S0-BFB-932

CONGRESSIONAL QUARTERLY

1999

ALMANAC®

106TH CONGRESS
1ST SESSION

VOLUME LV

Congressional Quarterly Inc.

1414 22nd Street N.W.
Washington, D.C. 20037

CONGRESSIONAL QUARTERLY 1999 ALMANAC

Congressional Quarterly Inc.

Congressional Quarterly Inc. is a publishing and information services company and the recognized national leader in political journalism. For more than half a century, CQ has served clients in the fields of business, government, news and education with complete, timely and nonpartisan information on Congress, politics and national issues.

The flagship publication is CQ Weekly, a news magazine on Congress and its legislative activities. The award-winning reporters and editors of CQ Weekly are widely considered top experts in their subject specialties. They track legislation as it is created in subcommittee, committee, floor, House-Senate conferences and leadership offices, providing detail and analysis unavailable anywhere else.

The CQ Daily Monitor is a morning news report on Congress and the scheduled hearings and markups of congressional committees. It provides a comprehensive breaking news report of everything that just happened or is about to happen on Capitol Hill.

CQ now offers the most comprehensive, detailed and up-to-the-minute legislative tracking information on the Internet. CQ.com On Congress is a web-based service with immediate access to exclusive CQ coverage of bill action, votes, schedules and member profiles, with direct links to relevant texts of bills, committee reports, testimony and verbatim transcripts.

CQ also publishes specialized publications on campaign politics and trends: Campaigns & Elections magazine is a monthly trade journal for candidates and campaign consultants, and Campaign Insider is a weekly fax newsletter for political professionals.

CQ serves the academic and education markets with a special weekly publication — The CQ Researcher — which focuses each week on a single topic of widespread interest.

Also CQ Press publishes a variety of books, including political science textbooks, to keep journalists, scholars and the public abreast of developing issues and events. This includes a line of print and web-based directories, such as the Congressional Staff Directory, plus reference books on the federal government, national elections and politics.

The Congressional Quarterly Almanac®, published annually, provides a legislative history for each session of Congress. Congress and the Nation, published every four years, provides a record of government for a presidential term.

Library of Congress Catalog Number 47-41081
ISBN: 1-56802-270-0 ISSN: 0095-6007

CONGRESSIONAL QUARTERLY OFFERS A COMPLETE LINE OF PUBLICATIONS AND RESEARCH SERVICES.

The CQ Almanac

"The story of Congress is the sum of the work of these members on the floor, in the lobbies, in committees in Washington and on the road, at home and abroad, in session and during recess."

A little more than 50 years ago, CQ founders Henrietta and Nelson Poynter prefaced the 1946 edition of the CQ Almanac with those words. They had only recently initiated the unprecedented task of compiling the only complete reference work on the actions of each session of Congress.

A half century later, Congressional Quarterly Inc. is proud to maintain the Poynter legacy and Poynter mission. This 1999 edition of the CQ Almanac, edited by CQ Weekly Senior Editor Jan Austin and Production Editor Melinda W. Nahmias, covers the actions, votes and other deeds of the first session of the 106th Congress. It provides a collection of articles from CQ Weekly, our award-winning, flagship news magazine, with stories tracking some 80 pieces of legislation that received action at the full committee, floor or conference level.

The Almanac also pulls together all the recorded votes in the House and Senate, important presidential statements and responses from members of Congress, and public laws. It includes the annual CQ Vote Studies, which provide exclusive statistical analyses of presidential support, party unity and voting attendance.

The bills covered in the 1999 edition — selected as the most significant of the year by Congressional Quarterly's editors — range from the historic overhaul of the financial services industry, to the year-end omnibus appropriations package, to congressional attempts to tighten security at the nation's nuclear weapons labs and unfinished efforts to reauthorize the Federal Aviation Administration.

The 1999 edition also includes the Senate's impeachment trial of President Clinton.

It covers the 13 regular appropriations bills, the budget resolution, authorization bills for the Defense and State departments and significantly different House and Senate bills to protect patients enrolled in managed-care health plans.

Most sections begin with a brief introduction, followed by articles from the CQ Weekly arranged in chronological order and marked with the date of the magazine in which they appeared.

In the back, you will find a number of appendixes, including:

- **Congress and Its Members:** A 11-page glossary of terms that arise in discussing Congress and legislation and a list of members of the House and Senate in the first session of the 106th Congress.
- **Vote studies.** CQ's popular study of the roll call votes cast in Congress during the year. Separate studies analyze the level of presidential support, party unity and member participation during the year.
- **Key votes.** An account of the votes chosen by the CQ editors as most critical in determining the outcome of congressional action on major issues during the year.
- **Texts.** Presidential statements, Republican responses and materials related to the impeachment proceedings against Clinton.
- **Public laws.** A detailed list of all the bills enacted into law during the year.
- **Roll call votes.** A complete set of roll call vote charts for both chambers.

CQ produces the Almanac for public policy specialists, scholars, journalists and all interested citizens and students of the U.S. legislative system. As the Poynters wrote at the very beginning: "Congressional Quarterly presents the facts in as complete, concise and unbiased form as we know how. The editorial comment on the acts and votes of Congress, we leave to our subscribers."

David Rapp
Executive Editor

CQ

"By providing a link between the local newspaper and Capitol Hill we hope Congressional Quarterly can help to make public opinion the only effective pressure group in the country. Since many citizens other than editors are also interested in Congress, we hope that they too will find Congressional Quarterly an aid to a better understanding of their government.

Foreword, Congressional Quarterly, Vol. I, 1945
Henrietta Poynter, 1901-1968
Nelson Poynter, 1903-1978

SUMMARY TABLE OF CONTENTS

Table of Contents

Chapter 1 – Inside Congress

Chapter 2 – Appropriations

Chapter 3 – Abortion

Chapter 4 – Agriculture

Chapter 5 – Banking & Finance

Chapter 6 – Budget

Chapter 7 – Commerce

Chapter 8 – Congressional Affairs

Chapter 9 – Defense

Chapter 10 – Education

Chapter 11 – Employment & Labor

Chapter 12 – Environment

Chapter 13 – Executive Branch

Chapter 14 – Foreign Policy

Chapter 15 – Government Operations

Chapter 16 – Health

Chapter 17 – Industry & Regulation

Chapter 18 – Law & Judiciary

Chapter 19 – Science

Chapter 20 – Social Policy

Chapter 21 – Taxes

Chapter 22 – Technology & Communication

Chapter 23 — Trade

Chapter 24 — Transportation & Infrastructure

Chapter 25 — Veterans Affairs

Appendixes

Congress and Its Members

Vote Studies

Key Votes

Texts

Public Laws

Roll Call Votes

General Index

Chapter 1

INSIDE CONGRESS

A Year of Grudging Compromises And Unfinished Business

SUMMARY

Congress may have reached the height of futility during the final week of October when Republican leaders spent days combining two long-overdue appropriations bills with a proposed across-the-board cut in discretionary spending.

President Clinton had already vetoed an earlier version of the District of Columbia portion of the package and had left no doubt that both the across-the-board cut and the second spending bill, for the departments of Labor, Health and Human Services (HHS), and Education, would meet with a similar fate.

But the Republican majority was determined to send Clinton all of the 13 annual spending bills before beginning the negotiations that both sides knew would be necessary to complete the budget process.

The methodical crafting of doomed bills, whether for tactical or political reasons, left the first session of the 106th Congress open to White House criticism that its leaders simply could not get their work done.

But with only a bare majority in the House and relentless Democratic pressure aimed at regaining control in the coming elections, GOP leaders were hard-pressed to keep their conservative wing satisfied while laying the groundwork for the 2000 campaigns.

Any prospect for getting much work done in in the first session was further undermined by the bitter partisanship left over from Clinton's impeachment by the House in December 1998 and his trial and acquittal in the Senate in early 1999.

Overhauling Financial Services

Though lawmakers were busy — they took 985 recorded votes, the third-highest number in the decade — bill signings were far less frequent. The number of bills enacted into law, 170, was the third-lowest in 10 years.

Arguably the biggest legislative accomplishment of the first session was enactment of a law (S 900 — PL 106-102) allowing banks, securities firms and insurance companies to compete on one another's traditional turf.

The most salient feature of that law may have been that it was 66 years in the making and occurred only after businesses already had found ways to legally circumvent many of the restrictions that the new statute eliminated. Once that happened, lobbyists for the competing interests settled several long-running disputes, and the House blessed the deal by passing its initial version of the measure (HR 10) by a 4-1 ratio in the summer. The Senate backed the final version by a 9-1 ratio in the fall.

The sessions' other achievements included enactment of a bill increasing Medicare reimbursements to health care providers and legislation granting extended federal health care benefits to the disabled when they return to work.

Also cleared was a package of business tax break extensions, legislation allowing satellite television providers to carry local stations' programming and a crackdown on software piracy.

More Process Than Progress

More often, however, the story in 1999 was one of fascinating process but little legislative progress, of maneuvering in an era in Washington when power between the parties is divided, congressional majorities are narrow, civility is on the decline — and a pivotal election is on the horizon.

The House and Senate, for instance, each passed bills designed to bolster the rights of people whose medical insurance is provided through managed-care plans. But their approaches had little in common, and the outlook for enactment of a law in the second session was murky at best. The House passed its more sweeping measure (HR 2723) with a solid, bipartisan majority that the GOP leadership was unable to tamp down. The Senate vote to pass its bill (S 1344) was almost exactly along party lines and was orchestrated by Majority Leader Trent Lott, R-Miss.

Something similar happened with the latest push for campaign finance legislation. GOP leaders could not prevent the House from passing a bill (HR 417) aimed at changing the role of money in national politics, but they were again able to stop Senate legislation (S 1593) when supporters could not come up with the votes to stop a threatened filibuster.

On gun control, the roles were reversed. A month after a high school shooting massacre in Littleton, Colo., the dam against new firearms restrictions appeared to be breaking. The Senate endorsed — albeit with Vice President Al Gore's tie-breaking vote

Session Highlights

Congress did:

- Bust the 1997 budget caps and, according to the Congressional Budget Office, dip into Social Security reserves to reach compromises on fiscal 2000 spending.
- Repeal decades-old banking laws to meet the needs of today's financial-services industry.
- Extend federal health insurance benefits for disabled workers once they return to the labor market.
- Agree to pay nearly $1 billion in back dues to the United Nations, while restoring some anti-abortion restrictions on international family planning aid.
- Limit liability for businesses responsible for year 2000, or Y2K, computer failures.
- Launch a program to subsidize 100,000 new teachers in public schools, while giving greater flexibility to school districts to determine how to use other federal aid.
- Resolve a long-running partisan dispute over the way the 2000 census will be conducted.
- Maintain current milk-pricing rules and extend the Northeast Dairy Compact, despite strong objections from Midwestern lawmakers.
- Create a special security unit within the Energy Department to deter thefts of nuclear secrets, after exposing spying attempts by the Chinese government.
- Call for, but not mandate, deployment of a national missile-defense system.
- Extend expiring tax breaks for research and other purposes.
- Double the next president's salary, to $400,000 a year.

Congress did not:

- Convict President Clinton in a Senate trial on House impeachment charges, brought in 1998, that he committed perjury and obstructed justice in testimony about his affair with a White House intern.
- Enact a $792 billion tax cut.
- Revise campaign finance laws.
- Reauthorize the Federal Aviation Administration; delivery of airport construction money was thus stalled.
- Stiffen penalties for juvenile offenders.
- Enact new curbs on gun sales.
- Kill the F-22 fighter jet.
- Revise personal bankruptcy guidelines.
- Increase the minimum wage.
- Decrease premiums that farmers pay for crop insurance.
- Move to protect the privacy of medical records, thus allowing the administration to enact its own regulations.
- Enact laws to expand trade.
- Complete work on an overhaul of the superfund hazardous waste cleanup program.
- Deregulate the electric power industry.
- Renew the independent counsel law.
- Impose import quotas on foreign steel, although the domestic steel industry won $1.5 billion in subsidized loans.
- Punish Russia or other nations that aid Iran's weapons development program.
- Send to the states a proposed constitutional amendment that would ban desecration of the flag.

— gun show regulations that the National Rifle Association emphatically opposed. It then passed the underlying juvenile crime bill (S 254) by a wide margin, suggesting that a new center on a long-polarized issue might have been found.

But a month later, the House soundly defeated a package (HR 2122) of more modest gun controls. To that end, Majority Whip Tom DeLay, R-Texas, employed a classic technique for stopping legislation: He arranged for enough "poison pills" that the final language was objectionable to ardent fans and ardent foes alike.

Foreign Policy Dynamics

Important measures were not always thwarted by parliamentary tactics or unbridgeable differences between the two chambers.

The Senate's resounding rejection of a treaty to expand restrictions on nuclear testing may be remembered as one of Clinton's most embarrassing foreign policy setbacks. It may be the best example to date of what many foreign policy experts see as a "neoisolationist" trend in Congress.

A more defensive nuclear policy was advanced by the Republicans early in the year, when the House passed a bill (HR 4 — PL 106-38) calling for, but not mandating, deployment of a national missile defense system. But it did so only after rejecting an amendment embodying Clinton's alternative.

Votes in the spring on both sides of the Capitol revealed ambivalence about the military deployment in Kosovo, although the messages about what U.S. policy should be were somewhat muddled by anti-Clinton sentiment and unwillingness to go too far out on a limb.

On a tie vote, the House rejected a symbolic resolution (S Con Res 21) to endorse the air bombing campaign that Clinton had launched five weeks before. A month later, the Senate narrowly squelched an amendment to the annual defense authorization bill (S 1059 — PL 106-65) that would have required Clinton to get express congressional permission before deploying ground troops.

There was evidence of isolationism on trade as well. The protectionist sentiment displayed in March when the House voted by a 2-1 ratio to pass a bill restricting steel imports (HR 975) portended the year's standoff on proposals designed to stimulate trade with Africa and the Caribbean.

On the other hand, there was a clear sign of growing congressional impatience with the policy of trying to isolate Cuba. Although it was dropped in conference, the Senate lined up overwhelmingly behind an amendment to its fiscal 2000 agriculture

First Session by the Numbers

DECEMBER 11— The first session of the 106th Congress closed at 12:03 p.m. on Nov. 22 when the House adjourned *sine die*. The Senate had adjourned *sine die* at 8:49 p.m. on Nov. 19. Both chambers started the year on Jan. 6.

The following is a statistical portrait of the two chambers of Congress over the past decade:

		1999	1998	1997	1996	1995	1994	1993	1992	1991	1990
Days in Session	Senate	162	143	153	132	211	138	153	129	158	138
	House	137	119	132	122	168	123	142	123	154	134
Time in Session (hours)	Senate	1,184	1,095	1,093	1,037	1,839	1,244	1,270	1,091	1,201	1,250
	House	1,125	999	1,004	919	1,525	905	982	857	939	939
Avg. Length Daily Session (hours)	Senate	7.3	7.7	7.1	7.9	8.7	9.0	8.3	8.5	7.6	9.1
	House	8.2	8.4	7.6	7.5	9.1	7.4	6.9	7.0	6.1	7.0
Public Laws Enacted		170	241	153	245	88	255	210	347	243	410
Bills/Resolutions Introduced	Senate	2,352	1,321	1,839	860	1,801	999	2,178	1,544	2,701	1,636
	House	4,241	2,253	3,662	1,899	3,430	2,104	4,543	2,714	5,057	2,769
	Total	6,593	3,574	5,501	2,759	5,231	3,103	6,721	4,258	7,758	4,405
Recorded Votes	Senate	374	314	298	306	613	329	395	270	280	326
	House[1]	611	547	640	455	885	507	615	488	444	536
	Total	985	861	938	761	1,498	836	1,010	758	724	862
Vetoes		5	5	3[2]	6	11	0	0	21[3]	4[3]	11

[1] includes quorum calls
[2] does not include line-item vetoes
[3] includes pocket vetoes

spending bill (S 1233) that would have allowed food and medicine shipments to the island.

How Things Change

The most ambitious GOP wish was to cut taxes $792 billion in the next decade. But votes in July to pass the House and Senate bills (HR 2488, S 1429) revealed that the effort had minimal Democratic support, and it never had the public enthusiasm that might have made Clinton think twice about stopping it in its tracks. He vetoed the final version with a fanfare normally associated with the enactment of tax cuts.

In many other ways, however, the agenda in the first session suggests how much had changed since the first year of revived Republican control of the Capitol. Managed care regulation, gun control, federal money to hire teachers — the GOP mentioned none of these in 1995, but the president succeeded in forcing Congress to address them.

Moreover, no Cabinet department received serious consideration for elimination in 1999. No federal cultural program got a drubbing. No sweeping "Contract With America" was drafted in the House, where the new Speaker, J. Dennis Hastert, R-Ill., settled for a year of meeting diminished expectations. He could aspire to little else, given that he ended 1999 with just four more lawmakers than he needed to form an absolute GOP majority.

So Republicans and Democrats spent much of the year blaming each other for what was not going to pass and fighting over credit for the rest.

Congress overwhelmingly backed, and Clinton signed, a measure (HR 800 — PL 106-25) giving localities greater latitude in spending education money from Washington. But the debate was filled with rancor, because Democrats saw themselves as the education party and were loath to share the label with the GOP. When the Senate took up its version of of the legislation (S 280), Democrats tried to make it a vehicle for their own education agenda, including the hiring of 100,000 new teachers.

In the House, Democrats used a bill to create a new federal education block grant (HR 1995) as their vehicle for funding the teachers. Although both efforts came up short, the votes were close enough to give Clinton incentive to push the teacher proposal in the year-end budget talks, and the provision made it into the omnibus spending law (HR 3194 — PL 106-113) for fiscal 2000.

Social Issues

Social conservatives had a mixed record in 1999. Anti-abortion forces opened a new offensive, ushering to passage in the House legislation (HR 2436) to declare that a fetus is an "unborn child" and elevate its standing under federal law; abortion rights groups said that would undermine the legal rationale for Roe v. Wade, the 1973 Supreme Court decision legalizing abortion. Abortion opponents also took heart when only 51 senators vot-

Vetoes by President Clinton

Bill	Description	Date	Response
		1995	
HR 1158	Rescissions/Supplemental	June 7	No override attempt
S 21	Lift Bosnia arms embargo	Aug. 11	No override attempt
HR 1854	Legislative appropriations	Oct. 3	No override attempt
HR 2586	Debt limit increase	Nov. 13	No override attempt
H J Res 115	Continuing appropriations	Nov. 13	No override attempt
HR 2491	Reconciliation	Dec. 6	No override attempt
HR 1977	Fiscal 1996 Interior spending	Dec. 18	House sustained, 239-177
HR 2099	Fiscal 1996 VA-HUD spending	Dec. 18	No override attempt
HR 2076	Fiscal 1996 Commerce-Justice-State spending	Dec. 19	House sustained, 240-159
HR 1058	**Securities litigation**	**Dec. 19**	**House overrode, 319-100; Senate overrode, 68-30**
HR 1530	Defense authorization	Dec. 28	House sustained, 240-156
		1996	
HR 4	Welfare overhaul	Jan. 10	No override attempt
HR1833	Partial-birth abortion ban	April 10	House overrode, 285-137; Senate sustained, 57-41
HR1561	State Dept. authorization	April 12	House sustained, 234-188
HR 956	Product liability	May 2	House sustained, 258-163
HR 743	TEAM Act	July 30	No override attempt
HR 2909	Silvio Conte Wildlife Refuge	Oct. 2	No override attempt
		1997	
HR 1469	Supplemental appropriations	June 9	No override attempt
HR 1122	Abortion procedure ban	Oct. 10	House overrode, 296-132; Senate sustained, 64-36
HR 2631	**Disapprove line-item vetos from HR 2016**	**Nov. 13.**	**House overrode, 347-69; Senate overrode, 78-20**
		1998	
S 1502	D.C. school vouchers	May 20	No override attempt
HR 2709	Punish missile aid to Iran	June 23	No override attempt
HR 2646	Education savings accounts	July 21	No override attempt
HR 4101	Fiscal 1999 agriculture spending	Oct. 7	No override attempt
HR 1757	State Dept. authorization	Oct. 21	No override attempt
		1999	
HR 2488	10-year tax-cut package	Sept. 23	No override attempt
HR 2587	Fiscal 2000 D.C. spending	Sept. 28	HR 3064 introduced
HR 2606	Fiscal 2000 foreign operations spending	Oct. 18	HR 3196 introduced
HR 2670	Fiscal 2000 Commerce-Justice-State spending	Oct. 25	No override attempt
HR 3064	Fiscal 2000 D.C./Labor-HHS-Education spending	Nov. 3	HR 3194 introduced

***Bold indicates successful override.** (Does not include "line-item" vetoes, which were permitted by PL 104-130 but overturned in* City of New York v. Clinton, *1998.)*

ed for non-binding language endorsing that landmark ruling.

A vote on a measure to block an Oregon law permitting physician-assisted suicide (HR 2260) forced the House to choose between the wishes of two GOP constituencies: those who advocated states rights and those who said the right to life is paramount. The House sided with the latter group.

But social conservatives were rebuffed on an amendment to a juvenile crime bill (HR 1501) that would have criminalized sales of explicitly violent or sexual material to young people. This time, the House sided instead with another longstanding GOP constituency: retailers such as bookshop owners and video rental outlets, who teamed up with movie and music producers to stop the proposal.

Environmentalists, who had had some success playing defense against the GOP Congress, were rebuffed when they tried to play offense. The auto industry persuaded the Senate to reject an amendment to the transportation spending bill (HR 2084 — PL 106-69) urging a reconsideration of automobile fuel-efficiency standards. And the House again sided with its public works promoters in their annual tussle with the budget hawks, defeating an amendment to strike from a bill (HR 1000) language dedicating revenue from airline ticket taxes to aviation projects.

Appropriations

Hastert had promised during his first year at the helm to bring "regular order" to the budget process, which he said meant enacting the 13 annual spending bills by the time fiscal 2000 began on Oct. 1.

Republicans were also determined to avoid repeating the previous year's endgame negotiations with the White House that yielded a mammoth spending package both sides viewed as a victory for Clinton. The Republicans' strategy for 1999 called for moving spending bills one at a time, while honoring the discretionary spending caps imposed by the 1997 Balanced Budget Act (PL 105-33) and pledging not to dip into the Social Security surplus.

After focusing in July on their tax package, Republicans turned in earnest to the spending bills in September. They started with the easiest bills, mostly small domestic spending measures and the defense budget, while deliberately underfunding some of the bigger domestic bills such as the Labor-HHS measure and the bill for veterans, housing, space and the environment.

To stay within the spending caps and pass the larger bills, Republicans exempted some of the funding as "emergency" spending and counted $14 billion in other spending as advance appropriations against the fiscal 2001 budget. Eventually, the caps were no longer mentioned and protecting the Social Security surplus emerged as the GOP's battle cry. By selectively choosing cost estimates for spending provisions, the Republicans produced a budget plan they said achieved their goal.

Negotiations with the White House in November added more spending and a package of offsets including, at GOP insistence, a small across-the-board cut in discretionary spending. The resulting year-end omnibus package included five spending bills, along with legislation that increased Medicare reimbursements, set dairy pricing policy, allowed satellite providers to carry local programming and reauthorizing the State Department.

Through History's Eyes

In assessing Congress' record for 1999, however, students of history will likely skip over all but one event: The Senate's resounding Feb. 12 acquittal of Clinton on charges that he committed perjury and obstructed justice, the two counts on which the House had impeached him in 1998. The first article was rejected, 45-55; the second was rejected, 50-50. A two-thirds majority would have been required to convict. It was second impeachment trial of a United States president and the first ever of an elected president. *(1998 Almanac, p. 12-3)* ◆

Chapter 2

APPROPRIATIONS

After a Year of Partisan Bickering, Congress and the President Agree On an 11th Hour Spending Package

SUMMARY

President Clinton got most of what he wanted for fiscal 2000 in end-of-session bargaining with Republican leaders.

In the end, the GOP found itself surrendering once again to many of Clinton's goals on appropriations: new money for teacher and police hiring subsidies; the release of back U.S. dues to the United Nations; and funding to purchase new federal lands.

At the same time, Republicans dropped most of their demands for conservative legislative "riders" that had been at the heart of many of their previous battles with Clinton. But they claimed to have made good on their top priority: limiting Clinton's penchant for even more new spending and tax increases in order to stop the practice of borrowing from Social Security surpluses to fund the rest of the government.

But as they sealed a deal with Clinton on appropriations, Republicans smashed "caps" on discretionary spending set barely two years ago (PL 105-33).

The key congressional participant was Speaker of the House J. Dennis Hastert, R-Ill., who vowed a return to "regular order" in the aftermath of the GOP's mishandling of the budget and appropriations bills in 1998, which produced a bloated "omnibus" fiscal 1999 spending bill (PL 105-277). Hastert vowed to pass all 13 of the annual bills separately, avoid year-end negotiations over an omnibus bill and leave Social Security surpluses untouched.

Hastert largely succeeded on the first goal, but after Clinton rejected five of the bills, negotiators began more than two weeks of talks over yet another omnibus measure. The bill encompassed new versions of bills to fund the District of Columbia (HR 3194); foreign aid (HR 3422); and the departments of Interior (HR 3423); Commerce, Justice and State (HR 3421); and Labor, Health and Human Services, and Education (HR 3424).

The omnibus followed months of difficult appropriations action. For most of the year, appropriators chafed under unrealistic spending caps set in 1997 that were reinforced by the fiscal 2000 budget resolution (H Con Res 68). To lift the caps earlier in the year would have reduced the size of the GOP tax cut bill.

Appropriators first advanced mostly small domestic bills and the defense budget bill (HR 2561), while deliberately underfunding bills for labor, health and education programs (Labor-HHS), foreign aid and a popular bill for veterans, housing, space and environmental programs (VA-HUD).

After the Republicans' tax bill (HR 2488) was vetoed, appropriators claimed almost all of the $14 billion fiscal 2000 non-Social Security-generated surplus for appropriations. They also took extraordinary advantage of controversial scorekeeping and accounting tactics to squeeze additional spending into the bills, outbidding Clinton on spending for education, health research and even the Environmental Protection Agency. According to the Congressional Budget Office, the GOP-passed bills exceeded the caps by $31 billion and dipped into Social Security surpluses by $17 billion.

After Clinton vetoed four bills and threatened to veto one other, more than two weeks of talks over an omnibus began. In the end, Clinton obtained more than $5 billion in year-end add-ons, financed by a package of offsetting savings that included: a 0.38 percent across-the-board cut ($1.2 billion); an administration-sponsored capture of surplus Federal Reserve funds ($3.8 billion); and moving the last federal payday for fiscal 2000 back one day, which would push $3.6 billion in outlays into fiscal 2001.

At the same time, the omnibus served as a vehicle for year-end deals to provide Northeastern lawmakers a big win on dairy policy, ease Medicare cuts enacted two years ago, boost the satellite television industry and reauthorize the State Department. ◆

Appropriations Mileposts

Fiscal 2000
(as of December 10, 1999)

Bill	House	Senate	Final
Agriculture (HR 1906 — Conference report: H Rept 106-354)	Adopted conference report 10/1/99	Cleared conference report 10/13/99	President signed (PL 106-78) 10/22/99
Commerce, Justice, State (HR 3421, incorporated in HR 3194 — Conference report: H Rept 106-479)	Adopted conference report 11/18/99	Cleared conference report 11/19/99	President signed (PL 106-113) 11/29/99
Defense (HR 2561 — Conference report: H Rept 106-371)	Adopted conference report 10/13/99	Cleared conference report 10/14/99	President signed (PL 106-79) 10/25/99
District of Columbia (HR 3194 — Conference report: H Rept 106-479)	Adopted conference report 11/18/99	Cleared conference report 11/19/99	President signed (PL 106-113) 11/29/99
Energy and Water Development (HR 2605 — Conference report: H Rept 106-336)	Adopted conference report 9/27/99	Cleared conference report 9/28/99	President signed (PL 106-60) 9/29/99
Foreign Operations (HR 3422, incorporated in HR 3194 — Conference report: H Rept 106-479)	Adopted conference report 11/18/99	Cleared conference report 11/19/99	President signed (PL 106-113) 11/29/99
Interior (HR 3423, incorporated in HR 3194 — Conference report: H Rept 106-479)	Adopted conference report 11/18/99	Cleared conference report 11/19/99	President signed (PL 106-113) 11/29/99
Labor-HHS (HR 3424, incorporated in HR 3194 — Conference report: H Rept 106-479)	Adopted conference report 11/18/99	Cleared conference report 11/19/99	President signed (PL 106-113) 11/29/99
Legislative Branch (HR 1905 — Conference report: H Rept 106-290)	Adopted conference report 8/5/99	Cleared conference report 8/5/99	President signed (PL 106-57) 9/29/99
Military Construction (HR 2465 — Conference report: H Rept 106-266)	Adopted conference report 7/29/99	Cleared conference report 8/3/99	President signed (PL 106-52) 8/17/99
Transportation (HR 2084 — Conference report: H Rept 106-355)	Adopted conference report 10/1/99	Cleared conference report 10/4/99	President signed (PL 106-69) 10/9/99
Treasury, Postal Service (HR 2490 — Conference report: H Rept 106-319)	Adopted conference report 9/15/99	Cleared conference report 9/16/99	President signed (PL 106-58) 9/29/99
Veterans Affairs, HUD (HR 2684 — Conference report: H Rept 106-379)	Adopted conference report 10/14/99	Cleared conference report 10/15/99	President signed (PL 106-74) 10/20/99
Eighth Fiscal 2000 Continuing Resolution (H J Res 83)	Passed H J Res 83 11/18/99	Cleared H J Res 83 11/18/99	President signed (PL 106-106) 11/19/99

Putting Differences Aside, Lawmakers Clear $69 Billion Agriculture Spending Bill

Box Score

Agriculture

- **Bill:** HR 1906 — PL 106-78
- **Legislative action: House** passed HR 1906 (H Rept 106-157), 246-183, on June 8.

Senate passed HR 1906 by voice vote Aug. 4, after substituting the text of S 1233 (S Rept 106-80).

House adopted the conference report (H Rept 106-354), 240-175, on Oct. 1.

Senate cleared the measure, 74-26, on Oct. 13.

President signed HR 1906 on Oct. 22.

SUMMARY

For the second straight year, significant controversy surrounded consideration of the agriculture spending bill. But lawmakers resolved their differences, added several billion dollars in emergency relief to farmers and sent the $69 billion bill to President Clinton, who signed it Oct. 22.

The measure followed a tortuous journey until the House and Senate grudgingly approved the final bill amidst attacks on a number of fronts — both for what it did and did not contain, and for the way it was negotiated. Making the bill irresistible, however, was a record-breaking $8.7 billion in relief to farmers who had been hurt by low commodity prices, bad weather and barriers to overseas markets. Another $576 million in emergency assistance was included in the fiscal 2000 omnibus measure (HR 3194) cleared Nov. 19.

The bailout package included $1.2 billion in direct assistance to farmers and livestock producers whose crops or animals were destroyed by drought or flooding. It also doubled, to $5.5 billion, the amount of money available to farmers through government contracts designed to help wean them off government subsidies and into a free-market economy. Despite the relief package's unprecedented size, numerous members said it still fell short of what was needed, and many Eastern lawmakers believed it was tilted in favor of Midwestern farmers.

Aside from relief money, two controversial provisions — on dairy pricing and the removal of sanctions on food and medicine exports to Cuba — were not included in the final measure. But they attracted considerable attention during a floor debate that also included charges that decisions on the issues were made by the House and Senate leadership in private talks after the conference committee was suspended.

New England members sought language to extend the Northeast Dairy Compact, which gives Northeastern farmers higher prices for their milk. Lawmakers from the Upper Midwest were able to keep it out of the agriculture conference agreement. It was, however, included in the omnibus. (*Dairy, p. 4-6*)

Various farm-state members also sought unsuccessfully to lift sanctions on food and medicine sales to nations such as Cuba, arguing that the embargo hurts American farmers without achieving foreign policy goals. The matter was dropped after House conservatives opposed the move. (*Sanctions, p. 14-11*)

The majority — $35 billion — of the measure's funding went to domestic food programs, including $21.1 billion for food stamps and $4 billion for the Women, Infants and Children supplemental food program.

House Panel OKs Relatively Unencumbered Bill

MAY 15 — Helping to get the fiscal 2000 appropriations season under way, the House Agriculture Appropriations subcommittee approved, by voice vote, a $60.8 billion spending measure May 13.

The unnumbered measure would fund the Agriculture Department (USDA), the Food and Drug Administration (FDA), and nutrition programs such as food stamps.

House Republican leaders are hoping to move the bill, along with two other spending measures, to the floor by Memorial Day. The Appropriations Committee is tentatively scheduled to mark up the Agriculture measure May 19.

The fiscal 1999 version was the first Agriculture spending package to be vetoed since 1919. The fiscal 2000 package is free of the type of policy riders that helped stall the bill last year, but subcommittee action pointed to other areas of dispute.

Panel Democrats complained that they had not had a chance to examine the draft prior to the nearly five-hour markup. Ranking Democrat Marcy Kaptur of Ohio said she had "never felt more uncomfortable" about a markup. "I'm not sure what's even in this bill," she complained.

Kaptur and other Democrats said it was ill-advised to proceed with the bill prior to completion of the House-Senate conference on a fiscal 1999 supplemental package (HR 1141), which contains $574 million in new budget authority for various agriculture aid programs.

Although Republicans argued that the supplemental money would ease the fiscal pressures on the fiscal 2000 Agriculture bill, Democrats complained that it was not enough to heal the ailing farm economy.

"This bill, coupled with that supplemental, is an inadequate response to the needs of farm country," said ranking House Appropriations Democrat David R. Obey of Wisconsin.

Last year, President Clinton vetoed the agriculture bill because he said it did not provide enough disaster relief for farmers. "Emergency" farm aid totalling $6 billion was then wrapped into the fiscal 1999 omnibus spending law (PL 105-277).

Amendments To Come

Agriculture Subcommittee Democrats said that at the full committee markup they would offer amendments to provide more farm aid as well as increase spending on child nutrition and youth tobacco prevention programs.

The fiscal 2000 Agriculture bill is nearly $6 billion larger than the fiscal 1999 package, with most of the increase attributable to mandatory payments to the Commodity Credit Corporation, which extends subsidy payments to farmers.

Subcommittee Chairman Joe Skeen, R-N.M., noted that the fiscal 2000 package provides $13.9 billion in new discretionary spending, an increase of $250 million over fiscal 1999 levels.

"The bill, so far, does not have any of the commodity provisions, such as dairy and sugar, that have caused trouble in the past," Skeen said.

Many members of Congress are angry at the USDA for a major change in dairy policy announced March 31. Senior subcommittee Republican James T. Walsh of New York said he refrained from offering amendments on dairy policy, which causes regional rifts, because bills to change the USDA plan (HR 1402, HR 1604) are moving through authorizing committees.

Most of the two dozen subcommittee amendments dealt with parochial issues, from funding "tick riders" who examine Mexican cattle crossing the Texas border, to a University of Georgia research farm.

Several members cut the bill's research programs to offset funding for projects in their home states.

The most heated debate came during consideration of an amendment by Jo Ann Emerson, R-Mo., to block the USDA from conducting climate research. Emerson said the research duplicates work at other agencies.

But other members argued that the research is necessary because farming is tied so closely to weather conditions. Emerson's amendment was defeated by voice vote.

The subcommittee later approved, by voice vote, her amendment to block funds in the bill from implementing the Kyoto Protocol on global warming.

Allen Boyd, D-Fla., won voice vote approval of two tobacco-related amendments. One would require the FDA to study the potential impact of machine-readable identification cards on retailers and on sales to minors. The other would create an FDA pilot program to speedily report to retailers on the results of anti-youth smoking compliance checks.

Full Committee Approves Bill; Floor Fight Looms

MAY 21 — The House Appropriations Committee May 19 approved a $60.8 billion spending bill (HR 1906) for agriculture and nutrition programs, but the panel's long and often bitter debate over spending priorities presaged difficult fights on the floor.

The measure, approved by voice vote, is expected to reach the House floor the week of May 24. The bulk of the bill's total price tag is mandatory spending on nutrition programs and U.S. Department of Agriculture (USDA) loans.

The bill includes discretionary funding levels of nearly $14 billion, $253 million more than was appropriated for fiscal 1999 and $530 million less than the amount President Clinton requested. Democrats complained the bill's spending levels would not provide adequate relief for ranchers and farmers devastated by falling prices and poor weather.

Last year, Clinton vetoed the agriculture bill because he said it did not provide enough disaster relief to farmers. A total of $6 billion in emergency aid was later included in the fiscal 1999 omnibus spending law (PL 105-277).

"The bill is simply unrealistic to address Depression-era conditions in rural America," said Agriculture Subcommittee ranking Democrat Marcy Kaptur of Ohio. "This is an exceedingly limited response to an extremely serious problem."

Kaptur offered two amendments, both defeated, that would have given the secretary of Agriculture emergency spending authority to aid farmers if an agriculture spending bill is not signed into law before the fiscal year begins Oct. 1. Kaptur signaled that she might offer the amendments on the floor.

One amendment, rejected 25-30, would have given the Agriculture Department $109.6 million in emergency loan authority that would not be offset by cuts in other areas. Kaptur argued the authority would be used if farmers need the assistance and if "Congress gets bound up in legislative gridlock."

The committee defeated, 23-28, another amendment that would have given the Agriculture secretary $500 million in emergency spending authority to buy surplus commodities to ease oversupplies and raise prices.

Sanctions Amendment Rejected

The issue launched the committee into a debate on the administration's disbursal of last year's emergency aid and the implementation of one of the Republicans' deregulatory victories, the 1996 farm overhaul (PL 104-127). Republicans, convinced administration policies are aggravating farmers' difficulties, were wary of giving the USDA more authority. *(1996 Almanac, p. 3-15)*

"I have little faith in the secretary of Agriculture's ability to address the farm crisis nationally," George Nethercutt, R-Wash., said at the markup.

The panel also rejected, 24-28, a Nethercutt amendment that would have allowed direct sales of U.S. agricultural products and medicines to markets closed because of sanctions.

Despite language that would allow the president to reimpose the sanctions if they are in the interest of national security, Nethercutt's amendment was opposed by members who feared that the provision would free Cuban President Fidel Castro from U.S. embargoes.

Majority Whip Tom DeLay, R-Texas, pointing to a group of former Cuban political prisoners assembled in the back of the room, argued that the United States should not give Castro any concessions because he would "use the food and medicine as political tools."

Amendments to boost spending on nutrition programs such as school lunches and the Women, Infants and Children (WIC) program are also likely. Rosa DeLauro, D-Conn., withdrew an amendment in committee that would have increased by $45 million the $4 billion allotted under the bill for WIC. That is $81 million more than fiscal 1999 levels but $100 million less than requested by the president.

Meanwhile, James T. Walsh, R-N.Y., told the panel that he would not rule out offering an amendment on the floor to address a new dairy pricing policy proposed March 31 by the USDA. But he said he held off in committee because bills (HR 1402, HR 1604) to modify the plan are being considered in authorizing panels.

Tom Coburn, R-Okla., also plans to offer an amendment that would prevent the Food and Drug Administration from approving abortion-inducing drugs. The House voted to include the language in last year's agriculture spending bill, but it was deleted in conference committee. In addition, a perennial battle over funding for sugar subsidies is very likely to be fought on the floor.

House Action Grinds to a Halt Over Amendments

MAY 29 — A bitter Republican feud over spending strategy spilled onto the House floor the week of May 24, bringing the $60.8 billion fiscal 2000 spending bill (HR 1906) for agriculture and nutrition programs to an abrupt halt.

Late on May 26, the House leadership shut down debate on the measure, bringing to an end a two-day crusade by Republican Tom Coburn of Oklahoma and other conservatives to slash more than $250 million from the bill.

The House is expected to return to the measure after the Memorial Day recess, assuming House leaders can bridge deep divisions in the GOP and come up with an overall appropriations strategy.

The explosive debate over spending cuts drowned out concerns voiced earlier in the process by Democrats, who claimed the bill would not adequately fund programs designed to prop up farmers hit by low prices and poor weather.

The fiscal 2000 measure calls for nearly $14 billion in discretionary spending, which is $253 million more than the fiscal 1999 measure. However, the proposed funding is $5.6 billion less than the fiscal 1999 level when "emergency" spending provided in last year's omnibus measure (PL 105-277) and the recently enacted midyear supplemental (HR 1141— PL 106-31) is included. *(1998 supplemental, 1998 Almanac, p. 2-117)*

The Agriculture appropriations measure is traditionally one of the first spending bills to the floor because it is generally the easiest to pass. That notion was put to rest on May 25 when Coburn circulated a letter to GOP colleagues outlining his intention to offer more than 115 amendments one at a time, to trim funding from a broad range of U.S. Department of Agriculture (USDA) administrative and research programs.

While overall discretionary spending levels in the bill were within the allocation set by the House Appropriations Committee, Coburn argued that the process was skewed so that early appropriations bills received generous allocations, thereby setting up Congress for the inevitability of breaking the budget caps with later, more difficult spending measures

Over two days of debate, Coburn and colleague Mark Sanford, R-S.C., offered a total of 10 amendments to cut the bill by nearly $84 million. They had only one success. On May 25, the House adopted, by a vote of 239-177, language reducing the budget of the USDA's chief information officer by $500,000. *(Vote 154, p. H-58)*

Separately, the House by voice vote adopted an amendment by Bernard Sanders, I-Vt., to cut the bill's overall funding level by $3 million. The amendment would reduce the Agricultural Research Service account by $13 million and increase commodity loan programs by $10 million.

Members of both parties denounced Coburn's effort. Republican Terry Everett of Alabama called Coburn's effort a "self-righteous indulgence," while Earl Pomeroy, D-N.D., said members should know that "hijacking the floor of this House is not the appropriate way to advance our convictions."

"Do not nitpick us to death," Agriculture Appropriations ranking Democrat Marcy Kaptur of Ohio said May 25. "We are not the [Senate]. We are not supposed to have filibusters here. We are supposed to move the people's business."

Attempts to dissuade Coburn and fellow fiscal conservatives from pushing the amendments were complicated by mixed messages from the GOP leaders.

As Appropriations Committee Chairman C.W. Bill Young, R-Fla., pleaded with the conservatives to allow the spending bill to move forward, other leaders voted for his amendments.

Majority Leader Dick Armey, R-Texas, supported all but one of Coburn's attempts to reduce spending. Majority Whip Tom DeLay, R-Texas, voted for all of the conservatives' funding cuts. By May 26, both Armey and DeLay started opposing his amendments but Coburn did not let up.

He even tried to cut $300,000 from research on peanuts, an important crop in Oklahoma. The effort failed, 119-308. *(Vote 161, p. H-58)*

The House also rejected, 35-390, an attempt by Coburn to wipe out the bill's $50.8 million budget increase for the Agricultural Research Service. *(Vote 158, p. H-58)*

By a vote of 143-274, the House rejected a Sanford amendment to reduce the USDA buildings and facilities account by $21.7 million. *(Vote 155, p. H-58)*

The bill itself contained major increases for agricultural research and food inspection services, but would scale back rural development programs, funds for crop insurance and USDA construction accounts.

Kaptur called on the leadership to provide more funding to head off "Depression-level conditions affecting many sectors of rural America" by providing additional funding for USDA price support and loan programs.

Under the measure, the Agriculture Research Service would receive $836.4 million, a $50.9 million increase over fiscal 1999 levels, while animal and plant inspections would receive $440 million, an $18.2 million increase over fiscal 1999 and nearly $9 million more than requested by the president.

The bill would provide $666.1 million for the program that funds grants for rural water, waste and other development programs, $56.6 million less than fiscal 1999 levels and $4 million less than the administration requested.

Funding for nutrition programs, such as school lunches and the Women, Infants and Children (WIC) program, make up the bulk of the measure's mandatory spending allocation. The bill would fund WIC at $4 billion, $81 million more than fiscal 1999 but $100 million less than the president's request.

Democrats were unhappy that the bill would provide no funding for a school breakfast pilot project called for in last year's reauthorization of nutrition programs (PL 105-336). They are expected to offer amendments increasing spending for nutrition programs when debate resumes. *(1998 Almanac, p. 20-3)*

House Passes Bill After Coburn Gets $103 Million Cut

JUNE 12 — By reversing course and cutting more than $100 million from the fiscal 2000 Agriculture appropriations bill, House Republican leaders were able to secure its passage June 8 on a largely party-line vote.

The victory may have been Pyrrhic, however, as the cuts angered Republican appropriators. And Democrats, who had previously found the bill's funding level acceptable, largely turned against it.

Even before the 246-183 vote to pass the bill (HR 1906 — H Rept 106-157), farm-state Republicans and Democrats alike were hoping that the bill's funding could be increased in conference with the Senate. The Senate Appropriations Agriculture Subcommittee is scheduled to mark up its version of the bill June 15. *(Vote 177, p. H-64)*

The House measure would provide $60.7 billion in new budget authority to fund the Agriculture Department (USDA), the Food and Drug Administration (FDA) and nutrition assistance such as food stamps and the Women, Infants and Children (WIC) program. All but about $13.9 billion of the bill's funding is devoted to mandatory spending.

GOP leaders had hoped that increasing the bill's total over its fiscal 1999 levels would ease its passage. But instead they found themselves negotiating spending cuts with Tom Coburn, R-Okla., who in the week before the Memorial Day recess blocked the bill's progress in anger about overall fiscal 2000 spending.

Democrats were angry that funding in the agriculture bill had become entangled in budget politics and castigated Republicans for cutting money for agriculture at a time when many farmers are suffering from low commodity prices.

"It's a terrible bill," said Maurice D. Hinchey, D-N.Y., a member of the House Appropriations Subcommittee on Agriculture, Rural Development, FDA and Related Agencies. "They [House Republicans] have internal difficulties that they're trying to address, and unfortunately rural America is being asked to bear that burden."

Coburn had led a filibuster by amendment May 25 and 26, seeking to cut the bill by $253 million to reduce it to the fiscal 1999 level. Most of his amendments were defeated handily.

Members Unhappy

As part of a plan to keep overall appropriations levels within the caps set in the 1997 budget agreement (PL 105-33), Coburn agreed June 8 to withhold dozens of amendments in exchange for a leadership proposal to cut spending in the bill by $102.5 million.

"That doesn't go far enough," Coburn told reporters after the final number was set. But, he added, "I still have to support cuts."

Farm-state Republicans agreed to accept funding cuts that could cause them political trouble back home. GOP leaders pressured them to accept reductions that were needed to make the first day of the new appropriations strategy a success.

"Frankly, I don't think they're going to like it," Appropriations Committee Chairman C.W. Bill Young, R-Fla., said as he headed into a meeting in Majority Whip Tom DeLay's office suite with several rural lawmakers who serve on the Agriculture Committee and Agriculture Appropriations Subcommittee.

"Well, I don't like it, obviously," said John Thune, R-S.D., after the meeting. "But the reality is the bill isn't going anywhere unless we address Coburn's problems with it."

Prices for many commodities, such as corn, wheat and pork, have for the past year fallen lower than they had been for decades because of a combination of weakened exports, overproduction and regional weather problems.

"Farmers are the one sector of the economy that haven't enjoyed the prosperity of the rest of the country, and we think it's pretty despicable that they've turned to the USDA budget to make those cuts," said Erika Hovland, a spokeswoman for the National Farmers Union.

Appropriations Agriculture Chairman Joe Skeen, R-N.M., refused a leadership request to present the amendment to cut the bill. "It isn't a killer, but it certainly doesn't help us any," Skeen said in a June 10 interview.

Presenting the amendment, Young maintained that farmers have already benefited from recent federal aid, including $6 billion in "emergency" funding in the fiscal 1999 omnibus spending law (PL 105-277), and $574 million in agriculture assistance included in the fiscal 1999 supplemental spending law (PL 106-31). *(Omnibus, 1998 Almanac, p. 2-117)*

Turning that argument around, Democrats noted that USDA programs stand to receive nearly $6 billion less in fiscal 2000 than in fiscal 1999 when the emergency spending is counted.

"Consideration of the agriculture appropriations bill has been an utter travesty," said Earl Pomeroy, D-N.D. "I cannot tell you how dispiriting it is to be an advocate for American agriculture and have the chairman of the Appropriations Committee propose a $100 million-plus cut."

Young's amendment passed, 234-195, with just four Republicans dissenting. Lamar Smith, R-Texas, said in an interview that his "no" vote had been a mistake. *(Vote 175, p. H-64)*

Ranking Appropriations Committee Democrat David R. Obey of Wisconsin subsequently offered a motion to recommit the bill to the committee with instructions to restore $20 million in FDA salaries and expenses cut by the Young amendment. The motion was rejected, 207-220. *(Vote 176, p. H-64)*

Ongoing Negotiations

Coburn met with Speaker J. Dennis Hastert, R-Ill., the evening of June 7. Hastert told Coburn that he had a plan to preserve the budget caps in part by reducing "smaller" spending bills such as agriculture.

"He's our leader, and he's come up with at least a strategy to keep us from going back where we were last year," Coburn said, referring to the omnibus spending law, which exceeded budget caps by $21 billion.

On June 8, in negotiations with Coburn that continued on and off the floor through much of the day, GOP leaders and their aides initially proposed cutting the agriculture bill by $50 million. Asked why they did not offer to cut the bill by $253 million, as Coburn wanted, Young said such a cut would be too drastic, given the "crisis in farm country."

"He's a very reasonable member," Young said of Coburn.

The bulk of the cuts came from USDA buildings and facilities accounts. Farm-state members rejected an earlier version of the amendment, which they felt cut too close to the bone, but were willing to live with the final $102.5 million reduction.

"This amendment is basically taking money out of brick and mortar," said Thomas W. Ewing of Illinois, a senior Agriculture Committee Republican. "When money is tight, that's a legitimate place to look."

Coburn also received help from the leadership on his amendment to block the FDA from spending funds to test or approve abortion-inducing drugs, such as the French-developed pill RU-486.

"There is something terribly wrong when we ask the taxpayers to spend money in a way that is designed to allow the [FDA] the ability . . . to approve drugs that are designed to kill unborn children," Coburn said.

Opponents of the amendment argued that it would interfere not only with abortion rights but with the FDA's ability to make sound judgments about medications that might induce abortion as a side effect.

"If abortion is legal, why should we not allow funds to be used by private enterprise to develop a drug that would lead to . . . earlier, safer abortions?" said Henry A. Waxman, D-Calif.

Coburn's amendment passed, 217-214, with DeLay pressing four Republicans — Herbert H. Bateman of Virginia, David Dreier of California, Charles H. Taylor of North Carolina and Michael G. Oxley of Ohio — to switch their votes to "aye" in the closing moments of its consideration. *(Vote 173, p. H-62)*

Coburn had offered essentially the same amendment to the fiscal 1999 Agriculture appropriations bill, stalling its progress. House GOP leaders maintained support for the provision in the face of opposition from the Senate and President Clinton, but it was eventually stripped out in the House-Senate conference. *(1998 Almanac, p. 2-5)*

Sidestepping Controversy

Appropriators and the Republican leadership managed to keep this year's agriculture spending bill free of other policy provisions that might have caused further headaches.

James T. Walsh, R-N.Y., withheld an amendment that would have blocked the USDA from implementing a proposed overhaul of federal dairy policy.

Walsh agreed not to offer the amendment after Agriculture Committee leaders pledged on the floor to hold a subcommittee hearing on the matter June 24 and to "expedite" consideration of legislation (HR 1402) that would overturn the USDA's new rules.

In the face of a threatened point of order against legislating on an appropriations bill, George Nethercutt, R-Wash., withdrew an amendment to block unilateral food and medicine embargoes against other countries. Although some farm-state members contend that such sanctions only hurt U.S. farmers who lose access to overseas markets, others argued that they are a necessary tool for punishing dictators such as Cuba's Fidel Castro.

A similar Nethercutt amendment held up the bill last year as appropriators negotiated language acceptable to foreign relations authorizers.

Many of the other amendments considered June 8 were also variations on themes heard in previous years.

Steve Chabot, R-Ohio, sought to eliminate funding for the $90 million Market Access Program, which helps pay for overseas advertising of American food products, calling it a "corporate welfare" program that benefited major corporations.

Several members of the Appropriations Agriculture subcommittee rose to defend the program, noting that increased exports are key to reviving the U.S. farm economy, and pointing out that other countries spend far greater amounts to promote their food products internationally.

The amendment failed, 72-355. *(Vote 174, p. H-62)*

Peter A. DeFazio, D-Ore., and Charles Bass, R-N.H., offered an amendment similar to one they proposed last year to cut funding for a USDA predator control program by $7 million.

"The question is, should federal taxpayers pay for predator control services on private ranches for profit in the Western United States?" DeFazio said.

But several members contended that the spending was necessary to control wildlife and prevent animal attacks on humans. The amendment was rejected, 193-230. *(Vote 172, p. H-62)*

Ranking Agriculture Appropriations Democrat Marcy Kaptur of Ohio won voice vote approval of an amendment to allow the USDA to shift up to $7 million from rural housing insurance accounts to outreach programs for socially disadvantaged farmers.

In April, the USDA won a federal court's blessing of its settlement of a class-action lawsuit brought by black farmers who had suffered discrimination at the hands of the department.

Senate Panels Give Quick Approval; Bill Heads to Floor

JUNE 19 — The fiscal 2000 agriculture appropriations bill easily cleared two hurdles the week of June 14, winning unanimous approval from two Senate spending panels.

But when the $60.7 billion package reaches the floor the week of June 21, it will be the subject of contentious amendments regarding financial aid to farmers and dairy policy that were deferred during committee action.

The Senate Appropriations Committee on June 17 approved the measure (S 1233), 28-0, en bloc with the fiscal 2000 foreign operations measure. The panel's subcommittee on Agriculture, Rural Development and Related Agencies had approved the package by voice vote on June 15.

The bill funds the Agriculture Department, Food and Drug Administration, Commodity Futures Trading Commission and nutrition programs such as food stamps and Women, Infants and Children (WIC).

The House passed its version of the bill (HR 1906) on June 8.

The Senate bill would provide $14 billion in new discretionary budget authority, with most programs "at or about a freeze level [compared] with last year's enacted level," said Thad Cochran, R-Miss., chairman of the Agriculture Appropriations Subcommittee. That represents a boost from the subcommittee's original allocation of $13.1 billion.

But Democrats said the bill was still too stingy to help farmers who are suffering because of low prices for commodities such as wheat, corn and pork.

In response, Tom Harkin, D-Iowa, offered an amendment at the subcommittee markup that would have provided $6.5 billion in "emergency" assistance to farmers. "This may sound like a lot of money, and it is a lot of money, but it's not, compared to the problem out there," Harkin said.

In a June 11 meeting with White House Chief of Staff John D. Podesta, representatives of 23 farm groups said farmers would need $6 billion to $8 billion in direct federal assistance this year to make up for lost income.

Senate Republicans did not dispute the assertion that national net farm income is plummeting and that farmers are going to need additional assistance. But they were wary of revisiting the bidding war that transpired during the legislative course of the fiscal 1999 agriculture bill, when the Senate's initial $500 million disaster provision grew into a $6 billion package.

Harkin's amendment was tabled, or killed, 6-5, on a party-line subcommittee vote. He did not offer it during the full committee markup but promised to bring it up again during floor consideration. Republicans called on the Clinton administration to submit a formal emergency budget request.

"The emergency clause has greater standing when it comes from the president," said Appropriations Committee Chairman Ted Stevens, R-Alaska.

The administration has signaled that it would support additional aid to farmers, but in a June 16 interview Agriculture Secretary Dan Glickman refused to comment on the timing or amount of money he might request.

Like Harkin, Patrick J. Leahy, D-Vt., acceded to pleas from senior Appropriations members to defer a controversial amendment regarding dairy policy until the bill reaches the floor.

Leahy had planned on June 17 to propose that Congress override USDA-proposed changes in the complex system of regional price supports known as milk marketing orders.

His amendment also would have authorized regional dairy compacts in the Northeast and Southeast. Leahy had inserted a provision into the 1996 farm law (PL 104-127) that created a regional dairy compact among six New England states. *(1996 Almanac, p. 3-15)*

A compact allows an interstate commission to raise the minimum price paid to dairy farmers for fluid milk above the federal level.

Leahy said that ending the Northeast compact and allowing rules changes in USDA milk marketing orders to take effect would make dairy farmers in his state an endangered species.

Dairy battles tend to be fought on a regional basis. Senators from the Midwest and Western states argued that Leahy's amendment would have hurt consumers and put dairy farmers in their regions at a disadvantage.

"I was confident I had the votes, but we would have been here until 11 tonight and still face the same fight on the floor," Leahy said after the full committee's afternoon markup.

The committee approved, by voice vote, an amendment sponsored by Mitch McConnell, R-Ky., to speed the application process for Labor Department approval of migrant farm workers.

Senate Passes Bill With Compromise On Farm Aid

AUGUST 7 — In reaching an agreement Aug. 4 about how to provide aid to struggling farmers, the Senate employed an unusual mode of compromise. Rather than hammering out a deal off the floor, senators voted on several competing plans before settling on one with a price tag that fell in the middle.

On Aug. 4, the Senate passed, by voice vote, a $70 billion agriculture appropriations bill (HR 1906) to fund the Agriculture Department (USDA), Food and Drug Administration (FDA) and nutrition aid such as food stamps and the Women, Infants and Children program.

The measure includes $7.4 billion in "emergency" assistance to farmers, who have been suffering from low commodity prices and regional weather problems. That package was approved, 89-8, on Aug. 4, but the lopsided vote masked the partisan bidding war that preceded it. *(Vote 257, p. S-50)*

Democrats and Republicans offered three different aid packages each, with the bottom lines of the Democratic amendments dropping down from a starting point of $10.8 billion and Republicans inching upwards from just under $7 billion.

Arguments about financial aid to farmers dominated the three days of debate on the bill, although the Senate also turned back a major amendment on dairy pricing and killed an effort to end the sugar price support program. It also approved an amendment to end unilateral sanctions involving sales of food and medicine to foreign countries.

The GOP's final emergency aid package was generous enough to win the support of farm-state Republicans, and was accepted as better than nothing by Democrats.

"They will win the day," Byron L. Dorgan, D-N.D., conceded just before the vote on the $7.4 billion package. "At least we go to conference with something."

The House version contains no emergency agriculture assistance, though House conferees are expected to agree to a multibillion-dollar bailout.

During the Senate's three days of give and take on the issue, even Republicans acknowledged that their bill would merely serve as the starting point for negotiations in the House-Senate conference.

Several senators expressed a desire to wait until later in the year to determine the size of the assistance package, because the scope of the agriculture sector's problems will be clearer after harvest.

"In this particular week, everything

we do will be like water washing over the beach," Agriculture Committee Chairman Richard G. Lugar, R-Ind., told reporters Aug. 3.

Adding to the confusion is the lack of information about how much money the Clinton administration believes is necessary to help farmers. Senate Republicans for much of the year have pressed the administration for a formal supplemental budget request, or at least for guidance. Senate Democrats have also complained that the administration has not been sufficiently specific.

"I don't want to be in a position to say you have to spend 'X' dollars or 'Y' dollars," Agriculture Secretary Dan Glickman told the Senate Agriculture Committee on Aug. 3. "It is a fair statement that the administration expects a multibillion-dollar package."

Even as Glickman was testifying, Vice President Al Gore appeared at a Capitol news conference to endorse the initial Senate Democratic $10.8 billion package, although he suggested that those funds should eventually be offset.

"The Republican proposal is clearly inadequate," White House spokesman Joe Lockhart said at an Aug. 4 news briefing.

Means of Delivery

Aside from cost, Republicans and Democrats differed over the mechanism for delivering the money to farmers. Noting that the USDA took months to deliver much of the $6 billion in emergency agriculture spending included in the fiscal 1999 omnibus spending law (PL 105-277), Republicans insisted on using an existing program known as transition payments. *(1998 Almanac, p. 2-3)*

The fixed transition payment program was created by the 1996 farm law (PL 104-127) in an effort to wean farmers off the old subsidy system. Rather than fluctuating with commodity prices, farmers are guaranteed a fixed amount of money that is scheduled to decline each year. *(1996 Almanac, p. 3-15)*

The payments were eventually supposed to be phased down, if not out. But Republicans have since embraced this particular payment system as the swiftest way to deliver aid directly to farmers.

"The purpose of this amendment is to provide direct income assistance to farmers and ranchers in the fastest way possible," said Pat Roberts, R-Kan., in introducing one of the Republican amendments, saying that transition checks could be cut within 10 days.

A Bidding War

All three of the GOP versions would have doubled the scheduled transition payments for fiscal 2000, at a cost of $5.5 billion, and included money to assist farmers who produce livestock or crops not eligible for the transition payments such as soybeans.

The $7.5 billion Roberts amendment would have provided additional disaster assistance to farmers suffering from bad weather, such as the drought in the mid-Atlantic states. His version also would have extended a $400 million subsidy program to assist farmers buying crop insurance that was included in the omnibus spending law.

The Roberts amendment was tabled, or killed, 66-33, on Aug. 4. *(Vote 253, p. S-50)*

Democrats complained that the transition payments are based on outdated historical formulas. Their initial $10.8 billion package would have delivered much of the money through loan deficiency payments. These payments are given to farmers when their crops fall below the bottom price set for each commodity through the government's marketing loan program.

The first Democratic package was tabled, 54-44, on Aug. 3. A trimmer version that would have cost $9.8 billion was tabled the next day, 55-44. *(Votes 250, 255, pp. S-49, S-50)*

Undaunted, Democrats then joined forces with Charles E. Grassley, R-Iowa, to offer an $8.8 billion package that used transition payments as the vehicle for sending money to farmers. Although the plan attracted support from a half-dozen Republicans, it was killed, 51-48. *(Vote 256, p. S-50)*

Democrats then reluctantly supported the revised version of a transition payment-based package offered by Agriculture Appropriations Subcommittee Chairman Thad Cochran, R-Miss. To attract sufficient support from his own caucus, Cochran enhanced his original $7 billion transition payment plan with $400 million for crop insurance.

Phil Gramm, R-Texas, complained about the dollar amounts involved in the "political bidding war," but conceded that his was a decidedly minority opinion. Other than Gore, no one suggested the need to offset the cost of aid to farmers.

"We need to come to grips as a country with what our farm policy is going to be," Lugar said at the Aug. 3 hearing. "There will come a year where the budget situation is not so favorable and the desire to go into emergency spending is not there."

House Agriculture Committee Chairman Larry Combest, R-Texas, has said he intends to hold hearings this fall about the best method for delivering aid to farmers.

Milk and Sugar

The Senate blocked a move to insert dairy policy provisions into the bill. A fight about proposed USDA changes to federal dairy policy has caused spats in both chambers, and senators on both sides of the issue had threatened to filibuster the agriculture spending bill if they did not get their way.

Dairy pricing policy splits the country into regions, and members from the Northeast and South are unhappy about the USDA's revisions, saying farmers in their states will be driven out of business.

Republican James M. Jeffords and Democrat Patrick J. Leahy, both of Vermont, wanted to amend the bill to overturn the USDA pricing changes. Their amendment would also have extended and expanded a dairy compact between six New England states that was authorized by the 1996 farm law but is set to expire Oct. 1.

The compact allows an interstate commission to raise milk prices within the region above the federally mandated level. Opponents of the compact say that it raises prices for consumers and unfairly blocks farmers who live in other states from having access to those consumers.

A motion to invoke cloture on the Jeffords-Leahy amendment fell well short of the 60 votes required, 53-47. But its supporters vowed to fight for the provisions in conference. *(Vote 252, p. S-50)*

John McCain, R-Ariz., offered an amendment to cut off funding for the

Backers of New Dairy Price Plan Are Confident Despite Losing House Vote

SEPTEMBER 25 — Rep. Paul D. Ryan, a Republican from dairy-rich Wisconsin, was surprisingly unfazed Sept. 22 after losing — by a lopsided margin — the biggest fight of his legislative career.

The House had just passed a bill (HR 1402) that is despised in the Upper Midwest but highly favored in the East and Southeast. It would block the Agriculture Department from installing a new dairy pricing formula for milk "marketing orders," the Depression-era scheme the government uses to ensure farmers in 31 regions a minimum price for their milk.

The 285-140 vote in favor of HR 1402 would have been enough in this instance to override an expected presidential veto. But Ryan and his Midwestern allies say not to worry. The most important fact to note, they say, is the date of the roll call — about a week away from Oct. 1, when the new plan will automatically go into effect unless blocked by Congress. *(Vote 436, p. H-142)*

With the session lurching toward a close and Senate opponents of the bill talking tough, HR 1402 is unlikely to go much further. The Senate has no thirst to take up the bill, and if it does, Wisconsin Sens. Russell D. Feingold and Herb Kohl, both Democrats, have promised a filibuster. They undoubtedly would be supported by Minnesota's two senators, Rod Grams, a Republican, and Paul Wellstone, a Democrat.

Prospects are similarly sour on other fronts. Members from New England and the South have been working to preserve the current pricing system by attaching language similar to HR 1402 to the fiscal 2000 agriculture appropriations bill (HR 1906), which is in a House-Senate conference.

The dairy question stalled the conference for two consecutive days the week of Sept. 20 as House members have so far complied with a request from Republican leaders to keep dairy provisions out of the conference report.

Ryan said he had personal assurances from House GOP leaders that the dairy issue would remain separate from the must-pass appropriations bill.

And finally, should the bill somehow get to the president's desk, Agriculture Secretary Dan Glickman said he would urge a veto.

All of that contributed to Ryan's upbeat outlook. "We accomplished two things," Ryan said. "We delayed the vote until today and we educated our colleagues . . . about an antiquated, Soviet style pricing scheme."

The Pricing Scheme

The goal of HR 1402, sponsored by Roy Blunt, R-Mo., is to preserve the status quo by prohibiting the Agriculture Department (USDA) from implementing a pricing system that essentially would flatten regional differentials built into the pricing scheme. The current system, designed in 1937, gives a bonus to farmers the farther they are from Eau Claire, Wis., the historical center of the dairy industry. The bonuses were intended to reflect different production and transportation costs.

The administration's new plan would minimize those bonuses. The approach, the USDA and its supporters say, would reduce the cost of a gallon of milk by 2 cents. But critics say it would funnel more money to producers in the Upper Midwest and push financially strapped dairy farmers, particularly those in the Northeast and South, over the edge.

"What we have been reduced to this time around is 48 states, or at least 40 states, being harmed for the benefit of two," said Republican James T. Walsh of New York, who, like most of his colleagues from the Northeast and South, supported HR 1402.

That argument carried the day in the House, but the debate exposed deeply entrenched regional, rather than partisan, differences over dairy policy.

Lawmakers from the East and Southeast said the new formula would drive thousands of dairy farmers out of business because it would shift $200 million in revenues and cause a contracting industry to consolidate even more.

"Does America really want a handful of [dairy] corporations to determine the price of dairy products?" asked Independent Bernard Sanders of Vermont, who strongly backed HR 1402.

Opponents of the bill, including scattered members from the West, such as Cal Dooley, D-Calif., and those from the greater Midwest, such as John A. Boehner, R-Ohio, argued that the rationale for regional pricing variations is invalid in an era of interstate highways and refrigerated transport. The entire country is now within reach of fresh milk, even if it is not locally produced, they said.

"This place is locked in a time warp," declared Mark Green, R-Wis. "This place is using a milk pricing mechanism that was created in the era of the manual typewriter."

As passed, the bill also would extend for another year the federal milk price-support program, which was scheduled to expire Dec. 31.

By including that language, the House backed away from the 1996 farm bill (PL 104-127), which called for the phaseout of such subsidies for a range of commodities, including milk.

sugar price support program, which keeps domestic prices above the world market rate through loans and import restrictions.

"Not too many average grocery shoppers realize they are paying at least 10 cents more per pound of sugar because of these costly sugar mandates," he said.

Defenders of the program said that it was necessary to keep domestic sugar farmers solvent and that killing it would merely cost jobs and leave the United States dependent on foreign sugar. Their position prevailed when the McCain amendment was tabled, 66-33. *(Vote 254, p. S-50)*

House Adopts Bill Despite Dismay Over 'Back Room' Deal-Making

OCTOBER 2 — A $69 billion spending bill won grudging final approval in the House on Oct. 1 despite bitter complaints from Republicans and Democrats that the House-Senate agreement ignored two critical farm-state issues and was negotiated in secret.

The House-Senate conference report on the bill (HR 1906), which includes $8.7 billion in emergency relief to farmers reeling from bad weather and historically low prices, was adopted, 240-175, but not before a stream of members berated the way it was assembled. *(Vote 469, p. H-154)*

The measure is likely to face similar criticism when the Senate takes it up the week of Oct. 4, but final adoption is expected, if only so disaster money can be distributed immediately to hard- hit farmers and livestock producers.

President Clinton is expected to sign the bill.

Many conferees did not hesitate to express their dismay about the way the deal was forged.

"Our rights to write this bill were stolen from us, and I'm angry about that," said Jo Ann Emerson, R-Mo., a House conferee whose authority was effectively usurped when House Speaker J. Dennis Hastert, R-Ill., and Senate Majority Leader Trent Lott, R-Miss., decided to broker the conference agreement themselves.

Hastert and Lott bypassed the deadlocked conference the week of Sept. 27 in order to resolve two issues that had put farm-state negotiators at loggerheads the week before: trade sanctions on terrorist states (mainly Cuba), and milk prices.

Agriculture conferees, who see promising new markets for U.S. farm goods, were eager to include a Senate provision that sought to lift trade sanctions on food and medicine to terrorist states by including special requirements that Cuba would have to meet in order to have sanctions lifted.

Key House GOP conservatives were adamantly opposed to that provision, and the Hastert-Lott deal, arranged in cooperation with Joe Skeen, R-N.M., chairman of the House conferees, and Majority Whip Tom DeLay, R-Texas, dropped that provision altogether.

That prompted a cry of foul from co-opted conferees. "Are we really going to close our eyes to the real problems [in agriculture], which are closed markets and low prices?" said Rep. Marcy Kaptur, D-Ohio.

Senators were also upset, though leaders on both sides said they expect the measure to pass. Senate Minority Leader Tom Daschle, D-S.D., said Sept. 29 that a filibuster is unlikely.

"As disappointed and frustrated as we are, we are also cognizant of how much economic pain there is out there, and we're not inclined to delay for one day providing at least some form of assistance to those who are going to get it," he said.

Eastern and Southern members wanted to include a provision, absent from the House and Senate bills but supported overwhelmingly in a separate House bill (HR 1402), to block the Clinton administration's plans to implement a new milk "marketing order" scheme on Oct. 1.

Wisconsin and other upper Midwest senators were determined to let the Clinton pricing plan proceed because it favors milk producers in their states. Hastert and Lott kept it out of the conference report.

"This bill was dictated by the Republican leadership," Rep. Bernard Sanders, I-Vt., said Oct. 1. "Deals were made in a back room."

Farm-State Relief

To win farm-state support, Lott and Hastert agreed to raise the ante on disaster relief, from $7.4 billion included in the Senate bill to $8.7 billion. The House bill had included no disaster relief. Included in the total is $1.2 billion for farmers whose crops were destroyed by drought or flooding.

Two Democratic conferees from Wisconsin, Rep. David R. Obey and Sen. Herb Kohl, both signed on after receiving inducements from the leadership. The bill includes $125 million in subsidies for dairy producers in Wisconsin.

Sen. Conrad Burns, R-Mont., said he would support the agreement because language was added requiring meatpackers to declare how much they pay livestock producers.

All of that nudged the bill toward the floor, despite complaints from farm groups and the U.S. Chamber of Commerce. Business groups favor lifting trade sanctions against Cuba and other nations with farm-export potential.

The Senate on Aug. 3 had voted 28-70 against a motion to table (kill) an effort to lift the sanctions.

"This is complete nonsense; it is buffoonery to take the will of 70 United States senators and say that doesn't count because we have a couple of people in the House leadership who say, 'We don't like this,' " said Chuck Hagel, R-Neb., on Sept. 29.

To Expedite Farm Relief, Senators Reluctantly Clear $69 Billion Bill

OCTOBER 16 — Congress sent President Clinton a $69 billion agriculture spending bill Oct. 13, despite complaints that the bill would shortchange growers in the East and sidestep a critical trade issue.

The fiscal 2000 bill (HR 1906 — conference report: H Rept 106-354) would provide a record-breaking $8.7 billion in emergency aid to farmers nationwide who have been hurt by low commodity prices, bad weather and barriers to overseas markets.

Agriculture Spending Highlights

Where the Money Goes

HR 1906 (Conference report: H Rept 106-354)

Spending Synopsis:

The $69 billion conference agreement, adopted by the House, 240-175, on Oct. 1, includes $8.7 billion in emergency aid to farmers. The measure, which funds agriculture and nutrition programs, increases discretionary spending by $296 million over the fiscal 1999 level. More than half the spending in the bill is for domestic food programs, including food stamps and other nutritional assistance. The agreement provides $649 million for the Food Safety and Inspection Service, a $32.4 million increase over fiscal 1999. The measure also funds the Food and Drug Administration (FDA), conservation programs, foreign agricultural assistance and rural economic development. About three-quarters of the bill's non-emergency spending is mandatory.

- **Agriculture programs**

The conference report provides $20 billion for agriculture programs, an increase of $5.6 billion over fiscal 1999 and $108 million less than President Clinton requested. Most of the increase reflects higher mandatory payments to the Commodity Credit Corporation, which finances commodity support programs and agricultural export subsidies. Low commodity prices have increased demand for Agriculture Department (USDA) loan programs.

- **Food and Drug Administration**

The bill provides the FDA with $1.1 billion, a $70 million increase over fiscal 1999 but $90 million less than the president's request. The FDA's tobacco program, enforcing age and photo identification requirements to buy tobacco products, was funded at $34 million, the same as in fiscal 1999.

- **Domestic food programs**

Child nutrition programs were funded at $9.6 billion, an increase of $377 million over fiscal 1999 and $11 million less than the president requested. The Women, Infants and Children (WIC) nutrition program was funded at $4 billion, an increase of $108 million over fiscal 1999 and $73 million less than Clinton's request. The school breakfast and lunch programs received $7 billion.

Hot-Button Issues

△ **Aid to farmers:** The agreement provides $8.7 billion in emergency aid to farmers facing declining prices for their produce or whose crops were destroyed by weather.

△ **Dairy policy:** Two provisions involving milk were not included. One would have extended the New England compact on milk pricing. The other would have prohibited USDA from ordering a new formula for milk subsidies.

△ **Sanctions:** The conference report did not include provisions that were in the Senate bill to lift sanctions against Cuba and allow exports of food and medicine.

△ **RU-486:** The report did not include House language that would have barred the FDA from approving abortion drugs, such as RU-486.

(figures are in thousands of dollars of new budget authority)

	Fiscal 1999 Appropriation	Fiscal 2000 Clinton Request	House Bill	Senate Bill	Conference Report
Agricultural programs	$14,481,998	$20,174,117	$19,961,493	$19,999,976	$20,066,454
Conservation programs	793,072	866,820	800,012	808,072	813,337
Rural economic and community development	2,175,234	2,194,349	2,136,508	2,184,449	2,213,135
Domestic food programs	34,817,199	41,381,688	35,530,668	35,546,075	35,044,275
Foreign assistance and related programs	1,196,718	1,056,853	1,157,191	1,062,908	1,063,686
Food and Drug Administration, related agencies	1,046,138	1,209,355	1,149,700	1,104,888	1,114,988
Other	–	–	1,000	3,250	2,250
Emergency farm aid	6,617,285	–	–	7,649,000	8,699,000
Loan authorizations	*(8,453,684)*	*(9,096,281)*	*(10,695,416)*	*(9,650,251)*	*(10,712,421)*
GRAND TOTAL	**$61,127,644**	**$66,883,182**	**$60,736,572**	**$68,358,618**	**$69,017,125**

TABLE: House and Senate Appropriations committees

The Senate cleared the report Oct. 13, 74-26. The House adopted the conference report Oct. 1, 240-175. Clinton is expected to sign it, opening the way for relief checks to begin flowing to farmers in a matter of weeks. *(Vote 323, p. S-64)*

Though the conference agreement was attacked on a number of fronts — both for what it did and did not contain and for the way it was negotiated — senators said they voted for it because they could not walk away from the aid for farmers even with the bill's flaws.

"This bill is not perfect, but it's fair," Herb Kohl, D-Wis., said Oct. 13.

Included in the $8.7 billion is $1.2 billion in direct assistance to farmers and livestock producers whose crops or animals were destroyed by drought or flooding. The emergency aid portion of the bill also would:

- Double the amount of money (to $5.5 billion) available to grain and cotton farmers through government contracts that are designed to help wean farmers from government subsidies and into a free-market economy.
- Provide $328 million to compensate tobacco growers for declining cigarette sales.
- Earmark $475 million for soybean and sunflower farmers to subsidize crop losses.
- Extend dairy price supports through fiscal 2001 so the government could continue buying surplus production.
- Provide $325 million in assistance to livestock and dairy producers to compensate them for low prices.
- Require meatpackers to start reporting the prices they pay for cattle and hogs to give ranchers more precise information about market prices.

"We think this is a generous response, but we know it's not enough to satisfy every single need," said Thad Cochran, R-Miss., chairman of the Appropriations Agriculture, Rural Development and Related Agencies Subcommittee.

Looking for More

Despite the relief package's unprecedented size, Democrats said it falls short of what is needed. They pledged to seek "at the very least" an additional $1 billion this year to help farmers in the mid-Atlantic states recover from a long drought.

That effort will be supported by Eastern lawmakers of both parties who said the aid package is tilted toward Midwestern farmers at a time when farmers in the East are recovering from a season of harsh weather.

"What is in this bill is not enough to take care of the needs of the farmers in my state," Rick Santorum, R-Pa., said Oct. 13 during floor debate. "The one time we ask for money, the answer is 'No.' "

Paul S. Sarbanes, D-Md., echoed Santorum: "The $1.2 billion that is in this bill is clearly inadequate."

Sarbanes and Santorum voted against the bill, in step with their colleagues from the region. All but six of the 26 senators who voted against the measure represent states stretching from Maine to Maryland.

In reality, however, the emergency money contained in the final version of the bill was a considerable step above the starting point for negotiators.

The Senate approved $7.4 billion in aid, while the House had included no relief money. The final amount — $8.7 billion — was a compromise between the original Senate position and the $10 billion in emergency aid that the Democrats had wanted.

Aside from relief money, two controversial provisions — on dairy pricing and the removal of sanctions on food and medicine exports to Cuba — were not included but attracted considerable attention during floor debate. The dairy debate pitted lawmakers from the Northeast against those in the Midwest who support a pricing plan advanced by the Clinton administration.

Pushing hardest were New England senators who wanted language extending the Northeast Dairy Compact. The compact, which expired Oct. 1 only to be extended by a federal judge, gave Northeastern farmers higher prices for milk and dairy products than the federal formula would allow. Producers from the Northeast insisted they would go out of business if the compact was dissolved.

Lawmakers from the upper Midwest, which is the center of the nation's dairy bucket, bitterly opposed the compact and succeeded in keeping it out of the conference agreement.

Senate negotiators also sought unsuccessfully to lift sanctions on selling food and medicine to nations such as Cuba. The matter was dropped after House conservatives opposed the move. Senators from farm states, including John Ashcroft, R-Mo., said the embargo hurts American farmers without achieving foreign policy goals.

"Farmers are getting, in my judgment, shortchanged," Ashcroft said. "They are getting short-term financial relief, but they have been robbed of good policy. Current U.S. policy favors foreign farmers not U.S. farmers."

The Senate on Aug. 3 had voted 28-70 against a motion to table (kill) a move to lift the sanctions.

On both the dairy and trade questions, critics complained that the matters were settled in private negotiations between Senate Majority Leader Trent Lott, R-Miss., and House Speaker J. Dennis Hastert, R-Ill. They forged the agreement after the conference committee was suspended.

Lost in much of the debate was the $60 billion in non-emergency spending for programs that have been used by farmers for generations.

The bill would provide $15.4 billion to the Commodity Credit Corporation to pay for a variety of farm price supports, programs to promote U.S. agricultural products overseas and the disposition of surplus commodities. The amount contained in the final report is $5.4 billion more than in fiscal 1999.

The agreement also approved $296 million for the Agricultural Credit Insurance Fund. The money would underwrite $3.1 billion in loans to farmers and ranchers to buy livestock, feed, seed and fertilizer, restructure debt and undertake environmentally responsible conservation practices.

Meat and Poultry

In another high-profile area, the final bill would provide $649 million for meat and poultry inspection. The total is 5 percent higher than in fiscal 1999 but $3.5 million less than the administration's request.

In a related area, the agreement called for $446 million for the Department of Agriculture's Animal and Plant Health Inspection Service. The service inspects and, if necessary, quarantines animals to protect livestock and plants from disease and pests. The total in the agreement would be $13 million more than in fiscal 1999 and $3.8 million more than the administration requested.

Conferees also provided $887 million for the Agricultural Research Service, which conducts and underwrites research related to plant and animal sciences; soil, water and air sciences; and agricultural engineering.

The total was a $45 million increase over fiscal 1999 and $5 million more than the administration requested.

Conferees also added money for conservation programs, but less than the administration requested.

The conference agreement called for $813 million in spending by the Agriculture Department's Natural Resources Conservation Service, $53 million less than Clinton wanted.

The agreement also contained $1.1 billion for direct housing loans to low-income families in rural areas, an amount equal to the administration's request but $238 million less than the House version.

Food Programs

While much of the attention over the $69 billion bill was directed to disaster relief, trade policy and dairy programs, the most expensive programs involved domestic food programs.

In all, the conference agreement would provide $35 billion in fiscal 2000, $227 million more than in 1999, for such programs as food stamps ($21.1 billion) and the Women, Infants and Children supplemental food program ($4.0 billion).

In another major account, the conferees provided $1.1 billion for the Food and Drug Administration (FDA). The total was $33 million less than approved by the House and $90 million less than the administration's request. It was $70 million more than in fiscal 1999.

One major loss for the administration was in tobacco policy. Conferees agreed to provide $34 million to implement FDA-approved programs to reduce youth smoking. The administration wanted $68 million.

But in a victory for abortion-rights supporters, conferees severed House language that would have prohibited the FDA from using any federal money to test, develop or approve abortion drugs such as RU-486.

Another little-noticed item that was slipped into the final bill prohibited the use of federal funds to implement the Kyoto Treaty on global warming.

The United States signed the treaty in 1997 along with 167 other nations, but it has yet to be ratified. The treaty, which has been bitterly attacked by critics in Congress, calls for the United States to reduce greenhouse gas emissions (which are primarily carbon) to 7 percent below 1990 levels no later than 2012. *(1998 Almanac, p. 2-101)*

Congressional critics were adamant that none of Kyoto's provisions be implemented before the treaty is ratified. ◆

After Initial Veto, GOP and Clinton Split the Differences On Commerce-Justice-State

SUMMARY

President Clinton vetoed the first appropriations bill (HR 2670) for the departments of Commerce, Justice and State (CJS), the federal judiciary and 14 agencies, complaining it would not have provided enough for his priorities and could have jeopardized the U.S. seat in the United Nations General Assembly. Negotiators then drafted a second bill that both sides said split the difference between Republican and presidential wishes. Congress cleared the $39.6 billion package as part of the comprehensive legislation that included five of the 13 fiscal 2000 appropriations measures.

Evidence that a middle ground had been found appears on the bottom line of the second CJS bill. The grand total is $625 million, or 1.6 percent, more than that of the vetoed version. It is also $669 million, or 1.7 percent, under what the president had requested, if scorekeeping adjustments agreed to by both sides are factored in. This accounting does not count, for example, the $9.3 billion Clinton wanted Congress to commit to spending now even though the money would not be needed until future years. On the CJS bill, most of this "forward funding" was sought for a sweeping plan to upgrade embassy security.

Absent scorekeeping adjustments, the final CJS measure allocated $39.6 billion, or 9 percent more than in fiscal 1999, which ended Sept. 30.

One of the last items settled by negotiators allowed the State Department to send $926 million to the United Nations, thereby making good on years of back dues. In return, Clinton agreed to support legislation (HR 3427), also rolled into the omnibus package, reviving some abortion restrictions on international family planning assistance. *(State Department authorization, p. 14-3)*

Clinton claimed as his biggest domestic policy victory in the bill its $595 million for the Community Oriented Policing Services program, created under the 1994 anti-crime law (PL 103-322) to fulfill Clinton's promise during his first run for president to boost the local police rolls by 100,000. The first CJS bill provided just 25 percent of what he requested; the second version gave him almost half. The Republicans claimed victory here, too, because they insisted on directing $523 million to the Local Law Enforcement Block Grant, to which the president had wanted to dedicate nothing.

The Commerce Department budget soared under the bill, from $5.2 billion to $8.7 billion, but only because all sides agreed to give the Census Bureau all $4.5 billion it requested to conduct the 2000 census.

How the census was to be conducted had been one of the biggest disputes over the CJS appropriations bill the previous two years. But the Supreme Court went a long way toward resolving the dispute with a ruling in January that while a direct head count must be used to apportion House seats among states, so-called statistical sampling could be used to generate population figures that would be used to allocate federal aid and draw political boundaries within states. Next year's census will draw up both sets of numbers.

The CJS bill the Senate passed in July (S 1217) would have expanded the federal jurisdiction to prosecute hate crimes, in part by making offenses motivated by a victim's sexual orientation, gender or disability subject to such prosecution. Only acts motivated by racial, religious or ethnic bias are now covered. Clinton endorsed this, but Republican negotiators on both sides of the Capitol insisted on dropping it.

The Legal Services Corporation, the quasi-public agency that provides lawyers for the poor, survived another year of GOP criticism; it got $305 million for fiscal 2000, a $5 million increase and $55 million more than originally approved by the House. The Small Business Administration got a 22 percent boost, some to pay for a disaster loan program the president pushed. The Advanced Technology Program, which gives businesses money to research potential technological breakthroughs, survived a GOP move to terminate it but with $143 million, a deep cut.

The bill also denied a $20 million request by Clinton to fund Justice Department litigation against tobacco companies; provided $10 million — Clinton sought $27 million — for a special counterterrorism fund; and increased funding for the National Oceanic and Atmospheric Administration by 8 percent, to $2.3 billion.

Box Score

Commerce-Justice-State

- **Bill:** HR 3421 (incorporated by reference in HR 3194) — PL 106-113
- **Legislative action: Senate** passed S 1217 (S Rept 106-76) by voice vote July 22.

House passed HR 2670 (H Rept 106-283), 217-210, Aug. 5.

House adopted the conference report on HR 2670 (H Rept 106-398), 215-213, and **Senate** cleared by voice vote Oct. 20.

President vetoed HR 2670 on Oct. 25.

House adopted conference report on HR 3194 (H Rept 106-479), incorporating HR 3421, 296-135, Nov. 18.

Senate cleared HR 3194, 74-24, Nov. 19.

President signed HR 3194 Nov. 29.

CJS Bill Runs Smoothly Through Senate Panels

JUNE 12 — Legislation to fund fiscal 2000 spending for programs run by the Commerce, Justice and State departments moved smoothly through the

Senate committee process the week of June 7. But the measure may hit choppy waters when it reaches the Senate floor, and it drew the Clinton administration's first appropriations veto threat of the year.

Voting 28-0, the Senate Appropriations Committee approved the $35.3 billion measure June 10, following voice vote approval by the Commerce, Justice, State Subcommittee the day before. According to Appropriations Chairman Ted Stevens, R-Alaska, it was the "earliest date on record" that the usually contentious measure has been ready for the Senate floor.

The committee did not release spending details, saying that specific amounts would be available the week of June 14. But according to numbers obtained from members' statements and staff aides, the bill would allocate $35.3 billion in total spending, with nearly half that designated for myriad law enforcement programs run by the Justice Department. The Commerce Department would receive $7.2 billion, while the State Department and its related agencies would get about $5.4 billion.

The hurried and mostly uneventful debate contrasted sharply with arguments last year over funding for the 2000 census. Then, appropriators were mired in a dispute over whether the Census Bureau should be allowed to use a method known as statistical sampling to augment traditional head counts.

The administration has argued that sampling, which relies on scientific population estimates, better accounts for hard-to-reach residents, including immigrants and minorities, who are sometimes missed by traditional counting methods. Republicans insist that sampling is not an "actual enumeration," as called for in the Constitution.

The Supreme Court ruled Jan. 25 that the Census Bureau could not use statistical sampling as a basis for apportioning congressional seats, but left open the possibility of using sampling for other purposes, such as determining the amounts of federal money states receive.

The Clinton administration has interpreted the ruling in a way that would allow sampling to provide population numbers for intrastate redistricting and for distributing federal funds.

During full committee markup of the measure, Richard J. Durbin, D-Ill., sharply questioned the $3 billion allocation for the census. "There are some glaring omissions in this bill," he said, arguing the funding shortfall would "virtually guarantee another undercount."

Money disputes are likely to continue. While subcommittee members touted a fully funded census, the panel did not provide the additional $1.7 billion requested by the White House; census officials and Democrats argue that amount is needed to pay for requirements that resulted from the court ruling. Subcommittee Chairman Judd Gregg, R-N.H., said he would hold hearings to determine whether all of the spending is needed, and whether offsets suggested by the administration to pay for the additional funds are legitimate.

COPS vs. Border Control

About half the spending in the bill would fund Justice Department law enforcement programs. That total includes $2.9 billion for the FBI, $1.2 billion for the Drug Enforcement Administration and $3.7 billion to run the federal prison system. More than $400 million was included for new embassy security and maintenance programs.

Subcommittee Democrats were disappointed that the bill would decrease funding for the Community Oriented Policing Service (COPS) program, providing about $650 million less than the $1.2 billion requested. The committee included $180 million for police officers in schools under the program, and about $375 million for crime-fighting technology, but Clinton requested more money to hire additional officers.

In a letter dated June 10, White House budget director Jack Lew threatened a veto recommendation, saying the bill's funding levels could not pay for current law enforcement staff and lamented the sharp reductions in COPS funding. The 1994 program was designed to enable local police departments to hire additional officers. *(1994 Almanac, p. 273)*

Gregg said Clinton proposed COPS funding at the expense of Border Patrol activities. The issue dominated full committee debate. The measure includes about $4 billion for the Immigration and Naturalization Service, which, along with the Customs Service and the Drug Enforcement Agency, conducts most border control activity. Some of the funds would be designated to hire 1,000 additional agents to beef up security along the U.S.-Mexico line.

Senate Passes Bill As House Panel OKs Its Version

JULY 24 — After several weeks in a stall, bills to finance the federal judiciary and the departments of Commerce, Justice and State in fiscal 2000 advanced with superficial ease on both sides of the Capitol within a few hours of one another July 22.

But both measures call for cutting spending on a wide array of programs below both this year's levels and President Clinton's budget request — foretelling a round of difficult negotiations by this fall among the House, the Senate and the administration.

The House Commerce-Justice-State (CJS) Appropriations Subcommittee approved its $35.8 billion draft measure on a voice vote. But that happened only after the House leadership decided to designate $4.5 billion needed to pay for the 2000 census as an "emergency" not subject to budgetary caps — even though the Constitution calls for a census every decade and this one has been in the planning stages throughout the 1990s.

The Senate passed its bill (S 1217) by voice vote after Majority Leader Trent Lott, R-Miss., decided against using the measure to force a vote on whether senators should be restricted in attaching policy legislation to appropriations. Instead, he cut a deal with Democrats to debate the question July 26.

The Senate bill includes a major victory for Clinton and congressional Democrats — language by Edward M. Kennedy, D-Mass., that would add crimes motivated by a victim's sexual orientation, gender or disability to the roster of federal hate crimes. Currently, race, color, religion or national origin are covered by a law (PL 90-284) enacted in 1968 that first authorized federal prosecution for hate crimes.

Clinton praised the Senate for adopting the amendment — it did so by voice vote and without debate — and urged the House to "meet its responsibility in combating violence that is fueled by hate" by endorsing Kennedy's language.

Still, the Office of Management and Budget said it would urge Clinton to veto the Senate bill. A similar threat will probably be delivered to the House when its version of the CJS bill reaches the floor — unless the measure is radically overhauled by the full Appropriations Committee, which is not likely.

In any event, aides in both chambers said the troublesome funding levels and policy disputes in the CJS bill mean it is likely to end up as part of a package of the most contentious spending bills that House and Senate leaders are expected to negotiate with the administration this fall.

Both the House and Senate bills would make big cuts in politically popular — and in some cases required — programs. Both, for example, call for the first cuts to major federal crime-fighting programs since the beginning of the Clinton administration.

The Senate bill would deny Clinton the request he made this spring for an additional $1.7 billion to conduct the census, although appropriators plan to convene a hearing the week of July 26 to consider that request.

The shortfalls are a consequence of the tighter caps on discretionary spending instituted by the law (PL 105-33) designed to carry out the 1997 deal between Clinton and Congress on how to ensure a balanced federal budget. The squeeze is made more acute in fiscal 2000 because the Census Bureau, an arm of the Commerce Department, says it needs an increase of approximately $3.4 billion to employ the armies of people necessary to count the nation's population next spring.

'Emergency' Escape Hatch

Other parts of the House bill would have been subject to even more draconian cuts had the funding for the census not been given its "emergency" designation, which exempts it from the caps. Prior to that GOP decision, the CJS subcommittee's allocation had already been raided to ease the spending shortfalls in several other spending bills that were further along in the legislative process.

Subcommittee Chairman Harold Rogers, R-Ky., said the emergency declaration was the only way of funding the census without gutting the rest of the bill. Appropriations Committee Chairman C.W. Bill Young, R-Fla., said the designation was necessary to create "a passable bill." They offered no other rationale for designating the census spending as an emergency.

David R. Obey of Wisconsin, ranking Democrat on the Appropriations Committee, replied that — even with this census spending maneuver — the cuts were so deep that widespread Republican support should be in doubt.

He did not object to the emergency designation for the census, but quipped that, "I guess this means we didn't see it coming."

Wide Array of Cuts

Overall the House bill would provide $18.1 billion to the Department of Justice, essentially the same as in fiscal 1999 but $314 million below what Clinton requested. The Commerce Department would receive $8.1 billion, a $3 billion increase above this year — and all of that related to the census. The State Department and related international programs would receive $5.7 billion, or $1.2 billion less than this year and $506 million less than Clinton's request. The federal judiciary would get $3.9 billion, a $272 million increase from fiscal 1999 but a $234 million decrease from what the president sought.

The bill would cut spending on dozens of programs. The Community Oriented Policing Service (COPS) program — created to carry out Clinton's campaign promise to allow local police departments to to hire 100,000 new officers — would receive only $268 million. With the violent crime trust fund created to support the COPS program as part of the 1994 crime law (PL 103-322) in its last year, the amount the House would appropriate is all that is authorized. *(1994 Almanac, p. 273)*

Clinton and most Democrats want to extend the program. The president requested $1.3 billion to do that, slightly less than this year's allocation.

The bill would restore funding for a host of block grant programs that Republicans favor as an alternative to the COPS program. This to-and-fro has taken place most of the years Republicans have controlled the House, with Clinton including nothing for block grants and the GOP restoring funds.

The opposite generally occurs with the Legal Services Corporation, which provides legal representation to the poor. Its funding would be more than halved under the House bill, to $141 million. If the pattern of past years is repeated, in the end the corporation budget will approximate Clinton's $340 million request.

The Advanced Technology Program, which provides grants to businesses to develop marketable technologies, would be eliminated. It received $203 million this year and Clinton sought $238 million for next year.

Many of these cuts are unpopular with Democrats, but influential Republicans are balking as well. Rogers said he was far from happy with the allocation he received. His bill's grand total needs to be $37.2 billion just to keep current services in fiscal 2000 while paying for the census, he said.

Senate Version

The Senate bill divides up its pot into amounts roughly equivalent to the House bill. Justice would receive $17 billion, Commerce would get $7.2 billion and the State total would be $5.4 billion.

Like the House bill, the Senate measure does not come anywhere near Clinton's request for the COPS program. In fact, Judd Gregg, R-N.H., chairman of the Senate CJS Appropriations Subcommittee, initially proposed no funding for the program.

But by voice vote senators adopted an amendment by Joseph R. Biden Jr., D-Del., to maintain funding.

Debate on the Senate measure was originally expected to take several days, but eventually was condensed to several hours once a critical mass of senators served notice they would not be in Washington July 23. Four attended services in New York for John F. Kennedy Jr., the son of the former president and a nephew of the senator, who died July 16 in a private plane crash.

In the end, some three dozen amendments were bundled together and approved, without debate, by voice vote.

The hate crimes language was the most significant of these. In addition to the sweeping Kennedy language, the package included a competing proposal by Orrin G. Hatch, R-Utah, that would create grants for the states to combat hate crimes.

"We'll do our best to have a meeting of the minds" before a conference with the House begins, Hatch said. "If not, they'll both be dropped."

Hatch has raised questions about the constitutionality of the Kennedy provision, because the Supreme Court has struck down a number of federal laws recently on grounds that Congress had overstepped its authority.

The Kennedy provision would expand federal jurisdiction over hate crimes. The 1968 law covers such crimes only if they take place on federal property or are committed against someone engaged in a federally protected activity, such as going to school. Kennedy would expand that jurisdiction to cover any activity that could be linked to interstate commerce. Supporters say the provision was crafted to avoid the types of federalism objections raised by the Supreme Court.

The House bill contains no hate crimes provision, and it is far from certain that the Senate language will survive in conference. But David Smith, a spokesman for the Human Rights Campaign, a group advocating gay rights, said after the Senate bill passed: "We're feeling pretty good this morning."

Violent Crime Fund

One amendment not included in the final package was one prepared by Gregg to reauthorize the violent crime trust fund, which pays for not only the COPS program but also for a competing Republican violent crime block grant and a host of other local law enforcement efforts.

The amendment was apparently designed as a vehicle for GOP efforts to overturn a Senate precedent set in 1995 making it easier to add legislative riders to appropriations bills — a move engineered by the GOP when it came to power but often used since by Democrats searching for a well-fueled legislative vehicle for their favorite policy initiatives. Gregg withdrew his amendments once Lott — after negotiations with Minority Leader Tom Daschle, D-S.D., that put the Senate into a quiet quorum call for much of July 22 — arranged for a showdown vote July 26.

The stall in the debate produced by this tussle — and the fact that the bill and all the amendments to it were endorsed by voice vote — masks the problems the CJS bill faces.

Before the Senate took up the bill, Clinton issued an eight-page laundry list of complaints, most of them dealing with inadequate funding levels.

He cited the census shortfall; the lack of complete COPS funding; a $165 million cut in the budget for the Economic Development Administration, which provides grants in low-income areas; the denial of the administration's request for funds to build an array of new U.S. embassies; inadequate funding to pay the U.S. debts to the United Nations and other international organizations; and a lack of funding to manage the national instant check system contained in the 1993 Brady law (PL 103-159).

Ignoring Veto Talk, House Committee Makes Major Cuts

JULY 31 — Putting aside charges that its unpalatable cuts and budget chicanery will spur a veto, the House Appropriations Committee approved a $35.8 billion bill July 30 to fund the departments of Commerce, Justice and State (CJS), and the federal judiciary.

The draft measure, endorsed by voice vote, is one of several fiscal 2000 spending bills that — because of the spending caps set by the 1997 budget-balancing law (PL 105-33) — would allocate billions less than what Democrats and many Republicans believe is prudent, let alone politically realistic. The CJS bill would cut spending on an array of crime-fighting programs and lower payments to international organizations, and would pay for next spring's census — which the Constitution called for two centuries ago — only by declaring it an unanticipated budgetary emergency exempt from the caps. Overall, the bill would allocate 8 percent less than President Clinton requested.

"I'm here to tell you that the piper is here to be paid," said Harold Rogers, R-Ky., chairman of the Appropriations CJS subcommittee, wondering aloud if Congress realized the consequences of the caps when it set them in 1997.

David R. Obey of Wisconsin, the top Democrat on the full committee, complained that the measure was only helping Congress procrastinate until fall on an inevitable increase in discretionary spending limits. He accused Republican leaders of forcing Appropriations Committee Chairman C.W. Bill Young, R-Fla., to move unrealistic bills based on the best available forecasts from the Congressional Budget Office, the Office of Management and Budget, or the Wizard of Oz. Young did not disagree with this assessment.

"I don't know if I'm the Wizard of Oz or the Wicked Witch of the West," he said. "But I can guarantee you I am going to click my heels three times and we are going to move on."

Among the biggest cuts in the bill would be an appropriation of $268 million — $1 billion less than Clinton asked — for the Community Oriented Policing Services (COPS) program, which the Justice Department says is unlikely to meet Clinton's goal of paying for 100,000 new local police by the end of his tenure. The president wants to extend the program; the committee allotment would fund COPS at its authorized level for its final authorized year.

The bill would more than halve, to $141 million, funding for the Legal Services Corporation, which provides counsels for the poor. Eliminated outright would be the Advanced Technology Program, which subsidizes research that may have commercial applications. For fiscal 1999, it received $203 million.

Jose E. Serrano, D-N.Y., proposed an amendment to partially lift the U.S. embargo on Cuba by allowing food and medicine sales. It was rejected, 23-29.

Obey proposed two amendments to remove the emergency designation for census funding, saying his aim was to force the House to make up its mind now to break the spending caps. Both were rejected on party-line votes.

And the Senate, after initially casting a wary eye on the emergency designation, may now be willing to go along. Chairman Ted Stevens, R-Alaska, indicated as much after a Senate Appropriations Committee hearing July 29. But Judd Gregg, R-N.H., chairman of the Senate CJS Appropriations Subcommittee, still opposes the designation, aides said the next day.

The president initially requested $2.8 billion but asked for $1.7 billion more in response to a Supreme Court ruling that, he said, requires one population count with the use of statistical sampling and another without sampling.

Nothing To Fight Cyber Sabotage

The House bill provides no money for the administration's desire for the FBI to begin a program to monitor government and private computer communications in a bid to curb cyberterrorism. The report accompanying the bill specifically prohibits spending on the effort.

The program has come under sharp criticism by both civil libertarians and congressional conservatives, who fear it could lead to invasions of privacy. The plan "raises the Orwellian possibility that unscrupulous government bureaucrats could use such a system to read our personal e-mail," House Majority Leader Dick Armey, R-Texas, said in a statement.

The House report on CJS is critical of an array of agencies and programs. It describes many administrative problems at the Immigration and Naturalization Service but does not propose restructuring it. Rogers supports dividing the agency in two but has decided to propose separate legislation (HR 2528) to that end.

House Passes Bill Despite White House Criticisms

AUGUST 7 — For the past two years, Republicans and Democrats in the House vehemently disagreed on the conduct of the upcoming census every time they took up legislation that would fund it. But in the fiscal 2000 appropriations bill for the departments of Commerce, Justice and State (CJS) and the federal judiciary, the census became the one thing the two sides agreed on.

During two days of debate on the $35.8 billion House version of the measure (HR 2670), camps that had been ideologically opposed on how the census should be conducted next spring banded together to thwart an attack on the funding mounted by fiscal conservatives.

But the vote to pass the bill was 217-210, largely along party lines, the night of Aug. 5. It was the 11th and last appropriations measure the House produced before leaving on its summer recess. *(Vote 387, p. H-126)*

That ballot illustrated that, while the census may have finally faded as the bellwether for controversy on this bill, there are plenty of other issues that congressional Democrats and President Clinton cannot abide. And the cuts in law enforcement, business regulation and diplomatic overhead have enough lawmakers in both parties — and on both sides of the Capitol — grumbling that assembling a conference agreement with the Senate would be difficult.

Since the GOP took control of Congress four years ago, only one CJS spending bill, for fiscal 1998, has been enacted as a distinct law. Appropriators had been preparing to wrap the fiscal 2000 bill, once again, into a package containing several of the most contentious appropriations bills. But Majority Whip Tom DeLay, R-Texas, said Aug. 5 that he would oppose creation of such an omnibus package.

As the House debate opened, the Clinton administration released what could only be called an epic-length veto threat: 40 separate criticisms of the bill, from its deep cut in the Community Oriented Policing Service (COPS) program; to its failure to heed the president's request for a big down payment on a massive capital improvement program for U.S. embassies; to its elimination of subsidies for research on technologies with potential commercial uses.

Rare Consensus

But CJS Appropriations Subcommittee Chairman Harold Rogers, R-Ky., and the panel's ranking Democrat, Jose E. Serrano of New York, tried to focus the debate on a rare accord. "The census is the one thing we worked on together, where we reached some agreement," Serrano said in an interview.

Since 1997, the fight has been about whether census-takers should limit themselves to a head count in which they sought to contact every household in the country — the GOP position — or whether to acknowledge the impossibility of that task and use extrapolation techniques known as statistical sampling to supplement it — the Democratic position. The dispute was settled this year by providing money for both. The decision was aided by a Supreme Court ruling that results of a head count must be used to apportion House seats among states for the next decade, but that redistricting within states and federal aid allocations could be based on a statistically adjusted census.

This year, the fight against census spending was led by Tom Coburn, R-Okla., a leading critic of the GOP leadership's fiscal policies. He sought to strip $2.8 billion from the $4.5 billion for the census to protest that the overall measure would breach the spending caps in the 1997 budget-balancing law (PL 105-33) — but would not violate that law because the census spending is classified as an "emergency" and therefore exempt from the caps.

Republican leaders opted for the emergency designation last month when it became clear they could not fund a $3.4 billion increase in census funding needed to hire an army of census-takers for next spring without gutting other portions of the bill.

"Dare we pull the wool over the American people's eyes by declaring an emergency?" Coburn asked. He said that by violating the spirit of the caps, if not the letter, Congress would spend money that should be reserved for shoring up Social Security.

That argument won the votes of GOP conservatives. His accusation of chicanery won the votes of Democrats eager to protest what they saw as a folly in describing an event mandated by the Constitution as an unanticipated emergency. But the amendment was defeated, 171-257, as a majority concluded that a rare agreement on the census should not be upended by a desire to make a statement on spending. *(Vote 374, p. H-122)*

Major Spending Cuts

Even with the emergency designation for the census, the bill stays nominally within its constraints — to allocate $400 million, or 1 percent, less than this year — only by making major cuts in crime-fighting, the Legal Services Corporation, the Small Business Administration and other programs.

"The problem with this bill is that it simply is not real," said David R.

Obey, of Wisconsin, ranking Democrat on the Appropriations Committee.

"This is the bare bones," replied Rogers. "It's based on a freeze, with reductions where we could."

Topping the administration's list of complaints about the bill was that it would cut the president's request for the COPS program by more than $1 billion, to $268 million. The program was designed to allow Clinton to fulfill his 1992 campaign promise to help local governments hire as many as 100,000 new police officers. It has remained his highest- profile plan to combat crime. Created by the 1994 omnibus crime law (PL 103-322) as a five-year program, without an extension it would be phased out in the next year. *(1994 Almanac, p. 273)*

Clinton wants to keep the program going, either by extending the violent crime trust fund that has been its main funding source — it also was created in the 1994 law — or by appropriating general Treasury revenue for it.

Many Republicans would like to see the program end, although they do not necessarily want to see anti-crime funding created by the 1994 law dry up. They have their own crime-fighting program, a more open-ended block grant, to which the bill would dedicate $523 million, the same as this year.

Minority Whip David E. Bonior, D-Mich., tried to send the bill back to the Appropriations Committee with orders to give Clinton what he wanted for COPS. His motion was rejected along party lines, 208-219. *(Vote 386, p. H-126)*

In addition to the cut in the COPS program, the administration also complained that the bill would prohibit the collection of any fee to fund the National Instacheck System, the database authorized by the 1993 Brady law (PL 103-159) to aid gun purchase background checks. Congress has consistently blocked collection of such a fee.

The database would get much more use if negotiators on juvenile justice legislation (HR 1501), who convened Aug. 5, decide that buyers at gun shows should be subject to such background screenings.

John D. Dingell, D-Mich., a leading gun rights advocate, offered but then withdrew an amendment to require states to provide more complete records for the Instacheck system.

Among the other reasons the administration objected to the House bill:

- It would cut to $10 million the administration's $27 million request for a counterterrorism fund. GOP say this fund, which is supposed to pay for unexpected missions to thwart terrorism, has instead been improperly used to develop new programs not authorized by Congress. The bill would block any spending on the Federal Intrusion Detection Network, or FIDNet, an FBI project to monitor government and private computers in order to stop cyber-terrorism.
- It would deny funding for the Justice Department to engage in litigation against tobacco companies in the absence of a law setting a new national tobacco policy. *(1998 Almanac, p. 15-3)*
- It would deny advanced appropriations of $3.6 billion for beefing up security at U.S embassies.
- It would freeze the Securities and Exchange Commission (SEC) budget at this year's level of $324 million, which the administration says would force the elimination of 300 positions and could slow prosecution of stock market malfeasance. With market activity at record levels because of the economic boom, the SEC sought a $37 million increase.
- It would eliminate the Advanced Technology Program, which is spending $203 million this year on research into technology with potentially marketable applications.
- It would cut the administration's request for the National Oceanic and Atmospheric Administration by $208 million, with major cuts to ocean research, Pacific coast salmon recovery and the Lands Legacy Initiative, which helps restore oceans and coastal areas.
- It would hold the Small Business Administration budget to $734.5 million, in part by not paying for an $85 million loan program to distressed inner cities and rural areas.

Points of Contention

Debate began with consideration of a perennial controversy: how much to help the Legal Services Corporation, a quasi-public agency that provides attorneys to the poor. Critics say the corporation is rife with abuse and too quick to take on politically charged causes like challenging labor laws or getting involved in abortion litigation. But by 242-178, the House raised the appropriation to $250 million from the committee's proposal of $141 million. The corporation is receiving $300 million this year. *(Vote 370, p. H-122)*

Despite that loss, Majority Leader Dick Armey, R-Texas, a longtime foe of the program, declared himself satisfied that the amendment did not ask for more money. "I think we were able to raise some serious questions about practices at LSC," Armey said.

United Nations funding was another flash point in the debate.

As in fiscal 1998 and 1999, the House bill would pay some of the United States' back dues to the United Nations, but the money — $244 million for fiscal 2000 — could not be spent unless separate legislation is enacted requiring the United Nations to trim its budget and otherwise revamp its bureaucracy. The Senate has passed such requirements in its State Department reauthorization bill (S 886), but the issue faces rough passage in conference with the House-passed bill (HR 2415) because conservatives want to use the bill to restrict aid to international family planning agencies.

Tony P. Hall, D-Ohio, a staunch anti-abortion lawmaker, nonetheless offered an amendment to remove the policy restrictions on the payment of arrearages. His amendment was rejected, 206-221. *(Vote 380, p. H-124)*

In another debate related to abortion, the House defeated, 160-268, an amendment by Diana DeGette, D-Colo., that would have stripped language from the bill that bars federal payments for abortions for federal prisoners in almost all circumstances. *(Vote 373, p. H-122)*

The House rejected, 169-256, an amendment by Dennis J. Kucinich, D-Ohio, and Charles Bass, R-N.H., directing the Federal Communications Commission (FCC) to enact a plan by March to slow the proliferation of telephone area codes by devising a more efficient way of assigning telephone numbers. *(Vote 381, p. H-124)*

But overall, the FCC was still another agency that did not get what the president requested. The bill would freeze current spending at $192 million, almost all of it derived from fee revenues. The administration sought a boost of $39 million, to pay for more broadcast regulators.

Congress Clears Compromise Bill; Confrontation With Clinton Looms

OCTOBER 23 — Enhanced by additional spending but still unacceptable to President Clinton, a $39 billion appropriations measure to finance the federal judiciary and the departments of Commerce, Justice and State (CJS) for the rest of fiscal 2000 has been cleared by Congress.

But the package (HR 2670) appears to stand no chance of surviving in its current form. If it is vetoed, as the president has threatened, Republicans are suggesting they will abandon some of the concessions to administration spending priorities that they made in a bid to make the bill more appealing to both Clinton and congressional Democrats. And the next round of deliberations will occur as part of horse-trading between the White House and GOP leaders on not only the CJS provisions but also on as many as four other spending bills.

Hanging over those talks will be the fact that the compromise CJS legislation survived by only the narrowest margin in the House. The vote to adopt the conference report on Oct. 20 was 215-213, and the outcome was only assured after a small cluster of Republicans who waited to cast their ballots late in the roll call broke narrowly in favor of the deal. *(Vote 518, p. H-168)*

But with no debate, the measure was cleared by the Senate on a voice vote later that day, masking the size of the reservoir of opposition to the package there. Senators were also not called upon to cast recorded votes on their original version of the CJS bill — making this the first spending measure since the fiscal 1998 District of Columbia bill, enacted two years ago, cleared by Congress without a Senate roll call.

Until GOP leaders begin bargaining in earnest with the administration, Senate Democrats said they would take a similarly passive approach to other appropriations conference reports. "Assuming that no agreement has been reached, we want to expedite the vetoes," Minority Leader Tom Daschle, D-S.D., said Oct. 21.

That strategy was not followed in the House, where 13 Democrats — including the party's four members on the CJS appropriations subcommittee — voted for the conference report. Seventeen Republicans — a combination of fiscal conservatives, who said the bill would spend too much, and border- state lawmakers opposed over an obscure immigration provision — voted against it.

The Democratic split, with the leadership opposing the bill and some appropriators supporting it, gave Republicans an easy opening.

"The Democratic leadership wants to do anything they can to stop progress," said John Feehery, spokesman for Speaker J. Dennis Hastert, R-Ill. "The president and congressional Republicans want to get something done in a bipartisan manner. The Democratic leadership is so desperate to take back the House, they'd rather do nothing."

But senior Democratic aides reported that Minority Leader Richard A. Gephardt, D-Mo., promised Clinton during a White House meeting Oct. 19 that he could rally sufficient Democratic support to sustain any veto of an appropriations bill.

Boosted Funding

Overall, the CJS conference report would allocate 8 percent more in spending than the comparable law for fiscal 1999, which lapsed three weeks ago. While the compromise would still appropriate $10.6 billion less than Clinton requested, it would spend $1.4 billion more than under the bill the House passed on Aug. 5 and $3.6 billion more than the version the Senate passed on July 22.

The Department of Commerce and a handful of related agencies would get a 68 percent increase, to $8.7 billion, although more than half would be used to conduct the 2000 census. As the House had proposed this summer, the entire $4.5 billion requested by the administration for that effort was declared an "emergency" so that the spending would not count toward the budget caps set by the 1997 law (PL 105-33) designed to ensure a balanced budget.

Next year's effort has been made especially complicated and expensive, because the Census Bureau is planning to end years of squabbling with parallel population counts, one with statistical sampling to augment the traditional head count. Nonetheless, the emergency declaration has been labeled by Democrats as ridiculous for an event the Constitution anticipated two centuries ago.

The judicial branch would receive an 8 percent funding increase under the bill, to $4 billion, including an 11 percent boost in spending on court security and a 3.4 percent raise for federal judges, a cost of living increase in line with what members of Congress have allowed themselves for next year.

The Justice Department would receive $18.5 billion, about 2 percent more than what was appropriated for the past year. Among the winners within the department was the Antitrust Division, which would gain a 12 percent increase to $110 million despite reportedly intense lobbying to cut the division's funding by the Microsoft Corp., whose software marketing practices have made it the defendant in one of the most significant antitrust case in decades.

The State Department would receive $6 billion, 8 percent more than during the past year.

It was the increases in spending that prompted Jose E. Serrano of New York, the top Democrat on the CJS subcommittee, to describe the final version as "improved dramatically" from what the House first passed. He specifically commended the conferees' provisions for the Legal Services Corporation, the quasi-public agency that provides lawyers to the poor. The final bill would allocate it $300 million, the same as in fiscal 1999 and $50 million more than in the House bill, albeit $40 million below Clinton's request.

Another winner in conference was the Small Business Administration (SBA), which had outlined a round of widespread layoffs it said it would be forced to make under the modest increases in the initial House and Senate versions. But the bill sent to Clinton would boost the agency's budget by 12 percent, to $804 million.

"While the bill is now a lot better for the SBA, it's still a long way from closure," said Debra Silimeo, the agency's top spokesman. "The problem is it's part of a bill that's part of a veto threat."

Connected to the Endgame

Clinton has threatened to veto the CJS bill and four other spending measures unless he becomes satisfied with the overall spending figures and policy decisions at the end of the budget process. But despite Clinton's urging that Congress work with him to develop a broad spending plan, Republicans pressed ahead the week of Oct. 18 with efforts to finish the last of the 13 spending bills as free-standing measures.

The morning after a bipartisan chorus of cooperative statements were voiced following an Oct. 19 White House meeting between Clinton and congressional leaders, House Democrats called the CJS measure an integral piece of a very flawed picture.

"Republicans cannot see the forest for the trees, and the president has said no more signing of the trees until we see the forest," Gephardt told the House. "If we insist in rolling out phony bills . . . we will be here at Thanksgiving and maybe even Christmas."

Democrats accused Republicans of using creative accounting to keep the spending measures under the budget caps, and they cited the census provision as Exhibit A. "This bill tries to fund a lot of worthwhile programs, but it does so with some pretty incredible gimmicks," David R. Obey of Wisconsin, the top Democrat on the Appropriations Committee, told the House.

"I'm a little tired of this carping," Senate Appropriations Committee Chairman Ted Stevens, R-Alaska, said on Oct. 18, when the CJS conferees met to ratify their agreement. "Our numbers are no more phony than the president's."

House Republicans later responded to Clinton's threat with one of their own. "If this bill is vetoed, I promise you it will come back in a much different form," CJS Appropriations subcommittee Chairman Harold Rogers, R-Ky., said on the House floor.

Asked later what he meant by that, Rogers replied: "We tried to accommodate the president's priorities as best we could within limited funds. . . . We will revert to our priorities on the new bill if this is vetoed."

Reasons for a Veto?

Even as the conferees restored some of the funding cuts that had been featured in earlier veto threats, they left out enough other presidential priorities to make the Democrats confident the final version would be rejected as well.

Topping that list is the $325 million appropriation for the Community Oriented Policing Service (COPS) program, which is barely 25 percent of what the president requested to maintain his highest-profile initiative for combating crime. Created by the 1994 crime law (PL 103-322) to fulfill Clinton's campaign promise to help boost the local police rolls by 100,000 officers, its authorization expires next year. *(1994 Almanac, p. 273)*

While largely spurning the COPS program, the conferees more than tripled spending, to $1.8 billion, on a collection of block grants to local police, state prison agencies, state border patrols and similar efforts.

The most controversial provision in the State Department section is language that would allocate $351 million to pay overdue U.S. dues to the United Nations. But the money could not be spent until separate legislation is enacted to require that the United Nations streamline its bureaucracy and its budget. The requisite language is in the State Department reauthorization bill (S 886) the Senate passed June 22, but negotiations to find a middle ground with the House-passed version of the bill (HR 2415) are stuck because of the unyielding aspiration of abortion opponents to make the bill a vehicle for restricting aid for family planning abroad.

If the money is not delivered to the United Nations by Jan. 1, the United States is liable to lose its vote in the General Assembly.

"Our ability to influence world decisions is at stake," Rep. Tony P. Hall, D-Ohio, said in the debate. "Our honor is at stake. Our position as a world leader will be diminished if we turn our back on the U.N."

House Democrats also used the issue to add to their criticism of the way congressional Republicans have been thwarting Clinton on foreign policy this fall, most recently with the Senate's defeat of the Comprehensive Test Ban Treaty on Oct. 13.

Republicans, who have long been critical of the United Nations for overspending, said the burden should be put on Clinton to work out a deal on the State Department reauthorization bill in time to free the money.

While this is the type of contentious policy rider that the administration and congressional Democrats lament is all too frequently added to spending bills, it is the absence of one such rider from the CJS conference report — one that would expand the definition of a federal hate crime — that has added to the bill's rough fortunes at the president's hand.

Currently, crimes motivated by a victim's race, color, religion or national origin are covered by the statute (PL 90-284) enacted in 1968 that first authorized federal prosecution for hate crimes. In its CJS bill, the Senate included grants to combat hate crimes; language to expand the law's reach to include crimes motivated by a victim's sexual orientation, gender or disability; and an expansion of federal authority to prosecute any hate crime that could be linked to interstate commerce. All of these provisions were dropped by the conference committee.

"Hate crimes legislation is important," Clinton said Oct. 19 during an anti-violence rally on Capitol Hill. "It embodies what I think is the biggest challenge facing not only our society, but societies all over the world."

Congressional Democrats said they would pursue the expansion of the hate crimes law as separate legislation before the end of the year. But the White House signaled it wanted to make the issue part of the agenda for deal-cutting on spending bills.

Other Issues

These are the resolutions to some of the additional proposals in the original House and Senate measures that have made enactment of the CJS package problematic:

- It would retain the current prohibition on the collection of fees to support the federal computer database used to assist law enforcement officials carrying out the background checks required on some would-be gun buyers — and on more customers at gun shows under the Senate version of a juvenile crime and gun control bill (HR 1501) stuck in conference.
- It would provide a compromise $143 million for the Advance Technology Program, which provides grants to businesses to develop marketable tech-

nologies. That would be $96 million below Clinton's request and $61 million below the fiscal 1999 level. The House bill would have cut off funding for the program; the Senate would have given it an 11 percent increase.

- It would allow pharmacists to refuse to fill prescriptions for contraceptives on moral or religious grounds. The provision had been a point of controversy in the debate on the Treasury-Postal appropriations bill but was dropped from the final version (HR 2490 — PL 106-58).
- It would provide just $10 million for a special counterterrorism fund, as the House wanted, instead of the $27 million requested by the president and provided by the Senate. Republicans say the fund, which is supposed to pay for unexpected missions to thwart terrorism, has instead been improperly used to develop unauthorized new programs.
- It would prohibit publication of any federal document referring to any place other than Jerusalem as Israel's capital and would require that any U.S. diplomatic outpost there be under the supervision of the ambassador to Israel. The city has become a major sticking point in Israeli-Palestinian peace negotiations, with both sides claiming it as their capital.
- It would provide $742 million for security and maintenance of missions abroad and other security upgrades worldwide, but it would deny Clinton the $3.6 billion he sought in advanced appropriations to boost embassy security.
- It would deny a $20 million request by Clinton to fund Justice Department litigation against tobacco companies.
- It would rebuff Clinton's request to pay for the FBI to begin a program to monitor government and private computer communications in a bid to curb cyberterrorism.The project had come under attack from conservatives and civil libertarians, who feared it would lead to invasions of privacy.
- It would give the National Oceanic and Atmospheric Administration an increase of about 1 percent, to $2.3 billion.
- It would boost spending on the Securities and Exchange Commission (SEC) by 14 percent, to $368 million — $7 million more than the president requested. When the House froze the agency's budget in its initial bill, the White House said the SEC would be forced to lay off 300 employees, thereby slowing enforcement of securities trading rules at a time of record volume.
- It would give the Federal Communications Commission $210 million, nearly splitting the difference between what the president requested and what the House had provided. The agency, which gets most of its money from fee collections, sought the boost to pay for more broadcast regulators.
- It would maintain a requirement in immigration law (PL 104-208) that by 2001 the Immigration and Naturalization Services establish an automated entry and exit system at all border crossings. *(1996 Almanac, p. 5-8)*

The Senate version of the bill would have blocked this move, and when the conferees dropped the language that apparently prompted several House Republicans with districts near the Canadian border to line up against the conference report. Fred Upton, R-Mich., said business groups keen on Canadian trade fear that a flawed system will cause massive traffic jams at border crossings.

Linking U.N. Dues To Family Planning Snags CJS Bill

NOVEMBER 13 — Negotiators came tantalizingly close the week of Nov.8 to finding common ground on the spending package for the departments of Commerce, Justice and State (CJS) and the federal judiciary. But, as is so often the case in year-end budget talks, the most nettlesome dispute was left for last.

Once again, the issue is whether to make payment of nearly $1 billion the United States owes the United Nations contingent on restrictions on funding for family planning programs abroad. The dues have not been paid in full because Republicans have been insisting on the family planning caveat since 1997. If $111 million does not arrive by Jan. 1, the United Nations says, it will consider taking away the U.S. seat in the General Assembly.

To appease President Clinton, however, Republicans sweetened the package by adding approximately $600 million, or 2 percent, to the $39 billion grand total in the legislation (HR 2670) Clinton vetoed Oct. 25.

Negotiators from the White House and Capitol Hill were planning to keep talking through the weekend of Nov. 13-14, and they could announce a comprehensive deal on the CJS provisions and those stalling enactment of the four remaining fiscal 2000 appropriations bills. The provisions would then be assembled in one final appropriations measure that would bring the first session of the 106th Congress to an end.

"We've got 90 percent of it done," Judd Gregg, R.-N.H., chairman of the Senate CJS Appropriations Subcommittee, said Nov. 9. "All the money is settled. It's just the U.N. to work out."

Aides said the White House initially asked for slightly more than $1 billion in boosted funding, but eventually agreed on a figure closer to splitting the difference The biggest winner will be the president's cherished Community Oriented Policing Service (COPS) program, created to fulfill his 1992 campaign pledge to put 100,000 more officers on the beat. COPS was given $325 million, barely 25 percent of what Clinton had requested, in the bill he vetoed. It would get $595 million under the funding deal, according to Harold Rogers, R-Ky., chairman of the House CJS Appropriations Subcommittee.

Clinton is also expected to win an additional $300 million for international peacekeeping operations; Congress included $200 million for that purpose in the vetoed CJS bill.

The deal would also provide more money for the Small Business Administration. In his veto message, Clinton said the $804 million originally appropriated — while 12 percent more than in fiscal 1999 — was inadequate for a loan program for disaster victims. Clinton wants an additional $108 million.

And Hill aides said Clinton is also likely to win more funding to implement an agreement between the United States and Canada on the protection and harvesting of salmon. Clinton requested $60 million; the initial CJS bill provided just $10 million.

United Nations and 'Mexico City'

The administration has been holding firm against conditioning the pay-

Parents' Pilgrimage to the Hill Fails To Revive Hate Crimes Measure

NOVEMBER 13 — Despite a flurry of lobbying by the parents of the most prominent recent victim of a hate crime, a campaign to revive legislation that would expand the federal role in prosecuting such offenses is coming to naught this year.

In July, the Senate amended its fiscal 2000 Commerce-Justice-State (CJS) appropriations bill to federalize crimes motivated by the dislike of gays or the disabled, or by gender bias; expand federal jurisdiction over hate crimes; and create new grants for states to prosecute such cases. But all those provisions were abandoned in conference. When President Clinton vetoed the bill (HR 2670), he lamented that the hate crimes proposals had been dropped, although he signaled that their revival was not essential to a year-ending budget agreement.

Still, several senior members of both chambers and both parties spent the week of Nov. 8 pressing to revive at least some of the language. They had as their main allies Dennis and Judy Shepard, whose 21-year-old son Matthew was beaten to death in Laramie, Wyo., in October 1998 primarily because he was gay. Both men convicted in the case have been given life sentences.

During two days of meetings on Capitol Hill and at the White House, the Shepards said that, had the hate crimes measure been law, it not only would have sent an important signal, but also would have allowed federal agents to help Wyoming law enforcement investigate their son's killing. The state has no hate crimes law.

The couple was accompanied to many of their meetings by three law enforcement officials on the case. The trip was orchestrated by the Human Rights Campaign, which lobbies for gay rights.

At a news conference Nov. 8, Commander David O'Malley of the Laramie police said that the Shepard case had reversed his longstanding view that there did not need to be a special hate crime designation on the law books.

The Shepards spoke at the weekly caucus lunch of Democratic senators Nov. 9 and met with the chairmen of the Senate and House Judiciary committees. But they said they were not granted a request to meet with Senate Majority Leader Trent Lott, R-Miss.

His spokesman, John Czwartacki, said unequivocally Nov. 10 that the Senate would not act on hate crimes legislation again this year.

Key GOP senators say they opposed the language all along but allowed it to be added to the CJS bill in order to speed its passage. Republican leaders in both the House and Senate say that all violent crimes are egregious and that special federal categories should not be created for some of them. Others object particularly to making crimes motivated by gender bias federal hate crimes, contending that that could federalize all rape cases.

Three GOP lawmakers have been prominent in pushing the legislation: Sen. Gordon H. Smith of Oregon, Sen. James M. Jeffords of Vermont and Rep. Mark Foley of Florida. "It's because it has to do with the issue of homosexuality," Smith said at a Nov. 8 news conference when asked about the GOP leadership's opposition. "Many people are uncomfortable with that."

Under a 1968 law (PL 90-284), hate crimes are now defined as assaults motivated by the victim's race, color, religion or national origin. Part of the Senate's CJS language — identical to companion measures (S 622, HR 1082) by Sen. Edward M. Kennedy, D-Mass., and Rep. John Conyers Jr., D-Mich. — would expand the definition to include gender, sexual orientation and disability. It also would allow federal prosecution of any hate crime linked to interstate commerce. The other proposal, by Sen. Orrin G. Hatch, R-Utah, would take an alternative approach, creating a $5 million federal grant to help states prosecute hate crimes.

Staff aides to Hatch and Kennedy tried to devise a compromise the week of Nov. 8 that could be slipped into an appropriations bill at the last minute. They did not succeed.

"I'd like to do something," Hatch said Nov. 10. "But getting something done in that area is very hard."

ment of U.N. dues on the reimposition of a ban on federal aid to international family groups that advocate on abortion overseas, even with their own funds. In congressional parlance that is the "Mexico City" language, because President Ronald Reagan announced it at the time of a 1984 population conference there. President George Bush retained the restriction.

In 1998 Clinton vetoed a bill to allow a retiring of the debt to the U.N. because it also contained "Mexico City" language. *(1998 Almanac, p. 16-3)*

This year, the spending bill said the only way a big portion of the U.N. debt could be paid was if Congress also enacted a measure requiring a U.N. budget overhaul. But that measure (S 886) is tied up because Rep. Christopher H. Smith, R-N.J., and his anti-abortion allies are insisting it be the vehicle for the "Mexico City" provision.

"Now, here's the thing about Mexico City," House Majority Leader Dick Armey, R-Texas, told reporters Nov. 11. "Why does it make it, as it were, a potential show-stopper? Because it is, what I call, an issue of the heart. And when you get issues of the heart in the process, as opposed to issues of money, and sometimes even policy, these things will have a commanding influ-

Commerce-Justice-State Spending

Where the Money Goes

HR 3421 (incorporated in HR 3194 — Conference report: H Rept 106-479)

Synopsis:
The Senate on Nov. 19 cleared a rewrite of the appropriations bill for the federal judiciary, 14 federal agencies and the departments of Commerce, Justice and State. President Clinton vetoed the first version (HR 2670) on Oct. 25. The new version, which Clinton has endorsed, would appropriate $39.6 billion overall. That is $625 million, or 1.6 percent, more than the total for the vetoed measure. It is also $669 million, or 1.7 percent, less than what the president had requested for fiscal 2000 if scorekeeping adjustments are factored in. This accounting reduces the total of Clinton's request, principally by not counting $9.3 billion he sought now for spending in future fiscal years. Most of that money would have been dedicated to embassy security.

Hot-Button Issues

Δ **COPS.** Clinton made a robust level of funding for the Community Oriented Policing Services (COPS) program — created to fulfill the main law enforcement promise of his 1992 campaign — a top priority in the CJS bill. The vetoed bill provided just 25 percent of Clinton's $1.3 billion request for the program. Under the revised version he will get 47 percent of what he wanted, but he nonetheless hailed the gain as a major victory.

Δ **Block grants.** Republicans, who favored block grants for states and cities to fight crime over the COPS program, were able to retain $523 million for the Local Law Enforcement Block Grant, the same amount provided in the vetoed version. The program had been zeroed out under Clinton's budget request. But the GOP had to take $130 million from a state and local enforcement assistance program in order to help Clinton's initiatives.

Δ **Spectrum.** The White House and Judd Gregg, R-N.H., chairman of the Senate CJS Appropriations Subcommittee, had sought to have the Federal Communications Commission (FCC) repossess a portion of the telecommunications spectrum purchased at auction by a company now in bankruptcy proceedings, Nextwave Telecom Inc., so that it could be sold for as much as $5 billion, which would have gone a long way to solving the need for offsets of additional year-end spending. But House GOP leaders refused, saying the government should not get involved in a private legal battle over bankruptcy.

Δ **Espy's bills.** Sen. Thad Cochran, R-Miss., wanted to use the bill to pay the $1.3 million legal bill of former Agriculture Secretary Mike Espy, acquitted last year after a four-year independent counsel investigation into charges he accepted illegal gratuities. The negotiators rebuffed the request.

Δ **FCC.** The agreement allotted the agency $210 million, the same amount as in the vetoed bill. The figure represents a nearly exact midpoint between the $231 million requested by the president and the $192 million originally approved by the House.

Δ **Counterterrorism.** Clinton failed to win additional money for a special counterterrorism fund under the Justice Department. The bill gives the fund $10 million; Clinton sought $27 million. Republicans say the fund, which is supposed to pay for unexpected missions to thwart terrorism, has instead been improperly used to develop unauthorized new programs.

Δ **Census.** Settling one of the most nettlesome recent disputes on the CJS bill, a Jan. 25 Supreme Court ruling gave legal justification for the Census Bureau to launch plans to conduct parallel population counts in 2000, one augmenting the traditional head counting methods with statistical sampling. The final bill gives the bureau all $4.5 billion it requested and declares it "emergency spending" in order to avoid breaching spending caps.

Δ **Hate crimes.** Clinton sought, but did not press hard for, the second conference agreement to include language expanding the federal role in prosecuting hate crimes. The Senate had passed such language, but GOP leaders on both sides of the Capitol were vehemently against it and it was dropped.

(figures are in thousands of dollars of new budget authority)

	Fiscal 1999 Appropriation	Fiscal 2000 Clinton Request	House Bill	Senate Bill	Conference Report
Department of Justice	$18,207,450	$18,542,949	$18,138,926	$17,098,025	$18,646,502
Commerce and related agencies	5,168,274	14,754,229	8,076,863	7,232,710	8,719,438
The Judiciary	3,652,049	4,163,972	3,900,273	3,813,685	3,959,292
Department of State	5,501,854	10,156,657	5,790,996	5,535,171	6,302,118
Related agencies	1,856,368	2,198,573	1,798,591	1,940,666	2,068,370
Rescissions, less other spending *	1,811,277	– 3,400	– 28,366	– 235,693	– 64,753
GRAND TOTAL	**$36,197,272**	**$49,812,980**	**$37,677,283**	**$35,384,564**	**$39,630,967**
Total adjusted for scorekeeping	**($33,752,277)**	**($39,048,564)**	**($36,309,836)**	**($34,264,377)**	**($38,379,346)**

* Includes emergency spending in the fiscal 1999 supplemental spending law (PL 106-31)

TABLE: House Appropriations Committee

ence over votes."

The next day, State Department spokesman James P. Rubin did not directly dispute reports that Secretary Madeleine K. Albright had persuaded the White House to at least partly give in on the issue, even though abortion-rights groups would be angry. And White House spokesman Joe Lockhart suggested that the president was willing to meet the GOP halfway.

"We are talking to the leaders on the Hill involved in this issue to find a way to pay our dues and accommodate their concerns," Lockhart said. But he also added: "We don't believe that a side issue of intentional family planning should hold up U.N. dues."

Espy and Spectrum Sales

A handful of other policy issues are still under discussion.

Hill aides said negotiations were continuing Nov. 12 on whether to include a rider on the Federal Communications Commission's spending section to take a telecommunications spectrum license away from Nextwave Telecom Inc. The company bought the license at a federal auction but has since filed for bankruptcy. Were it resold, it could bring more than $1 billion to the Treasury, advocates of the move say. But some GOP leaders, led by those from Texas, are balking at the idea.

Also at issue was a request by Sen. Thad Cochran, R-Miss. to appropriate $1.3 million to pay the legal bills of former Agriculture Secretary Mike Espy, acquitted last year after a four-year independent counsel investigation into charges he accepted illegal gratuities.

An effort failed to revive provisions from the original Senate CJS bill to combat hate crimes.

Both Sides Claim Win as Senate Clears Compromise

NOVEMBER 20 — Congressional Republicans and President Clinton are both claiming victory in the final spending package for the departments of Commerce, Justice and State (CJS) and the federal judiciary. And, at least by one reading of the numbers, the two sides nearly exactly split the difference in crafting the measure (HR 3421), which was incorporated in the omnibus fiscal 2000 appropriations package (HR 3194) that the Senate voted 74-24 to clear Nov. 19. The House had voted 296-135 to adopt the conference report the day before. *(Vote 610, p. H-198)*

The new grand total is $39.6 billion, which is $625 million — or 1.6 percent — more than the grand total in the initial CJS bill (HR 2670), which Clinton vetoed last month.

But the bill is just $669 million — or 1.7 percent — under what the president had requested, when budgetary scorekeeping adjustments agreed to by both sides are taken into account. These reduce the total of Clinton's request, principally by not counting $9.3 billion he sought for spending in future fiscal years. Most of that was requested to boost embassy security.

Without scorekeeping adjustments, the bill would allocate 9 percent more than the comparable law enacted for fiscal 1999. Under the alternate accounting, the boost is 14 percent.

While Clinton touted the increases in spending on his priorities, Republicans boasted that they had agreed to less than the president wanted.

But haggling over money was not what kept the negotiations alive. The last big issue settled was whether to condition payment of arrears to the United Nations on restrictions for overseas family planning groups. Here, too, the outcome was a split decision: Clinton will be allowed to deliver $926 million to the United Nations, but the GOP won restrictions on abortion advocacy abroad.

Clinton claimed his biggest victory on funding for the Community Oriented Policing Services (COPS) program, created to fulfill the main law enforcement promise of his 1992 campaign. The program would get $595 million, $270 million more than under the vetoed bill but still $680 million less than the president's request.

"The budget makes America a safer place," Clinton said of the funding deal Nov. 18. "This agreement will help to hire up to 50,000 more community police officers targeted to neighborhoods where crime rates are still too high."

Republicans, however, claimed their own victory, because the money they denied Clinton for COPS they used primarily to give block grants to state and local police, their preferred method for fighting crime but one that Clinton has not embraced. Still, they had to settle for $130 million less in these grant funds than under the vetoed measure.

Overall, the Justice Department would receive a 2 percent boost,to $18.6 billion, with small increases for the FBI, prison construction and the Immigration and Naturalization Service.

More for Other Departments

The other Cabinet departments covered by the measure would also get more than last year and more than was allotted in the vetoed bill.

The Commerce Department will get $8.7 billion, more than half of which will be spent to conduct next year's census. Since his veto, Clinton won $45 million more for the National Oceanic and Atmospheric Administration, in part to carry out an accord with Canada on salmon protection.

The State Department will get $6.3 billion, $347 million more than in the vetoed bill, mainly to pay dues to other international peacekeeping groups that were denied the first time.

Federal judiciary spending of $4 billion would be the same amount allotted in the vetoed bill.

In his Oct. 25 veto statement, Clinton attacked the funding allotted the Small Business Administration (SBA), particularly the money provided for the agency's disaster loan program. To accommodate him, negotiators agreed to boost spending for SBA salaries and expenses to $323 million, $46.5 million more than in the vetoed bill, and to allocate $276 million for disaster loans, $21 million more than before. *(Veto text, p. D-28)*

The negotiators also gave Clinton an additional $5 million for the Legal Services Corporation, the quasi-public agency that provides lawyers to the poor and is largely opposed by Republicans. The vetoed bill had allocated $300 million, the same as in fiscal 1999. Clinton had requested a $40 million increase.

Clinton was rebuffed on a few things he pressed for, including $20 million to assist the Justice Department's litigation against tobacco companies and language to enhance federal prosecution of hate crimes. ◆

Accounting Tricks Exempt $21 Billion of Defense Bill From Spending Caps

BoxScore
Defense

2000 Fiscal Year

- **Bill:** HR 2561 — PL 106-79
- **Legislative action: House** passed HR 2561 (H Rept 106-244), 379-45, July 22.

Senate passed S 1122 (S Rept 106-53), 93-4, on June 8.

House adopted the conference report on HR 2561 (H Rept 106-371), 372-55, on Oct. 13.

Senate cleared the bill, 87-11, on Oct. 14.

President signed HR 2561 on Oct. 25.

SUMMARY

The $267.8 billion defense appropriations bill for fiscal 2000 added $4.5 billion to President Clinton's budget request. It was cleared after House and Senate conferees agreed to allow the Air Force to buy additional F-22 fighters, which the House had rejected, but also to require additional testing before full-scale production of the plane can begin. Despite initial hints of a veto, Clinton signed the measure, which provides the first significant defense spending increase since 1985 and the largest military pay raise since 1981.

It was clear from the start that Congress would add billions to Clinton's defense budget request despite increasingly tight budget caps. Congress simply finessed the spending squeeze with budget gimmicks that exempted $21 billion in defense spending from the budget caps, allowing the House and Senate to increase outlays for other domestic programs by the same amount.

The total in the defense bill shielded from the caps included $6.6 billion for the lion's share of the pay raise and other routine operating expenses that were designated as "emergency" spending. Another $10.5 billion worth of the outlay reduction was based on the premise that the Pentagon would spend its budget more slowly than had been assumed.

The bill did not include funds to pay for U.S. forces serving with a NATO-led peacekeeping mission in the Serbian province of Kosovo. Clinton promised to request a supplemental appropriation to cover that operation, which was expected to cost between $2 billion and $3.5 billion.

As usual, the bill made hundreds of additions to Clinton's funding request — most of them small — for projects of local interest to lawmakers.

For instance, Daniel K. Inouye, ranking Democrat on the Senate Defense Appropriations Subcommittee, boasted of steering a total of $387 million to Hawaii. But some of the add-ons were not geographically specific: $175 million was added for research on breast cancer and $75 million for research on prostate cancer.

The bill included $375 million for a helicopter carrier to be built in the Mississippi hometown of Senate GOP Leader Trent Lott, $320 million for a high-speed cargo ship to be built either in San Diego or New Orleans, and a total of $372 million for a package of fringe benefits and bonuses intended to bolster sagging re-enlistments.

The most contentious issue was the Lockheed Martin F-22, intended by the Air Force to be its premier fighter in the next few decades, replacing the 1970-vintage F-15. Without warning to the Pentagon or Lockheed Martin, the House Defense Appropriations Subcommittee rejected the administration's budget request for $1.6 billion to buy six of the planes and an additional $277 million for components that would be used in 10 more F-22s to be purchased in fiscal 2001. The panel's position was backed by the full Appropriations Committee and then by the House.

The subcommittee cited cost increases and production problems to argue that it would be premature to commit to full-scale production of the F-22. The panel also complained that the Air Force's plan to buy 339 of the planes at a cost of about $70 billion was symptomatic of the Pentagon's tendency to sink too much money into high-tech weapons designed to do battle with the Soviet Union while shortchanging more mundane items more relevant to U.S. missions in the post-Soviet world.

But the Senate vigorously supported the F-22 production request, and it got strong backing from the White House, Defense Secretary William S. Cohen and the Air Force. Senate conferees insisted that the House overestimated the F-15's ability to deal with the types of fighters and anti-aircraft missiles that potential adversaries could field.

After unusually contentious negotiations, conferees agreed on a compromise that would allow the Air Force to begin building up to six F-22s — the number it had requested — but with the planes designated to conduct additional tests.

The conferees also approved the $277 million requested for components to build additional planes next year, with the stipulation that production could not begin until key electronic systems had been flight-tested in a prototype.

Joint Chiefs Say Clinton's Defense Budget Falls Short

JANUARY 9 — It took only gentle prodding for the Joint Chiefs of Staff to help Senate Armed Services Committee Republicans lay out the terms of this year's defense budget debate: President Clinton's promise to let the Pentagon spend $12 billion more in fiscal 2000 is not enough, the officers said during a Jan. 5 hearing.

Clinton is expected to propose $267 billion in budget authority for defense in fiscal 2000, instead of the $263 billion he had earlier projected. In addition, Clinton will allow the Pentagon to take more than $8 billion previously authorized in several areas of the defense budget and reallocate it for high-priority programs. The administration said the money is available because, for example, fuel prices and other costs have been lower than projected.

The administration counts this money as an addition to the Pentagon's purchasing power since such savings normally would be returned to the Treasury Department.

The proposed increase for fiscal 2000, which Clinton announced during his weekly radio address, would be the first in a series of annual increases in projected Pentagon purchasing power that would total $110 billion through fiscal 2005. The money would be primarily to boost military pay, combat readiness and weapons modernization.

Clinton agreed to increase future defense budgets last fall under heavy pressure from congressional defense hawks and senior Pentagon leaders who contend that the administration's spending plans were too stingy, given the large forces being sent overseas on peacekeeping and other missions.

The administration plan would be "the first, sustained, long-term increase in defense spending in a decade," Clinton said. Pentagon budgets have declined annually since fiscal 1985.

Joint Chiefs of Staff Chairman Gen. Henry H. Shelton told the Senate panel Jan. 5 that Clinton's proposed increases would "meet our most critical needs, and it will represent a major turnaround following years of decreased spending."

But the service chiefs restated the even larger budget increases they had called for during testimony before the Armed Services Committee Sept. 29. At that time, they asked $17.5 billion more in fiscal 2000 and a total of about $130 billion more through fiscal 2005.

"It does not meet the stated needs," Air Force Chief of Staff Gen. Michael E. Ryan said of Clinton's proposal, "but it's a good start."

Committee Republicans made it clear they would use the service chiefs' higher figure as a guide to drafting the annual defense authorization bill.

"There's still the benchmark of Sept. 29," newly installed Armed Services Chairman John W. Warner, R-Va., said.

Budget Camouflage

In fact, the gap between Clinton's proposal and the service chiefs' requests is larger than it appears.

The chiefs had emphasized in September that the $17.5 billion in added spending they were seeking did not include upward of $2 billion that would be needed to increase military pay and pensions. However, Clinton's $12 billion proposal includes those personnel costs, as well as more than $2 billion to pay for the continued presence of U.S. forces in Bosnia.

Several GOP senators said that deducting the pay and Bosnia funds from Clinton's proposal meant he was promising less than $8 billion for readiness and modernization programs.

The traditionally pro-Pentagon Armed Services Committee would be expected to push for a larger defense budget than Clinton will request. And support in the Senate as a whole seems widespread. In a Dec. 8 letter to Budget Committee Chairman Pete V. Domenici, R-N.M., Majority Leader Trent Lott, R-Miss., called for adding $20 billion a year to the projected defense budgets.

The outlook for stepped-up defense spending is less clear in the House. Speaker Dennis Hastert, R-Ill., included a vague call for a more robust defense in the speech he made Jan. 6 immediately after his election.

But any increase in defense spending apparently would have to be offset by cuts in domestic spending under the spending caps enacted by the balanced-budget law (PL 105-33) in 1997. *(1997 Almanac, p. 2-47)*

Congress has balked at significant additional domestic cuts, and GOP fiscal conservatives have dug in to support the spending caps.

"The defense hawks on the Hill have to talk to the deficit hawks on the Hill," National Security Council staff member Robert G. Bell told reporters Jan. 7.

Pay Increase Supported

The committee generally supported the administration's three-part package of proposed increases in military pay and pensions.

This includes a 4.4 percent increase in military pay, targeted additional pay raises for midlevel officers and all-but repealing a 1986 law (PL 99-348) under which, beginning in 2006, service members who retire after 20 years of active duty would get pensions equal to only 40 percent of their basic pay, rather than the current 50 percent.

Military leaders insist that the pay and retirement changes are essential to recruiting and retention. But as the administration's plan was taking shape last fall, senior Armed Services Democrat Carl Levin of Michigan and then-Chairman Strom Thurmond, R-S.C., told the Pentagon they wanted to see a detailed analysis of how such expensive changes in compensation were expected to improve the services' personnel woes.

During the Jan. 5 hearing, Rhode Island Democrat Jack Reed noted that experienced personnel are leaving the service for many reasons, including fewer opportunities for promotion to command since the services have been reduced by one-third since the end of the Cold War, and greater opportunities in the booming civilian economy for skilled military leaders and technicians.

"We have a very profound problem here that will not be easily remedied simply by raising pay and allowances," Reed warned.

The chiefs agreed that the personnel problems had many roots, principal among them the fact that the smaller, post-Cold War military is being used much more frequently overseas than was anticipated. But they insisted that the pay and retirement increases were important as a gesture of national support for military personnel.

"All of that sends a very clear signal as to whether or not a very heavily used force is appreciated for what it's doing," Shelton said.

Shelton also argued that the complaints about pay and the retirement system from personnel who are leaving made the need for the pay package too urgent and too obvious to await sophisticated analysis.

"Long, detailed studies might lead to the demise of the force at a time when we need to start fixing some of those things that are being reflected in every survey that we see as reasons . . . that are causing our people to depart," Shelton said.

Indeed, support for the pay and retirement package was so widespread among committee members from both parties that Warner suggested trying to enact it as free-standing legislation early in the year, before Congress buckles down to work on the annual defense funding legislation.

The last major overhauls of the Pentagon's pay and retirement systems, in 1981 and 1986 respectively, were enacted as separate legislation. *(1986 Almanac, p. 486; 1981 Almanac, p. 207)*

Though details of Clinton's plan were not final, it would increase funding for weapons procurement to $60 billion in fiscal 2001. This would meet the modernization funding requirement set by former Joint Chiefs of Staff Chairman Gen. John Shalikashvili, although later than he said was necessary.

Clinton Offers His Defense Initiatives In Annual Address

January 23 — President Clinton outlined numerous budget and tax proposals in his State of the Union address, many of which had been released in the days leading up to the Jan. 19 speech. Details will be officially unveiled Feb. 1 when Clinton sends his fiscal 2000 budget proposal to Congress. Highlights include:

- **Social Security.** A proposal to set aside 62 percent — or about $2.8 trillion — of projected budget surpluses over 15 years to shore up Social Security's cash reserves. Surpluses in the next 15 years are expected to total about $4.5 trillion. One-quarter of the set-asides would be invested in stock markets, marking the federal government's first investment in the markets. Clinton said his plan would extend Social Security's solvency by more than 20 years, to 2055. The New Deal retirement plan is now expected to run out of money after 2032 as Baby Boom retirees grow in number and live longer than previous generations.

Clinton proposed setting aside another 11 percent of surpluses – averaging about $33 billion a year, or $500 billion — to create subsidized retirement accounts, to be known as Universal Savings Accounts, similar to the 401(k) plans offered to employees by many businesses. These accounts would supplement but not replace Social Security. The government would provide a certain dollar amount to most Americans, and would match individual contributions to the accounts, with larger matches going to people with lower incomes.

- **Medicare.** A call to use 16 percent of surpluses to ensure the solvency of Medicare, the federal health insurance program for the elderly and disabled, until 2020. Clinton also revived last year's proposal to allow people between ages 55 and 65 who lose their health insurance to buy into Medicare, and said the program should cover prescription drugs.
- **Long-term care.** An annual tax credit of up to $1,000 for expenses of the elderly, ailing and disabled, and the families that care for them.
- **Family assistance.** A tax credit of up to $250 a year per child under one year old for parents who stay home to care for children.
- **Education.** Redirecting the $15 billion in annual federal spending on public schools to emphasize, as Clinton put it, "what works and to stop supporting what doesn't." Clinton said he would send Congress an "Education Accountability Act" later this year that would, among other things, require that states and school districts end automatic grade promotions, improve the worst schools or close them, administer teacher competency tests, and improve school discipline.
- **Labor.** Raising the minimum wage by $1 an hour over two years, to $6.15. Clinton also called for women and men to get equal pay for equal work through enforcement of equal pay laws. He has requested tax credits of up to $1,000 a year, and other assistance, for the working disabled.
- **Trade.** A call to expand trade and open markets, starting with legislation to renew the president's fast-track trade negotiating authority.
- **Defense.** Spending an additional $12 billion in fiscal 2000 and $110 billion over the next six years to improve military readiness, reversing the decade-long decline in defense spending.
- **Crime.** A request for $6 billion over five years to support police hiring subsidies, including up to 50,000 new officers in high crime areas. Clinton also called for expanded drug testing and treatment of prisoners, safe school programs, and restoring the five-day waiting period for handgun purchases.
- **Conservation.** More than doubling the money (to $1 billion) for land purchases and other conservation purposes, and $700 million in tax credits to finance bond initiatives to preserve open spaces.

Senate Committee Uses Authorization Bill as Guide

MAY 29 — The Senate Appropriations Committee marked up its first funding bill for fiscal 2000 on May 25, approving, 24-3, a $264.7 billion defense measure for fiscal 2000 that closely tracks the defense authorization bill (S 1059) the Senate passed May 27.

The appropriations bill (S 1122) has a narrower scope than the authorization, since it funds core Pentagon programs. The authorization bill covers the entire defense-related budget, including military construction, which is funded in a separate appropriations bill, and defense programs conducted by the Energy Department, which are funded in the energy and water appropriations bill. *(Defense authorization, p. 9-3)*

S 1122 would provide $1.4 billion more than President Clinton requested for the programs it covers. As approved May 24 by the Defense Subcommittee, the bill would have added $4.5 billion to the request. But to increase the amount that other subcommittees could spend without breaking the budget caps, the full Appropriations Committee cut $3.1 billion from the Defense Subcommittee's total.

That reduction will have no impact on any of the programs approved by the subcommittee, however, since the Pentagon will be able to make up the loss from the billions that Congress added to Clinton's request for the supplemental appropriations bill enacted May 21 (PL 106-31).

In only a few cases would S 1122 appropriate substantially more for a major weapons program than S 1059 would authorize. The appropriation measure would provide $500 million — rather than the $375 million the authorization bill would allow — for components of a large helicopter carrier to be built in Pascagoula, Miss., by

Litton Industries. Mississippi's Thad Cochran is the second-ranking Republican on the Defense Appropriations Subcommittee.

The appropriations bill also would add $200 million to the $837 million Clinton requested to continue work on an anti-missile defense for U.S. territory. The increase is intended to preserve the possibility of deploying the defense by 2003, the date that had been planned through early 1999. The Pentagon announced in January that the system likely would not be deployed until 2005.

As usual, the Appropriations Committee added to the defense bill hundreds of relatively small amounts for projects of special interest to individual senators. Ted Stevens, R-Alaska, who chairs both the full committee and its defense panel, and Daniel K. Inouye of Hawaii, the subcommittee's senior Democrat, fared particularly well. Among the many projects added to the bill for their states were $3 million to continue closing a landfill in Alaska and $1 million to keep military aircraft from inadvertently carrying brown tree snakes to Hawaii, where they would endanger native bird species.

The bill also includes funds for politically popular medical research, as has become routine. This year, the committee added to the bill $175 million for breast cancer, $75 million for prostate cancer and $50 million for other peer-reviewed medical research.

Senate-Passed Bill Provides $4 Billion For Pet Projects

JUNE 12 — The Senate on June 8 dispatched a $264.7 billion spending bill for the Pentagon that retains $4 billion in members' special projects, steers clear of any major policy disputes and leaves U.S. peacekeeping expenses for Kosovo for a separate bill.

The fiscal 2000 defense appropriations bill (S 1122) passed on a 93-4 vote. *(Vote 158, p. S-33)*

It includes no funds to pay for U.S. participation in the NATO-led peacekeeping force slated to move into Kosovo under the peace agreement hammered out between the alliance and Yugoslav President Slobodan Milosevic. President Clinton promised June 10 to request a supplemental appropriation to cover the cost of deploying about 7,000 U.S. personnel as part of a planned NATO force of 50,000. The operation could cost the Pentagon between $2 billion and $3.5 billion during fiscal 2000, according to the Center for Strategic and Budgetary Assessments, a Washington think tank.

But the appropriations bill did not pass free of Kosovo-related provisions. The Senate adopted by voice vote an amendment by Majority Whip Don Nickles, R-Okla., that would bar the use of funds to reconstruct Yugoslavia — battered by nearly three months of U.S.-led NATO airstrikes — while Milosevic remains the country's president.

Also winning voice vote approval was an amendment by Judd Gregg, R-N.H., to restrict the use of funds for the relief of Kosovar refugees included in the emergency supplemental funding bill (HR 1141 — PL 106-31) that Congress enacted in May. Gregg's amendment would bar the use of these funds for long-term Balkan economic reconstruction unless Congress authorizes such a program.

While the Senate adopted dozens of amendments to S 1122, most were minor in scope and few were controversial.

The bill would add about $1.4 billion in new budget authority to Clinton's budget request for most Defense Department programs. As originally drafted by the Defense Appropriations Subcommittee, the bill had topped Clinton's request by $4.5 billion. But to let other subcommittees spend more money without breaking the budget caps, the full Appropriations panel sliced $3.1 billion from the defense bill after Congress added more than $5 billion to Clinton's request for the emergency funding bill.

Otherwise, S 1122 would make few significant changes in Clinton's defense budget request. As usual, it adds small amounts for hundreds of projects of special interest to individual senators, but it makes no significant departures from the companion defense authorization bill, which the Senate passed May 27. The defense appropriations bill does not include funding for construction of military facilities or for defense-related projects of the Energy Department, which are funded in two separate appropriations measures.

Special Projects

In what has become a regular feature of appropriations debates, the Senate rejected, 16-81, an effort by John McCain, R-Ariz., to transfer billions of dollars from members' pet projects to the sections of the Pentagon's budget request that had been cut by the Appropriations Committee. *(Vote 156, p. S-33)*

This year, McCain sought to eliminate $3.1 billion in unspecified projects, which he insisted could be drawn from a list of more than 150 committee initiatives with a total price tag of $4 billion.

He singled out some committee additions for particularly scathing criticism, such as a $3.5 million earmark for a "smart truck" initiative. "Perhaps we will have trucks that gas themselves," he quipped. The Michigan-based Army project — backed by Armed Services Committee member Carl Levin, D-Mich. — would integrate flat-panel displays, night-vision equipment and other electronic gear in a cargo truck.

McCain allowed that some member projects might have merit. But he argued that Congress was short-circuiting the Pentagon's budgeting process, where these projects are supposed to compete for funds with other projects that might be more essential militarily, but less well-connected politically.

Appropriations Chairman Ted Stevens, R-Alaska, and ranking Democrat Daniel K. Inouye of Hawaii — who both unabashedly shoehorn projects for their states into the annual defense bill — insisted that many parochial initiatives merely give local communities relief from problems created by the Pentagon in the first place. Inouye cited as an example his annual addition of $1 million to ensure that military ships and planes do not inadvertently carry brown tree snakes from Guam to Hawaii, where they would decimate native bird species.

Executive Jets

The most heated dispute in the otherwise flaccid debate on S 1122 surrounded an amendment to eliminate a provision authorizing the Air Force to sign a long-term lease for six Gulfstream V executive jets for use by the commanders in chief — the senior generals and admirals who command U.S. forces.

The amendment, offered by Democrats Barbara Boxer of California and Tom Harkin of Iowa, would have required instead that the Pentagon do an analysis of alternative ways to provide transportation for these officers, who frequently travel long distances. Noting that the leases would cost more than $475 million over 10 years, Boxer and Harkin contended that the officers' travel needs could be met by some of the 300 executive planes already in the Pentagon's inventory or by smaller, much cheaper executive jets.

But Stevens cited a Pentagon study concluding that the Gulfstreams would be cheaper than the much larger and elderly jetliners, such as Boeing 707s, that the commanders currently use for long-distance travel. The study also asserted that only the Gulfstream could carry enough people over a far enough distance to let the commanders and their staffs operate efficiently.

On a 66-31 vote, the Senate tabled (killed) the amendment. *(Vote 157, p. S-33)*

Other Amendments

Among the dozens of amendments adopted by voice vote, with no debate, were three that would affect major weapons programs.

The one with the largest budgetary impact, sponsored by Christopher S. Bond, R-Mo., added $220 million to the bill to buy four F-15E jet fighters, built by The Boeing Co. The Air Force has not requested additional copies of the plane, but the company has said it may lay off workers at its St. Louis plant because of dwindling overseas sales.

The Bond amendment offsets the addition by slicing a total of $220 million from other items in the bill. Among those cuts is a reduction, from $200 million to $150 million, in the amount that the Appropriations Committee would have added to Clinton's request for $837 million to continue developing an anti-missile defense for U.S. territory.

The Senate also adopted, by voice vote, an amendment by Edward M. Kennedy, D-Mass., to give the Army discretion to use up to $35 million to modify existing Patriot missiles to have a better chance of destroying small cruise missiles. The Army, which is buying a new version of the Patriot, built in Dallas by Lockheed Martin Vought Systems, has not supported Kennedy's proposal, which would provide work for Massachusetts-based Raytheon Corp.

Also adopted by voice vote was an amendment by James M. Inhofe, R-Okla., to require the Army to test two small anti-aircraft missiles as potential anti-air armament for Apache helicopters. The two missiles are Raytheon's Stinger and the Starstreak, built by the British firm of Short Brothers PLC, which has teamed up with Lockheed Martin in a bid for U.S. sales.

Two other amendments have potentially significant foreign policy impact:

- By Sam Brownback, R-Kan., to suspend for five years economic sanctions imposed on India and Pakistan after they each conducted nuclear test explosions in 1998.
- By Majority Leader Trent Lott, R-Miss., to require the Pentagon to conduct a detailed review of the military balance between China and Taiwan.

Other Provisions

The bill would provide $73.9 billion for military pay and benefits, a net increase of $132 million over Clinton's request.

The bill would make two major additions to Clinton's personnel funding request: $165 million, to allow a 4.8 percent pay raise instead of the 4.4 percent raise Clinton proposed; and $27 million, to increase the number of full-time personnel performing administrative and maintenance work for National Guard and reserve units.

Those increases were partly offset by a reduction of $94 million to reflect that fact that the services had fewer active duty personnel than were budgeted.

Although S 1122 includes no funds for operations in or over Yugoslavia, it would provide $2.1 billion for operations in Bosnia and Iraq, which is $300 million less than Clinton requested. In its report on the bill, the Appropriations Committee complained that the services had been paying for routine overhead costs out of funds earmarked for these ongoing operations.

For the so-called Nunn-Lugar program, intended to help former Soviet republics dispose of the nuclear, chemical and biological arsenals they inherited, the bill would provide $476 million, the same as Clinton requested.

To continue cleaning up hazardous and toxic waste at current and former defense installations, the bill would provide $1.3 billion, an increase of nearly $40 million over the administration request.

The bill would make relatively few major changes in Clinton's request for major weapons programs.

Among the significant increases are:

- $201 million for 15 H-60 helicopters, built in Connecticut by United Technologies Corp.'s Sikorsky division. The administration requested $511 million for 26 of the aircraft.
- $123 million for two V-22 Ospreys, vertical takeoff craft used by the Marines as troop-carriers. The budget requested $796 million for 10 Ospreys.
- $151 million for two specialized variants of the C-130 cargo plane — one adapted to refuel Marine aircraft in midair, and one modified for psychological warfare broadcasts. Clinton had sought no funds for additional C-130s.
- $500 million for components to be used in a large helicopter carrier built to haul up to 2,000 Marines, along with more than 30 helicopters and three large hovercraft to haul them and their equipment ashore. The ship would be built by Litton Industries Inc. in Pascagoula, Miss., the hometown of Majority Leader Lott. The Navy has not planned to begin buying components for this ship until 2004.
- $46 million for components to be used in a Joint STARS ground surveillance plane to be paid for in the fiscal 2001 budget. The bill also includes $280 million requested to buy one of the planes in fiscal 2000, but the administration made no request for future purchases.

The bill also would authorize the Air Force to negotiate with Boeing for the possible purchase of 60 additional C-17 long-range cargo jets, beyond the 120 planes the Pentagon already plans to purchase.

House Committee Bars Purchases Of F-22 Fighter Jet

JULY 17 — California Republican Jerry Lewis, in his first run as chairman of the House Defense Appropriations Subcommittee, jolted the Pentagon on July 12 when he persuaded his panel in a closed-door markup not to buy the F-22 fighter plane, the Air Force's premier procurement program.

As Air Force generals fanned out across Capitol Hill to save the jet, which would cost $300 million each, the full House Appropriations Committee endorsed Lewis' decision by approving the unnumbered fiscal 2000 bill by voice vote July 16.

President Clinton had requested $1.8 billion to buy the first six production F-22s. The subcommittee decided to divert the money to other uses, including older-model planes and pilot incentives, while approving $1.2 billion for F-22 research and development.

The $266.1 billion defense bill is expected to reach the House floor the week of July 19. An extra $2.6 billion the government hopes to raise from an auction of electromagnetic spectrum would increase the budget authority available to $268.7 billion.

The Pentagon decided two years ago to limit spending on the advanced air-to-air F-22, which was conceived in the mid-1980s, and cut back its purchases from 438 to 339. The Air Force insists that the plane, which will not be flying in large numbers until late in the next decade, is needed to ensure U.S. pilots an edge over adversaries who may be flying modern jets that are becoming available in the international market.

But Lewis said the air war against Yugoslavia showed there is no need for such an advanced aircraft, since two similar planes — the Joint Strike Fighter and the F-18E/F — are being developed.

A March report by the General Accounting Office found that the F-22 was over budget and that some work was behind schedule. The plane is built by Lockheed Martin Corp. in Marietta, Ga.

The Defense Subcommittee has a history of taking strong steps to get the Pentagon's attention. But the F-22 decision may run more deeply. Lewis and other members are concerned that the military, while complaining that it does not have enough money for spare parts, maintenance and personnel retention, is pouring money into three different air-superiority fighter planes.

Congress in recent years has funded most of the military's main procurement requests, but Lewis said the F-22 decision shows that the House "is going to be in the middle of these procurement decisions."

Moving Fast

The Air Force responded quickly. "We're not taking this lightly," Lt. Gen. Gregory S. Martin, deputy Air Force Secretary for acquisition, told reporters at a July 15 Pentagon briefing.

Martin and other Air Force officials began discussions July 15 with individual House appropriators about the plane. The Air Force says the F-22 is necessary in deterring rogue nations from developing the types of weapons that could compete with U.S. defenses. The F-22 will not be used next year or the year after that, Martin said. "We're buying it to fight America's wars in 2010 to 2030 or beyond."

"The more people that get in our knickers, the less likely we are to maintain our dominance," Martin said.

Maj. Gen. Bruce Carlson, the Air Force deputy chief of operational requirements, said that although the 20-year-old F-15 may have proved successful in the recent air war against Yugoslavia, "asking a pilot to put his life on the line with a piece of equipment that is 26 years old doesn't make sense."

Martin added, "I don't think we'll lose the war in 2010, but I do believe a lot more people will be coming home in body bags."

The Senate version of the bill (S 1122) fully funds the F-22, setting up a potential showdown in conference.

The House bill would appropriate $440 million to buy eight F-15s. The administration requested none. It also would provide $350.6 million to buy 15 F-16 fighters, up from the administration's request of 10.

Missing from the bill is funding for the LHD-8 helicopter carrier. The Senate bill would provide $500 million for components for the ship, which would be built by Litton Industries Inc. in Pascagoula, Miss., the hometown of Senate Majority Leader Trent Lott. The Navy does not plan to begin buying components for this ship until 2004.

The bill would provide $167 million to supplement the amount included in a fiscal 1999 supplemental bill (PL 106-31) for a 4.8 percent military pay increase in fiscal 2000, rather than the 4.4 percent requested by the administration. The pay raise is meant to alleviate recruiting and retention problems throughout the services.

House Passes Bill Without Funding For F-22 Fighters

JULY 24 — A potentially bruising political battle shaping up over the F-22 fighter plane could spark debate over other big-ticket Pentagon weapons programs before it is resolved.

Although the House omitted $1.9 billion to begin production of the F-22 when it passed a $268 billion fiscal 2000 defense appropriations bill (HR 2561), 379-45, on July 22, there is little chance the Senate will agree to halt the program. *(Vote 334, p. H-110)*

The plane's friends include President Clinton, Defense Secretary William S. Cohen, Air Force leaders, prime contractor Lockheed Martin Corp. and members of the Georgia, Texas, Connecticut and Washington state congressional delegations whose states have a stake in the project.

There is no recent precedent for either the House or the Senate trying to kill off a major defense program that has come this close to production.

But Republican Jerry Lewis of California, chairman of the House Defense Appropriations Subcommittee, which cut funding for the plane, is after larger issues than the F-22.

Lewis picked this fight, blindsiding the Pentagon, to goad the Clinton administration and Congress into resolving what he and the committee insist are fundamental problems in the Pentagon's long-term plans — problems, they say, that are typified by the stealthy fighter plane.

For one thing, these critics contend, the armed services' long-range spending plans are affordable only with highly optimistic assumptions that future defense budgets will increase, despite pressure to reduce taxes and increase domestic spending.

Compounding this mismatch between plans and budgets, the critics say, is the continued insistence of the military services on developing highly sophisticated weapons, designed to overpower Soviet forces that no longer exist, while shortchanging personnel programs and equipment more relevant to the post-Cold War world.

The F-22 is the centerpiece of Air Force plans to retain air superiority through the first few decades of the next century. But Lewis and other critics contend that the plane is too costly and unnecessarily complex and that it is soaking up funds needed by more essential but less glamorous Air Force programs.

The House bill includes $1.2 billion, as requested, to continue developing the F-22. Thus, Lewis insisted, the House position would provide a "pause" to let Congress and the Pentagon ponder whether the plane fits into projected future defense budgets, in light of competing requirements.

"The Air Force has such tremendous needs in so many other areas — air tankers, airlift transports, aerial reconnaissance — that we believe it is imperative for the Air Force to reassess its priorities," Lewis said in a July 22 statement.

However, Cohen and other F-22 supporters maintained that the House action would delay production and run up costs to an extent that would destroy the Pentagon's plan to buy 339 of the planes over 16 years at an average cost of about $120 million apiece.

"If you take that amount of money out," Cohen warned during a Senate Armed Services Committee hearing on July 20, "you are in fact killing the program."

Symptom or Solution?

Though Lewis said he wanted to shift money to programs that would help the military services with their current missions, the House bill would sharply restrict some initiatives the Pentagon says would address those concerns.

For instance, at the urging of the House and Senate Armed Services committees, the U.S. Atlantic Command, headquartered in Norfolk, Va., is supposed to test radical changes in the services' war-fighting plans by conducting war games and simulations. But the Appropriations Committee cut $22 million from the $42 million requested for that program, complaining that the Atlantic Command's plans were too vague.

The bill also denied the Pentagon's request to sign multi-year production contracts for several weapons programs, including the new, larger "E" and "F" models of the Navy's F/A-18 fighter. Multi-year contracts typically offer lower unit prices but restrict Congress' ability to reshuffle budgets in future years.

The Pentagon's mismatch of plans and budget is exemplified, the critics say, by the services' plans to spend about $340 billion over the next two decades on three jet fighter programs:

- The enlarged version of the Navy's F/A-18, already in production.
- The F-22, slated to enter service in numbers late in the next decade.
- The Joint Strike Fighter, three versions of which are slated for production late in the next decade to replace several types of planes dating from the 1970s.

Since the new versions of the F/A-18 are already in production, that program would be very hard to stop, Lewis acknowledged to reporters after the House vote.

And as the Joint Strike Fighter is years from production, stopping it would give the House little leverage to force the Pentagon to make hard choices Lewis says have to be faced now. "It's too early in this process to make that point," he said.

The F-22, on the cusp of production, offered Lewis both the leverage to force a showdown with the Pentagon and, he insisted, an illustration of the way a handful of big-ticket items crowd other programs out of the budget.

Lewis and other critics put the F-22's average cost at nearly $200 million apiece for a planned fleet of 339 planes. However, Cohen and other supporters say that figure is inflated, since it includes for each plane a proportionate share of the $20 billion spent thus far to develop the aircraft. The only cost that is relevant to the Pentagon's future budget squeeze, they argue, is the price of buying the planes once they have been developed — a price currently planned to be about $120 million apiece.

Sharing the Wealth

Some of the $1.8 billion the House bill denied for new F-22s would be parceled out for needs the committee says the Air Force has underfunded in its zeal for the F-22.

"What we've done is take care of the short-term problems to make sure the people who are serving today will be safe," senior Defense Subcommittee Democrat John P. Murtha of Pennsylvania said July 22. Among those initiatives are:

- $300 million for bonuses to stem the exodus of pilots that is projected to leave the Air Force 1,600 short by 2003.
- $451 million for various air reconnaissance programs, including an additional $188 million to buy two JSTARS ground-surveillance radar planes rather than the one requested, and $102 million to upgrade the aging Rivet Joint electronic eavesdropping planes.
- $564 million to buy eight tanker versions of Lockheed Martin's C-130 cargo plane, which the Marine Corps uses to refuel its helicopters.

The House also put some of the money cut from the F-22 request toward the purchase of fighters already in production — $115 million for five F-16s in addition to the 10 requested, and $440 million for eight F-15s, of which the administration requested none.

Even if the F-15s are not as formidable as the F-22s, the committee argued, they could, with upgrades, defeat any plane U.S. pilots are likely to face in the next couple of decades, until the less-expensive Joint Strike Fighter enters service.

Whatever the merit of that argument, many of the committee's spending alternatives should lock in political support for its challenge to the F-22. That is particularly true for the proposal to buy additional F-15s. Because Israel, Greece and the United Arab Emirates each have opted in the last several months to buy cheaper F-16s rather than F-15s, several thousand jobs at Boeing's St. Louis, Mo., plant may be lost early next year unless the company can sell more F-15s to the U.S. government.

Cohen and other F-22 supporters insist the House committee grossly underestimates the quality of the weaponry that U.S. pilots might confront a decade and more from now. No feasible modifications to the F-15, designed in the late 1960s, can give it an edge on fighters and anti-aircraft missiles already on the international arms market or likely to become available, they contend.

"We are trying to develop technology . . . to make sure that we keep a generation or a step ahead of all the potential competition," Cohen said July 20.

The F-22 is intended to ensure combat domination with a combination of radar-evading "stealth," high-speed for sustained periods and a web of electronic sensors knitted together to give the pilot a comprehensive picture of the combat situation.

The Joint Strike Fighter is intended to be slower and less stealthy than the F-22. Moreover, it will depend on technology being developed for the F-22.

Shaping a Deal

Lewis indicated July 22 that he was ready to discuss alternatives to the House bill's handling of the F-22. "We're looking for serious responses from the Air Force and others as to how we can develop these programs and make sense out of our conflicting budgetary needs," he said.

A compromise may be easier than first appears. For one thing, acting Air Force Secretary F. Whitten Peters told the Senate Armed Services Committee on July 21 that Lockheed Martin had made "dramatic" efforts to cut costs and increase efficiency. That might allow the company to accept a price reduction on the F-22.

In theory, conferees could scrape together the $1.9 billion for F-22 production without having to fight for the money the House bill would give to the F-15 and other weapons programs. Lewis' bill would add more than $2 billion to the budget request for large funding categories such as spare parts or property maintenance.

Lewis, however, insists that the committee wants to see a long-term defense spending plan that looks more credible than the current one, not just a garden-variety compromise that would produce a spending bill for next year.

"The bill's purpose is to see that they know we're serious about it," he said.

Budget Debate May Delay Conference Until Fall

JULY 31 — The high-profile debate over whether to begin building the F-22 fighter plane masks a high-stakes battle over fundamental defense spending that could last well into September.

An unusually wide difference in total funding for fiscal 2000 has opened between the House-passed bill (HR 2561) and the Senate version (S 1122). At $268.7 billion in new budget authority, the House bill is nearly $4 billion larger.

The closer the final bill comes to the more generous House version, the easier it will be to accommodate the spending priorities of both chambers.

But the defense bill is caught up in the broader budget debate.

Acting under the overall limits of the 1997 balanced-budget law (PL 105-33), Senate Republican leaders allocated more money to some domestic spending bills than did their House colleagues, leaving less for the defense appropriations measure. As a consequence, the defense issue may not be resolved until the broader budget fight is settled. *(Balanced-budget law, 1997 Almanac, p. 2-18)*

Further complicating the picture, President Clinton will have to send Congress a supplemental appropriations request this fall to pay for U.S. participation in the NATO-led peacekeeping operation in Kosovo. In May, House and Senate appropriators used a similar fiscal 1999 supplemental, (PL 106-31), intended to pay for peacekeeping operations in Bosnia, to bootleg into the defense budget billions of dollars in "emergency" spending that did not count against the budget caps.

Members who want to increase the defense budget might be tempted to settle for a lower total in the regular fiscal 2000 defense bill if they can reap a similar windfall later this year.

Meanwhile, the F-22 remains a troublesome issue for appropriations conferees. The Air Force considers it a key to maintaining air supremacy for decades to come, but the House Appropriations Committee called it a symptom of the services' habit of pouring money into a handful of big-ticket weapons at the expense of more pressing requirements.

The F-22 funds are included in the Senate-passed version of the defense bill, and the plane has sufficient support to ensure that this issue alone could take some time to resolve.

The F-22 debate casts a long shadow across the rest of the defense bill not only because the amount in disagreement is so large — $1.9 billion for the first six planes — but because supporters of the program warn that they have little room to negotiate a reduction in the F-22 request. Any significant cut, they contend, would nullify some existing contracts and free F-22 builder Lockheed Martin Corp. and its subcontractors either to raise their prices or, in the case of some suppliers, leave the program altogether.

Here is a look at other key issues in the defense spending bills:

Personnel and Readiness

The Senate and House bills would continue through fiscal 2000 the drawdown in military manpower that has been going on for more than a decade, down to about 1.4 million active duty personnel and about 865,000 members of the National Guard and reserves, numbers that Clinton proposed.

Both bills would cut more than $200 million from the budget request on the grounds that the Pentagon will start the fiscal year with fewer people on its payroll than the administration assumed. The House bill would cut $212 million from the military personnel accounts, while the Senate bill would cut $209 million from the accounts that fund civilian pay. The Clinton administration objected to the Senate cut, arguing that no such shortfall is likely.

• **Pay raise.** With the U.S. economy booming, the military services have found it increasingly difficult to fill their ranks with recruits and hang on to those that the services have trained. Early in July, even the Air Force, which typically has an easy time attracting young people, predicted that it would fall 2,500 recruits short of its fiscal 1999 goal.

Some members of Congress have speculated that at least a limited resumption of the military draft might become necessary. But that idea is anathema to most senior military leaders, who have experienced both the last years of the draft, which ended in 1973, and the all-volunteer force that began to hit its stride in the mid-1980s.

The Pentagon is approaching its personnel problems on two fronts: trying to make overseas assignments less frequent and more predictable while increasing pay, benefits and pensions.

The House and Senate appropriations bills would add to Clinton's request about $165 million for a 4.8 percent military pay raise, instead of the 4.4 percent raise Clinton asked for. The $1.8 billion that will pay for the 4.4 percent increase was included in the supplemental appropriations bill passed in May.

• **Retirement.** The House bill would cut $392 million from the personnel account to reflect near-term savings expected to result from the more liberal military-retirement system that is all but certain to be established by the companion defense authorization bill (HR 1401). That bill would allow those planning to retire at 20 years a choice — 50 percent of their basic pay, which was the rule for those who joined up before 1986, or 40 percent but with a $30,000 bonus after 15 years of service.

• **Personnel retention.** The House bill includes three additions to the budget request that are not matched by the Senate:

• $225 million to accelerate a more generous housing allowance for personnel who do not live in government quarters.

• $300 million for higher bonuses to stem the exodus of Air Force pilots.

• 104 million — in addition to the $784 million requested by the administration — for recruiting and advertising.

Both bills would add funds to increase the number of high school ROTC programs, which the services view as a recruiting tool. The House bill would add $35 million, and the Senate bill $27 million.

In recent years, the House and Senate versions of the defense spending bills have added large amounts for broad categories ostensibly related to combat readiness. This time, both bills' "readiness" additions to the president's budget request are $2 billion. But the Senate would devote the entire amount to facilities maintenance. The House, by contrast, would divide the total among real property maintenance ($854 million), routine base-operating costs ($440 million), spare parts ($453 million) and major equipment overhauls ($298 million).

To improve combat training ranges for the services, the House would add $112 million to the request; the Senate, $49 million.

• **Balkans.** Over strong administration objections, both bills would cut back the $2.4 billion Clinton requested to pay for peacekeeping operations in Bosnia and military operations against Iraq. The House cut $575 million on the grounds that the air war against Yugoslavia is over and the tempo of operations against Iraq has slowed. The Senate cut $300 million, saying the services were using this "contingency" fund to pay for recurring annual expenses.

The administration insists that the fund includes no money for either the war against Yugoslavia or subsequent peacekeeping operations in Kosovo. Clinton has promised to request a supplemental appropriation to pay for the Kosovo mission in fiscal 2000.

• **Hazardous waste.** Both bills would make minor additions to the $1.3 billion requested to clean up waste at current and former defense installations. The House would add $10 million and the Senate $40 million.

• **Nunn-Lugar.** The Senate bill would approve the $475 million requested for the Cooperative Threat Reduction Program, also known as the Nunn-Lugar program, to help Russia and other former Soviet republics dispose of nuclear, chemical and biological weapons. The House bill would reduce that total by $19 million, but its real impact on the program would be larger because it would deny the entire $106 million designated to build a plant to dismantle Russian chemical weapons. That cut is largely offset by additions to the amounts requested for dismantling and safeguarding former Soviet nuclear weapons.

Ground Combat

Both bills include the $636 million Clinton requested to continue upgrading early-model M-1 tanks by installing digital communications and improved night-vision equipment.

The House bill also added $22 million to the $67 million requested to begin developing a lighter tank that could be airlifted to distant trouble more easily than the 70-ton M-1. The Senate bill added $5 million for this project.

• **Helicopters.** The Senate cut $12 million from the $765 million requested to equip Apache helicopters with Longbow target-finding radar. The House bill included the full amount. Both bills would add $45 million to replace electronic components in the Apache fleet that cannot be maintained because they are no longer in production.

The House bill would also add $81 million to better equip some Apaches for low-level missions behind enemy lines by giving them new night-vision equipment that could better detect telephone wires and other obstacles and high-frequency radios that could stay in contact with distant headquarters.

Those were two of the improvements recommended to a House Armed Services panel on July 1 by Brig. Gen. Richard Cody, who commanded the Apache unit deployed to Albania during the war with Yugoslavia this year. The helicopters were not used.

The House approved the $427 million requested to continue developing the Comanche — a stealthy reconnaissance helicopter. The Senate would add $56 million to the president's budget request to accelerate testing of a second Comanche prototype.

• **Artillery.** Both bills approve the $283 million Clinton requested to continue developing the Crusader mobile cannon, which the Army says promises rapid, accurate, long-range fire but which critics say is too heavy to be quickly deployable.

The Senate bill would add to the budget request $31 million to accelerate development of a lightweight launcher for Army artillery rockets. Unlike the current launcher, the new one could be carried in C-130 cargo planes.

Both bills provide the $172 million

requested for long-range artillery rockets and the $149 million for anti-tank warheads to be carried by the rockets.

Both measures would more than double, to $85 million, the $30 million requested to buy night-vision equipment for Army and Marine troops.

- **Mines.** The Senate turned down the $48 million the administration requested to gear up for producing an artillery shell designed to scatter anti-tank and anti-personnel mines. The weapon's purpose is to quickly deploy an anti-tank minefield that would be hard for enemy troops to clear. The House bill approved the request.

The administration objected to the Senate's action, which was led by Patrick J. Leahy, D-Vt., a leading supporter of a treaty to ban anti-personnel mines. Under pressure from the Pentagon, Clinton has declined to sign the treaty, but he has vowed to try to develop weapons that could replace anti-personnel mines. The administration contends that artillery shells will be needed if no "non-mine" alternative can be devised by 2001. *(1997 Almanac, p. 8-26)*

Air Combat

The two spending bills support plans to field two combat jets over the next decade, in addition to the F-22.

Both bills include $2.7 billion that the administration requested to buy 36 E and F model F/A-18s, to be used by the Navy as ground attack planes, with the Senate trimming $10 million.

Both bills would beef up the $477 million requested to continue developing the Joint Strike Fighter, to be built in three versions to replace 1970s-vintage jets used by the Navy, Marine Corps and Air Force. The House bill added $100 million and the Senate bill $15 million.

The administration requested $253 million to buy the Air Force 10 of the latest model F-16s, equipped to hunt anti-aircraft radar sites. The Senate bill added $50 million for two additional planes, while the House bill added a net of $98 million for five more.

While no additional F-15s were requested, the House bill added $440 million for eight planes, and the Senate bill added $220 million for four.

- **Bombers.** Praising the effectiveness of long-range bombers during the war with Yugoslavia, the House Appropriations Committee argued in its report that targets could be destroyed more cheaply with precision-guided bombs dropped from a stealthy airplane than with long-range cruise missiles. Criticizing the Pentagon's plan to defer efforts to develop a new bomber until 2013, the committee ordered the Air Force to prepare a rough budget and timetable by May 2000 for developing both a new bomber and a cheaper version of the stealthy B-2.

Meanwhile, the bills each would fund initiatives to beef up the existing bomber force. The House bill would add $142 million to the $202 million Clinton requested to develop improvements to the B-2 and an additional $16 million to buy portable hangars to protect the planes' skins when they are deployed away from their home base in Missouri.

The Senate bill would add $37 million to the budget request for the B-2 development program.

Both bills would add $15 million to develop improved radar for the venerable B-52s, built in the early 1960s. The Senate bill also would add $47 million to keep all 94 of those planes, blocking Air Force retirement plans. The provision was instigated by Senate Appropriations Committee member Byron L. Dorgan, D-N.D., whose state hosts half the B-52 fleet at Minot Air Force Base.

The bills would fund three major "smart" bomb programs.

To buy more than 6,000 bombs that use satellite guidance to hit within yards of preselected coordinates, the Senate bill approved the $162 million requested. The House bill added $50 million for additional production and $19 million to speed up the process of adapting various types of planes to use the weapon.

For more than 800 bombs that use satellite navigation to glide 20 miles to their targets, the Senate bill includes the $235 million requested, while the House bill would cut $38 million.

Both bills include the $166 million Clinton requested to develop a stealthy, air-launched missile.

- **Radar.** Besides approving the $280 million requested for a JSTARS ground-surveillance radar plane, the Senate bill would add $46 million for components to buy another of the aircraft in fiscal 2001. The House bill includes an additional $250 million to buy a second plane in fiscal 2000.

Both would add funds to the budget request for improvements in the aging force of about 100 Prowler radar-jamming planes, which were spread thin to support the war against Yugoslavia and attacks on Iraq. The Senate bill would add $40 million, while the House bill would add $227 million, including $40 million designated to explore the feasibility of modifying F/A-18 Es and Fs to take over the jamming mission.

Naval Forces and Transport

Neither bill would make significant changes in the budget request for major Navy ships and weapons. They would provide:

- $752 million for components to be used in an aircraft carrier, for which the administration plans to request about $4 billion in the fiscal 2001 budget.
- $2.7 billion for three destroyers equipped with the Aegis anti-aircraft system.
- $748 million for components of a nuclear-powered submarine slated for inclusion in the fiscal 2001 budget.

Both bills would add $13 million to draw up plans to convert four huge Trident missile-launching subs so each could carry more than a hundred Tomahawk long-range cruise missiles.

To continue developing a cheaper version of the Tomahawk that could more quickly be shifted from one target to another, the Senate bill would approve the $145 million requested. The House bill would trim $5 million from that request.

Both bills include $51 million to upgrade older Tomahawks, as requested. But neither includes the $50 million recommended by the House Armed Services Committee to resume production of the current model Tomahawk.

- **Shipbuilding.** The Senate bill would add $500 million for components of a helicopter carrier that would be built by Litton Industries Inc. in Pascagoula, Miss., the hometown of Senate Majority Leader Trent Lott. The House bill has no funds for the carrier, but would add $320 million for a large cargo ship to be built either in San Diego by National Steel and Shipbuilding Co., or in New Orleans by Avondale Industries Inc.

Both bills include $1.5 billion, as

requested, for two LPD-17-class cargo ships designed to carry Marine amphibious landing forces along with helicopters and air-cushion vehicles to haul them ashore.

- **Cargo planes.** In addition to approving the $796 million requested for 10 Osprey tilt-rotor aircraft, which the Marines plan to use as troop carriers, the House bill adds $60 million for one additional aircraft, while the Senate bill adds $123 million for two.

The $3.1 billion requested for 15 C-17 long-range, wide-body cargo jets was approved, though the House bill would shift nearly $400 million of that amount into another budget account for bookkeeping purposes. The Senate bill also would allow the Pentagon to negotiate with the Boeing Co. a multi-year contract to buy 60 additional C-17s, beyond the 120 currently slated for purchase.

Both bills would add funds for C-130 cargo planes, none of which were included in the fiscal 2000 budget request. The Senate bill includes $153 million for two aircraft, one equipped to refuel Marine helicopters in midair and the other packed with electronic eavesdropping equipment. The House bill would add $564 million for eight of the Marine Corps tankers.

The Air Force had planned to defer purchase of any additional C-130s until 2002. But acting Air Force Secretary F. Whitten Peters told the Senate Armed Services Committee on July 21 that the service might be willing to accelerate that schedule because C-130 builder Lockheed Martin Corp. has achieved some dramatic cost reductions.

Conferees Race Clock for a Deal On F-22 Money

SEPTEMBER 25 — Senior House and Senate conferees on the defense appropriations bill (HR 2561) huddled into Sept. 24, looking for a compromise on the Air Force's F-22 fighter, the most contentious issue before them.

The negotiators had agreed on some elements of a deal that would provide much of the $1.9 billion President Clinton requested to start buying the planes, while deferring a commitment to full production until more flight tests are performed.

But agreement on the details remained elusive and House Appropriations Committee Chairman C.W. Bill Young, R-Fla., told reporters Sept. 23 that time was running out for the defense conferees.

"They want to move; they have to move," Young said. "If this bill stays in limbo much longer, there are those who would like to take money from the defense bill to help solve the money problems with other bills."

The Senate had approved the production request; the House turned it down. However, House Defense Appropriations Subcommittee Chairman Jerry Lewis, R-Calif., has insisted all along that his intention was not to kill the program but to enforce a "pause," during which the Pentagon and Congress could review the new plane's necessity, cost and test performance.

Both versions of the bill approved the $1.2 billion requested to continue testing the F-22.

Behind Closed Doors

The Air Force and F-22 contractor Lockheed Martin, which have waged a strenuous lobbying effort to overturn the House action, insist that any significant reduction in the fiscal 2000 procurement request would be fatal to the program, since it would increase the cost of each plane.

According to sources familiar with the closed negotiations, Lewis offered to accept about $500 million that could be used to buy two F-22s, provided additional testing was required.

Senate Appropriations Committee Chairman Ted Stevens countered with an offer that would reduce the $1.9 billion request to $1.3 billion, of which $227 million would be used to buy components for planes to be paid for in the fiscal 2001 budget. Stevens would add the remaining $1.1 billion to the $1.2 billion F-22 research budget.

Lewis told reporters Sept. 22 that any additional spending must be linked to more testing, as his panel demanded. But Young told reporters the following day that, under Stevens' proposal, the added funds for the research budget actually could be used to build more planes.

Senate Appropriations Committee member Kay Bailey Hutchison, R-Texas, a staunch F-22 supporter whose state has a major Lockheed Martin facility in Fort Worth, predicted that the conference would eventually approve money for the F-22 that was closer to the Senate's position. But as a result of the House initiative, she added, the program would be closely scrutinized over the next year. "We need to have a full airing and then put it to bed, so we don't have this kind of uprising in the future," she said.

Back to the Future

In addition to the F-22, defense conferees remained at odds on some other key issues, most notably total funding for the Pentagon. On paper, the bills are nearly $4 billion apart — $268.7 billion in new budget authority in the House version; $264.7 billion in the Senate. Clinton requested $263.3 billion.

But those figures exaggerate the practical difference in spending because, in addition to the new budget authority, the Senate bill would let the Pentagon spend $3.1 billion from the fiscal 1999 supplemental bill (PL 106-31) enacted in May.

Using fiscal 1999 money gave the Senate more fiscal 2000 funds to allocate to other appropriations bills without breaching the 1997 budget caps.

House conferees insist that most of the supplemental funds are needed to pay for military operations earlier this year against Serbia.

Among other issues the defense conferees grappled with during the week of Sept. 20 was funding for a helicopter carrier to be built by Litton Industries in Pascagoula, Miss., the hometown of Senate Majority Leader Trent Lott.

The Navy had planned to buy this ship in 2004-5. But, in a Sept. 23 interview, John P. Murtha of Pennsylvania, the senior Democrat on the House Defense Appropriations Subcommittee, said most conferees now accept the Senate's argument that buying the ship sooner would save money. The Senate Armed Services Committee has said that early funding would reduce the helicopter carrier's price from $2.3 billion to $1.5 billion.

F-22 Compromise May Free Bill For Floor Votes

OCTOBER 2 — Both sides in the battle over the Air Force's F-22 fighter jet can claim a partial victory in the final version of the defense appropriations bill (HR 2561). House and Senate negotiators are expected to sign the conference report Oct. 4, with votes in each chamber possible later that week.

The F-22 compromise, reached by senior members of the House and Senate Defense Appropriations subcommittees, would provide $1.3 billion of the $1.9 billion the Clinton administration requested and the Senate approved for production of the radar-evading jet.

Thus, Senate conferees led by Appropriations Committee Chairman Ted Stevens, R-Alaska, would win their demand that Congress not interrupt the program for a year. The Air Force and F-22 contractor Lockheed Martin Corp. had warned that the program would be killed by the House proposal to "pause" production for a year by withholding the $1.9 billion.

At the same time, the deal also contains provisions reflecting the demand of House conferees, led by Defense Appropriations Subcommittee Chairman Jerry Lewis, R-Calif., that additional testing be conducted before the Pentagon commits itself to the planned purchase of 339 F-22s.

The program is projected to cost about $70 billion, of which about $20 billion has been spent developing the aircraft. House conferees such as retired Navy fighter ace Randy "Duke" Cunningham, R-Calif., contended that the program was crowding out of the budget funds needed to improve the quality of life for military personnel and to meet less glamourous needs, such as upgrading the Pentagon's aging fleet of radar-jamming planes.

The partial victory for the House on the F-22 is highlighted by the fact that at least a large part of the $1.3 billion would be designated as research and development money rather than procurement funds. That would be in addition to $1.2 billion in the defense bill that the administration requested and the House and Senate both approved to continue F-22 development in fiscal 2000.

Lewis and John P. Murtha of Pennsylvania, the senior Democrat on the House Defense Appropriations Subcommittee, complained that the Air Force had scaled back planned testing rather than delaying production of the F-22 until the testing was completed. The Air Force and Lockheed Martin countered that the program is on a sound technological footing, while saving time and money, because it exploits breakthroughs in computer simulation and mathematical modeling to verify that the plane will perform as advertised.

The House conferees were skeptical. "We made it clear that the testing was inadequate," Murtha told reporters Sept. 30. "The big player in this was Duke Cunningham, because of his experience in testing airplanes."

In addition to the $1.2 billion in research funding that was not disputed, the conference report is expected to include the following amounts for the F-22 program:

- About $725 million to build additional planes in fiscal 2000. This could be used to pay part of the cost of as many as six planes, which is the number requested. In that case, the Air Force would have to provide additional funds in its 2001 budget.
- $277 million, as requested, for components to be used in 10 F-22s slated for funding in the fiscal 2001 budget. The money could not be spent until specific test milestones were met.
- $300 million in a reserve fund to cover the cost of killing the program, in case Congress or the Pentagon cancels existing contracts. If the contracts are not canceled during fiscal 2000, this money could be used in the following year to cover part of the funding shortfall on the planes purchased with the $725 million.

Talks at the Top

One factor contributing to the unusually testy relationship between members of the two staunchly pro-defense committees was press reports early in the process that characterized the negotiations as a victory for the House side.

"Our principals have not been too happy when they see things reported by you scrounging reporters," Murtha quipped at one point.

The basic elements of the deal were settled Sept. 29 in a late afternoon meeting in the office of Senate Majority Leader Trent Lott, R-Miss., with Lewis, Stevens and the three top-ranking House Republicans: Speaker J. Dennis Hastert of Illinois, Majority Leader Dick Armey of Texas and Majority Whip Tom DeLay of Texas.

While the F-22 was the most controversial item holding up completion of the defense conference report, Murtha cautioned that other problems remain to be worked out. But most of those issues involve the broader political battle over the budget rather than the provisions of the defense bill.

For example, Murtha noted that the Senate, in order to find more money for other spending bills, had agreed to designate $8 billion of the money in the defense bill as "emergency" spending, which would not count under the budget caps. The House so far has rejected that approach.

Turning Point?

While the compromise would save the F-22 for this year, the unexpected battle raises questions about its future. Since the end of the Cold War, two other major Air Force programs have run into heavy flak on Capitol Hill because of their cost:

- The B-2 stealth bomber, designed to penetrate Soviet air defenses, was stopped dead despite the fervent support of influential congressional defense specialists.
- McDonnell Douglas Corp., now a part of The Boeing Co., solved technical problems with the C-17 cargo jet and cut its cost to the point that the Pentagon is considering buying more than it had planned.

Richard L. Aboulafia, who analyzes combat aircraft programs for Teal Group Corp., speculates that the F-22's situation may be closer to the B-2's in that the need for long-range airlift (the C-17) is more widely accepted than the need for a new air-superiority fighter.

The Air Force said the F-22 is essential if U.S. pilots are to dominate the air over future battlefields. The F-15s and F-16s currently in service could be matched by some fighters available in the world market, the Air Force insists.

But skeptics argue that the current U.S. planes, with some upgrades, could suffice, given the superiority of U.S. pilot training and the small number of front-line craft any prospective foe could afford.

"Congress might argue that we don't need the absolutely best fighter in the world, just as they decided that we don't need the absolutely best bomber," in the form of the B-2, Aboulafia said in an interview Oct. 1.

On the other hand, he predicted that if Congress cuts back the size of the F-22 program, it will not slash it as drastically as it had the B-2 because the fighter's cost is much lower.

Final Measure Funds F-22 But Also Requires More Tests

OCTOBER 9 — The conference report on the $267.7 billion defense appropriations bill approved Oct. 6 by House and Senate negotiators includes $1 billion of the $1.9 billion President Clinton had requested and the Senate had approved to buy F-22 jet fighters.

In all, the bill (HR 2561) would provide $4.5 billion more than Clinton requested for Pentagon spending in fiscal 2000 and $17.3 billion more than Congress appropriated for fiscal 1999.

A White House spokesman on Oct. 8 reportedly said that spending Congress added for defense might have to come from Social Security revenue.

The spokesman particularly criticized the addition of $375 million to begin work on a helicopter carrier that would be built by Litton Industries in Pascagoula, Miss., hometown of Senate Majority Leader Trent Lott. The Navy had planned to request funds for the ship beginning in 2004, but Litton said the price would drop from $2.3 billion to $1.5 billion if Congress funds it now.

Supporters of the F-22, meanwhile, said the funds provided would keep the program on track, allowing the Air Force to begin production of additional planes.

But House Defense Appropriations Subcommittee Chairman Jerry Lewis, R-Calif., at whose urging the House had rejected the F-22 production request, insisted that House conferees had achieved their aim because the conference report would require the Air Force to conduct additional testing before committing to full-scale production of the aircraft.

Lewis and senior House subcommittee Democrat John P. Murtha of Pennsylvania told reporters Oct. 7 that their skepticism about the F-22 foreshadowed the type of critical scrutiny their panel would give other high-priced weapons programs in the future.

"It sends a message to the services and the contractors that it's not going to be business as usual — that . . . Congress has a role in oversight," Lewis said. Such scrutiny is essential, the two members argued, because future defense budgets would require tough choices among competing priorities.

One potential target of the subcommittee's interest is the Army's effort to develop the Comanche helicopter. The conference report includes $467 million for that program, $40 million more than Clinton requested.

Begun as a lightweight, stealthy scout aircraft, the Comanche, Lewis said, has acquired "bells and whistles to the extent that there's some question as to whether it can fly." The subcommittee had "lots of homework to do" on the helicopter, Lewis acknowledged. But he added: "We intend to be asking the tough questions."

Budget Maneuvers

Final action on the defense appropriations conference report was delayed until Oct. 12 at the earliest, because it became a pawn in the wider battle between President Clinton and congressional Republicans over the fiscal 2000 budget.

As approved by conferees Oct. 6, the final bill included some accounting devices that would reduce the way it is counted against the spending caps set by the 1997 balanced-budget law (PL 105-33). For one thing, $7 billion of the $267.7 billion would not count because it is designated "emergency spending."

The total also does not include $1.8 billion in the fiscal 1999 supplemental appropriations bill enacted in May (PL 106-31), which would be used to cover most of the cost of the annual military pay raise in fiscal 2000.

The only funding for the pay raise in the fiscal 2000 bill is $165 million, the difference between a 4.8 percent raise and the 4.4 percent raise Clinton proposed.

But for at least a day after the conferees agreed on the defense bill, the measure hung in procedural limbo while House and Senate leaders and staff members considered additional accounting ploys that would reduce its fiscal 2000 outlays, thus making room under the spending caps for additional spending in other appropriations bills.

One of the devices reportedly under consideration was a delay in the final Defense Department payday for fiscal 2000 for a few days, until Oct. 1, 2000 — the first day of fiscal 2001— thus kicking into the next budget year upwards of $2 billion in outlays. An alternative being weighed would put the payday delay in some other bill and apply it to the entire federal work force.

Also being considered was a provision in the defense bill that would reduce outlays by $1.2 billion by slowing payments to defense contractors.

The conference report was slated to be filed before midnight Oct. 8, which would clear the way for final action on the bill the week of Oct. 11.

F-22 Deal

The $1 billion for the F-22 would be divided up this way:

- About $725 million in research money in lieu of $1.58 billion the White House requested to buy six planes. This could be used to start work on as many as six, though additional funds would be needed in fiscal 2001 to complete them. The planes would be specified for some of the additional testing the bill would require. However, F-22 supporters contended that, practically speaking, they would be the six planes the Air Force had requested.

Using research funds rather than production funds to pay for the planes was "not consequential," Senate Appropriations Committee member Kay Bailey Hutchison, R-Texas, told reporters Oct. 6. One of the major facilities that F-22 prime contractor Lockheed Martin Corp. would use to build the planes is in Fort Worth.

- $277 million, as the administration requested, for components to be used in 10 additional F-22s, most of the funding for which would be requested in the fiscal 2001 budget. Lewis said the bill would bar production of those 10 planes until the operational version of the F-22's sophisticated electronic system had been successfully flown in an F-22.

The Air Force, which contends that the F-22 is essential if U.S. pilots are to have the same advantage over future enemies that they do over current foes, touts the plane's avionics, or instrument system, as a key to its combat effectiveness. Built around a linked pair of computers with the combined power of two Cray supercomputers, the system is intended to perform many of the routine parts of flying the plane, leaving the pilot free to concentrate on trying to outsmart an enemy. In particular, the Air Force is betting heavily on the F-22's ability to integrate information from many different sources, so the pilot will be able to see on a single computer screen a "god's eye view" of the surrounding airspace, rather than looking at several different screens and trying to form a clear picture in his own mind.

Making all the electronics work together is the job of The Boeing Co., which has about a one-third share of the total F-22 program. Boeing and the Air Force insist they have been saving time and money by testing the avionics extensively in laboratories and in a jetliner modified to be a flying testbed for the F-22's radar and other detection gear.

Some F-22 opponents dismissed the conference agreement as a cave-in by Lewis to intense lobbying pressure by the Pentagon and by F-22 contractors. Council for a Livable World, a liberal group that favors smaller defense budgets and had applauded the initial House decision to deny production funds, dismissed the compromise as a "fig leaf," saying, "In essence, Congress has just redefined production models as testing models. . . . It just extends the F-22 debate into next year. And this time Lockheed and the Air Force will be ready."

In particular, critics lamented that House conferees had not followed through on the question they had raised earlier as to whether the F-22 could be dispensed with in favor of less expensive fighters.

But Lewis maintained that, besides ensuring that the plane would be more thoroughly tested, House conferees achieved some of their broader goals. For instance, they were able to include funds for other programs which, they argued, the Air Force had short-changed in its zeal to develop the F-22.

Lewis argued that this year's skirmish could benefit the program if the Air Force and its contractors keep a tighter rein on the F-22's cost, forestalling future congressional objections. "We're calling on the contractors to get their act together," Lewis said.

Congress Clears Bill, Swathed in Camouflage Green

OCTOBER 16 — Budget gimmicks appeared to reduce the bottom line of the fiscal 2000 defense appropriations bill cleared for the president Oct. 14. The changes allowed Republican congressional leaders to add $21 billion to other domestic appropriations bills while claiming they have not dipped into the Social Security surplus to pay for annual government operations.

The conference report on the bill (HR 2561) would appropriate $267.8 billion in new budget authority for the Defense Department, $4.5 billion more than President Clinton requested. The House adopted the report Oct. 13 by a vote of 372-55. The Senate adopted it Oct. 14 by a vote of 87-11. *(House vote 494, p. H-162; Senate vote 326, p. S-65)*

The $21 billion in accounting changes reduces the outlays that would be counted against the spending caps set by the 1997 balanced-budget law (PL 105-33).

In recent weeks, GOP leaders have used similar tactics to exempt billions of dollars in other appropriations bills from the spending caps.

But the breadth of the defense bill scorekeeping maneuvers is impressive:

- $7.2 billion in budget authority is designated emergency spending, as is $1.8 billion in budget authority to pay for most of the military's annual pay raise. Most of the pay raise funds are not included in the bill at all, but rather are drawn from the fiscal 1999 supplemental appropriations bill (PL 106-31) passed in May. All told, this exempts at least $6.6 billion in fiscal 2000 outlays from the budget caps.
- The bill assumes that a Federal Communications Commission auction of broadcast frequencies will net the government $2.6 billion, which is to be turned over to the Pentagon to offset that amount of budget authority and outlays in the bill. The Congressional Budget Office (CBO) predicts that the auction will be delayed and will net less money.
- Congress has ordered CBO to reduce its estimate of the bill's outlays by an additional $10.5 billion, on the premise that the Pentagon will spend the money more slowly than CBO assumed.
- The bill orders the Pentagon to slow the rate at which it pays contractors, reducing outlays by $1.2 billion.

David R. Obey of Wisconsin, ranking Democrat on the House Appropriations Committee, called that provision the "government deadbeat amendment."

"It will raise the cost of those contracts down the line," Obey said, "and, in the end, the taxpayers will pay for this foolishness."

Plane and Fancy

Despite such complaints, the conference report drew few objections. Conferees had solved the most contentious issue with a compromise on the F-22 fighter, agreeing to spend $1 billion that could be used to begin work on up to six planes, though more testing is required. Clinton had asked for $1.9 billion in procurement funds.

House opposition to the F-22 was a rare challenge to a major Pentagon program. In most cases, lawmakers were adding, rather than cutting, defense funds, particularly for their own favored projects.

For instance, conferees agreed with the Senate to add $375 million as partial payment for a helicopter carrier to be built by Litton Industries in Pascagoula, Miss., hometown of Senate Majority Leader Trent Lott.

Most of the add-ons involved much smaller amounts, one of the most modest being $250,000 to help conserve a cemetery at Fort Atkinson, Neb., an Army post in the 1820s.

Among the many projects funded in Alaska, home of Senate Appropriations Committee Chairman Ted

Army Speeds Up Plans To Travel Lighter, Hit Harder

OCTOBER 16 — The Army is accelerating its effort to field combat units that are easier to transport than its heavily armored tank battalions and more lethal than its current air-mobile forces.

Gen. Eric K. Shinseki, the Army chief of staff, told an audience of fellow officers and military contractors at a convention in Washington on Oct. 12 that 70-ton M-1 tanks may be replaced eventually by wheeled vehicles weighing one-third as much and able to shoot down attacking missiles rather than absorbing their impact.

At the same time he pushes for the technical breakthroughs that would yield such weapons, Shinseki said he will "jump-start" the Army's transformation this year by equipping two brigades at Fort Lewis, Wash., with lightweight fighting vehicles already available. The brigades will experiment with new tactics but also will be trained for deployment in future peacekeeping missions.

The goal, he said, is to field a combat-ready brigade of about 3,000 soldiers anywhere in the world within four days, a division of 15,000 within five days and five divisions within 30 days.

"We intend to get to trouble spots faster than our adversaries can complicate the crisis," Shinseki said. "If deterrence fails, we will . . . prosecute war with an intensity that wins at least cost to us and our allies."

Since becoming the Army's top officer in June, Shinseki has warned that the service must be "strategically relevant," his response to grumbling that it took too long for Army units to reach the Balkans during the Kosovo crisis and that some of their equipment was too unwieldy to operate in the mountainous terrain.

As Shinseki was speaking during the annual meeting of the Association of the U.S. Army, some off-the-shelf items he could buy were on display in a nearby exhibition hall. One is a light tank built by United Defense, which the Army was planning to buy in the mid-1990s but abandoned because of the budget squeeze. Another is a large armored car dubbed "The Generals' Solution" — the generals in question being General Motors, which builds the chassis, and General Dynamics, which makes the tank-sized cannon.

A key criterion for the interim equipment and any new weapons is whether they can be carried by the Air Force's ubiquitous C-130 cargo plane. The much larger C-5s and C-17s can carry M-1 tanks, but the Pentagon has many more C-130s, and they can land in rough terrain near a battlefield that could not accommodate the larger aircraft.

Getting There

With only weeks to go before the Army's fiscal 2001 budget request is locked up, officials are scrambling to translate Shinseki's vision into a concrete plan. Army officials have complained for years that their budgets have been $5 billion a year less than they need to equip and train the force as it is. So unless the service gets a greater share of the Pentagon pie, something may have to give to fund the new initiative.

The conference report on the fiscal 2000 defense appropriations bill (HR 2561) suggests there is congressional support for some of the light-weight weapons the Army wants to develop. But the picture may become more complicated if the service tries to fund new initiatives by canceling ongoing programs.

The conference report would add $10 million to the budget for work on a new combat vehicle. And it would add $31 million to accelerate development of a compact artillery rocket launcher small enough to fit in a C-130.

The report would provide $467 million, $40 million more than President Clinton requested, to develop the Comanche scout helicopter. And it would provide $273 million of the $350 million requested to develop the mobile, long-range Crusader cannon. The Army touts the Crusader's unprecedented combat versatility, but critics argue that its 70-ton weight compounds the Army's existing problems in deploying forces abroad.

Stevens, a Republican, were research on the aurora borealis ($10 million) and cleanup work at a landfill in the town of Barrow ($3 million).

In a news release, Daniel K. Inouye, ranking Democrat on the Senate Defense Appropriations Subcommittee, claimed credit for $387 million in projects for his home state of Hawaii. They include $47 million for facilities at a missile test range on the island of Kauai and $35 million, rather than the $15 million requested, to continue removing unexploded bombs and shells from the island of Kahoolawe, used by the Navy for target practice. It also includes $1 million to prevent brown tree snakes, which would devastate Hawaii's native birds, from being carried in by military ships and planes.

The conference report would add $630 million for medical research and treatment projects not requested, including $175 million for breast cancer research and $75 million for prostate cancer research.

House Defense Appropriations Subcommittee Chairman Jerry Lewis, R-Calif., who led the fight against the F-22, secured $15 million in the bill for a project at Loma Linda University Medical Center in his district. Lewis told reporters Oct. 7 that the medical programs were justified partly by the fact that the usual channels for federal funding of medical research are unduly influenced by a small group of institutions favored by the National Institutes of Health.

The bill also includes $15 million added for various projects around Fort Irwin, Calif., the Army's Mojave Desert tank training ground. One of Lewis' initiatives, which has become a fixture in defense bills, would require the Army to fly troops to Fort Irwin through a former air base in Victorville, Calif., rather than through Edwards Air Force Base. The bill includes the additional $2 million this would cost the Army.

Other highlights of the bill include the following:

Personnel Issues

The bill's $73.9 billion appropriation for military pay and benefits is a net increase of $171 million over Clinton's request and includes some cuts as well as additions designed to improve recruiting and the retention of experienced personnel.

Pentagon officials say the booming economy is the main reason the services have had trouble meeting their recruiting and retention goals. But they also say that the picture has improved recently because service personnel who were deciding whether to re-enlist became increasingly confident that Congress not only would approve a pay raise and other Clinton initiatives, but would sweeten the pot.

Both House and Senate versions of the appropriations bill included a 4.8 percent military pay raise rather than the 4.4 percent increase Clinton requested. The conference report would provide $165 million to fund the difference.

The conference report includes scaled-down versions of other retention incentives the House had approved, and would add to Clinton's request:

- $100 million to accelerate a more generous housing allowance for those who live off base; and
- $110 million for higher bonuses to stem the exodus of Air Force pilots.

It also would add $162 million to Clinton's request for bonuses to those who enlist or re-enlist in essential and hard-to-fill specialties.

Key to the personnel issue, but funded in another part of the report, is the budget for recruiting and advertising, for which the conference report would provide $105 million more than the $784 million Clinton requested.

Split between the personnel and operations sections of the bill is the $35 million the bill would add to Clinton's budget for high school ROTC programs. The services say that while these programs are not avowedly recruiting efforts, many graduates wind up joining the military.

The bill also would add $7 million to fund an Army program that would allow junior college students to defer the start of active-duty service for up to two years and collect a stipend while they complete their education.

These congressional add-ons would be partly offset by cuts to Clinton's personnel budget, including reductions of:

- $219 million because the services started the fiscal year with nearly 10,000 fewer active duty personnel than the budget assumed;
- $136 million because of near-term savings in the military pension system. Clinton and Congress agreed to essentially repeal a 1986 law (PL 99-348) that reduced pensions for those retiring after 20 years. But the retirement package written on Capitol Hill and enacted as part of the companion defense authorization bill (PL 106-65) will be cheaper than the administration's formula.

Operations and Readiness

The appropriations bill would give the Pentagon $92.2 billion for day-to-day operations, maintenance and training, $967 million more than Clinton requested, but $1.45 billion less than the House approved. It is $340 million more than the Senate version of the bill.

Clinton did not request and Congress did not include money for fiscal 2000 operations in Kosovo, which Clinton has promised to ask for in a supplemental.

For operations in Bosnia and Iraq, the bill would provide $1.7 billion of the $2.4 billion requested. Conferees said the $665 million reduction could be offset with funds left over because the air war against Serbia was halted before the end of fiscal 1999.

With the intention of improving morale and combat readiness, conferees added to Clinton's budget request:

- $289 million for spare parts;
- $222 million for overhauls of ships, planes, vehicles and other equipment;
- $223 million for routine base operations; and
- $362 million for facilities maintenance.

As in the past, the bill would partly offset those additions with cuts to Clinton's request which, the Appropriations committees insist, will have no effect on the services' combat readiness. The largest of these — $171 million — is because the dollar's strength will reduce the cost of supplies and services purchased overseas.

Other routine cuts called for in the bill include:

- $140 million to compel the services to slim down their management headquarters;
- $123 million because the Pentagon started the fiscal year with a smaller civilian payroll than Clinton's request assumed; and
- $50 million to force a reduction in the Pentagon's use of consultants.

The bill would provide $461 million of the $476 million requested for the so-called Nunn-Lugar program to help Russia and other former Soviet states dispose of their nuclear, chemical and biological weapons, and the long-range missiles and bombers that could carry them.

However, the bill would have a greater impact on the program than the relatively small reduction may suggest: It would deny the $130 million requested to continue building a chemical weapons destruction facility in Russia and would deny the $20 million requested for modifying three Russian reactors used to generate power to make it harder to use them to build nuclear weapons. The funds requested for those projects are parceled out to other parts of the Nunn-Lugar program.

Air Combat

The conference report would add $104 million to continue a long-running program to equip 1960s-vintage midair refueling tankers with more reliable and more powerful engines.

It also would include $60 million for new engines for two tankers that have been modified into electronic eavesdropping planes. To upgrade the fleet of 1970s-vintage Prowler radar-jamming planes, the bill would include

Defense Spending Highlights

Where the Money Goes

HR 2561— Conference report: H Rept 106-351

Spending Synopsis

The Senate cleared the conference report on the fiscal 2000 defense appropriations bill, 87-11, Oct. 14, after the House adopted it, 372-55, Oct. 13. The report provides $267.8 billion in new budget authority, $1.2 billion more than was appropriated in fiscal 1999, which included $16.1 billion in emergency and supplemental spending. It is $4.5 billion more than President Clinton requested, $3.1 billion more than the Senate passed but $866 million less than the House had passed. In order to stay within budget caps, congressional leaders designated $7.2 billion as "emergency" defense spending and ordered the Pentagon to slow down payments to contractors.

- **Personnel**

The $73.9 billion in the conference report is $171 million more than Clinton requested, largely to cover the difference between the 4.4 percent military pay raise Clinton proposed and the 4.8 percent raise Congress approved. The report adds $110 million to Clinton's request for bonuses to help retain pilots and $100 million for higher housing allowances. The report cut $219 million from Clinton's request because the number of military personnel was below projections.

- **Operations and maintenance**

The report provides $92.2 billion for operating costs, $967 million more than Clinton requested, $340 million more than the Senate version but $1.5 billion less than the House version. Among major additions to Clinton's request were $362 million for facilities maintenance, $223 million for base operations, $289 million for spare parts.

- **Procurement**

The report's $53 billion for buying weapons and equipment was $1.1 billion more than Clinton requested, virtually the same as the House bill but $1.6 billion less than the Senate bill. The largest additions were $375 million for a helicopter carrier built in Mississippi, $320 million for a roll-on/roll-off cargo ship and $275 million for five F-15 fighters.

- **Research and development**

The report provides $37.6 billion, a $3.2 billion increase over Clinton's request, $1.2 billion more than the Senate version and $431 million more than the House.

Hot-Button Issues

Δ **F-22 fighter.** In a careful compromise on the bill's hottest issue, conferees denied the $1.9 billion Clinton requested to buy six F-22 fighters, approved $1 billion for continued research and to purchase advance components of 10 planes. Some of the research money may be used to start building planes for testing.

Δ **Jets for generals.** Conferees went along with a Pentagon request to lease six Gulfstream V executive jets for its top commanders, an object of heated debate in the Senate. The report also approved buying one 737 that the administration requested.

Δ **Balkan reconstruction.** A Senate provision barring any aid to Serbia as long as Yugoslavia President Slobodan Milosevic remains in power was retained in the conference report. No funds were requested or appropriated for Balkan reconstruction.

Δ **Anthrax vaccine.** Conferees ordered the General Accounting Office to study the controversial anthrax immunization program, including its effect on military morale, retention and recruiting.

(figures are in thousands of dollars of new budget authority)

	Fiscal 1999 Appropriation	Fiscal 2000 Clinton Request	House Bill	Senate Bill	Conference Report
Military personnel	$70,607,566	$73,723,293	$73,850,403	$73,855,093	$73,894,693
Operation and maintenance	84,042,814	91,268,249	93,687,750	91,894,349	92,234,779
Procurement	48,590,420	51,851,538	53,025,397	54,592,016	52,980,714
Research and development	36,756,650	34,375,219	37,174,446	36,439,725	37,605,560
Other Defense Department programs	11,797,668	12,932,601	12,883,961	13,261,996	13,168,961
Miscellaneous and rescissions	14,821,379	– 884,941	– 1,960,454	–5,350,079	– 2,089,347
GRAND TOTAL	**$266,616,497 ***	**$263,265,959**	**$268,661,503**	**$264,693,100**	**$267,795,360**

* Includes emergency and supplemental appropriations

Table: House and Senate Appropriations committees

$240 million instead of the $161 million requested.

The House bill would have provided $468 million to buy two Joint STARS radar planes, converted jetliners able to find ground targets 150 miles away. The conference report would buy one of the planes, as Clinton requested. It also would add to the budget $36 million as a down payment on another Joint STARS plane, which Congress wants the Pentagon to buy in fiscal 2001.

The conference report includes $275 million for five Boeing F-15 fighters and $25 million for components of additional F-15s to be funded in fiscal 2001. The administration requested no F-15s. The Senate would have added $220 million for four, while the House would have added $440 million for eight.

The bill also would allot $246 million to buy 10 Lockheed Martin F-16s, for which the administration had requested $253 million. The House had added to that request $98 million for five additional F-16s.

Neither chamber had significantly changed the amounts requested for the Pentagon's two other new fighter jet programs. Accordingly, the conference report would appropriate $2.7 billion for 36 Boeing F/A-18 E and F model ground attack planes for the Navy. It also would provide $492 million — $15 million more than requested — to continue developing the Joint Strike Fighter, slated to enter service with the Navy, Air Force and Marine Corps late in the next decade. The Boeing Co. and a team of companies led by Lockheed Martin Corp. are competing for this contract.

Naval Forces and Transport

Neither chamber significantly changed the administration's requests for major warships, including components of a new aircraft carrier and submarine and three destroyers.

The largest single increase in the conference report was the $375 million added as partial payment for the helicopter carrier to be built in Mississippi. The Navy had planned to buy components for the ship in fiscal 2004, with the bulk of the funding to be requested in 2005. But the contractor said the price would drop from $2.3 billion to $1.5 billion if Congress funds the vessel immediately.

The bill also would add $320 million for a "roll on/roll off" cargo ship for trucks and other vehicles of a U.S.-based combat unit. Likely candidates for the contract are National Steel and Shipbuilding Co. in San Diego, a subsidiary of General Dynamics, and Avondale Industries in New Orleans, recently purchased by Litton Industries.

As requested, the bill would provide $1.5 billion for two ships to carry Marine amphibious landing forces. Avondale and General Dynamic's Bath Iron Works subsidiary build these vessels.

The provision in the bill with the greatest long-term budgetary impact may be one that would authorize the Air Force to sign a multi-year contract to buy 60 additional C-17 cargo planes, beyond the 120 currently planned, provided the additional planes are at least 25 percent cheaper than those being purchased under the current contract.

Like the Senate version, the final bill included $153 million for two Lockheed Martin C-130 cargo planes, neither of which Clinton requested. The House had added $564 million for eight of the planes, which long have been popular with Congress.

The conference report also would add:

- $60 million for one more V-22 Osprey tilt-rotor plane in addition to the $796 million requested by the Marine Corps for 10 of the craft, built by Boeing's Vertol division in Pennsylvania and Textron's Bell Helicopter division in Fort Worth; and
- $116 million for 11 additional H-60 helicopters, on top of the $510 million requested for 28 of the aircraft, built in Connecticut by the Sikorsky division of United Technologies Corp.

Post-Cold War Missions

The bill would require reports from the Pentagon on how well U.S. forces are matched with the new missions they have been taking on since the end of the Cold War.

One report is to analyze U.S. airstrikes against Iraq last December and NATO's war with Yugoslavia over the province of Kosovo, with attention to the effectiveness of U.S. forces and of NATO's command structure.

Another report is to review the Pentagon's plans to modernize and expand its inventory of electronic warfare planes, such as the Prowler radar jammers. Defense officials say there is such high demand for the limited number of these craft that planes and crews are wearing out.

In their statement on the compromise bill, conferees expressed particular concern that the Air Force's small fleet of aging U-2 reconnaissance planes might be worn out before a replacement enters service. The bill would add $19 million for U-2 upgrades.

The conference report would require a quarterly report on the costs the military incurs supporting resolutions of the United Nations Security Council. It also would require a report on Washington's efforts to persuade the United Nations to reimburse the United States for these costs.

It also would authorize the president to waive a section of the 1994 Arms Export Control Act (PL 103-236) that required the automatic imposition of sanctions on India and Pakistan last year, after those countries conducted nuclear test explosions.

And the final bill would prohibit the use of any defense funds to aid North Korea, unless specifically approved by Congress. It would prohibit any reconstruction aid to Serbia as long as Yugoslavia President Slobodan Milosevic remains in power. ◆

After Two Vetoes, D.C. Bill Becomes Vehicle for Omnibus Spending Package

District of Columbia

2000 Fiscal Year

- **Bill:** HR 3194 — PL 106-113
- **Legislative action: Senate** passed S 1283 (S Rept 106-88) by voice vote July 1.

House passed HR 2587 (H Rept 106-249), 333-92, July 29.

House adopted conference report on HR 2587 (H Rept 106-299), 208-206, on Sept. 9.

Senate cleared HR 2587, 52-39, on Sept. 16.

President vetoed bill Sept. 28.

House passed HR 3064, 211-205, on Oct. 14.

Senate passed HR 3064, amended, by voice vote on Oct. 15.

House adopted conference report (H Rept 106-419), 218-211, on Oct. 28.

Senate cleared HR 3064, 49-48, on Nov. 2.

President vetoed bill Nov. 3.

House passed HR 3194, 216-210, on Nov. 3.

Senate passed HR 3194, amended, by voice vote Nov. 3.

House adopted conference report (H Rept 106-479), 296-135, on Nov. 18.

Senate cleared the bill, 74-24, on Nov. 19.

President signed HR 3194 on Nov. 29.

SUMMARY

Congress cleared the fiscal 2000 District of Columbia appropriations bill Nov. 19 after President Clinton had vetoed two earlier versions. The D.C. spending measure, which has become a magnet for legislative riders in recent years, carried four other appropriations bills to final passage.

The first two D.C. spending bills triggered vetoes from the president for a number of reasons, including a provision to bar the city from using any federal or local funds to operate needle exchange programs.

The programs are intended to curb the spread of infectious diseases such as HIV by giving clean needles to drug users. Ultimately, conferees modified the provision by requiring groups that conduct such programs to account for public funds separately from the funds used for needle exchange programs.

The $435.8 million spending bill for the District of Columbia included $17 million for a college tuition program for city residents and $6.7 million for environmental cleanup at the Lorton Correctional Complex in Virginia. The prison is scheduled to close by 2002.

Senate Panel's Quick OK Belies Trouble Ahead

JUNE 26 — The Senate Appropriations Committee gave quick approval June 24 to a fiscal 2000 spending bill (S 1283) for the District of Columbia that would make a $410.7 million federal payment to the city, but D.C. officials say they are bracing for big fights ahead.

The panel's 28-0 vote was the first action on the D.C. spending bill this year. The Senate panel's District of Columbia Subcommittee never acted on the measure, and no action is scheduled in the House until after the July Fourth break.

The bill's total is significantly less than the $683.6 million that Congress provided to the District last year, but equals the amount President Clinton requested for the city.

Last year's allocation included several one-time appropriations, such as $125 million to implement the city's revitalization plan, which did not need to be funded in fiscal 2000.

While Democrats supported the bill in committee, the measure is not expected to have a smooth ride when it reaches the Senate floor.

The D.C. subcommittee's ranking Democrat, Richard J. Durbin of Illinois, said he had a "major" problem with the legislation's acceptance of the tax cuts for District residents that city officials approved in May. He vowed to bring the issue up on the floor. Durbin said it was unacceptable for the city to enact a tax cut he said would cost $59 million next year while law enforcement and other crucial services are lacking.

But the D.C. Subcommittee's new chairwoman, Kay Bailey Hutchison, R-Texas, defended the city's tax cut as "quite reasonable," saying it would account for only 1 percent of its budget.

Also sure to draw fire from Democrats and the administration are some of the contentious policy provisions that have become annual battles on the legislation.

Policy "riders" on the Senate bill include a prohibition on the use of federal or local funds to pay for abortions in most cases, a prohibition on extending health insurance to domestic partners, a limitation on attorneys' fees in special education cases and language preventing the city from using funds in the bill to support an ongoing lawsuit to win voting representation in the House.

Fighting Over Riders

The annual D.C. bill has often been a magnet for social policy riders that have resulted in bitter, divisive debates. Last year, the fiscal 1999 bill started out on a smooth course as well, but ran into trouble on the House floor, where Democrats objected to a number of such policy provisions.

The House passed the bill along party lines, but Senate leaders never brought it to the floor and the measure was ultimately folded into the omnibus appropriations bill (PL 105-277).

Paul Strauss, one of the city's non-voting, elected representatives in the Senate, said city officials found this year's Senate bill less objectionable than they had in previous years, but that he was concerned about Durbin's vow to offer amendments on the floor to revisit the tax cut.

In addition, Byron L. Dorgan, D-N.D., said he would offer amendments on the floor to stiffen penalties for District parolees who fail drug tests and to require a "comprehensive investigation" of the District's criminal justice system.

Strauss said that both Durbin and Dorgan's moves would erode the city's home rule. "If we're getting bashed by our friends like Durbin and Dorgan, we can't wait to see what our enemies will do," Strauss said.

Hutchison touted a provision she contends would help ensure that the city's finances stay on a secure footing and would boost the city's standing with investors.

It would require the city to maintain its current $150 million reserve fund. In addition, the provision would require the city to maintain any budget surplus equivalent to 4 percent of expenditures.

If the city runs a surplus beyond that amount, half would have to go to debt reduction, but the other half could be spent on "non-recurring" expenses.

"This should help improve the District's standing in the municipal finance markets," Hutchison said.

The bill also would provide $17 million for a program that would provide aid to District residents who attend state colleges and universities.

It also contains $5.8 million for increased drug testing of individuals on probation or supervised release from prison and $1 million for the city's police department to try to eliminate open-air drug markets.

The Senate measure would allow a 5 percent pay increase for the District's City Council members, a cut from the 15 percent increase the City Council had voted to give itself.

Senate-Passed Bill Includes Tax Cut For D.C. Residents

JULY 3 — Despite Democratic objections, the Senate endorsed a proposed $59 million tax cut for residents of the District of Columbia when it passed a fiscal 2000 spending bill that would make a $410.7 million federal payment to the capital city. The bill (S 1283 — S Rept 106-88) passed July 1 by voice vote.

D.C. Appropriations Subcommittee Chairman Kay Bailey Hutchison, R-Texas, called the City Council's plan for the tax cut "much-needed."

The panel's ranking Democrat, Richard J. Durbin of Illinois, said police, schools and other services should have a higher priority. "Tax cuts can be a part of the answer, but after you do the basics," he said. Senators adopted by voice vote his non-binding amendment calling for an evaluation of the city's social services.

The bill's total is less than the $683.6 million that Congress provided to the District for fiscal 1999, but it equals the amount President Clinton requested for the city. The current allocation includes several one-time appropriations, such as $125 million to implement the city's revitalization plan.

In addition to four minor amendments, senators agreed by voice vote to a proposal by Minority Leader Tom Daschle, D-S.D., that would allow wireless communication towers to be erected near Rock Creek and Potomac Parkway, a scenic thoroughfare.

Because senators were eager to finish the bill and depart for the July Fourth recess, a number of controversial amendments were withdrawn, including a GOP proposal that would have prohibited the city from administering a needle-exchange program for drug addicts and a Democratic amendment to strike $17 million in tuition assistance to allow D.C. students to attend public colleges and universities across the country at in-state costs.

An administration statement said the White House is "deeply concerned" about several provisions in the bill, including a prohibition on public funding of abortions.

House Panel OKs Draft Bill Despite Riders Controversy

JULY 17 — A House Appropriations panel July 14 approved a $453 million fiscal 2000 spending bill for the District of Columbia, including several policy riders likely to cause tension in full committee.

The District of Columbia Appropriations Subcommittee agreed by voice vote to send the draft bill to full committee, which has scheduled a markup for July 20.

The bill is almost $60 million more than President Clinton requested, but $231 million less than the fiscal 1999 measure, which included several one-time appropriations. With the federal payment, the District would have a fiscal 2000 operating budget of $6.8 billion.

While both sides hailed language to provide funding for a special tuition rate program for college-bound District residents and one to encourage the adoption of foster children, Democrats complained about several social policy riders.

The measure retains a provision from previous years' bills that would bar the city from using its own funds to pay for abortions for low-income women. The language includes exceptions for cases of rape and incest or when the woman's life is endangered.

District of Columbia Subcommittee ranking Democrat James P. Moran of Virginia said he would offer amendments in full committee to strike provisions that would prohibit the city from using non-federal funds for needle exchange programs or to count the ballots in a medicinal marijuana referendum.

He said such restrictions "tie the hands of the District to use its own funds to carry out its own prerogatives." Chairman Ernest Istook, R-Okla., noted that such provisions were in last year's omnibus spending measure (PL 105-277).

The bill would also prohibit the city from using its own funds to petition Congress or the courts for full voting rights in Congress and prevent the city from enforcing a law that would extend health insurance to domestic partners.

Many members are likely to try to add provisions next week aimed at parochial issues. For example, John E. Sununu, R-N.H., is expected to offer an amendment to prevent the city from imposing zoning or ordinance impediments to the planned construction of a new headquarters for the American Red Cross. Sununu withdrew a similar amendment in subcommittee.

But the full committee's top Democrat, David R. Obey of Wisconsin, has signaled that he and other Democrats would fight such efforts, calling them attempts to micromanage the city.

"We should spend more time being congressmen and less time being city council members," he said.

The panel adopted by voice vote an amendment by Alan B. Mollohan, D-W.Va., that would prohibit high- or medium-security prison inmates from being transferred to privately run corrections facilities. Under current law, the District's prison facilities in Lorton, Va., will close by 2002. Half its inmates will be transferred to private prisons and half placed in federal facilities.

Mollohan said more than 50 percent of the District's inmates are classified as either high or medium security, and are therefore not suitable for private facilities.

Moran attempted to add to Mollohan's initiative with an amendment to require the city to house at least 50 percent of its minimum- to low-security female and youth inmates. But Moran withdrew the proposal, saying he would bring it up in full committee.

Some of the funds for corrections would go toward beefing up the city's drug testing of parolees. Both Istook and Moran said repeat offenders are the most common criminals in the District and that putting them back in jail for violating parole could reduce the incidence of violent crimes.

The bill would endorse a $59 million tax cut passed by the City Council earlier this year. Congress could have disapproved the tax cut within 30 days of its implementation July 8, but Istook wanted to explicitly endorse it. The Senate did so in its bill, passed July 1.

House Amends Bill To Allow Marijuana Tally, Needle Exchange

JULY 24 — The House Appropriations Committee approved a $453 million fiscal 2000 spending bill for the District of Columbia on July 20, including amendments that would allow the city to use its own funds on needle- exchange programs and to count the ballots in a 1998 medicinal marijuana referendum.

The bill (HR 2587) would provide the city with almost $60 million more than the Clinton administration requested but $231 million less than the fiscal 1999 level. In addition, the bill authorizes the district to spend $6.8 billion of its own funds in fiscal 2000.

Voting 32-23, the committee adopted an amendment by the D.C. Subcommittee's ranking Democrat, James P. Moran of Virginia, that would allow the District to use non-federal funds for needle exchange programs.

The ban was included in the subcommittee bill and was part of the fiscal 1999 D.C. appropriation, which was folded into last year's omnibus spending law (PL 105-277). Opponents of such programs argue that they encourage drug use.

Proponents of the programs say they reduce the spread of infectious diseases, such as AIDS, without encouraging drug use. The bill also includes $45.2 million for drug testing and treatment.

Voting 24-13, the committee also adopted a Moran amendment that would allow the District to release the results of a recent referendum on the use of marijuana for medicinal purposes.

While objecting to the medical use of marijuana, committee ranking Democrat David R. Obey of Wisconsin said preventing the city from knowing the referendum results constitutes "an incredible display of congressional arrogance and authoritarianism."

Riders Retained

The panel rejected, 24-29, an amendment by Carolyn Cheeks Kilpatrick, D-Mich., that would have removed a provision preventing District residents from using local funds to seek a court ruling on voting representation for the District in Congress.

D.C. Subcommittee Chairman Ernest Istook, R-Okla., said the bill would restrict District residents only from using public funds for such a voting rights court case, and would not do "anything to restrict anyone's rights to the courts."

The bill retained provisions in current law that would prevent the city from enforcing a law that would extend health insurance to domestic partners and bar the city from using its own funds to pay for abortions for low-income women. Moran withdrew amendments to strike those provisions, but said he would offer them on the House floor. The House is expected to consider the measure the week of July 26.

The bill also includes $7.5 million to study traffic problems on the city's 14th Street bridge, $5 million toward cleanup of the Anacostia River and $17 million for education tuition grants.

House Passes Bill; Democrats Hope To Soften Riders In Conference

JULY 31 — House Republicans narrowly avoided a showdown with Democrats July 29 with bipartisan passage of a $453 million fiscal 2000 spending bill for the District of Columbia.

Although two social policy mandates that have provoked a White House veto threat were attached to the measure, members agreed to put aside some of their differences until conference with the Senate. The House vote was 333-92. *(Vote 347, p. H-114)*

"We had to make a split-second decision on whether or not to support this bill," James P. Moran of Virginia, the ranking Democrat on the House Appropriations D.C. Subcommittee, said after the vote. "We decided on balance this was a bill worthy of support."

The measure (HR 2587), which also would approve the District's $6.8 billion fiscal 2000 budget, contains about $422 million for District corrections trustee operations, courts and offender supervision; $17 million for tuition scholarships for the city's high school graduates; and $8.5 million for foster child adoption incentives.

After sharply partisan debate, the House adopted, 241-187, an amendment that would prevent the city from spending city or federal funds on needle exchange programs, which provide intravenous drug users with clean needles in order to cut down on the spread of infectious diseases. *(Vote 344, p. H-114)*

Democrats condemned the ban as an irresponsible and unfair usurpation of the District's prerogative to chart its own social policy course.

"Some on the Republican side treat D.C. like their own conservative petri dish," said Lynn Woolsey, D-Calif.

The House also adopted, by voice vote, an amendment that would prevent the District from legalizing marijuana for medicinal purposes. The amendment, offered by Bob Barr, R-Ga., would prohibit the District from legalizing or reducing penalties for the possession, use or distribution of certain drugs, including marijuana.

Democrat Eleanor Holmes Norton, the District's non-voting delegate, called Barr's amendment "prior restraint on democracy" and said his aim was to strike down a medicinal marijuana statute before it had even been passed.

But Barr said that if Congress did not adopt such language, it would "tell people that drug use in our nation's capital is okay."

Barr last year attached language to the D.C. bill (PL 105-277) to stop the District from counting the ballots from a 1998 referendum on the use of medicinal marijuana.

In what Norton called "the real breakthrough" of the day, the House narrowly rejected, 213-215, an amendment offered by Steve Largent, R-Okla., that would have prevented the District from using any fiscal 2000 funds to allow unmarried domestic partners to adopt a child jointly. *(Vote 346, p. H-114)*

When the bill is in conference, Democrats hope to weaken the needle exchange funding restrictions and to clarify the marijuana language to allow the District to formulate its own policy.

D.C. Subcommittee Chairman Ernest Istook, R-Okla., said he will work with Democrats to revise the drug provision so that it has no "unintended consequences" for the city.

The Senate measure (S 1283), passed July 1, contains neither provision. Majority Leader Trent Lott, R-Miss., indicated July 28 that he opposes needle exchange programs but might be willing to remove some other riders.

Moran said he believes needle exchange programs are important enough to Democrats that they can depend on the president's bully pulpit to help strip the prohibition out of the measure.

Another potential holdout for Dem-ocrats during conference is the issue of allowing the District to spend local funds on a lawsuit to obtain congressional voting representation. The House bill would bar expenditure of funds on such a legal challenge. The House rejected, 214-214, a Norton amendment to eliminate the restriction. *(Vote 345, p. H-114)*

Conferees Retain Riders Despite Veto Threats

AUGUST 7 — After tussling over social policy riders, House and Senate appropriators agreed Aug. 4 to a fiscal 2000 spending plan for the District of Columbia, including many provisions that the Clinton administration has said would prompt a veto.

Overall, the conference report would provide a federal payment of $429.1 million to the District and approve the city's budget of $6.8 billion. It also would endorse a $59 million tax-relief package approved earlier this year by the D.C. Council.

The D.C. appropriations bill is the smallest of the 13 regular spending bills Congress considers each year, yet is often one of the most contentious.

This year's measure proved no different. On the day the conferees met, Office of Management and Budget Director Jack Lew fired off a letter to C.W. Bill Young, R-Fla., chairman of the House Appropriations Committee, outlining the administration's concern about policy riders in the measure.

The outcome disappointed Democrat Eleanor Holmes Norton, the District's non-voting delegate, who has fought Republican efforts to put social policy mandates in the bill.

She and other Democrats argued that the final report intrudes too much on the city's ability to decide how to spend its own tax revenues.

They cited a prohibition on the use of federal or local funds for distributing hypodermic needles. The ban had been included in the House bill, but not the Senate measure. The Clinton administration has indicated its strong opposition to the ban.

"We are singling out one jurisdiction in America and saying, 'No, you can't use your own money for needle exchange programs,'" said Sen. Richard J. Durbin, D-Ill., who offered unsuccessful alternatives to the report language. "Let them use their own funds for this."

Republicans argue that needle exchange programs tacitly encourage intravenous drug use. Supporters cite studies showing that the programs can be successful in helping to stop the spread of infectious diseases.

The conference report also would provide $20 million for universal drug screening and testing, including $7 million for drug treatment services.

More Riders

Conference member Rep. James P. Moran, D-Va., echoed Durbin's concerns about local control when the committee turned to a provision that would bar the city from using federal or local funds for petition drives or civil actions seeking federal voting rights for its citizens. The ban had been included in both House and Senate bills.

"They're not talking about a revolution," said Moran, urging the committee to allow D.C. the ability to use its own money on the issue. "This is not an extremist position. We would never, ever do this to one of our own jurisdictions."

While Democrats attacked the spending proposal as intruding unfairly on internal city policies, Republicans countered that they have a constitutional mandate to oversee certain operations of the District.

"We do have a vested interest in this," said Rep. Todd Tiahrt, R-Kan.

Rep. Ernest Istook, R-Okla., the House Appropriations D.C. Subcommittee chairman, unsuccessfully offered an amendment to the report that would have allowed the city to use its own funds for voting rights issues in the future.

A similar measure was offered on the House floor July 29 and failed by a vote of 214-214. The voting rights change "was an easy one to give us, and they couldn't even do that one," Norton said after the conference meeting.

The committee also agreed to provide up to $17 million for a new program to provide tuition aid to D.C. residents attending college outside the city. The program would be authorized in a separate measure (HR 974) approved by the House in May and now awaiting Senate action.

While Norton supports the program, she criticized the funding level in the conference report, saying it did not account for D.C. students who are already in college.

In his letter, Lew also said the administration objected to a provision, in both House and Senate bills, that would prohibit the use of federal or local funds to pay for abortions, except in cases of rape, incest or if the woman's life is endangered. The conference report retained the ban.

The Clinton administration also opposes a prohibition on the use of federal or local money to provide health insurance benefits for domestic partners or to legalize or reduce the penalties for using controlled substances. The latter provision is aimed at preventing the District from legalizing marijuana for medicinal purposes.

Beyond the policy issues, the conference report would provide $5 million for community renewal tax credits, $5 million in incentives for the adoption of foster children, $2.5 million for Children's National Medical Center, $5 million for cleaning the Anacostia River, and $5 million for planning and designing work on the 14th Street Bridge.

House Adopts Bill That Democrats Call 'Tyrannical'

SEPTEMBER 11 — The House on Sept. 9 narrowly adopted a House-Senate conference agreement on a fiscal 2000 District of Columbia spending bill (HR 2587) that includes social policy riders that have prompted a veto threat.

Democrats, many of whom supported the measure when it passed the House on July 29, voted against the conference report, saying Republicans reneged on a commitment to tone down or remove some of the policy provisions during conference with the Senate.

The measure, which would appropriate $429 million in federal funds for District activities and approve a D.C. budget of $6.8 billion, was approved 208-206. *(Vote 404, p. H-130)*

Enraged by the outcome of the House-Senate conference, the District's non-voting delegate, Democrat Eleanor Holmes Norton, unleashed fierce criticism of the measure and asked House Democrats to support her.

"The District should not be asked to grovel to get its own money," Norton said. "I will never grovel before this House to get the money to which we are entitled — our own money."

Despite efforts by Democratic conferees to narrow the policy riders they considered objectionable, the conference agreement retained several provisions that Norton had hoped to eliminate during the talks.

The riders include provisions that would stop the District from spending federal or local funds on weakening marijuana laws or funding needle-exchange programs, and a prohibition against the use of District funds for court actions seeking D.C. voting representation in Congress.

Norton and James P. Moran, D-Va., the ranking member of the House Appropriations D.C. Subcommittee, supported the bill in July after receiving assurances that the riders they and the White House found most egregious would be addressed in conference. But they made little headway.

"So we walk in, and it is a done deal — virtually no room for maneuver, virtually no room for any kind of negotiation or compromise," Moran said.

"The bill has grown worse in conference as the Senate simply piled on with unrelated additions and the House made no improvements and kept no promises," Norton said.

Drug Issues

Two policy provisions dealing with drugs played prominently in the partisan debate, as Democrats argued that the District should be able to chart its own course with regard to needle-exchange programs and medicinal marijuana.

As passed by the House, the bill would lift a prohibition enacted in the fiscal 1999 omnibus spending law (PL 105-277) that stopped the District from counting the ballots from a voter referendum on the legalization of marijuana for medicinal use. But it would establish a new ban on spending money to legalize or reduce penalties for the use of marijuana.

Republican conferees rejected an attempt by Moran to clarify that the prohibition should not prevent prosecutors from reducing drug penalties as part of a plea bargain, or stop the legal use of marijuana derivatives.

D.C. Appropriations Subcommittee Chairman Ernest Istook, R-Okla., said limiting or eliminating the prohibition would start the city down a slippery slope.

"Where do you draw the line?" Istook said. "If you say it's OK for D.C. to legalize marijuana, then what's next? Legalizing cocaine? Or heroin? Or perhaps rape and murder?"

Democrats also objected to the sweeping nature of the ban on needle-exchange programs, saying the District should at least be allowed to enjoy the benefits of such a program if it were run by a private, nonprofit organization. Such programs are designed to stem the spread of diseases, but opponents say they encourage drug use.

Istook said the riders were nothing new, and that Democrats were searching for an excuse to push a liberal policy on drugs.

"They're just grasping so hard," Istook said. "For them to try to claim that it's on principle is a cover story for an extremist agenda."

In a letter to Moran dated Sept. 9, Istook blasted the Democrats' position on the drug issue as a "highly extremist" one designed to "promote a pro-drug agenda."

"I fear your position would bring D.C. back to the worst of the [former Mayor] Marion Barry days, when the loose attitude toward illegal drugs made the city the butt of late-night talk show jokes," the letter said.

Democrats seized on the issue of congressional voting rights for the District as another example of the ways in which they felt the bill oversteps its bounds.

The conference report retains provisions included in both the House and Senate measures that would prohibit the use of District funds for legal attempts to attain congressional representation for the District.

The provision is largely symbolic, since the District already is represented pro bono in its legal appeals for vot-

D.C. Spending Highlights

Where the Money Goes 

HR 2587 (Conference Report: H Rept 106-299)

Spending Synopsis

The House on Sept. 9 approved a conference report that included a $429.1 million payment to the city, about midway between the House and Senate bills. The president proposed a $393.7 million payment. The D.C. appropriations bill funds a federal payment to compensate the city for hosting the federal government, whose properties are not taxed. The bill funds some programs and agencies in the District as well as courts, corrections and the financial control board.

Hot-Button Issues

△ **Medicinal marijuana.** The conference report retains House language to prohibit the District from legalizing controlled substances or reducing penalties, a provision aimed at a District initiative to legalize marijuana for medicinal purposes.

△ **Needle-exchange program.** The conference report would bar the city from using federal or city funds for needle-exchange programs. The Clinton administration has said such a ban could lead to a veto.

△ **Abortion.** The Clinton administration strongly opposes a provision in the conference report that would bar the city from using federal or local funds to pay for abortions for low-income women.

(figures are in thousands of dollars of new budget authority)

	Fiscal 1999 Appropriation	Fiscal 2000 Clinton Request	House Bill	Senate Bill	Conference Report
Total federal funds	$683,639	$393,740	$453,000	$410,740	$429,100
TOTAL D.C. Budget	**$6,790,169**	**$6,745,279**	**$6,785,833**	**$6,749,883**	**$6,778,433**

TABLE: Conference report on HR 2587

ing rights by the large Washington law firm Covington and Burling. But Norton said the limitation is still "a personal insult to the District," and Maryland Democrat Steny H. Hoyer called the limitation "one of the most extreme, tyrannical, dictatorial provisions that I have ever seen."

Istook called the criticism "hogwash."

Other Programs

The measure funds a wide spectrum of District priorities.

The federal funding in the measure is $255 million less than the fiscal 1999 appropriation. It includes $404 million for District corrections trustee operations, courts, court-appointed lawyers and offender supervision; $20 million for universal drug screening and testing; $5 million for foster child adoption incentives; and funds for tuition scholarships for District high school graduates.

Congress currently is considering legislation (HR 974) to authorize the resident tuition aid program, which would allow D.C. to award up to $10,000 per year to eligible college-bound students who attend public colleges or universities.

While the House approved a version May 24 that would allow the payments to apply to any state university in the country, the Senate drafted a measure that would allow the scholarships to be used only in Maryland or Virginia. Under the agreement, the spending bill would scale down the tuition aid appropriation if the authorization was limited to the two neighboring states.

The measure also would endorse a $59 million tax cut measure passed by the D.C. City Council and give District charter schools access to construction and repair funds available to other District schools. It would also provide $5 million each for lane work on the 14th Street Bridge and for environmental cleanup of the Anacostia River.

Senate Adopts Conference Report

SEPTEMBER 18 — The fiscal 2000 District of Columbia spending bill cleared its final congressional hurdle Sept. 16, when the Senate adopted the conference report (HR 2587 — H Rept 106-299) by a vote of 52-39. *(Vote 279, p. S-54)*

The White House, however, has threatened to veto the bill over several social policy riders, including a provision that would bar the funding of needle-exchange programs.

The final bill, which would provide $429 million in federal funds for the District, won narrow House passage Sept. 9.

Sen. Richard J. Durbin of Illinois, the ranking Democrat on the D.C. Appropriations Subcommittee, opposed policy riders. He also questioned the wisdom of providing for a local tax cut at the expense of education and anti-crime programs.

Subcommittee Chairwoman Kay Bailey Hutchison, R-Texas, responded that Congress has a role in overseeing District policy.

Clinton Delivers Promised Veto

OCTOBER 2 — The District of Columbia spending bill became the first of the fiscal 2000 appropriations measures to meet with a veto. In his Sept. 28 veto message, Clinton said he was returning the bill (HR 2587) to Congress because it contained "a number of highly objectionable provisions that are unwarranted intrusions into local citizens' decisions about local matters." *(Text, p. D-25)*

Clinton said he had no problem with the $429.1 million in federal funding provided under the bill. But he singled out a number of social policy "riders," including provisions to restrict the city's use of its own funds for efforts to obtain voting representation in Congress, prohibit the use of federal or local funds to pay for abortions in most cases, and block implementation of a local law providing health benefits for domestic partners.

Clinton also cited provisions to prohibit the city from using federal or local funds for needle exchange programs and language to prevent the city government from legalizing marijuana for medicinal reasons.

Similar amendments prevented Congress from agreeing on a fiscal 1999 D.C. appropriations bill. In the end, most riders were dropped and the bill was rolled into an omnibus spending bill (PL 105-277). *(1998 Almanac, p. 2-32)*

House, Senate Pass Revised D.C. Measure

OCTOBER 16 — A second fiscal 2000 spending bill for the District of Columbia is headed for conference committee after House and Senate action the week of Oct. 11. Senate revisions to the bill could bring it out of veto territory.

The House passed the new bill (HR 3064), 211-205, on Oct. 14, and the Senate passed it by voice vote Oct. 15, after amending it to include some changes that House Democrats had proposed. *(House vote 504, p. H-164)*

While the House-passed legislation retained several controversial riders that sparked a veto of the first D.C. bill (HR 2587) on Sept. 28, the Senate amendment attempted to address two of the more contentious issues.

The bill includes a provision that would prevent the District from spending any funds on needle-exchange programs. Senate language would clarify that the provision does not apply to the use of private funds for such programs, in which clean needles are given to drug users to prevent the spread of disease.

The bill would also prohibit the city from spending its own funds to seek voting rights in Congress. The Senate-adopted amendment would clarify that city attorneys could review and comment on private legal briefs on the matter, to which the District is a party.

Both the House and Senate left untouched a provision that would prohibit the city from spending any funds to implement an approved ballot initiative on the use of medicinal marijuana.

The House and Senate are also at odds on a handful of smaller provisions the administration opposed. The House bill, for example, would remove a limit on the salary of certain D.C. council officials, thus allowing a pay increase to take effect. The Senate, however, maintained the limit. The Senate language also retained a limit on attorneys' fees in special education cases, even though the House bill would have increased the cap.

Conferees are expected to begin meeting the week of Oct. 18.

Conferees Ease Policy Riders In D.C. Bill

OCTOBER 30 — Congress has finally developed a District of Columbia spending bill that could have a chance of being signed into law if it were not for a bit of baggage: a Labor, Health and Human Services appropriations bill more than 700 times its size in dollar terms.

The District of Columbia appropriations bill (HR 3064) would make a $429.1 million federal payment to the city. President Clinton vetoed the first D.C. spending bill (HR 2587) on Sept. 28. After that, lawmakers removed some of the more contentious provisions from the measure in order to make it more palatable to the White House.

But House and Senate leaders then yoked to the D.C. bill a $317.1 billion spending measure for the departments of Labor, Health and Human Services and Education that has drawn a veto threat from the White House.

When Clinton vetoed the last D.C. bill, he cited several social policy riders, including language that would have prevented the city from using any funds on needle-exchange programs. The House passed a new bill that would have retained the ban, but the conferees agreed to Senate-passed language clarifying that the provision would not apply to the use of private funds for such programs.

The conference report retained several other policy riders the White House opposes, including a restriction on salaries of D.C. City Council members, a prohibition on using funds to provide health benefits for domestic partners and permission for the construction of cellular phone towers in Rock Creek Park. It also retained a House- and Senate-passed provision that would prohibit the city from spending any funds to implement an approved ballot initiative on the use of medicinal marijuana.

In addition to the $429.1 million federal payment, the D.C. measure approves the spending of $6.8 billion in local funds for the district.

Clinton Vetoes Second Bill; Lawmakers Produce A Third

NOVEMBER 6 — Almost simultaneously, President Clinton vetoed the second District of Columbia spending bill Nov. 3 and the House and Senate passed a third. Conferees are expected to produce a bill that Clinton will sign.

The measure (HR 3194) passed by the House, 216-210, included a controversial provision that would prohibit federal or local funds from going to groups that distribute needles to drug users in order to curb the spread of disease. *(Vote 562, p. H-182)*

The Senate amended the bill to say that local or federal funds cannot be used for needle exchange programs, but did not prohibit groups that run such programs from receiving federal or local funds for other activities. The amendment brought it in line with the last D.C. bill (HR 3064 — Conference report: H Rept 106-419) sent to Clinton.

Clinton vetoed that bill not because of the D.C. language, but because it contained appropriations for the departments of Labor, Health and Human Services, and Education, including a

0.97 percent across-the-board cut in all discretionary spending.

This time, the new D.C. bill was passed as a stand-alone measure. But that may not remain the case. The bill could be used as a vehicle for fixes to one or more of the remaining fiscal 2000 appropriations bills. That became clear when the House and Senate appointed GOP Appropriations chairmen to the conference committee.

House conferees are Appropriations Committee Chairman C.W. Bill Young, R-Fla., ranking Democrat David R. Obey of Wisconsin and Jerry Lewis, R-Calif. Senate conferees are Appropriations Chairman Ted Stevens, R-Alaska; ranking Democrat Robert C. Byrd of West Virginia; Kay Bailey Hutchison, R-Texas; Pete V. Domenici, R-N.M.; and Richard J. Durbin, D-Ill.

As in past years, policy riders, rather than funding, have stalled the D.C. measure, which would make a $429.1 million federal payment to the city.

Spending Bills To Piggyback On D.C. Measure

NOVEMBER 13 — House and Senate conferees have agreed to a $435.8 million fiscal 2000 spending bill for the District of Columbia. The measure is expected to be finalized the week of Nov. 15 and made the vehicle for the four other remaining appropriations bills.

House conferees have agreed to drop a controversial provision in the House-passed bill that would prohibit any federal or local funds from going to groups that conduct needle exchange programs, even if the funds are used for other purposes. In needle exchange programs, clean needles are given to drug users in order to curb the spread of disease.

The bill would still prohibit the use of federal or local funds for needle-exchanges, and staff aides said the conference report would probably include a requirement that such groups account for public funds separately from those used for needle exchange programs.

Conferees are also expected to add $6.7 million to the bill for environmental cleanup at the Lorton Correctional Complex near three proposed Virginia schools. The prison is scheduled to be completely closed by 2002. The addition would bring the bill's total from $429.1 million to $435.8 million.

The annual D.C. measure is usually controversial because of policy riders, but this year's bill has had an extraordinarily tortuous path. President Clinton vetoed the first D.C. bill (HR 2587), citing a prohibition on the use of public funds for abortions in most cases and a restriction on the use of city funds for efforts to obtain voting representation in Congress.

Lawmakers then reworked the bill to make it acceptable to the president. But the second bill (HR 3064) was vetoed because it contained, among other things, a 0.97 percent across-the-board cut in all discretionary spending.

The D.C. bill has been selected as the appropriations vehicle because it is the one spending measure in conference and therefore ready to be sent to both chambers for final passage. Also, conference reports cannot be amended in either chamber.

Lawmakers Clear Third D.C. Bill As Vehicle for Omnibus Package

NOVEMBER 20 — The Senate on Nov. 19 cleared a $435.8 million fiscal 2000 spending measure for the District of Columbia, including a compromise on the controversial issue of needle-exchange programs.

The measure was the vehicle for the omnibus budget package (HR 3194 — Conference report: H Rept 106-479). The House voted, 296-135, on Nov. 18 to adopt the conference report, and the Senate cleared it the next day, 74-24. *(House vote 610, p. H-198; Senate vote 374, p. S-74)*

President Clinton vetoed two previous versions of the D.C. bill. The first (HR 2587) contained several legislative "riders" that the White House opposed.

The second bill (HR 3064) was used as a vehicle for a $317 billion Labor, Health and Human Services, and Education appropriations measure. Clinton vetoed it not because of the D.C. provisions, but because it contained a 0.97 percent across-the-board cut in discretionary spending.

The third House bill included a controversial provision that would prohibit any federal or local funds from going to groups that conduct needle-exchange programs — even if the funds were used for other activities. In needle-exchange programs, clean needles are given to drug users in hopes of curbing the spread of diseases.

The compromise still prohibits the use of federal or local funds for needle exchanges, but groups running such programs could receive public funds for other programs. Under the compromise, such groups must account separately for needle-exchange programs and publicly funded activities.

The D.C. bill appropriates federal funds to the city and approves the spending of $6.8 billion in local funds. As in past years, disputes over social policy riders, rather than money, have held up the D.C. bill. The compromise includes some items Clinton had objected to, including language that prohibits the District from using any funds for abortions, except to save the life of the woman or in cases of rape or incest. ◆

Energy-Water Bill Clears After House Leaders Dredge Up More for Water Projects

BoxScore	2000 Fiscal Year
Energy and Water	

• **Bill:** HR 2605 — PL 106-60

• **Legislative action: Senate** passed S 1186 (S Rept 106-58), 97-2, on June 16.

House passed HR 2605 (H Rept 106-253), 420-8, on July 27.

House adopted the conference report (H Rept 106-336), 327-87, on Sept. 27.

Senate cleared the bill, 96-3, on Sept. 28.

President signed the bill into law Sept. 29.

SUMMARY

President Clinton signed the $21.3 billion fiscal 2000 energy and water development appropriations bill Sept. 29.

The legislation proceeded smoothly to passage after House Republican leaders gave energy and water conferees an extra $1.1 billion to use. Until that occurred, Senate Energy and Water Appropriations Chairman Pete V. Domenici, R-N.M., had warned that an agreement would prove impossible because the House-passed bill provided $1.1 billion less than the Senate version.

The conference report represented a $210 million increase over fiscal 1999 levels, but remained $303 million less than the Clinton administration's request. The legislation funds operations at the Department of Energy, the U.S. Army Corps of Engineers and some Interior Department programs.

At Domenici's behest, the conference agreement significantly increased funding for the Energy Department's nuclear weapons programs, which account for more than half the bill's total spending. Domenici's state is home to two of the three Energy Department nuclear weapons laboratories — Los Alamos and Sandia. The third facility, Lawrence Livermore, is in California.

But the bill still drew darts from Energy Department officials. In particular, Energy Secretary Bill Richardson complained that it omitted $35 million that the administration requested to upgrade computer security at 70 of his agency's facilities. The department had come under heavy criticism from Republicans for lax security, which may have allowed China to obtain highly classified nuclear weapons data.

Domenici responded that there was no way to accommodate the department's security needs in a comprehensive fashion in the energy and water spending bill but that he would consider a request next year for additional funding in a supplemental appropriations bill.

The energy and water bill included money for water projects that have long been popular with House members. The final agreement contained $4.1 billion for the Army Corps of Engineers, $246 million above the administration's request.

The conference agreement also struck House-passed language designed to speed up permits for construction in designated wetlands. Environmental groups decried the language, and the White House had threatened to veto the bill if the provisions were included.

Senate Committee Bolsters Nuclear Security Funds

MAY 29 — During a week in which a House report detailed security breaches at U.S. nuclear laboratories, senators ordered more money for security at the facilities but did not dictate how it should be spent.

The Senate Appropriations Committee on May 27 approved, 27-1, a $21.3 billion draft bill to fund the Energy Department and water projects across the nation. In the process, the panel heeded Energy and Water Development Subcommittee Chairman Pete V. Domenici's advice to allow authorizing committees to handle any legislative response to charges of Chinese nuclear espionage.

The appropriations bill, which includes funding for Energy Department agencies charged with maintaining and ensuring the security and reliability of U.S. nuclear stockpiles, would boost funding for security and counterintelligence activities at the nuclear facilities and laboratories on alert in the wake of the alleged theft of U.S. technology secrets by China.

Funding for security investigations would increase from $30 million to $45 million, and the counterintelligence budget would more than double, to $39 million. But appropriators did not include specific language ordering heightened security measures.

All told, the draft bill earmarked $12.6 billion for nuclear stockpile management programs and environmental cleanup at nuclear facilities.

Although there was no specific mandate to change how security is handled, Domenici — a New Mexico Republican whose state is home to the Los Alamos national laboratory and Sandia national laboratories — suggested that the Energy Department contract with the FBI to conduct security checks. An amendment to the fiscal 2000 defense authorization bill (S 1059), adopted by voice vote on the Senate floor May 27, would require such a relationship to be implemented within one year. Currently, security checks are conducted by independent contractors hired by the Energy Department.

Water Projects

Hanging over appropriators during the week of May 24 were complaints about a net reduction in funding for home-state water projects — cherished by lawmakers — most of which are carried out by the Army Corps of Engineers and the Bureau of Reclamation. Lawmakers blamed the tight limits on discretionary spending caps enacted in 1997, but the full committee's somewhat generous energy and water allocation did not mute the groans.

"Many very, very important projects and priorities are simply going to be overlooked," said Harry Reid, D-Nev., the panel's ranking member, during the markup. "Our ability to appropriate is extremely limited."

Even Domenici, chairman of the Senate Budget Committee, which helped establish the caps, lamented that the caps forced him to provide less money for water projects than was requested by the White House for the first time in his memory.

Overall, non-defense programs would be funded at almost $8.7 billion. The Army Corps was given about $3.8 billion, almost $350 million less than was enacted in fiscal 1999.

More Money

But for all of the talk about lower funding figures, Domenici's energy and water allocation is almost $2 billion more than was received by his House counterpart, Ron Packard, R-Calif., chairman of the House Appropriations Energy and Water Development Subcommittee.

Domenici had complained that defense spending was receiving a large boost at the expense of the other 12 subcommittees. Resulting meetings with Appropriations Chairman Ted Stevens, R-Alaska, produced a $400 million increase in non-defense budget authority, which surfaced in a last-minute change to proposed allocations for the energy and water panel.

The Senate committee bill also includes language that would cap Energy Department travel expenses at 80 percent of fiscal 1998 levels after Domenici argued that officials had abused travel expenditures. In 1998, Energy Department contractors sought $249 million in travel expenses.

"These travel costs are absolutely out of line and completely unacceptable," Domenici said in a statement after the full committee markup.

"This is one area where the labs are going to have to change the way they do business."

Domenici said he expects the energy and water bill to be the first appropriations measure to reach the Senate floor after action on the fiscal 2000 defense appropriations bill (S 1122).

Dianne Feinstein, D-Calif., was the sole "nay" vote, though her opposition was to a transportation appropriations measure considered at the same time as the energy and water bill.

Senate Passes Bill Tilted Toward Defense Programs

JUNE 19 — The Senate's overwhelming passage of its spending bill for energy and water programs indicates that nuclear weapons activities may end up prevailing over dams and other similar projects in the fight for scarce funds.

Senators voted 97-2 on June 16 to pass the $21.7 billion appropriations bill for fiscal 2000, which funds operations at the Energy Department, Army Corps of Engineers and some Interior Department programs. James M. Jeffords, R-Vt., and Paul Wellstone, D-Minn., cast the only dissenting votes. *(Vote 172, p. S-35)*

The bill would provide $12.4 billion for the Energy Department's defense-related activities, including nearly $4.6 billion for nuclear weapons programs and about $4.6 billion for environmental cleanups at the department's sites.

Lawmakers cited the need to maintain the Energy Department's weapon activities because of national security needs. But the Clinton administration expressed dismay that the result would hurt the agency's non-defense work.

"The bill would significantly reduce vital programs in energy research and other activities to fund unrequested enhancements to nuclear weapons and other defense activities that are also not related to counterintelligence and security concerns," the White House Office of Management and Budget said in a June 11 statement.

Such defense-related projects have long been a priority for Senate Energy and Water Development Appropriations Subcommittee Chairman Pete V. Domenici, R-N.M., whose state is home to two of the Energy Department's nuclear weapons laboratories, Los Alamos and Sandia. He has been such an ardent protector of the labs that he is affectionately known among agency employees as "St. Pete."

But Domenici's House counterpart, Republican Ron Packard of California, is expected to be more inclined to support House members' requests for new dams, beach repairs and other environmental restoration projects that usually are tacked on to the energy and water bill. Packard's subcommittee has yet to take up its bill.

Complicating matters for Packard is the fact that the House's fiscal 2000 allocation of $19.4 billion in budget authority is $1.7 billion less than last year's appropriated level.

"The House currently has an allocation that won't work — it's a huge cut," Domenici said in a June 15 interview. "I assume the House wants to do many, many water projects, so I assume it's going to be a very difficult conference."

Domenici Adds Money

As in previous years, Domenici succeeded in adding money for the Energy Department's initiative to manage and test the safety and reliability of the nuclear weapons stockpile without actually conducting explosive tests. Much of the work is done at Los Alamos.

The stockpile stewardship program, which uses a system of computer simulations to monitor nuclear weapons, would receive $2.35 billion, a $203.7 million increase from fiscal 1999.

To address revelations about security lapses at Los Alamos and other weapons labs, the bill increases funding for security investigations from $30 million to $45 million. Funding for the department's counterintelligence program would more than double, to $39.2 million, while security at Energy sites would increase from $55.2 million to $69.1 million.

But Domenici and Harry Reid of Nevada, the Energy and Water subcommittee's ranking Democrat, warned that the caps in the 1997 balanced-budget act (PL 105-33) forced them to provide less money for water projects than was requested by the White House for the first time in recent memory.

"I have already indicated that we don't have enough money," Reid said.

"But I would like to see anyone do a better job than we have done."

Reid and Domenici did allow a number of last-minute changes requested by senators seeking to save pet projects. They included setting aside $1.5 million for research on zebra mussels, sponsored by Democrats Carl Levin of Michigan and Daniel K. Akaka of Hawaii, and $4 million for a riverfront park sought by New Jersey Democrats Frank R. Lautenberg and Robert G. Torricelli.

But other senators were not as successful. Jeffords tried to add $70 million for solar and other renewable energy projects. The bill includes $353.9 million for such projects, $92.1 million less than the Clinton administration's request.

"Federal support for renewable energy research and development has been a major success story," Jeffords said. "Costs have declined, reliability has improved and a growing domestic industry has been born."

Domenici and Reid contended that renewable energy programs fared better in the bill than many other areas. The Senate voted 60-39 to table, or kill, an appeal of a ruling that Jeffords' amendment was out of order. *(Vote 171, p. S-35)*

House Panel Boosts Water Projects, Cuts Funds for Energy Department

JULY 17 — Setting the stage for a fight with both the Senate and the Clinton administration, a House subcommittee on July 15 approved steep cuts to the Department of Energy's budget while demanding that the agency reorganize itself to improve security.

The House Energy and Water Development Appropriations Subcommittee approved a $20.2 billion bill for fiscal 2000 by voice vote after its members urged Appropriations members to allocate an additional $800 million. The bill funds operations at the Energy Department (DOE) and Army Corps of Engineers and some programs at the Interior Department.

The legislation contains $880 million less than the amount appropriated in fiscal 1999 and $1.4 billion less than President Clinton's request. Despite the request for additional funds, the bill remains $1.5 billion below the Senate-passed version.

The Senate measure reduced funding for the Corps of Engineers and other environmental programs in favor of boosting the Energy Department's nuclear weapons programs. But the House measure takes the opposite approach.

It contains $4.19 billion for the Corps of Engineers, an increase of $400 million over the Senate bill. It also provides $784.7 million for the Bureau of Reclamation, which oversees federal dams and water supply projects, $23 million more than the Senate bill.

At the same time, the House bill provides $15.5 billion for the Energy Department, a cut of more than $1.5 billion from the Senate's amount. It contains $1.2 billion less for Energy's defense-related programs than the Senate's version.

Pete V. Domenici, R-N.M., chairman of the Senate's Energy and Water Development Subcommittee, has long defended Energy's nuclear weapons programs, which include two weapons laboratories in his state. But Domenici's House counterpart, Republican Ron Packard of California, said his sympathies lie with more than 400 House members who approached him with requests for water projects in their districts.

"We made clear publicly right up front that any cuts would come out of energy rather than water in my bill," Packard said July 15. "I really believe the infrastructure of this country is vital. . . . Sen. Domenici and I have different priorities."

Ranking subcommittee Democrat Peter J. Visclosky of Indiana declined to comment on the bill other than to say that Packard "has done a responsible job."

National Security

The most controversial portion of the House bill is a provision to withhold $1 billion in appropriated funds for fiscal 2000 until Congress restructures the Energy Department's national security programs or establishes an independent agency to oversee those programs.

The action comes in response to a continuing series of revelations about lax security at the department's weapons labs that most recently were highlighted in a stinging report last month by Clinton's Foreign Intelligence Advisory Board. The report concluded that "organizational disarray, managerial neglect and a culture of arrogance" warranted a legislative restructuring by Congress.

The board, chaired by former Sen. Warren B. Rudman, R-N.H. (1980-93), recommended that Congress consider either an independent agency similar to NASA or a semiautonomous agency within the Energy Department to run the weapons programs. Packard said he strongly prefers that a new agency be established.

"I'm going to push for a separate, independent agency," he said. "The DOE has not been a manager that can handle that problem."

Domenici and several other GOP senators have been negotiating with Energy Secretary Bill Richardson on a proposal to install a new agency within the department. Richardson has accepted that concept, but the senators said they have been unable to reach an agreement on details.

"Based on what I've seen, I'm not optimistic we will agree," Sen. Jon Kyl, R-Ariz., said in a July 14 interview.

Kyl, Domenici and Frank H. Murkowski, R-Alaska, plan to offer their proposal to restructure the Energy Department as an amendment to the fiscal 2000 intelligence authorization bill (S 1009 — S Rept 106-48), which the Senate is expected to begin debating July 19.

The Energy Department issued a statement July 16 saying it believes that Packard's plan for an independent agency would have no effect on the department's funding because of Richardson's expectation that the Senate will pass a restructuring bill.

Further complicating matters, a group of members that included the chairmen of the House Science and Commerce committees asked Speaker J. Dennis Hastert, R-Ill., on July 12 to allow them more time to develop legislation to restructure the department.

The lawmakers urged Hastert "to oppose hasty and haphazard efforts to legislate this matter on the defense or intelligence authorization bills."

Opposition Rises As Full Committee Approves Bill

JULY 24 — Environmentalists, administration officials and lawmakers supporting renewable energy have joined Senate appropriators in objecting to the House's fiscal 2000 spending bill for energy and water development programs.

Despite the objections, the House Appropriations Committee approved the $20.2 billion bill (HR 2605; H Rept 106-253) by voice vote July 20. The legislation funds operations at the Department of Energy, Army Corps of Engineers and some Interior Department programs.

The House is expected to consider the bill the week of July 26.

Senate appropriators already have expressed concern that the House bill too heavily favors water projects over Energy Department nuclear weapons activities.

The bill would provide $15.6 billion for the Energy Department, $1.5 billion less than the Senate-passed amount. Because of the vast difference in spending levels between the two bills, senators are warning of an extremely difficult conference.

"I don't think we could get a bill that we could send to the president based on the current energy and water appropriations bills," said Pete V. Domenici, R-N.M., chairman of the Senate Energy and Water Development Appropriations Subcommittee. "We're trying to get [House members] to understand how serious this is."

The House bill also includes a provision to withhold $1 billion in fiscal 2000 appropriated funds until Congress restructures the Energy Department's national security programs or establishes an independent agency to oversee those programs.

Even if the restructuring occurs, the House bill would not allow use of the $1 billion until after June 30, 2000. Domenici said the resulting delay would disrupt Energy's stockpile stewardship program, which assesses the safety and reliability of nuclear weapons without conducting underground tests.

Domenici's House counterpart, Republican Ron Packard of California, said the bill "maintains a vigorous civil works program." He asked members to speed its approval in committee by delaying amendments until the bill moves to the House floor or into conference.

Environmental Riders

But Peter J. Visclosky of Indiana, the Energy and Water Subcommittee's ranking Democrat, offered two amendments seeking to change two "anti-environmental riders" that he said would harm wetlands.

Visclosky's first amendment sought to remove language that would allow anyone building on designated wetlands to contest the designation in federal court before finishing the permit process with the Army Corps of Engineers. Visclosky predicted the language would "encourage more litigation."

Packard, however, said the language would merely give permit applicants the right to appeal decisions before going through a potentially time-consuming permit process. After a brief debate, Visclosky's amendment was rejected, 23-32.

Visclosky's other amendment sought to strike a provision commissioning a report from the Corps of Engineers on the cost of overhauling "Nationwide Permit 26," a part of the clean water act (PL 101-549). The permit allows for rapid approval of wetlands development, and environmentalists say the process has led to destruction of isolated wetlands and small streams.

Visclosky cited letters from Environmental Protection Agency Administrator Carol M. Browner and Federal Emergency Management Agency Director James L. Witt predicting the provision could delay ongoing efforts to overhaul the Permit 26 process. A coalition of six environmental groups also contended in a July 19 letter to House Appropriations Chairman C.W. Bill Young, R-Fla., that the language would lead to "unnecessary and inappropriate" interference.

But Packard said the provision "is not going to change anything." At his urging, committee members rejected Visclosky's amendment, 22-34.

In funding solar and renewable energy research programs, the House bill includes $326.5 million, a $39.5 million cut from the current fiscal year and $119.6 million less than the president requested.

Matt Salmon, R-Ariz., chairman of the House Renewable Energy Caucus, said he plans to offer an amendment to the bill on the House floor seeking to restore the money. Salmon joined more than 80 House members in signing a July 15 letter to Packard and Visclosky calling for increased funding.

"It represents badly needed research and development," Salmon said. "If research isn't happening at the federal level, it's not going to happen."

House-Passed Bill Is Far Apart From Senate's Version

JULY 31 — The House voted 420-8 on July 27 to pass a $20.2 billion spending bill for energy and water development programs in fiscal 2000, setting the stage for what lawmakers acknowledge will be a difficult House-Senate conference battle over water projects vs. nuclear weapons.

The bill (HR 2605) funds operations at the Department of Energy and U.S. Army Corps of Engineers and some Interior Department programs. The versions produced by the two chambers differ sharply: The House legislation emphasizes water development programs over Energy Department defense activities, while the Senate's (S 1186) takes the opposite approach. *(Vote 342, p. H-112)*

To further complicate matters, each chamber also passed its bill by an overwhelming margin, giving conferees on each side the ammunition they believe will help them prevail. The conference will take place some time after the August recess.

"It's going to be an interesting conference," said Ron Packard, R-Calif., who chairs the House Energy and Water Development Appropriations Subcommittee. "We've done everything we can to strengthen our position."

Looming over the House bill, however, is the threat of a presidential veto based on what the Clinton administration describes as several anti-environmental provisions relating to permits

Energy and Water Bill Highlights

Where the Money Goes

HR 2605 (Conference report: H Rept 106-336)

Spending Synopsis

The $21.3 billion conference report was adopted by the House, 327-87, Sept. 27, and cleared by the Senate, 96-3, on Sept. 28. Though the final version of the bill provides $303 million less than President Clinton requested, he signed it Sept. 29. Total spending is just $2.6 million more than the Senate passed but $1.1 billion more than the House version. House leaders raised their budget allocation for the popular bill by $1.1 billion just before the conference with the Senate. The measure provides money for the Army Corps of Engineers and projects in the Interior and Energy departments, as well as funding for such independent agencies as the Nuclear Regulatory Commission and the Appalachian Regional Commission. It also includes funding for atomic energy defense activities such as the nuclear weapons stockpile, defense waste management and counterintelligence. It has long been a popular way for lawmakers to finance water, dam and environmental projects for their districts. The conference report's total funding is $210.3 million more than the fiscal 1999 level.

- **Army Corps of Engineers**

The Corps' water projects, including flood control and conservation, are among the most popular with House members. The conference report provides $4.1 billion — $46.1 million less than the House but $408.5 million more than the Senate version and $246.4 million more than Clinton requested.

- **Interior Department**

The conference report provides $808.7 million for the department's water resource, reclamation and conservation programs, $13.1 million less than the House version, $8.1 million more than the Senate and $87.2 million less than Clinton requested.

- **Energy Department**

The report provides $16.7 billion, $1.1 billion more than the House but $407.6 million less than the Senate and $441.5 million less than Clinton requested. More than half the bill's total, $12 billion, went to the department's atomic energy defense activities — $849.7 million more than the House bill and $427.3 million less than the Senate version.

Hot-Button Issues

△ **Nuclear waste.** The conference agreement provides $353 million for defense and civilian nuclear waste disposal, $72 million more than the House wanted and $2 million less than the Senate, but lawmakers continued to grapple with where to store the waste — in temporary or permanent sites, or at the locations where it is generated.

△ **Weapons labs.** Conferees omitted a House provision that would have held up $1 billion for the Energy Department's nuclear weapons programs until Congress passed legislation restructuring them in the wake of an alleged spy scandal. A National Nuclear Security Administration was created by the fiscal 2000 defense authorization bill (S 1059).

△ **Energy Department expenses.** Disclosures that department contractors had racked up $249 million in government-paid travel costs in 1998 led lawmakers to impose limits. The House bill would have prevented the department from paying more than $95 million for contractor travel. The conferees were more generous and set the limit at $150 million.

(figures are in thousands of dollars of new budget authority)

	Fiscal 1999 Appropriation	Fiscal 2000 Clinton Request	House Bill	Senate Bill	Conference Report
Army Corps of Engineers (Defense Department)	$4,097,233	$3,895,800	$4,188,389	$3,733,718	$4,142,250
Interior Department	824,596	895,979	821,871	800,592	808,722
Energy Department	17,060,796	17,112,197	15,546,035	17,078,389	16,670,746
Independent Agencies	175,700	117,050	84,100	147,050	129,000
Appalachian Regional Commission	(66,400)	(66,400)	(60,000)	(71,400)	(66,400)
Nuclear Regulatory Commission	(20,200)	(23,000)	(23,000)	(23,000)	(23,000)
Tennessee Valley Authority	(50,000)*	(7,000)	(0)	(7,000)	(0)
Rescissions				–42,424	–20,749
Scorekeeping adjustments	–1,088,690	–438,300	–450,000	–440,000	–450,000
GRAND TOTAL	**$21,069,635**	**$21,582,726**	**$20,190,395**	**$2,277,325**	**$21,279,969**

*Provided in fiscal 1999 supplemental spending law (PL 105-277)

TABLE: Senate and House Appropriations committees

for wetlands development. House Democrats tried to amend the bill to eliminate the provisions but were rebuffed by Republicans who contended that the language would have no adverse effects.

The House legislation would provide $880 million less than in fiscal 1999 and more than $1.3 billion less than both the Senate version and the administration's request. Many House members who raised concerns over the low funding level voted for passage, explaining that they were optimistic that the amount will be raised in conference.

At issue is whether money will be added in conference for beach repairs, erosion control efforts and other environmental projects that House members are seeking, or the Energy Department nuclear weapons activities that senators favor.

The House bill contains $4.2 billion for the Corps of Engineers, an increase of $282.6 million over what the administration sought. It would provide $15.5 billion for the Energy Department, a cut of about $1.5 billion from the fiscal 1999 level, the Senate-passed version and the administration's request.

One of the largest differences between the House and Senate bills is the funding for the Energy Department's "stockpile stewardship" program, which seeks to assure the safety and reliability of nuclear weapons without conducting explosive tests through a series of computer simulations and other activities.

The Senate bill includes $2.35 billion for stockpile stewardship, an increase of $203.7 million over fiscal 1999 and $253 million more than the House figure. Senate Energy and Water Appropriations Chairman Pete V. Domenici, R-N.M., is an ardent advocate of the program. His state includes Los Alamos National Laboratory, where much of the work is done.

In response to revelations of lax security at the Energy Department's nuclear weapons laboratories, the House bill also includes a provision to withhold $1 billion in fiscal 2000 appropriated funds until Congress restructures the department's national security programs or sets up an independent agency to oversee those programs.

Although the Senate approved a restructuring of the department as part of the fiscal 2000 intelligence authorization bill (HR 1555 — H Rept 106-130), the House bill would not allow use of the $1 billion until after June 30, 2000.

Domenici has expressed concern that the delay would hurt the Energy Department.

Meanwhile, the House bill includes $1.41 billion for Corps of Engineers construction projects on rivers, channels, inlets, harbors and other areas. The amount is $52 million below the administration request, but $299 million above the Senate figure.

Most of the debate in the House over the energy and water bill centered on the wetlands provisions that have drawn the presidential veto threat.

Wetlands Debate

Peter J. Visclosky of Indiana, the Energy and Water Subcommittee's ranking Democrat, offered an amendment to remove language that would allow anyone who wants to build on designated wetlands to contest the designation in federal court before finishing the permit process with the Corps of Engineers.

Visclosky warned that the language would lead to more litigation. The White House Office of Management and Budget said in a statement that the provision "would short-circuit the review process for wetlands permits" by making the review of initial jurisdictional determinations on those permits appealable to the courts before the final permit decision.

But Packard and other backers of the provision said it would merely give permit applicants the right to appeal decisions before going through a potentially time-consuming permit process.

Visclosky's amendment also sought to strike a provision commissioning a report from the Corps of Engineers on the cost of overhauling "nationwide Permit 26," a controversial part of the clean water act (PL 101-549). *(1987 Almanac, p. 297)*

The permit allows for rapid approval of wetlands development, and environmentalists say the process has led to destruction of isolated wetlands and streams. They joined administration officials in arguing that the provision could delay ongoing efforts to overhaul the permit 26 process by delaying implementation until the report is completed.

In an effort to reach a compromise, Sherwood Boehlert, R-N.Y., offered a separate amendment calling for the Corps of Engineers to submit studies and analyses on the impact of the process 30 days before the final publication of proposed replacements for Permit 26 and no later than Dec. 30.

After lawmakers voted 426-1 to adopt Boehlert's amendment, Visclosky's amendment failed, 183-245, with lawmakers voting largely along party lines. *(Votes 340, 341, p. H-112)*

Lawmakers also adopted, by voice vote, an amendment by Matt Salmon, R-Ariz., to increase funding for solar and other renewable energy research by $30 million to $356 million. The money would come from an offsetting decrease in the travel budget for Energy Department contractors, a program that lawmakers already had reduced by half in response to allegations of contractor abuse.

During debate on the bill, a provision that would have terminated the Denali Commission in Alaska was struck on a point of order by Resources Committee Chairman Don Young, R-Alaska.

The commission, created last year, provides funding to rural parts of the state for road, sewer, sanitation and other infrastructure projects.

Bill Clears After House Leaders Add $1.1 Billion

OCTOBER 2 — A $21.3 billion energy and water development spending bill for fiscal 2000 was signed into law Sept. 29, a day after the Senate easily cleared the measure for President Clinton.

The House on Sept. 27 adopted the conference report on the bill (HR 2605), 327-87. The Senate cleared the measure the next day, 96-3. *(House vote 452, p. H-148; Senate vote 295, p. S-58)*

The bill funds operations at the Department of Energy, including its nuclear weapons activities, the U.S. Army Corps of Engineers and some Interior Department programs.

The legislation's smooth path to passage came after House Republican leaders gave energy and water conferees an extra $1.1 billion to work with. Until that occurred, the chairman of the Senate Energy and Water Appropriations Committee, Pete V. Domenici, R-N.M., had warned that an agreement would be impossible because the House-passed version (H Rept 106-253) provided $1.1 billion less than the Senate version (S Rept 106-58).

The conference report represents a $210 million increase over fiscal 1999 levels but remains $303 million below the administration's request.

At Domenici's behest, the agreement significantly increases funding for the Energy Department's nuclear weapons programs, which account for more than half the bill's total spending. But the $12 billion included for the weapons programs is still $247 million below what the administration sought.

Energy Secretary Bill Richardson issued a statement Sept. 27 complaining that the conference report "makes a number of severe cuts that will harm national security and basic scientific research programs."

Richardson pointed to the omission of $35 million the administration requested to increase computer security at 70 of his agency's facilities. The department has come under heavy criticism from Republicans for lax security that may have allowed China to obtain highly classified nuclear weapons data.

Domenici said in response that there was no way this year for appropriators to provide the $450 million that the department wants to upgrade computers at the department's three nuclear weapons laboratories — Los Alamos and Sandia in New Mexico and Lawrence Livermore in California.

"We leave it to the administration," Domenici said. "If they seek this in a supplemental next year, we will look at it carefully."

Domenici helped craft a controversial proposal to create a semi-autonomous agency within the Energy Department to shore up the security of its weapons programs.

The energy and water spending bill includes $69 million for the department's nuclear safeguard and securities program. The amount is $10 million above the administration's request.

Pocket Money

The extra $1.1 billion added by House leaders for the conference enabled negotiators to provide for water projects that have long been popular with House members. The final agreement contains $4.1 billion for the Corps of Engineers, which is $246 million more than the administration's request and $409 million more than the Senate-passed bill.

Sen. John McCain, R-Ariz., a persistent critic of what he considers wasteful spending, was not present for the Senate vote on the conference report. But McCain issued a statement criticizing conferees for adding $200 million "in pork barrel projects," particularly in the Corps of Engineers' budget.

Domenici's House counterpart, Republican Ron Packard of California, lamented that appropriators were unable to fund any new projects authorized in a $6.3 billion water resources development bill (PL 106-53) passed in August.

The conference agreement also leaves out House-passed language designed to speed up permits for construction in designated wetlands. The White House had threatened to veto the bill because of the provisions.

The only complication during floor debate in either chamber came when Bud Shuster, R-Pa., chairman of the House Transportation and Infrastructure Committee, complained that GOP leaders "snuck" the agreement onto the floor before lawmakers could review it. Shuster's committee has jurisdiction over some water programs.

Shuster cited past instances in which lawmakers have voted on legislation without knowing all of its details, only to be surprised later. He and 24 other Transportation Committee members subsequently voted against the conference report. ◆

President Accepts Limits on Family Planning Funds in Exchange for Other Priorities

Foreign Operations

- **Bill:** HR 3422 (incorporated by reference in HR 3194) — PL 106-113
- **Legislative action: Senate** passed S 1234 (S Rept 106-81), 97-2, on June 30.

House passed HR 2606 (H Rept 106-254), 385-35, on Aug. 3.

Senate passed HR 2606, by voice vote on Aug. 4, after substituting the text of S 1234.

House adopted the conference report on HR 2606 (H Rept 106-339), 214-211, on Oct. 5.

Senate cleared bill, 51-49, on Oct. 6.

President vetoed HR 2606 on Oct. 18.

House passed HR 3196, 316-100, on Nov. 5.

House adopted the conference report on the omnibus spending bill (H Rept 106-479), incorporating HR 3422, 296-135, on Nov. 18.

Senate cleared bill, 74-24, on Nov. 19.

President signed HR 3194 on Nov. 29.

SUMMARY

A last-minute compromise on debt relief for poor nations allowed Congress to finish the $15.3 billion fiscal 2000 foreign operations spending bill, which the Senate cleared Nov. 19 as part of the omnibus spending package (HR 3194). President Clinton is expected to sign the bill.

With congressional Republicans determined to hold down foreign aid spending as part of their overall budget plan and the White House equally intent on funding some key foreign policy initiatives, the foreign operations appropriations bill became a major battleground in the fiscal 2000 budget wars.

The conference report on the first foreign aid bill (HR 2606) was nearly $2 billion below Clinton's initial request, and did not include another $1.8 billion he sought to help Israel, Jordan and the Palestinian Authority implement the 1998 Wye River peace agreement.

In an attempt to wage the battle on budgetary terms alone, House Republicans steered clear of policy disputes. They removed a restriction on $25 million in U.S. funds to the United Nations Fund for Population Activities, which critics accused of helping fund compulsory abortions in China. The low spending level, however, prompted Clinton to veto the original legislation (HR 2606) on Oct. 18.

Republicans then backed down and moved a fresh bill (HR 3196) that included the $1.8 billion for the Wye River agreement plus another $800 million for various recipients, including the World Bank, republics of the former Soviet Union and bilateral debt relief. Negotiators removed the last sticking point the week of Nov. 15 with an agreement to allow the International Monetary Fund to use a rise in the value of the gold it holds in storage toward its share of an international debt-relief package.

At the last minute, GOP leaders appeased anti-abortion members by attaching restrictions on family planning assistance to the bill, clearing the way for other foreign policy legislation.

Senate Committee Approves Bill With Balkan Aid

JUNE 19 — Congress is taking its first steps to respond to the withdrawal of Serb forces from Kosovo, with the Senate Appropriations Committee moving legislation June 17 that would set aside more than a half-billion dollars for the postwar reconstruction of the Balkans.

The committee voted 28-0 to approve a $12.7 billion fiscal 2000 foreign aid spending bill (S 1234) that included $535 million for the region. That is $142 million more than President Clinton requested for the region in February and includes $105 million in unallocated funds, most of which would probably go to Bosnia.

The Senate bill includes funds for Kosovo ($150 million), Albania ($85 million), Romania ($60 million), Macedonia ($55 million), Bulgaria ($45 million) and Montenegro ($35 million), which is joined with Serbia in the Republic of Yugoslavia.

No funds would be allocated for Serbia itself, in accordance with a provision in the fiscal 2000 defense appropriations bill (S 1122 — S Rept 106-53) barring aid as long as Yugoslav President Slobodan Milosevic remains in power.

The Balkan recovery plan, drafted by Mitch McConnell, R-Ky., chairman of the Senate Foreign Operations Appropriations Subcommittee, is based on initial reconstruction estimates from European countries. His plan was written so that the United States would fund 15 percent to 20 percent of all recovery expenses, according to committee aides.

Members of Congress have so far shown little interest in paying for Balkan reconstruction.

"While I expect the Europeans to bear the lion's share of responsibility for reconstruction, we have concrete trade interests in regional economic recovery and security interests in promoting stability and democracy," McConnell said.

To increase funding for the Balkans, McConnell was forced to slash proposed spending on other foreign aid programs.

Less for Russia

Assistance for the countries of the former Soviet Union, a top administration priority amid the Russian economic crisis, was cut by about one-fourth from the president's request of $1 billion, to $780 million.

Aid for Russia is expected to fall by an even larger percentage, since McConnell continued to specify significant amounts for Ukraine ($210 million), Georgia ($95 million) and Armenia ($90 million).

The bill specifies that before aid would be given to Russia, Clinton would have to certify that Russian troops have not established an operational zone in Kosovo and that they are operating under NATO command. And the committee once again asked him to certify that Russia is not helping Iran build a nuclear power plant, a provision that the administration has managed to water down the past several years.

Another program cut significantly from Clinton's request was the State Department's international narcotics and law enforcement account: Clinton requested $295 million; the committee approved only $215 million.

Spending on that program increased markedly after Bill McCollum, R-Fla., chairman of the House Judiciary Subcommittee on Crime, and other key Republicans, including the current House Speaker J. Dennis Hastert, R-Ill., won $255 million in emergency supplemental funds for anti-drug efforts as part of the fiscal 1999 omnibus spending law (PL 105-277). Much of the money was to be spent helping Colombia mount more aggressive anti-drug efforts.

However, House appropriators will find it difficult to increase funds for that program as they struggle with severe budget constraints.

House Foreign Operations appropriators have $10.4 billion in discretionary spending to work with for fiscal 2000, $2 billion below the funds appropriated last

Both the House and Senate allocations are well below President Clinton's request of $14.6 billion.

Missing from the Senate bill and its likely House counterpart are $1.9 billion in budget authority that the president requested to buttress the 1998 Wye peace accords between Israel and the Palestinians.

The funds have been put on hold since Israel has elected a new prime minister, Ehud Barak, who has struggled to put together a new government coalition.

McConnell expressed concern, though, that appropriators might find it difficult to approve the funds when a new Israeli government is firmly in place.

"I don't know how we're going to accommodate that," McConnell said. "It's a big mystery."

Senate Passes Bill Handily Despite Clinton Objections

JULY 3 — Armenian-American and Cuban-American groups defeated efforts by business interests to lift economic sanctions affecting their homelands as the Senate passed a fiscal 2000 foreign operations appropriations bill (S 1234) June 30.

The Senate voted 97-2 for the $12.7 billion bill despite threats from the administration to veto the measure because its spending totals fall far short of President Clinton's request. *(Vote 192, p. S-39)*

The administration also is concerned about a provision that would effectively bar any aid to Yugoslavia unless President Slobodan Milosevic is driven from power.

The closest vote of the daylong debate, however, came on an attempt by Sen. Sam Brownback, R-Kan., to change U.S. policy toward Azerbaijan, which for a decade has been locked in a struggle with neighboring Armenia over the enclave of Nagorno-Karabakh. U.S. energy companies have invested heavily in the oil-rich region of the former Soviet Union between the Caspian Sea and the Caucasus Mountains, and they favor closer ties with Azerbaijan.

Brownback proposed allowing the president to waive a ban on most kinds of direct U.S. assistance to the government of Azerbaijan — the only former Soviet republic under such limitations. The attempt came as part of a broader amendment that incorporated Brownback's "Silk Road" bill (S 579 — S Rept 106-45), designed to encourage political and economic reform, economic development and the settlement of conflicts in the Caspian

Brownback said the United States needed to support the region to prevent it from coming under the thumb of neighboring Russia or Iran.

The Senate ultimately adopted Brownback's amendment by voice vote, but first agreed, 53-45, to a second-degree amendment by Mitch McConnell, R-Ky., chairman of the Foreign Operations Appropriations Subcommittee, and Spencer Abraham, R-Mich., to strip the change in policy toward Azerbaijan. *(Vote 191, p. S-38)*

Abraham argued that Azerbaijan had recently rejected a proposal by the United States, France and Russia to settle the dispute with Armenia and that lifting the U.S. sanctions would be "counterproductive in the extreme."

"It could not be more self-evident that if the one and only leverage we have in the peace process to bring an end to this blockade [by Azerbaijan] and to the hostile relationships is taken away, there will be no incentives whatsoever," Abraham said.

Brownback said he simply was seeking "evenhanded" treatment for Azerbaijan and pointed out the administration's support for the measure.

"If the administration thought it was such a sensitive time, I think they would be here saying, don't offer this amendment rather than supporting my position," he said.

Cuban Embargo

Lawmakers also squared off on an amendment by Democratic Sen. Christopher J. Dodd of Connecticut that would have allowed Americans to freely travel to Cuba.

"Let [Fidel Castro] be the one who shuts the door to U.S. citizens traveling there," Dodd said. "Let us not deny our own citizens the right to try and make a difference."

But Cuba's traditional supporters in Congress said that Castro's recent crackdown on overseas trips showed that U.S. policy, written into law (PL 104-114) in 1996, should be maintained. *(1996 Almanac, p. 9-6)*

Clinton earlier this year chose to maintain the longstanding embargo on U.S. trade with Cuba but allowed increased exchanges, including additional flights to the island.

"They hold hundreds of political prisoners, people are shot in the streets, people are held in secret trials, and our response is: Let's go for a visit," chided Robert G. Torricelli, D-N.J.

Tensions rose during the debate, with Sen. Robert C. Byrd, D-W.Va., at one point yelling to have Rep. Lincoln Diaz-Balart, R-Fla., a fervent Castro critic, removed from the well of the Senate for lobbying during a vote. Nonetheless, opponents succeeded in tabling the Dodd amendment, 55-43. *(Vote 189, p. S-38)*

Tight Money

The bill's total is $1.9 billion below Clinton's request, and the administration has recommended a veto if certain priorities are not met.

"A bill funded at this level would be grossly inadequate to maintain America's leadership around the world," said a statement of administration policy.

Among the key items missing from the bill, according to the administration, is $205 million for the State Department's share of a program aimed at halting a "brain drain" of Russian weapons scientists to unfriendly states such as Iran, Iraq or North Korea. The Senate did approve non-binding language calling for the money to be added in a House-Senate conference.

The bill also does not include $500 million the president requested for fiscal 2000 ($1.9 billion over three years) to buttress the 1998 Wye peace accords between Israel and the Palestinians. The importance of that aid was manifested when Egyptian President Hosni Mubarak, who hopes to see the distribution of aid to his country speeded up, made an impromptu appearance on the floor during debate, escorted by Foreign Relations Committee Chairman Jesse Helms, R-N.C.

Balkan Reconstruction

Helms persuaded the Senate to adopt, by voice vote, an amendment incorporating key provisions of his legislation (S 720) that would authorize $100 million over the next two fiscal years to aid democratic forces opposed to Milosevic.

But administration officials expressed concern about other provisions affecting the Balkans.

For example, the legislation designates Serbia a terrorist state under a 1985 law (PL 99-83), effectively cutting off the possibility of U.S. assistance of any kind until Milosevic is forced out of power. *(1985 Almanac, p. 41)*

Administration officials said the provision gives them no flexibility. They said it could also unintentionally force the United States to impose sanctions on neighboring states that provide humanitarian assistance to Yugoslavia.

The Office of Management and Budget, in a statement of the administration's position on the bill, also complained that $20 million specified to equip and train a security force in Kosovo "could be interpreted as aimed at training and equipping the Kosovo Liberation Army (KLA), a policy prescription diametrically at odds with the recent agreement by the KLA to disarm under NATO supervision."

But McConnell insisted that the provision was not a back-door means of aiding the insurgents.

"There is nothing in this bill which calls for arming or supporting the KLA," McConnell said. "Members of the KLA may very well be included in a security force, but that is not a decision for us to make. A Kosovo civilian government should make all decisions regarding recruitment standards, organization, and supervision of internal security."

House Panel OKs Bill That Falls $1.7 Billion Short Of Clinton Request

JULY 17 — The prospect of a 23 percent increase in their budget allotment helped put members of the House Foreign Operations Appropriations Subcommittee in a sunny mood July 14 as they approved a fiscal 2000 foreign aid bill by voice vote.

A $2.5 billion increase, which the Appropriations Committee was expected to act on July 19, raised the aid bill to $12.8 billion. That was about $100 million more than a version passed by the Senate on June 30 (S 1234) but still $1.7 billion less than President Clinton requested. The administration has threatened the Senate bill with a veto.

Neither bill includes what could amount to $2 billion to $3 billion that Clinton is expected to request to bolster peace in the Middle East, ease the debts of very poor countries and reconstruct the Balkans after the NATO air campaign against Yugoslavia. Lawmakers say that money will be added later in the year, perhaps in separate legislation.

The full House Appropriations Committee is scheduled to take up the foreign aid bill July 20.

During the July 14 markup, subcommittee members skirmished over funds for Israel and other countries in the Middle East.

But they held their fire on other major issues, preferring to fight those battles during the full committee markup or when the bill comes to the House floor.

Still, panel chairman Sonny Callahan, R-Ala., did not shy away from making substantial cuts to Clinton's request:

- Aid to the former Soviet republics would be $725 million, $307 million less than Clinton's request and $76 million below current spending. It is also below the Senate bill's $780 million. Aides said the low total would likely lead to severe cuts in a $241 million program aimed at halting a "brain drain" of Russian scientists to unfriendly states such as Iran, Iraq and North Korea.
- Support for the Global Environmental Facility, which provides aid to help developing countries cope with environmental problems, would be cut from Clinton's request of $143.3 million to $50 million. Still, that is double what the Senate bill calls for.
- Voluntary contributions to United Nations peacekeeping operations would be frozen at current levels of $76.5 million, $53.5 million below Clinton's request.

The subcommittee entirely eliminated funding for some agencies and overseas organizations, including:

- The Multilateral Investment Guarantee Agency, a World Bank affiliate that provides guarantees for private investors in developing countries. Clinton had requested $10 million, which the Senate would provide.
- The Multilateral Investment Fund, a program administered by the Inter-American Development Bank to provide grants and investments to promote private sector growth, labor force train-

ing and small enterprise modernization in Latin America and the Caribbean. Clinton had requested $25.8 million.

- The Inter-American Investment Corporation. Clinton had requested $25 million.
- The U.S. Community Adjustment and Investment Program, intended to provide loans to businesses negatively affected by the North American Free Trade Agreement (NAFTA). The program's legislative champion, Esteban E. Torres, D-Calif.(1982-99), retired from Congress after the 105th Congress. The Clinton administration had requested $17 million. *(1993 Almanac, p. 171)*

Also left out of the bill was $25 million Clinton requested for the United Nations Fund for Population Activities. Appropriators said they would see how a debate over that issue was resolved by the House on the State Department authorization bill (HR 1211— H Rept 106-122) before deciding how to tackle it in the spending measure.

Balkan Estimates

Appropriators also sidestepped another population controversy that has dogged them regularly in recent years, leaving a debate on international family planning assistance for another day.

Also left aside were new funds for the Middle East and the Balkans.

During his first visit to Washington as Israel's Prime Minister, Ehud Barak, was expected to press Congress to release more funds.

The House bill included $393 million that Clinton requested for the Balkans and Eastern Europe. But that is well below the $535 million that the Senate approved and probably below what Clinton will request for reconstruction.

Appropriators were pleasantly surprised by recent assessments by the World Bank and other international groups that Kosovo will not require as much reconstruction as earlier thought.

At a meeting in Brussels on July 13, representatives of European nations, which are expected to pick up the bulk of the cost, said they anticipated spending no more than $500 million on reconstruction this year. Original estimates were as much as $3 billion annually.

Like the Senate bill, the House measure prohibits aid to Serbia as long as Yugoslav President Slobodan Milosevic remains in power. But lawmakers and aides in both the House and Senate indicated the week of July 12 that they are rethinking the ban in light of growing opposition to Milosevic in Serbia. They might instead support aid to cities whose mayors have called for Milosevic's resignation.

"To be fluid and help the broad forces of democracy is more important than being rigid and missing opportunities," said Gordon H. Smith, R-Ore., chairman of the European Affairs Subcommittee of the Senate Foreign Relations Committee.

House Committee Cuts International Development Aid

JULY 24 — The House Appropriations Committee on July 20 ignored the heated complaints of Democrats and cut $200 million from a fiscal 2000 foreign operations spending bill.

David R. Obey of Wisconsin, ranking Democrat on the committee, issued a scathing attack on the panel's Republican leaders for proposing the cut, which brought the bill to $12.7 billion.

The Foreign Operations Subcommittee had approved a $12.8 billion version of the bill July 14 with the assumption that the full committee would increase its budget allocation by $2.5 billion. But when the new figures were issued July 19, foreign operations gained only $2.3 billion.

Obey complained that Republican appropriators had "welshed" on commitments they made to him in drafting the bill because of pressure from Republican conservatives to cut foreign aid.

"Are we a great committee of the Congress that tries to do the best job we can substantively?" Obey fumed. "Or are we simply a puppet mouthpiece of the most radical elements in the Republican caucus?"

Nancy Pelosi of California, ranking Democrat on the subcommittee, complained that the $200 million cut would come from funds for the International Development Association, a World Bank subsidiary that provides interest-free loans to the world's poorest countries.

The cut would lower U.S. contributions to the development agency to $577 million, $227 million below President Clinton's request.

GOP appropriators ignored the complaints, however, and the amendment by subcommittee Chairman Sonny Callahan, R-Ala., was approved on a largely party-line vote of 30-26.

The reduction is one of a series of cuts in contributions to international development banks — from the Asian Development Fund to the Global Environmental Facility — that allowed House appropriators to put together a bill nearly $2 billion below Clinton's request and $42.5 million below the Senate version of the legislation (S 1234).

But lawmakers are bracing for requests for more money later this year.

Clinton has said he will seek additional spending to help bring peace to the Middle East, rebuild Kosovo and friendly nations in the Balkans, and relieve the debt of poor countries.

In recent weeks, Barry R. McCaffrey, director of the Office of National Drug Control Policy, has been sounding out congressional leaders on the possibility of dedicating hundreds of millions of dollars to Colombia to help it fight the drug war and battle guerrillas.

All told, the additional spending could run as high as $2 billion to $3 billion, according to knowledgeable congressional aides. Yet the administration has formally submitted only a few of the proposals and has not specified how the additional funding would square with limits specified in the 1997 balanced-budget law (PL 105-33). *(1997 Almanac, p. 2-18)*

Middle East Peace

Speaking at a July 19 news conference with Israeli Prime Minister Ehud Barak, Clinton pledged "to work closely with our Congress for expedited approval" of $1.2 billion pledged to Israel between fiscal 1999 and fiscal 2001 to help implement last fall's Wye River peace agreement.

Barak, on his first trip to the United States as prime minister, pledged to move forward on the accord — a step his predecessor, Benjamin Netanyahu, was reluctant to take.

But appropriators included only $100 million of the proposed Wye funds in the fiscal 2000 bill — and that money is destined for Jordan, not Israel. It follows $100 million for Jordan included in the fiscal 1999 supplemental spending bill (PL 106-31).

Appropriators said the added money for Israel and the Palestinians would have to wait until later in the year.

"At this point, we don't have room in this budget we're operating under to meet that promise," Obey said. "Perhaps by the time we get to conference we can meet that need."

Callahan agreed and said he told Barak that Congress' attitude will depend on the actions taken by Israel and the Palestinians. "If Israel and the Palestinians reach agreement and organize the next steps, Congress will consider it," Callahan said.

In its only other roll call vote, the panel approved, 30-26, a Pelosi amendment to strike a prohibition on support for the United Nations Fund for Population Activities.

House GOP Vows To Hold Up Bill If Abortion Riders Are Challenged

JULY 31 — The House sent a mixed message with two abortion-related votes July 29 as it opened debate on a fiscal 2000 foreign aid bill. The votes could set up a contentious conference with the Senate and a battle with President Clinton.

The House is expected to vote on final passage of the $12.7 billion foreign operations spending bill (HR 2606) on Aug. 2.

In a perennial dispute, the House voted to reinstate some restrictions on aid to private international family planning groups that were part of the "Mexico City" policy of Presidents Ronald Reagan and George Bush. The policy is named for a 1984 world conference on population.

Clinton rescinded the restrictions in 1993 and has made opposition to their reinstatement a cornerstone of his foreign policy. He vetoed a State Department authorization bill over the issue last year and could be at loggerheads with Congress over a fiscal 2000 State Department bill (HR 1211; S 886) because it might contain similar restrictions.

The House voted 228-200 to adopt an amendment by Rep. Christopher H. Smith, R-N.J., to prohibit aid to international family planning groups that perform abortions — except where the life of the mother is in danger or in cases of forcible rape or incest — or that violate anti-abortion laws in other countries or try to change those laws. *(Vote 349, p. H-116)*

Smith said in an interview that he has a commitment from GOP leaders to tie up the foreign operations bill unless it retains the House-passed provisions in a future House-Senate conference.

The vote on Smith's amendment came after a struggle over both the provision and the process by which it was to be considered. Smith argued that the provision was needed to avoid having the United States entangled in overseas abortion debates.

"Do we want our representatives doing family planning and only family planning, or do we want them working overtime trying to topple pro-life laws in other countries?" he asked.

Rep. James C. Greenwood, R-Pa., countered that Smith's amendment would undermine a "good, wide, compassionate and enlightened program" on family planning. Greenwood and other opponents said that in any case, the provisions would not be enacted into law because Clinton would veto them. Senior administration officials have also recommended that Clinton veto the bill because it falls almost $2 billion short of the president's request.

Smith gained traction for his amendment by pushing for a debate rule the House passed, 256-172, largely along party lines. The rule rebuffed attempts by abortion rights supporters to use an amendment by Greenwood as a substitute for the Smith amendment. Instead, members decided to vote on both. *(Vote 348, p. H-114)*

Choice of Limits

The argument ultimately will be settled in a House-Senate conference. Greenwood's amendment would prohibit the use of U.S. aid by international groups to promote abortion as a means of family planning or to lobby for or against abortion. Such groups would have to certify that they would use the U.S. funds to reduce the incidence of abortion. Greenwood's amendment was approved 221-208. *(Vote 350, p. H-116)*

Greenwood contended that his provision, unlike the Smith amendment, would likely survive a conference committee. "The question is: What will remain in conference committee; what restriction do we want to have?" Greenwood said.

A conference committee also may have to deal with the House's decision, on a 230-197 vote, to cut off foreign operations funding for military training conducted at the School of the Americas at the Army's Fort Benning in Georgia. No such provision exists in the Senate bill. *(Vote 352, p. H-116)*

The House action, even if supported in conference, would not close the school, since the preponderance of its funding comes from the defense spending bill (HR 2561 — H Rept 106-244; S 1122 — S Rept 106-53).

Critics of the school, including Joe Moakley, D-Mass., have tried for several years to cut off its funding. They say that graduates of the military training school include some of the most notorious violators of human rights in Central and South America.

"If the School of the Americas had a reunion this weekend, it would be a gathering of some of the most unsavory elements in the Western Hemisphere," said Democrat Martin T. Meehan of Massachusetts.

Supporters of the school, including top Pentagon officials, say its graduates have promoted democracy and battled the drug trade at home. The school, they say, should not be condemned for a small number of problem graduates.

Sonny Callahan, R-Ala., chairman of the Foreign Operations Appropriations Subcommittee, said the school's curriculum now includes training on human rights.

"We can't blame the School of the Americas forever for something that happened 15 or 20 years ago," Callahan said. "The school has cleaned up its act."

The campaign against the school has gained support in recent years from religious groups, and some Central American countries have issued official reports in which the school is blamed for educating human rights violators.

House Passes Bill; Abortion Dispute Awaits Conferees

AUGUST 7 — When House and Senate negotiators sit down to patch together a fiscal 2000 foreign operations appropriations bill in September, they will find little to quarrel about on spending. Instead, they must resolve significant policy differences, particularly over abortion restrictions on international family planning aid.

Congress for the 14th straight year has not passed, or this year even introduced, a foreign aid authorization bill to address such issues.

The House cleared the way for the appropriations conference Aug. 3 when it passed, 385-35, its version of the foreign aid spending bill (HR 2606). *(Vote 362, p. H-120)*

On Aug. 2, the House soundly defeated an amendment that would have led to the eventual closing of the Overseas Private Investment Corporation (OPIC), which provides loan guarantees and insurance against political unrest to U.S. investors doing business in less-developed countries. Critics say the agency amounts to "corporate welfare."

As passed, the House foreign operations bill calls for spending $12.6 billion in fiscal 2000, only $100 million below the Senate bill (S 1234). Both are almost $2 billion below President Clinton's original request of $14.6 billion, and senior administration officials have said they would recommend a veto if the spending is not raised.

Specific programs are funded at different levels in the two bills. The House, for example, allocated $568.6 million for the International Development Association, a World Bank subsidiary that provides interest-free loans to the world's poorest countries. That is $208 million below the Senate total and $234.8 million less than Clinton requested.

The Senate bill contains $55 million more for the former Soviet republics, including a specified $210 million for Ukraine, $95 million for Georgia and $90 million for Armenia.

The House bill includes an amendment by James A. Traficant Jr., D-Ohio, that would limit aid to Russia to $172 million and would prohibit funds for the State Department's contribution to the Expanded Threat Reduction Initiative, which tries to provide civilian work for former Soviet weapons scientists. The Senate said it would try to include additional funds for the program in conference.

The Senate bill would provide $142 million more than Clinton requested and the House would provide for the Balkans, including $150 million for Kosovo.

Yet neither bill takes full account of the amount the administration is expected to request later this year for long-term reconstruction in the Balkans, including Kosovo. Last week, Clinton announced several elements of that program, including a new OPIC fund for the region.

Nor does either bill take account of additional funding that the administration is seeking for aid to Colombia, countries engaged in the Middle East peace process, or very poor countries seeking debt relief.

Making a Choice

The administration may try to have some money for such programs added in conference. But most of the debate there will be focused on resolving the issue of abortion restrictions on international family planning assistance, a debate that could scuttle the entire bill.

Conferees will have to decide whether to include either of two substantially different amendments on family planning aid that the House approved July 29.

Current law prohibits the use of U.S. aid to pay for abortions as a method of family planning or to "motivate or coerce" anyone to practice abortion. Neither amendment would change this prohibition.

One amendment the House adopted, offered by Christopher H. Smith, R-N.J., would reinstate elements of a Reagan and Bush administration policy — the "Mexico City" policy — that banned aid for international family planning groups that performed abortions, even if they used non-U.S. money.

Smith's amendment would bar U.S. aid for any international family planning organization unless it certified that it would not perform abortions, except when the life of the woman would be endangered or in case of forcible rape or incest. The amendment also would ban aid to family planning groups that try to change abortion laws in other countries — even if they use their own funds for the purpose.

The House also adopted an amendment by James C. Greenwood, R-Pa., that would require family planning groups to certify they will not use U.S. aid to promote abortion as a method of family planning or to lobby for or against abortion. The groups also would have to certify they would use the U.S. aid "to reduce the incidence of abortion as a method of family planning." The groups would be free to do what they wished with non-U.S. funds.

Greenwood argued that his provision took a stronger anti-abortion stance than current law and was more likely to endure in conference, and 22 House members voted for both.

The Clinton administration supports the Greenwood amendment, but not Smith's. The Senate bill does not include either version, but the Senate has generally resisted Smith's provision in the past, only narrowly approving it, 51-49, last year as part of a State Department authorization bill that was ultimately vetoed by Clinton. *(1998 Almanac, p. 16-3)*

Smith insists he has a commitment from the House leadership that the spending bill will not advance without his anti-abortion provision.

Smith says he wants a "universal settlement" with Clinton that will allow House-Senate conferences to produce a spending bill and a State Department authorization bill that would include the payment of U.S. debts to the United Nations. But he said such a settlement will require Clinton to agree to Smith's amendment.

School of the Americas

Conferees will also have to resolve foreign operations funding for the School of the Americas at the Army's Fort Benning in Georgia. The House bill cuts off funds for the school, which trains military officers from Latin America. Critics say it has trained dictators and military thugs.

The Army is working hard to ensure that the decision is reversed by a

House-Senate conference, although the bulk of the school's funding comes from the defense appropriations bill (HR 2561, S 1122).

In finishing its work on the bill, the House on Aug. 2 defeated, 315-103, an attempt by Rep. Robert E. Andrews, D-N.J., to prevent OPIC from insuring new investment in developing countries or making additional loans. *(Vote 359, p. H-118)*

Andrews and other critics said OPIC was providing large corporations with insurance they could obtain from the private sector. And they warned again that the U.S. government could be liable for billions of dollars of bad loans or insurance payments if OPIC-guaranteed investments go sour.

OPIC's defenders said that the agency has supported the expansion of U.S. industries into new markets and that it provides a service that could not be obtained commercially. And they pointed out that without OPIC, U.S. companies could be at a disadvantage in the global marketplace since most major U.S. competitors boast such services.

In 1996, OPIC's defenders lost that fight, when the House voted 260-157 to reject legislation reauthorizing the agency. It was continued thanks to funding in the fiscal 1997 foreign operations spending bill, part of an omnibus spending bill (PL 104-208). *(1996 Almanac, p. 2-60)*

Since then the agency and its corporate supporters have painstakingly garnered support for the program. In fact, 107 members who had opposed reauthorizing the agency three years ago supported its continued existence this year.

Rep. Sonny Callahan, R-Ala., the chairman of the Foreign Operations Appropriations Subcommittee, said that many members changed their position on OPIC because of grass-roots pressure exerted by business groups.

"The tentacles of OPIC benefits are spread nationwide," Callahan said, "Some of their constituents are totally dependent on these services."

Also among the converts to OPIC's cause were nine members of the Congressional Black Caucus.

The support of black members can be partly traced to OPIC's decision to open two investment funds for Africa, programs authorized by trade legislation for Africa pending before Congress (HR 434 — H Rept 106-19, Parts 1 and 2).

"Generally I would be on the other side of an issue like this one," voting against OPIC, said Rep. Danny K. Davis, D-Ill., who was elected to Congress after the 1996 vote. However, he said, "I find myself in opposition to this amendment because I want to see Africa have an opportunity to grow and develop."

Conference Stalls Over House Effort To Restrict Family Planning Programs

SEPTEMBER 25 — House and Senate negotiators, close to reaching a compromise on the fiscal 2000 foreign aid spending bill Sept. 22, were halted by a perennial roadblock — abortion-related restrictions on international family planning assistance.

Conferees had ironed out all the other details of a $12.6 billion foreign operations appropriations bill (HR 2606), despite significant policy differences.

It was unclear how long the population planning dispute would last, but some members thought it might only be resolved as part of a broader agreement between congressional leaders and President Clinton, who wants significantly more money for foreign aid.

"We may not have a foreign aid bill until the omnibus bill," said Rep. Nita M. Lowey, D-N.Y., one of the House conferees. "The bill is not adequate, and I'm not sure if the president would veto it."

"It's going to be a long wait," agreed Rep. Frank R. Wolf, R-Va.

The holdup came after a compromise proposal by House Foreign Operations Appropriations Subcommittee Chairman Sonny Callahan, R-Ala., was effectively rejected by Senate negotiators, 8-7, with Sen. Arlen Specter, R-Pa., crossing party lines.

House Appropriations Committee Chairman C.W. Bill Young, R-Fla., said House Republicans were surprised by the vote. "We thought the Senate had agreed to it, but they hadn't."

Callahan had attempted to bridge the gap between the slight anti-abortion majority in the House and the majority of senators opposed to further abortion restrictions on international family planning aid.

He proposed retaining the language included in the fiscal 1999 omnibus spending law (PL 105-277), which permits the president to spend $385 million a year on international family planning aid, but omits additional abortion-related restrictions supported by social conservatives that would restore anti-abortion policies of the Reagan and Bush administrations. Those restrictions are adamantly opposed by Clinton and most senators. *(1998 Almanac, p. 2-45)*

The House had adopted those restrictions for its foreign operations bill in an amendment by Rep. Christopher H. Smith, R-N.J., as well as a somewhat contradictory amendment by Rep. James C. Greenwood, R-Pa.

U.N. Fund Debate

At the same time, Callahan tried to appease abortion opponents by proposing to drop a $25 million contribution to the United Nations Fund for Population Activities (UNFPA). The House had agreed to reauthorize the contribution for fiscal 2000 after zeroing it out for this year.

Smith and other abortion opponents had managed to eliminate funds for the U.N. program for this year by arguing that the agency condoned the practice of coercive abortions in China.

On July 19, Smith sought to cut off the funds in fiscal 2000 through an amendment to the State Department authorization bill (HR 2415). But supporters of the U.N. fund, led by Rep. Tom Campbell, R-Calif., blocked his move by modifying his amendment.

Callahan's proposal was adopted by House negotiators, 8-6. But Senate negotiators, led by Patrick J. Leahy of Vermont, ranking Democrat on the Foreign Operations Appropriations Subcommittee, rejected the idea of removing the U.N. funds.

Leahy argued that the contribution should not be eliminated because the $25 million was approved by both the House and Senate. And he said the U.N. fund actually reduced abortions by helping women avoid becoming pregnant in the first place.

He was backed by abortion-rights supporter Rep. John Edward Porter, R-Ill., who said Callahan's plan "fails to recognize that this Congress is a different Congress than the one that voted to cut UNFPA."

Young said Callahan's plan was a fair effort at compromise. "These people have to get something," Young said of abortion opponents.

Falling Short

Before hitting the impasse over family planning, negotiators had agreed on a bill that would fall nearly $2 billion below Clinton's original request. The $12.6 billion total does not include billions more that Clinton has requested or is expected to request for foreign aid — from debt relief for the world's poorest countries to rewards for Israel, the Palestinians and Jordan for forging a peace agreement last year.

Leahy warned that "the president may well veto [the bill] because of the spending levels."

But Sen. Mitch McConnell, R-Ky., said that there was no way to meet the president's requests, given the spending allocation available to the panel.

"It reminds me of puppies wrestling in a sack for a bone," McConnell said. "It's pulled every which way, but the size of the bag doesn't change."

Nonetheless, McConnell said he expects many of the president's priorities to be met in a subsequent supplemental spending bill.

Alluding to recent earthquakes in Turkey and Greece and the hurricane that devastated portions of the U.S. Atlantic coast this month, McConnell said, "We've got earthquakes, we've got hurricanes, and the thought that there is not going to be some supplemental in the near future is nonsense."

Assuming that there would be a supplemental bill that would include much of the nearly $2 billion that Clinton pledged to Israel, Jordan and the Palestinians last year, House Republicans agreed to strip out $100 million they had previously set aside for Jordan.

The compromise bill included several other substantial cuts. Negotiators agreed to provide:

- $625 million for the International Development Association, a World Bank subsidiary that provides no-interest loans to poor nations. Clinton had requested $803 million. The House had cut the funding to $568.6 million.
- $180 million for Ukraine. The Senate had originally agreed to provide $210 million. The reduction came as overall aid to countries of the former Soviet Union was cut by about one-fourth amid criticism of the administration's policy toward the region, particularly Russia. No funds were provided for the State Department's share of the Expanded Threat Reduction Initiative, a plan that would increase U.S. support for programs that seek to employ former Russian scientists in civilian work.
- $35 million for the Korean Peninsula Energy Development Organization, a consortium formed primarily by the United States, Japan and South Korea to supply North Korea's energy needs as part of a 1994 agreement to curb North Korea's nascent nuclear energy program.

The administration could spend the full $55 million it requested if North Korea either fulfilled certain requirements or Clinton chose to waive those restrictions on national security grounds. Republicans have criticized Clinton's decision to lift some long-standing sanctions on North Korea in return for an oral agreement by the Pyongyang regime not to test a new long-range ballistic missile.

- $33 million for debt relief for the world's poorest countries. Clinton had initially sought $120 million and pledged further funding at a meeting of industrial countries earlier this year. On Sept. 21, Treasury Secretary Lawrence Summers said that Clinton was asking Congress for an additional $250 million for debt relief for fiscal 2000 and then $600 million spread over the three subsequent fiscal years.

Rep. Nancy Pelosi, D-Calif., sought to authorize Clinton's new full request for fiscal 2000 — $370 million — during the conference, but she was defeated by House Republicans on a 6-5 party-line vote.

"This is an appropriations bill, not an authorization bill," said Callahan, who said the matter would be handled by the Banking Committee.

At the same time, conferees voted to spend $285 million for anti-narcotics efforts, the full amount that the Clinton administration requested and more than was approved by either the House or Senate.

The increase came as Colombian President Andres Pastrana visited Washington seeking more anti-drug funds for his beleaguered nation.

Foreign Military Training

House conferees did resolve one controversial policy issue when they rejected, 7-8, a motion by Lowey that would have cut off about $2 million in International Military Education and Training funds for the Army's School of Americas at Fort Benning, Ga.

The House on June 30 voted to cut off foreign operations budget support for the school after some lawmakers, led by Joe Moakley, D-Mass., argued that some graduates of the training facility for Latin American military officers had violated human rights in the region.

Callahan said that he gave in to the Senate, which continued funding for the school, because Army officials indicated that if the House ban held, they would shift all funding for the school to the defense budget, which already provides most of the facility's support.

"It would have been a loss of jurisdiction by this committee over [foreign military training] programs," Callahan said. "In order to have standards for [the programs] it is better to have it here than in the defense subcommittee."

The conference did approve one cutoff in military aid — a version of legislation (S 1568) by Sen. Russell D. Feingold, D-Wis., that would cut off U.S. military and economic assistance to Indonesia until the situation in East Timor is peacefully resolved.

It calls on the administration to persuade the IMF and other multilateral organizations not to loan money to Indonesia.

House GOP Lacks Votes To Clear Foreign Aid Bill

OCTOBER 2 — Republican leaders hoped to execute a difficult three-step dance in winning House adoption of the conference report on a fiscal 2000 foreign aid bill, but ended up tripping over their own feet.

First, House Republican leaders, eager to see the $12.6 billion foreign operations spending bill (HR 2606) become law before the fiscal year began Oct. 1, yielded to Senate demands that they renew contributions to the United Nations Fund for Population Activities.

A House-Senate conference committee had bogged down Sept. 22 after Senate conferees objected to a House proposal to cut the funds — approved by both chambers — in a bid to win the support of anti-abortion lawmakers.

Second, Republicans led by Sonny Callahan of Alabama, chairman of the House Foreign Operations Appropriations Subcommittee, had tried to keep the overall price tag for the bill down, in an attempt to please fiscal conservatives and to employ the bill as part of their overall budget strategy.

That strategy sought to portray President Clinton as stealing money from Social Security to pay for spending initiatives.

"If the president says, 'I want to bend the caps and break into Social Security to fund the foreign aid budget,' then he can do that," Callahan said at a Rules Committee hearing Sept. 28.

In the third and final step, Callahan won support for the legislation from the American Israel Public Affairs Committee (AIPAC). Republican leaders counted on the renowned lobbying muscle of the pro-Israel group to win enough Democratic votes for the bill to counter any Republican losses.

But with the House poised to move toward consideration of the conference report Sept. 29, Republican leaders took a head count and realized they were far short of the number they had counted on for passage. They then pulled the bill from the floor calendar and began furiously twisting arms, hoping to win enough support to bring the bill up the week of Oct. 4.

They faced an uphill battle.

Growing Problems

Anti-abortion Republicans such as Rep. Christopher H. Smith of New Jersey objected to the conference report because, unlike the House-passed bill, it does not include any abortion-related restrictions on U.S. aid to international family planning groups. Nor does it include an end to contributions to the U.N. population fund that Callahan had proposed as an alternative in the conference committee.

Anti-abortion groups oppose helping the U.N. fund because of its involvement in China, which is alleged to practice coercive abortions in an attempt to limit population growth. The conference report includes a House-passed provision that deducts from the $25 million U.S. contribution to the U.N. fund any money that it spends in China.

Republicans also insisted that they could not yield to Clinton's demands for more foreign aid spending, because they would be forced to break the caps from the 1997 balanced-budget agreement (PL 105-33). *(1997 Almanac, p. 2-18)*

"We should not break the caps and spend more in every category," said GOP Rep. John Linder of Georgia at the Rules Committee hearing on the measure.

But to some fiscal conservatives, the final bill was already too expensive. It was listed by Republican leaders as costing $12.7 billion instead of the $12.6 billion total included in the House-passed version.

Aides say that a $77 million debt relief payment to the African Development Bank — technically not scored as part of what is called a $12.6 billion final bill — accounts for much of the difference.

Facing opposition in their own ranks, Republicans tried to push Democrats to support the bill, using AIPAC to win their support.

But although the pro-Israel group's board endorsed the measure, there was initial uncertainty about how intense an effort AIPAC was making in the bill's behalf.

"I don't think they've been that active," House Minority Whip David E. Bonior, D-Mich., said Sept. 30 in an interview.

Republicans pushed leaders of the pro-Israel group to make a stronger effort in support of the bill.

"They're taking a walk on this, and we're not going to let them do it," said a Republican leadership aide.

After several discussions, Republican aides said AIPAC had stepped up its efforts.

"We support the bill. Full stop," said AIPAC spokesman Ken Bricker.

The organization supports the legislation because it includes almost $3 billion in aid to Israel, including $960 million in economic assistance and $1.9 billion in military aid.

But at the same time, Israel's allies on Capitol Hill are concerned that the bill does not include $500 million the Clinton administration requested for fiscal 2000 — part of the nearly $1.8 billion requested through fiscal 2001— to help implement last year's Wye River peace accord between Israel and the Palestinians.

Clinton and congressional Democrats have used the lack of Wye River funds in the bill to dampen enthusiasm for the measure and drive a wedge between AIPAC's leadership and its traditional congressional supporters. For example, Bonior said that no Jewish Democrats are supporting the measure.

"Failure to provide any funding sends the worst possible message to Israel, Jordan and the Palestinians about our commitment to the peace process," Clinton said in a Sept. 30 letter to House Speaker J. Dennis Hastert, R-Ill.

Republicans say that the funds will be included in a future supplemental spending bill.

"It would take an idiot not to know that this Congress is going to have some kind of supplemental," Callahan said. He did acknowledge, however, that Congress might not take up a supplemental measure until next year.

Senate Adoption Likely

That message seemed to take hold in the Senate, where lawmakers and aides predicted that the measure would pass despite grumbling from Democrats such as Patrick J. Leahy of Vermont, ranking member of the Senate Foreign Operations Appropriations Subcommittee.

Leahy refused to sign the conference report, saying in a Sept. 28 interview that "this is just a ridiculously low level of funding for a great nation." But he predicted that if the House approved the conference report, the Senate would clear it.

In the House, aides and lawmakers gave credit to Democratic leaders, who, sensing the chance to score a major victory in the budget battle and bucked up by Clinton's threat to veto the bill, have held firm in opposition.

"If they want this bill, they're going to have to pass it on their own," Rep. Nancy Pelosi of California, ranking Democrat on the Foreign Operations Appropriations Subcommittee, said in a Sept. 29 interview, relishing the low number of Democratic defections.

One experienced GOP appropriations aide confessed admiration for the other party.

"Democrats see this as their chance to get back in the majority, and they are holding people. This is the tightest whip operation I've ever seen on this," the aide said.

In his letter to Hastert, Clinton complained of the bill's "woefully inadequate overall funding level" and said that "if Congress were to enact this conference report, I would have no choice but to veto it."

In addition to the Wye funds, Clinton complained of several other shortfalls in the conference report, including:

- No funds for the State Department's portion of the Expanded Threat Reduction Initiative, an enlarged effort to stem the threat of the spread of weapons of mass destruction from the nations of the former Soviet Union. Clinton had requested $241 million for a State Department program designed to help former weapons scientists shift to commercial work.
- Low funds for programs for poor countries, particularly those in Africa. "The bill dramatically underfunds debt relief, multilateral development bank financing, development programs, and the Economic Support Fund," Clinton wrote.

Short on Debt

Clinton complained that the measure would particularly hurt Africa because the conferees had refused to fund his pledge to write off much of the debt of the world's poorest countries.

Addressing the annual meeting of the International Monetary Fund and the World Bank on Sept. 29, Clinton expanded his promise. He pledged to cancel all $5.7 billion of debt that 36 very poor countries owe the U.S. government. Clinton had already promised U.S. participation in a program to write off the debt of poor nations to international agencies such as the World Bank.

All told, administration officials have requested that Congress approve $1 billion to write off the poor countries' debt over four fiscal years. That would suffice because many of the loans are now valued at only a portion of their original face value because lenders assumed they would not be fully repaid.

But even before Clinton's proposal, Congress has been balking at substantial debt relief for poor countries. The conference report includes only $33 million of the $120 million that Clinton requested in February.

Still, debt relief has some powerful supporters in Congress, including House Banking Committee Chairman Jim Leach, R-Iowa, who has introduced legislation (HR 1095) to support the Clinton initiative. Senate Republican Conference Chairman Connie Mack of Florida is planning to introduce a similar bill in that chamber.

Bill Clears, But Veto Is Likely Over Aid Levels

OCTOBER 9 — After GOP congressional leaders warned party members that their budget strategy and even their House majority hung in the balance, Republicans in the House and Senate buried their differences and united behind the conference report to the fiscal 2000 foreign operations appropriations bill (HR 2606), narrowly adopting it despite solid Democratic opposition.

The House adopted the report, 214-211, on Oct. 5, and the Senate cleared it, 51-49, the next day. *(House vote 480, p. H-156; Senate vote 312, p. S-61)*

With Republicans thus far short of the two-thirds majority they would need to override President Clinton's expected veto, a drawn-out struggle is still expected over foreign aid.

Clinton and congressional Democrats oppose the $12.7 billion legislation because it falls $1.9 billion short of his budget request. In particular, Clinton has complained that the bill includes few funds for debt relief for the world's poorest countries and does not designate any money for a State Department program designed to find work for former nuclear scientists in Russia.

Clinton also has said that the measure does not address an additional request he made for $500 million in fiscal 2000 — and nearly $1.8 billion over three years — to help implement last year's Wye River peace accord between Israel and the Palestinians.

Wye Opposition

House Democratic leaders, eager to shoot down one of the Republicans' spending bills, seized on the lack of Wye River funds as a reason for voting against the measure.

They were aided by Jewish Democrats, such as Sam Gejdenson of Connecticut and Howard L. Berman of California, senior members of the House International Relations Committee who sent a letter to their colleagues urging them to vote against the conference report because it did not contain the Wye funds.

Berman brushed aside promises from Republican leaders that the Wye River funds would be included in a supplemental spending bill sometime in fiscal 2000.

He said the money needs to be approved by Congress before February, when Palestinian and Israeli negotiators are scheduled to try to complete a framework for their permanent relationship.

"To not do the Wye supplemental, to not appropriate those monies before the February framework agreement, is to tell both parties that America's commitments cannot be accounted on, that the sacrifices and the compromises that need to be made cannot be carried out because the funding will not be there," Berman said on the House floor Oct. 5.

"Who knows what is going to happen next spring or next summer when the Republican leadership may choose to bring up a supplemental, and who knows what will be in that supplemental? This is the time to deal with it," he said.

Republican leaders want to hold off on the Wye River spending because it would undermine their budget strategy: Hold the line on spending — particularly foreign aid spending — and say that Clinton's requests for more money would have to be paid from funds set aside for Social Security.

By postponing action on the Wye River pledge until next year, Republicans could take advantage of what is expected to be a higher non-Social Security budget surplus.

"We do not have more money," said Sonny Callahan, R-Ala., chairman of the House Foreign Operations Appropriations Subcommittee. "The only way to get more money is through new taxes, through possibly jeopardizing Social Security or breaking the budget caps."

Callahan and other Republican leaders also brandished the support of the American-Israel Public Affairs Committee (AIPAC) to deflect criticism about the lack of funds for the Wye River agreement.

But that endorsement did not pack the punch they anticipated. Although Republican leaders had counted on the powerful pro-Israel lobbying group to help move the conference report, AIPAC was unable to budge House Democrats. Only two voted for the bill.

One dissident Democrat, Sanford D. Bishop Jr. of Georgia, said he backed the conference report because, unlike the House-passed bill, it contained funding for the Army's School of the Americas, at Fort Benning in his district.

"All politics is local," explained Bishop.

The other Democrat, Debbie Stabenow of Michigan, is running for the Senate.

Scramble for Votes

Short of votes after the conference concluded, Republicans on Sept. 29 pulled the report from the House floor. Then they began wooing Republicans who had previously opposed the measure.

The horse-trading even included concessions to Northeastern lawmakers worried about dairy pricing included in the fiscal 2000 agriculture appropriations conference report (HR 1906 — H Rept 106-354), which the House adopted Oct. 1.

The largest bloc of additional GOP votes came from those who had threatened to scuttle the legislation because it dropped a House-passed provision with abortion-related restrictions on aid to international family planning organizations and because it includes a contribution to the United Nations Fund for Population Activities, opposed by many social conservatives.

In the end, only a half-dozen anti-abortion Republicans voted against the measure.

Joseph R. Pitts, R-Pa., said he had initially opposed the conference report but was swayed by party leaders. "I don't think we have any other options," Pitts said in an Oct. 5 interview. "If we don't pass it, everything falls apart, and it just gets worse."

Another conservative, Rep. Steve Largent, R-Okla., said the foreign aid vote was a linchpin of the Republican budget strategy, which seeks to confront Clinton over spending levels rather than policy differences.

"I back the leadership's strategy that if he vetoes this, he should veto this over money rather than riders," Largent said in an Oct. 5 interview.

Even with the support of anti-abortion Republicans and days of prodding, GOP leaders still went into the vote unsure if they would win. House Speaker J. Dennis Hastert, R-Ill., cast a rare floor vote in favor of the report.

During the tally, Majority Leader Dick Armey, R-Texas, continued to lean on Roscoe G. Bartlett, R-Md., a perennial foreign aid opponent, until he supported the conference report.

Another regular opponent of foreign aid, Ron Paul, R-Texas, abstained from voting.

Solid Wall

Much the same situation existed in the Senate, where Republicans faced a solid wall of Democratic opposition — all 45 Democrats voted against the conference report.

Republicans again argued that passage of the legislation was essential for maintaining budget discipline.

Telling colleagues that Clinton's expected veto was "inexplicable," Sen. Mitch McConnell, R-Ky., chairman of the Foreign Operations Appropriations Subcommittee, said, "I don't know where the president wants to get more money for this bill. Are we going to take it out of the Social Security trust fund to spend it on foreign aid?"

Still, the conference report was initially opposed by four Republicans — George V. Voinovich of Ohio, Chuck Hagel of Nebraska, Gordon H. Smith of Oregon, Foreign Relations Committee Chairman Jesse Helms of North Carolina — and one former Republican, Robert C. Smith of New Hampshire, who is now an independent. Some opposed the measure because they said it called for too much spending; some because it called for too little.

Their opposition initially set up a 50-50 tie vote, which would have meant defeat for the conference report.

So Senate Majority Leader Trent Lott, R-Miss., went to work on the party dissidents. At first, he was rebuffed by Gordon Smith, who said the report did not adequately fund U.S. foreign aid needs. But Lott won the support of Helms, who has traditionally voted against foreign aid bills but did not want to hand an embarrassing defeat to the party's leadership.

Contentious Aftermath

That narrow victory sent the bill on its way to Clinton but may make it easier for him to veto, as he has repeatedly threatened to do.

Alternatively, Clinton and congressional leaders could find a way to include additional foreign aid funds in other legislation.

According to aides, Clinton raised three major objections to the spending bill in a Sept. 30 telephone conversation with Callahan — the lack of funds for the Wye River agreement, debt relief and the program to halt a "brain drain" of Russian scientists.

Yet, Clinton has or is expected to request billions more for other foreign aid initiatives — from aid to Colombia, the Balkans and East Timor, to earthquake relief for Turkey and Greece.

Speaking on the House floor Sept. 5, Callahan repeatedly complained about "this insatiable appetite for money that President Clinton has that he wants to hand out as he makes his travels.

"Every time the president meets with a foreign dignitary, they have a toast, [and] the president of the United States says, 'here is my commitment to you. I am going to give you some more money.' Then they run over here and say this is an obligation of the United States," Callahan said.

President Vetoes Foreign Aid Bill; GOP Digs in Heels

OCTOBER 23 — President Clinton vetoed the fiscal 2000 foreign aid spending bill Oct. 18, saying its $12.7 billion total was too low and part of a slide by Republicans toward isolationism.

In carrying out his threat to veto the foreign operations appropriations bill (HR 2606), Clinton not only struck back at congressional Republicans who had recently refused to ratify the Comprehensive Test Ban Treaty he signed in 1996, he also spurred a round of negotiations between Capitol Hill and the White House over the fiscal 2000 budget.

Yet, congressional aides said it is likely that when a final foreign aid bill emerges from the budget negotiations, it will not be significantly different from the one Clinton vetoed — and likely with far less money than he has sought.

The measure fell $1.9 billion below Clinton's budget request, and as much as $5.8 billion short of the total the White House is now said to be seeking.

Clinton told an Oct. 18 news conference, "I vetoed the foreign operations bill this morning because it seems to me to be the next big chapter in American isolationism, right after the Comprehensive Test Ban Treaty." *(Veto text, p. D-26)*

Clinton had dedicated most of a news conference on Oct. 14 to slamming the Republicans for rejecting the nuclear test ban treaty.

Immediately after the veto, Republicans shot back, saying Clinton's foreign policy goals could only be achieved by dipping into the Social Security surplus.

"The president vetoed this bill because it doesn't send more of the taxpayer's money overseas," said House Speaker J. Dennis Hastert, R-Ill., in a written statement. "We will not raid the Social Security trust fund to pay for more foreign aid."

Truce for Talks

Despite the rhetoric, when the White House and congressional Republicans agreed to an overall approach to budget negotiations, appropriators and administration officials were quick to seek a negotiated end to the impasse.

Aides said the most likely outcome is that a small portion of politically sensitive aid would be approved — $500 million for Israel, the Palestinians and Jordan to help carry out last year's Wye River peace accord. The aid would likely be designated as "emergency" spending, so that it could not be counted against budget caps.

The rest of the aid package might be included in a supplemental spending bill next spring, according to lawmakers and aides.

Earlier this year, Clinton requested $1.9 billion in supplemental appropriations for those countries in fiscal years 1999-2001 as a reward for making peace; $100 million for Jordan was included in a supplemental spending bill (PL 106-31) approved last spring. So the administration is still seeking $1.8 billion more for the region, in addition to about $5 billion already included for the Middle East in the foreign operations measure.

Democratic aides acknowledged that it will be difficult to muster their party's opposition to a new foreign aid bill that includes the Wye River funds but otherwise falls short of Clinton's foreign aid request. Opposition by Jewish Democrats to the legislation Clinton vetoed had nearly torpedoed the measure on the House floor.

Meanwhile, Republicans, such as Foreign Operations Appropriations Committee Chairman Sonny Callahan of Alabama, have told Clinton that they will stand firm on all other spending.

No Debt Relief

For example, GOP leaders are resisting including in the legislation the fiscal 2000 portion of nearly $1 billion that Clinton has sought to write off, over the next four fiscal years, the debt that 36 very poor countries owe the United States.

Secretary of State Madeleine K. Albright made a plea for debt relief and other foreign aid funds after visiting potential beneficiaries in West Africa Oct. 18-20.

"It is not that they expect a handout from the U.S. They expect help," she told reporters Oct. 20. It is "very hard to understand that we have the world's greatest economy and we have a huge budget surplus, and they are digging themselves out of garbage."

However, the House International Relations Committee on Oct. 19 put off a scheduled markup of a measure (HR 1095) that would have authorized the debt relief.

Republican House leaders told the committee they did not want the bill considered while they were in budget negotiations with the White House.

"The leadership called it off," said one GOP aide. "I couldn't think of a worse [budget] climate to launch something like this."

Colombian Tactics

Supporters of efforts to increase aid to Colombia to bolster the South American country's fight against drug traffickers also said it is unlikely additional money for that effort will be appropriated until the spring.

Part of the decision is tactical. House GOP leadership aides say the administration has been holding off on requesting those funds so they can be used as a bargaining chip with Hastert, who has consistently favored increasing aid to Colombia.

But Sen. Paul Coverdell, R-Ga., sponsor of a measure to authorize a $1.6 billion increase in spending in Colombia and surrounding countries over the next three fiscal years, said that Colombia would need the money in the spring, not now.

"There's enough money now in the pipeline, but later we have to pour more in," Coverdell said. "When we come back in January, that's when attention will focus on this. "

Additional foreign aid for the Balkans, East Timor and other countries may also be considered at that point, aides said.

Clinton administration officials were not giving up on getting extra funds.

For example, national security adviser Samuel R. Berger continued campaigning for money to be specifically designated for a State Department program that seeks to find civilian work for former Soviet weapons scientists.

The vetoed bill did not prohibit any of the $735 million in funds for the former Soviet Union from being spent on the State Department's Expanded Threat Reduction Initiative. But it did not specify $241 million that Clinton requested for the program, and it cut $297 million from his overall request for the region.

GOP Leaders Agree To Fund Wye River Aid

OCTOBER 30 — As GOP congressional leaders and Clinton administration officials battle publicly, lawmakers and top White House aides are working behind the scenes to fashion a compromise on foreign aid spending.

Picking up on similar remarks by President Clinton the previous week, Secretary of State Madeleine K. Albright returned from a trip to Africa and endorsed Clinton's Oct. 18 veto of the fiscal 2000 foreign operations appropriations bill (HR 2606 — Conference report: H Rept 106-339), because it fell far short of administration requests.

"The way that the foreign operations bill had been cut did the most amazing kind of damage to what our goals have been," Albright told reporters Oct. 25. "We need it. It's not a matter of sitting here and trying to make up budgets that ask for more than we need. We are down to bare bones."

As passed, the $12.7 billion bill called for spending about $1.9 billion less than Clinton originally requested. Since then, Clinton has added a number of other requests that could amount to as much as $6 billion above the bill approved by Congress.

Behind the scenes, Senate Foreign Operations Appropriations Committee Chairman Mitch McConnell, R-Ky., has been meeting with Jack Lew, director of the White House Office of Management of Budget, to seek a solution.

A senior Republican aide said that the negotiations have been making progress. "We are closing the gap," the aide said.

In particular, the aide said that Republicans were virtually certain to agree to include $1.3 billion of $1.9 billion that Clinton requested earlier this year to implement last year's Wye River peace accord between Israel and the Palestinians.

That total would mean that Congress would fully fund the fiscal 1999 and 2000 portions of aid to Israel, Jordan and the Palestinians, leaving the final year of the proposed three-year package to the fiscal 2001 budget cycle.

Failure to include the funds had been a particular sticking point on Capitol Hill, angering Jewish Democrats and almost causing the defeat of the legislation in the House.

But speaking to members of the powerful American-Israel Public Affairs Committee on Oct. 26, Senate Majority Leader Trent Lott, R-Miss., said he is "committed to funding Wye aid now."

The GOP aide also said it was likely that a final agreement would in a "modest way" address Clinton's request to begin writing off the debt that 36 very poor nations owe the United States. Clinton has requested nearly $1 billion over the next four fiscal years.

Sen. Connie Mack, R-Fla., who has sponsored a bill authorizing the debt relief (S 1690), said Oct. 26, "We are sure trying to find a way to do that. It doesn't really have any opponents."

He said lawmakers and the White House were trying to strike a deal on the language governing who would be eligible for debt relief, the amount of money that would be appropriated, and how the spending would be offset.

The proposal faces opposition from House Foreign Operations Appropriations Chairman Sonny Callahan, R-Ala., who fears the money would only support corrupt governments.

Congress is likely to grant Clinton's request for additional funds for humanitarian aid to Kosovo, Senate Appropriations Committee Chairman Ted Stevens, R-Alaska, said Oct. 26.

The GOP aide said the final package would also seek to boost the economies of Kosovo's neighbors, which were battered by the air campaign there earlier this year.

Among the issues still to be resolved is what, if any, additional funds Colombia and other nations will receive to help their anti-drug efforts.

House Government Reform Chairman Dan Burton, R-Ind., joined a chorus of Republicans demanding more funds for the South American nation in particular. "Something needs to be done now before it is too late," Burton said Oct. 26.

But some leading Senate Republicans have said that aid could wait until next year.

GOP Yields on Funding Levels; House Passes Revised Bill

NOVEMBER 6 — Republicans the week of Nov. 1 gave in to most of President Clinton's demands for higher foreign aid spending, perhaps clearing the way for a larger budget agreement.

After weeks of negotiations with the White House over the fiscal 2000 foreign operations appropriations bill — Clinton vetoed the original (HR 2606) Oct. 18 — GOP leaders agreed to $2.6 billion in additional aid, including more money for the Middle East, the former Soviet Union and the World Bank.

A revised foreign operations bill (HR 3196) won overwhelming support from Democrats and passed the House on Nov. 5 by a vote of 316-100. *(Vote 572, p. H-186)*

Republicans said they agreed to the compromise in an effort to wrap up the overall budget talks. In a Nov. 4 interview, House Appropriations Committee Chairman C.W. Bill Young, R-Fla., said White House budget director Jack Lew had promised him that "once we settle foreign aid . . . we'll settle everything else quickly."

But the concessions came grudgingly after several attempts by Republicans to split congressional Democrats from the White House over the foreign aid bill fell through.

Republicans first agreed to White House demands to fund the most politically sensitive assistance: $1.8 billion that Clinton had promised to carry out the 1998 Wye River peace agreement between Israel and the Palestinians.

That agreement won the enthusiastic support of the American Israel Public Affairs Committee, the powerful pro-Israel lobbying group, and led Republicans to believe they could gain the backing of pro-Israel Democrats in the House, whose opposition to the previous bill nearly killed it before it reached Clinton's desk and gave him political cover to veto the measure.

But House aides said that in a meeting of some pro-Israel Democrats on Nov. 4, only about one-third supported the bill. They continued to side with the administration and House Democratic leaders in urging a higher overall spending level. The vetoed bill had been almost $2 billion less than Clinton originally requested, not counting the Wye funds.

Meeting with Lew the night of Nov. 3, House Republicans made a small concession: With the Clinton administration asking for at least $1.4 billion in additional spending, Republicans said they would agree to spending an additional $216 million. That would include $150 million more for the International Development Association, the World Bank subsidiary providing no-interest loans to the world's poorest countries.

Dealing With Debt

But according to Rep. Nancy Pelosi of California, ranking Democrat on the Foreign Operations Appropriations Subcommittee, Republicans led by subcommittee Chairman Sonny Callahan of Alabama refused to take up three of the administration's priorities: additional funding for humanitarian and reconstruction efforts in Kosovo, debt relief for the world's poorest countries, and the Global Environment Facility, which provides grants to developing countries for environmental initiatives.

Republicans then planned to take the revised bill to the House floor Nov. 4. But when their efforts to win over enough pro-Israel Democrats failed, they postponed the vote and increased their offer to the administration by $545 million, setting off a new round of negotiations.

After a late night of talks, the two sides settled on a total increase — beyond the Wye funds — of $799 million.

"I hate this bill more than any other bill we've passed," Young said on the House floor Nov. 5. "But if we pass it, we can get on with the business of Congress."

The proposal includes an additional $90 million for debt relief, $3 million more than Clinton's original budget request of $120 million in bilateral debt relief. But Callahan continued to hold out against increasing the U.S. contribution to a multilateral debt relief effort led by the International Monetary Fund, for the most deeply indebted countries.

Callahan urged that the effort be considered only as part of a supplemental spending bill next year. And Republicans expressed concern about IMF plans to finance part of the effort through gold sales.

The issue remained unsettled as the bill was taken up by the House, but appropriators promised to continue working on it as the legislation was considered by the Senate and a House-Senate conference.

"We are in the anomalous position of having American taxpayers forgive debt to Africa without leveraging our ability to get the IMF to do the same thing," said David R. Obey of Wisconsin, ranking Democrat on the House Appropriations Committee.

"In that sense," Obey said, "this bill is still shortsighted and needs to be corrected as this bill moves through the process."

U.N. Debts

As White House officials and congressional Republicans continued to negotiate details of the foreign aid spending bill, they were also trying to reach a compromise on paying nearly $1 billion in U.S. debts to the United Nations.

Administration officials have warned that if the debts are not repaid soon, the United States could lose its vote in the U.N. General Assembly, though not its vote on the Security Council.

So White House officials and congressional Republicans are attempting to find a compromise on the two-year-old standoff, which has stalled the latest State Department authorization bill (HR 2415).

Prompted by discussions between Clinton and House Speaker J. Dennis Hastert, R-Ill., aides have been "exploring concepts" of how to get past a hurdle set up by anti-abortion Republicans, led by Rep. Christopher H. Smith, R-N.J.

Smith has insisted on restoring a Reagan and Bush administration policy that cut off funds to overseas family planning groups that try to change abortion laws in other countries, even if they use their own funds for the purpose. Clinton last year vetoed legislation that contained the restrictions and has said he would do so again. *(1998 Almanac, p. 16-3)*

The House leadership has promised Smith it will not support Senate legislation to repay the debts unless the Senate agrees to endorse Smith's effort to restore the abortion restrictions.

In an effort to break the impasse, Clinton has been meeting with women's groups, and Richard C. Holbrooke, the new U.S. ambassador to the United Nations, has been meeting with anti-abortion Republicans, including Smith, and pressing them to disconnect the two issues.

In a Nov. 4 interview, Smith said he has been discussing the "concepts" with administration officials but has so far found them unacceptable. Smith said the White House proposals include finding ways to better monitor funds that flow from the U.S. government to groups that promote family planning overseas.

"Bookkeeping isn't the issue," Smith said, insisting that it is easy for groups to shift the funds to different accounts.

Seeking Peace

Testifying before the Senate Foreign Relations Committee on Nov. 3, Holbrooke said the back payments to the United Nations and U.N. peacekeeping funds are essential to U.S. national security. Both are contained in the fiscal 2000 Commerce, Justice, State appropriations bill (HR 2670) that Clinton vetoed Oct. 25.

Peacekeeping funds, Holbrooke said, particularly constitute a "terrific bargain" because they allow the United States a say in such missions without paying the whole cost or putting U.S. troops in harm's way in places such as East Timor.

Holbrooke said also that U.N. reforms sought by Congress, such as holding down the U.N. budget and reducing the U.S. share of its costs, cannot be accomplished without repaying the U.N. debt.

"I hate to quote 'Jerry Maguire,' but [U.S. allies are] saying, 'Show me the money,' " Holbrooke said.

Committee members commended Holbrooke, who was confirmed in August, for quickly taking steps to advance U.S. interests at the United Nations, including regaining U.S. membership on a key budget committee and winning Israel a platform from which it might be eligible to launch a bid for membership in the U.N. Security Council.

But lawmakers and aides remained skeptical that a compromise would be worked out on the U.N. payments, given the passions surrounding the abortion issue.

"The problem with this issue is there's no 50 yard line," said one Senate Republican aide. "Every gain in yardage for one side is seen as a loss for the other side."

The most likely outcome, lawmakers said, would be just enough funds to avoid losing the General Assembly vote, which will happen if the United States owes more than two years' worth of contributions to the United Nations for peacekeeping and the regular budget.

With Debt Issue Unresolved, Bill Stalls in Senate

NOVEMBER 20 — Although the White House and congressional Republicans have reached agreement on foreign aid spending, the latest version of the fiscal 2000 foreign operations appropriations bill (HR 3196) remains stalled because of a dispute over debt relief for poor countries and efforts by Democrats to use the bill as leverage in winning support on other issues.

After a compromise between Congress and the White House following President Clinton's Oct. 18 veto of the original foreign aid bill (HR 2606), the House quickly passed the new, $15.3 billion version Nov. 5 — virtually the same but with an additional $2.6 billion for the Middle East, the states of the former Soviet Union and the World Bank.

But, unexpectedly, the Senate was unable to take up the legislation the week of Nov. 8. Attempts to pass the measure by voice vote ran into a series of objections from Democratic Sens. Robert C. Byrd of West Virginia, Mary L. Landrieu of Louisiana and Herb Kohl of Wisconsin, each of whom was pushing unrelated legislation.

Nonetheless, the foreign aid compromise itself held firm as the White House and Republicans made clear that further movement on aid totals was unlikely.

For example, despite pressure from some House Republicans, including Speaker J. Dennis Hastert, R-Ill., to quickly increase aid to the South American nation of Colombia, beleaguered by drug traffickers and guerrillas, the White House said Nov. 10 that such spending would have to wait until a supplemental spending bill in the spring.

"While we will continue to move forward to aid . . . Colombia with currently available funds," Clinton said, "more funding is needed if we are to gain the upper hand in the fight against drugs and help Colombia on the path to stable democracy. I have asked my senior advisers to work with Congress, following completion of the current budget process, to enhance our bilateral assistance programs — for counterdrug efforts and for other programs to help President [Andres] Pastrana deepen democracy and promote prosperity."

Going Into Debt

At the same time, Clinton administration officials and Republican leaders were working behind closed doors to clear up a lingering dispute over debt relief so they could produce a final bill in a future House-Senate conference.

The dispute is somewhat arcane, but important to House Majority Leader Dick Armey, R-Texas, and some other Republicans who only reluctantly agreed to provide $17.9 billion in credit to the International Monetary Fund (IMF) last year and are reluctant to allow IMF officials to get their hands on additional funds.

The dispute centers on U.S. support for an IMF proposal on how to finance part of a debt-relief plan agreed to by Clinton and the leaders of other wealthy nations at a summit in Cologne, Germany, in June. That plan would forgive $27 billion in foreign debt owed by some of the world's poorest countries.

Under the plan, wealthy nations are supposed to forgive bilateral debt owed by the poor countries and to contribute to a pool that will help write off some of the money the poor countries owe to multilateral agencies such as the IMF and the World Bank. At the same time, those agencies are supposed to use some of their own resources to write off a portion of the debt.

In reaching a compromise on foreign aid spending levels Nov. 4, lawmakers agreed to provide $123 million in bilateral debt relief in the fiscal 2000 foreign operations bill. But they put off discussions on an additional $1 billion in multilateral debt relief that Clinton has requested over four years.

The administration has shown some flexibility on when those additional funds are appropriated. But congressional aides say that administration officials insist that lawmakers agree to policy changes that would allow the IMF to tap more of its own resources to fund its share of the debt relief package.

Some Republicans say the changes would actually hurt U.S. taxpayers rather than making the institutions pay some of the price for poor loans.

One of the proposed changes would allow IMF officials to capture the value of gold reserves held by the Fund on a contingency basis. The gold stores, contributed by the United States and other IMF members, have rarely been tapped, but have been held in reserve in case IMF loans are not repaid.

IMF officials earlier this year planned to sell some of the gold to finance their portion of the debt relief package. But that brought howls of protest from Capitol Hill, where lawmakers feared it would further weaken gold prices. Under IMF rules, the U.S. government has an effective veto over gold sales, and U.S. law requires prior congressional approval of such sales.

IMF officials had considered the sale as a way of capturing some of the difference between how the gold deposits are valued on the IMF's books — about $47 per ounce, the price at which it was acquired decades ago — and its current market price of close to $300 an ounce.

The IMF, which has more than 100 million ounces of gold, had considered selling about 10 million ounces, which could yield $2 billion to $3 billion for debt relief. The United States has agreed to such sales in the past, such as in the late 1970s when the IMF sold gold to help poor countries.

Full Accounting

When the gold sale option was rejected this year, IMF officials hit upon an accounting maneuver that would similarly tap the difference between the market value of the gold and its current value on the IMF's books, without requiring an open market sale of the gold.

Acting through a complicated series of sales and purchases among member countries, the maneuver would revalue the gold on the IMF's books at market prices. That boost in assets would allow the IMF to write off some debt from poor countries at the same time, without affecting its balance sheet.

The new proposal calmed some opponents of the open market gold sales. But longtime IMF critics such as Armey and Joint Economic Committee Vice Chairman H. James Saxton, R-N.J., were not satisfied. They said the United States and other members, rather than the IMF, deserved to profit from the rise in gold values.

"The gold sales plans disguise the taxpayer cost amounting to about $2 billion," Saxton said earlier this year. "The essence of the gold sales proposal is the tapping of $2 billion of gold profits that should ultimately be returned to the contributing countries and their taxpayers."

According to congressional aides, IMF officials are also hoping to tap a special contingency account that was created in 1991 in case countries defaulted on their loans. It has never been needed. But congressional aides said that if it were used now it would mean a $300 million budgetary outlay.

Rush Hour

Armey and other Republican leaders are reluctant to approve the debt-relief funds in the closing weeks of this year's congressional session, saying the complicated proposal deserves thorough scrutiny by the relevant committees next year. Debt relief legislation (HR 1095) was approved by the House Banking and Financial Services Committee on Nov. 3 but has yet to be considered by the House International Relations Committee or any Senate panels.

But administration officials, particularly Treasury Secretary Lawrence H. Summers have argued in private meetings that the provisions are essential and urgent, saying that the whole international debt relief effort could crumble without the U.S. commitment.

Some developing countries, particularly in sub-Saharan Africa, have seen their foreign debt burden skyrocket in recent years.

Summers met Nov. 10 with Armey and Phil Gramm, R-Texas, chairman of the Senate Banking, Housing and Urban Affairs Committee, to press his case. But participants said there was little progress at the meeting.

Armey told reporters Nov. 11 that the gold sales question "is a fascinating issue and it's an issue where the heart says go, go, and the mind says, well, just wait a minute, a little because it's very complex."

"There are some members that need persuasion," Armey added. "There are some difficult things in terms of working out the language."

Free Hand

On other issues, the new version of the foreign operations legislation gives the administration a freer hand than the bill Clinton vetoed last month.

Most importantly, at this point, the measure does not contain many restrictions on military and economic assistance to Indonesia. The original bill would have cut off nearly all U.S. military and economic assistance to the Asian nation in retaliation for its violent treatment of the province of East Timor, which had voted for independence.

However, since the conference report was cobbled together last month, Indonesia has undergone major changes. East Timor has been granted independence, and a new Indonesian government has been elected and warmly welcomed by Congress and the White House. In fact, Indonesia's new president, Abdurrahman Wahid, visited Washington Nov. 12.

In addition, business groups and pro-business lawmakers such as Sen. Chuck Hagel, R-Neb., a Foreign Relations Committee member, have pressed to see the restrictions dropped, calling them an affront to a major trading partner.

Sen. Patrick J. Leahy, D-Vt., who inserted the provisions in the original spending bill, was willing to lift the economic sanctions, such as a provision calling for the United States to use its clout to prevent multilateral organizations such as the IMF from lending to Indonesia.

But Democratic aides said that Leahy, ranking Democrat on the Foreign Operations Appropriations Subcommittee, still wants restrictions on military aid or other contacts with the Indonesia military, such as human rights and non-operational training.

"The Indonesian military has not reformed itself in three weeks," an aide said.

Still those who favor a tougher approach to Indonesia are always looking for other vehicles. Sen. Russell D. Feingold, D-Wis., is planning to offer an amendment to a bankruptcy reform bill pending in the Senate (S 625) that would reimpose most of the restrictions on Indonesia.

The revised foreign aid bill addresses other administration concerns as well. It would specify $241 million for a State Department program that finds civilian work for former Soviet weapons scientists.

And the bill would dedicate $13 million out of a total of $123 million in bilateral debt relief for a program that calls on countries to use the funds to rescue tropical rain forests.

Compromise Bill Is a Success for Clinton Team

DECEMBER 4 — After months of bruising battles with Republican lawmakers over foreign policy, the Clinton administration's national security team finished the legislative year on a high note, winning congressional support to repay U.S. debts to the United Nations, provide debt relief to the world's poorest countries, and beef up security at U.S. embassies and consulates around the world.

The victories in the final days of budget negotiations between Capitol Hill and the White House were not cost free. President Clinton, who had stood fast against abortion restrictions on international family planning aid since he took office, accepted some limits this year.

Nonetheless, after the Senate's rejection last month of the Comprehensive Test Ban Treaty, Clinton and his foreign policy team were clearly elated by the new turn of events, which included a foreign aid bill with $2.6 billion more than a version Clinton vetoed last month and a broad trade agreement with China announced Nov. 15.

"This is a very good day for foreign policy," Clinton said Nov. 15 after an agreement on the World Trade Organization was announced and a breakthrough had been reached in negotiations about U.N. dues.

The fiscal 2000 omnibus budget package (HR 3194) included three key foreign policy initiatives:

- A State Department authorization bill (HR 3427) with $4.5 billion over five years to improve security at U.S. embassies and consulates, more than Clinton requested or either chamber initially passed.
- A Commerce-Justice-State spending bill (HR 3421) that would repay $926 million in U.S. debts to the United Nations over three years, potentially ending a long controversy with the international organization and with Congress.
- The foreign operations spending bill (HR 3422), which includes portions of the U.S. contribution to a global plan to forgive the debt of some of the world's poorest countries, including approval of the sale of some International Monetary Fund (IMF) gold reserves.

Ceding Ground

Critical to untangling the Gordian knot on foreign aid this year was a compromise on overseas family planning aid and abortion.

The issue has bedeviled lawmakers and the White House since 1997, when Rep. Christopher H. Smith, R-N.J., a leader of anti-abortion forces, persuaded GOP House leaders to bind the repayment of U.S. debts to the United Nations to the restoration of some anti-abortion restrictions on family planning aid. Presidents Ronald Reagan and George Bush had imposed such restrictions by executive order, but Clinton lifted them in 1993 as one of his first acts in office.

Clinton vetoed a bill last year that would have repaid the U.N. dues, because the bill also contained the anti-abortion restrictions. And in vetoing the Commerce-Justice-State appropriations bill (HR 2670) in October, Clinton cited the "unacceptable linkage" between the two issues as one of the main reasons. *(CJS veto text, p. D-28; 1998 CQ Almanac, p. 16-3)*

However, Clinton also was eager to curtail anti-American sentiment at the United Nations because of the debts, and last month he told House Speaker J. Dennis Hastert, R-Ill., that he would like to reach a compromise with congressional Republicans.

Lawmakers said Clinton changed his mind largely because he was running up against two deadlines:

- U.N. rules would have forced the United States to give up its seat in the U.N. General Assembly if Congress did not pay at least $111 million of the money it owes the world body.
- This is the last year, under the 1997 balanced-budget law (PL 105-33), that such spending could be written off as "emergency spending" without offsetting budget cuts. *(1997 Almanac, p. 2-18)*

Lawmakers also said Clinton had more leeway to negotiate on abortion than last year, when his impending impeachment trial in the Senate made him loath to anger women's groups.

After weeks of "exploring concepts," Hastert and White House negotiators reached a deal the weekend of Nov. 13-14.

The compromise provision, which will expire at the end of fiscal 2000, would bar any of the $385 million in U.S. international family planning assistance for organizations that perform abortions — except in cases of rape, incest or where the life of the woman is in danger — or lobby to change abortion laws or government policies in other countries.

Clinton could waive this restriction, but that would trigger a shift of $12.5 million in family planning aid to an account for child survival and disease prevention.

Both advocates and opponents of the new restrictions acknowledge that they will have little practical effect.

A 1997 Congressional Research Service report noted that although it is difficult to determine precisely who might be affected by the restrictions, the one group clearly involved, the International Planned Parenthood Federation, received less than $15 million a year.

Secretary of State Madeleine K. Albright emphasized this element, saying the compromise would "have minimal effect" on international family planning aid.

"It will not go into permanent law," Albright told reporters Nov. 15. "And it will allow the president to carry out U.S. family planning [policy] around the world."

But both abortion rights supporters and their opponents said that writing the proposal into statute, rather than executive order, would set an important precedent.

And they said that even though the proposal was for 10 months, such "temporary" prohibitions can have a long life.

"Once this kind of legislative language is adopted, it is very hard, if not impossible, to remove," Democratic Rep. Lynn Woolsey of California, an abortion rights supporter, told reporters Nov. 16.

In a Nov. 16 interview, Smith agreed, citing as inspiration the "Hyde Amendment," which is annually attached to appropriations bills to prohibit federal funding of abortions except in cases of rape, incest or to save the woman's life. The amendment, originally sponsored by House Judiciary Committee Chairman Henry J. Hyde, R-Ill., has never become permanent law. It first passed Congress in 1976 — three years after the Supreme Court decided *Roe v. Wade*, the landmark case that established a woman's right to choose an abortion.

Rather than blame Clinton, however, Democratic women trained their fire on congressional Republicans and served notice that they intend to use the agreement against GOP candidates in the 2000 congressional and presidential elections.

Rep. Nancy Pelosi of California, ranking Democrat on the Foreign Operations Appropriations Subcommittee, said the "insistence by the Republican Party" on the issue is "a demonstration of the extremism in this issue that has captured this party. The American people should remember that when they vote."

Unease at the U.N.

Nor will the compromise be entirely popular with U.N. members in New York. The legislation would repay $819 million in U.S. debts to the United Nations over three years and forgive $107 million the world body owes the United States. But the measure would require that the United Nations first agree to a number of changes in the way it operates.

"There's going to be weeping and gnashing of teeth" from other U.N. members, said Joseph R. Biden Jr. of Delaware, ranking Democrat on the Senate Foreign Relations Committee.

But at a Nov. 18 press conference, Biden and panel Chairman Jesse Helms, R-N.C., expressed confidence that the conditions would ultimately be accepted.

"This legislation takes away all the United Nations' excuses," Helms said. "We have heard, time and time again, the complaint that the United Nations is in financial crisis because Congress has refused to pay the U.S. arrears. Well today, Congress is ready to write a check. The only thing that could possibly prevent the United Nations from cashing it is an unwise refusal to enact common sense reforms."

The most important of these conditions, first written by Helms and Biden in 1997, would be cutting the U.S. share of the regular U.N. budget from 25 percent today to 20 percent in three years. The United Nations also would have to accept a unilateral decision that Congress made in 1994 (PL 103-236) to cut the U.S. share of the U.N.'s peacekeeping budget from 31 percent to 25 percent. *(1994 Almanac, p. 454)*

Helms tried to deflect criticism from fellow GOP conservatives about the debt repayment by noting that the measure would save U.S. taxpayers money over time.

"If the Helms-Biden reforms were already in place, they would have saved the American taxpayers between $180 million and $230 million this year alone," Helms said. "At that rate of savings, in less than five years, the U.S. will get back every penny we pay the U.N. in this legislation."

Biden also tried to please elements of his party dissatisfied with Clinton's concessions on international family planning aid. He called the deal worked out between Clinton and Hastert a "reasonable compromise" and said, "I think the president made the right decision."

Easing Debts

Biden said the agreement also provided a sizable amount of debt relief for the world's poorest countries. The possible cut in family planning aid "pales in comparison to forgiving international debt," Biden said.

A final agreement on that issue, a Clinton priority, was worked out at a Nov. 15 meeting between Treasury Secretary Lawrence H. Summers and two Texas Republicans: House Majority Leader Dick Armey and Senate Banking Committee Chairman Phil Gramm.

Summers had been pushing for congressional support for key portions of a debt relief plan drawn up by Clinton and the leaders of other wealthy nations at a summit in Cologne, Germany, in June. That plan would forgive $27 billion in foreign debt owed by poor countries.

Under the plan, wealthy nations are supposed to forgive bilateral debt owed by the poor countries and to contribute to a pool that will help write off some of the money that the poor countries owe to multilateral agencies such as the IMF and the World Bank. At the same time, those agencies are supposed to use their own resources to write off a portion of their debt.

Lawmakers already had agreed to meet the administration's request to forgive nearly all the bilateral debt owed to the United States by these poor countries — providing $123 million in the foreign operations bill. The administration and congressional Democrats, meanwhile, agreed to put off discussions on an additional $1 billion in multilateral debt relief over four years that Clinton requested. Lawmakers will consider that request again next year.

But the two sides had squared off over a somewhat esoteric policy change in how the IMF accounts for stocks of gold it holds in reserve as a contingency against defaults on its loans.

In order to finance its portion of the debt relief package, IMF officials had hoped to use a complex series of transactions to profit from the difference of value between the below-market prices the gold was valued at on the IMF's books — about $47 an ounce — and the current market price of close to $300 an ounce.

Armey, an IMF critic, had argued that those profits should flow to IMF members, such as the United States, which had deposited the gold and that the IMF should find other sources to finance its portion of the debt relief package.

As part of a broad agreement between Hastert and Clinton, Armey largely conceded to the administration.

Under the plan, the United States, which exercises what amounts to a veto at the IMF, would support freeing up about $3.1 billion for debt relief by revaluing 12.5 million ounces of the more than 100 million ounces of gold the IMF holds. Almost two-thirds of the funds would become available immediately for debt relief, while Congress would have to vote by May 1, 2000, to reauthorize the remainder.

In addition, the agreement would authorize the IMF to tap a special account created in 1991, but never used, in case countries defaulted on their loans.

In return, Armey received a number of commitments, which he said would further open up the often secretive IMF to international scrutiny. Most importantly, he said, the compromise would require the IMF to publish its budget for the first time.

Dodging Bullets

Agreement on debt relief, the United Nations debts and family planning allowed House and Senate negotiators to reach a compromise on the State Department authorization measure, which had been stuck for three years on such issues, and include it by reference in the omnibus budget bill.

Negotiators avoided final and possibly fatal battles by removing a few controversial proposals that were in either the House or Senate State Department bills.

For example, the compromise omits language that would have forced the administration to move the U.S. embassy in Israel from Tel Aviv to Jerusalem, in that way recognizing Jerusalem as the Mideast nation's capital. With Jerusalem's ultimate status a subject of current talks between Israel and the Palestinians aimed at a final peace settlement, the administration had threatened to veto the measure

Foreign Operations Spending

Where the Money Goes

HR 3422 (incorporated by reference in HR 3194 — Conference report: H Rept 106-479)

Spending Synopsis

As part of its overall budget agreement with the administration, Congress added $2.6 billion to the fiscal 2000 foreign aid bill vetoed by President Clinton on Oct. 18 (HR 2606 — Conference report: H Rept 106-339). The new measure provides $15.3 billion for foreign operations, the same amount as a compromise bill (HR 3196) the House passed Nov. 5. The largest addition was the $1.8 billion Clinton requested in the spring to help Israel, Jordan and the Palestinian Authority implement the Wye River peace accords. If the Wye River spending is excluded, the final foreign aid bill provides $1.4 billion less than Clinton requested but a net gain of $500 million for the White House during the final budget negotiations.

Hot-Button Issues

Δ **Abortion.** The main stumbling block for the bill was a demand by social conservatives in the House for further abortion-related restrictions on aid to international family planning groups, which already are barred from using government money to perform abortions. This year's final provision prohibits aid to groups that lobby for more lenient abortion laws overseas, even if they use their own funds for the purpose. The president can waive the restrictions, but funding then would be cut by 3 percent. The provision, which will be in effect for 10 months, is much the same language that caused Clinton to veto a State Department authorization bill in 1998. *(1998 Almanac, p. 16-3)*

Δ **Middle East peace.** Congress gave in to a key Clinton demand — $1.8 billion to help Israel, Jordan and the Palestinian Authority implement the 1998 Wye River peace accords. Republicans had wanted to include the money in a supplemental spending bill in 2000. The funds are designated "emergency" spending not subject to budget limits or offsets. The final bill quietly dropped language requiring the United States to move its embassy in Israel from Tel Aviv to Jerusalem, which would have been a tacit recognition of that city as the Israeli capital. The city's final status is still an issue in peace talks.

Δ **Russian aid.** Members came up with an additional $104 million for the republics of the former Soviet Union, for a total of $839 million, which still was $193 million less than Clinton wanted. However, Congress set aside $241 million for one Clinton priority it had ignored: a program to find work for Russian nuclear scientists to help stop any "brain drain" to unfriendly countries.

Δ **Debt relief.** Addressing another Clinton priority, negotiators included $123 million to help some of the world's poorest nations restructure debts they owe the United States, basically the amount Clinton requested. More important, Congress agreed to support an International Monetary Fund (IMF) plan to revalue some of its gold reserves, raising about $3.1 billion to help finance debt forgiveness of the most heavily indebted nations.

Δ **School of the Americas.** Conferees on the foreign operations bill Clinton vetoed Oct. 18 had restored $2 million that the House voted to cut from the Army's School of the Americas, at Fort Benning, Ga., and the money was included in the final agreement. Critics say the school has trained Latin American officers who later committed human rights abuses. Most of the school's budget comes from defense appropriations.

Δ **Silk road.** Legislation aimed at developing closer economic ties to former Soviet republics in central Asia and the Caucasus was added to the foreign operations bill, but not before the Senate defeated an attempt to give the president authority to waive a ban on direct aid to Azerbaijan, which is denied assistance because of its blockade of the disputed Armenian enclave of Nagorno-Karabakh. Azerbaijan, which is on the Caspian Sea, has vast oil reserves.

(figures are in thousands of dollars of new budget authority)

	Fiscal 1999 Appropriation	Fiscal 2000 Clinton Request	House Bill	Senate Bill	Conference Report
Export and investment assistance	$659,000	$685,000	$595,500	$620,500	$599,000
Bilateral economic assistance	9,664,629	8,591,037	7,418,397	7,469,337	8,470,917
Military assistance	3,507,500	3,956,000	3,585,500	3,534,000	4,992,000
Multilateral economic assistance	1,638,264	1,687,498	1,068,718	1,111,818	1,298,018
International Monetary Fund *	17,861,000	0	0	0	0
GRAND TOTAL	**$33,330,393**	**$14,919,535**	**$12,668,115**	**$12,735,655**	**$15,359,935**

* Special appropriation for loans and U.S. quota payment to IMF.

TABLE: House and Senate Appropriations committees

over the proposal.

The deal also stripped out a controversial provision inserted in the House version of the State Department bill by International Relations Committee Chairman Benjamin A. Gilman, R-N.Y. The provision would have held up assistance to North Korea until Congress enacted a joint resolution stating that the regime in Pyongyang has complied with international nonproliferation accords.

The proposal could well have stymied U.S. assistance to the Korean Peninsula Energy Development Organization, an international consortium created in 1994 to provide North Korea's energy needs while curbing its nuclear weapons programs. The Clinton administration has been working to improve relations with North Korea but has met fierce resistance from House Republicans.

Lawmakers also resolved a number of disputes between the House and Senate. For example:

- The agreement would take the Senate's lead and authorize State Department and related agencies' activities for fiscal years 2000 and 2001, as opposed to the House's recommendation of a one-year authorization. It would authorize $6 billion in fiscal 2000 and "such sums as may be necessary" for fiscal 2001; the second year's spending is expected to increase by 15 percent over the first year.
- The measure would authorize $4.5 billion over five years to improve security at U.S. embassies in the wake of bombings and attacks in Kenya and Tanzania last year. This represents a significant boost from the $3 billion the Senate bill would have authorized or the $1.4 billion in the original House bill. *(1998 Almanac, p. 2-117)*
- Negotiators put off until next year an effort to provide as much as $1.6 billion in aid to Colombia and neighboring nations in South America over the next three years. The funds, which are supported by Clinton and Republican congressional leaders, would be used to help that country counter narcotics traffickers who are often protected by a growing guerrilla insurgency.

Spoils of War

Negotiators also put off until next year a decision on what to do with billions of dollars in Iraqi assets that have been frozen in U.S. banks since the Persian Gulf War in 1991.

The House bill had included a provision, inserted by Rep. Lloyd Doggett, D-Texas, that would have given U.S. Gulf War veterans first claim on the frozen assets.

But Helms objected to the House provision. He said it would disadvantage U.S. companies, including tobacco companies, which are owed money by Iraq. Helms said it also would prevent U.S. government agencies, particularly the Commodity Credit Corporation, from recovering billions of dollars in loans they had extended to Iraq. Some observers also have questioned the precedent that could be set by giving veterans a type of "war booty."

As a possible compromise, Helms proposed giving the veterans legal standing in any settlement, which would give them an opportunity, but no guarantee, of gaining a share of the assets. But with time running out on the legislative calendar, discussion of the proposal was postponed until next year. ◆

President Wins on Lands Initiative, Elimination of Most Riders in Interior Bill

SUMMARY

After weeks of threats, cloistered negotiation and frantic compromise, Congress included a $14.9 billion fiscal 2000 Interior appropriations bill in the year-end omnibus spending package (HR 3194).

The final product marked a clear victory for the Clinton administration, which was able to add money for its high-priority Lands Legacy initiative, and delete or substantially neutralize a series of policy riders. The final bill was nearly $1 billion larger than the one initially passed by the House.

For a bill that traditionally has a bumpy ride, the fiscal 2000 Interior appropriations endured an especially rough journey. Most of the difficulty came in the Senate and then spilled into conference. The House and Senate cleared a conference report on the bill, but never sent it to the White House. Instead, they added a revised version of the bill (HR 3423) to the omnibus package.

The House initially passed a $13.9 billion version of the bill (HR 2466) in July, after two days of debate that had little of the volume or passion of recent years. But things ground to a crawl when the Senate took up the measure.

Among the contentious items in the Senate version (S 1292) were riders on mining waste, grazing permits and oil drilling on public lands. Some of the provisions, including a proposed moratorium on an Interior Department royalty formula for oil extracted from public lands, were dropped after Senate Republicans reinstated a longstanding rule barring policy riders on appropriations bills.

When Kay Bailey Hutchison, R-Texas, offered a revised version of the oil royalty moratorium on the floor, Barbara Boxer, D-Calif., launched a filibuster that slowed work on the bill for days. The Senate finally voted to include Hutchison's amendment, but the administration strongly opposed it, saying that failure to use the new formula had allowed companies to underpay the government by at least $68 million annually. In the end, negotiations with the White House produced an agreement to lift the moratorium on March 15.

Another issue that attracted attention from environmentalists concerned mining waste. The House voted overwhelmingly to include language in its version of the bill supporting an Interior Department legal ruling that required mining operations to limit waste sites on public lands to five acres. The Senate took the opposite stance, approving language that would nullify the ruling.

In conference, negotiators agreed to apply the five-acre limit to mining applications submitted after May 21, 1999. That language was ultimately dropped, however, making the ruling effective from the day it was issued in November 1997.

One of the biggest differences — in both money and policy — was funding for Clinton's Lands Legacy initiative, aimed at acquiring environmentally and culturally significant land threatened by development. Clinton made this a major priority in his fiscal 2000 budget request. The first conference report provided only $266 million. The final agreement, however, pushed the total to $470 million.

In all, the $14.9 billion bill was $873 million more than the Senate-passed measure and $994 million more than the House version, but $338 million less than the administration requested.

About half the funds were for the Interior Department, which received a total of $7.4 billion. Of that, $1.8 billion went to the National Park Service, $46 million more than the fiscal 1999 level but $249 million less than the administration requested. The department's main agency for managing federal lands, the Bureau of Land Management, got $1.2 billion, $52 million above last year but $33 million less than that requested.

Box Score 

Interior

- **Bill:** HR 3423 (incorporated by reference in HR 3194) — PL 106-113
- **Legislative action: House** passed HR 2466 (H Rept 106-222), 377-47, on July 15.

Senate passed HR 2466, amended to reflect S 1292 (S Rept 106-99), 89-10, on Sept. 23.

House adopted the conference report (H Rept 106-406), 225-200, on Oct. 21.

Senate cleared the bill by voice vote Oct. 21.

House adopted conference report on HR 3194 (H Rept 106-479), 296-135, on Nov. 18.

Senate cleared the bill, 74-24, Nov. 19.

President signed HR 3194 on Nov. 29.

Senate Committee Bill Easily Adheres To Budget Limits

JUNE 26 — With little fanfare, the Senate Appropriations Committee approved by voice vote June 24 the fiscal 2000 spending bill for the Interior Department, blocking an effort to implement air pollution rules for government agencies.

The $13.9 billion bill is $1.2 billion below President Clinton's request and $80 million less than fiscal 1999.

The committee approved by voice vote an amendment by Thad Cochran, R-Miss., that would prohibit funds from being used for what Cochran complained was a "device to implement the Kyoto Protocol."

That environmental treaty, which the Senate has not ratified, calls for cutting vehicle emission levels to reduce air pollution. And on June 3, Clinton issued an executive order to reduce government dependence on electric and coal-produced energy by utilizing renewable energy such as natural gas and solar power. *(1998 Almanac, p. 2-101)*

Nevertheless, the full committee's relatively trouble-free walk was foreshadowed June 22 by a subcommittee markup that was equally pedestrian.

During the markup, Chairman Slade Gorton, R-Wash., noted that money was tight, that the spending plan used all of the subcommittee's allocation, "and all amendments must be offset."

That left little room for mischief. For the largest and most visible programs, the committee came close to meeting the administration's request to maintain fiscal 1999 funding levels.

The National Park Service, for example, would receive $1.7 billon in fiscal 2000, about $337 million less than the president requested but comparable to fiscal 1999. The Bureau of Land Management would receive $1.22 billion (compared with a request of $1.27 billion).

The bill would provide a $40 million increase for the Indian trust fund that compensates American Indians for the use of their land. The fund is designed to collect royalties from the sale of oil and gas, minerals, timber and other resources and distribute the proceeds to the owners. The additional money is earmarked to address ongoing problems involving the fund.

According to the Interior Department and independent audits, $2.4 billion in transactions over two decades is unaccounted for and cannot be reconciled because records are poor or have been lost. The additional money for fiscal 2000 is intended to resolve some of these problems.

More Spending

The Senate plan would increase spending for the National Endowment for the Arts and the National Endowment for the Humanities by $1 million each, up from the $98 million and $110.7 million respectively that passed Congress last year for fiscal 1999.

The bill would also provide $19 million to the Smithsonian Institution to pay the federal government's portion of construction costs for the National Museum of the American Indian.

One notable area of decrease was in land acquisition, one of the administration's top initiatives.

The committee approved $237 million for the Land and Water Conservation Fund, $92 million less than the fiscal 1999 level and $175 million less than the administration's request.

"While the bill provides substantial funding for federal land acquisition and other programs that were part of the president's 'Lands Legacy' initiative, it does so at a more modest level and without providing funding for programs that are not authorized," Gorton said.

Unless the land acquisition gap is closed, it could become a problem. Both Clinton and Vice President Al Gore have mentioned the Lands Legacy program as a budgetary focal point for 2000. The money would be used to expand national parks, build urban parks and protect farmland and other land threatened by development.

Meanwhile, Gorton suggested that this year's Interior bill could break from tradition by carrying fewer controversial policy "riders" that have been flash points in the past.

Still, additional requests are likely. Gorton said he received more than 2,400 funding requests from members as the bill was being assembled.

The relative calm, however, is due to the fact that historically, many of the controversial items are added during floor debate. Another reason is that, unlike most years, the House has yet to consider its own bill.

An aide to Rep. Ralph Regula, R-Ohio, chairman of the Interior Appropriations Subcommittee, said June 22 that no progress is expected on the bill before the July Fourth recess.

The reason is money. Unlike the Senate, the allocation for Regula's committee was nearly $3 billion below fiscal 1999 spending. That has left lawmakers with a list of programs that deal with everything from mining to grazing to national parks, with far too little money to pay for them.

House Panel OKs Interior Bill

JULY 3 — Liberated by an infusion of $2.7 billion, the House Appropriations Committee on July 1 easily approved a fiscal 2000 spending plan for the Interior Department and related agencies.

Despite the windfall, the $14.1 billion bill (HR 2466) sparked complaints that it was bound by unreasonable budget caps that starve worthy programs. Those complaints will likely be vigorously voiced when the bill comes to the floor the week of July 12.

Foremost among the shortages is money to buy ecologically important land threatened by development. The Clinton administration asked for $900 million for high-priority purchases as part of its Lands Legacy initiative. The administration said the money would be used to buy property around national parks, protect farms and other open areas threatened by urban sprawl, and provide grants to states for conservation. The largest portion of that request was $579 million for the Land and Water Conservation Fund.

The committee, however, approved $205 million for the fund, which was below the fiscal 1999 amount of $329 million.

Norm Dicks of Washington, the Interior Subcommittee's ranking Democrat, said he hopes more money will be found for land acquisition as well as for the National Endowment for the Arts and the National Endowment for the Humanities. The House bill would maintain funding for the arts foundation at $98 million and for the humanities foundation at $110.7 million. The administration asked for $150 million for each.

Given the budget caps, however, all sides agreed that it will be difficult to find more money.

"People think this committee can perform miraculous acts," said the full committee's ranking Democrat, David R. Obey of Wisconsin.

Even so, the bill that came out of committee was considerably more generous than the $11.3 billion originally allocated. The additional $2.7 billion will come from the sale of electromagnetic spectrum, according to Appropriations Committee spokeswoman Elizabeth Morra. *(1997 Almanac, p. 3-34)*

Unlike the Senate bill (S 1292 — S Rept 106-99), the House version steers clear of such controversial topics as oil royalties and mining rights. The Senate bill would delay the imposition of a new royalty formula that the oil industry opposes.

It also would override a controversial interpretation by the Interior Department that could limit mining on federal lands.

The Funding Breakdown

All told, the House bill provides $193 million less than the fiscal 1999 level and $1.2 billion less than the administration's request.

It would supply $1.2 billion in funding for the Bureau of Land Management, slightly less than the administration's request of $1.27 billion; $327 million for National Wildlife Refuges, a $33 million increase from $294 million; $2.6 billion for the Forest Service, $154 million less than enacted in fiscal 1999 and $309 million less than the administration requested; and $7.1 billion for the Interior Department, a level comparable with this year's spending but $661 million less than outlined in the president's budget request.

The bill also provides a $217 million increase for American Indian programs, including health and education.

In presenting the bill, Ralph Regula, R-Ohio, chairman of the Interior Subcommittee, praised it as a bipartisan effort with an emphasis on maintaining national parks and other natural areas, and addressing pressing needs of American Indians.

The bill would provide $1.4 billion for national parks, $2.3 million less than the administration's request. As was the case last year, Regula said much of the increase should be used to whittle down the estimated $15 billion in backlogged park maintenance costs.

The bill also would provide $114 million for restoring the Everglades. But in a policy shift, $42.4 million for acquiring land around the Everglades would be withheld until there is a signed "binding agreement" guaranteeing water supply to the Everglades. "Without a guaranteed water supply, there is no true restoration," Regula said June 29.

House Passes Clean Bill; Senate Battles Ahead

JULY 17 — The House's relatively easy passage July 15 of its fiscal 2000 Interior appropriations bill is not likely to be repeated by the Senate.

While the House bill (HR 2466) was virtually stripped clean of controversial policy riders, the Senate bill (S 1292) is studded with controversial provisions dealing with mining on federal lands, oil royalties and logging in national forests.

The Senate version, which is expected to reach the floor the week of July 19, faces heavy criticism from environmental interests and a veto threat from the White House.

The $13.9 billion House bill was not without critics, but the complaints focused more on money than on policy. Passage of HR 2466 came during a midnight vote of 377-47 after two full days of debate that had little of the volume or passion of recent years. *(Vote 296, p. H-100)*

As it came to the floor, HR 2466 provided $363 million less than the fiscal 1999 level and $1.3 billion less than the administration's request.

Fulfilling a promise to fiscal conservatives who said the bill was too expensive, a manager's amendment to reduce total funding by $138 million was approved by voice vote. The savings were achieved by cutting the amount of money for land acquisition by $5 million, deferring $66 million in funding for clean coal research and imposing a 0.48 percent across-the-board cut on all discretionary programs.

Before the final vote was taken, $32 million was sliced from the bill, intensifying complaints that the bill failed to sufficiently fund a number of high-priority programs.

But while the amendment was necessary to ensure passage, even its sponsor, Appropriations Chairman C.W. Bill Young, R-Fla., ushered it through with little enthusiasm.

"In a year of very tight budget restraints . . . there are things that we might have to do that we do not like to do in order to get where we have to be," Young declared. "This amendment is part of that process."

David R. Obey, D-Wis., the committee's ranking member, chided Young for yielding to the "hard-core right wing members" who are "largely term-limited, who detest government and who want to have one last swing before they walk out the door."

In criticizing the cut, Obey was echoing the administration and other Democrats who complained that the bill fell short in funding such priority programs as land acquisition, energy conservation and protecting endangered species.

Environmental Amendments

Still, Democrats and environmental interests won some surprising gains. Foremost was an amendment offered by Nick J. Rahall II, D-W.Va., to limit hardrock mining companies to a single, five-acre site for dumping mine waste when using public land.

The amendment, which was adopted 273-151, would uphold a 1997 legal opinion by the Interior Department that has been bitterly condemned by Western lawmakers and mining interests. *(Vote 288, p. H-98)*

In approving the amendment, the House put itself directly at odds with the Senate, which is moving to nullify the ruling.

Two other amendments that were adopted with endorsements from environmental interests would add $30 million for state grants though the Land and Water Conservation Fund. That account, which had been zeroed out in committee, was replenished when the amendment was adopted, 213-202. *(Vote 281, p. H-96)*

The other amendment would increase funding to the low-income weatherization programs by $13 million, bringing the total for fiscal 2000 to the $133 million that was appropriated for this year.

The sharpest debate came on amendments concerning the Forest Service. An amendment by George Miller, D-Calif., to prohibit the use of funds to construct new timber access roads in national forests was approved by voice vote.

And the House rejected a GOP-backed amendment that would have cut $16.9 million from Forest Service research programs. The amendment failed, 135-291. *(Vote 292, p. H-98)*

For the second year in a row, funding for the National Endowment for the Arts was protected at the $98 million level recommended by the Appropriations Committee.

As passed, the bill would supply $1.2 billion in funding for the Bureau of Land Management, slightly less than the administration's request of $1.27 billion; $2.6 billion for the Forest Service, $154 million less than enacted in fiscal 1999 and $309 million less than the administration requested; and $7.1 billion for the Interior Department, a level comparable with this year's spending but $617 million less than the president's budget request.

Senate Drops Policy Riders, Prepares To Resume Debate

JULY 31 — After a halting start, the Senate is likely to resume consideration the week of Aug. 2 of the fiscal 2000 Interior spending plan, a $14.1 billion bill that historically has been a magnet for environmental policy riders that are now prohibited under Senate rules.

But with the Senate prepared to resume debate of HR 2466, the foremost question will be: What separates an illegal provision from one that can be included in the bill?

The answer will shape the bill that funds everything from national parks and museums to management of millions of acres of federal land. The bill is $1.2 billion less than President Clinton's request and $240 million less than the fiscal 1999 appropriation.

As it came to the floor July 27 for one day of debate, the bill was in clear violation of the new prohibition on riders, known as Rule XVI; the bill was stuffed with 13 provisions to which the White House objected.

Four of the riders were stripped from the bill when it was reconstituted to conform with the revised Senate rule, which forbids attaching policy provisions to appropriations bills.

Of the remaining provisions, the Senate dealt with only one before setting the bill aside for the week.

But that provision, a dispute over how much public land that mining companies can use to dump waste, was also one of the most controversial.

The fight involved a 1997 opinion by Interior Solicitor John Leshy that waste from mining operations is limited to a single, five-acre site and not to multiple five-acre tracts, as had been the practice. The change infuriated the mining industry, which argued that it could not operate with such a restriction. Larry E. Craig, R-Idaho, and Harry Reid, D-Nev., inserted language in the Senate bill that would permanently nullify Leshy's opinion.

Patty Murray, D-Wash., however, offered an amendment that would have upheld Leshy's ruling. Murray countered that the interpretation would protect public lands from being scarred and polluted by mining companies.

Craig said Leshy crafted a ruling that "he knew would bring the mining industry to its knees."

In the end, the Senate voted 55-41 on July 27 to table, or kill, Murray's amendment. *(Vote 223, p. S-44)*

As for the four items deleted from the bill, aides said that the problems were largely a question of language, and that if properly written the items could be included. The four items taken out were:

- A provision that would have prevented the federal government from reintroducing grizzly bears into Idaho and Montana without permission from the states' governors. Opponents said the provision would set a precedent requiring federal agencies to get state permission to implement federal law on federal land.
- A provision blocking Interior Secretary Bruce Babbitt from prohibiting lead mining in the Mark Twain National Forest in Missouri for the next two years.
- A provision by Thad Cochran, R-Miss., that would stop Interior from developing plans to increase energy efficiency in federal buildings. Critics said the language would derail programs that could save the federal government $1 billion a year in energy costs.
- A provision that would have delayed deployment of a new formula for determining royalties that oil companies pay for drilling on federal lands. The Interior Department said the new formula would bring in an estimated $68 million in additional revenue.

A New Trend?

Kay Bailey Hutchison, R-Texas, who has opposed the new royalty formula, has promised to revise the language to make it conform to Rule XVI. An aide said Hutchison would offer the new language as an amendment and is optimistic that it will pass.

If so, the royalty matter could usher in a trend in which items are changed and added back into a bill on the floor or in conference. *(1998 Almanac, p. 2-57)*

Rule XVI may help address anti-environmental riders, said Robert Dewey, director of habitat conservation for the environmental group Defenders of Wildlife. "But it's also troublesome," he said, "because it could provide perverse incentives for dealing with some of these issues in even stealthier fashion."

Before that point, however, there will be debate on riders relating to such issues as grazing on public lands and building logging roads in national forests.

Senate Bill Heavy With Environmental Amendments

AUGUST 7 — When the Senate returns from its August recess, waiting at the doorstep will be the fiscal 2000 Interior spending bill and a coordinated campaign by environmental groups to eliminate "extremely ugly" riders on topics ranging from forests to oil royalties to grazing.

Senate leaders had hoped to finish work on the $14.1 billion bill (HR 2466) before leaving but had only begun nibbling at the edges before time ran out.

The bill was called up to fill holes in the floor schedule during the last two weeks before the recess, so debate was sporadic, and only two noteworthy amendments were addressed.

On July 27, the Senate voted 55-41 to table, or kill, an amendment by Patty Murray, D-Wash., that would have written into law a 1997 opinion by Interior Solicitor John Leshy that waste from mining operations be limited to a single, five-acre site and not to multiple five-acre tracts, as had been the practice.

Then, on Aug. 5, the Senate easily brushed aside a perennial attempt by Robert C. Smith, I-N.H., to delete all funding for the National Endowment for the Arts (NEA). Smith's amendment was defeated as expected, 80-16. *(Vote 260, p. S-51)*

"I believe it is important we make a statement about this because I do not believe the federal government should be spending money on this," Smith said on Aug. 5.

Smith argued that it is unconstitutional to have the NEA funded by the federal government.

Left to be addressed are a host of amendments that environmental groups as well as the Clinton administration have condemned because they are trying to affect policy through appropriations bills.

"This is reminiscent of the last Congress," said Greg Wetstone, legislative director for the Natural Resources Defense Council, a Washington-based environmental group, bemoaning the use of legislative riders.

"Congress is moving away from the democratic process," said Wetstone, who called the environmental riders "extremely ugly."

The circumstances in the Senate contrast with the route taken in the House, which passed its fiscal 2000 Interior bill July 15 largely stripped of riders.

In the Senate, said Rep. Christopher Shays, R-Conn., "We're seeing riders that say, the law not withstanding, you cannot enforce the law."

To draw attention to legislative provisions that environmental groups charge would harm the environment and that were slipped in with little or no public comment, a coalition of groups including the Sierra Club, the Natural Resources Defense Council, Friends of the Earth and the National Audubon Society circulated a letter to all senators.

The July 27 letter highlighted 13 "pernicious riders" that "represent a sneak attack on our environmental protections."

Among the coalition's most worrisome provisions are:

- Language offered by Sen. Pete V. Domenici, R-N.M., that requires the Bureau of Land Management to renew expiring grazing permits under the same terms and conditions as the old permit. Environmental groups say the provision would undercut efforts to add environmental protections to grazing permits.
- Language that would limit funding for forest management plans not already being revised. A related provision would give "broad discretion" to the secretaries of Agriculture and Interior as to whether any new information relating to wildlife should be collected before revising management plans for national forests and Bureau of Land Management properties.
- A provision backed by Sen. Kay Bailey Hutchison, R-Texas, that would have delayed deployment of a new formula for determining royalties that oil companies pay for drilling on federal lands. The Interior Department said the new formula would bring in an estimated $68 million in additional revenue.

Hutchison's amendment was stripped from the bill for not conforming to a Senate rule outlawing policy riders on appropriation bills. But Hutchison has promised to rewrite the provision to make it comply with the rule and reintroduce it.

The $13.9 billion House bill was not without critics, but the complaints focused more on money than on policy. The Senate adopted HR 2466 as its vehicle and then substituted the Senate bill.

Aside from policy questions, the Senate will also face questions of money. The proposed spending limit, the administration said in a formal statement July 26, "is simply inadequate to make the necessary investments that our citizens need and expect."

Oil Filibuster Delays Senate's Work; Logging Limits Defeated

SEPTEMBER 11 — Refreshed by their August vacation, senators got an immediate and frustrating reminder of the snarl they left behind when debate resumed on the fiscal 2000 Interior appropriations bill.

As was the case before the break, work on the $14.1 billion measure (HR 2466) slowed to a crawl the week of Sept. 6. This time, the drag was caused by differences over a proposed change to the formula for calculating oil royalties, by fights over timber sales and by the perennial dispute over grazing on public lands.

The royalty question — which will determine how much companies pay for drilling on public land — was the most problematic. It prompted a filibuster from Barbara Boxer, D-Calif., and the prolonged debate dashed the hopes of Senate leaders to complete work on the bill by week's end. They now hope to finish the week of Sept. 13.

The fight revolved around an amendment by Kay Bailey Hutchison, R-Texas, that would prohibit for the fourth consecutive year the Interior Department from putting into effect a new formula for determining royalties that companies must pay for pumping oil from public land.

Hutchison argued from the floor Sept. 8 that the new formula is a "backdoor tax" that would hit oil producers at a time when they have been bloodied by low prices.

But Interior Secretary Bruce Babbitt has insisted that the new formula, which is based on market price, must be used to ensure that oil companies pay their fair share. According to Interior, oil companies shortchange the government $66 million each year by using the outdated formula.

In a debate that crackled with emotion, Boxer warned her colleagues: "If you vote for the Hutchison amendment, you are aligning yourselves with a planned effort to defraud taxpayers. . . . We have a chance to stand up for the consumer, for the taxpayers, against cheaters, against people who would knowingly defraud taxpayers."

Hutchison said the new formula is unfair because it does not allow for deductions for the cost of building pipelines to move oil from wellheads to market, which adds to the cost of refining and storing it.

But Boxer and her allies would not be swayed, launching an afternoon filibuster that carried weight because it blocked the way for more than 60 amendments that were awaiting action.

Ultimately, Boxer stepped aside to allow other amendments to be considered, but by then, the week was nearly over.

Moving on to other issues, however, did little to diminish the intensity of debate.

That was evident Sept. 9 when an amendment by Charles S. Robb, D-Va., to limit logging in national forests in Georgia and Washington state was defeated on a 45-52 vote. Robb's amendment would have deleted language in the bill designed to overturn federal district court decisions that have halted timber sales in the Southern Appalachian Forest in Georgia and in the Pacific Northwest. *(Vote 266, p. S-52)*

Federal judges in those two jurisdictions ruled this year that timber sales could not go forward until environmental assessments had been completed. The Senate Interior spending bill, however, would allow those sales to go forward before the studies are finished.

Environmental groups condemned the defeat of Robb's amendment.

"In a shameful move, the Senate voted to allow the Forest Service to ignore science and fire up the chainsaws," said Sean Cosgrove, a forest policy specialist for the Sierra Club.

Lead Mining Defended

In another vote criticized by environmental groups, the Senate approved an amendment to allow continued lead mining in a Missouri national forest. Offered by Christopher S. Bond, R-Mo., for Majority Leader Trent Lott, R-Miss., the amendment would require the Interior Department to conduct extensive reports before blocking lead mining in the Mark Twain National Forest.

Amendment opponent Richard J. Durbin, D-Ill., argued that the provision would benefit the lead mining industry at the expense of recreational uses of the forest.

The Senate on Sept. 9 approved Lott and Bond's language, 54-44, along party lines. *(Vote 265, p. S-52)*

In its last action Sept. 9, the Senate voted to table, or kill, an amendment by Durbin that could have delayed the renewal of grazing permits on federal lands until environmental reviews were completed by the Bureau of Land Management. The 58-37 vote protects language offered by Pete V. Domenici, R-N.M., that would prevent the bureau from delaying the permit renewals. *(Vote 269, p. S-52)*

Oil Royalty Debate Has Final Hold On Senate Bill

SEPTEMBER 18 — The Senate nudged the fiscal 2000 Interior appropriations forward the week of Sept. 13 by sidestepping one contentious question and by showering millions of dollars on parochial projects in Alaska and other states.

The approach left the Senate on the verge of finishing work on the $14.1 billion bill (HR 2466) that had lurched along for two weeks. Senate leaders hope to pass the bill during the week of Sept. 20. All that stands in the way is a thorny dispute concerning the royalties that companies must pay for drilling for oil and gas on public lands.

Despite being unable to break a filibuster on the royalty question, senators were able to clear away dozens of noncontroversial amendments on the bill to fund the Department of Interior, national parks and other land management agencies, a portion of the Forest Service as well as such recognizable fixtures as the Smithsonian Institution.

The amendments, which were approved en bloc by voice vote on Sept. 14, for the most part involved local projects such as improvements for Civil War battlefields and boundaries for national parks. The package also included an item inserted by Ted Stevens, R-Alaska, that would give his state an additional $11.6 million for previously approved timber sales in the Tongass National Forest.

Other amendments would add $4 million each to the National Endowment for the Humanities and the National Endowment for the Arts, budgeting a total of $115.7 million for the NEH and $103 million for the NEA.

The Senate also rejected an amendment, offered by Democrats Richard H. Bryan of Nevada and Ron Wyden of Oregon and Republican Peter G. Fitzgerald of Illinois, to cut $32 million from a $228.9 million annual subsidy program that the U.S. Forest Service offers to companies that clear timber in national forests.

The Senate tabled (killed) the amendment on a 54-43 vote. *(Vote 272, p. S-53)*

Environmentalists supported the measure because it would reduce subsidies that they contend are environmentally harmful and fiscally wasteful.

Larry E. Craig, R-Idaho, disputed those claims, saying that harvesting timber is important for the long-term health of forests and that logging companies could not afford to work in national forests without a subsidy.

Majority Leader Trent Lott, R-Miss., temporarily set aside the bill Sept. 14 after senators were unable to shut off a filibuster by Sen. Barbara Boxer, D-Calif. The 55-40 vote to invoke cloture on Sept. 13 came up five short of the 60 votes required. *(Vote 271, p. S-53)*

Boxer objects to language offered by Kay Bailey Hutchison, R-Texas, to prohibit the Interior Department from imposing a new royalty formula for companies that drill for oil on public lands. Interior officials estimate that the new formula would generate $68 million more in payments each year.

Hutchison maintains that the higher royalty is an illegal tax that would hit oil companies hard at a time of low prices.

Lott and other Senate leaders believe 60 votes for cloture are within reach because four Republicans and one Democrat were absent for the first vote. Lott could move early in the week of Sept. 20 to call for another vote, which would clear the way for a conference with the House.

Senate Passes Bill; Conferees Face Gaps Over Mining, Grazing, Drilling

SEPTEMBER 25 — The Senate's $14.1 billion spending bill for the Interior Department and Forest Service is headed for a conference with the House the week of Sept. 27, as broad policy questions over mining, grazing and oil drilling on public lands continue to weigh on appropriators.

Despite an 89-10 vote to pass the bill (HR 2466) on Sept. 23, the Senate has struggled since July to push the bill forward. Even if House and Senate conferees bridge their differences on the public lands disputes, advisers are expected to urge President Clinton to veto the bill unless the clutch of public lands provisions is deleted. *(Vote 291, p. S-57)*

The question for the Republican majority on each side of the conference is how much political capital they want to invest in the Interior bill as the fiscal deadline (Oct. 1) approaches for 12 still-unsigned appropriations bills.

Slade Gorton, R-Wash., chairman of the Senate Interior Appropriations Subcommittee, said the conferees should be able to work through their differences, but he declined to elaborate on the chances with the White House.

Meanwhile, conferees have few disagreements over money. The two versions are comparable in total dollars: The House-passed bill would provide $13.9 billion, $113 million less than the Senate and $1.3 billion less than the administration requested. The current-year appropriation is $14.3 billion.

The more difficult questions, however, revolve around a series of policy riders added by the Senate and opposed by the administration and environmentalists. On two issues — oil royalties and mining — the House and Senate enter the conference with starkly different philosophies.

The House bill does not address the oil royalty issue, which tied the Senate in knots for weeks. Barbara Boxer, D-Calif., launched a filibuster against an industry-supported amendment by Kay Bailey Hutchison, R-Texas, that would prevent the Interior Department from changing the formula it uses to calculate royalties.

Boxer's filibuster was finally squelched on Sept. 23, when the Senate voted 60-39 to invoke cloture. Five Western and oil-state Democrats joined 54 Republicans and independent Robert C. Smith of New Hampshire in support of cloture. And John McCain, R-Ariz., provided the necessary 60th vote after returning from a national speaking tour to promote his recently published memoirs. *(Vote 289, p. S-57)*

Hutchison's amendment was subsequently adopted on a much narrower, 51-47, vote. On that vote, seven Republican moderates — most from the East — switched and voted "no." Boxer said the slim margin should bolster conferees who want to slice the provision out during conference. *(Vote 290, p. S-57)*

If the prohibition stands, it will mark the fourth consecutive year that Congress has thwarted the Interior Department's attempt to update a formula that department officials say allows oil companies to underpay the Treasury by $66 million annually. The department's proposed revision would calculate a company's royalty fee based on the current market price of oil. Now the price is pegged to the oil's value at the wellhead as determined by the companies.

The Mining Dispute

A second House-Senate dispute centers on regulating mining on public lands.

The Senate wants to nullify a 1997 opinion by Interior Solicitor John D. Leshy, who ruled that waste from mining operations be limited to a single five-acre site, rather than multiple five-acre tracts as had been the practice. The change infuriated the mining industry, which argued that it cannot operate with such a restriction.

Larry E. Craig, R-Idaho, and Harry Reid, D-Nev., inserted language in the Senate bill that would permanently nullify Leshy's opinion.

The House, in a 273-151 vote on July 14, adopted the opposite position by backing the department's legal interpretation. Both House and Senate aides said their respective conferees will hold fast to their chamber's position.

Among other issues that must be reconciled in conference is a provision backed by Sen. Pete V. Domenici, R-N.M., that would require the Bureau of Land Management to renew expiring grazing permits under the same terms and conditions as the old permits. The House was silent on the grazing issue, but environmental groups say the provision would undercut efforts to add environmental protections to grazing permits.

The administration opposes the Domenici provision as well as one that would limit funding for forest management plans that have not already been initiated by the Agriculture Department's Forest Service.

Conferees Agree, But Clinton Objects To Riders, Freeze On Arts Spending

OCTOBER 16 — About the time conferees on the fiscal 2000 Interior spending bill were struggling to resolve the last remaining difficulty — funding for the arts — President Clinton sent an unambiguous signal that all their work on the $14.6 billion measure may be for naught.

"Let me be clear, if the Interior bill lands on my desk looking like it does now, I will give it a good environmental response — I will send it straight back to the recycling bin," Clinton said Oct. 13.

The conference report, expected to be filed the week of Oct. 18, looks slightly different than when Clinton made his remarks. But it has been changed in ways likely to anger the White House more and enhance prospects for a veto.

The bill would provide funding for the Department of Interior, a portion of the Forest Service and the nation's primary land management agencies.

But it contains at least three environmental provisions Clinton finds objectionable, and it would provide no additional funding for the National Endowment for the Arts (NEA).

Clinton's remarks and the outcome of the NEA debate signaled problems for Republicans, who had hoped the spending plan (HR 2466) would be acceptable.

It was distressing to conferees such as Sen. Ted Stevens, R-Alaska, who told colleagues that forging an Interior bill that Clinton would find acceptable would break the appropriations logjam and avoid an omnibus bill. And key to appeasing Clinton, Stevens said, was finding more money for the NEA.

The Interior agreement, reached Oct. 15, would freeze fiscal 2000 funding for the NEA at the 1999 level of $98 million. Clinton asked for $150 million. The conference did agree to boost spending for the National Endowment for the Humanities by $5 million (for a total of $115.7 million, less than the $150 million Clinton wanted).

The NEA decision, along with several environmental policy riders in the report, brought scorn from Democrats and environmentalists, as well as the White House.

David R. Obey of Wisconsin, ranking Democrat on the House Appropriations Committee, condemned the agreement, taking particular aim at a provision on oil royalties.

Those criticisms are certain to be fully voiced the week of Oct. 18, when the conference agreement is expected to be debated by the House and Senate.

The conference's outcome belied a promising start. In two days of work after convening Oct. 12, conferees resolved a host of issues ranging from a legal opinion governing mining waste to the renewal of grazing permits.

Conferees agreed to postpone for at least 180 days a new formula for determining the amount that oil companies must pay for oil and natural gas taken from public lands. The compromise called on the General Accounting Office to conduct a study of the new formula during that time.

The proposal has been opposed by the oil industry and its allies in Congress as an illegal tax. Congress has prevented the formula from going into effect for the past two years. Supporters, however, say the current formula allows oil companies to underpay royalties they owe the government. The administration calculated that underpayment is $68 million a year.

Grazing, Other Disputes

The conference resolved a dispute over the renewal of grazing leases by allowing expiring leases on federal lands to remain in place until the Bureau of Land Management completes required environmental assessments. Lease conditions can be rewritten after the studies are complete.

Conferees agreed to provide $22 million in aid over three years to help Alaskan communities hurt by mill closings and "economic dislocation." The money was added at the request of Stevens, the Senate Appropriations Committee chairman.

They also approved $68 million in emergency spending to underwrite a fund that provides health care to more than 60,000 retired mine workers. The request was made by Sen. Robert C. Byrd, D-W.Va.

Conferees also broke an impasse over terms connected with $10 million for land purchases around the Everglades National Park in Florida.

House conferees insisted that the state of Florida produce a signed contract guaranteeing sufficient water supply to the Everglades before the money is released. Senate members objected, arguing that the water needs of people might be affected. In the end, conferees agreed that any dispute would be heard and resolved by the appropriations committees.

Senate Clears Bill; President Promises To 'Recycle' It

OCTOBER 23 — A $14.5 billion fiscal 2000 spending bill for the Interior Department passed its last hurdle on Capitol Hill Oct. 21 — only to head to a near certain presidential veto over controversial environmental riders and funding levels for certain programs.

The Senate cleared the bill (HR 2466) by voice vote and with no debate, shortly after the House adopted the conference report by a vote of 225-200. The action brought an end to weeks of struggling over provisions on oil royalties, grazing, mining and support for the arts. *(Vote 528, p. H-172)*

But clearing the bill only sets the stage for a new round of bargaining to bend the measure more to the administration's liking. Still, provoking a veto fit in with Republicans' strategy of getting the last spending bills to the president's desk even if they have little chance of being signed into law.

House Appropriations Committee Chairman C.W. Bill Young, R-Fla., maintained on the floor Oct. 21 that the sole way to discern the administration's precise objections is through a veto message. "Our experience has been that the only way we find exactly what the president's opposition is, is in a veto message where he must be specific," Young said.

Even with that knowledge, however, retooling the Interior bill to please everyone will be a difficult task.

President Clinton had warned Oct. 13 that "If the Interior bill lands on my desk looking like it does now, I will give it a good environmental response — I will send it straight back to the recycling bin."

Republican-led House and Senate conferees responded by making modest changes to a number of the environmental riders — hardly enough to sway Democratic critics or the White House.

Indeed, David R. Obey of Wisconsin, ranking Democrat on the House Appropriations Committee, charged that the bill that came out of the House-Senate conference Oct. 15 was "in worse shape than it was when it left the House originally."

Obey and other Democrats also criticized House GOP conferees for ignoring a motion passed by the House Oct. 4 calling on them to add $5 million for the National Endowment for the Arts (NEA), and to reject a Senate provision dealing with mining waste.

One of the biggest issues — in terms of both money and policy — was funding for Clinton's so-called Lands Legacy initiative, aimed at acquiring environmentally and culturally significant land that is threatened by development.

Clinton made this a major priority in his fiscal 2000 budget request and asked for $1 billion in fiscal 2000, spread across a number of agencies, to carry it out.

The Interior bill was the engine for much of that funding. The administration, for example, asked that the Land and Water Conservation Fund, which is the primary account for land acquisition, be funded at $442 million. The conference agreement provided $246 million, which is $82 million less than the fiscal 1999 level.

That cut was one of many provisions that angered Democrats.

"This bill lacks vision," David E. Bonior, D-Mich., said during the House debate. "It cannot see the trees or the forests, and we should send it back to the dark ages."

Republicans countered that the bill was similar to the version that the House had passed in July by a lopsided vote of 377-47.

"I have heard five different reasons, none related, as to why this bill is bad all of a sudden, but no evidence," said John E. Peterson, R-Pa. "The agencies that are important to our environment have been thoughtfully funded."

Splitting the Difference

The $14.5 billion total is $478 million more than the Senate had passed and $600 million more than the House version, but $732 million less than the administration requested.

About half the funds are for the Interior Department, which would receive a total of $7.3 billion. Of that, $1.8 billion would go to the National Park Service, $45 million more than the fiscal 1999 level but $250 million less than the administration requested.

The department's main agency for managing federal lands, the Bureau of Land Management, would get $1.2 billion, a level that is $50 million more than in fiscal 1999 but $35 million less than that requested by the White House.

The bill would direct $2.8 billion to fund part of the Agriculture Department's Forest Service and $1.1 billion to the Energy Department for energy conservation programs and fossil fuels research.

The Bureau of Indian Affairs would receive $1.8 billion, a $70 million increase over fiscal 1999 but $85 million short of what the administration requested.

The bill would also extend for another year a moratorium on offshore drilling for oil and gas.

Despite the criticism, conferees worked to remove some of the bill's sharpest edges. The agreement softens — but does not eliminate — environmental riders that Clinton disliked.

House and Senate negotiators also added millions of dollars for local programs, such as $68 million to prop up a fund that pays for health care for 66,000 retired miners, a cause of Sen. Robert C. Byrd, D-W.Va.; $22 million to help distressed Alaska communities find alternatives to a timber-based economy to satisfy Senate Appropriations Chairman Ted Stevens, R-Alaska; and $40 million to purchase the Baca Ranch in New Mexico, a priority of the state's senators — Democrat Jeff Bingaman and Republican Pete V. Domenici — that was stripped from the original bill.

The conference agreement also added $30 million for the Millennium Program, a fund for historic preservation that was favored by many Democrats as well as first lady Hillary Rodham Clinton, and $2 million for urban parks and recreation that Republicans initially criticized as unnecessary.

And in a gift to coal-state lawmakers, the conference committee agreed to defer $156 million in funding for clean coal technology rather than $256 million as proposed by the House.

Points of Contention

The following are among the key issues that will have to be resolved before a final bill is enacted:

- **Mining waste.** One of the issues that has brought the greatest outcry from environmentalists concerns the amount of land that can be used by mining companies to dump waste from mines on public land.

The House voted overwhelmingly July 14 to include language in the appropriations bill supporting a Department of Interior legal opinion that limited such waste sites to five acres. The Senate took the opposite stance, approving language that would nullify the ruling.

Conferees agreed on language that would apply the five-acre limit only to mining applications that are submitted after May 21, 1999.

- **NEA.** Funding for the NEA, which in dollar terms was one of the smallest items, triggered the biggest debate in conference. House conferees rebuffed Senate efforts to add $5 million to the NEA budget, keeping fiscal 2000 funding for the endowment at the 1999 level of $98 million. Clinton asked for $150 million. The conference did agree to boost spending for the National Endowment for the Humanities by $5 million, for a total of $115.7 million, less than the $150 million Clinton wanted.

- **Oil royalties.** Also prompting objections from Democrats and the White House was language that would postpone for at least six months a new formula for calculating the payments oil companies must make for extracting oil and natural gas from public lands.

The compromise would call on the General Accounting Office (GAO) to conduct a study of the new formula during that time and for the Department of the Interior to "review thoroughly" any GAO recommendations.

The proposed formula has been opposed by the oil industry and its allies in Congress as an illegal tax, and Congress has prevented it from going into effect for the past two years. Supporters, however, say the current formula allows oil companies to underpay royalties they owe the government.

The administration calculated that the underpayment amounts to $68 million a year.

Democrats, as well as Clinton, denounced the delay. "This report continues to let the oil companies have a royalty holiday," said Rep. George Miller, D-Calif. "That should not be allowed to continue."

- **Grazing.** Another difference involves language that would renew expiring grazing leases on federal lands. The conference agreement would allow leases that expire in fiscal 2000 to be automatically renewed for 10 years while the Bureau of Land Management completes a required environmental assessment. Once the assessment is finished, the grazing lease could be modified to ensure environmental protection even if the lease has not expired.

Democrats charged that the language is tantamount to a huge hole in a fence that would allow ranchers to continue using practices that harm the environment. But Republicans insisted that without the full 10-year renewal, banks would not provide loans that ranchers need to stay solvent.

- **Global warming.** Another provision, pushed by the House, would prohibit the use of any funds for implementation of the Kyoto Treaty before it is ratified. The agreement, which is bitterly opposed in Congress, would require the United States to reduce the amount of greenhouse gas pollution in an effort to lessen global warming.

Congress, White House Near Deal On Interior Bill

NOVEMBER 13 — Reaping a reward from intense and at times infuriating talks, congressional and administration negotiators neared a tentative agreement Nov. 12 on the fiscal 2000 Interior spending bill.

Under the plan, the bill (HR 2466 — Conference report: H Rept 106-406) totaled an estimated $15 billion, an increase of $385 million over the original conference agreement. That agreement has been adopted by both chambers, but has never been sent to the White House.

The new plan also carried seven fewer environmental riders dealing with such issues as prohibiting grizzly bears from being reintroduced in Idaho and Montana and preventing the U.S.

Forest Service and the Bureau of Land Management from conducting wildlife surveys as part of management plans for public lands.

Those riders that remained, Republican aides said, "were substantially watered down" to satisfy administration objections. "They should be thrilled," one GOP aide said.

The measure would provide $7.35 billion for the Department of Interior, a $220 million increase over the fiscal 1999 level; $1.24 billion for the Bureau of Land Management, an increase of $52 million; and $1.81 billion for the National Park Service, an increase of $46 million for an agency sagging under the weight of $12 billion in unmet maintenance at national parks.

The bill also would direct $1.87 billion to the Bureau of Indian Affairs, an increase of $126 million over 1999 spending, and $2.8 billion for the Forest Service, which amounts to $74 million in increased funding.

Funding for such agencies as the U.S. Forest Service, the National Park Service and cultural institutions such as the Smithsonian Institution, is $949 million more than in fiscal 1999.

Much of the increase would be used to underwrite the administration's Lands Legacy program, a high priority in the president's fiscal 2000 budget that would go to purchase environmentally sensitive land threatened by development.

Roughly $210 million of the $385 million added during the latest negotiations would go to a variety of land acquisition programs sprinkled throughout the Interior bill.

But even as agreement was reached, aides acknowledged the shakiness of budget questions and the way new issues would spring to life, complicating efforts for approval.

That fear certainly rang true with the Interior bill, which had followed an arduous path involving a filibuster in the Senate over oil royalties, a bitter dispute in conference over funding for the National Endowment for the Arts and acrimonious debate in both the House and Senate over mining law.

Instability also seeped into the negotiating stage. Congressional Republicans and the White House said they reached agreement on a controversial matter dealing with grazing permits. Under the agreement, permits, which usually are valid for 10 years, would be automatically renewed for one year while federal environmental reviews of each lease are conducted.

That language, however, was not acceptable to Sen. Pete V. Domenici, R-N.M., who argued in conference that unless permits were renewed for the full 10 years, ranchers would have a hard time securing loans.

After hearing about the proposed one-year renewal, Domenici called President Clinton and persuaded him to agree to the longer term.

That change has angered environmentalists who complained that the language would allow ecological damage to continue.

Final Obstacles

The final barrier to agreement involved $30 million in additional funding requested by the administration and changing by one month the date on which a moratorium on a new formula on oil royalties would expire.

In the end, the administration relented on both counts, accepting the $385 million in additional money. Both sides compromised on the expiration date for the moratorium on the new royalty formula stayed at March 15, not March 1 as requested by the White House, according to GOP aides.

Despite the fights and eventual agreements on all sides, the fate of the Interior bill is unsettled. The reason has to do with two Interior-related issues — mining and revenue for offshore drilling — which were not part of the bill but which stand in the way of passage.

Appalachian Coal Mines

Sen. Robert C. Byrd, D-W.Va., vowed to stop legislation from moving until he could insert language overturning a court decision that declared that some coal mines in West Virginia violated the clean water act (PL 92-500).

The other obstacle was erected by Sen. Mary L. Landrieu, D-La., who wanted assurances that states such as her own would receive a guaranteed share of the royalties for offshore oil and gas drilling.

"The biggest problem is, what do you do with Sen. Byrd's problem with mining?" Majority Leader Trent Lott, R-Miss., said Nov. 9. He said the problems were magnified by expanding the language to include other mining issues. "It has a lot of reverberations."

The effort was sharply criticized by environmental groups that demanded Clinton veto any bill containing the language.

"Today's coal mining in Appalachia literally strips off hundreds of feet of the tops of mountains and fills long pristine valleys with waste and spoil from the mining operation. These mountaintop removal and valley fill operations are extremely controversial due to the permanent damage that is occurring to the creeks and rivers in Appalachia that are being filled with the spoils of mining," a coalition of 19 environmental groups wrote to Clinton on Nov. 2.

Conferees Remove Riders Opposed By the President

NOVEMBER 20 — Capping weeks of intense bartering, negotiators reached agreement Nov. 17 on a fiscal 2000 Interior spending bill studded with significant wins for the White House and relatively few for Republicans.

The $14.9 billion agreement (HR 3423), part of the omnibus spending bill (HR 3194 — Conference report: H Rept 106-479) is $873 million more than the version passed by the Senate and $994 million more than the bill passed by the House.

And more significantly, the final agreement is $395 million more than the agreement forged in October between House and Senate conferees and is free of a series of riders on mining, forest policy and wildlife issues that the White House and environmentalists found objectionable.

The House adopted the conference report on the omnibus bill, 296-135, on Nov. 18. The Senate cleared the bill, 74-24, on Nov. 19. *(House vote 610, p. H-198; Senate vote 374, p. S-74)*

The outcome clearly pleased the administration. George Frampton Jr., acting chairman of the White House Council on Environmental Quality, said in a Nov. 18 interview that the

Interior Spending Highlights

Where the Money Goes

HR 3423 (incorporated in HR 3194 — Conference report: H Rept 106-479)

Synopsis: The final Interior Department spending bill, wrapped into the fiscal 2000 omnibus appropriations package, contains $14.9 billion for Interior and related agencies — about $395 million more than the House and Senate had agreed to in the conference report on the first Interior bill (HR 2466 — H Rept 106-406). Congress cleared that bill but never sent it to the White House. The compromise is still $338 million less than the administration requested, but White House negotiators praised the addition of some $204 million for land acquisition.

Hot-Button Issues

Δ **Mining.** The final agreement contains a compromise on a 1997 Interior Department ruling that bars mining companies from using more than five acres of federal land to dump mine waste. Republicans, particularly those from the West, vehemently opposed the limits. Though the House backed the ruling, the Senate sought to nullify it. A compromise in the first conference report would have left it in force but exempted mining applications submitted prior to May 21, 1999. In the end, the White House was able to remove even that limited exception. Under the final bill, the limit would apply to all mine applications submitted after the date of the 1997 ruling, affecting an estimated 300 permits. The administration also won on another mining issue. Republican efforts to insert language preventing the Bureau of Land Management from implementing new mining regulations were also defeated.

Δ **Oil and gas royalties.** The agreement postpones until March 15, 2000, a new formula for determining royalties paid for drilling oil and gas on public land. The issue was one of the most contentious in the bill. The proposed new formula, which is expected to bring in at least $66 million more in payments annually, has been blocked in each of last two Interior spending bills. The Senate bill would have delayed it for another year. The first conference report would have blocked it pending a GAO report. The final negotiations came down to a one-month difference. Republicans wanted the delay in place until April 1; Democrats and the administration wanted it lifted March 1. They split the difference by lifting the moratorium on March 15.

Δ **Lands Legacy.** One of the biggest White House victories — in both money and policy — was funding for Clinton's so-called Lands Legacy initiative, aimed at acquiring environmentally and culturally significant land threatened by development. Clinton made this a major priority in his fiscal 2000 budget request. The first conference report would have provided $266 million, but the final agreement pushed the total to approximately $470 million. Included is $101 million to purchase the Baca Ranch in New Mexico, $45 million to buy land surrounding the Everglades in Florida and $15 million for the Catellus properties in the California desert. The package includes $40 million in grants to states for land acquisition, doubling the amount in the first conference report. The state money is also a significant reversal because state grants were eliminated during the 104th Congress despite bitter protests from environmental groups and many Democrats.

Δ **Grazing.** In one of the few clear victories for Republicans, the agreement allows expiring grazing permits to be renewed automatically for 10 years. Democrats and the White House wanted the renewal limited to a single year, while the Bureau of Land Management completes a required environmental impact study. Under the deal, forged by Sen. Pete V. Domenici, R-N.M., in a personal call with President Clinton, the permits will be renewed under the existing terms for the standard 10-year period. Once the environmental review is completed, however, the permit could be canceled, suspended or modified to comply with the findings.

(figures are in thousands of dollars of new budget authority)

	Fiscal 1999 Appropriation	Fiscal 2000 Clinton Request	House Bill	Senate Bill	Conference Report
Interior Department	$7,130,235	$7,768,930	$7,151,904	$7,120,673	$7,350,520
National Park Service	(1,764,224)	(2,058,943)	(1,755,324)	(1,749,917)	(1,810,363)
Forest Service	2,757,464	2,912,645	2,603,898	2,671,404	2,831,265
Energy Department	1,316,878	1,170,159	962,758	1,101,292	1,191,911
Strategic Petroleum Reserve	(160,120)	(159,000)	(146,000)	(159,000)	(159,000)
Other related agencies	3,093,226	3,414,403	3,285,049	3,210,341	3,289,215
GRAND TOTAL	**$14,297,803**	**$15,266,137**	**$13,934,609**	**$14,055,710**	**$14,928,411**
Total adjusted for scorekeeping	**($14,000,151)**	**($15,105,137)**	**($13,944,609)**	**($13,979,210)**	**($14,959,411)**

TABLE: House and Senate Appropriations committees

bill was brimming with "very significant wins."

Most of the additional money — $180 million — was directed to the Land and Water Conservation Fund, the nation's primary mechanism for buying environmentally sensitive land.

White House negotiators were able to eliminate or substantially water down a series of provisions they opposed. One of the most significant items deleted from the bill would have prevented the U.S. Forest Service and the Bureau of Land Management from conducting wildlife surveys as part of management plans for public lands.

Though environmental groups found some items to dislike, such as language dealing with grazing, they conceded that the final product was a vast improvement over earlier versions, which carried more than two dozen troublesome riders and prompted veto threats.

Also stripped from the final bill were provisions prohibiting grizzly bears from being reintroduced in Idaho and Montana, and language to reduce the noise from aircraft flying over the Grand Canyon.

The administration also scored a major victory by deleting language that would have created an exemption for some mining concerns from a recent interpretation of the 1872 Mining Law.

The interpretation, issued by the Interior Department in November 1997 and contested ever since by Western lawmakers and the mining industry, limits to five acres the amount of public land that can be used to dump waste from mining operations.

The final agreement would apply the legal interpretation to all mine applications submitted after the date of the 1997 ruling, affecting an estimated 300 permits.

Royalty Payments

The final agreement also postpones until March 15, 2000, a new formula for determining royalties paid for drilling oil and gas on public land.

Oil-state Republicans condemned the new formula as an illegal tax. Republicans in the Senate sought, but failed, to postpone the new formula for the entire fiscal year. In the end, Republicans pushed for the moratorium to extend until April 1, 2000, while the administration pushed for March 1. Negotiators ultimately agreed to lift the moratorium on March 15, 2000.

The spending measure would provide $7.4 billion for the Department of Interior, a $220 million increase over fiscal 1999; $1.24 billion for the Bureau of Land Management, an increase of $52 million; and $1.81 billion for the National Park Service, an increase of $46 million for an agency sagging under the weight of $12 billion in unmet maintenance at national parks.

The bill also would direct $1.9 billion to the Bureau of Indian Affairs, an increase of $126 million over 1999 spending, and $2.8 billion for the Forest Service, which amounts to $74 million in increased funding.

Funding for such agencies as the U.S. Forest Service, the National Park Service and cultural institutions such as the Smithsonian Institution is $147 million more than in fiscal 1999.

Much of the increase would be used to underwrite the administration's Lands Legacy program, a high priority in the president's fiscal 2000 budget that would go to purchase environmentally sensitive land.

The bill also carries a number of small programs important to individual lawmakers, including $22 million in economic aid to assist Alaskan timber communities, supported by Sen. Ted Stevens, R-Alaska, and, at the insistence of Democratic Sen. Robert C. Byrd of West Virginia, $68 million to underwrite a fund that provides health care to more than 60,000 retired mine workers. ◆

Dispute Over Education Leads to Veto; Final Deal Wrapped Into Omnibus Bill

Labor-HHS-Education

- **Bill:** HR 3424 (incorporated by reference in HR 3194) — PL 106-113
- **Legislative action: Senate** passed S 1650 (S Rept 106-166), 73-25, on Oct. 7.

House adopted the conference report on HR 3064 (H Rept 106-419), 218-211, on Oct. 28.

Senate cleared the bill, 49-48, on Nov. 2.

President vetoed the bill Nov. 3.

House adopted conference report on HR 3194 (H Rept 106-479), incorporating HR 3424, 296-135, on Nov. 18.

Senate cleared bill, 74-24, on Nov. 19.

President signed HR 3194 on Nov. 29.

SUMMARY

After a long struggle over education issues, Congress cleared a $318.5 billion fiscal 2000 spending bill for the departments of Labor, Health and Human Services (HHS), and Education on Nov. 19.

Agreement on a one-year extension of Clinton's plan to hire 100,000 new teachers cleared the way for passage of the Labor-HHS measure as part of the omnibus budget bill (HR 3194). The teachers issue was the most difficult provision in the negotiations.

As in 1998, the differing education priorities of Clinton and Congress were apparent during negotiations over the Labor-HHS bill. In the fiscal 1999 bill (PL 105-277), Clinton won $1.2 billion as a first installment on the administration's proposal to hire 100,000 new teachers in the next seven years to reduce class sizes. Republicans believed that acting on legislation this year would put them in a better position to bargain with Clinton and help them avoid a rerun of 1998, when the administration was able to score points on the politically important issue of education.

So in September, House appropriators decided to plow ahead with a gimmick-laden plan to increase funding for the National Institutes of Health (NIH) and for education of the disabled, while cutting hundreds of millions of dollars from training and jobs programs. The bill approved in subcommittee did not provide funding for many of Clinton's education priorities.

In full committee, the debate became even more partisan. The bill included an amendment by Majority Whip Tom DeLay, R-Texas, to save $9 billion by delaying payment of the earned-income tax credit for the working poor, a provision that prompted a veto threat from Clinton and sharp criticism from GOP presidential candidate George W. Bush, the governor of Texas.

The Senate advanced its own version of the bill (S 1650), which would have "borrowed" $11 billion from other appropriations bills and delayed more than $16 billion in spending until fiscal 2001. Senate Democrats tried unsuccessfully on the floor to increase funding for teachers and after-school programs.

Although the House never passed its bill, the House and Senate began negotiating a compromise. House Appropriations' ranking Democrat David R. Obey of Wisconsin refused to participate because it was not a formal conference. The product, which was attached to the conference report for the second District of Columbia spending bill (HR 3064), included a slew of special interest projects for lawmakers and a cut in all federal discretionary spending of 0.97 percent.

Clinton vetoed the bill, citing the across-the-board cut, among other things.

After the veto, the White House and appropriators began negotiating in earnest, and a final compromise (HR 3424) began to take shape. Clinton won $1.325 billion of the $1.4 billion he sought for more teachers. Republicans won provisions that would increase the amount of money allocated for teacher training and repeal Clinton's Goals 2000 program, which provides grants to help schools improve student achievement. The deal also imposes tougher standards for teacher quality.

Republicans and White House officials agreed to add $1.45 billion to the package to beef up some of Clinton's priorities, including after-school programs, aid to disadvantaged children, health care, and the Social Service block grant covering child care and other aid. The final deal included $17.9 billion for NIH, compared with $15.6 billion in fiscal 1999, reflecting both parties' interest in spending on medical research.

House Democrats added $86 million in special interest projects during talks with the White House. The final agreement also provides for an $8.6 billion package of offsets, including a 0.38 percent across-the-board cut in all discretionary spending.

House Panel Fills Measure With Accounting Tricks

SEPTEMBER 25 — For months, House GOP leaders have been struggling to pass a fiscal 2000 Labor, Health and Human Services and Education appropriations bill without busting tight spending caps or dipping into the Social Security trust fund.

They have not been able to find a way to do so. Desperate to avoid a repeat of last year's budget negotiations with President Clinton, where the White House scored politically by demanding and winning billions of dollars in new spending for education, Republicans decided to plow ahead with a bill anyway.

A House Appropriations subcommittee on Sept. 23 approved, 8-6, a gimmick-laden measure that would provide an 8 percent increase in funds for the National Institutes of Health (NIH) and a $500 million boost in education for the disabled, while cutting hundreds of millions of dollars from training and jobs programs. The bill would not provide funding for many of Clinton's education priorities.

The bill is still about $8 billion above its budget allocation, even though the panel deferred more than $20 billion in education, health and labor funds until fiscal 2001 — including postponing $3 billion in promised welfare payments to states. It also declared as "emergency spending" a decades-old program that pays the heating and cooling bills of low-income Americans, thereby making it exempt from budget caps enacted in 1997.

Subcommittee members said they were waiting for the House GOP leadership to tell them how the overrun would be addressed without tapping into the Social Security surplus.

"This bill . . . has come to epitomize how phony our legislative process has become, and how trivialized we have become in the process," said David R. Obey of Wisconsin, the ranking Democrat on the full Appropriations Committee.

"This bill is a fantasy, it is not real," he said, blaming House leaders, rather than Republican appropriators, for the spending morass.

Double Trouble

The accounting difficulties are rivaled only by the political troubles surrounding the measure.

Clinton on Sept. 23 wasted no time in issuing a veto threat, saying the bill would "seriously undermine our efforts to strengthen public education, protect workers and move people from welfare to work." The nation's governors, a majority of them Republicans, were deeply troubled over the welfare plan.

Committee members privately acknowledge that, with the Oct. 1 start of the fiscal year closing in, they are not likely to have time to move the bill to the House floor, and that action by the full committee may even be jeopardized. Senate appropriators have yet to act on their bill.

Furthermore, Democrats hope to get political mileage out of an amendment by Anne M. Northup, R-Ky., that would postpone for one year proposed Labor Department rules designed to revamp the claims process for the more than 124 million Americans enrolled in health plans regulated by the federal government under the 1974 Employee Retirement Income Security Act (PL 93-406). The amendment was adopted on an 8-6 party-line vote.

The regulations would, among other things, require a faster response time on claims and requests to see a specialist for care and liberalize the appeals process.

Northup argued the rules could significantly increase monthly premiums, and that small business would suffer as a result. Democrats said they were necessary to protect consumers. The controversy is tied into a larger debate over whether Congress should more tightly regulate managed care companies.

Still, subcommittee Chairman John Edward Porter, R-Ill., defended the measure as the best possible bill under the circumstances. He said the alternative was to let the White House and a select group of lawmakers get together behind closed doors and cut a deal.

"To [allow] the bill to be negotiated by the few, instead of shaped by the all . . . would be an affront," Porter said.

Level Funding

The overall bill includes $226.6 billion in mandatory spending for programs such as Medicare and Medicaid. It would provide $89.4 billion in discretionary funds, a reduction of about $300 million from the fiscal 1999 level.

Although Democrats accused Republicans of slashing money for education, the bill would allocate about $35.6 billion for the Department of Education. That is roughly the same level as fiscal 1999, but about $1.4 billion below Clinton's budget blueprint. The GOP decided not to fully fund some Clinton requests in order to increase the amount available for their priorities such as special education.

The bill would bump the maximum annual college Pell grant for low-income students to $3,275, a $150 increase from fiscal 1999, and also above the White House request. It would slightly increase funding for the Head Start program for low-income preschoolers, aid to school districts that have tax-exempt federal facilities in their tax base, and the TRIO program to prepare low-income students for college.

In some instances, "cuts" were in the eye of the beholder. For example, Democrats complained the GOP had cut after-school programs. The bill actually boosts such aid by $100 million to $300 million. The White House had asked for $600 million in overall aid, however.

"This bill doesn't reflect good judgment, good policy, and I would suggest to my friends in the majority, it is not good politics," said Democrat Steny H. Hoyer of Maryland.

Other changes were more substantive. Following the lines of a teacher training bill (HR 1995) passed by the House on July 20, the bill would roll Clinton's plan to hire 100,000 new teachers, the Eisenhower Professional Development program for teacher training and Goals 2000 grants for improving educational quality into one block grant.

The authorizing bill called for $2 billion a year for the block grant. The appropriations bill would provide $1.8 billion. Clinton has threatened to veto the authorizing bill, and Democrats say that the block grant includes so many loopholes, school districts would not be required to hire a single teacher.

The spending bill also would reduce literacy and education technology aid.

It would increase funding for NIH by $1.2 billion, to $16.9 billion. There is a bipartisan push in Congress to double funding for the institutes over five years. The Senate version of the bill is expected to include a $2 billion increase.

The measure would cut job training programs by more than 13 percent from fiscal 1999, reduce the National Labor Relations Board (NLRB) budget by $10 million, eliminate the $250 million school-to-work program and sharply reduce spending on the Occupational Safety and Health Administration.

"Under the circumstances we are doing a good job," said Dan Miller, R-Fla.

To finance the bill, the subcommittee proposed deferring release of about $15 billion in education, health and training programs until fiscal 2001. But that number does not tell the whole story. Because some programs, primarily the Title I education program for the disadvantaged, are already forward-funded, the overall bill pushes more than $20 billion in spending into fiscal 2001.

It would defer release of funds for teacher training and vocational education, Head Start and Job Corps, among other programs. The change is not expected to affect the operation of the programs. The bookkeeping ploy could make it harder next year, however, when appropriators sit down to write a fiscal 2001 bill under even tighter spending caps.

Welfare Blowup

The bill would rescind $3 billion in fiscal 2000 welfare payments to states, but reappropriate the funds in fiscal 2001. That move would essentially take the money off the books for a year but not eliminate it.

The 1996 welfare law (PL 104-193) replaced a 61-year entitlement to aid with a $16.4 billion annual block grant to states called Temporary Assistance to Needy Families (TANF). *(1996 Almanac, p. 6-3)*

Because welfare rolls have been falling faster than expected, and because some governors have not been spending all they could on child care and other benefits, states had built up a $4.2 billion surplus in TANF funds through the end of last year. The committee bill would defer aid only to states that have a surplus. Those that have spent their grants would not be affected, aides said.

The National Governors' Association (NGA) is vehemently opposed to any effort to rescind welfare funds, arguing that it violates the 1996 welfare deal. The governors say the money will be needed if the economy goes into a recession and the welfare rolls increase.

"Any rescission of these funds, even if they are to be reappropriated in a future year, would mark a drastic departure from the agreement made with the governors," NGA Chairman Michael O. Leavitt, a Utah Republican, and Vice Chairman Parris N. Glendening, a Maryland Democrat, wrote in a Sept. 23 letter to Porter.

Legislative Riders

The bill also includes some contentious legislative policy riders.

By an 8-6 vote, the subcommittee approved an amendment by Ernest Istook, R-Okla., that would increase the financial threshold at which the NLRB could intervene in a business-labor dispute.

The Istook amendment would index the financial thresholds, many set in the 1950s, to inflation. For example, the threshold for a non-retail business with gross receipts of more than $50,000 would be increased to $275,773 under an inflation adjustment.

By voice vote, the committee adopted a second Istook amendment to require software on federally purchased computers to filter out pornography.

The committee also adopted, by an an 8-6 party-line vote, a Northup amendment to delay Department of Labor regulations that are designed to clarify rules governing "helpers" who are not full-fledged apprentices, under the Davis-Bacon law. The law requires that the prevailing wage rate in a region be paid on federal construction projects.

The underlying bill would extend for another year a present ban on proposed HHS rules to revamp the national system of organ donations.

Bills on Course To Collide With White House

OCTOBER 2 — The House and Senate made great strides in moving the fiscal 2000 Labor, Health and Human Services (HHS), and Education appropriations bill during the week of Sept. 27 — straight toward a presidential veto and Republican Party implosion.

The House Appropriations Committee on Sept. 30 approved its version of the spending measure, which would provide about $90 billion in discretionary spending, only after adopting an amendment by Majority Whip Tom DeLay, R-Texas, that would save $9 billion by delaying payment of the earned-income tax credit (EITC) for the working poor.

President Clinton seized on the 32-27 party-line vote for the DeLay amendment to escalate his already sharp veto threats.

"Let me be clear: I will not sign a bill that turns its back on these hard-working families," Clinton said Oct. 1.

Complicating matters for the GOP, Texas Gov. George W. Bush, the Republican presidential front-runner, on Sept. 30 warned Congress not to "balance their budget on the backs of the poor." Senate Republicans also distanced themselves from the plan.

DeLay initially remarked that Bush "needs a little education on how Congress works." But by Oct. 1, House Republican leaders were mulling over whether to ditch the plan, worrying that they could not muster the votes to bring a bill to the floor as long as the EITC provision was attached.

The amendment would convert the current lump sum payment into 12 monthly installments. Because that would defer part of the payment until fiscal 2001, it would reduce fiscal 2000 spending.

The Senate, meanwhile, advanced a version of the bill (S 1650) that would increase funding for education programs and the National Institutes of Health by more than $4 billion from fiscal 1999, all the way through an appropriations subcommittee to floor debate.

To stay within tight spending caps and keep their promise not to tap into the Social Security trust fund for other federal programs, Senate GOP leaders "borrowed" $11 billion from the Commerce (HR 2670) and defense (HR 2561) appropriations bills, now in conference, and delayed more than $16 billion in spending until fiscal 2001. The House bill pushes more than $20 billion in spending to fiscal 2001.

"There's going to come a time when their house of cards, this Ponzi scheme, is going to fall apart," Sen. Harry Reid, D-Nev., said Sept. 28. "They're coming to the point where they can no longer do the fast shuffle."

GOP leaders hoped that moving the legislation would put them in a stronger bargaining position in expected end-of-year budget negotiations with the White House. Many Republican lawmakers complain they got rolled by Clinton in similar talks last year, especially on education, where he won more money, including $1.2 billion as a down payment on his plan to hire 100,000 teachers and reduce class sizes. *(1998 Almanac, p. 2-64)*

"The American people are fed up, really sick and tired of partisan bickering in Washington," said Sen. Arlen

Specter, R-Pa., chairman of the Appropriations Labor-HHS Subcommittee.

Spoiling for a Fight

The sharply partisan Senate debate and Clinton's veto threat, however, made it clear that as much as Republicans want to avoid a repeat of last year, Democrats crave a rerun. Instead of trying to work with Specter, whose bill would increase Education Department programs by $2.3 billion above fiscal 1999, the White House attacked the Senate measure as too stingy.

Clinton on Sept. 28 said that he would veto the Senate bill, asserting that it "still falls short of what we need to strengthen America's schools." Senate Democrats offered unsuccessful amendments on the floor to increase funding for teachers and after-school programs. *(Votes 298, 299, pp. S-58, S-59)*

Further, Republican leaders have tried to keep their troops united by arguing that unpopular moves to stretch out the earned-income tax credit or cut all domestic programs were necessary to keep their promise not to tap into the Social Security trust fund. As the Senate adjourned for the week on Oct. 1, the pending amendment was a sense of the Senate resolution by Majority Whip Don Nickles, R-Okla., to protect Social Security.

That argument was harder to sell as the week of Sept. 27 went on. After fending off Republican amendments to increase spending, the House Appropriations Committee by voice vote on Sept. 30 adopted an amendment by Rep. David E. Price, D-N.C., to provide $515 million in disaster relief to farmers hurt by Hurricane Floyd.

On the Senate side, Democrats and Republicans, after decrying the budgeting trick of forward funding, decided to embrace it. The Senate on Sept. 30 by voice vote approved Democratic amendments to increase fiscal 2001 spending on the social services block grant and child care block grant. *(Votes 302, 303, p. S-60)*

Some GOP lawmakers conceded that in the end they may not be able to keep their Social Security vow.

"We may fall short, but we're going to do everything we possibly can do not to spend more of it," said Rep. John Edward Porter, R-Ill., chairman of the Labor-HHS Appropriations Subcommittee, on Sept. 30.

Clinton has avoided the Social Security issue so far by advocating an increase in tobacco taxes to pay for new spending. Even while they attack the GOP for stinting education and labor, Democrats have helped exacerbate the budget difficulties by pushing for major increases in NIH spending.

Senate Gets Going

After weeks of delay on the Labor-HHS bill, the Senate got down to business. Members reported a bill from subcommittee on Sept. 27, from the full committee the following day and brought it to the floor Sept. 29. With dozens of amendments still pending, the Senate is expected to work on the bill into the week of Oct. 4.

It would increase the NIH budget by $2 billion above fiscal 1999 to $17.6 billion as part of a bipartisan effort to double funding over five years. The House bill included a $1.3 billion increase. The Senate measure also would create a $20 million matching fund that pharmaceutical firms and NIH-backed researchers could use for joint partnerships to develop antibiotics.

Specter's initial draft included language that would have given the NIH authority to conduct research using stem cells its scientists derived from embryos that were created as part of in vitro fertilization efforts, but were no longer needed for that purpose. Embryonic stem cells, which have the power to reproduce themselves and create more specialized cells, are a major focus of research efforts.

At the request of Senate Majority Leader Trent Lott, R-Miss. — acting on behalf of conservatives opposed to federal funding for such research — Specter deleted the language in full committee. Lott promised debate on a separate bill in February.

Sen. Tom Harkin of Iowa, ranking Democrat on the Labor-HHS Subcommittee, complained on the floor Sept. 29 that taking the stem cell language out "prohibits Congress from doing what I think is in the best interests of morality, ethics and science."

The House bill is silent on the issue. House GOP leaders quashed efforts by conservatives to offer amendments barring stem cell research.

The Senate bill would increase the maximum college Pell grant for low-income students by $200, to $3,325 per year; increase special education for the disabled by $912 million, which is more than the House bill and Clinton's request. The Senate bill would double after-school aid to $400 million. Clinton had requested $600 million. It would provide a program level of $11.4 billion for the Labor Department, an increase of $527 million from fiscal 1999, but $201 million less than Clinton's request.

The measure would cut the social services block grant, which provides money for child care and other social programs, by nearly $860 million in fiscal 2000. It would combine existing programs and devote new money to an $851 million initiative to combat school violence, including counseling and safety efforts.

The bill would provide $1.2 billion for Clinton's 100,000 teacher initiative, subject to authorization. The Senate on Sept. 29 by a 54-44 vote tabled (killed) an amendment by Patty Murray, D-Wash., to increase the appropriation to the $1.4 billion Clinton requested and authorize the program. It adopted an amendment by Slade Gorton, R-Wash., by 53-45, that would release $1.2 billion in July, if no authorization had been enacted, under rules giving schools broad flexibility. *(Votes 298, 297, p. S-58)*

The Senate bill would increase Head Start by $609 million from fiscal 1999 and boost funding for AIDS research, meals on wheels and the Job Corps.

During floor debate, the full Senate:

- By voice vote adopted a sense of the Senate amendment by Robert C. Smith, I-N.H., that conferees on the Interior Appropriations bill should deny funding to the Brooklyn Museum of Art unless it cancels a controversial exhibit titled "Sensation."
- By voice vote adopted an amendment by Michael B. Enzi, R-Wyo., to shift funding for Occupational Health and Safety Administration site inspections by $16.8 million.
- By voice vote adopted an amendment by Christopher J. Dodd, D-Conn., to increase funding for the child care block grant by $900 million in fiscal 2001.
- By voice vote adopted an amendment by Bob Graham, D-Fla., to provide $1.3 billion for the social services block grant in fiscal 2001.

Partisanship Reigns in House

The House Appropriations Committee on Sept. 30 marked up its companion measure, including DeLay's EITC plan. The amendment was designed to save up to $9 billion — roughly the amount that the House bill was over its spending allocation when reported out of subcommittee.

"This amendment does not cut one dime from what these people are eligible for," DeLay said. He said providing the credit in monthly increments would be responsible, "rather than getting one check and who knows what they do with it."

DeLay's amendment also would eliminate a provision of the House bill, as passed by subcommittee, that would have rescinded $3 billion in fiscal 2000 Temporary Assistance to Needy Families welfare payments to states. Governors vehemently opposed the plan to rescind TANF funds.

It would further overturn a recent Education Department decision to cut the origination fee on direct student college loans.

In other action, the House panel:

- Voted 27-32 against an amendment by Rosa DeLauro, D-Conn., that would have deleted a provision in the bill barring the Labor Department from implementing a rule to strengthen patients' rights for 124 million Americans in federally regulated health plans.

Anne M. Northup, R-Ky., who pushed the moratorium, said the rule would hurt business.

- By a 29-31 vote, defeated an amendment by Rep. Nancy Pelosi, D-Calif., to eliminate language in the bill that would bar the Labor Department from implementing a rule governing "helpers" hired under the Davis-Bacon law, which requires contractors on federal construction sites to pay the prevailing local wage.

Senate-Passed Bill Is Billions Richer Than House Bill

OCTOBER 9 — For only the second time in five years, the Senate on Oct. 7 managed to pass a free-standing Labor, Health and Human Services (HHS) and Education appropriations bill, after adopting amendments to add billions of dollars in new spending.

Now, congressional Republican leaders, intent on developing a unified bargaining position for expected budget negotiations with the White House, face the hard part — trying to take some of that money away.

Even before the final vote, Senate Majority Leader Trent Lott, R-Miss., had begun telling GOP senators that the fiscal 2000 measure (S 1650) would have to be cut to bring it closer to the version (HR 3037) moving through the House, which contains about $90 billion in discretionary spending.

The House bill "is way below where this bill is . . . we're going to have to come down some," Lott said in an Oct. 7 interview. "We've got to identify emergency [spending] if any, spending in the next fiscal year, if any, and cut back spending if we can."

The Senate bill, passed by a healthy 73-25 margin, would provide about $93 billion in fiscal 2000 discretionary funding, including increases of more than $2 billion each for education and the National Institutes of Health over fiscal 1999 levels. *(Vote 321, p. S-63)*

Depending on whose estimates are used, the Senate bill is $4 billion to $5 billion above the version approved by the House Appropriations Committee on Sept. 30. The gap is larger than the discretionary spending totals imply, because the two chambers use different assumptions to calculate overall spending in their bills.

Senate appropriators argue that their bill, which would defer more than $18 billion in spending until fiscal 2001, is within their budget allocation. Still, it is too big to squeeze into House and Senate GOP leaders' overall strategy of funding all fiscal 2000 spending measures without dipping into the Social Security surplus.

Further, there is worry on the part of House lawmakers that the Senate proposal could become the starting point for talks with Clinton — who on Oct. 8 reiterated his threat to veto the measure on the grounds that it shortchanges education — leading to an even more expensive measure.

"I don't intend on cutting anything," said Tom Harkin of Iowa, the ranking Democrat on the Labor-HHS Appropriations Subcommittee.

House Struggles

House leaders are trying to find a way to bring their bill to the floor during the week of Oct 11.

"The Senate is already . . . above my spending level," John Edward Porter, R-Ill., chairman of the Labor-HHS Appropriations Subcommittee complained Oct. 7. "If we don't pass the bill, we will have very little leverage."

So far, House lawmakers have been unable to come up with about $9 billion in spending offsets needed to replace a controversial provision in the bill that would convert a federal tax credit for low-income workers from a lump sum into monthly installments.

The proposal was criticized Sept. 30 by Republican presidential front-runner Texas Gov. George W. Bush, who warned his party not to balance the budget on the backs of the poor.

In a sign of the intense politicking around the question of finding offsets, senators on Oct. 6 adopted, 54-46, a sense of the Senate amendment by Majority Whip Don Nickles, R-Okla., calling for lawmakers to cut spending across the board if necessary to prevent any use of the Social Security surplus. *(Vote 313, p. S-62)*

Nickles later withdrew the amendment, but Democrats seized the opportunity to offer counterproposals. Frank R. Lautenberg of New Jersey advocated closing business tax loopholes instead. Edward M. Kennedy of Massachusetts sought to exempt key education programs. The amendments were tabled, or killed, by votes of 56-46 and 56-43, respectively. *(Votes 314, 316, p. S-62)*

The White House has proposed an increase in the federal tobacco tax to provide the needed revenue, an idea Republicans have steadfastly rejected.

"The Nickles amendment . . . says: rather than closing tax loopholes or asking the tobacco industry to pay its fair share, let's cut education, let's cut defense, let's cut the FBI," said Lautenberg.

On another front, the Senate bill would fund most of Clinton's request for labor programs. The House bill, by contrast, would cut hundreds of millions of dollars from the Labor Department and includes a series of policy riders.

During five days of floor debate, the Senate adopted dozens of amendments to the bill, including proposals to increase funding for child care, the Social Services Block Grant and mental health services.

Even with the changes, Clinton said in a statement that he would veto the bill on the grounds it "woefully shortchanges America's children."

With an eye toward national polls, which show that education is a top priority for voters, Democrats spent days railing against education funding levels in the bill. In the end, however, only five Democrats voted against the measure.

The amendments adopted by the Senate ranged from proposals to ban needle exchanges for drug addicts, to renaming the National Centers for Disease Control after Harkin and the National Library of Medicine after Labor, HHS subcommittee chairman Arlen Specter, R-Pa.

Among the changes:

- Spencer Abraham, R-Mich, won voice vote adoption Oct. 7 of an amendment to bar the use of federal funds for any program to provide clean needles to intravenous drug users. The vetoed District of Columbia appropriations bill (HR 2587) included a more limited ban on needle exchanges.

The Clinton administration has argued that such programs can prevent the spread of AIDS. Abraham and other opponents said needle exchanges encourage illegal drug use.

The underlying bill had included a provision to allow exchanges only if the administration certified such programs were effective and did not promote drug use.

- The Senate voted 59-40 on Oct. 7 to table an amendment by Robert C. Smith, I-N.H., to exempt federal disaster areas from requirements under the Davis-Bacon Act that contractors on federally funded jobs pay prevailing wage rates. *(Vote 320, p. S-63)*
- Paul Wellstone, D-Minn., won voice vote adoption Oct. 7 of an amendment to increase funding for the mental health services block grant by $50 million.
- The Senate voted 53-45 on Oct 7 to table an amendment by Jeff Bingaman, D-N.M., that would have dedicated $200 million under the Title I program of education for the disadvantaged to help turn around failing schools. *(Vote 317, p. S-63)*

Lawmakers Seek Vehicle To Carry Revised Bill

OCTOBER 23 — House and Senate negotiators have filled in most of the blanks on a fiscal 2000 Labor, Health and Human Services and Education appropriations bill that would provide about $95 billion in discretionary funds, including a 15 percent increase for the National Institutes of Health (NIH).

The question now is how to get the bill, which is about $5 billion above the fiscal 1999 levels, to the floor and, once it is there, how to come up with majority support.

The Senate passed its version (S 1650) of Labor-HHS on Oct. 7, but the House was never able to push its measure past full committee. Negotiators from the two chambers met anyway to work out a "pre-conferenced" package that GOP leaders planned to piggyback on a conference report for the District of Columbia appropriations measure.

House-Senate negotiations to resolve the D.C. bill broke down, however, over a dispute about whether the bill should prevent the district from using any funds on needle-exchange programs. Those programs distribute clean needles to drug users to prevent the spread of diseases such as HIV, the virus that causes AIDS. Supporters say such programs have proved successful in preventing disease transmission but opponents say they only encourage drug use.

The original version of the D.C. bill (HR 2587), vetoed by Clinton last month, would have barred the District from using local or federal funds for needle exchanges. *(Veto, D-25)*

In recent days, administration officials worked out a compromise with the Senate that would have allowed private groups to carry out needle exchanges if they used only their own funds. The Senate included that language when it passed the bill Oct. 15.

Rep. Ernest Istook, R-Okla., chairman of the Appropriations D.C. subcommittee, has resisted such a deal. His revised bill (HR 3064), which passed the House Oct. 14, retained the needle-exchange funding restriction.

Even if they can work out a consensus on the contentious needle exchange issue, lawmakers said other eleventh-hour changes could complicate matters.

On Oct. 21, for example, House and Senate negotiators on Labor-HHS were forced to rework their tentative agreement in order to cut $100 million from a proposed increase for after-school programs and $7 million from family planning aid. The changes were requested by congressional leaders to make the bill more palatable to conservatives.

Furthermore, in order to make the numbers fit while still preserving the $2.3 billion boost for NIH — higher than the House's suggested $1.3 billion increase and the Senate's original $2 billion rise — lawmakers deferred spending of about $1 billion in the bill.

Political Spinning

Even as the agreement was being worked out, Republicans, who took a beating from Clinton on education issues in fiscal 1999 spending talks, were touting the fact that they had provided about $300 million more for school spending than the White House requested. *(1998 Almanac, p. 2-64)*

"When the president says he's concerned about education — and I'm delighted he is — he's usually talking about spending," Rep. J.C. Watts Jr., R-Okla., chairman of the House Republican Conference said at an Oct. 19 news conference. "Even in that area, we've topped the president."

Democrats did some spinning of their own on the emerging package.

At an Oct. 22 Capitol news conference with first lady and Senate hopeful Hillary Rodham Clinton, Senate Democrats charged that the bill would gut the White House plan to hire 100,000 new teachers and reduce class sizes in the early grades.

"Unfortunately, the Republicans apparently still don't understand that it's not just how much money you spend on education, it's also how you use the money that matters," said Senate Minority Leader Tom Daschle, D-S.D. "Republicans want to give states a blank check with no accountability."

The bill worked out by House and Senate negotiators includes $1.2 billion of the $1.4 billion Clinton requested for his class-size initiative in fiscal

2000, but would allow states to use it for teacher training or other purposes.

Republicans argue that Clinton's program would provide too little latitude to schools, especially small ones that may not get enough money under the program to hire any teachers.

Thirty-eight Senate Democrats have signed a letter pledging to uphold a presidential veto of any bill that does not meet Clinton's priorities on class size. In the House, Education and the Workforce Committee Chairman Bill Goodling, R-Pa., wrote a letter to GOP leaders urging them to hang tough on teacher flexibility.

Cuts Across the Board

The final package is expected to include a 1.4 percent across-the-board cut in all federal agencies, which Republicans say is needed to fulfill their pledge to fund all fiscal 2000 appropriations bills without dipping into the Social Security surplus.

Education advocates said the across-the-board proposal would result in a $500 million reduction from education spending levels proposed in the bill, undercutting Republican boasts that they provided more for public schools than the president requested.

"It's far below what's necessary," said Edward R. Kealy, executive director of the Committee for Education Funding, an umbrella organization of education groups. "The conference has been a retreat."

The Labor-HHS proposal would provide some hefty increases for education spending, including boosting the maximum college Pell grant for a low-income student to $3,300 per year, a $175 increase from fiscal 1999. Education for the disabled, a top Republican priority, would receive a $700 million increase. The bill would provide $300 million for after-school programs, a $100 million increase but less than the $600 million Clinton requested.

It also includes $7.8 billion for Title I education of the disadvantaged, a slight increase from this year, and would fully fund Head Start at Clinton's requested level of $5.3 billion.

House and Senate negotiators were working on a compromise on the thorny issue of organ donations. HHS has been trying to overhaul the nation's system for allocating donated organs. Its proposed regulations, which were revised and reissued Oct. 18, have sparked a fierce regional battle.

Congress in the fiscal 1999 bill (PL 105-277) imposed a one-year moratorium on any new organ plan. The House recommended extending that moratorium through fiscal 2000. Negotiators were considering a plan that would allow what amounts to a four-month comment period on the administration's proposed organ-donor plan.

The House-Senate compromise would also drop a provision by Rep. Anne M. Northup, R-Ky., that would have barred the Labor Department for one year from implementing new rules designed to expand consumers' appeal rights in managed care health plans regulated under federal law. More than 124 million Americans are in such plans.

Negotiators dropped a second Northup amendment that would have delayed for one year Department of Labor rules intended to clarify the compensation of "helpers" at construction sites under the Davis-Bacon law. Davis-Bacon requires that workers be paid prevailing regional wages on federally funded projects.

The agreement also would eliminate a provision by Istook that would have indexed to inflation the financial threshold at which the National Labor Relations Board has jurisdiction in business-labor disputes. Istook had complained that thresholds had not been updated for decades, meaning that many small businesses were subject to NLRB intervention.

House Passes Spending Package, Looks to Post-Veto Revisions

OCTOBER 30 — Republican leaders are pulling out all the stops to clear a fiscal 2000 Labor, Health and Human Services, and Education spending bill — including stuffing it full of special interest projects — despite President Clinton's promised veto. In coming days, they will attempt to write a revised measure that can actually become law.

By a largely party-line vote of 218-211, the House on Oct. 28 approved a legislative package (HR 3064) that included the $317.1 billion Labor-HHS measure, the District of Columbia appropriations bill, and a set of budget offsets, including a nearly 1 percent across-the-board cut in discretionary federal spending. *(Vote 549, p. H-178)*

The Senate is scheduled to take up the bill Nov. 2.

Even as the House was debating the legislation, Clinton, in a speech to an education group, ran through the list of reasons he would veto it. One of his chief complaints was that the measure would water down his plan to hire 100,000 new teachers and reduce average class size in the early grades.

"I do not believe that the proper response to America's education challenge is fewer teachers, no accountability and across-the-board cuts in education," Clinton said.

John Edward Porter, R-Ill., chairman of the House Appropriations Labor-HHS subcommittee, said Republicans were ready to sit down with White House officials, post-veto, to draw up a new plan. They were not prepared, however, to let the administration dictate the terms of an agreement.

"We won't sit down and say, 'Let's write the bill together.' We're not going to do that," Porter said Oct. 28. "We're in the legislative branch. It's up to us to write the bill."

The measure, the largest of the fiscal 2000 spending bills, includes about $95.5 billion in discretionary spending. That is a roughly $5.5 billion increase over fiscal 1999. The remainder of the bill is mandatory spending on Medicare, Medicaid and other programs.

Consideration was delayed for months as GOP leaders tried to find a way to pay for the bill without breaking their promise not to tap into the Social Security trust fund. Drafting involved intricate negotiations, budget sleight of hand and some old-fashioned pork- barrel politics.

The final result was a mishmash that did not satisfy even some of its own authors.

For example, the bill included a proposed $2.3 billion increase for the National Institutes of Health, to $17.9 billion. The rise comes on top of a 15 percent boost in fiscal 1999. A broad coalition of lawmakers, colleges, patient advocacy groups and pharmaceutical companies are agitating to double the NIH budget over five years.

NIH Supporters Unhappy

In the end, however, NIH supporters were unhappy with the measure. That is because the committee, to guard against dipping into the Social Security trust fund, added a provision that would delay $7.5 billion of NIH funding until Sept. 29, 2000 — one day before the end of the fiscal year.

"It will be very difficult for the NIH to fund the critically important research it supports in an efficient and timely fashion when nearly one-half of its budget will not be available until the end of the fiscal year," the Coalition for Health Funding said in an Oct. 26 letter. The coalition is an alliance of 40 medical and research associations.

To blunt Democratic charges that they were soft on education, Republicans wrote a bill that would provide $37 billion for the Department of Education. That total is about $2 billion above fiscal 1999, and $322 million more than Clinton requested.

Once again, in an effort to steer clear of Social Security, Republicans approved a 0.97 percent across-the-board cut in discretionary spending that would bring the overall education total near or below the White House request.

The Committee for Education Funding, a coalition of 96 education groups, called for the defeat of the measure.

"The bill is below the president's request, a big step down from the Senate levels and far below what is needed for education," Joel Packer, president of the committee and senior professional associate at the National Education Association said in an Oct. 25 news release.

Overall, the bill would defer about $10 billion in spending until late in fiscal 2000. Aside from the NIH money, delayed obligations included nearly $1 billion for the Centers for Disease Control, $425 million for the Social Service Block Grant and $1.2 billion for Health Resources and Services Administration.

On top of the delayed funding, the bill pushed another $19 billion in spending into fiscal 2001. Sponsors acknowledged the difficulties with the bill, but defended it as the best that could be done given budget constraints.

"If this is another step in the legislative process, so be it. With the bill heading toward the president's desk if he signs it, great. If he vetoes it, we are prepared to go to work and try to move through what ought to be done," said Senate Labor-HHS Subcommittee Chairman Republican Arlen Specter of Pennsylvania on Oct. 27. "The objective is not touching Social Security."

In a further effort to lock up votes for the bill — which was extolled by GOP leaders as an example of budget discipline — lawmakers loaded it up with special interest projects.

Many of the more than 300 designations in the bill were for Republicans, but Senate Democrats got a share. Among the big winners were Porter's Illinois and Specter's Pennsylvania.

For example, the Labor-HHS bill that left the House Appropriations Committee in September included no money for construction or renovation of hospitals and other health facilities. The Senate-passed bill included $10 million.

The final measure had $104 million, set aside for work on facilities from Northwestern University/Evanston Hospital Center in suburban Chicago — which Porter had a hand in securing — to the Jackson Medical Mall Foundation in Mississippi.

Porter acknowledged that his home state did well, adding that many of the projects were not in his district. "A lot of them [Illinois projects] are multiple-member requests," Porter said.

The Fund for the Improvement of Education, a special discretionary fund at the disposal of Education Secretary Richard W. Riley, ballooned from $76 million in the House bill and $39.5 million in the Senate bill to $155.8 million in the conference report.

Riley got more money, but less discretion, after the fund was weighed down with projects including: $1 million for Washington, D.C.'s National Museum of Women in the Arts; $250,000 for the Rock School of Ballet in Philadelphia to expand programs for underprivileged youth in nearby Camden, N.J.; and $500,000 for Chicago's Shedd Aquarium and Brookfield Zoo for science education.

Sen. Conrad Burns, R-Mont., got $800,000 to help build a Hays/Lodgepole elementary school and $450,000 for a hospital in Billings.

Sen. Tom Harkin of Iowa, the ranking Democrat on the subcommittee, helped attach a $4 million provision creating and funding a program to screen newborns for possible hearing loss. Harkin, who has a deaf brother, has long fought for increased funding for people with disabilities.

Labor Department Fares Better

The legislation passed by the House was not a conference report in the technical sense. While the Senate had approved its version of the bill, the House measure never came to the floor of that chamber.

Instead, lawmakers met informally to work out an agreement, which was attached to the D.C. appropriations bill at an Oct. 27 conference. David R. Obey of Wisconsin, the ranking Democrat on the House Appropriations Committee, refused to take part in the talks, protesting that Congress was not following the proper order.

The measure that emerged was less generous than the Senate-passed bill, but provided more money than the House version.

The bill would provide $9.7 billion for the Labor Department, a $345 million increase from fiscal 1999 and more than $1 billion over the House proposal. The compromise version would restore money for job training and youth employment that the House bill would have cut.

The compromise would eliminate a series of Labor Department policy riders that had been attached by the House to delay new regulations regarding the Davis-Bacon prevailing wage law and greater consumer protections in managed care plans regulated under the federal Employee Retirement and Income Security Act (PL 93-406). It also eliminated a Senate-passed provision that would have dedicated half the increase in funds for the Occupational Safety and Health Administration to voluntary compliance, rather than federal enforcement efforts.

The final bill includes a compromise that would allow HHS to go forward, 90 days after enactment, with a proposed rule to revamp the national system for allocating hearts, kidneys and other donated organs.

Education at Issue

The legislation would provide $6 billion for education of the disabled, a $913 million increase above fiscal 1999. The program has been a priority for the GOP. Funding for after-school programs would increase to $300 million, less than the $600 million Clinton wanted but an increase from 1999.

The bill would provide $1.2 billion of the $1.4 billion Clinton requested for his plan to hire 100,000 teachers and reduce class size in early grades.

Under the bill, the money could be used to hire or train teachers or for other purposes. The White House contends the plan would undercut Clinton's teacher proposal.

Republicans say it would give schools needed flexibility, pointing out that many small districts would not get enough money under Clinton's plan to hire any teachers.

House Education and the Workforce Committee Chairman Bill Goodling, R-Pa., at the last minute requested changes in the language to ensure that schools had flexibility.

Clinton Vetoes Bill Over Teachers, NIH Funding

NOVEMBER 6 — President Clinton's Nov. 3 veto of a $317 billion fiscal 2000 Labor, Health and Human Services and Education spending bill (HR 3064) set the stage for negotiations on a compromise version, including a replay of last year's struggle over a White House plan to hire 100,000 new teachers.

Lawmakers and the Clinton administration held preliminary talks the week of Nov. 1, with the White House calling on Congress to add $2.2 billion in spending for education and health priorities. *(Veto text, p. D-30)*

Detailed discussions were expected to begin Nov. 6. While the class-size initiative will be the main political focus — Clinton wants dedicated funding for new teachers, Republicans favor a broad block grant for a host of purposes — there are other tough issues to be worked out.

For example, the bill would provide a $2.3 billion increase for the National Institutes of Health (NIH), but defer about $7.5 billion in actual NIH spending until Sept. 29, 2000. The Clinton administration said that policy would disrupt essential research grants. Eliminating the deferrals, however, would require appropriators to come up with other outlay savings for fiscal 2000.

"The NIH problem has to be worked out," said John Edward Porter, R-Ill., chairman of the House Appropriations Labor-HHS Subcommittee.

The administration also opposes a 90-day delay on issuing new Department of Health and Human Services rules governing organ donations.

The Senate bill included the Labor-HHS and District of Columbia appropriations along with a 0.97 percent across-the-board cut in discretionary spending.

The bill squeaked through the Senate on Nov. 2 on a 49-48 vote. Only two Democrats, Charles S. Robb of Virginia and Robert C. Byrd of West Virginia, voted for the bill. *(Vote 343, p. S-69)*

Majority Leader Trent Lott, R-Miss., had to work to round up enough Republican support to clear the measure, including persuading Chuck Hagel, R-Neb., to change his vote from nay to yea. John Ashcroft, R-Mo., and Rick Santorum, R-Pa. — both expected to face tough re-election battles — voted against the bill after it was clear that Lott had the votes to pass it. Others defended the across-the-board cut as a necessary price to keep the GOP promise not to dip into the Social Security surplus to fund other programs.

"I am stunned the other side will not step up to the plate and do what they promised also. That is, keep Social Security intact," said Kay Bailey Hutchison, R-Texas.

A Rerun of 1998

Lawmakers quickly sent the measure to the White House where Clinton, as promised, vetoed it. "We value education, yet this bill fails to invest the right way in education. It reneges on last year's bipartisan agreement to fund 100,000 new, highly trained teachers," Clinton said. "And . . . it opens the door for federal funds to be used for private school vouchers."

The debate looks a lot like a replay of 1998, when Clinton maneuvered Republicans into adding $1.2 billion to an omnibus spending bill (PL 105-277) as the down payment on his plan to help local schools hire 100,000 teachers over seven years and reduce class size. *(1998 Almanac, p. 2-64)*

That agreement required schools to devote 85 percent of their allocation to hiring teachers, including special education teachers. The rest could be used for training. Schools were allowed to hire only certified instructors. To address complaints that some smaller districts would not get enough money to hire any teachers, the bill allowed rural schools to form consortia. The Education Department has also approved waivers giving smaller schools more flexibility. About 30,000 teachers have been hired since the bill was enacted.

Clinton requested $1.4 billion for his teacher plan in fiscal 2000. The Labor-HHS bill would instead provide $1.2 billion and let districts use the money for class size reduction, training or any other purpose that would improve student performance. It does not include a current requirement that states put up matching funds in order to receive the aid.

The Education Department in a Nov. 1 memo said the bill's language was so vague that school districts could use the money to provide vouchers for private school instruction.

Republicans called Clinton's plan too rigid. House Education and the Workforce Committee Chairman Bill Goodling, R-Pa., wants a middle ground to give schools more latitude than the White House plan, but more accountability than the Labor-HHS bill. The House passed a Goodling measure along those lines, which was originally included in the House Labor-HHS bill, which Clinton had threatened to veto.

White House, GOP Reach Truce On Labor-HHS Bill

NOVEMBER 13 — The White House and GOP negotiators agreed to a one-year extension of President Clinton's plan to hire 100,000 new teachers, though Republicans signaled that they had not abandoned plans to write separate legislation that could eventually override the deal.

During Nov. 10 talks on a compromise fiscal 2000 Labor, Health and Human Services, and Education spending measure, Congress and the White House worked out a pact that would provide $1.325 billion of the $1.4 billion Clinton sought for the plan to hire more teachers and thereby reduce class sizes.

Republicans won provisions that would increase the amount of money allocated for teacher training and repeal Clinton's Goals 2000 program, which provides grants to help schools improve student achievement. The deal would also impose tougher standards for teacher quality.

"This is truly good news for our children and for their future. We know that school enrollments are exploding [and] record numbers of teachers are retiring," Clinton said Nov. 11 at the White House.

Though Republicans and the White House reached a truce on the Labor-HHS bill, the decision is not likely to be the final word. The House passed a bill July 20 that would roll the plan to reduce class sizes into a larger block grant. The bill (HR 1995) was part of an overall effort to reauthorize the Elementary and Secondary Education Act (PL 103-382). Staff aides said that bill was still alive. Conservatives have introduced a similar plan in the Senate.

During several days of steady talks the week of Nov. 8, negotiators worked out much of the compromise Labor-HHS package but did not nail down all the details.

Republicans and White House officials agreed to add $1.45 billion to the package to beef up some of Clinton's priorities, including after-school programs, aid to disadvantaged children, health care and the Social Service block grant covering child care and other aid.

House Democrats, who had refused to participate in negotiations last month on the vetoed bill, made up for lost time. They have added $86 million in special interest projects during talks with the White House.

Underscoring efforts by both parties to appeal to voters — who rank school quality as one of their primary concerns — the overall bill would provide nearly $1 billion more than Clinton originally requested for education.

"We've gone a long way toward meeting the president's requests," said Arlen Specter, R-Pa., chairman of the Senate Labor-HHS subcommittee. "This is a very, very good bill."

The measure contains about $7 billion more in discretionary spending than the fiscal 1999 measure. *(1998 Almanac, p. 2-64)*

Clearing up another thorny dispute, members in a Nov. 10 session with Health and Human Services Secretary Donna E. Shalala agreed to a deal that would allow her to proceed, after a final 42-day assessment, with controversial regulations to create a national system for allocating hearts, kidneys and other organs donated for transplant. Organs are now handled on a regional basis.

Opponents — who coalesce more on regional than party lines — had put a one-year moratorium on the organ donor changes in the fiscal 1999 Labor-HHS measure (PL 105-277) and proposed another 90-day delay in the current measure. Shalala wanted to proceed immediately.

The two sides split the difference, agreeing to a 21-day comment period and 21-day review before the rules take effect.

The original version of the bill would have delayed $7.5 billion in spending for the National Institutes of Health until Sept. 29, 2000, thereby pushing some of the outlays into the next fiscal year and helping Republicans meet their goal of not tapping into the Social Security surplus.

After the White House, colleges and researchers protested, negotiators were trying to reduce the amount of delayed spending to $4 billion.

Despite the progress, lawmakers cautioned that there could still be problems before a Labor-HHS deal is sealed.

Unresolved Issues

Among the outstanding issues, David R. Obey of Wisconsin, ranking Democrat on House Appropriations Committee, wants to require that any proceeds from a proposed federal lawsuit against the tobacco industry be reserved for Medicare and Social Security.

There was worry that the Senate's decision to recess until Nov. 16 — which forced the House to cancel a planned Nov. 12 session in which Republican leaders had hoped to vote on a package of spending measures — left ample time for mischief and efforts to reopen the bill.

For weeks, Democrats have been carrying out a coordinated public relations campaign accusing Republicans of trying to undermine Clinton's plan to hire 100,000 teachers over seven years and reduce average class sizes in grades one through three.

Research over the past decade, including a Tennessee study, have suggested that children perform better in classes with lower teacher-student ratios. Twenty states have approved initiatives to reduce class sizes, some of them more successful than others. California, for example, has come under criticism for hiring too many unqualified teachers in its push for a lower teacher-to-student ratio.

"My concerns [about any federal class-size plan] were that there be a requirement that they be qualified teachers," said Rep. George Miller, D-Calif., in a recent interview.

After a bruising battle last year, Republicans, who had resisted Clinton's proposal, agreed to provide $1.2 billion in the fiscal 1999 Labor-HHS bill as the first installment of the plan.The money was aimed at schools that had a large number of students in poverty.

The fiscal 1999 bill allowed states to spend 15 percent of the funding on training and other efforts to improve teacher quality. Schools that had already achieved a 1-18 ratio also had latitude to use the money for purposes other than hiring teachers.

In the fiscal 2000 Labor-HHS bill, the GOP included $1.2 billion of the $1.4 billion Clinton sought. They sought to rework the 1999 agreement by releasing aid to states through a block grant that would let schools spend the money for a wide array of purposes.

Quality vs. Quantity

The White House said the Republican proposal would gut its teacher initiative. The dispute is a prime reason that Clinton vetoed the original Labor-HHS bill (HR 3064) on Nov. 3.

"Class reduction is something that is so clearly beneficial to the ability of our students to learn and our teachers to teach, that I am bewildered by any effort to stand in its way," Education Secretary Richard W. Riley said at a news conference Nov. 8.

When negotiators began to discuss a second compromise bill Nov. 7, White House officials angered many Republicans by quickly announcing that the teacher plan was non-negotiable. Specter several times threatened to send a Labor-HHS bill to the White House that had a block grant plan.

"We are not going to negotiate with [Clinton] when he says something is non-negotiable," Specter said Nov. 10.

At the same time, however, House Education and the Workforce Committee Chairman Bill Goodling, R-Pa., was negotiating with White House officials on an agreement that would split the difference.

On Nov. 10, Goodling reached a deal that would provide $1.325 billion for the class-size initiative, up from the $1.2 billion originally offered. It would allow schools to spend up to 25 percent of the funds on training, as opposed to the 15 percent set aside in current law.

Clinton's signature Goals 2000 program, which he battled to get enacted in 1994, would be repealed Sept. 30, 2000. The Education Department, in its proposal to reauthorize the 1965 Elementary and Secondary Education Act, had recommended combining the Goals 2000 program, designed to improve academic achievement, with a separate block grant for teacher training. *(1994 Almanac, p. 397)*

Further, the compromise would allow states that had achieved a 1-20 student ratio to seek a waiver allowing them to spend the class-size money for professional development. Some state laws set a 1-20 goal, rather than Clinton's 1-18 target. School districts in which more than 10 percent of the teachers were not certified would also be allowed to apply for waivers to use money for training and other purposes.

A study by the Council of the Great City Schools, which represents urban districts, found that 10 percent of the teachers hired in such areas under the first installment of the plan were not fully qualified.

The bill would require teachers hired with federal funds to be certified and to demonstrate teaching skills and knowledge in their field of instruction.

"The agreement . . . will help provide more of our students with what they need most: well-qualified teachers," Kati Haycock, director of The Education Trust, said in a Nov. 11 statement. The trust advocates for better education of disadvantaged students.

The agreement would also require schools to report on the professional qualifications of teachers hired.

"I just want to say hooray for the kids," House Majority Leader Dick Armey, R-Texas, said at a Nov. 11 news conference.

Democrats, however, asserted they had not given up much. According to the Education Department, states to date have spent about 8 percent of class-size funds on training.

By the Numbers

Much of the discussion on the Labor-HHS bill revolved around a White House request to add $2.3 billion to the measure to fully fund a number of Clinton's priorities.

Republicans and administration officials settled on a $1.45 billion increase from the vetoed bill, with the money sprinkled throughout the measure.

The compromise version of the measure includes $450 million for after-school programs. That is less than the $600 million Clinton had sought, but a $150 million increase over the vetoed measure. Congress provided $200 million in fiscal 1999.

The bill would provide an additional $109 million for the Title I program for education of disadvantaged children and about $75 million more for disease research, including $44 million more for the Centers for Disease Control and Prevention.

The Labor Department would get $40 million over the amount in the vetoed bill, including more funds for enforcement of safety regulations. The Social Services Block Grant would receive an additional $75 million.

HHS would receive an additional $475 million in discretionary funds.

At the behest of Obey, the bill will include a $50 million program to help school districts reach a goal of ensuring that no high school has more than 1,000 students.

A shooting rampage at Colorado's Columbine High School this year, along with academic studies, have raised questions about the possible negative impacts of large high schools.

Cleared Measure Allows for Public School Transfers

NOVEMBER 20 — Education groups were buoyed by a major increase in funding in the fiscal 2000 Labor, Health and Human Services and Education bill (HR 3424) that cleared Congress on Nov. 19, but they worried about a provision that would give students in poorly performing institutions the right to transfer to another public school.

The Senate voted 74-24 to clear the Labor-HHS bill as part of the conference report on the fiscal 2000 omnibus spending bill (HR 3194). The House adopted the measure Nov. 18, 296-135. President Clinton is expected to sign the bill. *(House vote 610, p. H-198; Senate vote 374, p. S-74)*

The legislative rider, inserted in the measure by House Education and the Workforce Committee Chairman Bill Goodling, R-Pa., would apply to students in the $8 billion-a-year Title I program for low-income and disadvantaged students.

The language would allow Title I students at public schools that have been classified as "failing" to transfer to other public schools in the same district. The bill also would provide $134 million to help school districts comply with the new directive, as well as improve the performance of substandard Title I schools.

"Republicans in Congress have been looking forward to this day for years. School choice is finally poised to become a reality for thousands of students stuck in substandard learning environments," Goodling said in a Nov. 17 statement.

A similar provision was included in HR 2, which would reauthorize Title I of the Elementary and Secondary Education Act. That bill passed the House by 358-67 on Oct. 21, but has not yet been taken up by the Senate.

About 7,000 schools receiving Title I funds have been identified as substandard. Public school administra-

Labor-HHS-Education Spending

Where the Money Goes

HR 3424 (incorporated in HR 3194 — Conference Report: H Rept 106-479)

Synopsis

The final Labor, Health and Human Services (HHS) and Education appropriations bill, wrapped into the omnibus fiscal 2000 spending package, totals $318.5 billion — about $1.4 billion more than the House and Senate had agreed to in the first conference report (HR 3064 — H Rept 106-419). President Clinton vetoed that bill. The compromise is $5.5 billion more than Clinton requested and $27 billion more than appropriated in the fiscal 1999 measure (PL 105-277). In discretionary spending, the bill contains almost $3 billion more than last year's measure.

The conference report includes $9.7 billion for the Department of Labor, a 4.3 percent increase over the fiscal 1999 level and slightly less than the amount requested by Clinton; $237.2 billion for HHS, an 11.4 percent increase over last year and 2 percent more than Clinton requested; and $38 billion for the Department of Education, a 6.8 percent increase over last year and 2.7 percent more than the administration request.

Hot-Button Issues

Δ **Teachers.** Congress and the White House worked out a pact that would provide $1.325 billion of the $1.4 billion Clinton sought for his plan to hire more teachers and thereby reduce class sizes. Republicans won provisions that would increase the amount of money allocated for teacher training and repeal Clinton's Goals 2000 program, which provides grants to help schools improve student achievement. The deal would also impose tougher standards for teacher quality.

Δ **National Institutes of Health (NIH).** The conference report reflects both parties' interest in boosting funding for NIH, which received $17.9 billion, compared with $15.6 billion in fiscal 1999. The original version of the bill would have delayed $7.5 billion in spending for NIH until Sept. 29, 2000, thereby pushing some of the outlays into the next fiscal year and helping Republicans meet their goal of not tapping into the Social Security surplus. After the White House, colleges and researchers protested, negotiators agreed to reduce the amount of delayed spending to $3 billion.

Δ **Education programs.** The bill increases overall education spending over last year's levels. It includes $454 million for after-school programs, less than the $600 million Clinton had sought, but a $150 million increase over the vetoed measure.

Δ **Organ allocations.** The bill contains a provision that would allow Health and Human Services Secretary Donna E. Shalala to proceed, after a final 42-day assessment, with controversial regulations to create a national system for allocating hearts, kidneys and other organs donated for transplant. The administration first proposed the rules in 1998, but Congress in the fiscal 1999 Labor-HHS measure (PL 105-277) placed a moratorium on their implementation until October 1999. Organs are now handled on a regional basis; the administration wants them to be based more on medical need. Shalala, who issued revised rules Oct. 18, wanted to proceed with them immediately. Opponents of the rules had wanted a 90-day delay. The bill split the difference, agreeing to a 21-day comment period and 21-day review before the rules take effect. However, the provision appears to contradict one in a bill to expand health benefits for disabled workers (HR 1180). That bill would bar implementation of the administration's regulation for 90 days.

(figures are in thousands of dollars of new budget authority)

	Fiscal 1999 Appropriation	Fiscal 2000 Clinton Request	House Bill	Senate Bill	Conference Report
Department of Labor	$9,329,316	$9,779,919	$8,518,670	$9,785,840	$9,727,984
Department of Health and Human Services	212,956,423	232,533,478	230,875,507	237,853,159	237,175,802
Department of Education	35,614,815	37,050,870	35,659,674	37,632,509	38,041,212
Related Agencies	33,510,636	33,623,615	33,441,751	33,519,134	33,558,505
Other*			508,000		
GRAND TOTAL	**$291,411,190**	**$312,987,882**	**$309,003,602**	**$318,790,642**	**$318,503,503**
Total adjusted for scorekeeping	**($292,648,792)**	**($318,668,218)**	**($303,633,204)**	**($312,823,744)**	**($315,175,787)**
Trust Funds	$9,756,956	$9,971,057	$9,310,328	$9,822,199	$9,724,382

*House bill included agriculture disaster emergency funds

TABLE: House Appropriations Committee

tors, however, fear that they will be unable to accommodate all the students seeking to transfer under the new provision.

"Local school boards might find it very, very difficult to implement such a requirement," said Reginald M. Felton, director of federal relations of the National School Boards Association in Alexandria, Va.

There are also worries that school districts might have to resort to "lotteries" to decide which students get to transfer. Opponents of the provision also argue that allowing students to leave does nothing to help the failing schools.

Overall, the Labor-HHS measure provides $96.8 billion in discretionary spending for fiscal 2000 — $1.39 billion more than the version of the bill that was vetoed by President Clinton. The total funding includes $35.7 billion for the Education Department, a $2.2 billion increase above fiscal the 1999 level.

Beyond Education

The conference report would provide $17.9 billion for the National Institutes of Health (NIH), a 15 percent increase above fiscal 1999 levels. The earlier, vetoed version of the bill would have delayed $7.5 billion in NIH funding until Sept. 29, 2000. The delay was designed to limit fiscal 2000 spending and help Republicans keep their vow not to dip into the Social Security surplus to fund other federal programs.

NIH officials and colleges and universities that receive grants from the institution warned that the delay could derail vital research. After negotiations with the White House, the amount of money that would be held back until Sept. 29 was reduced to $3 billion.

The measure includes $1.3 billion for Clinton's plan to hire 100,000 new teachers over seven years and reduce average class size in grades one through three. Republicans won concessions that would give local school districts more autonomy to spend the funds.

Democrats were unsuccessful in including language in the conference that would designate any future revenues generated from lawsuits against tobacco companies for Medicare and Social Security. Appropriators argued that the issue should be considered by the House Ways and Means Committee, which would have jurisdiction over such a decision.

The agreement would provide $40 million in funding for pediatric medical education, subject to an authorization bill being approved. It includes $1.59 billion for the Ryan White AIDS program, an increase of $184 million over last year. ◆

$2.5 Billion Legislative Spending Bill Includes Funds for Staff Raises

Box Score

Legislative Branch

2000 Fiscal Year

- **Bill:** HR 1905 — PL 106-57
- **Legislative action: House** passed HR 1905 (H Rept 106-156), 214-197, on June 10.

Senate passed HR 1905, 95-4, on June 16, after adding provisions of S 1206 (S Rept 106-75).

House adopted the conference report (H Rept 106-290), 367-49, on Aug. 5.

Senate cleared the bill by voice vote Aug. 5.

President signed HR 1905 on Sept. 29.

SUMMARY

Hewing to recent tradition, the fiscal 2000 spending bill for the legislative branch, signed by President Clinton Sept. 29, was among the least contentious of the annual appropriations measures. The bill pays for congressional overhead — staff salaries, committee expenses, mail, security and upkeep of the Capitol complex — and an array of offices and agencies that serve Congress.

The law provides $2.5 billion, or 6 percent less than Clinton requested, although by law his budget simply retransmitted requests that the administration had received from Congress and its allied agencies. The total is 5 percent less than the appropriation from the previous year, when the shootings of two Capitol Police officers prompted Congress to spend an extra $207 million on security and plans for a new Capitol visitors' center. Without those funds, fiscal 2000 spending is 3 percent more than in fiscal 1999.

The bill had its roughest time in the House, where it passed only after Republican leaders moved to trim the committee-endorsed measure by $54 million to quell a revolt by fiscal conservatives. The biggest cut was $28 million from office accounts, a freeze that would have imperiled cost of living increases for House aides. (The House and Senate do not take part in drafting the portions of the bill covering one another's overhead.) After the Senate passed a bill to provide for 3 percent raises for its aides, and it became clear that members of Congress would accept their scheduled salary increases as well, the House shifted course. The conference agreement restored $21 million to the House office account.

While the bill saved money by blocking spending on projects for which design work is incomplete — the second phase of the Capitol Dome restoration, for example — it boosted spending 6 percent for the Library of Congress and 5 percent for the General Accounting Office.

Conferees dropped a Senate provision that would have doubled to two years the period that departed members must wait before lobbying Congress. It also would have expanded the reach of restrictions on lobbying by departed senior staff.

House Panel Stints On Legislative Branch Bill

MAY 15 — A House subcommittee kicked off the fiscal 2000 appropriations process May 12 by approving, in almost painless fashion, a $1.9 billion draft bill to fund congressional operations. The bill was kept $135 million below current levels to stay within tight budget caps, largely by deferring spending for projects that are still in planning stages.

The office of the Architect of the Capitol felt the biggest pinch, receiving $154.3 million, about $100 million below fiscal 1999 funding and its current request.

The draft legislative branch bill, approved by voice vote, includes $769 million for House operations, up from the fiscal 1999 level of $740.5 million. The Senate will determine its own level of spending when it takes up its version. House staff predicted about $589 million for the other chamber. Items funded by both bodies, such as the Congressional Research Service, would get $98.8 million.

Legislative Branch Subcommittee Chairman Charles H. Taylor, R-N.C., said the panel was building on four years of job cuts since his party took over the House, citing a 16 percent staff reduction, the equivalent of 4,412 slots, since 1994. The new bill would eliminate 98 jobs that are currently vacant, Taylor said.

The only hint of slight disagreement centered on denial of $1.8 million requested by the Capitol Police to develop its own information technology system, as recommended by a management audit by the Booz-Allen & Hamilton firm. The Senate currently provides those services.

Steny H. Hoyer, D-Md., offered an amendment asking for the money, but withdrew it in hope that budget limits would ease later in the process.

The police department's total allotment in the bill is $85.2 million, a $2.2 million increase. It got a 12 percent increase in the current fiscal year, after the deaths of two officers in a Capitol shootout in July 1998.

Other major components are $26.2 million for the Congressional Budget Office, $386.2 million for the Library of Congress, $107.7 million for the Government Printing Office and $372.7 million for the General Accounting Office.

Taylor told reporters afterward that the cuts for the architect's office did not stem from management problems such as a recent citation from the Office of Compliance for failing to monitor the level of the potentially deadly Legionella bacteria in the Capitol power plant's cooling towers. Instead, he said, "We are not funding anything that is not planned. In the past, we found that the funding, without adequate planning in the process, accelerated the costs."

For example, planning funds for a proposed Capitol visitors' center and the next phase of the Capitol Dome renovation were not included because the projects already have enough money to carry them into the next budget cycle, said Edward E. Lombard, the subcommittee's top aid. Proposed improvements to the Cannon House Office Building garage also were omitted from the spending bill, he added. Altogether, Lombard said, 13 of 60 requested projects were not funded.

However, the appropriations bill would put $18 million to $20 million in a reserve fund that can be tapped if projects run ahead of schedule, the subcommittee chairman said.

House Bill Would Boost Office Funds, Delay Renovations

MAY 22 — Spending on legislative operations would likely be trimmed about 3 percent in fiscal 2000 under a measure approved by voice vote May 20 by the House Appropriations Committee.

The legislative branch appropriations bill (HR 1905) allocates $1.9 billion for joint congressional operations and the House's spending on itself. By custom the House bill does not mention Senate operations, although at the markup House appropriators expressed confidence that the Senate would not seek more than $575 million. That would bring the bill's grand total to $2.5 billion, or $68 million less than in the current fiscal year.

Much of the savings would be derived from delaying spending on the next phase of the Capitol Dome renovation and other capital improvements until the designs are done. That decision would allow for a 7 percent increase in House members' office allowances, to $414 million; 8 percent more for the leadership offices and the party caucuses, to $14 million; 5 percent more for the Library of Congress, to $386 million; and 4 percent more for the General Accounting Office, to $373 million.

The measure is expected to be among the least contentious of the 13 regular spending bills for the fiscal year that opens Oct. 1.

Congressional salaries are provided for in another appropriations bill.

By voice vote, the committee adopted an amendment by Rep. Sam Farr, D-Calif., requiring House members to comply with the Architect of the Capitol's waste recycling program, with revenue from the sale of recycled material to aid operation of the House's child care center. Two years ago, Farr said, the House's 8,000 employees generated 4.4 million pounds of waste that recouped just $7.51 in revenue, while the Department of Agriculture raised $29,730 by recycling some of the 1 million pounds of trash generated by its 7,000 workers in Washington.

Legislative Branch Subcommittee Chairman Charles H. Taylor, R-N.C., opposed the amendment on the grounds that "it puts a legal requirement on the members to participate."

By voice vote, the committee adopted an amendment by Taylor directing the Government Printing Office to study ways to rely less on printed documents and improve its use of computer technology, particularly at its distribution center in Pueblo, Colo.

As he had at the subcommittee markup, Steny H. Hoyer, D-Md., offered but then withdrew an amendment to allocate $1.8 million to the Capitol Police to develop their own information technology system instead of relying on the Senate's. Hoyer said he hoped to win the funding in conference.

House Trims Its Own Budget Before Passing Bill

JUNE 12 — In a move characterized by conservative Republicans as a symbolic show of budgetary restraint, the House trimmed its own office accounts back to current levels before passing the legislative branch appropriations bill June 10.

Democrats, however, complained that the $54 million that was sliced from the $1.9 billion measure for fiscal 2000 (HR 1905 — H Rept 106-156) was a betrayal of the generally bipartisan appropriations process.

After a series of delays and procedural tussles, the House passed the bill just before midnight by 214-197, with eight Democrats voting for it, six Republicans opposed and 24 members not voting. *(Vote 203, p. H-70)*

Earlier the same day, the Senate Appropriations Committee approved its draft of the bill 27-0.

House floor action followed hours of off-and-on negotiations within the GOP Conference between fiscal conservatives and appropriators. The version approved May 20 by the Appropriations Committee met its budget targets. But conservatives, led by Tom Coburn, R-Okla., said cuts were necessary in this and other appropriations bills to make sure that an end-of-year squeeze did not result in a raid on Social Security funds.

"The least we can do is lead by example in our own offices," Coburn said. He maintained that by slicing Congress' own funds, money could be saved for later bills that traditionally are harder to pass, such as the Labor, Health and Human Services and Education measure.

Coburn had stalled the Agriculture appropriations bill May 26, and he helped get $103 million cut from that bill in floor action June 8.

On the legislative bill, Coburn demanded cuts totaling $90 million. Appropriations Committee Chairman C.W. Bill Young, R-Fla., resisted, but eventually agreed to cut up to $30 million. After a few hours of talks, Speaker J. Dennis Hastert, R-Ill., pulled together support for a $54 million reduction. The key element of that was a $28 million cut from members' office accounts, the amount that would be needed for cost of living adjustments.

"We don't use all that money anyway," Young said as the bill came to the floor. His own committee's budget was trimmed by $213,000.

"In Oklahoma, we think $54 million is a whole lot of money, and we think $54 million added to Labor-HHS might make a difference in somebody's life," Coburn said.

In addition to the office account cuts, $13.8 million was taken from the Architect of the Capitol's operations, originally set by the panel at $154 million.

Moderates, including Michael N. Castle, R-Del., backed the deal. "If you are in the position to cut appropriations, you have to look at your own House first," Castle said.

Democrats called the cuts a charade. They pointed out that two leadership offices, those of the majority whip and the minority leader, had each gotten increases of $333,000 in an emergency supplemental appropriations bill (PL 106-31) enacted May 21. Those funds were not affected by the cuts.

Democrats complained loudly that the Republicans, under pressure from conservatives, were undoing a committee's bipartisan work.

"It's a continuing to pander to the right wing in the Republican Conference," said Steny H. Hoyer, D-Md.

David R. Obey of Wisconsin, the ranking Democrat on the Appropriations panel, offered a series of unsuccessful stalling amendments to protest the third time in recent weeks that "we have had the Republican leadership unilaterally rewrite committee products with no consultation with the minority party."

After a test vote on the proposal won 232-182, Young's package was approved by voice vote. *(Vote 196, p. H-68)*

Senate Committee Action

The Senate Appropriations Committee's bill totaled $1.7 billion, but that did not include funds for House operations (as the House bill did not include Senate funding). Each chamber will adopt the other chamber's funds in the final version.

Senate appropriators recommended $246 million for their own office expense accounts, a $6.6 million increase from the current year.

Senate operational expense accounts include a 3 percent pay increase, less than other government employees are getting.

Appropriations Committee Chairman Ted Stevens, R-Alaska, said the Senate should pass its version of the bill by the July Fourth congressional recess.

Senate Passes Bill, Making It First To Go to Conference

JUNE 19 — The first fiscal 2000 appropriations bill ready for conference negotiations between the House and Senate covers Congress' own budget.

By 95-4, the Senate June 16 passed a $2.5 billion measure (HR 1905) to pay for congressional overhead — staff salaries, mail, security and maintenance of the Capitol complex — and an array of offices and agencies that serve Congress, the Library of Congress and General Accounting Office principal among them. *(Vote 173, p. S-35)*

In keeping with the tradition that each chamber acquiesces in the other's decisions on spending for its own operations, the Senate combined its own measure (S 1206) with the funding for House accounts contained in the version of the bill the House passed on June 10.

The fast pace for the bill gives a small ray of hope for Republicans, who have made enactment of most spending bills by the Oct. 1 deadline one of their top aspirations for the year. But recent history cautions against finishing the legislative branch bill too soon. When the fiscal 1996 version was the second spending bill to clear Congress, President Clinton vetoed it because Congress was taking "care of its own business before it takes care of the people's business." *(1995 Almanac, p. 11-61)*

During the brief debate, senators adopted one amendment by voice vote. It would double, to two years, the length of the prohibition on lobbying Congress by those who have just left the House or Senate. And it would expand the cooling-off period for senior staff. Aides earning $102,000 or more annually on their departure from Capitol Hill would be prohibited for two years from lobbying the chamber where they had most recently worked. Currently, departing senior aides are barred for one year from lobbying the committee or member for whom they last worked.

"A crucial part of the culture of special interest influence that pervades Washington is the revolving door between public service and private employment," said sponsor Russell D. Feingold, D-Wis. "We can send a message that those entering government employment should view public service as an honor and a privilege, not as another rung on the ladder to personal gain and profit."

No one spoke against the proposal.

As passed by the Senate, the bill would spend 5 percent less than this year overall, but sponsors say it could allow a 3 percent pay increase for Senate employees. The account covering House staff salaries was frozen by the House bill to save funds at the behest of GOP conservatives.

Both bills would deny funding for major construction projects, including the second phase of the Capitol Dome renovation. Chairman Robert F. Bennett, R-Utah, of the Senate Legislative Branch Appropriations Subcommittee said he would seek funding for that project in fiscal 2001.

Bill Clears After Conferees Restore House Staff Raises

AUGUST 7— A $2.5 billion appropriations measure to pay for legislative branch operations was cleared by Congress on Aug. 5. It was the second fiscal 2000 spending bill to be finished, and the last before the start of the congressional summer recess, which ends on Sept. 8. Eleven more appropriations bills are supposed to be done by Oct. 1, the start of the new budget year.

The legislative branch measure (HR 1905), against which President Clinton has raised no objections, would spend $124 million — or 5 percent — less overall than in this fiscal year. The bill pays the expenses of running the offices of members of Congress and their committees, security and maintenance of the Capitol complex, and an array of agencies that serve the lawmakers.

The final agreement would provide about 6 percent less than what was requested by the congressional agencies affected. The main reason for the drop in spending is that, after two Capitol Police officers were shot and killed one year ago, Congress appropriated an extra $207 million for fiscal 1999 (PL 105-277) to enhance security and to speed design of a new visitors center.

On a voice vote, the Senate agreed to clear the bill as soon as the House acted. A few hours later, the House voted 367-49 to adopt the conference report. *(Vote 389, p. H-126)*

The other completed spending bill, for military construction (HR 2465), cleared Aug. 3.

Legislative Branch Spending Highlights

Where the Money Goes

HR 1905 (Conference report: H Rept 106-290)

Spending Synopsis

The conference agreement was reached Aug. 4; the next day, the conference report was adopted by the House 367-49 and cleared by the Senate on a voice vote. Because the measure provides money for Congress and its affiliated operations, President Clinton has taken no position on it, as is customary. The total is $165 million, or 6 percent, less than Clinton requested, although by law his budget retransmitted the requests forwarded to the Office of Management and Budget by Congress and its aligned agencies. The fiscal 2000 total is also $124 million, or 5 percent, less than what was appropriated for this year, but that is somewhat misleading because the fiscal 1999 total includes $207 million in "emergency" funds in the omnibus appropriations law (PL 105-277) — written in the wake of the shooting deaths of two Capitol Police officers — to speed planning of a Capitol visitors' center and enhance security. Absent those funds, fiscal 2000 spending would be 3 percent more than in fiscal 1999.

• Payroll

The bill provides for staff salary increases averaging 3 percent. That is less than what executive branch workers expect but represents a victory for House aides; to placate GOP fiscal conservatives, the House bill would have frozen the account that covers staff pay. Salaries of members of Congress are covered by a permanent appropriation created in 1981; continuing a recent practice, the Treasury-Postal Service appropriations bill (HR 2490) has been the locus of debate on whether members should accept their automatic cost of living adjustment; it appears certain that they will.

• Other agencies

The bill appropriates $743 million for five agencies whose purposes are broader than the direct support of Congress. The Library of Congress would get a 6 percent increase; the General Accounting Office, a 9 percent increase.

Hot-Button Issues

△ **Revolving door.** Conferees dropped Senate language that would have doubled, to two years, the length of the prohibition on lobbying Congress by those who have just left it while also expanding the "cooling-off" period for departing senior staff.

△ **Capitol improvements.** The bill provides $10 million less than this year to maintain House buildings but $10 million more than this year to spend on Senate buildings. No projects were funded that did not have completed designs.

△ **Police communications.** The Capitol Police relies on the Senate for its information technology system and sought $1.8 million to start building its own. The bill allocates one-third of that.

(figures are in thousands of dollars of new budget authority)

	Fiscal 1999 Appropriation	Fiscal 2000 Clinton Request	House Bill	Senate Bill	Conference Report
House of Representatives	$740,481	$785,186	$739,884	$769,019	$760,884
Senate	474,891	517,580	—	489,406	489,406
Capitol Police	189,863	90,187	85,212	88,696	85,075
Other joint items	184,399	196,174	186,347	191,589	186,919
Architect of the Capitol	289,746	263,430	123,742	203,545	191,634
Library of Congress	296,516	312,408	308,853	308,414	314,702
General Accounting Office	359,268	387,048	371,181	382,298	379,000
Other related agencies	45,988	70,088	46,934	55,741	49,444
GRAND TOTAL	**$2,581,152**	**$2,622,101**	**$1,862,153**	**$2,488,708**	**$2,457,064**

TABLE: House Appropriations Committee

The most important decision made in conference on the legislative branch bill was to restore $21 million of the $28 million that the House had voted in June to cut from its own office accounts in a symbolic show of budgetary restraint. The cut was part of a $54 million package of trims to the bill that GOP leaders assembled in order to stanch a rebellion by a pivotal band of fiscal conservatives. They had demanded $90 million in cuts.

But since the House passed its bill, members across the political spectrum had become leery of the idea of essentially freezing spending on their office overhead — and thereby making it difficult to give cost of living raises to their aides — while allowing their own cost of living increase of 3.3 percent, or $4,600 for most members, to take effect.

Negotiators on the Treasury-Postal Service spending bill (HR 2490) — which House members have come to use to debate acceptance of their automatic annual pay raises — never met the week of Aug. 2, but there is no indication they will back away from the decision to allow the lawmakers' staffs to receive raises.

In a preliminary debate on the issue Aug. 4, fiscal conservatives complained about the House's decision not to put a tighter rein on its own spending.

"Stick with the numbers we gave you. . . . Let the legislative branch of this government lead in the fight for fiscal discipline by example," Patrick J. Toomey, R-Pa., urged negotiators, who at that hour had already decided to restore much of what the House had trimmed two months before.

Tom Coburn, R-Okla., argued that there was enough unused money in most lawmaker office accounts at the end of each year to allow staff raises.

But David R. Obey of Wisconsin, ranking Democrat on the Appropriations Committee, said, "It would be the height of outrageous behavior" if aides could not rely on salary increases in a year when their bosses were allowing themselves a raise.

Allocations

The measure provides $761 million for House overhead — staff salaries, mail, security and other operational expenses — and $489 million for Senate overhead. Money for Senate aide raises was never in doubt. In keeping with tradition, each chamber set its own budget.

The bill also funds an array of agencies that serve Congress. The Library of Congress would get $18 million more than this year and the General Accounting Office would get $20 million more, while the Architect of the Capitol would get $98 million less — partly by delaying spending on the next phase of the Capitol dome renovation and other improvements until designs are completed.

Conferees allocated $635,000 to the Capitol Police to develop an information technology system; the police, who now rely on the Senate system, sought triple that amount. Overall, the police will receive $85 million, 6 percent less than what they sought.

Conferees dropped language, adopted as a Senate amendment by Russell D. Feingold, D-Wis., which would have doubled, to two years, the length of the prohibition on lobbying Congress by those who have just left the House or Senate. It also would have expanded the "cooling-off" period required for departing senior staff. ◆

Congress Rejects Clinton's Incremental Spending Plan For Military Construction

Military Construction

- **Bill:** HR 2465 — PL 106-52
- **Legislative action: Senate** passed S 1205 (S Rept 106-74), 97-2, on June 16.

House passed HR 2465 (H Rept 106-221), 418-4, on July 13.

House adopted the conference report (H Rept 106-266), 412-8, on July 29.

Senate cleared the bill by voice vote Aug. 3.

President signed HR 2465 on Aug. 17.

President Clinton signed HR 2465, the military construction appropriations bill, on Aug. 17.

SUMMARY

The bill providing funds for military construction, family housing and the costs associated with closing surplus military bases was the first spending measure signed by the president. The bill's $8.4 billion total was $125 million less than Clinton requested and $81 million short of fiscal 1999. The bill allocated $4 billion for military construction, 15 percent more than Clinton's $3.5 billion request, because Congress rejected the president's plan to pay for construction projects incrementally. Congress cut Clinton's request for NATO construction funds by more than one-half, from $191 million to $81 million, and reduced his request for base closing funds by 48 percent, from $1.3 billion to $672 million.

Senate Military Construction Bill Advances

JUNE 12 — The Senate Appropriations Committee on June 10 approved an $8.27 billion military construction spending bill (S 1205) for fiscal 2000, rejecting a Clinton administration request to defer funding for some construction projects to future years.

Voting 28-0, the committee approved the draft bill, which would pay for building and repairing barracks and family housing as well as costs associated with closing military bases.

Although the military construction measure is typically one of the least controversial of the 13 annual spending measures, the administration touched off a debate this year by attempting to defer spending on some projects.

In past years, the administration has complied with Congress' insistence that it request funding for the full amount of each construction project, even though spending for such projects often is spread over several years. This year, however, it announced plans to fund some projects incrementally and requested a relatively low funding level of $5.4 billion.

Pentagon officials explained the "split funding" approach as a one-time action intended to make more funds available within the spending limits set by the 1997 balanced-budget law (PL 105-33). They contended that appropriations for some projects could be deferred until the years in which construction would occur.

But members of both parties criticized the approach, with some contending that it would delay construction of essential projects.

"We were faced with a unique challenge this year when the administration attempted to, in effect, juggle the books by seeking to incrementally fund military construction in an effort to free up more dollars for defense," said Patty Murray of Washington, ranking Democrat on the Senate Appropriations Military Construction Subcommittee. "The subcommittee quickly determined this was not a prudent course of action."

The committee-approved funding level remains $176 million less than the amount appropriated for fiscal 1999. Committee members reiterated longstanding concerns that budget constraints have limited funds for new construction.

The committee added funds for construction at National Guard and Reserve sites, approving an appropriation of $638 million — $561 million more than the administration's request and $133 million more than the fiscal 1999 level.

"When we look at the overall force structure of our military, over 50 percent of our force structure is found in the Reserve and the Guard," said Military Construction Appropriations Chairman Conrad Burns, R-Mont. "We're finding as we go to our home states . . . our infrastructure is lacking just a little bit."

As in past years, the bill would fund projects not sought by the administration. They include $17 million for work on a military operations training range at Fort Wainwright, Alaska, home of Republican Ted Stevens, the Appropriations chairman; $12.1 million for the second phase of a regional training institute at Bellows Air Force Station in Hawaii, home of Defense Subcommittee ranking Democrat Daniel K. Inouye; and $8.9 million for a C-130J simulator facility at Keesler Air Force Base in Mississippi, home of Appropriations Republican Thad Cochran and Majority Leader Trent Lott.

Senate Adds Nearly $3 Billion Before Passing Bill

JUNE 19 — Rejecting an administration accounting gambit intended to reduce the fiscal 2000 Pentagon budget, the Senate passed an $8.27 billion military construction appropriations bill June 16 that would add $2.8 billion to President Clinton's request.

The bill (S 1205 — S Rept 106-74) passed 97-2, with John McCain, R-Ariz., and Paul Wellstone, D-Minn., voting "nay." *(Vote 168, p. S-34)*

Most of the spending increase was to fully fund projects for which the administration requested only partial funding.

Congress normally appropriates the full amount of a project even if it would take several years to complete. In this case, the administration proposed appropriating only money that would be spent in fiscal 2000, putting off, and saving, the rest. Administration officials assured Congress it would seek the remaining money in future budgets and that this was a one-time departure from usual practice. The Senate Appropriations Committee — like the House and Senate Armed Services committees — rejected the proposal out of hand.

But the Senate bill also provides $687 million for 75 projects in 43 states that were not requested by the Pentagon — $334 million for projects for active-duty forces, $312 million for the National Guard and reserves, and $41 million for family housing.

McCain vs. Add-Ons

Continuing his crusade against such unrequested additions to appropriations bills, McCain issued a statement complaining that the add-ons reflected parochial interest rather than military priorities. As an example, he singled out the $6 million added to the bill for a visiting officers quarters for the Air Force Reserve at Niagara Falls.

McCain put the total for congressional additions at nearly $1 billion, but that erroneously included nearly $300 million that the Appropriations panel simply shifted from one part of the budget to another.

The administration had proposed using $42.8 million from the Pentagon's drug interdiction account to build bases in Ecuador, Costa Rica and Curaçao for U.S. forces trying to stem the flow of narcotics from South America into the United States. These missions have been flown from Howard Air Force Base in Panama, which U.S. forces are vacating under terms of the 1977 Panama Canal Treaty. *(1977 Almanac, p. 403)*

But the Senate's version of the defense appropriations bill (S 1122 — S Rept 106-53), passed June 8, which funds the drug interdiction program, omitted the money requested for the three bases. Instead, the Senate added to the military construction bill $5 million to design the new bases.

In its report accompanying S 1205, the Appropriations Committee said it would be premature to fund new drug-fighting bases until the Pentagon provided Congress with long-range plans for the operation and settled which of the armed services would be responsible for operating any bases that were built.

Other Highlights

The bill would provide $754 million to build or extensively renovate 47 barracks. Six of those projects, costing a total of $81 million, were not requested.

As requested, S 1205 also includes $706 million for environmental cleanup at military bases that are being closed and for construction to accommodate units that are vacating the installations.

The bill provides only $100 million of the $191 million Clinton requested for the annual U.S. contribution to NATO's fund for facilities used by all member countries, such as fuel pipelines. However, the Appropriations panel said it intended for the Pentagon to make up that reduction out of the $10.9 billion in defense-related spending that Congress included in the emergency supplemental appropriations bill passed in May (PL 106-31).

House Committee OKs Its Military Construction Bill

JULY 3 — The House Appropriations Committee approved by voice vote July 1 an $8.5 billion military construction spending bill (HR 2465) for fiscal 2000 that contains far less money than lawmakers of both parties want.

The spending total is virtually the same as for the current fiscal year but is $141 million less than the level authorized by the House version of the fiscal 2000 defense authorization bill (HR 1401 — H Rept 106-162). According to a committee report, the figure would be the lowest enacted level in 18 years.

As they have done in the past, committee members lamented the lack of available money for a backlog of new housing projects and upgrades of existing facilities.

"I wish we could do more," said John W. Olver of Massachusetts, ranking Democrat on the Military Construction Appropriations Subcommittee.

In particular, subcommittee Chairman David L. Hobson, R-Ohio, said he wanted more money for family housing. He and other members noted that the proportion of married military personnel has risen from 42 percent to 61 percent over the past four decades.

No Incremental Funding

The bill includes $3.6 billion for family housing, including $747 million for new units and improvements to existing housing. It also includes $4.2 billion for military construction projects and $706 million for costs associated with military base closures.

House members joined the Senate in spurning a Clinton administration request to incrementally fund military construction over two fiscal years — appropriating for fiscal 2000 only money that would be spent during the year, rather than funding the entire cost of projects.

The Pentagon said the one-time request would free up money for other military needs, but Hobson said the approach would create too many problems.

Full House Passes Bill With Little Discussion, Dissent

JULY 17 — With little debate, the House on July 13 easily passed a bill to provide $8.4 billion in fiscal 2000 for military construction and related projects.

The legislation (HR 2465) has been among the least controversial of the 13 annual appropriations bills. It was approved 418-4, with the dissenting votes coming from lawmakers who protested what they considered unnecessary spending. *(Vote 280, p. H-96)*

Military Construction Highlights

Where the Money Goes

HR 2465 (Conference Report: H Rept 106-266)

Spending Synopsis

The House adopted the conference report, 412-8, on July 29, after House-Senate conferees reached agreement July 27. The bill provides $8.4 billion in new budget authority, $760 million less than the $9.1 billion appropriated for fiscal 1999, which included $684.5 million in emergency military construction added by the fiscal 1999 supplemental spending bill (PL 106-31) passed in May. The conference agreement provides $75.7 million less than the House bill but $100.2 million more than the Senate version (S 1205). The conference agreement provides $125.3 million less than President Clinton requested, though his proposal was for an incremental approach, appropriating only what would be spent in fiscal 2000 — $5.4 billion — rather than the total, multiyear cost of projects: $8.5 billion. The proposal allowed Clinton to save $3 billion in his budget.

- **Military construction**

The conferees reduced the amount for general construction to $4 billion, $187.2 million less than the House bill and $135.3 million less than the Senate version, but it still was $249.4 million more than fiscal 1999 and $530.8 million more than Clinton requested. Construction for active duty forces was cut, while the total for National Guard and reserve projects was $198.7 million higher than the House bill and $56.9 million more than in the Senate version.

- **Family housing**

The conference report provides $3.6 billion, $21.6 million more than in fiscal 1999 and $64.8 million more than Clinton's request. The total is $13.9 million more than the House bill and $10 million more than the Senate. Concerned by reports that both the Navy and Air Force have used operations and maintenance funds to improve housing for flag and general officers, the report includes statutory language to prohibit the practice.

- **NATO infrastructure**

The conference report provides $81 million for the U.S. share of NATO construction, less than half the $191 million Clinton requested and $19 million less than the Senate bill included, but the same amount as the House bill. The conferees said the requirement for the NATO program had been reduced to $172 million since Clinton's budget was submitted.

(figures are in thousands of dollars of new budget authority)

	Fiscal 2000 Clinton Request	House Bill	Senate Bill	Conference Report
Military construction	$3,478,989	$4,196,989	$4,145,140	$4,009,798
NATO infrastructure	191,000	81,000	100,000	81,000
Family housing	3,546,067	3,597,019	3,600,820	3,610,891
Base closure and realignment	1,283,217	705,911	705,911	672,311
GRAND TOTAL	**$8,499,273**	**$8,499,742**	**$8,273,820**	**8,374,000**

Table: House and Senate Appropriations committees

The spending total is $141 million less than the level authorized by the House version of the fiscal 2000 defense authorization bill (HR 1401 — H Rept 106-162). It is the same amount enacted for fiscal 1999, not counting the $684.5 million added in a fiscal 1999 supplemental appropriations bill (PL 106-31).

Despite the broad bipartisan support for the bill, many lawmakers continued to lament the lack of available money for a growing list of new military housing projects and upgrades of existing facilities.

"We have a huge backlog with respect to operational and training facilities, the barracks for the single military personnel, the family housing, the day care centers, the health facilities," said John W. Olver of Massachusetts, ranking Democrat on the House Appropriations Military Construction Subcommittee.

House members joined the Senate in rejecting a Clinton administration request to incrementally fund military construction projects over two years. The request would have involved appropriating for fiscal 2000 only money that would be spent during the year rather than funding the entire cost of multi-year projects.

The Pentagon said the one-time request would free up money for other military needs, but lawmakers have said that the approach would create too many problems.

Subcommittee members have emphasized the importance of new construction and housing rehabilitation by noting that the ratio of married military personnel has risen from 42 percent to 61 percent since 1959.

"When we consider the number of people in our military that are married today, these quality-of-life issues, while they may not have defense subcontractor lobbyists from 40 states lobbying in their behalf, are at the heart and soul of building and strengthening our national defense structure," said subcommittee member Chet Edwards, D-Texas.

David L. Hobson, R-Ohio, chairman of the subcommittee, said he was pleased the bill includes $24 million for new construction and improvements to existing day care centers for military dependents, $22 million more than the administration's request.

"By targeting adequate resources for new child development centers, we are recognizing the changing makeup of our military force," Hobson said.

The legislation includes $4.2 billion for military construction, $3.6 billion for family housing and $706 million for costs associated with the last two rounds of military base closures.

It includes $789 million for new construction and modernization of existing barracks, $626 million more than President Clinton's request, and $165 million for construction of new hospitals and clinics, $101 million above the president's request.

In an attempt to save money in recent years, the administration has started a pilot program to privatize some family housing programs. But Olver said the program "has had significant problems" and cautioned against relying on it for future savings.

"Some people see privatization as a quick fix to address the unmet need for quality housing," he said. "But there have been false starts, and it is not at all clear that all the specific privatization proposals make long-term fiscal and budgetary sense for us."

House Adopts Conference Report

JULY 31 — With little comment, the House adopted a conference report July 29 for a fiscal 2000 military construction spending bill that would provide three-quarters of a billion dollars less than Congress appropriated for this year.

The report on the $8.4 billion bill (HR 2465 — H Rept 106-266) was adopted, 412-8, two days after House and Senate conferees reached agreement. *(Vote 343, p. H-114)*

The conferees lamented that their report would provide $760 million less than fiscal 1999 and $216 million less than the military construction portion of the House-passed, fiscal 2000 defense authorization bill (HR 1401).

David L. Hobson, R-Ohio, chairman of the House Appropriations Military Construction Subcommittee, said, "There's still not enough money, and it's not the Senate's fault and it's not our fault."

The final version includes $3.6 billion for family housing and $22 million for child development centers to address the needs of a growing number of dual-income or single-parent military households. The conferees added $3.6 million for a child development center at the Charleston Naval Weapons Station in South Carolina that was not in either bill.

Military construction spending has been on a steady decline in recent years, falling nearly $3 billion from a fiscal 1996 level of $11.2 billion. Lawmakers attribute the trend to budget restraints and competing demands in the overall defense budget.

The conference report would provide $672 million, about $34 million less than both the Senate and the House recommendations, for environmental cleanup and other costs for the latest round of base closings. It would appropriate $643 million, about $150 million less than the House and about $110 million less than the Senate, for the construction and renovation of military barracks.

Senate Vote Sends Bill to President

AUGUST 17 — The Senate on Aug. 3 adopted the conference report on the military construction spending bill (HR 2465 — H Rept 106-266), clearing the measure for the president.

The bill would provide $8.4 billion for fiscal 2000 military construction projects. It is generally the least controversial of the 13 annual appropriations bills. The House-passed bill provided $8.5 billion, while the Senate-passed measure provided $8.3 billion. The final compromise version is $760 million less than current funding and about $100 million less than the military construction portion of the fiscal 2000 defense authorization bill (Conference report: S Rept 106-301).

The conference report appropriates $643 million, about $150 million less than the House and about $110 million less than the Senate, to build and refurbish military barracks. ◆

Congress Grants Most Of Clinton's Requests in Transportation Spending Bill

Box Score — Transportation — 2000 Fiscal Year

- **Bill:** HR 2084 — PL 106-69
- **Legislative action: House** passed HR 2084 (H Rept 106-180), 429-3, June 23.

Senate passed the bill, amended, 95-0, on Sept. 16.

House adopted the conference report (H Rept 106-355), 304-91, on Oct. 1.

Senate cleared the conference report, 88-3, on Oct. 4.

President signed HR 2084 on Oct. 9.

SUMMARY

President Clinton signed the $50.2 billion fiscal 2000 transportation spending bill into law Oct. 9.

With more than two-thirds of the bill's spending set by the 1998 surface transportation law (PL 105-178), appropriators had limited flexibility to shore up funding for aviation, railroads and the Coast Guard. But predictions of dire spending cuts never came to pass.

The bill provided $3 billion more than in fiscal 1999 and nearly matched Clinton's budget request. The measure included $28.9 billion for highways, $5.8 billion for mass transit and $10.1 billion for the Federal Aviation Administration (FAA), including $5.9 billion for operations. It allocated $4 billion for the Coast Guard, an increase of $128 million over fiscal 1999. Amtrak received $571 million, matching Clinton's request.

The Senate got an early start on the bill, with the Appropriations Committee approving its version (S 1143) in late May. But a move by Richard C. Shelby, R-Ala., chairman of the Transportation Appropriations Subcommittee, to redistribute transit aid touched off a controversy, and Democrats from California and New York rallied colleagues to delay floor debate until Shelby dropped the provision.

On the House side, the appropriations bill began to move only after Bud Shuster, R-Pa., chairman of the Transportation and Infrastructure Committee, agreed to delay the effective date of his proposal in an FAA authorization bill (HR 1000) to take the Airport and Airway Trust Fund off-budget. Appropriators contended that the proposal would leave them even less leeway in funding transportation programs. (*FAA reauthorization, p. 24-3*)

During House floor debate, Tom Coburn, R-Okla., an ardent budget hawk, successfully struck the entire $5.9 billion FAA operating budget from the bill, in hopes of forcing a conference to adopt a lower, Senate-passed level. The money was restored in conference, though it will be paid for from the airport trust fund.

Under pressure from automakers, the Senate defeated an effort by Dianne Feinstein, D-Calif., and Richard H. Bryan, D-Nev., to overturn a provision preventing the Transportation Department from even studying the possibility of updating fuel-economy standards for cars and light trucks.

After the bill was cleared, controversy arose over a provision that cut off funding for the agency that regulates trucking and buses unless it was moved out of the Federal Highway Administration. Amid reports that the language would block the department from fining unsafe trucks or enforcing rules in court, Shuster moved briefly to repeal the bill, then worked on a compromise bill (HR 3036 — PL 106-73) to ensure that the transportation secretary has authority to enforce the laws. (*Trucking, p. 24-21*)

Senate Bill Caps Big States' Share Of Transit Funds

MAY 29 — The Senate Appropriations Committee has sent a fiscal 2000 transportation spending bill to the floor, setting aside concerns about a move to redistribute transit funds from California and New York to the other 48 states.

The panel approved the draft measure May 27 on a 27-1 vote. Dianne Feinstein, D-Calif., the sole dissenter, said language crafted by Transportation Subcommittee Chairman Richard C. Shelby, R-Ala., would cut unfairly into programs in the nation's two most transit-reliant states.

"Transit is, and should be, a needs-based program," Feinstein said. She said the impact of Shelby's plan would be "immediate" and "devastating."

Shelby said the language, dubbed the transit equity provision, was necessary to ensure "no states get left behind" in the face of "growing national demand on this account." It would place a 12.5 percent cap on any one state's share of Federal Transit Administration funds. Any grant in excess of the cap would be offset by reductions in other accounts, and that money would be redistributed equally to all 50 states.

New York received 15.9 percent of the transit money in fiscal 1999 — $813 million; and California received 13.6 percent — $696 million. But Feinstein said New York would lose $160 million and California would lose $117 million next year under the current funding formula. No other state would be affected. The White House opposes the provision.

Appropriations Chairman Ted Stevens, R-Alaska, said Feinstein would have a chance to fight for more money when House-Senate negotiators work out their differences over transportation spending.

Passenger Bill of Rights

In a manager's amendment adopted by voice vote, the panel dropped an airline passenger "bill of rights" provision authored by Shelby. The provision would have required airlines to inform passengers of expected delays, honor reservation ticket prices and give passengers more freedom to use a single portion of a round-trip ticket.

It also would have given airport executives more leeway in permitting planes lined up on a runway to unload passengers at any available open gates, "so that we can avoid the repeat of the Detroit hostage situation," Shelby said.

Federal rules were blamed for keeping dozens of planes grounded at Detroit Metro Airport for up to eight hours during a blizzard in January as harried passengers were stuck on planes with little food or other amenities.

Shelby said he would put aside the provision for now, after heavy lobbying by airline executives. "It felt like my office was a chalet at the Paris air show," he said, referring to an annual gathering popular with the executives. But Shelby said he might reintroduce the language as a floor amendment if the airlines did not move to meet his concerns.

In comments during the May 25 Transportation Appropriations Subcommittee markup, Slade Gorton, R-Wash., expressed strong disapproval of the Shelby provision.

"The inclusion of an airline passenger bill of rights will make it impossible to bring this measure to the floor," Gorton said.

A Boost for Airports

Shelby said his amendment also increases funding for the Federal Aviation Administration's Airport Improvement Program, from $1.3 billion to $2 billion.

A $300 million appropriation that would have been used to leverage a $2 billion loan program for larger airports was dropped. Before the May 27 full committee markup, two influential aviation groups, the American Association of Airport Executives and Airports Council International/North America, wrote to Stevens and said the loan program had "no significant value."

"Larger airports in the country already have access to the capital markets in the form of tax-exempt bond financing, and the smaller airports in the country cannot afford to repay loans," the groups wrote.

More dramatic increases in the Airport Improvement Program have been envisioned under a five-year FAA authorization bill (HR 1000).

Most appropriators say that bill, by taking aviation trust fund money off-budget, would have led to a tighter budget squeeze for other FAA programs, such as the Coast Guard and Amtrak.

Overall, the Senate bill would provide $11.2 billion for FAA programs, including $5.75 billion in operations.

Shelby noted he was able to craft a bill to boost airport funding without resorting to increased airport user fees, as recommended in the administration budget request.

Overall, the bill would provide $48.8 billion in fiscal 2000 funding. The president had requested $50.2 billion; current-year funding is $47.8 billion.

Senators were clearly strained by the so-called budget caps, spending limits agreed to in 1997 by President Clinton and Congress as part of a five-year deal to balance the federal budget. *(1997 Almanac, p. 2-66)*

"I wish we could be more enthusiastic about the transportation bill before us," said Frank R. Lautenberg, D-N.J.

The bill provides $12 billion in discretionary budget authority.

Senate appropriators also were aided by revised Congressional Budget Office (CBO) scoring after the May 25 markup. Shelby said the revised CBO figures enabled him to free up funds for the Airport Improvement Program.

Maintaining Highway Funding

The bill would provide $28.9 billion for the Federal Highway Administration, including $27.7 billion for highway projects. In fiscal 1999, the highway administration was granted $27.3 billion, including $25.5 billion for highway projects.

Robert C. Byrd of West Virginia, the ranking member on the committee, noted that the bill maintained a principle laid down in last year's transportation law (PL 105-178). That law states that future gas tax revenues that exceeded budget projections should be spent on highway construction. The Clinton administration, in its fiscal 2000 budget request, suggested using $1.5 billion of the excess gas tax revenue on anti-sprawl "livability" programs.

"I'm pleased that the subcommittee rejected these proposals," Byrd said.

On other programs, the bill would provide $4 billion for the Coast Guard, up from $3.9 billion in fiscal 1999. The Federal Transit Administration would be funded at $3.3 billion, up from $3 billion in fiscal 1999. The panel would allocate $376 million for the National Highway Traffic Safety Administration, up from $361 million in the previous year.

The committee would provide $730 million for the Federal Railroad Administration and Amtrak, down from $779 million in fiscal 1999. The panel maintained the subcommittee's $571 million allocation for Amtrak, matching the president's fiscal 2000 budget request. That is down from $609 million last year. Amtrak is in the second year of a five-year plan to wean the passenger railroad off its federal subsidies. *(1998 Almanac, p. 2-85)*

The committee also would trim funding for the office of the Transportation secretary to $59.3 million, down from $60.5 million in fiscal 1999.

House Subcommittee Action

Meanwhile, the House Appropriations Transportation Subcommittee received a more generous allocation to work with and approved its draft version of the fiscal 2000 transportation spending bill May 27.

Overall, the House bill would provide $50.7 billion in total budgetary authority. Highway spending was approved at $27.7 billion and transit programs were approved at $5.8 billion, as guaranteed by the firewalls created in last year's massive highways and public transport law. *(1998 Almanac, p. 24-22)*

Even with the relative generosity, some subcommittee members said they would have preferred more money than the $12.7 billion in discretionary funds they were allocated.

In addition, the subcommittee approved $10.5 billion for the Federal Aviation Administration, including $2.25 billion for the Airport Improvement Program. The panel would provide $4 billion for the Coast Guard and $571 million for Amtrak.

Appropriations Chairman C.W. "Bill" Young, R-Fla., offered and then withdrew an amendment that would have provided an additional $37 million for the Coast Guard, matching the Clinton administration's funding request.

The bill contains $16 million in additional funding for the Federal Highway Administration's Office of Motor Carriers for truck safety programs. But Transportation Subcommittee Chairman Frank R. Wolf, R-Va., included language to make the funds contingent on relocating the office elsewhere in the Department of Transportation.

Wolf has introduced a separate bill (HR 507) that would transfer the office to the National Highway Traffic Safety Administration. The office, which oversees truck safety, has been roundly criticized for being too friendly with the truck lobby and not diligent in enforcing safety rules. The bill contains funding for 42 additional truck safety inspectors at U.S. borders.

Measure Heads To House Floor; Airports Prime Target for Cuts

JUNE 12 — The overriding question as the House Appropriations Committee approved a fiscal 2000 transportation spending bill June 8 was how long it would retain $50.7 billion in funding.

The bill is tentatively scheduled for floor debate the week of June 14. At that point, lawmakers will have to reconfigure the bill to meet new budget targets being drawn up by House leaders.

Republican leaders have reversed course on their plan to spare such early, less controversial appropriations bills from cuts when they reach the floor.

At a GOP Conference meeting June 8, leaders told their conservative critics that they would scale back the transportation bill and four others. The savings, which could total $7 billion when combined with some new revenue sources, would be used to beef up later, more troublesome spending bills and, party leaders believe, give them a better chance of passing.

At the June 8 markup, Appropriations Committee members approved the transportation bill (HR 2084) by voice vote. But they did not know how much of a bite House leaders would take out of the measure.

Transportation Appropriations Subcommittee Chairman Frank R. Wolf, R-Va., said in a June 9 interview that it was still too early to say how much would be trimmed. He said he probably would not know the target until shortly before the bill comes to the floor.

Whatever figure House leaders decide on, Wolf said there would be no easy cuts. "We have a pretty tight bill," he said.

Some of the constraints upon appropriators result from last year's surface transportation bill (PL 105-178), which authorized large increases in highway and transit construction projects and made the spending mandatory. Those projects account for $33.5 billion, about two-thirds of the transportation appropriations bill's total. *(1998 Almanac, p. 24-3)*

Overall, the bill would provide $14.6 billion in new budget authority and $36.1 billion in obligational authority, which states and other recipients can use to contract for highway, transit and airport projects. They are reimbursed from highway and other trust funds.

The House bill's $50.7 billion cost is $3.5 billion more than was enacted in fiscal 1999, $541 million more than President Clinton requested and $1.2 billion more than was approved by the Senate Appropriations Committee in its bill (S 1143).

Static on the Airways

Like their Senate counterparts, House appropriators rejected a plan by the Clinton administration to redirect $1.5 billion in unexpected gasoline tax revenue from highway projects to anti-sprawl "livability" programs. The surface transportation law specifically called for any new gas tax money to be allocated to highway programs, and appropriators backed that policy.

Appropriators have not been receptive, however, to an attempt by the House Transportation and Infrastructure Committee to take the Airport and Airway Trust Fund off-budget and thus reserve it for airport construction in much the same way that the surface transportation law protected the Highway Trust Fund.

Transportation and Infrastructure Chairman Bud Shuster, R-Pa., has worked hard in recent weeks to assure skeptical appropriators that his bill would not further squeeze other programs left under their jurisdiction, including the Coast Guard and Amtrak.

At a May 27 markup, Shuster decried a "disinformation campaign" about the impact of his Federal Aviation Administration reauthorization bill (HR 1000). In a May 26 letter to all House members, Shuster, John J. "Jimmy" Duncan Jr., R-Tenn., James L. Oberstar, D-Minn., and William O. Lipinski, D-Ill., argued that "every penny" of a $14 billion boost in FAA spending "would be paid for by the $14 billion in unspent aviation taxes that, under historic funding patterns, would be collected but not spent" in fiscal years 2001 through 2004.

"No cuts will be required in other federal programs to pay for" the aviation bill, the lawmakers wrote.

The scaled-down version of HR 1000 reported by Shuster's committee May 27 did seem to address some of the concerns of appropriators. But senior members of the appropriations panel said the Shuster bill, and others like it, would change the budget process and reduce their flexibility to address budget problems.

David R. Obey of Wisconsin, ranking Democrat on Appropriations, called the FAA bill "another piece of candy" for the authorizing committee. The bill would pervert the budget process, he said, by beginning a trend of lawmakers trying to move their "pet programs" off-budget.

"If anybody in this room is interested in fiscal integrity," Obey said, "we need to take that bill head-on."

Appropriations Committee Chairman C.W. Bill Young, R-Fla., agreed with Obey, calling the Shuster bill "a serious attack on the budget process."

Even if it is approved by the full House the week of June 14, the FAA bill will not affect fiscal 2000 spending. With the onset of the appropriations process, the Transportation Committee redrafted the bill to make its off-budget provisions effective beginning in fiscal 2001.

Inviting Target

Aviation programs are the largest chunk of the $14.6 billion in new discretionary budget authority still under the control of the Appropriations panel. The House bill would provide a total of $10.5 billion for the FAA, an increase of $985 million over the fiscal 1999 spending level.

Within the FAA portion of the bill,

appropriators included $2.25 billion for the Airport Improvement Program, a $300 million boost over fiscal 1999 and $650 million more than was requested in the Clinton budget.

The Senate bill would provide $2 billion for the airport program. Given the limited number of options lawmakers will have on the floor, airport funding could be an inviting target to meet any reduction required by House leaders, despite the documented construction needs of airports to meet booming air traffic.

Lawmakers also increased the Clinton budget request for aviation safety programs by $66 million.

The House bill would provide $4 billion for the Coast Guard, an increase of $153 million over fiscal 1999 spending levels. That allocation includes an additional $200 million for Coast Guard readiness activities.

House appropriators also would fund Amtrak at the president's requested level of $571 million. That would be a 7 percent reduction from the fiscal 1999 allocation of $609 million. But the proposed allocation is consistent with a five-year plan to wean the passenger rail corporation off federal subsidies. *(1998 Almanac, p. 2-85)*

Amtrak has some vocal supporters in Congress, but there also are powerful lawmakers who want to eliminate its federal subsidy. Rail advocates are watching closely for attempts on the floor or in conference to speed up the elimination of the Amtrak subsidy.

Dangerous Cargo

Wolf continued to use the transportation spending bill to highlight his concern about truck safety. Wolf has been critical of the Federal Highway Administration's efforts to stem a rising number of truck-related traffic fatalities.

Last year during conference negotiations on the omnibus spending law (PL 105-277), Wolf tried to insert language that would have transferred the Office of Motor Carriers (OMC), which is in charge of truck safety, from the Federal Highway Administration to the National Highway Traffic Safety Administration (NHTSA). The provision was dropped after an intense lobbying campaign by the trucking industry. *(1998 Almanac, p. 2-84)*

Wolf has introduced a free-standing bill (HR 507) that would move the motor carrier office to NHTSA but he has refrained from trying to add the provision to the spending bill.

But Wolf did keep the issue alive. The spending bill includes language that would prevent the office from receiving any funds unless it is moved out of the highway administration.

The bill would provide $70.5 million for motor carrier safety operations, $9.3 million more than the Clinton administration requested. The bill also includes $105 million in motor carrier safety grants.

Specifically, the bill would provide $4 million for collecting data on truck-related crashes and $3 million for a safety system database. The legislation also includes $750,000 for new safety inspectors and staff to reduce the regulatory backlog and $816,000 for border enforcement activities. Beginning on Jan. 1, 2000, the U.S. border will be open to trucks from Mexico and Canada.

Wolf called the bill's relocation language a "placeholder" until Congress has a chance to debate the proper location of the motor carrier office. To date, the Clinton administration has preferred keeping it within the highway administration while beefing up its enforcement capabilities. In a statement, Wolf declared that option off the table. "The issue now is not 'should we move OMC,' but 'where should we move OMC,' " he said.

Leaders of the House Transportation and Infrastructure Committee, including Shuster, Ground Transportation Subcommittee Chairman Tom Petri, R-Wis., and Nick J. Rahall II, D-W.Va., have been working to draft truck safety legislation. That bill will be unveiled soon after the completion of the FAA authorization bill on the House floor, committee spokesman Scott Brenner said June 9.

House Passes Bill After Eliminating Funds for FAA

JUNE 26 — Despite a nearly unanimous vote for passage, the fiscal 2000 Transportation spending bill had a rough takeoff from the House floor June 23 after a huge hole was blown in its fuselage.

The hole: the $5.9 billion budget for operations of the Federal Aviation Administration (FAA), including the salaries of air traffic controllers and safety inspectors. Those who engineered its removal insisted it would not affect air travelers; they said they will reach agreement with Senate negotiators on an acceptable funding level in an upcoming conference.

The amended bill (HR 2084) passed, 429-3. *(Vote 250, p. H-86)*

The vote to strike the FAA funding was the unexpected climax to a drama that featured some familiar thorns in the sides of House leaders: Transportation and Infrastructure Committee Chairman Bud Shuster, R-Pa., and a band of fiscally conservative junior Republicans led by Tom Coburn, R-Okla.

The disappearance of the FAA funds began with a dispute between Shuster and Transportation Appropriations Subcommittee Chairman Frank R. Wolf, R-Va., over how to pay for FAA operations.

Shuster objected that the bill funded FAA operations entirely out of the Airport and Airway Trust Fund. Historically, Congress has taken about 30 percent of FAA operations from general funds, with the remainder covered by the trust fund.

During consideration of Shuster's aviation reauthorization bill (HR 1000) the week of June 14, the House had voted to continue a general fund contribution, rejecting an amendment by appropriators to remove it.

So Shuster raised a point of order alleging a rules violation against the section of the Transportation appropriations bill that called for total reliance on the trust fund. Shuster's move would have left the funding level at $5.9 billion, with the question of where the money would come from deferred for later negotiations, since the Rules Committee did not make in order the amendment by Shuster that would have spelled out the general fund/trust fund mix.

But Coburn expanded Shuster's point of order to include the entire section of the bill covering FAA operations. He argued that FAA operations had not been specifically subject to an authorization bill. When Coburn's point was accepted, $5.9 billion was struck from the bill.

"His intention is not to eliminate the FAA," Coburn spokesman John Hart said later. "It would be a mistake to say that the FAA will be harmed by this action."

Hart said Coburn hopes the House-Senate conference committee will settle on the Senate's funding level for FAA operations, which is about $245 million less than the original House level.

Transportation Secretary Rodney Slater said in a statement that he was "disappointed and concerned" by the FAA cut. "The continued safe performance of our national aviation system is vitally important, and I urge Congress to act quickly to resolve this matter," he said.

Heading Off the Conservatives

Coburn's dramatic gesture overshadowed what was expected to be the toughest floor issue: whether an amendment by Appropriations Chairman C.W. Bill Young, R-Fla., to cut $300 million in obligational authority from the FAA's principal airport-construction program would be enough to satisfy fiscal conservatives.

Young offered the amendment after extensive discussions with other House leaders, who had been trying to broker a deal to avoid a time-consuming package of amendments by fiscal conservatives. In May, Coburn had tied up floor debate on the agriculture spending bill (HR 1906) with dozens of amendments, delaying its passage until after the Memorial Day recess.

Coburn was working on a similar strategy for the Transportation bill, but he abandoned his "filibuster by amendment" after House leaders chose to make the challenge to FAA operations subject to a point of order in the rule for the bill.

Coburn went into the floor debate with a goal of trimming $570 million from the Transportation bill, a figure that would have brought the first four fiscal 2000 spending bills in line with fiscal 1999 levels.

"Wouldn't you love to see the committee stand up and defend every item in this bill?" Coburn said in an interview. "Wouldn't it be a nice thing for the American people . . . [if the appropriators were] able to defend a $300 million highway that replaces one we just spent $90 million on? And justify to the American public why we ought to enhance somebody's property that's a billionaire?"

The $300 million airport construction cut, adopted by voice vote, was described by aides as almost painless. They said it amounted to an accounting adjustment, bringing the program's funding level in line with the amount of money the FAA would be able to spend in contract authority for the fiscal year.

Martin Olav Sabo, D-Minn., described the Young amendment as a "pretend" cut. "The amendment really does not do any damage to the bill, because it does not cut any money that we were planning to spend in the year 2000," Sabo said. "If it makes someone feel good, I guess that is a plus. But it is also one of our pretend schemes which really is not doing anything."

Young said that because of the budgetary protection for highway programs under last year's highway law (PL 105-178), the only other realistic alternatives appropriators had for reducing outlays in the bill would be to cut deeply into Amtrak or the Coast Guard. He said neither of those options were politically acceptable to the House.

Because of the elimination of funding for FAA operations, the House bill now would provide only $2.4 billion for the FAA, compared with $7.6 billion in fiscal 1999 and $8.5 billion in President Clinton's fiscal 2000 budget request.

Before the cuts on the floor, the bill would have provided $8.3 billion for the FAA, a 9 percent increase over fiscal 1999. The Senate bill includes $8.1 billion, a 6 percent increase.

The potential $245 million in FAA savings that could emerge from conference committee, along with Young's $300 million reduction, would fall just short of Coburn's $570 million goal.

In other House floor action:

- Mark Sanford, R-S.C., offered an amendment, adopted by voice vote, that would cut $1 million from the Transportation Administrative Service Center, a program that provides support services for Department of Transportation employees.
- Robert E. Andrews, D-N.J., was successful with an amendment to reduce funding for the Amtrak Reform Council, from $750,000 to $450,000. The council was created under the last Amtrak authorization law (PL 105-134) as an independent body that would monitor Amtrak operations and suggest ways to save money. The amendment was adopted, 289-141. *(Vote 248, p. H-86)*

Andrews described the council as a superfluous body that had the potential to interfere with Amtrak, which he said had gone a long way toward solving its management problems. But Shuster countered that the House should not revisit the Amtrak issue on the spending bill, and he threatened to look anew at efforts to phase out federal funding for the national passenger railroad more quickly if the Andrews amendment were adopted.

Bill Provisions

Overall funding in the bill was reduced from $50.7 billion to $44.5 billion. Discretionary budget authority dropped from $14.6 billion to $8.7 billion.

The bill includes $27.7 billion in obligational authority for highway spending, an increase of $2.2 billion, or 9 percent, over fiscal 1999 spending levels. That budget target was mandated by last year's highway authorization. Transit spending would total $5.8 billion, a $407 million increase over fiscal 1999, or 7.5 percent. That spending level was also mandated by the highway law.

The bill would allocate $4 billion for the Coast Guard, an increase of $153 million, or 3.9 percent, over fiscal 1999. The Clinton administration requested $4.1 billion.

Amtrak would be funded at $571 million under the House bill, a level that matches the Senate bill and Clinton's budget request. That represents a 6 percent reduction from the fiscal 1999 allocation of $609 million, consistent with a five-year plan to wean the passenger rail corporation of its federal subsidy. *(1998 Almanac, p. 2-85)*

Provisions crafted by Wolf to highlight his concerns over truck safety remain intact. The bill would provide $70.5 million for motor carrier safety operations, $9.3 million more than the president requested. And it includes $105 million in safety grants.

But the bill would prevent the Office of Motor Carriers, the Department of Transportation's main truck safety unit, from receiving any money unless it is transferred out of the Federal Highway Administration. Wolf has charged that the highway agency has failed in its duty to deal with truck safety issues, since the number of deaths in truck-related accidents has risen dramatically over the past several years.

Wolf has introduced a free-standing bill (HR 507) that would move the motor carrier office to the National Highway Traffic Safety Administration. He said he would not make that language part of the appropriations bill until the Transportation and Infrastructure Committee has a chance to consider legislation. Adding it in conference remains a possibility.

Outlook in the Senate

The Senate is expected to take up its version of the Transportation bill (S 1143) soon after the July Fourth recess.

House members telegraphed one issue likely to come up in Senate debate and in conference: an effort by Republican Richard C. Shelby of Alabama to cap any one state's allocation of federal transit funds.

New York and California lawmakers argued that the Shelby provision would cost their states hundreds of millions of dollars. "New York has one-third of the nation's transit riders; California has about 14 percent. Combined, the two states make up almost half of the entire nation's transit users," said Rick A. Lazio, R-N.Y., noting that the Senate bill would limit any one state to 12.5 percent of the overall funds.

Since only two states would be affected by the provision, its chances of making it through the Senate are good. But in the House, the states' delegations comprise 83 of the chamber's 435 members — a significant bloc of votes.

The states are united in pressing their case even before House-Senate negotiations begin. The lawmakers outlined their concerns in a letter to Young and ranking House Appropriations Democrat David R. Obey of Wisconsin signed by every member of the two delegations.

According to the letter, written by John E. Sweeney, R-N.Y., New York is slated to receive 15.5 percent of federal transit funding in fiscal 2000, and California is slated for 14.6 percent. If the Senate provision were to become law, Sweeney estimated it would result in losses of $200 million for New York and $120 million for California.

Lazio said the provision would begin to unravel carefully negotiated formulas included in last year's highway bill — an effort that few members are ready to embark upon again so soon.

"For the millions of people who use mass transit, the environment and the economy, we should uphold the allocation formulas we worked so hard for in that historically crafted bill," Lazio said.

Senate Positioned For Showdown On Fuel Efficiency Standards

SEPTEMBER 11 — As the fiscal 2000 Transportation appropriations bill awaits Senate floor debate, it is becoming the vehicle for a growing number of heated policy debates.

During the week of Sept. 6, an old dispute re-emerged between automakers and environmentalists over fuel efficiency standards.

Dianne Feinstein, D-Calif., Slade Gorton, R-Wash., and Richard H. Bryan, D-Nev., are leading an effort to allow the government to study whether to raise the corporate average fuel economy (CAFE) standard for automobiles.

In each of the past four years, the transportation spending bill has included a provision, inserted by the House, that has prevented the Department of Transportation from working on updating the fuel efficiency standards.

The bill (HR 2084) passed by the House June 23 would again prohibit funds from being used to "prepare, propose or promulgate any regulations . . . prescribing corporate average fuel economy standards" different from existing standards.

To this point, the administration has not threatened a veto over the issue. But in a letter to President Clinton cosigned by 28 other senators, Feinstein, Gorton and Bryan urged the administration to push for "improved CAFE standards." The senators argued that because of the surging popularity of sport utility vehicles (SUVs) and other light trucks, the average fuel economy of all new passenger vehicles is now at its lowest point since 1980, while fuel consumption is at its highest.

"The freeze rider [in the House bill] denies the purchasers of SUVs and other light trucks the benefits of existing fuel saving technologies," the senators wrote.

The senators are planning to introduce an amendment to S 1143 that would call for a study on updating the standards. The group hopes to garner enough votes to counterbalance the freeze language in the House bill, which is backed by Majority Whip Tom DeLay, R-Texas, and a good number of House Republicans.

The senators will be close to their goal of 50 votes, said an aide involved in the push. The Senate would then be in a strong position to strike the House provision in conference. "I don't see how we couldn't prevail if we got 50," the aide said.

Current Standards

The fuel efficiency standards were last updated in 1990, but they have not changed significantly since the mid-1980s. The current requirements are that automakers' new fleets of cars average 27.5 miles per gallon. New fleets of light trucks must average 20.7 miles per gallon. Those fuel efficiency targets are in line with what was envisioned in the original 1975 legislation. *(1990 Almanac, p. 279)*

Environmentalists argue that technology has improved greatly since automakers hit the current standards in the mid-1980s. Since then, automakers, and American automakers in particular, have reaped enormous profits from a booming market in sport utility vehicles and minivans, which fall into the less efficient light truck category.

Those trends have occurred during an era of cheap gasoline. But the larger vehicles and increasing numbers of cars on the road and miles driven have boosted emissions of greenhouse gases, which accelerate global warming, environmentalists say.

Furthermore, the United States has become even more dependent on foreign oil, they say, importing 48 percent of its oil in 1997, up from 34 percent in 1973, according to the Environmental and Energy Study Institute.

Automobile manufacturers have responded to the Senate effort with a fierce lobbying campaign. They argue that new fuel efficiency standards would force them to build cars that do not fit the marketplace. Americans have consistently expressed a desire for bigger, more powerful vehicles, according to the Alliance of Automobile Manufacturers.

The industry alliance also argues that the bigger vehicles are safer to drive. That contention is questioned by some safety advocates, who point to government tests that indicate a higher flipover rate during accidents.

The automakers, in a statement, said they are working on new fuel economy technologies that will do more in the long run to reduce fuel consumption than "short-term CAFE increases that effectively limit consumer choice." The group said Congress would be more effective by supporting advanced technologies such as electric vehicles and fuel cells.

But automakers have already developed promising fuel-saving technology that is offered on selected mass market cars, according to Jason Mark, a transportation analyst for the Union of Concerned Scientists. The group developed a prototype Ford Explorer that uses variable valve timing, a technology offered on the 1999 Honda Accord. The prototype vehicle averages 28.4 miles per gallon, compared to 19.3 miles per gallon for a standard Explorer.

Test Vote on Transit Issue

The spending bill remained stalled after a cloture vote failed, 49-49, on Sept. 9. Four Republicans joined all 45 Democrats to defeat GOP leaders' push for a full floor debate on the measure, which was marked up by the Senate Appropriations Committee May 27. *(Vote 264, p. S-52)*

The failed attempt to invoke cloture was the first effort to gauge support on a controversial provision by Transportation Appropriations Subcommittee Chairman Richard C. Shelby, R-Ala. The language would place a 12.5 percent cap on any one state's share of Federal Transit Administration funds. Only two states, New York and California, would lose money under the provision.

GOP leaders hoped the provision might garner the support of some Democrats, since many, particularly those from more rural states, would stand to benefit under the Shelby language.

"If they stick together, some of their members get hurt badly," said Larry E. Craig, R-Idaho.

But many Democratic senators felt it had become a partisan issue, because Shelby had never approached them to sell his provision. Furthermore, Shelby has not attempted to compromise with the four senators whose states would be affected, all Democrats.

Minority Leader Tom Daschle, D-S.D., framed the issue as an important test of Democratic unity. "He presented it to the caucus as an issue of 'there but by the grace of God goes the next member,' " an aide said.

The Clinton administration issued a veto threat over the Shelby provision. In a Sept. 7 statement, the Office of Management and Budget said transit funding formulas enacted in the 1998 highway bill (PL 105-178) "should not be reopened in an appropriations bill."

GOP leaders may try another cloture vote the week of Sept. 13, said Majority Leader Trent Lott, R-Miss.

If the logjam cannot be broken, GOP leaders may hold the Transportation bill — which is usually one of the easiest spending bills to pass — as a sweetener for a catchall omnibus spending bill, as happened last year.

Air Passenger, Auto Fuel Provisions Rejected as Senate Passes Bill

SEPTEMBER 18 — The Senate toned down an effort to protect airline passengers from high fares and overbooked flights and rejected an effort to study stronger fuel economy standards for cars and trucks as it passed a $49.5 billion Transportation spending bill Sept. 16.

The bill (HR 2084) passed 95-0. *(Vote 278, p. S-54)*

Money was tight, except for highway programs authorized and required by last year's surface transportation law (PL 105-178). But Transportation Appropriations Subcommittee Chairman Richard C. Shelby, R-Ala., was able to avoid large-scale cuts in the Federal Aviation Administration (FAA), the Coast Guard or Amtrak that were predicted earlier in the year.

The bill would provide $27.7 billion for highways and $5.8 billion for mass transit. The FAA would receive $9.8 billion, including $5.9 billion for operations. The House struck $5.9 billion of operations funding from its bill June 23 in a procedural maneuver. The funds are expected to be restored in conference.

The bill would provide $4 billion for the Coast Guard, an increase of $93 million over the fiscal 1999 level. Amtrak would receive $571 million, matching President Clinton's request.

State Rebate

As the bill moves to conference, one possible point of contention is a provision that would redirect about $120 million of gas tax revenues to the states instead of to federal programs included in the highway law's funding formula, such as those for roads on American Indian reservations and public lands.

John H. Chafee, R-R.I., chairman of the Senate Environment and Public Works Committee, and Max Baucus of Montana, the panel's ranking Democrat, fought the language as an attempt to legislate on an appropriations bill. The Senate sided with Shelby, voting 62-35 that the language was germane to the bill. *(Vote 274, p. S-53)*

Amendments that aimed to bolster airline passengers' rights were highlights of the Senate debate. Ron Wyden, D-Ore., offered two that would have required the Department of Transportation to investigate complaints that an airline overbooked a flight or failed to provide a consumer with the lowest available fare.

Amendment opponents noted that the airline industry has recently unveiled an initiative to answer consumer complaints.

Wyden said the industry effort was "toothless." But he assuaged his opponents by changing the amendment to "sense of the Senate" language. The watered-down amendments passed on a voice vote.

Low Mileage

Controversy flared over an amendment that would have allowed the Transportation Department to study whether to change fuel efficiency standards for vehicles. It was defeated, 40-55. *(Vote 275, p. S-53)*

The effort was aimed at a provision the House has added to each transportation spending bill since 1995 prohibiting the Transportation Department from studying or implementing new corporate average fuel efficiency (CAFE) standards.

Slade Gorton, R-Wash., Dianne Feinstein, D-Calif., and Richard H. Bryan, D-Nev., argued that the prohibition has been tantamount to a gag order. They said that more efficient cars and trucks would save consumers money while reducing pollution, global warming and the U.S. trade deficit.

But the amendment drew opponents, backed by aggressive lobbying from the auto industry. Spencer Abraham, R-Mich., said the Transportation Department would raise overall mileage requirements 15 percent to 35 percent.

In a reprisal of heated, 1970s debates that proceeded the original CAFE standards, Abraham said the amendment would force American automakers to build smaller, lighter cars.

Citing a National Academy of Sciences study, Abraham said the fuel efficiency standards had caused thousands of deaths because more people were riding in lighter vehicles.

The easy passage of the overall bill belied some contentious issues, especially an early provision by Shelby that would have shifted transit funding from New York and California to other states. The controversy delayed floor consideration for three months.

Shelby withdrew the provision after losing a cloture vote 49-49 Sept. 9. Shelby said in an interview that he had given up on the provision for the year. "I can read the tea leaves," he said.

But Shelby added that the issue will return, because, he said, "when you have two states that are going to eat up most of the funding, a lot of states with fast-growing populations are going to be shortchanged."

House Adopts Report Over Shuster Objections

OCTOBER 2 — The House handed Transportation and Infrastructure Committee Chairman Bud Shuster a rare defeat Oct. 1 as it easily adopted the conference report on a fiscal 2000 Transportation spending bill he opposed.

Conferees on the legislation (HR 2084) ignored the Pennsylvania Republican's threat to lead a floor insurrection, partly over aviation funding in the bill. The House adopted the conference report, 304-91. The Senate is scheduled to vote the afternoon of Oct. 4. *(Vote 466, p. H-154)*

The conference report would provide $27.7 billion for highways and $5.8 billion for mass transit. Those levels reflect increases envisioned under the 1998 surface transportation law (PL 105-178). Both levels were preset by that law's "firewalls," which protected Highway Trust Fund money from being redirected to other purposes. *(1998 Almanac, p. 24-27)*

The Federal Aviation Administration (FAA) would receive $10.1 billion, including $5.9 billion for operations. The House had struck the $5.9 billion from its bill June 23 in a procedural maneuver. The funds were restored in conference.

The bill would provide $4 billion for the Coast Guard, an increase of $93 million over the fiscal 1999 level. Amtrak would receive $571 million, matching President Clinton's request.

Shuster's Charge

House and Senate leaders, under pressure to pass as many spending bills as possible before the new fiscal year began Oct. 1, pushed the transportation conferees to wrap up their work. But a long list of Shuster's objections slowed down the schedule.

Chief among the problems were two provisions in the Senate bill that authorizers in both chambers denounced as legislating on an appropriations bill.

The highest priority for Shuster was a difference over how to fund the FAA. Conferees agreed to keep Senate language to fund the agency entirely out of the Airport and Airway Trust Fund, eliminating any general fund contribution.

House appropriators had tried to do that in their version of the bill, but were thwarted by Shuster during floor debate in June. Shuster got the language thrown out on a point of order; House rules prohibit authorizing language in appropriations bills.

Shuster argued that the trust fund was created solely to finance construction, not FAA operations. In recent years, about 30 percent of FAA funding has come from the general fund. But appropriators in both chambers said there is ample money in the trust fund for both operations and construction.

"The Senate version frankly is a disaster," Shuster said during a meeting of his committee Sept. 23. He cited provisions that he classified as usurping authorizers' power, as well as a $90 million shortfall for special projects for lawmakers. He urged the 75 members of his committee to closely monitor the conference and fight the bill if necessary.

"If these problems are not fixed, we may find ourselves having to oppose the bill or the rule for its consideration," Shuster said. "We hope to work it out. If not, we should gird for battle."

On Sept. 22, Shuster and ranking committee Democrat James L. Oberstar of Minnesota pressed their case in a nine-page letter to House Speaker J. Dennis Hastert, R-Ill. The letter listed 43 provisions in the Senate bill they found objectionable. A week later, Shuster and Oberstar sent a letter to all House committee chairmen arguing that their authority was at stake unless all took a stand against the conference agreement.

In the end, Shuster found himself in a rare position: on the wrong side of a slew of high-priority local projects for fellow members. A vote with Shuster against the conference report would have been a vote to delay highly coveted federal transportation money for their districts. Not even Shuster, with his history of success in challenging House leaders, could stop such a train.

Gas Tax Windfall

Also at issue for House and Senate negotiators was what to do with a portion of a $1.5 billion gasoline tax windfall. Authorizers wrote into last year's surface transportation law language to direct higher-than-projected revenues back to the states and to various federal programs under the carefully crafted formulas contained in the law.

However, in the Senate-passed bill, Transportation Appropriations Subcommittee Chairman Richard C. Shelby, R-Ala., redirected $210 million of that windfall to the states alone, and away from federal programs such as road construction on public lands and American Indian reservations.

Senate Environment and Public Works Committee Chairman John H. Chafee, R-R.I., objected that this rewrote the highway law, legislating on an appropriations measure in violation of Senate rules. The Senate backed Shelby, 62-35.

As the conference prepared to meet, Shuster objected loudly on the issue, warning members of the Transportation Committee that the Shelby move would divert back to the states more than $90 million that could be earmarked by individual lawmakers.

Conferees scaled back the Shelby provision. Instead of redirecting $210 million to the states, conferees settled on $112 million. The funding to be sent back to the states did not include any from the accounts Shuster had targeted for special projects.

Favorite Projects

Individual projects requested by lawmakers also were a subject of extensive negotiations before the conference formally met Sept. 29.

Conferees divided up billions of dollars in federal transit funds. Shelby backed off from an attempt to rewrite the distribution formula for basic federal transit grants. But conferees did specify how to distribute $2.5 billion in discretionary funds for new rail projects and local bus systems. Since 1993, the allocations have been painstakingly detailed in conference.

Among the big winners this year were West Virginia, with a $12 million earmark for a facility in Huntington; Wisconsin, with $14.5 million for buses and bus projects; Minnesota, with two $10 million earmarks; Michigan, with $22.5 million for statewide bus service; and Florida, with $13.5 million for buses in Tampa.

Besides the designations for buses and new transit projects, lawmakers specified: $113 million for "intelligent" transportation projects; $59 million for transportation corridors; $50 million in projects aimed at getting welfare recipients into jobs; $50 million for roads on federal lands; $48 million for bridges; $25 million for community preservation projects; and $11 million for ferries.

The Clinton administration objected to the expansion of congressional involvement in the programs, most of which have been left to the discretion of the Transportation Department. But the administration stopped short of issuing a veto threat.

Truck and Bus Safety

The conference report also reflects the final decision on a number of contentious policies that had been fought out during floor debate.

Conferees kept language offered by House Appropriations Transportation Subcommittee Chairman Frank R. Wolf, R-Va., intended to spur the Transportation Department to beef up its truck and bus safety rules. The language would cut off funding for the Office of Motor Carriers unless it is moved out of the Federal Highway Administration. The provision has potentially wide-ranging implications for motor carrier safety.

The House Transportation Committee approved a bill (HR 2679) in August that would create a new Motor Carrier Administration. The Senate Commerce Committee has held one hearing on a similar bill (S 1501), sponsored by John McCain, R-Ariz.

But from the time the president signs the bill until the time the motor carrier measures clear Congress, the Transportation Department will have to come up with an interim truck safety plan, or face a cutoff of $70 million.

The Federal Highway Administration has faced increasing criticism on motor carrier safety this year. An April report of the Transportation Department's inspector general criticized the highway administration for collaborating with the trucking industry at the same time the number of trucking-related highway deaths was increasing to almost 5,400 in 1997.

As the number of deaths increased, the highway administration has conducted fewer inspections of trucking companies and has levied fewer fines.

CAFE Standards

The conference report also includes House language to prevent the Department of Transportation from spending any funds on updating fuel efficiency (CAFE) standards. The Clinton administration backed an effort in the Senate to fight the ban, but that effort failed on the Senate floor. Without that Senate language, conferees quickly agreed to keep the House ban in place.

The conference report kept "sense of the Senate" language that aims to bolster efforts to protect the rights of airline passengers.

Ron Wyden, D-Ore., sponsored two provisions designed to increase Department of Transportation efforts to investigate complaints that an airline overbooked a flight or failed to provide a consumer with the lowest available fare.

Opponents of the effort noted that the airline industry has recently unveiled an initiative to address consumer complaints.

The Wyden provisions were largely changed to "sense of the Senate" language that encourages the department to consider the overbooking and low-fare information as it prepares a report on unfair or deceptive practices of the airline industry. The department is still required by law to produce a report, Wyden aides noted.

Conferees kept the Wyden language in the conference report.

Privacy Concerns

At the only official meeting of the conference, on Sept. 29, House and Senate negotiators spent the bulk of their time trying to hash out a compromise on language by Shelby to crack down on the distribution of motor vehicle information for commercial purposes.

"I'm concerned that private information is too available," Shelby told the conferees.

Shelby said the thrust of his provision was to change the default setting for whether personal information would be available for sale for marketing purposes. Instead of individuals having the ability to "opt out" of databases available for purchases, Shelby said, they would now have to "opt in," choosing to allow their information to be available in such databases.

House negotiators said they were concerned that the Shelby language could have wide-ranging implications for a number of industries. But Wolf said most House concerns had been satisfied by narrowing the scope of the provision so that most of the protections centered on four categories of personal information: photographs, medical information, disability information and Social Security numbers.

Sonny Callahan, R-Ala., said the provision would have a devastating effect on Alabama's used-car warranty industry and pressed for an amendment giving the industry an exemption. Callahan's amendment was rejected by House conferees on a voice vote.

Final Bill Provides More Money But Limits Spending Options

OCTOBER 9 — Congress sent President Clinton a relatively generous fiscal 2000 Transportation appropriations bill Oct. 4, giving the administration virtually all of the record-level funding it sought but changing some of the priorities.

The Senate cleared the $50.2 billion conference report on the bill (HR 2084) by 88-3. *(Vote 306, p. S-61)*

The fate of the measure was never in doubt after conferees worked out compromises on contentious provisions, deciding to fund the Federal Aviation Administration (FAA) entirely from the Airport and Airway Trust Fund, keeping most driver license information private and sharing with states a $1.5 billion gasoline tax windfall.

The administration has not threatened to veto the bill, usually one of the easier spending measures to enact because of its public works spending. But the White House did raise concerns, including the large number of spending earmarks and a potential cut-off of authority to conduct truck safety activities.

The conference report would provide $28.9 billion for highways — $27.8 billion in obligation limits on the Highway Trust Fund and $1.1 billion in obligations for projects exempt from the limits under previous authorization bills. The $5.8 billion for mass transit includes $4.6 billion in obligation limits on the trust fund and $1.15 billion in new budget authority.

The highway total — which accounts for 57 percent of the final bill's spending — is a 6 percent increase over fiscal 1999 and a 1 percent increase over Clinton's budget request. The total was preset by the 1998 surface transportation law (PL 105-178) to prevent trust fund money from being spent elsewhere. *(1998 Almanac, p. 24-27)*

The greatest blow to the president's budget request was in a program intended to help welfare recipients reach jobs, primarily in the suburbs. The administration requested a doubling of funding, from the fiscal 1999 level of $75 million to $150 million. The final bill would keep funding at $75 million.

Limited Choices

For months, transportation appropriators have lamented their loss of control over highway and transit money. They also complained that spending limits in the 1997 balanced-budget law (PL 105-33), combined with the surface transportation law "firewalls," left them little flexibility to make decisions on aviation, rail and Coast Guard programs. *(1997 Almanac, p. 2-18)*

This was especially true of aviation programs. The FAA would receive a total of $10.1 billion, including $5.9 billion for operations and a $1.95 billion limit on trust fund obligations for airport grants-in-aid. The House had struck the $5.9 billion from its bill June 23 in a procedural battle over whether the money would come from the airport trust fund or the general fund. The money, all from the trust fund, was restored in conference, but at a level $139 million below the president's budget request. That led to complaints by administration officials.

On Sept. 29, the day the transportation conference met, Office of Management and Budget Director Jack Lew wrote Senate Transportation Appropriations Subcommittee Chairman Richard C. Shelby, R-Ala., that the FAA operations funding level Congress planned would not provide "sufficient resources to maintain current service levels, let alone meet increased demands."

When the Senate cleared the conference report, Transportation Secretary Rodney Slater said the final bill had "inadequate levels of funding for aviation operations and capital programs."

At the beginning of the year, appropriators said severe cuts might have to be made in the budget for the Coast Guard and Amtrak in order to meet the budget caps and the spending required for highways and transit. In the end, an increase in the House Transportation Appropriations Subcommittee's 302(b) allocation ensured that neither program took a severe hit.

The bill would provide $4 billion for the Coast Guard, an increase of $128.1 million over the fiscal 1999 level and close to what Clinton requested.

Amtrak would receive $571 million, matching Clinton's request. That is $38 million less than the rail carrier received in fiscal 1999, but it is consistent with Amtrak's five-year plan to phase out its federal subsidy. *(1998 Almanac, p. 2-85)*

Favored Spending

In his observations on the conference report, Slater was particularly critical of the growing number of projects for which Congress has stipulated spending, often skewing Transportation Department priorities. The final bill goes beyond traditional earmarks for highways, bridges and transit systems to include community preservation projects, "intelligent" transportation systems, ferries and even specific cities and towns in the access-to-jobs program.

Slater said he was concerned about "the widespread earmarking of vital highway and transit programs without regard to criteria established to ensure that these are sound investments."

Individual projects requested by lawmakers also were a subject of extensive negotiations before the conference formally met Sept. 29.

Conferees divided up billions of dollars in federal transit funds. Shelby backed off from an attempt to rewrite the distribution formula for basic federal transit grants. But conferees did specify how to distribute $2.5 billion in discretionary funds for new rail projects and local bus systems. Since

Transportation Spending Highlights

Where the Money Goes

HR 2084 (Conference report: H Rept 106-355)

Spending Synopsis

The Senate cleared the conference report Oct. 4, by a vote of 88-3, after the House adopted the report, 304-91, on Oct. 1. The total cost of the final bill was $50.2 billion, including $14.4 billion in new budget authority, a $34.7 billion ceiling on obligations from the highway and aviation trust funds, and $1.1 billion in obligations from the highway trust for programs exempt from the obligation ceiling. The total is nearly identical to President Clinton's request, but $5.7 billion more than the House bill and $674.5 million more than the Senate version. The main difference from the House bill is the inclusion of $5.9 billion for FAA operations that was eliminated on the House floor.

- **Federal Aviation Administration**

The agency is slated to receive all of its $8.1 billion in new budget authority from the Airport and Airway Trust Fund, with no general fund support for operations, a change from current practice. The final bill includes a $1.9 billion ceiling on obligations from the trust fund for airport grants in aid.

- **Federal Highway Administration**

The report provides $28.9 billion for road projects, including a $27.8 billion limit on obligational authority from the highway trust fund and $1.1 billion in obligations for programs exempt from the limit. The total is $1.6 billion more than in fiscal 1999, $389.1 million more than Clinton requested but almost the same as the House and Senate passed.

- **Federal Transit Administration**

The conference report provides $1.2 billion in new budget authority — exactly what Clinton asked for and the House and Senate passed — and a $4.6 billion limit on obligational authority for mass transit programs, $291.3 million less than Clinton requested but $386.2 million more than in fiscal 1999.

- **Coast Guard**

The report provides $4 billion, $128.1 million more than in fiscal 1999 but virtually the same as Clinton requested and the House and Senate passed.

Hot-Button Issues

Δ **Airline passenger rights.** Conferees kept non-binding Senate language on the investigation of complaints that airlines overbook flights and do not provide information on the lowest fares.

Δ **Fuel economy.** Despite complaints from the White House and environmental groups, the final bill continues a ban on any government move toward changing vehicle fuel economy standards.

Δ **Truck and bus safety.** The report cuts off funding for the Office of Motor Carriers unless it is immediately moved out of the Federal Highway Administration.

Δ **Amtrak.** The National Railroad Passenger Corp.'s subsidy declined 6 percent to $571 million, part of a five-year plan to eliminate federal aid. The Amtrak Reform Council's duties would be expanded to include identifying routes that should be closed or changed.

Δ **Driver information.** The final bill prohibits states from distributing, without express consent, an individual's driver's license photograph, Social Security number or medical or disability information. Only the name, address and phone number could be distributed.

(figures are in thousands of dollars of new budget authority)

	Fiscal 1999 Appropriation	Fiscal 2000 Clinton Request	House Bill	Senate Bill	Conference Report
Federal Aviation Administration	$7,612,558	$8,531,000	$2,373,000	$8,053,102	$8,131,495
Federal Highway Administration	332,000	0	0	50,000	0
Federal Railroad Administration	777,791	642,477	718,724	749,653	734,952
Federal Transit Administration	1,138,200	1,159,000	1,159,000	1,159,000	1,159,000
Coast Guard	3,895,465	4,084,574	4,048,039	3,988,203	4,023,653
National Highway Traffic Safety Administration	89,400	2,000	89,400	74,900	89,400
Miscellaneous and rescissions	–141,405	220,769	– 33,888	– 151,336	230,557
GRAND TOTAL	**$13,704,009**	**$14,639,820**	**$8,354,275**	**$13,923,522**	**$14,369,057**
Limits on obligations and exempt obligations	*($33,519,847)*	*($35,518,266)*	*($36,119,566)*	*($35,576,266)*	*($35,805,266)*

TABLE: House and Senate Appropriations committees

1993, the allocations have been painstakingly detailed in conference.

The new rail projects were the largest earmarks in the bill, including $99 million for New Jersey's Hudson-Bergen project, $65 million for an extension of San Francisco's Bay Area Rapid Transit to the airport, $54 million for a South Boston piers transitway, $53 million for the Houston regional bus plan and $50 million each for an extension of the Los Angeles North Hollywood line and light rail projects in Dallas and St. Louis.

Lawmakers also designated $12 million for the Florida Memorial Bridge, $9 million for the Hoover Dam in Nevada and $9 million for a bridge on U.S. 82 in Greenville, Miss.

Besides the designations for buses and new transit projects, lawmakers specified $113 million for "intelligent" transportation systems, $59 million for transportation corridors, $50 million in projects aimed at getting welfare recipients to jobs, $50 million for roads on federal lands, $48 million for bridges, $25 million for community preservation projects and $11 million for ferries.

In a Senate speech, John McCain, R-Ariz., decried the practice: "Bill after bill, year after year, earmarks continue to divert needed federal resources away from more meritorious and deserving projects." ◆

Treasury-Postal Service Bill Includes Pay Raise for Next White House Resident

- **Bill:** HR 2490 — PL 106-58
- **Legislative action: Senate** passed S 1282 (S Rept 106-87) by voice vote July 1.

House passed HR 2490 (H Rept 106-231), 210-209, on July 15.

House adopted the conference report (H Rept 106-319) on HR 2490, 292-126, on Sept. 15.

Senate cleared the bill, 54-38, on Sept. 16.

President signed HR 2490 on Sept. 29.

SUMMARY

President Clinton signed the $28.2 billion fiscal 2000 spending bill for the Treasury Department, Postal Service and general government agencies on Sept. 29.

The bill's total was about 4 percent higher than in fiscal 1999, generally allowing programs to continue operating at current levels. Thanks, largely to the bill's generous funding allocation, Congress and Clinton reached agreement with relatively few partisan spats.

The bill doubles the pay of the next president, bringing it to $400,000 a year. The proposal — the first presidential pay increase in three decades — drew bipartisan support in Congress and from high-ranking officials in previous administrations. The bill was silent on congressional pay, allowing an automatic annual pay increase to take effect; the Treasury bill traditionally has been the vehicle for blocking the increase. The bill also includes a 4.8 percent pay increase for federal employees. It maintains current law requiring federal employee health plans that cover prescription drugs to cover a full range of contraceptives, while prohibiting those plans from covering most abortions.

The most contentious fights were over guns. The bill stalled for weeks as Democrats threatened to attach gun control amendments. House appropriators postponed a planned markup in May, following a school shooting in Conyers, Ga. Seven weeks later, with school shootings in Georgia and Littleton, Colo., no longer front-page news, Republicans moved the bill out of committee July 13 after defeating Democratic amendments, including a proposal to tighten requirements for background checks at gun shows, on nearly party-line votes. *(Gun control, p. 18-3)*

Efforts by House conservatives to cut proposed funding for the IRS led to another partisan fight and to a one-vote margin of victory for the bill on the floor. But the cuts were restored in conference, and the final bill won by comfortable margins in both chambers.

House Panel OKs Measure, Omits Funds for New Courthouses

MAY 15 — A Treasury-Postal Service appropriations bill that closely follows President Clinton's budget proposal coasted quietly to House subcommittee approval May 14, but as in previous years, the bill will likely become a magnet for controversial policy proposals as it continues through the committee process.

The unnumbered bill, approved by voice vote, would increase fiscal 2000 funding for numerous drug programs and measures to enforce gun laws. But it contains no funding for federal courthouse construction, a situation bemoaned by both Democratic and Republican appropriators. Jim Kolbe, R-Ariz., chairman of the House Treasury-Postal Service-General Government Appropriations Subcommittee, said that if additional funds become available, courthouse construction will be a top priority. "I'm concerned that our nation's infrastructure needs are not being met," Kolbe said.

The bill would provide $28.2 billion in budget authority, an increase of 4.1 percent over fiscal 1999. The bill funds the Treasury Department, construction and repair of some federal buildings, several independent agencies and the Executive Office of the President. Much of the money is for the Treasury Department, which oversees the nation's tax collections and performs numerous law enforcement tasks.

Kolbe said he believed that Clinton "would happily sign this bill." However, Kolbe criticized the president's request as "negligent" on law enforcement. The administration's budget called for using funds from a proposed fee on importers and brokers to help fund U.S. Customs Service programs. The fee has not been enacted, which resulted in a shortfall that could force the agency to cut its staff by 28 percent, Kolbe said. The subcommittee made up the shortfall from other accounts.

Ranking Democrat Steny H. Hoyer of Maryland agreed that nobody on the committee "reasonably expected" any revenue from the proposed tax. Hoyer also praised Kolbe's bill. "You have come close to funding most of the president's request," Hoyer said.

Amendments

The committee approved by voice vote an amendment by Lucille Roybal-Allard, D-Calif., to give the Office of National Drug Control Policy the authority to warn youths about the dangers of alcohol use. Roybal-Allard called alcohol a "gateway drug" that leads young people to use illegal drugs, and Frank R. Wolf, R-Va., agreed.

Kolbe, who voiced dissent on the vote, said it would be wrong to make such a change until there was evidence that such a program would help reduce alcohol consumption, and that for now the office should stick to its mission of

Proposed Presidential Pay Raise Would Ease Others' Salary 'Compression'

MAY 29 — An all-star lineup of former top White House officials spanning presidential administrations from Lyndon B. Johnson to the present urged Congress to boost the paycheck for the leader of the free world. The president's annual salary, frozen at $200,000 since 1969, is holding down the pay of other federal officials and will eventually start driving well-qualified people from public service, the witnesses testified.

The issue also has implications for the pay of members of Congress, whose top leaders are just a few cost-of-living increases away from overtaking the president.

Although a presidential raise would represent little more than a rounding error in the $1.8 trillion federal budget, lawmakers are keenly aware that it is an issue that will draw public attention. Presidential pay would be doubled under a provision in the unnumbered fiscal 2000 Treasury-Postal Service Appropriations bill, which is headed for a markup in June in the House Appropriations Committee.

Several former presidential advisers suggested a boost to $500,000, plus a mechanism for regular review. They also agreed that the public would generally be receptive to a presidential raise. John H. Sununu, chief of staff for President George Bush, suggested the public might even accept a raise to $1 million a year.

Thomas F. McLarty III, former chief of staff to President Clinton, said members of Congress can sell the issue to the public if they are honest and direct. "I don't think most people realize the president's pay has not been raised in 30 years," McLarty said.

The panel testified May 24 before the House Government Reform Subcommittee on Government Management, Information and Technology. Several said that while people do not run for president for the money, the president should be paid a sum that dignifies the office. "I think the American people are ready to take this, if it's given to them with the factual data that's been presented at this hearing," said Alexander M. Haig Jr., chief of staff to President Richard M. Nixon.

The Constitution prohibits raising the pay of the current occupant of the office, so any pay increase could not take effect until 2001.

In 1969, the salaries of the vice president and the chief justice of the United States — $62,500 each — amounted to 31 percent of the president's salary. Currently those two officials are paid $175,400, or 88 percent of the president's salary. If Congress does not raise the president's pay this session, the salary will be frozen until at least 2005. Depending on inflation, the salary of the vice president, which has increased automatically since Congress passed the 1975 Executive Salary Cost of Living Adjustment Act (PL 94-82), could overtake the president's before 2005, according to the Congressional Research Service. *(1975 Almanac, p. 703)*

The president's current salary would rank him 785th on the list of the 800 highest paid corporate chief executive officers, according to Paul C. Light, director of the Center for Public Service at the Brookings Institution. Although the public would not want its president paid tens of millions annually, Light said, polling data suggests there is substantial public support for a presidential raise, particularly when the people surveyed are told the president's pay has not been increased in three decades.

Testimony at the hearing was not unanimous, however. A bit of fireworks erupted when Gary Ruskin, executive director of the Congressional Accountability Project, accused Congress of conspiring to raise presidential pay just to ease the "compression" that holds down congressional and judicial salaries.

Members of Congress currently make $136,700 a year. The Speaker of the House makes $175,400. The majority and minority leaders of each chamber make $151,800.

Rather than dispute the notion that higher congressional salaries are in the offing, subcommittee member Democrat Paul E. Kanjorski of Pennsylvania angrily asked Ruskin whether he knew how expensive it was to maintain two residences, among other congressional financial burdens.

Ruskin held his ground, insisting that members of Congress should take a pay cut because even with their special circumstances, they already are paid enough to live much better than most people. "You all seem to exist on a different planet," Ruskin said.

dealing with controlled substances.

The committee rejected, by a 4-6 party-line vote, a Hoyer amendment to approve $55.9 million for the first phase of construction for a new Food and Drug Administration building in Maryland. The total cost of the building, which would allow the FDA to consolidate operations currently scattered throughout the Washington area, is estimated at $500 million.

Riders

In 1998, with election-year pressure bearing down on lawmakers, the Treasury-Postal Service bill was one of eight appropriations bills rolled into an omnibus bill (PL 105-277) — which traditionally is used as a vehicle for controversial legislative proposals — that effectively broke through budget caps set in 1997. The version incorporated in the omnibus law included provisions requiring federal employee health plans that cover prescription drugs to cover a full range of contraceptives, and it permitted about

50,000 Haitian refugees to remain permanently in the United States.

Other issues that came up in the House and Senate included "emergency" funding to help federal agencies deal with year 2000 computer problems; cost of living adjustments for members, federal judges and high executive branch officials; and term limits for the top two staff officials at the Federal Election Commission.

Few such issues came up this year at the subcommittee markup. But like last year's measure, the bill would continue the prohibition on using funds to pay for abortions through the Federal Employees Health Benefit Program. It would also require that the program fund prescription contraceptive services.

Allison Herwitt, director of government relations for the National Abortion and Reproductive Rights Action League, said her organization would try to strip the abortion prohibition from the bill. Herwitt said she also expected her organization to fight likely Republican attempts to pull the contraception provision from the bill.

Senate Bill Heads To Floor; House Action Stalled

JUNE 26 — A measure intended to crack down on violations of intellectual property rights by establishing a new coordination center in the Executive Office of the President was added to a Senate spending measure Republicans hope will win floor approval the week of June 28.

The proposal was added by voice vote as an amendment to the fiscal 2000 appropriations bill (S 1282) that funds the Treasury Department, the Executive Office, construction and repair of some federal buildings, and several independent agencies. It was approved, 28-0, by the Senate Appropriations Committee on June 24. The bill calls for $27.7 billion in budget authority, which is $839 million more than President Clinton requested. The largest chunk is for the Treasury Department, which oversees the nation's tax collections and performs law enforcement tasks.

Action on the unnumbered House version of the spending bill remained stalled as Republicans refused to bring up the measure while Democrats were threatening to use it as a vehicle for amendments on gun restrictions. House Appropriations Committee spokeswoman Elizabeth Morra said June 25 that Republicans were hoping to bring up the bill for a full committee vote the week of June 28, "but there are a lot of leadership decisions to be made in association with that."

Like its House counterpart, the Senate spending measure generally continues current services, with funding boosts for some anti-crime programs.

At the markup, Chairman Ted Stevens, R-Alaska, said his intellectual property amendment would help combat more than $18 billion in revenue losses annually suffered by record companies, movie studios and software companies whose products are copied and resold illegally. The amendment calls for the president to establish a National Intellectual Property Coordination Center to coordinate activities among local, state and foreign law enforcement agencies using existing funds within the Executive Office budget for the new center.

The bill was taken up by the full committee without formal action by the Treasury and General Government Appropriations Subcommittee, although subcommittee members informally laid out the blueprint for the full committee. Subcommittee Chairman Ben Nighthorse Campbell, R-Colo., said tight budget caps on discretionary spending made the task difficult. "Overall, I think we have a good bill, given our constraints," Campbell said.

Echoing concerns raised in a House subcommittee markup of the Treasury spending measure May 14, Campbell complained that there was no money available for new courthouse construction, and that the administration had left a $312 million hole in its budget request by counting on revenues from a fee that was never enacted. The administration's budget called for using funds from a proposed fee on importers to help fund U.S. Customs Service programs.

Jon Kyl, R-Ariz., said he plans to offer an amendment on the floor to provide $50 million to be used to help fund 500 new Customs positions. Kyl said the administration has severely underfunded the Customs Service in recent years, resulting in spotty enforcement of illegal drug trafficking laws and lengthy waits at the Mexican border for truckers trying to move goods across the border. "There is a very urgent and immediate need for more Customs inspectors," Kyl said. He said he would come up with offsetting cuts to fund his proposal.

Neither the House nor the Senate bill would block a cost of living pay increase for members of Congress, whose $136,700 annual salaries would rise by about $4,600. The raises are automatic unless Congress votes to stop them. The House bill calls for boosting the president's pay from $200,000 to $400,000 annually. The Senate measure contains no presidential pay increase.

The House bill, which would provide $28.2 billion in new budget authority, has been stalled since May 14. Democrats have threatened to force votes on gun control amendments, and Republicans have balked at bringing up the bill at the full committee until Democrats back off.

In a June 22 interview, Rep. Nita M. Lowey, D-N.Y., said Democrats were willing to stand firm on the gun issue, even if it pushes Congress to a repeat of 1998, when the Treasury-Postal Service bill was one of eight measures rolled into an omnibus spending bill (PL 105-277) that effectively broke through budget caps set in 1997. *(1998 Almanac, p. 2-112)*

"If they're not going to work with us, we may end up with a great big omnibus bill," Lowey said.

Senate Passes Bill To Fund Treasury, Other Agencies

JULY 3 — After fighting a familiar battle involving federal workers and abortion, the Senate on July 1 easily passed a $27.7 billion spending plan that funds the Treasury and numerous other government agencies.

The fiscal 2000 appropriations bill (S 1282) that funds the Treasury Department, the Executive Office of the President, construction and repair of some federal buildings, and several independent agencies was approved on a voice vote July 1. An effort to kill the anti-abortion provision, which would extend current law that prohibits federal workers' health care plans from paying for most abortions, was rejected, 47-51. *(Vote 197, p. S-39)*

Action on the House version of the spending bill remained stalled, as Republicans refused to bring up the measure while Democrats threatened to use it as a vehicle for amendments that would restrict guns.

The Senate spending bill calls for for $27.7 billion in budget authority. Mandatory spending accounts for $14.5 billion of the bill. Like its unnumbered House counterpart, the Senate spending measure generally continues current services, with funding boosts for some anti-crime programs.

The Treasury Department, which oversees numerous law enforcement functions and tax collections, gets the largest chunk of funding, a total of $12.2 billion in budget authority under the Senate bill.

Ben Nighthorse Campbell, R-Colo., chairman of the Treasury and General Government Appropriations Subcommittee, praised the overall funding levels in the measure, although he expressed some concerns about the amount of money available for new facilities. "For the third year in a row, the administration has not requested funding for courthouse construction," Campbell said June 30 on the Senate floor. "Unfortunately, due to the very limited funding available to the committee, we have not included any new courthouse construction projects."

The bill includes a provision added by the Senate Appropriations Committee on June 24 to crack down on violations of intellectual property rights by establishing a new coordination center in the Executive Office of the President.

Neither the House nor the Senate bill would block a cost of living pay increase for members of Congress, whose $136,700 annual salaries would rise by about $4,600. The raises are automatic unless Congress votes to stop them. The House bill calls for boosting the president's pay from $200,000 to $400,000 annually. The Senate measure contains no such increase.

Jon Kyl, R-Ariz., offered an amendment on the floor to provide $50 million for 500 new Customs positions. Kyl said an underfunded Customs Service has had trouble enforcing drug-trafficking laws and has produced lengthy waits at the Mexican border for truckers trying to move goods. However, Kyl acknowledged the difficulty in implementing his plan while staying within budget caps.

The amendment was approved by voice vote after it was modified to say that the hirings would be funded by unspecified Customs Service programs, in addition to funds provided to the Customs Service under the fiscal 1999 supplemental spending bill (PL 106-31). *(1998 Almanac, p. 2-117)*

House Passes Bill By Single Vote; Still, Conference Should Be Smooth

JULY 17 — Despite controversial policy votes and a lack of bipartisan support in the House, reconciling the fiscal 2000 appropriations bill that funds the Treasury Department, Postal Service and other government agencies with its Senate counterpart should be relatively uncomplicated.

The versions of the bill that emerged from the two chambers — albeit by a single vote majority in the House — have similar spending blueprints and no major policy differences, although the Senate bill does not include a pay increase for the president.

Lawmakers from both parties and both chambers grumbled about the absence of funding for new courthouse construction, and House fights over gun amendments stalled the bill for weeks. In the latest action, the House voted 210-209 on July 15 to pass a $28 billion spending plan (HR 2490), including $13.5 billion in discretionary spending. *(Vote 305, p. H-102)*

The bill generally would allow programs to continue operating at current levels and would fund some anti-crime initiatives. It totals $460 million less in budget authority than President Clinton requested, but $878 million more than the fiscal 1999 plan.

Pay Raises

Under the House bill, the next president's pay would double to $400,000. The measure also continues to bar health-benefit plans for federal employees from paying for abortions under most circumstances, after an effort to eliminate the provision failed.

House members use the bill to position themselves for an automatic cost of living increase to their annual salaries (this year a $4,600 boost to their $136,700 pay). Members get the increase unless they vote to block it, and the Treasury appropriations bill traditionally has been the vehicle used to do so. But with almost no debate, the House members sidestepped an opportunity to block a pay raise for themselves on a 276-147 procedural vote that prevented the measure from being offered. *(Vote 300, p. H-100)*

In an interview July 14, Rep. Steny H. Hoyer of Maryland, the ranking Democrat on the Treasury-Postal Service Appropriations Subcommittee, said Congress enacted the automatic pay raise measure so members would get smaller, incremental raises rather than fight over big, infrequent boosts of $10,000 or $15,000. "I think members have come to grips with the fact that an annual cost of living adjustment is understandable," Hoyer said.

The House bill also would raise the president's annual pay from $200,000 to $400,000. An amendment offered by Pete Sessions, R-Texas, to strip the presidential pay raise from the bill was defeated, 82-334. *(Vote 302, p. H-102)*

Treasury-Postal Service Appropriations Subcommittee Chairman Jim Kolbe, R-Ariz., praised the bill on the floor as a bipartisan product.

However, Hoyer said Republicans destroyed Democratic support for the measure at the Appropriations markup July 13 when they approved a $240 funding reduction. "They are pandering to some of their most conservative members," Hoyer said after the July 15 floor vote.

The Senate passed its bill (S 1282), which calls for $27.7 billion in budget authority, on July 1.

The Treasury Department, which oversees tax collections and numerous law enforcement functions, would get the largest chunk of funding — $12.2 billion in both the House bill and the Senate bill. The bill also funds the Executive Office of the President, the upkeep of some federal buildings, and a small slice of the Postal Service budget, including services for the blind.

Gun Disputes

The bill stalled in the House for weeks after Democrats threatened to use it as a vehicle for amendments to toughen gun controls. The stalemate was solidified May 20 when news of a school shooting in Conyers, Ga., arrived just as the Appropriations Committee prepared to take up the spending plan. Republicans postponed the markup indefinitely.

Seven weeks later, with the school shootings in Georgia and Littleton, Colo., no longer front page news and juvenile justice legislation (S 254, HR 1501) nearing completion, House Republicans decided to move the spending bill. The Appropriations Committee approved it July 13 by voice vote.

At the markup, three Democratic amendments related to gun sales and safety were defeated on nearly partyline votes.

Hoyer offered an amendment to tighten requirements for background checks at gun shows. It failed, 24-35. Nita M. Lowey, D-N.Y., offered an amendment to restrict the import of high capacity magazines, which failed, 24-34. Rosa DeLauro, D-Conn., offered an amendment to require dealers to include child safety locks with handgun sales. It failed, 24-34.

Committee member and Majority Whip Tom DeLay, R-Texas, pleaded for the defeat of the amendments, saying conferees for the juvenile justice measures would be named soon. DeLay stressed that he expected some of the gun provisions to be included in the conference measure.

Controversial Cut

Democrats strongly objected at the markup to a GOP amendment by Kolbe to trim $240 million from proposed spending for the Internal Revenue Service and the General Services Administration, which is responsible for repairs and alterations of federal buildings. Democrats complained that House leaders were applying pressure on committee Republicans to make the cuts to appease a small band of conservatives led by Tom Coburn, R-Okla.

David R. Obey of Wisconsin, the ranking Democrat on the Appropriations Committee, complained that the cuts were big enough to hurt programs but not big enough to significantly affect overall federal spending. Several panel Republicans also complained about pressure from their leaders. Kolbe's amendment was adopted, 33-26.

The administration issued a statement saying it "strongly opposes" the cuts but did not threaten to veto the measure.

Both the House and Senate measures would continue current law by prohibiting federal health plans from paying for most abortions and requiring that such plans cover contraception.

On the floor, an amendment to strike the restriction on abortion coverage, offered by DeLauro, was defeated, 188-230. *(Vote 301, p. H-102)*

The Senate bill includes a measure that aims to bolster intellectual property rights by establishing a coordination center in the Executive Office of the President to fight the illegal reproduction of copyrighted materials. The House bill contains no such provision.

Conferees Add Presidential Pay Raise, Restore Funding for IRS

SEPTEMBER 11 — Controversial cuts in IRS funding, which Democrats said would undermine the agency's congressionally mandated modernization efforts, were rescinded in a compromise fiscal 2000 appropriations bill that could go to the floors of both chambers the week of Sept. 13.

House-Senate conferees also approved a pay boost for the president, doubling the annual salary to $400,000, a provision that was in the House version of the bill but not in the Senate's. If adopted, it will be the first presidential pay increase in more than three decades.

Conferees reached agreement Sept. 9 on the $28.2 billion spending bill (HR 2490), which funds the Treasury Department, Postal Service, executive office of the president and other government agencies. The bill also leaves the door open for a congressional pay raise. Members get an automatic annual pay increase unless they vote to block it, and the Treasury appropriations bill traditionally has been the vehicle used to do so. The spending plan would not block the increase, so members are likely to get a $4,600 increase above their $136,700 annual salaries. The bill also includes a 4.8 percent pay increase for federal employees, the same as for military employees under the pending defense appropriations bill (HR 2561).

The Treasury measure calls for $12.4 billion in budget authority for the Treasury Department, compared with $12.6 billion in fiscal 1999, and $8.3 billion for the IRS, down from $8.4 billion in fiscal 1999.

The conference measure also would continue current law on two controversial reproductive issues. It would bar health insurance plans for federal employees from paying for abortions under most circumstances and would require the plans to pay for contraceptives.

The bill calls for $13.7 billion in discretionary budget authority. The rest is for mandatory spending, mainly for federal workers' health and pension benefits. Most differences between the bills were reconciled by staff members before the Sept. 9 meeting. Conferees approved the measure by voice vote in a brief session in which only one amendment was offered, and defeated, 2-4, by Senate panel members. House conferees did not vote on the amendment.

The amendment, offered by Sen. Jon Kyl, R-Ariz., would have curtailed the president's ability to intervene in cases in which plaintiffs attempt to collect damages they have been awarded against foreign governments. The president has intervened occasionally in such cases for national security reasons.

House Treasury-Postal Service Appropriations Subcommittee Chairman Jim Kolbe, R-Ariz., said he agreed with the goal of the amendment but believed the appropriations bill was the wrong place for it.

Members of both parties from both chambers praised the bill as a bipartisan effort that accomplished much, given budgetary restraints. The bill was one of the more generously funded

Treasury-Postal Spending Highlights

Where the Money Goes

HR 2490 (Conference report: H Rept 106-319)

Spending Synopsis:

The fiscal 2000 Treasury-Postal Service conference report adopted by the House on Sept. 15 and cleared by the Senate on Sept. 16 provides $28.2 billion for the Treasury Department, Postal Service, Executive Office of the President, and independent agencies such as the General Services Administration, Office of Personnel Management and Federal Election Commission. Appropriators control only about half the money; the rest is mandatory spending, mainly for federal workers' health and pension benefits.

• Treasury Department

The Treasury Department received $12.4 billion in budget authority under the spending plan, including $8.2 billion for the IRS. Conferees restored about $135 million in controversial House cuts to the IRS. Other Treasury agencies include the Customs Service, bank regulators, the U.S. Mint and the Financial Management Service, which keeps the federal books. Treasury is also responsible for the Bureau of Alcohol, Tobacco and Firearms (ATF) and the Secret Service. In addition, the bill provides some payments under permanent authority that do not require congressional consideration. The largest is payment of net interest on the public debt, expected to be $222 billion in fiscal 2000.

• Postal Service

Although the quasi-private Postal Service funds its own operations, Congress provides an annual payment — $93 million in fiscal 2000 — to subsidize free or discounted delivery to qualified organizations such as nonprofit groups.

• Executive Office of the President

The Executive Office of the President, including the president's salary and White House agencies such as the Office of Management and Budget, received $645 million. The bill doubled the president's salary to $400,000.

• General Services Administration

The General Services Administration, which is responsible for maintaining and renovating federal buildings, got $152 million. The measure contains no funding for new courthouse construction.

Hot-Button Issues

Δ **Guns.** The bill's funding for the ATF has made the measure a target for gun control advocates. Democrats failed to attach gun restrictions.

Δ **Contraceptives.** The bill continues an existing requirement that federal employee health plans that cover prescription drugs cover a full range of contraceptives.

Δ **Abortion.** The bill continues a ban on federal employees receiving abortions through their taxpayer-subsidized health plans, except in cases of rape, incest or danger to the woman's life.

Δ **Pay increases.** In past years, the bill has carried an amendment blocking an automatic pay increase for members and judges. Leaders avoided that amendment this year, so congressional salaries are set to rise $4,600 above the current annual salary of $136,700. Federal employees were slated to get pay increases of 4.8 percent.

Δ **Breast feeding.** The bill mandates that women be allowed to breast feed on federal property.

(figures are in thousands of dollars of new budget authority)

	Fiscal 1999 Appropriation	Fiscal 2000 Clinton Request	House Bill	Senate Bill	Conference Report
Treasury Department	$12,637,225	$12,376,130	$12,189,648	$12,214,649	$12,354,616
Customs Service	(2,049,154)	(1,829,783)	(1,817,502)	(1,782,435)	(1,817,052)
IRS	(8,375,165)	(8,248,774)	(8,109,774)	(8,191,135)	(8,248,774)
Postal Service	100,195	93,436	93,436	93,436	93,436
Executive Office of the President	670,112	639,498	654,759	570,128	645,489
General Services Administration	643,960	158,316	146,006	156,297	151,781
Office of Personnel Management	13,480,640	14,355,105	14,354,105	14,355,105	14,354,105
Other Independent Agencies	390,580	374,569	362,151	364,982	372,991
GRAND TOTAL	$27,122,137	$28,460,249	$27,999,867	$27,933,949	$28,245,461

TABLE: House, Senate Appropriations committees

of the 13 annual appropriations measures. It generally would allow programs to continue operating at current levels and would fund some anti-crime initiatives.

"I think this bill is a responsible package," said Rep. Steny H. Hoyer of Maryland, ranking Democrat on the subcommittee.

The tone of the conference was far different from the debate on the House floor, where the spending plan passed by one vote. Hoyer voted against the bill on the floor because he and other Democrats strongly objected to a GOP-led cut in committee of $240 million from proposed spending for the IRS and the General Services Administration, which handles repairs and alterations of federal buildings. Democrats complained that House leaders pressured Republicans to make the cuts to appease a small band of GOP conservatives led by Tom Coburn of Oklahoma.

Hoyer said that because conferees had agreed to restore $135 million cut from IRS funds, he would support the conference measure on the floor.

Presidential Pay Raise

If enacted, the presidential pay raise would not take effect until the next president took office. In hearings in May, a panel of luminaries from administrations past and present endorsed the pay raise, including John H. Sununu, chief of staff to President George Bush; Thomas F. McLarty III, former chief of staff to President Clinton; and Alexander M. Haig Jr., chief of staff to President Richard M. Nixon.

Supporters of the increase argued that the president is underpaid, that not all presidents have substantial personal wealth while they are in office and that the public would be willing to accept an increase.

Final Bill Includes Pay Raises for All

SEPTEMBER 18 — President Clinton is expected to sign the fiscal 2000 spending plan for the Treasury Department, Postal Service and other government agencies, which the Senate cleared Sept. 16 after Internal Revenue Service funds cut in the bill were restored.

The measure includes a pay increase for the next president, doubling the annual salary to $400,000, and a 4.8 percent increase for federal employees. It would allow an automatic boost for members of Congress, raising their $136,700 salaries by $4,600.

It also would require that women be permitted to breast feed on federal property. The breast-feeding provision had been pushed by Rep. Carolyn B. Maloney, D-N.Y., who co-chairs the Congressional Women's Caucus, and by Treasury-Postal Service Appropriations Subcommittee member Lucille Roybal-Allard, D-Calif., among others. It was added on the House floor July 15.

The House adopted the conference report on the $28.2 billion bill (HR 2490) on Sept. 15 by a vote of 292-126. The Senate cleared it, 54-38, the next day. *(House vote 426, p. H-136; Senate vote 277, p. S-54)*

Final congressional action was eased by the decision of House-Senate conferees, who reached agreement on the plan Sept. 9, to restore about $135 million in IRS funding cuts made by the House Appropriations Committee at the request of a group of conservatives led by Tom Coburn, R-Okla. Rep. Steny H. Hoyer of Maryland, ranking Democrat on the Appropriations subcommittee, said there was broad agreement among conferees to restore the cuts.

Coburn was the only member to speak against the measure on the House floor.

He complained that a 4.8 percent pay increase for federal employees was excessive. Coburn said the increase was particularly unreasonable when compared with the 1.8 percent cost of living increase that Social Security recipients will be getting. Giving federal workers more than the 4.4 percent increase requested by Clinton will cost an additional $330 million at a time when Congress is on the verge of breaking the 1997 budget agreement (PL 105-33), Coburn said. *(1997 Almanac, p. 2-3)*

"So not only are we not supplying our seniors with what they should have through an equitable Social Security system, but what we are doing is we are taking $330 million that ultimately will come from Social Security," Coburn said.

In the Senate, Bob Graham, D-Fla., complained on the floor Sept. 16 that the bill would help push spending over the budget caps. Both Coburn and Graham voted against the spending plan.

But appropriators from both chambers and both parties praised the bill as a sensible, bipartisan product.

Rep. Jim Kolbe, R-Ariz., chairman of the Appropriations subcommittee, said that restoring the cuts to the IRS was necessary for the agency to meet its congressionally mandated obligation to improve efficiency and customer service.

Byron L. Dorgan of North Dakota, ranking Democrat on the Senate Appropriations subcommittee, said the spending plan required sacrifices, including no funding for new federal courthouse construction. "We are short of money, so we had to make some difficult choices," Dorgan said Sept. 16. ◆

Compromise Boosts Funds For Veterans' Health Care, Provides Hurricane Relief

- **Bill:** HR 2684 — PL 106-74
- **Legislative action: House** passed HR 2684 (H Rept 106-286), 235-187, on Sept. 9.

Senate passed HR 2684 by voice vote Sept. 24, after substituting the text of S 1596 (S Rept 106 161).

House adopted the conference report (H Rept 106-379), 406-18, on Oct. 14.

Senate cleared the bill, 93-5, on Oct. 15.

President signed HR 2684 on Oct. 20.

SUMMARY

The fiscal 2000 spending bill for the departments of Veterans Affairs (VA) and Housing and Urban Development (HUD) and independent agencies sailed to enactment once Republicans abandoned plans to hew to spending caps set by the 1997 Balanced Budget Act (PL 105-33) and the White House showed a willingness to find funding offsets for its spending priorities.

The measure provided a total of $99.5 billion for fiscal 2000, 4 percent more than in fiscal 1999 and just $150 million less than requested. The total included $4.2 billion in advance fiscal 2001 spending for HUD rental assistance and $2.5 billion in "emergency" disaster relief funding to help victims of Hurricane Floyd. It provided $28.6 billion, 6 percent more than in fiscal 1999, in programmatic funding for HUD; $44.3 billion for the VA, including a $1.7 billion increase for veterans health care; $7.6 billion for the EPA and $13.7 billion for NASA.

Although the final package won overwhelming bipartisan support, the bill had a rough start. To adhere to the 1997 spending caps, the bill's initial spending allocation was set well below the fiscal 1999 level. To soften the impact, House appropriators shifted $4 billion from the spending bill for the departments of Labor and Health and Human Services (HHS) and assumed $3 billion in savings from Tennessee Valley Authority borrowing authority. Still, the $92 billion bill was $3.3 billion below fiscal 1999 and $7.6 billion less than requested. The measure also would have eliminated funding for the Selective Service System and for President Clinton's AmeriCorps national service program.

House Democrats argued that Republicans were using the deep cuts in housing, space and other programs to make room for their proposed $792 billion tax cut, while Republicans defended the cuts as necessary to comply with the spending caps. After an acrimonious debate, the House passed the bill on a largely party-line vote after rejecting most attempts to restore funding.

In the Senate, appropriators shifted $7 billion from the Labor-HHS allocation to increase funding for housing and space programs and to fund the Selective Service and AmeriCorps, in the hope of averting a presidential veto. While $1.6 billion larger than the House version, it was still below fiscal 1999 funding and considered insufficient by the administration. To help stay within spending limits, the Senate used two budgetary devices rejected by House appropriators — "advance" fiscal 2001 funding for $4.2 billion in HUD rental assistance and the use of "emergency" designation for $600 million for VA health care, which meant the money did not count under the caps.

In conference, with Republicans eager to avert budgetary gridlock and a possible government shutdown, GOP leaders abandoned plans to adhere to the 1997 spending caps and focused instead on avoiding using any of the expected fiscal 2000 Social Security surplus. With the administration willing to provide offsets for requested funding increases, conferees completed negotiations swiftly.

Among other things, conferees agreed to the advance fiscal 2001 funding for housing and the emergency funding for disaster assistance, although the emergency designation for VA health care was removed. The administration agreed to $2.2 billion in rescissions of previously approved housing funds to offset increases in other high priority programs — including more than $340 million for 60,000 new housing vouchers to provide rental assistance to additional families.

The final bill funded the Selective Service and AmeriCorps, and it included provisions from a House-passed bill (HR 202) to enable elderly and disabled residents to remain in their homes when landlords discontinue participation in federal low-income housing programs.

House Panel OKs Bill; Challenges Await on House, Senate Floors

JULY 31 — House appropriators reduced a proposed cut in the space program and shifted money into a popular veterans' health care program, clearing the way for floor debate the week of Aug. 2 on the fiscal 2000 spending bill for the departments of Veterans Affairs (VA) and Housing and Urban Development (HUD) and independent agencies.

The tricky job of finding the right chemistry for the third-largest spending bill has been complicated in the 106th Congress by vociferous demands for increases in popular programs, ranging from veterans' services to initiatives to combat poverty.

Faced with competing demands from lobbying groups from the American Legion, a veterans advocacy group, to the National League of Cities, representing city government officials, lawmakers are struggling to craft a bill that can win support while complying with tight spending caps set by the balanced-budget act of 1997 (PL 105-33).

The House Appropriations Committee approved a $92 billion, fiscal 2000 VA-HUD spending bill by voice vote July 30. The unnumbered would provide a slight decrease over the fiscal 1999 funding level of $93.4 billion.

The vote came just four days after the bill was unveiled in a House Appropriations subcommittee markup. But the version that emerged from the full committee was much different from the original.

Despite the changes, the bill is likely to face major challenges on the House floor and in the Senate, as members continue to shift money between programs to attract votes and comply with the spending caps.

Senate Appropriations Committee Chairman Ted Stevens, R-Alaska, said July 27 that he would closely study the House bill and then decide on funding levels for programs under the bill.

"I just have to understand what it means to our allocations and see what we have to do to re-allocate money in the Senate to take care of the changes that they have suggested," Stevens said. The Senate Appropriations VA-HUD Subcommittee, chaired by Christopher S. Bond, R-Mo., is not expected to mark up the bill until September.

Take and Give

The House committee's vote came after adoption by voice vote of a manager's amendment that dramatically altered the bill.

The amendment kept the focus on increases in veterans' services, but reversed course on measures used to pay for the bill, including elimination of $5.5 billion in proposed "emergency" spending — $3 billion for veterans' health care and $2.5 billion for the Federal Emergency Management Agency (FEMA).

Instead of relying on the budgetary gimmick of emergency funding, which is not subject to the budget caps, the amendment provided additional funding to pay for the increases in veterans' health care.

The money was taken from the largest of the spending bills, for the departments of Labor, Health and Human Services, and Education.

Appropriations Committee Chairman C.W. Bill Young, R-Fla., said he believes that move will answer complaints about the bill and lay the groundwork for passage by the House.

"This is the last time we will rob Peter to pay Paul," Young said.

Alan B. Mollohan, D-W.Va., said the bill would make too many cuts in too many programs. "It does some good. But it does future harm," he said.

The manager's amendment addressed another key obstacle by providing $400 million for NASA, reducing a proposed cut in the agency's budget from $1.4 billion, or 10 percent, to $1 billion, or 7 percent.

It also shifted money from other VA-HUD programs, including $400 million from AmeriCorps, the federal volunteer service program, to the space program.

The amendment also incorporated other concessions designed to mollify critics, including $19 billion for veterans' health care, an increase of $1.7 billion over President Clinton's request and $700 million more than House appropriators originally proposed.

Faced with a potential revolt by fiscal conservatives, appropriators jettisoned the controversial provision calling for emergency funding.

The bill was attacked by editorial writers for several major newspapers. The New York Times accused lawmakers of using a loophole in the balanced-budget law to treat ordinary programs as if they were "a flood or earthquake."

Stephen Slivinski, a fiscal policy analyst at the Washington-based Cato Institute, a libertarian think tank, charged that the maneuver looked like a clear attempt to get around spending caps.

"It is not a good thing to use emergency spending for programs like this," he said.

Emergency funding was a linchpin of the original, draft bill unveiled at the House VA-HUD Appropriations Subcommittee markup July 26. The panel approved the bill by voice vote.

Republican James T. Walsh of New York, the subcommittee's chairman, initially defended the use of emergency funding, noting that it would help to pay for FEMA's assistance with disasters and avert layoffs in the Department of Veterans Affairs. Moreover, he argued, the cuts and other restraining measures were needed to pay for the bill.

"Everybody will feel a little pain," he said.

Appeal for Votes

With the issue of emergency funding taken care of, appropriators turned to the task of resolving objections to the bill and increasing funding for pet programs.

The bill would provide $258.6 million to pay for 118 water and waste water projects, including $7.5 million for drinking water infrastructure improvements in the district of Speaker J. Dennis Hastert, R-Ill. An additional $56 million would be provided for 26 environmental programs.

In another maneuver by appropriators to drum up support for the bill, a series of funding increases was proposed for veterans' health care.

The American Legion charged that the administration's request of $17.3 billion for veterans' medical care programs in fiscal 2000 was too small and called for an increase of $1.9 billion. Lawmakers of both parties agreed that the administration's request was too small.

And, on July 26, the same day as the subcommittee markup, the Clinton administration agreed with that assessment.

Vice President Al Gore announced that the administration would send an amended budget request to Congress, seeking an increase of $1 billion in the level of funding for veterans' health care.

"Our veteran population is aging — and with that fact, the need for high-quality health care becomes even more important," Gore said.

Facing criticism and uncertain prospects for the bill on the floor, the full committee elected to raise the increase to $1.7 billion in response to strong lobbying by the legion and other veterans groups.

"This will provide a needed shot in the arm. But we still feel there is not enough money," said Richard B. Fuller, a lobbyist for Paralyzed Veterans of America, which has 17,000 members.

Fight Over HUD

While both parties scrambled to find more money for veterans' health

NASA Wins Back Some Funding After Lobbying by Goldin

JULY 31 — Stung by criticism of a proposed 10 percent budget cut for NASA, House appropriators agreed July 30 to restore some funding to the agency. But space program supporters are continuing a push to restore more on the House floor and in conference with the Senate.

For the past seven years, NASA officials have stoically accepted declining budgets as they have sought to transform the agency from what critics in the 1980s described as a bloated bureaucracy into what NASA Administrator Daniel S. Goldin now hails as a "faster, better, cheaper" example of government.

But even the usually upbeat Goldin described the House VA-HUD Appropriations Subcommittee's decision July 26 to give NASA a $12.3 billion budget as "devastating." The amount would be $1.4 billion less than the fiscal 1999 appropriation and $1.3 billion less than the administration's request.

"The ultimate effect could be the loss of critical, long-term scientific and technological investment not only for space science, but also for the nation's national security and economic well-being," Goldin warned in July 29 letters to Appropriations Committee Chairman C.W. Bill Young, R-Fla., and ranking Democrat David R. Obey of Wisconsin.

In particular, Goldin said in a statement that the proposed cuts could force the closure of between one and three unspecified NASA space centers, as well as "significant" layoffs. He told Young and Obey the reductions would force him to furlough all agency employees for three weeks.

House Science Committee Chairman F. James Sensenbrenner Jr., R-Wis., took issue with such dire forecasts. Noting that NASA had not criticized past budget projections that called for giving the agency even less than the subcommittee recommendation, Sensenbrenner said Goldin's statements "are disingenuous at best and purposely inflammatory at worst."

Nevertheless, lobbying by lawmakers on NASA's behalf helped prompt the House Appropriations Committee to shift $400 million from President Clinton's AmeriCorps national service program to NASA.

Of the extra funds, $100 million would be used for the Space Infrared Telescope Facility, a project scheduled for launch in December 2001 that had been marked for cancellation by the subcommittee. In addition, $75 million would be used for planning future missions to Mars, and $225 million would go toward space science research and technology.

But Goldin said the committee's decision was not enough. "I appeal to members of Congress to fully restore the president's budget," he said in a statement.

One NASA backer, Republican Dave Weldon of Florida, is optimistic that such an action is possible. He said he has received assurances from House Speaker J. Dennis Hastert of Illinois and other senior Republicans that they will support restoring cuts in conference.

But Weldon, whose district includes Cape Canaveral's Kennedy Space Center, added, "Whether every penny is going to get restored, I don't know."

In fiscal 1999, senators gave NASA more money than the House or the administration sought, enabling the final House-Senate conference figure to be in line with the administration's initial request. To accomplish the task, however, Barbara A. Mikulski of Maryland, the Senate VA-HUD Appropriations Subcommittee's ranking Democrat, said the 1997 spending caps will need to be increased.

"I don't want to go below last year's funds," said Mikulski, a longtime protector of NASA's Goddard Space Flight Center in her state.

This year's funding reduction for NASA dashed hopes among some supporters that its recent achievements, such as the celebrated shuttle flight last fall of former astronaut and Sen. John Glenn, D-Ohio (1974-99), could translate into a financial windfall for the agency. *(1998 Almanac, p. 19-10)*

Some members have wondered if NASA has become a victim of its own success by faithfully demonstrating it can do more with less. Goldin has been criticized for not objecting more strenuously to previous White House efforts to downsize his agency, a situation that some lawmakers have attributed to Clinton's lack of leadership on space.

The situation with the president, the lawmakers said, has been offset by NASA's presence in many members' districts across the country, including such politically powerful states as Texas and Florida. In the past, it also drew support from former House Speaker Newt Gingrich, R-Ga. (1979-99), a space enthusiast.

In their defense, House VA-HUD appropriators acknowledged that their proposed funding reduction for NASA was significant but less severe than it appeared. The subcommittee's report said the projects it sought to cancel "are for the most part early in their development," so that long-term savings would be significant.

The subcommittee's proposed budget for human space flight, which includes the space shuttle and International Space Station, is $5.39 billion for fiscal 2000, a decrease of $92 million from fiscal 1999 and $250 million less than the administration request. *(1998 Almanac, p. 2-101)*

The subcommittee called for a $100 million cut for the space station. Members have been concerned about Russia's financial problems, which have led to cost overruns with the orbiting laboratory and living quarters.

care, they disagreed sharply on funding for the Department of Housing and Urban Development.

The bill would provide $2 billion less than Clinton's request and would roughly match the level of funding for programs in last year's bill. The fiscal 1999 funding level was reduced by a $2 billion rescission of funding for expiring contracts for Section 8 subsidized public housing.

HUD Secretary Andrew M. Cuomo charged that the bill would strike a "terrible blow against families and communities in need" because it reduced funding for some key programs and did not meet the administration's request for $347 million for housing vouchers.

The bill would provide $100 million less than the administration requested to renew expiring Section 8 contracts, and it would cut funding for community development block grants by $250 million.

The bill would provide $7.3 billion for the Environmental Protection Agency, about $106 million more than Clinton requested, but $278 million less than the fiscal 1999 funding.

The bill also would provide $1.2 billion for a clean water fund for states, $325 million more than Clinton requested.

But the bill would shrink a number of initiatives promoted by the administration. For example, it would provide $115 million for his climate change technology initiative, $111 million less than he requested.

Kyoto Ban

The committee's bill report included language similar to last year's report to ensure that funding in the bill is not used to implement the Kyoto treaty, a plan to reduce greenhouse gases in order to combat global warming. The report said the agency had "strayed across a fine line separating education and advocacy" on Kyoto issues in the last year.

The bill would pare other science programs. At the National Science Foundation, the bill would provide less than one-quarter of the $146 million requested by Clinton for an information technology initiative.

There will be some major cuts at other independent agencies.

Among them, the bill would eliminate the Selective Service System, providing $7 million for termination costs. The draft was eliminated in 1980 after the Vietnam War, but President Carter reinstated draft registration after the Soviet invasion of Afghanistan.

Lawmakers said the agency was no longer needed after the end of the Cold War.

House Passes Cuts, Sets Up Conflicts With Senators, Clinton

SEPTEMBER 11 — Defying a threatened veto over $3.3 billion in proposed spending cuts, the House on Sept. 9 passed a $92 billion fiscal 2000 spending bill (HR 2684) for veterans, housing, environmental and space programs.

The measure, which funds the departments of Veterans Affairs (VA) and Housing and Urban Development (HUD) and 17 independent agencies, passed 235-187 despite protests that it would cut housing, space and other programs to offset a 10 percent increase in veterans' medical care. *(Vote 403, p. H-130)*

The partisan battle now moves to the Senate, where appropriators plan to begin work the week of Sept. 13. With hopes of averting a presidential veto, Senate VA-HUD and Independent Agencies Appropriations Subcommittee Chairman Christopher S. Bond, R-Mo., and other senators are expected to push for a slightly larger bill that would restore some of the funds for housing, space, Selective Service and volunteer service programs.

If the Senate completes work on the bill during the week of Sept. 20, as expected, House and Senate conferees could begin their work quickly. House Republicans plan to defend the increase in veterans' medical care, but they expect opposition in the Senate.

"Things will be difficult in conference committee," said James T. Walsh, R-N.Y., who managed the House floor debate. "We have different priorities."

The White House's veto threat further complicates the outlook. Democratic lawmakers and administration officials contend that Republicans are using the cuts in housing, space and other programs to justify their tax cut.

"I will do my best to ensure this bill never becomes law," House Minority Leader Richard A. Gephardt, D-Mo., said at a Sept. 8 news conference with HUD Secretary Andrew M. Cuomo.

With the new fiscal year to begin Oct. 1, the VA-HUD debate captured heightening tensions between the White House and congressional Republicans over spending and taxes.

"The Republican tax cut hurts the poorest families in our nation to help the richest families in our nation," said Cuomo, who said he would urge President Clinton to veto the VA-HUD bill.

The bill's $92 billion total is $3.3 billion less than the fiscal 1999 appropriation and $7.6 billion less than the administration's request.

Because appropriators initially did not have enough money to support spending in the bill, they needed to find budget cuts, offsets and some extra money. Republicans shifted $4 billion previously allocated for the departments of Labor, Health and Human Services (HHS) and Education. And they reduced borrowing authority by $3 billion for the Tennessee Valley Authority, a marketer of federal hydropower.

The bill would trim spending for NASA by $1 billion and the Federal Emergency Management Agency (FEMA) by $2.5 billion. It would also cut $935 million from HUD programs; terminate the Selective Service, the agency that registers men aged 18 to 25 for a potential military draft; and eliminate Clinton's national volunteer service program, AmeriCorps.

In a final effort to scuttle the bill, some opponents, including ranking Appropriations Committee Democrat David R. Obey of Wisconsin, argued that the cut in TVA borrowing authority would not produce real savings and could not be used to offset spending in the bill. But Republicans insisted the TVA cut would ensure that the bill complied with spending caps under the the Balanced Budget Act of 1997 (PL 105-33). The House defeated, 207-215, an Obey motion to recommit the bill to the Appropriations Committee with instructions to specify another $3 billion in offsets. *(Vote 402, p. H-130)*

"We won all the battles we had to

win," Walsh said. He said the bill was designed to trim nearly all programs across the board while taking care of two "special needs:" improved veterans' medical care and higher rent subsidy payments for low-income families.

"Only the fat, and not the meat, was cut from each program," Walsh said.

The debate came more than a month after its originally scheduled starting date, Aug. 5. It was postponed to allow Alan B. Mollohan of West Virginia, the top Democrat on the subcommittee that wrote the bill, to attend the funeral for his father, former Rep. Robert H. Mollohan (1953-57 and 1969-83), who died Aug. 3.

Housing Woes

Returning from the summer recess, House Democrats and the White House were prepared for a contentious discussion of public housing policy. Democrats called for raising spending caps set in the 1997 budget law as an alternative to the cuts contained in the bill. Republicans defended cuts in HUD programs as necessary to comply with spending caps.

The bill would provide $26.1 billion in funding for HUD. That is $2 billion more than the net funding received by the agency in fiscal 1999, after factoring in budget scorekeeping adjustments to reflect a fiscal 1999 rescission of unspent appropriations for rent subsidies for low-income families living in private housing.

Democrats insist that in terms of the funds actually available for housing programs, the bill amounts to a cut of $935 million from fiscal 1999.

For the rental subsidy program, the bill would provide an increase of more than $200 million, mainly to pay higher rents needed to renew contracts for some private properties. But that increase would be offset by reductions in other housing programs, such as a $445 million cut in modernization of housing projects and a $250 million cut in community development block grants.

The battle over money for housing was in sharp contrast to the debate over housing policy last year. Lawmakers agreed in 1998 on an overhaul of HUD programs designed to shift more control to local officials and to reserve a large share of public housing for families with the lowest incomes. The fiscal 1999 VA-HUD spending law (PL 105-276) was one of just five separately enacted spending measures and included a 14 percent increase in funding for HUD. *(1998 Almanac, p. 2-101)*

On the floor, Obey charged that the cuts would accelerate a division of the country into "two separate societies," one rich and one poor.

While lawmakers of both parties agreed that the cuts were painful, they would only agree to a modest change in the bill to increase HUD funding.

With a spate of last-minute vote changes by a half-dozen lawmakers, the House on Sept. 8 narrowly passed, 212-207, an amendment by Jerrold Nadler, D-N.Y., to provide $10 million in housing subsidies for people who have AIDS. The amendment cut polar and Antarctic research by the National Science Foundation. *(Vote 394, p. H-128)*

Space Station

While Democrats planned to seek more money for low-income housing in the Senate, defenders of NASA deflected a series of attacks on the International Space Station.

The House defeated, 121-298, a perennial amendment offered by Tim Roemer, D-Ind., and Mark Sanford, R-S.C., to kill the project by eliminating $2 billion in funding and allocating it to veterans' medical care, housing and other NASA programs. *(Vote 392, p. H-128)*

A similar proposal offered by Roemer in 1993 lost by one vote on the House floor. *(1993 Almanac, p. 249)*

Support for the space station was striking in the wake of two General Accounting Office studies last month. The office questioned Russia's ability to participate in the project and found a "high degree of uncertainty" in NASA's original estimate for total operating costs of $13 billion from 2005 to 2014. If Russia cannot meet its obligations, the burden would fall on the United States and other partners in the project, including Canada and Japan.

The project is still five years from completion, but it enjoys broad support in part because construction contracts create jobs across the country. While the space station survived challenges on the floor, NASA supporters lost their battle to save other parts of the agency's budget from deep cuts.

The House defeated, 185-235, an amendment offered by James E. Rogan, R-Calif., to provide $95 million for space science research and technology programs by taking money from discretionary and other funds for the EPA. *(Vote 395, p. H-128)*

Finding Offsets

The defeat of efforts to provide more money for NASA was emblematic of the difficulty that lawmakers found in trying to carve out spending from targets such as the EPA to provide funding for pet programs.

The lack of support for more large budget cuts made it virtually impossible for supporters of the Selective Service to find offsets to save that agency from proposed termination.

The House voted, 187-232, to defeat an attempt to provide enough money to save the Selective Service System. *(Vote 391, p. H-128)*

Republican Thomas M. Davis III of Virginia said the amendment, by Randy "Duke" Cunningham, R-Calif., was rejected because it would have taken $17 million from FEMA and the EPA. "Nobody likes these cuts," he said.

The Selective Service was last challenged in 1995. *(1995 Almanac, p. 11-83)*

Cunningham predicted the service would survive in conference committee, with the help of Senate Appropriations Committee Chairman Ted Stevens, R-Alaska.

Supporters said a military draft could be required to respond to a surprise attack. But Walsh called the service "a mothballed program" in the post-Cold War era that could be quickly renewed to meet any new threats.

Senate Panel Uses Funds Squeezed From Labor-HHS

SEPTEMBER 18 — Using more than $7 billion once allocated for labor, health and social service programs, Senate appropriators smoothed the way for passage of a $91 billion fiscal 2000 spending bill (S 1596) for the departments of Veterans Affairs and Housing and Urban Development the week of Sept. 20.

Senate appropriators set the stage for floor action by agreeing Sept. 14 to shift $7.2 billion previously allocated for the departments of Labor and Health and Human Services.

With the extra money in hand, Senate VA-HUD Appropriations Subcommittee Chairman Christopher S. Bond, R-Mo., moved quickly on the bill. The subcommittee approved the bill by voice vote Sept. 15, and the full panel followed suit, 28-0, Sept. 16.

The Senate's efforts to quickly pass the VA-HUD bill were part of a broader push by Republicans to concentrate on appropriations after President Clinton's veto of their tax cut bill (HR 2488). But the funding cut from the Labor-HHS measure will complicate their task.

On the horizon, Bond is preparing for a conference committee where a key fight will be over the House's proposal to raise funding for veterans' medical care by $1.7 billion, about $600 million more than the Senate version of the bill would provide. Senators would prefer to spend more money on housing and space programs.

The Senate bill would virtually match funding levels that Clinton requested for many programs. Senators also adopted a gimmick that Clinton put in his own budget: $4.2 billion in "advance appropriations" for fiscal 2001, which would allow HUD to renew expiring contracts in its rental subsidy program. By appropriating the money for fiscal 2001, lawmakers stayed within spending caps and avoided deeper cuts in programs for fiscal 2000. The fiscal 2001 appropriation does not count against spending caps for fiscal 2000.

The House passed a $92 billion version of the bill Sept. 9 that faces strong Democratic opposition and a veto threat because it would cut housing, space programs and the Tennessee Valley Authority's borrowing power to pay for a big boost in medical care.

The Senate spending bill would provide $18.4 billion for veterans medical care, $1.1 billion more than Clinton sought. It would roughly match his request for NASA and for major HUD programs. And it would slightly exceed his requests for the Environmental Protection Agency (EPA) and the National Science Foundation.

The major difference from the Clinton request was the omission of $2.5 billion in contingency disaster funding for the Federal Emergency Management Agency (FEMA).

Although Appropriations Committee Chairman Ted Stevens, R-Alaska, said the costs from Hurricane Floyd recovery could require a separate funding bill, he said FEMA had adequate funding to meet current needs.

A Work in Progress

Apart from the uncertain cost of disaster relief to deal with Hurricane Floyd, which pounded the East Coast the week of Sept. 13, key lawmakers said the bill was designed to fund basic needs of existing programs.

Bond, the prime architect of the Senate bill, said there was no money to pay for many of the initiatives Clinton had requested, such as additional vouchers for the HUD rental subsidy program.

"We did change his priorities. We had to put more money into the VA," Bond said. "I would hope he understands."

Ranking Democrat Barbara A. Mikulski of Maryland said there were "yellow flashing lights" in the bill because of such items as a $100 million cut in the superfund program for cleaning up hazardous waste sites. But she predicted objections could be resolved by increasing funding for AmeriCorps, EPA, housing and science. "We are a work in progress," she said.

Overall, the bill would provide about $70 billion in discretionary spending. Both the House and Senate bills would provide more than $21 billion in mandatory spending for entitlement programs, which include veterans' pensions and benefits.

By providing a smaller increase in veterans' medical care, senators avoided several controversial cuts proposed by the House.

The Senate bill would provide $423.5 million, $2 million less than the fiscal 1999 appropriation, to AmeriCorps, the national volunteer service program championed by Clinton. The bill would rescind $80 million in reserve funds for AmeriCorps. The House bill would kill the program.

Another program that fared better in the Senate was the Selective Service, which would receive $25.3 million under the bill, matching Clinton's request. The House bill proposed to slash its budget to $7 million to pay only for the costs of eliminating the agency.

HUD Programs

Overall, the bill would provide $27.2 billion for HUD, retaining the same funding as fiscal 1999 for many housing programs.

Bond provided for an increase of about $700 million in all rental subsidy programs. The bill would offset the increase with cuts in other agencies, including FEMA, and in selected HUD programs, including a $125 million cut aimed at refurbishing severely distressed public housing.

The House-passed bill proposed to increase rental subsidy programs by $214 million, offset by big cuts in modernization of public housing and community development block grants.

HUD Secretary Andrew M. Cuomo initially charged that the House bill was part of a GOP strategy to cut vital programs for the poor in order to finance the Republicans' short-lived tax cut proposal. HUD officials said they were pleased that senators came much closer to the administration's requests for many HUD programs.

But they said the Senate bill would still provide too little for restoring public housing and for expanding the rent subsidy program.

Bond said there was simply not enough money to admit more families to the rent subsidy program. He said the administration should join lawmakers to try to find ways to increase the funding. Without more money, he said, as many as 1.3 million HUD-assisted families could be displaced if rent subsidy contracts are not renewed over the next 10 years.

Lawmakers say rents are increasing across the country because of a booming economy and a strong real estate market in many cities. That means that HUD must pay out more to renew long-term rental subsidy contracts for privately owned apartments and homes.

In a significant difference with the House, Senate appropriators dropped the practice of providing funding in the bill to cover the cost of renewing contracts for rental housing in the following fiscal year.

Although they included the funding — $4.2 billion — in the bill, they pushed it into fiscal 2001. Thus it does not count against the fiscal 2000 spending caps or contribute to the bottom line for the bill.

Bond said the caps left him little choice, but he acknowledged that the decision would cause headaches for VA-HUD appropriators next year since it would mean that $4.2 billion in discretionary funding for fiscal 2001 had already been claimed.

Potential Floor Amendments

While senators appeared to be closing the gap with Clinton on funding for housing programs, other battles surfaced in the full committee markup over the administration's plan to use $15 million in HUD funding to finance an anti-crime initiative.

Clinton announced a plan Sept. 9 to give HUD grants to police to buy guns for $50 each to try to get as many weapons as possible off the nation's streets.

Sen. Larry E. Craig, R-Idaho, said he would offer a floor amendment to require the return of any stolen guns and permit resale of guns worth more than $500. Democrats charged that his proposal would defeat the aim of gun removal.

Meanwhile, Democrats pledged to fight a provision that would cap HUD employment at 9,300, and eliminate more than 400 participants in a program that employs community builders to help market HUD programs. Republicans contended that the program is unnecessary.

While Democrats pledged a floor fight for more funding for community builders and other housing programs, Bond vowed to promote an accounting change in the bill to prevent possible cost increases in the International Space Station project from draining other programs.

The bill would make a separate account with $2.5 billion for the space station project and would prevent the diversion of shuttle program funding.

Bond said he was a strong supporter of the space station but added that precautions were needed in case bad management or financial woes prevented Russia, one the main partners, from paying its share of the project.

He predicted that critics of the space station, such as Tom Harkin, D-Iowa, would not succeed if they offered amendments to cut funding for the project. A longstanding critic of the space station, Harkin said he would like to shift money to other NASA programs, including exploration of Mars.

Despite ongoing criticism of the space station, Bond and other supporters of NASA said they would fight to retain the Senate's funding level for space programs on the floor and in conference.

James T. Walsh, R-N.Y., chairman of the House VA-HUD and Independent Agencies Appropriations Subcommittee, said he would support efforts to reduce a $1 billion cut in NASA programs contained in the House bill, but worried about other demands that may arise in conference. "We will have to see what the Senate finally comes up with," Walsh said in an interview Sept. 13.

Senate-Passed Bill Differs Sharply From House's On Rental Subsidies

SEPTEMBER 25 — Facing a showdown with the House over funding for a troubled low-income housing program, the Senate on Sept. 24 passed by voice vote a $97.8 billion fiscal 2000 spending bill for the departments of Veterans Affairs (VA), Housing and Urban Development (HUD), and independent agencies.

The bill (HR 2684) now moves to a House-Senate conference committee, which is expected to begin work the week of Sept. 27. The conferees' biggest challenge will be resolving major differences over how to deal with HUD's massive rental subsidy program.

Senate action came after Minority Leader Tom Daschle, D-S.D., and other Democrats sharply criticized Republicans for not providing more money for education in overall fiscal 2000 spending. The bill was completed with the addition of $7.2 billion from an allocation for a draft spending bill for the departments of Labor, Health and Human Services (HHS), and education.

Senate appropriators have been cutting other housing programs or other agencies' funds in order to cover rising costs in the rent subsidy program, known as Section 8, which helps 3 million families in privately owned houses and apartments.

Lawmakers fear that some participants in the program will be evicted when existing rent contracts expire, unless HUD gets more money to renew contracts and make higher rent payments. Housing costs are rising in many parts of the country because of the strong economy and heavy demand for rental units.

The Senate bill would provide an increase of more than $700 million, to $11 billion, for the rental subsidy program and offset the increase with cuts in other agencies, including the Federal Emergency Management Agency (FEMA), and in selected HUD programs, including a $125 million cut in a program to modernize severely distressed housing.

The House bill would increase funding for the rental subsidy program by about $214 million, to $10.5 billion, and offset the increase with cuts in modernization of public housing and community development block grants.

The housing issue is one of several differences between House and Senate measures. Others include a Senate provision to create a separate budget account to deal with potential cost increases for the International Space Station and a House provision to terminate the Selective Service, which registers men age 18 to 25 for a potential military draft.

Overall, the Senate bill would provide $1.6 billion more in budget authority for fiscal 2000 than the House bill.

Most of the gap between the two chambers can be found in NASA funding. The Senate would nearly match the agency's fiscal 1999 appropriation, while the House would cut $1 billion. Another big part of the gap is tied to Clinton's national volunteer service initiative, AmeriCorps. The House included no funding, while the Senate would provide $423.5 million.

In a Sept. 22 letter to Senate appropriators, the administration echoed its threat to veto the House bill. It criticized the Senate version for providing too little funding for housing, FEMA, national service and environmental programs.

Still, senators avoided some controversies that could have slowed passage of the bill, including disagreements over funding for the Environmental Protection Agency. The Senate bill would provide more money for the agency than Clinton's request, although it would cut $100 million from the superfund program to clean toxic waste sites.

The Senate averted another potential controversy in conference committee by approving by voice vote Sept. 22 an amendment to increase veterans' medical care by $600 million, to $19 billion, matching the House bill.

The Senate would pay for the $600 million increase with an emergency appropriation, which is not subject to spending caps. In all, both versions of the bill would provide $1.7 billion more than Clinton requested for veterans' medical care.

Senate VA, HUD and Independent Agencies Appropriations Subcommittee Chairman Christopher S. Bond, R-Mo., said lawmakers were on a "forced march" to complete work on the bill in order to continue funding for agencies after the end of the fiscal year Sept. 30.

Ranking Democrat Barbara A. Mikulski of Maryland said she agreed with complaints that Clinton's original proposal for veterans' health care was inadequate. She urged other Democrats to support the Senate bill, noting that it would provide for needs of "core constituencies," including veterans and low-income families, while preserving other programs such as space research and the Selective Service.

James T. Walsh, R-N.Y., chairman of the House VA, HUD and Independent Agencies Appropriations Subcommittee, praised the Senate for making sure it was "in sync" with the House on veterans' medical care.

"We won't have to fight over it in conference committee," Walsh said Sept. 22. "Now, we have to agree on other issues including housing."

He pointed to the House proposals to cut NASA funding and to a House decision to provide $300 million less than Clinton requested for the National Science Foundation.

Walsh said lawmakers would also have to reach agreement on a set of offsets to comply with spending caps.

Finding Offsets

The Senate bill would provide $93.6 billion in budget authority for fiscal 2000, about $1.7 billion less than Congress appropriated in fiscal 1999, and about $1.8 billion less than Clinton requested. The House bill, passed Sept. 9, would provide $92 billion in fiscal 2000 budget authority, $1.6 billion less than the Senate bill.

Overall, the Senate bill would provide $97.8 billion in appropriations, including a gimmick in the bill and in Clinton's budget: $4.2 billion in "advance appropriations" for fiscal 2001. The advance appropriation would allow HUD to renew expiring rent subsidy contracts. By appropriating that money for fiscal 2001, senators stayed within spending caps for fiscal 2000. A similar provision was not in the House bill.

Walsh echoed budget hawks in the House who are loath to set a precedent for skirting spending caps.

"We have not provided an advance appropriation for that program in the past, and I don't think we should start doing it," Walsh said. "It will create a huge hole to fill next year."

But he added that he would listen to arguments for the advance funding.

"We may not have other offsets," Walsh said. He and other House Republicans are considering whether to jettison an offset in the House bill: a reduction in borrowing authority for the Tennessee Valley Authority (TVA), a marketer of hydropower.

Democrats have charged that the proposed TVA accounting change will not produce real savings. Walsh said concerns about that House provision had yet to be resolved.

"The question of what to do about offsets is in the air," Walsh added.

While trying to resolve differences in offsets aimed at complying with spending limits, the conference committee must find common ground on housing programs and national service.

Housing Problems

Senate Republicans insisted on more money to pay for projected increases in rent payments for families in HUD's rent subsidy program. But Democrats said that more funding was needed to increase the number of families in the program.

Daschle said the nation was in the midst of an "affordable housing crisis." He and other Democrats said they would fight for more rent subsidies. They noted that Congress provided rent subsidies to an additional 50,000 families in the fiscal 1999 VA-HUD bill (PL 105-276). *(1998 Almanac, p. 20-12)*

The administration originally called for funding to provide rent subsidies to an additional 100,000 families. It has estimated that 5.3 million families need housing assistance.

But Republicans said funding increases should focus on dealing with rising costs for families already in the rent subsidy program. "Under this appropriations bill, unlike the course the administration is on, no one will lose their housing," Bond said.

John Kerry, D-Mass., offered but later withdrew an amendment to provide $288 million for new rent subsidies for 50,000 families. The Senate on Sept. 24 approved by voice vote another Kerry amendment to increase funding for housing assistance for the disabled and for persons with AIDS.

Other Priorities

In addition to dealing with demands for more housing aid, the conference committee will face the question of funding for FEMA. Neither version of the bill included $2.5 billion in "emergency" funds for potential disasters requested in Clinton's budget.

But Appropriations Committee Chairman Ted Stevens, R-Alaska, said Sept. 21 that he would likely seek additional money to help victims of Hurricane Floyd in a spending bill this year.

"We all know it's coming. But we don't know how much," Stevens said.

John Edwards, D-N.C., said Sept. 22 that the hurricane had devastated homes, businesses and farms across his state. In a news release, he called for at least $1 billion in disaster aid for his state.

More requests are expected. "Both parties will support more disaster relief because everyone has gone through something like this," said Ernest F. Hollings, D-S.C.

Conferees Increase Funding for Rental Subsidies, FEMA

OCTOBER 9 — House and Senate negotiators approved a fiscal 2000 spending bill (HR 2684) for veterans, housing, space and other programs Oct. 7, after reaching a compromise with the White House to add 60,000 families to a federal rental subsidy program.

Both chambers were expected to vote on the conference report the week of Oct. 11. The final bill would provide about $99.5 billion for the departments of Veterans Affairs (VA), Housing and Urban Development (HUD), and 17 independent agencies.

Senate VA, HUD and Independent Agencies Appropriations Subcommittee Chairman Christopher S. Bond, R-Mo., the chairman of the conference panel, said the funding plan would have strong support in both chambers. President Clinton is expected to sign it.

The voice vote by the conference committee came hours after appropriators reached agreement with the White House to provide $2.5 billion in emergency funding for the Federal Emergency Management Agency to deal with the damage caused by Hurricane Floyd and to provide reserve money for other potential disasters.

In addition, the deal provided an additional $764 million for housing, space and science and for a Clinton priority — national service programs. The spending would be offset by previously unspent funding for HUD, including money for a tenant protection program.

One of the centerpieces of the compromise was an agreement by lawmakers to meet one of the administration's top demands: $344 million to put an additional 60,000 low-income families in HUD's rental subsidy program, known as Section 8 housing. That would bring total funding for the program to $11 billion, including $4.2 billion in advance funding for 2002.

The administration said expansion of the program, which serves 3 million families, was needed to help more low-income families deal with increasing rents in many parts of the country.

Talks with the White House began after the House passed, 306-113, on Oct. 4 a motion to instruct House conferees to accept the higher levels of funding proposed in the Senate version of HR 2684. *(Vote 472, p. H-154)*

Office of Management and Budget Director Jack Lew worked out more than a dozen key issues with lawmakers over three days of negotiations that began on Oct. 5. The deal included $135 million in additional operating subsidies for public housing; $70 million for economic development aid to 20 HUD and Agriculture Department empowerment zones; $39 million for HUD salaries and other housing programs; $100 million for NASA space research; and $45 million for research by the National Science Foundation.

As part of the compromise, the conferees agreed to terminate funding on Sept. 1, 2000, for 400 HUD employees who market housing programs for the poor. Republicans charged that the program, started by HUD Secretary Andrew M. Cuomo, was wasteful.

In completing work on the bill, the conferees approved by voice vote an amendment by House Majority Whip Tom DeLay, R-Texas, to suspend until 2001 the launch of the $75 million Triana satellite, which would provide a live picture of the Earth for display on the Internet as part of a NASA education and science program. The measure would allow time for the National Academy of Sciences to conduct a study on the scientific value of the project, which has been supported by Vice President Al Gore and ridiculed by Republicans.

Lawsuit Ban

One final battle in conference committee was resolved when Bond agreed to revise his Senate provision to discourage recipients of federal grants from using federal funds to lobby or to file lawsuits against the government.

Bond agreed to delete a provision that would have required violators of the lobbying ban to forgo federal funding for five years. The conference report would require recipients of federal grants to certify that none of the money was used for lobbying or litigation against the government.

Bond's provision was inspired in part by a legal battle in his home state. The Sierra Club and the Missouri Coalition for the Environment filed suit in 1998 against the Environmental Protection Agency in U.S. District Court in Washington, D.C., to try to force the agency to impose sanctions on the St. Louis area for not meeting clean air standards.

Although environmental groups have denied using federal funds to pay for lawsuits, Bond said his provision was needed to ensure that the lobbying ban was enforced.

Final Bill Includes Hurricane Aid, Extra Money for Rental Subsidies

OCTOBER 16 — With strong bipartisan support, Congress gave final approval Oct. 15 to a fiscal 2000 appropriations bill (HR 2684) for veterans, housing and science programs, after House and Senate negotiators cut a deal with the White House to provide disaster relief for Hurricane Floyd and additional funding for a federal rental subsidy program.

President Clinton is expected to sign the bill the week of Oct. 18, providing $99.5 billion for the departments of Veterans Affairs (VA) and Housing and Urban Development (HUD) and for 17 independent agencies.

The House adopted the conference report on the bill Oct. 14, by a vote of 406-18, and the Senate cleared it, 93-5, on Oct. 15. *(House vote 500, p. H-164; Senate vote 328, p. S-66)*

Enactment became all but certain after House and Senate negotiators reached a compromise with the White House on Oct. 7, agreeing on funding levels for disaster aid, housing, space and national service programs.

Under the deal, the final bill contained $3.4 billion for the Federal Emergency Management Agency (FEMA), including $871 million in appropriations for operations and $2.5 billion in emergency funding for damage caused by Hurricane Floyd and for other potential disasters.

It also included an extra $764 million for other programs, with nearly half that money devoted to expanding HUD's rental subsidy program, known as Section 8. Funding for NASA programs was increased by $100 million over what conferees initially planned to provide, and public housing operating subsidies were up $135 million over Clinton's request.

The conferees initially opposed the funding for new housing initiatives proposed by Clinton, but it became clear that including the money was the only way to ensure the bill's final approval.

In addition to the increase for the Section 8 program, the deal with the White House helped to finance an increase in spending on veterans' medical care to $19 billion, about $1.7 billion more than Clinton's request. The increase is intended to help 3.4 million veterans who rely on VA hospitals and clinics for care.

The final bill would preserve two programs proposed for termination by the House: Clinton's national service program, AmeriCorps, and the Selective Service, which registers young men for a potential military draft.

Despite the bill's overall total, it would actually provide $95.3 billion in fiscal 2000. The remaining $4.2 billion is "advance appropriations" for fiscal 2001 to allow HUD to renew expiring contracts in its rental subsidy program.

Pushing the $4.2 billion into 2001, as the Senate and Clinton had proposed, removed a key obstacle to completing the bill: lack of room for increased spending under the fiscal 2000 spending caps set by the 1997 balanced-budget act (PL 105-33).

The change made room under the caps to provide $7.6 billion to the Environmental Protection Agency (EPA), $385 million more than Clinton requested; and $13.7 billion to NASA, $74 million more than Clinton requested for space programs such as shuttle missions, the International Space Station and space research. Most of the increase for EPA would be used for grants to states and tribes for sewers, drinking water systems and water treatment projects.

Despite strong bipartisan support for the use of advance funding this year, some lawmakers warned that it could set a bad precedent and cause serious problems when appropriators try to complete a VA-HUD spending bill next year.

"Republicans are playing a shell game," charged ranking House Appropriations Committee Democrat David R. Obey of Wisconsin.

Senate VA, HUD and Independent Agencies Appropriations Subcommittee Chairman Christopher S. Bond, R-Mo., said that using advance funding for the rental subsidy program would probably hurt HUD next year. He warned that appropriators would have little room under spending caps in fiscal 2001 to provide spending increases for housing programs.

Housing Woes

Bond noted that appropriators would likely face mounting costs in the Section 8 program because rents are rising in many areas of the country. As a result, Bond says, appropriators will have a "big hole" to fill next year.

While lawmakers and the White House agreed that the rental subsidy program should remain a priority, they disagreed on the best way to deal with the mounting cost. Republicans argued for putting money into existing housing projects and only renewing existing contracts for rental housing in the Section 8 program. But the White House insisted on adding more families to the rental subsidy program.

The bill would provide $26 billion to HUD, but housing programs would also get an additional $2.6 billion through rescissions and other means, bringing the total to $28.6 billion, 6 percent above the fiscal 1999 level.

The rental subsidy program would receive an increase of $1 billion, to about $11.4 billion.

About one-third of the additional Section 8 money would be used to bring 60,000 more low-income families into the rental subsidy program. The rest of the increase would pay for renewing soon-to-expire rental contracts for families already in the program.

The bill also includes a provision from a measure (HR 202) passed by the House, 405-5, on Sept. 27, to permit the use of rental subsidies for assisted living facilities, and to authorize about $900 million in funding to develop such facilities. *(Vote 451, p. H-146)*

Senate Banking, Housing and Urban Affairs Banking and Transportation Subcommittee Chairman Wayne Allard, R-Colo., initially balked but later accepted the provisions under a deal to allow his panel to review them next year, when it will consider other sections of HR 202 that would encourage wider availability of housing for the elderly.

While expanding the Section 8 program, the VA-HUD bill would cut $150 million from public housing modernization and rescind more than about $2.2 billion of unobligated funds for HUD. That money includes savings in the Section 8 program from rental subsidy contract expirations and reduced levels of subsidies for tenants with higher incomes.

The unspent money would be reallocated to offset increases in veterans' medical care, operating subsidies for public housing and space research.

Battle Over Space Projects

Under the final bill, NASA would receive $13.7 billion, $12.3 million less than in fiscal 1999.

The measure includes about $5.5 billion in funding for two of the agency's main programs, space shuttle missions and the International Space Station. The space station remains under scrutiny because of possible cost overruns and concern that Russia may be unable to finance its share of the project.

The bill would delay the launch of the $75 million Triana satellite program until early 2001. The satellite is part of a science and education program strongly endorsed by Vice President Al Gore, but it is viewed by Republicans as an example of wasteful spending. The bill would require a National Academy of Sciences study of the project's value.

Conferees added a controversial provision to create a demonstration program that would allow NASA to make deals with companies to launch commercial projects such as zero-gravity biological research and production of educational videos. NASA would be able to charge the companies fees and to retain some of the funds for investment in other commercial projects.

House Science Committee Chairman F. James Sensenbrenner Jr., R-Wis., charged that the provision would allow NASA to give "unequal access" to companies it favored, and he called for hearings to examine the program.

Final Deal

Like NASA, EPA came away with roughly the same funding as in fiscal

VA-HUD Spending Highlights

Where the Money Goes

HR 2684 (Conference rept: H Rept 106-379)

Spending Synopsis

The conference report on fiscal 2000 VA-HUD bill was cleared by the Senate on Oct. 15, 93-5, after it was adopted by the House, 406-18, on Oct. 14. It provides $99.5 billion for the departments of Veterans Affairs (VA) and Housing and Urban Development (HUD), as well as 17 independent agencies. The bill includes $4.2 billion in "advance appropriations" for HUD's rental subsidy program in fiscal 2001.

- **Veterans Affairs**

The bill provides $44.3 billion for veterans programs, about $1.8 billion more than President Clinton requested. A centerpiece of the bill is $19 billion for veterans' medical care, about $1.7 billion more than the fiscal 1999 appropriation. The increase is aimed at covering rising health care costs of aging veterans.

- **Housing and Urban Development**

The $26 billion in the bill for HUD programs in fiscal 2000 is about $1.9 billion more than in fiscal 1999. The bill provides $11.4 billion for HUD's troubled Section 8 rental subsidy program, about $1 billion more than was provided in fiscal 1999. The increase would pay for renewing soon-to-expire rental contracts and funding to add 60,000 families to the rental subsidy program. Total funding for rental subsidies includes $4.2 billion in advance appropriations in fiscal 2001.

- **NASA**

Under the bill, space programs receive $13.7 billion, about $12.3 million less than the fiscal 1999 appropriation but $74.3 million more than Clinton's request.

Hot-Button Issues

Δ **Environmental Protection Agency.** The bill provides $7.6 billion in funding for the EPA, about $385 million more than Clinton's request. But the administration opposed cuts in some programs, including a provision to reduce superfund toxic waste cleanup by $100 million. Environmental groups opposed a provision to require recipients of federal grants to certify that they are not violating an existing federal ban on using federal funding to lobby or to file lawsuits against the government. As in fiscal 1999, the report directs the EPA not to implement the Kyoto climate control treaty.

Δ **FEMA.** The bill provides an additional $2.5 billion in emergency funds requested by Clinton to deal with disasters such as Hurricane Floyd. But lawmakers say more money will probably be needed to deal with damage from Floyd. FEMA received $2 billion in emergency funds in fiscal 1999.

Δ **National and Community Service.** The bill maintains the volunteer programs promoted by Clinton, providing $434 million, about $9 million more than last year.

Δ **Selective Service System.** The bill retains the Selective Service, which the House proposed terminating.

Δ **Housing and development.** Advocates for the poor say the bill does not go far enough to help 5.3 million families eligible for federal housing assistance that are not currently served.

(figures are in thousands of dollars of new budget authority)

	Fiscal 1999 Appropriation	Fiscal 2000 Clinton Request	House Bill	Senate Bill	Conference Report
Veterans Affairs	$42,625,039	$42,538,434	$44,156,241	$44,350,684	$44,334,684
Housing and Urban Development	24,079,378	28,048,366	26,067,049	27,170,066	25,951,223
Independent Agencies	28,558,844	29,016,204	24,756,866	26,307,446	29,181,011
NASA	(13,665,000)	(13,578,400)	(12,653,800)	(13,578,400)	(13,652,700)
Environmental Protection Agency	(7,590,352)	(7,206,646)	(7,307,557)	(7,322,378)	(7,591,659)
Federal Emergency Management Agency	(2,870,254)	(3,401,725)	(880,737)	(854,580)	(3,351,155)
GRAND TOTAL	**$95,263,261**	**$99,603,004**	**$91,980,156**	**$97,828,196**	**$99,452,918**
Total adjusted for scorekeeping	**($92,117,459)***	**($93,313,004)****	**($89,890,156)**	**($9,538,196)**	**($93,162,918)**

* Does not include fiscal 1999 emergency funding for FEMA.
** Includes president's request for $2.5 billion in emergency funding for FEMA.

TABLE: Senate and House Appropriations committees

1999. The agency would receive $7.6 billion.

The bill would cut funding for the superfund toxic waste cleanup program by $97 million to $1.4 billion. It would shift $75 million of that money to state and tribal assistance grants — including grants for the construction of sewer systems and water treatment projects. These grants would total $2.6 billion, $629 million more than Clinton requested.

The bill includes language similar to last year's VA-HUD measure (PL 105-276), barring efforts by EPA to implement an international agreement on reduction of greenhouse gases known as the Kyoto Protocol. House report language to make the prohibition more sweeping was not included in the final conference report. *(1998 Almanac, p. 2-101)*

Selective Service would be preserved under the bill, thanks to strong support in the Senate. But Republican James T. Walsh of New York, chairman of the House VA-HUD and Independent Agencies Appropriations Subcommittee, said the program would likely remain a target for cuts. "I think that debate will continue next year," Walsh said. The Selective Service was last challenged in 1995. *(1995 Almanac, p. 11-83)*

Other provisions of the bill would:

- Cut funding for NASA research, including the study of propulsion systems, by $47 million, while increasing funding for shuttle missions by $31 million.
- Increase funding for the National Science Foundation by $241 million, or 7 percent, including $60 million for genetic plant research.
- Provide $44.3 billion to VA programs, $1.7 billion more than in fiscal 1999. ◆

GOP Leaders See Emergency Spending Bill as Opportunity To Beef Up Defense Budget

SUMMARY

Repeating the pattern of recent years, Congress cleared a substantial fiscal 1999 supplemental appropriations bill just months into the new session. The $14.5 billion measure, signed by the president May 21, included $10.9 billion in funding related to operations in Kosovo, emergency funds for recovery efforts associated with Hurricanes Mitch and Georges, and funding to back loans for U.S. farmers hurt by persistently low commodity prices.

The year's supplemental appropriations process started with a relatively routine funding request for hurricane-related relief in Central America and the Caribbean and for aid for U.S. farmers hurt by a steep drop in crop prices.

The House and Senate quickly passed versions of the bill in late March — measures whose main points of contention centered on how to reduce other spending to offset the bill's costs.

However, in response to Serb assaults against ethnic Albanians in the Yugoslav province of Kosovo, NATO began a massive bombing campaign at the end of March against Yugoslav forces. The administration subsequently requested $6 billion to pay for the NATO military operation.

Many Republicans viewed the new request as an opportunity to bolster what they considered to be dangerously underfunded defense readiness accounts. By providing additional defense spending in the fiscal 1999 supplemental — including the first of a multiyear pay increase for military personnel — House Republicans hoped to ease the "cash crunch" that was expected when the fiscal 2000 defense appropriations bill (HR 2561) ran up against the budgetary caps imposed by the 1997 Balanced-Budget Act (PL 105-33).

On May 6, the House passed a second supplemental bill (HR 1664) containing funds for the crisis in Kosovo. The Senate never acted on that bill. By the time conferees met to develop a single measure, most of the main Kosovo and defense funding questions had been settled.

Instead, negotiations on the first bill (HR 1141) threatened to break down over a series of Senate "riders" that House leaders pledged to oppose. Chief among these was a provision by Democratic Sen. Robert C. Byrd of West Virginia, to establish a $1 billion loan guarantee program for U.S. steel producers hurt by rising steel imports. Only after a pledge by House leaders to bring the loan guarantee measure to the House floor as a free-standing bill did Senate conferees agree to drop Byrd's provision.

All but $1.7 billion of the bill's funding was declared "emergency" spending, avoiding the need for offsetting cuts in other fiscal 1999 discretionary accounts. The bill instead relied on the projected budget surplus for its funding.

The final version appropriated close to $15 billion, about double the president's original request. The total included $10.9 billion for military operations in Kosovo and other defense spending, including $1.8 billion for an increase in military pay and retirement benefits. The bill provided $687 million for recovery efforts associated with Hurricanes Mitch and Georges; $1.1 billion for international economic, refugee and disaster assistance related to Kosovo; $574 million to support direct and guaranteed operating loans for U.S. farmers hurt by persistently low commodity prices; and $900 million for tornado victims in Oklahoma and Kansas.

The bill offset $1.7 billion of the new spending by rescinding previous appropriations that had yet to be spent, primarily for the food stamp program.

Box Score 

2000 Fiscal Year

Fiscal 1999 Supplemental

- **Bill:** HR 1141 — PL 106-31
- **Legislative action: House** passed HR 1141 (H Rept 106-64), 220-211, on March 24.

Senate passed HR 1141, amended, by voice vote March 25.

House adopted the conference report (H Rept 106-143), 269-158, on May 18.

Senate cleared the bill, 64-36, on May 20.

President signed HR 1141 on May 21.

Even a Modest Supplemental Faces Trouble

FEBRUARY 6 — Buried inside the budget tome are the seeds of an annual spring ritual that gives Congress fits: a supplemental appropriations bill.

The supplemental is a midyear addition of money for emergencies and other unanticipated needs. As a rule, conservative Republicans have bristled at having to pass these bills, particularly in the last couple of years when it has been harder and harder to find offsetting spending cuts to finance them.

Luckily for Republicans, President Clinton's request for added funds for fiscal 1999 is pretty measly — so far. Clinton will request $900 million in new 1999 spending to implement last year's Wye Peace Accords for the Middle East. Another $1 billion would be released in fiscal 2000 and 2001. In addition, the administration is poised to ask for about $800 million to $900 million in disaster assistance for Central American nations, such as Honduras, hit hard by recent hurricanes.

However meritorious, these are not the sort of proposals that speed a supplemental to passage. Foreign aid carries little urgency with Congress.

But with U.S. farmers in deep distress, powerful lawmakers such as Senate Minority Leader Tom Daschle, D-S.D., are preparing add-ons to help them, especially those raising livestock.

Clinton proposes cutting certain Pentagon accounts to finance the supplemental, and last year's omnibus spending bill (PL 105-277) includes other opportunities for rescissions, or cuts of money previously appropriated. Lawmakers last year added more money for items such as missile defense and intelligence than can be spent this year.

The White House proposes striking $652 million in intelligence and $230 million in missile defense spending that was added to last year's omnibus spending bill at the last minute.

The outlook for the supplemental is vague at best. Administration officials have made it clear that the Middle East funds are contingent on full implementation of the Wye accords reached between Israel and the Palestinians on Oct. 23. Israel agreed to turn over additional land to the Palestinians, in return for a clampdown on terrorism.

The accords helped provoke a political crisis in Israel that has forced Israeli Prime Minister Benjamin Netanyahu to call for parliamentary elections in May. The peace process has largely been put on hold in the meantime.

Promoting Peace

If it is implemented, the bill would provide $1.9 billion in budget authority for the Middle East.

In the current fiscal year, $900 million would be spent: $600 million in military aid for Israel to help move Israeli troops from the West Bank and build alternative security measures; $100 million in military aid for Jordan; and $200 million in economic support funds for Palestinians in the West Bank and Gaza.

Another $1 billion would be dedicated toward advance appropriations for fiscal years 2000 and 2001: $300 million each year in military assistance for Israel; $100 million each year for Jordan, evenly split between military and economic aid; and $100 million each year in economic aid for the West Bank and Gaza.

But administration officials, including Secretary of State Madeleine K. Albright, emphasized that the money is particularly important amidst political changes in Jordan. With the impending death of King Hussein, they are considering speeding up and increasing aid to the monarchy.

The aid for Central America and the Caribbean would help those nations recover from two recent hurricanes. State Department officials indicated that the package might also provide aid to help Colombia recover from its recent earthquake.

Meanwhile, a group of senators is offering legislation authorizing about $800 million in aid to the region.

That bill (S 371), the Central American and Caribbean Relief Act, is sponsored by a bipartisan group including Democrat Bob Graham of Florida and Republican Paul Coverdell of Georgia.

The bill would authorize $700 million in direct humanitarian assistance, and $25 million toward a multilateral fund, as well as a host of other programs.

Coverdell, who chairs the Western Hemisphere Subcommittee of the Senate Foreign Relations Committee, noted the longstanding ties between those countries and the United States, remarking that "these folks are in the 'hood."

But unlike the administration's forthcoming bill, Graham's legislation includes controversial trade preferences that could hurt its chances of passage.

Inserted at the request of Central American leaders who met with a bipartisan group of House and Senate leaders Dec. 10, the measure would grant Central American and Caribbean countries trade benefits comparable to those given Mexico under the North American Free Trade Agreement (NAFTA).

"This is a bill to help our neighbors help themselves," said Sen. Mike DeWine, R-Ohio, a key sponsor of the legislation.

Yet the Caribbean trade legislation has been stymied for the past few years by many of the same legislators who have prevented passage of other trade measures.

They have been particularly critical of NAFTA, saying it has led to a loss of U.S. jobs.

Clinton's Bid To Speed Aid To Jordan Meets Opposition

FEBRUARY 13 — Hoping to buoy Jordan after the death of King Hussein, President Clinton announced Feb. 6 that he would ask Congress to speed up the kingdom's share of a proposed Mideast aid package. Despite widespread congressional support for Jordan, efforts to accelerate the aid are running into obstacles on Capitol Hill.

The administration has been preparing to ask Congress for $1.9 billion over three years to reward Israel, Jordan and the Palestinians if they proceed with implementing last year's Wye River peace accords. Jordan's share was to be $300 million in military and economic aid in return for Hussein's help in sealing the pact.

The money was intended to augment $195 million in annual assistance that the United States currently provides Jordan.

But after Hussein's death on Feb. 7, Clinton said he would ask Congress to speed up the timetable for Jordan, providing that country with all of its funds in the current fiscal year.

Lawmakers, administration officials and pro-Israel interest groups disagree, however, on whether to seek aid to Jordan separately from the other Middle East aid or to include the entire Wye River package in a supplemental bill expected to be unveiled the week of Feb. 15.

Either bill is expected to include hundreds of millions of dollars for Central America to help countries struck by Hurricane Mitch last year, as well as funds to help Colombia recover from an earthquake last month.

Some lawmakers and pro-Israel groups believe the popular appeal of the Jordan aid would help the entire package coast through Congress.

Others are concerned that giving Congress an earlier chance to act might influence the Israeli elections in May and the peace process. Some senators could use the occasion to hold back U.S. aid to the Palestinians unless Palestinian Authority Chairman Yasser Arafat backs down from his threat to declare an independent state in May.

In a Feb. 10 interview, House Appropriations Chairman C.W. Bill Young, R-Fla., said that it was likely that the money for Jordan would move separately from the rest of the Wye River package.

However, Senate Appropriations Committee Chairman Ted Stevens, R-Alaska, expressed concern Feb. 9 about administration plans to shift money from emergency defense spending accounts, particularly anti-missile defense, to pay for the aid. Stevens, a strong supporter of anti-missile defense, said the Middle East aid should be offset by cuts in non-defense accounts.

Senate Committee OKs Bill; House Awaits Offsets

MARCH 6 — The Senate Appropriations Committee approved a $1.9 billion supplemental fiscal 1999 appropriations bill (S 544) on March 4 that would provide disaster relief for hurricane victims in Central America and the Caribbean, help for beleaguered U.S. farmers, and new economic and military aid for Jordan. The vote was 28-0.

Lawmakers agreed to fully offset costs by slicing more than $1 billion from last year's omnibus appropriations bill (PL 105-277) and by making other cuts. House appropriators also had planned to mark up a bill March 4, but they delayed action to find offsets.

Senate offsets included $262 million from food stamps, $210 million from defense, $350 million from welfare block grants and $314 million from community development block grants. Appropriations Chairman Ted Stevens, R-Alaska, indicated a willingness to reconsider the offsets later.

"The final offsets for this bill will be agreed to in conference on a bipartisan basis," Stevens said.

Floor debate is expected the week of March 15.

The House Appropriations panel had to go back to the drawing board March 3 when the leadership demanded that it find offsetting cuts for its $1.3 billion bill. The committee had planned to offset only the $100 million for Jordan.

Speaker J. Dennis Hastert, R-Ill., told Appropriations Committee Chairman C.W. Bill Young, R-Fla., that without offsets, there would be too little Republican support to pass the bill. Conservative and moderate Republicans have clamored for offsets, arguing that without them, the extra spending will come out of the budget surplus, which they want to use to shore up Social Security, cut taxes or both.

At the leadership's behest, the House also plans to include $152 million in aid to farmers hurt by tumbling crop prices. Leaders were unwilling to move ahead with a massive foreign aid package without including some relief for American farmers.

A markup is expected the week of March 8.

Internal wrangling over the supplemental revealed some tensions in Hastert's fledgling leadership team. Whip Tom DeLay, R-Texas, was given credit for forcing changes in the bill in a March 4 story in the Capitol Hill newspaper Roll Call, which cited unidentified sources close to the whip.

But the decision to order changes in the supplemental was made by Hastert, and he was supported by Majority Leader Dick Armey, R-Texas, as well as DeLay, said senior leadership aides. DeLay was chagrined by the story. "You don't force the Speaker to do anything," said Tony Rudy, DeLay's deputy chief of staff.

The Senate bill would appropriate more than $900 million to help nations devastated by hurricanes Mitch and Georges. The bill would provide $100 million for Jordan as well as aid to U.S. farmers.

Sen. Robert C. Byrd, D-W.Va., added a $1 billion loan guarantee program to support the domestic steel industry, which has been hurt by imports. Kay Bailey Hutchison, R-Texas, offered an amendment, approved by voice vote, to bar the federal government from taking part of the revenue from the $246 billion tobacco settlement negotiated by tobacco companies and the states.

House Panel Approves Bill; Both Chambers Delay Floor Votes

MARCH 13 — Momentum for a fiscal 1999 supplemental spending bill appeared to diminish the week of March 8.

The House Appropriations Committee approved a $1.3 billion unnumbered bill — and nearly equal cuts to foreign aid programs — by voice vote March 11. The bill differed broadly from the measure (S 544) approved March 4 by the Senate Appropriations Committee. To pay for its $1.9 billion bill the Senate panel opted to cut social programs, some of which have excess funding because of a drop in the number of beneficiaries.

The varying cuts, and a handful of contentious riders that senators attached to their bill, could make for a difficult House-Senate conference.

With Democrats maligning the proposed cuts in both bills, Senate Majority Leader Trent Lott, R-Miss., warned March 9 that "if people start playing political games with it . . . it could collapse." Lott called the measure — which would aid Jordan as it goes through leadership changes, farmers hurt by tumbling commodity prices, and Central American nations devastated by hurricanes Mitch and Georges — "a train with no engine pulling it." He added that there is "very little real pressure domestically to do this bill."

The difficulties seem to have prompted GOP leaders in both chambers to delay floor action until just before members leave for spring recess March 26. Scheduling votes on pressing bills when members want to leave town is a time-honored way to press for passage without long-winded debate.

Senate Minority Leader Tom Daschle, D-S.D., said March 11 that the bill would be the last thing the Senate took up before the recess, a statement Lott's office confirmed. Daschle added that Lott "doesn't anticipate bringing it up unless there is time." A senior House GOP aide said the House bill is expected on the floor the week of March 22 also.

House Markup

Whether and how to find offsetting spending cuts was the main problem when the House Appropriations Committee marked up its measure March 11. Panel Chairman C. W. Bill Young, R-Fla., had released a bill that would have granted most of Clinton's emergency spending requests without offsets.

But at the markup, Young introduced a manager's amendment to rescind $994.4 million in spending while adding $152.4 million in farm operating loans, a more recent Clinton request. The directive to make such cuts came from GOP leaders, not panel leaders. "We didn't have to have offsets. . . . However, it wasn't up to me," said Sonny Callahan, R-Ala., chairman of the Foreign Operations Appropriations Subcommittee.

Young said he had gone out of his way to find cuts that would hurt the least. "I don't think this is going to cause any heartburn anywhere," he said. But Democrats objected to the cuts, particularly the largest, which would rescind $648 million in "callable" capital that the United States pledged decades ago to back up international monetary institutions, such as the World Bank, in case loans went bad. Ranking panel Democrat David R. Obey of Wisconsin called the cut "a highly risky and dangerous and reckless thing to do," and he warned that it could "bring into question the basic credit-worthiness of the banks."

In a March 11 letter to Obey, Office of Management and Budget Director Jack Lew said he and other advisers would recommend that Clinton veto a House bill containing the offsets. The administration has not released a position on the Senate bill.

The panel approved the cuts in Young's amendment in a 34-26 party-line vote and approved the spending increases, mostly for the Agriculture and Interior Departments, by a vote of 57-0.

Young's amendment, however, did not offset the bill's entire cost. It allowed $195 million that the Defense Department already spent in aid for Central America to be considered "emergency" spending, needing no offsets.

Todd Tiahrt, R-Kan., offered an amendment to pay for that by rescinding $195 million from last year's end-of-session omnibus spending bill (PL 105-277). Tiahrt's amendment would have made cuts of $1 million or less to dozens of programs and bigger cuts to social programs. With Democrats and the panel's Republican leaders speaking against it, the amendment failed on a voice vote.

The panel also defeated by voice vote an amendment by Nancy Pelosi, D-Calif., that would have forgiven $66 million of the debt that Honduras and Nicaragua owe the United States. The underlying bill would provide $41 million for debt forgiveness.

The panel considered an amendment by Robert B. Aderholt, R-Ala., to set up a loan fund for steel companies adversely affected by high increases in imported steel. The Senate measure contains a similar provision. Aderholt withdrew the amendment but said he intends to offer it on the floor.

Bill Stalls in Senate, Stranding Aid To Central America

MARCH 20 — Despite the best efforts of Senate Appropriations Committee Chairman Ted Stevens, R-Alaska, Congress appears poised to go home for a spring recess without passing President Clinton's emergency relief package for Central America.

With his usual flair, the cantankerous Stevens put the Senate through its paces March 17-19, but Senate action on the $2 billion fiscal 1999 supplemental spending measure (S 544) will not be wrapped up until March 23 at the earliest. The House is expected to take up a $1.3 billion companion bill (HR 1141) on March 24.

The Senate measure would provide more than $977 million for Central American countries hit last year by Hurricanes Mitch and Georges, $100 million in aid to Jordan to implement the Wye River Middle East peace accord and $152 million to expand federal loans to U.S. farmers hurt by falling crop prices.

Like all supplemental spending bills, the measure proved to be a magnet for a variety of senators' mostly modest initiatives, such as additional aid to hog farmers and rules regarding native American hunting of the beluga whale in Alaska.

The bill closely tracks the White House request, but it has earned a veto threat because it would block the federal government from claiming a share of the states' $246 billion settlement with tobacco companies, extend a moratorium on revising royalties from federal oil leases, and postpone new Interior Department environmental regulations on hard-rock mining.

As the bill occupied the Senate off and on for three days, the chamber spent much of its time in quorum calls while Stevens worked to clear routine amendments and get rid of controversial ones.

The only votes came on amendments on matters unrelated to spending. By a 71-29 vote March 18, the Senate killed a proposal by Arlen Specter, R-Pa., and Tom Harkin, D-Iowa, to force states to devote at least 50 percent of last year's tobacco settlement to anti-smoking and tobacco-related health programs. *(Vote 53, p. S-14)*

The Senate also killed a move by Tim Hutchinson, R-Ark., to require congressional approval before the United States could support the entrance of China into the World Trade Organization. The amendment was tabled, 69-30. *(Vote 54, p. S-14)*

And the Senate rebuffed by voice vote a move by Harkin and Robert G. Torricelli, D-N.J., to cut off funding for any independent counsel — including impeachment investigator Kenneth W. Starr — who was appointed before mid-1996.

After Stevens announced that he would move to kill any amendment that did not have support on both sides of the aisle, politically challenging amendments vanished.

One troublesome amendment, offered by Kay Bailey Hutchison, R-Texas, would place restrictions on the use of U.S. troops in the war-torn Serbian province of Kosovo. But that issue is instead going to be debated as a separate measure March 22.

In the only significant substantive changes to the bill, Christopher S. Bond, R-Mo., obtained $150 million in aid to be directed to Midwestern hog farmers, who are suffering from low prices that have left them in or near bankruptcy.

Senate Rejects Tobacco Rider

MARCH 20 — The Senate delivered a blow March 18 to Clinton administration hopes of controlling billions of dollars in tobacco settlement money when it tabled, or killed, 71-29, an amendment that would have required states to spend half their money on public health and tobacco prevention programs. *(Vote 53, p. S-14)*

The vote preserved a rider to the fiscal 1999 supplemental appropriations bill (S 544) that would block the federal government from recouping any portion of the $246 billion that states will receive over 25 years from tobacco companies to settle lawsuits.

The administration has threatened a presidential veto of S 544 because of the tobacco rider. It also objects to spending rescissions in the legislation.

The administration contends that the federal government is entitled to 57 percent of the settlement because it pays that percentage of the costs of Medicaid, the health insurance program for the poor. However, the administration has offered to waive its claim to the settlement if the states devote the money to public health and anti-tobacco programs — an offer for which the states have shown no enthusiasm.

President Clinton's fiscal 2000 budget assumes that the federal government would receive $18.9 billion over five years from the settlements that the states have individually or collectively negotiated with the tobacco industry.

Senate Majority Leader Trent Lott, R-Miss., called the defeated tobacco amendment "typical federal government arrogance."

It would have required states to report annually to the Department of Health and Human Services (HHS) that they had expended at least half their settlement money on anti-tobacco and health programs.

"What do they have at HHS that the states don't have, to decide what is best for their own people?" Lott asked.

The House is not expected to take up the tobacco issue in its version of the supplemental bill (HR 1141). But House bills have been introduced that mirror either the provision to block federal recoupment or the one requiring that states pay for tobacco-related programs.

Some tobacco opponents have defended the federal claim to the money. "I certainly don't think that the states ought to be given money the federal government has paid for health care for tobacco-related disease, and then turn around and spend it on roads and prisons," said Rep. Henry A. Waxman, D-Calif., in a March 17 interview.

Legal Arguments

The National Governors' Association has called the effort to block federal recoupment of the settlement money its top priority for the 106th Congress.

Appearing at a March 15 hearing of the Appropriations subcommittee that funds HHS, Democratic Gov. Paul E. Patton of Kentucky said: "Although states will spend significant amounts of money on programs that improve the health, education and welfare of their citizens, states do not need to be told how to spend any portion of their money."

Many states have outlined their initial plans for the settlement money but have resisted writing any checks for fear HHS will withhold future Medicaid funds. The states have threatened to sue if the federal government prevents the distribution of federal Medicaid money to them.

The administration's claim to the money rests on a provision of Social Security law that requires the states to reimburse the federal government a pro rated share of any Medicaid money recouped from third parties.

"Existing federal law clearly requires states to share all Medicaid recoveries from third parties with federal taxpayers," Mike Hash, deputy administrator of the Health Care Financing Administration, which oversees Medicaid, said at the March 15 hearing.

Hash noted that states turned over $1.5 billion worth of such Medicaid recoupments to the federal Treasury from fiscal 1994 through fiscal 1998.

But the states and their allies in the Senate maintain that the Social Security law is meant to apply to excessive charges recovered from health care providers and insurance companies, not legal settlements.

They also note that the tobacco lawsuits centered on a number of issues aside from Medicaid, including possible fraud, racketeering and violations of consumer protection laws."Medicaid is not a major portion of the settlement, and therefore the federal government has no claim to it," Patton said.

The Defeated Amendment

The defeated Senate amendment would have waived any federal claim to the settlement money, but it required the states to spend at least 20 percent of the money on smoking prevention efforts and education for teenagers. It would also have required that at least 30 percent be spent on public health programs or assistance to tobacco farmers and communities economically damaged by reductions in smoking rates and demand for tobacco crops.

Tom Harkin, D-Iowa, who cosponsored the amendment, said that Medicaid law requires the states to pursue money from tobacco companies while precluding the federal government from doing so. The Justice Department is preparing a tobacco lawsuit centered on recovery of Medicare funds.

Still, some senators complained that requiring large states such as California and New York to expend 20 percent of their billions on anti-smoking efforts would lead to overkill.

"We could literally hire thousands of people and have a personal trainer for every person who's smoking and dipping snuff," said Phil Gramm, R-Texas.

And in response to criticism of a provision that delayed $350 million in welfare payments to states, Stevens replaced that language with delays in funding for Section 8 subsidized housing.

The bill includes $1.7 billion in rescissions of earlier appropriations. The Senate typically is less insistent than House Republicans on financing supplemental bills with cuts in previously appropriated spending. But in the wake of last year's omnibus appropriations bill (PL 105-277), in which lawmakers and Clinton were seen as abusing the appropriations process to evade tight budget caps established in the 1997 balanced-budget law (PL 105-33), senators agreed to include offsets.

Among the reasons for offsetting savings is that the bill came to the floor as Republicans and Democrats wrangled over the fiscal 2000 budget resolution. Republicans are intent on not appearing to raid the budget surplus — which depends exclusively on Social Security surpluses — to finance tax cuts or increases in spending.

Unlike most prior supplemental bills, this year's measure is not driven by a need to take care of a pressing domestic need, such as relief from a flood or other natural disaster. Nor is it needed to finance military peacekeeping missions such as those in Bosnia and the Middle East. As such, the foreign aid-heavy measure does not carry the urgency associated with previous supplementals.

Among the provisions driving the bill forward is the agricultural relief and a new $1 billion loan guarantee program for the steel industry.

Both Chambers Pass Bills; Tough Conference Likely

MARCH 27 — House and Senate appropriators will begin reconciling their divergent midyear spending bills when they return in mid-April from a two-week recess, a delay that proponents had hoped to avoid. The White House wanted aid to be on its way for Central American nations to rebuild after two devastating hurricanes in 1998, but the fiscal 1999 supplemental spending bills hit numerous snags on their way through the Senate and House on March 23-24.

Both bills include nearly $1 billion for disaster relief, expanded federal loans to U.S. farmers and $100 million to Jordan to implement the Wye River Middle East peace accord.

At times, though, both measures seemed headed in the wrong direction. Senate leaders feared that an amendment to restrict the use of U.S. troops in Kosovo would hold up their bill (S 544). After they dropped the Kosovo language, the bill passed by voice vote March 23. The next day, House leaders had to twist arms after time ran out to ensure passage of their measure (HR 1141). The final tally was 220-211. *(Vote 70, p. H-28)*

Members now face the formidable task of finding a compromise. "The two bills are vastly different," said House Appropriations spokeswoman Elizabeth Morra. "It's going to take time to conference this bill." Among significant differences is cost. Senators could not resist adding money during floor debate, and their measure costs about $2.4 billion. The House did not accept floor amendments. Its bill remains at $1.3 billion.

Jim Kolbe, R-Ariz., a senior House appropriator, said the Senate was "really mucking it up." As to whether the Senate's extra programs — additional money for domestic farmers (almost $600 million, compared with $152 million in the House bill), a loan program for the beleaguered steel industry, a loan program for the oil and gas industry, and rebates on the royalties the industry pays to the federal government — can remain part of the package, Kolbe said, "I don't think the House is going to stand for that stuff."

Complicating the debate is the question of offsets: how and whether to pay for the measures. The House left $195 million in defense spending without offsets, and senators might have left much of their bill without offsets had not Phil Gramm, R-Texas, spoken up. The White House's original request would have paid for only $123 million of the package, classifying the rest as "emergency" spending that does not require offsets.

Gramm offered an amendment, adopted by voice vote, that would offset more than $2 billion in budget authority by making across-the-board cuts from the fiscal 1999 omnibus spending bill (PL 105-277). But Appropriations Chairman Ted Stevens, R-Alaska, suggested that the provision would be dropped in conference.

The two chambers' offsets are quite different. The Senate included cuts in fiscal 1999 funding for food stamps, community development block grants and public housing accounts — the last replacing a $350 million delay in welfare money to states that governors had protested.

House appropriators included a $648 million cut in "callable capital" appropriations, an account used to back up international lending institutions in case loans go bad. Also, $150 million was taken from an account to be used to seek reductions in Russia's nuclear capacity. Aides said the money would not have been spent anyway, and Jerry Lewis of California, a key GOP appropriator, called the callable capital cut "an offset that really is not an offset." The Congressional Budget Office said the House bill would be about $800 million short in outlays over five years.

Whether Senate appropriators will accept the reduction in callable capital authority is unclear, especially since Treasury Secretary Robert E. Rubin said he would urge a presidential veto if the provision remained in the bill. But Sonny Callahan, R-Ala., chairman of the House Foreign Operations Appropriations subcommittee, insisted that callable capital would be used. "We're not going to give in on that," he said in an interview. "That's going to be the offset as soon as I explain it to them."

Floor Debate

Most of the House debate focused on offsets. Democrats charged that Republicans, in targeting foreign aid accounts, were sending an ominous signal to international markets. "Of all the times, this is the least desired moment for the United States' credibility to be questioned," said Appropriations ranking Democrat David R. Obey of Wisconsin. "This bill will bring into question our commitment to the financial institutions. . . . " But Obey's amendment to remove the offsets was rejected, 201-228, on a largely party-line vote. *(Vote 68, p. H-28)*

Republicans argued that both the callable capital and the funds to remove Russian uranium and plutonium from the market would not be spent in fiscal 1999. That logic prompted conservative Todd Tiahrt, R-Kan., to offer an amendment to increase the cuts in callable capital by $195 million, thus paying for the entire bill. His bid was rejected, 164-264. *(Vote 69, p. H-28)*

Still, conservatives sympathized with Tiahrt's effort, and the bill came up for a final vote with concerns from both the left and the right. Indeed, HR 1141, the House's first significant legislation in the 106th Congress, seemed to be on its way to defeat until GOP leaders persuaded some members to change their votes — including Republicans Donald Manzullo of Illinois, Lindsey Graham of South Carolina, Joe L. Barton of Texas and Scott McInnis of Colorado.

After the close call, Appropriations Chairman C.W. Bill Young, R-Fla., said the vote was a harbinger of things to come. "I expected to win by one vote," he said March 24. "This is going to be a very difficult year for appropriations."

The Senate passed S 544 by voice vote, masking Stevens' difficulties in marching it through. An amendment by Kay Bailey Hutchison, R-Texas, to require a peace agreement in Kosovo before spending money on troop deployment was among items that held up debate. Then Senate leaders decided March 23 to divorce Kosovo from the supplemental bill.

Pete V. Domenici, R-N.M., succeeded in including a $500 million guaranteed loan program for the oil and gas industry, which would cost about $125 million. Jeff Bingaman, D-N.M., added a provision to allow oil and gas companies to deduct the costs of certain drilling and exploring activities from royalties paid to the federal government, at an estimated cost of $60 million.

Charles S. Robb, D-Va., won floor approval of an amendment to allow the Defense Department to compensate the families of victims of the 1998 accident in Italy in which a U.S. military airplane clipped the cables of a gondola, killing 20 people. It could cost up to $40 million. A similar amendment was ruled out of order in the House.

The Interior Department has threatened to urge a veto over a provision by Frank H. Murkowski, R-Alaska, that would prevent the federal government from implementing restrictions on fishing in certain parts of Alaska's Glacier Bay National Park. A motion to table, or kill, the provision failed, 40-59. *(Vote 56, p. S-15)*

Appropriators Set To Grant Clinton's Kosovo Request — And Then Some

APRIL 24 — The House and Senate Appropriations committees have scheduled meetings the week of April 26 to mark up Clinton's $6 billion supplemental appropriations request, most of which is to pay for military operations against Yugoslavia.

The only issue to be settled on this bill, apparently, is how much money Republicans will add to Clinton's request. Pentagon officials insist their $6 billion request has been calculated to cover all the costs of the Yugoslavia operation, including replenishing the diminishing stockpiles of long-range, precision-guided cruise missiles used in some of the attacks.

But a phalanx of GOP leaders and defense specialists hope to add billions more in military spending to the supplemental bill, money they say would begin to shore up weak spots in the defense establishment that have resulted from Clinton giving the Pentagon too little money and too many missions.

Duncan Hunter, R-Calif., chairman of the House Armed Services Subcommittee on Military Procurement, called for increasing the bill to nearly $29 billion. But the prevailing view among GOP leaders by April 22 was that the final version of the supplemental would provide between $10 billion and $12 billion.

Republican leaders have not said just how the added money would be used. Lawmakers who patrol the limits of the federal budget say their pro-defense colleagues are trying to evade regular spending limits by pumping billions into the supplemental.

Of Clinton's $6 billion request, about $5.5 billion would go to the Defense Department. Most of the Pentagon funds would pay for the Kosovo operation, though it also includes $451 million to pay for military operations against Iraq since last November.

The Pentagon's Kosovo funding includes $287 million to cover personnel and operating costs incurred between March 24, when the attacks began, and the end of April, plus an additional $3 billion to pay for operations through the end of the fiscal year.

The Pentagon's other large slice of the supplemental request is $1.5 billion to replenish stocks of missiles and bombs. This includes $686 million for precision-guided missiles and bombs used in an attack on Iraq last December ($177 million) and in the Kosovo mission since March 24 ($521 million). The remaining $850 million is for weapons the Pentagon expects to use, assuming the Yugoslavia operation continues through the end of the fiscal year.

The supplemental request includes $686 million for refugee assistance. This total includes $335 million for the Pentagon to cover the cost of providing and transporting food, tents, blankets and other supplies for Kosovar refugees and $351 million for multilateral refugee assistance funded through the State Department and the Agency for International Development.

The request also would provide $185 million for assistance to Balkan states adjacent to Yugoslavia that have suffered because of the conflict.

Getting Around Outlay Caps

For Republicans, whose legislative agenda so far this year has been spare, the Kosovo spending measure represents an opportunity to advance one of their top priorities for the 106th Congress: Reversing the steady downward trend in defense spending.

"One of our four priorities from the get-go has been national security," said John Feehery, spokesman. for Speaker J. Dennis Hastert, R-Ill.

Under the budget resolution, domestic programs would be cut to shift money into defense and still stay within the caps. But the Kosovo bill will not count toward the caps, so anything added for the Pentagon would be "free" money.

"You've got some people who want to use it to cure all of the military's ills forever," said a GOP member of the House Appropriations Committee. "That probably isn't going to happen, but there will be some of that."

Every dollar above the Kosovo request that goes to the Pentagon in the fiscal 1999 supplemental is a dollar that eases the difficulty appropriators will face later this year when they try to pass the 13 fiscal 2000 spending bills. But it will still not be enough to get the bills passed and signed.

"Our outlay problems . . . are so severe that this will not make us well," said James W. Dyer, majority staff director of the House Appropriations Committee. "It will make us well on defense, but not on the other bills."

One reason the supplemental will help out on appropriations involves arcane but important nuances in the relationship between budget authority and outlays.

Among the thorniest difficulties facing appropriators are the tight caps on outlays, the funds that actually get spent each year. Budget authority represents new spending, which can take years to be spent as outlays — especially in the case of Pentagon procurement. The budget resolution gives the Pentagon lots of budget authority but not enough outlays.

To ease the outlay problems, Young and key Democrats such as Rep. John P. Murtha of Pennsylvania are pushing to add a military pay raise and retirement package to the supplemental measure, even though there is no direct link between military pay and the war. Young said that, especially with a war going, "the issue of recruitment and retention is an emergency."

The pay raise would free up about $4 billion a year for other purposes. But the idea has gotten a cool reception from the White House, and Senate Appropriations Committee Chairman Ted Stevens, R-Alaska, opposes adding it to the bill. The Senate passed a pay raise (S 4) in February.

"Stevens is apparently more disciplined; he does not want to put the pay-retirement bill in this package for good reason — that is not an emergency," said a senior Senate GOP aide.

If the Kosovo situation promises to give a little relief to appropriators, it does not advance the cause of Republicans who favor a big tax cut.

The money for Kosovo, as well as the appetite for additional defense and non-defense spending, threatens to eat into future "on-budget" surpluses that Republicans are reserving for a tax bill.

"I think that's a growing concern," Feehery said.

At the same time, it has become increasingly apparent that the war has overshadowed the domestic agendas of both parties. Said Nevada Democratic Sen. Richard H. Bryan: "The Kosovo thing has sucked all the energy out of this place."

House Committee Increases Amount To Cover Kosovo Operations

MAY 1 — Congress may be bitterly divided over the prudence of President Clinton's policy on Kosovo, but it has no alternative but to pay for it. Despite sweeping and fervent GOP opposition to "Clinton's war," a bulked up version of Clinton's emergency request for the mission is expected to pass the House with relative ease the week of May 3.

Republicans are nevertheless split over how much additional defense money to bestow upon the Pentagon through the must-pass vehicle, which Clinton has little choice but to sign.

The House Appropriations Committee approved a $12.9 billion draft measure April 29 that more than doubled Clinton's request. Voice vote approval belied the contentiousness of the markup, during which some top committee Democrats accused the Republicans of larding the fiscal 1999 supplemental bill with unnecessary spending to ease their pain later in the year when they must confront tight "caps" on fiscal 2000 spending.

At the same time, Republicans sharply rejected an attempt by one of their own to limit Clinton's options in carrying out the war.

Democrats will attempt to pare the bill on the floor. Regardless of what happens there, the House will have achieved its most important objective: getting the measure to the safety of a House-Senate conference.

That is where congressional leaders and other experienced lawmakers will regain firm control and shape a final bill that members have no choice but to pass and that Clinton is eager to sign.

The Appropriations Committee action represents the high-water mark for the bill, which will shrink in conference and, perhaps, on the House floor, where some GOP members are wary of borrowing from the Social Security-generated budget surplus to give Clinton more than he requested for a bombing mission they do not support. Some are worried that the additional money could ultimately be used to support the same ground war that they voted to block.

The floor vote will come after Republicans issued a sharp rebuke to Clinton on April 28 by passing a bill (HR 1569) to block the use of ground troops. Also, Clinton's Democratic allies could not muster enough GOP votes to adopt a resolution (S Con Res 21) to express approval of the ongoing air campaign.

Lawmakers of both parties will confront vexing choices when voting on the Kosovo spending bill. Republicans opposed to Clinton's Kosovo policy will be asked to vote to fund it. Many Democrats who support the policy are balking at the bill's cost but are likely to vote for it in the end.

The bill must pass because the alternative would be to appear unsupportive of the troops and to force the Pentagon to make brutal cuts in training and readiness — exactly the opposite statement Republicans want to make.

"Republicans and Democrats may agree to disagree over the policy in Kosovo," said Defense Appropriations Subcommittee Chairman Jerry Lewis, R-Calif. "But we must not — for a minute — send a message to our troops that we do not support them."

Clinton is unhappy with the current size of the House bill, but a letter from Office of Management and Budget (OMB) Director Jack Lew expressing the administration's views barely slapped Republicans' wrists. "Regrettably, the draft committee bill . . . goes well beyond the funding requirements of the mission in Kosovo," it said. "Regrettable" is among the weakest objections in the arcane but closely watched argot of OMB position papers. Lewis said Clinton signaled at a White House meeting the day before the markup that he would accept additional spending provided it would not slow down the bill.

Some of the president's most bitter enemies are among his most powerful allies in keeping the bill's price down: conservative Senate Republicans such as Majority Whip Don Nickles, R-Okla., and Larry E. Craig, R-Idaho. They left an April 28 Senate GOP meeting expressing reservations about going much higher than Clinton's $6 billion request.

Said Slade Gorton, R-Wash., a member of the Appropriations Committee: "I opposed getting into this adventure in the first place, and I don't see why I should signal my support for it by giving him more than he asked for."

On the other side of the Senate GOP Conference are old-timers such as Appropriations Committee Chairman Ted Stevens, R-Alaska, and senior committee member Pete V. Domenici, R-N.M., who support a higher figure. "I agree with what the House is doing," Stevens said. "I don't know how much of it the Senate's going to be willing to buy."

Several Republicans most skeptical of adding money above Clinton's request, such as Craig, Gorton, and Kay Bailey Hutchison of Texas, are members of Appropriations. But Stevens, who has a good relationship with panel Democrats, plans to sidestep a committee markup as well as floor debate, with the blessing of Majority Leader Trent Lott, R-Miss. "We're going to wait for [the House] to move a bill through the floor and then go directly to conference," said a top Stevens aide.

Smaller Supplemental

Stevens and Lott can skip floor debate because an earlier fiscal 1999 supplemental bill (HR 1141) is currently in conference and the Kosovo bill can be added to it. The earlier supplemental would provide emergency loans to U.S. farmers beset by low prices and give relief to Central American nations devastated last year by hurricanes Mitch and Georges.

The House and Senate have substantial differences over the earlier, smaller supplemental, which has earned a White House veto threat over GOP cuts in spending to offset, or "pay for," the humanitarian assistance. The $2.4 billion Senate bill is almost double the size of the House bill, and the two bodies have wholly different ideas about what programs to cut.

There has been no public progress on that measure since House conferees were named April 22, and not a lot more behind the scenes. The week of May 3 promises to be crucial.

Anxiety about inaction on the disaster and farm aid bill is growing among lawmakers from farm states whose constituents cannot get loans for spring planting and from Southern border states worried about a wave of Central American refugees fleeing the devastation of that region.

Kosovo Engine

The current Kosovo supplemental reflects an effort by House defense hawks to use it as an engine to pull other favored Pentagon spending into law. The measure, for example, contains $3.1 billion for improvements in readiness that the military had sought before the Kosovo mission began March 24. These include money for spare parts, depot maintenance, recruitment, and training and base operations. It contains $1.8 billion to finance a military pay raise and pension improvements.

The bill also includes a more controversial $1.1 billion for military construction projects concentrated in Europe. Democrats and White House aides scoffed at this request as nothing more than an attempt to use the Kosovo situation to help pay for more U.S.-based military construction projects, a favorite of lawmakers.

"They're trying to make room in the fiscal 2000 bill for their pork, and this is how they do it," charged top panel Democrat David R. Obey of Wisconsin. Obey noted that more than half the construction projects were slated for funding after fiscal 2000 or were not even in the Pentagon's long-range plans.

In countering criticism that they were stuffing the bill with money unrelated to the Kosovo mission, Republicans pointed out repeatedly that in order for any of it to be spent Clinton would have to officially certify it as emergency spending. "If there are some items in here that he doesn't approve of, all he has to do is nothing," said Appropriations Chairman C.W. Bill Young, R-Fla.

An Obey bid to trim $2.7 billion from the bill failed, 20-35. Four Democratic defense hawks joined Republicans in killing the amendment.

More revealing was a brief but intense debate over an amendment by Ernest Istook, R-Okla., that mirrored a bill (HR 1569) passed by the House on April 28 to require congressional approval before dispatching ground troops into the war. Istook said he was concerned that Clinton could use money in the bill for a ground war. "We want to restore military readiness but not expand the war," Istook said.

Reading the names of Appropriations members who voted less than 24 hours earlier for identical language on HR 1569, which the Senate will not consider, Istook challenged them to do the same on a live vehicle.

"When you voted yesterday, was that just for the cameras, or did you mean it?" Istook asked. "I'm frankly disturbed, Mr. Chairman, by hearing some people say, 'Well, maybe we ought to vote differently today.' If someone wants to flip-flop in 24 hours, people ought to know about it."

If it had been adopted, the amendment would have complicated the supplemental measure's prospects for passage and would have certainly earned a veto threat — an unthinkable step given the crisis.

Senior panel Republican Ron Packard of California implored Istook to withdraw the amendment. "Don't put us in a position to have to vote against what we voted yesterday," Packard said.

Istook's amendment was defeated by a resounding voice vote. Republicans rebuffed his request for a recorded vote.

Social Security Concerns

Besides uneasiness about the war, another issue will add pressure to reduce the bill's cost: Social Security. After spending weeks assuring voters that they would not tap into the Social Security-related surplus for tax cuts or new spending, lawmakers have no choice but to do so to pay for the bombing. It does not sit well with them.

"We finally got our message out about Social Security, and now it's going to hang us," said Mark Souder, R-Ind., who said he was recently upbraided by a constituent who complained that Congress was going to use Social Security to pay for the war.

Might Republicans be vulnerable to charges that they are loading up the Kosovo supplemental only a week after voting against U.S. participation in NATO airstrikes? Absolutely not, said John Feehery, spokesman for Speaker J. Dennis Hastert, R-Ill. "One vote is to support the president's policy; the second vote is to make the Pentagon whole again," Feehery said. "They're two different votes."

The markup's timing the day after the heated floor debate on the war ensured a sometimes lively debate. Among the liveliest remarks came from Obey and Randy "Duke" Cunningham, R-Calif., a decorated former fighter pilot.

Said Obey: "I also, frankly, find it mind-boggling that some of the same members who yesterday voted against the operation will today here, now vote to more than double the amount of spending that the president has asked for to conduct those operations. I think that is spectacularly inconsistent."

Said Cunningham: "This is the most inept, the most ill-planned, illogical war that I have ever been associated with. And for me to . . . put my fingerprints on what I consider a disgrace was the reason that I voted no."

House-Passed Bill Doubles Clinton's Kosovo Emergency Spending Request

MAY 8 — Republican leaders took no chances in briskly advancing through the House a $13.1 billion emergency spending bill to pay for U.S. participation in the war in Kosovo. Scores of Republicans who had cast mostly symbolic votes against airstrikes or a potential ground war only a week earlier changed their votes to support financing the war.

The House passed the fiscal 1999 supplemental spending bill (HR 1664) by a 311-105 vote May 6. A difficult conference awaits, and House-Senate negotiators are under pressure to quickly reach agreement on the bill. House Speaker J. Dennis Hastert, R-Ill., and Senate Majority Leader Trent Lott, R-Miss., said they want to get the measure to President Clinton by the end of the week of May 10. *(Vote 120, p. H-46)*

Such an ambitious timetable will prove difficult to meet. The House and Senate differ over how much additional Pentagon money to add to Clinton's $6 billion request, which was limited to Kosovo costs. To avoid a lengthy debate over Kosovo in the Senate, Lott has opted to attach the money for the war to an earlier fiscal 1999 supplemental bill (HR 1141) to provide disaster aid to Central America and relief to U.S. farmers. That will speed action, but it means the Senate will enter the conference without a concrete position from which to negotiate.

Meanwhile, great differences among the House, Senate and Clinton over the earlier emergency spending bill threaten a lengthier conference than everyone would like.

Resounding approval of the must-pass Kosovo funding bill came barely a week after House Republicans voted en masse against a resolution (S Con Res 21) expressing approval of the NATO air campaign against Yugoslavia. The turnaround came about because GOP leaders cast the vote on HR 1664 as a vote to support U.S. troops under fire and to restore a "hollowed out" military. Earlier votes were about the wisdom of Clinton policy in the Balkans.

"Last week, the House spoke on the president's policies in conducting the engagement in Kosovo. Clearly, the House had some misgivings about those policies," Hastert said. "But today, let there be no mistake. The United States Congress stands with its soldiers, sailors and airmen as they defend America."

In contrast to his hands-off approach on earlier votes, which Hastert depicted as votes of conscience, the Speaker took no chances in ensuring easy passage of the funding bill. Hastert had come under fire for sitting on his hands April 28 as Majority Whip Tom DeLay, R-Texas, engineered defeat of S Con Res 21, the Senate-passed resolution to authorize airstrikes.

By longstanding tradition, the Speaker usually votes only on major legislation. On that day, Hastert supported Clinton but cast his vote late in the tally. Many Republicans were unaware of his position; several subsequently told him they would have voted differently had they known where he stood. In a closed-door GOP meeting May 5, Hastert apologized for not sending a clearer signal.

No such mixed signal was sent during the May 6 debate. The GOP whip operation hummed, and Hastert worked the floor and voted early and often: He not only voted for the bill, but also for the rule (H Res 159) required to bring the bill to the floor and against a key amendment by Ernest Istook, R-Okla., aimed at blocking ground troops — a reversal of his vote for a largely identical bill (HR 1569) that passed April 28.

The only major hiccup in the days leading up to the vote came when farm-state lawmakers objected because HR 1664 did not contain emergency funds for federally guaranteed farm loans. The money is in the earlier supplemental bill, and there is a growing sense of urgency in farm country over the delay.

Those concerns were eased by an amendment by Tom Latham, R-Iowa, adopted by voice vote, to add $110 million for the loan guarantees. It would be financed by an equal amount in offsetting cuts from HR 1141. The vote did not speed up the farm aid, but it eased pressure on farm-state lawmakers who faced a potentially difficult vote on an amendment by top Appropriations Democrat David R. Obey of Wisconsin that contained the farm aid.

In the only other change to the bill, Republicans accepted by voice vote an amendment by Nancy Pelosi, D-Calif., to add $67 million in extra humanitarian assistance for Kosovar refugees.

Ground Troops

Debate grew heated on Istook's amendment to block U.S. ground troops in Yugoslavia, including in the province of Kosovo. On April 28, 203 Republicans voted for HR 1569, which would require congressional authorization for ground troops. That vote carried little weight because the Senate has no plans to take up HR 1569 and, even if it did, Clinton would veto it.

But when the vote on blocking ground troops really mattered, only 97 Republicans supported Istook, and his amendment failed, 117-301. Among those switching positions was a lead sponsor of the earlier ban, Tillie Fowler, R-Fla. She not only changed her vote but also stood at a House door to lobby colleagues as they entered the chamber. Republicans such as Majority Leader Dick Armey of Texas and leading defense hawk Randy "Duke" Cunningham of California — who had previously helped lead the fight against ground troops — warned that Istook's amendment would have delayed enactment of the bill and sent a signal to Yugoslav President Slobodan Milosevic that he would not have to worry about a land war. *(Vote 119, p. H-46)*

In other votes, the House:

- Defeated an amendment by conservative Tom Coburn, R-Okla., to finance the bill with across-the-board cuts in domestic appropriations. The vote was 101-322. *(Vote 117, p. H-46)*
- Rejected an amendment by Obey to pare the Kosovo portion of the bill to $10.2 billion and add $1.7 billion for items contained in the earlier emergency bill for farm loans and relief for Central America. The vote was 164-260. *(Vote 118, p. H-46)*

Obey was the most vocal of Democrats critical of the way Republicans have handled Kosovo in general and the emergency funding in particular. He and others accused Republicans of hypocrisy for voting against the war one week and then turning around and doubling Clinton's request the next.

Said Democratic Caucus Chairman Martin Frost of Texas: "I am at a loss to explain how the Republican Party can, on one hand, be so irresponsible as to abandon our troops in the midst of a military action to demonstrate its visceral hostility toward the commander in chief, and then, on the other, turn around and double his request for money for what they call 'Clinton's war.' "

Roles Reversed

Largely lost in the debate was the curious change of roles between the GOP-led House and Senate over the funding measure. Typically, House hard-liners exert pressure to limit the size of appropriations bills, particularly supplementals. The Senate's attitude on spending, although changing, is considerably more permissive. A supplemental presents an opportunity to address senators' parochial needs.

The earlier supplemental was typical, as the Senate version of HR 1141 is nearly twice the size of the House bill after senators added extra funding for agricultural aid, disaster relief, and relief for domestic steel, and oil and gas producers. But the Senate has generally displayed more restraint on the Kosovo bill, with a band of GOP conservatives working to keep costs down. Some advocate little if any funding above Clinton's $6 billion request.

At least two factors color the Senate's attitude on the current supplemental: Social Security and a sweeping distaste for Clinton's Kosovo policies. On Social Security, Republicans have spent much of the year assuring voters that they will not touch the portion of the surplus generated by surplus Social Security revenues (currently all of it) for tax cuts or new spending. But they have no choice but to do so to pay for the war.

"This isn't so much a change of mind on most basic things where the Senate of course uses any appropriations bill as a vehicle for a number of other goals . . . as it is a battle about one's attitude toward the war in the Balkans," said Slade Gorton, R-Wash.

Also at play, however, is the upcoming fiscal 2000 appropriations cycle, which is going to be extraordinarily difficult, given the tight "caps" on appropriations that lawmakers face. Those in favor of bulking up Clinton's request made no secret that they were seeking to use the Kosovo bill — which as an "emergency" measure does not count toward the caps — as a vehicle to make this year's task a little easier.

Even Gorton, among the group most firmly against adding money for the war, acknowledged the temptation, especially given his position as chairman of the Interior Appropriations Subcommittee: "I have not wanted to vote an extra dime for the war over what the president asks, but I also have to recognize as a subcommittee chairman how next to impossible it's going to be to meet those caps."

At the same time, Senate Democratic Leader Tom Daschle of South Dakota announced May 6 that he would like to add billions of dollars in additional farm relief to the bill.

Tough Conference Ahead

Conferees are tentatively scheduled to meet May 11, and GOP leaders have declared that negotiations may be wrapped up that day. But that will prove difficult.

Among the chief obstacles is Senate language, written by Kay Bailey Hutchison, R-Texas, to block the federal government from claiming a share of the $246 billion settlement between tobacco companies and the states. Along with spending cuts deemed objectionable by the White House and other Senate "riders" to extend a moratorium on revising royalties from federal oil leases and to postpone new Interior Department environmental regulations on hard-rock mining, the tobacco language has helped earn HR 1141 a veto threat from Clinton.

But since Kosovo was added to the mix, the administration has been careful not to hint of a veto. White House officials say they have a secret roster of offsets to replace spending cuts made by Republicans in HR 1141. Republicans are often eager to accept administration offsets, however dubious, and if that pattern persists, the offset obstacle could vanish.

On Pentagon spending, it may prove difficult for conferees to resist the temptation to err on the high side. That is the natural inclination of House Appropriations Committee Chairman C.W. Bill Young, R-Fla., who will head the conference.

Based on the sweeping House vote, it is also probably acceptable to lawmakers in both chambers. Senate Appropriations Committee Chairman Ted Stevens, R-Alaska, makes no secret that he would prefer a package like the House's, and even liberal Democrat Obey won 164 votes for his $10.2 billion Kosovo package.

Lott said May 6 that he wants to see a final bill of $9 billion to $10 billion for Kosovo alone. A top GOP Senate Appropriations aide predicted a combined final cost of $12 billion to $13 billion for Kosovo and the smaller supplemental bill.

Fireworks, Finesse Mark Conference On Supplemental

MAY 15 — A freewheeling conference on a $14.6 billion emergency spending bill exposed a rift between GOP leaders and their appropriators and featured a dramatic battle between a Senate legend and the new Speaker of the House. But after three days of contentious debate and a major blowup that threatened to derail the key bill, all elements slid into place with surprising ease May 13.

Final floor action on the supplemental spending bill (HR 1141) is expected in the House and Senate the week of May 17. All indications are that President Clinton will sign the bill, although it doubles his request for money to carry out the war over Kosovo.

The conference agreement, as expected, added funds for U.S. participation in the Kosovo mission (HR 1664) to a smaller — but more contentious — measure to give long-delayed relief to Central American nations devastated last year by Hurricanes Mitch and Georges and to provide help to U.S. farmers.

The accord resolves several issues that Congress and Clinton have maneuvered over for months, and paves the way for a difficult fiscal 2000 appropriations cycle. The additional supplemental funds promise to ease appropriators' headaches, if only slightly.

On the supplemental, the most difficult issue to resolve involved a plan by Sen. Robert C. Byrd, D-W.Va., to establish a loan guarantee program for steel producers, including one in his home state, harmed by subsidized imports. With the backing of Senate Appropriations Chairman Ted Stevens, R-Alaska, Byrd fought tenaciously and won an early decision May 13 to keep the loan guarantee program in the bill. Speaker J. Dennis Hastert, R-Ill., rallied later that day and forced two House Republican Appropriations subcommittee chairmen who had supported Byrd to reverse course and kill the provision.

The battle over Byrd's pet provision and a companion loan program for smaller oil and gas producers provided the most compelling conference drama, but the hotly debated question of what spending cuts to make to finance some non-defense items in the measure was finessed with remarkable ease.

At the last minute, the White House came forward with $1.6 billion in fiscal 1999 spending authority that cannot be used this year. Republicans quickly accepted those offsets and dropped controversial House- and Senate-passed spending cuts that had provoked veto threats. Offsets were a priority for House conservatives, but the chief offset — a $1.3 billion reduction of soon-to-expire money for food stamps — will not generate any savings that would not have accrued anyway.

Clinton won another major victory as House GOP leaders permitted full-year funding for the Commerce, Justice and State departments, whose budgets were held hostage to a quarrel between Clinton and House Republicans over the question of census "sampling."

But the administration was rebuffed in its bid to strip a provision, backed by all 50 governors, to forbid the federal government from claiming any of the $246 billion that states have won in a settlement with the tobacco industry. That Senate provision, sponsored by Kay Bailey Hutchison, R-Texas, was one of several Senate "riders" that had helped earn an earlier version of the bill a veto threat. Standing alone, however, the widely backed tobacco language will not provoke a veto, a top administration official said.

Getting Started

The conference convened May 11, a Tuesday, with negotiators spending the afternoon clearing away the legislative underbrush: They resolved relatively minor disagreements and identified more significant ones. A few major issues were settled, but the afternoon mainly provided a chance for lawmakers to debate issues, such as school safety and farm aid, which would be settled the next day.

From the start, Stevens was characteristically cantankerous. He blasted a House provision for $1.1 billion in Kosovo-related overseas military construction projects, many of which could not have been completed for years. He suggested killing all the projects, but later agreed to $475 million, provided the Pentagon was given latitude to determine the most critical ones.

House Appropriations Chairman C.W. Bill Young, R-Fla., who won kudos from his colleagues for running the conference with patience and aplomb, was generous in letting members debate issues at length. For the first time — and possibly the last — an appropriations conference was televised on C-SPAN. Speeches lengthened, however, and the fraternity-party atmosphere typical of the insular world of appropriations earned mixed reviews from the public and from congressional leaders.

For example, Senate Democrats launched a dramatic but futile bid for a $5 billion-plus increase in funds to ease the crisis in farm country, where low prices are threatening thousands with bankruptcy. "We are in a crisis situation," said Tom Harkin, D-Iowa. Harkin's bid was later killed by Senate conferees in a 14-14 vote on whether to present it to the House. The final farm aid figure was $574 million.

Sen. Richard J. Durbin, D-Ill., followed with a $1 billion plan for grants to school districts for programs to increase school safety and combat teen violence. In the wake of the Colorado school shootings April 20, the bid appeared to have momentum and Stevens signed off on a reduced $265 million offer to the House. But House conferees, already impatient with Senate add-ons, blocked the move. "It is nice the Senate has solved this without any consultation," said Rep. John Edward Porter, R-Ill.

The slow pace of the talks, while typical of conferences on supplemental bills, irritated Hastert and Senate Majority Leader Trent Lott, R-Miss., who issued a May 11 letter telling conferees to get busy and instructing them, in an unusually public fashion, on the size and scope of the final product.

The letter leaked to the media and rankled appropriators. But when the conference reconvened on the afternoon of May 12, negotiations began to inch forward. Conferees settled on a $10.9 billion figure for the Pentagon, nearly double Clinton's request to carry out the Balkan air war.

Other agreements included:

- **Tobacco.** As expected, the House accepted Senate language to block the federal government from obtaining any of the tobacco settlement money.
- **Glacier Bay.** Stevens and Alaska GOP colleague Frank H. Murkowski made an impassioned plea to keep the inland waters off Glacier Bay National Park open to commercial and subsistence fishing. That would have reopened a deal reached last year between the administration and the Alaska delegation, and could have prompted a veto. House conferees — who became impatient with the pre-

Congress Aims Extra Billions At Pentagon's Routine Costs

MAY 15 — Most of the $5.4 billion in defense-related spending that House-Senate conferees added to President Clinton's $5.5 billion supplemental appropriations request for the Kosovo air war is aimed at beefing up the Pentagon's budget for spare parts, maintenance and other routine operating costs.

The additional money for fiscal 1999 reflects the long-standing view of congressional defense specialists that Clinton has undermined the armed forces by giving them budgets that were too stingy even as he committed them to a wider range of overseas missions.

The increase also will give the congressional Armed Services and Appropriations committees some breathing room as they write the defense authorization and appropriations bills for fiscal 2000. Much of the defense-related funding in the fiscal 1999 supplemental (HR 1141) is designated "emergency" spending, exempt from the budget caps set by the 1997 balanced budget law (PL 105-33). *(1997 Almanac, p. 2-18)*

Insofar as it pays for items that otherwise would be included in fiscal 2000 bills, the supplemental provides room for congressional initiatives that otherwise would not fit under the budget caps.

The $13 billion version of the supplemental bill passed by the House (HR 1664) included about $3 billion for items that otherwise would have to be funded in the fiscal 2000 bills. In working out a final agreement, House-Senate conferees dealt only in amounts for broad budget categories, so it was not immediately clear how it will be apportioned among defense accounts in the fiscal 2000 bills. But the range is expected to be $2 billion to $3 billion of headroom in the fiscal 2000 bills.

Clinton Request

The conference report would provide, as Clinton requested, $5.46 billion to pay for military costs directly associated with both the Kosovo operation and the airstrikes against Iraq since last fall.

Of that total, $453 million would be for operations against Iraq and the replacement of cruise missiles fired at Iraqi targets. The balance — $5 billion — would be to pay for the U.S. share of NATO air strikes against Yugoslavia that began March 24 and for humanitarian operations to care for ethnic Albanian refugees driven out of the Serbian province of Kosovo.

Clinton's request for the supplemental assumed that the air war against Yugoslavia would continue at the current level of intensity through Sept. 30, the end of the fiscal year. If a cease-fire was reached before then, the Pentagon would have money left over. On the other hand, if NATO sent ground troops into Kosovo, the Pentagon would need more money.

The Kosovo-related amount in the conference report includes, as requested, $684 million to replenish stocks of precision-guided bombs and missiles that account for a much larger proportion of the weapons used against Yugoslavia than they did of those used against Iraq in the 1991 Persian Gulf war. The conference report would provide:

- $431 million to convert older Navy Tomahawk cruise missiles to the newest, most accurate version.
- $178 million to convert nuclear-armed missiles launched from Air Force bombers to conventionally armed weapons.
- $35 million for bombs that use Global Positioning Satellites to steer to within several yards of a target.
- $40 million for decoys used to lure enemy missiles away from U.S. planes.

The House had added $3.1 billion to Clinton's supplemental request for spare parts, maintenance, operating costs and recruiting. Of that amount, about $1 billion would have been included in the fiscal 2000 bills because it was for items in Clinton's fiscal 2000 budget request.

The conferees pared this House initiative down to $2.35 billion. As of May 13, it was not known how much of the conferees' reduction came from the $1 billion the House had drawn from the fiscal 2000 request.

Another major addition to the defense portion of the supplemental was $1.84 billion for a 4.8 percent increase in military pay and pensions. The Senate in February passed legislation (S 4 — S Rept 106-1) for a 4.8 percent increase, rather than the 4.4 percent Clinton proposed, and the increase was part of the defense authorization bills.

Although the raise would not take effect until Jan. 1, 2000, by including the funds in the supplemental, Congress would free up $1.8 billion from the fiscal 2000 legislation for other congressional initiatives.

Other Provisions

The conference report also includes $550 million for procurement that Clinton did not request. Of that amount, $250 million would be for missiles and bombs.

The remaining $300 million apparently is intended for items that could be put into service quickly enough to have an impact on the Kosovo operation.

For instance, one House aide suggested that some of the money could be used to buy additional radar jamming equipment to increase the effectiveness of the EA-6B Prowler electronic warfare planes that try to shield U.S. aircraft from Yugoslav radar detection.

The conference report also includes $475 million for unspecified military construction projects and $200 million for the Coast Guard.

sentation by Murkowski, a non-conferee — promptly killed the provision by voice vote.

Instead, Stevens obtained about $26 million in assistance for Alaskans who will be affected by the phasing out of fishing in the park. The money continued a trend in which Stevens has agreed to drop environmental riders opposed by Clinton in exchange for funding.

• **Commerce, Justice, State.** With little fanfare, Republicans yielded to the White House and extended fiscal 1999 funding for agencies whose budgets are included in the spending bill for the departments of Commerce, Justice and State and the federal judiciary. That measure has annually become mired in controversy over an administration plan to use census "sampling" techniques meant to produce a more accurate 2000 count, especially in urban areas. Republicans abhor the plan, which promises to produce a more Democratic tilt in the upcoming round of congressional redistricting, and they had insisted on a June 15 cutoff of Commerce, Justice, State funding as a way to pressure the White House into compromise. But Clinton refused to yield, and Republicans gave up rather than risk a partial government shutdown.

• **Kansas gas producers.** With little debate, conferees killed a Senate provision that would have given Kansas natural gas distributors an estimated $235 million windfall by letting them avoid interest penalties for overcharging consumers in 23 states. "This is a straight special interest versus public interest issue," said top House Appropriations Democrat David R. Obey of Wisconsin.

• **Refugee assistance.** Over the objections of Young and Rep. Sonny Callahan, R-Ala., chairman of the Foreign Operations Appropriations Subcommittee, ranking subcommittee Democrat Nancy Pelosi of California won an additional $141 million in aid for Kosovar refugees, bringing total aid to $1.1 billion, including $100 million for temporary resettlement of Kosovar refugees in the United States, added just before the conference closed.

• **FEMA.** Conferees added $900 million for the Federal Emergency Management Agency for disaster assistance for Oklahoma and Kansas in response to the recent tornadoes. Clinton requested $372 million.

• **Airport grants.** Lawmakers extended until Aug. 6 the authority of the Federal Aviation Administration (FAA) to issue airport improvement grants. A temporary authorization expires May 31 and the further extension will give Congress time to pass an FAA reauthorization bill (S 82, HR 1000).

Two Approaches

The conference vividly illustrated the divide between the House and Senate over how to approach an emergency appropriations bill. Young repeatedly stressed that the House had kept the legislation "clean," or free of members' parochial projects. He said he had refused many members' requests for help. The Senate used HR 1141 as a vehicle for lawmakers to tend to their states.

"We turned down many, many members of the House, including leadership," Young said as the House fought off Senate water projects.

The high-profile Senate loan guarantee programs were stripped, but other parochial provisions remained or were slipped into the bill with little debate. An example of Senate collegiality occurred when the House tried to strip $800,000, obtained by Senate Minority Leader Tom Daschle, D-S.D., to transfer federal land to Sioux Indian tribes. Stevens held fast and said that he had given Daschle his word the money would stay in the bill. "We are prepared . . . to stand by this amendment," Stevens bellowed.

Stevens was equally adamant about keeping Byrd's loan guarantee program for steel producers and a companion loan guarantee program for independent domestic oil and gas producers who operate relatively small "stripper" wells. Its chief advocate was powerful New Mexico Republican Sen. Pete V. Domenici. Lott and Republican Whip Don Nickles of Oklahoma opposed the add-ons, but Stevens and his fellow appropriators pressed for them anyway.

After approving Byrd's provision, House Republicans stunned and infuriated the Senate by rejecting Domenici's provision in the early morning hours of May 13. Stevens abruptly adjourned the conference.

For a while, it appeared that the conference had stalled. But with intense pressure to move the legislation, Republican leaders got the bill back on track by promising a stand-alone vote on the steel provisions. That was enough to get Reps. Ralph Regula, R-Ohio, and Joe Skeen, R-N.M., to reverse their previous votes for including the steel provisions in HR 1141. Byrd grudgingly accepted the result.

All that remained was the issue of offsets. Republicans are uneasy over the cost of the bill, which will be financed almost entirely by the budget surplus, currently made up entirely of surplus Social Security revenues. The Kosovo bill is advancing as Republicans tout their efforts to protect the portion of present and future surpluses that stem from Social Security.

The administration rescued House and Senate Republicans, who had passed two different but equally controversial sets of cuts in unused budget authority. Among the most contested were House plans to cut $150 million from a program to help Russia dispose of plutonium and $648 million in capital reserves for the World Bank and other international development banks.

The chief offset offered by the White House, $1.3 billion in mandatory appropriations for food stamps, was deemed by Obey to be "much preferable" to the earlier offsets. No food stamp recipients would lose benefits. But the food stamp rescission and a companion $350 million cut from housing subsidies gave House Democrats such as Marcy Kaptur of Ohio and Jose E. Serrano of New York a final chance, with C-SPAN cameras rolling, to lambaste Republicans for adding billions for the military while cutting programs for the poor.

C-SPAN coverage may have provided the public with an unusually intimate glimpse of the inner workings of Congress, but the experiment was distinctly unpopular with appropriators. Said a top GOP staff aide: "Never again."

Senate Clears Supplemental Spending Bill

MAY 22 — At long last, a $14.5 billion fiscal 1999 supplemental spending bill for defense, disaster relief and U.S. farmers cleared Congress on May

20. President Clinton signed it the next day.

The action cleared the way for the regular fiscal 2000 appropriations season to begin and rid congressional leaders of a legislative headache that had been pounding all spring. The Senate cleared the bill (HR 1141), 64-36, after the House adopted the conference report, 269-158, on May 18. The bill nearly doubled Clinton's $5.5 billion request to pay for the U.S. role in the NATO campaign against Yugoslavia. *(Senate vote 136, p. S-29; House vote 133, p. H-52)*

Several Senate Republicans spoke against the bill, complaining of its cost and policy provisions. But Majority Leader Trent Lott, R-Miss., prodded his colleagues to vote for it to provide funds needed by the military. "I said it sucks, but we ought to pass it," Lott told reporters May 19.

The bill includes $10.9 billion in defense-related spending for the war over Yugoslavia as well as money for the Pentagon for spare parts, maintenance and other routine operating costs. The defense money, passed in the House as HR 1664, was added to an earlier, smaller bill to help U.S. farmers ($574 million) and give long-delayed relief ($687 million) to Central American nations devastated by hurricanes.

The final measure also includes $900 million in disaster assistance for Oklahoma and Kansas in response to recent tornadoes.

Despite widespread reservations about the bill's cost and parochial provisions, lawmakers had little choice but to accept it. To reject it would have sent an unthinkable message to the troops and to Yugoslav President Slobodan Milosevic, and would have required another time-consuming effort to produce a replacement bill that would not necessarily have been more acceptable.

The House adopted the conference report by a comfortable margin, as GOP leaders and appropriators defended it against attacks from both sides of the aisle.

Democrats objected mainly to three environmental riders the Senate had attached to the bill. One allows the development of an open pit gold mine in Washington. The second extends until Oct. 1 a moratorium on regulations that would increase royalties on oil and gas pumped from federal lands. The third extends until at least December a moratorium on the issuing of a final rule concerning management and reclamation requirements on hard-rock mining on public land.

Republican opposition arose in the House, along with bitter GOP dissent in the Senate, because virtually all of the bill was designated as "emergency" spending to be paid for out of the budget surplus, which is made up of surplus Social Security revenues. But Senate Republican and Democratic leaders easily beat back, 70-30, an attempt by Phil Gramm, R-Texas, to force across-the-board cuts to fund $3.4 billion in domestic programs included in the bill. *(Vote 135, p. S-29)*

House leaders reminded members that a vote against the bill would be a vote against money for struggling farmers, hurricane and tornado victims, and a military engaged in battle. ◆

Fiscal 1999 Supplemental

MAY 15 — Conferees agreed May 13 to a $14.6 billion fiscal 1999 supplemental spending bill, about $6.8 billion more than President Clinton requested.

	Congress	Clinton
Defense		
Kosovo operations	$5.458 billion	$5.458 billion
Additional munitions	250 million	—
Additional procurement	300 million	—
Additional spare parts, maintenance	2.25 billion	—
Coast Guard	200 million	—
Recruiting	100 million	—
Pay and retirement	1.838 billion	—
Construction	475 million	—
Defense total	**$10.871 billion**	**$5.458 billion**
Kosovo humanitarian assistance		
International disasters	$163 million	$71 million
Economic Support Fund	105 million	105 million
Eastern Europe	120 million	170 million
Migration and refugees	431 million	220 million
Food assistance	149 million	—
Resettlement	100 million	—
Humanitarian total	**$1.068 billion**	**$566 million**
Kosovo security upgrades	$70.5 million	$25 million
Aid to farmers	$574 million	$152 million
Aid to Latin America	$687 million	$677 million
Aid to Jordan	$100 million	$300 million
FEMA relief	$900 million	$372 million
Other	$314 million	$269 million
Grand total	**$14.6 billion**	**$7.8 billion**

SOURCE: House Appropriations Committee

Supplemental Bill Provisions

MAY 22 — The conference report on the fiscal 1999 Emergency Supplemental Appropriations Act (HR 1141 — H Rept 106-143) appropriates a total of $14.5 billion in supplemental funds in fiscal year 1999. President Clinton signed HR 1141 May 21.

The Clinton administration asked Congress for $6.0 billion in supplemental funds to pay for current air operations against Yugoslavia through the end of fiscal 1999 on Sept. 30 at the current level of intensity. The United States currently is paying an estimated 75 percent of the cost of ongoing operations.

Military Equipment & Personnel

The agreement provides a total of $10.9 billion in additional funding for military equipment, personnel, and operations and maintenance, almost double the president's request. The total includes the president's request and House-passed level of $5.0 billion for Kosovo operations and munitions replacement, and $453 million for ongoing operations against Iraq.

• **Munitions procurement.** The agreement includes $984 million to replenish munitions, $300 more than the president's request, but $100 million less than the House bill. The total includes $431 million for Tomahawk cruise missiles, $178 million for Conventional air-launched cruise missiles for the Air Force and $40 million for Air Force decoys.

• **Personnel costs.** The measure provides the president's request of $439 million for personnel costs related to operations in and around Kosovo and $16 million for added personnel costs for service members deployed in ongoing operations against Iraq.

• **Readiness.** The report provides $2.3 billion in unrequested funds for various readiness accounts, compared with $3.1 billion in the House bill, including:

- $1.1 billion for spare parts and associated logistical support, largely for Navy and Air Force aircraft;
- $743 million for depot level maintenance and repair requirements;
- $182 million for base operations support, including facilities operations and maintenance and utilities services;
- $200 million for readiness-related training; and
- $100 million for recruiting and advertising costs.

• **Rapid response transfer fund.** The agreement, like the House bill, establishes a new account to enable the rapid transfer of equipment or other war-fighting systems between different theaters of operations. The agreement provides $300 million in unrequested funds for an Operational Rapid Response Transfer Fund, $100 million less than the House measure. The funds are available only if the president designates an emergency, and may be used only to rapidly develop or deploy equipment or systems in response to specific requests made by U.S. regional commands, and only if the obligation of funds is specifically approved by the Defense secretary.

• **Burden-sharing reports.** The agreement, like the House bill, requires the president to seek an equitable reimbursement from NATO for costs incurred by the U.S. government in connection with Operation Allied Force. The agreement directs the president to report to Congress by Sept. 30 on such efforts. However, the measure does not require any of its funds to be conditioned on such burden-sharing.

Military Pay Raise

The agreement, like the House measure, provides $1.8 billion in contingent emergency appropriations for increases in military basic pay, targeted pay increases and overhaul of the military retirement system.

However, since the president and the Senate have proposed substantively different approaches to these compensation issues, and the House Armed Services Committee has yet to make its recommendation to the House, release of these funds is conditioned upon enactment of authorizing legislation, as well as the funds being designated as emergency appropriations by the president. Such actions are expected in the fiscal 2000 Defense authorization bill (HR 1401, S 974) expected for floor consideration as early as the week of May 24. The increased spending is expected to fund a pay increase of at least 4.8 percent and a change in the military pension system that would allow 20-year veterans to retire at half pay, the system that existed before a 1986 law lowered the amount to 40 percent.

Military Construction Funding

The agreement includes a total of $475 million in unrequested funds for overseas military construction projects. The House bill provided $1.1 billion.

Unlike the House measure, which designated specific projects for funding, the conference agreement gives the Defense secretary the authority to determine which projects will be funded.

Coast Guard

The agreement contains $200 million for the Coast Guard, expected to be used for pay raises, compensation parity in the basic allowance for housing, military health care, recruiting, work force readiness tools, intermediate and depot-level maintenance, and additional staffing.

Kosovo Refugee Assistance

The report provides $1.1 billion for refugee, disaster and economic assistance to address the crisis in Kosovo. The president's original request was $566 million.

• **International disaster assistance.** The report, like the House bill, provides $163 million for international disaster assistance, $92 million more than the president's request. The added funds are provided for an expected increase in refugees in the Balkans.

• **Economic support fund.** The report appropriates the House level of $105 million in direct economic assistance to Albania, Bosnia, Bulgaria, Romania, Macedonia and Montenegro, the so-called front-line states. The total is $5 million more than the president's request. The assistance is designed to help these countries meet balance-of-payments shortfalls and to partially offset costs of refugee assistance.

The conferees strongly support additional resources to support Montenegro (a part of Yugoslavia), and expect that $13 million will be used to document war crimes and atrocities in Kosovo. The conferees noted that the number of victims of war crimes in Kosovo may far exceed what is currently known. The conferees believe that the administration's request of $5 million for the War Crimes Tribunal is inadequate and strongly recommended that up to $13 million be made available to meet the full request of the tribunal. In addition, the conferees strongly recommend that $10 million be provided to the State Departments Human Rights and Democracy Fund to promptly obtain information from fleeing refugee victims and witnesses, to assist in providing identity documents to refugees whose papers and property titles have been confiscated, and to provide counseling to rape victims. Funds for these purposes may be derived from other appropriation accounts provided under this chapter. The report also prohibits any economic stabilization funds from being used for reconstruction in Serbia.

• **Eastern Europe and the Baltic States.** The report provides $120 million for the

Eastern Europe account, $50 million less than the administration's request but $45 million more than in the House bill. These funds have been added to the Migration and Refugee Assistance Fund for Kosovo refugees. The conferees believe that the administration planned to use some of the requested funds for the Eastern Europe account for long-term reconstruction projects in the Balkans. The conferees contended that funding for Kosovo refugee assistance should be a higher priority than Balkan reconstruction, that such reconstruction planning is premature, and that European nations bear greater responsibility for the integration of these front-line states into Europe's economy and for reconstruction programs in the region.

- **Migration and refugee assistance.** The report provides $266 million for migration and refugee assistance, $151 million more than the president's original request. The measure also provides $165 million for the Emergency Migration and Refugee Assistance Fund, $70 million more than the president's original request.
- **Food for Peace.** The measure provides $149 million in unrequested funds for the Food for Peace foreign food aid and loan program. The aid is expected to go to the Balkans.
- **Temporary resettlement.** The report provides $100 million for the temporary resettlement of 20,000 Kosovar Albanians in the United States.

Diplomatic Security

The report provides $71 million for diplomatic security upgrades and evacuation costs related to the Kosovo crisis, $46 million more than the president's request. The total includes $36 million for a new secure embassy facility in Tirana, Albania.

Disaster and Agriculture

The conference report includes long-delayed aid to Central American nations hit by hurricanes, help for U.S. farmers and a number of miscellaneous provisions.

Hurricanes Mitch and Georges

The report, like the House bill, appropriates the president's request of $687 million in emergency funds for recovery efforts associated with hurricanes Mitch and Georges. The measure includes $216 million to replenish various Defense Department accounts drawn down to pay for emergency response efforts after the hurricanes hit, as well as funding to support planned National Guard and Reserve training in the region, including reconstruction, engineering and medical services.

The $687 million total also includes:

- 283 million to repair rural roads and to provide micro-credit loans and basic agricultural inputs;
- $136 million to rebuild hospitals and clinics and to provide water and sanitation services; $64 million for environmental management and disaster mitigation;
- $55 million to rebuild schools and to build 6,000 housing units;
- $41 million for debt restructuring and relief, including $25 million for the recently created Central America Emergency Trust Fund and $16 million for the cost of reducing Honduras' debt to the United States; and
- $10 million to help Colombia cope with the January 1999 earthquake.

Tornado Relief

The measure contains $900 million for the Federal Emergency Management Agency (FEMA) to aid victims of recent tornadoes in Oklahoma and Kansas.

Agricultural Assistance

The report includes a total of $574 million in a variety of emergency funds to help U.S. farmers who have been hurt by persistently low commodity and livestock prices, and who have sought additional economic support from the Agriculture Department (USDA). Included in this total is $105 million for the Agricultural Credit Insurance Fund to provide credit of roughly $1.1 billion to farmers through USDA's guaranteed and direct farm ownership and operating loan programs, and the department's emergency loan program.

Also included in the agricultural assistance total is $145 million for the Agricultural Marketing Service to strengthen agricultural markets; $43 million for USDA's Farm Service Agency salaries and expenses; $30 million for USDA's Rural Community Advancement Program; and $20 million in assistance to migrant and seasonal farmworkers adversely affected by natural disasters.

In addition, the report provides emergency funding for certain agricultural programs geared toward environmental protection and restoration, including $95 million for USDA's Emergency Watershed Program, and $63 million for the Conservation and Wetlands Reserve Programs. The measure also includes $28 million for the Emergency Conservation Program, which provides cost-sharing assistance to farmers and ranchers for farmland damaged by flooding, drought, tornadoes and other natural disasters.

Tobacco Settlement

The report includes a Senate provision prohibiting the federal government from recovering part of the $246 billion tobacco settlement between the states and tobacco companies. The report contains no restrictions on how states could use such funds.

Commerce-Justice-State Spending

The conference report includes language to remove the current restriction on fiscal 1999 funding for the departments of Commerce (including the Census Bureau), Justice and State and for the judiciary. Under the fiscal 1999 appropriations act for those departments and agencies (PL 105-277), funding is scheduled to end on June 15, but now, under the conference report, continues through the end of the current fiscal year on Sept. 30.

The funding for those agencies, including the Immigration and Naturalization Service, FBI and Supreme Court, was caught up in a dispute between Congress and the White House over how to conduct the 2000 census. On Jan. 25, the Supreme Court ruled that the Census Bureau could not use statistical sampling to determine the population count for congressional apportionment among the states (i.e., how many representatives each state would receive). However, the court was silent on the constitutionality of using sampling for congressional redistricting within each state and other demographic data collected through the census, citing a 1976 law that gives the Census Bureau the option to use statistical sampling should it be deemed feasible. The Republican majority in Congress opposes the use of statistical sampling and brought the lawsuit to force the bureau to use actual enumeration. The report also includes a supplemental appropriation of $45 million for the Census Bureau, which will be used to open more field offices and hire more enumerators, since a full head count must now be attempted in the 2000 census for congressional apportionment. The Census Bureau plans to attempt to count only 90 percent of the population and, through statistical sampling, estimate the remaining 10 percent for redistricting and other purposes.

Airport Funding Extension

The report extends through Aug. 6 the authority of the Federal Aviation Administration (FAA) to distribute federal airport improvement grants to airports. The FAA's current airport grant authority expires May 31. (Unlike funding for other FAA programs, airport grants may not be distributed without an enacted authorization; in March, Congress enacted a two-month extension in anticipation of congressional action on a long-term authorization.)

The measure also extends through Aug. 6 the FAA's authority to provide war-risk insurance coverage to commercial aircraft flying into high-risk areas for U.S. foreign policy and national security needs. (Current authority expired March 31.)

Finally, the measure allows the regional Washington, D.C., airports authority to collect an additional $30 million in passenger facility charges to pay for improvements to Dulles International and Reagan Washington National Airports. (Under the 1996 Federal Aviation Administration reauthorization law (PL 104-264), new passenger fees for the two airports may not be approved until federal nominees to the D.C. airport authority's board are confirmed by the Senate. The airport authority has requested fees for some $200 million in improvements at the two airports; the short-term airport grant extension enacted in March allowed passenger fees to be approved for $30 million in improvements.)

Public Lands Provisions

- **Moratorium on oil and gas royalties regulations.** The report includes Senate-passed provisions that were not in the House-passed measure that extend an existing moratorium on revising the way crude oil from federal lands is valued in order to determine federal royalties from the leases. (The fiscal 1999 Interior Appropriations law, part of the omnibus spending law (PL 105-277) imposed a moratorium on the new rules until June 1, 1999. The proposed new regulations are expected to increase the value of the federal oil reserves, and thus increase the prices oil companies pay the federal government for extracting the resources.)
- **Moratorium on new mining regulations.** The report includes Senate-passed provisions that were not in the House-passed measure that extend the existing moratorium on publishing final Interior Department regulations concerning management and reclamation requirements at hardrock mining sites on federal lands. Under the report, the new regulations could not be released until a 120-day comment period has passed after release of a National Academy of Sciences (NAS) study on the new regulations. (The fiscal 1999 Interior Appropriations law imposed a moratorium on the new regulations until the end of fiscal 1999, and required the NAS study to be completed by July 31, 1999. Thus, under the report, the new regulations could not be released until at least December 1999.)
- **Crown Jewel mine in Washington.** The report includes a Senate provision that would effectively exempt the proposed Crown Jewel mine in Washington state from a recent Interior Department ruling that would have blocked the mine's development. Under the department's March ruling, the Battle Mountain Gold Co. was denied a waiver of provisions of the General Mining Law of 1872 regarding the amount of land needed for disposal of its mining waste or tailings. Environmentalists have opposed the mine plan due to the potential effects of the large mine's waste, while supporters of the mine argue that the developers had invested $80 million over seven years in the project, had complied with all relevant environmental laws and that the Interior Department's actions would establish a new precedent for restricting mining on federal lands.

Immigration

The report, like the House bill, provides $80 million for the Immigration and Naturalization Service (INS) for increased border enforcement. The funds are for 2,945 additional beds for detaining of criminal aliens from Central America. The House committee report contended that the need for additional detention space is in large part a direct result of INS' failure to plan for such a contingency, and that such a failure represents the latest in a long and continuing series of management failures by the INS.

Jordan

The report, like the House bill, provides $100 million in economic support and foreign military financing for Jordan in conjunction with that nation's participation in the Wye River Peace Accords between Israel and the Palestinian Authority. The administration requested $300 million, including an advance appropriation of $200 million for fiscal 2000 and fiscal 2001.

Non-Emergency Domestic Funding

The report includes a total of $268 million in non-emergency funding, $178 million more than the president's request, for a variety of programs, including:

- **Credit union liquidity.** The report increases from $600 million to about $20 billion (for fiscal 2000 only) the cap on credit union borrowing from the National Credit Union Administration's Central Liquidity Fund. The increase is intended to ensure credit unions will have enough cash on hand for customers who withdraw funds near the end of the year because of concerns about the Year 2000 (Y2K) computer problem.
- **Mortgage insurance limits.** The measure increases by $30 billion (to $140 billion) the limit on loan guarantees under the Federal Housing Administration's Mutual Mortgage Insurance Program Account (which includes FHA single-family mortgage loans), and by $50 billion (to $200 billion) the guarantee commitments that may be made by the Government National Mortgage Association (Ginnie Mae) in guarantying principal and interest payments on mortgage-backed securities issued by Ginnie Mae.
- **Public Broadcasting.** The report appropriates $31 million in fiscal 1999 and $17 million in fiscal 2000 for the Corporation for Public Broadcasting and National Public Radio to replace the failed satellite that had served the Public Radio Satellite System.
- **House page dormitory.** The measure provides $3.8 million to renovate and furnish new dormitory space for House pages currently located in the O'Neill House Office Building. The report also contains $1.8 million to correct safety deficiencies in the O'Neill building.
- **Japanese reparations.** The measure authorizes the transfer of $4.3 million in existing Justice Department funds to pay remaining reparation claims of Japanese interned during World War II, including Latin American Japanese interned in U.S. camps.
- **Postal Service.** The report provides $29 million for the U.S. Postal Service as part of its annual appropriation for subsidized mail.
- **Indian affairs.** The measure appropriates $22 million for the Office of the Special Trustee for American Indians, largely to support costs associated with ongoing litigation involving the Interior Department and approximately 300,000 holders of Individual Indian Money Trust Accounts.
- **Russian leaders.** The report establishes a pilot program within the Library of Congress to bring up to 3,000 emerging Russian political leaders to the United States for up to 30 days each. The Senate is transferring $10 million of its own funds to finance the program during fiscal 1999.
- **Overseas religious persecution.** The measure provides $3 million for the U.S. Commission on International Religious Freedom established in the International Religious Freedom Act of 1998 (PL 105-292).
- **Export controls.** The report provides $2 million for the State Department's Office of Defense Trade Controls to improve scrutiny of export license applications.
- **Drug trafficking.** The measure provides $2.5 million for the High-Intensity Drug Trafficking Areas Program, and directs the funds to be used in New Mexico and Arizona, and for support of the Cross-Border Initiative between Washington, D.C., and Prince George's County, Md.
- **National Commission on Terrorism.** The report appropriates $840,000 for the National Commission on Terrorism.

• **Pan Am 103 trial.** The measure authorizes the use of funds for the families of victims of Pan Am Flight 103 to attend the upcoming Lockerbie bombing trial in the Netherlands.

Offsets

The report offsets $1.7 billion of new spending contained in the bill by rescinding previous appropriations that have yet to be spent. Unlike the first House-passed supplemental bill, the report does not rescind callable capital appropriations to various international development banks, nor does it rescind funding from the so-called Nunn-Lugar program that aids in the disarming of Russian nuclear weapons by buying and storing enriched uranium and plutonium from the weapons production.

• **Food stamps.** The report rescinds $1.25 billion in funding previously appropriated — but not spent — by individual states for food stamps.

• **Section 8 housing.** The measure rescinds $350 million from Section 8 housing subsidy programs for individuals receiving subsidies for private housing.

• **Community Development Block Grants.** The report rescinds $230 million of unobligated balances for disaster relief. The conferees note, however, that an identical amount has been included in FEMA's account to deal with issues relating to disaster relief.

• **Military construction.** The report rescinds $31 million in fiscal 1999 military construction funding. The total reflects inflation and foreign currency fluctuation savings of $25 million and $6 million from the Base Realignment and Closure Account, Part IV.

• **Global Environment Facility**. The report rescinds $25 million from the Global Environment Facility, a World Bank agency that funds environmental projects throughout the world.

• **Unemployment insurance funds.** The report rescinds $22 million from the Labor and Health and Human Services departments' funding for state unemployment insurance funds.

Based on continued low unemployment rates, the full amount of the unemployment insurance contingency fund is not needed to fund current administrative workloads.

• **USIA.** The report rescinds $20 million from the United States Information Agency (USIA). The reduction comes from the agency's buying power maintenance account, a reserve fund to help pay for international programs affected by exchange rate movements. The conferees note that because of exchange rate gains over the past few years, the program currently exceeds potential requirements. ◆

Chapter 3

ABORTION

House Passes Bill Making It a Crime To Help Minors Evade Parental Notification Laws

Box Score

- **Bills:** HR 1218, S 661
- **Legislative action: House** passed HR 1218 (H Rept 106-204), 270-159, June 30.

SUMMARY

Under a veto threat, the House passed legislation that would make it a federal crime to take a girl across state lines for an abortion in order to circumvent the parental consent or notification laws of her home state. The Senate took no action on its companion measure.

More than 20 states currently enforce laws requiring the consent or notification of at least one parent, or court authorization, before a minor may obtain an abortion. Under the bill, any adult other than the parent or legal guardian of someone younger than 18 who takes her from a state with parental involvement laws to one without such requirements to get an abortion would be subject to a fine of as much as $100,000 and one year in prison. The bill would bar prosecution when the abortion was necessary to save the girl's life and would exempt the girl who had the abortion from liability. It also would allow parents to file suits alleging that other adults abridged their rights under state notification laws.

Opponents argue that criminalizing abortion assistance to minors could actually endanger teenagers, because they might try to cross state lines on their own rather than risk having relatives or friends prosecuted for helping them. They also say the bill would be unconstitutional for two reasons: It would interfere with a woman's right to an abortion, and it would have the effect of imposing one state's laws on residents of other states.

Supporters say the bill is needed to bolster state efforts to ensure that parents are involved in such momentous decisions involving their children. They also say it would counter inducements such as advertising by abortion clinics in states without parental involvement laws. The White House has said exempting close relatives from liability under the bill is a precondition for the president's possible support.

There is little chance the bill will become law next year. A similar measure died in the Senate in 1998 after sponsors came up six short of the 60 votes required to overcome a filibuster. Seven votes beyond that would be needed to override a veto. And the House majority was 20 short of the number required to guarantee a veto override there. Still, anti-abortion groups say the measure remains high on their priority list, so it may be debated in an election year.

House Panel Votes To Criminalize Abortion Aid To Minors

JUNE 26 — Setting the stage for a highly charged floor battle over abortion before the July Fourth recess, the House Judiciary Committee approved a bill (HR 1218) that would make it a federal crime to transport a minor seeking an abortion across state lines to avoid parental consent laws in her home state.

Voting 16-13 along party lines, the committee approved the bill June 23. Sponsors said they hoped to bring it to the floor the week of June 28.

Echoing last year's debate over a similar measure, Republicans turned back nearly a dozen attempts by Democrats to amend the legislation. Proposals to exempt non-parental family members and other adults from the bill's penalties were defeated, as were efforts to make exceptions in cases of incest or when the health of the minor was jeopardized.

On a 14-16 vote, the panel rejected an "en bloc" amendment offered by Texas Democrat Sheila Jackson-Lee that would have exempted clergy, aunts, uncles, first cousins and godparents from criminal penalties.

A proposal offered by Jerrold Nadler, D-N.Y., to exempt grandparents was defeated on a 13-17 vote.

Nadler argued that Congress should not "penalize family members who come to a minor's aid in a time of crisis," and contended the bill "sends the wrong message by actually discouraging minors from seeking advice from adults."

But Judiciary Chairman Henry J. Hyde, R-Ill., argued against the provision: "I can think of nothing more destructive of the family unit than to have grandparents pulling one direction and parents in another."

Last year, the House passed a similar measure, but the Senate failed to reach cloture on the bill, voting 54-45, six votes short of the 60 needed. President Clinton had threatened to veto it.

Opponents argue that criminalizing abortion assistance to minors could actually endanger teens because they might try to cross state lines on their own rather than risk having relatives or friends prosecuted.

Supporters of the measure, however, say that it is important for parents to be involved in medical decisions involving their children. Parents, they argue, are most likely to have important medical information about their children that doctors may need before performing a surgical procedure.

"The law recognizes, and we should not usurp, the special role of parents in children's lives," said bill cosponsor and Constitution Subcommittee Chairman Charles T. Canady, R-Fla.

Democratic amendments to provide exceptions to the bill's prohibitions in cases of incest and when the health of the minor is in jeopardy were defeated, 12-15 and 11-17, respectively.

Republicans said the exceptions were not needed because minors could seek a judicial bypass of parental consent laws in such cases. But Democrats say that exceptions are often denied by judges who oppose abortion and that, in any case, a teenager who is reluctant to tell her parents about an abortion is not likely to tell a judge.

The bill would set penalties of up to a year in jail and $100,000 in fines.

House-Passed Bill Faces Procedural Hurdles in Senate

JULY 3 — Reigniting the abortion debate between congressional Republicans and President Clinton, the House passed legislation June 30 that would give parents the leverage of the federal criminal code when they want to prevent young daughters from ending a pregnancy.

The House voted 270-159 to pass a measure (HR 1218) that would make it a federal crime for anyone other than a girl's parent to take her across state lines in order to have an abortion and thereby avoid the parental consent or notification laws of her home state. *(Vote 261, p. H-90)*

The majority was 16 votes shy of two-thirds, the percentage that it would take to override the veto threatened by the White House unless the bill is changed to, among other things, exempt close family members from prosecution. The president raised the same objections in the 105th Congress, when Republicans won passage of a bill identical to this year's. The measure died in the Senate in 1998 after sponsors fell six votes short of overcoming a filibuster.

Ileana Ros-Lehtinen, R-Fla., sponsor of the House bill, said the companion version (S 661) faces similar obstacles in the Senate this year as well.

"If we were ever able to get it to the floor for the vote itself, we absolutely have the votes to pass it," she said in an interview July 1. "It's the procedural moves that are the difficult test."

Strategy sessions on how to win Senate passage will begin after the July Fourth recess, Ros-Lehtinen said. Aides to the main Senate sponsor, Spencer Abraham, R-Mich., said that he had not yet contemplated his next move.

No matter what the outcome, however, there seems little chance the bill could become law — and every chance that it will become a key focus of those on both sides of the abortion question in evaluating candidates in the 2000 elections.

The day after the House bill passed, senators waged their first abortion fight of the year, with opponents of abortion rights winning adoption of an amendment to the Treasury-Postal Service appropriations bill, which provides payments for federal worker medical plans.

Parental Rights

The House Judiciary Committee says more than 20 states are currently enforcing law requiring the consent or notification of at least one parent, or court authorization, before a minor may obtain an abortion. Under the legislation, any adult other than the parent or legal guardian of someone younger than 18 who takes her from a state with parental involvement laws to one without such requirements to get an abortion would be subject to a fine of as much as $100,000 and one year in prison.

The bill would prohibit such prosecutions when the abortion was necessary to save the girl's life, and would not allow the prosecution of the girl who had the abortion. It also would allow parents to file civil lawsuits alleging that other adults had abridged their rights under state notification laws.

"Grandma has no right to take that child across the state line, circumvent the state laws and dishonor her own children," said House Majority Leader Dick Armey, R-Texas. "It is not right to love yourself or love somebody more, or love some abstract devotion to abortion rights more, than the safety and security of that child and the honor of the parents."

Opponents said the legislation would prompt young women to seek abortions without the help of any adult, which they lamented would not only hurt a girl's emotional health but also would raise the likelihood that she would make decisions that could endanger her physical health.

"Young women are better served by talking through the decision and having someone to lean on than going through it alone," said David Wu, D-Ore. "This bill would make criminals out of people whose only crime is helping a young person in distress."

Democrats also said the legislation would be unconstitutional for two reasons: It would interfere with a woman's right to an abortion, and it would have the effect of imposing one state's laws on residents of other states.

"This bill would prosecute somebody for going to a state for conduct that is legal in that state," said Melvin Watt, D-N.C., who likened the provision to making it criminal to leave a state that bars gambling for a trip to Las Vegas.

Republicans said the bill would counter inducements to young people, such as advertisements for abortion clinics in states that do not require parental input. "These ads are telling young teens, 'We can end your baby's life, and your parents need never know,' " said Christopher H. Smith, R-N.J.

Democrats tried to return the bill to the Judiciary Committee to draft exceptions for close relatives and clergy, which the president said would be a precondition for his signature. Their motion to recommit the bill was rejected, 164-268. *(Vote 260, p. H-90)* ◆

Senate Passes Bill To Punish Doctors Who Perform 'Partial Birth' Procedure

Box Score

- **Bill:** S 1692
- **Legislative action: Senate** voted 63-34 to pass S 1692 on Oct. 21.

SUMMARY

The Senate passed a bill to make it a crime for doctors to perform a procedure they call "dilation and extraction," but which the legislation describes as "partial birth" abortion.

The bill would subject those who perform the procedure illegally to two years in prison. The woman who had the abortion would not be liable. While the bill would create an exception for doctors who use the procedure to save the woman's life, it would not provide the exception President Clinton has insisted on: use of the procedure to protect a woman's health.

Congress has considered such a measure each year since the GOP took control in 1995. Twice Clinton has vetoed it; twice the House has voted to override the veto; and twice the Senate has sustained it. Opponents of the ban say that its underlying purpose is to be a toehold in the campaign by abortion foes to outlaw virtually all abortion. To make that point, Barbara Boxer, D-Calif., and Tom Harkin, D-Iowa, proposed an amendment stating the sense of the Senate that Roe v. Wade, the 1973 decision establishing a constitutional right to abortion, was "appropriate" and should not be overturned. It was adopted 51-47. Sponsors said it was the first time Congress has ever taken a vote on whether to endorse Roe.

The House is expected to debate the legislation early in 2000. Proponents appear to have enough votes to override a veto in the House, but there are no signs the Senate would do anything other than sustain it.

Senate Again Passes 'Partial Birth' Ban

OCTOBER 23 — Following the latest Senate vote to pass legislation that would define "partial birth" abortion and make it a crime for physicians to perform the procedure, it was unclear which side had won the latest round in this emotional and politically charged debate. Anti-abortion lawmakers noted that they had moved closer to showing they could override a presidential veto, while abortion rights supporters said they were eager to use the legislation in the 2000 campaign.

Congress has considered such a measure each year since the Republicans took control in 1995. Twice a bill has been sent to President Clinton; twice he has vetoed the measure; twice the House has voted to override the veto; and twice the Senate has sustained it. In the short term, it appears none of those outcomes would be different in the 106th Congress.

But the 63-34 Senate vote on Oct. 21 to pass this year's version (S 1692) suggested that the measure had gained a net of one supporter since the 105th Congress. *(Vote 340, p. S-67)*

"Each time this bill has been voted on, succeeding Congresses picked up votes," noted Rick Santorum, R-Pa., the sponsor of the legislation. "I am hopeful we will continue that trend."

Had the three senators who were absent voted the way they have in the past, the outcome would have been 65-35, two short of the supermajority needed to guarantee an override. Last year, 64 senators voted to enact a partial-birth ban that Clinton vetoed; two years before that, 57 senators did so.

The House — which is expected to take up companion legislation in January, although it has not yet been introduced — seems certain to have more than enough votes to override a veto, as it has done in each of the previous two election years.

The Senate bill "contains the same serious flaws" as the two Clinton has vetoed, the White House budget office said in a statement Oct. 20. While the legislation would create an exception for doctors who perform a partial-birth abortion when the woman's life is endangered by the pregnancy, it does not provide the exception Clinton wants to allow use of the procedure to protect a woman's health.

The bill would subject those who perform the procedure illegally to two years in prison; the woman who had the abortion would not be criminally liable.

Abortion Rights Amendment

Perhaps more politically significant than the Senate's passage of the bill was its narrow endorsement of language that calls for maintaining the right to abortion.

Opponents of the ban say that its underlying purpose is to be a foothold in the campaign by abortion foes to outlaw virtually all abortion. To make that point, Barbara Boxer, D-Calif., and Tom Harkin, D-Iowa, proposed an amendment stating that Roe v. Wade, the Supreme Court's 1973 decision establishing a constitutional right to abortion, was "appropriate" and should not be overturned. It was adopted 51-47. Although the language was nonbinding, its sponsors said it marked the first time Congress has ever taken a vote on whether to endorse the historic ruling. *(Vote 337, p. S-67)*

"We know who they are," Boxer said of those who voted against the amendment: two Democrats, the one independent and 44 Republicans. She vowed to make the vote a campaign issue "in every one of the states" where one of those senators is seeking reelection next year.

"This has lifted the veil of moderation that a lot of Republican senators were hiding behind," said Harkin.

Gov. George W. Bush of Texas, the GOP presidential front-runner, applauded the Senate for voting to end "the inhumane practice of partial-birth abortion." Vice President Al Gore, the Democratic front-runner, called the vote a "wake-up call to all

Americans as to what is truly at stake in this election," and promised that "as president, I will always, always defend a woman's right to choose."

While fewer abortion restrictions than in the past several years have been pushed as riders on fiscal 2000 appropriations bills, abortion opponents are moving three other measures toward election-year confrontations with Clinton. The partial-birth ban is one of them. The House has passed the others. One (HR 1218) would make it a crime to help a girl cross state lines for an abortion in order to avoid state parental consent laws. The other (HR 2436) would elevate the legal standing of a fetus by making it a federal crime to harm a fetus during the commission of another federal crime.

The Senate Debate

By calling up the bill, Majority Leader Trent Lott, R-Miss., spurned a request made in a letter from abortion-rights supporters, who said they feared that debate so close to the Oct. 23 anniversary of a New York abortion doctor's high-profile murder has "the potential to inflame anti-abortion violence."

In an interview, Lott said he called up the bill at the request of its sponsors, who wanted to put senators on record before adjournment.

In the end, no senator switched sides from last year, although Bob Kerrey, D-Neb., said on the floor that he was troubled by the procedure and "keeping an open mind."

Of the eight freshman senators, three voted as their predecessors had. "Nay" votes were cast by two Democrats who defeated Republicans who had voted "yea" in the past. But "yea" votes were cast by three senators whose predecessors had voted "nay," creating the net gain of one vote for the legislation.

Even as they gained that vote, however, abortion opponents lost a powerful ally off Capitol Hill. The American Medical Association, while saying it still opposed use of the procedure, issued a statement Oct. 19 saying that it could not support legislation that would make doctors criminally liable for practicing medicine.

Santorum won voice-vote approval for an amendment changing the definition of the procedure to be when a person "vaginally delivers some portion of an intact living fetus until the fetus is partially outside the body of the mother" and then "performs the overt act that kills the fetus."

"This baby is now outside of the mother, almost outside of the mother," Santorum said during the debate. "I hope we all believe that once a baby is born, that baby is entitled to life."

He said he decided to change the language in response to a recent ruling by the 8th U.S. Circuit Court of Appeals, which held that various state laws banning the procedure were unconstitutionally vague.

Opponents said Santorum's new version would still be unconstitutional, because *Roe v. Wade* held that governments could not bar abortions before a fetus was able to live outside the womb. After viability, the court held, lawmakers could restrict abortions as long as exceptions were made to protect a woman's life and health.

Various types of partial-birth abortion bans exist in 29 states. But 19 of those laws have been blocked by the courts or otherwise limited in enforcement, according to the American Civil Liberties Union.

Democrats proposed an amendment that would have banned all abortions of viable fetuses, except to save the life or protect the health of the mother. But Santorum argued that those exceptions were too broad, and senators voted 61-38 to table, or kill, the proposal. *(Vote 335, p. S-67)* ◆

Chapter 4

AGRICULTURE

Crop Insurance Bill Wins Easy Passage in the House; Senate Postpones Action

Box Score

- **Bill:** HR 2559
- **Legislative action: House** passed HR 2559 (H Rept 106-300) by voice vote Sept. 29.

SUMMARY

The House on Sept. 29 passed legislation (HR 2559) to lower the premiums that farmers pay for crop insurance, the federally subsidized program that is supposed to avoid the multibillion-dollar "emergency" bailouts that Congress routinely funnels to farmers after droughts and other natural disasters. The Senate did not act.

The legislation, sponsored by Agriculture Committee Chairman Larry Combest, R-Texas, would authorize an additional $6 billion for federally subsidized crop insurance in fiscal years 2001 through 2004.

House Panel OKs Rewrite of Crop Insurance Law

JULY 24 — An effort to revamp the much- maligned federal crop insurance program appears to be on the fast track in the House, but it could run into trouble if its multibillion-dollar cost exceeds Agriculture Committee estimates.

The House Agriculture Subcommittee on Risk Management, Research and Specialty Crops gave voice vote approval on July 21 to a bill (HR 2559) intended to encourage more farmers to buy crop insurance by increasing subsidies.

The Agriculture Committee is scheduled to mark up the bill on July 27, and committee chairman and sponsor Larry Combest, R-Texas, hopes for House action before the August recess.

Subcommittee Chairman Thomas W. Ewing, R-Ill., predicted that the bill would pass the House "overwhelmingly," but cautioned that the measure may need major reworking if it exceeds its estimated cost of $6 billion over four years.

On top of current spending levels, the fiscal 2000 budget resolution (H Con Res 68) authorizes $6 billion more for crop insurance in fiscal 2001-04.

Some farm-state members — including Senate Agriculture Committee Chairman Richard G. Lugar, R-Ind. — argue that at least a portion of the $6 billion should go toward helping farmers through other programs. But most members of the House Agriculture Committee want to devote the funds to shoring up crop insurance.

Farmers have complained about the program's cost and the lack of protection it affords when they suffer setbacks because of bad weather or low prices.

"Basically, what we're seeing is that people can't afford the level of insurance that protects their investment," said Earl Pomeroy, D-N.D.

The federal government entered the crop insurance business in 1938, but it was a minor program until Congress created a subsidy system in 1980 (PL 96-365). *(1980 Almanac, p. 95)*

The last major revision of crop insurance law took place in 1994 (PL 103-354). *(1994 Almanac, p. 194)*

Farmers purchase policies from private insurance companies, with the federal government picking up a portion of the tab. For instance, the government currently pays 42 percent of the premium for crop insurance policies that have a 35 percent deductible. (The farmer pays the rest.) The bill would increase the government's share to 60 percent.

The government also reimburses the insurance companies for certain losses. The subsidies and administrative expenditures currently cost the government about $1.5 billion a year.

To offer deeper premium discounts to farmers this year, the Agriculture Department has devoted $400 million of the $6 billion farm "disaster" package in the fiscal 1999 omnibus spending law (PL 105-277) to the insurance program. *(1998 Almanac, p. 2-112)*

Agriculture Committee aides say the bill will consume all of the budget resolution's allocation, but the Congressional Budget Office has not yet made an official estimate of HR 2559's cost. Some members worry that the bill will exceed $6 billion in new spending.

"This may well have been the easy part," Ewing said. "When we get the figures on cost, we may have to make decisions about priorities."

Bill Highlights

HR 2559 would either increase or preserve the subsidies offered to farmers buying all levels of insurance coverage. The bill would also change the formula for setting a farmer's "actual production history," the baseline used for insurance purposes to determine how much a farmer produces in an average year.

The bill would limit the amount a farmer's baseline could drop after a bad year, so farmers suffering consecutive years of weather disasters or other problems can still buy adequate coverage.

The bill would also stiffen penalties against farmers and insurers for fraud and authorize $55 million a year for pilot programs to insure livestock.

Pomeroy offered an en bloc amendment to increase the federal subsidy for policies with 25 percent and 30 percent deductibles. His amendment, approved 15-7, would offer farmers a choice of formulas for determining their actual production histories, as well as extend a 20 percent premium subsidy provided by the omnibus spending law to farmers whose crops have been destroyed by the diseases scab and vomitoxin.

Currently, about 65 crops are eligible for coverage. The bill would devote $55 million a year to developing new kinds of insurance plans.

Ranking subcommittee Democrat Gary A. Condit of California won voice vote approval of an amendment that would designate $25 million from that pool to create insurance plans for "specialty crops," such as fruits, which he said were underserved by the program.

Spending Cuts Ensure Crop Bill Gets a Go-Ahead

JULY 31 — Having cleared the tallest hurdle — finding spending cuts totaling more than $2 billion — House Agriculture Committee Chairman Larry Combest, R-Texas, can confidently assume that his bill to expand the federal crop insurance program will win easy approval from the panel on Aug. 3.

A markup on Combest's bill (HR 2559) was delayed for three days as he scrambled to find the cuts. At the start of a July 30 markup, he offered an en bloc amendment that reduced the bill's size to just a hair below $6 billion.

"We have a final scoring now, and we're not going to take any more phone calls from CBO [the Congressional Budget Office]," Combest quipped.

Administration costs and subsidies to farmers and insurance companies currently cost the federal government about $1.5 billion a year. The fiscal 2000 budget resolution (H Con Res 68) provides for an increase of $6 billion in crop insurance spending from fiscal 2001-04.

Farmers have complained that the policies they purchase with federal subsidies from private insurance companies cost them too much money for too little coverage.

The bill seeks to encourage greater participation in the crop insurance program by increasing premium subsidies. The bill would also change the formula for setting a farmer's "actual production history," the baseline used for insurance purposes to determine how much a farmer produces in an average year.

In addition, the bill would stiffen penalties against farmers and insurers who engage in fraud.

Combest's amendment, approved by voice vote, made the bill's premium subsidy increases slightly less generous. It also decreased the bill's spending on pilot programs for livestock insurance, rewrote the formula for determining a farmer's actual production history and pushed back the starting dates for a variety of the bill's provisions.

Some farm-state members, notably Senate Agriculture Committee Chairman Richard G. Lugar, R-Ind., would like to see portions of the $6 billion budget allocation dedicated to other farm programs.

But an amendment offered July 30 by ranking Democrat Charles W. Stenholm of Texas to give farmers $550 million worth of direct cash payments under certain price conditions was turned back by voice vote. His amendment would have cut some premium subsidies by an equivalent amount.

"You don't establish a price protection program by diluting what you need for crop insurance," said Earl Pomeroy, D-N.D.

Several members expressed interest in pursuing Stenholm's formulas as part of a "disaster" aid package to agriculture considered all but certain this fall.

By voice vote, the committee approved an amendment to allow farmers to plant a second crop after collecting insurance claims for being unable to plant their originally intended crop.

"There's something that seems morally wrong to have productive land growing weeds when it could be growing a crop," said Democrat David Minge of Minnesota.

The committee defeated by voice vote an amendment to provide increased premium subsidies to farmers who "blow the whistle" on neighbors who cheat the program.

Still to come are fights about how much control private insurers, as opposed to the federal government, should have over various aspects of the program.

Full Committee Acts To Boost Farm Subsidies

AUGUST 7 — The House Agriculture Committee gave voice vote approval Aug. 3 to a bill (HR 2559) that would expand the federal crop insurance program by about $6 billion over four years.

Currently, about 65 percent of eligible farmland is enrolled in the crop insurance program. Many farmers balk at participating because they say the coverage is too low to justify paying the premiums.

The bill would provide higher subsidies for most levels of coverage. It also would stiffen penalties against farmers and insurers who cheat the system, devote $55 million to developing new coverage packages and create pilot programs for livestock coverage.

The federal government currently subsidizes the purchase of private crop insurance policies, at a cost of about $1.5 billion a year. Members of Congress hope to expand the program to offer more risk protection to farmers and wean them from multibillion-dollar bailouts during hard times.

The fiscal 2000 budget resolution (H Con Res 68) authorized $6 billion for additional crop insurance spending for fiscal 2001-04. To fit within that allocation, committee Chairman Larry Combest, R-Texas, cut more than $2 billion from his original bill. (His amendment to cut the bill was approved when the markup began July 30.)

The bill still exceeds the crop insurance allocation for fiscal 2000, and Combest announced that he would find further cuts before the bill comes to the floor after the August recess. If he can keep the bill within its allocation, it should have no trouble winning approval in the House.

The bill would allow farming cooperatives to pay for "catastrophic coverage," the minimum level of coverage available, and market those policies to farmers. Independent insurance agents have complained that this provision will cut them out of the action.

The committee approved, by voice vote, an amendment by John Thune, R-S.D., to require that anyone who sells crop insurance be licensed to do so.

Thune withdrew an amendment that would have stipulated that insurance companies must abide by state laws regulating their industry. Combest and others complained that the amendment would weaken the bill by allowing companies the option of abiding by sometimes less-stringent state laws, bypassing some of the bill's anti-fraud provisions.

Making Adjustments

The panel had dispensed with most of the major amendments to the bill during the first half of the markup on July 30; however, the committee adjusted one amendment that had been approved.

Saxby Chambliss, R-Ga., had won approval of an amendment that would allow farmers to plant a second crop after collecting insurance claims for being unable to plant their originally intended crop. (Farmers have to file their planting decisions with their insurers.)

Current law prevents farmers from planting a second crop on land for which they have already received insurance money. Members worried that allowing them to plant a second crop might lead to fraud, with farmers perhaps misrepresenting their original intentions, collecting the insurance and then planting another crop for additional income.

To address that possibility, Chambliss offered a second amendment, approved by voice vote, to stipulate that farmers could only take advantage of the "prevented planting" provision if other farmers in the area had experienced the same conditions and had been similarly unable to get their crops in the ground.

Much discussion centered on the formula for setting a farmer's "actual production history," the baseline used for insurance purposes to determine how much a farmer produces in an average year.

Charles W. Stenholm of Texas, the committee's ranking Democrat, offered an amendment to allow farmers to adjust their production history when pests such as gypsy moths, boll weevils and medflies had been eradicated and their crop yield had risen. It was approved by voice vote.

The committee rejected by voice vote an amendment by David Minge, D-Minn., that would have adjusted the production history formula to benefit new farmers. His amendment would have also have put a $300,000 cap on catastrophic insurance payoffs.

Farmers pay $60 per crop for catastrophic coverage, with the federal government subsidizing the rest of the cost. Minge said the program was intended to help smaller farms, but said large farms benefit most, paying $60 and sometimes receiving hundreds of thousands of dollars in return. Most members agreed that the program has been abused and needed changes, but they wanted to study the issue before imposing limits on payments.

Crop Insurance Bill Passes House

OCTOBER 2 — Besieged by bad weather, low commodity prices and a political maelstrom in Washington, farmers got a bit of encouraging news from Congress on Sept. 29.

The House, by voice vote, passed a bill (HR 2559 — H Rept 106-300) to lower the premiums that farmers pay for crop insurance, the federally subsidized program that is supposed to avoid the multibillion-dollar "emergency" bailouts that Congress routinely funnels to farmers after droughts and other natural disasters.

The legislation, sponsored by Agriculture Committee Chairman Larry Combest, R-Texas, would authorize an additional $6 billion for federally subsidized crop insurance in fiscal years 2001 through 2004.

It also would increase the government's share of the premium, an attempt to appeal to farmers who have insisted in past years that they could not afford the insurance. And it would direct the Agriculture Department to study ways of expanding the program to encourage more participation by farmers and ranchers.

A key component in that effort is recalculating the premiums paid by farmers. Under HR 2559, the government would pay a larger share. For example, a farmer covering 75 percent of his crop at 100 percent of the price would pay 46 percent of the premium. Current law calls for that farmer to pay 76.5 percent.

For a policy covering 50 percent of a farmer's crop at 100 percent of the cost, the government would absorb 67 percent of the premium under the bill, an increase from 57 percent under the current formula.

The bill would almost double the amount spent each year on crop insurance, from $1.7 billion to an expected $3.2 billion, according to congressional aides.

Crop insurance "is a safety net that assists the producer in managing risk on the farm," said Rep. Thomas W. Ewing, R-Ill. "It allows the producer, not the government, to decide how to manage this risk."

Among the more significant changes in the bill is a provision to allow farmers to exclude bad years from the formula used to calculate coverage. The measure also would provide discounted premiums to farmers who have a history of good production. ◆

Eleventh Hour Dealing Clears Way for Passage Of New Dairy Pricing Plan

Box Score

- **Bill:** HR 3428 (incorporated by reference in HR 3194)
- **Legislative action: House** passed HR 1402 (H Rept 106-239), 285-140, on Sept. 22.

House adopted conference report on HR 3194 (H Rept 106-479), incorporating HR 3428, 296-135, on Nov. 18.

Senate cleared HR 3194, 74-24, on Nov. 19.

President signed HR 3194 on Nov. 29.

SUMMARY

Congress cleared two dairy provisions benefiting other regions of the country at the expense of the Upper Midwest. The provisions, part of the omnibus fiscal 2000 appropriations package (HR 3194), maintain current milk pricing rules and extend the Northeast Dairy Compact. Midwestern lawmakers gave up end-of-session attempts to block the omnibus in exchange for a promise that Congress would address the dairy issue early in 2000.

Under the 1996 farm law (PL 104-127), the Department of Agriculture (USDA) was directed to streamline the federal government's complex system of regional price supports, known as milk marketing orders. These were designed during the Depression to ensure that all sections of the country have access to highly perishable dairy products. The resulting USDA changes, proposed March 31, would have cut the prices that processors pay for fresh milk outside Wisconsin and Minnesota.

The department was told to reduce the number of milk marketing orders from 31 to no more than 14 and not less than 10. The USDA settled on 11 regions in its proposed new system. But even before it announced its decision, lawmakers from the South, Southwest and Northeast were ready with legislation to block it.

Republican Rep. Roy Blunt of Missouri introduced a bill (HR 1402) to override the USDA's decision and maintain the status quo for many states. The bill quickly attracted 138 cosponsors, setting the stage for a regional dairy battle. The House voted 285-140 to pass the measure in September signaling that could also override President Clinton's threatened veto.

The Senate never acted on the companion measure (S 1265), introduced by Paul Coverdell, R-Ga., partly because of filibuster threats from Wisconsin's senators, Democrats Herb Kohl and Russell D. Feingold.

Advocates of dairy interests outside the Midwest also tried to move legislation to make permanent the Northeast Interstate Dairy Compact. The compact, created by Congress in 1996, established an interstate commission that raised prices paid to dairy farmers in six New England states above the federally mandated levels. But a bill to do so (HR 1604) saw no action after approval by the House Judiciary Subcommittee on Commercial and Administrative Law on July 29.

The dairy compact's authority was due to end Oct. 1 and the milk pricing rules were to change that day, but both actions were halted by lawsuits. At the same time, advocates of preserving both of them pressed negotiators to add language to the catch-all spending bill, at one point threatening to engineer defeat of the initial foreign operations appropriations conference report (HR 2606) unless they got their way.

Senate Majority Leader Trent Lott, R-Miss., said he opposed including the dairy provision, but he acquiesced when he concluded the provisions were necessary to get the package through the House. The dairy package was among the last items added to the omnibus measure. One section would block USDA from instituting its new rules, the other would keep the Northeast Compact alive until Sept. 30, 2001.

Midwestern lawmakers were furious that the language was included. They charged Republicans had inserted the language in order to give a political chit to Sen. James M. Jeffords, R-Vt., who faces a re-election fight next year. Kohl, Feingold, and the two Minnesota senators, Republican Rod Grams and Democrat Paul Wellstone, opened a parliamentary war against the year-end package. Even after the House had adopted the conference report and gone home for the year, the four threatened to use procedural moves to keep the Senate in session, perhaps until Thanksgiving. They relented just hours after a procedural vote went against them, 80-8.

Just before calling off their filibuster, lawmakers from the dairy states said, they received assurances from Senate leaders of both parties that the issue would be revisited in 2000. And Senate Agriculture Committee Chairman Richard G. Lugar, R-Ind., promised that his panel would vote on legislation early in 2000 addressing an overhaul of the current dairy pricing system.

Regional Rivalries Heat Up as House Panel OKs New Dairy Price Plan

JULY 3 — Setting the stage for a major floor fight, the House Agriculture Committee on June 30 approved a bill to overturn the Clinton administration's plan to revise federal dairy pricing policy.

The 32-15 vote offered a preview of what is to come on the floor, with members splitting into contentious regional factions. With dairy farmers going out of business all over the country, members have formed warring camps in trying to preserve pricing advantages for farmers in their home states.

The bill (HR 1402) would block the Agriculture Department (USDA) from implementing its proposal to flatten different regional prices paid to dairy farmers under the arcane federal "marketing order" system for milk.

The Depression-era system requires dairy processors within each marketing order, or region, to pay farmers a minimum price for their milk.

Currently, farmers are paid more for fluid milk the farther they are located from Eau Claire, Wis., the historic "center" of the dairy industry. The bonuses given to farmers outside the Upper Midwest were intended to reflect different production and transportation costs. The administration plan would minimize those bonuses.

HR 1402 would preserve the status quo in pricing for many Southern and Northeastern states.

The bill has attracted 225 cosponsors, seven more than a majority of the House. Members from the Northeast and South are concerned that the USDA's new pricing formula, if allowed to go into effect as scheduled on Oct. 1, would hit their farmers hard.

"I think it's a case where Congress is asserting its will," said John M. McHugh, R-N.Y., one of the many Northeastern critics of the USDA plan. "In this case, I think that's appropriate."

But members from the Upper Midwest and a few Western states, along with consumer and taxpayer groups, are adamantly opposed to HR 1402.

Agriculture Secretary Dan Glickman outlined his opposition to the bill in a June 29 letter to the committee.

Congressional opponents of the bill are hoping they can delay floor consideration until after the August recess.

They also hope the bill's chances have been complicated by amendments adopted by the committee. One would allow dairy farmers to sign pricing contracts with private entities for future delivery; another would overturn a new USDA formula for pricing milk used in cheese production.

But Roy Blunt, R-Mo., HR 1402's chief sponsor, remained sanguine.

"It's good to be headed to the floor [with 225 cosponsors], I'll tell you that," Blunt said in an interview June 30. "I don't see anything in these amendments that would complicate things for our cosponsors."

Marketing Milk

Dairy policy is notoriously complex, and during the markup members joked about the difficulty of untangling, or even understanding, all the issues.

"It's a wonder any gallon of milk gets from the cow to the marketplace," quipped John A. Boehner, R-Ohio.

Boehner offered an amendment to abolish milk marketing orders by 2001.

Several members expressed sympathy for Boehner's desire to move milk toward a market-oriented system but argued that U.S. dairy farmers could not compete against foreign producers whose milk is subsidized. Boehner's amendment was rejected, 11-35.

Much debate centered on an amendment by Cal Dooley, D-Calif., to allow dairy farmers to enter into forward contracts with private companies. Forward contracts allow farmers to lock in the current price for their commodity for delivery at a later date.

"The greatest challenge that our producers face today is [price] volatility in the market," said Richard W. Pombo, R-Calif. "This helps reduce some of that volatility."

But ranking Democrat Charles W. Stenholm of Texas argued that other commodities that are traded with forward contracts, such as pork and beef, have driven farmers out of business in droves.

The contracts amendment was adopted, 23-20.

The committee also adopted, 25-15, a Stenholm amendment to send the USDA back to the drawing board in setting the price formula for milk used in cheese production.

And the committee adopted, by voice vote, an amendment to extend the dairy price support program, which is set to expire on Dec. 31, by one year.

Collin C. Peterson, D-Minn., said an extension would save taxpayers money, because if the program were terminated, farmers would be eligible for certain government loans, resulting in a cost to taxpayers.

Some milk processors and taxpayer organizations warn, though, that extending the program leaves open the possibility that the federal government might again spend billions buying surplus cheese, as it did during the 1970s and 1980s, if dairy overproduction forced prices below the government's price-support guarantee.

House Judiciary Panel Approves Dairy Compacts

JULY 31 — The House Judiciary Subcommittee on Commercial and Administrative Law on July 29 approved, 7-3, a bill to authorize two regional dairy compacts. But that action may prove a high point for the measure (HR 1604), which is opposed by senior Republicans on the full committee and within the House leadership.

A compact allows a quasi-public interstate commission, made up of farm, processor and consumer representatives, as well as state officials, to set the price farmers are paid for milk above the federally mandated level. The nation's only dairy compact, in the Northeast, is set to expire on Oct. 1. HR 1604 would make it permanent and expand it into New York and the mid-Atlantic region. The bill would also authorize a new compact in the South.

On a procedural vote, the committee killed, 7-2, a bill (HR 744) that would have terminated the Northeast compact immediately. Compact proponents say that they provide stable incomes for struggling farmers, but opponents say the higher prices hurt consumers and farmers in states outside the compact regions.

Tammy Baldwin, D-Wis., won voice vote approval of several amendments requiring the Agriculture Department (USDA) to study the effects of compacts on farmers and consumers. But compact supporters expressed concern that imposing such new duties on the USDA would delay the bill's progress because it would be referred to the Agriculture Committee. (The Judiciary Committee has jurisdiction over legal agreements between states.)

An amendment to have the General Accounting Office perform the studies instead was approved by voice vote.

The Judiciary Committee is unlikely to act on the bill before the August recess. But the Senate the week of Aug. 2 may consider an amendment to the fiscal 2000 agriculture spending bill (S 1233) that contains identical language.

House Votes To Block New Dairy Pricing Plan

SEPTEMBER 25 — Rep. Paul D. Ryan, a Republican from dairy-rich Wisconsin, was surprisingly unfazed Sept. 22 after losing — by a lopsided margin — the biggest fight of his legislative career.

The House had just passed a bill (HR 1402) that is despised in the Upper Midwest but highly favored in the East and Southeast. It would block the Agriculture Department from installing a new dairy pricing formula for milk "marketing orders," the Depression-era scheme the government uses to ensure farmers in 31 regions a minimum price for their milk.

The 285-140 vote in favor of HR 1402 would have been enough in this instance to override an expected presidential veto. But Ryan and his Midwestern allies say not to worry. The most important fact to note, they say, is the date of the roll call — about a week away from Oct. 1, when the new plan will automatically go into effect unless blocked by Congress. *(Vote 436, p. H-142)*

With the session lurching toward a close and Senate opponents of the bill talking tough, HR 1402 is unlikely to go much further. The Senate has no thirst to take up the bill, and if it does, Wisconsin Sens. Russell D. Feingold and Herb Kohl, both Democrats, have promised a filibuster. They undoubtedly would be supported by Minnesota's two senators, Rod Grams, a Republican, and Paul Wellstone, a Democrat.

Prospects are similarly sour on other fronts. Members from New England and the South have been working to preserve the current pricing system by attaching language similar to HR 1402 to the fiscal 2000 agriculture appropriations bill (HR 1906), which is in a House-Senate conference.

The dairy question stalled the conference for two consecutive days the week of Sept. 20 as House members have so far complied with a request from GOP leaders to keep dairy provisions out of the conference report.

Ryan said he had personal assurances from House GOP leaders that the dairy issue would remain separate from the must-pass appropriations bill.

And finally, should the bill somehow get to the president's desk, Agriculture Secretary Dan Glickman said he would urge a veto.

All of that contributed to Ryan's upbeat outlook. "We accomplished two things," Ryan said. "We delayed the vote until today and we educated our colleagues . . . about an antiquated, Soviet style pricing scheme."

The Pricing Scheme

The goal of HR 1402, sponsored by Roy Blunt, R-Mo., is to preserve the status quo by prohibiting the Agriculture Department (USDA) from implementing a pricing system that essentially would flatten regional differentials built into the pricing scheme. The current system, designed in 1937, gives a bonus to farmers the farther they are from Eau Claire, Wis., the historical center of the dairy industry. The bonuses were intended to reflect different production and transportation costs.

The administration's new plan would minimize those bonuses. The approach, the USDA and its supporters say, would reduce the cost of a gallon of milk by 2 cents. But critics say it would funnel more money to producers in the Upper Midwest and push financially strapped dairy farmers, particularly those in the Northeast and South, over the edge.

"What we have been reduced to this time around is 48 states, or at least 40 states, being harmed for the benefit of two," said Republican James T. Walsh of New York, who, like most of his colleagues from the Northeast and South, supported HR 1402.

That argument carried the day in the House, but the debate exposed deeply entrenched regional, rather than partisan, differences over dairy policy.

Lawmakers from the East and Southeast said the new formula would drive thousands of dairy farmers out of business because it would shift $200 million in revenues and cause a contracting industry to consolidate even more.

"Does America really want a handful of [dairy] corporations to determine the price of dairy products?" asked Bernard Sanders, I-Vt., who strongly backed HR 1402.

Opponents of the bill, including scattered members from the West, such as Cal Dooley, D-Calif., and those from the greater Midwest, such as John A. Boehner, R-Ohio, argued that the rationale for regional pricing variations is invalid in an era of interstate highways and refrigerated transport. The entire country is now within reach of fresh milk, even if it is not locally produced, they said.

"This place is locked in a time warp," declared Mark Green, R-Wis. "This place is using a milk pricing mechanism that was created in the era of the manual typewriter."

As passed, the bill also would extend for another year the federal milk price-support program, which was scheduled to expire Dec. 31.

By including that language, the House backed away from the 1996 farm bill (PL 104-127), which called for the phaseout of such subsidies for a range of commodities, including milk.

Foes of New Price Policy Drop Effort To Tie Up Senate

NOVEMBER 20 — After the final deal had been cut and the House had been sent home for the year, Russell D. Feingold was still stalking the Senate floor Nov. 19. With his trusty file "All About Milk: A Dairy Filibuster" at his side and books of cheese recipes at the ready, the Wisconsin Democrat was the last vestige of the lost campaign by Midwestern lawmakers to win a victory for their region's dairy farmers.

Two dairy provisions benefiting other regions of the country at the expense of the Upper Midwest — both of which would undo victories that region thought it had won from the Agriculture Department (USDA) — were assembled as a bill (HR 3428) that was in turn incorporated into the catch-all appropriations legislation (HR 3194) for fiscal 2000. The Senate voted 74-24 to clear the bill a day after the House voted 296-135 on Nov. 18 to adopt the conference report. *(House vote 610, p. H-198; Senate vote 374, p. S-74)*

Midwesterners had delayed the final Senate vote for 24 hours, after finally giving up a parliamentary war against the measure that was doing nothing besides exacerbating an increasingly lactose intolerant Senate.

When the bill arrived on the floor the night of Nov. 18, Feingold insisted that clerks spend two hours reading it aloud. Then he forced a vote on whether to make the bill the pending business, losing 80-8. *(Vote 369, p. S-73)*

Still Feingold and three colleagues — Herb Kohl, D-Wis., Rod Grams, R-Minn., and Paul Wellstone, D-Minn. — pressed on, insisting overnight that they would keep senators in town at least through the weekend by employing procedures that could have forced at least one middle-of-the night roll call. But by then all hope of overturning the dairy decision was lost.

When they assembled a coalition with senators upset about different items in the spending package, GOP leaders mollified the others by arranging votes on their issues on other legislation. When Kohl threatened to block a continuing resolution, he quickly backed down when it was clear he would be blamed for any resulting partial government shutdown.

The Midwesterners officially lost the battle when the Senate voted 87-9 to invoke cloture, thereby limiting debate, on the conference agreement. At that point, they allowed the final Senate roll call of the year, claiming their protest had been rewarded with a leadership promise of a dairy debate early next year. "I feel real good. I feel terrific," Kohl told reporters.

Majority Leader Trent Lott, R-Miss., said he opposed the dairy provisions but concluded they were necessary to get the package through the House. Adding the language to the measure was among the last decisions reached by the negotiators, and at one point Nov. 17 the House floor resounded with a chorus of intolerant "moos" when GOP leaders referred to the dairy standoff.

Once the deal was cut, there were fewer dilatory options available to the House's angry Midwesterners. David R. Obey, D-Wis., delayed the inevitable for a few hours by arranging 11 procedural votes — a protest he said was as much against the dairy deal as against debating the year-end conference report just hours after its assembly was completed. *(Votes 598-609; pp. H-194–H-198)*

It All Started in Eau Claire

The fight centered on the complex system of regional price supports, known as milk marketing orders, begun in the Depression to guarantee farmers a higher price for fluid milk the farther it is produced from Eau Claire, Wis. — dairy's historical ground zero. Midwesterners say that unfairly depresses their fresh milk prices.The 1996 farm law (PL 104-127) told USDA to revamp the system, and it issued regulations this year to minimize the bonuses and thereby lower prices outside the Midwest. Lawmakers from the affected regions quickly coalesced behind a bill (HR 1402) to block the new rules, and the margin to pass it signaled the House would override a threatened presidential veto.

The bill added to the omnibus appropriations package similarly keeps the current system in place.

But that is not all that galled the Midwesterners. The spending package also would keep alive until Sept. 30, 2001, the Northeast Dairy Compact, a quasi-public commission that is allowed to set — at above the federally mandated level — the prices that farmers in six states are paid by bottlers for their milk. Critics say such compacts violate free-market principles and set a bad precedent for other industries.

Conceding defeat for the year, Feingold acknowledged that prospects for changing dairy policy may be no better in 2000. "There's a lot more people who live farther away from Eau Claire than who live closer," he said. ◆

Chapter 5

BANKING & FINANCE

Major Overhaul Enacted Of Rules Governing the Financial Services Industry

SUMMARY

After decades of failed efforts, Congress passed and President Clinton signed a historic overhaul of laws governing the financial services industry. The issue drew scant public attention and was little known outside of Washington and Wall Street, but it will rank among the key laws passed by the 106th Congress.

The measure repeals laws restricting cross-ownership among banks, brokerages and insurers, and establishes a new regulatory framework for maintaining the safety and stability of the financial industry.

The barriers to cross-industry activities were enacted in response to the Great Depression in the belief that they would help stem financial failures. The 1933 Glass-Steagall Act erected barriers between the banking and securities industries, and the 1956 Bank Holding Company Act imposed barriers between banking and insurance activities.

A consensus had emerged in Congress in recent years that the laws were outdated, and that widespread financial collapse could be averted through less restrictive regulations. Bill supporters also argued that repealing the barriers would improve customer service by offering one-stop shopping for financial products, and would help U.S. financial institutions better compete globally.

Recent court and regulatory decisions had already eroded the barriers among the industries, allowing some cross-sector affiliations to proceed. Still, the financial industry wanted new laws explicitly repealing the barriers and providing guidance for future consolidation.

Overhaul efforts had foundered repeatedly in previous Congresses as various industry sectors fought among themselves over the details. In 1999, the industries generally put aside their differences and united to get a bill enacted, and they repeatedly applied heavy pressure on GOP leaders to keep things moving.

The chief front-line strategists were Rep. Jim Leach, R-Iowa, and Sen. Phil Gramm, R-Texas, chairmen of their chambers' Banking committees. The two approached the issue with different leadership styles, and the bills that initially emerged from the two chambers differed dramatically.

Leach worked hard to win Democratic support for his bill (HR 10), seeking bipartisan consensus at every turn while trying to avoid divisive provisions. Gramm took a more partisan approach. He insisted on including controversial provisions that would have scaled back the 1977 Community Reinvestment Act (PL 95-128), an anti-redlining law intended to force banks to make loans in low-income areas. Democrats, the White House and community groups vehemently opposed those provisions, and the Senate bill passed on a party-line vote in committee and with only one Democratic vote on the floor.

In conference negotiations, Gramm made concessions on the reinvestment act that eventually helped seal a bipartisan agreement.

Gramm gave up a provision that would have exempted small, rural banks from complying with the law, but he was able to include a provision reducing the frequency of compliance reviews for most small banks. The final measure also contains a "sunshine" provision pushed by Gramm that requires community groups to disclose payments they receive from banks as part of arrangements in which the groups agree not to protest banks' reinvestment ratings. The provision also requires the groups to disclose how they spend the payments.

Privacy provisions were another partisan flash point. In the end, Democrats succeeded in placing some new restrictions on the ability of financial service companies to transfer customer data to third parties. Republicans fought off Democratic efforts to impose more sweeping privacy measures opposed by the industries.

Complicating matters further were several difficult provisions that did not divide lawmakers along party lines. For example, conferees haggled over whether savings and loans, also known as thrifts, should be barred from affiliating with commercial firms.

Legislators' positions on the issue had more to do with home district and philosophical concerns than partisanship. Conferees decided to bar such mergers in the future, although existing affiliations between commercial businesses and thrifts would be allowed to continue.

Another key turning point for the bill was an agreement between the Treasury Department and Federal Reserve over how the new financial conglomerates would be structured and who would regulate them.

The White House had threatened to veto the bill if Treasury's demands were ignored, but many legislators were reluctant to pass a bill over the objections of Fed Chairman Alan Greenspan. The two agencies settled their long-running feud during conference negotiations by agreeing to a framework in which both agencies would continue to play strong banking oversight roles.

Public and private conference negotiations were lengthy. The prospects for the bill appeared grim on several occa-

Box Score

- **Bill:** S 900 — PL 106-102
- **Legislative action: Senate** passed S 900 (S Rept 106-44), 54-44, on May 6.

House passed HR 10 (H Rept 106-74, Parts 1-3), 343-86, on July 1.

Senate adopted the conference report on S 900 (H Rept 106-434), 90-8, on Nov. 4.

House cleared the bill, 362-57, on Nov. 4.

President signed S 900 on Nov. 12.

sions, but industry lobbyists stepped up the heat whenever discussions appeared on the brink of collapse.

Fuzzy Battle Lines Complicate Overhaul Effort

FEBRUARY 27 — It would be difficult to find an issue with a more curious mix of interest-group conflict than the proposed overhaul of financial services regulations. Small banks agree with big banks on some issues but disagree on others. Insurance agents agree on oversight issues with the state officials who regulate them. Consumer groups echo some, but not all, positions voiced by insurance agents. Federal regulatory agencies are engaged in turf battles.

With the House and Senate financial services bills (HR 10, Senate draft) drawing a dizzying mix of praise and ire from the affected groups and industries, congressional leaders in both chambers face a tough task in meeting their goal of moving the measures quickly to floor votes. Committee markups are scheduled for March 3 in the Senate Banking, Housing and Urban Affairs Committee and March 4 in the House Banking and Financial Services Committee.

The bills call for repealing provisions of the 1933 Glass-Steagall Act and amending the 1956 Bank Holding Company Act, which erected barriers between the banking, securities and insurance industries under the belief that they would help avert widespread financial failures.

Similar bills have failed numerous times in recent years, but last year's version of HR 10 moved further than ever: It passed the House by one vote, then stalled in the Senate.

A consensus has emerged that the 1933 and 1956 laws are outdated and harmful to U.S. financial companies' ability to compete internationally. But the details involved in revamping financial services laws are complex.

Several prominent groups have given qualified support to HR 10. They see it as a delicate compromise that took months to negotiate. But Sen. Phil Gramm, R-Texas, the new chairman of the Senate Banking Committee, disagrees. During committee hearings Feb. 25, Gramm derided HR 10 as a timid "mass of compromises" that would erect new barriers in the process of knocking down old ones. Gramm said it would be "a waste of time" to go back to HR 10.

Legislative activity has prompted an avalanche of campaign contributions from industries angling to win market advantages or deny such advantages to competitors. In the 1997-98 election cycle, industries lobbying on the issue gave $45 million in political action committee (PAC) money, soft money and individual contributions to federal parties and candidates, according to the Center for Responsive Politics, a nonpartisan group that tracks campaign money. Of that amount, about 40 percent went to members of the three committees — including House Commerce — with jurisdiction over financial services.

The following is an issue-by-issue scorecard on where major players stand on key elements of the legislation:

Community Reinvestment Act

The overhaul process is generally viewed as a classic inside-the-Beltway battle among heavyweight lobbyists, federal regulators and interest groups. An exception is the debate over what to do with the 1977 Community Reinvestment Act (PL 95-128). The act requires banks to document their efforts to invest in all segments of their communities. An unfavorable review from federal regulators could bring sanctions.

Reinvestment supporters include community groups across the nation, who say the 1977 law has helped revitalize scores of neighborhoods by prodding banks to look for investment opportunities in poor neighborhoods. They add that banks have thrived in doing so.

Many Republicans view the reinvestment act as an inappropriate big-government intrusion on business. Gramm has been among the harshest critics, but he has softened his public stance since becoming Banking chairman. The Clinton administration supports the law, and in recent weeks has signaled that it will veto any overhaul legislation that is unfriendly to it.

The House bill (HR 10), sponsored by Banking Committee Chairman Jim Leach, R-Iowa, would maintain reinvestment requirements for banks. The Senate bill unveiled by Gramm would ease compliance requirements for banks.

The banking community generally wants to do away with the act in order to ease regulatory compliance burdens. But bankers view repeal as politically unrealistic and have held their fire.

Some consumer and community advocates have called for expanding the reinvestment act to cover financial operations of the new conglomerates that would be allowed under the overhaul legislation. A Republican aide said that was also politically unrealistic.

Banking and Commerce

The House and Senate bills differ widely on whether to allow banks to engage in commercial non-banking enterprises. Opponents worry that the failure of bank-owned commercial enterprises could threaten the banking system's safety and stability. They also fear that banks would be tempted to deny credit to commercial competitors.

Leach adamantly opposes any mix of banking and commerce. His bill would prohibit it. Treasury Secretary Robert E. Rubin and Federal Reserve Board Chairman Alan Greenspan support this position. But Greenspan has said that market forces and technological advancements are making the mixture of commercial and banking activities inevitable. He said Congress will likely have to address the issue a few years after a financial services overhaul is enacted.

Gramm's draft bill initially suggested support for a limited mix of commerce and banking, but that item was under revision Feb. 26.

A Democratic alternative bill (HR 665), sponsored by House Banking panel ranking member John J. LaFalce, D-N.Y., would allow bank holding companies to own commercial firms totaling up to 15 percent of the holding company's annual consolidated gross revenues. Rubin generally supports HR 665 but has cited this provision as Treasury's only major objection.

Smaller banks adamantly oppose any mix of banking and commerce. Kenneth A. Guenther, a lobbyist for the Independent Bankers Association of America, said the organization agrees that mixing banking and commerce poses bank safety concerns. Guenther also noted that the smaller banks the association primarily represents are unlikely to be big players in commercial activities, and would be at

Who Wants What

FEBRUARY 27— With financial services legislation scheduled for markups in the Senate Banking, Housing and Urban Affairs Committee on March 3 and the House Banking and Financial Services Committee on March 4, lobbyists, consumer groups and regulators will be working overtime to guard their interests. The following is a rundown of what major players want:

• **Banks.** Large banks want to use the legislation as a road map to move forward with consolidation of financial services. Small banks, which have less capacity to branch into other financial services, are not as enthusiastic. But large and small banks see the legislation as a way to scale back unitary thrifts, which they regard as competitors with unfair advantages.

Banks favor federal oversight of their insurance and securities activities rather than having to deal with 50 sets of state rules and regulators. At the federal oversight level, banks want bank regulators rather than the Securities and Exchange Commission to oversee banks' securities activities.

Small banks generally oppose the mixing of banking and commerce. Large banks support it on a limited basis.

• **Insurance.** State insurance agents and regulators want state oversight of bank insurance activities. State regulators say they are best able to protect consumers. Insurance agents fear that banks might gain a competitive advantage if they were subject to less rigorous federal controls. Insurance companies take a different view, and support language in HR 10 giving federal authorities a substantial role in regulating bank insurance activities.

• **Securities.** State securities regulators who currently share regulatory chores with the SEC want this dual oversight to include bank securities activities. Banks want to nudge state and federal securities regulators out of the picture and instead report to banking regulators. The SEC opposes giving federal banking regulators primary oversight of banks' securities activities.

• **Consumer groups.** Consumer groups want to protect and expand the 1977 Community Reinvestment Act. They also want state oversight of insurance because they generally perceive state officials as more friendly to consumers than federal officials.

• **Federal regulators.** The Federal Reserve and the Treasury disagree over how financial conglomerates should be structured, and thus who would regulate them. Also, federal banking regulators are wrangling with the SEC over who should oversee securities operations in banks, with both camps arguing that they are best suited for the job.

a disadvantage competing against larger banks that could buy large businesses and cross-market a wide variety of commercial and financial products.

Unitary Thrifts

Under current law, commercial companies are allowed to own one federal savings institution, which functions largely like a bank. These unitary thrifts are seen by banks as unfair competitors because banks generally cannot engage in commerce. Banks would like to see unitary thrifts eliminated.

Thrift groups oppose attempts to scale back the operation of unitary thrifts. Gramm's bill generally would leave the thrifts alone. Leach's bill would allow existing thrifts to continue but would halt new thrift charters.

Structure and Regulation

A big impediment to passage of an overhaul bill is an unusually high-profile spat between the Clinton administration and the Federal Reserve over how financial conglomerates should be structured and thus regulated.

Greenspan says that to preserve the safety and soundness of federally insured banking activities, non-banking financial activities should be conducted in separate holding companies. Rubin says banks should be allowed to organize non-banking financial services as subsidiaries of parent banks. The Federal Reserve regulates holding companies, and Treasury regulates banks and their subsidiaries.

Leach's bill embraces the holding company structure favored by Greenspan. Gramm's bill would allow national banks with assets of $1 billion or less to have operating subsidiaries, although real estate activities would be barred from subsidiaries.

The banking community is split. Small banks, which are unlikely to be major players in the development of financial services conglomerates, support the holding company requirement as written in HR 10. Guenther said his organization, which represents smaller banks, agrees with Greenspan's safety and security concerns, and said stability and consumer trust in banking are paramount. Large banks disagree. They believe the subsidiaries arrangement would be safe, and they want the flexibility to structure financial services that way.

Insurance Oversight

The insurance industry is regulated largely by state governments. There is a sharp division among interest groups over whether federal regulators should play a larger role in insurance regulation under a financial services overhaul. Gramm's bill generally leans toward federal regulation of banks' insurance activities. Leach offers more of a mix of state and federal oversight.

State insurance regulators want to maintain their oversight authority, and they have complained that HR 10 goes too far in limiting their ability to regulate insurance activities when those activities are conducted through banks. Consumer advocates have similar concerns. Consumers Union, which publishes Consumer Reports, has argued that federal regulators have shown a lack of interest in consumer protection.

These consumer groups and insurance regulators have found themselves allied with insurance agents, who have joined in the call to preserve comprehensive state regulatory oversight of the insurance industry. The agents want to make sure that banks do not have a competitive advantage in the insurance industry by operating under what they call less rigorous federal standards.

However, insurance companies have taken a different view than the people who sell and buy their services. The American Council of Life Insurance and the American Insurance Association, which represent insurance companies, support HR 10. Bank groups also support this position. Bankers fear that state regulators will favor local insurers over multistate banking operations, and that the regulators will lean harder on national banks selling insurance to help give local insurers a competitive edge.

Securities Oversight

Like their counterparts in the insurance industry, state securities regulators want to protect their oversight responsibilities. They want shared oversight with federal regulators in the Securities and Exchange Commission (SEC) over securities transactions, including those conducted by banks. The Securities Industry Association favors SEC regulation of securities.

State regulators have complained that HR 10 is too ambiguous in preserving joint oversight of financial conglomerates, that it would permit bank employees not licensed by state securities regulators to sell securities. In Feb. 11 testimony to the House Banking panel in behalf of the North American Securities Administrators Association Inc., Thomas E. Geyer, commissioner of the Ohio Division of Securities, warned that HR 10 could hurt consumer protections in securities transactions by creating a "parallel universe" of unregistered banks and their sales force.

Federal regulators are also wrangling over oversight duties. Gramm's bill would dilute the SEC's oversight of banks' securities activities in favor of federal bank regulators, which banks support.

Democrats Warn That Senate Panel's Bill Will Draw Veto

MARCH 6 — A Senate committee approved legislation March 4 to overhaul the financial services industry in a markup that was partisan from the outset, with Democrats warning that Republicans' insistence on scaling back community reinvestment laws would kill any chance of shaping a bill that President Clinton would sign.

The same day, a House committee began marking up its own measure (HR 10), a bill whose hallmark is Democratic and administration support. The panel disposed of 20 amendments before adjourning March 4, and planned to reconvene March 10.

Both bills call for repealing provisions of the 1933 Glass-Steagall Act and amending the 1956 Bank Holding Company Act, which erected barriers among the banking, securities and insurance industries. Last year the House passed a similar bill by one vote, but it stalled in the Senate.

In the Senate on March 4, Republicans on the Banking, Housing and Urban Affairs Committee held together on two 11-9 party-line votes to reject a minority-supported overhaul proposal offered by ranking Democrat Paul S. Sarbanes of Maryland, and then approve an unnumbered Republican-backed measure. The bill is expected on the floor in April, a GOP staff aide said.

Sen. John Kerry, D-Mass., asked Republicans why they were pushing ahead when they knew the two sides were at an impasse on key issues. Chairman Phil Gramm, R-Texas, did not dispute the use of "impasse," but said he believed Clinton was responsible for it. "I am increasingly convinced that the president does not want the bill," Gramm said.

Community Reinvestment

The most contentious issue of the day was an amendment by Richard C. Shelby, R-Ala., to exempt small, nonurban banks from the 1977 Community Reinvestment Act (CRA), which requires banks to document their efforts to invest in all segments of their communities. The law (PL 95-128) provides for sanctions if federal regulators issue a bank an unfavorable review. The amendment passed, 11-9, with one member of each party crossing the battle lines.

The Clinton administration has said it will veto any attempt to weaken the reinvestment act. Reinvestment supporters include community groups across the nation, who say the law has helped revitalize neighborhoods by prodding banks to look for investment opportunities in poor neighborhoods. Committee Republicans said the act has created heavy paperwork requirements that are particularly burdensome for small banks.

Shelby's amendment was targeted at banks with less than $250 million in assets located outside metropolitan areas. Gramm supported it, saying the law has little relevance to small banks. These banks, he argued, are often in tiny communities and generally do not need government pressure to spread their assets around because they must reinvest locally just to survive.

Democrats disagreed, saying small banks have a track record of using a large share of local bank deposits to invest in securities rather than the local community. Christopher J. Dodd, D-Conn., warned Republicans that they were heading down a path that would doom chances of enacting a financial services bill. "We're about to have a train wreck here over this issue," he said.

Gramm said Democrats' insistence on applying the reinvestment act to the smallest banks in the smallest communities signaled their unwillingness to compromise. "Maybe you're the extremists on this issue," Gramm said.

In an effort to sway votes, Gramm moved to reduce the cap in Shelby's measure from banks with $250 million in net assets to $100 million, which Shelby accepted. But when the vote was called only one Democrat, Tim Johnson of South Dakota, joined the Republicans. Johnson issued a statement afterward saying that although the reinvestment act was important, a "narrowly tailored CRA exemption for small, rural banks makes sense and gives our community banks a competitive break as we create vast new entities which will compete with them for increasingly scarce deposits."

The only Republican to vote against the amendment, Rick Santorum of

Pennsylvania, said he was concerned about the impact of changes to the reinvestment act on rural areas of his state.

Gramm also differed with Sarbanes on "unitary thrifts." Under current law, commercial companies are allowed to own one federal savings institution, which functions largely like a bank. These unitary thrifts are seen by banks as unfair competitors because banks generally cannot engage in commerce. Banks want unitary thrifts eliminated.

Gramm's and Sarbanes' overhaul proposals both call for freezing the number of unitary thrifts while allowing existing thrifts to continue. However, Sarbanes said his bill would do more to restrict the expansion of existing thrifts, a position that Gramm said would violate owners' rights.

House Action

While the Senate markup produced a bill that conservatives favor, House Banking and Financial Services Chairman Jim Leach, R-Iowa, and the panel's ranking Democrat, John J. LaFalce of New York, struggled to maintain bipartisan support for their measure.

The bill (HR 10) would allow banks with less than $10 billion in assets to organize their other financial services as operating subsidiaries, as favored by the Treasury Department. They would be prohibited, however, from underwriting insurance or funding real estate development through such a setup.

Leach and LaFalce generally were successful in holding their bill together, as the committee rejected the most threatening amendments.

As it had in the Senate markup, the Community Reinvestment Act played a prominent role in panel deliberations. The House bill would extend reinvestment requirements to banks included in the new financial conglomerates, but Democrats attempted to extend it further.

Luis V. Gutierrez, D-Ill., led three attempts to apply the act to insurance and securities portions of the conglomerates, but all three amendments were rejected, mostly along partisan lines.

Richard H. Baker, R-La., attempted to allow banks to comply with the law by investing in any improvements that would boost public health or the environment. Baker said he wanted to set some parameters for compliance, but Democrats said it would allow banks to invest in Fortune 500 companies and call it community reinvestment. Baker's amendment was defeated by voice vote.

The panel also touched on several other contentious issues, including:

- **Redlining.** The panel adopted, 28-27, an amendment by Barbara Lee, D-Calif., that would prevent an insurance company from merging with a bank or securities firm if it was involved in litigation over alleged redlining or if it had settled such a suit by consent decree. Redlining is the practice of denying people insurance because they live in a certain neighborhood.
- **Low-cost bank accounts.** After an emotional debate, the panel rejected, 27-31, an amendment by Maxine Waters, D-Calif., that would have required banks to have a "demonstrable record" of providing low-cost accounts. Proponents said that more than 12 million people do not have bank accounts, in part because they cannot afford them.
- **Privacy issues.** The panel adopted by voice vote an amendment by Ron Paul, R-Texas, and Tom Campbell, R-Calif., to prevent the executive branch from implementing certain proposed "know your customer" regulations. The regulations aim to enlist banks in stopping fraudulent cash transactions, such as laundering drug money. But members said they had received many letters from constituents concerned about the privacy of their financial records.

Before approving the amendment, the panel adopted by voice vote a secondary amendment by Baker and Bob Barr, R-Ga., that narrowed the proposals that could not be implemented. The original amendment would have prohibited federal agencies from requiring banks "to monitor the legality of the transaction activities of customers," but several members said it was too broad.

Some Republicans expressed concern about the bill's overall structure, saying that Leach had moved too far toward LaFalce and the administration.

High-ranking panel Republican Marge Roukema of New Jersey strongly opposed Leach's move to allow some financial conglomerates to organize as operating subsidiaries. Roukema favors an approach pushed by Federal Reserve Chairman Alan Greenspan that would require conglomerates to be set up as holding companies in which the bottom line of each business remained distinct. LaFalce and Treasury Secretary Robert E. Rubin favor allowing companies to set up operating subsidiaries in which additional businesses become part of the bottom line of the parent corporation, often likely to be a bank.

Roukema offered but withdrew an amendment that would have overturned the provisions, but she warned that the issue would not go away. "Perhaps we can only look to the Commerce Committee to save us from ourselves," she said. That panel has jurisdiction over several aspects of the bill, mostly involving securities.

Michael G. Oxley, R-Ohio, chairman of Commerce's Subcommittee on Finance and Hazardous Materials, said March 4 that panel leaders will likely wait for the Senate to act before they spend much time on HR 10. He said he felt that despite House-Senate differences, the bill was not necessarily doomed. "Most of the people who've been through it know that it's the usual drill of two steps forward and one step back," Oxley said.

Both Sides Cheer Measure Approved By House Panel

MARCH 13 — A financial services overhaul bill approved by a House committee with strong bipartisan support had members glowing about its prospects for becoming law, but the bill clashes with companion legislation in the Senate on some thorny issues that could derail progress.

The House bill (HR 10) was approved, 51-8, on March 11 by the House Banking and Financial Services Committee after a grueling three-day markup held March 4, March 10 and March 11. Committee Chairman Jim Leach, R-Iowa, painstakingly steered the panel through a minefield of partisan pitfalls and veto-triggering amendments to produce a bill that had members of both parties clapping and back-slapping upon approval.

Moments after the final vote, ranking Democrat John J. LaFalce of New York — who just 24 hours earlier during a procedural flap with Republicans was pounding on his desk and shouting that bipartisanship was on its deathbed — proudly proclaimed that he believed it was a bill President Clinton would sign if it reached his desk.

Both the House and Senate bills call for repealing provisions of the 1933 Glass-Steagall Act and amending the 1956 Bank Holding Company Act, which erected barriers among the banking, securities and insurance industries. There is widespread industry consensus that those laws are outdated and that they limit the international competitiveness of U.S. financial institutions.

But HR 10 differs substantially from the unnumbered Senate bill approved March 4 by the Banking, Housing and Urban Affairs Committee on at least two key issues: community reinvestment requirements for banks, and regulatory oversight of the new financial conglomerates that would be created under the legislation.

Further complicating matters, the House bill contains a provision on financial privacy despite efforts by Leach and others to keep it out. The Senate bill does not include anything comparable. Both parties tend to agree on the need for greater protection of bank customers' privacy, but they disagree on how it should be done.

Community Reinvestment

HR 10 largely avoids changes to the 1977 Community Reinvestment Act (PL 95-128), which aims to ensure that banks invest in poor and minority communities. It requires banks to document efforts to invest in all segments of the communities in which they collect deposits, and provides for sanctions if federal regulators issue a bank an unfavorable review.

The threat of a partisan showdown on community reinvestment hung in the air when Rep. Bill McCollum, R-Fla., submitted four amendments that would have scaled back the reach of the reinvestment act, but McCollum never called for their consideration. Democrats adamantly oppose any rollbacks of reinvestment requirements, and adoption of any of McCollum's amendments could have sunk the chances for widespread Democratic support of HR 10. Clinton has said he will veto any bill that weakens community reinvestment requirements.

The Senate bill contains a controversial GOP-backed exemption for banks with less than $100 million in assets located outside metropolitan areas. Senate Republicans argued that the reinvestment act creates a heavy compliance and paperwork burden, particularly for smaller banks.

Regulatory Oversight

The battle between Federal Reserve Board Chairman Alan Greenspan and the Clinton administration on regulatory oversight of financial services conglomerates appears to be shifting in both chambers toward the administration's position.

Greenspan strongly believes that all non-bank financial services should be conducted in holding companies that are separate from bank operations. Treasury Secretary Robert E. Rubin believes banks should be allowed to conduct those activities through subsidiaries. The disagreement has been characterized as a turf war because the Fed oversees holding companies while Treasury regulates bank subsidiaries, but Greenspan and Rubin say their positions are based on what they believe to be the safest ways to structure banks.

Both the House and Senate bills edge away from Greenspan's position, but they remain far apart in the details. HR 10 would allow banks with less than $10 billion in assets to organize their non-banking financial services as operating subsidiaries, as favored by the Treasury Department. Subsidiaries would be prohibited, however, from underwriting insurance or funding real estate development. Those would have to be conducted separately through a holding company. The Senate bill would allow banks with $1 billion or less in assets to organize non-bank financial services as subsidiaries, except for real estate activities.

Privacy

Rep. Jay Inslee, D-Wash., forced his colleagues to choose between dueling, hastily drafted banking privacy measures, even though many members of both parties were reluctant to do so. At the House committee markup March 10, Inslee offered an amendment that, among other things, would require banks to notify customers if they planned to release information about their depository transactions, such as check writing, to third parties. Customers would then have 30 days to inform the bank that they did not want such information released. "This is a privacy right," Inslee said. "We need to protect it."

Leach warned that while he agreed with Inslee's concerns, the amendment would raise "enormous" issues and have unintended consequences that could hurt consumers. He urged Inslee to withdraw the amendment so the issue could be considered more thoroughly later. Instead, Inslee's staff worked late into the night with majority staff members to produce a bipartisan revision unveiled the next day.

Leach, apparently sensing that he could not head off a vote on some kind of privacy measure, joined the fray with his own proposal. His staff and aides from the office of Bruce F. Vento, D-Minn., also toiled late into the evening March 10 to produce a 20-page Leach-Vento substitute amendment that would require consumer notification of banks' information-sharing practices.

The Leach-Vento amendment contained no "opt out" provision as required under Inslee's measure. At the markup March 11, with the two privacy measures competing, several members expressed unease with the timing. Rep. Brad Sherman, D-Calif., said, "It is very difficult for many of us to vote against having a privacy component of this bill now that this issue has come up."

The committee approved the Leach-Vento measure, 34-22, as a substitute for Inslee's amendment, and then approved the underlying amendment, 52-6.

Other issues tackled by the committee included:

- **ATM fees.** Rep. Bernard Sanders, I-Vt., attempted to win approval for a measure prohibiting banks from charging non-customers a fee to use automated teller machines (ATMs). But a substitute amendment by LaFalce and Leach requiring banks to disclose any such fees prior to an ATM transaction was approved, 35-10. The underlying measure was then approved, 48-1.
- **Unitary thrifts.** Rep. Ken Bentsen, D-Texas, succeeded in an effort to relax a provision in HR 10 that would have frozen the creation of new thrifts

and prohibited existing thrifts from affiliating with commercial companies. Thrifts are insured federal savings institutions that function much like banks. The banking community complains that thrifts have unfair market advantages over banks, such as the ability to affiliate with commercial businesses. Leach and others have worried about the mixing of banking and commerce that occurs when thrifts are sold to commercial firms.

Supporters of Bentsen's efforts argued strongly that there is no evidence that thrifts have caused a problem in the marketplace and that it would be unfair to change the rules for them. Bentsen's amendment, which would freeze the number of existing thrifts but continue to allow those thrifts to be sold to commercial firms, was approved, 29-26.

- **Bank mergers.** On March 4, the committee voted, 22-21, on an amendment to require the Federal Reserve Board to hold public hearings on big mergers in all major affected cities. On March 10, Republicans Paul D. Ryan of Wisconsin and John E. Sweeney of New York offered an amendment to give the Fed greater discretion in deciding whether to hold such hearings. Democrats angrily accused Republicans of trying to revisit an issue the Republicans had lost. The dispute led to an angry burst of parliamentary maneuvering, leading LaFalce to pound his desk and shout that bipartisanship was sinking fast.

Leach adjourned the session for the day, and the next morning a bipartisan amendment offered by Vento, Sweeney and Ryan was calmly adopted by voice vote, with a few members expressing dissent. The compromise measure would require the Fed to conduct public meetings in some of the affected cities on mergers involving depository institutions with $1 billion or more in assets.

Different Approaches

Throughout the House markup Leach calmly but doggedly tugged at the strings of both parties to keep factions from drifting away on key issues. Leach even occasionally broke with the Republican majority to support Democratic positions.

In contrast, the March 4 Senate markup struck a much more partisan tone. That markup lasted less than three hours and produced a much shorter bill that, while praised by some financial industries, drew fire from others that saw compromise sacrificed for brevity. Gramm has responded that HR 10 is so complicated that nobody really understands it, which is why fewer people oppose it.

Leach said that he has had only "preliminary" discussions with Gramm regarding the financial services overhaul, and the two have not yet had substantive discussions on key details. Nevertheless, Leach said, he believed the Senate and House bills had inched closer during the markup phase.

The House Commerce Committee, which has joint jurisdiction over HR 10 with the Banking Committee, has yet to take up the measure. A spokesman said the panel was waiting for Senate floor action, which is not expected in March.

Despite Rancorous Debate, Senate Passes Overhaul

MAY 8 — The Senate narrowly passed a financial services overhaul bill containing controversial provisions that would almost surely draw a veto, although a key Republican predicted compromises were likely to emerge in conference to rescue the measure. The most partisan and contentious floor battle involved a community lending law, and a split among Republicans over a regulatory issue nearly derailed a final vote.

Additional complications for the legislation have cropped up in the House, where deep differences are emerging between committees with joint jurisdiction.

Senate Banking, Housing and Urban Affairs Committee Chairman Phil Gramm, R-Texas, acknowledged on the floor that part of the reason for the partisan rancor over the bill (S 900) was that he had not worked well with the committee's ranking Democrat, Paul S. Sarbanes of Maryland. "I regret that I have not done a better job in working with Sen. Sarbanes," Gramm said. Sarbanes responded: "I share the regret expressed by the chairman that we have not been able to work this matter out this year in a way to avoid these sharp party differences."

The contrition was short-lived, however, and both men were soon accusing each other of making misleading statements. A Democratic substitute was voted down along party lines, and on May 6 the Senate voted, 54-44, to pass Gramm's bill with only minor changes. The only senator to cross party lines to vote for the bill was Ernest F. Hollings, D-S.C. *(Vote 105, p. S-24)*

Congress has struggled for years to undo Depression-era laws restricting cross-ownership among banks, brokerages and securities firms. These restrictions — contained in the 1933 Glass-Steagall Act and the 1956 Bank Holding Company Act — were enacted to help avert widespread financial failures, but a consensus has emerged in recent years that they are outdated.

Gramm told reporters that despite partisan disputes and veto threats over his bill, he believed agreements could be worked out in conference that President Clinton could support.

Community Reinvestment

The issue claiming the largest portion of the three-day Senate debate was the 1977 Community Reinvestment Act (PL 95-128), which requires banks to document efforts to invest in poor neighborhoods. A poor rating can result in denial of bank applications for mergers or expansions. The law has broad support among Democrats, who said it has improved poor and minority neighborhoods. "The dramatic increase in home ownership rates for minorities is attributable in large part to increased focus on banks' CRA performance," said Richard H. Bryan, D-Nev. Clinton has threatened to veto any bill scaling back the law. *(1977 Almanac, p. 126)*

Gramm said the law imposes a heavy regulatory burden, especially on smaller banks, and that community groups have used it to "extort" grants and loans from banks. His bill would make it more difficult for these groups to challenge a bank's reinvestment record if a bank had been in compliance with the law for the past three years, and it would exempt small, rural banks from reinvestment requirements.

Gramm said savvy community groups have learned that banks are particularly vulnerable to unfounded allegations of redlining and loan-

Where Gramm Draws the Line

APRIL 24 — What makes Phil Gramm fight the Community Reinvestment Act?

Gramm sounded eager a few months ago to prove he could get things done as the new chairman of the Senate Banking, Housing and Urban Affairs Committee. But Gramm, R-Texas, now appears willing to sink the biggest bill on the committee's agenda in a clash over an anti-redlining measure.

Banks, brokerages and insurance companies are pushing for financial services legislation (HR 10, Senate draft) that would establish a clearer set of rules for the cross-industry consolidation that is already under way.

Yet Congress finds itself hung up — again — on the 1977 Community Reinvestment Act (PL 95-128), which requires banks to document efforts to invest in all segments of the communities in which they collect deposits. Last year the Senate failed to take a final vote on a House-passed overhaul measure in large part because of Gramm's protests against the bill's reinvestment provisions. Gramm wants to loosen the requirements, especially on small banks.

This year Gramm has said he is willing to deal on the issue, but he also has said that he can live without a financial services overhaul if enactment requires too many compromises on key issues. Gramm has staked out positions on the reinvestment act that would draw a presidential veto on the underlying bill and that so far have helped prevent even a whiff of bipartisanship from emerging in the Senate. The banking industry, which is eager for financial services legislation, has remained relatively quiet on the 1977 law. So have most of Gramm's GOP Senate colleagues.

Observers say Gramm's passionate stand on the reinvestment issue is a logical component of his free-market conservatism. Government-forced credit allocation is anathema to conservatives such as Gramm, said John Heasley, general counsel and lobbyist for the Texas Bankers Association. American Bankers Association lobbyist Edward L. Yingling agreed, and said relatively little pressure was coming from interest groups or constituents.

Nevertheless, Gramm has plenty of home-state motivation to push for changes. Texas is home to about 840 state and nationally chartered banks, more than any other state in the nation and about 10 percent of the nation's total, Heasley said. Under Gramm's bill, about 150 to 200 of the state's banks would qualify for exemption from reinvestment requirements because they are rural banks with less than $100 million in assets.

Gramm has used the words "bribery" and "extortion" to describe how he believes some community housing groups abuse the law. When it comes to examples, Gramm and his staff generally have held their fire, saying they want to wait until the Banking Committee holds as-yet-unscheduled hearings this year.

But in committee hearings earlier this year, Gramm spoke of a case involving a small Southern bank company that invested heavily in efforts to reach out to a growing Spanish-speaking population. For example, Gramm said, the bank employed bilingual tellers and provided a free wiring service for bank customers to send money to Mexico. Gramm said bank regulators told the bank "they were doing the right things, but doing it the wrong way," and the only way to get a good reinvestment rating was to give money directly to community groups.

Gramm said the hearings will provide evidence that the law needs to be modified. "I find that in debating community groups, they don't take on these issues head on," Gramm said. "It's basically that if you're willing to stop any abuse, any one abuse, that you're against the CRA."

Community groups have few warm feelings for Gramm. On April 11, the National People's Action coalition, in Washington for its annual conference, sent 15 bus loads of members to Gramm's home to protest his efforts to scale back the reinvestment act. Gramm called police, and the crowd broke up with no arrests, leaving Gramm's lawn littered with fliers.

sharking when the banks are seeking to merge or expand, and thus banks feel pressure to cut deals with community groups even if they have done nothing wrong.

He produced copies of what he said were confidential reinvestment agreements between banks and community groups. The documents show, Gramm said, that community groups are promised cash payments in exchange for withdrawing complaints about bank loan practices so that the banks will get good reinvestment ratings. Some agreements require banks to send letters to lawmakers stating that they support the 1977 law, he said. "This is about abuse," Gramm said. "This is about a wrong going on in America."

Democrats countered that Gramm's reinvestment proposals were far more sweeping than necessary to deal with isolated cases of abuse. They sought to eliminate Gramm's reinvestment language with two amendments that were defeated May 5. An amendment by Bryan to strip the bill of its reinvestment provisions was tabled, or killed, 52-45. *(Vote 101, p. S-24)*

A Sarbanes substitute for S 900 also was tabled, 54-43. The substitute would have deleted Gramm's reinvestment measures, among other changes. The only substantial reinvestment change was a bipartisan "sunshine" measure approved by voice vote. It would require that reinvestment agreements be made public. *(Vote 100, p. S-23)*

Structure and Oversight

The bill was nearly derailed by a squabble among Republicans over how the new financial conglomerates should be structured. Gramm's bill generally would adhere to a position advocated by Federal Reserve Board Chairman Alan Greenspan, requiring that non-banking financial activities, such as insurance and securities underwriting, be conducted separately from bank operations under the umbrella of a holding company.

The Clinton administration and most Democrats favor giving banks the option of operating non-banking activities through bank subsidiaries, and Clinton has threatened to veto legislation that does not allow it. Richard C. Shelby, R-Ala., introduced an amendment to allow the subsidiary structure, saying it was more flexible and would make U.S. banks more globally competitive without endangering the banking system.

Gramm disagreed, saying federally insured bank operations must be separated from other financial services to ensure banking system safety. He added that he would pull S 900 from the floor if the Shelby amendment was adopted. It was tabled, 53-46, with six Democrats and seven Republicans crossing party lines. *(Vote 104, p. S-24)*

Like the House bill, Gramm's bill would prevent the creation of any new commercially owned savings and loans, also known as unitary thrifts. Tim Johnson, D-S.D., offered an amendment that would go a step further to prevent existing unitary thrifts from being bought by commercial companies. Johnson called current law a "loophole" allowing a dangerous mix of banking and commerce. Gramm said it would be unfair and unconstitutional to change the rules for existing thrifts, but Johnson's amendment was approved by voice vote.

House Prospects

The House bill (HR 10), approved by the Banking and Financial Services Committee in a bipartisan vote March 11, does not include the Senate's reinvestment rollbacks. The bill generally allows the subsidiary option for all but the largest banks.

Much of Banking's work could be undone by the Commerce Committee, however, which has joint jurisdiction over financial services. At Commerce, members of both parties have said they will seek substantial changes that could move the House bill closer to the Senate version, particularly on structural issues.

Committee Chairman Thomas J. Bliley Jr., R-Va., said he would try to overturn the subsidiary provision of HR 10. Failing to do so "would compromise the integrity of our financial markets," he said at a hearing April 28. Ranking Democrat John D. Dingell of Michigan also said that he wants changes.

GOP Thwarts Effort To Toughen Privacy Protections In House Bill

MAY 29 — Consumer privacy has grown into a major point of contention as Congress works to overhaul the laws governing the nation's financial service industries. With Democrats pushing hard for greater restrictions on the corporate use and sale of personal data, Republicans have been in the uncomfortable position of trying to placate a public increasingly concerned about privacy while defending industry demands that Congress not interfere with businesses' use of databases.

At a May 27 subcommittee markup, Democrats pushed for approval of the most far-reaching privacy measure offered so far in this year's debate over a financial services overhaul. The amendment failed, but Republicans approved a weaker privacy measure and Democrats vowed to continue pushing for more.

The markup by the House Commerce Subcommittee on Finance and Hazardous Materials was generally a bipartisan effort, and the underlying bill (HR 10) was approved, 26-1. The full committee is likely to mark up HR 10 the week of June 7, a Republican committee staff aide said.

The bill would undo Depression-era laws restricting cross-ownership among banks, brokerages and securities firms. These restrictions, contained in the 1933 Glass-Steagall Act and the 1956 Bank Holding Company Act, were enacted to help avert widespread financial failures, but a consensus has emerged that they are outdated and should be repealed.

The most powerful financial interests in the nation are keeping watchful eyes on every detail of the legislation, and they are lobbying hard to win competitive advantages. The subcommittee adopted by voice vote an amendment by Chairman Michael G. Oxley, R-Ohio, that would require companies to disclose their privacy policies to consumers. Oxley said that would let people "vote with their feet" if they did not like a company's policy. Several Democrats said it was a positive step, but insufficient.

The Commerce Committee shares jurisdiction on HR 10 with the House Banking and Financial Services Committee, which approved the bill March 11 with a similar privacy policy disclosure requirement, along with additional provisions to restrict the sharing of medical information.

The Senate financial services overhaul bill (S 900), which passed May 6, does not contain any such privacy requirements. The Senate Banking, Housing and Urban Affairs Committee will hold a series of hearings on privacy beginning June 9, said committee spokeswoman Christi Harlan.

Greater Restrictions Pushed

Rep. Edward J. Markey, D-Mass., said Oxley's amendment would not do enough, and he mocked financial services industry lobbyists — who stand to reap big profits from the legislation — for complaining that some privacy protections would ruin the bill.

He offered an amendment, which was defeated, 8-19, that would have required companies to get permission from customers before sharing information with third parties. It also would have required conglomerates to give consumers the right to opt out of information-sharing among affiliates of the same company. Markey said lobbyists were warning of "unintended consequences" if Congress passed strong privacy legislation, when what lobbyists were most concerned about was protecting their ability to make money from consumer information. "They don't want anybody to have the right to say no," Markey said.

John D. Dingell of Michigan, ranking Democrat on the full committee, said he supported Markey's amendment because without it, there would be nothing to prevent companies from selling personal and potentially embarrassing information to such media outlets as People magazine or radio personality Howard Stern.

Republicans said Markey's approach was too far-reaching and would invite litigation against companies that make honest mistakes.

"I think we need to work this through a lot more carefully," said W.J. "Billy" Tauzin, R-La. He added that sometimes consumers benefit from information-sharing when companies direct products and services at people who might want them.

Unitary Thrifts

A seesaw issue in the financial services debate this session has been whether to continue to allow federal savings and loan institutions, or "unitary thrifts," to be purchased by commercial companies. The issue, which cuts across party lines, was the subject of lengthy debates in the House Banking Committee and on the Senate floor.

There is general agreement that any new thrifts should be prohibited from affiliating with commercial firms. However, the thrift industry and its allies in Congress have fought strenuously against attempts to prohibit existing thrifts from affiliating with commercial firms. The House Banking version of HR 10 originally prohibited the sale of thrifts to commercial firms, but that restriction was stripped in a close vote at the March 11 markup. The Commerce panel's original bill would have allowed the sale of thrifts to commercial firms, but that was reversed, 15-13, by an amendment by Steve Largent, R-Okla.

In the Senate, S 900 originally would have allowed thrifts to affiliate with commercial firms, but that position was reversed by a floor amendment.

Operating Subsidiaries

The bill approved by the Commerce subcommittee would prohibit banks from conducting non-banking activities, such as insurance and securities underwriting, in operating subsidiaries. Instead, such activities would have to be operated in affiliates under the umbrella of a holding company, as favored by Federal Reserve Board Chairman Alan Greenspan.

The subcommittee position puts the bill more closely in line with the Senate bill, but contrasts sharply with the House Banking Committee version, which would allow the subsidiary arrangement for all but the largest banks. Whether to allow banks to operate non-financial activities in subsidiaries has been a key issue in the debate, but the Commerce subcommittee rejected the Banking Committee's position without a separate vote, by putting the holding company requirement in its underlying bill.

It places the bill in conflict with the Clinton administration, which has threatened repeatedly to veto any bill that does not allow banks to choose the subsidiary option. The disagreement has been characterized as a turf war between Greenspan and the Treasury Department because the Fed oversees holding companies while Treasury regulates bank subsidiaries. Both sides say their positions are based on what they believe to be the safest ways to structure banks.

The subcommittee bill also would give greater authority to states to regulate insurance activities conducted in nationally chartered banks than would the Banking Committee's version, a move that insurance agents favor but banks generally oppose.

House Panel Approves Bill; Industry Prepares For Floor Fight

JUNE 12 — House Republican leaders will face heavy pressure from banks and other financial industries in the weeks ahead over privacy protections recently added to a financial services overhaul bill headed for the floor. Financial industry representatives were seething over provisions added to the bill (HR 10) that would curtail businesses' ability to sell and share data about their customers.

Republicans have struggled in recent weeks to restrain Democratic-led efforts to add privacy provisions to the bill. Republicans said the provisions were too sweeping and could have unintended consequences that could hurt consumers, while Democrats accused Republicans of bending to big financial interests that hope to reap substantial profits from consumer data files.

The Commerce Committee approved HR 10 by voice vote June 10.

The bill would repeal restrictions on cross-ownership among banks, insurance companies and brokerages. Although the industries generally agree on the need for the legislation, they disagree on many details as each sector seeks to win competitive advantages or avoid disadvantages. However, the emergence of privacy as a significant factor in the debate this year has given the industries a common rallying point.

Brian C. Conklin, director of legislative affairs for the Financial Services Council, said the privacy provisions added to the bill are so onerous that "most, if not all" of the companies represented by his organization would oppose it. The council's membership includes several large banks and insurance companies.

Dan Zielinski, media relations director for the American Insurance Association, called the privacy provisions "disappointing," and said he also expects across-the-board industry opposition. The Securities Industry Association announced its objection to the privacy measures in a June 10 news release.

Markey Pushes Privacy

As he did at a May 27 markup in the House Commerce Subcommittee on Finance and Hazardous Materials, Edward J. Markey, D-Mass., offered an amendment to require companies to get "opt-in" permission from customers before sharing information with third parties, and to require conglomerates to give consumers the right to opt out of information-sharing among affiliates of the same company.

The measure failed in the subcommittee but had greater success in the full committee. It was softened with a substitute measure by Ohio Republican Paul E. Gillmor, which was approved by voice vote. The amendment as approved would require companies to give consumers the right to opt out of information sharing among affiliates and with third parties.

After the markup, Conklin said the financial services industries can support some privacy provisions, and he suggested they might be able to live with an "opt out" requirement for third party information-sharing if the measure were carefully crafted. However, he said proposals restricting information-sharing among affiliates of the same company were not acceptable. "Affiliate sharing is not a problem," Conklin said. "The horror stories are not there."

The committee also approved, 25-23, an amendment by Greg Ganske, R-Iowa, to limit companies' ability to disclose medical information about customers. Most Democrats opposed the measure, with some saying it contained so many loopholes it would hurt consumer privacy overall. For example, the committee's ranking Democrat, John D. Dingell of Michigan, said the amendment contained an exception for "research" that was so vague that it could include marketing studies.

Thrift Disagreement Persists

Congress enacted the barriers to cross-ownership among banks, brokerages and insurance companies in response to the Depression under the belief that they would help prevent widespread financial failures. A bipartisan consensus has emerged in recent years that those restrictions are outdated, but Congress has tried and failed numerous times to work out the details of an overhaul.

Regulation of savings and loan institutions has been a long-running point of contention. Unlike banks, these unitary thrifts, as they are also called, are allowed to affiliate with commercial firms. Many lawmakers believe that mixing banking and commerce is problematic and perhaps dangerous, and most support legislation to prohibit new thrifts from affiliating with commercial enterprises.

However, there are splits within both parties over whether existing thrifts should be prohibited from affiliating with commercial firms. Some members want to prevent those that are not already affiliated with commercial firms from doing so in the future, while opponents say it would be unfair to change the rules for existing thrifts. The dispute has prompted lengthy debates and close votes throughout the legislative process this session.

At the June 10 markup, Edolphus Towns, D-N.Y., sought to strip the bill of a provision restricting the ability of existing unitary thrifts to affiliate with commercial firms. The measure failed, 23-26.

Insurance Measure Fails

The committee also rejected a measure by Thomas M. Barrett, D-Wis., to require insurers to compile and publicly disclose demographic data about their policyholders and applicants.

Barrett said his measure would help curtail insurance "redlining," the practice of systematically denying insurance to specific geographic areas and groups of people. Opponents said it was well-intended, but would create a huge government-mandated invasion of privacy. Michael G. Oxley, R-Ohio, said if an insurer asked an applicant about his or her race, the insurer "would be in court before the ink was dry on the contract."

Barrett's proposal was defeated, 17-28, on a nearly party-line vote. A second, weaker amendment by Barrett, which would have required the Commerce Department to study whether insurers are discriminating and whether there is a need for greater data collection, also was defeated, 19-23.

Shared Jurisdiction

The Commerce Committee shares jurisdiction over HR 10 with the House Banking and Financial Services Committee, which approved the bill March 11. The two versions now head for the Rules Committee with differences on several key issues including unitary thrifts, privacy provisions and regulatory oversight. Republican leaders will have to sort out the differences before HR 10 heads to the floor.

The Senate financial services overhaul bill (S 900), which passed May 6, presents another set of positions to reconcile if the bills make it to conference. The Senate bill does not contain the privacy requirements of either House measure. The Senate bill also contains a controversial provision to scale back the reach of the 1977 Community Reinvestment Act (PL 95-128), which requires banks to document efforts to lend to all segments of the communities they serve. Both House committees generally avoided changes to the reinvestment act.

Leaders Soften Privacy Language As Bill Heads for House Floor

JUNE 26 — House leaders plan to hold a floor vote on a financial services overhaul bill before the July Fourth recess after spending weeks reconciling conflicts on privacy, regulatory oversight and other key issues that emerged from two committees with joint jurisdiction. Leaders decided to adopt much of the language from the Banking and Financial Services Committee version of the bill, which contains less stringent privacy language and an oversight structure favored by the administration.

Majority Leader Dick Armey, R-Texas, said in a June 22 news briefing that he expects the House to take up the bill (HR 10) the week of June 28. The reconciled bill would blend provisions from markups that took place in Commerce (H Rept 106-74, Part 3) on June 10 and in Banking (H Rept 106-74, Part 1) on March 11. If the full House passes a bill, further negotiations will be required in conference to settle differences with a Senate-passed overhaul bill (S 900 — S Rept 106-44).

The three versions differ significantly in numerous ways, but all of them call for repealing provisions of the 1933 Glass-Steagall Act and amending the 1956 Bank Holding Company Act, which erected barriers between the banking, securities and insurance industries. A consensus has emerged that the laws are outdated and harmful to U.S. financial companies' ability to compete internationally.

As Congress has attempted to sort out the details involved with repealing the legislation, numerous differences have emerged. Some have been partisan, others involve disputes among the affected industries, and still others have pitted businesses against consumer groups.

Armey said the leadership had worked hard to come up with a bill that respected both committees of jurisdiction. "We're not likely to pass this bill if either of the two chairmen are not in agreement," Armey said.

Preparing for Action

Financial businesses and industry groups, many of which have contributed substantially over the past several years to the campaigns of key players in the overhaul debate, have moved quickly in recent weeks to make clear their positions on specific provisions in each House bill. High-ranking members of the administration met at the White House on June 14 with representatives of the banking and financial services industries to exchange views. According to a participant at the meeting, White House officials said the administration cares most about two things: making sure banks are allowed to conduct new financial activities through operating subsidiaries, and preserving community reinvestment requirements.

Industry lobbyists at the meeting complained bitterly about the recent groundswell of congressional support for measures that would limit the ability of corporations to share personal data about their customers, and they urged the administration to put the brakes on this issue, according to the participant, who requested anonymity. The administration expressed a willingness to weigh the industries' privacy concerns, but also indicated there was a growing populist push for government to do more to help consumers protect their privacy.

Key areas of disagreement that House leaders had to reconcile included:

• **Regulatory oversight.** The Treasury Department has threatened to urge a veto of any bill that does not allow banks to conduct financial services in operating subsidiaries, and the House bill would allow subsidiaries. Federal Reserve Chairman Alan Greenspan, along with some influential members of Congress, has argued that the Treasury position is dangerous, and that new financial services should be conducted separately through affiliates under the umbrella of bank holding companies. The bill would allow subsidiaries for financial services except insurance underwriting and real estate development.

Majority Whip Tom DeLay, R-Texas, who was reported to be deeply involved in reconciling the Commerce and Banking bills, also has indicated he supports this position, according to the Independent Community Bankers of America, which represents smaller banks. The leadership likely will allow a floor amendment that would adopt the Greenspan position instead, a Republican Banking Committee staff member said.

• **Privacy.** The privacy push began in earnest at the House Banking markup. Members of both parties were reluctant to delve into the issue, but the committee approved a modest, bipartisan privacy amendment as a compromise to thwart a more sweeping privacy measure pushed by Democratic Rep. Jay Inslee of Washington. The adopted measure would require financial institutions to disclose their privacy policies.

The Commerce Committee added even stronger privacy language that would require companies to give consumers the right to opt out of information sharing among affiliates and with third parties. Business interests have grumbled loudly that this would hurt their ability to provide a wide range of services that their customers want.

House leaders opted to include the Banking Committee's notification requirement, and did not include the Commerce Committee's opt-out provisions. A Republican Banking staff aide said leaders planned to adopt a rule for the bill that would allow floor consideration of a stronger privacy amendment.

Democrat Edward J. Markey of Massechusetts, who pushed for even stronger language than what Commerce approved, said in a June 15 interview that Republicans are being forced to choose between the libertarians in their party, who are deeply concerned about privacy, and their business constituents, who hope to make billions of dollars by selling databases.

Markey said polls show Americans are concerned about privacy, and if House leaders refuse to allow a strong privacy amendment to be offered, they will face a "public firestorm" of outrage. Consumer groups have supported stronger privacy laws.

Republicans have tried to push privacy out of the financial services overhaul picture, pledging instead to take up the issue separately and hold hearings. They have complained that Congress is jumping into the issue too quickly without adequate study, and the hastily crafted privacy provisions could have unintended consequences.

The Senate Banking, Housing and Urban Affairs Committee already held a privacy hearing June 9, and the House Banking and Financial Services Committee is scheduled to hold hearings July 21-22.

Banks and thrifts are generally willing to live with the weaker privacy provisions in the Banking bill, but they objected to the stronger measures in the Commerce bill.

• **Thrifts.** House leaders have attempted to forge a compromise between the two committees over whether to allow new savings and loan institutions, or "unitary thrifts," to affiliate with commercial firms. Banks, which are not allowed to affiliate with commercial firms, see thrifts as having an unfair competitive advantage.

The Senate and Commerce measures also would prohibit existing thrifts from affiliating with commercial entities, which banks support but the thrift industry opposes. The thrift industry supported the more lenient Banking Committee bill on this issue.

House leaders chose to prohibit thrifts from affiliating with commercial firms unless such unions win the approval of the Federal Reserve. The Fed has historically opposed any mixing of banking and commerce, so it is unclear what this measure would mean for thrifts.

Community Reinvestment

The House bills agreed on community reinvestment, an area where the Senate bill diverges sharply. The 1977 Community Reinvestment Act (PL 95-128) requires banks to document their efforts to invest in all segments of their communities. An unfavorable review from federal regulators could bring sanctions. The administration has threatened to veto any bill that would scale back the reach of the reinvestment law.

While banks generally have been willing to live with the reinvestment provisions in the House bills, they are more supportive of the Senate bill on this issue because it relaxes some reinvestment requirements.

Houses Passes Bill By Wide Margin; Leaders Hope for Edge in Conference

JULY 3 — A strong, bipartisan vote for a financial services overhaul in the House on July 1 left leaders hopeful that they will have a strong hand on key issues such as customer privacy when they begin negotiations with the Senate on a final bill, possibly later this month.

Although Democrats and Republicans clashed over some elements of the bill (HR 10), lawmakers from both parties wore broad smiles and crossed the center aisle of the House floor to shake hands after the final vote passing the measure, 343-86, shortly before midnight. It was Congress' last major action before the July Fourth recess. *(Vote 276, p. H-94)*

The scene was in sharp contrast to the Senate, where a companion overhaul measure (S 900) was approved largely along party lines in the Banking Committee and on the Senate floor earlier this year.

While not abandoning his trademark caution and understatement, House Banking and Financial Services Chairman Jim Leach, R-Iowa, was clearly enthusiastic after the July 1 vote. "I'm optimistic, but I can give no assurances of anything," Leach said.

"I don't want to suggest that margins are the be-all and end-all of lawmaking, but they're helpful," he added when asked about House leverage in the conference negotiations. Leach said he hoped the two chambers would head to conference before the August recess.

The bills would repeal decades-old laws restricting affiliations among banks, brokerages and insurance companies, and establish a new regulatory framework for overseeing the conglomerates that would be created under the bill. Although Congress has worked for decades to repeal the restrictions, the House vote marked the first time both chambers approved an overhaul measure in the same session of Congress.

The administration issued a statement saying it supports the House bill, although it added that it would like to see numerous changes.

John D. Dingell of Michigan, ranking Democrat on the Commerce Committee, voted against the bill, predicting that the mega-mergers it would allow could re-establish the conditions that led to the stock market crash of 1929 and the hard times that followed.

Power To Deal on Privacy

John J. LaFalce, D-N.Y., the ranking member on the House Banking Committee, said the margin of victory would be particularly helpful in conference when debating the controversial issue of protecting customer privacy.

When it reached the House floor, the bill included limits on the sharing of medical information and bans on "pretext calling," the practice of using false pretenses to obtain financial information about someone from a bank. In addition, the House approved, 427-1, an amendment that would require financial institutions to give consumers the right to opt out of the disclosure of financial information to unaffiliated third parties. *(Vote 274, p. H-94)*

The Senate bill contains no similar provisions. LaFalce said the overwhelming House vote would make it unlikely that privacy protections would be stripped from the bill in conference.

Democratic Reps. Jay Inslee of Washington and Edward J. Markey of Massachusetts expressed disappointment on the floor that they were not allowed to go even further than the approved legislation. Markey wanted to offer a broader "opt out" amendment that would have applied to both affiliates and third parties but was prevented from doing so by the rule.

Still, LaFalce praised the two for taking the lead on privacy, saying that because of their efforts, Democrats were able to get everything possible on privacy issues without provoking widespread industry opposition to the bill. "We pushed them to the wall," LaFalce said.

The financial services industries have fought Democratic efforts to strengthen provisions in the bill that would limit the ability of financial institutions to share personal data with affiliates and third parties.

Democrats accused the industries of opposing privacy restrictions because they stand to make billions of dollars from consumer databases that contain everything from Social Security numbers to information about check-writing habits. The industries have argued that privacy provisions would have unintended consequences that could hurt their ability to serve consumers.

Though House Republicans tried to fend off an onslaught of Democratic privacy amendments in the Banking and the Commerce committees, as well as on the floor, they have softened their position in recent weeks and have been willing to accept some privacy measures.

Other amendments considered on the floor included:

- **Insurance and domestic violence.** Democrats assailed Republicans for tying a domestic violence proposal supported by Democrats into a single amendment with a provision that would make it easier for some mutual insurance companies to reorganize into stock companies.

LaFalce said the mutual insurance portion of the amendment was focused specifically on enriching the top executives of the companies at the expense of policyholders, who would have no say in the transactions. "It is a payoff to the mutual insurance industry, no more, no less," which would fail if acted on by itself, LaFalce said. Supporters said the change would have a limited impact and would help mutual companies raise capital.

The other part of the amendment would prohibit insurers from discriminating against victims of domestic violence. LaFalce failed in a procedural effort to separate the two items, and the amendment passed, 226-203. *(Vote 273, p. H-94)*

- **Bank insurance sales.** The House adopted by voice vote an amendment by Melvin Watt, D-N.C., to prohibit banks from requiring customers to purchase insurance products from an affiliate or subsidiary as a condition of a loan.
- **Bank customer profiling.** The House rejected, 129-299, an amendment by Ron Paul, R-Texas, Bob Barr, R-Ga., and Tom Campbell, R-Calif., that would have loosened banks' requirements to file "suspicious activity reports" about unusual bank transactions. The amendment came under withering

attack from members of both parties, who said it would make it easier for drug dealers to launder money. Leach called the amendment "an absolute assault on law enforcement." Bill McCollum, R-Fla., added, "This is no time to retreat in the war on drugs." Barr said his colleagues were overreacting. "It takes nothing away from law enforcement," he said. *(Vote 269, p. H-92)*

Working With the Senate

House and Senate conferees will have to resolve a number of important differences between the two bills. The Senate bill would scale back the 1977 Community Reinvestment Act (PL 95-128), which requires banks to document their efforts to invest in all segments of their communities. An unfavorable review from federal regulators could bring sanctions. The administration has threatened to veto any bill that would limit the reach of the reinvestment law.

The administration also favors the House bill on another key issue — the basic way that financial conglomerates should be structured. The House bill would permit banks to conduct most financial activities through subsidiaries. The Senate bill generally adheres to the position of the Federal Reserve, which believes banks should be required to conduct non-banking financial activities separately through affiliates under the umbrella of a holding company.

Both sides claim their positions are based on what is best for the safety and stability of financial institutions, but the two organizations also have a stake in the outcome. The Treasury Department regulates subsidiaries while the Fed regulates bank holding companies.

Phil Gramm, R-Texas, chairman of the Senate Banking Committee, has said the Senate's position on both the reinvestment issue and the regulatory dispute are important to him. He has said he is willing to compromise in conference, but he has not offered specifics.

"We now have it within our grasp to pass a good bill," Gramm said in a July 1 statement. "We face some very high hurdles, and negotiations will require a tremendous effort."

Difficult Start

House action on the bill got off to a rocky start when Democrats tried to rally their entire caucus against the rule that Republican leaders had crafted for floor debate. The rule allowed just 11 amendments and left Democrats fuming over items excluded from consideration. They were particularly angered over the exclusion of an amendment by Barbara Lee, D-Calif., to pre-empt state insurance laws and ban insurance "redlining," the practice of refusing to sell insurance in specific geographic areas, usually poor neighborhoods. The measure had been approved by the House Banking Committee, but was stripped by the Rules Committee.

"This is not a rule. It is a gag rule," Dingell said. Leach said he was "not a great enthusiast for this rule," and would have preferred allowing Lee to offer her amendment, but he said the bill would make progress on consumer protection in numerous other respects. The rule was adopted, 227-203, with six Democrats defecting to support it. *(Vote 264, p. H-92)*

At the end of the evening, the Democrats made one final push to reinsert the Lee amendment, along with two proposals to strengthen privacy provisions in the bill, in a motion to recommit. The move was defeated, 198-232. *(Vote 275, p. H-94)*

Although they have disagreed on many facets of the various overhaul bills considered in recent years, some financial services groups — including the American Insurance Association and the Securities Industry Association — quickly expressed support for the House action.

Conference-Bound Bill Gets Boost From Democratic Vote-Switching

JULY 10 — When House and Senate negotiators meet later this month to iron out differences between their competing financial services overhaul bills, it will be an unprecedented event in the decades-long effort to undo the Depression-era laws that restrict cross-ownership among the nation's banks, brokerages and insurance firms.

The very fact that a House-Senate conference is needed is perhaps the most remarkable development of all: Never before has an overhaul measure passed both chambers in the same legislative session. The House bill (HR 10 — H Rept 106-74, Parts 1-3) also marks the first time that a financial services rewrite has emerged from either chamber with overwhelming bipartisan support and the backing of the White House. This year also has been a turning point for the industries most affected by the legislation. They have been more willing to compromise than ever before to get a deal done.

Both HR 10 and the Senate bill (S 900 — S Rept 106-44) seek to repeal barriers among banks, brokerages and insurance firms that were enacted in response to the Depression in the belief that they would help stem widespread financial failures.

A broad consensus has emerged in recent years that the laws are outdated, and numerous efforts have been made to revise them. However, writing new laws to repeal the barriers while ensuring the safety and stability of the U.S. financial system has proved complicated and divisive. The affected industries have lobbied heavily to win competitive advantages, and members of Congress have fought over consumer protection, financial privacy measures and community reinvestment requirements, among other issues.

Groundswell in the House

The legislation gained significant momentum going into conference thanks to the lopsided, 343-86, House floor vote for HR 10 on July 1. Of the 343 members who voted "yes," 130 changed their positions from 1998, when the predecessor to HR 10 passed by only one vote. *(1998 Almanac, p. 5-3)*

Seventy-four of those voting "no" last year but "yes" this year were Democrats, including Minority Leader Richard A. Gephardt of Missouri and Minority Whip David E. Bonior of Michigan.

Democrats said their change of heart was due largely to provisions added to the bill intended to protect the privacy of financial and health records, and to the fact that the Clinton administration supports the bill.

Last year's legislation would have

Financial Services Bills Compared

JULY 10 — This chart compares the Senate-passed financial services overhaul bill (S 900) with the House-passed version (HR 10). The more bipartisan House bill passed, 343-86, on July 1. The Senate bill was approved, 54-44, on May 6 with only one Democrat joining the majority.

The administration has threatened to veto the Senate bill over community reinvestment issues.

ISSUE	S 900 (SENATE)	HR 10 (HOUSE)
Operating subsidiary vs. holding company	The bill would require banks to use a holding company structure with Federal Reserve oversight, as favored by Fed Chairman Alan Greenspan. Exception: Banks with less than $1 billion in assets would be allowed to conduct most activities through operating subsidiaries, which are regulated by the Treasury.	The House version would give banks the option of organizing financial services as operating subsidiaries, as favored by the Treasury. However, banks with more than $10 billion in assets would be required to establish holding companies in order to engage in non-banking financial activities, which would give the Federal Reserve oversight of these larger institutions.
Thrifts	The bill would prohibit new and existing thrifts from affiliating with commercial entities. Existing thrifts already affiliated with commercial firms would not be affected.	The bill would allow existing thrifts to affiliate with commercial firms only with the approval of the Office of Thrift Supervision and the Federal Reserve. New thrifts would be barred from affiliating with commercial firms. Existing thrifts already affiliated with commercial firms would not be affected.
Privacy	No provision.	Financial institutions would be required to let customers opt out of information-sharing activities with unaffiliated third parties. Financial institutions would be required to disclose their privacy policies. The bill would also restrict disclosure of medical information.
Community Reinvestment Act (CRA)	The bill would exempt rural banks with less than $100 million in assets from compliance with the CRA. It would require public disclosure of terms of agreements used to settle disputes and make it more difficult for community groups to challenge banks' past ratings.	The bill would generally maintain current reinvestment requirements. It would require banks to have a satisfactory reinvestment rating for proposed new affiliations to win approval, and would add new penalties for non-compliance.
Insurance regulation	The bill would provide broad authority for state regulation of insurance activities in national banks but would prohibit states from discriminating against national banks as opposed to state insurance providers.	Similar to Senate bill.
Securities regulation	Banks would be allowed to conduct many securities activities within the bank, thereby limiting oversight by the Securities and Exchange Commission (SEC).	The bill would place more restrictions on banks' securities activities and would create a stronger role for SEC oversight of securities activities than would the Senate version.
Pretext calling	The bill would make it a federal crime to use false pretenses to gather private information about an individual from a bank.	Same as Senate bill.
Automated teller machine (ATM) fees	The bill would require that ATMs provide notice of surcharges before a transaction is completed.	Same as Senate bill.

required the new financial conglomerates to organize in holding companies, a position vehemently opposed by the Treasury Department. This year's version would allow most companies to organize insurance and securities businesses as operating subsidiaries of the parent bank, a plan the department advocates.

But underlying the bill's change of fortunes in the House was the fact that most of the industries that had been feuding for decades over rewriting the so-called Glass-Steagall anti-affiliation laws had laid down their arms.

"We had much more consensus in the private sector," said Robert A. Rusbuldt, a lobbyist for the Independent Insurance Agents of America (IIAA). "You had the IIAA and the American Bankers Association supporting the bill. We have been throughout the last 20 years the two major players. Usually, it was one or the other supporting or opposing. That dynamic didn't exist this time."

Such disputes among the industries had often split the House and Senate along regional lines in votes on their issues. Midwesterners and Southerners, for instance, tended to side with the small bankers and insurance agents. Those on the coasts were more sympathetic to big banks and brokerages.

But this year, the divisions crumbled. Few industries opposed a bill whose rough points had mostly been smoothed out. One group that did oppose the measure, the Independent Community Bankers of America, spent much of its efforts trying to bring down the rule (H Res 235) that allowed the bill to come to the floor. It passed on a mostly party-line 227-203 vote.

"Really, that was the key vote," said Kenneth A. Guenther, a lobbyist for the group, which represents small, independent banks. "I don't think there was a fight from any quarter on final passage. I think the fight was over the rule."

While banks were angry that the Rules Committee had not allowed Republican Steve Largent of Oklahoma to offer amendments that would have blocked commercial firms from buying thrifts, they gave up their fight after the rule passed.

In contrast, last year most medium and small banks, joined by some large ones, fought passage of the bill tooth and nail. Republican leaders eked out a one-vote victory only after then-Speaker Newt Gingrich, R-Ga. (1979-99), twisted arms on the floor, causing half a dozen Republicans to switch from "no" to "yes" votes or to vote "yes" at the last minute.

Before that, the House had never passed an overhaul of the 1933 Glass-Steagall law. Then-GOP Conference Chairman John A. Boehner of Ohio, who was in charge of shepherding the bill to passage, declared that "a one-vote victory looks like a landslide."

New Leadership

Times have changed greatly since then. Gingrich and Boehner have been dethroned, and those who took their places have been more willing to compromise with the administration and win Democratic support than to twist the arms of their own members, at least on banking issues.

And the industries, sensing a chance for a historic overhaul that many say is critical if they are to compete with foreign financial services firms, have largely halted their bickering. "I am absolutely convinced a bill will be sent to the president," Rusbuldt said. "I'm not saying [it will happen] before the August recess, but I think it will happen this year. It's just too close; there's too much history, too much that's been accomplished" not to see it to enactment.

Brian C. Conklin, acting president for the Financial Services Council, agreed, saying he expects conferees will be named by the end of the week of July 12, and that a bill could be on President Clinton's desk before the August recess. "It's absolutely within the realm of reason," said Conklin, whose organization represents several large banks and insurance firms.

Groups that have praised the House bill include the American Bankers Association, the American Insurance Association, the Securities Industry Association, the Council of Insurance Agents & Brokers, the Financial Services Roundtable, and America's Community Bankers. Although some have complaints about specific provisions, most appear eager for the measure to pass.

Only one major financial industry group — the Independent Community Bankers of America — opposes the House bill. It objects to a provision that would allow savings and loan institutions to affiliate with commercial firms with the approval of federal regulators. Banks, which do not have the same ability to affiliate with commercial firms, complain that thrifts have an unfair competitive advantage. Banks support language in the Senate bill that would prohibit new and existing thrifts from affiliating with commercial firms. "We strongly oppose HR 10," Guenther said.

Although the American Bankers Association, which represents larger banks, has grumbled about the thrift provision in the House bill, it has not considered it sufficient cause to oppose the entire measure.

John J. LaFalce of New York was one of 13 Democrats on the House Banking and Financial Services Committee who switched his vote to support the bill this year after opposing it last year. LaFalce, ranking Democrat on the committee, said in a July 7 interview that the difference was that the Republican leadership pushed a bill last year that was opposed by the administration. With the White House supporting this year's House measure, he said it was much easier for many House Democrats to support it. "The administration was key," LaFalce said.

Conference Battles Ahead

Industry and interest groups ranging from banks to civil rights organizations are gearing up for what perhaps will be their last shot at influencing the legislation before it heads to the president's desk. Civil rights advocates, for example, object to proposed Community Reinvestment Act (CRA) rollbacks in the Senate bill. The act (PL 95-128) requires banks to document efforts to invest in all segments of the communities where they collect deposits.

"The CRA is a major civil rights issue," the Leadership Conference on Civil Rights declared in a July 2 news release. "Does the 106th Congress want to become known as the Congress that squelched the American Dream for millions of hard-working Americans?"

The fight over thrifts is expected to continue into conference, as is the issue of operating subsidiaries vs. holding companies.

Those three issues — thrifts, regulatory structure and community reinvestment requirements — will be the key points of disagreement and debate in conference, industry observers said.

The White House has threatened to veto any bill that does not allow banks to conduct most non-banking financial services in subsidiaries. It also has pledged to veto any bill that rolls back reinvestment requirements. Senate Banking, Housing and Urban Affairs Committee Chairman Phil Gramm, R-Texas, has stuck just as fiercely to the holding company requirement in the Senate bill, and he has offered no concrete proposals yet for a compromise on community reinvestment.

Gramm's Big Role

Although House leaders said they believe the big margin of support for their bill will give them leverage in conference negotiations, observers warned against underestimating Gramm, who has touted his Senate bill as a cleaner deregulation measure. They suggest that Gramm will likely be the strongest presence in the conference debate.

"I think the House will have, at least going into conference, the perceived upper hand," said Rusbuldt of the independent insurance agents' group. But he added, "Having worked closely with Phil Gramm, I wouldn't underestimate this guy in any way, shape or form. He will know his issues inside and out."

Conklin of the Financial Services Council noted that Gramm almost single-handedly derailed last year's overhaul bill in the Senate. "I don't underestimate Chairman Gramm and what he can accomplish," Conklin said. However, Rusbuldt and Conklin both said Gramm appears to want to pass a bill that Clinton would sign.

"Gramm has always said, 'Just get me to conference. . . . Give me the CRA provision I want and give me some wiggle room in conference committee,' " Rusbuldt said. "His implication always was, 'If the Senate gives me what I want, I am willing to compromise in conference committee.' He's positioned now for compromise. The question is how far will the administration and the Democratic leadership compromise on CRA."

Roster Dispute Marks Beginning Of Conference

AUGUST 7 — Deep fissures among Republicans have cast a pall of uncertainty over a House-Senate conference on legislation to overhaul the financial services industry, and negotiators who will resume work after the summer recess hope staff members can resolve some issues in their absence.

Financial industries will be watching nervously for more Republican defections on privacy issues after a key GOP senator came out in favor of tough new privacy laws for financial institutions.

Conferees met for the first time Aug. 3 to draw battle lines on the bill (S 900, formerly HR 10), which would repeal decades-old laws restricting affiliations among banks, brokerages and insurance companies. In the only official action, they named House Banking and Financial Services Chairman Jim Leach, R-Iowa, as conference chairman. A procedural flap prompted Senate Banking, Housing and Urban Affairs Chairman Phil Gramm, R-Texas, to declare that there would be no more meetings until the dispute was resolved.

Gramm complained that Leach allowed the committee to include more House Democrats than House Republicans. House conferees were drawn from four committees, including Judiciary and Agriculture. Most came from the Banking and Commerce panels, each of which was allotted eight Republican and six Democratic seats. To represent Banking, Leach selected the eight most senior Republicans. Democrats, however, chose to rotate their seats among lawmakers assigned to various sections of the bill. As a result, House conferees total 22 Democrats and 20 Republicans.

Gramm said all 22 Democrats would be entitled to a final vote on the conference report. "That problem needs to be resolved," he said.

House GOP Banking spokesman David R. Runkel said the conference roster should not be a problem because House Republicans will hold a majority on every section-by-section vote along the way to final passage. He said that if necessary, the House parliamentarian could settle what to do about the overall vote, perhaps by ruling that part-time conferees are entitled only to partial votes. But Gramm spokeswoman Christi Harlan said her boss was convinced that the matter is more serious and needs to be resolved before the conference resumes. Meanwhile, conferees agreed to push staff members to resolve policy disagreements between the House and Senate versions of the bill.

Shelby Joins Privacy Push

Privacy has become the most high-profile issue in the overhaul debate, particularly in the House, where Republicans fought in committee and on the floor to sink or weaken Democratic-led proposals to impose tough restrictions on the ability of financial institutions to sell or share customer data. The House bill would require financial institutions to let customers "opt out" of information-sharing with unaffiliated third parties. The Senate bill contains no such provisions.

At the Aug. 3 conference session, Sen. Richard C. Shelby, R-Ala., announced that he supports imposing substantial new limits on banks' ability to sell and share data about their customers. As the second-ranking GOP member of the Senate panel, Shelby represents a key Republican defection on the privacy issue. Several other Republicans have not yet announced positions.

The financial industries have grudgingly accepted some of the tamer privacy proposals discussed, such as the House "opt out" provision. However, they have vehemently opposed more stringent privacy measures offered by Democrats, such as "opt in" proposals that would require financial institutions to get permission from customers before sharing financial information.

The financial industries have complained that far-reaching privacy proposals could have unintended consequences, such as making it more difficult to cross-check data for fraud.

Shelby did not specify which privacy provisions he supported, but he made it clear that he would support strong measures. Congress should not pass a bill "just to satisfy Wall Street," he said.

Brian C. Conklin, acting president

for the Financial Services Council, said he was surprised by Shelby's statement. Conklin, whose organization represents several large banks, brokerages and insurance firms, said he did not know whether other Republicans might follow Shelby's lead.

Staff members also face a daunting task in finding compromises on several issues that generate sharp disagreements within both parties. Resolving them will require assembling bipartisan alliances likely to shift vote by vote in conference. Such issues include whether thrifts should be prohibited from affiliating with commercial firms and whether the Federal Reserve or the Treasury should oversee the new financial conglomerates that would be created under the bill.

Clamor Over Consumer Privacy Puts Banks On the Defensive

AUGUST 14 — When U.S. Bancorp was accused earlier this year of improperly selling information about customers' account balances, telephone numbers, addresses and credit card purchases to an outside marketing firm, CEO Jack Grundhofer defended the company by saying that such sales were an "industrywide practice." But Minnesota's attorney general had taken a dimmer view. He filed a complaint against Bancorp, the nation's 13th-largest bank holding company, alleging that it committed consumer fraud and engaged in deceptive advertising when it sold the information without customers' knowledge or consent.

Bancorp quickly sought to settle the matter, and the attorney general announced in June that the company would stop selling data to third parties. The bank admitted no wrongdoing, but it paid $3 million in fines and contributions to charities. Because the lawsuit was settled out of court, it did not answer the question of whether the bank's actions were illegal.

Nevertheless, the case could have a profound impact on the future of privacy laws and regulations. In the same way that state lawsuits against tobacco companies eventually led to sweeping federal involvement in the issue, the Minnesota case could be a catalyst for federal action on privacy. When tobacco litigators won the cooperation of Liggett Group Inc., which sells tobacco products, it helped expose previously confidential industry documents containing evidence that eventually pushed the tobacco industry toward a deal. *(Tobacco, 1998 Almanac, p. 15-3)*

In similar fashion, the Minnesota case laid out the kinds of information that can pass from bank to telemarketer, and some privacy advocates in Congress say it is something that ought to deeply concern the public. Consumer groups and their congressional allies, who want to curtail companies' ability to sell or trade customer data, have frequently cited the Minnesota case and Grundhofer's "everybody's doing it" defense as frightening evidence of the need for more federally mandated privacy protections.

Privacy Issues Spread

Indeed, consumer privacy has become a key issue in numerous legislative arenas, including regulation of the Internet and medical records. This year's financial services overhaul is another high-profile example. Congress is under heavy pressure from consumer groups to curtail the ability of financial institutions to sell or share customer data. The affected industries worry that their ability to cross-market products, detect fraud and perform routine transactions could be jeopardized by such restrictions.

Congress is struggling to balance the demands of consumer groups, regulators and industry groups who have sharply conflicting agendas on privacy issues. In the financial services arena, consumer groups demanding greater government-mandated privacy protections say they speak for a public increasingly wary of technology's potential intrusiveness. Industry groups and regulators say they cannot do their jobs if their ability to examine and share customer data is sharply curtailed.

Privacy is likely to play a prominent role in weeks to come in the ongoing House-Senate conference on the financial services overhaul bill (S 900, formerly HR 10). Both versions of the bill would repeal decades-old restrictions on cross-ownership among banks, brokerages and insurers. But the House and Senate versions differ sharply on several details, and privacy is among a handful of issues that could sink the entire bill.

The House bill includes a provision that would require banks to allow customers to "opt out" of allowing banks to share information with third parties. It also would require banks to disclose their privacy policies. The Senate bill contains no such provisions.

Democrats, knowing they have some reluctant Republican allies who fear voting against consumer privacy provisions, say they will not let up in their push for restrictions. In the House Commerce and Banking panels, which share jurisdiction on the overhaul, Democrats pushed hard on privacy issues, and Republicans countered by offering less far-reaching provisions as compromises.

The result was that although Democrats did not get as much as they wanted, they transformed a House bill that was largely silent on the privacy issue into one with several new measures. Industry lobbyists have groaned that a deregulation bill has become referred to as "the privacy bill" in some media outlets, including The Associated Press. A motion to instruct conferees was adopted, 241-132, on the House floor July 30, calling on negotiators to push for "the strongest consumer financial privacy protections possible." The Clinton administration also favors strong privacy language.

Industry representatives and their allies in Congress, primarily Republicans, have warned against moving too quickly with privacy restrictions. Senate Banking, Housing and Urban Affairs Committee Chairman Phil Gramm, R-Texas, would prefer to handle privacy in separate legislation. Lobbyists for financial institutions warn that even routine transactions, such as contracting with printers to produce check blanks for customers, require providing account numbers to third parties and could become cumbersome or even illegal if Congress enacted tough new privacy measures.

While groups representing banks, securities firms and insurers have bickered over numerous provisions in the bills, they have coalesced to fight against new privacy proposals.

In prepared remarks for a July 21 hearing on privacy before the House

Banking and Financial Services Subcommittee on Financial Institutions and Consumer Credit, Washington attorney L. Richard Fischer said excessive privacy rules would hurt consumers. Testifying on behalf of Visa USA, two major bank groups and the Financial Services Roundtable, which represents some of the nation's largest bank and thrift-centered financial service holding companies, Fischer said, "The ability to share information and out-source banking operations heightens efficiency and promotes competition in the financial services sector, to the ultimate benefit of consumers."

Consumer advocates and members of Congress who are arguing for strong privacy protections say financial institutions are concealing their reasons for opposing them. Democrat Rep. Edward J. Markey of Massachusetts said financial institutions are concerned mainly about the billions of dollars that can be made selling customers' personal data to marketers who prize detailed financial information.

Consumers Union believes the privacy provisions in the House version are "riddled with loopholes," and that the debate boils down to a matter of corporate profits vs. consumer privacy. "We believe that consumers have a right to decide whether their personal financial data is for sale to the highest bidder or can be shared with a multitude of affiliated companies," Consumers Union said in a July 20 news release. "Too often, information from consumers' financial transactions is used against them to market worthless or overpriced products, such as credit insurance or credit card protection."

Consumers have become increasingly aware that bank information can provide a detailed rundown of their financial status and spending habits. This has always been the case, but the information had little value other than for internal record-keeping until computers made it quick and easy to categorize, compile and transmit. "Technology takes the friction out of the movement of information," said Thomas P. Vartanian, an adjunct professor in the graduate law program at Georgetown University Law Center.

Balancing Act

In a meeting with journalists July 19 arranged by financial services interests, Vartanian and industry representatives said protecting privacy while giving consumers the services they want will require a delicate balancing act. Vartanian cautioned against placing enormous obstacles to information-sharing that could hurt financial services companies.

While databases have transformed customer information into organized, movable commodities, banking has undergone a transformation into a more automated, less personalized industry. Financial institutions have been consolidating, expanding the reach of large banks at the expense of traditional hometown banks. With the growth of Internet services and the use of automated teller machines (ATMs), face-to-face transactions between customers and bank employees have become less frequent. Markey argues that with depersonalization, bankers tend to see customers less as business partners and more as commodities to be exploited for maximum financial gain.

Industry representatives reject this notion, saying banks will always have to protect their reputations by treating customers and their information with respect. Robert R. Davis, director of government relations for America's Community Bankers, which represents the thrift industry, testified July 20 before the Financial Institutions Subcommittee that if financial institutions are reckless with their customers' personal information, they will lose business. "I can assure you that none of these community banks are making calls to their neighbors during dinner to offer products," Davis told the subcommittee.

Many industry groups have grudgingly accepted some of the tamer privacy proposals, such as requiring companies to honor customer requests to opt out of some information-sharing practices with third parties. They have vehemently opposed tougher measures, such as "opt in" proposals pushed by Markey and others that would require financial institutions to get permission from customers before sharing information.

Making matters more complicated for lawmakers trying to find a compromise, smaller banks represented by the Independent Community Bankers of America have staked out a position potentially putting them at odds with larger banks.

Robert N. Barsness testified July 20 on behalf of the community bankers group, saying small banks are less likely than larger banks to have non-bank affiliates and are more likely to contract with third parties to provide banking-related services. Thus, small banks would be at a competitive disadvantage if Congress imposed an opt-out requirement for third parties but not for affiliates, said Barsness, president of Prior Lake State Bank in Minnesota.

Public's Privacy Fears

Earlier this year, federal bank regulators provoked a powerful display of the public's concern over financial privacy when they announced a proposed set of "know your customer" regulations. The proposal would have required banks to report suspicious transactions to federal officials in an effort to detect money laundering and other crimes. It prompted thousands of angry responses from citizens, and several GOP lawmakers joined the protest. The rules were quickly dropped.

Voting for privacy provisions in the financial services overhaul could be trickier for Republicans than taking on the "know your customer" proposal. Instead of blasting federal regulators, Republicans who support tougher data-sharing restrictions for financial institutions would have to face down some of the most powerful groups that traditionally support the GOP, including insurance companies and large banks.

Nevertheless, Republican defections on privacy have already begun. When the conference opened Aug. 3, Sen. Richard C. Shelby of Alabama, the second-ranking GOP member on the Banking Committee, announced that he supported substantial new limits on banks' ability to disclose customer data. Shelby's move left lobbyists wondering how many more Republicans would follow him. And House Financial Institutions Subcommittee Chairwoman Marge Roukema, R-N.J., said July 20 that the bank privacy provisions were just a starting point for future action that would "set the stage for more comprehensive privacy legislation."

New Backroom Strategy Debated For Banking Bill

OCTOBER 2 — Unable to agree on any difficult issues despite days of debate, GOP negotiators working on legislation to overhaul the financial services industry planned to shift to a strategy of backroom deal-brokering among a handful of party leaders to break the logjam.

Conference Chairman Rep. Jim Leach, R-Iowa, who had hoped to solve issues one by one through open debate, reluctantly agreed to the more secretive approach over objections from Democrats.

Senate Banking, Housing and Urban Affairs Committee Chairman Phil Gramm, R-Texas, said at the Sept. 29 conference session that talks would stall unless GOP leaders exerted authority. Gramm suggested that he, Leach and House Commerce Chairman Thomas J. Bliley Jr., R.-Va., meet privately to merge the House and Senate versions of the bill (S 900). After a working proposal was on the table, other conferees could offer amendments. "I think if we're going to finish a bill this year, that's what we're going to have to do," Gramm said. "Part of being in the majority is having the obligation to lead."

The three met behind closed doors Sept. 30 with House Speaker J. Dennis Hastert, R-Ill., and Senate Majority Leader Trent Lott, R-Miss., and emerged with the leadership's blessing for Gramm's plan. GOP leaders in both chambers have been under heavy pressure from industry lobbyists to move the bill before Congress adjourns for the year.

Gramm promised that he would support the product that emerged from such a process, even if it included amendments he opposed. But Democrats objected to Gramm's plan, saying the bill would need support from the minority to avoid a presidential veto.

Leach, chairman of the House Banking and Financial Services Committee, said he wanted to continue open discussions on the difficult issues before meeting privately to produce a GOP agreement, which could be ready as early as Oct. 8. Conferees are tentatively scheduled to meet again Oct. 6.

The number of conferees is unusually large — 20 from the Senate and 46 from the House. A Senate GOP staff aide said Leach's goal of avoiding closed-door dealing does not mesh well with such a large group. "It's a noble objective, but it's a huge crowd," the aide said.

The bill would repeal decades-old laws restricting affiliations among banks, brokerages and insurance companies. Conferees on Sept. 29 approved by voice vote a list of 15 noncontroversial, mostly technical issues. On Sept. 29-30 they also discussed controversial issues, such as the privacy of consumer bank records and the 1977 Community Reinvestment Act (PL 95-128), but did not take votes.

The reinvestment act, a law intended to encourage banks to make loans in low-income neighborhoods, was a particularly contentious issue. Gramm said the law has been abused by community groups to extract grants and questionable loans from banks.

Gramm has proposed scaling back the law by exempting small, rural banks. He also wants to forbid community groups from striking confidential deals with banks in which loans or grants are given to the group in exchange for the group's silence or support of the bank's lending record. Democrats have objected to any attempts to curtail the law, and President Clinton has vowed to veto the bill if it contains anti-reinvestment provisions.

United at Last, Financial Industry Pressures Hill To Clear Overhaul

OCTOBER 9 — The House Banking Committee chairman wanted a lengthy, public debate with open votes to encourage bipartisanship. His Senate counterpart said such a strategy would never work, that the majority party needed to hammer out a deal behind closed doors or the bill would die. So financial industry lobbyists, sensing an eleventh-hour logjam on legislation they had doggedly pursued for three decades, started an all-out blitz to get Congress moving again on an overhaul of the laws governing financial services.

The industry's effort to jump-start progress on the bill (S 900) is a case study in how a well-heeled and well-organized interest group can swiftly prod Congress to move, even on an issue about which most people outside Washington and New York have little knowledge.

"This bill must pass," said Carroll A. Campbell Jr., president and CEO of the American Council of Life Insurance, a former Republican governor of South Carolina and former House member (1979-87).

Lobbyists could smell victory this year when, for the first time ever, both the Senate and the House passed overhaul legislation. Then the bill appeared to bog down in a House-Senate conference as negotiators bickered over process and failed to progress on substantive issues. So lobbyists leaned hard on the GOP leadership.

House Speaker J. Dennis Hastert, R-Ill., and Senate Majority Leader Trent Lott, R-Miss., personally intervened to force key Republican committee chairmen to get together and strike a deal. "The leadership turned up the heat, and that's when things started to move," said a top industry representative.

A consensus has long existed in Congress that the laws restricting cross-ownership among banks, brokerages and insurers are outdated and need to be repealed. The barriers, enacted in response to the Depression to stem widespread financial failures, are now considered a drag on the economy. But working out the details for a new regulatory framework has been excruciatingly complex, sparking numerous fights among the affected industries.

Lobbyist Kenneth A. Guenther of the Independent Community Bankers of America, which represents smaller banks, said industry lobbyists, congressional leaders and almost everyone else involved in the issue is weary of dealing with it. They want the bill enacted before the end of the year. "They're just sick and tired of this, and they want it off their backs," Guenther said, adding that all three major industries are eager to expand their affiliations.

Some affiliations are already under

way because of regulatory decisions favorable to the industry, but most major financial groups still want Congress to provide a more established legal framework for diverse financial conglomerates. The need for legislation was highlighted by the recent merger of the Travelers Group and Citicorp into the Citigroup financial conglomerate. Regulators allowed the merger to go through, but Citigroup must sell off its insurance activities within the next few years unless Congress approves an overhaul. *(1998 Almanac, p. 5-3)*

The financial industries have spent millions of dollars lobbying Congress and contributing to key election campaigns, only to see overhaul efforts die time after time. In the first six months of 1999, political action committees representing banks, brokerages and insurers gave at least $6.6 million to congressional candidates, according to Federal Election Commission records. Of that amount, $1.2 million went to members of the House Banking panel, and $480,000 went to Senate panel members.

Financial services companies argue that barriers against affiliation put them at a competitive disadvantage globally because overseas competitors do not face similar restrictions. The Financial Services Coordinating Council — which represents a broad swath of the affected industries, including bankers, insurance companies and securities interests — warned in a Sept. 30 statement that failure to pass a bill "would be a great disservice to our nation's consumers, investors and policyholders."

Roadblocks of Substance, Style

Negotiators have had great difficulties with certain provisions in S 900, several of them — such as whether banks should be required to keep affiliated insurance and securities businesses at arm's length under an umbrella holding company — relatively disconnected from party politics. Coalitions shift from issue to issue, making it difficult to broker deals. "There aren't going to be any clear winners or key losers in this bill," Sen. Phil Gramm, R-Texas, chairman of the Senate Banking, Housing and Urban Affairs Committee, said at a Sept. 23 conference session.

Conflicts in management style have also strained negotiations. Conference Chairman Jim Leach, R-Iowa, who chairs the House Banking and Financial Services Committee, faced resistance to his leadership style from key members of both parties, including Gramm and John D. Dingell of Michigan, the top Democrat on the House Commerce Committee, which shares jurisdiction with Banking.

At the Sept. 23 session, Leach pushed the need for a tight timetable to finish the bill this year. He has argued for open negotiations with public votes. But Gramm said progress could not be made unless GOP leaders struck a deal privately. Dingell agreed that an open conference would likely go nowhere, and he suggested letting staff aides hammer out agreements in private.

Gramm's ultimate intentions were unclear. In public comments he sometimes insisted that he wanted a bill and sometimes seemed to dismiss the possibility that the conference could finish its work this year.

As progress slowed, some legislators warned that the overhaul was lumbering toward hibernation for the year, and that it might be impossible to revive such a complex and contentious measure. Chuck Hagel, R-Neb., a member of the Senate Banking Committee, worried that "this thing will just die of its own weight" if Congress cannot move it within the next few weeks. "I don't think time is on our side here," Hagel said.

Guenther, the lobbyist for small banks, agreed that waiting until next year could doom the bill. Numerous players could decide to make new demands that would further complicate matters, and a drop in the stock market while Congress was in recess could change the dynamics for the legislation in unpredictable ways, Guenther said.

A remarkable blitz of lobbying, public relations and backroom arm twisting got things moving on the bill. At a Sept. 29 conference session, Gramm suggested that the entire overhaul was going to die if Leach did not alter his strategy. "I think we're fast coming to the moment of truth as to whether we're going to have a bill or not," Gramm said.

Gramm suggested that he, Leach and House Commerce Committee Chairman Thomas J. Bliley Jr., R-Va., meet privately to hammer out a bill, and then return with a proposal for the other conferees to amend, followed by a final vote.

Leach, who had gone out of his way throughout the bill's journey through the House to maintain bipartisan support, balked at the proposal and stuck with his plan to hold lengthy debates followed by up-or-down votes, issue-by-issue, in open session. Gramm said in an interview outside the conference that such an approach would never produce a bill.

Industry's Full-Court Press

Sensing that their best opportunity for legislation was losing momentum, industry lobbyists cranked up their efforts to get things moving again. On Sept. 29, the same day Leach and Gramm argued over procedure, a coalition of industry lobbyists visited Lott. They carried a simple, straightforward message: The financial industries want a bill this year, and they are willing to line up behind one even if they have to swallow some tough provisions they do not like.

Industry representatives also worked the media, stressing to reporters that the financial sectors interested in the bill, which have a history of squabbling over nearly every detail of the legislation, have put aside their differences in the interest of enactment.

On Sept. 30, the Financial Services Coordinating Council huddled with business reporters in a small Capitol Hill meeting room to present a united message. Seeing the finish line at last, they agreed to focus on the larger goal. There would be no talk of lines in the sand, and no provisions condemned as deal killers. "We now have a common front," said Marc E. Lackritz, president of the Securities Industry Association.

That same day, Lott, Hastert, Gramm, Bliley and Leach met behind closed doors to discuss strategies for the conference. The financial industry is an important GOP constituency, and House and Senate leaders apparently were feeling the heat.

The leaders leaned on the three committee chairmen to get a bill done, and they generally endorsed Gramm's way of doing it, according to staff aides and lobbyists. The three chairmen would put together a bill behind closed doors. Leach said the three wanted it done by Oct. 20, so Congress could act before adjourning for the year.

Later that day, at a scheduled conference session, Leach reluctantly explained the new plan, much to the chagrin of Democrats. Leach vowed to pay "as much attention to a consensus product as we humanly can," but Democrats generally were unmoved. "It's a lot of things, but it's not bipartisanship," said Paul S. Sarbanes of Maryland, the Senate panel's ranking Democrat.

Although many issues do not break down along party lines, two key matters — the level of customer privacy protections in the bill and the fate of a 1977 anti-redlining law — have been highly partisan. Leach appeared at pains to insist that however reluctant he might be about the plan, he would have to stand firm.

Industry sources said Gramm, despite his partisan reputation, was working hard with Leach and Bliley to produce balanced legislation that could garner at least some bipartisan support. Leach continued to hold public conference sessions Oct. 6 and Oct. 7, but the real work was being done behind the scenes. Industry lobbyists continued to maintain regular contact with GOP leaders, and the three chairmen met repeatedly the week of Oct. 4 to produce a merged bill, according to industry and congressional staff aides.

As Conferees Tackle Final Issues, Leaders Promise Quick Floor Votes

OCTOBER 16 — A bill to overhaul the federal regulatory structure for banking and financial services may go to the House and Senate floors for final approval as soon as Oct. 20, on the heels of breakthrough negotiations among congressional Republicans, on the one hand, and the Treasury Department and Federal Reserve, on the other.

The Clinton White House is still holding a veto threat over the bill (S 900) because of a continued dispute over anti-redlining laws. A surprise Capitol Hill visit by the Rev. Jesse Jackson at the House-Senate conference negotiations on Oct. 15 highlighted the pressure that consumer advocacy and civil rights groups are putting on the measure.

With only a handful of issues remaining, conferees are scheduled to finish merging the House and Senate versions of the bill when they reconvene Oct. 18, and GOP leaders have said they want a vote on the floors of both chambers almost immediately thereafter. The bill would overhaul the nation's financial services laws, removing barriers to cross-ownership among banks, brokerages and insurers.

Advocates of the bill were upbeat when the Federal Reserve and the Treasury Department announced on Oct. 14 that they had reached a truce in their long-running and potentially deal-killing dispute over how the new financial conglomerates that could be created under the bill should be structured and regulated.

And an agreement to include a provision prohibiting thrifts from affiliating with commercial firms removed another potentially veto-inducing issue.

Lobbying Fast Track

Rep. Jim Leach, R-Iowa, Sen. Phil Gramm, R-Texas, and Rep. Thomas J. Bliley Jr., R-Va., the three GOP committee chairmen who merged the House and Senate versions of the overhaul, unveiled their backroom handiwork on Oct. 12. They reconvened the formal conference committee only two days later, opening their draft bill to amendment.

Industry representatives, administration officials and consumer advocacy groups worked quickly to establish and work for their positions. Bank groups reiterated their longstanding plea for Congress to put a halt to the ability of thrifts to affiliate with commercial firms. The administration quickly stated that, despite some compromises by Gramm on the anti-redlining Community Reinvestment Act (PL 95-128), the bill was still veto material.

Finance industry groups warned conferees not to adopt far-reaching consumer privacy provisions, while consumer groups and their allies in Congress pushed in the opposite direction.

On Oct. 13, Sen. Richard C. Shelby, R-Ala., and Rep. Edward J. Markey, D-Mass., joined other lawmakers at a news conference announcing the formation of a new bipartisan Financial Privacy Coalition, with the stated goal of pushing for stronger laws restricting the transfer of individuals' financial data. The group's eclectic membership includes the American Civil Liberties Union, Phyllis Schlafly of Eagle Forum, and Ralph Nader of Public Citizen.

The conference draft generally adopted House-bill language placing some new privacy restrictions on banks, but those measures fell far short of what consumer groups and other privacy advocates wanted. The White House also wants stronger privacy provisions.

The provisions to amend the 1977 Community Reinvestment Act (CRA), which is intended to encourage banks to make loans in low-income neighborhoods, could spell trouble for the bill. The law allows regulators to block banks' applications for mergers or acquisitions if they do not have satisfactory CRA ratings.

The conference draft would reduce the frequency of CRA regulatory exams for rural banks and small urban banks. It also contains a "sunshine" provision that would prohibit banks and community groups from striking confidential deals intended to keep community groups from protesting a bank's reinvestment activities in exchange for loans or grants.

Democrats have accused Gramm of gutting the CRA's effectiveness and taking the first steps toward eliminating it. "The CRA is one of the most important tools that local communities have," said Bruce F. Vento, D-Minn., a member of the House Banking and Financial Services Committee.

John J. LaFalce of New York, the ranking Democrat on the House Banking Committee, sought to undo the CRA changes, but House conferees rejected his amendment, 12-15.

The LaFalce amendment also would have restored a House bill provision (dropped in the conference draft) that would have allowed civil penalties to be levied against banks for CRA non-compliance.

Gramm, chairman of the Senate Banking Committee, said the provision would have amounted to a dramatic expansion of the law, and he accused Democrats of unfairly characterizing his proposed changes. "Nothing in our bill undoes CRA," he said.

Democrats warned that even though the GOP draft dropped a highly contentious provision exempting small, rural banks from CRA compliance, the remaining CRA provisions were still unacceptable to the White House. Community groups also objected to the bill's CRA provisions.

In an Oct. 12 news release, the Leadership Conference on Civil Rights said that reducing the frequency of inspections would hurt CRA enforcement efforts and that the so-called sunshine provision would impose "onerous reporting requirements" on banks and community groups.

Jackson, a vocal proponent of the CRA, attended the conference for several hours Oct. 15, huddling with Gramm privately and talking strategy with supporters outside the conference. He was joined by John E. Taylor, president and CEO of the National Community Reinvestment Coalition and a strong CRA backer.

In an interview outside the conference, Taylor said he had been informed by the administration that a veto threat still hangs over the bill unless changes are made to the CRA provisions. Taylor also said CRA supporters were hoping to fix the problems with the bill. "We're working on Gramm, for what it's worth," Taylor said.

Turf War?

The eleventh-hour announcement by the Federal Reserve and the Treasury that they had settled their differences raised the spirits of overhaul proponents.

The compromise — to allow banks to operate most financial services, except insurance underwriting and real estate development, as subsidiaries regulated by Treasury — eliminated one of the administration's key veto-triggering concerns. And Gramm said he would support anything that Fed Chairman Alan Greenspan endorsed.

The Fed, which regulates bank holding companies, had argued that financial conglomerates should be required to keep non-bank affiliates at arms length by organizing them as affiliates under a holding company. The Treasury, with the strong backing of the White House, insisted that banks be allowed to organize non-banking financial activities in subsidiaries, which the Treasury oversees.

Some observers had complained that the Fed and the Treasury were engaged in a turf war because they argued for positions that protected and potentially expanded their respective regulatory responsibilities. But officials from the two agencies maintained that their positions were based on bank safety and soundness concerns.

Conferees on Oct. 18 will continue to debate proposed restrictions on the ability of financial institutions to share customer data. The draft produced by the three committee chairmen generally adopted the privacy provisions from the House-passed bill, albeit in somewhat weaker form. While banks are required to let customers "opt out" of information sharing activities with third parties, an exception was carved out for joint marketing activities.

The change was made at the request of small banks, who argued that large banks with numerous, diverse affiliates would be less encumbered by third-party privacy restrictions.

On Oct. 15, Senate conferees rejected, 6-14, a proposal by Shelby and Sen. Richard H. Bryan, D-Nev., to impose extensive restrictions on the ability of companies to share data. The amendment contained an "opt in" provision that would have required companies to get permission from customers before sharing data with affiliates or third parties. Shelby urged his colleagues not to give in to a show of power by the financial industry lobby, which threatened to oppose the bill if it contained opt-in provisions.

"I've never seen so many lobbyists in the hall," Shelby said.

Gramm countered that opt-in requirements were onerous and harmful to consumers because they would be denied information about services they might want. He also said the provision in the underlying measure requiring companies to disclose privacy policies would give consumers the information they needed to decide whether they were comfortable with financial companies' privacy policies, and they could take their business elsewhere if they had doubts.

After the defeat of Shelby's amendment, Gramm argued that the privacy debate should be closed, but conference Chairman Leach, who also chairs the House Banking panel, said he expected there would be more privacy amendments offered Oct. 18.

In an Oct. 13 letter sent to all conferees, a coalition of industry groups warned Congress against going too far with privacy proposals. Opt-in requirements would be so complex and cumbersome, it would be "the equivalent of a ban," the letter states. "Our associations will support legislation containing the privacy provisions in the print released [Oct. 12]. However, our associations will find it necessary to oppose any legislation that . . . imposes opt-in requirements and/or imposes new restrictions on the sharing of information among affiliates."

The letter was signed by the Securities Industry Association, the American Bankers Association, the American Council of Life Insurance, the American Insurance Association, the Financial Services Council and the Investment Company Institute.

White House, Conferees Reach Final Agreement

OCTOBER 23 — A historic measure that would radically alter the financial services world is ready for approval by Congress and President Clinton because of two committee chairmen with strong personal reasons for wanting a bill, as well as a powerhouse lobby united to an unprecedented degree and determined that this year's opportunity would not slip away.

As a result, the deal reached in the early morning hours of Oct. 22 eluded a number of pitfalls that doomed previous efforts. The path was not easy. Conference negotiations, both public and private, were lengthy and often contentious. But one by one, negotiators reached agreements that cleared the way for congressional approval of a bill likely to win Clinton's signature.

The chief strategists were Rep. Jim Leach, R-Iowa, and Sen. Phil Gramm, R-Texas, who chair their chambers' respective Banking committees. Leach has watched in frustration as previous overhaul plans evaporated despite his painstaking efforts to craft bipartisan agreements. Under House rules, he will have to relinquish his chairman-

Decades of Efforts To Change The Glass-Steagall Act

OCTOBER 23 — In response to thousands of bank failures and a deepening Depression, Congress enacted the Glass-Steagall Act in 1933 to separate the commercial and savings bank industries from investment banking.

The 1933 law (PL 73-66), named after Sen. Carter Glass, D-Va. (1920-46), and Rep. Henry Steagall, D-Ala. (1915-43), prohibited banks from underwriting or selling securities.

After enactment, support grew for regulation of bank holding companies to prevent bank monopolies. President Franklin D. Roosevelt requested legislation in 1938, and bills to regulate holding companies were introduced in nearly every Congress until the Bank Holding Company Act (PL 84-511) became law in 1956.

The law defined holding companies as those with at least a 25 percent share of two or more banks. It limited their activity to the ownership and management of banks and prevented them from controlling assets in non-banking enterprises. Certain companies, however, were exempt, including one-bank holding companies, some long-term investment trusts and certain registered investment companies. Those entities could own as many banks as they wanted and could also engage in non-banking businesses.

1965-66

The House passed legislation in 1965 that sought to eliminate virtually all exemptions from the 1956 law, including its exemption for one-bank holding companies. President Lyndon B. Johnson signed the bill (PL 89-485) in 1966. But by then it included Senate-passed provisions to restore many exemptions, including the one for one-bank holding companies.

1969-70

President Richard M. Nixon promised legislation to extend the 1956 law to one-bank holding companies. The House passed such a bill in 1969. The Senate cleared it in 1970, and Nixon signed it (PL 91-607).

1978

Amendments to the 1956 law to allow bank holding companies to engage in limited insurance activities were included in a 1978 omnibus financial services bill. But the House failed to complete work on the holding company provisions before the bill became law (PL 95-630).

1980

The House passed a bill to restrict certain bank hold-

ship at the end of the 106th Congress, and this year's bill represented his last shot at passing the most sweeping financial services legislation in decades.

For Gramm, a primary player in bringing down last session's overhaul in the Senate, taking the helm of the Banking, Housing and Urban Affairs Committee imposed a new set of responsibilities. Instead of playing spoiler over pet issues, Gramm found himself under heavy pressure from the GOP leadership to get a bill passed.

And although he stuck to his guns and won some of what he wanted on a controversial anti-redlining provision, Gramm ended up agreeing to a finished product that was far different from the legislation he set before his committee early this year.

Republican leaders were pushed by the financial services lobby, which was unwilling to let this year's effort get away, particularly after the legislation reached the conference stage for the first time ever. Banks, brokerages and insurance interests largely put aside their differences to get a bill, and they presented a united front, applying heat several times when conference negotiations seemed to be falling apart.

Long Road

Negotiators painstakingly cleared away land mines to merge the House and Senate versions of the bill (S 900), announcing at 2 a.m. on Oct. 22 that a deal was at hand. The bill would undo restrictions on cross-ownership among banks, brokerages and insurance companies.

The road had been a treacherous one.

First the Federal Reserve and the Treasury Department had to resolve a long-running feud over the structure and regulation of financial conglomerates by agreeing on a compromise. Negotiators then worked out language on the privacy of customer financial records, which left some consumer groups and Democrats unhappy but drew an approving nod from the White House. Negotiators also agreed to prohibit thrifts from merging with commercial businesses, eliminating another potential veto point.

But one sticking point lingered. Gramm was butting heads with the White House over the Community Reinvestment Act (CRA), a 1977 anti-redlining law (PL 95-128) aimed at forcing banks to make loans in poor neighborhoods. Gramm said the law was excessively coercive and a heavy regulatory burden for small banks, and he insisted on what he described as modest changes. The White House — backed by civil rights leaders such as the Rev. Jesse Jackson — drew a line in the sand, saying any retreat on community reinvestment was unacceptable.

Conferees resolved the issue in the early morning hours Oct. 22 in a biing companies from acting as insurance agents. Similar legislation never reached the Senate floor.

1983

President Ronald Reagan proposed to permit banks to engage in securities, real estate and insurance activities. But legislators had little incentive to act, as there was general agreement that a repeal of Glass-Steagall would adversely affect constituents in every district.

1984

House legislation was introduced to close loopholes in the 1956 law, including requiring banks to divest themselves of their non-banking activities within two years. It never saw floor action. The Senate passed legislation to allow bank holding companies to form subsidiaries to underwrite mortgage-backed securities and municipal bonds.

1987

A law to bail out the Federal Savings and Loan Insurance Corporation (PL 100-86) also amended the 1956 law to close loopholes on non-banking activities, through which some retailers and financial houses had opened limited banking operations.

1988

The Senate passed a bill to repeal portions of the Glass-Steagall Act to allow banks to participate in securities activities while restricting their insurance activities. Two House committees approved a similar bill but could not compromise on jurisdictional issues. *(1988 Almanac, p. 230)*

1991

The House rejected a bill to repeal parts of Glass-Steagall and to allow banks to open branch offices nationwide. The Senate passed a bill overhauling the deposit insurance system only after the Glass-Steagall language was stripped on the floor. *(1991 Almanac, p. 75)*

1995

A bill to deregulate the financial services industry, including Glass-Steagall changes, failed to reach the House floor after opposition from banks and others persuaded leaders to shelve it. *(1995 Almanac, p. 2-78)*

1996

The 1995 bill was redrafted several times, but banks opposed it because it included restrictions on selling insurance. Bill sponsors lost hope after it became clear that House leaders would not allow floor action. *(1996 Almanac, p. 2-51)*

1997

House leaders were again unable to bring a bill to repeal the Glass-Steagall Act to the floor because of disagreements between the banking and insurance industries. *(1997 Almanac, p. 2-73)*

1998

The House passed the bill by one vote. It sought to repeal the 1933 law and other laws separating the banking, securities and insurance industries. The bill stalled in the Senate because of disagreements over community reinvestment and operating subsidiaries. *(1998 Almanac, p. 5-3)*

partisan agreement that sent a euphoric cheer through the financial industry representatives who have been fighting for the measure for decades.

Cory N. Strupp, head of government relations for J.P. Morgan & Co., said the overhaul was the biggest financial industry bill ever passed by Congress, including the landmark Depression-era legislation it would overturn. "The scope of this bill is broader than anything that's been done before," Strupp said.

In an Oct. 22 statement praising conferees, the American Bankers Association, which represents many of the nation's largest banks, said outdated laws were crippling financial institutions' ability to compete. "For more than 20 years, banks and other financial institutions have been seeking the kind of legal reform that is contained in legislation now on the verge of enactment."

The administration is awaiting the drafting of final language before giving their final approval, but Treasury Secretary Lawrence H. Summers all but gave the administration's endorsement of the bill, clearing the way for likely floor approval and Clinton's signature before Congress adjourns for the year. "Nothing is done until the language is fully reviewed," Summers said in a handwritten statement distributed to reporters in the wee hours of Oct. 22. However, Summers said that "significant improvements" were made to the reinvestment provisions and that the administration was "very pleased" with some key elements.

Conference committee Democrats also were optimistic but awaited the final language before giving their assent. In a telephone interview Oct. 22, Paul S. Sarbanes of Maryland, the top Democrat on the Senate Banking Committee, called the agreement a "major accomplishment."

The Senate originally passed its version of the bill with only one Democrat joining Republicans in favor of it. Sarbanes said he expected the conference agreement to draw much more Democratic support because of the changes made in conference. "This bill is much better than the bill that passed the Senate," he said.

The agreement with its new language will be circulated among conferees for their signatures, said House Banking and Financial Services Committee spokesman David Runkel, so the report can be filed the week of Oct. 25.

Gramm a Key Player

Leach has been working on an overhaul bill for years, but it was Gramm who emerged as the key player in the debate. He was the focus of the White House's attention, and the bane of community groups opposed to his efforts to scale back reinvestment provisions.

Gramm thwarted Democrats in several areas, including consumer protection measures he considered unworkable and onerous for business, but he also lost on at least two big points. He had insisted that he would rather deal with consumer privacy in separate legislation, and he also opposed a provision preventing thrifts from affiliating with commercial firms. Winning some concessions on reinvestment appeared to be his line in the sand. In an Oct. 22 statement, Gramm said he was pleased with the final product, which he predicted would "pass both houses of Congress by large margins and . . . be signed by the president."

In relation to the bill's gigantic scope, the proposed reinvestment changes seemed relatively minor, but both sides dug in firmly on the issue for most of the week of Oct. 18, saying to compromise would be to sacrifice principles.

The law is intended to encourage banks to make loans in low-income neighborhoods, and it allows regulators to block banks' applications for mergers, expansions or acquisitions if they do not have satisfactory reinvestment ratings.

Leach, Gramm, and Rep. Thomas J. Bliley Jr. of Virginia, the three GOP committee chairmen who initially merged the House and Senate versions of the overhaul, unveiled their backroom handiwork Oct. 12.

Their bill sought to reduce the frequency of reinvestment regulatory exams for many small banks. It also contained a "sunshine" provision that would prohibit banks and community groups from striking confidential deals intended to keep community groups from protesting a bank's reinvestment activities in exchange for loans or grants. Those provisions were altered somewhat Oct. 22, but remained essentially intact in the final product.

Democrats warned that even though the GOP draft dropped a controversial provision to exempt small, rural banks from reinvestment compliance, the remaining provisions were still unacceptable to the White House. Community groups also objected.

Gramm's opponents accused him of trying to gut the 1977 law's effectiveness and take the first steps toward eliminating it. House Banking panel ranking Democrat John J. LaFalce of New York sought to undo the changes in the conference draft, but House conferees rejected his amendment.

With negotiations bogged down over community reinvestment, Summers paid a surprise late-night visit to Capitol Hill on Oct. 18. It appeared that Republicans were ready to push ahead with reinvestment provisions that the White House strongly opposed. Committee chairmen and ranking Democrats met with Summers for about two hours.

Over the next two days, fearing that the White House could be softening its stand on the reinvestment law and ceding ground to Republicans, supporters of the law swung into action. On Oct. 20, Democrats Maxine Waters of California, Melvin Watt of North Carolina, Stephanie Tubbs Jones of Ohio and Edward J. Markey of Massachusetts held a news conference to denounce the GOP's proposed reinvestment provisions. Watt said he was concerned about what the administration might be giving up in private negotiations with Gramm. "A group of men have retired into a back room to discuss the communities' business," Watt said. "I'm not happy about that."

Watt added that his discussion with administration officials had not satisfied his concerns.

Marathon talks among Gramm, Summers and other White House officials continued through Oct. 20, when Summers left Gramm's office late in the evening apparently believing he had reached a deal acceptable to the administration. But the White House rejected it, according to several industry sources and a Senate staff aide.

Gramm insisted he had compromised repeatedly on the community lending law, first by dropping a provision exempting small, rural banks from compliance, which he had done in the closed-door negotiations with Leach and Bliley. In his discussions with White House officials, Gramm said, he made further concessions.

Gramm said he had altered the sunshine provision and modified the regulatory relief provisions, among other changes, to move the bill toward the White House position.

In a somber news conference at 1 p.m. Oct. 21, Gramm said negotiations had failed to produce an agreement, but that the conference would push ahead on the bill anyway in hopes that the concessions he had made would be enough to avoid a veto.

In a conference session later that day, conferees discussed the reinvestment law but made little headway. Several Senate Democrats who were enthusiastic about passing an overhaul bill, including Christopher J. Dodd of Connecticut, Charles E. Schumer of New York and John Kerry of Massachusetts, urged Gramm to delay further proceedings in hopes that more talks could avoid a veto.

Kenneth A. Guenther, executive vice president of the Independent Community Bankers of America, a group of mostly small banks, said a large segment of the financial services industry wanted the bill, and it mobilized that day to urge conferees to hold off if Gramm and the administration could not reach a deal.

"There's a large group of people, financial services industry people, who do not want this bill going down over CRA for a second year running, and we are together conveying that message at the highest levels of the House and Senate leadership," he said.

But Republican leaders pushed ahead with the conference.

Break in Action Produces Deal

On the evening of Oct. 21, the conference session broke up for a series of House floor votes. As members drifted back to the conference room, impromptu backroom discussions among committee Democrats and Republicans appeared to be making headway. Leach recessed the conference so talks could continue.

Administration officials were present, but it was the Senate Democrats who had pushed for more time to get a deal who were instrumental in getting constructive talks going, Senate Banking Committee spokeswoman Christi Harlan said. "The White House had already pooh-poohed the proposal that Treasury was OK with on Wednesday [Oct. 20] night," Harlan said.

Again sensing that a key moment could be at hand, backers of the 1977 law restated their demands. At about 10 p.m., the Congressional Black Caucus distributed a copy of a letter sent to Clinton urging him "to maintain your strong support" of the law. The letter

Financial Services Accord

OCTOBER 23 — *The following are highlights of the conference report on the financial services overhaul bill (S 900 — H Rept 106-434):*

• **Privacy.** The conference agreement generally would follow the House provisions. It calls for banks to develop written privacy policies and disclose them conspicuously to customers, and to give consumers the right to opt out of information-sharing with unaffiliated third parties. In one exception, the measure would not require banks to let customers opt out of joint marketing agreements with other financial institutions. Small banks requested the exception, arguing that without it they would be at a competitive disadvantage because large banks were more likely to have in-house affiliates to participate in cross-marketing projects. Republicans thwarted Democratic-led attempts to pass stronger privacy measures, including an amendment that would have allowed customers to opt out of information-sharing with affiliates as well as third parties.

The bill would also make a crime of "pretext" calling, the practice of gathering personal information from a bank about a customer by using false information or deceptive tactics. The provision contains exceptions for law enforcement activities and for attempts to collect child support payments.

• **Community Reinvestment Act.** The Community Reinvestment Act (PL 95-128) is an anti-redlining law that requires banks to document efforts to invest in all segments of their communities. The conference agreement would require fewer reinvestment reviews by federal regulators for most banks with less than $250 million in assets unless they sought to merge, establish a new branch or relocate. Banks wishing to expand the scope of their businesses into insurance or securities activities would have to have satisfactory reinvestment ratings to do so.

The agreement also includes a "sunshine" requirement that is similar to a provision in the Senate bill. It would require banks and community groups to disclose deals in which grants or loans were offered by a bank to a community group in exchange for the group's support of the bank's reinvestment activities. Critics of reinvestment requirements said the confidential agreements allowed community groups to abuse the law by making deals with banks eager to avoid public opposition to their expansion plans.

• **Title insurance.** The agreement would allow federal bank subsidiaries to sell title insurance. The measure would also override any state laws prohibiting such sales by national bank themselves if state banks were allowed to sell title insurance.

• **Structure and regulatory oversight.** Negotiators adopted a compromise on the structure of new financial conglomerates worked out by the Federal Reserve and the Treasury Department, which share jurisdiction in bank regulation. The Fed had argued that financial conglomerates should be required to keep non-bank affiliates at arms' length by organizing them as affiliates under a holding company. The White House insisted that banks be allowed to organize non-banking financial activities as subsidiaries. Treasury now oversees banks and subsidiaries that are not part of a holding company, and the Fed regulates holding companies. Under the deal, banks generally would be allowed to operate most financial services, except insurance underwriting and real estate development, as subsidiaries. However, the total assets of a bank's subsidiaries could not exceed $50 billion or 45 percent of the bank's assets, whichever was less.

• **Regulation of insurance and securities.** The agreement, which hews more closely to the House bill, would require that insurance and securities activities be overseen by their respective state and federal regulators, even if the activities were conducted by a bank affiliate or subsidiary. Exceptions would be made for some traditional bank activities, such as trust management, which would continue to be overseen by bank regulators. The Senate bill would have placed more securities functions under the review of bank regulators, rather than the Securities and Exchange Commission.

• **Automated teller machine fees.** The agreement would require that automated teller machines give notice of transaction fees and allow customers to cancel transactions before any fees were imposed.

• **Thrifts.** The agreement follows the Senate version, which would forbid new and existing thrifts from affiliating with commercial firms. Opponents of affiliation argued that mixing banking and commerce places the financial industry at risk, and that it could be anti-competitive if thrifts refused to grant loans to potential competitors of their commercial affiliates. Banks also complained that existing thrifts have an unfair advantage because they are currently allowed to affiliate with commercial firms, and banks are not.

• **Wholesale financial institutions.** The agreement would allow the creation of a new type of bank called a wholesale financial institution, nicknamed a "woofie" because of the WFI acronym. These institutions would not be as heavily regulated as regular banks, and their deposits would not be federally insured. They would require a minimum deposit of $100,000 and would be geared toward the needs of institutional and large individual investors. These institutions could not be affiliated with federally insured banks, and the reinvestment act would not apply to them.

said, "Unless we maintain strong Community Reinvestment Act provisions, the ongoing consolidation of the banking industry will adversely affect disadvantaged low- and moderate-income communities."

At around 2 a.m. Oct. 22, conference Chairman Leach emerged to say negotiators had reached a deal. One key to the White House's support was a provision requiring that banks have a satisfactory reinvestment rating before expanding into securities or insurance activities.

Some members and consumer groups expressed their displeasure with the legislation later Oct. 22. In addition to their concerns about administration concessions on reinvestment, consumer groups were unhappy with the White House on another score — its endorsement of the privacy provisions adopted earlier in the week.

After wrangling for hours over privacy amendments, conferees settled Oct. 18 on provisions similar to those passed in the House.

The measure calls for banks to develop written privacy policies and disclose them conspicuously to customers, and to give consumers the right to opt out of information sharing with unaffiliated third parties. In one exception, banks would not be required to let customers opt out of joint marketing agreements with other financial institutions.

Republicans turned back several attempts by Democrats, some of them with some GOP support, to pass stronger privacy measures.

Privacy Provisions Endorsed

The White House quickly endorsed the privacy provisions, and Democrats who fought for stronger measures said they felt abandoned by an administration that previously had said it wanted strong provisions. They complained that even though conference negotiations were ongoing, the administration's public endorsement ended the debate. "In effect, they've cut our legs off," complained Sen. Richard H. Bryan, D-Nev.

Republicans had opposed an amendment by Markey that would have allowed customers to opt out of information sharing with affiliates as well as third parties, a position Markey said the administration supported in earlier statements. Markey encouraged the White House to veto the bill over privacy provisions.

Republicans who substituted weaker privacy language for Markey's amendment said his provision would have prevented companies from offering consumers a broad array of services.

Rep. W.J. "Billy" Tauzin, R-La., said provisions in Republican-backed privacy language offered by Michael G. Oxley, R-Ohio, would provide sufficient protections by requiring companies to disclose their information-sharing policies, allowing consumers to take their business to companies with privacy policies they could accept.

The amendment by Oxley closely followed language in the House bill, requiring companies to let customers opt out of information-sharing with third parties. The Oxley amendment also contained a provision not in the House bill, which would exempt joint marketing agreements from the opt-out requirement. Some Democrats called the exception a huge loophole rendering the entire provision nearly meaningless.

House conferees approved the Oxley substitute, 20-10. After a few small amendments were also accepted, Senate conferees approved the privacy measure by voice vote, and the House conferees adopted it, 22-7, with one abstention.

Title Insurance

The bill would allow bank subsidiaries to sell title insurance to home buyers.

Conferees rejected an amendment by Rep. Spencer Bachus, R-Ala., that would have expanded states' ability to regulate the sale of title insurance by national bank subsidiaries. Bachus said there were numerous potential problems with banks selling title insurance, including conflicts of interest because bank title insurance subsidiaries would be eager to clear potentially suspect titles so that their parent banks' loans would go through.

Gramm opposed the amendment, saying it would allow states to prohibit national banks from selling title insurance. He argued that such a move would undermine the bill's central purpose, which is to tear down barriers among the three industries.

"It makes absolutely no sense," Gramm said of the Bachus amendment. House conferees approved the measure by voice vote, but Senate conferees defeated it, 7-10.

Conferees rejected an amendment by LaFalce that would have stripped a provision from the bill allowing states to pre-empt federal consumer protection standards on insurance sales and set lower standards. LaFalce said federal consumer insurance protections should be a floor that states could exceed but not go below. Gramm said states should be trusted to set their own standards. "I think it is possible that we don't know everything," Gramm said.

Rep. Barney Frank, D-Mass., citing Gramm's positions on prohibiting state intervention in the sale of title insurance but supporting the right of states to reduce consumer protection standards, accused Gramm of switching positions on states' rights depending on the position most favorable for business.

Gramm said his position on title insurance was a matter of prohibiting states from discriminating against banks, which would happen if banks were denied the right to sell certain kinds of insurance while insurers could engage in banking.

One-Stop Shopping

Industry representatives who support the legislation see it as a boon for consumers and financial services companies. They say consumers will benefit from one-stop shopping for financial services, lower-cost financial products, special package deals, and increased competition as a growing number of financial conglomerates jump into new service areas and vie for customers. *(New world, p. 2504)*

But consumer advocates worry that consolidation will reduce competition and customer choice. They also have complained that the legislation fails to protect individuals from an assault on their privacy. They see a world where faceless financial conglomerates compile detailed digital files containing personal information, and then sell it to the highest bidder.

Industry supporters and consumer groups agree on at least two things though — the changes in the financial industry will be profound, and nobody is exactly sure how they will go.

With the help of favorable decisions by courts and regulators, the financial services industries have already been consolidating. Industry representatives said the legislation would not have an immediate, jarring impact on the evolution of the financial world. Instead, it would probably accelerate changes that have already been going on for years.

Some industry players will likely move aggressively to expand their reach, particularly large banks moving deeper into insurance and securities, but some financial sectors may have little interest in branching out into new areas of business.

The financial markets appeared to be pleased with the deal, although the reaction was subdued. Financial sector stocks generally rose during trading Oct. 22, but much of that rise could be attributed to a good day across the board for most stocks, said Raphael Soifer, a financial services analyst for Brown Brothers Harriman & Co. in New York.

Bill Clears After Final Skirmish Over Community Reinvestment

NOVEMBER 6— The financial world breathed a sigh of relief as Congress cleared a historic, bipartisan rewrite of the nation's banking, securities and insurance laws. President Clinton is expected to sign it.

Despite last-minute partisan sniping over the wording of the conference agreement, both chambers overwhelmingly adopted it Nov. 4. The Senate vote was 90-8. The House cleared the bill (S 900), 362-57. *(House vote 570, p. H-184; Senate vote 354, p. S-70)*

The bill would repeal key provisions of the 1933 Glass-Steagall Act, which erected barriers between the banking and securities industries, and the 1956 Bank Holding Company Act, which erected barriers between banking and insurance activities.

House-Senate conferees reached a bipartisan agreement in principle Oct. 22 that won tentative White House approval. But hammering out the final text of the bill and agreeing on report language proved daunting. Republican and Democratic House staff aides said Senate Banking Committee Chairman Phil Gramm, R-Texas, caused problems by seeking language that veered away from the Oct. 22 agreement.

Among points of contention was the 1977 Community Reinvestment Act (PL 95-128), a law intended to force banks to make loans in low-income areas. Gramm had fought to scale back the law, drawing the ire of community groups, congressional Democrats and the White House.

Gramm did little to dispel reports that he contributed to the ruckus in the final negotiations. He said he was proud of the finished product, had made concessions throughout the process and was going to fight to the end for whatever he could get. "All these people were telling me what they've got to have," Gramm said. "I thought it was a good time for me to start demanding more myself."

Gramm said the White House had tried to renege on the spirit of the Oct. 22 agreement, particularly on a reinvestment "sunshine provision." The provision would require disclosure of deals in which a bank offered grants or loans to a community group in exchange for the group's support of the bank's reinvestment activities. Gramm insisted that the community groups provide detailed reports on how they spend the grants or loans.

Despite lengthy fights, the bill emerged from conference with broad bipartisan support. In the House, 38 of 46 conferees signed the report. Some Democrats objected to what they called weak consumer privacy provisions or insufficient protection for the reinvestment act. All but two of 20 Senate conferees signed the report. Richard C. Shelby, R-Ala., and Richard H. Bryan, D-Nev., opposed it because, they said, it lacked sufficient privacy protections.

Some consumer and public interest groups also opposed the bill. Common Cause, a nonpartisan group that supports an overhaul of campaign finance laws, said in an Oct. 29 publication that the bill was a sop to big businesses, which have made millions in campaign contributions.

On the eve of passage, lobbyists and lawmakers celebrated. At a party in the House Banking hearing room, Federal Reserve Board Chairman Alan Greenspan and Treasury Secretary Lawrence H. Summers mingled with guests and congratulated House Banking Chairman Jim Leach, R-Iowa, who has spent years struggling to pass the bill.

Political Contributions

Bank, insurance and securities interests have made more than $30 million in "soft money," political action committee and individual contributions so far this year, with 60 percent going to Republicans, according to the Center for Responsive Politics, a nonprofit group that tracks campaign contributions.

The center noted that key events in this year's overhaul efforts coincided with heavy political contributions by Citigroup Inc., which would have had to sell some insurance operations if the bill were not enacted. On May 6, when the Senate passed its version, Citigroup made a $20,000 soft-money contribution to the 1999 Republican Senate-House Dinner and a $35,000 soft-money contribution to the Republican National Committee. On June 23, shortly before the House took up the overhaul, Citigroup gave $50,000 to the Democratic Congressional Campaign Committee.

Questions about Citigroup's involvement with the bill were heightened with the Oct. 26 announcement that the company had hired former Treasury Secretary Robert E. Rubin as co-chairman. The Independent Community Bankers of America, which represents smaller banks and has been lukewarm about S 900, said in an Oct. 29 newsletter, "The revolving door between high Treasury and White House officials and powerful financial firms is nothing new. But the timing of this one is particularly troublesome." ◆

Financial Services Overhaul

The following are provisions of the financial services overhaul bill (S 900 — PL 106-102) signed by President Clinton on Nov. 12, 1999.

Laws repealed

• **The 1933 Glass-Steagall Act.** The act's prohibitions on affiliations between the banking and securities industries are repealed.

• **The 1956 Bank Holding Company Act.** The act's prohibitions on affiliations between the banking and insurance industries are repealed.

Structure and oversight

• **Shared bank jurisdiction.** The Federal Reserve and the Treasury Department will continue to share oversight of national banks. The Fed will continue to regulate bank holding companies and will regulate new financial holding companies created under the law. The Treasury Department will continue to be the primary regulator of national banks.

• **Functional regulation.** Each affiliate or subsidiary of a financial conglomerate will be regulated by its "functional" regulator — banks by banking regulators, securities affiliates by the Securities and Exchange Commission (SEC), and insurance companies by state insurance regulators.

• **Safeguards.** The bill authorizes federal banking regulators to restrict relationships and transactions among insured banks and their affiliates or subsidiaries if needed to avoid conflicts of interest or to enhance the financial stability of banks and the general banking system.

Subsidiary activities and oversight

• **Bank and bank subsidiary activities.** National banks will be allowed to engage in, directly or through an operating subsidiary, activities that are "financial in nature or incidental to a financial activity." The Treasury will supervise bank activities, while the operations of individual bank subsidiaries will be supervised through functional regulation.

• **Exceptions to allowable bank subsidiary activities**. Banks or bank subsidiaries cannot conduct the following activities: insurance or annuity underwriting, insurance company portfolio investments, real estate development, real estate investment and merchant banking activities. Companies that want to engage in those activities will have to establish financial holding companies and organize the activities as affiliates, rather than as subsidiaries. However, subsidiaries could conduct merchant banking activities after five years if the Treasury and the Federal Reserve agree to allow them.

• **Subsidiary requirements.** The parent national bank and all affiliated banks must be well-capitalized and well-managed before financial activities can be conducted through a subsidiary. The parent bank also must obtain Treasury Department approval before initiating any eligible activity through subsidiaries. The consolidated total assets of all subsidiaries of any single bank will be limited to $50 billion, or 45 percent of the assets of the parent bank, whichever is less.

• **Large bank limitations.** The largest 100 banks in the nation by total asset size can conduct securities underwriting activities in subsidiaries only if the parent bank meets certain debt rating requirements.

Holding company activities and oversight

• **Other financial activities.** In addition to banking, insurance and securities activities, financial holding companies will be allowed to engage in activities that are "financial in nature," incidental to activities that are financial in nature, or complementary to such activities. This represents a significant expansion of previous law, which limited bank affiliates to activities "closely related to banking." The bill specifies that investment advisory activities, merchant banking and insurance company portfolio investments are financial in nature. It empowers the Federal Reserve Board — if the Treasury Department concurs — to define and authorize other eligible activities.

• **Limits on Fed oversight.** The Federal Reserve will not be allowed to examine functionally regulated non-bank affiliates unless it has reasonable cause to believe the affiliate is engaged in activities that pose a material risk to an insured bank, nor can it impose any capital adequacy rules, guidelines or other requirements beyond those already required by the affiliates' functional regulators. The bill limits the reach of the Fed's "source of strength" doctrine, which states that affiliates of insured banks may be considered part of the bank's enterprise with responsibility for financially supporting the institution. Under the new law, the SEC and state insurance regulators will be able to prevent the Fed from compelling securities, investment advisers and insurance affiliates to provide funds to an undercapitalized insured bank affiliate.

• **Fed enforcement of non-bank affiliates.** The Federal Reserve can take enforcement action against a non-bank affiliate only if needed to prevent or redress a practice that poses a material risk to the financial soundness of an affiliated bank or the U.S. or international payments systems, and only if it is not possible to guard against such risk through requirements imposed directly on the bank. In overseeing non-bank affiliates, the Fed generally will have to rely on reports from the affiliates, and on examinations conducted by other regulators.

• **Prohibited activities.** The measure does not allow banks to affiliate with commercial, non-financial entities, such as retail or manufacturing businesses.

• **Exceptions to prohibited activities.** Securities and insurance firms that already own, or are affiliated with, commercial non-financial companies can affiliate with banks under a financial holding company if they were engaged in commercial activities as of Sept. 30, 1999, as long as the commercial activities made up 15 percent or less of the company's gross revenue. Such commercial activities could not be expanded, and they would have to be terminated or divested within 10 years of the bill's enactment. Also, firms that own or are affiliated with companies engaged in commodities trading or investments can affiliate with banks under a holding company if they were engaged in such commodity activities as of Sept. 30, 1997, and if such commodity activities made up 5 percent or less of the company's total assets. The measure does not require the divestiture of these activities, but it prohibits cross-marketing of banking and commodities products.

Community Reinvestment Act

• **Confirms existing law.** The agreement generally preserves existing requirements of the 1977 Community Reinvestment Act (PL 95-128). The law is intended to spur loans in low-income areas by requiring banks to document their efforts to make loans in all areas where they collect deposits. Banks seeking to merge or open new branches must have reinvestment ratings of satisfactory or better.

• **Requirements expanded to cover new affiliations.** The bill requires that banks have a satisfactory or better reinvestment rating before they can affiliate with securities and insurance firms. It prohibits holding companies that have a bank with an unsatisfactory reinvestment rating from engaging in new financial services activities until the bank achieves a satisfactory rating.

• **"Sunshine" provision added.** The measure requires the public disclosure of any agreements made between banks and community groups involving more than $10,000 in grants or $50,000 in loans when the agreement is made in connection with the bank fulfilling its Community Reinvestment Act (CRA) requirements. This requirement applies only to parties that have commented on, testified about, or otherwise contacted the bank about the CRA.

• **Disclosure of expenditures.** Groups receiving funds under a CRA agreement with a bank must submit a detailed, itemized list reporting how the funds were used, including salaries, administrative expenses, travel, entertainment, consulting fees paid, and any other categories required by the banking regulator. Community groups can submit their annual reports directly to the bank, which is required to forward them to banking regulators.

• **Reduced regulatory reviews.** The bill reduces the frequency of CRA reviews for rural and small banks with less than $250 million in assets that have good CRA records. CRA regulatory reviews will be limited to every five years for such banks that have "outstanding" CRA ratings and every four years for banks that have "satisfactory" ratings. Banks will still be subject to CRA reviews whenever they propose to open a new branch or merge, and banking regulators can conduct reviews more or less frequently if they have reasonable cause.

• **Studies required.** The Treasury Department, in consultation with federal banking agencies, is required to study the extent to which services are being provided as intended by the CRA — including services in low- and moderate-income neighborhoods and for people of moderate means — as a result of the bill's enactment. The measure also requires the Federal Reserve to conduct a comprehensive study on the default rates, delinquency rates and profitability of loans made by banks in complying with the CRA.

Privacy

• **Disclosure.** The bill requires financial institutions to clearly and conspicuously disclose their policies regarding the sharing of customer information with other institutions. These disclosures must describe the type of customer information collected, the institution's policies and practices for sharing information with both affiliated institutions and non-affiliated third parties, and policies for protecting the confidentiality and security of confidential customer information. Such disclosures will have to be made to every new customer, and to all existing customers at least once a year.

• **Opt-out requirement.** Banks must allow consumers to opt out of their information sharing arrangements with unaffiliated third parties. The measure does not require companies to let consumers opt out of information-sharing with affiliates or subsidiaries.

• **Opt-out exception for marketing agreements.** Banks are not required to let consumers opt out of information-sharing with third parties made in association with a financial institution's joint marketing agreement, provided the institution discloses the arrangement with its customers and the third party agrees to keep the customer information confidential. The measure prohibits financial institutions from disclosing a customer's bank account or credit card numbers — or means of accessing such accounts — to third parties for purposes of telemarketing, direct mail marketing or electronic mail marketing.

• **Additional opt-out limitations.** Consumers cannot opt out of information sharing associated with the processing of consumer-initiated transactions, maintaining consumer accounts, or complying with consumer reporting requirements, legal requirements or law enforcement investigations.

• **Privacy rules.** The measure requires federal banking regulators, the Treasury Department, the SEC and the Federal Trade Commission (FTC), in consultation with state insurance authorities, to establish standards to ensure the security and confidentiality of customer financial records and information, and to protect against unauthorized access and use of such information. Each agency must conduct its own rulemaking, although agencies must coordinate with one another and, to the extent possible, make their regulations consistent.

• **Privacy study.** The bill requires the Treasury Department to conduct a study of information-sharing practices among financial institutions and their affiliates. Among other criteria, the study must examine the purposes for which confidential consumer information is shared, and the potential benefits of sharing for financial institutions and for customers; the potential risks to consumer privacy by sharing; the adequacy of existing laws to protect privacy; and the adequacy of security protections for shared information. The study must also explore the feasibility of approaches to privacy, including opt-out and opt-in policies that allow customers to control whether their confidential information can be shared with affiliates and third parties.

• **State privacy laws.** The bill's privacy provisions establish a floor, rather than a ceiling, for consumer privacy protection by allowing states to enact more stringent privacy provisions than those established in federal law.

Privacy and Fraud

• **Pretext calling.** The bill makes it illegal to obtain, or attempt to obtain, confidential information about a customer from a financial institution by fraudulent or deceptive means, or to request that another person obtain such information knowing that it will be done in a fraudulent manner. The most frequently noted example of such a prohibited activity is "pretext calling," in which an information broker impersonates the individual whose account information is sought or engages in other ruses designed to trick a financial institution into disclosing information. People found guilty of violations will be subject to criminal fines and imprisonment up to five years – with penalties doubled for certain aggravated cases.

• **Pretext calling exceptions.** Exceptions to this prohibition will be provided for certain law enforcement activities, for financial institutions that are testing their internal security procedures, for investigations of allegations of improper conduct by employees, for insurance companies and agents investigating insurance fraud or other misconduct, and for state-licensed private investigators authorized by a court to help collect delinquent court-ordered child support payments.

Automated teller machine fees

• **Disclosure.** The bill requires banks and other operators of automated teller machines (ATMs) to prominently disclose whether the machine will impose a fee on users who are not customers of the bank or other ATM operators. This must be done both through a sign on the ATM and a notice either on the ATM's screen or on a slip of paper dispensed by the machine. These provisions essentially codify procedures currently being followed voluntarily by most ATM operators. The disclosures must specify the amount of the surcharge, and the on-screen or dispensed-paper notice must provide the consumer with a chance to refuse the fee and cancel the transaction.

• **Fee disclosure exception.** The measure exempts from the on-screen or dispensed-paper requirement, until the end of 2004, any machines not technically able to display such messages on-screen or through dispensed paper.

• **Additional fee disclosure.** The bill requires ATM card issuers to notify consumers when cards are issued that surcharges may be imposed by other parties when using an ATM operated by a party other than the card issuer.

• **Liability protection.** The measure protects ATM operators from liability for violating the bill's disclosure requirements if the posted notice on the ATM has been removed, damaged or altered by other parties.

• **GAO study.** The bill requires the General Accounting Office (GAO) to study the feasibility, costs, benefits to consumers and competitive impact of requiring ATM operators to disclose to customers ATM fees that are being charged by the customer's bank.

Thrift holding companies

The bill prohibits new and existing savings and loans, also known as thrifts, from affiliating with commercial activities. It allows existing thrift-commerce affiliations to continue, including pending affiliations in which an application was filed on or before May 4, 1999.

SEC regulation

• **Banks as brokers and dealers.** The bill repeals the broad exemption for banks from regulation under federal securities laws, thereby providing for functional regulation of bank securities activities by the SEC. The bill extends SEC regulation of securities to the securities activities of banks by amending the definitions of "broker" and "dealer" under the 1934 Exchange Act to include banks. Subjecting banks to federal securities regulation will require banks either to register as securities broker-dealers or to move their securities activities out of banks and into registered securities affiliates or subsidiaries. However, the measure exempts specified types of bank securities activities, allowing banks to continue those activities without registering as broker-dealers.

• **Exempted securities activities.** The bill exempts certain bank securities activities from SEC broker-dealer regulation, including third-party brokerage arrangements in which a registered broker or dealer offers services on or off bank premises, but away from bank deposit-taking activities. It also exempts traditional bank trust activities, provided the bank receives no brokerage commissions and does not solicit brokerage business; transactions in commercial paper, bankers acceptances, commercial bills, and municipal and other exempted securities; certain stock purchase plans, such as those made in connection with 401(k) plans and dividend reinvestment plans, as long as the bank does not solicit transactions or provide investment advice on those transactions; and sweep accounts, in which banks invest customers' deposits in registered money market funds.

• **Exemption for low-volume securities activities.** Banks that perform fewer than 500 securities transactions per year of any kind are exempt from SEC broker-dealer regulation.

• **Exemption for private placements.** Banks will be permitted to perform private placements with "qualified investors" without SEC broker-dealer regulation. These are non-public securities sales made to certain large investors. Individuals and corporations will be classified as qualified investors for all private placements — except for asset-backed securities and loan participations — if they have at least $25 million in investments. The previous requirement was $10 million.

• **Mutual fund oversight.** The bill ends the exemption from the 1940 Investment Advisors Act for banks that sell mutual funds or advise mutual fund companies, thereby authorizing SEC oversight of such bank activities. Banks that advise mutual fund companies will be required to register with the SEC as investment advisers and will be subject to SEC examination of their mutual fund activities. If a bank establishes a separately identifiable department within the bank to act as the investment adviser, only that department will be required to register with the SEC.

• **Disclosure of mutual fund risk.** The measure requires banks that sell mutual funds to prominently disclose to customers that such investments are not federally insured or otherwise guaranteed.

• **Investment trust requirements.** The measure requires the SEC to issue rules on the conditions under which a bank or bank officer may serve as custodian of the assets of an affiliated management investment company or unit investment trust. It places restrictions on loans and other transactions between a bank and an affiliated investment company, and it limits the ability of bank officers to serve on the board of such affiliated companies.

• **Oversight of new products.** The measure empowers the SEC to determine if future "hybrid" products developed by banks are securities subject to SEC regulation. Before initiating a rulemaking process, the SEC would have to seek the concurrence of the Federal Reserve, and consider the history and purpose of the hybrid product and the likely impact that regulating the product as a security would have on the banking industry. If the Federal Reserve opposes an SEC rule declaring a hybrid to be a security, the measure provides for an expedited review in the U.S. Court of Appeals, with deference given to neither agency.

• **Securities holding companies.** The bill allows securities holding companies to be voluntarily supervised by the SEC. Before the bill was enacted, such holding companies — which besides a securities firm may include other financial and non-financial affiliates (but no federally insured banks or thrifts) — were not subject to any overall regulation. Allowing voluntary SEC oversight of the entire holding company is intended to enhance the ability of certain U.S. investment bank holding companies to do business in foreign nations that require consolidated holding company supervision.

• **Limitations on voluntary SEC oversight.** The voluntary SEC oversight will apply only to securities holding companies that do not include an insured depository institution. All holding companies that include insured banks are automatically subject to regulation by the Federal Reserve.

Bank insurance activities

• **State regulation of insurance.** The bill reaffirms the 1945 McCarron-Ferguson Act (PL 79-15), which provides that insurance is to be regulated by the states, not the federal government. It provides that no person or entity may underwrite or sell insurance in a state unless licensed by that state.

• **Insurance products defined.** The bill defines "insurance" to help delineate which products are to be regulated as bank products and which are to be regulated by states as insurance. Insurance products are defined as anything regulated by a state as insurance as of Jan. 1, 1999, including annuities. Future bank products will be classified as insurance if they are based on certain insurance concepts and are regulated by the state as insurance. Products based on core banking products —such as deposits, loans, trusts, derivatives and guarantees — will be treated as banking products unless they are treated as insurance for tax purposes by the IRS.

• **Dispute resolution.** For federal bank and state insurance regulators who disagree over the status of a product, the measure establishes a dispute resolution process under which either the banking or the insurance regulator may file a review petition directly to the U.S. Court of Appeals, bypassing U.S. district courts. The appeals court will have to examine the case's merits under both state and federal law, consider the nature and history of a product and its regulation, and make a decision within 60 days. No deference will be given to the opinion of either the state or federal regulator. Courts previously deferred to the opinion of the Office of the Comptroller of the Currency (OCC) in disputes concerning bank products. Court decisions could be appealed to the Supreme Court.

• **Restrictions on bank insurance underwriting.** The bill generally prohibits national banks and their subsidiaries from underwriting insurance, except for products that national banks were underwriting as of Jan. 1, 1999, or those the OCC had authorized banks to underwrite as of that date. Generally, any insurance underwriting will have to be conducted by insurance affiliates of banks under a financial holding company.

• **Title insurance restrictions.** The bill generally prohibits national banks or their subsidiaries from underwriting or selling title insurance. However, they can sell title insurance if the state allows state banks to sell title insurance, but only to the same extent and manner as allowed for state banks. In addition, existing title insurance activities by banks and subsidiaries will be allowed to continue, although such activities (including both underwriting and sales) will have to be moved out of the bank or subsidiary to an insurance affiliate, if one exists.

• **Consumer protections.** The bill requires federal banking regulators to develop consumer protection rules to govern the sale of insurance by banks. Among those to be developed are anti-tying and anti-coercion rules that prohibit banks from misleading consumers into believing that a loan or extension of credit is conditional upon the purchase of insurance; disclosure rules requiring that consumers be told orally and in writing that the insurance product is not FDIC-insured, that there may be an investment risk involved, and that the product may lose value (in the case of variable annuities); guidelines on the extent to which insurance transactions should be conducted in a location away from where bank deposits are made; consumer grievance procedures to address customers complaints; and a prohibition on discriminating against victims of domestic violence in providing insurance.

Pre-emption of state insurance laws

• **Pre-emption of state affiliation laws.** The bill provides that insurance is to be regulated by the states, but it specifically pre-empts state laws and rules that prevent or restrict affiliations between banks and insurance companies. State laws that regulate the "business side" of insurance (rather than sales, solicitation or cross-marketing activities) will not be pre-empted, however, and state regulators will be able to prohibit affiliations for managerial or solvency reasons. The bill authorizes state insurance regulators to gather certain information from parties proposing to acquire or merge with an insurance company to ensure that capital requirements for the company will be met and maintained. The bill pre-empts state laws that restrict the ability of banks and bank subsidiaries or affiliates to sell, solicit or cross-market insurance by codifying the standard set by the Supreme Court in its 1996 Barnett Bank decision (*Barnett Bank v. Nelson*). That decision held that no state laws or rules can "prevent or significantly interfere" with the rights of a national bank to engage in insurance sales or solicitation activities under federal banking law.

• **Court guidelines for review of state insurance laws.** In the case of state laws enacted before Sept. 3, 1998, the court — in deciding whether the state law meets the *Barnett* standard — will defer to the opinion of the federal bank regulator, as was previously the case in bank product disputes. For state laws enacted on or after Sept. 3, 1998, however, the court will not defer to the opinion of either state or federal regulators, but will consider four non-discrimination tests established by the measure (the agreement specifies four types of laws to be considered discriminatory against bank insurance sales).

• **"Safe harbors" for state insurance regulation.** The bill specifies 13 kinds of state insurance sales laws that are protected and will not be pre-empted, regardless of when they were enacted. These include state laws that prohibit banks from requiring customers to obtain coverage from an affiliated insurance company if insurance is required when taking out a loan; that require banks to provide written disclosures to customers that they may obtain insurance from third parties; that prohibit banks from charging fees for handling third-party insurance policies; that prohibit advertising or other materials that could lead customers to believe that bank loans or insurance policies are government-backed, and that require written disclosures stating that such policies are not federally backed; that prohibit insurance brokerage fees or commissions for non-licensed personnel; that prohibit the release of certain insurance information on customers; and that require credit and insurance transactions to be completed through separate documents.

Uniform insurance licensing

• **New standards and reciprocity.** States have different licensing and other requirements, which makes it difficult and expensive for insurance agencies to sell on a multistate basis. The bill calls for states to enact laws creating uniform state licensing standards that will provide reciprocity for licensed insurers to operate in other states.

• **Creation of federal standards.** If a majority of states fail to enact uniform licensing standards and reciprocity laws within three years, a private, nonprofit corporation called the National Association of Registered Agents and Brokers (NARAB) will be created to develop uniform standards to be applied on a multistate basis, pre-empting state licensing requirements. Insurance agents and brokers who join NARAB will be allowed to work in any state, with NARAB's licensing requirements overriding state requirements. The rights of states to license insurance agents and brokers will be preserved; however, those state requirements will apply only to state-licensed agents and brokers, and not to NARAB members.

• **NARAB guidelines.** In developing its standards, NARAB will have to make its licensing requirements comparable to the highest state licensing requirements, and its continuing education requirements will have to be comparable to, or greater than, the requirements of a majority of states. The measure requires that NARAB be created under the direction of the National Association of Insurance Commissioners (NAIC), the association of state insurance regulatory bodies. If the NAIC fails to implement NARAB, and a majority of states do not enact uniform licensing and reciprocity laws, the measure requires that NARAB be established by the president.

• **Rental car insurance.** The bill establishes a presumption that a state insurance license is not needed for employees of car rental companies who sell or market short-term insurance associated with a car rental or lease. This presumption will expire after three years and will not apply to states that have already established rules on whether car rental company employees are subject to state insurance licensing. This three-year presumption is intended to stem uncertainty in the car rental industry and give states time to determine how car rental companies should be treated.

Federal Home Loan Bank changes

• **Thrift membership.** The Federal Home Loan Bank (FHLB) System provides low-cost loans to local lenders for use in providing home mortgages. The measure makes membership in the system voluntary. Previously, federally chartered thrifts were required to join the system, but state-chartered savings and loans were voluntary members.

• **Participation requirements eased.** Under the law, small banks and thrifts will no longer be required to have at least 10 percent of their assets in mortgages or mortgage-backed securities in order to obtain FHLB advances.

• **Mission expanded.** The bill expands the mission of the home loan bank system by allowing small thrifts and banks with less than $500 million in assets to obtain advances for use in funding small businesses and small farms. As collateral for such FHLB advances, these small thrifts and banks will be allowed to pledge secured loans they previously made for eligible activities.

• **Management changes.** The bill sets the terms for both elected and appointed FHLB bank directors at three years. Previously, elected directors served two years and appointed directors served four.

'Limited purpose' banks

The bill lifts certain restrictions on cross-marketing and other activities for so-called limited purpose banks. These federally insured limited-service banks are owned by major financial and commercial firms, and they either accept demand deposits or make commercial loans, but not both. These institutions are also known as "non-bank" banks. The bill allows limited-purpose banks to cross-market products of affiliates and expands the types of overdrafts such banks may incur on behalf of an affiliate.

'Redomestication' of mutual insurers

The measure grants mutual insurance companies the authority to redomesticate (move) to another state and reorganize into a mutual holding company or stock company. This redomestication authority applies only to mutual insurers located in states that do not have laws providing reasonable terms and conditions for such reorganizations within the state. Such moves will be subject to approval by insurance regulators in the new state. All licenses of the insurer will be preserved, and all outstanding policies, contracts, and forms will remain in force.

Special thrift fund eliminated

The 1996 Deposit Insurance Act (PL 104-208) created a special reserve fund to augment the Savings Association Insurance Fund. The bill eliminates it. The reserve fund was intended to back up the SAIF and further protect taxpayers from thrift bailouts. It was established Jan. 1, 1999, using $1 billion in SAIF deposits that exceeded the SAIF's designated reserve ratio of 1.25 percent of estimated insured deposits. Critics of the reserve fund contended that it would be better to make these funds available to the regular SAIF account.

Microenterprise technical assistance

• **New grant program.** The bill establishes a new grant program to fund local nonprofit microenterprise development organizations and programs that help low-income and disadvantaged entrepreneurs. Grants could be provided to eligible organizations to provide training and technical assistance to entrepreneurs interested in starting or expanding their own businesses, to enhance the capacity of other organizations to serve low-income and disadvantaged entrepreneurs, and to support research and development of better training and technical assistance programs. Local organizations must match $1 for every $2 in federal assistance provided, and at least 50 percent of federal grant funding must be used to benefit people with extremely low incomes, defined as families living at 150 percent of the poverty line or below.

• **Grant funding authorized.** The measure authorizes $15 million a year through fiscal 2003 for the program, which would be administered by the Small Business Administration.

Miscellaneous provisions

• **Bank municipal bond activities.** The bill authorizes national banks to underwrite, purchase and deal in municipal bonds.

• **Plain language.** The bill requires federal banking agencies to use plain language in all rulemaking proposals published in the Federal Register after Jan. 1, 2000.

• **Interest rate cap exemption.** The measure allows local banks in states in which interest rates are capped to charge higher rates equal to those charged by an interstate bank that branches into the state.

• **Name rights.** Existing thrifts that convert to national or state banks will be permitted to keep the word "federal" in their names.

• **Bank board changes.** The bill amends utility law to permit officers and directors of public utilities to serve as officers or directors of banks, trust companies or securities firms.

• **Reserve bank audits.** The bill requires the Federal Reserve Board to contract for independent annual audits of the financial statements of each Federal Reserve Bank, as well as of the board itself.

• **Foreign bank powers expanded.** The bill allows a federal or state agency of a foreign bank to upgrade to a branch with the approval of the appropriate chartering authority and the Federal Reserve Board.

• **Grand jury access for state banks.** The bill authorizes U.S. attorneys to seek court orders to provide state banking regulatory agencies with access to certain grand jury material, thereby giving state agencies parity with federal bank regulatory agencies.

Additional studies

• Federal Reserve. The bill requires that the GAO study the conflict of interest faced by the Federal Reserve between its role as a primary regulator of the banking industry and its role as a vendor of services to the banking and financial services industry.

• Treasury Department. The bill requires the Treasury Department to study the extent to which credit is provided to small businesses and farms as a result of this legislation.

• "S" corporations. The measure requires the GAO to study the implications of revising rules concerning "S" corporations to allow greater access by community banks to S corporation treatment. An S corporation receives tax treatment similar to a partnership. ◆

Bankruptcy Overhaul Effort Loaded With Amendments, Stalls in the Senate

SUMMARY

The House passed a bill (HR 833) to overhaul the nation's bankruptcy laws. The Senate voted on several amendments to a companion bill (S 625) but then suspended debate shortly before adjourning for the year. A cloture vote was scheduled for Jan. 25, 2000.

Both the House and Senate bills seek to force more debtors to file under Chapter 13, which involves a reorganization of debts under a repayment plan, rather than under Chapter 7, which involves a liquidation of assets to pay creditors and the discharge of remaining unsecured debts.

The bill got off to a fast start in the House, despite partisan conflicts in committee, and passed on the floor May 5 by a veto-proof margin. Bill opponents got a surprise win when Republicans agreed to amend the measure to exclude Social Security and Medicare payments from calculations of filers' ability to repay debts.

The House and Senate also accepted amendments requiring credit card companies to more clearly disclose interest rates and other terms. However, Democrats in both chambers failed to attach amendments intended to temper provisions that many consumer groups said were too onerous for debtors. The Clinton administration warned in a statement May 5 that the House bill was tilted toward creditors and that President Clinton's advisers would recommend he veto it.

In the Senate, bill proponents made progress by winnowing more than 300 amendments to about a dozen, but the bill fell victim to Congress' eagerness to adjourn for the year after settling with Clinton on a budget package.

If the bill is revived in the Senate, prospects for passage will be uncertain. The bill was growing heavy with controversial amendments, and more were likely. It contains an increase of $1 an hour in the minimum wage over three years, added by Republicans to preempt a Democratic effort to raise the minimum wage by $1 over two years. Democrats also opposed $18.4 billion in tax cuts included in the GOP measure. The federal minimum wage is currently $5.15 per hour.

In addition, Charles E. Schumer, D-N.Y., had planned to offer an amendment that would prohibit people found guilty of violence at abortion clinics from discharging debts in bankruptcy court related to those violent activities. Carl Levin, D-Mich., planned to offer an amendment that would bar gun manufacturers from discharging debts arising from lawsuits filed against them by municipalities.

Creditors Push Congress To Revive Previous Year's Overhaul Effort

FEBRUARY 13 — As the rate of bankruptcy filings continues to climb despite a booming economy, lawmakers are under pressure to pick up a bankruptcy overhaul measure where they dropped it last year and do what it takes to pass a bill that President Clinton will sign.

Creditors are eager for Congress to pass bankruptcy overhaul legislation that will result in a greater percentage of debtors filing under a section of the bankruptcy code in which creditors may recoup more of what they are owed.

Bills that would make it more difficult to file under Chapter 7 of the code, in which debts are discharged after certain assets are liquidated, passed in both chambers in 1998. The House adopted a conference report on the bill in October, but it stalled in the Senate without coming up for a final vote after the Clinton administration threatened a veto, saying the bill was too heavily stacked against debtors.

The credit industry sees the 106th Congress as a prime opportunity to finish the job, using the conference report as a starting point.

The key sticking point relates to how courts should determine whether debtors should be allowed to proceed under Chapter 7. Creditors want legislation that would steer more people away from Chapter 7 and into Chapter 13, in which debts are restructured and repaid over time. Consumer advocates said last year's conference report erected excessive barriers to Chapter 7 filings, and Clinton agreed. But the credit industry objected to the changes requested by the administration.

Consumer advocate Gary Klein, a bankruptcy specialist with the National Consumer Law Center in Boston, said the conference report was so hostile to debtors that it should be scrapped, and Congress should start over. But the credit industry, which generally supported last year's plan and is eager for legislation, fears that starting over could mean Congress would run out of time again.

"We have a compromise that was worked out fairly carefully," said George J. Wallace, a lobbyist for the American Financial Services Association and a lawyer at the Washington firm of Eckert, Seamans, Cherin & Mellott. The association, which represents credit card companies, automobile finance companies and other consumer lenders, supported last year's conference report. Starting over would

Box Score

- **Bills:** HR 833, S 625
- **Legislative action: House** passed HR 833 (H Rept 106-123, Part 1), 313-108, on May 5.

  Senate debated S 625 (S Rept 106-49) between Nov. 4 and Nov. 17 but did not finish debate before adjourning for the year.

be a mistake, Wallace said.

Republican congressional leaders apparently agree. Rep. George W. Gekas, R-Pa., chairman of the Judiciary Subcommittee on Commercial and Administrative Law, plans to introduce a bankruptcy bill within the next two weeks that will be "fairly similar" to the conference report, said Carey Dearnley, Gekas' press secretary. The bankruptcy bill will be a high priority for Republican leaders, and efforts will be made to pass something quickly, said Dearnley, who predicted a markup within a month.

In the Senate, Charles E. Grassley, R-Iowa, chairman of the Judiciary Subcommittee on Administrative Oversight and the Courts, plans to introduce a bankruptcy overhaul bill in late February or early March, according to his staff. Grassley's bill will closely follow last year's conference report, although it is likely to contain provisions to give judges greater discretion than the House bill to deviate from provisions to use income and debt load criteria, or "means testing," to determine who can file under Chapter 7, staff members said.

More Bankruptcies Than Ever

The credit industry has watched with alarm as bankruptcy filings have increased dramatically in recent years. "Something wild is happening out there," Wallace said.

According to the American Bankruptcy Institute (ABI), a nonpartisan research organization, the annual number of consumer bankruptcy filings has increased from 284,517 in 1984 to 1.4 million in 1997, nearly a five-fold increase. During that time, business bankruptcy filings remained relatively constant, fluctuating between a low of 51,959 in 1995 and a high of 82,446 in 1987, according to the ABI. In 1984, consumer filings accounted for 81.6 percent of all filings. By 1997, consumer filings accounted for 96.2 percent.

Totals for the first nine months of 1998 indicate that it will mark the third consecutive year of a record-setting number of bankruptcy filings, although the rate of growth appears to be slowing.

Wallace and other credit-industry advocates say the numbers clearly point out a disturbing trend toward consumers being more inclined to walk away from their debts. Bankruptcy attorneys who in recent years have been aggressively advertising their services have helped fuel the rise in filings, Wallace said. "It's the success of marketing, I guess," he said.

Consumer groups see a different explanation for the rise in filings. Klein said the problem lies with credit card companies charging excessive interest rates and encouraging consumers to get too far into debt. "The truth here is that powerful credit industry interests are scapegoating the bankruptcy system for problems caused by their high-rate and high-risk lending," Klein said.

Another problem is the growth in home equity lending, with some creditors allowing equity loans that increase a borrower's debt to 125 percent of the home's value, Klein said. This increases the potential for mortgage default, which tends to push debtors toward bankruptcy to avoid foreclosure, Klein said.

He added that so far, the Clinton administration has been an advocate for consumers, and the Senate appears inclined toward a more debtor-friendly approach than the House.

Means-Testing Disagreement

The main obstacle to a bankruptcy overhaul in 1998 was a dispute over means-testing provisions for people seeking to file for Chapter 7 debt relief. It involved the amount of discretion judges would have to depart from the means-testing thresholds. Chapter 7 absolves much of the filer's unsecured debts, such as those generated by credit cards, after the sale of the debtor's assets. The credit industry believes many people filing under Chapter 7 should be required to file under Chapter 13, which involves a reorganization of debt under a repayment plan. Seventy-one percent of the 1.4 million consumer bankruptcy filings in 1997 were under Chapter 7, according to the ABI.

The 1998 agreement would have required a debtor with an income above the median to file under Chapter 13 if the person could pay at least 25 percent of debts within five years. The report language also gave judges discretion to permit debtors to file under Chapter 7 under special circumstances, such as a major illness in the family.

Clinton wanted to give judges greater leeway in granting exceptions to the means-testing provisions, but the credit industry objected.

"Judges are hostile to unsecured creditors' interests, the credit industry believes," said Samuel J. Gerdano, executive director of the ABI. Unsecured credit includes credit card debt and other forms of debt that are not backed by specific assets. With the bill facing a veto threat and the credit industry objecting to the president's requested changes, the legislation died.

Gerdano predicted that while Congress will start with last year's conference report, it will have to give ground to debtor interests to get a bill that can win Senate and presidential approval.

97 Percent Unaffected?

A study released late last year by the ABI suggested that haggling over means-testing limits may have a relatively small practical effect because only a small percentage of people who file under Chapter 7 can afford to repay their debt. The study used the needs-based test included in the bankruptcy bill that the House passed June 10. Under that bill, anyone who earned at least the national median income — about $51,000 for a family of four — and was able to repay 20 percent or more of unsecured debts over five years would be transferred into a Chapter 13 repayment plan.

The study, conducted by two Creighton University School of Law professors, found that only 3 percent of the people who filed under Chapter 7 met the criteria to be moved to Chapter 13. In other words, 97 percent would not have been affected by the requirements.

The ABI takes no position on the bankruptcy overhaul and includes members from the credit industry and debtor advocacy groups. Gerdano said the study lends support to arguments in both camps.

Opponents of tightening Chapter 7 criteria say the study shows there is no widespread abuse of Chapter 7 by people who can afford to pay off their debts, and thus there is no need for a far-reaching overhaul. The credit industry can argue that the study proves that the legislation is being carefully targeted at system abuses and would not erect unfair barriers to Chapter 7 filings. Creditors also can say that while 3 percent does not sound like much, it represents about 30,000 situations every year in which bankruptcy laws are used to avoid debts that people can afford to repay, Gerdano said.

He said overall consumer debt levels remain "very high," and there is a strong correlation between bankruptcy filings and overall household debt. Debt levels tend to go up during hot economic times as consumers feel freer to spend.

Despite the unresolved issues on means-testing and judicial discretion, Gerdano said he is expecting bankruptcy legislation in the 106th Congress. "As soon as the decks are cleared on impeachment, I think we'll have some action," he said.

Farm Bankruptcy

There appears to be little disagreement over at least one bankruptcy-related issue sure to come up this year — renewing the Chapter 12 family farm bankruptcy provisions.

Chapter 12, which allows farmers to continue operating while reorganizing their debts, was extended by Congress last fall in the omnibus appropriations bill (PL 105-277), but is set to expire April 1. Gekas wants to extend Chapter 12 again, and he favors a stand-alone bill rather than a provision in a broader bankruptcy bill, spokeswoman Dearnley said.

Grassley, a strong advocate of Chapter 12, has introduced legislation (S 260) to make it permanent. Grassley's bill also would broaden the criteria for who could file under Chapter 12. No markup date has been set on the legislation.

House Committee Debates Role of Credit Card Issuers

MARCH 27 — Republicans say a bankruptcy overhaul bill that is headed for a House Judiciary Committee markup within a few weeks is a fair, reasonable attempt to curb egregious abuses of the bankruptcy system. But several provisions face strong opposition from congressional Democrats, who say the bill is heavily stacked against low-income debtors. Among other issues, the parties are squabbling over the degree to which credit card companies are responsible for record numbers of bankruptcies in recent years.

On a party-line vote of 5-3, the House Judiciary Subcommittee on Commercial and Administrative Law approved a bankruptcy overhaul bill (HR 833) on March 25. The bill was introduced by subcommittee Chairman George W. Gekas, R-Pa., and amended with a substitute that made technical changes. The bill will likely be marked up by the full committee shortly after the spring recess, a Republican staff member said.

Last year, the House adopted a conference report on a bankruptcy overhaul bill, but the measure never came up for a vote in the Senate, in part because the Clinton administration threatened a veto, saying the bill was too pro-creditor. Gekas' bill generally follows the conference report, and he says that last year's 300-125 vote in favor of it shows that it had bipartisan backing.

But subcommittee ranking member Jerrold Nadler, D-N.Y., produced a letter from the Office of Management and Budget indicating that President Clinton would reject HR 833 unless Republicans accepted substantial changes. "We can still be confident that we are wasting our time on a bill that will be veto bait," Nadler said.

One of the bill's primary goals is to steer more debtors away from Chapter 7 bankruptcy filings, which involve liquidation of assets to pay off some creditors, with most remaining debts being discharged. Creditors want the courts to force more debtors to file under Chapter 13 of the bankruptcy code, which requires a reorganization of debts under a repayment plan.

Subcommittee Democrats pursued several debtor-friendly measures that Republicans rejected. Republicans mainly held together at Gekas' request to preserve the bill without major changes, although several defected to support a Democratic amendment that would dramatically curtail debtors' ability to shelter multimillion-dollar homes from bankruptcy liquidation.

Homestead Exemption

Democrats argued that current bankruptcy laws allow wealthy people to shelter assets by moving to a handful of states with laws that exempt homes from bankruptcy proceedings. People who plan to file for bankruptcy can move to those states, purchase expensive homes and then get their debts discharged while keeping their homes, Democrats said. Although numerous states place limits on the value of a home that can be sheltered — under $20,000 in some states — five states have no limit. Those states are Florida, Iowa, Kansas, South Dakota and Texas.

Bill Delahunt, D-Mass., called it a "gaping loophole" in the law, and proposed an amendment to place a nationwide cap of $100,000 on the homestead exemption. The cap was changed to $250,000 at the suggestion of Melvin Watt, D-N.C., in an effort to sway some Republican votes. "If ever there was a case for a national standard, this is it," Delahunt said.

Gekas called for rejection of the amendment, saying the bill already contained a measure to combat homestead abuses with a two-year residency requirement in a particular state before debtors could claim homestead protection. But Rep. Spencer Bachus, R-Ala., started a flow of Republican defections by saying he agreed that protecting multimillion- dollar homes was unfair. The amendment was approved, 10-2, with Gekas and Joe Scarborough, R-Fla., voting against it.

Credit Cards

Democrats also complained that the bill fails to recognize that credit card company practices deserve a large share of the blame for the increasing number of bankruptcy filings, which hit a record 1.4 million in 1998. Democrats have accused credit card companies of granting excessive credit lines to poor customers, luring customers into high-interest debts by offering low introductory interest rates, offering payment options that are too small to reduce principal balances and other practices designed to crank up consumer debt levels.

Delahunt said the bill "goes after lower- and middle-class debtors" while making it easier for credit card companies to collect their balances. The bill also would help credit card companies "leapfrog" their balances in front of other types of debts that should come first, such as child support, Delahunt said.

Republicans have countered that

their bill is targeted at the small number of people who abuse the bankruptcy system, and that advocates for the poor would complain loudly if credit card companies shut down the flow of credit to low-income people.

Delahunt proposed an amendment that would require greater disclosure of credit card terms and prohibit several credit card practices, such as charging fees for customers who pay their balance in full each month. It would also generally prohibit issuing credit cards to minors without parental permission.

Gekas said the issue of credit card practices belonged in the banking committees, and the amendment was defeated on a 5-4 party-line vote.

Means Testing

Democrats also object to the means-testing provisions in the bill, intended to prohibit some debtors from filing under Chapter 7. The House bill generally would require a debtor with an income above the median to file under Chapter 13 if he could pay at least 25 percent of his debts within five years. Clinton and congressional Democrats want to give judges greater leeway to take into account special circumstances before barring debtors from filing under Chapter 7, and Nadler sought an amendment to do that. Gekas said he believed the bill adequately dealt with special circumstances, and Nadler's amendment was rejected, 6-4, on a party-line vote.

At the end of the first day of the markup March 24, Watt called the procedure a "charade" that was failing to advance agreements on the issues.

In the Senate, the Judiciary Committee delayed a markup on a bankruptcy overhaul measure (S 625) sponsored by Charles E. Grassley, R-Iowa. That bill is similar to HR 833, but would give judges greater leeway in determining who could file under Chapter 7.

Both Chambers' Bills Slowed by Partisan Bickering

APRIL 24 — Committee leaders in both chambers, who failed to complete markups on bankruptcy overhaul bills by their April 22 goal, mapped out a tight schedule to resume efforts and send bills to the floor the week of April 26. But a long list of amendments remains unresolved, including a highly contentious abortion-related measure that failed in the House Judiciary Committee but is likely to reappear in the Senate.

In the House, a three-day markup of a bill (HR 833) to overhaul consumer bankruptcy laws alternated between partisan bickering and bipartisan progress before the Judiciary Committee left for the weekend on a note of confusion. The panel is scheduled to return April 27 to finish the markup, and the legislation is scheduled for House floor consideration April 28 or 29.

Opening statements at the markup April 20 included blistering attacks by Democrats, who called the Republican-sponsored bill a pro-lender assault on consumers. "This is a one-sided bill in the extreme," said ranking Democrat John Conyers Jr. of Michigan. "It's great for the credit card companies. It's bad for almost everyone else."

The House Judiciary Subcommittee on Commercial and Administrative Law approved the bill, introduced by subcommittee Chairman George W. Gekas, R-Pa., by a 5-3 party-line vote March 25.

One of the bill's primary goals is to steer more debtors away from Chapter 7 bankruptcy filings, which involve liquidation of assets to pay off some creditors, with most remaining debts being discharged. Creditors want the courts to force more debtors to file under Chapter 13 of the bankruptcy code, which requires a reorganization of debts under a repayment plan.

Democrats objected to a means test in the bill, which generally would require debtors with an income above the median to file under Chapter 13 if they could pay at least 25 percent or $5,000 of their debts (whichever was less) within five years.

Democrats and Republicans also argued over the method that should be used to calculate a debtor's disposable income available to repay debt. This calculation is a crucial part of the means test and helps determine whether debtors are eligible to file under Chapter 7. Democrats want to give judges greater leeway to take into account special circumstances before barring debtors from filing under Chapter 7. The Clinton administration also has pushed for greater judicial leeway, and a veto threat over the issue helped sink bankruptcy legislation in the 105th Congress.

Three Days in House Judiciary

At the full committee markup, the tone shifted toward conciliation after opening statements when Chairman Henry J. Hyde, R-Ill., offered the first three amendments, all of which the committee approved with the support of Democrats, who seemed surprised by Hyde's pro-debtor measures. The three amendments would:

- Exempt families below the regional median income from being forced out of Chapter 7 into Chapter 13. It was approved by voice vote with a few Republicans voicing dissent.
- Allow debtors to include bankruptcy-related administrative and legal fees in their list of expenses used to determine whether a debtor qualifies to file under Chapter 7. This amendment would also change the disposable income standard in the means test from $5,000 to $6,000 and eliminate the 25 percent alternative. It was approved, 18-11.
- Alter the way a debtor's monthly expenses are calculated. Expenses are used to determine the amount of a debtor's income available to apply toward debts. The underlying bill called for using an IRS calculation of estimated living expenses, which Democrats opposed. Hyde's amendment would remove this provision and give bankruptcy judges discretion in determining a debtor's ability to repay debt. The amendment was approved, 13-11.

Gekas said Hyde's amendment to eliminate the IRS standard would kill the bill, but Conyers called it "another very important step forward." Subcommittee ranking member Jerrold Nadler, D-N.Y., who in his opening statement called the subcommittee document "one of the most unbalanced special-interest bills" he had ever seen, was guarded but pleased by Hyde's moves.

Republicans quickly began searching for ways to undo some of Hyde's work. On April 22, the panel voted 20-17 to approve an amendment by Lindsey Graham, R-S.C., that would essentially strike the Hyde amendments and replace them with several minor changes to the original means test provision in the Gekas bill. Two Democrats — Rick Boucher of Virginia and Steven R. Rothman of New Jersey — voted to support the amendment, and three Republicans — Hyde, F. James Sensenbrenner Jr. of Wisconsin and Spencer Bachus of Alabama — voted against it.

The Graham amendment would restore the means test based on the IRS standards in the subcommittee-approved measure but would add private school tuition to the list of expenses exempt from the calculation of disposable income, and enable debtors to claim up to 5 percent more in food and clothing expenses than the standards allow. The amendment as drafted would repeal the three Hyde amendments, but Graham said he meant only to reinsert the provisions on IRS standards. Graham said he would offer an amendment to rectify this problem when the markup resumes.

On April 21, the GOP thwarted Democratic efforts to adopt amendments related to abortion and gun violence. Nadler offered an amendment aimed at people facing civil or criminal penalties for harassment or violence directed toward abortion clinics or their patients. The amendment sought to prevent people facing such penalties from discharging those debts in a bankruptcy filing. "This is a clear abuse of the bankruptcy laws," Nadler said.

Republicans said current law already covers the issue because debts arising from malicious conduct cannot be discharged in a bankruptcy proceeding. Charles T. Canady, R-Fla., said Democrats were injecting an emotional issue that does not belong in bankruptcy legislation. "This is a good way to derail this bill," he said. The amendment failed on an 18-13 party-line vote.

Martin T. Meehan, D-Mass., offered an amendment to prohibit gun manufacturers from discharging debts arising from civil lawsuits related to gun use. Some local governments have sued manufacturers to recover damages for gun-related crimes. Bob Barr, R-Ga., a board member of the National Rifle Association, called the amendment "so bogus as to hardly warrant debate." Barr has introduced legislation (HR 1032) to prohibit such lawsuits. Meehan's amendment failed, 19-8.

Another Nadler amendment related to reaffirmations was defeated, 12-16, with Hyde crossing party lines to support it. Nadler sought to remove a provision that would prohibit class-action lawsuits based on lender abuses of reaffirmations, which are private repayment agreements between debtors and lenders. Critics say lenders abuse them and take advantage of debtors who do not fully understand the law.

Also on April 21, the committee weakened a provision to cap the homestead exemption for bankruptcy filers at $250,000. Democrats say current laws allow wealthy people to shelter assets by moving to a handful of states with laws that exempt primary homes from bankruptcy proceedings. People who plan to file for bankruptcy can move to those states, purchase expensive houses and then get their debts discharged while keeping their homes, Democrats said. Most states limit the value of a home that can be sheltered, but Florida, Iowa, Kansas, South Dakota and Texas have no limit. Florida and Texas were cited repeatedly by some Democrats as the biggest havens for people seeking to shelter assets from creditors.

Sheila Jackson-Lee, D-Texas, introduced a measure to eliminate the cap, saying that states should have the right to set their own caps and that abuses were exaggerated. Ed Bryant, R-Tenn., offered an amendment to the Jackson-Lee amendment that would preserve the $250,000 cap, but would allow states to opt out of the restriction by passing state laws to do so. Bryant called his provision a compromise that would force states to reconsider the issue before retaining an unlimited homestead exemption. The Bryant measure was approved, 18-12, and Jackson-Lee's measure was approved as amended, 18-15. All six panel members from Texas or Florida — two Democrats and four Republicans — supported both measures.

Senate Plans

Senate Judiciary Committee Chairman Orrin G. Hatch, R-Utah, said he plans to continue work on S 625 on April 27. At the April 22 markup, panel members raised and pushed aside several issues. Some were withdrawn to work out compromises; others were set aside for lack of a quorum.

In interviews after the markup, Hatch and Charles E. Schumer, D-N.Y., said the Senate, like the House, is headed for debate over an abortion provision. Schumer said he will introduce a provision similar to the House measure. Hatch said he will meet with Schumer in an attempt to keep abortion out of the bankruptcy debate. "It shouldn't be on the bankruptcy bill," Hatch said.

Panels OK Bills, Save Showdowns For House and Senate Floors

MAY 1 — Bankruptcy overhaul bills are speeding toward potentially bruising floor fights as Democrats prepare to press their efforts to roll back or weaken the Republican measures. Floor votes could occur in both chambers the week of May 3.

The House Judiciary Committee approved a bill (HR 833) to overhaul consumer bankruptcy laws on April 28 after a five-day markup. The vote was 22-13, with Barney Frank, D-Mass., voting "present." In a nod to committee Democrats, Chairman Henry J. Hyde, R-Ill., who crossed party lines to support several Democratic amendments, said he would seek a rule to allow a limited number of floor amendments.

The Senate Judiciary Committee approved its overhaul measure (S 625), 14-4, on April 27. The Senate's more bipartisan vote came only by skirting disagreements on several key issues that will likely come up again on the floor. Chairman Orrin G. Hatch, R-Utah, successfully encouraged Democrats to withdraw several contentious amendments in hopes that compromises could be worked out.

Central Issues

Central to both bills is a new means test for determining whether a debtor is allowed to file under Chapter 7 of the bankruptcy code, which involves liquidation of assets to pay off some creditors, with most remaining debts being discharged. Creditors want courts to force more debtors to file un-

Temporary Extensions of Chapter 12

House Passes Extension

MARCH 13 — The House passed a bill March 11 to prevent the expiration of a section of the bankruptcy code used by family farmers to prevent foreclosures. The vote was 418-1. *(Vote 42, p. H-20)*

Chapter 12 of the bankruptcy code is set to expire on April 1, but the House bill (HR 808 — H Rept 106-45) would extend that deadline six months. Chapter 12, which has been extended twice previously, allows farmers to restructure their debts and continue operating.

The bill, sponsored by Nick Smith, R-Mich., originally called for a three-month extension, but amendments approved by the House Judiciary Committee on March 2 stretched the deadline to six months.

While there is widespread and bipartisan support in Congress for permanently authorizing Chapter 12, there are disagreements on whether to tackle the issue as a stand-alone measure or as part of the broader bankruptcy overhaul legislation that Congress will take up later this year.

In the Senate, Charles E. Grassley, R-Iowa, chairman of the Judiciary Subcommittee on Administrative Oversight and the Courts, has introduced a bill (S 260) to make Chapter 12 permanent. The fiscal 1999 supplemental appropriations measure approved by the Senate Appropriations Committee (S 544 — S Rept 106-8) would extend Chapter 12 for six months.

In the House, a broad bankruptcy overhaul bill (HR 833) sponsored by George W. Gekas, R-Pa., chairman of the Judiciary Subcommittee on Commercial and Administrative Law, includes a provision to make Chapter 12 permanent.

During floor debate March 9, Gekas urged enactment of HR 808 as a means of protecting farmers while Congress tackles other bankruptcy issues. Tammy Baldwin, D-Wis., called Chapter 12 "a safety net of last resort for our farmers."

Senate Clears Bill for President

MARCH 27 — President Clinton is expected to sign a measure (HR 808) to delay the expiration of a farmer-friendly provision of the bankruptcy code that cleared the Senate by voice vote on March 24, just days before the law was set to lapse.

Chapter 12 was set to expire April 1. The House passed the six-month extension (H Rept 106-45) on March 11.

HR 808 will keep Chapter 12 on the books while Congress takes up a broader bankruptcy overhaul this year. Clinton supports Chapter 12 and is expected to sign HR 808, a Democratic staff aide said.

Chapter 12 prevents foreclosure and allows a farmer to continue operating while seeking bankruptcy relief. A House bankruptcy overhaul bill (HR 833), which includes a provision to make Chapter 12 permanent, was approved by the Judiciary Subcommittee on Commercial and Administrative Law on March 25. At the markup, Rep. Bill Delahunt, D-Mass., sought to expand the reach of Chapter 12 to include small commercial fishermen. The effort was rejected, 6-4, on a party-line vote.

In the Senate, Charles E. Grassley, R-Iowa, has introduced a stand-alone bill (S 260) to make Chapter 12 permanent.

If Congress had allowed Chapter 12 to expire temporarily, it could have created legal headaches for bankruptcy courts, attorneys and filers, said Samuel J. Gerdano, executive director of the American Bankruptcy Institute.

Senate Passes Second Extension

OCTOBER 2 — A key senator vowed Sept. 28 that despite repeated delays, an overhaul of the nation's bankruptcy laws will make it to the floor this year. The previous day, the House salvaged a popular bankruptcy program for family farmers that has stalled as part of the broad overhaul.

The Senate overhaul bill (S 625 — S Rept 106-49) has been bogged down in partisan squabbling over whether to allow unrelated amendments on the floor.

Charles E. Grassley, R-Iowa, who has worked with Democrats to forge compromises on bankruptcy legislation, said on the Senate floor that the bankruptcy overhaul will move soon. "We are committed to bringing this bill to a vote, this year," he said.

The bill for family farmers (HR 2942), which passed by voice vote Sept. 27, would extend Chapter 12 of the bankruptcy code for three months past its current Oct. 1 expiration date. A similar Senate bill (S 1606), passed by voice vote Sept. 30, would provide a nine-month extension.

Chapter 12, enacted in 1986, allows bankrupt family farmers to keep operating while they reorganize their debts. It was last extended in March (PL 106-5).

House Clears

OCTOBER 9 — The House cleared legislation to extend a popular bankruptcy provision aimed at helping struggling family farmers continue operating. The bill (S 1606) would grant a nine-month extension for Chapter 12 of the bankruptcy code, which expired Oct. 1.

Chapter 12 allows family farmers to keep operating while they reorganize their debts. The temporary extension cleared the House Oct. 4 on a voice vote. The Senate approved the measure Sept. 30. A larger bankruptcy overhaul (S 625), which would make Chapter 12 permanent, is stalled and waiting for Senate floor time.

Sen. Charles E. Grassley, R-Iowa, sponsor of the broad bankruptcy overhaul, initially introduced S 1606 as a measure to make Chapter 12 permanent, but the legislation was amended to a nine-month extension.

der Chapter 13 of the code, which requires a reorganization of debts under a repayment plan.

Democrats and Republicans in both chambers wrangled over how the means test should be calculated and the amount of discretion judges should have to deviate from the rules. In the end, both bills generally retained their original means test, which would rely on a combination of income and expense factors, including an IRS calculation of estimated living expenses. Democrats strongly opposed the means test as too rigid. They also maintained that the IRS standards, which the IRS uses for tax collection purposes, do a poor job of measuring actual living expenses. The Clinton administration has pushed for greater judicial leeway, and a veto threat over the issue helped sink bankruptcy legislation in the 105th Congress.

Another key point of partisan division is whether credit card companies should be more closely regulated. Democrats argue that the companies bear a large share of the burden for the increasing number of bankruptcies in recent years, and they have argued unsuccessfully in both chambers for greater disclosure requirements for credit card terms and conditions.

Consumer groups generally have opposed the measures. Consumers Union, which publishes Consumer Reports magazine, issued a statement April 27 criticizing both bills, and the House bill in particular. It said the House measure would institute "dozens of anti-consumer practices while rewarding the credit industry's risky behavior."

House Committee Action

In the House, Hyde offered an amendment that would give judges more leeway in determining who is eligible to file under Chapter 7, a move that was endorsed by committee Democrats and approved, 13-11, by the committee April 20. However, other committee Republicans balked at the measure. On April 22 the committee approved by voice vote an amendment, introduced by Lindsey Graham, R-S.C., to undo Hyde's means test amendment and other amendments. On April 27, the committee approved by voice vote a Graham amendment that restored all but the Hyde means test.

Republicans turned back an effort by Jerrold Nadler, D-N.Y., to ensure that child support payments owed to spouses, family and the government would be given a higher priority in Chapter 13 repayment plans than any other debts owed to government entities. Bill sponsor George W. Gekas, R-Pa., opposed the measure, saying the underlying bill struck the proper balance among competing creditors. "Taxpayers should be able to benefit from some of the aspects of bankruptcy" overhaul, Gekas said. Gekas offered an amendment to Nadler's measure that stripped most of its provisions. It was approved, 17-10, and the underlying Nadler amendment then was approved by voice vote.

Republicans also thwarted numerous Democratic efforts to exempt certain categories of income, such as Social Security benefits and disaster relief payments, from the means test used to determine eligibility to file under Chapter 7.

Gekas argued repeatedly that a bill provision that would exempt families below the median income from the means test was sufficient protection for the poor, and that wealthier people whose incomes were supplemented by special categories of income should not have a portion of their income sheltered from the means test.

But the committee approved, 21-7, a Nadler amendment to exempt payments to victims of war crimes from the means test.

When the underlying bill came up for a vote, two Democrats, Rick Boucher of Virginia and Steven R. Rothman of New Jersey, joined Republicans in voting for it. Frank, who broke from his party on several amendments, voted "present." After the markup, Frank said in an interview that he supported an overhaul of bankruptcy laws, but he opposed several provisions of the committee bill, including the means test and the lack of disclosure requirements for credit card companies.

Senate Committee Action

There were fewer partisan splits in the Senate than in the House, but the comity came at the expense of leaving several difficult issues unresolved.

At the urging of Hatch, who labored to move a bill with bipartisan support, Democrats agreed to withdraw several amendments on controversial issues and said they would try to work out bipartisan agreements for floor consideration. Other amendments were defeated with a pledge from Republicans to try to work out compromises on the floor.

Senate Majority Leader Trent Lott, R-Miss., has promised floor time for the bill, an aide to a key committee Republican said, but no date has been set.

Unresolved issues include:

- **Means test.** Democratic efforts to soften the means test failed, but Hatch said a floor compromise was possible.

"The IRS standards . . . are cookie cutter," said Charles E. Schumer, D-N.Y. "They don't fit the needs here." Schumer offered an amendment to alter the means test by, among other things, replacing the IRS standard with calculations based on data from the Bureau of Labor Statistics. Democrats argue that such statistics provide a more accurate measure of living expenses. Schumer's amendment failed, 7-11, with Joseph R. Biden Jr., D-Del., joining Republicans in opposing it. Bill sponsor Charles E. Grassley, R-Iowa, and Hatch said Schumer's provision was too complex, but Hatch said a floor compromise might work.

- **Evictions**. Russell D. Feingold, D-Wis., withdrew an amendment to make it more difficult to evict a tenant during bankruptcy proceedings. Hatch pledged to work out an agreement for the floor.
- **Credit counseling.** The Senate bill would require credit counseling for Chapter 7 filers. Democrats argued that judges should have discretion to waive the requirement in special circumstances, but a Feingold amendment to accomplish that was defeated, 9-9.
- **Credit cards**. Democrats have pushed hard to hold credit card companies at least partially responsible for rising consumer debt levels, saying they use deceptive practices and aggressive mass-marketing techniques to lure consumers into building up excessive debt levels with high interest rates.

Schumer offered an amendment to require more thorough disclosure by credit card companies of late fees and introductory "teaser rates" that escalate automatically. The measure would also place rate and fee disclosure requirements on credit card solicitations on the Internet. Schumer agreed to withdraw the amendment after Republicans pledged to work on a compromise.

"There's no question some consumer protection is going to have to be in this bill," said Robert G. Torricelli, D-N.J. Grassley said Republicans would be willing to discuss consumer protection and credit card issues.

Abortion-Related Fines

Democrats in both chambers have pushed measures aimed at those responsible for violence or other unlawful acts directed at health care facilities that provide abortions. The amendments would prohibit debts arising from civil or criminal cases related to such acts from being discharged in bankruptcy proceedings. Democrats have said that militant factions in the anti-abortion movement have vowed to use the bankruptcy laws to avoid paying fines or penalties.

Republicans said current law already covers the issue because debts arising from malicious conduct cannot be discharged in a bankruptcy proceeding. They argued that Democrats were trying to inject an emotional, unrelated issue into the bankruptcy debate.

In the House committee April 21, the GOP thwarted Democratic efforts to adopt an abortion-related amendment by an 18-13, party-line vote.

In the Senate committee, Schumer pushed an abortion amendment, saying the law was not clear enough. Republicans again said the issue was unrelated, and Biden agreed. "We should keep this off the bill," Biden said. However, Biden voted for Schumer's amendment, which failed, 9-9.

In response to the Democratic efforts on abortion, Robert C. Smith, R-N.H., threatened to introduce an amendment that would bar debts arising from abortion-related malpractice cases from being discharged in bankruptcy proceedings.

Smith said he did not introduce his amendment because Schumer's abortion amendment failed. After the markup, Smith said he would offer his amendment on the floor if Democrats insisted on pursuing their abortion-related measures there.

House Passes Bill To Make It Harder To Erase Debts

MAY 8 — The House overwhelmingly passed a bill May 5 to make it more difficult for consumers and small businesses to file for bankruptcy protection, a measure favored by credit card companies, banks and other lenders.

The vote came after the House debated 11 amendments to the bill (HR 833), several of which aimed to temper provisions that many consumer groups and bankruptcy experts said were too onerous for debtors. The final tally was 313-108. *(Vote 115, p. H-46)*

The bill aims to force more debtors to file under Chapter 13 of the bankruptcy code, which requires some repayment of debt, and to limit access to Chapter 7, which erases debt after liquidation of assets.

In the next few weeks, the Senate is expected to take up a measure (S 625) similar in structure but less specific about when filers should be moved from Chapter 7 to Chapter 13. Creditors are bracing for attempts by Sens. Edward M. Kennedy, D-Mass., Charles E. Schumer, D-N.Y., and others to rein in credit card solicitations to young people and others thought to be at risk of amassing too much debt.

In the House, those siding with consumer groups made little headway as moderate Democrats teamed with nearly all Republicans in supporting the bill, an effort to stem the number of personal bankruptcies, which totaled 1.4 million in 1998, up 94 percent since 1990.

Bill opponents got a surprise win when Republicans agreed to amend the measure to preclude Social Security and Medicare payments from calculations of filers' ability to repay debts. The proposal, offered by John Conyers Jr., D-Mich., as part of a procedural motion, was adopted by voice vote.

The House also accepted by voice vote an amendment by Democrats James P. Moran of Virginia, Cal Dooley of California and Gary L. Ackerman of New York to require credit card companies to disclose in solicitations or applications how long it would take a consumer to pay off debt by paying the minimum each month. The amendment would also require credit card companies to disclose such information in Web site solicitations, to state clearly when "teaser" rates would expire and what interest rates would then apply, and to clearly disclose deadlines and late fees.

Sponsors said none of those requirements would unduly inconvenience credit card issuers, many of whom already provide such information. Moran said the proposal aimed to help consumers understand their obligations but not to "inappropriately load up" the credit card industry. Bill opponent Jerrold Nadler, D-N.Y., said the amendment should have required more of credit card companies, though he said it "may do a little bit of good."

The Clinton administration warned in a statement May 5 that it thought the bill was tilted toward creditors, and that President Clinton's advisers would recommend that he veto it. "The bill focuses on perceived abuse of the bankruptcy system by debtors without adequately addressing abuses by creditors," the statement said.

For Creditor or Debtor?

Throughout the debate a small but vocal group of liberal Democrats, and occasionally Republicans such as Judiciary Chairman Henry J. Hyde of Illinois, argued that the bill would crack down too hard on bankruptcy filers. Most Republicans and several conservative and moderate Democrats argued that it was fair to require those with the ability to pay their debts to do so.

Like a similar bill that made it to a House-Senate conference last year, HR 833 aims to restrict access to Chapter 7, which liquidates a filer's debts after the sale of many assets, and force more debtors into Chapter 13, which requires payment of debts in three to five years, while protecting many assets from repossession.

The bill would require courts to transfer debtors from Chapter 7 to Chapter 13 if it was determined that they could pay at least $100 a month of unsecured debts, such as credit card balances — after they had paid attorney fees, monthly living costs, a minor child's tuition, all secured debts (such as a mortgage) and any unsecured debts given priority by the court.

Trustees would consider a person's ability to pay for 60 months, so applicants judged likely to have $6,000 or more in disposable income over that period would be moved into Chapter 13. Monthly expenses would be determined by using IRS standards measuring the average expenditure for food, housekeeping supplies, clothing and other necessities.

An exception to this "means test" would be made for filers earning the median income or less for their geographic region. Debtors making less could file under Chapter 7, even if they had some disposable income. Median income varies throughout the country, but generally hovers around $50,000 a year for a family of four.

The bill would also make it harder for debtors to nullify debts. It would require filers to continue paying some credit card debts, something not now required, and it would prevent trustees from reducing the amount a filer owed on a secured debt, such as a car, acquired within five years of filing for bankruptcy.

Nadler attempted to change many of those provisions with a substitute amendment, but it failed, 149-272. *(Vote 114, p. H-44)*

The House also rejected, 184-238, an amendment by Hyde and Conyers that would have removed the IRS standards from monthly expense calculations, and required the Executive Office of the U.S. Trustees to draw up guidelines that courts and bankruptcy trustees would consider when judging the validity of monthly expense claims. *(Vote 110, p. H-44)*

Hyde voted for the final bill but argued vociferously for the change, saying it added "a little humanity" to the bill. The IRS statistics have long been criticized as parsimonious. Hyde worried that the standards would give distorted pictures of debtors' expenses, and force courts and trustees to require too much for debt repayment. "What will debtors, their spouses and their children be able to live on?" he asked.

But bill supporters such as House Majority Leader Dick Armey, R-Texas, disagreed. Armey said that "for too many years, what we've done is we have written law in this body to leave things . . . to the discretion to the court." And Rick Boucher, D-Va., said the amendment would "seriously undermine" the bill by allowing trustees and judges too much discretion. Under current law, trustees and judges can move debtors from Chapter 7 to Chapter 13 if they find "substantial abuse" in the filing, but bill proponents say that is not done frequently.

In other action, the House:

- Approved an amendment by Moran to require agencies providing bankruptcy assistance to make sure clients know they are in the business of filing bankruptcy cases. Moran said this would stop "mills" that funnel clients into bankruptcy, regardless of whether they want to file. Melvin Watt, D-N.C., said it would impose undue burdens on legitimate credit counselors and others. The vote was 373-47. *(Vote 111, p. H-44)*
- Adopted by voice vote an amendment by Lindsey Graham, R-S.C., to prevent bankruptcy filers from discharging private student loans. Under current law, debtors given bankruptcy protection must repay federally guaranteed and insured student loans.
- Defeated, 192-230, an amendment by Watt to remove requirements that bankruptcy applicants file three years of tax returns. The proposal would have required the returns only upon request by trustees, creditors or another party. Watt said it would otherwise create unnecessary paperwork for courts dealing with bankruptcy applications, most of which are never contested. *(Vote 113, p. H-44)*
- Defeated, 143-278, an amendment by Conyers to waive provisions requiring small businesses to file more information in a shorter time about a Chapter 11 reorganization, if the provisions could result in the loss of five or more jobs. *(Vote 112, p. H-44)*

Lott Seeks Action On Senate Bill

SEPTEMBER 18 — Senate Majority Leader Trent Lott, R-Miss., filed a cloture petition Sept. 16 to try to bring up the chamber's long-stalled bankruptcy overhaul bill (S 625) under rules limiting debate and amendments. A vote on the petition is scheduled for Sept. 21, raising the prospect that the bill could hit the floor later in the week if 60 votes are obtained.

Lott and his staff have repeatedly said that previous delays were related to scheduling conflicts. But Sen. Edward M. Kennedy, D-Mass., has angered Republicans by insisting that he will push an amendment that would increase the federal minimum wage by $1 an hour, to $6.15, by January 2001.

The House overwhelmingly passed it's bankruptcy bill (HR 833) on May 5.

Senate Measure Remains Mired In Amendments

NOVEMBER 13 — With lawmakers growing eager to adjourn for the year, the prospects for finishing Senate debate on an overhaul of the nation's bankruptcy laws looked increasingly shaky as the chamber struggled to make progress on more than 200 amendments.

Some amendments were dealt with on the floor and dozens were withdrawn, but the Senate still has many hours of work to do before reaching a final vote on the bill (S 625). The measure remained on the floor Nov. 8-10, while offstage GOP leaders wrangled with the White House to clear the logjam over unresolved fiscal 2000 spending bills.

The bankruptcy bill aims to force more debtors to file under Chapter 13 of the bankruptcy code, which requires some repayment of debt, and to limit access to Chapter 7, which erases debt after liquidation of assets.

John Czwartacki, spokesman for Senate Majority Leader Trent Lott, R-Miss., said Lott hoped to complete the bankruptcy overhaul before Congress adjourns, but he stopped short of promising that the Senate would continue to work on it if the spending bills were settled. Phil Gramm, R-Texas, said he did not think the Senate would stay in session just to finish a bankruptcy bill. "I'm not opposed to finishing it up, but I would be surprised," Gramm said Nov. 10.

Veto Threat

Even if the bill wins Senate passage, it faces a veto threat over a Republican-backed amendment to raise the minimum wage by $1 an hour over three years, while providing $18.4 billion in tax breaks for businesses. The current minimum wage is $5.15 an hour.

Democrats and the White House

complained that the amendment, offered by Pete V. Domenici, R-N.M., contained too much in tax breaks. They also favored a two-year phase-in for the minimum wage increase.

The administration also opposes an amendment by Orrin G. Hatch, R-Utah, on illegal drugs. The measure includes efforts to crack down on methamphetamine production and boost the minimum penalties for distributing powdered cocaine. It was approved, 50-49, on Nov. 10. *(Vote 360, p. S-71)*

The House passed its version of a bankruptcy overhaul (HR 833) on May 5. It also seeks to force more debtors to file under Chapter 13. Both bills contain a means test — based on income and ability to repay debt — that courts would use to determine whether debtors must be forced out of Chapter 7, although the Senate bill is less specific.

The Senate agreed by voice vote Nov. 9 to several amendments, including a measure that would allow judges to waive bankruptcy filing fees for people unable to pay them, and a provision that would allow courts to dismiss Chapter 7 filings by people convicted of violent crimes or drug trafficking if a victim or other interested party requested it.

However, Senate Republicans defeated Democratic attempts to ease the means test. They also rejected an amendment, sponsored by Democrats Christopher J. Dodd of Connecticut and Edward M. Kennedy of Massachusetts, that would make it more difficult for companies to issue credit cards to people under 21. The amendment was tabled, 59-38, on Nov. 9. *(Vote 359, p. S-71)*

Homestead Cap Approved

The Senate added a provision, sponsored by Herb Kohl, D-Wis., and Jeff Sessions, R-Ala., that would cap the so-called homestead exemption at $100,000. The amount of the exemption currently is set by states. The exemption allows bankruptcy filers to shield their primary residence from seizure during bankruptcy. Five states — Florida, Iowa, Kansas, South Dakota and Texas — have unlimited homestead exemptions, and many senators complained that wealthy debtors abused the system by moving to those locales, pouring their assets into expensive homes and then filing for bankruptcy. Sessions called the practice "an absolute scandal."

But senators from states with unlimited exemptions said a federal cap would needlessly trample on states' rights. Kay Bailey Hutchison, R-Texas, said the bankruptcy bill already deals with people who abuse the homestead exemption by imposing a two-year residency requirement on bankruptcy filers seeking to use it.

The Senate adopted the homestead cap, 76-22, after defeating, 29-69, a second-degree amendment by Hutchison and Sam Brownback, R-Kan., that would have allowed states to opt out of the federal cap. The House bill contains a $250,000 cap with an opt-out provision for states. *(Votes 364, 363, p. S-72)*

The Senate will return to the bankruptcy bill on Nov. 17 when it resumes debate on an amendment by Paul Wellstone, D-Minn., to impose a moratorium on large agribusiness mergers.

Bankruptcy Rewrite Dead For the Year

NOVEMBER 20 — An overhaul of the nation's bankruptcy laws lumbered to a halt in the Senate after weeks of debate and votes on amendments, leaving senators a massive piece of unfinished business when they return next year. They have scheduled a cloture vote for Jan. 25.

The House passed its version of a bankruptcy overhaul (HR 833) on May 5. Both the House and Senate bills seek to force more debtors to file under Chapter 13, which involves a reorganization of debts under a repayment plan, rather than Chapter 7, which involves a liquidation of assets to pay creditors and the discharge of remaining unsecured debts.

Senators made substantial progress on their bill (S 625) by winnowing more than 300 amendments to fewer than a dozen, but the bill fell victim to Congress' eagerness to adjourn for the year after settling on an appropriations agreement with President Clinton.

Senators on Nov. 17 approved by voice vote an amendment by Robert G. Torricelli, D-N.J., to require prominent disclosure of several types of credit card interest rate and payment information. They adopted, 82-16, a proposal by Dianne Feinstein, D-Calif., to require a Federal Reserve report on "the indiscriminate solicitation and extension of credit by the credit industry." Senators also agreed by voice vote Nov. 17 to an amendment by Edward M. Kennedy, D-Mass., that would make Social Security benefits off limits for debt repayment in bankruptcy proceedings. *(Vote 368, p. S-73)*

Even if the bankruptcy bill had reached a final vote, its prospects for passage were dicey. The bill was growing heavy with controversial germane and non-germane amendments, with more on the way. After it became clear that a budget deal was at hand and Congress could adjourn, Majority Leader Trent Lott, R-Miss., decided Nov. 18 to pull the bankruptcy bill rather than battle with Democrats over amendments.

Charles E. Schumer, D-N.Y., had planned to offer an amendment that would prohibit people found guilty of violence at abortion clinics from discharging debts in bankruptcy court related to those violent activities. An amendment by Carl Levin, D-Mich., would bar gun manufacturers from discharging debts arising from lawsuits filed against them by municipalities.

"I'm really surprised and disappointed," Minority Leader Tom Daschle, D-S.D., said Nov. 18 after learning that Lott had pulled the bill. "I hope that we can come back to it sometime very soon . . . these are clearly relevant bankruptcy amendments."

The amendments would have heated up partisan fights on an already troubled bill. It contains an increase of $1 an hour in the minimum wage over three years, added by Republicans to thwart a Democratic minimum wage increase of $1 over two years. Democrats also opposed $18.4 billion in tax cuts included in the GOP measure. The federal minimum wage is currently $5.15 per hour.

In addition, several Republican senators object to a bankruptcy amendment approved Nov. 10 that would override laws in their states that grant unlimited homestead exemptions for personal bankruptcy filers and would cap homestead exemptions nationwide at $100,000. ◆

Chapter 6

BUDGET

The President's Budget: Clinton's Strength Portends A Tough Season for the GOP

FEBRUARY 6 — President Clinton's fiscal 2000 budget is a well-aimed salvo across a battlefield of budget politics that has been dramatically changed by the stunning reversal of the nation's economic fortunes. For Clinton, whose presidency opened with a politically costly deficit-cutting effort and is currently stained by impeachment, the budget and its surplus predictions represent an opportunity to establish a legacy that could redeem his place in history.

Clinton has already presided over a budgetary turnaround and robust economy; now he wants to be the president who saved Social Security and prepared the nation for the retirement of Baby Boomers such as himself.

"With our economy expanding and our surplus rising, we have confidence that we can now look to the long-term challenges of our country to fulfill our obligations to 21st century Americans, both young and old," Clinton said Feb. 1 as he unveiled the budget.

For lawmakers of both parties, most of whom cut their teeth on the politics of deficit reduction that has preoccupied Washington for almost two decades, the upcoming debate over the budget, taxes and the fate of the surplus sets the stage for the next election and could potentially define the parties for years to come.

The fight comes at a time when Republicans and Democrats are searching for new ways to appeal to voters in the critical 2000 election, in which control of the White House and Congress is up for grabs.

The politics of deficit reduction has scuttled many political careers. A hard-fought 1985 vote to cut Social Security helped Republicans lose the Senate the next year. Voters sent President George Bush back to Texas in 1992 in part because he broke his "no new taxes" promise in 1990. And Clinton's 1993 deficit-cutting plan (PL 103-66) helped Democrats lose the House and Senate in the 1994 landslide.

Adapting to the politics of surplus is among the biggest challenges facing the parties, especially as issues such as crime, welfare and tax increases have faded from the political radar screen.

Clinton's $1.8 trillion blueprint for fiscal 2000 forecasts budget surpluses — about $827 billion over the next five years — that would have boggled lawmakers' minds only a year ago. White House officials were ecstatic over the turnaround.

"At the beginning of this administration . . . I could not have imagined that we would go from a period of the very high deficits of the '80s and early '90s to the remarkable period we're in right now, with large surpluses," Treasury Secretary Robert E. Rubin said Feb. 1.

Republicans pointed to their 1995 deficit-cutting drive and their 1997 deal with Clinton as they sought their share of the credit for the surplus figures — which they hope to use for a major tax cut.

"This budget has totally succeeded in drawing a bright line of distinction between the two great political parties in America," said Sen. Phil Gramm, R-Texas, at a Feb. 2 Senate Budget Committee hearing. "We want the family to spend the money, and you want the government to spend the money. . . . I want to thank President Clinton for defining the issue for this Congress, the presidential election and probably the debate for the next decade."

Early Signs of Conflict

Despite the requisite calls from both Republicans and the White House for high-minded bipartisanship, there was no immediate call for the type of split-the-differences deal that might have a chance to become law. Instead, both sides dug in for a battle over taxes.

At the outset, Republicans' chances of returning a big chunk of the surplus to taxpayers appear dim.

Similarly, the chances for much of Clinton's new spending appear dim. The plan is filled with a panoply of new spending and targeted tax cuts that he proposes to finance with an array of politically difficult tax increases, tax loophole closings, accounting gimmicks and new fees and savings. The budget calls for $213 billion in new spending over five years for discretionary programs such as defense, education, health, child care and medical and scientific research.

Still, Clinton, a self-proclaimed "New Democrat," wraps himself in the cloak of fiscal discipline by insisting that most of the surplus be dedicated to buying down the debt — even as he proposes a wave of new spending. His budget contains something for virtually every interest group except the GOP's tax-cutting wing. Instead, Clinton plans to sell the idea of paying down the debt by proposing to sock it away in the trust funds for Social Security and Medicare.

Republicans blasted the Clinton blueprint as a gimmick-loaded return of the Big Government monster, and they vowed that it was dead on arrival.

"In all my years in Congress, I have never seen such a kitchen-sink approach to government," said House Ways and Means Committee Chairman Bill Archer, R-Texas. "It's a throwback to the days when the government tried to solve problems by raising taxes and throwing money at problems."

And Republicans were dismayed at the almost complete lack of detail on Clinton's plans to fix Medicare and Social Security and to establish federally subsidized retirement accounts.

Top Republicans, such as House Budget Committee Chairman John R. Kasich of Ohio, responded with a proposed 10 percent across-the-board cut in tax rates that would consume the bulk of the surplus, at a 10-year cost of

The President's Budget Request

(in billions of dollars)

	1999	2000	2001	2002	2003	2004
Budget authority	$1,770.1	$1,781.1	$1,802.7	$1,833.4	$1,920.0	$1,976.8
Outlays	1,727.1	1,765.7	1,799.2	1,820.3	1,893.0	1,957.9
Revenues	1,806.3	1,883.0	1,933.3	2,007.1	2,075.0	2,165.5
Surplus	79.3	117.3	134.1	186.7	182.0	207.6

SOURCE: Office of Management and Budget

$743 billion. Clinton immediately brushed off the idea as "the latest in a rather long series of large and risky tax proposals."

The president holds a commanding tactical position. He may win only a small fraction of his proposed spending and tax initiatives, but the heart of his proposal — using the surplus to start paying off the debt — would begin to occur automatically should he and Congress come to a stalemate over taxes. And Congress may have to cave in to many of his discretionary spending demands anyway.

Paying Down the Debt

To blunt the GOP drive for tax cuts, the White House proposes to devote more than three-fourths of projected surpluses to buying back the national debt, a move that economists across the spectrum say would have a better effect on the economy than any tax cut. To make the politically unsexy idea of paying down the debt feasible, the administration draws a link between the sacrosanct Social Security and Medicare programs and the use of the surplus.

Clinton is not proposing to deposit the government's surplus cash into the Social Security and Medicare trust funds; government accounting does not work that way. The surplus would instead be used to reduce the amount of the federal debt held by corporations and the public. Such an arrangement would occur automatically even if Clinton and Congress took no action, as long as surpluses continued to materialize.

But paying down the debt, as Office of Management and Budget (OMB) Director Jack Lew told lawmakers Feb. 2, does not give politicians something tangible to deliver to voters. So the White House forged a political link to the hugely popular retirement and health insurance programs for senior citizens by proposing to deposit Treasury bonds equal to 62 percent of the surplus ($2.8 trillion over 15 years) into Social Security and 15 percent ($686 billion) into Medicare.

"Buying down the debt is a good thing, but it's very hard to sell," Lew told the Senate Budget Committee on Feb. 2. "I think it's much easier to promote a policy that is more straightforward than buying down the debt, and there's nothing more straightforward than saying, 'You can take a dollar and you could spend it, or you could take a dollar . . . and give Social Security and Medicare the first call on the good economic fortunes that we've built over the last six years.'"

Added former Congressional Budget Office (CBO) Director Robert D. Reischauer, now a senior analyst at the Brookings Institution: "Wrapping this policy in the protective cloak of Social Security and Medicare makes it politically sustainable."

Economics Lesson

Until recently, the idea of paying off the $5.6 trillion national debt has been an abstract debate mostly left to economists. A wide range of economists, from conservative Federal Reserve Board Chairman Alan Greenspan to liberal Robert Greenstein, director of the Center on Budget and Policy Priorities, agree that buying down the debt is the best single use of the surplus, preferable to new spending or big tax cuts.

Paying down the debt has many benefits. It puts downward pressure on interest rates because the government is doing less borrowing. Lower interest costs mean lower mortgage, car and credit card payments — which has the potential to put more in consumers' pockets than a tax cut.

"Balancing the budget, an idea that once seemed abstract, arcane or impossible, has made a real difference in the lives of our citizens," Clinton said Feb. 1. "Fiscal discipline has transformed the vicious cycle of budget deficits and high interest rates into a virtuous cycle of budget surpluses and low interest rates."

Cutting the debt would also increase savings and investment because capital that is now tied up in government bonds would be saved or invested in the private sector. And it would greatly reduce the amount of money in the federal budget required to pay interest, which would free up resources for other programs. Clinton's fiscal 2000 budget devotes 11 cents of every dollar to interest payments; by 2014, that would plummet to 2 cents.

"Politicians often talk about children and being responsible for the future," Greenstein said. "And increasing savings and paying down the debt are the best ways to do that."

Highlights

Amid the debate over the surplus, the debt, tax cuts and Social Security, there was little discussion of the budget's nuts and bolts. Among the highlights:

- **Vital statistics.** Clinton's budget calls for $1.77 trillion in spending in fiscal 2000, a $39 billion increase (2.2 percent) over fiscal 1999. Almost all of the increase, $35 billion, would go to mandatory entitlement programs, including Social Security (up $16 billion), Medicare (up $13 billion) and Medicaid grants to states (up $6 billion). However, interest payments on the national debt held by the public would decrease by $12 billion. Interest payments would continue to drop by about that amount each year through 2004.
- **Booming surpluses.** The budget forecasts a continuing turnabout in the government's fiscal health. The government ran a budget surplus of $69 billion, the first in three decades,

in fiscal 1998. For fiscal 1999, OMB predicts a $79 billion surplus, rising to $117 billion in 2000, $208 billion in 2004 and a whopping $393 billion in 2009.

These estimates are slightly less optimistic than those produced by the CBO: $769 billion from fiscal 1998 through 2003, compared with CBO's $877 billion. But the predictions are sharply higher than OMB forecast a year ago, when it projected surpluses totaling $209 billion from fiscal 1998 through 2003. Both OMB and CBO have consistently underestimated the size of the surplus. Their current projections rely on predictions of slow economic growth, averaging slightly over 2 percent, for the next five years.

• **New spending.** Clinton's budget proposes $18 billion in discretionary appropriations above the fiscal 2000 spending limits, or caps, set by the 1997 budget law (PL 105-33). To officially stay within the caps, Clinton claims offsetting savings or revenue increases — such as a 55-cents-per-pack cigarette tax — that are, at best, political long shots. He also proposes a "tobacco recoupment policy" to claim from the states another $16 billion through 2004 from settlement of their lawsuit against the tobacco companies.

Starting in fiscal 2001, assuming a Social Security overhaul, Clinton proposes raising the caps and spending $26 billion of the surplus in additional appropriations; such surplus-financed spending would total $138 billion from fiscal 2001 through 2004. About $4 billion in additional appropriations would be financed each year by new user fees, most of which are controversial.

In addition, Clinton proposes $21.8 billion in new mandatory entitlement spending over the next five years, focusing on child care subsidies and expanded health care. Offsetting savings would finance the initiatives.

The single biggest beneficiary of Clinton's new spending would be the Department of Defense, whose budget would steadily rise from $262 billion in fiscal 2000 to $301 billion in 2004.

• **Revenues.** In lieu of a big tax cut, Clinton proposes $33 billion over five years in targeted tax cuts, such as greater tax credits for child care and new tax credits for long-term care, energy efficiency and the subsidizing of school construction bonds. These would be financed by $33 billion in tax hikes and loophole closures, including a major assault on corporate tax shelters designed to raise $7.2 billion over five years.

He also proposes to devote 12 percent of the surplus ($96 billion over five years) to establish Universal Savings Accounts, a new federally subsidized retirement account to supplement Social Security. Lower-income people would receive a higher federal contribution.

• **Breaking the rules.** Clinton's team made the budget add up by violating budget rules, chiefly by using new taxes to pay for discretionary spending, which explicitly violates existing rules. Clinton also claims for the Pentagon $2.9 billion in mandatory savings that would flow from previously enacted bills. An additional $2.6 billion would come by claiming spectrum auction revenues in fiscal 2000 that will not be received until fiscal 2001 and 2002.

Building on an increasingly common practice, Clinton proposes $12 billion in an accounting gimmick to squeeze more money into the appropriations bills. He proposes to "advance fund" about $12 billion in fiscal 2001 appropriations to agencies for 2000, in effect borrowing from future years to finance additional spending.

Tactical Advantage

The biggest question confronting both Clinton and GOP lawmakers is whether this year's budget debate will produce a deal or a battle. The key factor favoring a deal is a bipartisan desire to overhaul Social Security, which, if successful, could provide a way to combine new spending with tax cuts. But there have yet to be any substantive discussions between the White House and Republicans in search of a deal.

Indeed, Clinton holds a commanding advantage, both politically and tactically, as the debate begins.

While he may not win a lot of his spending initiatives or limited tax cuts, his veto pen ensures that Republicans with designs to use the surplus for a broad tax cut will be thwarted — and that the bulk of the surplus will automatically be devoted to buying back debt, Clinton's biggest goal.

Public opinion polls have consistently shown that, when the question is framed as a choice between Social Security and Medicare or a tax cut, voters prefer using the surplus to bolster Social Security. In a New York Times/CBS News poll released Feb. 3, 64 percent of respondents favored using the surplus for Social Security vs. only 12 percent for tax cuts. Private polls done for Republicans and the White House show similar results.

Adding to the White House's confidence is Clinton's high job approval rating, accompanied by low approval ratings for congressional Republicans. The same New York Times/CBS News poll gave Clinton a 65 percent approval rating, while only 41 percent of respondents had a positive view of the Republican Party. The comparable figure for the Democratic Party was 56 percent.

Still, Republicans view tax cuts as a way to revive their dispirited faithful. No issue has as much resonance with their bedrock voters. "We're doing this because there is a core that is animated by this," said a top Senate GOP aide.

With such a narrow majority in the House, however, Republican leaders face an extraordinarily difficult budget year. The sequence of events in the upcoming debate works to their disadvantage.

First, they face intense pressure to produce the annual budget resolution, the blueprint for the separate budget and appropriations bills to follow. Producing the resolution is almost always partisan. Last year, because of divisions within Republicans ranks, Congress failed to pass a budget resolution for the first time since the Budget Act was enacted in 1974. The even narrower House majority this year and competing GOP factions promise another difficult struggle.

Next will come the round of 13 annual appropriations bills. The system bogged down last year amid opposition from Democrats, veto threats from the White House and soft support among GOP moderates. Each of those factors is likely to remain in place because of tight limits on how much money can be doled out in these bills. The bills will be difficult to pass if Congress holds to the caps, which would force severe cuts in spending. On the other hand, breaching the caps would cause heartburn among conservatives.

Republicans demonstrated last year that a healthy portion of their party, along with Democrats, could not live within the caps. There is little expectation among appropriations experts that this year will be any different. Add the desire to boost the Pentagon's budget — which under existing rules would have to come from domestic programs — and an already daunting job becomes impossible.

"Most of the members of their caucus and many members of my caucus don't have any idea what these numbers are," said top House Appropriations Committee Democrat David R. Obey of Wisconsin. "The Republicans are going to have a hell of a time not breaking the caps. It's going to be a long, hot summer."

Clinton has repeatedly proved adroit at extracting spending concessions on appropriations from Republicans, with last year's omnibus spending bill (PL 105-277) being the best example.

If there is no deal this year between Congress and Clinton on taxes and spending, the following scenario could play out: Clinton blocks Republicans on taxes, obtaining his overriding goal of buying down the debt, while at the same time he wages war on appropriations and gets some of his new spending anyway.

Stalemate may help the Democrats' drive to retain the White House and take back Congress. Without help from the White House and Democrats, congressional Republicans face a difficult year. Some Democrats are content to watch them suffer.

"From a purely political point of view, a split-the-differences kind of deal doesn't help us," said a prominent Democratic pollster and strategist. "Let them stew in their own juices."

Clinton Plan Pushes Limited Tax Cuts

FEBRUARY 6 — As has often been the case in the last 25 years of presidential budget plans, the tax proposals in President Clinton's fiscal 2000 package offer more of a confirmation of favored causes than a promising legislative blueprint.

The president's proposals, several of which recycle ideas that did not make it through prior Congresses, would largely benefit low- and middle-income taxpayers, addressing issues Clinton considers top priorities. For instance, taxpayers would receive tax credits to help care for elderly or disabled relatives, to pay for day care expenses, and to defray the cost of staying at home to raise infants or of installing energy saving devices in their homes.

The administration would cover the $32.6 billion cost of these initiatives by shutting down corporate tax shelters and tweaking the tax code to extract more revenue from wealthier taxpayers and businesses.

Republicans — who feel their vision of an across-the-board income tax cut looks more realistic in light of the budget surplus — were decidedly underwhelmed.

"To be candid, I find it incomprehensible that the president's plan would not allow for a wide-gauge tax cut in the next 15 years," Senate Finance Committee Chairman William V. Roth Jr., R-Del., said at a Feb. 2 hearing.

But Treasury Secretary Robert E. Rubin, testifying before Roth's committee, said tax burdens on working families were at "record lows for recent decades" — a point disputed by Republicans — and that the country would be better served by shoring up Social Security and paying down the national debt. "The core of this budget is fiscal discipline," he said.

The budget, like its predecessors, has no chance of passing through Congress intact. But it serves to lay out Clinton's agenda and, perhaps more than in recent years, highlight the differences between Republicans and Democrats, particularly on taxes.

With a budget surplus materializing for the first time in generations, providing a deep pocket for politicians' wish lists, Clinton's rejection of a big tax cut clearly would set him apart from the GOP Congress.

Though Republicans have agreed with Clinton that more than 60 percent of the surplus should be used to bolster Social Security, they are quick to claim the rest of it for the first across-the-board income tax cuts in more than a decade. The main question: How big?

"We're going to have huge surpluses, even beyond that that we're going to need for Social Security," House Budget Committee Chairman John R. Kasich, R-Ohio, said at a news conference Feb. 1, the day the president released his budget. "We can give, in my judgment, a 10 percent or 15 percent . . . 20 if we can get there. Whatever it is. We can give an across-the-board tax cut."

But before they spar with Clinton, Republicans must make sure their party is unified on tax issues. Consensus in the GOP for a broad tax cut is clearly stronger this year than last, when the Senate failed to take up a broad House bill and instead passed a small bill extending expiring tax breaks. But members have still not reached agreement on how much to cut.

At the Feb. 1 news conference with Kasich, Senate Budget Committee Chairman Pete V. Domenici, R-N.M., said he had "not found a way" to cut taxes by as much as 10 percent next year, though he could do so in 2003 or 2004, he said.

And Sen. John H. Chafee of Rhode Island, a GOP moderate, said repeatedly at the Finance Committee hearing Feb. 2 that he favored using as much of the surplus as possible to pay down the federal debt — an idea Federal Reserve Chairman Alan Greenspan endorsed at a hearing Jan. 28. "We should use nearly all the surplus that materializes for debt reduction," Chafee said.

Chafee's more conservative colleagues seem convinced that a tax cut is necessary, in part because many analysts blamed the GOP's lackluster showing in the 1998 election on the lack of such a cut. With a budget surplus materializing, Kasich said, "we're not going to blow this."

Republicans assume that the public is clamoring for a tax cut — an evergreen of politics — but many polls suggest that in this topsy-turvy political year the percentage of people interested in shoring up Social Security is far greater than the percentage that wants a tax cut. "Saving Social Security" has been Clinton's mantra, and if the early polls are borne out, he could once again win the war of public opinion — despite long odds and despite being impeached — and keep Republicans from a major victory on taxes.

Republicans' main complaints with Clinton's tax proposals are that certain people are targeted to encourage certain activities, and thus they are more like a government program than a tax cut.

Areas of Agreement

While Republicans — and several academics — believe such initiatives are making the tax code unnecessarily complicated, some of Clinton's individual proposals for tax credits do not face Republican opposition.

For instance, his plan to give up to $1,000 in annual tax credits to elderly or disabled people or their caregivers to supplement the cost of long-term care is similar to a GOP proposal included in the 1995 budget-reconciliation bill that Clinton vetoed for other reasons. The credit would be phased out for wealthier taxpayers. *(1995 Almanac, p. 2-66)*

Clinton's plan would also expand the child and dependent care tax credit, last increased in 1982, to cover 50 percent instead of 30 percent of child care costs for taxpayers with annual adjusted gross incomes of $30,000 or less. The credit would be phased down for higher-income filers, until it reached 20 percent for taxpayers with incomes greater than $59,000.

In response to GOP criticism that the child care proposals had not taken families with a stay-at-home parent into account, Clinton's plan would give all parents with a child up to one year old a $250 per child tax credit.

Among other initiatives included in the president's $32.6 billion in tax breaks and credits are:

- A plan similar to one in Clinton's fiscal 1999 budget that would enable state and local governments to issue $24.8 billion in bonds to build or renovate public schools, mostly in areas with lower-income children.
- Six separate credits for taxpayers who purchase energy-efficient homes, use solar energy, or purchase electric or fuel-efficient hybrid automobiles.
- More than a dozen proposals aimed at encouraging retirement savings, including simplifying pensions by allowing people to more easily consolidate different retirement accounts without adverse tax consequences.

A proposal certain to gain Republican support would extend five expiring tax credits that generally help businesses, including a credit for research and experimentation and a credit for hiring welfare recipients. A Ways and Means Committee staff member said Chairman Bill Archer, R-Texas, was committed to extending the provisions.

Clinton's budget would also extend a provision Congress enacted last year in the omnibus spending bill (PL 105-277) to allow taxpayers to benefit from tax credits, such as a $500 per child credit passed in 1997, even if they are required to file the alternative minimum tax (AMT). The AMT, a parallel income tax system, was created in 1969 (PL 91-172) to ensure that wealthy filers did not use exemptions and credits to wipe out their income taxes. But middle-income filers are now affected. Clinton's budget would extend Congress' fix for two years, but Archer wants a more comprehensive overhaul of the tax. Republicans may not like some of Clinton's tax credit proposals, but they do not oppose them as vehemently as his plan to raise money to pay for them. A major component aims to crack down on the use and marketing of corporate tax shelters — and raise an estimated $7.17 billion over five years.

The administration would also clarify or change the tax treatment of certain stock transactions and subject large trade associations to corporate income taxes on net investment income of more than $10,000.

Clinton aims to increase cigarette taxes by 55 cents a pack, and accelerate implementation of an increase of 15 cents per pack enacted as part of the 1997 budget-reconciliation package (PL 105-34). The administration estimates that the tobacco plan would raise $34.5 billion through 2004. It would be used to offset $42.3 billion in estimated tobacco-related costs to federal health care programs. *(1997 Almanac, p. 2-38)*

Experts Say Growth To Continue — At Slower Pace

FEBRUARY 6 — White House forecasters say the economy's performance in the past few years was so "extraordinary" that it inevitably must start to slow down. So the Office of Management and Budget (OMB) has based its budget for fiscal 2000 on more down-to-earth projections.

But the administration's predicted rate of growth and other indicators are still solid, and surpluses can be expected as far as the eye can see — or at least through 2014.

The White House projects inflation, interest rates and unemployment will remain low — though not as low as in the past couple of years — while income and other measures of productivity will continue to rise, though not quite so spectacularly as in 1997-98.

As a result, the White House expects government revenues from fiscal 1999 through 2004 to outpace spending by $906.7 billion or more — a black-ink phenomenon that seemed unthinkable just four years ago.

The Congressional Budget Office — which traditionally takes a more cautious view than the White House's team — has issued forecasts generally in line with the administration's.

But some private economists say both agencies may be underestimating the economy's continuing vigor.

"I think the [White House's] assumptions are quite reasonable. In fact, one can argue that they are a tad conservative," said Sung Won Sohn, senior vice president and chief economist for Wells Fargo & Co., in an interview Feb. 2. "I believe productivity gains are underestimated, and that means economic growth potential is also underestimated. I think the long-term economic growth potential is closer to 2.75 percent than 2 or 2.5 percent."

As measured by the output of goods and services, or gross domestic product, the economy expanded an estimated 3.9 percent in 1998, about the same rate as in 1997.

The White House projects "real growth" at 2 percent per year in 1999, 2000 and 2001, with an increase to 2.4 percent per year in 2002-04. CBO predicts 1.8 percent in 1999, 1.9 percent in 2000, 2.3 percent in 2001 and not less than 2.4 percent per year in 2002-04.

The so-called Blue Chip consensus forecast of 50 private-sector economists predicts 2.4 percent in 1999, 1.9 percent in 2000, 2.2 percent in 2001, and then a jump to 2.6 percent per year in 2002 through 2004.

Janet Yellen, chairman of the president's Council of Economic Advisers, said it is better to err on the side of

(Continued on p. 6-12)

Administration's Economic Assumptions

(Calendar years; dollar amounts in billions)[1]

	Actual	Projections						
	1997	1998	1999	2000	2001	2002	2003	2004
Gross domestic product								
Dollar levels:								
Current dollars	$8,111	$8,497	$8,833	$9,199	$9,582	$10,004	$10,456	$10,930
Real, chained (1992) dollars [2]	7,270	7,539	7,717	7,872	8,029	8,208	8,404	8,606
Chained price index (1992 = 100), annual average [2]	111.6	112.7	114.4	116.8	119.3	121.8	124.4	127.0
Percentage change, fourth quarter over fourth quarter:								
Current dollars	5.6	4.5	4.0	4.2	4.1	4.5	4.5	4.5
Real, chained (1992) dollars [2]	3.8	3.5	2.0	2.0	2.0	2.2	2.4	2.4
Chained price index (1992 = 100) [2]	1.7	0.9	1.9	2.1	2.1	2.1	2.1	2.1
Percentage change, year over year								
Current dollars	5.9	4.8	4.0	4.1	4.2	4.4	4.5	4.5
Real, chained (1992) dollars [2]	3.9	3.7	2.4	2.0	2.0	2.2	2.4	2.4
Chained price index (1992 = 100) [2]	1.9	1.0	1.5	2.1	2.1	2.1	2.1	2.1
Incomes								
Corporate profits before tax	$ 734	$ 721	$ 724	$ 739	$ 765	$ 787	$ 826	$ 867
Wages and salaries	3,890	4,146	4,349	4,526	4,701	4,892	5,106	5,331
Other taxable income	1,717	1,763	1,815	1,863	1,921	1,980	2,051	2,126
Consumer price index (all urban) [3]								
Level (1982-84 = 100), annual average	160.6	163.1	166.7	170.6	174.5	178.5	182.6	186.8
Percentage change, fourth quarter over fourth quarter	1.9	1.6	2.3	2.3	2.3	2.3	2.3	2.3
Percentage change, year over year	2.3	1.6	2.2	2.3	2.3	2.3	2.3	2.3
Unemployment rate, civilian (percent) [4]								
Fourth quarter level	4.7	4.6	4.9	5.1	5.3	5.3	5.3	5.3
Annual average	5.0	4.6	4.8	5.0	5.3	5.3	5.3	5.3
Federal pay raises, January (percent)								
Military [5]	3.0	2.8	3.6	4.4	3.9	3.9	3.9	3.9
Civilian [6]	3.0	2.8	3.6	4.4	3.9	3.9	3.9	3.9
Interest rates (percent)								
91-day Treasury bills [7]	5.1	4.8	4.2	4.3	4.3	4.4	4.4	4.4
10-year Treasury notes	6.4	5.3	4.9	5.0	5.2	5.3	5.4	5.4

1 Based on data available as of early December 1998.

2 In January 1996, the Commerce Department's Bureau of Economic Analysis replaced the traditional method of adjusting Gross Domestic Product calculations for inflation. Instead of using a price index based on the relative weights of certain goods from a single year, the calculation now uses a moving two-year average of relative prices, where the index is set at 100 for 1992. GDP has been recomputed using this method back to 1959.

3 CPI for all urban consumers. Two versions of the CPI are now published; the index shown here is used, as required by law, in calculating automatic adjustments to individual income tax brackets. Projections reflect scheduled changes in methodology.

4 Percent of civilian labor force, excluding military personnel residing in the United States.

5 Beginning with 1999 increase, percentages apply only to basic pay, not housing and subsistence allowances.

6 Overall average increases including locality pay adjustments.

7 Average rate on new issues within period.

SOURCE: President's fiscal 2000 budget

Budget Authority, Outlays by Agency

(Fiscal years, in millions of dollars)

Agency	BUDGET AUTHORITY 1998 Actual	1999 Estimate	2000 Proposed	OUTLAYS 1998 Actual	1999 Estimate	2000 Proposed
Legislative Branch	$2,656	$2,977	$3,043	$2,600	$2,850	$3,120
The Judiciary	3,551	3,799	4,291	3,467	3,913	4,133
Executive Office of the President	246	374	263	237	374	263
Agriculture	58,300	67,551	55,053	53,947	63,412	55,167
Commerce	4,110	5,139	7,272	4,046	4,767	6,647
Defense — Military	258,536	262,563	267,225	256,122	263,556	260,834
Defense — Civil	31,333	32,418	33,320	31,216	32,311	33,220
Education	35,502	34,269	36,284	31,463	34,360	34,971
Energy	14,396	15,898	15,941	14,438	15,544	15,756
Health and Human Services	359,536	379,284	403,654	350,568	375,532	400,327
Housing and Urban Development	21,022	20,776	25,056	30,227	32,324	32,533
Interior	8,198	7,645	8,616	7,218	8,426	8,470
Justice	18,753	19,006	19,220	16,168	16,458	19,794
Labor	33,190	36,572	39,567	30,007	34,923	38,652
State	6,060	8,128	6,961	5,382	6,791	6,959
Transportation	44,407	50,492	52,852	39,463	41,873	45,503
Treasury	392,651	387,656	378,933	390,140	385,976	377,916
Veterans Affairs	42,766	43,398	43,591	41,773	43,474	43,953
Corps of Engineers	4,215	4,143	2,915	3,845	4,209	3,065
Environmental Protection Agency	7,037	7,330	7,151	6,284	6,667	7,346
FEMA	2,439	761	856	2,096	2,668	2,744
General Services Administration	220	448	154	1,091	328	429
International Assistance Programs	7,144	28,525	9,557	8,974	10,130	10,401
NASA	13,649	13,666	13,580	14,206	14,043	13,357
National Science Foundation	3,476	3,743	3,999	3,188	3,259	3,629
Office of Personnel Management	47,360	49,644	52,080	46,305	48,266	50,531
Small Business Administration	243	–829	509	–77	–866	287
Social Security Administration	407,930	421,145	439,185	408,303	422,438	439,015
(On budget)	(36,608)	(41,073)	(40,726)	(38,134)	(41,122)	(40,794)
(Off budget)	(371,322)	(380,072)	(398,459)	(370,069)	(381,316)	(398,221)
Other independent agencies	24,361	16,402	20,997	10,990	6,341	14,802
Allowances	—	7,577	–307	—	3,118	2,631
Undistributed offsetting receipts	–161,035	–160,394	–170,768	–161,035	–160,394	–170,768
TOTAL	1,692,252	1,770,106	1,781,050	1,652,552	1,727,071	1,765,687
(On budget)	(1,368,253)	(1,443,651)	(1,441,914)	(1,335,948)	(1,404,015)	(1,429,830)
(Off budget)	(323,999)	(326,455)	(339,136)	(316,604)	(323,056)	(335,857)

Figures may not add due to rounding

SOURCE: President's fiscal 2000 budget

Fiscal 2000 Budget by Function

in millions of dollars

	BUDGET AUTHORITY			OUTLAYS		
	1998	1999	2000	1998	1999	2000
NATIONAL DEFENSE						
Military defense	$258,536	$262,563	$267,225	$256,122	$263,556	$260,834
Atomic energy defense activities	11,704	12,520	12,352	11,268	12,012	12,062
Defense-related activities	1,014	1,147	1,223	1,066	1,162	1,173
TOTAL	271,254	276,230	280,800	268,456	276,730	274,069
INTERNATIONAL AFFAIRS						
International development/humanitarian assistance	7,225	7,364	7,295	5,446	5,714	6,084
International security assistance	5,372	6,357	6,182	5,135	5,737	5,638
Conduct of foreign affairs	3,845	5,764	5,200	3,262	4,617	5,058
Foreign information and exchange activities	1,224	1,119	731	1,159	1,216	801
International financial programs	-2,897	16,949	-2,040	-1,893	-1,810	-1,479
TOTAL	14,769	37,553	17,368	13,109	15,474	16,102
GENERAL SCIENCE, SPACE AND TECHNOLOGY						
General science and basic research	5,674	6,378	6,771	5,353	5,738	6,316
Space flight, research and supporting activities	12,321	12,469	12,509	12,866	12,791	12,253
TOTAL	17,995	18,847	19,280	18,219	18,529	18,569
ENERGY						
Energy supply	-739	-1,302	-3,485	181	-894	-3,106
Energy conservation	584	628	838	621	560	722
Emergency energy preparedness	208	160	164	233	182	169
Energy information, policy and regulation	243	204	223	235	201	220
TOTAL	296	-310	-2,260	1,270	49	-1,995
NATURAL RESOURCES AND ENVIRONMENT						
Water resources	5,127	4,813	3,752	4,721	5,454	3,955
Conservation and land management	5,516	5,141	5,768	5,475	5,074	5,463
Recreational resources	3,857	3,365	3,628	2,984	3,952	3,510
Pollution control and abatement	7,197	7,530	7,364	6,422	6,855	7,552
Other natural resources	2,779	3,093	3,440	2,794	2,926	3,266
TOTAL	24,476	23,942	23,952	22,396	24,261	23,746
AGRICULTURE						
Farm income stabilization	9,845	21,241	10,982	9,297	18,405	12,044
Agricultural research and services	2,885	3,161	3,166	2,909	3,044	3,102
TOTAL	12,730	24,402	14,148	12,206	21,449	15,146
COMMERCE AND HOUSING CREDIT						
Mortgage credit	-1,465	-5,195	-81	-2,934	-1,112	-2,496
Postal Service subsidy (on budget)	86	—	164	86	—	164
Postal Service (off budget)	(6,359)	(5,607)	(4,874)	(217)	(964)	(1,833)
Deposit insurance	-33	2	—	-4,371	-5,047	-2,324
Other advancement of commerce	9,381	4,770	9,515	8,016	5,647	9,175
TOTAL	14,328	5,184	14,472	1,014	452	6,352
(On budget)	(7,969)	(-423)	(9,598)	(797)	(-512)	(4,519)
(Off budget)	(6,359)	(5,607)	(4,874)	(217)	(964)	(1,833)
TRANSPORTATION						
Ground transportation	31,099	35,851	38,168	26,004	28,333	31,056
Air transportation	10,394	11,231	11,251	10,622	10,559	11,090
Water transportation	3,637	3,932	3,799	3,507	3,502	4,103
Other transportation	207	218	205	199	246	186
TOTAL	45,337	51,232	53,423	40,332	42,640	46,435
COMMUNITY AND REGIONAL DEVELOPMENT						
Community development	5,492	5,502	5,669	5,118	5,437	5,373
Area and regional development	2,575	3,011	2,632	2,456	2,570	2,489
Disaster relief and insurance	2,562	578	806	2,146	2,421	2,372
TOTAL	10,629	9,091	9,107	9,720	10,428	10,234
EDUCATION, TRAINING, EMPLOYMENT, SOCIAL SERVICES						
Elementary, secondary and vocational education	18,794	16,821	20,821	16,571	16,989	20,102
Higher education	13,829	14,259	12,339	12,070	14,047	11,643
Research and general education aids	2,232	2,582	2,725	2,271	2,448	2,792
Training and employment	8,382	8,648	8,535	6,636	7,941	8,675
Other labor services	1,041	1,131	1,286	1,036	1,108	1,246
Social services	16,698	17,418	19,578	16,335	17,532	18,893
TOTAL	60,976	60,859	65,284	54,919	60,065	63,351

Fiscal 2000 Budget by Function

in millions of dollars

	BUDGET AUTHORITY			OUTLAYS		
	1998	1999	2000	1998	1999	2000
HEALTH						
Health care services	$118,726	$123,828	$137,013	$116,336	$126,190	$134,242
Health research and training	14,270	16,312	16,499	13,073	14,681	16,098
Consumer and occupational health and safety	2,112	2,228	1,971	2,031	2,224	1,930
TOTAL	135,108	142,368	155,483	131,440	143,095	152,270
MEDICARE	193,667	205,550	216,444	192,822	204,982	216,599
INCOME SECURITY						
General retirement and disability insurance	5,841	3,133	6,314	4,632	2,312	5,272
Federal employee retirement and disability	75,233	77,977	80,834	73,485	76,262	79,082
Unemployment compensation	22,130	25,106	28,135	22,070	25,178	28,151
Housing assistance	17,486	20,698	19,120	28,741	28,376	29,606
Food and nutrition assistance	37,840	36,764	37,323	33,585	35,271	36,205
Other income security	73,049	79,436	79,234	70,689	75,731	79,713
TOTAL	231,579	243,114	250,960	233,202	243,130	258,029
SOCIAL SECURITY	380,474	391,361	408,813	379,225	392,608	408,575
(On budget)	(9,152)	(11,289)	(10,354)	(9,156)	(11,292)	(10,354)
(Off budget)	(371,322)	(380,072)	(398,459)	(370,069)	(381,316)	(398,221)
VETERANS BENEFITS AND SERVICES						
Income security	21,517	22,819	22,753	21,322	22,640	23,316
Education, training and rehabilitation	1,168	1,002	1,261	1,102	1,337	1,290
Hospital and medical care	17,959	18,052	18,001	17,545	17,933	17,807
Housing	1,145	471	443	837	468	423
Other benefits and services	1,003	1,113	1,204	975	1,148	1,188
TOTAL	42,792	43,457	43,662	41,781	43,526	44,024
ADMINISTRATION OF JUSTICE						
Federal law enforcement activities	10,771	11,085	10,918	9,998	10,506	10,443
Federal litigative and judicial activities	6,773	7,223	8,185	6,683	7,030	7,951
Federal correctional activities	3,097	3,299	3,777	2,682	3,402	3,562
Criminal justice assistance	5,229	5,245	4,045	3,469	3,529	5,573
TOTAL	25,870	26,852	26,925	22,832	24,467	27,529
GENERAL GOVERNMENT						
Legislative functions	2,074	2,345	2,365	2,007	2,214	2,421
Executive direction and management	562	660	676	378	548	626
Central fiscal operations	8,725	9,869	8,621	7,906	9,466	8,593
General property and records management	264	693	373	1,030	553	618
Central personnel management	149	152	164	116	153	164
General-purpose fiscal assistance	2,121	1,836	1,804	2,117	1,846	1,804
Other general government	977	1,186	1,122	959	1,232	1,424
Deductions for offsetting receipts	-1,069	-1,160	-1,160	-1,069	-1,160	-1,160
TOTAL	13,803	15,581	13,965	13,444	14,852	14,490
NET INTEREST						
Interest on the public debt	363,793	353,429	346,504	363,793	353,429	346,504
Interest received by on-budget trust funds	-67,208	-67,233	-68,611	-67,208	-67,233	-68,611
Interest received by off-budget trust funds	-46,630	-51,869	-56,492	-46,630	-51,869	-56,492
Other interest	-6,592	-7,083	-6,214	-6,596	-7,083	-6,214
TOTAL	243,363	227,244	215,187	243,359	227,244	215,187
(On budget)	(289,993)	(279,113)	(271,679)	(289,989)	(279,113)	(271,679)
(Off budget)	(-46,630)	(-51,869)	(-56,492)	(-46,630)	(-51,869)	(-56,492)
ALLOWANCES	—	7,577	-307	—	3,118	2,631
UNDISTRIBUTED OFFSETTING RECEIPTS	-47,194	-40,028	-45,656	-47,194	-40,028	-45,656
(On budget)	(-40,142)	(-32,673)	(-37,951)	(-40,142)	(-32,673)	(-37,951)
(Off budget)	(-7,052)	(-7,355)	(-7,705)	(-7,052)	(-7,355)	(-7,705)
TOTAL	1,692,252	1,770,106	1,781,050	1,652,552	1,727,071	1,765,687
(On budget)	(1,368,253)	(1,443,651)	(1,441,914)	(1,335,948)	(1,404,015)	(1,429,830)
(Off budget)	(323,999)	(326,455)	(339,136)	(316,604)	(323,056)	(335,857)

Figures may not add due to rounding

SOURCE: President's fiscal 2000 budget

(Continued from p. 6-7)
caution in building the budget.

"We believe that it would not be wise, for budgetary purposes, to count on the continuation of growth at its recent extraordinary pace," Yellen said at a briefing for reporters after President Clinton released the budget Feb. 1.

"Looking ahead, we expect this economic expansion to continue, with new jobs created and real wages continuing to grow," Yellen said, but at more modest rates.

William Sharp, an economist at Chase Manhattan Corp., told Bloomberg News: "Those aren't too far-fetched projections over the long term, but a recession could derail them in the short term."

Chase is projecting a 1 percent growth rate for 1999. "Will one year's growth be much lower? Yes," Sharp said. "But the following year could be even higher" than predicted.

The administration's restraint does not satisfy everyone, however.

"Before rushing to spend the projected surpluses, the basic premise that they will exist should be questioned," said Robert Bixby, policy director of The Concord Coalition, a bipartisan budget watchdog group.

"It is astounding how quickly everyone has bought into the idea of massive surpluses over the next 15 years. . . . [Clinton and Congress] are dividing the winnings of a hypothetical jackpot."

Rolling Along

The budget notes that December was the 94th consecutive month of economic growth, making this "the longest period of continuous growth in peacetime. . . . If the expansion continues through February 2000, it will exceed the longevity record of 106 months set during the Vietnam War expansion of the 1960s."

Indeed, the U.S. economy has rolled along despite last year's turmoil in Asia and Brazil, and both government and private economists say it shows no sign of stopping — slowing, but not stopping.

Yellen attributed part of the administration's restrained expectations to "the view that tight labor markets are apt to constrain growth in the near term, while several components of domestic demand may be poised to grow at slower rates. Consumption in particular has been growing faster than income and may be likely to slow to a solid but sustainable pace."

Last year's economic expansion created about 2.9 million jobs, pushing unemployment down to 4.3 percent in December.

But the Clinton administration notes that the new jobs were not spread across all sectors. Industries dependent on exports, such as mining and manufacturing, did little or no hiring.

That trend is likely to push the unemployment rate up this year and beyond, administration aides predict, although only slightly. The White House forecasts a 4.8 percent rate this year, rising to 5 percent in 2000 and 5.3 percent per year in 2001-04.

CBO is slightly more optimistic about this year, predicting a 4.6 percent jobless rate. But then it expects a jump to 5.1 percent in 2000 and 5.4 percent or more in 2001 and beyond. The Blue Chip consensus forecast says the rate will be 4.7 percent for 1999, 5.2 percent for 2000, then rise to 5.4 percent in 2001 and 2002.

Counterbalancing that will be continued low inflation and low interest rates, according to all three forecasts of the Consumer Price Index (CPI) and yields on Treasury bills.

The CPI rose just 1.6 percent in 1998, beating the 2.3 percent rate of 1997. The administration predicts a return to the 2.3 percent inflation rate for this year, which will remain constant through 2004.

The CBO projects 2.7 percent this year, but 2.6 percent per year from 2000 to 2004.

The Blue Chip forecast is for 2 percent inflation this year, then a 2.7 percent annual average for 2000-04.

As for interest rates, both the administration and CBO predict short-term rates at 4.5 percent or below through 2004, while long-term rates hover around 5.4 percent per year.

However, the Blue Chip consensus forecast projects short-term rates at about 5 percent, with long-term rates closer to 6 percent per year.

The Unforeseeable

The chief problem with the government's dependence on economic forecasts, especially for the long term, is that they can be terribly wrong.

Administration officials took great delight, as they discussed their fiscal 2000 plan, in noting how unexpected the current geyser of black ink was just six years ago.

Harking back to 1993, Gene Sperling, chairman of the president's National Economic Council, gloated: "The Congressional Budget Office projected that the deficit that we would face this year when we came in was $404 billion. Instead, we now project a $79 billion surplus. That is a $483 billion difference in the amount of money available to our private markets, to homeowners, to people starting businesses."

In tight years, off-the-mark forecasts can cause great consternation for politicians and policy-makers. Last year, GOP leaders, especially in the House, were angry at the CBO for not anticipating the size of this year's surplus in time to help make the case for a big package of tax cuts. That, in large part, led to the departure of CBO Director June O'Neill.

But in truly flush times, it appears forecasts that fall short can be a source of bemusement, if not amusement.

Vice President Al Gore drew hearty laughs at the White House's budget unveiling when he told a joke about three economic forecasters who went deer hunting.

When they came upon a deer, Gore said, the first forecaster took a shot that whizzed past 10 feet to the right. Then the second forecaster tried, and his shot flew 10 feet to the left. The third economist jumped up and hollered, "We got him!"

Lower Share

Appearing before House and Senate committees in the first round of the annual budget debate, administration officials argued that the unanticipated increases in government revenues have not come out of the pocket of the average taxpayer.

Appearing before the Senate Budget Committee on Feb. 2, OMB Director Jack Lew said, "If you look at the typical family with a median income — $54,900 a year — that family is paying a lower share of its income in income and payroll taxes than at any time in the last 23 years.

"Income taxes alone are the lowest percentage of income since 1966. A family of four with one-half of the median income — that's about $28,000 — will pay the lowest share of its income in taxes since 1965. Even a family of four at twice the median income — that's nearly $110,000 — will pay less in combined income and payroll taxes than in any point since 1977," Lew said.

Appearing before the Senate Finance Committee the same day, Treasury Secretary Robert E. Rubin added, "Overall tax revenues have risen as a percentage of gross domestic product, but that is primarily because the most affluent individuals in our society have had large increases in income, in part from bonuses based on high stock prices and increased realizations of capital gains, and in part because of increased corporate earnings."

Given their expectations of more modest growth over the next six years, the effect of the administration's economic assumptions is a slight decline in the growth of federal receipts. When this year's economic assumptions are applied to last year's revenue forecasts, the growth in receipts drops from $27.9 billion in fiscal 1999, to $25.9 billion in 2000 and $24.4 billion in 2001.

A more significant slowdown would have more drastic implications, the forecasters warn.

Appearing before the Senate Budget Committee on Jan. 29, in advance of the release of the president's proposal, O'Neill warned on her last day as CBO director: "There is a significant danger . . . that a worsening international financial situation or other developments could lead to a more precipitous slowdown in the United States."

For example, in their budget analysis, the White House forecasters outlined a scenario under which an unforeseen shock from abroad this year slowed the rate of growth in gross domestic product by just 1 percent through 2004 and led to a one-half percentage point higher unemployment rate over the next five years.

That would take $9.8 billion out of the surplus this year, $33.4 billion out in 2000, $60.9 billion in 2001, $91.4 billion in 2002 and more than $125 billion in 2003 and 2004. ◆

Economy's Effect on the Budget

(Fiscal years, in billions of dollars)

	1999	2000	2001	2002	2003	2004
Previous Economic Forecast						
Receipts	$1,778.4	$1,857.0	$1,909.0	$1,988.9	$2,060.2	$2,154.5
Outlays	1,743.1	1,789.0	1,824.8	1,846.3	1,921.0	1,987.8
Surplus	35.4	68.1	84.1	142.6	139.2	166.8
Changes Due to New Economic Assumptions						
Receipts	+$27.9	+$25.9	+$24.4	+$18.1	+$14.8	+$11.0
Outlays						
Inflation	–4.9	–6.3	–6.6	–6.9	–7.3	–7.9
Unemployment	–3.5	–2.4	–1.6	–0.7	–0.9	–1.0
Interest rates	–6.4	–11.0	–11.4	–10.0	–9.2	–8.3
Reduced borrowing	–1.2	–3.6	–6.1	–8.4	–10.6	–12.7
Increase in surplus	43.9	49.2	50.0	44.1	42.9	40.9
Revised Economic Forecast						
Receipts	$1,806.3	$1,883.0	$1,933.3	$2,007.1	$2,075.0	$2,165.5
Outlays	1,727.1	1,765.7	1,799.2	1,820.3	1,893.0	1,957.9
Surplus	79.3	117.3	134.1	186.7	182.0	207.6

This table shows the effects of changed economic assumptions between President Clinton's fiscal 1999 and fiscal 2000 budget requests. Some numbers may not add due to rounding.

The changes in economic assumptions from year to year are primarily due to more favorable results in fiscal 1998 and the first part of fiscal 1999 than anticipated; economic growth was stronger, and inflation and unemployment were lower. As a result, the annual averages for fiscal 1999 for unemployment and inflation have been reduced slightly. Interest rates are again assumed to decline, but the decline is smaller in percentage terms because the surplus has increased so much faster than expected.

The greatest of the net effects of these modifications is higher receipts from 1999-2004 due to higher projected taxable incomes. In all years through 2004, there are lower outlays for interest as a result of the larger-than-expected decline in interest rates, plus lower outlays for cost of living adjustments for most federal programs due to lower rates of inflation.

SOURCE: President's fiscal 2000 budget

Congress Meets Deadline for Budget Resolution, Leaves Problems for Appropriators

SUMMARY

For only the fourth time since the Budget Act (PL 93-344) was created in 1974, Congress met the statutory deadline for passing its budget. To pave the way for a 10-year, $792 billion tax cut bill, the measure projected Congress could live within tight "caps" on appropriations set under the 1997 balanced-budget agreement (PL 105-33). In the end, however, Congress and President Clinton teamed up to exceed those caps by more than $30 billion, according to the Congressional Budget Office (CBO).

After the GOP-controlled Congress failed to pass a budget blueprint in 1998, new House Speaker J. Dennis Hastert, R-Ill., vowed a return to "regular order," which meant timely passage of the fiscal 2000 budget resolution.

Initially, Republicans considered raising the budget caps, which had been broken in 1998 when Clinton and Congress negotiated a year-end omnibus spending bill (PL 105-277). But after prominent Democrats such as Senate Minority Leader Tom Daschle of South Dakota said lawmakers should live within the caps, those efforts fell apart.

Instead, Republicans crafted a budget resolution that was aimed chiefly at clearing the way for a big tax bill. The blueprint was extended for 10 years for the first time, instead of the more customary five, to claim long-term surpluses in the second five years of the plan. The measure provided for a tax cut of $142 billion from 2000 through 2004, ballooning to $778 billion over 10 years.

All the while, Democrats and even many Republicans said the GOP budget blueprint called for untenable cuts in discretionary programs such as education, scientific research and housing. Just to maintain discretionary appropriations at a "freeze" level, appropriators said, would require breaking the caps by about $17 billion. Virtually no one believed such cuts could be achieved in an era of surging surpluses. Clinton's proposed budget stayed within the caps only by using proposed new revenues and fees, such as an increase in cigarette taxes.

After Clinton vetoed the tax bill in September, appropriators quickly claimed almost all of the projected $14 billion non-Social Security-generated budget surplus for appropriations. They also took advantage of an unprecedented array of accounting methods to pump more money into the 13 fiscal 2000 spending bills.

After this year, lawmakers could no longer pretend to live within the caps on appropriations. The question was how much the caps would have to be raised next year. At the same time, the flood of new spending promised to reduce the amount of money available for an election year tax bill.

Republicans Vow To Cut Taxes, Keep Caps

MARCH 20 — In an opening gambit in a budget debate that will not clarify itself until later this year, congressional Republicans are rallying around a fiscal 2000 blueprint that they say trumps President Clinton on Social Security, Medicare and education, while preserving GOP priorities such as tax cuts and smaller government.

In backing the plan, largely written by Senate Budget Committee Chairman Pete V. Domenici, R-N.M., Republicans appear to be preserving short-term unity while virtually guaranteeing gridlock when they turn in May to the 13 annual appropriations bills.

The non-binding blueprint, approved by both the House and Senate Budget committees the week of March 15, gives Republicans a chance to broadcast their response to Clinton's February budget submission, which they blasted as chock-full of funny numbers, phony assumptions and politically dead proposals such as a 55 cents-per-pack cigarette tax increase.

But the Republican plan also has its share of hard-to-believe assumptions, starting with the expectation that Congress can pass fiscal 2000 appropriations bills that would cut spending for popular domestic programs far below anything deemed realistic by the green-eyeshade appropriators, who are charged with distributing the approximately one-third of the federal budget that advances through Congress each year.

The House Budget Committee approved its measure March 17 on a party-line, 22-18 vote. The Senate panel approved an almost identical plan the next day on a 12-10 vote. Both chambers are expected to pass the plan the week of March 22.

The fiscal 2000 resolution, which does not go to the president nor carry the force of law, would set out the parameters for the tax and appropriations bills to follow over the next few months. The measure would dedicate to tax cuts almost $800 billion over 10 years in "on-budget" surpluses — those that do not depend on surplus Social Security revenues — while reserving the estimated $1.8 trillion Social Security surplus for reducing the national debt. It would also increase funding for education above Clinton's request

Box Score

- **Bill:** H Con Res 68
- **Legislative action: House** adopted H Con Res 68 (H Rept 106-73), 221-208, on March 25.

Senate adopted its version of H Con Res 68 (formerly S Con Res 20 — S Rept 106-27), 55-44, on March 25.

House adopted conference report (H Rept 106-91) on H Con Res 68, 220-208, on April 14.

Senate adopted conference report, 54-44, on April 15.

while significantly increasing Pentagon spending for the first time since the Bush administration.

"It is a good start on wisely and effectively using projected surpluses into the next century," Domenici said.

The White House quickly went on the attack, lambasting the plan for promoting tax cuts instead of using the surplus to shore up Social Security and Medicare. "We don't need more Republican 'retronomics,' " said Vice President Al Gore, the front-runner for the Democratic presidential nomination in 2000.

The GOP plan would hew to excruciatingly tight "caps" on appropriations, while shifting tens of billions of dollars from domestic programs to the Pentagon. The current caps, put in place under the 1997 budget law (PL 105-33), are a symbol of Congress' resolve to keep federal spending in check. They have been a successful deficit-reduction tool since first put in place in 1990. *(1997 Almanac, p. 2-3)*

Since the federal ledger started showing a surplus last year, however, lawmakers of both parties have yielded to the temptation to find ways around the caps, most obviously when they passed last year's omnibus spending bill (PL 105-277). That measure contained $21 billion in "emergency" spending that, in effect, permitted Clinton and Congress to evade the caps. Republicans have vowed to avoid a repeat of that embarrassing experience.

But to stick with the caps, say appropriators, would make it virtually impossible to pass all of the annual spending bills, especially the bill for the departments of Labor, Health and Human Services (HHS), and Education. According to estimates by the Senate Budget Committee, appropriators will have $20 billion less in new spending for domestic discretionary programs to distribute when they turn to the fiscal 2000 bills later this spring.

"The bottom line is, I don't think they can pass the appropriations bills," said a senior administration official monitoring the twin House and Senate markups.

What it would take to make it easier to pass the appropriations bills — raising the caps — was deemed a nonstarter by Republicans. Among other reasons, raising the caps would spark intra-party turmoil because budget hawks such as Sen. Phil Gramm, R-Texas, would revolt.

"I think there is reason for people to question our credibility on these caps. We broke them last year," Gramm said. "We've broken spending caps almost every time we've ever set them. . . . I just want to say that I am not going to vote to break these caps."

Holding Pattern

After failing to pass a budget resolution last year for the first time since the system was set in place in 1974, Republicans have redoubled efforts to get the fiscal 2000 budget completed early. But as they hurry to finish action on the plan, they are producing a document that will quickly become outdated.

Republicans acknowledge that the current plan is a placeholder while they await more favorable surplus figures from the Congressional Budget Office (CBO) this July. The chairmen of the tax-writing House Ways and Means and Senate Finance committees have both said they plan to hold off on advancing any major tax cut bills until August or September at the earliest.

"They're really banking on a windfall that will come this summer in the form of CBO re-estimates," said top House Budget Committee Democrat John M. Spratt Jr. of South Carolina.

Added House Budget Committee Chairman John R. Kasich, R-Ohio: "Come August, we expect to have better numbers."

The expectation of rosier surplus forecasts is of little immediate comfort to appropriators, who will begin bringing bills to the House and Senate floors in June, before the new numbers come out.

The companion House and Senate measures cruised through the Budget committees as Republicans swatted down Democratic amendments to block tax cuts until Congress finds a way to extend the solvency of the Social Security and Medicare trust funds. Other Democratic initiatives, such as decreasing school class sizes, were turned away.

The only significant change in the resolution occurred March 18 when the Senate panel approved, 19-1, a plan by Olympia J. Snowe, R-Maine, to establish a "reserve fund" that could pay for a prescription drug benefit under Medicare. But she abandoned plans to finance the plan through a tobacco tax after that threatened to unravel Republican support for the resolution.

Clinton Boundaries

The two parties differ on tax and spending priorities, but to a remarkable degree, Republicans are advancing their plan within boundaries set by Clinton and congressional Democrats. This is most obvious in their hands-off treatment of the Social Security surpluses. Republicans have accepted the argument, advanced most stridently by Sen. Ernest F. Hollings, D-S.C., that tapping the Social Security surplus for tax cuts or additional spending amounts to a raid on the program. As a result, the GOP plan would devote 100 percent of Social Security surpluses to paying down the national debt.

Other features of the plan include:

- **Taxes.** The plan would provide a $143 billion tax cut over the next five years and a $779 billion cut over 10 years. For fiscal 2000, however, no net tax cut would be allowed. One option would be to cut capital gains taxes again, which would provide a short-term increase in revenues.
- **Spending.** The plan sticks to the fiscal 2000 cap on discretionary outlays of $571 billion, $3 billion below this year's anticipated spending. Defense spending would increase by about $2 billion, to $276 billion in outlays, while the domestic ledger would shrink by almost $5 billion, to $295 billion. But to increase defense outlays by an additional $11 billion in 2001 would require domestic accounts to absorb an unrealistic hit of an equal amount.

Among the facets of the GOP plan most challenging to understand is the arcane relationship between the concepts of budget authority and actual budget outlays. Budget authority ("BA" in appropriators' parlance) is new spending, which typically may take several years for the government to fully digest, particularly in capital-heavy areas such as military procurement. Budget outlays represent the amount of money actually spent in any given year.

The GOP budget contains a significant flaw, say appropriators, because it does not adequately match budget authority and outlays. For example, the GOP plan would boost new budget authority for defense programs, from $280 billion this year to $290 billion next year, but outlays would tick up by only $1.5 billion. From fiscal 2000 through 2004, budget authority for defense would exceed outlays by $77 billion.

Kasich has "given us more BA for defense but no outlays to go with it," said a top House Appropriations Committee staff aide. "There's a BA/outlay mismatch totally there." But for domestic programs, budget authority would come in more than $200 billion under outlays over the next five years.

• **Debt reduction.** Under the plan, the $1.8 trillion in Social Security surpluses expected over the next decade would be used to retire debt held by the public, which would decline from $3.6 trillion to $1.9 trillion. Domenici has shelved for now plans to advance a bill to create a debt reduction "lockbox" by establishing by law steadily shrinking public debt limits. Treasury Secretary Robert E. Rubin said March 17 that he would recommend that Clinton veto any such plan.

Unity and Wishful Thinking Yield Budget Resolution

MARCH 27 — House and Senate passage of Republicans' fiscal 2000 budget plan gave lawmakers a fistful of talking points for the spring recess and patched up a schism between House and Senate Republicans over taxes and spending cuts that derailed the budget process last year.

But adoption of the blueprint (H Con Res 68) provided only a few clues about the ultimate fate of an unexpectedly big budget surplus that the booming economy has dropped in the laps of President Clinton and his congressional rivals.

At this stage, the budget debate is mainly a political, party-defining exercise, and at times both the House and Senate debates had a "going through the motions" feel.

The House adopted H Con Res 68 on March 25 by a 221-208 vote; the Senate followed suit hours later with a 55-44 endorsement of the plan. After the recess, the nearly identical measures are expected to be quickly reconciled, giving Republicans a realistic chance of making the rarely met April 15 statutory deadline for completing the budget. *(House vote 77, p. H-30; Senate vote 81, p. S-18)*

The annual budget resolution is a non-binding forecast of tax and spending priorities over the next decade. This year's debate gave lawmakers of both parties an opportunity to showcase their competing plans for the surplus. For Republicans, the focus is on cutting taxes, reducing the national debt and sticking to painful "caps" on discretionary appropriations, the one-third of the budget that advances through Congress every year to finance day-to-day government operations.

"The Republican budget does it all," said House Majority Whip Tom DeLay of Texas. "It cuts taxes, it reduces the debt, it saves Social Security, and it increases defense."

Democrats agree with Republicans on debt reduction, but they countered with proposals to use part of the estimated $2.6 trillion surplus over the next decade to shore up the Medicare and Social Security trust funds, while increasing spending for domestic programs such as agriculture and education.

"The budget that congressional Republicans passed today is a series of missed opportunities," Clinton said in a statement. "It fails to lock in debt reduction, fails to extend the solvency of Social Security and Medicare, and fails to protect key investments for the American people — from Head Start to clean water and law enforcement."

The plan forecasts an almost $800 billion tax cut over 10 years and steady spending increases for the Pentagon. But those GOP priorities depend — at least for now — on cuts in domestic programs and international aid that lawmakers admit they will not be able to stomach.

Indeed, the appropriations cuts that would be required to live within the caps — about $20 billion less in new budget authority for non-defense appropriations — would require drafting such austere domestic spending bills that many Republicans worry that they will not be able to pass them, much less get Clinton to sign them. That raises the potential for the type of appropriations gridlock that produced last year's much-maligned omnibus spending bill (PL 105-277).

For all their tough talk, Republicans have a history of caving in to Clinton's spending demands, and there is no reason to believe they will not do so again. "We don't negotiate with this president," Senate Appropriations Committee Chairman Ted Stevens, R-Alaska, groused recently. "We submit to this president."

Areas of Agreement

Despite sometimes overheated rhetoric, the debate showed that there is much upon which the two parties can agree: to devote most of the surplus to debt reduction, to boost funding for defense and education, and to cut taxes. "I think all of us see where the real resolution lies," said Sen. Christopher J. Dodd, D-Conn.

The question facing lawmakers is whether to seek a split-your-differences deal as already envisioned by Dodd and others, or whether to keep fighting for party principles.

For all of the passionate speechmaking about the parties' differing priorities, there are only two figures in the budget resolution that have immediate significance: the 10-year, almost $800 billion tax cut and the $571 billion in discretionary outlays for the fiscal 2000 appropriations cycle. Neither figure is realistic, and both will change later in the year when higher surplus estimates come in and negotiations begin between Republicans and the White House. The only sure outcome of those negotiations is that a tax cut will not be financed by borrowing from the Social Security trust funds.

For the immediate future, House and Senate GOP leaders face a difficult task in passing the 13 appropriations bills this summer. Back-of-the-envelope calculations by appropriators suggest that ultimately lawmakers will have to add at least $30 billion beyond the budget plan to obtain Clinton's signature on the upcoming bills.

But for now, unity is the overriding concern as Republicans seek to demonstrate that they can get the budget process back on track after failing to adopt a budget resolution last year for the first time since the system was put in place in 1974. The debate demonstrated the ability of House GOP factions to pull together behind a common alternative despite reservations, pass it and run the institution with a five-vote margin for error. It was also a signal of support for new Speaker J. Dennis Hastert, R-Ill. "That's a far larger issue than this budget," said Rep. Robert L. Ehrlich Jr., R-Md.

Hastert had to defuse a mini-crisis when Transportation Committee Chairman Bud Shuster, R-Pa., threatened to scuttle the budget unless he won an amendment to reserve $50 billion over 10 years in unspent aviation taxes for airport projects, instead of devoting them to tax cuts. Shuster ultimately dropped his amendment in exchange for a pledge of speedy floor consideration of his bill (HR 1000), which would devote all the money in the aviation trust fund to airport projects. Shuster will be permitted to bring the measure up without finding offsetting spending cuts that would otherwise be required under budget rules.

The episode illustrated a continued desire for more spending even as lawmakers profess to want to stick to the caps. Members are awaiting new and improved surplus figures this summer to help them escape the money crunch.

"The Republicans expect a big windfall in the fiscal 1999 surplus when the midsession review comes out this summer," said a veteran House Democratic Appropriations Committee aide. "They are promising everyone from Shuster to the domestic appropriations cardinals to the defense hawks that this will be the answer to their money problems."

Said Rep. Michael N. Castle, R-Del.: "I am fully convinced that before this year is over, these are not the caps we're going to be dealing with. These numbers are not going to hold up."

An Easier Season

For House Republicans, action on the budget was a breeze compared with last year, when Budget Chairman John R. Kasich, R-Ohio, devoted months to winning support for an austere plan to break the 1997 budget deal and cut taxes and spending by $100 billion over five years. It quickly died.

This year members, flush with even bigger surplus estimates, found putting together a budget fairly easy. The central element of the fiscal 2000 plan, largely crafted by Kasich's Senate counterpart, Pete V. Domenici, R-N.M., is to hold off on cutting taxes until "on-budget" surpluses — those that do not depend on Social Security revenues — start to show up in fiscal 2001.

After flirting with raising the appropriations caps, Republican leaders opted to stick to them — at least for now. Then they focused mainly on plugging in strictly advisory numbers for a host of spending categories, such as defense, education, veterans and the environment. Those figures provide the basis for competing claims about what the other side is doing for politically popular programs.

Before approving their plan, Republicans easily defeated two Democratic plans. First, by a 134-295 vote, the House rejected a plan drafted by moderate-to-conservative "Blue Dog" Democrats that would have devoted all of the Social Security surplus and half of future on-budget surpluses to reducing the national debt. The remaining 50 percent of on-budget surpluses would have been evenly divided between tax cuts and new spending. *(Vote 75, p. H-28)*

The House then killed, 173-250, a mainstream Democratic plan assembled by Budget Committee members. It would have blocked tax cuts or new spending until legislation was enacted to address the solvency of the Social Security and Medicare trust funds. After that, it would have provided for a 10-year tax cut of $116 billion and significantly higher spending than the GOP plan. It also would have deposited more than $2 trillion in additional bonds into the Medicare and Social Security trust funds. *(Vote 76, p. H-30)*

In the Senate, the budget passed after a two-day debate during which Domenici's blueprint emerged mostly unscathed. The only substantive changes to the plan came on Democratic amendments to add $2 billion to the GOP plan for fiscal 2000 for veterans' health care and to pare the tax cut by $10 billion over 10 years to finance additional child care block grants.

Meanwhile, Republicans killed numerous other Democratic amendments, including ones to delay tax cuts until after fixing Social Security and Medicare, increase agricultural subsidies, devote much of the surplus to Medicare, add funding for education and express Senate support for raising the minimum wage by $1 by September 2000, to $6.15 an hour.

Domenici also accepted an amendment by John H. Chafee, R-R.I., to strike a section of the measure that would have reserved any on-budget fiscal 2000 surplus for tax cuts; Chafee prefers debt reduction.

Medicare Spat

Debate grew heated during a vote on a non-binding "sense of the Senate" amendment to consider a plan by John B. Breaux, D-La., to overhaul Medicare. Breaux chaired a national bipartisan commission on Medicare that failed to produce a recommendation for Congress. After lobbying by the White House, all but two Democrats — Breaux and commission member Bob Kerrey of Nebraska — opposed the amendment, which was adopted, 56-43. *(Vote 65, p. S-16)*

In perhaps the most significant vote on a Republican amendment, a majority embraced a proposal by Olympia J. Snowe of Maine to raise tobacco taxes to pay for a prescription drug benefit under Medicare. Twelve Republicans joined all but three Democrats to produce a 54-44 vote, but that tally was not enough to waive a point of order against the measure. It did illustrate bipartisan sentiment in the Senate to raise tobacco taxes. *(Vote 76, p. S-17)*

In a vote that underscored the schism among Senate Republicans on taxes, the Senate, 67-32, killed an amendment by George V. Voinovich, R-Ohio, to scrap the GOP tax cut in favor of devoting more of the surplus to deficit reduction. Liberal Democrats who favor surplus-financed spending joined with all but five Republicans to kill the amendment. But those five Republicans illustrated GOP moderates' sense that the plans of the party's tax-cutting wing are too ambitious. *(Vote 71, p. S-17)*

Adoption of GOP Budget Resolution Is Small Victory With Big Asterisk

APRIL 17 — After embarrassing themselves by not passing a budget last year, congressional Republicans took great satisfaction in reversing course and adopting their fiscal 2000 budget resolution by the rarely met April 15 deadline.

But the accomplishment almost certainly will represent the high-water mark for the GOP's hopes to cut taxes and keep government spending down. It also sets up a difficult spring and summer for appropriators, who have to make the real-world spending decisions required to carry out the plan.

And a clash with President Clinton over taxes is looming.

Final action on the non-binding budget plan (H Con Res 68) is but the first, relatively easy step in what promises to be a standoff between congressional Republicans and Clinton that — so far at least — has been made no easier to resolve by budget surpluses that have federal coffers overflowing.

The GOP budget advanced after a strong push from House Speaker J. Dennis Hastert, R-Ill., who has made "making the trains run on time" a major goal of his tenure.

The House adopted the conference report on the budget resolution April 14 by a 220-208 vote; the Senate followed suit the next day, 54-44. Clinton does not need to act on it. *(House vote 85, p. H-34; Senate vote 86, p. S-20)*

The budget resolution is the official Republican response to Clinton's February budget submission, which called for targeted tax relief, modest spending on new programs and the deposit of $2.7 trillion in new IOUs into the Social Security trust funds.

The Republican plan envisions a tax cut of $142 billion over the next five years and $778 billion over 10 years, while significantly boosting the Pentagon's budget. But that would be possible only by making politically difficult and probably untenable cuts in domestic programs for veterans, farmers, the environment and crime prevention.

"We're pleased, No. 1, that we passed good legislation . . . a good blueprint for America's future," Hastert said. "We're also pleased that this Congress can get its work done."

Countered House Minority Leader Richard A. Gephardt, D-Mo.: "[Republicans'] obsession with irresponsible tax cuts leaves no room for other critical responsibilities. It will require draconian funding cuts for key programs in education, veterans affairs and environmental protection."

Only a Blueprint

In and of itself, the budget resolution is a non-binding blueprint that does little more than set the amount of discretionary money available for appropriations and pave the way for a filibuster-proof budget-reconciliation bill that will serve as the vehicle for a tax cut this summer.

The next step comes in May, when the House and Senate Appropriations committees — which are responsible for doling out the approximately one-third of the federal budget that has to pass Congress every year — begin voting on the 13 spending bills for fiscal 2000, which starts Oct. 1. Republicans insist that they will try to stay within excruciatingly tough caps on discretionary appropriations set by the 1997 balanced-budget law (PL 105-33). *(1997 Almanac, p. 2-18)*

However, it is an open secret among lawmakers both on and off the Appropriations committees that the caps are so stringent that it is impossible to abide by them in all of the bills, much less obtain Clinton's signature.

"As far as I can see . . . they're on a train-wreck course," said a top White House official.

In fact, House Appropriations Committee Chairman C.W. Bill Young, R-Fla., who favors raising the caps, made a plea to Clinton to lead the effort at an April 13 meeting at the White House on the Kosovo conflict.

"Bill Young said, 'We have to raise the caps,' and said, 'Mr. President, I wish you would take the lead in raising the caps,' " said Rep. John P. Murtha, D-Pa., who was in the room. Clinton did not respond, Murtha said.

There appears to be little incentive for Clinton and his Democratic allies to help the Republicans out of their jam on appropriations. Last year's chaotic appropriations process featured an end-of-session logjam that gave Clinton remarkable leverage, especially given the scandal in which he was embroiled. But by caving to Clinton's demands for new spending — and then adding some of their own — GOP leaders disappointed their base and that may have contributed to their disappointing showing in last year's elections.

Some Democrats are looking forward to a repeat of last year that would give them much of the spending they want, while blocking the Republican drive to cut taxes.

GOP leaders' public statements pay homage to the caps, and they insist they can stay within them. But if Congress and Clinton would not stay within the caps for fiscal 1999 — the end-of-session omnibus bill (PL 105-277) contained more than $20 billion in "emergency" spending — it is virtually inconceivable that they will hew to them this year, especially with a $111 billion budget surplus estimate.

Seeking to block a repeat of last year's debacle, Senate Republicans have installed a new point of order against any non-defense "emergency" spending that is not truly urgent. Waiving this point of order requires 60 votes.

Many Republicans acknowledge privately that the caps will ultimately be raised — or broken. Some do so publicly. "We need to raise the caps," said Rep. John Edward Porter, R-Ill., who is chairman of the Appropriations subcommittee with jurisdiction over health and education programs. "We need to do it in an honest, direct way."

Even a key architect of the budget, Senate Budget Committee Chairman Pete V. Domenici, R-N.M., knows that the caps, and therefore his budget, are unrealistic. Less than a year ago, as Domenici was battling his House counterpart, John R. Kasich, R-Ohio, over whether to cut discretionary spending, Domenici said that even at the caps, appropriators would not be able to pass all their bills, especially the Labor, Health and Human Services bill. He was right.

So, what makes Domenici think appropriators can now live within the caps when he accurately predicted that they could not last year?

"Look, all I can tell you is that you take things around here one step at a time," Domenici replied in an April 14 interview. "We have to end up going through a lot of other hoops, and the president has to get involved sooner or later."

When To Deal?

The great unanswered question is when — or whether — congressional Republicans and the White House will reach a split-their-differences agreement that would give Republicans tax cuts and more defense spending while providing Clinton and his allies additional domestic spending and targeted tax cuts.

With surpluses bulging, such a deal should not be too hard to reach by the numbers. But the politics are much trickier.

One obstacle to any such agreement is that the budget debate this year has featured a lot of hot rhetoric about Social Security. Lawmakers of both parties see a critical difference between the portion of the surplus that comes from excess Social Security revenues and future "on-budget" surpluses from general government operations that are projected to start appearing in 2001.

Republicans have accepted arguments by Democrats, such as Sen. Ernest F. Hollings of South Carolina, that spending Social Security surpluses on tax cuts amounts to a "raid" on the program, so they have tailored their budget to use only on-budget surpluses for tax cuts.

But additional spending that will flow when and if lawmakers break the caps, along with paying for the U.S. military's role in NATO airstrikes on Kosovo, promises to eat up the first several years' worth of future on-budget surpluses.

At present, the Congressional Budget Office predicts on-budget surpluses that start at $6 billion in fiscal 2001 and hover between $48 billion and $72 billion over the following four years. But those projections assume that lawmakers will abide by the spending caps, and appropriators warn that it will probably take $30 billion above the caps to get all of the fiscal 2000 spending bills passed and signed by Clinton. If discretionary spending grows in 2001 and beyond, on-budget surpluses will shrink rapidly or disappear.

What this means is that under current budget projections, any tax cut would probably be financed, at least in the first few years, by surpluses produced by Social Security.

Republicans are hoping, however, that new revenue estimates due in July will show even bigger surpluses. But any huge midyear jump in surplus estimates is probably not in the offing, economists in both the private and public sector say. "All the indications now . . . are that we're not going to have that revenue surprise," said a senior Senate Budget Committee GOP aide.

Little Drama

The April 13 budget conference was a ceremonial affair. The House- and Senate-passed budget resolutions were largely identical, and Republicans had ironed out most of their differences in private the previous day.

One difference was the timing for a tax bill. The House had set a deadline of Sept. 30 for the Ways and Means Committee to report a bill; the Senate had called for committee action in mid-June. The conference report set the deadline for mid-July, over the protests of Ways and Means Committee Chairman Bill Archer, R-Texas.

About the only drama involved the fate of an amendment by Sens. Christopher J. Dodd, D-Conn., and James M. Jeffords, R-Vt., to boost child care block grants by $1 billion per year over five years, financed by a corresponding reduction of the tax cut. At the private GOP meeting, the Senate agreed to dump the language, but after catching wind of the decision, Dodd forced and won a 66-33 vote to instruct the Senate conferees to keep it. *(Vote 85, p. S-20)*

Though non-binding, the vote pressured Domenici to insist on a compromise: $3 billion dedicated to tax cuts and $3 billion for the block grants. ◆

Senate Filibuster Stops Effort To Lock Up Social Security Revenues

SUMMARY

A bill that supporters said would put surplus Social Security revenues into a protected "lockbox" passed in the House but ran into a Democratic filibuster in the Senate.

The great lockbox debate of 1999 started as congressional Republicans sought to use Social Security as a political wedge to advance their budget and tax goals — while winning political points at the expense of Democrats. With surplus projections far surpassing prior estimates, the federal government in fiscal 2000 would no longer have to borrow from Social Security reserves to pay for other government programs, provided lawmakers' appetites for spending and tax cuts could be curbed. The lockbox bills aimed to erect procedural hurdles that would make it more difficult for lawmakers to cast votes to "spend" Social Security surpluses.

The idea originated in the Senate, where Budget Committee Chairman Pete V. Domenici, R-N.M., crafted a plan that would "protect" Social Security by ratcheting down the limit on the publicly held national debt each year by the amount of the Social Security surplus. But Finance Committee Chairman William V. Roth Jr., R-Del., opposed the measure, saying it could provoke a first-ever default on the national debt. Because of his objection and because Finance has jurisdiction over the matter, the measure came to the floor as an amendment to a bill (S 557) to make it more difficult to pass "emergency" spending bills. The lockbox measure would also effectively require 60 Senate votes to pass any bill or adopt any amendment that would spend the Social Security surplus. Existing Senate rules already imposed that hurdle for tax bills.

In the House, opposition from House Ways and Means Committee Chairman Bill Archer, R-Texas, killed any prospect for the Senate bill and its debt reduction component. Instead, the House passed HR 1259, which sought to establish points of order in both chambers against any bill that "spent" the Social Security-generated surplus for new spending or tax cuts. It essentially aimed to impose the 60 vote hurdle in the Senate for bills financed by Social Security surpluses.

Senate Democrats successfully filibustered the more stringent Domenici plan and also blocked the House bill from coming to the floor because Majority Leader Trent Lott, R-Miss., restricted their ability to offer amendments.

President Clinton endorsed the lockbox idea at a July 12 White House meeting. But further debate could prove embarrassing, because the Congressional Budget Office said that Congress and Clinton teamed up to "raid" Social Security yet again in the fiscal 2000 spending bills.

Cloture Vote Fails On 'Lockbox' Amendment

APRIL 24 — The Social Security Surplus Preservation and Debt Reduction Act came to the Senate floor April 20 carrying all the signs of a measure that GOP leaders were not particularly serious about passing.

It aimed to create a "lockbox" mechanism to make it more difficult for lawmakers to tap the "off-budget" Social Security-related budget surplus for new spending or a tax cut. Both parties consider protection of Social Security a top priority. This off-budget surplus is the portion of the surplus that appears because of extra Social Security revenues. It is responsible for all of the current budget surplus.

The measure would have done nothing in the short term to strengthen Senate rules against tapping the surplus to pay for calamities such as the war in Kosovo or anything else Congress officially declares an emergency. And existing rules block Social Security surplus-financed tax cuts anyway.

The measure came to the floor after Majority Leader Trent Lott, R-Miss., employed an unusual parliamentary end-run around Finance Committee Chairman William V. Roth Jr., R-Del., who opposed it. It was debated as an amendment to a related bill (S 557) to make it easier to block "emergency" spending. S 557 would do so by making it more difficult for lawmakers to take advantage of a budget rule that permits Congress to evade strict limits on spending by designating certain kinds of spending as emergencies.

Democrats killed the lockbox measure through a filibuster April 22 — a result that did not entirely displease Republican leaders, who immediately accused their rivals of not being serious about protecting the Social Security-related surplus.

The lockbox would have set a new limit on the allowable amount of publicly held debt and would ratchet those limits down by the amount of the annual Social Security surplus. Under

BoxScore

- **Bills:** HR 1259; amendment to S 557
- **Legislative action: Senate** failed to invoke cloture on the amendment to S 557, 54-45, on April 22. Sixty votes are required for cloture.

Senate failed to invoke cloture on the amendment, 49-44, on April 30.

House passed HR 1259, 416-12, on May 26.

Senate failed to invoke cloture on the amendment, 53-46, on June 15.

Senate failed to invoke cloture on HR 1259, 55-44, on June 16.

Senate failed to invoke cloture on the amendment, 52-43, on July 16.

such a law, any bill (with several major exceptions) that would tap the "off-budget" surplus could prompt a first-ever default on the national debt.

At the heart of the lockbox measure was a new Senate point of order that would effectively require 60 votes for any tax or spending bill that used the Social Security portion of the surplus — even though budget points of order under pay- as-you-go rules already place that obstacle in front of tax bills. "It will become very difficult when this legislation becomes law for us to ever again in a wholesale, willy-nilly manner spend Social Security trust fund money," said the measure's author, Budget Committee Chairman Pete V. Domenici, R-N.M.

Meanwhile, the measure would permit lawmakers to get around discretionary spending "caps" by continuing to use the controversial emergency designation. That designation allowed President Clinton and Congress to evade the caps by $21 billion in last year's omnibus spending bill (PL 105-277). The measure came to the floor just as lawmakers were acknowledging that the war in Kosovo was going to use up billions of dollars of the Social Security-generated surplus.

Republicans could have imposed the point of order when considering the recently passed budget resolution (H Con Res 68) — which does not require Clinton's signature and is not subject to a filibuster. But opposition from Roth and House Ways and Means Chairman Bill Archer, R-Texas, ended that idea. Instead, Republicans brought the lockbox measure to the floor on a bill that Democrats could easily stop.

Only seven senators spoke during a brief debate April 20, and Republicans turned to other matters before losing a cloture vote April 22. The vote to limit debate and proceed to the lockbox measure was 54-45, short of the 60 votes required for cloture. *(Vote 90, p. S-21)*

Roth remained silent during debate. He agrees with Treasury Secretary Robert E. Rubin that the lockbox measure could provoke a debt crisis that would damage U.S. standing with its creditors, aides said. Rubin warned that it could hinder distribution of Social Security checks if the government breached the debt limit. Had Republicans passed a lockbox measure, Rubin vowed to recommend a Clinton veto.

"The amendment could create a government default — a U.S. government default," said Frank R. Lautenberg of New Jersey, the top Budget Committee Democrat. "It could undermine our nation's credit standing, increase interest costs and ultimately lead to a worldwide economic crisis." Domenici countered that he had modified the idea to ensure that Social Security checks would never have been cut off.

The underlying bill to make it harder to pass "emergency" spending bills would have created in law a point of order against any such bill that did not consist solely of true emergencies. It would have required a majority to waive the point of order. The budget resolution changed Senate rules to impose a tougher, 60-vote point of order against non-defense spending that is not an emergency.

GOP Leaders Push Private Accounts, As Bill Again Stalls

MAY 1 — Even though GOP congressional leaders have made it clear that they do not want to debate a Social Security overhaul this year, key House Republicans on April 28 unveiled a plan that would create individual investment accounts to replace a portion of program benefits.

Ways and Means Committee Chairman Bill Archer, R-Texas, and Social Security Subcommittee Chairman E. Clay Shaw Jr., R-Fla., said the private accounts — which would be invested 60 percent in stocks and 40 percent in bonds — would generate significant new retirement earnings for Social Security beneficiaries, thereby relieving financial strain on the federal pension program.

Social Security is forecast to run a deficit beginning in 2034, as the Baby Boom generation retires, the proportion of the population paying into the system continues to decline and retiree life expectancy increases.

"Our [plan] does not cut benefits, it does not raise taxes, but it does save Social Security. Not just for a limited number of years, but for all time," Archer said.

The duo released their plan at a time when the politics of Social Security has become very complicated. The GOP congressional leadership, citing internal polls, has warned that the party could take a beating in the 2000 elections if it gets too far ahead in advocating major changes to the popular program. Democrats have attacked Republicans in the past for recommending reductions in annual cost of living increases.

President Clinton, who has said a Social Security overhaul is a top priority, would still very much like legislation to enhance his legacy. Any bipartisan plan that included private investment to replace program benefits could anger the liberal wing of his party. That could complicate Democrats' chances of retaking the House in 2000 and Vice President Al Gore's efforts to energize the party base for his presidential bid.

After the plan was announced, House Speaker J. Dennis Hastert, R-Ill., issued a statement that kept the proposal at arm's length, without publicly waving goodbye.

"I pledge that I will take a close look at this proposal," Hastert said, adding: "Make no mistake. Any efforts to enact a Social Security reform plan must be done in a bipartisan manner."

The Senate GOP leadership has been equally hesitant about moving ahead without bipartisan support. Senate Majority Leader Trent Lott, R-Miss., has said he does not believe Congress will act on the issue this year.

Administration Shows Interest

Archer and Shaw received a somewhat more encouraging response from the White House, where Clinton met with top aides April 30 to discuss possible changes to his own Social Security plan. Clinton's proposal, unveiled in his Jan. 19 State of the Union address, calls for the government to directly invest a portion of the program's trust fund in the stock market and would set up retirement accounts for low-income workers to supplement, not replace, basic benefits.

Administration officials said Clinton and his advisers ran through a list of possible options that could move the White House closer to Republicans and moderate Democrats who also favor private accounts, but came to no conclusion. Further meetings are planned.

"We're going to take a close look at what Chairman Archer put out," White House spokesman Joe Lockhart said April 28. "What's important here is this looks like a serious attempt to engage in a very important debate, and stands in some contrast to some others in the leadership who sought to dismiss this debate for political reasons."

Archer and Clinton talked by telephone April 27 about Archer's proposal. Archer and Shaw also briefed Ways and Means Democrats on April 28 after unveiling the plan.

Even if Clinton were to make overtures to the Republicans, overall reaction to the Archer-Shaw plan underscores the dim chances for enacting major legislation this session.

Conservatives, including the libertarian CATO Institute — the chief proponent of private accounts — said the plan was "not a serious attempt to reform" because individuals would not have ownership of the earnings.

Moderates warned that the plan, by using the Social Security surplus to create the accounts, imposed trillions of dollars in new government liabilities and sidestepped politically difficult decisions about cutting benefits or raising payroll taxes.

Liberals warned that the proposal was the first step toward "privatizing" the program, which provides retirement, disability and survivors' benefits to 44 million Americans.

"This has been an attempt to address the image problems of the Republican party, not [to address] Social Security," Rep. Rosa DeLauro, D-Conn., assistant to the minority leader, said April 28.

Archer responded to such comments by saying: "When you're getting criticized from the extremes, you're probably doing the right thing."

Nuts and Bolts

The Archer-Shaw plan would keep intact the current structure of Social Security, including survivors' and disability benefits.

It would impose major changes in the system's financing, however, by tapping into the federal budget surplus to create an annual, refundable tax credit for all those paying into the Social Security system. The program is now funded through a 12.4 percent payroll tax, half paid by employers and half by employees.

The credit would be equal to 2 percent of earnings up to the Social Security wage cap. The wage cap is currently $72,600, but is increased annually. That means the maximum credit provided in 1999 under the Archer-Shaw proposal would be $1,452.

The tax credit would be automatically deposited by the government into a mandatory personal account, called a Social Security Guarantee Account.

Individuals would have some ability to choose where to invest the money, selecting from a government-approved list of 50 investment funds. To limit the downside risk and ensure that the accounts realized a 5.35 percent annual rate of return, all the financial instruments would be based on 60 percent stock index funds and 40 percent bonds.

Except in the case of disability, workers would not be allowed to withdraw money from the accounts before retirement. At retirement, the accounts would be annuitized and used to replace a portion, or all, of the regular Social Security benefits an individual would be eligible to receive under current law.

If the account was insufficient to provide at least the same benefit as current law, the Social Security Administration would draw from the program trust fund to make up the difference.

Individuals whose account balance was worth more would realize the difference in the form of higher monthly benefits. At death, any money remaining in the account would go first to survivors' benefits and any balance would revert to the Social Security trust fund.

If an individual died before retirement, the account balance would be used first to pay survivors' benefits. Any remainder could then be passed on tax-free to an estate. Otherwise, individuals would not get any lump sum payment from the accounts.

The lack of private ownership is a key objection of CATO and other advocates of personal accounts. They argue that unless individuals can build wealth to be passed on to their families, accounts will not have popular support.

Others raise concerns about the complexity and administrative expense of managing tens of millions of individual accounts. The plan would limit administrative fees to 25 basis points, or one-quarter of 1 percent of interest earnings. Any costs over that level would be borne by general revenues.

Predicting that most individuals would not fare noticeably better under the new system, Dean Baker, senior research fellow of the Preamble Center, a moderate think tank, said in a statement that "all the administrative expenses . . . are simply transfers to the financial industry."

While Archer and Shaw stressed that no one would get a lower benefit under the new plan, Ways and Means aides added that over the next 75 years, few individuals were expected to earn higher monthly payments.

According to tables released by the Joint Committee on Taxation, low- to middle-income workers would get the most benefit from the tax credit.

The proposal would also repeal by 2006 the current earnings limit, whereby seniors who continue working face an initial reduction in Social Security benefits. In 1999, individuals age 65 to 69 who earn more than $15,500 a year lose $1 in Social Security benefits for every $3 in extra earnings.

If anything, the Archer-Shaw proposal showed the political limits of trying to fix Social Security. Lawmakers do not want to cut benefits, raise taxes or increase the retirement age — the most commonly recommended fixes, but the most unpopular. Clinton's proposal has run into similar criticisms.

On one level, the Archer-Shaw plan is a success. The Social Security Administration, in a detailed analysis on April 29, found that if the economic assumptions in the plan were correct, it would ensure the solvency of the program and allow for payroll tax cuts in 2050 and 2060.

That does not mean it is cost-free. The Social Security actuaries forecast that the plan would result in major increases in the public debt.

And, as in Clinton's proposal, the plan envisions for the first time using general government revenues to finance Social Security and the tax credit. The credit alone is forecast to cost $1 trillion over 10 years.

While the lawmakers' plan is the most visible, it is not the only one under consideration. Rep. Benjamin L. Cardin, D-Md., will soon introduce a bill. Reps. Charles W. Stenholm, D-

Texas, and Jim Kolbe, R-Ariz., are refining a plan, introduced last year, that would divert part of the Social Security payroll tax to private accounts, while making other benefit changes.

In the Senate, Republican Rick Santorum of Pennsylvania is working with Democrat Bob Kerrey of Nebraska, Republican Judd Gregg of New Hampshire and others on a plan.

House Passes 'Safe Deposit Box Act' To Guard Surplus

MAY 29 — House Republicans talked a good game on fiscal discipline in passing a bill that purports to lock away the budget surplus for Social Security. But their lack of a game plan to avert a looming impasse on appropriations exposed deep fissures within House GOP ranks and stalled the first fiscal 2000 spending bill.

Events the week of May 24 vividly illustrated how the daunting reality of the Republicans' budget dilemma is taking hold. The Republican rank and file is increasingly worried that the party will take another beating at the hands of President Clinton unless the leadership can figure out a successful strategy for the fiscal 2000 appropriations bills.

In the Senate, on the other hand, lawmakers made slow but steady bipartisan progress in getting their spending cycle started, as the Appropriations Committee approved subcommittee allocations and draft defense, transportation and energy spending bills.

It was a frustrating week for House Republicans of all stripes: Appropriators watched what should have been an easy-to-pass agriculture appropriations bill (HR 1906) stall at the hands of conservative renegades; GOP true believers accused their leaders of inviting a "train wreck" on appropriations; and Speaker J. Dennis Hastert, R-Ill. — faced with no easy choices — acknowledged that he has yet to devise a plan to avoid a repeat of last year's debacle on the omnibus spending bill (PL 105-277). *(1998 Almanac, p. 2-112)*

The difficulties on appropriations were but one element of a bad week for Hastert. The day after pulling the agriculture bill from the floor, GOP leaders again lost control of the floor and had to abruptly adjourn for the Memorial Day recess after it became apparent that they would not win the votes needed to proceed to the defense authorization bill (HR 1401).

House leaders had hoped to pass two or three appropriations bills before heading to their districts, but their single accomplishment came instead on the ambitiously titled Social Security and Medicare Safe Deposit Box Act. The House passed the bill (HR 1259) on May 26 by a vote of 416-12, after a sparsely attended debate during which bill proponents exaggerated the potential effectiveness of their "lockbox." *(Vote 164, p. H-60)*

Typical was bill sponsor Wally Herger, R-Calif., who said the bill "locks up the Social Security surpluses and allows them only to be used for Social Security and Medicare reform."

Actually, the most significant component of the measure would establish points of order in both chambers against any bill that "spends" the Social Security-generated surplus for new spending or tax cuts.

Existing Senate "pay as you go" rules and a new Senate point of order against domestic "emergency" spending already offer procedural protections almost identical to those that would be provided by the bill. And the House Rules Committee routinely waives points of order, which are objections raised by a lawmaker that the chamber is departing from its rules.

The main purpose of the bill appeared to be to make it more politically difficult for lawmakers to vote for bills that borrow from the Social Security trust fund surplus to pay for other programs. With 416 members on record as supporting the idea, sponsors hope to make it difficult to vote for fiscal 2000 bills that may bust through spending "caps" that are a pillar of the 1997 budget deal and the GOP fiscal 2000 budget resolution.

Rep. E. Clay Shaw Jr., R-Fla., chairman of the Ways and Means Subcommittee on Social Security, acknowledged that the measure would not prevent tapping trust fund-generated surpluses for other government programs such as defense or education. "But it sets up a barrier that you've got to cross over before you do that," Shaw said. "And that's going to be a very tough vote."

The lockbox bill came to the floor one week after Republicans voted to double Clinton's request for an emergency supplemental bill (PL 106-31) to pay for the Kosovo operation and provide aid to Central America and U.S. farmers. Before sending the supplemental to Clinton, lockbox supporters such as Senate Majority Leader Trent Lott, R-Miss., and Budget Committee Chairman Pete V. Domenici, R-N.M., voted to waive a lockbox-like point of order against a host of "emergency" provisions in that bill

"One week they double defense; this week they're trying to put Social Security in a lockbox, and in the end they're going to break the caps," said Rep. John P. Murtha, D-Pa.

Democrats voted for the bill even as they dismissed it as mostly toothless. "If members want to save Social Security, bring out a bill that saves Social Security," said Rep. David R. Obey of Wisconsin, ranking Democrat on Appropriations. "Do not bring out something which ought to be labeled the No. 1 legislative fraud of the year."

Republicans believe the issue will play well among voters. It was the topic of a May 22 GOP radio address by Rep. James E. Rogan of California, and Lott made it the centerpiece of a May 27 news conference. "This will help restore fiscal sanity, it will build a wall around the Social Security money, and it will help pay down the national debt and therefore lower interest rates," Lott said.

Lott said the lockbox bill would be the first order of business when the Senate returns the week of June 7. Democrats have successfully filibustered a more stringent version of the lockbox over a provision that would ratchet down the national debt by the amount of the annual Social Security surplus. At a May 27 meeting, Senate GOP leaders weighed whether to move the House bill or continue to debate the Senate measure. It appears they will adopt something similar to the House bill, said a senior GOP aide.

Spending Stalled

The lockbox debate came on the heels of a successful effort by conservative Rep. Tom Coburn, R-Okla., to stall the agriculture spending bill over his leadership's appropriations strategy. That strategy would tap big domestic spending bills that fund education, health, housing and veterans programs to free up enough money to pass smaller bills such as agriculture.

Conservatives complained that the strategy ensures that measures, such as the spending bill for the departments of Labor and Health and Human Services (HHS), will not have enough money to pass, and that the resulting impasse will lead to a negotiating atmosphere much like last year's, in which Clinton and Congress agreed to effectively break the caps by $21 billion.

"If we continue down this path, we will have another disaster like we had at the end of the last Congress," said Republican Rep. Steve Largent of Oklahoma. "What is the end game? Where are we going?"

To a remarkable degree, the debate on the agriculture measure had little to do with the underlying bill and everything to do with the broader issue of the caps, the lack of a plan and the overall amount of money that should go for appropriations.

Those issues were given relatively short shrift earlier this year when the House debated the fiscal 2000 budget resolution (H Con Res 68). Instead, the House and Senate crafted a measure that stuck with the caps, even though Congress and Clinton proved unable to live within them last year.

"Instead of debating agriculture appropriations . . . we were debating the overall scope of how much money should be for discretionary spending," said a top House Appropriations Committee Republican staff aide. "We should have had that . . . debate when we were doing the budget resolution."

Even the most die-hard supporters of the caps, such as Coburn, concede that given the narrow House GOP majority, at least some breach of the caps is inevitable. Coburn wants to freeze fiscal 2000 appropriations at this year's level, which is about $14 billion in outlays above the caps but $16 billion below Clinton's request.

Republican leaders are not counting on the administration to help them out of the bind. Office of Management and Budget Director Jack Lew turned the screws in a May 26 speech at the Brookings Institution.

"The fact of the matter is that Congress is considering a budget that severely underfunds critical programs. We have been down that road before, and we know where it leads," Lew said. "The Appropriations committees are now implementing an untenable budget resolution, which is a blueprint for chaos."

Lew urged lawmakers to take another look at the many new revenues and user fees laid out in Clinton's February budget, including $8 billion from an increase in cigarette taxes. If those revenue raisers were accepted, Lew said, Congress could stay within the caps and still fund administration priorities.

Republicans responded angrily to Lew's remarks, complaining that the White House sends up the same revenue raising proposals year after year and does not spend any political capital trying to get them enacted. Yet the White House assumes passage of these proposals when presenting its budget — which includes demands for new spending that, according to the Congressional Budget Office, is about $30 billion above the caps.

"The president's budget is full of accounting gimmicks and unrealistic user fee proposals," said House Appropriations Committee Chairman C.W. Bill Young, R-Fla., in a May 26 letter to Lew. "These gimmicks have been overwhelmingly rejected, even by [Democrats]."

The significance of the exchange had less to do with the merits of Clinton's offsets — many of which stir significant opposition among his Democratic allies — than with Lew's admonition to Republicans to stay within the caps. The administration is apparently not interested in a near-term budget summit to discuss raising the caps, leaving Republicans to fend for themselves.

A group of 13 mostly moderate House Republicans led by Michael N. Castle of Delaware wrote Clinton on May 26 to urge that "talks begin immediately [with the leadership of Congress] on a budget and appropriations agreement for this year to avoid a likely impasse at the end of the fiscal year. . . . Resolving these differences should not be left to last-minute negotiations in the fall."

But it is not just the White House that is cool to a summit; Republican leaders have displayed no enthusiasm either.

For their part, congressional Democrats are content to watch Republicans flounder. Many welcome an impasse that would give Clinton the type of leverage that produced last fall's bill.

"I'm an old quarterback. We ran this play last year and it worked," said House Democratic Whip David E. Bonior of Michigan. "Let's run it again."

Senate Side

Things are proceeding more smoothly in the Senate, where Appropriations Committee Chairman Ted Stevens, R-Alaska, has been maneuvering to add money to the fiscal 2000 bills. He snared $2.6 billion in offsets for additional spending by speeding up an auction of portions of the electromagnetic spectrum currently scheduled for 2001. He awarded this money to the Defense Subcommittee, which he chairs.

Stevens also shifted $4.6 billion in defense outlays that flowed from the two fiscal 1999 supplemental bills to a 14th panel called the Deficiencies Subcommittee, which is distributing the money to various non-defense subcommittees as those bills go forward.

Stevens issued subcommittee allocations on May 25, and the full committee approved them, 24-3. Generally, the Senate panels will have more money to work with than the House, which promises a smoother path in that chamber for bills to fund foreign aid and the departments of Commerce, Justice, State, Energy and Interior.

Stevens concedes that he is taking advantage of the recently passed Kosovo supplemental — which contained $10.9 billion in fiscal 1999 emergency defense funds — to squeeze additional money into the 2000 bills. "We had all of this in mind" when crafting the supplemental, Stevens said. "I do think beyond the next job."

The Pentagon accounts that Stevens is tapping to assist the domestic bills include readiness, munitions, spare parts and recruiting — the same areas that Republicans said needed such urgent replenishment when they doubled Clinton's request for Kosovo.

One senior Senate GOP aide predicted that the savvy Stevens would get all the money back in a future fiscal 2000 emergency supplemental.

Senate Bill Echoes Existing Rules

JUNE 12 — Senate Republicans, confident they have hit upon a winning issue, will take another run the week of June 14 at passing a bill designed to make it more difficult for lawmakers to borrow from the Social Security trust funds to fund new spending or tax cuts.

The political benefits of passing the so-called Social Security lockbox measure seem to outweigh the additional protections the bill would provide to the system's trust funds. The most significant element of the House bill (HR 1259), a modified version of which the Senate is expected to ultimately pass, would in effect require 60 votes in the Senate for any bill that used the Social Security-generated surplus to pay for new spending or tax cuts.

Existing Senate pay-as-you-go rules against Social Security surplus-financed tax cuts or spending that would violate budget "caps" provide procedural hurdles identical to those that would be established by the lockbox bill. And the Senate easily waived a new lockbox-like procedural device during debate on the recent emergency spending bill (HR 1141 — PL 106-31) for the Kosovo mission and other supplemental fiscal 1999 spending.

But Republicans think they are gaining political traction with the idea. It has twice been the topic of their Saturday radio addresses, and it was no coincidence that three participants in a June 9 GOP news conference on the lockbox were potentially vulnerable incumbents up for re-election in 2000: Spencer Abraham of Michigan, Rick Santorum of Pennsylvania and John Ashcroft of Missouri.

"This legislation will mandate, for the first time by federal law, that all Social Security surplus funds be used exclusively for Social Security," Santorum said in a June 4 radio address. Proponents may exaggerate the strength of the lockbox, but the idea does well in polls among voters of all stripes, said a senior Senate GOP aide. It has given Republicans a potent retort to President Clinton's vow to "save Social Security first" before tapping the surplus for tax cuts or new spending.

Senate Republicans have brought a stricter version of the lockbox measure to the floor as an amendment to a bill (S 557) to make it more difficult for Congress to evade the budget caps by designating new spending as an "emergency." Democrats have successfully filibustered the measure over a provision that would automatically ratchet down limits on the publicly held national debt by an amount equal to the Social Security-generated surplus. Treasury Secretary Robert E. Rubin said that could provoke a debt crisis and possibly hinder distribution of Social Security checks, a point that Republicans contested.

Majority Leader Trent Lott, R-Miss., wants to force at least one more cloture vote on the amendment to S 557 — there have already been two — the week of June 14. If that fails, as seems certain, then Lott will take up the House bill, which passed with bipartisan support, despite Democratic grumbling that it is mostly for show. Senate Democrats are likely to accept the House version of the bill, said Joseph I. Lieberman, D-Conn. If so, the measure will head to President Clinton, who will probably sign it. Once Clinton's signature is obtained, GOP reasoning goes, it will be politically difficult for him to turn around and try to press for new spending programs.

But the Congressional Budget Office (CBO) announced June 9 that the fiscal 1999 surplus will be "slightly higher" than the current official figure of $111 billion. When CBO issues its midyear review next month, the all-important re-estimate for fiscal 2000 may show a small on-budget surplus, one that is not dependent on Social Security, said a GOP aide who recently met with CBO Director Dan Crippen. The new procedural hurdles would not apply to any bill that only "spends" the on-budget surplus.

Senate Filibuster, Impasse Continue

JUNE 19 — On the face of it, the Senate Republicans' Social Security lockbox received a double blow the week of June 14. Democrats continued to filibuster the measure on substance and procedure. And it came to the floor just as lawmakers across the Capitol were voting for more surplus-financed spending.

But that appeared not to bother Republicans, who think they are on the winning side of a potent political issue and are content, for now, to cast Democrats as filibustering a bill aimed at making it more difficult to "raid" Social Security surpluses for new spending.

The idea behind the so-called lockbox is to make it more difficult to "spend" the budget surplus, which is now made up exclusively of surplus Social Security revenues, on new programs or tax cuts. Despite the ambitious moniker, the most significant element of the more widely backed House bill (HR 1259) would be to place procedural hurdles in front of surplus-financed spending that virtually duplicate existing rules.

But the debate has focused more on the politics of Social Security than on the merits of the lockbox. Senate Majority Leader Trent Lott, R-Miss., invited a Democratic blockade by using once rarely employed procedural devices to block floor amendments. Minority Leader Tom Daschle, D-S.D., has successfully led filibusters every time his 45-member caucus has been denied a chance to offer floor amendments.

The Senate on June 15 took up its more stringent lockbox proposal for a third time, as an amendment to a bill (S 557) that aims to make it more difficult to designate certain spending as an "emergency" not subject to budget caps. A move to invoke cloture, or limit debate, on the measure failed, 53-46. Sixty votes are required. *(Vote 166, p. S-34)*

The next day, Democrats again denied cloture, 55-44, on the weaker House-passed lockbox bill after complaining that the debate had been rigged to deny them a chance to offer amendments. "We have been locked out of the legislative process," said Frank R. Lautenberg, D-N.J. *(Vote 170, p. S-34)*

The main difference between the House and Senate measures is a Senate provision that would automatically ratchet down the statutory limit on the publicly held portion of the national debt by the amount of the Social Security-generated surplus. That idea has provoked a veto threat from the administration and is opposed by the GOP chairmen of the House Ways and Means and Senate Finance committees, who agree with Treasury Secretary

Robert E. Rubin that the proposal has the potential to spark a debt crisis.

Rubin's opposition, as well as internal GOP divisions over the proposal, virtually guarantees that any lockbox that becomes law will be constructed along the lines of the House bill. That bill would, in effect, require 60 Senate votes to pass any budget resolution or bill that would tap the Social Security surplus for new spending or tax cuts. It would also require both the administration and Congress to exclude Social Security when calculating budget surpluses or deficits.

In what Democrats say is a glaring loophole, Social Security surpluses could be used for Social Security "reform." They say any bill that is labeled as Social Security or Medicare reform, including a partial privatization of the Social Security program, could be used to allow lawmakers to tap Social Security-generated surpluses.

Timing

The first cloture vote of the week came June 15 at the same time the House was debating a five-year, $59 billion bill (HR 1000) to reauthorize the Federal Aviation Administration and boost funding for airport construction projects. That measure would provide $14 billion over five years — taken from the budget surplus — more than was called for in the fiscal 2000 budget resolution (H Con Res 68) for such projects. Critics said such spending would come from Social Security and break the budget caps.

Meanwhile, in the Senate, barely an hour after Republicans again failed to block a filibuster of their lockbox bill, lawmakers voted, 71-28, to invoke cloture on a bill (HR 1664) to create a loan guarantee program for the troubled steel, and oil and gas industries. That bill, while fully offset over time, would have tapped $108 million of the fiscal 1999 surplus to subsidize up to $1.5 billion in federally guaranteed loans. *(Vote 167, p. S-34)*

The timing of the vote on HR 1664, which is backed by three of the Senate's most powerful "old bulls" — Robert C. Byrd, D-W.Va., Pete V. Domenici, R-N.M., and Ted Stevens, R-Alaska — rankled some lockbox supporters.

"We just had a vote about an hour ago where we said we want to stop the plundering of the Social Security trust fund," said Phil Gramm, R-Texas. "In fact, Republicans have been pretty self-righteous about it. We have held up our little lockboxes, and we have had press conferences . . . but we keep supporting measures that knock the doors off, springs go flying, the combination thing goes rolling across the room. You cannot have it both ways. You either want to spend money or you don't want to spend money."

Gramm and Majority Whip Don Nickles, R-Okla., reversed the potential embarrassment during debate on the loan guarantee bill June 17, successfully striking a provision that labeled the loan program as an "emergency" appropriation that would have raised the budget caps and spent some of the surplus.

Spending the Surplus

In several instances this year, Congress has either voided existing procedural rules set in place to block surplus spending, or did not even consider them. For example:

- The Senate on Feb. 24 overwhelmingly passed a military pay raise measure (S 4) that over 10 years would reduce the surplus by $17 billion.
- During consideration May 20 of the supplemental spending bill (HR 1141 — PL 106-31) for Kosovo and other emergencies, the Senate turned back a move by Gramm, who raised a point of order to try to finance the bill with across-the-board domestic spending cuts instead of the surplus. Senators waived the point of order by a 70-30 vote, well above the required 60.
- During Senate debate on the defense authorization bill (S 1059) the week of May 24, senators added direct spending provisions for new pension, education and other benefits, totaling about $16 billion in surplus-financed spending over 10 years. They were subject to a point of order under existing pay-as-you-go rules that mirror those sought by lockbox supporters. Because of their popularity, however, no one challenged the amendments.

When asked why the lockbox is needed even though current rules offer identical protections, Santorum said that in voting to waive the lockbox rules, lawmakers would have to cast "a specific vote that says, 'We will spend Social Security money.' "

'Lockbox' Remains Stalled as Fifth Cloture Vote Fails

JULY 17 — Despite vows of cooperation at a July 12 meeting at the White House, bitter partisanship continued to stall an effort to build a so-called lockbox to block Social Security revenues from being used to finance tax cuts or new federal spending.

On July 16, Senate Democrats voted for the fifth time to deny cloture on a lockbox measure. They said GOP leaders constructed floor debate to limit Democrats' rights to offer amendments. The lockbox measure came to the floor as an amendment to a bill (S 557) to make it more difficult for lawmakers to pass "emergency" spending. The cloture motion failed, 52-43, with 60 votes required. *(Vote 211, p. S-42)*

Senate lockbox advocates continue to push a version that would ratchet down statutory limits on the national debt by the amount of the annual Social Security surplus. That approach is opposed by President Clinton and the House. ◆

Bipartisan Agreement Elusive As Committees Go Separate Ways On Budget Process Overhaul

SUMMARY

Efforts in the House and Senate to overhaul the congressional budget process advanced through several committees but stalled amid Democratic opposition and reservations from key Republicans.

Any attempt to dramatically change the way Congress does its budgeting and appropriations requires significant bipartisan support and a push from top leaders. A Senate bid early in the year to establish a two-year budget and appropriations cycle stalled amid opposition from appropriators and others concerned that the bill would erode Congress' power of the purse and weaken its oversight role.

The House budget process bill (HR 853) did not contain the "biennial budgeting" provision. But a provision to establish an automatic continuing resolution (CR) to keep the government running after the Sept. 30 end of the fiscal year proved just as controversial, and that bill stalled. The House measure also sought to give the annual budget resolution the force of law, ease pay-as-you-go rules to permit surpluses not generated by Social Security to be used for tax cuts or new entitlement spending, and establish a reserve fund to budget in advance for natural disasters and other emergencies.

Driving the Senate bill (S 92) was Budget Committee Chairman Pete V. Domenici, R-N.M., who said the Senate spent too much time on the annual budget resolution and appropriations bills, leaving too little time for other legislation. Appropriations Committee Chairman Ted Stevens, R-Alaska, made it clear he had little use for the measure.

In the House, Budget Chairman John R. Kasich, R-Ohio, and Jim Nussle, R-Iowa, led the effort, along with a small group of Democrats. Appropriators opposed the bill and made sure it stalled. They said the "automatic CR" would remove incentives to complete the appropriations bills and permit a minority in the Senate to stall any spending bill and keep the budget on automatic pilot.

Significant opposition within GOP ranks in both chambers means a budget process overhaul is probably dead for the 106th Congress.

GOP Leaders Endorse Senate Committee's Plan

MARCH 6 — The first tentative decisions as congressional Republicans embark on a difficult budget debate are aimed at getting their Balkanized rank and file to pass a budget blueprint while avoiding traps laid by rival Democrats and President Clinton.

To get the budget process rolling, top House and Senate GOP leaders quickly endorsed a plan March 4 by Senate Budget Committee Chairman Pete V. Domenici, R-N.M., to stick to excruciatingly tight spending caps and to block lawmakers from using surplus Social Security revenues to cut taxes.

In the short term, the plan — if acceptable to competing GOP factions — would allow Republicans to proceed to the first step in the annual budget process: passage of the fiscal 2000 budget resolution, which will lay out the blueprint for a tax cut bill and the 13 fiscal 2000 appropriations bills.

But the plan also shows that Republicans face few easy choices as they take the budget battle to Clinton. It seems to ensure the sort of gridlock on appropriations experienced last year, when end-of-session chaos allowed Clinton to win a big victory on spending.

And despite the ever-growing surplus, Republicans find themselves boxed in on taxes because of Clinton's warning to hold off on tax cuts until Social Security is overhauled. Moreover, Senate rules impose formidable procedural roadblocks that allow Democrats to block surplus-financed tax cuts.

Domenici's plan reflects a central feature of this year's budget climate — a bipartisan desire to end the practice of financing the government's day-to-day operations by borrowing from the Social Security trust fund. Despite a projected surplus of $133 billion in fiscal 2000, lawmakers are reluctant to touch it because it consists of surplus Social Security revenues that are supposed to be socked away for the retirement of Baby Boomers.

This political and tactical landscape ensures that in the early years of the budget plan, tax cuts will have to be more modest than many Republicans, especially in the House, would like. The key selling point for GOP tax cut advocates is that in the later years of the 10-year plan the cuts would grow swiftly as surpluses got even bigger.

The early stages of this year's budget process find Republicans in a holding pattern as they await what they hope will be even bigger surplus estimates this summer. The Congressional Budget Office (CBO), whose estimates lawmakers follow, has consistently underestimated the economy's strong performance and the bulging federal surplus.

CBO forecasts that the surplus for the current fiscal year will reach $111 billion, based on a forecast that the economy will grow by 2.3 percent. But first-quarter growth performance of 6.1 percent virtually guarantees a continued surge in tax revenues. Wall Street economists say the fiscal 1999 surplus might reach $150 billion, which would exceed the Social Security surplus by about $25 billion. If surpluses for fiscal 2000 and later years grow accordingly, lawmakers will have much more room to maneuver.

But in the short term, in vowing to stick to the discretionary spending caps, GOP leaders have dealt themselves an all-but-impossible hand when they turn to the appropriations bills later this spring. The decision to stick to the caps reflects a desire to regain fiscal conservatism lost last year when lawmakers passed an omnibus spending bill (PL 105-277) that designated $21 billion in appropriations as "emergency" spending not subject to the caps.

Virtually everyone familiar with the appropriations process acknowledges privately that Congress will not be able to pass all the appropriations bills unless the caps are eventually raised — a view held by many architects of the pending proposal. House Speaker J. Dennis Hastert, R-Ill., has said that among his top priorities is for the House to pass every appropriations bill by the August recess — a promise that will be difficult to keep.

"It's a strategy for dumping everything into September and October," said a top Republican House Appropriations aide.

But to unilaterally break the caps now would bite into the available pool of money for tax cuts and embroil Republicans in intra-party turmoil while inviting taunts from Democrats and Clinton — who profess to support the caps but nonetheless are pushing lots of new spending. A CBO analysis of Clinton's budget released March 3 determined that his plan would shatter the fiscal 2000 caps by $30 billion.

House GOP leaders recently floated the idea of breaching the caps but quickly fell back in line. Meanwhile, many Democrats are smirking at the Republicans' dilemma over the caps.

GOP Cease-Fire

For Republicans, the budget outline reflects a cease-fire between the House and Senate, whose impasse last year over tax and spending cuts resulted in gridlock and a failure to pass an annual budget resolution for the first time since the Congressional Budget Act (PL 93-344) was passed in 1974.

The House-Senate plan mirrors a draft put together by Domenici. House negotiators quickly abandoned a plan advocated by Rep. Wally Herger, R-Calif., to use part of Social Security interest income to pay for a tax cut in 2000 and 2001.

"Domenici's going to owe me a New York [strip steak] and a glass of wine at the Monocle [a Capitol Hill restaurant] for all the water I'm carrying for him," said House Budget Committee Chairman John R. Kasich, R-Ohio.

The key unknown as Republicans embark on the budget debate is at what juncture they will invite Clinton to enter the process. His signature is required on any tax bill and each of the appropriations bills. There is no sign they will invite him to engage early. They may wait until after he vetoes a party-defining tax bill, or, alternatively, seek a split-the-difference deal if they find themselves awash with on-budget cash in the summer. The only certainty is that negotiations will have to occur when the appropriations process comes to an impasse and the end of the fiscal year looms Sept. 30.

Regardless of whether Clinton and Congress come to terms on taxes and strengthening Social Security and Medicare, they are required to enact the appropriations bills. Since the budget began showing surpluses in fiscal 1998, discipline has eroded, and both Clinton and Republicans succumbed last year to the temptation to spend part of the surplus -- only one instance in a recent past replete with examples of Congress' inability to stay within the caps.

The Domenici plan reflects a budget climate dominated by surplus projections that were unthinkable only a year ago. But as these surplus estimates reach high enough to finance the government's operations without borrowing from revenues generated by near-term surpluses in Social Security, they ironically get more difficult to touch. The Social Security system is currently responsible for all of the government's "unified" surplus — the overall amount that federal revenues (including Social Security) exceed spending.

Congresses and presidents for years have routinely tapped surplus Social Security revenues to finance other spending or tax cuts. But now that the government is on the brink of running surpluses that do not depend on Social Security, lawmakers are loath to risk the appearance of "raiding" Social Security to finance tax cuts or additional spending.

If left alone, Social Security surpluses would be devoted to buying down the portion of the national debt held by the public. Paying off the national debt helps improve the posture of Social Security by placing the federal government on firmer fiscal ground when the retirement system is projected to start running a deficit in 2013 and bonds held by the trust fund must be cashed in.

To keep Social Security surpluses out of the hands of lawmakers who want to spend the money on tax cuts or new federal programs, Domenici has devised a "lockbox" plan that, by law, would require a steady reduction of debt held by the public, now $3.6 trillion. The mechanism is complicated and details have yet to be revealed, but the result would be to fence off Social Security surpluses by, in effect, imposing a 60-vote hurdle in the Senate for those seeking to tap that money for other purposes. Over 10 years, the Domenici plan would dedicate $1.8 trillion of Social Security surpluses to reducing public debt.

Sketchy Blueprint

Budget details were lacking beyond the commitment to Social Security and the spending caps. One crucial question is the as-yet-undetermined size of the tax component. Roughly speaking, the plan would permit a tax cut of about $15 billion in fiscal 2000 and at least $150 billion from fiscal 2000 through fiscal 2004. To placate the GOP's tax cut wing, the measure would take the unprecedented step of extending the budget window to 10 years, which would permit the tax-writing committees to produce an eye-popping tax cut of about $800 billion.

On the spending side, the plan envisions a boost of $9 billion over Clinton's request for the Pentagon. But to stay within the overall spending cap of $574 billion will require steep cuts in domestic programs. Even before the shift of money from domestic programs to defense, the caps require a $20 billion cut in outlays from fiscal 1999 levels, according to CBO.

The prospect of cuts of that magnitude has appropriators up in arms. Rep. John Edward Porter, R-Ill., chairman of the subcommittee that writes the annual spending bill that finances labor, health and education programs, said March 4 that to stick with the caps would require him to cut $5 billion from levels passed last year and $10 billion from Clinton's request.

"I could draw a bill that way, but I can't pass it," Porter said. "We will be right back in the situation where we lump bills into one big package and negotiate with the executive branch. It will be a disaster."

House Committee Approves Plan; Turf Wars Ahead

JUNE 19 — The House Budget Committee approved a proposal June 17 to dramatically reshape the much-maligned congressional budget process.

The bill (HR 853), approved 22-12, may have little chance of becoming law, but it sets the stage for a rousing battle between the rival Budget and Appropriations committees over a provision that aims to avoid future government shutdowns. This so-called automatic CR — a stopgap continuing resolution to fund agencies whose budgets have not been enacted by the Oct. 1 start of the new fiscal year — is but one controversial element of the bill, which would rewrite the 1974 Budget Act (PL 93-344).

The bill would also:

- Give the annual budget resolution, which is currently non-binding, the force of law. It would require the president's signature.
- Create a reserve fund for emergency spending.
- Relax pay-as-you-go (PAYGO) rules to permit non-Social Security-generated budget surpluses to be used for tax cuts or new entitlement spending.
- Create a "lockbox" device that aims to ensure that program cuts from appropriations bills made on the floor actually reduce spending instead of being restored later or used for other programs.

The measure could come to the floor as early as the week of June 21. If it passes, it will likely stall. The Senate Governmental Affairs Committee approved a set of bills (S 92, S 557, S 558) on March 4 that present that chamber's much different view of what constitutes budget "reform."

The central element of the Senate agenda is S 92, which would establish a biennial budget and appropriations process — an idea that House advocates of changing the budget process favor but know they cannot pass because it would be perceived as weakening Congress' power over the purse. And the Senate panel voted March 4 to reject having the president sign the annual budget resolution.

The House bill is a product of negotiations between senior Budget and Rules committee Republicans and a small group of Democrats, including Benjamin L. Cardin of Maryland, David Minge of Minnesota and Charles W. Stenholm of Texas.

But most Democrats will find much to dislike, especially the automatic CR and adjustments to PAYGO that would make it easier for Republicans to cut taxes — but raise the prospect of an across-the-board sequester of entitlement programs, such as Medicare, if surplus projections fall short of expectations.

Inter-Panel Battles

The bill also has the potential to prompt Republican-on-Republican fights by pitting the Appropriations Committee against the Budget Committee. Appropriators are generally against the automatic CR and are poised to vote to strip the language at a June 22 Appropriations markup of HR 853. Ultimately, such issues will have to be decided on the floor, where a close vote is expected.

The bill comes in response to a bipartisan sense that the current budget process does not work well. The system is structured with a timetable that, under a divided government, invites months of political games and partisanship before serious negotiations begin.

The president submits his budget, a document crafted to make his programs look as appealing and politically feasible as possible, in February. Congress responds in April with the budget resolution, a non-binding measure that sets the overall spending amount for appropriations bills and the parameters for a budget-reconciliation bill, which implements tax and spending goals.

Most years the budget resolution debate is more a contest of Republican and Democratic thrust and parry, with exaggerated claims and political pirouettes on both sides over a document that has little real meaning.

The budget resolution is binding only when it sets the amount available for appropriations. This year the House Appropriations Committee blasted the Budget Committee for not giving it enough money to complete its job; Budget members point out that the amounts were set at the cap levels called for in the 1997 balanced-budget law (PL 105-33). *(1997 Almanac, p. 2-27)*

In most years — 1997 was an exception — serious budget talks between the White House and Congress do not begin until the fall, much later than envisioned in 1974.

A central feature of HR 853 would change the format of the budget resolution from a non-binding concurrent resolution to a joint resolution, which would be submitted to the president to sign. The idea is to get the president involved earlier in the process, as he was in the successful 1997 negotiations. "It makes the opening play of the budget process negotiation rather than confrontation," said Jim Nussle, R-Iowa.

Ranking Budget panel Democrat John M. Spratt Jr. of South Carolina countered that requiring the president's signature has the potential to "delay the process rather than expedite it." James P. Moran, D-Va., said it would shift too much power to the White House and a few members of Congress, while cutting most everyone else out.

Automatic CR

A big fight looms between the Budget and Appropriations panels over the automatic CR. Under the provision, funding for agencies whose budgets have not become law would automatically continue to flow when the fiscal year runs out Sept. 30. It would wrest from the president much of the leverage that he has at the end of the appropriations process. A similar provision provoked a Clinton veto of a major 1997 disaster bill (HR 1469). *(1997 Almanac, p. 9-84)*

The House Appropriations Committee, which opposes the idea, has prepared a draft "Adverse Report" on the bill. It says: "No longer would appropriations bills be considered 'must pass' legislation. Inaction would favor the status quo." The committee plans to send the bill to the full House with the recommendation that it not pass. "The option of doing nothing or stonewalling appropriations bills would become a legitimate strategy." The report also says the use of the automatic CR would loosen Congress' power of the purse and deny chances to earmark money for specific projects or favored programs.

Critics added that it would potentially derail appropriations bills because Congress would lose incentive to work out agreements. The automatic CR would kick in, and that would allow a minority in the Senate, through a filibuster, to entirely derail appropriations.

The bill would also:

- Establish a reserve fund for supplemental spending for natural disasters and other emergencies and tighten the definition of "emergency" to make it more difficult for non-urgent items to be funded with such money.
- Modify the budget resolution to eliminate reconciliation instructions and to replace the 20 non-binding budget function categories (such as national defense, agriculture, and administration of justice) with aggregate spending and revenue levels.
- Relax PAYGO rules to permit "on-budget," or non-Social Security-generated, surpluses to be used for tax cuts. Under current law, all tax cuts must be financed with cuts in mandatory spending or new revenues. If PAYGO is violated, the White House must impose an across-the-board sequester of mandatory spending.

Republicans say it is only fair to make on-budget surpluses available for tax cuts. Democrats counter that Social Security should be overhauled first. And they say that if taxes are cut and then revenue projections do not meet expectations, and the budget slides back into an on-budget deficit, a huge sequester will result, forcing cuts in programs for the elderly, veterans and the poor.

House Measure Meets Discord At Starting Line

JUNE 26 — Any attempt to dramatically change the way Congress conducts its fiscal business needs sweeping bipartisan support and a big push from top leaders. The current bid to rewrite the rules governing the congressional budget process has neither.

That tells most of what happened the week of June 21 to a House bill (HR 853) that would greatly alter the process Congress has used to write its budget for the past 25 years.

The measure was blasted on June 22 by the relatively bipartisan House Appropriations Committee, which saw the bill as a direct assault on the appropriations process and its prerogatives. After voting to change the one provision it has jurisdiction over, the appropriators summarily dismissed the bill on a voice vote, sending it to the full House with a recommendation that it be voted down. "The bill is so flawed that it should not pass," said Chairman C.W. "Bill" Young, R-Fla.

The next day, the House Rules Committee, meeting in a rare legislative mode because it has jurisdiction over budget process issues, just as quickly gave the bill its voice vote approval.

Why the conflicting results? The bill's progress through three committees of jurisdiction — Appropriations, Rules and Budget, which approved it June 17 — has mirrored the political dynamics of those committees. The measure went through the highly partisan Budget and Rules committees without a hint of reservation on the part of Republicans, who are looking for a way to regain leverage from a Democratic president in the wake of the 1995-96 government shutdowns.

Since those shutdowns, President Clinton has exercised extraordinary leverage over Republicans, using veto threats on routine spending measures to force Congress to add money for his favored programs.

In the more collegial Appropriations Committee, however, members of both parties had little taste for the bill's most controversial provision, which would allow for an automatic continuing resolution (CR) to fund any agency into a new fiscal year if Congress failed to pass a spending bill by the Oct. 1 deadline.

Both Republicans and Democrats on Appropriations gave solid support to Young's proposal to strip the automatic CR provision from the bill.

The bill could come to the floor the week of June 28, but with opposition so strong, it may have to wait until after the July Fourth recess. Even if the House passes the measure, the Senate has opted for a much different, piecemeal approach to budget process "reform." And the Senate's effort has little momentum.

More Provisions

As approved by the Budget and Rules committees, the bill would also:

- Give the annual budget resolution, currently a non-binding "concurrent" resolution of both chambers, the force of law by making it a "joint" resolution requiring the president's signature.
- Ease the current "pay as you go" (PAYGO) budget rules to permit non-Social Security-generated budget surpluses to be used for tax cuts or new entitlement spending.
- Create a reserve fund so that Congress sets aside money for emergency spending in advance.
- Significantly weaken the Senate's "Byrd rule," named after Robert C. Byrd, D-W.Va., which requires 60 votes to retain non-spending items in a budget "reconciliation" bill, which implements tax and spending policies.
- Create a complicated "lockbox" procedure to try to ensure that cuts from appropriations bills made on the floor are not restored to other appropriations accounts later in the process.

With few exceptions, Democrats dislike the measure, and their leadership appears poised to aggressively oppose it. They join GOP appropriators in opposition to the automatic CR, but also have big objections to the proposed change in PAYGO procedures, which would remove a major procedural roadblock to Republican efforts to cut taxes.

The administration also opposes the bill, White House and congressional aides said.

But the immediate problem facing the measure are Republican pockets of opposition to it. Unhappy GOP appropriators, combined with almost monolithic Democratic opposition, would be enough to scuttle the bill. On top of that, powerful Transportation committee Chairman Bud Shuster, R-Pa., also has reservations about it, said a top aide.

Response to Crisis

The bill is the product of more than a year's work by a small, bipartisan band of current and former members of the Budget Committee and GOP members of the Rules Committee. Key participants included Jim Nussle, R-Iowa, Benjamin L. Cardin, D-Md., and Porter J. Goss, R-Fla. They want to clean up an often-messy budget process, and they want to take back some of the leverage that Congress has given to Clinton.

"Make no mistake, the current budget process does not work. It is a disorganized patchwork of decades-old rules and laws," said Rules Chairman David Dreier, R-Calif. "This comprehensive bill increases efficiency, improves accountability and strengthens enforcement in the budget process."

Outside of this group and their allies, however, there appears to be little enthusiasm for tackling a complex overhaul of the budget process, which was established by the 1974 Budget Act (PL 93-344) and modified by the 1985 and 1987 Gramm-Rudman-Hollings bills (PL 99-177, PL 100-119). The addition of "caps" on appropriations and PAYGO rules against new deficit spending came with the 1990 budget deal (PL 101-508). *(1990 Almanac, p. 111; 1987 Almanac, p. 604; 1985 Almanac, p. 459; 1974 Almanac, p. 145)*

Each of those budget laws, however, came in response to a crisis: President Richard M. Nixon's impoundment of congressional spending in 1974 and the intractable deficit problems and economic crises of the 1980s and early 1990s. The process works most smoothly when a single party controls government, such as the Democrats' 1993 deficit-reduction package (PL 103-66), or when the president and an opposition party Congress both want a deal, as in 1997. *(1993 Almanac, p. 107)*

But under a divided government, the system does not work as well — witness last year, when gridlock on many of the 13 fiscal 1999 spending bills produced a bloated and unpopular omnibus spending bill (PL 105-277).

"Under today's system, there is simply no incentive for the president to come to the table and negotiate in earnest with the Congress until the last few days of the session," Goss said.

While many lawmakers and budget experts agree that the budget process could use some change, the Nussle-Cardin-Goss bill has drawn numerous critics who say its fixes would never work as intended.

"This is a very well-meaning effort by people on both sides of the aisle who don't have any real experience in trying to put through legislation that deals with the budget or with appropriations or with revenue," said David R. Obey of Wisconsin, ranking Democrat on the Appropriations Committee and its former chairman.

"Most of the fixes create more problems than they solve," added Young. "Most of the problems they create would then come home to roost on the Appropriations Committee."

The automatic CR provision would be a disaster, these critics say, because it would shift power to those defending the status quo and would permit a minority in the Senate to stall any appropriations bill and therefore block any funding changes. In effect, they said, the budget could be put on autopilot.

Interior Appropriations Subcommittee Chairman Ralph Regula, R-Ohio, who has received more than 2,700 requests from members for projects in their districts, said that committee members should remind the rank and file that under an automatic CR, such earmarking opportunities would be forfeited.

The bill would also eliminate the current rule that allows the Appropriations committees to move the annual spending bills after May 15, if the final House-Senate budget resolution has not been adopted by then.

Defending PAYGO

Among Democrats, one of the chief objections is a provision that would relax PAYGO rules to permit on-budget surpluses (those that do not depend on Social Security) to finance tax cuts or new spending. Supporters of the idea say that PAYGO was designed for an era of deficits and that it needs to be changed to permit tax cuts such as the $778 billion, 10-year cut called for under the fiscal 2000 budget resolution (H Con Res 68).

But Democrats say that if revenue projections did not meet expectations, PAYGO would require across-the-board cuts in mandatory programs.

"It eliminates a useful budgetary tool [PAYGO] in order to facilitate tax cuts and, in doing so, could trigger massive across-the-board cuts in Medicare, student loans, farm price support programs, crop insurance, veterans' benefits, child support enforcement and other vital programs," said Martin Frost, D-Texas.

Requiring the president's signature on the annual budget resolution and giving that measure the force of law is seen by the bill's authors as a way to speed up the process. Currently, the congressional budget resolution sets non-binding guidelines that are fleshed out later with appropriations bills and a budget-reconciliation bill.

The idea is to get the president involved in the process earlier rather than later. If, under the new process, an impasse occurred between Congress and the executive, Congress would then pass the measure again as a non-binding resolution. In their report criticizing the bill, appropriators said the mere existence of this "escape hatch" would remove the very incentive for negotiation that the underlying provision seeks to establish.

In an attempt to assuage appropriators, Goss said, bill sponsors are leaning toward adding a "sunset" provision to the bill under which it would expire after four years. The idea is to see if the measure would work as intended and to limit the damage should it backfire. ◆

Chapter 7

COMMERCE

Congress Creates $1.5 Billion Loan Guarantee Program for Steel, Oil and Gas Industries

Box Score

- **Bill:** HR 1664 — PL 106-51
- **Legislative action: Senate** passed HR 1664, 63-34, on June 18.

House cleared HR 1664, 246-176, on Aug. 4.

President signed the bill Aug. 17.

SUMMARY

The domestic steel, oil and gas industries got a shot in the arm from Congress in the form of $1.5 billion in federally subsidized loans under a bill signed by President Clinton in August. At the same time, a drive by the steel industry to impose import quotas on steel died in the Senate.

The bill (HR 1664) established a $1 billion loan guarantee program for qualified midsize steel companies hurt by "dumping" of below-cost foreign steel on the U.S. market. It also set up a $500 million fund for small to medium-size domestic oil and gas companies operating "stripper" wells, which had been hard-hit by low oil prices. Authority to make loans under the program will expire at the end of 2001.

Bill champions Sens. Robert C. Byrd, D-W.Va., Pete V. Domenici, R-N.M., and Ted Stevens, R-Alaska, initially folded the loan subsidies into the Senate-passed version of a supplemental spending bill (HR 1141) for Central America and U.S. farmers, but it was stripped during conference in May after GOP leaders promised stand-alone floor votes on the loan guarantees. Byrd seized HR 1664, the House-passed Kosovo supplemental measure, which had not passed the Senate, as the vehicle for the loan guarantees.

Opponents, led by Majority Whip Don Nickles, R-Okla., and Phil Gramm, R-Texas, argued that the bill, albeit well-intentioned, was a poorly designed special-interest giveaway.

The legislation also appropriated $270 million to cover loan defaults, offset by equal cuts in administrative and travel accounts for non-defense federal agencies. The guaranteed loans must be repaid by the end of 2005 for steel companies and by the end of 2010 for oil and gas producers.

Sens. Rick Santorum, R-Pa., and John D. Rockefeller IV, D-W.Va., said Senate passage of HR 1664 contributed to their inability to pass tough steel quota legislation. The House passed the quota bill (HR 975 — H Rept 106-52), 289-141, on March 17, but an attempt to muster the 60 votes needed to invoke cloture in the Senate failed, 42-57, on June 22.

Senate Passes Loan Subsidies for Steel, Oil Companies

JUNE 19 — The old-timers faced off against the new breed as the Senate debated a bill to provide federally subsidized loans to the ailing steel industry and small to medium-size oil and gas producers.

For the most part, the veterans won, though GOP conservatives were able to win concessions before the Senate voted 63-37 on June 18 to pass the bill (HR 1664). It would subsidize up to $1.5 billion in federally guaranteed loans to the industries.

Three powerful senators backed the measure: Robert C. Byrd, D-W.Va., Pete V. Domenici, R-N.M., and Ted Stevens, R-Alaska. It had been included in the Senate-passed version of a supplemental appropriations bill (HR 1141 — PL 106-31) for disaster relief for Central America and U.S. farmers, but it was stripped during conference in May after intervention from House Speaker J. Dennis Hastert, R-Ill., who insisted it be taken out.

To speed the supplemental along, Hastert and Senate Majority Leader Trent Lott, R-Miss. — who also opposed the loan guarantees — promised stand-alone floor votes. Byrd seized HR 1664, the House-passed Kosovo supplemental measure, which had not passed the Senate.

The bill would establish a $1 billion loan guarantee fund for loans to qualified medium-size steel companies hurt by "dumping" of below-cost foreign steel on the U.S. market. A $500 million fund would be set up for small to medium-size domestic oil and gas companies that operate "stripper" wells in the oil patch. Authority to make loans would expire at the end of 2001. The measure contains an appropriation of $270 million to cover loan defaults, offset by cuts in executive branch travel.

To bill opponents, led by Majority Whip Don Nickles, R-Okla., and Phil Gramm, R-Texas, the measure, while well-intentioned, represented a poorly designed special interest giveaway. They noted that a similar loan guarantee program for steel, established in 1978, was a dismal failure. That fund made $290 million in loans, of which the steel industry defaulted on $222 million.

"We have tried it. It didn't work before," Nickles said. "I am afraid it won't work again."

Nickles and Gramm also objected to designating the $270 million appropriation as an "emergency," which meant that it would not be subject to budget spending limits and would tap into the budget surplus at the same time Republicans were touting their Social Security "lockbox" proposal.

After losing a bid June 15 to block cloture, 71-28, bill opponents won several changes to the measure June 17. They struck the emergency designation, shifted some of the loan risk back to the lender, and put the chiefs of the Federal Reserve Board and the Securities and Exchange Commission on the loan funds' governing boards instead of the secretaries of Labor and the Treasury. *(Vote 167, p. S-34)*

House Clears Bill To Guarantee Oil, Steel Loans

AUGUST 7 — A bill (HR 1664) that promises $1.5 billion in loan guarantees for the domestic steel, oil and gas industries cleared its last hurdle in Congress Aug. 4, passing the House by a vote of 246-176. *(Vote 375, p. H-122)*

The measure would create a $1 billion loan guarantee program for the steel industry and a $500 million program for oil and gas producers. It also would appropriate $270 million to cover loan defaults, offset by equal cuts in administrative and travel accounts for non-defense federal agencies

The loan guarantee program would be overseen by a three-member board headed by the chairman of the Federal Reserve. The secretary of Commerce and the chairman of the Securities and Exchange Commission would fill out the board.

All guaranteed loans would have to be repaid by the end of 2005 for steel companies and by the end of 2010 for oil and gas producers.

The main drivers of the legislation — Sens. Robert C. Byrd, D-W.Va., Pete V. Domenici, R-N.M., and Ted Stevens, R-Alaska — initially included the plan in the Senate-passed version of a supplemental spending bill for Central America and U.S. farmers, but it was stripped during conference in May after GOP leaders promised stand-alone floor votes on the loan guarantees.

The Senate passed the loan guarantees June 18. ◆

Chapter 8

CONGRESSIONAL AFFAIRS

Proponents Seek New Strategy After Filibuster Again Kills Campaign Finance Overhaul

Box Score

- **Bills:** HR 417; S 1593
- **Legislative action: House** passed HR 417 (H Rept 106-297, Part 1), 252-177, on Sept. 14.

Senate failed to invoke cloture Oct. 19 on two amendments to S 1593. It voted 52-48 on an amendment copying the text of HR 417, and 53-47 on an amendment essentially restating S 1593. (Sixty votes are required to limit debate.) The Senate voted 52-48 to take up other legislation Oct. 20.

SUMMARY

For the second straight year, the House passed legislation to revamp the laws governing the financing of presidential and congressional campaigns. And, as in 1998, Senate sponsors of a similar approach scaled back their bill in a bid to keep the momentum going, only to see it thwarted by a Republican filibuster — the fifth time in the past six years that campaign finance legislation has been stopped that way.

Soon after becoming Speaker, J. Dennis Hastert, R-Ill., promised that the House would vote on campaign finance legislation sometime in 1999. He eventually scheduled debate for the middle of September. That was not soon enough for advocates of legislation (HR 417) sponsored by Christopher Shays, R-Conn., and Martin T. Meehan, D-Mass., who argued that passage of that comprehensive bill by the House early in the 106th Congress was their best chance of overcoming a Senate filibuster. They gathered 202 signatures, six of them from Republicans, on a discharge petition to force the bill to the floor, 16 short of the number needed.

As in 1998, GOP leaders arranged a procedure for the House debate under which Shays and Meehan had to defeat a series of substitute proposals and what they termed "poison pill" amendments for their bill to survive until the final vote. But they did so again, then won 252 House votes to pass the bill — the same number as the year before.

The measure has two main features: It would ban "soft money," the unlimited and unregulated donations by corporations, unions and wealthy people that have become the fastest growing source of cash for the national party committees; and it would broaden the definition of advertising subject to federal regulation in a bid to curb "issue advocacy" ads, those sponsored by third parties in an attempt to promote candidates without making explicit endorsements. Advocates say these changes would appropriately limit the influence of well-moneyed special interests in politics; opponents say the proposals would unconstitutionally curtail political speech. And officials in each major political party say they fear the changes could work to the benefit of the rival party. The bill also would restrict the use of non-members' union dues for political purposes.

In the Senate, a similar measure (S 26) was the initial proposal put forward by John McCain, R-Ariz., and Russell D. Feingold, D-Wis. When McCain threatened to tie up the Senate in July in a bid to force its immediate consideration, Majority Leader Trent Lott, R-Miss., persuaded him to back down by promising to set aside five days in October for an unfettered debate.

Two days after the House passed its bill, McCain and Feingold shifted tactics. They introduced a bill (S 1593) containing a soft-money ban and the union dues restrictions. They dropped the issue ad provision, hoping to either gain GOP supporters or get a test vote on the proposal by having it put forward as a distinct amendment on the floor.

The debate did not really yield either. The Senate moved on to other business after parliamentary wrangling resulted in a pair of test votes, both of which showed that McCain and Feingold were nowhere close to stopping a filibuster again coordinated by Mitch McConnell of Kentucky, chairman of the National Republican Senatorial Committee. Their high-water mark was that 53 senators, all 45 Democrats and eight Republicans, voted to limit debate on an amendment containing the soft money ban. But two GOP senators who had voted in the past for the broader McCain-Feingold bill voted against the narrow measure.

McCain has made his efforts to change the campaign finance system central to his bid for the GOP presidential nomination, so he is likely to move to revive his and Feingold's bill early in 2000. On Nov. 4, McConnell announced that the Rules Committee, which he chairs, would mark up other campaign finance bills next spring, including a bill (S 1816) that would cap soft-money donations and raise the limits on "hard money," the regulated donations to candidates by individuals and political action committees.

Senators Consider 'Soft Money' Limit In Return for More 'Hard Money'

MARCH 6 — It sounds like such an obvious solution to the congressional campaign finance imbroglio that it is surprising nobody promoted it sooner.

To break the logjam that has stalled such legislation for years, why not simply raise the limits on "hard money" contributions to individual lawmakers — a longstanding goal of many Republicans — while clamping down on the donations of "soft money" to political parties, as Democrats demand?

Although it is not the newest idea for bridging the political chasm over how to revamp the nation's political fundraising laws, it has been attracting increased interest at the outset of the 106th Congress. Still, it faces a familiar obstacle: mustering the requisite 60 votes to overcome an expected Senate filibuster.

After a year in which campaign finance advocates won a surprise victory in the House and then were rebuffed, in predictable fashion, by a GOP-led filibuster in the Senate, the political landscape appears to have undergone modest but potentially significant changes.

A bipartisan coalition in the House, buoyed by its success in 1998, is demanding that Speaker J. Dennis Hastert, R-Ill., schedule a vote this spring on the leading campaign finance vehicle (HR 417), sponsored by Christopher Shays, R-Conn., and Martin T. Meehan, D-Mass. Theirs was the bill the House passed last summer.

"We have 229 returning supporters," Shays said recently. "And 21 freshmen are either cosponsors or have signed pledges to vote for it."

In the Senate, which has long been a graveyard for campaign finance measures, Rules and Administration Committee Chairman Mitch McConnell, R-Ky., has expressed willingness to explore a possible compromise, along the lines of the hard money for soft money trade-off, with Christopher J. Dodd of Connecticut, the panel's ranking Democrat.

But McConnell is playing down chances for a breakthrough, and many senators are skeptical. "As a practical matter, I have to admit it's very unlikely" that any campaign finance legislation will become law this year, said Sen. Robert G. Torricelli, D-N.J.

Democrats regard campaign finance legislation as such a low priority that the subject was never mentioned when President Clinton and Vice President Al Gore led a cheerleading session for the party's agenda at the Library of Congress on March 3.

Still, it is noteworthy that McConnell, who chairs the GOP organization responsible for electing senators, wants to hold talks with the opposition. In past years, he has been the point man in the GOP strategy to block all efforts to overhaul the law governing money in federal elections. McConnell and other opponents — backed by a diverse coalition that included the Christian Coalition and the American Civil Liberties Union — argued that all of them would abrogate the First Amendment rights of the politically active.

Some senators, while acknowledging that any compromise is a long way off, sense a new attitude as this year's debate heats up.

"We had a test of manhood last year, and that isn't going to work," said Republican Sen. Chuck Hagel of Nebraska. "We need to look at what's achievable, what's realistic."

New Attitude?

Like the Shays-Meehan bill, the leading campaign finance measure in the Senate (S 26), once again sponsored by John McCain, R-Ariz., and Russell D. Feingold, D-Wis., would eliminate soft money, the unlimited and unregulated contributions that the two parties raise from corporations, organized labor and individuals.

Both parties have collected soft money in record amounts in recent years. According to a recent report by the independent citizens' lobbying group Common Cause, such contributions have more than doubled in the past four years — to $193.2 million in the 1998 campaign cycle from $85.3 million before the 1994 elections.

Beyond eliminating those contributions, the Shays-Meehan and McCain-Feingold measures would place new restrictions on "issue advocacy" television advertising — the spots sponsored by unions, business coalitions, trade associations and other ostensibly independent groups that, critics claim, often amount to thinly veiled promotions of individual candidates.

All sides agree that while a Shays-Meehan bill might again pass the House, the companion Senate bill will again face a filibuster. In 1998, McCain and Feingold garnered 52 votes for their bill — all 45 Democrats and seven Republicans. That was eight short of the 60 needed to overcome McConnell's filibuster. The election of eight new senators last fall, four from each party, might end up slightly changing the arithmetic on this issue, but not enough to affect the final outcome.

Still, the prospect of another stalemate has prompted McConnell, with the blessing of Majority Leader Trent Lott, R-Miss., to consent to talks with Dodd that may ultimately produce a compromise.

In part, this new openness reflects some discomfort within GOP ranks over maintaining the status quo. Last fall, Hagel unsuccessfully challenged McConnell for the chairmanship of the National Republican Senatorial Campaign Committee, in part because he felt that organization had grown overly dependent on soft-money contributions.

Hagel has made it clear he is not a convert to McCain-Feingold. But he says he may favor raising the $1,000 ceiling on individual contributions, which has not been increased since it became law in 1974, in return for unspecified limits on donations of soft money.

Hagel and other supporters of this approach claim it would lead to greater accountability, by raising the amount of "hard money" individual contributions, which are subject to tighter regulations, while reducing the dependence of both parties on huge, unrestricted donations of soft money.

Freshman Republican George V. Voinovich, who was previously Ohio's governor, is among those in search of a campaign finance compromise. "What bothers me is any system in which you don't know where the money is coming from," he said in an interview.

He wants the GOP to come up with its own bill to rein in the worst fundraising abuses. "But if something like Shays-Meehan was all that was there, I'd vote for it," he said.

McCain and Feingold are considering scaling back their legislation to address soft money and raising the ceiling for individuals. But they have reached no decisions on how to proceed.

For his part, McConnell has long believed the $1,000 limits on individual donations to a primary and general- election campaign are ludicrously low. But it is hard to imagine him agreeing to limits on contributions of soft money as part of a bargain.

A key question is whether the 19 GOP senators facing re-election in 2000, particularly those in tough races, press McConnell and the leadership to cut a bipartisan agreement on campaign finance.

Many Senate Democrats, having tangled with McConnell over this issue in the past, are dubious his talks with Dodd will produce tangible results.

"The single advantage Republicans bring to the next election is financial," said Torricelli, who is chairman of the Democratic Senatorial Campaign Committee. "I can't imagine they'd relinquish that advantage."

The issue proved to have minimal political potency in last year's midterm elections, although the nation had just come off what was arguably the worst presidential fundraising scandal since Watergate.

Democrats, who used a legislative guerrilla strategy to force a vote on the McCain-Feingold bill in the last Congress, have given no indication they will expend a great deal of political capital in this year's battle.

If McCain and Feingold limit their bill to changes in the rules of hard money and soft money, some Democrats will have a justification — perhaps in some cases an excuse — to oppose the measure on grounds that it is too weak.

Hastert's Dilemma

In the House, Shays and Meehan are confident they have more than enough votes to pass their bill. But it is uncertain if the new GOP leadership will give them that opportunity early in the year, which would put more pressure on the Senate to conduct a full-scale debate.

At a Feb. 25 news conference that Shays and Meehan held to promote the bill, Rep. Jay Inslee, D-Wash., who was re-elected last fall after a four-year absence from Congress, said the timing will be crucial: "I am a freshman but I know something already. The end of the session is like the elephant's graveyard: It's where good bills go to die."

Last year, the House voted, 252-179, to pass the Shays-Meehan bill just before the summer recess began. Returning after Labor Day to face the end-of-session legislative crunch, senators debated the McCain-Feingold bill for one day — the day after Independent Counsel Kenneth W. Starr's impeachment report arrived at the Capitol — before killing it with little public notice.

Shays said that Hastert intends to bring up the bill this year. But John P. Feehery, the Speaker's press secretary, said that Hastert has only promised to permit a vote sometime during the 106th Congress. "We're trying to deal with our priorities first," Feehery said.

Last year, when House GOP leaders tried to block the bill, campaign finance advocates took successful advantage of a discharge petition — a rarely used procedure for bringing bills to the floor over the objections of the leadership. Meehan said supporters of his bill are ready to resort to the same tactic this year. "The 'Blue Dogs' will take the lead," he said, referring to a group of conservative Democrats who aggressively promoted the discharge petition last year.

Hastert will likely come under countervailing pressure from House Majority Whip Tom DeLay, R-Texas, his friend and close political ally, to delay action on the Shays-Meehan bill.

After the leadership relented and brought the issue to the floor last year, DeLay and other leaders arranged for the debate to occur sporadically and stretch through most of the summer — which pro-overhaul forces claimed was a backdoor way to scuttle the legislation.

There have been indications that DeLay may opt for a similar drag-it-out strategy this year, perhaps by loading up the bill with amendments. But that also would carry risks for the leadership, because 61 Republicans voted for the Shays-Meehan measure last year and many are demanding early action on the measure in 1999.

"After what we have been through with impeachment" and the earlier fundraising scandals, said Rep. Marge Roukema, R-N.J., "this is the kind of legislation we need to restore the credibility of Congress with the American people."

Six Republicans Defy Speaker, Sign Petition for Earlier Debate

MAY 29 — For weeks, more than two dozen House Republican advocates for altering the laws governing the financing of federal campaigns have been publicly pressuring Speaker J. Dennis Hastert, R-Ill., to schedule an early debate on the issue.

But so far, only six have been willing to back up that demand by standing with Democrats — and against Hastert — in a formal effort to move up that timetable. Frustrated at the Speaker's decision to put off the debate until the middle of September, they added their names May 26 to a Democratic-sponsored discharge petition aimed at forcing action on a campaign finance bill before the summer congressional recess.

The group included Christopher Shays of Connecticut, sponsor along with Massachusetts Democrat Martin T. Meehan of the most widely supported campaign finance bill (HR 417), and five other GOP moderates: Michael N. Castle of Delaware, Michael P. Forbes of New York, Greg Ganske of Iowa, Nancy L. Johnson of Connecticut and Constance A. Morella of Maryland.

Their signatures brought the number of names on the petition to 202. Sixteen more are needed to put a majority of the House on the petition, which would then circumvent the GOP leadership and move the Shays-Meehan bill toward the floor.

That legislation would ban unregulated "soft money" donations to political parties and place new curbs on "issue advocacy" advertising, which critics say is misused for political purposes.

The six Republicans, who have been at odds with the leadership on various issues in the past, insisted that an early House vote is essential if the legislation is to have any hopes in the Senate. "Delay sustains the greater possibility, even probability, that this bill won't become law," Castle said at a news conference May 26.

But while that view is widely shared among GOP supporters of Shays-Meehan, most have not yet been willing to sign the petition. It has been signed by 195 of the 211 House Democrats, as well as Independent Bernard Sanders of Vermont.

Some GOP campaign finance advocates say they are reluctant to show disloyalty to Hastert so early in his tenure as Speaker. Others say Hastert has been more accommodating than his predecessor, former Rep. Newt Gingrich, R-Ga. (1979-99), who denied campaign finance supporters any floor time last year until the threat of a successful discharge petition forced him to relent.

Finally, some appear to be fearful of the political consequences of defying the party's elders. "I don't think you put yourself on a leadership track by signing the petition," said Shays.

Shays suggested that members of the leadership have threatened retribution if he signed the petition. He said he had received vague warnings from a staff member of the House GOP political arm — the National Republican Congressional Committee (NRCC) — and indicated that campaign committee officials had been encouraging a primary challenge against him.

But Thomas M. Davis III, R-Va., who is chairman of the NRCC, insisted that the organization would support Shays' re-election. "The best way to bring Republicans into a minority is to start cannibalizing themselves," Davis told reporters May 26.

Building Pressure

During the Memorial Day recess, campaign finance advocacy groups will try to build public pressure on the 29 Shays-Meehan supporters who wrote Hastert in April to press him to schedule an early debate. But garnering 16 more discharge petition signatures is likely to be difficult. In part, that is because Hastert has made tactical concessions to campaign finance supporters, such as permitting campaign finance hearings this summer. The House Administration Committee will begin hearings in June, it announced May 25.

"They're doing what I've been screaming bloody murder about, they're moving it through committee," Rep. Brian P. Bilbray, R-Calif., said in an interview. A vocal advocate of the Shays-Meehan bill, he has been considered among the most likely petition signers, and he said he has not ruled out that action. "If they're not doing anything in committee, I walk up to that petition," Bilbray said.

In the 105th Congress, the House passed a similar campaign finance bill by a 73-vote margin, but a threatened filibuster thwarted the bill until the Senate adjourned three months later. *(1998 Almanac, p. 18-3)*

Senate Minority Leader Tom Daschle, D-S.D., warned May 26 that a similar scenario could unfold in the 106th Congress unless a House vote this summer raises the heat. For now, Daschle sees no hope of breaking the filibuster. "I don't see any real movement on this side, unfortunately," Daschle told reporters.

McCain Ponders Modifications As Lott Decides To Allow Debate

JULY 24 — With the decision by Senate Republican leaders to permit debate on campaign finance legislation, the stage is now set for pivotal battles this autumn on both sides of the Capitol.

After Republican Sen. John McCain of Arizona dropped his threat to tie up the Senate in a bid to force an immediate debate on his campaign finance bill (S 26), which he has cosponsored with Democratic Sen. Russell D. Feingold of Wisconsin, Senate Majority Leader Trent Lott, R-Miss., agreed July 20 to bring the matter to the floor not later than Oct. 12.

The deal seemed like a winner for everyone concerned: Lott removed a potential speed bump from the Senate's legislative track; McCain and Feingold, whose bill previously has come to the floor under restrictive procedures, won fairly favorable terms for a debate; and McCain, who is vying for the GOP presidential nomination, will have a high-profile and timely forum for promoting the signature issue of his campaign.

In the House, Republican leaders had previously scheduled a debate for the week of Sept. 13 on campaign finance legislation (HR 417) sponsored by Christopher Shays, R-Conn., and Martin T. Meehan, D-Mass. Their measure is nearly identical to the McCain-Feingold bill.

Nearly a year ago, the House passed the Shays-Meehan bill by 73 votes. But the Senate has long been a graveyard for campaign finance measures. Senate Republicans, led by Mitch McConnell of Kentucky, chairman of the Republican National Senatorial Committee, have successfully filibustered the McCain-Feingold measure for several years. *(1998 Almanac, p. 18-3)*

Chastened by that experience, McCain, Feingold and their allies are not about to chill champagne in anticipation of victory. But they are cautiously optimistic that Lott's willingness to permit an array of amendments could change the dynamics of the debate and give them a chance to garner the votes needed to break the filibuster.

"We have reason to believe that through an amending process we could get to 60 votes," McCain said. During the past few years, McCain and Feingold have never mustered more than 52, eight short of the requisite number.

Democratic Dilemma?

The agreement to bring the McCain-Feingold bill to the floor ran into one potentially troublesome hitch: Carl Levin, D-Mich., objected to the terms of the arrangement, complaining that campaign finance advocates will be permitted only one chance this year to break the filibuster.

Minority Leader Tom Daschle, D-S.D., and other Democrats supported Levin. "If Carl has problems, I have problems," said Harry Reid of Nevada. Still, Democrats will not stand in the way of the campaign finance debate; Levin and every other Democrat have repeatedly supported McCain-Feingold.

The larger question for Democrats, as McCain has observed, is whether to accept some changes that may be made to that legislation. McCain and Feingold have not yet decided whether to offer their original bill as the vehicle for debate, or to modify it first. Under the agreement, they must decide by Sept. 14.

As introduced, the McCain-Feingold bill has two main features: a ban on "soft money," the huge, unregulated donations from corporations, labor unions and wealthy individuals that have been flowing into the coffers of both parties in record amounts; and new restrictions on "issue advocacy" advertising — television campaigns that, critics charge, are often thinly veiled endorsements of candidates.

McCain and Feingold have expressed willingness to tinker with their basic bill in the interest of picking up GOP support. One change would be to raise the existing $1,000 limit on contributions to candidates by individuals — the so-called hard-money cap — which has not been changed since 1974. Such a tradeoff has been mulled over all year.

"There are some Republicans who have said that, 'If you lift hard-money limits, I would vote to ban soft money,' " McCain said July 20, adding that he could live with that approach.

Several Republicans have also indicated that they would be more amenable to the bill if it dropped the issue advocacy provision, which many regard as an unconstitutional infringement on political speech. But Daschle has reservations about scaling back the McCain-Feingold bill. "His position continues to be that he wants comprehensive campaign finance reform," said Daschle spokeswoman Ranit Schmelzer.

As they assemble their final proposal and sketch out possible amendments, McCain and Feingold will engage in a delicate balancing act as they try to woo Republicans without alienating Democrats. McCain said they have ruled out going ahead with a bare-bones bill that would include the ban on soft money and little else.

Whatever they decide, however, all sides agree that it will be a tall order for McCain and Feingold to break McConnell's stranglehold on the bill, particularly since the vote will come at a time when the priority of all candidates facing election in 2000 will be to raise as much money as possible.

House Leaders Set Rules for Debate

AUGUST 7 — For the second year in a row, House Republican leaders will force supporters of a popular bill to revamp campaign finance law to survive a difficult procedural gantlet before getting a vote on their measure.

Just before Congress departed for its summer recess shortly after midnight Aug. 6, the House Rules Committee — an agent of the majority leadership — approved procedures for a debate on the issue in September. The plan, which still must be endorsed by the full House, sets the stage for a vote on the campaign finance measure (HR 417) sponsored by Christopher Shays, R-Conn., and Martin T. Meehan, D-Mass. — but only if the House first rejects three alternatives.

The Shays-Meehan bill, a version of which passed the House by 73 votes last year, would ban contributions of "soft money," the unregulated donations to political parties from corporations and other sources, and would impose new restrictions on issue-oriented advertising and other campaign expenditures by non-candidates.

The biggest potential threat to the bill comes from a substitute amendment that House Administration Committee Chairman Bill Thomas, R-Calif., will be allowed to offer. That measure (HR 2668), which Thomas has described as "purposefully modest," would tighten disclosure requirements, streamline operations at the Federal Election Commission and crack down on political donations by foreigners.

Thomas' bill is relatively noncontroversial, and many of its provisions appear to have broad support. Under the procedures crafted by the Rules Committee, adoption of the Thomas amendment would make it the base bill, wiping out the Shays-Meehan legislation.

The committee's rule also would provide for votes on two other alternatives: one (HR 1867), by Asa Hutchinson, R-Ark., is less aggressive than Shays-Meehan in restricting soft money; the other (HR 1922), by John T. Doolittle, R-Calif., would eliminate limits on the size of campaign donations and mandate faster and more complete disclosure of contributions.

Thomas' committee marked up all four bills Aug. 2, endorsing the chairman's legislation, urging defeat of the Shays-Meehan bill and staying neutral on the others.

Democrats claimed that, as in 1998, GOP leaders have stacked the deck in trying to squash tough campaign finance legislation. Some were worried by the Rules Committee's proposal to permit votes on 10 other amendments aside from the three alternatives, only one by a Democrat. Some are "poison pills" designed to splinter support for Shays-Meehan, said a spokesman for Steny H. Hoyer of Maryland, the top Democrat on House Administration.

Last year, GOP leaders — who were more open in their determination to kill the Shays-Meehan bill — forced it to compete with 10 other substitutes in a debate that lasted for two months. Even though it survived, the companion Senate measure, by John McCain, R-Ariz., and Russell D. Feingold, D-Wis., was stopped by a filibuster.

A spokesman said Shays viewed the proposed procedures for this year as fair, although not ideal.

'Soft Money': Who Benefits?

The procedural maneuvering came as the battle over campaign finance heated up. On Aug. 4, Republican National Committee Chairman Jim Nicholson told the House GOP Conference that the Shays-Meehan bill's ban on soft money represents a serious threat to the party.

"His whole message was that soft money is a big part of what Republicans do, and it's not tainted," Shays said afterward.

In the Senate, where an autumn debate is also on the schedule, McCain and Feingold are considering modifying their measure (S 26) in a bid to break an anticipated GOP filibuster. No decisions have been made, but Democrats, who have unanimously supported the bill, appear worried that McCain and Feingold will opt to propose only a soft money ban, dropping other provisions. Senior Democrats believe the soft money that now flows to the GOP will ultimately find its way into the coffers of Republican-aligned interest groups, who would be free to underwrite independent campaigns for Republican candidates.

McCain seemed to take encouragement from the fact that both parties are discomfited by the prospect of a soft money ban. "Can we win? I don't know," he said in an interview Aug. 4. "But this could be a hell of a lot more exciting."

A Guide to the Campaign Finance Overhaul Debate

SEPTEMBER 4 — The upcoming congressional debate over campaign finance legislation will feature partisan fights, procedural brinkmanship and heated rhetoric about the evils of huge and unchecked political contributions, from one side, and the threats that various campaign finance proposals pose to the Constitution, from the other.

But the central question of the debate has not changed for more than a generation: Will lawmakers revamp the fundraising system for congressional and presidential campaigns that has been integral to their success and the survival of the two political parties?

History strongly suggests the answer is no, although advocates of an overhaul remain undaunted. No campaign finance legislation has become law since the parameters of the current system were finished with enactment of a law (PL 96-187) two decades ago. *(1979 Almanac, p. 558)*

Senate opponents are confident they can continue to block such legislation with a filibuster, as they did most recently in the 105th Congress. *(1998 Almanac, p. 18-3)*

The House is scheduled to take up an array of campaign finance proposals during the week of Sept. 13. But the focal point for the debate will be legislation (HR 417), sponsored by Reps. Christopher Shays, R-Conn., and Martin T. Meehan, D-Mass., which is similar to a measure that easily passed the House last year.

In the Senate, Majority Leader Trent Lott, R-Miss., has agreed to permit a campaign finance debate by Oct. 12. That will likely occur on a bill (S 26) sponsored by Sens. John McCain, R-Ariz., and Russell D. Feingold, D-Wis., that is the companion to the Shays-Meehan measure.

Both the Shays-Meehan and McCain-Feingold bills would ban "soft money," the unlimited and unregulated contributions from labor unions, corporations and wealthy individuals. That provision, along with proposals in the two bills to restrict so-called issue-advocacy advertising, will surely provoke the most vigorous debate.

Indeed, the battle has already taken a nasty turn. Sen. Mitch McConnell, R-Ky. — the leading foe of the McCain-Feingold bill and also the chairman of the National Republican Senatorial Committee — recently sent bluntly worded letters to several business executives urging them to resign from an organization that favors tightening campaign finance laws. Some members of that group, the Committee for Economic Development, suggested during the week of Aug. 30 that McConnell was trying to intimidate them.

Here is a guide to the policies, politics and process of the debate:

Q. Why has soft money become so controversial?

A. Because it is flooding the political system, say advocates of outlawing it. Common Cause, a nonpartisan group that strongly supports the soft money ban, recently released a report that found that the two parties are on pace to shatter all previous records for this sort of fundraising. The two parties raised more than $55.1 million in soft money between them during the first six months of this year — 80 percent more than in the comparable period before the 1996 presidential election.

The Common Cause report said both parties have received hundreds of thousands of dollars from groups with strong interests in pending legislation. Telecommunications and securities firms have been the leading GOP contributors; securities firms, labor unions and trial lawyers top the list of Democratic donors.

But McConnell and other defenders of the system say there is nothing intrinsically wrong with the flow of soft money into the political system. Donating to campaigns, McConnell has said, "is as American as apple pie." And many Republicans, who historically have raised more soft money than Democrats, are concerned that a soft money ban would place them at a severe disadvantage.

Q. What accounts for the increase in soft money?

A. Quite simply, the two parties have discovered it is much easier to solicit funds in large chunks rather than go after many small donations. Federal law places strict limits on the amount of money that individuals, companies and unions may donate to political candidates during each election season. Long-standing laws prevent corporations and unions from making direct donations at all — which is why they have to funnel such contributions through political action committees (PACs) that are federally regulated.

But since 1979, the two parties have been able to solicit unlimited amounts of soft money — that is, funds not covered by federal statutory caps — for party-building activities such as get-out-the-vote drives. Often, soft money finances much more than that, including issue-oriented television ads by the parties that look and sound like election ads.

Still, many observers believe the parties would not be so reliant on soft money if the federal limits on "hard money," such as the $1,000 limit on donations by individuals to candidates for each election, had been adjusted to keep up with inflation. And despite the significant increase in soft money contributions, those funds still accounted for only slightly more than 10 percent of all the money spent during the 1996 federal election campaign, according to an analysis by the Center for Responsive Politics, a nonpartisan research group.

Q. What is "issue advocacy"?

A. Any time a group or political party identifies or criticizes a position taken by a politician it is engaging in issue advocacy. The Supreme Court has ruled that such issue ads are constitutionally protected speech and may not be regulated by federal election laws. Only "express advocacy" advertisements that explicitly advocate the defeat or election of a candidate — by using so-called magic words such as "vote for congressman Smith" or "vote against Sen. Jones" — are subject to such laws.

In the campaign of three years ago, there was widespread outrage over a deluge of issue ads, particularly those that were indistinguishable from political attack ads. Both the Shays-Meehan bill and McCain-Feingold bill aim to restrict such ads, though in slightly different ways.

Supporters of the bills insist these provisions will clean up elections by eliminating some negative issue ads. Critics, including the American Civil Liberties Union (ACLU), maintain that the restrictions on issue ads are flatly unconstitutional and would force interest groups to scale back their political activity.

The Shays-Meehan bill would establish a broad, new standard on what constitutes express advocacy by imposing federal restrictions on ads that "can have no other reasonable meaning" than to advocate election or defeat of a candidate. Any issue advocacy ad that runs within 60 days of an election and refers to a candidate would also be subject to federal contribution limits under that legislation. The issue advocacy provision in the McCain-Feingold bill is narrower. Either proposal, if enacted, is sure to face a challenge on the grounds that it abridges the right to free speech.

Q. If issue advocacy restrictions are so controversial, why don't

overhaul advocates drop them from their bills?

A. That is the $64,000 question in the Senate. Under an informal agreement setting ground rules for the debate, McCain and Feingold have until Sept. 14 to decide on a vehicle for the debate. It might be the original text of their bill, or a modified version of that measure.

McCain and Feingold are now considering whether and how to change their bill to overcome an expected filibuster by McConnell and his allies. In recent years, they have garnered 52 votes for their bill, eight short of the 60 needed to break the delaying tactics that otherwise scuttle legislation.

Dropping the issue advocacy provision would help McCain and Feingold neutralize the argument that their bill tramples on the First Amendment. It might also make the bill somewhat more palatable to some conservatives, who have been concerned over the potential impact of the issue advocacy restrictions on the political activities of such organizations as the Christian Coalition.

But some Senate Democrats — who have unanimously supported the McCain-Feingold bill in the past — might defect if the issue advocacy provisions are dropped. Senior Senate Democrats are concerned that millions of dollars in soft money that now flows to the GOP might simply be diverted to conservative and pro-business interest groups to help them underwrite issue ads directed against the Democrats.

Q. How will the House debate unfold?

A. The most important point to remember is that the Shays-Meehan bill received 252 votes last year. It is difficult to defeat legislation that so recently attracted such widespread support.

But the procedures House GOP leaders set for the debate clearly do not favor Shays-Meehan and their supporters. The House will consider three major alternatives to the Shays-Meehan bill and 10 other amendments. Approval of any of the alternatives means the end for Shays-Meehan. In addition, some advocates for the legislation charge that many of the 10 amendments are "poison pills" designed to fracture support for Shays-Meehan.

Q. What are the alternatives to Shays-Meehan?

A. The proposal likely to attract the most support (HR 2668) is sponsored by House Administration Committee Chairman Bill Thomas, R-Calif. That bill, which Thomas has characterized as "purposefully modest," would expand the ban on political contributions by foreigners, mandate faster and more complete disclosure of contributions and strengthen the Federal Election Commission.

Under different circumstances, Thomas' bill would probably pass the House with an overwhelming vote. Its provisions are not controversial. But since it is pitted against Shays-Meehan, supporters of that bill will mount a furious effort to defeat the Thomas measure.

Another alternative (HR 1867), by Rep. Asa Hutchinson, R-Ark., is less aggressive in restricting soft money and issue ads than Shays-Meehan; the third (HR 1922), sponsored by Rep. John T. Doolittle, R-Calif., would take a radically different approach by removing all federal limits on political contributions and stiffening disclosure requirements.

Of the 10 other amendments, the one that has raised greatest concern among Shays-Meehan forces is another proposal by Doolittle aimed at exempting printed and on-line materials such as voter guides from the bill's issue advocacy provision.

The bill already provides some protections for voter guides, but Doolittle and other conservatives say they are insufficient. Supporters of Shays-Meehan say Doolittle's real goal is to gut their bill. Last year, a similar amendment by Doolittle was rejected by just 18 votes.

Q. What would it take to enact campaign finance legislation this year?

A. Pro-overhaul forces may well prevail in the House, but the Senate remains the stumbling block. In that chamber, the political dynamics will have to change dramatically for McCain and Feingold to succeed.

A new fundraising scandal could generate more public demand for new and tougher laws. But the 1996 campaign, with all of its sordid allegations of foreign fundraising and Lincoln Bedroom sleepovers, has not produced the needed legislative momentum.

In different ways, Hutchinson and Thomas have argued that as long as Congress is at loggerheads over more sweeping revisions, it should try to enact more modest legislation. "Too often over the years, and increasingly so it seems, the good has been seen as the enemy of the perfect when it comes to campaign finance reform," said the Administration Committee's report on Thomas' bill.

But those who back more ambitious changes argue they have already made significant concessions over the years. Besides, they say, Congress would be derelict if it enacted campaign finance legislation that does nothing to plug what they see as the biggest loopholes in current law — soft money and "sham" issue ads.

McCain, Feingold Narrow Senate Bill After House Passes Its Version

SEPTEMBER 18 — Adopting a tactic that they have been contemplating all year, the leading Senate sponsors of legislation to limit the influence of money in politics will push a narrow bill this fall that focuses on ending the unregulated and unlimited donations to the political parties.

By putting aside — at least for now — their aspiration to more closely regulate "issue advocacy" advertising by third parties, John McCain, R-Ariz., and Russell D. Feingold, D-Wis., hope to dilute Republican objections to revamping the federal campaign finance system at least enough to pick up the eight votes needed to overcome a filibuster when the Senate debate opens next month.

But as McCain and Feingold introduced their new measure (S 1593) on Sept. 16, there were few if any indications that the strategy would work, given the longstanding refusal of members on either side to budge on an issue that all lawmakers see as at the center of their political futures.

"I don't think there are 60 votes to pass anything," pronounced Majority Whip Don Nickles, R-Okla., who said he would oppose the narrow bill, as he had the previous version.

That remaining the case, the 106th Congress would be on course to replicate the record of the 105th Congress on the issue, with the House soundly passing a multifaceted bill, and McCain and Feingold failing in an effort to keep the momentum going by scaling back their companion offering.

This senators unveiled their newest strategy two days after the House passed, for the second time in 14 months, the campaign finance overhaul legislation sponsored by Christopher Shays, R-Conn., and Martin T. Meehan, D-Mass. On the 252-177 vote — the bill received precisely the same number of "yes" votes as last year — just 13 Democrats voted against the bill, while 54 Republicans voted for it in defiance of their leadership's wishes. *(Vote 422, p. H-136)*

The House measure (HR 417) closely mirrors the broad Senate bill (S 26) that McCain and Feingold have set aside.

"While I support a more comprehensive bill and hope a more extensive package will eventually pass the Senate, I am also a realist, and know that we must not let the perfect bill be the enemy of real reform," McCain said in a statement jointly issued with Feingold.

Their new bill retains the modest restrictions on the use of labor union dues for political purposes that were in their earlier version and are in the bill the House passed.

Other items, such as restrictions on issue-oriented ads that often are implicit endorsements of candidates, are not precluded from being offered as amendments under the new game plan. "The goal here is to let senators fashion a bill beyond this base," Feingold said in an interview Sept. 16.

Prospects for the New Tactic

Advocates of altering the laws that govern the financing of presidential and congressional campaigns have struggled for years to get a straightforward Senate vote because of repeated filibusters organized by Mitch McConnell of Kentucky, chairman of the National Republican Senatorial Committee, which recruits and helps finance GOP Senate candidates. Last year, McCain and Feingold drew an outright majority of 52 — seven Republicans and all 45 Democrats — but eight more Senate supporters were needed to cut off debate and compel a vote on the merits of the bill.

By recasting the issue as primarily a debate over "soft money" donations, Senate backers are counting on neutering McConnell's chief argument against past campaign finance bills: Their restrictions on issue advocacy advertising would unconstitutionally limit the types of political speech that the First Amendment protects.

But McConnell has not removed his threat of a filibuster. While Nickles conceded that dropping the curbs on issue ads is a "big thing," the House passed such a provision, so it would be subject to conference negotiations if the Senate passes any campaign finance measure.

But some Republicans who are seen by the bill's advocates as possible converts declined to commit on the new approach. Chuck Hagel, R-Neb., said he favors limits, but not an outright prohibition, on donations of soft money. Gordon H. Smith, R-Ore., agreed, saying, "A ban is unconstitutional."

Some Democrats grumbled at the move to drop the issue advocacy restrictions. They fear that if soft money to the parties is stopped, that money would flow instead into issue ad campaigns, which are outside the control of the two major political parties.

For some Democrats, the question is whether to hold out for the more comprehensive approach embodied in the original McCain-Feingold bill. But such a rigid position could backfire on them, especially after they railed against GOP opposition to any change in the system, said Thomas E. Mann, a senior fellow at the centrist Brookings Institution. "Democrats would have a very difficult time," he said, "to come back and say, 'Oh, just kidding. If we just have a soft money ban we are not going to support it.' "

House sponsors greeted the new approach of McCain and Feingold with a note of pragmatism. "There's only so much value in banging your head against the wall," said Eric Friedman, a spokesman for Shays. "They know what they have to do to pass it."

Under a deal struck between the bill's sponsors and Majority Leader Trent Lott, R-Miss., the Senate debate is set to begin by Oct. 12, but sponsors have promised to let the debate lapse until next year if they are thwarted on the first cloture vote.

Some advocates of a sweeping bill, including Sen. Carl Levin, D-Mich., want to force McConnell to mount a live filibuster to try and stop the legislation, saying they hope the nonstop speechmaking reminds voters of the similar tactics used — ultimately unsuccessfully — by the opponents of civil rights legislation.

Shays sees a strategic benefit to having the debate carry into 2000, "a year where it just sits around waiting for action, a year of a presidential race where a plethora of money is being spent."

Campaigners' Battle Cry

The money fueling the presidential campaign at this stage — "hard money" given directly to the candidates — would not be curbed under the Shays-Meehan or McCain-Feingold bills. But the campaign finance issue has become a part of the presidential campaign.

McCain has made the issue the centerpiece of his bid for the GOP nomination. Gov. George W. Bush of Texas, the Republican front-runner, has called for banning soft money contributions from corporations and unions. Echoing President Clinton, who has endorsed the Shays-Meehan bill, has been Vice President Al Gore. The other Democratic candidate, former Sen. Bill Bradley of New Jersey (1979-97), has offered to refuse help associated with soft money next year if the Republican nominee does the same.

Republicans have historically raised more soft money from corporations, and more overall. Democrats, who have received more soft money from labor, say that it accounts for a greater percentage of total party fundraising.

In the 1997-98 election cycle, Republican soft money donations totaled $131.6 million, 151 percent more than in the previous off-year election cycle, 1993-94, according to the Federal Election Commission. Democrats collected $92.8 million, an 89 percent increase.

Much of that money was funneled to candidates by political action committees (PACs) run for the benefit of congressional leaders, and giving to those PACs has surged again this year.

Shays maintained that — in contrast with the freshmen of the 105th Congress, who offered a limited campaign finance measure — this year's

Highlights of House-Passed Bill

SEPTEMBER 16 — But for three amendments, the campaign finance overhaul bill (HR 417) passed by the House Sept. 14 is substantively the same as the legislation the House passed in 1998. These are the major provisions of HR 417:

- **'Soft money.'** The bill would ban national party committees from soliciting, receiving or spending "soft money" donations. These are the currently unlimited and unregulated contributions from unions, corporations and wealthy people that are supposed to be used solely for party-building activities and not to promote individual candidates. It would also prohibit state parties and local parties from using soft money for any federal election activity, including voter registration drives within four months of a federal election.
- **Contribution limits.** The bill would increase, to \$30,000 from \$25,000, the aggregate annual limit on an individual's contributions. It would double, to \$10,000, the annual limit on an individual's gifts to state party committees. It would require unions to notify dues-paying nonmembers that they may disallow political use of their fees.
- **Foreign contributions.** The bill would prohibit donations by foreign nationals and set procedures for expulsion of House members who accept such contributions.
- **Issue advocacy.** The bill would broaden the definition of "express advocacy" advertising to include those ads that "can have no other reasonable meaning" other than to advocate a candidate's election or defeat, and to paid broadcasts that cite a candidate by name within 60 days of an election. It would require that express advocacy advertising be financed with contributions subject to federal limits and disclosures.
- **Independent expenditures.** The bill would tighten the definition of what expenditures by individuals and groups constitute coordination and cooperation with a campaign. It would increase the frequency of disclosure of large amounts of money spent in independent campaigns close to an election.
- **Wealthy candidates.** The bill would ban political parties from making coordinated expenditures for House candidates who exceed a \$50,000 voluntary limit on using their personal or family funds.
- **Disclosure.** The bill would permit the Federal Election Commission (FEC) to conduct random audits within a year of an election and give the agency more leeway to initiate enforcement. It would require all campaign committees to file electronically and the FEC to post those reports on the Internet within a day of receipt. It would lower the threshold for contributor name and address disclosure to \$50, from \$200. It would require nonreligious groups spending more than \$50,000 a year to sway federal elections to file monthly FEC reports.
- **Use of government facilities.** The bill would enhance curbs on the use of federal property for fundraising. It would prohibit franked mass mailings within 180 days of a general election. It would restrict use of the White House and Air Force One for fundraising and require those who do not hold federal office to reimburse for the use of any government vehicle for campaign purposes.

GOP freshmen were "locked in" to opposing a comprehensive overhaul "because the leadership is doling out money in large measure" to ensure their re-election. Ultimately, just two of the 19 Republican first-termers, Californians Steven T. Kuykendall and Doug Ose, voted for the Shays-Meehan bill.

For and Against

Supporters of the House bill rallied behind the theme that the electoral system has been seized by out-of-control special interests, and that it would be to the long-term benefit of both parties to reorder the balance of power. "It is just not good enough to have hearings and create an environment where Democrats attack Republicans, Republicans attack Democrats, on the abuses in the last campaign and then do nothing about it," Meehan said as debate began.

Opponents countered that the bill is unconstitutional because it would limit the ability of citizen groups to communicate with the public about upcoming congressional action. Majority Whip Tom DeLay, R-Texas, called the measure "the mother of all government regulation" and said it would "stifle free speech and end criticism of elected officials at critical stages of the election process."

Opponents of abortion rights — led by the National Right to Life Committee, which says its voter education efforts would be unfairly curbed under the bill — mounted an effort to sway their allies against the bill. But of the three House members who changed their votes to a "no" this year from a "yes" last year, only James A. Barcia, D-Mich., said the switch was at the urging of abortion rights opponents. Two Democrats and two Republicans, meanwhile, voted "yes" this year after voting "no" in 1998.

The bill was passed only after it overcame a series of legislative hurdles — amendments and substitutes opposed by Shays and Meehan — erected by GOP leaders as part of their effort to fracture the coalition behind the bill in order to defeat it. All six amendments labeled "poison pills" by Shays and Meehan were rejected. *(Votes 411, 412, 413, 415, 417, 418, pp. H-132, H-134)*

Three amendments were adopted, one of which appeared to be a clear swipe by Republicans at the expected Democratic Senate candidacy in New York of first lady Hillary Rodham Clinton. It would require candidates for federal office who are not federal officeholders to repay the government for the use of any federal property for transportation associated with the campaign. It was adopted, 261-167, with 46 Democrats voting in favor. *(Vote 416, p. H-134)*

Sponsor John E. Sweeney, R-N.Y., said his constituents had "raised concerns about the inequity that exists with an individual who may or may not be a candidate using the resources of Air Force One or a military jet to conduct what may or may not be a campaign."

Replied Zoe Lofgren, D-Calif.: "It is bad policy, it is unconstitutional, it is petty — and it is unchivalrous."

By voice vote, the House adopted a provision clarifying the right of American Samoans to make campaign donations. By 242-181, the House added language to strengthen the ban on gifts by non-citizens. *(Vote 414, p. H-134)*

But Shays and Meehan perceived as the greatest threat a substitute that Bill Thomas, R-Calif., designed to be "purposefully modest" in a bid to gain widespread support. Its central provisions were tighter requirements for finance reports to the Federal Election Commission and a crackdown on political donations by foreigners. While similar provisions were in the Shays-Meehan bill, adoption of Thomas' package would have taken the more sweeping bill off the table under the rules for debate arranged by GOP leaders. It was rejected, 173-256. *(Vote 421, p. H-136)*

A substitute by John T. Doolittle, R-Calif., that would have repealed all donation limits and ended presidential campaign public financing was defeated, 117-306. *(Vote 419, p. H-134)*

A substitute by Asa Hutchinson, R-Ark., proposing lesser curbs on soft money and issue advocacy was rejected, 99-327. *(Vote 420, p. H-136)*

Scaled-Back Senate Bill Vulnerable to Another Filibuster

OCTOBER 16 — For the better part of two decades, the battle in the Senate over revamping the nation's campaign finance system has been hard-fought and contentious, exposing deep philosophical divisions over whether and how to control the flow of money into politics. But it is hard to remember when that debate has ever been as confusing and downright nasty as this year's edition.

It opened in earnest on Oct. 14, when a pair of senior Republicans launched an extraordinarily pointed and personal attack on one of their own, John McCain of Arizona, who hopes his effort to push campaign finance legislation (S 1593) with Russell D. Feingold, D-Wis., will help him to win the GOP presidential nomination next year. By the next day, the debate had bogged down in a procedural morass, as both Republicans and Democrats deployed increasingly complex parliamentary maneuvers to gain a tactical edge.

But with a showdown coming on the bill during the week of Oct. 18, one element from past campaign finance struggles remains unchanged: McCain and Feingold still will need 60 votes to overcome a GOP filibuster led by Mitch McConnell of Kentucky — the leading opponent of the bill, a longtime McCain nemesis and also chairman of the National Republican Senatorial Committee.

And at this point, as in years past, McCain and Feingold appear to be well short of that magic number.

Still, it was hard to tell whether to describe the outcome as preordained, given the heat and passion of the opening stage of the debate and the intense procedural maneuvering that followed. Almost as soon as the debate began, McCain came under a furious assault from McConnell and Utah Republican Robert F. Bennett, who claimed that in attacking the current fundraising system McCain had impugned their integrity.

At issue was the central theme of McCain's campaign — namely, that Washington has been corrupted by the rapidly rising wave of special interest cash. But Bennett and McConnell contended that McCain, in stump speeches and on his campaign Web site, had gone too far in drawing a cause-and-effect relationship between the proliferation of unlimited donations of "soft money" to political parties and lawmakers' support for "pork barrel" spending. Bennett's ire was raised because a Utah project he had backed had been among those identified by McCain as an example of such pork.

Standing beside a placard where a line taken from one of McCain's speeches — "We are all corrupted" — was reproduced in giant letters, McConnell challenged his colleague with prosecutorial zeal. "Who is being corrupt?" McConnell repeatedly asked McCain. "Where is the corruption?"

McCain, struggling to keep his composure as he paced the floor, responded that his charge of corruption was not aimed at Bennett or any other lawmaker. "I'm trying to change a system that corrupts all of us," he said.

The Parliamentary Thicket

That contretemps, however, was but a prelude to the procedural maneuvering afterward, which appeared to stack the parliamentary deck against McCain and Feingold.

Having failed in their prior attempts to break McConnell's filibuster, McCain and Feingold shifted gears this year and scaled back their bill more dramatically than ever before. They dropped virtually all the provisions of their bill except for a ban on soft money, the unregulated and unlimited donations that have been flowing into both political parties at a record rate. Among the abandoned sections was one — denounced as an unconstitutional violation of free speech rights by its opponents — that would regulate issue-oriented television advertising by political advocacy groups. Similar curbs are in the legislation (HR 417) the House passed by a 75-vote margin one month ago.

Since unveiling that change in tactic, however, McCain and Feingold have done little overt work to boost the chances for their measure — or even to provoke much meaningful debate.

As the week of Oct. 11 began, the League of Women Voters announced that it would not support the narrow-gauge bill. Next, McConnell appeared to blind-side the proponents by proposing the seemingly innocuous requirement that senators report "credible information" of corruption to the Ethics Committee. The amendment, an obvious jab at McCain, was adopted by voice vote. Only later did most senators realize that, because it would change Senate rules, the new language raised the number of votes needed to overcome a filibuster of the underlying bill to 67 from 60. McConnell later promised, however, not to force McCain and Feingold to come up with the seven extra votes.

After that, it was the Democrats'

turn to reach deep into the procedural playbook. Minority Leader Tom Daschle, D-S.D., proposed the text of the House-passed bill as a substitute amendment. Then Minority Whip Harry Reid, D-Nev., offered an amendment containing the text of McCain and Feingold's modified bill, minus McConnell's rules change. The net effect was to set up a head-to-head matchup between those competing versions and, for a time at least, gain control over the floor from McConnell and the Republicans.

Daschle and Robert G. Torricelli of New Jersey, head of the Democratic Senatorial Campaign Committee, have long contended that banning soft money without taking any accompanying step to rein in issue advertising would open the door to a dramatic expansion of the influence of policy advocates — and a diminution of the power of the candidates and their parties to control the agendas of their campaigns.

Both proposals ultimately need 60 votes to survive. As the votes loomed, McCain's biggest worry was that the GOP — eager to halt any momentum for a bill — would join Democrats in backing the more comprehensive House approach. If that were to survive, McCain believes that it would be impossible to even get close to the needed 60 votes. "Simply put, if [Daschle's] amendment is accepted, campaign finance reform will be dead," he said on the floor Oct. 15.

By immediately arranging for votes to limit debate on both proposals, Daschle also seemed to foreclose any immediate chances for a freewheeling amendment process. All along, McCain and Feingold had been open to seeing their streamlined bill reconfigured on the floor, perhaps significantly. Proponents of the bill felt whipsawed by both sides.

"Sen. McCain figured that an open amending process might enable him to get to 60," said one of his aides. "Evidently the opponents of the bill on both sides of the aisle believe that might be so."

Finding a Center?

McCain and Feingold were intent on shaking up the political dynamics of the debate, which had been frozen in place in past years, with Majority Leader Trent Lott, R-Miss., blocking nearly all opportunities for amendments. The bill's previous high water mark was 52 votes, eight short of what is needed to trump a filibuster.

What had drawn some interest this year was a possible agreement under which the flow of soft money would be either shut off or capped in return for some significant increase in the caps on the amounts individuals may donate to candidates and political action committees. Those "hard money" limits, including the $1,000 ceiling on donations by individuals to a candidate during each election, have not been adjusted since their enactment with the centerpiece of the current campaign finance law (PL 93-443) a quarter-century ago. *(1974 Almanac, p. 611)*

Sen. Fred Thompson, R-Tenn., who has supported McCain-Feingold in the past, wants to triple the hard money limits, which would put the cap at about where it would be if adjusted for inflation. Sen. Chuck Hagel, R-Neb., has also proposed doing that, and has written an amendment that at the same time would cap soft money donations at $60,000 a year.

As the debate began, the expectation of extended deliberation on amendments was seen by some as a way for the Senate to locate a political middle-ground on the issue. "This is the best process we've had in years," said Sen. Olympia J. Snowe, R-Maine.

McCain has been open to raising the hard money limits, although only as part of a broader package that included the soft money ban. Feingold has been cool to that approach, as have been the most aggressive advocates for overhauling the campaign finance system.

"In this process, the system could actually get worse," said Ellen S. Miller, executive director of Public Campaign, an advocacy group that supports public financing of campaigns. "It could get tilted more toward hard money in larger increments."

It is uncertain when, or even whether, a vote to do that will occur this year. Votes on whether to limit debate on the Daschle and Reid amendments are expected Oct. 19. But under an informal agreement reached in July, Lott promised to allow five days of debate on the bill. Since the debate formally began the night of Oct. 13 and continued through Oct 15, Lott could claim that he has made good on his commitment the same day as those cloture votes — perhaps leaving Thompson and Hagel without an opportunity to push their proposals to a vote.

"We have been shut out by the other side," McConnell complained. But having been victimized by similar tactics employed by Lott and McConnell over the years, Democrats were hardly feeling sympathetic.

Small Victories

Virtually the only encouraging news for McCain and Feingold came when Sam Brownback, R-Kan., announced Oct. 12 that he would support the scaled-back version of their bill, bringing its roster of likely supporters to 45 Democrats and eight Republicans. McCain said other GOP senators were leaning toward supporting the measure, but he declined to name them.

The Senate also voted 77-20 to adopt an amendment by McCain that would speed up the disclosures of contributions by the Federal Election Commission and require national political parties to report to the election agency any transfer of funds to state or local parties. *(Vote 327, p. S-65)*

President Clinton weighed in with a letter in support of the soft money ban, but he also urged the Senate to use its "rare and fleeting opportunity to act" to restore the issue ad provision and other elements that McCain and Feingold had dropped.

But those developments were overshadowed by the unusually personal attacks on McCain by his two colleagues. Bennett was angry that McCain had cited a $2.2 million sewer project to help ready Salt Lake City for the 2002 Winter Olympic Games as an item in the "pork stew that is choking the American people." Bennett was particularly incensed by the suggestion that donations of soft money had influenced his decision to back the project.

"I have been accused on a Web site, for all the world to see, of caving in to soft money. I have been accused of being corrupt," Bennett complained.

McCain has been hammering away at the infusion of spending bills with lawmakers' pet projects for years, and he believes the "stop the pork" page on his

Web site is merely part of that crusade. But the entire episode provided him with some hard lessons: Not only are opponents of his and Feingold's legislation more determined than ever to stop it, but his own campaign rhetoric can provide them with inviting targets.

Even some of McCain's allies on the bill were a bit troubled by his sweeping allegations of corruption in Congress. Snowe, who has supported the McCain-Feingold bill in the past, said that "a lot of people have taken offense to it. You can say that there is too much money in the campaign process. But to say that 100 U.S. senators are corrupt is quite a different thing."

Campaign Finance Crusaders Regroup After Another Senate Defeat

OCTOBER 23 — With the most recent demise of campaign finance legislation, proponents of changing the way money influences politics are left to ponder what for them is both a familiar and frustrating question: What, if anything, can change the seemingly static political dynamics of this issue?

This year's Senate version (S 1593) was scuttled Oct. 20 after a pair of test votes showed that sponsors John McCain, R-Ariz., and Russell D. Feingold, D-Wis., were not even close to overcoming the type of Republican filibuster that has now stopped campaign finance bills in five of the past six years.

"I think it is safe to say there is no momentum whatsoever for this kind of measure," said Mitch McConnell of Kentucky, chairman of the National Republican Senatorial Committee. The leading opponent of changing campaign finance law, he maintains that the proposals put forth by McCain and Feingold would unconstitutionally restrict political speech.

McCain, whose campaign for next year's GOP presidential nomination seems to be gaining as other money-starved aspirants drop from the race, vowed that he and Feingold would keep up their fight. "We will take our case to the people and eventually — eventually — we will prevail," he declared.

Hoping to end years of futility, McCain and Feingold this fall dropped many of the provisions from their comprehensive package and focused primarily on banning political "soft money," the unregulated and unlimited donations that have been flowing to both parties in record amounts.

The new plan picked up the votes of three GOP senators, but that gain was nearly offset by the defections of two other Republicans, who supported the broader McCain-Feingold legislation. In the end, senators voted 53-47 on Oct. 19 to limit debate on an amendment embodying a soft money ban, seven short of the 60 votes needed to stop a filibuster. They had earlier voted 52-48 to limit debate on language copying the campaign finance bill (HR 417) that the House passed in September, again an outright majority but this time eight shy of what is required to stop a filibuster. *(Votes 331, 330, p. S-66)*

Opponents of changing the law insisted that the idea has gained no ground this year, despite continuing fallout from the worst presidential fundraising scandal (in 1996) since Watergate and the increasing media coverage of the proliferation of soft money.

"It is dead for the year," asserted Majority Leader Trent Lott, R-Miss.

Not enacting his proposal, McCain said, will only lead to more scandals, which in turn will ratchet up public demand for change. But campaign finance advocates have been awaiting such a surge of public outrage for years, without success. In a Gallup Poll Oct. 8-10 of 976 adults, 60 percent said overhauling campaign finance law should be a low priority or not a priority at all, while 39 percent rated the issue as either a high priority or the most important issue before Congress.

Glimmers of Hope

Still, while this year's campaign finance debate limped to a predictable impasse, there were developments that should give McCain, Feingold and their allies cause for hope, if not optimism:

- **Two in a row.** For the second year in a row, 58 percent of the House voted to pass campaign finance legislation sponsored by Christopher Shays, R-Conn., and Martin T. Meehan, D-Mass. Both times their bill got 34 votes beyond an absolute majority. The bill includes restrictions on "issue advocacy" advertising by independent groups, a provision McCain and Feingold dropped as part of their effort to keep their bill alive. The House vote did not put any identifiable new pressure on the Senate, as Shays and Meehan had hoped, but it did put 54 Republicans on record in support of such a broad measure and will provide a baseline for the House in the years to come.
- **The McCain factor.** McCain will keep campaign finance a front-burner presidential issue as long as he remains in the race. His campaign might have received a boost Oct. 20, when Elizabeth Dole said she was dropping her presidential quest because she had concluded she would never be financially competitive — a rationale that seemed to give credibility to McCain's argument that money has come to dominate politics.

As the surprisingly bitter floor debate on the bill highlighted, the down side for McCain is that his message exposes him to increased hostility from GOP colleagues at the very time he needs all the Republican support he can muster. McConnell and Robert F. Bennett, R-Utah, excoriated McCain for suggesting, in speeches and on his campaign Web site, that Congress had become corrupted by special interest money.

"This debate is being cast in the national press and over the Internet and indeed in the presidential campaign as a debate between the uncorrupt and the corrupt," McConnell said. "And I have been labeled as being on the side of the corrupt, and I don't like it."

- **Shift in the GOP?** In the Senate, a small but growing number of Republicans showed they are willing to seriously consider embracing campaign finance proposals, particularly if they are less sweeping than the Shays-Meehan bill — or previous iterations of the McCain-Feingold measure. Voting to limit debate on the soft money ban were all 45 Democrats and eight Republicans, including three who had in the past backed McConnell's filibuster: Sam Brownback of Kansas, Tim Hutchinson of Arkansas and William V. Roth Jr. of Delaware, who is facing a tough reelection race.

But two GOP senators who had backed more sweeping legislation in the past — John H. Chafee of Rhode Island and Arlen Specter of Pennsylvania — voted against the narrow proposal. Nor did it win over other Republicans, such as Chuck Hagel of Nebraska, who want to raise the federal "hard money" limits on direct contributions to candidates, which have not been adjusted since they were created in 1974. But Hagel's idea, which would make a ban or a cap on soft money more palatable for some Republicans, would draw objections from Democrats.

Blame Game

The biggest disappointment for McCain and Feingold was that there were never any votes on the various ideas, such as Hagel's, floated this year. Indeed, both parties seemed more interested in gaining a procedural advantage than in engaging in a meaningful legislating process.

Minority Leader Tom Daschle, D-S.D., seemed to take McConnell and other Republicans by surprise when he moved for the back-to-back test votes. That gambit enabled Democrats to control the floor, while McCain complained that Hagel and other senators had been effectively prevented from getting votes on their amendments. Democrats insisted that was not true, but Daschle's maneuver put the debate into a state of suspended animation.

McCain tried to force the action Oct. 18, with an unusual attempt to table, and thereby kill, the very amendment that included the soft money ban he and Feingold had put forward.

"There has been parliamentary maneuvering," McCain said in explaining his counterintuitive strategy. "There has been substitutes. There has been a filling up of the tree. There have been a lot of things that have been going on which have sort of not surprised me but disappointed me."

By moving to shelve his own proposal, McCain said he wanted to cut through the fog and force a "defining vote on whether or not we want to ban soft money." His maneuver came to naught, however. McConnell and the opponents of the soft money ban — confident they had the votes to sustain their filibuster — concluded there was no danger in allowing the amendment

The Rising Tide of 'Soft Money'

OCTOBER 23 — Whether to stem the flow of "soft money" is the central question in the campaign finance debate. But there is no question that this type of unlimited and unregulated giving by unions, corporations and wealthy people has burgeoned in the 1990s and is now the fastest growing source of cash for the Democratic and Republican national committees and the party committees that underwrite House and Senate campaigns.

The six main national party committees took in $57.3 million in the first six months of 1999, after which they all filed reports to the Federal Election Commission (FEC) for the 2000 election cycle. That is more than quadruple the $13.6 million they collected during the first six months of 1991, the comparable period before the 1992 presidential election.

That is when the party committees were first required by the FEC to disclose soft money receipts. But this type of giving has existed since 1978, when the agency first permitted state political party committees to use non-federal money to pay for certain expenses — for example, voter drives — that benefited federal and non-federal candidates. National party committees began raising soft money during the 1980 election cycle, but since it was used for non-federal purposes it was not initially subject to federal disclosure laws.

These charts compare soft money contributions during the first six months of the current and previous four election cycles. They illustrate that, after lagging far behind for the rest of the decade, the Democrats are now approaching soft money parity with the GOP.

(in millions of dollars)

Republican National Committee vs. Democratic National Committee

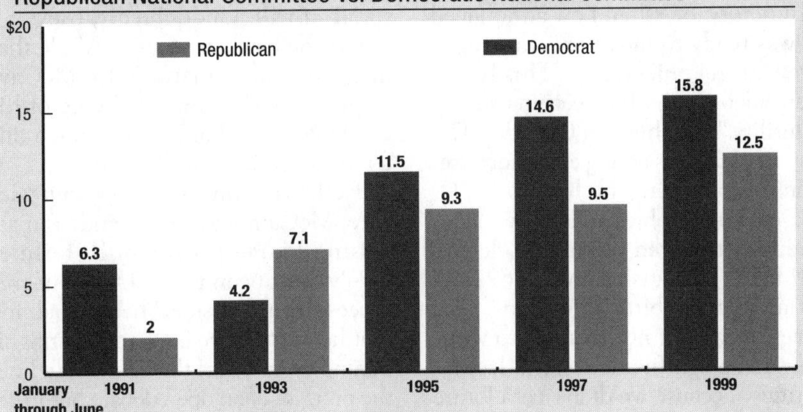

National Republican Senatorial Committee vs. Democratic Senatorial Campaign Committee

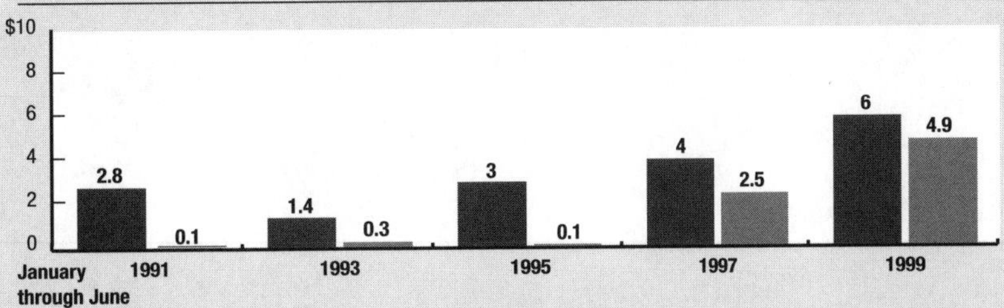

National Republican Congressional Committee vs. Democratic Congressional Campaign Committee

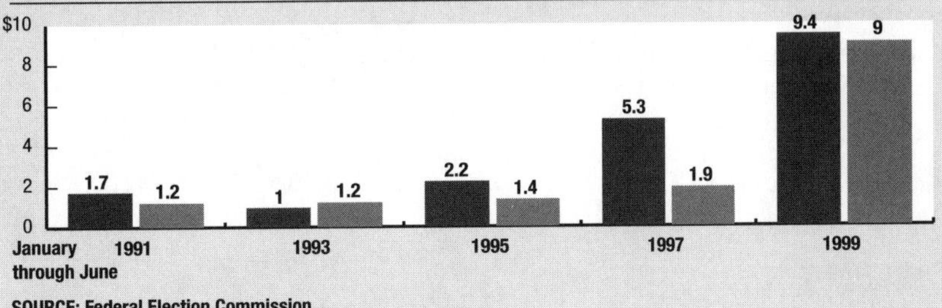

SOURCE: Federal Election Commission

to stay alive another day. In one of the more bizarre votes on this issue in recent years, McCain and McConnell were on the same side as the Senate voted 1-92 to reject the tabling motion. *(Vote 329, p. S-66)*

After the two cloture votes were taken the next day, it was the Democrats' turn to cry foul over procedures. Under an informal agreement reached in July, Lott had promised to allow five days of debate on the McCain-Feingold bill. And he lived up to the letter of that agreement, if not its spirit: The bill was put before the Senate on Oct. 13 and was the pending business for debate for at least part of the next four days that the Senate was in session.

But the Democrats and McCain felt cheated because the debate that began at dinnertime on Oct. 13 — a few hours after the Senate had rebuffed the nuclear test ban treaty — was brief and perfunctory. So when Lott announced he was ready to move on, they registered strong objections. "This hasn't been a debate, this has been an exercise in futility," Daschle said Oct. 19. "The majority leader is acting extremely irresponsibly in pulling this bill."

Democratic objections grew louder when Lott moved to end the debate and bring up legislation (S 1692) to outlaw "partial birth" abortions. "We have every right not to agree to withdraw campaign finance reform legislation just because we didn't get cloture on the first, second or third vote," said Carl Levin, D-Mich. "It took four votes to get civil rights legislation passed in the late 1960s and seven weeks to get that legislation passed."

But traditionally, such votes become a test of loyalty to the majority leader. Most Republicans had no interest in rolling Lott, and the motion to take up the abortion bill was approved 52-48, with the effect that the campaign finance bill had lost its place in the Senate's legislative pecking order. *(Vote 332, p. S-66)*

Last-Ditch Effort

McCain and Feingold have vowed to try to attach the soft-money ban to other legislation, perhaps in the waning weeks of this session. But it is hard to see what that would accomplish, other than to slow the path to adjournment and thereby generate more senatorial ill will. Undoubtedly, they will renew the battle next year. While that might provide a platform for McCain to promote the central theme of his campaign, it is hard to imagine a different outcome from this fall.

Reflecting on the most recent debate, McCain was even-handed in assessing blame for his bill's failure. "We've not been treated fairly in this process by either side," he said, adding that he might have been too trusting in signing on to a deal that seemed to hold the promise of an open debate but in reality left supporters of his bill in the same procedural bind they have been in for years.

Feingold, buoyed by the gain of the three additional GOP votes for the soft money ban, sees some vulnerability in McConnell's position. "He's slipping," Feingold claimed.

Even if that is so, however, the debate demonstrated that Democrats have deep reservations about ending soft money absent accompanying restrictions on issue advocacy ads. "We should ban big money contributions," said Robert G. Torricelli of New Jersey, chairman of the Democratic Senatorial Campaign Committee. "But we should do it for the political parties and these fringe groups on these issue advertisements."

McCain suspects that Democrats have other reasons for insisting on the broader package — namely, that a soft money ban will deal a crippling blow to the fundraising efforts of both parties. "The fact is this is a very cynical business we're in. Very, very cynical," he said.

But there is agreement on one point from nearly all the players in the debate — including McCain, McConnell and President Clinton. Until voters determine that campaign finance is a make-or-break issue, and punish those they believe are standing in the way of change, the status quo will likely persist. ◆

Leaders Name New Ethics Chairmen, But Little Action Taken in Either Chamber

SUMMARY

It was largely quiet on the congressional ethics front this year, with little public action or comment on the few cases known to be under investigation.

Republican leaders named new chairmen for the ethics panels. Lamar Smith, R-Texas, was named head of the House Committee on Standards of Official Conduct in January, and he has instituted a new degree of secrecy to the panel; it no longer announces when it meets. Pat Roberts, R-Kan., was put at the helm of the Senate Select Committee on Ethics in November, when the panel won adoption of new procedures (S Res 222) that streamline both the range of punishments and the method for investigating alleged senatorial misconduct.

Two cases involving senators came to light this year:

- On Nov. 5, the Ethics panel notified the Citizens Progressive Alliance that it had dismissed the group's complaint against Ben Nighthorse Campbell, R-Colo. The group alleged that Campbell broke Senate rules when he won passage of legislation in 1998 that would have given a federally owned reservoir to a group in which he was an investor. The House did not act on the bill. The committee would not release its letter to Campbell, but told the complainant the senator had created "the appearance of a conflict of interest."
- On Sept. 23, Christine M. Niedermeier, chief of staff to Max Baucus, D-Mont., from May 1998 to August 1999, announced that she was filing a complaint with the congressional Office of Compliance alleging that the senator had engaged in a "continuous course of conduct of sexual harassment" and had fired her when she complained. Baucus said he had not harassed Niedermeier "in any way" and had dismissed her "because she abused my staff, abused my constituents and abused other people she dealt with on the job." The compliance office is still reviewing the matter; under the rules, the Ethics Committee could investigate as well, but it has not announced if it is doing so.

The House ethics panel acknowledged opening two new inquiries and continuing one from the 105th Congress; it also wrote one letter of rebuke to a member:

- The committee has yet to announce its findings on a 1997 complaint by the Congressional Accountability Project that Transportation Committee Chairman Bud Shuster, R-Pa., has an inappropriate relationship with Ann Eppard, his chief of staff for 22 years until 1994. Eppard is now his top campaign fundraiser as well as a lobbyist representing several major transportation interests. In late 1998, the panel expanded its inquiry to include possible campaign finance improprieties in Shuster's past three reelection efforts.

The panel put the rest of its inquiry on hold in deference to the Justice Department in 1998, after Eppard was indicted on seven public corruption charges by a federal grand jury in Boston and it was widely reported that Shuster's dealings there were part of the inquiry. But on Nov. 1, federal prosecutors said their investigation was over after Eppard pleaded guilty to one misdemeanor charge of accepting an illegal payment while on the congressional payroll. The prospect that Eppard could be convicted on the more serious charges faded after the Supreme Court in April raised the standard for proving that a crime had been committed when a gratuity was given to a public official. The ethics committee declined to comment on the effect of Eppard's plea on its investigation.

- On Sept. 23, the committee announced it was beginning an inquiry into whether Earl F. Hilliard, D-Ala., complied with House financial disclosure rules and whether his campaign committee made improper payments and loans to businesses in which Hilliard had an interest. In 1997, the panel dismissed a complaint that Hilliard traveled to Libya without required State Department permission.
- On June 9, the panel said it was opening an inquiry into the relationship between Corrine Brown, D-Fla., and West African businessman Fountanga Dit Babani Sissoko. The St. Petersburg Times has reported that he provided Brown with free lodging and gave her adult daughter a car in 1997 in exchange for the congresswoman's help when he faced bribery charges. The committee essentially cleared Brown of another allegation — that she received $10,000 that she did not disclose from Henry J. Lyons, a former president of the National Baptist Convention USA.
- On May 11, the panel issued an advisory opinion warning that members and staff "are prohibited from taking or withholding any official action on the basis of the partisan affiliation or the campaign contributions or support of the involved individuals." It singled out for a special letter about such matters Majority Whip Tom DeLay, R-Texas, who in 1998 had threatened to retaliate against the Electronics Industries Alliance if it hired a Democrat as its president.
- On Sept. 24, the U.S. Court of Appeals for the District of Columbia voted 2-1 to reinstate a lawsuit in which Rep. John A. Boehner, R-Ohio, alleged that his right to privacy was violated when Rep. Jim McDermott, D-Wash., disclosed a 1996 telephone conversation among GOP leaders, allegedly in violation of federal law. A trial judge said McDermott had a First Amendment right to release the tape. The appeals panel disagreed. ◆

Speaker Hastert Gently Gavels In an Era of 'Order' In the House

FEBRUARY 27 — No doubt with relief, Republicans in Congress are emerging from the most tumultuous period of their majority — one in which they presided over a rare and unpopular presidential impeachment, survived a near-death election and saw their top leadership post in the House change with the frequency of an office temp.

So if the political establishment's main beef about the new Speaker of the House is his absence of charisma, members of an excitement-fatigued GOP could not be more pleased. When discussing J. Dennis Hastert, the new collective wisdom of the party's erstwhile political revolutionaries is: What's so bad about dull?

During the previous two months, while the attention of both Congress and the public was focused on the Senate impeachment trial of President Clinton, Hastert was busy behind the scenes doing just what his rank and file has informally charged him with doing: bagging up the confetti and the noisemakers of the Gingrich era and otherwise preparing the House for a new and unsensational phase of GOP rule.

Hastert and his supporters describe it as the return of "regular order" — a term of parliamentary art transformed into a salve for survivors of four years of high-stakes partisan standoffs.

The genial 57-year-old Illinoisan has put together a structure for running the House that should be as familiar to students of Congress as Newt Gingrich's was different. During his four-year tenure, the previous Speaker incorporated military doctrine into his leadership style and concentrated power in the Speaker's office and in an elite corps of Republican-only task forces he created. Hastert's style is right out of a civics textbook. He believes that policy ideas should bubble up from the ranks and be turned into legislation by the standing congressional committees. That will likely mean more involvement by the Democratic minority.

"The American people want Congress to work, and they don't want it to work exclusively in a Republican way or exclusively a Democrat way," Hastert said Feb. 21 on "Fox News Sunday," his first weekend talk show appearance since ascending to the speakership. "I stand for Republican values. But I think there's good ideas that come up on both sides of the aisle, and when they are good ideas and people want to support them, we ought to do it on a bipartisan basis."

In a series of recent interviews, Hastert has declined to be pinned down on such critical questions as how he believes the Republicans should allocate the budget surplus and what GOP proposal for cutting taxes he will embrace. He characteristically deferred to the committees, saying he would wait until they have had time to work their will.

The change is evident on K Street as well. Though conservative and Republican-leaning interests still enjoy a high level of special access to the leadership, lobbyists who once routinely headed for the Speaker's office to appeal decisions by committee chairmen say they are now being politely turned away at the door, instructed to take up their gripes with the committees.

The atmosphere is ripe for a less hierarchical and more decentralized House, with Hastert mediating between the GOP's competing interests. He says he will not dictate the final form of legislation, as Gingrich was wont to do, but will use his skills as a former high school coach to encourage compromises by rival factions and chairmen with overlapping jurisdictions.

And he has shown little interest in the type of epochal musings for which Gingrich was known.

"He's going to do what he needs to do to get 218 votes time after time, and that's going to drive most of his thinking," said Mark W. Isakowitz, a lobbyist who has allied himself with Hastert on health care issues. "That cuts out a lot of talk about inner-city kids with laptops."

In one sign of the shift, Hastert has dismantled Gingrich's policy planning shop, a group of aides charged with coming up with ideas for solving the potential problems of the new millennium. He has replaced it with a smaller policy team of eight that focuses on what might be brought to the floor in this Congress.

"Newt got up every day trying to figure out what the theme of the day was going to be," said Rep. Ray LaHood, R-Ill., a longtime friend of the new Speaker. "Denny gets up every day thinking about what is going on on the floor that day."

Hastert's inner circle is a reflection of the man at the top. It is an amalgam of loyal staff members, many of whom have been with him since his earliest days in the House; friends from the Illinois delegation; House colleagues who never completely bought into Gingrich's ideas about remaking Congress from the ground up; and a few lobbyists with ties to Hastert's home state.

One of their aims is to make the House a less polarized place, not only because members of both parties say they want that but also because the GOP is clinging to the narrowest margin of control in 46 years. Hastert, the chief deputy majority whip for the past four years, has made no bones about acknowledging the importance of Democratic votes to the fate of almost all important legislation coming out of a House divided by a breath.

Some Democrats remain skeptical that Hastert will govern the House in a significantly more bipartisan way. Some of the year's early legislative skirmishes, they say, have been just as polarized as in the previous Congress.

The GOP now has a dozen more votes than the Democrats: 223 to 211, with an independent who is a reliable Democratic vote. The newest House Republican, Johnny Isakson, won a Feb. 23 special election in Georgia to succeed Gingrich, who resigned before taking office for his 11th term.

Gingrich's disdain for the Democrats, coupled with his lack of interest in the minutiae of legislative sausage-making, meant that the House under his stewardship often failed to accomplish its basic tasks, such as producing a budget and passing the 13 annual appropriations bills on time.

Hastert has a Midwestern ethic that abhors the chaotic. Getting work done on time is a mantra for him, he says, and one of his priorities is to have a budget resolution out of committee and on the floor by March 27. He has also said he will not dismiss the House for its summer recess, set to start Aug. 7, unless it has passed all the spending bills.

Making the trains run on time is not the most tantalizing idea that the ruling power in Congress has ever had. But that is just fine with the GOP at the moment; at least the party's opponents will be hard-pressed to demonize Hastert the way they successfully used the flamboyant and gaffe-prone Gingrich against the Republicans in re-election campaigns.

"The fact is, if you don't like Denny Hastert, you ought to move to Siberia," said Ed Gillespie, a GOP consultant and a former top aide in the Gingrich era. "He's as solid a guy as you're ever going to come across."

Impeachment Beneficiary

Hastert is the principal short-term Republican beneficiary of the president's impeachment. It is unlikely he would have ascended to the speakership without it. And, while the GOP's move to remove the president has proved unpopular with the public, it at least held official Washington's nearly undivided attention for an eight-week period that was crucial for Hastert.

The House impeached Clinton on Dec. 19, just hours after the heir apparent to Gingrich, Robert L. Livingston of Louisiana, renounced his nomination for the speakership and said he would resign from the House in the wake of disclosures about his extramarital affairs.

Hastert emerged by the end of that day as the consensus GOP choice for election as the 51st Speaker, and he was elected when the 106th Congress convened Jan. 6.

But by then almost all the attention was on the Senate's trial, allowing Hastert some uninterrupted time to set an agenda and assemble a staff. Not only is Hastert the first person in 80 years to ascend to the speakership without holding another elected leadership job first, but also his tenure in the House — a dozen years — is the briefest preparation time for a Speaker since Charles F. Crisp, D-Ga., won the job in 1891 after just eight years in Congress.

The staff Hastert has assembled is made up mostly of longtime aides from his 14th District of Illinois and from his four years as chief deputy majority whip, an appointed but influential post in the leadership. He has kept on a few key aides from the Gingrich era, who serve as a link between the two administrations and can lend their battle-forged experience in dealing with the Senate and the Democratic White House. Gingrich's former policy director, Jack Howard, is Hastert's deputy chief of staff.

Among members, Hastert has sought advice from fellow Illinoisans, especially his closest friend in Congress, Rep. Thomas W. Ewing, and also from Majority Whip Tom DeLay of Texas, who picked Hastert as his chief deputy when the GOP came to power.

DeLay has been rewarded with an expanded portfolio that now includes the role of liaison to outside groups such as the influential Christian Coalition and National Federation of Independent Business, which represents small businesses. Under Gingrich the job belonged to the Republican Conference chairman, John A. Boehner of Ohio. He lost that job in the leadership shakeout that began with the House GOP setbacks in the election, which also led to Gingrich's resignation.

Aides are quick to note that Hastert also is relying heavily on Majority Leader Dick Armey of Texas, whom he leapfrogged on his way to Speaker. Hastert also has had the delicate task of repairing the split between Armey and DeLay, the two top elected leaders below Speaker. Once close, the two Texans have been barely on speaking terms since the unsuccessful attempt in 1997 to oust Gingrich. Each blamed the other for what came to look like a naked power grab at a time when disillusionment with Gingrich was at its peak. *(1997 Almanac, p. 1-11)*

Hastert — known for his ability to use a combination of tenacity and congeniality to bring warring factions to the table — has brought Armey and DeLay together frequently, and they are becoming increasingly comfortable working together again, said a Republican operative close to the leadership.

The new Speaker has developed a four-point agenda, which was vetted by House Republicans during their legislative retreat Feb. 5-6 in Williamsburg, Va. Without offering specifics, Hastert has said the House will take up legislation to shore up the financially rocky Social Security program, improve federal aide to public schools, cut taxes and boost defense spending.

Former Rep. Bill Paxon, R-N.Y. (1989-99), says he expects the new Speaker to stay focused on a "limited but important agenda" in part because, "If you can get the conference to agree on a common goal and theme, many of the obstacles become secondary."

Overcoming Partisanship?

To survive, Hastert's agenda will have to overcome the partisan bitterness left over from the yearlong investigation of Clinton's lack of candor about his affair with former White House intern Monica Lewinsky, which spawned the perjury and obstruction of justice charges of which Clinton was acquitted Feb. 12.

Hastert went to the White House on Feb. 23 along with the rest of the congressional leadership to discuss the legislative agenda for the year. It was the first such meeting in more than 18 months — since July 15, 1997.

Hastert and the other Republicans all supported the president's removal from office, but all sides pledged to try to put aside any bitterness left over from the impeachment battle in pursuit of areas of agreement.

"We all took an oath, and I think we intend to follow it," Clinton said over pastries and coffee in the Oval Office. "We owe it to the American people, and I'm looking forward to it."

Hastert and Senate Majority Leader

Trent Lott, R-Miss., declined to answer directly when reporters asked afterward whether they were ready to trust the president. "We're starting to work to put together ideas. That's the first step," Hastert said.

Hastert's insistence on passing legislation — even if that takes Democratic votes — may put him at odds with activist conservatives, who believe moderate proposals do little to define the GOP. But supporters say the new Speaker believes conservatives can be persuaded to go along because of the Republicans' need to re-establish goodwill with the electorate at a time when Democrats are within six seats of reclaiming control of the House.

"There is a new day here," declared Hastert's chief of staff, Scott B. Palmer. "There is a great deal of unity among House Republicans."

Terry Greene, Ewing's chief of staff, said: "Those who are overly anxious and believe the fire is not hot enough stand a good chance of leading this good cause back to the minority, and that's where reality sets in. Nothing clears the head quicker than a good look at the gallows."

Consummate Networker

Hastert has begun his tenure with an impressive stockpile of goodwill, just as Gingrich did — but for different reasons. Whereas Gingrich the revolutionary hero was imbued with power because he led his party to the majority after four decades, Hastert's power has been built from one-on-one relationships with members during the past 12 years. Even as a freshman in the 100th Congress, Palmer said, Hastert was a consummate networker, arriving early on the floor for votes and staying until most others had returned to their offices. Now, every Wednesday, he still attends meetings of the 11 remaining House Republicans first elected in 1986.

Hastert still lumbers onto the floor for every vote, though the Speaker by tradition does not vote. He makes himself accessible to members in the same way former Speaker Thomas P. "Tip" O'Neill, D-Mass. (1953-87), kept in touch with the rank and file, by parking himself in the same spot on the floor every legislative day. Hastert's friends in Congress say that O'Neill is serving as a model for his speakership.

Gingrich was said to have few genuine friends among Republicans; Hastert has many. Gingrich was trusted by neither moderates nor conservatives because both camps found it frequently difficult to tell which he truly was. Hastert is a bona fide conservative who, like the late O'Neill, can be highly partisan at times. For example, he has led the GOP resistence to the use of statistical sampling in the 2000 census, one of the nastiest partisan battles of recent years.

But he is also well-liked by moderates who have worked with him in legislative coalitions. "If the goal is to pass a bill that Bill Clinton can sign, that's what he'll do," Gillespie said. "If it is to pass a bill regardless of whether Clinton will sign it and to stand and fight on an issue, then he'll do that."

Hastert's mentor in the House was Robert H. Michel, R-Ill. (1957-95), who was pushed from minority leader into retirement by Gingrich, who thought Michel was too willing to cut deals with the Democratic majority. But Hastert was quickly adopted by the rebels, and when Gingrich was elected Speaker he brought Hastert into his head-counting operation. Hastert cemented his partisan credentials with the aggressive newcomers by enthusiastically rounding up votes to pass legislation that embodied major elements of the 1994 House GOP policy manifesto, the "Contract With America."

As a key member of the GOP whip operation in both the minority and the majority, Hastert has done so many good works for his colleagues that his credit with them runs deep. "He has done so many favors over the years, never asking any favors in return," said Paxon, once considered a leading contender for Speaker himself. "The difference with him is, unlike everyone else who wears their ambition on their sleeves, he was never ringing up chits with something else in mind. He was never looking to climb up the ladder. No one thought he was going to climb over them to grab the brass ring."

Significantly, Hastert was the only one among the top GOP leaders whose reputation was not sullied by the coup attempt against Gingrich. House Republicans say Hastert kept himself busy with activity on the floor the night that Armey, DeLay and others held secret discussions that led to the bungled ouster attempt.

Across the Aisle

Although Democrats are skeptical about the call for bipartisanship — "We've heard that before," is the common reaction from their camp — there are signs Hastert is serious about renewing old legislative coalitions between Republicans and moderate and conservative Democrats.

Tim Roemer of Indiana, ranking Democrat on Education and the Workforce's Postsecondary Education Subcommittee, met with Hastert this month at the Speaker's request to discuss chances for passing a bill (HR 800) to exempt public schools from some federal regulations to give them flexibility in solving problems unique to their school districts.

"It's the first time a Speaker has made an effort to talk with Democrats about legislation and to encourage some common ground," said Roemer. "It's a new experience for me since Republicans took over."

There has been little floor activity on which to judge Hastert's formula, but his early track record has been discouraging for some Democrats. Henry A. Waxman, D-Calif., said the Republican leadership passed up an ideal opportunity for bipartisanship on Feb. 10, when the House debated the first contentious bill of the year. The measure (HR 350) would create new procedural powers for members of Congress to stop legislation that would impose new costs on business and industry. It was passed after narrow votes to defeat an amendment by Waxman that would have added procedural powers to protect some environmental and public health mandates and to reject a similar amendment by Sherwood Boehlert, R-N.Y.

"On the floor, we saw Republicans doing everything they could to make sure neither Boehlert nor I could get our proposals through," Waxman said. "I haven't seen any evidence of bipartisanship yet. But I'm still hopeful."

Democrats are also unhappy with Hastert for allowing only modest increases in their ranks on committees, which they say do not reflect their near-parity with Republicans. They began the year with 48.6 percent of the House seats.

But asked about the committee assignment ratios Feb. 21, Hastert said bluntly, "It's not going to change."

Hastert enjoys more cordial relations with Minority Leader Richard A. Gephardt, D-Mo., than did Gingrich. The former Speaker met with Gephardt only a handful of times in four years. The new Speaker already has had three meetings and several telephone conversations with Gephardt.

"If the Republicans come halfway, we'll come halfway, and we'll meet them in the middle and get things done," Gephardt told reporters Feb. 25. But, he added, "there are a lot of angry feelings on both sides. Ultimately, it takes genuine intent and action to compromise."

Many Democrats still say there is little incentive to cooperate now that they are so close to retaking the House. But the new Speaker may be able to rely on those Democrats who believe impeding any GOP attempts to pass bills can backfire.

"If we're going to have Social Security reform, it is going to have to be bipartisan. If we're going to have tax cuts, it has to be bipartisan," said Rep. Gary A. Condit, D-Calif. "Somebody will be penalized at the voting booth in a couple of years if these things don't get done, and I couldn't tell you with any certainty who voters are going to take that out on."

DeLay: 'Hammer' That Drives House GOP

JUNE 5 — Every good politician knows that power abhors a vacuum. No one in the House has a sharper sense of that axiom than Majority Whip Tom DeLay.

Consider the way he worked the House floor on April 28, when the new Speaker, J. Dennis Hastert of Illinois, signaled to his troops that they could "vote their consciences" on a resolution supporting the U.S. airstrikes in Yugoslavia. While Hastert waited until the last moment to cast his own "yea" vote, DeLay saw the opportunity to strike another blow against President Clinton and bent just enough Republican arms to defeat the measure.

Or look what happened last fall when John A. Boehner of Ohio lost his bid for re-election as chairman of the House Republican Conference. DeLay immediately persuaded the new leadership team to allow him — the third-ranking man in the leadership, behind Hastert and Majority Leader Dick Armey of Texas — to become the new liaison to business and trade groups. J.C. Watts Jr. of Oklahoma, Boehner's replacement as conference chairman, simply did not move quickly enough to thwart DeLay.

It was the same with impeachment. When no other top Republican wanted to trumpet the president's sexual indiscretions and alleged deceptions, DeLay made it his cause to insist that ouster from office, not congressional censure, was the only just punishment.

"If you give Tom the opportunity to assert himself, he will," said Rep. Peter T. King, R-N.Y. "If there's a power vacuum, he fills it."

Authoritatively grabbing the reins like some mythical cowboy, and letting people know it, is part of how the native Texan DeLay works. He cultivates a tough-guy mystique as someone to be feared, and not to be trifled with. He perceives himself as quite able to deflect the arrows of critics. He always expects to win. He will cut the deals and raise the money he needs for victory. He takes matters into his own hands if he thinks he can do the job better. He relishes his nickname — "The Hammer" — and keeps a long leather bullwhip in his Capitol office.

To all this, he brings potent mixtures of anger and persuasiveness, partisan fervor and political practicality. Sometimes combative while rounding up votes, he wants it known that he will do most anything to keep fellow Republicans happy, from plying them with Texas barbecue during late votes to ensuring they are not cheated out of their share of pet projects in appropriations bills. Despite his conservative zeal, which has prompted him to push the GOP against the popular tide on an array of issues, one of DeLay's new campaign 2000 projects is designed to help re-elect GOP moderates in order to hold or expand the party's narrow House majority.

Now, with Hastert's blessing, the whip is aggressively expanding his reach outside Congress. Already known for his open eagerness to leverage K Street money and influence to achieve party goals — most recently the midyear boost in defense spending — he has broadened his boiler-room vote-counting operation by taking responsibility for keeping tabs on the influential business and ideological groups that are Republicans' natural allies.

DeLay's grasp on so much authority has led many to suggest he is the House's most powerful man. That may be too simplistic.

The Speaker has a comparable base of support, with his own network of lobbyists, fealty from a GOP rank and file eager for him to succeed, and stature as the highest legislative official under the Constitution. In addition, DeLay is showing respect for his former protégé by following Hastert's lead on two issues — gun control and campaign finance — that DeLay would rather throw in the trash.

Rather, DeLay seems clearly to be the second-most powerful lawmaker in the House, a reputation he does little to discourage while Armey struggles to rebuild from a slide in GOP confidence that spawned a bid to oust him from the leadership last year.

Asked recently how he managed to become what Republicans and Democrats alike consider to be the most effective whip in recent memory, DeLay, who began his career as an exterminator, flashed an "aw shucks" grin and confidently replied: "That would be like braggin' on myself. Let other people evaluate me on how I do it."

Deploying the Lobbyists

One way he has done it is by capitalizing on just about every advantage inherent in the job or given him by Hastert. And under the guidance of his chief deputy whip, Roy Blunt of Missouri, business lobbyists this year have become a de facto extension of DeLay's 67-member whip operation.

Brought together in clusters based on common interests, the lobbyists are deployed from the very beginning of a legislative push, and they are used both to identify members' positions and to pressure them to vote the leadership's way. At most strategy sessions, DeLay steps into the meetings just long enough to deliver a rallying pitch, then leaves while subordinates hone in on the details.

"He's efficient. He knows his stuff.

He doesn't like to fool around," said Lonnie Taylor, senior vice president for congressional affairs at the U.S. Chamber of Commerce. "We take on assignments and provide updates or feedback on an as-needed basis."

The marching orders given defense contractors during the drive to enact the $14.5 billion fiscal 1999 supplemental spending measure (HR 1141 — PL 106-31) were typical of DeLay's methods.

Several weeks before the initial May 6 House vote, lobbyists from such major defense contractors as the Boeing Co., Lockheed Martin Corp. and Northrop Grumman Corp. were called to meeting with Susan Hirschmann, DeLay's chief of staff, and top aides from the Appropriations Committee.

The message, according to participants, was that the defense industry must actively push the bill, designed principally to finance U.S. participation in the NATO mission in Kosovo, or risk losing coveted payouts in the fiscal 2000 defense spending bill, which had not yet begun to move.

The lobbyists were each given a form and told to return it to the whip's office indicating what efforts they had made to identify wavering members and to obtain their votes. Headed "Progress Report," the document asked for such details as whether the lobbyists had used letters, telephone calls or personal contacts.

Highly motivated to help out, the defense contractors targeted House groups seen to be wavering on the bill, including GOP fiscal conservatives and members of the Democratic "Blue Dog" group. In the end, the House passed the bill by 206 votes.

"It was very smart tactically and also from a policy standpoint," said defense consultant Pete Rose. "It absolutely was effective and contributed to the success of the bill."

Democrats briefly tried to ignite public sentiment against DeLay's tactics. Once again, they lamented, the Hammer was pounding heads, and they implied that such conduct was unbecoming of a leader of the House.

But longtime observers of Congress recognized not a new approach to vote getting, but a road-tested strategy borrowed from the Democrats in their majority days. One of DeLay's role models, in fact, is former Rep. Tony Coelho, D-Calif. (1979-89), now the new chairman of Vice President Al Gore's presidential campaign but in the 1980s a House majority whip known for hardball tactics — and a sometimes questionable merging of public policy with private enterprise and political consideration.

The Democrats' continuing success at getting unions, women's groups and other interests to mobilize for one another's issues has prompted DeLay to take the opposite tack: He organizes business groups around shared concerns.

Under Boehner, a compact group of lobbyists from an array of businesses generally met once a week. A drawback of that system, GOP aides say, was that executives at telecommunications companies, for example, would resist lobbying for the Republican health care plan out of concern that they would lose support for their own special interests if they started meddling in other controversies.

The Price of Doing Business

The strategy used for the defense supplemental bill was copied to win initial passage in March of the budget resolution (H Con Res 68) for fiscal 2000.

In that case, DeLay deployed representatives from two GOP-leaning powerhouses, the Chamber of Commerce and National Federation of Independent Business (NFIB), as well as from such smaller groups as the Food Marketing Institute, which represents supermarkets.

Again, the whip's orders were designed to appeal to the lobbyists' self-interest: Participants got the message that anyone interested in a tax cut down the road was expected to help out with the budget resolution.

John Motley, senior vice president of the Food Marketing Institute, said it made good political sense for his group to support a budget that could pave the way for tax legislation later in the year. A reduction in estate taxes is especially important to the association's many family-owned grocery chains.

Mark Isakowitz, a Republican lobbyist formerly with the NFIB, said DeLay's practice of checking on the commitments made by the groups keeps them on their toes.

"There is always a sense of accountability with Tom," he said. "But that's the way it ought to be. The truth of the matter is people respond if they are asked later, 'Did you do what I asked you to do?' He is very serious and task-oriented."

Not all move along so cheerfully, however. One May meeting of business lobbyists was marked by Republicans' frustration with polls showing gun control to be more important to voters than tax relief, the GOP's strong suit.

The DeLay operation told the business representatives that it was time to repay past favors by helping Republicans raise the public profile of their push for tax cuts. They were to report back on activities undertaken to meet this goal, said two lobbyists.

"If that was not an intimidation, then it's a failure of the English language to cover that," said one, who spoke on condition of anonymity. What was more galling, he added, is that his clients have little interest in helping on tax cuts, "because every time there's a targeted tax cut vote for some, it's the business community that has to pay."

That some lobbyists prefer to keep their complaints to themselves speaks volumes about the respect and occasional fear that DeLay engenders.

Under Hastert, power is much more decentralized than it was under the previous Speaker, Newt Gingrich, R-Ga. (1979-99), who seemed to have a finger in every legislative pie. When the party's business allies wanted to appeal a decision by a committee chairman during the 104th or 105th Congresses, they turned to Gingrich as a court of last resort. Hastert has signaled that he will not routinely open his Speaker's office doors to such entreaties, so lobbyists now are taking their appeals to those in the leadership with whom they have pre-existing relationships — or to Tom DeLay.

This is all part of doing business with DeLay, said former Rep. Steve Gunderson, R-Wis. (1981-97), a moderate who was once DeLay's chief deputy whip and lavishes praise on him as the "ultimate political and power broker."

"If you approach Tom DeLay, you have to be willing to play his game of politics in Washington, and that's everything from networking to fundraising," Gunderson said in an interview. "I don't know that Tom DeLay gives anyone . . . a free ride."

Clinton's Nemesis

The person in Washington least likely to get easy treatment from DeLay is the president.

Almost from the start of the Clinton scandal early in 1998, the whip positioned himself on the House floor and in network television talk shows as the conscience of conservatives angered by what they saw as moral decay in the White House. By year's end, DeLay was the only Republican leader willing to lead the congressional excoriation of Clinton. The election had cost the GOP five House seats and driven Gingrich to announce his resignation. Before quitting in the face of disclosures about his own sexual affairs, Robert L. Livingston, R-La. (1977-99), had been reluctant to make impeachment the hallmark of his tenure as Speaker-designate. And Armey was still recovering from a narrow escape from losing his post as majority leader. *(1998 Almanac, p. 7-4)*

DeLay led the Republicans to spurn a congressional censure as an alternative to impeachment, a move that catapulted him to national prominence and gave him folk hero status among social conservatives. Soon, his "in" box was stuffed with invitations to address local and state GOP groups. *(Impeachment, 1998 Almanac, p. 12-44)*

"Tom DeLay walks into rural America and people come up to him and call him their hero," said Ed Buckham, DeLay's former chief of staff.

This year, the fight against Clinton has played itself out in the ongoing debate over U.S. involvement in Kosovo.

DeLay's first visit to the White House after Clinton's acquittal occurred in early spring, when Clinton and his top advisors briefed congressional leaders on the Balkans. The GOP leader said he listened quietly for a couple of hours, then gave the president a piece of his mind.

"I told him that my daddy taught me how to use a gun when I was . . . 8 years old, and he told me that if I ever pointed that gun at anybody I better be ready to kill him," DeLay recalled in an interview May 27. "Then I told the president, 'You're about to go bomb Kosovo, but you're not committed to go all the way. It may get so bad that you have to go all the way, and it scares me because you don't know what you are doing.' "

Nothing personal against the president, DeLay said; they even politely shook hands. It is just that, in his view, the president "doesn't have the moral authority to lead" on either Kosovo or any other issue.

DeLay reinforced his point a few weeks after that White House briefing, when he sensed imminent defeat for a resolution supporting the military operation and talked to just enough members to ensure its defeat on a tie vote.

Raising Money and Controversy

DeLay earned the sobriquet "The Hammer" soon after Republicans won control in 1994. Having won a three-way election for whip, he worked quickly to acquire more contributors from K Street and to press trade associations to hire only Republicans for top positions.

His tactics have gotten him into trouble on occasion. In May, he was criticized by the House Committee on Standards of Official Conduct for attempting last year to pressure an electronics trade association to hire a Republican as its president.

In the past six years, DeLay's reelection effort and Americans for a Republican Majority (ARMPAC), his leadership political action committee (PAC), have raised a combined $5.5 million — the vast majority to help elect House GOP candidates. DeLay was the first member of the current majority hierarchy to begin raising money for a leadership PAC. While the combined fundraising total of his leadership and personal political groups through the end of last year is less than either Gingrich's or Armey's, it dwarfs that of the Speaker. And DeLay's totals do not include the unregulated "soft money" that ARMPAC is raising for activities not explicitly linked to a candidacy.

A new fundraising group DeLay is backing has stirred more controversy. Called the Republican Majority Issues Committee, it has a goal of raising $25 million to help elect House Republicans in two dozen competitive races in 2000. It is run by a former top aide to DeLay, Karl Gallant, who ran ARMPAC for three years. And it is using the party's top draws at fundraising events. Organizers say Hastert, Armey, DeLay and Watts all boarded the yacht of the DeVos family, the founders of Amway and longtime GOP contributors, for a fundraiser last month.

But even though the new group will act much like a campaign committee, it will neither register with the Federal Election Commission (FEC) nor disclose the names of its contributors.

Gallant said in an interview May 21 that the group need not register because it does not plan to expressly endorse candidates, give them money or coordinate with their campaigns. Rather, he said, it plans to copy the on-the-ground techniques that the AFL-CIO used to spur Democratic turnout last year, including sophisticated voter identification and get-out-the-vote efforts.

But on May 26, the Democratic Congressional Campaign Committee (DCCC) called on Attorney General Janet Reno to have the Justice Department's Campaign Finance Task Force investigate. The new GOP effort, said DCCC spokesman Erik Smith, "is pushing beyond all known legal boundaries."

A DeLay spokesman said that while the congressman is helping the organization by appearing at its fundraising events, he is not otherwise involved.

DeLay also has asked each of his whips to contribute $3,000 to an effort called Retain Our Majority Program, organized in late March, to help re-elect 10 House Republicans targeted by the Democrats. Lobbyists and business PACs also have been tapped for gifts.

DeLay bristles at any suggestion that money corrupts the political process. "People [call] us prostitutes and the mud splashes right back on them. I don't know of a dishonest member of Democrats or Republicans that allows money to affect their ultimate decision-making," he said.

Fighting Campaign Finance Bills

Efforts to overhaul the campaign finance law — to tighten reporting requirements and curb soft money — are adamantly opposed by DeLay, who calls the proposals a threat to free speech.

Last year, the whip was in charge of blocking such efforts from reaching the House floor. Once the debate began on the bill sponsored by Christopher Shays, R-Conn., and Martin T. Meehan, D-Mass., DeLay went to the floor day after day to push one GOP amendment after another in a bid to stop the bill. *(1998 Almanac, p. 18-3)*

This year, in deference to Hastert's decision to allow a House debate on campaign finance legislation in September, DeLay said he plans to take a slightly lower profile. But only slightly. "Don't get me wrong. I will be fighting as hard as I can to kill" this year's Shays-Meehan measure (HR 417).

Not only has Shays been pressing fellow Republicans to defy the leadership and sign a discharge petition to force an earlier House debate, but he also is attacking leadership PACs such as those of DeLay for "purchasing influence over their colleagues." At a news conference May 26, Shays predicted some of that PAC money would find its way into the coffers of a GOP primary challenger in his district next year.

DeLay said in a later interview that he does not intend to work for Shays' defeat, even if his actions are "disappointing."

"I can't explain why members make such comments," said DeLay. "I try to deal with the issues. . . . We have a very different philosophy. I try my best not to make it personal."

Another GOP renegade, King of New York, took it personally when he suspected DeLay of trying to strip him of his chairmanship of the Banking Subcommittee on Oversight. King — who with Shays and just two other House Republicans voted against every article of impeachment — had frequently criticized DeLay for his efforts to try and remove the president from office. But as the impeachment issue has faded, so has King's fear of retribution.

"Even with any trouble I have had, I walk up to him and say 'Hello,' and he says 'Hello,' " King said. "It's not that he has a mean streak. It's political. I have never heard people talk about a dark side, a nastiness. There is no dark side."

Fear or Trust?

Many members say that DeLay does not use fear tactics to instill loyalty. Rather he tries to cultivate a bond of trust with every member of the Republican Conference.

He respects a difference of opinion on issues but has little use for a member who promises to vote as the leadership wants and then switches sides without warning, current and past members said.

"Tom DeLay has a lot of personal and professional pride," Gunderson said. "He does not want to be embarrassed. He will at least respect you if you tell him where you are at. That's what makes vote counters good vote counters."

Several Republicans said the mutual trust between DeLay and his GOP colleagues was cemented in 1997, when DeLay plotted with restless conservatives in an unsuccessful attempt to remove Gingrich from the Speaker's chair. Unlike Armey, who also was involved, DeLay publicly apologized to the rank and file and subtly pointed the finger at others who also were involved but had denied complicity.

Afterward, DeLay retreated with his allies to his offices and prayed. He was interrupted by Rep. Ray LaHood, R-Ill., a Gingrich defender, who wanted to shake DeLay's hand and congratulate him for telling the truth. "He didn't try and weasel his way out of it. He really didn't," LaHood said recently.

In day-to-day matters, DeLay has made sure that his office is useful to members with problems, whether it is a pet provision in an appropriations measure or an out-of-town travel arrangement.

At the 1992 Republican Convention in Houston, just up the road from his home in Sugar Land, DeLay helped lawmakers with such seemingly trivial matters as hotel reservations, restaurant choices and arrangements for rental cars. "He was a full-blown concierge service," Robert Rusbuldt, a senior vice president of the Independent Insurance Agents of America, recalled appreciatively.

Such an accommodating style defies DeLay's reputation as a tart, tobacco-chewing conservative with no time for nonsense. But it was exactly that image that charmed Lindsey Graham, R-S.C., when he visited DeLay in 1994 to seek support for his first House campaign.

"He was talking about the 'Contract With America' and raising money," Graham recalled. "He would spin around in his chair, get all excited and spit. And I said, 'This will work. I can do this too.' "

Just how long DeLay intends to play the political game is uncertain. Those close to him say his goal is not to become Speaker, but to enjoy the legislator's luxury of being the majority whip working with a Republican in the White House.

For now, he just enjoys the victories. "All I can remember is time and time again, getting up in the morning and being 50 to 60 votes behind, and five or six hours later having the votes to pass," he said. "It's a huge rush, a huge rush. I'm very competitive, and I love winning."

Hastert Exhibits Staying Power As House Speaker

DECEMBER 11— When a list of Republican-endorsed defense projects made the rounds this spring, Rep. Sherwood Boehlert was stunned to see that an important Air Force project in his central New York district was not on it. Boehlert, a GOP moderate, viewed the slight as payback for his activism on environmental issues, which has found him continually at odds with Western conservatives such as Joel Hefley, R-Colo., chairman of the House Armed Services subcommittee that prepared the list. So Boehlert complained to Speaker J. Dennis Hastert, R-Ill.

The Speaker asked Hefley to restore a provision sought by New York's Rome Laboratory to the defense authorization bill. Hefley refused. So Hastert arranged for Jerry Lewis, R-Calif., chairman of the Defense Appropriations Subcommittee, to provide for the laboratory in the fiscal 2000 military spending bill instead.

It was one of the many occasions this year when Hastert's ability to deal with his factious troops and paper-thin majority has been tested. And in typical fashion, the mild-tempered Speaker chose the path of least resistance. Boehlert got what he wanted, and Hefley was not forced to back down — a win-win for Hastert, the GOP's Clark Kent of legislating.

As he has little by little put his stamp on the speakership, Hastert has revealed himself during his first year in the job to be effective in ways that his larger-than-life predecessor, Republican Newt Gingrich of Georgia, was not. But Hastert is still struggling with some aspects of leadership that have come to be expected of a modern Speaker, such as setting his party's agenda and articulating its beliefs to the public. Nevertheless, the likable Hastert has won broad if restrained support within the GOP caucus, from both activist conservatives and politically pragmatic moderates. No hint of a challenger has surfaced, so he seems destined to be returned as Speaker if Republicans hold their House majority in the 2000 elections.

Although he was drafted for the position under extraordinary circumstances one year ago — and is the first person in eight decades to become Speaker without first working his way up through the ranks by holding an elected leadership job — Hastert seems to have stemmed speculation that he would seek to be little more than a transitional figure in the history of the House. As the first session of the 106th Congress came to an end, he said in a Nov. 16 interview that he would like to be Speaker again in the 107th Congress.

"I think the people who did the most in Congress over a long period of time were steady. They laid out an agenda and they followed through on an agenda. They involved other members of their conference and in the Congress to get things done," he said.

"I'd rather start out slow and end up strong than not end up at all," he said. "It's a great job. I think you move the job to suit your personality."

Wins and Losses

Hastert gets credit for some admirable victories, particularly saving his party from another in a recent series of end-of-the-year drubbings in budget talks with President Clinton. He also effectively argued that Republican spending decisions did not require borrowing from Social Security reserves, which proved popular with the public even as its truthfulness was called into question by the Congressional Budget Office.

But there were some spectacular losses as well. Hastert pushed Congress to clear a massive tax cut bill, but when the public took little interest, Clinton vetoed the measure, and the GOP dropped it for the year. And the House defeated both a gun control bill and a patients' rights bill that Hastert championed.

Unlike Gingrich (Speaker 1995-99) and Democrat Jim Wright of Texas (Speaker 1987-89), both of whom sought to consolidate power, Hastert has delegated much responsibility to subordinates. That has allowed aggressive members of his leadership team and a few committee chairmen to create power centers of their own. Majority Whip Tom DeLay of Texas is especially prone to going his own way, to Hastert's consternation at times. The two others in the top tier of the House GOP hierarchy — Majority Leader Dick Armey of Texas, and GOP Conference Chairman J.C. Watts Jr. of Oklahoma — have been more loyal to the Speaker.

In business, Hastert's style would be called consensus building, said William Bleuel, a Pepperdine University expert on management strategies who has also studied political campaigns. A consensus builder "keeps things moving without making a judgment or taking a position," Bleuel said. "So what happens sometimes, as was apparently the case with the patient's bill of rights, Hastert just ran out of time. Consensus building is a long process."

By contrast, Bleuel said, Gingrich followed the "autocratic" model, which usually works only for a visionary leader who has the charisma to pull people in his direction.

Hastert's technique is to gather opposing sides together again and again, for meeting after meeting, until they wear down and find middle ground.

Last summer, for example, Hastert launched an effort to settle a long-running dispute between the Federal Reserve and the Treasury Department over which would regulate the conglomerates sure to emerge from an overhauled financial services industry. After meeting separately with Federal Reserve Chairman Alan Greenspan and Treasury officials in June and July, he called Greenspan and Treasury Secretary Lawrence H. Summers to his office in August. Hastert spokesman John Feehery said the meeting produced the beginnings of an agreement that was ultimately reflected in the law (S 900 — PL 106-102) allowing banks, brokerages and insurance into one another's businesses. It was the biggest legislative achievement of the year.

"He's an enhancer. He urges people along," James Thurber, director of American University's Center for Congressional and Presidential Studies, said of Hastert.

Nancy L. Johnson, R-Conn., a Ways and Means Committee member, said Hastert's mediating skills have helped restore civility to the House.

"When he took over, our caucus had broken down into rival factions that spent their time trying to see if they could defeat each other," she said. "Now factions spend their time figuring out how to work together. We even know each other better, because Denny brings people into the room together."

His supporters say Hastert did about as well as could be expected in 1999, considering that he took over not only a House plagued by the extreme bitterness of impeachment, but also a Republican Conference reeling from unexpected electoral setbacks; the loss of Gingrich, their strongest leader in decades; another leadership shake-up fueled by sexual indiscretions; and factional rivalries growing more intense by the week.

He came to the job with little preparation, and after only 12 years in the House. He was not groomed to be Speaker in the usual way; his only leadership training was as chief deputy whip under DeLay for the preceding four years. But his standing as a trusted and stabilizing figure made Hastert the consensus choice for Speaker just hours after the GOP nomination for the job was abandoned by Robert L. Livingston, R-La. (1977-99); he withdrew amid revelations of marital infidelity. *(1998 Almanac, p. 7-10)*

Hastert "has restored a modicum of respectability to the office and his party," said Wright, who resigned under a cloud a decade ago and now teaches political science at Texas Christian University. *(1989 Almanac, p. 36)*

"He's not going off on a witch hunt trying to impeach the president or doing other odd things," Wright said in an interview. "I think the public probably breathes a little easier with Dennis in the saddle, but they just don't see him going anywhere."

In eight Harris Polls this year, respondents who ventured an opinion about Hastert gave him consistently lukewarm ratings, and lower marks than congressional Republicans over-

The New Order

DECEMBER 11 — With a new Speaker at the helm, the personal and political dynamics among the other top leaders of the House Republican majority changed dramatically in 1999. Some of the leaders grew more powerful, while others receded into lesser roles. Here is a snapshot of how the other three at the top of the hierarchy fared:

Majority Leader DICK ARMEY of Texas

As the Gingrich era ended and the Hastert era began, Armey receded from the front lines to a less powerful place in the lineup. He spent the year mending fences after a bitter challenge to his leadership last fall. He had to fight for re-election to a third term as majority leader against Steve Largent of Oklahoma and Jennifer Dunn of Washington. Also, younger conservatives were still seething over Armey's role in a failed 1997 ouster attempt against Gingrich. Armey also had to repair his relationship with Hastert, who, before he was drafted to run for Speaker, had been urged by fellow Republicans to take Armey on. Hastert asked Armey to release him from an earlier pledge to support his re-election, but Armey refused. In a sign that their relationship was on the mend, Hastert put Armey in charge of the GOP's big tax cut drive this year.

Majority Whip TOM DeLAY of Texas

Hands down, DeLay has been the biggest winner in the new order. He and Hastert do not always agree, but the Speaker has given his No. 3 man an unprecedented amount of independence, which DeLay has used with effect to promote his views on bill after bill. Some students of Congress are calling DeLay the most powerful House whip in history. He and Hastert are good friends, although DeLay's tendency to ambush the Speaker could, over time, wear on the bond of trust between them. His downside at the moment is his sometimes controversial conservative views, which play into the hands of the enemy. For example, this year he advocated delaying tax credits for the poor — an idea that fed perceptions of Republicans as uncaring toward society's disadvantaged. His proposal was quickly withdrawn. But Democrats continue to use him as the poster boy for GOP extremism.

Conference Chairman J.C. WATTS JR. of Oklahoma

Because hopes for his performance had been so high, Watts is probably the House Republicans' biggest leadership disappointment. When he ousted Ohio's John A. Boehner as conference chairman, Watts' election was seen by his colleagues as a way to put a fresh face on the party and a chance to appeal to minority voters who usually align with Democrats. But he has proved unexpectedly weak in one key aspect of the position: dealing with the media and speaking for the GOP on television. National reporters stopped turning to him for interviews because his cautious comments failed to make news. And he had a tough time sticking to the Republican message on TV, instead being dragged into debates on Democratic territory. But Republicans say Watts, who had no leadership experience before this job, is improving every day.

all. But in each poll a large percentage of the public was too unfamiliar with him to rate his performance.

No Salesman

While credited with restoring a civil working environment to the House, Hastert has a more ambiguous record in two other important roles of the modern Speakers: setting an agenda for the House and being a readily identifiable spokesman for the party.

Gingrich and Wright were more typical in that they developed distinct policy agendas and were eager to sell them to the nation. Hastert's approach is more like that of Thomas S. Foley, D-Wash. (Speaker 1989-95), a conciliator who regularly deferred to the legislative wishes of committee chairmen.

Thomas P. O'Neill Jr., D-Mass. (Speaker 1977-87), was adept at providing a populist counterpoint to President Ronald Reagan in the 1980s. Wright was a gifted orator and engaged the media in daily briefings. Gingrich, a product of the television age, was a regular both in front of the cameras and on the national speaking circuit.

Hastert brought neither a grand policy vision to the job nor a natural ability to articulate his party's positions. His speeches often seem passionless, and he is admittedly ill at ease in the media spotlight.

"If you're going to compare me with Newt Gingrich, I'm not the visionary that Gingrich is. If you are going to compare me with the talking-head ability of Gingrich, I'm not there yet," Hastert said. But, he added, he brought to the job strengths lacking in his predecessor, including an ability to see ideas through to fruition by immersing himself in legislative mechanics — which never held Gingrich's fascination — and a knack for steering the House clear of debilitating partisanship.

"I said from the beginning that it was important for this Congress to get its work done, and get away from the animus that was around this place. And I think we've accomplished that," he said.

Every Speaker is also a product of his circumstances, said the University of Oklahoma's Ronald M. Peters Jr., who has written several books on the speakership. While Gingrich was the right Speaker for Republicans during their struggle to throw off the yoke of 40 years in the minority, Peters said, Hastert may be the right fit for Republicans as they try to convince the electorate they have the maturity to remain in the majority.

House Republicans, who just four years ago prided themselves on being the ideological vanguard of their party, say now that they expect their presidential nominee for 2000, not the Speaker, to assume responsibility for articulating the GOP agenda.

"If Republicans take the White House, the president is going to be our spokesman, so the Speaker's role as spokesman is diminished," said Jo Ann Emerson, R-Mo.

At least until then, Peters maintained, Hastert needs to become more comfortable as party spokesman. In the absence of an overarching Republican agenda, he noted, Democrats were effective this year in pushing their issues, and are sure to press for action next year on such issues as increasing the minimum wage and regulating managed health care providers.

"He is still the leader of the House Republicans and more than anyone else he has responsibility for ensuring their prospects," said Peters. "If Republicans are going to control the House, they need to move Republican agenda items, not Democratic ones."

Back to Order

Among his peers, Hastert may have passed the most difficult test as Speaker with his handling of the budget, which he said would be his highest priority for the year in order to show he was restoring "regular order" to the House.

He and Senate Majority Leader Trent Lott, R-Miss., agreed early on to send the 13 spending bills to Clinton one at a time to avoid a repeat of previous years, when Republicans wound up negotiating with the president over several incomplete bills, giving Clinton leverage to demand more funding for favored programs. Hastert insisted on sticking to "regular order" even as the clock ran out this fall, and Congress was compelled to keep the government running for the first seven weeks of fiscal 2000 with stopgap spending measures.

"Usually we'd get to this point and Gingrich's veins would be popping out of his head; he would be angry and talking war," Mark Souder, R-Ind., said as the appropriations end game neared its conclusion.

"In five years of Republican control, this is the strongest position Republicans have been in at the end of the budget process," said Ed Gillespie, a political consultant who was formerly a top aide to Armey.

"After debacle after debacle we saw ourselves involved in with the last speakership, most of us feel Denny is a breath of fresh air, said Matt Salmon, R-Ariz., one of the party's aggressive, young conservatives. "Our strategy now is more level-headed and patient. We don't always have to go for the knock-out punch."

But Hastert's soft touch means that sometimes he cannot, or will not, engage in old-fashioned head-banging when party imperatives are in jeopardy.

"Part of the job of leadership is to have a program, to schedule bills on the calendar, move them at an orderly pace and keep control of the ball," Wright said. "If that role goes unfilled, if the trumpet gives forth an uncertain sound, who will come to the battle?"

In a few high-profile debates where Hastert did assert a position, he suffered humiliating losses.

He urged the House to pass gun control legislation in the wake of the high school shootings in Colorado in April. But the measure he backed (HR 2122) was defeated overwhelmingly, in large part because DeLay teamed up with a Democrat, John D. Dingell of Michigan, to engineer its defeat.

Hastert tried again on legislation aimed at protecting patients from medically unsound decisions by their insurers — the issue on which he has had the most legislative experience. He named a task force to draft such a bill, but the committee chairmen with jurisdiction over the issue balked and insisted they could produce a bill themselves. While their efforts foundered, support built for a proposal by Dingell and Charlie Norwood, R-Ga. By the time of the floor debate, so many Republicans had declared their support for that bill (HR 2723) that the leadership version produced by the task force was doomed. Hastert did not even try to force the turf-conscious chairmen to fall in line for the good of the party.

"One of the things I said I was going to do is not throw my weight around," Hastert said. "We are going to do things in regular order and try to keep to those principles."

Hastert's supporters say he has done about as well as can be expected with a margin of control so small; just five GOP defectors can spell defeat. And Minority Leader Richard A. Gephardt, D-Mo., sensing a chance to win back control of the House for the Democrats next year, managed to keep his troops unified on issue after issue, blocking Hastert from picking up needed votes.

"I'd give him a B minus," Burdett A. Loomis, a University of Kansas scholar on Congress, said of Hastert. "But a B minus is a pretty good grade considering the potential for a D or an F was definitely there."

Who's in Control?

With Congress set to reconvene Jan. 24, Hastert is spending the recess in efforts to shore up his party's standing with the public, which no doubt will further endear him to the GOP rank and file. After leading a week-long congressional trip to New Zealand, Australia and Japan, he will spend the coming weeks on a series of speaking appearances and fundraisers for fellow House Republicans. He also has developed radio advertising touting the GOP accomplishments of 1999, which he hopes will be a model for other Republicans to follow.

Still, Democrats are fond of perpetuating the notion that Hastert is a weak Speaker and that DeLay controls of the House. "He's a nice guy, but he's not a strong Speaker," Joe Moakley of Massachusetts, the ranking Democrat on the Rules Committee," said of Hastert. "He's like a designated driver. He has people sitting in the back telling him where to go."

It is true that DeLay has become an enormously powerful No. 3 man, in part by making the most of his closeness to Hastert and by aggressively pursuing his own agenda whenever he has perceived a leadership void.

Hastert gives DeLay an unusually large amount of freedom, sharing power with his underling in a way that has allowed DeLay to become arguably the most powerful whip in history, the University of Oklahoma's Peters noted.

However, House Republicans say Hastert retains ultimate decision-making authority, and that DeLay poses little threat to the boss's job. "DeLay understands that he has gone as high as he's going to go," said a prominent GOP lawmaker. "So if he can't be king, the next best thing is to be king-maker."

Said Souder: "No one is going to depose Denny." ◆

Chapter 9

DEFENSE

Dispute Over Weapons Labs Nearly Shoots Down Defense Authorization

SUMMARY

The $288.8 billion defense authorization bill for fiscal 2000 added $8.3 billion to President Clinton's budget request. The bill was cleared only after a protracted standoff between Energy Secretary Bill Richardson and the Republican-led Congress over provisions intended to improve security at the Energy Department's nuclear weapons laboratories.

More than a third of the funds Congress added to Clinton's budget request — $3.1 billion — resulted from a bookkeeping dispute with the White House. Instead of following the usual practice of requesting the full amount needed for military construction projects that were scheduled to begin in fiscal 2000, Clinton tried to hold down the size of budget outlays by deferring funds that would not be spent during the year. It was clear from the start that Congress would not go along, and lawmakers added the total cost of such projects to the defense authorization and military construction appropriations bill.

The authorization bill also added money to the budget for several major weapons programs. The largest was $375 million for components of a helicopter carrier for the Marine Corps. The remaining cost of the ship — about $1.1 billion — is to be in the fiscal 2001 budget. The ship would be built by Litton Industries in Pascagoula, Miss., hometown of Senate Majority Leader Trent Lott, R-Miss., who vigorously promoted its inclusion in this year's budget. The Navy had planned to include funds for the ship in the fiscal 2004 and 2005 budgets, but Litton argued that buying it now would reduce the price to $1.5 billion from $2.3 billion.

Other major increases for weapons included $252 million for four Lockheed Martin C-130 cargo planes built in Marietta, Ga. (the White House requested none), and $157 million for 12 H-60 helicopters over and above the $511 million the administration requested for 28 helicopters. The helicopters are built in Connecticut by the Sikorsky division of United Technologies.

The bill authorized $4.2 billion for anti-missile defense programs, 9 percent more than Clinton sought. The increase was distributed across several projects. There was no significant debate over anti-missile defense on this bill, even though Republicans have made acceleration of such programs an issue in their critique of Clinton's defense program. The debate over anti-missile defenses was waged, instead, on separate legislation (HR 4 — PL 106-38), which Clinton signed in July.

The bill's most significant policy initiative is a slightly greater increase in military pay and pension benefits than Clinton recommended in hopes of improving recruiting and retention. The bill authorized a 4.8 percent increase in basic pay, rather than the 4.4 percent raise Clinton proposed, and mandated that any military pay raises through fiscal 2006 be 0.5 percent higher than the increase in private-sector wages as measured by a government survey.

The bill also included, as Clinton requested, additional raises of up to 5.5 percent for midcareer officers and enlisted personnel with key training or experience. And it replaced a 1986 law (PL 99-348), unpopular in the military, that reduced pensions by 10 percent for those who entered the military after 1986 and retire after 20 years of active duty. The new plan gave personnel a choice: Retire with 50 percent of basic pay or retire with 40 percent but receive a $30,000 lump-sum payment after 15 years of service.

Both the House and Senate rejected efforts to include in the bill a requirement that Clinton seek congressional approval before sending forces into the Serbian province of Kosovo.

Box Score

- **Bill:** S 1059 — PL 106-65
- **Legislative action: Senate** passed S 1059 (S Rept 106-50), 92-3, on May 27.

House passed HR 1401 (H Rept 106-162), 365-58, June 10.

House passed S 1059, by voice vote, on June 14, after substituting the text of HR 1401.

House adopted the conference report on S 1059 (H Rept 106-301), 375-45, on Sept. 15.

Senate cleared the conference report, 93-5, on Sept. 22.

President signed the bill into law Oct. 5.

Critics of the administration warned that a war with Serbia over the province — which was brewing as the bills were drafted and had started by the time they were debated — would undermine the combat readiness of U.S. forces by draining funds needed for training, maintenance and modernization. GOP skepticism of Clinton was underscored when leading House Republicans insisted that he put in writing a promise to seek supplemental appropriations to pay for the Kosovo operation before they would join Democrats to kill the anti-Kosovo provision in the House bill.

As enacted, the bill required Clinton to request a supplemental to pay for the deployment of U.S. units as part of the NATO-led peacekeeping force in Kosovo. It also authorized only $1.9 billion of the $2.4 billion he requested for air and naval patrols of Iraq and peacekeeping operations in Bosnia. The Pentagon has decided to reduce the number of troops in Bosnia.

Underscoring GOP complaints that Clinton had been sending too many military forces abroad, the bill terminated the deployment of troops in Haiti by May 31, 2000. The mission began in 1994.

In another swipe at Clinton, Congress rejected his request to include authority for two additional rounds of base closings. Only the Senate consid-

Proposed Pay Increase Aimed at . . .

JANUARY 9 — Nearly $3 billion of the fiscal 2000 defense budget that President Clinton will unveil next month is for a package of military pay and pension increases aimed at attracting new recruits and holding on to experienced personnel.

It would be the largest increase in military compensation since 1981 and would cost about $30 billion over the next six fiscal years.

Basic Pay

About two-thirds of the total would go for annual increases in the basic pay of service personnel.

It is an article of faith in the military that since 1981 — the last time there was a major increase — military pay has improved at a slower rate than private sector wages, creating a pay gap of 13.5 percent. Clinton's plan promises to narrow that gap with a series of annual pay raises that slightly exceed the rate at which private sector wages increase.

Clinton is proposing to increase basic pay by 4.4 percent in 2000 and by 3.9 percent in each of the following five years.

Some analysts challenge the notion that any gap exists, contending that, for the most part, military personnel fare well against civilians of comparable age, experience and responsibility.

But Joint Chiefs of Staff Chairman Gen. Henry H. Shelton and other top military leaders have lent their authority to the pay-gap argument, and there appears to be great political momentum behind the notion of an across-the-board increase in basic pay.

The only congressional debate on this part of Clinton's package may be over whether his proposed raise for 2000 is large enough. Because the government recently increased its estimate of how fast private-sector salaries will grow by 2000, Congress may consider a higher military pay increase.

In addition to basic pay, all service members receive either government-supplied housing or a tax-free housing allowance that varies with rank, years of service and location. Many personnel in critical, dangerous or hard-to-recruit specialties receive additional pay or one-time bonuses for joining or staying in the service.

Clinton's budget is expected to request increases for some of the bonuses and special pay. It also will propose a new category of special pay for Navy officers who serve on surface warships, like the additional pay given to submarine crew members and aviators.

Targeted Increases

Beyond the 4.4 percent basic pay raise for all service personnel, Clinton is proposing increases of as much as 5.5 percent for some midcareer commissioned officers and non-commissioned officers with the education, skills

ered the proposal, which it rejected. Many Republicans contended that Clinton improperly manipulated the last base closing round in 1995 in order to save jobs in vote-rich Texas and California.

Joint Chiefs Say Clinton's Defense Budget Increase Falls Short

JANUARY 9 — It took only gentle prodding for the Joint Chiefs of Staff to help Senate Armed Services Committee Republicans lay out the terms of this year's defense budget debate: President Clinton's promise to let the Pentagon spend $12 billion more in fiscal 2000 is not enough, the officers said during a Jan. 5 hearing.

Clinton is expected to propose $267 billion in budget authority for defense in fiscal 2000, instead of the $263 billion he had earlier projected. In addition, Clinton will allow the Pentagon to take more than $8 billion previously authorized in several areas of the defense budget and reallocate it for high-priority programs. The administration said the money is available because, for example, fuel prices and other costs have been lower than projected.

The administration counts this money as an addition to the Pentagon's purchasing power since such savings normally would be returned to the Treasury Department.

The proposed increase for fiscal 2000, which Clinton announced during his weekly radio address, would be the first in a series of annual increases in projected Pentagon purchasing power that would total $110 billion through fiscal 2005. The money would be primarily to boost military pay, combat readiness and weapons modernization.

Clinton agreed to increase future defense budgets last fall under heavy pressure from congressional defense hawks and senior Pentagon leaders who contend that the administration's spending plans were too stingy, given the large forces being sent overseas on peacekeeping and other missions.

The administration plan would be "the first, sustained, long-term increase in defense spending in a decade," Clinton said. Pentagon budgets have declined annually since fiscal 1985.

Joint Chiefs of Staff Chairman Gen. Henry H. Shelton told the Senate panel Jan. 5 that Clinton's proposed increases would "meet our most critical needs, and it will represent a major turnaround following years of decreased spending."

But the service chiefs restated the even larger budget increases they had called for during testimony before the Armed Services Committee Sept. 29. At that time, they asked $17.5 billion

. . . Making Services More Attractive

and talent the services particularly value.

Under the current basic pay tables, an officer's years of service, or longevity, typically account for nearly two-thirds of his or her total pay increases, while promotions account for one-third.

The administration wants to change the tables to put more emphasis on rewarding promotion. The assumption is that members who are promoted have demonstrated talent that makes them particularly worth keeping.

Defense Secretary William S. Cohen told reporters Dec. 21, "This is going to enable us to do a better job in rewarding performance, compensating people for their skills, their eduction, their experience, and also to encourage them to continue their military service. These targeted raises are also going to help narrow the wage disparity with the private sector."

The prime beneficiaries of these additional increases would be officers in the middle ranks — Army majors, lieutenant colonels and colonels and their Navy counterparts — who have been promoted more quickly than most of their peers.

For instance, Clinton's package would provide only the 4.4 percent across-the-board increase for a private with two years of service, whose monthly basic pay would increase from $1,076 to $1,123. But an officer who had reached the rank of major after only 10 years of service — the hallmark of a "fast burner" — would see his monthly basic pay increase by 9.9 percent, from $3,855 to $4,237.

Retirement Pay

Clinton's compensation plan would largely repeal a 1986 law (PL 99-348) that cut retirement pay for future retirees — those who enlisted after Aug. 1, 1986 and retired after 20 years would receive 40 percent of basic pay, rather than 50 percent. *(1986 Almanac, p. 486)*

The law also provided that such retirees would receive less generous cost-of-living pay increases than those given to personnel who joined the service before 1986.

The new formula was hotly debated when it was made, but it then faded from the political radar screen. The issue has resurfaced in the past year, as the first members covered by the new system, having served for 12 years, began weighing whether to stay in uniform for the 20 years that would make them eligible for retirement benefits.

Far more of these experienced personnel decided to get out than the services hoped, and many of them cited as a reason the reduced pension.

Clinton's proposal would provide that all 20-year retirees collect 50 percent of the basic pay. It also would make the cost-of-living increase for post-2006 retirees more generous than the law enacted in 1986, but less generous than the one in effect for those who joined before 1986.

more in fiscal 2000 and a total of about $130 billion more through fiscal 2005.

"It does not meet the stated needs," Air Force Chief of Staff Gen. Michael E. Ryan said of Clinton's proposal, "but it's a good start."

Committee Republicans made it clear they would use the service chiefs' higher figure as a guide to drafting the annual defense authorization bill.

"There's still the benchmark of Sept. 29," newly installed Armed Services Chairman John W. Warner, R-Va., said.

Budget Camouflage

In fact, the gap between Clinton's proposal and the service chiefs' requests is larger than it appears.

The chiefs had emphasized in September that the $17.5 billion in added spending they were seeking did not include upward of $2 billion that would be needed to increase military pay and pensions. However, Clinton's $12 billion proposal includes those personnel costs, as well as more than $2 billion to pay for the continued presence of U.S. forces in Bosnia.

Several GOP senators said that deducting the pay and Bosnia funds from Clinton's proposal meant he was promising less than $8 billion for readiness and modernization programs.

The traditionally pro-Pentagon Armed Services Committee would be expected to push for a larger defense budget than Clinton will request. And support in the Senate as a whole seems widespread. In a Dec. 8 letter to Budget Committee Chairman Pete V. Domenici, R-N.M., Majority Leader Trent Lott, R-Miss., called for adding $20 billion a year to the projected defense budgets.

The outlook for stepped-up defense spending is less clear in the House. Speaker Dennis Hastert, R-Ill., included a vague call for a more robust defense in the speech he made Jan. 6 immediately after his election.

But any increase in defense spending apparently would have to be offset by cuts in domestic spending under the spending caps enacted by the balanced-budget law (PL 105-33) in 1997. *(1997 Almanac, p. 2-47)*

Congress has balked at significant additional domestic cuts, and GOP fiscal conservatives have dug in to support the spending caps.

"The defense hawks on the Hill have to talk to the deficit hawks on the Hill," National Security Council staff member Robert G. Bell told reporters Jan. 7.

Pay Increase Supported

The committee generally supported the administration's three-part package of proposed increases in military pay and pensions.

This includes a 4.4 percent increase in military pay, targeted additional pay raises for midlevel officers and all-but repealing a 1986 law (PL 99-348) under which, beginning in 2006, service members who retire after 20 years of active duty would get pensions equal to only 40 percent of their basic pay, rather than the current 50 percent.

Military leaders insist that the pay and retirement changes are essential to recruiting and retention. But as the administration's plan was taking shape last fall, senior Armed Services Democrat Carl Levin of Michigan and then-Chairman Strom Thurmond, R-S.C., told the Pentagon they wanted to see a detailed analysis of how such expensive changes in compensation were expected to improve the services' personnel woes.

During the Jan. 5 hearing, Rhode Island Democrat Jack Reed noted that experienced personnel are leaving the service for many reasons, including fewer opportunities for promotion to command since the services have been reduced by one-third since the end of the Cold War, and greater opportunities in the booming civilian economy for skilled military leaders and technicians.

"We have a very profound problem here that will not be easily remedied simply by raising pay and allowances," Reed warned.

The chiefs agreed that the personnel problems had many roots, principal among them the fact that the smaller, post-Cold War military is being used much more frequently overseas than was anticipated. But they insisted that the pay and retirement increases were important as a gesture of national support for military personnel.

"All of that sends a very clear signal as to whether or not a very heavily used force is appreciated for what it's doing," Shelton said.

Shelton also argued that the complaints about pay and the retirement system from personnel who are leaving made the need for the pay package too urgent and too obvious to await sophisticated analysis.

"Long, detailed studies might lead to the demise of the force at a time when we need to start fixing some of those things that are being reflected in every survey that we see as reasons . . . that are causing our people to depart," Shelton said.

Indeed, support for the pay and retirement package was so widespread among committee members from both parties that Warner suggested trying to enact it as free-standing legislation early in the year, before Congress buckles down to work on the annual defense funding legislation.

The last major overhauls of the Pentagon's pay and retirement systems, in 1981 and 1986 respectively, were enacted as separate legislation. *(1986 Almanac, p. 486; 1981 Almanac, p. 207)*

Though details of Clinton's plan were not final, it would increase funding for weapons procurement to $60 billion in fiscal 2001. This would meet the modernization funding requirement set by former Joint Chiefs of Staff Chairman Gen. John Shalikashvili, although later than he said was necessary.

House Chairman Seeks $8.7 Billion More in Defense Budget Authority

MARCH 6 — House Armed Services Committee Chairman Floyd D. Spence, R-S.C., has called for enough headroom in the fiscal 2000 budget resolution for Congress to add at least $8.7 billion in budget authority to President Clinton's $281 billion defense budget request. But he may have to battle House and Senate leaders to do it.

The extra authority would cover the cost of projects that the armed services have listed as priorities that were not included in Clinton's request.

Many Republicans and centrist Democrats appear ready to support such an addition to the defense request. They had urged that the cap on discretionary spending set by the 1997 balanced-budget law (PL 105-33) be amended to allow for higher defense spending. *(1997 Almanac, p. 2-47)*

Indeed, when Defense Secretary William S. Cohen appeared before the Senate Budget Committee on March 2, Chairman Pete V. Domenici, R-N.M., said it was "very apparent" that it was time for Congress to review the annual spending caps.

But momentum for such a change disappeared two days after Spence made his recommendation in a letter to House Budget Committee Chairman John R. Kasich, R-Ohio. On March 4, Senate and House Republican leaders agreed jointly to craft a budget resolution that would retain the spending cap.

Since the law sets a single limit on all discretionary spending in fiscal 2000, Congress could, theoretically, add money to Clinton's defense request by cutting domestic programs. But Republicans were unable to do that in the 105th Congress, when they had a larger and more confident majority in the House than they do now.

In his March 2 letter to Kasich, Spence argued that Congress may have to add an even larger amount to Clinton's request to be able to buy the $8.7 billion worth of additional projects the services want. Like many other members of the House and Senate Armed Services committees, Spence expressed skepticism about some of the economic assumptions in Clinton's budget that reduce his fiscal 2000 Pentagon funding request.

For instance, critics have objected to Clinton's proposal to defer until 2001 the appropriation of $3.1 billion for military construction projects that would be started in 2000 — nearly two-thirds the total cost of the projects.

Moreover, the 2000 budget cap may have to absorb other defense increases besides those included in the services' $8.7 billion list of recommendations:

- The Senate has already approved a bill (S 4) that would give service personnel more generous pay and benefits than Clinton recommended, and the House is likely to consider similar increases.
- Sending U.S. troops to Kosovo as part of a peacekeeping force would cost $1.5 billion to $2 billion a year, which is not in Clinton's budget.

Shopping the Hill

The services' shopping lists of "unfunded priorities" have been a feature of congressional deliberations on the defense budget since Republicans took over Congress in 1995.

As in previous years, the requests for 2000 were mostly to improve training and facility maintenance, with relatively small amounts to upgrade existing equipment.

For instance, the Army's $2.6 billion request included 47 items ranked in order of priority. The top 10, costing $849 million, were for operations and maintenance accounts. The largest requests for equipment, at $149 million each, were for night-vision equipment and communications gear.

Similarly, the Navy's list included

53 items, for a total of $2.3 billion. Nearly $1 billion of that was for base operations and military construction. The largest single equipment request ($281 million) was to accelerate creation of a Navy-wide computer intranet. The Air Force list, totaling $2.5 billion, gave top priority to family housing and spare parts.

The Marine Corps request, for $1.3 billion, had a slightly stronger emphasis on major equipment. It included $130 million for two Lockheed-Martin C-130 tanker planes and $123 million for two V-22 Osprey tilt-rotor troop transport aircraft.

House, Senate Panels Beef Up Clinton's Defense Spending Requests

MAY 15 — Congressional defense hawks, who contend that President Clinton is hollowing out the U.S. military with budgets that are too small and missions that are too numerous, moved on two fronts the week of May 10 to bolster the Pentagon's budget.

While House-Senate conferees added $6 billion to a fiscal 1999 emergency spending bill (HR 1141) to pay for the war in Yugoslavia, the Senate and House Armed Services committees launched the fiscal 2000 defense authorization bill, which is likely to add $8.3 billion to Clinton's request of $280.5 billion.

The Senate committee finished work on its bill (S 974) on May 13. Some of the House panel's subcommittees drafted portions of the counterpart House measure (HR 1401) on May 12-13. The full House committee is scheduled to mark up the bill the week of May 17.

Leaders in both the Senate and House hope to pass the authorization bill before Memorial Day, by which date the Senate also hopes to pass the companion defense appropriations bill, which has not yet been drafted.

As has been true each year since 1995, when the GOP took control of Congress, most of the funds added to Clinton's request would be scattered across an array of accounts for such routine items as spare parts, maintenance and a military pay raise of 4.8 percent, rather than the 4.4 percent increase that Clinton proposed. There is no conspicuously different approach to shaping the U.S. military.

Senate Bill

As approved, 20-0, by Senate Armed Services, S 974 would authorize a fiscal 2000 budget of $288.8 billion. That includes $12.2 billion for defense-related projects of the Energy Department, most of which involve nuclear weapons or nuclear power plants for warships.

The committee added to the bill several provisions intended to better protect secrets at Energy Department laboratories.

The panel's largest addition to Clinton's weapons request was $375 million to continue work on a new helicopter carrier that would be built by Litton Industries in Pascagoula, Miss. The vessel, with a price of about $1.5 billion, would replace an older ship the Navy had planned to overhaul.

As it has done in the past two years, the committee added a provision barring the administration from reducing the number of long-range nuclear weapons in the U.S. arsenal until Russia ratifies the 1993 START II treaty. This time, however, the committee worded its provision so that the Navy could reduce from 18 to 14 the number of *Ohio*-class submarines that are used to carry Trident nuclear-armed missiles.

The Navy wants to retire the four oldest subs from nuclear patrol duty to save money. But the committee added $13 million to Clinton's request to study the feasibility of converting the four ships to carry hundreds of conventionally armed cruise missiles.

Despite a renewed push by Defense Secretary William S. Cohen and the Joint Chiefs of Staff for the expedited procedure that has been used four times since 1988 to close surplus military bases, the committee rejected two such proposals. By a vote of 12-8, it rejected the two additional rounds of closings that the administration had recommended, and then by a vote of 11-9 it refused to authorize a single round.

While acknowledging that more bases need to be closed, Armed Services Chairman John W. Warner, R-Va., said Congress would not authorize another round now because of widespread suspicions that Clinton manipulated the last round, in 1995, to save jobs in vote-rich California and Texas.

But senior committee Democrat Carl Levin of Michigan said the effort was failing because Majority Leader Trent Lott, R-Miss., and Minority Leader Tom Daschle, D-S.D., both oppose it.

Levin and committee member John McCain, R-Ariz., are expected to offer an amendment on the Senate floor that would authorize additional base closings.

House Panel Adds Billions to Budget, Saying Military Is Spread Too Thin

MAY 22 — The House Armed Services Committee reaffirmed its traditional, bipartisan support for the Pentagon on May 19, approving by a vote of 55-1 a defense authorization bill for fiscal 2000 that would add $8.3 billion to President Clinton's defense budget request. The bill (HR 1401) would authorize $288.8 billion for the Pentagon and for defense-related programs of the Energy Department.

The lone "nay" vote was cast by Cynthia A. McKinney, D-Ga., who argued in her dissent from the committee's report that the bill would spend too much on military forces at the expense of domestic needs.

The Armed Services panel's generally collegial, nine-hour markup session was punctuated by two contentious battles:

- On a near party-line vote, the committee rejected a Democratic effort to eliminate a provision that would bar Clinton from using funds authorized by the bill to pay for military operations in Yugoslavia, including the possible use of ground troops in the province of Kosovo.

Democrats complained that the provision would encourage Yugoslav President Slobodan Milosevic to hold out against the U.S.-led NATO airstrikes. Republicans insisted that the prohibition was needed to make Clinton seek supplemental funding for military operations in Yugoslavia rather than undermining combat readiness by dipping into other Pentagon accounts to pay those costs.

- In a series of votes, the committee liberalized one restriction on abortions in military hospitals overseas but turned back an effort to repeal the general ban. The fiscal 1996 defense authorization law (PL 104-106) bars female service members or military dependents stationed overseas from obtaining abortions in U.S. military hospitals abroad, even if they pay for the procedure, except in cases where the pregnancy threatens the woman's life. *(1995 Almanac, p. 9-3)*

Both issues likely will be revisited when the House takes up the defense bill, probably early in June.

The Senate is scheduled to take up its version of the $288.8 billion authorization bill (S 1059) the week of May 24 and also may act on its version of a defense appropriations bill.

Costs of Combat

By adding $8.3 billion to Clinton's defense request, the House committee's bill would bring the defense budget for fiscal 2000 to the ceiling allowed by the congressional budget resolution adopted in April (H Con Res 68). But the emergency supplemental appropriations law for fiscal 1999 (HR 1141 — H Rept 106-143), which Clinton signed May 21, includes an additional $1.8 billion to pay for increases in military pay and pensions in fiscal 2000. Thus, the total increase over Clinton's defense budget request would be more than $10 billion.

Some of the committee's specific additions to the budget request reflect shortfalls highlighted by the air war against Yugoslavia. For instance, the panel added $524 million to beef up stocks of precision-guided bombs and long-range missiles, most notably by restarting the production line for the Navy's Tomahawk cruise missile.

But most of the added funds were spread across a wide range of accounts, reflecting the view of most Republicans, and many committee Democrats, that Clinton has run down U.S. forces by giving them too few dollars and too many missions. So, for example, Armed Services added $1.5 billion to the amounts requested for operating military bases and maintaining facilities.

The most expensive decision the committee made was to reject the administration's proposal to save $3 billion by authorizing only the first year of housing and other military construction — $8.6 billion in fiscal 2000 — with a promise to request the remaining funds in future budgets.

The administration plan would violate Congress' long-established "full funding" rule for defense programs, under which committees authorize and appropriate the total cost of a project, even when the budget authority will be spent as outlays over a period of several years.

Kosovo Funding Limits

The fight over funding for military operations in Yugoslavia turned on a GOP-backed provision that would bar the president from using money in the bill for that purpose and require him to seek supplemental funding to cover the cost of operations in the Balkans.

"We have repeatedly gone into our ammunition accounts and our spare parts accounts and our operating accounts to pay for ongoing military contingencies," said Duncan Hunter, R-Calif. "If we have another war, we're going to be in very difficult shape."

The House bill includes a provision, drafted by committee member Tillie Fowler, R-Fla., that would prohibit the president from spending money on the peacekeeping mission in Bosnia beyond what he specifically requested and what was authorized. The president could waive that limit in the interest of national security.

Committee Democrats blasted the provision on Yugoslavia, which contains no waiver, saying that it would be read as a signal that the United States could pull the plug on combat operations in Yugoslavia, including the current air attacks, on Oct. 1, if Congress does not enact a supplemental funding bill.

"It specifically puts into law that there's a time certain to end our involvement in the Balkans," insisted Vic Snyder, D-Ark.

"Every time we say 'we're not going to do this' or 'we're going to be out by then,' we embolden the enemy," said Gene Taylor, D-Miss., likening the provision to the series of votes on April 28 in which the House refused to endorse any particular course of action in the Kosovo conflict. "It's getting to the point where it's bordering on treason," Taylor added.

Robert S. Rangel, the committee's deputy staff director, pointed out that the language would not bar Clinton from paying for the Yugoslavia mission in 2000 out of the $6 billion that Congress included in the emergency supplemental bill to prosecute the war for the rest of fiscal 1999. That was the amount Clinton asked for.

However, Democrats hammered at the provision's potential symbolic impact on the morale of friend and foe alike.

Taylor offered an amendment that would have replaced the Republican provision with a requirement that Clinton request, by the start of fiscal 2000, a supplemental spending bill to cover the expected cost of continued operations in Yugoslavia. But Republicans insisted that Clinton could not be trusted to submit such a request.

"The president is going to be reluctant to come to us with another supplemental unless we make him," Hunter said.

Taylor's amendment was rejected by a vote of 27-31 that broke almost along party lines. Roscoe G. Bartlett of Maryland was the only Republican at the markup who voted for Taylor's substitute, and McKinney was the only Democrat to vote against it.

Abortion Limitations

The stage was set for the committee's abortion debate when the Military Personnel Subcommittee voted May 13 to liberalize two limitations in current law. The panel proposed eliminating restrictions on privately funded abortions in overseas military hospitals and recommended that federally funded abortions in military hospitals be available in cases of rape and incest, as well as in cases where the woman's life was at risk. The latter is the only circumstance under which federally funded abortions can be obtained under current law.

Through most of the 1980s, after Congress barred most elective abortions in domestic military hospitals, service members and dependents overseas were allowed to get abortions in U.S. military hospitals, provided the procedures were paid for privately. The rationale was that many U.S. forces were stationed in countries where local medical services were not up to U.S. standards.

A relative handful of cases were involved, but the issue of using U.S. facilities for abortions became a lightning rod for both sides in the abortion rights debate. In 1988, President Ronald Reagan barred privately funded abortions at the military hospitals. In 1993, Clinton lifted that ban as one of his first official acts as president. Beginning in 1996, the Republican-led Congress wrote the prohibition into the annual defense authorization bills. The House has rejected several efforts to eliminate the ban.

During the May 19 committee debate, Personnel Subcommittee Chairman Steve Buyer, R-Ind., offered an amendment to reverse his panel's recommendation to drop the prohibitions on privately funded abortions. Loretta Sanchez, D-Calif., who had led the successful effort to have the prohibitions dropped in subcommittee, insisted that the issue was one of ensuring women in the military of rights enjoyed by all other female American citizens. "They shouldn't have to sacrifice their privacy, their health and rights for a policy with no military rationale," she argued.

Buyer's amendment was adopted, 33-26, largely along party lines. Of those voting, a handful of conservative Democrats voted for Buyer's amendment, and both Republican women — Fowler and Mary Bono of California — voted against it.

There followed two rounds in the committee's battle over broadening the exemptions from the ban on federally funded abortions in military hospitals. First, the committee rejected, 25-29, an amendment by Bartlett that would have dropped exemptions for rape and incest, allowing abortions only to save the life of the woman, the current law.

The committee then adopted, 30-29, an amendment by Buyer that would exempt from the general prohibition only cases of forcible rape and incest that were reported to a law enforcement agency. Buyer said his amendment was intended to prevent fraudulent claims of rape by women seeking a government-funded abortion. It also would exclude from the exemption cases of statutory rape.

The fundamental issue before the committee, said James M. Talent, R-Mo., was members' philosophical view of abortion. "If you view it as a good thing, you want it subsidized," he said. "If you view it as a bad thing — as a tragic taking of human life . . . then, if you can't prohibit it, you at least try to discourage it."

Other Issues

The committee adopted several other amendments to the bill May 19, most of them minor in scope and noncontroversial. Among the more notable were amendments:

- By Curt Weldon, R-Pa., to eliminate a provision that would have exempted from judicial review environmental impact statements filed in connection with a nationwide antimissile defense system.

At issue was a provision of the bill drafted by Republican John Hostettler of Indiana intended to eliminate potential delays in deploying the antimissile system. Besides barring judicial review of any environmental statement, the provision would have allowed the Defense secretary to waive a law (PL 101-189) requiring that a weapons system pass certain types of tests before it goes into production.

Objecting that Hostettler's exemptions went too far, Neil Abercrombie, D-Hawaii, proposed an amendment that would have struck the entire Hostettler provision. As a compromise, the committee adopted by voice vote Weldon's proposal to drop from the bill only the ban on judicial review of environmental statements.

- By Ellen O. Tauscher, D-Calif., reducing by $15 million the amount the committee cut from programs intended to help Russia and other former Soviet republics prevent terrorists or rogue nations from acquiring nuclear weapons material and other weapons of mass destruction. The effort is part of the Nunn-Lugar program for reducing the former Soviet nuclear arsenal.
- By Democrat Solomon P. Ortiz of Texas, dropping a provision that would have eliminated a longstanding law barring the government from trying to replace security guards who are federal employees with guards hired from private contractors.

Both the Tauscher and Ortiz amendments were agreed to by voice vote as part of separate packages.

Senate-Passed Bill Adds $8 Billion to Pentagon Budget

MAY 29 — The Senate the week of May 24 rejected efforts to limit President Clinton's military options in Kosovo, and Republicans dropped a far-reaching proposal to realign the Energy Department's nuclear weapons laboratories after allegations in a House committee report of Chinese espionage.

The moves came during four days of debate on the fiscal 2000 defense authorization bill (S 1059) that was passed, 92-3, on May 27. The bill would allow the defense budget to rise to $288.8 billion, $8.3 billion more than Clinton requested. *(Vote 154, p. S-32)*

The administration took some losses in the debate, most notably when the Senate rejected, for the third year in a row, a proposal for another round of military base closings. Defense Secretary William S. Cohen and the Joint Chiefs of Staff had promoted the initiative vigorously as a way to save money.

The debate was dominated by reaction to the release May 25 of a bipartisan House report critical of lax security at the weapons labs and at U.S. commercial satellite launches in China.

Faced with the dual threat of a Democratic filibuster and a presidential veto, Republicans dropped the most far-reaching of several amendments designed to tighten up security at the facilities. But the Senate adopted, by voice vote, another amendment by Majority Leader Trent Lott, R-Miss. — a watered-down measure designed to strengthen export control laws, improve counterintelligence and require closer monitoring of satellite launches and better notification to Congress of security breaches.

Partly because of the China debate, Senate Appropriations Committee Chairman Ted Stevens, R-Alaska, was thwarted in his hope of rapid Senate action on the defense appropriations bill (S 1122) before the Memorial Day recess.

In the House, a partisan battle over the espionage issue contributed to a deadlock that stalled, at least until early June, floor action on the

House version of the authorization bill (HR 1401).

Balkan Troubles

While the lion's share of S 1059 authorizes appropriations for the Defense Department, it also would authorize $12.2 billion for defense-related programs run by the Energy Department, which is $170 million less than Clinton requested. Of that total, $5.6 billion is for the management of toxic and nuclear waste, most of it a legacy of nearly a half century of nuclear weapons production and testing.

The funds the bill would add to Clinton's Pentagon spending request were distributed through all parts of the defense budget by the Senate Armed Services Committee. Of the increase, $3 billion would go to military construction projects, for which Clinton had requested only partial funding, as a ploy to hold down the cost of his budget request.

As usual, Senate debate ranged across such diverse issues as the government's purchase of items manufactured by federal prison inmates to the culpability of U.S. commanders for the American military debacle at Pearl Harbor.

The key Senate battle over U.S. policy in Kosovo came on an amendment by Arlen Specter, R-Pa., that would have barred the deployment of U.S. ground troops in that Serbian province unless Congress authorized the operation. The prohibition would not have applied to troops sent to police a peace agreement between the Serb-dominated government of Yugoslavia and the ethnic Albanians who made up a large majority of the Kosovar population until hundreds of thousands were driven into neighboring countries.

Clinton, who insists he has no intention of sending ground troops into Kosovo, had assured congressional leaders that he would consult with Congress before making such a move. However, like every other president since Congress enacted the War Powers Resolution of 1973 (PL 93-148) over President Richard M. Nixon's veto, Clinton has refused to be bound by any congressional vote against a given deployment. *(1973 Almanac, p. 95)*

Specter, who said Clinton might persuade him to vote for such an authorization, cast the issue as one more round in the 25-year effort to give Congress more control over whether U.S. forces should be sent into combat.

The only way Congress could be sure its views were respected, Specter argued, was to prohibit any deployment unless it was specifically authorized by law.

If Clinton were left alone and sent troops into Kosovo, it would be practically impossible for Congress to force their removal, Specter said. "We [would] face the impossible predicament of seeking to cut off funds for an ongoing military operation," he said.

Specter's amendment was tabled (killed) by a vote of 52-48. *(Vote 145, p. S-31)*

Subsequently, the Senate tabled, by a vote of 77-21, an amendment by Robert C. Smith, R-N.H., that would have cut off any funds for military operations in Yugoslavia — including NATO's U.S.-led bombing campaign — on Oct. 1 unless Congress authorized the mission. *(Vote 151, p. S-32)*

Pat Roberts, R-Kan., a critic of the administration's involvement in Kosovo, offered an amendment in an unsuccessful effort to force a debate on the broader issue of whether U.S. forces should be engaged in such missions.

Roberts, like many other opponents of the growing U.S. military engagement in the Balkans, contends that NATO has shifted its mission from one of defending members against outside attack to one of using military forces to reduce large-scale social turmoil in neighboring areas, such as Yugoslavia.

According to these critics, the change is embodied in NATO's new "strategic concept" adopted April 24, during the Washington summit meeting to commemorate the 50th anniversary of the alliance.

Roberts' non-binding amendment urged the president to seek Senate ratification of the strategic concept, as an amendment to the NATO Treaty, if he certified that it entailed new U.S. commitments.

But senior Armed Services Committee Democrat Carl Levin of Michigan insisted that he and the administration could live with the amendment since, in their view, NATO's new strategy involves no new commitments. The amendment was agreed to 87-12. *(Vote 143, p. S-30)*

Base Closings, Abortions

The amendment calling for more base closings, sponsored by John McCain, R-Ariz., and Levin, was rejected, 40-60. *(Vote 147, p. S-31)*

Drafted along the same basic lines as the law that set up four earlier base closing rounds, the amendment would have created an independent panel to identify bases that would be closed or consolidated, unless either the president or Congress rejected the entire list. Since many Republicans contend that Clinton improperly manipulated the last round in 1995, in order to save jobs in California and Texas, McCain and Levin noted that their amendment would not begin a new round until 2001, after Clinton leaves office. *(1996 Almanac, p. 8-6)*

However, Armed Services Chairman John W. Warner, R-Va., insisted that Clinton had poisoned the well on this issue, for now. "You cannot legislate trust," he declared. Although Cohen insisted that the Pentagon could save $3.6 billion annually by closing unneeded bases, 22 Democrats voted to block the McCain amendment, including Minority Leader Tom Daschle, D-S.D. The largest single employer in Daschle's home state is Ellsworth Air Force Base, near Rapid City.

Another emotionally charged battle the administration lost came on an amendment by Olympia J. Snowe, R-Maine, and Patty Murray, D-Wash., that would have allowed women stationed with the armed forces overseas and female dependents to obtain abortions in local U.S. military hospitals, provided they pay for the procedure. The amendment was tabled 51-49. *(Vote 148, p. S-31)*

Weapons Issues

As has been typical of the defense authorization debate for years, few amendments came up that had a significant impact on major weapons.

One that did, by Russell D. Feingold, D-Minn., would have capped Navy spending in fiscal years 2000-04 for F/A-18 "E" and "F" jets at $8.8 billion, the currently projected cost. After that amendment was tabled, 87-11, the Senate adopted, by voice vote, a Feingold amendment that would require the secretary of Defense to certify that the plane is performing adequately. *(Vote 153, p. S-32)*

Also tabled, 56-44, was an amendment by Bob Kerrey, D-Neb., that would have eliminated a provision that prevents the Pentagon from reducing the number of nuclear warheads deployed on long-range missiles and bombers. This is the third consecutive year the Armed Services Committee has added the provision to the bill, in hopes of pressuring Russia to ratify the 1993 START II treaty that would require the elimination of thousands of U.S. and Russian warheads. *(Vote 149, p. S-32)*

In drafting S 1059, the committee bowed to the Navy's desire to remove from service four of its 18 huge Trident submarines. But it would require the Pentagon to load more warheads on the remaining weapons to compensate for those now on the subs that would be retired.

Other Amendments

Reaching back nearly six decades to the start of World War II, the Senate adopted a hotly debated amendment by William V. Roth, R-Del., that would posthumously promote Rear Adm. Husband E. Kimmel and Maj. Gen. Walter C. Short, the senior officers in Hawaii when the Japanese attached on Dec. 7, 1941. Both were forced to retire with a loss of rank a few months after the Pearl Harbor attack. Kimmel's son is a Delaware resident.

Roth's amendment was adopted 52-47. *(Vote 142, p. S-30)*

The Senate's 10 World War II veterans split on the issue, with five voting for the amendment and five against.

On another proposal, the Senate changed its mind. It rejected, 49-51, an amendment by Phil Gramm, R-Texas, that would have eliminated a provision, supported by labor, making it more difficult for the Pentagon to buy furniture and other items made by prison inmates. After voting 51-49 to reconsider the issue, the Senate adopted Gramm's amendment by voice vote. *(Vote 146, p. S-31; vote 150, p. S-32)*

Military Personnel

The bill would increase military pay and pensions with provisions that basically duplicate S 4, military pay legislation the Senate passed in February.

The bill would provide a 4.8 percent military pay raise effective Jan 1, 2000, rather than the 4.4 percent raise Clinton requested. It also would require that future annual military pay raises through fiscal 2006 be one-half percent higher than the average increase in civilian pay, as measured by a government survey.

As requested by the administration, the measure also would provide additional, targeted raises of up to 5.5 percent for midcareer officers and enlisted personnel of certain ranks and experience whom the services see as key leaders.

And the bill would replace an unpopular 1986 law that reduced pensions for service personnel retiring after 20 years of service. That earlier law reduced the 20-year pension from half basic pay to 40 percent for those who joined up beginning in 1986. Now personnel would be offered a choice: Return to the 50 percent formula or stay with a 40 percent pension but receive a lump-sum payment of $30,000 after 15 years of service.

The bill also would authorize military personnel to deposit up to 5 percent of their pretax pay, as well as any lump-sum bonuses, in a tax-sheltered investment fund similar to civilian 401(k) plans. As a retention incentive, the bill would give the Pentagon discretion to match these contributions, just as many corporations do.

The legislation would renew authority for enlistment and re-enlistment bonuses and extra pay for personnel in essential and hard-to-fill specialties. It would fatten some existing bonuses — the maximum re-enlistment bonus would increase to $60,000 from $45,000 — and authorize some new ones, such as a bonus for naval officers specializing in surface warfare.

The bill would authorize an active-duty force of 1.38 million, a reduction of nearly 11,000 from the fiscal 1999 personnel ceiling. The only difference from Clinton's manpower request is that the bill would allow 92 additional Marines.

For National Guard and reserve units, the bill would set a manpower ceiling of slightly more than 874,000. This would be nearly 11,300 below the fiscal 1999 personnel ceiling, but 745 higher than the administration's request.

Several provisions are intended to make recruiting easier. For instance, the bill would authorize programs under which recruits could defer their active duty service while they complete college or vocational training.

It also would add $39 million to the $133 million Clinton requested for high school ROTC programs. "More than half of the young men and women who voluntarily participate in this . . . program affiliate with the military in some fashion after graduation," the committee said.

The bill also would require that a general or admiral approve the deployment of any member of the service for more than 180 days in a year, that a four-star general or admiral approve any deployment that would take a member of the armed forces away from home more than 200 days, and that personnel deployed for more than 220 days be paid an additional $100 a day.

This provision, which the secretary of Defense could waive in the interests of national security, is intended to pressure Pentagon leaders to reduce the frequent deployments that many armed forces members cite as the chief source of their dissatisfaction with military life.

Operations and Maintenance

The bill's $104.8 billion authorization for operations, maintenance and related accounts would add $1.15 billion to Clinton's budget request.

As usual, large chunks of that increase are dedicated to expenses that typically are underfunded in Pentagon budgets. The bill would add $554 million to the $5.2 billion requested for maintaining facilities, for instance, and it would add $420 million to the $13.8 billion requested for operating military bases.

On the other hand, the bill would make only modest additions to two other parts of the budget that, in the past, have received large congressional add-ons. For instance, it would add only $40 million to the $7.3 billion requested for depot maintenance — the major overhaul of ships, planes, vehicles and electronic equipment. The bill would add just $73 million to the $1.3 billion requested for aircraft spare parts.

The bill would make some hefty reductions in parts of Clinton's budget request that routinely are targeted by congressional budget writers. It would cut:

- $209 million because the Pentagon is reducing its civilian payroll faster than had been planned.
- $205 million because the dollar's strength compared with foreign currencies reduces the cost (in dollars) of goods and services purchased locally by U.S. forces stationed abroad.
- $40 million to make the Pentagon reduce the use of outside consultants.

The bill would approve, as requested, $2.39 billion to pay for ongoing operations in Bosnia and against Iraq. However, it includes no funds to pay for the U.S. share of any NATO air campaign against Yugoslavia in fiscal 2000, let alone for the cost of deploying any U.S. ground troops in Kosovo.

Ground Force Modernization

In its report on S 1059, the Armed Services Committee praised the Army's effort to equip its combat units with digital communications intended to give them the advantage of a detailed and coherent view of any battlefield. But the committee complained that the Army had not yet solved two serious problems — making its forces lighter and easier to deploy rapidly to distant trouble spots, and fitting modernization plans into its projected budgets.

The committee approved the current plan to upgrade the Army's Abrams tanks and Bradley troop carriers with digital communications and improved night-vision equipment, among other refinements. The bill would authorize $664 million for the tank program, nearly $28 million more than was requested, in order to cover escalating costs. And it would approve the $309 million requested to keep building new Bradleys.

But the committee also added to the bill $10 million to accelerate the development of much lighter combat vehicles.

By the same token, the committee included in the bill the authorizations requested to continue developing the Crusader mobile cannon ($283 million) and to buy additional launchers for missiles with a range of up to a couple of hundred miles ($115 million). However, the panel added $31 million to develop a much lighter version of the missile launcher that could be carried by smaller cargo planes.

The bill would authorize $172 million requested for ATACMS missiles that could be fired from both types of missile launchers, and $277 million requested to continue development and production of BAT warheads — yard-long gliders with tank-destroying warheads that could be dispensed from some of those missiles.

As requested, the bill would approve nearly $400 million to continue producing the Javelin, a shoulder-launched, anti-tank missile used by the Army and Marine Corps.

The bill would add funds to the amounts requested for the Army's two major combat helicopter programs:

- $816 million to equip Apache helicopters with digital communications links and Longbow target-finding radar. This includes $45 million more than the budget request in order to replace obsolescent parts in the 20-year old aircraft.
- $483 million to continue developing the smaller Comanche scout helicopter. This would add $56 million to the budget request to allow the Army to begin flying the second Comanche prototype, which currently is grounded by a lack of funds.

The committee report on S 1059 blasted the Army for not coming up with a long-range helicopter modernization plan it could afford. But it also complained that the service's plan to pay for Comanche production by cutting back on the number of Apaches it would modernize lacked any military rationale. So the committee added to the bill a provision fencing off 10 percent of the Army's $1.5 billion aircraft procurement budget for fiscal 2000 until the service sends Congress a comprehensive, long-range plan to modernize its helicopter fleet.

Air Combat

The Armed Services Committee expressed concern in its report about the long-term cost of the Pentagon's plan to buy three new types of fighter planes over the next two decades. Nevertheless, the panel approved the amounts requested in fiscal 2000 for all three programs.

The bill would authorize $1.2 billion to continue developing the Air Force's F-22 and $1.8 billion to buy six of the planes. But the committee warned the service not to take shortcuts in the testing program just to keep the program within established cost limits. The General Accounting Office (GAO) and a Pentagon cost-estimating agency, basing their analysis on the cost of earlier fighter programs, have argued that the Air Force and lead contractor Boeing are low-balling the likely cost of the F-22. But Boeing and the Air Force counter that they are using innovative design and production techniques that will make the F-22 cheaper to build than the historical record suggests.

The bill also would authorize $2.8 billion to buy 36 additional F/A-18 E and F model jets, which the Navy will use primarily to attack ground targets. It also would authorize the Navy to sign a contract for up to four additional years of F/A-18 E and F purchases, provided the plane passes a series of tests that are under way. The committee predicted that the multi-year contract would save $700 million compared with the cost of buying the same number of planes one year at a time.

For the third of the new jets — the Joint Strike Fighter to be built in versions for the Air Force, Navy and Marines — the bill would approve $492 million, $15 million more than was requested.

The bill also would approve the $253 million requested for 10 additional Air Force F-16s.

With the air war over Yugoslavia highlighting the importance of Prowler radar-jamming planes that protect U.S. bombers from detection, the committee questioned the Pentagon's assumption that its fleet of about 120 of the 1970s-vintage jets will remain serviceable through 2015. The panel told the Pentagon to send it a timetable for fielding a replacement jammer aircraft.

To modernize the Prowlers, the bill would authorize $186 million, which is $25 million more than requested.

The bill would authorize $326 million, as requested, for the 14th in the fleet of JSTARS ground surveillance planes — refurbished jetliners equipped with radar that can spot vehicles up to 100 miles away. It also would add to the budget $46 million that could be used as a down payment if the Pentagon decides to buy additional JSTARS planes.

Naval Forces

The bill would authorize the amounts requested for several naval vessels and for the design of new types of warships intended to be cheaper to build and operate. However, the Armed Services Committee warned that projected budgets would not buy enough new ships to keep a fleet of 300, as currently planned. It ordered the Pentagon to send Congress, along with its fiscal 2001 budget request, the department's shipbuilding plan through 2030 and an estimate of an annual budget necessary to build the eight to 10 ships a year required to sustain a 300-ship fleet.

The bill would authorize:

- $752 million for components of the 10th, and last, *Nimitz*-class aircraft carrier, for which the administration plans to request more than $4 billion in fiscal 2001.
- $25 million to continue designing the first ship of a cheaper class of carrier, slated for funding in the fiscal 2006 budget.
- $2.7 billion for three destroyers equipped with the Aegis anti-aircraft system.
- $270 million to continue designing a new destroyer that would carry hundreds of land-attack missiles.
- $749 million for components to be used in two *Virginia*-class nuclear-powered submarines slated for inclusion in the fiscal 2001 and 2002 budgets.
- $440 million for the first of a new class of supply ships intended to replenish a fleet's ammunition and food stocks in mid-ocean.

Air and Sea Transport

The priciest piece of hardware the bill would add to Clinton's request is a helicopter carrier to transport nearly 2,000 Marines, along with more than 30 helicopters and three hovercraft to take them ashore. The Senate bill would add $375 million to the budget for components to be used in the ship, which would be built by Litton Industries in Pascagoula, Miss., the home town of Senate Majority Leader Trent Lott, R-Miss.

At the strong urging of Lott, the contractor and the Marine Corps, Congress appropriated $50 million in fiscal 1999 to begin work on this ship to replace an older helicopter carrier, which the Navy had planned to refurbish. Officially, the Navy has not yet decided whether to refurbish the old ship or buy the new one. But it has tentatively planned to buy components for the new ship in fiscal 2004 and to pay for construction of the vessel beginning in fiscal 2005.

However, the Armed Services Committee accepted the company's argument that, if funding for a new ship were accelerated by four years, to begin in 2000, the vessel's projected $2.3 billion price could be slashed to $1.5 billion.

The bill also would authorize:

- $1.5 billion, as requested, for two slightly smaller transport ships designed to haul Marine units to amphibious landings.
- $990 million to buy 12 V-22 Ospreys — vertical takeoff airplanes the Marines want to use as a faster alternative to helicopters to carry troops ashore. This is an increase of two aircraft and $123 million over the request.

As requested, the bill would authorize $3.4 billion for 15 C-17 wide-body cargo jets. It would add $130 million to the budget to buy two modified C-130 cargo planes, which the Marines use to refuel other aircraft.

The budget requested $554 million for 28 H-60 helicopters of various versions, all of which are built by the Connecticut-based Sikorksy division of United Technologies.The bill would add $157 million for 12 additional helicopters.

Anti-Missile Defenses

The bill would add $399 million to the $3.3 billion Clinton requested for anti-missile defense programs. But none of that increase would go to the most politically contentious of those programs: the effort to develop a system to protect U.S. territory from a small number of attacking missiles, such as might be fired by a rogue state such as North Korea. The bill would approve Clinton's $837 million request for the national missile defense program.

The bill's largest increase for anti-missile defense would go to one of the least controversial — the PAC-3 version of the Patriot. Earlier versions of the Patriot, built in Massachusetts by Raytheon, are designed to destroy their targets with a cloud of shrapnel from an exploding warhead. The much smaller PAC-3 version, built by Lockheed Martin Vought Systems of Dallas, is designed to destroy an attacking missile by colliding with it.

The bill would authorize $542 million for PAC-3 — $212 million more than was requested — in order to deal with a funding shortfall. It also would authorize $60 million not requested to equip some of the larger Raytheon missiles with new guidance systems designed to intercept small cruise missiles.

For two anti-missile programs funded by the Air Force, the bill would authorize:

- $309 million, as requested, to develop a jumbo jet armed with an anti-missile laser.
- $89 million, which is $25 million more than requested, to continue work on a laser-armed space satellite.

House Passes Bill As GOP Questions Clinton's Defense Leadership

JUNE 12 — Even as President Clinton hailed the success of the bombing campaign against Yugoslavia, Republican mistrust of that operation and Clinton's stewardship of U.S. defenses suffused House debate on the annual defense authorization bill for fiscal 2000.

The House rejected proposals that would have limited Clinton's use of funds authorized by the bill to pay for the planned deployment of 7,000 U.S. troops as peacekeepers in Kosovo. But many of the Republicans who helped Democrats on those questions did so grudgingly and only after Clinton promised in a letter to request a supplemental appropriation to pay for the operation. He promised not to siphon funds out of budget accounts meant for training, maintenance and modernization.

The House also challenged Clinton on a related issue, adopting an amendment that would force him to withdraw by year's end the estimated 500

U.S. troops still in Haiti.

It has been more than four years since U.S. military intervention forced a military junta from power in Haiti. *(1994 Almanac, p. 449)*

The two-day debate, from June 9 to June 10, on the $288.8 billion defense authorization bill (HR 1401) was dominated by the Republican theme that Clinton is undermining U.S. forces with budgets that are too small and an agenda that swamps them with peacekeeping and humanitarian missions peripheral to national security interests.

The bill was passed by a vote of 365-58. *(Vote 191, p. H-68)*

The legislation would authorize a fiscal 2000 budget $8.3 billion larger than Clinton requested for the Defense Department and for defense-related programs run by the Energy Department. The Senate's counterpart bill (S 1059), passed May 27, would authorize nearly the same increase over Clinton's request.

Deployment Debates

The key battle over peacekeeping policy came June 10 on an amendment by Ike Skelton, D-Mo., to eliminate from the bill a provision that would have barred Clinton from using any funds authorized by the bill either for the air war against Yugoslavia that was under way when the bill was drafted in May, or for a peacekeeping operation in Kosovo.

Armed Services Committee Republicans insisted that the provision was intended to ensure that Clinton would separately request funding for future operations in Yugoslavia.

The military campaign there was launched weeks after Clinton sent Congress his fiscal 2000 budget request.

An emergency supplemental appropriations bill passed in May (PL 106-31) will fund operations only through fiscal 1999, which ends Sept. 30.

When the House took up Skelton's amendment, as Yugoslav forces were beginning to pull out of Kosovo and NATO troops were preparing to move in, Democrats contended that the committee's ban would pull the rug out from under U.S. forces just when their efforts had succeeded.

When Skelton, the Armed Services Committee's senior Democrat, noted that Clinton had promised to seek supplemental funding to pay for the Yugoslavia deployment, Republicans demanded that Clinton put it in writing. Once he did, Armed Services Chairman Floyd D. Spence of South Carolina and 76 other Republicans threw their support to Skelton, whose amendment was adopted, 270-155. *(Vote 189, p. H-66)*

An amendment by Mark Souder, R-Ind., that would have slightly broadened the committee's prohibition on operations in Yugoslavia was rejected 97-328. *(Vote 187, p. H-66)*

The amendment requiring an end to the permanent deployment of U.S. troops in Haiti was offered by Porter J. Goss, R-Fla., who pointed out that it paralleled a recommendation that Gen. Charles Wilhelm, commander of U.S. forces in Central and South America, had made to a congressional committee.

Wilhelm's proposal, made during a closed hearing, subsequently was leaked. The Goss amendment, which would allow periodic U.S. deployments in Haiti, so long as they did not amount to a continuous presence, was adopted 227-198. *(Vote 183, p. H-66)*

But the large majority that rejected another amendment suggested that House opposition to U.S. deployments abroad does not extend to traditional missions in Europe.

By a vote of 116-307, the House rejected an amendment by Christopher Shays, R-Conn., and Barney Frank, D-Mass., that would have reduced the number of U.S. troops stationed in Europe from 100,000 to 25,000 by fiscal 2002. *(Vote 190, p. H-66)*

China Spying

Responding to reports of Chinese espionage at U.S. nuclear weapons laboratories, the House adopted, 428-0, an amendment by Christopher Cox, R-Calif., and Norm Dicks, D-Wash., that would tighten secrecy at the labs and in the handling of U.S.-built satellites sent to China for launching. The amendment incorporates several recommendations of a bipartisan House commission led by Cox and Dicks, including a temporary moratorium on visits to the labs by citizens of certain potentially hostile countries. *(Vote 180, p. H-64)*

The House rejected, 159-266, an amendment by Jim Ryun, R-Kan., that would have imposed a two-year moratorium on lab visits by those from certain countries. *(Vote 181, p. H-64)*

Several related proposals were adopted by voice vote.

The only China-related amendment to spark a debate was a proposal by Majority Whip Tom DeLay, R-Texas, to sharply curtail visits by Chinese military officers to U.S. installations.

Senior U.S. officers argue that such exchanges foster Chinese respect for U.S. military power. But DeLay and his allies said that the Clinton administration had pressured the services to give Chinese officials too much access to U.S. technology and tactics.

"Why on earth would we want to share our most valuable secrets with any nation, let alone a potential aggressor?" DeLay demanded.

DeLay's amendment was adopted, 284-143. *(Vote 182, p. H-64)*

Personnel Issues

The bill would authorize a 4.8 percent military pay raise, rather than the 4.4 percent raise proposed by Clinton.

By a vote of 425-0, the House adopted an amendment by Steve Buyer, R-Ind., chairman of the Armed Services subcommittee on personnel, authorizing members of the armed forces to supplement their pensions by investing in the Thrift Savings Plan — a tax-deferred investment plan available to civilian federal employees and similar to the 401(k) retirement savings plans available in the private sector. *(Vote 185, p. H-66)*

Like Clinton's budget request and the Senate version of the authorization bill, HR 1401 would all but repeal a 1986 law (PL 99-348) that reduced pensions for military personnel retiring after 20 years of active duty. *(1986 Almanac, p. 436)*

The bill would allow retirees to choose between 50 percent of their basic pay — the rule for those who joined up before 1986 — or 40 percent but with a $30,000 bonus after 15 years of service, an option also in the Senate bill.

Buyer's amendment would allow service members to contribute such lump-sum bonuses to the Thrift Savings Plan, along with up to 5 percent of their pre-tax basic pay, up to the maximum amounts allowed by the tax code.

By a vote of 203-225, the House rejected an amendment by Carrie P. Meek, D-Fla., that would have allowed female service personnel or dependents stationed overseas to obtain abortions in U.S. military hospitals abroad, provided they paid for the procedure. *(Vote 184, p. H-66)*

An amendment by John Thune, R-S.D., that was part of a large package of amendments adopted en bloc by voice vote, would make a variety of changes in Tricare, the Pentagon's HMO-style medical insurance program for dependents and retirees. Beneficiaries contend that the system is slow and unresponsive.

Among other changes, Thune's amendment would encourage faster processing of claims; require a study of the program's reimbursement rates to participating physicians and hospitals; and eliminate the requirement for prior approval of preventive obstetric, urological and gynecological procedures and mammograms for women over the age of 35.

Other Amendments

By a vote of 242-181, the House adopted an amendment by James A. Traficant Jr., D-Ohio, that would allow the Pentagon, at the request of the attorney general or the secretary of the Treasury, to assign military personnel to assist immigration and customs officials in drug interdiction and counterterrorist operations along U.S. borders. *(Vote 186, p. H-66)*

An amendment by Dave Weldon, R-Fla., providing $7.3 million for space launch ranges and requiring a study of whether the ranges need to be expanded, was adopted 303-118, *(Vote 188, p. H-66)*

Among other proposals adopted as part of the en bloc package were amendments:

- By John E. Sweeney, R-N.Y., requiring the Pentagon to provide equipment and training to veterans groups and other private organizations that provide honor guards at veterans' funerals;
- By Bill Goodling, R-Pa., and Traficant, requiring the Pentagon's inspector general to investigate whether the Defense Department has violated the law by buying barbells from foreign manufacturers for U.S. personnel.

Defense Conferees Must Reconcile Status Quo With High-Tech Future

JUNE 26 — The U.S.-led air assault on Yugoslavia, which highlighted fundamental questions about the future shape of the U.S. military, will provide a new backdrop for House and Senate negotiators when they convene next month on a $289 billion budget blueprint for the Pentagon.

The question most clearly facing conferees on the defense bill (S 1059 – S Rept 106-50; H Rept 106-162) is whether all four services are transforming themselves quickly enough to exploit new technologies and take on new adversaries.

Some critics complain that the four are shortchanging new war-fighting tools while spending too much to update the big-ticket items that evolved during the 40-year military standoff with the Soviet Union: heavy tanks, huge aircraft carriers and supersonic jets.

The 11-week NATO bombing campaign, which forced Yugoslav President Slobodan Milosevic's Serbian-dominated regime to withdraw its forces from the province of Kosovo, demonstrated both the unparalleled power of the current force and some of the limits on its effectiveness.

For instance, despite some tragic miscues, U.S. forces racked up an impressive array of ground targets that they located with high-tech detection equipment and destroyed with precision-guided missiles and bombs, some of the latter dropped from radar-evading stealth planes.

But the operation in Yugoslavia also demonstrated, for example, how hard it is to quickly deploy a heavily armed Army force to an unplanned-for location; how short the services are of certain key types of airplanes and precision-guided munitions; and how an adversary can flummox high-tech air power — at least for a while — by dispersing troops among helpless civilians.

On its face, the war appeared to confound the many defense experts who had predicted that air power alone could not prevail. "You did prove that a sustained air campaign, under the right conditions, can stop an army on the ground," President Clinton on June 22 told a throng of U.S. Air Force personnel at Aviano, Italy, the air base that was the linchpin of the Yugoslavia campaign.

But all of NATO's cutting-edge air power could not directly shield the region's populace from their Serb tormentors during the weeks of bombing. Moreover, the airstrikes began taking a heavy toll of Yugoslav forces in Kosovo only when those units began massing to battle hostile ground troops — in this case, the separatist Albanian guerrillas of the Kosovo Liberation Army.

Rocking the Boat

For their part, the services insist they must remain ready to deal with adversaries such as Iraq and North Korea, which equip their forces along Soviet lines. But there is also a political basis to the Pentagon's conservatism: In an era of tight budgets, radical new weapons can be developed only at the expense of continued production and modernization of older types — activities that typically support far more jobs than do development programs.

Despite that political disincentive, the House and Senate Armed Services committees have backed significant efforts to rock the boat.

In the fiscal 1997 defense authorization bill (PL 104-201), they chartered the National Defense Panel — a blue-ribbon commission intended to review the Pentagon's own quadrennial review of long-term defense needs. The panel's report, issued Dec. 1, 1997, urged the services to test some of their novel concepts in large-scale, joint exercises. *(1997 Almanac, p. 8-19)*

In the fiscal 1999 authorization bill (PL 105-261), the committees included a provision making the Atlantic Command, headquartered in Norfolk, Va., responsible for the joint experiments recommended by the National Defense Panel.

This year, each Armed Services panel included in its version of the fiscal 2000 authorization bill a provision to give the Atlantic Command's commander in chief more bureaucratic clout for promoting new technologies. The House bill (HR 1401) would also add $8 million to the command's joint experimentation budget, an initiative pushed by William M. "Mac" Thornberry, R-Texas.

The Senate bill (S 1059) would require creation of a National Defense Panel every four years to review long-term defense needs. It also includes a package of provisions drafted by Joseph I. Lieberman, D-Conn., Pat Roberts, R-Kan., and Jeff Bingaman, D-N.M., to stimulate technical innovation in the Pentagon and in the defense industry.

The House and Senate bills, both of which would add $8.3 billion to Clinton's request, concur on funding levels that would support or accelerate several innovations planned by the services. While there are few disputes over large amounts of money, the conferees face some funding disagreements related either to the pace of innovation or to the trade-off between upgrading existing weapons and developing new ones. Following are some of the highlights.

Ground Combat

The House bill would authorize the $636 million requested for the Army's program to equip some of its older M-1 tanks with night-vision gear and digital communications links over which troops could share information about their whereabouts and the enemy's. The Senate bill would add $28 million.

Both would also approve the $309 million requested to similarly upgrade some older Bradley armored troop carriers. But the House would add $72 million and the Senate $74 million for more modest improvements to Bradleys assigned to the National Guard.

In their reports on the authorization bills, both Armed Services committees applauded the Army's plan to develop combat vehicles that would weigh less than the 70-ton M-1 tank and the 30-ton Bradley, thus making it easier to quickly deploy U.S.-based troops. But both panels ordered the Army to accelerate the project and to collaborate with the Defense Advanced Research Projects Agency (DARPA), a Pentagon organization designed to jump-start the development of high-tech weapons. The Army requested $67 million in fiscal 2000 to develop a future combat vehicle. The Senate bill would authorize $77 million, while the House bill calls for $135 million. House Armed Services ordered the Army and DARPA to aim at starting to develop a specific vehicle in 2006.

Both bills would approve the $730 million requested to equip missile-armed Apache helicopters with Longbow radars to find ground targets in bad weather. Both would also add $45 million to replace out-of-production electronic components in the Apaches.

To accelerate development of the smaller Comanche armed helicopter, both bills would authorize $56 million more than the $427 million requested. The Comanche has "stealthy" features, including an exhaust system that diffuses hot gases through a long, thin slot in the aircraft's side, thus providing a more difficult target for shoulder-launched, heat-seeking missiles like the ones that caused NATO leaders not to use Apaches against Serb forces in Kosovo.

Last year, both Armed Services committees objected to the Crusader mobile cannon being developed for deployment in 2005, contending that the 55-ton vehicle did not fit the Army's own plan to make its forces lighter and more easily deployable. But the Army countered that the new weapon was more mobile than the gun it would replace and would be far more effective, given the automation and digital communication links it would incorporate. This year, both bills would approve the $283 million requested to continue Crusader development.

The Senate bill would also approve the $115 million requested for MLRS long-range artillery rocket launchers. The House bill would add $56 million to buy additional launchers for the National Guard.

To accelerate development of a smaller version of the missile launcher, both bills would add about $31 million to the $6 million requested. While the larger MLRS can be carried by big C-5 and C-17 cargo planes, the smaller version, dubbed HIMARS (high-mobility artillery rocket system), could be carried in the much more numerous C-130 cargo planes.

The House bill would add to the budget $20 million for kits to allow bulldozers, trucks and other heavy vehicles to be driven by remote control, so they could be used to clear land mines without endangering the operators.

Smart Bombs

The most striking impact of the war over Kosovo on the authorization process was the House bill's addition of more than $500 million to increase the stockpiles of some of the precision-guided bombs and missiles that accounted for most of the U.S. weaponry loosed on Yugoslavia.

HR 1401 would add:

- $114 million to the $161 million requested for JDAM satellite-guided bombs;
- $110 million to the $235 million requested for JSOW glider-bombs, a "stand off" weapon intended to let a plane stay beyond the reach of enemy defenses;
- $300 million to the $51 million requested for Tomahawk ship-launched cruise missiles.

In each case, the Senate bill would authorize the amount requested.

The Tomahawk budget request is to upgrade older missiles, as is $210 million of the House add-on. But the remaining $90 million the House would add is earmarked to reconstitute Raytheon Co.'s mothballed Tomahawk production line in Tucson, Ariz., and begin building new copies of the current Tomahawk design.

The Navy planned to defer production of new Tomahawks until 2002, when Raytheon is slated to begin turning out a new version of the missile. This so-called Tactical Tomahawk is intended to cost $500,000 a copy — about half the price of the current model. Both bills would authorize the $145 million requested to continue developing the Tactical Tomahawk.

House Armed Services Committee member James V. Hansen, R-Utah, is a leading proponent of resuming production of the current Tomahawk, both to replace the hundreds fired in the past few years and to hedge against problems with the new version. Hansen has vigorously objected to the Navy's refusal to allow Williams International, a company in his district that supplies engines for the current Tomahawk version, to compete for the contract to make Tactical Tomahawk engines.

Combat Aircraft

Both bills would accelerate improvements to the Air Force's fleet of 21 B-2 stealth bombers, some of which flew 30-hour round-trip missions from their base in Missouri to drop satellite-guided JDAM bombs on targets in Yugoslavia. The planes scored some impressive successes during the conflict — and one horrendous failure, when erroneous targeting information caused a B-2 to destroy the Chinese Embassy in Belgrade.

The budget requested a total of $329 million for various B-2 upgrade projects. The Senate bill would add $37 million to speed the addition of a high-speed data link over which the bomber crew could receive up-to-the-minute targeting information. The House bill would add $187 million for the data link and other improvements.

In its report on HR 1401, House Armed Services decried the Air Force's plan to defer production of a new long-range bomber until 2037, by which time the bomber fleet would consist of 40-year-old B-2s, 50-year-old B-1s and nearly 80-year-old B-52s. The panel ordered the service to spend $2 million to report by next Feb. 15 on the basic concept of a new bomber that could be put into production by 2015.

Both bills would authorize the $130 million requested for B-1 modifications, and the Senate bill would approve the $48 million requested to update the B-52s. But the House bill sliced $15 million from the B-52 request, with the Armed Services Committee insisting that many other projects had a higher priority.

Both would approve the amounts requested for three smaller combat jets:

- $2.7 billion for 36 F/A-18 "E" and "F" model planes for the Navy;
- $1.6 billion for six F-22s for the Air Force;
- $477 million to continue developing the so-called Joint Strike Fighter (JSF), slated to be built in three versions to replace 1970s-vintage planes currently used by the Navy, Air Force and Marine Corps.

The Senate bill would add $15 million to continue developing a General Electric engine as an alternative to the United Technologies Corp. Pratt & Whitney engine selected to power the JSF. The House bill would transfer $30 million from another part of the budget to bolster the alternative engine project.

Though the F-22 is designed chiefly for aerial combat, it can also deal with ground targets, like the other two aircraft. But it can preserve its stealthy, radar-flummoxing profile only if any bomb load is carried internally, rather than being hung from the wings. The House bill would add to the budget $38 million to speed up development of small but pinpoint accurate bombs that would let the F-22 carry more bombs in its relatively small bays.

Both bills would authorize the $253 million requested for 10 F-16s. Neither would authorize the $220 million that the Senate version of the companion defense appropriations bill (S 1122) would add to the budget to buy six F-15s that were not requested. The Senate added the money at the behest of Missouri Republican Christopher S. Bond, who said that Boeing's F-15 production line in St. Louis was in danger of shutting down after the Greek government decided to buy a competing fighter instead of the F-15.

Electronic Warfare

Since the 1991 war with Iraq, the aging fleet of Prowler radar-jamming planes has been spread more thinly and worked much harder than had been anticipated. The Senate bill added $25 million and the House bill added $45 million to the $161 million requested to upgrade the planes' electronic gear.

Both Armed Services committees voiced skepticism about the Navy's plan to keep the Prowlers in service until 2015, asking for a detailed outline of how the Pentagon planned to keep the planes up to snuff until then. In addition, the House panel added to its bill $5 million to study possible replacement aircraft.

Both bills would authorize the $280 million requested for a J-STARS surveillance plane, a converted jetliner carrying a huge radar that can track ground vehicles more than 100 miles away. Both would also add $46 million, not requested, for components to be used in a J-STARS that could be funded in fiscal 2001.

The House bill would add $30 million to the $82 million requested and approved by the Senate to buy mobile terminals on which ground commanders could share a J-STARS' eagle-eyed perspective on the enemy.

Naval Forces

A new type of warship, slated to join the fleet in about 10 years, is being designed chiefly to rain precision-guided missiles and shells down on distant land targets. Both bills would authorize the $162 million requested to continue designing this ship, designated DD-21.

The Senate bill would approve the $38 million requested to develop an ultra-long-range guided shell for the 5-inch guns carried by most surface warships now in service. The House bill would add $14 million to the project.

The Senate bill would add $13 million to plan the conversion of four giant missile-launching subs so they could carry dozens of conventionally-armed, land-attack cruise missiles instead of the 24 nuclear-tipped Trident missiles they were built to carry.

As requested, both bills would authorize:

- $2.7 billion for three destroyers equipped with the Aegis anti-aircraft system; and
- $752 million for components of a nuclear-powered carrier, most of the funds for which will be included in the fiscal 2002 budget.

Air and Sea Transport

The largest single spending issue before the conferees is the amount to be authorized for components of a helicopter carrier that would be built by Litton Industries Inc. in Pascagoula, Miss. No funds were requested, but the House bill would authorize $15 million and the Senate bill $375 million.

The House bill would add to the budget $50 million for components of a high-speed cargo ship to be built by National Steel and Shipbuilding Co. in San Diego, hometown of House Armed Services Procurement Subcommittee Chairman Duncan Hunter, R-Calif.

Both bills would approve, as requested, $3.1 billion for 15 C-17 wide-body cargo jets and $1.5 billion for two ships to carry Marines and their combat equipment to amphibious landings.

Both bills would add $26 million to the $95 million requested to develop a new amphibious troop carrier designed to haul Marines ashore at 30 mph, four times as fast as the current vehicle.

The conferees will also have to reconcile these conflicts:

- The budget included no funds for Lockheed Martin C-130 cargo planes, but the Senate bill would authorize

$130 million for two of them, while the House bill would approve $252 million for four equipped to refuel Marine aircraft in midair.

- The House bill would add one V-22 Osprey troop-carrying aircraft ($60 million) and the Senate bill would add two ($123 million) to the 10 Ospreys requested by the Marine Corps ($796 million).
- To the $511 million requested for 28 H-60 helicopters built in Connecticut by United Technologies' Sikorsky division, the House bill would add $65 million for five additional aircraft; the Senate bill would add $157 million for 12.

Security Proposal Fails To Placate White House

AUGUST 7 — Last-minute negotiations among congressional Democrats, Republicans and Clinton administration officials failed to resolve differences over a controversial Republican proposal to restructure the Energy Department's nuclear weapons programs.

The continuing disagreements created uncertainty for the fiscal 2000 defense authorization bill (S 1059). Lawmakers used the conference version of that legislation as the vehicle to shore up security at the Department of Energy (DOE), even though the provision had been included in the fiscal 2000 intelligence authorization bill (HR 1555 — H Rept 106-30) passed by the Senate July 21. In response to revelations about security lapses that apparently allowed China to obtain secrets from U.S. nuclear weapons labs, the House and Senate conferees on the defense bill agreed to create a National Nuclear Security Administration within the Energy department to oversee all weapons-related activities.

But Energy Secretary Bill Richardson was prepared to recommend a presidential veto of the bill because of provisions that he fears would undermine his authority, a spokesman said.

In addition, some Democrats on the Senate Armed Services Committee refused to sign the conference report because of similar concerns. They said they were undecided about whether to vote for the report when it comes before both chambers in early September.

"The final product on DOE reorganization appears to go beyond creation of a new, separately organized entity within DOE, which I support," said Carl Levin of Michigan, ranking Democrat on Senate Armed Services.

In response, Republicans said that they tried to accommodate Democrats but that it was not practical for them to meet all of their demands.

"I don't think that if we recalled William Shakespeare from the grave that we could have written this Department of Energy provision to satisfy everyone," said an exasperated John W. Warner, R-Va., chairman of Senate Armed Services.

Increased Funding

The Energy Department reorganization was the most contentious of the hundreds of issues conferees had to resolve in crafting a compromise bill that would authorize $288.8 billion in defense-related appropriations for fiscal 2000. This would add $8.3 billion to President Clinton's budget request.

The increase includes $4.6 billion for procurement and research programs, for which spending dropped by 55 percent in inflation-adjusted terms between 1985 and 1996. Another $3.1 billion of the added spending would authorize full funding for construction projects for which Clinton had requested only partial funding as a budget-trimming ploy.

The largest amount the conferees added for a single program was $375 million specified for a helicopter carrier to be built by Litton Industries Inc. in Pascagoula, Miss., the hometown of Senate Majority Leader Trent Lott. The Navy had not planned to fund the ship until 2005.

Like both the House and Senate versions of the bill, the conference report would approve the $1.9 billion requested for production of the Air Force's F-22 fighter. Negotiations on the companion defense appropriations bill (S 1122, HR 2561) promise to be highly contentious because the House bill would deny production funds for the plane, which is the Air Force's top weapons priority.

Revising Energy

Three Republican senators initially offered a proposal to restructure the Energy Department's weapons programs in May as an amendment to the Senate defense authorization bill. But they withdrew the amendment after Richardson objected.

The senators then redrafted the amendment to conform to the recommendations of the President's Foreign Intelligence Advisory Board, which concluded in a report released June 15 that the Energy Department has had "a cavalier attitude" toward security.

After Richardson reluctantly endorsed the concept of a separate agency within his department, the Senate passed the restructuring plan, 96-1, as an amendment to the intelligence bill.

But defense conferees decided that their bill, not the intelligence measure, was the proper place to deal with the Energy restructuring because of the House Armed Services Committee's jurisdiction on nuclear weapons.

Despite resistance from House Commerce Committee members who wanted a stand-alone bill dealing with Energy security, House defense conferees drafted an initial proposal that was much stronger than what the Senate passed. The proposal drew a veto threat from Office of Management and Budget Director Jack Lew, who said in a July 29 letter that it did not provide the Energy secretary with enough authority.

Working against the clock for the August recess, conferees worked out another proposal. In the final version, the secretary "can tell [the new administrator] to do anything he wants to — he has no restraints," said Rep. William M. "Mac" Thornberry, R-Texas.

"How [Richardson] can object to that kind of authority, I don't know," added House Armed Services Chairman Floyd D. Spence, R-S.C.

But Levin said the conference report remained inadequate. In particular, he said it appeared to duplicate counterintelligence functions, while not permitting the Energy secretary direct control over the employees of the new agency, only its administrator.

Criticism of FBI

The wrangling over the issue came as a Senate Governmental Affairs Committee report released Aug. 5 accused the FBI, the Justice Department and the Energy Department of bungling an investigation into a former Energy employee suspected of providing nuclear weapons data to China.

Governmental Affairs Chairman Fred Thompson, R-Tenn., and ranking Democrat Joseph I. Lieberman of Connecticut, released a 32-page statement that found "investigatory missteps, institutional and personal miscommunications and . . . legal and policy misunderstandings and mistakes at all levels of government."

The committee conducted 13 hours of closed hearings to examine how the agencies handled the investigation of Wen Ho Lee, a Los Alamos National Laboratory scientist fired in March in the wake of revelations that China obtained classified information on how nuclear warheads work. Lee has not been charged with a crime and has denied any wrongdoing.

"The bottom line is that the investigation . . . was not a comedy of errors, but a tragedy of errors," Lieberman said at a news conference.

Among the committee's findings was that Lee had signed a waiver four years ago that might have allowed his computer to be monitored, but that Energy and FBI investigators did not learn of the waiver until this year.

House Adopts Conference Report; Bill Mandates New Nuclear Agency

SEPTEMBER 18 — Despite Energy Secretary Bill Richardson's vehement opposition to provisions that would reorganize his agency's nuclear weapons programs, the House adopted the conference report on the annual defense authorization bill Sept. 15.

The vote on the legislation (S 1059) was 375-45. *(Vote 424, p. H-136)*

The Senate is all but certain to approve the measure by a wide margin in a vote slated for Sept. 21. But Richardson has threatened since early August to urge President Clinton to veto the bill, so its fate is uncertain.

The conference report would authorize $288.8 billion for defense programs in fiscal 1999, $8.3 billion more than Clinton requested. The most contentious issue in the report, however, is the proposed creation of a National Nuclear Security Administration within the Energy Department to oversee its $12.1 billion defense program, primarily nuclear weapons. The undersecretary for nuclear security would report directly to the Energy secretary.

Before approving the conference report, the House rejected, 139-281, a procedural motion by John D. Dingell, D-Mich., that would have eliminated the Energy Department provisions. *(Vote 423, p. H-136)*

Besides warning that the proposed changes would dangerously insulate the nuclear weapons program from outside review, Dingell complained that the provisions had been added to the conference report with no debate in either the House or Senate and with no opportunity for other committees with jurisdiction over the Energy Department to weigh in. Dingell is ranking Democrat on the Commerce Committee.

Among the five Republicans backing Dingell's motion were Commerce Committee Chairman Thomas J. Bliley Jr., R-Va., and Science Committee Chairman F. James Sensenbrenner Jr., R-Wis.

But supporters of the reorganization said the 70 Democratic votes against Dingell were a sign of the proposal's strength, since the test came on what technically was a procedural vote. Such votes usually are "partisan by nature," House Armed Services Chairman Floyd D. Spence, R-S.C., commented afterward.

But Richardson argued that the vote boded well for his opposition to the conference provision. "Recognizing that we only had a few days to work this issue . . . we fared well," he said in a statement. "I hope to be meeting with the president soon to discuss these issues."

Because the public has been largely unconcerned about defense issues since the Soviet Union's collapse, Clinton paid no apparent political price when he vetoed the fiscal 1996 defense authorization bill (HR 1530) late in December 1995. *(1995 Almanac, p. 9-3)*

However, because of publicity about possible Chinese spying at U.S. nuclear weapons labs, several House Republicans said Clinton would not dare veto the current bill. "It would only give us an opportunity to highlight the tragedies that occurred," Steve Buyer, R-Ind., told reporters.

Priorities in Conflict

The nuclear security initiative is intended to create a simple chain of command in the weapons program that might prevent security lapses that may have allowed China to obtain nuclear secrets.

As Spence explained: "Nobody's in charge when too many people are trying to be in charge."

But Richardson and some leading Democrats warn that the changes would hamstring the application of environmental, health and safety requirements to the nuclear weapons program. Energy Department offices responsible for those issues could oversee weapons program facilities but could not directly order them to take action. Any orders would have to go from the secretary to the new weapons director.

Critics argued that the proposed change would shield the weapons program from outside oversight, which happened when the labs were under the Atomic Energy Commission until the mid-1970s. "We are going to have an agency focused on making bombs hidden from public sight, causing environmental havoc, public health catastrophes and then the same kind of . . . lying and concealment," argued Edward J. Markey, D-Mass.

Fearing that the change would undermine states' abilities to force weapons facilities to comply with their environmental and safety rules, the National Governors' Association opposed the Energy Department changes, as did the attorneys general of 46 states. One of the 46, Texas Attorney General John Cornyn, dropped his opposition after Spence and Senate Armed Services Committee Chairman John W. Warner, R-Va., detailed in a letter provisions of the bill intended to preserve the states' existing authority.

Highlights of the Conference Report

SEPTEMBER 4 — Conferees on the fiscal 2000 defense authorization bill added $8.3 billion to President Clinton's military budget request, most of it aimed at improving military combat readiness. But the lawmakers included some money and instructions to nudge the Pentagon into buying more high-tech weapons and equipment.

The House and Senate are expected to vote on the conference report (S 1059 — H Rept 106-301) soon after returning from their summer recess, but it was not on the House schedule for the week of Sept. 6.

Discussions were continuing over possible White House opposition to the proposed creation of a nuclear security agency within the Energy Department to keep tighter control of the national nuclear weapons laboratories. Energy Secretary Bill Richardson thinks the semi-autonomous agency would undermine his authority.

While defense authorizers sought to foster innovation in the services, they did not go so far as canceling the Air Force's F-22 fighter — something the House included in its version of the fiscal 2000 defense appropriations bill (HR 2561) to force the services to take a closer look at their big-ticket weapons programs.

Instead, the authorizers proposed accelerating the purchase of some high-tech weapons already in service, such as electronic warfare planes and precision-guided missiles and bombs. They also agreed to authorize more money for research and development, including a lighter and more transportable Army tank.

And the conferees approved several provisions aimed at encouraging innovative thinking in the military and among defense contractors, including proposals to:

- Require a quadrennial Pentagon report to Congress on new warfare concepts.
- Add $10 million to the $42 million the administration requested for multiservice exercises to test new concepts.
- Require the Pentagon to consider whether changing the rules on profit margins for defense contracts might encourage greater innovation by contractors.
- Allow the Pentagon to spend as much as $10 million annually on cash prizes to companies that develop promising military technologies.

Here is a closer look at the main elements of the conference report:

Military Personnel

The focus of the report's $72 billion authorization for military personnel is improving recruiting and retention.

In hopes of inducing experienced personnel to remain in uniform, the conferees approved a 4.8 percent raise in basic pay, rather than the 4.4 percent Clinton requested. The higher increase was in both the House and Senate bills.

The conference report would deduct from Clinton's budget request the $1.8 billion cost of a 4.4 percent raise, because it was paid for in the supplemental appropriations bill (PL 106-31) enacted in May. Since those were emergency funds, they did not count against the spending cap set by the 1997 balanced-budget act. *(1997 Almanac, p. 2-18)*

The 0.4 percent additional pay raise required another $156 million. The conference report also mandates that future annual pay raises through 2006 be 0.5 percent larger than the increase in private-sector wages, as measured by a government survey.

Both versions of the bill had approved the administration's request for additional targeted raises of up to 5.5 percent for mid-career officers and enlisted personnel.

Pension changes. The conference report would replace a 1986 law (PL 99-348) that reduced pensions for service members retiring after 20 years of active duty, from 50 percent of basic pay to 40 percent for those who joined up beginning in 1986. The conference report would offer members a choice: They could retire under the 50 percent formula or stay with the 40 percent pension, in which case they would receive a $30,000 lump-sum payment after 15 years of service.

Because the new pension system is expected to save money, the conference report offsets some of its add-ons by trimming $161 million from the personnel budget request. Conferees cut an additional $270 million from the total authorized on grounds that the services will start the fiscal year with fewer personnel than the budget assumed.

Military 401(k). The conference report would authorize military personnel to contribute up to 5 percent of their pre-tax basic pay to a tax-sheltered investment fund, similar to civilian 401(k) plans. This option would be available only if Congress enacted measures next year that would offset the loss in federal revenue.

As a retention incentive, the Pentagon would have discretion to match such contributions, as many private companies do.

Pay raise for generals. The services' 150 highest-ranking officers, who hold the ranks of general, admiral, lieutenant general or vice admiral, would get a hefty pay raise under the conference report, since it raises the $110,700 limit on military pay. The limit is set to keep military officers from making more than their civilian bosses.

The conference report would increase the pay cap to $125,900, so pay for the 35 generals and admirals would climb to that level, while pay for the next tier of senior officers would increase to nearly $120,000, the full amount provided by the Pentagon's pay formula.

Recruiting benefits. To accelerate the transition to more liberal military housing allowances, the conference report would add $225 million to the budget request. It does not include several Senate-passed provisions that would have provided more GI Bill education benefits.

The final bill would renew authority for enlistment and re-enlistment bonuses and extra pay for personnel in key, hard-to-fill specialties. It also would increase some existing bonuses and create new ones, such as a bonus for lawyers and Navy officers specializing in surface warfare.

It would add $71 million to the amount requested for recruiting and advertising, and increase from $150 to $200 the monthly stipend for college students enrolled in senior ROTC programs. It also would add $32 million to Clinton's request for high school ROTC programs, from which 40 percent of the graduates eventually join the service.

In their report, the conferees urged the Pentagon to review the medical and physical standards for joining the services, with an eye to easing the requirements.

"Persons with conditions heretofore considered disabling today make significant contributions in all walks of life," the conferees said.

The measure would also direct the Army to test a program allowing recruits to defer the start of their full-time service for up to two years and collect a stipend while they complete college or technical training.

To better understand why military personnel are leaving, the conferees directed the Pentagon to survey all those departing between Jan. 1 and June 30, 2000.

Addressing one likely reason — long overseas deployments —

the conferees approved a slightly revised version of a Senate-passed provision that would require a general or admiral to approve any deployment of more than 220 days and would give anyone sent overseas for more than 250 days a daily bonus of $100. Each service chief could suspend this provision, for his service, on grounds of national security.

The conference report would reduce the active-duty force by more than 10,000, setting a ceiling for fiscal 2000 of 1.39 million personnel. This is slightly larger than Clinton requested, with most of the increase aimed at providing more Marine guards at U.S. embassies.

Operations and Maintenance

The view of many lawmakers that far-flung peacekeeping missions have undermined the combat readiness of U.S. forces underpinned several provisions of the conference report.

The $2.4 billion Clinton requested for operations in the Persian Gulf and the Balkans was cut by $508 million. The conferees justified the cut by citing the Pentagon's decision to greatly reduce the number of U.S. troops deployed in Bosnia.

To prevent the cost of operations in Bosnia or Kosovo from siphoning funds from training and maintenance, the conference report would require Clinton to request a supplemental appropriation to pay for the deployment of U.S. forces in Kosovo and for any costs of the Bosnia mission in excess of the $1.82 billion Clinton requested.

The administration planned to unveil such a request the week of Sept. 6.

The Pentagon also would be required to report on how severely deployments in the Balkans would affect the avowed goal of having U.S. forces ready to win nearly simultaneous wars, for instance in Korea and the Persian Gulf.

Haiti withdrawal. The conference report would terminate by May 31, 2000, the deployment of U.S. forces in Haiti, a mission that began in 1994.

Though fewer than 500 active-duty U.S. troops remain in Haiti, most Republicans consider their presence an example of the type of humanitarian mission, peripheral to U.S. security, on which they contend that Clinton is frittering away military strength. Their opposition gained strength early this year when Marine Corps Gen. Charles E. Wilhelm, commander of U.S. forces in Latin America, recommended withdrawing the troops from Haiti because growing domestic turmoil in the country put them at risk.

The administration has announced that it will replace the current U.S. force with small contingents sent for brief periods to carry out specific projects, such as road building.

Targeting readiness. As has been customary in recent years, the conferees approved additions to budget accounts Congress deems particularly relevant to combat readiness. They agreed to authorize $868 million more than the $5.2 billion Clinton requested for facilities maintenance and $380 million more than the $13.8 billion requested for day-to-day base operating costs. They also proposed to add $184 million to the $7.3 billion requested for equipment overhauls and $145 million to the $1.3 billion requested for aircraft spare parts.

The conferees also added $110 million to amounts requested for major combat training ranges.

Those increases would be partly offset by reductions that lawmakers routinely make in Pentagon budgets, including:

- $205 million because the dollar's strength has reduced the cost of supplies and services purchased overseas.
- $176 million to reduce the number of people assigned to various headquarters.
- $100 million because the Pentagon has been reducing its civilian payroll faster than the budget assumed.

Ground Combat

The dilemma lawmakers face in wanting to upgrade current weapons while encouraging faster development of new arms is evident in their treatment of several types of land warfare equipment.

To upgrade early-model M-1 tanks with larger cannon and digital communications links, the conference report would authorize $636 million, as Clinton requested, rejecting the Senate's $28 million increase. But to the $309 million the administration requested to modernize early-model Bradley troop carriers, the conference report would authorize another $72 million to add improved night-vision equipment and other upgrades for older Bradleys assigned to National Guard units.

At the same time, following the lead of the House, the conference report would authorize an additional $12 million beyond the $65 million requested to develop a future combat vehicle that would weigh much less than the 70-ton M-1 tank. That is intended to make it much easier to quickly deploy U.S. forces to distant trouble spots. The conferees ordered the Pentagon to come up with a plan for such a radically new combat vehicle that would be ready to go into development by 2007.

Helicopters. Additions to the Clinton budget request for the Army's current and future armed helicopters, included in both the House and Senate bills, were retained in the conference report. To the $765 million requested to equip tank-hunting Apache helicopters with Longbow ground-target radar, the final version of the bill would authorize an additional $45 million to replace obsolete electronic components. It would authorize $56 million more than the $427 million Clinton requested to accelerate development of the Comanche scout helicopter.

Crusader cannon. The conferees approved the $283 million Clinton requested to develop the Crusader mobile cannon, criticized by some for its 70-ton bulk.

But they also added $31 million to accelerate development of a much lighter artillery rocket launcher that could be deployed in the Air Force's hundreds of C-130 cargo planes.

Small arms. The conference report would authorize $43 million more than the $31 million requested for three types of small arms. The House bill had authorized additional funds for two types of machine guns built by FN Manufacturing in Columbia, S.C., which is represented both by House Armed Services Committee Chairman Floyd D. Spence and Strom Thurmond, a senior member of the Senate Armed Services Committee. Both are Republicans.

The Senate bill added an authorization for grenade launchers built by Saco Defense, in Saco, Maine. The city is represented by Senate Armed Services member Olympia J. Snowe, a Republican, and House Armed Services member Tom Allen, a Democrat.

Air Combat

The Air Force request for $1.9 billion in production funds for the F-22 fighter was not an issue in the authorization conference, since both the House and Senate approved production and $1.2 billion to continue developing the plane.

The authorizers did not include the purchase of additional F-15 fighters, something included in both House and Senate versions of the defense appropriations bill. The House Appropriations Committee said the F-15 is a cheaper alternative to the F-22.

The conferees approved without change the administration requests for $253 million to buy 10 F-16 fighters for the Air Force and $2.7 billion to buy 36 F/A-18 E/F jets for the Navy. The conference report would authorize $30 million above the $477 million requested to continue developing the Joint Strike Fighter, slated to enter service in about 2007 as a lower-cost complement to the F-22.

The conference report would authorize adding $112 million to the $202 million requested to develop improvements to the B-2 stealth bomber. It would also authorize $15 million more than the $32 million requested to develop improvements in the 1960s-vintage B-52 fleet, which the Air Force expects to soldier on for nearly four more decades.

The conferees approved less than one-tenth of the $524 million the House version of the bill added to the budget request for three types of precision-guided bombs and missiles, which had accounted for most of the U.S. weaponry used against Yugoslavia earlier this year. The conference report would add $50 million to the $161 million requested for satellite-guided bombs, whereas the House had added $114 million. The final version would also authorize $235 million for glider bombs and $51 million for Tomahawk ship-launched cruise missiles, in both cases the amount requested. The House had authorized $110 million for glider bombs and $300 million for Tomahawks, including $90 million to restart Raytheon Corp.'s Tomahawk production line in Tucson, Ariz.

The conference report would authorize the $145 million requested to develop a cheaper version of the Tomahawk and the $166 million requested to develop a stealthy air-launched missile with a range of a few hundred miles. It would also require the Pentagon to explain how it plans to replace its diminishing supply of air-launched cruise missiles, which fly farther and carry a much larger warhead than the new, stealthy missile.

To upgrade the aging fleet of Prowler radar-jamming planes, the conferees would authorize $25 million more than the $161 million requested. The conference report would also authorize $5 million to begin designing a replacement for the Vietnam War-era Prowler.

The J-STARS ground-surveillance plane, a converted jetliner with radar that can track ground vehicles more than 100 miles away, also got a considerable boost from the conferees. In addition to endorsing the $282 million requested for the 14th of the big planes, they approved $46 million for components to be used in a 15th plane, to be funded in fiscal 2001. They also authorized adding $48 million to the $131 million requested to improve the J-STARS radar and $25 million more than the $82 million requested for mobile terminals on which ground commanders could view J-STARS data.

Naval Combat

Neither version of the authorization bill made significant changes to the budget request for combat vessels. Nor did the conference report, which approved, as requested:

- $2.7 billion for three Aegis destroyers.
- $748 million for components to be used in new submarines, to be funded in future years.
- $752 million for components to be used in a nuclear-powered aircraft carrier, most of the funds for which will be included in the fiscal 2001 budget.

The conferees approved the amounts requested to continue designing two new classes of warships: $195 million for a carrier, the first of which would be funded in fiscal 2006, and $270 million for a new destroyer intended to save money by using a crew of fewer than 100, about one-third the number aboard current destroyers.

The new destroyers, the first of which is slated for funding in fiscal 2004, are intended to strike land targets up to 150 miles away with guided missiles and rocket-boosted cannon shells that use Global Positioning Satellite signals to steer to their targets. The conference report would authorize $15 million more than the $102 million requested to develop these land-attack weapons.

The conference report incorporates a Senate initiative that would add $13 million to plan for equipping four large missile-launching submarines to carry 132 Tomahawk missiles apiece instead of the 24 nuclear-armed Trident missiles they currently carry.

Sea and Air Transport

The conferees followed the Senate's lead in approving $375 million for components to be used in a helicopter carrier designed to carry up to 2,000 Marines. The ship would be built by Litton Industries in Pascagoula, Miss., the home of Senate Majority Leader Trent Lott, a Republican. The authorization would leave about $1.1 billion of the ship's cost to be covered by future budgets. The Pentagon had planned to begin funding the ship in fiscal 2004. But an earlier start was avidly desired by the Marines, the Mississippi congressional delegation and Litton, which said the faster timetable would cut $780 million from the ship's projected $2.3 billion price tag.

The conferees also agreed to authorize $80 million, which Clinton had not requested, to begin work on a high-speed cargo ship.

The conference report would authorize $1.5 billion for two transport ships to carry Marine landing forces.

Like the House and Senate bills, the final version would authorize adding $26 million to the $95 million requested to develop an amphibious troop carrier that could haul Marines ashore at 30 mph, four times as fast as the Marines' current vehicle.

The budget included no funds for Lockheed Martin C-130s, but the conferees added $252 million for four of the planes equipped to refuel Marine aircraft in midflight.

For a dozen V-22 Osprey tilt-rotor aircraft, which the Marines will use to carry troops ashore from transport ships, the conferees approved $919 million, adding two aircraft and $123 million to the Clinton request.

To the $511 million requested for 28 H-60 helicopters built by United Technologies' Sikorsky division in Stratford, Conn., the conferees approved an additional $157 million for 12 additional aircraft.

The report would authorize $127 million, $56 million more than was requested, to modernize the Army's fleet of Chinook cargo helicopters, an increase that was one of the Army's top priorities. The upgrade project is run jointly by Boeing's helicopter division in Philadelphia and by Allied Signal in Phoenix.

The conferees also authorized adding $12 million to buy two of the three Cessna Citation executive jets that were a top Marine Corps priority. They would also authorize two Boeing 737 passenger jets at $49 million apiece, rather than the one plane requested. The Navy uses the 737s chiefly to shuttle reservists to and from training sites.

Russia and China

The conference report would authorize $476 million, the amount requested, for Cooperative Threat Reduction. This is the Pentagon's portion of the so-called Nunn-Lugar program intended to help Russia and other former Soviet republics dispose of nuclear, chemical and biological weapons.

Nevertheless, the conferees challenged an important aspect of the program by barring the use of Nunn-Lugar funds for construction of a storage facility in Russia to hold chemical weapons. The $130 million requested for the storage site would be allocated to other projects.

As requested, $145 million was approved for the Energy Department's Nunn-Lugar initiatives aimed at helping former Soviet states secure their stockpiles of nuclear material from theft. But the conferees agreed to authorize only $40 million of the $60 million requested for two other Energy Department programs aimed at getting Russia's nuclear weapons workers employed in commercial activities.

In addition to the Energy Department reorganization issue that could prompt an administration veto, the conference report included other provisions triggered by allegations that China had tried to obtain militarily useful information. Among these were provisions that would:

- Prohibit U.S.-Chinese military exchanges that would "inappropriately" expose certain U.S. military capabilities.
- Require an annual report on the transfer of militarily significant U.S. technology to China, Russia or terrorist states.
- Require the president to notify Congress of any alleged violation of export control laws by U.S. companies having their satellites launched from China.

Other Provisions

Among the hundreds of other items in the conference report were provisions that would:

- Expand Arlington National Cemetery, which is projected to fill its current burial plots by 2025, by adding 44 acres of adjacent Defense Department property.
- Require the armed services to provide, on request, at least a two-person honor guard for a veteran's funeral.
- Give top Pentagon officials the final say over whether the Defense Department would be required to surrender to other users portions of the radio-frequency spectrum currently reserved for defense use.

The conference report also includes a House provision that would require the Pentagon's inspector general to review whether the Defense Department is buying dumbbells and barbells that are American-made only. ◆

Senate Clears Bill; Popular Pay Raise May Forestall Veto

SEPTEMBER 25 — Brushing aside objections to provisions that would reorganize the Energy Department's nuclear weapons programs, the Senate on Sept. 22 followed the House in overwhelmingly approving a $288.8 billion defense authorization bill for fiscal 2000.

The bill (S 1059) would add $8.3 billion to President Clinton's budget request, providing the first inflation-adjusted increase in the Pentagon's budget since 1985 and the largest military pay raise in 18 years. The Senate vote was 93-5, with one member voting "present." *(Vote 284, p. S-56)*

For weeks, Energy Secretary Bill Richardson has threatened to ask President Clinton to veto the bill because it would consolidate his department's nuclear weapons functions into a new organization, the National Nuclear Security Administration. Richardson worries that the new agency, which would be insulated from the Energy Department's bureaucracy, would undermine his authority.

But White House spokesman Joe Lockhart indicated Sept. 23 that Clinton was balancing Richardson's arguments against other popular aspects of the bill, including the pay raise and provisions addressing military readiness.

"There are some complicated issues within . . . the [Energy Department] reorganization that remain of concern," Lockhart told reporters. "The problem is . . . there's some very important and needed things in that bill for the military, as far as readiness and pay raise."

Management Worries

The proposed reorganization, intended to shore up security at the Energy Department's nuclear weapons laboratories, was one of several initiatives sparked by reports of widespread Chinese efforts to obtain U.S. military secrets, and the subsequent revelations of lax security at the department. Other provisions in the defense bill would restrict visits by Chinese military officers to U.S. bases and tighten restrictions on the transfer to China of U.S. technology for computers, satellite-launching rockets and other militarily useful items.

Richardson and other critics argued that the Energy Department reorganization language would make oversight of the nuclear weapons establishment practically impossible."This proposal damages environmental protection, threatens worker health and safety, degrades national security and jeopardizes counterintelligence reforms," a department spokesman said.

But Senate Armed Services Committee Chairman John W. Warner, R-Va., insisted the controversial provisions explicitly give the Energy secretary full control of the weapons complex and that the new weapons agency would remain subject to existing environmental, health and safety laws.

Sen. Pete V. Domenici, R-N.M., who helped craft the reorganization, also said it would ensure that security at the nuclear weapons facilities was given a higher priority. "By creating a semiautonomous agency within the Energy Department, we expect to see more accountability for the work and actions of our national laboratories," Domenici said in a statement.

During Senate debate on the conference report Sept. 21, Carl Levin of Michigan, the Armed Services panel's senior Democrat, echoed Richardson's objections to the Energy Department provisions.

Citing a study by the Congressional Research Service, Levin contended that the provisions could be interpreted as undermining the Energy Secretary's authority over the weapons complex, thus having "the perverse effect of diffusing responsibility" for the weapons labs.

Nevertheless, Levin voted in favor of the conference report. He supported the military pay raise and other defense initiatives contained in the bill, and said he concluded that the Energy reorganization provisions might be workable: "There is language which can be construed to give authority to the secretary which might allow him to run this agency."

Supporters of the bill were cheered by Levin's support, and by the huge margin with which the Senate approved it.

All five votes against the conference report were cast by liberal Democrats: Paul Wellstone of Minnesota, Russell D. Feingold and Herb Kohl of Wisconsin, Barbara Boxer of California and Tom Harkin of Iowa.

Slade Gorton, R-Wash., a retired member of the Air Force Reserve, voted "present" because if the bill becomes law, one provision would increase his military pension.

Nuclear Arguments

The new National Nuclear Security Administration would be headed by an undersecretary for nuclear security, who would be subject to Senate confirmation. The idea for the agency grew out of a recommendation by the President's Foreign Intelligence Advisory Board, chaired by former Republican Sen. Warren B. Rudman of New Hampshire (1980-93).

The Rudman panel's report, released June 15, concluded that "organizational disarray, managerial neglect and a culture of arrogance" at the department have left it incapable of reforming itself.

The new agency would be responsible for nuclear weapons development, defense nuclear non-proliferation and the disposition of fissile materials.

The defense bill also would establish new Energy Department offices of counterintelligence and intelligence. In addition, it would direct the national nuclear security administrator to set up a separate counterintelligence program at each weapons laboratory or weapons production site.

Aside from the issue of reorganizing the nuclear weapons complex, there was relatively little controversy over the conference report. It would authorize a 4.8 percent military pay raise, rather than the 4.4 percent raise Clinton had recommended.

It would authorize $3.1 billion, as Clinton requested, to continue development and production of the Air Force's F-22 fighter. Production funds for the plane are an issue in the House-Senate conference on the companion defense appropriations bill (HR 2561).

Warner, who discussed the authorization bill with Clinton and Domenici during an hourlong meeting Sept. 20, downplayed the likelihood of a veto. "There is not much fervor down at the White House for a veto," he observed.

The House adopted the defense conference report Sept. 15 by a vote of 375-45 — a margin much larger than the two-thirds majority that would be needed to override a veto.

However, on a procedural vote that was, in effect, a Democratic-sponsored effort to delete the Energy Department reorganization, Richardson's allies came closer: They got 139 votes — seven short of the 146 they would need to sustain a veto if all 435 House members were voting.

Ratings Battle

In the days leading up to the Senate vote, Richardson tried to highlight the administrative reforms he has made in security at his agency. He released the results of an independent security review conducted by his new Office of Independent Oversight and Performance Assurance that found Los Alamos National Laboratory in New Mexico received a "satisfactory" rating, up from "marginal" one year ago.

The department's other two nuclear weapons labs, Sandia in New Mexico and Lawrence Livermore in California, each received a "marginal" rating.

"People are getting the message that we're serious about protecting our nation's secrets," Richardson said Sept. 20.

In response to reports of security lapses at the labs, the Energy and Justice departments have focused their investigation on a former Los Alamos scientist, Wen Ho Lee, who was fired in March. Lee has not been charged with a crime and has denied any wrongdoing.

A recent bipartisan Senate Governmental Affairs Committee report accused the two agencies of bungling the Lee investigation. FBI Director Louis J. Freeh and other Justice Department officials told lawmakers at a closed session Sept. 22 that their probe will be expanded to look at other potential suspects besides Lee.

Senate Intelligence Committee Chairman Richard C. Shelby, R-Ala., said that such a move was overdue.

"I've thought from the beginning that the investigation was botched," he said. "There was culpability, blame and lack of diligence on the part of the Justice Department. What they're doing now, they should have done a long time ago."

Reducing Contacts

In addition to the Energy Department reorganization, the defense authorization measure contains provisions in response to China's apparent success in improving its military capabilities at U.S. expense.

The conference report would prohibit contacts between U.S. and Chinese military personnel that would risk "inappropriate exposure" of sensitive information about U.S. military tactics or technologies.

The legislation also addressed high-technology exports to China and other nations, although in a less comprehensive fashion than a separate measure approved Sept. 23 by a Senate committee.

The defense bill added a series of provisions calling for tighter security in the launching of U.S. commercial satellites from other countries, such as China, and calling for greater consultation with the intelligence community on the national security impact of satellite exports.

The legislation also would direct the president to provide an annual report on the implications of exporting high-performance computers to China and to seek an agreement allowing the United States to verify that those computers are not used for weapons development.

Supporters of the China-related provisions pointed to a U.S. intelligence community report released this month that predicted Beijing would test a longer-range mobile ballistic missile within the next several years that would be targeted "primarily against the United States."

Richardson Relents; Clinton Signature Expected

OCTOBER 2 — A concession by Energy Secretary Bill Richardson on reorganizing his department removed the final hurdle to the fiscal 2000 defense authorization bill becoming law.

Richardson had warned for weeks that he would urge President Clinton to veto the $288.8 billion defense bill (S 1059 — Conference report: H Rept 106-301) because of language added to consolidate the Energy Department's nuclear weapons programs into a National Nuclear Security Administration, which would not be subject to the department's normal bureaucracy. Richardson had expressed concern that the agency would undermine his authority.

However, the conference report on the popular defense bill, which contains the largest military pay raise in 18 years, was adopted by overwhelming majorities in the House and Senate.

Richardson then reversed course and announced Sept. 26 that he would no longer oppose the bill.

"I recognize the importance to the troops of the pay raise, readiness and retirement legislation," he said in a prepared statement.

Richardson said he would try to prevent the reorganization from causing disruptions within the department's current operations.

Nevertheless, some lawmakers expressed concern over how swiftly and completely he would carry out the move. They vowed to closely monitor the new agency's creation.

"I'm concerned about the back-channel communications coming from the Department of Energy as to how they intend to implement this new law," said Senate Armed Services Committee Chairman John W. Warner, R-Va. "I intend to hold a hearing in about 60 days to determine exactly what has and what has not been done in compliance with the law."

The proposed reorganization was among the initiatives by Congress in response to reports of widespread Chinese efforts to obtain U.S. military secrets, and the subsequent revelations of lax security at the Energy Department.

The National Nuclear Security Administration would be headed by an undersecretary for nuclear security who would be subject to Senate confirmation.

Among those being discussed as possible nominees for the job is Roger Hagengruber, senior vice president for national security and arms control at Sandia National Laboratories in New Mexico, home state of Republican Sen. Pete V. Domenici.

Money To Follow

The new agency would be responsible for nuclear weapons development, defense activities to prevent the spread of nuclear weapons and the disposition of fissionable material.

Domenici called the agency's creation "the most significant reform in perhaps 28 to 30 years in a department that has grown like Topsy and is filled with programs that don't necessarily relate to one another."

Although there is no funding for the agency in the fiscal 2000 energy and water development appropriations bill (HR 2605 — Conference report: H Rept 106-336), Domenici said he is open to accommodating the department's needs. He chairs the Senate Energy and Water Development Appropriations Subcommittee.

Richardson had sought to deflect congressional criticism about security by proposing a number of administrative reforms, including widespread polygraph testing for Energy employees.

But Domenici and Jeff Bingaman, D-N.M., both raised concerns about the department's polygraph proposal. Domenici asked Richardson in a Sept. 20 letter to follow language in the defense bill that limits the use of the procedure. ◆

President Irks GOP By Appointing Richardson To Head Nuclear Agency

Box Score

- **Bill:** S 1059 — PL 106-65
- **Legislative action: Senate** passed the Energy Department restructuring plan as part of the fiscal 2000 intelligence authorization bill (HR 1555 — H Rept 106-130) by voice vote July 21.

House adopted the restructuring plan as part of the conference report on the fiscal 2000 defense authorization bill (S 1059 — H Rept 106-301), 375-45, on Sept. 15.

Senate cleared S 1059, 93-5, on Sept. 22.

President signed S 1059 on Oct. 5.

SUMMARY

A proposal to restructure the Energy Department's nuclear weapons programs by putting them under a new agency, the National Nuclear Security Administration, was included in the fiscal 2000 defense authorization bill, which President Clinton signed into law Oct. 5. But the action did not end the protracted dispute over nuclear weapons oversight between the administration and Congress. Republicans were incensed when they learned that Clinton appointed Energy Secretary Bill Richardson to assume the duties as head of the new agency.

The creation of the new weapons agency represented the most far-reaching congressional response to a bipartisan House committee's report detailing China's alleged attempts to steal highly classified information from the Energy Department's nuclear weapons laboratories.

The committee, chaired by Rep. Christopher Cox, R-Calif., generated waves of publicity when the declassified version of its report was released in May. The 1,016-page, three-volume document confirmed a stream of earlier newspaper revelations that China had used a network of spies, front companies and visitors to the United States to obtain military secrets and other technology. The report contained 38 recommendations, including tightening security at the department's labs.

The release of the committee's findings was followed by a stinging report from the President's Foreign Intelligence Advisory Board, which detailed the Energy Department's lax security measures. The board, chaired by former Sen. Warren B. Rudman, R-N.H. (1980-93), concluded in June that "organizational disarray, managerial neglect and a culture of arrogance" left the department incapable of reforming itself.

Some Republicans called for having the Defense Department assume the management of the nuclear weapons program, while others supported having a new agency entirely separate from the Energy Department, functioning in a manner similar to NASA. But most members believed that the agency should remain within — but insulated from — the Energy Department's normal bureaucracy.

The National Nuclear Security Administration will be responsible for nuclear weapons development, defense activities to prevent the spread of nuclear weapons, and the disposition of fissionable material. It is to be headed by an undersecretary of Energy for nuclear security who would be subject to Senate confirmation.

One of the proposal's chief architects, Sen. Pete V. Domenici, R-N.M., called the agency's creation "the most significant reform in perhaps 28 to 30 years in a department that has grown like Topsy and is filled with programs that don't necessarily relate to one another."

Background

Domenici and other Senate Republicans initially sought to create the agency through the fiscal 2000 defense authorization bill in July. They withdrew the plan after Richardson and Senate Democrats said that it would undermine the Energy secretary's authority and could compromise compliance with health, safety and environmental rules. After extensive negotiations, between the two sides, the fiscal 2000 intelligence authorization bill (HR 1555) became the vehicle.

But interest from Republicans on the House Armed Services Committee, which has jurisdiction over nuclear weapons programs, led to the issue's inclusion in the conference on the defense authorization bill instead. After questioning the need for a new "fiefdom" within his department, Richardson reluctantly endorsed the Senate's proposal. But he subsequently condemned new language added by House conferees as inadequate and threatened to recommend a presidential veto. He backed down after the authorization conference report cleared the House and Senate by overwhelming majorities.

Nevertheless, Richardson persuaded Clinton to allow him to assume the duties as head of the new agency until lawmakers could make some "very modest modifications" that he suggested in the new law. Republicans balked, however, and accused Richardson of flouting Congress' intentions. The House Armed Services Committee set up a panel chaired by Republican Rep. William M. "Mac" Thornberry of Texas to oversee implementation of the new law.

Domenici and Richardson began talking about solutions to the impasse in October but made little progress. Although those talks are likely to continue, a showdown will not come until March 1, 2000, when many of the organizational provisions of the law will take effect. If the issue is not resolved and an undersecretary is not appointed, Republicans could renew their threats to cut Richardson's travel budget or legislatively prohibit him from taking on the new role.

Report Released; Struggle for Consensus Begins

MAY 29 — A House committee report on China's theft of U.S. technology drew immediate cries for action on Capitol Hill and touched off a wave of proposed solutions. But Republicans learned that implementing the report's recommendations will be trickier than reacting to its revelations.

GOP attempts in the House and Senate to amend pending defense bills to tighten security stalled May 27 after Democrats objected.

"This does not bode well for us being able to deal with the China problem and security in a bipartisan way," said Senate Majority Leader Trent Lott, R-Miss., after withdrawing one proposal when Democrats threatened a filibuster.

The long-awaited declassified version of the House report — a 1,016-page, seven-and-a-half-pound document in three volumes, complete with color photographs — confirmed a stream of earlier newspaper revelations that China has used a network of spies, front companies and visitors to the United States to obtain nuclear secrets and other military technology over several decades. The report said the stolen secrets "give [China] design information on thermonuclear weapons on par with our own."

The thefts occurred at least as early as the late 1970s, according to the report, with significant secrets stolen in the mid-1990s and espionage "almost certainly" continuing today. It also said China "has stolen or otherwise illegally obtained" U.S. missile and space technology that has improved its military and intelligence capabilities.

The report of the bipartisan House Select Committee on U.S. National Security and Military/Commercial Concerns with the People's Republic of China contained 38 recommendations, including tightening export control laws, strengthening counterintelligence at the Department of Energy, sharpening oversight of U.S. satellite launches in China, improving the domestic U.S. space launch industry, and requiring more prompt notification of future security lapses to Congress and the executive branch.

"What we are doing here today, I hope, will be a beginning and not an end," said Rep. Christopher Cox, R-Calif., the committee's chairman, in releasing the report May 25. "I hope that we will be able to cooperate with the administration and with the committees in the Senate as well as in the House to enact our recommendations."

President Clinton echoed earlier statements by administration officials that by and large, the recommendations were acceptable. "The overwhelming majority of those recommendations we agree with and are in the process of implementing," Clinton said May 25.

Though Congress and the administration agree that security at nuclear weapons laboratories needs to be tightened, they are at odds over whether it should be done by the administration or Congress.

In addition, the report's calls for tightening export control laws have provoked fears among high-technology companies that have been campaigning for looser controls.

"There's a collective holding of the breath," said Marc Pearl, senior vice president of government affairs and general counsel for the Information Technology Association of America, a Washington group representing 11,000 high-tech companies. "This controversy has nothing to do with anything private companies have done. It would be unfortunate if there was a crackdown on exports."

Reviewing Relations

Political rhetoric over the report stayed hot. Some Republicans called for the resignations of Attorney General Janet Reno or national security adviser Samuel R. Berger, while Democrats countered by noting that security problems dated back to the Reagan and Bush administrations.

Some lawmakers said the report was a rationale for a fundamental re-examination of relations with China. House International Relations Chairman Benjamin A. Gilman, R-N.Y., called the Clinton administration's policy of "strategic partnership" with China "naive and misguided" in the wake of the report's revelations.

But other lawmakers foresaw little dramatic change in relations between the two countries. "There's too much mutual interest, too much mutual need, too much at stake," said Joseph R. Biden Jr. of Delaware, the Senate Foreign Relations Committee's ranking Democrat. "You can't ignore a billion people, and they can't ignore us."

Chinese officials denounced the House report as an inaccurate and misguided attempt to demonize their country. Their comments came three weeks after the accidental U.S. bombing of China's embassy in Belgrade further poisoned relations between the two nations.

Some experts, however, predicted that Beijing is aware enough of the impact of the report to seek to repair ties with the United States.

"There's a floor under this relationship in that neither side wants to let this thing deteriorate," said Peter W. Rodman, director of national security programs at the Nixon Center, a Washington think tank specializing in foreign policy. "What's happening is that the tone is souring and there's no new advances being made, but there's still a basic dialogue."

Agreeing to Disagree

In Congress, initial hopes of establishing a bipartisan consensus that might mirror the spirit in which the Cox committee operated proved elusive in both chambers.

The problems were first illustrated in the House on May 27, when Republican leaders abruptly pulled from the floor the rule governing debate on the fiscal 2000 defense authorization bill (HR 1401).

The move came after the China committee's ranking Democrat, Norm Dicks of Washington, joined party colleagues in arguing that the rule would not allow consideration of a proposed amendment stemming from the report and intended to shore up security at nuclear weapons labs.

The rule for the legislation did contain other proposed Republican amendments offered in reaction to the Cox report. Among them was a controversial initiative by Armed Services Committee Chairman Floyd D. Spence, R-S.C., to have the Defense Department prepare a plan to assume control of Energy Department national security programs, including weapons production sites and national laboratories.

Energy Secretary Bill Richardson has strenuously objected to what he sees as congressional micromanagement of security at his agency's labs, saying that he has moved aggressively to implement a series of reforms in recent months. But some Republicans contend such measures do not go far enough.

The House Science Committee also weighed in on the Energy Department's management. It approved, by voice vote, on May 26 an amendment to a bill (HR 1656) authorizing Energy Department projects dealing with commercial applications of energy technology.

The amendment, by Jerry F. Costello, D-Ill., and George Nethercutt, R-Wash., would put a moratorium on access by citizens of certain countries to classified areas of Energy labs, but would allow case-by-case waivers.

A New Agency?

In the Senate, a more ambitious security initiative faced a difficult struggle. Jon Kyl, R-Ariz., offered an amendment to the fiscal 2000 defense authorization bill (S 1059) to reorganize the Energy Department's Office of Defense Programs and create a new agency, the Nuclear Security Administration, to oversee nuclear weapons production.

The new agency would be a separate "stovepipe" within the department, insulated from normal bureaucracy and its procedures, accountable directly to the Energy secretary to ensure more accountability of nuclear weapons activities, Kyl said.

His amendment also would write into law the department's office of counterintelligence, whose director would report any security breaches directly to the president and Congress.

But the proposal provoked a rare public dispute between two of the Senate's leading voices on nuclear matters: Pete V. Domenici, R-N.M., chairman of the Energy and Water Appropriations Subcommittee, and his home-state colleague Jeff Bingaman, ranking Democrat on the Energy and Natural Resources Committee.

Domenici joined Kyl in supporting the amendment, saying the Energy Department suffers from a "one-size-fits-all syndrome" in which nuclear programs must work within the demands of other agency priorities. Bingaman said the amendment was being offered too hastily and would produce "substantial unintended consequences."

Richardson wrote in a letter to Bingaman that he would recommend that Clinton veto the bill if the amendment was included. "The security mission cuts across the entire department, not just defense programs facilities," Richardson wrote.

After Democrats threatened a filibuster over the amendment, Lott called a break for negotiations that stretched into several hours. Eventually, he announced that the proposal will be offered as an amendment to the fiscal 2000 intelligence authorization bill (S 1009 — S Rept 106-48), which aides said would come up in early June.

"Shame on us because our secrets were stolen, and shame on Democrats," a frustrated Domenici told reporters.

Lott did persuade senators to pass, by voice vote, a relatively modest amendment to the defense bill to strengthen U.S. export control laws, increase counterintelligence training and require greater monitoring of satellite launches and better notification to Congress of security breaches.

Apart from the intelligence bill, Lott said he still anticipates major legislation later in the year dealing with the issues raised by the report. "There's got to be some balance between commercial desire, trade and national security," he told reporters May 27.

Security Guard Lapses

Congress began investigating the administration's dealings with China after reports that two satellite companies — Loral Space & Communications Ltd. and Hughes Electronics Corp. — might have compromised national security in helping Beijing determine the causes of rocket failures in 1995 and 1996.

The report found shoddy monitoring of U.S. satellites launched in China, with private security guards sleeping on the job, reporting for work under the influence of alcohol and even consorting with prostitutes. It recommended a series of steps to improve security, including making the Defense Department responsible for hiring and screening security officers for the launches.

The report also called for giving the State Department enough workers and money to handle the processing of export licenses for companies sending satellites to China. In the fiscal 1999 defense authorization law (PL 105-261), Congress shifted oversight authority for satellites from the Commerce to the State Department last summer because of national security concerns. *(1998 Almanac, p. 8-3)*

The export control situation has led many business groups to call on Congress for action on long-stalled legislation to regulate "dual use" exports with both military and commercial value. The most recent Export Administration Act (PL 103-10) expired in 1994, and industries contend that a better legal framework is needed to reflect the end of the Cold War — a finding echoed in the Cox committee's report.

Past attempts to rewrite the legislation have become bogged down in a maze of committees with jurisdiction over the issue. Businesses also have tried to ensure their interests overseas remain protected.

"It is a very, very tough issue to deal with," said Willard A. Workman, vice president of the international division at the U.S. Chamber of Commerce. "It only seems we're able to come to a conclusion when the debate is precipitated by a crisis."

Michael B. Enzi, R-Wyo., chairman of the Senate Banking, Housing and Urban Affairs Subcommittee on International Finance and Trade, has been working for months on a bipartisan reauthorization of the act. He said he hopes to introduce legislation soon that will reflect about half of the 38 findings of the Cox committee.

Enzi said the bill will reflect the committee's conclusion that there should be multilateral rather than unilateral controls over exports. Cox said reauthorizing the act in such a way is probably the most important of the committee's recommendations.

"We need to talk, one nation at a time, to each of our allies and solicit support for a multilateral regime," he told the House International Relations Asia and the Pacific Subcommittee May 26. "This requires American leadership."

House Takes Step To Bolster Security Of Technology

JUNE 12 — This was the easy part: The House on June 9 put aside its partisan differences and lined up behind legislation to address China's apparent theft of nuclear weapons data and other military technologies.

Members voted 428-0 to adopt an amendment to the fiscal 2000 defense authorization bill implementing some of the recommendations of a bipartisan committee's report that detailed a decades-long effort by China to steal nuclear weapons secrets and other sensitive information. *(Vote 180, p. H-64)*

But formidable challenges remain. Lawmakers in both chambers now have to take up more controversial proposals to tighten security and restrict exports of high-tech products to China.

In the Senate, tensions continued between the administration and GOP over whether to create a new agency within the Energy Department to oversee security. And some Democrats predicted an uphill effort to speedily enact a new law regulating high-tech exports — an idea embraced by Senate Banking committee Chairman Phil Gramm, R-Texas.

"It's easy to get involved in a lot of exhortation, but much more difficult to actually legislate that into being," said Tim Johnson of South Dakota, ranking Democrat on the Senate Banking Subcommittee on International Trade and Finance, at a June 10 hearing.

House Bill

The wide-ranging House floor amendment, offered on the defense authorization bill (HR 1401 — H Rept 106-162), sought to bolster security and counterintelligence measures at the Department of Energy's nuclear weapons laboratories while implementing stricter satellite export and launch guidelines to avert illegal technology transfers. It was sponsored by Reps. Christopher Cox, R-Calif., and Norm Dicks, D-Wash., chairman and ranking Democrat of the House Select Committee on U.S. National Security and Military/Commercial Concerns with the People's Republic of China.

"We're pleased that we're seeing the beginning of deliberate action in response to our recommendations," Cox said after the vote.

The House also adopted, by voice vote, a series of amendments aimed at addressing Energy Department policies in response to the committee's report, including a proposal to establish a counterintelligence polygraph program for agency employees with access to high-risk programs or information, and another to require the Energy secretary to report to Congress each year on counterintelligence and security measures at national labs.

At the same time, the House rejected, 159-266, an amendment by Jim Ryun, R-Kan., to impose a two-year moratorium on scientific exchanges at the weapons labs. Administration officials strongly opposed the amendment because they said it would harm international cooperation. And many Democrats said the moratorium language in the Cox-Dicks amendment was sufficient. *(Vote 181, p. H-64)*

House Amendments

The House's united action on the Cox-Dicks amendment to the defense bill reflected the eagerness among lawmakers to respond quickly to revelations about security lapses at the weapons labs that apparently enabled China to obtain nuclear weapons designs. The committee's report said those designs give China the ability to put its weapons on par with the United States.

Dicks had attempted to offer an earlier version of the amendment to the bill in May, but the rule governing debate on the measure did not allow consideration of his proposal. He and other Democrats complained about the exclusion, prompting House Republican leaders to pull the bill from the floor.

Cox and Dicks then worked out a compromise over the Memorial Day recess. Although they said their amendment addresses 26 of their report's 38 recommendations, they decided to leave out a number of proposals because they did not fall within the jurisdiction of the defense bill.

Their amendment would put into law several aspects of a recent order by President Clinton to increase security at Energy Department facilities by creating an Office of Counterintelligence reporting directly to the Energy secretary. It also would require the secretary to assign at least one person responsible for assessing security and counterintelligence matters at each Energy Department site.

The amendment would require the department to put in place a polygraph program under which employees and contractors would be subject to examinations on a regular basis.

It also would establish a temporary moratorium on visits by certain foreigners to Energy Department labs until 45 days after the date that the department and FBI certify to Congress that all needed security measures have been implemented. It would allow the secretary to waive the moratorium on a case-by-case basis for national security purposes.

To deal with technology transfers to China, the amendment would require the president to give Congress a report on that nation's compliance with the Missile Technology Control Regime, a multilateral pact to limit the spread of missile technology. It also would require the president to give annual reports on what transfers to China have occurred and calls for a series of other regular reports on China's activities.

Congress began investigating the Clinton administration's dealings with China after reports that two satellite companies — Loral Space & Communications and Hughes Electronics Corp. — might have compromised national security in helping Beijing determine the causes of rocket failures in 1995 and 1996. The Cox report found shoddy monitoring of U.S. satellites launched in China.

The Cox-Dicks amendment would establish new procedures to prevent illegal technology transfers during satellite launches in foreign countries. It would require the presence of Defense Department monitors to provide around-the-clock launch security.

Dicks said some portions of the amendment will need to be worked out in conference with the Senate. In particular, he said he wants to ensure that it does not undermine any existing bilateral agreements with China and Russia, and that the work of the nuclear Navy — which already has stringent security procedures in effect — would not be affected by the new provisions.

Although there was decisive bipartisan support for the amendment, some Democrats voiced concerns about the eventual effects of legislation stemming from the Cox report.

"I am fearful that the entire process is leading to a frenzy that will shut down American industry," said Sam Gejdenson of Connecticut, ranking Democrat on the House International Relations Committee. "And if there is anything that would harm American national security, it is our leadership in these very high-tech fields."

Business groups already have begun mobilizing in an effort to block any unduly restrictive changes in the policy that could hamper trade relations with an important overseas market.

Energy Secretary Bill Richardson told reporters he "can live with" the provisions in the Cox-Dicks amendment. But he said he remains concerned about language dealing with the moratorium on foreign scientific visits, saying it could disrupt his agency's international scientific program.

Energy Responsibilities

Richardson also said he is troubled by language in the Cox-Dicks amendment that would require the president to report on whether the department should maintain its nuclear weapons responsibilities. Some lawmakers have called for the Defense Department to assume that task, pointing to the litany of Energy Department security lapses.

House Armed Services Chairman Floyd D. Spence, R-S.C., had planned to offer an amendment to the defense bill to have the Defense Department study taking over nuclear weapons maintenance, but withdrew his proposal and supported the Cox-Dicks amendment.

While the Senate has looked at keeping the nuclear weapons role within the Energy Department, several prominent Republican senators are advocating that the department restructure itself to deal with security. They want to create a new Nuclear Security Administration that would handle all security issues and be insulated from normal departmental bureaucracy and procedures.

At a June 9 Senate Intelligence Committee hearing, three Republican senators said they had made changes to their proposal to try to accommodate the department's objections. The initiative was pulled from the fiscal 2000 defense authorization bill (S 1059), but is expected to be offered as an amendment to the fiscal 2000 intelligence authorization bill (S 1009 — S Rept 106-9), which the Senate could take up as early as the week of June 14.

Jon Kyl, R-Ariz., said the senators added language to clarify that counterintelligence functions would continue to remain the responsibility of the department's counterintelligence director.

Kyl joined Republicans Pete V. Domenici of New Mexico and Frank H. Murkowski of Alaska in stressing that the proposal needs to be put in place immediately to elevate security above other concerns within the Energy Department.

The senators predicted that a forthcoming report on weapons lab security from former Sen. Warren B. Rudman, R-N.H. (1980-93), head of the Foreign Intelligence Advisory Board, will complement their proposal. Rudman is scheduled to appear at a June 22 joint hearing of several Senate committees to present his findings.

"The DOE bureaucracy has proven time and time again that no matter how diligent the secretary of Energy is . . . it can ignore the secretary," said Murkowski, chairman of the Energy & Natural Resources Committee. "As a result, we have seen that past DOE security plans have had the life span of a fruit fly."

Domenici said the new agency would be similar operationally to both the Energy Department's Federal Energy Regulatory Commission, which establishes and enforces electric power transmission and interstate oil pipeline rates, and the Defense Department's Advanced Research Projects Agency, charged with determining which proposals for future projects related to national security deserve further research.

Richardson, however, said he remains adamantly opposed to the idea and contended it would undermine the security reforms he has implemented in recent months. "To set up an agency, a new fiefdom, in the department of fiefdoms is not what I need," he told the Intelligence panel.

Regulating Exports

Although the Clinton administration has supported recommendations by Cox and Dicks to deal with controlling exports abroad, a June 10 hearing on the issue in the Senate Banking Committee illustrated some of the difficulties lawmakers face in achieving that task.

Since the most recent Export Administration Act (PL 103-10) expired in 1994, Clinton has regulated exports through executive orders and individual waivers, with little oversight and only occasional intervention from Capitol Hill.

Cox noted that the penalties under current law are a fraction of what was in the expired act, and he urged quick action to raise them.

Gramm announced that he and Republican Michael B. Enzi of Wyoming, chairman of the Banking Subcommittee on International Trade and Finance, plan to circulate an outline of a proposed reauthorization bill during the week of June 14. The committee will hold three public hearings and try to mark up the legislation June 29.

In the House, lawmakers also plan to meet next week to discuss a timetable to reauthorize the act, said Ileana Ros-Lehtinen, R-Fla., who is chairman of the International Relations Subcommittee on International Economic Policy and Trade. She said her committee has been forced to spend its time "settling turf battles" on whether it still has jurisdiction over the bill.

Enzi said he agreed with a recommendation by Cox and Dicks "that less focus should be on controlling those goods and technologies that have a marginal benefit to national security and more focus should be on the critical technologies." He also said he supports the lawmakers' call for a multilateral regime to involve other countries in ensuring military data does not flow into China.

But Democrats noted that a balance must be struck between national security in controlling "dual use" exports with both military and commercial value and the interests of businesses trying to compete globally.

"The difficulty in achieving that balance is reflected in the failure to enact a permanent reauthorization of the act since 1990," said Paul S. Sarbanes of Maryland, the Banking committee's ranking Democrat.

At the same time, Banking member Richard C. Shelby of Alabama signaled that he wants the balance to be weighted much more heavily toward national security.

"There's been a great deal of talking of balancing the interests of business with the interests of national security," said Shelby, who is chairman of the Intelligence Committee. "However, I believe that begs the question: Is it worth compromising just a little bit of national security for a fatter earnings quarter?"

Past Security Gaffes

Even as lawmakers begin to implement legislative remedies to deal with China, many Republicans are continuing to demand answers from Clinton administration officials about how past security lapses occurred. They are trying to use the Chinese espionage issue as a political weapon against Democrats in the 2000 elections.

Shelby said June 8 that Clinton's national security adviser, Samuel R. Berger, would be asked to appear before the Intelligence Committee to discuss what he told the president about the security breaches. Republicans have accused Berger of not responding quickly enough to reports that China acquired classified data on how U.S. warheads work.

The following day, however, White House spokesman Joe Lockhart said that "as far as I know, there are no plans now for any formal testimony" from Berger — a decision that angered Republicans.

Senate Majority Leader Trent Lott, R-Miss., has drafted a letter calling for Berger to resign. Other Republicans have demanded that Richardson fire top Energy Department employees, but Richardson said he would put off doing so for at least a month while he awaits a new investigation by his agency's inspector general.

House Government Reform Chairman Dan Burton, R-Ind., announced that he will hold a June 24 hearing to listen to testimony from Energy employees and others who Republicans believe may have been intimidated and punished for giving information about security lapses.

Proposal for New Nuclear Agency Gains Momentum

JUNE 19 — Members of Congress are coalescing behind a Republican proposal to better guard the nation's nuclear secrets by creating a separate security agency within the Energy Department.

The proposal to create a Nuclear Security Administration to oversee the weapons stockpile is expected to be offered as an amendment to the fiscal 2000 intelligence authorization bill (S 1009 — S Rept 106-48), which the Senate is likely to consider the week of June 21.

The push to create the new agency has been given momentum by President Clinton's Foreign Intelligence Advisory Board, which concluded in a report released June 15 that the Energy Department has "a cavalier attitude" about security at its nuclear weapons laboratories.

In unusually blunt language, the report said reorganizing the department "is clearly warranted to resolve the many specific problems with security and counterintelligence in the weapons laboratories, but also to address the lack of accountability that has become endemic throughout the entire department."

Clinton in March asked the board, chaired by former Sen. Warren B. Rudman, R-N.H. (1980-93), to study Energy Department security after revelations that China apparently acquired highly classified nuclear weapons secrets from the labs.

The board recommended creating either a semiautonomous security agency within the department or a completely separate agency similar to NASA to run the weapons program. But many Republicans said that only the former idea is now being taken seriously.

"This report makes it inevitable . . . I don't see how this can be resisted in Congress," said Sen. Pete V. Domenici, R-N.M., a co-author of the internal security agency plan, in a June 15 interview.

Energy Secretary Bill Richardson appeared to be softening his opposition to Congress taking the lead on making any changes to his agency. Although he told the Senate Intelligence Committee on June 9 that he did not want to create "a new fiefdom" within the department, Richardson said June 16 that he was willing to work with lawmakers on a way to ensure that security is dealt with in all areas of his agency, not just for nuclear weapons programs.

"We're not that far apart," Richardson told reporters. "I am willing to have an enhanced security structure within the department, but for the whole department."

Although some Republicans have called for the Defense Department to assume the management of the nuclear weapons program, the intelligence board report explicitly recommended against doing so.

Expectant Audience

Rudman is scheduled to present his board's findings June 22 at an unusual joint hearing of four Senate committees — Armed Services, Governmental Affairs, Intelligence, and Energy and Natural Resources. They each have looked into aspects of the Energy Department's security problems.

The intelligence board accused both Congress and the Clinton administration of resorting to "simplification and hyperbole" on security issues within recent months. It found "neither the dramatic damage assessments [by some members of Congress] nor the categorical reassurances of the [Energy] department's advocates to be wholly substantiated."

The effort by Domenici, Jon Kyl, R-Ariz., and Frank H. Murkowski, R-Alaska, to create the Nuclear Security Administration has faced strong opposition from Richardson. The proposal was pulled from the fiscal 2000 defense authorization bill (S 1059 — S Rept 106-50) by Senate leaders May 27 after Richardson threatened to recommend a veto if it was included.

Under the proposal, the new agency would function as a separate "stovepipe" within the Energy Department, insulated from normal bureaucracy and procedures and accountable directly to the Energy secretary. Kyl said the proposal would be redrafted to make it conform to the Rudman panel's recommendation.

Rudman Panel Excerpts

JUNE 19 — The Foreign Intelligence Advisory Board did not mince words in its assessment of security at national weapons laboratories and the Department of Energy (DOE). Here are some excerpts:

"Organizational disarray, managerial neglect and a culture of arrogance — both at DOE headquarters and the labs themselves — conspired to create an espionage scandal waiting to happen."

"Foreign agents could probably not shoot their way past the concertina wires and bolted doors to seize secrets from U.S. weapons laboratories, but they would not need to do so. They could probably apply for an access pass, walk in the front door and strike up a conversation."

"The predominant attitude toward security and counterintelligence among many DOE and lab managers has ranged from half-hearted grudging accommodation to smug disregard."

"Never have the members of the . . . panel witnessed a bureaucratic culture so thoroughly saturated with cynicism and disregard for authority. Never before has this panel found such a cavalier attitude toward one of the most serious responsibilities in the federal government — control of the design information relating to nuclear weapons. . . . Never before has the panel found an agency with the bureaucratic insolence to dispute, delay and resist implementation of a presidential directive on security."

"The Department of Energy is incapable of reforming itself — bureaucratically and culturally — in a lasting way, even under an activist secretary."

Richardson's Plan

As an alternative to the senators' initiative, Richardson has unveiled a series of reforms to improve security. In the latest, he announced June 16 that retired Air Force Gen. Eugene E. Habiger would be his agency's "security czar" as director of a new Office of Security and Emergency Operations.

But even as the Foreign Intelligence Advisory Board's report praised Richardson for his attention to the security problem, it concluded that creating such a position would not be enough to end the agency's enduring resistance to change.

"Under the Richardson plan, even if the new 'security czar' is given complete authority over the more than $800 million ostensibly allocated each year to security of nuclear weapons-related functions in DOE, he will still have to cross borders into other people's fiefdoms, causing certain turmoil and infighting," the report said.

Several Republicans agreed that a stronger legislative response was needed. "Secretary Richardson may have picked a good man, but he's pushing an inadequate solution," said Rep. William M. "Mac" Thornberry, R-Texas, who has introduced legislation (HR 2032) similar to the Kyl-Murkowski-Domenici proposal.

Kyl said Richardson's reluctance to accept lawmakers' suggestions "sounds an awful lot to me like an 'It wasn't invented here, and therefore I'm against it' kind of thing."

Cracking Down

Lawmakers already have taken a number of steps to tighten security in the wake of a bipartisan House committee's report that concluded that China obtained designs from Energy Department labs and other sources that give it the ability to put its nuclear weapons on par with those of the United States.

The Senate's fiscal 2000 appropriations bill for the departments of Commerce, Justice and State (S 1217 — S Rept 106-76) calls for 60 FBI agents to be reassigned "as soon as possible" to field offices in eight cities to augment counterintelligence efforts at the Energy Department's labs.

The Senate's fiscal 2000 energy and water appropriations bill (S 1168 — S Rept 106-58) also boosts funding for Energy's counterintelligence program.

At the same time, Senate Banking, Housing and Urban Affairs Chairman Phil Gramm, R-Texas, unveiled a draft bill June 17 to control high-technology exports to China and other nations that includes stiff penalties for those caught exporting sensitive materials to other nations. The bill increases the maximum penalty to 10 times the value of the export and/or 10 years in prison for each violation, whichever is greater.

Senate Intelligence Committee Chairman Richard C. Shelby, R-Ala., told reporters June 17 that his committee is negotiating with national security adviser Samuel R. Berger on having Berger appear to discuss his role in the Chinese espionage case. Some Republicans have accused Berger of not responding more aggressively to security lapses and have called for his resignation.

Senate Appears Likely To Pass Proposal for New Nuclear Agency

JUNE 26 — Continuing disagreements between Senate Republicans and Energy Secretary Bill Richardson appear to have dimmed prospects for a broad bipartisan agreement to restructure the Energy Department's nuclear weapons programs to improve security.

The standoff between Richardson and the Republicans increases the likelihood that the Senate will approve a strict GOP amendment on security as part of the fiscal 2000 intelligence authorization bill (S 1009 — S Rept 106-48), even though the amendment could lead to a presidential veto. The Senate may take up the legislation the week of June 28.

The GOP proposal would create a

new agency within the department to oversee weapons programs in the wake of revelations that China apparently has stolen highly classified secrets from U.S. nuclear weapons laboratories. But Richardson insists the plan would hinder or reverse a recent series of administrative changes that he has launched.

Richardson told the Senate Armed Services Committee on June 23 that he is "ready to accept a stronger structure" within the department to improve security. But he insisted that the proposed GOP amendment would undermine his authority.

"To say that I am troubled is to put it mildly," Richardson told committee members after reviewing one version of the draft amendment.

Republicans, in turn, accused Richardson of being unwilling to allow Congress to make statutory changes that would ensure that the improvements instituted under his watch remain in place after he leaves.

"They [department officials] are trying to make it more difficult than it is, because they don't want it — let's face it," Jon Kyl, R-Ariz., one of the co-authors of the Senate amendment, said in a June 23 interview.

To accommodate Richardson, Kyl and other Republicans submitted a reworked draft amendment that included a number of changes aimed at clarifying the authority of the Energy secretary. But some Democrats said the amendment continued to raise concerns, leading Kyl to predict that an agreement may not be reached before the intelligence bill goes to the Senate floor.

In an escalation of the clash between the two sides, Kyl joined Sens. Pete V. Domenici, R-N.M., and Frank H. Murkowski, R-Alaska, in issuing a harshly worded statement June 25 charging that their efforts "are being politicized and resisted by the Department of Energy at the expense of national security."

The senators said their concerns were "compounded" by news reports that Victor H. Reis, the assistant Energy secretary in charge of the nuclear weapons stockpile, had been forced to resign on June 25. The senators questioned whether the move was in response to Reis' support of their proposal. A department spokesman said he was unaware of any official pressure on Reis.

Momentum for Change

Republicans had hoped that a report from President Clinton's Foreign Intelligence Advisory Board would give them the momentum to initiate rapid changes at the Energy Department. The report, released June 15, contended that "organizational disarray, managerial neglect and a culture of arrogance" at the department warranted a legislative restructuring by Congress.

The board's chairman, former Sen. Warren B. Rudman, R-N.H. (1980-93), said that more than 100 reports issued over the past two decades by a variety of task forces, internal departmental groups and the General Accounting Office reached essentially the same conclusion. Still, Rudman said, "report after report has been tossed on the shelf to gather dust for a long time."

His board's report called for creation of either a semi-autonomous security agency within the department or a completely separate agency, similar to NASA, to run the weapons programs.

Although many senators of both parties warmed to the idea of a new agency inside the department, the reaction among some influential House members was skeptical.

House Commerce Committee Chairman Thomas J. Bliley Jr., R-Va., and ranking Democrat John D. Dingell of Michigan both cited problems with the board's recommendation for an agency within the department. They pointed to language in Rudman's report citing strong resistance among Energy employees to implementing a 1998 presidential order intended to bolster security.

"We are concerned that those same bureaucrats who are refusing to accept the president's security order would be the ones running this [new] agency with even less oversight than is currently in place," Dingell said in a June 22 statement. "None of us wants to use these serious security problems as an excuse to put the inmates in charge of the asylum."

Richardson, however, told lawmakers at a June 22 joint meeting of the Senate Armed Services, Intelligence, Energy and Natural Resources, and Governmental Affairs committees that he saw "a large patch of common ground" between his views and those of the advisory board. His comments left some lawmakers hopeful that a bipartisan solution was close at hand.

Richardson had objected to an earlier effort by Kyl and other Senate Republicans to create a semi-autonomous agency within the department, saying he saw no need for "a new fiefdom." That proposal was pulled from the fiscal 2000 defense authorization bill (S 1059 — S Rept 106-50) by Senate leaders May 27 after the secretary threatened to recommend a veto if it was included.

Kyl and other Republicans redrafted their proposal in an effort to make it conform to the advisory board's recommendations. The revision called for creation of an Agency for Nuclear Stewardship, to be headed by an undersecretary of Energy, that would be charged with overseeing all nuclear weapons programs, activities at the department's national security laboratories, production facilities and naval reactor sites.

But Richardson told Armed Services members at the June 23 hearing that the new GOP proposal represented a step backward. "We were close yesterday on core principles," he said. "I think this draft simply ignores that."

In particular, the secretary said, the revision "does not clarify the difference between roles and responsibilities of the undersecretary and secretary. It doesn't deal with where science and where environment is in this scheme."

Richardson raised other concerns, including whether the undersecretary's duties would overshadow some of those of the secretary. He pointed to language in the draft amendment calling for all of the new agency's personnel to be "subject to the supervision and direction of" the undersecretary.

"This basically says that the personnel of the agency doesn't report to anyone but the undersecretary," he said.

For More Information

For action on intelligence authorization bill, see p. 14-13.

For inclusion of nuclear labs provisions in defense authorization bill, see pp. 9-19, 9-20

"This is a total undermining of the secretary's authority."

Some lawmakers echoed Richardson's objections. Jeff Bingaman of New Mexico, the Senate Energy Committee's ranking Democrat, said he is worried about the effect that the GOP proposal would have on non-nuclear weapons scientific research being done at the weapons labs. Bingaman's state is home to two weapons labs, Sandia and Los Alamos, which do significant amounts of non-weapons work.

"I have real problems with the notion that we're going to put all of that under the direct and sole responsibility of this undersecretary whose job it is to worry about nuclear weapons," Bingaman said. "And my real concern is, what's that going to do to the possibility of these activities continuing, and flourishing, in these laboratories? . . . The only reason that these weapons labs are world-class is because they do a lot of science other than nuclear weapons work."

But Republicans insisted that their intention was not to affect the non-nuclear work at the labs or to subvert the secretary's authority.

"Secretary Richardson seems to be taking affront to the fact that there would be somebody in charge of nuclear weapons other than the secretary," said Domenici, chairman of the Senate Energy and Water Appropriations Subcommittee. "He shouldn't be worried about that. This amendment says, 'The ultimate authority is the secretary.' "

In an attempt to pacify Richardson, Kyl and Domenici reworked their draft amendment a second time. They added language stipulating that the secretary would be responsible for all agency policies and clarifying that employees of the new agency would still take orders from the secretary.

Nevertheless, Democratic aides said the proposal did not appear to fully address Richardson's concerns. They said the draft amendment could end up creating logistical problems by forcing the secretary to deal with trivial matters as well as leading to micromanagement of the new agency by Congress.

Technology Export Controls

As Richardson and Republicans continued to scrap over the Energy Department's restructuring, another dispute between GOP senators and the Clinton administration held up action on a separate legislative initiative.

Senate Banking, Housing and Urban Affairs Committee Chairman Phil Gramm, R-Texas, has decided to delay until after the July Fourth recess action on a proposal to control high-technology exports to China and other nations, a Gramm spokesman said. Gramm had hoped his committee could mark up legislation on June 29 to reauthorize the Export Administration Act (PL 103-10), which expired in 1994.

But administration officials expressed strong objections to a draft proposal crafted by Gramm and Michael B. Enzi, R-Wyo., chairman of the Banking Subcommittee on International Trade and Finance.

William A. Reinsch, undersecretary of Commerce for export administration, said at the June 23 hearing that the draft would "cripple" the licensing process by requiring consensus among departments and agencies through the Cabinet level before a decision could be reached on an application. He also said a provision to require congressional approval for future export arrangements with other nations would infringe on the White House's ability to conduct foreign policy.

GOP, Richardson Nose-to-Nose Over Nuclear Security

OCTOBER 23 — As a former House member and diplomat, Bill Richardson has successfully struck deals with the likes of Iraq's Saddam Hussein and Haiti's Raoul Cedras. But as secretary of Energy, Richardson has discovered that Senate Republicans pose a tough new negotiating challenge.

Richardson, a Democrat from New Mexico (1983-97), is urging lawmakers to fix what he considers flaws in a recent law creating an agency within his department to oversee nuclear weapons. Angry Republicans, however, will not budge as long as the Energy secretary himself is running the new agency. They want someone appointed who is subject to Senate confirmation.

The lack of available legislative vehicles and the end-of-session time crunch make it unlikely that any more legislation dealing with the department's restructuring will make it through Congress this year.

Republicans became incensed this month when they learned that President Clinton had appointed Richardson to assume the duties as head of the new National Nuclear Security Administration, created Oct. 5 when Clinton signed into law the fiscal 2000 defense authorization bill (PL 106-65).

Lawmakers who created the agency within — but insulated from — the Energy Department said it was necessary to address security lapses at the department's weapons laboratories that may have enabled China to obtain highly classified nuclear weapons information.

Richardson contends the language creating the new agency would undermine his authority as Energy secretary and erode compliance with health, safety and environmental rules.

At a testy Oct. 19 hearing, Richardson asked members of the Senate Energy and Natural Resources and Governmental Affairs committees to make "very modest modifications" in the law.

"The president was so troubled . . . and I am so troubled by the deficiencies in the act . . . that we felt until these clarifications took place that I would serve as his designee in this position," he said.

Intents and Purposes

A number of Republican senators, however, lashed out at Richardson and the administration, accusing them of flouting Congress' intentions. Some of them have advocated cutting Richardson's travel budget or forbidding him to take on the new role.

"It is as if the president has exercised a line-item veto, signing the overall bill but denying effect to certain provisions," said Governmental Affairs Committee Chairman Fred Thompson, R-Tenn. "That approach is unconstitutional."

The anger continued the following day, when the subject came up at a luncheon of Senate conservatives. Among those present was Majority Leader Trent Lott, R-Miss., who said he shared his colleagues' frustrations.

"I'm going to call Bill Richardson and say, 'Before you have any hope of getting any consideration of any modification in the law, you have got to undo what you have done by just ignoring it and saying, 'I'm going to wear both hats here,' " Lott said in an interview. "This is the kind of thing that really makes it very difficult to work with this administration."

Democrats say it would be premature to punish Richardson, noting that most provisions of the Nuclear Security Administration law do not take effect until March 2000.

"We need to step back and take a deep breath," said Jeff Bingaman of New Mexico, the Energy Committee's ranking Democrat. "The Department of Energy and the national security missions are extremely important . . . and they're too important to be treated as a battleground for partisan rancor."

Despite the harsh rhetoric, Sen. Pete V. Domenici, R-N.M., is talking with Richardson about possible solutions. But Domenici warned that lawmakers are unlikely to have enough time this year to make clarifying changes.

"I don't know what other piece of legislation we've got around here that we can do anything about," Domenici said. "And it might be a little premature."

White House Has Few Options, Study Concludes

NOVEMBER 6 — The Congressional Research Service (CRS) has concluded that President Clinton and Energy Secretary Bill Richardson would violate the law if they circumvent a bureaucratic wall between nuclear weapons laboratories and the rest of the Energy Department — a wall that Congress erected in the fiscal 2000 defense authorization bill (PL 106-65).

A showdown over the issue will not come until March 1, however, when many of the organizational provisions of the law will take effect.

Congress put the laboratories into a nearly autonomous National Nuclear Security Administration, which is within the Energy Department but insulated from it except through its administrator, who would report to the Energy secretary. The unusual arrangement was intended to foster tighter security at the laboratories, which have been the scene of suspected Chinese espionage.

Richardson opposed creating the agency, saying it would undermine his authority and erode the laboratories' compliance with health, safety and environmental rules. When Clinton signed the defense bill Oct. 5, he ordered Richardson himself to act as head of the new agency and to assign current Energy Department managers to run its supposedly independent operations.

In the Nov. 1 report, CRS legal specialist Morton Rosenberg said that current law forbids Clinton from leaving Richardson indefinitely in charge of the new agency as a "temporary" appointee in order to avoid seeking Senate confirmation of a nominee for the job. He also said it would be "plainly contrary to the letter and intent of the law" for Richardson to assign current Energy officials to run the new agency.

The CRS report was requested by Rep. William M. "Mac" Thornberry, R-Texas, an author of the disputed provisions and the chairman of a committee created to oversee implementation of the new law.

Richardson insists that he wants some "very modest modifications" to the law. But Senate Energy and Natural Resources Committee member Pete V. Domenici, R-N.M., has rejected out of hand one set of proposals Richardson sent him. ◆

Congress Clears Bill Calling For Deployment of National Anti-Missile Defense System

SUMMARY

Continuing a debate that has raged since President Ronald Reagan unveiled his Strategic Defense Initiative in 1983, Congress passed legislation calling for deploying a national anti-missile defense system "as soon as is technologically feasible." Signed by the president July 22, the bill does not mandate establishing such a system. It commits the United States to arms reduction talks with Russia.

The Clinton administration has argued that its missile defense plan is the most prudent and cost-effective: to develop and test a system now that any time from 2000 onward could be deployed within three years. Supporters of the administration's plan argue that none of the systems now envisioned have come close to meeting minimal requirements. A Defense Department panel headed by former Air Force chief of staff Gen. Larry Welch recently warned that the missile program's compressed schedule, aggravated by testing delays and management problems, carried a high risk of failure. The same panel of outside experts last year warned against a "rush to failure" in the program.

Proponents of speeding up deployment argue that the time lag between acknowledging a threat and actually deploying a system is far too great and that only a mandatory deployment will ensure adequate protection. An independent panel led by former Defense Secretary Donald Rumsfeld concluded in July 1998 that "rogue" nations such as Iran and North Korea could deploy, in as little as five years — much sooner than previously believed — ballistic missiles capable of reaching the United States.

The original, House-passed HR 4 simply declared that it is U.S. policy to deploy a national missile defense system. The Senate added language from its version (S 257) that called for deploying a national system "as soon as is technologically feasible."

Senate Committee OKs Anti-Missile Defense Bill

FEBRUARY 13 — The Senate Armed Services Committee on Feb. 9 approved, 12-7, a bill (S 257) that would mandate deployment of a national anti-missile defense system "as soon as is technologically possible."

One Democrat, Joseph I. Lieberman of Connecticut, who has supported similar measures in the past, crossed party lines to vote for the legislation.

President Clinton opposes any requirement that an anti-missile system be fielded, saying he wants to wait until June 2000 before making such a decision based on an assessment of threats. The White House has said he would veto the Senate bill. National security adviser Samuel R. Berger said technological readiness should not be the only basis for a deployment decision.

Congress tried to set a firm deadline for fielding an anti-missile defense system in the fiscal 1996 defense authorization bill. President Clinton vetoed it. *(1996 Almanac, p. 8-12)*

The administration and many Democrats have shied away from rushing a decision on national missile defense in recent years partly because they fear it could violate the 1972 Anti-Ballistic Missile (ABM) Treaty with Russia, necessitating amendments to the agreement or a possible U.S. withdrawal from the treaty.

The committee rejected, 7-12, a substitute proposal offered by ranking Democrat Carl Levin of Michigan, based on the administration's position. Levin's measure would have based any deployment decision on assessments of existing missile threats, the system's effectiveness and cost, and its potential impact on arms control agreements the United States signed with the now-defunct Soviet Union.

Mary L. Landrieu, D-La., voted "present" on both measures.

Box Score

- **Bill:** HR 4 — PL 106-38
- **Legislative action: House** passed HR 4 (H Rept 106-39), 317-105, March 18.

Senate passed HR 4, amended, by voice vote, on May 18.

House agreed to Senate amendments to HR 4, 345-71, on May 20.

President signed HR 4 on July 22.

House Panel Backs Defense System Without Setting Specifics

FEBRUARY 27 — The House Armed Services Committee approved a bill Feb. 25 calling for deployment of a nationwide anti-missile defense system but setting no date or particulars. The bill (HR 4) may come to the House floor early in March.

Committee Chairman Floyd D. Spence, R-S.C., said the 50-3 vote in favor of the bill reflected the panel's "strong, bipartisan belief that all Americans deserve to be protected against the growing threat of ballistic missile attack."

But the bill's practical significance is unclear. Republicans, with slight Democratic support, have been trying for several years to pressure the Clinton administration to commit to fielding a defense system as quickly as possible.

However, South Carolina Democrat John M. Spratt Jr., who joined Curt Weldon, R-Pa., in drafting HR 4, insisted that he supports it precisely because it sets no timetable. Thus, the measure does not directly challenge the administration's plan to develop a system that can shoot down incoming missiles but wait until mid-2000 to decide whether to deploy it.

Behind this seemingly fine distinction is a long-running and largely partisan battle over how to reconcile deployment of an anti-missile defense with the 1972 treaty limiting such systems, the cornerstone of U.S.-Russian nuclear relations.

The administration, backed by most Democrats, argues that Russian leaders will make large cuts in their missile force, as required by the 1993 START II arms reduction treaty, only if the 1972 Anti-Ballistic Missile (ABM) treaty remains in effect to assure Moscow that its reduced nuclear deterrent would still be effective.

Anti-missile advocates contend that the 27-year-old ABM treaty would impose crippling limitations on a U.S. system designed only to knock down isolated missiles.

In recent months, top administration officials, including Defense Secretary William S. Cohen, and some key Democrats such as Sen. Carl Levin of Michigan, have acknowledged that "rogue state" missile threats are developing sooner than anticipated. They have called for trying to negotiate amendments to the ABM Treaty that would make it easier to deploy a limited defense, while preserving the basic structure of the treaty.

Negotiating With Moscow

However, hoping to obtain Moscow's cooperation in modifying the ABM Treaty, administration officials have opposed a Senate bill (S 257), by Thad Cochran, R-Miss., that calls for deploying a nationwide anti-missile defense system "as soon as is technologically feasible." Since the measure cites technological feasibility as the sole determinant, the administration and its congressional allies argue that Russia would interpret passage of the measure as a declaration of U.S. intent to proceed, regardless of whether changes to the treaty could be negotiated. Thus, they contend, the bill could make it harder to obtain Moscow's agreement to amend the ABM pact.

Twice in 1998, debate on a very similar bill by Cochran was blocked by Democrats.

On Feb. 19, Levin, the senior Democrat on the Armed Services Committee, announced that he would try to block Senate action on the new bill because passage might be seen by Russia as a unilateral U.S. repudiation of the ABM Treaty.

During a Feb. 23 White House meeting between Clinton and congressional leaders, Senate Majority Leader Trent Lott, R-Miss., floated a proposal to move the anti-missile debate beyond the current stalemate.

Acknowledging that any deployment would have an impact on U.S.-Russian relations, Lott suggested the creation of a bipartisan congressional working group to discuss U.S. plans and their implications for the ABM Treaty with members of the Duma, Russia's legislature.

The group would try to explain to Russian officials "what we're trying to do and what the significance is . . . and what could be in it for them," Lott told reporters.

Senate Minority Leader Tom Daschle, D-S.D., applauded the proposal. But it is not clear whether it will go anywhere. For one thing, Senate Democrats want the working group to be a substitute for the Cochran bill, and Lott does not.

But if anything comes of the idea, it will be the first time either chamber of Congress has tried to come to grips with the anti-missile defense issue in a bipartisan way since 1995.

That year, key members of the Senate Armed Services Committee worked out a compromise on anti-missile deployment as part of the annual defense authorization bill. But in conference with the House, the compromise was replaced with GOP-backed provisions that led Clinton to veto the bill. *(1995 Almanac, p. 9-3)*

Congress Passes Bills but Sets No Schedule; No Funds Appropriated

MARCH 20 — The Republican-led campaign for a national anti-missile defense system received a symbolic lift the week of March 15 when the Senate and House passed similar bills calling for the deployment of such a system.

Neither measure would appropriate money, set a timetable or require specific actions. However, proponents insisted that the bills would make development of anti-missile defenses more likely by mandating their deployment regardless of other issues the administration wants to take into consideration.

Mississippi Republican Thad Cochran, who drafted the Senate bill, said that the Senate "grabbed [the administration] by the lapel and shook it and said, 'We've got to get on with it.' "

Cochran's bill (S 257) declares it national policy to deploy a nationwide defense against a limited missile attack "as soon as technologically possible." It was passed March 17 by a vote of 97-3, with Democrats Richard J. Durbin of Illinois, Patrick J. Leahy of Vermont and Paul Wellstone of Minnesota voting "nay." *(Vote 51, p. S-14)*

Facing certain defeat in its yearlong effort to block the legislation, the White House abandoned the effort after the Senate adopted, by identical votes of 99-0, two face-saving amendments. One, by Cochran, declared that the anti-missile program would be subject to the congressional appropriations process, as required by the Constitution. The other, by Mary L. Landrieu, D-La., stipulated that the United States would continue to negotiate nuclear arms reductions with Russia. *(Votes 49, 50, p. S-14)*

In a statement released after the final vote, President Clinton said the two amendments "significantly change" the bill, thus making it acceptable.

But Clinton's claim was derided both by victorious Republicans and by liberal arms control advocates. The arms control supporters warned that the bill might provoke Russia to back away from making large reductions in its nuclear missile force that are required by the already ratified START I nuclear arms treaty and by the START II treaty, which is awaiting ratification by Russia's legislature.

Concern that Russia might backpedal on arms reductions has been the linchpin of administration opposition to Cochran's bill.

"The meaningless amendments to [S 257] merely restate the obvious," declared veteran arms control lobbyist John Isaacs, president of the Council for a Livable World. "There is no policy compromise, only political cover."

On March 18, the House passed, by a vote of 317-105, a slightly more vaguely worded bill (HR 4) which simply declares it national policy to deploy an anti-missile defense. *(Vote 59, p. H-24)*

Growing Support

The large majorities by which the two bills were passed reflect the near unanimity of Republican support and the growing Democratic backing for a system that could shoot down a small number of attacking missiles that might be launched at U.S. territory by a rogue nation such as North Korea.

The administration insists it is moving as fast as possible to develop such a defense. But it wants to defer a decision on whether to deploy the system until June 2000, partly so it can try to reconcile deployment of the system with the 1972 treaty limiting anti-ballistic missile (ABM) defenses, which has been the cornerstone of U.S.-Russian nuclear relations — the doctrine of mutually assured destruction.

Russian leaders insist they will agree to large cuts in their nuclear missile force only if they believe that the continued effectiveness of their remaining weapons is assured by the ABM Treaty's strict limits on a U.S. anti-missile defense. But some of the treaty's limits likely would have to be relaxed to allow even the modest anti-missile defense that is at issue.

While both the Senate and House legislation would repudiate Clinton's plan to put off the official deployment decision, neither measure requires any concrete change in the current timetable for developing, testing and fielding a defense system. Indeed, Sen. Jon Kyl, R-Ariz., a leading anti-missile proponent, warned last December that the administration could co-opt the Senate bill, embracing it and declaring that its own program met the measure's undefined criteria.

Accept and Move On

Shortly before the Senate passed the bill on March 17, senior Foreign Relations Committee Democrat Joseph R. Biden Jr. of Delaware mused ruefully that the bill had become a major test of administration strength only because the administration and its allies had invested it with such great significance. "I wish I had been smart enough a month ago to say to the administration, 'Accept the whole damn thing, and go on,' " he said.

Instead, the White House took a very hard line against S 257 and the similar bill Cochran had offered in 1998, to the point of threatening to veto each measure.

Clinton's argument — echoed by many Senate Democrats — was that, because the legislation would peg a deployment decision solely to the defense system's technical feasibility, it would amount to a unilateral declaration of U.S. intent to disregard the ABM Treaty in order to deploy missile defenses. Thus, the argument went, Cochran's measure would undermine administration efforts to secure Russia's agreement to ABM Treaty amendments that would allow a limited anti-missile defense while preserving the basic structure of the pact.

Last year, 41 Senate Democrats — enough to sustain a filibuster — backed the White House position and blocked action on the 1998 version of Cochran's bill. But the sense that any foreign threat was decades away vanished last summer in two events. In mid-July, a bipartisan panel of experts led by former Defense Secretary Donald H. Rumsfeld warned that North Korea and Iran could deploy missiles able to reach U.S. territory within five years — much sooner than U.S. officials had estimated. Six weeks later, North Korea tried unsuccessfully to launch a satellite using a modified version of its Taepo-Dong missile, nearly powerful enough to carry a small warhead to Alaska or Hawaii.

In January, Clinton beefed up his anti-missile defense program by including deployment funds in the Pentagon's long-range budget plans, for the first time.

At a Jan. 20 news conference, Defense Secretary William S. Cohen cited the Rumsfeld report and the North Korean launch as evidence that a threat to U.S. territory was practically at hand.

While reaffirming the administration's plan to defer a deployment decision on missile defenses until June 2000, Cohen said that, in light of this, the deployment decision would turn largely on the question of whether the system was technically ready for deployment.

Winds of Change

When Cochran introduced his new version of the legislation early this year, the administration and Senate Democratic leaders reiterated their adamant opposition. By early March, however, Landrieu and several Democrats had made it clear that merely stiff-arming the Cochran initiative for the sake of arms control negotiations with Russia was not their preferred approach. Indiana's newly elected Democratic Sen. Evan Bayh said in a March 17 interview that he and others wanted to "toughen up the Democratic approach . . . in favor of defending the country. . . . We can't give the Russians veto power over our national security."

Since four of the 45 Democrats already supported the bill, the defection of one more would give Cochran the 60 votes he would need to break a filibuster. But White House officials and some of their key Senate allies worried that if they simply continued their flat opposition to the legislation, they could not even muster the 34 Democrats they would need to sustain Clinton's threatened veto.

"The bill probably would have passed and, perhaps, would have passed with a two-thirds vote," senior Armed Services Committee Democrat Carl Levin of Michigan later told reporters.

To stave off defeat, the White House and its allies embraced the Cochran amendment on the requirement for appropriations and the Landrieu amendment on continuing the effort to negotiate nuclear arms reductions with Russia.

Acknowledging that the Republicans would not accept an amendment to specifically affirm the value of preserving the ABM Treaty, Levin insisted that Landrieu's amendment affirming a commitment to continued negotiations for nuclear arms reductions amounted to an implicit endorsement of the ABM pact.

It was only because of the ABM Treaty that Russia had agreed to large cuts in its nuclear arsenal, Levin said. Thus by endorsing that goal, the Senate was endorsing the means to achieve it.

Durbin, one of the three who voted against the Cochran bill, rejected that argument. By calling for continued negotiations to cut nuclear arms and for deployment of an anti-missile defense, the bill simply became inconsistent, Durbin said. "I don't know what the negotiating partner would believe."

Lawmakers Clear Anti-Missile Defense Bill

MAY 22 — Proponents of a nationwide anti-missile defense system claimed a major, if symbolic, victory May 20 when the House approved without amendment a Senate-passed bill (HR 4) declaring a national policy to deploy such a system "as soon as technologically possible."

The bill would neither provide more money nor accelerate the timetable of President Clinton's anti-missile development program. But advocates, led by Republican Rep. Curt Weldon of Pennsylvania, insisted the legislation is significant because it repudiates Clinton's plan to defer until June 2000 a decision on whether to deploy the system under development. Clinton is expected to sign the measure.

Getting the bill to Clinton's desk was complicated. The version of HR 4 that the House passed May 20 had been passed by the Senate on March 17 as S 257. On March 18, the House passed an earlier version of HR 4, which merely affirmed that it was U.S. policy to deploy an anti-missile defense.

On May 18, the Senate passed HR 4 after substituting the language of S 257. It was that amended version of HR 4 that the House approved May 20 by a vote of 345-71, thus clearing the bill for the president's signature. *(Vote 144, p. H-54)*

When the Senate initially debated this legislation as S 257, the administration had threatened to veto it, insisting that the decision to deploy an anti-missile system should take into account not only the technical feasibility of the defense but also its cost and its likely effect on efforts to negotiate nuclear arms reductions with Russia.

The defensive system called for by the legislation and under development by the Pentagon is intended to fend off only a small number of attacking warheads, such as might be launched by a rogue nation or by accident.

But to deploy even this limited defense likely would require changes in the 1972 Anti-Ballistic Missile (ABM) Treaty, changes the Russian government vehemently opposes.

However, the campaign for anti-missile defenses has gained momentum in the past year, largely because of growing evidence that North Korea and other potentially hostile states are developing long-range ballistic missiles. Facing certain defeat if it opposed the legislation, the White House dropped its opposition in March after the Senate adopted two face-saving amendments declaring that the anti-missile program would be subject to annual authorization and appropriations, and stipulating that the United States would continue negotiating arms reduction agreements with Russia.

When the Senate first adopted this language in March as S 257, and when the House adopted it on May 20 as HR 4, Republicans ridiculed Democrats' claims that the two amendments softened the legislation's challenge to Clinton's policy.

"The president and his party are seizing on this language to conceal the fact that they have flip-flopped," Majority Leader Dick Armey, R-Texas, said during the House debate.

No Defense Yet

How difficult it may be to make a national anti-missile system work is suggested by the fact that Duncan Hunter, R-Calif., chairman of the House Armed Services Subcommittee on Military Procurement, is wondering if the interceptor missiles should use nuclear blasts to destroy attacking warheads.

The interceptors now being developed would collide with incoming warheads, but this "hit to kill" approach has been hard to perfect even in shorter-range anti-missile systems.

Nuclear-armed interceptors were briefly deployed in the mid-1970s. Hunter said he might hold a hearing on the subject. ◆

President Suffers Defeat With Senate's Partisan Rejection of Test Ban Treaty

Box Score

- **Bill:** Treaty Doc 105-28
- **Legislative action: Senate** rejected ratification resolution, 48-51, on Oct. 13.

SUMMARY

The Senate on Oct. 13 soundly rejected the Comprehensive Test Ban Treaty, a blow to President Clinton, whose administration negotiated the pact that would prohibit further nuclear testing. The treaty would take effect on the approval of the 44 nations with nuclear capability; so far, 26 have approved it.

A top foreign policy goal of the Clinton administration, the treaty would expand an existing ban on atmospheric nuclear tests to include underground tests and those for peaceful purposes. The treaty would be verified by monitoring stations and on-site inspections.

President Clinton signed the treaty on Sept. 24, 1996, and submitted it to the Senate a year later. Supporters hailed the treaty as the most effective means of halting the global arms race.

But Foreign Relations Committee Chairman Jesse Helms, R-N.C., refused to hold hearings until the administration submitted the 1997 Kyoto protocol on global warming and changes to the 1972 Anti-Ballistic Missile (ABM) Treaty. Helms and other conservative Republicans said the test ban treaty would be difficult to implement, would weaken U.S. defenses and would give nations outside the pact an unfair nuclear advantage.

As Senate Democrats in the early fall stepped up their demands that the treaty be considered, Majority Leader Trent Lott, R-Miss., surprised them in early October by scheduling a vote after a minimal number of hearings and 22 hours of debate. Realizing the treaty was doomed, Minority Leader Tom Daschle, D-S.D., and a small group of moderate Republicans asked Lott to put off the vote. Lott said he would withdraw the treaty from the Senate schedule only if the administration promised not to push it for the remainder of Clinton's term. The White House would not agree; Lott went ahead with the vote.

The administration vowed that the treaty was not dead, but analysts and leadership aides in both parties predict that it will not get another chance until a new president is sworn in. Democratic candidates Bill Bradley and Vice President Al Gore support the treaty; Texas Gov. George W. Bush, the Republican front-runner, opposes it.

Senate To Debate Treaty; Ratification Still a Long Shot

OCTOBER 2 — Senate leaders have agreed to begin debate Oct. 8 on a controversial treaty to ban nuclear weapons testing, with a vote scheduled for Oct. 12.

Meanwhile, Armed Services Committee Chairman John W. Warner, R-Va., who has announced his opposition to the Comprehensive Test Ban Treaty (Treaty Doc 105-28), said he would hold three days of hearings on the pact beginning Oct. 5.

Foreign Relations Committee Chairman Jesse Helms, R-N.C., who also opposes the treaty, may hold hearings as well.

Democrats were not entirely pleased with the schedule. Senate Minority Leader Tom Daschle, D-S.D., who had rejected the first Republican offer to hold 10 hours of debate beginning Oct. 6 — it was later raised to 22 hours — said each side will be allowed to offer one amendment.

President Clinton has been urging the Senate for two years to ratify the treaty, though it was unclear whether supporters have the necessary 67 votes. Although all 45 Senate Democrats have publicly supported the test ban, only a handful of Republicans have joined them.

"I think this treaty is bad — bad for the country and dangerous," Majority Leader Trent Lott, R-Miss., said. "But if there is demand that we go forward with it, as I have been hearing for two years, we are ready to go."

The Foreign Relations Committee's ranking Democrat, Joseph R. Biden Jr. of Delaware, acknowledged that it will be extremely difficult for treaty supporters to persuade about 15 uncommitted Republicans to join their cause. But he said he is not ready to concede defeat.

"The only hope I think we have of this treaty passing is . . . to bring it up, and . . . to get as much focused attention on it for it to break through even a little bit to the public, so that my colleagues have to think about whether they're going to vote [their] party or they're going to vote where they are on the issue," Biden told reporters.

Arms Race

Considered by some the Holy Grail of arms control, the test ban treaty has been touted by proponents as the most effective means of halting a global arms race. It has drawn increased attention over the past year after nuclear tests in India and Pakistan that have increased tension between the two countries. *(1998 Almanac, p. 8-18)*

The treaty is intended to ban underground tests, using an international network of 320 monitoring stations to verify compliance. It would allow tests of nuclear weapons components, including the high explosives used to trigger the weapons, as long as no radioactivity was released. It would also allow on-site inspections — on short notice, in some cases — where testing was suspected.

The treaty cannot take effect until it is approved by 44 nations that have either nuclear power plants or nuclear research reactors. Although 154 countries have signed the treaty, only 23 of the 44 nations with nuclear capabilities have ratified it.

Administration officials have lobbied sporadically for the treaty since Clinton submitted it for Senate ratification in September 1997. In recent weeks, they have stepped up their efforts in advance of an Oct. 6 conference in Vienna of treaty signatories to determine what might be done to get non-ratifying members to join. *(1997 Almanac, p. 8-28)*

"We need this treaty now," Secretary of State Madeleine K. Albright said in a Sept. 23 speech to a lawyers conference in New York. "Not because we believe, naively, that signatures on a piece of paper can, by themselves, end the threat of nuclear attack, but because we have understood, rationally, that part of our fight against proliferation is building the strongest legal framework we can."

Biden said the treaty affords the United States an opportunity to show that it takes seriously the prevention of nuclear tests. He pointed to a June poll showing that 82 percent of respondents support the pact.

"Every one of the signatories is looking at us," he said. "If we do not ratify, . . . the ability to get these other nations to sign on diminishes precipitously."

Strong Reservations

But conservative Republicans, led by Helms, still resist the pact, questioning the effects of a test ban on the long-term effectiveness of the U.S. nuclear arsenal.

The United States, which has test-fired more nuclear weapons than any other country, has refrained from testing for the past seven years. Some treaty critics contend that as a result, Clinton's desire to set an example for other countries is misguided.

Until Lott's Sept. 30 offer to bring up the test ban for debate, Helms had refused to consider the treaty in his committee unless Clinton first submitted to the Senate the global warming treaty that arose from the 1997 Kyoto summit and changes to an older arms-control agreement, the 1972 Anti-Ballistic Missile Treaty.

At a Sept. 28 hearing, Helms said the test ban treaty would give Iraqi leader Saddam Hussein "the very protections that he pursued but was denied in his efforts to undermine" a U.N. weapons inspection team. He cited the right of foreign treaty participants to veto the participation of the United States in inspections and the right to restrict access to certain sites.

Although treaty proponents have criticized Helms for refusing to hold hearings on the treaty in his committee, the Foreign Relations chairman responded that the panel has held 14 hearings at which the pact has been extensively discussed over the past two years.

Biden, however, said that none of those hearings dealt specifically with the test ban. "This ain't a fair way to play the game," he told reporters. "This is a cavalier way to deal with something important."

Until last month, Biden said, he opposed bringing up the treaty for debate before extensive hearings could be held. But he concluded that Helms is willing to let the treaty die in the 106th Congress "unless we forced the issue."

Recruiting Challenge

The challenge Biden now faces is persuading skeptical Republicans to support an international agreement that, unlike the Chemical Weapons Convention the Senate ratified in 1997, has not won support from both recent Democratic and Republican administrations. *(1997 Almanac, p. 8-13)*

That challenge was made even more difficult when Warner announced that he opposes the treaty, citing classified documents he has reviewed.

The hearings he announced for Oct. 5-7 will focus on U.S. ability to detect nuclear testing and the Energy Department's nuclear weapons program, with testimony from Defense Secretary William S. Cohen and the Joint Chiefs of Staff.

With Warner likely to influence many undecided senators, supporters must court other influential GOP lawmakers such as Pete V. Domenici of New Mexico. Domenici is the Senate's leading backer of a costly alternative to nuclear testing known as science-based stockpile stewardship, which replaces large-scale tests with micro-explosions and supercomputer simulations.

Domenici, however, has misgivings about both the test ban and the Democrats' desire to bring it to a vote and risk defeat.

"I'm very worried about whether we have sufficient willpower to keep stockpile stewardship going," Domenici said. "We've never gotten it up quite to where it ought to be, although the president's tried very hard."

"But I also am not sure we should vote on [the treaty] and kill it," Domenici said. "The best course of action is to do nothing and keep it there . . . because I think that even though we have committed unilaterally to not doing underground testing, the defeat of this sends a signal that's not so good."

Senators Struggle To Put Treaty Back in Bottle

OCTOBER 9 — The Senate opened debate Oct. 8 on a controversial treaty to ban nuclear weapons testing, but supporters lacked the votes to ratify it and were scrambling for a way to avoid the scheduled Oct. 12 decision.

The Comprehensive Test Ban Treaty (Treaty Doc 105-28), a long-sought prize for President Clinton and arms control advocates, became entangled in a series of partisan political skirmishes that left some senators worried about the potential international implications of its defeat.

But efforts to shelve the vote proved elusive. Senate Foreign Relations Committee Chairman Jesse Helms, R-N.C., one of the treaty's most ardent opponents, insisted that Clinton promise in writing that the pact would not come up again for the remainder of his presidency.

"I want it to be a matter of record that he put all of this pressure on, personal and political and every other way, and he woke up and found out he didn't have anything," Helms said Oct. 6.

The treaty's Democratic supporters, in turn, denounced as unreasonable the demand that Clinton forswear the treaty for the rest of the 106th Congress. Conceding that they remain as many as 17 votes short of the 67 needed for ratification, the Democrats expressed hope that the numbers could change if they are given more time to make their case.

Although Clinton probably would agree to state in writing his wish to put off a vote, said Minority Leader Tom Daschle, D-S.D., the president would not accept "an 18-month gag order on the Senate."

To avert a vote, Daschle said Oct. 8 that Democrats would offer a parliamentary motion to turn from the treaty to other business on the legislative calendar. The motion would be non-debatable and require support from only 51 senators.

"It basically shelves the deliberation on the treaty until we get a motion to bring the treaty back under executive session, but it doesn't encumber us from taking up other matters on the executive calendar," Daschle told reporters.

Change of Heart

The Senate's Republican leadership, which joined Helms in staunchly opposing the treaty, startled Democrats when on Oct. 1 they abruptly yielded to Democratic demands and proposed to schedule a vote after 22 hours of debate.

Democrats complained that the amount of time was inadequate — they compared it to last year's lengthy debate over renaming Washington National Airport for former President Ronald Reagan — but reluctantly accepted after some concluded it might be their best chance of getting a vote during the 106th Congress. *(Airport debate, 1998 Almanac, p. 13-8)*

The Democrats had been pressing for Senate consideration of the treaty in part because of an approaching international conference of treaty signatories in Vienna Oct. 6-8 to determine what might be done to persuade non-ratifying members to join.

Within days of getting an agreement for a vote, however, Democrats were caught off guard by their failure to dent an unyielding wall of Republican opposition.

A number of the Republicans that Democrats had counted on courting said flatly there was no way they could support the pact, especially given what they perceived as Clinton's halfhearted interest.

"Presidential leadership has been almost entirely absent on the issue," said Foreign Relations Committee member Richard G. Lugar, R-Ind., one of the Senate's leading voices on international affairs, who stunned Democrats by saying he would vote against the treaty.

"Despite having several years to make a case for ratification," Lugar said, "the administration has declined to initiate the type of advocacy campaign that should accompany any treaty of this magnitude."

Rushing for the Doors

Faced with such a situation, a bipartisan group of senators began struggling to craft a graceful exit strategy. They said they feared the treaty's defeat would send an alarming and unwelcome signal to other nations — mainly India, Pakistan and North Korea — that either have developed or are interested in developing nuclear weapons of their own.

"We hate to delay it, but frankly, most of us would hate even more to see it defeated — it would be a huge international blow to non-proliferation," said Carl Levin of Michigan, the Armed Services Committee's ranking Democrat, who nevertheless supported GOP efforts to keep the treaty from resurfacing during Clinton's term unless international circumstances change.

Several Republican senators agreed, citing an Oct. 6 Washington Post opinion column written by former Secretary of State Henry A. Kissinger, former Ford and Bush administration national security adviser Brent Scowcroft and former Clinton administration CIA director John Deutch. The three officials noted that the treaty cannot take effect until it is approved by 44 nations that have either nuclear power plants or nuclear research reactors. Although 154 countries have signed the treaty, only 26 of the 44 nations with nuclear capabilities have ratified it.

"The simple fact is that it is premature for the Senate to vote on the [treaty] — at least during the life of the present Congress — because the treaty is not coming into force any time soon whether or not the United States ratifies it," they wrote.

Nevertheless, several conservative opponents of the treaty served notice that they would object to a unanimous consent agreement to put off debate. They said the treaty's supporters would exploit the failure to act by continuing to press their case.

"As [Republican presidential candidate] Steve Forbes would say, 'Stick a knife in its heart and kill it,' " said Robert C. Smith, I-N.H.

Principle or Party?

The protracted haggling over a delay of the vote came during a turbulent week of public statements, rampant rumor and backroom arm-twisting over the treaty's fate.

The resulting political atmosphere may not have been quite as partisan as Clinton's recent impeachment, but nevertheless surpassed the level of the last major treaty considered by the Senate, the Chemical Weapons Convention, ratified in 1997 after negotiations between the White House and Helms. *(1997 Almanac, p. 8-13)*

After failing to muster the support of enough Republicans to back the test ban treaty, Democrats accused Majority Leader Trent Lott, R-Miss., of putting pressure on his caucus to reject the pact. Without that pressure, they argued, the treaty stood a reasonable chance of passing on its merits.

"This unfortunately has become a partisan matter," Daschle told reporters Oct. 7. "There are some [Republicans] who don't want to give President Clinton a victory."

Republicans responded that there was no need for internal strong-arm tactics, given the treaty's numerous flaws. But some of them acknowledged they found it difficult to trust Clinton on such an important international matter.

"If you had a serious president proposing something like this, you would take it more seriously," said Jon Kyl, R-Ariz., one of the treaty's harshest critics. "But given the fact that part of the problem is that the treaty can't be verified, and that this administration has a very poor record of enforcing existing treaties . . . then why would you believe that this is going to make anything better?"

In denying any partisan motivations, Lott said in an Oct. 7 interview that he warned Clinton's national security adviser, Samuel R. Berger, about the implications of Democrats' forcing a vote. At the time, the majority leader recalled, Democrats were threatening to block other legislation if he did not schedule floor time for the treaty.

"I called Sandy Berger a month ago and said, 'Sandy, speak to your friends over here. Don't do this because it's not ready and it will lose,' " Lott said.

The exchange of criticism between

Treaty Provisions

OCTOBER 9 — Nine years after the United States exploded its first atomic bomb in July 1945, efforts were under way to halt such testing. Proposals for an outright test ban have been under discussion since 1957, but not until 1994 were serious talks started on a Comprehensive Test Ban Treaty, which was finished and opened for signatures on Sept. 24, 1996.

Here are the main features:

All Nuclear Explosions Banned

Each nation that is a party to the treaty agrees not to conduct "any nuclear weapon test explosion or any other nuclear explosion," including those for peaceful purposes and those underground.

When Treaty Would Take Effect

The treaty would take effect six months after it is ratified by 44 nations that have nuclear power and research reactors, including these nuclear weapon states and "threshold" states: the United States, Russia, Britain, France, China, India, Israel and Pakistan.

Ratification

A nation cannot ratify the treaty with reservations.

Decision-Making Authority

An Executive Council of 51 member nations, elected from geographic regions by all member nations and based in Vienna, would make most decisions.

Monitoring Compliance

Treaty compliance would be monitored by a network of 50 primary and 120 auxiliary seismological stations, 80 radionuclide stations and 16 radionuclide laboratories that can sample radioactive particles in the atmosphere, and 71 listening stations that could pick up the sound of a nuclear explosion in the atmosphere or underwater. Data would be collected and analyzed by a data center.

Suspicious Events

Nations that are parties to the treaty would be encouraged to resolve possible instances of nuclear explosions among themselves. A nation that is asked to clarify a suspicious event must do so within 48 hours.

Inspections

If the circumstances of an "ambiguous" event cannot be resolved, any party to the treaty may request an on-site inspection, which must be approved by 30 members of the Executive Council. The council must act on any request within four days and an inspection team must arrive within six. Any drilling must be approved by 26 council members.

Frivolous Challenges

A nation found to have submitted a frivolous or abusive inspection request could be fined or lose its power to request inspections.

Test Notifications

Each party to the treaty would notify the council's technical office of any chemical explosion equal to 300 tons or more of TNT.

Enforcement

In cases of treaty violations, a conference of nations that are parties to the treaty could revoke a state's treaty rights, recommend sanctions to the other parties or bring it to the attention of the United Nations.

the two parties led some observers in the U.S. foreign policy community to lament the degree to which the debate had become so politicized.

"No one is taking this as seriously as they should," said Richard N. Haass, a National Security Council aide under former President George Bush who now is director of foreign policy studies at the Brookings Institution, a nonpartisan Washington think tank.

"In the Cold War, there was the sense that arms control was the centerpiece of American foreign policy," Haass said. "That's no longer the case . . . so people are freer to play around with it. It's like Las Vegas; when you reduce the size of the ante, more people come to the table."

To University of Minnesota political scientist Steven Smith, the situation in the Senate reflected "the absence of a personality with credibility on defense issues," such as former Armed Services Chairman Sam Nunn, D-Ga. (1973-97), a frequent intermediary between the parties during the 1980s.

"In the past, you had someone like Nunn who would find a way to bridge differences on major proposals," Smith said. "There's no one like that left."

Getting a Hearing

The discussion over the merits and drawbacks of the treaty mirrored the polarized atmosphere of the political maneuverings.

Both the Armed Services and Foreign Relations committees held hearings on the treaty at which Clinton administration officials made their case for the treaty, while an array of former Reagan and Bush administration officials outlined their arguments against it.

Helms noted in an Oct. 6 floor speech that Secretary of Defense William S. Cohen had objected to limitations placed on nuclear testing in 1992, when he served as a Republican senator from Maine (1979-97).

Cohen, however, told the Armed Services Committee that his objections have been addressed. He said many of the older weapons that had been in the nuclear weapons stockpile and that had safety deficiencies have been retired, and that the threat of missile and nuclear proliferation "is far more acute today" than it was in 1992.

"If the Senate lacks confidence in the scientific means to verify the reliability of our nuclear weapons, I guess I would have to ask the question: Does it follow then that we should return to a policy of nuclear testing?" Cohen said.

The treaty would ban underground tests, using an international network of monitoring stations to verify compliance. It would allow tests of nuclear weapons components, including the high explosives used to trigger the weapons, as long as no radioactivity is released. *(Treaty details, p. 9-43)*

But some senators questioned whether the United States' monitoring capability would be adequate. They cited news reports that the CIA concluded it cannot monitor low-level nuclear tests by Russia with enough accuracy to ensure compliance with the treaty.

"I don't want to take the lid off the nuclear genie," said Republican Gordon H. Smith of Oregon. "If I'm convinced this keeps it in a smaller bottle, I'll vote for it. . . . But I don't want to be sucker-punched, either."

Nuclear Stewardship

As an alternative to explosive testing, the United States has developed an expensive and ambitious program called "science-based stockpile stewardship" that replaces large-scale tests with supercomputer simulations and high-powered lasers at the Department of Energy's nuclear weapons laboratories.

But several GOP senators cited the concerns of former Defense Secretary James R. Schlesinger, who told Armed Services Committee members that the results of the program will not be significant for another decade. He said that the program could not properly substitute for nuclear testing.

"Even with an immense increase in computational power, such as is envisaged, computer modeling or simulation will not provide a perfect replica of reality for a long, long time," Schlesinger said.

In addition, Armed Services Committee Chairman John W. Warner, R-Va., argued that depending too heavily on the stockpile stewardship program could have ominous repercussions.

"Were we to go ahead with this treaty and several years hence, the computer systems fail or the scientists come to you and say, 'No matter how well the computers may work, the [nuclear] components are just deteriorating at a rate we never anticipated' and we pull out, where does that leave the rest of the world that followed the great leader and abstained from any participation on their own initiative in protecting their own self-interests as a nation?" Warner asked. "They're out there naked, and we're gone."

Senate Defeat of Pact Leaves GOP Moderates Groping For Arms Strategy

OCTOBER 16 — The Senate's stinging rejection of a nuclear test ban treaty signifies that any future arms control agreement will require the active — and early — support of a small but influential group of Senate moderates who voted "no" on Oct. 13.

Tactical blunders by the Clinton White House and Senate Democrats put "internationalist" Republicans such as John W. Warner of Virginia, Pete V. Domenici of New Mexico, Richard G. Lugar of Indiana and Ted Stevens of Alaska squarely in the camp of their more isolationist GOP colleagues.

All opposed the Comprehensive Test Ban Treaty because of serious doubts that it could be enforced or that it provided enough assurances for U.S. national security interests. When it became apparent that they could not sidestep or put off a ratification vote, however, they chose to reject it outright, all but scoffing at the attendant worldwide outcry over the Senate's repudiation of a major international agreement.

Yet these lawmakers and a handful of other centrist Republicans believe the United States should play a key role in international agreements. They are now trying to pick up the pieces in the backwash of bitter partisan recriminations. A bipartisan group of senators had dinner together after the vote to discuss how to cooperate.

"We really talked very frankly about how we pull together a very strong bipartisan majority for not only arms control, but for very constructive foreign policy activity," Lugar said Oct. 14 on PBS's NewsHour with Jim Lehrer. "I think that is the majority [view], and it has to be nourished. We have to get together and visit more often."

Sens. Chuck Hagel, R-Neb., and Joseph I. Lieberman, D-Conn., also have begun talks about how to better negotiate such terrain.

The subject of nuclear non-proliferation "is very much alive, and I think embraced . . . by a majority of members of Congress, including the Senate, if it's presented in the right way," Lieberman said at an Oct. 14 news conference.

Hagel, a Foreign Relations Committee member who voted against the treaty but strongly advocated delaying the vote, said he and Lieberman want to find "a way to come at this with some more accountability. This thing got snagged and dragged into the political swamp, and we couldn't rescue it."

Meanwhile, conservative Republicans were celebrating one of their few clear triumphs over President Clinton this year.

After months of careful groundwork, Majority Leader Trent Lott, R-Miss., and Foreign Relations Chairman Jesse Helms, R-N.C., found themselves with a clear shot at two things they despise — an arms control treaty and President Clinton — and the result was never in doubt.

Ratification of the pact (Treaty Doc 105-28) was rejected, 48-51, with only four Republicans voting in favor. *(Vote 325, p. S-65)*

"What today's treaty rejection does say . . . is that our constitutional democracy, with its shared powers and checks and balances, is alive and well," said Jon Kyl, R-Ariz., one of the pact's most outspoken opponents, in an Oct. 13 written statement. "Today's Senate action sends a clear message that the United States will not sign on to flawed treaties that are not in our national interests."

Arms Control Challenges

To the treaty's supporters, such objections should be interpreted as "a wake-up call," said John D. Steinbruner, a senior fellow at the Brookings Institution, a nonpartisan think tank.

The next big challenge for lawmakers on arms control, Steinbruner said, will be amendments to the Anti-Ballistic Missile (ABM) Treaty, which limits the scope of anti-missile systems. Helms has repeatedly called on the administration to submit revisions to that 1972 agreement for his committee's consideration.

The rejection of the test ban treaty "is sort of like an early infection that could kill you, that could really kill you," Steinbruner said in an interview. "Are you going to go to work on it, or are you going to mess around with it?"

If the ABM treaty revisions meet a fate similar to the test ban, arms control experts warned, it could imperil the 1968 Nuclear Non-Proliferation Treaty, which bans the transfer of nuclear weapons to nations that do not already possess them. *(1969 Almanac, p. 162)*

The test ban vote "has raised the prospect of the [non-proliferation] regime gradually unraveling, perhaps beginning at the April 2000 [treaty] review conference, with nuclear weapons spreading widely around the world," said Thomas Graham Jr., president of the Lawyers Alliance for World Security and a former Clinton administration arms control aide.

Opponents of the test ban treaty, however, dismiss the notion that the pact's defeat will have any negative ramifications. In fact, they countered, it should strengthen the hand of U.S. negotiators in future arms talks.

"Our negotiators will be able to say in the future, when they're negotiating treaties, 'We can't agree to that, because we can't get the Senate to confirm it,' " Lott told reporters.

Partisan Twilight

Lott was among the test ban treaty's staunchest opponents, creating an atmosphere where confrontation trumped cooperation.

The treaty aroused deep-seated partisan tensions that had remained buried since Clinton's impeachment trial over his involvement with former White House intern Monica Lewinsky. Helms even alluded to Lewinsky on the Senate floor in his closing remarks against the test ban.

Former Sen. Alan K. Simpson, R-Wyo. (1979-97), said such partisanship reflects his party's mistrust of Clinton, as well as its unwillingness to hand him any major foreign policy accomplishment in the twilight of his final term.

"The bitterness toward Clinton from a majority of Republicans, you couldn't even measure," Simpson said. "Some of them say, 'He has foiled us so many times, we look like a circus act.' "

The White House, Senate Democrats and arms control activists, in denouncing the vote, made it clear that they intend to try to resuscitate the treaty even as they attempt to use its defeat as a political weapon against the Republicans.

"We will continue to force it, in as many ways as we know how," Minority Leader Tom Daschle, S.D., told reporters Oct. 14.

Despite such talk, most advocates agree that action is unlikely as long as Clinton is in office. Several Republican presidential candidates, including the current front-runner, Texas Gov. George W. Bush, have spoken out against the test ban, but some arms control activists held out hope that if Bush or another Republican is elected, the treaty will get another chance. They cited Bush's stated willingness to continue Clinton's seven-year moratorium on nuclear tests.

Until then, the arms control activists promised to exert political pressure on Republicans who opposed the treaty, particularly incumbents up for re-election next year such as Michigan's Spencer Abraham and Montana's Conrad Burns. Vice President Al Gore has joined them, running television advertisements blasting the Senate's action the day after it occurred.

"We will certainly try to make [opponents] pay a price in the coming weeks and months before the 2000 election," said John Isaacs, executive director and president of the Council for a Livable World, one of the groups that lobbied for the treaty.

Nuclear Stewards

Opponents of the treaty said they voted on the merits of the treaty, not the politics. Lugar and other moderates agreed that if lawmakers are to be coaxed into revisiting the treaty, their concern over protecting the U.S. nuclear arsenal will have to be addressed.

In particular, some lawmakers worry about the Energy Department's stockpile stewardship program as an alternative to nuclear testing. The ambitious and costly program uses computer modeling and simulations to verify the safety and reliability of the weapons inventory. Critics of the treaty have said stockpile stewardship remains unlikely to be fully operational for another decade or so.

"Stockpile stewardship is as yet unproven," Domenici said. "We still do not fully understand the aging effects on our nuclear arsenal."

The directors of the three Energy Department weapons laboratories — Los Alamos and Sandia in New Mexico and Lawrence Livermore in California — told senators at an Oct. 7 Armed Services Committee hearing that the nuclear stockpile remains safe and reliable without testing under the program. But some lawmakers said the officials were more equivocal in private.

"Privately, they will say, 'If this [treaty] goes down, it's fine, because we've got a ways to go,' " said Gordon H. Smith, R-Ore., who put aside his concerns and joined Arlen Specter of Pennsylvania, John H. Chafee of Rhode Island and James M. Jeffords of Vermont as the only Republicans to back the treaty.

A related concern for lawmakers was continued funding for the stockpile stewardship program. House members tried to cut the program in the fiscal 2000 energy and water appropriations bill (PL 106-60) as part of an overall $1 billion reduction in the Energy Department's budget, but Domenici and Stevens worked to restore the cuts in conference.

"Senator Domenici and I had to fight like banshees to get the $1 billion this year," Stevens said.

While Stevens said he thinks the United States will need nuclear weapons indefinitely, he said he has no trouble backing a test ban in theory. Nevertheless, he added, stockpile stewardship could be proven to work at a faster pace if Clinton abandoned his argument that any tests should be "zero yield," with no release of radiation.

But perhaps the main stumbling block to arms control treaties in the Senate is verification — how to keep other countries from cheating.

Lugar and other moderate Republicans said the test ban treaty lacked a common definition of an actual nuclear test but contained a process for on-site inspections that would require the consent of 30 members of the treaty's 51-member executive council.

By contrast, Lugar noted, the Chemical Weapons Convention, which the Senate overwhelmingly adopted in 1997, requires an affirmative vote to stop an inspection, not permit one. Lugar, Warner, Stevens and Domenici all supported that treaty — negotiated by former President George Bush — despite opposition from Helms and other conservatives. *(1997 Almanac, p. 8-13)*

Rescue Squad

When other arms control agreements have run into trouble in the Senate, a bipartisan group has been able to rescue them, or at least shelve them for another day.

During the 1979 debate over the SALT II arms-reduction treaty with the former Soviet Union, Warner sent President Jimmy Carter a letter, signed by Domenici and 17 other senators, letting him know of their concerns. The letter became a factor in Carter's subsequent decision to ask the Senate to defer action on SALT II. *(1979 Almanac, p. 411)*

When it became clear that the test ban treaty would fail, it again fell to Warner to seek a deferral. He joined Daniel Patrick Moynihan, D-N.Y., in circulating a letter to Lott and Daschle urging a "statesmanlike initiative" to delay the vote until the 107th Congress. That letter was eventually signed by 62 senators — 24 Republicans and 38 Democrats.

But the rules of the Senate, as well as the tradition of senators' deference to their leaders, helped give the treaty's critics the upper hand in what escalated into a political game of chicken.

After Warner began circulating his letter Oct. 12, Daschle agreed in writing not to push for a vote until after a new president and Congress take office in 2001, "absent unforeseen changes in the international situation," such as renewed testing by nuclear-capable nations. He later agreed to change the language to "extraordinary circumstances."

Under Senate rules, however, Lott had to obtain the unanimous consent of all senators. And treaty critics such as Helms and Kyl told him they wanted to see the pact voted down. Those critics, as well as Lott, had reservations with the vagueness of the "extraordinary circumstances" language.

"You can drive a Mack truck through that," Lott said.

In addition, no matter what their views on delaying the treaty, all of the Republicans — including the internationalist moderates — felt compelled to support a procedural motion by Lott to turn from the agriculture appropriations conference report (HR 1906 — H Rept 106-354) back to the treaty. The Democrats objected, and the Senate returned to the treaty on a 55-45 party line vote. *(Vote 324, p. S-64)*

"We should never be put in a spot where we have to challenge the Republican leader," Warner said. "Our party's going to stick with our leader."

Before he could bring up the treaty for the final vote, however, Lott was subjected to a harsh rebuke on the Senate floor from Robert C. Byrd, D-W.Va., the Senate's guardian of rules and customs. Byrd complained that Lott would not permit him 15 minutes to speak on the non-debatable motion.

After Byrd spent more than 15 minutes criticizing Lott, he shook Lott's hand, and the march toward the treaty's defeat proceeded. Byrd voted "present," for the first time in more than 40 years, citing procedural concerns.

The results left some of the treaty's opponents jubilant, but the older GOP veterans were considerably more sober about the turn of events. An unusually subdued Stevens summed up his feelings in an interview just before he entered the chamber to cast his vote.

"I'm sad," he said. "I'm sad." ◆

Chapter 10

EDUCATION

House Passes Bills To Reauthorize Elementary And Secondary Education Act

Box Score

- **Bills:** HR 2, HR 2300, HR 1995
- **Legislative action: House** passed HR 1995 (H Rept 106-232), 239-185, July 20.

House passed HR 2 (H Rept 106-394), 358-67, and HR 2300 (H Rept 106-386), 213-208, on Oct. 21.

SUMMARY

With the landmark 1965 Elementary and Secondary Education Act expiring, Congress faced the need to reauthorize the law, which governs aid to public schools. Congress provides about $14 billion in annual education funding through the law, which was last rewritten in 1994 (PL 103-382), for everything from aid to disadvantaged and low-income children to arts education, literacy programs, teacher training and bilingual instruction.

The House moved its reauthorization as a series of smaller bills: HR 2, which would rewrite the Title I program; HR 2300, which would set up a 10-state pilot program allowing officials to convert most federal categorical aid into block grants; and HR 1995, a bill to combine teacher training and President Clinton's plan to hire 100,000 new teachers.

The Senate Health, Education, Labor and Pensions Committee planned to move the reauthorization as one large bill. Chairman James M. Jeffords, R-Vt., has unveiled a blueprint, but the committee did not plan to hold a markup until early in 2000.

The House-passed bills incorporate a two-track strategy. While HR 2 would tighten federal control over the $8 billion-a-year Title I program, the teacher training bill and the so-called Straight A's measure would give states more flexibility. The White House supports HR 2, but has threatened to veto the other two bills.

The teacher training bill would roll three programs into annual grants to states and school districts: the $335 million Eisenhower Professional Development program for teacher training; the $491 million Goals 2000 grants for improving the quality of education; and Clinton's plan to hire 100,000 new teachers over seven years and reduce average class size to 18 in grades one through three. Under the bill, localities would have to spend some of the grant money to hire new teachers unless doing so would result in the hiring of underqualified instructors. States would have to ensure that all teachers were fully qualified by the beginning of 2004. Some key Democrats, including George Miller of California, supported the bill.

The Title I bill would provide $9.9 billion a year to improve the performance of low-income and disadvantaged students. The overall bill would also extend a series of smaller programs such as bilingual education.

The House-passed measure would set tighter academic standards for students in the Title I program. It would allow parents of students in low-performing schools to transfer their children to other public educational institutions. During debate in committee and on the House floor, lawmakers decisively defeated proposals to set up pilot programs to test private school vouchers. The bill would freeze the number of teachers' aides hired under the program and increase training requirements. Title I schools would have to issue report cards on their students' performance. Data on student test scores would have to be broken down into subcategories, such as race or gender, in order to detail trends in student achievement.

The House, in a series of amendments, voted to continue the authorization for the $3 million-a-year Women's Educational Equity Act, which was designed to eliminate gender-based discrimination in schools. It added an amendment to reauthorize bilingual education programs, including proposals that would require parental consent before students were placed in bilingual programs, and would give states more latitude to use federal funds for English-only instruction. The Congressional Hispanic Caucus had major concerns about the plan.

The Straight A's legislation was designed as the centerpiece of Republican education efforts. House GOP leaders unveiled the bill with great fanfare in a June 22 campaign-style rally outside the Capitol. The original Straight A's bill would have let states convert a host of programs, including Title I, migrant education, technology aid and vocational education, into block grants. To qualify for the five-year grants, states would have to develop plans to improve student achievement.

When the bill came to the House floor, however, Michael N. Castle, R-Del., a moderate who had cosponsored the legislation, told Republican leaders he could not support it. Castle and other opponents worried that the bill might dilute the effectiveness of federal aid, particularly Title I. While the bill had the support of "family values" groups such as the conservative Eagle Forum and Family Research Council, it was opposed by major education groups such as the National Education Association. In a last-minute compromise, Castle offered an amendment that scaled back the bill from a nationwide initiative to a 10-state pilot program.

Because the law expires in 2000, Congress must reauthorize it. But given public opinion polls showing that voters rate education as a top issue — and that there are wide philosophical splits between Republicans and Democrats — the process promises to be contentious. Key areas of disagreement are likely to be the 100,000-teacher plan and block grants. The Senate, like the House, is not expected to have a majority in support of private school vouchers.

Democrats Decry Lack of Guidelines In House Bill

MAY 29 — House Republicans on May 27 unveiled a teacher training bill that includes a truncated version of President Clinton's plan to hire 100,000 new instructors and reduce average class sizes in the early grades.

The legislation quickly drew fire from Democrats who said it would give school districts too much money with too few guidelines. It is the first in a series of measures to reauthorize the 1965 Elementary and Secondary Education Act, the nation's main education law. It was last rewritten in 1994 (PL 103-382). *(1994 Almanac, p. 383)*

In a break with past years, the House GOP has decided to move the Elementary and Secondary reauthorization as a series of smaller bills, rather than one large package. The strategy allows Republicans to respond to public clamor for improvements in school quality and enables them to point to specific votes on education, which opinion polls show is a top priority for voters.

The teacher training bill would fold a series of programs into broad grants, including funding under the "Goals 2000" program (PL 103-227) to improve academic quality, an existing teacher training program and a version of Clinton's proposal to hire 100,000 new teachers. It would authorize $2 billion in funding annually for five years, 95 percent of which would be passed to local schools. *(1994 Almanac, p. 397)*

States and local schools could use the funds for a variety of purposes including improving teacher quality, reducing class size, hiring special education teachers or implementing programs to provide merit pay and teacher "signing" bonuses.

The bill would give schools broad latitude. While it would require districts to spend money on teacher training, for example, it does not specify funding levels. In a shot at Democratic efforts to impose stringent requirements on instructors, the bill would bar national certification of teachers.

"We don't try to tell schools what [their] approach should be. We don't want to impose any one system that every school must follow in order to upgrade the quality of its teachers," said the bill's main sponsor, Howard P. "Buck" McKeon, R-Calif., chairman of the House Education and the Workforce Subcommittee on Postsecondary Education, Training and Life-Long Learning.

Republicans said they had tried to develop a middle-ground measure that could draw Democratic support. Their May 27 news conference underscored the partisan division on education, however. No Democrats have endorsed the bill, which is cosponsored by House Speaker J. Dennis Hastert, R-Ill., and Majority Leader Dick Armey, R-Texas.

The focus on block grants and local control contrasts sharply with Clinton's own Elementary and Secondary Education Act proposal, announced May 19, that would impose a series of new federal requirements on states. Clinton would mandate that new teachers under the Title I program of aid to the disadvantaged be fully certified and that all newly hired secondary school teachers be certified in their subject.

"It's [the GOP bill] pretty soft. It looks to me like all they're doing is block granting the status quo," said George Miller, D-Calif., a senior member of the Education and the Workforce Committee. "They're handing more money over to the same people who are hiring unqualified teachers."

GOP aides said they would address such complaints when they wrote a Title I reauthorization bill.

How Much Flexibility?

Others complained that the legislation would undermine Clinton's plan to hire 100,000 teachers over seven years, a centerpiece of his education agenda. Congress approved $1.2 billion in the fiscal 1999 omnibus spending law (PL 105-277) as a down payment on the plan, but has not enacted a long-term authorization.

Under the bill, districts would have to use some portion of the funds to hire teachers and reduce average class sizes. Unlike Clinton's plan, the GOP proposal would give schools more latitude to use the funds to hire special education teachers and could obtain a waiver of the class-reduction requirement to meet other goals, such as reducing the number of instructors teaching out of their specialty fields. Schools would not have to use the money to hire new teachers if it meant having to hire underqualified teachers.

McKeon and Education and the Workforce Committee Chairman Bill Goodling, R-Pa., hope to achieve both committee and House floor passage by the August recess. A Senate version has not been introduced.

Compared with other programs covered by the act — such as the $8 billion-a-year Title I program, bilingual education and school safety — teacher training is expected to be one of the less controversial.

Of the $2 billion that would be provided each year under the proposal, a small percentage would be reserved for the secretary of Education to fund activities such as academies that promote alternative certification and professional development programs.

Of the remaining funds, 5 percent would be set aside for states and grants to fund partnerships between colleges and local schools. To apply for funds, states would be required to outline their plans to use the money to improve student achievement and teacher quality, including provisions to hold local schools accountable for student performance.

School districts would be required to maintain current levels of funding to train math and science teachers, with some exceptions. Schools districts that did not establish or meet teacher development goals after two years would have to direct funds through a "teacher opportunity payments" program. Teachers would have the ability to decide how to use funds under this program.

GOP Leaders Push To Convert Aid Into Block Grants To States

JUNE 26 — Republicans, unable to eliminate the Department of Education since they took over Congress in 1995, are now pursuing a new strategy — trying to get around the agency by giving more authority to states.

House and Senate GOP leaders on June 22 unveiled a proposal that would allow states or school districts to convert $13 billion a year in targeted federal education programs into block grants. Governors could spend the money as they saw fit, so long as they improved student performance.

Lawmakers announced the plan campaign-style, using a yellow school bus and a crowd of cheering children as a backdrop as they faced a bank of television cameras.

"Education is No. 1 on the agenda of Republicans," declared Senate Majority Leader Trent Lott, R-Miss.

The event signalled that the GOP, which has traditionally lagged Democrats in public opinion polls on education issues, is determined to respond to voter concerns about the quality of education. It also indicated that the coming debate about school quality will be highly partisan.

As Lott and House Speaker J. Dennis Hastert, R-Ill., announced the proposal, Education Department aides strolled through the crowd handing out statements from Education Secretary Richard W. Riley opposing it.

"This bill provides no commitment to raising standards or improving student achievement and destroys targeting resources to the children who need them most," the statement said.

Many Democrats have lined up behind a Clinton administration proposal for reauthorizing the Elementary and Secondary Education Act (ESEA), last rewritten in 1994 (PL 103-382), that would impose tougher guidelines for federal aid, including instituting disciplinary policies and ending "social promotion" by which students are advanced to the next grade even though they are not academically ready.

Republican leaders said they planned to make their new bill a priority, but have not decided how or when to move it. It is unclear whether the measure will be incorporated into the reauthorization or offered as a freestanding measure.

While introduced as a way to free the states from what many see as onerous federal regulations, the law would cover only a fraction of public school spending. The federal government provides less than 10 cents of every education dollar.

Absent from the news conference was Senate Health, Education, Labor and Pensions Committee Chairman James M. Jeffords, R-Vt. Jeffords said in an interview that he was concerned that the administration plan seeks too much federal control and the GOP initiative too little.

"There are parts of it [GOP plan] I don't have a problem with, but it moves attention from the more important ESEA reauthorization," he said.

The action comes as Congress begins work in earnest on the reauthorization. The House Education and the Workforce Committee, which has decided to consider the legislation as a series of smaller bills rather than one broad measure, plans to mark up legislation the week of June 28 to revamp the teacher training section of the law.

Teacher Training

The proposal includes a truncated version of President Clinton's plan to hire 100,000 new teachers and reduce class size to 18 in the early grades. The GOP version would let states use the money for other initiatives, such as reducing the number of instructors teaching outside their specialty field.

"The core of their bill is to get rid of Clinton's 100,000 teachers as a separate program," said Rep. George Miller, D-Calif.

Democrats are likely to offer a series of amendments during the markup to bring the bill closer to Clinton's teacher hiring plan.

The Republicans' new block grant plan builds on a more modest, bipartisan education flexibility measure (PL 106-25) passed by Congress on April 21.

That law allows states and school districts to apply for waivers of certain federal education regulations as long as they agree to waive state rules as well.

The latest proposal would go further, by letting states or school districts negotiate five-year performance agreements with the Education Department.

States would submit detailed plans for improving achievement. In return, they could decide how to spend money under the Title I program of aid to the disadvantaged, Clinton's 100,000 teachers plan, vocational and immigrant education, Goals 2000 aid for educational quality and other programs.

The proposal would not apply to federal aid to disabled students.

Governors, acting with their states' legislatures, could use the money for any purpose allowed by state law, but could not waive civil right requirements and would have to have a system in place to track student performance. States that did not show improvement would lose their block grant authority.

The proposal moves beyond the "ed-flex" measure in both the number of programs covered and the level of autonomy. Under ed-flex, for example, states must direct Title I money first to high-poverty schools. The proposed bill would specify that each school district would receive at least as much Title I money as in the preceding year, but states would have more power to move Title 1 money between schools.

Opponents of the new plan point to studies showing that the federal government does a better job than states of targeting education dollars to disadvantaged students. They worry that the plan could further erode the effectiveness of Title I. Despite decades of funding, low-income students still lag behind their more affluent peers in academic achievement.

The bill was designed with the participation of GOP governors, some state education officials and the Heritage Foundation, a conservative think tank. The news conference was organized in part by social conservative groups, such as the Traditional Values Coalition, which have a big influence on the GOP education agenda. Sen. Paul Coverdell, R-Ga., has introduced a bill for tax-deferred education savings accounts developed with the Family Research Council.

House Debates Teacher Quality As Block Grants Move Forward

JULY 3 — Republicans scored a preliminary victory June 30 in their push to fund education programs through block grants when the House Education and the Workforce Committee approved a bill that would consolidate teacher training and hiring programs.

The bill (HR 1995), which would authorize about $2 billion a year for five years, would consolidate the Eisenhower Professional Development Program, Goals 2000, and, to the chagrin of committee Democrats, President Clinton's class-size reduction program. Grants would be delivered to states, which would pass the money on to local school districts for professional development and class-size reduction.

HR 1995 was approved, 27-19, with two Democrats, Tim Roemer of Indiana and Rush D. Holt of New Jersey, crossing party lines to support it.

The bill was the first considered to reauthorize portions of the Elementary and Secondary Education Act (PL 103-382), which was last rewritten in 1994 and expires this year. House Republicans said they want to reauthorize the act in sections, allowing a better focus on each part. They also want to convert about $13 billion in targeted federal aid programs into block grants. Democrats said they would prefer to review the law as a whole, to better understand how all the pieces fit.

Democrats unsuccessfully tried to offer their own teacher improvement proposal, drafted by Matthew G. Martinez of California. The proposal, rejected by a party-line vote of 21-23, would have separated funding for class-size reductions from funding for teacher training and improvement.

"The bill reneges on the commitment we made to reduce class sizes," ranking Democrat William L. Clay, Mo., scolded the committee.

Republicans said the bill, drafted by Republican Howard P. "Buck" McKeon of California, the chairman of the Postsecondary Education, Training and Life-Long Learning Subcommittee, would require schools to use some of the money to hire additional teachers to ease classroom crowding.

However, it also contains provisions that would allow state education departments to grant waivers from the requirement if schools can demonstrate that they would use the funds to ensure all teachers are qualified in the subject area they teach. Waivers would also be allowed if reducing class size meant hiring underqualified teachers or if there was not enough space for more teachers.

Democrats also told Republicans that Clinton would veto any bill that does not make class-size reduction a top priority.

The omnibus spending bill passed last year (PL 105-277) set aside $1.2 billion to hire as many as 30,000 new teachers in the first year of Clinton's seven-year plan. Clinton began releasing that money July 1. *(1998 Almanac, p. 2-112)*

More Local Control

While most panel Republicans agreed that smaller classes are generally a good idea, they also argued that reduction is not guaranteed to improve education. A poor teacher instructing a small class, they said, could be more detrimental than a good teacher instructing a larger class.

For that reason, sponsors said they want to give states and local education agencies more control over how the money is spent to improve classroom instruction, mirroring the general theme of their block grant proposal.

"We allow schools to decide if they should reduce the class size, improve the quality of their teachers, or hire special education teachers," said committee Chairman Bill Goodling, R-Pa.

Democrats also contended that the legislation would not require schools to hire teachers of the same caliber that the Democratic proposal would. Democrats would have required schools to use the money to hire teachers "qualified" in the subject they teach, while Republicans would require "certified" teachers, those who may or may not be teaching in their subject area.

"Simply saying a teacher is 'certified' doesn't mean the teacher is qualified," said George Miller, D-Calif.

"We just don't want to troll through a shopping mall to find teachers," said Dale E. Kildee, D-Mich.

HR 1995 also includes a provision that would allow schools to create teacher professional-development programs as long as they meet state requirements. In addition, individual teachers could apply for school grants to attend professional development courses of their own choosing, so long as they, too, meet state standards.

Despite the different approaches on the teacher training and class-size proposal, members of the committee agreed that they were not as far from one another as the partisan votes might indicate.

"We're merely sentences or paragraphs apart. I think we're very, very close," Roemer said.

House Passes Block-Grant Plan Despite Veto Threat

JULY 24 — The House on July 20 voted to fold a trio of education programs into broad grants that states could use for teacher training or recruitment, acting despite a veto threat from President Clinton, who said the bill undercut his plan to hire 100,000 teachers and reduce class size.

The bill (HR 1995) passed 239-185. Twenty-four Democrats, including George Miller of California, a leading liberal on education issues, split with the White House to vote for the measure. *(Vote 320, p. H-106)*

Supporters said it would give needed flexibility to school districts, some of which have already met Clinton's goal of reducing average class size to 18 in the first through third grades. Opponents argued that the proposed $2 billion annual grant was so vague that there was no guarantee that any money would be spent on new teachers.

"This bill guts the class-size program," said Loretta Sanchez, D-Calif.

While the Democratic support was not strong enough to ensure the two-thirds vote needed to override a veto, it was greater than the GOP, or the administration, had expected.

White House officials were puzzled and angered by Miller's stance. Miller argues that provisions in the bill to improve teacher quality are more important than focusing solely on reducing class size, which he says can lead to hiring unqualified teachers.

Democrats scored a political coup last fall when they maneuvered Republicans into adding $1.2 billion to a fiscal 1999 omnibus spending bill (PL 105-277) as the first installment of the seven-year class-size reduction plan. *(1998 Almanac, p. 2-112)*

House Minority Leader Richard A. Gephardt, D-Mo., worked with the White House in the hours before the vote to ensure that most Democrats voted "nay." In a sign of the administration's determination to hold support for Clinton's 100,000 teacher plan, White House Chief of Staff John D. Podesta and Education Secretary Richard W. Riley met with Education and the Workforce Committee Democrats to underscore the president's opposition to the block grants.

Democrats were also supported by groups that opposed the measure, including the National Education Association, the large teachers' union.

Republicans, who lag Democrats in public polls on education — a top priority of voters — were buoyed by the vote. It follows congressional passage earlier this year of a bipartisan measure (PL 106-25) giving states more flexibility to spend federal education funds.

"The president feels very strongly about this, and I think he's hung up on it," said Howard P. "Buck" McKeon, R-Calif. "If the administration hadn't jumped in and weren't so tied to the 100,000 teachers, we could probably have 95 percent [of House members] voting for the bill."

Moving Toward Block Grants

Republicans wasted no time trying to implement the bill, despite the veto threat. A draft version of the fiscal 2000 Labor, Health and Human Services, and Education appropriations bill drafted by Rep. John Edward Porter, R-Ill., rolled the three education programs into a $1.8 billion block grant. Democrats criticized the move.

The House-passed legislation would consolidate the three programs into annual grants to states and school districts. They are the $335 million Eisenhower Professional Development program for teacher training, Clinton's $491 million Goals 2000 grants for improving education quality and the 100,000-teacher proposal.

Localities would have to spend some of the funds to hire new teachers. That provision could be waived, however, if it would result in hiring underqualified teachers or would have a negative effect on student achievement. The grants could also be used for training and other purposes, including merit pay, hiring special education instructors and revamping tenure.

The bill would require that districts spend the same amount of money on math and science education that they would have under the existing Eisenhower program. This provision, too, could be waived.

The measure was the first in a series of bills to be debated by the House to reauthorize the 1965 Elementary and Secondary Education Act, which governs the bulk of annual education spending. The Senate, which will move its reauthorization as one broad bill, is not expected to begin voting until the fall.

Studies have shown that teacher quality is one of the top factors in student achievement. Projected enrollment increases, along with existing efforts in many states to reduce class size, have given rise to warnings of a severe teacher shortfall in the coming decade.

Series of Amendments

Before approving the bill, the House adopted a bipartisan manager's amendment offered by Education and the Workforce Committee Chairman Bill Goodling, R-Pa.

The amendment, worked out with Miller and other Democrats, imposed tougher requirements on states than the original bill. It would require states to ensure that all teachers were fully qualified by the beginning of 2004 and mandate that local school districts report on efforts to raise the performance of poor and disadvantaged students. It was adopted 424-1. *(Vote 316, p. H-106)*

It would ensure that no school district would receive less money than it received in fiscal 1999 under existing programs.

Miller said that the manager's amendment was an important step.

"For the first time . . . we required that teachers be trained in their core subjects, that schools are measured against their ability to close the gap between rich and poor students," he said.

Among other action, the House:

- Voted 207-217 to defeat a substitute amendment by Matthew G. Martinez, D-Calif., that would have authorized $3 billion in annual funds — $1.5 billion for training and $1.5 billion for a separate class-size initiative. It would have directed $500 million to special education training and targeted more overall funding to low-income areas. *(Vote 319, p. H-106)*
- Defeated, 181-242, an amendment by Patsy T. Mink, D-Hawaii, to allow grants for teachers who take sabbatical leave. *(Vote 317, p. H-106)*
- Adopted by voice vote an amendment by Michael N. Castle, R-Del., to increase teacher technology training.
- By voice vote adopted an amendment by Dennis J. Kucinich, D-Ohio, and Robert E. Andrews, D-N.J., to set up a national clearinghouse for entrepeneurship education.
- By voice vote adopted an amendment by Tim Roemer, D-Ind., to create a competitive program to recruit math and science teachers.

House Committee Works Out Deal On Title I Program

OCTOBER 2 — While President Clinton and Republican leaders traded barbs over education spending bills during the week of Sept. 27, lawmakers on the House Education and the Workforce Committee worked behind the scenes on a compromise measure that would reauthorize the landmark Title I program of aid to the disadvantaged.

The still-emerging bill (HR 2), which could be marked up by the full committee on Oct. 5, would avoid divisive issues such as private school vouchers and block grants. Instead, it would build on changes in a 1994 rewrite of the Elementary and Secondary Education Act (PL 103-382) that required states to develop academic standards and tests to measure student progress. *(1994 Almanac, p. 383)*

The legislation would set tougher academic standards for teachers' aides employed under the $8 billion a year Title I program, allow students in poorly performing schools to transfer to other public institutions and require schools to issue "report cards" on their performance. It would set aside 25 percent of any increase in Title I funding to reward schools that close the gap between their highest and lowest performing students.

"The program, though well-intentioned, has not worked," committee Chairman Bill Goodling, R-Pa., said in a Sept. 30 interview. "We have to find a way to make sure the most disadvantaged get the [quality education] they were promised."

Title I is the guts of the 1965 education law. The program provides assistance to school districts based on their population of low-income and disadvantaged students. Despite federal spending of more than $120 billion on the program since its creation, the achievement gap between poor children and their more affluent peers remains stubbornly high.

The bill, which would rewrite Title I and a series of smaller programs, is part of a broader effort to reauthorize the act. Unlike past reauthorizations, Republicans decided to slice the bulky measure into a series of smaller bills.

The House has already passed a separate piece of the reauthorization (HR 1995) to revamp teacher training. Clinton has threatened to veto the bill.

Although Democrats and Republicans have worked out the outlines of a Title I deal, there are still enough problems that the committee has twice canceled briefings on its proposal.

The Clinton administration is also taking a wait-and-see attitude on the bill, with officials saying they want to know the final details before deciding whether they could support it.

A main sticking point is a separate section of the legislation that would reauthorize federal bilingual education programs. The Clinton administration and the Congressional Hispanic Caucus want more liberal program rules than the GOP sought.

One of the big Title I issues was what to do about teachers' aides. Nearly half the money under Title I has gone to hire teachers' assistants. Only 10 percent of aides in high poverty schools had college degrees.

Under the new bill, within three years, teachers' aides would have to have either two years of college education or an associate's degree or pass a competency test.

The Senate Health, Education, Labor and Pensions Committee is still developing a draft of its reauthorization.

While Senate Majority Leader Trent Lott, R-Miss., hopes to bring it to the floor before the end of the session, aides are skeptical of that timeline.

If the House does move a bipartisan bill, it would offer only a temporary respite. After it marks up the Title I bill, the committee will turn to the controversial "Straight A's" bill (HR 2300) that would let states turn a series of programs into block grants.

House Committee Spars Over Title I

OCTOBER 9 — The House Education and the Workforce Committee sparred the week of Oct. 4 over bipartisan legislation to revamp the 35-year-old Title I program of aid to low-income and disadvantaged schoolchildren but recessed without reaching a final vote.

The committee is scheduled to finish marking up the measure (HR 2) on Oct. 13. The bill, which remained mostly intact during three days of intense debate, still faces a slew of amendments.

There is a consensus that Title I must be reworked if it is ever to meet its promise of ensuring that poor children get a quality education. There are philosophical rifts, however, between Democrats who generally want greater federal involvement, and Republicans who favor state autonomy.

"Of all the children who need help, these are the children who need help the most," said Republican Michael N. Castle of Delaware.

Panel Chairman Bill Goodling, R-Pa., and ranking Democrat William L. Clay of Missouri fended off conservative amendments to turn the Title I funds into a "portable entitlement" that students could take to the public or private school of their choice.

The committee defeated Democratic efforts to provide Title I funds only to states that equalized funding or performance between poor and wealthy school districts. Lawmakers adopted an amendment, supported by the Clinton administration, that struck a provision of the bill that would have made it easier to use federal aid for schoolwide improvement efforts, rather than focusing on disadvantaged children.

Setting Standards

The $8 billion-a-year Title I program is the heart of the 1965 Elementary and Secondary Education Act (ESEA), the main federal law governing aid to public schools. It must be reauthorized during this Congress.

The proposed legislation would build on a 1994 rewrite (PL 103-382) that required states to set academic standards and test students to measure their achievement. Even as those changes take effect, the performance gap between low-income students and their more affluent peers remains stubbornly high. *(1994 Almanac, p. 383)*

"We have spent nearly $120 billion on Title I since its inception, yet it continues to be the subject of study after study pointing to its ineffectiveness," Goodling said Oct. 5. "For some reason, Congress and the administration seem to have become resigned to the conclusion that it is just not fair to expect Title I to produce results."

The bill under debate would make a number of changes aimed at improving the quality of teaching and setting more rigorous standards for Title I.

Schools receiving funds would have to issue annual "report cards" on their academic performance. Students in low-achieving schools would be allowed to transfer to other public or charter schools but not to private institutions. States would have to ensure that all segments of the population — minorities, those with disabilities or limited English and the poor — were meeting higher standards.

Teachers' aides, who absorb about half of Title I funds — and often have no college coursework under their belts — would have to complete within three years at least two years of higher education, obtain an associate's degree or pass a competency test.

Aides now are required to have only a high school diploma or equivalent degree. Advocates for children, lawmakers and the administration all argue that the minimal standards have created a situation where students who are the most deprived are being guided by the least-qualified instructors. "If you have poor teachers for poor students in poor schools, then you get poor education," said George Miller, D-Calif.

While lawmakers expect a healthy margin of support for the bill at the end of the process, the atmosphere in the committee room has been far from harmonious. Both Democrats and Republicans complained that the bill was drafted by a small core of members.

"There are clearly provisions in this bill designed to appeal to the liberal instincts of the Democratic Party," said Bob Schaffer, R-Colo., who said the bill contained hundreds of mandates. "Bipartisanship came at the expense of our Republican vision to rescue children from failing schools."

Some Democrats also expressed

frustration, though they acknowledged that the legislation was closer to their initial goals than they had expected. As long as the committee does not make major changes, they said they will support the bill in hopes of improving it down the line.

"The compromise was really between the chairman and the ranking member," said Matthew G. Martinez, D-Calif. "They [GOP members] are terribly angry, and I don't know if they're going to hold together."

In an Oct. 5 letter to the committee, Education Secretary Richard W. Riley applauded the bipartisan effort to reach a compromise, but said he was "very concerned" about a number of proposals in the legislation.

For example, Riley said provisions in the bill setting tougher academic standards were too "rigid" and would force virtually every state to rework their education standards.

HR 2 includes a series of smaller ESEA programs such as education of the gifted and talented, and magnet schools. The committee, which is reauthorizing the act as a series of bite-size bills, had planned to include language reauthorizing bilingual education. But it postponed action on a series of issues including federal funds for "immersion," English-only programs when it became clear that lawmakers would not reach a consensus.

The bill also would eliminate the Women's Education Equity Act, a $3 million program designed to promote gender equity in schools. Supporters, who have resurrected the program from near death time after time since its creation in 1974, are trying yet again.

Seeking Middle Ground

On ESEA so far, the committee has tried to find the political middle ground. It has not gone as far as President Clinton, who advocates more sweeping changes, such as an end to "social promotion" where students are advanced to the next grade even when not academically ready. Nor does it accept the proposals of Republican presidential front-runner Texas Gov. George W. Bush, who has suggested letting students take federal money and move to another public or private school.

"On balance, this is a bill we can support," Clay said. "It rejects the idea advocated by some of turning Title I into a private school voucher."

Immediately after voting on the bill, the committee plans to mark up legislation (HR 2300) that would let states roll a host of programs — including Title I — into block grants. Republicans call it their "Straight As" bill.

At a news conference Oct. 6 before the committee resumed its markup of the Title I bill, Riley and Democrats promised a presidential veto of the block grant measure. For his part, Goodling has implored Republicans to consider Title I in the context of broader efforts such as Straight As and a measure enacted earlier this year (PL 106-25), known as "ed flex," to give states more authority.

The panel has debated 33 amendments. Among its actions, the panel:

- Approved, 24-21, an amendment by Donald M. Payne, D-N.J., to eliminate a provision that would have allowed schools with 40 percent of children in poverty to use Title I funds for institution-wide programs rather than targeting aid to disadvantaged students. The amendment retained the current 50 percent poverty threshold for schoolwide programs.

Though conservatives unexpectedly supported the amendment, Van Hilleary, R-Tenn., on Oct. 6 offered, but withdrew, an amendment to reduce the threshold to 25 percent.

- Approved, 28-16, an amendment by Tim Roemer, D-Ind., to provide $20 million a year for programs to help school districts design different approaches to instruction, thereby giving students and families greater choice.
- Defeated, 13-28, an amendment by Tom Petri, R-Wis., that would have given states the option of turning Title I into a "portable" program, under which funds would follow students to the public or private schools of their choice.

"This amendment provides real power to the people and one of the strongest kinds — real purchasing power," Petri said. Roemer called portability a "'90s focus group phrase for vouchers."

- Defeated, 8-40, a Schaffer amendment to eliminate the tougher standards for teachers' aides.
- Defeated, 17-30, a Schaffer amendment that would have eliminated a provision setting aside 25 percent of any increase in Title I funds to reward schools that make progress in closing the performance gap between disadvantaged and other children.
- Defeated, 21-26, an amendment by Chaka Fattah, D-Pa., that would have barred Title I funds to states unless they certified either that per-pupil expenditures were substantially equal across school districts or that students were performing at equivalent levels.
- Defeated, 22-25, a Martinez amendment that would have altered language in the bill requiring schools to obtain parental consent before placing students in Title I bilingual education classes. Martinez wanted language letting parents opt out of such classes, arguing that such paperwork might have the effect of barring some students from needed instruction.

House Panel OKs Tighter Regulations For Public Schools

OCTOBER 16 — The House Education and the Workforce Committee voted to set tighter federal regulations for public schools — and then quickly moved to provide waivers to states that find them too restrictive.

Voting 42-6 on Oct. 13, the panel approved legislation (HR 2) that would set tougher academic standards and require better-trained teachers under the $8 billion-a-year Title I program for disadvantaged children.

Title I is the core of the Elementary and Secondary Education Act, which must be reauthorized during the 106th Congress. The law (PL 103-382) was last reauthorized in 1994. *(1994 Almanac, p. 383)*

The committee next switched gears to approve a bill (HR 2300) — promoted by GOP leaders and opposed by the White House — that would allow states to convert Title I and a host of other education programs into broad block grants. The 26-19 vote broke down along party lines.

Tim Roemer, D-Ind., said the committee's back-to-back actions — spending four days debating Title I only to quickly pass a second bill letting states opt out of the program — reminded him of the myth of Sisyphus, a Greek legend in which a greedy king is doomed to eternally roll a rock uphill, only to have it roll back down again.

"We've just blown up the rock and the mountain. . . . There's no moral to this story," Roemer said.

Republicans said the block grant legislation, dubbed "Straight A's," would give states needed ability to experiment with federal dollars.

"This may be an opportunity for those we want to help the most to improve [their performance] the most," said Johnny Isakson, R-Ga.

The debate illustrated the political state of play on education. Republicans are torn between the demands of conservatives who want to give states greater control, and the efforts of moderates and Democrats to reinforce current federal programs.

Committee Chairman Bill Goodling, R-Pa., had some difficulty keeping conservatives on board the compromise Title I bill. After winning approval for amendments that would loosen some of the mandates in the original bill, conservatives agreed to support the measure. The block grant legislation was also an important factor.

"Outside the context of Straight A's, the Title I bill would have been problematic. . . ." said Bob Schaffer, R-Colo. "Conservatives can swallow a certain amount of regulation and new mandates as long as there is an escape valve."

Setting Standards

The committee-approved Title I bill would set tighter academic standards for teachers' aides and freeze the number of such aides hired under the program. It would allow students in poorly performing schools to transfer to another public institution, require schools to issue report cards or similar information on their own performance, and set tougher standards for students.

The committee approved a Schaffer amendment to eliminate a provision that would have set aside 25 percent of any new Title I funds for a new program to reward high-quality schools. Instead, Schaffer's alternative would create an optional program for up to 30 percent of new funds.

In a move that angered Democrats, the committee voted 26-21 to allow schools with 40 percent of students in poverty to use their Title I funds for institutionwide improvement efforts, rather than focusing them on disadvantaged kids. The current threshold for schoolwide projects is 50 percent, which the panel had voted to retain during the week of Oct. 4. Four Republicans changed position, however.

The move was a major reason that five Democrats voted against the bill. Donald M. Payne, D-N.J., called it a "sneaky, kind of slippery" ploy.

The panel voted down a series of Democratic amendments, including an effort by Patsy T. Mink, D-Hawaii, to restore the authorization for the Women's Education Equity Act. The bill would repeal the decades-old program, which was intended to ensure equal opportunities for girls.

Major education groups support the Title I bill. They do not back Straight A's, which is supported by the Family Research Council and other self-described family values groups, but opposed by the White House, the National Governors' Association and the National Education Association.

HR 2300 would let states receive federal education dollars under existing guidelines or convert funds into a block grant, with standards for student performance. It covers Title I, technology programs, the Safe and Drug Free Schools program, immigrant aid, vocational education and other programs. Special education is not included.

House Passes Bill Minus Vouchers, Broad Block Grants

OCTOBER 23 — The House lurched toward a middle ground on education policy during the week of Oct. 18, rejecting conservative proposals to create private school vouchers and broad block grants while voting to improve teacher training and set more rigorous standards for student performance.

A compromise bill (HR 2) that would overhaul the keystone Title I program of aid to poor and disadvantaged children passed, 358-67, on Oct. 21. *(Vote 526, p. H-170)*

The action came after the House handily rejected, 166-257, a plan by Majority Leader Dick Armey, R-Texas, to create a $100 million program of federally funded vouchers for private school tuition. *(Vote 521, p. H-170)*

"Can we not reach out a heart and a hand of compassion?" said Armey, who has long been a crusader for vouchers. "That does not strike me as too much to ask."

In a second run at the issue, the House defeated, 153-271, an amendment by Tom Petri, R-Wis., that would have set up a 10-state pilot program in which students could use Title I funds to attend private or public schools of their choice. *(Vote 524, p. H-170)*

GOP leaders were also forced to significantly scale back a companion bill (HR 2300) that would have let states convert Title I and a host of other programs that make up the bulk of federal elementary and secondary aid into block grants.

Republicans had unveiled the "Straight A's" measure, backed by self-described family values groups, such as the Family Research Council, with great fanfare this summer, intending to make it — not Title I — the focus of a public relations message that stressed empowering states and families.

They ran into a problem: They did not have the votes to pass it. Michael N. Castle of Delaware, who had been an original cosponsor of HR 2300, joined other Republican moderates in opposing the bill, saying it could undermine services to Title I students. President Clinton had promised to veto the measure since its introduction. The bill was opposed by groups such as the National Education Association and National Governors' Association.

As a fallback position, Republican leaders agreed to Castle's plan to pare down the measure to a 10-state pilot program. Even after that, the bill squeaked through, 213-208, with five Democrats voting aye and nine Republicans voting no. *(Vote 532, p. H-172)*

"Some conservative members of Congress are just fed up, sick and tired, of one or two people joining forces with the minority and putting them in charge," said Bob Schaffer, R-Colo. "Title I had nothing to do with our message."

Moderates in Control?

House Minority Leader Richard A. Gephardt, D-Mo., called the debate evidence of conservatives' waning clout.

"It's another indication that moderate Republicans are beginning to leave some of their [leaders'] more extreme positions," he told reporters.

Speaker J. Dennis Hastert, R-Ill.,

played down the retreat at a news conference held just minutes after he met with disgruntled conservatives.

"Our job is finding what's doable and what can pass," Hastert said. "Whether it's a full step or three-fourths of a step is debatable."

Title I is just one part of overall efforts in the 106th Congress to reauthorize the 1965 Elementary and Secondary Education Act (ESEA), the main law governing federal aid to public schools. The House is considering the reauthorization as a series of smaller bills.

In the Senate, James M. Jeffords, R-Vt., chairman of the Health, Education, Labor and Pensions Committee, hopes to mark up an overall ESEA bill before the end of the month. He has distributed a draft that steers clear of Title I vouchers. It would authorize $7 billion over five years for early childhood education and give states more flexibility to decide how to spend money on programs, including Clinton's plan to hire 100,000 new teachers.

Although lawmakers came together on HR 2, Congress and the White House are sparring over Clinton's 100,000 teacher plan as part of the fiscal 2000 Labor, Health and Human Services spending bill.

The $8 billion-a-year Title I program is the guts of the ESEA. The program targets aid to low-income and educationally disadvantaged children, serving about 11 million students.

Independent studies have shown that low-income students still lag far behind their more affluent peers, despite government spending of more than $120 billion since the program was created. The main goal of legislators was to close that gap by building on a 1994 rewrite (PL 103-382) that required academic standards and assessments. *(1994 Almanac, p. 383)*

The legislation would allow parents of children in poorly performing public schools to transfer them to another public institution. About 7,000 schools receiving Title I funds have been identified as substandard. It would freeze the number of teachers' aides hired under Title I and beef up training requirements. The 77,000 aides now hired under Title I are required to obtain a high school diploma or equivalent within two years. The bill also would require schools to issue annual "report cards" and would mandate that test results be reported separately for subgroups of the student population based on categories such as race or gender.

"I am happy to say this is not a status quo piece of legislation. We had status quo . . . for the first 20 years of this program, and it was a disaster," House Education and the Workforce Committee Chairman Bill Goodling, R-Pa., said Oct. 20.

Clinton in an Oct. 21 statement called passage of HR 2 an important step but said he would seek changes in bilingual education and other areas.

Vouchers Go Down

Proposals for publicly funded private school vouchers have long been a defining issue between Republicans, who argue families need the power of choice, and Democrats, who say the proposal would bleed needed funds from public schools.

The issue was elevated in September, when GOP presidential front-runner Texas Gov. George W. Bush proposed a limited national voucher plan as part of his wider education proposals.

Armey's amendment would have created a five-year pilot program to provide vouchers for students who were in failing public schools or who had been the victims of school violence.

William L. Clay of Missouri, ranking Democrat on the Education and the Workforce Committee, called the plan a "reckless amendment that would divert funds from poor public schools to parochial schools."

In the end, 52 Republicans voted against Armey's proposal, while three Democrats voted for it. The strong vote means any effort to include vouchers in the ESEA is probably dead for this Congress. The GOP has in recent years lost ground on the voucher issue. A voucher proposal was defeated in the House in 1997 by a vote of 191-228. *(1997 Almanac, p. 7-7)*

Other Issues

The voucher plan was not the only point of contention. Members of the Congressional Hispanic Caucus were upset that a proposal to overhaul bilingual education programs was added to the bill as part of a manager's amendment Oct. 20. They were also angry about a Title I provision that would require parents to give consent before their children could be placed in bilingual programs.

About 1.8 million children with limited English are served under Title I, while about 430,000 receive aid under the bilingual education programs.

The bilingual education provision would give states more latitude to use the roughly $200 million in federal bilingual funds for English-only instruction, though it does not endorse any method of teaching. After three years, students in programs receiving federal funds would be required to move to mainstream classes.

Though Goodling thought the Hispanic Caucus had signed off on the plan, lawmakers said there was no formal agreement.

The National Association for Bilingual Education said the parental notification provisions would create bureaucratic confusion and could prevent some children from getting services.

"When you delay learning, you deny learning," said Delia Pompa, executive director of the association. "This permission is only required for limited English proficient students. We believe that's a civil rights issue."

In other action on HR 2, the House:

- Adopted, 311-111, an amendment by Patsy T. Mink, D-Hawaii, to restore authorization for the 25-year-old Women's Educational Equity Act. Republicans had wanted to eliminate the $3 million-a-year program, arguing that girls were consistently outperforming boys in reading, graduation rates and other indicators of academic achievement. *(Vote 519, p. H-168)*
- Rejected, 208-215, an amendment by Donald M. Payne, D-N.J., that would have retained a provision of current law allowing use of Title I funds for schoolwide improvement programs only if 50 percent of students were in poverty. The bill would cut that threshold to 40 percent. *(Vote 522, p. H-170)*
- Adopted, 243-181, an amendment by Tim Roemer, D-Ind., to increase the Title I authorization to $9.9 billion. The legislation had included an $8.4 billion authorization. *(Vote 523, p. H-170)*
- Adopted, 360-62, a plan by Vernon J. Ehlers, R-Mich., to require science standards and assessments for Title I. *(Vote 525, p. H-170)* ◆

New 'Ed-Flex' Bill Allows States To Grant Waivers from Some Federal Regulations

Congress cleared legislation to give local school systems greater autonomy in how they use federal education money. Debate on the bill was often rancorous, and exemplified how both parties wanted to seize the education debate. The president signed the legislation April 29.

SUMMARY

Modeled on a 12-state pilot program, the new law gives states the power to approve waivers from federal regulations at the local level. Some regulations, such as those concerning health and safety and civil rights, cannot be waived.

In order to qualify, local districts must demonstrate beforehand that they have an education plan in place or are developing one under Title I of the Elementary and Secondary Education Act, the $8 billion federal program to aid disadvantaged students. Schools also will have to demonstrate that existing federal regulations are impeding their ability to raise student achievement, and will have to describe specific, measurable goals for students and schools affected by the waivers. States can terminate local waivers if performance declines for two consecutive years.

In the Senate, Republicans stymied Democratic attempts to use the bill as a vehicle for many of President Clinton's education priorities, including more money for after-school programs and dropout prevention, and an end to promoting students not academically ready to advance. Republicans also pushed, but later backed away from, an amendment that would have allowed schools to use $1.2 billion designated for class-size reduction for educating disabled children instead. The money was in the fiscal 1999 omnibus spending law (PL 105-277).

On the House side, Democrats tried to reduce waivers for Title I programs, which they worried would be diluted by the legislation, and pushed for tighter accountability measures.

Senate Panel OKs More Flexible Use Of Federal Aid

JANUARY 30— Education is emerging as a potential political antidote to the poisonous impeachment debate that has sent Republican poll numbers tumbling and raised questions about President Clinton's ability to lead.

There was never any question that public school quality would be a major issue for the 106th Congress, which must reauthorize the mammoth 1965 Elementary and Secondary Education Act (PL 103-382) — the nation's main federal education law.

But the drawn-out impeachment process has elevated the importance, and visibility, of the issue for both sides.

Republicans, desperate to convince voters that Congress is proceeding with business as usual, plan to quickly move education legislation to the floor.

One of the first measures scheduled is the so-called ed-flex bill (S 280) that would give states greater autonomy in allocating federal education dollars. The Senate Committee on Health, Education, Labor and Pensions approved the measure by a 10-0 vote on Jan. 27.

"We need to get a burst of activity to show that we are attending to the people's business, and we are," Senate Majority Leader Trent Lott, R-Miss., told the U.S. Chamber of Commerce earlier that day.

The House has begun early hearings on reauthorization of the Elementary and Secondary Education law, which encompasses the Title I program of aid to disadvantaged students, bilingual education, safe and drug-free education, and teacher training.

In addition to those two bills, Speaker J. Dennis Hastert, R-Ill., a former teacher, said in a Jan. 28 letter to Education and the Workforce Committee Chairman Bill Goodling, R-Pa., that he was reserving bill number HR 2 for legislation that would roll a series of federal education programs into state block grants. The top House priority, a Social Security overhaul, will be HR 1.

The block grant measure was approved by the House last year.

Clinton, who has been an activist on education since his days as governor of Arkansas, has repeatedly returned to the issue as a refuge from the yearlong scandal over his relationship with a former White House intern. The president made school quality a main element of his Jan. 19 State of the Union address.

Expand Federal Role

In his speech, Clinton unveiled proposals that could greatly expand the federal role in education by tying aid to requirements to end "social promotion," where students are advanced to the next grade even if not academically ready; issue report cards on schools; craft new discipline policies; and improve failing schools.

The president is seeking a new infusion of federal funds in fiscal 2000, including $1.4 billion for the second installment of his seven-year plan to hire 100,000 new teachers.

On Jan. 28, Clinton recommended nearly $1 billion to retrain older workers, combat adult illiteracy and provide jobs to disadvantaged youth.

Box Score

- **Bill:** HR 800 — PL 106-25
- **Legislative action: House** passed HR 800 (H Rept 106-43), 330-90, on March 11.

Senate substituted provisions of its version of the bill (S 280) and then passed HR 800, 98-1, on March 11.

House adopted the conference report (H Rept 106-100), 368-57, on April 21.

Senate cleared the bill, 98-1, on April 21.

President signed HR 800 on April 29.

"We need a national campaign to dramatically increase our efforts at basic adult education and family literacy to help the millions and millions of adults who struggle with basic reading or math," Clinton said at a technological training facility in Oakton, Va.

Many of the tougher education standards proposed by Clinton in his State of the Union address have already been approved by states, though some, such as banning social promotion, are highly controversial.

"The president laid out some general approaches to helping reshape the education system and to move it forward," said Gary Marx, spokesman for the American Association of School Administrators.

"The association would like to sit with the administration and talk about the details and make sure that any program is constructive . . . of what local schools are trying to do," he said.

Despite calls from both sides for bipartisan cooperation, Clinton's State of the Union speech also made it clear that he and the Republicans remain far apart philosophically.

Although the federal government provides less than 10 cents of every public education dollar, Clinton wants to leverage that investment to force states to adopt major changes. Republicans, by contrast, have drafted policies to increase the autonomy of states and local school districts.

At a Jan. 26 Senate Health committee hearing, Democrats and Republicans outlined competing agendas. GOP lawmakers called for block grants and tax-preferred savings accounts for private school tuition and other education expenses. Democrats reiterated their support for Clinton's 1998 proposals to renovate aging public schools and hire 100,000 teachers.

Amid the political positioning were signs that some lawmakers were searching for a middle ground.

Sen. John Kerry, D-Mass., who is considering a run for the presidency in 2000, has been working with Sen. Gordon H. Smith, R-Ore., on an education initiative that would expand programs allowing families to choose their children's public school.

"Last session, we were caught in gridlock when it came to the question of fixing our schools — trapped in a debate of false choices with only education savings accounts and money for school construction on the agenda," Kerry said.

While the larger philosophical questions will play out during the education act reauthorization, the Senate debate on the flexibility bill will provide a preview of the battles to come.

Flexibility As a Framework

The flexibility legislation, sponsored by Sens. Bill Frist, R-Tenn., and Ron Wyden, D-Ore., has to date been relatively non-controversial. The committee passed a similar version last year, 17-1.

The measure would expand nationwide an existing 12-state pilot program that gives the Education Department authority to waive federal regulations so that schools can experiment with new instructional approaches or reallocate funds.

Under the committee bill and the existing pilot program, states must comply with civil rights, health and safety rules. Further, while states would have to suspend state education regulations to ensure local administrators have maximum flexibility, there must be a system of accountability to determine whether the new approaches work.

The waiver authority would not apply to all federal education programs; aid to disabled children would be excluded, for example. It would cover the $8 billion a year Title I program.

"Ed-flex would free remaining states from the bulk of unnecessary and time-consuming federal regulations," Frist said. He said that students in Texas, one of the states participating in the pilot program, posted higher academic achievement scores in districts that had received federal waivers.

Although demonstration waivers have been in effect since 1994, some Democrats caution that evidence about their impact on student performance is inconclusive.

A November 1998 study by the Congressional Research Service found that the majority of initiatives approved under the authority were not new experiments, but to make it easier for schools with a relatively low number of low-income students to receive Title I funding.

Governors' Priority

The flexibility bill is a priority of the National Governors Association (NGA).In a Jan. 25 letter to Frist, Delaware Democratic Gov. Thomas R. Carper, chairman of the NGA, and Utah Republican Gov. Michael O. Leavitt, who is vice chairman, said the pilot program "has changed the culture in states and in school districts regarding flexibility."

Clinton last year assured governors he would push for passage of the bill.

Education Department spokesman Julie Green said the administration supported the initiative but would prefer to see it debated as part of the Elementary and Secondary Education reauthorization rather than as a standalone bill.

Administration officials and some Democrats said they were not sure how Clinton's promise to the governors to relax regulations would mesh with his State of the Union call to expand federal requirements for aid.

Senate Democrats plan to use the measure as a vehicle for a wider- ranging education debate.

Democrats plan to offer floor amendments to implement Clinton's proposal for government-backed bonds to renovate aging schools and funding to hire additional teachers.

House Democrats are still studying the flexibility proposal.

While the markup was an effort to show that the Senate was not distracted by impeachment, it was only partially successful.

The Health committee initially could not muster a quorum because senators were preparing for caucuses on impeachment or attending other hearings and markups, which were also scheduled in an effort to show the Senate was proceeding with business as usual.

Several television camera crews showed up for the markup. They were interested not in the education bill, however, but in how committee Chairman James M. Jeffords, R-Vt., planned to vote on a pending motion to call witnesses in Clinton's trial.

The committee convened to approve the bill only after the impeachment trial adjourned for the day.

No Democrats attended. Aides said there was not an organized boycott, although there was grumbling about the decision to schedule the session right after the Senate vote on a unsuccessful Democratic motion to dismiss the trial.

House Panel, Senate Debate How States Can Spend Federal Funds

MARCH 6, NEW CASTLE, DEL. — For years, Washington poured money into public schools in this working-class town and across the nation hoping disadvantaged children would catch up with other students. They didn't.

Students in low-income schools lag woefully behind in most measures of academic success, despite decades of federal aid and numerous failed strategies. Now, the federal government is pinning its hopes on state efforts to completely remake their school systems.

At the Harry O. Eisenberg Elementary School here, where officials have hung an "Eisenberg Students Love to Read" banner in a valiant effort to spruce up a dingy yellow hall, teachers are preparing students for a battery of reading tests that will determine whether they advance to the next grade.

The tests are part of a broad education law that Delaware, responding to anxious state voters and prodding from the federal government, enacted in 1998 to hold schools accountable for raising test scores.

The state's schools have responded by trying to upgrade their curricula and use more interesting materials in the classroom. State data from initial tests allow administrators to pinpoint which students and schools need additional help.

Before, students in the federal Title I program for the disadvantaged were often pulled out of class for unchallenging, remedial work. Now schools are devoting millions of dollars to after-school and other special activities to help all students, regardless of their socioeconomic position, meet the more rigorous standards.

"In the past, Title I was a pull-out program. . . . What that often meant was you talked slower, louder, and if it didn't work, you did it again," said Mary Wright, supervisor of learning for the Colonial School District, which includes New Castle."This [new system] is not so much a mode of remediation as acceleration."

As Congress this session dives into a five-year reauthorization of the 1965 Elementary and Secondary Education Act, which includes Title I, policymakers are watching Delaware and other states for clues about whether the "accountability" approach is improving the performance of disadvantaged children — the greatest challenge facing the nation's schools.

When Congress last rewrote the law in 1994 (PL 103-382), it required states to set academic standards and test students to measure their performance. In return, it gave states more flexibility to use the $8 billion that the federal government sends to states each year under Title I for schoolwide projects benefiting all children, not just those labeled "at risk." *(1994 Almanac, p. 383)*

In implementing the law, Delaware has merged a dozen state and federal programs into one grant to local districts. Supported by Title I requirements, the legislature established testing of third, fifth, eighth and 10th graders, aided failing schools and is ending "social promotion," in which students are advanced without being academically ready.

Nearly all states now have academic standards, and some, such as Texas, have shown impressive gains. Underscoring the difficulty of turning around troubled schools, other states have backed off of promises of tough action, such as taking over failing schools.

President Clinton wants the federal government to push all states to enact comprehensive plans to improve education. In his Jan. 19 State of the Union address, the president called on Congress to build on the 1994 law by using Title I as a lever to expand the federal role in education of all children, not just the disadvantaged.

While there is no consensus, educators, lawmakers and administration officials all believe additional changes are needed.

Nearly 35 years and $120 billion after Title I was created as part of President Lyndon B. Johnson's Great Society, critics label the program an outright failure, and even ardent supporters call it a major disappointment.

Studies show children in poor schools lag behind students in the most affluent institutions by two grades in math and four in reading. Most Title I funds have gone to hire personnel. Nearly half of the money has been devoted to teacher aides. Of those, only 10 percent in high-poverty schools had college degrees.

"If we had our gifted and talented children [rather than the disadvantaged] being taught by someone with less than a college degree, we would have an uprising on our hands," said Mary Jean LeTendre, director of the Title I program at the Department of Education. Both the administration and Republicans want to limit use of aides.

Reauthorization of the act carries high political stakes, partly because this is the first time that a Congress led by Republicans — who generally oppose federal control over education — has considered rewriting the law. Now, with polls showing that Americans rate education as a top priority, both parties have tried to outbid each other in showing support for public schools.

The Federal Role

Though it is the nation's largest elementary and secondary education program, Title I provides only about 3 cents of every public school dollar spent nationwide. About half of all schools receive funds to hire instructors and buy books and other supplies for poor students and those who lag academically.

Trying to make Title I more effective, Congress has often reworked parts of the program. The 1994 rewrite represented more fundamental change and was based on the theory that the way to raise performance of all students, not just poor ones, was to improve schools as a whole. That meant imposing standards and tests to measure performance. The law was the outgrowth of a national standards movement begun by President George Bush and the nation's governors in 1989.

In his State of the Union address, Clinton raised the stakes by proposing a major expansion of the movement toward standards — and of the federal government's role. He called for ending social promotion, adopting disciplinary programs, establishing performance tests for new teachers, forcing states to intervene quickly to turn around failing schools and instituting federally mandated school "report cards."

To help meet the standards, Clinton's plan would increase money for after-school programs and provide $200 million a year to intervene with failing schools. States could lose Title I and other funds if they did not comply.

"No child should graduate from high school with a diploma he or she can't read," Clinton said. "We do our children no favors when we allow them to pass from grade to grade without mastering the material."

Administration officials point to a March 1 assessment of the 1994 rewrite, released by an Education Department panel, to bolster their arguments. The report, based on data from national studies and select states and school districts, found that nine-year-olds from the poorest schools had improved math and reading scores by nearly a full grade level since 1992. The improvement follows a previous decline, however, meaning students are now at 1990 levels.

Further, the assessment points out that implementation of the 1994 law has been spotty. Quality of state standards has been uneven. Despite Clinton's call for states to intervene with poor schools, about a third of those identified as failing have not received any additional help. Parental involvement, a component of the 1994 act, has not materialized.

The study is controversial, with critics saying that it is impossible to determine whether the 1994 changes, which are still being phased in, were a major factor in the higher scores.

"It's a bunch of bunk. It's the Clinton administration politicizing data," said Victor F. Klatt, education policy coordinator for the House Education and the Workforce Committee.

Some critics believe Title I in its current form cannot improve performance. They cite many competing analyses showing that the program has had only a marginal impact. They charge that federal funding restrictions have hampered state experiments such as charter schools, which are public schools given latitude to experiment with curriculum.

Chester E. Finn Jr., a former Bush education official now president of the Thomas B. Fordham Foundation, a conservative think tank, is blunt. "The program in its current form is 34 years of failure," he said.

Finn advocates turning Title I into an entitlement and increasing aid by billions of dollars, not a typically conservative plan. But his proposed entitlement would be portable, meaning students could use the money to attend the school of their choice. States would decide if the funds could be used at private schools, similar to vouchers, which Democrats have opposed.

Sen. Judd Gregg, R-N.H., a member of the Health, Education, Labor and Pensions Committee, plans to sponsor a portability plan. Republican governors want more flexibility to implement school improvement. For example, Texas Republican Gov. George W. Bush, a likely presidential contender, has aggressively used federal waivers of Title I and other programs to revamp schools in his state.

Republican lawmakers and aides said they do not sense any desire to dilute the 1994 law. At the same time, they do not want the federal government setting national policy on discipline or whether to hold back students.

Adding to the mix, many education groups agree with Clinton's goals, but worry that his plan goes too far.

"To say that stopping social promotion — no matter how you do it — is going to be a condition of receiving Title I aid is shortsighted, to say the least," said Kati Haycock, director of The Education Trust, a nonprofit organization that works with poor districts.

"It basically takes a 'we'll pound the kids on the head one more time' approach, but does nothing [to] the teachers who pass them along without learning something," she said.

The question is how hard Clinton wants to push his education plan and how closely it would be linked to Title I. The White House has not yet released a draft bill.

Controversy Everywhere

Title I constitutes the guts of the education act, which includes dozens of programs, but is far from the only point of controversy. The reauthorization in 1994 spawned more sideshows than a traveling carnival.

Home schoolers tied up lawmakers' phone lines, charging that Congress wanted to force parents to get government teaching certificates. Conservatives tried to bar use of federal funds for activities they said promoted homosexuality. There were skirmishes over school prayer and efforts to make educators identify illegal immigrant children.

Similar fights are expected this year over bilingual education, teacher training and Clinton's plan to hire 100,000 new teachers. The battles began the week of March 1 as the Senate and a House committee took up measures (S 280, HR 800) allowing states to seek waivers of federal regulations governing how they can spend federal funds.

But in some areas, consensus is developing. There is increased willingness by education groups and lawmakers to consolidate some smaller education programs into block grants or something that looks a lot like one.

The Council of the Great City Schools, a group that represents large urban districts, wants to consolidate 29 programs into nine broad categories and give schools ability to transfer funds.

"It's a middle ground between a categorical appropriation and a block grant," said Jeff Simering, the group's legislative services director.

Republicans appear less likely to push for federally funded vouchers, partly because they do not have the votes and partly because they are eager to find common ground. Despite increasing aid in 1998 and backing off efforts to eliminate the Education Department, Republicans got the political equivalent of a schoolyard whipping when they balked at Clinton's agenda.

GOP lawmakers do not want to make the same mistake this year. Some even grouse that the White House is being too stingy. Senate Budget Committee Chairman Pete V. Domenici, R-N.M., wants a 40 percent increase over five years in education spending.

"It took me a little too long, but I finally learned what the president does with a subject like education," Domenici said. "The president has found a way to talk about education . . . to make people think he's doing a lot when he's doing very little."

Delaware Shows the Stakes

Delaware is a microcosm of the political, as well as the policy stakes, in the reauthorization.

In many ways, turning around public schools in Delaware is an easier challenge than in other states. The state is small, and there are few schools with overwhelming concentrations of poverty. The state also has one of the highest concentrations of charter schools in the nation and allows students broad public school choice.

At the Morris Early Childhood Center in Milford, which serves preschoolers through first graders, Principal Nancy Hawpe has been ahead of the national curve. She and district officials have long advocated focusing Title I on early intervention with children and families — a policy change favored by both the administration and Congress.

For example, the 1994 law's increased flexibility has allowed the district to end special parents' nights just for Title I families, which were sparsely attended. Instead schools have moved to more inclusive schoolwide programs.

But in other ways Hawpe's practices would be frowned on by many lawmakers. One of her priorities is to protect Title I funding for six teacher aides who assist in the computer lab, participate in reading programs and, recently, helped students bake "George Washington Carver cookies" using peanut butter they made themselves.

"The more one-on-one you can give children early on, the better they will be later on," Hawpe said.

Hawpe and Judy Spiegel, director of elementary education for the Milford School District, worry that they will not be able to meet the state's tougher requirements, saying students are coming to school with fewer social and educational skills.

While the Delaware law is not fully implemented, state politicians are already discussing ways to toughen it. Democratic Gov. Thomas R. Carper wants to strengthen the state plan to add teacher accountability. Saying that other states pass tough programs, Carper, chairman of the National Governors' Association, is a visible advocate of Clinton's plan.

Carper and other Democratic governors held a news conference with Education Secretary Richard W. Riley at the association's winter meeting in Washington in February to tout Clinton's proposal. The event drew criticism from GOP governors, prompting Carper to say later that he would try to find middle ground.

Taking a different tack is moderate Republican Rep. Michael N. Castle, a former Delaware governor who is chairman of the Education and the Workforce Subcommittee on Early Childhood, Youth and Families. He is part of a group working on education with the Republican Governors' Association.

"I don't really have a problem with anything the president has proposed. The only question is at what level this should be done. Should social promotion be handled at the federal level or state? . . . We really can't become a sort of national school board," Castle said.

The issue could become even more political. Castle and Carper are considered potential opponents in a Senate race in 2000 if Senate Finance Committee Chairman William V. Roth Jr., R-Del., decides not to run for re-election.

Title I Over the Years

When Title I was created, the impetus of federal policy was to expand opportunity for the poor, disabled and minorities. President Johnson, a former teacher, hailed the program as "the greatest breakthrough in the advance of education since the Constitution was written."

Even critics of Title I, initially funded at $1 billion a year, admit that it has focused attention on poor children and those labeled as educationally disadvantaged, a need as current now as when the law was written.

The percentage of children living in poverty remains near the 1965 level. Problems of economic and social isolation have been magnified by demographic changes such as the rise of the suburbs and the resulting concentration of low-income populations in inner cities. That has produced a shift in Congress, where a majority of House members now represent suburban districts.

Advocates of the program say performance of poor children might have been worse without the program. After some early gains, disadvantaged children lagged in the 1980s and early 1990s.

"I don't buy the accusation that the program is a failure. What may be a failure is that Americans have not figured out how to provide a good education for all children," said Jack Jennings, head of the Center on Education Policy, which advocates federal aid. A former staff director of the House Education Committee, Jennings helped write Title I.

One factor that has hampered effectiveness is the way Title I funding is distributed. Due to vagaries in the formula, in 1993-94 about 45 percent of schools with a relatively low percentage of poor students received money, while nearly 20 percent of the poorest schools did not.

The Clinton administration tried to direct more money to poor students in 1994. Lawmakers from states such as California that fare poorly under the formula may try again this year to change it. While the administration's larger proposal failed, the law did direct more aid to schools with the highest concentrations of poor students. Today 95 percent of the poorest schools receive Title I.

Over the years, Congress has tried a variety of fixes. After complaints that Title I was not reaching intended students, lawmakers in the 1970s set up strict rules for spending funds. That led to complaints that the program was too rigid and that children were being pulled out of regular classrooms to do work that had been "dumbed down."

Beginning with Bush in the late 1980s, the federal government shifted its focus from ensuring aid for poor students to raising standards. The 1988 reauthorization let schools with more than 75 percent of children in poverty use funds for schoolwide programs and allowed states to intervene with failing schools.

The 1994 law let schools with 50 percent impoverished children implement institutionwide programs and consolidate federal aid. The number of schoolwide programs has since tripled, to 16,000. The law also required states to adopt academic standards, with tests to measure performance due by the 2000-01 school year. The Education Department has approved 48 state standards and 21 assessments.

Rep. Dale E. Kildee, D-Mich., a senior member of the Education and the Workforce Committee, supports Clinton's plan. But he worries that so many special waivers have been granted for schoolwide programs that it has diluted the effectiveness of Title I. He also has concerns about phasing out teacher aides.

Committee Chairman Bill Goodling, R-Pa., said he plans to focus the reauthorization on improving quality and ensuring that disadvantaged students continue to receive services even if they change schools.

Goodling angered Democrats by proposing to divide Title I and other programs into smaller pieces rather than moving the elementary and secondary reauthorization in one bill.

He criticized Clinton's proposals as impinging on state and local control.

The Education Department panel that evaluated Title I recommended that Congress focus the program on schools with 75 percent of children in poverty, increase after-school aid, improve teacher training and phase out use of teacher aides.

"The first, and our main, message is we need to stay the course with standards-based education," said Valena Plisko, of the Education Department's Elementary and Secondary Education Division, who headed the evaluation.

A recent report from the Citizens' Commission on Civil Rights, a nonprofit group advocating equal opportunity, said the Education Department had not been aggressive enough in implementing the law.

In Delaware, one school trying to chart a course to higher achievement is the Eisenberg Elementary School in the New Castle suburb of Wilmington, which serves grades three to five. About 63 percent of students are eligible for free- or reduced-price school lunches, the indicator used to measure a school's poverty rate.

Eisenberg, due to be renovated next year, is using Title I funds for general curriculum development and materials, moving away from hiring teacher aides.

Using detailed data from statewide exams last year, the district can now identify students who need extra help.

In the past, Delaware allocated Title I aid based on paltry data and an educated guess, said Ron Houston, director of school improvement and state Title I coordinator. Delaware receives about $18 million in annual Title I funds.

But the differences in approach between the Eisenberg and Morris schools show why it is so difficult to measure Title I's impact, even under a centrally directed state system.

About 11 percent of the 545 Eisenberg students this year have been placed in after-school reading programs. Principal Dorothy Linn and others argue that the effort is quantitatively different from previous remediation.

Despite Linn's efforts, realities at the school provide another reason the success of Title I will be hard to gauge here, even though the 1998 state law, which requires 10th graders to pass exams beginning in 2000 in order to graduate from high school, is forcing intense study and effort.

That is simply because 35 percent to 40 percent of Eisenberg children will move within the year, a level that is not unusual for students from poor families. That makes it hard to provide the long-term aid students need.

Still, experts argue that the success of some states shows change is possible. "The bottom line needs to be: Are poor kids learning more?" said The Education Trust's Haycock. "The news is hopeful, but by no means yet conclusive."

Both Chambers Pass 'Ed-Flex' Bills By Big Margins

MARCH 13 — Based solely on the lopsided vote tallies, House and Senate passage of bills on March 11 that would give states more freedom to spend federal education dollars seemed a promising sign that comity was making a comeback in Congress.

In reality, however, the ferocious political sparring that led to final approval was a clear warning of intense battles ahead, as both parties jockey for position on an issue that polls show is a top priority of voters.

After more than a week of acrimonious debate, the Senate, voting 98-1, passed the "ed-flex" legislation (S 280), with only Paul Wellstone, D-Minn., voting no. *(Senate vote 48, p. S-13)*

The House passed its version (HR 800) by 330-90. Opposition — which included most members of the Congressional Black Caucus — came from Democrats concerned that the bill could undermine federal programs for disadvantaged students. *(House vote 41, p. H-18)*

The bill now heads to a House-Senate conference. President Clinton previously endorsed the legislation. But he and Senate Democrats have raised concerns about a Republican amendment that would rewrite part of a fiscal 1999 omnibus spending law (PL 105-277) that provided $1.2 billion to hire new teachers.

Republicans had hoped to hustle the legislation through Congress in an effort to accomplish two goals: move past the partisan impeachment debate and burnish their credentials on education.

Senate Democrats blocked action until Republicans agreed to allow debate on a series of amendments designed to implement Clinton's broader education agenda. The partisan wrangling included a series of failed votes to invoke cloture, or limit debate, and a Republican news conference replete with signs that said, "Better Education Held Hostage! Free Ed-Flex Now."

On largely party-line votes, the Senate on March 11 effectively killed Democratic amendments that would have authorized $11.4 billion over six years for Clinton's plan to hire 100,000 teachers and reduce class size, expand after-school aid, increase dropout prevention assistance, and end social promotion, in which students are advanced to the next grade even though they are not academically ready.

Further, the Senate, by a vote of 60-39, passed an amendment by Majority Leader Trent Lott, R-Miss., that would give states the option of using the $1.2 billion in the omnibus spending law to fund education programs for the disabled rather than hiring new teachers. *(Senate vote 40, p. S-12)*

"The Republicans have pulled an anti-education hat trick. They have effectively fought and defeated the guarantee for smaller classrooms, they've repealed the action taken last fall . . . and have pitted disabled children against other children in local communities," said Sen. Edward M. Kennedy, D-Mass.

Clinton, in a March 10 statement, said he would "vigorously oppose" any Republican effort to revamp last fall's teacher plan.

Republicans have increased funding over the past several years under a 1975 law (PL 94-142) that guaranteed disabled individuals a free and appropriate public education. They pointed out that Congress was still far short of meeting its commitment to provide 40 percent of the cost of special education, an enormous expense for many school districts. *(1975 Almanac, p. 641)*

Saying it would be "very foolish" for the administration to veto the bill over the Lott amendment, Sen. Judd Gregg, R-N.H., charged that "the administration has been very irresponsible in special education." The federal government pays about 10 percent of special education costs.

The issue took on new urgency for the GOP after a March 3 Supreme Court decision that appeared to expand the scope of the law by requiring schools to provide intensive medical care for disabled children during the school day.

The partisan divisions were not confined to the Senate. The House operated under a rule for debate that prevented Rep. William L. Clay, D-Mo., and Rep. David Wu, D-Ore., from offering an amendment to add the 100,000 teacher authorization. Other Democratic amendments that would have required states to meet tougher standards for student performance in order to receive waivers were also defeated.

"This bill authorizes states to arbitrarily and capriciously waive provisions of important federal education programs," complained Clay, ranking Democrat on the House Education and the Workforce Committee.

The ed-flex debate was a clear sign of the deep divisions between Democrats, who want to expand the federal role in education, and Republicans, who have proposed more funding but fewer federal strings.

"They don't really want to do this bill," said Rep. John A. Boehner, R-Ohio, citing the House Democratic amendments. "We do policy and we do politics. This is politics."

The arguments are sure to play out again later this session, as Congress reauthorizes the mammoth 1965 Elementary and Secondary Education Act, the main law governing federal education aid.

Minimal Impact Expected

Despite the overcharged rhetoric from both sides, ed-flex sponsors conceded that the bill would likely have only a minimal impact on national education policy.

Both the House and Senate bills would expand nationwide a current 12-state pilot program that allows governors to seek waivers of federal rules in order to try innovative approaches to education.

The Senate bill was sponsored by Bill Frist, R-Tenn., and Ron Wyden, D-Ore. The House bill was introduced by Michael N. Castle, R-Del., and Tim Roemer, D-Ind. Clinton has endorsed the legislation, which is a priority of the National Governors' Association.

The legislation would apply to about $11 billion in annual elementary and secondary education funding, including the $8 billion Title I program of aid to the disadvantaged, teacher training funds, vocational education, technology assistance and immigrant education.

To receive federal waivers, states would first have to agree to waive their own regulations and develop accountability standards to measure student progress. Further, states would have to continue to comply with health, safety and civil rights rules.

"This ed-flex bill is an old value and a new idea," Roemer said on March 10. "The old value is local control. The new idea is flexibility. The status quo has not worked."

Some states, such as Texas, have aggressively used the pilot program to revamp teacher training and programs for the disadvantaged. Independent evaluations have shown improved test scores for Texas students.

Other states in the pilot program have made little use of it. Evaluations by the General Accounting Office and Congressional Research Service found many waivers were based on vague promises to improve education.

Further, the bulk of the waivers granted to date have been to allow schools in danger of losing Title I funds to continue in the program, or to allow schools with a relatively small number of low-income students to use Title I for schoolwide programs, rather than targeting funds on the disadvantaged.

The Congressional Black Caucus in a March 11 statement said the bill would dilute the Title I program. "The bill is being pushed at stampede speed for seemingly little reason other than the desire to establish a legislative precedent for block grants," said Rep. James E. Clyburn, D-S.C., chairman of the caucus.

In response to the complaints, House and Senate sponsors added more detailed requirements to the bill, such as a House provision ending waivers if student performance declined two years in a row. Some Democrats wanted to go further.

The House by a 196-228 vote on March 10 defeated an amendment by George Miller, D-Calif., and Dale E. Kildee, D-Mich., that would have required states to set specific goals for reducing achievement gaps between disadvantaged students and their peers and to have a detailed plan to assess performance. The amendment was based on Texas policies. *(House vote 39, p. H-18)*

On March 11, the House also defeated, 195-223, an amendment by Rep. Robert C. Scott, D-Va., and Rep. Donald M. Payne, D-N.J., that would have barred waivers for schoolwide Title I programs unless at least 35 percent of students were in poverty. Under current law, schools must have 50 percent of students in poverty to run schoolwide programs. *(House vote 40, p. H-18)*

In other action the Senate:

- By a 59-40 vote, tabled, or killed, an amendment by Dianne Feinstein, D-Calif., that would have authorized $500 million in annual grants in fiscal 2000-04 for remedial education programs and early intervention. To receive funding, states would have had to adopt policies ending social promotion. The amendment would have also required schools to issue detailed report cards on student achievement, class size and other quality indicators. *(Senate vote 46, p. S-13)*

In a sign that Clinton's controversial social promotion plan may have difficulty within his own party, several Democrats voted to table the plan.

- By a 55-44 vote, the Senate tabled an amendment by Patty Murray, D-Wash., to implement Clinton's class-size plan. *(Senate vote 41, p. S-13)*
- By a 55-44 vote, the Senate tabled an amendment by Barbara Boxer, D-Calif., that would have increased funding for an existing network of after-school programs to $600 million a year. *(Senate vote 44, p. S-13)*
- By a 55-44 vote, the Senate tabled an amendment by New Mexico Democrat Jeff Bingaman that would have authorized $150 million a year for programs aimed at reducing drop-out

rates in middle school and high school. The program would have included a national clearinghouse on effective prevention programs. *(Senate vote 43, p. S-13)*

- By a 57-42 vote, the Senate tabled an amendment by Wellstone that would have imposed tighter state accountability standards for waivers of vocational education and Title I regulations. *(Senate vote 47, p. S-13)*

'Ed-Flex' Bill Clears Amid Debate Over School Tragedy

APRIL 24 — Temporarily papering over sharp partisan differences about how to improve the nation's schools, Congress on April 21 passed and sent to the White House legislation giving states more flexibility in spending federal education dollars.

The compromise "ed-flex" conference report was adopted by the House, 368-57. Opposition came from Democrats who worried that it could undercut programs designed to assist low-income students. The Senate cleared the measure, 98-1. Paul Wellstone, D-Minn., voted no. President Clinton is expected to sign the bill. *(House vote 94, p. H-38; Senate vote 89, p. S-21)*

The measure expands nationwide a 12-state pilot program, in effect since 1994, that allows governors to seek waivers of federal rules in order to experiment with innovative approaches to instruction.

"It offers a deal no one can refuse — results rather than red tape," said Sen. James M. Jeffords, R-Vt., chairman of the Health, Education, Labor & Pensions Committee.

Some states, such as Texas, have aggressively used the flexibility. Other states in the pilot program have made little use of it.

Though the bill, which covers almost $11 billion in annual spending, is expected to bring about only modest changes in the nation's schools, lawmakers have made it a high priority. The GOP, especially, is eager to respond to polls showing voters want Congress to raise education standards.

Political rhetoric was muted, however. Action on the legislation came just one day after 14 students and a teacher were killed during a shooting rampage at a Colorado high school. Much of the floor debate and attention was focused not on the bill, but on the tragedy at Columbine High School in Littleton.

"Any solution has to involve a change in our gun laws," said Sen. Charles E. Schumer, D-N.Y., a longtime gun control proponent.

By coincidence, the final ed-flex measure included an amendment by Sen. John Ashcroft, R-Mo., that would expand the power of officials to discipline disabled students who brought weapons to school.

While the ed-flex measure was relatively non-controversial, the road to passage was far from smooth. During original Senate consideration, Democrats stretched out debate as they offered a series of unsuccessful amendments that would have implemented much of Clinton's education agenda.

Veto Threat

Education Secretary Richard W. Riley in an April 13 letter to conferees threatened a White House veto unless they dropped a Republican amendment in the Senate bill. The amendment, sponsored by Majority Leader Trent Lott, R-Miss., would have allowed states to use $1.2 billion designated for Clinton's plan to hire 100,000 teachers on existing special education programs instead. The money had been appropriated in the fiscal 1999 omnibus spending bill (PL 105-277).

Eager to get the bill passed, Senate Republicans jettisoned the Lott provision. The final compromise legislation does, however, include a provision making it easier for schools to use the $1.2 billion for teacher training if they have already reduced class size.

The bill would cover the $8 billion-a-year Title I program for aid to disadvantaged students, teacher training, vocational education, technology assistance, immigrant education and other programs. It does not cover federal assistance to disabled students.

To be eligible for the waivers, states must either have, or be working toward, standards for student performance required under Title I. Governors must also agree to waive their own state regulations.

The legislation would not apply to civil rights, health and safety rules. States could not seek waivers of a provision of the existing Title I law that requires funds to be targeted first toward schools with more than 75 percent of children in poverty.

Democrats pressed for, and won, tougher provisions to ensure that states receiving waivers actually make progress in improving student performance.

The bill would require states to lay out detailed objectives and goals in their waiver applications and to specify which students would be affected. The Education Department would have to monitor state programs and could terminate a waiver after three years if states had not made measurable progress. Waivers would be terminated if states showed a drop in student scores for two consecutive years.

President Signs Measure Into Law

MAY 1 — At a full-blown White House ceremony April 29, President Clinton signed legislation (HR 800) that would give states more flexibility to waive federal education rules.

The pomp and circumstance for what is essentially a minor bill underscores the importance that both political parties place on the education issue.

The "ed-flex" bill expands nationwide a current 12-state pilot program that allows states to seek waivers of federal rules covering about $11 billion in annual education spending. To receive waivers and experiment with new approaches to instruction, states will have to agree to lift their own education regulations.

While Texas has shown gains in student achievement under the pilot program, other states have made little use of it. Clinton and lawmakers praised the bill as the first in a series of education initiatives.

"This new law will allow states and school districts, not to just save administrative dollars with less headache and red tape, but actually to pool different funds from different sources in the federal government," Clinton said. "But by demanding accountability in return, it will make sure states and school districts focus on results." ◆

Provisions of the 'Ed-Flex' Bill

The so-called Ed-Flex bill (HR 800 — PL 106-25), as signed by President Clinton on April 29, contained the following provisions:

Process and Accountability

• **Authority.** The law gives the Education secretary authority to implement a nationwide program under which state educational agencies can receive waivers of federal rules relating to a list of federal programs, including Title I aid to the disadvantaged, teacher training or vocational aid for any local educational agency or school within the state.

To be named an eligible "Ed-Flex" state, state officials must have developed and implemented educational content and student performance standards and aligned tests as required by the 1994 reauthorization of the Elementary and Secondary Education Act (PL 103-382).

States that do not have the standards and assessments in place will still be eligible if they have developed and implemented content standards and pilot tests or other methods for measuring student performance and made substantial progress, as determined by the secretary of Education, in developing final standards and assessments and producing school profiles.

States must also have a procedure in place to hold districts and schools accountable for meeting educational goals outlined in their waiver applications and for taking corrective action in case schools do not meet the higher standards. As a third condition for receiving a waiver of federal regulations, states will have to agree to waive state statutory or regulatory requirements relating to education.

• **State application.** States that want to receive waivers must submit a formal application to the secretary of Education. The application must describe the process the state education agency will use to evaluate requests from local districts or schools requesting waivers, give a detailed description of state rules to be waived and clearly describe the objectives of the waiver.

Further, the application must include a description of how the increased flexibility will complement the state's overall education improvement plan, or, if the state does not have such a plan, how the waiver will mesh with education improvement requirements of the Elementary and Secondary Education Act.

States must describe how they will evaluate the performance of students and local education agencies affected by the waivers and how they will provide for public comment on their proposed plan.

• **Federal approval of state plans.** The secretary of Education will approve a state plan only if he or she determines that it would provide substantial promise of assisting the state, local districts and schools in carrying out educational improvements. The secretary will consider whether the state meets eligibility requirements, whether the plan is comprehensive and ensures accountability, whether the state goals are clear, and the significance of state laws and regulations to be waived.

• **Local applications.** Each district or school seeking a waiver will submit an application to the state educational agency. The application will list the affected federal programs and regulations and laws to be waived; describe the overall purpose of waivers; and describe specific, measurable education goals for each district or school.

States will not be able to approve the waivers unless the district or school develops a local improvement plan, the waiver will assist the district or school in meeting its educational goals, and the state is satisfied that the underlying purposes of the laws being waived will continue to be met.

• **State termination.** States will annually review district or schoolwide waivers. States will terminate waivers if school performance has been inadequate or a school's academic performance has decreased for two consecutive years — unless the state determines that the decline was due to "exceptional and uncontrollable circumstances."

• **Oversight.** Each state must submit an annual report to the secretary of Education describing its oversight and the schools receiving waivers. Not less than two years after the date that a state is designated an "Ed-Flex Partnership State" it must include, as part of its annual report, data outlining how waivers have contributed to state goals for improving education.

Required data includes: information on the total number of state and federal waivers granted; the effect of waivers on state education improvement plans and student performance; the relationship of the waivers to the performance of students and schools; and an assurance that the data reported is reliable, complete and accurate.

Not later than two years after enactment and annually thereafter, the secretary of Education must submit a report to Congress and the public that summarizes state reports and describes the impact of the act on state initiatives and student performance.

• **Authority to issue waivers.** The Ed-Flex authorization runs from fiscal 1999 through fiscal 2004. In general, the secretary of Education may not grant a state authority to issue waivers for longer than five years. The secretary could make exceptions if the state authority has been effective in helping to carry out education improvement plans such as proposals to revamp curriculum and testing, meet accountability standards or has improved student performance.

• **Performance review.** Three years after a state is designated an Ed-Flex state, the secretary of Education must review the performance of the state educational agency in granting waivers. The secretary must terminate a state's authority to grant waivers if it is determined, after notice and an opportunity for a hearing, that the state education agency has failed to adequately implement the law. When deciding whether to extend a state's waiver authority, the secretary of Education must review the progress of the state toward achieving student progress and determining that local districts or schools covered by waivers have moved toward the specific goals outlined in their applications.

• **Public notice.** Each state and school district seeking waiver authority must provide public notice of the proposal, including a description of the proposed waiver and specific expectations for improved student performance. The notice must be posted in a "widely read or distributed" medium. Parents, educators and community members must have an opportunity to comment. Comments will be submitted to the Education secretary as part of state waiver applications.

Scope of Law

The Ed-Flex law applies to the following programs:

• Title I of the Elementary and Secondary Education Act of 1965, which provides compensatory education for low-income and disadvantaged students, the Even Start literacy program, Migrant education and neglected, delinquent and at-risk youth programs.

• Part B of Title II of the Elementary and Secondary Education Act of 1965, the Eisenhower Professional Development Program of teacher training.

• Subpart 2 of Part A of Title III of the Elementary and Secondary Education Act of 1965 (other than section 3136), which applies to most education technology assistance programs.
• Title IV of the Elementary and Secondary Education Act of 1965, the Safe and Drug Free Schools and Communities Program.
• Title VI of the Elementary and Secondary Education Act of 1965, Innovative Education Program Strategies.
• Part C of Title VII of the Elementary and Secondary Education Act of 1965, Emergency Immigrant Education.
• The Carl D. Perkins Vocational and Technical Education Act of 1998.
• **Waivers not authorized.** The secretary of Education and states cannot waive statutory or regulatory requirements relating to the following:
  • State maintenance of effort regarding funding;
  • Comparability of services to all students;
  • Equitable participation of students and professional staff in private schools;
  • Parental participation and involvement;
  • Distribution of funds to states or to local education agencies;
  • The requirement to first serve schools under the Title I program where more than 75 percent of students are in poverty. However, the law allows schools that might not otherwise qualify for Title I to seek program waivers to participate if the percentage of low-income children in the attendance area or school seeking a waiver is not less than 10 percentage points below the lowest percentage of such children for any school or attendance area that meets Title I requirements.
  • Use of federal funds to supplement, not supplant, non-federal funds; and
  • Applicable civil rights statutes.

The law allows for exceptions if the secretary of Education is satisfied that the underlying purposes of the program for which a waiver is granted continue to be met.
• **Existing Ed-Flex states.** In general, the law will not apply to states already operating under the Ed-Flex pilot program. Exceptions include a provision that allows states to expand existing waivers to include programs under technology assistance programs that provide funding for computers and training in computer technology. States will come under the new law once existing waivers expire.

Further, a notice describing the secretary of Education's initial decision to authorize state educational agencies to issue waivers under the pilot program is to be published in the Federal Register. The notice is to be distributed to states, educators, advocacy groups and the general public.

Related Provisions

• **Class size reduction.** The act amends a provision of the fiscal 1999 omnibus spending bill (PL 105-277) that provided $1.2 billion to states as a down payment on President Clinton's long-term plan to hire 100,000 teachers and reduce average class size to 18 in the early grades. The Ed-Flex legislation allows school districts that have already met the class size goal to use their funds, instead, for professional development programs without having to form a consortium. The original omnibus law required schools that wanted to use the funds for teacher training to band with other, similar school districts to spend the money. That was because the amount of money provided to some districts was so small it would not otherwise be efficient to spend the funds. Lawmakers in rural areas complained, however, that the provision was so cumbersome that schools were unable to use the funds at all.
• **Education of the disabled.** The legislation clarifies a provision of the Individuals with Disabilities Education Act (PL 105-17) to make it clear that school officials may discipline disabled students who either carry or possess a weapon at a school, on school premises or at a school function. The provision is an effort to clarify what lawmakers criticized as vague draft regulations issued by the Department of Education. ◆

Chapter 11

EMPLOYMENT & LABOR

Parties Differ Over Measures To Help Employers Cover $1-an-Hour Wage Hike

Box Score

- **Bills:** HR 3081; amendment to S 625.
- **Legislative action: House** Ways and Means Committee approved HR 3081 (H Rept 106-467, Part 1), 23-14, on Nov. 9.

Senate adopted an amendment to S 625 to raise the minimum wage, 55-45, on Nov. 9.

SUMMARY

Republicans tried to head off a potent Democratic political issue by moving their own measures to increase the minimum wage, but with the House in disarray on the issue and with GOP leaders in both chambers only lukewarm in their enthusiasm, the effort stalled.

Republican leaders desperately wanted to avoid a repeat of 1996, when GOP moderates banded together with Democrats to force the chambers to pass a 90-cents-an-hour increase in the minimum wage (PL 104-188), bringing it to $5.15 an hour. But their efforts to re-create the wage increase and tax break package that the GOP had cobbled together to save face in 1996 proved more difficult than expected.

The main problems were in the House, where some moderate Republicans leaned toward voting for a Democratic bill (HR 325) and where conservative Democrats, normally reliable partners for the GOP on business issues, had scattered opinions on whether and how to increase the wage.

Nonetheless, leaders attempted to move a package that Republicans Rick A. Lazio of New York and John Shimkus of Illinois had put together with two conservative Democrats, Gary A. Condit of California and Robert E. "Bud" Cramer of Alabama.

The bill (HR 3081) would have raised the minimum wage from $5.15 to $6.15 an hour over three years. It would have cut taxes for a variety of businesses and individuals by more than $30 billion over five years.

The Ways and Means Committee approved the bill after changing some tax provisions, but leaders could never get enough support to bring the bill to the floor.

The Senate, largely out of the limelight for months on the issue, decided to take the lead late in the session. When the chamber considered a bill (S 625) to overhaul consumer bankruptcy laws, Republicans and Democrats offered competing amendments to increase the wage and cut taxes for affected businesses. The chamber voted, 50-48, to table, or kill, an amendment by Edward M. Kennedy, D-Mass., to increase the wage by $1 an hour over two years and to cut taxes by $11.5 billion over five years. It adopted an amendment by Pete V. Domenici, R-N.M., to raise the wage by $1 over three years and to cut taxes by $18.4 billion over five years. However, the bankruptcy bill stalled at the end of the session. *(Bankruptcy, p. 5-37)*

The House will probably move a minimum wage measure with tax cuts attached. It is unclear whether Republicans will continue to push HR 3081 and the increase the Senate has passed, or if leaders will have to revise the plans. With political tension growing, Congress is expected to clear a wage increase for the president's signature next year.

Bipartisan Group Introduces House Bill to Increase Minimum Wage

OCTOBER 16 — With the House GOP leadership still smarting from a drubbing by Democrats and moderate Republicans on health care legislation, a bipartisan group of lawmakers worked to head off such divisions when the chamber considers another simmering centrist issue — an increase in the minimum wage.

As the group introduced its bill (HR 3081) on Oct. 14, Democratic leaders and labor groups urged members to oppose the measure, making it unclear if a minimum wage bill would succeed. It appeared likely to come to the House floor the week of Oct. 18.

"I don't think anybody knows what a vote count on this bill will look like," said Lee Culpepper, senior vice president of government affairs and public policy at the National Restaurant Association, which opposes increasing the wage but has yet to take a position on the newly introduced measure.

The bill would raise the minimum wage by $1 an hour, from $5.15 to $6.15, over three years.

Lawmakers said the week of Oct. 11 that it appeared that many conservative and mainstream Republicans would set aside their disdain for the minimum wage and vote to increase it because it would be teamed with tax breaks, such as a cut in estate tax rates. Fiscally conservative Democrats in the "Blue Dog" coalition, who helped write the bill, also seemed likely to go along. But most Democrats and moderate Republicans were question marks.

Pivotal members such as Jack Quinn of New York, the most ardent Republican supporter of a wage increase, said they were still looking at details of the bill. "I'm hoping to be able to support it," said Quinn, adding that "there's a real fine line" between putting members off and getting enough support to pass a bill. Quinn and other moderate Republicans joined with Democrats in 1996 to pass a minimum wage increase (PL 104-188) over the objection of GOP leaders. *(1996 Almanac, p. 7-3)*

Quinn said he was worried about the same issues that prompted House Minority Leader Richard A. Gephardt, D-Mo., to say Oct. 14 that he hoped Democrats would vote against the plan: its $1 increase in the wage over three years was too small, and its numerous tax provisions should be paid for with offsets. Members involved in the negotiations said the tax provisions would cost $35 billion over five years.

Peggy Taylor, legislative director of the AFL-CIO, sent a letter to House members Oct. 12 encouraging them not to cosponsor the bill for the same reasons Gephardt had outlined.

Democratic leaders continued to rally around a bill (HR 325) by Minority Whip David E. Bonior, D-Mich., that would raise the wage by $1 over two years. Ways and Means Committee ranking Democrat Charles B. Rangel of New York and panel member John Tanner of Tennessee, a Blue Dog Democrat, are crafting a package of tax breaks to add to that bill. Bonior filed a discharge petition Sept. 23 that, if signed by 218 members, would require House leaders to allow HR 325 on to the floor. As of Oct. 15, he had 163 signatures, all Democrats.

On the Senate side, Susan Collins, R-Maine, said Oct. 13 that she and other moderate Republicans are putting together a minimum wage package that is also likely to include tax alternatives. The plan will be offered when Sen. Edward M. Kennedy, D-Mass., brings to the floor his proposal to increase the wage by $1 over two years. Kennedy has been looking for a vehicle to which to attach his measure since the Senate failed to take up a bankruptcy overhaul measure (S 625) on Sept. 21. Introduction of the bipartisan House bill (HR 3081) had been held up largely by "small potatoes," said Rep. John Shimkus, R-Ill., who worked on the measure with Rick A. Lazio, R-N.Y., Gary A. Condit, D-Calif., and Robert E. "Bud" Cramer, D-Ala.

Working out the details was not made any easier when Ways and Means Committee Chairman Bill Archer, R-Texas, said Oct. 13 that he would seek to refer the bill to his panel, instead of allowing it to go straight to the floor, if it contained any tax provisions not previously approved by the committee.

Tax Breaks

Tax breaks in the bill include a reduction in the estate tax, increases in deductions for some business meals and a quicker phase-in of deductibility of health insurance for the self-employed.

The bill would also specify that funeral directors and some computer professionals were exempt from the Fair Labor Standards Act, which sets hours and other working conditions. A Democratic aide said that provision would be controversial.

Condit said he believed the proposal was "balanced." Shimkus said the group worked to include provisions that would attract bipartisan support. Members wanted to avoid the splits within the GOP that occurred during the health care debate.

Shimkus said he felt as Rep. John Shadegg, R-Ariz., had when he tried to put together a compromise health care bill. Shimkus said Shadegg had recounted his experience in a GOP conference meeting, saying, "When you move to the middle, you get shot at from both sides."

Members of the group said they would work to keep the bill unified, instead of moving it as one bill to increase the minimum wage and another to cut taxes. Majority Leader Dick Armey, R-Texas, had hinted Oct. 12 that he would consider a strategy similar to that by which the House voted for a health-related tax bill (HR 2990) later linked by leaders to a patients' rights bill (HR 2723) that the House passed separately.

"I think we would not be supportive of splitting it apart," Shimkus said. "That would disrupt the whole good-faith effort we've made."

Senate Prepares For Vote on Minimum Wage

NOVEMBER 6 — In a move that surprised lobbyists and many lawmakers, the stage for moving legislation to raise the minimum wage appeared to shift from the House to the Senate virtually overnight as the week of Nov. 1 ended.

House leaders struggled to find the votes for a bipartisan bill (HR 3081) to raise the minimum wage by $1 an hour to $6.15 over three years and provide more than $30 billion in tax breaks for businesses over five years. But Senate Majority Leader Trent Lott, R-Miss., and Minority Leader Tom Daschle, D-S.D., announced Nov. 4 that, after a month of negotiations, they had agreed to allow both parties to offer minimum wage-related amendments to a bankruptcy overhaul bill (S 625).

As a result, the Senate is set to vote Nov. 9 on increasing the minimum wage by $1 over two years, as proposed by Edward M. Kennedy, D-Mass. Democrats will also offer a package of tax breaks that would cost $9.5 billion over five years to address concerns that some businesses may be adversely affected by a wage increase.

After the Democrats offer their amendments, Republicans plan to offer one that would give significantly more tax relief to businesses and raise the minimum wage by $1 over three years. Among other provisions, the amendment would repeal a 0.02 percent unemployment tax on businesses, move up by three years — from 2003 to 2000 — the date by which self-employed people would be able to deduct 100 percent of their health care premiums and increase from $20,000 to $30,000 the new equipment costs businesses could deduct from their taxes. The package would cost $18.4 billion over five years.

The Republican amendment, crafted by conservatives and moderates, is likely to be adopted along party lines. Kennedy said Nov. 2 that approving his amendment "probably would be an uphill battle today." Lott said Nov. 4 that if Kennedy's amendment were to be adopted, it would "not go to the president. I can guarantee you that."

Business lobbyists, who believe they would get more favorable minimum wage legislation this year than during next year's election season, said they hoped the Senate would pass a measure and send it through the House.

House members continued to struggle to win support for their bill the week of Nov. 1. Matters became more complicated when Ways and Means Committee Chairman Bill Archer, R-Texas, set out his own plan to cut taxes by $30 billion over five years as part of the package. That added jurisdictional fights to the list of concerns leaders faced, though it appeared Nov. 5 that Archer might schedule a markup of tax provisions.

GOP leaders also risked splitting the bipartisan group that had put together HR 3081 by insisting that the Democrats in the group — Gary A. Condit of California and Robert E. "Bud" Cramer of Alabama — needed to come up with more support from their party. Condit and John Shimkus, R-Ill., who also helped write the bill, said the problem was a lack of GOP votes.

With so many questions remaining, leaders "really can't bring it up," said Jack Quinn, R-N.Y., an ardent supporter of increasing the minimum wage.

But he, like many others in the party, believed the GOP would be better off tackling the issue in 1999. "What happens next year is that the temperature gets turned up. More and more Republicans find themselves under the gun . . . and proposals of higher wages and less taxes become possible."

Minimum Wage Bill Stalls Over Business Offsets

NOVEMBER 13 — Since the early days of the 106th Congress, Republicans have viewed increasing the minimum wage as tough medicine. They knew swallowing a raise this year, before election-year posturing took root, would be good for the health of the party, even if it was a bitter pill for many conservatives.

But with members rushing to wrap up the first session, GOP leaders appeared unlikely to capitalize on progress made in both the House and Senate the week of Nov. 8. Instead, they were prepared to put off decisions on minimum wage legislation until next year. "I don't see us resolving that before we complete the session," Senate Majority Leader Trent Lott, R-Miss., said Nov. 8.

Other Republican leaders said that resolving the issue depended on how long lawmakers stayed in Washington. "If we're here long enough, there's a good chance we'll get it done," Chief House Deputy Whip Roy Blunt, R-Mo., said Nov. 9.

But most Democrats said they believed the issue was dead for the year, and they warned that they would turn up the volume for a minimum wage increase in 2000. "This will not go away," Senate Minority Leader Tom Daschle, D-S.D., said Nov. 9. "This is an issue that really resonates out there."

Moderate Republicans and business lobbyists seemed most bothered by the delay. Moderates worried that constituents would criticize their failure to move a minimum wage increase and businesses worried that Republicans, to avoid a political hit, would be forced to pass a larger wage increase next year with fewer tax offsets for businesses.

Sen. Susan Collins of Maine, a moderate Republican, said Nov. 9 that the obstinacy of members in both parties was to blame for the wage increase's apparent death. "I would view it as a failure on the part of both Democrats and Republicans," she said.

Party positions were not far apart on the wage increase itself. In both the House and Senate, Democrats proposed a $1-per-hour increase over two years, while Republicans proposed a $1-per-hour increase over three years, consisting of 35 cents the first year, 35 cents the second year and 30 cents the third year. About 11 million Americans earn the minimum wage, which is now $5.15 an hour.

The parties were fighting only over how quickly to phase in the increase, but that was obscured in debates on the Senate floor Nov. 8-9 and in the House Ways and Means Committee markup Nov. 9. Instead, members focused on the two parties' widely different plans to offset businesses' costs for raising the wage.

House Republicans wanted to cut taxes by $30.2 billion over five years. That proposal was part of the minimum wage bill (HR 3081) that Ways and Means approved, 23-14, on Nov. 9. Senate Republicans wanted to cut taxes by $18.4 billion over five years. That was part of an amendment that Budget Committee Chairman Pete V. Domenici, R-N.M., offered to a bill (S 625) to overhaul consumer bankruptcy laws. The Senate adopted the amendment, 55-45, on Nov. 9. *(Vote 357, p. S-71)*

Democrats from both chambers shared the goal of cutting taxes — by about $9.5 billion over five years in the House and $11.5 billion in the Senate — paying for the cuts by closing corporate loopholes and making other tax code changes. Both GOP proposals included some revenue-raising provisions, but the measures would be mostly paid for with projected budget surpluses, not by offsets. President Clinton has threatened to veto any bill that is not paid for with offsets.

The Senate on Nov. 9 tabled, or killed, the Democratic proposal crafted by Max Baucus of Montana and Charles S. Robb of Virginia and included in a broader minimum wage amendment sponsored by Edward M. Kennedy of Massachusetts. The vote was 50-48. Four Republicans — Lincoln Chafee of Rhode Island, James M. Jeffords of Vermont, Olympia J. Snowe of Maine and Arlen Specter of Pennsylvania — voted with all Democrats against tabling. *(Vote 356, p. S-71)*

At the Ways and Means markup, an amendment sponsored by ranking Charles B. Rangel, D-N.Y., failed in a party-line vote of 12-23.

The many tax proposals and intense partisanship involved in both debates underscored the difficulty House leaders had in trying to move a minimum wage bill, a key factor in Republicans' likely decision to put off the issue until next year.

House leaders continued to measure support for HR 3081, which had been put together by Republicans Rick A. Lazio of New York and John Shimkus of Illinois and Democrats Gary A. Condit of California and Robert E. "Bud" Cramer of Alabama. But staff aides and lobbyists said GOP leaders needed "yes" votes from 40 Democrats to move the measure, a number that seemed impossible to reach given the hesitance of all but the most conservative Democrats to sign on to the bill.

The group of 29 conservative Democrats to which Condit and Cramer belong — the Blue Dogs — are generally reliable votes for the GOP on business-related issues. But the minimum wage is a sticky wicket for many Blue Dogs, and the group has not taken a position on the bill. Instead, members are scattered across the board on the issue. While Condit and Cramer have worked with Republicans to forge a compromise, Blue Dog John Tanner of Tennessee worked with Rangel on the tax components of his minimum wage plan. And other Blue Dogs, such as Charles W. Stenholm of Texas, pursued a third approach — allowing states to opt out of a federal wage increase.

The need to look for Democratic support from such a disparate group indicated that GOP whips expected dozens of Republicans to desert the party and vote with Democrats for their bill (HR 325) to increase the wage by $1 in the next two years and cut taxes by less than $10 billion.

Senate Tax Breaks

Though the parties agree that the minimum wage should be raised, members often returned to the partisan rhetoric that characterized debates in the early 1990s and before, when most Republicans opposed raising it and Democrats beat the drum for an increase.

Senate Majority Whip Don Nickles, R-Okla., argued that Kennedy's amendment to raise the wage by $1 by Jan. 1, 2001, would be "too quick. It would have economic ramifications that would cause some people to lose their jobs."

Kennedy called such arguments an excuse. "The fact is the Republicans are opposed to any increase in the minimum wage . . . even in a time of record prosperity," he said. Kennedy called the GOP bill "a Thanksgiving turkey with three right wings" because, he said, it put tax cuts before a quick increase in wages for poorer Americans.

Republicans who supported Domenici's amendment to raise the wage by $1 over three years and opposed Kennedy's proposal focused their arguments almost exclusively on the tax components of both bills.

Both amendments aimed to help businesses that could find the requirement to pay a higher wage burdensome.

Among the tax cuts in Domenici's plan were pension changes, such as increasing annual contribution limits for 401(k)s and other retirement plans from $10,000 to $15,000 by 2005; provisions to allow self-employed individuals and workers without employer-provided health insurance to deduct 100 percent of their insurance costs from income taxes; a proposal to repeal a 0.02 percent surtax on taxable wages that Congress imposed in 1976 on businesses to pay for unemployment programs (PL 94-566); and provisions to increase from 50 percent to 80 percent the amount of meal and entertainment tabs that small businesses could deduct from taxes. *(1976 Almanac, p. 359)*

The Democratic plan offered by Kennedy included an increase from $1.3 million to $1.75 million in the amount that a family-owned business or farm could be worth before estate taxes were due; a provision to allow employers who help workers with day care to deduct 25 percent of the expenses; a provision to advance from 2003 to 2000 the date by which the self-employed could deduct 100 percent of their health insurance expenses; and an increase in the business meals deduction for small companies from 50 percent to 60 percent.

House Tax Breaks

Proposals offered in the House Ways and Means markup had many elements in common with the Senate plans, and they drew similar partisan debate.

The Lazio bill (HR 3081) included pension law changes to remove regulations that make it difficult for employers to offer pensions or for workers to save for retirement; a plan to accelerate the date by which the self-employed could deduct their health insurance costs; and a provision to reduce the estate, gift and generation-skipping taxes by repealing rates above 50 percent and allowing more estates to pay the lowest rate of 18 percent.

The bill also included smaller items, some of which Ways and Means Chairman Bill Archer, R-Texas, opposed. Archer proposed removing some of them, including tax incentives to keep independent film and television production in the United States. His amendment also would make all businesses, not just small businesses, eligible for the increase in business meal deductions. It was approved by voice vote.

The failed Democratic amendment offered by Rangel would have raised the business meal deduction to 65 percent for small businesses; allowed employers a $2,000-per-child deduction for educating or training employees' children; and accelerated the date by which the self-employed could deduct health insurance costs. ◆

Chapter 12

ENVIRONMENT

Senate Postpones Action On Nuclear Waste Storage Until Second Session

Box Score

- **Bills:** HR 45, S 1287
- **Legislative action: House** Commerce Committee approved HR 45 (H Rept 106-155), 39-6, on April 21.

Senate Energy and Natural Resources Committee approved S 1287 (S Rept 106-98), 14-6, on June 16.

SUMMARY

A crowded end-of-session calendar and objections from Nevada senators prevented the Senate from debating nuclear waste storage legislation this year. But proponents say it will be among the first bills the Senate will consider in 2000. House members are awaiting the Senate's action before determining how to proceed.

Since Republicans took control of Congress in 1994, they have tried without success to pass legislation to accommodate nuclear power companies in 34 states that want the federal government to remove high-level, spent fuel accumulating at their reactor sites.

The most common legislative proposal has been to temporarily store the materials above ground near Nevada's Yucca Mountain, which is under study as the permanent U.S. burial site. The House Commerce Committee approved a bill (HR 45) in April that called for temporary storage in Nevada by 2003.

But the Senate Energy and Natural Resources Committee took a different approach, adopting an alternative (S 1287) suggested by Energy Secretary Bill Richardson that would keep the waste where it is generated and hand the legal title and responsibility for managing it to the government.

The Senate proposal ran into controversy, however, because of language added by Energy Committee Chairman Frank H. Murkowski, R-Alaska. His provision would transfer authority for setting radiation exposure standards for Yucca Mountain from the Environmental Protection Agency (EPA) to the Nuclear Regulatory Commission (NRC).

Murkowski and other Republicans said they fear EPA's proposed standards will prove impossible to meet, effectively killing permanent storage at Yucca Mountain. Democrats and the Clinton administration responded that it would be improper to take the power from an agency that has wielded it for three decades.President Clinton has pledged to veto nuclear waste legislation if the EPA-NRC transfer language remains in the bill.

Senate supporters will try to pass the measure with the 67 votes needed to overcome a veto override, but they have been unable to muster enough votes to do so in the past. Nevada lawmakers are confident they can prevent the measure from becoming law, but they face potential trouble after 2000 if a Republican is elected president.

Domenici Offers Nuclear Waste Plan As New Mexico Storage Site Opens

MARCH 27 — As a New Mexico repository opened its doors to begin storing waste generated by nuclear weapons production, an influential Republican senator floated a proposal to address the growing waste problem faced by commercial nuclear power plants nationwide.

The opening of the $2 billion Waste Isolation Pilot Plant (WIPP) in southeastern New Mexico — 26 miles east of Carlsbad — came after more than two decades of political, legal and bureaucratic delays and more than six years after Congress allowed it to clear its final major legislative hurdle.

Built in salt caverns 2,150 feet below the desert, the site was designed as a permanent repository for more than 6 million cubic feet of mid-level nuclear waste, considered relatively low in radiation but high in plutonium. Legislation to pave the way for the site's opening passed in the final hours of the 102nd Congress and was signed by President George Bush (PL 102-592). *(1992 Almanac, p. 259)*

The first truckload of waste from Los Alamos National Laboratory arrived at the plant March 26, four days after a U.S. district judge issued an opinion that a 1992 injunction did not prevent shipments of certain types of waste to the site. Environmentalists unsuccessfully filed three last-minute appeals.

"This is indeed historic — for DOE and the nation," said Energy Secretary Bill Richardson, a former Democratic House member from New Mexico (1983-97) who led the fight against allowing waste to be shipped until the Environmental Protection Agency (EPA) determined it would be safe.

The EPA certified last year that the site would remain safe for 10,000 years. But the opening had been held up because New Mexico was slow in processing a state permit regulating the flammable solvents and other non-radioactive but hazardous wastes to be sent to the site. The nuclear waste shipped from Los Alamos is not covered by the state permit.

Rep. Tom Udall, D-N.M., said the judge's ruling allowing the initial shipments was "good news for the state of New Mexico" because it made clear the state permit must be issued before any hazardous waste could be shipped to the site. As New Mexico's attorney general, Udall successfully sued the Energy Department in 1991 to obtain congressional approval prior to shipping waste.

Environmentalists are likely to continue to press their legal case against the plant. They contend EPA's certification remains rife with problems stemming from improper assumptions about future oil and gas drilling at the site. They fear that drilling could someday trigger a release of radiation from the stored waste.

Many lawmakers, especially those from such states as Idaho, Colorado, Tennessee, South Carolina and Washington where waste is currently stored, are eager to see the waste removed from temporary storage sites in their states. The Energy Department faces an April 30 deadline to move waste out of Idaho, and Idaho officials have made it clear they want the agency to keep its word.

But Energy spokesman Brad Bugger said it was unclear whether waste could go to the New Mexico site by that date. "The department is looking at alternatives to WIPP to meet the April 30 deadline," he said.

Domenici's Proposal

The opening of the plant took place as Sen. Pete V. Domenici, R-N.M., outlined a sweeping proposal intended to break a legislative deadlock over storage of the nation's high-level nuclear waste in Nevada.

At a March 24 Senate Energy & Natural Resources Committee hearing, Domenici said he plans to introduce legislation soon that would launch a new scientific pilot program in states willing to temporarily accept spent fuel from commercial nuclear power plants.

The program would involve building a device called a particle accelerator that would be used to reduce the level of radioactivity in waste by bombarding it with radiation. The device also would be used to produce tritium and radioactive isotopes for medical use.

"Some states may say that 'If we can build the accelerator there . . . [and] be the focal point for isotopes for the medical profession, we [the states] might consider being an interim storage site'," Domenici said.

Several Republicans greeted Domenici's idea cautiously. They agreed that it merits further discussion, but emphasized they are troubled by the high costs of the procedure.

Although environmentalists estimate a program could cost upwards of $40 billion, a Los Alamos official said a smaller-scale project could be put in place for between $4 billion and $5 billion.

Lawmakers also said they do not want the idea to detract from ongoing efforts to temporarily store waste in Nevada, a plan Domenici said he still supports.

Yucca Mountain, 100 miles northwest of Las Vegas, is not expected to be ready for permanent disposal of high-level wastes before 2010. In the meantime, Republicans in the House and Senate have introduced bills (HR 45, S 608) to locate an interim site there over strenuous objections by Nevada's congressional delegation and President Clinton.

Efforts to locate such a site in Nevada passed both chambers in 1997 but could not muster enough votes in the Senate to overcome a veto.

House Commerce Energy and Power Subcommittee Chairman Joe L. Barton, R-Texas, said he intends to mark up the interim storage measure when Congress returns from its spring recess.

Domenici, chairman of the Senate Appropriations Subcommittee on Energy and Water Development, said his proposal also would require a review of U.S. spent fuel disposal strategy in collaboration with other nations.

House Committee Pursues Deal On Interim Site

APRIL 17 — The House Commerce Committee may take up legislation as early as the week of April 19 to provide temporary storage in Nevada for high-level waste from commercial nuclear power plants, but only if committee members can reach agreement on a number of sticking points.

Over the past year, utilities have won lawsuits against the federal government for its failure to meet its legal obligation to accept waste that has been piling up at commercial reactors. The legislation would require that the waste be stored at the Nevada Test Site, 100 miles northwest of Las Vegas, until work is complete on a permanent repository at nearby Yucca Mountain.

Commerce's Energy and Power Subcommittee voted 25-0 on April 14 to send the bill (HR 45) to the full committee. President Clinton has threatened to veto the bill, which is opposed by Nevada's congressional delegation.

Commerce Chairman Thomas J. Bliley Jr., R-Va., said he is eager to move quickly on the bill, a priority for House and Senate GOP leaders. But some supporters disapprove of provisions added to try to gain the administration's support.

Energy and Power Subcommittee Chairman Joe L. Barton, R-Texas, pledged to work with committee members to smooth out differences.

The subcommittee approved a substitute offered by Barton authorizing the Energy Department to take responsibility for waste storage at the utilities' sites in exchange for the companies' dropping their remaining lawsuits against the department. Energy Secretary Bill Richardson floated a similar proposal in February but emphasized that the administration remains opposed to temporary storage.

Charlie Norwood, R-Ga., who supports the legislation, nevertheless complained that forcing utilities to abandon their right to file suit against the department "is nothing short of political blackmail."

Panel OKs Bill; Work Still Needed Before Floor Votes

APRIL 24 — Legislation to temporarily store nuclear waste in Nevada faces new hurdles that threaten to slow its path to passage, if not jeopardize its chances of receiving broad support.

The House Commerce Committee on April 21 approved, by a 40-6 vote, a bill (HR 45) to store high-level radioactive materials from commercial nuclear reactors in Nevada by 2003, but only after several of the bill's supporters acknowledged that the measure needs more work to gain support before it can go to the House floor.

Although committee members expressed doubts about portions of the bill, they agreed to withhold amendments in the hope of fashioning a compromise. "This issue is too important not to take action as soon as possible," said Charlie Norwood, R-Ga.

The issue is a priority for the Republican leadership in both chambers. But the bill still faces consideration by the House Resources Committee, and other committees may claim jurisdiction over it as well.

The bill would store waste at the Nevada Test Site, a federal nuclear weapons testing ground 100 miles northwest of Las Vegas, as work continues on a permanent high-level storage facility at Yucca Mountain, located on the same test site. Nevada's congressional delegation opposes the bill, and President Clinton has threatened a veto.

The legislation is intended to deal with the backlog of waste piling up at commercial reactors. Over the past year, utilities have won lawsuits against the federal government for failing to meet its legal obligation to accept the waste.

The committee version of the bill would authorize the Department of Energy to take responsibility for on-site storage of waste at power plants in exchange for agreements by utilities to drop future lawsuits against the agency.

Several members of both parties who support the bill said they remain troubled about giving the department liability protection against lawsuits. They expressed many of the same concerns earlier this month, when Commerce's Energy and Power Subcommittee approved the legislation.

The bill would also take "off-budget" the $8 billion Nuclear Waste Fund established in the 1982 Nuclear Waste Policy Act (PL 97–425) to collect fees from utilities to finance construction of a storage site. The fund comes from a surcharge on consumers of electricity generated by nuclear energy. *(1982 Almanac, p. 304)*

Taking the fund off-budget would enable it to avoid the discretionary spending caps included in the 1997 balanced-budget law (PL 105-34). The move is intended to allow the Energy Department to spend money from the fund without congressional approval on both the temporary storage site and the permanent one at Yucca Mountain.

Energy Secretary Bill Richardson has acknowledged that his agency will lack enough money in future years to build a permanent site without breaking the budget caps.

But some committee members raised concerns about the precedent set by such a move. Office of Management and Budget Director Jack Lew warned in an April 20 letter to House Commerce Committee Chairman Thomas J. Bliley Jr., R-Va., that the move would likely lead to requests for similar treatment of other programs. In particular, some Republicans have been eager to take the Highway Trust Fund off-budget.

"It would signal to the American people that the Congress is not sincere about controlling spending," Lew wrote in reiterating the administration's intention to veto the bill. "We think that is the wrong signal to send."

For now, House Budget Committee aides are looking at the budget issue to determine whether the bill requires their committee's consideration. A Democratic Commerce Committee aide said it is possible that other House committees, including Transportation and Infrastructure and Armed Services, may also seek jurisdiction over the bill.

The Resources Committee is already expected to consider the bill at some point this spring.

Other Storage Sites

The Commerce Committee did reverse itself on an amendment offered by Energy and Power Subcommittee Chairman Joe L. Barton, R-Texas, to prevent the Skull Valley Band of Goshute Indians from obtaining federal authorization to temporarily store nuclear fuel on its reservation in Utah. Eight utilities have contracted with the tribe to store the waste, but Utah's congressional delegation opposes the move.

After the committee adopted the Goshute amendment on a voice vote as part of a package of amendments offered by Barton, Bobby L. Rush, D-Ill., offered an amendment to strip the language. That amendment was adopted, 29-14.

Senate Proposal Would Keep Waste Out of Nevada — For the Time Being

JUNE 19 — Another showdown over where to store 40,000 metric tons of nuclear waste may be looming between Republicans and the Clinton administration, despite significant concessions by Senate Republicans on legislation to take the waste off the hands of commercial nuclear power plants.

The Senate Energy and Natural Resources Committee voted 14-6 on June 16 to approve a newly drafted proposal that would keep high-level spent fuel at reactor sites in 34 states — with the federal government assuming ownership and management of the waste — instead of sending the materials to Nevada.

The Senate's initiative represents the closest attempt at a bipartisan compromise on the nuclear waste issue since Republicans took control of Congress in 1994. Since then, the GOP has attempted to enact a law that would send waste to the Nevada Test Site, despite strenuous objections from Nevada's congressional delegation and President Clinton.

The House has put off floor action on its version (HR 45) until it sees how the Senate deals with the issue.

Serious differences also remain over a provision in the Senate bill that would allow the Nuclear Regulatory Commission (NRC) to set radiation exposure standards for the permanent nuclear waste burial site at Nevada's Yucca Mountain, 100 miles northwest of Las Vegas, scheduled to open as early as 2010. Democrats contend that the Environmental Protection Agency (EPA) should be allowed to continue its work on establishing the standards, but Republicans fear that the EPA's standard will prove impossible to meet.

Turning the responsibility over to the NRC "is a show-stopper with this administration and with me," warned Jeff Bingaman of New Mexico, the Energy Committee's ranking Democrat.

Bingaman released a letter at the June 16 hearing from Energy Secretary Bill Richardson indicating that the provision would lead Richardson to recommend a presidential veto.

Republicans expressed hope they can reach agreement to schedule Senate floor debate before the August recess. But they made it clear Bingaman and the administration must be agreeable to further compromise.

"If [Democrats] don't work it out, then they don't want a bill," Energy Chairman Frank H. Murkowski, R-Alaska, told reporters. "And they will have to bear the responsibility for killing it."

The nuclear waste legislation was

the outgrowth of months of discussions initiated by Bingaman, bringing together Energy officials, Republicans and officials from utilities with waste piling up at their reactor sites.

Richardson set the talks in motion by proposing that his agency take legal title and management responsibility for the waste as an alternative to building a temporary storage facility in Nevada.

Before Richardson's offer, many lawmakers — especially Republicans — contended that a temporary site was the only way to honor a commitment made by the federal government and upheld by recent federal court decisions to accept spent fuel from commercial plants. They reintroduced legislation (S 608) that called for shipping nuclear waste to Nevada.

But the Clinton administration has steadfastly maintained that a temporary site in Nevada would only interfere with work on the permanent site at Yucca Mountain.

Lawmakers have been unable to obtain the 67 votes needed to override a presidential veto. The version of the Nevada waste storage bill that the Senate passed in the 105th Congress received 65 votes. Critics of the bill said the November 1998 elections failed to give supporters the additional two votes they needed. *(1997 Almanac, p. 4-20)*

"We don't have the votes for a veto override," Murkowski acknowledged in a June 15 interview. "We've been there and done that. So the alternative is to say, 'OK, [the administration] proposes to take [the waste] on site.' We'll consider that as long as it's achievable."

Murkowski's Compromise

To that end, Murkowski unveiled a draft bill at the outset of the Energy Committee markup that he said incorporated many of the ideas discussed by Bingaman and others.

The new measure calls for the federal government to take custody of the waste, providing utilities with storage casks or compensating them for costs of on-site storage, until the construction permit for the Yucca Mountain site is issued. In exchange, utilities would drop lawsuits against the Energy Department for failing to take the waste.

To accommodate Sen. Pete V. Domenici, R-N.M., Murkowski's bill would authorize an Office of Nuclear Spent Fuel Research to study the "treatment, recycling and disposal" of high-level wastes.

As a potential alternative to burying waste at Yucca Mountain, Domenici has advocated further study of an experimental process that reduces the level of radioactivity in waste by bombarding it with radiation.

Murkowski's measure also would require Congress to approve any increase in the fee paid by electricity ratepayers to the $8 billion Nuclear Waste Fund and would bar any expenditure from the fund for utility compensation.

Murkowski's bill also called for developing guidelines to transport waste.

Unlike the nuclear waste bill that passed the House Commerce Committee in April, Murkowski's bill does not take the nuclear waste fund "off-budget" to allow the Energy Department to spend money without congressional approval.

Murkowski described his legislation as "a major concession." The Nuclear Energy Institute, the utility industry's lobbying arm, endorsed the approach, though in more measured language than it used in embracing the earlier GOP proposal.

"We are moving in the right direction to address one of the nation's top environmental challenges," said John Kane, the institute's vice president for governmental affairs.

Nuclear Waste Standards

The bill touched off fierce debate in the Energy Committee because of the language calling for authorizing the NRC to set a radiation protection standard for Yucca Mountain, consistent with the recommendations of the National Academy of Sciences.

The EPA currently is charged with developing the standards. It traditionally has sought more stringent standards than the NRC, including a requirement that the levels of radiation in groundwater near the site be within the limits for safe drinking water.

Environmentalists contend that the drinking water standard is justifiable because the nearest water wells are within 20 miles of Yucca Mountain. But Republicans and the nuclear industry argue that it would be impossible to achieve, in part because of the amount of nuclear weapons testing that has been done in the area. They accused the EPA of using the standard to try to kill the project.

"I don't trust the EPA," said Republican Sen. Larry E. Craig of Idaho. "They have a record of politicizing themselves."

Bingaman, however, said Republicans were being too quick to prejudge EPA's actions. "It's a fairly major change to say, 'We don't know what they're coming out with, but we aren't going to like it and therefore we should change it,' " he said.

In his June 15 letter to Murkowski, Richardson said the administration strongly objects to any provisions that would remove the EPA from its role in setting the standard.

"I would recommend a veto if legislation containing these provisions were presented to the president," Richardson wrote.

Environmentalists also cited the NRC language as a major reason for their opposition to the new bill.

"We couldn't support politicization of the radiation standard," said Auke Piersma, an energy policy analyst for Public Citizen's Critical Mass Energy Project.

Bingaman said he had other concerns with Murkowski's bill, including language he said would set an unrealistic timetable for shipping of defense-generated waste to Yucca Mountain.

As an alternative, Bingaman proposed an amendment based on an earlier draft of Murkowski's bill that would allow the EPA to continue its work by 2001, with a commission of Cabinet members to review and overrule the standard if necessary. If the EPA did not act by 2001, the NRC would be given the authority to set the standard.

Bingaman's amendment was defeated, 7-13, with all of the committee's Republicans voting against it. Murkowski's proposal was then adopted with support from Republicans as well as Democratic Sens. Bob Graham of Florida, Mary L. Landrieu of Louisiana and Blanche Lincoln of Arkansas. Ron Wyden, D-Ore., opposed both proposals.

In a sign of the frustration among bill supporters about the potential for future deadlock, some Republicans criticized Democrats who opposed

Murkowski's legislation.

"It's unbelievable that we have come so far from where we started," said Jim Bunning, R-Ky. "The fact is, we are now discussing a one-half of 1 percent difference of opinion on whether NRC or EPA can do certain things. We might as well let the minority write the bill."

In addition to the question over the standards, another issue remaining to be addressed in the bill is the timetable for the Energy Department to take title to waste from utilities.

Peter G. Fitzgerald, R-Ill., sought to offer an amendment that would have provided an updated time frame governing the agency's acceptance of waste from utilities. But Fitzgerald withdrew the amendment after Murkowski agreed to work with him to include the language in the bill when it reaches the Senate floor.

Despite having prevailed over Bingaman, Republicans acknowledged that the New Mexico Democrat still holds the key to their chances of overcoming a veto and getting a bill into law. "The test remains with Sen. Bingaman," Craig said. "He was the one who said, 'Hold my hand' . . . and we said, 'OK, you've got it. Now vote with us.' " ◆

Congress Sidesteps Regional Fight, Clears Flood Control And Water Projects Bill

Lawmakers skirted a bitter dispute over water distribution in California to produce a water projects bill authorizing $6.3 billion for an array of flood control, navigation and water resource projects.

SUMMARY

The Water Resources Development Act was hung up for more than a year by a single issue, even though the bill was full of popular projects, from deepening harbors in Baltimore, Savannah, Ga., and Oakland, Calif., to rebuilding beaches in Florida and providing additional flood protection along the Mississippi River.

Republican Rep. John T. Doolittle, of California sought to link more flood protection for Sacramento with additional water allocations for his fast-growing 4th District, which stretches eastward from Sacramento to the Nevada border.

Critics balked at connecting flood protection for the state capital with what they viewed as an incursion on delicate attempts to manage water in a dry state.

Neither the Senate bill nor the House version (HR 1480) included the water diversion, mainly because lawmakers said it should be settled by state and local water authorities, not Congress. In the eleventh hour, House and Senate conferees agreed on additional flood protection for Sacramento. But the level fell short of that sought by advocate Robert T. Matsui, D-Calif.

The legislation, which President Clinton signed on Aug. 17, is replete with long-sought-after projects to control flooding, bulk up eroding beaches, deepen harbors, provide hurricane protection and repair the environment.

Another feature is an initiative that encourages the U.S. Army Corps of Engineers to pursue environmentally friendly "non-structural" approaches to control floods.

Box Score

- **Bill:** S 507 — PL 106-53
- **Legislative action: Senate** passed S 507 (S Rept 106-34) by voice vote on April 19.

House substituted text of HR 1480 and passed S 507 by voice vote on July 22.

Senate adopted conference report (H Rept 106-298) by voice vote on Aug. 5.

House cleared bill by voice vote on Aug. 5.

President signed S 507 on Aug. 17.

Senate Passes Water Projects Bill; House Version Troubled

APRIL 24 — After drifting aimlessly for more than a year, a multibillion-dollar bill authorizing navigation and flood control projects was approved by the House Transportation and Infrastructure Committee on April 22. The largely party-line vote was 49-24.

But as the Water Resources Development Act of 1999 (HR 1480) moves to the House floor for an expected vote the week of April 26, there is no assurance it will become law in its current form, because it will be difficult to reconcile differences with the Senate bill.

Like the House bill, the Senate counterpart (S 507), which was easily approved April 19, would authorize U.S. Army Corps of Engineers' civil works projects. The bills also are similar in total spending: The Senate version calls for $2.5 billion in federal spending; the House bill, $3 billion. Actual spending is higher because states and local governments are required to pay a portion of the costs.

But while spending levels may be similar, the House version departs from the traditional scope of the bill by including highly contentious provisions that critics say will dictate the way water resources are distributed in fast-growing Northern California.

Critics, including some environmental groups and Democratic House members from California, condemned the language as an intrusion to the state's delicate attempt to fairly distribute water. The water, used for a variety of purposes from drinking to farming to industrial operations, is critical to the region's continuing development.

The House language, a longtime goal of John T. Doolittle, R-Calif., calls for modifying the Folsom Dam and tapping the American River, north of Sacramento.

Doolittle insists that plan would lessen the risk of Sacramento being flooded. The projects would also supply more water to Doolittle's rapidly growing 4th District, rolling eastward from Sacramento to the Nevada border.

Complaints Are Flowing

Democrat Ellen O. Tauscher of California, whose Bay Area district could lose water if the diversions are built, tried unsuccessfully to delete the provisions in subcommittee and again in full committee. In addition to stemming the flow, Tauscher argued, the diversions would result in dirtier water.

Calling the attempt an "unauthorized and audacious water grab," Tauscher vowed to fight the language on the floor, putting at risk dozens of popular projects that have already been delayed by the California dispute.

Tauscher and others critics complained that Congress is "meddling" in the state's business by allocating water rights.

Sherwood Boehlert, R-N.Y., chairman of the Water Resources and Environment Subcommittee, insisted that is not the case: "We are not allocating water in California. That is not our job."

Mindful of the potential for problems and the fact that the California impasse has already delayed the bill by a year, committee Chairman Bud Shuster, R-Pa., urged members to settle their differences.

"I can understand their strong feelings on this," Shuster said of the Californians, "but I want them to recognize this is a national bill. This is not a Northern California bill . . . I would implore members to view it that way."

Shuster's words failed to bridge the differences, but the bill is likely to pass the full House because Republican unity is likely to hold.

That will shift the focus to House and Senate negotiators, where Tauscher and other critics believe their chances of making changes are greater.

An aide to Senate Environment & Public Works Committee Chairman John H. Chafee, R-R.I., said there is little support for Doolittle's plan. Like others, the aide expressed a desire to finish the bill, which was left over from the 105th Congress.

The Clinton administration also opposes Doolittle and has threatened to veto the bill unless it is changed.

The usually non-controversial bill authorizes a host of popular projects nationwide, including controlling floods, deepening harbors and rebuilding eroded beaches.

The debate this time was reminiscent of fights in 1992 and 1996 when another Northern California project, the Auburn Dam, became a lightning rod. Construction on the dam began in the 1970s but stopped amid withering criticism from environmentalists who said it was too expensive.

The Auburn Dam was intended to control flooding along the American River but efforts by Doolittle to revive it in 1992 and 1996 failed. In all, it would have cost $1 billion.

In addition to the California projects, the House bill also authorizes $7.2 million in federal spending for a for flood control on Beargrass Creek in Kentucky; $19 million for work on Baltimore's harbor; and $28.8 million in federal spending for floor control on the Des Plaines River in Illinois.

House Breaks Logjam, Passes Flood Control Bill

MAY 1 — A popular flood control bill, bottled up for more than a year by a bitter California water dispute, was approved by the House, 418-5, on April 29. *(Vote 104, p. H-40)*

But to pass the $4.3 billion Water Resources Development Act (HR 1480), the House had to turn its back on John T. Doolittle, R-Calif., and his long-cherished goal of pumping additional water to his district east of Sacramento.

The House action follows the Senate's, which passed its version (S 507) by voice vote on April 19, without Doolittle's proposal. The otherwise uncontroversial bill now goes to conferees to be reconciled. It would include $3 billion in federal money and the remainder from the states.

Doolittle's quest to siphon water to his district was the sticking point in a bill that traditionally is a grab bag of popular projects that rebuild eroding beaches, deepen harbors and erect levees in flood-prone areas.

Critics, including some environmental groups and House members from both parties, criticized Doolittle's plan as an intrusion into the state's delicate attempt to distribute water fairly. Currently, water rights are determined by regional boards and by CALFED, a state-federal cooperative that studies water needs and supplies in California.

In pressing his case, Doolittle insisted his plan would lessen the risk of flooding in Sacramento. The projects would also supply more water to Doolittle's rapidly growing 4th District.

'Zero Sum Game'

"Water in California is a zero sum game. There's only so much, and everybody wants it," said an aide to Ellen O. Tauscher, a California Democrat who opposed Doolittle.

With the exception of Doolittle's proposal, the bill was warmly embraced by lawmakers because it would authorize dozens of projects to protect areas from flooding.

It also would authorize $100 million over four years for environmentally sensitive flood control projects and would reduce the federal share of beach renourishment projects from 65 percent to 50 percent over four years.

With so many popular projects at stake, Doolittle and his adversaries were under pressure to work out their differences so the bill could move forward. Once Doolittle's language was removed, the bill moved easily through the House.

But the margin of victory was misleading. The outcome was in doubt until the night before the vote because Doolittle resisted efforts to strip his provision, even though the White House threatened to veto any legislation that included the language.

More opposition came from environmental groups and taxpayer organizations, as well as from California lawmakers whose districts are downstream from Doolittle's district.

Doolittle's provision would have given Sacramento much needed protection from flooding, but it also called for diverting 200,000 acre-feet of water per year from the Sacramento and American Rivers to supply his fast-growing district. An acre-foot is equivalent to 325,851 gallons.

The diversion was opposed by the state's two Democratic senators, Diane Feinstein and Barbara Boxer, as well as by Democratic Gov. Gray Davis. Even some Republicans, such as Tom Campbell, lined up against Doolittle.

The tide seemed to turn when an amendment, offered by Tauscher and Tom Petri, R-Wis., to delete Doolittle's provision appeared to have enough votes to pass.

Even with the changes, some members had doubts. "Is this bill 100 percent perfect, free of controversy? I'm sure it's not," said Bud Shuster, R-Pa., chairman of the Transportation and Infrastructure Committee.

"In many cases, people are not getting everything they want. . . . But it is a balanced compromise," he said.

One of the unsatisfied lawmakers was Robert T. Matsui, D-Calif., who represents Sacramento, which is considered one of the nation's cities most vulnerable to flooding.

Dam Improvements

Matsui favored a plan that would have raised the Folsom Dam north of the city by 6.5 feet and punched additional outlets in the dam to better control flooding from the American River. Levees along the river would also have been improved at an estimated cost of about $345 million. If that had been done, the odds of Sacramento being flooded in any single year would have improved from 1 in 75 to 1 in 175, according to Matsui's office.

In the end, language authorizing the additional outlets in Folsom Dam was approved, but Matsui had to settle for "expedited studies" of raising the dam and improving the levees.

With both chambers passing legislation, the focus now turns to reconciling the bills and to piecing together a water resources bill for next year. Shuster said he hopes to begin work on that measure in the near future.

Water Projects Bill Cleared, Sent To President

AUGUST 7 — With hours to spare before the August recess, the House cleared and sent to President Clinton a conference agreement authorizing $6.3 billion for an array of flood control, navigation and water resource projects.

By agreeing to the compromise conference report on Aug. 5, both chambers set aside — for the time being — a dispute over water distribution in California and cleared the way for a host of popular projects. Clinton is expected to sign the bill.

Although the Water Resources Development Act (S 507) is studded with noncontroversial projects, ranging from deepening harbors in Baltimore, Savannah, Ga., and Oakland, Calif., to rebuilding beaches in Florida and providing additional flood protection along the Mississippi River, the bill was snagged for more than a year by a single issue.

That issue linked additional flood protection for Sacramento, a high priority for Rep. Robert T. Matsui, D-Calif., to additional water allocations to several counties east of the city.

Gaining the extra water has been a long-cherished goal of Rep. John T. Doolittle, R-Calif., and the same dispute prevented the bill from passing in 1998.

Neither the Senate bill (S 507) nor the House version (HR 1480) authorized the water diversion, in large part because lawmakers said that question should be settled by state and local water authorities, not Congress.

But in an effort to mollify Doolittle, conference Chairman Sen. John H. Chafee, R-R.I., granted California lawmakers five hours on Wednesday to reach agreement.

Prospects for an agreement, however, were never high. Sen. Barbara Boxer, D-Calif., a crucial figure in the negotiations, expressed disappointment that additional protection for Sacramento was linked to Doolittle's quest for more water.

"Sacramento is being held hostage by an extraneous water supply issue," she said. "It's not a good way to legislate."

When no agreement could be reached, conferees accepted the House language providing additional flood control for Sacramento. Despite the improvement, the outcome left neither side happy.

Under the compromise, steps would be taken to protect Sacramento from a flood of a magnitude likely to occur once every 135 years, instead of its current protection against a once-in-95-years flood. The additional protection would be achieved by modifying Folsom Dam on the American River, north of the city.

While that would provide more protection than Sacramento has now, it is far less than the level favored by Matsui, who wants the city protected against a once-in-200-years flood.

With both Doolittle and Matsui disappointed with the result, the battle is certain to be refought again next year.

Controlling Floods

Though the California question is unresolved, the bill is studded with long-sought projects to control flooding, bulk up eroding beaches, deepen harbors, provide hurricane protection and repair the environment.

Another feature is an initiative that encourages the U.S. Army Corps of Engineers to pursue environmentally friendly "non-structural" approaches to control floods. The bills authorized $200 million over five years to promote wetland restoration for flood control. ◆

House Panel Takes Step Toward Establishing National Lands Protection Program

SUMMARY

A measure (HR 701) that would distribute federal offshore drilling revenues to the states for conservation projects was approved by the House Resources Committee at the end of the session, with floor action expected in 2000. It spawned unusual alliances and marked the end of months of negotiations on the part of its sponsor, Don Young, R-Alaska, and George Miller, D-Calif., sponsor of a similar measure.

The bipartisan compromise that emerged from the two competing measures struck a delicate balance between many conflicting interests and was hailed by Young and Miller as "historic." However, the measure encountered opposition during the committee markup Nov. 10. While Democrats and moderate Republicans banded together, there was a small bloc of Western Republicans who feared that it would take too much land away from private property owners and localities.

The legislation carried an annual price tag of nearly $3 billion, which would be paid for from Outer Continental Shelf royalties. Currently, all such royalties go into the federal Treasury.

The measure has a long road ahead of it, however. Young and Miller deflected almost all the amendments during the full committee markup, providing a good indication that opponents will try again on the floor. In addition, not only will the Western lawmakers continue their opposition, but property rights advocates and House appropriators object to spending $3 billion from discretionary spending accounts. And some environmental groups oppose the bill because they say it will encourage additional offshore oil drilling.

The measure stands at the center of an effort by Congress to underwrite a national program to buy up and protect wilderness and other threatened lands. The Senate has been debating similar bills. The Senate Energy and Natural Resources Committee postponed action numerous times on one of the measures (S 25) because a consensus could not be reached.

Box Score

- **Bill:** HR 701
- **Legislative action: House** Resources Committee approved the bill, 37-12, on Nov. 10.

Land Deal Wins Approval of House Panel But Draws Major Criticism

NOVEMBER 13 — Propelled by an unusual alliance, the House Resources Committee approved a bill Nov. 10 that would set aside $3 billion annually primarily to buy and protect the nation's most environmentally sensitive land and for other conservation programs.

The bill (HR 701), approved 37-12, was a compromise forged by two opponents, committee Chairman Don Young, R-Alaska, and ranking Democrat George Miller of California, who steered the bill through a difficult markup. Funding for the bill would come from the proceeds of offshore oil and gas drilling. That revenue has averaged about $4 billion a year, mostly generated by wells in the Gulf of Mexico and off the California coast.

Young said he expects the bill to reach the House floor by next summer.

Young, a conservative recognized as an aggressive property rights advocate, supports the bill because it provides money for wildlife and recreation programs. He has come under harsh attack for sponsoring the bill. Chuck Cushman, the executive director of the American Land Rights Association, said the bill is a "billion-dollar land grab [that] is a threat to every property owner in the country. No one is safe."

Young also was attacked by Western Republicans on his committee.

"When did we conclude that the government can manage the land more responsibly and efficiently than the private property owner?" Helen Chenoweth-Hage, R-Idaho, said during the markup.

Chenoweth-Hage made her displeasure known by filing 39 amendments. Though she did not offer them all during the markup, which lasted more than four hours, she did present some amendments that Young clearly considered nuisances. Those included provisions to limit the government to purchases of less than 100 acres in Idaho; prohibit the introduction of grizzly bears in Idaho or Montana; and require state legislatures to approve the purchase of property within their borders.

Those amendments and all others except one minor one were defeated in committee by a solid block of Democrats, Young and handful of moderate Republicans.

Young said he decided to oppose all amendments because approving even one substantive amendment would upset the bill's delicate compromise.

Land Purchases and More

The bill would provide $900 million annually in guaranteed funding for the Land and Water Conservation Fund (PL 88-578) to acquire environmentally important but threatened land. The fund, underwritten by royalties from oil and gas pumped from offshore, has rarely been fully funded, and critics worried that appropriators would continue to short-change the account.

"This legislation does reclaim the promise that the Congress made to the American people 30 years ago to provide for full funding of land and water conservation, to provide for the replacement and protection of non-renewable resources," Miller said after the bill was approved.

The bill also would provide $125 million annually for urban parks and $150 million annually for conservation easements. It would disburse $1 billion a year to coastal states to offset the effects of offshore drilling and for the conservation of coastal ecosystems.

The amount a state would receive would be tied to how much oil and gas was drilled off its coast. California, for example, would collect $328 million under the bill based on an estimate of $2.8 billion from offshore drilling.

Louisiana would receive $313 million, and Texas, $236 million. Alaska would get $164 million and Florida $141 million under the formula outlined in the bill.

Despite the windfall and the unusual but successful alliance, obstacles remain. Property rights advocates and House appropriators objected to spending $3 billion from discretionary spending accounts.

Some environmental groups oppose the bill because they say it would encourage additional offshore oil drilling and because the funding for the Land and Water Conservation Fund would still be subject to annual appropriations.

A companion bill (S 25) in the Senate, sponsored by Frank H. Murkowski, R-Alaska, and Mary L. Landrieu, D-La., is also snarled over money and property rights issues.

Young tried to defend the bill against attack during months of negotiations, which included strong property rights advocates such as Rep. Richard W. Pombo, R-Calif. The bill, Young said, included protections for property owners. The government could buy land only from willing sellers, and Congress must approve all sales.

But the criticism only intensified, much to Young's dismay. "I'm somewhat disturbed by some of the distortions and frankly outright lies that are being spread about this bill from both sides of the political spectrum," he said. ◆

Superfund Overhaul Stalls; Narrow Exemption Included In Omnibus Spending Bill

SUMMARY

The Senate was unable to produce a bill to overhaul the superfund program, leaving the issue dead for the year. In the House, two versions were marked up, setting the stage for a showdown in 2000. Meanwhile, a provision exempting certain recycling businesses from superfund liability was added to the omnibus spending bill (HR 3194).

With the superfund bill in the Senate (S 1090) declared dead in August, the House took the lead. The House Transportation and Infrastructure Committee approved a bipartisan bill (HR 1300), sponsored by Sherwood Boehlert, R-N.Y. The measure included provisions on the redevelopment of abandoned industrial sites.

The House Commerce Committee crafted its own measure (HR 2580), sponsored by Republican James C. Greenwood of Pennsylvania.

Boehlert's bill called for reinstating a tax on industries, such as oil and chemical producers, whose products are often found in superfund sites. The tax collected nearly $1.5 billion a year until suspended in 1995. HR 2580 makes no mention of the tax.

HR 2580 was significantly changed by Commerce Finance and Hazardous Materials Subcommittee Chairman Michael G. Oxley, R-Ohio, to provide limited liability relief for small businesses and more authority to states and local governments to clean up sites. The committee approved the bill along party lines.

In the Senate, Majority Leader Trent Lott, R-Miss., included language in the omnibus to exempt certain recyclers — those that recycle paper, glass, metals, textiles, rubber and other materials — from superfund liability.

Boehlert said Republican leaders would bring the bill up in early 2000. House Ways and Means Committee Chairman Bill Archer, R-Texas, is likely to block reinstatement of the superfund tax. The new chairman of the Senate Environment and Public Works Committee, Robert C. Smith, R-N.H., wants to rewrite the law but has not provided details.

Box Score

- **Bills:** HR 1300, HR 2580
- **Legislative action: House** Transportation Committee approved HR 1300 (H Rept 106-353, Part 1), 69-2, on Aug. 5.

House Commerce Committee approved HR 2580, 30-21, on Oct. 13.

Subcommittee OKs Superfund Deal

JUNE 12 — The House Transportation, Water Resources and Environment Subcommittee approved a bill June 10 that would adjust portions of the nation's superfund toxic-waste cleanup program. Five Democrats joined Republicans to approve the bill 22-9, moving it to the full committee, where a markup is expected before the July Fourth recess.

The two-hour debate was free of the partisan rancor that has dominated superfund discussions in the past, although the full committee's top Democrat, James L. Oberstar of Minnesota, said a number of issues would have to be resolved before the committee's Democrats would support the bill.

The panel adopted by voice vote an amendment offered by subcommittee Chairman Sherwood Boehlert, R-N.Y., striking exemptions for large paper recyclers and controversial provisions on how to apportion costs in a damage case.

An amendment by Democrat Ellen O. Tauscher of California , adopted by voice vote, would require that a neutral party determine the division of liability at superfund sites when more than one party was responsible for the waste.

House Panel OKs Bill, But Its Future Remains Uncertain

AUGUST 7 — A key House committee overwhelmingly approved a bill Aug. 5 that sponsors insist would improve the beleaguered superfund program, the nation's primary tool for cleaning up the most contaminated and dangerous waste sites.

By a vote of 69-2, the House Transportation and Infrastructure Committee endorsed HR 1300, a narrow bill that would authorize funding for eight years, exempt small businesses from liability and accelerate cleanup of so-called brownfields — abandoned industrial sites in urban areas.

While the committee action was a notable step forward in the tortured process to reauthorize the law, its future remained in considerable doubt.

Supporters said the bill is the best chance to significantly update the superfund law (PL 96-510) since Congress first passed it in 1980. *(1980 Almanac, p. 585)*

The bill would:

- Provide $1.5 billion annually for superfund from fiscal 2000 through fiscal 2003, then decrease funding as the number of sites declined. The bill calls for $975 million in funding in fiscal 2007, the final year.
- Set aside $25 million annually to assist state-run, voluntary cleanups.
- Exempt from liability businesses with fewer than 75 employees and less than $3 million in revenues. The bill also would exempt municipal solid waste operators and those who contribute less than 200 pounds of waste to a superfund site.
- Streamline the regulatory process for redeveloping thousands of brownfields in cities where officials believe these prime locations could be cleaned up and redeveloped.

Those provisions won the support of influential business groups, including the National Association of Realtors, the American Insurance Association, the National Automobile Dealers Association and the National Federation of Independent Business, which praised the bill for removing "innocent small businesses from superfund prosecution and [focusing] resources on actual cleanup, rather than costly litigation."

Despite such praise, the future of superfund overhaul is far from assured. One of the most troublesome questions involves reinstatement of a tax on industries, such as oil and chemical producers, whose products are often responsible for creating superfund sites.

Rep. Robert A. Borski, D-Pa., who helped negotiate HR 1300 with Sherwood Boehlert, R-N.Y., said the tax collected $4 million a day until suspended in 1995. *(1995 Almanac, p. 5-11)*

The committee recommended that the tax be reinstated, but the tax-writing Ways and Means Committee must approve such a provision.

Borski said his support is contingent on the reinstatement of the tax.

"If Ways and Means drops support for the tax," Borski said in an interview Aug. 4, "the bill will lose my support."

Ways and Means Chairman Bill Archer, R-Texas, however, is highly unlikely to support reimposing the tax. He wants to find money from existing sources to pay for superfund cleanup.

Aside from that hurdle, the House bill would have to win approval from the more ideologically divided Commerce Committee, a step that House aides said is far from assured.

Environmental groups and the EPA lined up against the bill.

"The legislative proposal . . . falls significantly short of the mark," the EPA said in a statement.

Among its complaints, the EPA said the bill "does away with the critical principle of 'polluter pays at hundreds of toxic waste sites' and instead shifts the cost of cleanup to the . . . taxpayer."

In direct contradiction to supporters of HR 1300, who insist the bill would accelerate cleanups and bring fairness back to the program, the EPA charged that the bill "would delay cleanups, drive up their costs and bring lawyers and litigation back into the system."

Boehlert remained upbeat, pointing out that the bill was a result of bipartisan negotiation. Though he conceded differences lie ahead as the bill moves forward, Boehlert said he believes the bipartisan support for HR 1300 would provide a basis for compromise.

Tough Road in Senate

Even if those barriers are surmounted, darkness looms in the Senate.

The House action came a day after the Senate Environment and Public Works Committee declared defeat by withdrawing S 1090, a bill that in many ways paralleled the House bill.

Like the House, the chief sponsor in the Senate, John H. Chafee, R-R.I., offered a scaled-down bill this year in the wake of failures of more comprehensive efforts in the last two Congresses.

"Our goal was always to report a bill that enjoyed wide support," Chafee said Aug. 4 in declaring defeat. "We thought S 1090 was that bill. We were wrong."

Among the most troublesome issues was the question of how to clean up damages to natural resources and who would pay for it.

House Leaders Move Ahead With Limited Plan

OCTOBER 2 — A limited overhaul of the superfund program for cleaning up toxic waste sites moved through a House Commerce subcommittee Sept. 29, indicating Republicans' determination to push their business-oriented plan this year or early next.

The bill (HR 2580) moved out of the Subcommittee on Finance and Hazardous Materials on a 17-12 vote after nearly six hours of debate, in which votes on most amendments broke along party lines. Only one Democrat, Ralph M. Hall of Texas, voted for the final bill.

The full Commerce Committee is expected to mark up HR 2580 the week of Oct. 11. If it reaches the Rules Committee, it will compete with a separate superfund bill (HR 1300) approved by the House Transportation and Infrastructure Committee on Aug. 5.

Business interests, led by the U.S. Chamber of Commerce, immediately hailed the Commerce subcommittee's outcome, while environmental groups condemned it.

Subcommittee Chairman Michael G. Oxley, R-Ohio, and bill sponsor James C. Greenwood, R-Pa., geared HR 2580 toward providing limited liability relief for small business, streamlining site cleanups by giving states and local governments more authority, and spurring redevelopment of urban "brownfields," which are abandoned, vacant and heavily polluted urban industrial sites.

The bill would exempt small businesses from having to pay a portion of the cleanup cost. This language was a major goal of small businesses and their powerful voice, the National Federation of Independent Business, which have long argued that regulators have gone after small businesses that have contributed only a fraction of the contaminants and forced them to pay an excessive amount of the cleanup costs.

Under the bill, a small business is defined as one that has annual revenues of less than $3 million and fewer than 75 employees.

The bill would cap liability of municipal landfill owners on superfund's list of national priorities at 10 percent for small municipalities and 20 percent for larger municipalities. And it would allow states to keep a site off the list by obtaining an agreement from parties to conduct a voluntary cleanup.

Democratic amendments to toughen cleanup standards and ensure a robust federal presence in the cleanups were all rejected on party-line votes. A substitute amendment by Edolphus Towns, D-N.Y., based on his bill (HR 1750) to limit superfund revisions to brownfields, was defeated, 12-15, also on a party-line vote.

Republicans and Democrats joined to defeat, 13-14, an amendment by W.J. "Billy" Tauzin, R-La., to limit claims related to natural resource damages. Current law requires that any damaged public resource be restored or replaced by the acquisition of a new area.

Republicans and Democrats generally agree that the superfund law (PL 96-510) needs to be overhauled and updated. Congress has made few revisions to the program, which cleans up the nation's most contaminated sites. *(1980 Almanac, p. 585)*

But Democrats and environmental groups remain staunchly opposed to the Greenwood-Oxley initiative. "Today, I must ask whether we are engaged in a political exercise or a serious or competent attempt to legislate," said John D. Dingell, D-Mich., who complained that a "hasty markup" cut short promising negotiations. Like many other Democrats, Dingell pushed for a bill that was limited to brownfields.

"If you pass this bill you're endangering public health," said Grant Cope, a staff attorney for the Washington-based U.S. Public Interest Research Group. Cope complained that the bill particularly weakens cleanup standards for water, posing a threat to people downstream who might drink it.

Committee aides said they expect the Greenwood-Oxley bill to be approved by the full committee, although prospects for floor action remain uncertain. Moreover, the Senate appears to have no appetite for superfund revisions.

Sen. John H. Chafee, R-R.I., chairman of the Environment and Public Works Committee, withdrew his bill (S 1090) on Aug. 4 because his committee could not agree even on what Chafee said was a narrowly drawn measure.

If HR 2580 makes it to the House floor, it will join HR 1300, the bill by Republican Sherwood Boehlert of New York that was approved by the Transportation and Infrastructure Committee by a lopsided, 69-2 margin.

One difference is that Boehlert's bill calls for reinstating a generic superfund tax on industries, such as oil and chemical producers, whose products are often responsible for creating superfund sites. The tax, which largely financed superfund cleanups in the past, collected nearly $1.5 billion a year until suspended in 1995. *(1995 Almanac, p. 5-11)*

House Committee Approves Modest Superfund Bill

OCTOBER 16 — The House Commerce Committee has set up a possible showdown between competing versions of bills to overhaul the superfund program for cleaning up toxic waste sites.

The committee approved a narrow bill (HR 2580) on Oct. 13, despite strong opposition from panel Democrats and a suggestion of a presidential veto. The measure was approved, 30-21, during a markup that lasted past 8 p.m. Two Democrats, Ralph M. Hall of Texas and Bart Gordon of Tennessee, broke party ranks to vote in favor of the bill.

The measure will now have to compete with a separate bill (HR 1300) sponsored by Sherwood Boehlert, R-N.Y. That bill, which would make more sweeping changes to superfund, gained bipartisan support from the House Transportation and Infrastructure Committee in August.

GOP staff members were unable to predict whether the competing bills will be taken up by the Rules Committee and scheduled for floor action this session.

The Commerce-approved bill, sponsored by James C. Greenwood, R-Pa., and expanded slightly by panel Republican Michael G. Oxley of Ohio would authorize funding for superfund for five years, at $1.5 billion for each of the first three years, $1.4 billion in the fourth year and $1.35 billion in the last year. It would establish a $1 million loan fund for redevelopment of brownfields, which are abandoned, polluted industrial sites.

The bill also would change liability provisions by expanding exemptions from cleanup costs for buyers, sellers, innocent site owners and owners of contiguous property. It also would exempt small businesses, those with annual revenues of less than $3 million and fewer than 75 employees.

Democrats argued that the liability exemptions would be too broad. "This bill will let the polluter off the hook. . . . We need to stick with the 'polluter pays' principle," said Frank Pallone Jr., D-N.J.

Democratic amendments aimed at toughening standards and maintaining a strong federal role in cleanups were rejected. For example, Bart Stupak, D-Mich., introduced an amendment, rejected by voice vote, that would have reverted to language in the original law that allows the EPA to intervene in a state cleanup if there is an "imminent and substantial endangerment to public health."

Republicans said the amendment would weaken provisions that would allow states to certify that a site has been cleaned up under state programs. Federal enforcement would be prohibited if a state certified that its program, once enacted, has the resources to be implemented.

"The language in the amendment is overly vague and would go against everything we are trying to do," Greenwood said.

The panel also rejected, 17-26, an amendment by Thomas M. Barrett, D-Wis., that would have allowed localities to request that a site be placed on the national priorities list for cleanup.

Many environmentalists and the Clinton administration declared staunch opposition to the bill that emerged from Commerce. In a letter to ranking committee Democrat John D. Dingell of Michigan, EPA Administrator Carol M. Browner said, "Given the significant progress we have been able to achieve in the superfund program over the past six years, the administration cannot support legislation that would undermine that progress and therefore must oppose HR 2580."

Said Dingell: "This measure is not ready for prime time yet. We don't have a bipartisan bill here, because we are rushing it."

Lott Adds Recyclers' Exemption to Spending Package

NOVEMBER 20 — Undaunted by earlier failures, Senate Majority Leader Trent Lott, R-Miss., grafted language onto the fiscal 2000 omnibus appropriations bill that would exempt certain recycling businesses from superfund liability.

The language added by Lott to HR 3194 (Conference report: H Rept 106-479) is a modified version of a bill (S 1528) that Lott sponsored with Minority Leader Tom Daschle, D-S.D.

It is similar to a provision Lott tried, but failed, to attach to last year's omnibus spending bill (PL 105-277). *(1998 Almanac, p. 2-112)*

The language would effectively exempt companies that recycle such materials as paper, glass, metals and rubber from having to pay some of the cost of cleaning up contaminated sites. While the language has the support of environmentalists and the White House, it is opposed by some members who believe that providing individual exemptions will dim prospects for comprehensive superfund overhaul.

Rep. Sherwood Boehlert, R-N.Y., who sponsored a superfund overhaul bill (HR 1300), said the recycling provision could further cloud the murky politics of superfund. Exempting one group from liability, he said, would increase the costs for others.

"It is not fair any way you slice it," he said.

Still another objection was voiced by groups representing low-income areas. They argued that exempting recyclers could slow cleanup of sites often found in low-income areas.

"Under the liability carve-out, these communities will have no hope of having the health threats cleaned up; the communities most in need of health protection are left with the least funding for cleanup," the Center on Race, Poverty and the Environment wrote to President Clinton on Nov. 5. ◆

Chapter 13

EXECUTIVE BRANCH

President Clinton Survives Impeachment Trial; His Reputation Does Not

Box Score

- **Legislative action: House** adopted H Res 10, reappointing managers for the House's case in the impeachment trial, 223-198, on Jan. 6. (The **House** impeached Clinton on Dec. 19, 1998, adopting two articles in H Res 611 of the 105th Congress. That day it also adopted H Res 614, notifying the Senate of its actions and making initial appointment of its 13 trial prosecutors.)

  Senate rejected Article I, 45-55, and rejected Article II, 50-50, on Feb. 12. (A two-thirds majority was required to convict.)

SUMMARY

The second impeachment trial of a president of the United States, and the first of an elected president, ended when the Senate voted Feb. 12 to acquit Bill Clinton on both articles of impeachment brought by the House at the end of 1998. Under the Constitution, a two-thirds majority vote for either article would have convicted the president and thereby removed him from office.

Despite the obvious drama, Clinton's presidency was never seriously imperiled by the trial. A day after being sworn in, senators Jan. 8 took the first of several steps toward narrowing the scope of the proceedings — and at the same time set a tone much less rancorous and partisan than in the House the year before. By 100-0, senators decided on a procedure that put in doubt whether witnesses would ever be called, and that set the stage for an early test vote on the strength of the House's case.

After three days of presentations by the "managers" from the House Judiciary Committee, three days of presentations by the president's defense team and two days in which senators posed questions to both sides, the Senate voted Jan. 27 on a motion to dismiss the case. Forty-four senators, all Democrats, voted in favor of ending the trial at that point — a tangible demonstration that the prosecutors would be unable to produce the two-thirds majority required for conviction.

Though the president's approval rating approached 70 percent, and while many Republicans described their "impeachment fatigue," GOP conservatives insisted that the trial continue. Depositions were taken from three witnesses, and videotaped clips were played for the senators and shown on national television. But on Feb. 4, the Senate rejected, 30-70, the managers' motion to bring their key witness, former White House intern Monica Lewinsky, to the Senate floor for questioning.

As the Constitution stipulates, Chief Justice William H. Rehnquist presided over the 20-day trial, but he downplayed his own importance in the proceedings. He ruled Jan. 15, for example, that the senators were not "jurors" as in a regular courtroom — empowered to decide only the merits of the facts — but constituted a "court," with the power to determine matters of law as well as fact.

Several of the debates on the key procedural motions took place only after the Senate chamber's audio system was deactivated and its doors secured. The three days of final deliberation on Clinton's fate were similarly secret. A vote to open that debate was defeated, 59-41, eight votes short of the two-thirds needed to change Senate rules for the proceedings.

Many senators later released what they said were transcripts of their speeches during the deliberations. From those, it appeared that no senator had risen to defend the president's Democrats stood united in their view that his actions did not rise to the level of misconduct contemplated by the drafters of the Constitution's impeachment provision.

Shortly after noon on Feb. 12, senators served notice that they had reached verdicts, signaling the climax of the first presidential impeachment trial since 1868, when Andrew Johnson avoided removal from office by a single vote.

In this case, by contrast, the only suspense was whether either article would get a simple majority — a legally meaningless marker, but one that would have been a symbolic victory to the House Republicans who pushed the impeachment.

Ten Republicans joined with all 45 Democrats to vote "not guilty" on Article I. It alleged that Clinton provided "perjurious, false and misleading testimony" about the sexual nature of his relationship with Lewinsky to a federal grand jury convened by Kenneth W. Starr, an independent counsel.

Five of those Republicans joined with all Democrats to vote "not guilty" on Article II. It alleged that Clinton directed a "scheme designed to delay, impede, cover up and conceal" his affair with Lewinsky and other evidence unfavorable to him in a sexual harassment lawsuit against him by Paula Corbin Jones, a state employee when Clinton was governor of Arkansas.

A bipartisan group of senators, most of them Democrats, tried at that point to obtain a vote on a resolution censuring the president for "shameful, reckless and indefensible" conduct. But the resolution was quashed on a procedural vote.

"I want to say again to the American people how profoundly sorry I am for what I said and did to trigger these events and the great burden they have imposed on Congress and the American people," Clinton said after the votes.

On April 12, U.S. District Judge Susan Webber Wright issued the first civil contempt citation against a sitting president. In the Jones case, she wrote, "the record demonstrates by clear and convincing evidence that the president [gave] false, misleading and evasive answers that were designed to obstruct the judicial process" — phrases resonant of Article II. Clinton did not contest the finding and paid a $90,686 sanction.

Starr resigned Oct. 18. At his request, a panel of three federal judges named as his successor Robert W. Ray, a top official in the independent counsel's office. He said he would move in a "prompt, responsible and cost effective" way to end an inquiry that began in August 1994 as a probe of the Clintons' Whitewater land deal.

Senate Opens Impeachment Trial

JANUARY 9 — Bill Clinton is facing a Senate trial that could end his presidency. But the 91 men and nine women who will judge the president are facing the most formidable test of their political careers. With pomp in the foreground and partisanship in the shadows, the Senate on Jan. 7 opened the second presidential impeachment trial in the nation's history.

At stake is not only the president's fate, but also the prestige of the Senate and the reputations of the senators who serve as the jury in this case.

Over the next several weeks, these 100 senator-jurors will be rendering judgments on a host of complicated and explosive questions that will dictate the course of the trial: whether to call as a witness Monica Lewinsky, the pivotal figure in the case, and risk turning the Senate into a political theater of the absurd; whether to peremptorily end the trial altogether; and, ultimately, whether to convict the president and remove him from office.

In doing so, they must reconcile the competing desires of Republicans, Democrats and the White House to render impartial yet speedy justice to the president.

The Senate trial began just one day after the new Congress convened with major leadership changes in the House, heightening the sense of political uncertainty at both ends of the Capitol. Illinois Republican Dennis Hastert was sworn in as the new Speaker of the House, capping a remarkable shake-up in the upper echelons of the GOP leadership.

The Senate is attempting to write the final chapter to an inglorious saga in American history, which began nearly a year ago with the disclosure of Clinton's affair with Lewinsky. It is trying the president on two articles of impeachment — on charges of perjury and obstruction of justice stemming from that affair — approved by the House on Dec. 19.

While it is never possible to predict the outcome of a trial, virtually no one believes that the Senate will muster the two-thirds supermajority needed to convict Clinton and remove him from office — particularly if his poll ratings remain as strong as they have so far.

"I don't really envision the ability to get 67 votes now," said Alaska Republican Ted Stevens, although he indicated that in a trial, "surprises can develop."

The impeachment proceedings, which triggered such intense acrimony in the House, got off to a surprisingly smooth start in the Senate after some initial partisan jousting. After an extraordinary bipartisan caucus in the old Senate chamber Jan. 8, members of the two major parties embraced a plan for the trial developed by a pair of ideological opposites — Massachusetts Democrat Edward M. Kennedy and Texas Republican Phil Gramm.

"Stranger things have happened in politics," John McCain, R-Ariz., told CNN. "But the Kennedy-Gramm alignment is one of the strangest."

The compromise plan, formally adopted later that day on a 100-0 vote, fulfills the GOP's demand that witnesses be permitted. But it places tight conditions on the issuing of subpoenas and the introduction of new evidence.

Under the proposal, the Senate will vote on a motion to present witnesses, as well as on individual subpoena requests. That means that if the 13 members of the House Judiciary Committee who will prosecute the case want to call Lewinsky or others, the Senate will have two opportunities to vote on the matter.

As the trial begins to move, said Senate Majority leader Trent Lott, R-Miss., there is "no preclusion of witnesses, or inclusion of witnesses."

The plan allows the Senate to go ahead with opening arguments by House prosecutors and White House lawyers, while deferring the contentious question of witnesses. It also sets the stage for votes, later this month, on motions to dismiss the charges against Clinton and to adjourn the trial.

Clearly, the proposal by Kennedy and Gramm does not resolve all the potential sticking points — particularly because the White House was not a direct participant in the negotiations. There are likely to be vigorous objections from Democrats if House prosecutors succeed in calling Lewinsky and other witnesses. White House officials said if that occurs, the president's lawyers may extend the proceedings for months with depositions and motions.

Neither does the plan foreclose the possibility that the Senate trial could deteriorate into the sort of bruising partisanship that dominated the House impeachment proceedings. "There is every possibility that partisanship can raise its ugly head again," McCain said.

At the same time, the plan gives Democrats a shot at convincing Republicans of the futility of prolonged proceedings, which could be stopped after the first phase by a procedural motion or even a final vote on conviction or acquittal.

The plan will allow the trial to resume Jan. 13 with opening statements by the House prosecutors the next day. "This is a getting-to-second-base proposal," said Kansas Republican Sen. Sam Brownback.

Moving Toward a Vote

Senate Democrats, backed strongly by the White House, had originally expressed strong opposition to the idea of calling witnesses. "I think it's fair to say there is universal, unanimous opposition to witnesses in our caucus," Minority Leader Tom Daschle, D-S.D., said before the start of the trial.

Democrats felt strongly that the introduction of witnesses would lead to a protracted trial, and many were bitterly resentful that Judiciary Committee Chairman Henry J. Hyde, R-Ill., and the other House Republicans — who refrained from calling any witnesses during the panel's hearings — were now insisting on taking testimony on the floor of the Senate.

But under the Senate's rules for impeachment trials, Daschle and the Democrats were prohibited from threatening a filibuster over the issue

— a tactic they have deployed effectively in legislative battles in recent years. Republicans could have rammed through their plan for the trial on a party-line vote.

And despite Daschle's sweeping statement, several Democrats indicated that they are open to the idea of permitting at least some witnesses.

With that issue resolved, at least temporarily, by the Gramm-Kennedy agreement, Democrats are now preparing for an effort to pull the plug on a trial once the opening statements have been concluded. "I have already told my colleagues that at that point I will offer a motion on the threshold question of whether the president's offenses rise to the level of impeachable offenses," said Robert G. Torricelli, D-N.J.

At this point, it is far from certain whether a motion to stop the trial could garner the 51 votes needed to pass. But several Democrats suggested that many Republicans, facing the prospect of a trial with lengthy arguments, multiple motions and Lewinsky telling a lurid tale of her relationship with Clinton to the Senate, may choose to simply shut down the proceedings.

"I believe there are a number of moderate Republicans who don't want to see the debacle of Monica Lewinsky appearing on the floor of the Senate," said Iowa Democrat Tom Harkin.

Even if a motion to adjourn were to fail, said Delaware Democrat Joseph R. Biden Jr., Democrats could show that there is little chance of persuading at least 12 of them to form the two-thirds majority needed to convict Clinton. "If that happens, then the burden would be on Republicans to show why we need to proceed," he said in an interview.

This vote is likely to be influenced by a host of factors, including the strength of the argument that the House prosecutors make on behalf of calling witnesses.

But in the end, an impeachment trial is a political as well as a legal proceeding, and senators will approach this crucial early test with that in mind. What is certain is that any Republicans who back an effort to shut down the trial before a final vote on articles of impeachment will incur the full wrath of the party's conservative base.

"We're under a lot of pressure, no question about it," said Vermont Republican James M. Jeffords, a leading moderate. He suggested it was premature to consider when to end the trial, saying his overarching objective was to ensure "an orderly process."

Pomp and Politics

The Senate trial opened with a solemn ceremony not seen since the nation's only other presidential impeachment trial, of Andrew Johnson, 131 years ago.

Supreme Court Chief Justice William H. Rehnquist was sworn in as the trial's presiding officer by Strom Thurmond, R-S.C., the president pro tempore of the Senate. Rehnquist then swore in the senators, who promised to render "impartial justice, according to the laws and the Constitution."

But the historic proceedings seemed to produce little outcry from the public, much of which long ago grew weary of the Lewinsky scandal. And Daniel K. Inouye, D-Hawaii, was troubled to observe empty seats in the gallery as senators were sworn in.

Indeed, even some senators seemed less than awestruck by the first impeachment trial since Reconstruction. "It's fairly routine," said Craig Thomas, R-Wyo., "We knew it was coming for a while."

When the closely scripted ceremony ended, the profound substantive differences between the two parties surfaced, although leaders quickly backed away from a floor confrontation. Soon after the swearing-in, Republican leaders announced that competing GOP and Democratic plans would be decided by floor votes. Once it appeared that these would be party-line divisions, however, they restarted discussions that led to the Jan. 8 plan.

The efforts by the protagonists in this drama to avoid a replay of the hostility that consumed the House were strenuous and unusual. For now, at least, all sides see it in their interest to resist the impulse to "go nuclear."

White House officials, who seldom passed up an opportunity to bash the Republicans who drove the impeachment process in the House, have shown considerably more deference to the Senate. White House spokesman Joe Lockhart heaped blame on the 13 House prosecutors for insisting on witnesses, even though it is clear that many Senate Republicans also favor that course.

Lott and Daschle have seldom worked more closely. Meeting with reporters Jan. 7, the two seemed more like old pals than leaders of rival political operations.

Both men know that resorting to political warfare not only would tarnish the Senate's reputation, but also would make it impossible to work together on legislative issues when the impeachment crisis ends.

"We think that the best way to keep calm and cool and dignified is to look at each other and talk to each other," Lott said.

Lott has been under intense pressure from conservatives to move forward with a trial with numerous witnesses and detailed testimony. He had initially promoted a bipartisan plan to hold a four-day trial without a single witness, sponsored by his ally Slade Gorton, R-Wash., and Joseph I. Lieberman, D-Conn. But he quickly abandoned the proposal when it was met with a torrent of criticism from the right.

Still, he has been trying to reassure skeptical Democrats that merely providing an opportunity for each side to call witnesses does not mean the trial will result in a long parade of dirty laundry dragged across the floor of the Senate.

"I want somebody to show me why X, Y or Z witness might be needed, what they might testify to, and some justification," Lott told reporters Jan. 7. "And I have to tell you I have to be persuaded because I'm not, you know, all that excited about that prospect."

Lott's adept balancing act has won him praise from senior Democrats, including Daschle and Lieberman. Others were more cynical, suggesting that Lott had hard-headed political motives for trying to put some limits on a trial. "He's trying to save members of his party from themselves," said Torricelli.

The unity tableau struck by Lott and Daschle provided an example to members of both parties as they entered the old Senate chamber for the 100-member caucus behind closed doors.

Participants said the tone for that session was set by Robert C. Byrd of West Virginia, the 81-year-old former Democratic leader who engenders respect from both sides of the aisle for his

The Articles of Impeachment

H Res 611

Resolution Impeaching William Jefferson Clinton, President of the United States, for high crimes and misdemeanors.

Resolved, that William Jefferson Clinton, President of the United States, is impeached for high crimes and misdemeanors, and that the following articles of impeachment be exhibited to the United States Senate:

Articles of impeachment exhibited by the House of Representatives of the United States of America in the name of itself and of the people of the United States of America, against William Jefferson Clinton, President of the United States of America, in maintenance and support of its impeachment against him for high crimes and misdemeanors.

Article I

In his conduct while President of the United States, William Jefferson Clinton, in violation of his constitutional oath faithfully to execute the office of President of the United States and, to the best of his ability, preserve, protect, and defend the Constitution of the United States, and in violation of his constitutional duty to take care that the laws be faithfully executed, has willfully corrupted and manipulated the judicial process of the United States for his personal gain and exoneration, impeding the administration of justice, in that:

On August 17, 1998, William Jefferson Clinton swore to tell the truth, the whole truth, and nothing but the truth before a Federal grand jury of the United States. Contrary to that oath, William Jefferson Clinton willfully provided perjurious, false and misleading testimony to the grand jury concerning one or more of the following: (1) the nature and details of his relationship with a subordinate Government employee; (2) prior perjurious, false and misleading testimony he gave in a Federal civil rights action brought against him; (3) prior false and misleading statements he allowed his attorney to make to a Federal judge in that civil rights action; and (4) his corrupt efforts to influence the testimony of witnesses and to impede the discovery of evidence in that civil rights action.

In doing this, William Jefferson Clinton has undermined the integrity of his office, has brought disrepute on the Presidency, has betrayed his trust as President, and has acted in a manner subversive of the rule of law and justice, to the manifest injury of the people of the United States.

Wherefore, William Jefferson Clinton, by such conduct, warrants impeachment and trial, and removal from office and disqualification to hold and enjoy any office of honor, trust or profit under the United States.

Article II

In his conduct while President of the United States, William Jefferson Clinton, in violation of his constitutional oath faithfully to execute the office of President of the United States and, to the best of his ability, preserve, protect, and defend the Constitution of the United States, and in violation of his constitutional duty to take care that the laws be faithfully executed, has prevented, obstructed, and impeded the administration of justice, and has to that end engaged personally, and through his subordinates and agents, in a course of conduct or scheme designed to delay, impede, cover up, and conceal the existence of evidence and testimony related to a Federal civil rights action brought against him in a duly instituted judicial proceeding.

The means used to implement this course of conduct or scheme included one or more of the following acts:

(1) On or about December 17, 1997, William Jefferson Clinton corruptly encouraged a witness in a Federal civil rights action brought against him to execute a sworn affidavit in that proceeding that he knew to be perjurious, false and misleading.

(2) On or about December 17, 1997, William Jefferson Clinton corruptly encouraged a witness in a Federal civil rights action brought against him to give perjurious, false and misleading testimony if and when called to testify personally in that proceeding.

(3) On or about December 28, 1997, William Jefferson Clinton corruptly engaged in, encouraged, or supported a scheme to conceal evidence that had been subpoenaed in a Federal civil rights action brought against him.

(4) Beginning on or about December 7, 1997, and continuing through and including January 14, 1998, William Jefferson Clinton intensified and succeeded in an effort to secure job assistance to a witness in a Federal civil rights action brought against him in order to corruptly prevent the truthful testimony of that witness in that proceeding at a time when the truthful testimony of that witness would have been harmful to him.

(5) On January 17, 1998, at his deposition in a Federal civil rights action brought against him, William Jefferson Clinton corruptly allowed his attorney to make false and misleading statements to a Federal judge characterizing an affidavit, in order to prevent questioning deemed relevant by the judge.

Such false and misleading statements were subsequently acknowledged by his attorney in a communication to that judge.

(6) On or about January 18 and January 20-21, 1998, William Jefferson Clinton related a false and misleading account of events relevant to a Federal civil rights action brought against him to a potential witness in that proceeding, in order to corruptly influence the testimony of that witness.

(7) On or about January 21, 23 and 26, 1998, William Jefferson Clinton made false and misleading statements to potential witnesses in a Federal grand jury proceeding in order to corruptly influence the testimony of those witnesses. The false and misleading statements made by William Jefferson Clinton were repeated by the witnesses to the grand jury, causing the grand jury to receive false and misleading information.

In all of this, William Jefferson Clinton has undermined the integrity of his office, has brought disrepute on the Presidency, has betrayed his trust as President, and has acted in a manner subversive of the rule of law and justice, to the manifest injury of the people of the United States.

Wherefore, William Jefferson Clinton, by such conduct, warrants impeachment and trial, and removal from office and disqualification to hold and enjoy any office of honor, trust or profit under the United States.

love of the Senate and its precedents.

Byrd, as always, studded his speech with historical references. But his basic theme was that only the Senate could lead the nation out of the impeachment crisis. Clinton has sullied his office through his own personal conduct, he said, and the House has tarnished its reputation with partisan rancor.

"Byrd set the stage," McCain said. "He was very eloquent reminding us of our obligations and what the American people expect from us."

Connecticut Democrat Christopher J. Dodd hit the same theme — that the Senate, not the White House or the House of Representatives, should control this process and ensure it is conducted with dignity.

"The matter we're dealing with is not some product liability case," Dodd said later. "It is about the most lurid and salacious material."

Then came the most surprising moment in the closed-door session, when Kennedy and Gramm found common ground. Gramm suggested that the Senate's impeachment rules permitted the calling of witnesses, and neither party was proposing changing those rules. Kennedy agreed, and the deal became a reality a few hours later.

"Everyone had a sense that . . . the Senate was on trial. It wasn't just the president of the United States," Kennedy said later.

Underlying Strategies

Senators left that meeting ebullient, with many feeling they had somehow found the solution to the Rubik's Cube of impeachment. But the reality is that, behind the bonhomie and bipartisanship, the gap between the White House and its strongest supporters on one side, and hard-core conservatives on the other, could not be wider.

Democrats have been so adamant in objecting to witnesses partly because they know, as things now stand, that there are not enough votes in the Senate to remove Clinton from office. But that could change if the trial drags on and new evidence surfaces showing more misconduct by Clinton.

Conservatives who detest Clinton have long harbored the belief, or the hope, that a "magic bullet" would emerge in the form of a new scandal that would turn the public and Congress decisively against the president.

Indeed, some Senate conservatives are already expressing interest in reviewing material — which was never part of the impeachment record compiled by the House Judiciary Committee — that includes new allegations. "Those who have seen it, and I have not, say it is absolutely necessary for us to consider," said Oklahoma Republican Sen. James M. Inhofe.

House prosecutors have already signaled they want to introduce new evidence in the Senate trial. That caused a last-minute hitch in negotiations over the trial plan.

Democrats are outraged by suggestions that any new material could be brought against Clinton at this late stage in the process. Sen. Patrick J. Leahy, D-Vt., characterized the view of House Republican prosecutors this way: "We may want to find some new witnesses, we may want to find something." But Leahy said the Senate "should not be looking for something beyond the four corners of what is the evidence already."

Senate Confronts Two Constituencies: History — and the Voters in 2000

JANUARY 16 — When Rod Grams left yet another recent closed-door meeting of Republicans, he took one look at the crowd of reporters waiting to grill senators about President Clinton's impeachment trial, pivoted smartly — and then quickly walked in the opposite direction.

A former TV newscaster and a Republican senator from Minnesota for four years, Grams had good reason for wanting to beat a hasty retreat from his previous associates in the media on Jan. 12.

All 100 senators are struggling with their unfamiliar, difficult and complicated roles as both judges and jurors in the first presidential impeachment trial in 131 years. But for Grams and 32 other senators who face re-election in 2000, in particular, impeachment angst has been increased significantly by another, intensely political concern: The decisions they make in the next several weeks — on questions ranging from whether to call witnesses right up to the ultimate judgment on removing Clinton from office — may determine their political future.

The trial got under way in earnest on Jan. 14 when a team of "managers" from the House Judiciary Committee, who are serving as the prosecutors in the case, began laying out in exhaustive and occasionally compelling detail why the Senate should find Clinton guilty of perjury and obstruction of justice and remove him from office.

The managers' opening arguments also had a crucial short-term goal — to persuade the Senate to permit the House to call witnesses to buttress its case. And it was clear that, on that question, the House team made headway; Senate Majority Leader Trent Lott, R-Miss., and other senior Republicans seemed increasingly receptive to the idea of allowing witnesses to be called.

That question will be among the most important tests facing the Senate when it casts a series of pivotal votes during the week of Jan. 25, which will determine the scope and duration of the trial.

It is difficult to say how these issues will be resolved. With the start of the case, many senators have become far more circumspect in sharing their thoughts — a situation bolstered by the requirement that they stay silent in their Senate seats for hours at a time. Still, the Senate appears to be headed for party-line votes, perhaps even including on the final question of whether to acquit or convict the president.

Senators insist they are determined to keep politics out of the judgments they will make. But during intermissions in the opening statements, all sides found time to hone their political strategy.

Even as Republicans raised the prospect of prolonging the trial by calling witnesses, they sought to erase the unwanted image of the GOP as the "impeachment party" by focusing attention on their inchoate legislative agenda. The president unveiled more of his agenda as well, determined to press on with business as usual. *(State of the Union, p. D-5)*

Democratic senators, who sharply attacked the case presented by the House prosecutors, know that if all 45 of them stick together against the president's conviction, he will not be removed. The arithmetic of impeachment favors the White House, because the 55 Republicans need 12 Democratic votes to muster the two-thirds majority needed for conviction.

The senators who face re-election in 2000 are making their own political calculus. None want to follow in the footsteps of Marjorie Margolies-Mezvinsky, a one-term House Democrat from Pennsylvania (1993-95), for whom a single vote — in favor of Clinton's 1993 budget plan — proved politically fatal.

Will votes they cast in the Clinton trial turn any of next year's incumbents into the new Margolies-Mezvinsky? No one knows, but it is clear that Republicans are more at risk than Democrats.

Not only has the party taken a pounding in public approval polls since embarking on the impeachment process, but Republicans must defend 19 seats as opposed to only 14 for Democrats.

"The avoidance of controversy in this particular instance is impossible, particularly for Republicans," said Ross K. Baker, a professor of political science at Rutgers University.

Of the 19 GOP senators up in 2000, 13 represent states that Clinton carried in 1996. They include Grams, Spencer Abraham of Michigan, Rick Santorum of Pennsylvania and Slade Gorton of Washington. By contrast, only three of the Democrats — Kent Conrad of North Dakota, Bob Kerrey of Nebraska and Charles S. Robb of Virginia — face the challenge of running in states that Clinton lost two years ago.

Grams, who represents what currently might be the quirkiest electorate in the nation, may feel the political cross-currents more acutely than anyone. While Minnesota is solidly pro-Clinton — he carried the state by 11 percentage points over George Bush in 1992 and 16 points over Bob Dole in 1996 — its Republican Party is dominated by social conservatives. Then there is the new governor, Jesse Ventura, who embodies the state's penchant for political independence.

Grams, who won his seat with just 49 percent of the vote, has compiled a solidly conservative voting record and has been a sharp critic of the president. It would be out of character for him to vote to let Clinton off the hook.

But for now, he is not saying what he will do. "This process should be driven by principle and conscience, not politics or those who pander to the press," he said in a statement explaining his decision to refrain from public comments on the trial.

Yet politics seems as integral a part of the process as the rules the Senate has devised for the trial. What follows is a guide as to how the next crucial weeks in the trial might unfold.

The First Vote: Pull the Plug ?

A bipartisan agreement unanimously adopted on Jan. 8 (S Res 16) has set much of the timetable. *(Vote 1, p. S-4)*

The first vote will come on a motion by White House lawyers, or perhaps a Democratic senator, to dismiss the two articles of impeachment voted by the House on the grounds that they fail to meet the constitutional standard of "high crimes and misdemeanors."

A few weeks ago, some GOP senators felt the White House had an outside chance of gaining the six Republican votes needed for the requisite 51 votes to approve this motion and shut down the trial. But that seems less likely now, as GOP moderates have shown reluctance to conclude the trial before moving to the question of conviction or acquittal.

"My guess is there are not enough votes to dismiss the case," Robert F. Bennett, R-Utah, said. "Conventional wisdom says there are not two-thirds to convict."

John H. Chafee, R.I., is one Republican the White House must pick up to prevail. But even he favors a full trial and says he is "quite confident" a motion to dismiss the case early would fail.

Supporting a motion of dismissal would be an extremely risky step for Grams and other GOP senators facing re-election in 2000. Conservative activists have strongly advocated letting the trial proceed to a conclusion, and supporting such a motion might trigger a primary challenge from the right.

Indeed, this vote might be more important as an indicator for how Democrats are approaching the Clinton trial. Some senior Democrats appear to share the GOP view that ending the trial early would indicate that the Senate is not approaching the charges seriously enough.

"I think we ought to reach a judgment on the articles," Robert C. Byrd, D-W.Va., said in an interview on the "NewsHour with Jim Lehrer" on Jan. 12. "Naturally, that does, in my thinking, mean that we would not support a motion to dismiss prior to a vote on the articles."

The senators who will be watched closely on this vote are those Democrats who have been most sharply critical of Clinton's personal conduct, such as Joseph I. Lieberman of Connecticut and Bob Graham of Florida, and those who expect tough re-election challenges in two years, such as Robb.

Democratic leaders want to use this vote to show that the Senate would fall short of the two-thirds required for conviction. A strong vote for the motion, even if it does not carry, would bolster Democratic arguments that — since the final verdict appears preordained — in-person testimony need not be taken and the final votes on Clinton's fate should be taken as soon as possible

But if more than a few Democrats oppose the motion to dismiss the charges, the vote would likely spur GOP demands for a full-blown trial with numerous witnesses. That raises the question of whether the White House, if confronted with significant Democratic defections, would forgo offering the motion.

The Next Test: Witnesses

While outlining their case in exhaustive detail over three days, House prosecutors again and again returned to a central theme — they need witnesses to mount an effective prosecution.

"The important point to remember is that the place for live witnesses is at a trial, so the jury can see the witnesses' demeanor, so the jury can watch how the witness testifies, so the jury can gauge the witnesses' credibility," said Rep. James E. Rogan, R-Calif., who argued the perjury count for the prosecution. Like all but three of the 13 House managers, he has prosecutorial experience.

No issue related to the trial has become more important, or more fiercely contested. "They realize that without witnesses they have nothing," said Sen. Richard J. Durbin, D-Ill.

Under the Senate's trial plan, the motion for dismissal is closely linked to the question of witnesses. After the opening presentations by House managers and White House attorneys and a senatorial questioning of both sides, the Senate will hear arguments on the dismissal motion and then retreat behind closed doors for debate.

Then the House managers will have additional time to make the case for witnesses, followed by the White House's rebuttal and more closed-door deliberations. Under a proposal by Democrats Tom Harkin of Iowa and Paul Wellstone of Minnesota, the deliberations would be opened, but that faces significant opposition.

After that, the Senate will cast back-to-back votes, first on the dismissal motion, then on the question of whether to depose witnesses.

If the motion to dismiss the charges is rejected, as expected, several factors could affect the subsequent vote on whether to depose witnesses.

Before the opening arguments, senior Republicans, such as Ted Stevens of Alaska, were skeptical about requests by House managers for the opportunity to call witnesses. But their opposition seemed to soften in the face of the managers' opening arguments. Republicans appear to be moving beyond the question of whether to take testimony from witnesses and are now focusing on which witnesses to call.

Several GOP senators facing reelection, including Grams and Santorum, support the House managers on the witness question, even though a longer trial would seem to be antithetical to their interest in having Congress concentrate on policies of more pressing interest to the voters.

By contrast, a few Senate conservatives have been far more cautious, suggesting that their ideological soul mates on the House prosecution team will have a hard time justifying the need for witnesses. "We have an extraordinary factual record already," said Sam Brownback, R-Kan.

For its part, the White House continues to warn that calling witnesses would take up so much additional time that the delays would imperil any chance to accomplish legislative business.

Politically, the witness question is a double-edged sword for Democrats as well as Republicans. A lengthy trial could cause the GOP's public support to further nosedive; it also could yield new evidence of misconduct by Clinton or prompt the public to support his ouster as a way to resolve the crisis.

In a procedural twist that rankled the House managers, the bipartisan agreement on trial procedure requires a second vote before hearing live testimony from specific witnesses. Several variables will shape this debate, including the extent to which Republicans feel that depositions alone are sufficient to resolve matters in dispute.

Through all the maneuvering over trial procedures, Lott has walked a fine line between the desire of Democrats — and some in his own conference — for a quick trial, and the demands of conservative activists for a full-blown proceeding that gives House prosecutors the opportunity to present their best evidence and testimony against Clinton. Lott has balanced skillfully thus far, but the pressure is rising. House prosecutors have shown no sign they intend to scale back their demands. "The conservatives have gotten their way on this all along, and the more you succeed, the more you escalate your ambitions," said Thomas E. Mann, director of governmental studies at the Brookings Institution.

Conservative activists may view Lott's approach to the trial as the most important test of his leadership to date. Many were angered by Lott's past compromises with the president, from his decision to back the chemical weapons treaty in 1997 to his support for the massive omnibus appropriations package (PL 105-277) last fall.

Ralph Reed, the former executive director of the Christian Coalition, said conservatives expect the Senate to accede to the managers' requests for a handful of witnesses, at a minimum. "If there are no witnesses, I think conservatives will be very disappointed," he told National Public Radio. "If there are at least, say, a half-a-dozen witnesses, I think they will feel they were treated fairly, and they will have no complaints about the outcome no matter what it is."

Calling the Roll: Convict or Acquit

No obvious path has yet emerged leading to a conclusion of the yearlong crisis for the president stemming from his affair with former White House intern Monica Lewinsky. But most senators agree that it probably will end with Chief Justice William H. Rehnquist atop the Senate dais, intoning: "Senators, how say you? Is the respondent, William Jefferson Clinton, guilty or not guilty?"

Then the roll will be called alphabetically, and all senators will rise and declare, without elaboration, their verdicts: guilty or not guilty.

Before the opening arguments, senators from both parties said that their 55-45 partisan split makes it highly improbable that two-thirds of the Senate will vote to remove Clinton. But the conventional wisdom about the impeachment process has been wildly off the mark since the scandal broke. With the trial under way, senators are becoming far more hesitant to venture predictions on how the vote might turn out.

Most believe this choice — on conviction or acquittal — could define their political careers. And yet there is a paradox in this weighty decision, which will be billed as the ultimate "vote of conscience": Barring a stunning development or major shift in public opinion, it probably will break along party lines.

Even as Majority Whip Don Nickles, R-Okla., admonished Democrats for making statements demonstrating they had "prejudged" the case, a senior GOP senator, who asked not to be identified, acknowledged most of his colleagues will probably vote to convict Clinton. That should not be surprising, given that the facts of the scandal and Clinton's failure to come clean about his conduct have been known for almost a year.

The public has also apparently made up its mind. A Washington Post-ABC News poll released Jan. 12 found that 85 percent of respondents have a set opinion of the case, with 65 percent opposed to removing the president from office.

What might change these dynamics? Conservatives are hoping that live testimony might produce new allegations of misbehavior or misrepresentations by Clinton, or at least add some meat to the bones of old allegations.

That has been the conservative game plan for months, and it has yet to bear fruit. But at the same time, there has been no new outburst of public anger over the ongoing impeachment process, in spite of Clinton's buoyant poll ratings. That has undercut efforts by the president's supporters to generate momentum for short-circuiting the trial.

The biggest challenge for the president will be to prevent defections by Democrats. That was the main reason the White House brought on board former Senate Majority Leader George J. Mitchell, D-Maine (1980-95), as an adviser for the trial.

The current Democratic leader, Tom Daschle of South Dakota, continues to press for a vote on a censure resolution, which probably would include some admission by Clinton that he lied. It could take the form of a joint resolution, which the president would be given to sign.

Daschle wants to give his troops an opportunity to vote affirmatively for a measure that registers their revulsion at Clinton's personal conduct. That could provide some political cover for Democrats with tenuous holds on their seats.

But Republicans are insistent that censure not be considered until the trial is over. Even then, Republicans may not embrace the idea. Judd Gregg, R-N.H., believes the Constitution does not provide for censure as a form of punishment and has threatened to filibuster a censure resolution, even if that means Clinton goes formally unpunished. However, it is hard to imagine that GOP senators — particularly moderates who might vote to acquit the president — would be willing to pass up the chance to cast a censure vote.

After the trial ends and the punishment, if any, is meted out, voters will have to wait nearly two years to register their verdicts on one-third of the jury. That can be a lifetime in politics, but voters' memories of the government shutdown of 1995-96 haunted the GOP through the 1996 campaign.

Baker of Rutgers University said that Grams and other potentially vulnerable incumbents may escape fallout if they provide a compelling rationale for their votes, whether for acquittal or conviction.

Besides, as a well-known product of the state's conservative movement it should not come as a great surprise if Grams votes to convict Clinton. "The context means everything," the professor said. "A Republican voting to convict Bill Clinton is not a deviant act."

Beleaguered President Delivers State of the Union Message

JANUARY 23 — Bill Clinton's remarkable up-and-down presidency would end on a positive note if he obtained even a modest fraction of the ambitious agenda he laid out in his State of the Union address.

Clinton delivered the speech Jan. 19 in front of House members who impeached him and senators who are now sitting in judgment. It was the second address in two years given under unusual circumstances. Never before has an impeached president appeared before Congress.

Clinton gave last year's State of the Union speech only a week after the scandal over his relationship with former White House intern Monica Lewinsky had led many political pundits to declare his presidency on the brink of extinction. This year's pep rally came only hours after his defense began its case in the Senate trial.

Clinton did not mention impeachment in his 77-minute speech. Instead, he focused on the themes that have led the American people to elect him twice and give him extraordinary job approval ratings despite his alleged wrongdoings. At the heart of the roster of initiatives was a call to "save Social Security now." Clinton then outlined new — and old — proposals on health care, education, crime, trade, the environment and campaign finance reform.

For example, he suggested setting aside trillions of dollars over 15 years to bolster Social Security reserves, investing some of the set-asides in the stock market, creating subsidized retirement accounts to supplement Social Security, allowing tax credits to help families care for the elderly, shoring up Medicare, improving schools and raising the minimum wage.

"With our budget surplus growing, our economy expanding, our confidence rising, now is the moment for this generation to meet its historic responsibility to the 21st century," Clinton said.

But it is difficult to see how an administration under siege, a House in which Republicans hold a razor-thin majority and much contempt for the man they impeached, and a Senate hogtied by Democrats can come together to pass much at all — despite vows by all three not to let impeachment get in the way of doing the nation's business.

Many if not most of the politically pleasing initiatives that studded Clinton's speech are legislative long shots. But they give Democrats a poll-tested agenda to present to voters in the 2000 elections. Relatively little of it appears likely to become law, but it is the platform that Democrats hope will return control of Congress to them — and keep the White House in their hands.

Clinton's speech earned predictable plaudits from Democrats and grudging admiration from Republicans. "The president gave another good speech under difficult circumstances," said House Speaker J. Dennis Hastert, R-Ill.

Even the Rev. Pat Robertson, chairman of the conservative Christian Coalition, said Clinton "hit a home run" and that "from a public relations standpoint he's won." Then he added: "They might as well dismiss the impeachment hearing and get on with something else because it's over as far as I'm concerned."

Indeed, opinion polls conducted immediately after Clinton's address showed Clinton still riding high. His job approval rating was 66 percent in an ABC News poll and a record 76 percent in an NBC News poll.

Polls notwithstanding, Clinton's agenda landed with a resounding thud among the Republicans he called on to help pass it. The president's wish list of new programs was not accompanied by details on how to pay for them. And Clinton did not press for tax cuts, despite the escalating size of projected annual federal budget surpluses.

"A $4 trillion surplus and not a penny for tax cuts," said House Majority Leader Dick Armey, R-Texas, who, along with Majority Whip Tom DeLay, R-Texas, declined during the speech to clap even for the most obvious applause lines. "I welcome the president's admission that not all of the surplus is needed to save Social Security," Armey said. "He proposes to spend the rest on Washington programs, and we propose to return it to working Americans as tax relief."

A Clinton Favorite

Republicans also laid out their agenda Jan. 19 and in subsequent days, though they struggled to be heard over the din of impeachment, the publicity surrounding Clinton's address and the follow-up White House road show that rollicked in Democratic strongholds such as Buffalo, N.Y. The annual State of the Union ritual is clearly a Clinton favorite, and he resisted calls from Republicans and even some in his own party to delay the address or submit it in writing.

But his speech — filled with applause lines that prompted standing ovations and close to 100 interruptions — raised hackles with some Republicans, especially the senators weighing his fate. "It's kind of awkward to be in the Senate one afternoon talking about impeachment, hear a rah-rah speech that should have been made to the Democratic National Committee and then be back in tomorrow going over impeachment," said Majority Whip Don Nickles, R-Okla.

Republicans continued to try to show that they were not being sidetracked by impeachment. But their pursuit of impeachment against the wishes of a clear majority of Americans has taken its toll: The same polls that show Clinton remains popular show Republicans faring poorly among voters.

Central to reviving the party and at the core of the GOP's agenda is a 10 percent across-the-board cut in marginal income tax rates.

"Washington demonstrated last year that unless the surplus is given back to the taxpayer, it will be spent," said Senate Finance Committee Chairman William V. Roth Jr., R-Del. "The broad-based tax cut in our package will be the simplest, fairest and, I believe, the most productive way to give the money back."

As he did last year with his call to "save Social Security first," the president sought to use the sacrosanct retirement system to foil the Republican's tax cut plans.

"What I said last night is not as popular as what others can tell you," Clinton said Jan. 20 in Buffalo. "Others can say, 'We have got this surplus now. I just want a big tax cut. I'll give it back to you.'. . . But I believe, if we save 60 percent of this surplus for Social Security . . . we can protect Social Security for 55 years."

The budget surpluses over the next 15 years are anticipated to total about $4.5 trillion. Republicans quickly embraced Clinton's plans to save roughly 60 percent, or $2.8 trillion, for Social Security. What to do with the remaining $1.7 trillion — which may or may not accrue, depending on economic performance and federal spending — is at the core of the philosophical chasm separating Democrats and Republicans.

The public seems to be with Clinton, consistently supporting use of the surplus for Social Security and Medicare instead of for tax cuts. The ABC News poll found 62 percent of the public supporting Clinton's call to dedicate the bulk of the surplus for Social Security and Medicare vs. only 24 percent in favor of dedicating it to tax cuts. The public also gives Clinton a 50 percent to 32 percent edge over congressional Republicans when asked who it has more faith in to handle the nation's agenda.

Gridlock on the Horizon

The immediate outlook is gridlock of the kind that gripped last year's session, during which high-profile bills on taxes, a campaign finance overhaul, tobacco regulations and patients' rights all stalled.

"Ninety-some percent of his proposal was all more government," Nickles said of Clinton's plans. "I don't think you'll see this Congress pass it. Most of it I'll be working very aggressively to see it doesn't pass."

But Republicans know they cannot be content to kill Clinton's popular agenda. They must offer voters other options and at least get their bills to Clinton's desk. Last year, divided Republicans failed to get a tax bill through Congress when a five-year, $80 billion House-passed tax cut measure died in the Senate.

At no point last year did Republicans and Clinton engage in substantive negotiations on how to bridge their differences and agree on a budget plan. Instead, in the session's waning days, Clinton and Congress hammered out a budget-busting omnibus spending bill (PL 105-277) that tapped $21 billion of the surplus for "emergency" spending that, in effect, broke the 1997 budget agreement — and presented appropriators with enormous problems as they contemplate this year's round of spending bills.

Conspicuously absent during last year's budget debate was any realistic effort to strike a deal that could become law. The basis for such a deal would involve Clinton trading tax cuts for additional spending increases. With such a huge surplus, there is plenty of money to finance such an arrangement.

There is also plenty of incentive. Republicans do not want the 106th Congress and their party going into the 2000 elections with nothing to show except that they impeached Clinton and blunted his agenda.

Clinton's Senate trial adds uncertainty to the mix. On one hand, both the White House and Republicans want to demonstrate that they can do the "people's business" at the same time that the Senate debates whether to remove Clinton from office. The White House and most lawmakers assume that Clinton will not be removed, and both sides have expressed confidence that they will be able to work together once the debacle is over. "We must put aside the rhetoric and get down to work," Hastert said.

Others fear that the repercussions of impeachment may be impossible to shake. "If we spend several more weeks on [impeachment], I think the atmosphere is going to be so poisoned that even people with good friends across the aisle are going to have a hard time working together," said Sen. Patrick J. Leahy, D-Vt.

Something for Everyone

The speech carried no direct reference to impeachment, although in an oblique reference to his troubles, Clinton said: "Perhaps, in the daily press of events, in the clash of controversy, we do not see our own time for what it truly is — a new dawn for America."

Instead, Clinton focused on proposals new and old, offering something for everyone.

For senior citizens, Clinton proposed to extend the solvency of Social Security by using regular tax revenues to help shore up the program, which traditionally has been financed solely by a dedicated payroll tax and interest on bonds in the program's trust

For the first time, the government would invest some trust funds in the stock market, an idea that fell flat with Republicans who do not want the government holding stock in private companies. "No, no, a thousand times no," said House Ways and Means Committee Chairman Bill Archer, R-Texas.

In a bow to Republicans, Clinton proposed to eliminate the limit on earnings that seniors from ages 62 to 70 can make without losing their Social Security benefits.

In addition to strengthening the core Social Security program, the president said he wanted to use about $33 billion a year to create subsidized retirement accounts.

Clinton also proposed to use 16 percent of surpluses to extend to 2020 the solvency of the equally sacrosanct Medicare health insurance program for the elderly and disabled. He also wants a second chance for last year's failed plan to allow retirees as young as 55 to buy into Medicare. And he proposed to add coverage of prescription drugs to Medicare's basic benefits package.

Some criticized Clinton for proposing the new benefit and for promising part of the surplus to shore up Medicare, saying it undercut deliberations of the National Bipartisan Commission on the Future of Medicare, which is scheduled to report to Congress in March on ways to make the program stronger for future generations.

Clinton also urged both parties to work with him to pass legislation that would give patients more leverage with their health care insurers. "Last year, Congress missed that opportunity and we must not miss that opportunity again," Clinton said. "For the sake of our families, I ask us to join together across party lines and pass a strong, enforceable patients' bill of rights."

Concerning tobacco, Clinton announced that the Justice Department was preparing to take the tobacco companies to court over the medical costs of caring for smokers, with any recovered funds to be dedicated to Medicare. He also promised to put in place new federal regulations governing medical record privacy if Congress did not act by August 1999.

The president's proposals drew instant ire from the business community, which assailed him for again seeking unnecessarily to expand the federal government's role in the nation's health care system.

In proposals likely to win favor among both Republicans and Democrats, Clinton asked for tax credits for long-term care (up to $1,000 annually), for parents who stay home to care for children ($250 per child under age 1) and to help disabled people who work (up to $1,000 per year). Republicans have signaled that they like this menu of small tax breaks — though they want to go further.

Congressional Republicans are less likely to support Clinton's call to raise the minimum wage over two years by another dollar per hour, to $6.15. They displayed no fear on that issue last year, although they caved to Clinton during the 1996 campaign and raised the minimum wage by 90 cents. *(1996 Almanac, p. 7-3)*

Clinton's reiteration of his request for fast-track trade negotiating authority left most of his fellow Democrats sitting on their hands, though his call to pass an Africa free trade bill won approval from his allies in the Congressional Black Caucus.

Passing the so-called Brady bill to reimpose a five-day waiting period for the purchase of handguns is a dead letter in the GOP-led Congress. Republicans are also likely to resist his call for additional police hiring subsidies. The chances for a campaign finance overhaul remain dim, and prospects for a 55 cent-per-pack increase in cigarette taxes are uneven at best.

"It isn't enough that he spends the whole surplus," grumbled Senate Budget Committee Chairman Pete V. Domenici, R-N.M. "Now he has a cigarette tax — going to collect that and spend that too."

Clinton's speech marked the opening salvo for GOP lawmakers who have already seen their share of turmoil and surprise, from their disappointing showing in the November elections, to the resignation of House Speaker Newt Gingrich, R-Ga., to the stunning announcement by his presumed successor, Robert L. Livingston, R-La., that he, too, would step aside. The shake-up in GOP ranks leaves Republicans with an untested Speaker and a narrow House majority that promises to be an unrelenting headache to manage.

Moreover, Republicans are struggling to gain traction with an agenda of limited government that is more difficult to sell in an era of budget surpluses.

With the departure of Gingrich, Republicans are seeking to put a fresh face on their party. So it fell to the telegenic Reps. Jennifer Dunn, R-Wash., and Steve Largent, R-Okla., to present the official GOP response to Clinton.

"Next year, there will be a $63 billion surplus. Mr. President, give it back," Dunn said. "Last year, a typical mother and father who both work paid nearly 40 percent of their income in taxes . . . . That's the highest percentage of income ever paid in taxes by American families."

Added Largent: "We will continue our efforts to control Washington's wasteful spending and its insatiable appetite for your money."

Surplus Estimates

The next step in the annual budget ritual is the submission of Clinton's fiscal 2000 budget on Feb. 1. With it will come new surplus estimates. The Congressional Budget Office (CBO) will also issue revised surplus and economic forecasts Jan. 28.

But preliminary estimates by the Senate Budget Committee give Republicans hope that they can advance a budget blueprint with plenty of room for tax cuts. The unofficial numbers forecast that an on-budget surplus (as opposed to the larger unified budget surplus that includes Social Security revenues) would materialize in fiscal 2002. That would make cutting taxes much more politically palatable because Democrats could not cast it as an attack on Social Security.

When Clinton says he wants to dedicate the bulk of the surplus to Social Security, he is actually proposing to pay down a portion of the nation's $5.5 trillion national debt, which would help the economy by putting downward pressure on interest rates and boosting national savings.

Under Clinton's plan, the normal flow of Social Security surpluses into the system's trust funds would continue. Additional bonds equal to the $2.8 trillion influx into the system would be added to the trust funds.

"You are double-counting for a good cause — paying down the debt," said former CBO Director Robert D. Reischauer, now a senior fellow at the Brookings Institution. "If you didn't wrap that up in Social Security and Medicare, it wouldn't be politically viable."

Clinton Team Saves Constitutional Arguments for Summation

JANUARY 23 — Coming into the Senate trial, President Clinton's defense team was battling criticism that it had relied too heavily on constitutional arguments and avoided the factual allegations when the impeachment was before the House.

As the White House opened its defense before the Senate on Jan. 19, White House Counsel Charles F.C. Ruff and his colleagues were determined to have the facts of the case thoroughly considered. They came with briefcases full of facts. They held forth for hours at a time about details. They swarmed the Senate chamber like traveling salesmen, hawking their facts like housewares: "You want facts. We've got facts."

Ruff and the three others called on to present the factual case, Special Counsel Gregory B. Craig, Deputy Counsel Cheryl D. Mills and Clinton lawyer David E. Kendall, tore into the case with steely precision, attempting to disassemble the case made by the House managers fact by fact and reassemble the details in a totally different way.

Only at the end of each of their presentations did they turn to broad arguments. And only at the end of the entire presentation were constitutional issues explored in depth, when former Sen. Dale Bumpers, D-Ark. (1975-99), was called for closing arguments.

Democratic senators said the White House's presentations established how difficult it would be for House managers to make the case for removing Clinton, even if allowed to call witnesses.

While conceding that the White House defense team scored some points, Republicans said their presentation only highlighted the need for witnesses to clear up several instances where the record is unclear.

"It seems like the White House is almost terror stricken that they might have witnesses," said Republican Sen. Orrin G. Hatch of Utah after Ruff's presentation Jan. 20.

The defense may or may not lead to a speedy end to the trial. But it gave momentum to the White House, and by the end of the week, some lawmakers — including Republicans — were casting about for a satisfactory end point.

Amid talk of a dismissal motion to be offered the week of Jan. 25 by Sen. Robert C. Byrd, D-W.Va., House managers implored senators to avoid short-circuiting the process.

"I think by dismissing the articles of impeachment before you have a complete trial, you are sending a terrible message to the people of the country," Henry J. Hyde, R-Ill., said Jan. 22. "You're saying, I guess, perjury is OK if it's about sex, obstruction is OK even though it is an effort to deny a citizen her right to a fair trial."

No Apologies

The defense made technical and legal arguments in the case, which pertains to Clinton's affair with former White House intern Monica Lewinsky. Most of the lawyers were unapologetic, almost boastful, of what has been derided as "legal hair-splitting." Only Craig and Bumpers spent much time dwelling on the wisdom — or lack thereof — of proceeding with an impeachment without a popular mandate to do so.

This argument was perhaps best made by Clinton himself, who defiantly ignored the trial during the week. He started by delivering what many supporters said was his best State of the Union address ever Jan. 19, and then took what looked like a victory lap around the country to receive accolades from the public.

Back in Washington, Clinton's defense team hunkered down to a sober and methodic presentation. The lawyers bitterly complained that the two impeachment articles approved by the House were fatally flawed since they bundled multiple allegations. This, Ruff said, could lead to a vote to convict on a particular article even though no single allegation contained within it could garner two-thirds support for conviction.

On the obstruction article, he explained, one faction in the Senate could conclude that Clinton should be removed for engineering a job offer for Lewinsky, and another faction might conclude that he should be removed for concealing gifts. That could mean a two-thirds vote to remove with no consensus on why.

The defense lawyers complained that the perjury count was vague, saying it cited no specific language on Clinton's part. They attacked the House managers' motives, calling their work "a rush to judgment."

But mostly they focused on details.

Obstruction Allegations

The obstruction article had seven separate allegations, some of them coming from Independent Counsel Kenneth W. Starr's impeachment referral, and some having been created by the House managers.

Arguably the best known of the seven pertains to the gifts that Clinton gave Lewinsky and that were later retrieved by Clinton's secretary, Betty Currie. The House managers assert that Clinton conspired to hide these gifts, which had been subpoenaed by Jones' lawyers.

The allegation centers primarily on a meeting between Clinton and Lewinsky on Dec. 28, 1997, in which Lewinsky asked if she should hide the gifts.

During her testimony before Starr's grand jury, Lewinsky was asked about Clinton's response to the gift question on numerous occasions and gave 10 separate responses, Mills observed. And, according to Mills, the most definitive answer she ever gave was that Clinton said, "Let me think about it."

"No one claims he ordered, suggested, or even hinted that anyone obstruct justice," said Mills. "At most, the president says, 'Let me think about it.' That is not obstruction of justice."

Mills also returned to an argument made by Ruff before the House Judiciary Committee. The main purpose of the Dec. 28 meeting was to exchange more gifts. If Clinton were so concerned about this evidence, Mills asked, why would he be creating more?

The gifts were later retrieved by Currie, who hid them under her bed. The House managers say this action was taken at the urging of Clinton. Mills argued that it was Lewinsky who wanted the gifts hidden, pointing to Currie's testimony to that effect and Clinton's seemingly cavalier attitude as evidenced by the new gifts.

"Why would the president give Ms. Lewinsky gifts if he wanted her to give them right back?" Mills asked.

The managers argue that Clinton was confident Lewinsky would hide all her gifts without any prodding. Mills responded that he would not have ordered the retrieval of the gifts if he was confident Lewinsky would hide them.

On the allegation that Clinton conspired to find Lewinsky a job in return for her silence, the president's lawyers focused on the chronology. The critical issue on the job hunt is not whether it was designed to hide the affair from the public or the media — concealing an embarrassing affair is not illegal. Rather, the question is whether the job hunt was designed specifically to conceal the affair from the lawyers in the Paula Corbin Jones sexual harassment case.

Clinton has long argued that the job hunt had nothing to do with the Jones case, citing the fact that it commenced long before Jones' lawyers had ever heard of Lewinsky. The House managers counter that the search became serious only after it was clear that Lewinsky would be called to testify.

The decision to have Lewinsky testify was made on Dec. 11, 1997, by U.S. District Judge Susan Webber Wright. She ruled that Jones' lawyers could call witnesses, including Lewinsky, to testify about Clinton's sexual proclivities. On that day, Clinton friend Vernon E. Jordan stepped up his long-moribund efforts to find Lewinsky a job. He contacted two potential employers by telephone and met directly with Lewinsky.

White House lawyers argued that Wright's ruling, however, did not come down until late in the day, well after Jordan's telephone calls and the Lewinsky meeting. By the time Wright ruled, Ruff said, Jordan was on a flight to Amsterdam.

The House managers took to the airwaves to rebut this argument, saying the White House actually knew Dec. 5 that the Jones team was interested in hearing from Lewinsky. On that date, the Jones team released a list of witnesses it wanted to call.

Kendall followed by arguing that the Dec. 5 date was considerably less significant because it was still far from certain then that Lewinsky would be called.

"You put every witness you can think of who might conceivably be relevant, from Mr. Aardvark to Ms. Zanzibar, all of them go on the witness list," Kendall said. "It wasn't until you get something like a subpoena for a deposition that you know a witness is really going to be a significant player in a trial."

The Coverup Allegations

There were two allegations based on discussions with Lewinsky about the Jones case — the first, that Clinton tried to get her to fill out a false affidavit, and the second, that he tried to get her to lie in the deposition if called to testify.

The Clinton defense team asserted that the two were built on extremely thin evidence. Both Clinton and Lewinsky denied these allegations under oath.

The House managers argued that Clinton and Lewinsky had a tacit understanding she would lie, either in the affidavit, or in testimony if it came to that. The evidence, they asserted, is that Clinton remained silent about the topic, and she knew that he could not want her to testify truthfully.

Ruff countered this by saying the Senate could not remove the president because House managers chose to ascribe sinister motives to his silence.

Another charge was labeled "witness tampering" in Starr's report. It involves Clinton's alleged coaching of Currie after his own deposition, which, to Clinton's surprise, focused heavily on Lewinsky.

The conversation, according to Currie's testimony, consisted of a number of questions Clinton posed to her, such as: "I was never really alone with Monica, right?" and "You were always there when Monica was there, right?"

Mills argued that if he were really tampering with a potential witness, he would pressure her to agree with his view of things. But when later asked if she had felt such pressure, Currie testified, "None whatsoever," Mills said.

Beyond that, Clinton's lawyers said, it is hard to call this conversation witness tampering since Currie was not a witness in the Jones case and never became one.

And there was no presumption she would ever be a witness in the Jones case, Ruff has argued. By the time Clinton spoke with her the depositions in the Jones case were winding down.

The final two allegations — that Clinton allowed his attorney, Robert Bennett, to falsely speak during the Jones deposition, and that Clinton lied to aides John D. Podesta and Sidney Blumenthal so they would repeat the lies — were dealt with least by the Clinton defense team.

The Bennett allegation, Ruff said, requires the House managers to prove that Clinton was paying attention to Bennett's statement, something that is almost impossible to do since Clinton did not nod or otherwise indicate his agreement with the statement.

The alleged lies to Podesta and Blumenthal are predicated on the notion that Clinton knew that at some future date they would be called upon to testify on what Clinton told them regarding the nature of his relationship with Lewinsky.

A Defiant Stance

The article charging Clinton with perjury during his Aug. 17 grand jury appearance provoked the strongest attacks from Clinton's lawyers. They said the article contains no specifics about which statements Clinton made were false.

To ferret out which specific statements may be perjurious, the Clinton team had to turn to the report filed by the House Judiciary Committee (H Rept 105-830), and a brief filed by the House managers Jan. 11.

The president's lawyers argue that neither document totally resolves the question. They cited as an example the Jan. 11 brief, which provides some instances of alleged lying under oath, but does not purport to be exhaustive. The brief cites only some of the "more overt examples."

The article itself is broken into four parts. It charges that Clinton lied about the nature and specifics of his affair, that he repeated his false testimony from the Jones deposition, that he lied about whether he had been paying attention to a false statement made by attorney Bennett during the Jones deposition and that he lied when he denied obstructing justice.

The heart of the first part of the perjury article, and of the entire article, is the allegation that Clinton lied in saying he had not engaged in "sexual relations" as defined in the Jones case.

Clinton has asserted that his denial in the Jones case was factually accurate because the activities he and Lewinsky engaged in did not meet that specific definition of sexual relations. This, in turn, is predicated on an assertion that the entire affair was one-sided, that he had not gratified her, as she had him.

Lewinsky testified about numerous instances when he had aroused her, and Starr's referral included testimony from Lewinsky's friends who said she had told them about these instances.

When this allegation was before the House Judiciary Committee, the White House did not dispute it. Instead, Ruff essentially asked the representatives to assume it is true and then ask whether it is worth impeaching the president of the United States because he admitted to having an affair, but was a little wrong on the details of who touched whom.

In the Senate, Ruff and Craig took a more defiant stance, though again provided no evidence to refute the claim. Craig said this charge never should have been made, since the evidence is lacking. It is by its nature impossible to prove, he said, because there are only two parties in the affair, and they disagree.

"This is a classic oath-on-oath, he-says-she-says swearing match, that under ordinary custom and practice at the Department of Justice never would be prosecuted without substantial corroborative proof," Craig said.

What 'Is' Is

The second section of the article, pertaining to repetitions of Clinton's untruths in the Jones deposition, Craig said was nothing more than an attempt to revisit the deposition perjury article the House defeated.

Clinton did not repeat his previous testimony when he took the oath Aug. 17 before the grand jury, Craig said. He refuted it. He admitted an affair he had denied previously. He admitted to being alone with Lewinsky when before he denied it.

Perhaps the most damning thing Clinton said pertained to his motivations in the Jones testimony. Clinton said he was trying to be "truthful, but not particularly helpful," then went on to say he thought he had been truthful.

"I was determined to work through the minefield of this deposition without violating the law, and I believe I did," Clinton said in the grand jury testimony.

The Clinton team argued that this did not amount to a reaffirmation of his Jones testimony.

The third part of the article centers principally on what might be called the "is-is" defense. During the deposition, Bennett read a statement saying "there is no sex of any kind, shape or manner" between Clinton and Lewinsky. When Clinton was asked in front of the grand jury whether the statement was true he gave the now-famous response: "It depends on what the meaning of the word 'is' is."

Clinton said that if "is" means at any time, the statement was false. But he went on to say, if it means only at the time of the deposition, the statement was accurate, since the affair had concluded by then.

Clinton told a second lie, the managers assert, when he claimed that he had not been paying much attention to the Bennett statement. A videotape of the deposition shows him looking in Bennett's direction.

Craig argued the "is-is" response may have been irritating, but was, and still is, factually accurate. On the question of whether he was paying attention to Bennett at the time of the statement, Craig said there was no evidence of this. Though he may have been looking in the direction of Bennett, he offered no acknowledgments of his statement, such as a nod of the head, Craig said.

"The moment is fleeting," Craig added. "It goes by very quickly. The moment occurs not at the beginning of the deposition, but well into it, after President Clinton has, in fact, been subjected to questions about Monica Lewinsky."

The fourth and final part of the perjury article got almost no attention from Craig because it overlaps the obstruction article considerably. This part says Clinton lied about his attempts to cover up the affair. Whether this is perjury depends almost entirely on whether the Senate concludes his efforts at concealing amounted to obstruction of justice.

Senate Limits Witnesses, Begins Push Toward Finishing Trial

JANUARY 30 — President Clinton's crisis was supposed to have ended last summer, when all but his most vehement congressional critics began losing interest in his affair with Monica Lewinsky.

Then again, it was supposed to be over last fall, when Democratic gains in the elections presumably warded off any threat of impeachment by a House that the Republicans only narrowly controlled.

Now, after those prognostications proved to be dead wrong, Senate Majority Leader Trent Lott, R-Miss., is declaring that this will all be over — once again — by Feb. 12.

After a series of revealing and almost entirely partisan votes, most senators are all but certain they know how it will end. The roll-call Jan. 27 on a motion to end the president's trial clearly demonstrated that there are not the votes needed to convict Clinton on either of the two articles of impeachment, which allege that he perjured himself and obstructed justice. Forty-four senators, all Democrats, voted to dismiss the case altogether; at least one-quarter of that group, or 11 senators, would have to reverse position for the president to be removed from office, because the Constitution sets a two-thirds majority threshold for conviction. *(Vote 4, p. S-5)*

"We know, basically, the outcome already," said Richard C. Shelby, R-Ala. "You've seen more than likely the end of the movie, or you've read the end of the book, unless something drastic happens, which none of us foresee."

Joseph R. Biden Jr., D-Del., made the same point in more blunt terms. "This dog is dead; they just don't know it yet," he said of the Republicans.

But if the ultimate verdict appears clear, getting there promises to be a journey fraught with political peril. And even the most optimistic Republicans believe that it will take large measures of political skill, senatorial discipline and old-fashioned luck to meet Lott's deadline — which is the Friday that starts the Senate's scheduled weeklong Presidents Day recess.

After rejecting the Democratic bid to end the trial immediately, Republicans pushed through a motion Jan. 27 to take depositions from a trio of witnesses, including Lewinsky, the former White House intern who has been at the center of the impeachment maelstrom since her liaison with the president came to light more than a year ago. *(Vote 5, p. S-5)*

A Fuse in the Videotape?

The next day, the Senate approved on another party-line vote a GOP plan for a process for taking the depositions. *(Vote 8, p. S-5)*

The ground rules raised the possibility that videotaped testimony from Lewinsky and the other witnesses — to be taken in the first half of the week of Feb. 1 — will be viewed not only by the 100 senators sitting in judgment of Clinton, but also by the entire nation.

Democrats insist that by calling witnesses and permitting their testimony to be videotaped, Lott and other Republicans have lit a fuse that may explode in their faces. Among other things, Democrats are warning that this process will make Lewinsky's affair with Clinton — and the Senate's detailed examination of it — fodder for more national gossip and jokes by late-night comedians.

"What little dignity Monica Lewinsky has left we hope we can protect," said Senate Minority Leader Tom Daschle, D-S.D.

The rigid political battle lines evident in the votes and the sharp partisan barbs suggested that the spirit of bipartisanship that senators so proudly trumpeted a few weeks ago has all but evaporated.

Democrats indicated that they may resort to more aggressive tactics to demonstrate that the proceeding has now become what they label a "Republican trial." Before approving the deposition procedures, senators rejected Daschle's request that they take an immediate vote on the impeachment articles. Democrats indicated that they would offer the motion again, to highlight their differences with Republicans. "They're going to get it every single day," vowed Edward M. Kennedy, D-Mass.

Still Groping for Compromise

The Senate's skirmishes still look tame when compared with the brawls that marred the House impeachment process. Lott, Daschle and their aides negotiated for hours in the search for common ground, and impeachment has not strained personal relations among senators of opposing parties.

Indeed, just moments before Kennedy harshly criticized the GOP in an impromptu session with reporters near the Senate subway, he was walking arm-in-arm with Texas Republican Phil Gramm, with whom he has worked closely on trial-related matters.

The talks between the Senate's leaders yielded tangible benefits for Democrats. Daschle won the right to share with Lott approval of any requests by House prosecutors to call new witnesses, beyond the three whose depositions were already authorized: Lewinsky; White House aide Sidney Blumenthal; and Vernon E. Jordan Jr., a lawyer and confidante of Clinton's.

"It was a concession," Lott later acknowledged. "But there were a lot of concessions on both sides as we went back and forth."

The trial has turned into a major headache for Republicans, who admit they are afflicted with "impeachment fatigue." But like their counterparts in the House, they have found it more difficult politically to pull the plug on impeachment than to permit it to continue.

From Lott on down, Republicans have been reluctant to poke a finger in the eye of conservative activists, who have been driving the impeachment process from the start. "Rejecting witnesses would have set our base on fire," said a GOP staff aide.

While Republicans speak publicly about the need to bring the trial to a dignified and fair conclusion, many acknowledge privately they are hoping that the depositions yield nothing in the way of blockbuster material.

That would make it easier for Republicans to turn down the requests for live testimony expected from the 13 House Judiciary Committee Republicans who are prosecuting the case.

Senate Republicans, who voted unanimously in favor of taking the depositions, were openly skeptical of the need for Lewinsky and other witnesses to testify in person. "If I'm a betting man, I say, 'Yeah, it tilts against live witnesses,'" said Robert F. Bennett, R-Utah.

Yet all lawyers worth their law degrees know there is no such thing as a guaranteed result when a witness is deposed. If prosecutors turn up anything novel or intriguing that they believe could strengthen their case, the Senate will come under huge pressure to take live testimony, or at least publicly release tape of the depositions. Lott was careful not to foreclose the possibility that the videotaped depositions will be released.

Other potentially significant legal and political hurdles must be crossed before the trial climax, when all 100 senators stand at their desks and announce their decisions on the president's guilt or innocence when asked by Chief Justice William H. Rehnquist.

Will the White House mount an aggressive defense, with its own witnesses? If Clinton's acquittal is indeed a foregone conclusion, will the Senate register its disapproval of his conduct in some other way, perhaps with a "finding of fact" as the Republicans are now assembling?

Those questions are a long way from resolution. And that is why a Democrat who has lived through the impeachment process from the outset, first as a House Judiciary Committee member and now as a senator, cautions against predicting when it might end.

"Anyone who is certain we will only go another week or nine days hasn't looked at the history of this case," Sen. Charles E. Schumer, D-N.Y. told reporters Jan. 27.

'She Does Have a Story To Tell'

Under the Republicans' plan for depositions, Lewinsky will appear on Feb. 1. Jordan will be deposed the next day, and Blumenthal the day after that. They will be questioned for as long as four hours each by the House prosecutors and White House attorneys, with a senator from each party presiding.

Undoubtedly, Lewinsky is the star witness. As Ed Bryant, R-Tenn., the House manager who will take her deposition, put it in what may be the understatement of the trial: "She does have a story to tell."

Prosecutors formally told the Senate that they hope Lewinsky's testimony will show that the president concocted an elaborate scheme to obstruct justice in the Paula Corbin Jones sexual harassment lawsuit. He sought to accomplish that, say the prosecutors, in part by helping Lewinsky get a job in New York as an inducement for her to file a false affidavit in the case, in which she denied a sexual relationship with the president.

"Why did she get the job within 48 hours of the affidavit, after months of unsuccess?" Bryant asked in a floor debate with White House attorneys over the deposition request. "Wouldn't it be nice to hear Ms. Lewinsky's version of this when it is so important to the overall case of obstruction of justice?"

This case is not about sex, the prosecution team has insisted repeatedly. That is why they are downplaying the perjury count in the House impeachment resolution — which centers more directly on the precise nature of the president's sexual contacts with Lewinsky — while placing more emphasis on the obstruction charge. They are acutely aware of deep concerns among senators that her testimony could easily veer into salacious material.

Yet if the prosecutors also pursue the perjury charge with Lewinsky, as seems likely, it is hard to imagine how they might avoid seeking her detailed descriptions of her liaisons with the president in the White House West Wing. "If you believe Monica Lewinsky, the president lied to the grand jury and committed perjury in denying he had sexual relations with Monica Lewinsky," said House manager Bill McCollum, R-Fla., in a Jan. 15 presentation on the Senate floor.

A few moments later, McCollum had senators squirming in their seats as he recounted some of Lewinsky's more graphic testimony — under a grant of immunity from prosecution if she was truthful — before the grand jury convened by Independent Counsel Kenneth W. Starr. Senators from both parties now fear that the mixture of sex and alleged lies, all caught on videotape, will prove highly combustible.

"I don't want to get to the situation that existed on the House side," said Olympia J. Snowe, R-Maine, referring to the vote to release Starr's chapter-and-verse account of Clinton's sexual contacts with Lewinsky.

"You really want to start showing video in prime time, saying who touched whom where?" asked Patrick J. Leahy, D-Vt. David E. Kendall, Clinton's attorney, scoffed at the prosecutors' efforts to glean new information from Lewinsky, or the other two witnesses, all of whom have testified numerous times before the grand jury. "They are a little like a blackjack player who sees 20 on the table and has 19 and is going to try to draw that two," Kendall told the Senate on Jan. 26. "Here they are simply gambling."

Prosecutors said Blumenthal could show that Clinton "lied to his aides, knowing that they could be called to testify before the grand jury," according to their request for his deposition. In addition, they want to explore Blumenthal's previous testimony that Clinton had depicted Lewinsky as a "stalker" who made sexual demands on him.

Thus, even as Democrats attempt to portray Lewinsky as a victim of an out-of-control impeachment process, the prosecution — using Blumenthal's testimony — says it will try to show that the president attacked Lewinsky's character "in an effort to exculpate himself."

And prosecutors will attempt to prove that Jordan was "the primary catalyst" in the efforts by the president and his friends to find Lewinsky a job.

But it seems unlikely that Jordan, one of the capital's most polished trial lawyers, would contradict previous assertions that there was no "quid pro quo" between his efforts to aid Lewinsky's job search and her testimony in the Jones suit.

Why Not Betty Currie?

GOP senators are primarily hoping that the depositions would clear up unresolved questions they have about the job search and about the circumstances surrounding gifts that Clinton gave to Lewinsky and that later were retrieved by Betty Currie, the president's personal secretary.

Like the prosecution, Senate Republicans have shown increasing interest in the obstruction charge. In part, that reflects the effectiveness of the presentation of that part of the case by the prosecution team, led by Rep. Asa Hutchinson, R-Ark.

"Some of us feel very strongly about the second count," the one alleging obstruction of justice, said Gordon H. Smith, R-Ore. "There are open questions, there are contradictions, and we'd like to get some answers. Those can best be provided at this point through witnesses."

Senators' desire to learn more about this aspect of the case made the prosecutors' decision not to seek testimony from Currie all the more perplexing.

Several senators view her as the pivotal witness on various aspects of the obstruction charge, including the allegation — which she has denied — that she concealed the gifts at the president's behest. The gifts had been subpoenaed by Jones' attorneys in the harassment suit.

Prosecutors made what they described as a tactical decision not to call Currie. Hutchinson contended that the loss of her testimony was not significant and that the other witnesses, Jordan in particular, would bolster the obstruction case.

But the value of her testimony appeared to be only one of the considerations prosecutors weighed. As an African-American and a career government secretary, Currie is seen as a sympathetic figure. As a Clinton loyalist, her testimony might not have been all that helpful to the prosecution anyway.

But Sen. Susan Collins, R-Maine, who is still struggling with how to vote on the obstruction count, said she was disappointed with that decision. "It's going to be hard to resolve some of these allegations without her testimony," she said in an interview.

Showdown Votes After Secrecy

Ever since the Senate voted unanimously Jan. 8 for the ground rules for getting the trial under way, it was clear that the decisive votes would come on two motions: first by Democrats to dismiss the case, and then by the House managers to depose witnesses.

Before those roll calls, however, senators spent almost eight hours over two evenings Jan. 25-26 deliberating behind the locked doors of the Senate. Transcripts were kept confidential; aides were admitted only after signing a secrecy oath. The secrecy was prescribed by the Senate's special impeachment rules.

Before each session, senators voted soundly against motions to leave the galleries open and the television cameras on. *(Votes 2 and 3, p. S-5)*

For the president, the vote on the motion to dismiss was about the best outcome he could have hoped for. Two weeks earlier, the White House was fearing that a rash of Democrats would shy away from a preliminary end of the trial. But on Jan. 27 all but one Democrat backed the proposal, offered by Sen. Robert C. Byrd, D-W.Va.

And even Russell D. Feingold of Wisconsin, the lone Democrat to break ranks, suggested in a lengthy and nuanced statement afterward that his vote should not be interpreted as a sign that he has decided to vote for conviction.

While Democrats viewed the dismissal motion as the trial's defining moment to date, the motion on witnesses offered them their best hope to bring the trial to an early conclusion.

Indeed, in the days leading up to the Jan. 27 showdown, the deposition vote had dominated the spotlight, because Shelby and a handful of other Republicans were so public in their skepticism about the need for any witnesses at all.

All Democrats had to do was pick off six Republicans to muster the 51 votes needed to reject the motion. But for a variety of reasons, Republicans simply could not bring themselves to reject the motion and end the trial prematurely.

First, the prosecutors — who at one point had assembled a witness "wish list" with 15 names on it — "narrowed it down to three, a pitiful three," as House Judiciary Chairman Henry J. Hyde, R-Ill., said in closing the trial debate on the issue.

The House also requested permission to augment its record with two statements by seemingly tangential figures and with the record of one telephone call between the president and Lewinsky. And it asked the Senate to ask Clinton to sit for a deposition, an idea the White House immediately rejected. The president may not be subpoenaed under impeachment rules.

Like so much else in the impeachment process, the request was influenced as much by political factors as legal considerations. House prosecutors knew that GOP senators had a limited appetite for witnesses, a point driven home in their comments on television and reaffirmed by a pair of Republicans — Arizona's Jon Kyl and Pennsylvania's Arlen Specter — who were deputized by Lott to meet with House prosecutors.

"We said, 'OK, it's crunch time: Here are some of things the Senate Republicans are thinking about. You probably need to get this thing limited down to a number of witnesses, and think what you really need out of it,'" Kyl said in an interview. So when the prosecutors limited their request, Senate Republicans felt obliged to support it. All 55 GOP senators and Feingold voted "yes."

For more than 24 hours, Republicans and Democrats exchanged proposals for how to govern the trial's new phase. Prospects for another bipartisan compromise initially seemed bright, but the talks ran aground over the GOP's insistence on making videotapes and keeping alive the option of making a senatorial "finding of fact" later in the case that Clinton did wrong.

When the talks collapsed, Lott quickly brought the matter to the floor, where he knew he had the votes to prevail. Daschle sought to substitute the Democratic plan for the remainder of the trial, which barred videotaping the depositions and set a firm deadline of Feb. 12 for ending the trial. The Democrats' proposal was rejected, 44-54; the GOP plan was approved, 54-44. The votes were on party lines. Absent were Barbara A. Mikulski, D-Md., who was ill, and Wayne Allard, R-Colo., who was with his ailing father.

As both sides tried to put their spin on the outcome, Democrats warned that Lott's Feb. 12 deadline for ending the trial was in serious jeopardy.

"This procedure is riddled with loopholes," said Richard H. Bryan, D-Nev. "There is no ending to this. Feb. 12 is a mirage. We get there, and in point of fact we don't end."

No Filibuster Allowed

The partisan vote tallies again brought home to Democrats how the rules for the impeachment trial have robbed them of their most potent legislative weapon, the filibuster.

Except on the final question of conviction — or on changing the Senate's impeachment rules — a majority may govern an impeachment trial. So long as Lott keeps his troops together, as he has to this point, the GOP should prevail on procedural motions. But it is not in the interest of Republicans to use their numbers to simply run roughshod over Democrats. That would risk turning the Senate trial into a replay of the House impeachment, and could drive the GOP's abysmal public approval ratings still lower.

Schumer says that, while the process is demonstrably unfair to the president, Senate Republicans have tried to be more accommodating than their House counterparts. "The dynamic is very different, thank God," he said.

But tough decisions are coming that will ratchet up partisan tensions. In coming days, the Senate must decide whether to release the videotapes, call witnesses onto the Senate floor and resolve thorny constitutional questions related to the finding of fact motion.

Outside pressure on the GOP is growing. Even as the White House and Democrats claim that Senate Republicans are permitting the prosecutors to call the shots, Hyde has bitterly attacked GOP senators for giving too much ground to the Democrats.

"I'm glad that they weren't at the Alamo or Valley Forge," Hyde said on Jan. 27.

Senate Seeks Another Way To Condemn Clinton

FEBRUARY 6 — As the impeachment trial of President Clinton nears its climactic moment, anticlimax is in the air. The Senate is still struggling to find a fitting punishment for a president who seems certain to avoid the ultimate congressional sanction of conviction and removal from office.

It is an ironic conclusion for the second presidential impeachment proceedings ever to run the course prescribed by the Constitution. Even after the House impeached Clinton and the Senate put him on trial — and even after the nation made clear that it has learned more than it ever wanted to about his sexual transgressions and rhetorical contortions — many Republicans and Democrats agree on one point: They still need to do more, preferably in unison, to show their disapproval of his conduct.

But beyond that still lingers the partisanship that has shadowed Congress as it has considered Clinton's fate for the past year.

Republicans had been backing a "finding of fact" proposal under which the Senate would vote to summarize the charges against the president without quite formally embracing them. The approach lost much of its momentum during the week of Feb. 1, as Democrats joined the White House in fiercely opposing the idea and an increasing number of Republicans started shying away from it.

Meanwhile, most Democrats still favor a harshly worded resolution of censure, but Republicans generally complain that would be too weak a condemnation under the circumstances and be constitutionally suspect as well.

Despite the divisions, there is a widespread, though hardly universal, worry that Clinton will feel that he got off easy if, as now seems all but certain, the Senate votes to acquit him on the two articles of impeachment forwarded by the House. *(Articles, p. 13-6)*

"I would be amazed if the president is able to contain himself" after the verdict, said Sen. Larry E. Craig, R-Idaho.

The concern, and the GOP's anticipatory annoyance, that Clinton might gleefully play his saxophone at a post-verdict celebration underscores the extent to which senators are already assuming that his acquittal is a done deal. It is also enhanced by the memory of the president's pep rally with House Democrats on the White House lawn the afternoon of his impeachment on Dec. 19.

Expecting acquittal, administration officials have vowed that the White House will be a "gloat-free zone" after the Senate roll calls.

Heading for the Exits

The last thorny substantive issues of the trial were resolved in a series of votes Feb. 4, as the Senate permitted House prosecutors to present portions of videotaped testimony from the pivotal figure in the trial, Monica Lewinsky. Clinton's campaign to obscure the sexual nature of his affair with the former White House intern is at the core of the perjury and obstruction of justice charges he faces.

But in a rebuke to House Judiciary Chairman Henry J. Hyde, R-Ill., and his prosecution team, the Senate rejected, 30-70, their request to bring Lewinsky to the Senate floor for questioning. That vote marked a clear and unusually bipartisan turning point in the trial, as 25 Republicans — including eight committee chairmen and Paul Coverdell of Georgia, a member of the GOP leadership team — joined with all 45 Democrats in blocking her in-person testimony. *(Vote 10, p. S-6)*

"The message was twofold," said Sen. John B. Breaux, D-La. "We've heard enough, and she would have been a stronger witness for the president than against."

The trial's outcome has not been in doubt since Jan. 27, when 44 Democrats voted to dismiss the case and thus showed that prosecutors would be unable to muster the two-thirds majority needed to remove the president from office. "That was the handwriting on the wall," said Sen. Ted Stevens, R-Alaska.

But prosecutors harbored faint hopes that the closed-door depositions of Lewinsky and two other witnesses — lawyer and Clinton confidant Vernon E. Jordan Jr. and White House aide Sidney Blumenthal — would yield a "bolt of lightning," as Senate Majority Leader Trent Lott, R-Miss., put it.

Before video cameras and small clusters of House trial managers and Senate monitors Feb. 1-3, however, the three for the most part confirmed testimony they had delivered on numerous previous occasions. But their depositions did reveal discrepancies in their accounts of some key events — particularly between Jordan and Lewinsky concerning the steps he took to line up a job for her.

The transcripts were published in the Feb. 4 Congressional Record after the Senate voted, 100-0, to to admit them and videotapes of the depositions as evidence. *(Vote 9, p. S-6)*

The job search is at the heart of the second impeachment article, which alleges that Clinton obstructed justice by encouraging Lewinsky to submit a false affidavit in the Paula Corbin Jones sexual harassment suit.

But increasingly, House prosecutors appeared resigned to Clinton's acquittal. After the Feb. 1 deposition by Lewinsky failed to produce any bombshells, Hyde was left to concede: "It wasn't harmful, but it wasn't helpful."

The prosecutors prepared to present their best evidence on Feb. 6, including clips of videotape from the depositions that would give most senators — and the public watching on television — their first chance to see Lewinsky speak. But despite this last-minute peek at the scandal's central figure, senators acknowledged that the proceedings had become anticlimactic. Most looked forward wearily to the end of the trial, which Lott suggested could come on Feb. 11 — one day ahead of his tightly choreographed script.

"Everybody's looking for the exit door," Breaux said Feb. 4. "It's getting bigger and it's getting closer."

One of the last remaining questions is whether to debate Clinton's fate behind closed doors, as required by Senate rules. A move to open the deliberations — essentially 15-minute speeches by each senator — has picked up momentum from some influential backers; it will take 67 votes to succeed.

Many senators are hoping to publicly explain their votes, notwithstanding the strict prohibition on discussing what transpires in closed sessions. If the rules are not changed, said Robert F. Bennett, R-Utah, he will release the text of the speech he intends to deliver just before the doors are shut in a move to avoid violating secrecy rules.

"This will be my explanation to my constituents who won't like how I vote," Bennett said in an interview Feb. 3. He said he has changed his mind on how he will vote since the trial began, but he declined to discuss his decision.

Dueling Punishments

Senators agreed that if there is to be any condemnation beyond the stigma of the House's impeachment, it will have to come on a bipartisan basis. But the battle touched off by the GOP "finding of fact" idea showed how difficult it is to find common political ground in setting a presidential punishment.

A Republican task force, led by Pete V. Domenici of New Mexico and Olympia J. Snowe of Maine, struggled to hit the right balance — a firm enough rebuke to be meaningful, but not so harsh as to alienate Democrats.

The final draft of the group's proposal said that the president "willfully provided false and misleading testimony" to a federal grand jury, and "wrongfully engaged in conduct" aimed at obstructing the Jones suit.

But Democrats declared the idea to

be a non-starter, more because of its form and timing than its content. Led by their elder statesman and impeachment sage, Robert C. Byrd of West Virginia, Democrats claimed that the GOP was trying to end-run the Constitution in coming up with an unprecedented form of punishment within the context of an impeachment trial.

What Democrats found most galling is that the finding — whatever it said — would be a permanent blot on Clinton's record. And unlike conviction, it would require only a simple majority. "To me it's a gutless way of trying to get out of a vote on the issue," said Sen. Patrick J. Leahy, D-Vt.

Faced with the prospect of proceeding on a partisan basis, Snowe and Domenici shelved the effort. "Our group is finished if we can't get some bipartisan support; it's that simple," Domenici said Feb. 4.

That focused renewed attention on the attempt by Democrats, led by Californian Dianne Feinstein, to craft a censure resolution that can win broad support. But it did not take long for her plan, which was still in the draft stage at week's end, to take partisan hits.

Censure is nothing more than a "wet noodle," Craig declared, designed to provide vulnerable Democrats some political cover. That was essentially the same charge Leahy and other Democrats lodged against the finding of fact.

This debate might strike some as confusing, even silly, as the two parties borrow each other's rhetoric and trade accusations of political cowardice. Still, there is a genuine desire by many to show their unhappiness with Clinton, regardless of the form it takes.

If the Senate had approved the finding-of-fact proposal, Snowe said, "we would have been able to overshadow the president's claim of exoneration."

A similar battle over a Democratic proposal to censure Clinton unfolded in the House in December, but there the stakes were much higher. If GOP leaders had permitted a vote on a censure, it might have picked up enough GOP votes to thwart the articles of impeachment.

Lott will likely come under increasing Democratic pressure the week of Feb. 8 to permit a vote on censure soon after the trial ends. "It'd be almost a chemical reaction" if Lott rebuffed Democratic demands, said John D. Rockefeller IV, D-W.Va.

In the end, the fate of the Democratic censure plan, like the GOP finding-of-fact plan, will depend on the level of bipartisan support it attracts. Bennett is collaborating with Feinstein on the censure proposal, but it is unclear if that is a harbinger of broader GOP backing. "I just want to vote to condemn this guy for his sleazy behavior," Bennett said.

Many Republicans are cool to the idea, and Chuck Hagel of Nebraska suggested that his colleagues should face the reality that the proceedings will end, for good, with Clinton's acquittal. "For those who say that's not good enough, well, he's been impeached and that can't be expunged. That's lasting," Hagel said in an interview Feb. 4.

The Bulls Say No

Since the trial began, Republicans have resisted taking any action to undermine or denigrate the case brought by the House. That was clearly a factor in the united GOP vote Jan. 27 to permit depositions of Lewinsky, Jordan and Blumenthal. But when House prosecutors sought more — they wanted Lewinsky on the Senate floor for as many as eight hours of questioning — a broad cross-section of the party drew the line.

The most prominent opponents were GOP elders such as Appropriations Chairman Stevens, Budget Chairman Domenici, Armed Services Chairman John W. Warner of Virginia and Senate President Pro Tempore Strom Thurmond of South Carolina.

In contrast, among the 30 Republicans who voted to call Lewinsky to the floor were several who are potentially vulnerable to defeat for election to second terms in 2000, including Spencer Abraham of Michigan, Mike DeWine of Ohio and Rod Grams of Minnesota.

Lott also voted to bring Lewinsky to the floor, yet he hailed the bipartisan outcome. Indeed, senators abandoned the rigid partisanship that has prevailed for weeks as they set ground rules for the introduction of evidence.

The Senate voted 62-38 to permit House prosecutors and White House attorneys to use excerpts of the transcripts and videotaped depositions in their final presentations. *(Vote 12, p. S-6)*

The White House fought hard against release of the excerpts, raising familiar concerns about the propriety and fairness of permitting prosecutors to assemble what Special Counsel Gregory B. Craig called "the greatest hits" from the depositions of the three witnesses. But the prosecutors prevailed as nine Democrats, including Byrd and Daniel Patrick Moynihan of New York, broke with the White House on the issue. Republicans Snowe and James M. Jeffords of Vermont opposed the prosecutors' request.

The day's last important skirmish also went to Hyde's team, as the White House sought to force the prosecutors to disclose in advance the portions of the testimony they intended to cite in their presentations.

Arguing against the White House proposal, House manager James E. Rogan, R-Calif., recalled a line from Otto Kaus, a former justice of the California Supreme Court, who remarked, in similar circumstances: "I believe the appropriate legal response to your request is that it is none of your damn business what the other side is going to put on."

The Senate turned down the White House request on a largely party-line vote, 46-54. *(Vote 14, p. S-6)*

Looking Ahead

With its end in sight, senators began looking to the trial's potential political ramifications. Republicans are well aware that pursuing impeachment has been a political loser for the party.

But they were confronted with graphic new evidence in a New York Times / CBS News poll released Feb. 3. Of all those surveyed, 37 percent approved of the Senate's handling of the trial, while 56 percent disapproved. And of those polled who called themselves GOP conservatives — the party's base — about half said they believe the party's handling of impeachment will make it harder for Republicans to win next year.

The question now is whether this widespread antipathy toward impeachment factors into senators' votes on conviction. Some Republicans have suggested that their colleagues have become so dispirited that the Senate may fall short of a simple majority for either impeachment article, much less the two-thirds needed for removal.

Several of those with the most to lose politically, such as Grams and

Abraham, seem certain to vote for conviction. But based on their trial votes to date, moderates facing the voters in 2000, including Snowe and Jeffords, seem to be leaning toward acquittal.

Party leaders such as Kentucky's Mitch McConnell, who chairs the Senate GOP campaign committee, are counseling their colleagues not to panic about how voters will view the trial 21 months hence. And a veteran Democrat agrees it is far too early to be formulating an impeachment casualty list, no matter what the polls say now.

"What's up today can be down tomorrow," Breaux said. "We are about to get into Medicare, Social Security and a lot of other tough issues. Some of these political ups and downs are very temporary."

Impeachment Trial Ends With Senate Vote To Acquit President Clinton

FEBRUARY 13 — The second presidential impeachment trial in U.S. history has ended with Bill Clinton still in the White House — and still enjoying the phenomenal popularity ratings that have become the hallmark of his tenure. While the Senate's lopsided verdict in the president's favor was entirely predictable long before its formal declaration on Feb. 12, it hardly represented a victory or vindication for the nation's 42nd president.

As he emerged from the congressional crucible that has consumed him for the past year, his character and integrity were impugned by political allies and opponents alike. His personal conduct was condemned in the harshest terms possible. A leading Democratic senator said the president had behaved like "a pig." A Republican said the name "Clinton" will eventually become synonymous with liar.

The president launched a bid for rehabilitation when he appeared in the White House Rose Garden two hours after his acquittal and offered his most abjectly humble apology of the past year.

Yet for all that, his presidency was never seriously imperiled. It had been clear for weeks that the Senate would not even approach the two-thirds majority the Constitution requires for conviction on impeachment articles and removal from office.

"The Founders really didn't want us to be France," said Bob Kerrey, D-Neb., referring to a nation where regimes once fell with frequency. "They made it extremely hard to remove a popularly elected president."

For three long days, senators deliberated behind their chamber's closed doors on the twin articles of impeachment brought by the House, which alleged that Clinton committed perjury and obstruction of justice in trying to conceal his relationship with Monica Lewinsky, a former White House intern.

Then, shortly after noon on Feb. 12, the senators served notice that they were ready, the Senate's doors were opened and Chief Justice William H. Rehnquist posed the final question of the trial: "Senators, how say you? Is the respondent, William Jefferson Clinton, guilty or not guilty?"

When their names were called alphabetically, senators stood at their desks and delivered their verdicts. It was a moment last seen in 1868, when President Andrew Johnson survived equally fateful roll calls by a single vote.

In this case, by sharp contrast, the only real suspense centered on whether either article would garner a simple majority of Senate support. That would have provided a legally meaningless but symbolically important victory for the Republicans who pushed the House to impeach Clinton in December.

But the House prosecutors, who had chafed under limitations imposed by senators during the trial, failed to achieve even that modest goal. Article I, alleging Clinton committed perjury before a federal grand jury, steadily lost support as the trial progressed and was defeated, 45-55. Ten Republicans joined with all 45 Democrats in rejecting the charge. *(Vote 17, p. S-7)*

Article II, which alleged a scheme by the president to obstruct justice, was regarded by most senators as the far stronger count. But it was defeated on a vote of 50-50. Five Republicans, all of them moderates from the Northeast, joined unanimous Democrats in rejecting the charge. *(Vote 18, p. S-7)*

That means that the high water mark for conviction on either count was 17 votes short of conviction, so the House prosecutors won only three of every four votes that they needed.

The result still spared the prosecutors a measure of embarrassment by enabling them to claim they swayed half the Senate, if not a majority. Prosecutors themselves accepted defeat with resignation and a hint of bitterness. "We all have our opinion of the president," said Rep. Lindsey Graham, R-S.C. "But under our system, impeachment is hard. It was meant to be hard. And it's over."

The Fallout

In the immediate aftermath of the votes, senators were left to ponder a series of political and legal questions that will take months, if not years, to answer. Among them:

Will the five Republicans who voted against removing Clinton from office face retaliation from the party's conservative base? Will Democrats find it a mixed blessing to have voted unanimously to keep this president in office? How long will it take Washington, which has been preoccupied with Clinton's fate for months, to return to normal?

But as the curtain descended on the five-week proceeding, trial-weary senators were mostly focusing on a one-week Presidents Day recess and the chance to trade their special hybrid roles as judges and jurors for their more familiar jobs as politicians and legislators.

The trial itself was a quasi-judicial proceeding firmly fixed in the political milieu. That was made clear when senators, after voting Feb. 9 to conduct final deliberations in secret, resorted to their favored practice of speaking at length, both in the chamber and to waiting reporters outside.

It was hardly the freewheeling deliberations hoped for by Senate Majority Leader Trent Lott, R-Miss. "We're just droning through these speeches," Jeff Bingaman, D-N.M., said Feb. 10.

When it was all over, however, senators felt as if they were entitled to a pat on the back, if for no other reason than for resisting the rigid partisanship that marked the House impeachment proceeding. Senators shook hands across the aisle, with lawyers for the president and with House prosecutors.

How Senators Voted

Republicans voting guilty on both articles:
Abraham, Mich.
Allard, Colo.
Ashcroft, Mo.
Bennett, Utah
Bond, Mo.
Brownback, Kan.
Bunning, Ky.
Burns, Mont.
Campbell, Colo.
Cochran, Miss.
Coverdell, Ga.
Craig, Idaho
Crapo, Idaho
DeWine, Ohio
Domenici, N.M.
Enzi, Wyo.
Fitzgerald, Ill.
Frist, Tenn.
Gramm, Texas
Grams, Minn.
Grassley, Iowa
Gregg, N.H.
Hagel, Neb.
Hatch, Utah
Helms, N.C.
Hutchinson, Ark.
Hutchison, Texas
Inhofe, Okla.
Kyl, Ariz.
Lott, Miss.
Lugar, Ind.
Mack, Fla.
McCain, Ariz.
McConnell, Ky.
Murkowski, Alaska
Nickles, Okla.
Roberts, Kan.
Roth, Del.
Santorum, Pa.
Sessions, Ala.
Smith, N.H.
Smith, Ore.
Thomas, Wyo.
Thurmond, S.C.
Voinovich, Ohio

Republicans voting not guilty on both articles:
Chafee, R.I.
Collins, Maine
Jeffords, Vt.
Snowe, Maine
Specter, Pa.

Republicans voting not guilty on Article I, guilty on Article II:
Gorton, Wash.
Shelby, Ala.
Stevens, Alaska
Thompson, Tenn.
Warner, Va.

Democrats voting not guilty on both articles:
Akaka, Hawaii
Baucus, Mont.
Bayh, Ind.
Biden, Del.
Bingaman, N.M.
Boxer, Calif.
Breaux, La.
Bryan, Nev.
Byrd, W.Va.
Cleland, Ga.
Conrad, N.D.
Daschle, S.D.
Dodd, Conn.
Dorgan, N.D.
Durbin, Ill.
Edwards, N.C.
Feingold, Wis.
Feinstein, Calif.
Graham, Fla.
Harkin, Iowa
Hollings, S.C.
Inouye, Hawaii
Johnson, S.D.
Kennedy, Mass.
Kerrey, Neb.
Kerry, Mass.
Kohl, Wis.
Landrieu, La.
Lautenberg, N.J.
Leahy, Vt.
Levin, Mich.
Lieberman, Conn.
Lincoln, Ark.
Mikulski, Md.
Moynihan, N.Y.
Murray, Wash.
Reed, R.I.
Reid, Nev.
Robb, Va.
Rockefeller, W.Va.
Sarbanes, Md.
Schumer, N.Y.
Torricelli, N.J.
Wellstone, Minn.
Wyden, Ore.

The Senate earned the warm praise of Rehnquist, who presided over the 20-day trial with a quick wit and an even quicker gavel. Repaying the compliment, senators awarded Rehnquist a ceremonial gavel and passed by voice vote a resolution (S Res 37) praising his work as the presiding officer in the trial.

The camaraderie was soon halted, however, by a bomb threat that forced the evacuation of the Capitol for 75 minutes of the usually balmy winter afternoon.

Attention quickly turned to the president for his statement on the trial. For his part, Clinton defied predictions by Republicans that he would be less than gracious in victory. "I want to say again to the American people how profoundly sorry I am for what I said and did to trigger these events and the great burden they have imposed on the Congress and on the American people," he said. *(Clinton's reaction, p. 13-23)*

Harsh Rhetoric . . .

In all likelihood, the Senate's twin votes acquitting Clinton will stand as Congress' last statement on the presidential scandal that exploded onto the national scene 13 months ago. A bipartisan group of senators, most of them Democrats, were rebuffed in an attempt to force an up-or-down vote in a proposal to censure the president. That effort was rejected on a procedural vote moments after the trial ended.

But while the notion of an official censure might have died, the statements that senators delivered — either during the secret deliberations, or to the worldwide media throng waiting outside — left no doubt of their distaste for Clinton's behavior.

In some cases, that might have been at least partly designed for political effect. Those who voted to acquit, particularly Democrats, appeared determined to create some political distance from the president. Still, the vehemence with which Democrats denounced the president was surprising.

"The president has disgraced himself and dishonored his office," said Jack Reed of Rhode Island, a reliable ally of the president. Clinton's actions were "boorish, indefensible, even reprehensible," said Richard H. Bryan of Nevada.

And Kerrey accused the president of intentionally placing Lewinsky in legal jeopardy by permitting her to file a false affidavit in the Paula Corbin Jones sexual harassment lawsuit. That charge was not part of the impeachment articles.

"Removing him because he's a pig, that's not on our list," Kerrey remarked to reporters Feb. 10.

Republicans were not to be outdone in questioning the president's character and morals. Olympia J. Snowe of Maine voted to acquit because, she said, in some instances evidence was lacking and in others charges that were proved to her satisfaction still failed to meet the constitutional standard of "high crimes and misdemeanors." But Snowe also was withering in her criticism.

"As a woman who has fought long and hard for sexual harassment laws, I resent that the president has undermined our progress," she said. Referring to Clinton's White House affair with Lewinsky, she added: "No matter how consensual this relationship was, it involved a man with tremendous power, with authority over a 21-year-

Clinton's Public Reaction: Humility, Regret

FEBRUARY 13 — President Clinton's public response to the end of his impeachment ordeal was a contrite appeal for "reconciliation and renewal for America." Behind closed doors, he was said to be plotting revenge.

In brief remarks from the Rose Garden after the Senate vote Feb. 12, a somber Clinton made his most direct apology to date for his actions.

"I want to say again to the American people how profoundly sorry I am for what I said and did to trigger these events and the great burden they have imposed on the Congress and on the American people," Clinton said. "Now I ask all Americans, and I hope all Americans here in Washington and throughout our land, will rededicate ourselves to the work of serving our nation and building our future together."

The carefully choreographed response to the long-awaited news of his acquittal came only a day after a New York Times story depicted Clinton as itching for revenge against the House Republicans who impeached him. The story — "Clinton Vows Strong Drive to Win a House Majority, Advisers Say" — quoted unidentified "advisers" who described Clinton as viewing the 2000 elections as payback time.

Republicans, who have watched their political fortunes fall as they pursued Clinton's impeachment, reacted with predictable outrage. "It is deeply troubling that the president views closure of this constitutional process as an opportunity for revenge," Senate Majority Leader Trent Lott, R-Miss., said Feb. 11.

Speculation that Clinton would target political enemies such as House impeachment manager James E. Rogan, R-Calif., for defeat in 2000 conflicted with the White House message of the week: Let's get this behind us and get on to doing the nation's work.

If Clinton was taking any satisfaction from the political misfortunes of his enemies, he was determined not to let it show. Asked after his remarks whether he could "forgive and forget," Clinton paused and said, "I believe any person who asks for forgiveness has to be prepared to give it."

The White House — "a gloat-free zone," according to spokesman Joe Lockhart — took pains to avoid the appearance of celebrating the verdict. "There's nothing to celebrate here," White House aide Paul Begala had told reporters. "Saying that you win this is like saying you win an earthquake. You survive it and you rebuild."

Clinton made his remarks two hours after White House Chief of Staff John D. Podesta informed him of his acquittal. The scene — a humbled president standing alone at a Rose Garden lectern — differed from that of December after the House voted to impeach him. Then, two busloads of House Democrats went to the White House for a pep rally. In retrospect, even Democrats recoiled at the sight of a defiant Clinton amid a sea of Democrats vowing, despite his impeachment, to serve "until the last hour of the last day of my term."

"I thought it was wrong," said Rep. James P. Moran, D-Va., who did not attend the Dec. 19 event. "What were we celebrating? The fact that he was impeached?"

With Clinton's acquittal assured, Vice President Al Gore, who would immediately have become president if Clinton had been convicted, spent the day at events in Baltimore and Albany, N.Y. Clinton postponed a trip to Mexico to be in Washington for the vote.

Clinton still faces potential criminal charges for his wrongdoings. But even House Judiciary Committee Chairman Henry J. Hyde, R-Ill., relentless in his pursuit of impeachment, said the entire matter should be dropped. "I don't think indicting and criminally trying him, after what we have all been through, is going to be helpful to the country," Hyde said after the vote. "I think we should try to find areas we can agree on and get some legislation passed."

old subordinate, in the workplace — and not just any workplace."

Perhaps the toughest words of all came from Robert F. Bennett of Utah, who voted twice for conviction. "Bill Clinton will go down in history as the most accomplished, polished liar we have ever had serving in the White House," he said. "The name Clinton is entering the political lexicon . . . it's synonymous for an elegant and well-crafted lie."

Charles E. Grassley, R-Iowa, suggested that Clinton could stumble again into an ethical or moral thicket. "My suspicion is there's plenty of skeletons in this guy's closet and they're going to drop out from time to time, and shoes are going to fall and maybe even legs are going to fall."

. . . Followed by Votes To Acquit

For a variety of reasons, the case brought by the House never had a realistic chance of crossing the Constitution's formidable two-third barrier to conviction. Some Democrats challenged the trial's very legitimacy, on the grounds that impeachment was approved by the House on nearly party-line votes. Others maintained the case was flawed because it was based on allegations lodged by a biased, out-of-control prosecutor, Independent Counsel Kenneth W. Starr, whose conduct of the inquiry is now the subject of a Justice Department inquiry.

"Extreme partisanship and prosecutorial zealotry have strained this process in its critical early junctures," said Patrick J. Leahy, D-Vt. "Partisan impeachments are lacking in credibility."

Finally, all Democrats and a number of Republicans were troubled by the particulars of the case itself.

The Senate agreed with the president's lawyers, who took the position that Clinton's testimony before a federal grand jury, while clearly evasive, did not cross the high legal threshold to become perjurious.

Senators from both parties agreed that the prosecution had made a much stronger case that Clinton obstructed justice — a charged based primarily on the allegation that he encouraged Lewinsky to file a false affidavit in the Jones case. But several Democrats said the facts laid out by the prosecutors, while compelling, formed only a circumstantial case. To the vast majority of Republicans, such objections amount to legal nitpicking. Many focused on what they regarded as the totality of the president's wrongdoing in the Lewinsky affair. And some accused him of misdeeds that went well beyond the case brought by the managers.

Bennett said he had originally decided to vote to acquit Clinton for perjury but changed his mind because he felt the president's statement before the grand jury fit into what he called a pattern of "habitual mendacity." Underscoring the diverse factors that influenced senators, Bennett said Clinton's "stealth" decision in 1996 to create a national wilderness area in Utah fit into that pattern. He conceded that if this were a standard trial, such issues would not be relevant.

But the nation's founders, he contended, "were not naive enough to think that we would check our understanding of the history of the accused president at the door as we took up this burden."

The Final Test

The final act in the impeachment drama was dominated by the largely symbolic tussle for the minds of a handful of senators who might have been persuaded to create a simple majority for the obstruction charge. As senators went behind closed doors Feb. 9 for final deliberations, very little else was in doubt.

The prosecution and White House lawyers had just spent two days — Feb. 6 and Feb. 8 — largely restating the same arguments for conviction and acquittal they had been making since the trial began.

The Feb. 6 session was considered crucial for the House managers. While the Senate had voted previously against calling Lewinsky as a witness, prosecutors won permission to roll four television monitors onto the Senate floor and show clips from her videotaped deposition, taken Feb. 1, and from the depositions taped in the next two days by presidential confidant Vernon E. Jordan Jr. and White House aide Sidney Blumenthal.

But that presentation appeared to change no one's mind, as the trio generally stuck to previous statements and testimony.

Lewinsky's long-awaited testimony was ambiguous enough to provide ammunition to both sides, but Clinton's lawyers had a clip they were particularly eager to show.

"No one asked me or encouraged me to lie, but no one discouraged me either," she said, repeating for a national television audience the grand jury testimony she gave under Starr's grant of immunity from prosecution.

Then the lawyers for both sides returned for one final round of sparring, as anxious senators fidgeted and showed the strain of sitting silently through the proceedings. Judiciary Committee Chairman Henry J. Hyde of Illinois, the last of the 13 House prosecutors to speak, delivered a passionate, freewheeling address larded with quotes from Shakespeare, Saul Bellow and Charles de Gaulle, among others.

Failure to convict, he pleaded, would "raise the most serious questions of whether the president is in fact subject to the law or whether we are beginning a restoration of the divine right of kings."

Before the Senate could decide Clinton's fate, it had to decide whether to do so behind closed doors, as Senate rules require.

A proposal to open the debate drew backing from across a broad ideological spectrum but was defeated, 59-41, eight votes short of the 67 needed to change the impeachment rules. *(Vote 15, p. S-7)*

Political Context

The intense speculation over whether even one article would draw a 51-vote majority took on heightened political importance, especially for Republicans. Hyde and the managers aspired to that majority as some validation for their efforts. Conservative activists hoped to cite such a vote as a lasting rebuke that would show most members of both houses of Congress had believed the president's behavior met the constitutional test for removal from office.

"Everyone within the Republican Party understood the dynamics of failing to get a majority," said Marshall Wittmann, director of congressional relations at the Heritage Foundation. "That's the water level."

But Republican support for conviction began draining as moderates began delivering statements announcing their votes.

Not surprisingly, James M. Jeffords, the soft-spoken Vermonter who often finds himself in the cross-hairs of his party's conservatives — and who faces re-election next year — was first to break for acquittal. Removing Clinton on the House's charges would set a precedent that could imperil future presidents, regardless of party, he said.

A bid to render a unique verdict was contemplated by Arlen Specter, R-Pa. Saying he was citing Scottish legal precedent, he said Feb. 10 he planned to vote "not proven" instead of "guilty" or "not guilty," partly as a way to register his opinion that the trial had been too superficial.

But on decision day, Specter changed his mind, twice declaring, "Not proven, therefore not guilty."

Three other GOP moderates voted to acquit on both counts: Snowe, John H. Chafee of Rhode Island and Susan Collins of Maine.

Five other Republicans, including a quartet of committee chairmen, ended up rendering a split decision, voting to acquit on perjury but to convict on obstruction of justice: Slade Gorton of Washington, Intelligence Committee Chairman Richard C. Shelby of Alabama, Appropriations Committee Chairman Ted Stevens of Alaska, Government Affairs Committee Chairman Fred Thompson of Tennessee and Armed Services Committee Chairman John W. Warner of Virginia.

All are former prosecutors, a final signal that the Senate viewed the House's rationale for impeachment with both legal and political suspicion. ◆

Chapter 14

FOREIGN AFFAIRS

Congress Folds State Department Authorization Into Omnibus Spending Bill

SUMMARY

For the first time in five years, Congress cleared a State Department authorization bill that President Clinton was willing to sign, thanks to compromises on abortion restrictions and the payment of U.S. debts to the United Nations. The measure (HR 3427) was cleared as part of the fiscal 2000 omnibus spending bill (HR 3194).

The abortion issue has bedeviled foreign policy committees and the White House since 1997, when Rep. Christopher H. Smith, R-N.J., a leader of anti-abortion forces, persuaded House Republican leaders to link the repayment of U.S. debts to the United Nations to the restoration of some abortion restrictions on international family planning aid. Presidents Ronald Reagan and George Bush had imposed such restrictions by executive order, but Clinton lifted them in 1993 as one of his first acts in office. *(1997 Almanac, p. 9-37; 1993 Almanac, p. 530)*

Clinton vetoed a State Department authorization bill in 1998 that would have repaid the U.N. dues, because the bill also contained abortion restrictions. And in vetoing the fiscal 2000 Commerce-Justice-State appropriations bill (HR 2670) in October, Clinton cited the "unacceptable linkage" between the two issues as one of the main reasons. *(Fiscal 1999 bill, 1998 Almanac, p. 16-3)*

Since the abortion restrictions are now scheduled to run only until the end of fiscal 2000 under the foreign operations spending bill (HR 3422), supporters and opponents are likely to take up the debate again next year.

Clinton was also eager to curtail anti-American sentiment at the United Nations because of the debts, and told House Speaker J. Dennis Hastert, R-Ill., that he would like to reach a compromise with congressional Republicans. That agreement allowed House and Senate negotiators to reach a broader compromise on the overall State Department authorization measure and include it by reference in the omnibus budget bill.

Negotiators also avoided last-minute battles by removing a few controversial proposals that were in either the House or Senate versions of the State Department bills. For instance:

- The compromise omits language that would have forced the administration to move the U.S. Embassy in Israel from Tel Aviv to Jerusalem, which would have been a tacit recognition of Jerusalem as Israel's capital amid peace negotiations that are to determine Jerusalem's final status.
- Negotiators stripped out a controversial provision that would have held up assistance to North Korea until Congress enacted a joint resolution stating that the regime in Pyongyang has complied with international non-proliferation accords. The provision was inserted in the House version of the State Department bill by International Relations Committee Chairman Benjamin A. Gilman, R-N.Y.

Lawmakers also resolved a number of disputes between the House and Senate. For example:

- The agreement would take the Senate's lead and authorize State Department and related agencies' activities for fiscal years 2000 and 2001, as opposed to the House's recommendation of a one-year authorization. It would authorize $6 billion in fiscal 2000 and "such sums as may be necessary" for fiscal 2001; the second year's spending is expected to be 15 percent higher than the first year's.
- The measure would authorize $4.5 billion over five years to improve security at U.S. embassies in the wake of bombings and attacks in Kenya and Tanzania last year. This represents a significant boost from the $3 billion the Senate bill would have authorized or the $1.4 billion in the original House bill.

Negotiators also put off until next year a decision on what to do with billions of dollars in Iraqi assets that have been frozen in U.S. banks since the Persian Gulf War in 1991.

Box Score

- **Bill:** HR 3427 — PL 106-103 (incorporated by reference in HR 3194)
- **Legislative action: House** passed HR 2415 (H Rept 106-122) by voice vote July 21.

Senate passed S 886 (S Rept 106-43), 97-2, on June 22 and passed HR 2415 by unanimous consent Aug. 3 after substituting the text of S 886.

House voted 296-135 to adopt the conference report on HR 3194 (H Rept 106-479), which included HR 3427, Nov. 18.

Senate cleared the bill, 74-24, Nov. 19.

President signed HR 3194 on Nov. 29.

House Panel Approves Big Increase for Embassy Security

MARCH 27 — As Congress continues to prod the Clinton administration to make U.S. embassies safer, a House subcommittee on March 23 approved a two-year, $14.2 billion State Department reauthorization bill that includes a hefty funding increase for security upgrades at embassies and missions.

The House International Relations Subcommittee on International Operations and Human Rights approved the bill (HR 1211) by voice vote. The full committee is expected to take up the measure in April.

The bill would authorize $1.8 billion over two years for building new embassies and other related initiatives, including $904 million for fiscal 2000 — about $600 million more than the administration requested.

"If this subcommittee has one responsibility that can be singled out as even more important than our other responsibilities, it is to do whatever is possible to protect the lives of the people who work in our embassies and other missions," said Chairman Christopher H. Smith, R-N.J.

Smith said the amount that would be authorized was based on what State Department security experts believe is the most that can reasonably be spent over the next two years. Smith said that if the experts determine that more can be spent, he will support increasing the total.

A State Department review committee headed by retired Adm. William J. Crowe Jr., a former chairman of the Joint Chiefs of Staff, has recommended that the administration spend an average of $1.4 billion a year over the next decade to upgrade embassies. Crowe's panel was formed in the wake of terrorist bombings at U.S. missions last year in Kenya and Tanzania that killed more than 250 people and injured more than 5,500.

Secretary of State Madeleine K. Albright has said that the department originally sought $1.4 billion for fiscal 2000 but that the Office of Management and Budget scaled back the request. The department is reassessing the request.

The administration's proposal "was not real; it was the flim-flam plan," said Cynthia A. McKinney of Georgia, the subcommittee's ranking Democrat. "We have done better, a whole lot better."

McKinney Signs On

In an unusual move, McKinney signed on as a cosponsor of the State Department bill despite acknowledging strong misgivings about several of its provisions. Those provisions are likely to pose a severe threat to the bill's chances.

McKinney's main concern was language calling for withholding the U.S. contribution to the United Nations Fund for Population Activities unless it withdraws from China or unless President Clinton certifies that no compulsory abortions are being performed there. "If this effort succeeds, millions of women will continue to be deprived of services they ought to be able to receive," she said.

Concerned that the international agency was supporting coercive family planning programs in China, Congress cut off money for the U.N. fund in the fiscal 1999 omnibus spending bill (PL 105-277).

Smith, an outspoken opponent of abortion, said he has been dismayed by China's population quotas under the "one child per family" system. But abortion rights groups and their congressional allies are trying to gather support for legislation (HR 895) backed by the administration that would restore aid to the agency.

Despite her concerns, McKinney said the bill "as a whole will do more good than harm." She and other lawmakers expressed hope that a deal can be struck in committee or on the floor.

The subcommittee approved three amendments by voice vote. One, offered by Smith, would allow up to three months' pay in advance for State Department workers outside the United States who require medical attention. It also would grant a repatriation allowance to the spouse or dependents of an employee who dies outside the United States.

Another amendment, sponsored by McKinney, would direct the secretary of State to describe the extent to which nations meet a code of conduct on arms transfers.

A third amendment, offered by Rep. Brad Sherman, D-Calif., would set goals to expedite the processing of visas for relatives of U.S. citizens. It also would require non-U.S. citizens who visit the United States and request non-immigrant alien status to post a $25,000 bond.

U.N. Dues

The subcommittee's approval of the State Department bill came as a bipartisan group of House members introduced a bill (HR 1355) to pay $575 million of the back dues the U.S. owes the United Nations.

Congress last year passed a State Department authorization bill (HR 1757) that included nearly $1 billion for U.N. debts, but Clinton vetoed the legislation because it would have banned federal aid to international family planning groups that advocate or lobby on abortion.

The administration may have to scramble this fall to find enough money to keep the debts from costing the United States its seat in the U.N. General Assembly.

House Committee OKs $1.4 Billion For Embassies

APRIL 17 — Congress is notoriously stingy about spending money overseas. Yet, since last year's terrorist bombing of U.S. embassies in Tanzania and Kenya, it seems lawmakers can't spend money fast enough to upgrade security at U.S. missions around the world.

Marking up a fiscal 2000 State Department reauthorization bill (HR 1211) on April 14, the House International Relations Committee voted to increase spending to rebuild or renovate embassies and consulates by almost $500 million more than was approved last month by its International Operations and Human Rights Subcommittee. The new total of $1.4 billion would be almost $1.1 billion more than the Clinton administration requested. The vote came as the panel approved, by voice vote, the broader legislation, which authorizes $7.6 billion for the State Department.

In March, Subcommittee Chairman Christopher H. Smith, R-N.J., said his panel had approved the maximum amount that State Department security experts believe could be reasonably spent in fiscal 2000. The administration had proposed waiting until fiscal 2001 to begin the bulk of the spending on upgrading embassies and to spend only about $268 million for personnel and other recurring costs in fiscal 2000.

But Rep. Doug Bereuter, R-Neb., argued that next year's spending should be up to the standard proposed by a State Department review commission headed by retired Adm. William J. Crowe Jr. That panel recommended that the administration spend an average of $1.4 billion a year over the next decade to upgrade overseas missions.

Foreign Aid Cuts

Yet, aside from the embassy spending, lawmakers reverted to familiar patterns in marking up the authorization bill. Since the fiscal 2000 budget resolution (H Con Res 68) calls for cutting overseas spending, International Relations Committee Chairman Benjamin A. Gilman, R-N.Y., decided to scale back the proposed two-year State Department reauthorization to a one-year measure in order to lower the bill's tab.

In response, first lady Hillary Rodham Clinton has joined an alliance of business, humanitarian, and ethnic groups to try to block Republican plans to cut international funds by about 15 percent from the State Department, the United Nations and foreign aid programs.

"I don't think that this is a demonstration of responsible leadership," Mrs. Clinton said April 13 as she kicked off a lobbying effort by the Campaign to Preserve U.S. Global Leadership.

For example, lawmakers ignored a State Department plea to include funds in the legislation to repay more than $1 billion in U.S. debts to the United Nations.

Instead, ranking Democrat Sam Gejdenson of Connecticut said he and Gilman plan separate legislation that would repay the debts. Although the U.N. funds normally would be in the reauthorization measure, Gilman and Gejdenson are eager to keep them separate, because Smith is likely to add anti-abortion language — expected to draw a presidential veto — to any bill that provides U.N. funds.

Senate Prospects

In the Senate, meanwhile, squabbles over funds for the United Nations are delaying plans for a proposed State Department authorization bill. The Senate Foreign Relations Committee is slated to mark up its version of the legislation April 21.

Lawmakers and aides on the committee said Chairman Jesse Helms, R-N.C., planned to reintroduce legislation that passed the Senate two years ago but was ultimately vetoed by Clinton after Smith added anti-abortion restrictions on international family planning funds.

But lawmakers said the administration wants to renegotiate some of the terms of a previous deal on U.N. debts because it thinks the package is no longer acceptable to U.N. members.

Administration officials have said that a proposal to ultimately cut the U.S. share of the regular U.N. budget from 25 percent today to 20 percent over a two-year period is no longer realistic.

The House committee did take one small step to repair ties to the United Nations, however. The panel voted 23-17 to adopt an amendment by Rep. Tom Campbell, R-Calif., that would restore funds to the United Nations Fund for Population Activities as long as the president certified, and independent monitors confirmed, that the funds were not being used to support a policy of coercive abortions in China. The legislation would provide only $25 million in fiscal 2000, but the vote marked a victory for abortion rights supporters in the first major test vote on abortion in the 106th Congress.

Senate Committee Approves Bill Without Abortion, U.N. Restrictions

APRIL 24 — The Senate Foreign Relations Committee handed President Clinton a legislative victory April 21, approving a fiscal 2000-01 State Department reauthorization bill that would clear nearly $1 billion in U.S. debts to the United Nations without imposing what administration officials viewed as onerous conditions on the international organization.

But the administration's victory party could be a short one. Republican Christopher H. Smith of New Jersey may add anti-abortion restrictions to a similar bill (HR 1211) being considered by the House. Such restrictions led Clinton to veto a fiscal 1998-99 State Department reauthorization bill last year.

For the time being, though, the $13.6 billion measure drafted by Senate Foreign Relations Committee Chairman Jesse Helms, R-N.C., takes pains to avoid a confrontation with the White House: The 77-year-old conservative firebrand is eager to see a State Department authorization bill signed into law for the first time since he took command of the committee in 1995.

So Helms, though an ardent foe of abortion, has fended off attempts to include Smith's restrictions on international family planning funds in the authorization bill, knowing it would likely doom the measure.

The restrictions would ban federal aid to international family planning groups that advocate or lobby on abortion, reinstating part of a policy from the Reagan and Bush administrations that Clinton overturned as one of his first acts in office. *(1993 Almanac, p. 348)*

Helms also bowed to diplomatic reality and the insistence of Secretary of State Madeleine K. Albright and agreed to cut back on conditions that would be attached to the payment of debts to the United Nations.

As approved by the committee, 17-1, the skeleton of the U.N. package remains similar to one agreed to by Albright, Helms and ranking committee Democrat Joseph R. Biden Jr. of Delaware in 1997 as part of the previous effort to enact a State Department authorization bill. *(1997 Almanac, p. 8-32)*

The package would pay back debts of $819 million over three years and forgive $107 million that the United Nations owes the United States. In order to receive the money, the United Nations would have to agree to a number of conditions, most importantly a reduction in the U.S. share of the regular U.N. budget from 25 percent to 20 percent and a cut in the U.S. portion of the peacekeeping budget from 31 percent to 25 percent.

Bad Relations

Since these provisions were originally drafted, U.S. relations with the United Nations have nose-dived. At the same time, U.N. Secretary-General Kofi Annan has carried out his own reform effort.

The result has been a growing resistance to U.S. demands, something Helms tacitly acknowledged by backing off from some earlier demands. Most important, his bill would allow the president to waive the requirement that the debts can be paid off only if the U.S. share of the budget is reduced.

The bill's other major funding initiative calls for spending $3 billion over the next five fiscal years to enhance security at U.S. diplomatic missions overseas, in the wake of last year's attacks of U.S. embassies in Kenya and Tanzania. It is the same amount Clinton requested.

The House International Relations Committee took a different approach in its one-year State Department bill approved April 15 — a $1.4 billion authorization for embassy construction in fiscal 2000.

A special commission headed by retired Adm. William J. Crowe Jr. recommended that the administration spend an average of $1.4 billion a year over the next decade to upgrade overseas missions.

Easing a Merger

Like their House counterparts, Helms and Biden tried to mitigate some of the effects of the reorganization of the foreign affairs bureaucracy that they had pushed through last year, originally as part of the failed State Department authorization bill and ultimately as part of an omnibus spending bill (PL 105-277) in the waning days of the last Congress.

That reorganization will merge the U.S. Information Agency (USIA), the Arms Control and Disarmament Agency and part of the Agency for International Development (AID) into the State Department by the end of the current fiscal year.

But lawmakers have sought to ensure that programs they consider essential continue.

In the House, Smith, who is chairman of the International Relations Subcommittee on International Operations and Human Rights, sought to preserve a separation between the State Department's press functions and the overseas public relations efforts of the USIA by creating a new bureau of international information programs.

In the Senate, Biden and Helms wanted to guarantee that the arms control agency's ability to monitor and enforce international agreements is maintained. So the legislation would create the post of assistant secretary of State for verification and compliance, subject to Senate confirmation.

Middle East

The Senate also took the lead on several policy initiatives, particularly in the Middle East and China.

In a move that sparked some debate, lawmakers approved, by voice vote, an amendment to prohibit the Palestinian Authority from maintaining an office in Washington if its president, Yasir Arafat, carried out threats to declare an independent Palestinian state without a peace agreement with Israel.

Sen. Sam Brownback, R-Kan., chairman of the Near Eastern and South Asian Affairs Subcommittee, who offered the amendment, said it should serve as a warning to Arafat.

"If you do something that's extraordinarily unhelpful to the peace process, here's the consequences," Brownback said. Congress this month adopted a resolution (H Con Res 24) opposing any such unilateral declaration of a Palestinian state.

Biden criticized the amendment as "micromanagement of incredibly delicate negotiations" and said it was unnecessary. "Everybody knows if Arafat declares a Palestinian state, school's out," Biden said. "The Palestinians would be totally isolated from the U.S."

The legislation also includes several other provisions designed to bolster Israel's claim to Jerusalem as the permanent capital of Israel. In particular, the bill would authorize $50 million a year in fiscal 2000 and 2001 to build a new U.S. embassy in Jerusalem. Currently, the embassy is in Tel Aviv, in order not to prejudice negotiations over Jerusalem's final status.

China

Helms, an anti-communist crusader, is seeking to revive several anti-China measures that Sen. Tim Hutchinson, R-Ark., tried to include in the fiscal 1999 defense appropriations (PL 105-262) and authorization (PL 105-261) bills last year.

Some provisions would deny entry to the United States to any foreign official involved in religious persecution or a forced abortion or sterilization policy. Another would deny visas to Chinese officials involved in the trade in organs of executed prisoners.

The bill also would establish a registry to track political and religious prisoners in China and would specify $2 million a year for monitoring human rights and the economic and political climate in China and Tibet.

The bill also includes a controversial measure that seeks to prevent China from using its takeover of the former foreign colonies of Hong Kong and Macao to gain easier access to technology that could help its military efforts.

In particular, the bill would apply to these former colonies new requirements for export license inspections and certificates listing actual recipients of equipment such as high-speed computers, that can have both civilian and military uses.

Sen. Rod Grams, R-Minn., objected to the provisions, saying such issues were already being addressed by the Banking, Housing and Urban Affairs Committee as part of its markup of an export administration bill. But he held off on an attempt to strike the provisions, saying he hoped that the issue could be worked out between the committees before the State bill is taken up by the full Senate.

Despite a clamor from farm-state lawmakers, members also agreed to a Helms request to not include in the measure legislation designed to make it more difficult to apply unilateral sanctions overseas.

Helms said that in the coming weeks, he, Biden and other panel members would seek to draft a separate bill that would address the sanctions issue.

"I believe common ground can be found on it," Helms said.

But Biden, noting the failure of a similar effort last year, was skeptical. "I don't think we can get a consensus," Biden said.

U.N. Debt Deal Improves Chances For Senate Passage Of State Dept. Bill

JUNE 19 — The words could hardly have been more generous or the prospects for passage brighter as the Senate took up a fiscal 2000-01 State Department authorization bill June 18.

Joseph R. Biden Jr. of Delaware, the ranking Democrat on the Senate Foreign Relations Committee, praised panel Chairman Jesse Helms, R-N.C., for putting together a bipartisan bill (S 886) that won 17 of 18 votes on the panel.

"It is a solid, solid bill," Biden said. "It would not have gotten this consensus out of an ideologically divided committee."

Helms then returned the favor. "This would not have happened if it had not been for Joe Biden," he said. "I have not enjoyed any of my service in the Senate more than our cooperation."

Senate Assistant Minority Leader Harry Reid, D-Nev., said bipartisanship would ensure smooth passage of the legislation.

"I've been involved in this bill when we've taken a week to resolve it," Reid said. "Now we're going to do it in a matter of hours."

In fact, lawmakers left the serious legislating until June 21, when they expect to consider a number of amendments, including one from Helms and Biden, and then vote on the legislation.

Speaking after the June 18 session, Biden was upbeat. "I think we'll work out 80 percent of the amendments beforehand," he said.

The most significant debate is likely to center around an amendment by Paul S. Sarbanes, D-Md.

Sarbanes, the sole dissenter when the Foreign Relations Committee approved the legislation, hopes to restore funds that the bill would cut from some United Nations functions, such as peacekeeping.

The heart of the bill is a compromise between Helms, Biden and Secretary of State Madeleine K. Albright that would pay $819 million in U.S. debts to the United Nations over three years and forgive $107 million that the United Nations owes the United States.

In order to receive the money, the United Nations would have to agree to a number of conditions, most importantly a reduction in the U.S. share of its regular budget from 25 percent to 20 percent and a cut in the U.S. portion of the peacekeeping budget from 31 percent to 25 percent.

Former Battles

The package remains similar to one the Senate approved in 1997 as part of the fiscal 1998-99 State Department authorization. The Senate passed that legislation 90-5, but it was ultimately vetoed by President Clinton after anti-abortion provisions were inserted by the House in a conference report, which the Senate adopted, 51-49.

The legislation is once again expected to become entangled in the abortion debate.

The House is expected to take up its version of the bill (HR 1211) in July. It so far does not include the money to repay debts to the United Nations.

Rep. Christopher H. Smith, R-N.J., chairman of the House International Relations Subcommittee on International Operations and Human Rights, has said that when the legislation reaches a House-Senate conference, he will insist that the conferees either drop the provision repaying the U.S. debts or include anti-abortion provisions that he inserted in the previous legislation.

"The U.N. arrearages and Mexico City will travel together," said a Smith aide. "Mexico City" is congressional lingo for restrictions on abortion in international family planning assistance; it refers to an international conference that took place during the Ronald Reagan years.

In his floor remarks, Biden said that in the Senate, "a little bit of reason is seeping into this debate" over repaying U.S. debts to the United Nations.

"I guess I'm preaching to the choir," Biden said of his Senate colleagues. "But I hope that some of the congregation in the House will listen. It's long past time to put this issue to bed."

Aside from the U.N. issue, the other key initiative in the legislation is a provision calling for spending $3 billion over the next five fiscal years to enhance security at U.S. embassies overseas, in the wake of last year's attacks of U.S. embassies in Kenya and Tanzania. It is the same amount that Clinton requested.

Helms said the Senate bill makes a particular point of establishing a budgetary firewall between the embassy construction funds and other State Department funds to "ensure that embassy funds are not raided to pay for other State Department pet projects."

Senate-Passed Bill Includes U.N. Debt Compromise

JUNE 26 — It is a lonely fight — and he keeps losing — but Sen. Paul S. Sarbanes, D-Md., continues to insist that Congress is not treating the United Nations fairly.

His latest quixotic battle to win more money for the international organization that some lawmakers barely tolerate and others loathe came June 22, when he voted against a fiscal 2000-01 State Department authorization bill (S 886 — S Rept 106-43). The bill passed 97-2; Robert C. Smith, R-N.H., joined Sarbanes. *(Vote 180, p. S-37)*

The heart of the bill is a compromise between Senate Foreign Relations Committee Chairman Jesse Helms, R-N.C., ranking Democrat Joseph R. Biden Jr. of Delaware and Secretary of State Madeleine K. Albright over repaying U.S. debts to the United Nations.

Under the plan, Congress would pay over three years $819 million that the United States owes to the United Nations and forgive $107 million that the United Nations owes the United States.

In order to receive the money, though, the United Nations would have to agree to institute a number of reforms. The most important would lead to a reduction in the U.S. share of the U.N. budget from 25 percent to 20 percent and a cut in the U.S. portion of the peacekeeping budget from 31 percent to 25 percent.

Calling these conditions "arbitrary and burdensome," Sarbanes said the U.S. failure to pay its debts was "wasting our own influence, damaging our credibility and international respect."

Sarbanes said U.N. Secretary General Kofi Annan had instituted several reforms at the United Nations and wanted to pursue more, "but he is trying to run an organization that operates by consensus. . . . The United States can be more helpful in the reform effort. We do this by not being the biggest delinquent in dues paying, which only brings resentment against our calls for change."

Biden countered that "I began this process six years ago exactly where the senator is. . . . We have been noble, myself included, in our efforts. But we haven't gotten a penny for those arrears."

For his part, Helms told the Senate: "I am not in the mood to give away the store, and I haven't given it away regarding the United Nations yet."

This is not the first time Sarbanes has stood alone on the issue. He cast the sole vote against the measure when it was considered by the Foreign Relations panel.

But he did win a consolation prize. Helms and Biden did not object to including in the bill an amendment Sarbanes offered to increase the funds authorized for U.N. peacekeeping operations in fiscal 2000 to $235 million from $215 million.

They also supported an amendment he offered to roll back some of Helms' proposed changes to the Foreign Service personnel system. The amendment passed, 88-0. *(Vote 177, p. S-36)*

The amendment would grant Foreign Service employees more time after a questionable incident occurs to file a grievance. It also limited the amount of time damaging information could be kept in an employee's file.

In the only other roll call vote on an amendment, lawmakers beat back, 23-76 an attempt by Russell D. Feingold, D-Wis., to alter the grant-making practices of the National Endowment for Democracy. *(Vote 179, p. S-36)*

Currently, about two-thirds of the endowment's budget is dedicated to four overseas institutes affiliated with the Democratic and Republican parties, the U.S. Chamber of Commerce and the AFL-CIO. Feingold's amendment would have phased out this earmark over a five-year period, subjecting all funding to competitive bidding.

Feingold said that these groups "shouldn't be getting an automatic bonanza."

But Richard G. Lugar, R-Ind., a senior member of the Foreign Relations Committee and a board member of the National Endowment for Democracy, defended the allocation, saying it struck an ideological and partisan balance.

"For the last 18 years, grants have not been politicized," Lugar said. "It is a situation of trying to fix something that is not broke."

Having made it through the Senate with little controversy, the legislation is likely to face greater tests in the weeks and months ahead.

Christopher H. Smith, R-N.J., chairman of the House International Relations Subcommittee on International Operations and Human Rights, has said that when the legislation reaches a House-Senate conference, he will insist that the conferees either drop the provision repaying U.S. debts to the United Nations or include anti-abortion provisions that he inserted in previous legislation.

President Clinton vetoed a similar bill last year when those abortion restrictions were included.

House Passes Bill, Leaving Abortion, U.N. Debt Issues For Conferees

JULY 24 — By putting off debate on the most controversial issues, the House easily passed a fiscal 2000 State Department authorization bill July 21. But in the process, it set up a contentious conference with the Senate to draft a compromise.

The legislation (HR 2415), passed by voice vote, would authorize $2.4 billion in fiscal 2000, most of it for improving the security of U.S. missions overseas in the wake of last year's terrorist bombings at U.S. embassies in Kenya and Tanzania. *(1998 Almanac, p. 2-117)*

In debate scattered over nearly a week, House members adopted controversial amendments that would give Congress a greater say over U.S. assistance to North Korea and provide aid to a U.N. family planning agency.

But in order to speed passage of the bill, key lawmakers agreed not to debate the highly charged issues of U.S. debts to the United Nations and aid to international family planning programs.

Instead, Sam Gejdenson of Connecticut, ranking Democrat on the International Relations Committee, and Christopher H. Smith, R-N.J., chairman of the panel's International Operations and Human Rights Subcommittee, agreed to thrash out the issues in a future House-Senate conference.

The Senate's State Department reauthorization bill (S 886), passed June 22, would pay $819 million in debts to the United Nations and forgive $107 million that the United Nations owes the United States.

The House bill does not include the U.N. funds, despite a plea from President Clinton.

Gejdenson agreed not to push for those funds as long as Smith, the leader of anti-abortion forces in the House, agreed to hold off on abortion restrictions he has included in previous State Department legislation.

Both or Neither

Smith's provisions would ban federal aid to international family planning groups that advocate or lobby for abortion.

Last year, GOP leaders included the anti-abortion provisions in a State Department authorization bill, leading Clinton to veto the measure, which also would have authorized the payment of U.S. debts to the United Nations.

This year, Smith has said that he will insist that any compromise bill that emerges from conference either have both the U.N. funds and the anti-abortion restrictions or neither.

However, it is not clear if Smith's position commands majority support in the current Congress, since he lost a key abortion-related vote during House consideration of the State Department bill.

Smith offered an amendment July 19 to reverse an April 15 vote in the House International Relations Committee and eliminate a $25 million U.S. contribution to the United Nations Fund for Population Activities (UNFPA), unless the organization ends its programs in China. Smith argued that the funds indirectly support coercive abortion in China.

"For 20 years, the U.N. population fund has poured millions of dollars — about $157 million to be exact — provided technical assistance and given effusive praise to China's program that relies on forced abortion and forced sterilization to achieve its goals," Smith said. "It has provided cover and covered up for the Beijing hard-liners who oppress and victimize women and murder their children."

But before the House considered Smith's amendment, Rep. Tom Campbell, R-Calif., modified it with a second-degree amendment. Campbell's amendment would permit the contribution to the population fund but would deduct from the $25 million total any money that the fund spends in China.

Campbell won the support of House International Relations Committee Chairman Benjamin A. Gilman, R-N.Y., and 44 other Republicans who

State Department Bills Compared

After four years of fruitless wrangling with President Clinton, the House and Senate are trying again to enact a State Department authorization bill. The last one Clinton signed was in 1994 (PL 103-236). *(1994 Almanac, p. 454)*

This chart compares key features of bills passed by the Senate (S 886) and the House (HR 2415). The most contentious issues, including abortion and debts to the United Nations, have been deferred to a conference.

ISSUE	HOUSE	SENATE
State Department operations	The bill would authorize State Department activities for fiscal 2000, with no specified amount. For most programs, the bill would authorize "such funds as may be necessary."	The bill would authorize $6.4 billion in fiscal 2000 and $6 billion in fiscal 2001 for State Department activities and broadcasting.
Embassy security	The bill would authorize $1.4 million for security upgrades to U.S. missions abroad in fiscal 2000, including construction and relocation costs.	The bill would authorize $3 billion over five years for construction and major security improvements at U.S. missions abroad. Though that is the total President Clinton requested, the bill would begin the program a year earlier, in fiscal 2000, and the authorization would be limited to $600 million a year. U.S. missions would have to adhere to stricter security standards, including consolidation of facilities and training.
Debts to the United Nations	No provision.	The bill would authorize the payment of $819 million in U.S. debts to the United Nations — $575 million already appropriated for fiscal 1998 and 1999 and $244 million for fiscal 2000 — and would forgive $107 million the United Nations owes the United States. The United Nations would have to agree to lower the U.S. share of its budget from 25 percent to 22 percent and the U.S. share of the peacekeeping budget from 31 percent to 25 percent.
Refugee assistance	The bill would authorize $750 million for migration and refugee assistance, including $50 million for Kosovo refugees in neighboring countries, $60 million to resettle refugees in Israel, and $2 million each for those from Burma, Tibet and Sierra Leone.	The bill would authorize $660 million for migration and refugee assistance in fiscal 2000 and fiscal 2001.
U.N. Population Fund	The bill would restore a $25 million annual contribution to the U.N. Population Fund eliminated by the fiscal 1999 omnibus spending law (PL 105-277), though U.S. funds could not be used in China.	The bill contains no restriction on payments to the fund.
North Korea	The bill would restrict any nuclear cooperation between the United States and North Korea until the president certified that North Korea was abiding by nuclear proliferation agreements, had ended its nuclear weapons program and had allowed inspection of its nuclear sites.	No provision.
Peacekeeping	The bill would authorize "such sums as may be necessary" for assessed contributions for international peacekeeping.	The bill would authorize $215 million in fiscal 2000 and the same amount in fiscal 2001 for international peacekeeping activities under U.N. auspices.

support abortion rights. That helped his amendment pass, 221-198, despite the opposition of 28 anti-abortion Democrats. *(Vote 312, p. H-104)*

"This debate should not be about China; it should be about the programs in over 100 other countries where UNFPA operates," Gilman said, pointing out that Smith's amendment would have cut off support for U.N. population programs in Mexico.

North Korean Threat

Gilman on July 21 also succeeded on another amendment — but this time he was strongly opposed by the Clinton administration.

The House approved, 305-120, an amendment by Gilman and Democrat Edward J. Markey of Massachusetts rebuking Clinton's policy toward North Korea by giving Congress more control over relations with the nation. *(Vote 321, p. H-106)*

The amendment — the text of a bill that Gilman previously introduced (HR 1835) — would prevent any U.S.-North Korea agreement on nuclear cooperation from taking effect unless Congress enacted a joint resolution saying that North Korea had complied with international non-proliferation accords.

In particular, Gilman's amendment would require North Korea to implement a 1994 bilateral agreement with the United States to freeze its nuclear weapons program and allow international inspections before receiving international aid.

Under the 1994 accord, the United States, Japan and South Korea agreed to provide North Korea with fuel oil and assistance in building safer nuclear power reactors in exchange for a commitment to freeze its nuclear weapons programs. *(1995 Almanac, p. 10-24)*

Markey said North Korea has consistently violated the 1994 accord as well as other non-proliferation agreements. And he noted that U.S. intelligence officials believe the North Korean regime has provided nuclear and missile technology to other countries and is preparing to test a missile capable of hitting the West Coast of the United States.

"We should not help a country get weapons that could explode in our face," Markey said.

Gary L. Ackerman, D-N.Y., countered that ending the accord would only increase North Korea's isolation and forego any chance of halting the country's nuclear ambitions.

"The fastest way to unfreeze that [nuclear weapons] program is to abandon the agreed framework, as this amendment would do," Ackerman said.

New Nukes

At the same time that the House was trying to tighten control over one potential nuclear power, it agreed to relax restrictions against India and Pakistan, which only a year ago had drawn sharp criticism for testing nuclear weapons.

Included in the bill, and not debated by the House, was a one-year waiver of all sanctions imposed on India and Pakistan after they tested the weapons.

The fiscal 1999 omnibus appropriations bill (PL 105-277) allowed the president to waive sanctions on farm and humanitarian goods for fiscal 1999.

Still, the provision is considerably less generous than an amendment the Senate approved June 8 as part of the fiscal 2000 defense appropriations bill (S1122 — S Rept 106-53). That amendment would give India and Pakistan a five-year waiver from sanctions.

For More Information

For final passage of the State Department authorization, which was included in the omnibus appropriations bill, see p. 2-3.

State Department Bill Still Stalled Over Abortion

OCTOBER 2 — Leaders of the House and Senate foreign affairs committees met Sept. 28 to see if they could work out a compromise on the fiscal 2000 State Department authorization bill (HR 2415), but they reached the same impasse that has dogged the legislation for three years — abortion restrictions on international family planning aid.

The informal gathering of chairmen and ranking Democrats on the House International Relations and Senate Foreign Relations committees was "an attempt to lay out the landscape" on the bill, an aide said.

Though each chamber passed a version of the legislation this summer (HR 2415 — H Rept 106-122; S 886 — S Rept 106-43), the House has yet to name conferees.

House Republicans would first like to work out the abortion dispute that led President Clinton to veto last year's version. *(1998 Almanac, p. 16-3)*

Christopher H. Smith, R-N.J., a leader of anti-abortion forces in the House who would be included in any conference, said House leaders promised him they will not support Senate provisions that would repay nearly $1 billion in U.S. debts to the United Nations without concessions on the anti-abortion provisions.

Smith is even more adamant that those provisions be included after similar language was dropped from the conference report on the fiscal 2000 foreign operations appropriations bill (HR 2606 — H Rept 106-339) ◆

Senate Action Stalls on Bill To Penalize Russia for Aiding Iran in Arms Development

SUMMARY

A last-minute hitch prevented Senate action on House-passed legislation aimed at punishing those in Russia and other countries that aid Iran's weapons development. The Clinton administration opposed the bill, although the president could have waived any sanctions. The Senate is expected to take up the matter in 2000.

The House overwhelmingly passed legislation Sept. 14 targeting those that have helped Iran with weapons programs. The bill would require the president every six months to inform Congress of any countries, organizations, companies or individuals which, according to "credible information," have transferred to Iran technology related to missiles or other nuclear, chemical or biological weapons. The president would be authorized to impose penalties, such as economic sanctions or a cutoff of U.S. military aid, unless the foreign governments already had punished those involved. If he chose not to impose sanctions, he would have to explain why to Congress.

The bill also would withhold pending U.S. aid to the Russian Space Agency for the International Space Station unless Russia makes it national policy to eliminate nuclear proliferation and the space agency shows that it has not allowed anyone to transfer sensitive technology to Iran.

The legislation is popular in Congress but strongly opposed by the administration, which says Russia is making progress in controlling proliferation and that such legislation could harm rather than help the effort. Congress did not attempt to override Clinton's veto in 1998 after the administration asked for more time to negotiate with Russia on proliferation.

Republican claims that Clinton has ignored Russian sales of missile components to Iran to protect Russian President Boris Yeltsin's political standing were buttressed by a CIA report released in September that said Russia is probably willing to sell developing nuclear powers such as Iran technology that would allow missiles to overcome U.S. defenses.

The Senate might try to make sanctions mandatory next year, with no presidential leeway; the administration would have difficulty staving off the popular measure.

Committees Delay Action on Bill To Punish Russia For Aiding Iran

AUGUST 7 — At the request of the Clinton administration, Democratic lawmakers and the Israeli government, the House International Relations Committee on Aug. 4 postponed until early September consideration of a bill that seeks to punish Russia for assisting Iran's weapons development.

The House Science Committee also postponed an Aug. 4 markup of the bill (HR 1883), which would withhold U.S. payments to subsidize Russia's share of the International Space Station unless Russia certifies it is not transferring technology that would help Iran develop weapons of mass destruction or the missiles that carry them.

Israeli embassy officials met with International Relations Committee Chairman Benjamin A. Gilman, R-N.Y., and ranking Democrat Sam Gejdenson of Connecticut to ask the committee to hold off on considering the bill. Israeli officials worry the bill might deter Russia from limiting technology transfers to Iran.

The House Science Subcommittee on Space and Aeronautics approved the bill 19-3 on July 29.

Box Score

- **Bill:** HR 1883
- **Legislative action: House** passed HR 1883 (H Rept 106-315, Part 1), 419-0 on Sept. 14.

House Bill To Punish Russia For Iran Arms Aid Nears Passage

SEPTEMBER 11 — Despite objections from the State Department and NASA, the House appears poised to pass legislation aimed at punishing Russia and other countries for assisting Iran's weapons development.

The House International Relations Committee on Sept. 9 approved the bill (HR 1883), 33-0. A few hours later, the Science Committee approved the measure, 41-0.

The full House is expected to consider the bill the week of Sept. 13, probably under suspension of the rules, a procedure for relatively non-controversial legislation.

The bill has wide bipartisan support, with 222 cosponsors ranging from House Majority Whip Tom DeLay, R-Texas, to Sam Gejdenson of Connecticut, ranking Democrat on the International Relations Committee. Lawmakers have become concerned by recent reports of weapons technology spreading from Russia and other nations to Iran.

Clinton administration officials have said Russia is taking steps to check the spread of weapons. But International Relations Committee Chairman Benjamin A. Gilman, R-N.Y., said that "all available evidence indicates those efforts have failed. Proliferation is as bad today as it's ever been."

The bill would require the president to take punitive actions, such as imposing economic sanctions, against countries that have transferred sensitive nuclear, chemical or biological weapons technology to Iran. The president could exempt a country from punishment, but only if he explains the reason to Congress in writing.

At the behest of the administration and Israeli officials, the International Relations and Science committees agreed last month to postpone the bill. The Israelis were concerned it might deter Russia from limiting technology transfers to Iran.

Since then, lawmakers have made several changes, including eliminating one of the reporting requirements and giving the president greater latitude in imposing sanctions.

But a State Department official told International Relations members that his agency remains "strongly opposed" to the bill, in part because it might undercut Russia's recent reforms on technology transfers.

"The problem here is we will eliminate the incentive for countries to work with us," said John Barker, deputy assistant secretary of State for nonproliferation controls.

Barker also said the reporting requirements would be burdensome. "We want to make sure we put all our resources toward fighting proliferation rather than writing reports," he said.

Meanwhile, NASA officials object to a provision that would tie U.S. payments to Russia for the International Space Station to Russia's agreement not to send weapons technology to Iran.

NASA last year proposed sending Russia $650 million for goods and services related to space station construction. The House bill would prohibit the rest of the payment unless the president determines Russia has taken adequate steps to prevent proliferation to Iran.

Senate Majority Leader Trent Lott, R-Miss., is working with Joseph I. Lieberman, D-Conn., on an Iran sanctions measure, a leadership aide said.

Lott Seeks Debate On Sanctions Bill

NOVEMBER 6 — Senate Majority Leader Trent Lott, R-Miss., said Nov. 4 that he hopes to have the Senate debate a House-passed bill that aims to punish Russia and other countries for assisting Iran's weapons development.

The House passed the bill (HR 1883), 419-0, on Sept. 14. Members have become concerned over recent reports that weapons technology has spread from Russia and other nations to Iran. They have acted despite the threat of a presidential veto. Clinton administration officials have said Russia is taking steps to block the spread of weapons technology, and the Office of Management and Budget said in a statement that the bill "would undermine U.S. non-proliferation goals and objectives."

The bill would require the president to inform Congress about the international transfer of items that could benefit Iran's ability to develop nuclear, chemical and biological weapons. Countries found to be making transfers would face penalties, such as a cutoff of U.S. military aid or economic sanctions, unless the president exempted them.

NASA officials have objected to a provision in the bill that would tie U.S. payments to Russia for the International Space Station to Russia's agreement not to send weapons technology to Iran.

Levin Blocks Vote On Iran Sanctions

NOVEMBER 20 — A Democratic senator's concerns over a House-passed bill that aims to punish Russia and other countries for assisting Iran's weapons development has prevented Senate action on the measure this year.

Senate Majority Leader Trent Lott, R-Miss., said earlier this month that he hoped the Senate could debate the bill (HR 1883 — H Rept 106-315, Part 1) before adjournment. The House passed the measure, 419-0, on Sept. 14.

The bill would require the president to inform Congress about the international transfer of items that could benefit Iran's ability to develop missiles and nuclear, chemical or biological weapons. Countries found to be making transfers would face penalties, such as a cutoff of U.S. military aid or economic sanctions, unless the president exempted them.

Although administration officials have objected to the bill, Senate supporters said they received assurances the White House would not actively oppose the legislation if the Senate passed it by voice vote.

But Carl Levin of Michigan, ranking Democrat on the Armed Services Committee, wanted the chance to offer amendments, thus preventing a unanimous consent agreement.

Levin said Nov. 16 that his amendments are aimed at improving "some internal inconsistencies" in the legislation's language. "I don't think they're show stoppers," he said. "They're just clarifications that I think should be welcome."

But Lott spokesman John Czwartacki said the delay in debating the bill would deny giving President Clinton "an important tool to wage the battle against non-proliferation."

As a result of the delay, Lott now is likely to introduce tougher sanctions legislation in the next session similar to a measure that Congress cleared in 1998. Clinton vetoed that bill, drawing criticism from both parties. *(1998 Almanac, p. 16-16)* ◆

Lawmakers Boost Spending For Intelligence-Gathering Agencies, Drug War

Box Score

- **Bill:** HR 1555 — PL 106-120
- **Legislative action: House** passed HR 1555 (H Rept 106-130, Part 1) by voice vote May 13.

Senate passed HR 1555 by voice vote July 21 after substituting the text of S 1009 (S Rept 106-48).

House adopted the conference report (H Rept 106-457) by voice vote Nov. 9.

Senate cleared conference report by voice vote Nov. 19.

President signed HR 1555 on Dec. 3.

SUMMARY

After months of delay, Congress cleared legislation shortly before adjournment authorizing an increase in spending for intelligence activities. President Clinton signed the fiscal 2000 intelligence authorization bill into law Dec. 3.

Spending levels in the measure are classified, but sources said it authorizes a 2.4 percent increase over Clinton's request. The measure covers the intelligence-gathering activities of 11 agencies, including the Central Intelligence Agency and operations in the State, Defense and Energy departments.

The conference report contained a provision to impose economic and financial sanctions on international drug kingpins. Although the House had overwhelmingly endorsed that provision as a stand-alone bill (HR 3164), Senate conferees agreed to include the measure in the intelligence bill.

The drug kingpin provision would require U.S. officials to release an annual list of individuals who play a significant role in international drug trafficking. Those on the list would have their U.S. assets frozen and would be barred from entering the United States. Any U.S. businesses or individuals having dealings with those on the list could face penalties of up to 10 years in prison and $10 million in fines.

The conference had been held up for months not only because of the drug kingpin language, but also because of disputes between the House and Senate over funding for classified satellite programs.

The intelligence bill also creates a commission to conduct an independent review of the National Reconnaissance Office — the Defense Department agency that handles space-borne reconnaissance — to ensure that the intelligence community acquires the best possible satellite collection systems.

Senate Republicans initially sought to attach provisions to tighten oversight of Energy Department nuclear weapons programs., but the matter was handled in the defense authorization bill instead. *(Nuclear security, p. 9-26)*

Several lawmakers remain concerned that the drug kingpin language will allow officials to take property without due process of law. At the behest of Senate Intelligence Committee Chairman Richard C. Shelby, R-Ala., the conference report establishes a commission to review the legal authority under which the government can block assets. Sen. Carl Levin, D-Mich., also promised to introduce legislation next year to restore the original due process language. A Treasury Department official said his agency "can work with" the asset language inserted by conferees.

House Bill Raises Intelligence Budget

MAY 1 — Spending for intelligence activities in fiscal 2000 would increase slightly above President Clinton's request under an authorization bill that the House Intelligence Committee approved April 28.

The committee approved the bill (HR 1555) by a 14-0 vote during a brief markup in closed session. Committee Chairman Porter J. Goss, R-Fla., said the legislation could reach the House floor within two weeks.

"There's not a lot of controversy. It was very clear-cut," Goss said. "There's an understanding among all parties on the need to rebuild our intelligence capabilities."

The bill sets guidelines for intelligence activities of 11 federal agencies, including the Central Intelligence Agency, National Security Agency and FBI.

Although the spending total is classified, the authorization is higher than the $26.7 billion level enacted for fiscal 1998, the last year that the Clinton administration made public its spending for intelligence. The committee-approved authorization level for fiscal 2000 is less than 1 percent above what Clinton sought.

The authorization bill contains what a committee statement described as a "significant increase" in funding for counterintelligence programs. The Department of Energy has been hit by revelations in recent weeks that Chinese spies allegedly stole sensitive nuclear weapons data from the agency's national laboratories.

Goss also said the authorization bill seeks to build on the programs funded in the fiscal 1999 omnibus appropriations law (PL 105-277).

The bill emphasizes rebuilding human intelligence activities, developing innovative tools for covert action and strengthening airborne reconnaissance programs.

Senate Panel Seeks Tighter Lab Security

MAY 8 — Foreign visitors to U.S. nuclear laboratories would be subject to stricter security under legislation approved, 15-0, May 5 by the Senate Intelligence Committee.

The as-yet-unnumbered bill would reauthorize intelligence activities for fiscal 2000. It comes on the heels of admissions by the Clinton administration that a suspected spy working for the Chinese government obtained nuclear weapons information from Energy Department nuclear laboratories in Los Alamos, N.M.

The committee gave voice vote approval to two amendments related to espionage. One, by Chairman Richard C. Shelby, R-Ala., and ranking Democrat Bob Kerrey of Nebraska, would place a moratorium on access to nuclear labs by foreign visitors.

"We all benefit from the exchanges of technical data between our scientists all over the world, and we don't want to stop it at all," Shelby told reporters after the closed markup. "But [we want] to make sure that when they do come that there is proper security."

The second amendment, by Orrin G. Hatch, R-Utah, would expand the definition of an agent of a foreign power to anyone who enters the country under a false identity with the intent to conduct espionage. Shelby said the amendment was designed to give the FBI more legal leeway to search computers at the labs.

The bill would fund activities within the CIA, the National Reconnaissance Office, the National Security Agency and other intelligence organizations. Details of intelligence legislation usually are kept confidential. The Clinton administration released the total for its fiscal 1998 intelligence funding request — $26.7 billion — after a CIA watchdog group sued the agency for access to its budget under the Freedom of Information Act.

The House Intelligence Committee approved its version of the intelligence authorization measure (HR 1555) on April 28.

After Bombing Mistake, House Passes Bill That Boosts Funding

MAY 15 — After heaping criticism on the CIA and FBI for major intelligence and security lapses, lawmakers are moving to give both agencies more money than President Clinton requested in hopes of averting future mistakes.

The House on May 13 passed, by voice vote, an intelligence authorization bill for fiscal 2000 (HR 1555) that adds slightly to the administration's request, including funding to ensure that the analysis of raw intelligence keeps pace with its collection. The May 7 NATO bombing of the Chinese embassy in Belgrade, which killed three Chinese journalists and sparked several days of demonstrations and official recrimination in Beijing, was blamed on outdated CIA maps.

"Rather than simply blaming our intelligence entities for a bad call, we on the committee have to look further and ask, 'How did this actually happen?' " said House Intelligence Committee Chairman Porter J. Goss, R-Fla. "In part, this is unfortunately a predictable outcome of stretching our finite resources too thin."

To deal with allegations that Chinese spies have stolen U.S. technology secrets, the intelligence bill provides more money for FBI counterintelligence, adds money for computer security and foreign nuclear weapons analysis, and raises spending for foreign language training of intelligence officials. Specific amounts are classified.

The House vote came as the Senate Armed Services Committee included in its fiscal 2000 defense authorization bill (S 974) a series of measures aimed at curbing security breaches at the Department of Energy's nuclear weapons laboratories. Committee members have been alarmed by continuing revelations that China allegedly has stolen large amounts of computer code showing how U.S. warheads work.

A damage assessment by administration officials last month found that China has obtained information that probably accelerated its development of weapons, although it noted that Beijing has yet to deploy an improved nuclear missile. But The New York Times reported May 14 that intelligence officials suspect that China is within three or four years of unveiling such a weapon.

Congressional concern over Chinese espionage is expected to heighten later this month, when a bipartisan House committee releases a declassified version of its long-delayed report showing evidence that China tried to acquire sensitive data from satellite launches as well as other U.S. technology. The report of the House panel and by Chairman Christopher Cox, R-Calif., could be released as early as the week of May 17.

Database Blamed

The bombing of the Chinese embassy in Belgrade prompted apologies from President Clinton and other administration officials who candidly acknowledged that the CIA and the National Imagery and Mapping Agency incorrectly identified the building as belonging to the Yugoslav government.

Angry Chinese officials demanded an investigation and remained deeply suspicious that their building was deliberately targeted. Their reaction led some congressional Republicans to rebuke China for using the bombing mistake to stir up anti-U.S. sentiment.

Republican Sen. John McCain of Arizona on May 12 said the two countries had a "complex, important and very consequential relationship" and warned that "that relationship should not be jeopardized as cavalierly as Beijing has allowed it to be jeopardized over these last few days."

Although the resulting anti-U.S. protests in China are not likely to make it easier for the administration to reach agreement with Chinese negotiators on that country's entry into the World Trade Organization (WTO), several lawmakers predicted that the protests would not prevent Congress from approving permanent normal trading status for China, allowing it the same tariff treatment as other WTO nations.

"I don't think this alone will derail the whole thing," said Sen. Craig Thomas, R-Wyo., chairman of the Foreign Relations Committee's East Asian and Pacific Affairs Subcommittee.

But Rep. Sherrod Brown, D-Ohio, who opposes efforts to give China permanent normal trading status, said the delays that the protests may have caused on WTO negotiations may have given opponents in Congress at least two chances to threaten China's trading status this year.

The president annually extends normal trade status to China, and Congress gets a chance to overturn him, although it never has. Come June, Clinton will likely announce another yearlong extension of that status, with any congressional vote in July. If a WTO deal is reached at some point this year, as expected, Congress will then have to vote again, this time on whether to halt its annual review of China's trade status, essentially granting permanent normal trade status.

Rebuilding Process

The bombing of the Chinese embassy dominated House debate on the intelligence authorization bill, which provides policy guidance and spending levels for all or part of 11 agencies, including the State and Defense departments, the CIA, the National Security Agency and the FBI.

The overall funding level is kept classified, but The Associated Press quoted knowledgeable officials May 14 as estimating it at about $27 billion. That would be a slight increase over the $26.7 billion authorized in fiscal 1998, the last time the total for intelligence spending was made public.

The Intelligence Committee's ranking Democrat, Julian C. Dixon of California, said the fiscal 2000 funding is slightly less than the fiscal 1999 level. The committee added less than 1 percent to Clinton's request.

Goss, however, emphasized that the level "is about the right amount of money that we can absorb this year," and cautioned that intelligence programs are in the midst of a rebuilding that likely will take several more years.

The House did not take up a proposed amendment by Rep. Jim Ryun, R-Kan., that would establish a counterintelligence program at Energy Department laboratories, place a one-year moratorium on visits to such labs by visitors from some countries, and require more thorough background checks for employees.

Defense Initiatives

The Senate Armed Services Committee included less-restrictive versions of some of those proposals in its defense authorization bill, which includes the following initiatives to deal with Chinese espionage:

- A permanent oversight commission to assess and make recommendations on Energy Department security and counterintelligence.
- Making Energy Department contractor payments partly dependent on their compliance with security and counterintelligence requirements.
- A moratorium on collaborative programs between weapons labs unless Energy, FBI and CIA officials certify that such programs include adequate counterintelligence safeguards.

The Senate committee provided an additional $35 million to enhance computer security at Energy Department sites and an extra $17 million to upgrade the security clearances of employees at its weapons labs. It also called for enacting into law a 1998 presidential order intended to tighten Energy Department security.

Sources said Armed Services Committee member Jeff Bingaman, D-N.M., pressed to continue the foreign visitors program while it is under review. Bingaman also pushed for the Energy Department to be included in the multi-agency security reviews.

Energy Secretary Bill Richardson has tried to address the security breaches on his own. In his latest move, Richardson on May 11 unveiled a plan that included a new high-level Office of Security and Emergency Operations, increased accountability for nuclear materials, additional computer security and more training for employees.

Richardson's moves received a positive response from Republicans, although they continued to attack the Energy and Justice departments for not moving more aggressively to deal with the case of Wen Ho Lee, a former scientist at New Mexico's Los Alamos National Laboratory. Lee is suspected of providing highly classified information to China, although he has not been charged with a crime and has denied any wrongdoing.

Attorney General Janet Reno told Senate Intelligence Committee members May 12 that her agency denied an FBI request to search Lee's computer in 1996 because Justice Department officials were not convinced there was enough probable cause. Justice officials feared it could constitute an illegal search and place their criminal investigation of Lee in jeopardy.

"It's indefensible on the part of the attorney general," Senate Intelligence Chairman Richard C. Shelby, R-Ala., told reporters after the closed-door meeting with Reno.

Some senators, including Pete V. Domenici, R-N.M., have called for laws to be changed to prevent such problems from recurring. But ranking Intelligence Committee Democrat Bob Kerrey of Nebraska said the case also points to the need for the president to be kept better informed about espionage.

"No legislative fix is going to replace an urgency and direction of resources based on that urgency," Kerrey said. "I'm still sort of surprised and concerned that we may have been briefed and notified on this . . . prior to the president knowing about it. If that's the case, we've got things backwards."

GOP senators also aggressively questioned why the Energy Department did not conduct its own search of Lee's computer when it had the authority to do so. The department's general counsel, Mary Anne Sullivan, said the law called for her agency to consult with law enforcement officials before conducting a search, but senators rejected her argument.

The situation was "a classic case of bureaucratic bungling," said Senate Energy and Natural Resources Chairman Frank H. Murkowski, R-Alaska, who joined Shelby in promising further hearings on the issue.

Senate, White House Agree On Nuclear Agency

JULY 24 — After months of wrangling, the Senate and the Clinton administration came together July 21 on a plan to dramatically reshape the Energy Department to prevent nuclear weapons secrets from being stolen. But reluctant House members must be brought into the deal before any action is possible.

By a 96-1 vote, senators agreed to create an Agency for Nuclear Stewardship to oversee weapons programs within the Energy Department. The plan was in an amendment to the fiscal 2000 intelligence authorization bill (HR 1555 — H Rept 106-130). Ron Wyden, D-Ore., cast the only dissenting vote. *(Vote 216, p. S-43)*

The Senate subsequently passed

the authorization bill by voice vote. It covers intelligence-gathering activities of 11 agencies, including the Central Intelligence Agency and operations in the State, Defense and Energy departments.

The vote to create the nuclear security agency marked the most ambitious attempt by Congress to deal with revelations that China apparently stole highly classified data from the Energy Department's nuclear weapons laboratories by exploiting internal security flaws. The department has been criticized for resisting efforts at reform.

"This is the beginning of the reforms necessary to begin cleaning up this espionage mess and seeing to it that it doesn't happen again," said Jon Kyl, R-Ariz., who sponsored the amendment with Frank H. Murkowski, R-Alaska, and Pete V. Domenici, R-N.M.

New Convert

Immediately after the intelligence bill passed, Energy Secretary Bill Richardson issued a statement calling the Senate's action "a good start." Richardson initially had insisted that he be allowed to administratively reshape his department to improve security, but he relented and endorsed a legislative fix in order to avoid facing even more drastic alternatives, such as an independent nuclear programs agency organized like NASA.

"I believe it's critical that we pass legislation this year to codify reforms and accelerate security and counterintelligence improvements," Richardson said in the statement. "It is my hope that as the action moves to the House-Senate conference, we can work to clarify the provisions adopted today and further strengthen the counter-intelligence, security and environment, safety and health provisions."

Republican senators said a broad bipartisan vote in favor of creating the new agency was necessary to give the Senate leverage in conference with the House. The House version of the intelligence bill contains no similar language, and some influential members of the House Commerce and Science committees are pressing for more time to develop a stand-alone bill as an alternative.

In a July 12 letter to House Speaker J. Dennis Hastert, R-Ill., seven members — including Commerce Committee Chairman Thomas J. Bliley Jr., R-Va., and ranking Democrat John D. Dingell of Michigan — urged him "to oppose hasty and haphazard efforts to legislate this matter on the defense or intelligence authorization bills."

Other House members, including Ron Packard, R-Calif., chairman of the Energy and Water Development Appropriations Subcommittee, are demanding that nuclear weapons activities be split off from the Energy Department. Packard has included a provision in the fiscal 2000 energy and water spending bill (HR 2605 — H Rept 106-253) that would withhold $1 billion in appropriated funds until Congress restructures the department or sets up an independent agency.

To avoid a stalemate, Hastert has asked Christopher Cox, R-Calif., to meet with lawmakers in both chambers to try to develop a consensus on the issue. Cox was chairman of the special bipartisan committee that investigated China's efforts to steal U.S. technology.

Kyl, Domenici and Murkowski said the Agency for Nuclear Stewardship is needed to specialize in nuclear weapons activities, because such functions no longer fit within the broad patchwork of energy-related functions assigned to the department at its creation.

"We poured them all into this department and said, 'Make it work,' " Domenici said.

The three senators initially offered their proposal to restructure the Energy Department in May as an amendment to the fiscal 2000 defense authorization bill (S 1059 — S Rept 106-50) but withdrew the amendment after Richardson and Senate Democrats objected.

The three then reworked the amendment to conform to the recommendations of the President's Foreign Intelligence Advisory Board, whose chairman was former Sen. Warren B. Rudman, R-N.H. (1980-93). The board concluded in a harshly worded report released June 15 that the Energy Department has had "a cavalier attitude" about security.

The Intelligence Committee's ranking Democrat, Bob Kerrey of Nebraska, joined Kyl, Domenici and Murkowski in backing the concept. But in order to win broader support, the three had to pacify Jeff Bingaman of New Mexico and Carl Levin of Michigan, ranking Democrats on the Energy and Natural Resources and the Armed Services committees.

Bingaman's Amendments

After negotiating with Republicans, Bingaman won approval by voice vote of three amendments that he said would enable the Agency for Nuclear Stewardship to function within the Energy Department without interfering with other non-nuclear weapons activities.

One amendment would expressly grant the Energy secretary authority to continue to use the department's 11 field offices to conduct business with all agencies. The Rudman panel's report recommended streamlining the new nuclear agency's management structure by abolishing all ties between the weapons labs and the field offices.

The report said that about 6,000 employees work in the field offices in addition to 5,000 workers at Energy Department headquarters, creating a "convoluted and bloated management structure [that] has constantly transmitted confusing and often contradictory mandates to the labs."

A second amendment would require the Energy secretary to ensure that other departmental programs and other federal agencies continue to draw on the expertise and capabilities of the labs. Bingaman said he was concerned that the new agency would inhibit the labs' ability to conduct non-weapons-related research and to attract top scientists.

The third amendment calls for the new agency to meet all applicable environmental, safety and health requirements that remain under the Energy secretary's authority. Bingaman said he feared the agency essentially would be policing itself if such a provision was not approved.

"In recent years we've developed a system for monitoring these activities, and for that system to continue, the secretary needs to retain authority over compliance," Bingaman said.

Levin, meanwhile, offered an amendment seeking to ensure that the Energy secretary would retain the authority to develop department-wide policy. But his proposal was rejected, 44-54. *(Vote 215, p. S-42)*

In the end, however, several of Levin's concerns were addressed in the final bill, including clarifying that the Energy secretary would keep control over counterintelligence and security operations. He said he hopes his remaining concerns can be addressed in conference.

"We should have a semi-autonomous agency, but we should permit the secretary to control it," Levin told reporters. "There are still too many restrictions on that."

Classified Territory

The spending level in the intelligence authorization bill is classified. The Clinton administration released the total for its fiscal 1998 intelligence request — $26.7 billion — after a CIA watchdog group sued the agency for access to its budget under the Freedom of Information Act.

The Office of Management and Budget said in a July 20 statement that it would not support the bill until several of its concerns were addressed. Among them is a moratorium sought by Intelligence Chairman Richard C. Shelby, R-Ala., on visits to classified facilities at Energy Department laboratories by people from "sensitive" nations, meant to include China.

The administration said the moratorium "could negatively affect a number of vital national security programs," such as an Energy Department program to assist Russia in disposing of its nuclear weapons materials. Russia might restrict access to its nuclear sites.

The administration also objected to an Intelligence Committee proposal to delay funding for two major intelligence-gathering systems as well as a proposed reorganization of communications. It provided no additional details on those systems.

In addition to the amendments sought by Bingaman, the Senate adopted by voice vote two amendments by Daniel Patrick Moynihan, D-N.Y. They expressed the sense of Congress that it is in the public interest to declassify certain information, and called for an additional $1.5 million for the Information Security Oversight Office, which administers intelligence classification and declassification programs.

Richard H. Bryan, D-Nevada, offered an amendment seeking to ensure that fines assessed on nonprofit contractors working at Energy Department laboratories are in line with those assessed on private-sector contractors. Bryan withdrew the amendment after Shelby and others agreed to work with him on the matter.

House Adopts Conference Report; Senate Delays Vote

NOVEMBER 13 — The House on Nov. 9 swiftly adopted a conference report authorizing a spending increase for intelligence activities in fiscal 2000, but a leading Democratic senator's concerns about one of its provisions delayed final action on the measure.

The House adopted the conference report (HR 1555 — H Rept 106-457) by voice vote. The legislation covers the intelligence-gathering activities of 11 agencies, including the Central Intelligence Agency and operations in the State, Defense and Energy departments.

Spending levels in the bill are classified, but sources said the measure authorizes a 2.4 percent increase over President Clinton's request.

The last year in which the administration made spending figures public for intelligence and security-related activities was 1998, when officials announced that the fiscal 1998 budget was $26.7 billion. *(1998 Almanac, p. 8-25)*

The bill also contains a provision to impose economic and financial sanctions on international drug kingpins. The House on Nov. 2 overwhelmingly approved the legislation (HR 3164) as a stand-alone bill, but Senate conferees agreed to include the measure in the intelligence bill.

Nevertheless, the Senate held off taking action after the House's vote because of concerns by Carl Levin of Michigan, ranking Democrat on the Armed Services Committee, over the anti-drug provision. The Senate is expected to take up the report the week of Nov. 15 before adjourning for the year.

Targeting Drug Lords

The drug kingpin provision would require U.S. officials to release an annual list of individuals who play a significant role in international narcotics trafficking. Those on the list would have their U.S. assets frozen and would be barred from entering the United States. Any individuals or businesses in the United States having dealings with those on the list could face penalties of up to 10 years in prison and $10 million in fines.

Although the House bill received overwhelming bipartisan support, a handful of Democrats argued it would allow officials to take property without due process of law and presume people to be guilty by association with alleged drug kingpins.

In a Nov. 8 letter to Treasury Secretary Lawrence H. Summers, Levin said he shared those concerns. He asked Treasury officials to provide him with a legal opinion on whether U.S. citizens could contest having their assets frozen.

The provision "would seem to limit the opportunity that exists today for innocent American citizens and businesses to petition the courts to challenge the blocking of assets," Levin wrote.

The Treasury Department said in a Nov. 10 response that the House-passed language "presumably would foreclose U.S. citizens from bringing a claim" under the federal Administrative Procedure Act to challenge a blocking of assets. But the director of the Treasury Department's Office of Foreign Assets Control, R. Richard Newcomb, said citizens would still have other ways to mount a legal challenge.

Court Concerns

To ease Levin's concerns, however, Intelligence Committee Chairman Richard C. Shelby, R-Ala., and ranking Democrat Bob Kerrey of Nebraska said they would join Levin in introducing separate legislation the week of Nov. 15 attempting to clarify the availability of judicial review to U.S. citizens.

Shelby said he remains troubled that the language in the bill could leave the government vulnerable to lawsuits.

"If it comes out as I think it will, there will have to be protection of due process of constitutional rights," he said. "If we don't fix it, I think the courts will."

Shelby was criticized by some proponents of the drug kingpin provision earlier this month after The New York

Times and the Washington Post reported that a Senate Intelligence Committee aide who had worked on the issue claimed he had been fired for refusing to back changes sought by business interests in Mexico and the Caribbean island of Aruba. Shelby denied the accusation.

At Shelby's behest, House and Senate conferees included a provision in the intelligence authorization conference report establishing a congressionally appointed commission to review the legal authority under which the federal government can block assets as well as the legal remedies available to U.S. citizens.

The intelligence authorization bill also would create a commission to conduct an independent review of the National Reconnaissance Office — the Defense Department agency that handles spaceborne reconnaissance — to ensure the intelligence community acquires the best possible satellite collection systems.

The intelligence bill originally was intended as a potential vehicle for addressing security lapses at the Energy Department's nuclear weapons laboratories. But all of the Energy-related language was stripped out and included in the fiscal 2000 defense authorization law (PL 106-65).

Senate Clears Intelligence Bill

NOVEMBER 20 — The Senate on Nov. 19 cleared by voice vote legislation authorizing a spending increase for intelligence activities in fiscal 2000.

The conference report on the bill (HR 1555), along with other end-of-session legislation, had been held up by Midwestern lawmakers opposed to dairy provisions in the omnibus spending package (HR 3194 — H Rept 106-479).

The legislation covers the intelligence-gathering activities of 11 agencies, including the Central Intelligence Agency and operations in the State, Defense and Energy departments.

Spending levels in the bill are classified, but sources said the measure authorizes a 2.4 percent increase over Clinton's request.

The last year in which the administration made spending figures public for intelligence and security-related activities was 1998, when officials announced that the fiscal 1998 budget was $26.7 billion. *(1998 Almanac, p. 8-25)*

Bob Kerrey of Nebraska, ranking Democrat on the Senate Intelligence Committee, said on the floor Nov. 19, "It is time to increase spending. We have a much better sense of the threats facing America."

Kingpin Linchpin

Action in the Senate on the conference report had earlier been delayed because of objections by Carl Levin of Michigan, ranking Democrat on the Senate Armed Services Committee, over a provision to impose economic and financial sanctions on international drug kingpins.

The drug kingpin provision, passed by the House as stand-alone legislation (HR 3164), would require U.S. officials to release an annual list of individuals who play a significant role in international narcotics trafficking.

Those on the list would have their U.S. assets frozen and would be barred from entering the United States. Any individuals or businesses in the United States having dealings with those on the list could face penalties of up to 10 years in prison and $10 million in fines.

Levin said he fears the provision would allow officials to take property without due process of law and presume people to be guilty by association with alleged drug kingpins. A Treasury Department analysis said that although the provision would foreclose claims under the federal Administrative Procedure Act of 1946, citizens would have other ways to mount a legal challenge.

But Levin said Nov. 16 that such challenges would have to be made on constitutional grounds. He planned to introduce legislation to accompany the intelligence bill restoring the original due process language.

"You ought to be able to challenge the legality of the seizure without raising the constitutionality," he said. "All I want to do is preserve an existing remedy that an innocent person has, to claim his assets were illegally seized or blocked by government action."

In a Nov. 17 letter to Levin, a Treasury Department official said his agency "can work with" the asset language inserted by conferees. The director of Treasury's Office of Foreign Assets Control, R. Richard Newcomb, said his office's administrative mechanisms will assist citizens seeking due process in such cases. ◆

Lawmakers Conflicted Over U.S. Involvement in Kosovo Peacekeeping Effort

Box Score

- **Bills:** S Con Res 21, S J Res 20, H Con Res 42, HR 1569
- **Legislative action: House** adopted H Con Res 42, 219-191, on March 11.

Senate adopted S Con Res 21, 58-41, on March 23.

House passed HR 1569, 249-180, and rejected S Con Res 21, 213-213, both on April 28.

Senate tabled (killed) S J Res 20, 78-22, on May 4.

SUMMARY

Congress declined to limit President Clinton's authority to send U.S. ground forces to the Yugoslavian province of Kosovo as part of a NATO-led peacekeeping force, but neither would it give him a free hand to deal with the Balkan conflict. The House sent mixed signals, authorizing troops and later demanding a say in any deployment. The House also refused, on a tie vote, to back the NATO air war against Yugoslavia even after it had begun.

Republican leaders in the House and Senate had expressed reservations through the winter about U.S. involvement in the Kosovo crisis, particularly the use of ground troops. On March 11, amid peace negotiations with Kosovar Albanians and Yugoslav President Slobodan Milosevic, the House debated and adopted a resolution (H Con Res 42) authorizing Clinton to send troops as peacekeepers.

On March 23, the Senate adopted a resolution (S Con Res 21) in support of NATO airstrikes, which began the next day against Yugoslavia, designed to force a Serbian withdrawal from Kosovo. As the air campaign dragged on and talk increased that greater military intervention might be necessary, the House on April 28 by a tie vote rejected the Senate resolution in support of the bombing. The same day, the House passed legislation (HR 1569) prohibiting the use of U.S. ground forces in Kosovo unless authorized by law.

The Senate was of a different opinion. Not only did it decline to take up the House measure, but on May 25, the Senate tabled (killed) an amendment by Arlen Specter, R-Pa., to the fiscal 2000 defense authorization bill (S 1059) that would have prohibited the use of ground forces in Kosovo, except for peacekeepers, unless Congress authorized them by a joint resolution or declared war.

Though the Senate would not tie Clinton's hands, neither would it give him a free hand in the Balkans. On May 4, the Senate tabled a resolution (S J Res 20) that would have authorized the president to use "all necessary force" to prevail in Kosovo.

Republicans Warn Clinton on Use of U.S. Peacekeepers In Kosovo

FEBRUARY 6 — Some key congressional Republicans are raising concerns about suggestions from President Clinton and Pentagon officials that U.S. troops may be needed to police a peace settlement in Yugoslavia's rebellious province of Kosovo.

The lawmakers are particularly worried that Pentagon planners are considering the possibility that a European, rather than an American, may command the mission.

Pentagon officials have said that British Lt. Gen. Sir Mike Jackson, currently commander of NATO's Rapid Reaction Corps, may well head the mission, which could involve as many as 4,000 U.S. troops.

"Under no circumstances can we support the deployment of U.S. soldiers under a foreign flag," Sens. Gordon H. Smith, R-Ore., and Mitch McConnell, R-Ky., wrote Clinton on Feb. 1, saying that such an arrangement led to the death of 18 Americans on a peacekeeping mission in Somalia in 1993. *(1993 Almanac, p. 486)*

Smith is chairman of the European Affairs Subcommittee of the Senate Foreign Relations Committee. McConnell is chairman of the Foreign Operations Appropriations Subcommittee.

In the House, Republican Policy Committee Chairman Christopher Cox of California said he also is opposed to having a European commander and already was concerned that NATO members had given Secretary General Javier Solana authority to call in airstrikes on Kosovo without further orders from member states.

But some key senators supported the outlines of the emerging Kosovo deal. Senate Armed Services Committee Chairman John W. Warner, R-Va., said, "I would be satisfied if a British officer were to command the ground elements of any NATO force that goes in."

And Sen. Joseph I. Lieberman, D-Conn., said: "I believe that we can't have it both ways. If we're asking our European allies in NATO to shoulder a larger proportion of the burden of ground troops in the peacekeeping mission in Kosovo, we also have to accept the possibility that it may be one of their nationals who will be commanding those troops. That's just fair."

Kosovo Policy Gets a Medley Of Complaints

FEBRUARY 13 — As Serbian officials and ethnic Albanians try to work out a diplomatic solution for the future of Kosovo, Congress is debating the wisdom of U.S. policy in the region. Lawmakers are showing little appetite for challenging the Clinton administration's approach, which may include sending troops to the troubled province to monitor any peace agreement.

In fact, the administration has been criticized by lawmakers who think it should use military force to help resolve the crisis, and by some who think it is too willing to send troops.

That marks a sharp break with previous debates over Bosnia and Somalia, where the administration was widely criticized for being too willing to intervene.

The contrast was particularly apparent at a House International Relations Committee hearing on the issue Feb. 10. Chairman Benjamin A. Gilman, R-N.Y., who helped lead the charge against U.S. involvement in Somalia, urged the administration to press for the removal from power of Yugoslav President Slobodan Milosevic.

"Solutions that stop short of achieving that goal — including new diplomatic agreements and new peacekeeping operations in the Balkans — are nothing more than holding actions," Gilman said.

"This cannot be a very satisfactory outcome for the Congress, or for most of the American people, who, sooner or later, will begin to ask why we are investing our treasure, and perhaps our blood, in a part of the world that is remote indeed from our ordinary interests," he added.

Gilman's words echo those of other lawmakers, such as Republican Richard G. Lugar of Indiana, a senior member of the Senate Foreign Relations Committee, who have also called for Milosevic's overthrow.

"I think that American policy, which regards Milosevic as part of the solution, is misguided," agreed Rep. Eliot L. Engel, D-N.Y. But Engel took a different tack than Gilman, saying Feb. 10 that any agreement on the embattled province's political status must include a firm deadline for a referendum on its independence.

By taking that stance, Engel, a co-chairman of the Albanian Issues Caucus, backed the position pushed by representatives of Kosovo's Albanian majority at the peace talks being held at a château in Rambouillet, France.

Engel introduced an as-yet-unnumbered non-binding resolution that would call on the administration to support "self-determination" for Kosovo and a date for a self-determination referendum in the province.

Sending Troops

Several Republican lawmakers, meanwhile, questioned whether the administration has the constitutional right to send troops to Kosovo without a declaration of war or congressional resolution. President Clinton has said he is weighing whether to dispatch U.S. forces to help implement a peace settlement.

"I have enormous difficulties with the proposal to send troops to Kosovo," said Rep. Doug Bereuter, R-Neb., a senior member of the International Relations Committee.

"I'm concerned about the constitutional process," Bereuter said, "and whether it's a vital national interest to devote such a large portion of our military capabilities to keep the peace at two places in the Balkans."

Rep. Tom Campbell, R-Calif., told administration officials, "You are making what would be an ally into an unwilling adversary because our first duty is to the Constitution."

Campbell last year unsuccessfully tried to set up a court ruling on the 1973 War Powers Resolution (PL 93-148) with a resolution calling for the return of U.S. troops from Bosnia. The resolution was defeated.

Testifying before the committee, Under Secretary of State for Political Affairs Thomas A. Pickering defended the constitutionality of the administration's actions.

And he said that diplomatically, a U.S. troop deployment may be necessary to persuade Kosovo's Albanians to sign off on a deal. "Our presence adds a particular note of guaranteed certainty of commitment that this will take place," Pickering said.

House Votes in Support of U.S. Troops in Kosovo

MARCH 13 — As the House on March 11 debated whether to support the potential deployment of U.S. troops to the embattled Serbian province of Kosovo, lawmakers were indirectly considering a question that may have an even greater long-term impact on foreign policy: What role should Congress play in decisions about the use of troops overseas?

The Clinton administration won the immediate battle, gaining enough support from Republican moderates and human rights backers for the House to adopt, 219-191, a resolution (H Con Res 42) supporting the deployment of about 4,000 troops as part of a 28,000-member NATO peacekeeping operation. *(Vote 49, p. H-20)*

But for the long term, the decision by House Speaker J. Dennis Hastert, R-Ill., to take up the resolution may augur a new level of involvement by Congress in the use of the military for operations short of war. Hastert went ahead with the vote despite appeals from President Clinton and Secretary of State Madeleine K. Albright to postpone it while delicate peace negotiations were under way between the warring parties in Kosovo.

"My request this morning is that such a vote not be taken while we are at this critical time in our negotiations and in our attempts to secure a settlement," Albright told a House Appropriations subcommittee on the eve of the vote. "A congressional debate now, I can assure you, will complicate our efforts to get the Serbs and the Kosovar Albanians on board. I might add that a vote at any time to oppose an authorization would be taken by both sides as a green light to resume fighting."

At a March 11 news conference, Clinton called the vote "premature."

Pressing Ahead

The appeal for postponement drew support from former Senate Majority Leader Bob Dole, R-Kan., and former U.S. Ambassador to the United Nations Jeane J. Kirkpatrick at a March 10 hearing of the House International Relations Committee.

Dole, who is serving as a special U.S. envoy to Kosovo's Albanian population, said, "I'd rather have the vote come after an agreement. If you want to throw cold water on any possible agreement, you vote no."

But Hastert, opening the debate on the House floor, rebuffed these entreaties, pointing out that the British and German parliaments had recently voted on the issue.

"No one should fear the free expression of ideas and the frank expression of opinions in a representative democracy," Hastert said. "I believe Congress must have a meaningful role in this decision, no matter how difficult our choice, no matter how hard our task."

And he told reporters March 11 that he did not want to repeat the pattern of recent years, when Congress expressed its opinion only after troops had been deployed, making it difficult to oppose the mission without harming military morale. The most recent instance was Clinton's decision to send troops to police the Bosnia peace agreement in 1995. *(1995 Almanac, p. 10-10)*

"What we have continually done over the past six or seven years is, when the president has moved troops into some place, we have acquiesced, just nodded our heads and done it, and then we have an emergency supplemental for $1 or $2 billion to cover the cost," Hastert said.

Even some Democrats congratulated Hastert for forcing Republicans to take more responsibility for foreign policy decisions.

"At least it's a reversal of their usual tendency to throw bricks without stepping up to the plate," Howard L. Berman, D-Calif., said in an interview.

But Minority Leader Richard A. Gephardt, D-Mo., said the debate should wait until a peace agreement is signed by the warring parties.

"To conduct a divisive debate in Congress and perhaps fail to support our government's efforts is the height of irresponsibility and threatens the hope for an agreement to halt the bloodshed and prevent a widening war," Gephardt said on the House floor, urging his colleagues to defeat the rule that allowed debate on the resolution to proceed.

Gephardt's efforts failed, though, and the rule (H Res 103) was approved, 218-201. *(Vote 46, p. H-20)*

Warriors, Not Baby Sitters

The biggest fight came over an amendment by Tillie Fowler, R-Fla., that would have prohibited the deployment of U.S. ground forces to Kosovo. Fowler said the humanitarian crisis in Kosovo "does not rise to a level that warrants the deployment of U.S. ground troops."

Particularly, she and other Republicans argued, "Our service people have had it with these deployments," leading to poor morale and an inability to retain trained troops.

"American soldiers have been trained to be warriors, not baby sitters," said House Majority Whip Tom DeLay, R-Texas, who helped press Hastert into taking up the resolution.

Other critics said intervening in Kosovo would be unjustified under international law because the province lies in Serbia, a sovereign country.

"Once NATO starts intervening in sovereign nations, where does it stop?" asked DeLay.

Doug Bereuter, R-Neb., said such an intervention constituted an invasion and would require a formal declaration of war from Congress, not the non-binding resolution ultimately approved by the House.

Pat Danner, D-Mo., one of the five Democrats to support the Fowler amendment, argued that the intervention would be a repeat of what has happened in Bosnia where Clinton initially promised in 1995 that U.S. troops would be out of the region in one year.

"There is no reason to believe that the crisis could not drag on indefinitely with a high cost in human lives," Danner said.

The opponents also echoed criticism by former Secretary of State Henry A. Kissinger, who told the House International Relations Committee March 10, "We may end up bombing the Serbs to get them to agree and then fighting the Albanians to get them to disarm. I'm extremely uneasy about this."

But with the help of some key Republicans, such as International Relations Committee Chairman Benjamin A. Gilman of New York and Judiciary Committee Chairman Henry J. Hyde of Illinois, Democrats were able to defeat the Fowler amendment, 178-237. *(Vote 48, p. H-20)*

Hyde argued that supporting Fowler's approach could endanger the NATO alliance, especially if the fighting spread to NATO members Greece and Turkey.

Supporting the deployment, Hyde said, "boils down to a simple proposition: Is NATO worthwhile?"

And Frank R. Wolf, R-Va., said U.S. involvement was needed if peace were be realized in the troubled region.

"Without U.S. participation it won't work," Wolf said.

Rules of Engagement

Hoping to quell some of the concerns of their members, Gilman and Intelligence Committee Chairman Porter J. Goss, R-Fla., offered an amendment to address the issues that had been raised.

Among other provisions, the amendment would require the Clinton administration, before sending troops, to give Congress the rules of engagement under which U.S. troops would operate in Kosovo, a description of the cost of the mission, how the administration plans to pay for it and the deployment's effect on military readiness.

The measure also would require that U.S. forces serve under a U.S. military commander.

"We should support a deployment with our eyes wide open," Goss said. The Gilman-Goss amendment was adopted by voice vote. It modified an amendment by Sam Gejdenson, D-Conn., that would authorize the use of U.S. troops when a "fair and just" peace agreement is reached and would limit a U.S. deployment to 15 percent of the total peacekeeping force. That also was adopted by voice vote.

It is not clear whether the Senate will hold a similar debate. Republicans had been coalescing around a proposal by Sen. Kay Bailey Hutchison, R-Texas, that in many ways mirrors the Goss-Gilman amendment.

But, "now Republicans are unsure if they want to hand Clinton another victory," said one Democratic aide.

Senate Majority Leader Trent Lott, R-Miss., had said March 9 that he hoped the Senate would vote on the Hutchison proposal before the president decided to deploy troops to Kosovo.

"I don't think we should wait till the president presumes, without congressional approval, to put troops on the ground again," Lott said.

Aiming at Milosevic

As part of their efforts, some key lawmakers were planning to attach legislation that seeks to punish the man many lawmakers view as responsible for the conflict in the Serbian province: Yugoslav President Slobodan Milosevic.

The legislation, being drafted by Foreign Relations Committee Chairman Jesse Helms, R-N.C., and Gordon H. Smith, R-Ore., chairman of the European Affairs Subcommittee, would tighten existing sanctions on Serbia, one of Yugoslavia's two constituent republics, in an effort to buoy opposition to Milosevic.

The legislation, one GOP aide said, would "throw everything at him."

Provisions would further tighten sanctions, foster alternative broadcasting outlets and assist democratic opponents of the regime, and perhaps redistribute some former Yugoslav missions in the United States now claimed by Serbia, giving the property to other former republics of Yugoslavia, which largely disintegrated in the early 1990s.

Yet, changing circumstances may negate the need for a Senate vote. With both Kosovar Albanians and the Serbian government continuing to reject the peacekeeping plan proposed by the United States and five other countries, chances were dimming that a NATO force would be deployed at all. Peace talks are scheduled to resume in France on March 15.

As Crisis Escalates, Lawmakers Reconsider Use Of Ground Troops

APRIL 13 — Even before three U.S. soldiers were taken captive by Serbian forces on the border of Macedonia on March 31, some key lawmakers were considering reversing course and supporting the use of American ground troops to halt further violence in Kosovo, where hundreds of thousands of ethnic Albanians were fleeing attacks by the Serbian military and police.

When the Senate debated and, on March 23, adopted a resolution (S Con Res 21) authorizing U.S. participation in NATO airstrikes against the Republic of Yugoslavia, which includes Serbia, President Clinton and his congressional supporters denied suggestions that the bombing would inevitably lead to the use of U.S. ground forces. The president and his top aides said they did not intend to commit ground forces to anything other than a peacekeeping mission.

But after more than a week of NATO airstrikes failed to bring Yugoslav President Slobodan Milosevic any closer to accepting a peace agreement, a rising chorus of lawmakers, foreign policy analysts and former government officials said that U.S. political leaders and NATO generals need to consider the possibility of using ground forces.

Air attacks alone, they warned, may not be able to prevent Milosevic from carrying out his program of "ethnic cleansing," in which Serbs force ethnic Albanians out of parts of Kosovo.

John McCain of Arizona, a senior member of the Senate Armed Services Committee and a likely presidential candidate in 2000, took the lead on the Republican side.

In television appearances and other public statements, McCain did not call for such a troop deployment but said Clinton should not rule out the use of ground troops if they prove necessary to stopping ethnic cleansing and bringing peace to the region.

"We are in it; now we must win it," McCain said in a written statement. If NATO fails, "America's adversaries from Pyongyang [North Korea] to Baghdad [Iraq] will be encouraged to challenge our interests more aggressively."

Addressing the 41 senators who voted against the March 23 resolution, McCain said, "Whether one agrees or not that we initially had a strategic interest in the Balkans, we have one now. There is no alternative to success."

Democratic leaders had less to say on the issue, though Sen. Paul Wellstone, D-Minn., expressed concern about the loss of civilian lives in the NATO air attacks.

Rep. Lane Evans, D-Ill., a member of the House Armed Services Committee, said, "When we're engaged in hostilities, it's no time to question the president."

Immediate Planning

McCain's position was backed by several Senate Republicans who initially supported airstrikes, including Foreign Relations Committee members Gordon H. Smith of Oregon and Chuck Hagel of Nebraska. Joseph R. Biden Jr. of Delaware, ranking Democrat on the committee, also believes Clinton should consider a range of military options, aides said.

"Immediately, conspicuous planning for the use of NATO ground troops must commence in the numbers required to blunt the Serbian offensive, stabilize Kosovo and, if necessary, repel whatever elements of the Serbian armed forces that remain," Richard G. Lugar, R-Ind., a member of the Foreign Relations Committee, wrote in an April 1 opinion column in The Washington Post.

"President Milosevic should be indicted as a 'world class' war criminal," Lugar wrote. "Likewise, we should accelerate apprehensions of war criminals in Bosnia and finally stabilize that country, making clear that any further ethnic cleansing will not be tolerated."

Several top officials from former Republican administrations have chimed in with support for the ground option.

"We're in a war, and we need to recognize it's a war and allow our military to do what's necessary to prevail," said Frank C. Carlucci, a former Defense secretary and national security adviser to President Ronald Reagan. "If it means troops on the ground, then so be it."

In addition, two leading conservative intellectual organs, The Weekly Standard and the editorial pages of The Wall Street Journal, have inveighed against "GOP squeamishness" on Kosovo and the 38 Republicans who voted against airstrikes.

Senate Armed Services Committee Chairman John W. Warner, R-Va., did not agree that the use of ground troops should be considered, but he told reporters March 30 that the air attacks had changed strategic considerations.

"You must remember that the stakes, particularly for the United States, are very high here," Warner said. "It's not just the credibility of NATO; it's the credibility of the United States in other very troubled areas of the world."

That message seemed to be sinking in among some Republicans who were initially opposed to the airstrikes.

For example, Sen. Kay Bailey Hutchison of Texas, who also warned about using U.S. ground forces, has softened her opposition as the crisis has escalated.

"I think one of the problems we have is that Milosevic has heard everyone say, 'No troops on the ground,'" Hutchison said March 28 on CBS's "Face the Nation." "I think we're going to have to look at other options here, and troops on the ground for the NATO forces, perhaps without American participation, since we have taken the lion's share in the air campaign, might be something that should be considered."

With momentum shifting among Republicans, there even was talk among some GOP thinkers that Congress should consider following up the fairly narrow Senate resolution on airstrikes with a broader measure authorizing Clinton to take whatever steps he deems necessary to win the conflict.

Memories of Somalia

The willingness of some Republicans to consider sending U.S. ground troops to a combat environment in Kosovo marks a sharp turn from recent GOP practice.

Scarred by the death of 18 Army Rangers in Somalia in 1993, at the beginning of the Clinton administration, Republicans have since resisted any deployment. *(1993 Almanac, p. 486)*

A large number of Republican lawmakers still oppose sending troops to defend areas outside of the Persian Gulf and existing alliances with NATO, Japan and South Korea.

Speaking about the Kosovo intervention, Pat Roberts, R-Kan., a member of the Senate Armed Services Committee said, "This is a bad idea whose time has come, and it's getting worse."

Across the Capitol, some leading House Republicans were equally critical of the administration's handling of the situation.

Clinton and Secretary of State Madeleine K. Albright "bit off more than they planned for," said Appropriations Committee Chairman C. W. Bill Young of Florida. "I'm just afraid that the administration is making up its plans as it goes along."

Young also pointed out that the price tag for America's involvement is climbing steadily. Noting that last December's Operation Desert Fox airstrikes against Iraq had cost the United States about $400 million, Young estimated March 31 that the Yugoslavia operation had already cost "close to a billion dollars."

In an effort to appease such critics, administration officials have continued to insist that ground troops will not be sent to Kosovo, despite the swelling tide of refugees threatening to destabilize the neighboring countries of Macedonia and Albania.

Staying the Course

Backing up the White House, Warner said he would support airstrikes indefinitely, but saw no need to introduce ground troops into Kosovo.

"It is clear we should stay the course as planned," Warner said. "I think the air operations are being conducted effectively."

Gen. Henry H. Shelton, chairman of the Joint Chiefs of Staff, warned on NBC's "Meet the Press" March 28 that a ground operation "would involve hundreds of thousands of ground troops over a rather protracted period of time and in a very dangerous situation."

Some Democrats continued to hold out hope that a diplomatic solution could still be found.

"It's highly unlikely we're going to get an end to this fighting through military means alone," said Senate Armed Services Committee member Jeff Bingaman, D-N.M., an opponent of sending ground troops. "I believe the president should be pursuing whatever kind of negotiated end to the fighting might be possible. I'm not suggesting he meet with Milosevic, but to the extent we have diplomatic contact with Milosevic, we should be continuing to explore a possible negotiated end to the fighting."

But some independent strategists argued that victory would require U.S. troops.

"The only way to get Serbian ground forces out is to put NATO ground forces in," said Ivo H. Daalder of the nonpartisan Brookings Institution. "If we wait, there won't be a Kosovo anymore."

He and other analysts said air operations can destroy tanks and heavy armor, but they are slow and largely ineffective at preventing the kind of house-to-house brutality the Serbs were carrying out, according to refugee accounts.

Mortars and other small arms the Serbs have used in ethnic cleansing cannot be effectively attacked from the air, said Michael E. O'Hanlon of Brookings.

Even if the NATO air attacks diminish the capability of the Serbian military, O'Hanlon said, its forces still can outmuscle the rebellious Kosovo Liberation Army, even if it is supplied with arms from the United States, as some lawmakers have proposed.

By week's end, according to published reports, the Kosovo guerrilla army was in danger of collapse because of the Serbian assaults.

Moreover, O'Hanlon estimated that NATO air attacks would eliminate only about 1 percent of Serb armor every day, allowing Milosevic to conclude his program of ethnic cleansing before NATO had finished the air campaign.

O'Hanlon said a deployment of at least 100,000 NATO troops, including a substantial U.S. contingent, would be needed to defeat Milosevic's ground forces. U.S. commanders have estimated that it could take up to 200,000.

Time To Assemble

But congressional critics and military experts warned that to put in enough NATO forces could be as time-consuming as the air operation.

Warner said, "It would take a considerable period of time, perhaps up to a month, to assemble and then begin to move into position any ground force that would be able to interdict and deter the current operations being conducted by Milosevic with the professional Serbian army."

One military analyst agreed with Warner's assessment, estimating that it would take about a month to move a division of some 15,000 troops into Kosovo. If more troops were needed, the analyst estimated, it could take as long as five months.

The analyst noted that Kosovo's high-country terrain, poor roads and rainy weather could bog down ground forces. In addition, he said, "We don't have the Army we had a few years ago. You just don't flex your muscles like you used to."

Many Republicans making a case

for sending troops to Kosovo acknowledged such problems and said they posed a challenge for Clinton to shape public opinion in support of a ground war. But they insisted it was incumbent on the president to act decisively.

"President Clinton still has the chance as our commander in chief to produce victory," Lugar said, "even if what he advocated was based on a hopelessly incomplete vision of the end game and a dubious strategy to reach even severely limited aims."

War Powers Act Forces House Vote; Senate Buys More Time

MAY 1 — Forced to vote on U.S. strategy in the Balkans, the House found no strategy of its own April 28, demanding congressional approval for sending ground troops but neither endorsing nor condemning the current NATO air campaign against Yugoslavia. The Senate is likely to duck the issue altogether the week of May 3.

Senate Majority Leader Trent Lott, R-Miss., and Minority Leader Tom Daschle, D-S.D., will move to table, and thus kill, a resolution that would give President Clinton authority to use all necessary force to pursue NATO success in the Balkans. They said a divisive debate might send the wrong signals.

While lawmakers cannot make up their minds on Clinton's strategy, they feel no ambivalence about his soldiers. A supplemental fiscal 1999 defense spending bill ostensibly to cover operations in the Balkans could be twice the amount Clinton requested.

House appropriators on April 29 approved a $12.9 billion measure, and the Senate is all but certain to approve at least the $6 billion Clinton requested, if not substantially more.

The Senate will vote on the defense spending only after it has been attached to the conference report on an earlier supplemental (HR 1141) that would provide disaster relief for Central America and U.S. farmers. That vote may come the week of May 10.

Administration officials dismissed the significance of the House votes on the Balkans. "They seemed to take all sides of the issue without taking responsibility for promoting one policy," White House spokesman Joe Lockhart told reporters April 29.

Speaker J. Dennis Hastert, R-Ill., drew a different message from the House debate. Clinton, he told reporters, should "come to the Congress and lay out . . . why we are there, what his plan is, and what our end game on this thing is. . . . The rank and file need to have confidence that the vote yesterday shows they don't have."

An overwhelming majority of Republicans voted against Clinton's Balkans policy, goaded by Majority Leader Tom DeLay, R-Texas, who warned his colleagues not to "take ownership" of Clinton's policy by "voting to continue an unplanned war by an administration that is incompetent of carrying it out."

Among the 31 Republicans who broke with DeLay were leading members of defense committees who appealed to the party's traditional support for presidential discretion in the use of force.

"The principle of the commander in chief having the power to move quickly . . . will outlast the Clinton administration," warned Duncan Hunter, R-Calif.

War Powers

With NATO planes pounding targets in Serbia for a sixth week, congressional leaders had not been eager to debate Clinton's policy or, as some GOP lawmakers have taken to calling it, "Clinton's war."

But Rep. Tom Campbell, R-Calif., by invoking a section of the 1973 War Powers Resolution (PL 93-148), forced the House to take up two resolutions — H Con Res 82, ordering a withdrawal of U.S. forces, and H J Res 44, declaring war on Yugoslavia. Two others were added to the agenda to give members a broader policy choice — S Con Res 21, to authorize the current air operations, and HR 1569, to require authorization for any ground troops.

As it happened, only the measure on ground troops passed the House, 249-180. *(Vote 100, p. H-40)*

The other resolutions were defeated, including the endorsement of the air war, which lost on a tie vote, 213-213. *(Vote 103, p. H-40)*

The Senate, meanwhile, may have been trapped accidentally into taking up a resolution (S J Res 20) that would authorize the president to use "all necessary force" to achieve NATO's goal of forcing the Serb-dominated government of Yugoslavia to halt its persecution of ethnic Albanians in the province of Kosovo.

That resolution was designed by a bipartisan group led by John McCain, R-Ariz., to express support for NATO to begin planning how it would use ground troops to occupy Kosovo in case the current bombing campaign does not induce Yugoslav President Slobodan Milosevic to give in. There was no mention of the War Powers Resolution.

Senate Parliamentarian Bob Dove announced April 28, however, that the resolution fit the criteria for triggering the War Powers Resolution, even though it was not designed with that in mind.

A Foreign Relations Committee meeting to vote on the measure, scheduled for April 29, was canceled to allow time for Senate leaders to negotiate a compromise under which action on the McCain measure would be deferred until May 10.

Lott is one of many Republicans who do not want either to endorse what they see as a badly flawed Clinton policy or to cast a vote that could be taken as encouragement by the Milosevic regime. So the real meat of the negotiations concerned what other options senators would be offered, besides McCain's proposal, whenever the Senate took up the issue.

But the negotiations broke down, leaving the Senate on the procedural autopilot set by the War Powers Resolution. Under that timetable, the McCain resolution would have been discharged from the Foreign Relations Committee on May 1, if the panel had not reported the measure by then.

On April 30, the committee voted 14-4 to report McCain's resolution to the Senate without a recommendation.

Campbell's Gambit

The War Powers Resolution was passed to force presidents to get congressional approval for overseas missions longer than 60 days, though no chief executive has acknowledged its authority. The resolution requires expedited congressional consideration of war-related measures during that period.

Campbell set out deliberately to force a court test of the act, and on April 30 he led a bipartisan group of 17 House members in filing suit against Clinton, asserting that his commitment of forces to the NATO campaign violated the War Powers Resolution.

The suit seeks to force Clinton to either withdraw forces from the NATO mission or seek congressional authorization.

When the House International Relations Committee considered Campbell's two resolutions on April 27, it reported each to the floor with a recommendation that it not be passed:

- H Con Res 82, requiring the president to withdraw forces from combat against Yugoslavia was reported negatively by a vote of 30-19;
- H J Res 44, a declaration of war against Yugoslavia, was reported negatively by a vote of 49-0.

When the House took up the two Campbell resolutions April 28, it also considered the two other measures — HR 1569, cosponsored by Republicans Bill Goodling of Pennsylvania, Tillie Fowler of Florida and John R. Kasich of Ohio on ground troops, and S Con Res 21, endorsing the air campaign.

Clinton's Promise

At a White House meeting on April 28, with a bipartisan group of Senate and House leaders, Clinton insisted that he had no plans to use troops and that he would consult with Congress before committing them. However, like all of his recent predecessors, he refused to be bound by Congress on this point.

Minutes before the House voted on HR 1569, Clinton's assurances, embodied in a letter to Hastert, were circulated to all members. However, some administration allies said this came too late to make a difference. "That letter should have been here this morning, on the desk of every member," complained John M. Spratt Jr., D-S.C.

Shortly before the House refused to endorse the current air war, it rejected, 139-290, Campbell's resolution calling for withdrawal of U.S. forces — including air units — from the conflict. It also rejected, by a vote of 2-427, H J Res 44, which would have declared war on Yugoslavia. *(Votes 101, 102, p. H-40)*

Although the troop-authorization measure would be binding law if enacted, the House vote to pass it was essentially symbolic. There is little prospect that it would be passed by the Senate and even less that Congress could override the certain presidential veto.

Moreover, when Rep. Ernest Istook, R-Okla., tried April 29 to add a similar provision to the draft supplemental appropriations bill that would fund military operations against Yugoslavia through the rest of fiscal 1999, the House Appropriations Committee brushed him aside, refusing even to take a roll call vote on his amendment.

Military Spending

As for the supplemental funding bill, which is the lifeblood of U.S. operations against Yugoslavia, the only question seems to be how much money the House will add to the $6 billion Clinton requested to replenish the missiles and bombs, fuel and spare parts used up in the air war.

Most indications are that the House will approve the enlarged bill during the week of May 3.

Some House members who backed the administration on the key votes warned that even a symbolic repudiation of the administration's war policy might embolden Milosevic and encourage dissent within other NATO countries.

"This will encourage [Milosevic] to hunker down," said Eliot L. Engel, D-N.Y. "This will encourage him to think that, somehow or other, the Congress will step in and deny the president the right to win this war."

Defense Secretary William S. Cohen echoed that view during an April 29 press conference, commenting that the vote not to endorse the air campaign was "counterproductive."

Senate Kills 'All Necessary Force' Resolution

MAY 8 — Military and diplomatic pressure increased on Yugoslav President Slobodan Milosevic the week of May 3 to come to terms over the province of Kosovo, and the conflict appeared closer to a resolution.

The Group of Eight — the United States, Britain, Russia, Japan, Canada, Germany, France and Italy — announced agreement May 6 on the broad outlines of a policy for Kosovo that included a call for an international military force to protect refugees who returned to the region.

Russia's agreement with the broad principles had been telegraphed several days earlier when a bipartisan delegation of House members and members of the Duma, the lower house of the Russian Federal Assembly, reached agreement on several similar points.

The Group of Eight statement stopped short of endorsing NATO's demands that all Yugoslavian military and police forces leave Kosovo and that NATO forces provide the "core" of the international force.

Nevertheless, White House national security adviser Samuel R. Berger insisted it was significant that Russia — Milosevic's most powerful supporter in his conflict with NATO — had gone as far as it did. "Russia is moving toward the NATO position," Berger told reporters. "[The Yugoslavs] have to see that they're increasingly isolated."

But with Milosevic balking at key elements of NATO's demands, the immediate prospect was for a continuation of the bombing campaign, which began March 24 and reached new levels of intensity the week of May 3.

NATO strategists also continued updating their plans for sending ground forces into Serbia, if only as part of the force to protect returning Kosovars. Before the bombing started, alliance plans had called for sending a protective force of 28,000 troops, including about 4,000 Americans, provided the Yugoslav government removed its own forces from the province.

But Senate Armed Services Committee Chairman John W. Warner, R-Va., told reporters May 6 that a larger international force now would be needed in Kosovo — even if Milosevic did not oppose its presence — because the bombing campaign had destroyed so much of the region's infrastructure that the international force would need to provide much of its own water, electricity and transportation.

Meanwhile, U.S. forces suffered their first casualties of the operation against Yugoslavia: Two Army pilots were killed May 5 in the crash of their heavily armed Apache helicopter. It was the second aircraft lost out of a force of 24 Apaches based in Tirana, Albania, as part of a force of about 4,500 Army troops.

Ambivalent Congress

Congress continued to bob and weave on the question of how the war should be fought. On May 4, the Senate voted 78-22 to table, or kill, S J Res 20, which would have authorized Clinton to use "all necessary force" to prevail in the war over Kosovo. *(Vote 98, p. S-23)*

The tabling motion was backed by Majority Leader Trent Lott, R-Miss., and Minority Leader Tom Daschle, D-S.D., who considered the measure premature. Sponsors, led by John McCain, R-Ariz., said it was intended to pressure Clinton to plan for the use of ground troops.

McCain, who is running for the GOP presidential nomination in 2000, bitterly denounced the Clinton administration for lobbying against the bill.

"The president of the United States would prefer to lose a war rather than do the hard work — the politically risky work — of fighting it as the leader of the greatest nation on earth," McCain said. "Had they worked half as hard in support of it as they did to defeat it, the result would have been different."

As for the House, on May 6 it rejected an amendment to a military supplemental appropriations bill (HR 1664) that would have put teeth into a position the House had taken only a week earlier when it passed a bill (HR 1569) requiring congressional authorization for the use of ground troops in Kosovo.

This time, the House rejected, 117-301, an amendment by Ernest Istook, R-Okla., that would have barred the use of any funds in the supplemental bill for an invasion of Yugoslavia. *(Vote 119, p. H-27)*

Voting "nay" on the Istook amendment were 100 Republicans and 28 Democrats who had voted "aye" on the free-standing bill, which appears to have very little chance of becoming law.

Dealing With the Duma

Though Congress has been unable to find its voice on the conflict in the Balkans, it has found its feet. Individual members and delegations have hurried to the region, and to other places in Europe, to try personal diplomacy and entreaty.

A bipartisan group of 11 House members met in Vienna April 30-May 1 with three leading members of the Duma, in hopes of agreeing on some basic principles of a Kosovo settlement and thus reducing tensions between Moscow and Washington.

The House delegation was led by Russian-speaking Curt Weldon, R-Pa., who has developed contacts among Russian political leaders in the course of several years of discussions on such issues as the elimination of excess nuclear weapons and the creation in Russia of a home mortgage finance system.

According to Weldon, the three Russians in the meetings represent 90 percent of the political factions in the 450-member Duma.

The two delegations agreed on a joint report that condemned "ethnic cleansing" and terrorism in the Balkans and called for negotiations to achieve three goals: an end to NATO's bombing of Yugoslavia, a withdrawal of Yugoslav armed forces from Kosovo, and an end to terrorism by the Kosovo Liberation Army (KLA), a guerrilla group seeking independence for Kosovo.

The joint report also called for an armed international force that would administer Kosovo after Yugoslav forces departed.

In a May 4 news conference at the Capitol, Weldon and other members of the House group said their goal had been to get Russia involved in achieving NATO's goals. "The solution has to have Russia playing its trump card and using its influence over Milosevic," Weldon said.

Weldon and others insisted they had not been trying to negotiate a settlement with Russia or to undermine the administration. Weldon said he had consulted with State Department officials before the trip and during the meetings with the Russians and that a State Department official accompanied the delegation at every step.

While the Weldon group was meeting with Russians in Vienna, Rod R. Blagojevich, D-Ill., the only House member of Serbian decent, was sitting with the Rev. Jesse Jackson in Belgrade negotiating directly with Milosevic and other Yugoslav officials for the release of three U.S. soldiers who had been captured on the Macedonian border.

Blagojevich grew up speaking Serbo-Croatian with his Serbian-born father. In an interview, he said that shortly after the soldiers were captured March 31, he was approached by Serbian-Americans who said they were in contact with senior Yugoslav officials and who indicated that he might play an intermediary role between the two governments.

After senior administration officials disregarded his offer, Blagojevich said he sought out fellow Chicagoan Jesse L. Jackson Jr., D-Ill., on the House floor and offered to help his father, who was trying to set up a trip to Belgrade to try to secure the release of the three Americans. The elder Jackson welcomed the offer and Blagojevich quickly secured the necessary permission in Belgrade.

Blagojevich stressed that Jackson was the key figure in the meetings that secured the American solders' release, but said his presence and ability to speak Serbo-Croatian likely helped.

Armey Delegation

The plight of Kosovar refugees in Albania and Macedonia was the focus of another House delegation of 11 Republicans and eight Democrats headed by Majority Leader Dick Armey, R-Texas. The group visited refugee camps, as well as NATO headquarters in Brussels and U.S. air bases, during an April 30-May 2 trip.

"The scale of the humanitarian disaster is enormous," Armey told a May 3 news conference on Capitol Hill, arguing that it was urgent to get the refugees out of their tent villages and into more permanent quarters before winter.

At the same event, Christopher H. Smith, R-N.J., called for the Clinton administration to immediately authorize construction in Albania of two additional camps — each with a capacity of 20,000 persons — in addition to the 20,000-person facility currently under construction.

Brad Sherman, D-Calif., said the existing refugee sites were overcrowded partly because the humanitarian agencies that run them do not rent land for such purposes, and they had used up most of the available free sites. ◆

Peace Corps Reauthorization Calls for Biggest Increase In Volunteers Since 1960s

SUMMARY

Congress cleared and President Clinton signed a four-year reauthorization of the Peace Corps that allows the 38-year-old agency to expand to 10,000 volunteers by 2003, if appropriations match.

The measure authorizes $270 million for fiscal 2000, gradually increasing to $365 million in fiscal 2003. The agency, however, will actually have less money to spend in the fiscal year that began Oct. 1, not more.

The first version of the fiscal 2000 foreign operations appropriations bill (HR 2606), vetoed by President Clinton Oct. 18, would have cut $35 million from the president's Peace Corps request.

The second version (HR 3196), incorporated into the fiscal 2000 omnibus spending legislation (HR 3194), cut $25 million from the Peace Corps request.

The goal of once again fielding 10,000 Peace Corps volunteers — who are sent overseas for two years to work on educational, agricultural, health, environmental, urban planning or small business development projects — was first voiced by President Ronald Reagan and enacted into law (PL 99-83) in 1985. The goal was later endorsed by Clinton. The agency has not been able to afford that many volunteers since the 1960s. It now has about 6,700.

House Panel Easily Approves Increased Funding For Peace Corps

FEBRUARY 13 — Few foreign aid programs enjoy as much bipartisan support as the Peace Corps, as members of the House International Relations Committee demonstrated anew on Feb. 11.

By voice vote and with little discussion, the committee approved legislation (HR 669) that would authorize a 52 percent increase in the Peace Corps budget over the next four fiscal years, with the goal of reaching 10,000 volunteers overseas.

That goal, first stated by President Ronald Reagan, was put into law (PL 99-83) in 1985 and endorsed last year by President Clinton.

The Peace Corps was last reauthorized in 1993, and the number of volunteers now stands at 6,700. Its budget has crept up from $226 million in fiscal 1998 to $241 million today.

The legislation enjoys wide support from members of both parties. A House vote on the bill is scheduled for the week of Feb. 22.

The new measure would authorize $270 million for the Peace Corps in fiscal 2000 — President Clinton's budget request and a 12 percent increase. Authorized spending then would increase to $298 million in fiscal 2001, $327 million for fiscal 2002 and $365 million for fiscal 2003.

"This is a part of our foreign assistance program that works the hardest and gives the most back to our country," said Republican Rep. Tom Campbell of California, who sponsored the legislation. "I couldn't be prouder to lead this bipartisan effort to expand the Peace Corps."

"The popularity and success of the Peace Corps as an institution is a testament to the power of an idea that transcends both politics and partisanship," Peace Corps Director Mark D. Gearan said. Gearan has held the job since 1995.

In the Senate, Republican Paul Coverdell of Georgia, a former Peace Corps director, and Democrat Christopher J. Dodd of Connecticut, a former Peace Corps volunteer, are expected to sponsor companion legislation.

Box Score

- **Bill:** HR 669 — PL 106-30
- **Legislative action: House** passed HR 669 (H Rept 106-18), 326-90, on March 3.

Senate cleared HR 669 by voice vote on May 12.

President signed the bill on May 21.

House Passes Peace Corps Expansion Bill

MARCH 6 — The Peace Corps received a 38th birthday present from the House on March 3 — a four-year reauthorization bill that would allow the agency to expand to 10,000 volunteers by 2003.

The bipartisan measure (HR 669), which passed 326-90, would authorize $270 million for the organization in fiscal 2000 and gradually increase funding to $365 million in 2003, enough for its long-held goal of 10,000 volunteers. The vote came two days after the anniversary of the Peace Corps' founding during the early days of the Kennedy administration in 1961. *(Vote 31, p. H-16)*

The first Peace Corps reauthorization since fiscal 1993, the legislation has backers on both sides of Capitol Hill. Paul Coverdell, R-Ga., and Christopher J. Dodd, D-Conn., respectively the chairman and ranking Democrat on the Senate Foreign Relations subcommittee that oversees the agency, introduced a companion reauthorization bill (S 509) on March 2. Coverdell was Peace Corps director from 1989 to 1991, and Dodd was a volunteer in the Dominican Republic in 1966-68.

If appropriations follow, the Peace Corps will expand from its current 6,700 volunteers to its highest level since the 1960s. The agency's rolls peaked at 15,556 in 1966, then plummeted through the 1970s, finally bottoming out at 4,219 in 1987. That was two years after President Ronald Reagan set the goal of reaching 10,000 volunteers, a target written into the fiscal 1986 foreign aid authorization law (PL 99-83). But large-scale expansion never materialized. *(1985 Almanac, p. 41)*

Still Relevant

Peace Corps leaders hailed the House action as an indication that their program is still relevant.

"We're pleased by the strong, bipartisan vote, which demonstrates once again that the popularity and success of the Peace Corps is a testament to the power of an idea that transcends both politics and partisanship," said Director Mark Gearan.

The measure would provide a $29 million increase in next year's Peace Corps budget, enough for 8,000 volunteers. While the administration originally hoped to expand the corps to 10,000 by 2000, funding constraints required slower growth.

House International Relations Committee Chairman Benjamin A. Gilman, R-N.Y., said he moved the Peace Corps bill ahead of any other foreign operations measure because it is "the best part of our foreign assistance program."

"There is no American program that has been a better ambassador for America and its values than the Peace Corps," said International Relations ranking Democrat Sam Gejdenson of Connecticut.

The fiscal 2000 authorization would allow the Peace Corps to expand in South Africa, Jordan, China, Bangladesh and Mozambique, with primary growth areas in the Caucasus, Central Asia and Africa, according to an International Relations Committee report. Smaller increases would be dedicated to programs in North Africa, the Middle East, Central Asia, Eastern Europe, South America and the Pacific region.

The expansion would also allow additional volunteers to be devoted to hurricane relief missions in Central America and to the "Crisis Corps," a program formed in 1996 to send experienced, highly skilled volunteers to deal with emergencies in such areas as Central America or West Africa.

Senate Clears Peace Corps Bill

MAY 15 — The Peace Corps could expand to its highest level since the 1960s under legislation (HR 669) the Senate cleared May 12 for the president.

The bill would authorize $270 million for the Peace Corps in fiscal 2000, rising to $365 million in fiscal 2003, enough to enlist 10,000 volunteers. The actual number will depend on appropriations, however. The 38-year-old organization now has about 6,700 volunteers.

If the money is available, the Peace Corps plans to expand primarily in the Caucasus, Central Asia and Africa, a House International Relations Committee report said.

The House passed the reauthorization measure March 3. ◆

Chapter 15

GOVERNMENT OPERATIONS

House Passes Bill To Allow Census Count Verification, But Senate Takes No Action

Box Score

- **Bill:** HR 472
- **Legislative action: House** passed HR 472 (H Rept 106-71), 223-206, April 14.

SUMMARY

Seeking to place its imprint on the 2000 census, the House passed a bill in April that would allow local officials to verify head counts before numbers are made official. The measure was part of a broader fight between congressional Republicans and the White House over whether the Census Bureau could use a method called statistical sampling to adjust census figures to correct for undercounts.

Republicans argued that the measure would increase the accuracy of population figures gathered by enumerators. But Democrats and administration officials contended that the bill, sponsored by House Government Reform Census Subcommittee Chairman Dan Miller, R-Fla., would reduce the accuracy of the census by eating into the time allotted for sampling. The administration threatened a veto of the bill, but the Senate never considered it.

Miller's broader package included other bills aimed at improving the accuracy of the census without using sampling, an estimating method that the Supreme Court ruled in January cannot be used in apportioning among the states the 435 seats in the House of Representatives. The administration plans to use sampling to produce adjusted population figures for use in congressional redistricting within states and in formulas for distributing federal funds.

GOP leaders and the White House agreed as part of the omnibus fiscal 1999 spending law (PL 105-277) to cut off funding for the departments of Commerce, Justice and State and the federal judiciary as of June 15, 1999, if there was no agreement by then on sampling. Full-year funding was restored by a supplemental spending law (PL 106-31), but only after GOP leaders floated a compromise. They asked the White House to accept the local review bill in exchange for détente on the sampling issue. The proposal was rejected, and Republicans remained quiet on sampling through the summer and fall.

With the decennial count set to begin early in 2000, HR 472 is essentially dead. The Senate has no intention of considering the measure, and House Republicans have removed it from their agenda. Remaining questions over the use of sampling will be resolved by the courts.

High Court Ruling Offers Little Hope For Ending Sampling Debate

JANUARY 30 — When the fight over the 2000 census lurched into the Supreme Court last fall, Justice Antonin Scalia wondered why the court was dealing with a question that appeared to him to be far more political than legal.

Would it not be preferable, he asked during oral arguments Nov. 30, if Congress and the White House could "duke it out" in much the same way they would over a tax bill or housing legislation?

Scalia got his wish Jan. 25, when he was in the 5-4 majority that issued an equivocal decision about the methodology that may be used to conduct next year's census. And it did not take long for the fisticuffs to begin.

The justices held that the Census Bureau may not use sampling if the results are used to apportion congressional seats among the states. That pleased Republicans by upholding at least part of the party's argument against statistically adjusting the national head count.

But the GOP conceded that it had won only a partial and narrowly focused victory, which leaves open a collection of sticky questions. The result is that one of the most sustained policy battles of the last four years — in which a Republican Congress has been sparring with a Democratic president — is right back at the Capitol, with little hope for a collaborative or quick resolution.

In fact, the decision did almost nothing to calm the waters or lessen the partisanship that shrouds the issue. Democrats quickly seized on a section of the ruling that suggested statistical sampling could — or even must — be used next year to generate the population figures that will be used for all other endeavors beside reapportionment of House seats among the states for the next decade. Principal among these would be the redistricting of House seats within states, the redrawing of all other political boundaries and the allocation of an estimated $180 billion in federal funds a year among the states, counties and cities.

The court "did affirm the legality of using statistical sampling for other purposes," Robert J. Shapiro, the under secretary of Commerce for economic affairs, declared Jan. 27.

"In real life, that is never the end of the discussion; it is only the beginning of the discussion," he said. "You might wish it were otherwise. I wish it was otherwise, because then this debate would go away."

The next deadline for that to happen is June 15. Funding for the departments of Commerce, Justice and State, and for the federal judiciary, will be cut off then unless President Clinton and Congress have agreed on an authorization measure that settles — once and for all — whether and how sampling will be used in 2000 to augment the traditional head count used for the past two centuries. The deadline was included by the GOP in the law (PL 105-277) that wrapped up most fiscal 1999 spending decisions last fall.

A Twin Census?

Soon after the Supreme Court handed down its decision in *Department of Commerce v. House of Representatives*, congressional Democrats and the Clinton administration began talking about conducting one census that would produce two population counts.

Under this plan, the population figures used to allocate the 435 House seats among states would be derived the traditional way — with mail-in questionnaires sent to every household and census takers knocking on the doors of millions of homes from which no form was received.

But political redistricting and the allocation of federal funds would be based on numbers derived with the help of statistical sampling — in which the Census Bureau would use traditional methods to obtain information on about 90 percent of the homes in each of the nation's neighborhoods, or census tracts, then conduct a detailed examination of the demographics of 750,000 randomly selected homes nationwide to project the remaining population.

"Congress should change the law to allow the most accurate number possible for apportionment, but I don't think that will happen," Rep. Carolyn B. Maloney of New York, the ranking Democrat on the House Government Reform Census Subcommittee, told the U.S. Conference of Mayors on Jan. 27. "Instead, we will be forced to accept inaccurate numbers for apportionment and accurate numbers for everything else."

Even with the court's narrow ruling, Republicans said they will contest any effort to employ sampling, and they scoffed at the Democrats' talk of pressing for two sets of numbers.

"It will absolutely be a disaster if we have a two-number census. Everybody was waiting for the court ruling. The court has stated its position; let's move forward," said Rep. Dan Miller, R-Fla., chairman of the Census Subcommittee. "If we try to divide the census, we'll have two failed censuses."

Miller's Offer of Money

To advance his cause, Miller, with the backing of the House Republican leadership, unveiled a $400 million package Jan. 27 designed to improve the accuracy of a census taken with traditional methods.

The money would be used to boost an advertising campaign aimed at educating people about the importance of filling out and returning their census forms; hire at least 100,000 more census workers to track down those who do not return their forms; conduct a second mailing of census forms to people who do not return the original; and remove bureaucratic barriers that keep welfare recipients from working as census enumerators.

And in a break from Republican doctrine, Miller even suggested that AmeriCorps volunteers be enlisted to help count people. AmeriCorps, the National Service program that Clinton cites as one of his proudest domestic achievements, has been relentlessly attacked by Republicans since soon after its creation. By floating the idea, Miller said, Republicans are proving they are serious about making a traditional count work.

That is only the start, Miller said, pledging Republican support to fully finance a traditional count.

That promise may be difficult to keep, however. Democrats estimate that a traditional census would cost at least $1 billion more than one using statistical sampling. That would drive the cost beyond $5 billion. Republicans say the additional cost could be $800 million, pushing the price of a traditional count to $4.8 billion.

Whatever the cost, a census without sampling faces a treacherous road.

Clinton has proved his willingness to veto sampling restrictions. In 1997, he rejected a supplemental appropriations bill designed mainly for flood relief because it contained anti-sampling language. Republicans quickly dropped the provision and recleared the bill, which Clinton promptly signed (PL 105-18). *(1997 Almanac, p. 9-84)*

The desire to trump the threat of another veto — and the hope that the Supreme Court would render an unambiguous decision in their favor — prompted the Republicans to create the June 15 funding cutoff last fall. The federal operations under the deadline have been appropriated a combined $34.2 billion for fiscal 1999. But after the court's decision, Democrats said they believe Clinton would veto any legislation prohibiting sampling.

"It's a moral issue, it's a civil rights issue, and if the Republican majority comes forth and puts language on an appropriations bill or any bill that tries to stop the professionals in the Census Bureau from doing their job, President Clinton has a lot of ink in his veto pen," Maloney said.

Republicans, meanwhile, have said they are likely to stick with their campaign to prohibit any sampling — and that it is not beyond possibility that the impasse could shut down part of the government.

Supporters of sampling, including the National Academy of Sciences, insist that it is the only way to determine the nation's true population because it is no longer logistically possible to find every person in the United States. The lack of statistical adjustments in 1990, they say, made that year's census the least accurate in history by missing 4 million people — or 1.6 percent of the population.

Most of those missed were racial minorities, immigrants and the poor living in cities or remote rural areas — leading Democrats to characterize an accurate census is a civil rights matter. They would also expect to benefit politically, however, since the groups that tend to be undercounted by census enumerators also tend to vote Democratic.

House Republicans say the Constitution's call for an "actual enumeration" may be accomplished only by a head count. While generally declining to talk openly about how sampling could hurt them at the polls, they say sampling is vulnerable to political manipulation.

O'Connor's Split Decision

The ruling itself failed to provide the clarity that all sides said was needed to avert another partisan brawl or a potential government shutdown.

Justice Sandra Day O'Connor, in the majority opinion, did not specify whether sampling is unconstitutional, as the GOP maintains. Instead, she decided the case by declaring that amendments to the Census Act added in 1976 (PL 94-521) forbade "the use of sampling in calculating the population for purposes of apportionment." But the same law, she wrote, "required" that sampling be used for other purposes if the Census Bureau and the secretary of Commerce deem it "feasible."

The split decision produced a decidedly split interpretation.

"The administration should abandon its illegal and risky polling scheme and start preparing for a true head count," House Speaker J. Dennis Hastert, R-Ill., declared Jan. 25.

House Minority Leader Richard A. Gephardt, D-Mo., countered that "the new arena in this battle is the House of Representatives, and there are two certainties: The Republicans will try to block a fair count, and Democrats will fight them."

But there is one point of agreement: There does not seem to be a middle ground. "Once impeachment is over, this will be the partisan fight" of the year, predicted an aide to one House Democratic advocate of sampling.

House Panel OKs Census Bills Despite Democrats' Opposition

MARCH 13 — The House Government Reform Subcommittee on The Census approved four bills March 11 that Chairman Dan Miller, R-Fla. — a bitter opponent of the Clinton administration plan to use statistical sampling as part of the decennial count — says will foster more accurate numbers.

A bill (HR 1010) that would quadruple the bureau's budget for fiscal 2000 to $400 million to pay for an advertising campaign was endorsed by voice vote. A measure (HR 928) to require the bureau to mail a second round of census forms was backed, 5-2. Legislation (HR 929) requiring census forms to be printed in at least 33 languages advanced 6-4. And a bill (HR 1009) to set up a $26 million matching grant program for localities to conduct outreach efforts was approved by voice vote.

Democrats opposed all but the advertising measure, which they unsuccessfully tried to amend to target funding to communities that traditionally have been undercounted. "These bills will not do anything to reduce the racial differential and the undercount," said ranking member Carolyn B. Maloney, D-N.Y.

The administration has announced plans to use statistical sampling to create a second set of population data that it believes will be more accurate than the national head count next year that the Supreme Court has required for the apportionment of House seats among the states for the next decade.

Chairman Dan Burton, R-Ind., said the Government Reform committee will consider the four measures the week of March 15.

Bitter Debate Continues as House Committee Moves Slate of Bills

MARCH 20 — The House Government Reform Committee proved once again March 17 that when it comes to the 2000 census, no issue is too small to spark a full-throttle partisan brawl.

The sharp edges were fully evident as the committee spent six acrimonious hours debating and approving seven bills, mostly along party lines.

The committee managed to unify on some issues — approving a bill (HR 1010) on a voice vote to spend $300 million on advertising, in addition to the $4 billion the census is expected to cost.

The committee also came together on HR 683, approved 31-1, which would allow welfare recipients to continue receiving benefits while working as paid census enumerators.

"Mr. Chairman, today we will be attacked for being too political, when all we want to do is remove politics from the census," said Republican Rep. Dan Miller of Florida, chairman of the Census Subcommittee and sponsor of multibill "America Counts" legislation for an accurate census.

Democrats bitterly disagreed, charging that the bills were little more than "wolves in sheep's clothing," designed to so burden the Census Bureau that it would be unable to proceed with plans to use statistical sampling for part of the effort. Sampling is a methodology used to estimate a percentage of the population that otherwise might be missed.

The Supreme Court ruled Jan. 25 that the Census Bureau could not use statistical sampling as a basis for apportioning congressional seats, but it left open the possibility of using sampling for other purposes, such as determining the amount of federal money a district receives.

But Democratic Rep. Carolyn B. Maloney of New York said Republicans are now trying to "make matters worse by offering seven bills, most of which will do absolutely nothing to improve the accuracy of the decennial count."

In keeping with the harsh politics of the 2000 census, Commerce Department Secretary William M. Daley warned in a letter to the committee's ranking Democrat, Henry A. Waxman of California, that he would recommend a veto of three of the bills.

Those three would give local communities the right to challenge census results before they became final and to force the Census Bureau to recount areas (HR 472); require the printing of short census forms in 34 languages (HR 929); and mandate a second mailing of census forms (HR 928).

With the census scheduled to commence April 1, 2000, many questions remain, and there is little hope for any resolution to the differences that have buffeted the issue for years.

The net result is that Census Bureau officials and others fear that the political feud over how the count will be conducted will drag on until the commencement date.

Though even many Democrats said some of the ideas were good — such as involving schools in the census effort — they complained that Republicans were "micromanaging" the mammoth undertaking.

Formula for Disaster?

Those reservations were echoed by Census Bureau Director Kenneth Prewitt, who said the legislation would complicate, not simplify, the count.

"While I understand that these bills were introduced with a view to improving the 2000 census," Prewitt wrote in a memo analyzing the bills, "their consequences for an orderly, timely and accurate census in 2000 are just short of disastrous."

If the bills become law, Prewitt warned, "the Congress would either have to significantly delay the starting day of census 2000 or require the Census Bureau to field an operational plan, which in our judgment would decrease accuracy levels."

The rhetoric and raw feelings are nothing new. Republicans have long objected to plans by the Census Bureau to use statistical sampling in the 2000 census, charging that it is unconstitutional and subject to political manipulation.

Democrats respond that sampling is the only way to ensure an accurate count and to fix the problems of the last census, in which 8 million Americans were not counted and 4 million were counted twice.

Most of those missed were racial minorities, immigrants and the poor living in cities or remote rural areas — leading Democrats to characterize an accurate census as a civil rights matter. They would also expect to benefit politically, however, since the groups that are undercounted by census takers tend to vote Democratic.

House Republicans say the Constitution's call for an "actual enumeration" may be accomplished only with a head count.

House GOP Pulls Census Bill, Promises a Return After Recess

MARCH 27 — With Democrats bracing for an all-out fight, Republican leaders abruptly pulled a bill from the House floor March 24 that would have given local officials time to review and challenge census counts before they became final.

The GOP-backed bill (HR 472) was bitterly opposed by Democrats who charged that it would upset the delicate timetable for the 2000 census.

The White House had threatened to veto the bill, sponsored by Rep. Dan Miller, R-Fla., chairman of the House Government Reform Census Subcommittee.

Miller and other supporters, however, said giving local officials 45 days to contest preliminary numbers would ensure a more accurate count.

Democrats said the bill was pulled because some Republicans opposed it, which would have led to a messy fight on the floor. But the spokesman for the Census Subcommittee disputed that interpretation.

"With all the stuff that is going on, it was felt it would be best to wait until after the recess," said spokesman Chip Walker, referring to NATO military strikes against Serbia.

"But anybody who suggests this bill will not be brought back is seriously mistaken."

House Passes Census Bill On Party-Line Vote

APRIL 17 — Bitter partisanship marked the latest round in the congressional battle over how to conduct the 2000 census. The House passed, 223-206, a measure (HR 472) that would require the Census Bureau to allow local officials to verify tallies before numbers are made official. The party-line vote on April 14 once again underscored the tension between Republicans and Democrats over how the census should be conducted. *(Vote 89, p. H-36)*

Republicans said the bill would increase the accuracy of the census. Democrats asserted that GOP leaders do not want minorities to be counted and that the bill allowing local reviews after the census actually would reduce the accuracy of the count.

"The Republican bill is a Trojan horse," said Carolyn B. Maloney of New York, the ranking Democrat on the House Government Reform Subcommittee on the Census.

But House Majority Leader Dick Armey, R-Texas, said the Constitution requires that every person be counted, "not estimated, not guessed at and not eliminated because you didn't fit in somebody's statistical model."

The debate on the legislation is part of a larger battle about a controversial White House plan to use statistical sampling, an estimating method that would raise counts in hard-to-reach areas, such as inner cities. Republicans oppose the idea, saying it is illegal and citing a Supreme Court decision stating that it cannot be used for congressional apportionment, a key purpose of the census.

But the White House argues that the court's decision allows sampling to be used for other purposes of the census — redistricting and establishing the population formulas used to distribute billions in federal grants.

Lawmakers face a June 15 cutoff date for funding the departments of Commerce, Justice and State, including the Census Bureau. If no agreement is reached and no money is appropriated, there could be a partial government shutdown. But both sides say that is unlikely to happen.

[The June 15 cutoff was lifted as part of the fiscal 1999 supplemental spending bill signed May 21 (HR 1141— PL 106-31).] ◆

Bill Calling for Cost Analysis Of Federal Regulations Stalls After Passing House

Box Score

- **Bill:** HR 1074
- **Legislative action: House** passed HR 1074 (H Rept 106-168), 254-157, July 26.

SUMMARY

The House passed legislation that would require government agencies to detail the costs and benefits of proposed federal rules, while efforts to pass a similar measure stalled for the second consecutive year in the Senate.

The Regulatory Right-to-Know Act of 1999 (HR 1074), would direct the White House's Office of Management and Budget (OMB) to submit an annual account of the costs and benefits that federal regulations would have for different agencies and programs. The report would also detail the regulatory impact of federal rules on small business, consumer prices and economic growth.

As in previous years, many Democrats generally opposed the measure, saying it would place an undue burden on OMB, requiring information that is not currently generated by the agencies. They also argued that it would force federal agencies to place cost considerations above hard-to-quantify benefits such as environmental protection or lives saved.

The Senate did not act on its version of the legislation (S 59), which was sponsored by Republican Fred Thompson of Tennessee.

The Senate Governmental Affairs Committee expects to mark up a companion bill early next year.

House Panel OKs Bill Requiring Study Of Rules' Costs

APRIL 24 — A House Government Reform subcommittee gave voice vote approval April 20 to a bill (HR 1074) that would require the government to assess the impact of federal regulations on private businesses and other government entities.

The bill would direct the Office of Management and Budget (OMB) to prepare annual reports on the costs and benefits of federal regulatory programs. The reports would outline how those programs affect small businesses, local and state governments, consumer prices, and economic growth, among other criteria.

Under the bill, two or more nongovernmental organizations with experience in reviewing the effects of government regulations would examine the OMB reports.

The National Economic Growth, Natural Resources and Regulatory Affairs Subcommittee approved by voice vote a substitute amendment by Chairman David M. McIntosh, R-Ind., that would eliminate some of the required impact analyses, such as reports on the effects on productivity and the way products are distributed.

The panel adopted by voice vote an amendment by ranking Democrat Dennis J. Kucinich of Ohio, which would require OMB to study the impact of regulations on public health and safety, the environment, and consumer protections.

The panel rejected by voice vote a Kucinich amendment that would have prevented OMB from spending more than $1 million a year on impact analyses and clarified that agencies would not be required to generate new data or conduct new analyses.

House Passes Bill Directing OMB To Assess Impact Of Regulations

JULY 31 — The House voted July 26 to require the White House to give Congress a detailed report each year on the costs and benefits of federal rules and regulations. The Senate Governmental Affairs Committee is tentatively scheduled to take up the bill Aug. 3.

Under the measure (HR 1074 — H Rept 106-168), which passed 254-147, the White House Office of Management and Budget (OMB) would be required to estimate the costs and benefits of all federal regulatory programs, including paperwork requirements. The president would submit the report to Congress along with his annual budget. *(Vote 336, p. H-112)*

Supporters argue that the bill, dubbed the "Regulatory Right To Know Act," is necessary to fulfill the government's obligation to inform the public about the magnitude and impact of federal regulations. "What this really comes down to is simply a good-government act," said Paul D. Ryan, R-Wis.

The Clinton administration and most Democrats oppose the bill, saying it would place an undue burden on OMB, requiring information that is not currently generated by the agencies. They also argue that it would force federal agencies to place cost considerations above hard-to-quantify benefits such as environmental protection or lives saved.

"We do not need analysis for the sake of analysis," argued Henry A. Waxman, D-Calif.

Republicans successfully fought off a Democratic attempt to cap the annual cost of the proposed agency assessments at $1 million and to sunset the program after four years.

The amendment, by Joseph M. Hoeffel, D-Pa., also would have required OMB to report on the degree to which regulatory costs imposed on corporations are offset by government subsidies, including grants, preferential tax treatment and federally funded research. It was defeated by a vote of 192-217. *(Vote 335, p. H-112)*

As passed, the bill would require OMB to provide cost-benefit estimates in a number of formats: across all agencies, by agency and program, and by "major" rule — those that generate costs of $100 million or more.

The OMB report would also have to analyze the impact of federal rules and paperwork on federal, state and local governments; the private sector; small business; wages; consumer prices; economic growth; public health and safety; and the environment.

Before submitting the report to Congress, OMB would be required to consult with the Congressional Budget Office, submit the information to peer review and allow 60 days for public review and comment. The results would be included in the report.

OMB would be given nine months to issue guidelines to standardize cost-benefit measurements across federal agencies.

For the past few years — most recently in the fiscal 1999 omnibus appropriations act (PL 105-277) — Congress has required OMB to conduct cost-benefit analyses of rules that have an annual cost of more than $100 million. Federal agencies are already required to maintain cost-benefit data on those regulations.

The House-passed bill is sponsored by Commerce Committee Chairman Thomas J. Bliley Jr., R-Va. It began in the Governmental Reform Subcommittee on National Economic Growth, Natural Resources and Regulatory Affairs, which approved it by voice vote April 20. The full committee followed suit May 19, also by voice vote. ◆

Chapter 16

HEALTH

Lawmakers Agree on Need For Patients' Rights But Remain Divided on Methods

Box Score

- **Bills:** HR 2990, S 1344
- **Legislative action: Senate** passed S 1344, 53-47, on July 15.

House passed HR 2990, 227-205, on Oct. 6 and passed HR 2723, 275-151, on Oct. 7. The two were combined and sent to the conference committee as HR 2990.

SUMMARY

Both the House and Senate passed bills designed to protect patients who are enrolled in managed care plans, though the two chambers took substantially different approaches, leaving the issue for a House-Senate conference committee to resolve in 2000. The biggest difference was in the controversial area of liability. Under the House bill, patients would be allowed to sue their health plans in state court over coverage decisions; the Senate bill had no such language.

Senate leaders agreed to bring the issue to the floor in July after months of pressure from Democrats and consumer advocates who said federal laws were needed to protect patients from managed care abuses. They packaged a measure (S 326) approved in March by the Senate Finance Committee with a set of tax provisions designed to make it easier for Americans to buy health insurance.

The resulting bill (S 1344) was brought to a vote on July 15. After four days of bitter, partisan debate, the measure passed, 53-47, along party lines. It included some patient protections, but many of them would apply only to 48 million people in plans that are exempt from state regulations. Democrats were united against the bill, and two Republicans, Peter G. Fitzgerald of Illinois and the late John H. Chafee of Rhode Island, opposed it. The bill included a provision under which outside medical specialists would hear and decide appeals of health plans' decisions.

In the House, it had been clear for months that Republican Charlie Norwood of Georgia and Democrat John D. Dingell of Michigan had enough votes to pass a broad managed care bill (HR 2723) that included the right to sue in state courts. Under intense pressure to bring the popular measure to the floor for a vote, Speaker J. Dennis Hastert, R-Ill., scrambled to find an alternative bill that could draw votes away from Norwood-Dingell.

Hastert had begun the year saying he wanted to produce a bill through the regular committee process. But the one package (HR 2041-2047 and 2089) that had come through a committee — approved by the Education and Workforce Subcommittee on Employer-Employee Relations in June — generated little enthusiasm. So in August Hastert appointed a task force to devise a compromise. The group, led by Tom Coburn, R-Okla., and John Shadegg, R-Ariz., produced a bill (HR 2824) that included the right to sue in federal court, but the leadership endorsement was half-hearted and came late in the process.

When the bill came to the floor the week of Oct. 4, the Coburn-Shadegg measure was offered as a substitute, but was rejected, 193-238. Another alternative, authored by Amo Houghton, R-N.Y., was also rejected 160-269. That bill would have permitted lawsuits against health plans in federal court and would have capped non-economic damages.

None of these alternatives could overcome the success of the popular Norwood-Dingell bill, which passed 275-151. Under the rule, the Norwood-Dingell bill was then attached to a measure (HR 2990), passed a day earlier, of tax breaks and insurance marketing mechanisms to help small-business people and others who do not have access to corporate health plans.

The tax bill would allow all taxpayers to establish Medical Savings Accounts, which are tax-exempt accounts that can be used for medical expenses. It would also allow taxpayers who purchase their own health insurance to take a tax deduction equal to 100 percent of their premiums and allow the self-employed to deduct 100 percent of their premiums. Current law would phase in the 100 percent deduction by 2003. The bill also would allow creation of "health marts," which are regional alliances of employers, insurers and health care providers (hospitals, for example) that band together to develop insurance packages for workers. And it would also allow creation of "association health plans," in which church groups or trade associations could pool together to buy insurance at more affordable rates than could be purchased individually.

President Clinton and many other Democrats opposed the tax package and accused Republicans of pursuing a "poison-pill" strategy by combining the two. But the fact that the tax measure would be paired with the Norwood-Dingell bill did not appear to drive away many votes. All but two Democrats, along with 68 Republicans, voted for Norwood-Dingell. In addition to the liability provision, the bill included a broad set of patient protections such as a guarantee that doctors, not health plans, determine what kinds of treatments are "medically necessary."

Election-year politics could cut both ways in the managed care debate. Lawmakers may not want to touch the politically sensitive topic. Yet doing nothing could hurt incumbents who are under pressure from constituents to address a subject that polls show is among voters' top concerns. Sponsors of the House bill believe they have momentum and note that their bill, unlike the Senate measure, has the stamp of bipartisanship. The biggest obstacle to agreement, however, may be finding a middle ground between two very different bills, a task Rep. Bill Thomas, R-Calif., likened to crossing "a Chihuahua and a Great Dane."

Senate Committee Approves GOP Bill After Rejecting 18 Amendments

MARCH 20 — Senate Republicans and Democrats have drawn very clear battle lines for this year's debate over how to improve the managed health care system — setting up what is sure to be a lengthy and contentious fight.

Both parties agree on broad principles for overhauling the managed care system. Both say patients need greater protection when dealing with their health plans, such as better access to emergency care, more choice in selecting doctors, and the ability to appeal health plans' decisions to deny treatment.

But Republicans favor a market-based approach that would keep federal regulation to a minimum. Democrats want to set federal standards to crack down on negligent health plans and allow the threat of court action to make sure plans comply with federal regulations.

Their differences were clear during a 13-hour markup of a GOP version of the so-called patients' bill of rights that stretched over two days, March 17-18, in the Senate Health, Education, Labor and Pensions Committee.

Committee Democrats offered 18 amendments, which were all defeated by party-line votes. The bill (S 326) finally was approved 10-8, with all Republicans voting for it and all Democrats voting against it.

Last year, Republicans introduced a nearly identical bill that never went through the committee process. A GOP bid to bring it to the Senate floor died because the parties could not agree on ground rules for debate.

Chances for Senate floor action this year are slightly higher. Members from both parties agree the health care issue is too politically important for the Senate not to move.

"The public wants us to take action to protect them. When the public demands things, things get done," Committee Chairman James M. Jeffords, R-Vt., said after the markup. "There's an important election coming up. We all want to be in the best position possible, and that requires us to do something with health care."

Republicans have already suggested they want time limits on floor debate for this bill, which Democrats insist they will not accept — the same standoff that killed the bill last year.

But Massachusetts Sen. Edward M. Kennedy, the top Democrat on the committee, agreed with Jeffords that public pressure will force the Senate to debate a bill. "This is going to come to the floor," Kennedy said. "The American people are going to demand it. We've got a long session. We've got all kinds of opportunities."

The White House also entered the fray. President Clinton issued a statement after the first day of the committee's markup, saying the GOP bill "falls far short of the legislation the American people deserve."

Kennedy vowed to bring to the floor most, if not all, of the 18 amendments that were killed by Republicans in committee.

Adding to the difficulty of passing a bill is strong opposition from the insurance industry. Even though health insurers find Republican proposals less burdensome than Democratic legislation, they say they will work to defeat any bill that imposes new mandates on the industry.

"Whatever they are, we believe additional mandates will add to the cost," said Dan Danner, chairman of the Health Benefits Coalition, which represents businesses and insurance companies.

And, Danner said, additional costs will lead to more Americans who cannot afford health care.

The coalition plans to run a series of television, radio and newspaper advertisements in more than a dozen media markets across the country during the upcoming congressional recess warning consumers about the costs associated with federal regulations.

An Ugly Beginning

A sharp partisan tone was established quickly on the opening day of the Senate committee markup — the first in either chamber this year on a managed care bill. The committee's first order of business was to reject by a 10-8 party-line vote a Democratic substitute (S 6).

One of the biggest complaints Democrats have with the Republican version is its scope. S 326 would only extend protections to the 48 million Americans who are in self-insured health plans. Self-insured plans — those in which the employer rather than an outside insurance company assumes all financial risk — are exempt from state regulations, including patient protection laws.

But Democrats say there are 113 million Americans in managed care plans who also deserve the protection of the federal government. Those Americans — including state employees, workers who independently buy their health insurance, and those whose jobs provide fully insured health coverage — are currently covered by a patchwork of state regulations.

The Democratic bill would extend federal protections to all managed care patients by pre-empting current state laws if they are not as stringent as the federal provisions.

Republicans argue that states have the right to regulate their own health care systems.

"It's a question of whether we want the federal government to take over health care in this country," said Jeffords. "One size does not fit all."

A separate Democratic amendment to extend the scope of the GOP bill was defeated along party lines.

Lawsuits

Another problem Democrats have with the Republican bill is its failure to provide enough legal remedies for patients.

Currently, patients who are in employer-provided health plans and feel they have been injured by a plan's decision can sue in federal court for just the cost of the denied treatment.

Democrats want to allow patients to sue in state courts for compensatory damages as well as pain and suffering.

Republicans argue that opening health plans to expensive lawsuits will drive up premiums and hurt consumers. Instead, Republicans say disputes between patients and insurers should be settled by an external appeals process.

Democrats counter that the GOP appeals proposal is tilted in favor of insurers. The GOP bill would let health plans choose an outside entity — such as a state agency or other group accredited by the state — which would select an independent mediator to hear disputes.

Democrats oppose giving health plans the power to pick the outside entities. Democrats also want to expand the situations under which a patient can appeal.

"It's greed prevailing over need," Christopher J. Dodd, D-Conn., said of the GOP appeals process.

In particular, Democrats oppose a GOP provision that allows patients to seek an external appeal if a plan denies care that is "medically necessary." Under the GOP bill, there is no set definition of medical necessity; that determination is left up to the outside reviewer, who must be a physician.

Bill Frist, R-Tenn. — the Senate's only physician — argued that a statutory definition would limit health plans' abilities to offer the best care to patients. He said continuing scientific advances require a flexible definition.

"Don't lock it in to a definition," Frist said. "We set up a process where medical necessity can be determined and confirmed on an ongoing basis."

But Democrats argue that if there is no statutory definition of medical necessity, health plans can arbitrarily set limits in their contracts and later contend that the treatment was never a covered benefit.

"Without this protection, all the other safeguards are worthless," Kennedy said at the markup. "If health plans are making medical decisions, they should have to justify their decisions the same way a doctor does."

A Kennedy amendment to define medical necessity as any treatment that "is consistent with generally accepted principles of professional medical practice" was defeated along party lines.

Among the other Democratic amendments shot down during the markup was one by Dodd that would have prohibited employers from using genetic information to discriminate against workers.

Republicans also killed an amendment by Paul Wellstone, D-Minn., and Jack Reed, D-R.I., that would have provided federal grants to states for ombudsmen to assist patients confused about health insurance.

Wellstone lost on another amendment that would have required health plans to offer "point of service" coverage, which allows patients to see doctors outside the health plans' networks.

Wellstone, however, won passage of one amendment. Republicans joined with Democrats to prohibit health plans from preventing patients from paying out-of-pocket for mental health treatment when the plan denies coverage.

Some plans threaten to drop coverage for their patients who continue to seek treatment at their own cost after it has been denied. The plans fear if the treatment proves effective, they could be sued for denying appropriate care.

Moving Forward

After the markup, Frist called the bill a "major leap forward . . . that will benefit millions of Americans in terms of consumer rights and in terms of quality care."

Kennedy, however, blasted it as "a bill of wrongs, not of rights."

Before S 326 can reach the floor, the Senate Finance Committee must finish work on an economic package that would provide tax breaks for people seeking health insurance. That package calls for making the cost of health insurance for the self-employed fully deductible, and it would expand the use of tax-exempt medical savings accounts.

Democrats oppose both provisions, saying they would only help the wealthy and leave poor patients out in the cold.

It is unclear when the Finance Committee will be able to complete its work. GOP leaders plan to meld both bills into one before bringing it to the floor.

House GOP Split On Managed Care As Committees Take Up Bills

JUNE 19 — When J. Dennis Hastert was sworn in as House Speaker on Jan. 6, he gaveled the 106th Congress into session vowing to hand legislation back to the committees. His move to "regular order" was expected to have a significant impact on politically charged debate over managed care.

As chairman of a health care task force hand-picked by former Speaker Newt Gingrich during the 105th Congress, Hastert had seen for himself the perils of bypassing the committee process. After months of struggle, his group produced a bill that was immediately attacked by Democrats and even some Republicans. The measure passed the House, but by only a slim margin, and 12 Republicans voted against it. The issue died in the Senate. *(1998 Almanac, p. 14-3)*

Now, a year later, managed care legislation is in the hands of the committees, but the issue is in an almost identical place. Regular order has not been able to help bridge deep differences over the role of government in America's health care system.

House Republicans are still split on how — or even whether — to impose protections for patients on managed care plans. A package that looks remarkably similar to last year's task force bill is scheduled for markup the week of June 21 in the House Education and the Workforce Committee. Democrats — who picked up five House seats last November — will once again oppose the language, and, with the support of a small but pivotal group of Republicans, could even defeat it.

The situation is no more clear in the Senate, where the two parties are unable to reach agreement on limiting floor debate or amendments. Majority Leader Trent Lott, R-Miss., had pledged to bring legislation to the floor in June, a prospect that now seems unlikely.

Meanwhile, Democrats are planning a new offensive on the issue, which has in recent months taken a back seat to debates over war in the Balkans and gun control.

"The time has come," Senate Democratic leader Tom Daschle of South Dakota said at a news conference June 18. He vowed to offer Democrats' "Patients' Bill of Rights" as an amendment to every bill that hits the floor — even must-pass fiscal 2000 spending bills.

The continued polarization leads many lobbyists on the issue and some lawmakers to conclude that with each passing day, the prospects for managed health care legislation move closer to last year's fate — a flat line. Some lawmakers privately say there may be more political payoff in expanding

Medicare benefits, and say some Republicans on Capitol Hill are beginning to warm to calls for Medicare prescription coverage.

For his part, Hastert has a large personal stake in the issue. Because he spent so much effort last year on the task force, he has made passing a bill a matter of pride, and aides say he wants a bill on the floor before the August recess. Others believe the pressure for legislation will build as the 2000 campaigns heat up.

"This will not go away," said Rep. Greg Ganske, R-Iowa, a physician, who says there is a 50-50 chance for legislative action this session. "The question is: Do you want to deal with it now or later?"

Pressure From Democrats

The managed care issue has long been difficult for Republicans, who have had to balance their belief in limited government against withering Democratic criticism that the GOP is letting managed care companies make medical decisions that belong in the hands of doctors.

The Republicans are also under strong pressure from their constituents in the business and insurance community to avoid placing new mandates on health plans or employers.

If Republicans produce a limited package, Democrats will force votes on a long list of amendments — including language that would allow patients to sue their plans for punitive damages. Opposing such amendments could open Republicans to charges that they are anti-consumer.

"There's always the fear that if we do this, Democrats will be willing to spend more and do more," said Bill McInturff, a Republican pollster. "We will never be able to neutralize this issue."

Republicans are also acutely aware that if they do not bring up any managed care legislation, Democrats will attack them for ignoring consumers' interests.

Democrats are already turning up the pressure. In the House, John D. Dingell, D-Mich., the main sponsor of a Democratic "Patients' Bill of Rights," has threatened to use a discharge petition to force a bill out of committee and onto the floor.

But health insurers and Republicans charge that Democrats are refusing to negotiate because they know that managed care provides them with a good political issue for the 2000 campaigns.

"A lot of Republicans think that no matter what they do, the Democrats will win," said Mary Nell Lehnhard, senior vice president of the Office of Policy and Representation with the Blue Cross Blue Shield Association.

The debate has also forced Republicans to choose between two key constituencies: doctors and the insurance industry. Both are traditional GOP supporters but have taken opposing views on the managed care debate.

The American Medical Association (AMA), which gave 85 percent of its political contributions to Republicans during the 1995-96 election cycle, is now putting heavy pressure on GOP leaders to overhaul the industry.

But insurers, who also have contributed heavily to Republicans, are waging a war against government-imposed mandates.

During the first six months of 1998, insurance companies and business groups involved in the managed care debate spent $60 million on lobbying.

Rep. Thomas M. Davis III of Virginia, chairman of the National Republican Campaign Committee, acknowledged that Republicans face some hard decisions on managed care in the coming months.

"Does this issue force you to choose between constituencies? Yes, it probably does," Davis said.

Senate Tax Difficulties

In the Senate, a Republican package of health care tax breaks (S 300) that was intended to be paired with a limited patient protection bill (S 326) has been stalled in the Finance Committee because Republican John H. Chafee of Rhode Island has refused to support it.

Chafee has introduced his own managed care legislation (S 374) that is closer to Democratic proposals than that of his own leadership.

In the House, several Republican lawmakers have threatened to make waves if a broad patient protection bill — including liability — is not soon brought to the floor.

Charlie Norwood, R-Ga., who authored his own patient protection bill (HR 216) that is opposed by his leadership, is expected to put up a fight at the Education and the Workforce Committee's markup.

That panel's Subcommittee on Employer-Employee Relations, headed by John A. Boehner, R-Ohio, on June 16 approved, generally along party lines, a package of eight bills (HR 2041-2047, HR 2089) that provide a limited number of expanded protections for managed care patients.

The bills would: ban insurance company "gag rules" that prevent doctors from discussing expensive treatment with patients; guarantee direct access for children to pediatricians, and women to obstetricians and gynecologists without first having to get referrals; and require that patients be able to appeal health plans' decisions to an external panel.

The package, however, would not allow patients to sue health plans for damages. Norwood and some Democrats charge that it simply provides a Band-Aid for major problems within the managed care system.

During the full committee markup, Norwood is expected to offer several amendments to force the committee to vote on his broader patient protection bill.

But committee Chairman Bill Goodling, R-Pa., said he is considering procedural ways to ensure that amendments opening the door to lawsuits are ruled out of order.

"We are looking very carefully at that. I have to see the germaneness to our particular jurisdiction," Goodling said June 16.

Goodling was handed primary jurisdiction over the managed care debate at a meeting on June 10 with Hastert.

During the meeting, which included California Republican Bill Thomas, chairman of the Ways and Means Subcommittee on Health, and Michael Bilirakis, R-Fla., chairman of the Commerce Subcommittee on Health and Environment, Hastert told the lawmakers to stick closely to their committee jurisdictions.

Because Goodling's panel oversees the Employee Retirement Income Security Act (ERISA), the issue of liability was placed firmly in his hands. The law (PL 93-406) prevents employees from suing their health plans for damages under state laws.

Before the Hastert meeting, many

lawmakers, including Commerce Committee Chairman Thomas J. Bliley Jr., R-Va., believed Commerce would handle the liability issue. Panel members had spent months preparing for work on a broad managed care bill.

Earlier this spring, Bliley instructed Norwood and two other members of his panel to draft a broad managed care bill that could quickly pass the committee. The bill they produced would give managed care patients the ability to sue their health plans in state courts.

According to Norwood, Bliley accepted the language and was set to mark up the bill in late June or early July.

Hastert's decision to take the issue away from the Commerce Committee meant that Bliley could not move Norwood's liability proposal forward. Instead, Hastert handed it over to Goodling, who is opposed to the lawsuit provisions.

Bliley expressed some frustration with the jurisdictional jockeying.

"I would have preferred we would have been able to do a comprehensive bill, but the Speaker makes the decisions," Bliley said.

When asked about the maneuvering, a Hastert spokesman simply said the Speaker is opposed to opening the door to more lawsuits.

"The Speaker has reiterated time and again he wants to make sure patients get the care they need, when they need it, as opposed to standing in line for the court system," said Pete Jeffries, Hastert's communications director.

No Game Plan?

Some proponents of a broad managed care overhaul charge that Republican leaders have lost control of the debate.

"The Democrats are all too eager to clobber Republicans on their failure to act on this legislation, but Republicans are beholden to the managed care industry. They have no game plan," said Ron Pollack, executive director of Families USA, a consumer group lobbying for strong government protections."

Republicans also suffered a blow in the health care debate over the past year with an exodus of a dozen senior health care aides from the Hill.

Among the key aides who have left are Howard Cohen, a senior counsel on the Commerce Committee who had worked on health care issues in the House for a decade. Cohen, who left the Hill late last year to join the law firm of Greenberg Traurig, was a key architect of the Medicare and Medicaid provisions in the 1997 balanced-budget law (PL 105-33).

Also leaving the Hill last year to join the same firm was Russell J. Mueller, who had worked with the Education and the Workforce Committee for more than 20 years. During his time on the Hill, Mueller helped write ERISA and the Health Insurance Portability and Accountability Act of 1996 (PL 104-191). *(1996 Almanac, p. 6-28)*

Facing all these obstacles with managed care legislation, Republicans are looking elsewhere for a health care victory. One option is the growing debate over whether Medicare should cover the cost of prescription drugs.

The Clinton administration this spring turned back a Medicare overhaul package drafted by Sen. John B. Breaux, D-La., and Rep. Thomas, which included limited coverage of prescription drugs.

The administration said the package did not go far enough in providing medication to the poor — but now Republicans believe they have an opportunity to jump on the issue.

"You need something substantive to show you care about the health care issue," said former Rep. Bill Gradison, R-Ohio (1975-93), who served as president of the Health Insurance Association of America after leaving Congress.

"The odds for action on prescription drugs are rising, the odds for managed care legislation are somewhat diminished. Although prescription drugs is a completely different issue, politically it fills a need," he said.

Although both parties believe health issues offer them a potential political victory, public pressure to pass a managed care package has waned.

Last spring, the drive for passing a so-called patients' bill of rights had reached a fevered pitch. Patient advocacy groups and the managed care industry let loose a flood of advertising for and against congressional action.

Karen Ignagni, head of the American Association of Health Plans, an industry group, called 1998 "the deepest, darkest time" for managed care.

"The height of all this was the spring of last year," she said, but added she still fears Congress will increase government mandates on health care.

But today, Republicans point to post-election polls that show the issue did not top voters' lists in 1998 and is waning as a political issue for 2000.

Pollster Gary Ferguson, senior vice president for American Viewpoint in Virginia, conducted a number of post-election polls that showed that the issue never lived up to its political expectations.

According to Ferguson, who has BlueCross BlueShield as a client, only 2 percent of those polled said health care was a determining factor in their congressional voting. Only 1 percent said managed care reform was.

But Ferguson said that does not mean lawmakers can ignore the issue.

"I would tell Republicans to be engaged, but they shouldn't rush," he said. "The issue only hurts you if you're perceived as not doing anything on the process."

As long as the issue is being debated, insurers continue to fight.

"I consider it at a lull. Every piece of legislation has a lull," said BlueCross BlueShield's Lenhard. "I don't feel we can take that deep breath yet."

Senate Democrats Block Action; House Panel Postpones Markup

JUNE 26 — Democrats stalled action in the Senate the week of June 21, attempting to force votes on their proposals to regulate managed care companies, draw attention to the debate and expose fractures within GOP ranks on the issue.

In seeking to attach managed care legislation to a fiscal 2000 spending bill (S 1233) for the Department of Agriculture, the Democrats succeeded in blocking the Republicans from advancing their legislative agenda.

But the temporary struggle over control of the chamber represents a deeper one: the continuing tug of war between the parties over the confidence of the public before the 2000 elections.

In a week in which GOP presidential front-runner George W. Bush made his first campaign trip to the Capitol, the political overtones of the managed care debate seemed only natural.

On June 25, President Clinton, in a major domestic policy speech, called on Congress to move "patients' rights" legislation, saying the only group in America that opposes it is the insurance industry.

Although managed care may soon be overshadowed by other health care developments, such as Medicare proposals and health care tax credits, Democrats temporarily resurrected the issue by returning to parliamentary tactics that scuttled the schedule for days last year. *(1998 Almanac, p. 14-3)*

In the House, fissures in GOP ranks caused leaders to delay a June 24 markup by the Education and the Workforce Committee. Democrats pushed forward a discharge petition, which would force the bill out of committee and onto the floor. They gathered 180 signatures by June 25; 218 are needed.

Despite the high-profile calls for action, the debate has become so divisive that efforts to strike a deal may be futile. Democrats say Republicans want to maintain the status quo; Republicans say the stalemate indicated that Democrats are less interested in a deal than they are in keeping the issue alive for the 2000 campaigns.

"It looks like we're back in campaign mode," said Karen Ignagni, president and chief executive officer of the American Association of Health Plans, which represents managed care plans.

All the bills offer patients varying levels of new protections, such as coverage of some emergency room care at any hospital, the right for patients and doctors to talk openly about treatment options and the ability to appeal claim denials to both internal and independent reviewers. But the details vary widely.

Wrestling in the Senate

Senate Democrats lost a pair of procedural votes early in the week but succeeded in blocking Republicans from advancing their agenda. They negotiated with the GOP for four days starting June 21 to find a way to proceed on managed care after the July Fourth recess.

Republicans, aware of polls showing that the public trusts Democrats more in general than Republicans on health care, sought to avoid a floor fight.

"I don't want our members to go through a series of votes that could be misconstrued for political purposes," said Assistant Majority Leader Don Nickles, R-Okla., who led the talks.

Democrats surprised Majority Leader Trent Lott, R-Miss., on June 22 by attempting to attach their managed care bill (S 6) to the farm spending measure. Minority Leader Tom Daschle, D-S.D., had warned that this would be the Democrats' strategy, but Republicans assumed Daschle and other farm-state senators would not try to stall the agriculture bill. But Daschle opposes parts of the agriculture bill and wanted to get Republicans' attention.

Lott responded by introducing the GOP's committee-approved alternative (S 326), with tax provisions added, as a substitute to the Democratic amendment. Following that, Lott moved to table both amendments. By doing this, Lott could demonstrate support for the GOP bill. A move to table it failed, 45-55, along straight party lines. *(Vote 181, p. S-37)*

However, Lott knew that the next move would erase the quandary of tying up the spending bill. The Senate voted 53-47 to kill the Democrats' bill. Because the Republican measure would amend the Democratic bill, the second vote stripped the agriculture bill of both amendments. *(Vote 182, p. S-37)*

After the two amendments were tabled, Democrats regained leverage by putting forth another health care amendment. When they adjourned for the week, the pending amendment, by Dianne Feinstein, D-Calif., would allow doctors — not health plans — to determine which treatments were medically necessary.

Such maneuvering is expected to continue the week of June 28 if the parties do not reach agreement.

House Maneuvers

In the House, a small but determined cadre of moderates is also determined to force votes on the issue. Charlie Norwood, R-Ga., insists that leaders include new legal remedies for patients and allow patients to choose their own doctors if they pay more.

Education and the Workforce Chairman Bill Goodling, R-Pa., postponed a June 24 markup when it became clear that Norwood probably had the votes to substitute his bill for an eight-bill plan (HR 2041-2047; HR 2089) promoted by Employer-Employee Relations Subcommittee Chairman John A. Boehner, R-Ohio.

A GOP aide said June 25 that Boehner was considering adding some form of liability provisions to the package.

Speaker J. Dennis Hastert, R-Ill., said June 24 that he is still "intent" on passing a bill in July. Hastert said that he expects the Education panel to approve bills the week of June 28.

"This has gone on long enough. We either need to come out with a bipartisan bill or let everybody draw their sabers," Norwood said.

Democrats were clearly pleased with the machinations. They want to force Republicans to face votes on provisions that would, among other things, give patients greater access to specialists and allow them to sue their health plans for damages.

"I don't see right now the dynamic to even get to conference," said Chip Kahn of the Health Insurance Association of America, an industry group.

The House and Senate have been proceeding on markedly different tracks. The Senate GOP bill (S 326), with tax provisions to be added, offers a range of protections but would affect fewer patients than other plans. Some parts of the Republican bill affect only the 48 million people in self-funded plans that are exempt from state regulation.

Of all the major bills, the Boehner bills would impose the smallest range of mandates on health insurers. They focus largely on issues that have lost any hint of controversy, such as ensuring that doctors can discuss all treatments with patients, even if the plan does not cover it (HR 2043), or permitting women direct access to obstetricians and gynecologists (HR 2041). Many states already have similar laws.

Conservatives such as Boehner say they are concerned about driving up the costs of health care premiums and increasing the number of uninsured Americans, now numbering 43 million.

Clinton Pushes To Salvage Partial Victory On Health Care

JULY 3 — With his impeachment acquittal five months behind him and his declaration of victory in Kosovo still fresh in the air, President Clinton is turning his focus to domestic issues. And with just 18 months left to burnish his legacy, he has placed two ambitious health care proposals atop his wish list.

Clinton won the presidency in 1992 after promising to make medical care "a right, not a privilege" and "affordable for every family." But the comprehensive overhaul of the nation's health care system that he proposed the next year — drafted under the stewardship of first lady Hillary Rodham Clinton — was widely criticized as too big, too complex and too regulatory. Congressional Democrats declared the president's effort dead 11 months later. *(1994 Almanac, p. 319)*

Now, Clinton is moving to minimize that failure by pushing hard for at least one more big health care victory to salvage part of what he sought six years ago as the signature achievement in the White House: a revamping of Medicare that would for the first time make prescription drugs a benefit for the program's 39 million elderly and disabled beneficiaries, and new regulation of the managed care plans that provide coverage to more than 150 million Americans.

By doing so, Clinton also hopes to create a strong campaign issue to help Vice President Al Gore ascend to the White House and put Democrats back in control of Congress.

"He has more than the usual presidential incentives to end with a big finish," Steven Schier, chairman of the political science department at Carleton College in Minnesota, said of Clinton's dual push on health care. "He would like to eclipse some of the sorrier parts of his record," in which the failure of the initial health care overhaul ranks with impeachment, Schier said.

At Georgetown University on June 25, Clinton declared that this summer could be a "season of progress" if Congress worked with him on an array of issues — managed care regulation and a Medicare overhaul among them. Four days later, he unveiled the details of his Medicare plan, which aims to keep the program solvent for the Baby Boom generation by making it more like private medical insurance. It won a cautious reception from Republicans at the Capitol, who are pushing their own restructuring ideas.

The same day, the Senate's two party leaders broke a legislative logjam that the Democrats had created, thwarting work on fiscal 2000 appropriations bills in a bid to force action on legislation to increase federal regulation of managed care. Under the deal, the issue will be debated starting July 12 — the day Congress is scheduled to return from its Fourth of July recess — with no restrictions on amendments but a final vote no later than July 15. The deal paved the way for passage of three spending bills.

But even as the schedule became clarified in the Senate, it became more muddied in the House, where continued disagreements among Republicans prompted the Education and the Workforce Committee to again postpone plans to mark up an eight-bill managed care plan (HR 2041-2047; HR 2089).

Each week of delay is crucial. All sides in the debate — insurers, doctors and patient advocates — agree that unless Congress acts decisively this summer, managed care will probably fall off the table for the rest of the 106th Congress. Once autumn arrives, lawmakers will be too busy with appropriations, and next year the issue seems sure to stalemate under the rhetoric of the presidential and congressional campaigns.

"This is it," said Nancey McCann, co-chairman of the Patient Access to Specialty Care Coalition, which represents 130 physician, non-physician and patient groups pushing to revamp the managed care system. "The time has come. It needs to be done now, this summer."

By contrast, it appears a final deal on Medicare would still be possible as late as next year.

Political Maneuvering

Although Medicare and managed care are two very different policy issues, they have become politically linked.

Health insurers, in their fight against efforts to place more government mandates on managed care, have spent big money in a bid to shift the legislative focus to revamp Medicare. A poll commissioned by the American Association of Health Plans (AAHP) in May concluded that key blocs of voters put an overhaul of Medicare higher on their list of priorities than changing the managed care system.

The survey, by Republican pollster Whit Ayres, found 59 percent of those 65 and older said Congress should focus on making Medicare financially sound, while only 9 percent said the top priority should be managed care. Among those 45 to 54, 37 percent said Medicare should top Congress' to-do list, compared with 18 percent who put managed care first.

"Medicare is a much more significant issue than managed care could ever dream of being," said Mark Merritt, vice president and chief of strategic planning and public affairs for the AAHP. "Medicare could well determine who controls Congress and the White House. Managed care reform doesn't have a chance of doing that."

Many in Congress agree.

Sen. John H. Chafee, R-R.I., who has introduced his own bill (S 374) to expand the rights of patients under managed care, conceded in an interview June 29 that Medicare carries more political weight. "Medicare, as far as being politically sensitive, is very much more so than health maintenance organizations," he said. "Medicare hits every senior, and therefore, every seniors' children."

For Republicans, Medicare also appears to be a sturdier political platform than managed care.

The GOP leadership has consistently fought efforts to enact more government regulations of patient care, instead favoring ways that might allow the marketplace to solve inequities or unfairness in managed care plans. That has given Democrats the upper hand politically, allowing them to score points with voters by characterizing the GOP as uncaring about consumers while doing the bidding of the insurance industry.

On Medicare, Republicans hope to turn the tables, characterizing Democrats and the White House as caring more about the welfare of wealthy seniors than poor seniors. Clinton's Medicare package would give drug coverage to all seniors, regardless of incomes, while Republicans are pushing for a plan that would give free coverage to the poor but charge an extra fee to wealthier seniors.

"Why should a bricklayer in my district pay taxes to help a wealthy senior who can already afford prescription drugs?" asked Rep. Ernie Fletcher, R-Ky., a physician. "We need to look at prescription drugs for low-income people."

Such arguments will certainly make fodder for the 2000 campaign trail, and, in the interim, give Republicans incentive to focus on Medicare and away from managed care. But that does not guarantee that Congress will clear legislation to revamp the federal government's biggest social program after Social Security. Republican distrust of the president and his plan runs deep, making it unlikely a compromise will be found in the next 18 months.

"It's about 80 to 90 percent politics, about 10 to 15 percent legacy," Senate Majority Leader Trent Lott, R-Miss., said in characterizing the president's proposal in an interview June 30. "Zero percent policy."

Managed Care

Patient advocacy groups say they still are hopeful Congress will clear a managed care overhaul this session.

"Both Medicare and managed care are so incredibly powerful," said Ron Pollack, executive director of Families USA, a patient advocacy group that supports Democratic proposals on the issue. "Republicans can take managed care off the agenda, but if they do they will find their opponents will throw it back in their faces during the elections."

The hopes of patient advocacy groups were bolstered by the June 29 agreement between Lott and Minority Leader Tom Daschle, D-S.D., on the framework for bringing managed care legislation to the floor. The deal does not specify what bill will be the basis for the debate, and Lott declined to say whether he would put forward the GOP bill (S 326) approved by the Health, Education, Labor and Pensions Committee on March 18.

There are no limits on the number of amendments that may be offered, which should allow the Democrats to offer their "patients' bill of rights" package (S 6) — either in whole or in part — as a way of forcing a series of bellwether votes on whether to give patients and their doctors more control than insurers over decisions on care. The agreement calls for a vote on final passage of whatever survives July 15. To give the GOP some leverage, the agreement allows Lott to offer the final amendment of the debate.

But that was not a sufficient sweetener for Majority Whip Don Nickles of Oklahoma, who had been a pivotal Republican negotiator on the issue. Fearing Republicans would be forced to cast a series of votes against consumers' rights, Nickles resisted any agreement that allowed unlimited amendments, fearing the votes that ensued would "be misconstrued for political purposes."

Lott hatched the agreement, however, the day after Democrats signaled that they remained almost completely united in blocking any action on pending bills absent a promise for a managed care debate. On four motions by Republicans to invoke cloture, and thereby limit debate, on appropriations measures, only a combined total of three Democratic "yes" votes were cast, thereby guaranteeing that the bills would stay stalled. *(Votes 184-187, p. S-38)*

The Senate standoff had begun the week of June 21, when Democrats stalled action in order to highlight differences with the Republicans over managed care.

"Republicans have a deep need to do two things. One: show people they are running the place and getting legislation passed. Two: get [managed care] off their agenda," said Chip Kahn, president of the Health Insurance Association of America, which strongly opposes any such legislation.

Kahn's association is working with a coalition of business and insurance groups that planned a $750,000 radio and television advertising campaign during the July Fourth recess aimed at defeating the Democrats' managed care proposals. The ads — paid for by the Health Benefits Coalition and the Business Roundtable — say those proposals would greatly increase the cost of health insurance and cause 1.5 million Americans to lose coverage.

On the other side, dozens of patient advocacy and doctors groups met July 1 to formulate their own campaign strategy for the recess. Afterward, Pollack of Families USA said members of his group would seek to make appearances on radio and TV talk shows and arrange rallies across the country.

He also said his and other groups were considering running advertising in favor of the Democratic proposals in states represented by moderate Republicans up for re-election to the Senate next year.

Among the key amendments Democrats are expected to offer, one would give doctors — rather than health plans — the right to decide what is medically necessary. Another would allow patients to sue their health plans in state court when they allege they were harmed by their insurers' decisions to deny care. Under current law, they may only sue — in federal court — to recover the cost of the denied procedure.

But Lott sounded sanguine that the agreement for floor debate gives him the leverage to nullify such amendments, even if they are initially adopted. "That will not be what passes in the end," Lott said of the Democratic liability proposal in an interview. "In the end, I have the last amendment right, and it could be a package."

House Action

Patient advocates believe there is a much better chance of passing a broad managed care overhaul on the other side of the Capitol. "I think we're stronger in the House. All of those folks have got to run for re-election next year. Only one-third of the Senate has to run," said Pollack. "To come back to the voters empty-handed will not augur well for incumbents."

Speaker J. Dennis Hastert, R-Ill., has vowed to bring a bill to the floor in July, but the continued delay in committee action on the bill suggests that could be a tough pledge to keep.

Several Republicans on the Education and the Workforce Committee, led by Charlie Norwood of Georgia, have indicated they will vote with Democrats to allow lawsuits against health plans.

Chairman Bill Goodling, R-Pa., is adamantly opposed to the liability language. Hastert, who also opposes liability, gave Goodling primary jurisdiction over the managed care package last month with the understanding that liability would not be included.

With the committee stalled, Norwood and his GOP allies in favor of the liability provision — principally Tom Coburn of Oklahoma and Greg Ganske of Iowa — are pressing the leadership to allow the bill to be marked up in the Commerce Committee, on which all three of them sit. (Norwood is a dentist, Coburn is an obstetrician and Ganske is a maxillofacial surgeon.)

Norwood said Chairman Thomas J. Bliley Jr., R-Va., has told him that he would support liability language. And Ganske said: "Staff doesn't do much without the chairman's OK, and they are working on it."

A Democratic spokesman for the Commerce Committee said GOP staff have contacted Democratic aides about working together on a bill.

At the weekly meeting of House Republicans on June 30, Ganske made his pitch for passing a managed care package. He also handed out a four-color newsletter he has published detailing the story of a 6-month-old boy denied emergency room treatment by his health maintenance organization (HMO). A picture in the newsletter shows the boy after his hands and feet were amputated because of delay in his treatment. The newsletter — which Ganske plans to send to each member of Congress — urged adoption of the liability language as a way to ensure plans are held accountable for their treatment decisions.

"I'm seeing a shift in opinion in my conference. They know the political reality," Ganske said in an interview June 30. "If they are presented with this on the floor, what are they going to do, vote for the HMO?"

Still, it is unclear whether Hastert would allow Commerce to report a bill that includes the Democrats' bid to expand patients' rights to sue.

Another possibility would be to allow the Ways and Means Health Subcommittee to mark up a patient protection package. That panel in 1997 drafted language that was ultimately signed into law (PL 105-33) that expanded protections for Medicare patients. These included a requirement that health plans pay for emergency care if a "prudent layperson" would determine a trip to the emergency room was necessary and a ban on "gag clauses," which prevent doctors from discussing treatment that was not covered by the HMO. *(1997 Almanac, p. 6-3)*

It is unclear, however, whether the subcommittee or the full Ways and Means Committee would support a liability provision.

Even if the House and Senate pass bills this summer, the ultimate fate of managed care is still very much up in the air. Language that emerges from the two chambers will likely be very different from each other, and a conference will be long and contentious.

"As far as getting it passed by Congress and signed by the president, no more than a 50-50 chance," Lott predicted when asked to assess the odds. "And that's probably pretty high."

Senate Braces For Debate, as Lott Seeks To Derail Amendments

JULY 10 — The Senate on July 12 will begin the first floor debate this year on overhauling the nation's managed health care system — a debate certain to be packed with partisan rhetoric and procedural maneuvering.

The political positioning kicked off on July 8, when Majority Leader Trent Lott, R-Miss., introduced as the base legislation the Democratic "Patients' Bill of Rights," S 6, under a new bill number, S 1344.

The move was apparently aimed at preventing Democrats from introducing numerous amendments that would force Republicans to cast politically unpopular votes against a variety of patient protection proposals.

Republicans oppose the proposals, saying they would increase federal bureaucracy in the nation's health care system, push up health insurance premiums and force millions of Americans to drop their coverage.

The maneuvering, however, fell short when Democrats quickly vowed to offer their patient protection amendments anyway. They said they may simply change a few words in the provisions so as not to duplicate the language in the underlying bill.

Democrats, who are planning a July 13 rally with President Clinton, say they may offer up to 20 amendments. Republicans also plan to offer amendments that will allow them to vote for patient protection provisions they support.

Under a unanimous consent agreement reached between the party leaders June 29, Lott has the right to offer the final amendment in the debate.

That amendment will likely be a package combining the GOP patient protection bill (S 326) — which was voted out of the Health Committee on straight party lines on March 18 — and a variety of tax provisions aimed at making it easier for Americans to buy health insurance.

That package is expected to win ultimate passage; the final vote is scheduled on July 15.

Republicans say their bill would increase premiums by eight-tenths of 1 percent, while the Democratic version would boost costs more than 6 percent.

Democrats, however, say their bill would raise costs by less than 5 percent, resulting in only a $2 per month increase for the average worker.

Democrats have attacked the Republican package as not providing enough protections for patients in managed care plans.

Among their criticisms of the GOP package is that it would provide federal protections to 48 million Americans in "self-insured" health plans — those under which an employer rather than an outside insurance company assumes all financial risk. Such plans are exempt from state regulations, including patient protections. Not covered by the GOP plan would be more than 100 million Americans who belong to "fully insured," or employer-provided managed care plans; state and local government plans; and people who buy their own insurance.

Republicans argue that federal protections are not needed for those additional managed care patients because they are already regulated by the states.

Among their amendments, Democrats propose to allow patients to sue in state court for damages if they are harmed by a plan's denial of treatment. Under current law, patients can only sue in federal court to recover the cost of the denied treatment but not for damages. The Republican package does not change current liability law.

Another Democratic amendment would prevent health insurance plans from interfering with a doctor's determination of what is "medically necessary." The Republican package contains no such provision.

Political Pressure

In hopes of putting pressure on Senate Republicans to vote for the amendments, Democrats and their allies off Capitol Hill have launched a media campaign.

The American Medical Association on July 8 began running newspaper ads across the country asking voters to call senators in support of the liability and medical necessity amendments.

Among the GOP senators targeted in the ads are Rod Grams of Minnesota, Rick Santorum of Pennsylvania, John W. Warner of Virginia and Spencer Abraham of Michigan. The ads also target two moderate Democrats, John B. Breaux and Mary L. Landrieu, both of Louisiana.

The group, which will spend more than $200,000 on the media campaign, will also begin running radio ads the week of July 12.

And Senate Democrats beginning July 12 will set up an I.C.U. — "intensive communications unit" — in the Capitol, which will run eight hours a day throughout the Senate debate. The war room will be equipped with phones, television cameras and computers linked to the Internet to allow Democratic senators to speak with local voters and news outlets about the importance of passing their Patients' Bill of Rights.

House Action

While the Senate begins its debate on managed care, House action has been stalled by disagreements within the Republican conference.

The Education and the Workforce Committee has twice canceled a markup of legislation after several Republicans on the panel threatened to vote with Democrats to adopt amendments, including language to allow lawsuits against health plans. The markup has yet to be rescheduled.

Staff aides on the Commerce Committee are now working on language that could be marked up as early as the week of July 12. Chairman Thomas J. Bliley Jr., R-Va., has indicated he will support liability language, despite opposition from Speaker J. Dennis Hastert, R-Ill.

Senate Passes GOP Plan; Battle Now Shifts to House

JULY 17 — Senate Republicans easily won the first legislative battle this year over the nation's managed health care system, but Democrats claimed a strong political victory and vowed to keep the issue alive well into next year's elections.

After four days of bitterly partisan debate, the Senate on July 15 passed a GOP bill (S 1344) that would expand protections for a limited number of Americans in managed health care plans. The measure is aimed at providing greater protections for patients in health plans not already regulated by the states, while also making health insurance more affordable.

Democrats charged that the GOP bill would fall far short of providing adequate oversight of insurance companies and leave the majority of managed care patients without any federal protections.

The final vote was 53-47, with all but two Republicans supporting the bill. Republicans John H. Chafee of Rhode Island and Peter G. Fitzgerald of Illinois voted against final passage. Senate Democrats remained unified throughout the debate, voting as a bloc for all of their amendments and against all Republican language. *(Vote 210, p. S-41)*

President Clinton vowed to veto the Republican bill if it ever comes to his desk.

"If the Republican leadership insists on passing this bill of goods — this charade — President Clinton will veto it in a minute," Vice President Al Gore said during a visit to the Senate shortly before the bill's passage. "It has zero chance of getting past his desk because it's a fraud."

Republicans said their bill struck a proper balance between improving the quality of health care and keeping costs down. "

All the consumer rights in the world don't matter an aspirin if you aren't able to become a consumer," Majority Leader Trent Lott, R-Miss., said as he wrapped up debate on the floor. "The American people don't want the federal government to take over their health care. . . . Our job is to find ways for more Americans to have broader access."

Lott said the Democratic version of the bill (S 6) would significantly drive up health insurance costs, forcing 1.8 million Americans to lose their coverage. Democrats said their language would increase costs only two dollars a month — about the price of a Big Mac — per worker.

Democrats criticized the GOP measure because most of its protections would apply only to 48 million Americans who are enrolled in health plans exempt from state regulations. Another 113 million Americans in plans that are regulated by the states would not be covered by the regulations in the bill.

Political maneuvering played heavily into the debate, with Democrats predicting that the issue will be used against Republicans in next year's elections.

During the lengthy consideration of the bill, Republicans defeated every Democratic amendment aimed at expanding the patient protections.

"I think we're going to take a majority in the Senate, and these last few days are making that easier," Democrat Harry Reid of Nevada said during a rally for his party's bill.

Prospects Uncertain

The issue now moves over to the House, which has been stalled for weeks, unable to vote a bill out of committee. A number of House Republicans — particularly a group of lawmakers who are doctors — attacked the Senate measure as inadequate and threatened to vote with Democrats on several managed care provisions, including language that would allow patients to sue their health plans for damages.

Several House Republicans — including Charlie Norwood of Georgia, Tom Coburn of Oklahoma and Greg Ganske of Iowa — have drafted compromise language they think could win the needed support to pass.

Speaker J. Dennis Hastert, R-Ill., has pledged to bring a bill to the floor before Congress' August recess.

Commerce Committee Chairman Thomas J. Bliley Jr., R-Va., has been working with ranking Democratic Rep. John D. Dingell of Michigan in an effort to write a bipartisan consensus bill.

The measure, however, would likely include language allowing patients to sue their health plans for damages — language Hastert strongly opposes.

It is unknown whether Hastert would allow such a bill on the floor or if Democratic leaders would approve of Dingell signing on to a bill sponsored by Republicans.

With House committee Republicans unable to approve a bill, leaders may decide to take the Senate-passed bill directly to the floor. But without significant changes, it is unlikely supporters could garner enough Democratic and Republican votes to pass.

Tortuous Process

The process under which the Senate debated its managed care legislation was steeped in politics. Many Hill veterans charged that it was the most convoluted they had ever witnessed.

The debate began July 12 after Republicans introduced the Democratic bill and Democrats introduced the Republican version. By doing that, each side was able to offer a long series of amendments to the other's bill in an effort to highlight its faults.

Both bills were then debated at the same time, with alternating amendments being offered to each bill.

"The debate that's going on now is one of the most partisan and the most vacuous, the most devoid of effort to try to reach a solution that I've heard in a long time — and that's saying something," said Max Baucus, D-Mont.

Throughout the debate, Republicans routinely offered their own versions of Democratic amendments that had been defeated just hours earlier. Democrats charged — and a number of Republicans privately agreed — that the maneuver was aimed at allowing Republicans to claim victory on a variety of issues originally raised by Democrats.

Even the names of the underlying bills were strikingly similar. Democrats called theirs the "Patients' Bill of Rights." Republicans called theirs the "Patients' Bill of Rights Plus."

But the underlying amendments contained sharp differences. The Republican language generally offered more limited government oversight to a fewer number of patients — in keeping with the GOP philosophy of limited government control.

Amendment by Amendment

The partisan vote on final passage of the GOP managed care bill was foreshadowed early on in the debate when the first Democratic amendment was defeated largely along party lines.

That amendment, by Charles S. Robb of Virginia, which would have allowed women in managed care plans to designate their obstetrician or gynecologist as their primary care provider, was defeated, 48-52, on July 13. Three Republicans — Chafee, Arlen Specter of Pennsylvania and John W. Warner of Virginia, whose father was a prominent gynecologist — supported the amendment. *(Vote 198, p. S-40)*

The Robb amendment also would have required doctors and their patients — rather than insurance plans — to determine the length of hospital stays after mastectomies.

It was considered the least controversial of the Democratic amendments, and after its defeat, even Democrats admitted there was little chance any of their other proposals would win enough Republican support for adoption.

The next day, Republicans offered their own version of the women's health language.

Republican Olympia J. Snowe of Maine offered a proposal that nearly mirrored the Democratic language on mastectomies. That amendment was adopted 55-45 along straight party lines. *(Vote 203, p. S-40)*

Republicans later offered another women's health amendment that included a requirement that health plans allow women to see gynecologists and obstetricians for routine care without prior authorization.

The amendment, offered by Susan Collins of Maine, also would expand access to emergency medical treatment at hospitals that were outside a patient's managed care plan, ensured "timely access" to specialty care, and allowed people with no employer-subsidized long-term care to deduct 100 percent of such costs.

That amendment was adopted 54-46, with Chafee being the only Republican to oppose it. *(Vote 207, p. S-41)*

Democrats fought the amendment because it did not guarantee direct access to specialists without prior approval from health plans and did not protect patients from having to pay additional costs to see outside specialists if they were not available within the plan's network.

Democrats also opposed the amendment because it did not allow women to designate their gynecologists as primary care providers. It simply allowed women direct access to the doctors for routine care. Under the GOP language, if a routine exam revealed abnormalities, a woman could be required to go back to her primary care provider for a referral to a specialist.

And Democrats opposed the GOP emergency care provision because it would cover only the treatment needed to stabilize a patient, but not any subsequent treatment that might be needed.

An amendment that would have required health plans to cover "post stabilization" care was defeated 47-53. Only two Republicans — Chafee and Specter — joined with Democrats in supporting the proposal, sponsored by Bob Graham, D-Fla. *(Vote 201, p. S-40)*

Republicans also defeated, 47-53, an amendment by Jeff Bingaman, D-N.M. that would have guaranteed access to specialists outside a plan's network at no added costs if that specialty care was not provided within the network. It also would have allowed chronically ill patients to designate a specialist as their primary care provider. *(Vote 205, p. S-41)*

And Republicans defeated language introduced by Democratic Sens. Bob Kerrey of Nebraska and Barbara A. Mikulski of Maryland that would have allowed patients at least 90 days of continued treatment from their own doctor if their plan changed physicians. The amendment was defeated 48-52, with Snowe, Chafee, and Specter joining with all Democrats. *(Vote 209, p. S-41)*

The biggest complaint Democrats had with all the Republican language was the number of patients that it covers. The GOP bill covers only those patients in "self insured" health plans. Such plans — in which the employer, rather than an outside health care organization, assumes all financial risk — are not regulated by state laws. There are 48 million Americans in such plans.

There are, however, 113 million other Americans who are in managed care plans that would not be covered by the GOP bill. Republicans say these patients — who include the self-employed, state government workers and those whose jobs buy insurance coverage from outside companies — are already protected by state laws and do not need additional federal oversight.

Democrats say federal regulation is needed to provide consistent and adequate patient protections to the 161 million Americans who are covered by all kinds of plans.

Democrats offered an amendment to the Republican bill that would have expanded the scope to those 161 million patients. That amendment was defeated 48-52, with Republican Sens. John McCain of Arizona, Chafee, and Specter joining all Democrats in voting for the language. *(Vote 204, p. S-40)*

"Many of our colleagues on the other side . . . [think] that we ought to just leave this up to the states," said Edward M. Kennedy of Massachusetts, a main proponent of the Democratic bill. "My response is, the law of the jungle may be good in the jungle, but we do not accept that in the United States, when people are being exploited by the private sector."

Kennedy led Democratic debate on the floor, often yelling emotionally and waving his arms. On several occasions, Republicans chided him, and Majority Whip Don Nickles, R-Okla., suggested that if he was not careful he might need help from Republican and heart surgeon Bill Frist of Tennessee.

"I am glad my colleague is sitting down. We might need Dr. Frist on the floor," Nickles — who led Republicans during the debate — said on the floor after a Kennedy tirade.

Kennedy shot back: "We couldn't see a specialist like Dr. Frist under the Republican bill."

Republican Strikes

During four days of debate, Republicans adopted a number of amendments that expanded the protections contained in their original managed care bill (S 326) that was approved by the Health committee in March.

Among the added provisions were the prohibition of "drive-through mastectomies," in which women are discharged from the hospital within hours of breast cancer surgery, and the full tax deductibility of long-term care.

The biggest swipe made by Republicans at the underlying Democratic bill eliminated a provision that would have allowed patients to sue their health plans in state court for damages if they were harmed by a plan's refusal to provide treatment. Under current law, patients can only sue in federal court for the cost of the denied care.

By a vote of 53 to 47, Republicans adopted an amendment removing the liability language from the Democratic bill. Only Specter and Fitzgerald voted with all Democrats to maintain the language. *(Vote 206, p. S-41)*

Republicans charged that if patients are allowed to collect punitive and compensatory damages, health care costs will go up and small businesses will drop coverage for their workers for fear of being sued.

Democrats argued the threat of large financial damages is needed to ensure that plans give the best possible care.

Republicans also stripped from the Democratic bill its statutory definition of what kind of treatment is "medically necessary."

Democrats defined medical necessity as "generally accepted" principles of medical practice, giving doctors — rather than health plans — final say over the specific care patients receive.

Republicans struck the medical necessity definition from the Democratic bill by a vote of 52-48, with Chafee, Fitzgerald and Spencer Abraham of Michigan joining Democrats in opposing the amendment. *(Vote 199, p. S-40)*

Instead of defining medical necessity, Republicans adopted an amendment that created a process under which patients could appeal plans' treatment decisions to independent review boards. That board could consider doctors' recommendations in handing down its decision on the appeal but would not be bound by the recommendation.

Under the Republican language, which was approved 54 to 46, a plan could be fined $10,000 if it did not comply with the review boards' decisions within a timely manner. The amendment also provided coverage for cancer patients to participate in some clinical trials and provided 90 days of continued care for patients by their doctors if their plans change physicians. Chafee was the only Republican to vote against the amendment. *(Vote 208, p. S-41)*

Another successful Republican amendment expressed the sense of the Senate that states should regulate health plans and provide full deductibility of health premiums for the self-employed. That was approved 53-47, with Specter and Chafee voting with Democrats against it. *(Vote 202, p. S-40)*

And Republicans adopted an amendment that would have prevented the Democrats' bill from being implemented even if it passed Congress and was signed by the president. The amendment placed a 1 percent cost increase cap on the bill, saying none of the provisions could be implemented if costs broke the cap or if the increased costs caused more than 100,000 people to lose their insurance.

The Congressional Budget Office estimated the Democrats' bill would increase health insurance premiums 6.1 percent over five years.

The cost cap amendment was approved 52-48, with Chafee, Specter and Fitzgerald crossing party lines to vote against it. *(Vote 200, p. S-40)*

Because Republicans were able to offer the final amendment, they wrapped up the debate with a package combining all the GOP-backed patient protections with a variety of tax incentives aimed at making health insurance more affordable.

The tax incentives included expanding the number of people who can create medical savings accounts and increasing the amount of money that could be contributed to the tax-exempt accounts.

Although the Democratic proposals were soundly defeated, party leaders vowed to revisit the issue this year and next.

"They're winning some amendments but I think we're winning the debate," said Senate Minority Leader Tom Daschle of South Dakota. "We'll come back again and again and again until this Congress passes a good patients' bill of rights."

No Interest in Compromise

In an attempt to bridge the partisan gap, a bipartisan group offered a compromise measure that would have taken provisions from both sides and tried to find middle ground on the liability issue. Chafee tried to offer the proposal as an amendment but leaders of both parties prevented it from coming to the floor.

Under Chafee's language — which he modified slightly in hopes of attracting more Republican support — patients could not sue in state court for denied care but could get expanded rewards in federal court, including pain and suffering and economic damages.

At least a half-dozen Democrats backed the Chafee plan along with Republican Specter.

"The Senate is operating on a kind of partisan autopilot, producing a bill we know the president will veto," said Democrat Joseph I. Lieberman of Connecticut, a supporter of the compromise. "What we're offering today is a 70 percent solution. It includes roughly 70 percent of all the patient protection bills virtually all members agree on."

Lieberman called the debate "a classic congressional moment. Are we going to adopt the 70 percent we agree on . . . or just leave it as it is and do nothing?"

He said he plans to offer the compromise as an amendment to future bills on the floor.

Political Maneuvering

Although leaders from both parties called for bipartisanship and asked that politics be put aside, neither appeared willing to budge from their stands.

Democrats said passing the GOP bill would actually be a step backwards from the status quo.

"It may provide a false sense of security. We don't want our fingerprints on something that is just a shell," Daschle said of the GOP package.

Democrats also were not willing to accept more limited provisions than those contained in their bill.

In the end, congressional Democrats and the Clinton administration said they would accept nothing short of their bill.

"I think the Democratic bill is the minimum," said Health and Human Services Secretary Donna E. Shalala, appearing at a Capitol rally on July 14. "There is no room for compromise between an absolute sham and a real patient bill of rights."

Democrats released a poll the night of the Senate's final vote showing that their party earned higher ratings than the GOP in the managed care debate.

The poll, conducted by the Democratic firm of Penn, Schoen and Berland Associates, showed that 54 percent of those surveyed "trust" Democrats to provide more rights for managed care patients, compared with 24 percent who trust Republicans on the issue.

House Leaders Struggle To Bridge Divisions Over Managed Care

JULY 24 — House Republican leaders are scrambling to meet a self-imposed deadline to bring managed health care legislation to the floor before Congress adjourns for its August recess.

Although the Senate passed a patient protection bill (S 1344) on July 15 largely along party lines, House action has been stalled because of jurisdictional disputes and splits within the Republican ranks.

A number of House Republicans, including a prominent group of members who are doctors, are calling for broader protections than those in the Senate bill or in measures proposed by the House GOP leadership.

Specifically, they want the House to take up language that would allow managed care patients to sue their insurance companies for damages if they were harmed by the companies' decisions to deny treatment.

They also want to give doctors — rather than insurance companies — greater say in deciding what treatment is medically necessary.

House Republican leaders said they plan to hold a special GOP conference meeting the week of July 26 to discuss the managed care issue with members. They have invited GOP senators who led the floor debate in that chamber.

"They [senators] have already gone through it," said House Republican Conference communications director Lauren Maddox. "They did a great job. They know how to address the Democratic arguments."

Among the senators who are expected to speak to House Republicans are Assistant Majority Leader Don Nickles of Oklahoma, Susan Collins of Maine and Bill Frist of Tennessee, that chamber's only doctor.

In the meantime, House Speaker J. Dennis Hastert, R-Ill., on July 20 met behind closed doors with leaders of the committees that have health care jurisdiction to emphasize his desire to move a managed care package before the targeted August recess.

The meeting, however, did not produce an agreement on how to get the stalled legislation out of the committees that have been working on the issue.

The House Education and the Workforce Subcommittee on Employer-Employee Relations marked up a package of eight bills (HR 2041-2047, HR 2089) on June 16, but a full committee markup was postponed twice.

Republican committee member and dentist Charlie Norwood of Georgia has publicly opposed the package, saying it does not go far enough in providing patient protections. He also criticized the bill for not allowing patients to sue their managed care companies for damages.

He predicted that enough committee Republicans oppose the language to kill the package.

Most managed care patients are prohibited from suing their insurance companies for damages in state court under the Employee Retirement Income Security Act of 1974 (PL 93-406), known as ERISA. The law exempts large interstate companies from state regulations governing health plans and pensions. *(1974 Almanac, p. 244)*

Insurers say the ERISA pre-emption saves time and money, and gives workers uniformity of benefits regardless of the state they live in. But the pre-emption also protects insurers from having to pay out costly punitive damage awards.

About 122.5 million workers, dependents and retirees belong to health plans governed by ERISA and are therefore limited in the damages they can recover. Patients can sue their insurance companies in federal court, but can only recover the cost of the denied treatment, not punitive or compensatory damages.

Education and the Workforce Committee Chairman Bill Goodling, R-Pa., said in an interview that although he opposes allowing patients to sue — for fear it will drive up premium costs and force patients to drop their coverage — he is open to "some sort of liability."

Several options have been discussed by House leaders, including placing caps on state court awards or expanding the remedies available in federal court to include compensatory or pain and suffering — but not punitive — damages.

"We're trying to come up with liability language that won't uninsure the millions who are insured," Goodling said. "It's a very fine line."

Racing Committees

Goodling was handed primary jurisdiction over the managed care debate during a closed-door meeting with Hastert on June 10. During that meeting, Hastert took most of the health care jurisdiction away from the Commerce Committee, which had been working for months on its own comprehensive managed care package.

Despite Hastert's edict, the Commerce Committee staff has continued to work on a broad bill that Chairman Thomas J. Bliley Jr., R-Va., hopes can win bipartisan support.

Some members say privately that they fear the two committees are almost racing each other to be the first to produce a package.

Bliley met with ranking Democratic member John D. Dingell of Michigan on July 20 in an effort to come up with a bipartisan package.

Dingell said the meeting "went generally well," but said no final agreements had been reached. "We're in an area where small differences are very important," he said.

Dingell said "almost everything" is still being negotiated, including the liability issue, which Hastert said should be handled by Education and the Workforce.

Republicans and Democrats generally disagree on such issues as who has final say over what kind of care is medically necessary and how an external appeals process should be organized to hear patient complaints about managed care decisions.

After that meeting, Bliley said he and Dingell are "making progress" and that he is "feeling better" about their talks.

Both Dingell and Bliley said they have informed their respective party leaders about the talks and have been given leadership approval.

"That's fine," House Minority Leader Richard A. Gephardt, D-Mo., said of the Dingell-Bliley talks. "We want a bill. If he can work out a bill, we're for it."

Hastert said if the committees are unable to mark up a bill soon, he may simply bring the Senate-passed bill to the House floor, but he called that strategy "a last resort." "I would prefer to use regular order," he said.

Norwood and other GOP doctors in Congress — including Reps. Tom Coburn of Oklahoma and Greg Ganske of Iowa — have said the Senate bill would not pass the House.

"If they bring the Senate bill over and allow us to amend it, they could get a rule passed," Ganske said. "But if no amendments are allowed, I don't know if they could get a rule passed."

Hastert, Bliley and others said a decision on how to proceed will likely be made early the week of July 26.

House Leaders Postpone Action Until After Recess

AUGUST 7 — Shortly after he arrived in Congress this year, Rep. Ernie Fletcher, R-Ky., was handed a spot in the limelight that is rare for a freshman. A family physician, he was chosen by House GOP leaders to be a top spokesman for their position on managed care.

But now, as Republicans scramble to overcome deep schisms within the party over the politically volatile issue, Fletcher has come to regret all the attention.

On July 27, the American Medical Association (AMA) faxed letters to every physician in Fletcher's central Kentucky district accusing him of choosing "to ignore the concerns of local patients and physicians."

"Tell him that you are his constituent and a physician or a physician's spouse, resident or medical student," the letter said. "Ask him to support real reforms."

A day after the letter went out, Fletcher was clearly no longer a spokesman for his leadership. He was reluctant to discuss the issue, and he refused to say whether he would still support the GOP package (HR 2041-2047; HR 2089) that he helped steer out of subcommittee June 16.

"It's not realistic" to discuss the package, which will likely never reach the House floor, Fletcher said. "I'm just trying to bring consensus with a focus on what's good for patients."

The pressures on Fletcher are emblematic of those facing the House GOP leadership as it tries to find a compromise in the stalemate over managed care. The GOP is caught between two powerful, longtime constituencies: doctors, who want a broad bill to increase their leverage with health maintenance organizations, and the insurance industry, which argues that new regulations will raise health care costs and increase the number of people who are uninsured.

After months of trying to sell their plan, House Republican leaders are still struggling to keep their troops in line and are scrambling for ways to avoid what could quickly turn into an embarrassing floor defeat at the hands of their own rank and file. They conceded the week of July 26 that they would not be able to bring a managed care bill to the floor before the August recess, a goal of Speaker J. Dennis Hastert, R-Ill.

Democrats and their allies, including the AMA, have vowed to continue their attack on the Republican majority and to focus on the issue in next year's campaigns. They want a broad measure that would allow doctors — not insurers — to decide which treatments are medically necessary and would allow patients to sue for damages if they are injured by health plans' coverage decisions.

Republican leaders have been pushing less strict bills they say would allow the marketplace and consumer choice to weed out health plans that do not provide adequate patient protections.

A new survey by the Kaiser Family Foundation and the Harvard School of Public Health will likely bolster the Democrats' position. The survey of nearly 2,000 doctors and nurses, released July 28, found a high level of conflict between medical professionals and health insurers, with nine out of 10 doctors reporting that health plans have denied coverage of needed services over the past two years. About three-quarters of the doctors and nurses said managed care has decreased quality of care. Health insurers played down the report, saying it did not look at the appropriateness of coverage decisions or at patient satisfaction with their health plans.

Meetings With Democrats

In a sign of growing trouble for the leadership, an increasing number of rank-and-file Republicans — led by several other House GOP doctors — have started to actively work with Democrats on the issue.

Republican Greg Ganske, a reconstructive surgeon from Iowa, met with House Democratic leader Richard A. Gephardt of Missouri twice the week of July 26, while Charlie Norwood, a Republican dentist from Georgia, held continual discussions throughout the week with John D. Dingell of Michigan, dean of the House Democrats.

Norwood and Ganske say that in their medical practices, they have seen devastating injuries caused when health plans cut corners in order to save money.

Hastert also broke his pledge to use "regular order" and move a health care bill through the committee process. Instead, on July 27 he hastily appointed a task force of subcommittee chairmen to draft a limited patients protection bill that could garner enough Republican votes to pass the House.

In contrast to the deeply divided Republican Conference — Norwood and Ganske say they have the support of 30 to 60 Republicans — House Democrats appeared unified in their legislative efforts.

Marion Berry, D-Ark., a member of the conservative Democratic "Blue Dog" caucus, said about a dozen Democrats are wavering in their support for a bill that would allow patients to sue their health plans for damages.

"I will vote with whatever my leaders put up," said Berry, who is chairman of the Blue Dogs' task force on health care. "There are not that many [Democrats] who won't."

With a united Democratic front, and a slim majority in the House, Republican leaders cannot afford to lose many of their members.

Hastert is trying to keep his troops in line, but has been unwilling to compromise his opposition to broad government regulation and expanded liability for health insurance companies.

As former chairman of the GOP health care task force that drafted a narrow package that passed the House last July by just six votes, Hastert has a personal interest in moving the bill this year and a political desire to remove the issue as a potential campaign weapon for Democrats in the 2000 elections. *(1998 Almanac, p. 14-3)*

Hastert has not only been forced to put the debate off until September, he now faces the prospect of having to use the August recess to attempt to unify his conference, a challenge that some say is impossible.

Norwood and Ganske say that if Hastert does not compromise on managed care legislation, they will sign a Democratic discharge petition in September to bring a broad patients protection bill to the floor.

"It's not easy," said Porter J. Goss, R-Fla., a Rules Committee member on the Hastert task force. The group spent 10 hours July 28 trying to piece together a package, but found themselves in a frustrating exercise of trying to balance competing, and often conflicting, demands. It became almost impossible, participants said, to write a bill that could win support from both moderates and conservatives in their conference.

"If you pick the wrong piece, you get two votes but lose four," Goss said. "We want to pick the piece where you win four votes but lose two."

Few were surprised when Republican tensions boiled over into public view the week of July 26. Norwood had bumped heads with Hastert last year over the leadership's managed care bill and only grudgingly voted for it in hopes of expanding its provisions in conference committee.

Ganske was one of 12 Republicans to vote against the GOP bill last year, and this spring he began making weekly after-hour floor speeches to call for a broad patient protection bill.

"For two years, I have argued to my own Republican leadership that the best action would be a bipartisan agreement," Ganske said in a recent interview. "Hastert's cover for months was, 'Well, you know, we'll just let the committee process do its job.' But when it became obvious that we had the votes to bring out a good bill, all of a sudden that just goes by the wayside."

Bliley-Dingell Talks Fail

In recent weeks, Ganske and Norwood had pinned their hopes for a bipartisan agreement on intense negotiations between Commerce Committee chairman Thomas J. Bliley Jr., R-Va., and committee ranking Democrat Dingell. Staff aides for the two met throughout much of July and appeared close to agreement on the most controversial of the managed care issues — allowing patients to sue their health plans for damages in state court.

Under current law, patients can only sue in federal court, where awards are limited to attorneys' fees and the cost of the denied treatment.

"They came within a gnat's blink of having an agreement," Norwood said of the Dingell-Bliley negotiations.

Earlier this year, Bliley told Norwood he would accept right-to-sue language. Norwood, in fact, said he was told the two had reached a deal on July 23. But by July 27, Bliley and Dingell declared the negotiations dead.

"It is very disappointing that the House Democrat leadership has decided to play partisan politics with the managed care issue, pulling the rug out from negotiations at the eleventh hour," Bliley said after the talks were called off. "At the last minute, Democrats insisted on including costly provisions that would significantly increase the number of uninsured Americans. This was unacceptable and ultimately the reason negotiations failed."

But Ganske, Norwood and other rebellious Republicans blame their own leadership for halting the talks.

"This was jerked out from under them," Tom Coburn, R-Okla., an obstetrician who is working with Norwood, said of the bipartisan talks. "The bill coming out of the committee was not something the [Republican leadership] wanted."

Soon after the negotiations ended, Hastert announced the creation of a task force of several subcommittee chairmen who have long opposed expanding liability. Bill Thomas, R-Calif., chairman of the House Ways and Means Health Subcommittee, is heading the task force, and he is working with Goss, Michael Bilirakis, R-Fla., chairman of the Commerce Subcommittee on Health and Environment, and John A. Boehner, R-Ohio, chairman of the Education and the Workforce Subcommittee on Employer-Employee Relations.

Although the task force members oppose language that would expose health plans to large court damages, they have not ruled out a limited liability provision. For example, they might consider expanding the awards patients could win in federal court, or capping compensatory damages.

Task force members and leadership aides say the group will try to draft a bill that borrows elements from last year's House-passed bill, and from the managed care package that passed the Senate on June 15.

The Senate plan was passed largely along party lines and stuck to the Republican philosophy of limited government. It expanded patient protections in areas such as emergency room treatment and women's health care but limited those provisions to the 48 million patients who belong to health plans that are exempt from state regulation.

Leadership aides said the House task force wants to extend the protections to an additional 113 million patients in plans that are regulated by the states.

The task force is also looking at a proposal by John Shadegg, R-Ariz., that would create a variety of tax incentives aimed at making health insurance more affordable.

Shadegg said conservative members of the Republican Conference would not likely support a broad patient protection bill if it did not contain financial breaks such as expanded medical savings accounts, tax credits to help self-insured workers buy health coverage, and association health plans to allow groups of workers to purchase insurance at lower costs.

Looking for Compromise

The task force, members say, will also likely look to legislation approved by Boehner's subcommittee on June 16. The eight-bill package would provide a limited number of expanded protections for managed care patients, including allowing a woman to see her gynecologist without first getting a referral from her primary care physician; allowing parents to choose a pediatrician as their child's primary care provider; and establishing an external review process to which patients could appeal their health plans' treatment decisions. The package, however, would not allow patients to sue plans for damages.

Soon after Hastert appointed his task force, the Republican rebels let it be known that they were negotiating with Democrats.

"I made a plea for [Democrats] to consider a bipartisan effort when we get to the floor," Ganske said of his meetings with Gephardt. "I told them it would be in the best interest for patients to do that, and it would be a politically wise move for them."

Norwood on July 28 said that he and Dingell had reached a tentative agreement on a bipartisan package and were planning to spend the next several days lobbying their respective party members to sign on.

"I'm looking for 300 good men and women," Norwood said. "I would like to go to the Speaker and say, 'Here's your opportunity to pass a good piece of legislation, but you'll have to share the credit with the Democrats.' "

Democrats said they were willing to talk but agreed with the GOP doctors that they would not compromise with Republican leaders on two issues: allowing patients to sue and letting doctors decide medical necessity.

"If I compromise on those two issues, there's no sense having a bill," Gephardt told reporters July 29. "We really shouldn't spend any time on the floor fooling around with a fraud bill."

Even if a compromise is reached, many do not believe Hastert would allow such a bill to come to the floor.

Industry Lobbyists Frustrated by Lack Of House Bill To Rally Support

AUGUST 14 — With House leaders planning to bring a managed care bill to the floor in September, business groups and the insurance industry say they have a big problem: There is no bill that they can rally support around.

As a result, industry lobbyists have focused their recess lobbying efforts against bipartisan legislation (HR 2723) that would impose broad new government regulations on managed care plans. The measure — sponsored by Reps. Charlie Norwood, R-Ga., and John D. Dingell, D-Mich. — has the solid backing of the Democratic Party and has attracted support from nearly two dozen rank-and-file Republicans.

Despite a promise to vote on a managed care bill before the August break, House Speaker J. Dennis Hastert, R-Ill., could not pull together a bill. The day Congress left for recess, the leadership hastily issued a list of health care priorities they want to put in legislation to bring to the House floor this fall.

The Senate on July 15 passed a Republican-authored managed care bill (S 1344) that included a number of patient protections, though many of them would only apply to the 48 million Americans who are in health plans that are exempt from state regulation.

With Hastert planning a House debate after the August recess, business leaders say the lack of specifics has made it difficult for them to lobby members on the issue during the August break. Lawmakers, they say, would much prefer to have a positive alternative to present to voters who are concerned about the issue.

"We don't have anything to put in front of them and make them feel comfortable," Bruce Josten, executive vice president of governmental affairs with the U.S. Chamber of Commerce, said in an interview Aug. 11.

Democrats, on the other hand, have a concrete package their members can take home over the break and sell to the voters. The Norwood-Dingell measure has 21 Republican sponsors, meaning that if most Democrats voted for it — as Democratic Leader Richard A. Gephardt of Missouri predicts — the plan would win House passage.

Liability Still an Issue

The Norwood-Dingell measure would, among other things, allow patients to sue in state courts and collect a variety of compensatory damages as well as punitive damages in some cases.

Republican leaders, the insurance industry and the business community say such a measure would give the federal government a heavy hand in the nation's health care system. Instead, they say they want to let the market work by allowing consumer choice to weed out health plans that do not provide adequate coverage.

Republicans have strongly opposed legislation that would expose health insurance companies to large court damages. The liability provisions in the Norwood-Dingell measure, they say, would cause premiums to skyrocket and millions of Americans to lose their coverage.

Shortly before Congress adjourned Aug. 6, Hastert appointed a task force of subcommittee chairmen to draft a bill that would expand protections for managed care patients and provide a variety of tax breaks aimed at making health care more affordable. Working with the task force are Republicans John Shadegg of Arizona and Tom Coburn, a doctor from Oklahoma.

Although Shadegg and Coburn say they want to produce a measure that would allow patients to sue for damages when they are harmed by health plans' coverage decisions, Hastert has been cautious on the issue of liability.

The Speaker has said he would agree to language that would allow managed care plans to be "taken to court and held accountable," but he has refused to provide details such as what types of damages they could collect.

Under current law, patients can sue in federal court when they believe they are harmed by a plan's decision to deny treatment, but they can collect only the cost of the denied care, not punitive damages — which can far exceed compensatory awards.

The issue of liability has been a key difference between the two parties' approaches to the managed care issue. The Senate-passed bill does not include liability provisions. With the details of the House leadership bill uncertain, lobbyists are unsure how to frame their arguments.

"We don't know what the Shadegg-Coburn bill will be. That's the challenge," said Josten.

Business and insurance groups, which have branded the Norwood-Dingell measure the "Dingwood" bill, are attempting to paint the measure as a trial lawyer's dream.

"Trial lawyers and liability are not the direction the health care system should go in," said John Murray, director of public affairs with the American Association of Health Plans. The group is targeting 60 House Democrats and Republicans over the recess to persuade them to oppose any bill that expands liability.

Murray declined to say how much the group will spend on lobbying, but he said it will run television ads across the country and encourage business leaders to write members of Congress. The group is also planning to have its leaders participate in radio talk shows every day in the districts of the targeted House members.

"It's important for us to be very active in grass roots over the break because we want to know where members stand on liability," Murray said. "The reality of health care outside the Beltway is very different. When members go home, they are accountable to their constituents, not special interests inside the Beltway."

Targeting Moderates

The Chamber of Commerce is also targeting 50 House Democrats and Republicans it fears will vote for the Norwood-Dingell bill.

"We've collected information on all the town hall meetings in the targeted districts and we'll make our presence known at those events," Josten said.

Among the House Republicans who have signed onto the bipartisan bill are several who voted last year for their leadership's managed care package and against the Democratic alternative that contained many of the same provisions in this year's bipartisan bill. *(1998 Almanac, p. 14-3)*

They include E. Clay Shaw Jr. and Mark Foley of Florida, Barbara Cubin of Wyoming and Christopher Shays of Connecticut.

The Chamber of Commerce is planning to target members of the Blue Dogs — a group of 30 moderate-to-conservative House Democrats. Although the Blue Dogs have formally endorsed the Norwood-Dingell bill, the Chamber hopes to persuade members to oppose the bill's liability provisions.

Shortly before the August break, Chamber President Thomas J. Donohue sent 3,000 letters via e-mail to business leaders across the country asking them to lobby their representatives on the issue.

"Business people need to help lawmakers understand that providing affordable access to basic care for the uninsured is the issue, not creating additional benefits for those who already have insurance," the letter said. "It's probably a good thing lawmakers are soon going home, where you can give them a little perspective on this issue."

The Chamber has also hired a firm to conduct "patch-through" calls. Business leaders across the country who are members of the Chamber will be given a toll-free number to call. Those callers will then be directly connected to a House member's office so they can lobby against the liability provision. The idea is to make it free and easy for Chamber members to deluge lawmakers with phone calls.

On the other side of the issue, the American Medical Association (AMA) is planning to run radio, television and print ads in late August and early September.

During the August break, the AMA is also encouraging doctors across the country to attend town hall meetings to express their support for the Norwood-Dingell bill.

"This is certainly one of the top, if not the top issue for us," AMA President Dr. Thomas R. Reardon said in an interview Aug. 10.

Lobbyists on both sides are warning House members that their votes on managed care will be remembered well into next year's election season.

"For the business community, this is and will continue to be a defining issue. If people think they can get by with a blink on this, they need to think again. There clearly will be a price to pay," Josten said.

Coburn-Shadegg Bill Puts Hastert In Predicament

SEPTEMBER 11 — Just weeks after Senate Republicans won passage of their managed care legislation, Speaker J. Dennis Hastert, R-Ill., looked to Tom Coburn, an Oklahoma physician, and John Shadegg, an Arizona lawyer, to develop a managed care bill that House leaders could support.

The defection of nearly two dozen House Republicans to a competing, bipartisan health bill (HR 2723) made it essential for House Republican leaders to provide an acceptable alternative. In an Aug. 6 statement, Hastert praised Coburn and Shadegg's outline as "yeoman's work" and pledged to bring the proposal to a floor vote this month.

But now that Shadegg and Coburn have introduced their bill (HR 2824), it appears that Republicans are dangerously close to a political meltdown on managed care. The two lawmakers to whom leaders had looked for a health care strategy instead have challenged the leadership's handling of the issue.

At a Sept. 9 news conference, Coburn said he planned to explain the "political realities . . . very carefully" to Hastert. Some backers of the bill said GOP leaders had lost control of the managed care issue and had to act quickly or suffer the consequences.

"This is an issue that can hurt us because we're not taking it seriously politically," said Rep. Lindsey Graham, R-S.C., a backer of the Coburn-Shadegg plan. "We're trying to help the Republican party come to grips with an issue that is politically ripe."

While Coburn and Shadegg say they are confident Hastert will eventually back their bill, many Republicans say they feel that their leadership is more focused on other issues, such as tax cuts and the fiscal 2000 spending bills.

If those distractions continue, the leadership could find itself under pressure from its own rank and file, Coburn said. Some Republicans are concerned about the embarrassing prospect that a rival bill sponsored by Reps. Charlie Norwood, R-Ga., John D. Dingell, D-Mich., and Greg Ganske, R-Iowa, could get enough Republican votes to win on the floor. Already that bill has won the support of 21 Republicans.

"A vast majority of members on both the Democratic and Republican side think this is a problem that needs to be fixed," Coburn said. "If leadership does not put a bill on the floor, I can assure you there will be a bill on the floor."

But even if a measure does pass, there is little time left to reconcile it with the vastly different approach taken by Senate Republicans (S 1344).

Political Pressure

In a Sept. 8 White House address to health care groups, President Clinton called on Congress to act this year.

"There are a lot of pessimists who think that nothing's going to happen here this fall, that the parties are just going to fight and maneuver and get ready for next year," he said. "I think they're wrong."

Clinton, however, is likely to veto either Republican plan because of concerns they do not provide enough protections for consumers.

Democratic presidential hopefuls Bill Bradley and Vice President Al Gore both recently included health care proposals in their campaign platforms, signaling that Democrats may see the issue as a defining one in the 2000 elections.

Some Republicans say that posturing indicates that they should seize the issue now.

"This is an issue that can hurt us because we're not taking it seriously politically," Graham said. "We're trying to help the Republican party come to grips with an issue that is politically ripe."

Shadegg and Coburn said their measure represents the middle ground between the Senate-passed measure and the more liberal Norwood-Dingell approach.

"This bill, I think, is the common ground, common sense bill," Rep. Van Hilleary, R-Tenn., said at the Sept. 9 news conference.

Coburn, Shadegg and their supporters said the bill was designed to provide both access to care and choice of doctors without opening health plans up to frivolous lawsuits.

The 1974 Employee Retirement Income Security Act (PL 93-406), known as ERISA, prevents patients from suing their health plans in state court. They can sue in federal court, but damages are generally limited to the cost of the denied treatments. *(1974 Almanac, p. 244)*

While several managed care proposals would allow patients to appeal an insurer's coverage decision, only those that exceed a $100 threshold could be appealed under the Coburn-Shadegg proposal. That threshold would be waived if the denial threatened the patient's life or health. Like the Norwood-Dingell plan, Coburn-Shadegg would permit lawsuits against insurers, while the Senate plan would not.

In the Norwood-Dingell plan, as part of the external review process, physicians would play a prominent role in determining what treatment was medically necessary for the patient. In the Senate plan, insurers would have more control over the issue. In the Coburn-Shadegg bill, the issue of medical necessity is dealt with by requiring insurers to clearly specify in their policy what they do and do not cover.

"That creates a market force — if that plan's not good enough, get another plan," Coburn said.

Legislative Strategies

Backers of the Norwood-Dingell measure say it would provide a far broader array of patient protections than the Coburn-Shadegg plan. Even if half the Republicans now on board came back into the GOP fold to support the Coburn-Shadegg measure, the Norwood-Dingell bill could still pass. The leadership has no apparent strategy for dealing with that reality, but would likely permit numerous amendments to water down the Norwood-Dingell bill.

While Hastert was silent on his view of the proposal, Coburn predicted that the bill would be backed by the House GOP brass. "I expect the leadership to be here," he said.

On Sept. 9, however, House Education and Workforce Employer-Employee Subcommittee Relations Chairman John A. Boehner, R-Ohio, and Ways and Means Health Subcommittee Chairman Bill Thomas, R-Calif., said they had "serious concerns" about the bill but declined to elaborate. Both Boehner and Thomas have worked closely with Hastert in recent months to draft a leadership bill that could pass the House.

Some employer and insurance groups also expressed reservations about the bill. In news releases distributed just outside the Coburn-Shadegg news conference, the U.S. Chamber of Commerce called the plan "misguided" because it "threatens the availability and affordability of employer-provided health benefits by expanding liability and adding costly mandates."

The Health Insurance Association of America, an industry group, said the bill's chief beneficiaries would be trial lawyers, with consumers and employers picking up the tab of increased litigation. The National Association of Manufacturers urged Congress to focus on passing a tax cut rather than a managed care bill.

Several physician groups, such as the American Academy of Family Physicians and the American Academy of Dermatology, backed the proposal.

Liability Provisions

Resolving what power, if any, patients should have to sue their health plans is a key point of dispute in the managed care debate.

Many Republicans and business groups, along with some Democrats, fear that expanding the power to sue too broadly will drive up health insurance costs and curb innovation in health care. But patients-rights groups and more liberal lawmakers say that health plans, just like physicians, should be held legally accountable for their actions.

In trying to satisfy both camps, Coburn and Shadegg developed what they describe as a "very narrow provision" for lawsuits. Individuals who believe they have suffered serious injury could sue their health plans in federal court. Critics say the federal court system is already overloaded, so patients would not be able to get timely trials.

Employers would face legal action only if they were directly part of the decision to deny health care.

The Coburn-Shadegg bill would require individuals to exhaust internal and external appeals processes before filing a lawsuit. Non-economic, or pain and suffering damages, would be capped at $250,000 or two-times the economic damages awarded. Punitive damages, allowed only in some cases, would also be capped at the greater of $250,000 or two times economic damages. Those two provisions alone would guarantee a presidential veto, since Clinton has never favored such caps. Hastert and other House leaders also may reject the liability provisions over fear that they too easily grant the right to sue.

Karen Ignagni, president and chief executive officer of the American Association of Health Plans, a trade group representing managed care insurers, said the legislative debate has focused too much on the liability issue. "I am concerned that we are hearing . . . that liability is the route to great health care," she said.

As they push for a floor vote on their bill, Coburn and Shadegg face a troubling paradox: They must win support from both the 21 Republicans who have supported the Norwood-Dingell bill and the House leadership. How do they appease both groups without losing one or the other?

Growing tensions between Coburn, Shadegg and the leadership became clear during the Sept. 9 unveiling of their bill. The sponsors had hoped for leadership backing of their plan, but Hastert was not yet on board. Shadegg said that every day, members face "intense pressure" to join the Norwood-Dingell bill, so leadership must give members an alternative to support.

Both Shadegg and Coburn believe their measure will see action. "We were promised a vote by the end of this month, and we expect to get it," Coburn said.

House Nears Vote With GOP Leaders Still in a Bind

SEPTEMBER 25 — House Republican leaders, who for weeks have delayed consideration of managed care legislation while they devise a strategy on the issue, are finding that the longer they put it off, the messier it gets.

After declaring Sept. 17 that he would bring the issue to the floor for a vote the week of Oct. 4, Speaker J. Dennis Hastert, R-Ill., has yet to define a clear strategy for unifying Republicans behind one bill.

Complicating matters, Tom Coburn, R-Okla., a physician Hastert had hoped would help GOP leaders develop managed care legislation, threatened to throw his support behind a rival bill after a tiff with the Speaker.

Also during the week of Sept. 20, a former House GOP leader, John A. Boehner of Ohio, introduced a revamped version of his managed care bill, potentially dividing the Republican ranks even further.

And doctors and business executives, two traditional Republican allies, swarmed Capitol Hill pushing contradictory views on the pending legislation.

Some House Republicans fear their leadership's inability to come up with a unifying Republican alternative will allow Democrats to continue to dominate the issue. House GOP members are feeling increased pressure to pass legislation and convince voters that Republicans have found the best way of curbing the power of managed care insurers.

Hastert, who last year headed a House leadership task force on managed care, would like to claim victory. But to do so, he must steal support from the popular bipartisan measure (HR 2723), sponsored by Reps. Charlie Norwood, R-Ga., John D. Dingell, D-Mich., and Greg Ganske, R-Iowa, that has the backing of Democrats and 21 Republicans.

Broken Alliance?

Hastert had looked to Coburn and John Shadegg, R-Ariz., to develop a bill that the leadership could endorse. But that alliance, which had been strained in recent weeks, showed signs of fracturing during the week of Sept. 20. Coburn was frustrated with Hastert's reluctance to support the bill (HR 2824). Hastert has signaled that he is uncomfortable with a provision that would allow patients to sue their health plans in federal court for damages.

In his Sept. 17 statement announcing the timetable for floor action, Hastert stressed that he wanted managed care legislation to guard against "reckless, unlimited lawsuits." Yet he must reconcile those views with demands from some Republicans to include some form of expanded liability in a managed care measure.

In an attempt to answer Hastert's concerns and win over Republicans who may be uncomfortable with the broad liability provisions in the Norwood-Dingell bill, Shadegg has been working with Republicans James C. Greenwood of Pennsylvania and Nancy L. Johnson of Connecticut to find compromise language.

Greenwood said that a "carefully crafted" provision allowing lawsuits in federal courts and imposing caps on damage awards against health plans may be the preferred middle ground.

Advocates of such an approach say that allowing lawsuits only at the federal level, rather than at the state level, as the Norwood-Dingell bill intends, would give companies one uniform standard to abide by rather than a patchwork of state laws.

But federal courts also are often tougher on plaintiffs and on average grant smaller judgments than state courts. Reflecting the Republican Congress' view that large civil suits belong in federal court, the House on Sept. 23 passed a measure (HR 1875) that would allow federal courts to decide many class action cases.

Shadegg said Republicans must include some form of liability for health plans in whatever legislation the House passes. But many employers, insurers and business groups fear that taking such action will drive up health insurance premiums and may expose employers to lawsuits. Currently, the 1974 Employee Retirement Income Security Act (PL 93-406), known as ERISA, shields many health plans from costly punitive damages.

Allowing that to continue as the GOP pushes a message of personal responsibility for welfare mothers, parents and other elements of society is simply unfair, Shadegg said. Health insurers should be responsible for their actions, Shadegg said. "It's not conservative to favor absolute immunity," he said.

Shadegg also said that the legal community will fill in gaps left by ERISA if lawmakers do not take action. "If Congress doesn't deal with the issue, the courts will," he said.

Shadegg, however, may end up pursuing his bill alone. Coburn has been talking with Norwood and Dingell about abandoning his own measure to support theirs. Norwood said it was just a matter of time until Coburn switched.

"He'll come home when he's ready," Norwood said. Coburn could not be reached for comment.

Boehner's Plan

Boehner's plan (HR 2926), introduced Sept. 23, could win the backing of members who fear other pending bills would expose employers to lawsuits from employees who feel they have been harmed by health plans' coverage decisions.

Rather than permit lawsuits in state or federal courts, Boehner's measure would rely on an external appeals process, with fines of up to $5,000 a day for plans that do not comply with the appeal panel's decision.

"It's a better idea than lawsuits because people want access to care, not access to lawsuits," Boehner said Sept. 23 during a news conference to reintroduce his bill. His original package (HR 2041-2047; HR 2089) passed the House Education and the Workforce Employer-Employee Relations Subcommittee, which Boehner heads, on June 16.

Boehner's revamped plan also includes many provisions found in other pending managed care legislation, such as permitting women to see their gynecologists without having to first obtain a referral from their primary care physicians, and requiring health plans to cover emergency medical care when a so-called prudent layperson would deem it necessary.

But the measure also contains elements that Democrats and President Clinton have rejected. They include medical savings accounts, tax-free accounts that can be used to pay for medical care, and a cap of $250,000 on medical malpractice awards.

Hastert had no comment on Boehner's bill, but House Majority Leader Dick Armey, R-Texas, said the proposal was "a good bill that does the right thing in the right way." Armey said his support did not mean that the entire leadership backing would follow. "My presence signifies my support," he said.

Boehner was not even sure if his plan would come to a floor vote: "I'm hopeful this bill will be made in order," he said. While insurers gave Boehner's plan a muted reaction, it received a warmer reception from the U.S. Chamber of Commerce. Boehner said he hoped more business groups would follow.

Continued Pressure

As House Republicans fought over how to proceed on managed care, members of the American Medical Association and members of the Business Roundtable, an association of chief executive officers, crowded members' offices, staking out opposite positions.

AMA President Dr. Thomas R. Reardon said "hundreds" of doctors were coming to Washington to push for passage of the Norwood-Dingell measure. "It's the persistent voice of physicians and patients that will move this bill," Reardon said Sept. 23.

The CEOs, however, were just as adamant that if patients were allowed to sue their health plans, the risk of big court damages would make insurance so expensive that some employers would simply drop health benefits.

How those two opposing pressures will affect floor action is unclear, as is what strategy GOP leaders will embrace on amendments.

Norwood said he fears the leadership will not allow a straight up or down vote on the bill, but rather allow numerous amendments intended to weaken the bill, in particular its provision that would allow patients to sue their health plans in state courts for damages. If the bill were amended to include some provisions Republicans favor, such as a cap on medical malpractice awards or an expansion of current law governing medical savings accounts, that could drive away Democratic support.

"We don't need to attach poison pill amendments to this," Norwood said at a Sept. 23 news conference. "We want an honest debate; we want a clean vote."

House Ways and Means Health Subcommittee Chairman Bill Thomas, R-Calif., said allowing amendments to weaken the campaign finance bill (HR 417) failed to alter the measure, which passed the House by a vote of 252-177 on Sept. 14.

Thomas argued that using the same strategy on managed care will turn the discussion from substance to gimmicks. "No one will have a lucid discussion on the merits of the bill," he said.

Lobbyists Target House Members In Home Districts

OCTOBER 2 — In a national television ad sponsored by the managed care industry, Robert A. Bonifas, a security systems company owner in Aurora, Ill., offers one of those firsthand testimonials about how proposed regulations from Washington are going to hurt the little guy.

"We work hard to give our employees health insurance," Bonifas says earnestly to the camera as he strolls through his office suite past occupied workers. "And now some politicians are bashing HMOs and adding expensive new regulations."

Like most ads of its kind, this one was aimed at a mass audience in an attempt to sway public opinion. But it also targeted a select audience of one: Speaker J. Dennis Hastert, R-Ill.

Bonifas, who is a friend and constituent of the Speaker's, served on Hastert's campaign finance committee. It is not by accident that he wound up on national television in behalf of the managed care industry.

He was recruited by The Direct Impact Co. of Alexandria, Va., a grassroots firm that specializes in identifying opinion leaders for use in lobby campaigns. Direct Impact had been hired by the American Association of Health Plans (AAHP) to find people such as Bonifas who, because of their close ties to lawmakers or stature in their districts, carry more sway than the industry's hired guns on the Hill.

"So here you had a key constituent of Hastert's on national television, saying, 'Don't do this to me,' " said Mark Merritt, AAHP's vice president and chief strategist. "It's high-tech grassroots."

The recruitment of Bonifas demonstrates how far a well-financed industry will go these days in the ever more sophisticated and aggressive business of lobbying Capitol Hill. The ad is part of an intricate, full-bore lobbying blitz leading up to an expected House showdown vote on legislation that would tighten regulations on the managed care industry.

The effort, which industry officials estimate will cost at least $10 million, involves some of the heaviest hitters inside the Beltway: on one side, the health insurance industry, allied with small employers and members of the Fortune 500-studded Business Roundtable; on the other, doctors, the American Medical Association (AMA), the Association of Trial Lawyers of America and consumer groups.

In addition to national television ads, special interests have used targeted radio and TV advertising in the districts of key lawmakers as well as full-page print advertisements in the newspapers that members read back home. The health insurance industry also has paid for polls and studies supporting its contention that the legislation will result in cost increases, expose employers who provide insurance to costly lawsuits and ultimately force companies to stop providing insurance for employees. In the most recent statistical volley, the AAHP released a survey Sept. 29 that showed HMO regulation ranked 21st on the list of issues that people consider most important, far behind Social Security, Medicare and education.

Managed care's critics point to independent polls in recent months that show the majority of Americans believe there are problems in the health care delivery system. For instance, 61 percent of respondents in a CBS News survey in July said that health maintenance organizations have impeded doctors' control over medical decisions.

Both sides have employed grassroots techniques and increasingly popular "grass-tops" strategies involving local opinion leaders like Bonifas. Washington's revolving door has been spinning, with industry groups retaining former Hill staff-cum-lobbyists who have personal contacts with members on important committees and in the leadership.

Campaign contributions are also part of the mix. The Center for Responsive Politics reported Sept. 13 that during the first six months of this year the members of the Health Benefits Coalition, a leading business group, gave more than $1.3 million in political action committee (PAC) contributions to lawmakers, more than 80 percent of it to Republicans.

For its part, the AMA PAC has given nearly $200,000 to lawmakers this year. In the last election cycle in 1997 and 1998, the doctors' PAC contributed $2.4 million, about 70 percent of that to Republicans.

One of the easiest ways for a member to raise a buck at the moment is to hold a fundraiser and invite people from both sides of the issue. A $1,000-a-head event Sept. 29 for moderate and conservative "Blue Dog" Democrats attracted representatives from the AMA, the insurance industry and hospitals.

"This is a special-interest-driven debate," lamented Rep. Lindsey Graham of South Carolina, one of 21 Republicans who have crossed party lines to support tighter controls on managed care. "If you left it up to the doctors, we do away with managed care. If you left it up to the lawyers, they would have a litigation playground where employers could be sued for just offering health benefits."

Patients' Rights

The so-called patients' rights bills pending in the House aim to give patients more leverage in dealing with managed care firms that now control about 85 percent of the employer-based health insurance market. The most contentious issue is whether patients should be allowed to sue their managed care companies if they feel they have been harmed by insurers' coverage decisions.

The issue has split the old health care coalition of 1993 and 1994, when doctors, hospitals and insurers were united against President Clinton's proposal to impose sweeping regulations on the health care delivery system. This time around, doctors are opposing insurers and have allied with their old arch enemies, the trial lawyers. The doctors, lawyers and patients' groups, such as Families USA, contend that the threat of lawsuits would make health maintenance organizations and other managed care companies accountable to patients. *(1994 Almanac, p. 319)*

The insurers, knowing they are not the most loved interest group in town, are working in the Health Benefits Coalition with employers, who, as job providers, are more apt to have the sympathy of members.

"Congress is more interested in our members than they are in us," said Chip Kahn, president of the Health Insurance Association of America (HIAA), a coalition member.

The coalition includes several politically connected groups: the AAHP, The Business Roundtable (an association of chief executive officers), the U.S. Chamber of Commerce, the National Association of Manufacturers, the National Retail Federation, the National Restaurant Association, the Healthcare Leadership Council and the BlueCross BlueShield Association.

The intensity of the lobbying campaign on both sides may wind up contributing to the death of any legislation.

The managed care lobby probably will not be able to stop a bipartisan House bill (HR 2723), cosponsored by Charlie Norwood, R-Ga., and John D. Dingell, D-Mich., from passing the House. But they have a chance of winning in conference. Even if the House enters the talks in favor of allowing patients to sue their health plans, the Senate bill (S 1344) has no such provision. And any legislation coming out of the negotiations may well have provisions likely to be vetoed by Clinton, such as caps on penalties awarded in medical malpractice lawsuits.

Ronald G. Shaiko, director of The Lobbying Institute at American University in Washington, said the managed care debate demonstrates how difficult it is for Congress to pass "macropolicies" that have consequential real world effects.

"Getting nothing to happen is a winning strategy for most organized interests," Shaiko said.

The question for lawmakers facing re-election in 2000: Is the status quo the best deal for consumers of health care? If not, some Republicans fear that their failure to take action this Congress will hurt them with voters at a time when they are hanging on to the majority by a thread.

Rep. John Cooksey, R-La., who also defied his leadership to support the Norwood-Dingell bill, said: "I'm afraid there is not nearly enough attention being paid to the needs of the patients."

HIAA's Kahn and others on the managed care side have tried to assuage those concerns with arguments that the issue will not be a make-or-break one for candidates in 2000.

"Half the problems with managed care have nothing to do with managed care," Kahn said. "They're problems of people's resentment that they sometimes have to fill out a form if they have a claim. . . . There are no people dying in the streets."

August Immobility

To date, a whole lot of effort has gone into making nothing happen.

During the August recess, lawmakers were peppered with broadcast advertising that in some cases went beyond generic blandishments. Rep. Mark Foley, R-Fla., said that a Business Roundtable radio ad in his district depicted him as a friend of trial lawyers, an idea Foley called "silly."

The trial lawyers' association leans heavily to the left and gives most of its political money to Democrats, making it a useful bugbear against Republicans, who generally view the group as litigation-happy and eager to expand, rather than limit, the use of civil suits.

"You have to do things to get people to think about it," said one top insurance industry lobbyist. "When you have subcommittee chairmen and members of the Republican establishment getting on a bill that's good for trial lawyers, who want to do nothing but put them in the minority, you have to remind people of that."

Another television ad that ran in targeted congressional districts invoked about every lawyer cliché known to the lobbying world. It opens with a scene of lawyers and politicians mixing it up in a noisy smoke-filled room on election night. An announcer says, "American trial lawyers have spent millions to elect their friends to Congress. Now it's payback time."

The ad does not mention the millions of dollars in campaign contributions by managed care companies to support their friends in Congress. It ends with five smirking men with slicked back hair, standing cross-armed in a courtroom.

Carlton Carl, spokesman for the trial lawyers' association, said the group's strategy is not to respond publicly to such attacks but to work behind the scenes to promote the Norwood-Dingell bill.

"People may not like lawyers, but they don't like insurance companies either," Carl said. "Anyone who has ever had to file a claim knows you can get screwed by an insurance company."

The lobby campaign reflects some subtle changes in grass-roots methodology.

The activation of everyday people to call or write letters advocating a point of view has been a lobbying staple since the 1993-94 debate. And it certainly is being employed in the current battle. Most of the broadcast ads used toll-free numbers allowing people to pick up the phone and immediately be patched through to their representative's office in Washington.

But equally important this time is the use of opinion leaders, who either have a pre-existing relationship with a lawmaker or, by dint of their profession or standing in a member's district, have a greater degree of influence than the average constituent.

Members of Congress say lobbying from both sides has generated a moderate level of phone calls and letters to their offices. However, activity at the "grass-tops" level has been brisk. Many lawmakers, especially Republicans who have supported the bill, report getting visits from influential county medical societies or from the business leaders in their districts.

For instance, the Business Roundtable had its president, Samuel L. Maury, pay a call on Rep. Amo Houghton, R-N.Y., a former roundtable member himself and former head of Corning, Inc. And Houghton also heard from several small businesses in his district who are members of the National Federation of Independent Business (NFIB), which is active in the coalition.

The visit had an impact. Houghton said that while he still supports the leading managed care bill, he is worried about employers' possible exposure to lawsuits. "There is a glitch in the Norwood-Dingell bill, and unless we can fix that, it's not a good bill," he said Sept. 22.

On a single day recently, Foley participated in a telephone conference call with several members of the roundtable in his district; Rep. E. Clay Shaw Jr., R-Fla., met with six local chambers of commerce; and Rep. Lincoln Diaz-Balart, R-Fla., met in his office with the head of the Florida Medical Association and its former head lobbyist, Donald "Scotty" Fraser, a friend of Diaz-Balart's from his days as a Florida state legislator.

Rep. Wayne T. Gilchrest, R-Md., said that since the beginning of August, "I've probably met with every doctor in every county."

During the week of Sept. 20, 80 industry chieftains paid visits to members of Congress, while the AMA arranged to have 300 physicians fan out on Capitol Hill to talk to House members.

Doctors have jumped into the lobbying action in a big way. Although politically active doctors have long represented a high-end grass-roots group on their own, they are asking their patients to also get involved.

The tactic has been employed at the state level but is being used for the first time by the powerful doctors' lobby in a national debate, said AMA President Dr. Thomas R. Reardon. "It has taken very little effort to get patients to call," Reardon said. "We want to let members know that patients are going to hold them accountable for these decisions."

Ex-Staff Members Lobby

The managed care debate has also brought a number of former staff members back to Capitol Hill, recruited by special interests hoping to make use of both their policy expertise and their contacts with members and their top aides. All are lobbyists who once worked the health care issue from the other side.

Kahn, who heads HIAA, is the former staff director to the Ways and Means Health Subcommittee. The AAHP is getting help from Dan Meyer, who was chief of staff to former Speaker Newt Gingrich, R-Ga. (1979-99), and is now a lobbyist with the Duberstein Group Inc.; and Ed Kutler, who was Gingrich's top health policy aide and is now a lobbyist with Clark & Weinstock Inc.

AAHP in July also hired Howard Cohen, former counsel to the Commerce Committee, who has ties to Hastert and worked with the Speaker on a leadership health care task force in the 105th Congress.

Plugged-in former aides give the coalition enviable access to congressional leaders. Before the House vote, for instance, Kahn was scheduled for meetings with Majority Leader Dick Armey, R-Texas, Ways and Means Health Subcommittee Chairman Bill Thomas, R-Calif., and John A. Boehner, R-Ohio, an influential member of the subcommittee.

The coalition, which is headed by Dan Danner, vice president of the National Federation of Independent Business, has a budget of roughly $2.5 million and is run day-to-day by Mark Isakowitz, a former top lobbyist with NFIB, now with the lobby firm Fierce & Isakowitz.

The coalition has taken a hard line against any form of liability legislation, refusing to even consider compromise options. The strategy is a calculated risk, and could backfire with lawmakers if the business groups come to be viewed as too intransigent. But it is designed to keep the pro-liability forces from going even further, especially if a conference eventually agrees to some form of liability legislation.

Rep. Graham said he believes that despite the intensive lobbying, the final bill will go further than the Senate bill, which has no liability provision at all.

"Lobbying inside the Beltway is one thing," he said. "But trying to convince the American people there is no need for HMO reform is another. If we leave this Congress with our only statement being the Senate bill, we are going to get whacked at the polls."

Norwood-Dingell Patient Protection Bill Passes House

OCTOBER 9 — Patients' rights legislation passed by the House Oct. 6 is significantly different from a Senate-passed measure, indicating a difficult conference ahead. Most of its provisions are opposed by both the House and Senate leaderships. And the White House is adamantly opposed to tax provisions that have been attached to the bill.

But, as the week of Oct. 4 showed, the politics of health care is complicated, unpredictable and dynamic. The broad patient protection bill (HR 2723) whose fate was uncertain right up until the vote on Oct. 7 ended up winning the support of almost a third of House Republicans.

Sponsors of the legislation are hoping that the sheer momentum of their victory will propel the legislation through to enactment. At a time when Democrats have tapped into voters' concerns about managed care, a stalled conference committee could make Senate Republicans vulnerable to charges of obstructionism on an issue that has wide public appeal.

But sponsors of the measure face numerous, possibly overwhelming, obstacles before their bill could become law. For starters, the measure, which passed 275-151, is completely different from its Senate counterpart (S 1344). The cornerstone of the House bill, which is cosponsored by Charlie Norwood, R-Ga., and John D. Dingell, D-Mich., is a provision that would give patients the right to sue their health plans in coverage disputes. The Senate measure has no liability provision. *(Vote 490, p. H-160)*

The House bill is also much wider than the Senate's in scope. While the Norwood-Dingell bill would apply to all 161 million Americans in private insurance plans, the Senate bill parcels out its protections. For example, the Senate provision requiring insurers to pay for emergency medical care when a prudent layperson thought it necessary would apply to 48 million patients enrolled in health plans that are exempt from state regulations.

These policy differences could be easy compared to the political ones. President Clinton and Democrats are opposed to a package of so-called access provisions (HR 2990) passed by the House on Oct. 6, which Republicans said are critical to helping the 44.3 million Americans who have no health insurance. The patient protection bill was melded with the tax provisions and sent to the conference committee as HR 2990.

The president and the Democrats also accused Republicans of not finding budget offsets for the package and charged that the GOP will be forced to use the Social Security surplus to pay for the provisions, which include tax deductions and insurance pooling arrangements. Clinton even threatened a veto should the bill reach his desk.

"I will not sign it unless its costs are fully offset by the conference committee," the president wrote in an Oct. 7 letter to House Minority Leader Richard A. Gephardt, D-Mo. Republicans said the criticisms were a sign that Democrats and Clinton were more interested in keeping managed care as a campaign issue for the 2000 election campaigns than in passing a managed care overhaul measure to help patients.

House Ways and Means Health Subcommittee Chairman Bill Thomas, R-Calif., a veteran of Capitol Hill health care wars, said trying to merge the two approaches in conference will be highly difficult. "You don't see too many crossbreeds between a Chi-

House Passes Insurance Tax Breaks, Medical Savings Accounts

OCTOBER 9 — While GOP leaders were unable to defeat patient protection legislation, they managed to put a Republican imprint on the package with a set of tax breaks designed to help Americans who have no insurance.

Over the protests of Democrats, the House on Oct. 6 passed legislation (HR 2990) that Republicans said would make health insurance more accessible to the 44.3 million Americans who now lack it. The measure passed 227-205, with five Republicans voting no and 11 Democrats supporting it. *(Vote 485, p. H-158)*

The bill, sponsored by James M. Talent, R-Mo., and John Shadegg, R-Ariz., would allow all taxpayers to establish Medical Savings Accounts (MSAs), which are tax-exempt accounts that can be used for medical expenses. It would also allow taxpayers who purchase their own health insurance to take a tax deduction equal to 100 percent of their premiums and allow the self-employed to deduct 100 percent of their premiums. Under the tax portion of the 1997 budget law (PL 105-34), the self-employed may now deduct 60 percent of their premiums. Current law would phase in the 100 percent deduction by 2003. *(1997 Almanac, p. 2-30)*

In addition, the package would allow the establishment of "HealthMarts," regional alliances of employers, insurers and health care providers (hospitals, for example) who band together to develop health insurance packages for workers who might not otherwise benefit from coverage. And it would establish "association health plans," in which church groups, trade associations and other organizations could pool resources to purchase health insurance at more affordable rates than could be purchased individually.

Democrats argued that the provisions would primarily help the healthy and wealthy and do very little for the uninsured. They also argued that the bill's Republican sponsors had not found ways to offset its estimated cost of approximately $48 billion over 10 years.

The Clinton administration strongly opposed the measure, saying in a statement that it would expand coverage for less than 1 percent of the uninsured and citing the lack of budget offsets. The statement said that the president's advisers would recommend a veto of HR 2990. However, the bill was sent to conference committee in combination with the patient protection measure (HR 2723), which Clinton strongly supports.

For months, Republicans have tried to shift the health

huahua and a Great Dane," he said.

Gephardt also acknowledged that prospects for a final bill are slim. "I'm worried that this bill goes into file 13 . . . into a conference that never ends," he said.

On a Roll

The biggest weapon Norwood and Dingell have in the fight, however, is momentum. Their ability to win the support of 68 Republicans, they say, could help them put pressure on a House-Senate conference committee to move the discussions more toward the bipartisan House bill.

"Ladies and gentlemen, we are now on top of Hamburger Hill," Norwood told supporters shortly after his victory, referring to a bloody battle 30 years ago in the Vietnam War. The metaphor was fitting for Norwood, who served as a combat medic in Vietnam after graduating from dental school.

Supporters of the Norwood-Dingell bill acknowledge that getting to the president's desk is a long shot, but as Dingell noted, the political dynamics of conference committees can be strange and unpredictable.

Senate Republicans facing tough re-election races may want political cover on the managed care issue and push Senate GOP leaders to give ground in negotiations with the House. House Republicans, not wanting to look as if they are content to pass managed care legislation and then let the issue go, may also push their leadership to find compromise.

The certainty that Democrats and Clinton will continue to use a managed care overhaul as a cornerstone of the agenda for the 2000 elections may give Republican leaders incentive to pass a law. With the centerpiece of its legislative agenda, their tax package, having failed, the GOP may want an achievement going into 2000. Democrats may agree to accept some sort of tax breaks in exchange for patient protections.

At an Oct. 7 news conference crowded with reporters as well as doctors, nurses, therapists and others representing the 300 groups that had endorsed the Norwood-Dingell bill, the legislation's two cosponsors were jubilant. Norwood was gracious, thanking House Speaker J. Dennis Hastert, R-Ill., for permitting the measure to receive a floor vote.

"The Speaker could have stopped this and you know it," he said. But moments later, Dingell likened the campaign for passage to "pushing a great wheelbarrow up a hill" because "we didn't get a great deal of help from the leadership."

While the crowd of supporters relished their victory, Dingell, the 44-year Capitol veteran who understands the lengthy battle ahead, urged restraint. "The time for rejoicing is really not here," Dingell said, telling supporters to "go back to work" to help push for a bill that Clinton would sign. "And then we'll have a wingding," he said.

Defining Issue

The defining line between the Norwood-Dingell measure and the three care debate from patient protections to the uninsured. They argued that patients' rights legislation would raise costs and cause employers to reduce health benefits or drop coverage altogether.

Their cause was helped Oct. 4 as the Census Bureau released data showing that about 44.3 million people, or nearly one in six Americans, lacked health insurance in 1998. That was an increase of about 1 million people since 1997.

"This is the only bill that we're going to consider that does anything for the uninsured," Talent said on the House floor Oct. 6.

In July, the Senate passed a bill (S 1344) that would also expand the deduction for the self-employed and the use of MSAs.

Controversy Ahead

The Senate bill does not include HealthMarts or association health plans, both Republican concepts that were included in the 1998 House-passed measure. *(1998 Almanac, p. 14-3)*

While they have support in the House, both HealthMarts and association health plans are controversial. Consumer groups say they would attract the healthiest people, forcing insurers who are required to offer coverage to accept sicker and more expensive individuals.

"What you have left in your state insurance pool is just sicker people. Premiums go up," said Judy Waxman, director of government affairs for Families USA, an advocacy group.

HealthMarts would be subject to some regulations, such as licensing and solvency requirements, but not minimum benefit mandates that other state-regulated plans must meet.

House Commerce Committee Chairman Thomas J. Bliley Jr. said that eliminating state mandates would not siphon off healthier people "because people would have a smorgasbord of choices. . . . If you want a Cadillac, you can get one. If you want a Yugo, you would be able to get it."

The issue has also divided business groups that were united against patient protection legislation. The National Federation of Independent Business applauds the concept as an alternative for its small-business members. Insurance industry officials say such pools would skim away healthier people from the universal risk pool, increasing their costs.

Critics of the insurance industry charge that opposition is also based on the idea that insurers do not want to deal with large groups of businesses pooling together to demand discounted rates, as many large corporations now do.

Also included in the bill is a proposal by Commerce Health and Environment Subcommittee Chairman Michael Bilirakis, R-Fla., to allow the expansion of provider-organized community health center networks in medically underserved areas. The bill would allow the Department of Health and Human Services to give a three-year waiver from state licensing regulations for the networks under certain circumstances.

other substitutes considered by the House during the week of Oct. 4 was liability. In many patient protection areas, such as guaranteed access to emergency care or appeals procedures, the plans were quite similar.

The fact that House Republicans were debating how patients should be allowed to sue their health plans — rather than on how to block lawsuits — was a watershed moment for the GOP, which directed its efforts to restrict rather than expand liability for industry.

A 1974 law known as the Employee Retirement Income Security Act (PL 93-406), known as ERISA, permits health plans to be sued in federal courts and damages are generally limited to the cost of denied care. *(1974 Almanac, p. 244)*

Porter J. Goss, R-Fla., whom Hastert appointed to build a GOP consensus on managed care legislation, does not favor widening health plans' liability. But including it in a leadership-backed bill (HR 2824) sponsored by Goss, John Shadegg, R-Ariz., and Tom Coburn, R-Okla., was inevitable because a large number of House Republicans wanted it.

"I know that my bill is not my first preference, but it's the best choice for the House," Goss said. It was, he said, "the middle ground of all the pieces I could get."

John A. Boehner, R-Ohio, pushed a measure (HR 2926) that would have not allowed consumers to sue their health plans. It failed 145-284, with 76 Republicans opposing their former GOP Conference chairman. Boehner, who played the role of protector of business interests in the debate, warned that widening health plans' liability would expose employers as well to costly lawsuits. *(Vote 487, p. H-160)*

"Expanding lawsuits against employer-based health plans means expanding lawsuits against employers," he said. "And if employers are exposed to lawsuits, they're going to stop providing coverage for their employees. It means millions of workers are going to lose their health insurance at the very time Congress should be working to expand access to coverage."

Opponents of ERISA changes argue that federal and state judges are interpreting the federal law to allow health plans to be sued, so Congress does not need to make sweeping changes that have unintended consequences.

"Right now, members of health plans all around the country have the right to sue if something has gone wrong in the quality area," said Karen Ignagni, president and chief executive officer of the American Association of Health Plans, a trade group representing managed care insurers.

The Dingell-Norwood bill would make the broadest changes to ERISA, widening it so that health plans could be sued in state courts over coverage disputes. Proponents said the change was necessary to make insurers accountable for their actions, and to think twice before denying needed medical care.

"Understand this: The value of the right to sue is not in the lawsuit. It is in the deterrence," Albert R. Wynn,

Key Managed Care Provisions

Patient protections bill (HR 2723) passed by the House on Oct. 7.

Issue	Provision
Scope	The bill would cover all privately insured Americans, about 161 million people.
Liability	The bill would allow patients who claimed that they had been physically or mentally injured when wrongly denied care by their health plans to sue in state court for damages. Plans that had complied with the decision of an independent, external reviewer would not be subject to punitive damages, and any state caps on damages would apply. Employers could not be sued unless they made a decision on a benefits claim.
Emergency Care	Health plans that covered emergency room care would be required to pay for it without prior approval if a "prudent layperson" would deem it necessary. The patient could seek care at any hospital. The care would include medical screenings as well as any treatment needed to stabilize the patient's health.
Gag Rules	The bill would bar plans from restricting what a doctor could tell a patient about treatment options. Even if a treatment was not covered by a plan, medical professionals could not be prevented from discussing that option.
Internal Appeals	Plans would be required to respond within 14 days (with a possible14-day extension) to a patient's internal appeal of a denial of coverage, and within 72 hours in urgent cases. The reviewer would be chosen by the plan but could not have made the initial denial. If the decision involved medical judgment, the reviewer would have to be a doctor. Any patient whose internal review was rejected could appeal to an independent reviewer.
External Appeals	Any patient whose internal appeal was rejected could appeal to an independent, external reviewer who would have to issue a binding, final decision within 72 hours in case of an emergency or 21 days otherwise. Penalties could include federal court action such as civil fines of up to $1,000 per day. Plan officials who repeatedly violated external review decisions could be fined up to $500,000.
Medical Necessity	The bill would guarantee that doctors, not health plan officials, determined what treatment was medically necessary. Patients could appeal a decision that found a treatment medically unnecessary or experimental.
Women's Health	Women in plans that covered obstetrical and gynecological care would be able to visit ob/gyns without going through a "gatekeeper" primary care physician.
Access to Specialists	The bill would require plans that cover specialty care to provide referrals for such care when needed, including treatment by out-of-network providers if no appropriate specialist was available in the network. Parents could designate pediatricians as primary care doctors for their children. Patients with ongoing special conditions would have continued access to their specialists for up to 90 days after a health plan dropped that specialist for reasons other than fraud or failure to meet quality standards. In cases such as pregnancy, scheduled surgery or terminal illness, patients could see the doctor throughout the duration of the experience.
"Whistleblower" Protections	Medical professionals who reported any actions by a plan affecting quality of care for patients would be protected. No health plan could retaliate against a protected health care professional who disclosed health plan abuses to a regulatory agency or other oversight officials.
Choice of Plans	The bill would permit patients to choose a point-of-service option if their health plan did not offer access to non-network providers. The patient could pay additional costs associated with this option.

D-Md., said during floor debate Oct. 6. "Because when HMOs understand that they can be sued, they have a strong deterrent to provide . . . the best quality of health care."

The proposal Goss and other leadership members advocated was a revised version of legislation first proposed by Coburn and Shadegg. Fine-tuning by Goss, Thomas and James C. Greenwood, R-Pa., broadened the bill's liability provision to allow lawsuits in both federal and state courts, if states had their own laws to allow such lawsuits, as in Texas and California, for example.

While the measure would have permitted lawsuits in federal courts, patients would first have had to meet a tougher test than in the Norwood-Dingell bill, proving to a third party that they had been injured.

Despite Hastert's assessment just before the vote that the Coburn-Shadegg bill was "an excellent product," it failed 193-238, with 29 Republicans opposing it. Coburn, who had been at odds with Hastert over his reluctance to embrace the bill earlier, said political dynamics played a part in the bill's defeat. *(Vote 488, p. H-160)*

"Party politics is what's driving this," Coburn said just after the vote. "The House is going to pass a bill that protects patients, even if it's a poor one."

Another liability proposal from Republicans Amo Houghton of New York and Lindsey Graham of South Carolina would have allowed individuals to sue in federal court, or, if they chose, select binding arbitration. Like the Goss-Coburn-Shadegg measure, the Houghton-Graham bill would have capped damages. The measure failed on a 160-269 vote. *(Vote 489, p. H-160)*

Industry Opposition

Business and insurance groups that had battled both expanding liability for health plans and giving the federal government power to regulate health plans pledged to continue their opposition. Those efforts will be pushed with a renewed vigor in light of the large number of House Republicans voting for the Dingell-Norwood bill.

Ignagni, for instance, lingered outside the hallway of the news conference where Norwood, Dingell, Greg Ganske, R-Iowa, and dozens of their supporters talked with reporters about their victory. As the event ended, Ignagni greeted reporters as they trailed out, ready to give her view of the day's events.

The group launched a new television ad campaign Oct. 6 to continue their message that the Norwood-Dingell bill's liability provisions would benefit trial lawyers more than patients. The ad uses an old lawyer cliché —swimming sharks — to stress the point.

The spot features a shark mouth open, inching toward the camera then jumping out of the water to devour bait. An announcer urges viewers to call Congress and "tell them to protect your family's health care from the trial lawyers' feeding frenzy."

Another insurance trade group executive, Chip Kahn, president of the Health Insurance Association of America, issued a memo to members calling the Norwood-Dingell vote "not a good day for the home team."

Kahn, a former Capitol Hill staff aide, told his membership — the chairmen, presidents and chief executive officers of insurance companies — that politics paid a key part in the outcome.

"That the national elections are a mere 13 months away of course played a part in this result," Kahn wrote. The group is now examining its "policy and communications strategy" after the House vote and will "prepare for the next phase of activity."

Seeking Middle Ground

It is unclear when conferees will be appointed for a joint House-Senate conference to merge the two bills, but GOP leaders in both chambers said they wanted to convene a conference.

Ganske said the fact that his bill won 275 votes is a sign that there is enough bipartisan support to push for a bill to send to Clinton.

"Once in a while, when it's a really important issue, we can come together to address the needs of our constituents," Ganske said. Goss said Hastert wants a conference to convene quickly and Senate Republican leaders echoed that sentiment after the vote.

Boehner said he would be surprised if Congress could produce anything that Clinton would sign because "it's beyond my imagination that both sides of Congress would support" the liability provisions of the Norwood-Dingell bill.

Greenwood, a co-author of the revised Coburn-Shadegg bill, predicted their liability provision would be the one that comes out of the conference.

"We've established middle ground and I think the center will hold," Greenwood said.

Senate Democrats, including Edward M. Kennedy of Massachusetts, said they welcomed a second crack at the issue. The Senate GOP bill passed along party lines, 53-47, on July 15.

Kennedy and other Democrats want to strip the tax and insurance provisions in the conference bill, arguing that they are not paid for and will not benefit the uninsured.

Republicans want to revive the tax measures that were part of the tax bill (HR 2488) that Clinton vetoed Sept. 23. Medical savings accounts, tax-exempt accounts used for medical expenses, are backed by GOP members in both chambers but strongly opposed by Democrats, guaranteeing a conference showdown.

Hastert's Choice Of Conferees Diminishes Chances For House Bill

NOVEMBER 6 — House Speaker J. Dennis Hastert's appointment of managed care conferees Nov. 3 gives sponsors of a broad patient protection bill little hope that the conference committee will produce a bill that resembles the one passed by the House last month.

Of the 13 Republican conferees, only one voted for the House-passed bill (HR 2990). Democrats and some Republicans said Hastert's appointments represented an attempt to sabotage efforts to send sweeping patients' rights legislation to President Clinton.

The appointees did not include Charlie Norwood, a Georgia dentist who was the leading Republican cosponsor of the bill. Norwood declined an offer from Democrats to sit on their side, saying he would be better able to "continue my outspokenness" if he did not serve as a Democratic conferee.

Greg Ganske of Iowa, another chief

Republican sponsor, also was excluded. And he was furious as he looked at the list of conferees.

"Is that stacking the deck, is that trying to subvert the will of the House, or what?" he said in an interview.

Proponents of the managed care bill hope the conferees will abide by a "motion to instruct" that the House passed, 257-167, Nov. 3. *(Vote 558, p. H-182)*

The motion states that House conferees should "insist" on provisions included in HR 2990 and guarantee that they are "paid for." But motions to instruct are non-binding, and conference committees often ignore them.

The bill would impose new regulations on managed care companies to give patients better access to specialists and emergency medical care and greater opportunities to appeal denials of care. Patients also would be able to sue their health plans in state courts for damages, a provision the Senate leadership strongly opposes.

Norwood urged the GOP conferees to fight for his bill. "Our party has no credibility on HMO reform . . . but that fact can and should change if our conferees act with courage to enforce the will of this House," he said.

Ganske said the best recourse for advocates of the broad managed care bill may be to look beyond the House-Senate conference and make their case directly to the public. The fact that the majority of conferees Hastert appointed voted against the bill means supporters will be able to "take the debate outside the [conference] room," Ganske said. "I've always thought the prospects will get better as we get further into 2000. The political heat will build and build."

Political Risks

In a floor speech Nov. 3, Ganske suggested Hastert was making a politically risky move. "Your leadership rests on a small majority, and that rests on respect," he told Hastert. By denying Ganske and Norwood a spot on the conference, Ganske said Hastert was "endangering that respect."

John D. Dingell of Michigan, the leading Democratic cosponsor of the bill, which passed the House, 275-151, on Oct. 7 — with the support of 68 Republicans — said he saw "no reason to protest" the GOP's conferee list. But he said he will "remind" them that they should abide by the motion to instruct.

Sen. Edward M. Kennedy, D-Mass., said Hastert's choices signaled that the GOP leadership "intends to work hand in hand with the insurance industry to block HMO reform as much as possible."

In a statement, Hastert said he followed the procedure of "regular order" by appointing chairmen and members of committees with jurisdiction over health issues. He called his nominees were "fair-minded people that represent and understand the complexities of this issue and who also understand the importance of enacting a law to protect patients." Hastert said he planned to work with the Senate to send Clinton "a bill he should sign."

It is likely that the conferees will not get to work in earnest until next year. Senate conferees were appointed Oct. 15.

Some of the appointees were unexpected. Government Reform Committee Chairman Dan Burton of Indiana, known more for his attacks on Clinton than for health care, is a conferee. So is Government Reform Civil Service Subcommittee Chairman Joe Scarborough of Florida, who has been absent on medical leave since September and was absent when the House voted. Scarborough, who has had back surgery, may return the week of Nov. 8.

Commerce Health and Environment Subcommittee Chairman Michael Bilirakis of Florida is the only Republican conferee who voted for HR 2990.

In addition to liability, there are other major differences. For example, the House bill would apply to all 161 million Americans in private insurance plans, while the Senate bill would apply different provisions to different groups. ◆

Lawmakers Prescribe Partial Relief For Medicare Providers

SUMMARY

With overwhelming support, Congress cleared as part of the catch-all spending bill (HR 3194) legislation that would increase payment rates for Medicare providers.

All year, health care providers complained that payments set in the 1997 Balanced Budget Act (PL 105-33) are too low. Since estimates show that Medicare spending is much lower than expected, lawmakers had no trouble justifying the $16 billion, five-year cost ($27 billion over 10 years) of the relief package. The "givebacks" bill (HR 3426) is intended to help hospitals, nursing homes, rehabilitation therapists, managed care plans, home health agencies and other providers.

The measure does not address any of the underlying problems associated with Medicare, which faces insolvency by about 2015. Negotiators expressed hope that the system could be restructured soon, but many lawmakers predict a couple more years of incremental tinkering before Medicare will be overhauled. Lawmakers said the estimated cost of $1.2 billion in fiscal 2000 would come from the non-Social Security surplus.

The Office of Management and Budget estimates that the measure would cost about $12.4 billion over five years because it would not count the cost of a provision to erase a scheduled 5.7 percent cut for hospital outpatient departments. Lawmakers insisted they never intended to make that cut, which they blamed on a drafting error in the budget law. That provision alone, by Congressional Budget Office estimates, would cost about $3.9 billion over five years.

The following groups would be helped by the bill:

- **Teaching hospitals.** Teaching hospitals would benefit in several ways. Hospitals would receive a boost in payments for the indirect costs of medical education, such as additional tests that physicians-in-training might order. Under the current schedule, Medicare would pay hospitals 6 percent in fiscal 2000 extra payments for every level of increase in the ratio of trainees to patients. But under the bill, hospitals would get 6.5 percent in additional payments in 2000, 6.25 percent in 2001 and 5.5 percent in later years. Teaching hospitals also would benefit from a freeze of cuts in disproportionate share payments, which help shoulder the costs of treating low-income patients. In the current system, these payments were to be reduced by 3 percent in fiscal 2000, 4 percent in 2001, and 5 percent in 2002. The agreement would freeze the cut at 3 percent in 2001 and shift to 4 percent in 2002.
- **Home health agencies.** At a cost of about $1.3 billion over five years, agencies would get a delay in a 15 percent cut scheduled for Oct. 1, 2000. The new time frame would delay the cut until a year after a new system takes effect.
- **Skilled nursing facilities.** The bill would provide about $2.1 billion over five years for skilled-nursing homes. The measure would temporarily increase daily payment rates by 20 percent for 15 categories of high-cost patients. The extra payments would be available between April 1, 2000, and Oct. 1, 2000. In fiscal years 2001 and 2002 the overall rate also would rise by an additional 4 percent annually.
- **Therapy caps.** For two years, caps for outpatient rehabilitation therapy that were set in the 1997 law would be lifted at a cost of $600 million. Those two caps limited costs for physical and speech therapy to $1,500 and for occupational therapy to $1,500. The Health and Human Services secretary is required by January 2001 to recommend a new payment policy.
- **Managed care plans.** Insurers would receive about $4.8 billion over five years, including increases that plans receive indirectly because payments are affected by fee-for-service rates. Plans won a more gradual phase-in to a new "risk adjustment" system that would pay less for patients with relatively healthy enrollees. The measure also would provide a bonus payment for managed care plans that agree to serve counties that are not currently covered by a Medicare managed care plan. Lawmakers are concerned because many plans have refused to offer coverage in low-paying areas of the nation. So the bill would offer a 5 percent bonus in the first year for insurers that opened service in an area without a Medicare managed care plan. In the second year of serving a previously uncovered county, plans would get a 3 percent bonus. Currently, about 17 percent of Medicare beneficiaries use managed care plans instead of the traditional fee-for-service plans.

BoxScore

- **Bill:** HR 3426 (incorporated in HR 3194) — PL 106-113
- **Legislative action: House** approved the first version of the bill (HR 3075 —H Rept 106-436, Part I), 388-25, on Nov. 5.

House adopted the conference report on HR 3194 (H Rept 106-479), incorporating HR 3426, 296-135, on Nov. 18.

Senate cleared HR 3194, 74-24, on Nov. 19.

President signed HR 3194 on Nov. 29.

Bills Advance To Rescind Some Medicare Cuts

OCTOBER 16 — House and Senate lawmakers are moving forward on legislation to give hospitals, nursing homes and other health care providers relief from provisions of the 1997 balanced-budget act (PL 105-33) that cut payments more drastically than expected.

For months, health care providers and senior citizens have pushed lawmakers to revisit the landmark law, which mandated the greatest change to Medicare since it was created in 1965. Medicare is the federal health insurance program for elderly and disabled Americans. *(1997 Almanac, p. 2-52)*

The House Ways and Means Health Subcommittee on Oct. 15 approved by voice vote a plan (HR 3075) that would restore about $9.4 billion in funds over the next five years. The package also assumes that the Clinton administration will make regulatory changes that will result in $5.6 billion of additional funding, primarily for hospital outpatient departments.

"After all, both Congress and the president worked together to enact this historic legislation. It's only right that we now work together to refine it," said subcommittee Chairman Bill Thomas, R-Calif.

Separately, during the week of Oct. 11, Senate Finance Committee Chairman William V. Roth Jr., R-Del., and Daniel Patrick Moynihan of New York, the panel's ranking Democrat, worked on a package that would boost Medicare spending by $9.7 billion over five years.

The committee is tentatively scheduled to mark up the bill on Oct. 20.

While the House and Senate approaches differ somewhat, both steer clear of any major revisions, such as covering prescription drugs in Medicare's fee-for-service plan. They would instead target funds to hospitals, managed care plans and home health agencies.

The 1997 budget law was expected to reduce Medicare outlays by $112 billion over five years. Instead, it has cut nearly twice that from the program — primarily by limiting payments to a wide range of health care providers, including hospitals, nursing homes, physical therapists, home health agencies and managed care plans. They and senior citizens' groups have been lobbying lawmakers to address the issue this year.

Funding Issues

Over the next five years, Thomas' package would result in an additional $3 billion to hospitals, $1.3 billion to managed care insurers, $1.3 billion to home health care agencies and $1.8 billion to skilled nursing facilities.

It would also revise therapy caps in current law. Beneficiaries now must abide by a cap of $1,500 on outpatient physical and speech therapy for each facility they use, and a separate $1,500 cap on occupational therapy. The Thomas bill would create separate $1,500 caps for physical therapy and speech therapy, meaning there would be three caps. Rehabilitation providers could exempt 1 percent of their highest-cost cases from the caps for two years.

In addition, home health agencies would benefit from the delay of a 15 percent across-the-board payment cut, currently scheduled to go into effect Oct. 1, 2000. Thomas' plan would delay that for one year after a prospective payment system for home health agencies was implemented.

Financing for the package would come from the non-Social Security surplus, Thomas said. While funds are tight, he said, the GOP leadership has promised him funding that includes about $600 million for fiscal 2000.

Thomas expects that his measure will win bipartisan support and easily pass the House because lawmakers are eager to resolve constituents' complaints about the budget law.

At the Oct. 15 markup, Thomas asked subcommittee members to withhold their amendments until the full Ways and Means Committee considers the bill, probably during the week of Oct. 18. But Thomas said the package could go directly to the House floor.

Pete Stark, D-Calif., said Democrats were concerned that the bill has not been paid for and that it does nothing to boost the budget of the Health Care Financing Administration, the agency that administers Medicare and Medicaid, the federal health insurance program for the poor and disabled.

Senate Bill

Like the House bill, the Senate plan would increase payments to managed care plans, hospitals and home health agencies. According to cost estimates from the Congressional Budget Office, the Roth plan would provide $1.7 billion over five years for managed care plans in the Medicare+Choice program and $1.3 billion for home health agencies. Medicare+Choice is a program created by the budget law to expand managed care in Medicare.

The per-patient caps for occupational and physical rehabilitation therapy would be combined into a unified $3,500-per-patient cap. Hospital outpatient centers would get approximately $1.2 billion over five years under the Roth plan, with another $1.8 billion for teaching hospitals and about $400 million for other types of hospitals.

House, Senate Panels OK Bills; Democrats Object To Funding

OCTOBER 23 — Republicans on Oct. 21 advanced their proposals to reverse some of the payment reductions made to hospitals, nursing homes and other health care providers in the 1997 balanced-budget law. But the measures face opposition from Democrats and President Clinton, who say the revisions are not properly financed.

The Senate Finance Committee moved a draft measure that would cost approximately $15.4 billion over 10 years. The bill, sponsored by panel Chairman William V. Roth Jr., R-Del., was approved by voice vote.

The House Ways and Means Committee approved, 26-11, a bill (HR 3075) sponsored by Bill Thomas, R-Calif., that would increase payments by $17.2 billion. Democrats John Tanner of Tennessee, Richard E. Neal of Massachusetts, Benjamin L. Cardin of Maryland and Gerald D. Kleczka of Wisconsin voted with Republicans to approve the bill.

While the president and most Democrats favor many of the provisions in the House and Senate proposals, they argue the plans would take money from the Social Security surplus and hasten by one year the insolvency of the Medicare Part A trust fund, which pays hospital costs. Medicare is the federal health insurance program for elderly and disabled Americans. Its Part A trust fund is expected to become insolvent in 2015.

In an Oct. 19 letter to Roth, the president said he is eager to correct the "unintended consequences" of the

1997 budget law. The law was designed to curb spending in some of Medicare's fastest growing areas, such as hospital care, home health services and physical therapy. But the cuts have reduced Medicare outlays nearly double the expected amount. *(1997 Almanac, p. 2-52)*

Clinton also agreed to implement a series of regulatory changes that would result in $5.6 billion of additional Medicare funding, primarily for hospital outpatient departments. But he stressed that any plan "should be paid for and not undermine the solvency of the Medicare Trust Fund."

During both markups, Democrats cited an Oct. 20 memorandum from the Health Care Financing Administration (HCFA) to support their argument that the bill would take a year off the life of the Part A trust fund. HCFA administers the Medicare program.

The dispute over funding may slow the progress of measures to increase payments to the providers in the Medicare program, but it is unlikely to derail action. Members of both parties are under pressure from senior citizens' groups and health care providers to quickly pass legislation easing some of those cuts.

The House may act on the Thomas bill during the week of Oct. 25. The timetable for action on the Senate measure is unclear.

Separately, the House Commerce Committee may consider a Medicare payment proposal during the week of Oct. 25. The committee has jurisdiction over some parts of the Medicare program.

House Bill

After complaints from hospitals, Thomas, chairman of the House Ways and Means Health Subcommittee, revised his package before the markup to freeze for one year a cut in payments to hospitals that treat a large number of uninsured patients.

John Lewis, D-Ga., said he hoped those payments, known as "disproportionate share" payments, would increase, but Thomas said that should only occur as part of a larger debate about overhauling the Medicare program.

Thomas also incorporated a provision that would guarantee that Medicare beneficiaries' payments for hospital outpatient services would not exceed the Part A deductible, which is $768 a year.

In addition, the revised language would increase the mandated minimum reimbursement rate for pap smears to $14.60 from the current rate of $7.15.

Despite nearly a dozen attempts to change the package, Democrats failed to amend the bill during a seven-hour markup that was interrupted frequently by floor votes.

In a nod to Democrats, Thomas said he would work with Karen L. Thurman, D-Fla., to increase Medicare's coverage of immunosuppressive drugs that are necessary after an organ transplant.

But another attempt by Thurman to broaden the bill failed. She and Rep. Lloyd Doggett, D-Texas, offered an amendment that would have required prescription drugmakers to charge Medicare beneficiaries either the lowest negotiated price paid by the federal government or the best price offered to private-sector businesses. The amendment failed, 15-22.

Ways and Means Democrats, like their Senate Finance counterparts, accused Republicans of using the Social Security surplus to pay for the bill.

Pete Stark, D-Calif., offered a package of Medicare administrative changes and payment reductions to providers as a way to finance the package, but his amendment failed along party lines, 15-22.

Cardin unsuccessfully tried to prevent managed care companies that qualified for a bonus payment program in Medicare from coming into an area just to receive the bonus payment then leaving. Cardin's amendment, which would have required companies to stay for two years, failed by voice vote.

Several other Democratic amendments were offered, then withdrawn, including a proposal from Sander M. Levin, D-Mich., that would have postponed for a second year a scheduled 15 percent payment cut for home health care providers.

Senate Plan

The Senate Finance Committee's markup had far fewer fireworks than the Ways and Means session, mostly because Finance members resolved their disputes behind closed doors before the meeting. Democrats, including Daniel Patrick Moynihan of New York, were generally supportive of the measure.

Roth's package includes slightly more than $2 billion for managed care plans in the Medicare+Choice program and $1.5 billion for home health providers. Medicare+ Choice is a program created by the budget law to expand managed care in Medicare.

Hospitals would receive $4 billion in additional payments under Roth's plan, while skilled nursing facilities would receive another $2 billion.

Like the House bill, the Senate plan would freeze the disproportionate share payments to hospitals for one year. Both bills also would delay for one year a scheduled 15 percent payment reduction to home health providers and would increase payments to skilled nursing facilities.

The Senate bill would increase the mandated minimum reimbursement rate for pap smears but do so only for two years. It also would freeze for two years the current $1,500 caps on outpatient physical and speech therapy and occupational therapy, requiring the Health and Human Services secretary to study the system and recommend payment alternatives.

The House bill would create separate $1,500 caps for physical therapy and speech therapy, meaning there would be three caps. It would also allow the secretary to distribute additional payments to the most expensive 1 percent of cases.

Bob Graham, D-Fla., offered a series of offsets to finance Roth's package, but Roth ruled that the amendment was not germane, and panel members, voting 14-5, upheld his decision.

Who Goes First?

Kent Conrad, D-N.D., said the committee's refusal to allow a vote on Graham's amendment meant both parties were headed toward spending part of the Social Security surplus after promising they would not.

"We are about to do exactly what we say we will not do," Conrad said.

Republicans in both chambers said the proposals would be financed by the budget surplus and the additional money from lower-than-expected spending increases in Medicare.

Graham also tried to amend the package to allow HCFA to engage in competitive bidding to reduce what the program spends on items such as durable medical equipment. Both Democrats and Republicans said the proposal should wait until next year when Congress once again considers a possible overhaul of Medicare.

"These changes can't be adopted in a vacuum," said John B. Breaux, D-La., who along with Thomas co-chaired a bipartisan commission charged with strengthening Medicare for future generations. The panel disbanded after failing to win the needed supermajority vote for an overhaul plan.

Thomas suggested the House measure would be the likely vehicle for final action. "It's imperative that we put together a package and deal with this issue, because the chances that others will are reasonably slim," he said.

Senate GOP leaders are hesitant to bring a stand-alone Medicare bill to the floor because they are concerned Democrats will see it as a way to achieve other health care priorities, such as a prescription drug benefit in Medicare or legislation to give consumers more power with their health plans.

Senate Majority Whip Don Nickles, R-Okla., a member of the Finance panel, has said that the Medicare givebacks might have to be rolled into a year-end omnibus tax and spending package to protect it from amendments on the Senate floor.

House Passes Bill To Rescind Cuts; Priority Treatment Likely in Senate

NOVEMBER 6 — The House on Nov. 5 passed legislation (HR 3075) that would increase Medicare payments to hospitals, nursing homes and managed care companies, reversing some cuts in the 1997 balanced-budget law that have caused an outcry from health care providers nationwide.

The bill, which passed 388-25, would cost $11.8 billion over five years. It was slightly more generous than a bill approved by the House Ways and Means Committee on Oct. 21. *(Vote 573, p. H-186)*

The bill would increase Medicare payments to hospitals, managed care insurers, and skilled nursing facilities. It also would postpone a 15 percent across-the-board cut in payments to home health care agencies and create new caps for therapy services. These and some other providers have been lobbying Congress to restore some of the funds cut under the 1997 law (PL 105-33), which was designed to curb spending in some of Medicare's fastest growing areas.

But the cuts have reduced Medicare outlays by nearly twice the expected amount. Lower-than-expected Medicare spending also has lessened the need for the reductions. Medicare is the federal health program for 39 million elderly and disabled Americans. *(1997 Almanac, p. 2-52)*

The House action was taken under a suspension of the House rules, meaning members were not allowed to amend the package. That angered Democrats who had wanted to offer several amendments. For example, they wanted to provide about $2.7 billion over five years to teaching and rural hospitals, skilled nursing homes, and home health agencies. Democrats also had hoped to offer an amendment they said would have reduced drug prices for seniors by as much as 40 percent.

Charles B. Rangel of New York, the ranking Democrat on the House Ways and Means Committee, was furious that the Medicare bill was not open to amendment.

"It's almost an insult to take a bill of this importance and put it on the suspension calendar," which is usually reserved for non-controversial legislation, Rangel said during floor debate.

Knowing they had no chance to amend the bill — and that they would probably vote for it anyway — Democrats used their 20 minutes of floor time to criticize the package because it did not include a Medicare prescription drug benefit. Democrats and President Clinton have signaled that they will aggressively pursue a plan to broaden Medicare to cover prescription drugs next year. About 17 percent of Medicare's beneficiaries receive drug coverage as part of Medicare's managed care program.

Ways and Means Health Subcommittee Chairman Bill Thomas, R-Calif., the chief sponsor of the measure, described his bill as a "very narrow, very shallow canoe that cannot support" the weighty issue of prescription drugs.

The bill also came under fire for a new hospital payment formula that some members said would hurt hospitals in their districts. Democrat Eliot L. Engel of New York said the change would shift millions in direct graduate medical education payments from his district to hospitals in Thomas' district. Jack Kingston, R-Ga., also said the new formula would hurt hospitals in his district.

Some Democrats, including John D. Dingell of Michigan, also said the bill was rushed to the floor, is not properly paid for and would jeopardize the Medicare Part A trust fund, which pays for hospital costs. Thomas said the bill is financed with money from the non-Social Security surplus.

Senate Outlook

In the Senate, a similar measure (S 1788) is expected to be folded into another piece of must-pass legislation. Senate GOP leaders, like their House counterparts, want to avoid stand-alone consideration of the Medicare bill to protect it from Democratic amendments.

Thomas said he would begin discussions with the Senate Finance Committee and the administration the week of Nov. 8.

Senate Minority Leader Tom Daschle, D-S.D., said Nov. 3 that the Medicare bill will likely be considered as part of an omnibus measure.

Underscoring the political urgency associated with the issue, 59 Republican and Democratic senators sent a letter Nov. 2 to Daschle and Senate Majority Leader Trent Lott, R-Miss., asking them to make sure Congress finishes action on the bill before adjournment.

"With only limited legislative days available, we the undersigned believe that Congress has a responsibility to ensure that this issue is addressed," the senators wrote.

The Senate Finance Committee on Oct. 21 approved an $11.6 billion package to increase payments to Medicare health care providers over the next five years.

During the week of Nov. 1, Thomas worked to smooth differences with Democrats and strike a deal with House Commerce Committee Chairman Thomas J. Bliley Jr., R-Va., in order to prepare the bill for floor action.

Commerce members had hoped to prepare their own bill but instead folded their provisions into the Thomas bill, including more money for Medicaid, the federal health program for the poor, and the Children's Health Insurance Program, a federal-state health program for children that was part of the 1997 budget law.

Bill Changes

To satisfy Ways and Means Committee member Karen L. Thurman, D-Fla., Thomas incorporated an amendment she offered at the committee markup to extend Medicare's coverage of immunosuppressive drugs that are necessary after an organ transplant. Such drugs, which are expensive, are currently covered for a three-year period, but organ recipients sometimes need to take them for a longer period after a transplant. The bill would provide an extra $200 million for the Health Care Financing Administration, which runs Medicare, to determine how to improve availability of such drugs.

The House also added $200 million in payments over five years to managed care plans participating in the Medicare+Choice program, a program created by the budget law to expand managed care in Medicare.

Rural hospitals with fewer than 100 beds would also receive an additional $100 million over the next five years, raising their total share of the bill to about $800 million. The facilities would be allowed to choose to be paid by either the rate they received in 1996 or by a new, transitional payment system, whichever was higher.

"We're showing a real commitment to retaining rural hospitals," Thomas said.

The bill would also boost so-called disproportionate share payments, which are made to hospitals that treat a large number of uninsured patients, by $300 million over the next five years.

In another change from the committee bill, cancer hospitals would be exempted for two years from abiding by a prospective payment system.

One provision that threatens to slow action on the bill is a dispute over how to fix language in the budget law that, if not corrected, would result in $850 million per year in additional payment cuts to hospital outpatient departments beginning next spring.

In an Oct. 19 letter, Clinton said he would make the changes administratively. Under that assumption, Thomas deleted a provision in the bill to make the change. The language would have added $5.6 billion to the bill's cost.

But the issue has not been resolved. Officials at the Department of Health and Human Services (HHS) said the agency does not have authority to make the change. The Office of Management and Budget, however, asserted that HHS does have such power. The Congressional Budget Office has said that if the language is inserted into either the House or Senate measures it will add to the bill's price tag.

The House-passed bill did not contain any language to fix the hospital outpatient payment issue, but Thomas said he expected the administration would nonetheless take steps to resolve the problem.

Senate Clears Rescissions as Part Of Fiscal 2000 Spending Package

NOVEMBER 20 — Congress on Nov. 19 cleared a package of Medicare funding increases that provides just enough money to satisfy for now hospitals, nursing homes, managed care insurers and other providers who complained for months that the 1997 budget law cut their reimbursements too deeply.

The measure (HR 3426) was folded into the fiscal 2000 omnibus budget bill (HR 3194). The House adopted the conference report on the bill, 296-135, on Nov. 18. The Senate cleared it, 74-24, the next day. *(House vote 610, p. H-198; Senate vote 374, p. S-74)*

The $16 billion price tag was not a difficult call for many members: Reductions in the the 1997 balanced-budget law (PL 105-33) cut much deeper than expected. But it sidestepped the larger, more difficult task that legislators have been reluctant to tackle: a complete overhaul of Medicare, the federal health program for more than 39 million elderly and disabled Americans.

Many experts and some lawmakers say that until Medicare is restructured to reflect changes in the world of health care since the program was created in 1965, Congress will be in a perpetual state of making fixes such as the ones just passed.

The GOP Congress has increased the role of private managed care companies in Medicare on the theory that it will lower the program's cost and give beneficiaries more choices. But as long as the Congress continues to decide the reimbursement level for every element of the program, analysts say, providers will want more money.

Home health agencies want a complete repeal of a proposed 15 percent across-the-board cut in Medicare payments. Managed care companies, who believe their reimbursements are too low, will push to have the payments raised. Hospitals and nursing homes will threaten to close unless they get more Medicare funding.

Thomas A. Scully, president and chief executive officer of the Federation of American Health Systems, a group representing private hospitals, said rural hospitals, for example, will likely press Congress for assistance.

Some lawmakers think this year's fight will mark the beginning of an annual battle. "They'll be back next year just as ferociously," said Sen. John D. Rockefeller IV, D-W.Va. "They'll get relief any way they can get it."

Rockefeller and some other lawmakers find the process maddening and are pushing their colleagues to make broad changes to the program.

"It's insane how we continue to micro-manage the Medicare program," said Sen. John B. Breaux, a Louisiana Democrat who has introduced legislation (S 1895) to overhaul Medicare. "We just can't continue doing what we're doing."

Armies of Lobbyists

Like Breaux, House Ways and Means Health Subcommittee Chairman Bill Thomas, R-Calif., has said Congress must focus on long-term, rather than short-term, changes to Medicare. The two lawmakers were co-chairmen of a bipartisan commission, created in the 1997 budget law, to develop a blueprint to strengthen Medicare. But the panel disbanded in

March, unable to reach consensus.

Thomas' role in the current Medicare debate has been to keep House and Senate negotiators and White House aides at the table while keeping lobbyists away. Still, Thomas could not prevent narrow, targeted provisions to help individual facilities such as hospitals in Mississippi, North Carolina and Vermont.

The main winners of the Medicare package would be the program's major players. Hospitals would receive about $7.2 billion over five years, managed care plans would receive $2.2 billion, and skilled nursing facilities and therapy services would receive $2.7 billion, according to preliminary estimates from the Congressional Budget Office (CBO) and congressional staff.

Home health agencies would receive $1.3 billion, mostly through a one-year postponement of a 15 percent across-the-board payment reduction. The cut would not become law until one year after implementation of a prospective payment system, which would give agencies a fixed, predetermined payment based on a patient's diagnosis. The industry won a one-year postponement last year as well. *(Home health, 1998 Almanac, p. 14-16)*

The Medicare bill also would spend an additional $200 million to raise Medicare's reimbursement for pap smears and expand the program's coverage of immunosuppressive drugs that are necessary after an organ transplant.

Funding for Medicaid, the federal health program for the poor and disabled, would increase by $700 million, and an additional $200 million would be spent on a federal-state program created in the 1997 budget law to help provide health insurance for children.

A provision on hospital outpatient departments that threatened to derail the bill was remedied Nov. 15 in a letter from White House Chief of Staff John D. Podesta to House Speaker J. Dennis Hastert, R-Ill. The administration said it would not count the cost of a legislative fix toward the bill's final price tag, nor would the White House "characterize such legislation as having an adverse effect . . . on the Social Security surplus," Podesta wrote.

Industry officials said hospitals would lose an additional $850 million a year in Medicare funding unless the problem were fixed. CBO, however, said the new provisions added $3.9 billion to the bill over five years.

"There's a general consensus that we responded to the people who needed it most," said Sen. Connie Mack, R-Fla.

Breaux, however, offered a different assessment: "The ones who needed the most yelled the loudest," he said.

But some providers who spoke a bit more softly benefited as well, partly because of help from lawmakers. Senate Majority Leader Trent Lott, R-Miss., Sen. Jesse Helms, R-N.C., and Sen. James M. Jeffords, R-Vt., inserted language into the bill that would reclassify hospitals in their states to give them more Medicare money.

Senate Assistant Majority Leader Don Nickles, R-Okla., helped win higher reimbursements for oxygen providers. Two New York lawmakers, Sen. Daniel Patrick Moynihan, the Senate Finance Committee's ranking Democrat, and Charles B. Rangel, the ranking Democrat on the House Ways and Means Committee, pushed for changes in a hospital funding formula that Rangel said would bring an additional $250 million to New York hospitals that train medical residents and serve a large number of patients who do not have health insurance.

Thomas suggested that his colleagues in the Senate are more likely to slip in special provisions for favored groups.

"The House doesn't do rifle shots, but the Senate does," he said Nov. 16. In negotiations with the Senate, reconciling policy differences between the House (HR 3075) and Senate (S 1788) bills took "about five minutes," he said, but dealing with the special interest items took hours.

Thomas' frustration with members' demands for more Medicare money became publicly apparent shortly before the House voted overwhelmingly to pass Medicare legislation Nov. 5.

"One movie role most members of Congress would not have to audition for was the scene in 'Oliver,' where he holds his porridge bowl up and says, 'More, please.' It is always 'more, please.' But this is a refinement, not a reform," he said.

Television Blitz

Lobbying on the Medicare legislation began months ago with television and newspaper advertising campaigns, phone calls and personal visits to members' offices and rallies around the country and on Capitol Hill. Some Medicare providers said their payment cuts were so deep that they might go out of business.

"Hospitals and nursing homes were threatening to close. Those aren't idle threats. That gets people's attention," said Benjamin L. Cardin, D-Md., a member of the House Ways and Means Committee.

Lawmakers were bombarded with advertising campaigns that highlighted the impact of the budget bill. Television ads by managed care and nursing home groups accused legislators of cutting Medicare funding so deeply that seniors were suffering.

The American Association of Health Plans (AAHP), a group representing managed care insurers, aired a television ad that said lawmakers who cut payments to Medicare managed care plans would pay in next year's elections.

"Unless [politicians] do something more to save Medicare HMOs like mine, you can bet I'll have an answer for them. Forget it!" said a white-haired actor in one such ad.

Karen M. Ignagni, president and chief executive officer of the AAHP, said the television ads, as well as Capitol Hill rallies featuring seniors who are enrolled in managed care, were designed to "have Congress look at the broader implications" of the budget bill and take action to correct mistakes.

The tactics appeared to work. Medicare managed care insurers would benefit from several provisions, including slightly higher payments in fiscal 2002 and a slower phase-in period for a new payment system that is designed to gear managed care payments to the level of health or illness of seniors in that plan. Plans now receive a flat fee per patient, regardless of their health status.

Managed care plans also would be required to contribute less of the cost for a booklet sent each year to Medicare beneficiaries that explains their coverage options. That change would give the industry approximately $85 million more yearly, an amount not reflected in the CBO estimates.

The American Health Care Association, which represents nursing homes, accused Senate Finance Committee Chairman William V. Roth Jr., R-Del., House Republicans and Vice President Al Gore of not doing enough to improve Medicare's nursing home funding.

The commercials featured a middle-aged woman who stroked her ailing father's forehead as she told politicians that her father could not get the care he needs. The ads urged viewers to call Gore and lawmakers to urge them to "keep the promise" that Medicare would provide health care to seniors when they need it most.

Some lawmakers described the nursing home ads as obnoxious, but they may have contributed to the group's ability to win more money for some of its highest cost patients.

"I think the ads made the issues real," said Linda Keegan, vice president of the health care association.

The National Association for Home Care, which represents home health agencies, featured an 83-year-old stroke patient whose lower left leg had been amputated. The ad said unless Congress increased Medicare payments to home health agencies, the man's access to home health services would be jeopardized, likely leading to a hospital stay.

"How can you compare an $80 home health visit to the $4,000 average cost of a hospital admission?" the ad asked. "After all, didn't Congress and the president enact the balanced-budget act to save money?"

"We've been working on this since [the balanced-budget act] passed," said Jeff Kincheloe, deputy director of government affairs for the home care group. "We knew it would be a disaster from day one." ◆

In Absence of Legislative Action on Medical Privacy, HHS Rules To Take Effect

Box Score

- **Bills:** S 881, S 573, S 578
- **Legislative action:** None

SUMMARY

Faced with three competing bills, Congress missed a self-imposed Aug. 21 deadline to pass legislation to protect the privacy of patients' medical records. The lack of action allowed the Department of Health and Human Services (HHS) to implement its own regulations, which will take effect early next year.

There is currently no comprehensive federal law to protect the confidentiality of health records. Although lawmakers agree that Congress should pass medical privacy legislation, they have differed over the best approach.

Under the 1996 Health Insurance Portability and Accountability Act (PL 104-191), Congress was given until Aug. 21 to pass privacy legislation. If it did not, HHS would have six months to implement its own rules. President Clinton on Oct. 29 unveiled the administration's regulations, which would govern only electronically stored medical data. He also urged Congress to pass broader legislation.

In Congress, the biggest disputes have been whether federal law should override state privacy laws, and whether patients should have the right to sue if their privacy is violated. Lawmakers are also split over whether parents should have access to children's medical records and what restraints should be placed on law enforcement access to data.

Three differing bills were introduced in the Senate. One (S 881) by Robert F. Bennett, R-Utah, would pre-empt state laws. That bill was backed by insurers and researchers who said one federal standard is needed to ensure uniformity. A second bill (S 573), by Patrick J. Leahy, D-Vt., and Edward M. Kennedy, D-Mass., which was backed by patient advocacy groups, said federal law should serve as a "floor," not a "ceiling," for privacy protections. A third (S 578), by James M. Jeffords, R-Vt., and Christopher J. Dodd, D-Conn., would grandfather existing state laws that are stricter than federal laws.

Jeffords' Committee on Health, Education, Labor and Pensions repeatedly postponed committee action on the bills after it became clear that compromise was not in reach. House members were also unable to find common ground.

The administration's guidelines would limit the release of private health information without a patient's consent and require health plans to tell patients how their medical information is used, and to whom it is disclosed. Patients would be able to see and copy their own records and correct errors. HHS will begin implementing those guidelines in January.

Lawmakers are expected to push forward with broad medical confidentiality legislation next year to protect all patient records, not just those stored electronically.

Disagreements Confound Trio Of Senate Bills

MAY 1 — Senate sponsors of competing bills to protect medical records are trying to negotiate compromise legislation that could pass Congress in the coming months, but a number of deep divisions — and a quickly approaching deadline — are complicating their efforts.

Congress must approve legislation by Aug. 21 or the Department of Health and Human Services (HHS) will be able to implement its own rules governing the use and protection of patient information.

The department has proposed regulations designed to give patients more control over their medical records, but the rules have been criticized by insurers and health plans because they do not pre-empt more stringent state laws. Civil liberties groups, meanwhile, say the HHS proposals do not put enough restrictions on the use of medical records, especially by law enforcement agencies.

Currently, there are no comprehensive federal laws protecting the privacy of medical records.

Three separate privacy bills have been introduced in the Senate this year. The Health, Education, Labor & Pensions Committee plans to mark up final language May 19.

Authors of the three measures, including Senate health committee Chairman James M. Jeffords, R-Vt., say they are willing to seek common ground in an effort to thwart the HHS rules.

But a committee hearing April 27 showed strong disagreements over how to balance patient privacy with the need of researchers and health care providers to have access to medical information.

A Floor or Ceiling?

Perhaps most contentious was the issue of federal pre-emption of state-passed privacy laws.

"There is a patchwork of state laws," said Sen. Robert F. Bennett, R-Utah, who testified at the hearing and introduced his own medical privacy bill (S 881) April 27. "[Health care providers] want a degree of uniformity and predictability in this area that currently doesn't exist."

Bennett, whose bill would pre-empt state laws, said medical research would suffer without one federal standard.

But Patrick J. Leahy, D-Vt., and Edward M. Kennedy, D-Mass., said federal law should serve as a "floor," not a "ceiling," for patient protections. Their bill (S 573) would allow states to enact laws that provide stricter protections of medical information. Edward J. Markey, D-Mass., has introduced a companion bill (HR 1057) in the House.

The third bill (S 578) pending in the Senate, introduced by Jeffords and Christopher J. Dodd, D-Conn., would grandfather existing state privacy laws that are more strict than federal law and give states 18 months after federal enactment to pass stricter laws.

The three bills also differ on how much control patients would have over their medical records.

The Leahy-Kennedy bill would require patients to give additional authorizations for any use of their records beyond treatment and payment. The Bennett and Jeffords-Dodd bills would require a single authorization for a broader use of medical information, including "health care operations" such as auditing, performance evaluations or fraud investigations.

Supporters of the Leahy-Kennedy bill fear the term "health care operations" is too broad and opens medical information to a wide audience. Bennett, Jeffords and Dodd, however, say their bills offer adequate protection without requiring patients to give repeated consent for use of their medical records.

The health insurance and managed care industries have largely aligned behind the Bennett bill. Among the groups supporting that legislation are the Health Insurance Association of America, the American Association of Health Plans and the American Health Information Management Association.

Several large consumer groups favor the Leahy-Kennedy language, including the American Psychiatric Association, the Consortium for Citizens with Disabilities and the American Civil Liberties Union.

Law Enforcement

All three Senate bills would place restrictions on the use of patient information by law enforcement officials. But representatives from the Justice Department and the FBI testified against limiting their use of medical records.

"It would have a devastating impact on our ability to solve some crimes," John Bentivoglio, special counsel for health care fraud and chief privacy officer for the Justice Department, told the committee.

Bentivoglio gave an example of a rape case in Washington, D.C., where the victim slammed a car door on the assailant's hand. Bentivoglio said local police immediately contacted local hospitals to find out if anyone matching the assailant's description had been treated for a hand injury. Bentivoglio argued that all three Senate bills would prevent police from gathering such information.

But committee members expressed strong reservations about giving police unlimited access to medical records. Committee member Susan Collins, R-Maine, said court orders and subpoenas are currently required before police can sift through banking records.

"How can you justify providing less protection to the access of medical records than we do for bank records?" Collins asked. "We do not want to interfere with legitimate access . . . but neither do I want to give you unfettered access to the most sensitive information on individuals."

Currently, there are no federal limits on access to medical records by law enforcement. Hospitals and doctors are not required to hand over patient information to police, but are not prevented from doing so if they wish.

The proposed regulations by HHS would permit patients to obtain and correct their medical records, require health plans and insurers to give patients easy-to-understand explanations of how the information will be used and require those who legally receive health information to take real steps to safeguard it, among other things. They would not place any restrictions on law enforcement.

Besides agreeing to federal limits on law enforcement, some senators at the hearing expressed support for congressional action on medical privacy rather than leaving it up to HHS.

Under the 1996 Health Insurance Portability and Accountability Act (PL 104-191), Congress must pass legislation "governing the standards with respect to privacy of individually identifiable health information" by Aug. 21. If it does not, HHS has six months to implement its own regulations. But the law gives HHS authority to implement privacy laws governing only electronically stored medical information. *(1996 Almanac, p. 6-28)*

Many members of Congress want to pass a comprehensive bill protecting all medical information — whether kept on paper or computers. Dodd estimated that 90 percent of all medical information is kept in paper files.

Senate Panel Again Fails To Reach Compromise

JUNE 19 — Two months before a deadline for congressional action, a Senate committee stumbled the week of June 14 in attempting to move sensitive legislation to establish federal guidelines for protecting the privacy of medical records.

After a series of awkward postponements that have stalled the panel for nearly a month, Senate Health, Education, Labor and Pensions Committee Chairman James M. Jeffords, R-Vt., acknowledged that he still could not produce a bipartisan product. On June 15, Jeffords again delayed action, saying he needed one day to broker a compromise with Democrats. That effort faltered, leaving lawmakers wondering aloud whether medical confidentiality legislation would move this year.

GOP leaders had hoped the committee would produce a bipartisan bill to govern how health insurance companies, law enforcement officials, schools, and other entities could access and use the personal medical information of individuals. Currently, there are no federal standards.

Absent an agreement between Jeffords and panel Democrats, lawmakers have two alternatives: They could wait for a bipartisan effort in the House to gain momentum, or they could extend the Aug. 21 deadline in the 1996 Health Insurance Portability and Accountability Act (PL 104-191). That measure says that if Congress does not act by the deadline, the secretary of Health and Human Services (HHS) must begin a rulemaking process to implement the regulations six months later. *(1996 Almanac, p. 6-28)*

Many lawmakers oppose the HHS guidelines because they would not preempt state laws and would not limit law enforcement agencies' access to the records. The HHS guidelines would also govern only the privacy of electronic medical records, which make up a small fraction of the records in use.

"I think we have to extend the deadline, given the lack of consensus," said Robert F. Bennett, R-Utah, who sponsored a bill (S 881) that has the support of biotechnology companies, hospitals and medical researchers. Bennett suggested a two-year extension.

Debates on Liability, Abortion

Jeffords tried to meld three bills into a compromise, but the momentum collapsed, as senators encountered unanticipated issues. The main obstacle was Democrats' insistence that patients be able to sue health care providers, researchers or others who willfully and intentionally disclose their records.

A Jeffords draft released June 11 offered a potential compromise. Republicans, led by Jeff Sessions, R-Ala., agreed to allow patients whose records are disclosed illegally to sue, but wanted to cap non-economic damages at $50,000. Ranking Democrat Edward M. Kennedy of Massachusetts dismissed the provision as a "non-starter."

Another major dispute centered on the rights of minors to prevent their parents from seeing private medical information. Before the markup, Republicans and Democrats agreed to keep intact current federal and state laws regarding minors but continued debating details.

Some states require parental consent laws for abortion, for instance, and both parties want those state laws to remain in place. But Kennedy wanted to amend the bill to clarify that in states that allow young people to receive care independently, adolescents should have the same privacy rights as adults.

Other contentious issues include the ability of patients to require separate authorizations for sensitive information; the confidentiality of deceased individuals' records; and procedures for law enforcement agencies in getting access to individuals' personal records. Kennedy opposed a limit on the liability of law enforcement officials.

On pre-emption of state laws, the Jeffords draft would grandfather in more restrictive state laws on the enactment date, with certain exceptions.

Jeffords' ally Christopher J. Dodd, D-Conn., said that if the committee does not act, the issue could lose momentum. "The assumption is that if we can't get this done, no one else is really going to try," he said.

Clinton Issues Guidelines

OCTOBER 30 — Urging Congress to pass legislation that would secure Americans' medical privacy, President Clinton on Oct. 29 proposed his own set of guidelines to protect electronic medical records.

"Please help protect America's families from new abuses of their privacy. You owe the American people a comprehensive medical privacy law," Clinton said at a news conference.

Congress missed its Aug. 21 deadline to pass privacy legislation under the 1996 Health Insurance Portability and Accountability Act (PL 104-191), giving the Department of Health and Human Services (HHS) six months to implement its own regulations protecting medical privacy. The department, however, was given authority to issue regulations governing the privacy of electronic records only, not traditional paper records. *(1996 Almanac, p. 6-28)*

Congress has been stalled over the issue for three years. Points of contention include the question of whether federal law should override state-passed privacy laws, and whether patients should be able to sue if their medical privacy is invaded.

Clinton's 638-page proposed guidelines would limit the release of private health information without a patient's consent and require health plans to tell patients how their medical information is used, and to whom it is disclosed. Patients would be able to see and copy their own records and correct errors.

The proposed guidelines also would require researchers and others seeking access to health records to abide by new disclosure standards. Penalties for violation of the new guidelines could result in fines of up to $250,000 and 10 years in prison. The public will have 60 days to comment on the proposed regulations before HHS takes steps to finalize them, the president said.

Clinton said the new rules were needed because health care providers were sharing more patients' records and insurance companies were demanding more information before paying claims, creating possible abuses of private medical information.

"Today, with the click of a mouse, personal health information could easily, and now legally, be passed around without patients' consent, to people who aren't doctors, for reasons that have nothing to do with health care," he said.

But the issue has presented lawmakers with the challenge of balancing patient privacy with technological progress that allows health professionals to have quick access to patients' health histories and to share data with other doctors.

Republicans generally agree that patients' records should be protected from abuse, but they have resisted enacting new federal rules that employers and insurers view as burdensome. Democrats reacted positively to Clinton's plan.

"Congress gave itself a deadline to act on medical privacy, and then Congress quickly ignored its own deadline," said Sen. Patrick J. Leahy, D-Vt., calling the draft rules "an important step forward." Leahy has sponsored a bill (S 573) that would put strict limits on who can see medical records and require patient consent for all uses of such data.

Industry Opposition

Insurance industry officials were wary of the proposed regulations, fearing they would interfere with their use of such data and create a bureaucratic nightmare that would increase costs.

"To be effective, regulations and laws protecting the confidentiality of consumers' medical records also must allow this information to be used appropriately," said Chip Kahn, president of the Health Insurance Association of America, an industry trade group.

But the proposed regulations also mean that insurers, health plans, hospitals and other health care providers "face the prospect of having to comply with a federal rule, along with 51 other rules from the states and the District of Columbia," Kahn said.

Mary Nell Lehnard, a senior vice president at Blue Cross and Blue Shield Association, said insurers are concerned that new rules "could end up costing doctors, hospitals, consumers and health insurance companies billions of dollars per year." Industry officials also expressed concern that the regulations could hamper their efforts to track and analyze illness trends and the effectiveness of treatments. ◆

Determined Campaign by Advocates for the Disabled Wins Over Divided Congress

SUMMARY

Congress cleared legislation Nov. 19 to help individuals receiving Social Security Disability Insurance (SSDI) and Supplemental Security Income (SSI) keep their Medicaid and Medicare health benefits if they go back to work. The president is expected to sign the bill.

The measure is designed to end a paradox in current law under which individuals receiving SSI or SSDI risk losing Medicare and Medicaid health insurance coverage if they return to work. The bill would also revamp vocational rehabilitation and employment services.

About 8 million working-age individuals are on the federal disability rolls. While many are too severely impaired to work, computer technology and the enactment of civil rights protections under the 1990 Americans with Disabilities Act (PL 101-336) have improved opportunities for many.

The Senate measure (S 331) was introduced by William V. Roth Jr., R-Del., Daniel Patrick Moynihan, D-N.Y., Edward M. Kennedy, D-Mass., and James M. Jeffords, R-Vt. Sponsors of the House bill (HR 1180) were Rick A. Lazio, R-N.Y., and Kenny Hulshof, R-Mo. The bill rode a roller-coaster path to final passage. While it enjoyed bipartisan support, lawmakers had difficulty finding money to offset the bill's estimated cost of $500 million. Senate leaders were also concerned that wealthy people could get benefits. In the end, House Speaker J. Dennis Hastert, R-Ill., brought GOP lawmakers together to find a consensus, and the White House came up with offsets.

The legislation marks a significant expansion of the Medicaid program, which helps the poor and disabled. States provide Medicaid benefits to SSI recipients. To qualify for SSI, individuals must meet disability guidelines and make less than $700 a month. Under HR 1180, effective Oct. 1, 2000, states could offer Medicaid to individuals with disabilities whose incomes would otherwise disqualify them for SSI. States could also continue coverage to workers with disabilities whose medical condition had improved.

Individuals could buy into Medicaid under a sliding fee scale. Those making more than $75,000 a year would pay the full premium. Grants would be provided to states to conduct outreach campaigns and provide services, such as personal attendant care, to help people perform such daily activities as dressing or eating. The grants would be funded at $20 million in fiscal 2001. The purpose is to give states, which fund Medicaid jointly with the federal government, a financial incentive to expand aid.

Box Score

- **Bill:** HR 1180 — PL 106-170
- **Legislative action: House** passed HR 1180 (H Rept 106-220), 412-9, on Oct. 19.

Senate passed S 331 (S Rept 106-37), 99-0, on June 16.

House adopted conference report on HR 1180 (H Rept 106-478), 418-2, on Nov. 18.

Senate cleared the bill, 95-1, on Nov. 19.

President signed HR 1180 on Dec. 17.

Senate Bill Would Protect Health Coverage

MARCH 6 — Voting 16-2, the Senate Finance Committee on March 4 approved legislation (S 331) that would make it easier for disabled people to enter the work force without losing health coverage.

Under current law, disabled individuals receiving Supplemental Security Income and Social Security Disability assistance become eligible for federal Medicare or Medicaid health insurance. Despite improvements in technology and enactment of civil rights laws making it easier for the disabled to work, many do not try to find jobs because they fear losing their federal health benefits. The legislation would expand a provision in existing law that gives states the authority to let individuals buy into Medicaid if they go back to work. It would extend the length of time that disabled individuals would be eligible for Medicare after returning to work and set up a new program to improve rehabilitation and other services.

President Clinton in his Jan. 19 State of the Union address recommended expansion of health care for disabled people who go back to work, and the legislation has wide support. The Senate effort has been spearheaded by James M. Jeffords, R-Vt., and Edward M. Kennedy, D-Mass.

In one sign of possible trouble ahead, however, the two Finance Committee members voting against the bill were Majority Leader Trent Lott, R-Miss., and Majority Whip Don Nickles, R-Okla.

House Panel Backs Benefits for Disabled Workers

APRIL 24 — Moving quickly on an initiative that has broad bipartisan support, a House subcommittee April 20 approved by voice vote a bill (HR 1180) that would allow the disabled to enter the work force without losing their federal health insurance benefits.

The bill, sponsored by Rick A. Lazio, R-N.Y., and approved by the Commerce Health and Environment Subcommittee, would give states the option of allowing disabled individuals to buy Medicaid coverage after they return to work. States could charge a sliding-scale monthly premium for the insurance, based on income earned.

Currently, disabled individuals receiving Supplemental Security Income and Social Security Disability assistance are eligible for Medicare or Medicaid health insurance. While improvements in technology and enactment of civil rights laws have made it easier for the disabled to work, many do not try to find jobs because they fear losing those

Under the Lazio measure, workers moving from the disability rolls to employment could retain their Medicare hospital coverage for 10 years, up from a maximum of 48 months at present.

The measure also would provide grants for states to develop programs to encourage the disabled to return to work. The bill now goes to the full Commerce Committee. It must also be approved by the Ways and Means Committee, which would determine offsets to cover estimated cost of $791 million over five years.

A companion measure (S 331), approved by the Senate Finance Committee on March 4, has 73 sponsors. But it has been blocked from reaching the floor by Majority Leader Trent Lott, R-Miss., and Assistant Majority Leader Don Nickles, R-Okla. — both Finance members. Nickles sought the addition of a means test to determine the eligibility of disabled workers who seek to retain their federal insurance benefits.

House Committee Approves Bill; Lott Steps Up Negotiations

MAY 22 — In a clear sign of growing momentum behind legislation that would expand health benefits for the working disabled, the House Commerce Committee on May 19 approved the bill (HR 1180) by voice vote and without a single amendment.

"We're here today to remove people from the cycle of dependency," said Rep. Rick A. Lazio, R-N.Y., the primary author of the measure, which has more than 150 cosponsors. Illustrating the intensity of the support, the audience in the committee room burst into applause when the vote was completed. Some supporters were weeping.

Now, the question is whether the momentum will reach the other side of the Capitol, where Senate Majority Leader Trent Lott, R-Miss., and one of his top lieutenants have for weeks blocked floor debate on a companion measure (S 331) cosponsored by 75 senators.

The majority leader has expressed concern about a $300 million pilot program in the bill that would allow states to provide Medicaid to working individuals who have degenerative ailments but are not yet impaired enough to meet the stringent federal definition of disability.

In private meetings, his staff has told advocates for the disabled that they are specifically concerned it could cover individuals who have HIV, the virus that causes AIDS. With negotiations at a sensitive stage and bill sponsors refusing to back away from the pilot plan, the unexpected objections have created turmoil.

In a sign they want to end the impasse, Lott and Majority Whip Don Nickles, R-Okla., stepped up negotiations with bill authors in a bid to move the legislation through the Senate before the Memorial Day recess.

The bill is designed to address a Catch-22 in current law that means individuals receiving federal disability benefits lose Medicaid or Medicare health insurance if they make too much money. The threat of being left without health coverage is one reason nearly 75 percent of the disabled are unemployed, experts say.

Pressure on Lott

The bill would allow, but not require, states to expand Medicaid coverage for the working disabled. Medicaid is the joint state-federal insurance program for the poor, elderly and disabled. It also would establish a 10-year trial program to allow individuals covered by Medicare to receive benefits while working without paying hefty premiums. Current law provides 39 months of Medicare benefits for the disabled once they have gone to work.

Lott and Nickles have complained that the bill could benefit the wealthy.

"We don't need people with a million bucks getting Medicaid, unless we just want to tell people: 'Don't worry about anything. Everything is going to be fine,' " Lott said in an interview.

The voluntary state demonstration would test whether giving quicker Medicaid coverage of prescription drugs and other therapies would help people with certain ailments — such as arthritis, multiple sclerosis or HIV — stabilize their conditions, keep their jobs and stay off disability.

Lott said he is opposed to the "idea that you would say that people have a condition that's not disabling, but might become disabling."

Terje Anderson, director of policy at the National Association of People with AIDS, a Washington advocacy group, said that under the current structure, "you have to get sick and poor before you're eligible.

"For any number of groups, particularly people with HIV, there is something ludicrous about this," she said.

Sponsors of the bill are committed to the pilot program. Chief authors in the Senate are Finance Committee Chairman William V. Roth Jr., R-Del.; ranking Democrat Daniel Patrick Moynihan of New York; Health, Education, Labor and Pensions Committee Chairman James M. Jeffords, R-Vt.; and ranking Democrat Edward M. Kennedy of Massachusetts.

Lott is under increasing pressure. Disability groups earlier this month picketed his Mississippi offices. Senate Democrats — all 45 of whom have cosponsored the bill — had planned to publicly criticize Lott and Nickles during the week of May 17. They backed off to give negotiations more time.

There are other obstacles. In the House, the measure must next move through the Ways and Means Committee, where one major issue is money. The Commerce panel moved its bill, expected to result in $682 million in outlays over five years, without any spending offsets. That angered Ways and Means Chairman Bill Archer, R-Texas.

The bill would rewrite laws requiring that, in order to receive Social Security Disability Insurance (SSDI) or Supplemental Security Income (SSI) cash assistance, individuals must prove they are too impaired to work. SSDI beneficiaries are eligible for Medicare and SSI recipients for Medicaid.

Advances in technology and civil rights protections have made it easier for many disabled people to re-enter the job market. Yet less than 1 percent of federal disability recipients move off the rolls.

The House and Senate bills, which are nearly identical, build on a provision in the 1997 balanced-budget law (PL 105-33) that gave states the option of providing Medicaid to disabled workers with incomes below 250 percent of the federal poverty level. (Currently, a family of two living on $11,060 is considered to be at the poverty level.)

The new bills would eliminate the income cap. States that elect to expand their Medicaid programs could require participants to pay a higher or even the full premium, based on their income. States could also continue Medicaid coverage for individuals who had severe impairments, but whose condition had improved to the point that they had lost eligibility for SSDI or SSI.

The bill would authorize $150 million for states to set up programs to help people with disabilities move into jobs. It includes a "ticket to work" program to allow recipients to shop for vocational services from either state or private organizations and provides assurances that people could resume cash benefits if their jobs fell through.

Senate Passes Bill; House Is Left To Find Offsets

JUNE 19 — Without opposition, the Senate on June 16 passed legislation (S 331) that would expand federal health benefits for the working disabled, ending months of backstage maneuvering by Republican leaders and giving new momentum to a companion House effort.

The 99-0 vote clearly improved the odds that Congress will clear the legislation this session. It also presented a new hurdle, however. In order to get the bill to the floor, sponsors at the last minute agreed to jettison a package of tax increases that would have covered the bill's $1.7 billion, 10-year cost. That means lawmakers must find offsetting funds either in the House or in conference. *(Vote 169, p. S-34)*

Still, supporters hailed the measure as the most important legislation for the mentally and physically impaired since the 1990 Americans with Disabilities Act (PL 101-336), which guarantees access to employment and housing. *(1990 Almanac, p. 447)*

"If America means anything, it means not leaving people out or leaving people behind. Today's unanimous action is a real invitation . . . to be a part of the American dream," Edward M. Kennedy, D-Mass., told reporters.

After the vote, Kennedy and Health, Education, Labor and Pensions Committee Chairman James M. Jeffords, R-Vt., gathered with disability advocates, some in wheelchairs, off the Senate floor. There were cheers, hugs, a group photo and planning about how to move a House bill.

The measure addresses a Catch-22 in which individuals who leave the federal support rolls for work lose essential health coverage. More than 7.5 million adults receive Supplemental Security Income (SSI) or Social Security Disability Income (SSDI). Less than 1 percent of them move off assistance and into jobs.

The measure would provide six years of Medicare coverage, up from 39 months, for the disabled once they started working and allow individuals with salaries above Medicaid limits to buy into the program. Advocates estimate that as many as 2 million people might work if the bill became law.

Passage underscored the growing clout of the disability community, which is also waging a series of high-profile legal battles to expand employment and health care rights.

"You may have a permanent disability, but it doesn't mean you are permanently unable to work," said Paul J. Seifert, director of government affairs for the International Association of Psychosocial Rehabilitation Services.

Gramm Drops Objections

At the same time, it showed the difficulty of getting even popular bills through Congress in an era of spending limits. Phil Gramm, R-Texas, blocked the bill until the tax provisions were dropped. Gramm said June 16 that he supported the measure but did not want to raise taxes to pay for it.

"It has not been easy to stand in the way of this bill," Gramm said during floor debate.

Senate Majority Leader Trent Lott,

R-Miss., and Majority Whip Don Nickles, R-Okla., had held the bill off the floor for months until sponsors agreed to scale back coverage.

Kennedy said that President Clinton, who joined bill sponsors before the cameras at the Capitol on June 15 to push for its passage, had instructed the Office of Management and Budget to find a way to pay for it. Other chief authors include Finance Committee Chairman William V. Roth Jr., R-Del., and ranking Democrat Daniel Patrick Moynihan of New York.

Gramm said the agreement he worked out required that the measure be paid for through cuts in other entitlement programs. Kennedy and Jeffords disputed that. "I think we have enough problems already with Medicare and Medicaid," Jeffords said.

Kennedy's goal is to get a bill to Clinton's desk by July 4. Clinton set an outside deadline of July 26, the nine-year anniversary of the disabilities law.

"The full promise of the Americans with Disabilities Act will never be realized until we pass this legislation," Clinton said at the news conference.

The House Commerce Committee approved a similar bill (HR 1180) by voice vote May 19. That measure also does not have a funding mechanism. The Ways and Means Committee, which has jurisdiction over Medicare and job training provisions, must now act. Chairman Bill Archer, R-Texas, has expressed concerns about the bill's scope. Some committee members support a less sweeping measure by Kenny Hulshof, R-Mo.

The Senate-passed bill would:

- Allow, but not require, states to offer Medicaid to disabled workers who earned more than 250 percent of the poverty level. States could set a sliding fee scale for coverage, but once income reached $75,000, the full premium would be required.
- Allow states to cover individuals whose condition improved enough that they lost eligibility for SSI or SSDI, but were still medically impaired.
- Create a pilot program in which states could provide Medicaid to individuals who did not meet the federal disability definition, but had a condition such as multiple sclerosis or HIV, the virus that causes AIDS, that would render them disabled in the future.
- Beef up training and job search programs for the disabled and provide assurances that cash aid would resume if they became unemployed.

House Ways and Means OKs Bill; Search for Offsets Continues

OCTOBER 16 — After months of intensive lobbying and a push by the House GOP leadership, the Ways and Means Committee approved a bill Oct. 14 to expand federal health benefits and job training for the disabled.

The measure (HR 3070), approved 33-1, would revamp present law so that individuals receiving Social Security Disability and Supplemental Security Income could return to work without losing Medicare or Medicaid insurance. It would also create a system of vouchers that could be used to purchase job training and rehabilitation services from government or private sources.

"Current law still tends to chain individuals with disabilities to the system," committee Chairman Bill Archer, R-Texas, said at the markup. "In essence, individuals who try to work lose cash benefits, along with access to medical coverage they so desperately need."

The vote comes after months of bickering — not about the basic premise of the bill but, rather, how to pay for it. Advocacy groups for the disabled have had to fight to get the legislation through the House, despite wide support for the measure.

House GOP leaders weighed in to support the bill during a series of meetings in recent weeks, reacting to the strong support in the chamber.

The Senate passed a broader version of the legislation (S 331), 99-0, in June only after stripping out a package of revenue-raising offsets that were opposed by a handful of lawmakers, including Phil Gramm, R-Texas. The House Commerce Committee in May unanimously passed a bill (HR 1180) that closely resembled the Senate package but also was not paid for. The Commerce and Ways and Means bills must be reconciled before the legislation comes to the floor, possibly the week of Oct. 18.

The Ways and Means bill would include $349 million in mandatory spending and $477 million in discretionary spending over five years. It would be funded largely by cracking down on fraud and abuse in Medicaid, the federal health program for the poor.

Like the other versions of the legislation, the bill would let disabled workers buy into Medicaid even if their income exceeded program limits. Overall, however, the cost-conscious Ways and Means panel provided less generous benefits than the Commerce Committee or Senate.

Senate vs. House Bills

Under current law, for example, individuals on Social Security disability can try working for up to nine months in any five-year period without losing cash or health aid. They then have an extended, 39-month work period in which they can receive Medicare.

The Senate measure would expand those benefits by creating a six-year program in which anyone who returned to work would be guaranteed Medicare as long as they worked. The House bill, by contrast, would allow recipients to receive Medicare for a total of 10 years after returning to work.

Further, the Ways and Means bill, unlike the Senate plan, would provide discretionary, rather than mandatory, funding for two new Medicaid projects.

One of those affected is a pilot program under which states could offer benefits to individuals who are not yet disabled but have degenerative conditions such as HIV, the virus that causes AIDS.

The other is a system of grants to states to improve services to individuals on Medicaid. Supporters of the bill argue that states, which share the cost of Medicaid with the federal government, will not offer expanded services without a guarantee of greater aid.

Rep. Rick A. Lazio, R-N.Y., a Commerce Committee member and the chief sponsor of the bill, is working to find offsets for the Medicaid projects.

Health and Human Services Secretary Donna E. Shalala, in an Oct. 14 letter to Archer, said she had "serious concerns" about the Ways and Means Committee's approach.

Lawmakers and advocates for the

disabled had their own gripe — that the administration never made good on a promise by President Clinton to come up with funding.

Some Democrats were concerned that Ways and Means had chosen to pay for the bill in part by imposing a surcharge on attorney fees in Social Security appeals cases. California Democrats Robert T. Matsui and Pete Stark offered an unsuccessful amendment to eliminate that provision. Their efforts were hampered by the fact that the White House had a similar attorney-fee proposal in its fiscal 2000 budget plan.

"We are deeply concerned that time will run out on this session before the remaining few steps have been taken to pass this important legislation," the Consortium for Citizens with Disabilities said in an Oct. 13 letter to the White House, Senate and House.

House Passes Bill; Conferees Struggle To Pay for Benefits

OCTOBER 23 — Congress is close to clearing legislation that would allow people on the federal disability rolls to go back to work without losing vital health benefits. Supporters of the bill, however, continue to face a major hurdle: how to pay for it.

Scrambling to get a measure to the White House before Congress adjourns for the year, the House, voting 412-9, passed legislation (HR 1180) on Oct. 19 that would expand Medicaid and Medicare and create a new program of job training for the disabled. The bill was approved by the Commerce Committee in May. It was merged with one (HR 3070) approved Oct. 14 by the Ways and Means Committee, and passed as HR 1180. *(Vote 513, p. H-168)*

The Senate passed a similar measure (S 331) in June by a vote of 99-0. "Rarely do we have a group of people coming to us in Washington and saying, 'We want to be taxpayers,' " said Rep. Kenny Hulshof, R-Mo., sponsor of HR 3070.

While there is broad support for the measure, there has been little consensus on how to finance it. The Senate bill did not include a funding mechanism. The House would offset much of the bill's costs by clamping down on fraud in the Supplemental Security Income (SSI) program, imposing a surcharge on attorney fees in Social Security benefit cases and altering the formula for calculating interest rates on federal guaranteed student loans.

Before bringing the bill to the floor, sponsors made a series of changes to reduce its price tag. They eliminated a provision that would have allowed individuals whose incomes are 250 percent above the official poverty line to buy into Medicaid.

Lawmakers are also under pressure from the White House to ditch the student loan recalculation as well as a separate provision that would impose a surcharge on attorneys' fees in Social Security benefits cases.

The Clinton administration, in an Oct. 19 statement, praised the House for acting, but said it was "seriously concerned" that the bill did not include several provisions that were in the Senate bill.

Republicans said the administration had offered little assistance as they searched for offsets.

"We got zero help from the White House," said Rick A. Lazio, R-N.Y., sponsor of HR 1180. He called the administration's criticism "disingenuous."

Popular Bill, Tough Journey

The House and Senate bills are designed to end a contradiction in current law by which individuals receiving Social Security Disability or SSI benefits risk losing Medicaid or Medicare health coverage if they make over a set amount of money.

While the national unemployment rate is at a three-decade low of 4.2 percent, about three-fourths of those with severe disabilities are unemployed. Less than 1 percent of those who get on the SSI rolls leave for jobs.

Both bills would update vocational training programs by giving individuals vouchers that they could use to buy services from either public or private providers. Lawmakers estimate that the change would increase the number of people receiving rehabilitation services to 550,000, from the present 125,000.

The bills would also expand Medicare coverage. The Senate bill would create a six-year program under which individuals would receive a lifetime guarantee of coverage. The House bill would provide a total of 10 years of Medicare coverage to disabled individuals who work, up from the current four years. The House measure would expand Medicare coverage to an estimated 42,600 people over 10 years.

Both measures would provide grants to states as an incentive to expand Medicaid services to the disabled. To receive grants, states would have to provide personal attendant services to people who need help with everyday activities such as bathing and dressing. Before bringing the bill to the floor, the House changed its bill to provide mandatory funding for the program. The Senate bill calls for mandatory funding for the grants, which would gradually rise to $40 million a year.

Supporters argue that unless states are guaranteed more federal money, they may be unwilling to commit their own money to expand Medicaid services. The House also came up with needed cash to provide mandatory funding for a second pilot program that would let states provide Medicaid benefits to people who have chronic ailments such as HIV or multiple sclerosis. The House capped the program at $50 million.

Governors, who fund Medicaid jointly with the federal government, argue that by intervening earlier, particularly with Medicaid's prescription drug benefit, they could stabilize health conditions, prevent costly long-term care services and keep people on the job.

Action Delayed as Conferees Address Senators' Concerns

NOVEMBER 13 — Despite wide support, legislation (HR 1180, S 331) to expand federal health benefits for the working disabled stalled in conference as negotiators tried to figure out how to pay for it and a key Republican demanded further changes.

Sen. Edward M. Kennedy, D-Mass., a main sponsor of the bill, threatened during the week of Nov. 8 to work against it unless lawmakers found a substitute for the package of proposed offsets needed to cover its estimated five-year, $800 million cost.

Negotiators were also under pressure from Senate Assistant Majority Leader Don Nickles, R-Okla., to scale back some of the health benefits in the bill.

The recommended offsets include a provision that would eliminate a federal mortgage insurance rebate for low-income borrowers and a surcharge on attorney fees in Social Security appeals.

Another controversial proposal would change the formula for calculating the interest rate on federal student loans. The Congressional Budget Office has estimated that the provision, which has bipartisan backing, would save $20 million. The White House, however, has called it an unwarranted handout to banks that could generate windfall profits.

"If the Republicans insist on the offsets, this bill won't get passed," Kennedy said in an interview Nov. 10.

The legislation is designed to end a paradox in current law whereby individuals receiving Social Security Disability or Supplemental Security Income (SSI) payments to the low-income disabled risk losing Medicare and Medicaid health benefits if they go back to work.

Even though the bill has been a top priority of the disability community, some advocacy organizations sent letters to the White House during the week of Nov. 8 urging President Clinton to veto it unless it was changed.

Other organizations, such as The Arc, which represents people with mental retardation, were not happy with the offsets, but were not prepared to oppose the overall bill because of them.

"We didn't have the same problems with the pay-fors as some other organizations," said Marty Ford, assistant director of The Arc. "There's a difference of opinion."

At the same time, lawmakers trying to work out a final version of the measure were irritated that despite Clinton's repeated calls for Congress to pass the bill, the administration had done little to help lawmakers come up with acceptable offsets. Kennedy again during the week of Nov. 8 asked White House officials to become more involved.

"The problem continues to be pay-fors. If people don't like [the ones we have], what are they going to do?" said Rep. Rick A. Lazio, R-N.Y., the chief House sponsor of the measure.

Republicans were talking with Kennedy and the White House in an effort to move the bill, which had broad bipartisan support. The measure passed the Senate, 99-0, on June 16 and the House, 412-9, on Oct. 19.

Other Complications

Further complicating the picture, Republican leaders want to attach other must-pass bills to any disability conference report, including a measure (S 1792) to extend expiring tax breaks and possibly another (HR 3075) that would restore about $12 billion in Medicare spending cuts made in the 1997 balanced-budget law.

That has angered some in the disability community, given that Republicans are not requiring full offsets for either the extender or the Medicare bills.

"This [disability] bill is ready to move. That's the main reason" other measures may be added to it, Senate Majority Leader Trent Lott, R-Miss., said in an interview Nov. 9. "There's nothing sinister or Machiavellian about it."

Lott is a conferee on the bill.

There are also policy questions. As worked out by House and Senate negotiators, the bill would expand the number of years that disabled workers could collect Medicare, set up pilot programs allowing people to buy into Medicaid, and allow states to offer Medicaid benefits, including prescription drugs, more quickly to people with degenerative conditions who are not yet disabled.

The idea is that by intervening earlier, states could keep people in the workplace and avoid more costly long-term care.

The bill would also revamp rehabilitation and training programs to give the disabled access to private providers.

Under current law, individuals on SSI can receive Medicare for a nine-month work trial period and another 39 months after going to work. The original Senate bill would have expanded that by adding a six-year "window" in which individuals who took jobs would have been guaranteed Medicare as long as they worked. The House bill included a straight six-year extension of the current Medicare benefit.

House and Senate negotiators had agreed to accept the House language. In a Republican leadership meeting, Nickles, who is not a conferee, raised objections. In response, negotiators cut the six-year extension to four and one-half.

Nickles said he was worried that under the bill a disabled person could return to work, make a hefty salary and still be guaranteed health benefits.

"Maybe you have somebody who is disabled but capable of generating quite a bit of income. We're going to be asking taxpayers to foot the bill," Nickles said in an interview.

But Nickles, who is under pressure from other Republicans to drop his objections, added that the legislation "is going to get through. We're going to get it done."

Sponsors are also trying to get more funding for the Medicaid pilot program for early intervention, which is now funded at $100 million.

After a Little Push From Web-Footed Friends, Senate Clears Legislation

NOVEMBER 20 — All those business groups ginning up million-dollar, "grass-roots" lobbying campaigns could learn something from advocates of a bill expanding health care for disabled workers. Like passion. Or how to quack.

There was plenty of both last fall after Senate Majority Leader Trent Lott slipped a provision into a mammoth spending measure extending the duck hunting season in his home state of Mississippi. Advocates for the disabled, who were blocked from adding their own health plan to the bill (PL 105-277), were livid. They went gunning for Congress.

An angry missive titled "Dead Ducks and Disability" was e-mailed across the country. The response was immediate. GOP lawmakers were barraged with faxes and phone messages. Over and over, people quacked into the receiver in a coordinated chorus of duck calls.

The effort did not clinch passage,

but it did make a point: This was no polite, inside-the-Beltway policy discussion. It was a crusade.

"It really upset people," said Tony Young, manager of government affairs at NISH, a group that helps connect the disabled to jobs. "The word went out . . . to protest his priorities, ducks over people, or hunting over people. I guess it wasn't very good for the ducks."

The Senate on Nov. 19 cleared legislation (HR 1180) to end a Catch-22 in current law under which people receiving federal disability aid risk losing Medicare and Medicaid if they go to work. The measure would revamp job training, extend health care and allow states to intervene earlier under Medicaid to help people with chronic ailments. The House adopted the conference report, 418-2, on Nov. 18. The Senate cleared it, 95-1, the next day. *(House vote 611, p. H-198; Senate vote 372, p. S-74)*

The bill's tortuous journey demonstrates the perils of legislating in a Congress that is deeply partisan, pinching pennies at a time of plenty and divided in purpose. At the same time, it is a reminder that Mr. Smith still visits Washington — that personal experience and emotional commitment can matter as much as campaign contributions or polls.

"No one should be forced to choose between health care and employment," said Senate Finance Committee Chairman William V. Roth Jr., R-Del. on Nov. 19. "Robbing the individual of the ability to work becomes a double tragedy in the life of someone who is living with a disability."

On the surface, it seemed that passage was preordained, that this bill was so popular it could not fail. Its goals were consistent with the times: Companies were begging for workers, Congress was moving people off benefit rolls, as in the 1996 welfare law (PL 104-193), and the budget was in surplus. *(1996 Almanac, p. 6-3)*

There was nothing easy about it.

The bill nearly died a dozen times. Lawmakers battled over turf. Conservatives charged the measure would swell into a fat middle-class subsidy and give special benefits to people with HIV, the virus that causes AIDS. All sides squabbled over how to pay for the bill until just hours before it passed.

"I thought it would be something everybody would be for," said Sen. Jim Bunning, R-Ky., sponsor of one of the earliest versions. "Everybody is. But it became a victim of all the problems [in Congress] and anticipation of not getting everything you wanted."

Unexpected Passion

The bill's survival was due, foremost, to the determination of the disability community, with its united Washington coalition and grass-roots presence. The disabled, once isolated, have found new power in the Internet: a technology that enables people with limited physical mobility to mount a fast, agile lobbying campaign.

The measure's fate also depended on a core of dedicated, almost obsessive staffers, such as Connie Garner, a senior adviser on disability policy for Sen. Edward M. Kennedy, D-Mass., and Patricia Morrissey, who holds the same position for Sen. James M. Jeffords, R-Vt. Garner, who has a daughter with mental retardation, brought both a mother's protective instincts and an agitator's toughness to the fight. Morrissey, born with cerebral palsy, was a technician who had to fight expectations that her condition made her an automatic advocate.

Passage hinged on outsized tactics, including a decision by Kennedy to kill Bunning's bill, a move that ultimately forced debate on a broader measure he wrote with Jeffords, Roth, and Finance Committee's top Democrat, Daniel Patrick Moynihan of New York.

There was the drive of a trio of House members: Rick A. Lazio, R-N.Y., whose father suffered from the crippling effects of a stroke; Commerce Committee Chairman Thomas J. Bliley Jr., R-Va., whose family transported a wheelchair-bound worker to and from their business each day for decades; and Kenny Hulshof, R-Mo., who got hooked after a campaign debate led by disability groups.

"It becomes a personal mission," said Lazio. "My dad would have been too disabled to take advantage of this bill, but a lot of his friends could have."

In the final days, House Speaker J. Dennis Hastert, R-Ill., forced warring House members to compromise. The White House, which for months had refused pleas to help find funding, pressed hard for the bill in budget talks with the GOP. President Clinton twice pressed Hastert to restore $100 million to the measure during House-Senate negotiations.

Years of Debate

To understand why the debate is so intense, advocates say, you have to understand the stakes. To receive disability payments, an individual must be both seriously impaired and have scant income. For example, someone who makes more than $700 a month on Social Security Disability Insurance (SSDI) can lose benefits. Those who exceed Medicaid limits can lose personal attendant care to help them bathe, dress and eat — coverage not available in the private market.

Rep. Jim Ramstad, R-Minn., started working on the issue as a state legislator. When he came to Congress in 1991, he hired a friend, Tom Haben, who is disabled.

"He had to quit to keep medical assistance," Ramstad said. "The system is cruel and unusual."

Congress has altered the law in fits and starts for decades. The debate resurfaced in 1995, when the GOP took control of Congress and made a push to weed out fraud in federal disability programs. During hearings Bunning conducted on the issue, he found that the system tended to discourage people from leaving the rolls for work. Working closely with the disability community, he introduced a bill in 1996 to retool job training and Jeffords began a separate health care effort.

The current push accelerated in June 1997, when Bryon R. MacDonald made his first-ever lobbying visit to Washington.

MacDonald, of Oakland, Calif., is an advocate with the Center for Independent Living, which helps people with physical and mental impairments find housing and jobs. He and many of his colleagues were frustrated by chronic unemployment among the disabled. They spent months organizing meetings with consumers, educators and parents, an effort that evolved into a 1997 Houston conference on job barriers.

MacDonald immersed himself in the issue in 1980, when he was hired to supervise people with mental disabilities who had been placed in jobs in greenhouses and nurseries. One charge was a man who had been in a special work

Disability Bill Highlights

NOVEMBER 20 — About 8 million working-age individuals are on the federal disability rolls, a number that has been steadily growing. Right now, less than 1 percent leave the rolls for work. While many are too severely impaired to take jobs, a revolution in computer technology and the enactment of civil rights protections under the 1990 Americans with Disabilities Act (PL 101-336) have improved the overall outlook. *(1990 Almanac, p. 447)*

Legislation (HR 1180) cleared Nov. 19 would end a paradox in current law whereby individuals receiving Social Security Disability (SSDI) or Supplemental Security Income (SSI) risk losing Medicare and Medicaid health insurance coverage if they return to work. The bill would also revamp vocational rehabilitation and employment services.

Advocates expect that millions will take advantage of the measure, but some budget forecasts are far less optimistic.

Under current law, individuals receiving SSDI can work for nine months in a five-year period without losing cash aid or Medicare. They can then work an additional 39 months and keep Medicare. The bill would add another 4½ years of Medicare coverage, for a total of 8½ years.

The original House version had a six-year Medicare extension, while the Senate bill included a six-year "window" during which qualified individuals would be guaranteed Medicare for as long as they worked. Conferees had agreed to take the House language. Senate Assistant Majority Leader Don Nickles, R-Okla., pressed them to scale it back to a 4½-year extension.

The legislation marks a significant expansion of the Medicaid program for poor, disabled and low-income people. States provide Medicaid benefits to SSI recipients. To qualify for SSI, individuals must meet disability guidelines and make less than $700 per month.

Under HR 1180, effective Oct. 1, 2000, states could offer Medicaid to individuals with disabilities whose incomes would otherwise disqualify them for SSI. States could also continue coverage to workers with disabilities whose medical condition had improved.

Individuals could buy into Medicaid under a sliding fee scale. Those making more than $75,000 a year would pay the full premium.

Grants would be provided to states to conduct outreach campaigns and provide services, such as personal attendant care, to help people perform such daily activities as dressing or eating. The grants would be funded at $20 million in fiscal 2001. The purpose is to give states, which fund Medicaid jointly with the federal government, a financial incentive to expand aid.

The bill includes another pilot program, funded at $250 million over six years, that would let states provide Medicaid to individuals with degenerative conditions who do not yet meet the stringent definition of disability. State governors hope that by more quickly providing prescription drugs they can keep individuals in the work force.

Another provision would create a "Ticket to Work," allowing individuals to purchase rehabilitation and job services through state agencies or private providers. To give individuals reassurance that working would not endanger their benefits, the bill provides that taking a job would not automatically trigger a review of disability status.

The measure includes a pilot program to test the impact of gradually reducing SSDI benefits by $1 for every $2 of earnings over a salary level that would be set by the Social Security commissioner. People now on SSDI fall off an "earnings cliff," losing aid if they make more than $700 a month.

The bill would be financed in part by altering payments for the federal school lunch program and changing earned-income tax credit rules relating to payments for low-income foster children.

program for seven years. His salary had risen to 45 cents an hour.

"The program was from hell," MacDonald said. "It isn't the disability, it isn't the condition. It's the supports that are either non-existent, or incredibly badly applied, that keep people out of the workplace."

MacDonald's initial Washington appointment was with Garner, who had been detailed to Kennedy by the Education Department to work on the Individuals with Disabilities Education Act (IDEA) rewrite (PL 105-17). Led by Lott's chief of staff, David Hoppe, Congress in 1997 worked out a compromise reauthorization. *(1997 Almanac, p. 7-3)*

During the debate, Kennedy and Garner were troubled by statistics showing that, more than two decades after IDEA's enactment, children with special needs were leaving public schools with scant hope of training or jobs. The bleak outlook had special resonance for Garner, whose brood of seven includes 13-year-old Ashleigh, who has mental retardation.

Ashleigh, Garner's fourth child, was born without complications. When she was 6 weeks old, Garner went back to work, only to return from her first day on the job to find the baby with mottled blue skin and a high fever. After being rushed to the hospital, she was diagnosed with viral encephalitis.

Ashleigh survived. But in the days and weeks that followed, it became clear that she was not developing like other children. It was the beginning of struggles with schools and other families for acceptance and opportunity — and worries about what she would do when her education ends.

"What happens when the [school] bus doesn't come any more?" Garner said. "For people coming up through the ranks, those 5½ million kids [in IDEA] . . . we want to be able to offer them something more than absolute fear when they get to the point of quote, unquote, the rest of their lives."

Even before MacDonald's visit, Kennedy wanted to write a bill to improve the job outlook for the disabled. The meeting was the beginning of a close relationship between Garner and the grass-roots. Adding to the movement, the Clinton administration, had proposed its own job program and backed a 1997 budget law provision (PL 105-33) to expand Medicaid. *(1997 Almanac, p. 2-18)*

A Sophisticated Network

Kennedy has had a lifelong interest in disability issues. His sister Rosemary has mental retardation, and his son Ted Jr. lost a leg to cancer. His sister Eunice Kennedy Shriver, Special Olympics founder, encouraged his work.

Kennedy joined with Jeffords, who has championed expanded rights for the disabled since coming to Congress in 1975. They decided to take the Bunning bill and add an expansive menu of health options. The two decided the way to win passage was to connect with the existing grass-roots organization. That meant more than a year of twice-weekly meetings with activists. It meant hitching a ride on a sophisticated network of advocates. MacDonald developed an e-mail blast list with more than 1,400 addresses for the disability bill alone. There is a broader database, coordinated with Washington-based organizations, that can reach 20,000 people in a matter of hours.

"I don't know what we did before [the Internet]," said Veronica Brown, chairwoman of Kentucky's Developmental Disability Council, an advocacy group.

There were also surveillance missions. Garner and Jeffords' aide Christopher Crowley would go unannounced to Social Security Administration offices, sit quietly in waiting rooms, and watch as people on disability struggled to get help from overwhelmed employees.

"It was one step removed from the Department of Motor Vehicles," Garner said. Social Security officials concede they have been overloaded.

In mid-1998, Crowley left, and Morrissey took over. A former House Republican aide, Morrissey worked on the landmark 1990 Americans with Disabilities Act (ADA) (PL 101-336), designed to end housing and employment bias. *(1990 Almanac, p. 447)*

She was convinced that Congress had bobbled an opportunity to address insurance issues in the ADA. Because of her cerebral palsy, Morrissey brought her own insight and deep commitment to the issue. Unlike Garner, Morrissey is leery of in-your-face lobbying. She sees her job as getting the best possible deal, not pushing an impossible ideal.

"People always want you on their side. The thing that probably makes the disability community in this town uneasy is that just because I have a disability, they don't know that I am going to agree with them," Morrissey said. "They have to sell me."

The two very different aides worked out a bill that would have cost about $5 billion and vastly expanded Medicare and Medicaid.

Kennedy also made a decision. The Bunning measure, cosponsored by former Rep. Barbara B. Kennelly, D-Conn. (1982-99), passed the House, 410-1, on June 4, 1998, and was sent to the Senate. Kennedy was afraid the Finance Committee would approve the bill, which included a two-year Medicare extension, but not the richer benefits he wanted. He used Senate rules to keep it from being referred to committee, despite some objections from the disability community.

That infuriated Bunning and Finance members who refused to take up the Jeffords-Kennedy bill. The duo moved to Plan B, mounting an all-out campaign to attach their measure to the end-of-year omnibus bill.

That is when the duck calls started.

The White House began to push the Jeffords-Kennedy plan in talks on the spending bill. Republicans refused to go beyond the Bunning bill. In addition to cost, there were questions about whether the Senate bill was workable.

The result was stalemate and anger that extended into the fall elections, specifically to Bunning.

As chairman of the Ways and Means Social Security Subcommittee, Bunning was one of the first to hone in on the work issue. When his bill passed in 1998, it was backed by a slew of advocacy and business groups.

While they supported Bunning's efforts, many advocates — by this time invested in the Jeffords-Kennedy plan — saw it as a starting point. Others considered the disability community naive for abandoning a sure deal.

In the closing days of his tight 1998 Senate race against former Democratic Rep. Scotty Baesler (1993-99), Bunning's campaign and district offices received an organized chain of phone calls from people accusing him of taking away their health care. Some said they had been contacted and told to protest.

"We worked on it for two years," Bunning said. "If there were phone banks from the disability community, it was misdirected. Without me and Barbara Kennelly . . . there wouldn't have been a bill."

Starting Over

After the election, Kennedy and Jeffords regrouped, enlisting Roth and Moynihan as cosponsors. Working with committee aides, they scaled the bill down to a hybrid, priced at about $1 billion over five years, that included many of Bunning's work provisions and less expansive health benefits.

"He [Roth] and his staff became champions of this bill. To see that turnaround was heartening," said Susan Prokop, advocate with the Paralyzed Veterans of America.

The sponsors agreed to walk in lockstep, no one sending out even a press release without the consent of the others. Then they pulled out the political and emotional stops to move the bill.

Clinton included the issue in his Jan. 19 State of the Union address and fiscal 2000 budget. In a bid to woo conservatives, a main witness at a Feb. 4 Finance Committee hearing was former Senate Majority Leader Robert J. Dole, R-Kan., who has limited use of his arms due to a World War II injury.

They had extra help. Nancy Becker Kennedy, a Los Angeles actress/playwright who is a quadriplegic, worked behind the scenes. She had testified before Congress in the 1970s, and again in 1998, about her friend, Lynn Thompson, who committed suicide after being told she would lose Social Security for making $400 a month.

"Lynn gave her attendant the night off, took a bottle of pills and alcohol and, while waiting to die, left an audio-taped suicide message. She said, 'Social Security, I overcame everything, but you were the straw that broke the camel's back.' "

One of Becker Kennedy's college friends is John D. Podesta, White House chief of staff, who would leave meetings with members of Congress to take her calls on the issue, staff aides said.

Finance marked up the bill (S 331) on March 4, with Lott and Assistant Majority Leader Don Nickles, R-Okla., voting nay.

In the House, Lazio with Rep. Henry A. Waxman, D-Calif., and Robert T. Matsui, D-Calif., introduced a companion measure. When Lazio was a sophomore in college, his father had a severe stroke that left him paralyzed.

"One story my mom tells . . . is how my dad went to one of these chain restaurants with some other folks that were going through rehabilitation with him. The manager shooed them out because, I guess, they weren't aesthetically correct," Lazio said.

Bliley moved Lazio's bill through his panel in a brisk markup on May 19 without any amendments (though without spending offsets).

Bliley had a gut-level reaction to the issue. For decades, employees at his family's Joseph W. Bliley funeral home in Richmond, Va., stopped each morning at the apartment of Ruth Rich, drove her to her secretarial job, and took her home at night.

"She had the best attendance record of anybody. She was loyal, devoted and hard-working," Bliley said. "This was her only outlet. Without this, she had her TV and her apartment."

Then the sponsors hit a wall. The bill lingered off the Senate floor as Nickles sought a cap on benefits, worried that upper-income people would receive subsidies. Lott wanted to eliminate a pilot program that would let people with degenerative conditions such as HIV qualify more quickly for Medicaid. The two, still smarting over Kennedy's efforts to ram a much larger bill through on the fiscal 1999 omnibus, thought the legislation was an effort to expand Medicaid beyond those with disabilities.

Bunning, now in the Senate, repaid Kennedy's move to kill his bill by putting his own hold on the measure — which had about 80 cosponsors. He later lifted his objection.

Lott's tactics did not go unnoticed. Advocates staged protests at his offices in Jackson and Pascagoula, Miss.

"The focus was for him to bring the bill up, to deal with whatever his problems were," said Mark Smith, executive director of the Coalition for Citizens with Disabilities in Jackson.

Throughout the year, activists tapped into their vast e-mail network and held demonstrations. The efforts were often coordinated with Washington-based disability groups.

"We were hell-bent to get this. To have the grass roots . . . both parties, both houses and the administration. It's so difficult to achieve that," said Marty Ford of The Arc, which represents people with mental retardation. She is also a co-chairman of the Consortium for Citizens with Disabilities, an umbrella group that lobbies on disability issues.

Obstacles, Again

Just as sponsors worked out compromises with Lott and Nickles, they ran into another obstacle in the form of Sen. Phil Gramm, R-Texas, who opposed paying for the bill by increasing a tax on foreign business. He blocked the measure from coming to the floor.

Unable to get around him, sponsors stripped the spending offsets from the bill. The Senate passed it, 99-0, on June 16. As the votes were counted, advocates waited outside the chamber.

Still, the measure languished in the House. Ways and Means Committee Chairman Bill Archer, R-Texas, said he would not take it up until Bliley suggested offsets. Bill Thomas, R-Calif., who wanted less of an expansion, worried that the Senate Medicare provisions would be a nightmare to administer.

Hulshof, a Ways and Means member, agitated for a markup of his bill, which had less sweeping health benefits. Ramstad and Nancy L. Johnson, R-Conn., also pressed Archer. As the House delayed, anxiety within the disability community grew. It intensified when Ways and Means in July marked up a 10-year $792 billion tax cut bill, without offsets."It's sorry to hear how everyone is committed to the policy, but they can't find the money," MacDonald said.

After the August break, Hastert brought the principals together and told them to work out a deal. Ways and Means on Oct. 14 marked up a scaled-down bill that was further cut before coming to the House floor.

It also picked up some heavy baggage. For instance, one offset — which the administration called a handout to commercial banks — changes the interest rate formula for guaranteed student loans. Another offset would have ended, in 2004, a break on Federal Housing Administration mortgage insurance.

Lott appointed himself as a conferee, with an eye toward using the bill as a vehicle for towing other must-pass legislation — such as expiring tax breaks — that were not fully offset.

At a GOP leadership meeting during the week of Nov. 8, Nickles, though not a conferee, demanded a cut in the bill's Medicare benefits. They were scaled back. "What if they [the disabled] have incomes of half-a-million dollars a year?" said Nickles.

Kennedy, upset about the changes and the FHA offset, threatened to work against the bill and persuaded some disability groups on Nov. 9 to send letters to Clinton seeking a veto. At that point, the Senate coalition and disability groups split. The Consortium on Citizens with Disabilities sent a Nov. 13 letter to conferees saying it could accept the measure.

The White House, fearing the bill would die, came up with offsets, including changes in the earned income tax credit. GOP leaders, having taken a political drubbing for recent efforts to alter that program, were afraid they were being set up, but accepted the White House offsets — and Clinton's demand to add back $100 million for a Medicaid pilot program. Nickles refused to restore the Medicare cuts.

On Nov. 17 Nickles and Lott, taking a high-risk gamble that Clinton would not veto the bill, attached a provision to bar the administration from going forward, for 90 days, with a controversial organ donor program. The White House bitterly protested, but did not try to stop the bill. The last-minute brinkmanship seemed a fitting ending for a bill that had teetered on the edge so many times before. ◆

Lawmakers Fail To Rewrite Organ Transplant Policy But Delay New HHS Regulations

SUMMARY

Congress placed a 90-day moratorium on organ procurement rules that the Department of Health and Human Services (HHS) released Oct. 18. It was included in a bill to extend health benefits for the disabled.

Despite intense interest in rewriting the nation's policy on how organs for transplantation are distributed, Congress was unable to enact comprehensive legislation. Instead, members placed a 90-day moratorium on new HHS rules.

The 90-day moratorium in the disability bill was expected to negate a deal between congressional leaders and HHS to delay the rules for 42 days. The 42-day moratorium was included in the fiscal 2000 Labor, HHS, and Education appropriations portion of the omnibus budget bill. Leaders were planning to send the disability bill to the president after the omnibus so the 90-day extension would prevail.

Last year, the administration issued proposed rules that would have distributed organs on the basis of medical criteria rather than geography. Administration officials said the changes would make the current system fairer, distributing organs to the sickest patients first. Currently, organs are allocated first to people on each transplant center's waiting list, then regionally, and then nationally.

Lawmakers representing large transplant centers, which would stand to benefit from a national allocation system, supported the administration's proposal. But members representing regional centers, which have taken patients and revenue from the larger centers, fought the plan. As part of the fiscal 1999 omnibus spending law (PL 105-277), Congress blocked the new regulations until October 1999.

HHS on Oct. 18 unveiled revised transplant regulations that maintained the fundamental aim of its earlier proposal: to direct organs to the sickest patients first, regardless of where they live. The proposed rules also would give the HHS secretary final say over organ allocation policy.

House Commerce Health Subcommittee Chairman Michael Bilirakis, R-Fla., sponsored a bill (HR 2418) that would take power away from HHS to make allocation policy. The measure was approved by the House Commerce Committee on Oct. 13, but was not considered on the floor.

Box Score

- **Bill:** HR 1180 — PL 106-170
- **Legislative action: House** adopted the conference report on HR 3194 (H Rept 106-479), 296-135, on Nov. 18. HR 3194 incorporated the Labor-HHS appropriations bill (HR 3424), which included a 42-day moratorium.

Senate cleared the bill, 74-24, on Nov. 19.

House adopted the conference report on the disability bill (HR 1180 — H Rept 106-478), which contained the 90-day moratorium, 418-2, on Nov. 18.

Senate cleared the bill, 95-1, on Nov. 19.

President signed HR 1180 on Dec. 17.

GOP Opposes Agency Plan

JULY 24 — Republican lawmakers say they will continue to oppose a Department of Health and Human Services (HHS) plan to allocate organs for transplant to the sickest patients first, despite a new report that generally supported the administration plan.

The report, by the Institute of Medicine, recommended greater federal government oversight of the system and backed the HHS plan to move to an organ allocation system based on medical need, not geography.

Congress ordered the study last year. Many lawmakers oppose HHS's organ guidelines, and Congress has blocked implementation of the guidelines until October and asked the institute to study them.

Many in Congress want to maintain the current system, in which organs are given first to patients on local transplant centers' waiting lists, then regionally, and then nationally.

Transplant advocacy groups, as well as the United Network for Organ Sharing (UNOS) — the private contractor that runs the country's organ allocation program — also oppose the HHS guidelines, fearing they will put small organ centers out of business.

The Institute's report agreed with the HHS proposal for broader organ sharing, but stopped short of calling for a national system. It also backed the HHS recommendation for greater government oversight.

On July 1, Rep. Michael Bilirakis, R-Fla., chairman of the Commerce Subcommittee on Health and Environment, introduced an organ allocation bill (HR 2418) that is largely at odds with the HHS plan.

Bilirakis said he will continue to push his bill but is willing to work with HHS and the transplant centers to find common ground. Congress must act by Oct. 21, or the HHS rules will go into effect. Bilirakis plans to hold hearings on his bill in September.

Administration officials argue that the current system causes great regional disparities in waiting times for organs.

House Committee Approves Organ Transplant Bill

OCTOBER 16 — The House Commerce Committee approved a bill (HR 2418) on Oct. 13 that would block the implementation of a Department of Health and Human Services (HHS) regulation on organ transplantation.

The HHS rule would allocate organs to patients who are most in need of transplants regardless of geography. It was proposed in April 1998, but its implementation was blocked by a one-year moratorium enacted as part of the fiscal 1999 omnibus spending bill (PL 105-277).

The House version of the fiscal 2000 Labor, Health and Human Services, and Education appropriations bill (HR 3037) would extend the moratorium for another year.

The Commerce Committee bill, approved by voice vote, would go further, taking power away from the HHS secretary to make substantive policy changes in the organ allocation system. Instead, it would create an Organ Procurement and Transplantation Network, a nonprofit private entity charged with running the program.

The result would be to nullify the HHS regulation.

Committee Democrats objected, saying the plan would eliminate the government's role. "Private contractors should have some input, but not total control," said Sherrod Brown, D-Ohio.

The panel rejected an amendment by Henry A. Waxman, D-Calif., to clarify that HHS would have oversight responsibility for the program. Republicans said it would give the secretary veto power.

HHS Modifies Its Rules for Giving Priority To Sickest Patients

OCTOBER 23 — The Department of Health and Human Services (HHS) on Oct. 18 unveiled revised regulations governing how organs for transplant are distributed around the nation. But critics say the revised policy did not go far enough to address their concerns.

In the new rules, which will take effect Nov. 19 unless Congress intervenes, HHS maintained the fundamental aim of its earlier proposal: to direct organs to the sickest patients first, regardless of where they live. But it clarified that organs should not be wasted by transferring them excessive distances or by transplanting them into extremely ill patients who would probably not survive.

Under the current system, organs are distributed on the basis of geography rather than medical need. Organs are allocated first to recipients on transplant centers' waiting lists, then regionally, then nationally. HHS has long argued for the sickest-first policy, saying that the current regional system has resulted in wide disparities in waiting times for organs across the country. Critics of the current system also say that it favors wealthy people who can afford to travel to another region and stay there for recuperation and follow-up care.

Larger transplant centers, which stand to benefit from a national allocation system, back the administration's proposed change. But regional transplant centers, which have grown steadily over the years — often at the expense of the larger centers — can be expected to fight to make sure the HHS policy does not take effect.

Several transplant centers as well as the United Network for Organ Sharing (UNOS), the Richmond, Va.-based private contractor that runs the organ allocation program for HHS, argue that the proposed policy could force some smaller centers to close.

The dispute led Congress to impose a one-year moratorium on implementing rules it proposed in 1998. The moratorium, which was part of the fiscal 1999 omnibus spending bill (PL 105-277), may be extended.

During House-Senate talks over the fiscal 2000 Labor, Health and Human Services and Education spending bill (HR 3037), lawmakers were discussing enacting a four-month review period before the new rules could take effect. That bill could see final action the week of Oct. 25.

Who Gets Control?

In proposing the new rules, HHS Secretary Donna E. Shalala said Oct. 18 that the agency's organ regulations reflected "constructive input" from Congress, transplant doctors and facilities.

Shalala said the new regulations relied heavily on a study released in July from the Institute of Medicine, a division of the National Academy of Sciences. As part of the 1999 spending law, Congress asked the agency to evaluate the current organ allocation system for possible inequities.

In a news release, Shalala urged lawmakers to focus on how to get organs to the people who need them most.

At the center of the organ fight is the question of who has authority over the system. The proposed HHS rules would give the secretary final say over organ allocation policy.

On Oct. 13, the House Commerce Committee approved a bill (HR 2418) that would take power away from the secretary to make substantive policy changes in organ allocation. The measure, approved by voice vote, would create an Organ Procurement and Transplantation Network, a nonprofit private entity charged with running the program.

House Commerce Health and Environment Subcommittee Chairman Michael Bilirakis, R-Fla., the bill's chief sponsor, has requested a floor vote, but it is unclear whether that will happen this year. Some Democrats oppose the legislation, saying the plan would eliminate the government's role. UNOS also said it would work to block broader HHS control of the program.

Senate Leaders Act To Delay Implementation Of New Rules

NOVEMBER 20 — The Senate's two top Republicans made a last-minute move to stop the Clinton administration from implementing proposed new regulations that would allocate organs for transplant based on necessity rather than geography.

Majority Leader Trent Lott of Mississippi and Assistant Majority Leader Don Nickles of Oklahoma on Nov. 17 inserted language into disability and tax legislation (HR 1180) that would stop the new federal rules from going into effect for at least 90 days after passage and reopen them to public comment.

The move is expected to negate an

earlier agreement reached Nov. 10 with appropriators and Secretary of Health and Human Services (HHS) Donna E. Shalala that would have delayed the regulation for 42 days.

Senate GOP leaders argued that they had not endorsed the earlier agreement. Lott said that he wanted to give Congress more time to enact legislation to revise the proposed policy.

"My problem was with what was done in the appropriations bill," Lott said Nov. 19. "I didn't think that was fair. We should have some reasonable period of time, 90 days, to take one last look at it and to see if we can develop legislation."

The measure with the 90-day delay passed the House on Nov. 18 by a vote of 418-2. The Senate cleared the measure Nov. 19 by a vote of 95-1. *(House vote 611, p. H-198; Senate vote 372, p. S-74)*

But the overall debate over organ policy is far from over. Although the 90-day delay may become law, proponents of the new policy vow to implement it eventually.

The maneuvering "is just going to increase our incentive to make sure this regulation does go into effect and there's no [future] legislation to change this," said Labor-HHS Appropriations Subcommittee Chairman Arlen Specter, R-Pa. HHS proposed the new standards for allocating organs in April 1998. The United Network for Organ Sharing (UNOS), the private contractor that administers the program, looks for a recipient first locally, then regionally and then throughout the nation.

A Regional Battle

The issue has sparked a fierce debate that has broken down over regional rather than party lines. Administration officials say that under the current policy, some people wait up to five times longer than others for a transplant because the system favors geography over medical urgency.

Congress in the fiscal 1999 omnibus spending law (PL 105-277) delayed the regulations until October. HHS officials tweaked their proposal after an Institute of Medicine report was released this summer that suggested changes but supported many aspects of the administration's proposal. The agency released revised regulations Oct. 18.

White House officials accused Republican leaders of "bad faith" in changing the agreed-upon delay. But their leverage to change the delay was limited. GOP leaders attached the longer delay to a conference report (H Rept 106-478) on a bill to expand health benefits for disabled workers and extend tax breaks.

However, Republicans will have to work through a procedural difficulty. Because the spending and tax bills carried irreconcilably different timetables, the provision that Clinton signs last would prevail. Republicans said they planned to ensure that Clinton would sign their preferred approach because they would send the time-sensitive spending bill first, then wait to send the disability/tax bill until after the budget bill was signed.

The debate will shift to the legislative arena next year. House Commerce Committee Chairman Thomas J. Bliley Jr., R-Va., is leading efforts to revise the entire program. He pushed a bill (HR 2418) through the Commerce Committee on Oct. 13 to strengthen the power of UNOS. ◆

Chapter 17

INDUSTRY & REGULATION

Despite Progress in the House, Attempt to Open Electricity Markets Stalls

Box Score

- **Bill:** HR 2944
- **Legislative action: House** Commerce Energy and Power Subcommittee approved HR 2944 Oct. 27 by a vote of 17-11.

SUMMARY

Supporters of legislation to deregulate the nation's electric utility industry achieved a significant milestone Oct. 27 when the House Commerce Energy and Power Subcommittee approved legislation designed to spur competition and consumer choice. But the bill (HR 2944) failed to bridge any of the differences that have stalled progress on past electricity deregulation measures, leaving its fate in doubt for 2000.

As in past years, efforts to infuse competition and consumer choice into the nation's $220 billion electricity market failed. The difference in 1999 was that a bill was actually marked up for the first time.

Getting beyond that point, however, will not be easy. Though HR 2944, sponsored by Joe L. Barton, R-Texas, was approved, there was no consensus. The bill would give much of the power to states, rather than the federal government, to set the rules governing a competitive electric market.

Barton's bill drew the ire of the White House and House Commerce Committee Chairman Thomas J. Bliley Jr., R-Va., who said that the bill would give states too much power to set rules for a deregulated market. It also has been criticized by environmental groups and some Democrats. Edward J. Markey, D-Mass., called the legislation "a monopoly bill," and the Clinton administration opposed HR 2944 in its current form.

Opponents complained that without a stronger federal role, consumers would not be sufficiently protected. Environmental interests, supported by the White House, criticized HR 2944 for not requiring utilities to generate power from renewable sources. The administration's proposal would require that 7.5 percent of all power by the year 2010 be generated from renewable sources.

Barton's bill is intended to promote competition by ensuring that competitors have access to the electricity transmission system. It would also repeal the Public Utility Holding Company Act of 1935, which restricts big utilities from entering new markets. Barton's bill also would attempt to ensure the reliability of the transmission system. Those changes, however, would be largely orchestrated by the states. Barton's bill would provide no significant new authority to the Federal Energy Regulatory Commission to oversee a more competitive marketplace. Nor does the bill include a "date certain" by which time states must move to open competition. HR 2944 also would not require utilities to generate power from renewable sources such as wind.

The House Commerce Committee will mark up HR 2944 next year, and the Senate Energy and Natural Resources Committee will begin considering separate legislation early in the year.

Both face major opposition from the administration, various utility groups, and consumer and environmental interests. Progress will be slow and difficult.

Senate Panel Votes To Repeal PUHCA

FEBRUARY 13 — The Senate Banking, Housing and Urban Affairs Committee approved by voice vote Feb. 11 a bill (S 313) to repeal the Public Utility Holding Company Act of 1935 (PUHCA).

The measure would allow multistate power companies to expand beyond current geographic limits by repealing the Depression-era law that limits their growth and business activities. Consumer groups say it would create more competition and lower the price of electricity. *(1997 Almanac, p. 3-7)*

But Sen. Phil Gramm, R-Texas, the panel's chairman, said he did not plan to push the bill to the Senate floor immediately. Rather, he said he would prefer to see the bill coupled with a broader bill being developed in the Energy and Natural Resources Committee.

"It is my goal to see our bill married up with a similar bill out of the Energy Committee to deregulate the production of electric power in America," said Gramm.

A stand-alone proposal to repeal PUHCA was blocked in 1998 by the threat of a filibuster by former Sen. Dale Bumpers, D-Ark. Although Bumpers has retired, a stand-alone repeal of PUHCA continues to face opposition from lawmakers who want more comprehensive legislation. At the banking hearing, Jack Reed, D-R.I., said he opposed the bill.

House Commerce Committee Chairman Thomas J. Bliley Jr., R-Va., has staunchly opposed a simple repeal of PUHCA, saying that such reforms must be coupled with a bill that sets a deadline for states to deregulate the price of electricity.

The 1935 law restricts 16 companies registered with the Securities and Exchange Commission — 13 electric power companies and three gas companies — from diversifying into new businesses.

White House Plan Gets Warmer Reception on Hill

APRIL 17 — In an effort to get the debate moving on Capitol Hill, the Clinton administration April 15 unveiled its plan for bringing competition to the nation's $215 billion electric utility market.

And unlike last year, when an administration plan was greeted in Congress with little enthusiasm, the latest edition was more warmly received.

"This is an important step forward in moving toward a bipartisan electricity restructuring bill," said Rep. Steve Largent, R-Okla., who joined Energy Secretary Bill Richardson, Environmental Protection Agency Administrator Carol M. Browner and others at a news conference to present the proposal.

Despite the encouraging start, the road ahead for electricity deregulation will be long and arduous. Aside from the technical and economic complexity of dismantling monopolies, there are regional and political differences that often are hard to reconcile.

Sen. Frank H. Murkowski, R-Alaska, who chairs the Energy and Natural Resources Committee, said the new administration proposal raises many of the same concerns as the one last year.

Foremost is the requirement that 7.5 percent of all electricity sold by 2010 come from "non-hydroelectric renewable resources" such as wind or solar energy. That is higher than the 5.5 percent outlined by the administration last year that came under attack from Murkowski and other critics.

"Setting up a mandate to take this nation from its current two-tenths of 1 percent in renewable sources to 7.5 percent is a quantum leap that will be very expensive to consumers," Murkowski said.

While he supported some proposals, Murkowski said the new plan did not go far enough to allow real competition and expressed concern that "many of the provisions still involve more government manipulation and interference with the marketplace."

Rep. Edward J. Markey, D-Mass., who also appeared at the news conference, said chances are "50-50" that a bill will pass this year.

While similar to last year's plan in many respects, the new version bears the imprint of Richardson, a former congressman from New Mexico (1983-97) who used his political skills to create a bill that Republicans could at least consider.

The most notable difference from last year's proposal is the treatment of the federally owned electric suppliers such as the Tennessee Valley Authority and the Bonneville Power Administration, which serves the Pacific Northwest. Customers of those utilities enjoy some of the lowest prices in the country, and many in those regions fear that deregulation would lead to higher electric bills.

"The administration's Northwest-specific provisions treat our region fairly, and we must make the most of this opportunity to ensure that we come out ahead instead of being left behind," said Sen. Slade Gorton, R-Wash.

Electricity deregulation is a high priority in the House. Largent is drafting legislation, and House Speaker J. Dennis Hastert, R-Ill., has indicated he hopes a bill could come to the floor by late August or early September.

New Competition

Just as last year, at the center of the administration's plan is the advent of open competition among electricity suppliers nationwide by 2003. The proposal also contains a circuit breaker, allowing states to "opt out" if there is evidence competition would not yield savings for consumers.

Richardson said the average family of four would save $232 a year in lower electric bills if the administration's plan is adopted.

"By sending this bill to Congress today, we hope to jump-start action on Capitol Hill and to demonstrate the momentum that exists for federal action on the issue," Richardson said.

In addition to mandating open competition by 2003, the administration's plan would:

- Give the Federal Energy Regulatory Commission new oversight powers to ensure that utilities promote competition.
- Establish a $3 billion "Public Benefits Fund" to support continued funding for low-income energy assistance, energy conservation, and other programs that promote development of clean and efficient technologies.

Murkowski expressed concerns about the fund, calling it a $3 billion tax for a federal "slush fund" with virtually no clear direction regarding the disbursement of funds.

- Establish a grant program to ensure that people in remote and rural areas benefit from competition.

More criticism came from such disparate groups as the Sierra Club and the Edison Electric Institute, which represents big investor-owned utilities. Their comments underscore the difficulty facing lawmakers attempting to draft legislation that could win passage.

The Sierra Club expressed "deep disappointment" with the plan because it does not contain "concrete goals for reducing global warming and air pollutants."

Thomas R. Kuhn, president of the Washington-based Edison Electric Institute, said there are some elements his group can support, but the plan still falls short.

"In many respects, this bill amounts to re-regulation and not deregulation," he said.

Despite the concerns and competing interests, 20 states have acted on electricity deregulation, putting pressure on Congress and the administration to find a workable bill.

"Federal action is vital to the success of these restructuring programs. Electrons do not respect state borders," Richardson said. "Competition won't reach its potential without comprehensive federal electricity restructuring legislation."

House Panel Resumes Work Despite Calls To Slow Down

OCTOBER 9 — For the first time in months, legislation to deregulate the nation's $220 billion electricity market appeared to be emerging from a long political brownout.

Joe L. Barton, R-Texas, chairman of the House Commerce Energy and Power Subcommittee and a leader in the push for deregulation, held two days of hearings Oct. 5-6 on his bill (HR 2944). A full markup is scheduled the week of Oct. 18.

The Commerce Finance and Hazardous Materials Subcommittee followed Barton's committee on Oct. 7 with a hearing on repealing the Public Utilities Holding Company Act of 1935 (PUHCA). The law is widely viewed as a barrier to open competition in the electricity marketplace because it prohibits 16 large utilities from diversifying into new businesses.

Meanwhile, another key figure in the debate, Sen. Frank H. Murkowski, R-Alaska, chairman of the Energy and Natural Resources Committee, unveiled the contours of a bill he plans to sponsor. Although Murkowski did not say when he would introduce his plan, it was a narrower proposal than Barton's bill.

Both measures, however, held true to the path preferred by Republicans — giving authority to oversee a deregulated market primarily to the states rather than the federal government. Both call for repealing the 1935 law.

Despite the spasm of activity, the net result at the end of the week was negligible as legislative efforts to bring competition and consumer choice to the electric industry remained snarled by partisan differences.

That being the case, some on the subcommittee urged Barton to slow down.

"There is little merit in forcing a markup in order to meet an arbitrary deadline," John D. Dingell, D-Mich., said Oct. 5 during the first hearing on Barton's bill.

"The time for enactment of legislation that will serve the broad public interest may not yet have arrived," Dingell said.

At the center of the debate are several issues that have blocked any movement. Among them:

- How much authority to give the Federal Energy Regulatory Commission (FERC) to oversee and guide a new electric economy that spans state borders and is based on competition rather than monopolies.
- How to fold such enormous federal government electric utilities as the Tennessee Valley Authority and the Bonneville Power Authority into the new market without trampling competing utilities that did not enjoy the same federal subsidy. (Murkowski does not address the issue; Barton would limit TVA's reach and its ability to compete outside its service area.)
- How to ensure the reliability of the transmission system in an era of competition.
- How to protect consumers from being harmed in the new freewheeling environment by keeping large, well-financed utilities from snuffing out competitors.

Although those questions have surrounded all deregulation bills, they have a particular hold on HR 2944.

The administration opposes the bill, as do most Democrats on the subcommittee. Nor does the bill bridge factions within the electric industry, where there is tension between large investor-owned utilities and cooperatives and between urban utilities and those serving rural areas.

Consumer Savings

There is general agreement that deregulation would save consumers money. The administration estimates annual savings of $20 billion, or $232 a year for a family of four.

But Barton's bill, said Alan H. Richardson, executive director of the American Public Power Association, "falls short of even the minimum requirements necessary to . . . promote competition."

Rep. Edward J. Markey, D-Mass., was even more blunt. "Something seems to have gone very wrong with the product before us," Markey said during the Oct. 5 hearing.

"It deregulates the monopolies in a manner which will free them to engage in a wide array of unfair, predatory, and manipulative practices."

Murkowski was even less ambitious, choosing to put off action until next year.

"We will begin next year when Congress reconvenes with hearings," Murkowski said at the National Summit on Electricity and Natural Gas on Oct. 7 when he unveiled his proposal. "It would be foolish to rush this."

That leaves Barton as the only game in town, and there is plenty of gamesmanship over his bill. Barton has been sparring for weeks with Commerce Committee Chairman Thomas J. Bliley Jr., R-Va., over deregulation. Bliley has been pushing Barton to cede more power to federal regulators.

Barton's pace annoyed Bliley, who encouraged Barton to move quicker and if necessary, muscle Democrats to the side.

"Does the esteemed committee chairman expect me to deliver a corpse?" Barton complained in a Sept. 21 letter to Bliley.

Despite his best efforts, however, Barton's bill appears to be struggling.

"It is critical the Congress pass comprehensive electricity restructuring legislation sooner, rather than later," Deputy Energy Secretary T. J. Glauthier told Barton at the Oct. 5 hearing.

But he added, "The administration cannot support HR 2944 in its current form" because the federal role is too limited.

"The federal government needs to send the appropriate signals about what the rules of the road will be in this new world of competition," Glauthier said.

Rules of the Road

HR 2944 would establish two sets of rules for the transmission systems, with the states responsible for lines in their jurisdiction and FERC the rest — about 34 percent of the system.

Barton's bill would ask, but does not require, utilities to use renewable sources to generate electricity. The bill would also require utilities to form partnerships with other utilities to ensure that all consumers were served. The bill would limit FERC oversight of such arrangements.

The administration and consumer groups insist that FERC should have a more dominant role in approving any partnership to ensure that consumers are protected.

"If this bill were enacted, the crazy quilt of state and federal regulations that exist today would get even crazier," said Elizabeth Anne Moler, former FERC chairwoman who is counsel for Americans for Affordable Electricity, an umbrella organization of utilities, industry and consumer groups.

Democrats, environmental groups and some utilities would like mandates establishing a "date certain" for states to open their markets to competition; requiring a certain percentage of a utility's power supply come from renewable sources such as wind and hydro; and giving the federal government oversight of the interstate electric grid. Republicans are opposed to mandates.

"The legislation now under consideration may have the effect at any state line of suddenly turning an eight-lane superhighway for power into the equivalent of a bumpy country road," Lynne H. Church, executive director of the Electric Power Supply Association, told Barton's subcommittee Oct. 6.

The administration's proposal, unveiled in April, calls for states to pass legislation necessary to deregulate the electric market by 2003.

Another stumbling block is that neither Barton nor Murkowski would require utilities to generate a portion of their electricity using renewable sources.

The administration's bill would mandate that 7.5 percent of all electricity generated by 2010 come from renewable sources such as wind or solar energy. Utilities and other critics insist that that target is unreasonable and would make electricity more expensive, not cheaper as envisioned by supporters of deregulation.

The administration's proposal also differs from Barton and Murkowski's proposals because it would give FERC much more authority to dictate and enforce rules for increasing competition.

With 24 states having already passed legislation to deregulate utilities, many in Congress — particularly Republicans — say that the federal government should do little more than step out of the way.

Rep. John Shimkus, R-Ill., made clear the division on Oct. 5 when he told Glauthier: "You trust the federal regulator. I trust [a state's] public utility commission."

House Panel OKs Bill, But Big Issues Still Unresolved

OCTOBER 30 — In muscling his bill through subcommittee Oct. 27, Rep. Joe L. Barton, R-Texas, achieved a long-sought goal in his effort to open the nation's $220 billion electricity market to competition.

But whatever joy he felt as the Commerce Energy and Power Subcommittee approved his bill, 17-11, was tempered by the reality of what lies ahead. The marathon markup did nothing to bridge differences that have weighed down the bill (HR 2944).

Barton, who is chairman of the subcommittee, was opposed by most Democrats on the panel, as well as the Clinton administration and a web of consumer, environmental and industry interests.

"This is really not a competition bill any longer — it is a monopoly bill," Democrat Edward J. Markey of Massachusetts said Oct. 27 as the markup got under way.

"It deregulates the monopolies and gives them a green light to engage in a wide array of unfair, predatory and manipulative practices — practices which would . . . leave consumers paying more than they should for their electricity," he said.

The lack of consensus was reflected in the 51 amendments that were filed before the markup. Many of those amendments were withdrawn, including one that would make sweeping changes in how utilities are regulated and another that would impose tougher environmental standards. The sponsors of those amendments, Markey and Frank Pallone Jr., D-N.J., said they would offer them when the full committee considers the bill next year.

Even Commerce Committee Chairman Thomas J. Bliley Jr., R-Va., who might be expected to support his GOP colleague, expressed reservations.

"While I am pleased we are finally taking this initial step," Bliley said, "I would be remiss if I did not mention that I still have concerns about this particular bill. I don't know if this bill strikes the right balance for consumers. . . . I believe we still have a long way to go."

Despite the heavy lifting that lies ahead and doubts about whether agreement can ever be found, Barton said he is pleased with the markup.

"We created a cooperative, bipartisan atmosphere, and crafted the first major electricity restructuring bill to ever pass a . . . subcommittee. I am very proud of our work," Barton said.

Barton's bill is intended to promote competition by opening access to the transmission system, removing such barriers as the Public Utility Holding Company Act of 1935, which restricts big utilities from entering new markets. Barton's bill also would attempt to improve the reliability of the transmission system.

Those changes, however, would be largely orchestrated by the states. Barton's bill provides no significant new authority to the Federal Energy Regulatory Commission (FERC) to oversee a more competitive marketplace.

Nor does the bill include a "date certain" by which time states must move to open competition.

HR 2944 also would not require utilities to generate power from renewable sources such as wind. The administration's proposal would require that 7.5 percent of all power by the year 2010 be generated from renewable sources.

The subcommittee adopted an amendment by Richard M. Burr, R-N.C., requiring FERC review of utility company mergers within 180 days. If FERC fails to act, the mergers are automatically approved.

The subcommittee also adopted an amendment by Robert L. Ehrlich Jr., R-Md., giving precedence to state laws dealing with consumer protection, mergers and interconnecting power systems if the state laws are enacted within three years of HR 2944's enactment.

Bigger Issues

Those amendments did little, however, to address the larger disputes. Those include:

- How much authority FERC should have in overseeing a new electricity industry that spans state borders and is based on competition rather than monopolies.
- How to fold enormous federal government electric utilities, such as the Tennessee Valley Authority (TVA) and the Bonneville Power Administration, into the new market without trampling competing utilities that have not benefited from a federal subsidy. (Barton's bill would limit TVA's reach and its ability to compete outside its service area.)
- How to keep other large, well-financed utilities from snuffing out competitors.
- How to ensure the reliability of the transmission system in an era of competition. ◆

Chapter 18

LAW & JUDICIARY

Gun Control Agreement Eludes Conferees, Derails Juvenile Crime Legislation

SUMMARY

The fate of wide-ranging juvenile justice legislation, the main provisions of which would increase penalties for teen criminals and provide state grants for crime prevention, was uncertain as Congress adjourned. That is because House and Senate negotiators remained at an impasse on what — if any — gun control provisions should be in the legislation. The Senate passed a bill with modest new restrictions. The House passed a juvenile justice bill without any gun control language, after overwhelmingly defeating a bill with gun restrictions more limited than the Senate's.

On April 20, Dylan Klebold and Eric Harris killed a dozen schoolmates, a teacher and then themselves at Columbine High School in Littleton, Colo. Two days later, the House began moving its juvenile justice legislation. The next week, Majority Leader Trent Lott, R-Miss., a longtime opponent of gun control, promised to arrange a Senate debate on new firearms restrictions.

He picked as a vehicle a juvenile justice bill (S 254) that was a revision of legislation that died in the 105th Congress. Many Democrats and children's rights advocates had reservations about the measure, complaining that it emphasized punishment too emphatically over prevention. The bill's scope was significantly expanded during eight days of debate, in part with the adoption of several gun control amendments. These would ban imports of clips or magazines capable of holding more than 10 bullets; require that all handguns be sold with a child safety trigger lock or safety storage device; enhance federal regulation of gun shows; and expand the so-called Brady law, which requires background checks for buyers of handguns (PL 103-159) to cover anyone who wanted to buy a weapon at any gun show with more than 50 firearms for sale. The statute gives law enforcement officials three business days to complete the check.

The gun show amendment, by Frank R. Lautenberg, D-N.J., proved the most contentious, both in Senate debate and in the negotiations that were continuing at adjournment. Initially, a minimally different version was tabled, or killed. It was adopted six days later, but only when Vice President Al Gore cast the tie-breaking vote.

After that, however, the Senate voted overwhelmingly to pass the bill, which would also expand the number of juveniles tried as adults, increase an array of sentences and permit more drug testing by schools.

The next week, Speaker J. Dennis Hastert, R-Ill., said he would push the House to pass "common-sense" gun control. But among those working against him was Majority Whip Tom DeLay, R-Texas. GOP leaders decided to arrange for separate votes on juvenile justice and gun control legislation.

The juvenile crime bill (HR 1501) is in general tougher on teenage criminals than the Senate bill, and it would go further in attempting to modify the behavior of teenagers before they get into trouble. It would, for example, provide broader civil immunity to school officials who discipline students and allow the Ten Commandments to be displayed in public. But the House rejected an amendment that would have banned the sale to minors of violent or sexually explicit material.

The gun control bill (HR 2122) was defeated because many gun control advocates concluded it did not go far enough, while gun rights advocates concluded it went too far. The House bill was less restrictive than the Senate's; President Clinton charged it was "ghostwritten" by the National Rifle Association. It would have allowed just 24 hours for background checks at gun shows, and the types of events where buyers would be subject to the checks were much more narrowly defined than under the Senate bill. A requirement that guns be sold with safety devices defined such device as any part that, when removed, disabled the firearm.

Conferees met only once, and positions hardened quickly. Senate gun control advocates said they would accept nothing less than the Lautenberg gun show language. House gun rights advocates said such language could never pass the House. The chairmen of the two Judiciary committees, Rep. Henry J. Hyde, R-Ill., and Sen. Orrin G. Hatch, R-Utah, who both favor some new gun curbs, unveiled a compromise that was spurned by both sides.

Both House and Senate leaders say they will try again to push for a gun control agreement, but compromise seems unlikely in an election year. Democrats generally support more gun control, and polls show that the public does as well. But gun rights advocates say they can marshal committed, single-issue voters who can make the difference in a close election. Negotiators say that differences between the House and Senate on juvenile crime should be easy to resolve, but only once the gun control issue is settled.

Box Score

- **Bill:** HR 1501
- **Legislative action: Senate** voted 73-25 to pass S 254 on May 20.

House passed HR 1501, 287-139, on June 17.

House defeated HR 2122, 147-280, on June 18.

House Panel OKs Bill To Combat Juvenile Crime

APRIL 24 — Congressional debate about how to combat youth violence has been animated in the past two decades by the belief that Washington had many, if not all, of the answers to slowing the crime rate. But the school massacre in Littleton, Colo., has generated doubts about that supposition.

That murderous rampage April 20 is likely to generate momentum for measures that would limit children's access to guns. But it also has forced lawmakers to question whether their traditional ways of combating crime should have stopped the shooting and bombing spree at Columbine High School.

In taking their own lives after killing 13 others, seniors Eric Harris and Dylan Klebold belied the theory that tough sentencing is the best deterrent. And the boys' lack of a record for violent crime suggested that the worst criminal acts are not always committed by a small group of repeat offenders, often referred to by lawmakers as "super predators."

"It's an irrational, suicidal attack we have here," said Chairman Bill McCollum, R-Fla., of the House Judiciary Crime Subcommittee. "It may well be that no amount of law will be effective."

McCollum said he needs to know more about the Colorado case before reaching conclusions. More aggressive intervention after the two were caught stealing last year might have helped, he said. But he and his colleagues are taking an increasingly sober look at their ability to stop crimes like this one.

"There is no legislative response that is going to have an immediate impact," said Virginia's Robert C. Scott, the ranking Crime Subcommittee Democrat.

On a voice vote two days after the shootings, the panel approved legislation (HR 1501) that would authorize $1.5 billion in grants during the next three years to states for combating juvenile crime. In return for the funds, the measure would ask states to create a graduated system of penalties for juvenile crime so that potentially violent teens would come face to face with the criminal justice system as soon as they commit their first crime. But states could avoid that requirement if they gave the Justice Department a persuasive rationale.

Legislation (HR 1150) reauthorizing Justice Department crime prevention grant programs was also approved on a voice vote April 22, by the House Education and the Workforce Subcommittee on Early Childhood, Youth and Families. It would streamline the application process and give communities greater flexibility in how they spend the money.

Both bills are expected to advance in full committee the week of April 26.

The easy start for the Judiciary bill was in marked contrast to the 105th Congress. Then, McCollum insisted on provisions tying the funding to requirements that violent teens be tried in adult courts, that states keep extensive records on youth crime and that judges be allowed to take action against parents for the behavior of their children. The House passed the bill but the full Senate never took it up.

With those mandates dropped, this year's bill has key Democratic backers. Such bipartisanship is not yet evident in the Senate, where no juvenile crime bill has begun to move. After the Colorado shootings, the Health, Education, Labor & Pensions Committee promised hearings next month on school safety.

Gun Control Legislation

As anger after the worst school shooting in American history spurred victories for gun control legislation in several statehouses, gun control advocates in the capital drew attention to legislation (HR 1342, S 735) designed to prevent both criminal activity and accidents involving guns. Among other things, it would penalize gun dealers for selling to minors. It would penalize gun owners if their guns are used by a minor to commit a crime. It would also require a number of safety features on guns, including trigger locks. The measure is opposed by the National Rifle Association.

At an April 22 news conference, House sponsor Carolyn McCarthy, D-N.Y., who was elected in 1996 after her husband was killed by a gunman on a Long Island commuter train, said she was prepared to use the parliamentary device of a discharge petition in a bid to gain a vote on the measure over the objections of the Republican leadership.

The White House and Justice Department said April 22 that the administration would soon propose legislation that would take the same multipronged approach as McCarthy's bill, of which Edward M. Kennedy, D-Mass., is the Senate sponsor. Officials said the package would seek to consolidate a variety of gun control proposals, revive the waiting period for handgun purchases (PL 103-159) that expired last year, and attempt to help schools and police identify potentially troublesome situations before they become violent.

"We have to look at a comprehensive set of measures," Deputy Attorney General Eric H. Holder Jr. told reporters. "Everything from conflict resolution to trigger locks."

Juvenile Crime Bill Heads Straight To Senate Floor

MAY 8 — For most of the 105th Congress, legislation designed to prevent and punish juvenile crime languished in the Senate. After surviving a bruising markup, the bill sat untouched for 18 months because of opposition on both the political left, which found the bill too hard on teenage offenders, and the political right, which was afraid the measure's anti-gang provisions could be used to prosecute gun dealers or that the bill would become the vehicle for new federal gun-lock requirements. *(1997 Almanac, p. 5-3)*

This year, in the wake of the carnage at Columbine High School, the Senate's approach is radically different. A revised juvenile crime bill (S 254) is expected to be brought to the floor the week of May 10 — without so much as a hearing. Few senators had even been briefed on the bill until the past few weeks.

And advocates of the rights of gun owners — who were fearful last year that they might lose a vote on whether to require that trigger locks be sold with all handguns — now have a host of other amendments to look out for. Majority Leader Trent Lott, R-Miss., has promised advocates of gun control a shot at several amendments, one of which is sure to be the gun-lock idea.

This new trial-by-fire approach is a direct outgrowth of the events in Littleton, Colo., on April 20, when two teenagers — armed with pipe bombs and a cache of weapons — killed a dozen schoolmates and a teacher before shooting themselves.

Until that day, the juvenile crime bill was relatively free of discord. The language that gun rights groups had objected to last year had been abandoned. And while Democrats were still grumbling about some of the bill's provisions, enough other changes had been made that the bill's sponsors saw themselves as picking up more than enough Democratic support to pass.

Now the bill could be the battleground for as many as eight proposals. These include a ban on gun sales over the Internet; an expansion of federal criminal background checks for participants in gun shows; an increase in the minimum age for a firearms purchase to 21 from 18; and an import ban on high-capacity ammunition clips.

It is not clear how many of these will be offered, because Lott has not detailed his proposed ground rules for the debate, but the Democrats orchestrating the effort have already begun to winnow out proposals they see having little chance. Reviving the law setting a waiting period for gun purchases (PL 103-159) is an idea they have stopped touting. Also fading from their serious consideration is a proposal central to both the leading House gun control package (HR 1342), by Rep. Carolyn McCarthy, D-N.Y., and the gun control proposal of President Clinton: subjecting parents to criminal prosecution when their firearms are used in a crime by their children. Senate Minority Leader Tom Daschle, S.D., who has been a vocal gun control skeptic, opposes this idea.

Of those still likely to get a vote, the gun-lock amendment may still be the hardest sell, said Adam Eisgrau, a lobbyist with Handgun Control Inc.

Adoption of any amendments could change the political dynamics on final passage. Some Republicans, who would otherwise embrace a bill to get tough on juvenile crime, may spurn any bill with gun control provisions; some Democrats, who would otherwise reject the bill as too draconian for children, may endorse it if it embodies gun curbs.

Whatever the outcome, said Richard J. Durbin, D-Ill., a leader of the gun control forces, amendments that are adopted will not be abandoned. "Once the sentiment of the Senate is clear," he said May 6, "there will be other vehicles."

In a bid to assure the debate does not focus exclusively on Democratic gun control ideas, Lott on May 4 announced the creation of a 12-senator "Youth Violence Task Force," whose chairman is Wayne Allard, R-Colo. It was preparing to meet the weekend of May 8-9 to come up with a package of proposals to be offered as alternatives to the Democratic gun amendments.

Prevent and Punish

The underlying bill, sponsored by Judiciary Committee Chairman Orrin G. Hatch, R-Utah, is far from the bipartisan juvenile crime bill (HR 1501) approved without opposition in the House Judiciary Crime Subcommittee April 22. The full committee markup has been postponed until after a panel hearing on "teen violence and culture," scheduled for May 13.

The aim of the Senate bill is to prevent and punish youth crime at both the state and federal levels. Under the bill, federal prosecutors would be allowed to try the most violent of youth offenders as adults. This is opposed by children's rights advocates, who say that if anyone decides to try a child as an adult it should be the judge, not the prosecutor.

The bill would authorize $5 billion in grants to states in the next five years, with fewer strings attached than under the 1997 bill. The only requirements would be that states draft policies laying out a system of graduated sanctions, addressing drug testing and outlining victims rights. In return, they could use the money for both crime prevention and enforcement. At least half the money would be earmarked for enforcement. Some Democrats argue that too little would be guaranteed for prevention.

In other departures from the previous version of the bill, states would not be required to try teens 14 years or older as adults and would not be required to keep elaborate records and share them with other states, although 7.5 percent of the money in this version is designated for voluntary recordkeeping.

At the request of small towns, which cite budget constraints, the bill would relax current requirements for segregating youth and adult prisoners to allow some contact, although they would still be housed separately. The language is opposed by children's rights groups.

Struggle Over Gun Control Imperils Senate Crime Bill

MAY 15 — The April 20 shootings at Columbine High School in Littleton, Colo., have dramatically altered the debate on gun control, although no one is certain how the issue will shake out. The Senate's abrupt reversal of course May 12-14 to distance itself from the National Rifle Association offered powerful evidence that members were rethinking their positions.

In the span of two days following what appeared to be an NRA triumph, the Senate voted to close a loophole allowing juveniles to privately purchase assault weapons, ban the importation of large ammunition clips and restrict unlicensed sales at gun shows.

The action occurred on a juvenile crime measure (S 254) that Republican leaders had offered as a vehicle to test post-Littleton sentiment. The tumultuous debate that followed showed that the leadership was on unsure footing, and that the gun issue could sink the bill.

The Senate defeated a proposal May 12 that would have required background checks for all sales at gun shows, then two days later adopted language purported to do just that. Even this second vote appeared to resolve little. The amendment was adopted by a single vote, with surprising arm-twisting in support exercised by GOP leaders.

President Clinton blasted it as a ruse that would in practice enable more gun show sales without background checks. Both Republicans and Democrats said the gun provisions were still a work in progress and subject to further negotiations.

The events of the week were, at best, the beginning of a process likely to spread through the remainder of the year, if not the remainder of the 106th Congress. The House has yet to take up any of these proposals or its youth crime bill (HR 1501).

The events may presage the demise of juvenile justice legislation. The Senate left the bill May 14 with approximately 75 amendments pending. Judiciary Committee Chairman Orrin

G. Hatch, R-Utah, threatened to kill the bill if action was not complete by the evening of May 18, as leaders pressed to move to other legislation.

Even if the bill gets out of the Senate, it faces serious challenges in the House, where sentiment against gun control measures is strong. A distraught-looking House Majority Whip, Tom DeLay, R-Texas, registered his concern at what was happening in the Senate by visiting the floor the evening of May

Reversal of Course

The week started with a May 12 show of strength by the NRA, as the Senate voted 51-47 to table (and thus kill) an amendment by Frank R. Lautenberg, D-N.J., to require background checks for all purchases at gun shows. Democrats had thought this to be one of their more popular gun-control proposals. *(Vote 111, p. S-25)*

Instead, the Senate approved by a 53-45 vote an amendment offered by Larry E. Craig, R-Idaho, a member of the NRA board and a staunch foe of controls. It would allow, but not require, private gun sellers to use a national database to check the background of purchasers at gun shows. It would offer civil liability protection to those sellers. *(Vote 112, p. S-26)*

Scarcely had the votes been taken before a handful of Republicans began expressing misgivings. Susan Collins of Maine, who voted against Lautenberg's amendment, said she favored a mandatory check but was concerned about the language in his proposal. Gordon H. Smith, R-Ore., grew increasingly dismayed as he read through the text of what he had voted for. He said he had been given the impression that the Craig alternative would not be purely voluntary. By the following morning, he and a host of senators were hopping mad.

"I just woke up angry at what we had done," Smith said.

The consequences of the first votes became apparent when they were featured in newspapers the morning of May 13. Clinton and Attorney General Janet Reno used unusually sharp language in their public statements.

"For the life of me I can't figure out how they did it, or why they passed up this chance to save lives," Clinton said at the White House. "There is simply no excuse for letting criminals get arms at gun shows they can't get at gun stores."

"It shows we're all shocked by Littleton," said Sen. Patrick J. Leahy, D-Vt. "But not shocked enough to stand up to powerful lobbies."

Within a few hours, Craig had been forced by restive colleagues to draft new language to make the background checks mandatory. Hatch pressed to get a vote on the new Craig language as a rapid response to Clinton's objections, but the vote slipped back a day.

Democrats, meanwhile, attacked this new language with undiminished ardor, saying it was full of loopholes and concessions to gun dealers. Clinton on May 14 said the Craig proposal was "riddled with high-caliber loopholes."

The measure passed by only the slimmest of margins, 48-47. Seven Republicans refused to support the Craig proposal, either because they were diehard gun control foes who thought it went too far, or because they had voted for the Lautenberg proposal and felt this one did not go far enough.

Several Democrats were absent, allowing Republican leaders to scramble and achieve their goal of wiping out the first Craig amendment. Finally they prevailed upon gun control foes Richard C. Shelby, R-Ala., and Conrad Burns, R-Mont., to switch their votes to prevent the embarrassment of the amendment being killed.

Afterward, Leahy said that the GOP leaders had "orthopedic surgeons stand by" to twist arms.

Democrats vowed they would bring back Lautenberg's amendment for reconsideration the week of May 17.

Republicans exhibited their own indignation at the course of events. John McCain of Arizona, one of the senators who pressured Craig to modify his language, said Democrats were playing the issue for maximum partisan advantage. He said Hatch offered to modify the Craig language even further to address a Democratic concern that some gun show vendors would still be exempt from background checks, but was rebuffed by Democrats.

"This issue is clearly being exploited by the Democrats for fundraising," McCain said.

Gun Show Provisions

Both the Lautenberg and Craig proposals targeted gun show transactions that do not go through licensed dealers — roughly 40 percent, according to Craig. These transactions are conducted by private vendors and gun hobbyists who are not subject to the background check provisions of the 1993 Brady law (PL 103-159). *(1993 Almanac, p. 300)*

The Lautenberg proposal would have required these private vendors to take their customers to a licensed dealer at the show and ask him or her to run the background check using a nationwide computer database.

The proposal also would have required all gun show organizers and promoters to register their guns with the Treasury Department at least 30 days before the show and pay a registration fee to be set by the department.

The Craig counterproposal would allow unlicensed vendors to avail themselves of licensed dealers to do the background check. Alternatively, it would allow an unlicensed vendor to go to a "special registrant" — a person who was not licensed but who would be specifically authorized to do background checks.

The language would create something called a "special licensee," a new type of licensed federal dealer who operated primarily or solely at gun shows.

Whether or not these special licensees would be required to do background checks was the matter of some debate. Republicans said yes. Democrats said they could find no requirement. Hatch later offered an amendment that he said would clarify the matter. Leahy responded that they should discuss the language off the floor, and it was not resolved in public.

Further aggravating Democrats were several extra concessions given to the NRA. Anyone at a show who conducted a check or sold a firearm for which a check had been made would be granted immunity from civil prosecution.

Pawnbrokers would be exempt from conducting background checks when selling a gun back to the person who pawned it.

Information gathered in a background check, which includes sensitive personal information such as criminal records, mental health histories and military service records, would have to be destroyed immediately following the transaction unless it revealed a reason to prohibit the sale.

An official at the Justice Department said that while the department was also concerned about privacy, federal regulators needed to audit the checks to keep tabs on who is accessing these records and how they are being used.

Craig said his language was approved "grudgingly" by the NRA. A lobbyist for the group, James Jay Baker, termed the Craig language "a minimal inconvenience based on the trade-offs we've been able to gain."

Ammunition Clips

There was surprisingly little squabbling over details of an amendment by Democrat Dianne Feinstein of California to ban the importation of clips and magazines capable of handling more than 10 bullets.

The amendment was agreed to by unanimous consent after a tabling motion failed by a 39-59 vote. *(Vote 116, p. S-26)*

Feinstein picked up votes from 20 Republicans, including several who switched their votes as they saw how many of their GOP colleagues were bucking the party. Among those who switched mid-vote were Spencer Abraham of Michigan and Jeff Sessions of Alabama, both of whom waited until the last moment. Also switching were Richard G. Lugar of Indiana and Charles E. Grassley of Iowa.

The 1994 "assault weapon" legislation (PL 103-322) bans large ammunition clips but exempted those manufactured prior to the legislation. Feinstein asserted that the importation ban was necessary because it is difficult to distinguish the types of clips. *(1994 Almanac, p. 273)*

Republicans made two significant concessions without any prodding from Democrats. The first was language in the underlying bill sometimes called "juvenile Brady," referring to the Brady Act curbs on handguns. Current law prohibits felons from ever owning a firearm. This provision would extend that ban to juveniles who were convicted of a violent crime but were not felons because they were not adjudicated in adult courts.

Republicans also offered an amendment, sponsored by John Ashcroft of Missouri, that would close a loophole allowing juveniles to privately purchase semi-automatic assault weapons. Originally this language was to be part of Feinstein's amendment, but Republicans wanted to offer it themselves. The Ashcroft version, however, included more exemptions than Feinstein planned to propose. It would exempt the children of farmers and ranchers, and people who needed the firearms for their work.

An amendment restricting Internet sales of firearms, offered by Charles E. Schumer, D-N.Y., was tabled May 14, 50-43. *(Vote 119, p. S-27)*

Juvenile Crime Proposals

Almost lost in this gun debate was the underlying bill, designed to revamp the way federal prosecutors deal with youthful offenders and provide grant money to states to combat youth crime.

At the federal level, the legislation would allow U.S. attorneys to try youths 14 years or older in adult courts on serious federal charges.

A related provision dealing with violations of state law, which constitute the vast majority of crimes, centers on a five-year, $5 billion grant program. The funds would be used for a mix of prevention programs such as drug treatment regimes and after-school activities, as well as prosecuting violent teens. Funds in the latter category could be used to hire additional prosecutors, develop databases of youth offenders and build detention space.

Rarely has legislation been greeted on Capitol Hill with so much fanfare and such low expectations. Before the bill came to the floor, the White House held a "summit" on youth violence featuring religious leaders, entertainment industry representatives, gun manufacturers and others. Throughout the week, senators held multiple news conferences touting various amendments. The House Judiciary Committee jumped into the matter with a hearing May 13 on the root causes of youth violence.

But for all the sound and fury, senators of both parties were quick to admit they had limited expectations for the legislation and its impact on the kind of violence visited on Columbine High School.

"You're not going to change the culture with a series of amendments, or a series of bills," said Judd Gregg, R-N.H.

"As my grandfather would say, this is not the horse that can carry the whole sleigh," said Joseph R. Biden Jr., D-Del.

The legislation seemed to be based on the understanding that youths can be divided neatly into groups: serious and dangerous criminals, who would be dealt with harshly; teens who have run afoul of the law and could be encouraged to straighten up; and teens at risk of becoming criminals if not provided with something approaching a structured and nurturing environment.

But with Eric Harris and Dylan Klebold, the two perpetrators at Columbine, authorities say they have a case of teens progressing, in a single year, from law-abiding youths to petty thieves to mass murderers.

The low expectations were also the result of the rather modest scope of the bill. Its key provision of a $5 billion authorization is a tiny fraction of what is already being spent by communities around the country.

Original Aim: Drug Crime

If the debate could be reduced to a few words, it would be something like "Gun lobby vs. Hollywood."

The bill was scheduled for floor debate before the Littleton shooting. The bill is less the product of high-profile suburban mass shootings than the inner-city youth crime wave that hit in the mid-1980s, which was associated with an epidemic of crack cocaine usage.

Some senators focused on the gun lobby with their amendments, charging that the NRA was misusing the Second Amendment to defend dangerously easy access to firearms.

Others took aim with amendments at Hollywood for producing movies, music, video games and other products that glorify violence.

Democrats tended to blame youth violence on the availability of firearms, while Republicans wanted to look harder at deeper causes, which they saw as breakdowns in cultural norms and morality brought about in part by the mass media.

"I think it's a societal and cultural problem," said Majority Leader Trent

Lott, R-Miss. "It's not the result of guns."

While the gun lobby deflected the most onerous provisions of the Lautenberg proposal, Hollywood escaped the most restrictive amendment affecting their industries. By a vote of 60-39, the Senate on May 13 tabled an amendment by Ernest F. Hollings, D-S.C., that would have banned violent television programming during hours when children are "likely to comprise a substantial portion of the audience." *(Vote 114, p. S-26)*

The Senate did, however, adopt 100-0 a Hatch amendment encouraging Internet service providers to offer filtering software designed to allow parents to block access to objectionable sites. *(Vote 113, p. S-26)*

Senate Passes New Regulations On Firearms

MAY 22 — By unusually public fits and starts, a political center in the debate on gun control is emerging on Capitol Hill.

Although its final shape will not be clear before summer, the longstanding polarization on the topic — between those who would have almost no federal restrictions on firearms and those who would regulate weapons more strictly than virtually all other consumer goods — has yielded a rare middle ground in the past month. Since 15 people died during two teenagers' rifle-wielding rampage in Littleton, Colo., each side has pushed what it describes as a newly pragmatic approach.

The result is that gun control legislation has more momentum than at any time since Republicans took control of Congress more than four years ago. "I just sense for the first time there's a real sea change," said Sen. Joseph R. Biden Jr., D-Del.

At the same time, Democrats have so far confined themselves to measures on which they believe congressional consensus may emerge. They have, for instance, steered clear of the most contentious parts of President Clinton's gun control package, including restricting consumers to one handgun purchase a month and holding parents liable when their guns are used by their children.

By an overwhelming 73-25, the Senate voted May 20 to pass a bill to combat juvenile crime (S 254) that includes an array of gun control provisions. Passage came precisely one month after the Columbine High School massacre. *(Vote 140, p. S-29)*

It also came after a string of humiliating retreats and defeats by the Senate Republican leadership. Hoping to suggest a more sure footing, the House Republican leadership moved the same day to head off an insurgent move by Democrats to force the gun control debate on that side of the Capitol into the open. Instead, they promised the House version of the juvenile justice legislation (HR 1501) would be marked up by the Judiciary Committee after lawmakers return from the Memorial Day recess the week of June 8, with a floor debate the week after that. Democrats said that was not soon enough.

In the Senate, two proposals that were stopped soundly and with minimal public notice last year were added in slightly altered form to the juvenile justice bill. The new and solid majorities of support for them are a clear illustration of how the perception of galvanized public sentiment can change a lawmaker's mind. One would ban the importation of high-capacity ammunition clips. The other would require the sale of a lock or storage box with each gun.

And, in the climactic vote on the bill, the long uphill struggle by gun control forces to require background checks on all people who buy firearms at gun shows resulted in a level senatorial playing field. Vice President Al Gore walked onto it May 20, cast a tie-breaking "yes" vote and seized a spot in the national limelight.

Adoption of all three of those measures by the House, once considered unthinkable, is given reasonable odds now that Speaker J. Dennis Hastert, R-Ill., and Judiciary Committee Chairman Henry J. Hyde, R-Ill., have signaled a willingness to support more gun control and to abandon past parliamentary tactics they employed to thwart proposals to regulate weapons.

"Clearly, we need to tighten current laws to make it more difficult for kids to get guns," the Speaker told the House on May 20, a day after endorsing background checks at gun shows and an increase in the minimum age for a handgun purchase to 21 from 18.

Guardians of 2nd Amendment

In their first four years in the majority, Republicans succeeded in finessing gun control efforts, either by rounding up the votes to defeat them or erecting procedural obstacles to debating them. So emphatically did House GOP leaders take their role as guardians of the Second Amendment that they kept their juvenile crime bills of 1997 and this year free of any modifications of the criminal code, thereby making most gun control amendments nongermane and capable of being blocked. *(1997 Almanac, p. 5-3)*

The first casualty of the events in the Senate may be the notion that the House's restrictive — and selectively enforced — rules on germaneness may still be used to quash the gun control debate. Hastert has signaled to Democrats he will not use the tactic.

The second casualty may be House leaders' ability to control the debate. Majority Leader Trent Lott, R-Miss., had a hard time of it in the Senate after promising Democrats a freewheeling deliberation on gun control, and then standing by as his party was pilloried by Democrats. "Some people have been critical of me for, you know, allowing this debate to happen in the Senate," Lott said after the final roll call. "You don't *allow* debate to happen. It happens!"

Democrats were elated by Lott's setbacks, including failing in three attempts to give new regulations on gun shows a Republican imprimatur. They were pleasantly surprised, even stunned, that he ceded the headline-grabbing moment to Gore, the front-runner for the 2000 Democratic presidential nomination.

In the wake of the Senate debate, Republicans are worried that the perception of them as the party against gun control will jeopardize their standing in the polls as the dominant party for being tough on crime issues in general.

"Perhaps we served a purpose for the party in moving it toward a centrist position," said Sen. John W. Warner of Virginia, one of six Republicans to vote for the gun show language. So did all but one Democrat, Max Baucus of Montana. *(Vote 134, p. S-29)*

The debate also showed how gun control views fall along regional as well as partisan lines. Three moderate New England Republicans voted "no" on the climactic gun show vote, while four more conservative GOP Midwesterners — two of them former big city mayors — voted "yes."

Among Republican presidential candidates, Elizabeth Dole has gained considerable attention for her pro-gun-control platform. More quiet has been the shift of Sen. John McCain of Arizona, who voted against the 1993 handgun waiting period law (PL 103-159) and the 1994 assault weapons ban (PL 103-322) but voted during the juvenile crime debate for the gun lock requirement, the import ban on ammunition clips and an amendment, tabled May 14, to restrict gun sales over the Internet. The Senate's other aspirant for the 2000 GOP nomination, New Hampshire's Robert C. Smith, remains resolutely opposed to gun curbs.

Gov. George W. Bush of Texas, the apparent GOP front-runner, has not made any dramatic shifts on gun control but did play a behind-the-scenes role in the Senate debate. Sen. Larry E. Craig, R-Idaho, a National Rifle Association board member, telephoned May 12 to confer on the gun debate while Bush monitored the proceedings on C-SPAN. Contrary to an assertion made by Frank R. Lautenberg, D-N.J., Craig said later, Bush said he opposed the Democratic gun show language.

Gun Show Watershed

Momentum for tougher gun control laws began to form May 13 when the Senate adopted the ammunition clip language by voice vote after a motion to table (and thus kill) it failed 39-59. Momentum surged May 18 when the Senate voted 78 to 20 to adopt the gun lock amendment. *(Vote 122, p. S-27)*

But it was the gun show vote, on an amendment by Lautenberg that was truly the watershed moment. A similar proposal had been rejected eight days earlier by a vote of 51-47.

On the second vote, Lautenberg was able to pick up the two Democrats absent for the first vote and also Democrat Max Cleland of Georgia. Cleland succumbed to steady pressure from fellow Democrats after winning some modified language, including a narrower definition of what is a "gun show." Other Democrats said Cleland had signaled his switch the night before the balloting, which occurred three hours after a 15-year old constituent of his, armed with two guns, shot and wounded six schoolmates at Heritage High School in Conyers, Ga., an Atlanta suburb.

"Sometimes we think our vote doesn't matter. But today my vote mattered, and I was honored to be on the right side," Cleland said in an interview afterward.

The Republican and Democratic proposals on guns shows had differences that highlighted the remaining fault lines in the current gun control debate.

About three in five gun show vendors are federally licensed dealers; the rest are amateur vendors and hobbyists not subject to the background check requirement. The Lautenberg proposal would require these non-licensed vendors to take their transactions to a licensed vendor at the show to do the check.

The final GOP version, drafted by Craig and modified by Gordon H. Smith, R-Ore., would have created two new entities at guns shows capable of doing background checks using the National Instant Check System (NICS) created under the waiting period law: "special registrants," who would do nothing but run background checks, and "special licensees" empowered to both run checks and make sales. Both categories would be for people who did not have a federal firearms license. *(Brady law, 1993 Almanac, p. 300)*

Republicans said this approach would successfully walk the narrow line between restricting improper access to firearms while preserving legitimate access. "We are attempting to craft a very important constitutional line," said Craig. "What the other side won't say, but what they whisper loudly, is that they consider the Second Amendment a loophole."

As the week wore on, Republicans complained that nothing they could do would satisfy Senate Democrats, who they said were slowly but steadily ratcheting up their demands for concessions in a bid to leverage the debate to maximum political advantage. Democrats said their differences on the amendment were substantive.

Underlying Provisions

Throughout the eight days of debate, attention to the bill's underlying provisions was almost entirely eclipsed by the gun debate. The measure would authorize $5 billion during the next five years for states to both prosecute juvenile criminals and deter youthful criminal behavior. And it would allow federal prosecutors to try those 14 years or older as adults.

A bipartisan catchall amendment, adopted May 20 by voice vote, would alter the requirements on states seeking the bill's funds. The law now requires states to segregate incarcerated juveniles from adults. The initial version of the bill would have relaxed that to allow "brief and incidental" contact between adults and juveniles. The amendment changed the language to "brief and inadvertent or accidental."

A relaxation of the current rules has been pressed by small towns, where officials say they spend a fortune building new facilities to ensure that older prisoners never cast an eye on the youngest prisoners. Civil rights groups say that is as it should be.

The manager's amendment also retained an existing presumption that juveniles should be tried in state courts. The initial bill would have ended that presumption. As passed, the bill gives attorneys for juveniles an avenue for challenging a federal prosecutor wanting to try a case. If the case stays at the federal level, the bill as amended strengthens the defense attorney's chances of getting a client tried as a juvenile.

Other Amendments Debated

Senators voted 75-24 on May 20 to adopt an amendment by John Ashcroft, R-Mo., to allow local school officials to discipline federally defined special education students in the same manner as other students when they bring guns or bombs onto school grounds. *(Vote 137, p. S-29)*

Tom Harkin, D-Iowa, threatened for two days to jeopardize the wave of Democratic victories by filibustering Ashcroft's amendment. In the end, however, he relented after winning assurances the Ashcroft language would be visited if the bill ever gets to conference with the House.

Also debated the week of May 17 were amendments:

- By Wayne Allard, R-Colo., making a congressional finding that prayers at services or on a physical memorial at a public school to anyone slain at the school do not violate the First Amendment. The amendment would require that anyone suing to challenge the constitutionality of such a service pay all attorneys' fees. Allard said he pushed the language because the parents of a Columbine shooting victim, Cassie Bernall, were frustrated in their efforts to erect a memorial to their daughter. It was adopted 85-13 on May 18. *(Vote 121, p. S-27)*
- By Biden, to extend the authorization for the Community Oriented Policing Service. It was rejected, 48-0. *(Vote 139, p.S-29)*

Biden credited the failure to the program's association with Clinton. He also said GOP anger at Democrats for dragging out the gun votes may also have played a role.

- By Robert C. Byrd, D-W.Va., to allow state attorneys general to sue in federal court if the state "has reasonable cause to believe" that someone has violated, is violating or may violate state liquor transportation laws. It was adopted 80-17 on May 18. *(Vote 124, p. S-27)*

An alternative by Feinstein was also adopted, by voice vote. It would require an adult to sign for deliveries of liquor.

House Republican Leaders Propose Gun Curb Bill

MAY 29 — Until the massacre this spring at Columbine High School, the notion that the House Republican leadership would propose its own gun control package would have been widely considered a fantasy.

But in a vivid example of the dynamic nature of politics, that is exactly what happened the week of May 24. The House Judiciary Committee plans to mark up the GOP gun curbs the week of June 7 as part of a revamped and expanded bill (HR 1501) to curb juvenile crime, with debate on the House floor expected the week after.

Republicans promise their bill will call for mandatory background checks at gun shows, require that trigger locks or similar safety devices be sold with handguns and ban the importation of high-capacity ammunition clips. Provisions to those ends were included as amendments to the juvenile crime bill (S 254) the Senate passed May 20, although House GOP aides say that the measure they are drafting will not necessarily include language identical to the Senate's.

The decision to move a GOP gun control bill, announced in a speech on the House floor May 25 by Speaker J. Dennis Hastert, R-Ill., ranks as one of the most remarkable political adjustments of recent congressional vintage. It also marks one of the most decisive moves yet by the new Speaker to navigate his narrow majority past a potentially severe public relations problem, although the Democrats continued to insist that the Republicans were offering to do too little, too slowly.

"This is one of those rare times when the national consensus demands that we act, but it does not require us to rush to judgment, to risk compounding the situation by stampeding toward what sounds like the best way to score points against each other," Hastert said.

Four years ago, House Republicans took control pledging to try and repeal the ban on so-called assault weapons enacted as part of the 1994 crime-fighting law (PL 103-322). At Memorial Day this year, a chamber still loaded with self-described defenders of the Second Amendment appears devoid of anyone willing to vocally oppose the modest new gun controls the GOP is offering.

Even Bob Barr, R-Ga., a board member of the National Rifle Association (NRA) who has led past fights against gun restrictions, characterizes the proposed gun locks requirement as ineffectual. Requiring background checks for those who want to buy weapons at gun shows, he says, is "a good idea in need of some work." Like many other Republicans, he has stopped arguing that gun curbs are not the solution to reducing violence. "No matter how important these are, they are just a small part of the whole solution," he said in an interview May 26.

Meanwhile, many Democrats, who until now would have considered themselves fortunate to pass a gun locks measure, are emboldened enough by the changed climate to declare themselves dissatisfied with the House GOP promises and the Senate-passed bill.

"I think that even more needs to be done than what was done in the Senate," Vice President Al Gore said at a Capitol rally with Democratic leaders May 27. "And what should be done here in the House is a tougher bill with tougher restrictions related to guns."

The Clinton administration is pushing a number of other items, including a purchasing limit of one gun each month and making parents criminally liable when their guns are misused by their children.

The House's shift seems inextricable from the fallout after the April 20 killings in Littleton, Colo. GOP leaders say they will not allow a repeat of the situation in the Senate, where Democrats prodded Republicans into a public retreat — first portraying the GOP as overly responsive to the NRA, then winning a steady series of amendments to the juvenile crime bill.

"The Democrats think they have a hot issue," House Judiciary Committee Chairman Henry J. Hyde, R-Ill., said May 25. "They think they can put us at a disadvantage. They can't. This is our issue too."

Democrats Press the Issue

Democrats were not in a sharing mood, and they tried without success the week of May 24 to use several avenues to force the issue of guns and juvenile crime to the fore. But their plan to attempt to add gun control language to fiscal 2000 appropriations bills was set back when the draft legislation for the Treasury and Postal Service was not marked up, and the legislative branch measure (HR 1905) did not make it to the floor.

Democrat John Conyers Jr. of Michigan tried to call up the juvenile crime bill at a May 26 Judiciary Committee meeting. His motion to overturn a ruling by Hyde that the bill could not be taken up since it had not been placed on the committee's agenda was rejected, 13-19.

The Democrats' last attempt was a

bid that evening to defeat the routine measure (S Con Res 35) allowing Congress to recess for Memorial Day. "We shouldn't leave town before acting to deal with the national crisis of youth violence," said Minority Leader Richard A. Gephardt of Missouri. His protests notwithstanding, the resolution was adopted, 249-178. *(Vote 165, p. H-60)*

Gore sounded a more political theme the next day, declaring that Republicans "are hoping against hope that if they can slow-walk this whole measure, then the American people will lose the sense of urgency that is now so obvious and so palpable."

Democrats generally were unwilling to express any measure of surprise at the GOP concessions. "I don't find it hard to believe public officials would take into consideration public sentiment," said Rep. Barney Frank, D-Mass.

Off Capitol Hill, some gun control advocates said they were stunned at how quickly their requests have gained currency since the Littleton shooting. Adam M. Eisgrau, a lobbyist for Handgun Control Inc., compares the GOP shift to the fall of the Berlin Wall in 1989, which happened so rapidly that it caught many in the West by surprise.

"Speaking for myself, the speed with which the walls may be coming down is breathtaking," Eisgrau said May 26.

Outlines of the Bill

The bill House Judiciary will call up was to be written the week of May 31 by committee attorneys, while many Republican lawmakers were planning to spend the recess speaking at commencements and gauging the views of constituents. But its broad parameters were sketched by Hyde and Crime Subcommittee Chairman Bill McCollum, R-Fla., in a news conference May 25 and in an outline distributed afterward.

In addition to the gun show, ammunition clip and and trigger lock provisions, the GOP has also promised language to ban violent teenagers from ever owning a firearm. This provision, known by the shorthand "Juvenile Brady," would expand those covered by a federal lifetime ban on gun purchases to include violent felons who are convicted as juveniles.

How the language is drafted will make all the difference both to skeptical Democrats — who say that they fear the GOP proposals will be full of loopholes or combined with concessions to the NRA — and to those Republicans who are still skeptical of gun control.

"The devil is in the details," said Charles T. Canady, R-Fla., a previous opponent of gun control. "I'm not going to make a judgment based on an outline."

For Democrats, the gun show provision prompts the greatest apprehension. It caused the longest and most complicated fight during the Senate debate, where Democrats accused Republicans of drafting a series of alternatives so full of loopholes as to be meaningless. In the end, a Democratic version passed because of the vice president's tie-breaking vote.

Of particular concern is whether Republicans will include language setting a deadline for such a background check. The Justice Department estimates that in about one-quarter of transactions, the national database created under the law (PL 103-159) named for former presidential press secretary James S. Brady fails to provide complete information on a potential gun buyer. In that case, authorities have 72 hours to call state record offices. Many Republicans would like to see that period shortened to 24 hours. The Senate bill made no changes. President Clinton has proposed lengthening the deadline to five days. *(1993 Almanac, p. 300)*

Of even greater concern to Democrats is that the GOP, while making substantive moves toward gun control, will also fill the bill with measures the Democrats cannot abide. These "poison pill" provisions might include federally mandated minimum sentences and requirements that states try people as young as 14 as adults in order to qualify for federal funding to combat juvenile crime.

Controversial Areas

As outlined, the GOP package already touches on some areas sensitive to Democrats. It would set mandatory minimums for, among other things, firing a gun on school property. It would call for the death penalty for anyone who kills a witness in retaliation for testimony. It promises a section on trying youths as adults. And it will have a section on the impact of the entertainment industry on youth violence, including Senate-passed provisions calling for a study on the effects of violent entertainment on the national culture and language allowing the federal government to ban the filming of violent films on its property.

The measure will be an expansion of a bill the Crime Subcommittee approved two days after the Littleton shootings.

Devoid of both gun restrictions and the sort of contentious provisions that prevented enactment of a juvenile crime bill by the 105th Congress, the original measure had broad bipartisan support. It did just one thing: authorize $1.5 billion for states, with few strings attached, to combat juvenile crime. *(Background, 1998 Almanac, p. 17-15)*

Also part of the mix is a measure (HR 1768) that incorporates the proposals made by the Clinton administration after the Littleton shootings.

That bill would do everything the Senate bill does, and more. It also includes the parental liability provision; a prohibition on buying more than one handgun a month; a prohibition on dealers from selling more than one handgun to any one person each month; an increase to 21 from 18 in the minimum age for purchasing a handgun; and reinstitution of the Brady law's cooling-off period — shortened to three days — before any transaction could be completed for the purchase of a handgun or assault weapon. This would cover all sales and would take place before the background check. If there were a discrepancy in the check, the purchaser could be compelled to wait an additional five days.

These provisions and others are likely to be turned into Democratic amendments in committee and on the floor. Of these, raising the minimum age for handguns is the most likely to pass. Hastert said May 20 that he supported the idea, but it did not make it into the Republican package.

Hyde may emerge as the biggest champion of gun restrictions among House Republicans. Gun control has been an area where he has strayed from the GOP mainstream in the past, supporting both the assault weapons ban and the Brady law.

He describes the Senate gun control provisions as having been crafted in a state of legislative near-chaos. But that, he said, should not detract from the fact they appear to be reasonable.

Crime Panel Hearing

While Democrats professed intolerance for the GOP schedule for the debate, Republicans arranged an unusually courteous response to Clinton's plan.

The bill embodying the president's package was the focus of a Crime Subcommittee hearing May 27 — an unusual gesture to Clinton from one of the most partisan committees under GOP control. Deputy Attorney General Eric H. Holder Jr. and Assistant Treasury Secretary James E. Johnson were the principal witnesses and were given wide latitude to pitch Clinton's proposals, although McCollum did use their appearance to criticize the administration's enforcement of existing gun control laws.

Panel members also heard from an unusual array of criminologists, police officers and crime victims — whose views stretched across a wide spectrum in the gun control debate.

Even while McCollum was outlining his party's response to the Littleton massacre, Darrell Scott, the father of one of its victims, said that lax gun laws were not to blame for the death of his 17-year-old daughter, Rachel Joy Scott. He placed all the responsibility with Eric Harris and Dylan Klebold, who took their own lives after killing a dozen schoolmates and one teacher.

"There are people behind those instruments of death," Scott said. "We do not need more restrictive laws. . . . No amount of gun laws can stop someone who spends months planning this kind of massacre."

Hastert's Gun Control Package Faces Criticism From Both Parties

JUNE 12 — As the House prepares for a debate the week of June 14 on an array of proposals to control the spread of firearms, curb juvenile crime and regulate media violence, Speaker J. Dennis Hastert is in exactly the position he hoped not to be in: struggling with both a lack of consensus among his fellow Republicans and rancorous opposition from a solid majority of Democrats.

Two weeks of effort by the Speaker to exert control over the Republican rank and file on gun control have come to naught, and what appeared before Memorial Day to be strong momentum behind a GOP package of weapons regulations has now dissipated.

As a result, Hastert appears to have been unable to lay the groundwork for a floor debate in which his party might avoid the rhetorical drubbing from Democrats that Republican senators took before passage of the Senate juvenile crime and gun control legislation (S 254) on May 20.

Despite concessions he has already made — and also because of them — Hastert, R-Ill., is facing a hailstorm of criticism over the package he plans to bring to the floor. As a result, he said June 10 that he would not lean on Republicans to support any portion of the package, since doing so would alienate at least one faction.

"Everybody has their points of view on this, and I think they will be able to work their will in the House," he told reporters. "I think even within our conference there are two or three different points of view, and legitimately so."

The announcement came after Hastert's top two lieutenants in the GOP leadership, Majority Leader Dick Armey and Majority Whip Tom DeLay, served notice that they were disavowing the Speaker's positions supporting several gun control measures, including mandatory background checks for buyers at gun shows and mandatory sales of safety devices with every handgun.

The moves by the two Texans undercut the promise to the House that Hastert had made May 25, when he said he was advocating gun controls "on behalf of the entire elected Republican leadership."

It also showed once again the limits of Hastert's powers to lead a House in which any half-dozen of his own troops can threaten an effective rebellion. It took all the Speaker's powers of persuasion the week of June 7 to postpone an explosion of Republican discord on fiscal 2000 spending priorities.

Democrats, meanwhile, spent the week alleging that the language the House GOP has drafted regarding gun locks and gun shows is the handiwork of the National Rifle Association (NRA). "It is a bill plainly ghostwritten by the NRA," President Clinton said June 9. "I think it is wrong to let the NRA call the shots on this issue. They've been calling the shots on this issue for decades now, and we have failed to do what is manifestly in the interest of our children and our communities."

Democrats struck this same theme in the Senate, where a leader of the Republicans in the gun control debate was Larry E. Craig of Idaho, an NRA board member. So the revival of the Democrats' theme came much to the consternation of House Judiciary Committee Chairman Henry J. Hyde, R-Ill., who shares many of Hastert's views on gun control. The NRA and GOP officials conceded, however, that the gun rights group had participated in drafting the House language.

"The Democrats have one overarching goal — and it transcends gun control — and that is to see us fail," Hyde said in an interview June 10.

Hastert and Hyde had tried to steer around much of this. They agreed, at least in principle, to accept much of the language Democrats had won in the Senate. They had also hoped to avoid some of the political fireworks of debate by taking the GOP proposals straight to the floor, thereby bypassing Hyde's own panel, which is one of the most ideologically polarized in Congress. But that decision only prompted bipartisan criticism that they were not allowing the type of full and measured debate that Hastert had promised as a rationale for not pushing gun controls through the House sooner.

And, in addition to criticism by Clinton and most Democrats that the GOP gun package is too weak, a solid group of Republicans and about 30 Democrats were preparing to oppose the proposals as too much.

But even Republican opponents of gun control worried that their party was in danger of a political miscalculation now that the massacre at Columbine High School has revived public support for tighter regulations of weapons. "They say Social Security is the third rail of politics," said Jack Kingston of Georgia. "They haven't been in a gun control debate."

Complex Procedure

The procedural road for the legislation on the House floor will be complex in large part because the Republicans involved in drafting it were unable to agree even on a starting point. The underlying vehicle will probably be a noncontroversial measure (HR 1501) authorizing $1.5 billion in grants to states for crime fighting during the next three years. It was approved by Judiciary's Crime Subcommittee on April 22, two days after 15 people died in the Littleton, Colo., high school rampage.

But the measure was put on hold after that while both Republicans and Democrats in the House reassessed their strategies, both in light of polling that showed growing sentiment for gun control and in the knowledge of the messy Senate debate.

The bulk of the Republican response to Littleton is contained in legislation (HR 2037) that Hyde and Crime Subcommittee Chairman Bill McCollum, R-Fla., introduced June 8. It will most likely be debated as an amendment to the juvenile justice bill.

The package includes several provisions that conservatives advocate as essential to fighting crime by young people, including a new set of mandatory minimum sentences — 10 years for discharging a firearm at a school, life if someone is killed in a school shooting, for example — and allowing teens to be tried as adults in federal court. The Democrats oppose much of this, and their ire at similar provisions thwarted a juvenile crime package in the 105th Congress. *(1998 Almanac, p. 15-17)*

For now, however, Democrats have focused their anger on the Hyde-McCollum gun language, which they said was a pale and inadequate imitation of the Senate's.

High on their list of complaints was the provision on gun locks, under which the "safety device" that must be sold with each handgun could be any piece that is already part of the weapon but that — once removed — would render the gun inoperable. Democrats said that would put almost every gun now manufactured in compliance, because it could be disarmed by partial disassembly.

The GOP gun show background-check proposal also is opposed by the Democrats. While it appears at first glance to be similar to the Senate's, which was adopted only with Vice President Al Gore's tie-breaking vote, its much narrower definitions would allow sales without background checks any time fewer than 10 vendors assembled, no matter how many guns were sold.

McCollum said the gun show language emerged from negotiations among lawmakers and with outside groups, including the NRA. Its lobbyists, he said, "knew what we were doing. There was a dialogue. But I'm sure you will find many things in there they don't like."

In one important respect, the Hyde-McCollum package goes well beyond what was in the Senate bill and adopts a key tenet of the gun control package that Clinton unveiled after the Littleton shootings. It would subject adults to criminal culpability, and as long as three years in prison, if their firearms fell into the hands of a young person who used them to kill or injure someone.

That one provision would be enough for Rep. Bob Barr, R-Ga., to oppose the entire bill — no matter how attractive the get-tough-on-crime and popular culture provisions are. Barr, an NRA board member, had suggested earlier this spring that he was inclined to acquiesce to what Hastert was advocating.

Hyde has two other gun control measures that he plans to offer as amendments separate from the main package. One would ban the importation of high-capacity ammunition clips, as the Senate bill would. The other would raise to 21 from 18 the minimum age for a handgun purchase, a proposal Hastert has been advocating. These measures are backed by most Democrats.

Target: Mass Media

The GOP package on gun control was not the only proposal that drew an array of criticism. Hyde will also propose an amendment, embodied in legislation (HR 2036) he introduced June 8, that is designed to curb violence in the mass media, which he perceives as the root cause of much youth violence.

His proposal would make it a federal crime to sell, lend or display to a minor material with any explicitly violent content. It would do this by applying to violence a standard similar to what the Supreme Court crafted in *Miller v. California*. That 1973 decision denied First Amendment protections to sexually explicit material that appealed only to a "prurient interest," was "patently offensive" and lacked "serious literary, artistic, political or scientific value."

The proposals also would require retailers to let adults review in the store the lyrics of any recording for sale.

The proposals touched off a firestorm of controversy from civil liberties groups, the entertainment industry and lawmakers who represent the industry. Many expressed confidence that the provision would be struck down as unconstitutional if enacted.

Rep. Mark Foley, R-Fla., chairman of the GOP Task Force on Entertainment, said the bill would have "dangerous implications" for the free flow of information and entertainment. He even suggested it could cause video stores and libraries to be prosecuted for lending such films as "Schindler's List," the grimly graphic but award-winning Holocaust movie. "As a Republican, I thought our party was committed to lessening government interference in the affairs of commerce and our personal lives," Foley said in a statement June 9.

Debate Bypassed

The Judiciary Committee has been bypassed on several occasions in recent years, often with Hyde's acquiescence.

This time, the decision to cancel a markup angered Democrats on and off the committee, and many Republicans on the panel, who lamented that their views were not being solicited or that the complexities of the proposals were not being fully aired.

While GOP leaders have "more control" by taking a bill directly to the floor, said Asa Hutchinson, R-Ark., a Judiciary member, "the disadvantage is you don't have the education process."

The move constituted something of a broken promise by Republicans, who had vowed a thorough airing of the issues but who are now moving many proposals to the floor without a single hearing. But Democrats too could be accused of a change in tune. Before Memorial Day, they insisted that gun control measures be brought to the floor immediately. Now, they are complaining about the absence of a committee debate.

And the Republican maneuver did not put the order and calm into the debate that Hyde and Hastert sought. As GOP lawmakers rewrote details of their proposals, doing behind closed doors what is normally done in committee, their secrecy only contributed to the ample unhappiness in many quarters about the emerging proposals.

Democrats, meanwhile, are promoting an alternative that would adopt the Senate language on gun shows, include new regulations for gun locks, raise the minimum age for handgun purchases to 21, order a federal study on the effects of violence in entertainment and reauthorize the Community Oriented Policing Service program. Clinton cites the program as one of his signature achievements but it is already facing cuts in the early rounds of drafting the fiscal 2000 spending bill.

Other amendments, to do portions of this and to resurrect other gun control ideas thwarted in the Senate, are also being circulated by Democrats, although how wide-ranging a debate the GOP will allow remains uncertain.

In the end, many of the votes on gun control could be close, with the bloc of Democratic opponents — mostly from the South and rural Midwest — offset by Republican advocates of gun control, who traditionally are from suburban districts. This faction's confidence that Littleton would allow them to pick up crucial new GOP allies has now begun to wane.

"I'm surprised we haven't learned our lesson from the Senate debate, and from pubic opinion," Marge Roukema of New Jersey said June 10.

House Passes Juvenile Crime Bill But Rejects Gun Control Measure

JUNE 19 — In five quick days the Littleton-inspired contest over gun control turned into a crucible for effective control of the House. In the process, the gun lobby and its allies in the Republican leadership managed to shift an emotion-laden drive to expand federal regulation of firearms into a debate over responsibility for the nation's culture of violence.

Now, in the coming days and weeks, the test will be whether the GOP or President Clinton and his Democratic allies at the Capitol can use these questions to sway voters as they go to the polls in 2000.

"A lot of Democrats think they can take back the Congress on guns," said Rep. James C. Greenwood, R-Pa. "A lot of Republicans think they can hold the Congress on culture."

Senate-passed provisions that would tighten background checks of buyers at gun shows, among other steps, ran aground in a House riven by partisan politics. A watered-down package of gun curbs (HR 2122) was resoundingly defeated on June 18 — the 147-280 vote coming 59 days after the slayings at Columbine High School in Littleton, Colo., renewed momentum for gun control, which had been stalled during the four years of revived Republican control of Capitol Hill. *(Vote 244, p. H-84)*

But the House's passage the night before of legislation (HR 1501) proposing tougher juvenile crime standards and a mix of anti-violence steps assures that there can be conference negotiations between the House and the Senate, which had passed a bill (S 254) combining juvenile justice and gun controls in May. That hands the Republican leadership — which had seemed to have a balky hold at best on the management of the debate on both sides of the Capitol — a renewed and strengthened measure of control, given their ability to name the members of the negotiating teams.

But the end product will face the scrutiny of the president and his congressional allies, who already are on the attack. Republicans are once again being labeled the lap dogs of the National Rifle Association (NRA), which lobbied intently to stanch the momentum for gun control that had seemed to be welling up on both sides of the House aisle in recent weeks.

"One more time, the Congress of the United States . . . said, 'We don't care what's necessary to protect our children. We can't possibly bear to make anyone in the NRA mad,' " Clinton said after the House votes. He spoke to reporters while at a summit in Germany, and he was scheduled to take the matter up again during his June 19 radio address.

At issue is whether to add the first new gun control law to the federal books in half a decade.

Even before the House took up its measures, Democrats threatened to add gun control amendments to fiscal 2000 appropriations bills as they come to the floor. The bill funding the Department of the Treasury and the Postal Service is expected to be their prime target, because it covers the federal agency that conducts background checks on potential gun buyers. Republican leaders say they want to move that bill through the Appropriations Committee before the July Fourth recess, set to start in two weeks.

If that plan does not work, they hope to make an election issue out of gun control. This was presaged by Patrick J. Kennedy, D-R.I., chairman of the Democratic Congressional Campaign Committee, during debate June 17 on the NRA-backed gun proposal that proved pivotal in the debate.

As the proposal edged toward a razor-thin victory, much to the dismay of most Democrats, Kennedy started a chant that sought to put a positive long-term political spin on the short-term legislative defeat.

"Six seats! Six seats!" he chanted, citing the number of House districts that Democrats must pick up to take back control, and many of his colleagues soon chimed in.

Partisan Tensions

After the defeat on final passage June 18, Republican leaders were bitter over what they considered the politicization of the gun vote. Though 82 Republicans — or 37 percent — voted against the measure, the bulk of the opposition came from Democrats. Their 197 "no" votes account for 93 percent of the Democratic Caucus membership.

Speaker J. Dennis Hastert, R-Ill., who had promised that the GOP leadership would work to "expedite" a gun control bill, blamed the setback on Democrats "who put partisanship over progress." At a news conference, Majority Whip Tom DeLay, R-Texas, said that "the bill had four of five things they wanted [and] still was not good enough for them. So it's quite obvious to me that they're just interested in politics."

While DeLay expressed disappointment over the outcome on gun control, however, he said "I've had a great time this week," owing to the victories he won in pushing to strengthen the juvenile justice bill.

Not only was the juvenile crime bill amended to add a new collection of mandatory minimum sentences for young people who commit gun crimes, but it also was enlarged to include several provisions pushed by cultural conservatives. First among them was a provision allowing the Ten Commandments to be displayed in public settings. The bill would also bar federal judges from addressing state prison overcrowding, create nine new federal judgeships in three states, express criticism of the entertainment media for gratuitous violence and provide civil immunity to teachers who discipline students.

"None of this," said a highly skeptical John P. Murtha, D-Pa., "is going to make any difference."

The vote to pass the juvenile crime bill was a resounding 287-139, although a majority of Democrats voted against it as well. *(Vote 233, p. H-80)*

Judiciary Committee Chairman Henry J. Hyde, R-Ill., pushed a provision that would have banned the sale to minors of certain violent and sexually explicit material. But his measure was rejected when civil libertarians raised First Amendment objections, retailers of videos and music complained they would not know what they could and could not legally sell — and the combined appeals won the ears of a pivotal group of Republicans. It was defeated, 146-282. *(Vote 213, p. H-74)*

The Senate bill contains several modest gun control provisions, some mandatory minimums and only a few minor provisions to address the theory that cultural decline has boosted youth violence. For the Republican leaders, their ability to shape a final bill, and possibly their ability to hold their majorities in the 107th Congress, will depend on how successfully they can present their message. They argue that an effective approach to incidents such as the shooting in Littleton, Colo. — in which two teenagers killed themselves after slaying 12 schoolmates and a teacher — should deal more with the underlying cultural issues behind youth crime, and less with gun control.

Background Checks

The most controversy was generated on the gun control bill, which called for background checks of prospective buyers at gun shows but would narrow the definition of what constitutes such a show from what was passed by the Senate. The Senate measure defined a show as any event in which 50 guns were offered for sale. The House measure would have required that there be at least 10 vendors present to constitute a gun show.

Gun control supporters argued the House definition would allow a handful of gun vendors to sell huge numbers of weapons without customer checks. Opponents said it was necessary to prevent triggering the background checks for simple transactions, such as an estate sale of someone who owned at least 50 guns.

On what both sides had described as the pivotal vote, the House toned down its bill by adopting an amendment by John D. Dingell, D-Mich., that had been sanctioned by the NRA. That Dingell would promote such an amendment — and describe how he had agreed to do so after negotiating with DeLay — infuriated many Democrats and served to highlight the complicated cultural and political forces that still buffet the gun control debate.

Dingell's language stipulated that any background check at a gun show be completed within 24 hours. Current law allows for three business days. The issue comes into play in approximately one quarter of the background checks when a computerized database created by the 1993 Brady law (PL 103-159) is unable to provide complete information on the purchaser. In these cases federal authorities are called on to contact courthouses and state records offices by telephone.

The amendment was adopted late in the night of June 17, 218-211. *(Vote 234, p. H-80)*

After that, gun control supporters offered the alternative that they had rallied behind. Sponsored by Carolyn McCarthy, D-N.Y., it would have adopted language similar to the Senate's. It was rejected 193-235. *(Vote 235, p. H-80)*

The series of options was designed to keep Republicans from voting for the McCarthy amendment by allowing them choices that might fit their political needs.

For a while it looked as though DeLay and Hastert had successfully negotiated the turbulent waters of gun control, in a classic example of how victory often goes to those who frame the debate. Blocking McCarthy would have been almost impossible had they not been able to present competing options.

Only 33 Republicans — or 15 percent of those voting — voted for the McCarthy amendment, fewer than the 54 (or 31 percent) who voted for the Brady law in 1993 and fewer even than than the 38 (or 22 percent) who voted for the assault weapons ban of 1994.

In contrast, Democrats cut their defectors from 69 who voted against Brady to 49 who voted against McCarthy. *(1993 Almanac, p. 300; 1994 Almanac, p. 276)*

One important difference was that the Democratic House of 1993 presented lawmakers with a choice of voting for the Brady legislation or nothing at all. This time, DeLay endeavored to give members in swing districts alternatives. They could vote for the underlying proposal by opposing both the Dingell and McCarthy amendments, or they could vote only for the Dingell language.

By voting for Dingell's language, they were given a rare chance to finesse the competing views of constituents. They could tell their gun control advocates that they voted for background checks, while telling gun control foes that they voted for a measure drafted by the NRA.

But in the end, all the package of amendments did was ensure that almost everyone had a gripe with the final bill. Despite support of the NRA, Dingell's plan was not enough for the staunchest gun control foes. And gun control supporters were not about to support an NRA-backed measure.

The final vote showed there will not be much cover for moderate Republicans. Christopher Shays, R-Conn., said the party has to distance itself from the NRA if it is going to portray itself as responsive to the public. "It's clear this marriage between the NRA and the Republican Party must come to an end," he said.

But Democrats' ability to score political points off the issue was dampened somewhat by the fact that DeLay handed the job of sponsoring the NRA amendment to Dingell. "The message is mixed when the senior Democrat offers the weakening amendment," said James P. Moran, D-Va.

On the other side of the equation, some Democrats may find themselves targeted by the NRA and angry gun owners for their votes for McCarthy. In the 1994 Republican sweep, a handful of Democratic losses were attributed specifically to votes to ban assault weapons.

Suburban Voters

The key to who ultimately wins on the gun control issue is how the House action plays in suburban districts. Lawmakers from suburban districts, as defined by a Congressional Quarterly study of the demographics of each of the 435 districts, have always been pivotal on gun issues. Representatives of rural areas as a rule tend to oppose gun control measures, while those from urban districts tend to support them.

The lawmakers who represent suburban districts are often the most whipsawed by gun control votes. No matter how they vote, no matter what the outcome, these issues make some of their constituents unhappy, whether they be soccer moms or weekend hunters.

The defeat of the McCarthy amendment in the House was largely the result of the fact that gun control opponents were able to hold on to most of the suburban Republican members. In the 1994 assault weapons ban, 67 suburban Republicans voted no. *(1994 Almanac, p. 48-H)*

In this year's debate, 68 suburban Republicans voted against the McCarthy amendment.

Suburban and mixed district members often have to walk a fine line between the soft majority support for gun control and intense minority opposition to it. Greenwood said most of the people he actually hears from are motivated by letters they receive from the NRA.

"My district as a whole is about 75 percent in favor of common sense gun issues," said Greenwood. "Having said that, we get about 50 or 100 calls a day against these measures. They are almost without exception NRA members who receive the letters and pretty much follow the script."

Greenwood waited until the last minute to decide. He voted against Dingell's amendment and for McCarthy's.

But for all of the suburban Republicans who supported McCarthy, there were many more who voted against her measure. Emblematic of McCarthy's opposition was Rob Portman, R-Ohio. While he has traditionally voted against gun control measures, he is the type of member McCarthy would have to convince to prevail in a Republican controlled House.

Portman said his suburban Columbus voters are much more aware of the availability of guns. But he said they have heavily nuanced opinions on how to approach the issue of teen violence.

"They are much more acutely aware of the issue," he said. "But they don't believe in a silver bullet."

Even some of the most conservative members noticed an uptick of interest in gun measures. "The Columbine tragedy . . . was real heartbreak for the country," Majority Leader Dick Armey, R-Texas, said at a news conference June 15. "It was catalytic on a lot of fronts, and one of them was on guns."

Surprise Defeat for Hyde

The overwhelming defeat for the Hyde proposal to ban sales of violent material to minors came as something of a surprise. Though most Democrats were expected to vote against it, it held an appeal to many Republicans eager to take on Hollywood. In his news conference, Armey referred to it as if it were the underlying bill that would be brought to the floor, not an amendment.

But then the lobbying heated up, and it did not come just from the movie industry. Retailers, a group generally supportive of Republican policies, started calling their biggest supporters in Congress. The U.S. Chamber of Commerce actively lobbied on the issue as well.

The measure may have also suffered from a little posturing. Hyde said some of his colleagues told him that if they voted against his measure based on protecting the First Amendment, they would more easily vote against gun control by portraying themselves as defenders of the Constitution.

Indeed, a number of members of both parties invoked both the First and Second Amendments during the debate. "By the Fourth of July," said Dingell, "we will probably have successfully trampled upon the entirety of the Bill of Rights."

The Hyde measure would have provided penalties of up to five years in prison for selling or lending material to a minor that contains certain violent or sexually explicit material. In doing so it attempted to create a new standard of violence that could be constitutionally restricted. The Supreme Court has carved out a free speech exemption for obscenity, but there is no corresponding exemption for extreme violence.

The criminal sanctions would apply to violent or sexually explicit material that "the average person" would find appealing to "prurient, shameful or morbid interest," and was "patently offensive with respect to what is suitable to minors." The material would have to lack "serious literary, artistic, political or scientific value for minors," as defined by "a reasonable person." The language is similar to that in the 1973 Supreme Court case *Miller v. California* defining obscenity.

Given that the motivation for the language was ostensibly the Columbine shooting, some members found it ironic that the amendment emphasized sex over violence, giving a much broader and graphically explicit definition of sexual material than of violence.

The amendment listed acts and parts of the human anatomy that would be considered "sexually explicit" if presented. These included "actual or simulated" displays of "human male or female genitals, pubic area or buttocks with less than a full opaque covering"; "a female breast with less than a fully opaque covering of any portion thereof below the top of the nipple"; "acts of masturbation, sodomy and or sexual intercourse"; and "covered male genitals in a discernibly turgid state."

Displays of "violent material" would have been defined as those acts that include "sadistic or masochistic flagellation by or upon a person"; "torture by or upon a person"; "acts of mutilation upon the human body"; or "rape." The specificity in both cases of sex and violence, Hyde said, was necessary to prevent vagueness, which could have a chilling effect on free speech.

McCollum's Proposal

The guts of the juvenile crime provisions were not in the bill as it came to the floor. The language the House started with merely called for a $1.5 billion authorization to states for combating teen crime.

By far the most significant amendment adopted was an omnibus juvenile crime package, sponsored by Crime Subcommittee Chairman Bill McCollum, R-Fla., that would have created a number of mandatory minimum sentences and allowed juveniles to be tried as adults in federal court. It was approved 249-181. *(Vote 211, p. H-74)*

The amendment was, in effect, the underlying bill. Thirty-eight of the 44 amendments offered were amendments to the McCollum amendment.

McCollum's proposal spawned a classic split, with conservatives and some moderates accepting the "get-tough" approach while traditional liberals attacked it as counterproductive and inhumane.

McCollum said the juvenile justice system in American simply has not caught up with the fact that many teens are exceptionally violent and dangerous people. Democrats countered that treating teens as adult criminals will only ensure that they continue to behave violently into their adulthood.

"Lock up a 13-year-old with a murderer, a rapist and a robber, and guess what he'll want to be when he grows up?" said Melvin Watt, D-N.C.

The vote represented a complete reversal from the approach pursued earlier this year and a return to the approach used in the 105th Congress, when the House passed a tough juvenile crime bill only to see it stall in the Senate. Until the Columbine shooting, McCollum and Robert C. Scott, D-Va., had been collaborating on the bipartisan, if somewhat limited, approach espoused in HR 1501.

Indeed, the initial responses to Columbine from McCollum and Scott were that Congress should not overreact and that the federal government's ability to combat crime is limited.

But the Columbine shooting caused an outpouring of ideas and plans to address the social decline thought to be behind it. In fact, as the debate continued, it became a forum for members' frustrations and aspirations about contemporary society and its governance.

Running through the debate were two contradictory themes: that federal government cannot possibly have much effect on the forces that would create a Littleton-like shooting, and that it should try to do just about anything it can think of.

Because gun control advocates seized immediately on the issue after the shooting, Republican members felt they needed to come up with alternatives to gun control, Greenwood said.

"The Congress would have done a lot better had it not waded into a lot of these gun and culture issues," Greenwood said. "I think things went downhill when Republicans perceived Democrats were trying to win points on guns. That's when we came up with this 'best defense is an offense' strategy."

Amendments adopted include:

- **Ten Commandments.** By Robert B. Aderholt, R-Ala., to allow the Ten Commandments to be displayed in public places. Adopted 248-180. *(Vote 221, p. H-76)*
- **Federal judges.** By DeLay, to limit federal judges' ability to order the release of inmates on the grounds of prison crowding. Adopted 296-133. *(Vote 215, p. H-74)*
- **Prison funding.** By Matt Salmon, R-Ariz., to penalize states whose convicts commit crimes in other states after release. The cost of incarcerating the criminal in the second state would be docked from the first state's federal crime assistance fund and transferred to the second. Adopted 412-15. *(Vote 212, p. H-74)*
- **Hollywood.** By Jo Ann Emerson, R-Mo., criticizing the entertainment industry for the use of pointless acts of brutality in movies, television, music and video games. Adopted by voice vote.
- **Disabled children.** By Charlie Norwood, R-Ga., to allow schools to discipline children with mental or physical disabilities the same way that other children are disciplined if they come to school with a weapon or illegal drugs. Adopted 300-128. *(Vote 227, p. H-78)*
- **Religious programs.** By Mark Souder, R-Ind., to ensure that religious organizations cannot be discriminated against when they seek to get government grants to provide juvenile services. Adopted 346-83. *(Vote 222, p. H-78)*

The House defeated, 161-266, an amendment by Zach Wamp, R-Tenn., to create a uniform system of ratings covering television, music videos and other forms of entertainment. *(Vote 224, p. H-78)*

Lott Attempts To Jump Start Stalled Bill

JULY 24 — Senate Majority Leader Trent Lott, R-Miss., took steps July 22 to get the stalled juvenile justice bill (HR 1501) to conference over the objections of Robert C. Smith, I-N.H.

Lott first tried the usual procedure, seeking unanimous consent for a series of steps that include calling up the House bill, inserting the text of the Senate version (S 254) and requesting a conference. But Smith, who has vowed to use every available parliamentary maneuver to block the bill, objected.

That forces Lott to begin a step-by-step process, beginning with a cloture vote July 26 to cut off debate on a motion to take up HR 1501.

Smith opposes the Senate bill and prefers the House-passed version. While both measures address youth crime, only the Senate bill includes gun control language promoted by Democrats. Provisions include mandatory background checks for sales of firearms at gun shows, a ban on imports of high-capacity ammunition clips and a requirement that handguns be sold with locks or other safety devices.

A less restrictive version of the gun provisions (HR 2122) drew sharp attacks from House Democrats and was defeated on the House floor June 18.

Both Chambers Name Conferees

JULY 31 — Pressure to at least show progress on juvenile crime legislation before schools reopen was apparently sufficient to force Congress to take several small procedural steps the week of July 26. But continuing disagreement about what gun control provisions — if any —should be in the final version of the bill means that House and Senate negotiators almost certainly will still be at work when the fall semester starts.

After a lopsided cloture vote on July 28, Sen. Robert C. Smith, I-N.H., agreed to delay his plans to try to stop, or at least slow, enactment of new federal gun controls.

By 77-22, or 17 votes more than were needed, senators voted to limit debate on the usually routine procedural question of whether to insert the text of the Senate-passed juvenile crime bill (S 254) into the House-passed measure (HR 1501) before seeking to begin conference negotiations with the House. *(Vote 224, p. S-44)*

After that, Smith dropped his threat to call for as many as a half-dozen more votes on such procedural questions, and Senate conferees were named.

"I see no reason to burn up the good will of the Senate by demanding vote after vote," said Larry E. Craig of Idaho, who as chairman of the GOP Policy Committee and a board member of the National Rifle Association (NRA) is perhaps Smith's most powerful ally.

The naming of House negotiators, which Speaker J. Dennis Hastert, R-Ill., had been promising for weeks, occurred July 30, a day after a securities day trader, after killing his family, shot nine people dead at two Atlanta brokerage firms before committing suicide.

Since the two chambers passed their bills this spring, progress has been glacial. The main reason had been Smith, who is considering a third-party presidential run and who vowed to use every parliamentary tool available to thwart gun control. He now says he may mount a filibuster against any conference report that contains gun control language. That underscores the difficulty conferees will have in finding a compromise that can win President Clinton's signature and also overcome the opposition of gun rights advocates.

The Senate voted to require background checks of weapons purchasers at gun shows, ban imports of high-capacity ammunition magazines and require that gun locks or safety devices be sold with handguns.

The House measure contains no such provisions, but limits itself to language like the Senate's to deter or harshly punish crimes by youngsters. Legislation (HR 2122) containing a watered-down version of many of the Senate's gun provisions was defeated June 18 by a combination of Democrats who said it did not go far enough and Republicans who said it went too far.

Senate Judiciary Committee Chairman Orrin G. Hatch, R-Utah, said July 27 that some gun control language is likely to emerge from conference. But Clinton has threatened to veto a bill that he concludes would weaken current law. That could be the effect, for example, of the middle ground between the Senate gun show language and the provision the House endorsed as an amendment before the underlying bill's defeat.

The House voted 305-84 on July 30 for a non-binding motion to instruct conferees to include unspecified gun show language in the final bill. *(Vote 354, H-118)*

After the worst schoolhouse killing spree in American history — on April 20 in Littleton, Colo., where two students killed a dozen Columbine High School students, a teacher and then themselves — both Hastert and Senate Majority Leader Trent Lott, R-Miss., pushed for Congress to craft a response before the next school year starts.

With that unlikely, the NRA will be "using every last minute of the August recess" to lobby lawmakers against supporting gun control provisions in either the juvenile crime bill or a wrapup spending package, said James Jay Baker, the top NRA lobbyist. "We've got a lot of grass-roots activities ahead to keep our members on alert."

Conferees Begin Quest for Deal On Gun Control

AUGUST 7 — Pressed to produce legislation that might have prevented the high school carnage in Littleton, Colo., and other highly publicized shootings, House and Senate negotiators began work Aug. 5 on a compromise version of juvenile justice legislation (HR 1501). The top Republican conferees announced agreement on two things: Some gun control proposals will be in the final bill, and the deal will not be done quickly.

"There is pressure to do it before school opens, but the complexity and volatility of these issues doesn't lend itself to rapid resolution," said House Judiciary Committee Chairman Henry J. Hyde, R-Ill.

By far the most contentious issues are the gun control measures in the version of the bill (S 254) that the Senate passed in May. These include a requirement that sales at gun shows be subject to background checks, a ban on the importation of large-capacity ammunition magazines and a requirement that gun locks or storage devices be sold with handguns.

The House measure has no gun control language, and a bill with more modest gun restrictions than the Senate passed (HR 2122) was defeated when it was opposed by both gun rights defenders — House Majority Whip Tom DeLay, R-Texas, the most influential among them — who said it went too far, and gun control stalwarts who said it would weaken current gun laws.

The Senate measures would serve as "the good beginning" for the talks, said Hyde, who supports gun control and counts Speaker J. Dennis Hastert, R-Ill., on his side. "But it is a beginning. Compromises are necessary, because as you know, we did not have the votes in the House to pass it. I want to get those votes."

Hyde and his Senate counterpart, Judiciary Committee Chairman Orrin G. Hatch, R-Utah, indicated that the Senate gun show language, as written, could not pass the House. Neither gave any indication how much it would have to be altered to get a majority. But both said dropping all gun provisions was not an option.

"We have an obligation to defend our institutions' respective positions," Hatch said. "More importantly, we have an obligation to reconcile these firearm-related provisions in this conference."

As they try to craft a middle ground that is politically palatable, Hyde and Hatch have their work cut out for them. On the one hand, polls show solid support for the types of gun controls the Senate endorsed, and if Congress does not enact similar language the Democrats are promising to make a campaign issue out of it. But gun rights defenders, while a minority, appear far more adamant in their position, and GOP strategists see their votes as potentially pivotal to their success in tight races for Congress next year.

Sen. Charles E. Schumer, D-N.Y., said Aug. 3 that he would help mount a filibuster if the conference report contains much less than the Senate gun show language. President Clinton has threatened a veto if he concludes that the final bill could weaken current law.

The Senate bill would require background checks of all prospective buyers at guns shows. Only some sales are subject now. The bill would give federal authorities three business days to call records offices to complete checks if the new, national computerized database produces incomplete information.

The defeated House bill would have allowed just one day for finishing background checks. One group of opponents of the bill said its effect would still be to shut down most gun shows. Another group of opponents said a one-day limit is inappropriate since most gun shows are on weekends, when public records offices are closed.

With all the political pressure on them to act, some opponents of gun control fear the conference report will contain tough restrictions. Rep. Jack Kingston, R-Ga., predicted Aug. 2 that the final bill would have language similar to what the Senate passed.

The first meeting of the conference was limited to opening statements, and several motions offered by Democrats were ruled out of order. There will be no more meetings until after Labor Day, although staff aides were ordered to begin informal discussions on issues considered less controversial.

Gun Compromise Remains Distant, But Hyde Vows To Keep Trying

SEPTEMBER 25 — Key Democratic and Republican lawmakers continued to search for common ground on gun control the week of Sept. 20, more than three months after the House and Senate passed vastly different versions of a juvenile crime bill.

But little progress was made, and as the session enters its final weeks, players on both sides of the aisle expressed doubt that a deal can be reached on the politically polarized issue.

Even if House-Senate conferees could come up with a deal this year, most believe it would be defeated in either the House or the Senate.

"I'll bet you at the end of this Congress, it's unlikely that something will happen because the NRA doesn't want anything to happen," House Minority Leader Richard A. Gephardt, D-Mo., said Sept. 22, referring to the National Rifle Association.

On May 20, the Senate passed a juvenile justice bill (S 254) that includes a variety of provisions aimed at making it more difficult to buy guns. One month later, the House passed its version of the bill (HR 1501) without any gun control measures. Conferees on the bill have met only once since they were named in July.

"This is a laborious process," said House Judiciary Committee Chairman Henry J. Hyde, R-Ill. "I don't think either party can pass a bill without both parties pitching in. We're all fighting for votes."

Hyde, however, was a bit more optimistic than Gephardt. "I'm not going to abandon my quest," Hyde said. "We'll do the best we can with what we have."

Hyde has offered what he calls a "compromise" package on gun controls to Democratic leaders who back more stringent gun regulations than GOP leaders do. The package includes a two-step process for background checks at gun shows. Most sales could be cleared in 24 hours, but others could be delayed for up to three business days.

Under the Senate-passed language, all background checks at gun shows could take up to three days.

Hyde's proposal, according to GOP aides, would also ban importing certain large-capacity ammunition clips and prohibit juveniles convicted of gun-related felonies from ever buying handguns. It would also require safety devices for handguns and prohibit minors from possessing assault weapons.

Gephardt met privately Sept. 23 with fellow Democrats Michigan Rep. John Conyers Jr., ranking member on the Judiciary Committee, and New York Rep. Carolyn McCarthy, whose husband was shot and killed on a Long Island commuter train, to review Hyde's proposal. Democratic sources said the proposal was rejected as inadequate.

Calls for Action

On Sept. 23 and 24, the House voted on four different non-binding motions to instruct conferees on the juvenile justice bills.

The outcome of the votes was somewhat conflicting. Two measures sponsored by gun control advocates easily passed, but broad support was given to a measure sponsored by gun control opponents.

The first motion, introduced by gun control advocate Rep. Zoe Lofgren, D-Calif., was adopted 305-117. That motion calls on conferees to support language that does not weaken current gun control laws, closes "loopholes" that allow criminals to obtain guns and strengthens enforcement of current laws against criminals who use guns. *(Vote 438, p. H-142)*

The measure won support from both Democrats and Republicans, including Hyde.

"While I support these laudable objectives, I do not support using them as a Trojan horse for more invidious goals," Hyde said of Lofgren's motion.

The next day, Lofgren offered a second motion instructing conferees to include language that would require unlicensed gun dealers at gun shows to conduct background checks, ban juvenile possession of assault weapons, require child safety locks to be sold with handguns and prohibit juvenile felons from ever buying guns.

That motion was adopted 241-167. *(Vote 447, p. H-146)*

McCarthy then offered a motion to instruct conferees to have their "first substantive meeting" within the next week and to meet every weekday in public session until a final bill is drafted. "Every day Congress fails to advance juvenile justice legislation is another day that we lose 13 children to gun violence," McCarthy said.

That motion failed, 190-218. *(Vote 445, p. H-146)*

Opponents of strict gun control measures offered their own motion to instruct conferees to reject all Senate provisions that "impose unconstitutional restrictions on the Second Amendment rights of individuals" to keep and bear arms.

(Continued on p. 18-24)

Juvenile Crime Bills Compared

ISSUE	HOUSE (HR 1501)	SENATE (S 254)
Juvenile justice grants	The bill would authorize $1.5 billion through fiscal 2002 for block grants for state and local projects to strengthen the juvenile justice system; purposes include imposition of graduated sentences, jail construction, youth witness assistance, enhancing records systems for young violent offenders, mental health and drug treatment, or "activities to encourage character education and development."	The measure would authorize $2.7 billion through fiscal 2004 for block grants with similar purposes. Under both bills, these grants would replace juvenile crime grants first established in 1968.
'Aimee's Law'	The bill would allow federal reimbursements to states that prosecute and imprison murderers, rapists and violent sexual offenders with prior convictions for similar crimes in states with lax sentencing laws. Funding would come from federal law enforcement aid otherwise allocated to the state of the prior conviction.	Similar provision.
Sexual offenders	The bill would require life sentences, if not the death penalty, for repeat convictions of sexual offenses involving children. It would prohibit the transfer of obscene material to those younger than 18.	No similar provision.
New judgeships	The bill would create five new United States District Court judgeships in Florida, three in Arizona and two in Nevada.	Similar provision.
Gun tracing	The bill would direct the Bureau of Alcohol,Tobacco & Firearms to expand to 75, from 27, the cities where it traces guns used in youth crimes and would authorize $50 million in fiscal 2000, and additional funds as needed through fiscal 2004, for that expansion.	The bill would order expansion of the program to 250 cities and counties by fiscal 2004 but makes no mention of additional authorization.
Violence in media	The measure would urge the entertainment industry to curb production of violent fare and require a federal study of the effect of mass media violence on juveniles.	The bill urges the entertainment industry to set guidelines to limit violence and other "harmful influences" on children. It would require federal studies of impact of violent music and video games on children and of practices of marketing violent and sexually explicit material to minors.
Internet advertising	No similar provision.	In general, unlicensed dealers would be prohibited from using the Internet to advertise guns or explosives for sale to juveniles or others not eligible to own guns or explosives.
Children's Internet protection	Schools and libraries that fail to place an obscenity filtering or blocking device on computer terminals with Internet access would be ineligible to receive federal aid to pay for high-speed access to the Internet.	Internet service providers would be required to offer their customers access to filtering or screening software.
Crimes against juveniles	The FBI would be authorized to help state or local police investigate deaths of those younger than 13. The U.S. Sentencing Commission would be directed to lengthen minimum sentences for crimes against those younger than 13. But a requirement of the 1994 crime law (PL 103-322) requiring the commission to lengthen sentences for crimes against the elderly would be repealed.	No similar provision.
Drug testing	No similar provision.	Drug testing of students by local school districts would be allowed with parental or legal guardian consent.

ISSUE	HOUSE (HR 1501)	SENATE (S 254)
Federal prosecution of minors	The bill would end the existing preference for trying federal offenses by juveniles 13 and older in state court.	The presumption of state proceedings for juveniles would be preserved, and federal proceedings for minors 14 and older would be authorized only when no state was willing to exercise jurisdiction and there was a substantial federal interest in the case.
Punishing juvenile delinquents	The bill would increase the maximum term of detention to 10 years, to the juvenile's 26th birthday,or to the maximum term available had the juvenile been convicted as an adult, whichever is less. The current maximum is the lesser of the 21st birthday or the adult maximum. The U.S. Sentencing Commission would be ordered to develop possible new sanctions for delinquent juveniles.	The maximum term would be the lesser of the date of the 26th birthday or the maximum term available had the juvenile been convicted as an adult. The Sentencing Commission would be instructed to set sentencing guidelines for juveniles convicted as adults or found to be delinquent.
Juvenile probation	Adult probation and supervised release rules would be applied to juvenile delinquents.	Similar provision.
Trying juveniles as adults	The bill would require adult trials for those 14 or older — down from 16 years or older — when they allegedly committed serious federal violent crimes, drug crimes or weapons offenses. It would give the attorney general discretion to try those as young as 13 as adults.	The bill would permit adult trials for juveniles previously tried as adults or for those 14 years or older when they allegedly committed a violent or serious drug felony. It would allow juveniles several grounds for petitioning to keep a case as a juvenile delinquency matter.
Trial deadlines	The bill would extend to 45 days, up from the current 30, the general deadline for starting a juvenile trial.	The deadline would be extended to 70 days.
Record-keeping	The bill would order that records of juvenile proceedings be kept in the same manner as adult criminal records. It would allow disclosure of juvenile criminal records to victims and schools. And it calls for the FBI to receive information on any juvenile found delinquent for a felony or firearms possession.	The bill would require that juvenile proceedings records be sent to the FBI and that records of violent juvenile delinquents be maintained as part of the FBI system of adult records. Federal criminal records of juveniles tried as adults would be made public to the same extent as adult records, but juveniles could petition to have the records — except for serious violent crimes — expunged after five years.
Segregation of imprisoned adults from juveniles	The "sight and sound" separation requirement would be altered to permit incidental and supervised contact, while still prohibiting regular contact. In rural areas, youths could be held in an adult facility if parents and the court agree.	The prohibition on incidental or accidental communication, or by sounds that cannot reasonably be considered speech, would be relaxed. Physical contact and sustained oral communication — rather than "regular" contact as in current law — would be prohibited. Segregation of violent and non-violent juveniles would be required to the extent practicable.
Disproportionate Confinement	The bill would bar states from setting numerical standards and quotas to meet requirements that they try to reduce the disproportionate imprisonment of minority youth.	The bill would require that efforts to reduce disproportionate incarceration look at "segments of the juvenile population," rather than at minorities.
Public juvenile proceedings	No provision.	The bill would require that juvenile proceedings generally be open to the public.
Gang activity	Those convicted of a new federal crime of recruiting for a criminal street gang would be subject to 1 to 10 years in prison, and a minimum of four years if the recruit is a minor. A street gang would be defined as a group of three or more, down from five currently. The roster of prohibited gang activities would be expanded to include gambling, use of explosives, immigrant smuggling and obstruction of justice.	Similar provision.

ISSUE	HOUSE (HR 1501)	SENATE (S 254)
Prison conditions	The bill would deny federal judges jurisdiction to order release of a felon based on prison conditions and would terminate any prison condition consent decree entered into before 1995.	No similar provision.
Drug trafficking to minors	For those convicted of distributing drugs to minors, using minors to distribute drugs or distributing drugs near schools, the bill would increase the mandatory minimum sentence from one year to three years for first time offenders, and to five years for subsequent convictions.	Similar provision.
Background checks of buyers at gun shows	No provision.	The bill would require background checks of all buyers at events where 50 or more firearms are offered for sale. The checks would be governed by the Brady law (PL 103-159), which gives law enforcement officials three business days to contact state and local records offices if the records in the national computer database are incomplete.
Gun show record-keeping	No provision.	Organizers would be required to register with the Treasury and verify the identity of vendors before each show. Unlicensed vendors would be absolved of any new federal record-keeping but federally licensed dealers would have to keep records of transactions with unlicensed dealers.
Ammunition clips	No provision.	The bill would ban importation of any ammunition feeding device capable of holding more than 10 rounds.
Handgun locks	No provision.	The bill would bar manufacturers, importers or dealers from selling a handgun unless it was accompanied by a disabling mechanism, trigger lock or lockable storage container. Owners of handguns who used such devices would be given civil liability immunity if their guns were stolen and used to commit a crime.
Gun ownership by juvenile convicts	No provision.	Those previously convicted of a violent juvenile crime would be barred from possessing a firearm.
Attorneys' fees	Federal courts would be barred from awarding attorney fee payments in cases involving a claim that a public school violated the constitutional prohibition against the establishment of religion by permitting, facilitating or accommodating student religious expression.	No similar provision.
Religious expression	The bill would give states and municipalities authority to display the Ten Commandments on their property and would expand the rights of individuals to express their religious faith on state or municipal property.	No similar provision.
School shootings	Those convicted in federal court of recklessly firing a gun in a school zone would be subject to as long as 20 years in prison or 25 years if serious injury resulted. If a death occurred, those 16 or 17 years old would be subject to life imprisonment; those 18 or older could be sentenced to death.	No similar provision.
Disabled students	The measure would permit the expulsion of, and denial of federal education aid to, disabled students who bring firearms to school.	Similar provision.

ISSUE	HOUSE (HR 1501)	SENATE (S 254)
Gun possession at schools	The maximum prison term for juveniles would be increased to as long as five years for simple possession in a school zone, but 20 years if the gun was intended for use in the commission of a violent felony. The maximum term for adults would be five years for possession, but 20 years if the weapon was intended for a juvenile's use or for use in the commission of a violent felony.	Similar provision.
Enhanced sentences for gun crimes	The maximum prison terms would be increased for firing a gun during a violent federal crime, lying in order to acquire a gun to be used by another for a violent felony, lying in order to give a gun to anyone prohibited from owning one, or removing the serial number from a gun. Gun dealers' licenses could be revoked before the appeal of a felony conviction.	The maximum prison sentence would be increased for firing a gun during a violent federal crime and making false statements to acquire a gun to be used by another to commit a violent felony.
Other enhanced sentences	The bill would increase prison terms for traveling across state lines in order to commit a variety of crimes, including burglary, assault with a deadly weapon and shooting at an occupied home or automobile.	The bill contains similar provisions and would also increase the maximum sentences for threatening a federal witness and assaulting or threatening a federal worker. It would make all carjackings federal crimes; now, they are federalized only if there is intent to cause death or serious injury. The bill would allow the government to confiscate a criminal's real estate or other property used in connection to the crime.
Teacher liability	The bill would bar plaintiffs from getting punitive damages from teachers, administrators and school board members in civil cases, so long as the school official acted within the scope of "responsibility" to a school or government entity. It would make exceptions for crimes of violence, sexual offenses, civil rights violations or misconduct while intoxicated.	The bill contains a similar provision, but would not apply the shield to school board officials.
Filming on federal land	No provision.	The bill would prohibit use of federal property, equipment or personnel to make commercial films that glorify or endorse violence. News programs and public service announcements would be exempt.
Body armor	No provision.	The bill would instruct the U.S. Sentencing Commission to issue enhanced penalties for the use of body armor during the commission of a crime and would prohibit convicted violent felons from owning body armor.
Prevention programs	The bill would eliminate the existing incentive grants for local delinquency prevention programs but would allow states to use the new block grants that would be established under the bill to create prevention programs.	The bill would eliminate the incentive grants for local delinquency prevention programs but would require states to set aside a minimum of 25 percent of new block grant funding for juvenile crime prevention programs. The bill also would authorize funds for the creation of a national "parenting as prevention" program.
Liquor sales	No similar provision.	The bill would allow states to go to federal court to enforce state liquor laws and require adults to sign for shipped liquor deliveries. The language is aimed at curbing liquor sales via the Internet or by mail.
Background checks for explosives	The bill would establish a system for checking the backgrounds of would-be explosives buyers.	No similar provision.

(Continued from p. 18-19)

"The Second Amendment is a precious and personal right of every American," John T. Doolittle, R-Calif., author of the motion, said on the floor. "We continue to see efforts by the left wing . . . intended to take away our fundamental rights."

Doolittle's motion was adopted, 337-73. *(Vote 446, p. H-146)*

The debate over gun violence also will likely rise up when senators begin work on a special task force on America's "cultural crisis."

Sen. Sam Brownback, R-Kan., first proposed creating a one-year special committee with subpoena power to look into the issue.

That proposal, however, was later downgraded to a task force without subpoena power that will disband next July.

Democrats say they will insist that gun violence be included in the task force's jurisdiction.

"If we're going to look at anything, we ought to be looking at violence and how we can curtail it," said Senate Minority Leader Tom Daschle, D-S.D.

Conferees Prepare To Reconvene; Optimism Rises For Compromise

OCTOBER 2 — Congressional leaders are promising that after nearly four months of delay, conferees on the juvenile justice bill (HR 1501) will finally meet to begin substantive deliberations the week of Oct. 4, whether or not any deals have been worked out beforehand — or even appear possible in the future.

Senate Judiciary Committee Chairman Orrin G. Hatch, R-Utah, has held off calling the conference back together to give House Republicans time to negotiate — both with Democrats and, at least as importantly, among themselves — on gun control proposals.

Those talks had produced little progress until near the end of the week of Sept. 27, when the top House conferees said they were near an agreement they believed they could sell to their respective parties' leaders.

"We're within striking distance," John Conyers Jr. of Michigan, the top Democrat on the House Judiciary Committee, said Sept. 30 after one in a series of unpublicized meetings with Chairman Henry J. Hyde, R-Ill., that they said focused entirely on gun control. But the issues Hyde listed as still under discussion have been the most nettlesome all year on both sides of the Capitol: the minimum size of a gun show at which a new requirement for background checks of purchasers would be applied, the time limit for those checks and the procedures for maintaining records of those checks.

The Senate version (S 254) includes a handful of gun controls, including language, added as an amendment only because of Vice President Al Gore's tie-breaking vote, which would require background checks at any show with more than 50 guns for sale and would allow law enforcement officers three business days to finish reviews of records.

After passing its juvenile justice bill, the House defeated a bill (HR 2122) with more limited gun controls, including looser gun show language. The bill was spurned by gun control proponents, who said it would not do enough, and gun rights advocates, who said it would do too much.

That same dynamic now faces Hyde and Conyers, who said they hoped to present their leadership with a gun compromise on Oct. 4. Minority Leader Richard A. Gephardt, D-Mo., is pushing for tough curbs. Majority Whip Tom DeLay, R-Texas, wants no new gun controls. Speaker J. Dennis Hastert, R-Ill., is eager for a compromise.

"By Monday, we'll know" if one is at hand, Hyde said.

Regardless, negotiators agreed that it is time to convene for a second meeting; the first was Aug. 5. "We've given the House quite a bit of time to come to a deal," said Hatch, who favors some gun controls. "We have to move forward."

Both Ends Against the Middle

The situation is not much different in the Senate. There, as in the House, negotiators must bridge the gap between factions both ardently for and against gun curbs.

Rep. Bob Barr, R-Ga., a conferee and board member of the National Rifle Association, said he could accept several of the gun control provisions included in the Senate language, including a requirement that safety devices be sold with all handguns. But he said he could not accept a three-day period for gun show background checks and would push to redefine gun shows subject to the checks to events where at least 10 different vendors do business.

"Everyone knows it's dead on arrival," Hatch said of the Senate gun show language Sept. 28. "It clearly has to be modified."

But Democratic proponents of gun control say they will not budge.

"This is far and away the most important provision of the gun provisions," said Sen. Charles E. Schumer, D-N.Y. "The focus of the entire bill is on the gun show loophole. That's the make-or-break issue."

Although conferees have focused their attention on gun issues, many outside groups are focusing on the hundreds of other provisions in the bill aimed at curbing juvenile violence, and on several more — from limiting teachers' civil liability to changing the way Internet liquor sales are conducted to limiting federal judges' powers to control prison conditions — that have a more tenuous connection to the bill's stated purpose.

Last month, the Children's Defense Fund and the Children's Welfare League of America took out newspaper advertisements in the districts of many House conferees attacking the bill for "draconian provisions" that "will cause more harm to kids who are already troubled, instead of holding them accountable and helping to turn their lives around."

In particular, the groups oppose provisions that would allow those as young as 13 to be held in adult prisons, require regular federal trials — rather than juvenile delinquency proceedings — for those as young as 14 who commit violent felonies or drug crimes, impose tougher mandatory sentences on juveniles and allow their crime records to go to schools and colleges. The groups also support the Senate gun control measures and said neither the House nor Senate bill provide enough money for preventive crime programs.

On Aug. 5, more than four dozen groups sent a letter urging conferees to soften the juvenile prosecution provisions. Among the signatories were the

Children's Defense Fund, the Children's Welfare League, the Girl Scouts of the U.S.A., the National Council of Churches, the American Academy of Pediatrics and the NAACP.

Conyers said he felt that if a deal could be struck on gun issues, Democrats and Republicans could find common ground on the juvenile justice provisions.

"If we can get past guns, we could reconcile our differences rather easily on juveniles," he said. "But until we reconcile this big Roman numeral one, we can't get to number two."

No Breakthroughs In Quest for Gun Compromise

OCTOBER 16 — Half a year has passed since the shooting rampage at Columbine High School made gun control an unanticipated addition to the agenda for the 106th Congress. But Republican leaders — who initially seemed ready to use public outrage after the incident to find a middle ground on what has long been one of Washington's most polarized topics — still find themselves boxed in by hardened positions on both sides.

That was the only consensus that emerged the evening of Oct. 14 from a meeting of nine members of the Republican leadership in the office of Senate Majority Leader Trent Lott, R-Miss. They convened in the hope of settling on what — if any — gun control provisions they could sell to majorities in both the House and the Senate. They broke up after an hour with no answer.

"These are real sensitive negotiations," Senate Judiciary Committee Chairman Orrin G. Hatch, R-Utah, said as he left the meeting. "It's a real struggle . . . very complex."

On May 20 — precisely one month after two teenagers from suburban Littleton, Colo., killed a dozen schoolmates, a teacher and then themselves — the Senate passed a juvenile crime control measure (S 254) with a collection of gun control provisions that carved out a new middle ground on the issue.

"This is one of those rare times when the national consensus demands that we act," Speaker J. Dennis Hastert,R-Ill., said in urging the House to pass gun controls, too. But a month after that, positions had hardened in the House. Gun control stalwarts, mostly Democrats, and gun rights advocates, mostly Republicans, combined to defeat a package of gun controls weaker than the Senate's (HR 2212). The juvenile justice legislation the House passed (HR 1501), the bill now in conference, contains no gun control language.

Negotiators have met only once since, and any talks on the broad array of cultural and anti-crime provisions in the measures was postponed until a deal on gun curbs was struck.

At the leadership meeting, House Republicans said they would not bring a compromise to the floor unless they were assured that enough Democrats would support it to offset the cadre of GOP lawmakers who would vote against any gun controls, according to participants. A top leadership aide said that House leaders also signaled they would not make their troops vote on a politically sensitive compromise unless they were sure the deal would also be endorsed by the Senate.

Key Compromise Outlined

At the meeting, Hatch and House Judiciary Committee Chairman Henry J. Hyde, R-Ill., who both favor some new gun controls, outlined a compromise proposal that would allow as long as three days to finish background checks for buyers at gun shows — an amount of time pivotal to gun control advocates — but would define a gun show as an event with at least five vendors. The Senate bill defined gun shows as events with 50 or more guns for sale, regardless of the number of vendors.

Hyde said that he thinks common ground may still be found on the remaining Senate gun provisions, which would ban imports of high-capacity ammunition clips, require safety locks on all guns sold and prohibit juveniles convicted of serious crimes from ever owning a gun.

But the gun show language is a "very tough, difficult issue," he conceded, because "there are many special interest groups that have a vital interest in what we're doing." He mentioned both the National Rifle Association and Handgun Control and the Center to Prevent Handgun Violence as two such groups. "This is very complicated."

The GOP leaders did not dismiss Hyde's and Hatch's compromise proposal outright, participants in the meeting said, although they said there was fear among the GOP leaders that Democrats would balk at it and accuse the GOP of proposing a poor alternative to what the Senate adopted, albeit by a single vote.

Senate GOP Policy Committee Chairman Larry E. Craig of Idaho, an NRA board member who attended the meeting, said House leaders agreed to reach out to Democrats in hopes of forging an alliance on modified gun provisions. Craig said House Majority Whip Tom DeLay of Texas promised to lead the effort by arranging a meeting with Rep. John D. Dingell, D-Mich., a former NRA board member. The two of them had teamed up this summer on gun show language that was adopted as an amendment before the underlying bill was rejected.

But Dingell rejected the compromise. "Five or more vendors? Hell, I got that many members at my skeet club on Sunday," he said in an interview. "They're harassing law-abiding citizens like me, and I'm up to here with it."

Six Months Since Columbine

Even before Dingell spurned the compromise, Craig predicted only a 50-50 chance of finding gun language that can pass both the House and Senate this year. And even if that happens, President Clinton has said he will veto any bill that he concludes would weaken existing law.

Craig said that the leaders discussed the possibility of eventually dropping all gun control language and simply pushing for a compromise on the other provisions in the juvenile crime bills. The conferees met once, on Aug. 5, and no date has been set for another meeting.

The delays prompted House Democrats to move Oct. 14 to instruct the conferees to meet immediately and to agree on final language by the six-month anniversary of Columbine. The motion, by Sheila Jackson-Lee, D-Texas, was defeated 174-249, although 19 Republicans voted for it and 51 Democrats voted against it. *(Vote 502, p. H-164)*

Only Agreement Is To Postpone Action Until 2000

NOVEMBER 6 — Political skittishness combined with partisan snappishness to take over the gun control debate the week of Nov. 1. In their wake, all sides in the Byzantine maneuvering over legislation to boost firearms regulations and cut down on juvenile crime acknowledged that the bill (HR 1501) would stay on the shelf until next year.

But the intensified public bickering also cast doubt on the prospects that House and Senate negotiators would get any closer next year to coming to an agreement, let alone that such a deal would be cleared by Congress and win a presidential signature.

Democratic leaders are refusing to consider any GOP compromise proposal, Republicans who favor some new gun controls maintain, because they would rather be able to blame Republicans for the standoff during next year's campaign.

GOP leaders are blocking the legislation, the Democrats maintain, in order to ensure both campaign contributions and grass-roots enthusiasm from advocates of liberal gun ownership, groups such as the National Rifle Association (NRA) and its membership.

But GOP leaders on both sides of the Capitol who oppose new gun controls concede that they fear the political consequences of putting the issue back in the congressional limelight.

House Majority Whip Tom DeLay, R-Texas, said he does not want to force lawmakers who are similarly opposed to more restrictive gun regulations to cast another vote on the issue unless they are confident that whatever compromise is put before them would be endorsed by the Senate as well.

"The plan was to go first in the Senate," DeLay said in an interview Nov. 4. "We don't want our members to vote on something that would die in the Senate."

But Larry E. Craig of Idaho, the chairman of the Senate Republican Policy Committee and an NRA board member, said the Senate GOP leadership wants the House to take the more politically risky first vote in the next round of the legislative debate — also in order to protect pro-gun rights members from taking a disproportionate share of the political fallout.

"Do we want to walk the line again?" Craig said Nov. 2, referring to Senate passage in May of legislation expanding background checks of would-be buyers at gun shows. That language was added as an amendment despite vigorous opposition from GOP leaders, and only after Vice President Al Gore cast a tie-breaking vote in favor of it.

Majority Leader Trent Lott, R-Miss., suggested at the time that Gore would rue the day he cast that vote. That has not happened during Gore's campaign for the Democratic presidential nomination, which included headlining a Nov. 4 news conference at the Capitol. "The Republican Speaker and the leadership in the House have paid attention to the National Rifle Association instead of to the American people," Gore said. "This is going to be a national issue."

The event was arranged after back-to-back office shootings — on Nov. 2 in Honolulu and Nov. 3 in Seattle — left nine people dead.

Lawmakers who support tougher gun restrictions say such safeguards are needed to prevent further gun violence, and their campaign gained an early surge of momentum after 15 people died in the massacre at Columbine High School in April. Opponents say there are already enough gun regulations on the books, and lawmakers should instead focus on enforcing existing laws.

Juvenile Crime Curbs in Limbo

The gun control legislation under negotiation is part of a broader juvenile justice bill (S 254) the Senate passed in May.

The House passed its juvenile justice bill one month later. But a package of modest gun curbs (HR 2122) was soundly defeated when it was spurned by a combination of gun control stalwarts, who said it would not go far enough, and gun control opponents, who said it would go too far.

The House and Senate bills contain dozens of non-gun control provisions aimed at cracking down on juvenile violence, ranging from tougher sentences for teen criminals to drug testing of students to state grants for crime prevention to permission to post the Ten Commandments in government buildings.

So far, talks have focused nearly exclusively on the gun language, and on the gun show provision in particular. The Senate bill would also prohibit teenagers convicted of violent crimes from ever owning guns, ban imports of high-capacity ammunition clips and require that guns be sold with trigger locks or another disabling mechanism.

In a Nov. 4 letter, Rep. Carolyn McCarthy, D-N.Y., Sen. Charles E. Schumer, D-N.Y., and Sen. Richard J. Durbin, D-Ill., urged President Clinton to make GOP agreement to the Senate gun show provision a precondition to finishing the end-of-the-session budget negotiations.

"The president should hold up all the appropriations because I know the American people want to see us do something," said McCarthy, whose own version of that gun show regulation was narrowly rejected by the House.

Also on Nov. 4, House Judiciary Committee Chairman Henry J. Hyde, R-Ill., formally unveiled a compromise gun control package endorsed by Senate Judiciary Committee Chairman Orrin G. Hatch, R-Utah. Hyde has met several times with Rep. John Conyers Jr. of Michigan, the Judiciary Committee's top Democrat, in hopes of finding common ground with the Democratic leadership.

"I know gun control is an explosive and politically divisive issue within your party," Hyde said in a letter to House Minority Leader Richard A. Gephardt, D-Mo. "As you review this proposal, please keep in mind that we must not allow perfect to become the enemy of the good. . . . Please do not let a desire to exploit a political issue undermine this unique opportunity to protect America's children."

Hyde's proposal would, among other things, allow up to three days to conduct background checks at guns shows — similar to the language passed by the Senate. Hyde's proposal, however, would define gun shows as any event with 50 or more guns for sale and at least five vendors. The Senate gun show definition included only the 50 gun requirement.

Schumer and McCarthy criticized the Hyde language as having too many loopholes. Schumer has said he would filibuster any deal with weaker gun language than what the Senate passed. ◆

In Wake of Presidential Probe, Independent Counsel Law Allowed To Expire

Box Score

- **Bills:** HR 117, HR 2083, S 1297, S 1427

SUMMARY

The independent counsel law lapsed June 30, when the current version (PL 103-270) expired without Congress taking any steps to reauthorize it. Attorney General Janet Reno then issued guidelines for how she would name special prosecutors to probe alleged executive branch malfeasance.

In hearings in the aftermath of President Clinton's acquittal in his impeachment trial, most witnesses argued against reviving the law because they disagreed with its basic premise — that the independent counsel must be almost entirely free of oversight in order to avoid the possible conflicts of interest that gave rise to the position's creation after Watergate. The Justice Department and Kenneth W. Starr, the independent counsel who investigated the president, agreed that such a level of independence was unnecessary and created the potential for abuse.

Four senators offered a bill (S 1297) that would retain the expired law's procedure by which federal judges name independent counsels at the attorney general's request, although with tight new restrictions: They could not expand their jurisdiction beyond their original scope, would generally have two years to finish their inquiries and would need to hew to federal prosecutorial procedures. Another bill (S 1427) would allow the Justice Department to appoint a special counsel only with congressional approval.

One House bill (HR 117) would limit the scope of independent counsel probes and subject them to more congressional financial oversight. Another (HR 2083) would reaffirm the attorney general's power to name special counsels.

A grandfather clause in the law allowed the five independent counsels still in office to keep working. Advocates of independent counsels say they hope the current "cooling off" period builds support for reviving the debate next year. The law that expired this year took effect in 1994, 18 months after the previous version had lapsed.

Senators Say Statute Should Lapse if Not Radically Changed

FEBRUARY 27 — Out of the great partisan bloodletting spawned by Independent Counsel Kenneth W. Starr's investigation is coming at least one more surprising development: a bipartisan accord in Congress. Senators of both parties now believe the statute that authorized Starr's probe of President Clinton should be stripped from the books in the absence of a quick and radical overhaul.

Even as Starr and Attorney General Janet Reno continue to spar over whether and how Starr's own investigatory methods should be formally investigated, the mood at the Capitol has become considerably more thoughtful and less combative.

A hearing on the independent counsel law (PL 103-270) conducted by the Senate Governmental Affairs Committee on Feb. 24 frequently sounded like a college seminar on the separation of powers doctrine. At other times it took on the quality of a therapy session for Democrats who supported the law in past but are now repenting.

"I made a mistake," said Sen. Richard J. Durbin, D-Ill. "Four years ago, I voted to reauthorize this law."

Committee aides said that the most likely scenario by far is that the statute will be allowed to lapse when its authorization expires on June 30. Only between 30 and 40 senators have expressed interest in continuing the law, said a senior Democratic staff assistant to the panel. But allowing the law to expire would not necessarily mean that it has been condemned to an irreversible death. Before its current authorization, the law did not exist for 18 months between December 1992 and June 1994.

Proponents of sunsetting the statute include the powerful Senate pair of Kentucky's Mitch McConnell, the chairman of the National Republican Senatorial Committee, and Connecticut's Christopher J. Dodd, a former general chairman of the Democratic National Committee. They announced Feb. 23 that they would filibuster any attempt to reauthorize the law. A number of other Republicans and Democrats are committed to this approach or leaning in its direction, aides said.

But an equally bipartisan Senate group believes that the law needs to be continued in some form. This camp includes Joseph I. Lieberman, D-Conn., Carl Levin, D-Mich., and Susan Collins, R-Maine. Each was instrumental in writing previous versions of the law — Lieberman and Levin as members of the Senate, and Collins when she was an aide to former Sen. William S. Cohen, R-Maine (1979-97).

"I'm not ready to abandon the independent counsel law altogether," said Collins, "for the attorney general will always have conflicts of interest, whether perceived or actual, in investigating his or her boss."

The statute may also have some additional support in the House. Its formal examination of the law in preparation for a debate on reauthorization is set to begin March 2, with a hearing featuring Deputy Attorney General Eric H. Holder Jr. But he has signaled that he will defer unveiling the Clinton administration's position to Reno, who is expected to testify before the Senate later in the month. And she said Feb. 25 that she has not yet made up her mind what to propose.

Jerrold Nadler of New York, ranking Democrat on the House Judiciary Subcommittee on Commercial and Administrative Law, which will conduct the Holder hearing, said few minds have been made up about the law's future, including his own. But he predicted that in the House debate, as well, the camps that form will not be partisan.

"I don't know where people are," Nadler said in an interview Feb. 26. "I'm not sure I'm in favor of abolishing the law, though I'm leaning in that direction. To the extent people dissent on that question, I don't know that it goes along party lines."

But it appears clear that only a greatly rewritten law — one that either puts considerable restrictions on future independent counsels or puts them under more direct supervision by the Justice Department — would have any chance of enactment. And even enacting a substantially rewritten statute, said Senate Governmental Affairs Committee Chairman Fred Thompson, R-Tenn., would be an uphill battle.

"The tinkering approach of earlier reauthorizations will not pass muster this time," said Thompson. "The burden of persuasion rests with those who desire to retain the statute, even with significant changes."

If the law lapses, however, Starr and four other independent counsels still investigating alleged Clinton administration malfeasance would be allowed to keep operating for as long as they need.

The law grandfathers all existing independent counsels — including allowing them to spend whatever they say they need. So they would be unrestricted in their spending unless Congress acted, which it could probably do only by limiting funding as a provision in a fiscal 2000 appropriations bill. Sen. Robert G. Torricelli, D-N.J., said he would try to limit the remaining time of Starr's investigation with such a rider. But with Republicans in charge of Congress, he is unlikely to succeed.

'Saturday Night Massacre' Legacy

The first version of the independent counsel act was enacted in 1978 in the wake of the Watergate scandal and its "Saturday Night Massacre," when President Richard M. Nixon dismissed Archibald Cox, the special prosecutor investigating him. The law stemmed from a conclusion that high officials in the executive branch could not be appropriately investigated by career Justice Department prosecutors, or even special prosecutors reporting directly to the attorney general.

Initially the law was seen as an improvement to the old system, in which the attorney general named a special prosecutor whenever the public clamor for one was great enough.

As currently written, the law provides for the mandatory appointment of an independent counsel if two preliminary tests are met. If the attorney general concludes there is "specific and credible" information that a high government official has violated a law, an initial inquiry is conducted. At the end of that, an attorney general finding "reasonable grounds to believe that further investigation is warranted" is to inform a panel of three federal judges picked by the chief justice of the United States; this panel picks the counsel. *(1994 Almanac, p. 295)*

The most sustained criticisms of the statute have come from conservatives such as former Reagan administration Justice Department officials Theodore B. Olson and Terry Eastland. Perhaps the most articulate statement of the problems of the law was contained in Supreme Court Justice Antonin Scalia's lone dissent in *Morrison v. Olson,* which upheld the law's constitutionality in 1988. "I fear," he wrote "the Court has permanently encumbered the Republic with an institution that will do it great harm." *(1988 Almanac, p. 123)*

But the Starr episode changed the dynamics dramatically. Many Democrats, the party that has given the law the bulk of its support in the past two decades, now have become unusually candid about the error of that position.

Lack of Accountability

The principal criticism of the law is that the independence given to the counsels creates a paucity of accountability. Once appointed, independent counsels have no limits on their spending, may expand their jurisdictions through a relatively easy process — applying to the attorney general or the three-judge panel — and may be fired only for "good cause."

Starr used these powers to take an exhaustive investigation of Clinton's Arkansas land deals and expand it to include the president's affair with former White House intern Monica Lewinsky. That probe could only be characterized as no-holds-barred; he even subpoenaed the store credit card records reflecting Lewinsky's book purchases. Between his appointment in August 1994 and March 1998, before the Lewinsky probe reached its zenith, Starr had already spent $33.5 million to operate offices in Little Rock and Washington.

In the other most controversial independent counsel probe, Lawrence E. Walsh came under fire for indicting Defense Secretary Casper W. Weinberger and other senior Republicans on the eve of the 1992 presidential election. His final report, a massive compendium of everything he thought went wrong during the Iran-contra arms deal, was highly critical of a number of officials who were not indicted. This came under fire from prosecutors who argue their role is to indict or not indict, but to otherwise keep quiet.

The probes have prompted criticism that too many minor officials, or even people unconnected with government, have had to pay too much in legal bills and in future political promise because they have had the misfortune of being in the line of fire between independent counsels and their targets.

Constitutionally, the main criticism of independent counsels is that they do not fall neatly into one of the three branches of government — most certainly not the executive branch, which had previously been charged with the sole power to prosecute.

The Justice Department and the three-judge panel frequently clash over the little enforcement there is over independent counsels. For example, when Independent Counsel Donald C. Smaltz asked Justice in 1996 to expand his jurisdiction to investigate matters related to former Agriculture Secretary Michael Espy, the department balked. So he went to the three judges and got their permission instead.

A similar fight is now unfolding over whether the department has the authority to review Starr's conduct of the Lewinsky inquiry.

In a move reminiscent of the Smaltz episode, the Landmark Legal Foundation, a conservative group sympathetic to Starr, went to the three-judge panel and asked it to halt the probe. The panel announced Feb. 23 that it would consider the case and render a decision in the next few weeks.

The question of the Justice Department's authority goes to the heart of the statute. The department will argue that the attorney general needs latitude for such a review if her dismissal of an independent counsel is to have credibility. It will also likely refer to the majority opinion in the Morrison case, which held the law constitutional by declaring that an independent counsel was an "inferior officer" of the executive branch. The attorney general's ability to fire an independent counsel means Justice "retains ample authority to assure that the counsel is competently performing her statutory responsibilities," the court held.

The department's case may be countered by the argument that the areas of Starr's behavior Justice wants to review do not rise to the level of firing offenses, even if true. One aspect of Starr's probe that the department reportedly wants to look into is the interview of Lewinsky in a Virginia hotel on Jan. 16, 1998, during which Starr's deputies allegedly urged Lewinsky not call her lawyer. While such tactics no doubt seem unsavory to some, they are not uncommon among conventional prosecutors.

The other proposed line of department inquiry is whether Starr was as forthcoming as he should have been about his contacts with lawyers for Paula Corbin Jones when he asked for jurisdiction to look into the truthfulness of Clinton's deposition in Jones' sexual harassment lawsuit.

Return to the Old System?

To many in Congress, this fight further underscores the problems of the independent counsel law. The final straw was Starr's suggestion that if the department wanted to investigate him it should appoint a special prosecutor, perhaps Griffin B. Bell, President Jimmy Carter's first attorney general.

"Where will it end?" Durbin asked in discussing the prospect of a special prosecutor for an independent counsel.

If the law lapses, the old system of special prosecutors would be revived. That would remove some of the criticisms of unaccountability but also would mean these prosecutors could be fired at any time by their bosses — as Cox was in 1973 — simply because someone above does not like the nature of an investigation.

An ardent advocate of this approach is Bell. He testified at the Senate hearing that special prosecutors worked well in Watergate, because after Cox was dismissed, Leon Jaworski picked up where he left off and won a spate of convictions that set the stage for Nixon's resignation. Bell said this system has worked well from the Teapot Dome oil scandal in the 1920s to the early days of Whitewater, when Robert B. Fiske Jr. was appointed to look into the matter during the law's hiatus; Starr replaced him when the law was revived.

A variation being considered in the Senate is creation of a special office at the Justice Department and headed by someone with a fixed term. This person would be responsible for screening allegations against top executive branch officials and could choose to appoint an outside special prosecutor or refer the case to department lawyers. The fixed tenure would presumably give this new official some autonomy, but the office would be subject to Justice's budgetary constraints.

The idea was first floated by former Sen. Howard H. Baker Jr., R-Tenn. (1967-85). But Baker testified at the Senate hearing that he has not yet decided whether he still supports the idea.

Among those who want to keep the concept of an independent counsel, Levin suggested at the hearing that their investigations be limited to three years. If the object of a probe tried to stall until the deadline, Levin said, the investigation could be turned over to the Justice Department.

He also proposed requiring that all future counsels have prosecutorial experience and that alleged crimes to be investigated be limited to those committed while in office.

Sen. Arlen Specter, R-Pa., proposed limiting independent counsels to 18 months. But he also proposed beefing up the statute in one significant way: allowing members of Congress a court challenge to an attorney general's decision after a preliminary review not to appoint an independent counsel.

Baker said Congress should allow the law to lapse to let the passions of impeachment recede.

"I recommend . . . that we cool it," he said. "We think about it for a while. We let the temper of these times subside. There's no absolute urgency in passing anything."

Administration Opposes Renewal, Citing Diminished Public Trust

MARCH 6 — With the Clinton administration now in the forefront, the roster of those reversing longstanding positions to declare opposition to the independent counsel law continues to grow.

The most important and dramatic change of stance so far is the administration's, which was announced by the Justice Department on March 2.

In 1993, Attorney General Janet Reno told the House Judiciary Committee of her "firm conviction" that the statute had been effective in preventing both real and perceived conflicts of interest in investigations of high executive branch officials. The next year Congress enacted a measure (PL 103-270) renewing the independent counsel law after an 18-month lapse.

But on March 2, Deputy Attorney General Eric H. Holder Jr. told Judiciary's Commercial and Administrative Law Subcommittee that the statute now does more harm than good and should be allowed to die when it expires on June 30. "The act was supposed to increase trust in our government," he said. "Unfortunately, it has diminished it."

Holder was not specific about which counsel investigations were instrumental in the administration's change of heart. Doing so, he said, could undermine the five still under way — including that of Kenneth W. Starr. Rather, Holder testified, the change of position came after a Justice Department task force he directed concluded that the law was not giving independent counsels genuine independence. Instead, he said, "It creates an artificial process that divides responsibility and fragments accountability."

White House Counsel Charles F.C. Ruff endorsed Justice's position after a brief review but had "no substantive role in the formulation of the change in policy," Holder told reporters March 4.

Reno has named seven independent counsels, and her department has had significant institutional disputes with at least two of them. It tried unsuccessfully to limit the jurisdiction of Donald C. Smaltz, whose investigation of former Agriculture Secretary Mike Espy climaxed with Espy's acquittal Dec. 2, and it is now arguing with Starr over whether it has authority to investigate some of the tactics that led to the report that launched the impeachment of President Clinton.

If the independent counsel law lapses, investigations of alleged misdeeds by administration officials would generally be assigned to Justice's Public Integrity unit. But an outsider could be hired if the attorney general believed the move would heighten public confidence. These outside counsels could be fired by the president or Justice Department officials.

In his testimony, Holder resisted suggestions that as an alternative to retaining the independent counsel act the Public Integrity unit could be expanded, made semi-autonomous within the department and put under the direction of an official subject to Senate confirmation. He said those ideas are logistically unworkable and would not do enough to remove politics from the process.

Changes of Heart

The next day Robert Bennett, the lawyer who defended Clinton in the Paula Corbin Jones sexual harassment lawsuit, told the Senate Governmental Affairs Committee that he had turned against the statute.

Bennett credited his reversal not to his role in Starr's inquiry but to Lawrence E. Walsh, the independent counsel who investigated the Reagan administration's Iran-contra arms deal. Bennett, who at that time represented former Defense Secretary Casper W. Weinberger, said he concluded then that the law creates too much power while imposing too little accountability. He also faulted the competence and experience of many lawyers who work for independent counsels. Weinberger was indicted near the end of the six-year inquiry, but the charges were nullified by a presidential pardon six months later. *(1992 Almanac, p. 571)*

Another group that has had a quiet change of heart is Common Cause.

The independent citizens' lobbying group had been one of the few organizations not affiliated with conservative issues that was willing to support the concept of independent counsels during the Starr investigation. But over the weekend of Feb. 27-28, the group's board of directors endorsed a radical change in the way top officials are investigated: Giving the job to career prosecutors in the Justice Department's Criminal Division.

To help insulate these civil servants from political pressures, Common Cause suggests that the head of the division serve not at the president's pleasure, as is the case now, but have a fixed term coinciding with a president's term. Decisions to investigate or indict could be overruled only by an attorney general willing to publicly state the reason. And, under the group's plan, in some cases a decision to close a case would require a public accounting of the investigation and the final decision.

Last month the American Bar Association also endorsed allowing the statute to expire.

There are still some holdouts for maintaining the law — albeit with great restrictions on future counsels. At the House hearing, three panel members, all of whom were managers in the Senate impeachment trial of Clinton — George W. Gekas, R-Pa., Lindsey Graham, R-S.C., and Asa Hutchinson, R-Ark. — all suggested they would endorse a revamping of the statute, although none offered a proposal.

"I'm worried sick about the prospect of it dying without a developed mechanism in place," Gekas said.

At the Senate hearing, Joseph I. Lieberman, D-Conn., urged Congress not to decide too quickly to let the law lapse, which he said could further increase skepticism of integrity in Washington. "It's too early to begin preparing eulogies," he said.

Attorney General Latest To Oppose Independent Counsel Law

MARCH 20 — Janet Reno, who has requested more independent counsels than any other attorney general, on March 17 became the latest in a string of witnesses urging Congress to let the independent counsel law die.

"We at the department have come to believe that the act's goals have not been well-served by the act itself — and that we could do better without a statute," she told the Senate Governmental Affairs Committee.

Reno's deputy, Eric H. Holder Jr., delivered the same message to a House panel March 2. A host of other witnesses, some of them once firm believers in the law (PL 103-270), have trooped to Capitol Hill in recent weeks to express their opposition to its renewal. It is scheduled to lapse June 30.

The statute has almost no support outside Congress; groups that once championed it, such as Common Cause, have turned against it.

On Capitol Hill, no one has endorsed renewal of the statute without significant changes. But several members of Governmental Affairs have signaled their wish to create a new way to prescribe the method for investigating high government officials.

Chairman Fred Thompson, R-Tenn., has never been a firm supporter of the law but also said he has reservations about letting it expire without a replacement. He told Reno he was reluctant — given her decision not to appoint an independent counsel to investigate the financing of President Clinton's 1996 re-election campaign — to leave the decision on how to investigate high officials entirely to her, or to her successors. "When the attorney general says, 'Give me even more discretion' . . . that causes me some concern," Thompson said.

Other members are intent not only to see the law die, but also to stop existing investigations, which would otherwise be allowed to continue after the law lapses. On March 18, Sen. Robert

G. Torricelli, D-N.J., offered an amendment to the supplemental fiscal 1999 spending bill (S 544) that would have ended the three investigations begun before June 30, 1996: Kenneth W. Starr's probe into allegations against the president, as well as investigations of former Agriculture Secretary Mike Espy and former Housing and Urban Development Secretary Henry G. Cisneros. It was tabled, and thereby killed, by a voice vote.

Meanwhile, on March 18, the panel of three federal judges that appoints independent counsels dismissed a request by the conservative Landmark Legal Foundation that the court halt the Justice Department inquiry into possible misconduct by Starr.

Kenneth W. Starr Holds No Brief For Law That Empowered Him

APRIL 17 — Had there been even a slight chance that the independent counsel law would be reauthorized by its June 30 expiration deadline, it was eliminated April 14 when Kenneth W. Starr — the most controversial personification of the statute in its 21-year history — told Congress of his opposition to the law.

Although he opposed the statute as long ago as the 1980s, while working in the Justice Department during the Reagan administration, Starr's testimony was portrayed by some on the Senate Governmental Affairs Committee as one of the great ironies of recent years. With his characteristic air of dispassion, the lawyer who has spent nearly five years leading the inquiry that imperiled Bill Clinton's presidency told the committee, in effect, that he never should have had the powers he has.

"I don't know if it was an act of repentance or reflection," said Joseph I. Lieberman, D-Conn.

Richard J. Durbin, D-Ill., said it appeared that Starr had come to Capitol Hill to beg Congress to "stop me before I prosecute again."

Starr formally announced his opposition two days after another event that did not bode well for the future of independent counsels. On April 12, U.S. District Court Judge Susan Webber Wright found Clinton in contempt of court for his deposition testimony in the Paula Corbin Jones sexual harassment lawsuit — the very statements at the heart of the groundwork that Starr laid for the president's impeachment.

Critics of the independent counsel law (PL 103-270) cited that ruling as evidence that misconduct by high government officials can be appropriately punished without using the unwieldy and blunt instrument of an independent counsel inquiry.

But it was Starr's testimony that appeared to foreclose the last chance that the measure's defenders would even start to push to renew the law before it lapses in 11 weeks. Starr has been one of the most assertive independent counsels ever. His probe, which is now estimated to have cost $39.2 million, started in 1994 with a look at the Whitewater land deals that Clinton engaged in while governor of Arkansas. It peaked with a referral to the House in which he said Clinton committed 11 separate impeachable offenses stemming from his affair with former White House intern Monica Lewinsky, which Clinton denied in his testimony in the Jones case. The House impeached the president, but the Senate acquitted him.

Reauthorization Draft

"I fully expect the current independent counsel statute will expire on June 30," Lieberman told reporters after Starr's testimony. "Perhaps when it expires we will get a little distance from all the passions and partisanship that were aroused."

Still, Lieberman has joined with three others on the panel — Susan Collins, R-Maine, Arlen Specter, R-Pa., and Levin — to begin drafting a reauthorization bill. The details remain largely unformed, he said, but the measure would create some sort of special prosecutor who could not be fired at will by the attorney general. Lieberman said it had not been decided whether this person would operate within or independent from the Justice Department. He did say the group had decided to propose dropping the law's current requirements that independent counsels tell the House about any "substantial and credible information" that may warrant impeachment and to submit a final report on every inquiry.

These changes would not be enough to win the support of the administration. The Justice Department on March 2 urged Congress to let the law expire.

"This committee, at least in one regard, has been able to bring about perfect harmony between you and the administration," Senate Governmental Affairs Committee Chairman Fred Thompson, R-Tenn., told Starr.

Joining the law's bipartisan roster of opponents was former Speaker Newt Gingrich, R-Ga. (1979-99), who was forced into retirement after being blamed when a GOP electoral strategy that emphasized impeachment resulted in a loss of House seats last year.

"Not modified. Not improved. Not partial. Kill it," he said at a dinner in his honor April 14. "Get rid of it. Go back to the system we had before 1978."

Starr's Testimony

Starr's appearance was, by and large, far more congenial than his testimony to the House Judiciary Committee on Nov. 19, at the height of the House's impeachment inquiry, when he faced a barrage of hostile questions from Democrats.

Democrats Durbin, Carl Levin of Michigan and Robert G. Torricelli of New Jersey criticized Starr for his conduct of the probe. Other Democrats confined their participation at the hearing to comments or questions on Starr's views of the law. On the Republican side, only Judd Gregg of New Hampshire served up the kind of questions that gave Starr easy opportunities to defend his record.

Absent institutional support from the Justice Department, Starr said, independent counsels "are especially vulnerable to partisan attack. In this fashion, the legislative effort to take politics out of law enforcement sometimes has the ironic effect of further politicizing it."

He enumerated a number of problems with how the statute is triggered: The attorney general must initiate an internal inquiry after finding "sufficient and credible evidence" that a high-level official may have violated the law; and appointment of an independent counsel by a panel of three

Independent Counsel Inquiries

Hamilton Jordan
Arthur H. Christy (1979-80)
Timothy Kraft
Gerald Gallinghouse (1980-82)
Raymond J. Donovan
Leon Silverman (1981-82; 1985-88)
Edwin Meese III
Jacob A. Stein (1984)
Theodore B. Olson
James C. McKay (1986)
Alexia Morrison (1986-89)
Michael K. Deaver
Whitney North Seymour Jr. (1986-89)
Iran-contra
Lawrence E. Walsh (1986-93)
Wedtech Corp.
James C. McKay (1987-88)
Undisclosed
Carl S. Rauh (1986-87)
James R. Harper (1987)
Department of Housing and Urban Development
Arlin M. Adams (1990-95)
Larry D. Thompson (1995-98)
Janet Mullins
Joseph E. diGenova (1992-95)
Michael F. Zeldin (1996)
Whitewater, Monica Lewinsky
Kenneth W. Starr (1994 —)
Mike Espy
Donald C. Smaltz (1994 —)
Henry G. Cisneros
David M. Barrett (1995 —)
Ronald H. Brown
Daniel S. Pearson (1995-96)
Eli Segal
Curtis E. von Kann (1996-97)
Bruce Babbitt
Carol Elder Bruce (1998 -1999)
Alexis M. Herman
Ralph I. Lancaster (1998 —)

NOTE: The names of two independent counsels, one in 1989 and one in 1991-92, are sealed, as are the names of their targets. Other independent counsel probes also could be under seal.

federal judges must be sought if the internal inquiry finds "reasonable grounds" of wrongdoing. *(1994 Almanac, p. 295)*

"Rarely if ever had Congress tried to regulate so specifically such unquantifiable matters," Starr said. "And rarely had Congress sought to tell the attorney general precisely how, and how not, to reach a professional judgment."

Most broadly, Starr concluded, the law unconstitutionally tries to "cram a fourth branch of government into our three-branch system."

The White House joined Senate Democrats in expressing amazement that Starr opposes the law. "It is still somewhat difficult to see how you reconcile the investigation that took place with the constitutional views that he expressed," spokesman Joe Lockhart told reporters.

But in his testimony, Starr said he saw no inconsistency in opposing the law while at the same time exercising its powers, because it had been upheld by the Supreme Court. *(1988 Almanac, p. 123)*

Starr is now prosecuting his indictments of former Associate Attorney General Webster L. Hubbell — ruled valid by a federal judge on April 14 — and Julie Hyatt Steele, a friend of Kathleen Willey, a former White House worker who alleged that Clinton groped her.

Asked whether he believed he had statutory authority to indict Clinton after the president leaves office in 2001, Starr pointedly answered with one word: "Yes." But later in the questioning he raised doubts about how long he will continue. Although the statute has a grandfather clause allowing Starr and the other four existing independent counsels to continue their work even if it lapses June 30 — and to spend whatever they need unless Congress moves to cut off funding — Starr said he would use "professional judgment" in assessing whether and how to proceed.

Sentelle on the Stand

Starr was followed to the stand by the three judges now assigned to choose independent counsels: David B. Sentelle of the U.S. Court of Appeals for the District of Columbia Circuit, Peter Fay of the 11th Circuit and Richard D. Cudahy of the 7th Circuit.

Sentelle and Fay were on the panel that selected Starr in 1994, and Sentelle spent much of his time defending the selection. Starr's selection was controversial from the outset because he was seen by many Democrats as too closely associated with Republican causes to be fair.

Sentelle was active in GOP politics before being nominated to the federal bench by President Ronald Reagan in 1985. Shortly before Starr's selection, he had lunch with his home-state senators, North Carolina Republicans Jesse Helms and Lauch Faircloth (1993-99), and Democrats have accused Sentelle of making an inappropriate selection at their behest. Sentelle vigorously denied this in his testimony.

"There was no substantive discussion about the independent counsel process whatsoever" at that lunch, Sentelle said. Had they been conspiring, he said, they would not have done so in a Senate restaurant: "We're not that dumb."

Contempt Citation

Wright's civil contempt citation was the first ever against a sitting president, and in it she ordered Clinton to compensate the federal court and Jones for expenses incurred as a result of his false deposition. The citation could result in Clinton's disbarment. The matter will be referred to the Professional Conduct Committee of the Arkansas Supreme Court. The judge had signaled soon after the president's Senate acquittal that her ruling was coming.

"The record demonstrates by clear and convincing evidence that the president responded to plaintiff's questions by giving false, misleading and evasive answers that were designed to obstruct the judicial process," she wrote.

Some Democratic opponents of the president's impeachment said the ruling showed that Clinton could be held accountable for his behavior like any other citizen, without the work of an independent counsel. "It's what we said all along," said Rep. Thomas M. Barrett, D-Wis. "There are mechanisms in place to deal with individuals who defy the courts."

Some Republicans said the ruling gave credence to their view that Clinton's behavior merited removal from office. "It counts as a strong reaffirmation of our work," said Sen. Larry E. Craig, R-Idaho.

But the major Republican sentiment was one of weary unease in revisiting the issue that caused so much political damage. "I'm not going there," said Sen. Mike DeWine of Ohio, when asked to comment about the ruling. He had been one of the most vigorous supporters of a full airing of evidence and witness testimony in the Senate trial.

The same day as Wright's ruling, a federal jury in Little Rock acquitted former Clinton business partner Susan McDougal of an obstruction of justice charge brought by Starr after she refused to cooperate with his probe. The jury deadlocked on two counts of contempt of court, prompting a mistrial.

"If anything should put a stake through the heart of Ken Starr, this should be it," said McDougal's attorney, Mark Geragos, who argued that his client was being unfairly prosecuted by the independent counsel.

Special Counsel Rules Unveiled

JULY 3 — The independent counsel law (PL 103-270) died June 30 amid a flurry of activity that sets the stage for how malfeasance in the executive branch will be investigated for the foreseeable future.

The Justice Department unveiled guidelines July 1 for how special counsels will take up their job, returning the country to a system similar to that before the first independent counsel law's enactment in 1978. Whether to appoint a counsel, whom to appoint and the areas for inquiry will be dictated exclusively by the attorney general. In a bid to prevent an administration from quashing worthy inquiries, attorneys general may fire a special counsel only for "good cause." They would be required to place great weight on counsels' views. And they would be required, to the extent consistent with law, to file a report when they deemed any action of a special counsel inappropriate.

Deputy Attorney General Eric H. Holder Jr. said the regulations "strike the proper balance between accountability and independence."

Four senators who find the new rules lacking introduced a bill (S 1297) June 29 to revive the law for five years while modifying some of its most contentious provisions, including setting a near prohibition on when a counsel could expand the initial scope of an investigation.

Otherwise, the regulations were well received in Congress, where there has been widespread interest in letting the law lapse.

Sen. Fred Thompson, R-Tenn., may offer legislation requiring the Justice Department to get congressional approval for the rules. A measure (HR 2083) by Rep. George W. Gekas, R-Pa., would codify the "good cause" requirement for firing a counsel.

Independent Counsel Kenneth W. Starr said June 30 that he is seeking an "orderly completion" for his five-year investigation of allegations surrounding President Clinton. He made that statement after former Associate Attorney General Webster L. Hubbell, in return for a suspended sentence, pleaded guilty to a felony charge of concealing his and first lady Hillary Rodham Clinton's legal work on a fraudulent Arkansas land project. Starr said he was "mindful" that the law empowering him was lapsing, although he and the four other active independent counsels may continue working under a grandfather clause in the law. ◆

House Passes Fetal Protection Bill; Senate Panel Does Not Act

Box Score

- **Bills:** HR 2436, S 1673
- **Legislative action: House** passed HR 2436 (H Rept 106-332, Part I), 254-172, on Sept. 30.

SUMMARY

The House passed a bill that for the first time would recognize the fetus as an entity distinct from the pregnant woman, although by a margin insufficient to override a veto threatened by President Clinton.

The measure would make it a separate federal crime to harm a fetus while committing any of 68 existing federal offenses or a crime under military law, regardless of whether the assailant knew the woman was pregnant or intended fetal harm. Doctors who perform consensual abortions would be exempt from prosecution, as would women whose actions harm the fetuses they carry.

Sponsors described their proposal principally as a crime-fighting bill. But it was drafted with the help of anti-abortion groups, which said they would welcome the codification of their belief that a fetus has distinct rights.

Abortion rights groups said the bill would undermine the Supreme Court's 1973 ruling in *Roe v. Wade*, which legalized abortion after concluding "the unborn have never been recognized in the law as persons in the whole sense."

The Senate Judiciary Committee has not said if or when it will consider its version of the measure.

Democrats See House GOP Bill As Attack on Abortion Rights

SEPTEMBER 18 — Opening a new venue for the abortion debate, House Republicans have begun pushing legislation that for the first time would recognize the fetus under federal law as an entity distinct from the pregnant woman.

Supporters say enactment of the

measure would help to protect "unborn children" from violent crime. Opponents maintain that the principal goal of the bill is to curb abortion rights.

The measure (HR 2436), sponsored by Rep. Lindsey Graham, R-S.C., would establish criminal liabilities and punishments for those who harm a fetus in utero while committing a federal crime, regardless of whether they intended that harm or even knew the woman involved was pregnant. The maximum punishments would be the same as for the assault or murder of the woman, except that no death penalty could be imposed. The measure would also apply to crimes by military personnel.

The bill was approved 14-11 along party lines by the House Judiciary Committee on Sept. 14. It is expected to reach the House floor in October.

No companion measure has yet been introduced in the Senate, but Sen. Tim Hutchinson, R-Ark., said Sept. 14 that he would soon write a letter to the Judiciary Committee calling for quick action on similar language.

The Justice Department said Sept. 9 that it opposes the bill, both because it may be unconstitutional and because its identification of a fetus as a separate and distinct victim of crime is "unprecedented" and "unwise to the extent that it may be perceived as gratuitously plunging the federal government into one of the most — if not the most — difficult and complex issues of religious and scientific consideration."

As a need for the bill, sponsors cited the 1995 bombing of an Oklahoma City federal building, in which three pregnant women died. Under this bill, the bombers could be charged not only with the death of the women, but also with the death of their fetuses.

"This legislation is not about abortion but rather holding criminals accountable for their actions," Graham said during committee debate.

The bill "exemplifies humanity at its best," said Chairman Henry J. Hyde, R-Ill. "A pregnant woman is two special persons. . . . She is carrying a tiny member of the human family."

The bill would exempt from prosecution anyone who treats a pregnant woman or performs a consensual abortion and any woman whose voluntary activities harm the fetus.

Eleven states have laws providing for prosecutions similar to those that would be authorized under Graham's legislation; 19 other states extend some sort of legal protection to fetuses. The National Right to Life Committee, which worked with Graham to draft the bill, praised the measure as a "major new pro-life initiative."

The First Step

Democrats and groups that support abortion rights said the bill was a first step toward outlawing abortion. "Recognizing the fetus as an entity with legal rights independent of the pregnant woman," said John Conyers Jr. of Michigan, the panel's senior Democrat, "could create future fetal rights that could be used against the pregnant woman. This is the real intent of the bill."

Zoe Lofgren, D-Calif., offered substitute legislation to establish sentences of as long as 20 years for a person convicted of interrupting "the normal course of the pregnancy" by attacking a woman during the commission of a federal crime, and up to life in prison if "the pregnancy is terminated." But her language would not have created a separate charge for harming the fetus.

"Oppose violence against women," Lofgren said. "Don't use that violence as an excuse to eliminate personal choice about reproduction for American women."

But her amendment was defeated, 8-20. It was opposed by all Republicans and Maxine Waters, D-Calif.

Democrats also said they would oppose the bill because its enactment would add to the federal law books the definition of an "unborn child" as "a member of the species homo sapiens, at any stage of development, who is carried in the womb." That definition, they said, could be used by abortion rights opponents to argue that federal law says life begins at conception.

Melvin Watt, D-N.C, offered an amendment to remove "unborn child" from the bill and replace it with "pregnancy" in an attempt to make the measure "less abortion-charged." His proposal was defeated, 11-14, along party lines.

The Planned Parenthood Federation of America, the National Abortion and Reproductive Rights Action League (NARAL) and the American Civil Liberties Union all oppose the bill. "As we strive to protect women from violence and prosecute those who assault them, we must not create a foundation that can be used to mount a future legal assault on *Roe v. Wade*," the 1973 Supreme Court ruling that established a constitutional right to abortion, said NARAL President Kate Michelman.

House Passes Bill; Further Progress Is Unlikely

OCTOBER 2 — Legislation that would grant an unprecedented measure of federal legal protection to the human fetus passed the House on Sept. 30. But opponents of abortion rights, who are among the biggest promoters of the measure (HR 2436), concede that its chances to advance further this year are minimal, because their allies at the Capitol are more likely to concentrate on other abortion-related bills.

In addition, the bill has so far garnered far fewer supporters than would be needed to override the veto President Clinton has threatened. The vote for the bill was 254-172, and 290 is an absolute two-thirds majority of the House. *(Vote 465, p. H-152)*

"I certainly wouldn't anticipate any movement on this in the Senate" before next year, Douglas Johnson, the legislative director at the National Right to Life Committee, said after the House vote, which occurred the same day that a companion bill (S 1673) was introduced in the Senate by Mike DeWine, R-Ohio.

Johnson predicted that any legislative push on the anti-abortion agenda this fall would come on two other proposals: A bill (HR 1218), passed by the House in June, that would make it a crime to help a girl cross state lines for an abortion in order to evade her state's parental consent laws, and legislation that has not yet begun to move (S 928) that would outlaw a procedure that its critics call "partial-birth" abortion. Clinton blocked such a bill with a veto in the 105th Congress. *(1998 Almanac, p. 3-7)*

Crimes Against Fetuses

As passed by the House, the bill would make it a separate federal crime to injure or kill a fetus while committing another federal offense, regardless of the assailant's knowledge of the pregnancy or intent to harm the fetus. Charges could not be brought against anyone involved in a consensual abortion or because of any act by a woman pertaining to her pregnancy.

Abortion opponents say this would have the welcome effect of codifying their belief that, from conception, a fetus is a human with rights independent of the woman carrying it.

"I think most Americans buy it, that there's a difference between a consensual abortion and a criminal attack," said sponsor Lindsey Graham, R-S.C., who dubbed his bill the Unborn Victims of Violence Act.

"There should be a way of defending the rights of a murdered unborn child," said Graham, who called the issue of fetal rights "a 2000 election issue."

Abortion rights advocates say the bill's enactment would undermine the right to abortion that the Supreme Court found in 1973 in *Roe v. Wade*, which was based in part on the conclusion that "the unborn have never been recognized in the law as persons in the whole sense."

"Let us confess that we are taking another little few baby steps forward to eat away at the fundamental premises" of that decision, said John Conyers Jr. of Michigan, ranking Democrat on the Judiciary Committee.

Opponents of the bill proposed an alternative that would have stiffened federal penalties for attacks on a pregnant woman that resulted in the injury or death of her fetus but would not have recognized the offense against the fetus as a separate crime. It was defeated, 201-224. *(Vote 464, p. H-152)*

The bill applies the legal principle of "transferred intent" — the notion that an individual who intends to harm one person is just as responsible for harming another in the process — to a pregnant woman and her fetus, but only when involved in one of 68 federal crimes or a crime under military law.

Because most states have some form of "fetal protection" statute, and none of them has been struck down by the Supreme Court, sponsors said their bill could "exist in harmony" with the acceptance of abortion rights.

Abortion rights advocates strenuously disagreed. They said the existing state laws were limiting the reach of the constitutional right granted 26 years ago, and that the bill before the House would go much further. The National Abortion Federation cited a 1984 South Carolina statute that considers killing a fetus after viability as homicide, which the group says opened the door to a 1997 state law that allows a pregnant woman to be punished for any behavior that could endanger her fetus.

"This legislation is really part of an endless crusade to strike down *Roe v. Wade*," said the federation's executive director, Vicki Saporta.

Most supporters argued that the bill should be considered as a crime-prevention measure, while others said it should be part of the debate over reproductive rights.

"Because an issue is difficult and creates heartburn on all sides is no reason that we should not address it," said Judiciary Committee Chairman Henry J. Hyde, R-Ill. "That little child in the womb is a member of the human family." ◆

House Passes Bill To Bar Doctor-Assisted Suicide; No Senate Action Taken

Box Score

- **Bills:** HR 2260, S 1272
- **Legislative action:** House passed HR 2260 (H Rept 106-378, Parts 1 and 2), 271-156, on Oct. 27.

SUMMARY

The House passed legislation that would bar doctors from helping patients kill themselves with prescription drugs — in effect thwarting the only state law allowing physician-assisted suicide, in Oregon. The Senate did not act on the bill.

After a court challenge ended and Oregon's law took effect in 1997, three years after its initial approval by referendum, the Drug Enforcement Administration (DEA) barred doctors from dispensing drugs for suicides, declaring that would not be a "legitimate medical purpose." But Attorney General Janet Reno said she would not enforce the ruling.

The House bill would explicitly permit prescriptions of federally controlled substances to alleviate pain, even if they "may increase the risk of death," and would authorize $5 million annually for a federal program to promote education and training in "palliative care," or pain management for the terminally ill. Those provisions helped the bill win the American Medical Association's backing, but critics say the result would be to give the DEA power to judge whether doctors were dispensing medicines to ease suffering or hasten death.

The bill would compel Reno to follow the DEA's ruling and says she "shall give no force and effect" to any state law permitting assisted suicide or euthanasia. Oregon allows lethal prescriptions to be issued to the terminally ill after they consult with physicians and if they administer the drugs themselves. The state says that 15 people took their lives with lethal medication last year.

Polls suggest a majority of people believe doctors should have leeway to help their patients die. Anti-abortion groups favor the bill, saying it would help codify a "right to life."

While the Justice Department "strongly opposes" doctor-assisted suicide, it said Oct. 19 that the provisions thwarting Oregon's law are "heavy-handed" and "intrusive."

Ron Wyden, D-Ore., says he will filibuster the Senate measure on the grounds that Congress has no business acting to countermand his state's law. But aides to the bill's sponsor, Majority Whip Don Nickles, R-Okla., say they are increasingly confident he could marshal the 60 votes needed to limit debate and pass the bill next year. Reno says she would like to work with the Senate to write a bill the Justice Department could embrace.

Assisted Suicide Measure Slows In House Judiciary

SEPTEMBER 11 — After two hours of partisan rhetoric and attacks, the House Judiciary Committee on Sept. 9 postponed final action on a bill aimed at overturning Oregon's assisted suicide law.

The committee is slated to meet again on Sept. 14 to finish marking up the legislation (HR 2260) as well as another bill (HR 2436) that would make it a crime to kill an unborn fetus during an assault against a pregnant woman.

The assisted suicide bill, introduced by Judiciary Committee Chairman Henry J. Hyde, R-Ill., would make it illegal for doctors to use controlled substances in order to cause death or to help another person cause death. However, it would expressly permit doctors to prescribe medication to relieve pain "even if the use of such a substance may increase the risk of death."

"I'm interested in medical doctors being healers," Hyde said during the markup, "not social engineers serving as executioners."

The Hyde bill comes in response to an Oregon law that took effect in 1997, allowing doctors for the first time in the United States to provide lethal doses of drugs to terminally ill patients.

Democrats on the committee charged Hyde and other Republican supporters of the bill with trying to usurp states' rights. "You are imposing the government over the right of people to make decisions in their lives," said Barney Frank, D-Mass. "Some of us believe an individual has the right to make a decision that life has become unbearable."

During the brief committee session, three Democratic amendments were defeated on party-line votes.

The first two, offered by Melvin Watt of North Carolina, would have preserved the Oregon law and allowed other states to pass laws permitting doctors to prescribe lethal doses of drugs to patients. They were rejected by votes of 13-15 and 12-15.

The third amendment, offered by Robert C. Scott of Virginia, would have struck from the bill all language prohibiting assisted suicide. It was defeated 12-16.

House Panel OKs Suicide Bill; Senate Filibuster Threatened

SEPTEMBER 18 — Legislation that would bar physicians from helping patients kill themselves with prescription drugs — thereby thwarting the only state law legalizing doctor-assisted suicide — was approved Sept. 14 by the House Judiciary Committee.

But the bill (HR 2260) still faces a substantial climb toward enactment. There is ample Democratic opposition on both sides of the Capitol. While Republicans may have the votes to push it through the House, a filibuster of the companion Senate measure (S 1272) is being threatened by Democrat Ron Wyden of Oregon, who says Congress has no business acting to countermand his state's assisted-suicide law.

After a long partisan markup that began Sept. 9, the Judiciary Committee vote for the bill was 16-8, with all Republicans voting for the measure and all Democrats voting against it. Sponsors, led by Chairman Henry J. Hyde, R-Ill., say they hope for a House floor vote this fall. No action has been taken on the Senate measure, sponsored by Majority Whip Don Nickles, R-Okla.

Hyde and Nickles pushed legislation in the 105th Congress to deter doctors from assisting in suicides, but it faltered when medical professionals protested that the bill would also deter doctors from prescribing pain-relief medication for the terminally ill.

To overcome that opposition, this year their legislation would make it legal for doctors to prescribe federally controlled substances to treat the pain and suffering of their dying patients, even if such drugs "increase the risk of death." The bill would also authorize an increase of $5 million for federal programs to promote "palliative care," or vigorous pain management for terminally ill patients.

Republicans said enacting the bill would help the dying by encouraging doctors to use aggressive pain treatment. The measure has the backing of two key groups that opposed the previous version, the American Medical Association (AMA) and the National Hospice Organization. The bill "strikes a fair balance of opposing assisted suicide while reaffirming physicians' ability to aggressively manage patients' pain and discomfort," the AMA said Sept. 14.

But Democrats attacked the bill for a provision that would amend the 1970 Controlled Substances Act (PL 91-513) to prohibit doctors from using federally controlled drugs for euthanasia or assisted suicide.

While the bill does not specifically mention Oregon, it would have the effect of overturning that state's 1994 law, enacted through a referendum, authorizing doctors to prescribe drugs to help terminally ill people end their lives. After a court challenge ended and the law took effect in 1997, the federal Drug Enforcement Administration (DEA) prohibited doctors from dispensing drugs for suicides, declaring that would not be a "legitimate medical purpose." When Attorney General Janet Reno said she would not enforce the DEA ruling, the GOP drafted legislation designed to countermand her.

"This is a patients' rights measure — it was so voted by the people," Barney Frank, D-Mass., said of the Oregon law in declaring his rationale for opposing the Hyde bill. "Are the patients in control of their own lives or is the federal government going to step in?"

Republicans countered that the bill had a purpose worthy of federal action. "It will help protect vulnerable people in this country from the misuse of controlled substances," said Charles T. Canady, R-Fla.

Doctors' Protection Debated

When the markup resumed Sept. 14, Democrats tried to bolster the bill's legal protections for doctors. They argued that the bill could have a "chilling effect" on physicians' decisions to prescribe pain treatment.

The panel's ranking Democrat, John Conyers Jr. of Michigan, offered an amendment to require that a doctor's intent to kill a patient with drugs be established "beyond a reasonable doubt" for a criminal conviction and that "clear and convincing evidence" be shown in a civil proceeding. Republicans argued that since the bill did not create any new criminal liability for doctors, the amendment was not needed, and it was defeated 9-15 along party lines.

On a 10-16 party-line vote, Conyers was defeated when he offered an amendment to allow doctors to argue as an "affirmative defense" that they used controlled substances with the sole intent of alleviating pain. Republicans called the amendment "nonsensical" because the bill would allow doctors to use drugs to alleviate pain even if it increased the risk of death.

Sheila Jackson-Lee, D-Texas, proposed an amendment that would have grandfathered the Oregon assisted-suicide measure under the federal law. It was rejected, 9-14.

"We come in with this Big Brother attitude that we should overcome the Oregon law," Jackson-Lee said. "I believe what we will do is increase suicide. . . . [Patients] will use their own means."

Assisted Suicide Bill Approved By House Panel

OCTOBER 16 — The House Commerce Committee on Oct. 13 approved a measure (HR 2260) that would effectively overturn Oregon's physician-assisted suicide law and ban the practice in other states.

The bill, which was approved by the House Judiciary Committee on Sept. 14, would amend the 1970 Controlled Substances Act by disallowing the use of a number of federally controlled drugs for euthanasia or assisted suicide. The measure instead promotes "palliative care," or vigorous pain management for the terminally ill.

Bart Stupak, D-Mich., won voice vote adoption of an amendment to ensure that the measure would apply to patients under all types of medical care, not just those with terminal diseases.

The bill still faces significant obstacles, including a threatened filibuster in the Senate.

House Passes Bill To Ban Assisted Suicide

OCTOBER 30 — Doctors who prescribe drugs knowing that they will be used in a suicide would be committing a federal crime under legislation the House passed Oct. 27. Advocates of the proposal are now focusing their campaign on the Senate, where Majority Whip Don Nickles, R-Okla., is promising to push for passage of such a measure in the closing weeks of the session and suggests he has the votes to do so.

Opponents — led by the delegation from Oregon, the only state where physician-assisted suicide is legal — took solace in the fact that the 271-156 vote in the House suggested that support was not great enough to overcome a veto by President Clinton, even though the White House has not yet weighed in on the measure (HR 2260). *(Vote 544, p. H-180)*

While the Justice Department "strongly opposes" doctor-assisted suicide, it said in a letter to the House Judiciary Committee on Oct. 19, provisions in the bill that would have the effect of overturning Oregon's law are "heavy-handed" and "intrusive."

"We were disappointed in the vote, and we will be working in the Senate to see what can be done," Attorney General Janet Reno told reporters Oct. 28.

Nickles may try to add an assisted-suicide ban to another bill that he concludes is likely to clear this fall, and he is increasingly confident he has the votes to overcome the threatened filibuster by Democrat Ron Wyden of Oregon, Nickles' spokeswoman Gayle Osterberg said.

The Senate companion (S 1272) has three Democratic cosponsors. But a spokesman for one, Joseph I. Lieberman, D-Conn., said the senator would probably side with his party's leadership — and against the bill — on a vote that would allow Nickles to pursue that strategy.

Supporters and opponents agree on one thing: The bill could dramatically change the way physicians treat terminally ill patients in extreme pain. But the accord ends there.

The bill would explicitly permit prescriptions of federally controlled substances to alleviate pain, even if they "may increase the risk of death," a provision that proponents say would create an important new legal safe haven for doctors. The measure also would authorize $5 million annually for a federal program to promote education and training in "palliative care," or pain management in the terminally ill.

The bill is technically an amendment to the 1970 law (PL 91-513) that regulates the use of narcotics. As such, opponents said, enactment would give Drug Enforcement Administration (DEA) agents the job of deciding whether a doctor's intent in writing prescriptions was to hasten a patient's death or ease suffering.

Overturning Oregon Law

The bill says the attorney general "shall give no force and effect" to any state law permitting assisted suicide or euthanasia. Opponents say that would in effect overturn the Oregon law, which allows lethal prescriptions to be issued to the terminally ill after they consult with physicians and if they administer the drugs themselves. The state says that 15 people took their lives with lethal medication last year.

The same section of the bill would countermand Reno's 1998 decision to reverse the DEA and allow doctors in Oregon to abide by their state law. The House voted 160-268 to reject an amendment that would have stricken the entire section. *(Vote 542, p. H-176)*

Lawmakers also voted 188-239 to reject a substitute measure that would have been limited to the promotion of palliative care. *(Vote 543, p. H-176)*

The public appears to want doctors to have leeway to help their patients die. In a Gallup Poll in March, 61 percent said they support allowing doctors "to assist the patient to commit suicide."

Sponsors said public sentiment must come second. "Facilitating the intentional killing of a human life is the opposite of healing," said Judiciary Committee Chairman Henry J. Hyde, R-Ill. "There is a sanctity of life that must be respected and defended."

Opponents, including some Republicans, complained that the bill's move to pre-empt state law undermines the GOP boast that it is the party of states' rights and the diminution of federal power.

A similar bill faltered last year, chiefly because it was opposed by medical professionals. But the American Medical Association supports this year's version, president Thomas R. Reardon said in an interview, because its language is akin to the group's own policy on the subject.

"Physicians have an obligation to relieve pain and suffering and to promote the dignity and autonomy of dying patients in their care. This includes providing effective palliative treatment, even though it may foreseeably hasten death," that policy says.

But it also says: "The societal risks of involving physicians in medical interventions to cause patients' deaths is too great to condone euthanasia or physician-assisted suicide at this time." ◆

Senate Panel Endorses Amending Constitution To Ensure Victims' Rights

Box Score

- **Bills:** S J Res 3; H J Res 64
- **Legislative action: Senate:** Judiciary Committee approved S J Res 3, 12-5, Sept. 30.

SUMMARY

A constitutional amendment enumerating some rights for the victims of violent crime was endorsed by the Senate Judiciary Committee. The House took no action.

The proposal would give victims the rights to be notified of and attend all proceedings related to the crime; to speak or submit statements at each public hearing in the case, including parole or other early release hearings; to reasonable notice if those convicted in their cases are released or escape; and to restitution. A similar proposal was endorsed by the Senate panel in 1998 and backed by the White House, which could aid its path in Congress even though presidents neither sign nor veto constitutional amendments.

But a section added this year gives the Justice Department pause, especially in light of President Clinton's controversial offer of clemency to 16 Puerto Rican independence activists. It would give victims the right to be notified before any state or federal grant of clemency and to submit a statement about it for the record.

Sponsor Jon Kyl, R-Ariz., is pushing for a floor debate by spring. Judiciary Committee Chairman Orrin G. Hatch, R-Utah, may seek amendments then to ensure that trial verdicts are not routinely undone if victims' rights are shirked. The House Judiciary Committee has not signaled whether it will consider a companion proposal next year.

Subcommittee Approves Victims' Rights Proposal

MAY 29 — A Senate Judiciary subcommittee approved May 26 by a 4-3 vote a resolution (S J Res 3) that proposes a constitutional amendment guaranteeing certain rights to victims of violent crimes.

The measure, approved by the Constitution Subcommittee, would establish the right of victims to participate in public hearings related to the criminal proceeding. It would stipulate that the safety of the victim be considered when the offender was released from custody.

However, state legislatures could create certain exceptions to these rights if they found a "compelling interest" to do so.

By a vote of 7-0, panel members adopted an amendment to the resolution offered by Chairman John Ashcroft, R-Mo., to give victims the additional right to testify at proceedings relating to pardons of their attackers or commutation of their sentences.

Panel Democrats objected to the resolution. Ranking Democrat Russell D. Feingold of Wisconsin called the resolution a "blunt instrument" that would needlessly alter the Constitution over an issue that states already are able to address.

In addition, he said state and federal statutes would be more effective at addressing victims' rights because they are more easily enacted and modified. But Ashcroft said such statutory rights "are of little help when they conflict with the constitutional rights of the accused."

"Until crime victims are protected by the United States Constitution, the rights of victims will be subordinate to the rights of the defendant," said resolution cosponsor John Kyl, R-Ariz.

Senate Judiciary Endorses Resolution

OCTOBER 2 — A constitutional amendment to guarantee certain rights to victims of violent crime took an important step Sept. 30, winning the bipartisan endorsement of the Senate Judiciary Committee.

But the panel's 12-5 vote for the measure (S J Res 3) belies a long road ahead. Committee Chairman Orrin G. Hatch, R-Utah, said that next spring is the earliest he could envision a Senate floor debate. And no action at all has been scheduled on the allied resolution (H J Res 64) before the House. To be added to the Constitution, an amendment must win two-thirds majorities on both sides of the Capitol, then the ratification of three-quarters of the states.

After more than five dozen revisions, Senate sponsors Jon Kyl, R-Ariz., and Dianne Feinstein, D-Calif., unveiled language last year that won the Clinton administration's blessing and bipartisan support from the Judiciary Committee. That version was the core of what Judiciary approved Sept. 30. The proposal would give victims the right to be notified of and attend all proceedings related to the crime; the right to speak or submit statements at each public hearing in the case, including parole or other early release hearings; the right to reasonable notice if those convicted in their cases are released or escape; and the right to restitution.

But a provision added this year has prompted the administration to reverse its position. President Clinton has no power to sign or veto constitutional amendments, but his views may still hold sway in Congress. And in this case, the provision at issue touches on a matter that has recently polarized Congress: his offer of clemency to 16 Puerto Rican independence activists and his claim of executive privilege in declining to detail his rationale.

The provision, added in subcommittee before the Puerto Rico imbroglio began, would give victims the right to be notified before any state or federal grant of clemency and to submit a statement about it for the record. The sponsor, John Ashcroft, R-Mo., said the Justice Department told the Senate on Sept. 22 that it believes this provision would improperly curb presidential power.

The objection may cause a rift between the cosponsors of the underlying measure and threaten to weaken its bipartisan support. Both Kyl and Feinstein said they continue to support the clemency provision, but there were indications Feinstein may end up advocating its removal in deference to Clinton.

Beyond that, supporters say the only way to ensure that victims' rights are protected is to guarantee them in the Constitution. Federal statutes are ineffective because they apply only to about 10 percent of all cases, Feinstein said, and state laws to help crime victims are ineffective because they are regularly trumped by the constitutional rights of the accused when conflicts arise.

Opponents said that the constitutional change could overcompensate in favor of the rights of the victims. The panel defeated, 5-11, language by Russell D. Feingold, D-Wis., that was designed to ensure that the new constitutional language could not be cited to curb the rights of the accused — by subjecting them to a second trial, for example, if a court ruled that the victims' rights had been abridged at the first one.

Feinstein said her proposal would provide this guarantee but that Feingold's change would "effectively gut" the measure. ◆

House Again Supports Amendment To Protect Flag; No Senate Vote Taken

Box Score

- **Bills:** H J Res 33; S J Res 14
- **Legislative action: House** voted 305-124 to pass H J Res 33 (H Rept 106-191) on June 24.

  Senate Judiciary Committee voted 11-7 to approve S J Res 14 on April 29.

SUMMARY

The House voted to send to the states a proposed constitutional amendment to permit federal laws against flag desecration. There was no vote by the Senate, where reaching the required two-thirds majority is unlikely.

As in the 104th and 105th Congresses, more than 300 House members voted to initiate a change to the Constitution to permit laws against flag desecration. But Senate supporters could count on no more than 65 votes. Their hopes had been buoyed early in the year when North Dakota's two Democrats, Kent Conrad and Byron L. Dorgan, briefly signaled that they were reconsidering their previous opposition.

Each state except Vermont has signaled it would ratify such a constitutional change. The campaign began after the Supreme Court ruled in 1989 that state laws against flag burning violate the First Amendment and in 1990 that a federal law to that end (PL 101-131) was unconstitutional as well. The Congressional Research Service has found 43 incidents of flag desecration in the United States between 1995 and 1998.

Supporters are seeking a Senate vote next spring.

Flag Amendment Moves Through Subcommittees

APRIL 24 — A constitutional amendment to allow federal laws to prohibit the desecration of the American flag has begun to work its way through the Senate, amid signs that it is edging closer than have past such proposals to adoption by Congress.

The Senate Judiciary Subcommittee on the Constitution approved the measure (S J Res 14) April 21 on a 5-3 vote along party lines. An identical measure (H J Res 33) was endorsed April 14 by the House Judiciary Subcommittee on the Constitution.

Of a long list of constitutional amendments promoted in recent years — including those that would create congressional term limits, permit prayer in schools, guarantee certain rights to crime victims, mandate balanced federal budgets and require two-thirds majorities in Congress to raise taxes — the flag amendment has emerged as the one with the best chance of clearing Congress. It would then become the 28th Amendment upon ratification by three-quarters, or 38, of the state legislatures.

With margins comfortably beyond the requisite two-thirds majority, the House endorsed such an amendment in the previous two Congresses. Both times the proposal died in the Senate.

In 1995, the Senate vote was three short of the two-thirds threshold. *(1995 Almanac, p. 6-22)*

In the 105th Congress, the measure was not brought up for a Senate vote after head counts showed it would win no more than 64 votes, still three short of adoption.

Vote counts taken by proponents and opponents suggest the amendment has gained a net of one supporter since the 1998 election. Three of the eight new senators — Blanche Lincoln, D-Ark., Peter G. Fitzgerald, R-Ill., and George V. Voinovich, R-Ohio — are expected to break with their predecessors and vote yes. Two — Charles E. Schumer, D-N.Y., and John Edwards, D-N.C. — are expected to break with their predecessors and vote no. The others are expected to vote as their predecessors did.

But such tentative head counts often mask an important legislative dynamic: Members will often reconsider their opposition to a popular proposal when its fortunes surge — or when their vote could be portrayed as pivotal to passage.

"If it got to be one vote, there are certain senators that won't want to be the one vote to go against it," said a Democratic senatorial aide, requesting anonymity. "There are other senators that don't want to be the one vote that lets it pass."

To muster support, both sides have been parading heroes. At an April 20 Senate hearing, proponents arranged for appearances by several Medal of Honor winners. At a hearing set for April 28, opponents have arranged for testimony by astronaut and former Sen. John Glenn, D-Ohio (1974-99), and Sen. Bob Kerrey, D-Neb., himself a Medal of Honor recipient.

The amendment has been under discussion since 1989, when the Supreme Court held that flag burning was constitutionally protected free speech. Congress enacted a law to curb flag desecration (PL 101-131), but it too was struck down. *(1990 Almanac, p. 524)*

The arguments have not changed much over the years. At the Senate markup, Orrin G. Hatch, R-Utah, said the amendment was necessary since the Stars and Stripes "symbolizes the love of liberty that Americans hold so dear in their hearts." Patrick J. Leahy, D-Vt., said there was no need to restrict the right of free expression.

Becalmed Amendments

The flag amendment's fortunes may be improving, but there is little momentum for the other amendments promoted by the Republican majority. The term limits, school prayer and balanced-budget amendments are moribund. The crime victims' amendment (S J Res 3) has nowhere near two-thirds support. And the amendment to require a supermajority for tax increases (H J Res 37) was rejected for a fourth time by the House on April 15.

Marshall Wittman, director of congressional relations for the Heritage Foundation, a conservative think tank, says that the GOP has been pushing amendments to make symbolic statements, with little expectation of success.

Those amendments that are still alive have nearly unanimous support among conservative activists. The school prayer and term limits amendments, in particular, have prompted divisions among conservatives.

One of the few conservative constituencies to oppose the flag amendment are the libertarians. Roger Pilon, director of the Center for Constitutional Studies at the libertarian Cato Institute, says the amendment was designed to curry favor with veterans at the expense of individual rights.

"One just despairs at their craven desertion of principle," Pilon said of the Republicans, who dispute the libertarians' characterization.

Senate Judiciary Votes in Favor Of Resolution

MAY 1 — The proposed constitutional amendment to allow federal laws against desecration of the American flag was adopted, 11-7, by the Senate Judiciary Committee on April 29. Chairman Orrin G. Hatch, R-Utah, said he expected the measure would be on the Senate floor before Memorial Day.

Vote counts this year suggest that the measure (S J Res 14) has 65 Senate supporters, just two short of the two-thirds majority required for passage.

Supporters had hoped to win votes from North Dakota Democrats Kent Conrad and Byron L. Dorgan, who both voted "no" on the last Senate ballot in 1995. But their offices released statements April 30 that they would not switch positions.

The House has twice adopted the amendment since the Republicans took control. Congress has been debating the issue since a 1989 Supreme Court ruling that flag burning was constitutionally protected free speech. *(1990 Almanac, p. 524; 1995 Almanac, p. 6-22; 1997 Almanac, p. 5-10)*

At the markup, Hatch said the proposed amendment would "simply restore the Bill of Rights to the form it enjoyed prior to the Supreme Court's drastic change." But ranking committee Democrat Patrick J. Leahy of Vermont said the one-sentence amendment — "The Congress shall have power to prohibit the physical desecration of the flag of the United States" — would be the "first-ever cutback on American civil liberties" enshrined in the Constitution.

Dianne Feinstein, D-Calif., was the only panel member to cross party lines. She voted "yes," she said, because the flag "is a monument in fabric that hangs as a symbol of our nation" and its values.

At a hearing April 27, John H. Chafee, R-R.I., a Marine in World War II, joined a panel of Senate combat veterans testifying against the proposal. "It trivializes the Constitution," he said. "None of us can even imagine James Madison taking this proposed amendment seriously."

House Panel OKs Flag Amendment

MAY 29 — The move to add flag desecration to a short list of acts that could be constitutionally prohibited has advanced another step, but the future of this perennial proposal remains adrift as supporters' head counts in the Senate continue to come up short.

By voice vote May 26, the House Judiciary Committee approved a resolution (H J Res 33) proposing a constitutional amendment to allow Congress to prohibit desecration of the American flag. On April 29, the Senate Judiciary Committee approved an identical measure (S J Res 14).

The next step remains uncertain. Plans to put the resolutions on the House and Senate floors before the Memorial Day recess were scrapped, at least in part because Judiciary Committee members in both chambers became unexpectedly consumed by the burgeoning gun control debate. Chairman Charles T. Canady, R-Fla., of House Judiciary's Constitution Subcommittee, which has jurisdiction over the issue, said May 26 that the House might debate the amendment by the end of June but that "other things could push it off the schedule."

Republican leaders appear confident of winning the requisite two-thirds majority in the House, which has adopted flag protection constitutional amendments twice since Republicans became the majority. The debate began after the Supreme Court struck down, as a violation of the First Amendment, state laws banning flag desecration in 1989 and then a federal law (PL 101-131) designed to overcome the initial court ruling. *(1990 Almanac, p. 524; 1995 Almanac, p. 6-22; 1997 Almanac, p. 5-10)*

The Senate has never endorsed a flag constitutional amendment, although this year it appeared that might change because of the chamber's changing membership and because two senators who voted no in the past, North Dakota Democrats Kent Conrad and Byron L. Dorgan, said they were reconsidering. They decided April 30 to continue opposing the amendment while endorsing a bill (S 931) that would make it a federal crime to damage a U.S. flag in a bid to "produce imminent violence or a breach of the peace." Neither that bill nor its House counterpart (HR 1081) has seen any legislative action.

Most of the committee members at the House markup made the same points they have been making for years. Supporters of the amendment said the American flag is so synonymous with the nation that its destruction is, in effect, a crime against the state.

Opponents said that the amendment would curtail one of the bedrock liberties — freedom of political speech — that the flag embodies. "Through this amendment you are elevating a symbol of freedom over freedom itself," said John Conyers Jr., D-Mich.

To that end, Democrat Melvin Watt of North Carolina offered an amendment declaring the amendment "not inconsistent" with the First Amendment. It was rejected, 7-17.

Zoe Lofgren, D-Calif., drew giggles from the audience by proposing a substitute constitutional amendment mandating that American flags be made of flame-retardant materials. That way, "people who want to exercise their freedom to burn the flag can try, but they won't succeed," she said. "Our flag would be protected and the Bill of Rights, too."

It was defeated by voice vote.

House Passes Flag Amendment for The Third Time

JUNE 26 — Three times now, more than 300 members of the House have voted for amending the Constitution in a bid to stop people from burning or otherwise desecrating the American flag. And for a third time, the Senate is standing as a formidable obstacle to that effort advancing any further.

The House voted 305-124 on June 24 to pass a resolution (H J Res 33) proposing a constitutional amendment that would permit federal laws against flag desecration — 19 votes more than the two-thirds majority required to advance a constitutional change. *(Vote 252, p. H-86)*

Similar amendments permitting laws to protect the flag won 310 votes in the House two years ago and 312 votes two years before that. But the high-water mark in the Senate was in 1995, a 63-33 tally that left the proposal three votes short of being sent to the states for ratification. *(1997 Almanac, p. 5-10; 1995 Almanac, p. 6-22)*

Senate Republicans did not arrange for a vote on such a constitutional amendment last year when they became convinced it would fall short. That forecast has not changed, but John Czwartacki, chief spokesman for Majority Leader Trent Lott, R-Miss., said June 23 that a Senate debate is "expected by late summer."

Rep. Charles T. Canady, R-Fla., a leading proponent of the flag amendment, said after the House vote: "Right now, we are facing an uphill battle in the Senate."

Backers of the amendment say they will continue to focus their lobbying efforts on North Dakota Democrats Kent Conrad and Byron L. Dorgan. Both said earlier this year that they were reconsidering their past opposition to the amendment, but both announced April 30 that instead of voting for the amendment this year they would promote a bill (S 931) to outlaw some flag desecration because they believed it could withstand constitutional scrutiny.

The Citizens' Flag Alliance Inc., a coalition supported by the American Legion, has organized a campaign of newspaper and television advertising in North Dakota, featuring the entertainers Pat Boone and Wayne Newton, designed to press those senators into voting for the amendment after all.

"We hope, as we always do, that if they hear from enough people before they pull the lever, they will change their minds," said retired Army Maj. Gen. Patrick Brady, chairman of the coalition. "We would all like it to be done by statute, but it cannot be done. The Supreme Court struck it down."

Fiery Debate

The court ruled in 1989 that state laws against flag-burning are unconstitutional and in 1990 that a federal law to that effect (PL 101-131) was unconstitutional as well. *(1990 Almanac, p. 524)*

Ever since, arguments for and against amending the Constitution to settle the question have sounded like the two days of House debate this year.

Rep. Randy "Duke" Cunningham, R-Calif., a highly decorated Navy fighter pilot in the Vietnam War, appeared to fight back tears as he spoke of the symbol of American freedom.

"This is not a matter of freedom of speech. There is free speech. There is nothing in this amendment that prevents someone from speaking or writing or doing any of the other things, but just the radical burning of the symbol that we hold dear," he said.

"The American flag is not just a piece of cloth. It is a symbol that reflects the values, the struggles and the storied history of our great country," said Rep. Joe Knollenberg, R-Mich.

Countered Gary L. Ackerman, D-N.Y.: "Burning one flag or burning 1,000 flags does not endanger it. It is a symbol. But change just one word of our Constitution of this great nation, and it and we will never be the same."

Melvin Watt, D-N.C., likened his opposition to the amendment to his law firm's defense of the Ku Klux Klan. "We may not agree with the ideas they express, but we will defend until the end their right to express them," he said.

Watt proposed altering the amendment to allow federal laws against flag desecration "not inconsistent with the First Amendment." His amendment was rejected, 115-310. *(Vote 251, p. H-86)*

In a report prepared for Sen. John H. Chafee, R-R.I., the Congressional Research Service found 43 reported incidents of flag desecration in the United States from 1995 through 1998 — not only protest burnings but also acts of vandalism, disorderly conduct by drunken teenagers and the case of a boy who used a flag to wipe oil from his car's dipstick.

Presidents play no formal role in amending the Constitution, but President Clinton reiterated his opposition to the flag proposal. "Efforts to limit the First Amendment to make a narrow exception for flag desecration are misguided," presidential spokesman Joe Lockhart said after the House vote. ◆

House Passes Bill To Limit States' and Localities' Power To Curb Religious Activities

Box Score

- **Bill:** HR 1691
- **Legislative action: House** passed HR 1691 (H Rept 106-219), 306-118, July 15.

SUMMARY

With the backing of the Clinton administration, the House voted overwhelmingly to pass legislation that attempts to resurrect a new form of federal protection for the practice of religion, even in the face of countervailing state laws or local regulations. But the vote came a month after a Supreme Court ruling that legal experts say casts doubt on the enforceability of the measure.

The bill seeks to stop states and cities from intruding on religious expression — for example, by citing an anti-alcohol ordinance to prohibit wine at communion, or a zoning rule to bar a church expansion.

The last effort by Congress to shield religious practice (PL 103-141) was struck down by the Supreme Court in 1997 as an unconstitutionally broad effort to impose restrictions on the states.

In a bid to overcome the high court's objection, the legislation would require states or cities to have a "compelling governmental interest" before imposing a "substantial burden" on individuals' practice of faith in cases that involve interstate commerce or federal funding, or where the federal government was trying to remedy past violations of religious freedom. Religious groups would have to be treated like nonreligious groups in local land use cases.

The bill was endorsed by groups ranging from the liberal People for the American Way to the conservative Christian Coalition. But it was opposed by a similarly diverse group ranging from the American Civil Liberties Union, on the left, to the Eagle Forum, on the right.

Civil rights groups, especially, view the measure as a potential legal justification for discrimination — for example, for a landlord to cite religious belief in refusing to rent to a gay person.

The House defeated an amendment designed to prevent the bill from being cited as a defense for violating existing civil rights law.

Republican Orrin G. Hatch of Utah, chairman of the Senate Judiciary Committee hopes to unveil a compromise version with Democrat Edward M. Kennedy, of Massachusetts.

Even if Congress clears a bill, however, a stumbling block to enforcement was created June 23, when the Supreme Court held that a state may not be sued in state court for breaching a federal law predicated on the Constitution's interstate commerce clause.

House Panel Tries Another Tack To Protect Religion

MAY 29 — The House has renewed its effort to craft a law to protect religion without running afoul of the First Amendment. By voice vote May 26, the Judiciary Subcommittee on the Constitution approved legislation (HR 1691) to limit the ability of state and local governments to restrict religious expression.

The effort began after the Supreme Court's 1990 ruling, in Employment Division v. Smith, that local governments could pass laws that interfere with religious expression so long as that was not the statute's principal intent. A county, for instance, could ban wine at communion as part of an ordinance making the entire county dry.

That ruling so shocked lawmakers at both ends of the political spectrum that in 1993 Congress enacted the Religious Freedom Restoration Act (PL 103-141), which said local governments would need a compelling interest in limiting religious expression, even as part of a broader aim. *(1993 Almanac, p. 315)*

Four years later, that law was struck

down by the Supreme Court in *City of Boerne v. Flores*, which said Congress could not make such an edict to states. *(1997 Almanac, p. 5-23)*

To get around such restraints of federalism, this year's bill would limit the "compelling interest" edict to matters involving federal funding or interstate commerce. Regulating interstate commerce is one of the broadest, and most nebulously defined, powers assigned to the federal government by the Constitution.

Sponsored by Charles T. Canady, R-Fla., chairman of the subcommittee, the bill has bipartisan support. There are still some skeptics, however. Democrat Barney Frank of Massachusetts, who supported the earlier act, now has second thoughts. The new bill, Frank said at the markup, is vague and would create a host of decisions for the courts to wade through.

Religious Rights Measure Heads For House Floor

JUNE 26 — State and local governments would be required to meet stringent legal standards before enforcing laws that could infringe on religious practices under a bill approved on a voice vote June 23 by the House Judiciary Committee. The markup began June 15.

The legislation (HR 1691) is expected on the House floor before the August recess. No companion Senate measure has yet been introduced, although the Senate Judiciary Committee held a hearing June 23 on ways legislation might be crafted to protect "the exercise of religious liberties."

The House bill would prohibit local or state governments from imposing a "substantial burden on a person's religious exercise" — where interstate commerce was involved or in the actions of local governmental entities that receive federal funding — unless they could demonstrate a "compelling governmental interest" in doing so. The measure specifically addresses the application of local land-use ordinances, stating that religious institutions must be treated the same as nonreligious institutions.

The bill is an attempt by Congress to circumvent the Supreme Court's 1997 decision in Boerne v. Flores striking down the latest effort by Congress to protect religious freedom. The court said that 1993 statute (PL 103-141), known as the Religious Freedom Restoration Act, was unconstitutionally broad in imposing limits on the states.

But on the same day that the Judiciary panel approved the bill, the Supreme Court issued three rulings on federalism that, some legal scholars said, could make its enforcement difficult.

Sponsor Charles T. Canady, R-Fla., said the legislation is needed to remedy a "pervasive pattern of discrimination and abusive treatment suffered by religious individuals and organizations." He cited cases in which church renovations were blocked by local zoning boards and in which Roman Catholic prisoners were warned that what they said in the confessional could be reported to police.

Several Democrats expressed concern that the bill would be held unconstitutional because it singles out religious practices for special consideration, and at times, exemption from local laws. Also of concern to Democrats is how the bill would impact the enforcement of civil rights laws. "It wasn't long ago that religion was used to justify all kinds of abominable views like slavery and segregation," said Barney Frank, D-Mass.

The National League of Cities said it would oppose the bill because it "establishes a class of landowners and business operators that are given the right to ignore . . . valid municipal regulation simply because they profess a religious belief." The American Civil Liberties Union backed the bill in the 105th Congress, when it did not get beyond a subcommittee markup, but opposes the bill this time "because of the potentially severe consequences that it may have on state and local civil rights laws."

Jerrold Nadler, D-N.Y., offered an amendment to limit the bill's protections to single-family homeowners, the smallest businesses and organizations that meet specific religious criteria. Others would be barred from raising claims related to housing, employment or public accommodation discrimination. It was defeated on a voice vote after Canady argued the provision would make religious rights subordinate to other civil rights.

House Passes Bill To Restore Federal Protections for Religious Practices

JULY 17 — The House ventured back into the thorny issue of protecting religious liberties June 15, setting off a debate on civil rights and firing the latest volley in the intensifying tussle between Congress and the Supreme Court over which powers are granted to the legislative branch by the Constitution.

The vehicle was a bill (HR 1691) that attempts to resurrect some new form of federal protection for the practice of religion even in the face of countervailing state or local regulations. With majorities of both parties voting "yes," the legislation passed, 306-118. *(Vote 299, p. H-100)*

The last such effort to shield the practice of religion (PL 103-141) was struck down by the Supreme Court two years ago as an unconstitutionally broad effort by Congress to impose restrictions on the states. That decision was part of a trend by the justices to rein in congressional powers, most recently in three decisions last month that cast doubt on the enforceability of the legislation that the House passed.

Both the 1993 law and the new bill attempt to prevent states and localities from interfering with individual religious expression — by adopting an anti-alcohol ordinance that bars wine at communion, for example, or zoning rules that prevent expansion of a church. In an effort to overcome the Supreme Court's previous objections, the new measure would prohibit the imposition of a "substantial burden" on individuals' practice of faith in cases involving interstate commerce or federal funding — or where the federal government was trying to remedy past violations of religious freedom.

The measure won a ringing endorsement from the Clinton administration, which said July 14 that the measure would "protect the religious liberty of all Americans."

But the bill provoked an odd split on both the left and right. The American Civil Liberties Union (ACLU) and the Human Rights Campaign, which lobbies for gay rights, joined such conservative groups as the Eagle Forum and the Home School Legal Defense Association to oppose the bill, while its supporters ranged from the liberal People for the American Way to the conservative Christian Coalition.

But in the days before the bill reached the floor, opposition from civil rights groups began to mount. The NAACP Legal Defense and Education Fund Inc. came out against the measure July 14, and support from other groups began to falter. These groups came to view the bill as creating a potential legal justification for discrimination or violation of existing federal civil rights laws. Landlords might use the measure, they said, to claim a religious justification for refusals to rent to gays, single parents or people who were not members of a particular faith or denomination.

"It's meant as a shield to protect religious free exercise against state intrusion," said Christopher Anders, legislative counsel for the ACLU. "What we are concerned about is people taking this shield and turning it into a sword to be used against other people's civil rights."

To address this issue, Rep. Jerrold Nadler, D-N.Y., offered an amendment designed to prevent the legislation from being cited as a defense for violating existing civil right laws. But bill sponsors said Nadler's proposal would undermine the bill's main aim. It "would subordinate religious liberty to all other civil rights, perpetuating [its] second-class status," said Rep. Charles T. Canady, R-Fla.

Nadler's amendment was rejected, 190-234. *(Vote 298, p. H-100)*

Nadler and civil rights groups said that vote would give momentum to their effort in the Senate. No bill has been introduced there, but Judiciary Committee Chairman Orrin G. Hatch, R-Utah, and Sen. Edward M. Kennedy, D-Mass., are in discussions about a bipartisan measure.

Problems With Enforcement?

Opposition was more muted on the right, because most conservative groups supported the bill. Rep. Ron Paul, R-Texas, said the measure still constituted an attempt by his colleagues to claim new powers. "Congress has been granted no power to protect religious liberties," he said.

Conservative opponents expressed concern that the bill would claim for Congress a broad new authority over religion by connecting it to interstate commerce. Construction at a church could be federally regulated under the bill, they said, because it involves not only an act of religious expression but also the use of materials that are likely to have been shipped across state lines.

This reasoning may be a stretch for a court that has been on a recent federalist tear. "There are some constitutional law professors who think this bill has constitutional problems," Nadler said. "I hope they're wrong."

Even if the bill becomes law and is not entirely struck down, a recent ruling suggests it might be rendered meaningless. On June 23, the court ruled in *Alden v. Maine* that a state government may not be sued in state court on the basis of a federal law predicated on the Interstate Commerce Clause and other powers enumerated in Article I of the Constitution. In 1996, the court made a similar ruling affecting federal courts. Cumulatively those rulings cast doubt on whether an individual would have a chance to sue over a perceived violation of religious liberties, legal experts say. ◆

House Backs Hyde's Effort, Passing Bill To Curb Abuse In Federal Property Seizures

Box Score

- **Bills:** HR 1658; S 1701
- **Legislative action: House** passed HR 1658 (H Rept 106-192), 375-48, June 24.

SUMMARY

The House overwhelmingly passed legislation to make it more difficult for federal agents to seize private property that they suspect is linked to a crime. The practice nets millions of dollars annually for the Treasury, but critics say it has led to abuse of innocent people. The Clinton administration opposes the bill, saying it would hurt crime-fighting efforts. Senate negotiations this fall to find a middle ground did not come to fruition.

The law now requires the government to show only probable cause of a criminal connection before seizing property, regardless of whether the owner was criminally involved. To avoid seizure, owners must prove their property has no criminal connection.

The House bill would transfer that burden of proof to the government; require that it link property to criminal activity with "clear and convincing evidence" before seizing it; bar seizures from people unaware of the ill-gotten nature of their possessions; and authorize court-appointed lawyers for the poor to fight civil asset forfeiture proceedings.

Senate Judiciary Committee leaders say they will resume their talks early next year. They say the bill by Jeff Sessions, R-Ala., is unacceptable, in part because it would expand federal asset seizure powers in some cases.

House Passes Bill To Limit Seizures Of Private Assets

JUNE 26 — It had been a while since Judiciary Committee Chairman Henry J. Hyde enjoyed such sweet legislative success, and he showed it. He took the sheet of paper bearing the final House tally on a pet bill and kissed it.

"I am ecstatic," the Illinois Republican said of the 375-48 House vote June 24 to pass a bill (HR 1658) that would make it more difficult for federal agents to seize private property that they suspect is linked to a crime. *(Vote 255, p. H-88)*

The bill caps a six-year crusade for Hyde, who has suffered setbacks this year on impeachment and juvenile crime. He wrote a 1995 book about civil forfeitures after studying cases of innocent people having their property taken by the federal government because of vague suspicions the assets were criminally tainted.

He got a bill through his committee in 1997, but that attempt to broker a compromise with the Justice Department, which sees forfeitures as a key weapon in its war on drugs, did not make it to the floor.

In this Congress — Hyde's last as chairman — he returned to his original approach to force the government to show "by clear and convincing evidence" that confiscated property was tied to illegal misuse. The 1997 bill would have set a lower standard, requiring a "preponderance of the evidence."

Within his own committee, whose sharp partisan divide was highlighted by the question of President Clinton's impeachment in 1998, the bill was carried by an odd coalition that included ranking Democrat John Conyers Jr. of Michigan, conservative Republican Bob Barr of Georgia and liberal Democrat Barney Frank of Massachusetts.

Noting the equally divergent support from outside groups representing lawyers, real estate agents, bankers, the American Civil Liberties Union and the National Rifle Association, Hyde said he hoped to rally them into pressuring senators to take up the measure. Currently, no companion bill exists in the Senate.

Powerful law enforcement groups oppose the measure, arguing that it would hinder drug interdiction efforts such as seizing cash profits at airports and on highways.

The International Association of Chiefs of Police vowed to block Senate consideration.

"We were very disappointed with the House vote. We had hoped that the needs of law enforcement might have been recognized," said Gene Voegtlin, legal counsel for the police chiefs' group.

Hyde said he hopes to resolve differences with law enforcement groups.

Burden of Proof

Forfeiture rules date back to English admiralty law involving seizure of smugglers' cargoes. In recent years they have been used more aggressively by prosecutors as part of the war on drugs. Under current law, the government need only show "probable cause," the lowest standard of proof, to take property with a suspected crime connection, regardless of whether the owner was criminally involved. The burden of proof is on the owner to establish that it is not subject to forfeiture.

Hyde's bill would not affect forfeiture of assets as part of a criminal proceeding against a convicted defendant.

Hyde said the current rules have been abused by the government, which collects millions of dollars each year from the sale of the property. Proponents complain that innocent parties or their heirs often have to undergo great expense to recover property seized without even an arrest or a hearing.

They cite the example of the Red Carpet Motel in Houston, which was seized by the government in 1998 because the owners had not done enough to stop drug activity in some of the rooms. The property was returned to the owners after several months of expensive legal wrangling.

The bill would require the government to show "by clear and convincing evidence" that the confiscated property was related to a crime. Other key provisions would define a defense for "innocent owners" who did not know of illegal conduct or reported it to police; allow assets to be returned in cases of substantial hardship while review was pending; allow owners to sue if the assets were damaged or lost; and provide government-paid lawyers to those who could not afford a legal defense.

The Judiciary Committee approved the bill, 27-3, on June 15.

Opponents complained in floor debate that the government's war on drugs would be set back by requiring a higher standard of proof. They also maintained that the bill would make it easier for drug kingpins to file frivolous claims against the government.

"This is not the time to disarm our soldiers and to demoralize our police on the front line, and it is certainly not the right time to signal to the drug dealers that we are weakening our resolve," said Republican Asa Hutchinson of Arkansas, a former prosecutor.

Hutchinson's amendment, which would have raised the current standard to the 1997 proposal to require a preponderance of evidence, failed, 155-268. *(Vote 254, p. H-88)*

Senate Action Postponed

NOVEMBER 13 — It will be next year before the Senate considers legislation to make it more difficult for federal agents to seize private property that they suspect is linked to a crime. The Senate Judiciary Committee, which had scheduled and postponed debate on the issue three times this fall, announced Nov. 10 that no markup will be held this year. Aides cited as reasons the lack of a committee agreement on the issue and the short time before Congress adjourns for the year.

Chairman Orrin G. Hatch, R-Utah, and ranking Democrat Patrick J. Leahy of Vermont have been working to draft what they hope will be a compromise between two bills. One measure is a narrow attempt (S 1701) by Jeff Sessions, R-Ala., that has been embraced by a bipartisan group of four other committee members; the other is a more sweeping approach (HR 1658) by House Judiciary Committee Chairman Henry J. Hyde, R-Ill., which the House passed overwhelmingly in June.

The House bill is supported by groups ranging from the American Civil Liberties Union to the National Rifle Association. But the Clinton administration opposes it, as do many law enforcement groups. They say the House measure would hinder drug interdiction and other crime-fighting efforts.

Both the Hyde and Sessions bills, as

well as the emerging Hatch-Leahy proposal, would change the burden of proof in such cases to require that the government prove the property targeted for seizure was connected to a crime. Currently, the owner must prove that it is not. Hyde's bill would require "clear and convincing evidence" that confiscated property was tied to crimes. Both Senate measures would require the lower standard of a "preponderance" of the evidence.

Hyde's bill would bar seizures from "innocent" owners, such as spouses or children unaware of the ill-gotten nature of their property. Both Senate measures have more narrowly written provisions in this area.

One key difference between the Sessions and the Hatch-Leahy bills is that the latter would modify one of the most controversial of Hyde's provisions, to allow courts to appoint lawyers for aggrieved property owners who cannot afford them. Hatch and Leahy would restrict such appointments to instances in which real property, such as a house, was at risk or when an individual has been charged with a crime and already has qualified for court-appointed counsel.

Another key difference is that the Sessions legislation would expand federal power to seize assets under some circumstances. The Hatch-Leahy plan would not. ◆

House Passage of Bill To Federalize Many Class Actions Heartens Supporters

Box Score

- **Bills:** HR 1875, S 353
- **Legislative action: House** passed HR 1875 (H Rept 106-320), 222-207, on Sept. 23.

SUMMARY

The House passed a bill that would divert most class-action litigation to federal court. The White House threatened a veto, saying the bill would hurt consumers, curb states' rights and add to an already overcrowded federal docket.

Sponsors said the bill was needed to curb abuse of the current system, in which plaintiffs' attorneys may seek out the state court most sympathetic to their claim.

Under the bill, class action cases with more than 100 plaintiffs or more than $1 million at stake could be moved to federal court whenever one plaintiff was from a state different from any defendant. If a federal judge declined to certify a suit as a class action, it could be refiled in state court.

Both sides agree that the bill would benefit nationwide businesses by consolidating in one place the similar cases in which they must defend themselves. And there is general accord that federal courts are more sympathetic than most state courts to corporate defendants in class action cases.

As a result, proponents say the bill would give businesses appropriate relief from spiraling legal costs; opponents say the effect would be to limit consumers' legal remedies for perceived wrongdoing and boost their costs by requiring them to fight in court far from where they live.

The House defeated amendments that would have exempted tobacco companies, gun makers and ammunition companies from the bill's easier standard for mounting their class action defenses in U.S. District Court.

A Senate Judiciary subcommittee held hearings on the companion bill, but senior Republicans have been noncommittal about their intentions for the legislation.

House Panel OKs Bill That Would Help Defendants

AUGUST 7 — Many more class-action lawsuits would be heard in federal court under legislation approved 15-12 by the House Judiciary Committee on Aug. 3. Both sides in the debate said the bill (HR 1875) would benefit businesses, which are most often the defendants in such litigation.

Republican supporters said federal judges are more likely than state judges to rule in favor of nationwide companies, both when considering whether a suit is eligible for class-action status and at trial. They say the bill is needed to restrict groups of plaintiffs from around the country from shopping around for a state most likely to rule favorably on their particular claim.

Democrats — except for Rick Boucher, D-Va., a cosponsor — argued that the bill would make it too easy for companies to defend themselves far from where their alleged misbehavior occurred. They also said the bill would result in an unnecessary federal trumping of state power.

The bill would grant federal jurisdiction to most class-action suits in which any plaintiff is from a state different than the defendant's state. Cases could be moved to federal court by any defendant without the consent of the others and by any plaintiff without the consent of the others. If a federal judge declined to certify a suit as a class action, plaintiffs could refile their claims in a state court. Cases with fewer than 100 plaintiffs or where less than $1 million was at issue would not be covered by the bill.

Democrats tried unsuccessfully to raise those thresholds to 200 people and $5 million. The panel also rejected Democratic amendments to exempt cases involving the gun, tobacco or health industries from the bill's reach.

The bill is the first attempt to change the rules of class-action litigation to move in Congress this year. Last year Congress and President Clinton came together after three years of disagreement on a law (PL 104-67) to limit such suits against companies whose earnings do not meet expectations. *(1998 Almanac, p. 5-30)*

House Narrowly Passes Bill; Clinton Threatens Veto

SEPTEMBER 25 — Legislation that could have sweeping implications for the kind of class action lawsuits aimed at tobacco and gun makers and health care providers won narrow passage in the House on Sept. 23, raising the hopes of its Republican supporters and Democratic detractors.

The 222-207 vote to pass the bill (HR 1875) was hailed as a breakthrough by House sponsors, even as it drew a noncommittal response from Senate leaders and a strong veto threat from the White House. *(Vote 443, p. H-144)*

As passed by the House, the bill would subject most proposed class actions to stringent federal rules, instead of allowing them to be handled at the state level, where it can be easier for a group of plaintiffs to qualify as a "class." Most proposed class actions in which at least one of the plaintiffs and the defendant live in different states would be subject to removal from state court and transferred to federal jurisdiction.

The GOP-led initiative, backed by a small group of Democrats, was pushed as a way to guard against abuse of the class action system, which they argue gives plaintiffs and attorneys incentive to seek out the state court most sympathetic to their cause.

The bill "ends the abuse of nationwide forum shopping to find the one judge in the one state in the one county . . . that thinks that anything goes regarding class actions," said sponsor Robert W. Goodlatte, R-Va.

HR 1875 was opposed by most Democrats and 15 Republicans, who said it would deprive injured parties of access to their own state courts, making it less convenient, more expensive and in some cases impossible to remedy wrongs done by business and industry.

"The bill will benefit only one class of litigants: corporate wrongdoers," said Michigan's John Conyers Jr., ranking Democrat on the House Judiciary Committee.

The White House issued a statement threatening a veto on the grounds that the bill "will limit the availability of class actions as a viable remedy for those with bona fide claims who are unable to afford a suit of their own; it will infringe significantly on state courts' ability to offer redress and provide a convenient forum for their citizens; and it will expand the already overloaded federal docket . . . ."

The close vote presages an uncertain future for the measure in the Senate, where a companion bill (S 353), cosponsored by Charles E. Grassley, R-Iowa, and Herb Kohl, D-Wis., has not gone past the hearing stage.

Senate Judiciary Chairman Orrin G. Hatch, R-Utah, has not committed to acting on S 353. "I don't know that we're close or not close" to a markup of the legislation, Hatch said Sept. 23. "I have not looked at it yet."

Rep. Rick Boucher, D-Va., a cosponsor of HR 1875, said the Senate has been waiting for a signal from the House, and he expects Hatch's panel to take up the issue in October.

But opponents suggested that the signal sent by the vote was a negative one. "This vote should send a very strong message to the Senate that it would be a waste of time to do this, because it isn't going to pass," said Carlton Carl, director of media relations for the Association of Trial Lawyers of America.

Tobacco, Gun Makers, HMOs

Many Democrats and consumer groups are concerned about the bill's consequences for class action lawsuits against such businesses as tobacco companies, gun manufacturers and health maintenance organizations, which have been parties to massive settlements in recent years. Under the House-passed bill, most, if not all, of such suits in the future would be decided by the federal courts.

Democratic efforts to carve out exceptions for suits against certain industries were soundly defeated. The House rejected, 152-277, an amendment by Jerrold Nadler, D-N.Y., to exempt suits against gun and ammunition makers from the new standard for sending cases to federal court. *(Vote 439, p. H-142)*

More than 20 cities and the NAACP have filed such class actions, Nadler said. "We should not handicap these important civil suits just as they are beginning. . . . We should not stack the deck against victims of gun violence."

Bill supporters argued that it would be unfair to single out members of a certain group and deprive them of the right to have their cases heard in federal court.

Also rejected, 162-266, was an amendment by Sheila Jackson-Lee, D-Texas, that would have exempted tobacco suits. *(Vote 440, p. H-144)*

Democrats also failed, 205-225, on an amendment by Barney Frank, D-Mass., to ensure that once a federal judge rejected a class action suit, it could be returned to the state court permanently for all further actions. *(Vote 441, p. H-144)*

The amendment aimed to eliminate what proponents called the bill's "merry-go-round effect," in which a class action rejected by a federal court could face several more trips between the federal and state levels before being allowed to qualify as a class action. ◆

Both Chambers Take Action To Criminalize Possession, Sales of 'Date Rape' Drugs

SUMMARY

The House and Senate passed slightly different versions of a bill to add substances — known as "date rape drugs" because they are used with alcohol to render women unconscious and vulnerable to sexual assault — to the roster of narcotics subject to federal regulation and criminal prosecution.

Both bills would add gamma hydroxybutyric acid (GHB), known colloquially as "liquid ecstasy," to the roster of Schedule I drugs — those with no current lawful purpose — making its possession or sale subject to the most stringent federal criminal penalties. An exception would be made for use in clinical studies of sleep disorders. Because it has commercial uses, possession of gamma butyrolactone, a substance converted into GHB when consumed, would be subject to less stringent security requirements than GHB. The House version would make ketamine, an animal tranquilizer known on the street as "Special K," a Schedule III drug.

House sponsors will move next year to clear the Senate version; they expect President Clinton will sign it.

House Committee Approves Penalties For Possession

AUGUST 7 — A bill to stiffen criminal penalties for possession of so-called date-rape drugs won voice vote approval Aug. 5 from the House Commerce Committee. The measure (HR 2130) would require that gamma hydroxybutyric acid (GHB) and ketamine be classified as controlled substances, making those convicted of possessing the drugs subject to mandatory minimum sentences similar to those for possession of marijuana, cocaine and heroin.

Taken in excessive amounts or combined with alcohol, the drugs can reduce respiration and heartbeat to dangerously low levels, resulting in seizures, coma or death. The drugs have been used to render victims unconscious and vulnerable to sexual assault.

Bill sponsor Republican Fred Upton of Michigan said both drugs are currently legal to possess and that people are able to buy them over the Internet with a credit card.

House Passes Measure Targeting 'Date Rape' Drugs

OCTOBER 16 — With overwhelming bipartisan support, the House on Oct. 12 passed a bill aimed at cracking down on so-called date rape drugs.

The measure (HR 2130), which passed 423-1, would amend the Controlled Substances Act to tighten regulation of drugs that have been used to render victims unconscious and more vulnerable to sexual assault. *(Vote 493, p. H-162)*

Under the bill, gamma hydroxybutyrate (GHB), also known as Liquid Ecstasy, would be classified as a Schedule I drug. This is the most tightly regulated classification, reserved for substances such as heroin that have no accepted medical use.

Regulations would also be tightened for gamma butyrolactine, a substance commonly found in paint strippers that is converted into GHB when it is consumed. And the bill would confirm a recent Drug Enforcement Administration (DEA) decision to regulate another abused substance, ketamine, known as Special K.

While some states control these drugs, none of them are regulated under federal law. The proposed change is the result of growing concern over the availability and use of date rape drugs at nightclubs and parties. The bill is named for Hillory J. Farias, a 17-year-old Texan who died in 1996 after GHB was slipped into her drink. According to the Commerce Committee report, the DEA has documented 32 deaths associated with GHB since 1990.

"Without this bill, illicit use of GHB would increase drastically," said Rep. Sheila Jackson-Lee, D-Texas. "It's being made in bathtubs. It's being made on the Internet."

However, the bill would provide exemptions for scientific research using GHB. The drug is being investigated as a possible treatment for the sleeping disorder narcolepsy.

The bill was approved by the Commerce Committee (H Rept 106-340, Part 1) on Aug. 5.

Tauzin noted that in 1998, more Americans bought wireless telephones than traditional phones. "People count on those phones to be their lifeline in emergencies," he said.

Senate Passes Bill, Which is Expected To Clear in 2000

NOVEMBER 20 — The Senate passed a bill (HR 2130) by voice vote Nov. 19 that would stiffen criminal penalties for possession of several drugs associated with date rape.

But before doing so, the Senate inserted its own, slightly different version of the measure (S 1561), setting up negotiations with the House next year. Still, sponsors on both sides of the Capitol predicted a compromise

Box Score

- **Bill:** HR 2130
- **Legislative action: House** passed HR 2130 (H Rept 106-340, Part I), 423-1, on Oct. 12.

Senate substituted the text of S 1561 and passed HR 2130 by voice vote Nov. 19.

would be reached and said they expected President Clinton to sign it early next year.

The Senate Judiciary Committee had endorsed S 1561 by voice vote Nov. 17. The House passed its bill Oct. 12.

Both bills would classify gamma hydroxybutyric acid (GHB), a central nervous system depressant, as a Schedule I drug, the most closely regulated category of controlled substances. Drugs on the list have no medical purpose, making their possession or sale subject to the most stringent federal criminal penalties.

Taken in large doses or combined with alcohol, GHB — known colloquially as liquid ecstacy — can render victims unconscious. The bills would create an exemption for GHB possession by participants in clinical studies of sleep-related disorders.

The House bill would also classify ketamine, an animal tranquilizer known by the street name "Special K," as a Schedule III drug. ◆

Partisan Impasse Blocks Judicial Confirmations For Most of the Year

SUMMARY

The Senate confirmed 34 federal judges but also voted to reject a judicial nominee for the first time in 12 years. Judiciary Committee Chairman Orrin G. Hatch, R-Utah, declined to hold hearings on nominees until President Clinton agreed in June to nominate Ted Stewart, who drew the enmity of environmentalists as Republican official in Utah, for a U.S. District Court seat in Salt Lake City.

Confirmations stopped for much of the fall after the Senate voted 45-54 along party lines Oct. 5 to reject Ronnie L. White, the first black on Missouri's Supreme Court, for a federal district judgeship in St. Louis; the last judicial nomination defeated on the floor was Robert H. Bork's, for the Supreme Court. Democrats said the White vote was evidence that the GOP is tougher on women and minority judicial nominees. Republicans countered, saying their opposition was to judicial liberals, regardless of their race or gender.

Majority Leader Trent Lott, R-Miss., promised votes by March 15, 2000, on seven nominees who were endorsed by the Judiciary Committee in 1999, including long-stalled Richard A. Paez and Marsha L. Berzon for the 9th U.S. Circuit Court of Appeals. Some Republican senators said they would try to block all confirmations if the president used his recess appointment powers too liberally to fill executive branch jobs before Congress reconvened for the second session of the 106th Congress. There were no nominees for 21 of 56 vacancies, out of 844 judgeships nationwide, and odds were long that a Republican Senate would allow a Democratic president to fill them in his last year in office.

Clinton's Deals On Judges Stir Discontent Among Democrats

APRIL 10 — Ted Stewart has devoted his entire career to getting Republicans elected to office and then serving under them. An avowed conservative, he rose from congressional aide in the early 1980s to his current post as chief of staff to Gov. Michael O. Leavitt of Utah. Along the way, he was an ardent defender of mining and development interests while directing the state Department of Natural Resources.

In other words, he is not the first person who would generally come to mind for a Democratic president to nominate for a federal judgeship.

But with the fervent backing of Republican Orrin G. Hatch of Utah, chairman of the Senate Judiciary Committee, Stewart may well win such an appointment. His name is in the pre-nomination vetting process in Utah, which normally involves a series of discreet discussions among a state's top lawmakers and members of the legal establishment. In this case, however, these deliberations have exploded into the open, with environmental groups outraged that President Clinton might name Stewart, and Hatch outraged that the president might not.

The standoff has implications well beyond Utah. In a bid to put leverage behind his protégé, Hatch has not scheduled a single hearing on judicial nominations so far in the 106th Congress and threatens not to as long as Stewart is in limbo. Just how far he is willing to go is unclear, but he is certainly making his feelings known to the Clinton administration and to the public. "I'm not going to like that," Hatch told television station KSL in Salt Lake City when asked how he would react if Stewart is not picked by the president. "Things can get rough around here."

The Stewart situation is also emblematic of the quandary Clinton is in over his judicial nominations. Now in the seventh year of his presidency, he is in a position to fill two out of every five seats on the United States district and appeals courts by the time he leaves office in 21 months — which would allow him to influence federal jurisprudence well into the next century. But his strategy of trying to shape the judiciary in a quiet and noncontroversial way has now come under increasing criticism from liberal advocacy groups and some Democrats, who say Clinton has become too quick to cut deals with

Trials of the Unconfirmed: A Look at Stalled Nominations

APRIL 10 — A federal judgeship may be a position of great power and prestige, but getting there can be a lonely and tiring process.

It involves waiting months, sometimes years, just to get a hearing before the Senate Judiciary Committee. Confirmation often comes near the end of a Congress, if at all.

If a nominee is not confirmed by the time the two-year Congress ends, he or she needs to be renominated at the outset of the new session.

Republican senators have been particularly hard on nominees to the 9th U.S. Circuit Court of Appeals, which includes nine Western states and two Pacific territories.

That circuit has a reputation as the most liberal and is often overruled by the Supreme Court. The population it covers is more than twice the size of most circuits, and some Republicans from the Mountain States are trying to break it in two. Keeping the bench understaffed may be a way of convincing skeptics that the circuit is too large to be workable.

In addition to nominees to the 9th Circuit, women and minority nominees are more likely to wait for lengthy periods. Some of the nominees who have waited the longest include:

- **James A. Beaty Jr.** His wait may be over, but not because he is about to be confirmed. The Clinton administration may be ready to give up on him. His name was absent when the White House announced its first round of nominations in late January.

A federal district judge in North Carolina, Beaty was first nominated for a promotion to the 4th Circuit in December 1995. The 104th and 105th Congresses refused to bring him up for a vote. His nemesis: North Carolina Republican Sen. Jesse Helms.

- **Richard Paez.** A district judge in California hoping for a spot on the 9th Circuit, Paez has been anonymously blocked since January 1996.

Republicans grumble that he is too liberal and has activist tendencies. In 1997, he struck down a local ordinance banning panhandling near automated teller machines, for instance. But the specifics of his case remain something of a mystery. No one has come forward to say why his nomination is being held up.

- **Helene White.** A state court of appeals judge, White is hoping for a promotion to the 6th Circuit, which includes her home state of Michigan and three others. She has been waiting since January 1997.

Her nomination has stalled, apparently because Sen. Spencer Abraham, R-Mich., is trying to make her part of a package deal with Gerald E. Rosen, a conservative Republican-appointed district judge Abraham is touting for the 6th Circuit.

- **Timothy Dyk.** A Washington, D.C., attorney up for a spot on the U.S. Court of Appeals for the federal circuit, which reviews some decisions of lower courts and agencies, he has been waiting since April 1998.

Dyk represented television networks challenging indecency standards drafted by the Federal Communications Commission. He is also a former board member of People for the American Way, a liberal organization. It is unclear who is holding up his nomination.

- **Ronnie White.** A justice on the Missouri Supreme Court, White is hoping for a district judgeship. He was nominated in June 1997.

Sen. John Ashcroft, R-Mo., one of the most vociferous critics of Clinton's nominees, has complained that White may be too much of an "activist" on the federal bench, though Ashcroft says he is not the one who placed the hold on him.

Republican senators and too unwilling to stand up and push for nominees that are not part of such deals.

A Stewart nomination would not be the first time Clinton has agreed to a conservative jurist. Last year Clinton nominated Barbara Durham, a Republican in Washington state, for the influential 9th U.S. Circuit Court of Appeals, which reviews trial court decisions in California, eight other Western states and two Pacific territories. Her nomination was made in exchange for Senate confirmation to the same court of longtime Clinton friend William A. Fletcher, a former law professor at the University of California.

Another deal is under discussion in Michigan, where U.S. District Judge Gerald E. Rosen of Detroit, a former Republican congressional candidate and a close friend of Sen. Spencer Abraham, R-Mich., is being considered for a promotion to the 6th U.S. Circuit Court of Appeals as part of a package that would include confirmation of Helene White to the same court. White, a Michigan Court of Appeals judge, was first nominated in January 1997 — one of a growing roster of Clinton picks whose confirmations have been stalled by determined opposition. Some have waited as long as three years in a kind of judicial limbo. *(Nominees, above)*

Aside from deals in which the president is promoting a GOP pick and one of his own simultaneously, critics say, Clinton has made few efforts on behalf of his nominees. And at times — particularly in 1996 and 1997 — the Republicans in control of the Senate have slowed confirmations to a trickle. Clinton's most visible effort to draw attention to this was a brief mention in his 1998 State of the Union address.

"This is clearly a secondary issue for him, which is a shame because he is the first constitutional law professor to be president," said Stephan Kline, legislative counsel for the Alliance for Justice, which pushes for more judges who would rule in favor of its consumer, civil rights and environmentalist group members.

Moreover, Kline said, liberal groups are increasingly annoyed by Clinton's quiescence and his propensity to make deals. "People are beginning to say that is certainly not what we put this guy in the White House for," he said.

When Ronald Reagan took office in 1981, by contrast, his administration put great weight on molding a more conservative federal bench. His aides announced they would seek to fill the courts with "strict constructionists," those who would base their rulings on what they saw as the original intent of the Founding Fathers, and the effort did not let up in the ensuing eight years. Reagan succeeded in part because he was working with a GOP Senate for the first six of those years. *(1986 Almanac, p. 59)*

The process of filling judgeships, in which the Senate must vote on every presidential choice, is most difficult in the type of divided government Clinton is now operating — and in an era when congressional attacks on the judiciary are on the rise.

But confirmations are always complicated by parochial considerations and the often divergent views of a state's two senators. Until recently, the power of any senator to put an anonymous "hold" on a nomination obscured almost all the intrigue from public view, but even under a new procedure, senators may keep secret from the president and the public their decision to thwart a nominee's progress.

Negotiating Behind the Scenes

Assistant Attorney General Eleanor D. Acheson, the person in charge of the Justice Department's judicial screening, says the administration does go to the mat for its nominees, but that much of it is done through quiet negotiation rather than public confrontation. She says she is at a loss for why she receives so much criticism from groups such as Kline's.

"We have worked as hard and effectively as we can to push the people the president has nominated," she said. "It may well be that what they are looking for is a more public, in-your-face drawing of lines."

Overall, the numbers appear to bear out her argument. Clinton has won confirmation of 306 judges, which puts him on track to match the 385 people Reagan put on the bench. (There are 844 seats nationwide.) Last year the Senate confirmed 73 judges, an exceptionally high number for a party that does not control the White House. The number was especially notable at a time when the case leading to Clinton's impeachment was building and the White House legal counsel, Charles F. C. Ruff, was busy defending the president rather than assisting in judicial selection.

"Frankly, I'm impressed they've been able to do what they've done," said Sen. Patrick J. Leahy of Vermont, ranking Democrat on the Judiciary Committee.

"The administration has been as good as one could expect under those circumstances," said Sheldon Goldman, political scientist at the University of Massachusetts at Amherst and author of "Picking Federal Judges: Lower Court Selection from Roosevelt Through Reagan." "It didn't have a lot of capital to expend here."

But critics say last year's confirmations were mostly the result of pressure applied by Chief Justice William H. Rehnquist, whose complaints about longstanding vacancies on the lower courts — and the delays in criminal trials and civil litigation that result — were prominent in his annual State of the Judiciary reports for 1996 and 1997.

But liberal groups want judges who will do more than keep the court dockets moving swiftly. They pushed hard, for example, to persuade Clinton to make a public campaign for the confirmation of James A. Beaty, who would have been the first black judge on the 4th U.S. Circuit Court of Appeals, which stretches from Maryland to South Carolina. Instead, Beaty's nomination languished for three years and has not been renewed in the 106th Congress.

The Hard-Line Approach

Clinton's Democratic critics realize that with the Republicans in comfortable control of the Senate, some nominees are not going to be confirmed. But many liberals are convinced of the adage about negotiating with adversaries: If you give an inch, they will take a mile.

Elliott Mincburg, legal director of People for the American Way, a liberal civil liberties organization, said that Presidents Reagan and George Bush always fought to the last for even nominees who appeared doomed. They also were weary of making deals, at least ones that were made public. The rationale was that if they gave in to one senator's demands, that would encourage other senators to throw up roadblocks.

"In the Bush administration, there were few if any of these kinds of deals, and Bush would go forward with people who clearly wouldn't get confirmed," said Mincburg. "That helped the administration in the overall process."

Acheson said the argument that making deals with senators will only beget more deals has not been borne out. "You can't say it is crazy on its face," she said. "But it just hasn't resulted in that so far."

That Clinton is under fire from his own Democratic base of support for his limited commitment to his judicial nominees may not be surprising, given that his record for persistence in promoting non-judicial nominees has been mixed.

In 1993 Clinton enraged the party faithful when he withdrew the nomination of Lani Guinier as assistant attorney general for civil rights. After her writings on race and affirmative action drew vociferous criticism from conservatives, Clinton declined to push for confirmation in order to husband his political capital for other purposes early in his tenure. *(1993 Almanac, p. 307)*

But Clinton has won modest praise from liberals for his steadfast support of Bill Lann Lee, whom the president made acting assistant attorney general for civil rights after the Senate blocked his nomination. And despite continued GOP criticism, Clinton has formally nominated Lee again.

A Limited Audience

On judicial nominations, Clinton's apparent lack of passion has caused grumbling within the party ranks. But groups that follow the issue realize it is not one that resonates much outside Washington among grass-roots liberals.

Ironically, Clinton might not be receiving so much criticism from within his own party these days had he been less successful last year in getting judges confirmed. Until then, liberal groups specializing in judicial politics had their hands full criticizing conservative Republican senators such as John Ashcroft of Missouri, Jeff Sessions of Alabama and Majority Leader Trent Lott of Mississippi for blocking nominees for lengthy periods.

But a Stewart nomination would be a bitter bill for Democrats, particularly those focused on environmental issues.

Environmental groups in Utah have written to White House Chief of Staff John D. Podesta and filled the state's airwaves and newspaper op-ed columns with harsh criticism of Stewart, who earned their enmity when he was the state's top natural resources regulator.

Standing up to Hatch would enable the president to win praise from some of his most loyal allies. And if Hatch continues to delay the entire senatorial judicial nomination schedule, that could redraw the battle lines for confirmation politics in a more traditional form, with liberal Democrats attacking conservative Republicans instead of their own president.

On the other hand, standing up to Hatch could mean that Clinton would not be seeing many more of his judges confirmed. The pace of confirmations almost always slows in the last year of a president's term, no matter what the other factors.

It is a difficult choice. If history is any guide, an act of presidential defiance may not be in the cards.

Senate Panel Holds First Confirmation Hearings of Year

JUNE 19 — For the first time in the 106th Congress, the Senate Judiciary Committee is back in the business of considering President Clinton's nominees for the federal courts.

Judiciary Committee Chairman Orrin G. Hatch, R-Utah, had declined to schedule any nomination hearings this year as he pressed Clinton to nominate Ted Stewart, a political ally of the senator's and chief of staff to GOP Gov. Michael O. Leavitt of Utah, to a federal judgeship.

But Hatch told the Deseret News of Salt Lake City on June 15 that the president intends to nominate Stewart. And the next day, the Judiciary Committee held its first confirmation hearing of the year, for six nominees to the U.S. District courts and two nominees for U.S. Courts of Appeal vacancies.

Hatch has never explicitly acknowledged that Stewart's nomination was his price for re-engaging the confirmation process, but the timing of the developments was more than coincidental. Both the White House, which would not officially confirm that the president intends to nominate Stewart, and Senate Democrats were cautiously encouraged that Hatch's panel is finally moving nominees.

"We've made some progress in the last couple of weeks," said Senate Minority Leader Tom Daschle, D-S.D., who has been critical of the slow pace of the nominations process.

Clinton, Hatch Again Spar Over Judgeships

AUGUST 14 — The long-running dispute between President Clinton and Senate Republicans over the confirmation rate of federal judges broke into the open again Aug. 9, when Clinton and Judiciary Committee Chairman Orrin G. Hatch, R-Utah, exchanged gibes.

Clinton made his case in a speech before the American Bar Association, where he complained of the 67 vacancies on the federal bench. "We cannot expect our society to do justice without enough judges to handle the rising number of cases in our courts," he said. "Despite the high qualifications of my nominees, there is a mounting vacancy crisis in the courts."

Clinton singled out vacancies on the 4th U.S. Circuit Court of Appeals, which covers five states from Maryland to South Carolina, and the 7th Circuit, which covers Indiana, Illinois and Wisconsin. Neither has ever had a black judge, and Clinton has nominated African-Americans for vacancies on each.

In a letter to Clinton the previous day, Hatch said 67 is hardly a huge vacancy list. Instead, he maintained, it approaches "full employment" given that it will always take some time for the Senate to carefully consider each nominee. There are 844 seats on the federal courts.

Hatch and Clinton have often worked fairly well together on this topic. While hardly speeding Clinton's nominees along, Hatch has stood up to conservatives who routinely vote against the president's picks and who at one point two years ago almost succeeded in limiting the chairman's powers. *(1997 Almanac, p. 5-19)*

But Hatch refused to hold any judicial confirmation hearings this year until Clinton picked Ted Stewart, a longtime GOP operative, for a judgeship in Salt Lake City. The day after Clinton said he planned to nominate Stewart, hearings got under way. Three days after the nomination was formalized, it was endorsed July 29 by the Judiciary Committee.

So far this year, the committee has endorsed 24 judicial nominees, 11 of whom have been confirmed by the Senate. Among those still waiting are Richard A. Paez, whose initial nomination for the 9th Circuit was made in the 104th Congress.

Historically, 67 vacancies is not particularly high. In 1996, the number topped 100. In 1991, it reached 148, although that was after Congress created 85 new judgeships. But in a presidential election year, confirmations usually plummet. So unless the confirmation pace quickens this fall, the vacancies could ascend to triple digits by the end of the Clinton presidency.

Partisan Impasse May Block Confirmations For Rest of Session

SEPTEMBER 25 — A bitter partisan showdown over judicial nominees on the Senate floor Sept. 21 left both Republicans and Democrats predicting that few, if any, confirmation votes will occur in the remaining weeks of this session.

Democrats said they will continue to hold hostage a top GOP pick until floor votes are scheduled on their own choices for judgeships. That strategy, warned Judiciary Committee Chairman Orrin G. Hatch, R-Utah, "sets a bad precedent."

It is an ally of Hatch's that Democrats are holding hostage. Ted Stewart, a former congressional aide and long-time GOP operative who was most recently chief of staff to Gov. Michael O. Leavitt of Utah, was nominated for a U.S. District Court seat in Salt Lake City on July 27. President Clinton made the nomination at Hatch's insistence; the administration hoped it would break the logjam in the Senate. The Judiciary Committee endorsed Stewart's nomination three days later.

But Democrats have filibustered Stewart's nomination since. And when the GOP leadership finally called for a cloture vote Sept. 21, it fell short of the 60 votes required. The vote was 55 to 44. *(Vote 281, p. S-55)*

"If there is no cloture, there won't be any more judgeships that will pass without 60 votes," Hatch said shortly before the vote.

But Democrats said they will not allow a floor vote on Stewart until two of their nominees are brought up for confirmation:

- Richard A. Paez was first nominated for the 9th Circuit Court of Appeals in January 1996. He has been approved twice by the Judiciary Committee but has never reached a vote on the floor.
- Marsha Berzon was first nominated for the 9th Circuit in January 1998. She has also been approved by the Judiciary Committee but has been blocked on the floor.

"All one has to do is look at the terrible unfairness of someone having to wait 1,300 days, 25 times longer than Ted Stewart, . . . to see how unfair this system is," Minority Leader Tom Daschle, D-S.D., said.

Immediately after defeating the cloture motion, Daschle made two procedural moves to call up the Paez and Berzon nominations. Both were defeated along party lines. *(Votes 282, 283, p. S-55)*

There appears to be little hope for negotiation. "That's not going to happen," Majority Whip Don Nickles, R-Okla., said of a floor vote on Paez. "He's very liberal in an activist way."

Democrats, too, have dug in their heels. Shortly before the cloture vote on Sept. 21, Hatch, Daschle and Patrick J. Leahy of Vermont, the top Democrat on the Judiciary Committee, held a heated discussion on the Senate floor. Hatch offered to bring up five nominees supported by Democrats — but not Paez or Berzon. Daschle, with arms firmly crossed, repeatedly shook his head no.

Slow To Confirm?

During Clinton's seven years in office, 321 judicial nominees have been confirmed. That puts him on track to match the 385 judges President Ronald Reagan appointed during his eight years in office. Still, Democrats charge that the process of confirming judges has become more partisan since Republicans took control of Congress in 1995.

During the 105th Congress, the Senate confirmed 101 judicial nominees. During the 104th Congress, the Senate confirmed 75 nominees.

The last time the Democrats controlled the Senate, during the 103rd Congress, they confirmed 128 of Clinton's nominees.

Hatch says he has tried to work closely with Democrats and the White House to move nominees along.

The Senate has confirmed 15 judges since June. During the first six months of the year, two judicial nominees were confirmed. Thirty-eight nominations are pending in committee, and seven others are awaiting floor votes.

Senate Rejection Of Jurist Draws Charges of Racism

OCTOBER 9 — President Clinton's chances of winning confirmation of judicial nominees in the remaining 15 months of his term are in doubt, after a week filled with charges ranging from racism to political gamesmanship.

The partisan fighting reached a fevered pitch Oct. 6, when Clinton accused Senate Republicans of racism after the chamber rejected the nomination of a black Missouri judge, Ronnie L. White, to a seat on the U.S. District Court.

Clinton's comments capped months of Democratic complaints that the GOP-controlled Senate has unfairly delayed confirmation votes on his nominees, especially women and minorities.

Republicans, in turn, accused Clinton of intentionally nominating unqualified minorities and women to the bench in hopes of painting the GOP as bigoted.

Conservative Republicans also say that Clinton is nominating judges who are too liberal, and they vow to continue delaying confirmations until more "mainstream" nominees are sent to the Senate.

Instead of prodding Republicans into quicker action, furious GOP leaders said Clinton's attack may prompt them to take even longer to review nominees for federal courts.

"They don't get my attention by slapping me in the face," said Idaho Sen. Larry E. Craig, chairman of the Republican Policy Committee. "[Clinton] has clearly tainted the water."

The bitter fighting does not bode well for the 45 judicial nominees who are still awaiting Judiciary Committee or floor action.

In the first 10 months of this session, the Senate has confirmed 21 of Clinton's nominees to the federal bench. Congress is scheduled to adjourn within a month, and observers say there is realistically only a six-month window of opportunity in 2000 before the confirmation process is stalled by election-year politics.

"This seems to be, if not the all-time low, an all-time low," said Sheldon Goldman, a political science professor at the University of Massachusetts at Amherst and author of the book "Picking Federal Judges: Lower Court Selection From Roosevelt Through Reagan."

The partisan bickering "has been ratcheted up to an extent we've never seen before," Goldman said, and it could linger into the first term of the next president.

Rising Tempers

Democratic complaints in recent months have centered on the treatment of two nominees who have been awaiting Senate action for years.

Richard A. Paez, a Hispanic, was first nominated for the 9th Circuit Court of Appeals in January 1996. He has been approved twice by the Judiciary Committee, but his nomination has never come to a vote on the floor.

Marsha Berzon was first nominated for the 9th Circuit in January 1998. She has also been approved by the Judiciary Committee, but her nomination has been blocked on the floor.

To protest the delays, Democrats in late September held a Republican-backed nominee hostage from floor consideration. Ted Stewart, a longtime GOP operative and close friend of Judiciary Committee Chairman Sen. Orrin G. Hatch, R-Utah, was nominated for a District Court seat July 27. He was approved by the Judiciary Committee three days later, and Republican leaders sought to bring him to the floor this fall.

On Sept. 21, Democrats defeated a cloture motion to bring Stewart's nomination to a floor vote.

Hatch attacked the cloture defeat as unprecedented and a dangerous move that could permanently taint the judicial process.

But on Oct. 1, Democrats agreed to allow the Stewart vote in exchange for floor consideration of several other nominees, including White, who was appointed by Democratic Gov. Mel Carnahan in 1995 as the first black on Missouri's Supreme Court.

But Missouri GOP Sen. John Ashcroft took to the floor Oct. 4 to attack White's dissents in death penalty cases and cited opposition to his nomination from several Missouri law enforcement organizations. Democrats countered with statements of support from Carnahan — who is set to challenge Ashcroft in 2000 — and others.

The 45-54 vote on Oct. 5 followed party lines. Several Republicans who supported White in the Judiciary Committee, including Hatch, switched on the floor. Stewart was then confirmed, 93-5. *(White, vote 307; Stewart, vote 308, p. S-61)*

White's rejection marked the first time the full Senate had defeated a judicial nomination since Robert H. Bork was blocked from taking a seat on the Supreme Court in 1987. *(1987 Almanac, p. 271)*

"I am hoping . . . the United States has not reverted to a time in its history when there was a color test on nominations," Sen. Patrick J. Leahy of Vermont, the top Democrat on the Judiciary Committee, said after White's defeat.

Clinton leveled his own charges against Senate Republicans in a Rose Garden ceremony the following day. "The Republican-controlled Senate is adding credence to the perceptions that they treat minority and women judicial nominees unfairly and unequally," Clinton said.

Angry Republicans responded that it was not racism, but rather a fear of overly liberal judges that led to White's defeat and the delay in action on Clinton nominees.

"These are left [wing] appointments," said Sen. Jeff Sessions, R-Ala. Sessions said he is particularly concerned about Clinton's nominations to the 9th Circuit and has placed "holds" on Paez and Berzon. A hold can indefinitely prevent nominations from coming to the Senate floor.

"I don't want them voted on, and I don't want them on the bench," Sessions said.

Sessions said that an inordinately high number of judges on the 9th Circuit Court of Appeals are liberals first nominated by Democratic Presidents Clinton and Jimmy Carter. There are eight Republican-appointed judges and 13 Democratic judges now serving on the court. There are six vacancies, although one will soon be filled by Associate Attorney General Raymond C. Fisher, who won confirmation Oct. 5 by a 69-29 vote. *(Vote 309, p. S-61)*

"This is a legitimate thing for senators to consider," Sessions said. "I hope the White House would start sending mainstream nominees. I'm inclined to believe that until they get the message, we don't intend to vote unless we get some nominees that are more mainstream."

Minority Nominees

The flap over minority nominees has prompted both Democrats and Republicans to dig in their heels.

"We've been real sweet about it. Now we're entering a new phase," said Sen. Barbara Boxer, D-Calif. "Now we're playing hardball."

Boxer, Leahy and Minority Leader Tom Daschle, D-S.D., have threatened to use any means necessary to bring Paez, Berzon and other Clinton nominees to the floor. They have declined to say what their strategy will be, but Daschle said Democrats "will do all we can to see those votes are taken before the end of the year."

Republicans say Democrats are using the race card in order to score political points during next year's elections.

"It's the president's and his party's attempt to set up a series of scenarios that they can then charge the Senate next year as being racist," Craig said. "Maybe they're putting up a lot of nominations they know are unqualified but they think will shape this into a political issue for next year's elections."

Craig and many other Republicans insisted that they did not even know that White was black when they voted against his nomination.

"I can look you in the eye and swear on a Bible that I didn't know what his race was," said Sen. James M. Inhofe, R-Okla., who voted against White.

Senate Majority Leader Trent Lott, R-Miss., noted that of the 21 judges confirmed this year, four were women, one was black and four were Hispanic. "Their records and the kind of judges that the men and women would make are the only thing that has been a factor," Lott said.

A recent study by the bipartisan group Citizens for Independent Courts showed that the Senate in recent years has in fact been slower to confirm women and minorities.

According to the report released Sept. 22, the GOP Senate took an average 33 days longer to confirm female than male nominees in the 104th Congress, and an average of 65 days longer to confirm women in the 105th Congress.

The study also showed that the Senate took an average of 60 days longer to act on minority nominees than whites.

But the study also levied blame against Clinton for delays in filling judicial vacancies. The study found that Clinton has taken longer to nominate judges to fill vacancies than any of his predecessors since Carter.

The Clinton administration has taken an average of 315 days to nominate federal judges to vacancies, compared with 240 days for Carter, 254 days for President Ronald Reagan and

296 days for President George Bush, the study found.

"It's silly for the Congress and the president to be pointing fingers at each other for this judicial crisis — and it is a crisis — when neither has performed well in this area on behalf of the American people," said former Rep. Mickey Edwards, R-Okla. (1977-93), co-chairman of the group.

Future Nominations

Even if Republicans and Democrats can smooth over their differences in the next several months and clear the path for Clinton's nominations, many say a dangerous precedent has been set that could hurt the judicial process for years to come.

Goldman blasted the use of holds to prevent votes on nominees as a "perversion of the judicial process." He added that stalling on nominations will likely continue — and possibly worsen — if Republicans win control of the White House.

"The Democrats are fuming," he said. "If the Republicans get the White House, Democrats will not be in any mood to cooperate — certainly not on judicial nominations."

Standoff on Nominations Intensifies

OCTOBER 30 — Not only did partisan fighting continue to prevent the confirmation of federal judges the week of Oct. 25, but it also intensified to the point that the fates of dozens of others nominated by President Clinton are now in doubt.

Majority Leader Trent Lott, R-Miss., says he will block all civilian nominations until Democrats lift a "hold" on a home-state ally of his, Tupelo Mayor Glenn McCullough, nominated for a six-year term on the Tennessee Valley Authority board.

"It is a package. They all go or none go," Lott told the Senate on Oct. 28, after Democrats objected to his request to launch a procedure leading to the likely confirmation of three federal judges and 27 other midlevel executive branch officials, McCullough among them.

Barbara Boxer, D-Calif., placed a hold on McCullough on Oct. 21, she said, to protest the absence of action on two nominees for seats on the 9th U.S. Circuit Court of Appeals: Richard A. Paez, a federal trial court judge in Los Angeles first nominated in January 1996, and Marsha L. Berzon, a San Francisco attorney first nominated in January 1998.

Democrats have made the Berzon and Paez cases a key exhibit for their contention that Republicans are less inclined to vote to confirm women and racial minorities. But they point chiefly to the Oct. 5 vote against confirming Ronnie L. White, the first black ever on the Missouri Supreme Court, for the federal bench. It was the first time the Senate had defeated a judicial nominee in a dozen years.

"I have no problem with Sen. Lott's nominee," Boxer said of McCullough, "as long as Sen. Lott and the Republican majority also consider those who have been waiting years for a vote."

Republicans say they are blocking Paez and Berzon solely because they view them as too liberal. They emphatically rebut any suggestions their motives are tinged with racism.

Lott said he would not relent in the face of the Democratic move, which he termed shortsighted.

"I do not think it is reasonable to try to hold up one six-year term nominee to try to get two lifetime nominees to the 9th Circuit Court of Appeals, a circuit that already has too many activist judges in it, a circuit that is the most liberal in this country, a circuit . . . basically that is out of control," Lott said on the floor.

The Judicial Conference of the United States terms 21 vacancies on the federal bench — including six on the 9th Circuit — "judicial emergencies." Lott's Oct. 28 proposal included votes to confirm Seattle attorney Ronald M. Gould for the 9th Circuit and women nominees for trial court vacancies in Texas and California.

Those nominees will continue to languish, as will new ones forwarded by committees, until Boxer relents. Lott did, however, allow the confirmation by voice vote Oct. 29 of a roster of routine military and Defense Department nominees.

"Sugar gets you a lot more than sticks," he said in an interview.

Lott Strikes Deal With Democrats, Ending Standoff

NOVEMBER 13 — A three-week partisan standoff over the Senate's priorities for acting on President Clinton's judicial and executive branch nominees ended Nov. 10, allowing six federal judges, a dozen ambassadors and 74 others to win confirmation.

The logjam was broken after Majority Leader Trent Lott, R-Miss., promised Minority Leader Tom Daschle, D-S.D., that by March 15 he would move to begin debate on two of the president's long-stalled picks for the 9th U.S. Circuit Court of Appeals, which has sweeping jurisdiction to review federal trial court rulings from California, seven other Western states and the Pacific territories.

Democrats in turn dropped a countervailing "hold" they had placed on a nominee backed by Lott: Glenn McCullough, the mayor of Tupelo, Miss. He was then confirmed for a seat on the Tennessee Valley Authority board.

Barbara Boxer, D-Calif., moved to block McCullough on Oct. 21 to protest the lack of votes on the nominations of Richard A. Paez, a federal trial court judge in Los Angeles first nominated in 1996, and Marsha L. Berzon, a San Francisco attorney first nominated in 1998. At that point, Lott said he would block all civilian nominations until McCullough's was put to a vote.

Republicans say they have been thwarting votes on Paez and Berzon because they believe the 9th Circuit is already too liberal and the two would only add to its judicial activism. Democrats say their stalled nominations are part of a pattern in which women and racial minorities face a tougher path to confirmation. The racial overtones of the debate peaked Oct. 5 when the Senate rejected the nomination of Ronnie L. White, the first black on the Missouri Supreme Court, for a federal District Court judgeship.

But among the judges Lott called up to be confirmed Nov. 10 were four women, two blacks and a Hispanic. Five were to fill District Court vacancies and one, U.S. District Judge Ann Claire

Williams of Chicago, was promoted to the 7th U.S. Circuit Court of Appeals.

Lott also agreed to push for votes by March 15 on any other judicial nominees forwarded by the Judiciary Committee before the end of this session, even if that means pressing to break a GOP colleague's filibuster. "I do not believe that filibusters of judicial nominations are appropriate," he said.

After that, many more confirmations are unlikely; historically, a president in his last year in office has little success winning confirmations of life-tenured judges from a Senate controlled by the other party.

Among the ambassadors confirmed under the deal was Joseph W. Prueher for China. A separate vote confirmed Carol Moseley-Braun as ambassador to New Zealand.

Before Lott and Daschle struck their deal, other Republicans pressed Clinton not to use his recess appointment powers after Congress adjourns, as some Democrats were advocating.

In a Nov. 10 letter, 17 GOP senators threatened to place holds on all judicial nominees next year if they concluded Clinton had abused his recess appointment powers. "The result would be a complete breakdown in cooperation between our two branches of government on this issue which could prevent the confirmation of any such nominees next year," they wrote.

And Assistant Majority Leader Don Nickles, R-Okla., threatened to move to keep the Senate in session until January in order to prevent recess appointments.

Clinton has used recess appointments in the past to install problematic nominees such as Assistant Attorney General Bill Lann Lee, who was criticized for his views on affirmative action, and James C. Hormel, the first openly homosexual ambassador. After Hormel was installed as envoy to Luxembourg, Clinton agreed to inform Senate leaders when he planned to make recess appointments. ◆

Lawmakers Vote To Overhaul Patent Process, Expedite Publication of Applications

SUMMARY

Congress cleared legislation to overhaul the nation's patent system. including it in the omnibus spending bill (HR 3194). The measure would allow publication of some patents within 18 months of filing, cut some patent filing fees and restructure the U.S. Patent and Trademark Office.

The push to reform the patent system was driven by big businesses, including IBM Corp. and Dow Chemical Co., as a means of resolving disputes between inventors and companies over the ownership of new technology.

In the House, Howard Coble, R-N.C., worked out a deal with a longtime defender of the rights of inventors, Dana Rohrabacher, R-Calif. The key to the deal was an agreement to narrow a provision requiring patent applications to be published within 18 months of filing. The requirement would apply only in cases where similar applications had been filed in a country, such as Japan, that had similar requirements for publishing patent applications.

Some inventors argued that early publication of patent applications would allow foreign companies to take American ideas. But Rohrabacher and other supporters said the bill would protect inventors by giving them the option of keeping applications secret by not filing them abroad.

In the Senate, Judiciary Committee Chairman Orrin G. Hatch, R-Utah, and ranking Democrat Patrick J. Leahy, D-Vt., agreed on a compromise similar to the House bill.

To expedite passage, House and Senate negotiators put patent reform language similar to HR 1907 in the conference report for satellite television bill (HR 1554). The satellite language was later inserted in another bill, HR 1948, which was, in turn, incorporated by reference in the omnibus. It included a House provision calling for a clear separation of the patent and trademark units under the umbrella of the U.S. Patent and Trademark office.

Box Score

- **Bill:** S 1948 (incorporated by reference in HR 3194 — PL 106-113)
- **Legislative action: House** passed HR 1907 (H Rept 106-287), 376-43, Aug. 4.

House adopted conference report on HR 1554 (H Rept 106-464), 411-8, Nov. 9.

House adopted conference report on HR 3194 (H Rept 106-479), 296-135, Nov. 18.

Senate cleared HR 3194, 74-24, on Nov. 19.

President signed HR 3194 on Nov. 29.

House Panel OKs Bill To Speed Up Patent Process

MAY 29 — With opposition evaporating, a bill to revamp the U.S. patent system won the approval of the House Judiciary Committee on May 26 and will move to the House for debate after the Memorial Day recess.

The committee approved the bill (HR 1907) by voice vote two days after the bill's sponsor, Republican Howard Coble of North Carolina, worked out a deal with two opponents, California Republicans Dana Rohrabacher and Tom Campbell. It would be the first overhaul of the patent process since 1952 (PL 82-593).

"We were at each other's throats. But we have now found common ground," Rohrabacher said in an interview May 25.

He and Campbell endorsed the bill

after agreeing with Coble to alter a provision that was intended to speed up patent approvals.

Orrin G. Hatch, R-Utah, who plans to introduce a similar patent overhaul in the Senate, said the compromise in the House would help clear the way for passage of legislation.

"The fact that Rohrabacher is on board will undermine the opposition. Frankly, opponents of this legislation have sometimes not been willing to listen to reason," Hatch said May 26.

Publication Compromise

The key to the House compromise was an agreement by Coble to revise a provision on publication of patent applications. Under current law, patent applications are not released to the public until a patent is issued. This prevents opponents from challenging the patents and big companies from stealing the ideas of independent inventors.

Originally, the bill would have required publication of patents within 18 months after applications were filed. The compromise would require publication within 18 months only when inventors filed duplicate applications in the United States and another country.

Patent applications would continue to remain private until a patent was approved in cases where an application was filed only in the United States.

Rohrabacher said the compromise would give inventors the option of protecting sensitive ideas by filing patent applications in the United States, avoiding the prospect of public disclosure by filing applications abroad.

The bill is intended to protect U.S. patents from foreign inventors who might steal ideas before they are protected, and it brings U.S. patent law in line with that of many foreign nations.

The requirement for publication of patent applications was a prime obstacle to passage of patent overhaul legislation in the 105th Congress. The House passed a bill by voice vote in April 1997, but it died in the Senate. *(1997 Almanac, p. 3-14)*

The Eagle Forum, a conservative group headed by Phyllis Schlafly, warned that the publication of patent applications would effectively give away American technology to foreign manufacturers.

But supporters of an overhaul, including the Intellectual Property Owners Association, which represents about 450 large and small manufacturers, have argued that requiring publication of applications within 18 months of filing would streamline the process, discouraging inventors from trying to delay approval in the hope of collecting greater royalties as new technology makes their inventions more versatile.

"We are hoping Congress will pass this compromise bill. We think it will speed up the system, provide certainty and reduce costs," said Herbert C. Wamsley, executive director of the association.

The bill also would keep the current 20-year life for patents but would set deadlines for patent approval by the Patent and Trademark Office and establish rules for companies to challenge patent applications. It would help companies seek re-examination of existing patents and defend themselves against patent-infringement lawsuits.

Small-Business Opposition

While the bill is expected to win easy passage in the House, it faces continued opposition from Republican Christopher S. Bond of Missouri, chairman of the Senate Small Business Committee. "I still have a number of concerns about the effect of the bill on small business," Bond said May 26. He helped to block a similar bill in the Senate in 1997.

Among the opponents are Nobel Prize-winning scientists and economists, including Franco Modigliani, an economics professor at the Massachusetts Institute of Technology, and the Alliance for American Innovation, a group that represents small inventors and some universities.

Some opponents have questioned the need for an overhaul, including a provision to move the patent office outside the control of the Commerce Department and transform it into a government corporation.

Supporters say that such a move would help ensure that the patent office could keep and use revenue that it raised from fees and eliminate the possibility that the revenue would be diverted to other agencies.

House Passes Bill After GOP Deal On Intellectual Property Rights

AUGUST 7 — The Senate Judiciary Committee will begin work in September on a House-passed bill to overhaul the nation's patent system, amid growing efforts in Congress to help high-tech companies stay competitive in the global marketplace.

House passage of HR 1907, 376-43, on Aug. 4 came after a flurry of negotiations to close a rift among Republicans over measures aimed at protecting intellectual property rights of independent inventors.

The bill would provide the first major overhaul of the nation's patent system since 1952 (PL 82-593).

Despite sporadic opposition, the patent bill is likely to win strong support from both parties this year as they vie for campaign contributions from high-tech firms, which support patent overhaul in order to speed up resolution of disputes over the ownership of new technology.

Senate Majority Leader Trent Lott, R-Miss., included patent reform on an agenda the GOP will pursue to help the high-tech industry.

Lott referred to the need to nurture the growth of companies in the electronics business. "The future of the economy in this country is going to be so tremendously positively impacted by what's happening in this high-tech area," he said Aug. 3.

It is regarded by manufacturers, such as IBM Corp. and Dow Chemical Co., as vital to speed up patent approvals and to help U.S. businesses beat foreign rivals in the race to get patent protection for new products, including computer chips and pharmaceuticals.

But advocates for independent inventors argued that the bill would make their inventions more vulnerable to theft by revealing details about their applications within 18 months of filing and before patents are granted.

"This is a historic bill. I think people will energetically support it when they see what's in it," said Dana Rohrabacher, R-Calif.

He said he would fight to keep key provisions in the House bill, including the earlier publication of some patent applications.

"I want to make sure that we will firmly stand behind the text of this bill in the event of contrary action by the Senate," Rohrabacher said.

Changing the Law

The bill would revise current law, which keeps patent applications confidential until they are approved. Companies have argued change is needed to resolve patent disputes quickly and avoid infringement lawsuits.

The bill would require publication of applications for new patents within 18 months after they are filed, to help companies get advance warning of patent applications that could affect their businesses. It also matches the disclosure policies in Japan and many European nations.

The requirement would not apply if the inventor filed an application only in the United States, or filed in a country that does not publish applications.

In the Senate, provisions in the bill will face close scrutiny from Christopher S. Bond, R-Mo., who has long expressed concern that changes in patent law could hurt small businesses that do not have the resources to defend their patents against larger rivals. A patent system overhaul proposal passed the House by voice vote in 1997, but died in the Senate. *(1997 Almanac, p. 3-14)*

Other critics of patent reform include the Eagle Forum, a conservative group led by political activist Phyllis Schlafly, which says the bill could hurt national security by divulging U.S. technology before it is patented.

Wall Street's Concerns Slow Senate Action

NOVEMBER 6 — Completion of a bill (HR 1907) that would overhaul the nation's patent system and bring it in line with laws in Japan and Europe is likely to be delayed until next year as a result of a push by Wall Street to clarify patent protection of business practices in the financial services industry.

The Senate Judiciary Committee added its own language to the bill by voice vote and then approved HR 1907, 18-0, on Nov. 2. But two Democrats, Charles E. Schumer of New York and Robert G. Torricelli of New Jersey, raised strong concerns about the need for language in the bill to clarify rules for patent protection of practices used in the financial services industry, including formulas used to calculate the value of certain investments.

A 1998 decision by the U.S. Court of Appeals in Washington, D.C., found that patents could be granted for business methods, including data processing systems for operating investment funds for Signature Financial Group Inc., a Boston mutual fund manager. But the ruling left unclear what other types of practices in the financial services industry could be covered by patents.

"We need to get this problem resolved," Schumer said. He said investment bankers were concerned that rival companies could get patents on formulas used to calculate the value of investments and then charge fees for the use of similar formulas.

Judiciary Chairman Orrin G. Hatch, R-Utah, said that he still hoped to move the bill to the Senate floor in the final days of this session. But Schumer and Torricelli hinted they could block the bill if they were not satisfied. The Senate version (S 1798) was sponsored by Hatch and Patrick J. Leahy, D-Vt.

Schumer said one way to resolve confusion about patents on practices used by Wall Street would be to exempt companies using similar financial investment formulas from paying patent royalties. The exemption would apply to companies that could prove they had been using similar practices prior to the granting of a patent.

Both versions of the bill already contain an exemption from patent royalties for companies that can prove they used certain business methods before a patent was granted. But the provisions do not specify whether business methods would include financial investment formulas.

Among the companies with an interest in the patent issues are Merrill Lynch & Co., which has been considering patents related to its consumer cash management program, and investment banker Goldman Sachs & Co., which has expressed concern about patents on financial investment formulas.

One of the main differences in the two bills is that the Senate version would require a study by the General Accounting Office of the effect of patents on business methods on innovation, competition and electronic commerce. Opponents of business method patents contend they could prevent competition in financial services, and in newly developed businesses for retail sales and auctioning of products on the Internet. They hope the study will provide ammunition for restrictions on business method patents. But supporters of such patents contend further study of the issue is not needed.

Another key difference is that the House bill would provide for a restructuring of the U.S. Patent and Trademark Office, separating the patent and trademark operations within the office and providing for separate managers.

Hatch has already begun discussing differences in the two bills with a key sponsor of the House version, Dana Rohrabacher, R-Calif.

Both the House and Senate versions of the bill would require publication of patent applications within 18 months of filing, matching similar requirements in Europe and Japan. But applications filed only in the United States would remain confidential. Both bills would also guarantee patents would last at least 17 years from the time they are issued, resolving complaints about delays in the approval of patents that shorten their effective life. Currently, patents last 20 years from the time the application is filed, but can last less than 17 years from the time a patent is granted if the patent approval process lasts longer than three years. ◆

Lawmakers Compromise On Sentencing Guidelines For Intellectual Property Theft

SUMMARY

The Senate cleared a bill to increase statutory damages for copyright infringement in order to deter software piracy. President Clinton signed the bill (HR 3456 — PL 106-160) on Dec. 9.

Key lawmakers resolved differences between House- and Senate-passed versions of copyright infringement legislation (S 1257). The key compromise was a deal on language calling for development of sentencing guidelines to enforce a 1997 law (PL 105-147) that prohibits software piracy. The bill had been delayed to allow time for Senate confirmation of new members of the U.S. Sentencing Commission, which develops sentencing guidelines for federal judges. The compromise was inserted into a new bill (HR 3456) at the end of session.

The bill would provide for statutory damages ranging from $750 to $30,000 for copyright infringement. The new minimum and maximum amounts for statutory damages would be about 50 percent higher than those in current law.

House Panel Votes To Raise Damages For Copyright Infringement

MAY 22 — The House Judiciary Subcommittee on Courts and Intellectual Property approved by voice vote May 20 a bill (HR 1761) that would increase the amount of statutory damages in copyright infringement cases.

Bill sponsor James E. Rogan, R-Calif., said the current damage amounts have not been adjusted since 1988 and do not accurately reflect inflation. The bill would establish a higher level of damages for those who repeatedly infringe on copyrights — subjecting them to $250,000 in fines, up from $100,000 in current law.

The panel also approved by voice vote May 20 a bill (HR 354) to provide 15-year copyright protection for collections of electronic information such as stock quotes and real estate listings.

House Passes Tougher Penalties For Intellectual Property Theft

AUGUST 7 — In an effort to clamp down on piracy of computer software, music videos and other intellectual property, the House passed a bill Aug. 2 that would increase the statutory penalties in copyright infringement cases.

The bill (HR 1761 — H Rept 106-216), passed by voice vote, would raise the limit on individual statutory damage awards, with even stiffer penalties for repeat offenders.

The measure also would clarify that the overall value of any pirated work should be determined by its retail value — not its street value, which is often lower.

Supporters say the measure is needed because copyright piracy of intellectual property has skyrocketed, made easier by the Internet and other advanced technologies. Industry groups estimate that counterfeiting and piracy of computer software cost the affected copyright holders more than $11 billion last year.

After passing the bill, the House called up a similar Senate bill (S 1257) and inserted the text of HR 1761 — a procedural move that returns the amended bill to the Senate for final action. The Senate had passed its version July 1 by voice vote.

Box Score

- **Bill:** HR 3456 — PL 106-160
- **Legislative action: Senate** passed S 1257 by voice vote July 1.

House passed S 1257 by voice vote Aug. 2, after substituting the text of HR 1761 (H Rept 106-216).

House passed HR 3456 by voice vote Nov. 18.

Senate cleared HR 3456 by voice vote on Nov. 19.

President signed HR 3456 on Dec. 9.

Senate Clears Bill To Target Software Piracy

NOVEMBER 20 — The Senate cleared a bill (HR 3456) by voice vote Nov. 19 to increase statutory damages for copyright infringement by about 50 percent in an effort to crack down on software piracy. The action came after Senate Judiciary Committee Chairman Orrin G. Hatch, R-Utah, and other key lawmakers agreed to a compromise on the bill.

The House passed HR 3456 by voice vote Nov. 18. The bill incorporated many provisions of another bill (HR 1761) passed by the House on Aug. 2.

Like HR 1761, the compromise bill would provide for statutory damages ranging from $750 to $30,000 for copyright infringement. The new minimum and maximum amounts for statutory damages would be about 50 percent higher than the current figures of $500 and $20,000.

The key compromise leading to final passage was a deal on language calling for development of sentencing guidelines to enforce a 1997 law (PL 105-147) that prohibits software piracy.

The earlier House-passed bill called for tougher penalties for software piracy that would be based on the retail price of copyright-protected software, not the value of bootleg copies. But that provision was not included in HR 3456. (*1997 Almanac, p. 3-15*)

The completion of the bill was delayed until this month to allow time for Senate confirmation of new members of the U.S. Sentencing Commission, which develops sentencing guidelines for federal judges. The Senate confirmed seven voting members for the commission Nov. 10, clearing the way for HR 3456. The bill would require the commission to develop sentencing guidelines for software piracy within four months of enactment. ◆

Chapter 19

SCIENCE

Despite Progress in Both Chambers, NASA Funding Authorization Remains Stalled

SUMMARY

Both chambers passed legislation to authorize $41 billion over three years for NASA, but the bill did not get to the stage of a House-Senate conference in the first session.

The House easily passed its NASA reauthorization bill May 19, though the measure drew sharp criticism from the White House and NASA Administrator Daniel S. Goldin. Key objections included the proposed termination of a $75 million satellite that would beam images of Earth to the Internet, a project proposed by Vice President Al Gore. The issue became moot, however, under a provision in the VA-HUD spending bill (HR 2684) that suspended the project pending a study. *(VA-HUD, p. 2-135)*

The Senate on Nov. 5 amended HR 1654, passed it by voice vote and appointed conferees. The bill would cap costs of the International Space Station at $21.9 billion through assembly; the House defeated a similar proposal.

Prospects for a final bill are tempered by the fact that Congress has not completed a NASA reauthorization measure since 1992, preferring to leave funding and policy decisions to be made as part of the VA-HUD spending bill.

Box Score

- **Bill:** HR 1654
- **Legislative action: House** passed HR 1654 (H Rept 106-145), 259-168, May 19.

Senate passed HR 1654, amended, by voice vote Nov. 5.

Senate Committee Approves NASA Reauthorization

MAY 8 — As lawmakers continue to bemoan the rising cost of the International Space Station, the Senate Commerce, Science and Transportation Committee on May 5 clamped a price cap on NASA's share of the project.

The committee approved the spending limit as part of legislation (S 342) to reauthorize the space agency for fiscal years 2000 through 2002. The measure was approved by voice vote.

Congress has not sent a NASA reauthorization bill to the White House since 1992. Since then, funding and policy decisions have been left largely in the hands of appropriators, who provide money for the agency through annual spending bills for veterans and housing programs.

The House Science Committee is scheduled to take up its own NASA authorization bill (HR 1654) May 13.

The Senate bill, sponsored by Science, Technology and Space Subcommittee Chairman Bill Frist, R-Tenn., calls for funding NASA at $13.4 billion in fiscal year 2000, $13.8 billion in fiscal 2001 and $13.9 billion in fiscal 2002.

The authorization bill limits NASA space station costs to $21.9 billion through the assembly phase. It also limits space shuttle launch costs in connection with the station's assembly to $17.7 billion.

During the 105th Congress, Commerce Chairman John McCain, R-Ariz., added a space station cap to a NASA authorization bill (S 1250) that passed the committee in March 1998 but never reached the Senate floor. McCain and other lawmakers have repeatedly criticized the schedule delays and cost overruns that have plagued the project, and some opponents have cited those problems in trying for years without success to kill the station during the appropriations process.

The space station, NASA's showcase project, is the most complex structure ever planned for orbit. A laboratory and living quarters roughly the size of two football fields, it is being built by a partnership of the United States, Russia and 14 other nations. The first U.S. and Russian components were launched last year.

Frist noted at an April 29 hearing that the estimated price for the station's assembly has grown from $17.4 billion in 1997 to as much as $26 billion. The nearly $9 billion difference, he said, is about equal to the original total estimate for the station in 1984.

"While we should continue to applaud many of NASA's achievements in 1998, management and financial problems continue for the International Space Station," Frist said.

Limiting the Cost

NASA officials have expressed reservations about a price cap, emphasizing that the project is a research program and that it is difficult to anticipate future expenses.

But Frist said the legislation gives NASA flexibility. The measure would allow the cap to increase to reflect any costs attributed to inflation or to new technologies that would either improve safety or reduce station costs once assembly was complete.

Many of the space station's problems have been attributed to Russia's inability to deliver crucial components on time because of its ongoing financial crisis. The situation has led NASA to develop backup contingency plans to reduce its primary partner's role.

Some lawmakers want Russia's involvement to be greatly reduced, perhaps to subcontractor status.

"Defending and maintaining the fiction that Russia is capable of discharging its responsibilities gets [the station] nowhere," House Science Committee Chairman F. James Sensenbrenner Jr., R-Wis., wrote in a commentary in the May 10 issue of Space News, a space trade newspaper.

But the costs of delaying the station's assembly until the United States can fully assume Russia's obligations for the space station "would be significant," NASA administrator

Daniel S. Goldin said in testimony to Frist's subcommittee. "The prudent course is to continue to seek Russia's contributions."

Problems with the station have also stemmed from cost overruns by Boeing, the project's prime contractor. The General Accounting Office said last month that Boeing's projected overrun has grown since June from $783 million to $986 million.

The Commerce Committee adopted two amendments to the NASA authorization bill by voice vote. The first, offered by Sens. Conrad Burns, R-Mont., and John D. Rockefeller IV, D-W.Va., would increase funding for the Experimental Program to Stimulate Competitive Research by $45 million over three years. The program provides grants to academic centers for scientific research projects in rural states.

The second amendment, which was offered by Majority Leader Trent Lott, R-Miss., would add over three years: $95 million for space shuttle safety and performance upgrades, $92.7 million for academic programs and $580 million for planning of future shuttle launches.

House Panel Rejects Gore's Satellite Proposal

MAY 15 — A satellite that would transmit images of Earth to the Internet — a project proposed by Vice President Al Gore — has led to a showdown over legislation to reauthorize NASA.

The House Science Committee on May 13 voted along party lines, 21-18, to terminate the $75 million Triana project and transfer the funding to other space research programs. Democrats described the vote as a political shot at Gore, while Republicans dismissed the project as a waste of money.

The vote was on an amendment to legislation to authorize NASA (HR 1654) for fiscal years 2000 through 2002. The committee subsequently approved NASA's reauthorization, 27-13.

But the Republican victory over Gore may be short-lived. The Senate's NASA authorization bill (S 342) does not include the Triana amendment, and the space agency considers the project important enough to recommend a veto to President Clinton if the amendment remains in the bill.

Science Committee members are eager to have Clinton sign a NASA bill. Congress has not sent reauthorization legislation for the agency to the White House since 1992, leaving funding and policy decisions in the hands of appropriators, who provide money to NASA through annual spending bills for veterans and housing programs.

Science Committee Chairman F. James Sensenbrenner Jr., R-Wis., said the House may consider the bill as early as the week of May 17. The Senate Commerce, Science & Transportation Committee approved its version (S 342) earlier this month.

The House bill, sponsored by Space and Aeronautics Subcommittee Chairman Dana Rohrabacher, R-Calif., would fund NASA at $13.6 billion in fiscal year 2000, $13.7 billion in fiscal 2001 and $13.8 billion in fiscal 2002.

The Triana project calls for sending a camera-equipped satellite into orbit next year that could transmit a color image of the entire sunlit side of Earth to the Internet. NASA selected the Scripps Institution of Oceanography to undertake the mission after the vice president suggested it last year.

Although some space policy analysts have dismissed the mission as a campaign stunt, NASA officials maintain that the project would help scientists better understand global climate patterns and the degree to which the sun's energy is absorbed in the atmosphere.

"This is a real important scientific experiment," NASA Administrator Daniel S. Goldin said in an April 14 interview. "If the vice president of the United States happened to come up with the idea, instead of criticizing him, maybe we ought to say, 'Thank you, Mr. Vice President.' "

But committee members Dave Weldon, R-Fla., and George Nethercutt, R-Wash., who offered the amendment to terminate Triana, argued that the project was never subject to advance review and that NASA has better ways to spend its money.

"Is this the best science NASA can get for $75 million in taxpayers' money?" Weldon said. "That question has not ever been answered. It has not even been asked."

Nethercutt said canceling Triana would help other scientific endeavors. "If we cut this one project, we're enabling hundreds of new primary investigators to receive funding," he said.

Not a Pretty Picture

But Bart Gordon, D-Tenn., accused GOP members of wanting only to score political points against Gore, the current Democratic front-runner to succeed Clinton. Gore has been ridiculed for saying he invented the Internet.

The Republican National Committee has sought to make an issue of Triana, noting that images of Earth already are available on the Internet. NASA officials say those images are not as useful because they have been stitched together from different satellites.

Gordon said Goldin told him he would recommend a veto if the Triana amendment is included. "This really is a political effort to sink this program, which, in turn, will sink this bill," Gordon said.

On another area, Gordon and other Democrats expressed concern over language in the House bill that would prohibit NASA from spending money on an inflatable module called TransHab as a home for astronauts on the International Space Station. NASA is testing the module as an alternative to the planned aluminum quarters.

Sensenbrenner said the language was added because GOP members are concerned that TransHab might lead to a redesign of the station. "If the station is going to stay on schedule, we've got to stick with the existing design," he said.

Unlike the Senate bill, the House version does not contain a price cap on the space station, NASA's showcase project. House members have joined senators in criticizing the schedule delays and cost overruns that have plagued the station, but have heeded NASA's assertion that a price cap could hurt its flexibility in building the orbiting laboratory and living quarters.

House Passes NASA Bill; Tough Conference Awaits

MAY 22 — Congressional supporters of the space program won a victory May 19 with House passage of legislation to reauthorize NASA for the next three years. But the legislation still faces a controversial conference with the Senate — and a possible presidential veto — because of several partisan sticking points left in the bill.

The measure (HR 1654), passed 259-168, would provide the space agency with $13.6 billion in fiscal 2000, $13.7 billion in fiscal 2001 and $13.8 billion in fiscal 2002, including $6.9 billion for the International Space Station, NASA's showcase project. *(Vote 139, p. H-54)*

But the bill exposed the raw partisan tensions that have engulfed the House in recent months. Many Democrats who strongly support NASA's activities cast votes against it.

The Democrats cited language sought by House Science Committee Republicans to cancel a $75 million satellite project proposed by Vice President Al Gore. Although Republicans described the Triana project as a waste of money, Democrats and the Clinton administration complained that targeting the project amounted to a political shot at their party's front-runner for the 2000 presidential nomination.

"We strongly object to the [Science] committee's arbitrary and partisan recommendation to terminate the Triana science mission," NASA Administrator Daniel S. Goldin wrote in a May 20 letter, warning that he would recommend a veto if the Triana language was included.

Goldin and the Office of Management and Budget also cited objections to other parts of the bill, including restrictions on the use of space station research funds as well as language prohibiting NASA from spending money on TransHab, an inflatable module, as a home for astronauts on the space station. The Senate's NASA authorization bill (S 342) does not contain those initiatives.

The resulting vote left some House Republican critics of Triana aware they are unlikely to prevail. Nevertheless, they expressed satisfaction that they got to register their objections to the project.

Science Committee members are anxious to have President Clinton sign a NASA authorization bill into law. No reauthorization of the agency has been sent to the White House since 1992, leaving funding and policy decisions in the hands of appropriators, who provide money to NASA through annual spending bills for veterans and housing programs.

"The onus should be on the president to get [the Triana language] put back in," said Rep. Dave Weldon, R-Fla. "If it gets restored, we know it's Clinton and Gore who got it restored. I can live with that."

Triana, named for the sailor aboard Christopher Columbus' ship who first saw the New World in 1492, is designed to study global climate and solar energy patterns. It calls for sending a camera-equipped satellite into orbit next year that could transmit a full-color image of the entire sunlit side of Earth to the Internet.

Although some Republicans and space policy analysts have noted that images of Earth already are available on the Internet, NASA officials said those images have been stitched together from various satellites. Other than a few short-duration missions, they said, NASA has not had a spacecraft provide a full view of Earth since the days of the Apollo program.

NASA selected the Scripps Institution of Oceanography in San Diego to undertake the mission after Gore suggested it last year, reportedly after coming up with the idea at home one night.

Weldon joined George Nethercutt, R-Wash., in offering the amendment to kill Triana that passed the Science Committee in a vote along party lines. The amendment called for transferring $32.6 million in proposed spending for Triana to research involving the low-gravity environment in space.

"We think it is more important to spend $32 million on medical research than on funding the vice president's late-night inspiration for a multimillion-dollar screen saver called Triana," said House Science Committee Chairman F. James Sensenbrenner Jr., R-Wis. He lamented a statement by a Gore spokesman in The Washington Post on May 19 calling Republicans "the party of troglodytes" for opposing the project.

Weldon noted that NASA was forced to lay off 600 workers at the Kennedy Space Center in his district around the time Gore came up with the inspiration for the project. "To do nothing and say nothing about this, in light of what happened to the men and women who got laid off in my district, would be an insult," he said.

But Bart Gordon of Tennessee, the ranking Democrat on the Space and Aeronautics Subcommittee, dismissed such remarks as "totally parochial, totally partisan. . . . This bill and this committee deserve better."

Other Problems

Gordon pointed to several other problems with the NASA bill in citing his opposition to the measure. Among them was the TransHab prohibition language, which Republicans said they included because of fears it would lead to a redesign of the space station.

TransHab is being developed at NASA's Johnson Space Center southeast of Houston. Rep. Nick Lampson, D-Texas, whose district includes the space center, said he decided not to offer an amendment to restore funding for the project after Sensenbrenner held open the possibility that the Science Committee would hold a separate hearing on it.

But other Democrats did not shy away from offering amendments to challenge other features of the bill. One of them was Rep. Tim Roemer, D-Ind., who used the NASA authorization bill as an opportunity to renew his criticism of the space station.

A laboratory and living quarters the size of two football fields, the station is being built by a partnership of the United States, Russia and 14 other nations. The first U.S. and Russian components were launched last year.

Roemer and other critics have noted the estimated price for the station's assembly has grown from $17.4 billion to as much as $26 billion.

The nearly $9 billion difference, they say, is about equal to the original total estimate for the station in 1984.

Roemer offered three unsuccessful amendments related to the space station. One would have imposed a price cap on the project of $21.9 billion through assembly and capped space shuttle launch costs in connection with assembly at $17.7 billion.

The Senate's authorization bill includes similar price cap language added at the insistence of Commerce, Science and Transportation Committee Chairman John McCain, R-Ariz., a space station supporter. But the House voted to kill Roemer's amendment, 114-315. *(Vote 135, p. H-52)*

Roemer's other two proposals also were resoundingly rejected. An amendment to remove Russia as a primary partner in the station was defeated, 117-313. *(Vote 136, p. H-52)*

Another amendment to terminate the project lost 92-337 — a margin of victory that station supporters said was so dramatic it should lay to rest any doubts about Congress' enthusiasm for the project. *(Vote 137, p. H-52)*

"The ground-based hardware [for the station] is 82 percent complete," Sensenbrenner said. "If we adopt this amendment . . . that hardware will not go to orbit but will end up in museums around the country as an exhibit of Congress' foolishness in defunding the program when it was close to completion."

But the House approved an amendment offered by Anthony Weiner, D-N.Y., to add an average of $10 million over each of the next three years for aircraft noise reduction research. The amendment was narrowly adopted on a 225-203 vote. *(Vote 134, p. H-52)*

Sensenbrenner and other Republican critics of the amendment noted that NASA already has added $25.3 million to the original $46 million dedicated for noise reduction research over the next three years and that it would be fiscally irresponsible to spend any more.

Weiner and other Democrats argued, however, that more research needs to be done to make airports quieter in light of action on pending legislation (HR 1000) to reauthorize the Federal Aviation Administration.

"We are going to be passing an FAA reauthorization bill that I believe is going to, regardless of how it emerges, increase air traffic," Weiner said. "There are proposals to almost entirely deregulate all of our airports. That is going to mean another increase in air noise."

Another Investigation

The NASA authorization bill includes funding to continue the agency's ongoing work on advanced space transportation technologies. Sensenbrenner pointed to a recent string of six military and commercial launch failures "that have reminded us how critical reliable, low-cost access to space is for our economy, our scientific endeavors and our national security."

Clinton on May 19 directed Defense Secretary William S. Cohen to provide a report on why the space launches failed. "It is vitally important that we fully understand the root causes behind the recent launch vehicle failures and take corrective action," Clinton said in a memo to Cohen.

In another space-related development, the General Accounting Office released a report May 20 showing that NASA's computer systems are vulnerable to attack. The GAO found that 135 of 155 systems reviewed did not meet all of the space agency's requirements for risk assessment and that NASA has not conducted an agency-wide review of its security since 1991.

"These findings are troubling," said Senate Governmental Affairs Chairman Fred Thompson, R-Tenn. "NASA spent more than $1 billion last year on information systems to support a wide range of critical missions. . . . Now we're learning that the security and integrity of many of these computing systems is vulnerable to attack. At the same time, there is no security training system in place and security incidents are not being reported. That's unacceptable."

Senate Passes Three-Year NASA Authorization

NOVEMBER 6 — After months of delay, the Senate on Nov. 5 passed legislation to reauthorize NASA for fiscal years 2000-02. But Senate aides said a House-Senate conference on the bill appears unlikely this year.

The Senate passed the bill (HR 1654) by voice vote. The Commerce, Science and Transportation Committee had approved it in May. But the bill encountered a series of delays. Most recently, it had been held up for weeks after Paul Wellstone, D-Minn., insisted on the right to offer an unrelated amendment to pending Senate legislation that would impose a moratorium on mergers and acquisitions among large agribusinesses.

To ensure that GOP leaders would comply, Wellstone blocked Senate floor action on several bills that Republicans hoped to pass by unanimous consent. Wellstone subsequently lifted his objection.

Another space-related bill that Wellstone had blocked is likely to pass the Senate before adjournment this year. That measure (S 832) would renew government indemnification of commercial U.S. space launch companies, allowing them to keep their prices competitive with foreign launch facilities. ◆

Lawmakers Vote To Extend Risk-Sharing Arrangement For Space Launches

SUMMARY

The House passed a five-year extension of the government-industry arrangement for sharing the risk of space launches (HR 2607), but the Senate did not vote on a companion bill (S 382). A one-year extension was included in the the fiscal 2000 spending bill for the departments of Veterans Affairs and Housing and Urban Development (HR 2684 — PL 106-74). *(VA-HUD, p. 2-135)*

The risk-sharing arrangement, known as indemnification, is one of the aerospace industry's top legislative priorities. Enacted in 1984 (PL 98-375), the law requires launch companies to insure each commercial launch privately for up to $500 million, with the government covering liability claims beyond that. Without the law, which was set to expire Dec. 31, U.S. launch providers say they could not buy insurance at rates that would allow them to compete with foreign companies. The Senate is expected to take up the long-term extension as a separate bill next year.

Box Score

- **Bill:** HR 2684 — PL 106-74; HR 2607, S 832
- **Legislative action: Senate** Commerce Committee approved S 832 (S Rept 106-135) by voice vote on June 23.

House passed HR 2607 by voice vote on Oct. 4.

President signed HR 2607 on Oct. 20.

Senate Committee OKs Bill To Help Aerospace Industry

JUNE 26 — The Senate Commerce, Science and Transportation Committee approved a bill (S 832) on June 23 that would limit for 10 years the amount of liability insurance coverage needed by commercial launch companies.

The proposal, approved by voice vote, is a priority of the U.S. aerospace industry. Under current indemnification law, if the federal government licensed a company or contractor before Dec. 31, 1999, to conduct space launches, the government would pay for third-party claims in excess of $500 million for deaths, injuries and other damages resulting from a launch.

Industry officials have warned that if the indemnification law is not renewed when it expires at the end of the year, U.S. launch providers would not be able to obtain greatly reduced insurance rates, placing them at a competitive disadvantage with space manufacturers in other countries.

"The importance of this congressionally sanctioned risk-sharing arrangement in encouraging technology innovation and increasing U.S. competitiveness cannot be overstated," Patricia A. Mahoney, chairman of the Satellite Industry Association, told the House Science Committee's Space and Aeronautics Subcommittee on April 21.

Senate Commerce Chairman John McCain, R-Ariz., has noted that space launches of U.S.-made satellites in China apparently enabled the Chinese to gain access to sensitive technology. He said lawmakers must do more to encourage companies to launch in the United States.

A bipartisan House committee led by Rep. Christopher Cox, R-Calif., which recently investigated China's acquisition of U.S. technology, recommended that Congress pass legislation to stimulate the expansion of the U.S. space launch industry.

"If we expect a more competitive commercial U.S. space launch industry to evolve, we must extend indemnification," McCain said.

But Ernest F. Hollings of South Carolina, the committee's ranking Democrat, criticized the program as "a 10-year subsidy to the richest industry there is." Hollings offered an amendment seeking to limit the extension of indemnification to three years. But Hollings withdrew his amendment after McCain promised to seek a compromise of between three years and 10 years.

The House has not begun work on the issue. Space and Aeronautics Subcommittee Chairman Dana Rohrabacher, R-Calif., said June 10 that he plans within a month to introduce a five-year renewal of indemnification authority "along with a process for guiding its future, longer-term renewal."

Bipartisan Deal Readies Bill For Senate Floor

JULY 24 — An agreement is at hand between Senate Commerce, Science and Transportation Committee Republicans and Democrats on one of the aerospace industry's top legislative priorities, clearing the way for floor action before the recess.

The legislation (S 832) would renew government indemnification of commercial U.S. space launch companies, allowing them to keep their prices competitive with foreign launch facilities. Unless Congress acts, the indemnification provisions of the Commercial Space Launch Act of 1984 (PL 98-575) will expire Dec. 31. *(1984 Almanac, p. 195)*

Under that law, launch companies must insure each commercial launch privately for up to $500 million. The government covers liability claims beyond that amount.

When the Commerce Committee approved the bill June 23, ranking Democrat Ernest F. Hollings of South Carolina objected to extending the indemnification for 10 years. Hollings offered an amendment to cut the time to three years, but he withdrew it after

Chairman John McCain, R-Ariz., promised to seek a compromise.

A GOP Commerce aide said both sides appear ready to agree to a five-year extension. The aide said the legislation could pass the Senate by unanimous consent before the August recess.

Republican Dana Rohrabacher of California, chairman of the House Science Committee's Space and Aeronautics Subcommittee, said he, too, expects to introduce legislation soon that calls for a five-year extension of indemnification authority, "along with a process for guiding its future, longer-term renewal."

Hollings has criticized the legislation as "a subsidy to the richest industry there is." But industry officials contend that, without the measure, U.S. launch providers would face sky-high insurance rates, putting them at a competitive disadvantage with space companies abroad.

House Panel Gives Thumbs Up To Space Launch Bill

JULY 31 — The House Science Space and Aeronautics Subcommittee on July 29 approved a bill to renew government indemnification of commercial U.S. space launch companies for five years.

The bill (HR 2607), approved by voice vote, is one of the aerospace industry's top priorities. Science Committee Chairman F. James Sensenbrenner Jr., R-Wis., said he expects the full panel to act on it the week of Aug. 2.

Unless Congress acts, the indemnification provisions of the Commercial Space Launch Act of 1984 (PL 98-575) will expire Dec. 31. Under that law, launch companies must insure each commercial launch privately for up to $500 million, with the government covering liability claims beyond that amount. *(1984 Almanac, p. 195)*

Space launch companies say the indemnification measure allows them to keep their prices competitive with foreign launch facilities.

House Passes Bill To Extend Aerospace Deal

OCTOBER 9 — The aerospace industry won House passage Oct. 4 of one of its top legislative priorities: an extension of the government-industry arrangement for sharing the risk of space launches, known as indemnification. The House passed the bill (HR 2607) by voice vote.

Without new legislation, the indemnification provisions of the Commercial Space Launch Act of 1984 (PL 98-575) will expire Dec. 31. Under that law, launch companies must insure each commercial launch privately for up to $500 million, with the government covering liability claims beyond that amount. *(1984 Almanac, p. 195)*

The House-passed bill would authorize $31.4 million in fiscal years 1999-2002 for the Transportation Department's Office of Commercial Space Transportation, and $1.7 million in fiscal 2000-02 for the new Office of Space Commercialization at the Commerce Department.

The Transportation secretary would be required to give Congress a long-term report on risk sharing, aimed at ensuring future U.S. competitiveness in the international launch market.

Bill supporters say that if the indemnification law is not renewed, U.S. launch providers will be unable to obtain the reduced insurance rates that allow them to remain competitive with foreign companies.

A similar bill (S 832 — S Rept 106-135) was approved by the Senate Commerce Committee on June 23. It would provide a 10-year extension of the law. ◆

Chapter 20

SOCIAL POLICY

Jobs Program for Seniors Snags Reauthorization Of Older Americans Act

Box Score

- **Bill:** HR 782
- **Legislative action: House** Education and the Workforce Committee approved HR 782 (H Rept 106-343) by voice vote Sept. 15.

SUMMARY

House efforts to reauthorize the Older Americans Act (PL 89-73) came to a halt in October, a month after the House Education and the Workforce Committee marked up the bill. There was no Senate action.

The Older Americans Act, which covers programs such as Meals on Wheels, nursing home assistance, legal aid and subsidized senior centers, has not been reauthorized since 1995. Many lawmakers viewed 1999 as an opportunity to finally complete a rewrite, as Congress looked for ways to court the seniors' vote in 2000. Also, two conservatives who are willing to work across party lines —Republican Rep. Howard P. "Buck" McKeon of California and Republican Sen. Mike DeWine of Ohio — were leading the effort.

But despite the promising outlook early in the year, the bill became caught up in turmoil, mostly over a seniors' jobs program, which places people 55 and older in part-time, community service jobs. The program has been the target of many conservative Republicans who view it as an inefficient handout to liberal groups. The jobs program has been run for decades by 10 nonprofit organizations, including Green Thumb and affiliates of the AARP and the National Council of Senior Citizens.

Funding was allocated under a formula that gave 78 percent to the community organizations and 22 percent to states. The bill approved by the Education and the Workforce Committee would have gradually changed that formula to a 55-45 group-state split. Faced with losing part of their quasi-entitlement, the groups launched a campaign to kill the bill.

Democrats blamed Republicans in part for the setback. Others cited concerns about provisions that would have rewritten a nursing home ombudsman program and cut legal aid services.

The jobs program has been a major sticking point on the Senate side as well.

A reauthorization is not likely next year unless members can find a way to bridge their differences over the jobs program. Some members have said a straight continuation of existing programs may be a fallback position.

House Panel Approves Rewrite Of Popular Program For Seniors

SEPTEMBER 18 — The House Education and the Workforce Committee on Sept. 15 approved an Older Americans Act rewrite (HR 782) that would reduce funds for 10 nonprofit groups that have long operated jobs programs for seniors. The money would instead be shifted to the states.

The bill, approved by voice vote after five years of partisan bickering, includes a provision for a new $125 million-per-year family caregiver program. The program, based on a proposal by President Clinton, would give states grants to provide counseling and information to people who care for elderly relatives. It would help provide respite care and help families find needed services.

Despite bipartisan support for the bill, which authorizes Meals on Wheels, senior centers, transportation and legal services for millions of the elderly, it faces a fight when it reaches the floor, possibly the week of Sept. 20.

Labor Secretary Alexis M. Herman, in a Sept. 15 letter to lawmakers, said the cuts in the employment program were "unacceptable" and would "significantly diminish" its effectiveness. More than 120 members have signed a separate letter opposing the changes.

Committee Chairman Bill Goodling, R-Pa., said an overhaul was essential, noting that the same organizations, including the AARP Foundation (an affiliate of the AARP), National Senior Citizens Education and Research Center, National Urban League and Green Thumb — have automatically received funds every year under the current $440 million program.

"How can you tell 10 groups that from now until the end of time — with no competition whatsoever — you should just continue to receive this money?" Goodling said.

The situation is complicated by antipathy on the part of some Republicans to one specific group — the National Senior Citizens Education and Research Center, which is affiliated with the National Council of Senior Citizens. The council has been a vociferous opponent of GOP plans to revamp Medicare. Further, a recent Department of Labor audit questioned how the council had accounted for millions of dollars of health benefits under its annual job program grant.

Democrats Fight Back

The committee by voice vote defeated an amendment by Rep. Robert E. Andrews, D-N.J., that would have continued the current funding formula for the program. Andrews argued that existing grantees had a better job placement record than states.

A similar amendment is expected when the House debates the bill, as is a possible effort to exempt Green Thumb — the largest provider — from cuts.

Andrea Wooten, president of Green Thumb, said the group has not taken a position on the plan.

"We are not working for an exemption. . . ." Wooten said after the markup. "We are in a difficult position on this."

Currently, funds for the part-time employment program are distributed under a formula, developed by appropriators, that gives 78 percent to nonprofits and 22 percent to states. The committee bill would, over five years, phase in a new formula providing 55 percent of annual grants to the groups and 45 percent to states.

The program's contractors have been working together to stave off cuts. Some of the top Democrats on the committee, including ranking member William L. Clay of Missouri and Matthew G. Martinez of California, have agreed to support the rewrite in order to get the larger bill moving.

Further, the Senate Health, Education, Labor and Pensions Committee is moving more slowly on reauthorization.

The Older Americans Act (PL 89-73) may be one of the most popular laws ever passed by Congress. For the past five years it has also been one of the most controversial. The program's authorization lapsed in 1995, though appropriators have continued to provide about $1.5 billion in annual funding. *(1995 Almanac, p. 7-54)*

While there is broad support for the basic intent of the law, Republicans have tried to rewrite portions of it, including an unsuccessful effort to turn Meals on Wheels into a state block grant. There was also an effort to eliminate a provision that gives low-income minority seniors priority for aid on the grounds it was affirmative action. This time around, Martinez, Howard P. "Buck" McKeon, R-Calif., and Bill Barrett, R-Neb., teamed up to work out a compromise.

The bill would continue the minority-targeting language. The panel also approved an amendment by voice vote to give preference to seniors in rural areas in determining who receives aid. It would direct more aid to native Americans; would give states more flexibility to shift funds from congregate meals served in senior centers to home delivered meals; and consolidate programs for long-term care ombudsmen and elder abuse prevention.

House Drops Bill After Outcry Over Jobs Program

OCTOBER 9 — House Republicans have abruptly abandoned efforts to reauthorize the Older Americans Act for the remainder of the year, and possibly the rest of this Congress.

A bill (HR 782) to reauthorize the 35-year-old law (PL 89-73), which governs Meals on Wheels, senior centers, transportation services and other popular programs, had been scheduled for the suspension calender on Oct 4.

GOP leaders yanked the bill, however, after receiving dozens of phone calls from lawmakers worried about provisions to reduce funding for a longstanding seniors' jobs program.

The employment program, which places people 55 and older in part-time, community service jobs, has been run for decades by 10 nonprofit groups, including Green Thumb and affiliates of the AARP and the National Council of Senior Citizens.

The groups automatically receive annual funding and do not compete to provide services. In fiscal 1999, Congress appropriated $440 million for the program. The money was allocated under a formula that gave 78 percent to the groups and 22 percent to states.

The bill reported out of the Education and the Workforce Committee would have gradually changed that formula to a 55-45 group-state split.

Faced with losing part of their quasi-entitlement, the groups launched a campaign to kill the bill.

"They [job sponsors] have so much clout here and they're just at the trough. . . . They want the money to come continually to them," said Rep. Howard P. "Buck" McKeon, R-Calif., one of the chief sponsors of the measure. He said he and committee chairman Bill Goodling, R-Pa., had agreed to drop efforts to move the bill.

Democrats blamed Republicans in part for the setback, saying they never should have tried to bring up the bill on the suspension calender. Bills considered under suspension need a two-thirds majority to pass. No amendments are allowed.

Rep. Jo Ann Emerson, R-Mo., had hoped to offer an amendment on the floor to ensure that Green Thumb, which concentrates on helping rural senior citizens, was exempt from the cuts.

In an Oct. 4 letter, the senior citizens group AARP urged lawmakers to vote against the bill, calling it "seriously flawed" and urging Congress to pass a straight reauthorization of existing law. Others cited concerns about provisions that would have rewritten a nursing home ombudsman program and cut legal aid services. Some lawmakers said a straight continuation of existing programs may be a fallback option.

The House dustup is just the latest in a series of complications for the act, which has been without a reauthorization since 1995. The two parties have fought over Republican efforts to turn Meals on Wheels into a block grant, end funding to what GOP lawmakers called left-leaning groups and eliminate provisions of the law giving low-income minority seniors first priority for aid. Some Republicans consider that affirmative action.

With McKeon and Sen. Mike DeWine, R-Ohio, leading the effort this year, many had hoped that a reauthorization would finally move. Both have reputations as conservatives who are willing to work across party lines.

DeWine, chairman of a Health, Education, Labor and Pensions subcommittee, said on Oct. 6 that he had not given up efforts to rewrite the act. "What the House has done is irrelevant to us. We intend to proceed," he said.

He has his own obstacles, however. The jobs program is a major sticking point on the Senate side as well. In particular, some members are opposed to inclusion of the National Council of Senior Citizens. The council, which has close ties to organized labor, has been one of the most vociferous opponents of GOP Medicare proposals. It is the subject of a Department of Labor audit questioning payment of some health benefits under the job program. ◆

Congress, White House At Odds Over How Best To Protect Social Security

SUMMARY

This was supposed to be the year lawmakers and President Clinton joined together to tackle the tough issue of Social Security's long-term solvency. Instead, as they have so many times before, legislative efforts foundered while Republicans and Democrats sparred over which party was more dedicated to protecting the retirement program.

Social Security, which provides retirement, disability and survivors' benefits for 44 million Americans, is now running a trust fund surplus. Because of the aging of the Baby Boom generation and increased life expectancies, however, the program's long-term fiscal outlook is bleak. Beginning in 2014, it will begin paying out more in benefits than it collects through its 12.4 percent payroll tax. Unless there are changes to the program, the trust fund will be depleted by 2034.

Clinton in 1998 launched a broad public relations effort, including a series of national "town hall" meetings, that was supposed to build public awareness of and support for overhaul efforts. In his Jan. 19, 1999, State of the Union address, the president outlined a proposal that called for the government to directly invest about 15 percent of the program's trust fund in the stock market in an effort to realize higher financial returns. The plan envisioned "reinvesting" the projected Social Security surplus in the program, a sharp break from the traditional practice of using the surplus to pay for other domestic programs. *(Text, p. D-5)*

House Republicans were critical of Clinton's plan for direct investment, many pushing instead to allow individuals to invest all or a portion of their payroll taxes in the financial markets. During congressional hearings, the GOP and some Democrats charged that Clinton's plan would, in effect, double-count Social Security revenues.

On April 28, House Ways and Means Committee Chairman Bill Archer, R-Texas, and Social Security Subcommittee Chairman E. Clay Shaw, R-Fla., unveiled an alternative that would let individuals invest, through a refundable tax credit, a portion of their payroll taxes in the private markets. Individuals would choose from a government-approved list of investment vehicles. The plan would ensure that no one got a lower benefit under the proposed system than they would have gotten under current law. A bill was never formally introduced.

Instead of a broad rewrite of the program, Republican leaders concentrated on ensuring that Congress did not tap into the Social Security surplus in the fiscal 2000 spending bills. They pushed a bill to create a so-called lockbox. On Oct. 28, at the White House's request, Democrats introduced an altered version (HR 3165) of Clinton's original plan that dropped direct investment, but would continue caps on discretionary spending. *(Lockbox, p. 6-20)*

Shaw has been trying to build support for a Ways and Means Committee markup. With the 2000 elections approaching, supporters see little chance for major action.

Clinton's Plan Stirs Controversy, As Well as Hope For Compromise

JANUARY 23 — On its face, President Clinton's proposal to channel hundreds of billions of dollars in Social Security revenues into the stock market represented a bold stroke to harness the power of Wall Street to shore up the popular retirement program.

Underneath the plan, however, lies the cautiousness of a first-time investor.

The president's proposal would leave the basic structure of the Social Security program intact. For some people — such as poor widows — he even proposed increasing benefits. Most significantly, he veered away from what administration officials believe is a riskier proposition of replacing a portion of Social Security with private retirement accounts that individuals could invest as they saw fit.

Since he called on Congress to "save Social Security" in his 1998 State of the Union address, Clinton has been under pressure from Republicans to come up with a blueprint on how to do that.

The result was a proposal that satisfied many Democrats, who had worried that the White House would embrace calls from GOP lawmakers and private industry for using the market-based accounts as a substitute, not a supplement, for basic program benefits. It angered many Republicans, who said the plan would amount to an unsustainable, big-government approach that did not address the program's long-term solvency.

Under the plan, about $2.8 trillion of the projected budget surplus would be used to bolster Social Security over the next 15 years. The government would invest a quarter of that amount in the stock market. It would use another $33 billion a year to create federally funded retirement savings accounts for low- and middle-income workers separate from Social Security.

The plan goes only about halfway toward the goal of keeping Social Security solvent for 75 years. Rather than proposing benefit cuts or tax increases to fill the remaining gap, the White House issued a vague call for Congress to make "difficult but fully achievable choices" on a bipartisan basis.

"The president is standing on the diving board instead of jumping in the pool," said Republican Sen. Charles E. Grassley of Iowa.

Democrats protested that Clinton had met GOP demands to unveil a detailed plan and said that despite the differences, it could form the basis for bipartisan negotiations.

"They [Republicans] have to stop setting the president up for failure," said Robert T. Matsui of California, the ranking Democrat on the House Ways and Means Social Security Subcommittee.

Opening the Debate

Republicans have been at the forefront of efforts to tie Social Security to the stock market, saying the government is wasting an opportunity to increase the program's financial returns. But they want individuals — not Washington — to make investment decisions.

"The president's suggestion that Social Security reform starts with government intervention in the stock market is plain wrong," said House Speaker J. Dennis Hastert, R-Ill.

Republican criticisms were seconded Jan. 20 by influential Federal Reserve Board Chairman Alan Greenspan. In testimony before the Ways and Means Committee, Greenspan reiterated his argument that it would be impossible to insulate federal investments from politics.

But he generally endorsed the administration's effort to reserve the surplus for Social Security first.

Moderates of both parties worried that instead of preparing Americans for difficult reductions in Social Security and other entitlement programs as the Baby Boom generation ages, the White House had made an impossible promise of increased retirement aid.

"His proposal established a bipartisan framework for dealing with long-term reforms," said Rep. Charles W. Stenholm, D-Texas. "The bad part is he ducked all the heavy lifting. Depending on surplus projections that may not materialize . . . that's not going to find bipartisan support."

Complicating the debate — but possibly providing an opening for compromise — is the fact that the future of Social Security is tangled up in a larger, emerging fight over the budget surplus.

Democrats attacked House Republicans in the 1998 election campaigns for voting for an $80.1 billion tax cut that would have been funded largely through the surplus, calling it an attack on Clinton's proposal to save Social Security first. The Senate did not take up the tax cut.

This year, the House and Senate GOP are so far working in unison. They hope to tap into the surplus to fund an across-the-board tax cut of at least 10 percent.

Aside from Social Security, the administration has proposed reserving part of the surplus to shore up Medicare, which is projected to run short of funds in 2010, and pay for defense and education initiatives.

"We're going to have a big argument about this, and we should," Clinton said at a rally in Buffalo, N.Y., on Jan. 20.

House Ways and Means Committee Chairman Bill Archer, R-Texas, who has criticized Clinton's plan for market investment, offered an olive branch of sorts on Jan. 21.

"We would be willing to reserve 62 percent of the surplus until Social Security has been saved," Archer said. House Minority Leader Richard A. Gephardt, D-Mo., welcomed the GOP overture, but reiterated that the White House wanted to use some of the surplus for the personal savings accounts and for ensuring the long-term solvency of Medicare.

The political positioning showed that, while the two parties are far apart on specifics, they are eager to move beyond the divisive impeachment debate to reach a deal on Social Security.

Some Republicans praised Clinton for at least moving toward individual retirement accounts and said they hoped to build on the proposal. Analysts said that by channeling most of the surplus back into the Social Security trust fund, rather than spending it on tax cuts or new programs, the plan would have the important, secondary benefit of reducing the massive federal debt.

And both sides believe that after making Social Security a top priority, they cannot afford to let it die.

The fact that Congress is even debating proposals to shore up the Social Security system, which provides retirement, disability and survivors benefits to 44 million Americans, is in itself a remarkable development.

Created by President Franklin D. Roosevelt in 1935, Social Security faces no imminent crisis; rather, there is a looming, long-term crunch as the Baby Boom generation retires, life expectancy increases and fewer workers remain in the economy to pay benefits.

Payroll taxes and trust fund balances are sufficient to cover benefits through 2032. After that point, the 12.4 percent payroll tax, half paid by workers and half by employers, will cover only about three-fourths of commitments.

Acting now would allow Congress to phase in changes over a longer period of time, allowing for more gradual policies and more equity across generations. It would also allow lawmakers to take advantage of the emerging surplus and a strong economy.

Market Intervention?

Of all the provisions in the administration's plan, the most controversial is market investment.

"Direct investment of any of the surplus by the government . . . is socialism," said Rep. E. Clay Shaw Jr., R-Fla., chairman of the House Ways and Means Social Security Subcommittee.

The idea behind direct investment is to get better earnings for the Social Security trust fund, and therefore minimize the need for benefit cuts, by realizing the higher returns of the market.

The stock market has historically averaged a 7 percent rate of return. Currently, Social Security trust funds are invested in lower-yielding, but less volatile, Treasury bonds.

While market-based proposals were unthinkable even a decade ago, booming stock prices and increasing investor sophistication have fueled the move toward private investment.

Republican opposition to the concept of direct government investment in the market is no surprise to the administration. What is troubling, White House officials say, is the degree of vitriol. They argue that their plan was designed with safeguards to prevent government abuse.

While some members of the 1994-96 Advisory Council on Social Security, for example, called for investing 40 percent of the trust fund in the stock market, the Clinton plan calls for investing about $700 billion over 15 years. That would represent about 4 percent of the total equity market and less than 15 percent of the Social Security trust fund.

The administration has yet to work out a final proposal, but officials envision an independent government board that would contract with private investment houses. To minimize market disruption, overhead costs and the potential for abuse, investments would go into broad-based investment instruments, such as mutual funds, rather than specific stocks.

Greenspan warned that it would be impossible to insulate the federal government from pressure to turn to more politically palatable, but less financially sound, investments. That would both distort the market and reduce the expected rate of return to the program.

"I am fearful that we would use those assets in a way that would create a lower rate of return for Social Security recipients and . . . create sub-optimal use of capital and a lower standard of living," Greenspan said.

In response, the White House sent Treasury Secretary Robert E. Rubin on a tour of the morning television talk shows Jan. 21 to promote the plan.

"There will be no — zero — no government involvement in the investment of the funds," Rubin said on NBC's "Today."

While the proposal to invest in the stock market has received the bulk of attention, it was not the key element in Clinton's plan for keeping the program solvent.

The administration estimates that transferring a portion of the surplus to Social Security and realizing higher market rates of return would extend the solvency of Social Security by 23 years, through 2055. The bulk of the improvement, however, would come from the transfer of the surplus, not from the stock market investment. Administration officials said the stock plan by itself accounted for about five of the additional 23 years of solvency.

Private Accounts

A second area of both division and hope for compromise is the White House's plan to create so-called Universal Savings Accounts (USAs), financed through the surplus, to supplement the basic Social Security benefit.

The plan would dedicate $33 billion a year, or about 11 percent of the projected surplus, for the next 15 years to the accounts, which would operate like 401(k) accounts. While the details are still to be worked out, White House officials said the accounts would be intended to help low- and middle-income workers create savings pools for retirement.

In a theoretical example laid out by White House officials, a family making $40,000 a year could receive a $100 flat contribution from the federal government to set up an account. If the family contributed $600 on its own, the government could match $300 of that amount, for a total investment of $1,000. The administration has not made final decisions on how the funds would operate.

The idea already has some powerful advocates. Senate Finance Committee Chairman William V. Roth Jr., R-Del., on Jan. 20 re-introduced similar legislation. Roth's plan would use half the federal budget surplus from 2000 to 2004 to set up individual accounts. A minimum-wage earner making $12,400 a year in adjusted gross income would receive about $1,850 annually. The accounts would have to be invested in federally specified plans.

"Let's get these accounts up and running, proven and tested, while Congress considers carefully protecting and preserving Social Security for the long term," Roth said.

Harvard economist Martin Feldstein also has proposed a plan that would require individuals to invest two percent of earnings in the market. Proceeds from the accounts would be used to reduce Social Security benefits.

Many lawmakers want to go further, allowing individuals to use some or all of the Social Security payroll tax to set up individual accounts. Earnings from the accounts would be used to replace basic program benefits.

Social Security Commissioner Kenneth S. Apfel said in an interview Jan. 21 that the administration looked at such proposals but rejected them as too risky.

"We need to have more savings, but not to replace parts of the Social Security system," Apfel said. "You've got to have that benefit you can count on, whether you outlive your savings or your spouse. The creation of individual accounts as a replacement to Social Security puts individuals at risk."

Still, advocates of greater privatization hope to build on the White House proposal.

Leanne Abdnor, executive director of the Alliance for Worker Security, which represents the National Association of Manufacturers, Business Roundtable and U.S. Chamber of Commerce, said her group would lobby hard for individual accounts to replace some program benefits, and against direct government investment.

"The members are very skeptical and cautious about an additional retirement program. I love the idea of giving workers back their money. I'm not sure it needs to be a new program," Abdnor said.

Despite Apfel's opposition, some Democrats worry that the White House's proposal is the first step toward private accounts that would replace program benefits.

And there is broad concern that, although the accounts are envisioned to last only 15 years, they would turn into a new entitlement program. Supporters said they will cross that bridge down the road.

"If you have a 10 percent across-the-board income tax rate cut . . . at the end how do you finance it? That is a much bigger problem" than extending individual accounts, said Robert Greenstein, director of the Center on Budget and Policy Priorities, a liberal think tank.

Expanding Aid

Clinton believes that the overhaul would provide an opportunity to improve the basic program. One major concern is widows, who account for nearly two-thirds of elderly women in poverty.

Under the current Social Security system, after a married individual dies, the survivor — usually a woman — receives 100 percent of the deceased spouse's benefit or her own benefit, whichever is higher. Many experts say the amount should be increased to 75 percent of the higher, joint benefits the couple received when both were alive.

While Clinton called for greater protection for women in his State of the Union address, he is not advocating funding an enhanced widow's benefit through the surplus. Rather, Congress and the White House would have to come up with billions of dollars in additional savings to pay for it.

The plan calls for eliminating the so-called Social Security earnings test. Under current law, individuals ages 65 to 70 who earn above $15,500 in 1999 will have their benefits reduced $1 for every $3 of income.

GOP Critiques President's Plan

FEBRUARY 13 — Republican opposition to President Clinton's Social Security overhaul plan hardened during the week of Feb. 8, leading lawmakers from both parties to question whether Congress could reach a compromise on the politically contentious issue.

The president's proposal, unveiled in his Jan. 19 State of the Union address, called for direct government investment of 15 percent of Social Security funds in the stock market to generate higher earnings. It would dedicate about 60 percent of projected budget surpluses to the program.

House Ways and Means Committee Chairman Bill Archer, R-Texas, opposes Clinton's call for direct government investment, but is encouraged by the president's willingness to use the stock market to improve Social Security earnings.

"I think he [Clinton] just put a placeholder out there that he could speak for that really offers no plan to save Social Security," Archer said Feb. 11. He said the GOP was examining proposals to create some type of Individual Retirement Accounts as an alternative to Clinton's plan.

Others suggested that proposed meetings between Clinton and congressional Republican leaders, designed to move the parties beyond the divisive impeachment debate, could serve as a catalyst to get things moving.

Rep. Robert T. Matsui of California, ranking Democrat on the Ways and Means Social Security Subcommittee, said House Democrats were generally satisfied with Clinton's plan. He added that instead of criticizing the White House proposal, Republicans needed to come up with alternatives.

"No one at this time knows how we can get this thing going, how we can find some common ground," he said. "Unless we begin talking some, we as Democrats will be asking Republicans to come up with their own plan."

Some moderate Senate Democrats have been critical of Clinton's initiative. Treasury Secretary Robert E. Rubin met with the Senate Democratic caucus Feb. 11, during a break in Clinton's impeachment trial, to explain the initiative. Aides said the briefing was intended to bring senators up to date before the weeklong recess.

Republicans dislike directly investing Social Security trust funds on the grounds it could lead to government manipulation of the stock markets.

Furthermore, there is growing criticism of Clinton's complex proposal for crediting budget surpluses to Social Security. The White House plan, for the first time, envisions using general revenues to fund the retirement system, in addition to the dedicated 12.4 payroll tax.

Coming To Account

Social Security payroll taxes are included in calculations of the unified budget. They will account for about $2.7 trillion of the projected surpluses over the next 15 years.

Under current law, payroll taxes over the amount needed to pay program benefits are converted into Treasury bonds, which make up the program trust fund. The trust fund is not locked away, however. Rather, when the government runs a deficit, Social Security revenues are used to finance other programs with the understanding the government will, in the future, make good on the bonds. In times of surplus, excess funds are automatically used to pay down public debt.

Under Clinton's plan, the government would issue a second set of bonds that also would be credited to Social Security, basically doubling the trust fund.

The White House has said that mechanism would ensure that the surplus was used to buy down debt and protect Social Security, rather than pay for new spending programs or tax cuts.

By using bonds to give Social Security "first choice" on the surplus, the White House estimates that the program's projected date of insolvency would be put off from 2032 to 2049. Clinton's stock market proposal could add another six years — still short of Clinton's goal of keeping the program solvent until 2075.

Some outside experts argue that while Clinton's plan would reduce public debt, it would increase overall government debt. Taxpayers, through general revenues, would have to redeem the additional bonds, starting early in the next century, when Social Security payroll taxes will no longer be sufficient to cover promised benefits.

At a Feb. 9 Senate Finance Committee hearing, Federal Reserve Governor Edward M. Gramlich, former chairman of the 1994-96 Advisory Council on Social Security, criticized the plan. He said the council at one point debated, but rejected, using general revenues to fund Social Security.

"Using general revenues to fund Social Security puts the Social Security system in competition with other spending programs," Gramlich said. That is because tax revenues that support general programs would be used to redeem the bonds and pay for benefits.

David M. Walker, comptroller general of the General Accounting Office, said the White House proposal would not improve Social Security's projected cash flow imbalance. Further, because Clinton did not recommend structural changes in the program — such as benefit cuts or tax increases, the proposal "does not represent a Social Security reform plan."

The accounting dispute may be dry, but it is serious. Republicans have agreed in general terms to set aside 62 percent of the surplus for Social Security. If they reject Clinton's accounting, however, such a move by itself would not extend program solvency past 2032. That widens the gap, since neither party wants to cut benefits or raise payroll taxes to shore up the system.

"You can dislike the Clinton policy, but the numbers add up," said Robert Greenstein, head of the liberal Center on Budget and Policy Priorities.

GOP Leaders Oppose Private Investment Plan

APRIL 24 — House Republican leaders are trying to put the brakes on a high-profile plan to create individual investment accounts within Social Security, exposing deep splits within the party and all but assuring that an overhaul of the retirement system will not move this session.

In a series of private meetings over the past two weeks, House Speaker J. Dennis Hastert, R-Ill., and other leaders have warned Ways and Means Chairman Bill Archer, R-Texas, and Social Security Subcommittee Chairman E. Clay Shaw Jr., R-Fla., against moving forward with a plan that would create individual accounts to replace a portion of Social Security benefits.

Citing polls, the leaders argued that voters, particularly senior citizens, are skeptical of private accounts.

Republicans and moderate Democrats who have been briefed on the Archer-Shaw proposal, still under revision, have been lukewarm. The business community and conservative organizations have expressed concerns, with some groups saying it does not go far enough.

"We're not there yet," Hastert said recently. He cautioned that Republicans, who have been burned in the past on the issue, needed bipartisan support for any bill.

There is also little appetite among Senate Republicans for getting out ahead in proposing major changes to the popular program, which provides retirement, disability and survivors' benefits to 44 million Americans.

Many senators, including Majority Leader Trent Lott, R-Miss., were in the House in the 1980s when Republicans took a political drubbing on Social Security. "We need to have some agreement with the Senate," Hastert said.

Despite the bleak odds, Shaw and Archer still plan to introduce their proposal within the next several weeks.

"There are no commitments out there and there have been no commitments out there, but there has been a desire by the leadership to do the right thing," Shaw said April 21.

Shaw said that he interpreted recent opinion polls to mean that Americans wanted Congress to act, and quickly, on Social Security. Lawmakers who advocate action worry that Republicans will be more susceptible to political attacks if they do not develop a plan.

Individual Accounts

Congressional aides who have been briefed on the Archer-Shaw proposal said it would tap into the budget surplus to provide Americans with a tax credit, equal to about 2 percentage points of the current 12.4 percent Social Security payroll tax.

The tax credit would be deposited into individual accounts, which would then be invested in a specified mix of 60 percent stock index funds and 40 percent bonds, aides said.

At retirement, the Social Security Administration would convert the accounts into annuities that would be used to replace a portion of the regular Social Security benefit.

Individuals would be assured of receiving monthly payments at least equal to what they would get under the current Social Security system. If accounts provided greater earnings, individuals would realize the difference.

The plan would avoid unpopular alternatives such as raising the retirement age or increasing taxes.

Archer and Shaw reached out to a number of lawmakers, including moderates such as Rep. Jim Kolbe, R-Ariz., and Rep. Charles W. Stenholm, D-Texas, who are retooling legislation they introduced last year that includes individual accounts.

Some lawmakers familiar with the plan do not like the idea of using the surplus to finance accounts. Other conservatives said individuals would not have enough control.

Rep. Earl Pomeroy, D-N.D., who has been spearheading his party's efforts on Social Security, said Democratic opposition to individual accounts was so intense Archer and Shaw would likely find only token support.

In the Senate, Finance Committee Chairman William V. Roth Jr., R-Del., has made it clear that Social Security is not his top priority. Instead, Roth's committee has started a series of hearings on Medicare.

House Republicans also have been talking to the White House, trying to gauge whether Clinton, who has said that Social Security overhaul is a top priority, would be willing to make concessions to get a bill moving. So far they have little encouragement.

"Just one week after passing a budget that promises a massive $800 billion tax cut, the Republican leadership is sending a message that Congress is either unable or unwilling to face up to the challenge of strengthening Social Security," Clinton said in a statement April 23.

Clinton's Social Security plan calls for the government to directly invest a portion of the Social Security surplus in the stock market. The White House proposal falls short of Clinton's goal of ensuring the system stays solvent for 75 years. Clinton has been unwilling to recommend benefit cuts or tax increases to fill the gap.

Both parties have been active in selling their plans. The Republican-drafted budget resolution (H Con Res 68) would put the Social Security portion of the federal budget surplus off limits.

The Senate during the week of April 19 stalled on Republican legislation that would set up a "lockbox" that would make it more difficult to dip into the Social Security trust fund to finance other programs. The White House had threatened to veto the bill on the grounds it could impede the government's ability to manage debt.

The war in Kosovo will increase pressure on Congress to use the budget surplus, including Social Security, to finance the armed forces.

Archer, Shaw Push Private Accounts as Overhaul Stalls

MAY 1 — Even though GOP congressional leaders have made it clear that they do not want to debate a Social Security overhaul this year, key House Republicans on April 28 unveiled a plan that would create individual investment accounts to replace a portion of program benefits.

Ways and Means Committee Chairman Bill Archer, R-Texas, and Social Security Subcommittee Chairman E. Clay Shaw Jr., R-Fla., said the private accounts — which would be invested 60 percent in stocks and 40 percent in bonds — would generate significant new retirement earnings for Social Security beneficiaries, thereby relieving financial strain on the federal pension program.

Social Security is forecast to run a deficit beginning in 2034, as the Baby

Boom generation retires, the proportion of the population paying into the system continues to decline and retiree life expectancy increases.

"Our [plan] does not cut benefits, it does not raise taxes, but it does save Social Security. Not just for a limited number of years, but for all time," Archer said.

The duo released their plan at a time when the politics of Social Security has become very complicated. The GOP congressional leadership, citing internal polls, has warned that the party could take a beating in the 2000 elections if it gets too far ahead in advocating major changes to the popular program. Democrats have attacked Republicans in the past for recommending reductions in annual cost of living increases.

President Clinton, who has said a Social Security overhaul is a top priority, would still very much like legislation to enhance his legacy. Any bipartisan plan that included private investment to replace program benefits could anger the liberal wing of his party. That could complicate Democrats' chances of retaking the House in 2000 and Vice President Al Gore's efforts to energize the party base for his presidential bid.

After the plan was announced, House Speaker J. Dennis Hastert, R-Ill., issued a statement that kept the proposal at arm's length, without publicly waving goodbye.

"I pledge that I will take a close look at this proposal," Hastert said, adding: "Make no mistake. Any efforts to enact a Social Security reform plan must be done in a bipartisan manner."

The Senate GOP leadership has been equally hesitant about moving ahead without bipartisan support. Senate Majority Leader Trent Lott, R-Miss., has said he does not believe Congress will act on the issue this year.

Administration Shows Interest

Archer and Shaw received a somewhat more encouraging response from the White House, where Clinton met with top aides April 30 to discuss possible changes to his own Social Security plan. Clinton's proposal, unveiled in his Jan. 19 State of the Union address, calls for the government to directly invest a portion of the program's trust fund in the stock market and would set up retirement accounts for low-income workers to supplement, not replace, basic benefits.

Administration officials said Clinton and his advisers ran through a list of possible options that could move the White House closer to Republicans and moderate Democrats who also favor private accounts, but came to no conclusion. Further meetings are planned.

"We're going to take a close look at what Chairman Archer put out," White House spokesman Joe Lockhart said April 28. "What's important here is this looks like a serious attempt to engage in a very important debate, and stands in some contrast to some others in the leadership who sought to dismiss this debate for political reasons."

Archer and Clinton talked by telephone April 27 about Archer's proposal. Archer and Shaw also briefed Ways and Means Democrats on April 28 after unveiling the plan.

Even if Clinton were to make overtures to the Republicans, overall reaction to the Archer-Shaw plan underscores the dim chances for enacting major legislation this session.

Conservatives, including the libertarian CATO Institute — the chief proponent of private accounts — said the plan was "not a serious attempt to reform" because individuals would not have ownership of the earnings.

Moderates warned that the plan, by using the Social Security surplus to create the accounts, imposed trillions of dollars in new government liabilities and sidestepped politically difficult decisions about cutting benefits or raising payroll taxes.

Liberals warned that the proposal was the first step toward "privatizing" the program, which provides retirement, disability and survivors' benefits to 44 million Americans.

"This has been an attempt to address the image problems of the Republican party, not [to address] Social Security," Rep. Rosa DeLauro, D-Conn., assistant to the minority leader, said April 28.

Archer responded to such comments by saying: "When you're getting criticized from the extremes, you're probably doing the right thing."

Nuts and Bolts

The Archer-Shaw plan would keep intact the current structure of Social Security, including survivors' and disability benefits.

It would impose major changes in the system's financing, however, by tapping into the federal budget surplus to create an annual, refundable tax credit for all those paying into the Social Security system. The program is now funded through a 12.4 percent payroll tax, half paid by employers and half by employees.

The credit would be equal to 2 percent of earnings up to the Social Security wage cap. The wage cap is currently $72,600, but is increased annually. That means the maximum credit provided in 1999 under the Archer-Shaw proposal would be $1,452.

The tax credit would be automatically deposited by the government into a mandatory personal account, called a Social Security Guarantee Account.

Individuals would have some ability to choose where to invest the money, selecting from a government-approved list of 50 investment funds. To limit the downside risk and ensure that the accounts realized a 5.35 percent annual rate of return, all the financial instruments would be based on 60 percent stock index funds and 40 percent bonds.

Except in the case of disability, workers would not be allowed to withdraw money from the accounts before retirement. At retirement, the accounts would be annuitized and used to replace a portion, or all, of the regular Social Security benefits an individual would be eligible to receive under current law.

If the account was insufficient to provide at least the same benefit as current law, the Social Security Administration would draw from the program trust fund to make up the difference.

Individuals whose account balance was worth more would realize the difference in the form of higher monthly benefits. At death, any money remaining in the account would go first to survivors' benefits and any balance would revert to the Social Security trust fund.

If an individual died before retirement, the account balance would be used first to pay survivors' benefits. Any remainder could then be passed on tax-free to an estate. Otherwise, individuals would not get any lump sum payment from the accounts.

The lack of private ownership is a key objection of CATO and other advocates of personal accounts. They argue that unless individuals can build wealth to be passed on to their families, accounts will not have popular support.

Others raise concerns about the complexity and administrative expense of managing tens of millions of individual accounts. The plan would limit administrative fees to 25 basis points, or one-quarter of 1 percent of interest earnings. Any costs over that level would be borne by general revenues.

Predicting that most individuals would not fare noticeably better under the new system, Dean Baker, senior research fellow of the Preamble Center, a moderate think tank, said in a statement that "all the administrative expenses . . . are simply transfers to the financial industry."

While Archer and Shaw stressed that no one would get a lower benefit under the new plan, Ways and Means aides added that over the next 75 years, few individuals were expected to earn higher monthly payments.

According to tables released by the Joint Committee on Taxation, low- to middle-income workers would get the most benefit from the tax credit.

The proposal would also repeal by 2006 the current earnings limit, whereby seniors who continue working face an initial reduction in Social Security benefits. In 1999, individuals age 65 to 69 who earn more than $15,500 a year lose $1 in Social Security benefits for every $3 in extra earnings.

If anything, the Archer-Shaw proposal showed the political limits of trying to fix Social Security. Lawmakers do not want to cut benefits, raise taxes or increase the retirement age — the most commonly recommended fixes, but the most unpopular. Clinton's proposal has run into similar criticisms.

On one level, the Archer-Shaw plan is a success. The Social Security Administration, in a detailed analysis on April 29, found that if the economic assumptions in the plan were correct, it would ensure the solvency of the program and allow for payroll tax cuts in 2050 and 2060.

That does not mean it is cost-free. The Social Security actuaries forecast that the plan would result in major increases in the public debt.

And, as in Clinton's proposal, the plan envisions for the first time using general government revenues to finance Social Security and the tax credit. The credit alone is forecast to cost $1 trillion over 10 years.

While the lawmakers' plan is the most visible, it is not the only one under consideration. Rep. Benjamin L. Cardin, D-Md., will soon introduce a bill. Reps. Charles W. Stenholm, D-Texas, and Jim Kolbe, R-Ariz., are refining a plan, introduced last year, that would divert part of the Social Security payroll tax to private accounts, while making other benefit changes.

In the Senate, Republican Rick Santorum of Pennsylvania is working with Democrat Bob Kerrey of Nebraska, Republican Judd Gregg of New Hampshire and others on a plan.

Archer Mounts Last-Ditch Effort

JUNE 12 — House Ways and Means Committee Chairman Bill Archer, R-Texas, is one of the few lawmakers in Washington who refuses to concede that efforts to overhaul Social Security are dead for the year. He is also one of the few in a position to do something about it.

During a June 10 committee hearing, Archer invited panel Democrats to begin meeting privately with Republicans in the next few weeks to see if they can work out a compromise bill that would ensure the long-term solvency of the federal retirement program.

"We have the opportunity to prove something historic. It's not easy, but we can prove that a democracy can address a difficult problem far ahead of the drop-dead date," Archer said. "We don't have to wait until we're at the edge of a cliff."

Charles B. Rangel of New York, the panel's ranking Democrat, said his party would be willing to engage in the closed-door discussions.

But even as the two agreed to begin the new effort, they acknowledged that it faced long odds. Archer, who is retiring at the end of the 106th Congress, has the ability and the desire to push his powerful committee forward. Still, he can only go so far without a strong show of support from Republican leaders. Likewise, President Clinton and congressional Democratic leaders have shown little desire to make concessions to the GOP in order to get a bill passed.

"If you're going to make history and not political points, you've got to have everyone on board. Not on the solution, but on the spirit [that] we're working together to reach a solution," Rangel said.

Rangel said that House Minority Leader Richard A. Gephardt, D-Mo., and Speaker J. Dennis Hastert, R-Ill., needed to issue a joint call for the House to act. For his part, Archer asked Clinton to sit down with Ways and Means Republicans to talk through policy options. The president has met with Democratic committee members.

The cautionary tone of the two lawmakers reflects the current political dilemma. Opinion polls show that Social Security is an important issue with the public, particularly senior citizens who make up a large and active voting bloc.

Both Clinton and Republican leaders have pledged to make a Social Security overhaul their top priority this year. Costs of the program, which provides retirement, disability and survivors' benefits to 44 million Americans, are forecast to begin exceeding payroll taxes in 2014. The trust fund will be depleted, and the program will run a deficit, in 2034 without action.

A Waiting Game

Given the long history of demagoguery on the issue and the difficulty of coming up with a solution, neither party has been willing to go first — and they trust each other too little to move together.

The lack of bold action has created a vacuum that Archer and a core of other lawmakers committed to a Social Security overhaul are trying to fill.

House Budget Committee Chairman John R. Kasich, R-Ohio, seeking his party's presidential nomination, on June 9 unveiled his own Social Security plan. Kasich's proposal would reduce guaranteed benefits but would try to make up the difference by allowing individuals to invest a portion of the program's 12.4 percent payroll tax in stocks, bonds and other financial instruments.

Kasich said the private accounts would generate a high enough rate of return to make up for much, though possibly not all, of the lost program benefits. Still, he admitted that some individuals could fare worse under his plan than present law.

"I would hope that the politicians of both parties would look at this and rally behind this plan. If we do nothing, we're going to melt down," he said.

Archer tried to generate additional momentum by holding two days of hearings June 9 and 10 on a wide range of Social Security proposals drafted by lawmakers, ranging from plans to increase taxes and raise the retirement age to proposals to create individual accounts.

Archer even left the committee dais to appear at the witness table with Social Security Subcommittee Chairman E. Clay Shaw Jr., R-Fla. The two answered sometimes tough questions from Democrats about their own plan to use the federal budget surplus to fund a new system of personal investment accounts. Their plan would not reduce current program benefits.

Hastert and other top Republicans have refused to endorse the Archer-Shaw bill and at one point discouraged them from unveiling it.

There did appear to be general agreement on several points during the hearings. Lawmakers in both parties seem to be increasingly open to the idea of using general government revenues, rather than the dedicated payroll tax, for the first time, to underwrite the Social Security program.

And both parties put forward plans that would involve private investment, though Democrats and Republicans have major differences about how much control individuals should have over any investments.

Lockbox: The Political Key

The GOP leadership is concentrating its efforts on legislation that would make it more difficult to borrow from the Social Security trust fund to pay for other programs, the so-called lockbox. The measure (HR 1259) is seen as a way to inoculate the GOP against a repeat of the 1998 election when Democrats accused them of raiding the trust fund to pay for a proposed tax cut.

"In the short-term, it trumps Clinton on Social Security," said Robert L. Ehrlich Jr., R-Md. "And that's good. That's the first time we've done that since I've been here."

The lockbox strategy has created a new set of problems. By trying to place the Social Security trust fund off limits, Republicans have painted themselves into a budget corner. Many lawmakers concede that Congress will have no choice but to tap into the trust funds to get around spending caps imposed in the 1997 budget deal (PL 105-33) that are forcing deep cuts in domestic spending. Even some of the most ardent supporters of the lockbox have privately pleaded with the leadership to back off, worried that it will exacerbate problems with appropriations bills.

Clinton Unveils Revised Proposal

OCTOBER 30 — President Clinton delivered his much ballyhooed Social Security overhaul plan to Congress on Oct. 26 after dropping a controversial provision that called for the federal government to directly invest a portion of the program's trust fund in the stock market.

Clinton's original plan, unveiled in his Jan. 19 State of the Union address, called for the government to directly invest about 15 percent of the Social Security surplus in broad stock index funds to generate higher returns. The proposal was opposed by many Republicans, who favor individual investment accounts, and many Democrats, who are leery of tying the program to the financial markets.

Clinton's new plan is designed to delay the projected insolvency date of the federal retirement program by 16 years, to 2050, through a complicated scheme that essentially transfers general government revenues to the program. Social Security is now funded through a dedicated 12.4 percent payroll tax.

The scheme, touted by Clinton in his Oct. 23 weekly radio address, would also set aside one-third of the non-Social Security portion of the federal budget surplus through 2009 to shore up the Medicare health program for the elderly and disabled.

The White House decision to finally send a plan to Capitol Hill generated a flurry of partisan rhetoric, but little hope for action. Both Democrats and Republicans said there was little chance that this Congress would grapple with the long-term financing problems of Social Security. Even Clinton, in an Oct. 28 session with reporters, acknowledged Congress would not address the issue this year.

Republicans were quick to criticize the proposal. Senate Budget Committee Chairman Pete V. Domenici, R-N.M., dubbed it the "Godzilla of all gimmicks" and said it was a political move designed to counter a GOP promise not to tap into the Social Security surplus to pay for other programs.

Republicans have made their promise to place the Social Security surplus in a legislative "lockbox" the centerpiece of their political and legislative strategy.

"Frankly, I do not understand why, in the waning moments of this year . . . the president came up with a new idea about Social Security," Domenici said in an Oct. 26 floor speech. "I speculate maybe the idea of the lockbox and not spending any Social Security money was starting to take hold."

House Republicans recently started running ads in the districts of selected Democrats, accusing them of raiding the retirement program. Democrats are firing back with ads of their own on Social Security and Clinton's proposal for a Medicare prescription drug benefit.

Democrats' Concerns

House Democrats introduced Clinton's bill on Oct. 28, touting it as a counter to the lockbox and proof that their party was the one that was most committed to protecting Social Security. Some lawmakers had concerns, however, after looking at the fine print. Among other things, the proposal would extend current caps, or limits, on discretionary spending, that are now set to expire in 2002.

It also includes budget enforcement mechanisms that would make it more difficult for Congress to use the Social Security surplus — or the portion of the general budget surplus the White House wants to reserve for Medicare —for other domestic spending.

White House officials said the bill would hold discretionary spending at about fiscal 1999 levels, plus inflation.

The Center on Budget and Policy Priorities, a liberal think tank, said the caps were actually tighter.

Congress has had a difficult time complying with the caps. According to the Congressional Budget Office, appropriations bills for fiscal 2000 exceed spending targets by $31 billion.

"The key test on Social Security is whether the life of the trust fund is extended," said Rep. Earl Pomeroy, of North Dakota, co-chair of a Democratic task force on Social Security. "Whether the caps are at levels that would be appropriate would be something that needs careful evaluation."

Rep. E. Clay Shaw Jr., R-Fla., chairman of the Ways and Means Social Security Subcommittee, said the bill would at least serve as the basis for another round of hearings. The committee will hold a hearing on Clinton's proposal before Congress adjourns this year.

The revised plan would mandate that future Social Security surpluses be dedicated to debt reduction. Cutting the debt would in turn reduce projected interest savings. Those interest savings would be returned to the Social Security trust fund in the form of government bonds — essentially a promise to transfer general revenues at a future date.

According to the White House, during the next 15 years Social Security surpluses will total $3.1 trillion. Under Clinton's plan, that would be dedicated to debt reduction. Critics said the plan did not address underlying problems — increasing life expectancy and the aging of Baby Boomers — that threaten the program. It does not alter the 2014 date at which Social Security spending is expected to exceed payroll taxes. ◆

Congress Doubles Federal Aid for Teens Who Must Leave Foster Care at Age 18

SUMMARY

In an effort to attack widespread problems such as unemployment and unwanted pregnancy, Congress cleared legislation to double federal aid to adolescents who are now forced to leave foster care at age 18.

Though some of the 500,000 children in foster care are eventually adopted or reunited with their biological parents, about 20,000 turn 18 and leave the system each year, expected to fend for themselves. Bleak statistics show that many cannot.

The legislation (HR 3443) would double federal aid to expand education, counseling and other services to youths up to age 21; let states extend Medicaid coverage to teenagers moving off foster care; and allow foster children to accumulate up to $10,000 in assets, up from the current limit of $1,000. The legislation incorporated the language of HR 1802, which was passed by the House on June 25.

The measure was sponsored by Republican Nancy L. Johnson of Connecticut, the chairman of the House Ways and Means Human Resources Subcommittee.

States try to prepare foster children for adult life through the Independent Living Program, now authorized at $70 million a year. Independent Living includes education, counseling and basic life skills such as cooking, balancing a checkbook and doing laundry. The bill would rename the program the John H. Chafee Foster Care Independence Program, to honor the late Republican senator from Rhode Island.

Experts have said that the Independent Living Program, which is meant to help youths ages 16 to 18, is too limited. The legislation would let states expand the services to include room and board and to cover youths aged 18 to 21. It would also require states to certify that prospective foster parents will be given training and other aid.

Lawmakers had originally wanted to require states to make extended Medicare health insurance coverage mandatory, but they could not find a way to pay for it. The bill would be financed partially by altering a federal child-support enforcement program. States finance child-support enforcement through state collections and federal aid.

The 1996 welfare law (PL 104-193) made a number of changes to the system and instituted a "hold harmless" guarantee that no state would receive less in federal money than its fiscal 1995 level.

BoxScore

- **Bill:** HR 3443 — PL 106-169
- **Legislative action: House** passed HR 1802, 380-6, on June 25.

House passed HR 3443, by voice vote, on Nov. 18.

Senate cleared HR 3443, by voice vote, on Nov. 19.

President signed HR 3443 on Dec. 14.

House Panel Votes To Double Foster Care Grants

MAY 22 — In an effort to better prepare foster children to live on their own when they become adults, a House subcommittee May 20 approved legislation (HR 1802) that would double federal funding for programs that serve them.

The Ways and Means Human Resources Subcommittee approved the measure by voice vote. It would allow states to use money from the federal grants to tailor their programs to help foster children live independently when they turn 18 and are no longer covered by state programs.

The bill, sponsored by Human Resources Subcommittee Chairman Nancy L. Johnson, R-Conn., would increase annual federal funding for state programs from $70 million to $140 million. The bill is scheduled for consideration by the full House Ways and Means Committee on May 26.

Teens who leave foster care often have a higher rate of homelessness and are more likely to be victims of abuse or to have children out of wedlock, according to supporters of the legislation. They say children in foster care are often not provided the same kind of social education and training that children in traditional families receive.

Although the extent of the problems is not clearly known, bill supporters said, Congress should give states greater latitude in running their foster child programs.

Under the measure, states could qualify for additional foster care money if they demonstrate that their programs meet several objectives, including:

- Identifying children likely to be in foster care through age 18.
- Providing job training and education to foster children.
- Preparing foster children for education beyond the high school level.
- Providing personal help such as mentors for foster children.
- Helping foster children after they leave the system until they turn 21.

The bill also would allow states to provide Medicaid to the 20,000 foster children who leave the system annually. The bill could provide $195 million over five years in state Medicaid grants.

"I would like to see that [Medicaid] mandatory coverage instead of permissive," said cosponsor and ranking member Benjamin L. Cardin, D-Md. However, subcommittee members estimated it would cost $400 million over five years to make the coverage mandatory.

Though there was no opposition on the subcommittee, some Republicans said they were concerned about costs.

One of the bill's provisions would repeal a provision in the 1996 welfare overhaul (PL 104-193) that requires the federal government to ensure states receive at least as much money each year as the amount they received in 1995 from the portion of child support collections they could retain. *(1996 Almanac, p. 6-3)*

"I have some grave concerns with the funding mechanisms," said Republican Dave Camp of Michigan. "To eliminate this provision would be wrong and would hurt states."

Despite the concerns of their colleagues, Cardin and Johnson were not convinced.

"The states have effectively been making a profit off this program," Johnson said. "We are saving the states lots of money through" this foster care legislation.

House Ways and Means Approves Foster Care Bill

MAY 29 — The House Ways and Means Committee on May 26 approved legislation (HR 1802) that would expand federal programs designed to prepare foster-care teenagers to live on their own when they leave the system at age 18.

The measure, approved by voice vote, is an attempt to address what many lawmakers say is a major shortcoming in the current system: Thousands of youths are discharged from foster care even though they may not be prepared to become self-sufficient. Sponsors say that rates of homelessness, unemployment and unplanned pregnancy are especially high among these youths.

The bill, sponsored by Human Resources Subcommittee Chairman Nancy L. Johnson, R-Conn., would double funding to states for training, education and other services for individuals and allow the money to be used for youths up to age 21.

"We are their parents. The government is their parents. How many parents cut off all support when their child turns 18?" said Rep. Benjamin L. Cardin of Maryland, the subcommittee's ranking Democrat, who cosponsored the bill.

The measure is expected to reach the House floor quickly, in part because of strong support from Majority Whip Tom DeLay, R-Texas, himself a foster parent. DeLay testified in support of the bill earlier this month.

The Clinton administration has strongly supported the measure. The Senate Finance Committee has not yet scheduled a markup.

Unprepared for Adult Life

According to the Department of Health and Human Services, even though some foster care children are adopted or reunited with their biological parents, about 20,000 leave the system each year on the assumption that they will be able to live on their own. Federal subsidies for foster children end when a child turns 18. While some may remain with their foster families, others have been turned out when payments end.

A 1990 study of former foster care youths in the San Francisco Bay Area found that 55 percent left foster care without a high school degree. A 1991 survey of youths in eight states who had been out of the system for up to four years found that one-quarter had been homeless at least one night, half were unemployed and 42 percent had given birth or fathered a child.

States and the federal government are supposed to prepare foster children for the rigors of adult life through the Independent Living Program, which provides short-term training, education and supervised housing. Currently, the program serves mainly youths ages 16 to 18.

The bill would increase annual funding for the program from $70 million to $140 million and allow states to intervene with children far earlier.

"You can't start talking to kids at 16 and expect them to succeed at 18," Johnson said.

The bill recommends, but does not require, that states extend Medicaid health coverage to those ages 18 to 21. Johnson and Cardin originally made the coverage mandatory, but could not come up with the necessary spending offsets. Still, half of eligible youths are expected to be covered under the voluntary program.

Pete Stark, D-Calif., offered but withdrew an amendment to mandate Medicaid coverage. Johnson and others said they hoped to expand coverage during later negotiations with the Senate. The House measure also would allow foster care children to compile as much as $10,000 in assets, up from the current $1,000 limit, before losing eligibility for federal foster care payments.

The committee had planned to pay for the bill, in part, by reducing federal payments to states under a program that requires them to establish the paternity of children receiving welfare. That was dropped after states protested.

Despite objections by the National Governors' Association, the committee kept a second provision that would reduce federal child support payments to states by $230 million over five years.

The bill would eliminate a "hold harmless" provision of the 1996 welfare law (PL 104-193) that guarantees states would receive no less in federal funds than in 1995. Johnson argues that overall, states have made a profit under the child support program by collecting more than their operational costs. But some states, such as Wisconsin, have not realized a surplus. *(1996 Almanac, p. 6-3)*

Gerald D. Kleczka, D-Wis., offered an amendment to rewrite the committee plan, but withdrew it after Johnson promised to work with him.

The committee by voice vote approved minor amendments, including one by J.D. Hayworth, R-Ariz., that would require the government to consult with American Indian tribes about the new foster care aid and allow tribes to use excess federal welfare payments in the following fiscal year.

House Passes Bill To Help Youths As They Leave Foster Care System

JUNE 26 — The House on June 25 voted to double federal aid to adolescents who are now forced to leave foster care abruptly at age 18, in an effort to attack widespread problems such as unemployment and unwanted pregnancy.

The House voted 380-6 to pass a bill (HR 1802) that would mandate $140 million a year to expand education, counseling and other services to youths up to age 21; let states extend Medicaid coverage to teenagers moving off foster care; and allow foster children to accumulate up to $10,000 in assets. *(Vote 256, p. H-90)*

"With just good care and common sense and concern these kids can fulfill their dreams like all American children should be able to," said Nancy L. Johnson, R-Conn., chairman of the Ways and Means Human Resources Subcommittee.

Johnson and ranking Democrat Benjamin L. Cardin of Maryland are the chief sponsors of the bill. The Senate Finance Committee is expected to mark up a companion measure soon. The legislation is a priority of House Majority Whip Tom DeLay, R-Texas, a foster parent of two.

"My foster daughter turned 18 yesterday and she, by all rights, should be out on the streets. But she's staying at our home, getting ready to go to college," DeLay said during debate.

While some of the 500,000 children in foster care are adopted or reunited with their biological parents, about 20,000 turn 18 and leave the system each year, expected to fend for themselves. Bleak statistics show that many cannot.

A 1991 survey of 810 youths who had been out of foster care for up to four years found a quarter had been homeless at least one night, more than half were jobless and 42 percent had either fathered a child or given birth.

States try to prepare foster children for adult life through the Independent Living Program, now authorized at $70 million a year. Independent Living includes education, counseling and basic life skills such as cooking, balancing a checkbook and doing laundry.

"These children are very vulnerable," Cardin said. "In many cases they were removed from their natural parents because of abuse [or] neglect."

Experts have said that the Independent Living Program, which is meant to help youths ages 16 to 18, is too limited. The House-passed bill would let states intervene earlier and expand the services to include room and board.

Lawmakers had originally wanted to require states to make extended Medicaid coverage mandatory, but they could not find a way to pay for it. Instead, the bill urges states, which jointly run Medicaid with the federal government, to extend benefits to youths up to age 20. It would let foster children accumulate as much as $10,000 in assets, up from the current $1,000 limit.

Amendments Added

Before approving the bill, the House by voice vote approved a manager's amendment offered by Johnson that would expand a provision of the original bill allowing Filipino veterans of World War II to continue receiving Supplemental Security Income (SSI) benefits, though at a reduced rate, if they returned to the Philippines. The amendment would extend the same treatment to any World War II veteran who leaves the United States.

The House by voice vote approved an amendment by Mike Thompson, D-Calif., to require states to certify that prospective foster parents will be given training and other aid.

Lawmakers by voice vote approved an amendment by Steve Buyer, R-Ind., to require the Social Security Administration to study the impact of denying SSI benefits to family farmers with resources of less than $100,000 who care for disabled relatives in their homes.

The bill would be financed partially by altering a federal child-support enforcement program. States fund child-support enforcement through state collections and federal aid. The 1996 welfare law (PL 104-193) made a number of changes to the system and instituted a "hold harmless" guarantee that no state would receive less in federal money than its fiscal 1995 level. *(1996 Almanac, p. 6-3)*

Johnson said that states, overall, are making a profit under the child-support program, so she proposed ending the hold-harmless plan. That brought howls from states such as Wisconsin that — in part because they share as much child support as possible with families rather than holding any for the state — did not realize a surplus.

Johnson addressed the issue in her manager's amendment by guaranteeing states that passed child-support collections back to families would receive partial protection.

The bill would crack down on abuse in the SSI program by holding families of deceased recipients liable for overpayments and by letting the Social Security Administration use private debt collection agencies. ◆

Legislation Enacted To Ensure Affordable Housing For Senior, Disabled Citizens

SUMMARY

The House overwhelmingly passed a bill (HR 202) in September aimed at preserving existing affordable housing for the elderly and disabled. Many of the provisions were later attached to the fiscal 2000 spending bill (HR 2684) for the departments of Veterans Affairs (VA) and Housing and Urban Development (HUD). The VA-HUD provisions aim to keep residents of federally assisted housing from being forced out of their homes if landlords give up federal housing contracts, and expands housing and housing services for the elderly and disabled. *(VA-HUD, p. 2-135)*

In the past 25 years, the federal government has expanded its Section 8 rental subsidy program to make more housing available for low-income residents, including senior citizens. In recent years, many of these housing units have been taken off Section 8 rolls as 20-year contracts offered through the program expired, or as owners paid off federally insured mortgages. Such "opt out" moves by landlords allow them to rent apartments at fair market value, in effect pushing rents out of reach of low-income tenants. The House Banking and Financial Services Committee estimates that contracts covering 1 million Section 8 units nationwide will expire by 2004, with half of those in jeopardy of being lost through owner opt-outs.

The parts of HR 202 included in the VA-HUD bill will keep current residents of federally assisted housing from losing their homes by offering "enhanced" vouchers with higher subsidies, allowing tenants to remain in their homes if landlords opt out of Section 8 or pay off Federal Housing Administration mortgages. It also allows funds to be used to convert housing projects for the elderly into assisted-living facilities where residents could continue to live when they are no longer entirely independent.

The Senate is expected to review components of HR 202 not included in the VA-HUD law, including refinancing old Section 202 projects for the elderly and authorizing matching grants to help preserve affordable housing. ◆

Box Score

- **Bill:** HR 2684 — PL 106-74
- **Legislative action: House** passed HR 202, 405-5, on Sept. 27.

House adopted the conference report on HR 2684 (H Rept 106-379), which included sections of HR 202, 406-18, on Oct. 14.

Senate cleared the bill, 93-5, on Oct. 15.

President signed the bill Oct. 20.

Chapter 21

TAXES

Annual Exercise in Extending Expiring Tax Provisions Is Anything But Routine

Box Score

- **Bill:** HR 1180 — PL 106-170
- **Legislative action: House** Ways and Means Committee approved HR 2923 (H Rept 106-344), 23-14, on Sept. 24.

Senate passed S 1792 (S Rept 106-201) by voice vote on Oct. 29.

House adopted conference report on HR 1180 (H Rept 106-478), 418-2, on Nov. 18.

Senate cleared the bill, 95-1, on Nov. 19.

President signed HR 1180 on Dec. 17.

SUMMARY

Extending tax provisions that expire annually is generally considered the equivalent of keeping the trains running on time, but Republicans faced obstacles to moving the package time and again this year.

The measure, which contains $21 billion worth of extended provisions, was among the last major bills to clear Congress this session.

After President Clinton vetoed their broad-based tax cut bill (HR 2488), Republicans set their sights on using a portion of the projected budget surplus to grant long-term extensions of expiring tax provisions.

But GOP leaders soon found that the surplus did not make their task of renewing the "extenders" — so called because they expire almost annually and need to be renewed — any easier.

Businesses that benefited from the tax breaks stepped up their requests, aiming for long-term or even permanent extensions. And Democrats and the White House demanded that the costs of any tax bill, even an extenders package, be offset with other changes to the tax code.

Because of the divergent forces, the House Ways and Means Committee and Senate Finance Committee approved substantially different bills. The House measure (HR 2923), which would have cost $23.3 billion over five years, would have extended the research and experimentation credit for five years and made permanent a fix that allows taxpayers subject to the Alternative Minimum Tax to claim personal tax credits to reduce their income taxes, in addition to extending a number of other provisions. Its revenue loss was to be covered with offsetting changes only in fiscal 2000.

The Senate measure (S 1792) would have extended all provisions through Dec. 31, 2000, and would have cost $8.5 billion over 10 years. All revenue losses would have been offset with other changes to the tax code, a product of panel Chairman William V. Roth Jr., R-Del., working closely with ranking Democrat Daniel Patrick Moynihan of New York to craft a measure after Roth's original $75.5 billion proposal was rejected in a private meeting of the committee.

With the session coming to a close, Roth and Moynihan reached agreement with Ways and Means Committee Chairman Bill Archer, R-Texas, the committee's ranking Democrat, Charles B. Rangel of New York, and Treasury Secretary Lawrence H. Summers on a package that extended the research and development credit for five years and all other provisions through Dec. 31, 2001. The package's $21 billion cost over 10 years was offset with $2.9 billion in changes to the tax code.

The measure was attached to a bill (HR 1180) to help the disabled keep health insurance while working.

With their multi-year bill, members have made it possible to avoid doing an extenders measure next year and to concentrate on a larger tax bill instead.

House Committee Votes To Extend Tax Provisions

SEPTEMBER 25 — With the year's big tax package officially dead, members of Congress turned their attention to the tax equivalent of keeping the trains running — extending a handful of popular tax breaks for businesses and other interest groups.

The action came quickly after President Clinton vetoed the GOP's $792 billion tax bill (HR 2488) on Sept. 23. Clinton said he was willing to discuss a smaller tax cut bill than the one he rejected, but the chances for such a deal appeared increasingly slim. Instead of focusing on negotiating another tax bill, Republicans placed their hopes for cutting taxes on attaching some business tax breaks to a minimum wage bill. *(Veto text, p. D-24)*

After the veto, the House Ways and Means Committee voted 23-14 on Sept. 24 to approve a bill (HR 2923) that would extend six expiring tax provisions, known as "extenders" because they are renewed annually.

The markup was timed to ensure that Congress could meet an Oct. 7 deadline that IRS Commissioner Charles O. Rossotti had set for printing next year's tax forms. But progress on the extenders bill, a measure that would likely have garnered bipartisan support in the past, will be slow at best.

House Majority Leader Dick Armey, R-Texas, said Sept. 24 that he did not think the House would take up the extenders bill in September, and several senators said they did not see how the bill would proceed in that chamber's partisan atmosphere. Finance Committee member Charles E. Grassley, R-Iowa, said Sept. 21: "Under this environment . . . it isn't going to be very possible."

Because the extenders bill would not have the protection from Senate amendments that HR 2488 had as a reconciliation bill, it would likely get bogged down in partisan battles in that chamber. And even if it made it through, Clinton would veto it if Republicans did not find offsets for the bill's entire cost, Deputy Assistant Treasury Secretary for Tax Policy Jonathan Talisman told the Ways and Means Committee.

The bill's $1.5 billion cost in fiscal 2000 would be more than offset by narrowing the "safe harbor" for taxpayers who underpay their estimated tax and have adjusted gross incomes greater than $150,000. However, the $23.3 billion in revenue expected to be lost through 2004 would not be offset by changes in tax law but would be paid for with projected budget surpluses.

Ways and Means Committee Democrats objected to that because extender bills have been paid for in the past. "If you decide for political reasons that you're going to go into the off-budget surplus to pay for extenders, then you really want the veto," said the panel's ranking Democrat, Charles B. Rangel of New York. "I hope that this committee will find some way to discuss with the administration what we can get signed into law."

The bill would extend the research and experimentation credit for five years, permanently allow taxpayers subject to the Alternative Minimum Tax to claim child and education credits and extend for two-and-a-half years tax credits for businesses that hire hard-to-place workers and welfare recipients.

Despite partisan differences, some members predicted that the extenders would find their way into an end-of-year omnibus spending bill.

John B. Breaux, D-La., a Senate Finance member, described Republican suggestions that they might not do extenders as "posturing" and predicted that the provisions would be on "the last train leaving the station."

Breaux said he thought Democrats would cooperate with Republicans to ensure passage. "Finance members know we have to get these things done," he said.

Both Ways and Means Chairman Bill Archer, R-Texas, and Finance Chairman William V. Roth Jr., R-Del., have consistently committed to a "seamless" extension of the provisions, a number of which expired June 30. Roth sent a letter to Senate Majority Leader Trent Lott, R-Miss., on Sept. 22, reminding him that he needed $3.2 billion in fiscal 2000 to pay for extenders.

Paying the Price

Much of the discussion in Ways and Means, and among panel leaders writing the extender bill, centered on how to pay for it.

As approved, the bill's major offset is the provision to narrow the "safe harbor" for wealthy taxpayers who underpay their estimated taxes. The provision would raise $1.5 billion in fiscal 2000, the only year it would be in effect. Lindy L. Paull, chief of staff for the Joint Tax Committee, said the provision would accelerate tax payments that would normally be made in fiscal 2001.

The only other offset is a provision to impose an excise tax of 75 cents per dose on a new streptococcus pneumonia vaccine. Under current law, vaccines routinely given to children are taxed and proceeds are deposited in a fund to pay for injuries caused by the vaccines. Paull said the vaccine, which is expected to win approval from the Centers for Disease Control and the Food and Drug Administration this fall, could not go straight to market if it was not included in this program. The provision is estimated to generate $4 million in fiscal 2000 and $39 million from fiscal 2000 through 2004. The provision and two other non-controversial changes were included in an amendment offered by Archer and adopted by voice vote.

The two provisions combined would more than cover the fiscal 2000 cost of the bill, but they would barely make a dent in its five-year cost.

Rangel offered a substitute that included the extenders in the Republican bill, an extension of school construction credits and bonds and an extension of tax credits for employers who pay for workers' educations. The bill was to be paid for by shutting down corporate tax shelters as outlined in the president's February budget submission and in bills (HR 2255, HR 2705) introduced by Lloyd Doggett, D-Texas, and Richard E. Neal, D-Mass., respectively. The amendment was defeated on a 14-23 party-line vote.

Archer objected to Rangel's offsets, saying that the committee should wait before acting on the issue until it holds hearings on tax shelters later this year and until the Treasury Department releases a long-awaited report. Talisman said the report could come out by the end of the month.

Archer objected to the president's insistence that an extender bill be entirely paid for by offsets. He said it would "foreclose any net tax relief to the people of this country for the rest of this year."

He also said he had heard that the White House would soon send a $300 billion tax package to Congress and that it would not be paid for with offsets, but Talisman and Rangel said they did not know of such plans.

Pushing the Envelope

Though money is tighter now than it was in July when members put together the $792 billion bill that Clinton vetoed, business lobbyists still made strides in the extenders bill.

High-tech, biotechnology and manufacturing lobbyists won a five-year extension of the research and experimentation credit, instead of the usual one year. However, the bill included an unusual adjustment to ensure that the provision was paid for in fiscal 2000.

Businesses eligible for the credit, which generally covers 20 percent of a company's research and development costs above a certain baseline, will not be able to claim it until Oct. 1, 2000.

Financial services companies also won a five-year extension of a provision that allows them to delay paying interest on active investments overseas until the money comes to the United States.

And retailers and restaurateurs won a two-and-a-half year extension of two provisions that help them employ hard-to-hire workers and welfare recipients. Both tax credits had expired June 30.

With Little Debate, Senate Panel Approves Bill

OCTOBER 23 — With the curtain poised to fall on the first session of the 106th Congress, the Senate Finance Committee easily approved an $8.5 billion draft bill Oct. 20 that would extend expiring tax provisions.

Taking care of the so-called extenders, a dozen business tax breaks that generally expire annually, is considered a necessity before Congress adjourns. The panel's five-minute debate and voice-vote approval of the measure raised hopes that moving it would be easy.

But it was unclear whether the legislation — and its substantially different House Ways and Means counterpart (HR 2923) — could move as standalone bills or would be folded into a larger, session-ending spending measure.

Senate Majority Leader Trent Lott, R-Miss., did not make the situation clearer Oct. 22 when he introduced his own $33 billion extenders bill. An aide said Lott was "keeping his options open."

Earlier in the week, committee member Richard H. Bryan, D-Nev., said, "I don't think we have the lay of the land yet." He said the entreaties of panel Chairman William V. Roth Jr., R-Del., and ranking Democrat Daniel Patrick Moynihan of New York to hold off on amendments to avoid smothering the bill may not work on the Senate floor.

Unlike most tax bills, it would not have the status of a budget-reconciliation bill to protect it from amendments. That protection was already given to the GOP's $792 billion tax measure (HR 2488), which President Clinton vetoed Sept. 23.

"This is such a tempting vehicle," Bryan said. "I think [members] are going to find it irresistible." Panel member Bob Kerrey, D-Neb., said he was considering offering a floor amendment to cut payroll taxes, which fund Social Security, but would "probably yield" to panel leaders' wishes.

Senate floor action on the measure does not appear imminent, however, and the House also has had little enthusiasm for taking up its version, which would cost $1.5 billion in fiscal 2000 and $23.3 billion through fiscal 2004. The Senate measure would cost $3.5 billion in fiscal 2000 and $7.6 billion over five years. Unlike the House measure, its overall costs would be offset by other changes to the tax code. The cost of the House bill would be offset only in fiscal 2000.

Scaled-Back Bill

The bill Roth presented Oct. 20 was substantially less costly and ambitious than a measure he unveiled to members privately the week of Oct. 4.

That measure would have made three extenders permanent: a research and experimentation tax credit favored by high technology, biomedical and manufacturing companies; a tax credit for employers who cover graduate and undergraduate education costs for workers; and a provision to allow taxpayers subject to the alternative minimum tax to claim personal credits such as the $500-per-child tax credit.

The measure was estimated by the Joint Tax Committee to cost $1.7 billion in fiscal 2000 and $75.5 billion over 10 years. It did not include offsetting tax code changes.

After that measure met resistance from both Republicans and Democrats, Roth and Moynihan worked to scale it back to a level more in line with past extenders bills, and to pay for it.

The bill that resulted, which the panel approved, is narrower than the original. It would extend a dozen expiring provisions through Dec. 31, 2000, including the research and experimentation credit, the education credit and the alternative minimum tax fix. And it would extend the provisions without employing cost-saving stratagems, such as the House bill's provision to extend the research and experimentation credit but not allow companies to claim it until Oct. 1, 2000.

The Senate bill would be paid for largely with changes to the tax code that the committee has considered before, such as a provision to shorten the time frame in which taxes paid to foreign countries can be counted as a credit on U.S. income taxes. That provision would raise $87 million in fiscal 2000 and $3.5 billion over 10 years.

Other Tax Measures

In other action on taxes, the House leadership on Oct. 19 brought up a measure (HR 3085) by Rep. Lee Terry, R-Neb., incorporating the tax and fee increases that President Clinton included in his fiscal 2000 budget proposal. The bill failed, 0-419, with five Democrats voting present. The move was largely an effort to rule out raising tobacco and other taxes as a way to pay for spending bills. *(Vote 511, p. H-166)*

The House also voted along party lines, 215-203, to table a motion by Benjamin L. Cardin, D-Md., that would have prompted a vote to override Clinton's veto of the large tax bill. *(Vote 512, p. H-166)*

Senate Passes Bill To Extend Tax Provisions Through 2000

OCTOBER 30 — The Senate passed an $8.5 billion bill (S 1792) on Oct. 29 to extend expiring tax provisions. The House is expected to pass its own measure the week of Nov. 1.

An aide to Senate Majority Leader Trent Lott, R-Miss., said negotiators from the two chambers plan to convene a conference committee shortly after the House measure passes, to resolve considerable differences between the two bills.

The House measure (HR 2923 — H Rept 106-344) would cost $23.3 billion over five years, including $1.5 billion in fiscal 2000. The $1.5 billion would be offset by increasing penalties on taxpayers who inaccurately estimate their taxes, but the rest would not be offset.

The cost of the Senate bill, which passed by voice vote, is entirely offset by changes to the tax code. The bill is estimated to cost $3.5 billion in fiscal 2000, $7.6 billion over five years and $8.5 billion over 10 years.

The Senate bill costs less because it would extend all provisions only through Dec. 31, 2000. The House bill, which the Ways and Means Committee approved Sept. 24, would extend most provisions longer, including a five-year extension for a research and experimentation credit for businesses and a permanent extension of provisions that allow taxpayers subject to the alternative minimum tax to claim personal tax credits, such as the $500-per-child credit.

But the two bills are unlikely to be the only ones on conferees' agenda. Lott introduced his own $33 billion measure (S 1770) on Oct. 22. It would permanently extend the research and experimentation credit and would extend the other expiring provisions for 30 months. Lott is likely to be a conferee.

The research credit will be a key issue in conference. The high-technology, biomedical and manufacturing industries are pushing for a permanent or lengthy extension of the credit, and both parties are vying for the high-tech industry's favor.

Bill Clears Despite 11th Hour Debate Over Additions

NOVEMBER 20 — Extending a dozen tax breaks that expire annually has become almost second nature to Congress over the years. But this year's measure ran up against hurdles time and again, and it was one of the last major bills to clear Congress before it adjourned.

The House endorsed a legislative package (HR 1180) that included extensions of 13 expiring provisions, 418-2, on Nov. 18. The Senate cleared the measure, 95-1, on Nov. 19, with Republican George V. Voinovich of Ohio voting no. *(House vote 611, p. H-198; Senate vote 372, p. S-74)*

The action had been far from certain because of provisions in and out of HR 1180, which deals with health benefits for workers with disabilities. The Senate was tied in procedural knots over issues such as coal mining regulations and milk prices, and Senate GOP leaders had raised Democrats' ire when they inserted a provision on organ donations in HR 1180.

The organ provision, which would delay by at least 90 days a new regulation on donations, disregarded a 42-day delay that both parties had agreed to and that was included in the omnibus spending bill (HR 3194).

Sen. Edward M. Kennedy, D-Mass., and other Democrats lambasted the provision's inclusion in the bill, but they did not hold up consideration. A House leadership aide said President Clinton could negate the provision in the extenders package if he signed it before the spending bill, but Senate leaders indicated that they would delay sending HR 1180 to the White House until Clinton signed the spending bill.

Both congressional Republicans and Democrats supported the extenders package, and the White House voiced no objections, after the camps reached agreement on $2.9 billion to partially offset the bill's $21 billion cost over 10 years. The White House and congressional Democrats had been pushing to offset the entire measure, but they dropped any significant opposition after Republicans agreed to extend a set of provisions that Democrats wanted.

Members have generally extended the expiring provisions for a year or two, but with a projected budget surplus, this year's bill was broader. The measure would extend for five years the research and experimentation credit, which generally benefits high-tech, biotechnology and manufacturing companies. It would extend most other provisions through Dec. 31, 2001, a 24- or 30-month extension in most cases.

Bill Provisions

The major provisions in the extenders measure were more like those in the $23.3 billion bill (HR 2923) that the Ways and Means Committee approved in September than the $8.5 billion measure (S 1792) that the Senate passed in October, but it contained something for everyone involved in the process. The House bill's costs were measured over five years; the Senate's over 10. Cost estimates came from the Joint Committee on Taxation. The following tax breaks would be extended:

- **Research.** The major win for the House was the five-year extension of the research and experimentation credit, worth about 20 percent of a company's research and development costs, above a fixed average. The bill also would increase the credit for those businesses that use an alternate rate calculation that generally allows companies to claim more credits but at a lower rate. Both the House and Senate bills contained this provision.

The credit would be extended through June 30, 2004, but businesses could not claim it until Oct. 1, 2000, a qualification that had been included in the House bill to make the measure more affordable. The research and experimentation provisions would cost $13.1 billion over 10 years.

- **Alternative minimum tax.** The provision would allow the millions of taxpayers subject to the alternative minimum tax, a parallel tax system designed to ensure that taxpayers do not wipe out all tax liability through deductions and credits, to continue claiming personal tax credits, such as the $500-per-child credit. The extension would cost $2.9 billion over 10 years. Including it was considered a win for all parties because no one wanted to be blamed for raising taxes on the estimated 1 million taxpayers who would have been affected without the extension.
- Overseas investment. The bill includes a top priority of financial services companies: extending their exemption from so-called Subpart F rules, which require them to pay taxes on interest earned in other countries before the money is returned to the United States. The provision would cost $1.7 billion over 10 years.
- **Employment tax credits.** The bill would extend two provisions that give tax credits to employers who hire workers from certain hard-to-place groups, such as the disabled and young people age 18-24 from disadvantaged neighborhoods — the work opportunity tax credit and the welfare-to-work tax credit. Extending the provisions had been a priority of the retail and restaurant industries. The extensions would cost $1.4 billion over 10 years.
- **Education.** The bill would extend a provision that lets employers who pay for workers' undergraduate classes deduct those expenses from income taxes, at a cost of $584 million over 10 years. It would not expand the provision to graduate courses, as the Senate Finance Committee had proposed. The bill also includes a provision important to Democrats that would extend a program that gives tax credits to financial institutions that invest in bonds to improve schools in needy areas. The provision would cost $242 million over 10 years.
- **Environmental issues.** The measure would extend a program that provides tax credits to those who use wind or burn plant matter, known as biomass, to generate electricity. It would expand the program to include facilities that use poultry waste to generate power, a priority of Finance Chairman William V. Roth Jr., R-Del., whose state is home to many poultry producers. The provision would cost $318 million over 10 years.

The bill contained several provisions that did not extend tax programs. One would extend through Sept. 30,

2001, the generalized system of preferences, which lowers tariffs on goods imported from developing countries, at a cost of $798 million over 10 years.

And it included a provision that would ban the disclosure of advanced pricing agreements, confidential information that businesses must file with the Internal Revenue Service.

Offsets to pay for a portion of the bill included more than a dozen provisions. The one that would raise the most revenue — $2.1 billion over 10 years — would change accounting methods for some taxpayers who work on contract, such as architects and consultants. The bill also included changes to clarify the taxable status of Real Estate Investment Trusts, essentially mutual funds made up of property investments. ◆

GOP Offers Party-Defining Tax Cut Proposal; Clinton Responds With Veto

SUMMARY

The $792 billion Republican tax bill, which included something for everyone in the GOP, was viewed by outsiders and even by Republicans as more of a party-defining document than a potential law. After Republicans failed during the August recess to sell the bill to people back home, President Clinton vetoed it. Clinton had proposed more limited and targeted tax breaks in February. (*Text, p. D-24*)

Republicans knew that history was against them when they began the year calling for a 10 percent across-the-board cut in income taxes. Such an idea, pushed most vociferously by then-presidential candidate and House Budget Committee Chairman John R. Kasich, R-Ohio, had never been a political winner during good economic times — and the United States was experiencing record-breaking prosperity. Kasich and Senate Budget Committee Chairman Pete V. Domenici, R-N.M., reserved $792 billion of the projected non-Social Security budget surplus over 10 years for tax cuts, but their plans for the grandest reduction in taxes since the Reagan administration did not come to fruition.

Early on, when Republican moderates signaled that they were not comfortable with a large tax cut, it appeared that the party's divisions might prove too deep for them to unite even on their most prized issue. Some Republicans advocated waiting until 2000, when elections loomed, to push the issue. But leaders pressed on. In midsummer, when budget surplus projections came in higher than expected, both the House Ways and Means Committee and the Senate Finance Committee marked up big tax-cutting measures. Both chambers passed them, but only after leaders made a few changes to placate moderates.

The two bills differed greatly. The House measure was more tilted toward business. House lawmakers were also less concerned about charges that their bill would disproportionately help the wealthy. For instance, it would have cut income taxes across the board by 10 percent — which benefits most those who pay the most taxes — and it also would have reduced capital gains taxes and phased out estate taxes. To gain the support of GOP moderates, authors included a provision that would have cut personal income tax rates contingent upon reducing the interest paid on the national debt after 2001.

The Senate bill (S 1429) would have reduced income taxes only for those in the lowest — 15 percent — tax bracket. It included more provisions than the House bill to mitigate the so-called marriage penalty, which requires some married couples to pay more taxes than they would pay if they were single. It focused heavily on changing pension and retirement benefits, in an effort to add to the legacy of Finance Chairman William V. Roth Jr., R-Del., as a proponent of Individual Retirement Accounts. To get around Senate procedural hurdles, leaders agreed to sunset the bill's tax changes on Sept. 30, 2009.

It looked as if the bills were headed to a tough House-Senate conference committee, but differences evaporated with relative ease when GOP leaders appointed themselves to the panel. House Majority Leader Dick Armey, R-Texas, and Senate Majority Leader Trent Lott, R-Miss., were heavily involved in shaping the bill. The final product included a broad-based cut in personal income taxes, though its method of reducing each of the five tax brackets by 1 percentage point by 2005 was less advantageous to the rich than an across-the-board percentage cut. A broad cut had been a Lott priority. The final measure also contained $117 billion in marriage penalty relief over 10 years. Lawmakers said Armey had demanded that the bill include at least $100 billion in such relief, a priority of religious conservatives.

Most economists said the hodgepodge bill would do little to reduce tax complexity, but Republicans pushed forward with the measure, believing it would give them a potent political issue.

Republicans expect it will be harder for Clinton to veto a large tax cut bill in an election year, when Vice President Al Gore and several congression-

Box Score

- **Bill:** HR 2488
- **Legislative action: House** passed HR 2488 (H Rept 106-238), 233-208, on July 22.

Senate passed S 1429 (S Rept 106-120), 57-43, on July 30.

House adopted conference report on HR 2488 (H Rept 106-289), 221-206, on Aug. 5.

Senate cleared the bill, 50-49, on Aug. 5.

President vetoed HR 2488 on Sept. 23.

al Democrats will need political help. A similar version of the bill is likely to resurface next year, though the GOP knows it could meet the same fate as this year's bill.

President's Budget Doesn't Mesh With GOP's Tax Plan

FEBRUARY 6 — As has often been the case in the last 25 years of presidential budget plans, the tax proposals in President Clinton's fiscal 2000 package offer more of a confirmation of favored causes than a promising legislative blueprint.

The president's proposals, several of which recycle ideas that did not make it through prior Congresses, would largely benefit low- and middle-income taxpayers, addressing issues Clinton considers top priorities. For instance, taxpayers would receive tax credits to help care for elderly or disabled relatives, to pay for day care expenses, and to defray the cost of staying at home to raise infants or of installing energy saving devices in their homes.

The administration would cover the $32.6 billion cost of these initiatives by shutting down corporate tax shelters and tweaking the tax code to extract more revenue from wealthier taxpayers and businesses.

Republicans — who feel their vision of an across-the-board income tax cut looks more realistic in light of the budget surplus — were decidedly underwhelmed.

"To be candid, I find it incomprehensible that the president's plan would not allow for a wide-gauge tax cut in the next 15 years," Senate Finance Committee Chairman William V. Roth Jr., R-Del., said at a Feb. 2 hearing.

But Treasury Secretary Robert E. Rubin, testifying before Roth's committee, said tax burdens on working families were at "record lows for recent decades" — a point disputed by Republicans — and that the country would be better served by shoring up Social Security and paying down the national debt. "The core of this budget is fiscal discipline," he said.

The budget, like its predecessors, has no chance of passing through Congress intact. But it serves to lay out Clinton's agenda and, perhaps more than in recent years, highlight the differences between Republicans and Democrats, particularly on taxes.

With a budget surplus materializing for the first time in generations, providing a deep pocket for politicians' wish lists, Clinton's rejection of a big tax cut clearly would set him apart from the GOP Congress.

Though Republicans have agreed with Clinton that more than 60 percent of the surplus should be used to bolster Social Security, they are quick to claim the rest of it for the first across-the-board income tax cuts in more than a decade. The main question: How big?

"We're going to have huge surpluses, even beyond that that we're going to need for Social Security," House Budget Committee Chairman John R. Kasich, R-Ohio, said at a news conference Feb. 1, the day the president released his budget. "We can give, in my judgment, a 10 percent or 15 percent . . . 20 if we can get there. Whatever it is. We can give an across-the-board tax cut."

But before they spar with Clinton, Republicans must make sure their party is unified on tax issues. Consensus in the GOP for a broad tax cut is clearly stronger this year than last, when the Senate failed to take up a broad House bill and instead passed a small bill extending expiring tax breaks. But members have still not reached agreement on how much to cut.

At the Feb. 1 news conference with Kasich, Senate Budget Committee Chairman Pete V. Domenici, R-N.M., said he had "not found a way" to cut taxes by as much as 10 percent next year, though he could do so in 2003 or 2004, he said.

And Sen. John H. Chafee of Rhode Island, a Republican moderate, said repeatedly at the Finance Committee hearing Feb. 2 that he favored using as much of the surplus as possible to pay down the federal debt — an idea Federal Reserve Chairman Alan Greenspan endorsed at a hearing Jan. 28. "We should use nearly all the surplus that materializes for debt reduction," Chafee said.

Chafee's more conservative colleagues seem convinced that a tax cut is necessary, in part because many analysts blamed the GOP's lackluster showing in the 1998 election on the lack of such a cut. With a budget surplus materializing, Kasich said, "we're not going to blow this."

Republicans assume that the public is clamoring for a tax cut — an evergreen of politics — but many polls suggest that in this topsy-turvy political year the percentage of people interested in shoring up Social Security is far greater than the percentage that wants a tax cut. "Saving Social Security" has been Clinton's mantra, and if the early polls are borne out, he could once again win the war of public opinion — despite long odds and despite being impeached — and keep Republicans from a major victory on taxes.

Republicans' main complaints with Clinton's tax proposals are that certain people are targeted to encourage certain activities, and thus they are more like a government program than a tax cut.

Areas of Agreement

While Republicans — and several academics — believe such initiatives are making the tax code unnecessarily complicated, some of Clinton's individual proposals for tax credits do not face Republican opposition.

For instance, his plan to give up to $1,000 in annual tax credits to elderly or disabled people or their caregivers to supplement the cost of long-term care is similar to a GOP proposal included in the 1995 budget-reconciliation bill that Clinton vetoed for other reasons. The credit would be phased out for wealthier taxpayers. *(1995 Almanac, p. 2-66)*

Clinton's plan would also expand the child and dependent care tax credit, last increased in 1982, to cover 50 percent instead of 30 percent of child care costs for taxpayers with annual adjusted gross incomes of $30,000 or less. The credit would be phased down for higher-income filers, until it reached 20 percent for taxpayers with incomes greater than $59,000.

In response to GOP criticism that the child care proposals had not taken families with a stay-at-home parent into account, Clinton's plan would give all parents with a child up to one year old a $250 per child tax credit.

Among other initiatives included in the president's $32.6 billion in tax breaks and credits are:

- A plan similar to one in Clinton's fiscal 1999 budget that would enable state and local governments to issue $24.8 billion in bonds to build or renovate public schools, mostly in areas with lower-income children.
- Six separate credits for taxpayers who purchase energy-efficient homes, use solar energy, or purchase electric or fuel-efficient hybrid automobiles.
- More than a dozen proposals aimed at encouraging retirement savings, including simplifying pensions by allowing people to more easily consolidate different retirement accounts without adverse tax consequences.

A proposal certain to gain Republican support would extend five expiring tax credits that generally help businesses, including a credit for research and experimentation and a credit for hiring welfare recipients. A Ways and Means Committee staff member said Chairman Bill Archer, R-Texas, was committed to extending the provisions.

Clinton's budget would also extend a provision Congress enacted last year in the omnibus spending bill (PL 105-277) to allow taxpayers to benefit from tax credits, such as a $500 per child credit passed in 1997, even if they are required to file the alternative minimum tax (AMT). The AMT, a parallel income tax system, was created in 1969 (PL 91-172) to ensure that wealthy filers did not use exemptions and credits to wipe out their income taxes. But middle-income filers are now affected. Clinton's budget would extend Congress' fix for two years, but Archer wants a more comprehensive overhaul of the tax.

Republicans may not like some of Clinton's tax credit proposals, but they do not oppose them as vehemently as his plan to raise money to pay for them. A major component aims to crack down on the use and marketing of corporate tax shelters — and raise an estimated $7.17 billion over five years.

The administration would also clarify or change the tax treatment of certain stock transactions and subject large trade associations to corporate income taxes on net investment income of more than $10,000.

Clinton aims to increase cigarette taxes by 55 cents a pack, and accelerate implementation of an increase of 15 cents per pack enacted as part of the 1997 budget-reconciliation package (PL 105-34). The administration estimates that the tobacco plan would raise $34.5 billion through 2004. It would be used to offset $42.3 billion in estimated tobacco-related costs to federal health care programs. *(1997 Almanac, p. 2-38)*

GOP Tax Plans Yield to Political Reality: Not Much And Not Now

FEBRUARY 27 — With Republican leaders' dreams of a Reaganesque, 10 percent across-the-board income tax cut appearing to fade, the party found itself in familiar territory the week of Feb. 22 — in search of a tax plan that would fit both its political needs and its budget.

There was no shortage of suggestions from GOP Conference members. Moderates pushed their package of targeted tax cuts aimed at married couples, senior citizens and people who buy their own health insurance. Others renewed calls to phase out or eliminate the estate tax or trim payroll taxes. Others tried to rejuvenate talk of replacing the income tax with a sales tax or flat tax.

With all the chatter inside Congress — and pressure from Republican governors and others outside the Capitol to pass as broad a tax cut as possible — GOP leaders appeared likely to put off decisions on specific tax cuts until after they pass a budget resolution. "We don't have to decide that now," Senate Majority Whip Don Nickles, R-Okla., said Feb. 23, "and we don't even have to decide that by the budget."

The budget resolution, a non-binding blueprint for federal spending and revenue goals, sets the overall parameters of any tax bill. The Senate Budget Committee may take up its resolution the week of March 8 — panel Chairman Pete V. Domenici, R-N.M., released highlights of his proposal Feb. 23 — and the House Budget Committee plans to take up its version the next week.

Domenici's aides said the senator's plan would provide $787 billion to $900 billion in tax relief from fiscal 2000 through fiscal 2010, most of it toward the end. More immediate projections show that Republicans will have to choose among several proposals, and perhaps pare them down, to fit their budget. Domenici's plan could fund $154 billion in tax cuts over five years, but just $5 billion in fiscal 2000.

That is not much in the trillion-dollar federal revenue system. Moderate Republicans' targeted tax plan, sponsored by Rep. Nancy L. Johnson, R-Conn., is estimated to cost $8 billion in fiscal 2000. The across-the-board income tax cut proposed by House Budget Committee Chairman John R. Kasich, R-Ohio, would cost $59 billion in fiscal 2000, according to the Joint Committee on Taxation.

Republican leaders could not implement Kasich's plan without creative accounting or without breaking a pledge to reserve 62 percent of the budget surplus — about $2.8 trillion over 15 years — for Social Security. And some experts say the cost was only the nail in the tax cut's coffin, not the killer.

Tax cuts have long been thought to be political winners in both good times and bad, but public opinion polls taken in the last year consistently showed tax cuts ranking lower on Americans' priority list than shoring up Social Security or spending more on education.

Republicans, eager to find a way into the public's good graces after the unpopular impeachment trial, did not want to risk a costly gaffe by pushing a fiscally unwieldy tax cut for which the public was not clamoring.

"I'm jaded enough to believe that politics is why it died," said William Gale, a senior fellow at the Brookings Institution, a public policy think tank that predicted the across-the-board tax cut's demise several weeks ago. "Having said that, the economics of it were atrocious."

But Gale believes the proposal had a good side. "The surplus is a lobbyist's dream and one of the advantages of having the across-the-board cut there was [that], on some grounds, it trumped all other targeted tax cuts. To have that disappear from the scene so quickly . . . might ultimately make the outcome much worse," he said.

He said the vacuum left by the apparent death of the broader tax cut will energize lobbyists and interest groups to pressure lawmakers to give their friends in the business community and elsewhere targeted relief.

The tax-writing committees will be left to sort it out, perhaps with fewer leadership dictates than if the 10 percent proposal were still in the forefront. Ways and Means Committee spokesman Ari Fleischer said panel Chairman Bill Archer, R-Texas, is likely to unveil a tax proposal in early May. The House traditionally moves tax measures first. That gives members and lobbyists two months to duke it out for a piece of the surplus.

Marriage Penalty

A plan to eliminate the so-called marriage penalty is an early front-runner for the tax bill. It has support from both the left and right wings of the Republican Party and increasing support from Democrats.

The marriage penalty is a quirk of the tax code that leaves some married couples with a higher tax bill than unmarried couples with the same income. This is largely because married couples are sometimes pushed into the next tax bracket. The tax code establishes lower bracket thresholds for married people than it does for single filers.

In a 1997 study, the Congressional Budget Office (CBO) estimated that 21 million married couples were affected by the penalty in 1996, with the average paying $1,400 more than an unmarried couple with the same income.

Many lawmakers believe changing the penalty is necessary to help newlyweds financially and to remove any tacit government condemnation of marriage. Reducing or removing the penalty is mentioned in hundreds of bills introduced this year, but the one most likely to see action is a measure (HR 6) sponsored by Reps. Jerry Weller, R-Ill., David M. McIntosh, R-Ind., and Pat Danner, D-Mo.

The bill, which has more than 200 cosponsors, would widen tax brackets for married couples, allowing them to remain in the 15 percent, or lowest, bracket if their taxable annual income was $51,500 or less. Currently, the limit is $41,200 for married couples and $24,650 for single people. The bill would also increase the standard deduction for married couples from $6,900 to $8,300. Standard deductions for single people would remain at $4,150.

Speaker J. Dennis Hastert, R-Ill., has endorsed the plan, and Johnson plans to make a portion of it the centerpiece of her bill. She has not yet introduced the measure, though nearly 20 Republicans have already signed on to it.

Johnson's measure would address the marriage penalty by increasing the standard deduction. It is also expected to include several other provisions, which she says mostly aim to give relief to middle-income taxpayers. Fixing the marriage penalty would help high- and middle-income taxpayers the most, according to CBO studies, but would also help some lower-income people.

Likely to be included in Johnson's proposal are provisions to increase from $15,500 to $30,000 the income that workers age 65 to 69 could earn without losing Social Security benefits, to allow self-employed people to deduct 100 percent of health insurance premiums from their taxable income, and to make permanent some business tax credits, including those for research and development and for hiring welfare recipients.

Estate Tax and Other Contenders

Johnson's bill will likely not touch on one tax that is anathema to many Republicans — the estate tax.

Opponents like to call it the "death tax" because it is the children or the estate of the deceased who must pay this inheritance tax. The first $650,000 of inheritance is exempt, but beyond that level it is taxed at 55 percent. The exemption is set to increase annually until 2006, when it will be $1 million.

Two recently introduced bills would eliminate that penalty, though on different schedules. A measure (HR 8) sponsored by Reps. Jennifer Dunn, R-Wash., and John Tanner, D-Tenn., would phase out the tax by 5 percent each year, until it was eliminated in 2010. A bill (HR 86) sponsored by Rep. Christopher Cox, R-Calif., House Majority Leader Dick Armey, R-Texas, and Majority Whip Tom DeLay, R-Texas, would repeal the tax immediately.

Though eliminating the tax is popular with many business and farm groups whose members want to pass the family operations on to their children, it is likely to come under Democratic attacks because many beneficiaries would have high incomes. It also could be expensive. Sen. Orrin G. Hatch, R-Utah, who favors eliminating the tax, said recently that an outright repeal would cost $16 billion a year in lost revenue.

Another Republican proposal likely to come under attack is a plan to cut capital gains taxes, particularly for corporations.

Some Republicans, such as Nickles, are interested in cutting the payroll tax, which funds Social Security and Medicare. Nickles said he hopes for some Democratic support, because low-income people are often hit harder by the payroll tax than the income tax. But cutting the payroll tax would be highly controversial because of the revenues lost for Social Security and Medicare.

While most members are pushing specific tax cut proposals, at least one — Ways and Means member Jim Nussle, R-Iowa — is urging the party to rejuvenate plans to scrap the current tax code and start over. "I just don't want to see this issue gone by the wayside," Nussle said Feb. 23. "I think this can be more important than reducing taxes."

Nussle said he has not chosen sides between the flat income tax advocated by Armey and the sales tax on goods and services that Archer advocates. Armey and Archer plan to meet to see whether they can find common ground in their proposals, Fleischer said, but they have not set a date.

Concern for the Future

Nussle is not the only one who hopes to rekindle Republicans' interest in broader tax policy.

All of the announced or anticipated candidates for the party's presidential nomination in 2000 — including Kasich — are pushing a tax cut, hoping to reclaim taxes as the party's main issue.

And congressional Republicans are relying on tax relief for their 2000 reelection campaigns. "I believe tax relief will happen in the next two years in a big way," Dunn said Feb. 22. "I truly believe this is our wedge issue."

That is why reports that Republicans had abandoned an across-the-board tax cut so early this year were met with scorn from many party faithful outside Congress or the Beltway.

Several Republican governors, in town for the annual conference of the National Governors' Association, urged party leaders in Congress to stand firm on tax cuts, and not to fear a veto from President Clinton.

Others from organizations on the party's conservative side used harsher tones. "It's truly a shame to watch," Larry Klayman, chairman of Judicial Watch, a conservative legal group, said in a statement Feb. 23. "This is a party that . . . has managed to become ashamed of pushing the centerpiece of the conservative agenda."

Emotional Archer Shepherds Bill Through House Ways and Means

JULY 17 — Congressional Republicans are moving the largest tax cut proposal since the Reagan administration in a post-Deficit Era bid to reclaim the tax issue's unifying power over their tentative and still-fractious majority.

But as an $864 billion House plan and a $792 billion Senate proposal came into view the week of July 12, the question was whether the ambitious GOP game plan could produce the second coming of the tax-cut strategy that became the centerpiece of Ronald Reagan's 1980 election to the White House.

Reagan's victory and subsequent push for a $749 billion tax cut in 1981 unified the "austerity" and "supply side" wings of the party, which then enabled Republicans to dominate the issue through most of the 1980s. But the GOP lost that advantage after former President George Bush's backslide in 1990 from his "no new taxes" pledge and the subsequent election of Bill Clinton in 1992. Ever since then, Democrats have been able to keep Republicans on the defensive. Witness former Senate Majority Leader Bob Dole's attempts to use tax cuts as a springboard to the presidency in 1996: It was an utter failure.

Now, working with slim majorities in both the House and Senate and a promising presidential candidate in Bush's son, Texas Gov. George W. Bush, Republicans are trying to reclaim a successful tax cut strategy for 1999 and 2000.

Bill Archer, R-Texas, chairman of the House Ways and Means Committee, sounded the clarion call as he moved his bill (HR 2488) through the committee July 13-14. This is the "defining difference between Republicans and Democrats," he said. "Democrats believe the government can spend money more effectively and more wisely than people can spend their own money. We believe people can spend their own money more wisely. . . . That is the issue that is before us here today with this bill."

Rep. Jennifer Dunn of Washington reflected Republicans' newfound optimism as the Archer plan moved through Ways and Means with solid GOP support (and equally solid Democratic opposition). "It's exciting," Dunn said. "Tax cuts are just the meat and bones of the party. I want people to know we're different."

But the GOP's tax cut fever may cool off when confronted by economic realities: tax cuts almost always happen in bad economic times. And many economists say the nation, in a period of record fiscal prosperity, is not in need of a stimulus. Such a large plan may be offset almost immediately by an interest rate increase from a Federal Reserve board of governors already nervous about inflation.

Moreover, public opinion polls in recent years have consistently shown that respondents put education, Social Security and other issues ahead of tax cuts on their list of national priorities.

And House Republican leaders face a challenge from 15 to 20 party moderates who are threatening to vote against the measure if it is not changed to provide more money for debt reduction. In addition, the Christian Coalition is angry that Republican leaders did not do more in the bill to correct the code's so-called marriage penalty.

Nonetheless, many lawmakers and observers believe that a tax bill will likely be forthcoming this year, though not the bill that Ways and Means approved July 14 nor the one the Finance Committee is expected to take up July 20 and 21. "The president wants tax cuts. . . . The Republican Congress wants tax cuts. It's going to happen," Sen. Richard H. Bryan, D-Nev., said July 14.

"If the Republicans wanted to, they could write a tax bill that the president would sign," said Wendell Primus, director of income security for the Center for Budget and Policy Priorities, a group concerned with low- and middle-income Americans. "There's a pretty big gulf between the two parties at the moment, but I'm not willing to say that the gulf can't be bridged."

Ever more optimistic predictions for an on-budget surplus — one that does not depend on Social Security revenues — have defused Democratic arguments that a tax cut would raid Social Security, although Democrats are still quick to point out that the Social Security program has not been overhauled to ensure long-term solvency.

Some Democrats privately say they fear that Clinton, who has already offered to work on a tax plan with Republicans despite his threat to veto the House bill, will sign on to a bigger bill than Democrats want. They are leery of his track record of switching positions on key issues such as the 1996 welfare overhaul bill (PL 104-193). And while House Democrats have remained united in calling for shoring up Social Security and Medicare and paying down the national debt before cutting taxes, some of their Senate counterparts are more willing to go along with a cut early on.

Republicans touted their bills as embodying what the party stands for, but they will have to work to keep party members on the same page. The Senate bill, unveiled July 16, does not include cuts in capital gains taxes — a cornerstone of the House bill. In the House, some moderate Republicans met with conservative Democrats the week of July 12 to devise strategies to dedicate more of the on-budget surplus to debt reduction.

Some of these House moderates said they thought there was enough party opposition to the bill to delay its expected floor consideration the week of July 19. One member said at least 15 moderate Republicans were prepared to vote against the Ways and Means bill. The Senate Finance Committee is expected to take up a bill by Chairman William V. Roth Jr., R-Del., on July 20 and 21.

Senate Democrats, eager to keep their sometimes unruly flock together, are preparing a $295 billion alternative plan for the markup, and House Democrats will offer an alternative to

History of Recent Tax Bills

1981 Economic Recovery Tax Act (PL 97-34)

Inheriting a sluggish economy and promising sweeping tax cuts, President Ronald Reagan proposed a largely untested "supply-side" economic plan at the start of his administration. The theory, dubbed "Reaganomics," held that restricting government growth and returning taxes to businesses and workers would inspire Americans to work harder and save more. Congress adopted Reagan's plan, which included $749 billion in tax cuts for businesses and individuals over five years. The plan reduced individual income tax rates by about 25 percent over 33 months and reduced the maximum capital gains tax rate from 28 percent to 20 percent. *(1981 Almanac, p. 91)*

1986 Tax Reform Act (PL 99-514)

At the end of 1985, the nation faced its largest budget deficit and a slowing economy. Reagan avoided endorsing a tax boost but made overhauling the tax code his No. 1 domestic priority. The tax law, which projected $121.9 billion in individual taxpayer savings over five years, reduced tax rates and, against the president's wishes, closed many tax "loopholes." It eliminated the traditional lower tax rate on capital gains, making them taxable at the same rate as ordinary income. The law reduced the top individual marginal tax rate from 50 percent to 28 percent and put 85 percent of Americans into the bottom rate of 15 percent. It reduced the top corporate tax rate from 46 percent to 34 percent but generally shifted tax liability from individuals to corporations. *(1986 Almanac, p. 491)*

1990 Omnibus Budget-Reconciliation Act (PL 101-508)

Reversing his "no new taxes" campaign pledge, President George Bush signed a measure to reduce the deficit largely by increasing revenues. The law included a gasoline tax increase, an increase in the income tax rate for people in the highest tax bracket from 28 percent to 31 percent, a phasing out of personal exemptions for upper-income taxpayers, and an increase in alcohol and tobacco excise taxes. The five-year plan aimed to reduce the deficit by $236 billion, including $137 billion in revenue increases. *(1990 Almanac, p. 111)*

1993 Omnibus Budget-Reconciliation Act (PL 103-66)

Less than a month after taking office, President Clinton unveiled an ambitious plan for pairing deficit reduction with a renewed government role in spurring the economy. The five-year, $496 billion bill targeted the wealthiest taxpayers. No Republicans voted for it, and some Democrats were skeptical. The Office of Management and Budget estimated that $250 billion of the proposed deficit reduction would come from taxes. The law created a fourth tax bracket (between 35 percent and 36 percent) and additional surtaxes for corporations and upper-income families. It also imposed a permanent 4.3-cents-per-gallon excise tax on most transportation fuels. Democrats hoped deficit reduction would yield lower interest rates and trigger job growth. *(1993 Almanac, p. 107)*

1997 Tax-Payer Relief Act (PL 105-34)

Building on a strong economy, Congress and Clinton enacted the deepest tax cut since 1981, including $275 billion in cuts over 10 years. The bill and its companion balanced-budget law (PL 105-33) aimed to eliminate the federal deficit by 2002. The tax bill included a $500-per-child tax credit. It generally cut capital gains tax rates by 8 percent and created tax-preferred individual retirement accounts named after Sen. William V. Roth Jr., R-Del. The tax cuts were partially offset by revenue raisers, including a tax on air travel. *(1997 Almanac, p. 2-30)*

Archer's bill on the floor.

GOP leaders are equally eager to rally their party around the issue, and to use the bills to foreshadow arguments likely to be heard on the 2000 campaign trail.

Archer's bill contains tax-cutting proposals that Republicans have long hoped to enact: a 10 percent across-the-board reduction in income tax rates over the next 10 years, a cut in capital gains taxes, progress on eliminating the so-called marriage penalty and a phase-out of inheritance taxes within 10 years.

The ranking Democrat on Archer's panel, Charles B. Rangel of New York, agreed that the bill showcased both parties' positions well. "There's a great difference between us," he said at the markup July 13. "From the beginning, you never supported Social Security . . . Medicare . . . health care." He added, "I had no idea that you were going to kick off the year 2000 campaign in this committee."

Senate Plans

While several conservative Senate Republicans also want to highlight such differences, many chamber Democrats will not make it easy. Unlike in the House, where Minority Leader Richard A. Gephardt of Missouri and other party leaders have persuaded even the most conservative Democrats to oppose the Archer bill, at least for now, Senate Democrats have been more independent.

In an interview July 15, Sen. Bob Kerrey, D-Neb., said he would likely vote for Roth's bill when it came up in committee.

"I'm not troubled by the size of it," he said, adding that he thought it possible to shore up Medicare and cut taxes at the same time. "My guess is I will not be alone."

Roth's bill would cut the lowest income tax rate from 15 percent to 14 percent, phase out portions of the marriage penalty and make it easier for more people to set aside retirement funds at favorable tax rates.

It is more palatable to Democrats than Archer's bill because it does not include rate cuts on capital gains from the sale of stocks, bonds or property, which tend to favor wealthier taxpayers. But its $792 billion price tag over 10 years is too high for some. Panel member John B. Breaux, D-La., said of the tax reductions, "I think that Roth's is too high and that the Democrats' is too low."

Roth continued to work with Democrats and moderate Republicans such as James M. Jeffords of Vermont and John H. Chafee of Rhode Island, who favors more debt reduction, but it was unclear how many would support the measure. The Senate plan is more likely than the House bill to be to Clinton's liking, but it costs too much to keep available enough of the on-budget surplus for discretionary spending and other programs the administration is likely to insist upon.

Many Congress-watchers believe that GOP leaders and Clinton will reach a middle ground for tax cuts between the $250 billion Clinton has suggested and the $800 billion to $900 billion Republicans want.

"It's obvious that they're going to $500 billion," said Kevin Hassett, an analyst for the American Enterprise Institute, a business-oriented Washington think tank. Hassett does not think a tax cut of that size would hurt the economy, but other economists say it may not be the right time for such a stimulus.

"They'll increase consumption substantially and lower our savings rate, and we don't need that," said Primus of the budget and policy center.

Said William G. Gale, a senior fellow at the Brookings Institution: "The economy is already screaming along and the Fed is already putting on the brakes. It's quite plausible that the Fed would want to counteract any stimulative effect further and raise interest rates."

Many economists are skeptical about positive effects from the voluminous GOP tax cut, but they also say it would be preferable to a bill filled with tax credits, similar to what the president has consistently proposed. They say tax credits clog up and complicate the tax code, especially because many credits enacted in recent years are phased out at different income levels. "I don't think we could do worse than we've done in recent years," said Alan J. Auerbach, an economics and law professor at the University of California at Berkeley.

Many economists say they are disappointed that lawmakers have not proposed more radical changes. "That's what's so disappointing about this whole episode, and I think frankly both sides are to blame," Gale said.

"Even with the sort of changes that are being tossed around in the House, they're still sort of in the box," Hassett said. "It's a really, really ornate box that everybody dislikes, but they're not really willing to try to clean things up at all. . . . It shows the deep fear that the Republicans have that the money will get spent. They are, in some sense, giving up the goal of getting the tax system they really want in order to make sure the money leaves town as fast as possible."

Archer, who has long declared his desire to "rip the tax code out by its roots," admitted as much during his panel's 15-hour markup over two days. He said the contentiousness had convinced him "even more that we will never fix the income tax. . . . As changes are made, it will create demand for greater changes."

House Markup

But despite his passion for replacing the income tax with a surtax on the purchase price of goods and services, the retiring chairman was emotional about his bill when he addressed the party conference July 14. "He said this is the bill he's been wanting to write for 29 years," said Rep. Robert L. Ehrlich Jr., R-Md. In unveiling details July 13, Archer said abolishing the income tax was "another issue for another day."

Archer's immediate task was to move his mammoth bill through his committee, highlighting the differences between the two parties. The differences were evident from the beginning of opening statements at 6 p.m. July 13 to the 23-13 party-line vote to approve the bill around 9 p.m. July 14.

Republicans of all political stripes offered praise for Archer, a 28-year veteran in his last term in Congress. They then offered amendments targeted at specific industries that made his bill, which already contained dozens of provisions to appeal to all facets of the party and the population, even more of a repository for the party's ideas on how to change the tax system.

Democrats, from liberals such as Pete Stark of California to conservatives such as John Tanner of Tennessee, offered amendments to reduce the tax cut to pay for social spending or debt reduction.

Among the industry-related amendments adopted were proposals by Dunn and Mac Collins, R-Ga., to allow certain people in the timber industry to deduct more costs from their income taxes and to cut their capital gains taxes. Both were approved by voice vote.

The committee also accepted by voice vote an amendment by Wes Watkins, R-Okla., and William J. Jefferson, D-La., to allow oil and gas producers to deduct more costs from their income taxes, and an amendment by Nancy L. Johnson, R-Conn., to increase the amount of tax credits states could offer low-income housing developers. It would cost $3.8 billion over 10 years. Johnson's amendment was adopted despite Archer's opposition to her plan to pay for it by scaling back Archer's cut in corporation tax rates on capital gains.

The panel approved by voice vote an amendment by Collins to require wholesalers of distilled spirits to collect and pay taxes on domestic and imported liquor, instead of requiring producers and importers to pay the taxes directly.

The committee defeated by voice vote an amendment to include a measure (HR 957) by Kenny Hulshof, R-Mo., to allow family farmers to deduct up to 20 percent of their net income from their income tax if they set the money aside in Farm and Ranch Risk Management Accounts designed to be drawn upon in bad times. Distributions from the accounts would have been taxed as regular income.

While Republicans attempted to help constituent businesses, Democrats tried to cut the bill and direct the funds to their priority programs. All their amendments were defeated on party- line votes, including:

- A plan by Robert T. Matsui, D-Calif., to cut all provisions in the bill except the extension of certain expiring business tax credits and a few revenue offsets. Matsui said this would have preserved a portion of the non-Social Security surplus to help the retirement program stay solvent for 75 years. It was defeated, 13-23.

- An amendment by Richard E. Neal, D-Mass., to postpone the tax cuts until the Office of Management and Budget certifies that the budget is balanced, Social Security will be solvent for 75 years and the Medicare Trust Fund will be solvent until 2027. It was defeated, 13-22.
- A plan by Tanner to halve the tax plan and dedicate $400 billion-plus to paying down the national debt. It was defeated, 13-23.

Democrats also proposed cutting $375 billion from the bill to pay for the president's Medicare prescription drug benefit plan — a Stark amendment to do so was defeated, 13-22 — but Republicans pre-empted action on the issue by addressing it first.

At the beginning of the markup, Archer introduced a plan to allow Medicare recipients to deduct premiums for prescription drug insurance from income taxes. Enactment of the proposal was tied to conditions: The federal government would have to subsidize prescription drug coverage for low-income Medicare recipients and drug coverage would have to be provided through health plans that compete with each other. The latter provision was supported by a majority of the Medicare Commission, which was charged with finding a way to shore up the troubled health insurance program. The panel, headed by Breaux and Rep. Bill Thomas, R-Calif., disbanded after failing to reach agreement in March.

Democrats charged that the conditions were "a back-door approach" to enact the Breaux-Thomas plan and pre-empt Clinton's. But Thomas said the provision was a placeholder "for the possibility of using deductions as a way to assist seniors." The two parties argued over Medicare throughout the markup. Stark offered an amendment to give Medicare beneficiaries tax credits of up to $1,000 a year to cover the cost of prescription drugs, starting in 2002 and increasing to $2,500 a year by 2008. He estimated its cost at $270 billion over 10 years. It was defeated, 11-23.

The next day, Thomas said the panel's adoption of Archer's amendment had laid "to rest once and for all that Democrats are interested in taking care of seniors and Republicans are interested in cutting taxes. As a matter of fact, Republicans are interested in both."

House Passes Bill; Republicans Forge Ahead Toward Certain Veto

JULY 24 — With House passage and Senate committee approval of a $792 billion tax measure, congressional Republicans forged ahead on their goal of sending members home in August to tout their tax-cutting accomplishments — and overshadow the problems that appropriators are having in advancing their bills.

No one believes that a tax bill the size of the current ones (HR 2488, Senate draft) is headed anywhere except toward a presidential veto. That even appeared to be one of the lubricants in the legislative process enabling wary House moderates to vote for it.

The battle over taxes will be fought on terrain much different from what combatants faced in earlier skirmishes. With budget surpluses projected to fill federal coffers to overflowing, Republicans have conceded to Democrats that Social Security surpluses, which are roughly two-thirds of the total surplus over the next decade, will not be used to finance tax cuts. President Clinton has accepted that some of the rest of the surplus will be given back to taxpayers.

Clinton has a commanding tactical advantage in that his veto pen can kill any tax bill. But he may need to cooperate with Republicans if he is to win the domestic policy initiatives that will define his legacy, which has been tarred by impeachment.

For now, the competing sides are not expected to focus on the kind of split-the-differences deal that would win passage but blunt their message. Asked July 18 on Fox News Sunday whether he would "cut a deal in the middle," Senate Majority Leader Trent Lott, R-Miss., said, "Nope."

Privately, however, GOP leaders gave a different pitch: "You know this is not going to be the final product. We're moving the process forward," said moderate Sherwood Boehlert, R-N.Y., quoting pleas he received from the GOP leadership team, including Lott.

The Senate bill will come to the floor the week of July 26. With a reduction of the lowest tax rate from 15 percent to 14 percent as its centerpiece, it has been fashioned to repel Democrats' complaint that most GOP-crafted tax benefits flow to the rich.

As they did in committee, however, Democrats will charge on the floor that the benefits of the Senate bill would "explode" in the second five years of the plan. Democrats also criticize the Senate bill for "backloading" provisions that mainly benefit the wealthy, such as cuts in the estate tax, into the second five years of the bill.

Still, the House bill, with its 10 percent across-the-board tax rate cut, capital gains tax cuts and elimination of inheritance taxes, is more susceptible to charges that it favors the wealthy.

Among the big questions is how many Democrats and moderate Republicans will support a tax cut of about $500 billion, about halfway between the House bill and Clinton's budget proposal. Five non-Finance Committee Democrats signaled support for such a plan in a July 20 letter to moderates John B. Breaux, D-La., and Bob Kerrey, D-Neb., who assembled it. But Breaux said Democratic Leader Tom Daschle of South Dakota immediately registered his alarm.

Itching for Debate

Republicans in Congress have been itching all year for a grand, party-defining debate over tax cuts — hoping to showcase their differences with Clinton and the Democrats.

But first they had to bridge a rift between the GOP mainstream and the moderate wing. At one point, House moderates were in open revolt, and passage of the bill (HR 2488) appeared in peril.

Losing was not an option, however.

After a relentless whip effort, the moderates yielded, though only upon winning a provision that would condition the bill's marquee, 10 percent across-the-board cut in tax rates on achieving promised levels of savings elsewhere in the budget.

In the end, the bill passed, 223-

208, on July 22, giving House Speaker J. Dennis Hastert, R-Ill., his biggest win in an often difficult year. Four Republicans voted against the bill and six Democrats voted for it. *(Vote 333, p. H-110)*

"This is a great win for the American people — people that go to work every day, that punch a time clock . . . people who make this country work every day, day in and day out," Hastert said at a rally after passage.

Hastert had staked his speakership on the bill, and the pressure on GOP members to support it was intense. Losing the vote would have been a political debacle that would have threatened to rob Republicans of one of the last issues that vividly separate them from Democrats.

"Tax cuts for the American people . . . are an important part for us being able to move forward" as a party, Hastert said in an interview July 22. "I just said, 'If you want to be part of the team, this is a pretty important part of the process.' "

On the other side of the Capitol, at a markup by the Senate Finance Committee, the split between Republican moderates and conservatives was equally public but decidedly low-key. Two prominent GOP moderates and two moderate Democrats — Kerrey and Breaux — despite voicing reservations, voted to approve a $792 billion, 10-year tax cut. The prized Democratic support gave the bill a 13-7 vote.

"What we're doing, in my mind, is pretty precarious," said James M. Jeffords, R-Vt. He said he hoped ultimately to vote for a tax bill that split the differences between Clinton and Republicans.

Veto Promised

Clinton promised a veto at almost every public appearance the week of July 19. He opened a July 21 news conference, for example, with a lengthy statement on taxes.

"We're not debating whether to have tax cuts or not. We should have tax cuts, but tax cuts that provide for us first to save Social Security and Medicare, not undermine them," Clinton said. "Tax cuts we can afford, not ones that would demand drastic cuts in defense, education, agriculture or the environment. . . . If Congress passes the wrong kind, of course, I will not sign it. I will not allow a risky plan to become law."

Polls suggest voters want a tax cut. But when voters are asked whether they prefer cutting taxes instead of shoring up Social Security and Medicare and spending more on education, the environment, health care and defense, they consistently put taxes near the end of the list. For example, a Pew Research Center poll released July 22 found that 60 percent of respondents wanted a tax cut as opposed to generic "new government programs." But that slid to just 22 percent when the programs were identified.

Clinton is using the presidential spotlight to cast the debate in those terms. At a July 22 rally in Michigan for his Medicare prescription drug benefit, for example, Clinton asked voters to tell Congress they would settle for a smaller tax cut "if the money goes to save Medicare and Social Security, and keep up our investment in the education of our children, and pay the debt off." His proposed benefit may have been set back, however, when the Congressional Budget Office said it would cost $168 billion over 10 years, instead of the $118 billion the administration estimated.

Republicans hope the visceral appeal of a big dose of tax relief will create a public climate in which voters demand tax cuts from their lawmakers in Washington.

"If the power company or the phone company overbilled their customers, the customers would rightfully go berserk," said House Ways and Means Committee Chairman Bill Archer, R-Texas, sponsor of HR 2488. "The exact same thing is happening in Washington, and the American people expect and deserve their money back."

Archer's bill would, among other provisions, phase in a 10 percent across-the-board income tax rate cut; ease but not erase the so-called marriage penalty — in which certain couples pay more than they would pay if they remained single; trim and ultimately repeal estate taxes; lower tax rates on gains from the sale of real estate, stocks and other investments; and expand medical and education savings accounts.

Clinton backs only targeted tax breaks, although White House officials hinted that he would embrace Democratic ideas such as increasing taxpayers' standard deduction.

Moderates Hang Tough

Boehlert was among a group of members, mostly moderates, who initially held fast in opposition to the bill. The group, which at one point numbered about 20, was concerned that the tax cut would eat up almost all the $1 trillion portion of the non-Social Security-generated surplus over the next decade. They wanted more of that money available for debt reduction, fixing Social Security and Medicare and adding money to cash-starved discretionary programs.

"This tax cut is too large and it's based upon totally optimistic assumptions," Boehlert said. "It does not factor in the necessity of adjusting the spending caps."

House GOP moderates have earned a reputation for folding up their tents under pressure from the leadership. They are typically persuaded to support conservative measures such as the annual budget resolution or tax bills with assurances that the final proposal will move their way. But this time the moderates, relatively speaking, held tough.

"At the start there were 15 to 20 'no' votes and up to 25 with concerns. That dwindled to about 12 who demanded some language," said a staff aide to Rep. Michael N. Castle, R-Del. "The lobbying by the leadership was very consistently applied, but much more civilized than past experiences. They just met constantly with the reluctant members, but it was more urging; there were no threats." Hastert made personal pleas.

The compromise that turned the tide would condition most of the proposed 10 percent tax cut on whether interest payments on the national debt go up or down. The first 1 percent of the rate cut would automatically take effect in 2001. Additional cuts scheduled to start in 2004 would only take effect if the annual interest expense on the debt is going down.

The provisions, reluctantly accepted by Archer, were championed by moderates such as Fred Upton, R-Mich., and debt hawk Nick Smith, R-Mich., who worried that if future congresses failed to curb spending or if budget projections failed to match expectations, the non-Social Security portion of the budget could slide back into a deficit.

Leaders sealed the deal the evening of July 21 to include the moderate-backed language, and the relief felt by both leaders and the recalcitrant moderates was palpable. In the end, the only Republican moderates to oppose the bill were Castle, Greg Ganske of Iowa, Constance A. Morella of Maryland and Jack Quinn of New York.

In addition, Archer scaled back his original $864 billion bill to $792 billion, the size of the Senate measure and the amount set forth in the budget resolution (H Con Res 68). The cut was ostensibly made to placate moderates, but would have been made anyway because of Senate rules that make it easy for Democrats to block any bill that exceeds the budget resolution's tax cut figure. The cost was trimmed in part by delaying the phase-in of the 10 percent tax rate cut.

After moderates got on board, the debate July 22 was anti-climactic. Before passing the bill, Republicans turned back a $250 billion Democratic substitute that would have eased the marriage penalty, increased per-child tax credits, subsidized state and local school construction bonds and permanently extended the research and development tax credit and other expiring tax credits. The Democratic alternative failed, 173-258. *(Vote 331, p. H-110)*

On final passage, Democrats stayed unified in their opposition to the bill, surprising some Republicans who predicted that up to two dozen would ultimately vote for it. Instead, only six Democrats broke ranks: Sanford D. Bishop Jr. of Georgia, Gary A. Condit of California, Pat Danner of Missouri, Virgil H. Goode Jr. of Virginia, Ralph M. Hall of Texas and Ken Lucas of Kentucky.

Finance Markup

In the Senate, Finance Committee Chairman William V. Roth Jr., R-Del., pushed a draft bill that would change the tax code while walking a fine line between the two wings of the GOP.

Its main component, for example, would cut the lowest income tax rate bracket from 15 percent to 14 percent, at an estimated cost of $216 billion over 10 years. That would appeal to moderates who are concerned about helping those with lower incomes; conservatives generally would prefer an across-the-board cut, such as the one in the House bill.

At the July 21 markup, two bids by Senate conservatives to alter the broad-based rate change were defeated, with the key votes being cast by Roth, Jeffords and John H. Chafee, R-R.I.

On the first, Phil Gramm, R-Texas, offered a substitute amendment that contained the House's 10 percent tax rate cut. It failed, 7-13.

Later, Don Nickles, R-Okla., offered an amendment to replace the 15 percent to 14 percent rate change with an increase in the income level before the 15 percent rate is replaced by a 28 percent rate. The amendment, patterned after a bill (S 593) cosponsored by Paul Coverdell, R-Ga., and Robert G. Torricelli, D-N.J., would raise the income limit for the 28 percent bracket by $5,000 for single filers, to $30,750, and by $10,000 for joint filers, to $52,250.

This approach aims to direct a greater portion of the tax cut to the middle class and could be the basis for a middle ground in whatever bill emerges from a House-Senate conference. Finance rejected it, however, 8-12. Roth said changing his new 14 percent tax bracket provision would have left the bill without enough support to get out of committee.

Conservatives favored the Senate's marriage penalty provisions over the House version. The Senate measure would allow married couples to file separate schedules on a joint basis, at a cost of $112 billion over 10 years. The $44.5 billion House version would increase the standard income tax deduction for married couples filing jointly — $7,200 now — to double that of a single taxpayer, or $8,600.

Most provisions in Roth's bill return to a common theme of his career: promoting retirement savings. They include increasing from $2,000 to $5,000 a year the amount that could be contributed to all Individual Retirement Accounts (IRAs). The provisions would cost almost $70 billion over 10 years.

In a setback for Roth, the committee approved by voice vote an amendment by Orrin G. Hatch, R-Utah, to permanently extend the research and development tax credit, perhaps the most popular of the so-called tax extenders that Congress passes every year. *(Extenders, 1998 Almanac, p. 21-14)*

Roth proposed to extend the credit through 2004. The $17 billion cost of extending it through 2009 and beyond was absorbed by delaying until 2008 proposed increases in the income cap for contributions into traditional deductible IRAs.

As an ideological exercise, the Finance markup had a going-through-the-motions feel. Neither conservatives seeking to move the bill in their direction nor moderates interested in cutting it put much behind their efforts. "If we stay locked into positions, we don't legislate; we'll just have an issue to beat each other over the head with for the next election," Breaux said. "Ultimately, we are going to have to come together or nothing will be accomplished." Breaux, along with Kerrey and GOP moderates Jeffords and Chafee, backed a sketchy $500 billion tax cut plan but did not press for a vote, which they would have lost.

Senate Passes Bill; Leaders Plan for Speedy Conference

JULY 31 — As the Senate debated its $792 billion tax cut measure, there was perhaps no greater sign of the bill's questionable future than the lack of lobbyists parading up and down Senate hallways.

Though advocates from some major business groups pressed the flesh with senators, the number surrounding the chamber floor was greatly diminished from the "war rooms" that accompanied work on the 1997 tax law (PL 105-34). And at least one senator, freshman Democrat John Edwards of North Carolina, said he could not recall being lobbied on the tax bill.

Many lobbyists also stayed in the office because the outcome was never in much doubt, said one who ventured out: Dorothy B. Coleman, director of tax policy for the National Association of Manufacturers. The Senate passed the bill, 57-43, on July 30. Coleman and others expect they will get more of a workout the week of Aug. 2, when tax writers are expected to push ahead with plans to reconcile the House (HR 2488) and Senate (S 1429) bills. *(Vote 247, p. S-49)*

Their task — to give Republicans an accomplishment to take to constituents during the nearly monthlong summer recess — may not be an easy one. The House and Senate measures share little more than their $792 billion bottom lines. Members will be hard pressed to resolve many of the issues before Congress leaves, unless leaders dictate the outcome. "I don't see them concluding this easily," said Sen. John B. Breaux, D-La., who favors tax cuts but has proposed a $500 billion plan. "It's Republicans fighting Republicans."

As the Senate took its final votes, Majority Leader Trent Lott, R-Miss., said the conference was expected to agree to a final bill in time for an Aug. 5 vote in the House and an Aug. 6 vote in the Senate. To reach agreement so quickly, the leadership will likely dictate most decisions. Lott began that process July 30 when he said he would rather have the House's 10 percent across-the-board tax cut than anything else in either bill. "Clearly, it's going to have to be something different than what's in the Senate bill," he said. *(Bill comparison, p. 21-18)*

During floor debate on S 1429, the Senate GOP held together easily. Several moderates said they were concerned that the bill, sponsored by Finance Committee Chairman William V. Roth Jr., R-Del., used too much of the projected $1 trillion non-Social Security budget surplus, but only two Republicans — Arlen Specter of Pennsylvania and George V. Voinovich of Ohio — voted against it.

Four Senate Democrats voted for it: Breaux, Bob Kerrey of Nebraska, Mary L. Landrieu of Louisiana and Robert G. Torricelli of New Jersey. They had pushed the alternative $500 billion tax cut but withdrew it after party leaders peeled off supporters. Several GOP moderates had also supported the proposal.

Minority Leader Tom Daschle, D-S.D., worked to keep his party together, much as had House GOP leaders when passing their measure July 22. In the House, moderate Republicans had threatened to vote against the final bill if steps were not taken to reduce the national debt. Only four Republicans voted against the final measure, which was amended to make its 10 percent across-the-board income tax rate cut contingent upon reducing interest payments on the national debt. Six Democrats voted for HR 2448.

Both the Senate Democratic Caucus and House Republican Conference appeared on the verge of splintering during debate on their bills, but GOP leaders and President Clinton seemed dedicated to pulling their respective parties together and polarizing the debate, at least for now.

Lott said the final bill will not likely reach the president's desk until Congress returns from its break in September. "I don't want him to veto it either in the quiet of the night or with great fanfare when we're not here," Lott said July 28.

Clinton, boarding a plane to Sarajevo on July 29, reiterated that a veto was certain. "I hope, again, that we can get a bipartisan agreement that will save Social Security, save and reform Medicare, continue to invest in education and get this country out of debt. If we do those big things first, there's still money left for a good-sized tax cut," he said. "But what is being done now is wrong."

The polarization was frustrating to moderates such as Breaux who warned both parties that arguing over who killed something was a less successful strategy than vying for credit. But Breaux insisted, "There's a deal out there to be had."

House Speaker J. Dennis Hastert, R-Ill., also expressed faith that a deal could come later. "It's early in the process," he said July 30. "I think the president ultimately will come around on this issue." Such deals will likely come sometime after Congress returns from its break the week of Sept. 6 and before the fiscal year ends Sept. 30.

On to Conference

The House and Senate bills would cost $792 billion over 10 years, but major similarities end there.

The House bill is more tilted toward business interests, and its sponsor, Ways and Means Committee Chairman Bill Archer, R-Texas, was less concerned about charges of disproportionately helping the wealthy. The bill's most prominent feature is a 10 percent across-the-board cut in income tax rates, which accounts for half the bill's costs.

The bill also would reduce individual income tax rates on capital gains — the profits from the sale of stocks, bonds or other assets — and would allow corporations to pay an alternative to capital gains taxes, which are now as high as 35 percent.The alternative would ratchet down corporate capital gains rates to 25 percent after 2009.

The Senate bill takes a different tack. Its broadest component would reduce income tax rates, but only for the lowest bracket. It would reduce the rate from 15 percent to 14 percent and increase the number of people subject to the lowest rate. In 1999, single people in the lowest bracket earned up to $25,750. Married couples filing jointly earned up to $43,050. Under S 1429, single people could make $2,500 more and married couples $5,000 more and still pay the lowest rate. The increase would be phased in by 2007.

The Senate bill, as amended shortly before it passed, includes a provision to exempt the first $1,000 of capital gains from individual income taxes, beginning in 2006. The amendment, by Paul Coverdell, R-Ga., was accepted by voice vote. The Senate's "marriage penalty" provision goes farther than the House bill toward resolving a quirk in the tax code in which many married couples pay more in taxes than single people with the same income. In addition, the Senate bill does not go as far as the House bill in reducing inheritance taxes. The House bill would eliminate them by 2009.

Those issues are expected to be hurdles for the conference, but two of the most difficult provisions will be ones that were added on the floors.

The House's 10 percent tax rate cut is tied to reducing interest on the national debt after 2001. Moderates insisted on it.

And the Senate bill would expire and taxes would revert to current levels after Sept. 30, 2009, unless future Congresses intervened. The sunset provision had always been a part of the bill, but its effect had been negated by a subsequent provision to restart the bill's tax code changes the following day. The two provisions had been included to get around the so-called Byrd rule, which requires a supermajority of 60 votes to pass measures that are not offset by spending cuts or revenue increases.

When Democrats began to complain that the bill would cost trillions of dollars after 2009 (surplus projections have not been calculated beyond 2009), Lott issued a point of order against the provision extending the

Tax Bills Compared

JULY 31 — The House passed a $792 billion tax cut package (HR 2488) by a vote of 223-208 on July 22, after the Senate Finance Committee approved a $792 billion package (S 1429) by a vote of 13-7 on July 21. Senate floor debate began July 28 and the Senate passed S 1429, 57-43, on July 30. A House-Senate conference is expected to convene the week of Aug. 2. (Cost estimates are for each category, over 10 years.)

ISSUE	HOUSE	SENATE
Bill implementation	The bill would make reductions in personal income tax rates contingent upon reductions in the interest paid on the national debt after 2001.	All tax code changes in the bill would expire on Sept. 30, 2009.
Rate cut	The bill would reduce personal income tax rates by 10 percent by 2009. Rates for the five tax brackets would eventually stand at 13.5 percent, 25.2 percent, 27.9 percent, 32.4 percent and 35.64 percent. Cost: $405 billion.	The bill would reduce the lowest personal income tax rate from 15 percent to 14 percent, beginning in 2001, and expand the bracket gradually so more people would pay the lowest tax rate. Cost: $298 billion.
Marriage penalty	The bill would increase the standard deduction for married couples filing jointly — now $7,200 — to double that of a single taxpayer, or $8,600, effective Dec. 31, 2000. It would also allow more married couples to deduct student loan interest and convert to Roth Individual Retirement Accounts (IRAs). Cost: $47.5 billion.	The bill would allow married taxpayers to file a joint return that included two separate schedules, thus eliminating the "penalty" that often appears when people with differing incomes get married. It would also increase the standard deduction for married couples. Cost: Not available.
Inheritance taxes	The bill would phase out estate, gift and generation-skipping taxes by 2009. Tax rates of up to 55 percent are now applied to gifts handed down before or after death and to contributions above $1 million made to heirs other than children, such as grandchildren. Cost: $75.3 billion.	The bill would lower the highest tax rates — 55 percent and 53 percent — on estates, gifts and generation-skipping taxes to 50 percent beginning in 2001 and increase from $1 million to $1.5 million exemptions on estate taxes by 2007. Cost: $63 billion.
Capital gains	The bill would cut tax rates on profits from the sale of stocks, bonds and property. The 10 percent rate for individuals would drop to 7.5 percent, and the 20 percent rate would drop to 15. It would repeal 8 and 18 percent rates on certain gains from property held more than five years, retroactive to June 30. Cost: $51.6 billion.	The bill would exempt up to $1,000 in capital gains from taxes for individuals or married couples filing jointly, beginning in 2006. Cost: Not available.
Health care	The bill would allow self-employed taxpayers to deduct 100 percent of their health care and long-term care insurance expenses from income taxes, beginning in 2001, and others to deduct health and long-term care insurance costs in cases in which employers paid no more than 50 percent of the premium, effective Dec. 31, 2000. Cost: $51 billion.	The provisions are similar to the House bill, but deductions for health insurance premiums not paid by employers would be phased in through 2006, when 100 percent of such costs would be tax deductible. Cost: $55 billion.
Education	The bill would increase from $500 to $2,000 the amount that could be set aside before taxes in Education Savings Accounts, formerly education IRAs. Taxpayers could use the funds for elementary and secondary school expenses. Cost: $7.2 billion.	The bill would allow prepaid tuition programs for private colleges and would allow taxes to be deferred on interest earned. It would allow many withdrawals to be made tax-free from prepaid programs and education IRAs. Cost: $12 billion.
Retirement	Among other changes, the bill would increase allowable contributions to defined benefit plans from $30,000 to $40,000 annually. Cost: $14.5 billion.	Among changes, the bill would increase from $2,000 to $5,000 the annual amount that could be put into IRAs and would remove income limits on eligibility for Roth IRAs, starting in 2001. Cost: $69 billion.

cuts after 2009. Had he not done so, Democrats could have filed a point of order against the entire bill, jeopardizing its passage.

On July 28, Roth lost a motion to waive Lott's point of order, 51-48, with 60 votes required. Three Republicans — Specter and Susan Collins and Olympia J. Snowe, both of Maine — voted with all Democrats against the motion. Democratic solidarity was hard to maintain: Breaux voted no only after a stern floor lecture from Daschle; Torricelli, another tax cut supporter, voted no after being counseled by Robert C. Byrd of West Virginia, author of the Byrd rule. *(Vote 225, p. S-45)*

Several senators were disappointed that the bill was to expire. Breaux decried it as "terrible policy," and Connie Mack, R-Fla., expressed hope that business interests might pressure some Democrats to change their minds before voting on the conference report. "It's a provision that obviously I hate," Mack said.

Rep. Jim Nussle, R-Iowa, a member of the Ways and Means Committee, said his gut reaction was similar to Mack's. "At the end of the 10 years, basically what we're saying is there is an automatic tax increase," he said.

But at least one Republican, Sen. Phil Gramm of Texas, said he thought the development could work to Republicans' advantage both in removing Democratic arguments that the tax bill would re-create a budget deficit in the later years and in giving Republicans an impetus to pass future tax cuts. "From a political standpoint, I don't think they did themselves any favors," Gramm said.

The House provision tying a 10 percent tax rate cut to debt reduction is also expected to raise some ire. Gramm said he expected that the provision would be dropped in conference, but Nussle said he thought it should stay.

Senate Consideration

The Senate's 20-hour debate on the tax bill centered largely on Democrats trying to divert some of its funding toward such programs as Medicare and education, and Republicans trying to make the cut more generous.

Nearly all efforts failed.

An exception was an amendment by Kay Bailey Hutchison, R-Texas, to make the standard deduction for married couples double that of singles and to phase in that change beginning in 2001, three years earlier than provisions in the underlying bill. The amendment was approved, 98-2, on July 30, with Voinovich and Democrat Ernest F. Hollings of South Carolina voting no.

The Senate bill had already been considered stronger than the House bill on the marriage penalty issue, and the adoption of Hutchison's amendment pleased conservative religious groups, such as the Christian Coalition.

The Senate also adopted, by voice vote, an amendment by Snowe that would give tax credits of up to $1,500 a year for interest on college loans.

Other amendments offered during debate were:

- A substitute by Finance Committee ranking Democrat Daniel Patrick Moynihan of New York. It would have cut taxes by $290 billion over 10 years and would have expired in 2009. It would have increased the income tax's standard deduction, expanded the child care tax credit and made more health care expenses deductible. It was defeated, 39-60, with six Democrats joining all Republicans present in voting no. They were: Evan Bayh of Indiana, Byrd, Edwards, Joseph I. Lieberman of Connecticut, Torricelli and Paul Wellstone of Minnesota. Some who voted no, such as Lieberman and Wellstone, opposed any tax cut. Others, such as Torricelli, favored larger tax cuts. *(Vote 226, p. S-45)*
- A substitute by Gramm that included the House's 10 percent across-the-board tax rate cut, an elimination of the marriage penalty and inheritance taxes, and indexing of capital gains tax rates. It was defeated when the Senate voted, 46-54, against waiving a point of order and declaring the amendment germane. Nine Republicans voted against it: Christopher S. Bond of Missouri, John H. Chafee of Rhode Island, Collins, Snowe, Budget Committee Chairman Pete V. Domenici of New Mexico, James M. Jeffords of Vermont, Roth, Specter and Voinovich. All Democrats voted no. *(Vote 230, p. S-46)*
- A proposal by Bob Graham, D-Fla., and Charles S. Robb, D-Va., to delay implementation of the tax bill until legislation had been enacted to extend the Social Security trust fund through 2075 and the Medicare trust fund through 2027. A motion to waive a point of order declaring it non-germane was defeated, 46-54, with Breaux voting against waiving the motion and Snowe and Voinovich voting for it. *(Vote 229, p. S-46)*
- Two plans to establish "lockboxes" for entitlement programs. The first amendment, by Spencer Abraham, R-Mich., fell 54-46. Abraham's amendment, which aimed to put Social Security trust funds into a lockbox, was similar to an amendment Republicans have offered repeatedly this year and Democrats have consistently blocked. The vote on Abraham's amendment was party line, with the exception of Roth, who voted no. *(Vote 227, p. S-45)*

The second amendment, by Max Baucus, D-Mont., would have "locked away" the Social Security trust fund and one-third of the remaining non-Social Security surplus — or about $300 billion — for Medicare. It fell when a motion to waive a point of order against it was defeated, 42-58. Three Democrats — Breaux, Hollings and Kerrey — joined all Republicans in voting against the waiver. *(Vote 228, p. S-45)*

The chamber also took votes on other amendments, many of them Democratic attempts to push other issues. It defeated, 45-55, a motion to waive a point of order on an amendment by Edward M. Kennedy, D-Mass., to send the bill back to committee until it had included a plan to cover prescription drugs for Medicare beneficiaries. *(Vote 231, p. S-46)*

It voted, 46-54, against waiving a point of order on a Kennedy amendment to increase the minimum wage to $6.15 an hour in 2000. It also defeated, 35-65, a motion to waive a point of order on Specter's plan for a flat tax. An amendment by Jon Kyl, R-Ariz., to eliminate inheritance taxes, was ruled out of order. *(Vote 239, 240, pp. S-47, S-48)*

The Senate voted on more than 20 amendments during debate, but did not vote on one of the most anticipated proposals. Breaux withdrew his $500 billion substitute plan July 29, after it became clear he would not have the votes.

Though many of the bill's bipartisan supporters were disappointed that the measure would not come to a vote, they said it was necessary to withdraw it to preserve its viability when Congress and the administration finally get down to negotiating a plan. The president's advisers have said he would veto a $500 billion bill, but Breaux pointed out that Clinton had not said it himself. "It's still a viable option," Breaux said.

Senate Clears Bill; GOP Content To Show It Off Back Home

AUGUST 7 — With their prized $792 billion tax bill in the bag, Republicans launched a monthlong effort to convince voters that they need the package of cuts the Senate cleared Aug. 5.

But even before members left for their districts and states, it was becoming increasingly clear that their focus was not on pressuring President Clinton to sign the bill (HR 2488) this fall but rather on planting the seeds and hoping that public interest in a large, surplus-financed tax cut would germinate nearer to the November 2000 presidential and congressional elections.

Hints of the Republican strategy emerged the week of Aug. 2, though leaders and the rank and file continued to insist that they thought Clinton would abandon his veto threat and sign the legislation once he saw its potential popularity.

They consistently mentioned as precedent Clinton's 1996 decision to reverse two previous vetoes and sign the welfare overhaul bill (PL 104-193). House Majority Leader Dick Armey, R-Texas, called the example "a good model for where the president will be a year from now on tax cuts." In a news briefing Aug. 3, Armey added, "We're not interested in lowering the tax reductions [in the bill]. . . . We've got another year. We'll try another year." *(1996 Almanac, p. 6-3)*

Clinton left little doubt about his intentions at a news conference Aug. 4. "Members of the majority have been at work on a tax plan that is risky and plainly wrong for America. Let me repeat what I have said many times — if they conclude this plan and send it to me, I will have to veto it." Clinton also joined congressional Democrats in a Capitol Hill rally against the bill Aug. 5.

The House adopted the conference report on the bill, 221-206, on Aug. 5, and the Senate cleared it, 50-49, a few hours later. Clinton will not get a chance to veto the bill until Congress returns from its summer recess. Senate Majority Leader Trent Lott, R-Miss., decided to hold it at the enrolling desk until September so Clinton cannot rain on Republicans' many August town-hall meetings and events devoted to touting the tax bill. *(House vote 379, p. H-124; Senate vote 251, p. S-49)*

While it once appeared that Republicans might try to pick up the pieces of their bill after Clinton's veto and use it as a wedge in negotiations on Medicare and Social Security, it now appears they have little interest in a deal on taxes this year, the pleas of moderates in both chambers notwithstanding.

Early in the week, Senate Budget Committee Chairman Pete V. Domenici, R-N.M., proposed bridging the gap between Republicans and Clinton by considering a smaller tax cut, but leaders did not cotton to the idea. By the end of the week, Domenici was exhorting Clinton to sign the $792 billion bill.

"The guys in the middle don't count right now," said Clint Stretch, director of tax policy for accounting giant Deloitte & Touche. "Everybody seems to be winning, at least with their core constituencies. We're sort of in the season of grand theater. . . . Maybe the real time for compromise is next summer."

Republicans seemed to have thoughts of far-flung political dramas in their heads as the Senate prepared to clear the bill the evening of Aug. 5. John Czwartacki, Lott's spokesman, said that "if this does turn into a political issue next year" it will pit the tax-cutting desire of congressional Republicans and George W. Bush, the front-runner for the GOP presidential nomination, against Democrats, led by vice president and likely party presidential nominee Al Gore. Gore cast a tie-breaking vote in favor of the 1993 budget reconciliation bill (PL 103-66). That measure added a high-income tax bracket and otherwise increased taxes in an effort to reduce the budget deficit and pay for spending. *(1993 Almanac, p. 107)*

Republicans would gladly stand behind their bill, Czwartacki said. "It's good policy, and good policy always makes good politics," he said.

But House Speaker J. Dennis Hastert, R-Ill., denied that politics was on Republican minds. "This is not a political issue at all," he said. "This is an issue that's important to the American people. . . . That's why we put a lot of our capital and time and energy to make it happen."

The final package included a host of changes Republicans had long wanted to make to the tax code. It would cut the five individual income tax brackets by 1 percentage point each; make the standard deduction for married couples double that for singles and take other steps to alleviate the so-called marriage penalty; phase out estate, gift and generation-skipping taxes; cut individual capital gains rates; eliminate the Alternative Minimum Tax for individuals; raise limits on contributions to Individual Retirement Accounts (IRAs) and 401(k)s; and give tax relief to several targeted industries and multinational corporations.

A Grab Bag

Despite Hastert's commitment of capital and energy, the package produced does not make a strong statement about changing the tax code, liberal and conservative economists agree.

"It's a grab bag of little tax changes," said William A. Niskanen, chairman of the libertarian Cato Institute and chairman of the Council of Economic Advisers under President Ronald Reagan.

"A hodgepodge sounds probably like a good characterization," said Harvey S. Rosen, an economics professor at Princeton University and President George Bush's deputy assistant Treasury secretary for tax analysis. But Rosen added: "It doesn't necessarily mean it's a bad bill." Rosen favors cuts in the brackets and the phaseout of the Alternative Minimum Tax, but Niskanen finds less to his liking.

"I think this is not a coherent tax package with a clear vision in mind of where they want to go," Niskanen said. "I think that's better . . . than spending the money, but it's fairly far down my priority list."

Highlights of the Tax Bill

AUGUST 7 — The House adopted the conference report on HR 2488, 221-206, on Aug. 5, and the Senate cleared the bill, 50-49, a few hours later. President Clinton plans to veto it. (Cost estimates are for each category over 10 years.)

Issue	Conference Report
Broad-based income tax cut	The bill would reduce each of the five income tax brackets by 1 percentage point by 2005. The 15 percent bracket, for example, would fall to 14 percent, and the 39.6 percent bracket would fall to 38.6 percent. That reduction would result in a 7 percent tax cut for the 15 percent bracket — the lowest bracket — and less for the other brackets. It would expand the lowest bracket in 2006, allowing single filers and heads of household to earn $3,000 a year more than current limits — now $25,750 and $34,550 respectively — and still file in the lowest bracket. Implementation of this broad-based tax cut is contingent upon reducing interest paid on the national debt. The bill would sunset in 2009. Estimated cost: $283 billion.
Marriage penalty	The bill would gradually make the standard income tax deduction for married filers $8,600, or double that of an individual taxpayer, phased in beginning in 2001. It would increase the amount that a married couple could earn annually and still file under the lowest income tax bracket. Estimated cost: $117 billion.
Alternative Minimum Tax	The bill would allow taxpayers subject to the Alternative Minimum Tax (AMT), a parallel tax system that aims to ensure that no one avoids income taxes, to claim credits, such as the $500 per child tax credit, against their taxes. The phaseout in individual AMTs would occur from 2005 through 2008. Corporate AMTs would remain, but, beginning in 2002, corporations would be allowed to credit 100 percent of income taxes paid in foreign countries against their taxes. Currently, they can credit 90 percent. Estimated cost: $103 billion.
Estate taxes	The bill would eliminate estate, gift and generation-skipping taxes, phasing in the cut through 2009. It would also repeal laws that now effectively set beginning tax rates for estates at 38 percent. As a result, initial tax rates for estates worth more than $650,000 — when estate taxes now kick in — would be 18 percent. However, beginning in 2008, recipients of estates worth more than $2 million, except for spouses, would be required to pay higher capital gains taxes than under current law if they sold the estate. Estimated cost: $65 billion.
Health care	The bill would allow self-employed taxpayers and those whose employers pay no more than 50 percent of health care insurance premiums to deduct 100 percent of their premiums from income taxes. The self-employed could claim the deduction beginning in 2000; others could claim a portion of it beginning in 2002 and the full deduction in 2007. Those who care for an elderly relative in their home could exempt about $2,750 from taxes beginning in 2000. Estimated cost: $37 billion.
Retirement	The bill would increase contribution limits for Individual Retirement Accounts from $2,000 to $5,000 by 2008. The limit would revert to $2,000 in 2009. It would allow couples making as much as $200,000 annually to convert standard Individual Retirement Accounts (IRAs), in which contributions are not taxed but withdrawals are, to Roth IRAs, in which contributions are taxed but withdrawals are not. Estimated cost: $28 billion.
Capital gains	The bill would make cuts to individual capital gains rates but would not change corporate capital gains taxes. The 20 percent and 10 percent rates, which are based on a taxpayer's income, would be cut in 1999 to 18 percent and 8 percent, respectively. Capital gains would be indexed for inflation, beginning in 2000. Estimated cost, offset by revenue: $32 billion.
International taxes	The bill would make several changes to taxes on international business. The most expensive provision, estimated to cost $24 billion over 10 years, would let U.S. companies deduct interest expenses incurred in foreign businesses of which they own more than 50 percent. Current law requires them to own 80 percent to claim the deduction. Estimated cost: $31 billion.
Other provisions	The bill would increase allowable annual contributions to 401(k)s and other retirement accounts. It would increase from $500 to $2,000 the limit on contributions to Education IRAs, renamed Education Savings Accounts. Estimated cost: $9 billion.

Niskanen and the Cato Institute continue to press leaders to dedicate the surplus to a more radical change in government policy — privatizing the Social Security system and cutting the payroll tax, which affects low-income Americans more than those with high incomes. From Niskanen's viewpoint, it may be good if Congress reaches no tax agreement for a few years and pays down the national debt instead. "What may save us is gridlock," he said.

Both agree that the bill's provisions to sunset the tax changes and revert to the current code after fiscal 2009, and to cut the income tax brackets only if interest on the national debt remains steady or declines, are "really weird," as Niskanen said, and probably unprecedented for a tax bill.

Republican leaders were not enthusiastic about either provision but included the so-called debt trigger to win enough support from moderates to pass their original House bill and included the sunset after a vote to withhold it failed in the Senate. Even before members went to conference, it was clear a tax bill could not pass without both.

Because of the sunset provision and because leaders had to massage numbers to keep the bill within its $792 billion limit, almost all provisions in the bill would take effect and expire at different times. Many economists say that will make the tax code more complicated, and one critic said he would need to buy a new computer tax program every year if the bill became law. "It will make the tax code more complex — something that I think you could get right and left to agree is the wrong direction for tax policy," said Iris J. Lav, deputy director of the Center on Budget and Policy Priorities, a liberal-leaning think tank.

Others say the varying phase-in and phaseout times are unfair. In a floor speech Aug. 5, Sen. John McCain, R-Ariz., chided conferees for making cuts for businesses effective earlier than those for average Americans. "If this bill had any chance of becoming law, perhaps it would have been prioritized somewhat differently," he said.

Bridging Differences

Priorities in the conference agreement were set quickly: Conferees were appointed Aug. 2 and announced an agreement by 10:30 p.m. on Aug. 3 — with hands-on participation from party leaders. Lott, a member of the Finance Committee, and Armey, who is not on the Ways and Means Committee, were both conferees. They and their staffs actively participated in the daylong negotiations Aug. 3.

Armey had reportedly insisted that the conference dedicate at least $100 billion to alleviating the marriage penalty, a quirk of the tax code that requires many married couples to pay more in income taxes than they would as individuals. Funding for the marriage penalty provision, a main priority of conservative religious groups, had been a sticking point. Lindy Paull, chief of staff for the Joint Committee on Taxation, termed it a "very difficult compromise to be reached."

The final agreement included $117 billion to increase the standard deduction for couples who do not itemize deductions, and to increase the number of married couples who could file in the lowest tax bracket and the number of couples eligible for the Earned Income Tax Credit, which seeks to help the working poor.

Lott's favored issues — the 10 percent across-the-board income tax cut included in the House bill and a cut in capital gains tax rates — were not included in the final bill, but the majority leader enthusiastically backed the final product. Lott made sure the bill included some help for his home state. For instance, when sponsors of a Senate provision to establish tax-deferred savings accounts for farmers and ranchers tried to insert the provision in the conference report, Lott insisted that catfish farmers also be eligible for the accounts. Missouri Republican Kenny Hulshof, the main House proponent of the plan, emerged from the room where House conferees were meeting to announce that the provision had been included. When asked about the catfish addition, he said, "Certainly in Mississippi there are a lot of catfish farmers."

The bill also included a favorite of Senate Finance Chairman William V. Roth Jr., R-Del., to extend a tax credit for wind- or biomass-generated electricity to companies that burn poultry waste for their power. Delaware is a major poultry producer.

The bill also specified that seaplane operators do not have to pay aviation excise taxes. Many areas in Alaska are accessible only by seaplane, and the state is represented by Republican Sens. Frank H. Murkowski, a Finance member, and Appropriations Chairman Ted Stevens.

The measure would also repeal a 10 percent excise tax on fishing tackle boxes. Hastert's district is home to a tackle box maker.

Lawmakers were not the only ones to get special provisions, said lobbyist Stretch. "If you were a lobbyist and you didn't get your provision in this tax bill, you're in pretty dire straits with your client because everybody got their provisions in," he said.

Floor Debate

Rhetoric was plentiful when the House and Senate took up the conference agreement in rapid succession Aug. 5. In both debates, Democrats depicted the tax bill as irresponsible or reckless in spending much of a projected budget surplus, which has yet to materialize. Republicans charged that Democrats wanted to spend the surplus instead of giving 25 percent of it back to taxpayers.

"I urge members to reject instant gratification and save money for the future," said House Minority Leader Richard A. Gephardt, D-Mo.

Ways and Means Committee Chairman Bill Archer, R-Texas, charged that Democrats "have put every hurdle in the way of tax relief . . . and they fight ferociously to keep money in Washington."

The House adopted the conference report with support from five Democrats — Gary A. Condit of California, Pat Danner of Missouri, Virgil H. Goode Jr. of Virginia, Ralph M. Hall of Texas and Ken Lucas of Kentucky. Four Republicans voted against it: Michael N. Castle of Delaware, Greg Ganske of Iowa, Constance A. Morella of Maryland and Jack Quinn of New York.

Senate debate was similar, though the outcome was much closer. Republican leaders believed they could get the votes they needed, but they knew they had to work at it.

After GOP conferees reached an agreement the night of Aug. 3, Lott and others reopened the bill Aug. 4 and inserted provisions to attract votes from moderate Senate Republicans. Among the provisions added were $4 billion to give married couples who qualify for the Earned Income Tax Credit a bigger benefit and $4 billion to allow states to issue more low-interest bonds to developers of housing for the poor. Leaders also added funding to give more tax credits for child and dependent care.

As a result, moderates considered to be wavering, such as James M. Jeffords of Vermont and John H. Chafee of Rhode Island, voted for the conference report, which cleared by one vote Aug. 5. Republicans who voted against it were Susan Collins and Olympia J. Snowe of Maine, Arlen Specter of Pennsylvania and George V. Voinovich of Ohio. Specter and Voinovich had also voted against the Senate's original bill (S 1429) on July 30.

But the four Democrats who had voted for the original Senate bill — John B. Breaux of Louisiana, Bob Kerrey of Nebraska, Mary L. Landrieu of Louisiana and Robert G. Torricelli of New Jersey — voted against the conference report. They said the final agreement was much more like the House bill, which they felt was too weighted toward cutting taxes for businesses and for individuals with higher incomes.

Czwartacki said Lott had made appeals to the Democrats, but they "apparently have fallen on deaf ears." Democrats had little incentive to vote for the conference report because their conferees were left out of all but the committee's short opening meeting.

Impending Veto Fails To End Tax Cut Debate

SEPTEMBER 18 — President Clinton plans to veto the long-touted, $792 billion tax bill that congressional Republicans sent to the White House on Sept. 15.

But the veto, expected the week of Sept. 20 as part of both parties' design to showcase the differences in their policy stands, may not accomplish Republican leaders' goal of cementing the party on one of its core issues. Instead, Republicans appear fractured. Some House Ways and Means Committee members are pushing for a smaller but significant tax cut, and some senators say time for such action has run out. Lobbyists said the GOP did not appear to know which way it would go.

Senators made a compelling argument that a second attempt at a tax cut bill would not go far, pointing out that under Senate rules a sequel measure would not receive the protections from filibuster that the first measure received because it was a reconciliation bill. "I don't see it practically happening in the next few weeks" before the target adjournment in late October, said Sen. Paul Coverdell, R-Ga., who has sponsored bipartisan alternatives to the GOP bill. "It's a matter of pragmatic reality that it can't."

The veto will mark the official death of the bill (HR 2488). House Speaker J. Dennis Hastert, R-Ill., said he would not seek to override the president's action.

Rep. Philip M. Crane, R-Ill., the second-ranking member on Ways and Means and a candidate for the chairmanship being vacated by the retiring Bill Archer, R-Texas, said he was "a little doubtful that we'll get any significant tax relief . . . either in the remaining time of this session or next session."

Archer said he was committed to extending existing tax code provisions that have expired, including a research and experimentation tax credit for businesses and a provision allowing taxpayers subject to the Alternative Minimum Tax to claim child and education tax credits. "This does not preclude a big tax bill. All I'm saying is I'm committed to doing extenders," Archer said. *(Extenders, 1998 Almanac, p. 21-14)*

It was clear that several members of his committee, and some business lobbyists, were not happy to let go of a chance for a tax cut of about $450 billion over 10 years without a fight. "To say, 'Absolutely nothing if the president vetoes,' I think is absolutely crazy," said high-ranking panel member Amo Houghton, R-N.Y. "I don't think we should let this thing go."

House Majority Leader Dick Armey, R-Texas, seemed to recognize such sentiment at a news briefing Sept. 14, when he said that if the GOP completed work on spending bills and maintained "the integrity of the Social Security system," it should be "prepared to talk seriously with the president about tax relief." But Senate Majority Leader Trent Lott, R-Miss., said he did not think Congress could do another major tax bill this year. Republicans would give the president "another chance next year," Lott said.

Democrats said they were willing to negotiate a new bill with Republicans. Vice President Al Gore said at a Capitol Hill rally Sept. 15: "We're ready to work with them. We extend the hand of bipartisanship." Democrats were clearly pleased to be calling for a tax cut, albeit a targeted one such as Clinton included in his February budget submission, when Republicans seemed ready to give up on their plans, at least for now.

"The most heartening thing of all is that the American people really get it," said House Minority Leader Richard A. Gephardt, D-Mo. "They want a tax cut, but they want the right kind of tax cut." Democrats have charged that the GOP tax bill would cater to the rich, who pay a proportionally larger share of income taxes and therefore would see larger cuts than lower income taxpayers.

Most Republicans' political attention had already shifted to a more pressing issue — how to move the 13 appropriations bills before adjourning. "Basically, the tax debate is over in Congress with this president," said GOP Sen. Phil Gramm of Texas. "Now the battle becomes holding the line on spending." ◆

Chapter 22

TECHNOLOGY & COMMUNICATIONS

Lawmakers Vote To Allow Satellite TV Companies To Broadcast Local Programs

SUMMARY

Congress cleared legislation permitting satellite television companies to deliver local broadcast stations in cities across the country, matching the services provided by rival cable television systems. President Clinton signed the bill, which was made part of the omnibus spending measure (HR 3194), on Nov. 29, 1999.

Lawmakers feared that the end of cable television rate regulation on March 31 under the Telecommunications Act of 1996 (PL 104-104) would lead to higher prices and wanted to enact legislation to help satellite television companies compete with cable. The centerpiece of their effort was a measure to permit satellite television companies, for the first time, to carry the same local broadcast stations that are routinely offered on cable television.

Supporters of the legislation quickly reached agreement in the House and Senate on key provisions to permit delivery of local stations via satellite and to require satellite providers by 2002 to carry all local stations — if they carry any — in areas they serve.

But lawmakers disagreed on conditions for retransmission agreements and proposals by satellite providers to carry network affiliates nationally to some suburban customers.

In the House, lawmakers retained a ban in current law on the satellite delivery of broadcast stations from other cities to customers who receive local stations via antenna. The House measure instructed the Federal Communications Commission to develop a new standard to determine whether viewers could qualify to receive stations from other cities.

In the Senate, Commerce, Science and Transportation Committee Chairman John McCain, R-Ariz., came up with other proposals. The Senate version of the measure would give satellite providers a temporary waiver to allow them to continue delivering the same level of service that they provided to customers in July 1998, while conducting tests to determine if they violated the ban on providing programming from other cities that competes with local stations.

House and Senate negotiators cleared the way for completing a conference report for the satellite television bill (HR 1554) by reaching a compromise to let satellite television providers carry local broadcast stations immediately, even before they complete negotiations on retransmission agreements with local station owners. The agreements would have to be signed within six months of enactment.

Lawmakers overcame the last obstacle to final floor action when they deleted a $1.25 billion loan guarantee program to improve service for rural viewers. They added the remaining provisions to another bill (S 1948), which was then incorporated in the omnibus spending measure and cleared Nov. 19.

The bill also renewed licenses for satellite providers to carry copyright-protected broadcast programming. The copyright licenses would have expired Dec. 31, 1999, without action by Congress.

Box Score

- **Bill:** S 1948 (incorporated by reference in HR 3194 — PL 106-113)
- **Legislative action: House** passed HR 1554, 422-1, on April 27.

Senate substituted provisions of its own version of the bill (S 247 — S Rept 106-42) and passed HR 1554 by voice vote on May 20.

House adopted conference report on HR 1554 (H Rept 106-464), 411-8, on Nov. 9.

House voted, 296-135, to adopt conference report on HR 3194 (H Rept 106-479), incorporating S 1948, on Nov. 18.

Senate cleared HR 3194, 74-24, on Nov. 19.

President signed HR 3194 on Nov. 29.

Senate Panel Fires First Shot in Battle Over Satellite TV

FEBRUARY 27 — The Senate Judiciary Committee cleared the way for a battle over the future of satellite television Feb. 24, by approving a bill (S 247) by voice vote to make it easier for satellite television companies to deliver local network affiliates to customers.

Judiciary Committee Chairman Orrin G. Hatch, R-Utah, sponsor of S 247, said the bill faced little opposition, but it sets the stage for a fight over a companion bill (S 303) in the Senate Commerce, Science and Transportation Committee that would allow satellite companies to provide distant as well as local network affiliates.

In a growing conflict with cable, satellite television broadcasters are not allowed to beam local network programming to customers. They may only send distant network programming to customers in remote areas with no access to local network broadcasts.

Facing a court order requiring them to stop, effective Feb. 28, providing distant network programming to customers living near major cities, satellite television companies argued that changes were necessary to protect their customers. They said their inability to deliver local and distant station programming makes it hard to compete with cable giants, such as Tele-Communications Inc. and Time Warner Inc., that routinely provide them. But local broadcasters argued that loosening restrictions on distant stations could cut into their base of viewers and advertising revenue.

While stepping around the controversy over distant affiliates, Hatch said his bill would help satellite companies provide "real head-to-head competition to the cable industry for the first time." He and other lawmakers of both parties want to nurture competition to keep cable rates low, because cable rate regulation will end after March 31 under a provision of the Telecommunications Act of 1996 (PL 104-104). *(1996 Almanac, p. 3-43)*

The Hatch bill, aimed at helping satellite television companies deliver local stations to customers, will be combined with S 303 on the Senate floor. The bills amend and extend portions of the Satellite Home Viewer Act (PL 102-369). *(1994 Almanac, p. 216)*

The panel approved S 247 after passing an amendment by voice vote that made technical corrections to clarify that royalty rates paid by satellite companies will be reduced by 30 percent for superstations and by 45 percent for network affiliates, compared with rates in January 1998.

Although there is broad agreement on the Hatch bill to amend copyright-related portions of the Satellite Home Viewer Act, local broadcasters are marshaling opposition to a proposal in S 303 to allow satellite companies to deliver distant affiliates.

Senate Commerce Committee Chairman John McCain, R-Ariz., said at a Feb. 23 hearing on S 303, which he is sponsoring, that local broadcasters should negotiate a deal with satellite television companies on the issue of distant affiliates.

McCain said he would hold a March 3 markup for the bill. It would allow satellite companies to deliver distant affiliates to consumers just outside the core markets of local stations, provided that federal regulators found there was no material harm to local broadcasters.

Court Order Impetus

McCain and other lawmakers were pushing for quick action because of a federal court order requiring PrimeTime 24, a provider of programming to satellite companies, to stop delivering distant network affiliates to customers effective Feb. 28. His bill would provide a six-month moratorium on cutting off services to satellite customers,

Andrew S. Fisher, an executive vice president of Georgia-based Cox Broadcasting Co., said the National Association of Broadcasters strongly opposed changing restrictions on distant network affiliates, and said that satellite companies could deliver network programming to customers by providing local affiliates.

Eddy W. Hartenstein, president of DirecTV Inc., said it was technically not possible to get feeds of local network affiliates and deliver them to customers in every small town. Satellite companies say there are not enough channels to deliver all local stations to customers.

Local signals delivered by satellite will be available "in a limited number of television markets — those with the very largest number of households," Hartenstein said.

McCain urged broadcasters and satellite companies to resolve their dispute over satellite delivery of distant stations. Lawmakers of both parties said they were concerned about the court-ordered shutdown of distant network affiliates provided by PrimeTime 24 to its estimated 700,000 customers.

McCain called the battle a "showdown between corporate benefit and consumer welfare."

Bills To Foster TV Competition Move To House Floor

MARCH 27 — The debate over allowing satellite television companies to provide local network programming to city viewers moves to the House floor after Congress' spring recess.

For the first time, lawmakers could approve legislation to permit satellite companies to carry local stations not only in isolated rural areas but also in cities, where they compete with local broadcasters and cable television.

The House Commerce Committee approved by voice vote March 25 a bill, HR 851, to open competition in the broadcasting industry.

Satellite providers, which serve 10.8 million households, have long argued that their ability to carry local stations is essential to their survival. Rival cable television companies serve six times as many customers and routinely offer local programming with no restrictions.

There is broad support in Congress for helping satellite television companies, because lawmakers are concerned that cable companies will increase their charges when a law regulating cable rates expires March 31.

Instead of trying to impose restrictions on cable or extend the expiration date for rate regulation set in the Telecommunications Act of 1996 (PL 104-104), lawmakers are trying to work out a deal to strengthen satellite television companies.

"Cable will be deregulated. And there will be some price increases," said John Conyers Jr., D-Mich., ranking member on the House Judiciary Committee. "Now more than ever, we need to promote competition."

He spoke during a March 24 markup by the committee, which approved by voice vote on a companion bill (HR 1027) to revise copyright law to allow satellite companies to carry local television stations.

The Judiciary Committee adopted by voice vote an amendment to HR 1027 to prohibit any satellite company from transmitting distant network affiliates into areas where another satellite company offers at least two local stations. That provision was seen as a victory for Colorado-based EchoStar Communications Corp., which serves about 2 million households and is racing to offer local television programming to its customers.

The action by the two committees sets the stage for negotiations that are intended to produce a single, combined bill on the House floor soon after Congress returns April 12.

Compromise Reached

Both bills contain a compromise intended to resolve a battle that sets satellite companies against broadcast and cable companies.

The first part of the deal would end a ban in an 11-year-old satellite television law (PL 100-667) that prevents satellite companies from carrying network programming in areas where viewers can receive local stations with an antenna. *(1988 Almanac, p. 584)*

But in order to gain access to local programming, both bills would require satellite companies to accept provisions that would require them to carry all local stations in all markets they serve by 2002.

The requirement to carry all local stations matches one that cable television companies must meet. But satellite companies say they lack the capacity to carry all local stations. At best, lawmakers were told that each company might be able to transmit local stations to between 20 and 70 of the 200 major television markets in the country.

After the recess, lawmakers from the two committees are expected to focus on resolving questions about satellite service in rural areas and in areas near cities where consumers complain about fuzzy reception from antennas.

Rep. W.J. "Billy" Tauzin, R-La., said he would support negotiations between satellite television companies and local broadcasters to resolve a dispute over satellite customers living in or near cities that have been receiving distant network affiliates despite the ban. On March 12, California-based DirecTV Inc., a satellite provider serving about 4 million subscribers, reached a deal with four broadcast networks to allow DirecTV to continue to temporarily receive network broadcasts until June 30, giving customers time to buy antennas so they can receive local network affiliates.

Another fight looms in the Senate, where Commerce Committee Chairman John McCain, R-Ariz., has argued to lift the ban on distant network programming for satellite customers who live near cities and who now receive distant network affiliates.

Rep. Cliff Stearns, R-Fla., said he was concerned that satellite companies might exclude small towns from service territories if there is not enough satellite capacity to carry all local stations. Tauzin said the 2002 deadline allow time to increase capacity on satellites for more stations.

House Passes Bill To Let Satellite TV Transmit Local Programming

MAY 1 — A debate looms in the Senate this month over a bill that would give satellite television companies greater freedom to transmit news, sports and other programming to their customers.

The legislation (S 303) is the first step toward increasing competition in the cable and satellite television industries by expanding services to nearly 11 million satellite viewers. It would allow satellite viewers to receive local channels over their satellite dishes, lifting an 11-year-old ban (PL 100-667) that limited the kinds of programming they could receive. *(1988 Almanac, p. 584)*

On April 27, by a vote of 422-1, the House passed HR 1554, a similar measure that would allow satellite providers to deliver local channels and network shows such as NBC's "Frasier" and Fox's "The Simpsons" for the first time. *(Vote 97, p. H-40)*

The House bill would allow satellite viewers to get any show carried on local stations. The Senate version would allow satellite viewers to see local stations, and would direct the Federal Communications Commission to consider whether to allow them to also see programming from different regions of the country.

Congress is trying to help infuse competition in the pay television industry to keep cable rates down. The lack of local programming is the prime reason viewers choose cable instead of satellite services.

At present, satellite television viewers must have a separate antenna attached to their homes to pick up the local news or other programming from their local stations, an added expense and an eyesore for customers.

Grandfather Clause Dispute

Satellite television stations provide specialty programming, such as movies and sporting events, but with few exceptions are not allowed to beam programs from network television to many parts of the country.

The law does permit satellite companies to beam network signals to viewers who cannot receive local stations using rooftop antennas, a problem primarily in rural areas.

To protect the viewers in his home state and other rural areas, Sen. Conrad Burns, R-Mont., said in an interview April 26 that he would support a grandfather clause to allow satellite customers to keep their current level of service if they live outside cities.

Local stations and networks have gone to court to enforce the ban on beaming programs to satellite customers, except in certain circumstances.

Allies of the satellite television industry in the Senate, including Commerce Committee Chairman John McCain, R-Ariz., are supporting efforts to prevent court orders from cutting off network programming to satellite television customers.

For example, under one court order in February, satellite companies were forced to stop providing network programming to 700,000 customers. Other court cases could cause satellite customers to lose similar services.

Supporters of both bills are concerned that the decision by lawmakers to let regulation of the cable industry expire March 31, as provided in the Telecommunications Act of 1996 (PL 104-104), could lead to higher cable rates. They want to make sure that satellite television companies can compete and match prices offered by cable companies. *(1996 Almanac, p. 3-45)*

Nevertheless, Mark N. Cooper, research director for the Consumer Federation of America, said Congress erred in ending cable regulation. "They deregulated before there was competition. Now, they are scrambling to create it," Cooper said.

W.J. "Billy" Tauzin, R-La., defended the decision to deregulate in a speech on the House floor April 27. He said the legislation would "provide cable with a real competitor."

Democratic Rep. Edward J. Markey of Massachusetts said the bill represents a "revolution" that would instantly allow satellite companies to offer more varied services.

The lone vote against HR 1554 was cast by Robert A. Brady, D-Pa. He cited concerns by the 679,000-member International Brotherhood of Electrical Workers that local stations with union workers might lose viewers and advertising to satellite television.

Other Issues

The Senate and House bills would require satellite television companies to deliver all local stations in all markets they serve by 2002. The House bill would require a study by the Commerce Department to determine where there is adequate satellite television service in small towns.

Andrew R. Paul, senior vice president of the Satellite Broadcasting and Communications Association, praised the House bill but said he would seek more provisions to prevent networks and local stations from imposing onerous conditions for retransmission deals. "We need better protection," he said.

Senate Passes Satellite TV Bill

MAY 22 — The Senate passed legislation (HR 1554) by voice vote May 20 intended to broaden satellite TV programming and promote competition between the cable and satellite TV industries.

The bill would allow satellite television providers to transmit more programming from local broadcast television stations, lifting an 11-year-old law (PL 100-667) that limited the kinds of satellite programming customers could get.

Senate passage set the stage for a conference to resolve differences between the House and Senate on the Senate-passed version of the bill.

Both bills would allow satellite viewers to see any show carried on local broadcast stations. And they would require satellite television companies, which serve 11 million households, to deliver all local stations in areas they serve by 2002.

The Senate agreed to strip out the text of a similar House bill and insert a substitute amendment that incorporated a Senate bill (S 247), sponsored by Senate Judiciary Committee Chairman Orrin G. Hatch, R-Utah.

Hatch said on the floor May 20 that the bill is essential to help satellite television companies win new customers. "I want satellite TV to directly compete with cable TV. The only way they can do that is to be able to offer local TV stations."

Conferees Near Accord on Bill

NOVEMBER 6 — House and Senate negotiators set the stage for final passage of a bill (HR 1554) the week of Nov. 8 to broaden programming for satellite television after agreeing to provide a loan guarantee for a new orbiter to deliver service to rural customers.

Negotiators decided Nov. 4 to include a $1.25 billion Agriculture Department loan guarantee to support rural television service. The deal set the stage for conference committee approval, resolving lawmakers' fears that satellite television companies might focus on cities and abandon rural areas.

The loan guarantee would help finance a satellite to deliver programming in rural areas. Potential beneficiaries would be rural telephone cooperatives that plan to deliver satellite television service.

A conference committee has been working to finish the bill since Sept. 28. The bill would permit satellite television providers to deliver local broadcast channels to customers for the first time.

The agreement on the loan guarantee was designed to ensure that rural customers get the same benefits as city dwellers from a provision that would require satellite television companies to provide all local channels in all areas they serve by 2002. Some satellite television providers said it would be hard to meet that deadline in small towns.

The cable television industry opposed the loan guarantee, on grounds it would subsidize a competitor.

Other unrelated provisions were being added to the conference report, including a bill (HR 486) to require the Federal Communications Commission to create a new license for low-power television stations. The bill would also waive a mandatory delay in the effective date of a presidential order issued in July allowing exports of powerful, new personal computers. Companies would be allowed to sell the computers overseas as soon as the bill is signed by the president, instead of waiting until Jan. 23.

House Adopts Conference Report; Trouble in Senate

NOVEMBER 13 — The Senate was expected to consider a plan the week of Nov. 15 to salvage the conference report for HR 1554, a bill that would broaden programming for satellite television and send more television signals to rural viewers.

Senate leaders agreed reluctantly Nov. 10 to try to kill a proposed loan guarantee program for developing rural television service, in order to satisfy the objections of Banking, Housing and Urban Affairs Committee Chairman Phil Gramm, R-Texas.

The battle over the loan guarantees erupted just as the Senate was preparing to clear the conference report, filed Nov. 9 after six weeks of negotiations. The bill also included measures for low-power television and restricting public television stations from sharing their donor lists with political campaigns.

Gramm argued that the conference report did not offer enough details about companies and nonprofit groups eligible for the loan guarantees. He complained that the proposal was developed without his panel's consent.

The loan guarantee program was a key element in a conference report that had strong bipartisan support. It was adopted by the House, 411-8, on Nov. 9. *(Vote 581, p. H-190)*

The bill would allow satellite television providers to deliver local broadcast stations for the first time to customers living in cities across the country. President Clinton is expected to sign it once the Senate clears it. But the battle over the loan guarantees could delay final action on the bill.

"Our concern is for Congress to get it done as quickly as possible," said Jake Siewert, a spokesman for the White House. "We support the bill because it will create competition."

Gramm vowed to delay action on the conference report until the loan guarantee program is killed.

"I don't take bills hostage unless I'm willing to shoot them," he said in an interview Nov. 9. "I don't want to shoot this bill, but I will if I have to."

In order to satisfy Gramm, Senate leaders agreed Nov. 10 to a series of parliamentary maneuvers to kill the loan guarantee program, while saving the rest of the conference report. They came up with a plan to defeat the conference report when the Senate returns to work on Nov. 16. The Senate would then vote on a revised version of the bill that passed the Senate by voice vote May 20, containing the text of the conference report and excluding the loan guarantee program.

The plan was approved by Gramm and by Conrad Burns, R-Mont., who sponsored the loan guarantee program. But Democrats planned to insist on a cloture vote on the conference report.

Burns said he was assured that Gramm would be able to develop a bill early next year to create a similar loan guarantee program.

Patrick J. Leahy, D-Vt., and other Democrats questioned whether eliminating the loan guarantee program would threaten adoption of the conference report this year and prevent satellite viewers from getting access to expanded services.

"I would hate to be a Republican if this bill doesn't pass. Satellite television viewers want this bill," Leahy said.

Latest Compromise

Until Gramm objected, the conference report appeared to be cruising smoothly toward adoption.

House and Senate negotiators reached informal agreement Nov. 8 after a flurry of meetings to resolve disputes over satellite television and unrelated provisions inserted in the bill.

The agreement came after a compromise to permit satellite television providers to deliver local channels immediately, while they negotiate formal retransmission agreements with local station owners.

Lawmakers were hoping that pressure from satellite television viewers would force satellite and local owners to resolve differences dating to passage of the Satellite Home Viewer Act (PL 103-369) five years ago. *(1994 Almanac, p. 216)*

Commerce, Science and Transportation Committee Chairman John McCain, R-Ariz., said there was a deadline for satellite companies to complete retransmission agreements with local broadcasters within six months of enactment. He said the bill would force satellite companies to accept unfair terms. But he stopped short of joining Gramm's effort to block it.

Despite McCain's concerns about the satellite television industry, the final report included a number of provisions favorable to satellite providers. For example, it would allow them to deliver broadcast stations from big cities to a national audience in suburban areas unable to receive strong signals from local broadcast stations.

The report also directed the Federal Communications Commission (FCC) to study a new signal-reception standard used to determined whether consumers are living in areas "unserved" by local stations and should be eligible to receive broadcast stations from other cities by satellite.

Supporters of the conference report said the bill would usher in a new era of intensified competition between satellite and cable television providers. They said the bill was needed to ensure low rates for television subscription services following the end of cable rate regulation on March 31 under terms of the Telecommunications Act of 1996 (PL 104-104). *(1996 Almanac, p. 3-45)*

Lawmakers were afraid that cable companies, which already offer local stations, would charge higher prices after rate regulation ended.

While satellite television companies were primed to begin offering local stations to cities across the country, they face a challenge in trying to comply with another key requirement in the bill — that they deliver all local stations, or none at all, to every town they serve by 2002.

That requirement is intended to ensure that satellite companies provide more than minimal service to rural areas, instead of focusing only on providing local stations and winning new subscribers in big cities.

On-line Video Services

Although many lawmakers of both parties agreed with major provisions in the bill, a potential obstacle emerged in the House while senators debated the fate of the loan guarantee program.

Strong opposition emerged to a provision inserted in the conference report by Judiciary Courts and Intellectual Property Subcommittee Chairman Howard Coble, R-N.C.

Members of the Commerce Committee complained that the provision would exclude on-line video services from being automatically permitted to carry the same television programming as satellite television providers.

The provision was strongly opposed by some Internet service providers, including America Online Inc. (AOL).

Defenders of the provision said it was intended to protect the movies and programs owned by Hollywood studios and television production companies. But opponents said it would stifle development of new on-line video services.

Rep. Robert W. Goodlatte, R-Va., said Nov. 9 that he would continue efforts to modify or delete Coble's provision. "We're going to try to do something in another bill this year," he said.

Patent and Trademark Reforms

While Goodlatte tried to help America Online and other Internet businesses get access to video programming, Coble and other architects of the conference report worked to preserve other provisions in the text of their bill.

House and Senate negotiators included in their conference report the text of a bill (HR 1907) to overhaul the patent system. The bill was intended to resolve disputes between inventors and manufacturers over the ownership of new technology.

The bill would require publication of some patent applications within 18 months of filing. The requirement would apply only to applications filed in nations such as Great Britain, France and Japan that have similar requirements for publishing applications.

Sen. Charles E. Schumer, D-N.Y., said he was concerned that the report did not clarify rules for the use of business-method patents on Wall Street. He warned that the patents could put limits on the use of formulas used to calculate the value of financial investments and other business practices. "I'm not satisfied. But I think my concerns will be addressed later," Schumer said.

Negotiators inserted provisions of a bill (S 1255) to prevent the unauthorized use of brand names protected by trademark. Negotiators broadened the provisions to bar unauthorized use of the personal names of individuals in Internet addresses.

Other Issues

The conference report included other provisions dealing with a range of issues that had been pending before the Commerce and Judiciary committees in both chambers.

The report would require public broadcasting stations to get the permission of donors before sharing their names with any third parties including marketing companies. The report would bar federal funding for stations that share any donor lists with political parties and candidates.The report also included a measure (HR 486) to authorize a new FCC license for low power television.

Senate Compromise On Rural TV Clears Way for Satellite TV Bill

NOVEMBER 20 — The Senate completed work on legislation to expand programming for satellite television, after leaders of both parties hastily crafted a compromise to delay until next year debate on a $1.25 billion loan guarantee program to improve service for rural viewers.

Majority Leader Trent Lott, R-Miss., worked out a deal Nov. 18 to postpone action on the loan guarantee program, which would pump money to rural satellite and cable systems to help them deliver local broadcast stations to viewers who do not have access to local television channels.

Lott's plan ended objections from Democrat Max Baucus of Montana, who had threatened to block passage of a stopgap funding bill (H J Res 82).

Baucus had been angered by House and Senate leaders who decided to delete the loan guarantees from the conference report for the satellite television bill (HR 1554 — Conference report: H Rept 106-464).

Banking, Housing and Urban Affairs Committee Chairman Phil Gramm, R-Texas, insisted that the guarantees be deleted from the conference report because it was developed outside his committee.

And Senate leaders agreed to a series of parliamentary maneuvers to comply with his demand. The compromise requires debate to begin on the proposal by March 30, 2000.

The Baucus compromise was the final action on the satellite television bill.

Virtually all other provisions of the conference report for HR 1554 were put into a new Senate bill (S 1948). That bill, in turn, was included in the omnibus spending bill (HR 3194 — Conference report: H Rept 106-479).

The bill would allow satellite television providers to deliver local stations across the country for the first time. And it would require satellite providers to carry all local stations — or none — in areas they serve by 2002.

The House adopted the report on the omnibus spending bill, 296-135, on Nov. 18. The Senate cleared it, 74-24, on Nov. 19 after resolving a dispute over dairy prices. *(House vote 610, p. H-198; Senate vote 374, p. S-74)*

Loan Guarantee Fight

While final passage of the legislation appeared to be assured, the Senate debate of the satellite television issue exposed deep divisions on the question of how to improve television services in rural America.

The loan guarantee proposal won broad support after it emerged for the first time in the conference committee to resolve differences between House and Senate versions of the satellite TV bill.

The sponsors of the proposal, Sen. Conrad Burns, R-Mont., and Rep. Rick Boucher, D-Va., argued that rural residents would not benefit from improved service under the bill unless loan guarantees were available to deliver local stations in rural areas via satellite. They said rural residents were often unable to receive local programming because of uneven terrain and a dearth of local stations in some parts of the country.

Boucher and Republican Robert W. Goodlatte of Virginia collected 239 signatures from House members supporting the loan guarantees.

The loan guarantees were originally intended to promote development of satellite television service by rural telephone cooperatives. But the proposal was broadened by negotiators to support companies using a range of technologies, including cable television.

Gramm argued that the program favored cable and satellite television. He linked his criticism of the loan guarantee program to other controversial provisions that were deleted from the conference report for HR 1554. Those provisions would have prevented on-line video services from obtaining the same rights to broadcast programming as cable and satellite systems.

Hollywood movie studios and Major League Baseball backed these provisions to prevent possible piracy of copyright-protected movies and sports events.

But the provisions were strongly opposed by Internet-related businesses, including America Online. Gramm said he believed on-line video services could eventually deliver local stations in rural areas and pledged to include them in the debate of loan guarantees.

Other Issues

In another last-minute effort to clear the way for the omnibus spending bill, Senate and House leaders agreed to include provisions of a patent system overhaul (HR 1907). The bill would require publication of some patent applications within 18 months of filing.

The bill also includes provisions of a bill (S 1255) to bar unauthorized use of trademark-protected brand names in Internet addresses. ◆

Law Enacted To Limit Firms' Liability From Y2K-Related Computer Glitches

Box Score

- **Bill:** HR 775 — PL 106-37
- **Legislative action: House** passed HR 775 (H Rept 106-131), 236-190, on May 12.

Senate passed HR 775, 62-37, on June 15, after substituting the provisions of S 96 (S Rept 106-10).

House adopted the conference report (H Rept 106-212), 404-24, on July 1.

Senate cleared the bill, 81-18, on July 1.

President signed HR 775 on July 20.

SUMMARY

Five months before the arrival of the new millennium, President Clinton signed a bill July 20 aimed at resolving lawsuits over potential computer breakdowns caused by so-called Year 2000, or Y2K, problems. The high-tech industry argued that liability limits in the law were essential to prevent companies from being crippled by lawsuits.

In an age of growing dependence on computers, a wide range of businesses expressed concern that they could be held liable by their customers for damages if they were unable to deliver products or perform services because of a computer glitch on Jan. 1, 2000. High-tech firms were part of a coalition of business groups that pushed for legislation to limit liability for losses caused by computer breakdowns.

The Y2K bug is the result of flaws in computer programming that promised to cause many computers to recognize only the final two digits of each year and assume that the first two digits were "19." As a result, those computers would mistake the year 2000 for the year 1900.

In congressional hearings, representatives of high-tech companies testified that many newer computer systems did not contain the Y2K flaw and would not malfunction. But high-tech firms were still concerned that older computers and software would stop operating properly. Lawmakers heard tales of problems ranging from a grocer's cash register system that would not accept credit cards with expiration dates in 2000, to a doctor's office management software that would not make appointments beyond December 1999.

But the legislation ran into opposition from trial lawyers who feared it would set a precedent for broader product liability reform. Opponents argued that liability limits would remove pressure for companies to fix defective computers.

Two Republicans from Virginia, Thomas M. Davis III and Robert W. Goodlatte, helped shepherd the bill through the House over the trial lawyers' opposition.

Senate passage came after motions to invoke cloture failed 52-47 on April 29 and 53-45 on May 18. Commerce Committee Chairman John McCain, R-Ariz., worked out a compromise with Democrats to drop protection from liability for corporate officers and to narrow a cap on damages so that it applied only to small businesses. The compromise helped to solidify the support of 12 Democrats and to overcome staunch opposition from Ernest F. Hollings, D-S.C.

In conference committee, Republicans ended an impasse by agreeing with a White House demand to narrow federal jurisdiction for larger legal claims. The compromise required lawsuits seeking more than $10 million in damages to be filed in federal court. A Senate provision would have set the threshold for federal cases at $1 million.

The administration also insisted on a provision to protect plaintiffs by requiring solvent defendants to pay up to twice their share of damages if a codefendant was unable to pay. Before agreeing to these concessions, Republicans demanded a letter from the White House pledging that Clinton would sign the bill. Christopher J. Dodd, D-Conn., who helped to broker a compromise after private conversations with Clinton, made sure the missive was delivered to seal the deal.

The high-tech industry got much of what it wanted. The law applies to lawsuits in state or federal courts brought after Jan. 1, 1999, that allege actual or potential Y2K-related computer failures that occur or cause harm before 2003. It provides that defendants are liable only for their share of blame for any Y2K damage. That language was designed to prevent big companies from being held liable for the lion's share of damages in Y2K lawsuits.

The law gives companies up to 90 days to fix problems before a lawsuit can be brought. Punitive damages are limited to $250,000 or three times the amount of compensatory damages, whichever is less, for companies with fewer than 50 employees or individuals with a net worth of $500,000 or less.

Senate Backs Y2K Loans; Liability Protections Also Advance

MARCH 6 — Displaying a twinge of panic about the possibility of a year 2000 computer problem, the Senate moved on several fronts the week of March 1 to prepare for the immovable deadline less than 10 months away.

On March 2, the Senate passed by a vote of 99-0 a bill (S 314) that requires the Small Business Administration to guarantee loans to businesses to help them update computers to avoid the Y2K problem. *(Vote 28, p. S-10)*

The next day, the Commerce, Science and Transportation Committee approved S 96 to extend liability protections to businesses unable to update their computer systems on time.

"It is in our economic best interest to make sure that all of our small businesses — some 20 million, if we include the self-employed — are up and running soundly and effectively, creating jobs and providing services, on and after Jan. 1," said John Kerry, D-Mass., the Small Business Committee's ranking member.

"We have 10 short months now to become completely Y2K compliant, and national studies have found that the majority of small businesses . . . are not ready, and they are not even preparing," Kerry said.

Studies have found that small businesses are lagging in efforts to update their computers and may have a hard time financing repairs.

A 1998 survey by the Arthur Andersen Enterprise Group and National Small Business United found that 94 percent of all small and midsize businesses have computers, but only 64 percent have begun taking steps to fix the problem.

"The consequences of Congress not taking action to assist small businesses with the Y2K problems are too severe to ignore," said the bill's sponsor, Christopher S. Bond, R-Mo., chairman of the Small Business Committee.

In hearings before his committee, Bond said senators "received information indicating that approximately 750,000 small businesses may either shut down due to the Y2K problem or be severely crippled if they do not take the action to cure their Y2K problems."

Under the bill, the Small Business Administration is expected to guarantee about $500 million in loans through the end of the program on Dec. 31, 2000.

The year 2000 glitch is caused by a software engineering quirk. Early designers saved storage space by representing years with the last two digits rather than four. Because of that, many computers will interpret "00" as 1900 rather than 2000.

Discounting Armageddon

It is no small matter. The GartnerGroup, an international consulting firm, has estimated that it will cost $30 billion to fix the problem for the federal government alone and $600 billion to make the adjustments worldwide.

The consequences of not addressing the problem were outlined hours after S 314 passed, when the Special Committee on the Year 2000 Technology Problem released its interim report.

The report, presented by Chairman Robert F. Bennett, R-Utah, and ranking member Christopher J. Dodd, D-Conn., concluded that U.S. industries are well-prepared, though some problems will arise. The most vulnerable sector, the report said, is the health care industry, while telecommunications and financial services are in the best shape.

"We have tried to discount what I call the Y2K survivalist mentality somehow that this is going to be Armageddon," Dodd said, dismissing predictions that Jan. 1 will bring widespread power failures, food shortages and chaos.

Bennett and Dodd did warn, however, that many foreign countries are far behind in efforts to make their computer system immune to the Y2K bug.

Key oil supplying countries, including Venezuela and parts of the Middle East, are behind in repairing the problem, as are important trading partners, including China and South Korea.

On March 3, the bipartisanship and cordiality ended as the Commerce Committee considered a bill to extend limited liability protection to companies that are unable to update their computer systems to cope with the Y2K problem.

The bill, S 96, was sponsored by committee Chairman John McCain, R-Ariz., who said, "The purpose of the bill is to provide incentives to prevent Y2K failures, to fix the problems that do occur, and to avoid costly litigation."

Committee Democrats, however, sharply criticized the bill, charging that it provides an escape for "irresponsible" companies that ignore the threat. "This is a 'Get out of jail free' card," said ranking Democrat Ernest F. Hollings, D-S.C. "It's a bad, bad bill, and I hope we can kill it."

Hollings could not deliver the wish, however, as the committee approved the bill 11-9 on a party-line vote.

Senate Reaches Bipartisan Pact On Y2K Liability

APRIL 17 — A bipartisan deal was struck on April 15 to narrow the scope of a Senate bill (S 96) to cap liability for breakdowns caused by the Year 2000 computer glitch. It sets the stage for a showdown vote as early as April 26 on an expected Democratic filibuster.

Commerce, Science and Transportation Committee Chairman John McCain, R-Ariz., and Ron Wyden, D-Ore., confirmed April 15 that they would unveil on April 19 details of a compromise they had brokered. It was unclear how many other Democrats would support the deal, which included a key provision to exclude cases of fraud from any limit on liability.

Wyden's support signaled an end to unified Democratic opposition on McCain's panel, amid reports that other Democrats were wavering under heavy lobbying from business constituents.

"We are pleased . . . to address the Democrats' concern and move forward in a bipartisan fashion," said Pia Pialorsi, a spokeswoman for McCain.

The Clinton administration has opposed a cap on liability contained in the bill. The bill would limit damages for the "Y2K" problem at $250,000, or if there were greater losses, at three times the amount of actual damages.

In the compromise worked out by Wyden and McCain, the amount of the cap would remain the same, but an exemption would allow unlimited punitive and non-economic damages to be collected when a plaintiff could establish by "clear and convincing evidence that the defendant intentionally defrauded the plaintiff."

Wyden and other Democrats had strongly opposed the bill when it was approved by the Commerce, Science and Transportation Committee on March 3 on a party-line vote of 11-9. But Wyden worked out a deal that resolved his objections to the bill.

David E. Seldin, a spokesman for Wyden, said he was convinced that the compromise version of the bill would "address the concerns that the initial bill was unfair to consumers."

Lawmakers are under pressure from business groups to pass a Y2K liability protection bill, because businesses are worried about a potential flurry of litigation if the computer glitch causes substantial losses. The problem is the result of a software design quirk that causes computers to recognize only the last two digits of any year. Because of that, the year "00" could be interpreted by computers as 1900, not 2000.

Sunset Provision

Wyden and McCain were continuing to discuss other provisions in their compromise, including a possible sunset date for the bill, 10 to 20 years after the date of final passage of the law. In cases where there were multiple defendants, the bill would limit the liability of each to his proportional share of responsibility for damages. But the compromise would allow a judge to make adjustments six months after a final judgment in cases where some defendants could not pay for their share of damages.

While the negotiations continued, business lobbyists were quietly proclaiming victory.

One lobbyist familiar with the talks said that supporters of the compromise believed it would get 57 votes, including those of Wyden and Democratic Sens. Dianne Feinstein of California and Joseph I. Lieberman of Connecticut. Other Democrats being targeted as possible swing votes were Patty Murray of Washington, Richard H. Bryan and Harry Reid of Nevada, Charles S. Robb of Virginia and Herb Kohl of Wisconsin.

Other lobbyists said they were optimistic that the bill would narrowly pass the Senate and easily clear the House, setting the stage for a possible veto.

"The fact that Wyden has come on shows there's major momentum. We are feeling more encouraged that we will be able to overcome a filibuster," said Lonnie P. Taylor, senior vice president of congressional and public affairs for the U.S. Chamber of Commerce, representing 200,000 businesses.

For their part, opponents pledged to fight against the compromise, which is expected to be offered by McCain as a manager's amendment to the bill.

"There's no way we will support this. It is not a compromise, and it is anti-consumer," said Mark S. Mandell, president of the 55,000-member Association of Trial Lawyers of America.

Cloture Vote Fails To Stop Senate Debate

MAY 1 — A battle will continue behind the scenes in the Senate the week of May 3 over a bill (S 96) to limit the liability of companies for problems caused by the Year 2000 computer glitch.

The Senate voted 52-47 on a motion to invoke cloture April 29, falling eight votes short of the number needed to end a Democratic filibuster. Three Republicans crossed over to help block cloture: Richard C. Shelby of Alabama, Arlen Specter of Pennsylvania and Thad Cochran of Mississippi. *(Vote 95, p. S-22)*

The vote marked a victory for trial lawyers and consumer groups that opposed the bill.

"We won the first round of the fight today. But the fight is not over," said Gene Kimmelman, co-director of the Washington office of Consumers Union.

Business groups say the legislation is essential to avert a potential wave of lawsuits linked to expected "Y2K" computer problems on Jan. 1, 2000.

But trial lawyers and consumer groups charge that supporters are trying to establish a precedent to limit damage awards in product liability lawsuits.

Senate Commerce Committee Chairman John McCain, R-Ariz., said April 29 that he believed he could negotiate a deal to win more support to salvage the bill in another possible cloture vote the week of May 3.

But Senate Majority Leader Trent Lott, R-Miss., said in an interview April 29 that he did not want another vote until there is a clear sign that Democrats are willing to compromise.

"It may never be voted on again," Lott said. "Let them explain to Silicon Valley and to small businessmen and women and to AOL [America Online Inc.] in Northern Virginia why they oppose Y2K liability."

Lott and other Republicans are betting that pressure from the computer industry will force Democrats to cut a deal.

"There is a dilemma for Democrats on this one. Traditionally, they have been supportive of both the information technology community and the [plaintiff]. This is putting a Democrat at odds with himself or herself," said Marc Pearl, general counsel of the Information Technology Association of America, representing 11,000 software and computer service companies.

Lott and other Republicans insisted that they would not surrender on key elements. Sen. Edward M. Kennedy, D-Mass., replied in an interview April 29 that business groups were trying to lay the groundwork for broader product liability reform.

"They have refused to give ground. We have a stalemate," Kennedy said.

Fight Over the Cap

Meanwhile, battle lines hardened as Democrats prepared a series of controversial amendments. On April 28, they lost a party-line vote when the Senate agreed 55-44 to table (kill) a procedural motion to allow consideration of Kennedy's proposal to raise the minimum wage by a dollar, to $6.15 an hour. *(Vote 94, p. S-22)*

The administration's Office of Management and Budget, in a written statement April 27, threatened a veto of McCain's bill, as well as a substitute amendment he offered with Ron Wyden, D-Ore. The administration opposed a provision capping punitive damages in Y2K liability suits at $250,000 or three times the amount of actual damages, whichever is greater.

Alternatives

The administration supported an alternative, backed by Democrats John Kerry of Massachusetts and Charles S. Robb of Virginia, to encourage negotiated settlements.

In a final bid to resolve the impasse before the vote, McCain reached a compromise with Christopher J. Dodd, D-Conn., to narrow the cap on punitive damages to cover only small businesses. The Dodd compromise won the backing of several Democrats, including Dianne Feinstein of California, but it was strongly opposed by other Democrats. Critics said the compromise would limit the liability of big companies to their proportional share of responsibility.

In the House, allies of trial lawyers tried April 29 to revamp a Y2K liability bill (HR 775) in the Judiciary Committee. The panel voted 14-17 to reject an amendment to delete a section of the bill that included a cap on attorney fees and other restrictions on lawsuits.

Asa Hutchinson, R-Ark., offered another, narrower amendment to delete a cap to prohibit attorney fees of more than $1,000 an hour. The amendment could be considered May 4. The House bill, which includes a provision similar to the McCain bill's cap on punitive damages, is strongly opposed by trial lawyers and consumer groups.

"We have a lot of work to do," said Bill McCollum, R-Fla. "But we will reach agreement. The bill is important for a lot of businesses."

House Panel Votes To Cap Damages On Y2K Lawsuits

MAY 8 — The House appears poised to pass a bill (HR 775) the week of May 10 to cap damages in liability lawsuits for losses caused by the Year 2000 computer problem, against strong objections of the Clinton administration and trial lawyers.

The House Judiciary Committee approved the bill, 15-14, May 4. The vote came after the panel agreed by voice vote to sweeten the package by deleting a cap on attorneys' fees in Y2K liability cases.

The panel also approved, 15-13, an amendment adding language to make a plaintiff pay the defendant's legal fees if the plaintiff got less money in a court judgment than he would have in settlement offers.

The committee debate was deeply divided. "I can tell you that this bill will not become law. It will be stopped," said Zoe Lofgren, D-Calif.

In a letter to Judiciary Committee Chairman Henry J. Hyde, R-Ill., the Justice Department warned that Attorney General Janet Reno would recommend a presidential veto because of the cap on punitive damages and other limits on lawsuits.

Supporters say the bill is needed to prevent a flood of lawsuits resulting from computer breakdowns caused by the Y2K problem. But Democratic opponents of the bill say it is politically motivated and that it includes features, such as the cap on damages, that are intended to set a precedent for broader limits on product liability suits.

The bill would limit damages in Y2K lawsuits to $250,000 for large businesses, or three times the amount of actual damages, whichever is greater. The cap would be set at no more than $250,000 for small businesses (those with fewer than 25 employees), or three times actual losses, whichever is less.

Lindsey Graham of South Carolina, a former prosecutor, was the lone Republican to vote no in committee, saying there were too many restrictions on liability lawsuits.

Mark S. Mandell, president of the Association of Trial Lawyers of America, said May 5 that he was hopeful that his group would get revisions in the bill or block it.

"We are outnumbered. But it is a fluid situation. And we are trying as hard as we can to get changes," Mandell said.

Key House Republicans, including Robert W. Goodlatte of Virginia, said they believe the bill will have strong support.

"The bill has very good chances of passing, and then we will look to the Senate to get something done," Goodlatte said in an interview May 4.

But in the Senate, lawmakers are divided, and Democrats have vowed to block legislation unless a compromise can be reached.

While supporters of the bill prepared for the House vote, consideration of a similar bill in the Senate (S 96) was blocked April 29 by the objection of Ernest F. Hollings, D-S.C.

Some senators were skeptical that a bill would be completed soon. "The bill is in big limbo," said Patty Murray, D-Wash., on May 4.

"The bill may rise again, but it may not rise very far," said Richard C. Shelby of Alabama the same day. Shelby was one of a handful of Republicans critical of the bill.

Democrat Ron Wyden of Oregon disagreed May 4 with those who were predicting a long battle. "If we can get a vote on the bill in the Senate, we will get enough votes," said Wyden, a bill supporter.

The Barbs Fly

Leaders of both parties accused the other side of causing a stalemate. "Democrats are blocking it," Senate Majority Leader Trent Lott, R-Miss., said May 4.

He repeated his challenge to Democrats to accept a deal reached April 28 by Republican John McCain of Arizona, chairman of the Commerce, Science and Transportation Committee, and Christopher J. Dodd, D-Conn. Their compromise would narrow a cap on punitive damages to cover only lawsuits against small businesses.

Senate Minority Leader Tom Daschle, D-S.D., replied that Republicans have not been willing to compromise. "They are acting irresponsibly," Daschle said in an interview May 4.

With both sides trading barbs, and the Senate bill stalled, some lawmakers and staff aides said privately that final legislation could be delayed indefinitely until a compromise is reached.

Supporters hope the legislation will gain momentum later this year if there is more demand from consumers, as well as businesses, for limits on losses related to the anticipated glitch.

"Lawmakers know this must get done. There is a natural deadline, after all, to deal with this problem by the end of the year," said Richard P. Diamond, a spokesman for House Majority Leader Dick Armey, R-Texas.

House Passes Bill, Despite Opposition From White House

MAY 15 — With less than eight months remaining until the new millennium, the White House is quietly seeking to avert a political collision with supporters of a House-passed bill to limit lawsuits over year 2000 computer breakdowns.

The House voted May 12 mostly along party lines, 236-190, to approve a bill (HR 775) to limit damage claims for Y2K computer problems. The bill's key provisions were strongly opposed by the administration and by trial lawyers. It would cap punitive damages at $250,000 for businesses with 25 or more employees, or if losses were greater, at three times the amount of losses. *(Vote 128, p. H-50)*

While business trade groups supporting the bill proclaimed victory after the House vote, it will likely be a short-lived triumph. The bill fell short of winning a veto-proof majority in the House, and it faces a certain Clinton veto, increasing the likelihood that both sides will have to make concessions to resolve a stalemate in the Senate.

Supporters say the bill would stop a

wave of potential lawsuits to recover damages for losses — ranging from malfunctioning home appliances to the loss of electronic business files in computers — caused by Y2K computer malfunctions. Opponents say the bill included provisions sought by the business lobby to set the stage for other product liability limits.

Outline of a Deal

Senate Majority Leader Trent Lott, R-Miss., said May 14 that he hoped to have a floor vote on the Senate version of the Y2K liability bill (S 96) on May 18. He urged Democrats to end procedural objections and permit a vote on a bipartisan compromise reached April 28 by John McCain, R-Ariz., and Christopher J. Dodd, D-Conn.

Behind the scenes, the White House worked to avert Democratic defections in the Senate and to reshape the McCain-Dodd compromise. It encouraged a new round of negotiations focusing on a proposal floated May 14 by Democrat John Kerry of Massachusetts.

The core of the Kerry plan is a concession sought by the high-tech industry that would limit the liability of companies that took action to prevent Y2K problems. The Kerry plan resembles a proposal laid out by the White House in a May 11 letter sent to congressional leaders.

Liability Limits

The centerpiece of that outline, and of the new Kerry plan, is a provision to limit the liability of big high-tech companies — such as Intel Corp. and Microsoft Corp. — to their proportional share of responsibility for any damage caused by a Y2K computer problem. The measure would prevent the giant high-tech companies from being forced to pay for damages caused by suppliers, distributors and other companies in cases involving multiple defendants.

The concession on proportional liability reflected a new White House strategy for focusing on meeting specific demands of high-tech companies while resisting other provisions that it opposes, including a broad cap on punitive damages similar to the one in the House bill.

The May 11 letter was signed by Bruce J. Lindsey, deputy counsel in the White House, and Gene B. Sperling, director of the National Economic Council. It outlined nine policies that Clinton would support but made no mention of any cap on punitive damages.

The letter expressed a desire to provide proportional liability for high-tech companies that take "specific, appropriate steps to prevent or minimize harm" from Y2K failures.

While the White House tried to promote the Kerry plan, Senate Republicans said they would press for a vote on the McCain-Dodd plan.

"We have pared away everything that is not necessary, and now we have a reasonable, practical and supportable bill," McCain said at a news conference May 13.

"The clock is ticking," he added. "This legislation cannot wait."

With the sides sharply divided in the Senate, lawmakers from both parties predicted that a final deal would likely have to wait until a conference committee after Senate passage. On the House floor on May 12, some charged that the Y2K liability issue had become too partisan.

"What they are really doing is swatting a fly with a sledgehammer," said Joe Moakley, D-Mass.

The House voted, 190-236, to reject a Democratic substitute amendment that would have removed the punitive damage cap. *(Vote 126, p. H-50)*

Robert W. Goodlatte, R-Va., said May 12 that he believed the House vote would help prod both sides to compromise. "There is a tremendous amount of pressure now on the Senate and on the White House to make more concessions," he said.

Senate Bill Gains Momentum With Backing From Tech Industry

MAY 22 — Senate Commerce Committee Chairman John McCain got good news by e-mail from the chairman of Intel Corp. on May 18 — just before a Senate cloture vote on a McCain bill to limit companies' liability for year 2000 computer problems.

In the electronic note, Andrew S. Grove of Intel, a $26 billion-a-year computer chip manufacturer, told Arizona Republican McCain that he had found a "lack of specifics" in a competing proposal by Sen. John Kerry, D-Mass. That draft bill is designed to attract the support of high-tech companies, which could face lawsuits over Y2K computer problems.

With those three words, Grove signaled that he would stay behind McCain's bill (S 96) and a compromise worked out with Sen. Christopher J. Dodd, D-Conn. It would provide limited liability protection to companies if they are unable to fix their computer problems by Jan. 1, 2000.

The decision by Grove and executives of other technology companies was a clear defeat for an informal campaign by the White House and some Senate Democrats to peel away technology companies from a broad business coalition supporting the McCain-Dodd compromise.

Supporters of the bill say it would protect high-tech companies and other businesses from potential damage claims if they were sued for losses caused by Y2K computer malfunctions. But critics of the bill, including consumer groups, say the bill goes beyond what the high-tech industry wants.

The McCain-Dodd plan would cap damages for businesses with 50 or fewer employees at $250,000, or three times the actual damages, whichever was less. The cap is opposed by trial lawyers, and the White House threatened to veto the plan in a May 18 letter to Senate leaders. The Clinton administration has opposed punitive damage caps in the past, but the letter did not mention that longstanding position.

Supporters of the McCain bill are hoping that omission is a signal of a willingness to sign a bill that includes a narrow cap on punitive damages for small businesses.

While leaders of both parties continued to stake out opposite sides on the Y2K liability bill in public, they appeared to be laying the groundwork privately for reconsideration of the bill in June.

Rep. Zoe Lofgren, D-Calif., who represents the district that includes the Santa Clara headquarters of Intel, questioned whether Intel and other technology companies actually want a cap on punitive damages, as the Mc-

Cain bill provides.

In fact, Grove has not stressed punitive damage caps in lobbying on Capitol Hill, but he has emphasized other priorities, including a strong federal law that would pre-empt state laws and a guarantee that a company would be held liable only for losses that its products caused, not for damages caused by computer suppliers and other manufacturers.

Nevertheless, McCain was exultant May 18. "Andy Grove is supporting my bill, not the Kerry plan," he said. He carried a copy of Grove's e-mail onto the Senate floor to offer proof to anyone who wanted it that his bill was backed by one of the most influential corporate leaders in the high-tech industry.

The Senate failed to invoke cloture May 18 by a vote of 53-45, seven votes short of the number needed to end a Democratic filibuster. *(Vote 120, p. S-27)*

A number of Democrats were clearly willing to move to a vote on McCain's bill. However, they held ranks to oppose cloture in order to prevent an interruption in the debate that began the week of May 10 on the juvenile justice bill (S 254).

Democrats Get on Board

As the consideration of the juvenile justice bill neared an end later in the week, the political tide turned strongly in favor of McCain's compromise with Dodd. On May 19, the McCain-Dodd supporters released a letter signed by 13 Democrats, who said they would vote "yea" on any subsequent motion for cloture, virtually assuring that the motion would pass.

The letter was also a victory for Senate Majority Leader Trent Lott, R-Miss., who had insisted after the first of two cloture votes on the bill April 29 that Democrats should give ground and support the McCain-Dodd bill.

Hours after the May 18 cloture vote, Lott warned in a news conference that he was willing to let the Y2K liability bill wither.

"The Y2K bill is dead for the year," Lott said. "The Democrats apparently don't want a bill. When they come to me and say, 'We'll go to the substance and we'll produce enough votes to break a filibuster,' we'll bring it back up."

After receiving the letter from the 13 Democrats, Lott said he would schedule a new cloture vote, but he did not signal how soon it would be on the Senate calendar.

Sen. Ernest F. Hollings, D-S.C., who led opposition to the McCain-Dodd proposal, was gloomy about the prospects for continuing to block the effort.

"People are rushing for Silicon Valley [campaign] money. That's what this is all about. They've got all this money there, and people want to get some of it," Hollings said in an interview May 19.

Both sides argued that they had the best interests of high-tech companies at heart.

Sen. Dianne Feinstein of California said she believed that the McCain-Dodd compromise, which she and two other Democrats — Joseph I. Lieberman of Connecticut and Ron Wyden of Oregon — support, would remain the centerpiece of the Y2K bill.

Feinstein said Grove had expressed his opposition to the Kerry plan to her in a telephone conversation May 15, a day after Intel's lawyers reviewed a written draft of the Kerry plan.

The Kerry plan would offer a key concession to business by limiting the liability of a company to its proportionate share of blame for any losses, in cases where the company tried to remedy problems in advance. But Intel officials concluded that the Kerry plan would leave too much power with the states, allowing state law to dictate whether companies could be held responsible and leaving companies vulnerable to damage awards without limits.

The Price of Protection

The Y2K problem could result in a huge liability for Intel. The company has estimated that it may need to spend as much as $175 million just to fix potential Y2K problems involving its products. The company is also worried that it could become the target of a barrage of lawsuits filed by plaintiffs seeking millions of dollars in damages for business losses related to problems that affect personal computers, whether or not they were caused by Intel's products. Intel's microprocessor chips are in millions of personal computers, more than any other computer company's.

While Grove and other high-tech executives were willing to entertain and at least listen to new entreaties from Democrats, they elected finally not to switch sides and to stay within a broad business coalition that includes the U.S. Chamber of Commerce and the National Association of Manufacturers.

Grove has been perhaps the most outspoken and active corporate leader from Silicon Valley in trying to promote legislation and action by the federal government to prevent Y2K problems.

According to Public Disclosure Inc., a campaign finance watchdog group, Intel spent $1.1 million on lobbying last year and accounted for about $81,000 in campaign contributions, with three-quarters of the donations going to Republicans.

Democratic efforts to win Grove over reached their peak just before the May 18 cloture vote, with Kerry competing with Dodd and other supporters of the McCain-Dodd compromise.

Dodd privately told aides and lobbyists that he was concerned about reports saying Kerry had been circulating word that Grove and other high-tech executives were ready to back Kerry's proposal.

Kerry and Dodd had a face-to-face conversation about their differences after a Democratic caucus just before the May 18 vote. With both sides claiming to have Grove's ear, several Democrats and McCain asked the Intel chairman to clarify his position. Grove supplied a letter that was circulated among Democrats, saying he supported the McCain-Dodd compromise.

And Grove fired off his e-mail to McCain.

"Things are heating up," Grove told McCain dryly in his electronic message, referring to intensified efforts by Kerry and the administration to win his support.

Kerry continued scrambling to win support from Grove after the cloture vote. "I've got a call in to him. I'm waiting for his call back," Kerry said May 19.

Kerry got a call back from Grove, but got no support.

United We Stand

To counter Kerry's campaign, Republicans and a handful of Democratic allies urged leaders of high-tech companies to stay behind the McCain-

Dodd bill and to wait for Democratic opposition to collapse.

"It would be a big mistake for any of the advocates of this legislation to think they can cut a separate deal that just helps them," Spencer Abraham, R-Mich., said in an interview May 18. "I think that will cost votes on the other side and not bring anything to the table."

Feinstein agreed with this assessment May 19. "Frankly, we are not close to an agreement. We need to stand firm behind the Dodd-McCain compromise."

McCain was confident of victory in an interview May 18. "I think the Democrats are going to have to give ground. There is just too much pressure from businesses all across the country," he said.

Senate Leaders Postpone Vote on Y2K Compromise

JUNE 12 — After months of false starts, a bill to limit companies' liability for potential Year 2000 computer meltdowns was finally moving in the Senate on June 10. Liberated from the most controversial amendments and backed by bipartisan support, the end of the bill's difficult journey was in sight.

So it came as a surprise when Senate Republican leaders announced that passage of the bill (S 96) would be delayed until June 15.

"I'm very disappointed," Senate Minority Leader Tom Daschle, D-S.D., said on June 10. "I do not know why we cannot find a way to resolve all the other outstanding issues there are with regard to this bill this afternoon."

While the decision changed the timing, it will have little effect on the outcome. Passage of a reconstituted S 96 is assured because of a compromise worked out by primary sponsor John McCain, R-Ariz., and Democrats Christopher J. Dodd of Connecticut, Dianne Feinstein of California and Ron Wyden of Oregon.

While S 96 is almost certain to pass June 15, obstacles remain. It must be reconciled with a House bill (HR 775) that provides even stronger industry protections and with a White House that insists it will veto either bill.

The McCain compromise would eliminate caps on punitive damage awards against any company with more than 50 employees, while insulating municipalities and governments from such liability. It also would uphold the primacy of state legal standards and provide for proportional damages — sharing punitive damage costs among the companies held liable in any federal lawsuit.

McCain also agreed to strip out controversial language that would have protected corporate directors and officers from punitive damage liability.

The changes effectively broke a logjam that had been in place since April, when Democrat Ernest F. Hollings of South Carolina threatened to filibuster the bill.

Though Hollings continued to oppose the bill, he allowed debate to move forward. The last big obstacle was surmounted June 9 when a counterproposal, backed by the administration, from Democrat John Kerry of Massachusetts, Daschle and others, was defeated over a procedural question. The vote was on a motion to table, 57-41. Kerry's amendment would have provided additional protections for consumers. Critics charged that it would promote frivolous lawsuits. *(Vote 159, p. S-33)*

And, conveniently for supporters of the bill, final passage will come on the same day that executives from computer and other high-technology companies, including Microsoft Corp.'s Bill Gates, will be in Washington for a technology summit. Passage of so-called Y2K liability limits is one of the industry's highest legislative priorities.

The urgency was underscored June 8 by Thomas J. Donohue, president of the U.S. Chamber of Commerce, which has pushed hard to protect businesses from lawsuits.

"The Y2K bill will let companies put their money into fixing the problem rather than spend it paying lawyers to deal with frivolous litigation," Donohue said. "We need a comprehensive solution that encourages remediation, not litigation."

Veto Warning

But while the high-tech industry supports the bill, the Clinton administration does not. Administration officials have threatened a presidential veto because the bill favors industry rather than consumers.

Some senators were not intimidated by the threat, however, given that the year 2000 is less than six months away.

"He is not going to veto this bill. He would be nuts to veto it. This is a bipartisan bill," declared Orrin G. Hatch, R-Utah.

In addition to limiting liability and providing for proportional damages, the measure would require a 90-day waiting period before any lawsuit could be filed. Companies have been pushing for protection, fearing that they might be overwhelmed with Y2K lawsuits unless Congress provides some protection.

The Senate also tabled an amendment by Democrat Barbara Boxer of California that would have required companies to provide free software upgrades to any computer or software purchased after Dec. 31, 1994, that is affected by the Y2K problem. The vote was 66-32. *(Vote 163, p. 34)*

Likewise, two amendments offered by Democrat John Edwards of North Carolina, a former trial lawyer, were defeated. In both cases, opponents charged that the amendments would trigger more lawsuits, not fewer. *(Votes 161, 162, p. S-33)*

Meanwhile, an immovable deadline is drawing ever closer.

"The point here is that this is a complex technical problem with no easy, cheap solution," McCain said June 9.

Senate Passes Bill; GOP Fails To Win Veto-Proof Majority

JUNE 19 — Setting the stage for a showdown with President Clinton, the Senate passed a bill to limit businesses' liability in the event of year 2000 computer breakdowns.

For Republicans, the outcome was a sweet triumph that coincided with efforts by both parties to woo political support from computer and software company executives, including Microsoft Corp. Chairman Bill Gates.

The executives were in town for a three-day "high-tech summit" on Capitol Hill, sponsored by the Joint Economic Committee.

"There is no doubt it was a victory for us," Sen. Slade Gorton, R-Wash., said in an interview June 15 after the Senate passed HR 775, 62-37. *(Vote 165, p. S-34)*

"To have all these executives in town on the day of the vote provided a graphic illustration that Republicans are closer to the high-tech industry on economic issues," Gorton added.

The Senate passed HR 775 after inserting provisions of its own version (S 96). The bill now will go to negotiators, who must resolve its differences with the House version, which includes tougher language to limit lawsuits.

But while Republicans were able to claim a political victory, their celebration was muted by the failure to win a veto-proof majority. It takes 67 votes to override in the Senate.

Members of both parties warned that the heated debate surrounding the bill could impede efforts to cope with the real threat of breakdowns caused by programming in computers that fails to properly recognize the year 2000 and succeeding years.

Joseph I. Lieberman, D-Conn., one of 12 Democrats to vote in favor of the bill, urged both sides to negotiate a deal.

"There is a real deadline here, the end of the year. We're playing Russian roulette with this bill. Make that Silicon Valley roulette," Lieberman said.

Hours after the final vote, supporters began plotting a strategy to quickly resolve differences between the House and Senate versions of the bill, in order to avoid negotiations.

Supporters considered urging House members to accede to the Senate bill and accept compromises worked out by that bill's chief sponsor, Commerce Committee Chairman John McCain, R-Ariz., and Democrats Christopher J. Dodd, of Connecticut and Ron Wyden of Oregon.

But House members resisted the idea of simply adopting the Senate version.

Robert W. Goodlatte, R-Va., said he believed the House bill was stronger in some respects and should be considered in conference committee.

"It's too soon to tell what will happen. . . . We have a good chance to come up with a compromise," he said.

While trying to work out differences in the two bills, Goodlatte and other Republicans were adamant that they are not willing to make major concessions to the White House.

"If the president wants to veto this bill, that's his problem. And I think it is a problem. He's wrong on this issue," said Senate Majority Leader Trent Lott, R-Miss.

He added that the Senate is unlikely to support efforts by the White House to water down provisions in the Senate bill that would reduce lawsuits.

"I think we've already conceded a little bit too much," Lott said.

Veto Threat

The White House joined other Democrats in urging Republicans to be more accommodating.

"We will veto the bill as it stands because it goes well beyond what is needed to fix the Y2K problem. If we can scale back this bill to focus on litigation problems for high-tech, we will sign a reasonably balanced bill," said Jake Siewert, deputy White House press secretary, on June 16.

The White House objects to both the House and Senate bills because they would impose caps on damages and possibly discourage companies from fixing the problem.

A new, White House-backed proposal, released June 16 by Senate Minority Leader Tom Daschle, D-S.D., called for outright elimination of any cap on punitive damage awards, on the premise that caps would not benefit large technology companies.

Privately, the White House signaled that it might be willing to support a cap on punitive damages for small businesses, if it were limited to "good citizens" that can prove they took measures to fix or avoid Y2K problems.

The tech industry is more interested in bill provisions that would limit a company's liability to its proportional share of responsibility for any damages.

But Daschle said the limit on proportional liability should apply only to companies that "acted responsibly" to resolve Y2K problems.

Daschle urged conferees to give ground in order to "bridge the gap on the few remaining differences between S 96 and a bill that can garner much broader, bipartisan support."

White House Seeks Allies

While members sought to work out differences between the House and Senate versions, the administration and Democratic leaders in Congress looked for ways to neutralize the broad business coalition supporting the effort in Congress.

"We were willing to give the high-tech industry 80 percent of what it wanted," said Sen. John D. Rockefeller IV, D-W.Va. "They wanted 100 percent. No one gets 100 percent around here."

White House aides urged high-tech companies to support a narrower bill. The administration pursued a similar strategy during the Senate floor debate last month, but tech company executives, including Intel Chairman Andrew S. Grove, would not switch sides to endorse proposals backed by the White House.

In private discussions with industry lobbyists and executives during the week leading up to the vote, the administration tried to dispel any doubt about Clinton's resolve to veto the bill, according to an administration source.

In a June 16 meeting with a half-dozen representatives of the software industry, including Gates, John D. Podesta, the White House chief of staff, said that further delay would help no one, urging quick passage of a conference report. The administration wants to expedite the process toward a veto-override vote and, if an override fails, a new bill.

For bill supporters, victory was tinged with disappointment, because many of them believed they had a veto-proof margin of victory in the hours leading up to the June 15 Senate vote.

"I suspect it will be pretty overwhelming, probably veto-proof," Lott said June 14.

Lott was forced to delay the vote for five days, from June 10 until June 15, because of scheduling conflicts involving several senators, including presidential campaign commitments of McCain. The timing, coincidentally, put many Democrats in the uncomfortable position of voting against the bill in the midst of the high-tech summit.

On June 14, Lott took his friend

and fellow Mississippi native, James L. Barksdale, the former chief executive officer of Netscape Communications, Corp., into a hallway outside the summit to describe the Democrats' predicament. "We ground them down. You should have heard them whine when we delayed the vote," Lott said.

But the five-day delay may have played into the hands of opponents of the bill, allowing extra time for the White House and the Association of Trial Lawyers of America, which opposed the legislation because of its caps on damages, to match a lobbying blitz by business groups.

Supporters face a tough challenge in trying to work out a compromise and attract five more votes for a two-thirds majority. One vote will be easy to pick up. Sen. John H. Chafee, R-R.I., a supporter of the bill, missed the floor vote because he was in his home state on personal business.

But other votes may be hard to come by. Potential vote-switchers are Republicans Richard C. Shelby of Alabama, Thad Cochran of Mississippi, Fred Thompson of Tennessee and Arlen Specter of Pennsylvania, according to an industry source.

Another key vote belonged to Democrat Harry Reid of Nevada, who expressed support for a compromise worked out by McCain, but who voted no at Daschle's urging.

"It was a tough vote," said Democrat Kent Conrad of North Dakota, who voted against the bill after closely watching how a number of other Democrats voted. "There was a lot of political gamesmanship by Republicans on this one."

CEOs Make the Rounds

While both sides prepared for a conference compromise, high-tech industry executives increased the pressure for Congress to act on other measures.

Gates made the rounds on Capitol Hill. He ate lunch June 15 with House Republican leaders and urged passage of measures including a bill (HR 850) to loosen export controls on software used to encode sensitive information.

After the lunch, House Majority Leader Dick Armey, R-Texas, said he would unveil an "e-Contract" the week of June 21 that will include measures to ensure that the high-tech industry "will be free to continue innovating." It is expected to include proposals to loosen controls on the export of business computers to China and other countries and to increase H-1B visas for foreign workers sought by high-tech employers.

Sen. Connie Mack, R-Fla., chairman the Joint Economic Committee, said he believes the executives have improved the chances for passage of a range of measures, including the visas.

Eric Schmidt, chairman of Utah-based software maker Novell Inc., agreed with Mack's assessment but said he does not expect rapid action.

"High-tech time is a lot faster than time in Congress," he said. "I know that things take time here."

GOP, White House Talk After Plea To Avert Y2K 'Catastrophe'

JUNE 26 — Republican leaders and White House aides sat down for the first time June 24 to discuss a possible compromise to avoid a veto on a bill to limit liability for Year 2000 computer problems.

With time running out, it appeared that lawmakers and Larry Stein, the chief White House lobbyist, were trying to resolve key disputes over HR 775. The White House has opposed the Senate-passed version of the bill as well as a House version because they contain limits on punitive damages. But lawmakers have put the legislation on a fast track to passage and hope to avoid a presidential veto.

The White House has insisted on limiting a cap on punitive damages to $250,000, or three times compensatory damages, whichever is less, for businesses with 50 or fewer employees. It wants to cap only those companies that take strong measures to resolve Y2K problems.

One unresolved issue involves the definition of strong measures that those companies, or "good citizens," must take to get protection from Y2K lawsuits. The bill would reward them by limiting their liability to their proportionate share of blame for a Y2K problem.

Committee Chairman John McCain, R-Ariz., emerged from the conference committee negotiating session to say resolution of disagreements with the White House would be delayed until another conference meeting on June 29.

Of the White House, he said, "Sure, they're trying to open up the bill. It depends what they have to offer." Nonetheless, he said he would oppose attempts to "further emasculate" the bill.

Shifting Waters

The conciliatory tone of McCain and other negotiators was a sharp contrast with political bluster on both sides in days leading up to the meeting.

The mood in the House shifted dramatically during the week after the discovery of a controversial provision buried in the Senate-passed version of the bill.

Supporters of the bill had hoped to push that bill through the House and to force a presidential veto, setting the stage for veto override votes in the House and Senate.

But they changed course after discovering a provision inserted by Ernest F. Hollings, D-S.C., that would prevent banks and other financial institutions from collecting debts from consumers with Year 2000 computer problems. The provision was part of an amendment sponsored by James M. Inhofe, R-Okla., that the Senate approved by voice vote June 10.

Despite concern about that measure, Republicans were convinced a presidential veto would hurt Vice President Al Gore in the 2000 presidential race, while helping Republican candidates for president and Congress.

But Republicans abandoned their veto-defying strategy after federal regulators, including Comptroller of the Currency John D. Hawke Jr. and Federal Reserve Chairman Alan Greenspan, warned that the Hollings provision could leave banks insurers, utilities and other companies holding unpaid debts.

Meanwhile, a broad business coalition representing more than 50 trade groups sent a letter June 22 to House Republican leaders urging them to avoid "a catastrophe." In their letter, the groups said: "We are convinced that if such a bill were vetoed, the momentum to legislate on this important matter would be lost. A legislative process that terminates in a veto would be viewed as a complete failure."

Sen. Christopher J. Dodd, D-Conn., one of the conferees, said the business groups had had a major impact. "They really want this bill," he said.

House Minority Leader Richard A. Gephardt, D-Mo., echoed the lobbyists' lament, accusing Republicans of trying to "waste time and spin wheels."

In what amounted to a small victory for Gephardt and other critics of the bill, the House passed, 426-0, a motion to instruct conferees to get "substantive inputs" from the White House and Democratic leaders. *(Vote 253, p. H-88)*

On June 24, lawmakers supporting the bill sharply criticized White House negotiators for making vague lists of "principles" instead of proposals in bill language. "I thought we were going to have a meltdown. But the final 15 minutes were productive," said Sen. Ron Wyden, D-Ore.

In a key concession, the White House agreed to work from the Senate-passed bill, not from a June 16 proposal unveiled by Senate Minority Leader Tom Daschle, D-S.D.

Conferees quickly resolved the dispute over Hollings' provision by narrowing it to cover only cases clearly caused by a Y2K glitch. In an interview June 23, Hollings said he opposed the bill because it did not protect consumers, but he could not stop it. "I can't block it. They've got it."

Clinton Agrees to Damage Caps; Lawmakers Clear Legislation

JULY 3 — Just six months before computer systems might break down upon the arrival of the year 2000, Congress sent President Clinton a bill (HR 775) to limit the liability of companies that fail to fix the high-tech flaw.

The House adopted the conference report, 404-24, on July 1. Hours later, the Senate cleared it, 81-18. Clinton is expected to sign the bill the week of July 5. *(House vote 265, p. H-92; Senate vote 196, p. S-39)*

The bipartisan votes came after weeks of delays and then a final round of feverish negotiations, culminating in intervention by Clinton and a deal that prevented a threatened veto.

After resisting any limit on punitive damages, Clinton ultimately agreed to accept the cap for small businesses in the Senate's version of the the bill: $250,000 or three times compensatory damages, whichever is less, for businesses with 50 or fewer employees.

In return, he won revisions to keep some class action lawsuits in state courts, and to make defendants liable for economic losses if they intentionally cause damages.

Some Republicans grumbled that the bill was too watered down. Nonetheless, they claimed the lion's share of the credit for the final product, noting that Democrats were belatedly supporting provisions — including the cap on punitive damages — that the White House once opposed.

"Republicans in Congress are doing everything we can to ensure that Jan. 1, 2000, is a time for celebration and not litigation," said J.C. Watts Jr. of Oklahoma, chairman of the House GOP Conference.

Democrats expressed a combination of resignation and outrage that the White House had been forced to make concessions during five days of private talks that came after the only meeting of the conference committee, on June 24.

"I won't support it with enthusiasm, but I will support it," said Senate Minority Leader Tom Daschle, D-S.D.

Patrick J. Leahy, D-Vt., one of 18 senators who voted against the deal, said it went well beyond the changes needed to protect high-tech companies and tinkered unnecessarily with the civil justice system.

But such criticism was drowned out by overwhelming support for the bill on both the House and Senate floors. Lawmakers were eager to complete action on the bill before the July Fourth recess, and it had broad support from a wide range of businesses and trade groups, including the U.S. Chamber of Commerce.

Trial lawyers, who bitterly opposed the bill, were consoled only by a sunset provision in the bill to take the law off the books after Jan. 1, 2003. "It is positive that this unique response to a unique situation will be in law for only three years," said Mark S. Mandell, president of the Association of Trial Lawyers of America.

The final negotiations began with big obstacles, with House Republicans reluctant to make concessions beyond simply acceding to the Senate's bipartisan version of the bill. But a coalition of business leaders sent a June 22 letter to House GOP leaders urging them not to pursue a strategy of forcing a veto, and instead to negotiate with the White House.

A breakthrough began when Senate cosponsor Christopher J. Dodd, D-Conn., accompanied Clinton to a Democratic National Committee meeting in Westport, Conn., on June 28. Dodd discussed ways to resolve disputes over the bill while riding with Clinton on a helicopter from Connecticut to New York.

The talks continued in a telephone conversation between Dodd and Clinton about 1 a.m. June 29. "Obviously, he had strong feelings about parts of this bill," Dodd said. "He very graciously listened . . . as I tried to explain what I felt the differences were, and where some common ground might emerge."

Dodd said Clinton insisted on revamping one provision. He wanted to require that all class action lawsuits seeking more than $10 million in damages be filed in federal court. The Senate bill set the threshold for federal cases at $1 million, and Republicans initially resisted raising it to anything more than $5 million.

Final negotiations began June 29 among Virginia Republican Reps. Robert W. Goodlatte and Thomas M. Davis III, Senate Commerce Committee Chairman John McCain, R-Ariz., and administration officials led by chief White House lobbyist Larry Stein.

In a final negotiating session, Davis referred to his recent reading of a non-fiction book, "Shadow: Five Presidents and the Legacy of Watergate," by Washington Post reporter Bob Woodward. Davis said it was his impression based partly on the book that the Clinton White House used tough negotiating tactics that stressed delay, increasing pressure for a deal and demands for big concessions at the end. Davis insisted he would not allow such concessions to be made on the Y2K liability bill.

While Goodlatte and Davis discussed options with one group of White House aides, Dodd, McCain and Sen. Ron Wyden, D-Ore., began a separate round of discussions with other White House officials.

By 2 p.m., House Republicans agreed to accept Clinton's demand that the threshold be raised to $10 million for class-action suits to be filed in federal courts. They also acceded to a White House demand to provide more protection to plaintiffs by requiring solvent defendants to pay up to twice their share of damages if a codefendant is unable to pay.

In exchange for those concessions, Republicans demanded a letter from the White House pledging that Clinton would sign the bill. Otherwise, they said, they would not take the deal to the House or Senate floor for final votes.

Within a half-hour, White House Chief of Staff John D. Podesta, visiting Capitol Hill to discuss Clinton's Medicare plan, ordered the letter typed, signed it and had it delivered.

With Podesta's letter clutched in one hand, a relieved McCain announced that the deal was done. "I have to tell you that it was my view that we probably would not get an agreement because of the lack of progress in the last month or so," McCain said.

But, he said, "I think there was a realization on both sides that this was so critical to American business. As much as a trillion dollars could have been taken out of the economy in the form of frivolous lawsuits. It would have had a crippling effect on our economy."

The final deal resolved several other key differences. Among them, it drastically narrowed a provision inserted by Ernest F. Hollings, D-S.C., in the Senate version of the bill that would have stopped financial institutions from collecting debts if computer problems delayed bill payments.

The conferees narrowed the provision to prevent only foreclosure of residential mortgages because of a Y2K failure that disrupted mortgage payment processing.

In the hours leading up to the final votes, there was a last round of disputes as White House aides and some Democrats raised questions about the drafting of the bill and whether it conformed to terms of the deal reached June 29.

The disputes did not center on provisions at the core of the deal, however. For example, one trouble spot was over the White House's view that the deal required that defendants who caused intentional damage should be held liable for three times actual damages in certain cases. The provision in the final draft required that such defendants be held liable for 250 percent of their share of damages in these cases. The penalty would apply in cases of unpaid or uncollectible damages, owed by insolvent codefendants.

McCain insisted the bill was drafted in good faith. "I would like to dispel any misconceptions or misinformation that there was any underhandedness in the final negotiation and drafting of revisions to this bill," he said July 1.

Despite the last-minute wrangling, White House aides and Daschle said Clinton would sign the bill.

On the Senate floor, Hollings complained that conferees were left out of decisions made by key lawmakers in the private negotiations with Clinton.

"This is a shabby performance," Hollings said. Referring to Dodd's late-night telephone chat with the president, Hollings asked, "Who can call the president after midnight other than Monica?" Clinton's relationship with former White House intern Monica Lewinsky and his attempts to hide it led to the impeachment drive against him.

Hollings and other critics charged that the bill was a response to exaggerated fears of lawsuits. And he said supporters were rushing to back the bill in part because of efforts by both parties to raise campaign donations from the high-tech industry.

Republicans replied that more than 80 lawsuits had already been filed and more would follow.

But lawmakers on both sides acknowledged that many questions about the Y2K glitch remained unresolved.

"This represents our best shot at it today," Daschle said. "I think we can improve upon it at some point in the future." ◆

Year 2000 Bill Highlights

JULY 3 — These are the key provisions of the conference report for HR 775 (Conference report: H Rept 106-212):

Scope

The bill would cover lawsuits in state or federal courts involving actual and potential computer-related failures that occur or cause harm before Jan. 1, 2003. The plaintiff would be required to state the nature, amount and factual basis for damages and to prove a product or service was defective.

Punitive damages

The bill would limit punitive damages to $250,000 or three times the amount of compensatory damages, whichever was less, for individuals with a net worth of $500,000 or less and companies with fewer than 50 employees.

Proportionate damages

Defendants would be liable for damages proportionate to their share of fault for losses, except in cases of fraud or recklessness.

Notice to defendants

Defendants would get 30 days' notice and an additional 60 days to fix Y2K problems before litigation.

Class action lawsuits

Federal courts would have jurisdiction over major Y2K-related class action lawsuits. The bill would give state courts jurisdiction for lawsuits seeking less than $10 million in damages or involving fewer than 100 plaintiffs.

Year 2000 Liability Provisions

The following are major provisions of the year 2000 liability bill (HR 775 — PL 106-37), as signed by President Clinton on July 20.

Applicability of the New Law

• **Scope.** The law applies to lawsuits in state or federal courts brought after Jan. 1, 1999, that allege actual or potential Y2K-related computer failures that could occur or cause harm before Jan. 1, 2003.

• **Existing warranties and contracts.** The law preserves the terms of existing contracts, including any contractual limits on liability or warranty disclaimers. Such terms are to be strictly enforced, unless enforcement would contravene applicable state law in effect on Jan 1, 1999.

• **State law pre-emption.** The new federal law establishes national standards for dealing with Y2K lawsuits. However, nothing in the law alters or diminishes a state's ability to defend itself against any claim on the basis of sovereign immunity. And the new federal law does not pre-empt state laws that provide stricter limits on damages and liabilities, affording greater protection to defendants in Y2K lawsuits.

• **Detailed claims.** In all Y2K cases in which damages are sought, the plaintiff is required to file a detailed statement of the nature, amount and factual basis for calculating damages and to provide proof of any alleged material defect in the product or service.

• **Duty to mitigate.** A plaintiff must try to avoid or limit a Y2K problem. The law specifies that damages in a Y2K lawsuit must exclude any compensation for damages a plaintiff could reasonably have avoided because of the availability of information, including information provided by the defendant to purchasers or users of the product.

This requirement does not apply if the plaintiff relied on intentionally misleading information supplied by the defendant.

Punitive Damages

• **Caps on damages.** Punitive damages are limited to $250,000 or three times the amount of compensatory damages, whichever is less, for individuals with a net worth of $500,000 or less and companies with fewer than 50 employees.

• **Intentional injury.** The caps do not apply if the plaintiffs prove that the defendant intended to cause them injury.

• **Government exemption.** Punitive damages in a Y2K suit cannot be awarded against a government entity.

Proportionate Liability

• **Limitation on liability.** Defendants in suits other than those involving a contract claim are liable only for damages proportionate to their share of fault for losses, except in cases of fraud or intentional injury.

• **Determining responsibility.** In such cases, the court or the jury will determine each defendant's share of the liability, based on the defendant's conduct and the extent to which it was responsible for causing the damages incurred by the plaintiff.

• **Intentional injury or fraud.** Defendants who knowingly committed fraud or deliberately caused injury are subject to "joint and several liability," meaning they can be held liable for the total damages claimed by the plaintiff, not merely a portion of the damages. Fraud is defined as having occurred when a defendant knowingly made an untrue statement and knew that the plaintiff was reasonably likely to rely on the false information.

• **Uncollectible damages.** If a court determines within six months after a final judgment that damages cannot be collected from a defendant, the uncollectible damages can be collected from other co-defendants as follows:

• In cases where the plaintiff has a net worth of less than $200,000 and the recoverable damages are equal to more than 10 percent of the plaintiff's net worth, the remaining defendants are subject to joint and several liability; thus one of them can be tapped for the entire uncollectible amount.

• In cases that do not fit the above requirements, the remaining defendants are liable for the uncollectible share in proportion to their responsibility for the damage. However, co-defendants found to have acted with reckless disregard for the injury caused by their acts are liable for an additional portion of the uncollectible damages equal to 50 percent of their percentage of the responsibility. In any case, the total payments by all defendants cannot exceed the uncollectible damages owed.

• If the plaintiff is a consumer whose suit alleges a defect in a product, and who is not part of a class action lawsuit, the remaining defendants are subject to joint and several liability.

• Any defendant required to make an additional payment to cover uncollectible damages may recover contributions from the defendant originally responsible for those damages, or from any other defendant who is jointly and severally liable, or from any other defendants who have not paid their proportionate share of uncollectible damages or from any person who was responsible for the conduct that caused the losses.

• The standard for allocating damages and the procedure for reallocating uncollectible damages cannot be disclosed to the jury.

• **Settlement discharge.** A defendant who settles a Y2K lawsuit before the final verdict or judgment is to be discharged from all claims for contributions brought by others. The final judgment must be reduced by an amount corresponding to the percentage of responsibility of the defendant who settled or the amount paid by that defendant, whichever is greater.

• **General right of contribution.** A defendant who is jointly and severally liable for damages in any Y2K action, excluding contract-related lawsuits, may recover a contribution from any other persons who would have been liable for damages if they had been cited in the original action. The lawsuit seeking such a contribution must be brought not later than six months after the entry of a final, non-appealable judgment in a Y2K lawsuit.

• **State laws.** The proportionate-liability rules do not pre-empt any state law that limits the liability of a defendant in a Y2K suit to a lesser amount, or that affords a greater degree of protection from joint or several liability.

Pre-Litigation Notice

• **Timing.** Potential defendants must be given 30 days' notice before legal action can begin. However, if the defendant fails to respond to the notice within 30 days, the plaintiff can begin legal action immediately.

If the prospective defendant does respond, the defendant then has an additional remediation period of 60 days to complete the proposed corrective action or alternative dispute resolution before a legal action can begin.

• **Notification.** Except for cases that seek only injunctive relief, a prospective plaintiff in any Y2K lawsuit is required to send a written notice by certified mail to each prospective defendant. The notice must give specific information about the defect; the harm or loss allegedly suffered; how the plaintiff would like the defendant to remedy the problem; and the name, title, address and telephone number of any individual who has authority to negotiate a resolution of the dispute on behalf of the plaintiff. The notice must be sent to the registered agent of the prospective defendant, or to the chief executive officer of a corporation, to the managing partner of a partnership or to the proprietor of a sole proprietorship.

● **Defendant's response.** The prospective defendant has 30 days after receiving the notice to reply by certified mail describing the actions the company has taken or would take to resolve the problems in the complaint, and stating whether the company is willing to engage in alternative dispute resolution. The statement cannot be used as evidence in a Y2K suit.

● **Failure to notify.** If a plaintiff files suit without providing notice, the court is required to delay all discovery and other proceedings until the notification and response period has occurred.

● **Contractual waiting period.** The waiting period does not supersede a period of delay provided by a contract, or by a statute enacted before Jan 1, 1999.

● **Alternative resolution.** Nothing in the law supersedes a state law or rule of civil procedure regarding alternative dispute resolution of a Y2K lawsuit.

● **Special masters.** Any federal district court in which a Y2K lawsuit is pending may appoint a special master or magistrate judge to hear the matter and make findings of fact and conclusions of law.

Class Action Lawsuits

● **Material defect.** A claim that a product or service is defective can be maintained as a class action lawsuit in federal or state court only if it satisfies all other state and federal legal prerequisites and the court finds there was a material defect for the majority of members of the class.

● **Notification.** The court is required to notify every member of the class in any class action lawsuit, providing a concise and clear description of the nature of the lawsuit; the jurisdiction where the case is pending; and fee arrangements with counsel for the class, including the hourly fee and the percentage of the final award to be paid as a contingency fee.

● **Federal jurisdiction.** Federal courts are given jurisdiction over large Y2K-related class action lawsuits. State courts have jurisdiction for lawsuits seeking less than $10 million in damages or involving fewer than 100 plaintiffs. State courts also have jurisdiction over lawsuits in which the substantial majority of the plaintiffs and the primary defendants are citizens of a single state.

'Y2K Upset' Defense

● **Definition and application.** The law includes a "Y2K upset" defense for cases involving temporary failure by a computer user to comply with a federally enforceable measurement, monitoring or reporting requirement, if the non-compliance is caused by a Y2K problem and is beyond the reasonable control of the user. In order to claim a Y2K upset defense, the computer user must show that he had previously made good-faith efforts to resolve a Y2K problem. He also must try to correct the violation and give 72 hours' notice to a regulator.

This provision applies only to cases involving agencies that are enforcing regulations.

● **Exceptions.** This defense does not apply in cases where there is an imminent threat to the public health, safety or the environment, where there is a threat to the safety and soundness of the banking system or the integrity of national securities markets, or where there is operational error or negligence or lack of reasonable preventive maintenance.

Limits of Applicability

● **No new cause of action.** The law creates no new cause of action and does not expand any liability or limit any defense otherwise available under federal or state law.

● **Personal injury.** The law does not apply to a claim for personal injury or for wrongful death.

● **Other remedies.** Any person liable for damages in a civil lawsuit to which this law does not apply because of the exemption for personal injury and wrongful death lawsuits may pursue any remedy otherwise available under federal or state law against the person responsible for any Y2K failure that caused the damages. Such a remedy can be pursued to the extent of recovering the amount of damages owed.

● **Contract limits.** In any Y2K lawsuit for breach of contract, no party may claim damages unless such damages were allowed by the terms of the contract, or if the contract was silent, by the operation of state or federal law in effect when the contract was signed.

● **Economic losses.** A plaintiff in a Y2K lawsuit making a wrongful injury claim may not recover damages for economic loss unless recovery of such losses was provided for in a contract, or unless such losses resulted directly from damage to a property caused by a Y2K failure. Recovery of such losses also must be permitted by state and federal law.

The provision does not apply to cases of intentional injury that are independent of a contract. Economic losses include lost profits or sales, losses indirectly suffered as a result of the defendant's wrongful act or omission, losses that arise because of the claims of third parties, special damages and consequential damages as defined in the Uniform Commercial Code or state commercial law.

● **Residential mortgage protection.** A mortgage holder cannot foreclose on a consumer as a result of a Y2K failure that made it impossible to process a mortgage payment on time. The consumer is required to notify the mortgage service company in writing within seven business days of becoming aware of the problem.

However, four weeks after Jan. 1, 2000, or four weeks after the consumer notifies the service company of the Y2K problem, whichever comes later, the mortgage can be foreclosed if the consumer has not made the mortgage payment and the service company has not granted a time extension.

The residential mortgage protection provision does not apply to mortgage defaults that occur before Dec. 15, 1999, or to cases where the consumer notifies the mortgage service of a problem on or after March 15, 2000.

● **Small-business exemption.** Agencies may not impose a civil fine on any business with fewer than 50 employees for a first-time violation of a federal rule or regulation caused by a Y2K failure that occurs on or before Dec. 31, 2000. To qualify for the exemption, a business must show it made good-faith efforts to anticipate, prevent and correct the Y2K failure; it must also notify the appropriate agency within five business days.

The exemption does not apply to any rule that relates to the safety of the banking and monetary systems and the securities markets. Civil penalties may be applied if the rule violation poses an imminent threat to public health and the environment, or the business fails to correct the violation within a month of notifying the agency.

● **Defendant's state of mind.** For a Y2K lawsuit in which a defendant's awareness of a Y2K failure is an element of the claim, the defendant is not liable unless the plaintiff establishes proof of that awareness.

● **Bystander liability.** In a Y2K lawsuit in which the defendant was not the manufacturer, seller, distributor or provider of the product or service and was not in a contractual or business relationship with the plaintiff, the defendant is not liable unless the plaintiff proves that the defendant actually knew or recklessly disregarded the risk of a failure.

● **Control and liability.** The fact that a Y2K failure occurs in an entity, facility, system, product or component that was sold, leased, rented or controlled by a defendant cannot constitute the sole basis for recovery of damages in a lawsuit.

Congress Suspends Efforts On Encryption After Clinton Decides To Ease Controls

The White House sought to preempt congressional action in September by announcing that its policy for restricting exports of strong technology to encode communications would be loosened.

SUMMARY

The new policy is to exclude exports to seven nations: Cuba, Iran, Iraq, Libya, North Korea, Sudan and Syria.

The White House decided to relax export controls as the House was preparing to pass legislation that would lift most export controls on encryption technology used to scramble telephone calls and on-line communications.

Rep. Robert W. Goodlatte, R-Va., sponsored the House bill (HR 850) to allow American software firms to compete with foreign companies that sell similar products overseas. The bill had 258 co-sponsors.

Law enforcement officials, including the FBI, complained that the legislation could put strong encoding technology in the hands of criminals, making it harder to wiretap their telephone calls.

Supporters replied that the House bill was designed to prevent illegal acts by setting penalties of up to five years in prison for using encryption to try to hide a crime.

Senate Commerce, Science and Transportation Committee Chairman John McCain, R-Ariz., proposed a compromise (S 798) that would have allowed the export of some stronger encryption products and permitted exports of other products if they were found by the Commerce Department to be generally available. Despite the support for the two bills, some senior lawmakers in the House and Senate strongly opposed the weakening of export controls.

Congress will wait to see the White House plan before considering any further work on legislation.

House Panel OKs Bill To Ease Access To Encryption Technology

MARCH 13 — A House subcommittee approved a bill (HR 850) by voice vote March 11 that would give businesses and individuals easier access to more sophisticated technology to protect sensitive information.

The House Judiciary Courts and Intellectual Property Subcommittee sent the bipartisan bill, with 210 cosponsors, to the full committee for action the week of March 15. Robert W. Goodlatte, R-Va., who sponsored the bill, said he was confident that it would have strong support in the House, noting that it is backed by a broad coalition of businesses and some consumer groups.

"I feel very good about the bill. I think we have a very good chance," Goodlatte said March 11 after the panel's vote.

But Goodlatte and Zoe Lofgren, D-Calif., a cosponsor of the bill, acknowledged that they had yet to resolve opposition from the administration, which fears the bill could make it easier for terrorists and other criminals to cover their tracks by encoding messages with sophisticated encryption software. Encryption is the electronic scrambling, or coding, of computer messages and telecommunications signals for privacy and security purposes.

Protection From Thieves

Goodlatte argued that law enforcement would not be hurt by his bill, and he said it is needed to protect consumers from criminals who would try to steal personal and financial information from computer networks.

"This legislation is needed because every American is vulnerable to online predators," Goodlatte said. "Credit card numbers can be stolen, personal medical records can be exposed, and bank deposits can be rerouted, all because of the administration's restrictive encryption policy."

Despite the strong House support, similar legislation on encryption was stymied last year by opposition from law enforcement.

Like last year's bill, HR 850 would limit the government's ability to restrict the export, manufacture or use of encryption technology.

It contains several new provisions, including language designed to ease law enforcement worries. The bill would allow Commerce Secretary William M. Daley to review encryption technology for 15 days and to prohibit export of products to certain buyers overseas.

The bill would also make clear that it does not weaken embargoes against hostile nations such as Cuba and Iraq.

The key parts of the bill would give Americans the right to buy and use the best encryption technology and prevent the government from requiring manufacturers to give federal officials the ability to unlock encrypted data.

Box Score

- **Bills:** HR 850; S 798
- **Legislative action: House** Judiciary Committee approved HR 850 (H Rept 106-117, Part 1) by voice vote on March 24; Commerce approved HR 850 (H Rept 106-117, Part 2) by voice vote June 23; International Relations approved the bill HR 850 (H Rept 106-117, Part 3), 33-5, July 13; Select Intelligence approved HR 850 (H Rept 106-117, Part 5) July 15; Armed Services approved HR 850 (H Rept 106-117, Part 4), 47-6, July 21.

Senate Commerce Committee approved S 798 (S Rept 106-142) by voice vote June 23.

Lofgren said the concerns of law enforcement authorities had effectively kept the bill from reaching the floor last year. This year, she said, she is optimistic about a floor vote because the legislation has the backing of Rules Committee Chairman David Dreier, R-Calif.

"David Dreier is a supporter. That is an important difference this year," Lofgren said. Dreier's predecessor as rules chairman, Republican Gerald B.H. Solomon of New York (1979-99), opposed encryption legislation that did not include tougher provisions sought by law enforcement.

While backers of the bill have Dreier's support, they are still likely to face strong Clinton administration opposition to scaling back export controls on encryption technology.

Administration's Position

William A. Reinsch, an under secretary for export administration at the Commerce Department, told the Judiciary subcommittee at a hearing March 4 that the administration strongly opposes provisions in the bill that appear to preclude export controls on encryption technology.

Reinsch said the administration loosened export controls at the urging of business advocates last year, but now believes the current controls are vital to national security. He said the administration is sympathetic to the needs of consumers and businesses and does not support restraints on manufacture or use of encryption in the United States.

But some supporters of the Goodlatte bill said the administration has not gone far enough toward allowing exports.

Former Democratic Rep. Dave McCurdy of Oklahoma (1981-95), president of the Electronic Industries Alliance, which represents makers of encryption technology, told the subcommittee March 4 that export controls could ultimately weaken American companies if they are not able to sell encryption products as freely as foreign rivals.

"The net effect of this policy is to damage the global competitiveness of the U.S. high-tech industry, as well as to jeopardize the security of individuals and companies which operate internationally," McCurdy said.

House Judiciary Approves Measure

MARCH 27 — A battle is expected in the House International Relations Committee after the spring recess over a bill to ease restrictions on the export of the American technology for encrypting information to protect privacy on the Internet.

The House Judiciary Committee approved the bill (HR 850) by voice vote on March 24. Although the bill has 246 cosponsors, it faces challenges in other panels, including the Select Intelligence Committee.

The administration has argued that easing export controls could allow terrorists and other criminals overseas to get coding technology to scramble communications. Rep. Robert W. Goodlatte, R-Va., replied that criminals can already buy foreign-made products to encrypt computer messages.

Rep. Bill McCollum, R-Fla., a member of the Select Intelligence Committee, said March 24 that he wanted to revise the bill to make sure police and the National Security Agency can decode messages sent by criminals. "We need to make sure we do not erode our law enforcement capability," McCollum said.

If the bill is sent to the Intelligence Committee, he said, he hoped to offer an amendment that would require that encryption software include a feature to allow authorities, armed with a court order, to get immediate access to the data in "plain text" form.

A bill to relax export controls for encryption technology in the 105th Congress was approved by five committees before it was held up in the Rules Committee because of law enforcement concerns.

House Panel OKs Revised Version Of Encryption Bill

JUNE 19 — Facing opposition from advocates of law enforcement, the House Commerce Telecommunications Subcommittee approved by voice vote June 16 a revised version of a bill (HR 850) that would loosen controls on the export of software used to encode credit card numbers and other sensitive information on the Internet.

The panel's vote set the stage for a markup on the bill in full committee later this month. Commerce Committee Chairman Thomas J. Bliley Jr., R-Va., said June 16 that the bill was vital to protecting electronic commerce on the Internet.

"Consumer confidence in electronic commerce is important. The Internet must be safe, secure and private," Bliley said.

The bill has strong bipartisan support, but it has been held up by opposition from the Clinton administration and the reservations of some Republicans, including House International Relations Committee Chairman Benjamin A. Gilman of New York.

The administration has argued that current export controls are needed to keep powerful encryption software away from terrorists and countries that are potential enemies.

The panel adopted, 19-4, an amendment sponsored by Michael G. Oxley, R-Ohio, a former FBI agent, to allow the Commerce Department to deny an export license for encryption software if it believes that doing so would interfere with national security by aiding drug trafficking, espionage or organized crime.

The panel also adopted by voice vote a substitute amendment by W.J. "Billy" Tauzin, R-La., that would direct the Commerce Department to delegate more authority over encryption exports to the National Telecommunications and Information Administration, which is part of the Commerce Department and advises the administration on telecommunications policy.

In other action, the panel adopted by voice vote an amendment sponsored by Oxley and Heather A. Wilson, R-N.M., which would double from 15 days to 30 days the time limit for the Commerce Department to make a decision on whether to permit the export of an encryption product.

"A perfunctory 15 calendar days is simply insufficient to thoroughly consider whether the export of a new product will harm national security," Oxley said.

Executives Weigh In

On the day of the subcommittee vote, a dozen top executives of software companies, including Microsoft Chairman Bill Gates, sent a letter to Bliley praising him for his support and urging "expeditious passage" of the bill.

The software companies are counting on Bliley and Republican Robert W. Goodlatte of Virginia, a co-chairman of the Congressional Internet Caucus, to help push the bill through the House.

On June 8, Gilman, Select Intelligence Committee Chairman Porter J. Goss, R-Fla., and Armed Services Committee Chairman Floyd D. Spence, R-S.C., sent a letter to House Speaker J. Dennis Hastert, R-Ill., urging him to extend his deadline for dealing with the bill from July 2 to Sept. 30. But Goodlatte argued June 16 for quick action, not an extension. "It's not necessary for them to have more time," he said.

Bill Approved By Committees In House, Senate

JUNE 26 — Over strong objections of senior Republican Ted Stevens, who warned of looming threats to national security, the Senate Commerce, Science and Transportation Committee approved a bill June 23 that would ease export controls on technology that encodes sensitive data on the Internet.

Commerce Chairman John McCain, R-Ariz., the chief sponsor of S 798, said he was confident that the bill, which was approved by voice vote, would make its way past potential obstacles in three other committees — Armed Services, Intelligence and Foreign Relations — to reach the Senate floor.

McCain described S 798 as a modest effort to help U.S. companies compete in the global economy.

"It is completely illogical to deny U.S. producers the ability to compete globally if similar products are already being offered by foreign companies," McCain said.

John Kerry, D-Mass., endorsed the bill as an improvement over the Clinton administration's current policy, which has tough rules on encryption exports to keep the technology out of the hands of criminals and terrorists. But Kerry warned that even S 798 may be too late. "The fact is our companies are just getting clobbered," he said.

The bill would allow companies to get exemptions from export controls if an advisory board determined that similar products were generally available overseas.

The Clinton administration currently prevents the export of any encryption technology to potential enemies, including China and Russia, that encodes messages by using a mathematical "key" longer than 56 bits, or binary digits.

McCain's bill would relax the standard to 64 bits and permit further increases within three years. The more bits, the stronger the encryption.

The McCain bill has gained only lukewarm support from software and computer companies, many of which argue that the standard needs to be expanded even more.

A House bill (HR 850), which the House Commerce Committee approved by voice vote June 23, would allow export of much stronger encryption technology — products that use keys of at least 128 bits. But that bill faces even stronger opposition from the administration.

On the week of June 28, Speaker J. Dennis Hastert, R-Ill., must decide whether to extend his July 2 deadline for floor passage of HR 850 to work out disputes over protection of technology.

Stevens Stands Alone

In the Senate, Stevens stood alone in strongly opposing McCain's bill at the June 23 markup. He hinted at a possible filibuster.

"I'm going to be heard loud and clear when we get to the floor," Stevens said.

Stevens predicted that enemy nations would one day use coded electronic communications to attack computers in the United States.

"We will give up hope that industry can find a way to preserve our capabilities of the future to decode the traffic that will come at a time when we are entering 'cyber-warfare.' I think it's very shortsighted," Stevens said.

Supporters of the bill countered Stevens' criticism by arguing that export controls do little to prevent the spread of strong encryption technology. They said that foreign customers are already able to buy powerful, foreign-made encryption technology.

"The genie is out of the bottle," said Ernest F. Hollings, D-S.C.

McCain echoed some of Stevens' concerns about the need to protect national security, but he said his bill would achieve that goal by relying on the "profound power of the president" to veto any export license.

The passage of a bill to loosen controls on encryption technology is a priority for computer and software companies. Top executives for high-tech companies, including Microsoft Corp. Chairman Bill Gates, made the case for looser controls during a "high-tech summit" in the capital sponsored by the Joint Economic Committee on June 14-16.

On June 15, William Larson, chairman and chief executive officer of California-based Network Associates Inc., told the Joint Economic Committee that the company had probably lost several big deals because of export controls. His company's Pretty Good Privacy software is one of the most popular encryption products.

"Once customers select foreign security systems and build networks around them, there will be no opportunity for U.S. companies to regain that market leadership," Larson said.

Deeply Divided Over Encryption, House Looks to Clinton for a Deal

JULY 17 — Faced with a bitter feud between the high-tech industry and law enforcement, House Select Intelligence Committee Chairman Porter J. Goss has asked President Clinton to develop a compromise bill on the export of encryption products — technology used to encode information ranging from credit card numbers to national security plans.

Goss, R-Fla., made his plea as his panel tried to mollify critics of HR 850, which would loosen export controls on encryption products and which has broad bipartisan support. The bill, however, faces opposition from law enforcement and the Clinton administration.

The committee — one of five considering HR 850 — approved a watered-down version of the bill by voice vote in a closed session July 15.

A former CIA agent and a longtime ally of law enforcement, Goss said he is not optimistic about the ability of members to shape a bill that would be acceptable to both industry and police. He urged Clinton to follow the example of British Prime Minister Tony Blair, who recently began meeting with industry leaders to develop a policy on encryption technology.

Goss said he was "amazed that the president has not taken a stronger public stand in defense of national security and public safety. . . . His silence on these issues is deafening."

The approval of the bill by the Intelligence Committee and by the House International Relations Committee, 33-5, on July 13 cleared two more obstacles on a twisted legislative path.

Three committees— Armed Services, Intelligence and International Relations — failed to meet a July 2 deadline set by Speaker J. Dennis Hastert, R.-Ill., for finishing work on the bill. Hastert has set a new deadline of July 23 for the three committees to complete work and clear the way for a floor vote. The House Judiciary Committee approved its version of HR 850 by voice vote on March. 24 (H Rept 106-117, Part 1). The House Commerce Committee approved HR 850 on June 23 (H Rept 106-117, Part 2).

Meanwhile, the House Armed Services Committee will mark up its version of the same bill July 21.

A floor vote is expected by next month, after Rules Committee Chairman David Dreier, R-Calif., a strong supporter of HR 850, finishes shaping the final bill from competing versions.

But lawmakers have expressed deep reservations about the legislation, echoing concerns of law enforcement and national security officials.

International Relations Committee Chairman Benjamin A. Gilman, R-N.Y., cited his own memories of World War II, when he served on the crew of a B-29 bomber, as a reason for opposing the bill.

He said the bill could be harmful if the nation went to war against an enemy armed with powerful encryption technology. "Our ability to decode enemy communications was one of the reasons that we won the war," Gilman said July 13.

The high-tech industry has made the bill a priority, saying encryption legislation is needed to ensure privacy for credit card purchases and other financial transactions on the Internet.

But supporters are running into stiff resistance from law enforcement officials who argue that the legislation will encourage wider use of encryption by those attempting to evade detection.

At the heart of the dispute is the rapid growth in the use of encoding technology. It is integrated into some computer networks and World Wide Web browsers, providing security for electronic communications and for computer files. Similar technology is also incorporated on chips in personal computers and other electronic devices, such as some wireless telephones.

Opponents Join Forces

Law enforcement leaders, including FBI Director Louis J. Freeh, have opposed loosening export controls, citing the growing use of telephones that can scramble voices and prevent police investigators from eavesdropping.

In testimony before the Intelligence Committee on July 14 and before the Armed Services Committee on July 13, Freeh said electronic surveillance is vital in fighting drug dealers, terrorists and other criminals.

He warned that the bill would encourage wider use of devices that keep law enforcement from investigating and apprehending criminals.

"This bill will harm law enforcement," Freeh said July 13. He cited the example of Ramzi Yousef, a suspected terrorist whose laptop computer was confiscated by police when he was arrested in Pakistan in 1995. His laptop contained files, including some that were encoded, which provided clues allowing investigators to track down other terrorists. Yousef was convicted and sentenced to life imprisonment for masterminding the 1993 bombing of the World Trade Center in New York.

Marc Rotenberg, executive director of the Electronic Privacy Information Center, a public interest research group that has been following the encryption debate, said his group's informal review of committee votes on HR 850 and committee votes on similar legislation in the 105th Congress showed there was significant opposition from some senior lawmakers of both parties.

"There's a generational gap on this bill," he said. "The opponents tend to be people who have built careers on protection of national security. They tend to be more senior. Many of them have backgrounds in law enforcement or in the military."

In addition, opposition has mounted from some groups supporting Israel, including B'nai B'rith International, a Jewish human rights advocacy group.

Some supporters of Israel have argued that easing export controls could put the technology in the hands of Israeli adversaries in the Mideast.

Pushing for a Summit

Faced with potent political opposition, some key lawmakers have slowed the progress of the bill.

Privately, Republican leaders have been telling lobbyists they hope to finish work on the bill and send it to the Senate in August.

But leaders of both parties will face tough choices in coming weeks because of continued opposition from law enforcement officials. A conference with the White House, suggested by Goss, could give both sides of the debate a chance to resolve differences.

But Jake Siewert, a White House spokesman, said July 15 the administration had not yet made a decision on whether to meet with lawmakers to discuss the bill.

"We haven't received any sort of formal request on this," he said. "The bottom line is we testified. . . . We will probably leave it at that for now."

While supporters of the bill search for a way to resolve objections in the House, further debate looms in the Senate, where the administration has been less critical of a bill (S 798) sponsored by Senate Commerce, Science and Transportation Committee Chairman John McCain, R-Ariz.

It would allow companies to get exemptions from export controls if an advisory board determined that similar products were generally available overseas. The Clinton administration currently prevents the export of encryption technology to potential enemies, including China and Russia, that encodes messages using a mathematical "key" longer than 56 bits, or binary digits.

The administration has quietly hinted that middle ground might be found between the current policy and McCain's bill. One of the issues in such a compromise would be the composition of the advisory board that would determine whether encryption products were generally available overseas. But the tech industry has so far rejected such a compromise.

Manufacturers of encryption technology are hoping that supporters of the bill will be able to win a veto-proof majority in the House, which would force the White House to make more concessions.

Kelly Blough, the director of government affairs for California-based Network Associates Inc., the maker of PGP, or "Pretty Good Privacy," encryption software for personal computers, said that her company is still hopeful that the industry-supported version of the bill, approved by the Judiciary Committee by voice vote March 24, would be passed by the House. That version of the bill was passed with few revisions and is close to the original version supported by the tech industry.

"We are hoping it will have strong support," Blough said.

While high-tech companies are promoting their version of the bill, lawmakers are seeking compromises on some issues to satisfy critics.

Other Provisions

International Relations adopted by voice vote July 13 an amendment to lengthen the deadline, from 15 days to 30 working days, for the Commerce Department to complete its review of export license applications for encryption technology.

It also adopted by voice vote an amendment to allow the Commerce Department to prohibit export of encryption products if there was evidence they would be used to import illegal drugs, to sexually exploit minors or to assist in the proliferation of weapons of mass destruction.

A substitute amendment adopted by the Intelligence Committee on July 15 included several measures supported by law enforcement but opposed by industry.

One of them would allow the export of stronger encryption products after a 45-day review and would give law enforcement access to information needed to decipher encoded messages.

Security-Minded House Panel Votes To Limit Exports

JULY 24 — The battle over a bill to ease export controls on technology used to encode electronic communications will move to center stage on the House floor in September, amid growing efforts by lawmakers to negotiate a compromise with the White House.

The House Armed Services Committee passed a watered-down version of HR 850 (H Rept 106-117, Part 5) by voice vote July 21, in what amounted to a temporary victory by opponents of the bill. The panel's handiwork, and a similar version approved by the House Select Intelligence Committee on July 15, are not expected to survive in the Rules Committee, which must combine five versions of the bill approved by five separate committees.

The Armed Services bill would allow limits on encryption exports. But Rules Committee Chairman David Dreier, R-Calif., has long been an ally of the technology industry and is expected to support a version similar to one approved by the Judiciary Committee on March 24. That version would relax export controls and has been strongly endorsed by the high-tech industry.

The Judiciary Committee's bill (H Rept 106-117, Part 1) would require the Commerce Department to permit the export of encryption technology that is generally available to the public, after a technical review.

Supporters of the Judiciary bill say strong encryption is vital to protecting credit card numbers and other private information submitted when making purchases on the Internet.

But opponents argue that similar technology built into chips in telephones will hurt efforts by law enforcement and intelligence agencies to eavesdrop on conversations as part of criminal investigations.

Armed Services Committee Chairman Floyd D. Spence, R-S.C., acknowledged the likely outcome in the Rules Committee in an interview July 21. He said his panel's version is not likely to be the one that moves to the House floor. But he said he would insist on a rule for floor debate that would allow amendments to be offered.

"We want to be heard," Spence said. But he acknowledged that opponents have little chance of reshaping the bill. "For now, it seems like it's wired that way."

Revision Is Approved

In a symbolic victory for critics of HR 850, Republican Curt Weldon of Pennsylvania won approval in the Armed Services markup of a substitute amendment to curb the authority given to Commerce under the Judiciary Committee's bill. The substitute would authorize the president to set limits on the export of encryption products to potential enemies such as China and Russia.

Despite the overwhelming, 47-6 vote on the amendment, some committee members clearly had mixed feelings. "We're going to have to find a balance," said J.C. Watts Jr. of Oklahoma, the chairman of the House Republican Conference, who voted for the panel's sharply revised version.

The "no" votes came from supporters of the high-tech industry: Democrats Loretta Sanchez and Ellen O. Tauscher of California; Adam Smith, D-Wash.; Mary Bono, R-Calif.; Baron P. Hill, D-Ind.; and Martin T. Meehan, D-Mass.

Robert W. Goodlatte, R-Va., a sponsor of the Armed Services version of the bill, said the substitute reflects the views of a minority of House members.

"This is horrible. It guts the bill," he said July 21. He said he is confident that the House will pass legislation similar to the Judiciary bill, backed by more than 250 cosponsors, including 10 former prosecutors.

Administration Stands Aside

With little hope of winning floor votes in the House, critics of HR 850 sought intervention by President Clinton. On July 21, Weldon echoed a July 14 request by House Select Intelligence Committee Chairman Porter J.

Goss, R-Fla., that Clinton play a more prominent role in brokering a compromise. Weldon urged Clinton to convene an international summit to discuss efforts to limit the spread of encryption technology.

For now, the White House appears to be determined to let Congress resolve the dispute on its own. "We've made our views known. We hope lawmakers will coalesce around a balanced approach," said Jake Siewert, a White House spokesman, on July 22.

Barbara A. McNamara, deputy director of the National Security Agency, told a closed session of the Armed Services Committee before the July 21 vote that the bill would help potential enemies of the United States. According to Weldon, McNamara told lawmakers that the legislation "would drive a stake through the heart of U.S. security."

Republican Duncan Hunter of California another sharp critic of the bill, said the fight puts lawmakers in a difficult spot. "It's a classic conflict between security interests and commercial interests," he said.

White House Drops Most Controls On Encryption

SEPTEMBER 18 — The Clinton administration agreed on Sept. 16 to end most controls on the export of technology used to encode wireless telephone calls, e-mail and on-line credit-card purchases, heading off a possible showdown with Congress.

The House was expected later this month to pass a bill (HR 850) to force an end to strict controls on export of encoding, or encryption, technology. That bill, which had 258 House cosponsors, was expected to win strong support in the Senate, despite vociferous opposition by some senior lawmakers, including Appropriations Committee Chairman Ted Stevens, R-Alaska.

At a news conference with House Majority Leader Dick Armey, R-Texas, on Sept. 16, GOP Rep. Robert W. Goodlatte of Virginia, the chief sponsor of HR 850, said he believed the administration's policy would give high-tech companies most of what they wanted. But he and Armey said they would wait for more details of the administration's proposal before deciding what to do with the bill. "We want to be sure that everything that's been worked on so hard is well covered," Armey said.

The administration said it was changing its policy to allow U.S. companies to compete with foreign rivals. The controls were originally designed to keep encoding technology out of the hands of enemy nations and criminals.

The administration plans to issue new rules by Dec. 15 to allow the export of any encryption technology, after a technical review, to individuals and businesses in any nation except seven that the United States regards as supporters of terrorism: Cuba, Iran, Iraq, Libya, North Korea, Sudan and Syria. The administration also asked Congress to authorize $80 million over four years to support the FBI's code-breaking unit.

Deputy Secretary of Defense John J. Hamre said his agency still opposes HR 850. He said the bill would not prevent sales to spies and criminals. ◆

Lawmakers Vote To Expand Trademark Protections To Include Internet Usage

SUMMARY

Congress moved to crack down on the practice of "cyber-squatting," the unauthorized use of trademark-protected names in Internet addresses. A measure to extend protection of trademarks to such addresses was included in the conference report for the omnibus spending bill (HR 3194). President Clinton signed the bill on Nov. 29.

Lawmakers of both parties sought to end the practice of individuals registering and using choice Internet addresses that feature trademark-protected names such as Microsoft and Coca-Cola.

The problem arose when companies tried to establish Internet addresses and discovered that others had already registered their trademark as part of an Internet address. In some cases, investors marked up prices for these addresses and offered to sell them back to the trademark owners for a profit. Supporters said a Senate-passed bill (S 1255) would stop confusion about the ownership of trademark names and ensure that consumers would be able to find official Web sites with information about companies. Opponents said the bill could allow companies to intimidate Internet users for incorporating everyday terms in their Internet addresses.

The Senate measure would permit trademark owners to collect civil damages of $1,000 to $100,000 for unauthorized use of their brand names in Internet addresses. In the House, lawmakers inserted provisions to cover unauthorized use of the names of famous persons and to prevent civil damages in cases of inadvertent use of trademarks. James E. Rogan, R-Calif., added

Box Score

- **Bill:** S 1948 (incorporated by reference in HR 3194 — PL 106-113)
- **Legislative action: Senate** passed S 1255 (S Rept 106-140) by voice vote on Aug. 5.

House passed S 1255 by voice vote Oct. 26 after substituting provisions of a similar bill (HR 3028 — H Rept 106-412).

House adopted the conference report on HR 3194 (H Rept 106-479), which included S 1948, 296-135, on Nov. 18.

Senate cleared the bill, 74-24, on Nov. 19.

President signed HR 3194 on Nov. 29.

a requirement that the Commerce Department help develop special Internet addresses for political candidates and elected officials.

The domain-name language was first added to the conference report on a satellite television bill (HR 1554). It was later included in a new Senate bill (S 1948), which was added to the omnibus.

Senate Judiciary OKs Bill Targeting Misuse on Internet Of Brand Names

JULY 31 — The Senate will try to end a trademark dispute over Internet addresses the week of Aug. 2 with a bill that would prevent unauthorized use of brand names such as "Coca-Cola" and "Porsche."

The Judiciary Committee approved S 1255 by voice vote July 29 and set the stage for Senate passage before the August recess. The bill would establish statutory damages in civil suits of at least $1,000, but not more than $100,000, for "cybersquatting" — the unauthorized use of a brand name in an Internet address.

The legislation is designed to solve a growing problem on the Internet — individuals registering popular names for Internet addresses.

In recent years, corporations have been forced to negotiate for the use of their corporate names already registered or used by individuals. For example, computer giant Gateway 2000 Inc. paid $100,000 for the rights to a pornography site which was capitalizing on its name.

The bill, sponsored by Spencer Abraham, R-Mich., appears to be headed for quick passage in the Senate the week of Aug. 2. And it is likely to win strong support in the House.

But some lawmakers, as well as the Clinton administration, have questioned whether the bill is too tough and whether companies need more time to develop a procedure to resolve disputes on their own.

Rules on cybersquatting are being developed as part of a system to assign Internet addresses by the nonprofit Internet Corporation for Assigned Names and Numbers (ICANN). But advocates for companies that own trademarks argue that legislation is needed to protect their property and head off lengthy court battles in court.

The Senate panel approved the bill after adopting by voice vote a substitute amendment, sponsored by Judiciary Committee Chairman Orrin G. Hatch, R-Utah, and Patrick J. Leahy, D-Vt. It eliminated proposed criminal penalties of up to six months in jail for fraudulent use of a trademark. It also would allow trademark owners to seek forfeiture of infringing Internet addresses in cases where defendants could not be found.

Hatch said the changes are needed to resolve concerns that the bill is too punitive. He predicted the bill would win strong bipartisan support. "I can't imagine why anyone would oppose it," he said July 29.

But advocates representing investors who have bought rights to Internet names, and the Virginia-based Domain Names Rights Coalition, a nonprofit group representing Internet users, have questioned whether the bill is needed. The coalition has argued that Internet addresses should be treated as a form of speech and should not be strictly regulated.

Gregory D. Phillips, a Salt Lake City lawyer who represents a half-dozen companies, including German sports car maker Porsche A.G., said the bill is needed to deter investors from staking claims on the Internet to names that belong to companies.

"This bill will make what these guys have done illegal," Phillips said.

Phillips has been trying to eliminate the "Porsche" name from a California Web site featuring pornography.

Broader Trademark Protection

In a related issue, the House completed work on another trademark issue July 26, clearing by voice vote a bill (S 1259) to allow quicker resolution of trademark disputes. That bill would allow owners of trademark-protected brand names to file petitions with the U.S. Patent and Trademark Office to prevent rivals from getting approval of new trademarks for similar-sounding names.

But key lawmakers in the House are still studying the narrower subject of trademarks on the Internet.

The House Judiciary Courts and Intellectual Property Subcommittee held a hearing July 28 to consider the issue.

Republican Howard Coble of North Carolina, the panel's chairman, said he is not yet convinced that legislation is needed and noted that ICANN's new system for governing Internet addresses is just getting started.

Consumer groups and others have also questioned the need for extending trademark restrictions to cover Internet addresses.

Andrew J. Pincus, general counsel of the Department of Commerce, criticized cybersquatters but called for private measures, not legislation.

Michael A. Daniels, chairman of Virginia-based Network Solutions Inc., which previously held an exclusive contract with the federal government to register Internet addresses, said a range of measures may be needed to stop "cyberpiracy" of some of the 7.2 million names registered worldwide. He said Congress would have to decide whether legislation would solve the problem.

Senate Passes Bill To Penalize 'Cyber-Squatting'

AUGUST 7 — In a burst of legislative energy before beginning its August recess, the Senate passed a bill by voice vote Aug. 5 that would impose fines for the unauthorized use over the Internet of trademark names such as Gateway 2000 or Coca-Cola.

The legislation (S 1255) is aimed at curtailing "cyber-squatting," the practice among some Internet users of registering World Wide Web addresses that suggest a connection with a major company or even a political candidate.

The problem first surfaced when some companies tried to establish an on-line presence using their brand names. They discovered that others already had registered their trademark as part of a domain name, as Internet addresses are known. And in some instances, companies paid squatters thousands of dollars to buy back a name to use as an Internet address.

The bill would establish civil penalties of $1,000 to $100,000 for cyber-squatting. If a court found that the trademark use was "willful," it could impose fines of $3,000 to $300,000.

The House is expected to consider the matter this fall. Republican James E. Rogan of California, a member of the House Judiciary Committee, plans to introduce a companion bill.

The Senate version, sponsored by Judiciary Committee Chairman Orrin G. Hatch, R-Utah, and ranking Democrat Patrick J. Leahy of Vermont, was one of the last bills passed before Congress broke for its August recess.

The administration opposes the bill, saying disputes over domain names should be settled in court.

Senate aides said there was no organized lobby against the bill, though a group of Internet users has criticized it.

First Amendment Rights

The Domain Name Rights Coalition, based in Herndon, Va., represents individuals and small businesses that have bought rights to Internet names. The group argues that the legislation threatens free speech on the Internet and that trademark names are already protected by current law.

Coalition President Mikki Barry said big corporations often harass and try to intimidate individual Internet users for inserting everyday terms in their Web addresses. In most complaints by companies against cyber-squatters, the courts have ruled in favor of the companies, she said.

"There is simply no need for a bill that would squash First Amendment rights the way this one would," Barry said.

But bill supporters maintain that longstanding trademark law does not address all the problems in the brave, new world of the Internet. They cite a growing practice among cyber-squatters of posting pornographic images at sites that are only slight variations on trademark names.

For instance, computer giant Gateway 2000 Inc. paid $100,000 to obtain the rights to a domain name incorporating its trademark — www.gateway2000. The site was being used to peddle pornography.

"For the enterprising cyber-squatter, holding out a domain name for extortionate compensation is a tried-and-true business practice," said Sen. Spencer Abraham, R-Mich., a bill cosponsor. "And the net effect of this behavior is to undermine consumer confidence [and] discourage consumer use of the Internet."

A few corporate powerhouses that support the bill have joined together as the Private Sector Working Group. They include Microsoft Corp., Porsche A.G., Bell Atlantic Corp., AT&T Corp., Disney, Viacom Inc. and America Online Inc.

Politicians also have been burned by cyber-squatters, including bill sponsor Hatch. A squatter registered an address called www.hatch2000.org, which is not related to his fledgling presidential campaign but sounds as though it could be.

Cyber-squatting is one of a host of new problems confronting Congress with the growing use of the Internet.

Registering a domain name is relatively simple. All it takes is choosing a name and paying a fee to a Web site registrar such as Network Solutions Inc.

House Passes Bill To Protect Brand Names on Web

OCTOBER 30 — The House passed by voice vote Oct. 26 a bill to resolve a dispute over who owns famous names in cyberspace. The bill, S 1255 (H Rept 106-412), would prevent the unauthorized use of trademark names such as Coca-Cola and Microsoft in Internet addresses.

The bill now heads to a conference committee to resolve differences between House and Senate versions. Both would provide for trademark holders to be awarded civil damages of between $1,000 and $100,000 for unauthorized use of their names. The damages would apply to cases in which a person registered an Internet address knowing it resembled a name protected by a trademark.

In addition to protecting brand and company names, the House version would provide similar damage awards for unauthorized use of a famous person's name in an Internet address. The Senate bill does not include such a protection, but language similar to the House provision is expected to win support in conference. The Senate bill was passed by voice vote Aug. 5.

Rep. James E. Rogan, R-Calif., the bill's sponsor, said he believes House-Senate negotiators will quickly resolve other differences. They are expected to begin work the week of Nov. 1.

Besides the issue of whether to protect names of persons as well as trademarks, the conferees must also decide whether to include several House provisions not related to "cybersquatting."

The House bill would preserve names of buildings listed with the National Register of Historic Places. Rep. Ileana Ros-Lehtinen, R-Fla., said that would allow well-known buildings such as the art deco Tiffany Hotel in Miami Beach, Fla., to keep names that resemble names of companies or brands.

"To lose one's name is to lose one's identity," Ros-Lehtinen said Oct. 26 on the House floor.

The House bill would also allow specialized Internet addresses for political candidates.

(*For final action on the bill, see satellite TV, p. 22-3.*) ◆

Both Chambers Pass Bills To Honor On-line Signatures; Conferees To Meet in 2000

SUMMARY

The Senate passed its version of the bill this year, setting the stage for a contentious conference committee next year over electronic signatures. A coalition of Democrats joined Republicans in carrying the measure to a wide victory in the House, but a bipartisan Senate version has significant differences that will have to be worked out.

The measure would confer legal validity on electronic signatures, thus effectively superseding state laws that require written records to be kept.

A priority of the high-tech industry, HR 1714 was passed by the House on Nov. 9. This version would authorize the use of electronic signatures and records in business transactions on the Internet.

House Commerce Committee Chairman and bill sponsor Thomas J. Bliley Jr., R-Va., said this was "perhaps the most important pro-technology vote that this Congress will take." But the White House and Democratic leaders objected to the House bill, which they said would allow businesses to run roughshod over important consumer protections, including requirements for written notice of such actions as foreclosure on a house or termination of electrical service.

The House defeated, 126-278, a Democratic substitute amendment backed by the White House, which would have conferred legal validity on electronic signatures only for transactions affecting interstate commerce and that did not contain records provisions.

The substitute was virtually identical to a Senate deal reached between Commerce Manufacturing and Competitiveness Subcommittee Chairman Spencer Abraham, R-Mich., and Ranking Judiciary member Patrick J. Leahy, D-Vt. That compromise (S 761) was then passed by the Senate to clear the way for negotiations with the House.

Key differences separate the House version and Senate version, which has the blessing of Democrats and the administration. That leaves the battle for a conference, which will have election-year momentum behind it.

Box Score

- **Bills:** S 761; HR 1714
- **Legislative action: House** passed HR 1714 (H Rept 106-341, Parts 1 and 2), 356-66, on Nov. 9.

Senate passed S 761 (S Rept 106-131) by voice vote on Nov. 1.

House Panel OKs E-Signatures Bill

OCTOBER 16 — The House Judiciary Committee approved by voice vote Oct. 13 a bill (HR 1714) to allow use of electronic signatures and electronic records on the Internet, setting the stage for a floor debate over whether states should have the authority to require businesses and individuals to keep written records.

The bill has been promoted by the high-tech industry as essential to establish rules of the road for commerce on the Internet. The original version of the bill would have pre-empted existing state laws that require written records for business transactions and official documents, such as medical and tax records or marriage licenses.

But the panel adopted, 15-14, a substitute amendment, sponsored by Howard L. Berman, D-Calif., that would require states to recognize electronic contracts to finalize business deals. The amendment would allow states to require written records for other purposes, such as court orders and medical records. Supporters, including Republicans Bob Barr of Georgia and Lindsey Graham of South Carolina, said the amendment was needed to preserve the right of states to set recordkeeping standards.

Opponents of the amendment, including Howard Coble, R-N.C., and Robert W. Goodlatte, R-Va., said it would prevent development of uniform standards for electronic commerce.

"It's a big loophole," Goodlatte said Oct. 13. He predicted floor amendments would be offered to narrow the exemption for states to require written records.

The House Commerce Committee had approved the bill Aug. 5 by voice vote.

House Passes Bill

NOVEMBER 13 — The House passed a bill (HR 1714 — H Rept 106-341, Parts 1 and 2) on Nov. 9 to authorize the use of electronic signatures and records in business transactions on the Internet, setting the stage for floor action on a similar bill in the Senate. The vote was 356-66. *(Vote 579, p. H-188)*

The Senate was expected to consider a compromise bill (S 761) by Spencer Abraham, R-Mich., and Patrick J. Leahy, D-Vt., the week of Nov. 15. But members said it is unlikely that work could be completed on the measure this year because of differences in the two bills.

House Commerce Committee Chairman Thomas J. Bliley Jr., R-Va., criticized the Clinton administration for opposing HR 1714, which was strongly supported by high-tech companies.

But he added that he will try to work out differences if the Senate passes S 761, which is backed by the White House and does not include provisions to use electronic records.

"This bill — perhaps the most important pro-technology vote that this Congress will take — should not fall prey to partisan battles," Bliley said.

The administration said the bill would pre-empt existing state laws and might create problems for consumers who are unfamiliar with the procedures for receiving records by e-mail.

The House defeated, 126-278, a Democratic substitute amendment that resembled the Senate compromise bill. *(Vote 578, p. H-188)*

A group of Democrats, led by Jay Inslee of Washington, tried to broker a compromise with Republicans. They sponsored an amendment that was adopted, 418-2, to ensure that businesses get permission from consumers to use electronic records instead of written documents to provide notice of business practices. *(Vote 577, p. H-188)*

White House spokesman Jake Siewert said Nov. 11 that the administration strongly opposed the House bill. "We hope lawmakers will move in the direction of the Senate bill," he said.

Senate Passes Bill

NOVEMBER 20 — The Senate passed by voice vote Nov. 19 a compromise version of a bill (S 761) to authorize the use of electronic signatures to make financial transactions on the Internet, setting the stage for a contentious conference committee next year.

The White House has strongly backed the Senate bill, which would establish a national standard for the use of electronic signatures in on-line commerce. The Clinton administration has threatened to veto a broader bill (HR 1714) passed by the House, 356-66, on Nov. 9. The House bill would allow the use of electronic records, such as marriage licenses, as well as electronic signatures.

The administration has opposed HR 1714 on grounds it would allow businesses to notify consumers about business practices by e-mail rather than in letters. Democrats have argued that many Americans are not yet familiar with the use of e-mail and might not be able to get important consumer information that is provided only over the Internet and not by regular mail.

Supporters of HR 1714 including House Commerce Committee Chairman Thomas J. Bliley Jr., R-Va., intend to press in conference committee for language to authorize the use of electronic records. They are pointing to the strong bipartisan support for HR 1714 in the House and suggesting that the White House cannot count on enough Democratic votes to sustain a veto.

In the Senate, objections by Ranking Judiciary Committee Democrat Patrick J. Leahy, R-Vt., and other Democrats forced Republicans to develop a compromise version of S 761 that focused only on authorizing the use of electronic signatures, ranging from passwords to signatures written on touch-sensitive computer screens. Such devices are used to authenticate the identity of credit card buyers on the Internet.

Spencer Abraham, R-Mich., sponsor of S 761, said he would try to help negotiate a solution to the electronic records dispute. "Businesses and consumers must have the freedom to agree to the types of documents and information they receive electronically. This right to choose to receive records electronically must be provided by Congress," Abraham said in a floor statement Nov. 19. ◆

Senate Passes Bill To Ban On-Line Gambling; House Likely To Follow Suit in 2000

Box Score

- **Bills:** S 692; HR 3125
- **Legislative action: House** Judiciary Subcommittee on Crime approved HR 3125, 5-3, Nov. 3.

Senate passed S 692 (S Rept 106-121), by voice vote, on Nov. 19.

SUMMARY

The Senate passed legislation to ban gambling on the Internet, and the House is expected to pass similar legislation next year.

The Senate passed the Internet gambling ban at the end of the session, after resolving a dispute over online gambling operations owned by Indian tribes. In a compromise worked out by the sponsor, Sen. Jon Kyl, R-Ariz., and Indian Affairs Committee Chairman Ben Nighthorse Campbell, R-Colo., the bill would permit tribes to collect bets from online gambling customers physically located on Indian reservations in states where games were allowed.

A House Judiciary subcommittee approved a similar bill (HR 3125) but did not include the same language on Indian tribes.

Both bills would bar gambling businesses from using the Internet to place or receive a bet. They would set penalties of up to four years in prison and up to a $20,000 fine.

Senate Panel Votes To Ban Most On-Line Betting

MAY 15 — A Senate panel took the first step May 12 toward opening a broad debate on how to control gambling, approving a ban (S 692) on most domestic on-line betting.

Many World Wide Web sites featuring gambling are already located offshore, and they would not be affected by the ban. Nonetheless, lawmakers are hoping to promote a crackdown on gambling Web sites operating inside the United States and to increase public awareness of the lack of federal control over offshore on-line gambling.

The Senate Judiciary Subcommittee on Technology, Terrorism and Government Information approved the on-line betting ban by voice vote, setting the stage for a potentially contentious markup in full committee this month.

The bill has bipartisan support but could face difficulties in committee and on the Senate floor, where it could become a vehicle for amendments by anti-gambling advocates who want to put more restraints on gambling businesses.

Commission's Report Due

Gambling control is expected to be a high-profile topic this year. In June, lawmakers will receive a comprehensive report on the $50 billion gambling industry from the National Gambling Impact Study Commission, created by Congress three years ago (PL 104-169). The commission is expected to call for a moratorium on the expansion of the $50 billion gambling industry. Though the moratorium is unlikely to win support in Congress, other anti-gambling proposals are expected to surface this year. *(1996 Almanac, p. 5-44)*

Sen. Jon Kyl, R-Ariz., said in an interview May 12 that he would try to keep the bill narrowly focused on the Internet gambling industry, which takes in more than $1 billion in revenue each year.

"We are hoping to get the [gambling] bill marked up in full committee and on the floor. We have already resolved most issues," he said.

The bill is backed by the casino industry, which regards on-line gambling as an unregulated rival, but on-line betting businesses and other critics say the bill is too restrictive.

Sue Schneider, chairman of the Interactive Gaming Council, a group based in Canada that represents Internet gambling companies, told senators in written testimony March 23 that Congress should regulate the industry instead of banning it. She predicted that the ban would have little impact on access to offshore Web sites.

Feinstein Seeks Changes

While opponents tried to derail the ban, Democratic Sen. Dianne Feinstein of California said at the May 12 markup that she generally supported the bill but would press for revisions to protect companies that provide network space for on-line gambling. She said she would offer an amendment to ensure that such providers are given a set time to respond to requests from law enforcement to shut down the Web sites.

She would also try to protect the Internet providers, she said, by offering an amendment to make sure the ones that simply transmit advertising for gambling are not subject to penalties.

Despite her concerns, Feinstein praised the bill as an effort to "close the loophole which allows Internet gambling to flourish."

Kyl said he was confident of reaching a compromise with Feinstein. He predicted passage with the support of the National Association of Attorneys General, which is trying to find ways to curb Internet gambling in states.

Kyl's bill would extend a 1961 wire communications law (87-216) that prohibited the taking of wagers on sporting events by phone. The bill would set penalties of as much as four years in prison and $20,000 in fines for taking bets over the Internet.

The 1999 version of the bill is narrower than a bill that Kyl proposed last year, which passed the Senate but was deleted in conference from the omnibus spending law (PL 105-277).

Kyl deleted penalties of as much as $500 per bettor this year. He also made a deal with operators of fantasy sports games, which award prizes to customers based on the performance of professional sports teams and players. He exempted fantasy games that impose only administrative fees. Figures on the number of fantasy game players are not available, but Internet services sponsor the games mainly as a service, not to generate income.

Rep. Robert W. Goodlatte, R-Va., said a similar ban was being drafted by Rep. Bill McCollum, R-Fla., and would get strong support. "We will have a good opportunity to work something out with Sen. Kyl," he said.

Senate Judiciary Approves Bill

JUNE 19 — Gamblers would no longer be able to place bets with just a computer and a credit card under a bill (S 692) the Senate Judiciary Committee approved 16-1 on June 17.

The bill would prohibit the operation of gambling sites on the Internet, closing a loophole in federal gambling laws that ban betting over phone lines. Some sports gambling over the Internet is already banned.

Russell D. Feingold, D-Wis., cast the lone vote against the bill. His spokesman, Michael Jacobs, said Feingold does not believe gambling legislation should "single out" one type of technology to alleviate the broad problems created by gambling.

Owners of businesses that offer sports betting or casino games on the Internet could face fines of up to $20,000 and prison terms of up to four years. States would decide whether to take action against customers of the sites.

The bill would not affect sports fantasy leagues, state-operated lotteries, or betting on some horse and dog races. But the bill would prohibit gambling Web sites operated by Indian reservations.

National Indian Gaming Association Chairman Richard Hill objected to the provision involving Indian-operated Web sites. He said Indian casinos are "not phantom operators" on the Internet because, unlike many gambling Web sites, their physical location is known.

Hill said he expects Senate Indian Affairs Committee Chairman Ben Nighthorse Campbell, R-Colo., to add protections for Indian casinos in conference. However, a House bill has not yet been introduced. A similar bill passed the Senate last year but died in the final days of the 105th Congress. *(1998 Almanac, p. 22-7)*

Other anti-gambling measures are expected to surface following release June 18 of a report by the National Gambling Impact Study Commission. The 200-page report to Congress urged a moratorium on the spread of gambling, but industry supporters will fight proposals for taxes or restrictions aimed at casinos.

House Panel Moves Internet Gambling Ban

NOVEMBER 6 — A bill (HR 3125) to prohibit on-line gambling cleared its first subcommittee hurdle on Nov. 3, but it will not be moving further until next year.

The House Judiciary Crime Subcommittee approved the bill, 5-3, setting the stage for full committee action. But bill sponsor Robert W. Goodlatte, R-Va., said he did not expect another markup this year because time is running out on the 1999 session.

"I'm sure we will get to it early next year," Goodlatte said. A similar bill (S 692) is waiting for a floor vote in the Senate, and the sponsor, Jon Kyl, R-Ariz., said he expected a floor vote this year.

One key difference between the bills, Goodlatte said, was language in the House measure to permit on-line advertising for legal gambling operations. It is not in the Senate version.

All three Democrats in the subcommittee markup voted against the bill: Robert C. Scott of Virginia, Martin T. Meehan of Massachusetts and Steven R. Rothman of New Jersey. They cited the need for further study and expressed concern about whether the ban would stop offshore gambling operations.

Scott offered but then withdrew an amendment that would have created penalties for online bettors. But Judiciary Crime Subcommittee Chairman Bill McCollum, R-Fla., said the penalties on bettors should be left to the states where they lived.

The bill would set penalties of up to four years in jail and $20,000 in fines for operators of on-line gambling but would set no penalties for gamblers.

The bill would provide an exemption from the on-line betting ban for closed-circuit gambling operations regulated by states that take bets on horse and dog races and on jai alai.

Goodlatte predicted bipartisan support for the bill.

But Meehan expressed concern the bill did not exempt Indian gambling operations.

Senate Passes Bill To Ban Gambling On Internet

NOVEMBER 20 — The Senate passed by voice vote Nov. 19 a bill (S 692) to prohibit on-line gambling, clearing the way for House action on a similar bill (HR 3125) next year.

Sen. Jon Kyl, R-Ariz., said Nov. 18 there was broad bipartisan support for a ban on Internet gambling. And he predicted lawmakers would complete legislation next year.

Both bills would prohibit gambling businesses from using the Internet to place, receive or make a bet. They would provide criminal penalties of up to $20,000 in fines and four years in prison for an Internet gambling offense. Both bills would exempt closed-circuit gambling on horse and dog racing from the on-line gambling ban.

One key difference between the bills is language in the House bill, but not in S 692 to permit on-line advertising for legal casinos.

Another potential area of dispute is the issue of restricting on-line gambling by Indian tribes. The Senate bill included compromise language developed by Kyl and Indian Affairs Committee Chairman Ben Nighthorse Campbell, R-Colo. The bill would permit on-line gambling operations owned by tribes to collect bets from customers who were physically located on Indian reservations in states where on-line games were allowed. ◆

Chapter 23

TRADE

House Defeats Bill To Deny Normal Trade With China; Senate Does Not Act

Box Score

- **Bill:** H J Res 57
- **Legislative action: House** rejected H J Res 57, 170-260, on July 27.

SUMMARY

The House rejected a resolution (H J Res 57) that would have denied China normal trade status. The annual ritual may be coming to an end, however. The Clinton administration reached a broad trade deal with Beijing on Nov. 15 that would pave the way for China's entry into the World Trade Organization (WTO), provided Congress approves permanent normal trade status in 2000.

The outcome of the annual debate on normal trade relations with China was never really in doubt despite a sharp downturn in relations between Washington and Beijing. Supporters fretted about allegations of spying at U.S. nuclear weapons laboratories, the apparently accidental bombing of the Chinese embassy in Belgrade by NATO planes during the Kosovo conflict and disputes over Taiwan. But the strong interests of both countries in trade ties and a powerful pro-China U.S. business lobby managed to overcome those tensions and lingering disputes over human rights and other issues. A resolution seeking to overturn President Clinton's decision to renew China's normal trade status picked up only four more votes than in 1998. Because both houses of Congress would have to agree to reverse the president's decision, the Senate did not take up the measure.

The disputes took a toll on U.S.-China trade ties for a time. Clinton and Chinese Premier Zhu Rongji came close to a deal on Beijing's accession to the WTO during Zhu's April visit to Washington. But with tensions flaring because of the spy scandal, Clinton backed off. At the time, Clinton was criticized by many lawmakers for letting an opportunity for more trade slip by. On Nov. 15, after months of arduous talks, U.S. and Chinese officials reached an agreement in which the United States will support China's bid for WTO membership, in return for China lowering barriers to U.S. products and firms.

Though Congress has approved normal trade status for China annually since 1980, making the relationship permanent is not a foregone conclusion. Critics of China's record on human rights, trade and arms sales likely will oppose the plan, and labor unions are unhappy with the new trade deal.

China Policy: U.S. Struggles To See Clearly

MAY 1 — Wyoming Republican Craig Thomas, the chairman of the Senate Foreign Relations Subcommittee on East Asian and Pacific Affairs, closely follows the unfolding drama of China. Yet even with his frequent trips to the country, he has trouble figuring out which of China's many faces is genuine.

"You talk to some of the party leadership, and they are rigid communist ideologues with little flexibility," Thomas said. "And then you go in the streets of Shanghai or other cities and you see this incredibly vibrant, bustling society, and all this change going on. It's hard to tell what's happening."

Thomas is not alone. Policy-makers and members of Congress find it extraordinarily difficult to comprehend what China is today and what kind of nation it will become tomorrow. Will it follow Asian countries such as South Korea and Taiwan — whose dictatorships became economic powerhouses and evolved into democracies? Or will it become like the former Soviet Union, an "evil empire" in President Ronald Reagan's famous phrase, posing a threat to U.S. national interests that must be contained?

President Clinton outlined the problems in an April 7 speech to the U.S. Institute for Peace.

"I believe we should not look at China through rose-colored glasses, nor should we look through a glass darkly to see an image that distorts China's strength and ignores its complexities," Clinton said. "We need to see China clearly — its progress and its problems, its system and its strains, its policies and its perception of us, of itself, of the world."

Yet, the administration's policy of trying to influence China's course from within a close economic and diplomatic relationship has been frayed by criticism from the left and the right.

As Stanley O. Roth, assistant secretary of State for East Asian and Pacific Affairs, remarked at an April 21 hearing of the House International Relations Committee: "One of the joys of working on China policy is that we face bipartisan opposition on almost any issue."

Beijing's apparent theft of sensitive U.S. nuclear weapons secrets, its buildup of missiles aimed at Taiwan and the accusations that Chinese officials made illegal contributions to U.S. political campaigns have strengthened the hand of Beijing's opponents, who were already concerned about China's poor human rights record and sales of weapons and nuclear technology to other countries.

Beijing's opposition to NATO military action in Yugoslavia and the Persian Gulf have further poisoned relations and brought into question the "strategic partnership" that Clinton has proclaimed with China.

Yet China's critics in and out of Congress have been unable to shake the administration policy or to come up with a viable alternative. A key reason is that the economic ties at the heart of the Sino-U.S. relationship have never been stronger. China has become America's sixth-largest foreign market and the fastest-growing overseas destination for U.S. goods among major trading partners.

President Clinton and other officials have repeatedly applauded Beijing for not devaluing its currency, helping to keep a lid on the Asian financial crisis.

And meeting in Washington earlier this month, Clinton and Chinese Premier Zhu Rongji came close to signing an agreement that would have allowed China to enter the World Trade Organization and would have given U.S. companies broader access to the vast Chinese market. The pact would have provided an additional boost to the bustling trade between the two countries.

Trouble Ahead

Those trade ties offer long-term hope for relations between Washington and Beijing.

But U.S.-China relations could face some rocky times in the next few months.

Congress must digest the results of investigations by the Clinton administration, the House and the Senate into a decades-long effort by the Chinese to penetrate U.S. nuclear weapons laboratories. Lawmakers also may debate U.S. trade relations with China — always a testy subject — twice within six months. The Justice Department and congressional committees will continue their probes of alleged campaign contributions by Chinese officials to Clinton's 1996 reelection campaign, a source of embarrassment to the White House.

Meanwhile in China, the 10th anniversary of the June 4, 1989, Tiananmen Square massacre could spur major protests, as could the 50th anniversary of the founding of the communist government in China on October 1.

"This is a low point of Sino-American relations as far as Congress is concerned," said Rep. Doug Bereuter, R-Neb., who is chairman of the Asia and the Pacific Subcommittee of the House International Relations Committee. "I could hardly imagine how things could be worse"

In fact, each of the flash points in Sino-American relations has mobilized different constituencies.

"Each issue involves different groups," said Richard N. Haass, director of the foreign policy studies program at the Brookings Institution, a nonpartisan Washington think tank. "So there is a constellation of forces critical of China."

On the right, religious conservatives attack China for what they say is a stepped-up campaign of persecution against Catholics and Protestants who worship outside of government-controlled churches.

They rail against instances of forced abortion, and they claim that the Chinese government is selling organs from executed prisoners for transplants overseas. Senate Foreign Relations Committee Chairman Jesse Helms, R-N.C., has attached several anti-China provisions to a fiscal 2000-01 State Department authorization bill in an attempt to pressure the administration into action.

Liberal critics attack China for backing off promises to discuss the future of Tibet with the Dalai Lama, for taking advantage of labor and for polluting the environment. They also complain about China's soaring trade surplus with the United States.

Both groups are angered by a recent Chinese government crackdown on pro-democracy dissidents. Both the House and Senate adopted resolutions (S Res 45, H Con Res 28) this year that called on the administration to press for a condemnation of China at the annual meeting of the U.N. Human Rights Commission in Geneva in April. The administration agreed but failed to muster enough support from other delegations, and the measure was killed.

But the most troubling allegations to many members of Congress, particularly Republicans, concern the alleged thefts of U.S. military secrets from weapons labs, as well as China's ability to obtain civilian technology with potential military uses, such as satellites and supercomputers.

Military Maneuvers

Lawmakers fret that through espionage, China has leaped ahead in its efforts to rival the United States as a military power.

"China has made a very aggressive effort in military modernization," said Tim Hutchinson, R-Ark., a leader among China's critics in the Senate. "It's a grave error to view them as a strategic partner. They view us as a hostile power, and they are expansionist."

China's espionage may have allowed it to acquire U.S. technology for miniaturizing nuclear warheads, allowing several to be launched by the same missile and effectively doubling or tripling its strategic nuclear force. But the most immediate and likely threat it poses to U.S. interests, analysts say, is less direct — an attack on Taiwan.

U.S. officials say China has beefed up the number of missiles it has aimed at the island, which it considers a renegade province. With the former British colony of Hong Kong already under Beijing's control and the Portuguese colony of Macau due to revert by the end of the year, some lawmakers fear that China will make a new effort to reclaim Taiwan.

Taiwan and Taiwanese-Americans also are a powerful lobby in Washington, famous for generous campaign contributions and free trips to the island nation for lawmakers and their staffs.

Taiwan also can count on the support of powerful longtime allies such as Helms and Robert G. Torricelli, D-N.J., chairman of the Democratic Senatorial Campaign Committee. The two recently introduced the "Taiwan Security Enhancement Act" (S 693).

Helms portrayed the measure as a follow-up to his 1979 Taiwan Relations Act (PL 96-8), the basic law that defined U.S.-Taiwan relations after the United States decided that Beijing, not Taipei, was the legitimate government of China.

The new bill would enhance U.S.-Taiwan military exchanges and allow Taipei to buy a broad range of defense systems, including satellite early warning data, diesel submarines and advanced air-to-air missiles.

The legislation also would allow Taipei to acquire missile defense systems, consistent with the administration's pledge to provide a theater missile defense to protect Taiwan, South Korea and Japan from an attack by North Korea. The Chinese government has objected strongly to the potential deployment of a missile defense system.

Campaign Season

The charges of China's spying have resonated in part because the 2000 presidential election is getting under way. A number of Republican presidential candidates — particularly social conservatives such as Steve

Forbes, Gary Bauer and Pat Buchanan — are seeking to exploit the growing rift with Beijing.

Forbes for instance, said recently, "We need a strong and honest China policy, not a sellout. . . . If China continues to choose the path toward confrontation, instead of a fair and honest relationship, it must realize that everything, including trade, is at stake."

Robert Kagan, a contributing editor at the conservative magazine Weekly Standard and a senior associate of the Carnegie Endowment for International Peace, said China is a "juicy target" politically and predicted that it would be a major issue in the 2000 presidential elections.

Tying together the espionage allegations with the claims of illegal campaign contributions, Kagan said, allows a "nice linkage of high and low politics."

That is particularly so because Clinton and Vice President Al Gore repeatedly attacked then-President George Bush in 1992 for "coddling" China.

"Anti-China rhetoric gets applause right up there with anti-Clinton and black helicopters [alleged United Nations military infiltration of the United States]," Kagan said. "None of the candidates will be wanting to avoid it."

But Clinton warned in his April 7 speech that these potshots could damage an important relationship and steer China toward a dangerous future.

"As the next presidential election approaches, we cannot allow a healthy argument to lead us towards a campaign-driven Cold War with China, for that would have tragic consequences," Clinton said.

"While we cannot know where China is heading for sure, the forces pulling China toward integration and openness are more powerful today than ever before," Clinton said.

Clinton and Zhu did reach agreement to remove significant barriers to U.S. exports of wheat, citrus, and meat products to China.

But Clinton held back on a final comprehensive deal, in part, Zhu contended, because the American president feared that a political firestorm might break out on Capitol Hill if he signed an agreement.

Yet the politics of relations with China are more complex than some campaign rhetoric would indicate. Many Republican lawmakers and GOP presidential candidates, especially front-runners such as Texas Gov. George W. Bush, face a dilemma.

"Republicans want to make a growing issue out of China, which is a hot opportunity," Kagan said, "but they also want the continued support of American business."

So, he said, Republican candidates and congressional leaders often seem more intent on offering fresh rhetoric than alternative policy.

"I'm not convinced, for all the railing and moaning about China, that they are willing to hit home at all in districts and states," he said.

Policy of Engagement

Nearly all of the GOP presidential candidates have taken aim at Clinton's phrase that the United States is pursuing a "strategic partnership" with China, even those such as Sen. John McCain of Arizona, who largely favor Clinton's policy of engaging Beijing.

"Virtually at the speed of light, the president's view of Chinese leaders has changed from the 'bloody butchers of Beijing' to our 'strategic partners,' " McCain said in a March 15 speech at Kansas State University. "They are neither. They are determined, indeed, ruthless, defenders of their regime, who will do whatever is necessary, no matter how inhumane or offensive to us, to pursue their own interests. And they lead a nation of extraordinary potential, that is, whether we like it or not, becoming a military power."

Even Democrats have piled on.

"It's hard to think about China as a total strategic partner when they are railing against our action in Kosovo or not supporting our actions to enforce the no-fly zone in Iraq," said Howard L. Berman of California, ranking Democrat on the House International Relations Subcommittee on Asia and the Pacific.

Yet many, perhaps most, lawmakers say the United States is better off engaging than trying to contain China.

"It is not in our best interests not to deal with them. If we make them villains, we will make them enemies," said Chuck Hagel, R-Neb., a member of the Senate Foreign Relations Committee. "We are better off enlarging markets, giving opportunity."

Hagel pointed out that nearly all countries try to spy on the United States and said the fault for the security lapses lies more with Washington than Beijing.

"The problem with security is ours," Hagel said. "This wasn't invented by the Chinese. Sure they're spying on us. We're spying on China. Even our allies are spying on us."

Independent analysts also said that some Republican presidential candidates have exaggerated the national security threat that China poses.

"China is a poor, developing country with huge potential, but tremendous problems." said Michael Armacost, president of the Brookings Institution and an expert on Asia. "The military has antiquated equipment and lacks a . . . [deep] water navy and is no closer to being able to launch an amphibious assault on Taiwan than they were 20 years ago," he added.

Berman and others also point out that China's record on the proliferation of weapons of mass destruction has been improving. Beijing has signed such key arms control accords as the Chemical Weapons Convention and the Comprehensive Test Ban Treaty.

Power of Economics

China's defenders remain confident that in the long term, open markets will lead to broader changes in Chinese society.

"The single most positive force for change in the 5,000-year history of China has been economic reform, and trade with the U.S. has helped make that possible," said House Rules Committee Chairman David Dreier, R-Calif.

In fact, even as troubles plague other aspects of Sino-American relations, the economic ties between the two countries continue to grow, including the deal to open markets to more farm products.

"From the perspective of U.S. agriculture, this trade deal looks like a home run," said Earl Pomeroy, D-N.D., a member of the House Agriculture and International Relations Committees.

Technology companies also are eager to see restrictions lifted that they say impede U.S. exports to China while doing little to enhance U.S. national security.

For example, computer companies say U.S. restrictions on their exports — based on the power of their machines — are out of date and could soon affect exports of ordinary personal computers.

"They are not limiting the few and the powerful. They are limiting the many, the weak, and the cheap," said Dan Hoydysh, director of the Washington office of Unisys Corporation and co-chairman of the Computer Coalition for Responsible Exports, a new group that was formed to change laws and existing government policies regulating export controls.

Still, despite the hopes of business groups and their congressional supporters, trade issues could well take a back seat to human rights, weapons proliferation, regional security and other concerns when China's trade status is debated later this year.

As Berman put it, "The debate won't just be on the [tariff] treatment of soybeans."

Clinton Staffers Meet With Senate Intelligence Panel

JULY 3 — Two separate meetings between senators and top Clinton administration officials during the week of June 28 failed to close the rift between the two sides over security at the Department of Energy's nuclear weapons laboratories.

President Clinton's national security adviser, Samuel R. Berger, made a rare appearance before the Senate Intelligence Committee on June 30 to explain his actions in response to China's apparent theft of highly classified weapons data. Although Democrats said Berger acquitted himself well, Republicans expressed dismay over his answers and indicated that they will continue talking to him.

Meanwhile, Energy Secretary Bill Richardson sat down July 1 with three GOP senators who have crafted a plan to restructure the department's nuclear weapons programs that Richardson strongly opposes. The two sides were unable to resolve their differences, but they agreed to continue seeking a compromise.

The meetings with Richardson and Berger occurred against a highly charged political backdrop, as Republicans doggedly pursued the issues of Chinese espionage and lax security at the weapons labs.

Berger on the Hot Seat

Berger, in particular, has come under heavy criticism from Republicans who have accused him of not responding aggressively to reports of security lapses that apparently allowed China to acquire details of how nuclear warheads work.

Senate Majority Leader Trent Lott, R-Miss., last month drafted a letter calling for Berger's resignation. But he decided not to send the letter until Republicans had a chance to listen to Berger's side of the story.

Presidential aides do not normally testify before Congress, and the White House initially rebuffed a Republican invitation to have Berger appear before the Intelligence Committee. But the national security adviser eventually consented to an informal, closed-door question-and-answer session.

The meeting came four days after The New York Times reported that senior White House officials were informed in July 1995 that China might have stolen nuclear weapons information, nearly a year earlier than administration officials originally had disclosed.

At the meeting, Berger outlined how he responded in 1996 and 1997 to security breaches at the weapons laboratories. But his explanations left some Republicans unimpressed.

"I still have a lot of concerns about how this was handled, who was notified, who was not notified, when did the president know this," Lott said in an interview after the session. "I presume he's going to have to come back for another meeting."

Intelligence Committee member Jon Kyl, R-Ariz., was more blunt. "I was very disappointed. He was very defensive about the administration's actions," Kyl said in an interview.

In particular, Kyl cited "the mantra that 'Well, the Republican administrations weren't so hot [on security] either.' That kind of approach doesn't help you a lot. There were a lot of things that came up that are going to have to be pursued."

But ranking committee Democrat Bob Kerrey of Nebraska said Berger presented a strong enough case to quash the GOP effort to oust him.

Any serious talk of Berger's resignation "is over," Kerrey said in an interview. "You may not like everything he's done, but he's got a reasonable explanation for why he did it."

Lott would not say whether he still intends to press for Berger's resignation. "We'll have to see," he said.

The meeting between Richardson and the Senate Republicans was aimed at breaking an impasse over a GOP proposal to create a new agency within the Energy Department to oversee nuclear weapons programs. The measure's authors — Kyl, Pete V. Domenici, R-N.M., and Frank H. Murkowski, R-Alaska — plan to offer it as an amendment to the fiscal 2000 intelligence authorization bill (S 1009 — S Rept 106-48) when lawmakers take up the legislation after the July 4th recess.

Changing the Energy Level

Clinton's Foreign Intelligence Advisory Board, chaired by former Sen. Warren B. Rudman, R-N.H. (1980-93), has advocated such a proposal to end what it said is resistance among Energy Department employees to tightening security.

Richardson has objected to the plan, contending that the creation of a new undersecretary to head the agency would hinder or reverse a recent series of administrative changes that he has launched.

Several other administration officials, however, have expressed a willingness to reorganize the department in a fashion similar to the GOP proposal. And two Democratic senators, Kerrey and Dianne Feinstein of California, said they have agreed to support it.

Richardson, in the meeting with Kyl, Murkowski and Domenici, pledged to cooperate and to have his staff meet with the senators' aides to try to reach a quick agreement.

But Kyl said the Republicans' room for compromise remains limited. "At the end of the day, we are going to do what we have proposed essentially one way or another, and I think we'll succeed on that," he said.

As Senate Republicans engaged the administration on nuclear security,

House Commerce Committee members also pursued the subject.

Several Commerce members criticized the Energy Department after a new internal assessment found security flaws at California's Lawrence Livermore National Laboratory, one of the three nuclear weapons labs.

House Votes To Keep Doors To Trade Open

JULY 31 — Members of Congress have decried Chinese espionage and defense buildups for months, but the annual debate over the United States' trade relationship with China once again centered on how best to promote political and economic changes in the world's most populous nation.

Once again proponents of keeping the trade doors open won handily, with the House on July 27 rejecting a proposal (H J Res 57) that would have reversed President Clinton's decision to extend normal trade relations status to China for another year. The vote was 170-260. Last year, only four fewer members voted to overturn the president's decision. *(Vote 338, p. H-112)*

But members on both sides of the issue, which annually pits the two parties' wings against pragmatists in the middle, said the vote should not be taken as a sign that Congress would easily approve a permanent extension of normal trade relations. "A permanent vote is much more difficult," said Robert T. Matsui, D-Calif., a proponent of free trade.

If the Clinton administration and the Chinese government reach a deal in August or September on China's entry into the 134-member World Trade Organization (WTO), Congress will be asked to vote on permanent trade status before it adjourns, likely in late October.

Technically, members would vote on permanently waiving the 1974 Jackson-Vanik amendment (PL 93-618), which gives favorable tariff treatment to products from communist countries only if the president certifies that the country allows free emigration and if Congress does not reject the certification. China could enter the WTO without Congress' approval of permanent trade relations, but neither China nor the United States would reap the full benefits of China's membership. *(1974 Almanac, p. 553)*

It is unclear whether the administration can reach such an agreement with Chinese officials. Key Chinese leaders, such as Premier Zhu Rongji, favor opening the country to more trade, but others have been hesitant, given chilly relations exacerbated by NATO's bombing of the Chinese embassy in Belgrade on May 7 during the war over Kosovo. NATO said it was an accident.

Rep. Doug Bereuter, R-Neb., chairman of the International Relations Committee's panel on Asia and the Pacific, said Chinese officials are expected to signal their feelings after an August retreat. Proponents of China's entry into the WTO interpreted a cordial visit July 25 in Singapore between Chinese officials and Secretary of State Madeleine K. Albright as an encouraging sign.

Business groups, including the Business Roundtable and the U.S. Chamber of Commerce, have lobbied heavily for the annual trade extension and would step up their efforts should a WTO agreement be reached.

But the House may be more likely to again take up the trade debate in relation to another country this year — Vietnam. U.S. Trade Representative Charlene Barshefsky is expected to reach a deal on trade with Vietnamese leaders this summer. If so, the House will be asked to vote on a Jackson-Vanik waiver for Vietnam. Many members expect a controversial vote with debate featuring two former prisoners of war in Vietnam — Rep. Sam Johnson, R-Texas, and former Rep. Pete Peterson, D-Fla. (1991-97). Johnson said he would oppose such a waiver, while Peterson, now the U.S. ambassador to Vietnam, would be its strongest proponent.

Annual Trade Extension

A laundry list of concerns about China — from allegations that the country stole secrets from U.S. nuclear labs to continuing threats to Taiwan — has dominated recent discussion. But with espionage addressed in other measures, including the spending bill for energy programs (HR 2605), the House's debate on trade status returned to its usual focus: human rights abuses.

With the Chinese government's recent decision to outlaw a non-political meditation movement known as Falun Gong and issues such as religious persecution still unresolved, members of both parties argued that U.S. "engagement" with China has failed. "They want to play us for a sucker because we are willing to let them do it," said House Minority Leader Richard A. Gephardt, D-Mo.

But Ways and Means Committee Chairman Bill Archer, R-Texas, said, "The most valuable export to China is American ideals." He warned members not to hurt the two countries' "fragile" relationship by rejecting the trade benefits of normal relations.

Tim Roemer, D-Ind., agreed with Archer, saying that a rejection of normal trade status would demonize China. "The choice is clear. Are we going to have a constructive engagement policy with China or a new evil empire?"

Frank R. Wolf, R-Va., citing the plight of 13 jailed Chinese bishops, retorted, "They are the evil empire."

Clinton Faces Tough Selling Job On U.S.-China Trade Deal

NOVEMBER 20 — Free-trade lawmakers generally reacted favorably to the Clinton administration's landmark trade agreement with China. But they warned that the White House faces a formidable task persuading House Democrats to support legislation next year to implement the accord.

At the same time, leading House Republicans called for delaying a congressional vote on Beijing's trade status, even though such a move could risk embroiling the issue in election-year politics.

U.S. and Chinese negotiators reached agreement Nov. 15 on a pact that calls for China to slash tariffs and open a wide range of markets, paving the way for China to join the World Trade Organization (WTO) after 13 years of trying. U.S. Trade Representative Charlene Barshefsky said the deal was "of both profound and historic importance."

In return for China lowering its trade barriers, President Clinton must get Congress to grant Beijing permanent normal trade relations (NTR), formerly known as "most favored nation" status, the lowest tariffs enjoyed by nearly all U.S. trade partners.

China's trade status now is reviewed, and often hotly debated, each year because China is a communist nation without a true market economy.

A number of prominent lawmakers such as Senate Majority Leader Trent Lott, R-Miss., withheld judgment on the U.S.-China agreement until they could study the details. But other free-trade advocates said they were pleased with it.

"The early indications are that it's a good agreement," said House Rules Committee Chairman David Dreier, R-Calif. "But we're going to have to work very hard."

The debate over U.S. trade with China has been an annual House ritual since the 1989 Tiananmen Square massacre of dissidents. Critics have charged Beijing with human rights abuses, military threats and, most recently, nuclear spying. *(1989 Almanac, p. 518)*

Higher Stakes

This time, though, some lawmakers said the permanency of normal trade relations would color the debate. "There's more at stake," said Rep. Sander M. Levin, D-Mich., who was reserving judgment on the agreement. "There will be a sharper focus on the economics of this."

Some lawmakers who support permanent normal trade relations with China said the lobbying campaign must reach the level of the successful White House endeavor in 1993 to pass legislation (PL 103-182) approving and implementing the North American Free Trade Agreement (NAFTA). *(1993 Almanac, p. 171)*

"The president himself is going to have to sell this — he is going to have to dig deep into his political capital," said Chuck Hagel, R-Neb., a member of the Senate Foreign Relations and Banking committees.

To assist Clinton, business groups intend to throw their considerable political weight behind getting normal trade relations enacted.

"American business will explain to Congress the tremendous benefits that China's entry into the WTO would mean for this country in terms of future economic growth and job creation," said Thomas J. Donohue, president and chief executive officer of the U.S. Chamber of Commerce.

But labor unions and their congressional allies are mobilizing to defeat the effort. Some China WTO supporters conceded the unions will be more effective than Washington-based business groups in grass-roots lobbying during the winter congressional recess.

"Their side doesn't have any passion . . . their side has all the money," said Rep. Sherrod Brown, D-Ohio, an opponent of the China deal. "Our side has passion."

Before Congress votes on normal trade relations, Brown and other critics prefer to impose a deadline on China to improve its human rights situation and correct other problems. "I would like us to say, 'Show us for a year you can behave according to the norms of the rest of the world,' " Brown said.

To placate unions as well as environmentalists, Clinton has proposed creating a working group on labor issues and mandating a thorough environmental review of policies in any agreement between China and WTO members after talks expected to begin at the world trade conference Nov. 29 in Seattle. Seventy to 80 members of Congress are expected to attend the Seattle trade meeting.

Ensuring the Bet

But House Ways and Means Committee Chairman Bill Archer, R-Texas, and Trade Subcommittee Chairman Philip M. Crane, R-Ill., said the administration's labor proposal could divert energy from the goals of opening markets to U.S. products.

Archer also told reporters Nov. 17 that he would not bring up China's trade status until all WTO members complete their negotiations with China and until WTO officials bring China into the organization — a process that could take up to six months.

Although Archer said he would consider holding hearings early next year, he believes it would be unwise to press for action until the agreement is finalized. "It would make it more difficult to pass permanent NTR," he said.

Any delay could complicate the situation in Congress. But Archer said that if the current Democratic and Republican presidential front-runners, Vice President Al Gore and Texas Gov. George W. Bush, receive their parties' nominations and endorse proceeding with the vote, the process could go more smoothly. ◆

Full Calendar, Members' Objections Stall Action on Export Act Reauthorization

SUMMARY

The Senate is expected to take up the reauthorization of the Export Administration Act early in 2000.

Despite a select House committee's recommendation that a new export control law could help stem the loss of sensitive technology to China and other countries, the measure did not reach the Senate floor.

The legislation would rewrite Cold War-era laws regulating "dual use" exports, those with both military and commercial value. Since the most recent Export Administration Act (PL 103-10) expired in 1994, President Clinton has regulated exports through executive orders and individual waivers. The Senate Banking Committee bill would reduce the number of items under export control while imposing stiffer penalties on those guilty of export violations.

Even if the Senate can pass an export control bill early next year, the measure is likely to face objections from House and Senate Republicans alarmed by the central role that the measure would give the Commerce Department in regulating exports.

Senate Committee Backs Shorter List Of Exports Subject To Controls

SEPTEMBER 25 — A long-stalled proposal to license high-technology exports won unanimous support from a key Senate committee, but even sponsors acknowledge that it faces a difficult path in Congress.

The legislation that would rewrite Cold War-era laws regulating "dual use" exports — those with both military and commercial value — could be derailed by debates over allowing sales to Cuba and over which federal agencies should have a role in regulating U.S. exports.

"There are some very difficult issues out there yet," said Michael B. Enzi, R-Wyo., chairman of the Senate Banking, Housing and Urban Affairs Subcommittee on International Finance.

Nevertheless, Banking Committee members voted 19-0 on Sept. 23 to adopt Enzi's proposal to reauthorize the Export Administration Act. Enzi said he will work to address lawmakers' concerns before the measure reaches the Senate floor.

The bill would reduce the number of products under export control. It aims "to reduce or eliminate controls on items that don't have security implications and tighten controls on those that do," said Tim Johnson of South Dakota, the International Finance Subcommittee's ranking Democrat.

Worries Over China

Since the most recent Export Administration Act (PL 103-10) expired in 1994, President Clinton has regulated exports through executive orders and individual waivers, with little regular oversight and only occasional intervention from Congress. But the widely publicized findings of two recent committees have given renewed legislative momentum for a new export act.

A bipartisan House committee chaired by Christopher Cox, R-Calif., concluded earlier this year that weak export laws have contributed to China's apparent success in obtaining sensitive U.S. technology from the satellite, missile, telecommunications and machine tool industries.

A subsequent commission headed by former Director of Central Intelligence John M. Deutch that looked into the proliferation of nuclear, chemical and biological weapons strongly recommended revising the export act.

Banking Committee members said the proposal they adopted addresses the findings of the Cox and Deutch panels without hurting U.S. exporters.

"It's a tough task, trying to blend national security with economic growth," said Banking Committee Chairman Phil Gramm, R-Texas. "I think we have done it successfully with this bill."

At the heart of the bill, Gramm said, is a provision giving the secretary of Commerce the power to determine whether an export item is "mass market" and exempt from export licensing. Business groups say such an approach is intended to clarify that products with wide commercial availability overseas are not held up by a potentially lengthy licensing process.

The legislation follows recommendations from the Cox and Deutch commissions to impose stringent penalties on those guilty of export violations. Under the bill, corporations violating the licensing rules could be fined up to $10 million and individuals $1 million. Those convicted of multiple violations could be sent to prison for life, instead of the current maximum of 10 years.

White House Concerns

Administration officials did not object to the Banking Committee's proposal, but they said they are troubled by some provisions. In particular, they have cited language that would require consensus among all agencies reviewing an export license before it is granted.

"We're willing to go along with [the bill] as it is," said William A. Reinsch, undersecretary of Commerce for export administration. But Reinsch added, "I wouldn't say we're happy with it."

Some Republican senators said they also are unhappy with the central role the act would give the Commerce Department in regulating exports. They have accused the department of paying

Box Score

- **Bill:** S 1712
- **Legislative action: Senate** Banking, Housing and Urban Affairs Committee approved S 1712 (S Rept 106-180), 20-0, on Sept. 23.

more attention to business development than to national security.

"Their natural bias has to be toward getting a product out of the United States," said Connie Mack, R-Fla.

Another Banking Committee Republican, Richard C. Shelby of Alabama, said he may offer a floor amendment giving the directors of Central Intelligence and the FBI a more pronounced role in the licensing process.

The current legislation would not permit the future restriction of exports of agricultural commodities, medicine or medical supplies for foreign policy purposes. The provision would not lift the trade embargo on Cuba. However, the Senate included in its agriculture appropriations bill (S 1233 — S Rept 106-80) a provision allowing such sales to Cuba. That provision has helped stall a conference on the agriculture bill.

Further Action Unlikely in 1999

NOVEMBER 6 — Nearly a year after a bipartisan House committee said that a new export control law could help stem the loss of sensitive technology to China and other countries, Congress appears ready to adjourn for the year without taking up the legislation in either chamber.

Despite a bipartisan push in the Senate to reauthorize the Export Administration Act, the crowded end-of-session legislative calendar and objections from some lawmakers apparently will prevent the bill from being considered this year, said Senate Banking, Housing and Urban Affairs Committee Chairman Phil Gramm, R-Texas.

The measure (S 1712 — S Rept 106-180) would rewrite Cold War-era laws regulating "dual use" exports — those with both military and commercial value. The Banking Committee approved the bill 20-0 on Sept. 23.

Since then, Gramm and Michael B. Enzi, R-Wyo., chairman of the Banking Subcommittee on International Finance, have tried without success to get an agreement with Democrats to bring up the bill for debate. On Nov. 2, they joined with Tim Johnson of South Dakota, the International Finance subcommittee's ranking Democrat, to offer the legislation as an amendment to the bankruptcy overhaul measure (S 625).

"We've reconciled ourselves to having to begin in January," Gramm said in a Nov. 4 interview.

In the House, which has been awaiting the Senate's action before proceeding with its own bill, lawmakers also expressed frustration at having to wait until 2000.

"If there was any year in which this bill was going to happen, this would have been it," said Ileana Ros-Lehtinen, R-Fla., chairman of the House International Relations Subcommittee on International Economic Policy and Trade.

Since the most recent Export Administration Act (PL 103-10) expired in 1994, President Clinton has regulated exports through executive orders and individual waivers, with little regular oversight and only occasional intervention from Congress.

Gaining Momentum

But the widely publicized findings of a select House committee on China's alleged theft of U.S. technology gave momentum to a new export bill. In a report completed in December and made public in May, Chairman Christopher Cox, R-Calif., and his committee concluded that weak export laws contributed to China's apparent success in obtaining U.S. technology from the satellite, missile, telecommunications and machine tool industries.

A subsequent commission headed by former Director of Central Intelligence John M. Deutch that looked into the proliferation of nuclear, chemical and biological weapons also strongly recommended revising the export act.

Even before those two panels issued their reports, Enzi had met with industry representatives, lawmakers and Clinton administration officials to build support for a new export act.

The bill that emerged from the Senate Banking committee would reduce the number of items under export control while imposing stiffer penalties on those guilty of export violations.

The legislation also would give the secretary of Commerce the power to determine whether an export item is "mass market" and exempt from export licensing. Business groups say such an approach would clarify that products with wide commercial availability overseas are not held up by a potentially lengthy licensing process.

But Majority Leader Trent Lott, R-Miss., said that when he tried to schedule the export bill for debate, several prominent Republicans raised concerns about the bill's potential effect on national security. Some Republicans are wary of the central role the act would give the Commerce Department in regulating exports.

"This issue about national security and Commerce's kind of conflict of interest [in regulating exports with military uses] is a concern of many members," said Banking Committee member Connie Mack, R-Fla.

Super Sellers

The debate over the export act comes as some industry groups are eager to see the time reduced in which high-performance computer exports are subject to review by Congress.

In July, the Clinton administration loosened controls on such computers by increasing the performance level of those subject to government review before they can be exported. But under a law (PL 105-85) passed by Congress in 1997, lawmakers have six months to review changes to exports destined for countries that pose a potential proliferation risk, such as China. *(1997 Almanac, p. 8-3)*

Dan Hoydysh, co-chairman of the Computer Coalition for Responsible Exports, an industry group, called for a 30-day review period. He told the House Armed Services Committee at an Oct. 28 hearing that the six-month period "is longer than the life cycle of many of our products."

A day earlier, Harry Reid, D-Nev., sought to offer an amendment to African trade legislation (HR 434) that would shorten the computer review period to 30 days. Reid withdrew his amendment after Enzi promised to work with him on the issue.

Enzi said he supports shortening the review period, but he wants to see it done within the framework of reauthorizing the export act. Failing to do so, he said, could dissolve the coalition that currently supports the measure.

"There is a very delicate balance that is maintained through this bill," he said. "If one person gets everything he or she wants, there is no reason for them to participate in the rest of the bill." ◆

House, Senate Pass Bills To Boost Trade With Africa, Caribbean

Box Score

- **Bills:** HR 434; HR 984
- **Legislative action: House** Ways and Means Committee approved a Caribbean trade bill (HR 984) — H Rept 106-19, Part 2) by voice vote June 10.

House passed HR 434 (H Rept 106-19, Part 2), 234-163, on July 16.

Senate passed HR 434, 76-19, on Nov. 3, 1999, after amending it to reflect its own bill (S 1387 — S Rept 106-112) and incorporating its Caribbean trade bill (S 1389 — S Rept 106-160), among others.

SUMMARY

The House and Senate passed significantly different versions of a bill (HR 434) aimed at boosting U.S. investment in, and trade with, the 48 nations of sub-Saharan Africa.

The Senate version also contained a proposal to lift tariffs on most goods made in the Caribbean and Central America. The House Ways and Means Committee had approved a similar Caribbean trade bill (HR 984), but the full House never voted on it.

Textile manufacturers fought to limit favorable quota and duty treatment for the Caribbean to apparel and fabric made from U.S.-made fabrics or yarns. The Senate bill included the position, but the House measure included provisions to allow textiles and apparel made with Caribbean Basin-made yarns and fabric to enter the U.S. without quotas and with reduced duties.

Last-minute efforts by top leaders to reach a deal collapsed, and the bills are expected to go to a House-Senate conference in 2000.

The House sub-Saharan Africa trade bill (HR 434) passed with bipartisan support in July. It would allow goods from the region to enter the United States with no quotas or duties, if the president certified that the nations had met several conditions, including a commitment to human rights and economic structuring such as tariff reduction. Before duties could be lifted on textiles and apparel, the U.S. International Trade Commission would have to analyze the effects on U.S. industries.

The Senate version, passed in November, was far more restrictive. While the bill, which incorporated the language approved by the Finance Committee (S 1387), proposed to remove tariffs on most goods made in sub-Saharan Africa, the only eligible textile and apparel items would be those assembled from U.S.-made fabric and yarns. That provision still did not satisfy a number of Southeastern lawmakers, including Ernest F. Hollings, D-S.C., who still warned of job losses in the U.S. textile industry.

Both the House and Senate bills included language aimed at preventing other countries from shipping products through sub-Saharan nations to get a better tariff rate with the United States — a practice known as "transshipment." But textile-state lawmakers said it was inadequate.

The Senate version was also amended to include three other trade bills: trade preferences for certain Caribbean goods (S 1389), extension of the generalized system of preferences (S 1388) and reauthorization of trade adjustment assistance programs (S 1386).

House Panel Approves Bill To Foster Trade With Africa

FEBRUARY 13 — House members' mixed feelings on free trade, which have doomed broader trade legislation for two years, surfaced again as the International Relations Committee took up a bill Feb. 11 that would encourage trade with sub-Saharan Africa. But concerns about potential U.S. job losses and African environmental degradation were not strong enough to stop the measure.

The panel approved the bill (HR 434), 24-8. Republicans Bill Goodling of Pennsylvania and Cass Ballenger and Richard M. Burr, both of North Carolina, voted against it, as did Democrats Sherrod Brown of Ohio, Pat Danner of Missouri, Bill Delahunt of Massachusetts, and Brad Sherman and Barbara Lee, both of California.

The Ways and Means Committee, which has jurisdiction over large portions of the bill, may mark up the measure the week of Feb. 22. International Relations Committee Chairman Benjamin A. Gilman, R-N.Y., said Speaker J. Dennis Hastert, R-Ill., has taken an interest in the measure and wants it on the House floor the same week.

The bill, which has strong support from the Clinton administration, aims to help African nations overcome poverty. It would remove U.S. tariffs on many goods imported from 48 African countries located south of the Sahara, remove quotas on textiles and clothing imported to the United States from sub-Saharan Africa, and open the door for negotiation of an U.S.-Africa free-trade agreement. It would encourage U.S. businesses to invest in Africa by increasing the Overseas Private Investment Corporation's (OPIC) loan and loan guarantee programs. Mark Sanford, R-S.C., offered an amendment to remove the OPIC provision, but it was defeated by voice vote.

African countries could qualify for the favorable tariff and quota treatment if they did not engage in "gross violations of internationally recognized human rights" and had established or were moving toward a market-based economy. The determination would be made by the president. The bill outlines several actions that could be interpreted by the president as signs of moving toward a free market, including promoting free trade with the United States or establishing labor protections, such as a minimum wage or ban on slave labor.

Ranking member Sam Gejdenson, D-Conn., proposed the labor provision as an amendment to the list of qualifying actions. It was approved by voice vote. Gejdenson acknowledged that the language did not go as far as many of his Democratic colleagues wanted but said he hoped the amendment "increases the focus on these issues." He vowed, "We need to let no bill pass this committee that doesn't recognize environmental rights and labor rights."

Gejdenson also offered an amendment that would have included meeting "international environmental norms" as a sign that a country was moving toward a free market. It was defeated by voice vote, after several members said it would be unfair to Africa.

"We are superimposing our standards," said Amo Houghton, R-N.Y., a strong supporter of the measure. He added that the provisions would "impose on the poorest countries of the world a higher standard than we would be imposing on any other country."

Debt Forgiveness Proposal

Several committee members found themselves torn over the bill, particularly those in the Congressional Black Caucus.

Many caucus members agreed with Jesse L. Jackson Jr., D-Ill., who is not a panel member, that a better way to help Africa would be to forgive billions of dollars in loans that the countries owe to the United States. Cynthia A. McKinney, D-Ga., introduced an amendment similar to Jackson's proposal but withdrew it when jurisdictional issues arose. She said she would try to offer it on the House floor. Jackson, McKinney and Lee said they were concerned that the bill would allow multinational corporations to exploit Africans and their environment, providing little benefit in return.

But McKinney voted for the trade measure in the end, joining several other African-American members, led by Donald M. Payne, D-N.J., who said a perfect bill may be the enemy of a good bill.

Susan E. Rice, assistant secretary of state for African Affairs, had echoed Payne's remarks in testimony to the International Relations Subcommittee on Africa before the markup began. Noting support from all sub-Saharan African governments that have issued positions, Rice said, "I don't think we should allow our concerns for sovereignty to be greater than those of the countries themselves."

North Carolina Republicans Ballenger and Burr worried that the agreement would hurt the U.S. textile industry. Textile interests oppose the bill, and managed to kill a similar measure last year. They believe Asian nations would use Africa to transport cheap clothing to the United States and avoid the duty and quotas now imposed on them.

Clinton Promises Relief for Africa On Trade and Debt — Again

MARCH 27 — Meeting with ministers from 46 African countries March 16, President Clinton promised to move forward on legislation that would provide qualified Sub-Saharan countries with new trade benefits, and he unveiled a proposal to help forgive some of their foreign debt.

But the ministers could be forgiven for taking the pledges with a grain of salt, since Clinton made the same promises during a visit to Africa last year but failed to push the measures through Congress.

This year, Clinton is promising to do better. "No one is saying it will be easy, but we are resolved to help lower the hurdles left by past mistakes," he said.

But Clinton acknowledged that difficulties remain. "There are many friends of Africa in Congress and many strong opinions about how best to help Africa," he said. "I hope they will quickly find consensus. We cannot afford a house divided. Africa needs action now."

Lawmakers have expressed several different concerns about the measures. Textile-state lawmakers oppose a trade bill (HR 434), expected to be marked up soon by the House Ways and Means Committee, because they believe Asian nations would use Africa to transport cheap clothing to the United States while avoiding duties and quotas.

Budget hawks are concerned about a recent Congressional Budget Office estimate that placed a surprisingly high value on the revenues that the U.S. Treasury would forgo by lowering tariffs on African nations.

And some liberal members of the Congressional Black Caucus favor an alternative to the trade bill by Rep. Jesse L. Jackson Jr., D-Ill. That bill (HR 772) would forgive billions of dollars in loans that African countries owe the United States.

Clinton took a step in their direction by proposing a program under which the world's richest nations could forgive an additional $70 billion in loans to the most heavily indebted poor African countries, provided they carry out political and economic reforms. That would be in addition to $30 billion in loans, already eligible for such relief.

Trade Measure Inches Forward In the House

MAY 22 — A House Ways and Means panel approved a measure May 18 to open U.S. markets to more goods made in Caribbean and Central American nations. But with Congress' lack of enthusiasm for free-trade measures, it is unclear whether the bill, which the Trade Subcommittee approved by voice vote, will see further action.

Like similar measures introduced in the past three Congresses, the bill (HR 984), sponsored by Trade panel Chairman Philip M. Crane, R-Ill., would extend favorable tariff and quota treatments to products made in Caribbean and Central American nations with free-market economies that recognize labor rights and meet other standards certified by the president.

Under the 1983 Caribbean Basin Economic Recovery Act (PL 98-67), about 70 percent of goods imported to the United States from 27 Central American and Caribbean island nations already face no duties. *(1983 Almanac, p. 252)*

The bill aims to give the remaining 30 percent of the goods such treatment or the same declining duty rates for which certain goods from Mexico qualify under the 1993 North American Free Trade Agreement (PL 103-182). *(1993 Almanac, p. 171)*

Central American and Caribbean goods that are now excluded from such treatment include textiles and clothing, canned tuna, petroleum and petroleum products, footwear, handbags, luggage and work gloves. The U.S. textile industry has been the main obstacle to expanded trade, because it believes the legislation would hurt its already declining business.

Under the bill, Central American and Caribbean textile and clothing-makers would still face some requirements in order to avoid duties and quotas on their products. Textiles and apparel would qualify for the favorable treatment only if they originated in a Caribbean Basin country, as spelled out by NAFTA rules. It would also be acceptable if the apparel were made from U.S. yarns or fabric.

Those provisions will be controversial should the full committee take up the bill or should the Senate pass a Caribbean Basin measure. No House full committee markup has been scheduled. Senate Finance Committee Chairman William V. Roth Jr., R-Del., will likely include his version of the bill in a larger trade measure being compiled by his staff. A markup on that bill, which may include a languishing free-trade measure for sub-Saharan Africa and an extension of the president's fast-track trade negotiating authority, has not been scheduled.

Michigan Rep. Sander M. Levin, ranking Democrat on the Trade Subcommittee, worried that the two chambers were not on the same page with legislation such as the Caribbean Basin Initiative.

Because the textile industry has strong support from key senators, such as South Carolina Democrat Ernest F. Hollings and North Carolina Republican Jesse Helms, any measure that does not limit benefits to Caribbean apparel and textiles made with U.S. yarns and fibers is likely to be held up.

Levin warned that House leaders should have worked out their measure with Democrats and the Senate beforehand if they hoped to avoid past failures. "Unless we approach matters differently this time the result will be the same — a dead end," he said.

House Ways and Means Approves Trade Bills

JUNE 12 — Measures to broaden U.S. trade with Caribbean, Central American and African nations received voice vote approval from the House Ways and Means Committee on June 10, but they face an uphill climb to enactment.

Both the Caribbean Basin Initiative (HR 984) and the sub-Saharan Africa measure (HR 434) face opposition from the textile industry — a political force particularly in the Senate — and possibly from the Clinton administration.

U.S. Trade Representative Charlene Barshefsky told the committee June 10 that the administration wants the Caribbean Basin bill to include more restrictions on textile and apparel imports but does not want the bill to die. She supported the Africa measure.

House floor action on the Africa bill is likely to come before the August recess. The schedule for the Caribbean Basin bill, which faces more opposition, is less certain.

The Senate Finance Committee plans to mark up its version of the Caribbean bill and four other measures, including bills to reauthorize the Customs Service (HR 1833), deal with a steel import crisis, and extend the Trade Adjustment Assistance program and the Generalized System of Preferences, on June 16. It is not clear when the panel will mark up an Africa bill.

The House Africa and Caribbean Basin measures aim to increase both U.S. penetration into foreign markets and to allow nations in some of the world's least-developed regions more access to U.S. consumers.

HR 434 would allow goods from the 48 countries of sub-Saharan Africa to enter the United States with no quotas or duties if the president certified that the nations had met several conditions, including a commitment to human rights and economic restructuring, such as tariff reduction.

Before duties could be avoided on products now subject to them, including textiles and apparel, the U.S. International Trade Commission would have to analyze the effects such trade would have on U.S. industries. The bill would expire in June 2009.

HR 984 would expand upon a 1990 trade law (PL 101-382) that extended aid and trade preferences to the island nations of the Caribbean and to Central American countries. It would allow textiles and apparel to enter the United States free of quotas and duties if the products were assembled from U.S.-made yarns or fabrics. The bill, however, would allow the administration to establish separate "tariff preference levels," after consulting with the domestic industry, to allow specified amounts of fabrics and apparel not made with U.S. components to enter without tariffs or with lower tariffs. The bill, as amended by the committee by voice vote, would expire Aug. 1, 2002. *(1990 Almanac, p. 211)*

Ways and Means Committee Chairman Bill Archer, R-Texas, who introduced the amendment, said he had hoped to authorize the measure for five years but could not find enough funds to offset costs. The Joint Tax Committee estimates that the bill would cost $677 million from fiscal 1999 through fiscal 2004. The Africa bill is estimated to cost $259 million over the same period. Both bills would be offset with tax changes that the Senate Finance Committee has already used to pay for a draft education savings initiative that it marked up May 19.

The Africa bill would be financed by limiting the use of the non-accrual method of accounting — used mostly by people who operate on contract — to certain taxpayers in the service industry, and by denying charitable deductions to taxpayers who purchase life insurance policies through charities. The charities would have to pay an excise tax on any such policies they issued. Members and administration officials say a growing number of taxpayers are using such policies to portray life insurance payments as charitable contributions.

The Caribbean bill would be paid for by changing the tax treatment when certain employers make payments into workers' benefit funds before they are used.

The committee amended HR 984 to allow Puerto Rico and the Virgin Islands to keep for three months an excise tax on liquor, a portion of which usually goes to the U.S. Treasury. The cost of the change, proposed by committee ranking Democrat Charles B. Rangel of New York and approved by voice vote, was $16 million in fiscal 1999, an amount covered by the offset.

Several Democrats spoke against the bills, which they said did not do enough to protect domestic textile and apparel industries or to ensure that the countries involved meet international labor standards. The Senate bills are expected to be more to the textile industry's liking. Previous Senate bills have not allowed duty-free goods to enter the country if they are made from fabrics or yarns not made in the United States.

Senate Finance OKs Trade Bills To Benefit Africa and Caribbean

JUNE 26 — The Senate Finance Committee approved two bills long sought by free-traders to extend Africa's and the Caribbean's access to U.S. markets, but panel leaders were less than enthusiastic about pushing the measures further.

Despite voice vote approval of the Caribbean Basin Initiative and trade bill for sub-Saharan Africa on June 22, floor action on the unnumbered measures did not appear imminent.

Majority Leader Trent Lott, R-Miss., a committee member, asked Chairman William V. Roth Jr., R-Del., whether Roth thought the bills should move separately or in a package.

Roth responded: "It would be my thought that we should look and see what the House does and if we can match it with their action." When Lott asked what would happen if the House did not act, Roth said, "I don't like to consider that possibility."

It is unclear when the House will move its Caribbean Basin and Africa bills (HR 984, HR 434), which the Ways and Means Committee approved June 10. The House is thought likely to take up the Africa bill before the July Fourth recess, a House Republican aide said, but the Caribbean bill will not move until later. The Africa bill appears to have a more solid base of support because it is backed by free-traders as well as by most of the Congressional Black Caucus.

One reason for Roth's trepidation over moving the bills is that the two chambers' versions contain competing provisions on textiles and apparel that have stymied the legislation in the past.

Both Senate measures would require that apparel imported to the United States from the Caribbean Basin — 25 Caribbean and Central American nations — and from the 48 nations of sub-Saharan Africa be made of U.S. yarns or fabric in order to enter the country free of duties and tariffs.

The House would allow apparel assembled from Caribbean Basin-made fabrics or yarn into the United States with reduced tariffs. The House Africa bill contains no restrictions on yarns or textiles. It would allow all qualifying African nations quota- and duty-free treatment on apparel.

The textile industry, which has strong support in the Senate, has been adamant that U.S. yarns and fabric be required to ensure a market for the domestic industry. But apparel makers, retailers and others oppose the provisions.

Offsets

Neither bill drew much discussion nor any amendments, but some Caribbean Basin supporters were disappointed that the trade benefits in both the House and Senate versions would expire in 2002. Roth and Ways and Means Committee Chairman Bill Archer, R-Texas, included such sunsets because they could not find enough offsets in the tax code to pay for the extended trade benefits indefinitely.

The Joint Taxation Committee estimates the Senate bill would cost $664 million from 2000 through 2003. It estimates the House bill would cost $677 million. Both chambers' versions would be paid for by changing the tax treatment when certain employers make payments into workers' benefit funds before they are used.

The Senate's Africa bill would cost an estimated $228 million from 2000 through 2004. It would expire Sept. 30, 2006. The House bill is estimated to cost $259 million over the same period, and would expire in June 2009.

Both bills have two offsets. Each would limit the use of the non-accrual method of accounting — used mostly by people who operate under contract — to certain taxpayers in the service industry. The Senate bill would also require finance and credit card companies to report discharges of debt as part of their income and pay fines if they fail to do so. The House bill would instead prevent taxpayers from claiming charitable deductions on their income taxes if their contributions go toward purchasing a life insurance policy through a charity.

Other Trade Measures

The panel also approved by voice vote two other unnumbered trade bills.

- The first would reauthorize through June 30, 2004, the general system of preferences (PL 93-618), which is set to expire June 30. The program, established in 1974, allows certain goods from developing countries to enter the U.S. market duty-free. *(1974 Almanac, p. 553)*
- The other bill would reauthorize the Trade Adjustment Assistance (TAA) Act (also PL 93-618), enacted to help workers and industries adversely affected by trade. Its precursor program was created in the 1962 Trade Expansion Act (PL 87-794), a favored bill of President John F. Kennedy. *(1962 Almanac, p. 262)*

Under the program, workers can receive extended unemployment benefits and training assistance if the Labor Department certifies that their jobs were lost because of import competition. Affected companies can receive technical assistance. The program is set to expire June 30.

The bill also would extend a similar program — Transitional Adjustment Assistance — established under the 1993 North American Free Trade Agreement (PL 103-182) that will also expire June 30. *(1993 Almanac, p. 171)*

The programs would be authorized through Sept. 30, 2001, at a cost of $87 million over four years.

Charles E. Grassley, R-Iowa, and Kent Conrad, D-N.D., tried unsuccessfully to amend the bill to allow family farmers to receive payments of up to $10,000 each under the trade adjustment program if the price of a commodity they produced dropped more than 20 percent compared with the average price in the previous five years and if imports "contributed importantly" to that reduction. The Agriculture Department would have administered the program and could have given out only $100 million in assistance a year.

The two said the amendment would put farmers on a level playing field with workers in other industries. As the trade adjustment program now operates, workers qualify if they are laid off or in danger of being laid off because of trade. Those who own farms may be forced to sell, but they would not be technically laid off.

Others said the amendment would have made too big a change to the program. "It's quite a departure from the TAA as we know it," said John H. Chafee, R-R.I. He also opposed making retraining voluntary for farmers, as the amendment proposed. Retraining is mandatory for workers who now receive trade adjustment assistance.

But Conrad said, "The reason it's different is because circumstances are different. . . .The farm is still there, the farmer is still there, but they're being devastated economically."

Conrad and several other committee members said the amendment was important to retaining agricultural support for free trade, but the panel defeated the proposal, 9-11. All Republicans but Grassley and Frank H. Murkowski of Alaska voted against it, and all Democrats but ranking member Daniel Patrick Moynihan of New York and Charles S. Robb of Virginia voted for it.

House Passes Africa Trade Bill Despite Dissension In Black Caucus

JULY 17 — Encouraged by the backing of the Clinton administration and all 48 governments in sub-Saharan Africa, the House on June 16 passed legislation that aims to boost trade with and investment in the region. The vote was 234-163. (*Vote 307, p. H-104*)

The endorsements and the bipartisan House vote for the bill (HR 434) may not be enough to overcome opposition in the Senate, where lawmakers from textile-producing states will try to kill or substantially alter the measure, which they say would open the door to a flood of cheap imports. A similar measure passed in the House last year only to die in the Senate. (*1998 Almanac, p. 23-10*)

The Senate Finance Committee approved a similar draft trade bill for Africa in June, and Senate Majority Leader Trent Lott, R-Miss., has said he wants to move the bill, although a date for floor action has not been set.

It is possible the Senate will combine the Africa measure with a separate draft bill to expand access to U.S. markets for nations in the Caribbean.

The House bill on Africa aims to increase the flow of U.S. goods to markets there and allow nations in one of the world's least-developed regions more access to U.S. consumers.

The measure would allow goods from the 48 countries of sub-Saharan Africa to enter the United States with no quotas or duties if the president certified that the nations had met several conditions, including a commitment to human rights and economic restructuring, such as tariff reduction.

Before duties could be lifted on specific products, including textiles and apparel, the U.S. International Trade Commission would have to analyze the effects on U.S. industries.

The law would expire in June 2009.

The House debate was marked by strong disagreement over the bill among members of the black caucus, which split 19-15 on the measure.

Maxine Waters, D-Calif., and Jesse L. Jackson Jr., D-Ill., charged that the bill would do more to help multinational corporations than the countries in the region. "We're not going to support the rape of Africa a second time in a more sophisticated way," Waters said.

Killing With Kindness

Waters objected to some of the conditions that countries would have to meet to be eligible for the trade benefits and said the legislation should do more to ensure that stringent labor and environmental standards are met.

However, Charles B. Rangel of New York, ranking Democrat on the Ways and Means Committee, said the bill was designed to help African countries compete in global markets. Rangel said colleagues who wanted to do more for Africa by loading on provisions to improve health, education and other services would only doom the measure.

"We love [Africans] so much that we want to put so much in this bill that it will never get off the ground," Rangel said.

Some lawmakers from textile-producing areas, particularly in the Southeast, opposed the bill mainly because they believe China and other textile areas in Asia will avoid U.S. duties by trans-shipping goods through Africa.

"It will be a national holiday in China when we pass this bill," said Lindsey Graham, R-S.C.

"Seldom on the House floor have I ever seen such a blatant attempt to eliminate U.S. jobs," added Richard M. Burr, R-N.C.

The bill would direct the administration to ensure that any country in Africa that intends to export textiles or clothing to the United States have effective laws and enforcement to stop trans-shipment. The measure also would require the administration to deny all trade benefits under the bill for two years to any exporter determined to have engaged in illegal trans-shipment.

The rule on floor debate (H Res 250) prevented Sanford D. Bishop Jr., D-Ga., and Sue Myrick, R-N.C., from offering an amendment that aimed to protect U.S. textile workers by requiring that products receiving preferential duties be made from U.S. fabric. The rule was adopted 263-141.

The House defeated, by voice vote, an amendment offered by Jackson that would have required that assistance to sub-Saharan countries by the Overseas Private Investment Corporation be targeted for certain purposes, including health care, sanitation, schools, rural electrification and transportation. Opponents of Jackson's amendment said it was unrealistic and unworkable and would stifle the efforts of entrepreneurs in the region.

President Clinton issued a statement July 14 supporting the bill as a way to promote peace and democracy in the region. "The United States must do everything we can right now to support the efforts Africans are making to build democracy and respect for human rights, advance peace and lay the foundation for prosperity and growth," Clinton said.

Senate Poised To Vote on Bills To Expand Trade

OCTOBER 23 — Senate leaders will attempt the week of Oct. 25 to bring up measures that would expand U.S. trade with impoverished nations in the Caribbean and sub-Saharan Africa.

A cloture vote is scheduled Oct. 26 on a motion to proceed to a House-passed Africa trade measure (HR 434). Supporters of the bill say they will have the 60 votes they will need to proceed.

The cloture vote is necessary because textile-state senators led by Ernest F. Hollings, D-S.C., blocked consideration of the trade legislation Oct. 21.

If the bill is formally brought up, the floor managers said they will attempt to attach as an amendment a package of legislation reported out by the Senate Finance Committee, including a different Africa trade measure (S 1387), a bill granting trade benefits to Caribbean-made apparel (S 1389), a five-year extension of the Generalized System of Preferences (S 1388), and a multi-year extension of the Trade Adjustment Assistance program for workers and companies harmed by imports (S 1386).

Hollings and other Southeastern lawmakers contend that the Africa and Caribbean trade bills' tariff and quota reductions would hurt the domestic textile industry and eliminate jobs in their region.

Hollings likened these measures to the North American Free Trade Agreement "without the advantages." He said South Carolina has lost more than 30,000 textile jobs since 1993, and added: "We have got to maintain these manufacturing jobs."

Both the Africa and Caribbean trade bills would limit their trade preferences to apparel constructed from U.S.-made components. The House versions are more lenient, allowing a greater variety of apparel products to enter the United States duty- and quota-free.

Supporters say that the measures would create more jobs than they cost in this country and argue that export-producing jobs are generally higher paying. They also contend that both trade bills would be good first steps in helping the economies of two depressed regions.

Progress on Senate Measure is Tied to Minimum Wage, Bankruptcy Bills

OCTOBER 30 — A month before the United States will host a major international trade event, the Senate on Oct. 29 failed to bring up a package of measures that offered the best chance of the year for moving pro-trade legislation.

But Senate Majority Leader Trent Lott, R-Miss., and Minority Leader Tom Daschle, D-S.D., said later that day that the proposals may yet have more life. "We are still very hopeful we can get this done," Lott said.

In an exchange on the Senate floor, Lott and Daschle said they would continue to talk about ways to resolve their largely procedural differences over how to consider the bill. And Lott filed two cloture motions on the measure, which will result in votes Nov. 2 on whether to stem debate on the bill (HR 434) to expand trade with sub-Saharan African nations and a substitute package by Finance Committee Chairman William V. Roth Jr., R-Del.

But progress on the bill is also tied to reaching agreement on a measure (S 625) to overhaul bankruptcy laws and on a plan (S 192) by Edward M. Kennedy, D-Mass., to raise the minimum wage by $1 over two years. Lott and Daschle said they were very close to an agreement that would allow Kennedy to offer his bill as an amendment to the bankruptcy measure and would give Republicans a chance to offer their own minimum wage plan.

While Lott and Daschle appeared optimistic that they would reach an agreement on the disparate bills, it could be difficult to move the trade legislation even if they reach agreement on procedure. Ernest F. Hollings, D-S.C., whose home state has lost many textile jobs in part because of cheap imports, has vowed to fight the bill, and he could slow progress to a snail's pace on his own.

Hollings had help from other Democrats in slowing the bill the week of Oct. 25, despite the fact that passing the measure was a high priority for President Clinton. Clinton made calls to members — including at least six to Lott — to urge the Senate to pass the bills and help salvage his trade agenda, but neither he nor Cabinet members nor the African diplomatic corps watching eagerly from the visitors' gallery could break the Senate logjam.

The difficulty started when Democrats said they would offer a number of amendments to HR 434, and Hollings used every opportunity to stall.

After Hollings and Paul Wellstone, D-Minn., objected to Lott's effort to limit amendments, he resorted to a technique known as "filling the tree," or offering so many amendments that other senators' were blocked.

That led to testy exchanges between Lott and Daschle, who previously had seemed poised to work together on the bills. The standoff slowed Senate action to a crawl much of the week, despite the chamber's 90-8 vote on Oct. 26 to proceed to consideration of HR 434. The measure, which the House passed in July, would have lifted or reduced tariffs on most goods made in the 48 countries of sub-Saharan Africa, including textiles and apparel. *(Vote 341, p. S-68)*

Roth moved immediately after that vote to strip the House language from the bill and substitute four measures that had passed his panel: S 1387, which would lift U.S. tariffs on most goods made in sub-Saharan African nations but remove tariffs and quotas on textiles and apparel assembled from U.S.-made yarns and fabric or if they were handmade, folklore items; S 1389, to similarly eliminate tariffs and quotas on many products made in the Caribbean and Central America; S 1388, to extend through June 30, 2004, the Generalized System of Preferences, which waives duties on products imported from many developing nations; and S 1386, which would reauthorize through Sept. 30, 2001, Trade Adjustment Assistance programs.

The Senate voted 45-46 against invoking cloture on Roth's substitute Oct. 29, falling 15 votes short of the 60 votes necessary. All Democrats present, five Republicans and Independent Robert C. Smith of New Hampshire voted "no." *(Vote 342, p. S-69)*

The difference between the House and Senate bills' textile language would have made it difficult to reach agreement in a conference committee, but Roth and ranking Finance Committee Democrat Daniel Patrick Moynihan of New York chastised the Senate for letting politics come before trade policy, despite Moynihan's vote with other Democrats against invoking cloture on Roth's substitute.

Roth said a positive vote by the Senate would have been "a victory for an outward-looking, forward policy," and the negative vote sent the "wrong signal." But Hollings said Roth's exhortations about the job-creating possibilities of trade were all wrong. "Don't give me anything about jobs," he said. "There ought to be ashes in their mouths."

Free Trade Backers Celebrate as Bill Passes Senate

NOVEMBER 6 — Advocates of trade expansion won a rare victory Nov. 3 when the Senate passed a measure to eliminate tariffs and duties on many goods from sub-Saharan Africa, the Caribbean and Central America.

The 76-19 vote also broke a dry spell for the Senate, which had not passed significant pro-trade legislation in six years. *(Vote 353, p. S-70)*

The victory was largely symbolic because members are unlikely to reconcile differences between the House and Senate versions of the bill (HR 434) until Congress reconvenes next year, but it gave the Clinton administration a hard-fought win on its trade agenda.

Passing the measure had been a major priority for the administration, which lobbied vigorously for the bill in large part because it did not want to go to the World Trade Organization (WTO) meeting in Seattle later this month without positive movement on initiatives to expand trade.

After members passed the bill, U.S. Trade Representative Charlene Barshefsky waited outside the chamber to congratulate them. "The passage of this bill demonstrates the absolute commitment to U.S. leadership on trade policy," Barshefsky said. Had the bill failed, the effect on the WTO meeting and U.S. trade efforts would have been "quite negative," she added.

The bill's easy passage came less than a week after the measure appeared likely to die on the Senate floor, the victim of partisan procedural fights.

But after Majority Leader Trent Lott, R-Miss., and Minority Leader Tom Daschle, D-S.D., agreed on which amendments would be offered, the Senate dramatically reversed course. Senators voted 74-23 on Nov. 2 to stem debate, or invoke cloture, on an amendment by Finance Committee Chairman William V. Roth Jr., R-Del., that substituted four Senate bills for the version the House had passed in July. *(Vote 344, p. S-69)*

Roth and Finance Committee ranking Democrat Daniel Patrick Moynihan of New York were relieved by the outcome. "Now at least we can go to Seattle and say, 'Here are our bona fides,' " Moynihan said.

As amended by the Senate, HR 434 would lift U.S. tariffs on most goods made in sub-Saharan African nations but only remove tariffs and quotas on textiles and apparel items if they were handmade folklore items or assembled from U.S.-made fabric and yarns. That measure originally was approved in committee as S 1387. The Senate-passed bill also included S 1389, which would eliminate tariffs and quotas on many products made in the Caribbean and Central America; S 1388, to extend through June 30, 2004, the generalized system of preferences, which waives duties on products imported from many developing nations; and S 1386, to reauthorize trade adjustment assistance programs through Sept. 30, 2001. Trade assistance aims to retrain industrial workers who lose their jobs because of trade.

The House version of HR 434 would have lifted or reduced tariffs on most goods, including textiles and apparel, made in the 48 countries of sub-Saharan Africa.

Hollings Backs Off

Had the Senate not voted to invoke cloture, which limits debate to 30 minutes and amendments to those that are germane, bill opponents led by Ernest F. Hollings, D-S.C., could have talked the measure to death.

Hollings opposed the bill throughout the debate, saying it was unfair to U.S. workers and would lead to more job losses in his state's textile industry. But after most other Democrats abandoned their opposition to debate and voted for cloture, Hollings began to run out of steam, especially after the chamber voted Nov. 2 to table, or kill, his three amendments.

One, which the Senate tabled 54-43, would have required the president to negotiate a side agreement on labor to accompany the measure, as had been done in the 1993 North American Free Trade Agreement (NAFTA). Another Hollings amendment would have required the president to negotiate a side agreement on environmental issues as had been done in NAFTA. It was tabled, 57-40. *(Votes 345, 347, p. S-69; 1993 Almanac, p. 171)*

A third would have withheld the bill's tariff-reducing benefits from countries that did not establish tariff "rates identical to the tariff rates applied by the United States to that country." It was tabled, 70-27. *(Vote 348, p. S-69)*

The Senate also tabled:

- A proposal by Russell D. Feingold, D-Wis., to establish fines and prison sentences for importers and retailers who bring goods into the United States that are made in other countries but shipped through African, Caribbean or Central American countries to avoid U.S. quotas and tariffs. Such a practice is known as "transshipment." The vote was 53-44. *(Vote 346, p. S-69)*
- A proposal by Arlen Specter, R-Pa., to allow U.S. individuals and companies harmed by imports "dumped" at below-market prices to sue foreign companies and countries for redress. It was tabled, 54-42. *(Vote 350, p. S-70)*

The Senate adopted, 96-0, a far-reaching amendment by Tom Harkin, D-Iowa, that would require countries to "meet and effectively enforce" an International Labor Organization convention that aims to eliminate child labor. *(Vote 351, p. S-70)*

Amendments adopted by voice vote included:

- One by Roth to, among other changes, establish a trade representative specifically for agriculture issues and extend permanent normal trade status to goods from Albania and Kyrgyzstan.

• A proposal by Kent Conrad, D-N.D., and Charles E. Grassley, R-Iowa, to extend trade adjustment assistance to farmers and fishermen, giving them cash benefits of up to $10,000 a year.

• An amendment by Conrad and Grassley that would set goals for agricultural negotiations in the next round of WTO talks and require the administration to seek prior approval from Congress before negotiating a reduction in U.S. tariffs on imported farm goods. ◆

House Seeks To Aid Steel Industry by Passing Bill To Impose Import Quotas

Box Score

- **Bill:** HR 975
- **Legislative action: House** passed HR 975 (H Rept 106-52), 289-141, March 17.

Senate failed to invoke cloture on HR 975, 42-57, on June 22. Sixty votes are required for cloture.

SUMMARY

The House overwhelmingly passed a bill to impose quotas on steel imports, but the Senate failed to limit debate, or invoke cloture, on taking up the measure. With steel industry supporters shifting gears to deal with imports by strengthening U.S. trade laws, the measure seems unlikely to resurface.

Congress' concerns about the financial crisis facing the steel industry rose and fell with import statistics. Early in the year, with several steel companies declaring bankruptcy and laying off thousands of workers, steel supporters in the House, led by Peter J. Visclosky, D-Ind., and Ralph Regula, R-Ohio, introduced a measure they said would heal the industry's wounds. It would have required the president to impose quotas on steel imports within 60 days, with the quotas set at the average of the monthly import volume from July 1994 to June 1997, before the import surge. The quotas would have expired after three years. Foreign steelmakers would have been required to give the Commerce Department advance notice of planned steel shipments.

House supporters pushed the bill through the chamber with a majority so large it surprised them, but the measure stalled in the Senate. Senators were lobbied by the administration, which said the bill would violate international agreements, and by agricultural interests, which worried that countries would retaliate against them for steel quotas. Also, many members did not feel a need to do more for steel, because they had just voted for $1 billion in loan guarantees (HR 1664 — PL 106-51) to the industry.

With imports in many categories of steel abating, the industry and its congressional supporters are focusing less on imposing import quotas than on strengthening U.S. trade laws to make it easier for affected industries to petition for tariffs on nations that dump goods or whose products cause injury to domestic industries. But if imports surge again, the industry may turn again to the quota approach.

House Bill Puts Free-Traders Between Big Steel And a Hard Place

MARCH 13 — The nation's 170,000 steelworkers and their bosses continue to clamor for congressional action to curb the amount of foreign-made steel entering the United States, even though government figures show imports beginning to abate.

As a result, the House is likely to consider a measure (HR 975) the week of March 15 that would require the president to impose quotas and tariffs when steel imports reach certain levels. It also would set up a monitoring system requiring the executive branch to pay more attention to steel imports.

The bill is unlikely to be signed into law — the Clinton administration and Republican leaders both oppose it — but its consideration, and likely passage, on the House floor promises a lively debate and a dilemma for those caught between steel lobbyists and free-trade instincts.

Members from the Rust Belt and other highly unionized districts will have a chance to rail against the results of free-trade agreements, highlighting the devastation that they believe a glut of imports has caused. Three steel mills have filed for bankruptcy and 10,000 workers have been laid off in the past year as imports doubled from economically distressed countries, such as Japan, Russia and Brazil.

For free-traders, it will be a time to appeal for the United States to stick to the same laws it expects other countries to live by. They are likely to ask: How can the United States expect Europe to remove barriers to sales of U.S. companies' bananas or hormone-treated beef if the United States closes its doors to imported steel?

There are Democrats and Republicans on either side, but when the measure comes to the floor, it is likely to bring with it the strains of partisanship.

The bill, sponsored by Peter J. Visclosky, D-Ind., and including proposals from appropriator Ralph Regula, R-Ohio, moved through the Ways and Means Committee on March 10 at the request of Speaker J. Dennis Hastert, R-Ill., and Majority Leader Dick Armey, R-Texas. They requested that Ways and Means mark up the bill and send it to the floor with a recommendation that the House defeat it.

Committee Chairman Bill Archer, R-Texas, complied with the request, and the panel agreed by voice vote to send the bill to the floor with an unfavorable recommendation.

Archer said Hastert and Armey made the request to prevent bill sponsors, who had garnered more than 200 House cosponsors for a similar measure (HR 506) introduced by Visclosky, from bringing the bill to the floor by alternative means, such as a discharge petition. A successful discharge petition brings a bill to the floor, relieving a committee from jurisdiction over it.

But Sander M. Levin of Michigan, ranking Democrat on the panel's Trade Subcommittee, said he believed there was little danger of such action. He said he thought GOP leaders were calling up the measure to highlight divisions within the Democratic Party while claiming credit for moving a bill, even though they are unlikely to vote for it.

Floor debate also will present an opportunity for nearly all members to criticize the Clinton administration, which many believe did not move fast enough to use current laws to stem steel imports. In 1998, steel imports increased 33 percent, before beginning to subside in December.

HR 975 would cap steel imports at the average amount imported between June 1994 and June 1997. Phil English, R-Pa., a bill supporter, said that would be about 12 million metric tons less than the 35 million metric tons of steel imported in 1998, a gap which he said domestic producers could easily fill. Nancy L. Johnson, R-Conn., objected to those numbers, saying she believed that the amount allowed into the United States would be less than English described.

In a letter to Archer on March 10, White House Chief of Staff John D. Podesta said he will recommend that the president veto the bill if it reaches his desk. Podesta's main objections are that the bill would breach provisions to which the United States agreed when it became part of the World Trade Organization (WTO) in 1994. The organization is the successor to the General Agreement on Tariffs and Trade and was created by the most recent round of those trade talks. *(1994 Almanac, p. 123)*

On the other side of the Democratic Party are House Minority Leader Richard A. Gephardt of Missouri and Minority Whip David E. Bonior of Michigan; they support HR 975, which has 196 cosponsors, including 43 Republicans. By showing that prolabor Democrats support the bill, Republicans may be trying to make life difficult for President Clinton — and especially for Vice President Al Gore, the front-runner to be the Democratic Party's presidential nominee in 2000. Bob Ney, R-Ohio, a cosponsor of HR 975, said in an interview March 10 when asked whether Clinton would veto such a measure in the unlikely event that it makes it through the Senate: "Let's just see what they really do. . . . Mr. Gore better be walking down to the Oval Office, pleading his case."

Bipartisan Opportunity

Floor debate will pit Democrats against each other, but the Ways and Means debate may have opened the door for bipartisan cooperation on amending U.S. trade laws.

Archer strongly opposed the steel bill, but he told Susan Esserman, counsel for the U.S. trade representative, that if her office quickly came up with a plan that "would walk this fine line" between protecting the U.S. steel industry and complying with WTO rules, his committee would "review it and act on it."

Archer's comments followed a discussion in which members suggested that the nation's laws to counter "dumping" of imports on the U.S. market were not as strong as they could be under WTO rules.

The rules, enumerated in Section 201 of the Trade Act of 1974 (PL 93-618), allow the president to place duties on imports in an attempt to help domestic producers, if the International Trade Commission determines that the product is being imported in such high quantities that it is a "substantial cause of serious injury" to the U.S. industry.

A bill that Levin planned to introduce would require only that imports "cause or threaten to cause" serious injury to U.S. industry to prompt duties or other executive action. It would also require the International Trade Commission to make quicker determinations that such a case existed. Currently, such determinations often take into consideration imports over five years, a period so long that Amo Houghton, R-N.Y., said "you're practically out of business" before the administration can take antidumping measures.

Levin said he has talked with Houghton, the trade representative's office and other administration officials in devising his bill. He expects it will be the bill the administration submits, if it submits any. Houghton said he is also working on a bill to amend Section 201.

Neither Levin nor Houghton will be able to offer his bill as an amendment to HR 975, because the Rules Committee is expected to issue a closed rule for floor debate, blocking all amendments.

House Passes Steel Quotas Despite Veto Threat

MARCH 20 — The House easily passed a bill March 17 that would limit the amount of steel imported into the United States, despite worries by some members that the measure sets a bad precedent.

While steel-state and pro-labor members hailed passage of the bill (HR 975) as a victory for workers and "fair trade," the lopsided vote — 289-141 — was prompted, at least in part, by members' knowledge that the measure had little possibility of becoming law. Ninety-one Republicans and 197 Democrats voted for it. *(Vote 56, p. H-22)*

The Senate is not expected to take up a bill including quotas, although Arlen Specter, R-Pa., John D. Rockefeller IV, D-W.Va., and other steel-state senators are likely to try to attach some remedies for the steel industry to a supplemental appropriations measure (S 544). Specter said March 16 that the amendments were unlikely to focus on steel quotas because "it's very hard to get that passed and signed."

The Clinton administration signaled its opposition to the House bill March 10, when White House Chief of Staff John D. Podesta sent a letter to Ways and Means Chairman Bill Archer, R-Texas, threatening a veto, largely because the administration believes the bill would violate international trade agreements.

But members who support the bill, sponsored by Peter J. Visclosky, D-Ind., and Ralph Regula, R-Ohio, charged that the administration had not taken every step it could to stem a flood of imported steel into the country and thereby stop industry job losses. Labor leaders estimate 10,000 U.S. jobs have been lost in the past few years.

Marcy Kaptur, D-Ohio, said it was "unforgivable" that the administration had not moved more quickly to stem imports. "If we . . . cannot stand up for our own when they are being unfairly dumped on . . . when do we stand up for anyone?" But Amo Houghton, R-N.Y., said the bill could hurt U.S. workers by fueling international trading disputes. "We're doing unto others what we do not want others to do unto us," Houghton said. "This bill has a heart, but it does not have a head."

Free-Trade Fallout

The bill would require the president to impose quotas on steel imports within 60 days. The quota would be set at the average of the monthly import volume from July 1994 through June 1997. Quotas would expire after three years. In addition, foreign steelmakers seeking to export their goods to the United States would be required to give the Commerce Department advance notice of the amount of steel they were planning to ship, its origin and other details. The department would have to publish statistics on the advance notices once a week. The department now publishes once a month general import statistics compiled by the Census Bureau.

Archer said the measure would work "like a sledgehammer," but bill supporter Jack Quinn, R-N.Y., said that "of all the other solutions that might be out there, none are taking place. . . .We've not been given any other choice."

Under U.S. laws, which comply with World Trade Organization rules, the president can impose quotas or tariffs on certain imported goods if he determines they are being "dumped" on the U.S. market at prices lower than the price in their own country or if they are sold for less than they cost to make. The president can impose further remedies if the U.S. International Trade Commission finds that the imports have come in such quantities as to cause serious injury to a domestic industry.

In the past month, the Clinton administration took a step to curtail imports by issuing preliminary findings that Japanese and Brazilian companies were selling steel for as much as 71 percent less than it cost to produce, and by finding that the Brazilian government may have illegally subsidized its industry. The Commerce Department has worked with both countries and Russia to stem imports. As a result, imports have dropped in recent months.

But steel-state legislators say other countries have quickly stepped in to fill the vacuum, with China, South Africa and Indonesia doubling their steel exports to the United States. "This is a shell game," said Ron Klink, D-Pa. "We are kidding ourselves."

Philip M. Crane, R-Ill., said the volume of imports was declining and that "what happened in the steel industry is basically history at this moment."

Bill supporters said the issue was not dead for those who have been laid off or companies that have filed for bankruptcy. They said there has been a double standard, with the administration standing up for some business interests in trade disputes, such as Cincinnati-based banana giant Chiquita Brands International, but not for the U.S. steel industry.

"Bananas did not build America. Steel did," said Dennis J. Kucinich, D-Ohio. "Such a trade policy is, in a word, bananas."

Senate Panel OKs Alternative To Quotas

JUNE 19 — The Senate Finance Committee began to move its trade agenda June 16, approving a draft measure that aims to address a steel industry crisis by making it easier for the government to take action against countries with rapidly growing exports to the United States.

Panel Chairman William V. Roth Jr., R-Del., said he intended the bill, approved 9-2, to be a "constructive alternative" to a House-passed steel quota bill (HR 975) headed for the Senate floor. Rick Santorum, R-Pa., the chamber's main GOP proponent of HR 975, said the Senate would hold a cloture vote on it June 22. If cloture fails, the Senate may turn to Roth's bill.

The same day, the Finance Committee plans to mark up four more trade measures, including draft bills to reduce U.S. duties and quotas on goods made in Africa and in the Caribbean and Central America.

Roth said he expected more action on trade bills later in the session and that he had put renewal of fast-track trade negotiating authority for the president "on the top of the list." Fast track mandates that Congress consider trade agreements within 90 days and cast up-or-down votes with no amendments allowed. Roth said he could "think of nothing more disastrous than for the United States to turn our back on the global economy."

Panel members from the right and left urged Roth to move fast track, despite its recurrent failures in the House in recent years. "I think we need to take the initiative," said Connie Mack, R-Fla. But Max Baucus, D-Mont., said senators "must realize . . . it will not be easy. There are other interests that we must pay attention to," such as labor and environmental groups that oppose fast track.

Besides the steel bill, the panel approved by voice vote a House-passed measure (HR 1833) to authorize $2.26 billion for the Customs Service in fiscal 2000 and $2.3 billion in fiscal 2001. Customs was last reauthorized in 1990 (PL 101-382).

Steel Restrictions

The draft steel measure would require the U.S. trade representative to devise a strategy for dealing with "market-distorting practices" that may have contributed to a glut of imported steel on the U.S. market in 1997 and 1998.

The bill also would amend the 1974 Trade Act (PL 93-618) to require that domestic industries requesting relief from imports prove only that imports "cause or threaten to cause serious injury" instead of that imports be a "substantial cause of serious injury, or the threat thereof," as in current law. This has been interpreted to mean that imports must have caused most of the damage to the industry for the administration to take reciprocal steps, such as imposing duties on imports.

The change would bring U.S. law in line with World Trade Organization (WTO) standards that most other nations use, but Phil Gramm, R-Texas, argued that the change would lead to greater protectionism and cause more long-term damage than the House bill.

He called it a "gratuitous change in permanent trade law that is very dangerous," adding that it "does virtually nothing for steel but changes the standards we set by denying Americans the right to buy imports permanently."

Deputy U.S. Trade Representative Richard Fisher told the committee that there "is some room for improvement" in the statute, although he said the flood of imports that caused steel prices to drop drastically has largely abated. That did not stop the Senate from passing a measure (HR 1664) on June 18 that would establish a $1 billion loan guarantee program for steel companies.

John D. Rockefeller IV, D-W.Va., said HR 1664 and the Finance draft bill failed to "address the real problem of steel imports," and he continued to push for a quota measure, which would limit steel imports to pre-1997 levels for 36 months. Rockefeller and Gramm opposed the Finance bill.

The committee defeated, 5-14, an attempt by Gramm to remove the more liberal import injury standards. The panel approved, 11-8, an amendment by Orrin G. Hatch, R-Utah, and ranking Democrat Daniel Patrick Moynihan of New York to require that at least half the members of an affected industry, as determined by the Commerce Department, approve before the president enters into voluntary import reductions with a country.

The administration often uses such negotiations to reduce imports when domestic industries are hurt. Voluntary limits are less likely to trigger a trade war than duties or other legal restrictions. But Moynihan argued that such agreements circumvent stronger laws written to help domestic industries. Others said the provision would set a bad precedent. It would be "giving an industry that has a vested interest a veto," Mack said.

Senate Cloture Vote Fails

JUNE 26 — Supporters of a bill to set quotas on imported steel could not overcome the opposition of other industries and the Clinton administration as the Senate took a vote June 22 that likely marks the ends of the line for the legislation. Senators voted 42-57 against limiting debate and proceeding to the bill (HR 975). *(Vote 178, p. S-36)*

The House passed it, 289-141, on March 17. It would limit the amount of steel imported into the United States to pre-1997 levels for 36 months. The bill's main Senate supporters, Rick Santorum, R-Pa., and John D. Rockefeller IV, D-W.Va., said three factors hurt their efforts, despite the presence of hundreds of steelworkers lobbying legislators that day:

- Strong opposition from the administration, which feared political repercussions for Vice President Al Gore if President Clinton were forced to choose between free-trade interests, which opposed the bill, and unions, which supported it.
- Surging opposition from farm groups, which worried that they would make an easy target for other countries' retaliation against steel quotas.
- Senate passage June 18 of a bill (HR 1664) that would guarantee $1 billion in loans to struggling steel companies. Because members had already voted to help the steel industry, some did not feel pressure to do more.

Senate rules require 60 votes to limit debate, or invoke cloture. To reach that level, supporters would have needed the votes of all 45 Democrats and at least 15 Republicans. Santorum provided the 15 GOP votes but 17 Democrats voted against the bill, including some, such as Edward M. Kennedy, D-Mass., who generally side with labor leaders. "The White House pulled out every single stop," Rockefeller said.

Two days after the vote, however, monthly import statistics showed that the amount of steel entering the country had increased 30 percent from April to May, which may breathe new life into other steel measures.

Majority Leader Trent Lott, R-Miss., said yet another steel-related measure, a draft bill the Senate Finance Committee approved June 16 to make it easier for the government to take action against countries whose imports are hurting U.S. companies, may come to the floor the week of June 28.

Santorum and Rockefeller would not rule out offering HR 975 as an amendment to the Finance measure, or working to incorporate aspects of it.

But Rockefeller said most action is now likely to come outside Congress. Commerce Secretary William M. Daley said June 21 that his department was opening investigations into allegations that 12 countries "dumped" steel into the United States in the last two years at prices lower than it costs to make the steel, or less than it costs in the originating country. The Commerce Department imposed duties on Japan in June after officials determined steel had been dumped. It is negotiating with Brazil and Russia to reduce steel imports. ◆

Lawmakers Vote To Develop Trade With Asian Nations Along Historic 'Silk Road'

In its second go-around, legislation expanding aid to central Asia became law despite complications with the vehicle it used to get to the White House. The Senate deleted the most controversial part of the bill, which would have allowed the president to permit direct aid to the oil-rich nation of Azerbaijan.

SUMMARY

The House in August passed a stand-alone bill (HR 1152) by voice vote to expand U.S. aid to countries along the historic "Silk Road" trade route in central Asia and the South Caucasus region. The Senate attached a similar measure (S 579) to the fiscal 2000 foreign operations appropriations bill (HR 2606), which was vetoed by President Clinton, reborn in a fresh package (HR 3196) and eventually included in the fiscal 2000 omnibus appropriations package (HR 3194).

The Silk Road measure aims to develop economic cooperation and U.S. trade and resolve regional conflicts in the former Soviet states of Armenia, Georgia, Kazakhstan, Kyrgyzstan, Tajikistan, Turkmenistan and Uzbekistan. Each has suffered turmoil since the breakup of the Soviet Union.

Rep. Doug Bereuter, a Nebraska Republican, and Sen. Sam Brownback, a Kansas Republican, the primary sponsors, say the region is a national security priority because of its proximity to Russia, China, Iran, Afghanistan and Turkey. The region also holds as much as $4 trillion in oil and gas reserves. Similar legislation failed to reach the floor in the 105th Congress.

The legislation authorizes no new funds, but directs some previously appropriated aid for former Soviet states in the Balkans and Eastern Europe.

The Senate defeated an attempt to give the president authority to waive a ban on direct aid to Azerbaijan, which is denied assistance because of its food blockade against the disputed Armenian enclave of Nagorno-Karabakh.

Box Score

- **Bill:** HR 3194 — PL 106-113
- **Legislative action: House** passed HR 1152 by voice vote Aug. 2.

House adopted the conference report on HR 2606 (H Rept 106-339), 214-211, on Oct. 5.

Senate cleared HR 2606, 51-49, on Oct. 6.

President vetoed HR 2606 on Oct. 18.

House passed HR 3196, 316-100, on Nov. 5.

House adopted the conference report on HR 3194, 296-135, on Nov. 18.

Senate cleared HR 3194, 74-24, on Nov. 19.

President signed HR 3194 on Nov. 29.

House Panel OKs Central Asian Trade Measure

JUNE 26 — A bill that would expand U.S. aid to countries along the historic "Silk Road" trade route won the approval of a House International Relations subcommittee on June 23.

The Asia and Pacific Subcommittee approved the bill (HR 1152) by voice vote. The measure aims to strengthen democratic governments, resolve regional conflicts and promote U.S. business interests in Armenia, Azerbaijan, Georgia, Kazakstan, Kyrgyzstan, Tajikistan, Turkmenistan and Uzbekistan.

Those countries together hold as much as $4 trillion in oil and gas reserves and have been embroiled in political and social conflict since the breakup of the Soviet Union. They also have not been fully included in aid programs aimed at the Balkans and Eastern Europe.

Rep. Richard M. Burr, R-N.C., offered and then withdrew an amendment designed to strengthen the bill's non-proliferation requirements. As written, the bill would prohibit aid to any country that developed weapons of mass destruction. Burr's amendment, which he plans to offer again at full committee, would also deny aid to any country that knowingly allowed technology or material destined for nuclear, biological or chemical weapons to pass through its territory.

Unlike similar legislation (S 579) pending in the Senate, the House bill omits a controversial provision that would repeal a ban on certain types of aid to Azerbaijan. Some lawmakers have insisted that the United States deny aid to Azerbaijan as long as that country continues its food blockade against Nagorno-Karabakh, an Armenian enclave in Azerbaijan.

(For Senate committee action, see sanctions, p. 23-26; for inclusion of "Silk Road" provisions in foreign operations appropriations, see p. 2-62.)

Full Committee Approves Bill

JULY 24 — The House International Relations Committee voted July 22 to expand U.S. aid and support to central Asian countries along the ancient "Silk Road" trade route, but not before attaching a provision that would ensure the aid goes only to nations with democratically elected leaders.

The panel approved, by voice vote, a bill (HR 1152) meant to promote economic cooperation and U.S. business and to resolve regional conflicts in the former Soviet states of Armenia, Georgia, Kazakstan, Kyrgyzstan, Tajikistan, Turkmenistan and Uzbekistan.

These countries, which have vast oil and gas reserves, have suffered political and social turmoil since the breakup of the Soviet Union in 1991 and have not been included in other regional aid programs.

Doug Bereuter, R-Neb., who sponsored the bill and chairs the panel's Asia and the Pacific Subcommittee, said the countries' shared borders with Iran, Afghanistan and China make them "front-line states in the effort to combat counterfreedom."

Prompted by concerns raised by Dana Rohrabacher, R-Calif., the committee adopted, by voice vote, an amendment requiring the president to certify that countries receiving aid hold free and fair elections, free of substantial criticism by international organizations.

However, the committee struck language that would have required the president to also certify that the countries have adequate judicial systems or are undergoing judicial reform.

The panel defeated by voice vote another Rohrabacher amendment that would have limited any U.S. peacekeeping operations in the region.

The Senate attached similar legislation to its fiscal 2000 foreign operations spending bill (S 1234 — S Rept 106-81) after deleting a provision that would have allowed the president to waive restrictions on aid to Azerbaijan.

House Passes 'Silk Road' Bill

AUGUST 7 — The House passed legislation (HR 1152) Aug. 2 authorizing support for economic reform, democracy and regional integration in the Caucasus and Central Asia. Along with similar Senate legislation, the measure marks a new U.S. commitment to a region rich in natural resources but bedeviled by ethnic conflicts and threatened by powerful neighbors.

The Senate bill (S 579) has been incorporated in the Senate version of the fiscal 2000 foreign operations spending bill (S 1234).

Doug Bereuter, R-Neb., chairman of the House International Relations Subcommittee on Asia and the Pacific, said, "There is much at stake for our national security" in the region, which he noted is "strategically located at the geographic nexus of Russia, China, Iran, Afghanistan and Turkey."

"Given the region's clear importance," Bereuter said, "it is time for the United States to become more energetically and effectively engaged in the region."

The bill passed by voice vote, under suspension of the rules, the process used to consider non-controversial legislation. Such bills are subject to limited debate and must pass by a two-thirds majority.

Yet, the measure was not entirely without controversy. The Clinton administration has objected to an amendment added by the International Relations Committee in its July 22 markup. The amendment would require the president to certify that countries receiving aid hold free and fair elections, with no substantial criticism by international organizations.

Such a requirement could effectively bar aid to some countries, given the region's less-than-stellar record in conducting elections. The bill would apply to the former Soviet states of Armenia, Georgia, Kazakstan, Kyrgyzstan, Tajikistan, Turkmenistan and Uzbekistan, which lie along the ancient "Silk Road" trade route.

Lawmakers steered clear of the most sensitive issue for U.S. policymakers in the region: the dispute between Armenia and neighboring Azerbaijan over Nagorno-Karabakh, a majority Armenian enclave in the mountains of western Azerbaijan. The area has seen sporadic fighting over the past 10 years.

In 1992, prodded by pro-Armenian lawmakers, Congress included Section 907 of the Freedom Support Act (PL 102-511), which banned government-to-government assistance to punish Azerbaijan for its blockade of landlocked Armenia. Armenia says the blockade continues to hamper shipments of food, medicine and other vital supplies. *(1992 Almanac, p. 523)*

Since a fragile, Russian-mediated cease-fire took hold in 1994, however, energy companies have been pushing for the ban to be overturned, in order to improve relations with oil-rich Azerbaijan. Congress already has loosened the restrictions to allow trade-related assistance.

The Senate, in considering the fiscal 2000 foreign operations appropriations bill, debated and ultimately defeated a proposal to allow the president to waive the current ban.

The House shied away from a similar debate after voting last year, 231-182, to retain the ban. *(1998 Almanac, p. 2-45)* ◆

Lawmakers, Administration Take Steps To Ease Sanctions On Exports to Select Nations

Box Score

- **Bills:** S 757, HR 1906, HR 2561, HR 2606

SUMMARY

A Senate-passed provision that would have lifted sanctions from exports of food and medicine was dropped from the fiscal 2000 agriculture appropriations bill (HR 1906) in conference, but a waiver of sanctions on India and Pakistan was included in the fiscal 2000 defense appropriations bill (HR 2561) that President Clinton signed into law (PL 106-79) on Oct. 25. Legislation calling for a cost-benefit analysis of all sanctions (S 757) was not considered. The first version of a fiscal 2000 foreign operations spending bill (HR 2606 — Conference report: H Rept 106-339) included broad sanctions against Indonesia because of its actions in East Timor, but the bill was vetoed by Clinton. The final version of the foreign operations bill (HR 3422) did not include the East Timor sanctions language. *(Foreign operations, p. 2-62)*

With business and agriculture groups complaining that selective U.S. export sanctions deprived them of markets overseas, Congress and the White House took steps to roll back some sanctions but stopped short of major changes, such as lifting limits on food and medicine shipped to Cuba.

Sanctions opponents such as Sens. Richard G. Lugar, R-Ind., and Christopher J. Dodd, D-Conn., appeared to have some momentum early in the year. Lugar reintroduced a sweeping measure (S 757) that would force Congress to weigh the costs and benefits of new sanctions and automatically terminate those not renewed by Congress.

Sanctions opponents scored their biggest victory when the defense appropriations bill (HR 2561) gave Clinton permanent authority to waive sanctions on India and Pakistan imposed last year after both tested nuclear weapons.

The Senate on Aug. 4 adopted an amendment to its version of the agriculture spending bill to exempt exports of food and medicine from current and future U.S. sanctions, but the provision was removed in conference.

On his own, Clinton eased food and medicine sanctions on Iran, North Korea, Sudan, Libya and, to a much more limited extent, Cuba.

Clinton Eases Trade Restrictions On Cuba

JANUARY 9 — President Clinton on Jan. 5 unveiled several small steps to increase contacts with Cuba. But he stopped short of calling for a major review of the U.S. embargo on Fidel Castro's regime, because of criticism from Cuban-American groups and the political concerns of Vice President Al Gore.

Clinton's decision to ease restrictions on travel, mail and financial transfers won support from key lawmakers in both parties, although it prompted criticism from others who thought the measures went too far or not far enough.

Among the supporters was Senate Foreign Relations Committee Chairman Jesse Helms, R-N.C., co-author of a 1996 law (PL 104-114) that tightened the longstanding U.S. embargo on trade with Cuba. *(1996 Almanac, p. 9-6)*

Helms spokesman Marc Thiessen said Clinton's decision was "a strong reaffirmation of current U.S. law and a rejection of those who want to lift the embargo." He noted that the proposals include some elements Helms put forward in legislation (S 2080) last year. Helms kept the bill in his committee.

By executive order, Clinton took steps that would:

- Allow any U.S. resident to send up to $1,200 a year to Cuban citizens and non-governmental organizations.
- Authorize more exchanges of academics, athletes and scientists. As a first step, Clinton said he would allow the Baltimore Orioles to explore the possibility of playing two exhibition baseball games against the Cuban national team this spring, one in Baltimore and one in Cuba, as long as the proceeds go to Cuban charities rather than the Castro government.
- Allow sales of food, fertilizer and pesticides to religious groups, privately owned restaurants and private farmers in Cuba.
- Permit routes for charter flights for family members between the United States and Cuba beyond the current Miami-Havana route.
- Seek to establish direct mail service between the United States and Cuba as called for in the 1992 Cuban Democracy Act, which was part of the fiscal 1993 defense authorization bill (PL 102-484). *(1992 Almanac, p. 483)*
- Strengthen Radio and TV Marti, the U.S. government's surrogate broadcasters to Cuba.

Secretary of State Madeleine K. Albright said Jan. 5 that the policy "is designed to promote closer ties between our people and those of Cuba without providing aid and comfort to a repressive and backward-looking regime."

No Full Review

When Pope John Paul II visited Cuba a year ago, he called for an end to the U.S. embargo and for political and social change in Cuba, including an enhanced role for the Catholic Church. Clinton announced some steps to ease the embargo in March, after the Pope's visit.

But the president decided not to back a call from 18 senators, led by Armed Services Committee Chairman John W. Warner, R-Va., to establish an independent national commission to review U.S. policy toward Cuba.

"I think it's a real lost opportunity," Warner said. "Now it will be difficult for the president to form the commission without bumping up against the 2000 election."

Many critics of the proposal, such as Sen. Bob Graham, D-Fla., considered the plan for a review commission a backdoor means of ending the embargo, which would undermine Albright's authority and paralyze U.S. policy toward Cuba while the commission met.

Knowledgeable aides and lawmakers said the White House had been ready to sign off on a commission but had been persuaded not to by Gore, who recently announced that he would run for president in 2000.

A Gore spokesman would not comment on the vice president's role, saying he could not disclose Gore's views in internal policy discussions.

But Republican and Cuban-American groups had already started to call the panel "the Gore commission" as a warning of the political consequences.

Rep. Robert Menendez of New Jersey, an influential Cuban-American Democrat, said he warned Gore that if the commission was approved, Gore might lose the key electoral states of New Jersey and Florida, which boast large Cuban-American populations.

Nonetheless, Warner and Democratic colleague Christopher J. Dodd of Connecticut hope to revive the commission idea later.

They also intend to press forward with a revised version of a bill they championed last year (S 1391) to allow the widespread sale of food and medicine to Cuba.

Vocal Opponents

Yet, Cuban-American lawmakers said Clinton already has gone too far.

"This doesn't send a message of real hope for the slave population of Cuba," said GOP Rep. Ileana Ros-Lehtinen of Florida. "They [administration officials] are nibbling at the edges because they are not willing to deal with the heart of the problem, which is Fidel Castro."

She and other Cuban-American members complained that the "incredibly absurd" provisions allowing the sale of food and agricultural products would violate the 1996 law, would do little for impoverished Cubans, and could easily be circumvented by the Castro regime.

Joseph R. Biden Jr. of Delaware, ranking Democrat on the Senate Foreign Relations Committee, said the response of Ros-Lehtinen and others showed there was little political gain in taking such limited actions.

"Partial measures don't satisfy anybody," Biden said.

Senators Promote Bills To Reduce Trade Sanctions

JANUARY 30 — Pressed by agricultural groups eager to open overseas markets at a time of low crop prices, lawmakers are drawing up a series of bills that would limit the scope of economic sanctions against other nations.

First out of the box is legislation (S 315) by Sens. John Ashcroft, R-Mo., and Tom Harkin, D-Iowa, that would establish a new process to limit food embargoes on foreign countries.

The bill would require Congress within 100 days to approve or disapprove an embargo instituted by the president or it would expire. Embargoes approved by Congress, on the other hand, would have a maximum life of one year, but could be terminated earlier by the president.

That bill was cosponsored by Sen. Chuck Hagel, R-Neb., who also is cosponsoring three other anti-sanctions measures.

A bill (S 327) he cosponsored with Sen. Christopher J. Dodd, D-Conn., would exempt food and medicine from all sanctions. Dodd managed to pass similar legislation last year as part of the fiscal 1999 agricultural appropriations bill, which later became part of the omnibus spending bill (PL 105-277).

However, lawmakers who were determined to keep all existing sanctions on Cuba and Iran persuaded Congress to continue the ban on sales of food and medicine to countries the State Department says sponsor terrorism. The Hagel-Dodd bill would eliminate that exception.

Dodd and Hagel also are teaming up on legislation that would allow the president to waive existing congressionally imposed sanctions, while giving Congress 90 days to overturn such a decision.

And Hagel intends to cosponsor legislation that Sen. Richard G. Lugar, R-Ind., will reintroduce aimed at forcing a cost-benefit analysis of proposed sanctions and limiting sanctions to two years unless renewed.

House Panel OKs Bill That Would Let Congress Veto Embargoes

FEBRUARY 13 — Warning that an increase in the use of export sanctions to achieve foreign policy goals is threatening the livelihood of American farmers and ranchers, the House Agriculture Committee gave voice vote approval on Feb. 10 to a bill (HR 17) that would require congressional approval of agricultural embargoes ordered by the president.

Thomas W. Ewing, R-Ill., who sponsored the measure, said Congress must play an oversight role because farmers are "bearing a disproportionate share of the burden of American foreign policy decisions."

Under the bill, Congress would have 100 days to approve or disapprove any farm export embargo. Embargoes approved by Congress would be limited to a year, and the president could end them sooner.

The bill would not apply to agricultural products that are part of a total embargo on a particular country such as Cuba.

Rep. Cal Dooley, D-Calif., contended that the bill is too limited in scope to affect most of the embargoes imposed on agricultural products. Dooley challenged committee members to support broader legislation that would require Congress to approve any economic sanction that "could have a significant and adverse impact on our economy."

A companion measure (S 315) was introduced in the Senate by John Ashcroft, R-Mo.

Members Seek To Extend Waiver Of Sanctions On India, Pakistan

MARCH 6 — In the name of protecting U.S. farmers, some House members are trying to extend the president's authority to waive agricultural and humanitarian sanctions against India and Pakistan.

President Clinton imposed trade and credit sanctions on both countries shortly after they exploded nuclear weapons in May 1998. His action was required by the Arms Control Export Act contained in the 1994 State Department authorization law (PL 103-236).

Lawmakers responded to pressure from U.S. agricultural interests with an amendment to the fiscal 1999 omnibus appropriations bill (PL 105-277) by Republican Sen. Sam Brownback, of Kansas that allowed the president to waive the sanctions until Sept. 30, 1999. *(1998 Almanac, p. 2-112)*

This year, a provision in a House bill (HR 973) that aims to increase congressional tracking of U.S. military arms sales also would allow the president to waive sanctions against Pakistan and India for another year, until September 2000. The House International Relations Committee approved the measure by voice vote on March 4.

Lawmakers have said that imposing agricultural sanctions hurts American farmers and does little to deter foreign nations from developing nuclear weapons.

Republican Rep. Doug Bereuter, of Nebraska said extending the waiver authority is especially important with respect to Pakistan, which buys nearly one-third of the winter wheat produced by farmers in the Pacific Northwest.

Bereuter said the sanctions waiver also could greatly affect other agricultural sales, such as those of processed food.

Estimates of total savings to U.S. farmers from waiving the sanctions reach as high as $1 billion a year.

Anti-Sanctions Movement Builds In Both Chambers

MARCH 26 — Under pressure from business and agricultural groups, key lawmakers are making new efforts to restrict the use of unilateral economic sanctions overseas.

A bipartisan group of senators and House members introduced legislation that seeks to make it more difficult for Congress to impose restrictions on trade or foreign aid.

The Senate bill (S 757), introduced March 26, is sponsored by Agriculture, Nutrition and Forestry Committee Chairman Richard G. Lugar, R-Ind., as well as Nebraskans Chuck Hagel, a Republican, and Bob Kerrey, a Democrat. It also enjoys the support of Majority Leader Trent Lott, R-Miss.

The House version (HR 1244), introduced March 24, is sponsored by Philip M. Crane, R-Ill., chairman of the Trade Subcommittee of the Ways and Means Committee, as well as by Bill Archer, R-Texas, chairman of the full committee. Crane said he hopes to have his subcommittee mark up the bill in April, with consideration by the full committee shortly thereafter.

Crane expressed optimism that Republican House leaders, who share a free-trade ideology and large numbers of agricultural constituents, would back the measure.

Farm groups anxious for overseas markets are pushing particularly hard for the legislation. "There is a dire emergency throughout rural America to raise commodity prices," said Earl Pomeroy, D-N.D., a member of the House Agriculture Committee. "In a global marketplace, enacting sanctions makes as much sense as saying, 'Knock it off or I'll knock *my* block off.' "

The bills make special provisions for farmers. For example, they would exclude food and medicine, including U.S. government financing for such exports, from future export sanctions. And they would authorize the Agriculture Department to increase export promotion programs to compensate farmers when they lose markets because of U.S. economic sanctions.

The bills would also give the president permanent authority to exempt agricultural and humanitarian exports from sanctions required by the Arms Export Control Act contained in the 1994 State Department authorization law (PL 103-236).

Congress gave the president that authority for one year after he was forced to cut off U.S. credits and loans, including agricultural export credits, as part of sanctions against India and Pakistan for testing nuclear weapons.

Grain for Iran

Farmers may also benefit from other pending legislation. A supplemental fiscal 1999 spending bill (S 544 — S Rept 106-8), passed by the Senate on March 23, included a sense-of the-Senate amendment encouraging the administration to grant a license for the sale of $500 million of wheat and other commodities to Iran — sales that are generally prohibited by law now.

The amendment, by Republican Policy Committee Chairman Larry E. Craig of Idaho, was approved March 18 by unanimous consent and without debate.

Pomeroy said he is hoping to offer a similar proposal in the House. "I think it will be easy to cobble together a bipartisan coalition on the House side," he said.

Still, these and other anti-sanctions efforts must overcome the opposition of Senate Foreign Relations Chairman Jesse Helms, R-N.C., and House International Relations Chairman Benjamin A. Gilman, R-N.Y.

"We have a few mountains to climb, and the two chairmen are mountains," said Hagel.

Last year, Helms led a successful effort in the Senate to block a provision similar to the Lugar-Hagel-Kerrey bill in the fiscal 1999 agricultural spending bill.

During the same debate, Helms and Robert G. Torricelli, D-N.J., crippled an amendment that would have exempted food, fertilizer, medicine and medical equipment from sanctions.

On March 23, however, Helms did support another anti-sanctions measure when the Foreign Relations Committee approved by voice vote legislation (S 579) by Sam Brownback, R-Kan., designed to bolster development and improve relations with countries in the oil- and gas-rich region of the Caspian Sea.

The most controversial provision of the "Silk Road" bill, strongly backed by U.S. energy companies that have invested heavily in the region, would eliminate a ban on most kinds of direct U.S. aid to Azerbaijan. The oil-rich nation is locked in a longstanding struggle with neighboring Armenia over the disputed enclave of Nagorno-Karabakh.

The committee approved the bill last year, but it never reached the Senate floor because of opposition from Mitch McConnell, R-Ky., chairman of the Foreign Operations Appropriations Subcommittee. The ban was lifted by the fiscal 1999 foreign operations appropriations bill in the House, but was reinstated on the floor.

Clinton Eases Some Sanctions Against Iran, Libya and Sudan

MAY 1 — Partly in response to farm-state lawmakers and agribusiness groups, President Clinton ordered a major policy change April 28, easing sanctions on the sale of food and medicine to Iran, Libya and Sudan.

Clinton's executive order will permit case-by-case consideration of food and medicine sales to those countries, administration officials said. U.S. companies have been banned from exporting to those nations.

Clinton chose to sidestep some political trouble spots, retaining current restrictions on sales to Cuba, North Korea and Iraq. And he refused to lift restrictions on investment and trade in energy with Libya and Iran, both oil-rich nations.

The decision brought near-unanimous approval from Capitol Hill, where support has been growing for legislation (S 757, HR 1244) to ease unilateral U.S. sanctions on trade with other countries, particularly in food and medicine.

Senate Agriculture Committee Chairman Richard G. Lugar, R-Ind., who has spearheaded the anti-sanctions movement on Capitol Hill, welcomed the administration's decision.

"I do not believe that food and medicine should be used as a tool of foreign policy," Lugar said in a statement.

The action also drew surprising support from Senate Foreign Relations Committee Chairman Jesse Helms, R-N.C., a staunch defender of sanctions.

Helms said he had been assured by Stuart E. Eizenstat, undersecretary of State for economic, business and agricultural affairs, that exports to those countries would not receive any U.S. government assistance. Helms also said the administration would work with Congress to ensure that pesticides and other items with potential military use would not be exported.

"If Iran wants to pay cash-on-the-barrel for American grain, that is fine with me," Helms said in a statement. "Every dollar Iran spends on U.S. farm products is a dollar that Iran cannot spend on terrorism or weapons of mass destruction."

Eizenstat told reporters that the decision sprang from a two-year review of U.S. sanctions policy that concluded that allowing food and medicine sales to rogue states "doesn't enhance a nation's military capability or ability to support terrorism."

The change could permit Niki Trading Co., for instance, to sell 3.5 million tons of wheat and other commodities to Iran, valued at about $500 million. The Senate expressed its support for the sale during consideration of a supplemental fiscal 1999 spending bill (S 544 — S Rept 106-8) passed by the Senate on March 23.

Warmer Climate

The change comes amid a possible thaw in U.S.-Iranian relations after the 1997 election of moderate Iranian President Mohammad Khatami.

Administration officials said the sanctions decision was not made as a gesture to Khatami, but in recognition that sanctions on food and medicine had often backfired as a foreign policy tool. As if to illustrate the point, the Treasury Department April 28 turned down Mobil Corp.'s request for a license to swap crude oil from the Caspian Sea region with Iran.

Libya won wider acceptance in the international community and in the United States after its April 5 surrender of two suspects in the 1988 bombing of Pan Am Flight 103 over Lockerbie, Scotland.

Business groups, such as the U.S. Chamber of Commerce, complained that because of opposition from Helms and others, Clinton did not ease sanctions on Cuba. Those sanctions were written into law in 1996 (PL 104-114). *(1996 Almanac, p. 9-6)*

Rep. Jose E. Serrano, D-N.Y., and Sen. Christopher J. Dodd, D-Conn., introduced bills (HR 1644, S 926) April 29 to allow the sale of food, medicines, and medical products to Cuba.

House Panel Approves Bill To Limit Food Embargoes

JUNE 12 — A measure aimed at limiting the president's ability to embargo exports of U.S. farm products was approved by the House International Relations Committee by voice vote June 10.

Under the bill (HR 17), the president would have to notify Congress within five days of imposing an embargo on farm products and explain its purpose and time period. Congress then would have 100 days to approve or disapprove his action. An embargo approved by Congress would be limited to one year but could be terminated earlier by the president. He could waive the requirements in case of war or national emergency.

Identical legislation sailed through the House during the 105th Congress but died in the Senate when the session ended. The House Agriculture Committee approved HR 17 by voice vote Feb. 10.

Agriculture and business groups have been lobbying against the use of trade sanctions to punish other countries, saying they hurt U.S. industries more.

In most cases, the president imposes sanctions using the authority of previous legislation.

Though he supported the bill, House International Relations Committee Chairman Benjamin A. Gilman, R-N.Y., said it would not substantially change current U.S. policy on economic sanctions.

Agriculture Secretary Dan Glickman has estimated that food sanctions reduce exports by about $500 million a year, a tiny fraction of total sales. But staunch supporters of the bill from farming districts said agriculture-specific sanctions unfairly hurt U.S. farmers and do little to prevent a foreign country from engaging in terrorism or building up militarily.

"U.S. farmers have a right to be angry that they are being used by both executive and legislative branches to carry out symbolic acts so foreign-policy makers appear to be doing something about our toughest foreign policy problems," said Rep. Doug Bereuter, a Republican who represents Nebraska farmers and who has questioned the effectiveness of economic sanctions in the past.

"When Congress and the president point the unilateral sanctions gun at a foreign country," Bereuter said, "that gun more often than not gets pointed at the American farmer, on the tractor, who is simply trying to provide for his family."

The bill would not affect current sanctions or embargoes imposed by the United States in cooperation with other countries. It also would apply only to embargoes on certain agricultural products. Bereuter said the measure aims to protect U.S. farmers from product-specific embargoes such as the Soviet grain embargo in 1979.

Senate Foreign Relations Committee Chairman Jesse Helms, R-N.C., plans to hold hearings this month on trade sanctions. Committee aides said Helms hopes to formulate a compromise bill sometime this year.

President Clinton on April 28 eased sanctions on the sale of food and medicine to Iran, Libya and Sudan.

House Passes Agriculture Sanctions Bill

JUNE 19 — A bill designed to give Congress more authority over agricultural trade embargoes passed the House by voice vote June 15.

Farm-state interests that felt damaged by past trade embargoes had lobbied for the legislation (HR 17). "Unfortunately, agriculture often gets caught up in a sanctions policy that does not work," said Bill Barrett of Nebraska, the second-ranking Republican on the House Agriculture Committee.

Ray LaHood, R-Ill., another Agriculture Committee member, added, "Put quite simply, embargoes can be the death knell for agriculture."

Barrett called the bill a "minor, reasonable change in sanctions policy."

The Agriculture Department estimates that sanctions reduced U.S. agricultural exports by $500 million in 1996, a small fraction of total sales. But bill sponsors say the possibility that the White House can invoke its sanctions privilege without congressional say-so discourages potential foreign buyers from investing in the U.S. market. About 40 percent of U.S. domestic agricultural production is sold abroad.

The measure would require the president to tell Congress within five days of imposing an agricultural embargo. Congress then would have 100 days to approve or disapprove the action. Congressionally approved embargoes would be limited to one year, but the president could waive that during a war or national emergency. If Congress disapproved the action, the embargo would terminate at the end of the 100-day period.

Though not opposing the bill, the administration pointed out that President Clinton on April 28 said he would generally exempt farm products and medicine from future unilateral sanctions.

The Office of Management and Budget expressed concern that the bill would restrict the president's ability to use sanctions as a foreign policy tool and could force their termination whether or not a country had complied with U.S. demands.

Members said the bill would not affect current sanctions or multilateral embargoes, and would apply only to embargoes on certain agricultural products. Agriculture Committee Chairman Larry Combest, R-Texas, said the measure aims to protect U.S. farmers from actions such as the Soviet grain embargo in 1979, which Combest said destroyed this country's reputation in the international market. He said the United States "can't be considered a reliable supplier of wheat" because of the threat of an embargo.

Included in an arms control bill (HR 973), passed by the House by voice vote on June 10, is another provision aimed at reducing agriculture sanctions. The provision extends for one year, until September 2000, the president's authority to waive food and medicine sanctions against India and Pakistan for conducting nuclear tests last summer. Under current law, the United States must automatically impose economic and aid sanctions on any non-nuclear weapons state that detonates a nuclear device.

The sanctions would particularly hurt U.S. winter wheat farmers in the Northwest, who sell nearly one-third of their crop to Pakistan.

Senate Foreign Relations Committee aides said Chairman Jesse Helms, R-N.C., plans to hold hearings later this month on trade sanctions in hopes of formulating a compromise this year.

Senate Panel Poised To Mark Up Sanctions Bill

JULY 31 — The Senate Foreign Relations Committee is drafting legislation on overseas economic sanctions that could be marked up as soon as the week of Aug. 2, said Sen. Joseph R. Biden Jr. of Delaware, the panel's ranking Democrat, on July 28.

"It's either going to happen quickly, or it's not going to happen at all," Biden said. Aides from both parties were negotiating details of the bill.

The measure would include elements of legislation introduced by Richard G. Lugar, R-Ind. (S 757), John Ashcroft, R-Mo. (S 315), and Christopher J. Dodd, D-Conn. (S 926).

Those bills had previously been opposed by panel Chairman Jesse Helms, R-N.C. But after holding two recent hearings, and under pressure from business and agricultural groups, Helms agreed to help draft a compromise.

The bill would lift current U.S. sanctions on trade in humanitarian goods, including food, medicine, and medical equipment, if the sanctions were imposed by executive order.

The provision would put into law Clinton's recent executive order lifting restrictions on the sale of such items to Iran, Libya and Sudan.

But it would retain the embargo and sanctions on Cuba that Helms wrote into law (PL 104-114) in 1996.

(1996 Almanac, p. 9-6)

The House Appropriations Committee July 30 rejected, 23-29, an amendment to the Commerce, Justice State spending bill by Jose E. Serrano, D-N.Y., to allow sales of food and medicine to Cuba.

The Foreign Relations measure would call for Congress to periodically review existing sanctions, but stop short of Lugar's proposal that sanctions be automatically ended unless reauthorized by Congress.

Senate Votes To Halt Food Sanctions

AUGUST 7 — The Senate on Aug. 4 adopted an amendment that would exempt exports of food and medicine from current and future U.S. sanctions, a challenge to the efforts of Senate Foreign Relations Committee Chairman Jesse Helms, R-N.C., to control debate on the issue.

Helms is drafting legislation on unilateral economic sanctions that, among other provisions, would lift U.S. sanctions on trade in humanitarian goods, including food, medicine and medical equipment, if the sanctions were imposed by executive order.

But during debate on the fiscal 2000 agriculture appropriations bill (S 1233), the Senate adopted by voice vote an amendment by John Ashcroft, R-Mo., to eliminate virtually all current and future restrictions on the export of medicine and agriculture products, unless specifically authorized by Congress in a joint resolution. Only exports to countries at war and exports that also have a potential military use would be restricted. *(Agriculture spending, p. 2-5)*

If enacted, the legislation would severely weaken a 1996 law (PL 104-114) Helms co-wrote to tighten pressure on Fidel Castro's regime in Cuba. That law did not exempt food and medicine from the longstanding U.S. embargo on trade with Cuba. *(1996 Almanac, p. 9-6)*

Helms tried to ward off Ashcroft's amendment, moving Aug. 3 to table it. But lawmakers, under pressure from pharmaceutical companies and farmers, rejected Helms' motion, 28-70. *(Vote 251, p. S-49)*

Helms and Robert G. Torricelli, D-N.J., argued that the Ashcroft amendment would hurt U.S. efforts to punish nations, such as Cuba and North Korea, that allegedly support terrorism.

"These people are outlaws. Every one of these nations is on the terrorist list," Torricelli said. "Is our policy to put nations on the terrorist list because they kill our citizens, bomb our embassies, destroy our planes, and then to say: It is outrageous, but would you like to do business?"

He also noted that the Clinton administration had already agreed to ease restrictions on the sale of food and medicine to some countries on the list: Iran, Libya, Sudan, and, to a much more limited extent, Cuba.

Ashcroft countered that he would prefer that terrorist nations spend their cash on humanitarian goods than on more nefarious activities.

But to defuse potential opposition, Ashcroft modified his amendment — countries on the U.S. list of terrorist states would be allowed only one-year licenses for exports and could not receive any U.S. export assistance.

Still, Ashcroft said, "It is important for us to say to our farmers that we are not going to make them a pawn in the hands of people for international diplomacy."

It is not clear what will ultimately happen to the Ashcroft provision, which faces fierce opposition in the House from Cuban-American lawmakers. The House Appropriations Committee on July 30 rejected a similar amendment to the Commerce, Justice, State spending bill.

Senators' Cuba Trip Highlights Hill Debate

SEPTEMBER 4 — With House and Senate negotiators on the fiscal 2000 agriculture appropriations bill facing a dispute over food and medicine sales to Cuba, two key farm state Democrats — Senate Minority Leader Tom Daschle of South Dakota and Sen. Byron L. Dorgan of North Dakota — traveled to Havana to meet with President Fidel Castro and other Cuban officials the weekend of Aug. 13-15.

Daschle, the highest-level U.S. official to visit Cuba in years, said the trip was meant to highlight the Senate's approval of an amendment Aug. 4 to its agriculture spending bill (S 1233 — S Rept 106-80) that would lift virtually all restrictions on exporting medicine and farm products to Cuba, unless specifically authorized by Congress in a joint resolution.

"It serves neither the U.S.'s nor Cuba's interest to continue the embargo on vital supplies like food and medicine," Daschle said in a joint, written statement with Dorgan.

"To continue such an embargo only hurts U.S. family farmers who are prevented from serving that market, and the citizens of Cuba who need the food and medicine," Dorgan added.

The senators said Cuban officials claimed the country now imports nearly $1 billion in food and that Cuban food imports could double in five years — a potential market for U.S. farmers hurt by lower commodity prices. The senators also said they were told by Cuban officials that there would be strong demand for pharmaceuticals.

In addition to discussions on food and medicine sales, the senators said they also asked Cuban officials to expand their cooperation on drug interdiction by allowing the U.S. Coast Guard to pursue traffickers' boats into Cuban territorial waters.

Daschle and Dorgan's visit followed another high-profile trip to Cuba in July by Thomas J. Donohue, president of the U.S. Chamber of Commerce. Donohue also said the embargo should be scaled back and urged the United States to seek ties with the island's limited private sector.

During Senate debate on the agriculture spending bill, Democrat Robert G. Torricelli of New Jersey and some other anti-Castro legislators had opposed the embargo amendment by John Ashcroft, R-Mo., because it would lift restrictions on Cuba first imposed in the early 1960s by executive order and codified by the 1996 Helms/Burton law (PL 104-114), named for Senate Foreign Relations Committee Chairman Jesse Helms, R-N.C., and Rep. Dan Burton, R-Ind.

But an attempt by opponents to table the amendment was defeated, 28-70.

Opposition to the amendment is stronger in the House, led by the three Cuban-American representatives. The House agriculture spending bill (HR 1906 — H Rept 106-157) has no such amendment, and House members have defeated past attempts to ease restrictions on Cuba.

Rep. Lincoln Diaz-Balart, R-Fla., criticized Daschle and Dorgan's "love fest" meeting with Castro, pointing out that it occurred on the same weekend that a prominent pro-democracy dissident, Oscar Elias Biscet, was jailed by Cuban authorities. In their statement, Daschle and Dorgan said they had been unsuccessful in their effort to visit dissidents.

"I would hope that, at the very least, Sens. Daschle and Dorgan would hold an eight-hour protest upon their return to Washington to denounce Dr. Biscet's arrest and to demand democracy and freedom for the Cuban people," Diaz-Balart said.

Nonetheless, in an interview, Diaz-Balart appeared to concede that the Senate provision is likely to become law because of a strong push from agribusiness.

But he said he is not too concerned, because the amendment as it was reworked on the Senate floor does not stray too far from current law: It still requires licenses for exports and prohibits sales from being financed through U.S. export assistance programs.

"What Castro is seeking is financing," Diaz-Balart said. "This is a lot of fuss over nothing."

[For inclusion in agriculture appropriations, see p. 2-5.]

Food Sanctions Bill Stalls

NOVEMBER 6 — Farm-state Republicans in the Senate who hoped to revive a bill that would curb the use of sanctions on food and medicine sales abroad now say they may have to wait until next year.

Facing efforts to derail the legislation from both the left and the right, Pat Roberts of Kansas, Chuck Hagel of Nebraska and other advocates of the bill have decided not to press Senate Majority Leader Trent Lott, R-Miss., to bring it up this year.

Lott had promised the lawmakers a new vote on the legislation (S 315), sponsored by Republican John Ashcroft of Missouri after it was stripped from the conference report on the fiscal 2000 agriculture appropriations bill (HR 1906 — PL 106-78) when House and Senate leaders could not reach a compromise.

The provision, which was overwhelmingly approved by the Senate, would have expanded a current ban on most food and medicine sanctions to include countries that the State Department accuses of supporting terrorism. But because it would have lifted restrictions against Cuba, the measure provoked an uproar from Cuban-American lawmakers in the House who strongly oppose Cuban President Fidel Castro.

Supporters had considered but dropped the idea of attaching the bill to trade legislation (HR 434 — H Rept 106-19, Parts 1 and 2) that the Senate passed Nov. 3.

They also were considering moving the bill by itself. Paul Wellstone, D-Minn., threatened to filibuster the measure unless he was given the opportunity to amend it to include a moratorium on certain kinds of agribusiness mergers. But Senate leaders on Nov. 5 gave Wellstone a chance to amend a bankruptcy reform bill (S 625) instead.

Supporters feared they would not be able to muster the 60 votes needed to cut off debate if Wellstone united with anti-Castro diehards such as Senate Foreign Relations Committee Chairman Jesse Helms, R-N.C.

"To get into this at this time would be very counterproductive," Roberts said in Nov. 2 interview. He also said he concluded that the legislation was less important than forcing the administration to take full advantage of current law.

For example, he pointed out that President Clinton in April eased restrictions that had prevented sales of food and medicine to Iran

But he said the administration failed to offer the export financing that would have allowed the United States to compete for a major grain sale with Iran. ◆

Chapter 24

TRANSPORTATION & INFRASTRUCTURE

Disputes Over Funding Leave FAA Negotiators Still Circling at Adjournment

Box Score

- **Bill:** HR 1000
- **Legislative action: House** passed HR 1000 (H Rept 106-167, Parts 1 and 2), 316-110, on June 15.

Senate passed HR 1000 (S Rept 106-9), by voice vote, Oct. 5.

SUMMARY

A bill to reauthorize the Federal Aviation Administration (FAA), including an airport construction program, remained stalled in a conference committee at session's end.

Unable to bridge a deep divide over how to fund aviation programs, House-Senate negotiations on a long-term reauthorization bill for the FAA broke up for the year Nov. 10. The House refused to consider a six-month extension (S 1916) passed by the Senate.

House Transportation and Infrastructure Committee Chairman Bud Shuster, R-Pa., had declared 1999 the year of aviation and put together a five-year authorization bill that would triple airport construction grants and erect budgetary fences to guarantee aviation spending levels. But Shuster's Senate counterpart, John McCain, R-Ariz., chairman of the Commerce, Science and Transportation Committee, focused more on trying to increase airline competition by relaxing restrictions on the number of flights allowed at four busy airports: Chicago's O'Hare International, New York's John F. Kennedy and LaGuardia, and Washington's Ronald Reagan National. McCain's bill (S 82) was silent on the issue of taking the Airport and Airway Trust Fund "off-budget," as Shuster proposed.

Though McCain's committee marked up its bill Feb. 11, months of delay followed as some senators pressed objections to additional flights at the crowded airports. Virginia senators strongly opposed the new flights at Reagan National; those from New York and Illinois also delayed floor consideration as the provisions to add new flights were renegotiated.

Shuster's committee approved an $89 billion proposal by voice vote on March 11. The bill also included added flights at the four busy airports, provoking challenges from lawmakers from the affected cities. And the bill's off-budget treatment of the aviation trust fund drew strong opposition from House appropriators and fiscal conservatives. Taking the fund off-budget would exclude the money from overall budget calculations and guarantee aviation funding.

As tensions mounted, Shuster convened an unusual, second markup of HR 1000 on May 27. The bill was scaled back by $16.5 billion, and in order to conform with the fiscal 2000 budget resolution, the off-budget treatment of the aviation trust fund was delayed until fiscal 2001. Appropriators decried the likely effects of the bill on other transportation programs, but Shuster pressed ahead.

When the full House debated the measure June 15, Shuster won a decisive victory over his foes, who had grown to include Appropriations Committee Chairman C.W. Bill Young, R-Fla.; Budget Committee Chairman John R. Kasich, R-Ohio; Ways and Means Committee Chairman Bill Archer, R-Texas; and Majority Whip Tom DeLay, R-Texas. On a 179-248 vote, the House rejected the conservatives' attempt to strip the bill of its off-budget provisions. HR 1000 passed the House easily, 316-110.

McCain, meanwhile, was able to work through the problems of the Virginia, New York and Illinois delegations. The Senate amended and passed the bill by voice vote Oct. 5. The Senate measure would have authorized $35 billion for three years.

Conference negotiations barely narrowed the gap over budget issues. Shuster's demands for an aviation spending guarantee were too much for Senate budget hawks, led by Budget Committee Chairman Pete V. Domenici, R-N.M. A verbal agreement brokered by Senate Majority Leader Trent Lott, R-Miss., would have tied aviation authorization levels to the receipts and interest earnings of the aviation trust fund. Shuster's demand for additional spending from general revenue would have been backed by a letter from GOP leaders. But the two sides could never agree on written language to implement the agreement, and Shuster broke off the talks Nov. 10.

Proponents of the House measure hope to build support over the congressional recess, but there are no indications that Senate opposition to aviation funding guarantees will decrease. With McCain expected to be on the campaign trail in 2000, it may be hard to close a deal without the emergence of a new Senate champion.

Shuster's Plan for Trust Fund Sets Stage for Battles With Senate

JANUARY 9 — House Transportation and Infrastructure Committee Chairman Bud Shuster, R-Pa., got off to a quick start in an expected showdown with Senate Commerce Committee Chairman John McCain, R-Ariz., over aviation policy when Shuster's committee approved a $10.1 billion reauthorization of the Federal Aviation Administration (FAA).

The one-year bill (HR 99) would provide $5.6 billion for FAA operations, $2.1 billion for facilities and $2.3 billion for airport improvement grants that expire March 31.

In addition to the one-year reauthorization bill, approved by voice vote Jan. 7, the panel approved by voice vote a five-year reauthorization of the insurance program (HR 98) that covers commercial airlines carrying troops and cargo into war zones.

While the insurance bill faces little opposition, the one-year FAA bill may reopen a battle with McCain, who blocked a full-year FAA reauthorization last year by insisting on linking it to measures aimed at increasing airline competition, including additional flights at four crowded airports: LaGuardia and John F. Kennedy airports in New York, O'Hare International Airport in Chicago and Ronald Reagan Washington National Airport near the nation's capital. McCain also wants to extend the 1,250-mile limit on flights to and from Reagan National, allowing more direct flights servicing his home state.

Two-Part Game Plan

Shuster and ranking committee member James L. Oberstar, D-Minn., appear to have a strategy for dealing with McCain.

First, they are hoping he will agree to a one-year bill, now that it appears the Senate may be distracted by the impeachment trial and unable to move quickly on legislation.

Shuster's game plan calls for a broader bill (HR 111) that could incorporate the centerpiece of his "year of aviation" agenda for 1999: a proposal to move the Airport and Airway Trust Fund, along with two trust funds for harbor maintenance and inland waterways, off budget, meaning they would not be counted as part of the federal government's annual budget.

"Taxpayers will send $10 billion to the aviation trust fund next year, and they will only get $5.6 billion in return," Shuster said Jan. 6. "Every day, more people are flying, delays are increasing, and we are not doing enough to replace dangerous, outdated facilities and air-traffic control equipment."

On the following day, Shuster suggested the bigger bill might contain plans to allow more flights at the four crowded airports and to make all or part of the FAA an independent agency, as well as a five-year reauthorization.

A McCain aide said the lawmaker wanted a catch-all bill with multiyear funding and likely would oppose a one-year bill.

Oberstar said spending on airport facilities should increase by $1 billion a year.

The trust fund collects money from an 8 percent airline ticket tax, a $2 fee for each leg of a trip, and a $24 arrival and departure fee on international round trips. The off-budget proposal envisions no increases in those taxes, but President Clinton is expected to propose an increase in the current passenger facility fee, which goes directly to airports, in his fiscal 2000 budget — from $3 per trip to $4 or $5.

Shuster agreed to a compromise provision in the 1998 highway and mass transit law (PL 105–178) to create guaranteed highway funding, similar to an entitlement that cannot be touched for other purposes.

It is unclear whether Shuster can head off opposition to the off-budget plan, which would guarantee funding for aviation. One difference is that the FAA relies on general revenue for more than one-fifth of its budget, unlike road-building projects financed by the gas tax.

Appropriators and budget hawks have opposed the off-budget proposal as an intrusion on their turf, and some have questioned the need for increased aviation spending.

Despite possible resistance from McCain and others, Shuster appears to have key allies, including Speaker Dennis Hastert, R-Ill. Hastert reversed a plan endorsed by Rep. Robert L. Livingston, R-La., to reduce the number of members of Shuster's panel, and instead kept the number at 75.

Heavy demand for seats on Shuster's committee is being generated by the possibility of a "midcourse correction" bill for the highway law, if gas tax receipts exceed projections.

House Passes Bill; Fight Lies Ahead Over Flight Expansions

FEBRUARY 6 — The House moved toward a showdown with the Senate on aviation policy, voting on Feb. 3 to pass a $10.2 billion reauthorization of the Federal Aviation Administration (FAA).

The one-year bill (HR 99), approved 408-3, would provide $5.6 billion for FAA operations and $2.1 billion for facilities. It also would provide $2.4 billion for airport improvement grants. The House also voted 407-1 to approve a five-year reauthorization of the war risk insurance program (HR 98), which covers commercial airlines carrying troops and cargo into war zones. *(Votes 9, 10, p. H-6)*

The overwhelming votes of approval came after House Republican leaders on Feb. 3 reassured Judiciary Committee Chairman Henry J. Hyde, R-Ill., that they would staunchly oppose, for now, any compromise in conference committee to add flights at four crowded airports. They are Ronald Reagan Washington National Airport, LaGuardia and John F. Kennedy airports in New York, and O'Hare International Airport in Chicago.

Hyde said he was concerned that the bill would become a vehicle for senators to insert additional provisions, including flights at the four airports, that were demanded by Senate Commerce, Science and Transportation Committee Chairman John McCain, R-Ariz., last year. When negotiations on this issue broke down in a conference committee, McCain insisted on a short-term FAA reauthorization contained in the omnibus budget law (PL 105-277) to increase pressure for a compromise early this year.

Hard Line Now, Deal Later?

"I have raised this concern with the Speaker, the majority leader and the majority whip. It is my understanding they will not allow HR 99 to become a vehicle for such a broader conference," Hyde said on the floor Feb. 3. His congressional district is close to O'Hare.

Although the added flights would provide more connections to smaller cities across the country, they are strongly opposed by lawmakers representing constituents near the airports, who complain that more flights would increase noise, traffic congestion and pollution.

While Hyde had the backing of House Republican leaders to block revisions in the short-term House bill, that united front will probably not hold later this year.

Key opponents of adding flights at the four airports said they expected a compromise on that issue in other legislation this year. One possible vehicle would be the bill (HR 111), offered by House Transportation and Infrastructure Committee Chairman Bud Shuster, R-Pa., to move the Airport and Airway Trust Fund off budget, so that its revenues and expenditures are not counted toward the overall federal budget surplus.

John P. Feehery, press secretary for Speaker J. Dennis Hastert, R-Ill., said his boss was looking for a compromise "on additional flights in other legislation later this year. He wants to do whatever is best for his constituents and for the city of Chicago. It means probably adding some flights. The number is negotiable."

While Hastert offered qualified support for Hyde, McCain continued to prepare his own two-year FAA reauthorization (S 82). He has scheduled a markup for Feb. 10.

McCain has insisted on reaching an agreement with the House on the added flights and on his proposal to extend the 1,250-mile limit on flights to and from Reagan National — partly to allow more direct flights to his home state by smaller carriers such as Arizona-based America West Airline. He insisted on a short-term reauthorization as part of the omnibus law last year to force debate of the issue this year, but his plan for quick action was delayed by the Senate impeachment trial.

Shuster and James L. Oberstar of Minnesota, the ranking Democrat on the House committee, both said they would seek a clean short-term extension in order to assure there is no disruption in improvement grants for airports, which are set to expire March 31. Oberstar said the House bill should not be "sidetracked."

Shuster and his committee are also seeking to act quickly on HR 111 so it will be ready in case there is a breakdown in negotiations with McCain, who has been opposing the short-term bill and demanding a broader compromise on key issues.

A final agreement on the added flights will likely require a compromise among airlines as well as lawmakers.

United Air Lines is one of the key players in the talks. Additional flights by rivals would dilute its dominance at O'Hare. But the airline's concern about competition at Reagan Airport has been tempered by its proposal to acquire a rival that wants to compete there — America West.

McCain Pledges To Fight for Added Flights At Major Airports

FEBRUARY 13 — Republican Sen. John McCain of Arizona pledged Feb. 11 to force a showdown with major airlines over his proposal to add flights at crowded airports, including flights to his home state.

The Senate Commerce, Transportation and Science Committee, of which McCain is chairman, approved a two-year $24.2 billion reauthorization (S 82) of the Federal Aviation Administration (FAA) by voice vote . It set the stage for a likely confrontation on the Senate floor with opponents who represent constituents near the four crowded airports where flights would be added: John F. Kennedy and LaGuardia airports in New York, O'Hare International in Chicago, and Ronald Reagan Washington National Airport.

Although the McCain bill is expected to pass the Senate — which approved a similar bill last year — it faces opposition in conference committee from House leaders and major airlines.

The flights are opposed by residents of communities near the airports who complain that the flights would create more noise, traffic congestion and air pollution. Major airlines have been lukewarm to the proposal, which could create competition from smaller airlines which get access to the airports with more slots for airplanes.

House Transportation and Infrastructure Committee Chairman Bud Shuster, R-Pa., is backing a stripped-down, one-year $10.2 billion reauthorization of the FAA (HR 99), passed by the House on Feb. 3. That bill does not include new flights at the four airports.

McCain acknowledged that he might ultimately lose the argument over whether to approve the House version, which calls for a simple one-year reauthorization.

"If we don't win, it will be another victory for the major airlines and for special interests," McCain said. He accused airlines of quietly continuing an effort they began last year to kill proposals to increase airline competition.

He cited an Oct. 22 private memorandum circulated to heads of major airlines by Carol B. Hallett, president and chief executive officer of the Air Transport Association. She claimed a "significant victory" in winning provisions in the 1999 omnibus budget law (PL 105-277) that require congressional review of tough guidelines proposed by the Transportation Department aimed at attacking alleged predatory pricing by airlines at regional hub airports.

In the memo, Hallett wrote, "As we enter 1999, it is important to remember that the guidelines fight is not over, and we've won the battle but the war remains."

McCain said the limits on flights at the four airports and a cap on the length of flights allowed at Reagan airport are "artificial and unnecessary barriers to competition."

But McCain's proposal could face opposition on the floor. Ernest F. Hollings of South Carolina, ranking Democrat on the Commerce panel, opposed an amendment approved by voice vote to double from 24 to 48 the additional daily flights allowed at Reagan airport. Half the flights would be inside the 1,250-mile limit on flights, and half would be outside the limit. Hollings said additional slots for flights would cause delays at the airport.

Proposals Coming In

While McCain prepared to defend his bill on the Senate floor, new proposals emerged from the administration and from Shuster, which broadened the debate over consumer complaints about ticket prices and airline service.

The administration unveiled a draft bill Feb. 8 calling for a five-year reauthorization of the FAA. It included the administration's proposal to allow airports to increase passenger facility charges from $3 to $5 per stop, and it would remove limits on flights at three of the four airports, excluding Reagan airport.

Sen. John D. Rockefeller IV, D-W.Va., said Feb. 11 that he would introduce the administration's bill, which he said could be part of a broader compromise bill.

Rockefeller said he was concerned about an impending March 31 expiration of airport improvement grants that were extended for six months in the omnibus budget law last year.

While echoing Rockefeller's concern about the deadline, Shuster fired a few shots of his own at airlines, criticizing them for poor treatment of passengers. He unveiled a draft bill Feb. 10 that would require airlines to pay passengers twice the value of their tickets if they are stranded in planes for more than two hours.

Shuster's proposal came five days after McCain and Ron Wyden, D-Ore., unveiled a bill (S 383) to require that passengers be given information about overbooking of certain flights and full refunds within 48 hours of ticket purchase and be allowed to use parts of round-trip tickets when traveling.

House Committee Approves FAA Reauthorization

MARCH 13 — House Transportation and Infrastructure Committee Chairman Bud Shuster, R-Pa., steered his $89 billion, five-year aviation bill (HR 1000) through his own panel March 11, setting up a fight with those who want to keep a tighter rein on federal spending.

Shuster's reauthorization of the Federal Aviation Administration (FAA) would sharply increase spending on air transportation by moving the Airport and Airway Improvement Trust Fund off-budget, so that its revenues and expenditures are not counted toward the overall federal budget surplus.

The committee's approval of the bill also sets up a likely conference committee showdown with the Senate, where the Commerce, Science and Transportation Committee passed a $24.2 billion, 18-month FAA reauthorization (S 82) on Feb. 11 and where Chairman John McCain, R-Ariz., has opposed moving the trust fund off-budget.

A conference committee also will likely be needed to work out differences over another bill (HR 99), passed by the House on Feb. 3, that would reauthorize the FAA through Sept. 30 in order to avoid a cutoff of airport improvement grants March 31.

Shuster hoped to pass that short-term bill before considering a longer-term reauthorization, but McCain wants a longer-term measure that would increase flights at four crowded airports.

More Competition

HR 1000, approved by voice vote, contains several provisions to increase airline competition. But as McCain can attest, increased competition often is opposed because of the noise and crowding it can create.

Rep. Jerrold Nadler, D-N.Y., scolded Shuster for not asking for input from New York members about his proposal to end limits on flights, or "slots," at John F. Kennedy and LaGuardia airports, as well as at Chicago's O'Hare, by March 2000.

"Adding dozens of flights a day can only make things worse," Nadler told Shuster during the March 11 markup.

Shuster defended his plan, which is similar to a Clinton administration proposal, to enhance competition, and he said noise and traffic-control technology has become more sophisticated.

The situation with the New York delegation foreshadows differences between Shuster and McCain on similar plans to increase flights at Ronald Reagan Washington National Airport. Shuster mollified Washington-area members with a proposal to allow six additional daily, short-range flights at the airport, far short of the 48 daily flights proposed in McCain's bill.

Like Shuster, McCain had little trouble getting his bill through his committee in February.

McCain's proposal includes granting 24 daily exemptions to the "perimeter" rule, which bars direct flights of more than 1,250 miles from Reagan National Airport.

The proposals leave room for compromise, unlike Shuster's plan to take the Airport and Airway Improvement Trust Fund off-budget.

As he did with the Highway Improvement Trust Fund in the 1998 surface transportation reauthorization law (PL 105-178), Shuster wants to ensure that the airport money is not included in determining budget deficits or surpluses. McCain has traditionally opposed the idea.

James L. Oberstar of Minnesota, the ranking Democrat on the House Transportation Committee, predicted, "It will be a very intense conference, no doubt about that."

Shuster's bill also contains bipartisan language supported in both chambers to establish a procedure to license air tours over national parks.

The proposal, also introduced separately (HR 717, S 81) and approved by the House committee, directs the National Park Service and the FAA to cooperatively set permit guidelines on a park-by-park basis.

Past Differences

Differences between the House and Senate goals for aviation last year led to an impasse and a six-month authorization of the FAA in the omnibus appropriations bill (PL 105-277) that will expire at the end of March.

Shuster said Thursday that it is up to House leaders to act on the short-term reauthorization before spending authority expires. "We've done our work; we've acted responsibly," he said.

McCain's bill would fund the FAA through the end of the fiscal year at roughly the same level proposed in the HR 1000, with funding for an additional year at about $5.8 billion. Overall, Shuster's five-year bill would authorize funding FAA operations at $5.6 billion through fiscal 1999 and would increase authorizations yearly, culminating at about $8.8 billion in fiscal 2004.

FAA Reauthorized For 60 Days By Unanimous Senate Vote

MARCH 20 — The Senate unanimously voted March 17 to reauthorize the Federal Aviation Administration (FAA) for 60 days, a move that supporters said was necessary to keep safety and improvement programs running.

The reauthorization bill (S 643) covers FAA operations and management, the Airport Improvement Program (AIP), the Airway Facilities Program, the Aviation Insurance Program and the Military Airport Program. *(Vote 52, p. S-14)*

Sponsor John McCain, R-Ariz., said action was needed because the current authorization for the AIP, an airport capital improvements grant program, is to expire March 31.

Senators adopted by voice vote an amendment by John W. Warner, R-Va., that would allow Ronald Reagan Washington National and Dulles International airports to spend $30 million of the $200 million reserved in an escrow account under the AIP. The money would fund delayed safety and capacity-related projects, McCain said.

The measure would also remove a $300 million cap on the FAA's discretionary fund. The provision affects both small and large airports. Currently, if the account goes over the cap, the excess funds are divided among small airports and other programs.

With the extension, lawmakers can continue negotiations on the more contentious full FAA reauthorization bill (S 82), McCain said.

House Clears Extension of Airports Program

MARCH 27 — Buying time to work on a long-term compromise, the House has cleared for President Clinton a bill (S 643) that extends authorization of the Airports Improvement Program until May 31.

House passage was by voice vote on March 24. The Senate had passed the bill March 17.

The House and the Senate are working on longer-term Federal Aviation Administration authorization bills (HR 1000, S 82). Both measures have been approved by committees and are awaiting floor action.

But the authority for the FAA to make airport improvement grants was set to expire March 31.

The short-term bill, which Clinton is expected to sign, would also authorize work to begin on $30 million in improvements at Ronald Reagan Washington National and Dulles International airports, funded by passenger facility charges; more than $200 million in projects have been held up because the Senate has not yet confirmed federal appointments to the Washington Metropolitan Airports Authority board of directors.

Budget Conferees Aid Shuster Effort To Protect Airport Funding

APRIL 17 — House Transportation Chairman Bud Shuster, R-Pa., won another round in his campaign to protect funding for airports as part of this year's reauthorization of the Federal Aviation Administration (HR 1000).

Conferees on the fiscal 2000 budget resolution (H Con Res 68) dropped "sense of the Senate" language that "no additional firewalls should be enacted" for transportation spending.

As he did with the Highway Improvement Trust Fund in the 1998 transportation authorization law (PL 105-178), Shuster is proposing that the Airport and Airway Trust Fund be taken off-budget, or used exclusively for airport projects and not counted in calculations of the overall federal surplus or deficit.

Last year, Shuster settled for "firewalls" on highway funding, meaning that the money must be used for transportation but still is counted as part of the overall federal budget.

In order to get Shuster to drop a threat to oppose the budget resolution on the House floor, House Republican leaders in March promised him a separate vote on his aviation bill with the trust fund proposal and said they would keep billions of dollars in aviation trust fund money out of the calculations during budget talks.

The Senate language that was dropped in conference stated, "Domestic firewalls greatly limit funding flexibility as Congress manages budget priorities in a fiscally constrained budget."

The Senate added that if Shuster's proposal were enacted, many activities would be "drastically cut or eliminated," including Coast Guard searches, rescues and drug interdiction; programs of the National Highway Traffic Safety Administration; and federal support of Amtrak.

But Shuster, with the assistance of House leaders, insisted that the Senate provision be dropped. They argued that it was inconsistent with the deal struck in March.

"By dropping this provision, Congress can freely decide the best use of aviation taxes without the constraints of the Senate provision," Shuster said in a statement.

Shuster said that, contrary to the Senate's findings, his proposal to take aviation trust funds off-budget would not result in program reductions.

"Any budget increases would be outside the caps and would be fully paid for by the aviation taxes deposited into the aviation trust fund," he said.

Small Airports' Ambitions Steer Transportation Bill

MAY 1 — The fate of this year's big transportation battle in Congress may hinge not on the clout of the nation's largest airports but on the needs of some of the smallest. In Des Moines, Iowa, they are looking to Washington for help. Despite its name, Des Moines International Airport is a small facility that has not shared in the increased competition and lower prices that deregulation in 1978 brought to some large airports. Business travelers pay high fares going to and from the Iowa capital.

Even so, passenger and cargo traffic has grown dramatically in Des Moines, and projections are that it will grow so much that a third runway will be needed within 20 years.

But at the moment, the vagaries of Washington politics and Congress' fitful history of reauthorizing the Federal Aviation Administration (FAA) have made planning difficult for officials in Des Moines.

"With smaller airports, uncertainty is the biggest problem," said Scott Brockman, the airport's assistant aviation director of finance and administration.

This year, places such as Des Moines are getting a lot of attention in Congress. Both the House and Senate are expected to move to the floor legislation (S 82, HR 1000) to reauthorize the FAA before a temporary authorization expires May 31. And each chamber, led by its Transportation Committee chairman, has something to offer Des Moines.

On April 30, the Senate Commerce, Science and Transportation Committee, led by chairman and presidential aspirant John McCain, R-Ariz., held a field hearing in Des Moines on the Senate's FAA reauthorization bill. That measure, in an effort to boost airline competition, proposes relaxing the rules that restrict the number of flights at four of the nation's busiest airports.

Des Moines would benefit under McCain's bill if a small, low-cost airline such as Midwest Express could add service to Des Moines from Chicago's O'Hare or Ronald Reagan Washington National Airport. Since deregulation, studies have shown that ticket prices have fallen the most at airports where major airlines face competition from low-cost carriers.

In the House bill, Transportation and Infrastructure Committee Chairman Bud Shuster, R-Pa., also has embraced the idea of increasing competition, in his case by completely eliminating restrictions on the number of flights at O'Hare and two New York City airports, La Guardia and John F. Kennedy International.

But it is another aspect of Shuster's bill that is likely to spark the biggest debate in Congress: special budgetary treatment for aviation funding in an effort to guarantee a bigger pot of money for airport construction.

The Shuster plan, like last year's surface transportation reauthorization law (PL 105-178), which guaranteed higher spending levels for highways, is sure to be a flashpoint between House authorizers and budget hawks in both chambers if the legislation moves into a conference committee later this month.

Des Moines International has received about $30 million from the federal government over the last four fiscal years for an $84 million runway extension project. But funding has been uncertain, since most of it comes from discretionary grants made by the FAA through the Airport Improvement Program, which provides money based on the number of passengers at each airport. The availability of these grants during any given year depends on how much money Congress has made available overall and how many other airports are applying for the same kind of grant.

Shuster's legislation would greatly expand the Airport Improvement Program, increasing overall funding for the program from $2.4 billion in fiscal 1999 to $5 billion in fiscal 2000. It would authorize another $5 billion for each year through fiscal 2004. Total funding for the FAA would jump from $10.2 billion in fiscal 1999, to $15.3 billion for fiscal 2000, and to $20.3 billion in fiscal 2004.

Most important for airlines, airports and local governments — all of which are pushing for the Shuster bill — are the proposed funding guarantees.

For Des Moines International, the construction allotment would more than triple, from $1.9 million to $5.7 million each year. And the pot of money for discretionary FAA grants to address problems such as capacity and noise abatement at small airports would grow, too. "Clearly, every airport would support a properly funded, long-term [improvement program]," said Brockman.

Keeping Up With Capacity

Airline traffic is at an all-time high — more than 611 million passengers a year. The FAA estimates that will rise to more than 1 billion passengers by 2007.

Airports must go through a painstaking planning and review process to build new runways, gates and passenger facilities to accommodate such a surge in passengers. It generally takes more than seven years from conception to reality, according to Jeffrey Goodell, vice president for government relations of the Airports Council International – North America.

"There are tremendous needs in our aviation system," Goodell said. "We need to make the investments now."

To handle the projected level of passenger traffic will require the equivalent of 10 new big-city airports, Goodell said.

Since local politics make it extremely difficult to find sites for new airports — no one wants to live beside one — the most likely solution is to expand existing airfields.

Shuster has offered an $89 billion, five-year authorization bill. Using last year's $217.9 billion surface transportation bill as a model, he has proposed special budgetary treatment for airport funding. *(Aviation trust fund, p. 24-9)*

With the highway bill, Shuster was able to boost road and transit spending by 40 percent over six years. He originally sought to take the Highway Trust Fund off-budget, meaning that the proceeds from gasoline and other federal road taxes would be spent only on highway and transit projects and would not be included in calculations of the federal budget surplus or deficit.

Some lawmakers and highway interests have complained in the past that budget officials prefer to keep high balances in trust funds because they make any federal deficit appear smaller.

Shuster settled instead for "firewalls" around the trust fund, meaning that the money would be reserved for highway and transit spending, but still would be counted when figuring the federal surplus or deficit.

Shuster has proposed taking the Airport and Airway Trust Fund off-budget, but many believe he would settle for the same kind of firewalls he got for highway spending.

Before including the trust fund language in the overall FAA bill, Shuster drafted a separate, narrowly focused measure (HR 111) — dubbed the "Truth in Budgeting Act." The bill would take the aviation trust fund and two other transportation trust funds off-budget. As of April 29, there were 156 cosponsors. Last year, the highway bill had 118 cosponsors and passed the House on April 1, 337-80.

Shuster's success on the highway bill depended a great deal on the scope and personal impact of the legislation. Every congressional district was affected to some extent, and individual members of Congress could select road projects important to their districts.

It will be more difficult to make the case for aviation funding. There are fewer airports than highways. And Airport Improvement Program grants are determined by an established formula and at the discretion of the FAA. That means fewer lawmakers are likely to fight for them if there are charges that the bill is too generous.

On-Budget or Off? Aviation Trust Fund Has Lawmakers Calculating

MAY 1 — The key battleground of aviation policy this year is a government bank account few airline passengers have every heard of — the Airport and Airway Trust Fund.

Created in 1970 (PL 91-258) to help pay for the nation's airports and airway system, the fund is financed mostly through a tax on domestic airline tickets (8 percent in fiscal 1999, dropping to 7.5 percent in fiscal 2000) and a flight segment tax ($1 per segment in fiscal 1998, rising to $3 by fiscal 2002). Other money comes from taxes on aviation fuel, cargo and international departures and arrivals.

House Transportation and Infrastructure Committee Chairman Bud Shuster, R-Pa., has proposed that the trust fund be taken off-budget, meaning that the money would be dedicated exclusively to aviation capital projects and that any balance in the trust fund would not count toward the federal surplus or deficit.

Moving the fund off-budget shifts control to authorizers such as Shuster at the expense of appropriators, who bitterly oppose any such change and say that it makes balancing the budget more difficult. Besides, they say, general tax revenue subsidizes the aviation system. *(Background, 1995 Almanac, p. 3-72)*

The Congressional Budget Office (CBO) calculates that the unobligated trust fund balance — money not already committed to future projects — will grow from $8.5 billion in fiscal 1999 to $45.6 billion in 2009.

Rising Tide

The growing balance in the aviation trust fund can be traced to several policy debates in recent years.

In the 1980s, transportation authorizing committees won restrictions on the use of the aviation trust fund to finance operations of the Federal Aviation Administration. *(1987 Almanac, p. 339)*

House and Senate authorizers felt that the trust fund was for capital improvements, not to underwrite FAA operating costs.

Delays in modernizing the FAA's air traffic control computer system have helped pile up trust fund money intended to pay for the project.

Some of these gains were offset by lapses in aviation taxes. For almost eight months in 1996 and about two months in 1997, authority to collect the aviation taxes expired, costing the trust fund an estimated $5 billion.

Shuster has made his case for taking the trust fund off-budget by using numbers that far exceed CBO projections, in part because he is assuming that more money for FAA operations will come from the general fund.

Shuster argues that if historical spending patterns hold, the unobligated trust fund balance will rise to $91.3 billion in fiscal 2009. His projections rely on an average 30 percent contribution from the treasury for FAA activities, to cover costs associated with public and Defense Department use of airports.

A provision in the fiscal 1999 omnibus spending law (PL 105-277) lowered that 30 percent contribution to 15 percent for the duration of the current authorization. Senate budget hawks, such as Budget Committee Chairman Pete V. Domenici, R-N.M., would like to keep the 15 percent level.

The Clinton administration advocates eliminating the general fund contribution, arguing that the Defense Department air traffic control services paid for through the general fund are a big enough contribution by the general taxpayers.

Dire Budget Predictions

The debate over aviation funding is likely to draw out the same opponents who fought Shuster's highway spending efforts — budget hawks who feel the spending is excessive, and appropriators who see Shuster as encroaching on their turf.

On April 15, Rep. Frank R. Wolf, R-Va., chairman of the Appropriations Transportation Subcommittee, circulated a letter urging colleagues to consider that guaranteed aviation funding might result in budget cuts for the Coast Guard and Amtrak.

"Last year, the Congress provided record investment in aviation spending, and did it in the context of a unified budget — every additional dollar of investment requires an equal reduction somewhere else," Wolf wrote.

Wolf also sent House members an April 12 letter from Transportation Secretary Rodney Slater outlining the ramifications of passing Shuster's FAA bill. Slater estimated that the additional $1.1 billion in spending Shuster calls for above Clinton's request could result in a 21 percent cut in non-aviation transportation programs.

While noting that Congress has discretion over how the budget cuts would be distributed, Slater said it could mean elimination of Amtrak funding and severe reductions to the Coast Guard or the Federal Railroad Administration.

"We estimate that an across-the-board, 21 percent funding cut in fiscal 2000 would mean severe reductions to Coast Guard's drug interdiction, fisheries enforcement and safety missions, the likely closure of a number of Coast Guard facilities, and the laying up of ships and aircraft," Slater added.

Slater made the projections assuming that the FAA reauthorization bill would make no changes to the highway bill's firewalls and the highway spending they compel. Slater also assumed that the current spending caps would remain in place and that there would be no new user fees.

Shuster has said that any funding increases for the FAA under HR 1000 would fall outside the spending caps and would be fully paid for by the aviation taxes deposited in the aviation trust fund.

There is no provision to take the aviation trust fund off-budget in the McCain bill, and McCain has opposed the special treatment for the trust fund.

But McCain, distracted by the war in Yugoslavia and his nascent presidential campaign, may not be as eager to fight Shuster as he was a few months ago. "During the conference, everything will be on the table," said McCain spokeswoman Pia Pialorsi.

Strategy in the Senate

The fate of Shuster's budget proposal could rest with the determination of a few senators likely to participate in any conference committee.

Aides say that Senate Budget Committee Chairman Pete V. Domenici, R-N.M., wants to block any special budgetary treatment for the Airport and Airway Trust Fund and has the backing of Majority Leader Trent Lott, R-Miss., who has grown weary of the way Shuster wields power.

Domenici would participate in any conference on legislation that would take a program off-budget. Lott would participate because he is the fourth-ranking Republican on the Senate Commerce, Science & Transportation Subcommittee on Aviation.

Lott joined Domenici and Appropriations Transportation Subcommittee Chairman Richard C. Shelby, R-Ala., in pushing for "sense of the Senate" language in the fiscal 2000 budget resolution (H Con Res 68) opposing special budgetary treatment for aviation funding. The language was included when the Senate passed the budget resolution March 25, but it was dropped in conference.

The provision stated that trust fund firewalls "greatly limit funding flexibility as Congress manages budget priorities in a fiscally constrained budget." It also cited programs likely to be "drastically cut or eliminated," including the Coast Guard, National Highway Traffic Safety Administration and Amtrak.

Shuster, with the support of House Speaker J. Dennis Hastert, R-Ill., pushed to drop the language, saying it would violate an agreement they had made to set aside aviation trust fund money until the full House took a clean vote on the FAA authorization bill.

Domenici agreed to drop the firewall language out of deference to Hastert, since it was non-binding and had already served its purpose of attracting attention. But Domenici is determined to press his views in conference committee on any FAA legislation, aides said.

There are a few factors that give Domenici a better bargaining position than he had during the highway bill conference last year. At that time, Domenici faced tremendous pressure not to oppose special budgetary treatment for the highway trust fund. Almost two-thirds of the Senate had signed on to an amendment by Robert C. Byrd, D-W.Va., and Phil Gramm, R-Texas, that called for steep increases in highway spending. There is no similar group of senators calling for airport funding.

"Domenici feels he will have a position of strength in negotiations," said a senior GOP budget committee aide.

It also is unlikely that conferees will get relief on tight budget spending caps. The latest projection by the Congressional Budget Office for fiscal 2000 is for a $4.6 billion deficit.

Lawmakers anxious to reduce the federal budget also are likely to raise questions about FAA management, in light of the agency's difficulty implementing a 23-year, $42 billion upgrade of the nation's air-traffic control system. The project has suffered delays, cost overruns and accounting problems.

Added to these problems are concerns about the time it took the agency to work out its year 2000 computer problems. A test of the air-traffic control computer system in April was successful, but the agency will miss its March 31 deadline for full Y2K compliance by at least three months.

With these management concerns, some lawmakers may be hesitant to heap billions of extra dollars on the FAA each year.

If Shuster loses the battle to take the trust fund off-budget, it may be all but impossible to find the funds to increase aviation spending.

Last year, lawmakers were able to parlay one huge off-setting budget cut — ending disability payments for veterans with smoking-related ailments not directly related to military service — into a $15.5 billion boost for highway spending.

Lawmakers will be hard-pressed to come up with a similar offset that is politically acceptable this year.

McCain's Priority

While the battle over the Airport and Airway Trust Fund will take place in conference committee, another major policy dispute has been significantly narrowed.

Both FAA reauthorization bills relax slot restrictions — rules limiting the total number of takeoffs and landings — at three of the four major airports where they apply: O'Hare, JFK and LaGuardia.

The rules that govern the other slot-controlled airport, Reagan National, will be the subject of heated negotiations in the Senate and in conference committee.

McCain has long advocated relaxing the so-called perimeter rule, an FAA requirement that any flight into or out of Reagan National be within a 1,250-mile radius.

The rule, which has been amended in the past to permit longer flights, was intended to promote Washington Dulles International Airport as the Washington area's long-haul airport. As Dulles has prospered and filled up with flights, some have questioned whether the regulation has outlived its usefulness.

McCain is one of those doing the most questioning. The rule is hindering America West, a growing air carrier based in McCain's home state of Arizona. America West would like to fly directly into Reagan National from Phoenix, its main hub, and compete with the seven major airlines whose main hubs are within the 1,250-mile perimeter of National.

"We would be a tremendous pro-competitive force," said America West lobbyist John Timmons.

In Des Moines, officials hope that some of the new long-distance flights would be filled by Midwest Express, a low-cost carrier that would like to offer non-stop service from Reagan National to Des Moines, which is outside the 1,250-mile perimeter.

McCain is also seeking to boost

competition at National by adding 48 slots each day.

That provision is being fought by Republican Sen. John W. Warner of Virginia, where National is located, across the Potomac River from Washington. Warner favors a more limited slot expansion. But no senator has put a hold on the bill, which would prevent it from being considered on the floor.

In the House bill, Shuster would allow six additional daily flights at National in addition to removing the restrictions on the number of flights at O'Hare, JFK and LaGuardia. The Senate bill would add 30 flights at O'Hare and would allow the Department of Transportation to permit exemptions at O'Hare, JFK and LaGuardia for flights to underserved communities with fewer than 2 million passengers per year.

While airlines and airports generally support Shuster's bill, they part company on another issue prominent in the FAA authorization debate — whether to increase the passenger facility charge.

The Shuster bill includes a provision that would double the maximum fee from $3 to $6, which would raise prices for passengers but give airports a reliable stream of cash.

Airports levy the charge, authorized in the 1990 budget-reconciliation legislation (PL 101-508), on each arriving or departing passenger and keep the money to finance airport development. Airlines are responsible for collecting the fees and distributing them directly to the airports. The fees often finance additional gates or terminals — measures aimed at boosting traffic and competition, which are goals not necessarily shared by the airlines. *(1990 Almanac, p. 111)*

Airlines prefer increasing the Airport Improvement Program, over which they have more influence. They argue that the funding increase Shuster has proposed for that program is sufficient to cover the system's capital needs.

Work on the FAA reauthorization began in 1998 but has been delayed twice by differences in House and Senate priorities. The current authorization was extended for six months, until March 1999, as part of last year's omnibus spending bill (PL 105-277). A two-month extension (PL 106-6) will expire May 31.

The clear policy differences in the House and Senate have narrowed little in the intervening months, so it may be the power of airports, such as Des Moines, and their ability to press their case that determines the outcome of the huge budget fight.

But for every federally dependent small airport like Des Moines, there is a nearly autonomous San Francisco International.

San Francisco, in order to meet its huge and growing passenger demand, is in the midst of a major expansion, including a new international passenger terminal, an airport passenger train and new access roads.

San Francisco International would be one of Shuster's biggest winners under the expanded Airport Improvement Program, with its basic grant increasing from $11 million to $33 million each year. But the $2.4 billion expansion was financed mostly through the airport's own funds and bonding authority.

"We wouldn't turn it away," said airport spokesman John Ballesteros of the possibility of more federal money.

But it may be difficult for lawmakers to bust the budget caps or put the Coast Guard in peril to guarantee San Francisco International what amounts to 1 percent of its expansion plan.

Conferees Agree To Extend FAA For Two Months

MAY 15 — Lawmakers working on a long-term Federal Aviation Administration (FAA) authorization bill got some breathing room in the fiscal 1999 supplemental spending bill approved by conferees May 13.

House-Senate negotiators on the supplemental bill (HR 1141) added a provision authorizing the FAA's Airport Improvement Program through Aug. 6. They also added language to release $30 million for Ronald Reagan Washington National and Dulles International airports near Washington.

The FAA is operating under a two-month extension that will expire May 31.

Both chambers had been scheduled to act on long-term authorization measures by the end of May. But the failure of House Transportation Committee Chairman Bud Shuster, R-Pa., and Senate Commerce Committee Chairman John McCain, R-Ariz., to bridge their differences led House and Senate leaders to conclude that a conference committee could not complete its work before the Memorial Day recess.

The length of the extension was the subject of protracted negotiations between House and Senate Republican leaders, McCain and Shuster.

On May 6, Shuster wrote House Speaker J. Dennis Hastert, R-Ill., to oppose including a short-term FAA extension in the supplemental spending bill. The May 6 letter, also signed by about 66 others on the 75-member panel, said the extension would amount to authorizing on an appropriations bill. Shuster dropped his resistance in return for a commitment from House leaders to schedule a vote on his long-term FAA authorization during the week of June 14.

A range of options was under discussion, according to committee aides. Senate leaders initially proposed a longer, one-year extension. By May 12, the Senate position was a six-month extension. Shuster fought against any extension that would take the authorization beyond fiscal 1999, which ends Sept. 30, a position supported by Aviation Subcommittee Chairman John J. "Jimmy" Duncan Jr., R-Tenn.

"That would certainly take the pressure off and give people less incentive to work out some of the controversies," Duncan said.

Keeping the Pressure On

Shuster had been pushing to complete work on the FAA bill by May so that it would be finished before the fiscal 2000 appropriations process begins.

In order to get Shuster to drop his threat to oppose the fiscal 2000 budget resolution (H Con Res 68), House leaders in March promised him a separate vote on his five-year aviation bill, with its controversial provision to take the Airport and Airway Trust Fund off-budget, removing the fund from federal budget calculations.

As he did with the Highway Trust Fund in a multiyear surface transportation law last year (PL 105-178), Shuster is pushing for special budgetary rules which would ensure that aviation taxes are spent only on aviation programs.

Such special, off-budget treatment is vigorously opposed by appropriators.

Reports that House Appropriations aides are keeping track of those who support Shuster's proposal to take the airport trust fund off-budget added to the tension of negotiations. Shuster is said to be taking seriously threats that his supporters could have difficulty getting favored projects through the appropriations process if they back his plans.

A House Appropriations Committee aide explained that Shuster's trust fund proposal would reduce the discretionary budget and create a spending squeeze. One option to help mitigate that squeeze would be to cut back designated spending, or "earmarks," favored by individual members. And supporters of the Shuster bill would be the likely targets.

"We expect members, if they are making it more difficult for us to provide funding for federal agencies, . . . to be consistent and not make it doubly difficult by earmarking programs," the aide said.

The Senate bill (S 82) has no such special treatment for aviation programs.

House Committee Approves Revised Shuster Bill

MAY 29 — Tensions over the Federal Aviation Administration reauthorization bill erupted May 27 as the House Transportation and Infrastructure Committee approved special treatment for the aviation trust fund that finances airport improvement projects.

The committee approved the multiyear bill on March 11 but had never produced a report. That gave Transportation Committee Chairman Bud Shuster, R-Pa., a chance to recraft the bill to garner more support before it moves to the floor.

The revised bill (HR 1000), approved by the committee on a voice vote May 27, is a smaller measure that reflects an agreement Shuster made with House leaders during consideration of the fiscal 2000 budget resolution (H Con Res 68). In order to get Shuster to drop a threat to oppose the budget measure, GOP leaders promised him a clean up-or-down floor vote on the aviation bill, with its special budgetary treatment of aviation trust fund money intact.

As Shuster opened the May 27 markup, he let it be known that he was irritated with his colleagues on the Appropriations Committee.

Shuster read a news account about appropriations staff aides keeping track of cosponsors of a Shuster bill to take the aviation trust fund off-budget (HR 111), with a threat of retribution on the Transportation Appropriations bill.

"It looks like it's heating up," Shuster said. "But there's no doubt in my mind that we are on the side of the angels on this issue."

Appropriators, meeting on the fiscal 2000 transportation spending bill only a few minutes earlier two floors above in the Rayburn office building, had let it be known that they did not buy Shuster's argument that the aviation bill would not adversely affect other transportation programs.

The aviation proposal "makes a mockery of the entire budget process," fumed ranking House Appropriations Democrat David R. Obey of Wisconsin.

But Shuster and James L. Oberstar, of Minnesota, his Democratic counterpart on the Transportation and Infrastructure Committee, warned of a "disinformation campaign" and dismissed the appropriators' claim that the plan could reduce spending on other programs. "That is simply false. If anyone doubts that, read the bill," Shuster said.

Money Levels

The level of proposed authorizations for fiscal 2000 was largely unchanged from the original proposal. From fiscal 2001 through 2004, the bill would authorize a total of $57.4 billion, a $16.5 billion cut.

As approved by the panel, Shuster's bill maintains the special budgetary treatment for aviation funding, which is intended to make more money available for airport construction. The bill proposes to take the Airport and Airway Trust Fund off-budget, meaning that the money could be tapped only for aviation spending and would not be counted against the federal surplus or deficit.

That mechanism would give appropriators less say over how aviation money is spent, and it would reduce the size of the pot of money in their domain.

The bill would cap future funding of aviation programs from the general fund. Oberstar cited this as a concession to the appropriators, since future increases in operations would come from the trust fund for the first time.

The bill also would fund FAA operations at $28.6 billion from fiscal 2001 through 2004, a reduction of $2 billion from the committee's March 11 version.

The measure would authorize the Airport Improvement Program at $16.7 billion, a cut of $3.3 billion; facilities and equipment at $11.5 billion, a cut of $1.3 billion; and research, engineering and development at $600 million, a cut of $400 million.

In addition, the latest Shuster proposal does not include any funding for the Aviation Systems Accelerated Program. That program had been proposed at $10.2 billion from fiscal 2000-04. The program would have funded projects to reduce congestion and delays at airports, airport construction to increase airline competition, and projects to enhance air service to small- and medium-size communities.

Transportation Secretary Rodney Slater, in a letter to the committee, said he "would be unable to recommend that the president sign the bill" if it included the off-budget and guaranteed funding provisions.

The House is expected to consider the legislation the week of June 14.

Speaking after the markup, Shuster said he thought the appropriators' threats had "backfired," stiffening the resolve of his supporters. Asked whether he thought the spending panel would follow through on its pledge of retribution, Shuster said, "I would hope not. That's not the way we should do business."

House Passes Five-Year FAA Reauthorization

JUNE 19 — Despite an overwhelming victory in the House, proponents of a five-year reauthorization of the Federal Aviation Administration (FAA) that would take the Airport and Airway Trust Fund off-budget and limit the options of appropriators, face anything but a smooth glide-path.

Bud Shuster, R-Pa., chairman of the House Transportation and Infrastructure Committee, capped weeks of careful lobbying June 15 with a 316-110 vote in favor of his $59.3 billion reauthorization of the FAA (HR 1000). *(Vote 209, p. H-72)*

The focus now shifts to the Senate, where John McCain, R-Ariz., chairman of the Commerce, Science and Transportation Committee, has sponsored a two-year bill (S 82) that lacks Shuster's controversial, off-budget treatment for aviation funding, which would exclude the money from overall budget calculations.

But divisions remain among senators over such issues as landing slots at Ronald Reagan Washington National Airport. If the Senate does not act by early July, there is little hope of reaching a House-Senate conference agreement to bridge the huge differences between the two bills before the current, temporary authorization expires Aug. 6.

Dedicated Funding

Shuster's House floor victory June 15 may be the high-water mark in his quest to provide a dedicated funding stream for aviation programs. But it is likely to give him a position of strength going into any conference with the Senate.

Shuster successfully fought off a coalition of the House's most powerful chairmen as he shepherded his bill past a series of amendments that would have wiped out key sections.

The most significant vote of the day occurred on an amendment offered by Appropriations Committee Chairman C.W. Bill Young, R-Fla., and House Budget Committee Chairman John R. Kasich, R-Ohio, that would have stripped the bill of its off-budget treatment of the airport trust fund. It also would have eliminated a guaranteed $3.4 billion contribution from the general Treasury toward FAA activities — a matter contested by authorizers and appropriators of both parties for several decades.

The House rejected the amendment, 179-248. *(Vote 207, p. H-72)*

During the weeks leading up to the vote, Shuster decried what he described as a "disinformation campaign" about the impact of his bill. On June 14, he sent out four separate "dear colleague" letters to House members rebutting, charge by charge, arguments that his legislation would restrict the oversight functions of appropriators or that it would have a detrimental effect on other fiscal 2000 appropriations, the Social Security trust fund balance and GOP tax-cutting plans.

But Shuster was unable to sway the appropriators and their allies, and as the vote approached, House observers were treated to a titanic floor struggle between some of the chamber's most powerful members.

Kasich and Young were joined by other appropriators and budget hawks, including Ways and Means Chairman Bill Archer, R-Texas, Majority Whip Tom DeLay, R-Texas, and ranking Appropriations Committee Democrat David R. Obey of Wisconsin. In speech after speech, the group said Shuster's bill would set a dangerous precedent, throwing a wrench into the federal budget process.

Young noted that the quest to find $10 billion in order to shore up a few fiscal 2000 spending bills had brought the House to a standstill over the past few weeks. The aviation bill would authorize $14.3 billion in spending above the level in the fiscal 2000 budget resolution (H Con Res 68), he said. "We have to maintain fiscal discipline in this House," said Young. "This is a budget-busting bill."

DeLay called the off-budget provision "irresponsible." Archer said the bill would eliminate any tax cuts for fiscal 2001, the last chance to provide relief before lawmakers face voters in November 2000.

Obey said it would be wrong to put airports ahead of all other budget priorities, including health research, veterans' benefits and education.

"Airports are high priorities, but I don't see why we should insulate them from cuts and require deeper cuts in other programs," Obey said.

But Shuster countered that the bill simply would ensure that aviation taxes are spent on their intended purpose, and that his bill did not boost aviation spending in any amount greater than the trust fund.

He said it was "morally wrong" to spend aviation taxes on non-aviation purposes, such as a general tax cut. In the end, Shuster won a surprisingly easy victory.

Lindsey Graham, R-S.C., led another conservative charge against the bill, sponsoring an amendment to strip language that would allow airports to double a fee tacked on to airline tickets to finance construction projects, from $3 to $6. Graham attacked the provision as a tax increase, adding "This bill already spends more than it should."

Shuster assured lawmakers that the increase would not apply to every airport and that airports would have to justify any increase in terms of how it would boost competition or reduce congestion. The amendment was defeated, 183-245. *(Vote 208, p. H-72)*

The defeat of the Graham amendment was another slap at the airline industry, which had lobbied to reduce the fee increase.

The industry also has been reeling from news accounts of mistreated passengers, which have bolstered efforts in the House by Shuster and Democrat John D. Dingell of Michigan and in the Senate by McCain and Richard C. Shelby, R-Ala., to enact an airline passengers' "bill of rights."

Simmering Over Slots

Whether any long-term FAA authorization emerges at all could depend on how quickly McCain can resolve a dispute with Senate colleague John W. Warner, R-Va., over increasing the number of flights into Reagan National, a busy urban airport across the Potomac River from Washington and just minutes from the Capitol.

Senate GOP leaders are wary of scheduling a floor debate for the aviation bill until these two powerful senators work out their dispute. The leaders do not want to be sidetracked by any open-ended floor fights during a month that will be filled with appropriations and a tax bills.

McCain's bill would allow an additional 48 flights a day into and out of National. That would more than double the number negotiated last year with Warner, who has been wary of the impact of the added air traffic on his Northern Virginia constituents.

In the House, the slot issue emerged in the days before the June 15 vote. Members of the New York and Illinois delegations threatened to tie up the floor debate with amendments addressing the noise and safety effects of any added flights at Chicago's O'Hare International and New York's La Guardia and John F. Kennedy International airports. Along with National, they are the only airports in the country where the number of takeoff and landing slots are restricted in the interest of controlling congestion and noise. Slot restrictions also can hinder competition.

Shuster was able to forge an agreement with the two states' sizable congressional delegations to postpone the bill's slot provisions in return for dropping the amendments.

The agreement, adopted by voice vote as part of Shuster's manager's amendment, would postpone the complete elimination of slot restrictions from March 1, 2000, until March 1, 2002 for O'Hare and until March 1, 2007, for the New York airports. But an unlimited number of new flights would be permitted at the three airports by small, regional jets beginning in 2000.

The House bill would allow six additional flights per day at National airport. Maryland and Virginia lawmakers representing areas near Washington generally opposed the bill.

Senate Critics

Aviation supporters lack a Senate champion of the guaranteed spending approach — unlike debate on last year's surface transportation authorization law (PL 105-178), when key senators worked to help overcome fiscal-related objections. *(1998 Almanac, p. 3-23)*

During that debate, Phil Gramm, R-Texas, and Robert C. Byrd, D-W.Va., teamed up on an amendment that guaranteed funding levels for highway programs. That amendment eventually garnered nearly two-thirds of the Senate as cosponsors, leaving budget hawks such as Pete V. Domenici, R-N.M., little room to maneuver in conference.

Domenici has already identified himself as a firm opponent of any attempt to create special budgetary treatment for FAA funding, either through the off-budget protections in HR 1000 or guaranteed spending levels such as in the highway law.

In a statement June 16, Domenici condemned the House vote. "I strongly believe this action is short sighted and does nothing to improve our nation's air-traffic control system or our airport infrastructure," he said.

Domenici argued that Congress has historically given the FAA its full budget request, so any shortfalls are more likely to rest with management problems that special budget guarantees would not solve. The House bill "responds to the problems at the FAA the old-fashioned way: throwing more money after bad," Domenici said.

The Clinton administration also opposes the off-budget treatment found in the House bill. The Office of Management and Budget said in a statement June 15 that it would recommend the president veto HR 1000 in its current form.

FAA Showdown Imminent as Senate OKs Short-Term Extension

JULY 31 — The Senate passed a 60-day extension of the Federal Aviation Administration's (FAA) airport construction program July 30 (S 1467), setting up a pre-recess showdown with House Transportation Committee Chairman Bud Shuster, R-Pa.

The current authorization for the Airport Improvement Program will expire Aug. 6. Without an extension, airports would be unable to begin new construction. Increasingly, that looks like a price that many members may be willing to pay as positions harden in the debate over a long-term reauthorization. Specifically, the two chambers are at odds over whether to dedicate the Airport and Airway Trust Fund exclusively to the FAA and take it out of regular budget calculations.

House Transportation Committee spokesman Scott Brenner said July 30 that Shuster has grown tired of the cycle of short-term extensions while the House waits for the Senate to consider the full, long-term bill (HR 1000, S 82). The program has operated all year under a series of stopgap measures.

"There won't be another short-term extension out of this chamber," Brenner said. He said Shuster would be willing to let the airport improvement program lapse rather than do another extension.

On the Senate side, aides to Commerce Committee Chairman John McCain, R-Ariz., said he, too, is frustrated by the delay in debating his long-term bill, which the committee marked up Feb. 11.

A group of senior senators, including Pete V. Domenici, R-N.M., Ted Stevens, R-Alaska, and Robert C. Byrd, D-W.Va., sent a letter to Majority Leader Trent Lott, R-Miss., on July 22 outlining their objections to the House bill's off-budget provisions and urging Lott to close off any attempt to go straight to conference on the long-term FAA authorization. The group fears that a short-term extension could serve as a vehicle for such a step.

Shuster, McCain Square Off as House Votes for Substitute Text

AUGUST 7 — A confrontation between the House and Senate over aviation policy has left the government's airport construction program without authority to operate this month, and probably until the end of the fiscal year Sept. 30.

Although the legislation in dispute would authorize the Federal Aviation Administration (FAA) for either two or five years, the agency's only program that cannot function this year without the authorization is the Airport Improvement Program.

The Senate had offered another in a series of short-term extensions that had kept the airport program going all year (S 1467), but Bud Shuster, R-Pa., chairman of the House Transportation and Infrastructure Committee, refused to go along. He persuaded the House to substitute the text of his full authorization bill (HR 1000) and send the measure back to the Senate.

But by the time that happened, the Senate had gone home for the summer recess.

At the core of the maneuvering are

two powerful Republican lawmakers who have long been at odds over aviation: Shuster and Senate Commerce Committee Chairman John McCain of Arizona.

Shuster has used his bill to try to shield aviation trust funds from the general budget, much as he has protected the Highway Trust Fund.

McCain has stressed in his bill (S 82) the need to boost airline competition by relaxing flight restrictions at four of the nation's busiest airports, including Washington's Ronald Reagan National Airport.

Their different priorities have made an agreement unlikely, but they were in agreement the week of Aug. 2 about going straight to conference to work out a compromise.

Since McCain's panel marked up S 82 on Feb. 11, the bill has been bogged down in disputes over so-called slot restrictions — federal rules that limit the number of takeoffs and landings at Reagan National as well as Chicago's O'Hare International and New York's John F. Kennedy International and La Guardia airports.

But with some last-minute developments on Aug. 4 and 5, it looked as if the Senate would be in position to go to conference on the long-term bill without a full floor debate.

When the Senate passed its 60-day extension, which would have allowed the program to continue to operate through the remainder of the fiscal year, Shuster declared that he would not allow the House to act on another short-term bill. He said he would go forward only on the long-term measure.

Shuster failed in his first attempt to call up S 1467 on the House floor Aug. 2. He failed to get recognition from the chair, apparently because the move had not been cleared with House leaders.

Shuster reportedly told House leaders he would not go along with a move to attach the FAA extension to another must-pass bill. He even threatened to sink the GOP's centerpiece tax bill (HR 2488) rather than let the extension go through as an amendment, lobbyists tracking the issue said.

In an Aug. 3 interview, Shuster said House leaders were supportive of his efforts. "The House leadership has said let's get this [FAA authorization] done," he said.

David R. Obey, D-Wis., who has fought against Shuster's attempts to create budgetary fences for transportation trust funds, was prepared to block any request for unanimous consent, forcing Shuster to go to the leadership for a rule for floor consideration.

In an Aug. 4 interview, Obey said he continued to object to the bill's special protections of the aviation trust fund and its spending levels, $39 billion over the level agreed to in the bipartisan 1997 balanced-budget agreement (PL 105-33).

"I do not give up my right to oppose legislation I think is wrong at every step of the way in the legislative process," Obey said. He argued that it was Shuster, by trying to go to conference on a bill the Senate had not debated, who was using an "irregular process."

Transportation Committee Chief of Staff Jack Schenendorf called the attempt at delay "petulance."

"The Appropriations Committee had a chance on the floor, and they lost," Schenendorf said in an interview. "They're attempting to achieve by guerrilla warfare what they couldn't achieve by the rules of the House."

The delay was enough to kill any window of opportunity for the Senate to appoint conferees. By the time the House acted, just before midnight on Aug. 5, the Senate had been shut down for three hours.

Obey, in the only floor speech as the House considered S 1467, accused Shuster of using the Airport Improvement Program as a "pawn."

"There is no need to deny airports funding," Obey said. "There is no need to shut airports down."

Senate Passes on Conference

On the Senate side, McCain has tired of the negotiations. In particular, he has had to deal with objections from John W. Warner, R-Va., and Charles S. Robb, D-Va., over lifting flight restrictions at Reagan National, and from Peter G. Fitzgerald, R-Ill., and Richard J. Durbin, D-Ill., over adding flights at O'Hare.

Asked Aug. 3 if he would like to go to conference with the House on the multi-year FAA bill, McCain said, "I would love to do that."

McCain might be ready to deal with Shuster, but it was not clear whether some of the Senate's budget hawks were ready to.

A bloc led by Budget Chairman Pete V. Domenici, R-N.M., has argued vociferously that the House bill would shortchange the budget process. In its view, giving aviation programs special protection might force appropriators to pinch other transportation programs such as the Coast Guard and Amtrak.

Domenici and four other senators sent Majority Leader Trent Lott, R-Miss., a letter July 22 expressing concern about any move to go to conference before full Senate debate and outlining objections to budgetary protection for aviation programs.

The other senators were Appropriations Chairman Ted Stevens, R-Alaska, ranking Appropriations Democrat Robert C. Byrd of West Virginia, Richard C. Shelby, R-Ala., and Frank R. Lautenberg, D-N.J.

But negotiations since then may have put some of those objections to rest. Some senators with concerns may be content to try to work them out in conference rather than continuing to delay floor debate.

McCain said he would urge Lott to appoint Domenici and Stevens to any conference committee. "I would want their advice," he said.

Those assurances might be enough to get to the next level. Budget Committee spokeswoman Amy Call said Domenici would not block that step. "We'll go to conference, but we're not going to agree to do off-budget," she said, referring to Shuster's desire to reserve the Airport and Airway Trust Fund for aviation programs.

Slade Gorton, R-Wash., chairman of the Commerce Subcommittee on Aviation and another opponent of budgetary protections, would also probably be a conferee. McCain was reportedly also considering Shelby. And McCain himself was firmly in that camp earlier in the year.

However, a conference weighted with opponents of budgetary protections has brought forth other opponents. Senators who favor Shuster's position, including Ernest F. Hollings, D-S.C., were considering blocking the move to conference, aides said.

A number of other Democrats concerned about flight restriction issues also were considering blocking the appointment of conferees. "Slots for us still remain an issue of great concern," said Robb spokesman John DiBiase.

Other Senate staffers said their bosses were uncertain about going to conference. The complexity of the Senate positions would not square well with the House's strong, focused stance and a 316-110 vote June 15 backing its bill.

"Bud Shuster has the proxies of all the House members," said a Senate GOP staffer. "When you get to conference, people can evolve."

To the relief of many senators on the fence, the House did not act until the Senate had left town. No one had to formally declare his opposition.

Construction Program Lapses

The short-term casualty is the Airport Improvement Program, which Shuster has worked to boost in his five-year bill. The last short-term extension (PL 106-6) expired Aug. 6. That freezes some $290 million in grants that would have been available for the rest of fiscal 1999.

"The $290 million question is whether the Senate will appoint conferees in September," said Todd Hauptli, a lobbyist for the American Association of Airport Executives.

But airport lobbyists said the lapse will cause some hardship for facilities that were planning new runway or terminal upgrades. Airports will have to delay beginning such projects until Congress acts. Also at risk are cargo facility projects. "Clearly, airports are going to be losing something," said Jeff Goodell, vice president for government relations at the Airports Council International-North America.

Airport officials said the larger concern is that the lack of a long-term authorization is putting a crimp in planning for airports anxious to deal with growing passenger traffic.

The FAA projects traffic to grow from its current level of 611 million passengers a year — an all-time high — to more than 1 billion by 2007. Because of multi-year environmental and community reviews, airports are pressing Congress to act now so they don't fall behind in their efforts to keep up with the growing traffic.

Congressional delays are frustrating local officials as well. In an Aug. 5 letter, the executive directors of the National Governors' Association, the National League of Cities, the National Association of Counties and the National Conference of State Legislatures urged Senate leaders to appoint conferees as soon as possible.

"There are approximately 3,300 city, county and state airports that are eligible for AIP funds, and it is essential that a multi-year bill be passed prior to the end of this session of Congress," the officials wrote.

Senate Passes Bill, Setting Up Fight Over Trust Fund In Conference

OCTOBER 9 — The Senate passed a wide-ranging reauthorization of the Federal Aviation Administration (FAA) on Oct. 5, completing months of behind-the-scenes wrangling over efforts to increase airline competition by adding flights at four congested airports.

Passage of the Senate measure, by voice vote, as a substitute for the House version (HR 1000) set up what is likely to be a contentious conference between Senate budget hawks and Bud Shuster, R-Pa., the determined chairman of the House Transportation and Infrastructure Committee.

Shuster wants to use the bill to reserve the Airport and Airway Trust Fund only for aviation-related construction.

The Senate bill would authorize $35 billion for aviation activities for three years, fiscal 2000-02, including $7.3 billion for the Airport Improvement Program, $8.4 billion for facilities and equipment, and $18.2 billion for FAA operations.

The bill as passed by the House would authorize aviation programs for five years, fiscal 2000-04, and is more generous, permitting $59.3 billion of spending. The authorization would increase dramatically in fiscal 2001, the first year the Airport and Airway Trust Fund would be taken "off-budget" — dedicated solely to aviation activities and not included in calculations of the federal budget surplus or deficit.

The Senate bill says nothing about the budgetary treatment of the aviation trust fund.

The expected Senate Republican conferees listed by Commerce Committee Chairman John McCain, R-Ariz., the bill's sponsor, would include Ted Stevens of Alaska, Slade Gorton of Washington and Pete V. Domenici of New Mexico, all strong opponents of the House's trust fund position. As of Oct. 8, no Democratic conferees had been named.

Unlike during the conference over the 1998 surface transportation bill (PL 105-178), in which the Senate went along with Shuster's push to take the Highway Trust Fund off-budget, there is no widespread movement among senators in favor of such guarantees for aviation spending.

In surface transportation negotiations, Senate budget hawks were constrained by a floor amendment to take the trust fund off-budget. Close to two-thirds of the Senate supported that language. There has been no similar effort on the aviation bill.

Preliminary maneuvering by McCain and Shuster over the multi-year authorization made it necessary for Congress to pass two short-term extensions of the authorization for the Airport Improvement Program this year. The most recent expired Aug. 6, and Shuster would not go along with a third delay.

Slot Troubles

The two days of Senate floor debate on the full authorization bill were dominated by provisions to relax restrictions on the number of flights allowed at four of the nation's busiest airports.

Federal law restricts the number of takeoff and landing "slots" available each day at Ronald Reagan Washington National Airport, LaGuardia and John F. Kennedy airports in New York, and O'Hare International Airport in Chicago. When enacted in the late 1960s, the restrictions were intended to enhance safety at the crowded airports and cut down on noise in surrounding neighborhoods.

Proponents of additional flights at the airports say they are critical to increasing airline competition. They say low-cost carriers that want to begin service to small and medium-size cities are locked out by the slot restrictions.

Senators from states with slot-controlled airports have opposed any changes. Most had agreed to work out their objections on the floor or in a manager's amendment. But freshman Peter G. Fitzgerald, R-Ill., who campaigned in part on O'Hare issues in his 1998 race against incumbent Democrat Carol Moseley-Braun, objected to a substitute bill introduced by Gorton.

Besides adding new flights for the four busy airports, the Gorton substitute would have phased out slot restrictions for the two New York airports by Dec. 31, 2006, and O'Hare by Dec. 31, 2003.

Fitzgerald blocked a move to adopt the substitute by voice vote, saying he had not been included in discussions about lifting the slot restrictions and that the inclusion of O'Hare in the scheme broke an agreement made last year with Moseley-Braun to keep the restrictions in place.

"Going back to the 1960s, the FAA has had a rule in effect that limits operations at O'Hare to 155 operations an hour," Fitzgerald said. "The reason for that rule was that the airport was at capacity, and adding more operations per hour would add to delays and jeopardize the safety of the flying public."

On Oct. 5, Fitzgerald adopted a filibuster-by-amendment strategy, filing 304 amendments for consideration. McCain challenged Fitzgerald: "He is jeopardizing, literally, the safety of airline passengers across the country, perhaps throughout the world."

In a testy exchange, Fitzgerald replied that he had not been able to reach McCain with his objections in the days leading up to floor debate. "I am sorry we have missed each other in recent days," he said. "Obviously [McCain] has dual responsibility now as a candidate for president of the United States."

McCain replied that he and Fitzgerald had discussed the O'Hare issue ever since Fitzgerald arrived in the Senate. "The senator knows full well. . . . [that] it has nothing to do with any presidential campaign or anything else," McCain said. "The senator should know that and correct the record."

Fitzgerald did not back down. After extensive behind-the-scenes negotiations, he was allowed to offer a second-degree amendment to the Gorton substitute to keep the slot restrictions in place at O'Hare, while permitting 30 new flights a day by 2003.

Before that blowup, McCain's greatest challenge had been to navigate differences with Virginia Sens. John W. Warner, a Republican, and Charles S. Robb, a Democrat, over restrictions at Reagan National. Warner had objected when McCain doubled the number of new flights that would be permitted, from 24 to 48, at the February markup of the Senate's FAA bill (S 82).

Warner and McCain had negotiated 24 new flights during consideration of an aviation authorization bill (PL 105-277) last year. The Gorton substitute brought the number back down to 24, a number acceptable to Warner. *(1998 Almanac, p. 24-34)*

Robb was in a more difficult position. Engaged in a close re-election campaign, Robb said he would oppose any additional flights at National. But by blocking the bill, Robb also was blocking money for other Virginia airports.

In the end, Robb settled for a roll call vote on an amendment to eliminate the new slot exemptions at National. It failed, 37-61. *(Vote 310, p. S-61)*

Robb did win voice-vote adoption of an amendment to ensure that the new flights at Reagan National would not take off or land between 10 p.m. and 7 a.m.

Slot issues could present another problem for House and Senate negotiators. The House bill differs on how to add new flights at the four busy airports. It would postpone elimination of flight restrictions at O'Hare until March 1, 2002, and at Kennedy and LaGuardia until March 1, 2007. The bill would allow unlimited access to the three airports by small jets by March 1, 2000. The bill would allow up to six additional flights a day at Reagan National.

Air Traffic Control

Gorton and John D. Rockefeller IV, D-W.Va., cosponsored an amendment, adopted by voice vote, aimed at speeding up an overhaul of the nation's air-traffic control system.

The amendment included a $100 million emergency authorization. It also would institute management changes, including a new FAA executive as a chief operating officer for the air-traffic control system. And it would enable the FAA to enter into joint ventures to ensure that new equipment is installed more quickly.

Rockefeller said changes were urgently needed to keep up with growth in the aviation system. "It is no secret that the FAA has a history of problems controlling costs and schedules on large-scale projects," he said. "We hope the creation of the chief operating officer position, with the responsibility for running and modernizing our air-traffic control system, will inject the necessary discipline into that system."

The Clinton administration supports the changes in the air-traffic control system, but it did not completely endorse the Gorton-Rockefeller amendment.

The language "could become the basis for a dialogue on achieving necessary management reform of the air-traffic control system," according to an Office of Management and Budget statement.

Transportation Secretary Rodney E. Slater added in an Oct. 4 written statement, "As three national commissions have clearly stated, air-traffic control is in urgent need of efficiency and capacity reform if we are to turn the tide on the system's growing gridlock."

Passenger Protection

The legislation incorporated a number of initiatives that address growing interest in airlines' treatment of passengers.

The bill incorporated a bill (S 383 — S Rept 106-162), cosponsored by McCain and Ron Wyden, D-Ore., that passed the Senate on March 25 and is now awaiting House action. Originally a wide-ranging passenger "bill of rights," the measure was scaled back to require the Department of Transportation's inspector general to monitor a voluntary agreement announced by the airlines June 17 and to report to Congress by June 15, 2000.

The airlines agreed to voluntarily offer the lowest fares available through phone reservations, notify passengers in advance of delays and cancellations, and allow reservations to be held free of charge for 24 hours.

The measure also would require the Transportation Department to issue regulations increasing airlines' financial responsibility for lost baggage, increase civil penalties against airlines that violate aviation consumer-protection laws, and require the General Accounting Office to study the incidence of widely varying ticket prices for the same flight.

While the Senate agreed to create a committee to study the airline industry, it rejected, on a 30-68 roll call vote, an amendment by Frank R. Lautenberg, D-N.J., to increase penalties on airlines that involuntarily "bump" passengers with paid reservations. *(Vote 311, p. S-61)*

Conferees Hope To 'Unlock' Trust Fund For Long-Term Needs

OCTOBER 23 — Conferees on a key transportation bill took the first steps the week of Oct. 18 toward resolving a two-year impasse over how to pay for aviation programs.

A long-term reauthorization of the Federal Aviation Administration (HR 1000) has been stalled because of vast differences over how the government should use money piling up in the Airport and Airway Trust Fund, primarily revenue from airline ticket taxes.

After conference meetings on Oct. 18 and 20, lawmakers and aides began to look at ways to ensure an increase in aviation funding while limiting the impact of that increase on the appropriations process.

Appropriators have loudly complained about last year's surface transportation law (PL 105-178), which requires certain spending levels. *(1998 Almanac, p. 24-3)*

Both House and Senate versions of the FAA bill would authorize more money for air traffic control improvements and airport construction. The FAA predicts that airline traffic will grow from the current level of 611 million passengers a year to 1 billion by 2007.

The House, led by Transportation and Infrastructure Committee Chairman Bud Shuster, R-Pa., has focused on ensuring a stream of aviation funding by taking the Airport and Airway Trust Fund "off budget," meaning the funds could be spent only on aviation and would not be subject to limits by appropriators.

The Senate version of the bill is silent on the issue, and many senators vehemently oppose off-budget treatment of the trust fund as an affront to the integrity of the appropriations process.

An aviation lobbyist said the negotiations would probably yield a new scheme for aviation financing. The Senate is unlikely to accept off-budget treatment or the "firewalls" that guarantee highway and transit spending. Instead, the lobbyist said, FAA conferees will probably look at creating "firewalls by another name."

At an Oct. 20 meeting of the conference, Shuster said he wanted members to focus on ways to "unlock the aviation trust fund" to address the growing needs of the aviation system.

Senate conferee Pete V. Domenici, R-N.M., the Budget Committee chairman, said that could be a basis of negotiations.

"If we can stay by the word 'unlock,' we can continue to talk for a while," Domenici said. "I do believe we can look at ways to define the word 'unlock.' "

Shuster and John McCain, R-Ariz., sponsor of the Senate bill, directed aides to look at the issue and report back early the week of Oct. 25. Shuster said the conference would meet again in the middle of the week.

But while the two sides began talks amid new optimism, it was unclear exactly how they might write funding guarantees acceptable to the House without alienating Senate budget hawks.

Filling Aviation Needs

In opening statements Oct. 18, lawmakers from both chambers spoke about their hopes that the bill would deal with specific airport or airline problems. Shuster said the legislation would be able to address few of the problems without adequate funding.

Rep. John E. Sweeney, R-N.Y., picked by Shuster to help push any deal through the House, said he was optimistic. "Everyone will try to come up with a funding figure for the long-term needs for aviation," he said. "The question is how to find it."

In an interview, Domenici said he opposes off-budget treatment of any trust fund and said he was concerned that providing "automatic expenditures" would put a squeeze on other programs. He also said he was worried about lawmakers following suit with other trust funds.

Slade Gorton, R-Wash., chairman of Commerce's Aviation Subcommittee, said he supported Domenici's efforts to block "walling off the aviation money." But Gorton said he was interested in increasing aviation funding. "I am for more generous treatment of airports and aircraft infrastructure in general," he said.

But Gorton noted that any aviation funding increases would have to be accompanied by offsetting budget cuts — another pitfall. In 1998, negotiations over the six-year surface transportation law nearly failed over opposition to an offsetting cut in veterans' health benefits.

Until the funding issues are settled, conferees are unlikely to address two other areas of controversy: how to relax restrictions on the number of flights at four of the nation's busiest airports and whether to allow an increase in a surcharge on airline tickets.

Conferees Throw In the Towel On Long-Term FAA Funding

NOVEMBER 13 — House-Senate negotiations on a long-term authorization bill for the Federal Aviation Administration broke down Nov. 10 over how to guarantee increased funding.

Financing aviation programs in the face of projected growth in air travel has been at the center of negotiations over the bill (HR 1000), which also includes management changes at the FAA, proposals to increase airline competition and funding for an airport construction program.

In a strongly worded statement Nov. 10, House Transportation and Infrastructure Committee Chairman Bud Shuster, R-Pa., said the latest Senate proposal would actually cut aviation spending and allow an additional $3 billion to build up in the Airport and Airway Trust Fund.

"The Senate proposal simply fails to recognize the growing needs in aviation," Shuster said. "I pledge that I will renew my efforts next year to unlock the aviation trust fund and fulfill our commitment to make our skies as safe as they can be."

John McCain, R-Ariz., chairman of the Senate Commerce, Science and Transportation Committee, replied in a Nov. 11 statement that he was "disappointed" by the breakdown in negotiations.

"The air traveling consumer will have to wait once again for crucial competition enhancement provisions to take effect," McCain said.

With the two sides having given up on an agreement before Congress goes home for the year, the question was whether the House will go along with a stopgap authorization. The Senate passed a six-month extension (S 1916) on Nov. 10.

The short-term bill would allow airports to receive construction grant money through March 31. No grants have been authorized since the beginning of the fiscal year Oct. 1.

Shuster said he would oppose any short-term bill. He has grown frustrated with the series of short-term extensions that have kept airport grants flowing since 1997, aides said, because little progress has been made on the long-term bill.

"This Band-Aid approach can only delay the significant investments that the flying public has paid for and deserves," Shuster said.

But it is not clear that House leaders will back Shuster in his effort to hold airport construction money hostage. If they decide to sidestep the combative chairman, it is likely the short-term FAA extension will be attached to a must-pass appropriations bill the week of Nov. 15.

The Elusive Guarantee

Shuster and McCain began the year with aviation legislation among their most important goals. But their different priorities made a deal elusive for the second year in a row.

Nowhere was this more apparent than on the future of the 30-year-old Airport and Airway Trust Fund, financed primarily by taxes on domestic airline tickets and flight segments.

Shuster proposed taking the trust fund "off budget," meaning that the money would be available only for aviation and would not be counted toward the federal surplus or deficit. He sought to give aviation financing protection similar to that he won for highways and mass transit in the 1998 surface transportation authorization law (PL 105-178). *(1998 Almanac, p. 24-3)*

The House backed Shuster's position during floor debate on June 15, defeating an amendment offered by Appropriations Committee Chairman C.W. Bill Young, R-Fla., and Budget Committee Chairman John R. Kasich, R-Ohio, to remove the off-budget provision. And despite the opposition of those two powerful committee chairmen, along with Majority Whip Tom DeLay, R-Texas, and Ways and Means Committee Chairman Bill Archer, R-Texas, the House passed the bill, 316-110.

When conference discussions began, Shuster dropped his call for off-budget treatment of the trust fund. But he demanded some other kind of guarantee that aviation trust fund money would not be appropriated for other purposes.

Shuster proposed that aviation funds be treated the same way transit funds are under the surface transportation law — by a "firewall" that guarantees the appropriation while counting the spending toward the overall federal surplus or deficit.

Senate Republican conferees were adamantly against ceding much ground to Shuster on the issue. There was no budgetary provision in the Senate legislation (S 82), and many said special budget fences for aviation would not garner the 60 votes required to pass the conference report under budget rules.

Even senators who wanted to increase spending on aviation, such as Slade Gorton, R-Wash., were concerned that the budgetary protections Shuster sought would erode the integrity of the appropriations process.

Last-Ditch Efforts

Shuster's Nov. 10 declaration marked the abrupt end of a week of intense negotiations during which the two sides appeared to be narrowing their differences.

Throughout the week, Shuster's staff traded proposals with their Senate counterparts. They were attempting to implement a verbal agreement Shuster reached Nov. 8 with McCain, Senate Majority Leader Trent Lott, R-Miss., and Senate Budget Committee Chairman Pete V. Domenici, R-N.M.

The senators had proposed allowing the authorization for aviation spending to grow as receipts in the aviation trust fund increased. They also proposed that the interest generated by the trust fund, estimated at about $1 billion a year, could be authorized for aviation. The trust fund money would be protected against being spent on other purposes by a point of order.

The senators promised that Shuster would be backed by House and Senate GOP leaders in his quest to ensure that some general tax revenues would also be available for aviation.

Shuster directed his staff Nov. 8 to draft language that would implement his verbal agreement with the senators. The language they produced Nov. 9 was rejected by Senate staff members. One aide, citing its explicit guarantee of general fund money, described the language as "a huge step backward."

After more discussions between Shuster and Lott, Senate aides were directed to come up with their own implementing language.

But Shuster said Nov. 10 that the Senate language did not live up to the verbal agreement. He said the Senate plan would reduce current baselines on aviation spending, and that the promises on general fund money did not go far enough.

James L. Oberstar, the ranking Democrat on the House Transportation Committee, said the point of order offered by the Senate would provide little guarantee for aviation, since the Rules Committee could structure floor debate in such a way as to make it irrelevant.

Oberstar added that the leadership promises reminded him of pledges made during the debate on aviation legislation in 1990 (PL 101-508). Funding was delivered for a few years, but after leaders and chairmen changed, the promises quickly faded away. *(1990 Almanac, p. 384)*

Even if Shuster were to succeed in the negotiations with Lott, Oberstar said, the resulting package might not be enough for the House. "We might be better off with current law," he said.

Other Issues

Without an agreement on the aviation budget, House and Senate conferees never finalized agreements on other contentious issues, such as whether to allow additional flights into the four airports where the number of takeoff and landing slots are federally controlled — Chicago's O'Hare International, Ronald Reagan Washington National, and New York's John F. Kennedy and La Guardia international airports.

Supporters of the additional flights argued that they were essential to help increase competition among airlines, which would in turn lower prices for passengers. But lawmakers who represent areas surrounding the airports fought the new flights as a safety hazard and an imposition on their constituents.

The increases in the number of slots were McCain's highest priority. The Arizona Republican fought for months with senators from Illinois, New York and Virginia to win the new flights at the busy airports.

America West, an airline based in Phoenix, would have been one of the biggest winners of the increased access to the airports. The Arizona airline also would have benefited from McCain's attempt to eliminate the so-called perimeter rule, which prohibits flights of more than 1,250 miles from Reagan National.

"I will continue to fight for better access to the nation's largest airports so that new entrants can compete with the major airlines and bring enormous benefits to consumers," McCain said in his Nov. 11 statement.

Conferees also deferred a decision on whether to allow an increase in the passenger facility charge, which airports can levy. The House bill proposed allowing an increase in the maximum permissible fee from $3 to $6.

The increase is vigorously supported by airports, which rely on the charge to help finance development. But airlines oppose the fee increase because it would raise the price of tickets. Airports can also use the money to build additional gates, which can help to bring in competition not necessarily welcomed by airlines.

House Balks On Stopgap FAA Funding

NOVEMBER 20 — The House wrapped up its business for the year without acting on a six-month reauthorization of the Federal Aviation Administration and airport improvement grants, though FAA operations will continue under an appropriations law.

The Senate on Nov. 10 passed the stopgap bill (S 1916) because a full reauthorization measure (HR 1000 — H Rept 106-167, Parts 1 and 2; S Rept 106-9) is deadlocked in conference.

Without the six-month extension, airport construction projects around the country will not receive additional federal money until Congress enacts some type of reauthorization.

House Transportation and Infrastructure Committee Chairman Bud Shuster, R-Pa., refused to consider a short-term remedy in order to keep the pressure on negotiations on the long-term bill. House leaders went along with him.

"We feel that the best thing we can do is not have any extension," Shuster said Nov. 18.

Negotiations on the long-term reauthorization bill broke down Nov. 10 over how to guarantee increased funding for airport construction and other aviation programs.

Shuster wants to take the Airport and Airway Trust Fund "off budget," meaning that the money would be available only for aviation and would not be counted toward the federal surplus or deficit. He has been willing to consider other methods of guaranteeing that trust fund revenue, primarily from ticket taxes, would be used only for aviation.

Senate negotiators, led by John McCain, R-Ariz., chairman of the Commerce, Science and Transportation Committee, have refused to go along with Shuster's plan.

Shuster said the two sides had reached a verbal compromise Nov. 8, but the conference halted when aides tried to reduce the deal to writing.

A series of short-term extensions have kept airport grants flowing since 1997, but authority expired Oct. 1. ◆

Congress Creates Agency, Modeled on the FAA, To Oversee Truck Safety

Box Score

- **Bill:** HR 3419 — PL 106-159
- **Legislative action: House** passed HR 2679 (H Rept 106-333), 415-5, on Oct. 14.

House passed HR 3419, by voice vote, on Nov. 18.

Senate cleared HR 3419, by voice vote, on Nov. 19.

President signed HR 3419 on Dec. 9.

SUMMARY

HR 3419 would create a Federal Motor Carrier Safety Administration to oversee truck and bus safety. The bill was cleared for President Clinton on Nov. 19, and he signed it Dec. 9. The fiscal 2000 transportation appropriations act (HR 2084) had cut off the budget of the existing Office of Motor Carriers unless it was moved out of the Federal Highway Administration. (*Transportation appropriations, p. 2-116*)

Rising concern over highway deaths in truck and bus accidents drew increasing congressional attention to federal regulation of motor carriers. There were five separate House hearings to explore aspects of the issue.

On April 27, the Transportation Department's inspector general testified before the Senate Commerce, Science and Transportation Committee that the department had dramatically scaled back the enforcement activities of the Office of Motor Carriers even as the death toll was on the rise.

Such shortcomings fueled efforts to strip regulatory authority from the highway administration, which had inherited many safety and regulatory functions of the Interstate Commerce Commission when Congress shut that agency down in 1995 (PL 104-88). Lawmakers and consumer advocates argued that the safety mission had become buried in an agency that was primarily concerned with a $29 billion highway construction program. Critics also said the Office of Motor Carriers sided too often with the trucking industry.

In early August, Senate Commerce Committee Chairman John McCain, R-Ariz., and Bud Shuster, R-Pa., chairman of the House Transportation and Infrastructure Committee, unveiled separate bills to create a new agency to regulate trucks and buses outside the highway administration.

The Shuster bill (HR 2679) would have created a National Motor Carrier Safety Administration, patterned on the Federal Aviation Administration, to conduct compliance reviews of trucking companies and to transfer money to the states for roadside inspections. The House passed the bill on Oct. 14.

McCain's proposal (S 1501) would have required a Motor Carrier Safety Administration to implement all of the inspector general's recommendations on strengthening enforcement activities and overhauling data collection methods.

Meanwhile, the transportation appropriations act (HR 2084 — PL 106-69) jumped ahead and prohibited spending for the Office of Motor Carriers unless it was shifted out of the highway administration. The Clinton administration quickly did so.

In the final days of the session, Shuster put together a new bill (HR 3419) combining elements of his and McCain's measures, informally worked out differences with Senate Commerce Committee members and quickly moved the measure through both houses.

Report on Safety, Road Deaths Spurs Congress Into Action

MAY 29 — A scathing inspector general's report on the federal agency that regulates interstate trucks, coupled with the rising carnage on the highway, has given new impetus to the truck safety issue on Capitol Hill.

More lawmakers are showing interest in legislation by Rep. Frank R. Wolf, R-Va., chairman of the House Appropriations Transportation Subcommittee, that would move truck regulation out of the Federal Highway Administration and into the chief highway safety agency.

Transportation Secretary Rodney Slater, who wants to leave truck regulation where it is, unveiled an initiative on May 25 to reduce truck fatalities by half over the next 10 years — the second time since February he has set a new goal.

After years of lobbying to be left alone, the trucking industry now has come out in favor of a separate agency for truck regulation, but one that the industry could help shape. Some trucking executives think their industry deserves its own regulatory bureau, much as airlines have the Federal Aviation Administration and railroads have the Federal Railroad Administration.

Prospects are good that Congress will act on truck safety this year.

"The atmosphere has definitely changed," said Michael J. Scippa, executive director of Citizens for Reliable and Safe Highways, a grass-roots group. "It feels like the rest of the country is catching up to our agenda."

The new dynamic has led Congress to engage in more truck safety oversight activities than at any point since the Republican takeover in 1995. The turning point perhaps came on April 27, when Transportation Department Inspector General Kenneth Mead delivered a blistering report to the Senate Commerce, Science and Transportation Committee on the failings of the Office of Motor Carriers in the highway administration.

Mead painted a picture of an agency that has become too close to the industry it regulates. The report showed a dramatic fall-off in enforcement even as the number of deaths in truck-related accidents was rising — fewer trucks inspected, fewer cited for safety violations, and fewer fines collected.

"Sanctions imposed by [the Office of Motor Carriers] for noncompliance are too often minimal or non-existent, suggesting a certain tolerance level for violation of safety regulations," the report stated.

Mead's probe found that only 11 percent of violations cited by federal safety investigators in fiscal 1998 resulted in fines, and that the cases were settled for, on average, 46 cents on the dollar — averaging about $1,600. Many motor carriers viewed these fines as little more than a cost of doing business, rather than as a deterrent, the inspector general concluded.

Most damaging of all, Mead found in January that officials of the Office of Motor Carriers were improperly encouraging trucking firms to lobby Congress against proposals to relocate the agency. Shortly after the revelations, the head of the motor carrier office, George Reagle, was replaced by Julie Anna Cirillo, a 30-year veteran of the Federal Highway Administration who recently led a top-to-bottom restructuring of the highway agency.

Carrying the Freight

Three congressional committees are looking at efforts to improve truck safety, and all of those panels are considering ways to shake up the Office of Motor Carriers.

Last year, Wolf tried unsuccessfully to attach legislation to the omnibus spending bill (PL 105-277) that would have transferred truck regulation to the National Highway Traffic Safety Administration (NHTSA). *(1998 Almanac, p. 2-84)*

"I think it's an issue that people are very, very concerned about," Wolf said in a May 17 interview. "I think you have to beef up [the Office of Motor Carriers] and move it out of the Federal Highway Administration."

Wolf said truck regulation tends to get lost in an agency whose primary mission is to spend billions of dollars on road construction. But more than the location of the office, Wolf said any legislation must make the agency focus on safety rather than on promoting the trucking industry.

"Whatever we do, we need to make sure it is locked into law," Wolf said.

Wolf's move on the omnibus spending bill was quashed after an aggressive lobbying campaign by the trucking industry, including the hiring of former Republican National Chairman Haley Barbour to lobby congressional leaders.

Wolf's move also frustrated Senate Commerce Committee Chairman John McCain, R-Ariz., who helped strip the provision from the bill because it had never been aired in committee.

But after Mead's critique of the Office of Motor Carriers, McCain shot off a strongly worded letter to Slater calling for immediate action by the Transportation Department (DOT).

"The [inspector general's] audit provides little reassurance to the traveling public that DOT is working to get unsafe motor carriers off our nation's roads and highways," McCain wrote. "These findings are of serious concern and lead me, and many others, to question the seriousness of DOT's commitment to safety enforcement."

McCain spokeswoman Pia Pialorsi said the senator would evaluate the Transportation Department's plan before deciding on legislation.

The House Transportation and Infrastructure Committee has held three hearings on truck safety and one session on bus safety.

Committee Chairman Bud Shuster, R-Pa. — traditionally a friend of the trucking industry — said at a Ground Transportation Subcommittee hearing May 26 that "virtually everyone except DOT agrees that the placement of the [motor carrier] office handicaps it in its mission."

"There's no question that we have to strengthen that office," Shuster said. "The Federal Highway administrator has too many issues on his plate."

Subcommittee Chairman Tom Petri, R-Wis., said at the hearing that he would work with ranking Democrat Nick J. Rahall II, D-W.Va., on legislation that he believed would move this summer. Aides said a bill could be ready as early as the week of May 31.

Wolf, for his part, in February reintroduced his proposal (HR 507) to move truck regulation to NHTSA and the bill enjoys the fervid support of safety groups. Wolf has leverage: If the authorizing committee does not act, he will attach a rider to his spending bill.

Getting on Board

Trucks are increasingly the vehicles of choice for moving goods through a booming U.S. economy, and the number on the roads is likely to increase steadily, according to the American Trucking Association Inc. In 1997, trucking was a $372 billion industry. It moved 81 percent of the nation's freight by economic value, and 60 percent by volume. Trucks traveled 170 billion miles and used more than 42 billion gallons of fuel in 1997.

But as the amount of goods being shipped by truck has increased, so has the death toll. There were 5,302 people killed in truck-related accidents in 1998, which was 20 percent more than the 4,422 in 1992.

By comparison, there were no deaths on U.S. commercial air carriers in 1998.

Safety advocates say the number of deaths — roughly equivalent to a major plane crash every two weeks — is a crisis that has been virtually ignored by the federal government.

Federal Highway Administration inspectors concentrate on auditing trucking firms for compliance with federal regulations. Through grants, the agency funds roadside inspection programs that are administered by the states. Thirty-eight states currently have such inspection programs, according to the Commercial Vehicle Safety Alliance.

News coverage of truck-related deaths and the administrative failures of the Office of Motor Carriers have helped push the trucking industry to embrace a number of safety initiatives, including the establishment of a separate agency and a substantial increase in resources for enforcement of federal safety regulations.

Earlier this year, industry officials called for a restructuring of regulatory offices. The American Trucking Associations, the Motor Freight Carrier Association, the National Private Truck Council and the Owner-operator Independent Drivers Association all support the concept of a Motor Carrier Safety Administration within the Department of Transportation.

The groups argue that the size of the trucking industry is on a par with aviation. Truckers say that their concerns are buried in the Transportation Department's bureaucracy.

Testifying before the Senate Commerce Committee, American Trucking Association President Walter B. McCormick Jr. said, "The trucking industry and the motoring public deserve a federal agency that has truck and bus safety as its core mission. This would allow an administrator to sit with administrators from the other modes as an equal."

When Congress eliminated the Interstate Commerce Commission (ICC) in 1995 (PL 104-88), it capped two decades of trucking deregulation. Trucking organizations now say the pendulum may have swung too far, according to Timothy Lynch, president and CEO of the Motor Freight Carriers Association, which represents six major unionized trucking companies. *(1995 Almanac, p. 3-36)*

"We need more visible enforcement activity, so the whole community knows they had better play by the rules," Lynch said. The unionized companies believe that work rules and grievance procedures make their drivers safer.

Monitoring the Details

Accidents involving trucks have led to the creation of a number of private groups lobbying for stricter regulation. Scippa's group, Citizens for Reliable and Safe Highways, for instance, counts about 43,000 members who support the group's truck safety agenda, mainly to bolster federal efforts to limit truck size and weight, reduce driver fatigue and improve vehicle maintenance standards. The core members of the group are about 2,500 survivors of truck crashes, Scippa said.

"We're seeing, nationwide, little community groups popping up, trying to somehow affect the truck traffic where it's never been before," Scippa said.

One group seen on Capitol Hill earlier this year, the Maine-based Parents Against Tired Truckers, emerged from one of those local efforts. The group's co-chairman, Daphne Izer, told a House subcommittee in March about the 1993 death of her 16-year-old son, Jeffrey, killed with three teenage friends when an 80,000-pound truck smashed his Ford Escort.

Most safety groups prefer Wolf's plan to move the Office of Motor Carriers to NHTSA, rather than creating a new, independent agency. They say the only way to ensure that the motor carrier office does not simply continue its old ways under a new name is to merge it with an agency that has a different culture.

"The culture of the [motor carrier office] is a do-nothing agency," said Joan Claybrook, president of consumer watchdog Public Citizen and a board member of Advocates for Highway and Auto Safety.

Claybrook, a former NHTSA administrator, said the agency has a strong and proven safety focus. An independent motor carrier administration would not necessarily have a strong safety focus, she said. The trucking industry "realized there was momentum to do something," she said. "But they are interested in a promotional agency."

Trucking groups argue that NHTSA is smaller than the Office of Motor Carriers and is a more centralized agency focusing on design standards for cars and trucks. Safety concerns arising from trucking operations are an entirely different matter, and NHTSA does not have a proven field operation for enforcement, they say.

Mead, the Transportation Department inspector general, testified before the House Transportation Committee that NHTSA "does not have the field structure necessary to execute and support an effective motor carrier oversight program."

Wolf said he is open to the idea of an independent agency focused on safety. The key would be the legislative language creating such an agency.

"You would have to have in organic language requirements with regard to safety, so that it is not a promotional agency," he said.

Administration Efforts

Wolf said he hopes the Clinton administration will take a more active role in the debate in Congress. "I think history will judge them very harshly unless they propose something soon and actively work for it on the Hill," Wolf said.

Wolf got part of his wish May 25, when Slater announced his department-wide initiative to reduce truck-related deaths by half.

For years, the trucking industry and the Federal Highway Administration have evaluated progress on truck safety by focusing on the rate of fatalities compared with overall truck traffic. That rate has fallen from 3.7 per 100 million vehicle miles in 1989 to 2.8 in 1997.

In the Transportation Department's fiscal 2000 budget request, the primary highway safety goal is a reduction in the truck fatality rate from 2.8 to 2.5.

But the purported increase in safety has been offset by an ever-increasing number of trucks on the road, so that even as the death rate has gone down, the number of deaths has gone up. Recently, the department has begun focusing on the total death toll.

The safety goal was revised to a 20 percent decrease in the number of deaths in a plan submitted to Congress after the budget proposal. On May 25, Slater announced the 50 percent goal. To do that, he said, the Transportation Department would:

- Write new rules allowing the department to shut down unfit carriers.
- Limit negotiated settlements and eliminate the backlog of enforcement cases by Jan. 1.
- Double the number of compliance reviews for the department's 230 safety investigators, increasing the annual total per inspector from 24 to 48.
- Aggressively pursue criminal and civil actions against law-breaking carriers.
- Ask Congress for $55.8 million in additional resources for safety activities in fiscal 2000.

"As a department, we're stepping up to the plate," Slater said. "We're not just rearranging the organizational boxes."

Capitol Clout

To Wolf, it seems the industry's power in the Capitol has served mainly to slow the pace of change in safety initiatives. "They have too much clout," he said.

Figures from lobbying reports filed with the secretary of the Senate indicate that the trucking lobby spent $1.5 million in lobbying fees over the last half of 1998, including $160,00 with Barbour, Griffith & Rogers, the high-profile firm that includes former Republican official Barbour.

In terms of political action committee contributions, the industry has an even greater impact. The American Trucking Associations alone contributed to 239 congressional candidates in the 1997-98 election cycles, according to FEC figures.

Individuals and political action committees with ties to trucking contributed $818,586 to members of the Senate Commerce Committee over the last six years, according to a study by the Center for Responsive Politics.

But publicity from truck crash victims and their growing network of safety-oriented groups has countered that Capitol Hill clout. Those grassroots watchdogs helped shine light on the Clinton administration when the motor carrier office fell into some regulatory lapses.

"I think the average person thought the truck lobby was so powerful that there was nothing they could honestly do," Wolf said. "Now, I think, there's a little hope."

House Bill Would Create National Motor Carrier Administration

AUGUST 7 — House Transportation and Infrastructure Committee Chairman Bud Shuster, R-Pa., jump-started debate on truck safety Aug. 3, unveiling a bill that would create a National Motor Carrier Administration patterned on the Federal Aviation Administration.

The agency would take truck and bus regulation out of the Federal Highway Administration, where it is now, but not put it in the National Highway Traffic Safety Administration (NHTSA), where some lawmakers would like it.

The Transportation Committee approved the legislation (HR 2679) by voice vote Aug. 5, a day after the Ground Transportation Subcommittee approved it, also by voice vote.

In the Senate on Aug. 5, Commerce, Science and Transportation Committee Chairman John McCain, R-Ariz., unveiled his own truck safety legislation to transfer most of the current Office of Motor Carriers to a new Motor Carrier Safety Administration.

McCain's bill would limit the budget and staff of the agency to levels endorsed by the Clinton administration in May 1999 — including a $50 million boost for motor carrier safety and data collection programs.

The quick House markup came after several months of debate on how best to monitor the trucking industry. The number of people killed in truck-related accidents rose steadily over five years beginning in 1992, peaking at 5,398 in 1997. Over the same period, the fatality rate has remained constant.

"Let me be clear that there is not a major safety crisis," Shuster said. "But there is room for improvement."

But safety issues have been a subject of much interest on Capitol Hill. The House Transportation Committee held four hearings and the Senate Commerce Committee also looked into the issue. Department of Transportation Inspector General Kenneth Mead concluded in an April 27 report that the highway administration's Office of Motor Carriers had scaled back its inspection efforts and negotiated minimal fines even as the number of fatalities increased.

McCain's bill would require the new Motor Carrier Administration to implement Mead's recommendations.

Frank R. Wolf, R-Va., chairman of the House Appropriations Transportation Subcommittee, tried to address the issue last October by inserting a provision into the omnibus spending bill (PL 105-277) to move the Office of Motor Carriers from the highway administration to NHTSA. The provision was dropped after Shuster and McCain objected.

Stress on Safety

The Shuster bill would transfer personnel and funds for motor carrier safety from the Federal Highway Administration to the new Motor Carrier Administration. The charter of the new agency, stressing safety, is modeled after the legislation that created the Federal Aviation Administration in 1958.

The agency would be in charge of conducting compliance reviews of trucking companies and funneling money to the states for roadside inspections. It would be in charge of rule-making for the industry, including setting standards for commercial drivers' licenses. And it would conduct research on safety issues.

The trucking industry has embraced the Shuster proposal as a good way to put its industry on equal footing with aviation, railroads and maritime shipping industries, each of which has a separate administration within the Transportation Department.

Highway safety advocates expressed concern that the new agency would focus as much on the economics of the industry as on safety. Just before the subcommittee markup, the staff removed a section of the bill that would have directed the agency to encourage "sound economic conditions in the transportation industry and sound economic condition of carriers."

The American Insurance Association, which allied itself with safety advocates to support Wolf's proposal last year, endorsed Shuster's bill.

The legislation calls for the secretary of Transportation to develop a motor carrier safety strategy.

The agency would be funded by transferring money authorized under the 1998 surface transportation law (PL 105-178) for the Office of Motor Carriers. *(1998 Almanac, p. 24-3)*

The bill also would provide for an additional $550 million for motor carrier safety grants to state and local governments. A $250 million portion of these funds is guaranteed by the surface transportation law.

The bill would add new rules for suspending the licenses of commercial drivers who cause fatal accidents. And it would require the Transportation secretary to ensure there will be an adequate number of safety inspectors along the U.S. border.

Congress Meets Trucker Fatigue Issue Head-On

SEPTEMBER 25 — For James E. York, a truck driver from Columbus, Ohio, there is no real mystery why the Department of Labor now considers his occupation the nation's most lethal.

"In trucking, there's a lot of talk of safety," York said, "but the real bottom line is on-time delivery."

To meet tight, competitive schedules and cover the mileage on which their pay depends, truckers frequently bend or just ignore the federal government's 60-year-old rule that they take eight hours of rest for every 10 behind the wheel.

But with 5,000 people killed in truck-related accidents in each of the past three years, grieving families and highway safety groups have stepped up demands that either the Transportation Department or Congress do something about a contributing cause for some accidents — tired truckers.

Both have avoided the issue, and for a simple political reason — the two sides in the debate are pulling in opposite directions. Safety groups want drivers to have more time for rest and think they should be paid by the hour, not by the mile. The trucking industry thinks drivers can safely work the same or longer hours, but with schedules tailored to body rhythms.

Another case for caution is the likely economic impact of any change that affects trucking schedules. The just-in-time deliveries that help keep industries humming have turned trucks into rolling warehouses and drivers into clock-watchers.

"Eighty percent of the country's goods move on trucks," said Timothy Lynch, president and CEO of the Motor Freight Carrier Association. "We're wrapped around the economy."

The Transportation Department's Federal Highway Administration began looking into a new rule on driver rest in 1989, but the process turned into a battle of sleep scientists.

When Congress in 1995 passed legislation (PL 104-88) to shut down the Interstate Commerce Commission, which once regulated much of the trucking industry, it gave the Transportation Department three deadlines to draft new rules on truck driver hours of service, the most recent March 1. The department has missed all three. *(1995 Almanac, p. 3-36)*

"It has gotten to the point where the agency can miss deadlines with impunity," complained Jerry Donaldson, senior research director for Advocates for Highway and Auto Safety, a consumer group.

While Congress has gotten an earful of testimony on truck safety this year — five House hearings, two in the Senate and another scheduled for Sept. 29 by the Senate Commerce, Science and Transportation Subcommittee on Surface Transportation and Merchant Marine — neither of the truck safety bills being considered this year (HR 2679, S 1501) addresses the question of driver rest.

"They know it's a hornet's nest. They didn't feel taking on that controversy will get them anywhere," said Joan Claybrook, president of consumer watchdog group Public Citizen and former head of the National Highway Traffic Safety Administration.

Pressure for some action is building, however. The Highway Administration may issue a preliminary rule on driver rest in October, under prodding from Transportation Secretary Rodney Slater, who unveiled a broad truck safety program in May.

The House bill, which would create a National Motor Carrier Administration to regulate truck and bus safety, is likely to reach the floor in the coming weeks, and tired drivers could be an issue.

At a House Transportation and Infrastructure subcommittee hearing on March 25, Daphne Izer testified how the 1993 death of her teenage son and three friends when their car was hit by a truck led her to help found Parents Against Tired Truckers.

"I couldn't be angrier at the lack of movement on new hours-of-service rules and enforcement actions," Izer told the subcommittee. "I couldn't be more disheartened and denigrated as a parent of a child who lost his life to a truck driver who was violating outdated hours-of-service regulations."

Depression Rules

No one involved in the truck safety issue is satisfied with the current regulations, adopted during the Great Depression. Aside from the rule of eight hours' rest for 10 at the wheel, drivers are allowed to be "on duty" for another five hours, for paperwork or preparation at a terminal. Some use the time to load or unload. Others may work more than five hours loading but don't record the extra time in order to give themselves more hours at the wheel, according to York, who has worked with Parents Against Tired Truckers.

"There are a lot of tired drivers because they are not compensated like they should be," York said.

Truck drivers are exempted from the Fair Labor Standards Act, so 90-hour workweeks are common throughout the industry, York said.

Safety groups advocate shorter driving time limits, as well as restrictions on loading and unloading. They also advocate the European system of paying drivers by the hour rather than by the mile.

The groups often cite 1995 findings of the National Transportation Safety Board (NTSB) that driver fatigue and lack of sleep were factors in up to 30 percent of truck crashes that resulted in fatalities to truck occupants. A 1992 report of the safety board found that 19 percent of truck drivers surveyed said they had fallen asleep at the wheel during the previous month.

Trucking industry associations say the safety groups overstate the NTSB statistics. A truer measure, they say, is a safety board study of all truck accidents reported by police, which concluded that fatigue was a factor in 2.8 percent to 6.5 percent of all fatal truck crashes.

Circadian Rhythms

The trucking industry, through the powerful American Trucking Associations, is pushing for a "science based" rule on driver rest, one that presumably would allow longer shifts.

The association said that current rules can take safe drivers off the road well before they tire. A driver observing the government's 10-hours-on-eight-hours-off regulations will inevitably end up driving in the middle of the night or during the late afternoon. Industry-funded sleep scientists say this 18-hour cycle ignores the body's circadian rhythms, putting the driver on the road when his body will want to rest.

"We want a rule that assures adequate rest, but also one that assures that our industry can continue to operate," said trucking association spokesman Mike Russell. "We need to meet the needs of our shippers."

The trucking industry has proposed a longer work shift. A recent trucking association study concluded that drivers working a 14-hour shift with a lunch break do not get significantly more tired than those working shorter shifts.

Association President Walter B. McCormick Jr. argued that reducing hours of service will hinder safety efforts by forcing companies to hire more drivers.

"In a tight labor market, trucking companies already have difficulty recruiting the 80,000 new drivers that are needed every year," McCormick wrote in an op-ed piece in The Washington Post. "Does anyone really believe a flood of inexperienced drivers will improve truck safety?"

This view is echoed by Margaret Peterson, a Southern California-based truck driver with Roadway Express. Like many truckers, Peterson said adequate rest is a matter of personal responsibility, not government regulation. She said increasing trucks' idle time is likely to have an impact — but not the one safety advocates hope for.

"You have to be realistic. You've got to get food on the table," Peterson said. "I don't think there would be any increase in safety, but there would be economic problems."

Black Boxes for Trucks?

The Highway Administration is circulating among its personnel a proposed rule that would limit driving during any 24-hour period to 12 hours. The rule would require 10 consecutive hours of rest during any 24 hours and would require a trucker to have two more hours off during that period, either at the end of a driving shift or in shorter breaks.

The department would require at least two of the rest periods during a seven-day period to occur at night, since many scientists have concluded the body must have rest at specific times of day to recover properly.

More controversially, the department is considering requiring trucks to carry data recorders similar to the black boxes found on airliners. The NTSB has pushed this technology as a means of verifying the hours drivers work.

Currently, truckers are required to maintain log books for their hours of service. But truckers routinely falsify records, industry observers say, to the point that they are often referred to as "comic books."

The insurance industry wholeheartedly endorses the black-box idea, because there are grave doubts among insurers that the department could enforce any new rules without the devices. "The current log system is termite-ridden," said David F. Snyder, assistant general counsel of the American Insurance Association. "Without the black boxes, other reforms could be undermined to the point of being completely ineffective."

The trucking industry vehemently opposes the black-box proposal because of the added costs, estimated at between $500 and $2,500 per truck. Industry officials said many companies already equip their trucks with devices that could measure hours of service.

Transportation Spending Bill Creates Trouble On Highway

OCTOBER 9 — A provision in the fiscal 2000 transportation spending bill designed to force the Clinton administration to be more aggressive on truck safety instead may prevent federal authorities from enforcing some existing rules on trucks and buses.

Lawmakers and officials of the Transportation Department are trying to figure out how to remedy the situation.

The conference report on the bill (HR 2084), now on its way to President Clinton after the Senate cleared it Oct. 4, includes a section that would cut off funding for the Office of Motor Carriers — which regulates trucks and buses — unless it is moved out of the Federal Highway Administration.

Critics of the motor carrier office, including Frank R. Wolf, R-Va., chairman of the House Transportation Appropriations Subcommittee and the author of the provision, think it gets little attention from the highway administration and would be better off in an agency such as the National Highway Traffic Safety Administration. The trucking industry would prefer an independent agency.

But the provision in the final bill could cripple truck safety efforts because even if the Transportation secretary moves the motor carrier office to another area, which he plans to do, he cannot transfer or delegate all authority in civil actions against safety violators.

"Essentially, we would not be able to force a [motor] carrier to comply with federal law and regulation," Transportation Department General Counsel Nancy E. McFadden told a hastily arranged hearing before the House Transportation and Infrastructure subcommittee on ground transportation Oct. 7.

The motor carrier office could still issue safety rules, conduct compliance reviews and inspect trucks, including those at border crossings, and put drivers and vehicles out of service for serious safety violations, McFadden said. But without the ability to enforce civil actions, the department would become a "paper tiger," said committee member James L. Oberstar, D-Minn.

"The consequence really is that the department is not only handcuffed but leg-shackled as well," Oberstar said.

House Transportation and Infrastructure Committee Chairman Bud Shuster, R-Pa., and John McCain, R-Ariz., chairman of the Senate Commerce, Science and Transportation Committee, are each pushing bills (HR 2679, S 1501) to create a new truck and bus safety administration within the Transportation Department. The House bill is awaiting floor action; the Senate bill has had one hearing before the Commerce Committee.

Placing Blame

At the Oct. 7 hearing, Transportation Committee members blamed Republican leaders for allowing the conference report on the spending bill to come to the floor with the legislative provision and giving authorizers little chance to read the report before a floor vote.

Shuster said the final bill had created a legislative "emergency."

"We may find that this provision may not be able to be fixed at all and should be repealed," Shuster said. "It's a shameful situation."

Shuster introduced legislation (HR 3036) Oct. 7 that would undo the spending bill provision on the motor carrier office. The House is scheduled to take up the bill on Oct. 12.

Wolf sees no emergency and said any remedy could be added to other legislation headed for the White House. "If there is a minor thing that needs to be done," he said, "we can do it."

House Passes Bill To Create Agency For Truck and Bus Safety Oversight

OCTOBER 16 — In an effort to improve safety regulation of trucks and buses, the House passed legislation Oct. 14 that would establish a National Motor Carrier Safety Administration on the same footing as agencies that oversee aviation, highways and railroads.

The bill (HR 2679), which passed on an easy 415-5 vote, was promoted as an answer to the rising number of truck and bus accidents on the nation's highways. About 5,300 people have died in such wrecks in each of the past two years — 20 percent more than in 1992. *(Vote 501, p. H-164)*

The bill would remove the Office of Motor Carriers from the Federal Highway Administration and give it coequal status within the Transportation Department. The highway administration has come under increasing fire this year after a Transportation Department inspector general's report detailed a dramatic dropoff in enforcement actions at the same time the death toll from truck and bus accidents was on the rise.

"The bottom line was that truck safety was just not getting the level of attention it should," said Tom Petri, R-Wis., chairman of the House Transportation and Infrastructure Subcommittee on Ground Transportation.

The highway administration has had custody of motor carrier regulation since Congress abolished the Interstate Commerce Commission (ICC) in 1995 (PL 104-88) and moved its remaining functions to the Transportation Department. *(1995 Almanac, p. 3-36)*

The bill also would more than double the authorized funding level for federal and state enforcement, from $354 million to $774 million over three years. It also would require suspending the commercial driver's license of any truck or bus driver who causes a fatal accident.

The Senate Commerce, Science and Transportation Committee is expected to consider similar legislation (S 1501) at its next markup.

Transportation Secretary Rodney Slater commended the House for passing the bill.

Safety First

The bill is a step toward reregulating the trucking industry. Congress first moved to deregulate trucking in 1980, and House Republicans made abolition of the ICC one of their key aims after taking control of Congress in 1995.

During debate Oct. 14, the House adopted, by voice vote, a Shuster amendment to strengthen some of the powers and penalties that would be available to the new motor carrier administration. Among other things, it would authorize the agency to suspend the registration of a motor carrier for failing to pay a civil penalty.

In response to widespread concern about safety problems with trucks crossing into the United States from Mexico, Shuster's amendment would increase the fine for non-compliance from $500 to $10,000 for the first offense and $25,000 for the second.

The limited floor debate belied the controversial nature of some of the issues. The trucking industry and a number of consumer groups have battled over the causes of fatal accidents and proposed solutions.

The trucking industry hailed the passage of HR 2679. American Trucking Associations President Walter B. McCormick called the House action "the culmination of a 15-year effort . . . to see motor carrier safety given the same priority as air carrier safety."

Consumer groups called the bill "at best a tentative first step toward comprehensive motor carrier safety reform." In a joint letter to House members, six leading safety groups, including Advocates for Highway and Auto Safety and Public Citizen, expressed concern that the bill would assign the new agency the oversight of economic laws and regulations, "commingling" safety goals with economic concerns.

The Senate version of the bill also would create a motor carrier administration and is preferred by some safety advocates because it would require the agency to implement all of the recommendations of the inspector general's report.

Closing Loopholes

The House action concluded a hectic week for the Transportation Department and lawmakers who scrambled to close a loophole created by a provision of the fiscal 2000 Transportation appropriations bill (PL 106-69) that halted funding for the motor carrier office unless it was moved out of the highway administration. There was concern that the provision might prevent some enforcement of truck and bus safety rules.

On Oct. 14, the Senate cleared a measure (HR 3036) by voice vote giving the secretary of Transportation authority to issue fines and enforce regulations by taking motor carriers to court.

The bill, which the House passed by voice vote, Oct. 12, was a compromise in the earlier plan to rescind the appropriations bill language.

Senate Clears Rewritten Truck Safety Measure

NOVEMBER 20 — House Transportation and Infrastructure Committee Chairman Bud Shuster, R-Pa., rewrote a major truck safety initiative (HR 3419) at the last minute and shepherded it through House passage by voice vote Nov. 18. The Senate cleared the measure by voice vote Nov. 19.

The new bill, negotiated between Shuster's panel and the Senate Commerce, Science and Transportation Committee, would create a Federal Motor Carrier Safety Administration within the Transportation Department and require stepped-up truck and bus safety enforcement.

Aides said the bill combined elements of legislation (HR 2679) that passed the House Oct. 14 and a measure (S 1501) drafted by Sen. John McCain, R-Ariz., chairman of the Senate Commerce Committee.

There was no House debate on the measure. The White House strongly supported the earlier House bill.

The 5,300 highway deaths in truck-related accidents each of the past two years has raised concern in Congress about the effectiveness of the Office of Motor Carriers, which oversees truck and bus safety programs from within the Transportation Department's Federal Highway Administration.

A report in April by the Transportation Department's inspector general concluded that the motor carrier office had cut its enforcement activities at a time when the death toll was rising and that its relations with the trucking industry were too close.

One reason Shuster moved at the last minute, rather than waiting until next year to work out a compromise with the Senate, was that a section of the fiscal 2000 transportation appropriations law (PL 106-69) cut off funding for the Office of Motor Carriers unless it was moved out of the highway administration.

A Transportation Department official testified that although the spending bill allowed the transportation secretary to transfer motor carrier inspections and certification to another agency, he could not transfer enforcement authority, which would lapse.

Congress addressed the problem in separate legislation (PL 106-73), but Shuster's bill takes a broader approach by establishing the new agency.

New Home

The Motor Carrier Safety Administration, which would be modeled on the Federal Aviation Administration, would concentrate on improving safety in the trucking and bus industries.

The bill would increase funding for state roadside inspection programs, and it would toughen the requirements for commercial driver's licenses.

The bill would require the new agency to set fines for violations of safety and commercial driver's license laws high enough to ensure compliance. The inspector general found that some companies consider the fines just another cost of doing business.

The agency would be authorized to suspend the registration of a truck or bus company for failing to pay a civil penalty.

Borrowing from the Senate bill, the new measure would require the motor carrier agency to implement all of the recommendations of the inspector general's April report. ◆

Chapter 25

VETERANS AFFAIRS

Lawmakers Vote To Expand Long-Term Health Care Benefits for Veterans

SUMMARY

The president signed legislation to expand long-term health care services to U.S. veterans. The bill would create a four-year plan requiring the Department of Veterans Affairs (VA) to provide extended care services to veterans needing it for a service-connected disability and to any veteran who is 70 percent disabled by service-related injuries. The House bill would have lowered the threshold to 50 percent. The bill would expand non-institutional care for all enrolled veterans and allow the VA to offset some costs by setting co-payments on certain services.

House Passes Bill To Expand Health Care for Vets

SEPTEMBER 25 — In a lopsided, 369-46 vote, the House on Sept. 21 passed a bill to expand long-term health care for veterans. The measure (HR 2116) would authorize the Department of Veterans Affairs (VA) to operate a national program of extended care services, including geriatric evaluations, nursing home care, home visits, adult day health care and respite care. *(Vote 427, p. H-138)*

The services would be available to veterans whose disabilities are at least 50 percent service-related, as well as to any veteran who needs care for a service-connected condition. Veterans in the latter group could get extended care for non-service-related disabilities but only if they made co-payments.

The Congressional Budget Office (CBO) estimated that the expanded care could increase VA spending by about $200 million annually until it reached $1.4 billion in 2004.

House Veterans' Affairs Committee Chairman Bob Stump, R-Ariz., said the increased costs could be offset because the measure would expand the department's flexibility to generate new revenue.

For example, it would allow the VA to raise co-payments on prescription drugs for illnesses not related to military service and to assess new co-payments on devices such as hearing aids.

The measure also would address the use of unnecessary VA property. In the wake of a General Accounting Office report that 25 percent of VA funds are spent maintaining unneeded facilities, the VA has considered closing several facilities to consolidate space.

Cliff Stearns, R-Fla., said the bill would require the VA, when it closes one of its hospitals, to "reinvest savings in a new, improved treatment facility or improved services in the area."

Louise M. Slaughter, D-N.Y., who voted against the bill, said many lawmakers from the Northeast fear the measure could lead to an "end road" for facilities in the region that the VA has threatened to close down.

"It opens a door that I'm a little nervous about," said Slaughter, who also voiced concern about the proposed increase in co-payments.

The legislation also would extend the length of time the VA could lease facilities, space or land to private companies from 35 years to 75 years. Sponsors said the extension would encourage more local hospitals and nursing homes to lease the under-utilized property, allowing the VA to raise revenue.

The bill would specify that, if the federal government gleans any money from settlements with tobacco companies, the VA would receive an amount proportionate to its costs of providing care for tobacco-related illnesses. The money would go to a revolving veterans health care fund that could not be used until after fiscal 2004.

The bill also would reauthorize until Dec. 31, 2002, a VA program that provides counseling and medical treatment to veterans who were sexually abused or raped while in the service. It is estimated that at least 35 percent of female veterans report at least one incident of sexual harassment while on duty in the military.

Also under the bill, recipients of the Purple Heart would have automatic access to treatment at VA hospitals. Combat veterans who earned the Purple Heart but have less than 10 percent service-connected injuries do not now qualify for immediate VA health care.

The House Veterans' Affairs Committee approved the bill (H Rept 106-237) by voice vote July 15. Several veterans' groups, including the American Legion and Veterans of Foreign Wars, endorse the measure.

Box Score

- **Bill:** HR 2116 — PL 106-117
- **Legislative action: House** passed HR 2116 (H Rept 106-237), 369-46, Sept. 21.

Senate passed HR 2116, amended, by voice vote Nov. 5.

House adopted the conference report (H Rept 106-470) by voice vote Nov. 16.

Senate cleared the bill by voice vote Nov. 19.

President signed HR 2116 on Nov. 30.

Conferees Finish Work on VA Long-Term Care Expansion

NOVEMBER 13 — House and Senate conferees completed work Nov. 10 on a bill (HR 2116) that would expand long-term care for veterans.

The accord would create a four-year plan that would require the Department of Veterans Affairs (VA) to provide institutional care, mostly nursing home services, to veterans with 70 percent and higher service-connected disabilities. Under current law, the VA may provide institutional care to any enrolled veteran, but it is not required to do so.

Sens. Arlen Specter, R-Pa., and John D. Rockefeller IV, D-W.Va., expressed concern that creating more VA programs could squeeze the department's budget and eventually force some veterans out of the VA health care system.

Congress will review the plan after three years and determine before the program expires whether to eliminate it, expand it or leave it as is. But conferees said that eliminating the long-term nursing care in 2003 is unlikely. "Once you get people in there, it's going to be hard to stop them," said House Veterans Affairs Committee Chairman Bob Stump, R-Ariz.

House conferees agreed to the Senate's request to expand non-institutional care for all enrolled veterans. The bill would allow the VA to offset many of the costs of expanded care by setting co-payments on some services, which could bring in as much as $200 million a year.

Conferees avoided further delays by withdrawing several controversial provisions. The House dropped a provision that would have further restricted eligibility for burial in Arlington National Cemetery.

House conferees also dropped a provision that would have required that VA, when closing old facilities, reinvest the money in local VA projects. Northeast lawmakers, fearful of the potential effects of VA closings, especially opposed the provision. But Rep. Cliff Stearns, R-Fla., said the language actually would make it more difficult for VA to close a facility. Investigations have revealed that about 25 percent of VA dollars are spent on facilities that are either outdated or unneeded.

The House passed its version of the bill (H Rept 106-237) on Sept. 21. The Senate passed HR 2116, amended, by voice vote Nov. 5.

Senate Clears Vets' Health Care Bill

NOVEMBER 20 — The Senate on Nov. 19 cleared a bill aimed at improving long-term health care for veterans. The House had adopted the conference report on the bill (HR 2116 — Conference report: H Rept 106-470) on Nov. 16. Both chambers acted by voice vote.

The bill would require the Department of Veterans Affairs (VA) to increase home and community-based options for veterans needing extended care. It would provide nursing home care to veterans with service-related disabilities.

Other provisions would lift a six-month limit on VA adult day care, increase mental health services and start a pilot program for contracting assisted-living services.

In addition, the bill would authorize $57.5 million for fiscal 2000 and 2001 for construction and $2.2 million for leasing VA medical facilities. The measure also would cover uninsured veterans who need emergency care and do not have access to a VA facility.

The House passed its original version of the bill (H Rept 106-237) on Sept. 21. The Senate amended and passed the bill Nov. 5. Senate adoption of the conference report would clear the bill for the president's signature. ◆

Appendix A

CONGRESS AND ITS MEMBERS

Glossary of Congressional Terms

Act — The term for legislation once it has passed both chambers of Congress and has been signed by the president or passed over his veto, thus becoming law. Also used in parliamentary terminology for a bill that has been passed by one house and engrossed. *(Also see engrossed bill.)*

Adjournment sine die — Adjournment without a fixed day for reconvening — literally, "adjournment without a day." Usually used to connote the final adjournment of a session of Congress. A session can continue until noon Jan. 3 of the following year, when, under the 20th Amendment to the Constitution, it automatically terminates. Both chambers must agree to a concurrent resolution for either chamber to adjourn for more than three days.

Adjournment to a day certain — Adjournment under a motion or resolution that fixes the next time of meeting. Under the Constitution, neither chamber can adjourn for more than three days without the concurrence of the other. A session of Congress is not ended by adjournment to a day certain.

Amendment — A proposal by a member of Congress to alter the language, provisions or stipulations in a bill or in another amendment. An amendment usually is printed, debated and voted upon in the same manner as a bill.

Amendment in the nature of a substitute — Usually an amendment that seeks to replace the entire text of a bill by striking out everything after the enacting clause and inserting a new version of the bill. An amendment in the nature of a substitute can also refer to an amendment that replaces a large portion of the text of a bill.

Appeal — A member's challenge of a ruling or decision made by the presiding officer of the chamber. A senator can appeal to members of the Senate to override the decision. If carried by a majority vote, the appeal nullifies the chair's ruling. In the House, the decision of the Speaker traditionally has been final; seldom are there appeals to the members to reverse the Speaker's stand. To appeal a ruling is considered an attack on the Speaker.

Appropriations bill — A bill that gives legal authority to spend or obligate money from the Treasury. The Constitution disallows money to be drawn from the Treasury "but in Consequence of Appropriations made by Law."

By congressional custom, an appropriations bill originates in the House. It is not supposed to be considered by the full House or Senate until a related measure authorizing the funding is enacted. An appropriations bill grants the actual budget authority approved by the authorization bill, though not necessarily the full amount permissible under the authorization.

If the 13 regular appropriations bills are not enacted by the start of the fiscal year, Congress must pass a stopgap spending bill or the departments and agencies covered by the unfinished bills must shut down.

About half of all budget authority, notably that for Social Security and interest on the federal debt, does not require annual appropriations; those programs exist under permanent appropriations. *(Also see authorization bill, budget authority, budget process, supplemental appropriations bill.)*

Authorization bill — Basic, substantive legislation that establishes or continues the legal operation of a federal program or agency either indefinitely or for a specific period of time, or which sanctions a particular type of obligation or expenditure. Under the rules of both chambers, appropriations for a program or agency may not be considered until the program has been authorized, although this requirement is often waived.

An authorization sets the maximum amount of funds that can be given to a program or agency, although sometimes it merely authorizes "such sums as may be necessary." *(Also see backdoor spending authority.)*

Backdoor spending authority — Budget authority provided in legislation outside the normal appropriations process. The most common forms of backdoor spending are borrowing authority, contract authority, entitlements and loan guarantees that commit the government to payments of principal and interest on loans — such as guaranteed student loans — made by banks or other private lenders. Loan guarantees result in actual outlays only when there is a default by the borrower.

In some cases, such as interest on the public debt, a permanent appropriation is provided that becomes available without further action by Congress.

Bills — Most legislative proposals before Congress are in the form of bills and are designated according to the chamber in which they originate — HR in the House of Representatives or S in the Senate — and by a number assigned in the order in which they are introduced during the two-year period of a congressional term.

"Public bills" deal with general questions and become public laws if they are cleared by Congress and signed by the president. "Private bills" deal with individual matters, such as claims against the government, immigration and naturalization cases or land titles, and become private laws if approved and signed. *(Also see private bills, resolution.)*

Bills introduced — In both the House and Senate, any number of members may join in introducing a single bill or resolution. The first member listed is the sponsor of the bill, and all subsequent members listed are cosponsors.

Many bills are committee bills and are introduced under the name of the chairman of the committee or subcommittee. All appropriations bills fall into this category. A committee frequently holds hearings on a number of related bills and may agree to one of them or to an entirely new bill. *(Also see clean bill.)*

Bills referred — After a bill is introduced, it is referred to the committee or committees that have jurisdiction over the subject with which the bill is concerned. Under the standing rules of the House and Senate, bills are referred by the Speaker in the House and by the presiding officer in the Senate. In practice, the House and Senate parliamentarians act for these officials and refer the vast majority of bills. *(Also see discharge a committee.)*

Borrowing authority — Statutory authority that permits a federal agency to incur obligations and make payments for specified purposes with borrowed money.

Budget — The document sent to Congress by the president early each year estimating government revenue and expenditures for the ensuing fiscal year.

Budget Act — The common name for the Congressional Budget and Impoundment Control Act of 1974, which established the current budget process and created the Congressional Budget Office. The act also put limits on presidential authority to spend appropriated money. It has undergone several major revisions since 1974. *(Also see budget process, impoundments.)*

Budget authority — Authority for federal agencies to enter into obligations that result in immediate or future outlays. The basic forms of budget authority are appropriations, contract authority and borrowing authority. Budget authority may be classified by (1) the period of availability (one-year, multiple-year or without a time limitation), (2) the timing of congressional action (current or permanent) or (3) the manner of determining the amount available (definite or indefinite). *(Also see appropriations, outlays.)*

Budget process — The annual budget process was created by the Congressional Budget and Impoundment Control Act of 1974, with a timetable that was modified in 1990. Under the law, the president must submit his proposed budget by the first Monday in February. Congress is supposed to complete an annual budget resolution by April 15, setting guidelines for congressional action on spending and tax measures.

Budget rules enacted in the 1990 Budget Enforcement Act and updated in 1993 and 1997 set caps on discretionary spending through fiscal 2002. The caps can be adjusted annually to account for changes in the economy and other limited factors. In addition, pay-as-you-go (PAYGO) rules require that any tax cut, new entitlement program or expansion of existing entitlement benefits that would increase a deficit be offset by an increase in taxes or a cut in entitlement spending.

The rules hold Congress harmless for budget-deficit increases that lawmakers do not explicitly cause — for example, increases due to a recession or to an expansion in the number of beneficiaries qualifying for Medicare or food stamps. PAYGO does not apply if there is a budget surplus.

If Congress exceeds the discretionary spending caps in its appropriations bills, the law requires an across-the-board cut — known as a sequester — in non-exempt discretionary spending accounts. If Congress violates the PAYGO rules, entitlement programs are subject to a sequester. Supplemental appropriations are subject to similar controls, with the proviso that if both Congress and the president agree, spending designated as an emergency can exceed the caps.

Budget resolution — A concurrent resolution that is passed by both chambers of Congress but does not require the president's signature. The measure sets a strict ceiling on discretionary budget authority, along with non-binding recommendations about how the spending should be allocated. The budget resolution may also contain "reconciliation instructions" requiring authorizing and tax-writing committees to propose changes in existing law to meet deficit-reduction goals. The Budget Committee in each chamber then bundles those proposals into a reconciliation bill and sends it to the floor. *(Also see reconciliation.)*

By request — A phrase used when a senator or representative introduces a bill at the request of an executive agency or private organization but does not necessarily endorse the legislation.

Calendar — An agenda or list of business awaiting possible action by each chamber. The House uses six legislative calendars. They are the Consent, Corrections, Discharge, House, Private and Union calendars. *(Also see individual listings.)*

In the Senate, all legislative matters reported from committee go on one calendar. They are listed there in the order in which committees report them or the Senate places them on the calendar, but they may be called up out of order by the majority leader, either by obtaining unanimous consent of the Senate or by a motion to call up a bill. The Senate also has one non-legislative calendar, which is used for treaties and nominations. *(Also see executive calendar.)*

Call of the calendar — Senate bills that are not brought up for debate by a motion, unanimous consent or a unanimous consent agreement are brought before the Senate for action when the calendar listing them is "called." Bills must be called in the order listed. Measures considered by this method usually are non-controversial, and debate on the bill and any proposed amendments is limited to five minutes for each senator.

Chamber — The meeting place for the membership of either the House or the Senate; also the membership of the House or Senate meeting as such.

Clean bill — Frequently after a committee has finished a major revision of a bill, one of the committee members, usually the chairman, will assemble the changes and what is left of the original bill into a new measure and introduce it as a "clean bill." The revised measure, which is given a new number, is referred back to the committee, which reports it to the floor for consideration. This often is a timesaver, as committee-recommended changes in a clean bill do not have to be considered and voted on by the chamber. Reporting a clean bill also protects committee amendments that could be subject to points of order concerning germaneness.

Clerk of the House — An officer of the House of Representatives who supervises its records and legislative business. Many former administrative duties were transferred in 1992 to a new position, the director of non-legislative and financial services.

Cloture — The process by which a filibuster can be ended in the Senate other than by unanimous consent. A motion for cloture can apply to any measure before the Senate, including a proposal to change the chamber's rules. A cloture motion requires the signatures of 16 senators to be introduced. To end a filibuster, the cloture motion must obtain the votes of three-fifths of the entire Senate membership (60 if there are no vacancies), except when the filibuster is against a proposal to amend the standing rules of the Senate and a two-thirds vote of senators present and voting is required.

The cloture request is put to a roll call vote one hour after the Senate meets on the second day following introduction of the motion. If approved, cloture limits each senator to one hour of debate. The bill or amendment in question comes to a final vote after 30 hours of consideration, including debate time and the time it takes to conduct roll calls, quorum calls and other procedural motions. *(Also see filibuster.)*

Committee — A division of the House or Senate that prepares legislation for action by the parent chamber or makes investigations as directed by the parent chamber.

There are several types of committees. Most standing committees are divided into subcommittees, which study legislation, hold hearings and report bills, with or without amendments, to the full committee. Only the full committee can report legislation for action by the House or Senate. *(Also see standing, oversight, select and special committees.)*

Committee of the Whole — The working title of what is formally "The Committee of the Whole House [of Representatives] on the State of the Union." The membership is composed of all House members sitting as a committee. Any 100 members who are present on the floor of the chamber to consider legislation comprise a quorum of the committee. Any legislation, however, must first have passed through the regular legislative or appropriations committee and have been placed on the calendar.

Technically, the Committee of the Whole considers only bills directly or indirectly appropriating money, authorizing appropriations or involving taxes or charges on the public. Because the Committee of the Whole need number only 100 representatives, a quorum is more readily attained and legislative business is expedited. Before 1971, members' positions were not individually recorded on votes taken in the Committee of the Whole.

When the full House resolves itself into the Committee of the Whole, it replaces the Speaker with a "chairman." A measure is debated and amendments may be proposed, with votes on amendments as needed. *(Also see five-minute rule.)*

When the committee completes its work on the measure, it dissolves itself by "rising." The Speaker returns, and the chairman of the Committee of the Whole reports to the House that the committee's work has been completed. At this time, members may demand a roll call vote on any amendment adopted in the Committee of the Whole. The final vote is on passage of the legislation.

In 1993 and 1994, the four delegates from the territories and the resident commissioner of Puerto Rico were allowed to vote on questions before the Committee of the Whole. If their votes were decisive in the outcome, however, the matter was automatically re-voted, with the delegates and resident commissioner ineligible. They could vote on final passage of bills or on separate votes demanded after the Committee of the Whole rises. This limited voting right was rescinded in 1995.

Committee veto — A requirement added to a few statutes directing that certain policy directives by an executive department or agency be reviewed by certain congressional committees before they are implemented. Under common practice, the government department or agency and the committees involved are expected to reach a consensus before the directives are carried out. *(Also see legislative veto.)*

Concurrent resolution — A concurrent resolution, designated H Con Res or S Con Res, must be adopted by both chambers, but it is not sent to the president for approval and, therefore, does not have the force of law. A concurrent resolution, for example, is used to fix the time for adjournment of a Congress. It is also used to express the sense of Congress on a foreign policy or domestic issue. The annual budget resolution is a concurrent resolution.

Conference — A meeting between representatives of the House and the Senate to reconcile differences between the two chambers on provisions of a bill. Members of the conference committee are appointed by the Speaker and the presiding officer of the Senate.

A majority of the conferees for each chamber must agree on a compromise, reflected in a "conference report" before the final bill can go back to both chambers for approval. When the conference report goes to the floor, it is difficult to amend. If it is not approved by both chambers, the bill may go back to conference under certain situations, or a new conference may be convened. Many rules and informal practices govern the conduct of conference committees.

Bills that are passed by both chambers with only minor differences need not be sent to conference. Either chamber may "concur" with the other's amendments, completing action on the legislation. Sometimes leaders of the committees of jurisdiction work out an informal compromise instead of having a formal conference. *(Also see custody of the papers.)*

Confirmations — *(See nominations.)*

Congressional Record — The daily, printed account of proceedings in both the House and Senate chambers, showing substantially verbatim debate, statements and a record of floor action. Highlights of legislative and committee action are given in a Daily Digest section of the Record, and members are entitled to have their extraneous remarks printed in an appendix known as "Extension of Remarks." Members may edit and revise remarks made on the floor during debate, although the House in 1995 limited members to technical or grammatical changes.

The Congressional Record provides a way to distinguish remarks spoken on the floor of the House and Senate from undelivered speeches. In the Senate, all speeches, articles and other matter that members insert in the Record without actually reading them on the floor are set off by large black dots, or bullets. However, a loophole allows a member to avoid the bulleting if he or she delivers any portion of the speech in person. In the House, undelivered speeches and other material are printed in a distinctive typeface. The record is also available in electronic form. *(Also see Journal.)*

Congressional terms of office — Terms normally begin on Jan. 3 of the year following a general election. Terms are two years for representatives and six years for senators. Representatives elected in special elections are sworn in for the remainder of a term. Under most state laws, a person may be appointed to fill a Senate vacancy and serve until a successor is elected; the successor serves until the end of the term applying to the vacant seat.

Consent Calendar — Members of the House may place on this calendar most bills on the Union or House Calendar that are considered non-controversial. Bills on the Consent Calendar normally are called on the first and third Mondays of each month. On the first occasion that a bill is called in this manner, consideration may be blocked by the objection of any member. The second time, if there are three objections, the bill is stricken from the Consent Calendar. If fewer than three members object, the bill is given immediate consideration.

A member may also postpone action on the bill by asking that the measure be passed over "without prejudice." In that case, no objection is recorded against the bill and its status on the Consent Calendar remains unchanged. A bill stricken from the Consent Calendar remains on the Union or House Calendar. The Consent Calendar has seldom been used in recent years.

Continuing resolution — A joint resolution, cleared by Congress and signed by the president, to provide new budget authority for federal agencies and programs until the regular appropriations bills have been enacted. Also known as "CRs" or continuing appropriation, continuing resolutions are used to keep agencies operating when, as often happens, Congress fails to finish the regular appropriations process by the start of the new fiscal year.

The CR usually specifies a maximum rate at which an agency may incur obligations, based on the rate of the prior year, the president's budget request or an appropriations bill passed by either or both chambers of Congress but not yet enacted.

Contract authority — Budget authority contained in an authorization bill that permits the federal government to enter into contracts or other obligations for future payments from funds not yet appropriated by Congress. The assumption is that funds will be provided in a subsequent appropriations act. *(Also see budget authority.)*

Corrections Calendar, Corrections Day — A House calendar established in 1995 to speed consideration of bills aimed at eliminating burdensome or unnecessary regulations. Bills on the Corrections Calendar can be called up on the second and fourth Tuesday of each month, called Corrections Day. They are subject to one hour of debate without amendment, and require a three-fifths majority for passage. *(Also see calendar.)*

Correcting recorded votes — Rules prohibit members from changing their votes after the result has been announced. Occasionally, however, a member may announce hours, days or months after a vote has been taken that he or she was "incorrectly recorded." In the Senate, a request to change one's vote almost always receives unanimous consent, so long as it does not change the outcome. In the House, members are prohibited from changing votes if they were tallied by the electronic voting system.

Cosponsor — *(See bills introduced.)*

Current services estimates — Estimated budget authority and outlays for federal programs and operations for the forthcoming fiscal year based on continuation of existing levels of service without policy changes but with adjustments for inflation and for demographic changes that affect programs. These estimates, accompanied by the underlying economic and policy assumptions upon which they are based, are transmitted by the president to Congress when the budget is submitted.

Custody of the papers — To reconcile differences between the House and Senate versions of a bill, a conference may be arranged. The chamber with "custody of the papers" — the engrossed bill, engrossed amendments, messages of transmittal — is the only body empowered to request the conference. By custom, the chamber that asks for a conference is the last to act on the conference report.

Custody of the papers sometimes is manipulated to ensure that a particular chamber acts either first or last on the conference report. *(Also see conference.)*

Deferral — Executive branch action to defer, or delay, the spending of appropriated money. The 1974 Congressional Budget and Impoundment Control Act requires a special message from the president to Congress reporting a proposed deferral of spending. Deferrals may not extend beyond the end of the fiscal year in which the message is transmitted. A federal district court in 1986 struck down the president's authority to defer spending for policy reasons; the ruling was upheld by a federal appeals court in 1987. Congress can prohibit proposed deferrals by enacting a law doing so; most often, cancellations of proposed deferrals are included in appropriations bills. *(Also see rescission.)*

Dilatory motion — A motion made for the purpose of killing time and preventing action on a bill or amendment. House rules outlaw dilatory motions, but enforcement is largely within the discretion of the Speaker or chairman of the Committee of the Whole. The Senate does not have a rule barring dilatory motions except under cloture.

Discharge a committee — Occasionally, attempts are made to relieve a committee of jurisdiction over a bill that is before it. This is attempted more often in the House than in the Senate, and the procedure rarely is successful.

In the House, if a committee does not report a bill within 30 days after the measure is referred to it, any member may file a discharge motion. Once offered, the motion is treated as a petition needing the signatures of a majority of members (218 if there are no vacancies). After the required signatures have been obtained, there is a delay of seven days.

Thereafter, on the second and fourth Mondays of each month, except during the last six days of a session, any member who has signed the petition must be recognized, if he or she so desires, to move that the committee be discharged. Debate on the motion to discharge is limited to 20 minutes. If the motion is carried, consideration of the bill becomes a matter of high privilege.

If a resolution to consider a bill is held up in the Rules Committee for more than seven legislative days, any member may enter a motion to discharge the committee. The motion is handled like any other discharge petition in the House. Occasionally, to expedite non-controversial legislative business, a committee is discharged by unanimous consent of the House, and a petition is not required. In 1993, the signatures on pending discharge petitions — previously kept secret — were made a matter of public record. *(For Senate procedure, see discharge resolution.)*

Discharge Calendar — The House calendar to which motions to discharge committees are referred when they have the required number of signatures (218) and are awaiting floor action. *(Also see calendar.)*

Discharge petition — *(See discharge a committee.)*

Discharge resolution — In the Senate, a special motion that any senator may introduce to relieve a committee from consideration of a bill before it. The resolution can be called up for Senate approval or disapproval in the same manner as any other Senate business. *(For House procedure, see discharge a committee.)*

Discretionary spending caps — *(See budget process.)*

Division of a question for voting — A practice that is more common in the Senate but also used in the House whereby a member may demand a division of an amendment or a motion for purposes of voting. Where an amendment or motion can be divided, the individual parts are voted on separately when a member demands a division. This procedure occurs most often during the consideration of conference reports.

Enacting clause — Key phrase in bills beginning, "Be it enacted by the Senate and House of Representatives . . ." A successful motion to strike it from legislation kills the measure.

Engrossed bill — The final copy of a bill as passed by one chamber, with the text as amended by floor action and certified by the clerk of the House or the secretary of the Senate.

Enrolled bill — The final copy of a bill that has been passed in identical form by both chambers. It is certified by an officer of the chamber of origin (clerk of the House or secretary of the Senate) and then sent on for the signatures of the House Speaker, the Senate president pro tempore and the president of the United States. An enrolled bill is printed on parchment.

Entitlement program — A federal program that guarantees a certain level of benefits to people or other entities who meet requirements set by law. Examples include Social Security and unemployment benefits. Some entitlements have permanent appropriations; others are funded under annual appropriations bills. In either case, it is mandatory for Congress to provide the money.

Executive Calendar — A non-legislative calendar in the Senate that lists presidential documents such as treaties and nominations. *(Also see calendar.)*

Executive document — A document, usually a treaty, sent to the Senate by the president for consideration or approval. Executive documents are referred to committee in the same manner as other measures. Unlike legislative documents, treaties do not die at the end of a Congress but remain "live" proposals until acted on by the Senate or withdrawn by the president.

Executive session — A meeting of a Senate or House committee (or occasionally of either chamber) that only its members may attend. Witnesses regularly appear at committee meetings in executive session — for example, Defense Department officials during presentations of classified defense information. Other members of Congress may be invited, but the public and news media are not allowed to attend.

Filibuster — A time-delaying tactic associated with the Senate and used by a minority in an effort to prevent a vote on a bill or amendment that probably would pass if voted upon directly. The most common method is to take advantage of the Senate's rules permitting unlimited debate, but other forms of parliamentary maneuvering may be used.

The stricter rules of the House make filibusters more difficult, but delaying tactics are employed occasionally through various procedural devices allowed by House rules. *(Also see cloture.)*

Fiscal year — Financial operations of the government are carried out in a 12-month fiscal year, beginning on Oct. 1 and ending on Sept. 30. The fiscal year carries the date of the calendar year in which it ends. (From fiscal 1844 to fiscal 1976, the fiscal year began July 1 and ended the following June 30.)

Five-minute rule — A debate-limiting rule of the House that is invoked when the House sits as the Committee of the Whole. Under the rule, a member offering an amendment and a member opposing it are each allowed to speak for five minutes. Debate is then closed. In practice, amendments regularly are debated for more than 10 minutes, with members gaining the floor by offering pro forma amendments or obtaining unanimous consent to speak longer than five minutes. *(Also see Committee of the Whole, hour rule, strike out the last word.)*

Floor manager — A member who has the task of steering legislation through floor debate and amendment to a final vote in the House or the Senate. Floor managers usually are chairmen or ranking members of the committee that reported the bill. Managers are responsible for apportioning the debate time granted to supporters of the bill. The ranking minority member of the committee normally apportions time for the minority party's participation in the debate.

Frank — A member's facsimile signature, which is used on envelopes in lieu of stamps for the member's official outgoing mail. The "franking privilege" is the right to send mail postage-free.

Germane — Pertaining to the subject matter of the measure at hand. All House amendments must be germane to the bill being considered. The Senate requires that amendments be germane when they are proposed to general appropriations bills or to bills being considered once cloture has been adopted or, frequently, when the Senate is proceeding under a unanimous consent agreement placing a time limit on consideration of a bill. The 1974 budget act also requires that amendments to concurrent budget resolutions be germane.

In the House, floor debate must be germane, and the first three hours of debate each day in the Senate must be germane to the pending business.

Gramm-Rudman-Hollings Deficit Reduction Act — *(See sequester.)*

Grandfather clause — A provision that exempts people or other entities already engaged in an activity from rules or legislation affecting that activity.

Hearings — Committee sessions for taking testimony from witnesses. At hearings on legislation, witnesses usually include specialists, government officials and spokesmen for individuals or entities affected by the bill or bills under study. Hearings related to special investigations bring forth a variety of witnesses. Committees sometimes use their subpoena power to summon reluctant witnesses. The public and news media may attend open hearings but are barred from closed, or "executive," hearings. The vast majority of hearings are open to the public. *(Also see executive session.)*

Hold-harmless clause — A provision added to legislation to ensure that recipients of federal funds do not receive less in a future year than they did in the current year if a new formula for allocating funds authorized in the legislation would result in a reduction to the recipients. This clause has been used most often to soften the impact of sudden reductions in federal grants.

Hopper — Box on House clerk's desk into which members deposit bills and resolutions to introduce them.

Hour rule — A provision in the rules of the House that permits one hour of debate time for each member on amendments debated in the House of Representatives sitting as the House. Therefore, the House normally amends bills while sitting as the Committee of the Whole, where the five-minute rule on amendments operates.

House as in the Committee of the Whole — A procedure that can be used to expedite consideration of certain measures such as continuing resolutions and, when there is debate, private bills. The procedure can be invoked only with the unanimous consent of the House or a rule from the Rules Committee and has procedural elements of both the House sitting as the House of Representatives, such as the Speaker presiding and the previous question motion being in order, and the House sitting as the Committee of the Whole, with the five-minute rule being in order. *(See Committee of the Whole.)*

House Calendar — A listing for action by the House of public bills that do not directly or indirectly appropriate money or raise revenue. *(Also see calendar.)*

Immunity — The constitutional privilege of members of Congress to make verbal statements on the floor and in committee for which they cannot be sued or arrested for slander or libel. Also, freedom from arrest while traveling to or from sessions of Congress or on official business. Members in this status may only be arrested for treason, felonies or a breach of the peace, as defined by congressional manuals.

Joint committee — A committee composed of a specified number of members of both the House and Senate. A joint committee may be investigative or research-oriented, an example of the latter being the Joint Economic Committee. Others have housekeeping duties; examples include the joint committees on Printing and on the Library of Congress.

Joint resolution — Like a bill, a joint resolution, designated H J Res or S J Res, requires the approval of both chambers and the signature of the president, and has the force of law if approved. There is no practical difference between a bill and a joint resolution. A joint resolution generally is used to deal with a limited matter such as a single appropriation.

Joint resolutions are also used to propose amendments to the Constitution. In that case they require a two-thirds majority in both chambers. They do not require a presidential signature, but they must be ratified by three-fourths of the states to become a part of the Constitution. *(Also see concurrent resolution, resolution.)*

Journal — The official record of the proceedings of the House and Senate. The Journal records the actions taken in each chamber, but, unlike the Congressional Record, it does not include the substantially verbatim report of speeches, debates, statements and the like.

Law — An act of Congress that has been signed by the president or passed, over his veto, by Congress. Public bills, when signed, become public laws and are cited by the letters PL and a hyphenated number. The number before the hyphen corresponds to the Congress, and the one or more digits after the hyphen refer to the numerical sequence in which the president signed the bills during that Congress. Private bills, when signed, become private laws. *(Also see bills, private bills.)*

Legislative day — The "day" extending from the time either chamber meets after an adjournment until the time it next adjourns. Because the House normally adjourns from day to day, legislative days and calendar days usually coincide. But in the Senate, a legislative day may, and frequently does, extend over several calendar days. *(Also see recess.)*

Line-item veto — Presidential authority to strike individual items from appropriations bills, which presidents since Ulysses S. Grant have sought. Congress gave the president a form of the power in 1996 (PL 104-130), but this "enhanced rescission authority" was struck down by the Supreme Court in 1998 as unconstitutional because it allowed the president to change laws on his own.

Loan guarantees — Loans to third parties for which the federal government guarantees the repayment of principal or interest, in whole or in part, to the lender in the event of default.

Lobby — A group seeking to influence the passage or defeat of legislation. Originally the term referred to people frequenting the lobbies or corridors of legislative chambers to speak to lawmakers.

The definition of a lobby and the activity of lobbying is a matter of differing interpretation. By some definitions, lobbying is limited to direct attempts to influence lawmakers through personal interviews and persuasion. Under other definitions, lobbying includes attempts at indirect, or "grass-roots," influence, such as persuading members of a group to write or visit their district's representative and state's senators or attempting to create a climate of opinion favorable to a desired legislative goal.

The right to attempt to influence legislation is based on the First Amendment to the Constitution, which says Congress shall make no law abridging the right of the people "to petition the government for a redress of grievances."

Majority leader — Floor leader for the majority party in each chamber. In the Senate, in consultation with the minority leader, the majority leader directs the legislative schedule for the chamber. He or she is also his party's spokesperson and chief strategist. In the House, the majority leader is second to the Speaker in the majority party's leadership and serves as the party's legislative strategist. *(Also see Speaker, whip.)*

Manual — The official handbook in each chamber prescribing in detail its organization, procedures and operations.

Marking up a bill — Going through the contents of a piece of legislation in committee or subcommittee to, for example, consider the provisions, act on amendments to provisions and proposed revisions to the language, and insert new sections and phraseology. If the bill is extensively amended, the committee's version may be introduced as a separate (or "clean") bill, with a new number, before being considered by the full House or Senate. *(Also see clean bill.)*

Minority leader — Floor leader for the minority party in each chamber.

Morning hour — The time set aside at the beginning of each legislative day for the consideration of regular, routine business. The "hour" is of indefinite duration in the House, where it is rarely used. In the Senate, it is the first two hours of a session following an adjournment, as distinguished from a recess. The morning hour can be terminated earlier if the morning business has been completed.

Business includes such matters as messages from the president, communications from the heads of departments, messages from the House, the presentation of petitions, reports of standing and select committees and the introduction of bills and resolutions.

During the first hour of the morning hour in the Senate, no motion to proceed to the consideration of any bill on the calendar is in order except by unanimous consent. During the second hour, motions can be made but must be decided without debate. Senate committees may meet while the Senate conducts the morning hour.

Motion — In the House or Senate chamber, a request by a member to institute any one of a wide array of parliamentary actions. He or she "moves" for a certain procedure, such as the consideration of a measure. The precedence of motions, and whether they are debatable, is set forth in the House and Senate manuals.

Nominations — Presidential appointments to office subject to Senate confirmation. Although most nominations win quick Senate approval, some are controversial and become the topic of hearings and debate. Sometimes senators object to appointees for patronage reasons — for example, when a nomination to a local federal job is made without consulting the senators of the state concerned. In some situations a senator may object that the nominee is "personally obnoxious" to him. Usually other senators join in blocking such appointments out of courtesy to their colleagues. *(Also see senatorial courtesy.)*

One-minute speeches — Addresses by House members at the beginning of a legislative day. The speeches may cover any subject but are limited to one minute's duration.

Outlays — Actual spending that flows from the liquidation of budget authority. Outlays associated with appropriations bills and other legislation are estimates of future spending made by the Congressional Budget Office (CBO) and the White House's Office of Management and Budget (OMB). CBO's estimates govern bills for the purpose of congressional floor debate, while OMB's numbers govern when it comes to determining whether legislation exceeds spending caps.

Outlays in a given fiscal year may result from budget authority provided in the current year or in previous years. *(Also see budget authority, budget process.)*

Override a veto — If the president vetoes a bill and sends it back to Congress with his objections, Congress may try to override his veto and enact the bill into law. Neither chamber is required to attempt to override a veto. The override of a veto requires a recorded vote with a two-thirds majority of those present and voting in each chamber. The question put to each chamber is: "Shall the bill pass, the objections of the president to the contrary notwithstanding?" *(Also see pocket veto, veto.)*

Oversight committee — A congressional committee or designated subcommittee that is charged with general oversight of one or more federal agencies' programs and activities. Usually, the oversight panel for a particular agency is also the authorizing committee for that agency's programs and operations.

Pair — A voluntary, informal arrangement that two lawmakers, usually on opposite sides of an issue, make on recorded votes. In many cases the result is to subtract a vote from each side, with no effect on the outcome.

Pairs are not authorized in the rules of either chamber, are not counted in tabulating the final result and have no official standing. However, members pairing are identified in the Congressional Record, along with their positions on such votes, if known. A member who expects to be absent for a vote can pair with a member who plans to vote, with the latter agreeing to withhold his or her vote.

There are three types of pairs:

(1) A live pair involves a member who is present for a vote and another who is absent. The member in attendance votes and then withdraws the vote, announcing that he or she has a live pair with colleague "X" and stating how the two members would have voted, one in favor, the other opposed. A live pair may affect the outcome of a closely contested vote, since it subtracts one "yea" or one "nay" from the final tally. A live pair may cover one or several specific issues.

(2) A general pair, widely used in the House, does not entail any arrangement between two members and does not affect the vote. Members who expect to be absent notify the clerk that they wish to make a general pair. Each member then is paired with another desiring a pair, and their names are listed in the Congressional Record. The member may or may not be paired with another taking the opposite position, and no indication of how the members would have voted is given.

(3) A specific pair is similar to a general pair, except that the opposing stands of the two members are identified and printed in the Congressional Record.

Pay-as-you go (PAYGO) rules — *(See budget process.)*

Petition — A request or plea sent to one or both chambers from an organization or private citizens' group seeking support for particular legislation or favorable consideration of a matter not yet receiving congressional attention. Petitions are referred to appropriate committees. In the House, a petition signed by a majority of members (218) can discharge a bill from a committee. *(Also see discharge a committee.)*

Pocket veto — The act of the president in withholding his approval of a bill after Congress has adjourned. When Congress is in session, a bill becomes law without the president's signature if he does not act upon it within 10 days, excluding Sundays, from the time he receives it. But if Congress adjourns sine die within that 10-day period, the bill will die even if the president does not formally veto it.

The Supreme Court in 1986 agreed to decide whether the president could pocket veto a bill during recesses and between sessions of the same Congress or only between Congresses. The justices in 1987 declared the case moot, however, because the bill in question was invalid once the case reached the court. *(Also see adjournment sine die, veto.)*

Point of order — An objection raised by a member that the chamber is departing from rules governing its conduct of business. The objector cites the rule violated, with the chair sustaining his or her objection if correctly made. Order is restored by the chair's suspending proceedings of the chamber until it conforms to the prescribed "order of business."

Both chambers have procedures for overcoming a point of order, either by vote or, what is most common in the House, by including language in the rule for floor consideration that waives a point of order against a given bill. *(Also see rules.)*

President of the Senate — Under the Constitution, the vice president of the United States presides over the Senate. In his absence, the president pro tempore, or a senator designated by the president pro tempore, presides over the chamber.

President pro tempore — The chief officer of the Senate in the absence of the vice president — literally, but loosely, the president for a time. The president pro tempore is elected by his fellow senators. Recent practice has been to elect the senator of the majority party with the longest period of continuous service.

Previous question — A motion for the previous question, when carried, has the effect of cutting off all debate, preventing the offering of further amendments and forcing a vote on the pending matter. In the House, a motion for the previous question is not permitted in the Committee of the Whole, unless a rule governing debate provides otherwise. The motion for the previous question is a debate-limiting device and is not in order in the Senate.

Printed amendment — A House rule guarantees five minutes of floor debate in support and five minutes in opposition, and no other debate time, on amendments printed in the Congressional Record at least one day prior to the amendment's consideration in the Committee of the Whole.

In the Senate, while amendments may be submitted for printing, they have no parliamentary standing or status. An amendment submitted for printing in the Senate, however, may be called up by any senator.

Private bill — A bill dealing with individual matters such as claims against the government, immigration or land titles. When a private bill is before the chamber, two members may block its consideration, thereby recommitting the bill to committee. The backers still have recourse, however. The measure can be put into an "omnibus claims bill" — several private bills rolled into one. As with any bill, no part of an omnibus claims bill may be deleted without a vote. When the private bill goes back to the House floor in this form, it can be deleted from the omnibus bill only by majority vote.

Private Calendar — The House calendar for private bills. The Private Calendar must be called on the first Tuesday of each month, and the Speaker may call it on the third Tuesday of each month as well. *(Also see calendar, private bill.)*

Privileged questions — The order in which bills, motions and other legislative measures are considered on the floor of the Senate and House is governed by strict priorities. A motion to table, for instance, is more privileged than a motion to recommit. Thus, if a member moves to recommit a bill to committee for further consideration, another member can supersede the first action by moving to table it, and a vote will occur on the motion to table (or kill) before the motion to recommit. A motion to adjourn is considered "of the highest privilege" and must be considered before virtually any other motion.

Pro forma amendment — *(See strike out the last word.)*

Public Laws — *(See law.)*

Questions of privilege — These are matters affecting members of Congress individually or collectively. Matters affecting the rights, safety, dignity and integrity of proceedings of the House or Senate as a whole are questions of privilege in both chambers.

Questions involving individual members are called questions of "personal privilege." A member rising to ask a question of personal privilege is given precedence over almost all other proceedings. For instance, if a member feels that he or she has been improperly impugned in comments by another member, he or she can immediately demand to be heard on the floor on a question of personal privilege. An annotation in the House rules points out that the privilege rests primarily on the Constitution, which gives members a conditional immunity from arrest and an unconditional freedom to speak in the House.

In 1993, the House changed its rules to allow the Speaker to delay for two legislative days the floor consideration of a question of the privileges of the House unless it is offered by the majority leader or minority leader.

Quorum — The number of members whose presence is necessary for the transaction of business. In the Senate and House, it is a majority of the membership. In the Committee of the Whole House, a quorum is 100. If a point of order is made that a quorum is not present, the only business that is in order is either a motion to adjourn or a motion to direct the sergeant-at-arms to request the attendance of absentees. In practice, however, both chambers conduct much of their business without a quorum present. *(Also see Committee of the Whole House.)*

Reading of bills — Traditional parliamentary procedure required bills to be read three times before they were passed. This custom is of little modern significance. Normally a bill is considered to have its first reading when it is introduced and printed, by title, in the Congressional Record. In the House, a bill's second reading comes when floor consideration begins. (The actual reading of a bill is most likely to occur at this point, if at all.) The second reading in the Senate is supposed to occur on the legislative day after the measure is introduced, but before it is referred to committee. The third reading (again, usually by title) takes place when floor action has been completed on amendments.

Recess — A recess, as distinguished from adjournment, does not end a legislative day and therefore does not interrupt unfinished business. (The rules in each chamber set forth certain matters to be taken up and disposed of at the beginning of each legislative day.) The House usually adjourns from day to day. The Senate often recesses, thus meeting on the same legislative day for several calendar days or even weeks at a time.

Recognition — The power of recognition of a member is lodged in the Speaker of the House and the presiding officer of the Senate. The presiding officer names the member to speak first when two or more members simultaneously request recognition. The order of recognition is governed by precedents and tradition for many situations. In the Senate, for instance, the majority leader has the right to be recognized first.

Recommit to committee — A motion, made on the floor after a bill has been debated, to return it to the committee that reported it. If approved, recommittal usually is considered a death blow to the bill. In the House, the right to offer a motion to recommit is guaranteed to the minority leader or someone he or she designates.

A motion to recommit may include instructions to the committee to report the bill again with specific amendments or by a certain date. Or the instructions may direct that a particular study be made, with no definite deadline for further action.

If the recommittal motion includes instructions to "report the bill back forthwith" and the motion is adopted, floor action on the bill continues with the changes directed by the instructions automatically incorporated into the bill; the committee does not actually reconsider the legislation.

Reconciliation — The 1974 budget act created a "reconciliation" procedure for bringing existing tax and spending laws into conformity with ceilings set in the congressional budget resolution. Under the procedure, the budget resolution sets specific deficit-reduction targets and instructs tax-writing and authorizing committees to propose changes in existing law to meet those targets. Those recommendations are consolidated without change by the Budget committees into an omnibus reconciliation bill, which then must be considered and approved by both chambers of Congress.

Special rules in the Senate limit debate on a reconciliation bill to 20 hours and bar extraneous or non-germane amendments. *(Also see budget resolution, sequester.)*

Reconsider a vote — Until it is disposed of, a motion to reconsider the vote by which an action was taken has the effect of putting the action in abeyance. In the Senate, the motion can be made only by a member who voted on the prevailing side of the original question or by a member who did not vote at all. In the House, it can be made only by a member on the prevailing side.

A common practice in the Senate after close votes on an issue is a motion to reconsider, followed by a motion to table the motion to reconsider. On this motion to table, senators vote as they voted on the original question, which allows the motion to table to prevail, assuming there are no switches. That closes the matter, and further motions to reconsider are not entertained.

In the House, as a routine precaution, a motion to reconsider usually is made every time a measure is passed. Such a motion almost always is tabled immediately, thus shutting off the possibility of future reconsideration except by unanimous consent.

Motions to reconsider must be entered in the Senate within the next two days the Senate is in session after the original vote has been taken. In the House, they must be entered either on the same day or on the next succeeding day the House is in session. Sometimes on a close vote, a member will switch his or her vote to be eligible to offer a motion to reconsider.

Recorded vote — A vote upon which each member's stand is individually made known. In the Senate, this is accomplished through a roll call of the entire membership, to which each senator on the floor must answer "yea," "nay" or "present." Since January 1973, the House has used an electronic voting system for recorded votes, including yea-and-nay votes formerly taken by roll calls.

When not required by the Constitution, a recorded vote can be obtained on questions in the House on the demand of one-fifth (44 members) of a quorum or one-fourth (25) of a quorum in the Committee of the Whole. Recorded votes are required in the House for appropriations, budget and tax bills. *(Also see yeas and nays.)*

Report — Both a verb and a noun as a congressional term. A committee that has been examining a bill referred to it by the parent chamber "reports" its findings and recommendations to the chamber when it completes consideration and returns the measure. The process is called "reporting" a bill. In some cases, a bill is reported without a written report.

A "report" is the document setting forth the committee's explanation of its action. Senate and House reports are numbered separately and are designated S Rept or H Rept. When a committee report is not unanimous, the dissenting committee members may file a statement of their views, called minority or dissenting views and referred to as a minority report. Members in disagreement with some provisions of a bill may file additional or supplementary views. Sometimes a bill is reported without a committee recommendation.

Legislative committees occasionally submit adverse reports. However, when a committee is opposed to a bill, it usually fails to report the bill at all. Some laws require that committee reports — favorable or adverse — be made.

Rescission — Cancellation of budget authority that was previously appropriated but has not yet been spent.

Resolution — A "simple" resolution, designated H Res or S Res, deals with matters entirely within the prerogatives of a single chamber. It requires neither passage by the other chamber nor approval by the president, and it does not have the force of law. Most resolutions deal with the rules or procedures of one chamber. They are also used to express the sentiments of a single chamber, such as condolences to the family of a deceased member, or to comment on foreign policy or executive business. A simple resolution is the vehicle for a "rule" from the House Rules Committee. *(Also see concurrent and joint resolutions, rules.)*

Rider — An amendment, usually not germane, that its sponsor hopes to get through more easily by including it in other legislation. A rider becomes law if the bill to which it is attached is enacted. Amendments providing legislative directives in appropriations bills are examples of riders, though technically legislation is banned from appropriations bills.

The House, unlike the Senate, has a strict germaneness rule; thus, riders usually are Senate devices to get legislation enacted quickly or to bypass lengthy House consideration and, possibly, opposition.

Rules — Each chamber has a body of rules and precedents that govern the conduct of business. These rules deal with issues such as duties of officers, the order of business, admission to the floor, parliamentary procedures on handling amendments and voting, and jurisdictions of committees. They are normally changed only at the start of each Congress.

In the House, a rule may also be a resolution reported by the Rules Committee to govern the handling of a particular bill on the floor. The committee may report a rule, also called a special order, in the form of a simple resolution. If the House adopts the resolution, the temporary rule becomes as valid as any standing rule and lapses only after action has been completed on the measure to which it pertains.

The rule sets the time limit on general debate. It may also waive points of order against provisions of the bill in question such as nongermane language or against certain amendments expected on the floor. It may even forbid all amendments or all amendments except those proposed by the legislative committee that handled the bill. In this instance, it is known as a "closed" rule as opposed to an "open" rule, which puts no limitation on floor amendments, thus leaving the bill completely open to alteration by the adoption of germane amendments. *(Also see point of order.)*

Secretary of the Senate — Chief administrative officer of the Senate, responsible for overseeing the duties of Senate employees, educating Senate pages, administering oaths, overseeing the registration of lobbyists and handling other tasks necessary for the continuing operation of the Senate. *(Also see Clerk of the House.)*

Select or special committee — A committee set up for a special purpose and, usually, for a limited time by resolution of either the House or Senate. Most special committees are investigative and lack legislative authority: Legislation is not referred to them, and they cannot report bills to their parent chambers. The House in 1993 terminated its four select committees.

Senatorial courtesy — A general practice with no written rule — sometimes referred to as "the courtesy of the Senate" — applied to consideration of executive nominations. Generally, it means that nominations from a state are not to be confirmed unless they have been approved by the senators of the president's party of that state, with other senators following their colleagues' lead in the attitude they take toward consideration of such nominations. *(Also see nominations.)*

Sequester — Automatic, across-the-board spending cuts, generally triggered after the close of a session by a report issued by the Office of Management and Budget. Under the 1985 Gramm-Rudman anti-deficit law, modified in 1987, a year-end sequester was triggered if the deficit exceeded a pre-set maximum. However, the Budget Enforcement Act of 1990, updated in 1993 and 1997, effectively replaced that procedure through fiscal 2002.

Instead, if Congress exceeds an annual cap on discretionary budget authority or outlays, a sequester is triggered for all eligible discretionary spending to make up the difference. If Congress violates pay-as-you-go rules by allowing the net effect of legislated changes in mandatory spending and taxes to increase the deficit, a sequester is triggered for all non-exempt entitlement programs. Similar procedures apply to supplemental appropriations bills. *(Also see budget process.)*

Sine die — *(See adjournment sine die.)*

Speaker — The presiding officer of the House of Representatives, selected by his party caucus and formally elected by the whole House. While both parties nominate candidates, choice by the majority party is tantamount to election. In 1995, House rules were changed to limit the Speaker to four consecutive terms.

Special session — A session of Congress after it has adjourned sine die, completing its regular session. Special sessions are convened by the president.

Spending authority — The 1974 budget act defines spending authority as borrowing authority, contract authority and entitlement authority for which budget authority is not provided in advance by appropriation acts.

Sponsor — *(See bills introduced.)*

Standing committees — Committees that are permanently established by House and Senate rules. The standing committees of the House were reorganized in 1974, with some changes in jurisdictions and titles made when Republicans took control of the House in 1995. The last major realignment of Senate committees was in 1977. The standing committees are legislative committees: Legislation may be referred to them, and they may report bills and resolutions to their parent chambers.

Standing vote — A non-recorded vote used in both the House and Senate. (A standing vote is also called a division vote.) Members in favor of a proposal stand and are counted by the presiding officer. Then members opposed stand and are counted. There is no record of how individual members voted.

Statutes at large — A chronological arrangement of the laws enacted in each session of Congress. Though indexed, the laws are not arranged by subject matter, and there is no indication of how they changed previously enacted laws. *(Also see law, U.S. Code.)*

Strike from the Record — A member of the House who is offended by remarks made on the House floor may move that the offending words be "taken down" for the Speaker's cognizance and then expunged from the debate as published in the Congressional Record.

Strike out the last word — A motion whereby a House member is entitled to speak for five minutes on an amendment then being debated by the chamber. A member gains recognition from the chair by moving to "strike out the last word" of the amendment or section of the bill under consideration. The motion is pro forma, requires no vote and does not change the amendment being debated. *(Also see five-minute rule.)*

Substitute — A motion, amendment or entire bill introduced in place of the pending legislative business. Passage of the substitute kills the original measure by supplanting it. The substitute may also be amended. *(Also see amendment in the nature of a substitute.)*

Supplemental appropriations bill — Legislation appropriating funds after the regular annual appropriations bill for a federal department or agency has been enacted. Supplemental appropriations bills often arrive about halfway through the fiscal year, when needs that Congress and the president did not anticipate (or may not have wanted to fund) become pressing. In recent years, supplementals have been driven by spending to help victims of natural disasters and to carry out peacekeeping commitments.

Suspend the rules — A time-saving procedure for passing bills in the House. The wording of the motion, which may be made by any member recognized by the Speaker, is: "I move to suspend the rules and pass the bill . . ." A favorable vote by two-thirds of those present is required for passage. Debate is limited to 40 minutes, and no amendments from the floor are permitted. If a two-thirds favorable vote is not attained, the bill may be considered later under regular procedures. The suspension procedure is in order every Monday and Tuesday and is intended to be reserved for non-controversial bills.

Table a bill — Motions to table, or to "lay on the table," are used to block or kill amendments or other parliamentary questions. When approved, a tabling motion is considered the final disposition of that issue. One of the most widely used parliamentary procedures, the motion to table is not debatable, and adoption requires a simple majority vote.

In the Senate, however, different language sometimes is used. The motion may be worded to let a bill "lie on the table," perhaps for subsequent "picking up." This motion is more flexible, keeping the bill pending for later action, if desired. Tabling motions on amendments are effective debate-ending devices in the Senate.

Treaties — Executive proposals — in the form of resolutions of ratification — which must be submitted to the Senate for approval by two-thirds of the senators present. Treaties are normally sent to the Foreign Relations Committee for scrutiny before the Senate takes action. Foreign Relations has jurisdiction over all treaties, regardless of the subject matter. Treaties are read three times and debated on the floor in much the same manner as legislative proposals. After approval by the Senate, treaties are formally ratified by the president.

Trust funds — Funds collected and used by the federal government for carrying out specific purposes and programs according to terms of a trust agreement or statute such as the Social Security and unemployment compensation trust funds. Such funds are administered by the government in a fiduciary capacity and are not available for the general purposes of the government.

Unanimous consent — A procedure used to expedite floor action. Proceedings of the House or Senate and action on legislation often take place upon the unanimous consent of the chamber, whether or not a rule of the chamber is being violated. It is frequently used in a routine fashion, such as by a senator requesting the unanimous consent of the Senate to have specified members of his or her staff present on the floor during debate on a specific amendment. A single member's objection blocks a unanimous consent request.

Unanimous consent agreement — A device used in the Senate to expedite legislation. Much of the Senate's legislative business, dealing with both minor and controversial issues, is conducted through unanimous consent or unanimous consent agreements. On major legislation, such agreements usually are printed and transmitted to all senators in advance of floor debate. Once agreed to, they are binding on all members unless the Senate, by unanimous consent, agrees to modify them. An agreement may list the order in which various bills are to be considered; specify the length of time for debate on bills and contested amendments and when they are to be voted upon; and, frequently, require that all amendments introduced be germane to the bill under consideration.

In this regard, unanimous consent agreements are similar to the "rules" issued by the House Rules Committee for bills pending in the House.

Union Calendar — Bills that directly or indirectly appropriate money or raise revenue are placed on this House calendar according to the date they are reported from committee. *(Also see calendar.)*

U.S. Code — A consolidation and codification of the general and permanent laws of the United States arranged by subject under 50 titles, the first six dealing with general or political subjects, and the other 44 alphabetically arranged from agriculture to war. The U.S. Code is updated annually, and a new set of bound volumes is published every six years. *(Also see law, statutes at large.)*

Veto — Disapproval by the president of a bill or joint resolution (other than one proposing an amendment to the Constitution). When Congress is in session, the president must veto a bill within 10 days, excluding Sundays, after he has received it; otherwise, it becomes law without his signature. When the president vetoes a bill, he returns it to the chamber of origin along with a message stating his objections. *(Also see pocket veto, override a veto.)*

Voice vote — In either the House or Senate, members answer "aye" or "no" in chorus, and the presiding officer decides the result. The term is also used loosely to indicate action by unanimous consent or without objection. *(Also see yeas and nays.)*

Whip — In effect, the assistant majority or minority leader, in either the House or Senate. His or her job is to help marshal votes in support of party strategy and legislation.

Without objection — Used in lieu of a vote on non-controversial motions, amendments or bills that may be passed in either chamber if no member voices an objection.

Yeas and nays — The Constitution requires that yea-and-nay votes be taken and recorded when requested by one-fifth of the members present. In the House, the Speaker determines whether one-fifth of the members present requested a vote. In the Senate, practice requires only 11 members. The Constitution requires the yeas and nays on a veto override attempt. *(Also see recorded vote.)*

Yielding — When a member has been recognized to speak, no other member may speak unless he or she obtains permission from the member recognized. This permission is called yielding and usually is requested in the form, "Will the gentleman (or gentlelady) yield to me?" While this activity occasionally is seen in the Senate, the Senate has no rule or practice to parcel out time.

In the House, the floor manager of a bill usually apportions debate time by yielding specific amounts of time to members who have requested it. ◆

Members of the 106th Congress, 1st Session . . .

(As of Nov. 22, 1999, when the first session of the 106th Congress adjourned sine die.)

Representatives
R 222; D 212; I 1

— A —

Abercrombie, Neil, D-Hawaii (1)
Ackerman, Gary L., D-N.Y. (5)
Aderholt, Robert B., R-Ala. (4)
Allen, Tom, D-Maine (1)
Andrews, Robert E., D-N.J. (1)
Archer, Bill, R-Texas (7)
Armey, Dick, R-Texas (26)

— B —

Baca, Joe, D-Calif. (42)
Bachus, Spencer, R-Ala. (6)
Baird, Brian, D-Wash. (3)
Baker, Richard H., R-La. (6)
Baldacci, John, D-Maine (2)
Baldwin, Tammy, D-Wis. (2)
Ballenger, Cass, R-N.C. (10)
Barcia, James A., D-Mich. (5)
Barr, Bob, R-Ga. (7)
Barrett, Bill, R-Neb. (3)
Barrett, Thomas M., D-Wis. (5)
Bartlett, Roscoe G., R-Md. (6)
Barton, Joe L., R-Texas (6)
Bass, Charles, R-N.H. (2)
Bateman, Herbert H., R-Va. (1)
Becerra, Xavier, D-Calif. (30)
Bentsen, Ken, D-Texas (25)
Bereuter, Doug, R-Neb. (1)
Berkley, Shelley, D-Nev. (1)
Berman, Howard L., D-Calif. (26)
Berry, Marion, D-Ark. (1)
Biggert, Judy, R-Ill. (13)
Bilbray, Brian P., R-Calif. (49)
Bilirakis, Michael, R-Fla. (9)
Bishop, Sanford D. Jr., D-Ga. (2)
Blagojevich, Rod R., D-Ill. (5)
Bliley, Thomas J. Jr., R-Va. (7)
Blumenauer, Earl, D-Ore. (3)
Blunt, Roy, R-Mo. (7)
Boehlert, Sherwood, R-N.Y. (23)
Boehner, John A., R-Ohio (8)
Bonilla, Henry, R-Texas (23)
Bonior, David E., D-Mich. (10)
Bono, Mary, R-Calif. (44)
Borski, Robert A., D-Pa. (3)
Boswell, Leonard L., D-Iowa (3)
Boucher, Rick, D-Va. (9)
Boyd, Allen, D-Fla. (2)
Brady, Kevin, R-Texas (8)
Brady, Robert A., D-Pa. (1)
Brown, Corrine, D-Fla. (3)
Brown, Sherrod, D-Ohio (13)
Bryant, Ed, R-Tenn. (7)
Burr, Richard M., R-N.C. (5)
Burton, Dan, R-Ind. (6)
Buyer, Steve, R-Ind. (5)

— C —

Callahan, Sonny, R-Ala. (1)
Calvert, Ken, R-Calif. (43)
Camp, Dave, R-Mich. (4)
Campbell, Tom, R-Calif. (15)
Canady, Charles T., R-Fla. (12)
Cannon, Christopher B., R-Utah (3)
Capps, Lois, D-Calif. (22)
Capuano, Michael E., D-Mass. (8)
Cardin, Benjamin L., D-Md. (3)
Carson, Julia, D-Ind. (10)
Castle, Michael N., R-Del. (AL)
Chabot, Steve, R-Ohio (1)
Chambliss, Saxby, R-Ga. (8)
Chenoweth-Hage, Helen, R-Idaho (1)
Clay, William L., D-Mo. (1)
Clayton, Eva, D-N.C. (1)
Clement, Bob, D-Tenn. (5)
Clyburn, James E., D-S.C. (6)
Coble, Howard, R-N.C. (6)
Coburn, Tom, R-Okla. (2)
Collins, Mac, R-Ga. (3)
Combest, Larry, R-Texas (19)
Condit, Gary A., D-Calif. (18)
Conyers, John Jr., D-Mich. (14)
Cook, Merrill, R-Utah (2)
Cooksey, John, R-La. (5)
Costello, Jerry F., D-Ill. (12)
Cox, Christopher, R-Calif. (47)
Coyne, William J., D-Pa. (14)
Cramer, Robert E. "Bud," D-Ala. (5)
Crane, Philip M., R-Ill. (8)
Crowley, Joseph, D-N.Y. (7)
Cubin, Barbara, R-Wyo. (AL)
Cummings, Elijah E., D-Md. (7)
Cunningham, Randy "Duke," R-Calif. (51)

— D —

Danner, Pat, D-Mo. (6)
Davis, Danny K., D-Ill. (7)
Davis, Jim, D-Fla. (11)
Davis, Thomas M. III, R-Va. (11)
Deal, Nathan, R-Ga. (9)
DeFazio, Peter A., D-Ore. (4)
DeGette, Diana, D-Colo. (1)
Delahunt, Bill, D-Mass. (10)
DeLauro, Rosa, D-Conn. (3)
DeLay, Tom, R-Texas (22)
DeMint, Jim, R-S.C. (4)
Deutsch, Peter, D-Fla. (20)
Diaz-Balart, Lincoln, R-Fla. (21)
Dickey, Jay, R-Ark. (4)
Dicks, Norm, D-Wash. (6)
Dingell, John D., D-Mich. (16)
Dixon, Julian C., D-Calif. (32)
Doggett, Lloyd, D-Texas (10)
Dooley, Cal, D-Calif. (20)
Doolittle, John T., R-Calif. (4)
Doyle, Mike, D-Pa. (18)
Dreier, David, R-Calif. (28)
Duncan, John J. "Jimmy" Jr., R-Tenn. (2)
Dunn, Jennifer, R-Wash. (8)

— E —

Edwards, Chet, D-Texas (11)
Ehlers, Vernon J., R-Mich. (3)
Ehrlich, Robert L. Jr., R-Md. (2)
Emerson, Jo Ann, R-Mo. (8)
Engel, Eliot L., D-N.Y. (17)
English, Phil, R-Pa. (21)
Eshoo, Anna G., D-Calif. (14)
Etheridge, Bob, D-N.C. (2)
Evans, Lane, D-Ill. (17)
Everett, Terry, R-Ala. (2)
Ewing, Thomas W., R-Ill. (15)

— F —

Farr, Sam, D-Calif. (17)
Fattah, Chaka, D-Pa. (2)
Filner, Bob, D-Calif. (50)
Fletcher, Ernie, R-Ky. (6)
Foley, Mark, R-Fla. (16)
Forbes, Michael P., D-N.Y. (1)
Ford, Harold E. Jr., D-Tenn. (9)
Fossella, Vito J., R-N.Y. (13)
Fowler, Tillie, R-Fla. (4)
Frank, Barney, D-Mass. (4)
Franks, Bob, R-N.J. (7)
Frelinghuysen, Rodney, R-N.J. (11)
Frost, Martin, D-Texas (24)

— G —

Gallegly, Elton, R-Calif. (23)
Ganske, Greg, R-Iowa (4)
Gejdenson, Sam, D-Conn. (2)
Gekas, George W., R-Pa. (17)
Gephardt, Richard A., D-Mo. (3)
Gibbons, Jim, R-Nev. (2)
Gilchrest, Wayne T., R-Md. (1)
Gillmor, Paul E., R-Ohio (5)
Gilman, Benjamin A., R-N.Y. (20)
Gonzalez, Charlie, D-Texas (20)
Goode, Virgil H. Jr., D-Va. (5)
Goodlatte, Robert W., R-Va. (6)
Goodling, Bill, R-Pa. (19)
Gordon, Bart, D-Tenn. (6)
Goss, Porter J., R-Fla. (14)
Graham, Lindsey, R-S.C. (3)
Granger, Kay, R-Texas (12)
Green, Gene, D-Texas (29)
Green, Mark, R-Wis. (8)
Greenwood, James C., R-Pa. (8)
Gutierrez, Luis V., D-Ill. (4)
Gutknecht, Gil, R-Minn. (1)

— H —

Hall, Ralph M., D-Texas (4)
Hall, Tony P., D-Ohio (3)
Hansen, James V., R-Utah (1)
Hastert, J. Dennis, R-Ill. (14)
Hastings, Alcee L., D-Fla. (23)
Hastings, Richard "Doc," R-Wash. (4)
Hayes, Robin, R-N.C. (8)
Hayworth, J.D., R-Ariz. (6)
Hefley, Joel, R-Colo. (5)
Herger, Wally, R-Calif. (2)
Hill, Baron P., D-Ind. (9)
Hill, Rick, R-Mont. (AL)
Hilleary, Van, R-Tenn. (4)
Hilliard, Earl F., D-Ala. (7)
Hinchey, Maurice D., D-N.Y. (26)
Hinojosa, Rubén, D-Texas (15)
Hobson, David L., R-Ohio (7)
Hoeffel, Joseph M., D-Pa. (13)
Hoekstra, Peter, R-Mich. (2)
Holden, Tim, D-Pa. (6)
Holt, Rush D., D-N.J. (12)
Hooley, Darlene, D-Ore. (5)
Horn, Steve, R-Calif. (38)
Hostettler, John, R-Ind. (8)
Houghton, Amo, R-N.Y. (31)
Hoyer, Steny H., D-Md. (5)
Hulshof, Kenny, R-Mo. (9)
Hunter, Duncan, R-Calif. (52)
Hutchinson, Asa, R-Ark. (3)
Hyde, Henry J., R-Ill. (6)

— I, J —

Inslee, Jay, D-Wash. (1)
Isakson, Johnny, R-Ga. (6)
Istook, Ernest, R-Okla. (5)
Jackson, Jesse L. Jr., D-Ill. (2)
Jackson-Lee, Sheila, D-Texas (18)
Jefferson, William J., D-La. (2)
Jenkins, Bill, R-Tenn. (1)
John, Chris, D-La. (7)
Johnson, Eddie Bernice, D-Texas (30)
Johnson, Nancy L., R-Conn. (6)
Johnson, Sam, R-Texas (3)
Jones, Walter B. Jr., R-N.C. (3)
Jones, Stephanie Tubbs, D-Ohio (11)

— K —

Kanjorski, Paul E., D-Pa. (11)
Kaptur, Marcy, D-Ohio (9)
Kasich, John R., R-Ohio (12)
Kelly, Sue W., R-N.Y. (19)
Kennedy, Patrick J., D-R.I. (1)
Kildee, Dale E., D-Mich. (9)
Kilpatrick, Carolyn Cheeks, D-Mich. (15)
Kind, Ron, D-Wis. (3)
King, Peter T., R-N.Y. (3)
Kingston, Jack, R-Ga. (1)
Kleczka, Gerald D., D-Wis. (4)
Klink, Ron, D-Pa. (4)
Knollenberg, Joe, R-Mich. (11)
Kolbe, Jim, R-Ariz. (5)
Kucinich, Dennis J., D-Ohio (10)
Kuykendall, Steven T., R-Calif. (36)

— L —

LaFalce, John J., D-N.Y. (29)
LaHood, Ray, R-Ill. (18)
Lampson, Nick, D-Texas (9)
Lantos, Tom, D-Calif. (12)
Largent, Steve, R-Okla. (1)
Larson, John B., D-Conn. (1)
Latham, Tom, R-Iowa (5)
LaTourette, Steven C., R-Ohio (19)
Lazio, Rick A., R-N.Y. (2)
Leach, Jim, R-Iowa (1)
Lee, Barbara, D-Calif. (9)
Levin, Sander M., D-Mich. (12)
Lewis, Jerry, R-Calif. (40)
Lewis, John, D-Ga. (5)
Lewis, Ron, R-Ky. (2)
Linder, John, R-Ga. (11)
Lipinski, William O., D-Ill. (3)
LoBiondo, Frank A., R-N.J. (2)
Lofgren, Zoe, D-Calif. (16)
Lowey, Nita M., D-N.Y. (18)
Lucas, Frank D., R-Okla. (6)
Lucas, Ken, D-Ky. (4)
Luther, Bill, D-Minn. (6)

— M —

Maloney, Carolyn B., D-N.Y. (14)
Maloney, Jim, D-Conn. (5)
Manzullo, Donald, R-Ill. (16)
Markey, Edward J., D-Mass. (7)
Martinez, Matthew G., D-Calif. (31)
Mascara, Frank R., D-Pa. (20)
Matsui, Robert T., D-Calif. (5)
McCarthy, Carolyn, D-N.Y. (4)
McCarthy, Karen, D-Mo. (5)
McCollum, Bill, R-Fla. (8)
McCrery, Jim, R-La. (4)
McDermott, Jim, D-Wash. (7)
McGovern, Jim, D-Mass. (3)
McHugh, John M., R-N.Y. (24)
McInnis, Scott, R-Colo. (3)
McIntosh, David M., R-Ind. (2)
McIntyre, Mike, D-N.C. (7)
McKeon, Howard P. "Buck," R-Calif. (25)
McKinney, Cynthia A., D-Ga. (4)
McNulty, Michael R., D-N.Y. (21)
Meehan, Martin T., D-Mass. (5)
Meek, Carrie P., D-Fla. (17)
Meeks, Gregory W., D-N.Y. (6)
Menendez, Robert, D-N.J. (13)
Metcalf, Jack, R-Wash. (2)
Mica, John L., R-Fla. (7)
Millender-McDonald, Juanita, D-Calif. (37)
Miller, Dan, R-Fla. (13)
Miller, Gary G., R-Calif. (41)
Miller, George, D-Calif. (7)
Minge, David, D-Minn. (2)
Mink, Patsy T., D-Hawaii (2)
Moakley, Joe, D-Mass. (9)
Mollohan, Alan B., D-W.Va. (1)
Moore, Dennis, D-Kan. (3)
Moran, James P., D-Va. (8)
Moran, Jerry, R-Kan. (1)
Morella, Constance A., R-Md. (8)
Murtha, John P., D-Pa. (12)
Myrick, Sue, R-N.C. (9)

— N —

Nadler, Jerrold, D-N.Y. (8)
Napolitano, Grace F., D-Calif. (34)
Neal, Richard E., D-Mass. (2)
Nethercutt, George, R-Wash. (5)
Ney, Bob, R-Ohio (18)
Northup, Anne M., R-Ky. (3)
Norwood, Charlie, R-Ga. (10)
Nussle, Jim, R-Iowa (2)

— O —

Oberstar, James L., D-Minn. (8)
Obey, David R., D-Wis. (7)
Olver, John W., D-Mass. (1)
Ortiz, Solomon P., D-Texas (27)
Ose, Doug, R-Calif. (3)
Owens, Major R., D-N.Y. (11)
Oxley, Michael G., R-Ohio (4)

— P —

Packard, Ron, R-Calif., (48)
Pallone, Frank Jr., D-N.J. (6)
Pascrell, Bill Jr., D-N.J. (8)
Pastor, Ed, D-Ariz. (2)
Paul, Ron, R-Texas (14)
Payne, Donald M., D-N.J. (10)
Pease, Ed, R-Ind. (7)
Pelosi, Nancy, D-Calif. (8)
Peterson, Collin C., D-Minn. (7)
Peterson, John E., R-Pa. (5)
Petri, Tom, R-Wis. (6)
Phelps, David, D-Ill. (19)
Pickering, Charles W. "Chip" Jr., R-Miss. (3)
Pickett, Owen B., D-Va. (2)
Pitts, Joseph R., R-Pa. (16)
Pombo, Richard W., R-Calif. (11)
Pomeroy, Earl, D-N.D. (AL)

. . . Governors, Justices, Cabinet-Rank Officers

Porter, John Edward, R-Ill. (10)
Portman, Rob, R-Ohio (2)
Price, David E., D-N.C. (4)
Pryce, Deborah, R-Ohio (15)

— Q, R —

Quinn, Jack, R-N.Y. (30)
Radanovich, George P., R-Calif. (19)
Rahall, Nick J. II, D-W.Va. (3)
Ramstad, Jim, R-Minn. (3)
Rangel, Charles B., D-N.Y. (15)
Regula, Ralph, R-Ohio (16)
Reyes, Silvestre, D-Texas (16)
Reynolds, Thomas M., R-N.Y. (27)
Riley, Bob, R-Ala. (3)
Rivers, Lynn, D-Mich. (13)
Rodriguez, Ciro D., D-Texas (28)
Roemer, Tim, D-Ind. (3)
Rogan, James E., R-Calif. (27)
Rogers, Harold, R-Ky. (5)
Rohrabacher, Dana, R-Calif. (45)
Ros-Lehtinen, Ileana, R-Fla. (18)
Rothman, Steven R., D-N.J. (9)
Roukema, Marge, R-N.J. (5)
Roybal-Allard, Lucille, D-Calif. (33)
Royce, Ed, R-Calif. (39)
Rush, Bobby L., D-Ill. (1)
Ryan, Paul D., R-Wis. (1)
Ryun, Jim, R-Kan. (2)

— S —

Sabo, Martin Olav, D-Minn. (5)
Salmon, Matt, R-Ariz. (1)
Sanchez, Loretta, D-Calif. (46)
Sanders, Bernard, I-Vt. (AL)
Sandlin, Max, D-Texas (1)
Sanford, Mark, R-S.C. (1)
Sawyer, Tom, D-Ohio (14)
Saxton, H. James, R-N.J. (3)
Scarborough, Joe, R-Fla. (1)
Schaffer, Bob, R-Colo. (4)
Schakowsky, Jan, D-Ill. (9)
Scott, Robert C., D-Va. (3)
Sensenbrenner, F. James Jr., R-Wis. (9)
Serrano, Jose E., D-N.Y. (16)
Sessions, Pete, R-Texas (5)
Shadegg, John, R-Ariz. (4)
Shaw, E. Clay Jr., R-Fla. (22)
Shays, Christopher, R-Conn. (4)
Sherman, Brad, D-Calif. (24)
Sherwood, Donald L., R-Pa. (10)
Shimkus, John, R-Ill. (20)
Shows, Ronnie, D-Miss. (4)
Shuster, Bud, R-Pa. (9)
Simpson, Mike, R-Idaho (2)
Sisisky, Norman, D-Va. (4)
Skeen, Joe, R-N.M. (2)
Skelton, Ike, D-Mo. (4)
Slaughter, Louise M., D-N.Y. (28)
Smith, Adam, D-Wash. (9)
Smith, Christopher H., R-N.J. (4)
Smith, Lamar, R-Texas (21)
Smith, Nick, R-Mich. (7)
Snyder, Vic, D-Ark. (2)
Souder, Mark, R-Ind. (4)
Spence, Floyd D., R-S.C. (2)
Spratt, John M. Jr., D-S.C. (5)
Stabenow, Debbie, D-Mich. (8)
Stark, Pete, D-Calif. (13)
Stearns, Cliff, R-Fla. (6)
Stenholm, Charles W., D-Texas (17)
Strickland, Ted, D-Ohio (6)
Stump, Bob, R-Ariz. (3)
Stupak, Bart, D-Mich. (1)
Sununu, John E., R-N.H. (1)
Sweeney, John E., R-N.Y. (22)

— T —

Talent, James M., R-Mo. (2)
Tancredo, Tom, R-Colo. (6)
Tanner, John, D-Tenn. (8)
Tauscher, Ellen O., D-Calif. (10)
Tauzin, W.J. "Billy," R-La. (3)
Taylor, Charles H., R-N.C. (11)
Taylor, Gene, D-Miss. (5)
Terry, Lee, R-Neb. (2)
Thomas, Bill, R-Calif. (21)
Thompson, Bennie, D-Miss. (2)
Thompson, Mike, D-Calif. (1)
Thornberry, William M. "Mac," R-Texas (13)
Thune, John, R-S.D. (AL)
Thurman, Karen L., D-Fla. (5)
Tiahrt, Todd, R-Kan. (4)
Tierney, John F., D-Mass. (6)
Toomey, Patrick J., R-Pa. (15)
Towns, Edolphus, D-N.Y. (10)
Traficant, James A. Jr., D-Ohio (17)
Turner, Jim, D-Texas (2)

— U, V —

Udall, Mark, D-Colo. (2)
Udall, Tom, D-N.M. (3)
Upton, Fred, R-Mich. (6)
Velázquez, Nydia M., D-N.Y. (12)
Vento, Bruce F., D-Minn. (4)
Visclosky, Peter J., D-Ind. (1)
Vitter, David, R-La. (1)

— W —

Walden, Greg, R-Ore. (2)
Walsh, James T., R-N.Y. (25)
Wamp, Zach, R-Tenn. (3)
Waters, Maxine, D-Calif. (35)
Watkins, Wes, R-Okla. (3)
Watt, Melvin, D-N.C. (12)
Watts, J.C. Jr., R-Okla. (4)
Waxman, Henry A., D-Calif. (29)
Weiner, Anthony, D-N.Y. (9)
Weldon, Curt, R-Pa. (7)
Weldon, Dave, R-Fla. (15)
Weller, Jerry, R-Ill. (11)
Wexler, Robert, D-Fla. (19)
Weygand, Bob, D-R.I. (2)
Whitfield, Edward, R-Ky. (1)
Wicker, Roger, R-Miss. (1)
Wilson, Heather A., R-N.M. (1)
Wise, Bob, D-W.Va. (2)
Wolf, Frank R., R-Va. (10)
Woolsey, Lynn, D-Calif. (6)
Wu, David, D-Ore. (1)
Wynn, Albert R., D-Md. (4)

— X, Y, Z —

Young, C.W. Bill, R-Fla. (10)
Young, Don, R-Alaska (AL)

Delegates

Christensen, Donna M.C., D-Virgin Is.
Faleomavaega, Eni F.H., D-Am. Samoa
Norton, Eleanor Holmes, D-D.C.
Romero-Barceló, Carlos A., D-P.R.
Underwood, Robert A., D-Guam

Senators
R 55; D 45

Abraham, Spencer, R-Mich.
Akaka, Daniel K., D-Hawaii
Allard, Wayne, R-Colo.
Ashcroft, John, R-Mo.
Baucus, Max, D-Mont.
Bayh, Evan, D-Ind.
Bennett, Robert F., R-Utah
Biden, Joseph R. Jr., D-Del.
Bingaman, Jeff, D-N.M.
Bond, Christopher S., R-Mo.
Boxer, Barbara, D-Calif.
Breaux, John B., D-La.
Brownback, Sam, R-Kan.
Bryan, Richard H., D-Nev.
Bunning, Jim, R-Ky.
Burns, Conrad, R-Mont.
Byrd, Robert C., D-W.Va.
Campbell, Ben Nighthorse, R-Colo.
Chafee, Lincoln, R-R.I.
Cleland, Max, D-Ga.
Cochran, Thad, R-Miss.
Collins, Susan, R-Maine
Conrad, Kent, D-N.D.
Coverdell, Paul, R-Ga.
Craig, Larry E., R-Idaho
Crapo, Michael D., R-Idaho
Daschle, Tom, D-S.D.
DeWine, Mike, R-Ohio
Dodd, Christopher J., D-Conn.
Domenici, Pete V., R-N.M.
Dorgan, Byron L., D-N.D.
Durbin, Richard J., D-Ill.
Edwards, John, D-N.C.
Enzi, Michael B., R-Wyo.
Feingold, Russell D., D-Wis.
Feinstein, Dianne, D-Calif.
Fitzgerald, Peter G., R-Ill.
Frist, Bill, R-Tenn.
Gorton, Slade, R-Wash.
Graham, Bob, D-Fla.
Gramm, Phil, R-Texas
Grams, Rod, R-Minn.
Grassley, Charles E., R-Iowa
Gregg, Judd, R-N.H.
Hagel, Chuck, R-Neb.
Harkin, Tom, D-Iowa
Hatch, Orrin G., R-Utah
Helms, Jesse, R-N.C.
Hollings, Ernest F., D-S.C.
Hutchinson, Tim, R-Ark.
Hutchison, Kay Bailey, R-Texas
Inhofe, James M., R-Okla.
Inouye, Daniel K., D-Hawaii
Jeffords, James M., R-Vt.
Johnson, Tim, D-S.D.
Kennedy, Edward M., D-Mass.
Kerrey, Bob, D-Neb.
Kerry, John, D-Mass.
Kohl, Herb, D-Wis.
Kyl, Jon, R-Ariz.
Landrieu, Mary L., D-La.
Lautenberg, Frank R., D-N.J.
Leahy, Patrick J., D-Vt.
Levin, Carl, D-Mich.
Lieberman, Joseph I., D-Conn.
Lincoln, Blanche, D-Ark.
Lott, Trent, R-Miss.
Lugar, Richard G., R-Ind.
Mack, Connie, R-Fla.
McCain, John, R-Ariz.
McConnell, Mitch, R-Ky.
Mikulski, Barbara A., D-Md.
Moynihan, Daniel Patrick, D-N.Y.
Murkowski, Frank H., R-Alaska
Murray, Patty, D-Wash.
Nickles, Don, R-Okla.
Reed, Jack, D-R.I.
Reid, Harry, D-Nev.
Robb, Charles S., D-Va.
Roberts, Pat, R-Kan.
Rockefeller, John D. IV, D-W.Va.
Roth, William V. Jr., R-Del.
Santorum, Rick, R-Pa.
Sarbanes, Paul S., D-Md.
Schumer, Charles E., D-N.Y.
Sessions, Jeff, R-Ala.
Shelby, Richard C., R-Ala.
Smith, Gordon H., R-Ore.
Smith, Robert C., R-N.H.
Snowe, Olympia J., R-Maine
Specter, Arlen, R-Pa.
Stevens, Ted, R-Alaska
Thomas, Craig, R-Wyo.
Thompson, Fred, R-Tenn.
Thurmond, Strom, R-S.C.
Torricelli, Robert G., D-N.J.
Voinovich, George V., R-Ohio
Warner, John W., R-Va.
Wellstone, Paul, D-Minn.
Wyden, Ron, D-Ore.

Governors
R 31; D 17; I 1; Reform 1

Ala. — Donald Siegelman, D
Alaska — Tony Knowles, D
Ariz. — Jane Dee Hull, R
Ark. — Mike Huckabee, R
Calif. — Gray Davis, D
Colo. — Bill Owens, R
Conn. — John G. Rowland, R
Del. — Thomas R. Carper, D
Fla. — Jeb Bush, R
Ga. — Roy Barnes, D
Hawaii — Benjamin J. Cayetano, D
Idaho — Dirk Kempthorne, R
Ill. — George Ryan, R
Ind. — Frank L. O'Bannon, D
Iowa — Tom Vilsack, D
Kan. — Bill Graves, R
Ky. — Paul E. Patton, D
La. — Mike Foster, R
Maine — Angus King, I
Md. — Parris N. Glendening, D
Mass. — Paul Cellucci, R
Mich. — John Engler, R
Minn. — Jesse Ventura, Reform
Miss. — Kirk Fordice, R
Mo. — Mel Carnahan, D
Mont. — Marc Racicot, R
Neb. — Mike Johanns, R
Nev. — Kenny Guinn, R
N.H. — Jeanne Shaheen, D
N.J. — Christine Todd Whitman, R
N.M. — Gary E. Johnson, R
N.Y. — George E. Pataki, R
N.C. — James B. Hunt Jr., D
N.D. — Edward T. Schafer, R
Ohio — Bob Taft, R
Okla. — Frank Keating, R
Ore. — John Kitzhaber, D
Pa. — Tom Ridge, R
R.I. — Lincoln C. Almond, R
S.C. — Jim Hodges, D
S.D. — William J. Janklow, R
Tenn. — Don Sundquist, R
Texas — George W. Bush, R
Utah — Michael O. Leavitt, R
Vt. — Howard Dean, D
Va. — James S. Gilmore III, R
Wash. — Gary Locke, D
W.Va. — Cecil H. Underwood, R
Wis. — Tommy G. Thompson, R
Wyo. — Jim Geringer, R

Supreme Court

Rehnquist, William H. — Va., Chief Justice
Breyer, Stephen G. — Mass.
Ginsburg, Ruth Bader — N.Y.
Kennedy, Anthony M. — Calif.
O'Connor, Sandra Day — Ariz.
Scalia, Antonin — Va.
Souter, David H. — N.H.
Stevens, John Paul — Ill.
Thomas, Clarence — Ga.

Cabinet

Albright, Madeleine K. — State
Babbitt, Bruce — Interior
Cohen, William S. — Defense
Cuomo, Andrew M. — HUD
Daley, William M. — Commerce
Glickman, Dan — Agriculture
Herman, Alexis M. — Labor
Holbrooke, Richard C. — U.N. Representative
Reno, Janet — Attorney General
Richardson, Bill — Energy
Riley, Richard W. — Education
Shalala, Donna E. — HHS
Slater, Rodney — Transportation
Summers, Lawrence H. — Treasury
West, Togo D. Jr. — Veterans Affairs

Other Executive Branch Officers

Gore, Al — Vice President
Baily, Martin N. — Chairman, Council of Economic Advisers
Barshefsky, Charlene — U.S. Trade Representative
Berger, Samuel R. — National Security Adviser
Browner, Carol M. — EPA Administrator
Lew, Jack — OMB Director
Podesta, John D. — Chief of Staff
Sperling, Gene — Chairman, National Economic Council
Tenet, George J. — Director of Central Intelligence

Appendix B

VOTE STUDIES

Clinton Comes Up Short In a Year of Politics Over Substance

President Clinton took a pounding on Capitol Hill in 1999. In the wake of his Senate impeachment trial, he and the Republican-controlled Congress found little room for compromise. For the most part, they didn't even try.

In this atmosphere, Clinton's ability to persuade Congress fell to near record lows. None of the major initiatives outlined in his State of the Union address — overhauling Social Security and Medicare, raising the minimum wage, tightening regulation of health maintenance organizations (HMOs) or raising tobacco-related revenue — became law. Few ever came up for a vote.

On those issues that did prompt votes, Clinton fared poorly, achieving a 37.8 percent overall success rate — the second-lowest since Congressional Quarterly began evaluating presidential success in Congress 47 years ago. The lowest-ever success score, 36.2 percent, also belongs to Clinton. It came in 1995, when the Republican revolution was in high gear.

Though Clinton was acquitted in the Senate in February, the drawn-out impeachment fight shattered his already tenuous relationships with top GOP leaders and contributed to an extraordinarily partisan and polarized climate in Congress.

"Not only do the Republicans have policy problems with him, they have personal problems with him. This is not a recipe for presidential effectiveness in the House or Senate," said Steven Schier, chairman of the political science department at Carleton College in Minnesota. "Given the narrow majority in the House and Senate, given an impeachment and conviction vote, how could you expect anything other than this?"

Clinton himself made no major effort to seek compromise with Republicans, as he had in 1997 when he pushed hard for a balanced-budget pact. And many Republicans made little secret of their dislike for the president. "Nobody trusts him, Republican or Democrat," maintained House Majority Leader Dick Armey, R-Texas. "He does not make much of an effort."

CQ Vote Studies

Clinton's fortunes fell most dramatically in the Senate, where Republican leaders had unusual success in keeping moderates from abandoning the GOP fold. Only three Republican moderates — James M. Jeffords of Vermont, the late John H. Chafee of Rhode Island and Arlen Specter of Pennsylvania — supported Clinton more than half the time, far fewer than usual.

Overall, Clinton won on 42.2 percent of the Senate votes on which he staked a clear position. Excluding votes on nominations — nine of the 10 nominees that reached the floor were confirmed — Clinton had only a 28.6 percent success rate. The comparable figure for 1998 was 57.1 percent.

"The impact of the House impeachment and the trial in the Senate set the stage for the poor working relationship throughout the year," said a senior Senate GOP aide.

It was not just impeachment. GOP leaders frequently used procedural tactics to deny Democrats opportunities to offer non-germane amendments to bills. Democrats responded with filibusters to force Republicans to give them votes on Democratic priorities such as HMO changes and lifting the minimum wage. In that environment, GOP moderates tended to stick with their leaders and support alternative Republican plans.

"In part, that's a consequence of the success that [Minority Leader Tom] Daschle [D-S.D.] has had in the use of holds and the filibuster and so forth," said Charles O. Jones, professor emeritus at the University of Wisconsin at Madison. "That hardens the partisanship on the majority side."

Added Sen. Patrick J. Leahy, D-Vt.: "It has never been so partisan around here than the past year or so. Impeachment obviously added to that."

In the House, Clinton prevailed 35.4 percent of the time on presidential success votes, about level with the past two years. It had been the higher Senate scores — 67 percent in 1998 and 71.4 percent in 1997 — that brought Clinton's overall success rate to levels of 50.6 percent and 53.6 percent, respectively, in those years.

Lawmakers and staff aides attributed Republicans' ability to keep Clinton's success rate down in the House despite the ultra-slim GOP majority to Speaker J. Dennis Hastert, R-Ill., whose patient, team-building style inspired remarkable loyalty. "It's trust, the reserve of good faith that's unquantifiable in this town" said Hastert ally Robert L. Ehrlich Jr., R-Md.

Not Budging

The president's low score in 1999 was consistent with the indifference toward compromise shown by both sides.

"The president and Congress want different things, and there's not much room — or at this point, incentive — for compromise," said David W. Rohde, professor of political science at Michigan State University. "Both want to use the disagreements as a ba-

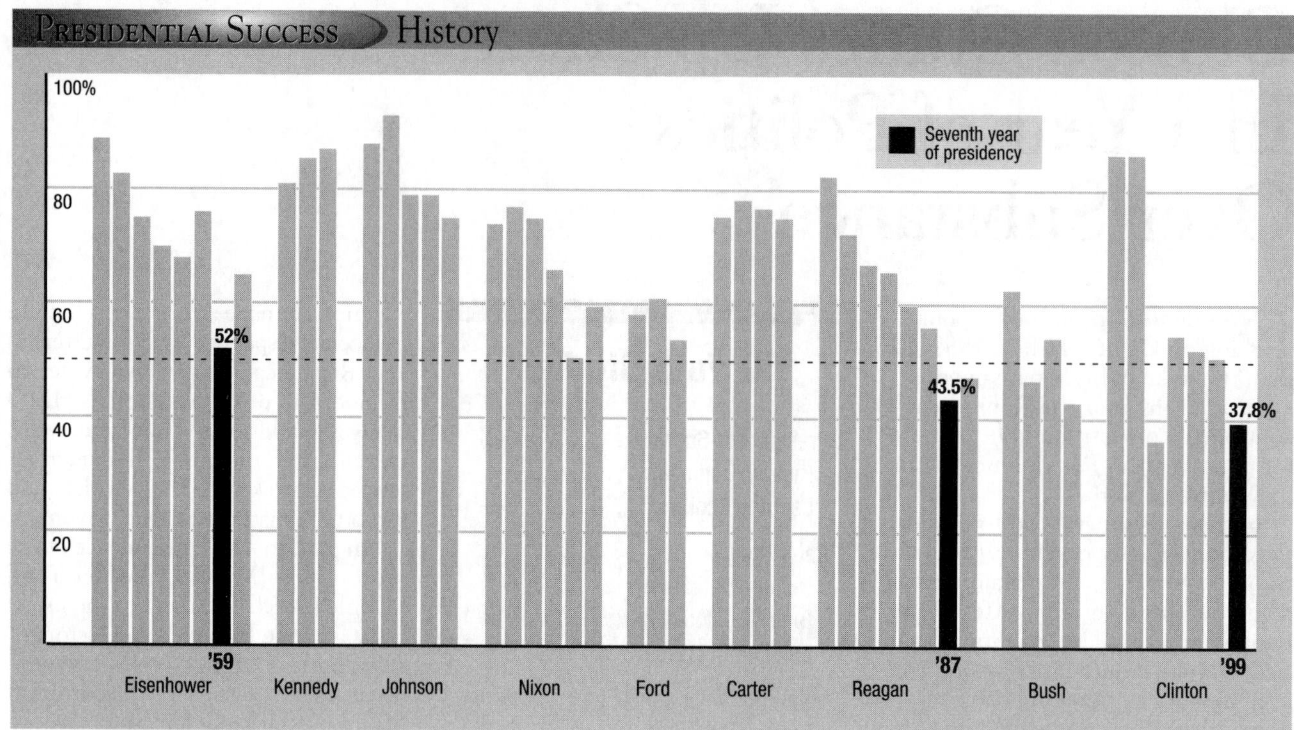

sis for altering the political balance. That is, they want to go to the country with the disagreements."

For example, Clinton and the Republicans offered significantly different tax plans. Yet at no point during the year did either side actively seek the kind of split-their-difference compromise that might have given them each policy victories.

Republicans made it clear that the huge 10-year, $792 billion tax cut bill they put at the top of their agenda was a party-defining issue designed to appeal to their political base — not an invitation to negotiate.

In that case, Clinton lost the battle — Congress cleared the bill (HR 2488) in August — but won the war. Though he got no tax cuts of his own, he vetoed the GOP bill, and there was no backlash from the public.

Clinton did not fight for a broad agenda in 1999, and Republicans, for the most part, kept tight control of the House and Senate floors as they pressed ahead with their own relatively modest proposals. Nor did the public seem to demand major legislative action.

"You've got a narrowly divided, highly polarized situation in Congress. And then we have a [situation] right in the country in which there is little or no pressing demand for public policy," said Professor George C. Edwards III, director of the Texas A&M University Center for Presidential Studies. "When times are good, you typically don't have those kinds of demands. And times are really good now."

At the same time, House Democrats made no secret of their lack of interest in helping Republicans develop a roster of accomplishments. They opted instead to portray the 106th as an inept, do-nothing Congress. "They are not of a mind to get too many accomplishments in the Congress," a senior White House official said of the House Democrats.

Neither Clinton nor Congress displayed any eagerness to tackle the lightning rod issues of Social Security and Medicare. Republicans dismissed without votes Clinton's proposals to, in effect, add general fund revenues to the Social Security trust fund, to overhaul Medicare and to provide a prescription drug benefit.

At the same time, Clinton undercut the deliberations of the National Bipartisan Commission on the Future of Medicare. The chairman, Sen John B. Breaux, D-La., co-authored an overhaul plan with Republicans, but Clinton's allies on the commission denied him the supermajority vote required to report it to Congress. Republicans declined to press ahead on their own.

"They've taken all the good stuff that's easy to do off the top, and what's left is just exceedingly difficult to do," said Stephen Hess, a senior fellow at the Brookings Institution. "Some of these questions really need another election to resolve."

"You have a majority party whose agenda is quite disparate from the president's. And the president hasn't sought out a lot of ways to overlap his agenda with our agenda," said Eric Ue-

Definition

How often the president won on roll call votes on which he took a clear position.

1999 Data

Senate	19 victories 26 defeats
House	29 victories 53 defeats

Total Clinton success rate: 38%

For More Information

Individual leaders B-5
Background and data B-12
List of House votes.................... B-13
House members' scores B-14
List of Senate votes B-16
Senators' scores....................... B-17

Leading Scorers: Presidential Support

Support indicates those who in 1999 voted most often for President Clinton's position; **opposition** shows those who voted most often against the president's position.

Scores are based on actual votes cast; members are listed alphabetically when their scores are tied. Members who missed half or more of the votes are not listed.

SENATE

Support				Opposition			
Jeffords, Vt.	56%	Graham, Fla.	93%	Smith, N.H.	84%	Byrd, W.Va.	30%
Chafee, J. R.I.	54	Kennedy, Mass.	93	Helms, N.C.	82	Conrad, N.D.	27
Specter, Pa.	53	Kerry, Mass.	93	Allard, Colo.	77	Dorgan, N.D.	27
Collins, Maine	49	Lautenberg, N.J.	93	Inhofe, Okla.	77	Breaux, La.	23
Snowe, Maine	49	Harkin, Iowa	91	Bunning, Ky.	76	Johnson, S.D.	22
Voinovich, Ohio	45	Kerrey, Neb.	91	Burns, Mont.	76	Hollings, S.C.	20
Roth, Del.	44	Kohl, Wis.	91	Enzi, Wyo.	76	Lincoln, Ark.	20
Smith, Ore.	43	Schumer, N.Y.	91	Hutchinson, Ark.	76	Baucus, Mont.	19
Ashcroft, Mo.	40	Wyden, Ore.	91	Sessions, Ala.	76	Feingold, Wis.	18
Lugar, Ind.	40	Akaka, Hawaii	89	Thurmond, S.C.	76	Leahy, Vt.	18
Thompson, Tenn.	40	Bayh, Ind.	89	Nickles, Okla.	73	Reid, Nev.	18
Warner, Va.	39	Biden, Del.	89				
		Bryan, Nev.	89				
		Levin, Mich.	89				
		Lieberman, Conn.	89				
		Reed, R.I.	89				
		Rockefeller, W.Va.	89				

HOUSE

Support				Opposition			
Morella, Md.	68%	Berman, Calif.	90%	Bartlett, Md.	91%	Goode, Va.	84%
Johnson, Conn.	54	Sawyer, Ohio	89	Hilleary, Tenn.	91	Hall, Texas	69
Boehlert, N.Y.	52	Gephardt, Mo.	88	DeMint, S.C.	89	Peterson, Minn.	61
Porter, Ill.	50	Kilpatrick, Mich.	88	Hostettler, Ind.	89	Taylor, Miss.	61
Castle, Del.	49	Matsui, Calif.	88	Scarborough, Fla.	89	Danner, Mo.	59
Houghton, N.Y.	49	Millender-McDonald, Calif.	88	Coble, N.C.	88	Lucas, Ky.	59
Gilman, N.Y.	48	Olver, Mass.	88	Metcalf, Wash.	88	Traficant, Ohio	56
Shays, Conn.	48	Payne, N.J.	88	Pombo, Calif.	88	Barcia, Mich.	54
		Weiner, N.Y.	88	Rohrabacher, Calif.	88	McIntyre, N.C.	54
				Burton, Ind.	87	Forbes, N.Y.	50
				Pease, Ind.	87	Shows, Miss.	49

land, chief of staff to Assistant Majority Leader Don Nickles, R-Okla.

A Step Up, a Step Back

Clinton did manage to win a few big votes, although victories in one chamber were often undone in the other. The House passed a popular, bipartisan bill (HR 2723) to give patients greater rights to challenge decisions made by their HMOs, and it once again passed legislation (HR 417) to overhaul campaign finance laws. Both were victories for the president.

In the Senate, however, Clinton absorbed losses on both issues as Republicans passed their own HMO bill (S 1344) and blocked debate on campaign finance reform (S 1593).

On gun control, Clinton won a dramatic, 51-50 Senate vote on restricting handgun purchases at gun shows (S 254), but a companion gun control effort (HR 2122) in the House failed entirely.

On perhaps the most significant bill enacted into law during the session — overhauling Depression-era financial services laws (PL 106-102) — Clinton stayed mostly on the sidelines. While he submitted his own proposal and signed the final bill in a White House ceremony, he did not actively push the measure, and Treasury officials became actively involved only at the end of the process, when it became clear the bill was about to pass.

The final bill contained several provisions the administration was uncomfortable with. As a result, CQ did not assign a presidential position to the final vote.

In one area — appropriations — Clinton's lack of success on individual votes contrasts significantly with his effect on the final outcome. Clinton opposed several of the fiscal 2000 spending bills as too parsimonious or too filled with GOP policy "riders." In the opening legislative round, he lost a host of votes on these bills. But in the end, as he and Congress negotiated over a year-end omnibus spending package (HR 3194), Clinton won reversals on many of those issues, getting additional funding for foreign aid, teacher and police hiring subsidies, and release of funding for U.S. arrears to the United Nations.

From a statistical perspective, Clinton fared better on foreign policy issues than he did on domestic policy. For example, he survived attempts in both the House and Senate to restrict his options in conducting the peacekeeping mission in Kosovo, as lawmakers debated a fiscal 1999 supplemental appropriations bill (HR 1664) and the defense authorization bill (HR 1401; S 1059).

But one of Clinton's biggest losses of the year also came on defense, when the Senate defeated the Comprehensive Test Ban Treaty. And the House undercut him as he pursued air operations over Kosovo, rejecting a non-binding resolution (S Con Res 21) to authorize the bombing. Republicans, however, took political hits for both votes.

Clinton's success rate in Congress has fluctuated wildly. In his first two years in office, with Congress under Democratic control, Clinton had near-record success scores of 86.4 percent. But those votes belied a major failure: Clinton's inability to win passage of a national health care bill.

After Republicans took over Congress in 1995, Clinton's score sank to a record low 36.2 percent as the House GOP ignored his views and pressed ahead with its "Contract With America." His scores recovered somewhat in 1996, as he and Republicans sought election year common ground on a few issues, such as overhauling welfare and raising the minimum wage. He hovered slightly above 50 percent in 1997 and 1998, before plummeting again this year.

The decline in Clinton's success with Congress in the seventh year of his presidency follows a historic pattern. Presidents Ronald Reagan and Dwight D. Eisenhower — both of whom, like Clinton, faced a Congress controlled by the opposition party — saw their success scores dip sharply in their seventh years in office. Eisenhower's 1959 presidential success score of 52 percent was his lowest ever, as was Reagan's 1987 score of 43.5 percent.

Add the bitter saga of impeachment to the mix, and the fact that Clinton's lame-duck score was even lower is no surprise.

"There is a diminished appeal to offending party colleagues and helping Bill Clinton, given what Republicans went through in the impeachment process," said Schier. "That's one of the key votes in their whole congressional careers, and that had to produce a chilling effect for a lot of Republicans on the possibility of walking the plank to aid Bill Clinton." ◆

Partisan Voting Holds Steady, Belying Fractious Tone Of Debates

Congress fought numerous partisan battles in 1999, ranging from education priorities early in the year to the bitter appropriations struggle that delayed adjournment for weeks. Some observers called it one of the most partisan years in recent decades, an atmosphere soured by the effort to impeach President Clinton a year ago. Still, Congress somehow managed to hold its percentage of partisan floor votes down to a moderate level compared with recent years.

The rate of partisan voting in the House actually declined in 1999 compared with the previous year, and rose only modestly in the Senate, according to Congressional Quarterly's annual vote analysis. The study defines partisan votes as those in which a majority of one party voted against a majority of the other party.

Academic observers cited a combination of factors to explain why the partisan atmosphere in 1999 was not more apparent in the percentage of partisan floor votes.

Floor votes do not tell the whole story. The GOP's thin margin in the House may have made Republican leaders reluctant to bring issues to a vote unless they were confident of the outcome. Moreover, the worst partisan fighting often occurred in committee battles, conference negotiations and in relations between the GOP and the White House. Indeed, the level of congressional support for President Clinton's favored positions in 1999 hit near-record lows. *(Presidential support, p. B-3)*

Perceptions of Partisanship

As defined by CQ, the rate of partisan voting in the House declined from 55.5 percent in 1998 to 47.1 percent in 1999, its lowest level in a decade. And despite the upward blip of partisan voting in the Senate, from 55.7 percent in 1998 to 62.8 percent in 1999, the rate was still lower than at other times during the 1990s.

Rep. Marge Roukema, R-N.J., said that in the wake of impeachment, the media decided 1999 was destined to be a highly partisan year for Congress, feeding a broad public misconception about the level of partisanship on Capitol Hill.

"People jumped to that conclusion, and it proved wrong," said Roukema. "It was a miscalculation of what would ensue after the impeachment." Roukema said the debate in Congress on many issues, such as agriculture and the environment, were more regional than partisan.

John R. Hibbing, a political science professor at the University of Nebraska-Lincoln, agreed that partisanship tends to be exaggerated by the media. Even though empirical data on voting trends show that partisanship has been

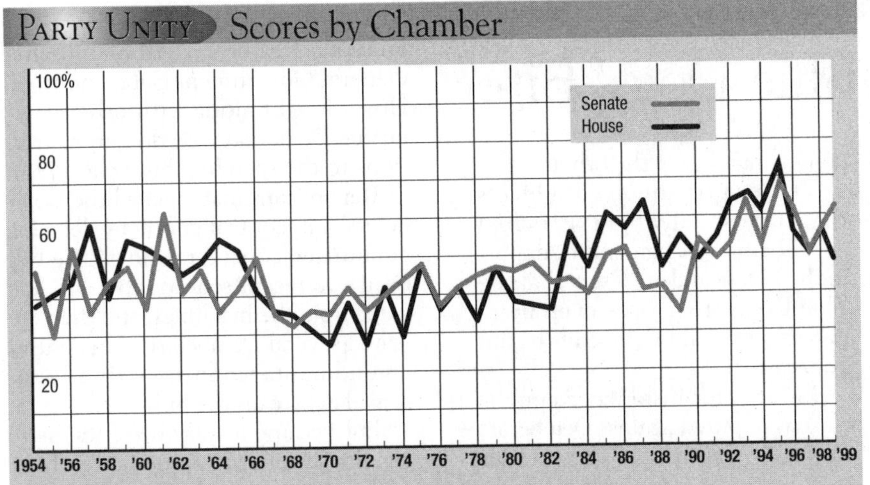

Definition

The percentage of recorded floor votes in each chamber on which a majority of one party voted against a majority of the other party.

1999 Data

	Partisan Votes	Total Votes	Percent
Senate	235	374	63
House	288	611	47

For More Information

Individual leaders........................ B-9
Background and data................. B-18
List of votes............................... B-19
House members' scores B-20
Senators' scores......................... B-22

relatively high over the past few decades, the differences on many big issues between the parties have actually narrowed in recent years, Hibbing said.

For example, even though Republicans and Democrats frequently argue about Social Security, they actually agree much more on the issue than they did a few decades ago. Republicans and Democrats used to fight over whether the program should exist at all; now they fight over how the annual cost of living adjustment should be calculated, Hibbing said.

Rep. Steny H. Hoyer, D-Md., a co-chairman of the Democratic Policy and Steering Committee, disagrees with the notion that partisanship was no worse than usual this year. "It was a hard-line, 'we're not going to go your way' attitude," he said.

The climate may have been fed by the fact that some of the most partisan battles were on high-profile issues. In some cases, floor action gave issues a glow of compromise that belied more difficult legislative histories.

For example, the huge and historically difficult rewrite of the nation's financial services laws, which finally became law (PL 106-102) in 1999 after decades of efforts, was billed as a bipartisan product by its proponents. The conference report was easily cleared in both chambers, and Clinton signed the bill with a large cast of Republicans and Democrats beaming proudly at his side.

But that scene masked intense partisan dogfights over consumer privacy, banks' community lending requirements and other side issues that jeopardized the entire bill at a number of points.

And during negotiations over the fiscal 2000 appropriations bills, the House recorded eight nearly unanimous votes on or related to continuing resolutions to keep the government running while Democrats and Republicans fought over the budget. While those votes were counted as bipartisan ones, they actually were a side effect of the underlying partisanship.

On the Margins

One possible explanation for the decrease in the percentage of partisan votes in the House is the loss of seats suffered by Republicans in the 1998 elections, which left them only a five-member voting majority. Roger H. Davidson, visiting professor of political science at the University of California, Santa Barbara, said he suspects that the Republicans' "razor thin" margin forced GOP leaders to back off from pushing their agenda at times.

With such a thin majority, all it takes is a handful of conservative or moderate Republicans to obstruct their party's agenda if they do not get what they want from the leadership. In other words, a relatively low level of partisan voting in such a climate can be more a matter of strategy and necessity than an indicator of goodwill and comity.

There were some vote patterns which more clearly illustrated the level of partisanship. Of the 235 partisan votes in the Senate, Democrats voted unanimously 100 times and Republicans voted unanimously 63 times. That is up substantially from the previous year, when Senate Republicans voted unanimously 33 times on partisan votes and Democrats voted unanimously 46 times on partisan votes.

Senate Minority Leader Tom Daschle, D-S.D., has a reputation for being able to pull his troops together, and the number of unanimous votes by Senate Democrats is a clear indicator of that, Davidson said. "Look at the performance that he put on in the impeachment," Davidson noted.

Although it is more difficult to achieve party unanimity in the House — simply because there are so many more members than in the Senate — House Republicans managed to muster unanimous coalitions on 59 of the 288 party unity votes in that chamber in 1999. House Democrats voted unanimously 11 times on partisan votes.

Republicans praise Speaker J. Dennis Hastert, R-Ill., for keeping their fractious caucus together. Hoyer and other Democrats argue that the Speaker was largely bending to the will of the most conservative GOP members, rather than seeking bipartisan consensus.

Hoyer pointed to education and health care as examples of issues where GOP leaders generally stuck to highly partisan positions and were willing to let little or nothing happen rather than seek consensus.

Hoyer also cited gun control as an issue where the level of partisanship would be drastically understated on an analysis of floor votes alone. As the ranking member of the House Appropriations Treasury, Postal Service and General Government Subcommittee, Hoyer fought along with other committee Democrats to add gun restrictions to the spending bill (HR 2490).

Republicans first blocked the Democrats' gun control efforts by delaying committee consideration of the bill until two recent school shootings had faded from the headlines, and then defeated several Democratic gun control amendments when they finally resumed debate on the bill.

But because it was one of the more generously funded appropriations bills, and fights over spending priorities were minimal, the conference report on the Treasury-Postal bill was easily adopted on the floors of both chambers, masking the highly partisan fights that preceded the final votes.

As another example of heated partisanship not reflected in floor votes, Hoyer said the fight over the Labor, Health and Human Services, and Education spending bill also was overwhelmingly partisan. Clinton and congressional Democrats argued with the GOP for weeks over numerous provisions in the bill (HR 3064) and never came to an agreement on it as a stand-alone measure. In, the end, the bill was wrapped into the end-of-year fiscal 2000 omnibus spending package (PL 106-113).

Hoyer said that because of the upcoming elections, he expects the GOP to soften its positions in 2000 to make its message more moderate and palatable for voters.

Influence of Moderates

David R. Mayhew, a political science professor at Yale University, said a shift of power in the House from the Speaker to Majority Whip Tom DeLay, R-Texas, in the post-Newt Gingrich era has had important ramifications for how Congress has functioned.

Despite his reputation as a partisan bulldog, Gingrich, R-Ga., (1979-99) was more willing than DeLay to accommodate the moderate wing of his party, which gave Gingrich more leverage for pushing the GOP agenda, he added.

However, Mayhew said he believes the GOP's thin majority probably forces the leadership to be more receptive to party moderates, who as a result

Democrats Feel Blue Dogs' Bite

Since wresting control of the House in 1994, Republican leaders have had to deal with a small but significant group of moderates who often stray from the party line on crucial votes. Constance A. Morella of Maryland, Christopher Shays of Connecticut and Sherwood Boehlert of New York are among the Republicans who have bucked the leadership on campaign finance, managed care and other measures.

A collection of centrist Democrats could give their party leaders even bigger headaches if the Democrats win a majority in the House next November — or even if it stays Republican. The 30-member group, which calls itself the Blue Dog Coalition, provided the margin of difference on a handful of votes during 1999 and very rarely nullified its votes by splitting down the middle.

"We understand our position in this with the narrowness of the majority," Chris John, D-La., one of three Blue Dog co-chairmen, said in an interview Nov. 29. "We understand how we can drive this process."

John was especially hopeful that the group could make a difference on budget policy, the common thread among the geographically diverse membership, which includes Loretta Sanchez of California, Ralph M. Hall of Texas and Harold E. Ford Jr. of Tennessee.

"We talk a lot about issues, but the centerpiece is our fiscal conservatism," John said. "I think you're going to see the Blue Dogs take a serious role in the budget process." If so, the coalition could find itself opposing fellow Democrats on spending bills, with the numbers to make a difference.

Four times during 1999, a majority of Blue Dogs voted against a majority of Democrats in situations where agreement between the two camps would have changed the outcome of the vote. All were "party unity" votes, defined by Congressional Quarterly as occurring when a majority of one party opposes a majority of the other.

These votes involved subjects that traditionally have attracted overwhelming Democratic support in the House and are a sign that the Blue Dog vote may be even more important should Democrats regain power in 2001.

In June, for instance, Republicans were pitted against Democrats in a high-profile vote on whether to impose a 24-hour limit for background checks at gun shows (HR 2122). Twenty Blue Dog members voted for the amendment, helping it pass, 218-211. In another case, a proposal to increase funding for the National Endowment for the Arts under the fiscal 2000 Interior appropriations bill (HR 2466) failed by 10 votes — in large part because 19 Blue Dogs voted "no."

Even when they sided with Republicans and lost, the Blue Dogs narrowed the margin on controversial votes. An amendment to the District of Columbia appropriations bill (HR 2587) to ban the adoption of children in the District by people who are not related by blood or marriage was narrowly defeated by Democrats, though 22 Blue Dogs voted for it.

The Blue Dogs almost never failed to unite on a key tally. They split their votes just eight times this year — all but once in situations where even a unanimous Blue Dog vote would not have altered the outcome.

The group takes an official position on a bill or amendment only if two-thirds of the group decides to endorse a particular position before a House vote, John said.

Despite that, most Blue Dogs tended to agree with the position taken by a majority of coalition members. Norman Sisisky, D-Va., voted with a majority of Blue Dogs on 96 percent of roll-call votes in 1999. The lowest such score was for Virgil H. Goode Jr., D-Va., who agreed with a majority of fellow members 70 percent of the time.

Leading Scorers: Party Unity

Support indicates those who in 1999 voted most consistently with their party's majority against the other party; **opposition** shows how often members voted against their party's majority. Scores are based on votes cast; members are listed alphabetically when their scores are tied. Members who missed half or more of the votes are not listed.

Support				Opposition			
SENATE							
Murkowski, Alaska	98%	Boxer, Calif.	97%	Specter, Pa.	36%	Breaux, La.	25%
Nickles, Okla.	98	Harkin, Iowa	97	Jeffords, Vt.	33	Byrd, W.Va.	20
Allard, Colo.	97	Kennedy, Mass.	97	Snowe, Maine	31	Landrieu, La.	19
Coverdell, Ga.	97	Levin, Mich.	97	J. Chafee, R.I.	30	Lincoln, Ark.	17
Craig, Idaho	97	Sarbanes, Md.	97	Collins, Maine	26	Moynihan, N.Y.	15
Crapo, Idaho	97	Akaka, Hawaii	96				
Gramm, Texas	97	Lautenberg, N.J.	96				
Kyl, Ariz.	97	Mikulski, Md.	96				
Lott, Miss.	97	Reed, R.I.	96				
Mack, Fla.	97	Wellstone, Minn.	96				
HOUSE							
Armey, Texas	97%	Cummings, Md.	98%	Morella, Md.	51%	Goode, Va.	78%
DeLay, Texas	97	Filner, Calif.	98	Boehlert, N.Y.	40	Hall, Texas	70
DeMint, S.C.	97	Kilpatrick, Mich.	98	Gilman, N.Y.	38	Traficant, Ohio	57
Hastings, Wash.	97	Nadler, N.Y.	98	Porter, Ill.	37	Taylor, Miss.	56
Herger, Calif.	97			Shays, Conn.	34	Lucas, Ky.	54
Johnson, Texas	97			Campbell, Calif.	33	Stenholm, Texas	51
Pitts, Pa.	97			Johnson, Conn.	33	Peterson, Minn.	49
Ryun, Kan.	97			Horn, Calif.	32	Cramer, Ala.	47
Stump, Ariz.	97			Castle, Del.	31	John, La.	47
				Frelinghuysen, N.J.	31	McIntyre, N.C.	46
				Kelly, N.Y.	31	Shows, Miss.	44

will become more prominent players in the months ahead.

With GOP members, such as Nancy L. Johnson and Christopher Shays of Connecticut, willing to buck the party on a regular basis, Mayhew said, the Republican leadership will continue to have a difficult time mustering majority votes without bringing moderates on board.

"There's no way to shut them up," Mayhew said.

The roster of Democrats and Republicans in both chambers who were most likely to buck their party on partisan votes remained remarkably stable in 1999 compared with 1998. Arlen Specter, R-Pa., and James M. Jeffords, R-Vt., remained the two Senate Republicans most likely to vote against their party on partisan votes. Robert C. Byrd of West Virginia and John B. Breaux of Louisiana were the Democrats most likely to side with the Senate Republicans on partisan votes.

In the House, Ralph M. Hall of Texas, Virgil H. Goode Jr. of Virginia, James A. Traficant Jr. of Ohio and Gene Taylor of Mississippi remained the GOP's top Democratic allies on partisan votes.

House Republicans Johnson, Shays, Constance A. Morella of Maryland, and Sherwood Boehlert and Benjamin A. Gilman of New York topped the list of the most frequent GOP defectors. All had been at or near the top of last year's list as well. ◆

In Demanding Session, Voting Participation Hits Record 96.6 Percent

Members of Congress set a record for overall voting participation in 1999, despite the fact that both chambers took a relatively large number of roll-call votes. Congress' 96.6 percent mark was the highest in the 47 years Congressional Quarterly has tracked roll-call votes. This year's score topped the previous record of 96.5 percent set in 1995 and 1997.

The House had an overall voting rate of 96.5 percent; the Senate scored even higher at 97.9 percent. In the House, 10 members earned perfect scores, each casting "yea" or "nay" votes 609 times. Eighteen senators participated in all 374 roll-call votes in 1999.

Perhaps this year's voting diligence could be summed up in the effort of 97- year-old Sen. Strom Thurmond, R-S.C., who, despite prostate surgery in August, participated in all 374 recorded votes. Over the past five years, Thurmond has missed just six votes.

Voting participation — defined by CQ as how often a member voted "yea" or "nay" on roll-call votes on the floor of the House or Senate — was more, not less, demanding than in most recent sessions.

The total number of votes (983) recorded in both chambers in 1999 was the third-highest this decade — although the number of bills enacted into law was among the lowest.

In the Senate, Charles E. Grassley, R-Iowa, maintained his perfect participation score for the sixth consecutive year. Grassley's streak, the longest active run in the Senate, began July 20, 1993, and now stands at 2,433 consecutive votes.

In the House, Jesse L. Jackson Jr., D-Ill., maintained his active voting streak. Jackson, who has not missed a vote since taking office in December 1995, joined Grassley this year in topping the 2,000 consecutive-votes plateau. Yet Jackson's mark of 2,252 is still 16,149 short of the all-time record set by Rep. William Natcher, D-Ky. (1953-94).

Grassley trails Sen. William Proxmire, D-Wis. (1957-89), who ended his career with a 22-year perfect participation streak.

Three House freshmen, Judy Biggert, R-Ill., Joseph M. Hoeffel, D-Pa., and Jay Inslee, D-Wash., had perfect scores, as did two first-year senators, Evan Bayh, D-Ind., and Blanche Lincoln, D-Ark. Overall, freshman members voted 98.1 percent of the time.

Rep. Dale E. Kildee, D-Mich. — whose participation streak of nearly 12 years ended in June 1998 when he, along with 67 other House members, voted "present" instead of "yea" or "nay" on a substitute amendment to a campaign finance bill — finished 1999 with a 100 percent participation score.

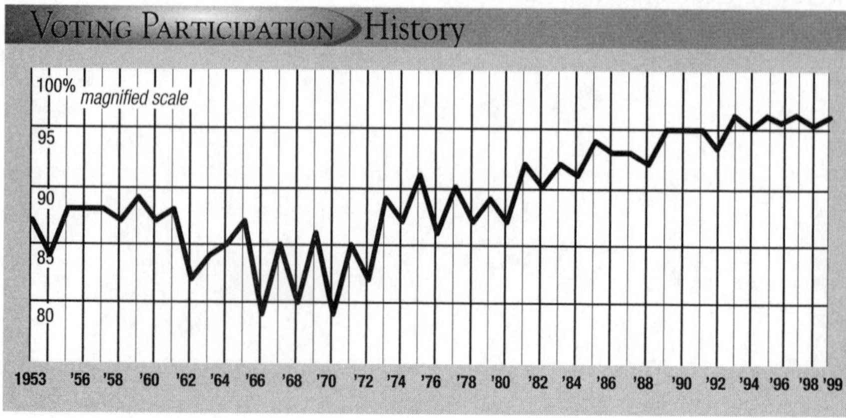

Voting and Campaigns

The 2000 presidential contest has dramatically affected one lawmaker's voting participation. GOP presidential contender Sen. John McCain, who maintained attendance rates above 90 percent throughout his Senate career, skipped more votes in 1999 than he had during the previous nine years. The Arizona Republican dropped to a career-low 64 percent and missed 134 votes. McCain's percentage was the lowest in the chamber this year, with retiring Sen. Daniel Patrick Moynihan, D-N.Y., a distant second at 85.6 percent.

McCain missed, and did not announce a position on, some major votes, including final passage of the financial services overhaul (S 900), an amendment to the fiscal 2000 transportation spending measure (HR 2084) concerning whether to raise the corporate average fuel economy (CAFE) standards for vehicles, and an amendment to the "partial birth" abortion bill (S 1692) expressing the sense of Congress that the Supreme Court's 1973

Definition

How often individual members voted "yea" or "nay" on roll call votes on the floor of the House or Senate.

1999 Data

	Recorded Votes	Percentage
Senate	374	97.9
House	609	96.5
Total Congress	983	96.6

For More Information

Senators' scores B-23
House members' scores........... B-24

Roe v. Wade decision was "appropriate" and "should not be overturned."

"Overall, Sen. McCain regrets having to miss even one vote," said Nancy Ives, McCain's press secretary. "No one has found a way to maintain embarking on this historic mission and being present for votes in the Senate."

Excluding illness-related absences, McCain's tally is the lowest in the Senate since Al Gore (1985-93) campaigned on Bill Clinton's presidential ticket in 1992. Gore's score that year was 56 percent. For non-election years, McCain's score is the lowest since 1987, when Gore and Sen. Paul Simon, D-Ill. (1985-1997), dipped below the 50 percent mark while campaigning for the 1988 Democratic presidential nomination.

Republican Sen. Orrin G. Hatch of Utah, who has also launched a presidential bid, missed 11 votes this year for a 97.1 percent rating.

What It Means on the Stump

Though voting participation is only one measure of a member's dedication to the job, candidates have been known to use it, with varying success, to cast doubt on an opponent's legislative record.

In 1998, New York Republican Sen. Alfonse M. D'Amato (1981-99) criticized his Democratic opponent, then-Rep. Charles E. Schumer, for missing House votes during the campaign. Schumer, who succeeded in taking D'Amato's seat, improved on his 1998 House score of 79 percent by making all but two votes in the Senate this year.

Six senators facing tough re-election battles in 2000 protected themselves from such criticisms, at least for 1999. Spencer Abraham, R-Mich., Charles S. Robb, D-Va., Rod Grams, R-Minn., John Ashcroft, R-Mo., William V. Roth Jr., R-Del., and Lincoln Chafee, R-R.I., missed a combined total of only six votes this year. Abraham has not missed a vote during his first term in the Senate.

Chafee, who was sworn in Nov. 4 to replace his father, the late Sen. John H. Chafee, R-R.I. (1976-99), was eligible for just 21 votes. The elder Chafee voted 93.5 percent of the time until his death Oct. 24.

Four current House members fell below the 80 percent mark. Jim McDermott, D-Wash., scored 79.8 percent; William J. Jefferson, D-La., voted 76.7 percent of the time; and Joe Scarborough, R-Fla., had a score of 67.0 percent. Scarborough missed seven weeks of votes after suffering a back injury in September that required surgery.

By tradition, House Speakers tend to vote only on symbolic or party-defining issues. Speaker J. Dennis Hastert, R-Ill., cast just 137 votes this year, netting a 22.5 percent participation score. ◆

Guide to CQ's Voting Analyses

Since 1945, Congressional Quarterly has analyzed the voting behavior of members of Congress. These studies have become references for academics, journalists, politicians and students who want information on how Congress behaves as an institution and how individual members vote.

What votes are used: CQ bases its vote studies on all roll call votes on which members were asked to vote "yea" or "nay." In 1999 there were 374 such votes in the Senate and 609 in the House. The CQ study excludes quorum calls, which require only that members vote "present." There were two quorum calls in the House in 1999, for a total of 611 roll calls.

The totals used by CQ do include votes in the House to approve the Journal (29 in 1999) and in the Senate to instruct the sergeant at arms to request members' presence in the chamber (two in 1999).

The studies on presidential support and party unity cover specific votes selected from the total according to the criteria described on pp. B-12 and B-18.

Individual scores: In the charts that follow, a member's scores are calculated based only on the votes he or she actually cast. The same method is used for leading scorers on pp. B-5 and B-9.

Overall scores: For consistency with previous years, graphs and breakdowns of chambers, parties and regions are based on all yea-or-nay votes. In those cases, absences lower scores. *(Methodology, 1987 Almanac, p. 22-C)*

Rounding: Scores are rounded to the nearest percentage point, except that rounding is not used to bring any score up to 100 percent.

Regions: Congressional Quarterly defines regions of the United States as follows: **East:** Conn., Del., Maine, Md., Mass., N.H., N.J., N.Y., Pa., R.I., Vt., W.Va. **West:** Alaska, Ariz., Calif., Colo., Hawaii, Idaho, Mont., Nev., N.M., Ore., Utah, Wash., Wyo. **South:** Ala., Ark., Fla., Ga., Ky., La., Miss., N.C., Okla., S.C., Tenn., Texas, Va. **Midwest:** Ill., Ind., Iowa, Kan., Mich., Minn., Mo., Neb., N.D., Ohio, S.D., Wis.

References to Northern Democrats and Northern Republicans include all members who do not represent the 13 Southern states, as defined by CQ.

Presidential Support Background

Congressional Quarterly determines presidential positions on congressional votes by examining the statements made by President Clinton or his authorized spokesmen.

Support measures the percentage of the time members voted in accord with the position of the president. **Opposition** measures the percentage of the time members voted against the president's position. **Success** measures the percentage of the contested votes on which the president prevailed. Absences lowered parties' scores. Scores for 1998 are given for comparison.

Success Scores by Issue

Following are presidential success scores by category. "Economic affairs" includes votes on trade and on omnibus and supplemental spending bills, which may fund both domestic and defense/foreign policy programs.

	Defense/Foreign Policy		Domestic		Economic Affairs		Average	
	1999	1998	1999	1998	1999	1998	1999	1998
Senate	33%	75%	44%	63%	43%	75%	42%	67%
House	50	31	22	36	56	50	35	37
Average	**46**	**58**	**31**	**48**	**52**	**57**	**38**	**51**

	Support				Opposition			
	Republicans		Democrats		Republicans		Democrats	
	1999	1998	1999	1998	1999	1998	1999	1998
Senate	34%	41%	84%	82%	64%	56%	14%	13%
House	23	26	73	74	74	71	24	21

Regional Averages

Support

	East		West		South		Midwest	
	1999	1998	1999	1998	1999	1998	1999	1998
Republicans								
Senate	48%	53%	30%	41%	29%	35%	36%	40%
House	32	34	22	24	20	22	24	26
Democrats								
Senate	85	84	84	81	83	81	84	83
House	76	77	78	79	68	68	72	73

Opposition

	East		West		South		Midwest	
	1999	1998	1999	1998	1999	1998	1999	1998
Republicans								
Senate	51%	43%	66%	55%	69%	61%	63%	59%
House	65	64	75	72	77	74	74	72
Democrats								
Senate	13	12	14	14	16	17	16	13
House	21	19	19	16	29	27	26	23

Success-Rate History

Average score for both chambers of Congress:

Eisenhower	
1953	89.0%
1954	82.8
1955	75.0
1956	70.0
1957	68.0
1958	76.0
1959	52.0
1960	65.0

Kennedy	
1961	81.0%
1962	85.4
1963	87.1

Johnson	
1964	88.0%
1965	93.0
1966	79.0
1967	79.0
1968	75.0

Nixon	
1969	74.0%
1970	77.0
1971	75.0
1972	66.0
1973	50.6
1974	59.6

Ford	
1974	58.2%
1975	61.0
1976	53.8

Carter	
1977	75.4%
1978	78.3
1979	76.8
1980	75.1

Reagan	
1981	82.4%
1982	72.4
1983	67.1
1984	65.8
1985	59.9
1986	56.1
1987	43.5
1988	47.4

Bush	
1989	62.6%
1990	46.8
1991	54.2
1992	43.0

Clinton	
1993	86.4%
1994	86.4
1995	36.2
1996	55.1
1997	53.6
1998	50.6
1999	37.8

1999 House Presidential Position Votes

The following is a list of House votes in 1999 on which there was a clear presidential position. Votes are categorized by topic and listed by roll-call number with a brief description.

Domestic Policy

10 Victories

Vote Number	Description
32	Transportation
35	Health care
137	Space station
256	Foster care
299	Religious expression
358	Federal construction
370	Legal Services
422	Campaign finance
490	Health care
552	Electronic commerce

36 Defeats

Vote Number	Description
17	Federal mandates
20	Paperwork reduction
89	2000 census
128	Y2K liability
139	NASA
173	Abortion
209	Transportation
232	Crime
234	Gun control
235	Gun control
243	Gun control
255	Law enforcement
261	Abortion
301	Abortion
319	Education
320	Education
336	Federal mandates
341	Environment
344	Needle exchange
347	D.C. appropriations
366	OSHA regulations
386	Crime
387	CJS appropriations
403	VA-HUD appropriations
436	Agriculture
443	Class action suits
444	Environment
465	Fetal harm
485	Health care
504	D.C. appropriations
518	CJS appropriations
528	Interior appropriations
532	Education
549	Labor-HHS appropriations
560	Environment
579	Electronic commerce

Defense and Foreign Policy

10 Victories

Vote Number	Description
69	Multilateral aid
101	Kosovo
119	Kosovo
187	Kosovo
189	Kosovo
304	Foreign aid
314	U.N. peacekeeping
324	Military aid
350	Abortion
353	Family planning

10 Defeats

Vote Number	Description
59	Anti-missile defense
68	Multilateral, bilateral aid
100	Kosovo
103	Kosovo
310	Iran nuclear sanctions
321	North Korea
349	Abortion
362	Foreign aid
409	Iran-Russia sanctions
480	Foreign aid

Economic Affairs and Trade

9 Victories

Vote Number	Description
90	Tax limit amendment
117	Supplemental appropriations
269	Financial services
307	Sub-Saharan Africa trade
322	AIDS drugs
338	China trade status
359	OPIC
365	Vietnam trade
610	Omnibus appropriations

7 Defeats

Vote Number	Description
56	Steel quotas
70	Supplemental appropriations
114	Bankruptcy overhaul
115	Bankruptcy overhaul
118	Supplemental appropriations
333	Taxes
379	Taxes

House Success Score

Victories	29
Defeats	53
Total	**82**
Success rate	35.4%

Presidential Support and Opposition: House

1. Presidential Support Score. Percentage of recorded votes cast in 1999 on which President Clinton took a position and on which the member voted "yea" or "nay" in agreement with the president's position. Failure to vote did not lower an individual's score.

2. Presidential Opposition Score. Percentage of recorded votes cast in 1999 on which President Clinton took a position and on which a member voted "yea" or "nay" in disagreement with the president's position. Failure to vote did not lower an individual's score.

3. Participation in Presidential Support Votes. Percentage of the 82 recorded House votes on which President Clinton took a position and on which a member was present and voted "yea" or "nay."

[1] *Joe Baca, D-Calif., was sworn in Nov. 18, replacing George E. Brown Jr., D-Calif., who died July 15. Baca was eligible for one presidential support vote in 1999. Brown was eligible for 14 presidential support votes; his presidential support score was 92 percent.*

[2] *Johnny Isakson, R-Ga., was sworn in Feb. 25, replacing Newt Gingrich, R-Ga., who resigned effective Jan. 3, 1999. Isakson was eligible for 80 presidential support votes in 1999.*

[3] *J. Dennis Hastert, R-Ill., as Speaker of the House, voted on 36 presidential support votes at his discretion in 1999.*

[4] *David Vitter, R-La., was sworn in June 8, replacing Robert L. Livingston, R-La., who resigned effective Feb. 28, 1999. Vitter was eligible for 60 presidential support votes in 1999. Livingston was eligible for two; his presidential support score was 0 percent.*

[5] *Michael P. Forbes, D-N.Y., switched his party affiliation from Republican to Democrat on July 17.*

Key

Democrats ***Republicans***
Independents

	1	2	3
ALABAMA			
1 ***Callahan***	26	74	98
2 ***Everett***	15	85	96
3 ***Riley***	19	81	99
4 ***Aderholt***	14	86	96
5 Cramer	54	46	99
6 ***Bachus***	17	83	100
7 Hilliard	78	22	96
ALASKA			
AL ***Young***	16	84	98
ARIZONA			
1 ***Salmon***	27	73	94
2 Pastor	83	17	99
3 ***Stump***	17	83	100
4 ***Shadegg***	15	85	98
5 ***Kolbe***	40	60	99
6 ***Hayworth***	15	85	99
ARKANSAS			
1 Berry	60	40	100
2 Snyder	78	22	100
3 ***Hutchinson***	24	76	98
4 ***Dickey***	17	83	95
CALIFORNIA			
1 Thompson	76	24	100
2 ***Herger***	22	78	100
3 ***Ose***	37	63	100
4 ***Doolittle***	17	83	100
5 Matsui	88	12	99
6 Woolsey	78	22	100
7 Miller	74	26	98
8 Pelosi	81	19	99
9 Lee	76	24	100
10 Tauscher	77	23	100
11 ***Pombo***	12	88	100
12 Lantos	83	17	87
13 Stark	75	25	94
14 Eshoo	85	15	100
15 ***Campbell***	40	60	100
16 Lofgren	84	16	94
17 Farr	85	15	99
18 Condit	55	45	100
19 ***Radanovich***	18	82	96
20 Dooley	72	28	100
21 ***Thomas***	31	69	95
22 Capps	80	20	96
23 ***Gallegly***	24	76	98
24 Sherman	78	22	99
25 ***McKeon***	22	78	98
26 Berman	90	10	89
27 ***Rogan***	20	80	98
28 ***Dreier***	30	70	99
29 Waxman	86	14	96
30 Becerra	85	15	95
31 Martinez	80	20	96
32 Dixon	86	14	98
33 Roybal-Allard	86	14	99
34 Napolitano	77	23	96
35 Waters	87	13	96
36 ***Kuykendall***	38	62	96
37 Millender-McD.	88	12	100
38 ***Horn***	39	61	100
39 ***Royce***	16	84	100
40 ***Lewis***	33	67	96
41 ***Miller***	21	79	99
42 Baca[1]	100	0	100
43 ***Calvert***	30	70	99
44 ***Bono***	25	75	96
45 ***Rohrabacher***	12	88	100
46 Sanchez	75	25	98
47 ***Cox***	18	82	87
48 ***Packard***	20	80	96
49 ***Bilbray***	39	61	88
50 Filner	85	15	100
51 ***Cunningham***	20	80	98
52 ***Hunter***	21	79	98
COLORADO			
1 DeGette	84	16	100
2 Udall	80	20	100
3 ***McInnis***	20	80	96
4 ***Schaffer***	21	79	100
5 ***Hefley***	17	83	99
6 ***Tancredo***	18	82	100
CONNECTICUT			
1 Larson	83	17	99
2 Gejdenson	83	17	99
3 DeLauro	82	18	100
4 ***Shays***	48	52	99
5 Maloney	72	28	100
6 ***Johnson***	54	46	98
DELAWARE			
AL ***Castle***	49	51	100
FLORIDA			
1 ***Scarborough***	11	89	77
2 Boyd	67	33	100
3 Brown	83	17	99
4 ***Fowler***	28	72	98
5 Thurman	78	22	94
6 ***Stearns***	18	82	100
7 ***Mica***	18	82	98
8 ***McCollum***	27	73	96
9 ***Bilirakis***	17	83	99
10 ***Young***	31	69	90
11 Davis	79	21	99
12 ***Canady***	22	78	100
13 ***Miller***	30	70	98
14 ***Goss***	28	72	100
15 ***Weldon***	16	84	100
16 ***Foley***	32	68	100
17 Meek	86	14	98
18 ***Ros-Lehtinen***	27	73	96
19 Wexler	84	16	98
20 Deutsch	80	20	100
21 ***Diaz-Balart***	33	67	100
22 ***Shaw***	37	63	96
23 Hastings	82	18	94
GEORGIA			
1 ***Kingston***	14	86	96
2 Bishop	64	36	99
3 ***Collins***	14	86	98
4 McKinney	71	29	96
5 Lewis	84	16	93
6 ***Isakson***[2]	29	71	100
7 ***Barr***	16	84	99
8 ***Chambliss***	26	74	99
9 ***Deal***	16	84	96
10 ***Norwood***	14	86	99
11 ***Linder***	18	82	100
HAWAII			
1 Abercrombie	71	29	98
2 Mink	74	26	98
IDAHO			
1 ***Chenoweth-Hage***	19	81	84
2 ***Simpson***	24	76	98
ILLINOIS			
1 Rush	86	14	94
2 Jackson	82	18	100
3 Lipinski	58	42	95
4 Gutierrez	76	24	93
5 Blagojevich	81	19	96
6 ***Hyde***	31	69	98
7 Davis	84	16	100
8 ***Crane***	16	84	99
9 Schakowsky	82	18	100
10 ***Porter***	50	50	98
11 ***Weller***	24	76	100
12 Costello	63	37	96
13 ***Biggert***	37	63	100
14 ***Hastert***[3]	17	83	44

ND Northern Democrats SD Southern Democrats

	1	2	3
15 ***Ewing***	23	77	99
16 ***Manzullo***	15	85	100
17 Evans	80	20	99
18 ***LaHood***	26	74	98
19 Phelps	63	37	100
20 ***Shimkus***	21	79	99
INDIANA			
1 Visclosky	77	23	100
2 ***McIntosh***	19	81	96
3 Roemer	62	38	100
4 ***Souder***	16	84	100
5 ***Buyer***	24	76	95
6 ***Burton***	13	87	95
7 ***Pease***	13	87	100
8 ***Hostettler***	11	89	98
9 Hill	65	35	100
10 Carson	81	19	90
IOWA			
1 ***Leach***	38	62	100
2 ***Nussle***	22	78	100
3 Boswell	67	33	99
4 ***Ganske***	39	61	96
5 ***Latham***	23	77	94
KANSAS			
1 ***Moran***	18	82	100
2 ***Ryun***	17	83	99
3 Moore	77	23	99
4 ***Tiahrt***	18	82	95
KENTUCKY			
1 ***Whitfield***	24	76	100
2 ***Lewis***	17	83	100
3 ***Northup***	28	72	100
4 Lucas	41	59	100
5 ***Rogers***	21	79	100
6 ***Fletcher***	19	81	98
LOUISIANA			
1 ***Vitter***[4]	20	80	100
2 Jefferson	85	15	80
3 ***Tauzin***	21	79	93
4 ***McCrery***	25	75	99
5 ***Cooksey***	24	76	87
6 ***Baker***	17	83	93
7 John	58	42	96
MAINE			
1 Allen	86	14	99
2 Baldacci	82	18	100
MARYLAND			
1 ***Gilchrest***	41	59	93
2 ***Ehrlich***	26	74	99
3 Cardin	83	17	100
4 Wynn	82	18	89
5 Hoyer	82	18	100
6 ***Bartlett***	9	91	100
7 Cummings	85	15	100
8 ***Morella***	68	32	100
MASSACHUSETTS			
1 Olver	88	12	95
2 Neal	78	22	98
3 McGovern	82	18	100
4 Frank	80	20	96
5 Meehan	84	16	98
6 Tierney	79	21	100
7 Markey	79	21	100
8 Capuano	81	19	99
9 Moakley	79	21	98
10 Delahunt	81	19	98
MICHIGAN			
1 Stupak	70	30	94
2 ***Hoekstra***	15	85	100
3 ***Ehlers***	29	71	100
4 ***Camp***	23	77	96
5 Barcia	46	54	100
6 ***Upton***	32	68	100
7 ***Smith***	22	78	99
8 Stabenow	78	22	99
9 Kildee	71	29	100
10 Bonior	79	21	100
11 ***Knollenberg***	30	70	100
12 Levin	87	13	100
13 Rivers	62	38	99
14 Conyers	84	16	98
15 Kilpatrick	88	12	99
16 Dingell	77	23	100

	1	2	3
MINNESOTA			
1 ***Gutknecht***	18	82	100
2 Minge	77	23	94
3 ***Ramstad***	34	66	100
4 Vento	81	19	98
5 Sabo	86	14	98
6 Luther	79	21	94
7 Peterson	39	61	100
8 Oberstar	73	27	95
MISSISSIPPI			
1 ***Wicker***	22	78	99
2 Thompson	82	18	96
3 ***Pickering***	21	79	99
4 Shows	51	49	99
5 Taylor	39	61	98
MISSOURI			
1 Clay	84	16	94
2 ***Talent***	22	78	96
3 Gephardt	88	12	93
4 Skelton	64	36	94
5 McCarthy	80	20	96
6 Danner	41	59	96
7 ***Blunt***	19	81	99
8 ***Emerson***	21	79	100
9 ***Hulshof***	22	78	95
MONTANA			
AL ***Hill***	20	80	100
NEBRASKA			
1 ***Bereuter***	35	65	98
2 ***Terry***	21	79	99
3 ***Barrett***	30	70	99
NEVADA			
1 Berkley	79	21	99
2 ***Gibbons***	20	80	100
NEW HAMPSHIRE			
1 ***Sununu***	18	82	98
2 ***Bass***	27	73	100
NEW JERSEY			
1 Andrews	76	24	98
2 ***LoBiondo***	18	82	100
3 ***Saxton***	32	68	100
4 ***Smith***	27	73	99
5 ***Roukema***	42	58	98
6 Pallone	79	21	100
7 ***Franks***	38	62	100
8 Pascrell	80	20	96
9 Rothman	82	18	100
10 Payne	88	12	100
11 ***Frelinghuysen***	45	55	100
12 Holt	79	21	99
13 Menendez	81	19	99
NEW MEXICO			
1 ***Wilson***	32	68	100
2 ***Skeen***	23	77	99
3 Udall	78	22	100
NEW YORK			
1 Forbes[5]	50	50	98
2 ***Lazio***	39	61	98
3 ***King***	32	68	99
4 McCarthy	77	23	96
5 Ackerman	87	13	96
6 Meeks	86	14	96
7 Crowley	81	19	98
8 Nadler	84	16	100
9 Weiner	88	12	98
10 Towns	79	21	95
11 Owens	85	15	98
12 Velázquez	76	24	100
13 ***Fossella***	26	74	94
14 Maloney	82	18	98
15 Rangel	81	19	98
16 Serrano	70	30	96
17 Engel	84	16	98
18 Lowey	86	14	98
19 ***Kelly***	41	59	100
20 ***Gilman***	48	52	100
21 McNulty	77	23	89
22 ***Sweeney***	25	75	98
23 ***Boehlert***	52	48	99
24 ***McHugh***	29	71	100
25 ***Walsh***	32	68	100
26 Hinchey	87	13	91
27 ***Reynolds***	25	75	99
28 Slaughter	81	19	82
29 LaFalce	78	22	100

	1	2	3
30 ***Quinn***	38	62	99
31 ***Houghton***	49	51	91
NORTH CAROLINA			
1 Clayton	83	17	95
2 Etheridge	67	33	100
3 ***Jones***	19	81	99
4 Price	74	26	100
5 ***Burr***	17	83	99
6 ***Coble***	12	88	89
7 McIntyre	46	54	99
8 ***Hayes***	17	83	99
9 ***Myrick***	14	86	93
10 ***Ballenger***	25	75	98
11 ***Taylor***	16	84	93
12 Watt	83	17	100
NORTH DAKOTA			
AL Pomeroy	73	27	99
OHIO			
1 ***Chabot***	22	78	100
2 ***Portman***	30	70	99
3 Hall	71	29	98
4 ***Oxley***	28	72	100
5 ***Gillmor***	24	76	100
6 Strickland	63	37	100
7 ***Hobson***	29	71	98
8 ***Boehner***	27	73	96
9 Kaptur	68	32	96
10 Kucinich	63	37	100
11 Jones	87	13	94
12 ***Kasich***	17	83	95
13 Brown	80	20	100
14 Sawyer	89	11	100
15 ***Pryce***	38	62	87
16 ***Regula***	32	68	100
17 Traficant	44	56	100
18 ***Ney***	16	84	98
19 ***LaTourette***	31	69	99
OKLAHOMA			
1 ***Largent***	21	79	93
2 ***Coburn***	14	86	94
3 ***Watkins***	21	79	99
4 ***Watts***	22	78	96
5 ***Istook***	19	81	99
6 ***Lucas***	17	83	99
OREGON			
1 Wu	78	22	98
2 ***Walden***	22	78	100
3 Blumenauer	80	20	99
4 DeFazio	73	27	99
5 Hooley	79	21	98
PENNSYLVANIA			
1 Brady	82	18	100
2 Fattah	86	14	99
3 Borski	78	22	99
4 Klink	73	27	96
5 ***Peterson***	19	81	65
6 Holden	54	46	93
7 ***Weldon***	29	71	93
8 ***Greenwood***	44	56	96
9 ***Shuster***	16	84	93
10 ***Sherwood***	20	80	99
11 Kanjorski	72	28	100
12 Murtha	58	42	99
13 Hoeffel	85	15	100
14 Coyne	83	17	99
15 ***Toomey***	28	72	98
16 ***Pitts***	17	83	99
17 ***Gekas***	24	76	100
18 Doyle	67	33	99
19 ***Goodling***	20	80	99
20 Mascara	65	35	98
21 ***English***	24	76	96
RHODE ISLAND			
1 Kennedy	78	22	89
2 Weygand	65	35	99
SOUTH CAROLINA			
1 ***Sanford***	21	79	99
2 ***Spence***	22	78	100
3 ***Graham***	18	82	98
4 ***DeMint***	11	89	98
5 Spratt	74	26	99
6 Clyburn	85	15	98
SOUTH DAKOTA			
AL ***Thune***	22	78	100

	1	2	3
TENNESSEE			
1 ***Jenkins***	16	84	100
2 ***Duncan***	16	84	100
3 ***Wamp***	14	86	99
4 ***Hilleary***	9	91	98
5 Clement	63	37	100
6 Gordon	62	38	95
7 ***Bryant***	17	83	100
8 Tanner	62	38	98
9 Ford	81	19	95
TEXAS			
1 Sandlin	68	32	99
2 Turner	60	40	100
3 ***Johnson***	17	83	99
4 Hall	31	69	99
5 ***Sessions***	21	79	99
6 ***Barton***	16	84	96
7 ***Archer***	22	78	98
8 ***Brady***	21	79	95
9 Lampson	77	23	100
10 Doggett	82	18	100
11 Edwards	79	21	95
12 ***Granger***	26	74	94
13 ***Thornberry***	20	80	100
14 ***Paul***	30	70	98
15 Hinojosa	78	22	98
16 Reyes	78	22	93
17 Stenholm	53	47	99
18 Jackson-Lee	78	22	96
19 ***Combest***	19	81	99
20 Gonzalez	84	16	100
21 ***Smith***	19	81	98
22 ***DeLay***	23	77	99
23 ***Bonilla***	20	80	98
24 Frost	76	24	93
25 Bentsen	79	21	100
26 ***Armey***	23	77	100
27 Ortiz	65	35	96
28 Rodriguez	79	21	100
29 Green	69	31	94
30 Johnson	81	19	99
UTAH			
1 ***Hansen***	24	76	98
2 ***Cook***	16	84	98
3 ***Cannon***	15	85	100
VERMONT			
AL Sanders	76	24	95
VIRGINIA			
1 ***Bateman***	32	68	100
2 Pickett	66	34	100
3 Scott	83	17	100
4 Sisisky	65	35	100
5 Goode	16	84	100
6 ***Goodlatte***	16	84	100
7 ***Bliley***	25	75	99
8 Moran	75	25	99
9 Boucher	67	33	96
10 ***Wolf***	32	68	100
11 ***Davis***	39	61	100
WASHINGTON			
1 Inslee	78	22	100
2 ***Metcalf***	12	88	98
3 Baird	77	23	99
4 ***Hastings***	16	84	99
5 ***Nethercutt***	23	77	99
6 Dicks	84	16	96
7 McDermott	87	13	63
8 ***Dunn***	28	72	100
9 Smith	75	25	96
WEST VIRGINIA			
1 Mollohan	58	42	88
2 Wise	70	30	98
3 Rahall	69	31	99
WISCONSIN			
1 ***Ryan***	21	79	99
2 Baldwin	79	21	95
3 Kind	76	24	100
4 Kleczka	75	25	99
5 Barrett	85	15	100
6 ***Petri***	22	78	100
7 Obey	80	20	99
8 ***Green***	21	79	100
9 ***Sensenbrenner***	21	79	100
WYOMING			
AL ***Cubin***	18	82	96

Southern states - Ala., Ark., Fla., Ga., Ky., La., Miss., N.C., Okla., S.C., Tenn., Texas, Va.

1999 Senate Presidential Position Votes

The following is a list of Senate votes in 1999 on which there was a clear presidential position. Votes are categorized by topic and listed by roll-call number with a brief description.

Domestic Policy

5 Victories

Vote Number	Description
17	Impeachment
18	Impeachment
134	Gun control
169	Disability benefits
260	NEA

17 Defeats

Vote Number	Description
39	Education
40	Education
41	Education
159	Y2K liability
165	Y2K liability
197	Abortion
210	Health care
223	Environment
279	D.C. appropriations
290	Environment
291	Interior appropriations
298	Education
299	Education
321	Labor-HHS appropriations
330	Campaign finance (cloture)
340	Abortion
343	D.C.-Labor-HHS appropriations

Defense and Foreign Policy

2 Victories

Vote Number	Description
145	Kosovo
151	Kosovo

4 Defeats

Vote Number	Description
147	Base closings
192	Foreign aid
312	Foreign aid
325	Nuclear test ban

Economic Affairs and Trade

3 Victories

Vote Number	Description
178	Steel quotas (cloture)
353	Sub-Saharan Africa, Caribbean trade
374	Omnibus appropriations

4 Defeats

Vote Number	Description
100	Financial services
105	Financial services
247	Taxes
261	Taxes

Nominations

9 Victories

Vote Number	Description
190	District Court judges
195	Lawrence H. Summers
259	Richard C. Holbrooke
262	Adalberto Jose Jordan
263	Marsha J. Pechman
308	Ted Stewart
309	Raymond C. Fisher
361	Carol Moseley-Braun
362	Linda Joan Morgan

1 Defeat

307 Ronnie L. White

Senate Success Score

Victories	19
Defeats	26
Total	**45**
Success rate	42.2%

	1	2	3
ALABAMA			
Shelby	38	62	100
Sessions	24	76	100
ALASKA			
Stevens	36	64	100
Murkowski	29	71	93
ARIZONA			
McCain	38	62	71
Kyl	34	66	98
ARKANSAS			
Hutchinson	24	76	100
Lincoln	80	20	100
CALIFORNIA			
Feinstein	87	13	100
Boxer	84	16	100
COLORADO			
Campbell	32	68	98
Allard	23	77	98
CONNECTICUT			
Dodd	86	14	98
Lieberman	89	11	100
DELAWARE			
Roth	44	56	100
Biden	89	11	98
FLORIDA			
Mack	28	72	87
Graham	93	7	100
GEORGIA			
Coverdell	31	69	100
Cleland	84	16	100
HAWAII			
Inouye	86	14	93
Akaka	89	11	100
IDAHO			
Craig	29	71	100
Crapo	30	70	89
ILLINOIS			
Fitzgerald	37	63	96
Durbin	87	13	100
INDIANA			
Lugar	40	60	100
Bayh	89	11	100
IOWA			
Grassley	33	67	100
Harkin	91	9	98
KANSAS			
Brownback	31	69	100
Roberts	29	71	100
KENTUCKY			
McConnell	33	67	100
Bunning	24	76	100
LOUISIANA			
Breaux	77	23	98
Landrieu	86	14	93
MAINE			
Snowe	49	51	100
Collins	49	51	100
MARYLAND			
Sarbanes	86	14	96
Mikulski	86	14	96
MASSACHUSETTS			
Kennedy	93	7	93
Kerry	93	7	98
MICHIGAN			
Abraham	36	64	100
Levin	89	11	98
MINNESOTA			
Grams	33	67	100
Wellstone	84	16	98
MISSISSIPPI			
Cochran	38	62	100
Lott	32	68	98
MISSOURI			
Bond	34	66	98
Ashcroft	40	60	100
MONTANA			
Burns	24	76	100
Baucus	81	19	96
NEBRASKA			
Hagel	36	64	100
Kerrey	91	9	100
NEVADA			
Reid	82	18	100
Bryan	89	11	100
NEW HAMPSHIRE			
Smith[1]	16	84	100
Gregg	33	67	96
NEW JERSEY			
Lautenberg	93	7	100
Torricelli	84	16	100
NEW MEXICO			
Domenici	33	67	100
Bingaman	84	16	100
NEW YORK			
Moynihan	86	14	96
Schumer	91	9	98
NORTH CAROLINA			
Helms	18	82	98
Edwards	87	13	100
NORTH DAKOTA			
Conrad	73	27	100
Dorgan	73	27	98
OHIO			
DeWine	38	62	100
Voinovich	45	55	93
OKLAHOMA			
Nickles	27	73	100
Inhofe	23	77	98
OREGON			
Smith	43	57	98
Wyden	91	9	100
PENNSYLVANIA			
Specter	53	47	100
Santorum	30	70	98
RHODE ISLAND			
Chafee[2]	100	0	100
Reed	89	11	100
SOUTH CAROLINA			
Thurmond	24	76	100
Hollings	80	20	100
SOUTH DAKOTA			
Daschle	84	16	98
Johnson	78	22	100
TENNESSEE			
Thompson	40	60	100
Frist	33	67	100
TEXAS			
Gramm	29	71	100
Hutchison	29	71	100
UTAH			
Hatch	30	70	96
Bennett	31	69	100
VERMONT			
Jeffords	56	44	100
Leahy	82	18	100
VIRGINIA			
Warner	39	61	98
Robb	87	13	100
WASHINGTON			
Gorton	36	64	100
Murray	88	12	91
WEST VIRGINIA			
Byrd	70	30	98
Rockefeller	89	11	98
WISCONSIN			
Kohl	91	9	100
Feingold	82	18	100
WYOMING			
Thomas	31	69	100
Enzi	24	76	100

Key

Democrats *Republicans*
Independents

ND Northern Democrats SD Southern Democrats

Southern states - Ala., Ark., Fla., Ga., Ky., La., Miss., N.C., Okla., S.C., Tenn., Texas, Va.

Presidential Support and Opposition: Senate

1. Presidential Support Score. Percentage of recorded votes cast in 1999 on which President Clinton took a position and on which the senator voted "yea" or "nay" in agreement with the president's position. Failure to vote did not lower an individual's score.

2. Presidential Opposition Score. Percentage of recorded votes cast in 1999 on which President Clinton took a position and on which the senator voted "yea" or "nay" in disagreement with the president's position. Failure to vote did not lower an individual's score.

3. Participation in Presidential Support Votes. Percentage of the 45 recorded Senate votes in 1999 on which President Clinton took a position and on which the senator was present and voted "yea" or "nay."

[1] *Robert C. Smith, R-N.H., switched his party affiliation from Republican to independent on July 13. He switched back Nov. 1.*

[2] *Lincoln Chafee, R-R.I., was sworn in Nov. 4, replacing his father, John H. Chafee, R-R.I., who died Oct. 24. Lincoln Chafee was eligible for three presidential support votes in 1999. John Chafee was eligible for 40; his presidential support score was 54 percent.*

Party Unity Background

Party unity votes. Recorded votes that split the parties, with a majority of Democrats who voted opposing a majority of Republicans who voted. Members who switched parties are accounted for.

Party unity support. Percentage of party unity votes on which members voted "yea" or "nay" *in agreement* with a majority of their party. Failures to vote lowered scores for chambers and parties.

Opposition to party. Percentage of party unity votes on which members voted "yea" or "nay" *in disagreement* with a majority of their party. Failures to vote lowered scores for chambers and parties.

Average Scores by Chamber

	Republicans		Democrats	
	1999	1998	1999	1998
Party Unity	**86%**	**86%**	**84%**	**83%**
Senate	88	86	89	87
House	86	86	83	82

	Republicans		Democrats	
	1999	1998	1999	1998
Opposition	**11%**	**12%**	**13%**	**13%**
Senate	10	12	9	10
House	12	11	14	13

Sectional Support, Opposition

Senate	Support	Opposition
Northern Republicans	86%	12%
Southern Republicans	93	6
Northern Democrats	90	8
Southern Democrats	85	14

House	Support	Opposition
Northern Republicans	84%	14%
Southern Republicans	90	8
Northern Democrats	86	11
Southern Democrats	75	22

1999 Victories, Defeats

	Senate	House	Total
Republicans won, Democrats lost	177	211	388
Democrats won, Republicans lost	58	77	135

Unanimous Voting by Parties

The number of times each party voted unanimously on party unity votes:

	Senate		House		Total	
	1999	1998	1999	1998	1999	1998
Republicans voted unanimously	63	33	59	42	122	75
Democrats voted unanimously	100	46	11	8	111	54

Party Unity Average Scores

Average score for each party in both chambers of Congress:

Year	Republicans	Democrats
1964	69%	67%
1965	70	69
1966	67	61
1967	71	66
1968	63	57
1969	62	62
1970	59	57
1971	66	62
1972	64	57
1973	68	68
1974	62	63
1975	70	69
1976	66	65
1977	70	67
1978	67	64
1979	72	69
1980	70	68
1981	76	69

Year	Republicans	Democrats
1982	71%	72%
1983	74	76
1984	72	74
1985	75	79
1986	71	78
1987	74	81
1988	73	79
1989	73	81
1990	74	81
1991	78	81
1992	79	79
1993	84	85
1994	83	83
1995	91	80
1996	87	80
1997	88	82
1998	86	83
1999	86	84

1999 Party Unity Votes

Following are the votes, by roll call number, on which a majority of Democrats voted against a majority of Republicans.

House

(288 of 609 "yea/nay" votes)

2	57	90	132	183	216	251	290	324	356	391	423	487	529	582
3	58	99	134	184	218	252	291	325	360	393	437	488	530	583
4	60	100	139	186	219	259	292	326	366	394	439	489	531	584
5	64	101	140	189	220	260	293	330	369	395	440	490	532	585
6	65	103	141	192	221	261	294	331	370	396	441	497	542	590
15	66	109	142	194	223	264	295	332	371	397	442	498	543	602
16	68	110	152	195	224	266	298	333	372	402	443	502	544	608
17	69	112	153	196	227	268	301	335	373	403	445	503	547	609
19	70	113	154	197	229	269	303	336	375	404	447	504	549	
20	72	114	156	198	232	272	304	339	377	411	463	512	552	
36	73	115	162	199	233	273	305	341	378	412	464	516	558	
37	75	116	163	201	234	275	306	344	379	413	465	517	559	
39	76	118	165	202	235	281	307	345	380	414	467	518	560	
40	77	123	172	203	239	283	312	346	382	415	468	519	561	
45	84	124	173	207	240	284	313	348	383	416	469	521	562	
46	85	125	175	208	241	285	315	349	385	417	473	522	564	
47	86	126	176	210	243	286	317	350	386	418	480	523	566	
48	87	127	177	211	244	287	319	352	387	419	483	524	567	
49	88	128	181	213	248	288	320	353	388	421	484	527	568	
56	89	131	182	215	249	289	321	355	390	422	485	528	578	

Senate

(235 of 374 "yea/nay" votes)

2	19	56	79	109	139	165	191	211	232	255	282	303	331	350
3	30	57	80	111	142	166	194	215	234	256	283	304	332	352
4	32	59	81	112	144	167	197	217	235	258	285	307	333	356
5	34	61	83	114	145	170	198	218	236	261	286	309	334	357
6	35	64	84	116	146	171	199	219	237	264	287	310	335	358
7	36	65	85	118	147	174	200	220	239	265	288	311	336	359
8	37	66	86	119	148	175	201	221	240	266	289	312	337	360
10	39	69	90	120	149	176	202	222	241	268	290	313	338	365
11	40	70	94	125	150	178	203	223	242	269	293	314	339	366
12	41	71	95	127	157	181	204	225	243	271	294	315	340	367
13	42	72	96	128	159	182	205	226	244	272	297	316	342	370
14	43	73	100	130	160	184	206	227	245	274	298	317	343	
15	44	74	101	131	161	185	207	228	247	275	299	320	345	
16	46	75	104	132	162	186	208	229	249	279	300	324	346	
17	47	76	105	134	163	187	209	230	250	280	301	325	347	
18	55	77	107	138	164	189	210	231	253	281	302	330	349	

Proportion of Partisan Roll Calls

How often a majority of Democrats voted against a majority of Republicans:

Year	House	Senate	Year	House	Senate	Year	House	Senate	Year	House	Senate
1956	44%	53%	1967	36%	35%	1978	33%	45%	1989	55%	35%
1957	59	36	1968	35	32	1979	47	47	1990	49	54
1958	40	44	1969	31	36	1980	38	46	1991	55	49
1959	55	48	1970	27	35	1981	37	48	1992	64	53
1960	53	37	1971	38	42	1982	36	43	1993	65	67
1961	50	62	1972	27	36	1983	56	44	1994	62	52
1962	46	41	1973	42	40	1984	47	40	1995	73	69
1963	49	47	1974	29	44	1985	61	50	1996	56	62
1964	55	36	1975	48	48	1986	57	52	1997	50	50
1965	52	42	1976	36	37	1987	64	41	1998	56	56
1966	41	50	1977	42	42	1988	47	42	1999	47	63

Party Unity and Party Opposition: House

1. Party Unity. Percentage of recorded party unity votes in 1999 on which a member voted "yea" or "nay" in agreement with a majority of his or her party. (Party unity roll calls are those on which a majority of voting Democrats opposed a majority of voting Republicans.) Percentages are based on votes cast; thus, failure to vote did not lower a member's score.

2. Party Opposition. Percentage of recorded party unity votes in 1999 on which a member voted "yea" or "nay" in disagreement with a majority of his or her party. Percentages are based on votes cast; thus, failure to vote did not lower a member's score.

3. Participation in Party Unity Votes. Percentage of the 288 recorded House party unity votes in 1999 on which a member was present and voted "yea" or "nay."

[1] *Joe Baca, D-Calif., was sworn in Nov. 18, replacing George E. Brown Jr., D-Calif., who died July 15. Baca was eligible for two party unity votes in 1999. Brown was eligible for 45 party unity votes; his party unity score was 97 percent.*

[2] *Johnny Isakson, R-Ga., was sworn in Feb. 25, replacing Newt Gingrich, R-Ga., who resigned effective Jan. 3, 1999. Isakson was eligible for 278 party unity votes in 1999.*

[3] *J. Dennis Hastert, R-Ill., as Speaker of the House, voted on 92 party unity votes at his discretion in 1999.*

[4] *David Vitter, R-La., was sworn in June 8, replacing Robert L. Livingston, R-La., who resigned effective Feb. 28, 1999. Vitter was eligible for 215 party unity votes in 1999. Livingston was eligible for 10; his party unity score was 100 percent.*

[5] *Michael P. Forbes, D-N.Y., switched his party affiliation from Republican to Democrat on July 17. His party unity score is based on the 135 party unity votes he was eligible for as a Democrat. While he was a Republican, Forbes was eligible for 153 party unity votes; his support score as a Republican was 65 percent.*

Key

Democrats ***Republicans***
Independents

	1	2	3
ALABAMA			
1 ***Callahan***	92	8	99
2 ***Everett***	95	5	99
3 ***Riley***	96	4	99
4 ***Aderholt***	95	5	99
5 Cramer	53	47	99
6 ***Bachus***	90	10	99
7 Hilliard	88	12	99
ALASKA			
AL ***Young***	91	9	92
ARIZONA			
1 ***Salmon***	93	7	93
2 Pastor	91	9	99
3 ***Stump***	97	3	100
4 ***Shadegg***	95	5	99
5 ***Kolbe***	80	20	99
6 ***Hayworth***	96	4	99
ARKANSAS			
1 Berry	67	33	97
2 Snyder	84	16	99
3 ***Hutchinson***	90	10	99
4 ***Dickey***	91	9	99
CALIFORNIA			
1 Thompson	85	15	99
2 ***Herger***	97	3	99
3 ***Ose***	78	22	99
4 ***Doolittle***	93	7	99
5 Matsui	94	6	98
6 Woolsey	97	3	99
7 Miller	93	7	96
8 Pelosi	96	4	95
9 Lee	94	6	100
10 Tauscher	84	16	100
11 ***Pombo***	93	7	99
12 Lantos	96	4	87
13 Stark	95	5	92
14 Eshoo	90	10	99
15 ***Campbell***	67	33	99
16 Lofgren	87	13	93
17 Farr	96	4	97
18 Condit	61	39	99
19 ***Radanovich***	95	5	98
20 Dooley	77	23	99
21 ***Thomas***	89	11	92
22 Capps	90	10	96
23 ***Gallegly***	88	12	97
24 Sherman	87	13	99
25 ***McKeon***	93	7	99
26 Berman	94	6	93
27 ***Rogan***	92	8	97
28 ***Dreier***	91	9	99
29 Waxman	96	4	97
30 Becerra	96	4	95
31 Martinez	92	8	94
32 Dixon	95	5	98
33 Roybal-Allard	97	3	99
34 Napolitano	92	8	96
35 Waters	97	3	97
36 ***Kuykendall***	76	24	99
37 Millender-McD.	97	3	96
38 ***Horn***	68	32	99
39 ***Royce***	92	8	99
40 ***Lewis***	85	15	97
41 ***Miller***	96	4	99
42 Baca[1]	100	0	100
43 ***Calvert***	92	8	99
44 ***Bono***	85	15	96
45 ***Rohrabacher***	94	6	100
46 Sanchez	90	10	99
47 ***Cox***	93	7	91
48 ***Packard***	95	5	100
49 ***Bilbray***	72	28	90
50 Filner	98	2	100
51 ***Cunningham***	95	5	99
52 ***Hunter***	91	9	98
COLORADO			
1 DeGette	95	5	99
2 Udall	93	7	98
3 ***McInnis***	93	7	99
4 ***Schaffer***	91	9	99
5 ***Hefley***	90	10	98
6 ***Tancredo***	94	6	100
CONNECTICUT			
1 Larson	93	7	98
2 Gejdenson	96	4	99
3 DeLauro	97	3	100
4 ***Shays***	66	34	98
5 Maloney	80	20	99
6 ***Johnson***	67	33	98
DELAWARE			
AL ***Castle***	69	31	100
FLORIDA			
1 ***Scarborough***	88	12	75
2 Boyd	70	30	99
3 Brown	93	7	99
4 ***Fowler***	88	12	99
5 Thurman	87	13	92
6 ***Stearns***	93	7	99
7 ***Mica***	91	9	99
8 ***McCollum***	89	11	98
9 ***Bilirakis***	90	10	99
10 ***Young***	89	11	94
11 Davis	81	19	98
12 ***Canady***	92	8	100
13 ***Miller***	87	13	99
14 ***Goss***	91	9	99
15 ***Weldon***	95	5	99
16 ***Foley***	78	22	99
17 Meek	95	5	97
18 ***Ros-Lehtinen***	83	17	94
19 Wexler	93	7	98
20 Deutsch	88	12	99
21 ***Diaz-Balart***	78	22	98
22 ***Shaw***	86	14	95
23 Hastings	97	3	92
GEORGIA			
1 ***Kingston***	93	7	95
2 Bishop	73	27	99
3 ***Collins***	95	5	99
4 McKinney	92	8	97
5 Lewis	96	4	97
6 ***Isakson***[2]	87	13	99
7 ***Barr***	91	9	98
8 ***Chambliss***	94	6	99
9 ***Deal***	92	8	99
10 ***Norwood***	94	6	99
11 ***Linder***	95	5	98
HAWAII			
1 Abercrombie	89	11	99
2 Mink	92	8	99
IDAHO			
1 ***Chenoweth-Hage***	90	10	89
2 ***Simpson***	91	9	97
ILLINOIS			
1 Rush	97	3	93
2 Jackson	95	5	100
3 Lipinski	66	34	94
4 Gutierrez	93	7	95
5 Blagojevich	91	9	97
6 ***Hyde***	89	11	98
7 Davis	97	3	98
8 ***Crane***	96	4	99
9 Schakowsky	95	5	100
10 ***Porter***	63	37	97
11 ***Weller***	88	12	99
12 Costello	73	27	99
13 ***Biggert***	78	22	100
14 ***Hastert***[3]	95	5	32

ND Northern Democrats SD Southern Democrats

	1	2	3
15 ***Ewing***	88	12	98
16 ***Manzullo***	92	8	99
17 Evans	94	6	99
18 ***LaHood***	83	17	97
19 Phelps	68	32	100
20 ***Shimkus***	92	8	99
INDIANA			
1 Visclosky	87	13	98
2 ***McIntosh***	93	7	95
3 Roemer	66	34	99
4 ***Souder***	94	6	99
5 ***Buyer***	92	8	93
6 ***Burton***	94	6	95
7 ***Pease***	90	10	100
8 ***Hostettler***	91	9	99
9 Hill	74	26	99
10 Carson	97	3	92
IOWA			
1 ***Leach***	70	30	99
2 ***Nussle***	87	13	99
3 Boswell	69	31	99
4 ***Ganske***	72	28	97
5 ***Latham***	91	9	97
KANSAS			
1 ***Moran***	86	14	100
2 ***Ryun***	97	3	99
3 Moore	82	18	100
4 ***Tiahrt***	95	5	99
KENTUCKY			
1 ***Whitfield***	89	11	99
2 ***Lewis***	95	5	100
3 ***Northup***	89	11	100
4 Lucas	46	54	99
5 ***Rogers***	93	7	100
6 ***Fletcher***	93	7	98
LOUISIANA			
1 ***Vitter***[4]	92	8	99
2 Jefferson	91	9	81
3 ***Tauzin***	93	7	97
4 ***McCrery***	92	8	98
5 ***Cooksey***	81	19	91
6 ***Baker***	94	6	97
7 John	53	47	95
MAINE			
1 Allen	96	4	99
2 Baldacci	91	9	99
MARYLAND			
1 ***Gilchrest***	72	28	97
2 ***Ehrlich***	86	14	98
3 Cardin	92	8	98
4 Wynn	91	9	91
5 Hoyer	89	11	98
6 ***Bartlett***	94	6	99
7 Cummings	98	2	99
8 ***Morella***	49	51	99
MASSACHUSETTS			
1 Olver	96	4	99
2 Neal	91	9	96
3 McGovern	96	4	100
4 Frank	92	8	97
5 Meehan	96	4	98
6 Tierney	95	5	99
7 Markey	96	4	99
8 Capuano	95	5	100
9 Moakley	91	9	98
10 Delahunt	95	5	97
MICHIGAN			
1 Stupak	83	17	94
2 ***Hoekstra***	93	7	99
3 ***Ehlers***	83	17	99
4 ***Camp***	90	10	94
5 Barcia	62	38	99
6 ***Upton***	80	20	100
7 ***Smith***	90	10	99
8 Stabenow	87	13	99
9 Kildee	87	13	100
10 Bonior	94	6	99
11 ***Knollenberg***	90	10	100
12 Levin	93	7	99
13 Rivers	86	14	94
14 Conyers	97	3	93
15 Kilpatrick	98	2	98
16 Dingell	85	15	99
MINNESOTA			
1 ***Gutknecht***	94	6	99
2 Minge	87	13	95
3 ***Ramstad***	77	23	100
4 Vento	97	3	99
5 Sabo	92	8	99
6 Luther	87	13	92
7 Peterson	51	49	99
8 Oberstar	88	12	99
MISSISSIPPI			
1 ***Wicker***	95	5	99
2 Thompson	94	6	98
3 ***Pickering***	95	5	99
4 Shows	56	44	99
5 Taylor	44	56	99
MISSOURI			
1 Clay	95	5	91
2 ***Talent***	91	9	99
3 Gephardt	94	6	94
4 Skelton	61	39	97
5 McCarthy	94	6	95
6 Danner	61	39	99
7 ***Blunt***	95	5	98
8 ***Emerson***	88	12	99
9 ***Hulshof***	88	12	98
MONTANA			
AL ***Hill***	92	8	99
NEBRASKA			
1 ***Bereuter***	79	21	96
2 ***Terry***	92	8	99
3 ***Barrett***	88	12	99
NEVADA			
1 Berkley	89	11	99
2 ***Gibbons***	91	9	99
NEW HAMPSHIRE			
1 ***Sununu***	95	5	95
2 ***Bass***	83	17	99
NEW JERSEY			
1 Andrews	86	14	99
2 ***LoBiondo***	80	20	100
3 ***Saxton***	80	20	98
4 ***Smith***	76	24	98
5 ***Roukema***	75	25	98
6 Pallone	94	6	99
7 ***Franks***	73	27	99
8 Pascrell	86	14	97
9 Rothman	89	11	98
10 Payne	97	3	97
11 ***Frelinghuysen***	69	31	99
12 Holt	91	9	99
13 Menendez	91	9	99
NEW MEXICO			
1 ***Wilson***	84	16	99
2 ***Skeen***	89	11	99
3 Udall	92	8	99
NEW YORK			
1 Forbes[5]	68	32	99
2 ***Lazio***	76	24	99
3 ***King***	79	21	99
4 McCarthy	89	11	95
5 Ackerman	97	3	97
6 Meeks	96	4	97
7 Crowley	91	9	98
8 Nadler	98	2	98
9 Weiner	95	5	98
10 Towns	94	6	91
11 Owens	97	3	98
12 Velázquez	95	5	99
13 ***Fossella***	89	11	96
14 Maloney	93	7	97
15 Rangel	96	4	91
16 Serrano	93	7	97
17 Engel	94	6	95
18 Lowey	94	6	98
19 ***Kelly***	69	31	100
20 ***Gilman***	62	38	99
21 McNulty	89	11	92
22 ***Sweeney***	86	14	99
23 ***Boehlert***	60	40	99
24 ***McHugh***	81	19	98
25 ***Walsh***	78	22	99
26 Hinchey	94	6	95
27 ***Reynolds***	88	12	99
28 Slaughter	96	4	91
29 LaFalce	84	16	100
30 ***Quinn***	74	26	96
31 ***Houghton***	70	30	90
NORTH CAROLINA			
1 Clayton	94	6	97
2 Etheridge	79	21	99
3 ***Jones***	91	9	99
4 Price	87	13	99
5 ***Burr***	93	7	98
6 ***Coble***	92	8	93
7 McIntyre	54	46	99
8 ***Hayes***	94	6	100
9 ***Myrick***	92	8	96
10 ***Ballenger***	94	6	99
11 ***Taylor***	96	4	97
12 Watt	94	6	99
NORTH DAKOTA			
AL Pomeroy	80	20	99
OHIO			
1 ***Chabot***	89	11	99
2 ***Portman***	89	11	99
3 Hall	76	24	98
4 ***Oxley***	89	11	94
5 ***Gillmor***	88	12	100
6 Strickland	84	16	98
7 ***Hobson***	85	15	99
8 ***Boehner***	93	7	98
9 Kaptur	87	13	97
10 Kucinich	83	17	99
11 Jones	96	4	95
12 ***Kasich***	93	7	88
13 Brown	95	5	99
14 Sawyer	95	5	99
15 ***Pryce***	84	16	89
16 ***Regula***	83	17	100
17 Traficant	43	57	99
18 ***Ney***	89	11	99
19 ***LaTourette***	77	23	98
OKLAHOMA			
1 ***Largent***	94	6	93
2 ***Coburn***	90	10	96
3 ***Watkins***	94	6	98
4 ***Watts***	94	6	96
5 ***Istook***	96	4	98
6 ***Lucas***	93	7	99
OREGON			
1 Wu	87	13	95
2 ***Walden***	90	10	100
3 Blumenauer	90	10	99
4 DeFazio	92	8	98
5 Hooley	87	13	97
PENNSYLVANIA			
1 Brady	94	6	99
2 Fattah	97	3	99
3 Borski	87	13	98
4 Klink	82	18	99
5 ***Peterson***	91	9	81
6 Holden	68	32	94
7 ***Weldon***	84	16	92
8 ***Greenwood***	71	29	99
9 ***Shuster***	92	8	94
10 ***Sherwood***	88	12	99
11 Kanjorski	83	17	98
12 Murtha	67	33	98
13 Hoeffel	91	9	100
14 Coyne	97	3	99
15 ***Toomey***	91	9	99
16 ***Pitts***	97	3	99
17 ***Gekas***	91	9	98
18 Doyle	77	23	98
19 ***Goodling***	89	11	98
20 Mascara	76	24	97
21 ***English***	84	16	98
RHODE ISLAND			
1 Kennedy	96	4	93
2 Weygand	86	14	98
SOUTH CAROLINA			
1 ***Sanford***	84	16	99
2 ***Spence***	93	7	100
3 ***Graham***	89	11	94
4 ***DeMint***	97	3	99
5 Spratt	82	18	99
6 Clyburn	95	5	99
SOUTH DAKOTA			
AL ***Thune***	91	9	100
TENNESSEE			
1 ***Jenkins***	91	9	98
2 ***Duncan***	85	15	100
3 ***Wamp***	90	10	99
4 ***Hilleary***	93	7	95
5 Clement	72	28	99
6 Gordon	68	32	98
7 ***Bryant***	96	4	100
8 Tanner	67	33	99
9 Ford	90	10	97
TEXAS			
1 Sandlin	74	26	98
2 Turner	64	36	100
3 ***Johnson***	97	3	99
4 Hall	30	70	100
5 ***Sessions***	96	4	99
6 ***Barton***	95	5	94
7 ***Archer***	96	4	96
8 ***Brady***	94	6	96
9 Lampson	84	16	100
10 Doggett	90	10	100
11 Edwards	80	20	99
12 ***Granger***	92	8	98
13 ***Thornberry***	93	7	98
14 ***Paul***	75	25	99
15 Hinojosa	89	11	95
16 Reyes	83	17	90
17 Stenholm	49	51	99
18 Jackson-Lee	96	4	94
19 ***Combest***	95	5	95
20 Gonzalez	94	6	99
21 ***Smith***	96	4	96
22 ***DeLay***	97	3	99
23 ***Bonilla***	90	10	99
24 Frost	85	15	93
25 Bentsen	84	16	96
26 ***Armey***	97	3	100
27 Ortiz	70	30	97
28 Rodriguez	90	10	99
29 Green	80	20	93
30 Johnson	93	7	99
UTAH			
1 ***Hansen***	93	7	99
2 ***Cook***	88	12	99
3 ***Cannon***	96	4	99
VERMONT			
AL Sanders	96	4	99
VIRGINIA			
1 ***Bateman***	89	11	99
2 Pickett	64	36	99
3 Scott	91	9	99
4 Sisisky	65	35	100
5 Goode	22	78	99
6 ***Goodlatte***	95	5	100
7 ***Bliley***	93	7	99
8 Moran	79	21	99
9 Boucher	75	25	96
10 ***Wolf***	84	16	99
11 ***Davis***	79	21	99
WASHINGTON			
1 Inslee	88	12	100
2 ***Metcalf***	87	13	99
3 Baird	89	11	99
4 ***Hastings***	97	3	100
5 ***Nethercutt***	92	8	96
6 Dicks	90	10	96
7 McDermott	96	4	76
8 ***Dunn***	88	12	98
9 Smith	75	25	98
WEST VIRGINIA			
1 Mollohan	64	36	90
2 Wise	75	25	99
3 Rahall	75	25	97
WISCONSIN			
1 ***Ryan***	90	10	99
2 Baldwin	96	4	93
3 Kind	82	18	100
4 Kleczka	87	13	99
5 Barrett	93	7	99
6 ***Petri***	86	14	99
7 Obey	87	13	98
8 ***Green***	90	10	99
9 ***Sensenbrenner***	92	8	100
WYOMING			
AL ***Cubin***	94	6	98

Southern states - Ala., Ark., Fla., Ga., Ky., La., Miss., N.C., Okla., S.C., Tenn., Texas, Va.

	1	2	3
ALABAMA			
Shelby	89	11	98
Sessions	94	6	99
ALASKA			
Stevens	90	10	99
Murkowski	98	2	96
ARIZONA			
McCain	90	10	65
Kyl	97	3	100
ARKANSAS			
Hutchinson	95	5	97
Lincoln	83	17	100
CALIFORNIA			
Feinstein	91	9	100
Boxer	97	3	97
COLORADO			
Campbell	88	12	99
Allard	97	3	99
CONNECTICUT			
Dodd	90	10	96
Lieberman	87	13	98
DELAWARE			
Roth	85	15	99
Biden	93	7	98
FLORIDA			
Mack	97	3	92
Graham	88	12	98
GEORGIA			
Coverdell	97	3	100
Cleland	92	8	100
HAWAII			
Inouye	91	9	94
Akaka	96	4	100
IDAHO			
Craig	97	3	99
Crapo	97	3	97
ILLINOIS			
Fitzgerald	87	13	96
Durbin	95	5	100
INDIANA			
Lugar	88	12	98
Bayh	88	12	100
IOWA			
Grassley	90	10	100
Harkin	97	3	99
KANSAS			
Brownback	95	5	99
Roberts	94	6	99
KENTUCKY			
McConnell	95	5	100
Bunning	95	5	98
LOUISIANA			
Breaux	75	25	98
Landrieu	81	19	98
MAINE			
Snowe	69	31	100
Collins	74	26	100
MARYLAND			
Sarbanes	97	3	100
Mikulski	96	4	98
MASSACHUSETTS			
Kennedy	97	3	95
Kerry	95	5	99
MICHIGAN			
Abraham	86	14	100
Levin	97	3	99
MINNESOTA			
Grams	95	5	100
Wellstone	96	4	99
MISSISSIPPI			
Cochran	94	6	98
Lott	97	3	99
MISSOURI			
Bond	93	7	99
Ashcroft	96	4	99
MONTANA			
Burns	94	6	99
Baucus	87	13	99
NEBRASKA			
Hagel	92	8	99
Kerrey	87	13	100
NEVADA			
Reid	92	8	100
Bryan	91	9	100
NEW HAMPSHIRE			
Smith[1]	94	6	100
Gregg	94	6	95
NEW JERSEY			
Lautenberg	96	4	97
Torricelli	91	9	96
NEW MEXICO			
Domenici	93	7	99
Bingaman	88	12	99
NEW YORK			
Moynihan	85	15	89
Schumer	94	6	100
NORTH CAROLINA			
Helms	94	6	99
Edwards	92	8	99
NORTH DAKOTA			
Conrad	87	13	100
Dorgan	88	12	99
OHIO			
DeWine	84	16	99
Voinovich	87	13	97
OKLAHOMA			
Nickles	98	2	100
Inhofe	95	5	97
OREGON			
Smith	86	14	99
Wyden	91	9	100
PENNSYLVANIA			
Specter	64	36	100
Santorum	91	9	99
RHODE ISLAND			
Chafee[2]	56	44	100
Reed	96	4	100
SOUTH CAROLINA			
Thurmond	92	8	100
Hollings	89	11	97
SOUTH DAKOTA			
Daschle	93	7	99
Johnson	93	7	100
TENNESSEE			
Thompson	94	6	100
Frist	96	4	99
TEXAS			
Gramm	97	3	99
Hutchison	90	10	99
UTAH			
Hatch	92	8	98
Bennett	93	7	99
VERMONT			
Jeffords	67	33	98
Leahy	94	6	99
VIRGINIA			
Warner	87	13	99
Robb	90	10	100
WASHINGTON			
Gorton	92	8	98
Murray	93	7	95
WEST VIRGINIA			
Byrd	80	20	99
Rockefeller	94	6	99
WISCONSIN			
Kohl	90	10	97
Feingold	88	12	100
WYOMING			
Thomas	96	4	97
Enzi	95	5	100

Key

Democrats *Republicans*
Independents

ND Northern Democrats SD Southern Democrats

Southern states - Ala., Ark., Fla., Ga., Ky., La., Miss., N.C., Okla., S.C., Tenn., Texas, Va.

Presidential Support and Opposition: Senate

1. **Presidential Support Score.** Percentage of recorded votes cast in 1999 on which President Clinton took a position and on which the senator voted "yea" or "nay" in agreement with the president's position. Failure to vote did not lower an individual's score.

2. **Presidential Opposition Score.** Percentage of recorded votes cast in 1999 on which President Clinton took a position and on which the senator voted "yea" or "nay" in disagreement with the president's position. Failure to vote did not lower an individual's score.

3. **Participation in Presidential Support Votes.** Percentage of the 45 recorded Senate votes in 1999 on which President Clinton took a position and on which the senator was present and voted "yea" or "nay."

[1] *Robert C. Smith, R-N.H., switched his party affiliation from Republican to independent on July 13. He switched back Nov. 1.*

[2] *Lincoln Chafee, R-R.I., was sworn in Nov. 4, replacing his father, John H. Chafee, R-R.I., who died Oct. 24. Lincoln Chafee was eligible for three presidential support votes in 1999. John Chafee was eligible for 40; his presidential support score was 54 percent.*

	1	2
ALABAMA		
Shelby	98	98
Sessions	98	98
ALASKA		
Stevens	99	99
Murkowski	95	95
ARIZONA		
McCain	64	64
Kyl	99	99
ARKANSAS		
Hutchinson	98	98
Lincoln	100	100
CALIFORNIA		
Feinstein	99	99
Boxer	97	97
COLORADO		
Campbell	99	99
Allard	99	99
CONNECTICUT		
Dodd	95	95
Lieberman	99	99
DELAWARE		
Roth	99	99
Biden	96	96
FLORIDA		
Mack	93	93
Graham	98	98
GEORGIA		
Coverdell	100	100
Cleland	99	99
HAWAII		
Inouye	94	94
Akaka	100	100
IDAHO		
Craig	99	99
Crapo	96	96
ILLINOIS		
Fitzgerald	95	95
Durbin	100	100
INDIANA		
Lugar	97	97
Bayh	100	100
IOWA		
Grassley	100	100
Harkin	98	98
KANSAS		
Brownback	98	98
Roberts	99	99
KENTUCKY		
McConnell	100	100
Bunning	98	98
LOUISIANA		
Breaux	98	98
Landrieu	98	98
MAINE		
Snowe	100	100
Collins	100	100
MARYLAND		
Sarbanes	99	99
Mikulski	98	98
MASSACHUSETTS		
Kennedy	93	92
Kerry	99	99
MICHIGAN		
Abraham	100	100
Levin	99	99
MINNESOTA		
Grams	99	99
Wellstone	98	98
MISSISSIPPI		
Cochran	99	99
Lott	99	99
MISSOURI		
Bond	98	98
Ashcroft	99	99
MONTANA		
Burns	99	99
Baucus	99	99
NEBRASKA		
Hagel	99	99
Kerrey	100	100
NEVADA		
Reid	100	100
Bryan	100	100
NEW HAMPSHIRE		
Smith[1]	100	100
Gregg	96	96
NEW JERSEY		
Lautenberg	95	95
Torricelli	97	97
NEW MEXICO		
Domenici	98	98
Bingaman	99	99
NEW YORK		
Moynihan	86	86
Schumer	99	99
NORTH CAROLINA		
Helms	98	98
Edwards	99	99
NORTH DAKOTA		
Conrad	99	99
Dorgan	99	99
OHIO		
DeWine	99	99
Voinovich	97	97
OKLAHOMA		
Nickles	99	99
Inhofe	97	97
OREGON		
Smith	98	98
Wyden	99	99
PENNSYLVANIA		
Specter	99	99
Santorum	99	99
RHODE ISLAND		
Chafee[2]	100	100
Reed	99	99
SOUTH CAROLINA		
Thurmond	100	100
Hollings	97	97
SOUTH DAKOTA		
Daschle	99	99
Johnson	100	100
TENNESSEE		
Thompson	100	100
Frist	99	99
TEXAS		
Gramm	99	99
Hutchison	99	99
UTAH		
Hatch	97	97
Bennett	99	99
VERMONT		
Jeffords	98	98
Leahy	98	98
VIRGINIA		
Warner	99	99
Robb	100	100
WASHINGTON		
Gorton	97	97
Murray	95	95
WEST VIRGINIA		
Byrd	99	99
Rockefeller	99	99
WISCONSIN		
Kohl	98	98
Feingold	99	99
WYOMING		
Thomas	96	96
Enzi	99	99

ND Northern Democrats SD Southern Democrats

Southern states - Ala., Ark., Fla., Ga., Ky., La., Miss., N.C., Okla., S.C., Tenn., Texas, Va.

Key

Democrats *Republicans*
Independents

Voting Participation: Senate

1. Voting Participation. Percentage of the 374 recorded votes in 1999 on which a senator voted "yea" or "nay."

2. Voting Participation (without motions to instruct). Percentage of 372 recorded votes in 1999 on which a senator voted "yea" or "nay." In this version of the study, two votes to instruct the sergeant at arms to request the attendance of absent senators were excluded.

Absences due to illness. *Congressional Quarterly no longer designates members who missed votes due to illness. In the past, notations to that effect were based on official statements published in the Congressional Record, but these were found to be inconsistently used.*

Rounding. *Scores are rounded to nearest percentage, except that no scores are rounded up to 100 percent. Members with a 100 percent score participated in all recorded votes for which they were eligible.*

[1] *Robert C. Smith, R-N.H., switched his party affiliation from Republican to independent on July 13. He switched back again on Nov. 1.*

[2] *Lincoln Chafee, R-R.I., was sworn in Nov. 4, replacing his father, John H. Chafee, R-R.I., who died Oct. 24. Lincoln Chafee was eligible for 21 votes in 1999. John Chafee was eligible for 340; his voting participation score was 94 percent.*

Voting Participation: House

1. Voting Participation. Percentage of 609 recorded votes in 1999 on which a representative voted "yea" or "nay."

2. Voting Participation (without Journal votes). Percentage of 580 recorded votes in 1999 on which a representative voted "yea" or "nay." In this version of the study, 29 votes on approval of the House Journal were not included.

Absences due to illness. *Congressional Quarterly no longer designates members who missed votes due to illness. In the past, notations to that effect were based on official statements published in the Congressional Record, but these were found to be inconsistently used.*

Rounding. *Scores are rounded to the nearest percentage, except that no scores are rounded up to 100 percent. Members with a 100 percent score participated in all recorded votes for which they were eligible.*

[1] *Joe Baca, D-Calif., was sworn in Nov. 18, replacing George E. Brown Jr., D-Calif., who died July 15. Baca was eligible for seven votes in 1999. Brown was eligible for 102 votes; his voting participation score was 83 percent.*

[2] *Johnny Isakson, R-Ga., was sworn in Feb. 25, replacing Newt Gingrich, R-Ga., who resigned effective Jan. 3, 1999. Isakson was eligible for 583 votes in 1999.*

[3] *J. Dennis Hastert, R-Ill., as Speaker of the House, voted 137 times at his discretion in 1999.*

[4] *David Vitter, R-La., was sworn in June 8, replacing Robert L. Livingston, R-La., who resigned effective Feb. 28, 1999. Vitter was eligible for 441 votes in 1999. Livingston was eligible for 26; his voting participation score was 73 percent.*

[5] *Michael P. Forbes, D-N.Y., switched his party affiliation from Republican to Democrat on July 17.*

Key

Democrats ***Republicans***
Independents

	1	2
ALABAMA		
1 ***Callahan***	97	97
2 ***Everett***	98	98
3 ***Riley***	97	97
4 ***Aderholt***	98	98
5 Cramer	98	98
6 ***Bachus***	99	99
7 Hilliard	98	98
ALASKA		
AL ***Young***	89	92
ARIZONA		
1 ***Salmon***	94	94
2 Pastor	99	99
3 ***Stump***	100	100
4 ***Shadegg***	99	98
5 ***Kolbe***	98	99
6 ***Hayworth***	99	99
ARKANSAS		
1 Berry	97	97
2 Snyder	99	99
3 ***Hutchinson***	97	97
4 ***Dickey***	96	96
CALIFORNIA		
1 Thompson	99	99
2 ***Herger***	98	98
3 ***Ose***	99	99
4 ***Doolittle***	98	98
5 Matsui	98	98
6 Woolsey	98	98
7 Miller	94	94
8 Pelosi	95	95
9 Lee	98	99
10 Tauscher	99	99
11 ***Pombo***	99	99
12 Lantos	87	87
13 Stark	93	93
14 Eshoo	99	99
15 ***Campbell***	99	99
16 Lofgren	94	94
17 Farr	96	97
18 Condit	99	99
19 ***Radanovich***	96	96
20 Dooley	98	98
21 ***Thomas***	91	91
22 Capps	93	93
23 ***Gallegly***	98	98
24 Sherman	99	99
25 ***McKeon***	99	99
26 Berman	89	89
27 ***Rogan***	95	96
28 ***Dreier***	99	99
29 Waxman	95	95
30 Becerra	92	93
31 Martinez	92	92
32 Dixon	97	98
33 Roybal-Allard	99	99
34 Napolitano	96	96
35 Waters	95	96
36 ***Kuykendall***	98	98
37 Millender-McD.	95	95
38 ***Horn***	99	99
39 ***Royce***	98	98
40 ***Lewis***	96	97
41 ***Miller***	97	97
42 Baca[1]	100	100
43 ***Calvert***	98	98
44 ***Bono***	94	94
45 ***Rohrabacher***	99	100
46 Sanchez	98	98
47 ***Cox***	90	91
48 ***Packard***	99	99
49 ***Bilbray***	90	91
50 Filner	99	99
51 ***Cunningham***	98	98
52 ***Hunter***	96	97
COLORADO		
1 DeGette	98	99
2 Udall	98	98
3 ***McInnis***	97	97
4 ***Schaffer***	99	99
5 ***Hefley***	99	99
6 ***Tancredo***	98	99
CONNECTICUT		
1 Larson	97	97
2 Gejdenson	97	98
3 DeLauro	99	99
4 ***Shays***	99	98
5 Maloney	99	99
6 ***Johnson***	95	95
DELAWARE		
AL ***Castle***	99	99
FLORIDA		
1 ***Scarborough***	67	68
2 Boyd	99	99
3 Brown	95	95
4 ***Fowler***	96	96
5 Thurman	94	94
6 ***Stearns***	99	99
7 ***Mica***	98	98
8 ***McCollum***	94	95
9 ***Bilirakis***	99	99
10 ***Young***	94	94
11 Davis	98	98
12 ***Canady***	99	100
13 ***Miller***	99	99
14 ***Goss***	99	99
15 ***Weldon***	99	99
16 ***Foley***	99	99
17 Meek	96	97
18 ***Ros-Lehtinen***	93	93
19 Wexler	96	96
20 Deutsch	98	98
21 ***Diaz-Balart***	97	97
22 ***Shaw***	96	96
23 Hastings	91	92
GEORGIA		
1 ***Kingston***	94	95
2 Bishop	97	97
3 ***Collins***	98	98
4 McKinney	94	95
5 Lewis	93	93
6 ***Isakson***[2]	99	99
7 ***Barr***	97	97
8 ***Chambliss***	99	99
9 ***Deal***	98	98
10 ***Norwood***	96	96
11 ***Linder***	98	98
HAWAII		
1 Abercrombie	97	97
2 Mink	98	98
IDAHO		
1 ***Chenoweth-Hage***	87	88
2 ***Simpson***	97	97
ILLINOIS		
1 Rush	86	88
2 Jackson	100	100
3 Lipinski	93	93
4 Gutierrez	93	94
5 Blagojevich	96	97
6 ***Hyde***	98	99
7 Davis	96	97
8 ***Crane***	97	98
9 Schakowsky	99	99
10 ***Porter***	96	96
11 ***Weller***	99	99
12 Costello	99	99
13 ***Biggert***	100	100
14 ***Hastert***[3]	22	23

ND Northern Democrats SD Southern Democrats

	1	2
15 ***Ewing***	96	96
16 ***Manzullo***	98	98
17 Evans	99	99
18 ***LaHood***	97	97
19 Phelps	99	99
20 ***Shimkus***	99	99
INDIANA		
1 Visclosky	98	98
2 ***McIntosh***	92	92
3 Roemer	99	99
4 ***Souder***	99	99
5 ***Buyer***	91	91
6 ***Burton***	94	96
7 ***Pease***	99	99
8 ***Hostettler***	98	98
9 Hill	99	99
10 Carson	86	87
IOWA		
1 ***Leach***	98	98
2 ***Nussle***	97	97
3 Boswell	99	99
4 ***Ganske***	97	97
5 ***Latham***	97	97
KANSAS		
1 ***Moran***	100	100
2 ***Ryun***	99	99
3 Moore	98	98
4 ***Tiahrt***	96	97
KENTUCKY		
1 ***Whitfield***	98	98
2 ***Lewis***	99	99
3 ***Northup***	99	99
4 Lucas	99	99
5 ***Rogers***	97	98
6 ***Fletcher***	97	97
LOUISIANA		
1 ***Vitter***[4]	99	99
2 Jefferson	77	78
3 ***Tauzin***	95	96
4 ***McCrery***	96	96
5 ***Cooksey***	88	89
6 ***Baker***	95	95
7 John	96	96
MAINE		
1 Allen	99	98
2 Baldacci	99	99
MARYLAND		
1 ***Gilchrest***	95	95
2 ***Ehrlich***	96	97
3 Cardin	99	99
4 Wynn	92	92
5 Hoyer	97	97
6 ***Bartlett***	99	99
7 Cummings	98	99
8 ***Morella***	98	98
MASSACHUSETTS		
1 Olver	97	97
2 Neal	91	92
3 McGovern	99	99
4 Frank	95	95
5 Meehan	94	94
6 Tierney	97	97
7 Markey	98	99
8 Capuano	98	98
9 Moakley	94	94
10 Delahunt	95	95
MICHIGAN		
1 Stupak	95	95
2 ***Hoekstra***	98	98
3 ***Ehlers***	99	99
4 ***Camp***	95	96
5 Barcia	98	98
6 ***Upton***	100	100
7 ***Smith***	97	97
8 Stabenow	99	99
9 Kildee	100	100
10 Bonior	97	98
11 ***Knollenberg***	99	99
12 Levin	99	99
13 Rivers	96	96
14 Conyers	92	93
15 Kilpatrick	95	96
16 Dingell	97	97
MINNESOTA		
1 ***Gutknecht***	99	99
2 Minge	96	96
3 ***Ramstad***	99	99
4 Vento	99	99
5 Sabo	97	97
6 Luther	94	94
7 Peterson	99	99
8 Oberstar	97	97
MISSISSIPPI		
1 ***Wicker***	98	98
2 Thompson	97	97
3 ***Pickering***	98	98
4 Shows	98	98
5 Taylor	98	98
MISSOURI		
1 Clay	90	90
2 ***Talent***	99	99
3 Gephardt	90	91
4 Skelton	98	98
5 McCarthy	96	96
6 Danner	95	96
7 ***Blunt***	97	98
8 ***Emerson***	98	99
9 ***Hulshof***	95	96
MONTANA		
AL ***Hill***	98	98
NEBRASKA		
1 ***Bereuter***	96	96
2 ***Terry***	99	99
3 ***Barrett***	99	99
NEVADA		
1 Berkley	99	99
2 ***Gibbons***	99	99
NEW HAMPSHIRE		
1 ***Sununu***	97	96
2 ***Bass***	98	98
NEW JERSEY		
1 Andrews	99	99
2 ***LoBiondo***	100	100
3 ***Saxton***	98	98
4 ***Smith***	97	97
5 ***Roukema***	97	97
6 Pallone	98	98
7 ***Franks***	99	99
8 Pascrell	96	96
9 Rothman	98	98
10 Payne	95	96
11 ***Frelinghuysen***	99	99
12 Holt	99	99
13 Menendez	97	97
NEW MEXICO		
1 ***Wilson***	99	99
2 ***Skeen***	99	99
3 Udall	99	99
NEW YORK		
1 Forbes[5]	98	98
2 ***Lazio***	99	99
3 ***King***	99	99
4 McCarthy	95	95
5 Ackerman	91	91
6 Meeks	92	93
7 Crowley	98	98
8 Nadler	97	97
9 Weiner	96	96
10 Towns	88	89
11 Owens	95	96
12 Velázquez	98	99
13 ***Fossella***	94	94
14 Maloney	96	97
15 Rangel	90	91
16 Serrano	95	95
17 Engel	93	93
18 Lowey	96	96
19 ***Kelly***	99	99
20 ***Gilman***	99	99
21 McNulty	92	92
22 ***Sweeney***	96	96
23 ***Boehlert***	99	99
24 ***McHugh***	98	98
25 ***Walsh***	97	97
26 Hinchey	94	94
27 ***Reynolds***	99	99
28 Slaughter	92	92
29 LaFalce	99	99
30 ***Quinn***	97	96
31 ***Houghton***	90	90
NORTH CAROLINA		
1 Clayton	95	96
2 Etheridge	99	99
3 ***Jones***	98	98
4 Price	99	98
5 ***Burr***	97	97
6 ***Coble***	94	93
7 McIntyre	98	98
8 ***Hayes***	99	99
9 ***Myrick***	95	95
10 ***Ballenger***	99	99
11 ***Taylor***	92	93
12 Watt	98	98
NORTH DAKOTA		
AL Pomeroy	99	99
OHIO		
1 ***Chabot***	99	99
2 ***Portman***	99	99
3 Hall	97	97
4 ***Oxley***	94	94
5 ***Gillmor***	98	99
6 Strickland	98	98
7 ***Hobson***	99	99
8 ***Boehner***	98	98
9 Kaptur	96	97
10 Kucinich	99	99
11 Jones	94	95
12 ***Kasich***	85	86
13 Brown	98	98
14 Sawyer	99	99
15 ***Pryce***	86	86
16 ***Regula***	99	99
17 Traficant	99	99
18 ***Ney***	99	99
19 ***LaTourette***	99	99
OKLAHOMA		
1 ***Largent***	90	91
2 ***Coburn***	94	95
3 ***Watkins***	95	96
4 ***Watts***	95	95
5 ***Istook***	97	97
6 ***Lucas***	98	98
OREGON		
1 Wu	94	94
2 ***Walden***	99	99
3 Blumenauer	97	97
4 DeFazio	96	96
5 Hooley	97	97
PENNSYLVANIA		
1 Brady	97	98
2 Fattah	94	95
3 Borski	96	96
4 Klink	97	97
5 ***Peterson***	84	84
6 Holden	96	96
7 ***Weldon***	92	93
8 ***Greenwood***	98	98
9 ***Shuster***	94	94
10 ***Sherwood***	99	99
11 Kanjorski	97	98
12 Murtha	98	98
13 Hoeffel	100	100
14 Coyne	98	98
15 ***Toomey***	99	99
16 ***Pitts***	98	98
17 ***Gekas***	97	97
18 Doyle	97	98
19 ***Goodling***	98	98
20 Mascara	95	95
21 ***English***	97	98
RHODE ISLAND		
1 Kennedy	93	93
2 Weygand	96	96
SOUTH CAROLINA		
1 ***Sanford***	98	98
2 ***Spence***	98	99
3 ***Graham***	94	94
4 ***DeMint***	99	99
5 Spratt	97	97
6 Clyburn	98	99
SOUTH DAKOTA		
AL ***Thune***	99	99
TENNESSEE		
1 ***Jenkins***	98	98
2 ***Duncan***	99	99
3 ***Wamp***	99	99
4 ***Hilleary***	95	95
5 Clement	98	99
6 Gordon	97	98
7 ***Bryant***	99	99
8 Tanner	98	98
9 Ford	97	97
TEXAS		
1 Sandlin	98	98
2 Turner	99	99
3 ***Johnson***	96	96
4 Hall	99	99
5 ***Sessions***	98	98
6 ***Barton***	95	95
7 ***Archer***	96	97
8 ***Brady***	95	96
9 Lampson	99	99
10 Doggett	99	99
11 Edwards	98	98
12 ***Granger***	94	94
13 ***Thornberry***	98	98
14 ***Paul***	97	98
15 Hinojosa	93	93
16 Reyes	90	90
17 Stenholm	99	99
18 Jackson-Lee	94	94
19 ***Combest***	96	97
20 Gonzalez	99	99
21 ***Smith***	95	95
22 ***DeLay***	97	97
23 ***Bonilla***	98	98
24 Frost	93	94
25 Bentsen	98	98
26 ***Armey***	98	99
27 Ortiz	95	94
28 Rodriguez	98	98
29 Green	94	94
30 Johnson	99	99
UTAH		
1 ***Hansen***	97	97
2 ***Cook***	98	98
3 ***Cannon***	96	97
VERMONT		
AL Sanders	96	97
VIRGINIA		
1 ***Bateman***	98	98
2 Pickett	97	97
3 Scott	98	99
4 Sisisky	99	99
5 Goode	99	99
6 ***Goodlatte***	99	99
7 ***Bliley***	97	97
8 Moran	98	98
9 Boucher	96	96
10 ***Wolf***	99	99
11 ***Davis***	98	98
WASHINGTON		
1 Inslee	100	100
2 ***Metcalf***	97	97
3 Baird	99	99
4 ***Hastings***	99	99
5 ***Nethercutt***	98	97
6 Dicks	97	97
7 McDermott	80	80
8 ***Dunn***	96	96
9 Smith	98	98
WEST VIRGINIA		
1 Mollohan	90	91
2 Wise	93	94
3 Rahall	97	98
WISCONSIN		
1 ***Ryan***	99	99
2 Baldwin	95	95
3 Kind	99	99
4 Kleczka	97	98
5 Barrett	99	99
6 ***Petri***	99	99
7 Obey	97	97
8 ***Green***	99	99
9 ***Sensenbrenner***	100	100
WYOMING		
AL ***Cubin***	96	97

Southern states - Ala., Ark., Fla., Ga., Ky., La., Miss., N.C., Okla., S.C., Tenn., Texas, Va.

Appendix C

KEY VOTES

The President's Acquittal Overshadows Year's Modest Legislative Accomplishments

SUMMARY

Since 1945, Congressional Quarterly has selected a series of key votes on major issues of the year.

An issue is judged by the extent to which it represents:

- A matter of major controversy.
- A matter of presidential or political power.
- A matter of potentially great impact on the nation and lives of Americans.

For each group of related votes on an issue, one key vote is usually chosen — one that, in the opinion of CQ editors, was most important in determining the outcome.

Charts showing how each member of Congress voted on these issues begin on p. C-15.

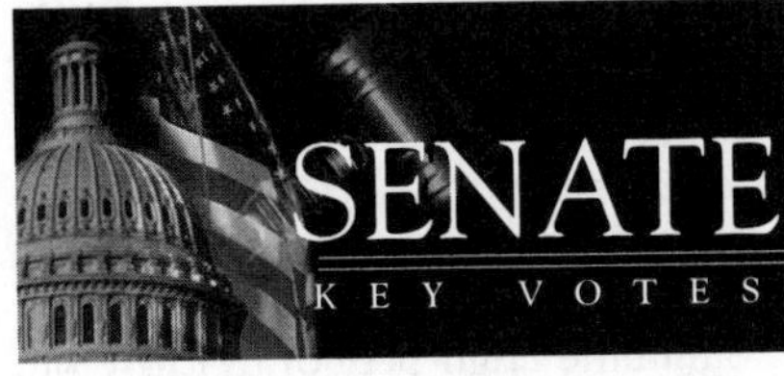

4 Impeachment: Motion To Dismiss

The Constitution stipulates that a two-thirds Senate majority is required to remove a president from office. Even as President Clinton's trial was convened as the first order of business for the 106th Congress, it was widely assumed that fewer than 67 senators would vote for either of the articles of impeachment the House had adopted a month earlier. *(1998 Almanac, p. 12-3)*

The first empirical, and emphatic, evidence to support that assumption came on Jan. 22, the ninth day of the trial, when Robert C. Byrd, D-W.Va., announced that he would lead the effort to dismiss both charges and adjourn the trial. The president was charged with committing perjury in testimony to a federal grand jury about his relationship with Monica Lewinsky while she was a White House intern, and with leading a campaign to cover up the affair. Even if true, Byrd said, those offenses did not constitute grounds for removal.

Such a motion had been expected, but the fact that Byrd had offered it was a clear indication that the 13 Republican House "managers" were making no headway in their effort to build a bipartisan majority for conviction. As one of the harshest Democratic critics of the president's behavior during the previous year — and as someone legendary for both guarding senatorial prerogative and promoting propriety in public life — Byrd was central to the prosecution strategy. Were he to announce for conviction, the managers believed, other Democrats would be sure to follow.

Instead, the opposite occurred. In the bellwether vote of the trial, on Jan. 27 Byrd's motion was defeated, 44-56: R 0-55; D 44-1 (ND 36-1 SD 8-0). *(Senate key vote 1, p. C-15)*

While the vote kept the proceedings alive, it also signaled, in the words of Sen. Richard C. Shelby, R-Ala., that "you've read the end of the book, unless something drastic happens, which none of us foresee." That is because every Democrat except Russell D. Feingold of Wisconsin voted to dismiss the case before any witnesses had been deposed, let alone heard from. At least one-quarter of them, or 11 Democratic senators, would have had to reverse position for there to have been a chance of conviction.

The proceedings lumbered on for two more weeks. But the atmosphere was palpably different, with many who wanted Clinton out of the White House clearly against dragging out the trial any longer. The House prosecutors harbored a faint hope that one dramatic moment — Lewinsky giving sworn testimony against the president from the well of the Senate — could galvanize senatorial sentiment against Clinton.

But on Feb. 4, that hope was dashed when 25 GOP senators joined all 45 Democrats to defeat a motion to send her a subpoena. Instead, she was only heard on snippets of deposition videotape played near the trial's end on television monitors.

18 Impeachment: Acquittal

Historic by its very occurrence — the first impeachment trial of an elected president and the only such trial since Andrew Johnson's 131 years earlier — the Senate proceedings of 1999 nonetheless ended not with a bang but a whimper. Acquittal was universally expected by the time Chief Justice William H. Rehnquist posed the final question of the trial on Feb. 12: "Senators, how say you? Is the respondent, William Jefferson Clinton, guilty or not guilty?"

From early on, it was clear that a Senate majority agreed with the president's lawyers, who argued that while Clinton's testimony before a federal grand jury about his relationship with White House intern Monica Lewinsky was evasive, it did not cross the high legal threshold to become perjurious, as Article I alleged. All 45 Democrats and 10 Republicans, seven of them former prosecutors, formed the majority that rejected the charge.

That left the only real suspense for the last vote of the trial, on Article II, which alleged that the president obstructed justice, primarily by encouraging Lewinsky to file a false affidavit in a sexual harassment lawsuit against Clinton filed by an Arkansas woman.

The 13 GOP prosecutors, or "managers" — who had drafted the articles and won their endorsement by the

House at the end of 1998 — were hoping to spare themselves a measure of embarrassment by persuading at least a simple majority of senators to vote to convict the president on this charge. But even that symbolic victory narrowly eluded them. The vote was a 50-50 tie: R 50-5; D 0-45 (ND 0-37 SD 0-8). *(Senate key vote 2, p. C-15)*

Because a two-thirds majority was required for conviction, the prosecutors were 17 votes shy of the mark. Put another way, the prosecutors garnered the support of only three of every four senators they needed.

The vote also reflected what many predicted would happen once a political entity like the Senate was converted to a court. Democrats were united and were joined by a small but pivotal group of GOP moderates. In addition, the five Republicans who voted to acquit on Article II all represented states Clinton carried both in 1992 and 1996.

That there was a vote at all amounted to something of a victory for Clinton's harshest critics. From the night of the 1998 election, when Democrats unexpectedly gained five House seats, pundits, congressional scholars and many in Congress assumed that the House's GOP leaders were sufficiently chastened that they would settle on an "exit strategy" to stop the process before impeachment. That did not happen. While the House prosecutors felt they were not granted permission to put on the comprehensive case that the situation demanded, however, they at least were able to make their arguments to the Senate and the nation. And they were able to hear the verdict rendered in an official — albeit disappointing to them — climax.

41 Education

If voters have been consistent about any one issue in recent years, it is education — more specifically, their demand that Congress enact policies to improve the quality of instruction in public schools.

President Clinton and Democrats have seized on the issue with a broad-based program that includes funding for school construction and renovation, beefing up after-school programs, providing aid to turn around failing public schools, and a seven-year plan to help local districts hire 100,000 new teachers and reduce class size in the early grades.

Republicans at first resisted Clinton's calls for more federal activism. After a bitter debate, however, they provided the first $1.2 billion installment of his 100,000-teacher plan in the fiscal 1999 omnibus spending bill (PL 105-277).

The GOP this session took a more activist approach on education, with an agenda designed to define the differences between the two parties as an issue of control, not money. Republicans argued that states and local schools, not the federal government, should decide spending priorities.

Democrats, arguing that states in the past have done a poor job of directing aid to low-income students, wanted the federal government to direct how funds are spent. The split came into focus on March 11, when the Senate took up the "ed-flex" bill (S 280), designed to allow states to waive federal regulations in order to carry out school improvement programs. While most Democrats supported the ed-flex legislation, they used it as the vehicle for highlighting Clinton's education priorities, especially his class-size reduction plan.

Sen. Patty Murray, D-Wash., announced she would offer an amendment to the bill that would authorize $11.4 billion over six years to carry out Clinton's program.

Republicans fought back during the debate, with Majority Leader Trent Lott, R-Miss., offering an amendment to instead let local schools redirect the $1.2 billion already appropriated for Clinton's plan to other programs, including special education for the disabled. The GOP has provided major funding increases for special education programs during the past several years.

Murray's amendment was tabled (killed) by the Senate on a 55-44 party-line vote: R 55-0; D 0-44 (ND 0-36, SD 0-8). *(Senate key vote 3, p. C-15)*

But the vote was not the final word. The 100,000-teacher issue resurfaced in November as part of the debate on the fiscal 2000 Labor, Health and Human Services and Education spending bill (PL 106-113). After intense negotiations, Congress and the White House worked out a deal to provide an additional $1.3 billion for the second year of the plan, while giving states more flexibility to use the money for teacher training and other purposes.

134 Gun Control

For sheer drama, no vote the Senate took in 1999 could match the May 20 cliffhanger on an amendment to the juvenile justice bill (S 254) by Frank R. Lautenberg, D-N.J.

It was adopted by one vote — only the fourth ballot cast by Al Gore during his vice presidency — reversing the outcome on a similar amendment eight days before. The tally was 51-50: R 6-49; D 44-1 (ND 36-1, SD 8-0), with Gore voting "yea." *(Senate key vote 4, p. C-15)*

Gun control advocates claimed the amendment's adoption as their most significant achievement since Republicans regained control of the Senate in 1995. It would set a requirement that all sales at almost all gun shows be subject to criminal background checks. Currently, only those prospective buyers who are doing business with federally licensed dealers are subject to such a requirement.

Momentum allowing such a vote was created by the April 20 shooting at Columbine High School in Littleton, Colo., which left 15 people dead and put great pressure on Congress to address the relative ease with which children, convicted felons and others may obtain firearms.

The vice president has touted the importance of his role ever since, while GOP leaders say Gore will come to regret the vote if he wins the Democratic presidential nomination and has to explain it in several key states next fall. But, either way, Gore would have been unable to make his entry on to the scene had it not been for some intense backroom arm-twisting. On May 12, a virtually identical version of the measure was tabled, or killed, when it garnered only 47 votes, with two sympathetic senators absent.

Needing one vote to set up a tie, Democrats focused on the two in their caucus who had voted to table Lautenberg's first proposal. They found their convert in Max Cleland of

Georgia, who was offered some modest changes in the language and some heavy persuasion. His switch was made easier when, on the morning of the second vote, a 15-year-old walked into a high school near Atlanta and shot six classmates.

The vote vindicated the Democratic tactic of limiting their gun control proposals to a few for which there was broad public support. They did not, for instance, put forward a Clinton administration proposal that would have limited purchasers to one gun a month. Ultimately, all their proposals were adopted, with Lautenberg's the marquee item. It remains the main sticking point in negotiations with the House.

The vote also proved a valuable lesson for Majority Leader Trent Lott, R-Miss., who went out of his way to allow an unusually open debate. He soon returned to his customary style of managing debates with near-military precision.

145 Kosovo

The quarter-century duel between Congress and the White House over a president's unilateral right to commit U.S. military forces to battle was played out again in the Senate on May 25. As on several other occasions since Congress enacted the 1973 War Powers Resolution (PL 93-148) over President Richard M. Nixon's veto, most members declined to challenge the president's insistence that his constitutional power as commander in chief gives him the right to deploy forces without congressional approval. *(War powers, 1973 Almanac, p. 905)*

This time, the test came on an amendment to the fiscal 2000 defense authorization bill (PL 106-65) by Arlen Specter, R-Pa., that would have barred the deployment of U.S. ground troops in the Serbian province of Kosovo unless Congress authorized it in advance. The amendment would not have affected the U.S.-led NATO air campaign against Yugoslavia, which began on March 24 with the aim of halting the repression of ethnic Albanians. Nor would Specter's amendment have applied to the deployment of U.S. ground troops in Kosovo to enforce any peacekeeping agreement that might be negotiated.

From the outset of the bombing campaign, Clinton had insisted that he had no intention of committing ground forces to combat in Kosovo and that he would consult with Congress before making such a move. Indeed, he stressed his aversion to sending in ground troops to the point that some members of Congress and foreign policy experts warned that he was squandering the leverage that even an unspoken threat of a NATO ground invasion might have on Yugoslav President Slobodan Milosevic.

But Specter insisted that Congress could ensure its rightful role in such a portentous decision only by writing the requirement into law. His argument rested on the same facts of political life that the 1973 legislation was intended to circumvent: Once U.S. troops are sent into harm's way, members of Congress are loath to force a withdrawal that might expose the troops to enemy attack.

Specter insisted that Clinton might be able to persuade him to vote to authorize a ground invasion of Kosovo. But opponents contended that the amendment would bolster Milosevic's determination to wait out the NATO air attacks by reassuring him he need not fear ground troops. The amendment was tabled, and thus killed, by a vote of 52-48: R 17-38; D 35-10 (ND 29-8; SD 2-6). *(Senate key vote 5, p. C-15)*

The complexity of Senate views on the Kosovo operation was mirrored in the crazy-quilt vote. In the GOP camp, some veteran centrists joined the tabling motion, while, among Democrats, liberals historically leery of military intervention abroad were found on both sides of the vote.

210 Managed Care

It may have been the most convoluted and politically tortuous Senate debate of the legislative year.

The delicate politics of managed care were apparent as the Senate took up the issue in July. Majority Leader Trent Lott, R-Miss., introduced language from the Democrats' "patients' bill of rights" (S 6) as the underlying bill for debate. It was given a new number (S 1344).

The Democratic language was used to prevent Democrats from offering a long series of amendments on the floor that would force Republicans to cast politically unpopular votes against a variety of patient protections, such as expanding the number of patients who would be guaranteed certain coverage and allowing patients to sue if they were harmed by the decisions of their health plans.

In turn, Democrats introduced the GOP managed care bill as a substitute, so that they could introduce their list of managed care provisions as secondary amendments. Both bills were then debated at the same time, with alternating amendments being offered to each — allowing ample opportunity for political gamesmanship.

"The debate that's going on now is one of the most partisan and the most vacuous, the most devoid of effort to try to reach a solution that I've heard in a long time — and that's saying something," grumbled Max Baucus, D-Mont.

Throughout the debate, Republicans repeatedly offered amendments similar to ones offered by Democrats and defeated along party lines just hours earlier. Democrats charged — and several Republicans privately agreed — that the maneuver was aimed at allowing the GOP to claim victory for enacting certain patient protections. But Republican amendments generally offered more limited government oversight to a fewer number of patients — in keeping with the GOP philosophy of less government regulation.

As their final amendment, Republicans offered a package that combined all the GOP-backed patient protections with a variety of tax incentives aimed at making health insurance more affordable. Democrats charged that the provisions would only help the rich and hurt the poor.

In an attempt to bridge the partisan divide, a bipartisan group of lawmakers, led by the late John H. Chafee, R-R.I., offered a compromise that would have taken provisions from both sides. But those efforts proved futile.

After four days of partisan debate and procedural contortion, the Republican package passed, 53-47: R 52-2;

D 0-45 (ND 0-37, SD 0-8) I 1-0. *(Senate key vote 6, p. C-15)*

The final, party-line outcome demonstrated just how entrenched both sides are on managed care. It also suggests that a compromise with the House, which passed a bipartisan managed care bill in October, will be difficult next year as a conference committee takes up the issue.

247 Tax Cuts

Senate Republicans had long been more cautious than their House counterparts about passing a huge tax cut. In 1998, for instance, they managed to whittle the House's $80.1 billion proposal down to $9.2 billion. But in 1999, with a projected budget surplus of $1 trillion over 10 years, the Senate agreed to move a major package. *(1998 Almanac, p. 21-14)*

After the Budget Committee reserved nearly $800 billion for a tax cut, Finance Committee Chairman William V. Roth Jr., R-Del., unveiled a $792 billion measure (S 1429). The bill would have cut the lowest income tax rate bracket from 15 to 14 percent, taken steps to ease the so-called marriage penalty, and made changes to pension and retirement laws to give more favorable tax rates to those who saved.

Roth had always worked well with panel Democrats, but he focused this time on ensuring that the bill would appeal to both moderate and conservative Republicans. Meanwhile, President Clinton threatened consistently to veto the bill and its House counterpart (HR 2488), and most Senate Democrats backed the president. *(House key vote, p. C-12)*

The polarizing situation led to parliamentary maneuvers when the Senate took up the bill the week of July 26. First, Republicans had to contend with the so-called Byrd rule, which requires a supermajority of 60 votes to pass measures that are not offset by spending cuts or revenue increases. The Senate bill was not paid for beyond the first 10 years, so when the Senate did not waive the Byrd rule, the bill's provisions were set to expire Sept. 30, 2009. The vote was 51-48. Party leaders, particularly Minority Leader Tom Daschle, D-S.D., worked hard to keep their troops in line. Daschle succeeded, but three Republicans — Arlen Specter of Pennsylvania and Susan Collins and Olympia J. Snowe, both of Maine — voted no with the Democrats.

Meanwhile, moderates of both parties led by John B. Breaux, D-La., began formulating a $500 billion tax measure that they said was a workable, responsible compromise between the main GOP measure and Democrats' $290 billion proposal. It appeared for a time that the moderate measure might garner enough support to challenge the bills, but Daschle and Majority Leader Trent Lott, R-Miss., began peeling supporters off the effort. By the time the Senate was ready to vote on the Republican bill, moderates withdrew their plan, all the while charging that partisanship should not keep Congress from agreeing to a tax bill.

The Senate passed S 1429 on July 30, 57-43: R 52-2; D 4-41 (ND 2-35, SD 2-6); I 1-0. Only two Republicans — Specter and George V. Voinovich of Ohio — voted against it, while four Democrats — Breaux, Bob Kerrey of Nebraska, Mary L. Landrieu of Louisiana and Robert G. Torricelli of New Jersey — voted for it. *(Senate key vote 7, p.C-15)*

251 Cuba Sanctions

For years, a powerful lobbying group, the Cuban American National Foundation, has played a key role in maintaining a hard-line U.S. policy toward Cuba.

Not only has the group helped sustain political support for maintaining the nearly 40-year trade embargo on Fidel Castro's Cuba, it has directed considerable financial resources toward further hardening that embargo after the end of the Cold War, when Cuba lost the support of its Soviet patron.

In 1992, the foundation rallied behind legislation (PL 102-396) by then-Rep. Robert G. Torricelli, D-N.J., now a senator, to tighten the Cuba embargo and strengthen opposition to Castro's rule. And in 1996, the foundation helped push through a bill (PL 104-114) by Senate Foreign Relations Committee Chairman Jesse Helms, R-N.C., and Rep. Dan Burton, R-Ind., to write the embargo into permanent law. That meant it would be up to Congress rather than the White House to decide if and when to lift the restrictions on Cuba. *(1996 Almanac, p. 9-6; 1992 Almanac, p. 557)*

Support for the embargo remains strong in the Cuban-American communities of Miami and New Jersey. But the end of the Cold War and the 1997 death of the foundation's charismatic leader, Jorge Mas Canosa, weakened its influence in Washington, and encouraged business and farm interests eager to ease the embargo.

In January, President Clinton, influenced by Pope John Paul II's 1998 visit to the island, took several small steps to increase contacts with Cuba. Clinton's decision to ease restrictions on travel, mail and financial transfers won support from key lawmakers in both parties.

But the clearest illustration of changing congressional sentiment came on Aug. 3, during debate on the fiscal 2000 agriculture appropriations bill (PL 106-78), when the Senate refused to table (kill) an amendment by John Ashcroft, R-Mo., that would have allowed the export of food and medicine to Cuba. The vote on Helms' motion to table was 28-70: R 17-36; D 10-34 (ND 8-28, SD 2-6); I 1-0. *(Senate key vote 8, p. C-20)*

The Ashcroft amendment was aimed at broadening a law enacted last year (PL 105-194) banning trade sanctions on food and medicine, except for countries — such as Cuba — on the State Department's list of terrorist states. At the time, an amendment to keep the sanctions in place on such states, including Cuba, was backed by 67 senators, including Ashcroft. This year, only 28 senators supported a continued embargo on food and medicine to Cuba.

The provision was ultimately pulled out of the agriculture spending bill in conference at the insistence of Cuban-American members of the House. But supporters said they would probably make another try in 2000.

275 CAFE Standards

Even the possibility of a study of new fuel-efficiency standards for cars and light trucks was too much for the auto industry to take. Pressure from the industry wilted an effort to lift a ban on the Clinton administration launching the study.

Automakers came out in force to lobby the vote, which occurred on a sense of the Senate amendment to the fiscal 2000 transportation spending bill (HR 2084 — PL 106-69).

Each year since Republicans took control of Congress in 1995, the House has inserted a rider in the transportation bill to block the Transportation Department from developing new fuel standards, and the Senate has gone along.

But this year, a bipartisan group of senators — concerned about the rising number of fuel-hungry trucks, sport utility vehicles (SUVs) and vans on the road — vowed to reverse the policy on environmental grounds. The debate reprised themes brought up in the 1970s, when CAFE standards were introduced — environmental and economic costs weighed against safety factors and consumer preferences.

Slade Gorton, R-Wash., Dianne Feinstein, D-Calif., and Richard H. Bryan, D-Nev., wrote President Clinton in March: "The freeze rider denies the purchasers of SUVs and other light trucks the benefits of existing fuel-saving technologies." The letter was signed by 27 Democrats and four Republicans.

Gorton, Feinstein and Bryan argued on the floor that more efficient cars and trucks would save consumers money while reducing pollution, global warming and the U.S. trade deficit. They said their language stopped short of advocating new fuel standards, which would come about only after the Transportation Department was allowed to review current data.

Groups such as the Union of Concerned Scientists, the Sierra Club and the League of Conservation Voters published pamphlets and other material outlining technology already employed on popular cars that could help manufacturers meet more stringent standards.

But opponents, led by Spencer Abraham, R-Mich., and Carl Levin, D-Mich., said the amendment would lead inexorably to a fuel standard increase, and that would force manufacturers to market smaller, lighter cars that are not as safe or as popular. Abraham cited National Academy of Sciences findings that current fuel-efficiency standards had contributed to thousands of deaths because the victims were driving in lighter vehicles.

Gorton's amendment would have allowed the Transportation Department to study changing the CAFE standards and would have encouraged the Senate to reject the House rider. His amendment failed, 40-55: R 6-45; D 34-9 (ND 29-7, SD 5-2); I 0-1. *(Senate key vote 9, p. C-20)*

325 Nuclear Test Ban Treaty

The Senate's rejection Oct. 13 of a treaty to ban nuclear weapons testing likely will go down as one of President Clinton's most embarrassing foreign policy defeats, as well as one of the clearest triumphs of conservative Republicans over his administration.

The Comprehensive Test Ban Treaty (Treaty Doc 105-28) became entangled in a series of partisan political skirmishes that left it with support from just four GOP senators.

Administration officials had lobbied sporadically for the treaty since Clinton submitted it for ratification in September 1997. But Senate Democratic proponents intensified their efforts in the weeks leading up to an Oct. 6 conference in Vienna of treaty signatories. *(1997 Almanac, p. 8-28)*

After learning of Democratic tactics to force consideration of the treaty, Majority Leader Trent Lott, R-Miss. — a staunch opponent of the test ban — abruptly agreed to schedule 22 hours of debate and a vote. Lott's move startled treaty advocates, who had hoped for more time to build political support for the measure.

Once debate began, it became clear that supporters would fall far short of the 67 votes needed for ratification. The administration had failed to win over some of the Senate's influential internationalist Republicans, including Armed Services Committee Chairman John W. Warner, R-Va., and Richard G. Lugar, R-Ind.

Warner led a group of lawmakers in seeking to delay the vote. He and Democrat Daniel Patrick Moynihan of New York circulated a letter urging that the issue be postponed until the 107th Congress. The letter was signed by 62 senators — 24 Republicans and 38 Democrats. But the rules of the Senate, as well as pressure to support the Republican leadership, helped give the treaty's critics the upper hand. Several Republicans objected to a unanimous consent agreement, proposed by Minority Leader Tom Daschle, D-S.D., to shelve the vote. A procedural motion by Lott to turn from other legislation back to the treaty passed on a 55-45 party-line vote.

The treaty was then rejected, 48-51: R 4-50; D 44-0 (ND 36-0, SD 8-0); I 0-1. *(Senate key vote 10, p. C-20)*

The rejection led Clinton and other Democrats to accuse Republicans of playing politics, a charge that the treaty's GOP critics denied. They said the treaty simply contained too many flaws and was unverifiable.

331 Campaign Finance

If there has been one constant in the story of campaign finance legislation during the past decade, it has been the role played by Mitch McConnell of Kentucky in leading Senate Republicans against such measures. He mounted his first successful filibuster in the 100th Congress; by his count, his most recent effort, in October, was the 20th time that he has marshaled most of his GOP colleagues to stop such a bill.

In order to prevail this year, McConnell had to triumph over a strategy advanced by John McCain, R-Ariz., and Russell D. Feingold, D-Wis., who led the effort to limit the influence of money in politics.

Convinced that their comprehensive proposal could not overcome a McConnell filibuster, they wrote a narrower measure (S 1593). Its central element was a ban on "soft money," the unlimited and unregulated donations from unions, corporations and wealthy people that are the fastest-growing source of cash to the Republican and Democratic committees that underwrite presidential and congressional campaigns. If they could win 60 votes for this narrow approach, they reasoned, they stood a chance of reassembling their original proposal — or perhaps finding a new bipartisan consensus — through the amendment process. Ultimately, McCain and Feingold aspire to win passage of a bill, like the measure (HR 417) the House passed on Sept. 14, that would not only ban soft money but would also regulate "issue advocacy" advertising, the campaigns paid for by third parties that promote a candidacy without ever explicitly urging a vote for or against anyone. *(House key vote, p. C-13)*

After a dizzying round of parliamentary chess, in which proponents and opponents in both parties sought to frame the debate to their liking, the key vote came on Oct. 19. It was on a motion to invoke cloture on an amendment by the Democratic leadership that essentially restated the text of the underlying bill. The vote was 53-47, seven short of the number needed to bring debate to a close. All Democrats and eight Republicans voted to limit debate; 46 Republicans opposed it (ND 37-0, SD 8-0). *(Senate key vote 11, p. C-20)*

The ballot showed the quicksand through which McCain and Feingold continue to labor. On the one hand, they won a net of one more ally than their previous best showing. And they did so with the help of three Republicans who had voted with McConnell in the past: Sam Brownback of Kansas, Tim Hutchinson of Arkansas and William V. Roth Jr. of Delaware. But they also lost the votes of two Republicans who were on record as supporting a sweeping approach: Arlen Specter of Pennsylvania and John H. Chafee of Rhode Island, who has since died. And their strategy failed to win over several other Republicans who, the sponsors hoped, would see the narrow bill as a vehicle for testing the Senate's sentiment for other approaches.

337 Abortion

Legislation to ban a procedure that opponents call "partial birth" abortion has been a hardy perennial in Congress every year since Republicans took over, although the bill has never become law because proponents have been unable to muster the two-thirds vote necessary to override President Clinton's veto. In that sense, this fall's debate was no exception, as the Senate vote for this year's measure (S 1692) passed 63-34.

The key vote in the debate, however, came on what was essentially an effort by two Democratic senators to make a point. During the debate, Tom Harkin of Iowa and Barbara Boxer of California offered a non-binding amendment to express the sense of Congress that the Supreme Court's 1973 Roe v. Wade decision that found that women have the right to abortion was "an appropriate decision" that "secures an important constitutional right" and "should not be overturned." Boxer and Harkin said they offered the amendment in hopes of "smoking out" those Republicans who argued that the "partial birth" ban had nothing to do with the broader issue of abortion rights.

"This is the first time, that I know of, that we have had the opportunity to vote up or down on whether or not we believe that Roe v. Wade should stand and should not be overturned, and that it is, indeed, a good decision," Harkin said.

After a Republican move to table the amendment failed, on Oct. 21 the amendment was adopted, 51-47: R 8-44; D 43-2 (ND 36-1, SD 7-1); I 0-1. *(Senate key vote 12, p. C-20)*

Abortion rights supporters expressed shock and dismay at their narrow victory, in which only one more senator than an outright majority took their side. They said the tally showed that anti-abortion forces wield growing power in Congress, and were within striking distance of pushing far more sweeping abortion bills through the Senate. And they said the tally demonstrated that Congress is out of step with the American people, citing polls showing that a solid majority believe abortion should remain legal.

Opponents of abortion rights said the vote revealed less than enthusiastic support for abortion on demand.

Both sides indicated that they would use the tally in the 2000 campaign. While non-binding, the amendment is expected to carry some some political weight. Vice President Al Gore issued a statement saying that if elected president next year he will "always, always defend a woman's right to choose." Noting that only eight Republicans voted against the amendment, Democrats vowed to make the vote a campaign issue in "every one of the states" where those senators are seeking re-election next year. "We know who they are," Boxer said.

354 Financial Services

Lawmakers had agreed for years that the United States needed to repeal decades-old laws restricting cross-ownership among the banking, securities and insurance industries. Supporters said it would help businesses compete globally and provide consumers with one-stop shopping for financial services. But partisan fights, along with battles among the industries over details, had made consensus in the Senate elusive.

Early in the year it looked as if 1999 would be no different. The new Banking Committee chairman was Phil Gramm, R-Texas, a key player in preventing a financial services overhaul from getting a floor vote in 1998. He was known for partisanship, and indeed, partisanship prevailed in May when the Senate passed an overhaul bill (S 900), 54-44, with only one Democrat, Ernest F. Hollings of South Carolina, on board.

Gramm plowed over Democratic opposition in committee and on the floor by insisting on inclusion of controversial changes to the 1977 Community Reinvestment Act (PL 95-128), an anti-redlining measure aimed at forcing banks to make loans in low-income neighborhoods. Gramm insisted on including a provision to exempt small, rural banks from the act, drawing sharp objections from Democrats and a veto threat from the White House.

In the House-Senate conference, Gramm continued to make waves, saying he was willing to pass a partisan bill and dare the White House to veto it. But behind closed doors, Gramm was playing ball. He fought for days with Democrats and the White House but never walked away from the table. Negotiators say each time a deal was on the verge of collapse, industry representatives stepped up pressure on Gramm, the White House and others to keep working. *(House key vote, p. C-11)*

Gramm eventually agreed to drop the reinvestment law exemption for small rural banks, but he won a provision to ease the law's regulatory requirements for most small banks. He also was able to include a "sunshine provision" to require disclosure of deals in which a bank offers grants or loans to a community group in exchange for the group's support of the bank's reinvestment activities.

After the protracted conference, the Senate voted overwhelmingly Nov. 4 to adopt the conference report on S 900. The vote was 90-8: R 52-1; D 38-7 (ND 30-7, SD 8-0). The House cleared the bill the same day, and President Clinton signed it Nov. 12 (PL 106-102). *(Senate key vote 13, p. C-20)*

Although it was little noticed outside Washington and Wall Street, the overhaul was one of the most important pieces of legislation signed in 1999. Many analysts said it will alter the basic structure of the financial services industry and change the way a broad array of services are provided to customers.

56 Steel Restrictions

In the six years since passage of the North American Free Trade Agreement (PL 103-182), debate over its impact on the nation's economy continued between free-trade advocates and supporters of protection for U.S. businesses. That debate sharpened in early 1999, when the steel industry found itself in a two-year slump. Prices for most steel products dropped sharply; several steel manufacturers filed for bankruptcy, and at least 10,000 of the nation's 170,000 steelworkers were laid off. Steelmakers and their workers blamed the troubles on a 33 percent increase in the volume of steel imported into the United States, much of it from Japan, Brazil and Russia.

Lawmakers cheered President Clinton when he said Jan. 19 in his State of the Union address that if Japan did not reverse the surge of steel imports, "America will respond." Members of the Congressional Steel Caucus went a step further. They introduced a bill (HR 975), sponsored by Peter J. Visclosky, D-Ind., to allow the president to limit steel imports for three years through quotas, tariffs or other measures. The limits would have kept steel imports at their average monthly level as calculated between August 1994 and July 1997.

The proposal sent a shudder through the nation's leading economists, who tend to strongly favor free trade. Then-Treasury Secretary Robert E. Rubin warned that such a bill would run "a very real risk of triggering protectionist interests around the world." Federal Reserve Chairman Alan Greenspan warned that a "drift toward protectionist policies, which are always difficult to reverse, is a much greater threat than is generally understood."

And Rep. Philip M. Crane, R-Ill., chairman of the Ways and Means Subcommittee on Trade, announced a series of hearings to counter what he called "protectionist temptations" in Congress. Free-traders called for the United States to stick to the same laws it expected other countries to live by.

With such opposition, it was unlikely that the Steel Caucus — supported by organized labor — would see its legislation enacted. But its vocal anti-import stance laid bare the public's angst over free trade, and underscored how difficult it would be for the president and GOP leaders to enact major trade legislation.

In the end, the margin of victory for protectionism was so wide that even bill supporters were surprised. The House passed HR 975 on March 17 by a vote of 289-141: R 91-128; D 197-13 (ND 146-9, SD 51-4), I 1-0. Republicans split between those defending home-state industries and free-traders who felt they had done enough for steel manufacturers by approving $1 billion in loan guarantees for the industry (PL 106-51). The steel import bill died in the Senate on June 22 when a motion to invoke cloture failed, 42-57. *(House key vote 1, p. C-16)*

58 Missile Defense

The push for a small-scale national anti-missile defense gained momentum in 1998 when North Korea tested a rocket with nearly enough range to strike Alaska or Hawaii, when India and Pakistan tested nuclear weapons, and when a commission chaired by former Defense Secretary Donald H. Rumsfeld warned that a missile threat to U.S. territory could materialize within five years — much sooner than the Clinton administration had projected.

In February, the administration included deployment funding for a national missile defense in its long-range budget plans for the first time. Defense Secretary William S. Cohen said the threat of a limited missile attack clearly warranted deployment, but he and other officials reiterated the administration's position that a decision also should be based on the technical success of the anti-missile system, its projected cost and its impact on arms reduction efforts. The administration emphasized the last point particularly, since any nationwide defense would require amending the 1972 Anti-Ballistic Missile (ABM) Treaty, a step Russia opposes.

To challenge the administration's conditional commitment to deployment, Curt Weldon, R-Pa., introduced a one-sentence bill (HR 4 — PL 106-38) declaring it to be national policy to deploy a national missile defense. John M. Spratt Jr., D-S.C., cosponsored the bill, arguing that it was vague enough that it did not threaten the ABM Treaty. However, the White House opposed the bill as an attack on the pact.

The GOP-led campaign for a limited nationwide anti-missile defense system received a symbolic lift March 18 from a House vote that showed growing Democratic support for the idea.

The vote, which came on a procedural motion, amounted to a test of President Clinton's policy of delaying a decision on deploying the anti-missile system until the summer of 2000 and basing the decision on many factors, including whether a deployment would undercut talks with Russia.

More than a quarter of the Democrats who voted on the motion joined all but two voting Republicans to reject Clinton's position, thus backing an immediate and unconditional endorsement of an anti-missile deployment.

The key vote was on a motion by Tom Allen, D-Maine, to recommit the bill to committee with instructions that it be amended to endorse Clinton's policy of basing a deployment decision on several factors, including any possibly adverse impact on arms reduction negotiations. The motion was rejected 152-269: R 2-212; D 150-56 (ND 125-28; SD 25-28). *(House key vote 2, p. C-16)*

The Weldon bill then was passed, 317-105, with Democrats splitting 103-102 in favor of the measure.

103 Kosovo

In the weeks before and during the NATO bombing campaign against Yugoslavia, intended to end the oppression of ethnic Albanians in the province of Kosovo, the House took a series of votes relating to the issue without defining a clear policy.

The most conspicuous of the lot was on April 28, when 26 Democrats joined all but 31 voting Republicans — led by Majority Whip Tom DeLay, R-Texas — in a tie vote that defeated a resolution (S Con Res 21) to authorize the air operations that had been under way for five weeks. The vote was symbolic, since the House was moving swiftly toward passing a supplemental spending bill (PL 106-31) to pay for the Kosovo campaign. But it underscored the House GOP's contempt for Clinton, whom they had voted to impeach four months earlier, and their mistrust of his stewardship of U.S. armed forces.

GOP disdain for Clinton's handling of defense issues, rooted in his avoidance of the draft and his 1993 effort to allow openly gay persons to serve in the armed forces, came to focus on his commitment of troops to peacekeeping and humanitarian missions rather than training for war. In late 1995, Clinton overrode those objections and deployed U.S. troops as the backbone of a NATO-led peacekeeping force in Bosnia. But congressional critics were further outraged when the administration's promise to end that mission in a year was brushed aside only a few days after the 1996 election.

Against that backdrop, when Yugoslavia's ethnic Serb majority began brutalizing Kosovo's Albanians late in 1998, congressional sentiment about a U.S. response was chaotically divided. Once military operations against the Serbs began on March 24, the prevailing sentiment among GOP leaders seemed to be that Congress should avoid any votes that would require members either to endorse what they saw as Clinton's flawed leadership or to vote against the U.S. involvement and thus strengthen the hand of Yugoslav President Slobodan Milosevic.

But Republican Tom Campbell of California invoked provisions of the 1973 War Powers Resolution (PL 93-148) to force the House to vote on a declaration of war against Yugoslavia and a resolution ordering the withdrawal of U.S. forces from the conflict. Though both were defeated, Democrats insisted that the House vote on the Senate-passed resolution authorizing the air war. *(War powers, 1973 Almanac, p. 905)*

Speaker J. Dennis Hastert, R-Ill., supported the resolution but declined to lobby Republicans on it, calling it a vote of conscience. But DeLay strenuously opposed the measure, urging members not to "take ownership" of an "incompetent" administration's policy. The resolution was rejected on a tie vote of 213-213: R 31-187; D 181-26 (ND 131-21; SD 50-5); I 1-0. *(House key vote 3, p. C-16)*

207 FAA

For the second year in a row, House Transportation and Infrastructure Committee Chairman Bud Shuster, R-Pa., confronted a coalition of powerful fiscal conservatives intent on stopping his plans for transportation spending. In a June 15 showdown on the House floor, Shuster again won big.

In the 1998 surface transportation law (PL 105-178), Shuster won a guarantee that gasoline tax revenues would be reserved for highway and transit spending. He beat Republican deficit hawks, who argued that the six-year measure short-circuited the appropriations process and was full of pork-barrel spending. *(1998 Almanac, p. 24-3)*

This year, Shuster targeted the Airport and Airway Trust Fund, financed primarily by airline ticket taxes. The fund was intended for aviation spending, but Shuster said that, in practice, appropriators underfunded aviation and spent part of the money on other purposes. With his five-year, $59.3 billion proposal (HR 1000), Shuster proposed taking the trust fund "off budget," keeping the money only for aviation projects.

Shuster built support for his bill by talking about the need to keep up with skyrocketing air passenger traffic. He argued that current spending levels would leave aviation wanting while unspent trust fund balances would grow to tens of billions of dollars. And he produced a chart showing how much every airport in the country would benefit from the tripling of the basic federal construction grant.

But Appropriations Committee Chairman C.W. Bill Young, R-Fla., and Budget Committee Chairman John R. Kasich, R-Ohio, said Shuster's bill would erode the checks and balances built into the federal budget process. Further, Young said Shuster's bill would authorize $14.3 billion in spending above the level set in the fiscal 2000 budget resolution (H Con Res 68).

Young and Kasich were backed by two other powerful lawmakers, Ways and Means panel Chairman Bill Archer, R-Texas, and Majority Whip Tom DeLay, R-Texas, on an amendment to remove the off-budget language from the bill. A bloc of fiscal conservatives, led by Tom Coburn, R-Okla., and Lindsey Graham, R-S.C., also backed the effort, as did Appropriations panel Democrats.

In the end, Shuster's opponents were overmatched by lawmakers eager to bring home the benefits of the bill. Airport construction projects have an impact on every congressional district, and added capacity can promote airline competition and lower ticket prices.

The Young-Kasich amendment was defeated, 179-248: R 111-108; D 68-139 (ND 49-106, SD 19-33); I 0-1. *(House key vote 4, p. C-16)*

But the House decision did little to influence the Senate, whose version of the bill did not include Shuster's plan. A conference on the bill broke down for the year on Nov. 10.

213 Media Sex and Violence

Days after a shooting rampage left 15 people dead at a Colorado high school, gun control advocates were on the offensive, hoping that public dismay could be leveraged into tighter restrictions on firearms. Cultural conservatives had a similar strategy — that the carnage would build support for proposals to address the "root causes" of youth violence. They pointed to what they perceive to be declining social values and the pernicious effects of sex and violence in the mass media.

Their most ambitious aspiration was adoption of an amendment that House Judiciary Committee Chairman Henry J. Hyde, R-Ill., offered to a bill (HR 1501) designed principally to crack down on juvenile criminals. It called for five-year prison terms for selling or lending to minors a wide array of violent or sexually explicit material. In doing so, it attempted to create a new legal definition of violence that could be constitutionally restricted, much the way obscenity has been since the Supreme Court's 1973 Miller v. California ruling.

With media attention at a fever pitch in the days before the vote, Hyde's proposal appeared poised to pass. But furious lobbying by an array of interests across the ideological spectrum caused support to implode. The vote June 16 to defeat the amendment was a lopsided 146-282: R 127-92; D 19-189 (ND 10-143, SD 9-46); I 0-1. *(House key vote 5, p. C-16)*

Hollywood's lobbyists alone probably did not have sufficient clout to stop the proposal, as many conservatives wear their differences with the movie and television industries as a badge of honor. But on this vote, they were allied not only with civil libertarians but with Main Street business groups, including bookstore owners, movie rental outlets and video game arcades. The U.S. Chamber of Commerce, which had beefed up its lobbying staff this year in an effort to have a bigger impact on legislation, got onto their side as well.

On a vote that pitted two key GOP constituencies against each other, business won. Social conservatives — who have had far less legislative success than they had expected since the Republicans took over Congress in 1995 — were dealt another setback. The outcome also suggested how much more lobbying clout is wielded by established retailers than by players in the new economy. Three years ago the House agreed to enact an overhaul of telecommunications law (PL 104-104) with similar penalties for disseminating certain sexually explicit material to minors over the Internet. It was struck down the next year by the Supreme Court. *(1997 Almanac, p. 5-25)*

Hyde attributed his defeat in part to posturing by colleagues who, he said, wanted to be perceived as equally fervent defenders of the First Amendment and the Second Amendment, the latter of which is raised as the main rationale for opposing gun control.

244 Gun Control

It would take someone as clever as Machiavelli to sort out the political dynamics that led the House to reject gun control legislation (HR 2122) on June 18. But in the end, the measure was defeated by an unusual coalition: defenders of the Second Amendment, who declined to vote for any new gun restrictions, and proponents of gun control, who said that a "poison pill" was dropped in to make the measure weaker than current law.

The vote halted the momentum toward increased gun restrictions that had been building since the April 20 massacre at Columbine High School in Littleton, Colo., and the May 20 vote in the Senate to require background checks of would-be buyers at gun shows. *(Senate key vote, p. C-4)*

The House bill would have required such checks, too, but with a 24-hour time limit — down from three business days under current law, which covers fewer gun show transactions. On one-quarter of checks, a national computer database provides incomplete records, forcing law enforcement officers to telephone courthouses and state records offices. A one day limit would do little good, Clinton administration officials argued, since most gun shows are on weekends when government offices are closed.

Majority Whip Tom DeLay, R-Texas, arranged a series of votes on different versions of the gun control proposals so that some lawmakers could vote "yes" on some without crossing the National Rifle Association (NRA). Language by Carolyn McCarthy, D-N.Y., that was similar to the Senate gun show provision was defeated, 193-235. It lost out to the amendment that limited the background check, which was offered — at DeLay's request — by John D. Dingell, D-Mich. That prevented President Clinton or Democratic leaders from getting much partisan mileage out of the issue.

With the Dingell provision added, 218-211, the bill became so onerous to gun control advocates that they deserted it in droves. Gun control foes, meanwhile, were never comfortable with some of the other provisions in the bill, including a requirement that gun locks be sold with all handguns.

On the key vote, on June 18 the legislation was defeated 147-280: R 137-82; D 10-197 (ND 6-146, SD 4-51); I 0-1. *(House key vote 6, p. C-16)*

Perhaps the biggest winner was the NRA and its allies, which got what it wanted most: nothing. Such a solid vote to defeat a gun control bill puts its advocates in a position of weakness in conference with the Senate on the juvenile justice bill (HR 1501). When a gun show compromise was floated by negotiators this fall, it was spurned both by gun control advocates, who refused to settle for less than the Senate language, and by gun control opponents, who refused to endorse anything.

276 Financial Services

Efforts to rewrite laws governing banks, brokerages and insurers foundered repeatedly for decades, usually before a bill even reached a floor vote in either chamber. So when the House passed a financial services overhaul for the first time ever in 1998, GOP Conference Chairman John A. Boehner of Ohio quipped that the bill's one-vote margin of victory "looks like a landslide."

Still, GOP leaders had to twist arms and wring out last-minute vote switches on the floor to overcome Democratic opposition. And the measure died in the 105th Congress, as it had many times before. *(1998 Almanac, p. 5-3)*

In 1999, things changed. The financial sectors toned down their long-running squabbles over details of the legislation, which sought to remove barriers between the banking, securities and insurance industries. As veteran banking lobbyist Kenneth A. Guenther of the Independent Community Bankers of America noted, almost everyone involved was "just sick and tired of this, and they want it off their backs."

On July 1, the House passed a financial services overhaul bill (HR 10) by a wide margin, sparking a can-do spirit that had been lacking in previous years and sending a signal that the measure's time had come. Bipartisan support for the measure had been painstakingly nurtured by House Banking and Financial Services Committee Chairman Jim Leach, R-Iowa. Under House rules, Leach has to leave the banking chairmanship at the end of the 106th Congress, and after years of effort he wanted to pass an overhaul before surrendering the gavel. The vote was 343-86: R 205-16; D 138-69 (ND 95-58, SD 43-11). After the vote, House members from both parties smiled broadly and crossed the center aisle of the floor to shake hands. *(House key vote 7, p. C-16)*

The House vote gave the bill momentum, though getting it to the president's desk was still not easy. It traveled a tougher, more partisan road in the Senate. Conference negotiations dragged on for days as lobbyists ordered pizza for dinner and nervously paced the hallways late into the evening. Senate Banking, Housing and Urban Affairs Chairman Phil Gramm, R-Texas, seemed content at times to craft a partisan bill and dare President Clinton to veto it, but Leach labored to keep everyone talking and on board. *(Senate key vote, p. C-8)*

The conference report was adopted overwhelmingly in both chambers Nov. 4 and signed by Clinton on Nov. 12 (PL 106-102).

Many analysts said the legislation will have a dramatic impact on financial companies, allowing large cross-industry mergers to proceed. Advocates say this will make U.S. companies more competitive globally, and consumers will be able to do one-stop shopping for a broad array of financial services.

319 Education

As the House began the difficult task of reauthorizing the 1965 Elementary and Secondary Education Act (ESEA), the main law governing federal aid to public schools, President Clinton's seven-year plan to hire 100,000 teachers became central to the debate.

The act, rewritten every five years, has historically been a lightning rod for controversial issues from private school vouchers to prayer in the classroom. This year was no exception, with the two parties sparring over Clinton's efforts to use the ESEA as a vehicle for authorizing his teacher hiring plan, designed to reduce class sizes in grades one through three.

The House addressed the issue in July when it took up a bill (HR 1995) that would create a new education block grant, including the current Eisenhower teacher training program, Clinton's 100,000-teacher plan and the administration's Goals 2000 program of grants to help states improve educational quality. The bill would also set standards to ensure that teachers are qualified in the subject area for which they are hired.

House Education and the Workforce Committee Chairman Bill Goodling, R-Pa., decided to rewrite the ESEA as a series of smaller bills, rather than one enormous measure. The teacher training package was the first to reach the floor.

Some Democrats, such as George Miller of California, supported the block grant plan. Miller believed that Congress should provide local districts with flexibility to use the money for either training or hiring new teachers.

White House officials, worried that other Democrats would follow Miller's lead, met with committee members before the floor vote and urged them to remain united behind Clinton's class-size reduction proposal. Clinton threatened to veto the Goodling bill on the grounds that it was too open-ended and provided no assurances that schools would use any of the $2 billion authorized under the block grant each year to hire new teachers.

Eager to get a vote on the teacher-hiring plan, Matthew G. Martinez, D-Calif., offered a substitute that would have increased funding for professional development, while providing a separate authorization for the 100,000-teacher program. The amendment would have authorized $1.5 billion for class-size reduction in fiscal 2000, increasing to $3 billion in fiscal 2005.

The Martinez amendment died on a 207-217 vote, with three Republicans voting "yea" and two Democrats voting "nay." R 3-215; D 203-2 (ND 151-0; SD 52-2); I 1-0. *(House key vote 8, p. C-18)*

The 100,000-teacher proposal resurfaced in November, when Congress provided $1.3 billion for it in the fiscal 2000 Labor, Health and Human Services and Education appropriations measure (PL 106-113).

333 Tax Cuts

Republican leaders faced a difficult decision early in 1999. They could attempt to unite their often fractious party around the traditional GOP magnet of massive tax cuts. Or they could pursue a deal with President Clinton that would probably get them a tax cut, but not as much as they wanted.

They took the former route. Budget writers reserved about $800 billion of the projected surplus over the next 10 years for tax-cutters.

The House Ways and Means Committee used that opportunity to forge an $864 billion tax cut package in July. The bill (HR 2488) included something for every Republican. Among its many provisions were several that conservatives had long waited to consider: a 10 percent across-the-board cut in income tax rates, a phaseout of the estate tax and a reduction in the capital gains tax rate.

The bill achieved one leadership goal — defining differences between the parties. Democrats, even moderates often attracted to tax cuts, vilified the bill as a sop to the rich, and the president repeatedly threatened to veto it.

But as GOP leaders attempted to

move the bill, about 20 moderate Republicans said the measure did not contain what they wanted most — an assurance that tax cuts would not defer paying down the national debt.

With the bill scheduled to come to the House floor the week of July 19, Republican leaders met with the moderates to win support for their plan. And Speaker J. Dennis Hastert, R-Ill., who often refrained from pressuring members on votes, staked his leadership on moving the bill.

Hastert met with wavering members and eventually persuaded Ways and Means Chairman Bill Archer, R-Texas, to accept a provision that conditioned the portion of the 10 percent across-the-board cut scheduled to take place in 2004 on a reduction in the interest accrued on the national debt.

That change, and Archer's decision to trim the bill to the Senate's proposed total tax cut of $792 billion, swayed most moderates back in the leaders' direction. *(Senate key vote, p. C-6)*

When the bill came to the floor July 22, the vote was 223-208: R 217-4; D 6-203 (ND 2-152, SD 4-51); I 0-1. Only four moderate Republicans — Michael N. Castle of Delaware, Greg Ganske of Iowa, Constance A. Morella of Maryland and Jack Quinn of New York — voted against it. Democrats also stayed largely united, with only six moderates voting for the measure. *(House key vote 9, p. C-18)*

On the day of the vote, Hastert said he had asked Republicans to vote for the bill because it was important "for us being able to move forward" as a party. "I just said, 'If you want to be part of the team, this is a pretty important part of the process.' "

422 Campaign Finance

It took six years for those who advocate a revamped system of federal campaign finance to push legislation through the House. But having finally accomplished that goal in the 105th Congress, they were able to replicate it with remarkable exactitude 14 months later.

The key vote was on Sept. 14, when the House passed a bill (HR 417) by Christopher Shays, R-Conn., and Martin T. Meehan, D-Mass. The vote was 252-177: R 54-164; D 197-13 (ND 148-8, SD 49-5); I 1-0. *(House key vote 10, p. C-18)*

The measure has two principal provisions. It would bar the political party committees that underwrite presidential, House and Senate campaigns from taking or spending "soft money," the term for the unlimited and unregulated donations from corporations, unions and wealthy people that are the fastest-growing source of campaign financing. And it would tighten federal regulation of "express advocacy" advertising, in which third-party groups try to sway voters without explicitly calling for a vote for or against anyone.

Shays and Meehan won an identical number of votes for similar legislation in 1998, showing that another round of congressional campaigns fueled by soft money and supplemented by advocate advertising had not changed the chamber's sentiment in favor of limiting either practice. In 1999, as the year before, 58 percent of the House voted for the bill, and both times the measure garnered a comfortable 34 votes beyond a majority. The second time around, 24 percent of Republicans defied their leadership and supported the bill.

To win, Shays and Meehan again had to navigate their legislation through a parliamentary obstacle course set up by GOP leaders, this year by defeating six amendments they called "poison pills" as well as three alternative campaign finance packages.

But there were two small salves this year for the bill's opponents. This year's measure received seven fewer GOP votes than last year's, and only two of the 19 first-term GOP members voted for it. Shays said that — in contrast with the freshmen of the 105th Congress, who pushed their own campaign finance bill — these newcomers were against changing a system from which many have already reaped big donations.

Four lawmakers voted "yes" in 1999 after voting "no" in 1998; three switched to "no" in 1999 from "yes" in 1998.

Still, the vote gave Shays and Meehan what they had said all year they desired: a solid House endorsement of their proposals early enough in the 106th Congress to raise the profile of the issue in the Senate and thereby make it more difficult for vulnerable GOP incumbents there to support a filibuster against the proposals by Shays and Meehan's allies, John McCain, R-Ariz., and Russell D. Feingold, D-Wis.

But a month after House passage, senators rejected attempts to limit debate on both a sweeping and a more narrow bill by McCain and Feingold. *(Senate key vote 11, p. C-7)*

465 Fetal Protection

House Republicans opened a new venue for the abortion debate this fall, pushing to passage legislation that, for the first time, would recognize the fetus under federal law as an entity distinct from the pregnant woman.

Although sponsors of the bill (HR 2436) acknowledged that the National Right to Life Committee had helped draft the language, they said that the measure's purpose was not to restrict abortions. Instead, they said, it was designed to create a new way to punish criminals.

The measure would make it a federal offense to harm an "unborn child" while committing any of 68 existing federal offenses or a crime under military law, regardless of whether the accused intended that harm or even knew the woman was pregnant. Those performing or undergoing an abortion would be explicitly exempt from prosecution.

Still, opponents argued that a vote for the bill was a vote to create a legal rationale for undermining the right to an abortion found by the Supreme Court in its 1973 *Roe v. Wade* decision, which was based in part on the conclusion that "the unborn have never been recognized in the law as persons in the whole sense." The bill defines "unborn child" as a "member of the species homo sapiens, at any stage of development, who is carried in the womb." Abortion rights advocates said that language could be cited in litigation to support the argument that federal law is that life begins at conception.

In explaining the rationale for the bill, sponsors cited the 1995 bombing of an Oklahoma City federal building. Under the bill, the bombers could have been charged not only with killing the three pregnant women inside, but also in the deaths of their fetuses. "A pregnant woman is two special persons, said Henry J. Hyde, R-Ill. "She is carrying a tiny member of the human family."

Opponents proposed an alternative that would have stiffened federal penalties for attacks on pregnant women that resulted in harm to the fetus but would not have recognized the offense as a separate crime. Sponsors of the bill argued that without creating a separate protection for the fetus, criminals would get away with murder. The amendment was defeated, 201-224.

On the key vote, the House overwhelmingly passed the bill on Sept. 30, but the majority would not be sufficient to override the veto promised by President Clinton. The vote was 254-172: R 198-21; D 56-150 (ND 40-113, SD 16-37); I 0-1. *(House key vote 11, p. C-18)*

In announcing its opposition, the Justice Department said the bill may be unconstitutional, and that its identification of a fetus as a separate and distinct victim is both "unprecedented" and "unwise to the extent that it may be perceived as gratuitously plunging the federal government into one of the most — if not the most — difficult and complex issues of religious and scientific consideration."

490 Managed Care

After promising for months to take up legislation to expand protections for 161 million Americans enrolled in private health insurance plans, the House GOP leadership in October finally agreed to bring the issue to a vote. It was a rare instance in which floor consideration of high-profile legislation was unscripted in advance by the leadership.

Speaker J. Dennis Hastert, R-Ill., had been looking for an alternative to a measure sponsored by Charlie Norwood, R-Ga., and John D. Dingell, D-Mich. Right up until Oct. 7, the Speaker's scheduled date for consideration, however, none of the alternatives proposed generated enough enthusiasm to overcome the popularity of the Norwood-Dingell bill. The GOP leadership opposed that measure, mostly because it would allow people to sue their health plans for damages in state courts.

The debate started on Oct. 6 with consideration of a Republican package of tax provisions (HR 2990) designed to ensure access to health insurance. That bill passed along party lines, 227-205.

The following day, the House took up a series of patient protection measures under a rule that made the Norwood-Dingell legislation the base bill. If any of the substitutes won a majority, debate would end and the passed bill would be combined with the tax measure and sent to a conference committee as one bill (HR 2990).

President Clinton and some Democrats had accused the Republican leadership of using the combined-bill rule as a "poison pill" strategy. Democrats, they said, would not want to vote for any managed care bill that would then be combined with a tax package they opposed. It did not turn out that way. When the votes were tallied, three alternatives were defeated, and Norwood-Dingell prevailed. The substitute to receive the most votes, a bill sponsored by Republicans Porter J. Goss of Florida, Tom Coburn of Oklahoma and John Shadegg of Arizona, was defeated 193-238. Some backers of the alternative blamed Hastert because he did not endorse the bill until the day the House voted on the measure.

While passage of the Norwood-Dingell bill was predicted, no one could have guessed the margin: 68 Republicans bucked their leadership position to vote for the bill, which passed 275-151: R 68-149; D 206-2 (ND 153-1, SD 53-1); I 1-0. *(House key vote 12, p. C-18)*

Conferees face the difficult challenge in 2000 of reconciling the House bill with a very different one passed by the Senate in July. *(Senate key vote, p. C-5)*

544 Assisted Suicide

A debate this fall on outlawing doctor assisted suicide forced House Republicans to choose between two fundamental tenets of their party: Federal intrusion into state matters should be limited, and the sanctity of human life should be preserved.

In this case, the GOP overwhelmingly sided with groups — including the National Right to Life Committee — that supported legislation (HR 2260) to effectively overturn a 1997 Oregon law that resulted from a referendum. The only state statute of its kind, it authorizes physicians to prescribe drugs to help terminally ill people end their lives.

When the House passed the bill Oct. 27, only a score of Republicans opposed it, while 90 percent of the House's GOP members supported it. The vote was 271-156: R 200-20; D 71-135 (ND 48-104, SD 23-31); I 0-1. *(House key vote 13, p. C-18)*

The solid majority also suggested the power of the American Medical Association (AMA), which endorsed the measure. Opposition by the doctors' lobby to a similar bill prompted sponsors to shelve the proposal in the 105th Congress.

Several Democratic lawmakers who opposed the bill this year said they were doing so in a bid to defend both state and individual rights. "This is a patients' rights measure — it was so voted by the people," Barney Frank, D-Mass., said of the Oregon law at a Judiciary Committee markup Sept. 14. "Are the patients in control of their own lives or is the federal government going to step in?"

The bill says the attorney general "shall give no force and effect" to any state law permitting assisted suicide. Supporters said helping the sick is a cause worthy of federal action. "It will help protect vulnerable people," said Charles T. Canady, R-Fla. "Facilitating the intentional killing of a human life is the opposite of healing," said Henry J. Hyde, R-Ill.

The bill would allow doctors to prescribe controlled substances to alleviate pain, even if that "may increase the risk of death," and would authorize $5 million annually to promote education and training in pain management for the dying. These "palliative care" provisions helped win over the AMA, and the House defeated amendments that would have essentially limited the legislation to those sections. ◆

Senate Key Votes 1, 2, 3, 4, 5, 6, 7

	1	2	3	4	5	6	7
ALABAMA							
Sessions	N	Y	Y	N	Y	Y	Y
Shelby	N	Y	Y	N	Y	Y	Y
ALASKA							
Murkowski	N	Y	Y	N	N	Y	Y
Stevens	N	Y	Y	N	N	Y	Y
ARIZONA							
Kyl	N	Y	Y	N	Y	Y	Y
McCain	N	Y	Y	N	Y	Y	Y
ARKANSAS							
Hutchinson	N	Y	Y	N	N	Y	Y
Lincoln	Y	N	N	Y	Y	N	N
CALIFORNIA							
Boxer	Y	N	N	Y	Y	N	N
Feinstein	Y	N	N	Y	Y	N	N
COLORADO							
Allard	N	Y	Y	N	N	Y	Y
Campbell	N	Y	Y	N	N	Y	Y
CONNECTICUT							
Dodd	Y	N	N	Y	Y	N	N
Lieberman	Y	N	N	Y	Y	N	N
DELAWARE							
Roth	N	Y	Y	N	Y	Y	Y
Biden	Y	N	N	Y	Y	N	N
FLORIDA							
Mack	N	Y	Y	N	Y	Y	Y
Graham	Y	N	N	Y	Y	N	N
GEORGIA							
Coverdell	N	Y	Y	N	N	Y	Y
Cleland	Y	N	N	Y	N	N	N
HAWAII							
Akaka	Y	N	N	Y	Y	N	N
Inouye	Y	N	N	Y	Y	N	N
IDAHO							
Craig	N	Y	Y	N	N	Y	Y
Crapo	N	Y	Y	N	N	Y	Y
ILLINOIS							
Fitzgerald	N	Y	Y	Y	N	N	Y
Durbin	Y	N	N	Y	N	N	N
INDIANA							
Lugar	N	Y	Y	Y	Y	Y	Y
Bayh	Y	N	N	Y	Y	N	N
IOWA							
Grassley	N	Y	Y	N	N	Y	Y
Harkin	Y	N	N	Y	Y	N	N
KANSAS							
Brownback	N	Y	Y	N	N	Y	Y
Roberts	N	Y	Y	N	N	Y	Y
KENTUCKY							
Bunning	N	Y	Y	N	N	Y	Y
McConnell	N	Y	Y	N	Y	Y	Y
LOUISIANA							
Breaux	Y	N	N	Y	Y	N	Y
Landrieu	Y	N	N	Y	Y	N	Y
MAINE							
Collins	N	N	Y	N	N	Y	Y
Snowe	N	N	Y	N	N	Y	Y
MARYLAND							
Mikulski	Y	N	N	Y	Y	N	N
Sarbanes	Y	N	N	Y	Y	N	N
MASSACHUSETTS							
Kennedy	Y	N	N	Y	Y	N	N
Kerry	Y	N	N	Y	Y	N	N
MICHIGAN							
Abraham	N	Y	Y	N	N	Y	Y
Levin	Y	N	N	Y	Y	N	N
MINNESOTA							
Grams	N	Y	Y	N	N	Y	Y
Wellstone	Y	N	N	Y	N	N	N
MISSISSIPPI							
Cochran	N	Y	Y	N	Y	Y	Y
Lott	N	Y	Y	N	Y	Y	Y
MISSOURI							
Ashcroft	N	Y	Y	N	N	Y	Y
Bond	N	Y	Y	N	N	Y	Y
MONTANA							
Burns	N	Y	Y	N	Y	Y	Y
Baucus	Y	N	N	N	Y	N	N
NEBRASKA							
Hagel	N	Y	Y	N	Y	Y	Y
Kerrey	Y	N	N	Y	Y	N	Y
NEVADA							
Bryan	Y	N	N	Y	Y	N	N
Reid	Y	N	N	Y	Y	N	N
NEW HAMPSHIRE							
Gregg	N	Y	Y	N	N	Y	Y
Smith [1]	N	Y	Y	N	N	Y	Y
NEW JERSEY							
Lautenberg	Y	N	N	Y	Y	N	N
Torricelli	Y	N	N	Y	N	N	Y
NEW MEXICO							
Domenici	N	Y	Y	N	N	Y	Y
Bingaman	Y	N	N	Y	Y	N	N
NEW YORK							
Moynihan	Y	N	N	Y	Y	N	N
Schumer	Y	N	N	Y	Y	N	N
NORTH CAROLINA							
Helms	N	Y	Y	N	N	Y	Y
Edwards	Y	N	N	Y	Y	N	N
NORTH DAKOTA							
Conrad	Y	N	N	Y	N	N	N
Dorgan	Y	N	N	Y	N	N	N
OHIO							
DeWine	N	Y	Y	Y	Y	Y	Y
Voinovich	N	Y	Y	Y	N	Y	N
OKLAHOMA							
Inhofe	N	Y	Y	N	N	Y	Y
Nickles	N	Y	Y	N	N	Y	Y
OREGON							
Smith	N	Y	Y	N	Y	Y	Y
Wyden	Y	N	N	Y	Y	N	N
PENNSYLVANIA							
Santorum	N	Y	Y	N	N	Y	Y
Specter	N	N	Y	N	N	Y	N
RHODE ISLAND							
Chafee	N	N	Y	Y	Y	N	Y
Reed	Y	N	N	Y	Y	N	N
SOUTH CAROLINA							
Thurmond	N	Y	Y	N	N	Y	Y
Hollings	Y	N	N	Y	N	N	N
SOUTH DAKOTA							
Daschle	Y	N	N	Y	Y	N	N
Johnson	Y	N	N	Y	N	N	N
TENNESSEE							
Frist	N	Y	Y	N	N	Y	Y
Thompson	N	Y	Y	N	N	Y	Y
TEXAS							
Gramm	N	Y	Y	N	N	Y	Y
Hutchison	N	Y	Y	N	N	Y	Y
UTAH							
Bennett	N	Y	Y	N	N	Y	Y
Hatch	N	Y	Y	N	Y	Y	Y
VERMONT							
Jeffords	N	N	Y	N	N	Y	Y
Leahy	Y	N	N	Y	Y	N	N
VIRGINIA							
Warner	N	Y	Y	Y	Y	Y	Y
Robb	Y	N	N	Y	Y	N	N
WASHINGTON							
Gorton	N	Y	Y	N	N	Y	Y
Murray	Y	N	?	Y	Y	N	N
WEST VIRGINIA							
Byrd	Y	N	N	Y	N	N	N
Rockefeller	Y	N	N	Y	Y	N	N
WISCONSIN							
Feingold	N	N	N	Y	N	N	N
Kohl	Y	N	N	Y	Y	N	N
WYOMING							
Enzi	N	Y	Y	N	N	Y	Y
Thomas	N	Y	Y	N	N	Y	Y

ND Northern Democrats SD Southern Democrats

Southern states - Ala., Ark., Fla., Ga., Ky., La., Miss., N.C., Okla., S.C., Tenn., Texas, Va.

Key

- Y Voted for (yea).
- # Paired for.
- + Announced for.
- N Voted against (nay).
- X Paired against.
- – Announced against.
- P Voted "present."
- C Voted "present" to avoid possible conflict of interest.
- ? Did not vote or otherwise make a position known.

Democrats • ***Republicans***
Independents

Following are Senate votes from 1999 selected by Congressional Quarterly as key votes. Original roll call vote number is in parentheses.

1. Impeachment of President Clinton/Motion To Dismiss. Byrd, D-W.Va., motion to dismiss impeachment proceedings against President Clinton. Motion rejected 44-56: R 0-55; D 44-1 (ND 36-1, SD 8-0). Jan. 27, 1999. *(Senate vote 4)*

2. Impeachment of President Clinton/Article II — Obstruction of Justice. Conviction on Article II, which would find President Clinton guilty of obstruction of justice, concealing evidence and delaying proceedings in the Paula Jones federal sexual harassment civil lawsuit. Acquitted 50-50: R 50-5; D 0-45 (ND 0-37, SD 0-8). Feb. 12, 1999. A two-thirds majority of those present and voting (67 in this case) is required to convict the president and remove him from office. A "nay" was a vote in support of the president's position. *(Senate vote 18)*

3. S 280. Educational Flexibility/New Teachers. Jeffords, R-Vt., motion to table (kill) the Murray, D-Wash., amendment. The Murray amendment would authorize $11.4 billion over six years to fund President Clinton's proposal to hire 100,000 new teachers to reduce class size. Motion agreed to 55-44: R 55-0; D 0-44 (ND 0-36, SD 0-8). March 11, 1999. A "nay" was a vote in support of the president's position. *(Senate vote 41)*

4. S 254. Juvenile Crime/Gun Show Checks. Lautenberg, D-N.J., amendment to require criminal background checks on all gun sales at gun shows, bar non-federal licensees from transferring a firearm to a buyer at gun shows and direct the U.S. attorney general to destroy background records within 90 days for purchasers who can legally purchase a firearm. Adopted 51-50: R 6-49; D 44-1 (ND 36-1, SD 8-0), with Vice President Gore casting a "yea" vote. May 20, 1999. A "yea" was a vote in support of the president's position. *(Senate vote 134)*

5. S 1059. Fiscal 2000 Defense Authorization/Ground Troops in Kosovo. Warner, R-Va., motion to table (kill) the Specter, R-Pa., amendment that would bar the use of Defense Department funds for deployment of U.S. ground troops in Yugoslavia, except for peacekeeping personnel, unless Congress declares war or enacts a joint resolution authorizing the use of military force. Motion agreed to 52-48: R 17-38; D 35-10 (ND 29-8, SD 6-2). May 25, 1999. A "yea" was a vote in support of the president's position. *(Senate vote 145)*

6. S 1344. Managed Care Revisions/Passage. Passage of the bill to provide federal protections, such as access to emergency care, continuing care and approved clinical cancer trials, primarily for those in self-insured health plans. The bill also would create internal and external appeals processes, bar denials based on predictive genetic data, allow self-employed individuals to deduct the full cost of health insurance premiums and expand access to medical savings accounts. Passed 53-47: R 52-2; D 0-45 (ND 0-37, SD 0-8); I 1-0. July 15, 1999. (Before passage, the Senate adopted a Lott, R-Miss., substitute amendment by voice vote.) A "nay" was a vote in support of the president's position. *(Senate vote 210)*

7. S 1429. Tax Package/Passage. Passage of the bill to reduce federal taxes by $792 billion over 10 years. The measure would reduce the lowest income tax bracket from 15 percent to 14 percent beginning in 2001, increase the maximum income levels for the lowest bracket, allow couples to calculate their taxes as individuals on the same form, reduce estate and gift taxes, increase the annual amount transferable to an Individual Retirement Account and extend the research and development tax credit. Passed 57-43: R 52-2; D 4-41 (ND 2-35, SD 2-6); I 1-0. July 30, 1999. A "nay" was a vote in support of the president's position. *(Senate vote 247)*

[1] *Robert C. Smith, N.H., switched his party affiliation from Republican to Independent on July 13. He switched back on Nov. 1.*

Senate key votes continued on p. C-20

House Key Votes 1, 2, 3, 4, 5, 6, 7

Following are House votes from 1999 selected by Congressional Quarterly as key votes. Original roll call vote number is in parentheses.

1. HR 975. Steel Imports/Passage. Passage of the bill to direct the president, within 60 days of enactment, to take necessary steps — including imposing quotas, tariff surcharges or negotiated enforceable voluntary export restraints — to ensure that the volume of steel products imported into the United States (based on tonnage) during any month does not exceed the average of monthly import volumes during the three years preceding July 1997. Passed 289-141: R 91-128; D 197-13 (ND 146-9, SD 51-4); I 1-0. March 17, 1999. A "nay" was a vote in support of the president's position. *(House vote 56)*

2. HR 4. Anti-Missile Defense/Recommit. Allen, D-Maine, motion to recommit the bill to the Armed Services Committee with instructions to report it back with an amendment that it is the policy of the United States to deploy a missile defense system that is demonstrated to be effective, does not diminish overall national security by jeopardizing other efforts to reduce threats to the United States, is affordable and does not compromise U.S. ability to provide for other military priorities. Motion rejected 152-269: R 2-212; D 150-56 (ND 125-28, SD 25-28); I 0-1. March 18, 1999. *(House vote 58)*

3. S Con Res 21. Kosovo Conflict — Air Operation/Adoption. Adoption of the concurrent resolution to authorize military air operations and missile strikes against Yugoslavia. Rejected 213-213: R 31-187; D 181-26 (ND 131-21, SD 50-5); I 1-0. April 28, 1999. A "yea" was a vote in support of the president's position. *(House vote 103)*

4. HR 1000. FAA Reauthorization/Off-Budget Funds. Young, R-Fla., amendment to strike the provisions of the bill that would take the Airport and Airway Trust Fund off budget and thereby permit all aviation tax revenue to be spent on aviation programs, exempt from budgetary restrictions but still subject to annual appropriations. Rejected 179-248: R 111-108; D 68-139 (ND 49-106, SD 19-33); I 0-1. June 15, 1999. *(House vote 207)*

5. HR 1501. Juvenile Justice/Media Violence. Hyde, R-Ill., amendment to prohibit the sale, loan or exhibition to juveniles of any material that contains sexual or violent depictions or detailed verbal descriptions, including any picture, drawing, sculpture, video game, motion picture, book, magazine or sound recording. Offenders would face fines and/or up to five years in prison for a first offense and 10 years for a second offense. Rejected 146-282: R 127-92; D 19-189 (ND 10-143, SD 9-46); I 0-1. June 16, 1999. *(House vote 213)*

6. HR 2122. Gun Shows/Passage. Passage of the bill to require background checks for purchasers at gun shows, defined as any event with 10 or more vendors and where 50 or more guns are offered for sale; background checks would have to be completed in 24 hours; gun show organizers would be required to destroy background records of those who pass background checks. Rejected 147-280: R 137-82; D 10-197 (ND 6-146, SD 4-51); I 0-1. June 18, 1999. *(House vote 244)*

7. HR 10. Financial Services Overhaul/Passage. Passage of the bill to eliminate barriers against cross ownership among banks, securities firms, insurance companies and other firms. The bill would prohibit banks from selling private customer financial information to telemarketing firms and allow customers to "opt out" of having information shared with other companies; allow mutual insurance companies to move their businesses to a different state when reorganizing into a stock company; and bar financial companies from conditioning the sale of products on the purchase of other financial products. Passed 343-86: R 205-16; D 138-69 (ND 95-58, SD 43-11); I 0-1, July 1, 1999. *(House vote 276)*

[1] *David Vitter, R-La., was sworn in June 8, replacing Robert L. Livingston, R-La., who resigned effective Feb. 28, 1999.*

Key

- Y Voted for (yea).
- # Paired for.
- \+ Announced for.
- N Voted against (nay).
- X Paired against.
- – Announced against.
- P Voted "present."
- C Voted "present" to avoid possible conflict of interest.
- ? Did not vote or otherwise make a position known.

•

Democrats ***Republicans***
Independents

	1	2	3	4	5	6	7
ALABAMA							
1 ***Callahan***	Y	N	Y	Y	Y	N	Y
2 ***Everett***	Y	N	N	Y	Y	N	Y
3 ***Riley***	Y	N	Y	Y	Y	N	Y
4 ***Aderholt***	Y	N	?	Y	Y	N	Y
5 Cramer	Y	N	Y	Y	N	N	Y
6 ***Bachus***	Y	N	N	N	Y	N	Y
7 Hilliard	Y	Y	Y	N	N	N	N
ALASKA							
AL ***Young***	Y	N	N	N	N	N	Y
ARIZONA							
1 ***Salmon***	N	N	N	Y	N	?	Y
2 Pastor	Y	Y	Y	Y	N	N	Y
3 ***Stump***	N	N	N	Y	Y	N	Y
4 ***Shadegg***	N	N	N	Y	Y	N	Y
5 ***Kolbe***	N	N	Y	Y	N	Y	Y
6 ***Hayworth***	N	N	N	Y	N	N	Y
ARKANSAS							
1 Berry	Y	Y	Y	N	N	N	Y
2 Snyder	Y	N	Y	Y	N	N	Y
3 ***Hutchinson***	N	N	N	N	N	Y	Y
4 ***Dickey***	Y	N	N	Y	N	N	Y
CALIFORNIA							
1 Thompson	Y	Y	Y	N	N	N	Y
2 ***Herger***	N	N	N	Y	Y	N	Y
3 ***Ose***	N	N	N	Y	N	N	Y
4 ***Doolittle***	N	?	N	N	N	N	Y
5 Matsui	Y	Y	Y	N	N	N	Y
6 Woolsey	Y	Y	N	N	N	N	N
7 Miller, George	Y	Y	Y	Y	N	N	N
8 Pelosi	Y	Y	Y	Y	N	N	?
9 Lee	Y	N	N	N	N	N	N
10 Tauscher	Y	N	Y	N	N	N	Y
11 ***Pombo***	Y	N	N	N	N	N	Y
12 Lantos	Y	Y	Y	N	N	N	N
13 Stark	Y	+	N	N	N	N	N
14 Eshoo	N	Y	Y	Y	N	N	N
15 ***Campbell***	N	N	N	N	N	N	N
16 Lofgren	N	Y	N	Y	N	N	N
17 Farr	Y	Y	Y	Y	N	N	N
18 Condit	Y	N	N	Y	N	N	N
19 ***Radanovich***	N	N	N	N	Y	Y	Y
20 Dooley	N	Y	Y	Y	N	N	Y
21 ***Thomas***	N	N	N	Y	?	?	Y
22 Capps	Y	Y	Y	N	N	N	N
23 ***Gallegly***	Y	N	N	N	Y	Y	Y
24 Sherman	Y	Y	Y	N	N	N	Y
25 ***McKeon***	N	–	N	Y	Y	Y	Y
26 Berman	N	Y	Y	Y	N	–	Y
27 ***Rogan***	Y	N	N	Y	N	Y	Y
28 ***Dreier***	N	N	N	Y	N	Y	Y
29 Waxman	Y	Y	Y	Y	N	N	N
30 Becerra	Y	Y	Y	Y	N	N	Y
31 Martinez	Y	Y	Y	N	N	N	N
32 Dixon	Y	Y	Y	Y	N	N	Y
33 Roybal-Allard	Y	Y	Y	Y	N	N	N
34 Napolitano	Y	Y	Y	N	N	N	Y
35 Waters	Y	Y	Y	N	N	N	N
36 ***Kuykendall***	N	N	N	N	N	Y	Y
37 Millender-McD.	Y	Y	Y	N	N	N	Y
38 ***Horn***	Y	N	N	N	Y	Y	Y
39 ***Royce***	N	N	N	Y	N	Y	Y
40 ***Lewis***	N	N	N	Y	N	?	Y
41 ***Miller***	N	N	N	N	Y	Y	Y
42 Brown	Y	Y	Y	?	?	?	?
43 ***Calvert***	N	N	N	Y	Y	Y	Y
44 ***Bono***	N	N	N	N	N	Y	Y
45 ***Rohrabacher***	N	N	N	Y	N	Y	Y
46 Sanchez	Y	Y	Y	N	N	N	Y
47 ***Cox***	N	N	N	Y	N	Y	Y
48 ***Packard***	N	N	N	Y	Y	Y	Y
49 ***Bilbray***	N	N	N	N	Y	N	Y
50 Filner	Y	Y	Y	N	N	N	N
51 ***Cunningham***	N	N	N	Y	Y	Y	Y
52 ***Hunter***	Y	N	Y	Y	Y	Y	Y
COLORADO							
1 DeGette	Y	Y	N	N	N	N	N
2 Udall	Y	Y	Y	N	N	N	Y
3 ***McInnis***	Y	N	N	Y	N	N	Y
4 ***Schaffer***	N	N	N	Y	N	N	Y
5 ***Hefley***	Y	N	N	Y	Y	N	N
6 ***Tancredo***	N	N	N	Y	Y	Y	N
CONNECTICUT							
1 Larson	Y	N	Y	N	N	N	Y
2 Gejdenson	Y	Y	Y	N	N	N	N
3 DeLauro	Y	Y	Y	Y	N	N	N
4 ***Shays***	N	N	N	Y	Y	N	Y
5 Maloney	Y	N	Y	N	Y	N	Y
6 ***Johnson***	N	N	N	Y	Y	N	Y
DELAWARE							
AL ***Castle***	N	N	Y	Y	N	N	Y
FLORIDA							
1 ***Scarborough***	N	N	N	Y	N	N	Y
2 Boyd	Y	N	Y	Y	N	N	Y
3 Brown	Y	Y	Y	N	N	N	Y
4 ***Fowler***	N	N	N	N	N	Y	Y
5 Thurman	Y	Y	Y	Y	N	N	N
6 ***Stearns***	Y	N	N	Y	Y	Y	Y
7 ***Mica***	Y	N	N	N	Y	N	N
8 ***McCollum***	N	N	N	N	N	Y	Y
9 ***Bilirakis***	Y	N	N	Y	Y	Y	Y
10 ***Young***	Y	N	N	Y	Y	Y	Y
11 Davis	N	N	Y	Y	N	N	Y
12 ***Canady***	N	N	N	Y	Y	Y	Y
13 ***Miller***	N	N	N	Y	N	Y	Y
14 ***Goss***	N	N	N	Y	N	Y	Y
15 ***Weldon***	N	N	N	N	Y	Y	Y
16 ***Foley***	N	N	N	Y	N	Y	Y
17 Meek	Y	Y	Y	N	N	N	Y
18 ***Ros-Lehtinen***	Y	N	N	N	N	Y	Y
19 Wexler	Y	N	Y	N	N	N	Y
20 Deutsch	Y	N	Y	N	N	N	Y
21 ***Diaz-Balart***	Y	N	Y	N	N	Y	Y
22 ***Shaw***	N	N	N	Y	N	Y	Y
23 Hastings	Y	Y	Y	N	N	N	Y
GEORGIA							
1 ***Kingston***	N	N	N	Y	Y	Y	Y
2 Bishop	Y	N	Y	N	N	N	Y
3 ***Collins***	Y	N	N	N	Y	N	Y
4 McKinney	Y	Y	N	N	N	N	N
5 Lewis	Y	Y	Y	?	N	N	N
6 ***Isakson***	N	N	N	N	Y	Y	Y
7 ***Barr***	Y	N	N	N	N	Y	Y
8 ***Chambliss***	N	N	N	Y	Y	N	Y
9 ***Deal***	N	N	N	N	Y	N	Y
10 ***Norwood***	Y	N	N	N	Y	Y	Y
11 ***Linder***	N	N	N	Y	N	Y	Y
HAWAII							
1 Abercrombie	Y	N	N	N	N	N	N
2 Mink	Y	Y	N	N	N	N	N
IDAHO							
1 ***Chenoweth-Hage***	Y	N	N	N	Y	N	N
2 ***Simpson***	N	N	N	N	Y	Y	Y
ILLINOIS							
1 Rush	Y	Y	Y	N	N	N	Y
2 Jackson	Y	Y	N	Y	N	N	N
3 Lipinski	Y	N	N	N	Y	Y	?
4 Gutierrez	Y	Y	Y	N	N	N	Y
5 Blagojevich	Y	Y	?	N	N	N	Y
6 ***Hyde***	N	N	Y	Y	Y	Y	Y
7 Davis	Y	Y	Y	N	–	N	Y
8 ***Crane***	N	N	N	N	N	Y	Y
9 Schakowsky	Y	Y	Y	N	N	N	N
10 ***Porter***	N	N	Y	Y	N	N	Y
11 ***Weller***	Y	N	N	Y	N	Y	Y
12 Costello	Y	Y	Y	N	N	N	N
13 ***Biggert***	N	N	N	Y	N	Y	Y
14 ***Hastert***			Y			Y	Y

ND Northern Democrats SD Southern Democrats

		2	3	4	5	6	7
15 ***Ewing***	Y	N	N	N	Y	Y	Y
16 ***Manzullo***	N	N	N	N	N	Y	Y
17 Evans	Y	Y	Y	N	N	N	N
18 ***LaHood***	N	N	N	N	Y	Y	N
19 Phelps	Y	N	Y	N	N	Y	N
20 ***Shimkus***	Y	N	N	N	Y	N	Y
INDIANA							
1 Visclosky	Y	N	N	Y	N	N	Y
2 ***McIntosh***	Y	N	N	Y	Y	N	Y
3 Roemer	Y	N	Y	Y	N	N	Y
4 ***Souder***	Y	N	N	N	Y	N	Y
5 ***Buyer***	Y	?	N	N	Y	N	Y
6 ***Burton***	Y	–	N	N	N	Y	Y
7 ***Pease***	Y	N	N	N	N	N	Y
8 ***Hostettler***	Y	N	N	?	Y	N	Y
9 Hill	Y	Y	Y	N	N	N	Y
10 Carson	Y	Y	Y	N	N	N	Y
IOWA							
1 ***Leach***	N	N	N	N	N	N	Y
2 ***Nussle***	Y	N	N	N	N	Y	Y
3 Boswell	Y	N	Y	N	N	N	Y
4 ***Ganske***	Y	N	N	N	N	N	Y
5 ***Latham***	N	N	N	Y	N	Y	Y
KANSAS							
1 ***Moran***	N	N	N	N	N	N	N
2 ***Ryun***	N	N	N	Y	Y	N	Y
3 Moore	Y	N	Y	N	N	N	Y
4 ***Tiahrt***	N	N	N	Y	Y	N	Y
KENTUCKY							
1 ***Whitfield***	Y	N	N	N	Y	N	Y
2 ***Lewis***	Y	N	N	N	Y	N	Y
3 ***Northup***	N	N	N	N	N	Y	Y
4 Lucas	Y	N	Y	N	Y	N	Y
5 ***Rogers***	Y	N	N	Y	Y	Y	Y
6 ***Fletcher***	N	N	N	N	N	Y	Y
LOUISIANA							
1 ***Vitter***[1]				N	Y	N	Y
2 Jefferson	Y	Y	Y	?	N	N	Y
3 ***Tauzin***	N	N	?	N	N	Y	Y
4 ***McCrery***	N	N	N	Y	Y	Y	Y
5 ***Cooksey***	N	Y	N	N	N	N	Y
6 ***Baker***	N	N	N	N	Y	Y	Y
7 John	N	N	Y	N	N	N	Y
MAINE							
1 Allen	Y	Y	Y	N	N	N	Y
2 Baldacci	Y	Y	Y	N	N	N	Y
MARYLAND							
1 ***Gilchrest***	Y	N	Y	N	Y	Y	Y
2 ***Ehrlich***	Y	N	Y	Y	N	Y	Y
3 Cardin	Y	Y	Y	Y	N	N	Y
4 Wynn	Y	Y	+	N	N	N	Y
5 Hoyer	Y	N	Y	Y	N	N	Y
6 ***Bartlett***	Y	N	N	N	Y	Y	Y
7 Cummings	Y	Y	Y	N	N	N	N
8 ***Morella***	N	Y	Y	Y	N	N	Y
MASSACHUSETTS							
1 Olver	Y	Y	Y	Y	N	N	N
2 Neal	Y	Y	Y	N	N	N	Y
3 McGovern	Y	Y	Y	N	N	N	Y
4 Frank	Y	Y	Y	N	N	N	N
5 Meehan	Y	Y	Y	Y	N	N	N
6 Tierney	Y	Y	Y	N	N	N	N
7 Markey	Y	Y	Y	N	N	N	N
8 Capuano	Y	Y	Y	N	N	N	N
9 Moakley	Y	Y	Y	N	N	N	Y
10 Delahunt	Y	Y	Y	N	N	N	N
MICHIGAN							
1 Stupak	Y	?	Y	N	N	N	N
2 ***Hoekstra***	N	N	N	Y	N	Y	N
3 ***Ehlers***	N	N	N	N	Y	Y	Y
4 ***Camp***	N	N	N	N	N	Y	Y
5 Barcia	Y	N	Y	N	N	N	Y
6 ***Upton***	N	N	N	N	Y	N	Y
7 ***Smith***	N	N	N	Y	Y	Y	Y
8 Stabenow	Y	Y	Y	N	N	N	Y
9 Kildee	Y	Y	Y	N	N	N	Y
10 Bonior	Y	Y	Y	N	N	N	Y
11 ***Knollenberg***	N	N	Y	N	Y	Y	Y
12 Levin	N	Y	Y	Y	N	N	Y
13 Rivers	Y	Y	N	N	N	N	N
14 Conyers	Y	Y	Y	Y	N	N	N
15 Kilpatrick	Y	Y	Y	N	N	N	Y
16 Dingell	Y	Y	Y	N	N	N	N
MINNESOTA							
1 ***Gutknecht***	Y	N	N	N	Y	Y	Y
2 Minge	Y	Y	Y	Y	N	–	Y
3 ***Ramstad***	N	N	N	Y	Y	N	Y
4 Vento	+	Y	Y	Y	N	N	Y
5 Sabo	Y	Y	Y	Y	N	N	Y
6 Luther	Y	Y	Y	Y	N	N	N
7 Peterson	Y	N	N	N	Y	N	N
8 Oberstar	Y	Y	Y	N	N	N	Y
MISSISSIPPI							
1 ***Wicker***	N	N	N	Y	Y	Y	Y
2 Thompson	Y	Y	Y	Y	N	N	Y
3 ***Pickering***	N	N	N	Y	Y	Y	Y
4 Shows	Y	N	Y	N	Y	N	Y
5 Taylor	Y	N	N	N	Y	Y	N
MISSOURI							
1 Clay	Y	Y	Y	N	N	N	N
2 ***Talent***	N	N	N	N	Y	Y	Y
3 Gephardt	Y	Y	Y	N	N	N	Y
4 Skelton	Y	Y	Y	Y	Y	N	Y
5 McCarthy	Y	+	Y	N	N	N	N
6 Danner	Y	Y	N	N	N	N	Y
7 ***Blunt***	N	N	N	Y	Y	Y	Y
8 ***Emerson***	Y	N	N	Y	Y	N	Y
9 ***Hulshof***	N	N	N	Y	N	N	Y
MONTANA							
AL ***Hill***	N	N	N	N	Y	N	Y
NEBRASKA							
1 ***Bereuter***	N	N	N	N	Y	Y	Y
2 ***Terry***	N	N	N	N	N	Y	Y
3 ***Barrett***	N	N	N	Y	N	Y	Y
NEVADA							
1 Berkley	Y	Y	Y	N	N	N	Y
2 ***Gibbons***	Y	N	N	Y	N	N	Y
NEW HAMPSHIRE							
1 ***Sununu***	N	N	N	Y	N	Y	Y
2 ***Bass***	N	N	N	N	N	Y	Y
NEW JERSEY							
1 Andrews	Y	N	Y	N	N	N	Y
2 ***LoBiondo***	Y	N	N	N	Y	Y	Y
3 ***Saxton***	N	N	N	N	Y	Y	Y
4 ***Smith***	Y	N	N	N	Y	N	Y
5 ***Roukema***	Y	N	N	Y	Y	N	Y
6 Pallone	Y	Y	Y	N	N	N	Y
7 ***Franks***	Y	N	Y	N	Y	Y	Y
8 Pascrell	Y	N	Y	N	N	–	Y
9 Rothman	Y	Y	Y	N	N	N	Y
10 Payne	Y	Y	Y	N	N	N	N
11 ***Frelinghuysen***	N	N	Y	Y	Y	N	Y
12 Holt	Y	Y	Y	Y	N	N	Y
13 Menendez	Y	Y	Y	N	N	N	Y
NEW MEXICO							
1 ***Wilson***	N	N	N	N	Y	Y	Y
2 ***Skeen***	Y	N	N	Y	N	Y	Y
3 Udall	Y	Y	Y	N	N	N	Y
NEW YORK							
1 ***Forbes***	Y	N	Y	N	N	N	Y
2 ***Lazio***	Y	N	N	Y	Y	Y	Y
3 ***King***	Y	N	N	Y	N	N	Y
4 McCarthy	Y	Y	Y	N	N	N	Y
5 Ackerman	Y	Y	Y	N	N	N	Y
6 Meeks	Y	Y	Y	N	N	N	Y
7 Crowley	Y	Y	Y	N	N	N	Y
8 Nadler	Y	Y	Y	N	N	N	N
9 Weiner	Y	Y	Y	N	–	N	Y
10 Towns	Y	Y	N	N	N	N	Y
11 Owens	Y	Y	Y	N	N	N	Y
12 Velázquez	Y	Y	Y	N	N	N	Y
13 ***Fossella***	N	N	N	Y	N	Y	+
14 Maloney	Y	Y	Y	N	N	N	Y
15 Rangel	Y	Y	Y	N	N	N	Y
16 Serrano	Y	Y	N	Y	N	N	N
17 Engel	Y	Y	Y	N	N	N	Y
18 Lowey	Y	Y	Y	Y	N	N	Y
19 ***Kelly***	Y	N	N	Y	N	Y	Y
20 ***Gilman***	Y	N	Y	N	N	N	Y
21 McNulty	Y	Y	Y	N	N	N	Y
22 ***Sweeney***	Y	N	N	N	Y	Y	Y
23 ***Boehlert***	Y	N	Y	N	Y	N	Y
24 ***McHugh***	Y	N	Y	N	Y	Y	Y
25 ***Walsh***	Y	N	Y	Y	N	Y	Y
26 Hinchey	Y	Y	Y	Y	N	N	N
27 ***Reynolds***	N	N	N	N	Y	Y	Y
28 Slaughter	Y	N	+	N	N	N	Y
29 LaFalce	Y	Y	Y	Y	N	N	Y
30 ***Quinn***	Y	N	Y	N	N	Y	Y
31 ***Houghton***	N	N	Y	?	?	Y	Y
NORTH CAROLINA							
1 Clayton	Y	Y	Y	Y	N	N	Y
2 Etheridge	Y	N	Y	Y	N	N	Y
3 ***Jones***	Y	N	N	Y	Y	N	Y
4 Price	Y	Y	Y	Y	N	N	Y
5 ***Burr***	N	N	N	Y	N	N	Y
6 ***Coble***	Y	N	N	N	N	Y	Y
7 McIntyre	Y	N	Y	N	Y	N	Y
8 ***Hayes***	Y	N	Y	N	Y	N	Y
9 ***Myrick***	+	–	N	Y	N	Y	Y
10 ***Ballenger***	N	N	N	Y	N	Y	Y
11 ***Taylor***	N	N	N	Y	Y	Y	Y
12 Watt	Y	Y	Y	Y	N	N	Y
NORTH DAKOTA							
AL Pomeroy	Y	Y	Y	N	N	N	Y
OHIO							
1 ***Chabot***	N	N	N	Y	Y	N	Y
2 ***Portman***	N	N	N	Y	Y	Y	Y
3 Hall	Y	Y	Y	Y	Y	N	Y
4 ***Oxley***	N	N	Y	Y	Y	Y	Y
5 ***Gillmor***	Y	N	N	Y	Y	Y	Y
6 Strickland	Y	Y	Y	N	N	N	Y
7 ***Hobson***	Y	N	N	Y	Y	Y	Y
8 ***Boehner***	N	?	N	Y	N	Y	Y
9 Kaptur	Y	Y	Y	Y	N	N	N
10 Kucinich	Y	N	N	N	N	N	N
11 Jones	Y	Y	Y	N	N	N	Y
12 ***Kasich***	Y	N	N	Y	?	Y	Y
13 Brown	Y	Y	Y	Y	N	N	N
14 Sawyer	Y	Y	Y	Y	N	N	Y
15 ***Pryce***	N	N	N	?	N	Y	Y
16 ***Regula***	Y	N	N	Y	Y	Y	Y
17 Traficant	Y	N	Y	N	Y	Y	Y
18 ***Ney***	Y	N	N	N	N	N	Y
19 ***LaTourette***	Y	N	N	N	N	Y	Y
OKLAHOMA							
1 ***Largent***	Y	N	N	N	Y	Y	Y
2 ***Coburn***	Y	–	N	Y	Y	N	N
3 ***Watkins***	N	N	N	Y	Y	Y	Y
4 ***Watts***	N	N	N	N	Y	Y	Y
5 ***Istook***	N	N	N	Y	Y	N	Y
6 ***Lucas***	N	N	N	N	Y	N	Y
OREGON							
1 Wu	Y	Y	Y	Y	N	N	Y
2 ***Walden***	N	N	N	N	Y	Y	Y
3 Blumenauer	Y	Y	Y	N	N	N	Y
4 DeFazio	Y	Y	N	N	N	N	N
5 Hooley	Y	Y	Y	N	N	N	Y
PENNSYLVANIA							
1 Brady	Y	N	Y	N	N	N	N
2 Fattah	Y	Y	Y	N	N	N	N
3 Borski	Y	Y	Y	N	N	N	Y
4 Klink	Y	Y	Y	N	N	N	Y
5 ***Peterson***	Y	N	N	N	Y	N	Y
6 Holden	Y	N	Y	N	Y	N	Y
7 ***Weldon***	Y	N	N	N	Y	Y	Y
8 ***Greenwood***	Y	N	Y	N	Y	Y	Y
9 ***Shuster***	Y	N	?	N	Y	Y	Y
10 ***Sherwood***	Y	N	N	N	Y	N	Y
11 Kanjorski	Y	Y	Y	N	N	N	Y
12 Murtha	Y	N	Y	Y	N	N	Y
13 Hoeffel	Y	Y	Y	Y	N	N	Y
14 Coyne	Y	Y	Y	N	N	N	N
15 ***Toomey***	Y	N	N	Y	N	Y	Y
16 ***Pitts***	?	N	N	Y	Y	Y	Y
17 ***Gekas***	Y	N	N	N	N	Y	Y
18 Doyle	Y	N	Y	N	N	N	Y
19 ***Goodling***	Y	N	N	N	Y	Y	Y
20 Mascara	Y	N	Y	N	N	N	Y
21 ***English***	Y	N	N	N	Y	Y	Y
RHODE ISLAND							
1 Kennedy	Y	Y	Y	N	N	N	Y
2 Weygand	Y	Y	Y	Y	N	N	Y
SOUTH CAROLINA							
1 ***Sanford***	N	N	N	Y	N	N	Y
2 ***Spence***	N	N	N	N	Y	Y	Y
3 ***Graham***	Y	N	N	Y	N	Y	Y
4 ***DeMint***	N	N	N	N	Y	Y	Y
5 Spratt	Y	P	Y	Y	N	N	Y
6 Clyburn	Y	?	Y	Y	N	N	Y
SOUTH DAKOTA							
AL ***Thune***	N	N	N	N	N	N	Y
TENNESSEE							
1 ***Jenkins***	Y	N	N	N	Y	N	Y
2 ***Duncan***	Y	N	N	N	Y	Y	Y
3 ***Wamp***	Y	N	N	Y	N	N	Y
4 ***Hilleary***	Y	N	N	N	Y	N	Y
5 Clement	Y	N	Y	N	Y	Y	Y
6 Gordon	Y	N	Y	N	N	N	Y
7 ***Bryant***	Y	N	N	N	Y	Y	Y
8 Tanner	Y	N	Y	N	N	Y	Y
9 Ford	Y	Y	Y	N	N	N	Y
TEXAS							
1 Sandlin	Y	Y	Y	N	N	N	Y
2 Turner	Y	N	Y	N	Y	N	N
3 ***Johnson, Sam***	N	N	N	Y	Y	N	Y
4 Hall	N	N	N	Y	Y	N	Y
5 ***Sessions***	N	N	N	Y	Y	Y	Y
6 ***Barton***	N	N	N	Y	Y	N	N
7 ***Archer***	N	N	N	Y	Y	Y	?
8 ***Brady***	N	N	N	N	Y	N	N
9 Lampson	Y	Y	Y	N	N	N	N
10 Doggett	Y	Y	N	Y	N	N	Y
11 Edwards	Y	Y	Y	Y	N	N	N
12 ***Granger***	N	N	N	Y	Y	Y	N
13 ***Thornberry***	N	N	N	Y	N	N	N
14 ***Paul***	N	N	N	N	N	N	N
15 Hinojosa	Y	Y	Y	N	N	N	Y
16 Reyes	Y	N	Y	N	N	N	Y
17 Stenholm	Y	N	Y	Y	Y	N	N
18 Jackson-Lee	Y	Y	Y	N	N	N	Y
19 ***Combest***	N	N	N	N	Y	N	N
20 Gonzalez	Y	Y	Y	N	N	N	Y
21 ***Smith***	N	N	N	Y	Y	Y	Y
22 ***DeLay***	N	N	N	Y	Y	Y	Y
23 ***Bonilla***	N	N	N	Y	N	?	N
24 Frost	Y	Y	Y	N	N	N	Y
25 Bentsen	Y	Y	Y	Y	N	N	Y
26 ***Armey***	N	N	N	Y	Y	Y	Y
27 Ortiz	Y	N	Y	N	N	N	N
28 Rodriguez	Y	Y	Y	Y	N	N	N
29 Green	Y	N	Y	N	N	N	+
30 Johnson, E.B.	Y	Y	Y	N	N	N	Y
UTAH							
1 ***Hansen***	Y	N	?	N	Y	Y	Y
2 ***Cook***	Y	N	N	N	Y	Y	Y
3 ***Cannon***	Y	N	N	N	N	Y	Y
VERMONT							
AL *Sanders*	Y	N	Y	N	N	N	N
VIRGINIA							
1 ***Bateman***	N	N	N	N	N	Y	Y
2 Pickett	Y	N	Y	N	N	N	Y
3 Scott	Y	N	Y	N	N	N	Y
4 Sisisky	Y	N	Y	N	N	Y	Y
5 Goode	Y	N	N	N	Y	N	Y
6 ***Goodlatte***	N	N	N	Y	Y	Y	Y
7 ***Bliley***	N	N	Y	Y	Y	Y	Y
8 Moran	N	N	Y	Y	N	N	Y
9 Boucher	Y	N	Y	?	N	N	Y
10 ***Wolf***	N	N	Y	Y	Y	Y	Y
11 ***Davis***	N	N	Y	N	N	Y	Y
WASHINGTON							
1 Inslee	Y	Y	N	N	N	N	N
2 ***Metcalf***	Y	N	N	N	Y	N	Y
3 Baird	Y	Y	Y	N	N	N	Y
4 ***Hastings***	N	N	N	N	N	N	Y
5 ***Nethercutt***	N	N	N	Y	N	N	Y
6 Dicks	N	Y	Y	Y	N	N	Y
7 McDermott	N	Y	Y	N	N	N	N
8 ***Dunn***	N	N	N	Y	N	Y	Y
9 Smith	N	N	Y	Y	N	Y	Y
WEST VIRGINIA							
1 Mollohan	Y	N	?	Y	Y	N	Y
2 Wise	Y	N	Y	N	Y	Y	Y
3 Rahall	Y	Y	Y	N	N	Y	Y
WISCONSIN							
1 ***Ryan***	Y	N	N	Y	N	Y	Y
2 Baldwin	Y	Y	N	Y	N	N	N
3 Kind	N	Y	Y	Y	N	N	Y
4 Kleczka	Y	Y	N	N	N	N	N
5 Barrett	Y	Y	Y	Y	N	N	N
6 ***Petri***	Y	N	N	N	N	Y	Y
7 Obey	Y	Y	Y	Y	N	N	N
8 ***Green***	N	N	N	Y	N	Y	Y
9 ***Sensenbrenner***	N	N	N	Y	N	Y	Y
WYOMING							
AL ***Cubin***	N	N	N	N	Y	N	Y

Southern states - Ala., Ark., Fla., Ga., Ky., La., Miss., N.C., Okla., S.C., Tenn., Texas, Va.

House Key Votes **8, 9, 10, 11, 12, 13**

8. HR 1995. New Teachers and Training Programs/Funding Increases. Martinez, D-Calif., substitute amendment to increase funding for professional development and class-size reduction activities, with a separate authorization for the class-size reduction program. The amendment would authorize $1.5 billion in fiscal 2000 for the class-size reduction program, increasing to $3 billion by fiscal 2005; it would authorize $1.5 billion for teachers' professional development, increasing to $3 billion by fiscal 2004. Rejected 207-217: R 3-215; D 203-2 (ND 151-0, SD 52-2); I 1-0. July 20, 1999. A "yea" was a vote in support of the president's position. *(House vote 319)*

9. HR 2488. Tax Reconciliation/Passage. Passage of the bill to reduce federal taxes by $792 billion over 10 years. The bill would reduce individual income tax rates by 10 percent over 10 years, contingent on annual progress in reducing interest on the nation's debt. It would increase the standard deduction for married couples to double that for singles; cut the capital gains tax rate to 15 percent for individuals and to 30 percent for corporations; phase out estate and gift taxes by 2009; accelerate the phase-in of a 100 percent deduction for health insurance premiums for the self-employed, and allow taxpayers to deduct health care and long-term care insurance if employers pay 50 percent or less of the premium; increase the annual contribution limit for Education Savings Accounts from $500 to $2,000 and permit tax-free withdrawals to pay for public and private elementary and secondary tuition and expenses. Passed 223-208: R 217-4; D 6-203 (ND 2-152, SD 4-51); I 0-1. July 22, 1999. A "nay" was a vote in support of the president's position. *(House vote 333)*

10. HR 417. Campaign Finance Overhaul/Passage. Passage of the bill to ban all contributions of soft money — money used for party-building activities as opposed to supporting a specific candidate — and impose restrictions on issue advocacy communications. The bill would raise the individual aggregate contribution limit from $25,000 to $30,000 per year and raise the limit on individual contributions to state political parties from $5,000 to $10,000. House candidates who receive coordinated party contributions could not spend more than $50,000 in personal funds. Labor unions would have to notify dues-paying non-members of any portion of their dues used for political purposes. Passed 252-177: R 54-164; D 197-13 (ND 148-8, SD 49-5); I 1-0. Sept. 14, 1999. A "yea" was a vote in support of the president's position. *(House vote 422)*

11. HR 2436. Criminal Penalties for Harming a Fetus/Passage. Passage of the bill to make it a criminal offense to injure or kill a fetus during the commission of a violent crime, regardless of the perpetrator's knowledge of the pregnancy or intent to harm the fetus. The bill states that its provisions should not be interpreted to apply to consensual abortion or to a woman's actions with respect to her pregnancy. Passed 254-172: R 198-21; D 56-150 (ND 40-113, SD 16-37); I 0-1. Sept. 30, 1999. A "nay" was a vote in support of the president's position. *(House vote 465)*

12. HR 2723. Managed Care Patient Protection/Passage. Passage of the bill to require health plans to cover emergency care when a "prudent layperson" could reasonably believe such care was required. Health plans would have to allow direct access to gynecological and pediatric care. The bill would establish an internal and external appeals process to review denial of care. Patients or their estates would have the right to sue their health plan in state courts when they believe plan decisions result in injury or death of patients. Passed 275-151: R 68-149; D 206-2 (ND 153-1, SD 53-1); I 1-0. Oct. 7, 1999. A "yea" was a vote in support of the president's position. *(House vote 490)*

13. HR 2260. Physician-Assisted Suicide/Passage. Passage of the bill to allow doctors to use controlled substances aggressively to alleviate pain, while barring them from using such drugs for the purpose of assisted suicide. The measure would supersede state law, effectively overturning an Oregon law that allows lethal prescriptions to be issued to the terminally ill, and preventing such laws from going into effect in other states. Passed 271-156: R 200-20; D 71-135 (ND 48-104, SD 23-31); I 0-1. Oct. 27, 1999. *(House vote 544)*

[1] *George E. Brown Jr., D-Calif., died July 15.*

Key

- Y Voted for (yea).
- # Paired for.
- + Announced for.
- N Voted against (nay).
- X Paired against.
- – Announced against.
- P Voted "present."
- C Voted "present" to avoid possible conflict of interest.
- ? Did not vote or otherwise make a position known.

•

Democrats ***Republicans*** *Independents*

	8	9	10	11	12	13
ALABAMA						
1 ***Callahan***	N	Y	N	Y	Y	Y
2 ***Everett***	N	Y	N	Y	N	Y
3 ***Riley***	N	Y	N	Y	N	Y
4 ***Aderholt***	N	Y	N	Y	N	Y
5 Cramer	Y	N	Y	Y	Y	Y
6 ***Bachus***	N	Y	Y	Y	Y	Y
7 Hilliard	Y	N	Y	N	Y	N
ALASKA						
AL ***Young***	N	Y	N	Y	N	Y
ARIZONA						
1 ***Salmon***	N	Y	N	Y	N	Y
2 Pastor	Y	N	Y	N	Y	N
3 ***Stump***	N	Y	N	Y	N	N
4 ***Shadegg***	N	Y	N	Y	N	Y
5 ***Kolbe***	N	Y	N	N	N	N
6 ***Hayworth***	N	Y	N	Y	N	Y
ARKANSAS						
1 Berry	Y	N	Y	Y	Y	Y
2 Snyder	Y	N	Y	N	Y	N
3 ***Hutchinson***	N	Y	N	Y	N	Y
4 ***Dickey***	N	Y	N	Y	N	Y
CALIFORNIA						
1 Thompson	Y	N	Y	N	Y	N
2 ***Herger***	N	Y	N	Y	N	Y
3 ***Ose***	N	Y	Y	N	N	Y
4 ***Doolittle***	N	Y	N	Y	N	Y
5 Matsui	Y	N	Y	N	Y	N
6 Woolsey	Y	N	Y	N	Y	N
7 Miller, George	Y	N	Y	N	Y	N
8 Pelosi	Y	N	Y	N	Y	N
9 Lee	Y	N	Y	N	Y	N
10 Tauscher	Y	N	Y	N	Y	N
11 ***Pombo***	N	Y	N	Y	N	Y
12 Lantos	Y	N	Y	N	Y	N
13 Stark	?	N	Y	N	Y	N
14 Eshoo	Y	N	Y	N	Y	N
15 ***Campbell***	N	Y	Y	N	N	N
16 Lofgren	Y	N	Y	N	Y	N
17 Farr	Y	N	Y	N	Y	N
18 Condit	Y	Y	Y	N	Y	N
19 ***Radanovich***	N	Y	N	Y	N	Y
20 Dooley	Y	N	Y	N	Y	N
21 ***Thomas***	N	Y	N	Y	N	Y
22 Capps	Y	N	Y	N	Y	N
23 ***Gallegly***	N	Y	Y	Y	Y	Y
24 Sherman	Y	N	Y	N	Y	N
25 ***McKeon***	N	Y	N	Y	N	Y
26 Berman	Y	N	Y	N	Y	N
27 ***Rogan***	N	Y	N	Y	N	Y
28 ***Dreier***	N	Y	N	Y	N	Y
29 Waxman	Y	N	Y	N	Y	N
30 Becerra	Y	N	Y	N	Y	N
31 Martinez	Y	N	Y	N	Y	Y
32 Dixon	Y	N	Y	N	Y	N
33 Roybal-Allard	Y	N	Y	N	Y	N
34 Napolitano	Y	N	Y	N	Y	N
35 Waters	Y	N	Y	N	Y	N
36 ***Kuykendall***	N	Y	Y	N	N	Y
37 Millender-McD.	Y	N	Y	N	Y	N
38 ***Horn***	N	Y	Y	N	Y	N
39 ***Royce***	N	Y	N	Y	N	Y
40 ***Lewis***	N	Y	N	Y	N	Y
41 ***Miller***	N	Y	N	Y	N	Y
42 Vacant [1]						
43 ***Calvert***	N	Y	N	Y	N	Y
44 ***Bono***	N	Y	N	N	Y	Y
45 ***Rohrabacher***	N	Y	N	Y	N	N
46 Sanchez	Y	N	Y	N	Y	N
47 ***Cox***	N	Y	N	Y	N	Y
48 ***Packard***	N	Y	N	Y	N	Y
49 ***Bilbray***	Y	Y	Y	Y	Y	Y
50 Filner	Y	N	Y	N	Y	N
51 ***Cunningham***	N	Y	N	Y	N	Y
52 ***Hunter***	N	Y	N	Y	Y	Y
COLORADO						
1 DeGette	Y	N	Y	N	Y	N
2 Udall	Y	N	Y	N	Y	N
3 ***McInnis***	N	Y	N	Y	N	Y
4 ***Schaffer***	N	Y	N	Y	N	Y
5 ***Hefley***	N	Y	N	Y	Y	Y
6 ***Tancredo***	N	Y	N	Y	N	Y
CONNECTICUT						
1 Larson	Y	N	Y	N	Y	N
2 Gejdenson	Y	N	Y	N	Y	N
3 DeLauro	Y	N	Y	N	Y	N
4 ***Shays***	N	Y	Y	N	Y	N
5 Maloney	Y	N	Y	N	Y	Y
6 ***Johnson***	N	Y	Y	N	N	N
DELAWARE						
AL ***Castle***	N	N	Y	Y	Y	N
FLORIDA						
1 ***Scarborough***	N	Y	N	?	?	?
2 Boyd	Y	N	Y	N	Y	N
3 Brown	Y	N	Y	N	Y	N
4 ***Fowler***	N	Y	N	Y	N	Y
5 Thurman	Y	N	Y	N	Y	N
6 ***Stearns***	N	Y	N	Y	N	Y
7 ***Mica***	N	Y	N	Y	N	Y
8 ***McCollum***	N	Y	N	Y	Y	Y
9 ***Bilirakis***	N	Y	N	Y	Y	Y
10 ***Young***	?	Y	N	Y	Y	Y
11 Davis	Y	N	Y	N	Y	Y
12 ***Canady***	N	Y	N	Y	Y	Y
13 ***Miller***	N	Y	N	Y	N	Y
14 ***Goss***	N	Y	N	Y	N	Y
15 ***Weldon***	N	Y	N	Y	Y	Y
16 ***Foley***	N	Y	Y	N	Y	Y
17 Meek	Y	N	Y	N	Y	N
18 ***Ros-Lehtinen***	N	Y	?	Y	Y	Y
19 Wexler	Y	N	Y	N	Y	N
20 Deutsch	Y	N	Y	N	Y	N
21 ***Diaz-Balart***	N	Y	N	Y	Y	Y
22 ***Shaw***	N	Y	?	Y	Y	Y
23 Hastings	Y	N	?	N	Y	N
GEORGIA						
1 ***Kingston***	N	Y	?	Y	N	Y
2 Bishop	Y	Y	N	N	Y	Y
3 ***Collins***	N	Y	Y	Y	N	Y
4 McKinney	Y	N	Y	N	Y	N
5 Lewis	?	N	Y	N	Y	N
6 ***Isakson***	N	Y	N	Y	N	Y
7 ***Barr***	N	Y	N	Y	Y	Y
8 ***Chambliss***	N	Y	N	Y	Y	Y
9 ***Deal***	N	Y	Y	Y	N	Y
10 ***Norwood***	N	Y	N	Y	Y	Y
11 ***Linder***	N	Y	N	Y	N	Y
HAWAII						
1 Abercrombie	Y	N	Y	N	Y	N
2 Mink	Y	N	N	N	Y	N
IDAHO						
1 ***Chenoweth-Hage***	N	Y	N	+	N	Y
2 ***Simpson***	N	Y	N	Y	N	Y
ILLINOIS						
1 Rush	Y	N	Y	N	Y	?
2 Jackson	Y	N	Y	N	Y	N
3 Lipinski	Y	N	Y	Y	Y	Y
4 Gutierrez	Y	N	Y	N	Y	N
5 Blagojevich	Y	N	Y	N	Y	N
6 ***Hyde***	N	Y	N	Y	Y	Y
7 Davis	Y	N	Y	N	Y	N
8 ***Crane***	N	Y	N	Y	N	Y
9 Schakowsky	Y	N	Y	N	Y	Y
10 ***Porter***	N	Y	Y	N	Y	N
11 ***Weller***	N	Y	N	Y	N	Y
12 Costello	Y	N	Y	Y	Y	Y
13 ***Biggert***	N	Y	N	N	N	N
14 ***Hastert***		Y	N		N	

ND Northern Democrats SD Southern Democrats

Member	8	9	10	11	12	13
15 ***Ewing***	N	Y	N	Y	N	Y
16 ***Manzullo***	N	Y	N	Y	N	Y
17 Evans	Y	N	Y	N	Y	N
18 ***LaHood***	N	Y	N	Y	N	Y
19 Phelps	Y	N	Y	Y	Y	Y
20 ***Shimkus***	N	Y	Y	Y	N	Y
INDIANA						
1 Visclosky	Y	N	Y	N	Y	Y
2 ***McIntosh***	N	Y	N	Y	N	Y
3 Roemer	Y	N	Y	Y	Y	Y
4 ***Souder***	N	Y	N	Y	N	Y
5 ***Buyer***	N	Y	N	Y	N	Y
6 ***Burton***	N	Y	N	Y	N	Y
7 ***Pease***	N	Y	N	Y	N	Y
8 ***Hostettler***	N	Y	N	Y	N	Y
9 Hill	Y	N	Y	Y	Y	Y
10 Carson	Y	N	Y	N	Y	N
IOWA						
1 ***Leach***	N	Y	Y	Y	Y	Y
2 ***Nussle***	N	Y	N	Y	N	Y
3 Boswell	Y	N	Y	N	Y	Y
4 ***Ganske***	N	N	Y	Y	Y	Y
5 ***Latham***	N	Y	N	Y	N	Y
KANSAS						
1 ***Moran***	N	Y	N	Y	Y	Y
2 ***Ryun***	N	Y	N	Y	N	Y
3 Moore	Y	N	Y	N	Y	Y
4 ***Tiahrt***	N	Y	N	Y	N	Y
KENTUCKY						
1 ***Whitfield***	N	Y	N	Y	N	Y
2 ***Lewis***	N	Y	N	Y	N	Y
3 ***Northup***	N	Y	N	Y	N	Y
4 Lucas	Y	Y	Y	Y	Y	Y
5 ***Rogers***	N	Y	N	Y	N	Y
6 ***Fletcher***	N	Y	N	Y	N	Y
LOUISIANA						
1 ***Vitter***	N	Y	N	Y	Y	Y
2 Jefferson	Y	N	Y	?	Y	Y
3 ***Tauzin***	N	Y	N	Y	N	Y
4 ***McCrery***	N	Y	N	Y	N	Y
5 ***Cooksey***	N	Y	N	Y	Y	N
6 ***Baker***	N	Y	N	Y	N	Y
7 John	Y	N	N	Y	Y	Y
MAINE						
1 Allen	Y	N	Y	N	Y	N
2 Baldacci	Y	N	Y	N	Y	Y
MARYLAND						
1 ***Gilchrest***	N	Y	Y	Y	Y	N
2 ***Ehrlich***	N	Y	N	Y	N	N
3 Cardin	Y	N	Y	N	Y	N
4 Wynn	Y	N	Y	N	Y	Y
5 Hoyer	Y	N	Y	N	Y	Y
6 ***Bartlett***	N	Y	N	Y	N	Y
7 Cummings	Y	N	Y	N	Y	N
8 ***Morella***	Y	N	Y	N	Y	N
MASSACHUSETTS						
1 Olver	Y	N	Y	N	Y	N
2 Neal	Y	N	Y	Y	Y	Y
3 McGovern	Y	N	Y	N	Y	N
4 Frank	Y	N	Y	N	Y	N
5 Meehan	Y	N	Y	N	Y	N
6 Tierney	Y	N	Y	N	Y	N
7 Markey	Y	N	Y	N	Y	N
8 Capuano	Y	N	Y	N	Y	N
9 Moakley	Y	N	Y	Y	Y	Y
10 Delahunt	Y	N	Y	N	Y	?
MICHIGAN						
1 Stupak	Y	N	N	Y	Y	Y
2 ***Hoekstra***	N	Y	N	Y	N	Y
3 ***Ehlers***	N	Y	N	Y	N	Y
4 ***Camp***	N	Y	N	Y	N	Y
5 Barcia	Y	N	N	Y	Y	Y
6 ***Upton***	N	Y	Y	Y	N	Y
7 ***Smith***	N	Y	Y	Y	N	Y
8 Stabenow	Y	N	Y	N	Y	N
9 Kildee	Y	N	Y	Y	Y	Y
10 Bonior	Y	N	Y	Y	Y	N
11 ***Knollenberg***	N	Y	N	Y	N	Y
12 Levin	Y	N	Y	N	Y	N
13 Rivers	Y	N	Y	N	Y	N
14 Conyers	Y	N	Y	N	Y	N
15 Kilpatrick	Y	N	Y	N	Y	N
16 Dingell	Y	N	Y	Y	Y	N
MINNESOTA						
1 ***Gutknecht***	N	Y	N	Y	N	Y
2 Minge	Y	N	Y	Y	Y	N
3 ***Ramstad***	N	Y	Y	Y	N	Y
4 Vento	Y	N	Y	N	Y	N
5 Sabo	Y	N	Y	N	+	N
6 Luther	Y	N	Y	Y	Y	N
7 Peterson	Y	N	N	Y	N	Y
8 Oberstar	Y	N	Y	Y	Y	Y
MISSISSIPPI						
1 ***Wicker***	N	Y	N	Y	N	Y
2 Thompson	Y	N	Y	N	Y	N
3 ***Pickering***	N	Y	N	Y	N	Y
4 Shows	Y	N	Y	Y	Y	Y
5 Taylor	Y	N	Y	Y	Y	Y
MISSOURI						
1 Clay	Y	N	Y	N	Y	N
2 ***Talent***	N	Y	N	Y	N	Y
3 Gephardt	Y	N	Y	N	Y	N
4 Skelton	Y	N	Y	Y	Y	Y
5 McCarthy	Y	N	Y	N	Y	N
6 Danner	Y	Y	Y	Y	Y	Y
7 ***Blunt***	N	Y	N	Y	N	Y
8 ***Emerson***	N	Y	N	Y	N	Y
9 ***Hulshof***	N	Y	Y	Y	–	Y
MONTANA						
AL ***Hill***	N	Y	Y	Y	N	Y
NEBRASKA						
1 ***Bereuter***	N	Y	Y	Y	N	Y
2 ***Terry***	N	Y	N	Y	N	Y
3 ***Barrett***	N	Y	Y	Y	N	Y
NEVADA						
1 Berkley	Y	N	Y	N	Y	N
2 ***Gibbons***	N	Y	N	Y	Y	Y
NEW HAMPSHIRE						
1 ***Sununu***	N	Y	N	Y	N	Y
2 ***Bass***	N	Y	Y	N	N	N
NEW JERSEY						
1 Andrews	Y	N	Y	N	Y	Y
2 ***LoBiondo***	N	Y	Y	Y	Y	Y
3 ***Saxton***	N	Y	Y	Y	Y	Y
4 ***Smith***	N	Y	N	Y	Y	Y
5 ***Roukema***	N	Y	Y	N	Y	Y
6 Pallone	Y	N	Y	N	Y	N
7 ***Franks***	N	Y	Y	Y	Y	Y
8 Pascrell	Y	N	Y	N	Y	Y
9 Rothman	Y	N	Y	N	Y	N
10 Payne	Y	N	Y	N	Y	N
11 ***Frelinghuysen***	N	Y	Y	N	Y	Y
12 Holt	Y	N	Y	N	Y	N
13 Menendez	Y	N	Y	N	Y	N
NEW MEXICO						
1 ***Wilson***	N	Y	N	Y	Y	Y
2 ***Skeen***	N	Y	N	Y	N	Y
3 Udall	Y	N	Y	N	Y	N
NEW YORK						
1 Forbes [2]	Y	N	Y	Y	Y	Y
2 ***Lazio***	N	Y	Y	Y	N	Y
3 ***King***	N	Y	N	Y	Y	Y
4 McCarthy	Y	N	Y	N	Y	Y
5 Ackerman	Y	N	Y	N	Y	N
6 Meeks	Y	N	Y	?	Y	N
7 Crowley	Y	N	Y	Y	Y	Y
8 Nadler	Y	N	Y	N	Y	N
9 Weiner	Y	N	Y	N	Y	N
10 Towns	Y	N	Y	N	Y	N
11 Owens	Y	N	Y	N	Y	N
12 Velázquez	Y	N	Y	N	Y	N
13 ***Fossella***	N	Y	N	Y	N	Y
14 Maloney	Y	N	Y	N	Y	N
15 Rangel	Y	N	Y	N	Y	N
16 Serrano	Y	N	Y	N	Y	N
17 Engel	Y	N	Y	N	Y	N
18 Lowey	Y	N	Y	N	Y	N
19 ***Kelly***	N	Y	Y	Y	N	Y
20 ***Gilman***	N	Y	Y	N	Y	Y
21 McNulty	Y	N	Y	Y	Y	Y
22 ***Sweeney***	N	Y	N	Y	Y	Y
23 ***Boehlert***	N	Y	Y	N	Y	Y
24 ***McHugh***	Y	Y	Y	Y	Y	Y
25 ***Walsh***	N	Y	Y	Y	Y	Y
26 Hinchey	?	N	Y	N	Y	N
27 ***Reynolds***	N	Y	N	Y	Y	Y
28 Slaughter	Y	N	Y	N	Y	N
29 LaFalce	Y	N	Y	Y	Y	Y
30 ***Quinn***	N	N	Y	Y	Y	Y
31 ***Houghton***	N	Y	Y	N	N	Y
NORTH CAROLINA						
1 Clayton	Y	N	Y	N	Y	N
2 Etheridge	Y	N	Y	N	Y	Y
3 ***Jones***	N	Y	N	Y	Y	Y
4 Price	Y	N	Y	N	Y	N
5 ***Burr***	N	Y	N	Y	N	Y
6 ***Coble***	N	Y	N	Y	Y	Y
7 McIntyre	Y	N	Y	Y	Y	Y
8 ***Hayes***	N	Y	N	Y	N	Y
9 ***Myrick***	N	Y	N	Y	N	Y
10 ***Ballenger***	N	Y	N	Y	N	Y
11 ***Taylor***	N	Y	N	Y	N	Y
12 Watt	Y	N	Y	N	Y	N
NORTH DAKOTA						
AL Pomeroy	Y	N	Y	Y	Y	Y
OHIO						
1 ***Chabot***	N	Y	N	Y	N	Y
2 ***Portman***	N	Y	N	Y	–	Y
3 Hall	Y	N	Y	Y	Y	Y
4 ***Oxley***	N	Y	N	Y	N	Y
5 ***Gillmor***	N	Y	Y	Y	N	Y
6 Strickland	Y	N	Y	N	Y	Y
7 ***Hobson***	N	Y	N	Y	N	Y
8 ***Boehner***	N	Y	N	Y	N	Y
9 Kaptur	Y	N	Y	Y	?	N
10 Kucinich	Y	N	Y	Y	Y	Y
11 Jones	Y	N	Y	N	Y	N
12 ***Kasich***	N	Y	N	Y	N	Y
13 Brown	Y	N	Y	N	Y	N
14 Sawyer	Y	N	Y	N	Y	N
15 ***Pryce***	N	Y	?	Y	N	Y
16 ***Regula***	N	Y	Y	Y	N	Y
17 Traficant	Y	N	N	Y	Y	Y
18 ***Ney***	N	Y	N	Y	N	Y
19 ***LaTourette***	N	Y	Y	Y	Y	Y
OKLAHOMA						
1 ***Largent***	N	Y	N	Y	N	Y
2 ***Coburn***	N	Y	N	Y	Y	Y
3 ***Watkins***	N	Y	N	Y	N	Y
4 ***Watts***	N	Y	N	Y	N	Y
5 ***Istook***	N	Y	N	Y	N	Y
6 ***Lucas***	N	Y	N	Y	N	Y
OREGON						
1 Wu	Y	N	Y	?	Y	N
2 ***Walden***	N	Y	N	Y	N	N
3 Blumenauer	Y	N	Y	N	Y	N
4 DeFazio	Y	N	Y	N	Y	N
5 Hooley	Y	N	Y	–	Y	N
PENNSYLVANIA						
1 Brady	Y	N	Y	N	Y	Y
2 Fattah	Y	N	Y	N	Y	N
3 Borski	Y	N	Y	Y	Y	Y
4 Klink	Y	N	Y	Y	Y	Y
5 ***Peterson***	?	?	N	Y	N	Y
6 Holden	?	N	Y	Y	Y	Y
7 ***Weldon***	N	Y	Y	Y	Y	Y
8 ***Greenwood***	N	Y	Y	N	Y	Y
9 ***Shuster***	N	Y	N	Y	?	N
10 ***Sherwood***	N	Y	N	Y	Y	Y
11 Kanjorski	Y	N	Y	Y	Y	Y
12 Murtha	Y	N	N	Y	Y	Y
13 Hoeffel	Y	N	Y	N	Y	Y
14 Coyne	Y	N	Y	N	Y	N
15 ***Toomey***	N	Y	N	Y	N	Y
16 ***Pitts***	N	Y	N	Y	N	Y
17 ***Gekas***	N	Y	N	Y	N	Y
18 Doyle	Y	N	Y	Y	Y	Y
19 ***Goodling***	N	Y	N	Y	N	Y
20 Mascara	Y	N	Y	Y	Y	+
21 ***English***	?	Y	N	Y	N	Y
RHODE ISLAND						
1 Kennedy	+	–	Y	N	Y	?
2 Weygand	Y	N	Y	Y	Y	Y
SOUTH CAROLINA						
1 ***Sanford***	N	Y	Y	Y	N	N
2 ***Spence***	N	Y	N	Y	Y	Y
3 ***Graham***	N	Y	Y	Y	Y	Y
4 ***DeMint***	N	Y	N	Y	N	Y
5 Spratt	Y	N	Y	Y	Y	Y
6 Clyburn	Y	N	Y	N	+	N
SOUTH DAKOTA						
AL ***Thune***	N	Y	Y	Y	N	Y
TENNESSEE						
1 ***Jenkins***	N	Y	N	Y	Y	Y
2 ***Duncan***	N	Y	Y	Y	Y	Y
3 ***Wamp***	N	Y	Y	Y	Y	Y
4 ***Hilleary***	N	Y	N	Y	N	Y
5 Clement	Y	N	Y	Y	Y	Y
6 Gordon	Y	N	Y	Y	Y	Y
7 ***Bryant***	N	Y	N	Y	N	Y
8 Tanner	Y	N	Y	Y	Y	N
9 Ford	Y	N	Y	–	Y	N
TEXAS						
1 Sandlin	Y	N	Y	N	Y	N
2 Turner	Y	N	Y	Y	Y	Y
3 ***Johnson, Sam***	N	Y	N	Y	N	Y
4 Hall	N	Y	N	Y	Y	Y
5 ***Sessions***	N	Y	N	Y	Y	Y
6 ***Barton***	N	Y	N	Y	N	Y
7 ***Archer***	N	Y	N	Y	N	Y
8 ***Brady***	N	Y	N	Y	Y	Y
9 Lampson	Y	N	Y	N	Y	Y
10 Doggett	Y	N	Y	N	Y	N
11 Edwards	Y	N	Y	N	Y	N
12 ***Granger***	N	Y	N	Y	?	Y
13 ***Thornberry***	N	Y	N	Y	Y	Y
14 ***Paul***	N	Y	N	N	N	N
15 Hinojosa	Y	N	Y	N	Y	–
16 Reyes	Y	N	Y	N	Y	Y
17 Stenholm	Y	N	Y	Y	Y	Y
18 Jackson-Lee	Y	N	Y	N	Y	N
19 ***Combest***	N	Y	N	Y	N	Y
20 Gonzalez	Y	N	Y	N	Y	N
21 ***Smith***	N	Y	N	Y	N	Y
22 ***DeLay***	N	Y	N	Y	N	Y
23 ***Bonilla***	N	Y	N	Y	N	Y
24 Frost	Y	N	Y	N	Y	N
25 Bentsen	Y	N	Y	N	Y	N
26 ***Armey***	N	Y	N	Y	N	Y
27 Ortiz	Y	N	Y	Y	Y	Y
28 Rodriguez	Y	N	Y	N	Y	N
29 Green	Y	N	Y	N	Y	Y
30 Johnson, E.B.	Y	N	Y	N	Y	N
UTAH						
1 ***Hansen***	N	Y	N	Y	N	Y
2 ***Cook***	N	Y	Y	Y	Y	Y
3 ***Cannon***	N	Y	N	Y	Y	Y
VERMONT						
AL *Sanders*	Y	N	Y	N	Y	N
VIRGINIA						
1 ***Bateman***	N	Y	N	Y	Y	Y
2 Pickett	Y	N	Y	N	Y	N
3 Scott	Y	N	N	N	Y	N
4 Sisisky	Y	N	Y	N	Y	Y
5 Goode	N	Y	N	Y	N	Y
6 ***Goodlatte***	N	Y	N	Y	N	Y
7 ***Bliley***	N	Y	N	Y	N	Y
8 Moran	Y	N	Y	N	Y	N
9 Boucher	Y	N	Y	N	Y	N
10 ***Wolf***	N	Y	Y	Y	Y	Y
11 ***Davis***	N	Y	N	Y	Y	Y
WASHINGTON						
1 Inslee	Y	N	Y	N	Y	N
2 ***Metcalf***	N	Y	Y	Y	N	N
3 Baird	Y	N	Y	N	Y	N
4 ***Hastings***	N	Y	N	Y	N	Y
5 ***Nethercutt***	N	Y	N	Y	N	Y
6 Dicks	Y	N	Y	N	Y	N
7 McDermott	+	–	Y	N	Y	N
8 ***Dunn***	N	Y	N	Y	N	Y
9 Smith	Y	N	Y	N	Y	N
WEST VIRGINIA						
1 Mollohan	Y	N	N	Y	Y	Y
2 Wise	Y	N	Y	N	Y	Y
3 Rahall	Y	N	N	Y	Y	Y
WISCONSIN						
1 ***Ryan***	N	Y	N	Y	N	Y
2 Baldwin	Y	N	Y	N	Y	N
3 Kind	Y	N	Y	Y	Y	N
4 Kleczka	Y	N	Y	Y	Y	Y
5 Barrett	Y	N	Y	N	Y	N
6 ***Petri***	N	Y	Y	Y	N	Y
7 Obey	Y	N	Y	Y	Y	N
8 ***Green***	N	Y	N	Y	N	Y
9 ***Sensenbrenner***	N	Y	N	Y	N	Y
WYOMING						
AL ***Cubin***	N	Y	N	Y	N	Y

Southern states - Ala., Ark., Fla., Ga., Ky., La., Miss., N.C., Okla., S.C., Tenn., Texas, Va.

Senate Key Votes 8, 9, 10, 11, 12, 13

	8	9	10	11	12	13
ALABAMA						
Sessions	N	N	N	N	N	Y
Shelby	N	N	N	N	N	N
ALASKA						
Murkowski	Y	N	N	N	N	Y
Stevens	Y	N	N	N	Y	Y
ARIZONA						
Kyl	Y	N	N	N	N	Y
McCain	Y	?	N	Y	?	?
ARKANSAS						
Hutchinson	N	N	N	Y	N	Y
Lincoln	N	N	Y	Y	Y	Y
CALIFORNIA						
Boxer	N	Y	Y	Y	Y	N
Feinstein	N	Y	Y	Y	Y	Y
COLORADO						
Allard	N	N	N	N	N	Y
Campbell	N	N	N	N	Y	Y
CONNECTICUT						
Dodd	N	Y	Y	Y	Y	Y
Lieberman	Y	Y	Y	Y	Y	Y
DELAWARE						
Roth	N	N	N	Y	N	Y
Biden	N	N	Y	Y	Y	Y
FLORIDA						
Mack	Y	N	N	N	N	Y
Graham	Y	Y	Y	Y	Y	Y
GEORGIA						
Coverdell	Y	N	N	N	N	Y
Cleland	N	Y	Y	Y	Y	Y
HAWAII						
Akaka	N	Y	Y	Y	Y	Y
Inouye	N	Y	Y	Y	Y	Y
IDAHO						
Craig	N	N	N	N	N	Y
Crapo	N	N	N	N	N	Y
ILLINOIS						
Fitzgerald	N	N	N	N	N	C
Durbin	N	Y	Y	Y	Y	Y
INDIANA						
Lugar	N	N	N	N	N	Y
Bayh	N	N	Y	Y	Y	Y
IOWA						
Grassley	N	N	N	N	N	Y
Harkin	N	Y	Y	Y	Y	N
KANSAS						
Brownback	N	N	N	Y	N	Y
Roberts	N	N	N	N	N	Y
KENTUCKY						
Bunning	Y	N	N	N	N	Y
McConnell	Y	N	N	N	N	Y
LOUISIANA						
Breaux	N	?	Y	Y	N	Y
Landrieu	N	N	Y	Y	Y	Y
MAINE						
Collins	N	Y	N	Y	Y	Y
Snowe	Y	Y	N	Y	Y	Y
MARYLAND						
Mikulski	N	N	Y	Y	Y	N
Sarbanes	Y	Y	Y	Y	Y	Y
MASSACHUSETTS						
Kennedy	?	Y	Y	Y	Y	Y
Kerry	N	Y	Y	Y	Y	Y
MICHIGAN						
Abraham	N	N	N	N	N	Y
Levin	N	N	Y	Y	Y	Y
MINNESOTA						
Grams	N	N	N	N	N	Y
Wellstone	N	Y	Y	Y	Y	N
MISSISSIPPI						
Cochran	N	N	N	N	N	Y
Lott	Y	N	N	N	N	Y
MISSOURI						
Ashcroft	N	N	N	N	N	Y
Bond	N	N	N	N	N	Y
MONTANA						
Burns	N	N	N	N	N	Y
Baucus	N	Y	Y	Y	Y	Y
NEBRASKA						
Hagel	N	N	N	N	N	Y
Kerrey	N	Y	Y	Y	Y	Y
NEVADA						
Bryan	Y	Y	Y	Y	Y	N
Reid	Y	Y	Y	Y	N	Y
NEW HAMPSHIRE						
Gregg	Y	Y	N	N	?	Y
Smith[1]	Y	N	N	N	N	Y
NEW JERSEY						
Lautenberg	Y	Y	Y	Y	Y	Y
Torricelli	Y	Y	Y	Y	Y	Y
NEW MEXICO						
Domenici	?	N	N	N	N	Y
Bingaman	N	Y	Y	Y	Y	Y
NEW YORK						
Moynihan	N	Y	Y	Y	Y	Y
Schumer	N	Y	Y	Y	Y	Y
NORTH CAROLINA						
Helms	Y	N	N	N	N	Y
Edwards	N	Y	Y	Y	Y	Y
NORTH DAKOTA						
Conrad	N	N	Y	Y	Y	Y
Dorgan	N	Y	Y	Y	Y	N
OHIO						
DeWine	Y	N	N	N	N	Y
Voinovich	N	N	N	N	N	Y
OKLAHOMA						
Inhofe	N	N	N	N	N	Y
Nickles	N	N	N	N	N	Y
OREGON						
Smith	N	Y	Y	N	N	Y
Wyden	N	Y	Y	Y	Y	Y
PENNSYLVANIA						
Santorum	Y	N	N	N	N	Y
Specter	N	N	Y	N	Y	Y
RHODE ISLAND						
Chafee[2]	N	#	Y	N	Y	Y
Reed	N	Y	Y	Y	Y	Y
SOUTH CAROLINA						
Thurmond	Y	N	N	N	N	Y
Hollings	N	Y	Y	Y	Y	Y
SOUTH DAKOTA						
Daschle	N	?	Y	Y	Y	Y
Johnson	N	Y	Y	Y	Y	Y
TENNESSEE						
Frist	N	N	N	N	N	Y
Thompson	Y	N	N	Y	N	Y
TEXAS						
Gramm	Y	N	N	N	N	Y
Hutchison	N	N	N	N	N	Y
UTAH						
Bennett	N	N	N	N	N	Y
Hatch	N	N	N	N	N	Y
VERMONT						
Jeffords	N	Y	Y	Y	Y	Y
Leahy	N	Y	Y	Y	Y	Y
VIRGINIA						
Warner	N	X	N	N	Y	Y
Robb	Y	Y	Y	Y	Y	Y
WASHINGTON						
Gorton	N	Y	N	N	N	Y
Murray	N	Y	Y	Y	Y	Y
WEST VIRGINIA						
Byrd	Y	N	P	Y	Y	Y
Rockefeller	N	Y	Y	Y	Y	Y
WISCONSIN						
Feingold	N	Y	Y	Y	Y	N
Kohl	Y	N	Y	Y	Y	Y
WYOMING						
Enzi	N	N	N	N	N	Y
Thomas	N	N	N	N	N	Y

Key

- Y Voted for (yea).
- \# Paired for.
- \+ Announced for.
- N Voted against (nay).
- X Paired against.
- – Announced against.
- P Voted "present."
- C Voted "present" to avoid possible conflict of interest.
- ? Did not vote or otherwise make a position known.

Democrats **_Republicans_**
Independents

ND Northern Democrats SD Southern Democrats

Southern states - Ala., Ark., Fla., Ga., Ky., La., Miss., N.C., Okla., S.C., Tenn., Texas, Va.

8. S 1233. Fiscal 2000 Agriculture Appropriations/Unilateral Food and Medicine Sanctions. Helms, R-N.C., motion to table (kill) the Ashcroft, R-Mo., amendment to the Daschle, D-S.D., amendment. The Ashcroft amendment would end U.S. unilateral sanctions on agricultural and medicinal goods and bar the president from imposing such sanctions against a country without congressional approval, with certain exceptions. Motion rejected 28-70: R 17-36; D 10-34 (ND 8-28, SD 2-6); I 1-0. Aug. 3, 1999. (Subsequently, the Ashcroft amendment was adopted by voice vote.) *(Senate vote 251)*

9. HR 2084. Fiscal 2000 Transportation Appropriations/Fuel Efficiency Standards. Gorton, R-Wash., amendment to express the sense of the Senate that the Department of Transportation should be allowed to study whether to raise the corporate average fuel economy (CAFE) standard for vehicles. It also would urge the Senate not to accept House-passed language that would prohibit an increase in CAFE standards. Rejected 40-55: R 6-45; D 34-9 (ND 29-7, SD 5-2); I 0-1. Sept. 15, 1999. *(Senate vote 275)*

10. Nuclear Test Ban Treaty/Adoption. Adoption of the resolution to ratify the Comprehensive Nuclear Test Ban Treaty (Treaty Doc 105-28), which would ban nuclear weapons testing six months after the pact is ratified by the 44 nations that have either nuclear power plants or nuclear research reactors. Rejected 48-51: R 4-50; D 44-0 (ND 36-0, SD 8-0); I 0-1. Oct. 13, 1999. A two-thirds majority of those present and voting (66 in this case) is required for adoption of resolutions of ratification. A "yea" was a vote in support of the president's position. *(Senate vote 325)*

11. S 1593. Campaign Finance Revisions/Soft Money Donations and Union Dues/Cloture. Motion to invoke cloture (thus limiting debate) on the Reid, D-Nev., amendment to the Daschle, D-S.D., substitute amendment. The Reid amendment would prohibit national party committees from collecting "soft money" donations, which currently are unlimited and unregulated, and labor unions would have to notify dues-paying non-members of any portion of their dues used for political purposes. It includes the previously adopted McCain, R-Ariz., amendment on disclosure requirements. Motion rejected 53-47: R 8-46; D 45-0 (ND 37-0, SD 8-0); I 0-1. Oct. 19, 1999. Three-fifths of the total Senate (60) is required to invoke cloture. *(Senate vote 331)*

12. S 1692. Abortion Procedure Ban/*Roe v. Wade*. Harkin, D-Iowa, amendment to the Boxer, D-Calif., amendment. The Harkin amendment would express the sense of Congress that the Supreme Court's 1973 *Roe v. Wade* decision was appropriate, secures an important constitutional right and should not be overturned. The Boxer amendment would express the sense of Congress that lawmakers must protect a woman's life and health in any reproductive health legislation Congress passes. Adopted 51-47: R 8-44; D 43-2 (ND 36-1, SD 7-1); I 0-1. (Subsequently, the Boxer amendment as amended was adopted by voice vote.) Oct. 21, 1999. *(Senate vote 337)*

13. S 900. Financial Services Overhaul/Conference Report. Adoption of the conference report on the bill to eliminate current barriers erected by the 1933 Glass-Steagall Act and other laws that impede affiliations between banking, securities, insurance and other firms. Adopted (thus sent to the House) 90-8: R 52-1; D 38-7 (ND 30-7, SD 8-0). Nov. 4, 1999. *(Senate vote 354)*

[1] *Robert C. Smith, N.H., switched his party affiliation from Republican to Independent on July 13. He switched back to Republican on Nov. 1.*

[2] *John H. Chafee, R-R.I., died Oct. 24, 1999. Lincoln Chafee, R-R.I., was sworn in on Nov. 4, 1999.*

Appendix D

TEXTS

'Solutions to Problems Cannot Be Found in a Pool of Bitterness,' New Speaker Hastert Declares

Following is a transcript of remarks by House Minority Leader Richard A. Gephardt, D-Mo., and Speaker Dennis Hastert, R-Ill., before Hastert was sworn in on Jan. 6:

Gephardt: Mr. Speaker and members of the House, before I hand the gavel over to our new Speaker, let me say to him simply, let's bury the hatchet.

First, I want to say to the new Speaker that Jane Gephardt and I would like to invite him and his wife Jean to our congressional district in Missouri, and I hope that in the days ahead Jane and I can come to your congressional district in Illinois.

The only problem I have with this new Speaker is that, as I understand it, he's a Chicago Cubs fan and —

Hastert: But my wife's a Cardinals fan.

Gephardt: And all of you know that I'm a St. Louis Cardinals fan — and he tells me his wife is a St. Louis Cardinals fan, which gives me real hope. But if Sammy Sosa and Mark McGwire can figure it out, so can we.

Now, Mr. Speaker, you know that over the next two years I am going to work hard to win a majority back for Democratic values and ideas. But I want to shift the focus today away from politics to other ideas, to other efforts that we can make together to do us all proud. Let's put to rest finally the poisonous politics that has infected this place.

Let's join together, not only in words but in deeds, to do right by the people to live up to our oaths, and to move our nation forward into a new century of prosperity. This is hallowed ground. This is a precious place where we have nurtured and protected for generations our democracy. We have a burden — all of us — and we have a responsibility to live up to those who have gone before us, and today and in the future to reach toward the sky and to listen to our better angels. It is in this spirit that I am proud to hand the gavel to the new Speaker of the House, to our new Speaker of the House, the gentleman from Illinois, Dennis Hastert.

Hastert: Thank you, Mr. Speak — Mr. Leader — for your kind and thoughtful remarks. I'm going to break tradition, and at this point I am going to ask you to hold the gavel so that I may go down to the floor.

Customarily a new Speaker gives his first remarks from the Speaker's chair. And while I have great respect for the traditions of this House and this institution, I am breaking tradition this once because my legislative home is here on the floor with you, and so is my heart.

To you, the members of the 106th Congress, to my family and friends and constituents, I say thank you. This is not a job that I sought, but one that I embrace with determination and enthusiasm. In the next few minutes I will share with you how I plan to carry out the job that you have given me.

But first I think we need to take a moment — and I want to say goodbye to a member of this House who made history. Newt [Gingrich], this institution has been forever transformed by your presence, and for years to come all Americans will benefit from the changes that you've championed — a balanced budget, welfare reform, tax relief. And in fact this week families all over America are beginning to calculate their taxes. And to help them they'll find a child tax credit made possible by the Congress that you led. Thank you, Newt, good luck, and God bless you in your new endeavors.

Those of you here in this House know me. But Hastert is not exactly a household name across America. So our fellow citizens deserve to know who I am and what I am going to do. What I am is a former high school teacher, a wrestling and football coach, a small businessman and a state legislator. And for the last 12 years I've been a member of this House. I am indebted to the people of the 14th congressional district of Illinois who continue to send me here to represent them.

I believe in limited government. But when government does act it must be for the good of the people. And serving in this body is a privilege — it is not a right — and each of us was sent here to conduct the people's business. And I intend to get down to business. That means formulating, debating and voting on legislation that addresses the problems that the American people want solved.

In the turbulent days behind us, debate on merits often gave way to personal attacks. Some have felt slighted, insulted or ignored. That is wrong, and that will change. Solutions to problems cannot be found in a pool of bitterness. They can be found in an environment which we trust one another's word, where we generate heat and passion, but where we recognize that each member is equally important to our overall mission of improving life for the American people. In short, I believe all of us, regardless of party, can respect one another, and even as fiercely as we disagree on particular issues.

And speaking of people who find ways to work together across the political fence, let me bring an analogy to a personal level. Two good Illinois friends of mine — George Ryan, the Republican governor-elect and Richard Daley, the Democratic mayor of Chicago — are in the visitors' gallery side by side, and I will ask them to stand to be recognized.

Those who know me well will tell you that I am true to my word. To me a commitment is a commitment, and what you see and hear today is what you will see and hear tomorrow.

Nobody knows me better than my family. My wife Jean and our sons Josh and Ethan are here today. They are my reason for being, and Jean, she keeps me — helps me keep my feet on the ground. And she and the boys are my daily reminder that home is on the Fox River and not the Potomac River. To Jean, Josh and Ethan, thank you for everything, and I love you.

As a teacher I explained the story of America year after year, and I soon came to realize that it was a story, but a story that keeps changing, for we Americans are restless people, and we like to tackle and solve problems. And we are constantly renewing our nation, experimenting and creating new ways of doing things. And I like to work against the backdrop of American basics — freedom, liberty, responsibility and opportunity. You can count on me to be a workhorse.

My experience as a football and wrestling coach taught me some other lessons that apply here. A good coach knows when to step back and let others shine in the spotlight.

President [Ronald] Reagan for years had a plaque in his office that said it all: "There is no limit to what can be accomplished if you don't mind who gets the credit." A good coach doesn't rely on only a few star players, and everyone on the squad has something to offer. And you never get to the finals without a well-rounded team, and above all, a coach worth his salt will instill in his team a sense of fair play, camaraderie, respect for the game and for the opposition. Without those, victory is hollow and defeat represents opportunities lost. I found that to be true around here too.

So where do we go from here? Some media pundits say that we'll have two years of stalemate because the Republican majority is too small. And some say that the White House, bent on revenge, will not give us a moment's peace. And some say the minority in this House will prevent passage of serious legislation so that they can later claim this was a do-nothing Congress. Washington is a town of rumors and guesses and speculation. So none of this comes as a surprise. But none of it needs to come true — that is, if we really respect the voters that sent us here.

To my Republican colleagues, I say it's time to put forward the major elements of our legislative program. We will succeed or fail depending upon how sensible a program we offer. And to my Democratic colleagues, I will say I will meet you halfway — maybe more so on occasion. But cooperation is a two-way street, and I expect you to meet me halfway, too.

The president and a number of Democrats here in the House have been saying it's time to address several issues head-on. I'll buy that. But I think we should agree that stalemate is not an option; solutions are.

And to all my colleagues I say, we must get our job done, and done now. And we have an obligation to pass all the appropriations bills by this summer, and we will not leave this chamber until we do.

I intend to be a good listener, but I want to hear ideas and the debate that flows from them. And I will have a low tolerance for campaign speeches masquerading as debate, whatever the source.

Our country faces four big challenges which we must address. And not next month or next year or the year after that, but now. And each challenge involves an element of our security. And first is retirement and health security.

Both our Social Security and Medicare programs will run into brick walls in a few years if we don't do something about them now. And we must make sure that Social Security is there for those who depend on it and those who expect to. We also must consider options for younger workers, so that they can look forward to an even brighter retirement.

Nearly a year ago, President Clinton came here to give his State of the Union address. He called for reform of Social Security. This year I invite him to return to give us his reform plan. And he has my assurance that it will be taken seriously.

Second, we must ensure a secure future for America's children by insisting that every child has a good school and a safe, drug-free environment. In my 16 years as a teacher I learned that most of the decisions having to do with education are best left to the people closest to the situation — parents, teachers, school board members. What should the federal government's role be? It should be to see that as many education dollars go directly to the classroom where they will do the most good.

And the next is economic security. In the early '80s we adopted policies that lay the foundations for long-term growth. And except for one brief period, that growth has continued ever since. And we want our economy to keep on growing. Well, toward that end it's time for us in Congress to put a microscope to the ways that government takes money from our fellow citizens and how it spends it.

There is a culture here in Washington that has grown unchallenged for too long. It combines three notions. One is that government has prior claim to the earnings of all Americans, as if they work for the government and not the other way around. Another notion is that a government program once it's begun will never end. And a third notion is that every program must grow each passing year. Well, to borrow a musical line, it just ain't necessarily so — at least it won't be as long as I am around here and have something to say about it.

We must measure every dollar we spend by this criterion: Is it really necessary? This is important. For most Americans money doesn't come easy. When I was a kid, to make ends meet my dad had a feed business, and he worked nights in a restaurant. My mom raised chickens and sold the eggs. And I still remember when tax time came around, our family really felt it. What we need is a leaner, more efficient government, along with tax policies that spur and sustain growth by giving tax relief to all working Americans.

And finally there's the challenge of America's security in a world of danger and uncertainty. Without it, other elements of our security won't be possible. And we no longer worry about Soviet nuclear bombs raining down on us. Today there are different worries: the sudden violence of a terrorist bomb, the silent threat of biological weapons, or the rogue state that aims a deadly missile at one of our cities. We need a defense capability that matches these turn-of-the-century threats. And we have asked the men and women of our armed forces to take on assignments in many corners of the earth, yet we have not given them the best equipment or preparation that they need to match those assignments. That must be corrected.

These are not Democratic or Republican issues. They are American issues. We should be able to reach agreement quickly on the goals. And, yes, we are going to argue about the means. But if we are in earnest about our responsibilities, we will find common ground to get the job done. In the process we will build the people's faith in this great United States Congress.

As a classroom teacher and a coach I learned the value of brevity. I learned that it's work, not talk, that wins championships. In closing, I want you to know just how proud I am to be chosen to be your Speaker. And there's a big job ahead for all of us. And so I ask that God bless this House as we move forward together.

Thank you very much. ◆

Urging Nation To 'Aim Higher,' Clinton Offers Proposals on Education, Retirement Security, Health Care

Following is the Federal News Service transcript of the text of President Clinton's Jan. 19 State of the Union address.

Clinton: Thank you. Thank you. Thank you. Please be seated. Thank you.

Mr. Speaker, Mr. Vice President, members of Congress, honored guests, my fellow Americans. Tonight I have the honor of reporting to you on the State of the Union.

Let me begin by saluting the new Speaker of the House and thanking him especially tonight for extending an invitation to two guests sitting in the gallery with Mrs. Hastert. Lynn Gibson and Wei Ling Chestnut are the widows of the two brave Capitol Hill police officers who gave their lives to defend freedom's house.

Mr. Speaker, at your swearing in, you asked us all to work together in a spirit of civility and bipartisanship. Mr. Speaker, let's do exactly that.

Tonight I stand before you to report that America has created the longest peacetime economic expansion in our history, with nearly 18 million new jobs, wages rising at nearly twice the rate of inflation, the highest homeownership in history, the smallest welfare rolls in 30 years and the lowest peacetime unemployment since 1957. For the first time in three decades, the budget is balanced. From a deficit of $290 billion in 1992, we had a surplus of $70 billion last year, and now we are on course for budget surpluses for the next 25 years.

Thanks to the pioneering leadership of all of you, we have the lowest violent crime rate in a quarter-century and the cleanest environment in a quarter-century. America is a strong force for peace, from Northern Ireland to Bosnia to the Middle East.

Thanks to the pioneering leadership of Vice President [Al] Gore, we have a government for the Information Age; once again, a government that is a progressive instrument of the common good, rooted in our oldest values of opportunity, responsibility and community, devoted to fiscal responsibility, determined to give our people the tools they need to make the most of their own lives in the 21st century, a 21st century government for 21st century America.

My fellow Americans, I stand before you tonight to report that the state of our union is strong.

America is working again. The promise of our future is limitless. But we cannot realize that promise if we allow the hum of our prosperity to lull us into complacency. How we fare as a nation far into the 21st century depends upon what we do as a nation today.

So with our budget surplus growing, our economy expanding, our confidence rising, now is the moment for this generation to meet our historic responsibility to the 21st century.

Our fiscal discipline gives us an unsurpassed opportunity to address a remarkable new challenge: the aging of America.

The Coming 'Senior Boom'

With the number of elderly Americans set to double by 2030, the Baby Boom will become a "senior boom." So first and above all, we must save Social Security for the 21st century. Early in this century, being old meant being poor. When President [Franklin D.] Roosevelt created Social Security, thousands wrote to thank him for eliminating what one woman called the "stark terror of penniless, helpless old age." Even today, without Social Security, half our nation's elderly would be forced into poverty.

Today Social Security is strong. But by 2013, payroll taxes will no longer be sufficient to cover monthly payments. By 2032, the trust fund will be exhausted and Social Security will be unable to pay the full benefits older Americans have been promised.

The best way to keep Social Security a rock-solid guarantee is not to make drastic cuts in benefits, not to raise payroll tax rates, not to drain resources from Social Security in the name of saving it. Instead, I propose that we make the historic decision to invest the surplus to save Social Security.

Specifically, I propose that we commit 60 percent of the budget surplus for the next 15 years to Social Security, investing a small portion in the private sector just as any private or state government pension would do. This will earn a higher return and keep Social Security sound for 55 years.

But we must aim higher. We should put Social Security on a sound footing for the next 75 years. We should reduce poverty among elderly women, who are nearly twice as likely to be poor as our other seniors, and we should eliminate the limits on what seniors on Social Security can earn.

Now, these changes will require difficult but fully achievable choices over and above the dedication of the surplus. They must be made on a bipartisan basis. They should be made this year. So let me say to you tonight, I reach out my hand to all of you in both houses and both parties and ask that we join together in saying to the American people: We will save Social Security now.

Now, last year, we wisely reserved all of the surplus until we knew what it would take to save Social Security. Again, I say we shouldn't spend any of it, not any of it, until after Social Security is truly saved. First things first.

Second, once we have saved Social Security, we must fulfill our obligation to save and improve Medicare. Already, we have extended the life of the Medicare Trust Fund by 10 years, but we should extend it for at least another decade. Tonight I propose that we use one out of every six dollars in the surplus for the next 15 years to guarantee the soundness of Medicare until the year 2020.

But again, we should aim higher. We must be willing to work in a bipartisan way and look at new ideas, including the upcoming report of the bipartisan Medicare commission. If we work together, we can secure Medicare for the next two decades and cover the greatest growing need of seniors: affordable prescription drugs.

Third, we must help all Americans from their first day on the job to save, to invest, to create wealth. From its beginning, Americans have supplemented Social Security with private pensions and savings. Yet today, millions of people retire with little to live on other than Social Security. Americans living longer than ever simply must save more than ever.

New Pension Initiative

Therefore, in addition to saving Social Security and Medicare, I propose a new pension initiative for retirement security in the 21st century. I propose that we use a little over 11 percent of the surplus to establish Universal Savings Accounts — USA Accounts — to give all Americans the means to save. With these new accounts, Americans can invest as they choose, and receive funds to match a portion of their savings, with extra help for those least able to save. USA Accounts will help all Americans to share in our nation's wealth and to enjoy a more secure retirement. I ask you to support them.

Fourth, we must invest in long-term care. I propose a tax credit of $1,000 for the aged, ailing or disabled and the families who care for them. Long-term care will become a bigger and bigger challenge with the aging of America, and we must do more to help our families deal with it.

I was born in 1946, the first year of the Baby Boom. I can tell you that one of the greatest concerns of our generation is our absolute determination not to let our growing old place an intolerable burden on our children and their ability to raise our grandchildren. Our economic success and our fiscal discipline now give us an opportunity to lift that burden from their shoulders and we should take it.

Saving Social Security, Medicare, creating USA Accounts — this is the right way to use the surplus. If we do so — if we do so — we will still have resources to meet critical needs in education and defense.

And I want to point out that this proposal is fiscally sound. Listen to this: If we set aside 60 percent of the surplus for Social Security and 16 percent for Medicare, over the next 15 years that saving will achieve the lowest level of publicly held debt since right before World War I, in 1917.

So, with these four measures — saving Social Security, strengthening Medicare, establishing the USA Accounts, supporting long-term care — we can begin to meet our generation's historic responsibility to establish true security for 21st century seniors.

Now, there are more children from more diverse backgrounds in our public schools than at any time in our history. Their education must provide the knowledge and nurture the creativity that will allow our entire nation to thrive in the new economy. Today we can say something we could not say six years ago: With tax credits and more affordable student loans, with more work-study grants and more Pell grants, with education IRAs and the new HOPE Scholarship tax cut that more than 5 million Americans will receive this year, we have finally opened the doors of college to all Americans.

With our support, nearly every state has set higher academic standards for public schools, and a voluntary national test is being developed to measure the progress of our students. With over $1 billion in discounts available this year, we are well on our way to our goal of connecting every classroom and library to the Internet.

Last fall you passed our proposal to start hiring 100,000 new teachers to reduce class size in the early grades. Now I ask you to finish the job.

You know, our children are doing better. SAT scores are up. Math scores have risen in nearly all grades. But there is a problem: While our fourth-graders outperform their peers in other countries in math and science, our eighth-graders are around average, and our 12th-graders rank near the bottom. We must do better.

Now each year, the national government invests more than $15 billion in our public schools. I believe we must change the way we invest that money, to support what works and to stop supporting what does not work.

Accountability in Education

First, later this year, I will send to Congress a plan that for the first time holds states and school districts accountable for progress and rewards them for results. My Education Accountability Act will require every school district receiving federal help to take the following five steps:

First, all schools must end social promotion.

Now, no child should graduate from high school with a diploma he or she can't read. We do our children no favors when we allow them to pass from grade to grade without mastering the material.

But we can't just hold students back because the system fails them. So my balanced budget triples the funding for summer school and after-school programs to keep a million children learning. If you doubt this will work, just look at Chicago, which ended social promotion and made summer school mandatory for those who don't master the basics. Math and reading scores are up three years running, with some of the biggest gains in some of the poorest neighborhoods. It will work, and we should do it.

Second, all states and school districts must turn around their worst-performing schools, or shut them down. That's the policy established in North Carolina by Gov. [James B.] Hunt [Jr]. North Carolina made the biggest gains in test scores in the nation last year. Our budget includes $200 million to help states turn around their own failing schools.

Third, all states and school districts must be held responsible for the quality of their teachers. The great majority of our teachers do a fine job. But in too many schools, teachers don't have college majors — or even minors — in the subjects they teach.

New teachers should be required to pass performance exams, and all teachers should know the subjects they are teaching.

This year's balanced budget contains resources to help them reach higher standards. And to attract talented young teachers to the toughest assignments, I recommend a sixfold increase in our program for college scholarships for students who commit to teach in the inner cities and isolated rural areas and in Indian communities. Let us bring excellence to every part of America.

Fourth, we must empower parents with more information and more choices. In too many communities, it's easier to get information on the quality of the local restaurants than on the quality of the local schools. Every school district should issue report cards on every school.

And parents should be given more choice in selecting their public schools. When I became president, there was one independent, public charter school in all America. With our support, on a bipartisan basis, today there are 1,100. My budget assures that early in the next century, there will be 3,000.

Fifth, to assure that our classrooms are truly places of learning, and to respond to what teachers have been asking us to do for years, we should say that all states and school districts must both adopt and implement sensible discipline policies.

Now, let's do one more thing for our children. Today too many schools are so old they're falling apart, are so overcrowded students are learning in trailers. Last fall Congress missed the opportunity to change that. This year, with 53 million children in our schools, Congress must not miss that opportunity again. I ask you to help our communities build or modernize 5,000 schools.

Now if we do these things — end social promotion; turn around failing schools; build modern ones; support qualified teachers; promote innovation, competition and discipline — then we will begin to meet our generation's historic responsibility to create 21st century schools.

Now we also have to do more to support the millions of parents who give their all every day at home and at work. The most basic tool of all is a decent income. So let's raise the minimum wage by $1 an hour over the next two years. And let's make sure that women and men get equal pay for equal work by strengthening enforcement of equal pay laws. . . .

Working parents also need quality child care. So again this year, I ask Congress to support our plan for tax credits and subsidies for working families, for improved safety and quality, for expanded after-school programs. And our plan also includes a new tax credit for stay-at-home parents too. They need support as well.

Parents should never have to worry about choosing between their children and their work. Now, the Family Medical Leave Act — the very first bill I signed into law — has since 1993 helped millions and millions of Americans to care for a newborn baby or an ailing relative without risking their jobs. I think it's time, with all the evidence that it has been so little burdensome to employers, to extend family leave to 10 million more Americans working for smaller companies. And I hope you will support it.

Finally, on the matter of work, parents should never have to face discrimination in the workplace. So I want to ask Congress to prohibit companies from refusing to hire or promote workers simply because they have children. That is not right.

'Patients' Bill of Rights'

America's families deserve the world's best medical care. Thanks to bipartisan federal support for medical research, we are now on the verge of new treatments to prevent or delay diseases from Parkinson's to Alzheimer's to arthritis to cancer, but as we continue our advances in medical science, we can't let our health care system lag behind.

Managed care has transformed medicine in America, driving down costs, but threatening to drive down quality as well. I think we ought to say to every American: You should have the right to know all your medical options, not just the cheapest. If you need a specialist, you should have a right to see one. You have a right to the nearest emergency care if you are in an accident. These are things that we ought to say, and I think we ought to say you should have a right to keep your doctor during a period of treatment, whether it's a pregnancy or chemotherapy treatment or anything else. I believe this.

Now, I have ordered these rights to be extended to the 85 million Americans served by Medicare, Medicaid and other federal health programs.

But only Congress can pass a Patients' Bill of Rights for all Americans. Now, last year Congress missed that opportunity, and we must not miss that opportunity again. For the sake of our families, I ask us to join together across party lines and pass a strong, enforceable Patients' Bill of Rights.

As more of our medical records are stored electronically, the threats to all our privacy increase. Because Congress has given me the authority to act if it does not do so by August, one way or another, we can all say to the American people we will protect the privacy of medical records and we will do it this year.

Now, two years ago, the Congress extended health coverage to up to 5 million children. Now, we should go beyond that. We should make it easier for small businesses to offer health insurance. We should give people between the ages of 55 and 65 who lose their health insurance the chance to buy into Medicare, and we should continue to ensure access to family planning. No one should have to choose between keeping health care and taking a job. And therefore, I especially ask you tonight to join hands to pass the landmark bipartisan legislation proposed by Sens. [Edward M.] Kennedy [D-Mass.] and [James M.] Jeffords [R-Vt.], [William V.] Roth [Jr., R-Del.] and [Daniel Patrick] Moynihan [D-N.Y.], to allow people with disabilities to keep their health insurance when they go to work.

We need to enable our public hospitals, our community, our university health centers to provide basic, affordable care for all the millions of working families who don't have any insurance. They do a lot of that today, but much more can be done. And my balanced budget makes a good down payment toward that goal. I hope you will think about them and support that provision.

Let me say we must step up our efforts to treat and prevent mental illness. No American should ever be afraid, ever, to address this disease. This year we will host a White House Conference on Mental Health. With sensitivity, commitment and passion, Tipper Gore is leading our efforts here, and I thank her for what she's done on it.

As everyone knows, our children are targets of a massive media campaign to hook them on cigarettes. Now I ask this Congress to resist the tobacco lobby, to reaffirm the FDA's [Food and Drug Administration] authority to protect children from tobacco, and to hold the tobacco companies accountable while protecting tobacco farmers.

Federal Litigation on Tobacco

Smoking has cost taxpayers hundreds of billions of dollars under Medicare and other programs. You know, the states have been right about this: Taxpayers shouldn't pay for the costs of lung cancer, emphysema and other smoking-related illnesses, the tobacco companies should. So tonight I announce that the Justice Department is preparing a litigation plan to take the tobacco companies to court, and with the funds we recover, to strengthen Medicare.

Now, if we act in these areas — minimum wage, family leave, child care, health care, the safety of our children — then we will begin to meet our generation's historic responsibility to strengthen our families for the 21st century.

Today, America is the most dynamic, competitive, job-creating economy in history. But we can do even better in building a 21st century economy that embraces all Americans.

Today's income gap is largely a skills gap. Last year, the Congress passed a law enabling workers to get a skills grant to choose the training they need, and I applaud all of you here who were part of that. This year, I recommend a five-year commitment to the new system so that we can provide over the next five years appropriate training opportunities for all Americans who lose their jobs and expand rapid response teams to help all towns which have been really hurt when businesses close. I hope you will support this.

Also, I ask for a dramatic increase in federal support for adult literacy, to mount a national campaign aimed at helping the millions and millions of working people who still read at less than a fifth-grade level. We need to do this.

Here's some good news: In the past six years, we have cut the welfare rolls nearly in half. Two years ago from this podium, I asked five companies to lead a national effort to hire people off welfare. Tonight, our Welfare to Work Partnership includes 10,000 companies who have hired hundreds of thousands of people. And our balanced budget will help another 200,000 people move to the dignity and pride of work. I hope you will support it.

We must do more to bring the spark of private enterprise to every corner of America, to build a bridge from Wall Street to Appalachia to the Mississippi Delta to our Native American communities, with more support for community development banks, for empowerment zones, for 100,000 more vouchers for affordable housing. And I ask Congress to support our bold new plan to help businesses raise up to $15 billion in private sector capital to bring jobs and opportunities to our inner cities and rural areas — with tax credits and loan guarantees, including the new American Private Investment Companies modeled on the Overseas Private Investment Company.

Now, for years and years and years we've had this OPIC, this Overseas Private Investment Corporation, because we knew we had untapped markets overseas. But our greatest untapped markets are not overseas; they are right here at home, and we should go after them.

We must work hard to help bring prosperity back to the family farm. As this Congress knows very well, dropping prices and the loss of foreign markets have devastated too many family farms. Last year the Congress provided substantial assistance to help stave off a disaster in American agriculture, and I am ready to work with lawmakers of both parties to create a farm safety net that will include crop insurance reform and farm income assistance.

I ask you to join with me and do this. This should not be a political issue. Everyone knows what an economic problem is going on out there in rural America today, and we need an appropriate means to address it.

We must strengthen our lead in technology. It was government investment that led to the creation of the Internet. I propose a 28 percent increase in long-term computing research.

Y2K Computer Problem

We also must be ready for the 21st century, from its very first moment, by solving the Y2K computer problem. Remember, this is a big, big problem. And we've been working hard on it. Already we've made sure that the Social Security checks will come on time. But I want all the folks at home listening to this to know that we need every state and local government, every business, large and small, to work with us to make sure that this Y2K computer bug will be remembered as the last headache of the 20th century, not the first crisis of the 21st.

Now, for our own prosperity, we must support economic growth abroad. You know, until recently, a third of our economic growth came from exports. But over the past year and a half, financial turmoil overseas has put that growth at risk. Today much of the world is in recession, with Asia hit especially hard.

This is the most serious financial crisis in half a century. To meet it, the United States and other nations have reduced interest rates and strengthened the International Monetary Fund. And while the turmoil is not over, we have worked very hard with other nations to contain it.

At the same time, we have to continue to work on the long-term project, building a global financial system for the 21st century that promotes prosperity and tames the cycles of boom and bust that have engulfed so much of Asia. This June I will meet with other world leaders to advance this historic purpose. And I ask all of you to support our endeavors.

I also ask you to support creating a freer and fairer trading system for 21st century America.

I'd like to say something really serious to everyone in this chamber and both parties. I think trade has divided us and divided Americans outside this chamber for too long. Somehow we have to find a common ground on which business and workers, and environmentalists, and farmers and government can stand together. I believe these are the things we ought to all agree on. So let me try.

First, we ought to tear down barriers, open markets and expand trade. But at the same time, we must ensure that ordinary citizens in all countries actually benefit from trade — a trade that promotes the dignity of work and the rights of workers — and protects the environment. We must insist that international trade organizations be open to public scrutiny instead of mysterious, secret things subject to wild criticism.

When you come right down to it, now that the world economy is becoming more and more integrated, we have to do in the world what we spent the better part of this century doing here at home — we have got to put a human face on the global economy.

Now, we must enforce our trade laws when imports unlawfully flood our nation. I have already informed the government of Japan that if that nation's sudden surge of steel imports into our country is not reversed, America will respond.

We must help all manufacturers hit hard by the present crisis with loan guarantees and other incentives to increase American exports by nearly $2 billion.

I'd like to believe we can achieve a new consensus on trade based on these principles, and I ask the Congress again to join me in this common approach and to give the president the trade authority long used, and now overdue and necessary, to advance our prosperity in the 21st century.

Tonight, I also issue a call to the nations of the world to join the United States in a new round of global trade negotiation to expand exports of services, manufacturers and farm products.

Tonight I say we will work with the International Labor Organization on a new initiative to raise labor standards around the world. And this year, we will lead the international community to conclude a treaty to ban abusive child labor everywhere in the world.

If we do these things — invest in our people, our communities, our technology, and lead in the global economy — then we will begin to meet our historic responsibility to build a 21st century prosperity for America.

You know, no nation in history has had the opportunity and the responsibility we now have to shape a world that is more peaceful, more secure, more free.

Peacekeeping and Arms Control

All Americans can be proud that our leadership helped to bring peace in Northern Ireland. All Americans can be proud that our leadership has put Bosnia on the path to peace. And with our NATO allies, we are pressing the Serbian government to stop its brutal repression in Kosovo, to bring those responsible to justice and to give the people of Kosovo the self-government they deserve.

All Americans can be proud that our leadership renewed hope for lasting peace in the Middle East. Some of you were with me last December as we watched the Palestinian National Council completely renounce its call for the destruction of Israel. Now I ask Congress to provide resources so that all parties can implement the Wye Agreement, to protect Israel's security, to stimulate the Palestinian economy, to support our friends in Jordan. We must not, we dare not, let them down. I hope you will help.

As we work for peace, we must also meet threats to our nation's security, including increased dangers from outlaw nations and terrorism. We will defend our security wherever we are threatened, as we did this summer when we struck at Osama bin Laden's network of terror. The bombing of our embassies in Kenya and Tanzania reminds us again of the risks faced every day by those who represent America to the world. So let's give them the support they need, the safest possible workplaces, and the resources they must have so America can continue to lead.

We must work to keep terrorists from disrupting computer networks. We must work to prepare local communities for biological and chemical emergencies, to support research into vaccines and treatments.

We must increase our efforts to restrain the spread of nuclear weapons and missiles, from Korea to India and Pakistan. We must expand our work with Russia, Ukraine and the other former Soviet nations to safeguard nuclear materials and technology so they never fall into the wrong hands.

Our balanced budget will increase funding for these critical efforts by almost two-thirds over the next five years.

With Russia, we must continue to reduce our nuclear arsenals. The START II Treaty and the framework we have already agreed to for START III could cut them by 80 percent from their Cold War height.

It's been two years since I signed the Comprehensive Test Ban Treaty. If we don't do the right thing, other nations won't either. I ask the Senate to take this vital step: Approve the Treaty now, to make it harder for other nations to develop nuclear arms and to make sure we can end nuclear testing forever.

For nearly a decade, Iraq has defied its obligations to destroy its weapons of terror and the missiles to deliver them. America will continue to contain [Iraqi President] Saddam [Hussein], and we will work for the day when Iraq has a government worthy of its people.

Now, last month, in our action over Iraq, our troops were superb. Their mission was so flawlessly executed that we risk taking for granted the bravery and the skill it required. Capt. Jeff Taliaferro, a 10-year veteran of the Air Force, flew a B-1B bomber over Iraq as we attacked Saddam's war machine. He is here with us tonight. I'd like to ask you to honor him and all the 33,000 men and women of Operation Desert Fox.

Building Up the Defense Budget

It is time to reverse the decline in defense spending that began in 1985. Since

April, together we have added nearly $6 billion to maintain our military readiness. My balanced budget calls for a sustained increase over the next six years for readiness, for modernization, and for pay and benefits for our troops and their families.

You know, we are the heirs of a legacy of bravery represented in every community of America by millions of our veterans. America's defenders today still stand ready at a moment's notice to go where comforts are few and dangers are many, to do what needs to be done as no one else can. They always come through for America. We must come through for them.

The new century demands new partnerships for peace and security. The United Nations plays a crucial role, with allies sharing burdens America might otherwise bear alone. America needs a strong and effective U.N. I want to work with this new Congress to pay our dues and our debts.

We must continue to support security and stability in Europe and Asia, expanding NATO and defining its new missions, maintaining our alliance with Japan, with Korea, with our other Asian allies, and engaging China.

In China last year, I said to the leaders and the people what I'd like to say again tonight: Stability can no longer be bought at the expense of liberty. But I'd also like to say again to the American people: It's important not to isolate China. The more we bring China into the world, the more the world will bring change and freedom to China.

Last spring, with some of you, I traveled to Africa, where I saw democracy and reform rising, but still held back by violence and disease. We must fortify African democracy and peace by launching Radio Democracy for Africa, supporting the transition to democracy now beginning to take place in Nigeria, and passing the African Trade and Development Act.

We must continue to deepen our ties to the Americas and the Caribbean, our common work to educate children, fight drugs, strengthen democracy and increase trade. In this hemisphere, every government but one is freely chosen by its people. We are determined that Cuba, too, will know the blessings of liberty.

The American people have opened their hearts and their arms to our Central American and Caribbean neighbors who have been so devastated by the recent hurricanes. Working with Congress, I am committed to help them rebuild. When the first lady and Tipper Gore visited the region, they saw thousands of our troops and thousands of American volunteers. In the Dominican Republic, first lady Hillary [Clinton] helped to rededicate a hospital that had been rebuilt by Dominicans and Americans working side by side. With her was someone else who has been very important to the relief efforts.

You know, sports records are made, and sooner or later, they are broken. But making other people's lives better — and showing our children the true meaning of brotherhood — that lasts forever. So for far more than baseball, Sammy Sosa, you are a hero in two countries tonight. Thank you.

So I say to all of you, if we do these things — if we pursue peace, fight terrorism, increase our strength, renew our alliances — we will begin to meet our generation's historic responsibility to build a stronger 21st century America in a freer, more peaceful world.

As the world has changed, so have our own communities. We must make them safer, more livable and more united. This year, we will reach our goal of 100,000 community police officers ahead of schedule and under budget. The Brady bill has stopped a quarter- million felons, fugitives and stalkers from buying handguns. And now, the murder rate is the lowest in 30 years, and the crime rate has dropped for six straight years. Tonight I propose a 21st century crime bill, to deploy the latest technologies and tactics to make our communities even safer.

Our balanced budget will help put up to 50,000 more police on the street in the areas hardest hit by crime and then to equip them with new tools, from crime-mapping computers to digital mug shots. We must break the deadly cycle of drugs and crime. Our budget expands support for drug testing and treatment, saying to prisoners, "If you stay on drugs, you have to stay behind bars," and to those on parole, "If you want to keep your freedom, you must stay free of drugs."

Gun Control

I ask Congress to restore the five-day waiting period for buying a handgun and extend the Brady bill to prevent juveniles who commit violent crimes from buying a gun.

We must do more to keep our schools the safest places in our communities. Last year every American was horrified and heartbroken by the tragic killings in Jonesboro, Paducah, Pearl, Edinboro, Springfield. We were deeply moved by the courageous parents, now working to keep guns out of the hands of children, and to make other efforts so that other parents don't have to live through their loss.

After she lost her daughter, Suzann Wilson of Jonesboro, Ark., came here to the White House with a powerful plea. She said, "Please, please, for the sake of your children, lock up your guns. Don't let what happened in Jonesboro happen in your town." It is a message she is passionately advocating every day. Suzann is here with us tonight with the first lady. I'd like to thank her for her courage and her commitment.

In memory of all the children who lost their lives to school violence, I ask you to strengthen the Safe and Drug-Free School Act, to pass legislation to require child trigger locks, to do everything possible to keep our children safe.

A century ago, President Theodore Roosevelt defined our "great, central task" as "leaving this land even a better land for our descendants than it is for us." Today, we are restoring the Florida Everglades, saving Yellowstone, preserving the red-rock canyons of Utah, protecting California's redwoods and our precious coasts. But our most fateful new challenge is the threat of global warming. 1998 was the warmest year ever recorded. Last year's heat waves, floods and storms are but a hint of what future generations may endure if we do not act now.

Tonight, I propose a new clean air fund to help communities reduce greenhouse and other pollution, and tax incentives and investment to spur clean energy technologies. And I want to work with members of Congress in both parties to reward companies that take early, voluntary action to reduce greenhouse gases.

Now, all our communities face a preservation challenge as they grow and green space shrinks. Seven thousand acres of farmland and open space are lost every day. In response, I propose two major initiatives. First, a $1 billion Livability Agenda to help communities save open space, ease traffic congestion and grow in ways that enhance every citizen's quality of life. And second, a $1 billion Lands Legacy Initiative to preserve places of natural beauty all across America, from the most remote wilderness to the nearest city park.

These are truly landmark initiatives which could not have been developed without the visionary leadership of the vice president, and I want to thank him very much for his commitment here.

Now, to get the most out of your community, you have to give something back. That's why we created AmeriCorps — our national service program that gives today's generation a chance to serve their communities and earn money for college. So far, in just four years, 100,000 young Americans have built low-income homes with Habitat for Humanity, helped to tutor children with churches, worked with FEMA [the Federal Emergency Management Agency] to ease the burden of natural disasters, and performed countless other acts of service that have made America better. I ask Congress to give more young Americans the chance to follow their lead and serve America in AmeriCorps.

We must work to renew our national community as well for the 21st century.

Last year, the House passed the bipartisan campaign finance reform legislation sponsored by Reps. [Christopher] Shays [R-Conn.] and [Martin T.] Meehan [D-Mass.] and Sens. [John] McCain [R-Ariz.] and [Russell D.] Feingold [D-Wis.]. But a partisan minority in the Senate blocked reform. So I'd like to say to the House: Pass it again, quickly.

And I'd like to say to the Senate, I hope you will say yes to a stronger American democracy in the year 2000.

Initiative on Race

Since 1997, our Initiative on Race has sought to bridge the divides between and among our people. In its report last fall, the initiative's advisory board found that Americans really do want to bring our people together across racial lines. We know it's been a long journey. For some it goes back to before the beginning of our republic, for others back since the Civil War, for others throughout the 20th century. But for most of us alive today, in a very real sense this journey began 43 years ago when a woman named Rosa Parks sat down on a bus in Alabama and wouldn't get up. She's sitting down with the first lady tonight, and she may get up or not, as she chooses.

We know that our continuing racial problems are aggravated, as the presidential initiative said, by opportunity gaps. The initiative I have outlined tonight will help to close them. But we know that the discrimination gap has not been fully closed, either.

Discrimination or violence because of race or religion, ancestry or gender, disability or sexual orientation is wrong and it ought to be illegal. Therefore, I ask Congress to make the Employment Non-Discrimination Act and the Hate Crimes Prevention Act the law of the land.

Now, since every person in America counts, every American ought to be counted. We need a census that uses [the] most modern scientific methods to do that.

Our new immigrants must be part of our one America. After all, they're revitalizing our cities, they're energizing our culture, they're building up our new economy. We have a responsibility to make them welcome here, and they have a responsibility to enter the mainstream of American life. That means learning English and learning about our democratic system of government. There are now long waiting lines of immigrants that are trying to do just that. Therefore, our budget significantly expands our efforts to help them meet their responsibility. I hope you will support it.

Whether our ancestors came here on the Mayflower, on slave ships, whether they came to Ellis Island or LAX in Los Angeles, whether they came yesterday or walked this land a thousand years ago, our great challenge for the 21st century is to find a way to be one America. We can meet all the other challenges if we can go forward as one America.

You know, barely more than 300 days from now, we will cross that bridge into the new millennium. This is a moment, as the first lady has said, to honor the past and imagine the future. I'd like to take just a minute to honor her for leading our Millennium Project, for all she's done for our children, for all she has done in her historic role to serve our nation and our best ideals at home and abroad. I honor her.

Last year I called on Congress and every citizen to mark the millennium by saving America's treasures. Hillary has traveled all across the country to inspire recognition and support for saving places like Thomas Edison's invention factory or Harriet Tubman's home. Now we have to preserve our treasures in every community. And tonight, before I close, I want to invite every town, every city, every community to become a nationally recognized "millennium community" by launching projects that save our history, promote our arts and humanities, prepare our children for the 21st century.

Already, the response has been remarkable, and I want to say a special word of thanks to our private sector partners and to members in Congress, of both parties, for their support. Just one example: Because of you, the Star Spangled Banner will be preserved for the ages.

In ways large and small, as we look to the millennium, we are keeping alive what George Washington called "the sacred fire of liberty."

Six years ago, I came to office in a time of doubt for America, with our economy troubled, our deficit high, our people divided. Some even wondered whether our best days were behind us. But across this country, in a thousand neighborhoods, I have seen, even amidst the pain and uncertainty of recession, the real heart and character of America. I knew then that we Americans could renew this country.

Tonight, as I deliver the last State of the Union address of the 20th century, no one anywhere in the world can doubt the enduring resolve and boundless capacity of the American people to work toward that "more perfect union" of our founders' dreams. We're now at the end of a century when generation after generation of Americans answered the call to greatness, overcoming Depression, lifting up the dispossessed, bringing down barriers to racial prejudice, building the largest middle class in history, winning two world wars and the "long twilight struggle" of the Cold War.

We must all be profoundly grateful for the magnificent achievements of our forebears in this century. Yet perhaps in the daily press of events, in the clash of controversy, we do not see our own time for what it truly is: a new dawn for America.

A hundred years from tonight, an American president will stand in this place to report on the State of the Union. He — or she — will look back on a 21st century shaped in so many ways by the decisions we make here and now. So let it be said of us then that we were thinking not only of our time, but of their time; that we reached as high as our ideals; that we put aside our divisions and found a new hour of healing and hopefulness; that we joined together to serve and strengthen the land we love.

My fellow Americans, this is our moment. Let us lift our eyes as one nation, and from the mountaintop of this American century, look ahead to the next one, asking God's blessing on our endeavors and on our beloved country.

Thank you, and good evening. ◆

GOP Response: Tax Relief, Social Security Overhaul Are 'Practical' Priorities

Following is the Federal News Service transcript of the text of the Republican response to President Clinton's Jan. 19 State of the Union address, delivered by Reps. Jennifer Dunn of Washington and Steve Largent of Oklahoma.

Dunn: Good evening. I'm Jennifer Dunn. I represent the people of the Eighth District of Washington state.

Largent: And I'm Steve Largent, from the First District of Oklahoma.

Dunn: As you might imagine, if you had been sitting with us in the House chamber tonight as the president was giving his speech, you could have felt the swirl of history. These are disturbing and controversial times in our nation's capital. A couple of weeks ago, I even heard a network anchor say the capital is in chaos. Another proclaimed we are in the midst of a constitutional crisis.

Ladies and gentlemen, our country is not in crisis. There are no tanks in the streets. Our system of government is as solid as the Capitol dome you see behind me. Our democracy is sound. Our economy is prosperous. The state of our union is strong. And no matter what the outcome of the president's situation, life in America will go on. Our lives will continue to be filled with practical matters, not constitutional ones.

I've been a single mother since my boys were little, 6 and 8. My life in those days was taken up with meeting — trying to make ends meet, trying to get to two soccer games at the same time on two different fields, worrying about dropping the boys off early at school in order for me to get to work on time. I know how that knot in the pit of your stomach feels. I've been there.

I'm still a practical person. You heard the president make a lot of promises to a lot of people tonight. But I'd like to talk to you about two very practical Republican priorities: tax relief and Social Security reform.

Our current tax system is a burden on the economy and on the American people. Let me tell you a story about a fellow I represent from North Bend, Wash., whose name is Robert Allen. A few years ago the IRS denied his right to file a joint return with his wife because they said his wife Shirley was deceased. Well, I've seen Shirley. She looks pretty good for a dead person. Robert took Shirley to the IRS office in Seattle. The IRS was not convinced. So the Allens brought in their family doctor, and in his medical opinion he pronounced Shirley alive. The IRS was still not convinced. It took intervention by a member of Congress — me — to resolve this comedy, which in truth is a tragedy, because it's symbolic of how removed our entire tax system has become from reality and from common sense.

Last year we passed legislation reining in the IRS so that taxpayers are now considered innocent until proven guilty. But so much more needs to be done. Next year there will be a $63 billion budget surplus. Mr. President, give it back.

Last year a typical mother and father who both worked paid nearly 40 percent of their income in taxes. That means 40 cents out of every dollar they earned went to the government in federal, state or local taxes. That's the highest percentage of income ever paid in taxes by American families.

I don't know about you, but that really bothers me. No wonder so many American families are struggling. Get married and your taxes go up. Save for your children's education and your taxes go up. And when you die — that's right — your taxes go up. The government gets a bigger piece of your life's work than all your children put together.

So what can you expect from Republicans? Expect action.

First, tonight, we're proposing a 10 percent, across-the-board cut in tax rates for every working American. That's the down payment on a simpler, fairer, flatter tax system.

Second, we must end the marriage penalty. We should honor commitment, not tax it.

And third, we must cut death taxes so that families don't have to sell their businesses and farms when Mom and Dad die.

In all of our tax policies, we start from this premise: The people's money belongs to the people, not to the government.

The second thing I want to talk about is Social Security. A year ago, in his State of the Union speech, the president said he was committed to saving Social Security.

I'm glad to hear him discuss it again this evening. Unfortunately, spending the surplus as he proposes will not save Social Security; it just temporarily props it up with some extra cash. Mr. President, we're still waiting for real legislation. We've reserved HR 1, the very first bill of this Congress, for the president's Social Security plan.

There's one thing we can all agree on, one non-negotiable principle: We must keep our contract with our senior citizens who depend on Social Security for part or all of their retirement income. This nation made that promise long ago and we will keep that promise.

But Social Security needs not just to be patched up, it needs to be updated for the 21st century. People today want and expect to have more control over their lives and over their money. But President Clinton's approach, as you just heard, gives the government more control of your retirement income. The Social Security dollars deducted from your paycheck currently earn less than 3 percent a year. That's not enough of a return. That's not going to keep Social Security solvent. And it's especially not fair to young people and to women.

For example, the current system works against mothers who choose to step out of their job for a while, away from their career, to raise children or to care for parents. It works against wives, who more often than not survive their husbands and they end up living for more years on fewer dollars.

And it works against young people, who believe they'll never see a Social Security check.

Here's a better way: Give working Americans the choice to invest some of their Social Security dollars in personal retirement accounts. We can do this without touching a dime in Social Security funds, without raising one nickel in taxes, and without touching one penny of current benefits.

A new century requires a new beginning in approaches, in ideas, and yes, in civility and cooperation between political parties.

I'd like to close on a personal note. I'm a mother, a gardener, a Republican and a member of Congress. Believe me, all four take patience. My boys, thankfully, turned out to be wonderful young men. My plants at home, unfortunately, need a lot of work. And as for my efforts in the Congress, I am constantly planting and watering.

As one citizen to another, in spite of all the troubling things you hear about our nation's capital, I believe that good ideas can take root here. Good things can grow here, and good things can blossom here.

And now, my friend, Steve Largent.

Largent: Thanks, Jennifer. First, let me say what a special privilege it is to speak to you and give my response and the Republicans' response to the president's remarks.

Let me tell you a bit about myself. I grew up in Oklahoma and was born in the very district I'm now proud to represent. I was raised in a broken home, and thanks to my mom, I stayed in school, stayed out of most trouble and went to college.

I married my high school sweetheart, Terry, a cheerleader. And for the next 14 years I got to live every boy's dream: playing in the National Football League, for the Seattle Seahawks. After I concluded my career in the NFL, I started my own marketing and advertising business back in Tulsa.

But in 1994, I campaigned for the first elective office in my life — and won. I came to Washington with a group of Republicans committed to balancing the budget, slowing the growth of government, cutting taxes, reforming welfare and saving Medicare. And that's exactly what we did.

But as Babe Ruth once said, yesterday's home runs don't win today's games. It's time to step up to the plate once again.

Prior to 1994, my wife and I, we weren't political. We were like most families — raising four kids, hustling from one school or sports event to another, our car littered by fast-food wrappers and french fries. In fact, it wasn't until after I was elected that I attended a Republican function where a banner hung that read, "GOP." I had to ask someone what those letters stood for. They said, "Grand Old Party, of course."

I believe tonight is an appropriate time to ask once again, what does the GOP stand for? What does the party of Lincoln and Reagan stand for today? What are the lasting bedrock principles that personify and distinguish the Republican Party? It's these questions I want to answer tonight, because the answer is why I ran for office in the first place.

Here's the 15-second sound bite answer: The Republican Party's mission is to promote, preserve and protect individual liberty, free enterprise and limited government. But what does that mean to my family and your family?

Let's start with individual liberty. We must preserve the notion that true liberty and freedom come from God and are his blessing on this land, and that freedom reigns only as we act responsibly — toward God, each other and his creation. Our freedom was bought at a great price, and our most important responsibility is to defend this sacred gift and to keep our country secure.

Tonight we support our troops that are stationed in Bosnia, the Middle East and around the world. And the good news is that after six years of cutting spending for our armed forces, the president has signaled that he's ready to join us in strengthening our national defense. We must never be complacent in what is still a dangerous world. Terrorists and rogue nations are rapidly acquiring technology to deliver weapons of mass destruction to our very doorstep. Most Americans are shocked to discover that our country is unshielded from the accidental or ruthless launch of even a single missile over our skies. Mr. President, we urge you, join Congress in establishing a viable missile defense system to protect the United States.

Protecting individual liberty also means protecting the unborn. Again, this year, overwhelming majorities in both houses will urge the president to end the dreadful and unwarranted practice of "partial-birth" abortion. We must uphold the sanctity of life amidst the tragedies of abortion, euthanasia and assisted suicide.

Republicans also promote free enterprise. We believe market principles like competition really work.

At the heart of free enterprise is good education. For far too long we've allowed Washington to dictate how our children are taught. One of our priorities is to give control of our schools to local communities. We want the most important election affecting your children's education to be the one that decides who sits on the school board, not who you send to Washington. Parents deserve the opportunity to choose the best school with the best curriculum, the best teachers and the safest environment for their children.

I recently met with a room full of teachers in Jenks, Okla. I came out of that meeting convinced, more than ever, that teachers like these know best how federal education dollars should be spent. That's why Republicans are leading the effort that will ensure 90 cents of every federal education dollar goes directly to the classroom, empowering parents and teachers, not bureaucrats.

And if we really want to "free" enterprise and the economy, let's scrap the Internal Revenue tax code. The 8,000-plus pages of confusion, contradiction and confiscation are choking small business and driving the average taxpayer mad.

Republicans want to establish a date by which the tax code will be abolished and replaced by something that's simple, fair and takes a smaller bite from the family's pocketbook.

Finally, Republicans stand for limited government. Ronald Reagan reminded us that a government that is big enough to give you everything you want is also big enough to take everything you have. And tonight, the federal government is still too big and taking more than it should. We will continue our efforts to control Washington's wasteful spending and its insatiable appetite for your money.

Well, this is what the Grand Old Party stands for, and if this represents your hopes and dreams, we ask not that you pull for us, but that you push with us. Back in my district, Oklahomans are steeped in America's deep tradition of faith, family, hard work and strong neighborhoods. They represent the values that hold communities together, and they believe in the power of a better tomorrow.

There's still a lot to be done, but I too am more optimistic than ever. These last four years have given me the unique opportunity to witness the grit and determination of the American people — our greatest resource.

Yesterday marked the 70th year since the birth of a great American leader and hero, Dr. Martin Luther King. In one of his last sermons, in 1968, Dr. King warned that while the world is a closer neighborhood, we are experiencing less brotherhood. That's equally true today. It is no longer the aggression from without that is America's greatest threat, but alienation from within; alienation at every level — husband from wife, mother from father, parent from child, black from white, Republican from Democrat, liberal from conservative. And there's only one solution: reconciliation. Ironically, the word Congress itself is made of two Latin words that mean "to walk together." Reconciliation requires the humility and courage to say, "I'm sorry. I was wrong. Will you forgive me?" Therein lies the healing salve for the wounded soul of our nation. You see, the body of our country is strong. It's the heart that needs attention.

On Christmas Eve, my family and I packed up our kids and gifts and headed to grandma's house. In the car, we sang along with Vince Gill's Christmas tape. As we sang one particular song, I was struck by the words and by their poignancy for our country tonight. The chorus went, "Let there be peace on Earth and let it begin with me."

So, let there be peace on Earth and let it begin with me. And let it begin with Republicans and Democrats and blacks and whites and moms and, yes, especially dads. Let there be peace on Earth and let it begin with all of us who comprise one nation, under God, indivisible.

And if we work together and walk together and if we have a Congress motivated not by the maintenance of power, but by principle, then I believe historians will tell our children's children, "There walked a great people — a nation that preserved the wonderful promise that we call America."

May God bless you and your family, and may God continue to bless this great nation.

Dunn: Thank you for listening. Good night. ◆

Hyde's Summation: 'We Must Never Tolerate One Law for the Ruler And Another for the Ruled'

Following is the Federal Document Clearing House transcript of the remarks to the Senate on Jan. 16 by House Judiciary Committee Chairman Henry J. Hyde, R-Ill., that concluded the initial presentation of the House managers in the impeachment trial of President Clinton:

Hyde: Mr. Chief Justice, counsel for the president, distinguished members of the Senate: 139 years ago — 136 years ago — at a small military cemetery in Pennsylvania, one of Illinois' most illustrious sons asked a haunting question: Whether a nation conceived in liberty and dedicated to the proposition that all men are created equal can long endure.

America is an experiment never finished; it's a work in progress. And so, that question has to be answered by each generation for itself, just as we will have to answer whether this nation can long endure.

This controversy began with the fact that the president of the United States took an oath to tell the truth in his testimony before the grand jury, just as he had on two prior occasions, sworn a solemn oath to preserve, protect and defend the Constitution and to faithfully execute the laws of the United States.

One of the most memorable aspects of this entire proceeding was the solemn occasion wherein every senator in this chamber took an oath to do impartial justice under the Constitution. But I must say, despite massive and relentless efforts to change the subject, the case before you, Senators, is not about sexual misconduct, infidelity, adultery. Those are private acts and are none of our business.

It's not even a question of lying about sex. The matter before this body is a question of lying under oath. This is a public act. The matter before you is a question of the willful, premeditated, deliberate corruption of the nation's system of justice through perjury and obstruction of justice.

These are public acts. And when committed by the chief law enforcement officer of the land, the one who appoints every United States district attorney, every federal judge, every member for the Supreme Court, the attorney general, they do become the concern of Congress. And that's why your judgment, respectfully, should rise above politics, above partisanship, above polling data.

This case is a test of whether what the Founding Fathers described as "sacred honor" still has meaning in our time 222 years after those two words, "sacred honor," were inscribed in our country's birth certificate, our national charter of freedom, our Declaration of Independence.

Every school child in the United States has an intuitive sense of the sacred honor that is one of the foundation stones of the American house of freedom, for every day in every classroom in America, our children and grandchildren pledge allegiance to a nation under God.

That statement is not a prideful or arrogant claim. It's a statement of humility. All of us as individuals stand under the judgment of God or the transcendent truths by which we hope finally to be judged. So does our country.

The presidency is an office of trust. Every public office is a public trust, but the office of the president is a very special public trust. The president is the trustee of the national conscience. No one owns the office of the president — the people do. The president is elected by the people and their representatives in the Electoral College. And accepting the burdens of that great office, the president in his inaugural oath enters into a covenant, a binding agreement of mutual trust and obligation with the American people.

Shortly after his election and during his first few months in office, President Clinton spoke with some frequency about a new covenant in America. In this instance, let's take the president at his word that his office is a covenant, a solemn pact of mutual trust and obligation with the American people. Let's take the president seriously when he speaks of covenants, because a covenant is about promise-making and promise-keeping.

For it's because the president has defaulted on the promises he made, it's because he has violated the oaths he has sworn, that he has been impeached. The debate about impeachment during the constitutional convention of 1787 makes it clear that the framers regarded impeachment and removal from office on conviction as a remedy for a fundamental betrayal of trust by the president.

The framers had invested the presidential office with great powers. They knew that those powers could be and would be abused if any president were to violate in a fundamental way the oath he had sworn to faithfully execute the nation's laws.

'The Covenant of Trust'

For if the president did so violate his oath of office, the covenant of trust between himself and the American people would be broken. Today, we see something else, that the fundamental trust between America and the world can be broken if a presidential perjurer represents our country in world affairs.

If the president calculatedly and repeatedly violates his oath, if the president breaks the covenant of trust he's made with the American people, he can no longer be trusted. And because the executive plays so large a role in representing our country to the world, America can no longer be trusted.

It's often said we live in an age of increasing interdependence. If that's true — and the evidence for it is all around us — then the future will require an even stronger bond of trust between the president and the nation, because with increasing interdependence comes an increased necessity of trust.

This is one of the basic lessons of life. Parents and children know it; husbands and wives know it; teachers and students know it; as do doctors, patients, suppliers, customers, lawyers, clients, clergy and parishioners.

The greater the interdependence, the greater the necessity of trust.The greater the interdependence, the greater the imperative of promise-keeping.

Trust, not what James Madison called the parchment barriers of laws, is the fundamental bond between the people and their elected representatives; between those who govern and those who are governed.

Trust is the mortar that secures the foundations of the American house of freedom. And the Senate of the United States, sitting in judgment on this impeachment trial, should not ignore or minimize or dismiss the fact that that bond of trust has been broken, because the president has violated both his oaths of office and the oath he took before his grand jury testimony.

In recent months, it's often been asked: So what? What is the harm done by this lying under oath, by this perjury?

Well, what is an oath? An oath is an

asking almighty God to witness to the truth of what you're saying. Truth telling, truth telling, is the heart and soul of our justice system. I think the answer would have been clear to those who once pledged their sacred honor to the cause of liberty. The answer would have been clear to those who crafted the world's most enduring written constitution.

No greater harm can come — can come than breaking the covenant of trust between the president and the people, between the three branches of our government, and between our country and the world, for to break that covenant of trust is to dissolve the mortar that binds the foundation stones of our freedom into a secure and solid edifice. And to break the covenant of trust by violating one's oath is to do grave damage to the rule of law among us.

That none of us is above the law is a bedrock principle of democracy. To erode that bedrock is to risk even further injustice. To erode that bedrock is to subscribe to a divine right of kings theory of governance in which those who govern are absolved from adhering to the basic moral standards to which the governed are accountable.

We must never tolerate one law for the ruler and another for the ruled. If we do, we break faith with our ancestors from Bunker Hill, Lexington and Concord to Flanders Fields, Normandy, Hiroshima, Panmunjom, Saigon and Desert Storm.

Let's be clear: The vote you are asked to cast is in the final analysis a vote about the rule of law. The rule of law is one of the great achievements of our civilization, for the alternative to the rule of law is the rule is the rule of raw power.

'We're The Heirs'

We here today are the heirs of 3000 years of history in which humanity, slowly and painfully, and at great cost, evolved a form of politics in which law, not brute force, is the arbiter of our public destinies.

We're the heirs of the Ten Commandments and the Mosaic law, moral code for a free people, who having been liberated from bondage, saw in law a means to avoid falling back into the habits of slaves. We're the heirs of Roman law, the first legal system which peoples of different cultures, languages, races and religions came to live together to form a political community.

We're the heirs of the Magna Carta, by which the free men of England began to break the arbitrary and unchecked power of royal absolutism. We're the heirs of a long tradition of parliamentary development in which the rule of law gradually came to replace royal prerogative as the means for governing a society of free men and free women.

Yes, we're the heirs of 1776 and of an epic moment in human affairs — when the founders of this republic pledged their lives, their fortunes and yes, their sacred honor to the defense of the rule of law.

Now we're the heirs of a tragic civil war which vindicated the rule of law over the appetites of some for owning others. We're the heirs of the 20th century's great struggles against totalitarianism in which the rule of law was defended at immense cost against the worst tyrannies in human history.

The rule of law is no pious aspiration from a civics textbook. The rule of law is what stands between us and the arbitrary exercise of power by the state. The rule of law is the safeguard of our liberties. The rule of law is what allows us to live our freedom in ways that honor the freedom of others while strengthening the common good.

Lying under oath is an abuse of freedom. Obstruction of justice is a degradation of law. There are people in prison for such offenses. What in the world do we say to them about equal justice if we overlook this conduct by the president?

Some may say, as many have in recent months, that this is to pitch the matter too high. The president's lie, it is said, was about a trivial matter; it was a lie to spare embarrassment about misconduct on a private occasion.

The confusing of what is essentially a private matter and none of our business with lying under oath to a court and a grand jury has been only one of the distractions we've had to deal with.

Senators, as men and women with a serious experience of public affairs, we can all imagine a situation in which a president might shade the truth when a great issue of national interest or national security is at stake. We've been all over that terrain.

We know the thin ice on which any of us skates when blurring the edges of the truth for what we consider a compelling, demanding public purpose.

Morally serious men and women can imagine the circumstances at the far edge of the morally permissible when, with the gravest matters of national interest at stake, a president could shade the truth in order to serve the common good. But under oath for a private pleasure?

In doing this, the office of the president of the United States has been debased and the justice system jeopardized. In doing this, he's broken his covenant of trust with the American people.

The framers also knew that the office of the president could be gravely damaged if it continued to be unworthily occupied. That's why they devised the process of impeachment by the House and trial by the Senate.

It is in truth a direct process. If on impeachment the president is convicted, he's removed from office and the office itself suffers no permanent damage. If on impeachment the president is acquitted, the issue is resolved once and for all and the office is similarly protected from permanent damage.

But, if on impeachment the president is not convicted and removed from office despite the fact that numerous senators are convinced that he has, in the words of one proposed resolution of censure, "egregiously failed the test of his oath of office, violated the trust of the American people, and dishonored the office by which they entrusted to him," then the office of the presidency has been deeply and perhaps permanently damaged.

And that is a further reason why President Clinton must be convicted of the charges brought before you by the House and removed from office. To fail to do so, while conceding that the president has engaged in egregious and dishonorable behavior, that has broken the covenant of trust between himself and the American people, is to diminish the office of president of the United States in an unprecedented and unacceptable way.

Now, Senators, permit me a word on my own behalf and on behalf of my colleagues in the House. I want to clarify an important point. None of us comes to this chamber today without a profound sense of our own responsibilities in life and of the many ways in which we have failed to meet those responsibilities to one degree or another. None of us comes to you claiming to be a perfect man or a perfect citizen.

Just as none of you imagines yourself perfect, all of us, members of the House and Senate, know we come to this difficult task as flawed human beings under judgment. That is the way of this world — flawed human beings must, according to the rule of law, judge other flawed human beings.

But the issue before the Senate of the United States is not the question of its own members' personal moral condition, nor is the issue before the Senate the question of the personal moral condition of the members of the House of Representatives.

The issue here is whether the president has violated the rule of law and thereby broken the covenant of trust with the American people. This is a public issue involving the gravest matter of public interest. And it's not affected one way or another by the personal moral condition of any member of either House of Congress or by whatever expressions of personal chagrin the president has managed to express.

Senators, we of the House don't come before you today lightly. And if you will permit me, it is a disservice to the House to suggest that it has brought these articles of impeachment before you in a mean-spirited or irresponsible way. That is not true.

We have brought these articles of impeachment because we're convinced in conscience that the President of the United States lied under oath, that the president committed perjury on several occasions before a federal grand jury. We have brought these articles of impeachment because we are convinced in conscience that the president willfully obstructed justice and thereby threatened the legal system he swore a solemn oath to protect and defend.

'These Are Not Trivial Matters'

These are not trivial matters. These are not partisan matters. These are matters of justice, the justice that each of you has taken a solemn oath to serve in this trial.

Some of us have been called Clinton-haters. I must tell you distinguished senators, that this impeachment trial is not, for those of us from the House, a question of hating anyone. This is not a question of who we hate, it's a question of what we love.

And among the things we love are the rule of law, equal justice before the law and honor in our public life. All of us are trying as hard as we can to do our duty as we see it; no more and no less.

Senators, the trial is being watched around the world. Some of those watching thinking themselves superior in their cynicism wonder what it's all about.

But others know, political prisoners know, that this is about the rule of law, the great alternative to arbitrary and unchecked state powers. The families of executed dissidents know that this is about the rule of law, the great alternative to the lethal abuse of power by the state. Those yearning for freedom know this about the rule of law — the hard, one structure by which men and women can live by their God-given dignity and secure their God-given rights in ways that serve the common good.

If they know this, can we not know it?

If across the river in Arlington Cemetery there are American heroes who died in defense of the rule of law, can we give less than the full measure of our devotion to that great cause?

I wish to read you a letter I recently received that expresses my feelings far better than my poor words:

Dear Chairman Hyde: My name is William Preston Summers. How are you doing? I am a third-grader in room 504 at Chase elementary school in Chicago.

I am writing this letter because I have something to tell you. I have thought of a punishment for the president of the United States of America. The punishment should be that he should write a 100 word essay by hand. I have to write an essay when I lie. It is bad to lie because it just gets you in more trouble. I hate getting in trouble.

It's just like the boy who cried wolf, and the wolf ate the boy. It is important to tell the truth. I like to tell the truth because it gets you in less trouble. If you do not tell the truth people do not believe you.

It is important to believe the president because he is a important person. If you cannot believe the president, who can you believe. If you have no one to believe in, then how do you run your life. I do not believe the president tells the truth anymore right now. After he writes the essay and tells the truth, I will believe him again.

William Summers

Then there's a P.S. from his dad:

Dear Representative Hyde: I made my son William either write you a letter or an essay as a punishment for lying. Part of his defense for his lying was that the President lied. He's still having difficulty understanding why the President can lie and not be punished.

Bobby Summers

Mr. Chief Justice and Senators, on June 6, 1994, it was the 50th anniversary of the American landing at Normandy, and I went ashore at Normandy and walked up to the cemetery area where, as far as the eye could see, there were white crosses, Stars of David. And the British had a bagpipe band scattered among the crucifixes, the crosses, playing Amazing Grace with that pierceful, mournful sound that only the bagpipe can make.

And if you could keep your eyes dry you were better than I. But I walked up to one of these crosses marking a grave because I wanted to personalize the experience. I was looking for a name. But there was no name. It said, "Here lies in honored glory a comrade in arms known but to God."

How do we keep faith with that comrade in arms? Well, go to the Vietnam memorial and the national mall and press your hands against the 58,000, a few of the 58,000 names carved into that wall and ask yourself how we can redeem the debt we owe all those who purchased our freedom with their lives. How do we keep faith with them?

I think I know. We work to make this country the kind of America they were willing to die for. That's an America where the idea of sacred honor still has the power to stir men's souls.

My solitary, solitary hope is that 100 years from today people will look back at what we've done and say, "they kept the faith."

I'm done. ◆

Bumpers' Conclusion: The People 'Are Calling on You To Rise Above Politics . . . Above Partisanship'

Following is the Federal Document Clearing House transcript of the summation for President Clinton's impeachment defense delivered Jan. 21 by former Sen. Dale Bumpers, D-Ark.

Bumpers: Mr. Chief Justice, distinguished House managers from the House of Representatives, colleagues, I have seen the look of disappointment on many faces because I know a lot of people thought you were rid of me once and for all.

And I've taken a lot of ribbing this afternoon, but I have seriously negotiated with some people, particularly on this side by an offer to walk out and not deliver this speech in exchange for a few votes. I understand three have it under active consideration.

It is a great joy to see you, and it is especially pleasant to see an audience which represents about the size of the cumulative audience I had over a period of 24 years.

I came here today for a lot of reasons. One was that I was promised a 40-foot cord — and I've been shorted 28 feet. [Sen.] Chris[topher J.] Dodd [D-Conn.] said that he didn't want me in his lap, and I assume that he arranged for the cord to be shortened.

I want to especially thank some of you for your kind comments in the press when it received some publicity that I would be here to close the debate on behalf of the White House counsel and the president. I was a little dismayed by Sen. [Robert F.] Bennett's [R-Utah] remark. He said, "Yes, Sen. Bumpers is a great speaker, but I never — he was never persuasive with me because I never agreed with him." I thought he could have done better than that.

You can take some comfort, colleagues, in the fact that I'm not being paid. And when I'm finished you will probably think the White House got their money's worth.

I have told audiences that over 24 years that I went home almost every weekend and returned usually about dusk on Sunday evening. And you know the plane ride into National Airport, when you can see the magnificent Washington Monument and this building from the window of the airplane. And I've told these students at the university, in a small, liberal arts school at home, Hendricks, after 24 years of that, literally hundreds of times, I never failed to get goosebumps. Same thing is true about this chamber.

I can still remember as though it were yesterday the awe I felt when I first stepped into this magnificent chamber so full of history, so beautiful.

And last Tuesday as I returned after only a short three-week absence, I still felt that same sense of awe that I did the first time I walked in this chamber.

Colleagues, I come here with some sense of reluctance. The president and I have been close friends for 25 years. We've fought so many battles back home together in our beloved Arkansas. We tried mightily all of my years as governor and his, and all of my years in the Senate when he was governor, to raise the living standards in the Delta area of Mississippi, Arkansas and Louisiana, where poverty is unspeakable, with some measure of success — not nearly enough. We tried to provide health care for the lesser among us, for those who are well-off enough they can't get on welfare, but not making enough to buy health insurance.

We have fought, above everything else, to improve the educational standards for a state that, for so many years, was at the bottom of the list or near the bottom of the list of income, and we have stood side-by-side to save beautiful, pristine areas in our state from environmental degradation.

We even crashed a twin-engine Beech Bonanza trying to get to the Gillette coon supper, a political event that one misses at his own risk. And we crashed this plane on a snowy evening on a rural airport, off the runway, sailing out across the snow, jumped out, jumped out and ran away unscathed, to the dismay of every budding politician in Arkansas.

The president and I have been together hundreds of times — at parades, dedications, political events, social events. And in all of those years, and all those hundreds of times we've been together, both in public and in private, I have never one time seen the president conduct himself in a way that did not reflect the highest credit on him, his family, his state, and his beloved nation.

The reason I came here today with some reluctance — please don't misconstrue that. It has nothing to do with my feelings about the president, as I've already said. But it's because we are from the same state and we are long friends, and I know that that necessarily diminishes to some extent the effectiveness of my words.

Constitutional Punishment

So if Bill Clinton the man, Bill Clinton the friend, were the issue here, I'm quite sure I would not be doing this. But it is the weight of history on all of us, and it is my reverence for that great document you heard me rail about for 24 years that we call our Constitution, the most sacred document to me next to the holy Bible.

These proceedings go right to the heart of our Constitution where it deals with impeachment, the part that provides the gravest punishment for just about anybody, the president, even though the framers said we're putting this in to protect the public, not to punish the president.

Ah, colleagues, you have such an awesome responsibility. My good friend, the senior senator from New York, has said it well. He says this: A decision to convict holds the potential for destabilizing the office of the presidency.

And those 400 historians — and I know some have made light of that; about those historians, are they just friends of Bill? And last evening, I went over that list of historians, many of whom I know, among them C. Van Woodward. In the South we love him. He is the pre-eminent Southern historian in the nation. I promise you, he may be a Democrat, he may be even a friend of the president. [But] when you talk about integrity, he is the walking personification, exemplification of integrity.

Historic Proceedings?

Well, colleagues, I have heard so many adjectives to describe this gathering and these proceedings. Historic, memorable, unprecedented, awesome — all of those words, all of those descriptions are apt. And to those I would add the word "dangerous" — dangerous not only for the reasons I just stated, but because it's dangerous to the political process, and it's dangerous to the unique mix of pure democracy and republican government Madison and his colleagues so brilliantly crafted and which has sustained us for 210 years.

Mr. Chief Justice, this is what we lawyers call "dicta." This costs you nothing. It's extra. But the more I study that document and those four months in Philadelphia in 1787, the more awed I am.

And you know what Madison did? The brilliance was in its simplicity. He simply said: Man's nature is to get other people to dance to their tune. Man's nature is to abuse his fellow man sometimes.

And he said, the way to make sure that the majorities don't abuse the minorities, and the way to make sure that the bullies don't run over the weaklings, is to provide the same rights for everybody.

And I had to think about that a long time before I delivered my first lecture at the University of Arkansas last week. And it made so much sense to me. But the danger, as I say, is to the political process. And dangerous for reasons feared by the framers about legislative control of the executive.

That single issue and how to deal with impeachment was debated off and on for the entire four months of the constitutional convention. But the word dangerous is not mine. It's Alexander Hamilton's — a brilliant, good-looking guy [White House Counsel] Mr. [Charles F.C.] Ruff quoted extensively on Tuesday afternoon in his brilliant statement here. He quoted Alexander Hamilton precisely, and it's a little arcane, it isn't easy to understand. So if I may, at the expense of being slightly repetitious, let me paraphrase what Hamilton said.

He said the Senate had a unique role in participating with the executive branch in appointment. And too, it had a role in participating with the executive in the character of a court for the trial of impeachments.

But he said — and I must say this, and you all know it — he said it would be difficult to get what he called a well-constituted court from wholly elected members. He said passions would agitate the whole community and divide it between those who were friendly and those who had inimical interest to the accused, namely the president.

And then he said, and this is his words, the greatest danger was that the decision would be based on the comparative strength of the parties rather than the innocence or guilt of the president.

Why Are You Here?

You have a solemn oath. You have taken a solemn oath to be fair and impartial. I know you all, I know you as friends, and I know you as honorable men, and I'm perfectly satisfied to put that in your hands under your oath.

This is the only caustic thing I will say in these remarks this afternoon, but the question is, "How did we come to be here?" We are here because of a five-year, relentless, unending investigation of the president. Fifty million dollars, hundreds of FBI agents fanning across the nation examining in detail the microscopic lives of people — maybe the most intense investigation not only of a president but of anybody ever.

I feel strongly just because of my state, and what we have endured. So you'll have to excuse me, but that investigation has also shown that the judicial system in this country can and does get out of kilter unless it's controlled. Because there are innocent people who have been financially and mentally bankrupted. One woman told me two years ago that her legal fees were $95,000. She said, "I don't have $95,000, and the only asset I have is the equity in my home, which just happens to correspond to my legal fees of $95,000." And she says, "The only thing I can think of to do is to deed my home." This woman was innocent — never charged, testified before the grand jury a number of times. And since that time, she has accumulated an additional $200,000 in attorney fees.

Javert's pursuit of Jean Valjean in "Les Miserables" pales by comparison.

I doubt that there are few people, maybe nobody in this body, who could withstand such scrutiny. And in this case, those summoned were terrified not because of their guilt, but because they felt guilt or innocence was not really relevant. But after all of those years and $50 million of Whitewater, Travelgate, Filegate, you name it, nothing, nothing, the president was found guilty of nothing, official or personal.

You're here today because the president suffered a terrible moral lapse, a marital infidelity. Not a breach of the public trust, not a crime against society, the two things Hamilton talked about in Federalist Paper number 65 — I recommend it to you before you vote — but it was a breach of his marriage vows. It was a breach of his family trust.

The Human Element

It is a sex scandal. H.L. Mencken said one time, "When you hear somebody say, 'This is not about money,' it's about money." And when you hear somebody say, "This is not about sex," it's about sex.

You pick your own adjective to describe the president's conduct. Here are some that I would use: indefensible, outrageous, unforgivable, shameless. I promise you the president would not contest any of those or any others.

But there's a human element in this case that has not even been mentioned, and that is the president and Hillary and Chelsea are human beings. This is intended only as a mild criticism of our distinguished friends in the House, but as I listened to the presenters — to the managers — make their opening statements, they were remarkably well-prepared, and they spoke eloquently, more eloquent than I really had hoped. But when I talk about the human element, I talk about what I thought was, on occasion, unnecessarily harsh and pejorative descriptions of the president. I thought that language should have been tempered somewhat, to acknowledge that he is the president. To say constantly that the president lied about this and lied about that, as I say, I thought that was too much for a family that has already been about as decimated as a family can get.

The relationship between husband and wife, father and child has been incredibly strained, if not destroyed. There's been nothing but sleepless nights, mental agony for this family for almost five years. Day after day, from accusations of having assassinated, or [having] had Vince Foster assassinated, on down. It has been bizarre. But I didn't sense any compassion, and perhaps none is deserved.

The president has said for all to hear that he misled, he deceived, he did not want to be helpful to the prosecution. And he did all of those things to his family, to his friends, to his staff, to his Cabinet and to the American people.

Why would he do that? Well, he knew this whole affair was about to bring unspeakable embarrassment and humiliation on himself, his wife whom he adored, and a child that he worshiped with every fiber in his body, and for whom he would happily have died to spare her this or to ameliorate her shame and her grief.

The House managers have said shame and embarrassment is no excuse for lying. Well, the question about lying, that's your decision. But I can tell you, you put yourself in his position, and you've already had this big moral lapse, as to what you would do.

We are none of us perfect. Sure, you say, he should have thought of all that beforehand. And indeed he should. Just as Adam and Eve should have. Just as you and you and you and you, and millions of other people who have been caught in similar circumstances, should have thought of it before.

And I say none of us are perfect.

I remember, Chaplain, the — the chaplain's not here, is he? That's too bad. He ought to hear this story: This evangelist was holding this great revival meeting, and at the close of one of his meetings he said, "Is there anybody in this audience who has ever known anybody who even comes close to the perfection of our Lord and Savior, Jesus Christ?" Nothing.

He repeated the challenge, and finally an itty bitty guy in back of the audience kind of held up his hand, and he said, "You — are you saying you've known such a person? Stand up." He stood up, and he said, "Tell us, share it with us. Who was it?" He said, "My wife's first husband."

Make no mistake about it, removal from office is punishment, it is unbelievable punishment, even though the framers didn't quite see it that way.

Again they said, and it bears repeating over and over again, they said they wanted to protect the people. But I can tell you this: The punishment of removing Bill Clinton from office would pale compared to the punishment he has already inflicted on himself.

There's a feeling in this country that somehow or other Bill Clinton's gotten away with something. Mr. Leader, I can tell you, he hasn't gotten away with anything. And the people are saying, "Please don't protect us from this man, 76 percent of us think he's doing a fine job. Sixty-five to seventy percent of us don't want [him] removed from office."

And some have said, "We're not respected on the world scene." The truth of the matter is, this nation has never enjoyed greater prestige in the world than we do right now. You saw Carlos Menem, the president of Argentina, just here recently, say to the president, "Mr. President, the world needs you."

The war in Bosnia is under control. The president has been as tenacious as anybody could be about Middle East peace. And in Ireland, actual peace, and maybe the Middle East will make it. And he has the Indians and the Pakistanis talking to each other as they've never talked to each other in recent times.

[Czech President] Vaclav Havel said, "Mr. President, for the enlargement of the North Atlantic Treaty Organization there's no doubt in my mind that it was personal leadership that made this historic development possible." [Jordan's] King Hussein: "Mr. President, I've had the privilege of being a friend of the United States and presidents since the late President Eisenhower. And throughout all the years that have passed, I've kept in touch. But on the subject of peace, the peace we're seeking, I have never — with all due respect and all the affection I held for your predecessors — have known someone with your dedication, clearheadedness, focus and determination to help resolve this issue in the best way possible."

Well, I'm not — I've got Nelson Mandela and other world leaders who have said similar things in the last six months. Our prestige, I promise you, in the world is as high as it's ever been.

Perjury?

When it comes to the question of perjury, you know, there's perjury and then there's perjury. Let me ask you if you think this is perjury: On Nov. 23, 1997, President Clinton went to Vancouver, British Columbia. And when he returned, Monica Lewinsky was at the White House at some point, and he gave her a carved marble bear. I don't know how big it was.

Question before the grand jury Aug. 6, 1998: "What was the Christmas present or presents that he got for you?"

Answer: "Everything was packaged in a big Black Dog, or big canvas bag from the Black Dog store in Martha's Vineyard. He got me a marble bear's head carving, sort of, you know — a little sculpture, I guess you'd call it, maybe."

"Was that the item from Vancouver?"

"Yes."

Question on the same day of the same grand jury: "OK, good. When the president gave you the Vancouver Bear on the 28th, did he say anything about what it means?"

"Mmm-hmmm."

"Well, what did he say?"

Answer: "I think he — I believe he said that the bear is the, maybe, Indian symbol for strength, you know, and to be strong like a bear."

"And did you interpret that to be strong in your decision to continue to conceal the relationship?"

"No."

House Judiciary Committee report to the full House: "On the other hand, knowing the subpoena requested gifts, his giving Ms. Lewinsky more gifts on Dec. 28 seems odd, but Ms. Lewinsky's testimony reveals why he did so. She said that she 'never questioned that we would ever do anything but keep this private, and that meant to take whatever appropriate steps needed to be taken to keep it quiet.'

"The only logical inference is that the gifts, including the bear symbolizing strength, were a tacit reminder to Ms. Lewinsky that they would deny the relationship even in the face of a federal subpoena."

She just got through saying "No," and yet this report says that's the only logical inference.

And then the brief that came over here accompanying the articles of impeachment said, "On the other hand, more gifts on Dec. 28. . . . Ms. Lewinsky's testimony reveals the answer. She said that she 'never questioned that we were ever going to do anything but keep this private, and that meant to take whatever appropriate steps needed to be taken to keep it quiet.' "

Again, they say in their brief, "the only logical inference is that the gifts, including the bear symbolizing strength, were a tacit reminder to Ms. Lewinsky that they would deny the relationship even in the face of a federal subpoena."

Is it perjury to say the only logical inference is something when the only shred of testimony in the record is, "No, that was not my interpretation. I didn't infer that"? And yet here you have it in the committee report and you have it in the brief.

Now, of course that's not perjury. First of all, it isn't under oath, but as a trial lawyer, I'll tell you what it is: It's wanting to win too badly. I tried 300, 400, maybe 500 divorce cases — incidentally, you're being addressed by the entire South Franklin County, Ark., Bar Association. I can't believe there were that many cases in that little town, but I had a practice in surrounding communities, too. And in all those divorce cases, I would guess that in 80 percent of the contested cases, perjury was committed. And you know what it was about? Sex. Extramarital affairs.

But there's a very big difference in perjury about a marital infidelity in a divorce case, and perjury about whether I bought the murder weapon or whether I concealed the murder weapon or not. And to charge somebody with the first and punish them as though it were the second stands justice, our sense of justice on its head.

There's a total lack of proportionality, a total lack of balance, in this thing. The charge and the punishment are totally out of sync.

All of you have heard or read the testimony of the five prosecutors who testified before the House Judiciary Committee. Five seasoned prosecutors. And each one of them, veterans, said under the identical circumstances, the identical circumstances of this case, we would never charge anybody because we'd know we couldn't get a conviction. And in this case, the charges brought and the punishment sought are totally out of sync. There is no balance, there is no proportionality.

Historically Speaking

But even stranger, you think about it, even if this case had originated in the courthouse rather than the Capitol, you would never have heard of it. How do you reconcile what the prosecutors said with what we're doing here?

Impeachment was debated off and on in Philadelphia for the entire four months, as I said. The key players were Gouverneur Morris — Sen. Specter, a brilliant Pennsylvanian — [and] George Mason, the only man reputedly to have been so brilliant that Thomas Jefferson actually deferred to him. And he refused to sign the Constitution, incidentally, even though he was a delegate, because they didn't deal with slavery, and he was a strict abolitionist. And then there was Charles Pinkney — Sen. Hollings, from South Carolina — just a youngster, 29 years old, I believe. Edmund Randolph from Virginia, who had a big role in the Constitution in the beginning; the Virginia Plan. And then there was, of course, James Madison, the craftsman.

They were all key players in drafting this impeachment provision. And uppermost in the mind during the entire time they were composing was, they did not want any kings. They had lived under despots, they had lived under kings, they had lived under autocrats, and they didn't want any more of that. And they succeeded very admirably. We've had 46 presidents, and no kings.

But they kept talking about corruption — maybe that ought to be the reason for impeachment, because they feared some president would corrupt the political process. That's what the debate was about. Corrupt the political process and ensconce himself through a phony election, maybe as something close to a king. They followed the British rule on impeachment, because the British said, the House of Commons may impeach, and the House of Lords must convict. And every one of the colonies had the same procedure: House, Senate.

Though in all fairness, House members, Alexander Hamilton was not very keen on the House participating.

But here was the sequence of events at Philadelphia that brought us here today. They started out with "maladministration," and Madison said that's too vague. What does that mean? So they dropped that. They went from that to "corruption," and they dropped that. Then they went to "malpractice." And they decided that was not definitive enough.

And they went to "treason, bribery and corruption." And they decided that still didn't suit them. But bear in mind one thing: During this entire process, they are narrowing — they are narrowing the things you can impeach the president for. They were making it tougher. Madison said, if we aren't careful, the president will serve at the pleasure of the legislature — the Senate, he said.

And then they went to "treason and bribery," and somebody said that's still not quite enough. And so they went to "treason, bribery," and George Mason added, "or other high crimes and misdemeanors against the United States." And they voted on it, and on Sept. 10 they sent the entire Constitution to a committee.

They called a committee on style and arrangement, which was the committee that would draft the language in a way that everybody would understand; it would be well-crafted from a grammatical standpoint. But that committee, which was dominated by Madison and Hamilton, dropped "against the United States." And historians will tell you that the reason they did that was because of redundance, because that committee had no right to change the substance of anything. They would not have dropped it if they hadn't felt that it was redundant.

And then, they put in for good measure — we can always be grateful — the two-thirds majority.

Now, this is one of the most important points of this entire presentation: The term — first of all — "treason and bribery," nobody quarrels with that, and we're not debating treason and bribery here in this chamber. We're talking about "other high crimes and misdemeanors."

And where did "high crimes and misdemeanors" come from? It came from the English law, and they found it in an English law under a category which said, "distinctly political offenses against the state." Let me repeat that, they said, "high crimes and misdemeanors was to be," because they took it from English law, where they found it in the category that said, "offenses distinctly political against the state."

So colleagues, please, for just one moment, forget the complexities of the facts and the tortured legalisms. And we've heard them all brilliantly presented on both sides, and I'm not getting into that. But ponder this: If "high crimes and misdemeanors" was taken from English law by George Mason, which listed high crimes and misdemeanors as political offenses against the state, what are we doing here?

If, as Hamilton said, it had to be a crime against society or a breach of the public trust, what are we doing here? Even perjury. Concealing or deceiving. An unfaithful relationship does not even come close to being an impeachable offense.

Nobody has suggested that Bill Clinton committed a political crime against the state. So, colleagues, if you honor the Constitution, you must look at the history of the Constitution and how we got to the impeachment clause. And if you do that and you do that honestly according to the oath you took, you cannot — you can censure Bill Clinton, you can hand him over to the prosecutor for him to be prosecuted, but you cannot convict him. And you cannot indulge yourselves the luxury or the right to ignore this history.

A Look Back

There's been a suggestion that a vote to acquit would be something of a breach of faith with those who lie in Flanders Field, Anzio and Bunker Hill and Gettysburg and wherever. I didn't hear that; I read about it. But I want to say — and, incidentally, I think it was Chairman Hyde who alluded to this and said, those men fought and died for the rule of law.

I can remember a cold Nov. 3 morning in my little hometown of Charleston, Ark., I was 18 years old. I had just gotten one semester in at the university when I went into the Marine Corps. And so, I reported to Little Rock to be inducted.

My, it was cold. The drugstore was the bus stop. I had to be there by 8 o'clock to be sworn in, and I had to catch the bus down at the drugstore at 3 o'clock in the morning, so my mother and father and I got up at 2 o'clock, got dressed, and went down there.

I'm not sure I can tell you this story.

And the bus came over the hill — I was rather frightened anyway about going in. I was quite sure I was going to be killed, only slightly less frightened that Betty would find somebody else while I was gone.

When the bus came over Schoolhouse Hill, my parents started crying. I had never seen my father cry. I knew I was in some difficulty.

Now, as a parent at my age, I know he thought he was giving not his only begotten son, but one of his begotten sons. Can you imagine? You know that scene. It was repeated across this nation millions of times.

And then happily, I survived that war; saw no combat; was on my way to Japan when it all ended. I'd never had a terrible problem with dropping the bomb, though that's been a terrible moral dilemma for me, because the estimates were that we would lose as many as a million men in that invasion.

But I came home to a generous government who provided me, under the GI Bill, an education in a fairly prestigious law school which my father could never have afforded. And I practiced law in this little town for 18 years; loved every minute of it. But I didn't practice constitutional law, and I knew very little about the Constitution. But when I went into law school, I did study constitutional law, though Mr. Chief Justice, it was fairly arcane to me.

And trying to read The Federalist Papers and Tocqueville — all of those things law students are expected to do, that was tough for me, I confess. So after 18 years in law practice, I jumped up and ran for governor, and I served as governor for four years. And I still — I guess I knew what the rule of law was, but I still didn't really have much reverence for the Constitution. I just did not understand any of the things I just got through telling you.

No. My love for that document came day after day and debate after debate right here in this chamber.

Some of you perhaps read an op-ed piece I did a couple of weeks ago, when I said I was perfectly happy for my legacy of a 24-year senator to be I never voted for a constitutional amendment. And it isn't that I wouldn't. I think they made a mistake not giving you fellows four years. You're about to cause me to rethink that one.

And the reason I developed this love of it is because I saw Madison's magic working time and time again, keeping bullies from running over weak people, keeping majorities from running over minorities. And I thought about all the unfettered freedoms we had. The oldest organic law in existence made us the envy of the world.

Mr. Chairman, we've also learned that the rule of law includes presidential elections. That's a part of the rule of law in this country. We have an event, a quadrennial event in this country which we call presidential elections. And that's the day when we reach across this aisle and hold hands, Democrats and Republicans. And we say, "Win or lose, we will abide by the decision."

It is a solemn event, presidential elections, and it should not — they should not be undone lightly. Or just because one side has the clout and the other one doesn't. And if you want to know what men fought for in World War II, for example, or in Vietnam, ask Sen. [Daniel K.] Inouye [D-Hawaii]. He left an arm in Italy.

He and I were in the presence at Normandy on the 50th anniversary. But we started off on Anzio. Sen. [Pete V.] Domenici [R-N.M.], were you with us? It was one of the most awesome experiences I've ever had in my life — certified war hero. I think his relatives were in an internment camp, so ask him what he was fighting for.

Or ask [Sen.] Bob Kerrey [D-Neb.], certified Medal of Honor winner, what was he fighting for. You'll probably get a quite different answer.

Or Sen. [John H.] Chafee [R-R.I.], one of the finest men ever to grace this body and certified Marine hero of Guadalcanal — ask him. And Sen. [John] McCain [R-Ariz.], a genuine hero — ask him.

You don't have to guess. They're with us, and they're living. And they can tell you. And one who is not with us here in the Senate any more, Robert Dole [R-Kan.]. Ask Sen. Dole what he was fighting for. Sen. Dole had what I thought was a very reasonable solution to this whole thing that would handle it fairly and expeditiously.

Voting the Polls?

The American people are now and for some time have been asking to be allowed a good night's sleep. They're asking for an end to this nightmare. It is a legitimate request. I'm not suggesting that you vote for or against the polls. I understand that. Nobody should vote against the polls just to show their mettle and their courage. I have cast plenty of votes against the polls, and it's cost me politically a lot of times.

This has been going on for a year, though. And in that same op-ed piece I talked about meeting [former President] Harry Truman my first year as governor of Arkansas. Spent an hour with him; an indelible experience. People at home kid me about this, because I very seldom make a speech that I don't mention this meeting. But I will never forget what he said: "Put your faith in the people. Trust the people. They can handle it." They have shown conclusively time and time again that they can handle it.

Colleagues, this is easily the most important vote you will ever cast. If you have difficulty because of an intense dislike of the president — and that's understandable — rise above it. He is not the issue.

He will be gone. You won't. So don't leave a precedent from which we may never recover and almost surely will regret.

If you vote to acquit, Mr. Leader, you know exactly what's going to happen. You're going to go back to your committees; you're going to get on this legislative agenda; you're going to start dealing with Medicare and Social Security and tax cuts and all those things which the people of the country have a non-negotiable demand that you do.

If you vote to acquit, you go immediately to the people's agenda. If you vote to acquit, you go immediately to the people's agenda. But if you vote to convict, you can't be sure what's going to happen.

James G. Blaine was a member of the Senate when Andrew Johnson was tried in 1868, and 20 years later he recanted. And he said: "I made a bad mistake." And he says, "As I reflect back on it, all I can think about is having convicted Andrew Johnson would have caused much more chaos and confusion in this country than Andrew Johnson could ever conceivably have tried."

And so it is with William Jefferson Clinton. If you vote to convict, in my opinion you're going to be creating more havoc than he could ever possibly create. After all, he's only got two years left. So don't, for God's sake, heighten people's alienation that is at an all-time high toward their government.

The people have a right, and they are calling on you to rise above politics, rise above partisanship. They're calling on you to do your solemn duty. And I pray you will.

Thank you, Mr. Chief Justice. ◆

House's Rationale for Witnesses: Testimony 'Will Lend Greater Coherence and Understanding'

Following are excerpts from the memorandum the House filed in the Senate on Jan. 26 laying out its rationale for seeking to depose three potential witnesses in the impeachment trial of President Clinton; asking to add three new pieces of evidence to the trial record; and asking the Senate to ask the president to sit for a deposition.

The witnesses will provide information concerning the specific instances in which the President lied under oath, encouraged others to lie under oath, or otherwise obstructed justice as part of a premeditated and calculated scheme to prevent a fellow American citizen from vindicating her rights in a court of law. . . .

Because President Clinton continues to deny that he perjured himself or obstructed justice through his testimony or other actions, and because the President has proposed that the Senate draw inferences from the factual record which support his denials of the charges brought in the Articles of Impeachment being exhibited by the House, obtaining testimony from the witnesses named in the motion, and additionally from the President himself, will greatly assist the Senate in resolving credibility issues, and in its obligation to determine the proper inferences to be drawn from the facts. In turn, these witnesses will enable the Senate to decide whether the President has fulfilled his constitutional responsibility to take care that the laws be faithfully executed, to honor his oath before the grand jury and, consequently, whether he should be removed from office.

In sum, the testimony of the witnesses will lend greater coherence and understanding to the narrative of events leading to Impeachment, allowing this body to determine the truth. The testimony will demonstrate the gravamen of the House position: namely, that the chief law enforcement officer of the country committed perjury and obstructed justice in a calculated and premeditated manner warranting removal.

Monica Lewinsky

. . . Ms. Lewinsky's contact with President Clinton is highly relevant within the context of the President's obstruction of the *Jones [v. Clinton]* lawsuit. Once she appeared on the witness list in that case, President Clinton, directly and through his subordinates and agents, sought her help to conceal the nature of their relationship by illegal means. The President meant to garner her cooperation by acting quickly on her request for help in obtaining a job in New York. When the false affidavit he encouraged Ms. Lewinsky to file did not succeed in precluding questions related to Ms. Lewinsky in the *Jones* case, the President obstructed the proceedings by lying in his civil deposition in using the cover story he had urged Ms. Lewinsky to use if she were called to testify personally. Additionally, he injected Ms. Currie into the proceeding by identifying her as the person with knowledge, even for matters about which he, not she, had personal knowledge. He then proceeded to obstruct justice by coaching others, including Ms. Currie, to corroborate his perjured testimony. He then perjured himself before the grand jury.

Ms. Lewinsky's testimony is relevant to resolve the discrepancies in the record and the different inferences drawn by the House and the President. Her live testimony will rebut the following inferences drawn by White House counsel on key issues, among others:

A. That President Clinton did not encourage Ms. Lewinsky to file a false affidavit.

B. That President Clinton did not lie about not having a "sexual affair," "sexual relations," or a "sexual relationship" with Ms. Lewinsky.

C. That President Clinton did not encourage Ms. Lewinsky to conceal any gifts he had given her.

D. That President Clinton did not instruct or encourage Ms. Currie to pick up the gifts he had given Ms. Lewinsky from her personal residence.

E. That President Clinton did not have an "understanding" with Ms. Lewinsky that the two would lie under oath. That President Clinton did not encourage Ms. Lewinsky to file a false affidavit.

In sum, given the almost complete disconnect between Ms. Lewinsky's testimony, offered under grant of immunity that would be lost if she committed perjury, and President Clinton's, and the inferences drawn by the parties from the factual record, Ms. Lewinsky's appearance would resolve the proper inferences surrounding the facts, assisting the Senators in fulfilling their constitutional duty to find the truth. . . .

Vernon Jordan

. . . Mr. Jordan's live testimony will help to prove that President Clinton obstructed justice by encouraging Ms. Lewinsky to file a false affidavit and by helping her to obtain employment in the private sector at a time when she was a witness in the *Jones* case.

According to Ms. Lewinsky, the President informed her on December 17, 1997, that her name had been placed on a witness list for the *Jones* case (he had been notified through his attorney). To avoid having to testify, Ms. Lewinsky claimed the President suggested she execute an affidavit.

In other words, Mr. Jordan's live testimony can effectively demonstrate that President Clinton knew the contents of her affidavit at least 10 days prior to his own deposition. This action was consistent with President Clinton's initial desire that Ms. Lewinsky file an affidavit in lieu of testifying, and, as Ms. Lewinsky's grand jury testimony reveals, that she coordinate her story with the President's by denying the existence of a sexual relationship. Ms. Lewinsky's false affidavit, in turn, permitted the President to lie in response to document requests answered two days before he testified and permitted the President to lie in his deposition without contradiction. President Clinton's manipulation of these events constitutes evidence to support both the perjury and obstruction Articles.

Mr. Jordan can also speak to another charge which helps to sustain the obstruction Article and which President Clinton's counsel disputes vigorously: the effort by the President to secure employment for Ms. Lewinsky in order to garner her cooperation in his efforts to suborn perjury and obstruct justice.

Although Ms. Lewinsky began her job search before December 7, 1997 —the day after President Clinton discovered her name had been placed on the *Jones* witness list — no effort to obtain private employment in New York had been made in earnest prior to the appearance of her name. His efforts to assist her intensified, however, after the appearance of her name on the *Jones* witness list.

The following time line is illustrative of how Ms. Lewinsky's appearance on a witness list in the *Jones* case drove White House efforts to obtain a job for Ms. Lewinsky. On December 11, 1997, the presiding Judge in the *Jones* case ordered President Clinton to answer certain interrogatories, including whether he had engaged in sexual relations with government employees. Five days later (December 16), his attorneys received a request for production of documents that mentioned Ms. Lewinsky by name. These events triggered the intensified efforts to accommodate Ms. Lewinsky in her job search, consistent with Mr. Jordan's anticipated testimony as set forth in points seven through 12, supra.

Mr. Jordan was the primary catalyst in obtaining Ms. Lewinsky's job in New York. It is expected that Mr. Jordan's testimony will lead to the reasonable and logical inference from the evidence that the timing and level of effort devoted to obtaining a desired job for Ms. Lewinsky — especially by powerful men such as Mr. Jordan — was intended to ensure Ms. Lewinsky's gratitude and thereby discourage her from providing any damaging information about her relationship with the President to the Jones attorneys. The live testimony of Mr. Jordan on this issue will therefore help the Senate as it considers the allegations against the President. . . .

Sidney Blumenthal

Through the testimony of Sidney Blumenthal, the House expects to prove, among other things, that . . . the President lied to his aides knowing that they may be called to testify before the grand jury. In addition, his testimony proves that President Clinton embellished his previous explanations to the public, his aides, and authorities, by depicting Ms. Lewinsky as a "stalker," thereby attacking her character in an effort to exculpate himself. This evidence is an important component of the obstruction charges set forth in Article II. . . .

Law Clerk's Sworn Statement

The House respectfully moves that that United States Senate admit into evidence the sworn declaration of Barry Ward, Law Clerk to the Honorable Susan Webber Wright, United States District Judge for the Eastern District of Arkansas. . . .

[Ward] assisted in the adjudication of *Jones v. Clinton*, which was filed in the Eastern District of Arkansas in 1994. . . . The President was deposed on January 17, 1998. . . . [Ward] was present at the deposition.

At one point in the questioning, the President's attorney, Robert Bennett, urged the Judge to preclude inquiries pertaining to alleged "sexual relations" between Monica Lewinsky, a former White House intern, and President Clinton. The basis for Mr. Bennett's argument was that Ms. Lewinsky had executed an affidavit "saying that there is absolutely no sex of any kind of any manner, shape or form, with President Clinton." Mr. Bennett further represented that President Clinton was ". . . fully aware of Ms. Lewinsky's affidavit. . . . " President Clinton did not contradict Mr. Bennett's assertion. . . .

When confronted with Ms. Lewinsky's admission during his grand jury appearance on August 17, President Clinton did not repudiate his January 17 testimony regarding the veracity of the Lewinsky affidavit. Among other justifications, President Clinton stated that he did not correct Mr. Bennett's characterization of the affidavit as true and accurate because he did not pay "any attention" to the colloquy between Mr. Bennett and the presiding Judge. In contrast, a videotape of President Clinton during the January 17 deposition clearly shows him looking directly at Mr. Bennett while he told the presiding Judge that there was "absolutely no sex of any kind in any manner, shape or form, with President Clinton."

From his seat at the conference table next to the Judge, he saw President Clinton listening attentively to Mr. Bennett's remarks ("absolutely no sex of any kind . . ." etc.) while the exchange between Mr. Bennett and the Judge occurred.

Mr. Ward's declaration would lend even greater credence to the argument that President Clinton lied on this point during his grand jury testimony and obstructed justice by allowing his attorney to utilize a false affidavit in order to cut off a legitimate line of questioning. Mr. Ward's declaration proves that Mr. Ward saw President Clinton listening attentively while the exchange between Mr. Bennett and the presiding Judge occurred. Such testimony would offer greater support for the obstruction charge in Article II.

Jones' Lawyer's Sworn Statement

The House respectfully moves that the United States Senate admit into evidence the sworn declaration of T. Wesley Holmes, one of the counsels for Paula C. Jones in the case of *Jones v. Clinton*.

Attached to the sworn declaration . . . is a photocopy of a subpoena issued to Betty Currie on January 22, 1998, and served on her on January 27, 1998. Also attached is a supplemental witness list filed in the case of *Jones v. Clinton*, containing the name of Betty Currie. . . .

During his January 17, 1998, deposition in the case of *Jones v. Clinton*, President Clinton made a number of references to Ms. Currie, his Personal Secretary. In effect, the President was suggesting that Ms. Currie, in certain instances, could corroborate his testimony. . . . It therefore became clear to Mr. Holmes that Ms. Currie was an important potential witness, and that she should be called to testify in the case.

The resulting subpoena for Ms. Currie, issued on January 22, and the supplemental witness list, become highly relevant in light of this factual background. Counsel for the President has repeatedly argued that Ms. Currie was not a potential witness in the *Jones* case and therefore that the President's January 18, 1998 statements to her were not intended to influence her anticipated testimony.

The subpoena and supplemental witness list undermine the President's claim and establish the House's position. That is, given the President's numerous references to Ms. Currie in his testimony, he knew that the Jones attorneys would want to depose her. She was, in fact, subpoenaed, thereby demonstrating that President Clinton's attempts to coach her to be a witness who would corroborate the President's lies. . . .

Records of Telephone Talks Between Clinton and Lewinsky

The House respectfully moves that the United States Senate admit into evidence telephone records which document certain conversations between Monica S. Lewinsky and William Jefferson Clinton.

The telephone records will prove that:

On December 5, 1997, the attorneys for Paula C. Jones faxed a witness list in the case of *Jones v. Clinton* to President Clinton's attorney.

After seeing President Clinton at a Christmas reception on December 5, 1997, Ms. Lewinsky composed a letter to him in which she expressed her disappointment that he was distancing himself from her. The next day, December 6, she went to the White House to deliver the letter and some gifts. . . . Ms. Lewinsky waited in a guard booth with uniformed Secret Service officers. One of them mentioned that Eleanor Mondale was in the White House. Ms. Lewinsky correctly deduced that President Clinton was visiting with Ms. Mondale and not his lawyers. Ms. Lewinsky became "livid," left, placed a telephone call to Betty Currie in which she berated her, and went home.

Later that same day, President Clinton called her. While portions of their exchange were testy, the President invited Ms. Lewinsky back to the White House. During their meeting, Ms. Lewinsky mentioned that Mr. Jordan had done nothing to help her with her job search. The President promised he would speak to Mr. Jordan. Ms. Lewinsky characterized the visit as "really nice" and "affectionate." The next day, December 7, Mr. Jordan met with the President in the White House. On December 11 Ms. Lewinsky met with Mr. Jordan to discuss her job search. After the meeting Mr. Jordan placed phone calls on Ms. Lewinsky's behalf to corporate officials with Young & Rubicam, MacAndrews & Forbes, and American Express.

Taken as a whole, these events establish that once President Clinton knew that Ms. Lewinsky was a named witness in the *Jones* litigation, he and his subordinates and agents made a concerted effort to obtain a job for her in New York. . . .

Request for the Appearance Of President Clinton

Additionally, the House petitions the Senate to request the appearance of William Jefferson Clinton, President of the United States, at a deposition, for the purpose of providing testimony related to the Impeachment Trial.

The President is the one person who possesses direct and personal knowledge of the course of all of the events which together constitute the charges of perjury and obstruction of justice being exhibited by the House. His credibility is critical in order for the Senate to resolve different inferences from the factual record in his favor. It is only appropriate that the President appear so that the Senate, sitting as a Court of Impeachment, may compare his responses and credibility against that of the other witnesses who have given testimony and who the House now seeks to depose. ◆

Clinton Says GOP Tax Bill 'Would Leave America Permanently in Debt'

Following is the text of President Clinton's Sept. 23 veto message on HR 2488, the "Taxpayer Refund and Relief Act of 1999":

TO THE HOUSE OF REPRESENTATIVES:

I am returning herewith without my approval H.R. 2488, the "Taxpayer Refund and Relief Act of 1999," because it ignores the principles that have led us to the sound economy we enjoy today and emphasizes tax reduction for those who need it the least.

We have a strong economy because my Administration and the Congress have followed the proper economic course over the past 6 years. We have focused on reducing deficits, paying down debt held by the public, bringing down interest rates, investing in our people, and opening markets. There is $1.7 trillion less debt held by the public today than was forecast in 1993. This has contributed to lower interest rates, record business investment, greater productivity growth, low inflation, low unemployment, and broad-based growth in real wages — and the first back-to-back budget surpluses in almost half a century.

This legislation would reverse the fiscal discipline that has helped make the American economy the strongest it has been in generations. By using projected surpluses to provide a risky tax cut, H.R. 2488 could lead to higher interest rates, thereby undercutting any benefits for most Americans by increasing home mortgage payments, car loan payments, and credit card rates. We must put first things first, pay down publicly held debt, and address the long-term solvency of Medicare and Social Security. My Mid-Session Review of the Budget presented a framework in which we could accomplish all of these things and also provide an affordable tax cut.

The magnitude of the tax cuts in H.R. 2488 and the associated debt service costs would be virtually as great as all of the on-budget surpluses the Congressional Budget Office projects for the next 10 years. This would leave virtually none of the projected on-budget surplus available for addressing the long-term solvency of Medicare, which is currently projected by its Trustees to be insolvent by 2015, or of Social Security, which then will be in a negative cash-flow position, or for critical funding for priorities like national security, education, health care, law enforcement, science and technology, the environment, and veterans' programs.

The bill would cause the Nation to forgo the unique opportunity to eliminate completely the burden of the debt held by the public by 2015 as proposed by my Administration's Mid-Session Review. The elimination of this debt would have a beneficial effect on interest rates, investment, and the growth of the economy. Moreover, paying down debt is tantamount to cutting taxes. Each one-percentage point decline in interest rates would mean a cut of $200 billion to $250 billion in mortgage costs borne by American consumers over the next 10 years. Also, if we do not erase the debt held by the public, our children and grandchildren will have to pay higher taxes to offset the higher Federal interest costs on this debt.

Budget projections are inherently uncertain. For example, the Congressional Budget Office found that, over the last 11 years, estimates of annual deficits or surpluses 5 years into the future erred by an average of 13 percent of annual outlays — a rate that in 2004 would translate into an error of about $250 billion. Projections of budget surpluses 10 years into the future are surely even more uncertain. The prudent course in the face of these uncertainties is to avoid making financial commitments — such as massive tax cuts — that will be very difficult to reverse.

The bill relies on an implausible legislative assumption that many of its major provisions expire after 9 years and all of the provisions are repealed after 10 years. This scenario would create uncertainty and confusion for taxpayers, and it is highly unlikely that it would ever be implemented. Moreover, this artifice causes estimated 10-year costs to be understated by about $100 billion, at the same time that it sweeps under the rug the exploding costs beyond the budget window. If the tax cut were continued, its budgetary impact would grow even more severe, reaching about $2.7 trillion between 2010 and 2019, just at the time when the baby boomers begin to retire, Medicare becomes insolvent, and Social Security comes under strain. If the bill were to become law, it would leave America permanently in debt. The bill as a whole would disproportionately benefit the wealthiest Americans by, for example, lowering capital gains rates, repealing the estate and gift tax, increasing maximum IRA and retirement plan contribution limits, and weakening pension anti-discrimination protections for moderate- and lower-income workers.

The bill would not meet the Budget Act's existing pay-as-you-go requirements, which have helped provide the discipline necessary to bring us from an era of large and growing budget deficits to the potential for substantial surpluses. It would also automatically trigger across-the-board cuts (or sequesters) in a number of Federal programs. These cuts would result in a reduction of more than $40 billion in the Medicare program over the next 5 years. Starting in 2002, they would also lead to the elimination of numerous programs with broad support, including: crop insurance, without which most farmers and ranchers could not secure the financing from banks needed to operate their farms and ranches; veterans readjustment benefits, denying education and training to more than 450,000 veterans, reservists, and dependents; Federal support for programs such as child care for low-income families and Meals on Wheels for senior citizens; and many others.

As I have repeatedly stressed, I want to find common ground with the Congress on a fiscal plan that will best serve the American people. I have profound differences, however, with the extreme approach that the Republican majority has adopted. It would provide a tax cut for the wealthiest Americans and would hurt average Americans by denying them the benefits of debt reduction and depriving them of the certainty that my proposals for Medicare and Social Security solvency would provide as they plan for their retirement.

I hope to work with Members of Congress to find a common path to honor our commitment to senior citizens, help working families with targeted tax relief for moderate- and lower-income workers, provide a better life for our children, and improve the standard of living of all Americans.

WILLIAM J. CLINTON
THE WHITE HOUSE,
September 23, 1999

Clinton Rejects D.C. Spending Bill's 'Unwarranted Intrusions' in Local Decisions

Following is the text of President Clinton's Sept. 28 veto message on HR 2587, the fiscal 2000 District of Columbia appropriations bill:

TO THE HOUSE OF REPRESENTATIVES:

I am returning herewith without my approval H.R. 2587, the "District of Columbia Appropriations Act, 2000." Although the bill provides important funding for the District of Columbia, I am vetoing this bill because it includes a number of highly objectionable provisions that are unwarranted intrusions into local citizens' decisions about local matters.

I commend the Congress for developing a bill that includes requested funding for the District of Columbia. The bill includes essential funding for District Courts and Corrections and the D.C. Offender Supervision Agency and goes a long way toward providing requested funds for a new tuition assistance program for District of Columbia residents. I appreciate the additional funding included in the bill to promote the adoption of children in the District's foster care system, to support the Children's National Medical Center, to assist the Metropolitan Police Department in eliminating open-air drug trafficking in the District, and for drug testing and treatment, among other programs.

However, I am disappointed that the Congress has added to the bill a number of highly objectionable provisions that would interfere with local decisions about local matters. Were it not for these provisions, I would sign the bill into law. Many of the Members who voted for this legislation represent States and localities that do not impose similar restrictions on their own citizens. I urge the Congress to remove the following provisions expeditiously to prevent the interruption of important funding for the District of Columbia:

- **Voting Representation.** H.R. 2587 would prohibit not only the use of Federal, but also District funds to provide assistance for petition drives or civil actions that seek to obtain voting representation in the Congress for residents of the District of Columbia.
- **Limit on Access to Representation in Special Education Cases.** The bill would cap the award of plaintiffs' attorneys' fees in cases brought by parents of District schoolchildren against the District of Columbia Public Schools under the Individuals with Disabilities Education Act (IDEA). In the long run, this provision would likely limit the access of the District's poor families to quality legal representation, thus impairing their due process protections provided by the IDEA.
- **Abortion.** The bill would prohibit the use of not only Federal, but also District funds to pay for abortions except in those cases where the life of the mother is endangered or in situations involving rape or incest.
- **Domestic Partners Act.** The bill would prohibit the use of not only Federal, but also District funds to implement or enforce the Health Care Benefits Expansion Act of 1992.
- **Needle Exchange Programs.** The bill contains a ban that would seriously disrupt current AIDS/HIV prevention efforts by prohibiting the use of Federal and local funds for needle exchange programs. H.R. 2587 denies not only Federal, but also District funding to any public or private agency, including providers of HIV/AIDS-related services, in the District of Columbia that uses the public or private agency's own funds for needle exchange programs, undermining the principle of home rule in the District.
- **Controlled Substances.** The bill would prohibit the District from legislating with respect to certain controlled substances, in a manner that all States are free to do.
- **Restriction on City Council Salaries.** The bill would limit the amount of salary that can be paid to members of the District of Columbia Council.

I urge the Congress to send me a bill that maintains the important funding for the District provided in this bill and that eliminates these highly objectionable provisions as well as other provisions that undermine the ability of residents of the District of Columbia to make decisions about local matters.

WILLIAM J. CLINTON
THE WHITE HOUSE,
September 28, 1999

President Says Foreign Operations Bill Endangers National Security

Following is the text of President Clinton's Oct. 18 veto message on HR 2606, the fiscal 2000 foreign operations appropriations bill:

TO THE HOUSE OF REPRESENTATIVES:

I am returning herewith without my approval HR 2606, the "Foreign Operations, Export Financing and Related Programs Appropriations Act, 2000."

The central lesson we have learned in this century is that we cannot protect American interests at home without active engagement abroad. Common sense tells us, and hard experience has confirmed, that we must lead in the world, working with other nations to defuse crises, repel dangers, promote more open economic and political systems and strengthen the rule of law. These have been the guiding principles of American foreign policy for generations. They have served the American people well and greatly helped to advance the cause of peace and freedom around the world.

This bill rejects all of those principles. It puts at risk America's 50-year tradition of leadership for a safer, more prosperous and democratic world. It is an abandonment of hope in our nation's capacity to shape that kind of world. It implies that we are too small and insecure to meet our share of international responsibilities, too shortsighted to see that doing so is in our national interest. It is another sign of a new isolationism that would have America bury its head in the sand at the height of our power and prosperity.

In the short term, HR 2606 fails to address critical national security needs. It suggests we can afford to underfund our efforts to keep deadly weapons from falling into dangerous hands and walk away without peril from our essential work toward peace in places of conflict. Just as seriously, it fails to address America's long-term interests. It reduces assistance to nations struggling to build democratic societies and open markets and backs away from our commitment to help people trapped in poverty to stand on their feet. This, too, threatens our security because future threats will come from regions and nations where instability and misery prevail and future opportunities will come from nations on the road to freedom and growth.

By denying America a decent investment in diplomacy, this bill suggests we should meet threats to our security with our military might alone. That is a dangerous proposition. For if we underfund our diplomacy, we will end up overusing our military. Problems we might have been able to resolve peacefully will turn into crises we can only resolve at a cost of life and treasure. Shortchanging our arsenal of peace is as risky as shortchanging our arsenal of war.

The overall funding provided by HR 2606 is inadequate. It is about half the amount available in real terms to President [Ronald] Reagan in 1985, and it is 14 percent below the level that I requested. I proposed to fund this higher level within the budget limits and without spending any of the Social Security surplus. The specific shortfalls in the current bill are numerous and unacceptable.

For example, it is shocking that the Congress has failed to fulfill our obligations to Israel and its neighbors as they take risks and make difficult decisions to advance the Middle East peace process. My administration, like all its predecessors, has fought hard to promote peace in the Middle East. This bill would provide neither the $800 million requested this year as a supplemental appropriation nor the $500 million requested in FY [fiscal year] 2000 funding to support the Wye River Agreement. Just when [Israeli] Prime Minister [Ehud] Barak has helped give the peace process a jump start, this sends the worst possible message to Israel, Jordan, and the Palestinians about America's commitment to the peace process. We should instead seize this opportunity to support them.

Additional resources are required to respond to the costs of building peace in Kosovo and the rest of the Balkans, and I intend to work with the Congress to provide needed assistance. Other lifesaving peace efforts, such as those in Sierra Leone and East Timor, are imperiled by the bill's inadequate funding of the voluntary peacekeeping account.

My administration has sought to protect Americans from the threat posed by the potential danger of weapons proliferation from Russia and the countries of the former Soviet Union. But the Congress has failed to finance the Expanded Threat Reduction Initiative (ETRI), which is designed to prevent weapons of mass destruction and weapons technologies from falling into the wrong hands and weapons scientists from offering their talents to countries, or even terrorists, seeking these weapons. The bill also curtails ETRI programs that help Russia and other New Independent States strengthen export controls to avoid illicit trafficking in sensitive materials through their borders and airports. The ETRI will also help facilitate withdrawal of Russian forces and equipment from countries such as Georgia and Moldovia; it will create peaceful research opportunities for thousands of former Soviet weapons scientists. We also cannot afford to underfund programs that support democracy and small scale enterprises in Russia and other New Independent States because these are the very kinds of initiatives needed to complete their transformation away from communism and authoritarianism.

A generation from now, no one is going to say we did too much to help the nations of the former Soviet Union safeguard their nuclear technology and expertise. If the funding cuts in this bill were to become law, future generations would certainly say we did too little and that we imperiled our future in the process.

My administration has also sought to promote economic progress and political change in developing countries, because America benefits when these countries become our partners in security and trade. At the Cologne Summit, we led a historic effort to enable the world's poorest and most heavily indebted countries to finance health, education and opportunity programs. The Congress fails to fund the U.S. contribution. The bill also severely underfunds Multilateral Development Banks, providing the lowest level of financing since 1987, with cuts of 37 percent from our request. This will virtually double U.S. arrears to these banks and seriously undermine our capacity to promote economic reform and growth in Latin America, Asia, and especially Africa. These markets are critical to American jobs and opportunities.

Across the board, my administration requested the funding necessary to assure American leadership on matters vital to the interests and values of our citizens. In area after area, from fighting terrorism and international crime to promoting nuclear stability on the Korean peninsula, from helping refugees and disaster victims to meeting its own goal of a 10,000-member Peace Corps, the Congress has failed to fund adequately these requests.

Several policy matters addressed in the bill are also problematic. One provision would hamper the Export-Import Bank's ability to be responsive to American exporters by requiring that the Congress be notified of dozens of additional kinds of transactions before the bank can offer financing. Another provision would allow the Export-Import Bank to operate without a quorum until March 2000. I have nominated two individuals to the Bank's Board, and they should be confirmed.

A third provision could be read to prevent the United States from engaging in diplomatic efforts to promote a cost-effective, global solution to climate change. A fourth provision places restrictions on assistance to Indonesia that could harm our ability to influence the objectives we share with the Congress: ensuring that Indonesia honors the referendum in East Timor and that security is restored there, while encouraging democracy and economic reform in Indonesia. Finally, this bill contains several sections that, if treated as mandatory, would encroach on the President's sole constitutional authority to conduct diplomatic negotiations.

In sum, this appropriations bill undermines important American interests and ignores the lessons that have been at the core of our bipartisan foreign policy for the last half century. Like the Senate's recent vote to defeat the Comprehensive Test Ban Treaty, this bill reflects an inexcusable and potentially dangerous complacency about the opportunities and risks America faces in the world today. I therefore am returning this bill without my approval.

I look forward to working with the Congress to craft an appropriations bill that I can support, one that maintains our commitment to protecting the Social Security surplus, properly addressing our shared goal of an America that is strong at home and strong abroad, respected not only for our leadership, but for the vision and commitment that real leadership entails. The American people deserve a foreign policy worthy of our great country, and I will fight to ensure that they continue to have one.

WILLIAM J. CLINTON
THE WHITE HOUSE,
October 18, 1999

Clinton Objects To Provisions On U.N., Community Policing In Commerce-Justice-State Bill

Following is the text of President Clinton's veto message on HR 2670, the fiscal 2000 appropriations bill for the federal judiciary and the departments of Commerce, Justice and State.

TO THE HOUSE OF REPRESENTATIVES:

I am returning herewith without my approval HR 2670, the "Departments of Commerce, Justice, and State, the Judiciary, and Related Agencies Appropriations Act, 2000."

This legislation should embody the continuing commitment of this administration on a broad range of fundamental principles. First and foremost amongst these tenets is the notion that the United States of America should be the safest country in the world. Our families must feel secure in their neighborhoods. Since 1993, the progress realized toward that end has been impressive and must not be impeded.

Moreover, America must continue to lead the community of nations toward a safer, more prosperous and democratic world. This guidepost has for generations advanced the cause of peace and freedom internationally, and an erosion of this policy is untenable and unacceptable at this critical moment in history.

This great nation serves as [an] example to the world of a just and humane society. We must continue to lead by our example and maintain a system that vigorously protects and rigorously respects the civil rights of individuals, the dignity of every citizen, and the basic justice and fairness afforded to every American.

Unfortunately, this bill fails to uphold these principles.

Specifically, and most notably, the bill fails to adequately fund the proposed 21st Century Policing Initiative, which builds on the success of the Community Oriented Policing Services (COPS) program. I requested $1.275 billion in new appropriations, and this bill provides only $325 million. To date, the COPS program has funded more than 100,000 additional police officers for our streets. The 21st Century Policing initiative would place an additional 30,000 to 50,000 police officers on the street over the next 5 years and would expand the concept of community policing to include community prosecution, law enforcement technology assistance, and crime prevention. Funding the COPS program required a bipartisan commitment, and it paid off; recently released statistics show that we have the lowest murder rate in 31 years and the longest continuous decline in crime on record. I strongly believe we must forge a similar commitment to support the COPS program's logical successor.

The bill would also threaten America's ability to lead in the world by failing to meet our obligation to pay our dues and our debts to the United Nations. This is a problem I have been working with the Congress to resolve for several years, but this bill fails to provide a solution.

Though the bill does include adequate funds to support our annual contribution to the United Nations regular budget, it conditions the funding on separate authorizing legislation, continuing an unacceptable linkage to an unrelated issue. For this reason, because of additional provisions, and because the bill is inconsistent with provisions agreed to by the authorizing committees, the bill would still cause the United States to lose its vote in the United Nations. It would undercut efforts that matter to America in which the U.N. plays an important role, from our fight against terrorism and proliferation, to our efforts to promote human rights, the well-being of children, and the health of our environment. It would undermine our ability to shape the U.N.'s agenda in all these areas and to press for reforms that will make its work more effective. All this is unacceptable. Great nations meet their responsibilities, and I am determined that we will meet ours.

In addition, the bill includes only $200 million for International Peacekeeping Activities, a reduction of almost 60 percent from my request. The requested level of $485 million is necessary to meet anticipated peacekeeping requirements in East Timor, Sierra Leone, the Democratic Republic of the Congo, Ethiopia, and Eritrea. In each of these places, the United States has worked with allies and friends to end conflicts that have claimed countless innocent lives and thrown whole regions into turmoil. In each case, the U.N. either has been or may be asked to help implement fragile peace agreements, by performing essential tasks such as separating adversaries, maintaining cease-fires, enabling refugees to go home, training police forces, and overseeing civilian institutions. In each case, as in all U.N. peacekeeping missions, other countries will pay 75 percent of the cost and provide virtually all the military personnel.

It is clearly in America's national interest to support an institution through which other countries share the burden of making peace. Refusing to do our part would be dangerous and self-defeating. It could undermine fragile peace agreements that America helped forge, and spark new emergencies to which we could only respond later at far greater cost. It would leave America with an unacceptable choice in times of conflict and crisis abroad: a choice between acting alone and doing nothing.

The bill includes a number of provisions regarding the conduct of foreign affairs that raise serious constitutional concerns. Provisions concerning Jerusalem are objectionable on constitutional, foreign policy, and operational grounds. The actions called for by these provisions would prejudice the outcome of the Israeli-Palestinian permanent status negotiations, which have recently begun and which the parties are committed to concluding within a year. The bill also includes a provision that could be read to prevent the United States from engaging in diplomatic efforts regarding the Kyoto protocol [on global warming]. Applying restrictions to the president's authority to engage in international negotiations and activities raises serious constitutional concerns.

Other provisions that should be deleted from the bill because they would unconstitutionally constrain the president's authority include provisions on Haiti, Vietnam, and command and control of United Nations peacekeeping efforts. My administration's objections to these and other language provisions have been made clear in previous statements of administration policy regarding this bill.

This bill does not contain a needed hate crimes provision that was included in the Senate version of the bill. I urge the Congress to pass legislation in a timely manner that would strengthen the federal government's ability to combat hate crimes by relaxing jurisdictional obstacles and by giving federal prosecutors the ability to prosecute hate crimes that are based on sexual orientation, gender, or disability, along with those based on race, color, religion and national origin.

The bill freezes the funding level for the Legal Services Corporation. Adequate funding for legal services is essential to ensuring that all citizens have access to the nation's justice system. I urge the Congress to fully fund my request, which provides an increase of $40 million over the fiscal 1999 enacted level. Also, funding for the Equal Employment Opportunity Commission (EEOC) is frozen at the enacted level. This level would undermine EEOC's progress in reducing the backlog of employment discrimination cases.

Similarly, inadequate funding is provided for the United States Commission on Civil Rights and the Civil Rights Division of the Department of Justice. The bill does not fund my requested $13 million increase for the Civil Rights Division, including increases for law enforcement actions related to hate crimes, the Americans with Disabilities Act, and fair housing and lending. I ask the Congress to restore requested funds for these law enforcement enhancements.

The bill contains adequate funding for the decennial census, but I oppose language that could inhibit the Census Bureau's ability to actually conduct the census. The bill would require the Census Bureau to obtain approval from certain committees if it chooses to shift funds among eight functions or frameworks. This approval process would impose an unnecessary and potentially time-consuming constraint on the management of the decennial census. It is imperative that we move forward on the census; this legislation could impede it.

The United States has recently entered into the U.S.-Canada Pacific Salmon Agreement. The agreement ends years of contention between the U.S. and Canada regarding expired fishing harvest restrictions and provides for improved fisheries management.

This bill includes extraneous legislative riders that would hinder the implementation of that important agreement. These riders would prohibit the application of the Endangered Species Act to Alaskan salmon fisheries and would change the voting structure of the Pacific Salmon Commission, the decision-making body established by the agreement. In essence, the voting-structure rider would prevent the federal government from negotiating agreements that balance the interests of all States.

In addition to the riders, the bill provides only $10 million of the $60 million requested to implement the Salmon Agreement. Similarly, funding for the Salmon Recovery Fund falls far short of that needed to work cooperatively with the States of Washington, Oregon, California, and Alaska and with treaty tribes to help them mount effective State-based plans to restore Pacific coastal salmon runs. These shortfalls together would severely inhibit our ability to recover this important species.

In addition, the enrolled bill does not provide my request for a number of other environmental programs, including my Lands Legacy Initiative, Endangered Species Act activities, the Clean Water Action Plan, and the Global Learning and Observations to Benefit the Environment program. The additional funds required to bring these programs to my requested levels are small compared to the benefits they provide to our natural resources.

The bill does not include $100 million in new funding for the Drug Intervention Program, which would have provided critical assistance to state and local governments developing and implementing comprehensive systems for drug testing, drug treatment, and graduated sanctions for drug offenders. These resources are critical to reducing drug use in America.

The bill does not provide additional requested funding to the Justice Department for tobacco litigation. Smoking-related health expenses cost taxpayers billions of dollars each year through Medicare, veterans' and military health, and other Federal health programs. The Department of Justice needs the $20 million I requested to represent the interests of the taxpayers, who should not have to bear the responsibility for these staggering costs.

This bill would also hurt our Nation's small businesses. The level provided for the Small Business Administration's (SBA's) operating expenses would inhibit my administration's ability to provide service to the nation's 24 million small businesses.

The bill also fails to provide sufficient funds for the disaster loan program within the SBA. Without additional funding, the SBA will not be able to respond adequately to the needs arising from Hurricane Floyd and other natural disasters. In addition, the bill does not include funds for my New Markets Initiative to invest in targeted rural and urban areas.

The bill fails to include a proposed provision to clarify current law and protect taxpayer interests in the telecommunications spectrum auction process. Currently, $5.6 billion of bid-for-spectrum is tied up in bankruptcy court, with a very real risk that spectrum licensees will be able to retain spectrum at a fraction of its real market value. The requested provision would maintain the integrity of the Federal Communications Commission (FCC) auction process while also ensuring speedy deployment of new telecommunications services. The bill would also deny funds needed by the FCC for investments in technology to better serve the communications industry. Also, the bill does not provide sufficient funds for the continued operations of the FCC. The commission requires additional funds to invest in technology to serve the communications industry more effectively.

In conference action, a rider was added that would amend the recently enacted Treasury and General Government Appropriations Act [PL 106-58] to expand the prohibition of discrimination against individuals who refuse to "prescribe" contraceptives to individuals who "otherwise provide for" contraceptives (all non-physician providers) in the Federal Employees Health Benefits Program. As an example, this language could allow pharmacists to refuse to dispense contraceptive prescriptions. This action violated jurisdictional concerns and is also unacceptable policy.

The bill underfunds a number of high-priority programs within the Department of Commerce. My administration sought an additional $9 million to help public broadcasters meet the federal deadline to establish digital broadcasting capability by May 1, 2003. The bill would provide less than half of last year's funding level for the Critical Infrastructure Assurance Office. The bill also fails to fund the department's other programs to protect critical information and communications infrastructures. The Congress must restore these funds if the department is to continue performing its important and emerging role in coordinating activities that support our economic and national security.

The bill does not include any funds to reimburse Guam and other territories for the costs of detaining and repatriating smuggled Chinese aliens. These entities deserve our support for assisting in this interdiction effort.

I look forward to working with the Congress to craft an appropriations bill that I can support, and to passage of one that will facilitate our shared objectives.

WILLIAM J. CLINTON
THE WHITE HOUSE,
October 25, 1999

Clinton Condemns Labor-HHS-Education Bill for Cutting Education Money, Delaying Medical Research

Following is the text of President Clinton's Nov. 3 veto of HR 3064, the fiscal 2000 appropriations bill for the District of Columbia and the departments of Education, Labor, and Health and Human Services.

TO THE HOUSE OF REPRESENTATIVES:

I am returning herewith without my approval HR 3064, the fiscal 2000 District of Columbia and departments of Labor, Health and Human Services, and Education, and related agencies appropriations bill.

I am vetoing HR 3064 because the bill, including the offsets section, is deeply flawed. It includes a misguided 0.97 percent across-the-board reduction that will hurt everything from national defense to education and environmental programs. The legislation also contains crippling cuts in key education, labor and health priorities and undermines our capacity to manage these programs effectively. The enrolled bill delays the availability of $10.9 billion for the National Institutes of Health, the Centers for Disease Control, and other important health and social services programs, resulting in delays in important medical research and health services to low-income Americans. The bill is clearly unacceptable. I have submitted a budget that would fund these priorities without spending the Social Security surplus, and I am committed to working with the Congress to identify acceptable offsets for additional spending for programs that are important to all Americans.

The bill also fails to fulfill the bipartisan commitment to raise student achievement by authorizing and financing class-size reduction. It does not guarantee any continued funding for the 29,000 teachers hired with fiscal 1999 funds, or the additional 8,000 teachers to be hired under my fiscal 2000 proposal. Moreover, the bill language turns the program into a virtual block grant that could be spent on vouchers and other unspecified activities. In addition, the bill fails to fund my proposed investments in teacher quality by not funding Troops to Teachers ($18 million) and by cutting $35 million from my request for Teacher Quality Enhancement Grants. These programs would bring more highly qualified teachers into the schools, especially in high-poverty, high-need school districts.

The bill cuts $189 million from my request for Title I Education for the Disadvantaged, resulting in 300,000 fewer children in low-income communities receiving needed services. The bill also fails to improve accountability or help states turn around the lowest-performing schools because it does not include my proposal to set aside 2.5 percent for these purposes. Additionally, the bill provides only $300 million for 21st Century Community Learning Centers, only half my $600 million request. At this level, the conference report would deny after-school services to more than 400,000 students.

The bill provides only $180 million for GEAR UP, $60 million below my request, to help disadvantaged students prepare for college beginning in the seventh grade. This level would serve nearly 131,000 fewer low-income students. In addition, the bill does not adequately fund my Hispanic Education Agenda. It provides no funds for the Adult Education English as a Second Language/Civics Initiative to help limited English proficient adults learn English and gain life skills necessary for successful citizenship and civic participation. The bill underfunds programs designed to improve educational outcomes for Hispanic and other minority students, including Bilingual Education, the High School Equivalency Program (HEP), the College Assistance Migrant Program (CAMP), and the Strengthening Historically Black Colleges and Universities program.

The bill underfunds education technology programs, including distance learning and community technology centers. In particular, the bill provides only $10 million to community based technology centers, $55 million below my request. My request would provide access to technology in 300 additional low-income communities. The bill provides $75 million for education research, $34 million less than my request, and includes no funding for the Department of Education's share of large-scale joint research with the National Science Foundation and the National Institutes of Health on early learning in reading and mathematics, teacher preparation and technology applications.

The bill does not fund the $53 million I requested to provide job finding assistance to 241,000 unemployment insurance claimants. This means that these claimants will remain unemployed longer, costing more in benefit payments. The bill also provides only $140 million of my $199 million request to expand services to job seekers at One-Stop centers as recently authorized in the bipartisan Workforce Investment Act. The bill funds $120 million of the $149 million requested for efforts to improve access to One-Stops as well as continued support for electronic labor exchange and labor market information. It funds only $20 million of the $50 million requested for work incentive grants to help integrate employment services for persons with disabilities into the mainstream One-Stop system.

The bill also does not provide funding for Right Track Partnerships (RTP). I requested $75 million for this new, competitive-grant program. Designed to help address youth violence, RTP would become part of the multi-agency Safe Schools/Healthy Students initiative, expanding it to include a focus on out-of-school youth.

The bill provides $33 million less than my request for labor law enforcement agencies, denying or reducing initiatives to ensure workplace safety, address domestic child labor abuses, encourage equal pay, implement new health law, and promote family leave. In particular, the bill provides an inadequate level of funding for the Occupational Safety and Health Administration, cutting it by $18 million, or 5 percent below my request.

The bill also fails to provide adequate funding for the Bureau of International Labor Affairs (ILAB). The bill funds ILAB at $50 million, $26 million below my request. The bill would prevent ILAB from carrying out my proposal to work through the International Labor Organization to help developing countries establish core labor standards, an essential step toward leveling the playing field for American workers.

The bill's funding level for the Bureau of Labor Statistics is $11 million less than my request. The enrolled bill denies three important increases that would: (1) improve the Producer Price Index, which measures wholesale prices; (2) improve measures of labor productivity in the service sector; and, (3) improve the Employment Cost Index, used to help set wage levels and guide anti-inflation policy. It also denies funding for a study of racial discrimination in labor markets.

The bill denies my request for $10 million to fund AgNet, even though the Senate included report language that supports AgNet in concept. AgNet, an Internet-based labor exchange, would facilitate the recruitment of agricultural workers by growers and the movement of agricultural workers to areas with employment needs.

The bill would cut the Social Services Block Grant (SSBG) by $209 million below fiscal 1999 and $680 million below my request. The SSBG serves some of the most vulnerable families, providing child protection and child welfare services for millions of children. In addition, the failure to provide the Senate's level of $2 billion in advance appropriations for the Child Care and Development Block Grant would mean 220,000 fewer children receiving child care assistance in fiscal 2001. The bill also fails to fund my National Family Caregiver Support program, which would provide urgently needed assistance to 250,000 families caring for older relatives.

By funding the Title X Family Planning program at last year's level, family planning clinics would be unable to extend comprehensive reproductive health care services to an additional 500,000 clients who are neither Medicaid-eligible nor insured. The bill also fails to fund the Health Care Access for the Uninsured Initiative, which would enable the development of integrated systems of care and address service gaps within these systems.

The bill fails to fully fund several of the Centers for Disease Control and Prevention's (CDC) critical public health programs, including:

- Childhood immunizations (–$44 million), so that approximately 300,000 children may not receive the full complement of recommended childhood vaccinations;
- Infectious diseases (–$36 million), which will impair CDC's ability to investigate outbreaks of diseases such as the West Nile virus in New York;
- Domestic HIV prevention (–$4 million);
- Race and health demonstrations (–$5 million), which will impair better understanding of how to reduce racial disparities in health; and,
- Health statistics (–$10 million) for key data collection activities such as the National Health and Nutrition Examination Survey and health information on racial and ethnic population groups.

The Congress has failed to fund any of the $59 million increase I requested for the Mental Health Block Grant, which would diminish states' capacity to serve the mentally ill.

In addition, the Congress has underfunded my request for the Substance Abuse Block Grant by $30 million, and has underfunded other substance abuse treatment grants by a total of $45 million. These reductions would widen the treatment gap in fiscal 2000 and jeopardize the Federal Government's ability to meet the National Drug Control Strategy performance target to reduce the drug treatment gap by 50 percent by fiscal 2007.

The bill provides only half of the $40 million requested for graduate education at Children's Hospitals, which play an essential role in educating the Nation's physicians, training 25 percent of pediatricians and over half of many pediatric subspecialists.

The bill underfunds the Congressional Black Caucus' AIDS Initiative in the Public Health and Social Services Emergency Fund by $15 million, thereby reducing current efforts to prevent the spread of HIV. By not fully funding this program, the scope of HIV/AIDS prevention, education, and outreach activities available to slow the spread of HIV/AIDS in minority communities will be more limited.

The bill fails to fund Health Care Financing Administration (HCFA) program management adequately. These reductions would severely impede HCFA's ability to ensure the quality of nursing home care through the Nursing Home Initiative. The bill does not adequately fund the request for Medicare+Choice user fees. This decrease would force HCFA to scale back the National Medicare Education Campaign. The Congress has not passed the proposed user fees totaling $194.5 million that could free up resources under the discretionary caps for education and other priorities.

The bill includes a provision that would prevent funds from being used to administer the Medicare+Choice Competitive Pricing Demonstration Project in Kansas and Arizona. These demonstrations, which are supported by MEDPAC and other independent health policy experts, were passed by the Congress as part of the Balanced Budget Act in order to provide valuable information regarding the use of competitive pricing methodologies in Medicare. The information that we could learn from these demonstrations is particularly relevant as we consider the important task of reforming Medicare.

The bill contains a highly objectionable provision that would delay the implementation of HHS' final Organ Procurement and Transplantation rule for 90 days. This rule, which was strongly validated by an Institute of Medicine report, provides a more equitable system of treatment for over 63,000 Americans waiting for an organ transplant; its implementation would likely prevent the deaths of hundreds of Americans. Since almost 5,000 people die each year waiting for an organ transplant, we must be allowed to move forward on this issue and implement the rule without further delay.

The bill does not provide any of the $9.5 million I requested for HHS' Office of the General Counsel and Departmental Appeals Board to handle legal advice, regulations review, and litigation support, and to conduct hearings and issue decisions on nursing home enforcement cases as part of my Nursing Home Initiative. This would increase the backlog of nursing home appeals and impair federal oversight of nursing home quality and safety standards. A reduction in funds for enforcement is inconsistent with the concerns that the GAO and the Congress have raised about this issue.

The bill cuts funds to counter bioterrorism. It funds less than half my request for CDC's stockpile, limiting the amount of vaccines, antibiotics, and other medical supplies that can be stockpiled to deploy in the event of a chemical or biological attack. In addition, the bill does not include $13.4 million for critical FDA expedited regulatory review/approval of pharmaceuticals to combat chemical and biological agent weapons.

The bill provides full funding of $350 million in fiscal 2002 for the Corporation for Public Broadcasting. However, the bill provides only $10 million of the $20 million requested for the digital transition initiative in fiscal 2000. This funding is required to help the public broadcasting system meet the federal deadline to establish digital broadcasting capability by May 1, 2003.

The enrolled bill delays the availability of $10.9 billion of funding until September 29, 2000. While modest levels of delayed obligations could potentially be sustained without hurting the affected programs, the levels in the enrolled bill are excessive, resulting in delays in NIH research grants, delays in CDC immunizations for children, and delays in the delivery of health services to low-income Americans through community health centers and rural health clinics.

The bill also seriously underfunds critical departmental management activities in the departments of Labor and Education and the Social Security Administration (SSA). For Education, these reductions would hamstring efforts to replace the department's accounting system and undermine the new Performance-Based Organization's plans to streamline and modernize student aid computer systems. Reductions to the Department of Labor would undercut the agency's ability to comply with the requirements of the Clanger-Cohen and Computer Security Acts, adjudicate contested claims in several of its benefits programs, and examine and update the 1996 study on Family and Medical Leave policies. For SSA, the reductions would result in significantly longer waiting times for disability applicants and millions of individuals who visit SSA field offices.

In adopting an across-the-board reduction, the Congress has abdicated its responsibility to make tough choices. Governing is about making choices and selecting priorities that will serve the national interest. By choosing an across-the-board cut, the Congress has failed to meet that responsibility.

This across-the-board cut would result in indiscriminate reductions in important areas such as education, the environment, and law enforcement. In addition, this cut would have an adverse impact on certain national security programs. The indiscriminate nature of the cut would require a reduction of over $700 million for military personnel, which would require the military services to make cuts in recruiting and lose up to 48,000 military personnel.

In adopting this cost-saving technique, the Congress is asserting that it will not have to dip into the Social Security surplus. However, this cut does not eliminate the need to dip into the Social Security surplus.

For these reasons, this across-the-board cut is not acceptable.

In addition to the specific program cuts and the 0.97 percent across-the-board reduction, the bill contains a $121 million reduction in salaries and expenses for the agencies funded by this bill, exacerbating the problems caused by the bill's underfunding of critical departmental management activities. If, for example, the $121 million reduction were allocated proportionately across all agencies funded in the Labor/HHS/Education bill, HHS would have to absorb an approximately $55 million reduction to its salaries and expenses accounts, Labor would be cut by about $14 million, Education by about $5 million, and SSA by some $45 million. This would dramatically affect the delivery of essential human services and education programs and the protection of employees in the workplace.

With respect to the District of Columbia component of the bill, I am pleased that the majority and minority in the Congress were able to come together to pass a version of the District of Columbia Appropriations Bill that I would sign if presented to me separately and as it is currently constructed. While I continue to object to remaining riders, some of the highly objectionable provisions that would have intruded upon local citizens' right to make decisions about local matters have been modified from previous versions of the bill. That is a fair compromise. We will continue to strenuously urge the Congress to keep such riders off of the fiscal 2001 D.C. appropriations bill.

I commend the Congress for providing the federal funds I requested for the District of Columbia. The bill includes essential funding for District Courts and Corrections and the D.C. Offender Supervision Agency and provides requested funds for a new tuition assistance program for District of Columbia residents. The bill also includes funding to promote the adoption of children in the District's foster care system, to support the Children's National Medical Center, to assist the Metropolitan Police Department in eliminating open-air drug trafficking in the District, and for drug testing and treatment, among other programs. However, I continue to object to remaining riders that violate the principles of home rule.

I look forward to working with the Congress to craft an appropriations bill that I can support, and to passage of one that will facilitate our shared objectives.

WILLIAM J. CLINTON
THE WHITE HOUSE,
November 3, 1999

Clinton Signs Omnibus Bill, Says It Funds Crucial Programs While Upholding Fiscal Discipline

Following are remarks that President Clinton made Nov. 29 in the White House Rose Garden, just before he signed the fiscal 2000 omnibus appropriations bill (HR 3194 — PL 106-113). Transcript provided by Federal News Service:

PRESIDENT CLINTON: Thank you. Thank you. Good afternoon. Please be seated.

I want to welcome the members of Congress who are here, members of the Cabinet, the police officers and teachers, who are shielding me from the cold wind — [laughter] — and who represent the big winners in this year's budget.

I would like to say a special word of thanks to Jack Lew, Sylvia Mathews, Larry Stein and Martha Foley, for the work that they did on this budget. [Applause.]

And I know that many members of the Senate and the House who are here brought their staff members who worked on the budget. I want to thank them for their work as well.

Last January, in my State of the Union address, I asked our Congress to use this truly historic time of peace and prosperity to meet our generation's responsibilities to the new century, to extend our economic prosperity, improve our education system, make our streets safer, protect our environment, move more Americans from welfare to work, prepare for the aging of our nation and strengthen our leadership in the world.

The first budget of the 21st century was a long time in coming, but it goes a very long way toward fulfilling those historic responsibilities.

Though it leaves some challenges unmet, it represents real progress. It is a budget for a government that lives within its means and lives up to the values of the American people.

We value prosperity, and this budget will help to extend it. It maintains the fiscal discipline that has turned deficits into surpluses and gives us what will be in February the longest economic expansion in the history of the United States. It avoids risky tax cuts that would have spent hundreds of billions of dollars from the Social Security surplus and drained our ability to advance education and other important public purposes. The budget keeps us on track toward paying down the debt, so that in 15 years our nation will be debt-free for the first time since 1835. This will mean lower interest rates and greater growth for a whole generation of Americans.

We value education, and this budget truly puts education first, continuing our commitment to hire 100,000 highly qualified teachers to lower class size in the early grades, which common sense and research both tell us leads to improved learning.

The budget also helps to fulfill another promise I made last winter: to encourage more accountability for results in our nation's schools. Under this budget, for the first time we will help states and school districts turn around or shut down their worst-performing schools, schools that year after year fail to give our most disadvantaged students the learning they need to escape poverty and reach their full potential.

And the budget provides further help for students to reach higher standards by doubling funds for after-school and summer school programs which will enable us to reach hundreds of thousands of more students, and by increasing support for mentoring programs, including the Gear-Up Program to help students go on to college.

We value the safety of our families, and this budget will make America a safer place. It invests in our COPS program, which already has funded 100,000 community police officers and helped to give us the lowest crime rate in 25 years. This agreement will help to hire up to 50,000 more community police officers targeted in neighborhoods where the crime rates still are too high.

We value the environment, and this budget protects the environment and preserves our precious natural heritage. It includes our historic Lands Legacy Initiative to set aside more of our magnificent natural areas and vital green spaces, and does not include destructive anti-environmental riders.

We value quality health care, and this budget includes historic investments in biomedical research, mental health, pediatric training and other areas. And it ensures that hospitals and other medical providers will have the resources they need to provide the 39 million elderly and disabled Medicare beneficiaries with the quality health care they need and deserve.

Finally, we value America's role of leadership in the world, and this budget strengthens that role with greater investments in our nation's strong defense and our nation's diplomacy by paying our dues and arrears to the United Nations, meeting our commitments to the Middle East peace process, providing debt relief for the poorest countries of the world, and funding efforts to safeguard nuclear weapons and expertise in Russia.

Let me thank the leaders of both parties for their roles in this agreement. We had a lot of late-night, long phone calls which led to it. I thank the leaders of the relevant committees and subcommittees for their special efforts in this regard. And, of course, I want to say a special word of thanks to the leaders and members of my party in both houses who strongly supported my efforts for the 100,000 teachers, the 50,000 police, investments in the environment and paying the U.N. dues.

As we celebrate what we have accomplished, I ask us all to be humble and mindful of what we still have to accomplish. To give all Americans in all health plans the protections they need, we still need a strong, enforceable Patients' Bill of Rights. To curb gun violence and keep firearms out of the hands of criminals and children, we still need sensible gun safety legislation to close the gun-show loophole in the Brady law, to ban the importation of large ammunition clips, to include the requirement for child trigger locks and a juvenile Brady bill. To build one America with freedom and justice for all, we should pass the Hate Crimes Prevention Act.

To meet the challenge of the aging of America, we must extend the life of the Social Security trust fund well beyond the years of the Baby Boomers' retirement, lift the earnings limitation and alleviate poverty among older women on Social Security. To ensure the health of our seniors in the years to come, we must secure and modernize Medicare, including a voluntary prescription drug benefit. To make sure hard-working Americans have a place at the table of our prosperity, we must pass a New Markets Initiative to give Americans the same incentives to invest in poor areas [in the United States that] they have to invest in poor areas around the world. We must raise the minimum wage and increase our support for quality child care.

In the weeks and months ahead, we can achieve these vital goals if we keep in mind that the disagreements we have are far less important than our shared values and our shared responsibility to the future. With this budget, we have helped to begin that future.

Again let me thank the leaders and the members in Congress in both parties that contributed to a budget that passed with large majorities in both houses, in both parties. I am proud to sign a bill that I believe will give us a stronger, better America in the 21st century.

I'd like to now invite the members of Congress to come up and stand with me. And then I'd like to ask the police officers and the teachers to come in behind the members of Congress and we'll sign the budget.

Thank you very much. ◆

Appendix E

PUBLIC LAWS

Public Laws

PL 106-1 (HR 433) Restore the management and personnel authority of the mayor of the District of Columbia. Introduced by DAVIS, R-Va., on Feb. 2, 1999. House Government Reform discharged. House passed Feb. 9. Senate passed Feb. 23. President signed March 5, 1999.

PL 106-2 (HR 882) Nullify any reservation of funds during fiscal year 1999 for guaranteed loans under the Consolidated Farm and Rural Development Act for qualified beginning farmers or ranchers. Introduced by COMBEST, R-Texas, on March 1, 1999. House passed, under suspension of the rules, March 2. Senate passed March 8. President signed March 15, 1999.

PL 106-3 (S 447) Deem the applications submitted by the Dodson School Districts for certain Impact Aid payments for fiscal year 1999 as filed on time, and process for payment. Introduced by BURNS, R-Mont., on Feb. 23, 1999. Senate Health, Education, Labor and Pensions discharged. Senate passed March 2. House passed March 10. President signed March 23, 1999.

PL 106-4 (HR 540) Amend Title XIX of the Social Security Act to prohibit transfers or discharges of residents of nursing facilities as a result of a voluntary withdrawal from participation in the Medicaid program. Introduced by DAVIS, D-Fla., on Feb. 3, 1999. House Commerce reported March 8 (H Rept 106-44). House passed, under suspension of the rules, March 10. Senate passed March 15. President signed March 25, 1999.

PL 106-5 (HR 808) Extend for three additional months the period for which Chapter 12 of Title 11 of the United States Code is re-enacted. Introduced by SMITH, R-Mich., on Feb. 23, 1999. House Judiciary reported, amended, March 9 (H Rept 106-45). House passed, amended, under suspension of the rules, March 11. Senate passed March 24. President signed March 30, 1999.

PL 106-6 (S 643) Authorize the Airport Improvement Program for two months. Introduced by McCAIN, R-Ariz., on March 17, 1999. Senate passed, amended, March 17. House passed March 24. President signed March 31, 1999.

PL 106-7 (HR 1212) Protect producers of agricultural commodities who applied for a Crop Revenue Coverage PLUS supplemental endorsement for the 1999 crop year. Introduced by COMBEST, R-Texas, on March 22, 1999. House passed, amended, under suspension of the rules, March 23. Senate passed March 25. President signed April 1, 1999.

PL 106-8 (S 314) Provide for a loan guarantee program to address the Year 2000 computer problems of small businesses. Introduced by BOND, R-Mo., on Jan. 27, 1999. Senate Small Business reported Feb. 23 (S Rept 106-5). Senate passed March 2. House passed, under suspension of the rules, March 23. President signed April 2, 1999.

PL 106-9 (HR 68) Amend Section 20 of the Small Business Act and make technical corrections in Title III of the Small Business Investment Act. Introduced by TALENT, R-Mo., on Jan. 6, 1999. House Small Business reported Jan. 19 (H Rept 106-1). House passed, amended, under suspension of the rules, Feb. 2. Senate Small Business discharged. Senate passed, with amendment, March 22. House agreed to Senate amendment, under suspension of the rules, March 23. President signed April 5, 1999.

PL 106-10 (HR 92) Designate the federal building and U.S. courthouse at 251 N. Main St. in Winston-Salem, N.C., as the "Hiram H. Ward Federal Building and United States Courthouse." Introduced by COBLE, R-N.C., on Jan. 6, 1999. House Transportation and Infrastructure reported Feb. 23 (H Rept 106-20). House passed, under suspension of the rules, Feb. 23, Senate Environment and Public Works reported March 17 (no written report). Senate passed March 23. President signed April 5, 1999.

PL 106-11 (HR 158) Designate the federal courthouse at 316 N. 26th St. in Billings, Mont., as the "James F. Battin Federal Courthouse." Introduced by HILL, R-Mont., on Jan. 6, 1999. House Transportation and Infrastructure reported, amended, Feb. 23 (H Rept 106-21). House passed, amended, under suspension of the rules, Feb. 23. Senate Environment and Public Works reported March 17 (no written report). Senate passed March 23. President signed April 5, 1999.

PL 106-12 (HR 233) Designate the federal building at 700 E. San Antonio St. in El Paso, Texas, as the "Richard C. White Federal Building." Introduced by REYES, D-Texas, on Jan. 6, 1999. House Transportation and Infrastructure reported Feb. 23 (H Rept 106-22). House passed, under suspension of the rules, Feb. 23. Senate Environment and Public Works reported March 17 (no written report). Senate passed March 23. President signed April 5, 1999.

PL 106-13 (HR 396) Designate the federal building located at 1301 Clay St. in Oakland, Calif., as the "Ronald V. Dellums Federal Building." Introduced by MILLER, D-Calif., on Jan. 19, 1999. House Transportation and Infrastructure reported Feb. 23 (H Rept 106-23). House passed, under suspension of the rules, Feb. 23. Senate Environment and Public Works reported March 17 (no written report). Senate passed March 23. President signed April 5, 1999.

PL 106-14 (H J Res 26) Provide for the reappointment of Barber B. Conable Jr. as a citizen regent of the Board of Regents of the Smithsonian Institution. Introduced by JOHNSON, R-Texas, on Feb. 9, 1999. House Administration discharged. House passed March 23. Senate passed March 24. President signed April 6, 1999.

PL 106-15 (H J Res 27) Provide for the reappointment of Dr. Hanna H. Gray as a citizen regent of the Board of Regents of the Smithsonian Institution. Introduced by JOHNSON, R-Texas, on Feb 9, 1999. House Administration discharged. House passed March 23. Senate passed March 24. President signed April 6, 1999.

PL 106-16 (H J Res 28) Provide for the reappointment of Wesley S. Williams Jr. as a citizen regent of the Board of Regents of the Smithsonian Institution. Introduced by JOHNSON, R-Texas, on Feb. 9, 1999. House Administration discharged. House passed March 23. Senate passed March 24. President signed April 6, 1999.

PL 106-17 (HR 774) Amend the Small Business Act to change the conditions of participation and authorize appropriations for the women's business center program. Introduced by VELÁZQUEZ, D-N.Y., on Feb. 23, 1999. House Small Business reported March 10 (H Rept 106-47). House passed, amended, under suspension of the rules, March 16. Senate passed March 24. President signed April 6, 1999.

PL 106-18 (HR 171) Authorize appropriations for the Coastal Heritage Trail Route in New Jersey. Introduced by LoBIONDO, R-N.J., on Jan. 6, 1999. House Resources reported Feb. 11 (H Rept 106-16). House passed, under suspension of the rules, Feb. 23. Senate Energy and Natural Resources reported March 17 (S Rept 106-24). Senate passed March 25. President signed April 8, 1999.

PL 106-19 (HR 705) Make technical corrections with respect to the monthly reports submitted by the Postmaster General on official mail of the House of Representatives. Introduced by THOMAS, R-Calif., on Feb. 11, 1999. House Administration discharged. House passed Feb. 11. Senate Governmental Affairs discharged. Senate passed March 25. President signed April 8, 1999.

PL 106-20 (HR 193) Designate a portion of the Sudbury, Assabet and Concord rivers as a component of the National Wild and Scenic Rivers System. Introduced by MEEHAN, D-Mass., on Jan. 6, 1999. House Resources reported Feb. 8 (H Rept 106-10). House passed, amended, under suspension of the rules, Feb. 23. Senate Energy and Natural Resources reported March 17 (S Rept 106-25). Senate passed March 25. President signed April 9, 1999.

PL 106-21 (HR 1376) Extend the tax benefits available with respect to services performed in a combat zone to services performed in the Federal Republic of Yugoslavia (Serbia/Montenegro) and certain other areas. Introduced by ARCHER, R-Texas, on April 13, 1999. House Ways and Means reported, amended, April 13 (H Rept 106-90). House passed, amended, April 15. Senate passed April 15. President signed April 19, 1999.

PL 106-22 (HR 440) Make technical corrections to the Microloan Program. Introduced by TALENT, R-Mo., on Feb. 2, 1999. House Small Business reported Feb. 8 (H Rept 106-12). House passed, amended, under suspension of the rules, Feb. 9. Senate Small Business discharged. Senate passed, amended, March 25. House agreed to Senate amendment, under suspension of the rules, April 12. President signed April 27, 1999.

PL 106-23 (HR 911) Designate the federal building at 310 New Bern Ave., Raleigh, N.C., as the "Terry Sanford Federal Building." Introduced by ETHERIDGE, D-N.C., on March 2, 1999. House passed, amended, under suspension of the rules, April 12. Senate passed April 15. President signed April 27, 1999.

PL 106-24 (S 388) Authorize the establishment of a disaster mitigation pilot program in the Small Business Administration. Introduced by CLELAND, D-Ga., on Feb. 8, 1999. Senate Small Business discharged. Senate passed March 25. House passed, under suspension of the rules, April 12. President signed April 27, 1999.

PL 106-25 (HR 800) Provide for education flexibility partnerships. Introduced by CASTLE, R-Del., on Feb. 23, 1999. House Education and the Workforce reported, amended, March 8 (H Rept 106-43). House passed, amended, March 11. Senate passed, amended, March 11. Conference report filed in the House April 20 (H Rept 106-100). House agreed to conference report April 21. Senate agreed to conference report April 21. President signed April 29, 1999.

PL 106-26 (S 531) Authorize the president to award a gold medal on behalf of the Congress to Rosa Parks in recognition of her contributions to the nation. Introduced by ABRAHAM, R-Mich., on March 4, 1999. Senate Banking, Housing and Urban Affairs discharged. Senate passed April 19. House passed April 20. President signed May 4, 1999.

PL 106-27 (S 453) Designate the federal building at 709 W. 9th St. in Juneau, Alaska, as the "Hurff A. Saunders Federal Building." Introduced by MURKOWSKI, R-Alaska, on Feb. 24, 1999. Senate Environment and Public Works reported March 17 (no written report). Senate passed March 23. House Transportation and Infrastructure reported April 27 (H Rept 106-113). House passed, under suspension of the rules, May 4. President signed May 13, 1999.

PL 106-28 (S 460) Designate the U.S. courthouse at 401 S. Michigan St. in South Bend, Ind., as the "Robert K. Rodibaugh United States Bankruptcy Courthouse." Introduced by LUGAR, R-Ind., on Feb. 24, 1999. Senate Environment and Public Works reported March 17 (no written report). Senate passed March 23. House Transportation and Infrastructure reported March 24 (H Rept 106-114). House passed, under suspension of the rules, May 4. President signed May 13, 1999.

PL 106-29 (HR 432) Designate the North/South Center at the University of Miami as the "Dante B. Fascell North-South Center." Introduced by GILMAN, R-N.Y., on Feb. 2, 1999. House passed Feb. 2, under suspension of the rules. Senate Foreign Relations reported March 23 (no written report). Senate passed May 5. President signed May 21, 1999.

PL 106-30 (HR 669) Amend the Peace Corps Act to authorize appropriations for fiscal 2000 through 2003. Introduced by CAMPBELL, R-Calif., on Feb. 10, 1999. House International Relations reported Feb. 16 (H Rept 106-18). House passed March 3. Senate Foreign Relations reported May 11 (S Rept 106-46). Senate passed May 12. President signed May 21, 1999.

PL 106-31 (HR 1141) Make emergency supplemental appropriations for the fiscal year ending Sept. 30, 1999. Introduced by YOUNG, R-Fla., on March 17, 1999. House Appropriations reported March 17 (H Rept 106-64). House passed March 24. Senate passed, amended, March 25. Conference report filed in the House May 14 (H Rept 106-143). House agreed to conference report May 18. Senate agreed to conference report May 20. President signed May 21, 1999.

PL 106-32 (HR 1034) Declare a portion of the James River and Kanawha Canal in Richmond,Va., to be non-navigable waters of the United States for purposes of Title 46, U.S. Code, and the other maritime laws of the U.S. Introduced by BLILEY, R-Va., on March 9, 1999. House Transportation and Infrastructure reported, amended, under suspension of the rules, April 27 (H Rept 106-107). House passed, amended, April 27. Senate Commerce, Science and Transportation reported May 18 (no written report). Senate passed May 26. President signed June 1, 1999.

PL 106-33 (HR 1121) Designate the federal building and U.S. courthouse at 18 Greenville St. in Newnan, Ga., as the "Lewis R. Morgan Federal Building and United States Courthouse." Introduced by COLLINS, R-Ga., March 16, 1999. House Transportation and Infrastructure reported April 27 (H Rept 106-111). House passed, under suspension of the rules, May 4. Senate Environment and Public Works discharged. Senate passed May 26. President signed June 7, 1999.

PL 106-34 (HR 1183) Amend the Fastener Quality Act to strengthen protections against the sale of mismarked, misrepresented and counterfeit fasteners and eliminate unnecessary requirements. Introduced by SENSENBRENNER, R-Wis., March 18, 1999. House Science reported, amended, April 29 (H Rept 106-121, Part 1). House Commerce discharged. House passed, amended, under suspension of the rules, May 11. Senate passed May 25. President signed June 8, 1999.

PL 106-35 (HR 1379) Amend the Omnibus Consolidated and Emergency Supplemental Appropriations Act of 1999 to make a technical correction relating to an emergency supplemental appropriation for international narcotics control and law enforcement assistance. Introduced by GILMAN, R-N.Y., April 13, 1999. House passed, amended, April 20. Senate Foreign Relations discharged. Senate passed May 27. President signed June 15, 1999.

PL 106-36 (HR 435) Make miscellaneous and technical changes to various trade laws. Introduced by ARCHER, R-Texas, Feb. 2, 1999. House passed, under suspension of the rules, Feb. 9. Senate passed, with amendment, May 27. House agreed to Senate amendment, under suspension of the rules, June 7. President signed June 25, 1999.

PL 106-37 (HR 775) Establish certain procedures for civil actions brought for damages relating to the failure of any device or system to process or otherwise deal with the transition from the year 1999 to the year 2000. Introduced by DAVIS, R-Va., Feb. 23, 1999. House Judiciary reported, amended May 7 (H Rept 106-131, Part 1). Small Business discharged. Commerce discharged. House passed, amended, May 12. Senate passed, with amendment, June 15. Conference report filed in the House on June 29 (H Rept 106-212). House agreed to conference report July 1. Senate agreed to conference report July 1. President signed July 20, 1999.

PL 106-38 (HR 4) Declare it to be the policy of the United States to deploy a national missile defense. Introduced by WELDON, R-Pa., Feb. 4, 1999. House Armed Services reported March 2 (H Rept 106-39, Part 1). International Relations discharged. House passed March 18. Senate passed, with amendment, May 18. House agreed to Senate amendment May 20. President signed July 22, 1999.

PL 106-39 (HR 2035) Correct errors in the authorizations of certain programs administered by the National Highway Traffic Safety Administration. Introduced by TAUZIN, R-La., June 8, 1999. House Commerce reported June 25 (H Rept 106-200). House passed, amended, under suspension of the rules, July 12. Senate passed July 15. President signed July 28, 1999.

PL 106-40 (S 880) Amend the Clean Air Act to remove flammable fuels from the list of substances with respect to which reporting and other activities are required under the risk management plan program. Introduced by INHOFE, R-Okla., April 26, 1999. Senate Environment and Public Works reported, amended, June 9 (S Rept 106-70). Senate passed June 23. House passed, amended, July 21. Senate agreed to House amendment Aug. 2. President signed Aug. 5, 1999.

PL 106-41 (S 604) Direct the secretary of Agriculture to complete a land exchange with Georgia Power Co. Introduced by COVERDELL, R-Ga., March 15, 1999. Senate Agriculture, Nutrition and Forestry reported June 21 (no written report). Senate passed June 28. House passed, under suspension of the rules, July 26. President signed Aug. 5, 1999.

PL 106-42 (S 1258) Authorize funds for the payment of salaries and expenses of the Patent and Trademark Office. Introduced by HATCH, R-Utah, June 22, 1999. Senate Judiciary reported July 1 (no written report). Senate passed July 1. House passed, under suspension of the rules, July 26. President signed Aug. 5, 1999.

PL 106-43 (S 1259) Amend the Trademark Act of 1946 relating to dilution of famous marks. Introduced by HATCH, R-Utah, June 22, 1999. Senate Judiciary reported July 1 (no written report). Senate passed July 1. House passed, under suspension of the rules, July 26. President signed Aug. 5, 1999.

PL 106-44 (S 1260) Make technical corrections to Title 17, U.S. Code, and other laws. Introduced by HATCH, R-Utah, June 22, 1999. Senate Judiciary reported July 1 (no written report). Senate passed July 1. House passed, under suspension of the rules, July 26. President signed Aug. 5, 1999.

PL 106-45 (HR 66) Preserve the cultural resources of the Route 66 corridor and authorize the secretary of the Interior to provide assistance. Introduced by WILSON, R-N.M., Jan. 6, 1999. House Resources reported, amended May 13 (H Rept 106-137). House passed, amended, June 30. Senate passed July 27. President signed Aug. 10, 1999.

PL 106-46 (HR 2565) Clarify the quorum requirement for the board of directors of the Export-Import Bank of the United States. Introduced by LEACH, R-Iowa, July 20, 1999. House passed, amended, under suspension of the rules, July 26. Senate Banking, Housing and Urban Affairs discharged Aug. 5. Senate passed Aug. 5. President signed Aug. 11, 1999.

PL 106-47 (S 1543) Amend the Agricultural Adjustment Act of 1938 to provide for the release of tobacco production and marketing information. Introduced by McCONNELL, R-Ky., Aug. 5, 1999. Senate passed Aug. 5. House passed Aug. 5. President signed Aug. 13, 1999.

PL 106-48 (HR 211) Designate the federal building and U.S. courthouse at West 920 Riverside Ave. in Spokane, Wash., as the "Thomas S. Foley Federal Building and United States Courthouse," and the plaza at the south entrance of such building and courthouse as the "Walter F. Horan Plaza." Introduced by NETHERCUTT, R-Wash., Jan. 6,

1999. House passed, amended, under suspension of the rules, Aug. 2. Senate passed Aug. 5. President signed Aug. 17, 1999.

PL 106-49 (HR 1219) Amend the Office of Federal Procurement Policy Act and the Miller Act, relating to payment protections for persons providing labor and materials for federal construction projects. Introduced by MALONEY, D-N.Y., March 23, 1999. House Government Reform reported, amended, July 30 (H Rept 106-277, Part 1). House passed, amended, under suspension of the rules, Aug. 2. Senate passed Aug. 5. President signed Aug. 17, 1999.

PL 106-50 (HR 1568) Provide technical, financial and procurement assistance to veteran-owned small businesses. Introduced by TALENT, R-Mo., April 27, 1999. House Small Business reported, amended, June 29 (H Rept 106-206, Part 1). House Veterans' Affairs discharged June 29. House passed, amended, under suspension of the rules, June 29. Senate Small Business reported, amended, Aug. 4 (S Rept 106-136). Senate passed, amended, Aug. 5. House agreed to Senate amendment Aug. 6. President signed Aug. 17, 1999.

PL 106-51 (HR 1664) Make emergency supplemental appropriations for military operations, refugee relief and humanitarian assistance relating to the conflict in Kosovo, and for military operations in southwest Asia for the fiscal year ending Sept. 30, 1999. Introduced by YOUNG, R-Fla., May 4, 1999. House Appropriations reported May 4 (H Rept 106-125). House passed, amended, May 6. Senate Appropriations reported, amended, May 25 (no written report). Senate passed, with amendments, June 18. House agreed to Senate amendments Aug. 4. President signed Aug. 17, 1999.

PL 106-52 (HR 2465) Make appropriations for military construction, family housing, and base realignment and closure for the Department of Defense for the fiscal year ending Sept. 30, 2000. Introduced by HOBSON, R-Ohio, July 2, 1999. House Appropriations reported July 2, 1999 (H Rept 106-221). House passed July 13. Senate passed, with amendment, July 14. Conference report filed in the House on July 27 (H Rept 106-266). House agreed to conference report July 29. Senate agreed to conference report Aug. 3. President signed Aug. 17, 1999.

PL 106-53 (S 507) Provide for the conservation and development of water and related resources, and authorize the Army Corps of Engineers to construct various projects for improvements to rivers and harbors of the United States. Introduced by WARNER, R-Va., March 2, 1999. Senate Environment and Public Works reported, amended, March 23 (S Rept 106-34). Senate passed, amended, April 19. House passed, with amendment, July 22. Conference report filed in the House on Aug. 5 (H Rept 106-298). Senate agreed to conference report Aug. 5. House agreed to conference report Aug. 5. President signed Aug. 17, 1999.

PL 106-54 (S 606) Direct the secretary of the Treasury to pay specified funds to the Global Exploration and Development Corp., Kerr-McGee Corp. and Kerr-McGee Chemical LLC, in settlement and compromise of claims. Introduced by NICKLES, R-Okla., March 15, 1999. Senate Judiciary reported, amended, June 10 (no written report). Senate passed, amended, July 1. House passed, amended, under suspension of the rules, Aug. 2. Senate agreed to House amendment Aug. 4. President signed Aug. 17, 1999.

PL 106-55 (S 1546) Amend the International Religious Freedom Act of 1998 to provide additional administrative authority to the U.S. Commission on International Religious Freedom, and to make technical corrections to that act. Introduced by NICKLES, R-Okla., Aug. 5, 1999. Senate passed Aug. 5. House passed Aug. 5. President signed Aug. 17, 1999.

PL 106-56 (HR 457) Amend Title 5, U.S. Code, to increase the amount of leave time available to a federal employee in any year in connection with serving as an organ donor. Introduced by CUMMINGS, D-Md., on Feb. 2, 1999. House Government Reform reported June 8 (H Rept 106-174). House passed, under suspension of the rules, July 26. Senate Governmental Affairs reported Aug. 27 (S Rept 106-143). Senate passed Sept. 8. President signed Sept. 24, 1999.

PL 106-57 (HR 1905) Make appropriations for the legislative branch for the fiscal year ending Sept. 30, 2000. Introduced by TAYLOR, R-N.C., on May 24, 1999. House Appropriations reported May 21 (H Rept 106-156). House passed, amended, June 10. Senate passed, with amendments, June 16. Conference report filed in the House on Aug. 4 (H Rept 106-290). House agreed to conference report Aug. 5. Senate agreed to conference report Aug. 9. President signed Sept. 29, 1999.

PL 106-58 (HR 2490) Make appropriations for the Treasury Department, the U.S. Postal Service, the Executive Office of the President and certain independent agencies for the fiscal year ending Sept. 30, 2000. Introduced by KOLBE, R-Ariz., on July 13, 1999. House Appropriations reported July 13 (H Rept 106-231). House passed, amended, July 15. Senate passed, with amendment, July 19. Conference report filed in the House on Sept. 14 (H Rept 106-319). House agreed to conference report Sept. 15. Senate agreed to conference report Sept. 16. President signed Sept. 29, 1999.

PL 106-59 (S 1637) Extend through the end of the current fiscal year certain expiring Federal Aviation Administration authorizations. Introduced by LOTT, R-Miss., on Sept. 24, 1999. Senate passed Sept. 24. House passed, under suspension of the rules, Sept. 27. President signed Sept. 29, 1999.

PL 106-60 (HR 2605) Make appropriations for energy and water development for the fiscal year ending Sept. 30, 2000. Introduced by PACKARD, R-Calif., July 23, 1999. House Appropriations reported July 23, 1999 (H Rept 106-253). House passed, amended, July 27. Senate passed, with amendment, July 28. Conference report filed in the House Sept. 27 (H Rept 106-336). House agreed to conference report Sept. 27. Senate agreed to conference report Sept. 28. President signed Sept. 29, 1999.

PL 106-61 (H J Res 34) Congratulate and commend the veterans of foreign wars. Introduced by STUMP, R-Ariz., on Feb. 25, 1999. House Veterans' Affairs reported June 29 (H Rept 106-205). House passed, under suspension of the rules, June 29. Senate passed Sept. 28. President signed Sept. 29, 1999.

PL 106-62 (H J Res 68) Make continuing appropriations for fiscal year 2000. Introduced by YOUNG, R-Fla., Sept. 27, 1999. House passed Sept. 28. Senate passed Sept. 28. President signed Sept. 30, 1999.

PL 106-63 (S 380) Reauthorize the Congressional Award Act. Introduced by CRAIG, R-Idaho, on Feb. 4, 1999. Senate Governmental Affairs reported March 26 (S Rept 106-38). Senate passed April 13. House passed, under suspension of the rules, Sept. 13. President signed Oct. 1, 1999.

PL 106-64 (HR 2981) Extend energy conservation programs under the Energy Policy and Conservation Act through March 31, 2000. Introduced by BLILEY, R-Va., on Sept. 30, 1999. House Commerce discharged. House passed Sept. 30. Senate passed Sept. 30. President signed Oct. 5, 1999.

PL 106-65 (S 1059) Authorize appropriations for fiscal year 2000 for military activities of the Department of Defense, for military construction, for defense activities of the Department of Energy, and to prescribe personnel strengths for the Armed Forces. Introduced by WARNER, R-Va., on May 17, 1999. Senate Armed Services reported May 17 (S Rept 106-50). Senate passed, amended, May 27. House passed, with amendment, June 14. Conference report filed in the House on Aug. 6 (H Rept 106-301). House agreed to conference report Sept. 15. Senate agreed to conference report Sept. 22. President signed Oct. 5, 1999.

PL 106-66 (S 293) Direct the secretaries of Agriculture and Interior to convey certain lands in San Juan County, N.M., to San Juan College. Introduced by DOMENICI, R-N.M., on Jan. 21, 1999. Senate Energy and Natural Resources reported March 16 (S Rept 106-17). Senate passed, amended, March 25. House passed, under suspension of the rules, Sept. 27. President signed Oct. 6, 1999.

PL 106-67 (S 944) Amend Public Law 105-188 to provide for the mineral leasing of certain Indian lands in Oklahoma. Introduced by INHOFE, R-Okla., on May 3, 1999. Senate Indian Affairs reported Aug. 2 (S Rept 106-132). Senate passed Aug. 5. House Resources reported Sept. 27 (H Rept 106-338). House passed, under suspension of the rules, Sept. 27. President signed Oct. 6, 1999.

PL 106-68 (S 1072) Make certain technical and other corrections relating to the Centennial of Flight Commemoration Act. Introduced by DeWINE, R-Ohio, on May 18, 1999. Senate Governmental Affairs reported July 8 (S Rept 106-105). Senate passed, amended, Aug. 5. House passed, under suspension of the rules, Sept. 27. President signed Oct. 6, 1999.

PL 106-69 (HR 2084) Make appropriations for the Department of Transportation and related agencies for the fiscal year ending Sept. 30, 2000. Introduced by WOLF, R-Va., on June 9, 1999. House Appropriations reported June 9 (H Rept 106-180). House passed, amended, June 23. Senate passed, with amendment, Sept. 16. Conference report filed in the House Sept. 30 (H Rept 106-355). House agreed to conference report Oct. 1. Senate agreed to conference report Oct. 4. President signed Oct. 9, 1999.

PL 106-70 (S 1606) Extend for nine additional months the period for which Chapter 12 of Title 11, U.S. Code, is enacted. Introduced by GRASSLEY, R-Iowa, on Sept. 21, 1999. Senate passed, amended, Sept. 30. House passed, under suspension of the rules, Oct. 4. President signed Oct. 9, 1999.

PL 106-71 (S 249) Provide funding for the National Center for Missing and Exploited Children and reauthorize the Runaway and Homeless Youth Act. Introduced by HATCH, R-Utah, on Jan. 19, 1999. Senate Judiciary reported, amended, March 4 (no written report). Senate passed, amended, April 19. House passed, with amendment, under suspension of the rules, May 25. Senate agreed to House amendment Sept. 28. President signed Oct. 12, 1999.

PL 106-72 (S 559) Designate the federal building located at 33 East 8th St. in Austin, Texas, as the "J.J. 'Jake' Pickle Federal Building." Introduced by GRAMM, R-Texas, on March 8, 1999. Senate Environment and Public Works reported May 12 (no written report). Senate passed June 16. House passed, under suspension of the rules, Oct. 5. President signed Oct. 19, 1999.

PL 106-73 (HR 3036) Provide for interim continuation of administration of motor carrier functions by the Federal Highway Administration. Introduced by SHUSTER, R-Pa., on Oct. 7, 1999. House passed, amended, under suspension of the rules, Oct. 12. Senate passed Oct. 14. President signed Oct. 19, 1999.

PL 106-74 (HR 2684) Make appropriations for the departments of Veterans Affairs and Housing and Urban Development, and for various independent agencies, boards, commissions, corporations and offices for fiscal 2000. Introduced by WALSH, R-N.Y., on Aug. 3, 1999. House Appropriations reported Aug. 3 (H Rept 106-286). House passed, amended, Sept. 9. Senate Appropriations discharged. Senate passed, with amendment, Sept. 24. Conference report filed in the House Oct. 13 (H Rept 106-379). House agreed to conference report Oct. 14. Senate agreed to conference report Oct. 15. President signed Oct. 20, 1999.

PL 106-75 (H J Res 71) Make further continuing appropriations for fiscal 2000. Introduced by YOUNG, R-Fla., on Oct. 18, 1999. House passed Oct. 19. Senate passed Oct. 19. President signed Oct. 21, 1999.

PL 106-76 (S 323) Redesignate the Black Canyon of the Gunnison National Monument as a national park and establish the Gunnison Gorge National Conservation Area. Introduced by CAMPBELL, R-Colo., on Jan. 28, 1999. Senate Energy and Natural Resources reported, amended, June 8 (S Rept 106-69). Senate passed, amended, July 1. House Resources reported, amended, Sept. 8 (H Rept 106-307). House passed, with amendment, under suspension of the rules, Sept. 27. Senate agreed to House amendment Oct. 1. President signed Oct. 21, 1999.

PL 106-77 (HR 560) Designate the federal building located at 300 Recinto Sur St. in Old San Juan, P.R., as the "Jose V. Toledo United States Post Office and Courthouse." Introduced by ROMERO-BARCELÓ, D-P.R., on Feb. 3, 1999. House Transportation and Infrastructure reported, amended, April 27 (H Rept 106-108). House passed, amended, under suspension of the rules, May 4. Senate Environment and Public Works reported Sept. 29 (no written report). Senate passed Oct. 8. President signed Oct. 22, 1999.

PL 106-78 (HR 1906) Make appropriations for agriculture, rural development, the Food and Drug Administration, and related agencies for fiscal 2000. Introduced by SKEEN, R-N.M., on May 24, 1999. House Appropriations reported May 21 (H Rept 106-157). House passed, amended, June 8. Senate Appropriations discharged. Senate passed, with amendment, Aug. 4. Conference report filed in the House on Sept. 30 (H Rept 106-354). House agreed to conference report Oct. 1. Senate agreed to conference report Oct. 13. President signed Oct. 22, 1999.

PL 106-79 (HR 2561) Make appropriations for the Department of Defense for fiscal 2000. Introduced by LEWIS, R-Calif., on July 20, 1999. House Appropriations reported July 20 (H Rept 106-244). House passed, amended, July 22. Senate passed, with amendment, July 28. Conference report filed in the House Oct. 8 (H Rept 106-371). House agreed to conference report Oct. 13. Senate agreed to conference report Oct. 14. President signed Oct. 25, 1999.

PL 106-80 (S 322) Amend Title 4, U.S. Code, to add the Martin Luther King Jr. holiday to the list of days on which the flag should especially be displayed. Introduced by CAMPBELL, R-Colo., on Jan. 28, 1999. Senate Judiciary reported April 29 (no written report). Senate passed June 14. House passed Oct. 12. President signed Oct. 25, 1999.

PL 106-81 (S 800) Promote and enhance public safety through the use of 911 as the universal emergency assistance number, further deploy wireless 911 service, support states in upgrading 911 capabilities, and encourage construction and operation of seamless, ubiquitous and reliable networks for personal wireless services. Introduced by BURNS, R-Mont., on April 14, 1999. Senate Commerce, Science and Transportation reported Aug. 4 (S Rept 106-138). Senate passed, amended, Aug. 5. House passed, under suspension of the rules, Oct. 12. President signed Oct. 26, 1999.

PL 106-82 (HR 356) Provide for the conveyance of certain property from the United States to Stanislaus County, Calif. Introduced by CONDIT, D-Calif., on Jan. 19, 1999. House passed, under suspension of the rules, Oct 4. Senate passed Oct. 13. President signed Oct. 27, 1999.

PL 106-83 (HR 1663) Designate as a national memorial the memorial being built at the Riverside National Cemetery in Riverside, Calif., to honor recipients of the Medal of Honor. Introduced by CALVERT, R-Calif., on May 4, 1999. House Veterans' Affairs reported, amended, Sept. 30 (H Rept 106-351). House passed, amended, under suspension of the rules, Oct. 5. Senate Armed Services discharged. Senate passed Oct. 20. President signed Oct. 28, 1999.

PL 106-84 (HR 2841) Amend the Revised Organic Act of the Virgin Islands to provide for greater fiscal autonomy consistent with other United States jurisdictions. Introduced by CHRISTENSEN, D-Virgin Is., on Sept. 13, 1999. House Resources reported Sept. 27 (H Rept 106-337). House passed, amended, under suspension of the rules, Sept. 27. Senate Energy and Natural Resources discharged. Senate passed Oct. 19. President signed Oct. 28, 1999.

PL 106-85 (H J Res 73) Make further continuing appropriations for fiscal 2000. Introduced by YOUNG, R-Fla., on Oct. 27, 1999. House passed Oct. 28. Senate passed Oct. 28. President signed Oct. 29, 1999.

PL 106-86 (HR 659) Authorize appropriations for the protection of the Paoli and Brandywine Battlefields in Pennsylvania, direct the National Park Service to conduct a special resource study of the Paoli and Brandywine battlefields, authorize the Valley Forge Museum of the American Revolution at Valley Forge National Historical Park. Introduced by WELDON, R-Pa., on Feb. 9, 1999. House Resources reported May 13 (H Rept 106-139). House passed, amended, June 22. Senate Energy and Natural Resources discharged. Senate passed, with amendments, Oct. 14. House agreed to Senate amendments, under suspension of the rules, Oct. 18. President signed Oct. 31, 1999.

PL 106-87 (HR 2367) Reauthorize a comprehensive program of support for victims of torture. Introduced by SMITH, R-N.J., on June 29, 1999. House passed, amended, under the suspension of the rules, Sept. 21. Senate passed Oct. 21. President signed Nov. 3, 1999.

PL 106-88 (H J Res 75) Make further continuing appropriations for fiscal 2000. Introduced by YOUNG, R-Fla., on Nov. 3, 1999. House passed Nov. 4. Senate passed Nov. 4. President signed Nov. 5, 1999.

PL 106-89 (HR 1175) Locate and secure the return of Zachary Baumel, an American citizen, and other Israeli soldiers missing in action. Introduced by LANTOS, D-Calif., on March 18, 1999. House passed, amended, under suspension of the rules, June 22. Senate Foreign Relations reported with amendment June 30 (no written report). Senate passed, with amendments, Aug. 5. House agreed to Senate amendments, under suspension of the rules, Oct. 26. President signed Nov. 8, 1999.

PL 106-90 (H J Res 62) Grant the consent of Congress to the boundary change between Georgia and South Carolina. Introduced by LINDER, R-Ga., on July 22, 1999. House Judiciary reported Sept. 8 (H Rept 106-304). House passed, under suspension of the rules, Sept. 21. Senate Judiciary reported Oct. 21 (no written report). Senate passed Oct. 26. President signed Nov. 8, 1999.

PL 106-91 (S 437) Designate the U.S. courthouse under construction at 338 Las Vegas Blvd. South in Las Vegas, Nev., as the "Lloyd D. George United States Courthouse." Introduced by REID, D-Nev., on Feb. 22, 1999. Senate Environment and Public Works reported March 17 (no written report). Senate passed March 23. House passed, under suspension of the rules, Oct. 26. President signed Nov. 9, 1999.

PL 106-92 (S 1652) Designate the Old Executive Office Building at 17th St. and Pennsylvania Ave. N.W., in Washington, D.C., as the Dwight D. Eisenhower Executive Office Building. Introduced by CHAFEE, R-R.I., on Sept. 28, 1999. Senate Environment and Public Works reported Sept. 29 (no written report). Senate passed Oct. 19. House passed, under suspension of the rules, Oct. 26. President signed Nov. 9, 1999.

PL 106-93 (H J Res 76) Waive certain enrollment requirements for the remainder of the first session of the 106th Congress with respect to any bill or joint resolution making general appropriations or continuing appropriations for fiscal 2000. Introduced by THOMAS, R-Calif., on Nov. 8, 1999. House Administration discharged. House passed Nov. 9. Senate passed Nov. 9. President signed Nov. 10, 1999.

PL 106-94 (H J Res 78) Make further continuing appropriations for fiscal 2000. Introduced by YOUNG, R-Fla., on Nov. 9, 1999. House Appropriations discharged. House passed Nov. 9. Senate passed Nov. 10. President signed Nov. 10, 1999.

PL 106-95 (HR 441) Amend the Immigration and Nationality Act with respect to the requirements for the admission of non-immigrant nurses who will practice in health profession shortage areas. Introduced by RUSH, D-Ill., on Feb. 2, 1999. House Judiciary reported May 12 (H Rept 106-135). House passed, under suspension of the rules, May 24. Senate Judiciary reported June 24 (no written report). Senate passed with amendments Oct. 22. House agreed to Senate amendment, under suspension of the rules, Nov. 2. President signed Nov. 12, 1999.

PL 106-96 (HR 609) Amend the Export Apple and Pear Act to limit the applicability of the act to apples. Introduced by WALDEN, R-Ore., on Feb. 4, 1999. House Agriculture reported March 2 (H Rept 106-36). House passed, under suspension of the rules, March 2. Senate Banking, Housing and Urban Affairs discharged. Senate passed Nov. 3. President signed Nov. 12, 1999.

PL 106-97 (HR 915) Authorize a cost of living adjustment in the pay of administrative law judges. Introduced by GEKAS, R-Pa., on March 2, 1999. House Government Reform reported, amended, Oct. 18 (H Rept 106-387). House passed, amended, under suspension of the rules, Oct. 25. Senate Governmental Affairs reported Nov. 4 (no written report). Senate passed Nov. 8. President signed Nov. 12, 1999.

PL 106-98 (HR 974) Establish a program to afford high school graduates from the District of Columbia the benefits of in-state tuition at state colleges and universities outside the District of Columbia. Introduced by DAVIS, R-Va., on March 4, 1999. House Government Reform reported, amended, May 24 (H Rept 106-158, Part 1). House Ways and Means discharged. House passed, amended, under suspension of the rules, May 24. Senate Governmental Affairs reported, amended, Sept. 9 (S Rept 106-154). Senate passed, with amendment, Oct. 19. House agreed to Senate amendment, under suspension of the rules, Nov. 1. President signed Nov. 12, 1999.

PL 106-99 (HR 2303) Direct the Librarian of Congress to prepare the history of the House of Representatives. Introduced by LARSON, D-Conn., on June 22, 1999. House passed, amended, under suspension of the rules, Oct. 25. Senate Rules and Administration discharged. Senate passed Oct. 29. President signed Nov. 12, 1999.

PL 106-100 (HR 3122) Permit the enrollment in the House of Representatives Child Care Center of children of federal employees who are not employees of the legislative branch. Introduced by THOMAS, R-Calif., on Oct. 21, 1999. House passed, under suspension of the rules, Oct. 25. Senate Rules and Administration discharged. Senate passed Nov. 4. President signed Nov. 12, 1999.

PL 106-101 (H J Res 54) Grant the consent of Congress to the Missouri-Nebraska Boundary Compact. Introduced by DANNER, D-Mo., on May 12, 1999. House Judiciary reported Sept. 8 (H Rept 106-303). House passed, under suspension of the rules, Sept. 21. Senate Judiciary reported Nov. 4 (no written report). Senate passed Nov. 5. President signed Nov. 12, 1999.

PL 106-102 (S 900) Enhance competition in the financial services industry by providing a framework for the affiliation of banks, securities firms and other financial service providers. Introduced by GRAMM, R-Texas, on April 28, 1999. Senate Banking, Housing and Urban Affairs reported April 28 (S Rept 106-44). Senate passed, amended, May 6. House passed, with amendments, July 20. Conference report filed in the House Nov. 2 (H Rept 106-434). Senate agreed to conference report Nov. 4. House agreed to conference report Nov. 4. President signed Nov. 12, 1999.

PL 106-103 (HR 348) Authorize the construction of a monument to honor those who have served the nation's civil defense and emergency management programs. Introduced by BARTLETT, R-Md., on Jan. 19, 1999. House Resources reported Oct. 27 (H Rept 106-416). House passed, under suspension of the rules, Nov. 1. Senate passed Nov. 8. President signed Nov. 13, 1999.

PL 106-104 (HR 3061) Amend the Immigration and Nationality Act to extend for an additional two years the period for admission of an alien as a non-immigrant under section 101(a)(15)(S), and authorize appropriations for the refugee assistance program under Chapter 2 of Title IV of the act. Introduced by SMITH, R-Texas, on Oct. 12, 1999. House passed, under suspension of the rules, Oct. 26. Senate passed Nov. 8. President signed Nov. 13, 1999.

PL 106-105 (H J Res 80) Make further continuing appropriations for fiscal 2000. Introduced by DREIER, R-Calif., on Nov. 16, 1999. House passed Nov. 17. Senate passed Nov. 17. President signed Nov. 18, 1999.

PL 106-106 (H J Res 83) Make further continuing appropriations for fiscal 2000. Introduced by YOUNG, R-Fla., on Nov. 17, 1999. House passed, amended, Nov. 18. Senate passed Nov. 18. President signed Nov. 19, 1999.

PL 106-107 (S 468) Improve the effectiveness and performance of federal financial assistance programs, simplify the application and reporting requirements, and improve the delivery of services to the public. Introduced by VOINOVICH, R-Ohio, Feb. 25. Senate Governmental Affairs reported, amended, July 1 (S Rept 106-103). Senate passed, amended, July 15. House passed, with amendment, under suspension of the rules, Nov. 2. Senate agreed to House amendment Nov. 4. President signed Nov. 20, 1999.

PL 106-108 (HR 2454) Assure the long-term conservation of midcontinent light geese and the biological diversity of the ecosystem upon which many North American migratory birds depend, by directing the secretary of the Interior to implement rules to reduce the overabundant population of midcontinent light geese. Introduced by SAXTON, R-N.J., July 1, 1999. House Resources reported, amended, July 29 (H Rept 106-271). House passed, amended, under suspension of the rules, Aug. 2. Senate Environment and Public Works reported, with amendments, Oct. 14 (S Rept 106-188). Senate passed, with amendments, Nov. 8. House agreed to Senate amendments, under suspension of the rules, Nov. 10. President signed Nov. 24, 1999.

PL 106-109 (HR 2724) Make technical corrections to the Water Resources Development Act of 1999. Introduced by SHUSTER, R-Pa., Aug. 5, 1999. House passed Aug. 5. Senate Environment and Public Works reported, amended, Oct. 13 (S Rept 106-183). Senate passed, with amendment, Nov. 8. House agreed to Senate amendment, under suspension of the rules, Nov. 10. President signed Nov. 24, 1999.

PL 106-110 (S 1235) Amend Part G of Title I of the Omnibus Crime Control and Safe Streets Act of 1968 to allow railroad police officers to attend the Federal Bureau of Investigation National Academy for law enforcement training. Introduced by LEAHY, D-Vt., on June 17, 1999. Senate Judiciary reported Oct. 21 (no written report). Senate passed Oct. 26. House passed, under suspension of the rules, Nov. 17. President signed Nov. 24, 1999.

PL 106-111 (HR 100) Establish designations for U.S. Postal Service buildings in Philadelphia. Introduced by FATTAH, D-Pa., on Jan. 6, 1999. House passed, under suspension of the rules, May 24. Senate Governmental Affairs reported Nov. 4 (no written report). Senate passed Nov. 19. President signed Nov. 29, 1999.

PL 106-112 (HR 197) Designate the building of the U.S. Postal Service at 410 North 6th St. in Garden City, Kan., as the "Clifford R. Hope Post Office." Introduced by MORAN, R-Kan., on Jan. 6, 1999. House passed, under suspension of the rules, May 24. Senate Governmental Affairs reported Nov. 4 (no written report). Senate passed Nov. 19. President signed Nov. 29, 1999.

PL 106-113 (HR 3194) Make appropriations for the government of the District of Columbia for fiscal 2000. Introduced by ISTOOK, R-Okla., on Nov. 2, 1999. House passed Nov. 3. Senate passed, with amendment, Nov. 3. Conference report filed in the House Nov. 18 (H Rept 106-479). House agreed to conference report Nov. 18. Senate agreed to conference report Nov. 19. President signed Nov. 29, 1999.

PL 106-114 (S 278) Direct the secretary of the Interior to convey certain lands to the county of Rio Arriba, N.M. Introduced by DOMENICI, R-N.M., on Jan. 21, 1999. Senate Energy and Natural Resources reported March 16 (S Rept 106-16). Senate passed March 25. House Resources reported Oct. 27 (H Rept 106-418). House passed, under suspension of the rules, Nov. 17. President signed Nov. 29, 1999.

PL 106-115 (S 382) Establish the Minuteman Missile National Historic Site in South Dakota. Introduced by JOHNSON, D-S.D., on Feb. 4, 1999. Senate Energy and Natural Resources reported March 17 (S Rept 106-23). Senate passed March 25. House Resources reported Oct. 18 (H Rept 106-391). House passed, under suspension of the rules, Nov. 17. President signed Nov. 29, 1999.

PL 106-116 (S 1398) Clarify certain boundaries on maps relating to the Coastal Barrier Resources System. Introduced by HELMS, R-N.C., on July 20, 1999. Senate Environment and Public Works reported, amended, Oct. 6 (S Rept 106-171). Senate passed, amended, Nov. 8. House passed, under suspension of the rules, Nov. 17. President signed Nov. 29, 1999.

PL 106-117 (HR 2116) Amend Title 38, U.S. Code, to establish a program of extended care services for veterans and to make other improvements in health care programs of the Department of Veterans Affairs. Introduced by STEARNS, R-Fla., on June 9, 1999. House Veterans' Affairs reported, amended, July 16 (H Rept 106-237). House passed, amended, under suspension of the rules, Sept. 21. Senate Veterans' Affairs discharged. Senate passed, with amendments, Nov. 5. Conference report filed in the House Nov. 16 (H Rept 106-470). House agreed to conference report, under suspension of the rules, Nov. 16. Senate agreed to conference report Nov. 19. President signed Nov. 30, 1999.

PL 106-118 (HR 2280) Amend Title 38, U.S. Code, to provide a cost of living adjustment in compensation rates paid for service-connected disabilities, enhance the compensation, memorial affairs and housing programs of the Department of Veterans Affairs, and improve retirement authorities applicable to judges of the U.S. Court of Appeals for Veterans Claims. Introduced by STUMP, R-Ariz., June 18, 1999. House Veterans' Affairs reported, amended, June 25 (H Rept 106-202). House passed, amended, under suspension of the rules, June 29. Senate Veterans' Affairs discharged. Senate passed, with amendment, July 26. House agreed to Senate amendment with amendments pursuant to H Res 368 on Nov. 9. Senate agreed to House amendments to Senate amendment Nov. 19. President signed Nov. 30, 1999.

PL 106-119 (HR 20) Authorize the secretary of the Interior to construct and operate a visitor center for the Upper Delaware Scenic and Recreational River on land owned by the state of New York. Introduced by GILMAN, R-N.Y., on Jan. 6, 1999. House Resources reported Oct. 4 (H Rept 106-361). House passed, under suspension of the rules, Oct. 12. Senate Energy and Natural Resources reported, with amendment, Nov. 2 (S Rept 106-211). Senate passed Nov. 19. President signed Dec. 3, 1999.

PL 106-120 (HR 1555) Authorize appropriations for fiscal 2000 for intelligence and intelligence-related activities of the U.S. government, the Community Management Account, and the Central Intelligence Agency Retirement and Disability System. Introduced by GOSS, R-Fla., on April 26, 1999. House Intelligence reported, amended, May 7 (H Rept 106-130, Part 1). House Armed Services discharged. House passed, amended, May 13. Senate passed, with amendment, July 21. Conference report filed in the House Nov. 5 (H Rept 106-457). House agreed to conference report Nov. 9. Senate agreed to conference report Nov. 19. President signed Dec. 3, 1999.

PL 106-121 (HR 459) Extend the deadline under the Federal Power Act for FERC Project No. 9401, the Mount Hope Waterpower Project. Introduced by FRELINGHUYSEN, R-N.J., on Feb. 2, 1999. House Commerce reported April 28 (H Rept 106-119). House passed, under suspension of the rules, May 4. Senate Energy and Natural Resources reported June 24 (S Rept 106-97). Senate passed Nov. 19. President signed Dec. 6, 1999.

PL 106-122 (HR 1094) Amend the Federal Reserve Act to broaden the range of discount window loans that may be used as collateral for federal reserve notes. Introduced by LEACH, R-Iowa, on March 11, 1999. House passed, amended, under suspension of the rules, Aug. 2. Senate Banking, Housing and Urban Affairs discharged. Senate passed Nov. 19. President signed Dec. 6, 1999.

PL 106-123 (HR 1191) Designate certain facilities of the U.S. Postal Service in Chicago. Introduced by DAVIS, D-Ill., on March 18, 1999. House passed, under suspension of the rules, May 24. Senate Governmental Affairs reported Nov. 4 (no written report). Senate passed Nov. 19. President signed Dec. 6, 1999.

PL 106-124 (HR 1251) Designate the U.S. Postal Service building at 8850 South 700 East, Sandy, Utah, as the "Noal Cushing Bateman Post Office Building." Introduced by COOK, R-Utah, on March 24, 1999. House passed, under suspension of the rules, May 24. Senate Governmental Affairs reported Nov. 4 (no written report). Senate passed Nov. 19. President signed Dec. 6, 1999.

PL 106-125 (HR 1327) Designate the U.S. Postal Service building at 34480 Highway 101 South in Cloverdale, Ore., as the "Maurine B. Neuberger United States Post Office." Introduced by HOOLEY, D-Ore., on March 25, 1999. House passed, under suspension of the rules, June 29. Senate Governmental Affairs reported Nov. 4 (no written report). Senate passed Nov. 19. President signed Dec. 6, 1999.

PL 106-126 (HR 3373) Require the secretary of the Treasury to mint coins in conjunction with the minting of coins by the Republic of Iceland in commemoration of the millennium of the discovery of the New World by Leif Ericson. Introduced by LEACH, R-Iowa, on Nov. 16, 1999. House passed, under suspension of the rules, Nov. 16. Senate passed Nov. 19. President signed Dec. 6, 1999.

PL 106-127 (H J Res 85) Appoint the day for the convening of the second session of the 106th Congress. Introduced by ARMEY, R-Texas, on Nov. 18, 1999. House passed Nov. 18. Senate passed Nov. 19. President signed Dec. 6, 1999.

PL 106-128 (S 574) Direct the secretary of the Interior to make corrections to a map relating to the Coastal Barrier Resources System. Introduced by BIDEN, D-Del., on March 10, 1999. Senate Environment and Public Works reported March 26 (S Rept 106-39). Senate passed April 22. House Resources discharged. House passed Nov. 18. President signed Dec. 6, 1999.

PL 106-129 (S 580) Amend Title IX of the Public Health Service Act to revise and extend the Agency for Healthcare Policy and Research. Introduced by FRIST, R-Tenn., on March 10, 1999. Senate Health, Education, Labor and Pensions discharged. Senate passed, amended, Nov. 3. House passed Nov. 18. President signed Dec. 6, 1999.

PL 106-130 (S 1418) Provide for the holding of court at Natchez, Miss., in the same manner as court is held at Vicksburg, Miss. Introduced by COCHRAN, R-Miss., on July 22, 1999. Senate Judiciary reported Nov. 4 (no written report). Senate passed Nov. 5. House passed, with amendment, under suspension of the rules, Nov. 17. Senate agreed to House amendment Nov. 19. President signed Dec. 6, 1999.

PL 106-131 (HR 449) Authorize the Gateway Visitor Center at Independence National Historical Park. Introduced by BORSKI, D-Pa., Feb. 22, 1999. House Resources reported March 17 (H Rept 106-66). House passed, under suspension of the rules, April 12. Senate Energy and Natural Resources reported June 7 (S Rept 106-68). Senate passed Nov. 19. President signed Dec. 7, 1999.

PL 106-132 (HR 592) Redesignate Great Kills Park in the Gateway National Recreation Area as "World War II Veterans Park at Great Kills." Introduced by FOSSELLA, R-N.Y., on Feb. 4, 1999. House Resources reported, amended June 16 (H Rept 106-188). House passed, amended, June 30. Senate Energy and Natural Resources reported Nov. 2 (S Rept 106-212). Senate passed Nov. 19. President signed Dec. 7, 1999.

PL 106-133 (HR 747) Protect the permanent trust funds of the state of Arizona from erosion due to inflation and modify the basis on which distributions are made from those funds. Introduced by STUMP, R-Ariz., on Feb. 11. House Resources reported May 13 (H Rept 106-140). House passed, under suspension of the rules, Aug. 2. Senate passed Nov. 19. President signed Dec. 7, 1999.

PL 106-134 (HR 748) Amend the act that established the Keweenaw National Historical Park to require the secretary of the Interior to consider nominees of various local interests in appointing members of the Keweenaw National Historical Parks Advisory Commission. Introduced by STUPAK, D-Mich., on Feb. 11, 1999. House Resources reported, amended, Oct. 7 (H Rept 106-367). House passed, amended, under suspension of the rules, Oct. 12. Senate Energy and Natural Resources discharged. Senate passed Nov. 19. President signed Dec. 7, 1999.

PL 106-135 (HR 791) Amend the National Trails System Act to designate the route of the War of 1812 British invasion of Maryland and Washington, D.C., and the route of the American defense, for study for potential addition to the national trails system. Introduced by GILCHREST, R-Md., on Feb. 23, 1999. House Resources reported, amended, June 17 (H Rept 106-189). House passed, amended, June 30. Senate passed Nov. 19. President signed Dec. 7, 1999.

PL 106-136 (HR 970) Authorize the secretary of the Interior to provide assistance to the Perkins County Rural Water System Inc. for the construction of water supply facilities in Perkins County, S.D. Introduced by THUNE, R-S.D., on March 3, 1999. House Resources reported, amended, Oct. 20 (H Rept 106-405). House passed, amended, under suspension of the rules, Oct. 26. Senate passed Nov. 19. President signed Dec. 7, 1999.

PL 106-137 (HR 1794) Require the secretary of State to report to Congress on efforts to more actively support Taiwan's participation in the World Health Organization. Introduced by BROWN, D-Ohio, on May 13, 1999. House passed, amended, under suspension of the rules, Oct. 4. Senate Foreign Relations reported Nov. 3 (no written report). Senate passed Nov. 19. President signed Dec. 7, 1999.

PL 106-138 (HR 2079) Provide for the conveyance of certain National Forest System lands in the state of South Dakota. Introduced by THUNE, R-S.D., on June 8, 1999. House Resources reported July 26 (H Rept 106-261). House passed, under suspension of the rules, Sept. 21. Senate Energy and Natural Resources discharged. Senate passed Nov. 19. President signed Dec. 7, 1999.

PL 106-139 (HR 2886) Amend the Immigration and Nationality Act to provide that an adopted alien who is less than 18 years of age may be considered a child under the act if adopted with or after a sibling who is a child under the act. Introduced by HORN, R-Calif., on Sept. 21, 1999. House Judiciary reported Oct. 14 (H Rept 106-383). House passed, under suspension of the rules, Oct. 18. Senate Judiciary discharged. Senate passed Nov. 19. President signed Dec. 7, 1999.

PL 106-140 (HR 2889) Amend the Central Utah Project

Completion Act to provide for acquisition of water and water rights for Central Utah Project purposes, completion of Central Utah project facilities and implementation of water conservation measures. Introduced by CANNON, R-Utah, Sept. 21, 1999. House Resources reported Oct. 27 (H Rept 106-417). House passed, under suspension of the rules, Nov. 1. Senate passed Nov. 19. President signed Dec. 7, 1999.

PL 106-141 (HR 3257) Amend the Congressional Budget Act of 1974 to assist the Congressional Budget Office with the scoring of state and local mandates. Introduced by REYNOLDS, R-N.Y., on Nov. 8, 1999. House passed, amended, under suspension of the rules, Nov. 16. Senate passed Nov. 19. President signed Dec. 7, 1999.

PL 106-142 (H J Res 65) Commend the World War II veterans who fought in the Battle of the Bulge. Introduced by SMITH, R-N.J., on Aug. 5, 1999. House Veterans' Affairs reported, amended, Sept. 30 (H Rept 106-352, Part 1). House passed, amended, under suspension of the rules, Oct. 5. Senate Judiciary reported Nov. 2 (no written report). Senate passed Nov. 19. President signed Dec. 7, 1999.

PL 106-143 (S 28) Authorize an interpretive center and related visitor center within the Four Corners Monument Tribal Park. Introduced by HATCH, R-Utah, on Jan. 19, 1999. Senate Indian Affairs reported, amended, Aug. 27 (S Rept 106-144). Senate passed, amended, Sept. 9. House passed Nov. 18. President signed Dec. 7, 1999.

PL 106-144 (S 416) Direct the secretary of Agriculture to convey the city of Sisters, Ore., a certain parcel of land for use in connection with a sewage treatment plant. Introduced by SMITH, R-Ore., on Feb. 11, 1999. Senate Energy and Natural Resources reported, amended, June 2 (S Rept 106-60). Senate passed, amended, July 1. House Resources reported, with amendment, Nov. 5 (H Rept 106-453). House passed, with amendment, under suspension of the rules, Nov. 17. Senate agreed to House amendment Nov. 19. President signed Dec. 7, 1999.

PL 106-145 (HR 15) Designate a portion of the Otay Mountain region of California as wilderness. Introduced by BILBRAY, R-Calif., on Jan. 6, 1999. House Resources reported March 17 (H Rept 106-65). House passed, under suspension of the rules, April 12. Senate Energy and Natural Resources reported July 21 (S Rept 106-116). Senate passed Nov. 19. President signed Dec. 9, 1999.

PL 106-146 (HR 658) Establish the Thomas Cole National Historic Site in New York as an affiliated area of the National Park System. Introduced by SWEENEY, R-N.Y., on Feb. 9, 1999. House Resources reported, amended, May 13 (H Rept 106-138). House passed, amended, under suspension of the rules, Sept. 13. Senate passed Nov. 19. President signed Dec. 9, 1999.

PL 106-147 (HR 1104) Authorize the secretary of the Interior to transfer administrative jurisdiction over land within the boundaries of the Home of Franklin D. Roosevelt National Historic Site to the Archivist of the United States for the construction of a visitor center. Introduced by SWEENEY, R-N.Y., on March 11, 1999. House Resources reported May 13 (H Rept 106-141). House passed, under suspension of the rules, Aug. 2. Senate passed Nov. 19. President signed Dec. 9, 1999.

PL 106-148 (HR 1528) Reauthorize and amend the National Geologic Mapping Act of 1992. Introduced by CUBIN, R-Wyo., on April 22, 1999. House Resources reported Oct. 18 (H Rept 106-389). House passed, under suspension of the rules, Oct. 26. Senate passed Nov. 19. President signed Dec. 9, 1999.

PL 106-149 (HR 1619) Amend the Quinebaug and Shetucket Rivers Valley National Heritage Corridor Act of 1994 to expand the boundaries of the Corridor. Introduced by GEJDENSON, D-Conn., on April 29, 1999. House Resources reported, amended, Sept. 8 (H Rept 106-306). House passed, amended, under suspension of the rules, Sept. 13. Senate Energy and Natural Resources reported Nov. 2 (S Rept 106-213). Senate passed Nov. 19. President signed Dec. 9, 1999.

PL 106-150 (HR 1665) Allow the National Park Service to acquire certain land for addition to the Wilderness Battlefield in Virginia, as previously authorized by law, by purchase or exchange as well as by donation. Introduced by BATEMAN, R-Va., on May 4, 1999. House Resources reported, amended, Oct. 4 (H Rept 106-362). House passed, amended, under suspension of the rules, Oct. 12. Senate passed Nov. 19. President signed Dec. 9, 1999.

PL 106-151 (HR 1693) Amend the Fair Labor Standards Act of 1938 to clarify the overtime exemption for employees engaged in fire protection activities. Introduced by EHRLICH, R-Md., on May 5, 1999. House passed, under suspension of the rules, Nov. 4. Senate passed Nov. 19. President signed Dec. 9, 1999.

PL 106-152 (HR 1887) Amend Title 18, U.S. Code, to punish the depiction of animal cruelty. Introduced by GALLEGLY, R-Calif., on May 20, 1999. House Judiciary reported, amended, Oct. 19 (H Rept 106-397). House passed, amended, under suspension of the rules, Oct. 19. Senate passed Nov. 19. President signed Dec. 9, 1999.

PL 106-153 (HR 1932) Authorize the president to award a gold medal on behalf of Congress to Father Theodore M. Hesburgh in recognition of his outstanding and enduring contributions to civil rights, higher education, the Catholic Church, the nation and the global community. Introduced by ROEMER, D-Ind., on May 25, 1999. House passed, under suspension of the rules, Oct. 12. Senate passed Nov. 19. President signed Dec. 9, 1999.

PL 106-154 (HR 2140) Improve protection and management of the Chattahoochee River National Recreation Area in the state of Georgia. Introduced by DEAL, R-Ga., on June 10, 1999. House Resources reported, amended, Oct. 7 (H Rept 106-369). House passed, amended, under suspension of the rules, Oct. 18. Senate passed Nov. 19. President signed Dec. 9, 1999.

PL 106-155 (HR 2401) Amend the U.S. Holocaust Assets Commission Act of 1998 to extend the period by which the final report is due and to authorize additional funding. Introduced by LAZIO, R-N.Y., on June 30, 1999. House passed, under suspension of the rules, Oct. 4. Senate Banking, Housing and Urban Affairs discharged. Senate passed Nov. 19. President signed Dec. 9, 1999.

PL 106-156 (HR 2632) Designate certain federal lands in the Talladega National Forest in the state of Alabama as the

Dugger Mountain Wilderness. Introduced by RILEY, R-Ala., on July 29, 1999. House Resources reported Oct. 28 (H Rept 106-422, Part 1). House Agriculture discharged. House passed, under suspension of the rules, Nov. 1. Senate passed Nov. 19. President signed Dec. 9, 1999.

PL 106-157 (HR 2737) Authorize the secretary of the Interior to convey to the state of Illinois certain federal land associated with the Lewis and Clark National Historic Trail to be used as a historic and interpretive site along the trail. Introduced by COSTELLO, D-Ill., on Aug. 5, 1999. House Resources reported, amended, Nov. 1 (H Rept 106-427). House passed, amended, under suspension of the rules, Nov. 1. Senate passed Nov. 19. President signed Dec. 9, 1999.

PL 106-158 (HR 3381) Reauthorize the Overseas Private Investment Corporation and the Trade and Development Agency. Introduced by MANZULLO, R-Ill., on Nov. 16, 1999. House passed, under suspension of the rules, Nov. 17. Senate passed Nov. 19. President signed Dec. 9, 1999.

PL 106-159 (HR 3419) Amend Title 49, U.S. Code, to establish the Federal Motor Carrier Safety Administration. Introduced by SHUSTER, R-Pa., on Nov. 17, 1999. House Transportation and Infrastructure discharged. House passed Nov. 18. Senate passed Nov. 19. President signed Dec. 9, 1999.

PL 106-160 (HR 3456) Amend statutory damages provisions of Title 17, U.S. Code. Introduced by COBLE, R-N.C., on Nov. 18, 1999. House Judiciary discharged. House passed Nov. 18. Senate passed Nov. 19. President signed Dec. 9, 1999.

PL 106-161 (H J Res 46) Confer status as an honorary veteran of the U.S. Armed Forces on Zachary Fisher. Introduced by MALONEY, D-N.Y. on April 28, 1999. House passed, under suspension of the rules, Nov. 2. Senate passed Nov. 19. President signed Dec. 9, 1999.

PL 106-162 (S 67) Designate the headquarters building of the Department of Housing and Urban Development in Washington, D.C. as the "Robert C. Weaver Federal Building." Introduced by MOYNIHAN, D-N.Y., on Jan. 19, 1999. Senate Environment and Public Works reported March 17 (no written report). Senate passed March 23. House passed Nov. 18. President signed Dec. 9, 1999.

PL 106-163 (S 438) Provide for the settlement of the water rights claims of the Chippewa Cree Tribe of the Rocky Boy's Reservation. Introduced by BURNS, R-Mont., on Feb. 22, 1999. Senate Indian Affairs reported July 22 (S Rept 106-200). Senate Energy and Natural Resources discharged. Senate passed, amended, Nov. 4. House passed Nov. 18. President signed Dec. 9, 1999.

PL 106-164 (S 548) Establish the Fallen Timbers Battlefield and Fort Miamis National Historical Site in the state of Ohio. Introduced by DeWINE, R-Ohio, on March 4, 1999. Senate Energy and Natural Resources reported, amended, June 7 (S Rept 106-64). Senate passed, amended, Oct. 14. House Resources discharged. House passed Nov. 18. President signed Dec. 9, 1999.

PL 106-165 (S 791) Amend the Small Business Act with respect to the women's business center program. Introduced by KERRY, D-Mass., on April 14, 1999. Senate Small Business reported, amended, Nov. 2 (S Rept 106-214). Senate passed, amended, Nov. 5. House passed Nov. 18. President signed Dec. 9, 1999.

PL 106-166 (S 1595) Designate the U.S. courthouse at 401 West Washington St. in Phoenix as the "Sandra Day O'-Connor United States Courthouse." Introduced by KYL, R-Ariz., on Sept. 16, 1999. Senate Environment and Public Works reported Sept. 29 (no written report). Senate passed Oct. 8. House Transportation and Infrastructure discharged. House passed Nov. 18. President signed Dec. 9, 1999.

PL 106-167 (S 1866) Redesignate the Coastal Barrier Resources System as the "John H. Chafee Coastal Barrier Resources System." Introduced by SMITH, R-N.H., on Nov. 4, 1999. Senate passed Nov. 4. House Resources discharged. House passed Nov. 18. President signed Dec. 9, 1999.

PL 106-168 (S 335) Amend Chapter 30 of Title 39, U.S. Code, to provide for the non-mailability of certain deceptive matter relating to sweepstakes, skill contests, facsimile checks, administrative procedures, orders and civil penalties relating to such matter. Introduced by COLLINS, R-Maine, on Feb. 3, 1999. Senate Governmental Affairs reported, amended, July 1 (S Rept 106-102). Senate passed, amended, Aug. 2. House passed, with amendment, under suspension of the rules, Nov. 9. Senate agreed to House amendment Nov. 19. President signed Dec. 12, 1999.

PL 106-169 (HR 3443) Amend Part E of Title IV of the Social Security Act to provide states with more funding and greater flexibility in carrying out programs designed to help children make the transition from foster care to self-sufficiency. Introduced by JOHNSON, R-Conn., on Nov. 18, 1999. House Ways and Means, House Commerce discharged. House passed Nov. 18. Senate passed Nov. 19. President signed Dec. 14, 1999.

PL 106-170 (HR 1180) Amend the Social Security Act to expand the availability of health care coverage for working individuals with disabilities, and establish a Ticket to Work and Self-Sufficiency Program in the Social Security Administration to provide meaningful opportunities to work. Introduced by LAZIO, R-N.Y., on March 18. House Commerce reported, amended, July 1 (H Rept 106-220, Part 1). House passed, amended, under suspension of the rules, Oct. 19. Senate passed, with amendment, Oct. 21. Conference report filed in the House Nov. 17 (H Rept 106-478). House agreed to conference report Nov. 18. Senate agreed to conference report Nov. 19. President signed Dec. 17, 1999. ◆

Appendix H

HOUSE ROLL CALL VOTES

House Roll Call Votes By Bill Number

House Bills

Senate Bills

Key

Y Voted for (yea).
Paired for.
+ Announced for.
N Voted against (nay).
X Paired against.
– Announced against.
P Voted "present."
C Voted "present" to avoid possible conflict of interest.
? Did not vote or otherwise make a position known.

•

Democrats ***Republicans***
Independents

1. **Quorum Call.*** 427 responded. Jan. 6, 1999.

2. **Election of the Speaker.** Nomination of J. Dennis Hastert, R-Ill., and Richard A. Gephardt, D-Mo., for Speaker for the 106th Congress. Hastert elected 220-205: R 220-0; D 0-204 (ND 0-149, SD 0-55); I 0-1. Jan. 6, 1999. A "Y" on the chart represents a vote for Hastert; an "N" represents a vote for Gephardt. A majority of the votes cast for a person by name (213 in this case) is needed for election. All members-elect are eligible to vote for Speaker.

3. **H Res 5. Rules of the House/Previous Question.** Dreier, R-Calif., motion to order the previous question (thus ending debate and the possibility of amendment) on the resolution containing the House rules for the 106th Congress, which extends House rules from the 105th Congress except for changes recommended by the Republican Conference. Motion agreed to 216-207: R 216-0; D 0-206 (ND 0-151, SD 0-55); I 0-1. Jan. 6, 1999.

4. **H Res 5. Rules of the House/Motion To Commit.** Moakley, D-Mass., motion to commit the resolution to a select committee composed of the majority and minority leaders with instructions to report it back to the House with an amendment to revise distribution of committee assignments to allow Democrats more seats and to prohibit spending of any budget surplus until the Social Security program is financially stable. Motion rejected 201-218: R 0-218; D 200-0 (ND 147-0, SD 53-0); I 1-0. Jan. 6, 1999.

5. **H Res 5. Rules of the House/Adoption.** Adoption of the resolution to adopt House rules for the 106th Congress, which extends the rules of the 105th Congress except for changes recommended by the Republican Conference. The changes include: allowing committees to add a sixth subcommittee if one deals with oversight; permitting certain House employees to receive honoraria; extending the life of the Government Reform Committee's Census Subcommittee and the select committee on technology transfers to China; and allowing the Budget Committee chairman to establish multiyear spending allocations as if Congress had enacted a fiscal 1999 budget resolution. Adopted 217-204: R 217-0; D 0-203 (ND 0-148, SD 0-55); I 0-1. Jan. 6, 1999.

6. **H Res 10. Impeachment of President Clinton/Reappointment of Managers.** Adoption of the resolution to reappoint and reauthorize managers, drawn from the Republican membership of the House Judiciary Committee, to conduct the impeachment trial against President Clinton in the Senate. Adopted 223-198: R 218-0; D 5-197 (ND 0-147, SD 5-50); I 0-1. Jan. 6, 1999.

**CQ does not include quorum calls in its vote charts.*

	2	3	4	5	6
ALABAMA					
1 ***Callahan***	Y	Y	N	Y	Y
2 ***Everett***	Y	Y	N	Y	Y
3 ***Riley***	Y	Y	N	Y	Y
4 ***Aderholt***	Y	Y	N	Y	Y
5 Cramer	N	N	Y	N	N
6 ***Bachus***	Y	Y	N	Y	Y
7 Hilliard	N	N	Y	N	N
ALASKA					
AL ***Young***	Y	Y	N	Y	Y
ARIZONA					
1 ***Salmon***	Y	Y	N	Y	Y
2 Pastor	N	N	Y	N	N
3 ***Stump***	Y	Y	N	Y	Y
4 ***Shadegg***	Y	Y	N	Y	Y
5 ***Kolbe***	Y	Y	N	Y	Y
6 ***Hayworth***	Y	Y	N	Y	Y
ARKANSAS					
1 Berry	N	N	Y	N	N
2 Snyder	N	N	Y	N	N
3 ***Hutchinson***	Y	Y	N	Y	Y
4 ***Dickey***	Y	Y	N	Y	Y
CALIFORNIA					
1 Thompson	N	N	Y	N	N
2 ***Herger***	Y	Y	N	Y	Y
3 ***Ose***	Y	Y	N	Y	Y
4 ***Doolittle***	Y	Y	N	Y	Y
5 Matsui	N	N	Y	N	N
6 Woolsey	N	N	Y	N	N
7 Miller, George	?	?	?	?	?
8 Pelosi	N	N	Y	N	N
9 Lee	N	N	Y	N	N
10 Tauscher	N	N	Y	N	N
11 ***Pombo***	Y	Y	N	Y	Y
12 Lantos	N	N	Y	N	N
13 Stark	?	?	?	?	?
14 Eshoo	N	N	Y	N	N
15 ***Campbell***	Y	Y	N	Y	Y
16 Lofgren	N	N	Y	N	N
17 Farr	?	?	?	?	?
18 Condit	N	N	Y	N	N
19 ***Radanovich***	Y	Y	N	Y	Y
20 Dooley	N	N	Y	N	N
21 ***Thomas***	Y	Y	N	Y	Y
22 Capps	N	N	Y	N	N
23 ***Gallegly***	?	?	?	?	?
24 Sherman	N	N	Y	N	N
25 ***McKeon***	Y	Y	N	Y	Y
26 Berman	N	N	Y	N	N
27 ***Rogan***	Y	Y	N	Y	Y
28 ***Dreier***	Y	Y	N	Y	Y
29 Waxman	N	N	Y	N	N
30 Becerra	N	N	Y	N	N
31 Martinez	N	N	Y	N	N
32 Dixon	N	N	Y	N	N
33 Roybal-Allard	N	N	Y	N	N
34 Napolitano	N	N	Y	N	N
35 Waters	N	N	Y	N	N
36 ***Kuykendall***	Y	Y	N	Y	Y
37 Millender-McD.	N	N	Y	N	N
38 ***Horn***	Y	Y	N	Y	Y
39 ***Royce***	Y	Y	N	Y	Y
40 ***Lewis***	Y	Y	N	Y	Y
41 ***Miller, Gary***	Y	Y	N	Y	Y
42 Brown	N	N	Y	N	N
43 ***Calvert***	Y	Y	N	Y	Y
44 ***Bono***	Y	Y	N	Y	Y
45 ***Rohrabacher***	Y	Y	N	Y	Y
46 Sanchez	N	N	Y	N	N
47 ***Cox***	Y	Y	N	Y	Y
48 ***Packard***	Y	Y	N	Y	Y
49 ***Bilbray***	Y	Y	N	Y	Y
50 Filner	N	N	Y	N	N
51 ***Cunningham***	Y	Y	N	Y	Y
52 ***Hunter***	Y	Y	N	Y	Y
COLORADO					
1 DeGette	N	N	Y	N	N
2 Udall	N	N	Y	N	N
3 ***McInnis***	Y	Y	N	Y	Y
4 ***Schaffer***	Y	Y	N	Y	Y
5 ***Hefley***	Y	Y	N	?	?
6 ***Tancredo***	Y	Y	N	Y	Y
CONNECTICUT					
1 Larson	N	N	Y	N	N
2 Gejdenson	N	N	Y	N	N
3 DeLauro	N	N	Y	N	N
4 ***Shays***	Y	Y	N	Y	Y
5 Maloney	N	N	Y	N	N
6 ***Johnson***	Y	Y	N	Y	Y
DELAWARE					
AL ***Castle***	Y	Y	N	Y	Y
FLORIDA					
1 ***Scarborough***	Y	Y	N	Y	Y
2 Boyd	N	N	Y	N	N
3 Brown	N	N	Y	N	N
4 ***Fowler***	Y	Y	N	Y	Y
5 Thurman	N	N	Y	N	N
6 ***Stearns***	Y	Y	N	Y	Y
7 ***Mica***	Y	Y	N	Y	Y
8 ***McCollum***	Y	Y	N	Y	Y
9 ***Bilirakis***	Y	Y	N	Y	Y
10 ***Young***	Y	Y	N	Y	Y
11 Davis	N	N	?	N	N
12 ***Canady***	Y	Y	N	Y	Y
13 ***Miller***	Y	Y	N	Y	Y
14 ***Goss***	Y	Y	N	Y	Y
15 ***Weldon***	Y	Y	N	Y	Y
16 ***Foley***	Y	Y	N	Y	Y
17 Meek	N	N	?	N	N
18 ***Ros-Lehtinen***	Y	Y	N	Y	Y
19 Wexler	N	N	Y	N	N
20 Deutsch	N	N	Y	N	N
21 ***Diaz-Balart***	Y	Y	N	Y	Y
22 ***Shaw***	Y	Y	N	Y	Y
23 Hastings	N	N	Y	N	N
GEORGIA					
1 ***Kingston***	Y	Y	N	Y	Y
2 Bishop	N	N	Y	N	N
3 ***Collins***	Y	Y	N	Y	Y
4 McKinney	N	N	Y	N	N
5 Lewis	N	N	Y	N	N
6 Vacant					
7 ***Barr***	Y	Y	N	Y	Y
8 ***Chambliss***	Y	Y	N	Y	Y
9 ***Deal***	Y	Y	N	Y	Y
10 ***Norwood***	Y	Y	N	Y	Y
11 ***Linder***	Y	Y	N	Y	Y
HAWAII					
1 Abercrombie	N	N	Y	N	N
2 Mink	N	N	Y	N	N
IDAHO					
1 ***Chenoweth***	Y	Y	N	Y	Y
2 ***Simpson***	Y	Y	N	Y	Y
ILLINOIS					
1 Rush	N	N	Y	N	N
2 Jackson	N	N	Y	N	N
3 Lipinski	N	N	Y	?	?
4 Gutierrez	N	N	Y	N	N
5 Blagojevich	N	N	Y	N	N
6 ***Hyde***	Y	Y	N	Y	Y
7 Davis	N	N	Y	N	N
8 ***Crane***	Y	Y	N	Y	Y
9 Schakowsky	N	N	Y	N	N
10 ***Porter***	Y	Y	N	Y	Y
11 ***Weller***	Y	Y	N	Y	Y
12 Costello	N	N	Y	N	N
13 ***Biggert***	Y	Y	N	Y	Y
14 ***Hastert***	P				Y

ND Northern Democrats SD Southern Democrats

	2	3	4	5	6
15 ***Ewing***	Y	Y	N	Y	Y
16 ***Manzullo***	Y	?	N	Y	Y
17 Evans	N	N	Y	N	N
18 ***LaHood***	Y	Y	N	Y	Y
19 Phelps	N	N	Y	N	N
20 ***Shimkus***	Y	Y	N	Y	Y
INDIANA					
1 Visclosky	N	N	Y	N	N
2 ***McIntosh***	Y	Y	N	Y	Y
3 Roemer	N	N	Y	N	N
4 ***Souder***	Y	Y	N	Y	Y
5 ***Buyer***	Y	Y	N	Y	Y
6 ***Burton***	Y	Y	N	Y	Y
7 ***Pease***	Y	Y	N	Y	Y
8 ***Hostettler***	Y	Y	N	Y	Y
9 Hill	N	N	Y	N	N
10 Carson	N	N	Y	N	N
IOWA					
1 ***Leach***	Y	Y	N	Y	Y
2 ***Nussle***	Y	Y	N	Y	Y
3 Boswell	N	N	Y	N	N
4 ***Ganske***	Y	Y	N	Y	Y
5 ***Latham***	Y	Y	N	Y	Y
KANSAS					
1 ***Moran***	Y	Y	N	Y	Y
2 ***Ryun***	Y	Y	N	Y	Y
3 Moore	N	N	Y	N	N
4 ***Tiahrt***	Y	Y	N	Y	Y
KENTUCKY					
1 ***Whitfield***	Y	Y	N	Y	Y
2 ***Lewis***	Y	Y	N	Y	Y
3 ***Northup***	Y	Y	N	Y	Y
4 Lucas	N	N	Y	N	Y
5 ***Rogers***	Y	Y	N	Y	Y
6 ***Fletcher***	Y	Y	N	Y	Y
LOUISIANA					
1 ***Livingston***	Y	Y	N	Y	Y
2 Jefferson	N	N	Y	N	N
3 ***Tauzin***	Y	Y	N	Y	Y
4 ***McCrery***	Y	Y	N	Y	Y
5 ***Cooksey***	Y	Y	N	Y	Y
6 ***Baker***	Y	Y	N	Y	Y
7 John	N	N	Y	N	N
MAINE					
1 Allen	N	N	Y	N	N
2 Baldacci	N	N	Y	N	N
MARYLAND					
1 ***Gilchrest***	Y	Y	N	Y	Y
2 ***Ehrlich***	Y	Y	N	Y	Y
3 Cardin	N	N	Y	?	?
4 Wynn	N	N	Y	N	N
5 Hoyer	?	?	?	?	?
6 ***Bartlett***	Y	Y	N	Y	Y
7 Cummings	N	N	Y	N	N
8 ***Morella***	Y	Y	N	Y	Y
MASSACHUSETTS					
1 Olver	N	N	Y	N	N
2 Neal	N	N	Y	N	?
3 McGovern	N	N	Y	N	N
4 Frank	N	N	Y	N	N
5 Meehan	N	N	Y	N	N
6 Tierney	N	N	Y	N	N
7 Markey	N	N	Y	N	N
8 Capuano	N	N	Y	N	N
9 Moakley	N	N	Y	N	N
10 Delahunt	N	N	Y	N	N
MICHIGAN					
1 Stupak	N	N	Y	N	N
2 ***Hoekstra***	Y	Y	N	Y	Y
3 ***Ehlers***	Y	Y	N	Y	Y
4 ***Camp***	Y	Y	N	Y	Y
5 Barcia	?	N	Y	N	N
6 ***Upton***	Y	Y	N	Y	Y
7 ***Smith***	Y	Y	N	Y	Y
8 Stabenow	N	N	Y	N	N
9 Kildee	N	N	Y	N	N
10 Bonior	N	N	Y	?	N
11 ***Knollenberg***	Y	Y	N	Y	Y
12 Levin	N	N	Y	N	N
13 Rivers	N	N	Y	N	N
14 Conyers	N	N	Y	N	N
15 Kilpatrick	N	N	Y	N	N
16 Dingell	N	N	Y	N	N
MINNESOTA					
1 ***Gutknecht***	Y	Y	N	Y	Y
2 Minge	N	N	Y	N	N
3 ***Ramstad***	Y	Y	N	Y	Y
4 Vento	N	N	Y	N	N
5 Sabo	N	N	Y	N	N
6 Luther	N	N	Y	N	N
7 Peterson	N	N	Y	N	N
8 Oberstar	N	N	Y	N	N
MISSISSIPPI					
1 ***Wicker***	Y	Y	N	Y	Y
2 Thompson	N	N	Y	N	N
3 ***Pickering***	Y	Y	N	Y	Y
4 Shows	N	N	Y	N	N
5 Taylor	N	N	Y	N	Y
MISSOURI					
1 Clay	N	N	Y	N	N
2 ***Talent***	Y	Y	N	Y	Y
3 Gephardt	P	N	Y	N	N
4 Skelton	N	N	Y	N	N
5 McCarthy	N	N	Y	N	N
6 Danner	N	N	Y	N	N
7 ***Blunt***	Y	Y	?	?	?
8 ***Emerson***	Y	Y	N	Y	Y
9 ***Hulshof***	Y	Y	N	Y	Y
MONTANA					
AL ***Hill***	Y	Y	N	Y	Y
NEBRASKA					
1 ***Bereuter***	Y	Y	N	Y	Y
2 ***Terry***	Y	Y	N	Y	Y
3 ***Barrett***	Y	Y	N	Y	Y
NEVADA					
1 Berkley	N	N	Y	N	N
2 ***Gibbons***	Y	Y	N	Y	Y
NEW HAMPSHIRE					
1 ***Sununu***	Y	Y	N	Y	Y
2 ***Bass***	Y	Y	N	Y	Y
NEW JERSEY					
1 Andrews	N	N	Y	N	N
2 ***LoBiondo***	Y	Y	N	Y	Y
3 ***Saxton***	Y	Y	N	Y	Y
4 ***Smith***	Y	Y	N	Y	Y
5 ***Roukema***	Y	Y	N	Y	Y
6 Pallone	N	N	+	N	N
7 ***Franks***	Y	Y	N	Y	Y
8 Pascrell	N	N	Y	N	–
9 Rothman	N	N	Y	N	N
10 Payne	N	N	Y	N	N
11 ***Frelinghuysen***	Y	Y	N	Y	Y
12 Holt	N	N	+	N	N
13 Menendez	N	N	Y	N	N
NEW MEXICO					
1 ***Wilson***	Y	Y	N	Y	Y
2 ***Skeen***	Y	Y	N	Y	Y
3 Udall	N	N	Y	N	N
NEW YORK					
1 ***Forbes***	Y	Y	N	Y	Y
2 ***Lazio***	Y	Y	N	Y	Y
3 ***King***	Y	Y	N	Y	Y
4 McCarthy	N	N	Y	N	N
5 Ackerman	N	N	Y	N	N
6 Meeks	N	N	?	N	N
7 Crowley	N	N	Y	N	N
8 Nadler	N	N	Y	N	N
9 Weiner	N	N	Y	N	N
10 Towns	N	N	Y	N	N
11 Owens	N	N	Y	N	N
12 Velázquez	N	N	Y	N	N
13 ***Fossella***	Y	Y	N	Y	Y
14 Maloney	N	N	Y	N	N
15 Rangel	N	N	Y	N	N
16 Serrano	N	N	Y	N	N
17 Engel	N	N	Y	N	N
18 Lowey	N	N	Y	N	N
19 ***Kelly***	Y	Y	N	Y	Y
20 ***Gilman***	Y	Y	N	Y	Y
21 McNulty	N	N	Y	N	N
22 ***Sweeney***	Y	Y	N	Y	Y
23 ***Boehlert***	Y	Y	N	Y	Y
24 ***McHugh***	Y	Y	N	Y	Y
25 ***Walsh***	Y	Y	N	Y	Y
26 Hinchey	N	N	Y	N	N
27 ***Reynolds***	Y	Y	N	Y	Y
28 Slaughter	N	N	Y	N	N
29 LaFalce	N	N	Y	N	N
30 ***Quinn***	Y	Y	N	Y	Y
31 ***Houghton***	Y	Y	N	Y	Y
NORTH CAROLINA					
1 Clayton	N	N	Y	N	N
2 Etheridge	N	N	Y	N	N
3 ***Jones***	Y	Y	N	Y	Y
4 Price	N	N	Y	N	N
5 ***Burr***	Y	?	N	Y	Y
6 ***Coble***	Y	Y	N	Y	Y
7 McIntyre	N	N	Y	N	N
8 ***Hayes***	Y	Y	N	Y	Y
9 ***Myrick***	Y	Y	N	Y	Y
10 ***Ballenger***	Y	Y	N	Y	Y
11 ***Taylor***	Y	Y	N	Y	Y
12 Watt	N	N	Y	N	N
NORTH DAKOTA					
AL Pomeroy	N	N	Y	N	N
OHIO					
1 ***Chabot***	Y	Y	N	Y	Y
2 ***Portman***	Y	Y	N	Y	Y
3 Hall	N	N	Y	N	N
4 ***Oxley***	Y	Y	N	Y	Y
5 ***Gillmor***	Y	Y	N	Y	Y
6 Strickland	N	N	Y	N	N
7 ***Hobson***	Y	Y	N	Y	Y
8 ***Boehner***	Y	Y	N	Y	Y
9 Kaptur	N	N	Y	N	N
10 Kucinich	N	N	Y	N	N
11 Jones	N	N	Y	N	N
12 ***Kasich***	Y	Y	N	Y	Y
13 Brown	N	N	Y	N	N
14 Sawyer	N	N	Y	N	N
15 ***Pryce***	Y	Y	N	Y	Y
16 ***Regula***	Y	Y	N	Y	Y
17 Traficant	N	N	Y	N	N
18 ***Ney***	Y	Y	N	Y	Y
19 ***LaTourette***	Y	Y	N	Y	Y
OKLAHOMA					
1 ***Largent***	Y	Y	N	Y	Y
2 ***Coburn***	Y	Y	N	Y	Y
3 ***Watkins***	Y	Y	N	Y	Y
4 ***Watts***	Y	Y	N	Y	Y
5 ***Istook***	Y	Y	N	Y	Y
6 ***Lucas***	Y	Y	N	Y	Y
OREGON					
1 Wu	N	N	Y	N	N
2 ***Walden***	Y	Y	N	Y	Y
3 Blumenauer	N	N	Y	N	N
4 DeFazio	N	N	Y	N	N
5 Hooley	N	N	Y	N	N
PENNSYLVANIA					
1 Brady	N	N	Y	N	N
2 Fattah	N	N	Y	N	N
3 Borski	N	N	Y	N	N
4 Klink	N	N	Y	N	N
5 ***Peterson***	Y	Y	N	Y	Y
6 Holden	N	N	Y	N	N
7 ***Weldon***	Y	Y	N	Y	Y
8 ***Greenwood***	Y	Y	N	Y	Y
9 ***Shuster***	Y	Y	N	Y	Y
10 ***Sherwood***	Y	Y	N	Y	Y
11 Kanjorski	N	N	Y	N	N
12 Murtha	N	N	Y	N	N
13 Hoeffel	N	N	Y	N	N
14 Coyne	N	N	Y	N	N
15 ***Toomey***	Y	Y	N	Y	Y
16 ***Pitts***	Y	?	N	Y	Y
17 ***Gekas***	Y	Y	N	Y	Y
18 Doyle	N	N	Y	N	N
19 ***Goodling***	Y	Y	N	Y	Y
20 Mascara	N	N	Y	N	N
21 ***English***	Y	Y	N	Y	Y
RHODE ISLAND					
1 Kennedy	N	N	Y	N	N
2 Weygand	N	N	Y	N	N
SOUTH CAROLINA					
1 ***Sanford***	Y	Y	N	Y	Y
2 ***Spence***	Y	Y	N	Y	Y
3 ***Graham***	Y	Y	N	Y	Y
4 ***DeMint***	Y	Y	N	Y	Y
5 Spratt	N	N	Y	N	N
6 Clyburn	N	N	Y	N	N
SOUTH DAKOTA					
AL ***Thune***	Y	Y	N	Y	Y
TENNESSEE					
1 ***Jenkins***	Y	+	–	+	+
2 ***Duncan***	Y	Y	N	Y	Y
3 ***Wamp***	Y	Y	N	Y	Y
4 ***Hilleary***	Y	Y	N	Y	Y
5 Clement	N	N	Y	N	N
6 Gordon	N	N	Y	N	N
7 ***Bryant***	Y	Y	N	Y	Y
8 Tanner	N	N	Y	N	N
9 Ford	N	N	Y	N	N
TEXAS					
1 Sandlin	N	N	Y	N	N
2 Turner	N	N	Y	N	N
3 ***Johnson, Sam***	Y	Y	N	Y	Y
4 Hall	N	N	Y	N	Y
5 ***Sessions***	Y	Y	N	Y	Y
6 ***Barton***	Y	Y	N	Y	Y
7 ***Archer***	Y	Y	N	Y	Y
8 ***Brady***	Y	Y	N	Y	Y
9 Lampson	N	N	Y	N	N
10 Doggett	N	N	Y	N	N
11 Edwards	N	N	Y	N	N
12 ***Granger***	Y	Y	N	Y	Y
13 ***Thornberry***	Y	Y	N	Y	Y
14 ***Paul***	Y	Y	N	Y	Y
15 Hinojosa	N	N	Y	N	N
16 Reyes	N	N	Y	N	N
17 Stenholm	N	N	Y	N	Y
18 Jackson-Lee	N	N	Y	N	N
19 ***Combest***	Y	Y	N	Y	Y
20 Gonzalez	N	N	Y	N	N
21 ***Smith***	Y	Y	N	Y	Y
22 ***DeLay***	Y	Y	N	Y	Y
23 ***Bonilla***	Y	Y	N	Y	Y
24 Frost	N	N	Y	N	N
25 Bentsen	N	N	Y	N	N
26 ***Armey***	Y	Y	N	Y	Y
27 Ortiz	N	N	Y	N	N
28 Rodriguez	N	N	Y	N	N
29 Green	N	N	Y	N	N
30 Johnson, E.B.	N	N	Y	N	N
UTAH					
1 ***Hansen***	Y	Y	N	Y	Y
2 ***Cook***	Y	Y	N	Y	Y
3 ***Cannon***	Y	Y	N	Y	Y
VERMONT					
AL *Sanders*	N	N	Y	N	N
VIRGINIA					
1 ***Bateman***	Y	Y	N	Y	Y
2 Pickett	N	N	Y	N	N
3 Scott	N	N	Y	N	N
4 Sisisky	N	N	Y	N	N
5 Goode	N	N	Y	N	Y
6 ***Goodlatte***	Y	Y	N	Y	Y
7 ***Bliley***	Y	Y	N	Y	Y
8 Moran	N	N	Y	N	N
9 Boucher	N	N	Y	N	N
10 ***Wolf***	Y	Y	N	Y	Y
11 ***Davis***	Y	Y	N	Y	Y
WASHINGTON					
1 Inslee	N	N	Y	N	N
2 ***Metcalf***	Y	Y	N	Y	Y
3 Baird	N	N	Y	N	N
4 ***Hastings***	Y	Y	N	Y	Y
5 ***Nethercutt***	Y	Y	N	Y	Y
6 Dicks	N	N	Y	N	N
7 McDermott	N	N	Y	N	N
8 ***Dunn***	Y	Y	N	Y	Y
9 Smith	N	N	Y	N	N
WEST VIRGINIA					
1 Mollohan	?	?	?	?	?
2 Wise	N	N	Y	N	N
3 Rahall	N	N	Y	N	N
WISCONSIN					
1 ***Ryan***	Y	Y	N	Y	Y
2 Baldwin	N	N	Y	N	N
3 Kind	N	N	Y	N	N
4 Kleczka	N	N	Y	N	N
5 Barrett	N	N	Y	N	N
6 ***Petri***	Y	Y	N	Y	Y
7 Obey	N	N	?	N	N
8 ***Green***	Y	Y	N	Y	Y
9 ***Sensenbrenner***	Y	Y	N	Y	Y
WYOMING					
AL ***Cubin***	Y	Y	N	Y	Y

Southern states - Ala., Ark., Fla., Ga., Ky., La., Miss., N.C., Okla., S.C., Tenn., Texas, Va.

7. HR 68. Small Business Investment Act/Passage. Talent, R-Mo., motion to suspend the rules and pass the bill to modify the Small Business Investment Company (SBIC) Program, including revising the test for eligibility for SBIC financing. Motion agreed to 402-2: R 209-2; D 192-0 (ND 143-0, SD 49-0); I 1-0. Feb. 2, 1999. A two-thirds majority of those present and voting (270 in this case) is required for passage under suspension of the rules.

8. HR 432. Dante B. Fascell North-South Center/Passage. Gilman, R-N.Y., motion to suspend the rules and pass the bill to rename the North-South educational institution in Florida as the Dante B. Fascell North-South Center. Motion agreed to 409-0: R 213-0; D 195-0 (ND 146-0, SD 49-0); I 1-0. Feb. 2, 1999. A two-thirds majority of those present and voting (273 in this case) is required for passage under suspension of the rules.

9. HR 99. Federal Aviation Administration Short-Term Extension/Passage. Passage of the bill to reauthorize programs and activities of the Federal Aviation Administration (FAA), including the Airport Improvement Program, through Sept. 30, 1999. The measure would authorize a total of $10.2 billion in additional and new funding for the improvement program and other FAA aviation programs in fiscal 1999. Passed 408-3: R 207-1; D 200-2 (ND 146-2, SD 54-0); I 1-0. Feb. 3, 1999.

10. HR 98. Federal Aviation War Risk Insurance Program/Passage. Shuster, R-Pa., motion to suspend the rules and pass the bill to reauthorize the federal aviation war risk insurance program, through Dec. 31, 2003. Motion agreed to 407-1: R 204-1; D 202-0 (ND 148-0, SD 54-0); I 1-0. Feb. 3, 1999. A two-thirds majority of those present and voting (272 in this case) is required for passage under suspension of the rules.

11. Procedural Motion/Journal. Approval of the House Journal of Tuesday Feb. 2, 1999. Approved 383-18: R 196-8; D 186-10 (ND 137-7, SD 49-3); I 1-0. Feb. 3, 1999.

Key

- Y Voted for (yea).
- # Paired for.
- \+ Announced for.
- N Voted against (nay).
- X Paired against.
- – Announced against.
- P Voted "present."
- C Voted "present" to avoid possible conflict of interest.
- ? Did not vote or otherwise make a position known.

•

Democrats ***Republicans***
Independents

	7	8	9	10	11
ALABAMA					
1 ***Callahan***	Y	Y	Y	Y	Y
2 ***Everett***	Y	Y	Y	Y	Y
3 ***Riley***	Y	Y	Y	Y	Y
4 ***Aderholt***	Y	Y	Y	Y	Y
5 Cramer	Y	Y	Y	Y	Y
6 ***Bachus***	Y	Y	Y	Y	Y
7 Hilliard	Y	Y	Y	Y	N
ALASKA					
AL ***Young***	Y	Y	Y	Y	Y
ARIZONA					
1 ***Salmon***	Y	Y	Y	Y	Y
2 Pastor	Y	Y	Y	Y	Y
3 ***Stump***	Y	Y	Y	Y	Y
4 ***Shadegg***	Y	Y	Y	Y	Y
5 ***Kolbe***	Y	Y	Y	Y	Y
6 ***Hayworth***	Y	Y	Y	Y	Y
ARKANSAS					
1 Berry	Y	Y	Y	Y	Y
2 Snyder	Y	Y	Y	Y	Y
3 ***Hutchinson***	Y	Y	Y	Y	Y
4 ***Dickey***	Y	Y	Y	Y	Y
CALIFORNIA					
1 Thompson	Y	Y	Y	Y	Y
2 ***Herger***	Y	Y	Y	Y	Y
3 ***Ose***	Y	Y	Y	Y	Y
4 ***Doolittle***	Y	Y	Y	Y	Y
5 Matsui	Y	Y	Y	Y	Y
6 Woolsey	Y	Y	Y	Y	Y
7 Miller, George	Y	Y	Y	Y	Y
8 Pelosi	Y	Y	Y	Y	Y
9 Lee	Y	Y	Y	Y	Y
10 Tauscher	Y	Y	Y	Y	Y
11 ***Pombo***	Y	Y	Y	Y	Y
12 Lantos	?	?	?	?	Y
13 Stark	Y	Y	Y	Y	Y
14 Eshoo	Y	Y	Y	Y	Y
15 ***Campbell***	Y	Y	Y	Y	Y
16 Lofgren	Y	Y	Y	Y	Y
17 Farr	Y	Y	Y	?	?
18 Condit	Y	Y	Y	Y	Y
19 ***Radanovich***	Y	Y	Y	Y	?
20 Dooley	Y	Y	Y	Y	Y
21 ***Thomas***	Y	Y	Y	Y	Y
22 Capps	Y	Y	Y	Y	Y
23 ***Gallegly***	Y	Y	Y	Y	Y
24 Sherman	Y	Y	Y	Y	Y
25 ***McKeon***	Y	Y	Y	Y	Y
26 Berman	Y	Y	Y	Y	Y
27 ***Rogan***	Y	Y	?	?	?
28 ***Dreier***	Y	Y	Y	Y	Y
29 Waxman	Y	Y	Y	Y	Y
30 Becerra	Y	Y	Y	Y	Y
31 Martinez	Y	Y	?	Y	Y
32 Dixon	Y	Y	Y	Y	Y
33 Roybal-Allard	Y	Y	Y	Y	Y
34 Napolitano	Y	Y	Y	Y	Y
35 Waters	Y	Y	Y	Y	N
36 ***Kuykendall***	Y	Y	Y	Y	Y
37 Millender-McD.	Y	Y	Y	Y	Y
38 ***Horn***	Y	Y	Y	Y	Y
39 ***Royce***	Y	Y	Y	Y	Y
40 ***Lewis***	Y	Y	Y	Y	?
41 ***Miller, Gary***	Y	Y	Y	Y	Y
42 Brown	?	?	Y	Y	Y
43 ***Calvert***	Y	Y	Y	Y	Y
44 ***Bono***	Y	Y	Y	Y	Y
45 ***Rohrabacher***	Y	Y	Y	Y	Y
46 Sanchez	Y	Y	Y	Y	Y
47 ***Cox***	Y	Y	Y	Y	Y
48 ***Packard***	Y	Y	Y	Y	Y
49 ***Bilbray***	Y	Y	Y	Y	Y
50 Filner	Y	Y	Y	Y	N
51 ***Cunningham***	Y	Y	Y	Y	Y
52 ***Hunter***	Y	Y	Y	Y	Y
COLORADO					
1 DeGette	Y	Y	Y	Y	Y
2 Udall	?	Y	Y	Y	Y
3 ***McInnis***	Y	Y	Y	Y	Y
4 ***Schaffer***	Y	Y	Y	Y	N
5 ***Hefley***	Y	Y	Y	Y	N
6 ***Tancredo***	Y	Y	Y	Y	Y
CONNECTICUT					
1 Larson	Y	Y	Y	Y	Y
2 Gejdenson	Y	Y	Y	Y	?
3 DeLauro	Y	Y	Y	Y	Y
4 ***Shays***	Y	Y	Y	Y	Y
5 Maloney	Y	Y	Y	Y	Y
6 ***Johnson***	Y	Y	Y	Y	Y
DELAWARE					
AL ***Castle***	Y	Y	Y	Y	Y
FLORIDA					
1 ***Scarborough***	Y	Y	Y	Y	Y
2 Boyd	Y	Y	Y	Y	Y
3 Brown	Y	Y	Y	Y	Y
4 ***Fowler***	Y	Y	Y	Y	Y
5 Thurman	Y	Y	Y	Y	Y
6 ***Stearns***	Y	Y	Y	Y	Y
7 ***Mica***	Y	Y	Y	Y	Y
8 ***McCollum***	Y	Y	Y	Y	Y
9 ***Bilirakis***	Y	Y	Y	Y	Y
10 ***Young***	?	?	Y	Y	Y
11 Davis	Y	Y	Y	Y	Y
12 ***Canady***	Y	Y	Y	Y	Y
13 ***Miller***	Y	Y	Y	Y	Y
14 ***Goss***	Y	Y	Y	Y	Y
15 ***Weldon***	Y	Y	Y	Y	Y
16 ***Foley***	Y	Y	Y	Y	Y
17 Meek	Y	Y	Y	Y	Y
18 ***Ros-Lehtinen***	Y	Y	Y	Y	Y
19 Wexler	Y	Y	Y	Y	Y
20 Deutsch	+	+	+	+	+
21 ***Diaz-Balart***	Y	Y	Y	Y	Y
22 ***Shaw***	Y	Y	Y	Y	Y
23 Hastings	Y	Y	Y	Y	Y
GEORGIA					
1 ***Kingston***	Y	Y	Y	Y	Y
2 Bishop	Y	Y	Y	Y	Y
3 ***Collins***	Y	Y	Y	Y	Y
4 McKinney	Y	Y	Y	Y	Y
5 Lewis	Y	Y	Y	Y	Y
6 Vacant					
7 ***Barr***	Y	Y	Y	Y	Y
8 ***Chambliss***	Y	Y	Y	Y	Y
9 ***Deal***	Y	Y	Y	Y	Y
10 ***Norwood***	Y	Y	Y	?	Y
11 ***Linder***	Y	Y	Y	Y	Y
HAWAII					
1 Abercrombie	Y	Y	Y	Y	Y
2 Mink	Y	Y	Y	Y	Y
IDAHO					
1 ***Chenoweth***	Y	Y	Y	Y	Y
2 ***Simpson***	Y	Y	Y	Y	Y
ILLINOIS					
1 Rush	?	?	?	?	?
2 Jackson	Y	Y	Y	Y	Y
3 Lipinski	Y	Y	Y	Y	Y
4 Gutierrez	Y	Y	Y	Y	?
5 Blagojevich	Y	Y	Y	Y	Y
6 ***Hyde***	Y	Y	Y	Y	Y
7 Davis	Y	Y	Y	Y	Y
8 ***Crane***	Y	Y	Y	Y	N
9 Schakowsky	Y	Y	Y	Y	Y
10 ***Porter***	Y	Y	Y	Y	Y
11 ***Weller***	Y	Y	Y	Y	N
12 Costello	Y	Y	Y	Y	Y
13 ***Biggert***	Y	Y	Y	Y	Y
14 ***Hastert***					

ND Northern Democrats SD Southern Democrats

	7	8	9	10	11
15 ***Ewing***	Y	Y	Y	Y	?
16 ***Manzullo***	Y	Y	Y	Y	Y
17 Evans	Y	Y	Y	Y	Y
18 ***LaHood***	?	?	Y	Y	Y
19 Phelps	Y	Y	Y	Y	Y
20 ***Shimkus***	Y	Y	Y	Y	Y
INDIANA					
1 Visclosky	Y	Y	Y	Y	Y
2 ***McIntosh***	Y	Y	Y	Y	Y
3 Roemer	Y	Y	Y	Y	Y
4 ***Souder***	Y	Y	Y	Y	Y
5 ***Buyer***	Y	Y	Y	Y	Y
6 ***Burton***	Y	Y	Y	Y	?
7 ***Pease***	Y	Y	Y	?	Y
8 ***Hostettler***	Y	Y	Y	Y	Y
9 Hill	Y	Y	Y	Y	Y
10 Carson	+	+	Y	Y	P
IOWA					
1 ***Leach***	?	?	Y	Y	Y
2 ***Nussle***	Y	Y	Y	Y	Y
3 Boswell	Y	Y	Y	Y	Y
4 ***Ganske***	Y	Y	Y	Y	Y
5 ***Latham***	Y	Y	Y	Y	Y
KANSAS					
1 ***Moran***	Y	Y	Y	Y	N
2 ***Ryun***	Y	Y	Y	Y	Y
3 Moore	Y	Y	Y	Y	Y
4 ***Tiahrt***	Y	Y	Y	Y	Y
KENTUCKY					
1 ***Whitfield***	Y	Y	Y	Y	Y
2 ***Lewis***	Y	Y	Y	Y	Y
3 ***Northup***	Y	Y	Y	Y	Y
4 Lucas	Y	Y	Y	Y	Y
5 ***Rogers***	Y	Y	Y	Y	Y
6 ***Fletcher***	Y	Y	Y	Y	Y
LOUISIANA					
1 ***Livingston***	Y	Y	?	?	?
2 Jefferson	?	?	Y	Y	Y
3 ***Tauzin***	Y	Y	Y	Y	Y
4 ***McCrery***	Y	Y	Y	Y	Y
5 ***Cooksey***	?	?	?	?	?
6 ***Baker***	Y	Y	Y	Y	Y
7 John	Y	Y	Y	Y	Y
MAINE					
1 Allen	Y	Y	Y	Y	Y
2 Baldacci	Y	Y	Y	Y	Y
MARYLAND					
1 ***Gilchrest***	Y	Y	Y	Y	Y
2 ***Ehrlich***	Y	Y	Y	Y	Y
3 Cardin	Y	Y	Y	Y	Y
4 Wynn	Y	Y	Y	Y	Y
5 Hoyer	Y	Y	Y	Y	Y
6 ***Bartlett***	Y	Y	Y	Y	Y
7 Cummings	Y	Y	Y	Y	Y
8 ***Morella***	Y	Y	Y	Y	Y
MASSACHUSETTS					
1 Olver	Y	Y	Y	Y	N
2 Neal	Y	Y	Y	Y	Y
3 McGovern	?	?	Y	Y	Y
4 Frank	Y	Y	Y	Y	?
5 Meehan	Y	Y	Y	Y	Y
6 Tierney	?	?	Y	Y	Y
7 Markey	Y	Y	Y	Y	Y
8 Capuano	Y	Y	Y	Y	Y
9 Moakley	?	?	Y	Y	Y
10 Delahunt	?	?	?	?	?
MICHIGAN					
1 Stupak	Y	Y	Y	Y	Y
2 ***Hoekstra***	Y	Y	Y	Y	Y
3 ***Ehlers***	+	+	Y	Y	Y
4 ***Camp***	Y	Y	Y	Y	Y
5 Barcia	?	Y	Y	Y	Y
6 ***Upton***	Y	Y	Y	Y	Y
7 ***Smith***	Y	Y	Y	Y	Y
8 Stabenow	Y	Y	Y	Y	Y
9 Kildee	Y	Y	Y	Y	Y
10 Bonior	Y	Y	Y	Y	Y
11 ***Knollenberg***	Y	Y	Y	Y	Y
12 Levin	Y	Y	Y	Y	Y
13 Rivers	Y	Y	Y	Y	Y
14 Conyers	Y	Y	Y	Y	?
15 Kilpatrick	Y	Y	Y	Y	Y
16 Dingell	Y	Y	?	?	?

	7	8	9	10	11
MINNESOTA					
1 ***Gutknecht***	+	+	Y	Y	Y
2 Minge	Y	Y	Y	Y	Y
3 ***Ramstad***	Y	Y	Y	Y	N
4 Vento	Y	Y	Y	Y	Y
5 Sabo	Y	Y	Y	Y	N
6 Luther	+	+	Y	Y	Y
7 Peterson	Y	Y	Y	Y	Y
8 Oberstar	Y	Y	Y	Y	N
MISSISSIPPI					
1 ***Wicker***	Y	Y	Y	Y	Y
2 Thompson	Y	Y	Y	Y	Y
3 ***Pickering***	Y	Y	Y	Y	?
4 Shows	Y	Y	Y	Y	Y
5 Taylor	Y	Y	Y	Y	N
MISSOURI					
1 Clay	Y	Y	Y	Y	Y
2 ***Talent***	Y	Y	Y	Y	Y
3 Gephardt	Y	Y	Y	Y	Y
4 Skelton	Y	Y	Y	Y	Y
5 McCarthy	Y	Y	Y	Y	Y
6 Danner	Y	Y	Y	Y	Y
7 ***Blunt***	Y	Y	Y	Y	?
8 ***Emerson***	Y	Y	Y	Y	Y
9 ***Hulshof***	Y	Y	Y	Y	Y
MONTANA					
AL ***Hill***	Y	Y	Y	Y	Y
NEBRASKA					
1 ***Bereuter***	Y	Y	Y	Y	Y
2 ***Terry***	Y	Y	Y	Y	Y
3 ***Barrett***	Y	Y	Y	Y	Y
NEVADA					
1 Berkley	Y	Y	Y	Y	Y
2 ***Gibbons***	Y	Y	Y	Y	N
NEW HAMPSHIRE					
1 ***Sununu***	Y	Y	Y	Y	Y
2 ***Bass***	Y	Y	Y	Y	Y
NEW JERSEY					
1 Andrews	Y	Y	Y	Y	Y
2 ***LoBiondo***	Y	Y	Y	Y	N
3 ***Saxton***	Y	Y	Y	Y	Y
4 ***Smith***	Y	Y	?	?	?
5 ***Roukema***	Y	Y	Y	Y	Y
6 Pallone	Y	Y	Y	Y	Y
7 ***Franks***	Y	Y	Y	Y	Y
8 Pascrell	Y	Y	Y	Y	Y
9 Rothman	Y	Y	Y	Y	Y
10 Payne	Y	Y	Y	Y	Y
11 ***Frelinghuysen***	Y	Y	Y	Y	Y
12 Holt	Y	Y	Y	Y	Y
13 Menendez	Y	Y	Y	Y	Y
NEW MEXICO					
1 ***Wilson***	Y	Y	?	Y	Y
2 ***Skeen***	Y	Y	?	?	?
3 Udall	Y	Y	Y	Y	Y
NEW YORK					
1 ***Forbes***	Y	Y	Y	Y	Y
2 ***Lazio***	Y	Y	Y	Y	Y
3 ***King***	Y	Y	Y	Y	Y
4 McCarthy	Y	Y	Y	Y	Y
5 Ackerman	Y	Y	Y	Y	?
6 Meeks	Y	Y	Y	Y	Y
7 Crowley	Y	Y	Y	Y	Y
8 Nadler	Y	Y	Y	Y	Y
9 Weiner	Y	Y	Y	Y	Y
10 Towns	?	?	Y	Y	Y
11 Owens	Y	Y	Y	Y	?
12 Velázquez	Y	Y	Y	Y	Y
13 ***Fossella***	Y	Y	Y	Y	Y
14 Maloney	Y	Y	?	Y	Y
15 Rangel	Y	Y	Y	Y	Y
16 Serrano	Y	Y	Y	Y	Y
17 Engel	Y	Y	Y	Y	Y
18 Lowey	Y	Y	Y	Y	Y
19 ***Kelly***	Y	Y	Y	Y	Y
20 ***Gilman***	Y	Y	Y	Y	Y
21 McNulty	Y	Y	Y	Y	Y
22 ***Sweeney***	Y	Y	Y	?	Y
23 ***Boehlert***	Y	Y	Y	Y	Y
24 ***McHugh***	Y	Y	Y	Y	Y
25 ***Walsh***	Y	Y	Y	Y	Y
26 Hinchey	Y	Y	Y	Y	Y
27 ***Reynolds***	Y	Y	Y	Y	Y
28 Slaughter	Y	Y	Y	Y	Y
29 LaFalce	Y	Y	Y	Y	Y

	7	8	9	10	11
30 ***Quinn***	+	Y	Y	Y	Y
31 ***Houghton***	Y	Y	Y	Y	Y
NORTH CAROLINA					
1 Clayton	Y	Y	Y	Y	Y
2 Etheridge	Y	Y	Y	Y	Y
3 ***Jones***	Y	Y	Y	Y	Y
4 Price	Y	Y	Y	Y	Y
5 ***Burr***	Y	Y	Y	Y	Y
6 ***Coble***	Y	Y	Y	Y	Y
7 McIntyre	Y	Y	Y	Y	Y
8 ***Hayes***	Y	Y	Y	Y	Y
9 ***Myrick***	Y	Y	Y	?	Y
10 ***Ballenger***	Y	Y	Y	Y	Y
11 ***Taylor***	Y	Y	Y	Y	Y
12 Watt	Y	Y	Y	Y	Y
NORTH DAKOTA					
AL Pomeroy	Y	Y	Y	Y	Y
OHIO					
1 ***Chabot***	Y	Y	Y	Y	Y
2 ***Portman***	Y	Y	Y	Y	Y
3 Hall	Y	Y	?	?	Y
4 ***Oxley***	Y	Y	Y	Y	Y
5 ***Gillmor***	Y	Y	Y	Y	Y
6 Strickland	Y	Y	Y	Y	Y
7 ***Hobson***	Y	Y	Y	Y	Y
8 ***Boehner***	?	Y	Y	Y	Y
9 Kaptur	Y	Y	Y	Y	Y
10 Kucinich	Y	Y	Y	Y	N
11 Jones	Y	Y	Y	?	Y
12 ***Kasich***	Y	Y	?	?	?
13 Brown	Y	Y	Y	Y	Y
14 Sawyer	Y	Y	Y	Y	Y
15 ***Pryce***	Y	Y	Y	Y	Y
16 ***Regula***	Y	Y	Y	Y	Y
17 Traficant	Y	Y	Y	Y	Y
18 ***Ney***	Y	Y	Y	Y	Y
19 ***LaTourette***	Y	Y	Y	Y	Y
OKLAHOMA					
1 ***Largent***	Y	Y	?	Y	Y
2 ***Coburn***	Y	Y	Y	Y	Y
3 ***Watkins***	Y	Y	Y	Y	Y
4 ***Watts***	Y	Y	Y	Y	Y
5 ***Istook***	Y	Y	Y	Y	Y
6 ***Lucas***	Y	Y	Y	Y	Y
OREGON					
1 Wu	Y	Y	Y	Y	Y
2 ***Walden***	Y	Y	Y	Y	Y
3 Blumenauer	Y	Y	Y	Y	Y
4 DeFazio	Y	Y	Y	Y	Y
5 Hooley	Y	Y	Y	Y	Y
PENNSYLVANIA					
1 Brady	Y	Y	Y	Y	Y
2 Fattah	Y	Y	Y	Y	Y
3 Borski	Y	Y	Y	Y	Y
4 Klink	Y	Y	Y	Y	Y
5 ***Peterson***	Y	Y	Y	Y	Y
6 Holden	Y	Y	Y	Y	Y
7 ***Weldon***	Y	Y	Y	Y	Y
8 ***Greenwood***	Y	Y	Y	Y	Y
9 ***Shuster***	Y	Y	Y	Y	Y
10 ***Sherwood***	Y	Y	Y	Y	Y
11 Kanjorski	Y	Y	Y	Y	Y
12 Murtha	Y	Y	Y	Y	Y
13 Hoeffel	Y	Y	Y	Y	Y
14 Coyne	Y	Y	Y	Y	Y
15 ***Toomey***	Y	Y	Y	Y	Y
16 ***Pitts***	Y	Y	Y	?	?
17 ***Gekas***	Y	Y	Y	Y	Y
18 Doyle	Y	Y	Y	Y	Y
19 ***Goodling***	Y	Y	+	Y	Y
20 Mascara	Y	Y	Y	Y	Y
21 ***English***	Y	Y	Y	Y	Y
RHODE ISLAND					
1 Kennedy	Y	Y	Y	Y	Y
2 Weygand	Y	Y	Y	Y	Y
SOUTH CAROLINA					
1 ***Sanford***	N	Y	Y	Y	Y
2 ***Spence***	Y	Y	?	?	?
3 ***Graham***	Y	Y	+	?	?
4 ***DeMint***	Y	Y	Y	Y	Y
5 Spratt	Y	Y	Y	Y	Y
6 Clyburn	Y	Y	Y	Y	Y
SOUTH DAKOTA					
AL ***Thune***	Y	Y	Y	Y	Y

	7	8	9	10	11
TENNESSEE					
1 ***Jenkins***	Y	Y	Y	Y	Y
2 ***Duncan***	Y	Y	Y	Y	Y
3 ***Wamp***	Y	Y	Y	Y	Y
4 ***Hilleary***	Y	Y	Y	Y	Y
5 Clement	Y	Y	Y	Y	Y
6 Gordon	Y	Y	Y	Y	Y
7 ***Bryant***	Y	Y	Y	?	Y
8 Tanner	?	?	Y	Y	Y
9 Ford	Y	Y	Y	Y	Y
TEXAS					
1 Sandlin	Y	Y	Y	Y	Y
2 Turner	Y	Y	Y	Y	Y
3 ***Johnson, Sam***	Y	Y	Y	Y	Y
4 Hall	Y	Y	Y	Y	?
5 ***Sessions***	Y	Y	Y	Y	Y
6 ***Barton***	Y	Y	Y	Y	Y
7 ***Archer***	Y	Y	Y	Y	Y
8 ***Brady***	Y	Y	Y	Y	Y
9 Lampson	Y	Y	Y	Y	Y
10 Doggett	Y	Y	Y	Y	Y
11 Edwards	Y	Y	Y	Y	Y
12 ***Granger***	Y	Y	?	?	?
13 ***Thornberry***	Y	Y	Y	Y	Y
14 ***Paul***	N	Y	N	N	Y
15 Hinojosa	Y	Y	Y	Y	Y
16 Reyes	Y	Y	Y	Y	Y
17 Stenholm	Y	Y	Y	Y	Y
18 Jackson-Lee	Y	Y	Y	Y	Y
19 ***Combest***	Y	Y	Y	Y	Y
20 Gonzalez	Y	Y	Y	Y	?
21 ***Smith***	Y	Y	Y	Y	Y
22 ***DeLay***	?	?	?	?	?
23 ***Bonilla***	Y	Y	Y	Y	Y
24 Frost	Y	Y	Y	Y	Y
25 Bentsen	Y	Y	Y	Y	Y
26 ***Armey***	Y	Y	Y	Y	Y
27 Ortiz	Y	Y	Y	Y	Y
28 Rodriguez	Y	Y	Y	Y	Y
29 Green	Y	Y	Y	Y	Y
30 Johnson, E.B.	Y	Y	Y	Y	Y
UTAH					
1 ***Hansen***	Y	Y	Y	Y	Y
2 ***Cook***	Y	Y	Y	Y	Y
3 ***Cannon***	Y	Y	Y	Y	Y
VERMONT					
AL *Sanders*	Y	Y	Y	Y	Y
VIRGINIA					
1 ***Bateman***	?	?	Y	Y	Y
2 Pickett	?	?	Y	Y	N
3 Scott	?	?	Y	Y	Y
4 Sisisky	?	?	Y	Y	Y
5 Goode	Y	Y	Y	Y	Y
6 ***Goodlatte***	Y	Y	Y	Y	Y
7 ***Bliley***	Y	Y	Y	Y	Y
8 Moran	Y	Y	Y	Y	Y
9 Boucher	Y	Y	Y	Y	Y
10 ***Wolf***	Y	Y	Y	Y	Y
11 ***Davis***	Y	Y	Y	Y	Y
WASHINGTON					
1 Inslee	Y	Y	Y	Y	Y
2 ***Metcalf***	Y	Y	Y	Y	Y
3 Baird	Y	Y	Y	Y	Y
4 ***Hastings***	Y	Y	Y	Y	Y
5 ***Nethercutt***	Y	Y	Y	Y	Y
6 Dicks	Y	Y	?	?	?
7 McDermott	+	Y	Y	Y	N
8 ***Dunn***	Y	Y	Y	Y	Y
9 Smith	Y	Y	N	Y	Y
WEST VIRGINIA					
1 Mollohan	Y	Y	Y	Y	Y
2 Wise	Y	Y	Y	Y	Y
3 Rahall	Y	Y	Y	Y	Y
WISCONSIN					
1 ***Ryan***	Y	Y	Y	Y	Y
2 Baldwin	Y	Y	Y	Y	Y
3 Kind	Y	Y	Y	Y	Y
4 Kleczka	Y	Y	Y	Y	Y
5 Barrett	Y	Y	Y	Y	Y
6 ***Petri***	Y	Y	Y	Y	Y
7 Obey	Y	Y	N	Y	Y
8 ***Green***	Y	Y	Y	Y	Y
9 ***Sensenbrenner***	Y	Y	Y	Y	Y
WYOMING					
AL ***Cubin***	Y	Y	Y	Y	Y

Southern states - Ala., Ark., Fla., Ga., Ky., La., Miss., N.C., Okla., S.C., Tenn., Texas, Va.

12. HR 440. Microloan Program Corrections/Passage. Talent, R-Mo., motion to suspend the rules and pass the bill to make several changes to the Small Business Administration's Microloan Program. The bill would clarify language to allow more intermediaries to reduce their cash reserve requirement to as little as 10 percent after five years of participating in the program with low default rates. Motion agreed to 411-4: R 213-4; D 197-0 (ND 143-0, SD 54-0); I 1-0. Feb. 9, 1999. A two-thirds majority of those present and voting (277 in this case) is required for passage under suspension of the rules.

13. HR 439. Electronic Filing for Small Businesses/Passage. Kelly, R-N.Y., motion to suspend the rules and pass the bill to provide small businesses the option of filing paperwork electronically. Motion agreed to 413-0: R 216-0; D 196-0 (ND 143-0, SD 53-0); I 1-0. Feb. 9, 1999. A two-thirds majority of those present and voting (275 in this case) is required for passage under suspension of the rules.

14. HR 435. Trade Law Corrections/Passage. Crane, R-Ill., motion to suspend the rules and pass the bill to streamline current customs laws, make technical corrections to trade laws and temporarily suspend duties for certain imported products that are not manufactured by U.S. firms. The majority of the products covered by the temporary duty suspension provisions are chemicals, including certain chemicals used to develop drugs to fight AIDS and cancer. Motion agreed to 414-1: R 216-1; D 197-0 (ND 143-0, SD 54-0); I 1-0. Feb. 9, 1999. A two-thirds majority of those present and voting (277 in this case) is required for passage under suspension of the rules.

Key

Y Voted for (yea).
\# Paired for.
\+ Announced for.
N Voted against (nay).
X Paired against.
– Announced against.
P Voted "present."
C Voted "present" to avoid possible conflict of interest.
? Did not vote or otherwise make a position known.

Democrats ***Republicans*** *Independents*

	12	13	14
ALABAMA			
1 ***Callahan***	Y	Y	Y
2 ***Everett***	Y	Y	Y
3 ***Riley***	Y	Y	Y
4 ***Aderholt***	Y	Y	Y
5 Cramer	Y	Y	Y
6 ***Bachus***	Y	Y	Y
7 Hilliard	Y	Y	Y
ALASKA			
AL ***Young***	Y	Y	Y
ARIZONA			
1 ***Salmon***	Y	Y	Y
2 Pastor	Y	Y	Y
3 ***Stump***	Y	Y	Y
4 ***Shadegg***	Y	Y	Y
5 ***Kolbe***	Y	Y	Y
6 ***Hayworth***	Y	Y	Y
ARKANSAS			
1 Berry	Y	Y	Y
2 Snyder	Y	Y	Y
3 ***Hutchinson***	Y	Y	Y
4 ***Dickey***	Y	Y	Y
CALIFORNIA			
1 Thompson	Y	Y	Y
2 ***Herger***	Y	Y	Y
3 ***Ose***	Y	Y	Y
4 ***Doolittle***	Y	Y	Y
5 Matsui	Y	Y	Y
6 Woolsey	Y	Y	Y
7 Miller, George	?	?	?
8 Pelosi	Y	Y	Y
9 Lee	Y	Y	Y
10 Tauscher	Y	Y	Y
11 ***Pombo***	Y	Y	Y
12 Lantos	Y	Y	Y
13 Stark	Y	Y	Y
14 Eshoo	Y	Y	Y
15 ***Campbell***	Y	Y	Y
16 Lofgren	?	?	?
17 Farr	Y	Y	Y
18 Condit	Y	Y	Y
19 ***Radanovich***	Y	Y	Y
20 Dooley	Y	Y	Y
21 ***Thomas***	Y	Y	Y
22 Capps	Y	Y	Y
23 ***Gallegly***	Y	Y	Y
24 Sherman	Y	Y	Y
25 ***McKeon***	Y	Y	Y
26 Berman	Y	Y	Y
27 ***Rogan***	Y	Y	Y
28 ***Dreier***	Y	Y	Y
29 Waxman	Y	Y	Y
30 Becerra	Y	Y	Y
31 Martinez	Y	Y	Y
32 Dixon	Y	Y	Y
33 Roybal-Allard	Y	Y	Y
34 Napolitano	Y	Y	Y
35 Waters	Y	Y	Y
36 ***Kuykendall***	Y	Y	Y
37 Millender-McD.	Y	Y	Y
38 ***Horn***	Y	Y	Y
39 ***Royce***	N	Y	Y

	12	13	14
40 ***Lewis***	Y	Y	Y
41 ***Miller, Gary***	Y	Y	Y
42 Brown	Y	Y	Y
43 ***Calvert***	Y	Y	Y
44 ***Bono***	Y	Y	Y
45 ***Rohrabacher***	Y	Y	Y
46 Sanchez	Y	Y	Y
47 ***Cox***	Y	Y	Y
48 ***Packard***	Y	Y	Y
49 ***Bilbray***	Y	Y	Y
50 Filner	Y	Y	Y
51 ***Cunningham***	Y	Y	Y
52 ***Hunter***	Y	Y	Y
COLORADO			
1 DeGette	Y	Y	Y
2 Udall	Y	Y	Y
3 ***McInnis***	Y	Y	Y
4 ***Schaffer***	Y	Y	Y
5 ***Hefley***	Y	Y	Y
6 ***Tancredo***	Y	Y	Y
CONNECTICUT			
1 Larson	Y	Y	Y
2 Gejdenson	Y	Y	Y
3 DeLauro	Y	Y	Y
4 ***Shays***	Y	Y	Y
5 Maloney	Y	Y	Y
6 ***Johnson***	Y	Y	Y
DELAWARE			
AL ***Castle***	Y	Y	Y
FLORIDA			
1 ***Scarborough***	Y	Y	Y
2 Boyd	Y	Y	Y
3 Brown	Y	Y	Y
4 ***Fowler***	Y	Y	Y
5 Thurman	Y	Y	Y
6 ***Stearns***	Y	Y	Y
7 ***Mica***	Y	Y	Y
8 ***McCollum***	Y	Y	Y
9 ***Bilirakis***	Y	Y	Y
10 ***Young***	Y	Y	Y
11 Davis	Y	Y	Y
12 ***Canady***	Y	Y	Y
13 ***Miller***	Y	Y	Y
14 ***Goss***	Y	Y	Y
15 ***Weldon***	Y	Y	Y
16 ***Foley***	Y	Y	Y
17 Meek	Y	Y	Y
18 ***Ros-Lehtinen***	Y	Y	Y
19 Wexler	Y	Y	Y
20 Deutsch	Y	?	Y
21 ***Diaz-Balart***	Y	Y	Y
22 ***Shaw***	Y	Y	Y
23 Hastings	Y	Y	Y
GEORGIA			
1 ***Kingston***	Y	Y	Y
2 Bishop	Y	Y	Y
3 ***Collins***	Y	Y	Y
4 McKinney	Y	Y	Y
5 Lewis	Y	Y	Y
6 Vacant			
7 ***Barr***	Y	Y	N
8 ***Chambliss***	Y	Y	Y
9 ***Deal***	Y	Y	Y
10 ***Norwood***	Y	Y	Y
11 ***Linder***	Y	Y	Y
HAWAII			
1 Abercrombie	Y	Y	Y
2 Mink	Y	Y	Y
IDAHO			
1 ***Chenoweth***	N	Y	Y
2 ***Simpson***	Y	Y	Y
ILLINOIS			
1 Rush	?	?	?
2 Jackson	Y	Y	Y
3 Lipinski	Y	Y	Y
4 Gutierrez	Y	Y	Y
5 Blagojevich	Y	Y	Y
6 ***Hyde***	Y	Y	Y
7 Davis	Y	Y	Y
8 ***Crane***	Y	Y	Y
9 Schakowsky	Y	Y	Y
10 ***Porter***	Y	Y	Y
11 ***Weller***	Y	Y	?
12 Costello	Y	Y	Y
13 ***Biggert***	Y	Y	Y
14 ***Hastert***			

ND Northern Democrats SD Southern Democrats

	12	13	14
15 ***Ewing***	Y	Y	Y
16 ***Manzullo***	Y	Y	Y
17 Evans	Y	Y	Y
18 ***LaHood***	Y	Y	Y
19 Phelps	Y	Y	Y
20 ***Shimkus***	Y	Y	Y
INDIANA			
1 Visclosky	Y	Y	Y
2 ***McIntosh***	?	?	?
3 Roemer	Y	Y	Y
4 ***Souder***	Y	Y	Y
5 ***Buyer***	Y	Y	Y
6 ***Burton***	Y	Y	Y
7 ***Pease***	Y	Y	Y
8 ***Hostettler***	Y	Y	Y
9 Hill	Y	Y	Y
10 Carson	+	+	+
IOWA			
1 ***Leach***	Y	Y	Y
2 ***Nussle***	Y	?	Y
3 Boswell	Y	Y	Y
4 ***Ganske***	Y	Y	Y
5 ***Latham***	Y	Y	Y
KANSAS			
1 ***Moran***	Y	Y	Y
2 ***Ryun***	Y	Y	Y
3 Moore	Y	Y	Y
4 ***Tiahrt***	Y	Y	Y
KENTUCKY			
1 ***Whitfield***	Y	Y	Y
2 ***Lewis***	Y	Y	Y
3 ***Northup***	Y	Y	Y
4 Lucas	Y	Y	Y
5 ***Rogers***	Y	Y	Y
6 ***Fletcher***	Y	Y	Y
LOUISIANA			
1 ***Livingston***	Y	Y	Y
2 Jefferson	Y	Y	Y
3 ***Tauzin***	Y	Y	Y
4 ***McCrery***	Y	Y	Y
5 ***Cooksey***	Y	Y	Y
6 ***Baker***	Y	Y	Y
7 John	Y	Y	Y
MAINE			
1 Allen	Y	Y	Y
2 Baldacci	Y	Y	Y
MARYLAND			
1 ***Gilchrest***	Y	Y	Y
2 ***Ehrlich***	Y	Y	Y
3 Cardin	Y	Y	Y
4 Wynn	Y	Y	Y
5 Hoyer	Y	Y	Y
6 ***Bartlett***	Y	Y	Y
7 Cummings	Y	Y	Y
8 ***Morella***	Y	Y	Y
MASSACHUSETTS			
1 Olver	Y	Y	Y
2 Neal	Y	Y	?
3 McGovern	Y	Y	Y
4 Frank	Y	Y	Y
5 Meehan	Y	Y	Y
6 Tierney	Y	Y	Y
7 Markey	Y	Y	Y
8 Capuano	Y	Y	Y
9 Moakley	Y	Y	Y
10 Delahunt	Y	Y	Y
MICHIGAN			
1 Stupak	Y	Y	Y
2 ***Hoekstra***	Y	Y	Y
3 ***Ehlers***	Y	Y	Y
4 ***Camp***	Y	Y	Y
5 Barcia	Y	Y	Y
6 ***Upton***	Y	Y	Y
7 ***Smith***	Y	Y	Y
8 Stabenow	Y	Y	Y
9 Kildee	Y	Y	Y
10 Bonior	Y	Y	Y
11 ***Knollenberg***	Y	Y	Y
12 Levin	Y	Y	Y
13 Rivers	Y	Y	Y
14 Conyers	Y	Y	Y
15 Kilpatrick	Y	Y	Y
16 Dingell	Y	Y	Y

	12	13	14
MINNESOTA			
1 ***Gutknecht***	Y	Y	Y
2 Minge	Y	Y	Y
3 ***Ramstad***	Y	Y	Y
4 Vento	Y	Y	Y
5 Sabo	Y	Y	Y
6 Luther	Y	Y	Y
7 Peterson	Y	Y	Y
8 Oberstar	Y	Y	Y
MISSISSIPPI			
1 ***Wicker***	Y	Y	Y
2 Thompson	Y	Y	Y
3 ***Pickering***	Y	Y	Y
4 Shows	Y	Y	Y
5 Taylor	Y	Y	Y
MISSOURI			
1 Clay	Y	Y	Y
2 ***Talent***	Y	Y	Y
3 Gephardt	?	?	?
4 Skelton	Y	Y	Y
5 McCarthy	Y	Y	Y
6 Danner	Y	Y	Y
7 ***Blunt***	Y	Y	Y
8 ***Emerson***	Y	Y	Y
9 ***Hulshof***	Y	Y	Y
MONTANA			
AL ***Hill***	Y	Y	Y
NEBRASKA			
1 ***Bereuter***	Y	Y	Y
2 ***Terry***	Y	Y	Y
3 ***Barrett***	Y	Y	Y
NEVADA			
1 Berkley	Y	Y	Y
2 ***Gibbons***	Y	Y	Y
NEW HAMPSHIRE			
1 ***Sununu***	Y	Y	Y
2 ***Bass***	Y	Y	Y
NEW JERSEY			
1 Andrews	Y	Y	Y
2 ***LoBiondo***	Y	Y	Y
3 ***Saxton***	Y	Y	Y
4 ***Smith***	Y	Y	Y
5 ***Roukema***	Y	Y	Y
6 Pallone	+	+	Y
7 ***Franks***	Y	Y	Y
8 Pascrell	Y	Y	Y
9 Rothman	Y	Y	Y
10 Payne	Y	Y	Y
11 ***Frelinghuysen***	Y	Y	Y
12 Holt	Y	Y	Y
13 Menendez	Y	Y	Y
NEW MEXICO			
1 ***Wilson***	Y	Y	Y
2 ***Skeen***	Y	Y	Y
3 Udall	Y	Y	Y
NEW YORK			
1 ***Forbes***	Y	Y	Y
2 ***Lazio***	Y	Y	Y
3 ***King***	Y	Y	Y
4 McCarthy	Y	Y	Y
5 Ackerman	?	?	?
6 Meeks	Y	Y	Y
7 Crowley	Y	Y	Y
8 Nadler	?	?	?
9 Weiner	Y	Y	Y
10 Towns	Y	Y	Y
11 Owens	Y	Y	Y
12 Velázquez	Y	Y	Y
13 ***Fossella***	Y	Y	Y
14 Maloney	?	?	?
15 Rangel	Y	Y	Y
16 Serrano	Y	Y	Y
17 Engel	Y	Y	Y
18 Lowey	Y	Y	Y
19 ***Kelly***	Y	Y	Y
20 ***Gilman***	Y	Y	Y
21 McNulty	Y	Y	Y
22 ***Sweeney***	Y	Y	Y
23 ***Boehlert***	Y	Y	Y
24 ***McHugh***	Y	Y	Y
25 ***Walsh***	Y	Y	Y
26 Hinchey	Y	Y	Y
27 ***Reynolds***	Y	+	Y
28 Slaughter	Y	Y	Y
29 LaFalce	Y	Y	Y

	12	13	14
30 ***Quinn***	Y	Y	Y
31 ***Houghton***	Y	Y	Y
NORTH CAROLINA			
1 Clayton	Y	Y	Y
2 Etheridge	Y	Y	Y
3 ***Jones***	Y	Y	Y
4 Price	Y	Y	Y
5 ***Burr***	Y	Y	Y
6 ***Coble***	Y	Y	Y
7 McIntyre	Y	Y	Y
8 ***Hayes***	Y	Y	Y
9 ***Myrick***	Y	Y	Y
10 ***Ballenger***	Y	Y	Y
11 ***Taylor***	Y	Y	Y
12 Watt	Y	Y	Y
NORTH DAKOTA			
AL Pomeroy	Y	Y	Y
OHIO			
1 ***Chabot***	Y	Y	Y
2 ***Portman***	Y	Y	Y
3 Hall	Y	Y	Y
4 ***Oxley***	Y	Y	Y
5 ***Gillmor***	Y	Y	Y
6 Strickland	Y	Y	Y
7 ***Hobson***	Y	Y	Y
8 ***Boehner***	Y	Y	Y
9 Kaptur	Y	Y	Y
10 Kucinich	Y	Y	Y
11 Jones	Y	Y	Y
12 ***Kasich***	Y	Y	Y
13 Brown	Y	Y	Y
14 Sawyer	Y	Y	Y
15 ***Pryce***	Y	Y	Y
16 ***Regula***	Y	Y	Y
17 Traficant	Y	Y	Y
18 ***Ney***	Y	Y	Y
19 ***LaTourette***	Y	Y	Y
OKLAHOMA			
1 ***Largent***	Y	Y	Y
2 ***Coburn***	Y	Y	Y
3 ***Watkins***	Y	Y	Y
4 ***Watts***	Y	Y	Y
5 ***Istook***	Y	Y	Y
6 ***Lucas***	Y	Y	Y
OREGON			
1 Wu	Y	Y	Y
2 ***Walden***	Y	Y	Y
3 Blumenauer	Y	Y	Y
4 DeFazio	?	?	?
5 Hooley	Y	Y	Y
PENNSYLVANIA			
1 Brady	Y	Y	Y
2 Fattah	Y	Y	Y
3 Borski	Y	Y	Y
4 Klink	Y	Y	Y
5 ***Peterson***	Y	Y	Y
6 Holden	Y	Y	Y
7 ***Weldon***	Y	Y	Y
8 ***Greenwood***	Y	Y	Y
9 ***Shuster***	Y	Y	Y
10 ***Sherwood***	Y	Y	Y
11 Kanjorski	Y	Y	Y
12 Murtha	Y	Y	Y
13 Hoeffel	Y	Y	Y
14 Coyne	Y	Y	Y
15 ***Toomey***	Y	Y	Y
16 ***Pitts***	Y	Y	Y
17 ***Gekas***	Y	Y	Y
18 Doyle	Y	Y	Y
19 ***Goodling***	Y	Y	Y
20 Mascara	Y	Y	Y
21 ***English***	Y	Y	Y
RHODE ISLAND			
1 Kennedy	Y	Y	Y
2 Weygand	+	+	+
SOUTH CAROLINA			
1 ***Sanford***	N	Y	Y
2 ***Spence***	Y	Y	Y
3 ***Graham***	Y	Y	Y
4 ***DeMint***	Y	Y	Y
5 Spratt	?	?	?
6 Clyburn	Y	Y	Y
SOUTH DAKOTA			
AL ***Thune***	Y	Y	Y

	12	13	14
TENNESSEE			
1 ***Jenkins***	?	Y	Y
2 ***Duncan***	Y	Y	Y
3 ***Wamp***	Y	Y	Y
4 ***Hilleary***	Y	Y	Y
5 Clement	Y	Y	Y
6 Gordon	Y	Y	Y
7 ***Bryant***	Y	Y	Y
8 Tanner	Y	Y	Y
9 Ford	Y	Y	Y
TEXAS			
1 Sandlin	Y	Y	Y
2 Turner	Y	Y	Y
3 ***Johnson, Sam***	Y	Y	Y
4 Hall	Y	Y	Y
5 ***Sessions***	Y	Y	Y
6 ***Barton***	Y	Y	Y
7 ***Archer***	Y	Y	Y
8 ***Brady***	Y	Y	Y
9 Lampson	Y	Y	Y
10 Doggett	Y	Y	Y
11 Edwards	Y	Y	Y
12 ***Granger***	?	?	?
13 ***Thornberry***	?	?	?
14 ***Paul***	N	Y	Y
15 Hinojosa	Y	Y	Y
16 Reyes	Y	Y	Y
17 Stenholm	Y	Y	Y
18 Jackson-Lee	Y	Y	Y
19 ***Combest***	Y	Y	Y
20 Gonzalez	Y	Y	Y
21 ***Smith***	Y	Y	Y
22 ***DeLay***	Y	Y	Y
23 ***Bonilla***	Y	Y	Y
24 Frost	Y	Y	Y
25 Bentsen	Y	Y	Y
26 ***Armey***	Y	Y	Y
27 Ortiz	Y	Y	Y
28 Rodriguez	Y	Y	Y
29 Green	Y	Y	Y
30 Johnson, E.B.	Y	Y	Y
UTAH			
1 ***Hansen***	Y	Y	Y
2 ***Cook***	Y	Y	Y
3 ***Cannon***	Y	Y	Y
VERMONT			
AL *Sanders*	Y	Y	Y
VIRGINIA			
1 ***Bateman***	Y	Y	Y
2 Pickett	Y	Y	Y
3 Scott	Y	Y	Y
4 Sisisky	Y	Y	Y
5 Goode	Y	Y	Y
6 ***Goodlatte***	Y	Y	Y
7 ***Bliley***	Y	Y	Y
8 Moran	Y	Y	Y
9 Boucher	Y	Y	Y
10 ***Wolf***	Y	Y	Y
11 ***Davis***	Y	Y	Y
WASHINGTON			
1 Inslee	Y	Y	Y
2 ***Metcalf***	Y	Y	Y
3 Baird	Y	Y	Y
4 ***Hastings***	Y	Y	Y
5 ***Nethercutt***	Y	Y	Y
6 Dicks	Y	Y	Y
7 McDermott	Y	Y	Y
8 ***Dunn***	Y	Y	Y
9 Smith	Y	Y	Y
WEST VIRGINIA			
1 Mollohan	Y	Y	Y
2 Wise	?	?	?
3 Rahall	Y	Y	Y
WISCONSIN			
1 ***Ryan***	Y	Y	Y
2 Baldwin	Y	Y	Y
3 Kind	Y	Y	Y
4 Kleczka	Y	Y	Y
5 Barrett	?	?	?
6 ***Petri***	Y	Y	Y
7 Obey	Y	Y	Y
8 ***Green***	Y	Y	Y
9 ***Sensenbrenner***	Y	Y	Y
WYOMING			
AL ***Cubin***	Y	Y	Y

Southern states - Ala., Ark., Fla., Ga., Ky., La., Miss., N.C., Okla., S.C., Tenn., Texas, Va.

15. HR 350. Federal Mandates on the Private Sector/Modify Point of Order. Boehlert, R-N.Y., amendment to modify the effect of the new point of order contained in the bill. Rather than triggering a vote on whether to proceed on the legislation, as in the bill, the point of order would provide an additional 20 minutes to debate the private sector mandates of the legislation. Rejected 210-216: R 34-187; D 175-29 (ND 141-9, SD 34-20); I 1-0. Feb. 10, 1999.

16. HR 350. Federal Mandates on the Private Sector/Public Health, Safety and Environment Protections. Waxman, D-Calif., amendment to permit points of order against provisions in legislation that would remove or make less stringent private sector mandates established to protect public health, safety and the environment. Rejected 203-216: R 19-196; D 183-20 (ND 144-5, SD 39-15); I 1-0. Feb. 10, 1999.

17. HR 350. Federal Mandates on the Private Sector/Passage. Passage of the bill to place certain new procedural limitations on legislation imposing federal mandates on the private sector. The bill would provide for points of order in the House — to be resolved by a majority vote — to block consideration of legislation that contains private sector mandates in excess of $100 million. Passed 274-149: R 207-11; D 67-137 (ND 34-117, SD 33-20); I 0-1. Feb. 10, 1999. A "nay" was a vote in support of the president's position.

18. S Con Res 7. Honor King Hussein of Jordan/Adoption. Adoption of the concurrent resolution to honor King Hussein ibn Talal al-Hashem, the recently deceased monarch of Jordan. The resolution extends condolences to the family of King Hussein, expresses admiration and appreciation for his leadership and support for the new government of Jordan, and reaffirms the U.S. commitment to strengthen the relationship between the United States and Jordan. Adopted 420-0: R 216-0; D 203-0 (ND 150-0, SD 53-0); I 1-0. Feb. 10, 1999.

19. HR 391. Small Business Paperwork Reduction Act Amendments/Waiver Replacement. Kucinich, D-Ohio, amendment to replace the bill's civil fine waiver with a requirement that agencies develop policies that reduce or waive penalties against first-time violators. Rejected 210-214: R 13-204; D 196-10 (ND 149-2, SD 47-8); I 1-0. Feb. 11, 1999.

20. HR 391. Small Businesses' Paperwork Reduction Act Amendments/Passage. Passage of the bill that waives civil fines on small businesses for first-time paperwork violations, with exceptions in certain cases such as violations that cause serious harm to public health and safety. Passed 274-151: R 210-7; D 64-143 (ND 37-115, SD 27-28); I 0-1. Feb. 11, 1999. A "nay" was a vote in support of the president's position.

21. HR 437. Chief Financial Officer in Office of the President/Passage. Passage of the bill to require the president to appoint a chief financial officer (CFO) within the Executive Office of the President. The measure permits the president to establish the position within any office of the Executive Office, including the Office of Administration. Passed 413-2: R 210-2; D 203-0 (ND 150-0, SD 53-0); I 0-0. Feb. 11, 1999.

Key

- Y Voted for (yea).
- # Paired for.
- + Announced for.
- N Voted against (nay).
- X Paired against.
- – Announced against.
- P Voted "present."
- C Voted "present" to avoid possible conflict of interest.
- ? Did not vote or otherwise make a position known.

•

Democrats ***Republicans***
Independents

	15	16	17	18	19	20	21
ALABAMA							
1 ***Callahan***	N	N	Y	Y	N	Y	Y
2 ***Everett***	N	N	Y	Y	N	Y	?
3 ***Riley***	N	N	Y	Y	N	Y	Y
4 ***Aderholt***	N	N	Y	Y	N	Y	Y
5 Cramer	N	N	Y	Y	N	Y	Y
6 ***Bachus***	N	?	Y	Y	N	Y	Y
7 Hilliard	Y	Y	N	Y	Y	N	Y
ALASKA							
AL ***Young***	N	N	Y	Y	N	Y	Y
ARIZONA							
1 ***Salmon***	N	N	Y	Y	N	Y	Y
2 Pastor	Y	Y	N	Y	Y	N	Y
3 ***Stump***	N	N	Y	Y	N	Y	Y
4 ***Shadegg***	N	N	Y	Y	N	Y	Y
5 ***Kolbe***	N	N	Y	Y	?	?	?
6 ***Hayworth***	N	N	Y	Y	N	Y	Y
ARKANSAS							
1 Berry	N	N	Y	Y	Y	Y	Y
2 Snyder	Y	Y	Y	Y	Y	N	Y
3 ***Hutchinson***	N	N	Y	Y	N	Y	Y
4 ***Dickey***	N	N	Y	Y	N	Y	Y
CALIFORNIA							
1 Thompson	Y	Y	Y	Y	Y	N	Y
2 ***Herger***	N	N	Y	Y	?	Y	Y
3 ***Ose***	N	N	Y	Y	N	Y	Y
4 ***Doolittle***	N	N	Y	Y	N	Y	Y
5 Matsui	Y	Y	N	Y	Y	N	Y
6 Woolsey	Y	Y	N	Y	Y	N	Y
7 Miller, George	Y	Y	N	?	Y	N	Y
8 Pelosi	Y	Y	N	Y	Y	N	Y
9 Lee	Y	Y	N	Y	Y	N	Y
10 Tauscher	Y	Y	Y	Y	Y	Y	Y
11 ***Pombo***	N	N	Y	Y	N	Y	Y
12 Lantos	Y	Y	N	Y	?	?	?
13 Stark	Y	Y	N	Y	Y	N	Y
14 Eshoo	Y	Y	N	Y	Y	N	Y
15 ***Campbell***	N	Y	Y	Y	N	N	Y
16 Lofgren	?	?	?	?	?	?	?
17 Farr	Y	Y	N	Y	Y	N	Y
18 Condit	N	N	Y	Y	Y	Y	Y
19 ***Radanovich***	N	N	Y	Y	N	Y	Y
20 Dooley	N	Y	Y	Y	Y	Y	Y
21 ***Thomas***	N	N	Y	Y	N	Y	Y
22 Capps	Y	Y	Y	Y	Y	Y	Y
23 ***Gallegly***	N	N	Y	Y	N	Y	Y
24 Sherman	Y	Y	N	Y	Y	N	Y
25 ***McKeon***	N	N	Y	Y	N	Y	Y
26 Berman	Y	Y	N	Y	Y	N	Y
27 ***Rogan***	N	N	Y	Y	N	Y	Y
28 ***Dreier***	N	N	Y	Y	N	Y	Y
29 Waxman	Y	Y	N	Y	Y	N	Y
30 Becerra	Y	Y	N	Y	Y	N	Y
31 Martinez	Y	Y	N	Y	Y	N	Y
32 Dixon	Y	Y	N	Y	Y	N	Y
33 Roybal-Allard	Y	Y	N	Y	Y	N	Y
34 Napolitano	Y	Y	N	Y	Y	Y	Y
35 Waters	Y	Y	N	Y	Y	N	Y
36 ***Kuykendall***	N	N	Y	Y	N	Y	Y
37 Millender-McD.	Y	Y	N	Y	Y	N	Y
38 ***Horn***	Y	Y	N	Y	N	Y	Y
39 ***Royce***	N	N	Y	Y	N	Y	N
40 ***Lewis***	N	N	Y	Y	N	Y	Y
41 ***Miller, Gary***	N	N	Y	Y	N	Y	Y
42 Brown	Y	Y	N	Y	Y	N	Y
43 ***Calvert***	N	N	Y	Y	N	Y	Y
44 ***Bono***	N	N	Y	Y	N	Y	?
45 ***Rohrabacher***	N	N	Y	Y	N	Y	Y
46 Sanchez	Y	Y	Y	Y	Y	Y	Y
47 ***Cox***	N	N	+	Y	N	Y	Y
48 ***Packard***	N	N	Y	Y	N	Y	Y
49 ***Bilbray***	Y	Y	N	Y	Y	Y	Y
50 Filner	Y	Y	N	Y	Y	N	Y
51 ***Cunningham***	N	N	Y	Y	N	Y	Y
52 ***Hunter***	N	N	Y	Y	N	Y	Y
COLORADO							
1 DeGette	Y	Y	N	Y	Y	N	Y
2 Udall	Y	Y	N	Y	Y	N	Y
3 ***McInnis***	N	N	Y	Y	N	Y	Y
4 ***Schaffer***	N	N	Y	Y	N	Y	Y
5 ***Hefley***	N	N	Y	Y	N	Y	Y
6 ***Tancredo***	N	N	Y	Y	N	Y	Y
CONNECTICUT							
1 Larson	Y	Y	N	Y	Y	N	Y
2 Gejdenson	Y	Y	N	Y	?	N	Y
3 DeLauro	Y	Y	N	Y	Y	N	Y
4 ***Shays***	Y	Y	N	Y	Y	N	Y
5 Maloney	Y	Y	Y	Y	Y	N	Y
6 ***Johnson***	Y	Y	Y	Y	Y	Y	Y
DELAWARE							
AL ***Castle***	Y	Y	Y	Y	N	Y	Y
FLORIDA							
1 ***Scarborough***	Y	Y	Y	Y	N	Y	Y
2 Boyd	N	Y	Y	Y	N	Y	Y
3 Brown	Y	Y	N	Y	Y	N	Y
4 ***Fowler***	N	N	Y	Y	N	Y	Y
5 Thurman	Y	Y	Y	Y	Y	N	Y
6 ***Stearns***	N	N	Y	Y	N	Y	Y
7 ***Mica***	N	N	Y	Y	N	Y	+
8 ***McCollum***	N	N	Y	Y	N	Y	Y
9 ***Bilirakis***	N	N	Y	Y	N	Y	Y
10 ***Young***	N	N	Y	Y	N	Y	Y
11 Davis	N	Y	Y	Y	Y	Y	Y
12 ***Canady***	N	N	Y	Y	N	Y	Y
13 ***Miller***	N	N	Y	Y	N	Y	Y
14 ***Goss***	N	N	Y	Y	N	Y	Y
15 ***Weldon***	N	N	Y	Y	N	Y	Y
16 ***Foley***	N	N	Y	Y	N	Y	Y
17 Meek	Y	Y	N	Y	Y	N	?
18 ***Ros-Lehtinen***	N	N	N	Y	Y	N	Y
19 Wexler	Y	Y	N	Y	Y	N	Y
20 Deutsch	Y	Y	Y	Y	Y	N	Y
21 ***Diaz-Balart***	N	N	N	Y	Y	Y	Y
22 ***Shaw***	N	N	Y	Y	N	Y	Y
23 Hastings	Y	Y	N	Y	Y	N	Y
GEORGIA							
1 ***Kingston***	N	N	Y	Y	N	Y	?
2 Bishop	N	Y	Y	Y	Y	Y	Y
3 ***Collins***	N	N	Y	Y	N	Y	Y
4 McKinney	Y	Y	N	Y	Y	N	Y
5 Lewis	Y	Y	N	Y	Y	N	Y
6 Vacant							
7 ***Barr***	N	N	Y	Y	N	Y	Y
8 ***Chambliss***	N	N	Y	Y	N	Y	Y
9 ***Deal***	N	N	Y	Y	N	Y	Y
10 ***Norwood***	N	N	Y	Y	N	Y	Y
11 ***Linder***	N	N	Y	Y	N	Y	Y
HAWAII							
1 Abercrombie	Y	Y	N	Y	Y	N	Y
2 Mink	Y	Y	N	Y	Y	N	Y
IDAHO							
1 ***Chenoweth***	N	N	Y	Y	N	Y	Y
2 ***Simpson***	N	N	Y	Y	N	Y	Y
ILLINOIS							
1 Rush	?	?	?	?	?	?	?
2 Jackson	Y	Y	N	Y	Y	N	Y
3 Lipinski	Y	Y	Y	Y	Y	N	Y
4 Gutierrez	Y	Y	N	Y	Y	N	Y
5 Blagojevich	Y	Y	N	Y	Y	N	Y
6 ***Hyde***	N	N	Y	Y	?	?	Y
7 Davis	Y	Y	N	Y	Y	N	Y
8 ***Crane***	N	N	Y	Y	N	Y	Y
9 Schakowsky	Y	Y	N	Y	Y	N	Y
10 ***Porter***	Y	N	Y	Y	N	Y	Y
11 ***Weller***	N	N	Y	Y	N	Y	Y
12 Costello	Y	Y	Y	Y	Y	N	Y
13 ***Biggert***	N	N	Y	Y	N	Y	Y
14 ***Hastert***	N		Y		N		

ND Northern Democrats SD Southern Democrats

	15	16	17	18	19	20	21
15 ***Ewing***	?	N	Y	Y	N	Y	Y
16 ***Manzullo***	N	N	Y	Y	N	Y	Y
17 Evans	Y	Y	N	Y	Y	N	Y
18 ***LaHood***	Y	N	Y	Y	N	Y	Y
19 Phelps	Y	Y	N	Y	Y	N	Y
20 ***Shimkus***	N	N	Y	Y	N	Y	Y
INDIANA							
1 Visclosky	Y	Y	N	Y	Y	N	Y
2 ***McIntosh***	N	N	Y	Y	N	Y	Y
3 Roemer	N	Y	Y	Y	Y	Y	Y
4 ***Souder***	N	N	Y	Y	N	Y	Y
5 ***Buyer***	N	N	Y	Y	?	?	?
6 ***Burton***	N	N	Y	Y	N	Y	Y
7 ***Pease***	N	N	Y	Y	N	Y	Y
8 ***Hostettler***	N	N	Y	Y	N	Y	Y
9 Hill	N	Y	Y	Y	Y	Y	Y
10 Carson	+	+	−	+	Y	N	Y
IOWA							
1 ***Leach***	Y	Y	Y	Y	N	Y	Y
2 ***Nussle***	N	N	Y	Y	N	Y	Y
3 Boswell	Y	Y	Y	Y	Y	Y	Y
4 ***Ganske***	Y	N	Y	Y	N	Y	Y
5 ***Latham***	N	N	Y	Y	N	Y	Y
KANSAS							
1 ***Moran***	N	N	Y	Y	N	Y	Y
2 ***Ryun***	N	N	Y	Y	N	Y	Y
3 Moore	Y	Y	Y	Y	Y	Y	Y
4 ***Tiahrt***	N	N	Y	Y	N	Y	Y
KENTUCKY							
1 ***Whitfield***	N	N	Y	Y	N	Y	Y
2 ***Lewis***	N	N	Y	Y	N	Y	Y
3 ***Northup***	N	N	Y	Y	N	Y	Y
4 Lucas	N	N	Y	Y	Y	Y	Y
5 ***Rogers***	N	N	Y	Y	N	Y	Y
6 ***Fletcher***	N	N	Y	Y	N	Y	Y
LOUISIANA							
1 ***Livingston***	N	N	Y	?	N	Y	Y
2 Jefferson	Y	Y	N	Y	Y	N	Y
3 ***Tauzin***	N	N	Y	Y	N	Y	Y
4 ***McCrery***	N	N	Y	Y	N	Y	Y
5 ***Cooksey***	N	N	Y	Y	N	Y	Y
6 ***Baker***	N	N	Y	Y	N	Y	Y
7 John	N	N	Y	Y	N	Y	Y
MAINE							
1 Allen	Y	Y	N	Y	Y	N	Y
2 Baldacci	Y	Y	N	Y	Y	N	Y
MARYLAND							
1 ***Gilchrest***	Y	Y	N	Y	N	Y	Y
2 ***Ehrlich***	N	N	Y	Y	N	Y	?
3 Cardin	Y	Y	N	Y	Y	Y	Y
4 Wynn	Y	Y	N	Y	Y	N	Y
5 Hoyer	Y	Y	N	Y	Y	N	Y
6 ***Bartlett***	N	N	Y	Y	N	Y	Y
7 Cummings	Y	Y	N	Y	Y	N	Y
8 ***Morella***	Y	Y	N	Y	Y	N	Y
MASSACHUSETTS							
1 Olver	Y	Y	N	Y	Y	N	Y
2 Neal	Y	Y	N	Y	Y	N	Y
3 McGovern	Y	Y	N	Y	Y	N	Y
4 Frank	Y	Y	N	Y	Y	N	Y
5 Meehan	Y	Y	N	Y	Y	N	Y
6 Tierney	Y	Y	N	Y	Y	N	Y
7 Markey	Y	Y	N	Y	Y	N	Y
8 Capuano	Y	Y	N	Y	Y	N	Y
9 Moakley	Y	Y	N	Y	Y	N	Y
10 Delahunt	Y	Y	N	Y	Y	Y	Y
MICHIGAN							
1 Stupak	Y	Y	N	Y	Y	N	Y
2 ***Hoekstra***	N	N	Y	Y	N	Y	Y
3 ***Ehlers***	Y	N	Y	Y	N	Y	Y
4 ***Camp***	N	N	Y	Y	N	Y	Y
5 Barcia	Y	Y	Y	Y	Y	Y	Y
6 ***Upton***	Y	N	Y	Y	N	Y	Y
7 ***Smith***	Y	N	?	Y	N	Y	Y
8 Stabenow	Y	Y	Y	Y	Y	Y	Y
9 Kildee	Y	Y	N	Y	Y	N	Y
10 Bonior	Y	Y	N	Y	Y	N	Y
11 ***Knollenberg***	N	N	Y	Y	N	Y	Y
12 Levin	Y	Y	N	Y	Y	N	Y
13 Rivers	Y	Y	Y	Y	Y	Y	Y
14 Conyers	?	Y	N	Y	Y	N	Y
15 Kilpatrick	Y	Y	N	Y	Y	N	Y
16 Dingell	Y	Y	N	Y	Y	N	Y
MINNESOTA							
1 ***Gutknecht***	N	N	Y	Y	N	Y	Y
2 Minge	Y	Y	Y	Y	Y	Y	Y
3 ***Ramstad***	Y	Y	Y	Y	N	Y	Y
4 Vento	Y	Y	N	Y	Y	N	Y
5 Sabo	Y	Y	N	Y	Y	N	Y
6 Luther	Y	Y	Y	Y	Y	Y	Y
7 Peterson	N	Y	Y	Y	Y	Y	Y
8 Oberstar	Y	Y	N	Y	Y	N	Y
MISSISSIPPI							
1 ***Wicker***	N	N	Y	Y	N	Y	Y
2 Thompson	Y	Y	N	Y	Y	N	Y
3 ***Pickering***	N	N	Y	Y	N	Y	Y
4 Shows	N	Y	Y	Y	Y	Y	Y
5 Taylor	Y	Y	Y	?	N	Y	?
MISSOURI							
1 Clay	Y	Y	N	Y	Y	N	Y
2 ***Talent***	N	N	Y	Y	N	Y	Y
3 Gephardt	Y	Y	N	Y	Y	N	Y
4 Skelton	N	Y	Y	Y	Y	Y	Y
5 McCarthy	Y	Y	Y	Y	Y	Y	Y
6 Danner	N	N	Y	Y	N	Y	Y
7 ***Blunt***	N	N	Y	Y	N	Y	Y
8 ***Emerson***	N	N	Y	Y	N	Y	Y
9 ***Hulshof***	N	N	Y	Y	N	Y	Y
MONTANA							
AL ***Hill***	N	N	Y	Y	N	Y	Y
NEBRASKA							
1 ***Bereuter***	Y	N	Y	Y	N	Y	Y
2 ***Terry***	N	N	Y	Y	N	Y	Y
3 ***Barrett***	N	N	Y	Y	N	Y	Y
NEVADA							
1 Berkley	Y	+	N	Y	Y	Y	Y
2 ***Gibbons***	N	N	Y	Y	N	Y	Y
NEW HAMPSHIRE							
1 ***Sununu***	N	N	Y	Y	N	Y	Y
2 ***Bass***	N	N	Y	Y	N	Y	Y
NEW JERSEY							
1 Andrews	Y	Y	−	Y	Y	N	Y
2 ***LoBiondo***	N	N	Y	Y	N	Y	Y
3 ***Saxton***	Y	Y	N	Y	N	Y	Y
4 ***Smith***	Y	Y	Y	Y	N	N	Y
5 ***Roukema***	Y	Y	Y	Y	N	Y	Y
6 Pallone	Y	Y	N	Y	Y	N	Y
7 ***Franks***	Y	N	Y	Y	N	Y	Y
8 Pascrell	Y	Y	N	Y	Y	N	Y
9 Rothman	Y	Y	N	Y	Y	N	Y
10 Payne	Y	Y	N	Y	Y	N	Y
11 ***Frelinghuysen***	Y	N	Y	Y	N	Y	Y
12 Holt	Y	Y	N	Y	Y	N	Y
13 Menendez	Y	Y	N	Y	Y	N	Y
NEW MEXICO							
1 ***Wilson***	N	N	Y	Y	N	Y	Y
2 ***Skeen***	N	N	Y	Y	N	Y	Y
3 Udall	Y	Y	N	Y	Y	N	Y
NEW YORK							
1 ***Forbes***	Y	Y	N	Y	N	Y	Y
2 ***Lazio***	N	Y	Y	Y	Y	Y	Y
3 ***King***	N	N	Y	Y	Y	Y	Y
4 McCarthy	Y	Y	Y	Y	Y	Y	Y
5 Ackerman	Y	Y	N	Y	Y	N	?
6 Meeks	Y	Y	N	Y	Y	N	Y
7 Crowley	Y	Y	N	Y	Y	N	Y
8 Nadler	Y	Y	N	Y	Y	N	Y
9 Weiner	Y	Y	N	Y	Y	N	Y
10 Towns	Y	Y	N	Y	Y	N	Y
11 Owens	Y	Y	N	Y	Y	N	Y
12 Velázquez	Y	Y	N	Y	Y	N	Y
13 ***Fossella***	N	N	Y	+	N	Y	Y
14 Maloney	?	?	?	?	?	?	?
15 Rangel	Y	Y	N	Y	Y	N	Y
16 Serrano	Y	Y	N	Y	Y	N	Y
17 Engel	Y	Y	N	Y	Y	N	?
18 Lowey	Y	Y	N	Y	Y	N	Y
19 ***Kelly***	Y	Y	Y	Y	N	Y	Y
20 ***Gilman***	Y	N	Y	Y	N	Y	Y
21 McNulty	Y	Y	N	Y	Y	N	Y
22 ***Sweeney***	N	N	Y	Y	N	Y	Y
23 ***Boehlert***	Y	Y	N	Y	Y	N	Y
24 ***McHugh***	N	N	Y	Y	N	Y	Y
25 ***Walsh***	Y	N	Y	Y	N	Y	Y
26 Hinchey	Y	Y	N	Y	Y	N	Y
27 ***Reynolds***	N	N	Y	Y	N	Y	Y
28 Slaughter	Y	Y	N	Y	Y	N	Y
29 LaFalce	Y	Y	N	Y	Y	N	Y
30 ***Quinn***	Y	N	Y	Y	Y	N	Y
31 ***Houghton***	Y	N	Y	Y	N	Y	Y
NORTH CAROLINA							
1 Clayton	Y	Y	N	Y	Y	N	Y
2 Etheridge	Y	Y	Y	Y	Y	Y	Y
3 ***Jones***	N	?	Y	Y	N	Y	Y
4 Price	Y	Y	Y	Y	Y	Y	Y
5 ***Burr***	N	N	Y	Y	N	Y	Y
6 ***Coble***	N	N	Y	Y	N	Y	Y
7 McIntyre	N	N	Y	Y	Y	Y	Y
8 ***Hayes***	N	N	Y	Y	N	Y	Y
9 ***Myrick***	N	N	Y	Y	N	Y	Y
10 ***Ballenger***	N	N	Y	Y	N	Y	Y
11 ***Taylor***	N	N	Y	Y	N	Y	Y
12 Watt	Y	Y	N	Y	Y	N	Y
NORTH DAKOTA							
AL Pomeroy	Y	Y	Y	Y	Y	Y	Y
OHIO							
1 ***Chabot***	N	N	Y	Y	Y	Y	Y
2 ***Portman***	N	N	Y	Y	N	Y	Y
3 Hall	Y	Y	N	Y	Y	Y	Y
4 ***Oxley***	N	N	Y	Y	N	Y	Y
5 ***Gillmor***	N	N	Y	Y	N	Y	Y
6 Strickland	Y	Y	Y	Y	Y	N	Y
7 ***Hobson***	N	N	Y	Y	N	Y	Y
8 ***Boehner***	N	N	Y	Y	N	Y	Y
9 Kaptur	Y	Y	N	Y	Y	Y	Y
10 Kucinich	Y	Y	N	Y	Y	N	Y
11 Jones	Y	+	N	Y	Y	Y	Y
12 ***Kasich***	N	N	Y	Y	N	Y	Y
13 Brown	Y	Y	N	Y	Y	N	Y
14 Sawyer	Y	Y	N	Y	Y	N	Y
15 ***Pryce***	N	N	Y	Y	N	Y	Y
16 ***Regula***	N	N	Y	Y	N	Y	Y
17 Traficant	N	N	Y	Y	Y	Y	Y
18 ***Ney***	N	N	Y	Y	N	Y	Y
19 ***LaTourette***	Y	N	Y	Y	N	Y	Y
OKLAHOMA							
1 ***Largent***	N	N	Y	Y	N	Y	Y
2 ***Coburn***	N	N	Y	Y	N	Y	Y
3 ***Watkins***	N	N	Y	Y	N	Y	Y
4 ***Watts***	N	−	Y	Y	N	Y	Y
5 ***Istook***	N	N	Y	Y	N	Y	Y
6 ***Lucas***	N	N	Y	Y	N	Y	Y
OREGON							
1 Wu	Y	Y	N	Y	Y	Y	Y
2 ***Walden***	N	N	Y	Y	N	Y	Y
3 Blumenauer	Y	Y	N	Y	Y	N	Y
4 DeFazio	Y	Y	N	Y	Y	N	Y
5 Hooley	Y	Y	Y	Y	Y	N	Y
PENNSYLVANIA							
1 Brady	Y	Y	N	Y	Y	N	Y
2 Fattah	Y	Y	N	Y	Y	N	Y
3 Borski	Y	Y	N	Y	Y	N	Y
4 Klink	Y	?	N	Y	Y	N	Y
5 ***Peterson***	N	N	Y	Y	N	Y	Y
6 Holden	Y	Y	Y	Y	Y	Y	Y
7 ***Weldon***	Y	Y	Y	Y	Y	Y	Y
8 ***Greenwood***	Y	N	N	Y	N	Y	Y
9 ***Shuster***	N	N	Y	Y	N	Y	Y
10 ***Sherwood***	N	N	Y	Y	N	Y	Y
11 Kanjorski	Y	Y	N	Y	Y	N	Y
12 Murtha	N	N	Y	Y	Y	Y	Y
13 Hoeffel	Y	Y	N	Y	Y	N	Y
14 Coyne	Y	Y	N	Y	Y	N	Y
15 ***Toomey***	N	N	Y	Y	N	Y	Y
16 ***Pitts***	N	?	Y	Y	N	Y	Y
17 ***Gekas***	N	N	Y	?	N	Y	Y
18 Doyle	Y	Y	Y	Y	Y	Y	Y
19 ***Goodling***	N	N	Y	Y	N	Y	Y
20 Mascara	Y	Y	N	Y	Y	N	Y
21 ***English***	N	N	Y	Y	N	Y	Y
RHODE ISLAND							
1 Kennedy	Y	Y	N	Y	Y	N	Y
2 Weygand	Y	Y	Y	Y	Y	Y	Y
SOUTH CAROLINA							
1 ***Sanford***	N	N	Y	Y	N	Y	Y
2 ***Spence***	N	N	Y	Y	N	Y	Y
3 ***Graham***	N	N	Y	Y	N	Y	?
4 ***DeMint***	N	N	Y	Y	N	Y	Y
5 Spratt	?	?	?	Y	Y	Y	Y
6 Clyburn	Y	Y	N	Y	Y	N	Y
SOUTH DAKOTA							
AL ***Thune***	N	N	Y	Y	N	Y	Y
TENNESSEE							
1 ***Jenkins***	N	N	Y	Y	N	Y	Y
2 ***Duncan***	N	N	Y	Y	N	Y	Y
3 ***Wamp***	N	N	Y	Y	N	Y	Y
4 ***Hilleary***	N	N	Y	Y	N	Y	Y
5 Clement	N	N	Y	Y	Y	Y	Y
6 Gordon	N	N	Y	Y	Y	Y	Y
7 ***Bryant***	N	N	Y	Y	N	Y	Y
8 Tanner	N	N	Y	Y	Y	Y	Y
9 Ford	Y	Y	Y	Y	Y	N	Y
TEXAS							
1 Sandlin	N	N	Y	Y	Y	Y	Y
2 Turner	N	N	Y	Y	Y	Y	Y
3 ***Johnson, Sam***	N	N	Y	Y	N	Y	Y
4 Hall	N	N	Y	Y	N	Y	Y
5 ***Sessions***	N	N	Y	Y	N	Y	Y
6 ***Barton***	N	N	Y	?	N	Y	Y
7 ***Archer***	N	N	Y	Y	N	Y	Y
8 ***Brady***	N	−	+	Y	?	?	?
9 Lampson	Y	Y	N	Y	Y	N	Y
10 Doggett	Y	Y	N	Y	Y	N	Y
11 Edwards	N	Y	+	Y	Y	Y	Y
12 ***Granger***	N	N	?	Y	N	Y	Y
13 ***Thornberry***	N	N	Y	Y	N	Y	Y
14 ***Paul***	N	N	Y	?	N	Y	N
15 Hinojosa	Y	Y	Y	Y	Y	Y	Y
16 Reyes	Y	Y	Y	Y	Y	N	Y
17 Stenholm	N	N	Y	Y	N	Y	Y
18 Jackson-Lee	Y	Y	Y	Y	Y	N	Y
19 ***Combest***	N	N	Y	Y	N	Y	Y
20 Gonzalez	Y	Y	N	Y	Y	N	Y
21 ***Smith***	N	N	Y	Y	N	Y	Y
22 ***DeLay***	N	N	Y	Y	N	Y	Y
23 ***Bonilla***	N	N	Y	Y	N	Y	Y
24 Frost	Y	Y	N	Y	Y	Y	Y
25 Bentsen	Y	Y	Y	Y	Y	N	Y
26 ***Armey***	N	N	Y	Y	N	Y	Y
27 Ortiz	Y	Y	Y	+	Y	N	Y
28 Rodriguez	Y	Y	N	Y	Y	N	Y
29 Green	Y	Y	Y	Y	Y	N	Y
30 Johnson, E.B.	Y	Y	N	Y	Y	N	Y
UTAH							
1 ***Hansen***	N	N	Y	Y	N	Y	Y
2 ***Cook***	Y	N	Y	Y	N	Y	Y
3 ***Cannon***	N	N	Y	Y	N	Y	Y
VERMONT							
AL *Sanders*	Y	Y	N	Y	Y	N	?
VIRGINIA							
1 ***Bateman***	N	N	Y	Y	N	Y	Y
2 Pickett	N	N	Y	Y	Y	Y	Y
3 Scott	Y	Y	N	Y	Y	N	Y
4 Sisisky	N	N	Y	Y	N	Y	Y
5 Goode	N	N	Y	Y	N	Y	Y
6 ***Goodlatte***	N	N	Y	Y	N	Y	Y
7 ***Bliley***	N	N	Y	Y	N	Y	Y
8 Moran	Y	Y	Y	Y	Y	Y	Y
9 Boucher	Y	Y	N	Y	Y	N	Y
10 ***Wolf***	Y	N	Y	Y	N	Y	Y
11 ***Davis***	N	?	Y	Y	N	Y	Y
WASHINGTON							
1 Inslee	Y	Y	N	Y	Y	N	Y
2 ***Metcalf***	N	N	Y	Y	N	Y	Y
3 Baird	Y	Y	N	Y	Y	N	Y
4 ***Hastings***	N	N	Y	Y	N	Y	Y
5 ***Nethercutt***	N	N	Y	Y	N	Y	Y
6 Dicks	Y	Y	N	Y	Y	N	Y
7 McDermott	Y	Y	N	Y	Y	N	Y
8 ***Dunn***	N	N	Y	Y	N	Y	Y
9 Smith	Y	Y	Y	Y	Y	Y	Y
WEST VIRGINIA							
1 Mollohan	?	N	N	?	N	Y	Y
2 Wise	Y	Y	Y	Y	Y	Y	Y
3 Rahall	Y	Y	N	Y	Y	N	Y
WISCONSIN							
1 ***Ryan***	N	N	Y	Y	N	Y	Y
2 Baldwin	Y	Y	N	Y	Y	N	Y
3 Kind	Y	Y	Y	Y	Y	Y	Y
4 Kleczka	Y	Y	N	Y	Y	N	Y
5 Barrett	Y	Y	N	Y	Y	N	Y
6 ***Petri***	N	N	Y	Y	N	Y	Y
7 Obey	Y	Y	N	Y	Y	N	Y
8 ***Green***	N	N	Y	Y	N	Y	Y
9 ***Sensenbrenner***	N	N	Y	Y	N	Y	Y
WYOMING							
AL ***Cubin***	N	N	Y	Y	N	Y	Y

Southern states - Ala., Ark., Fla., Ga., Ky., La., Miss., N.C., Okla., S.C., Tenn., Texas, Va.

22. HR 171. Coastal Heritage Trail/Passage. Hansen, R-Utah, motion to suspend the rules and pass the bill to extend for five years the authorization for the Coastal Heritage Trail Route in New Jersey. The bill also increases — from $1 million to $4 million — the existing funding authorization for developing the route. Motion agreed to 394-21: R 194-21; D 199-0 (ND 147-0, SD 52-0); I 1-0. Feb. 23, 1999. A two-thirds majority of those present and voting (277 in this case) is required for passage under suspension of the rules.

23. HR 193. National Wild and Scenic Rivers/Passage. Hansen, R-Utah, motion to suspend the rules and pass the bill to designate a portion of the Sudbury, Assabet and Concord rivers as part of the National Wild and Scenic Rivers System. Motion agreed to 395-22: R 195-22; D 199-0 (ND 147-0, SD 52-0); I 1-0. Feb. 23, 1999. A two-thirds majority of those present and voting (278 in this case) is required for passage under suspension of the rules.

24. HR 438. 911 as National Emergency Number/Passage. Passage of the bill to designate 911 as the universal national emergency telephone number for both wireless and wireline emergency calls. The bill allows location information on wireless calls to be provided to 911 centers and other emergency service providers, but prohibits the disclosure of this information to other parties. Passed 415-2: R 214-2; D 201-0 (ND 147-0, SD 54-0); I 0-0. Feb. 24, 1999.

Key

- Y Voted for (yea).
- # Paired for.
- + Announced for.
- N Voted against (nay).
- X Paired against.
- – Announced against.
- P Voted "present."
- C Voted "present" to avoid possible conflict of interest.
- ? Did not vote or otherwise make a position known.

•

Democrats ***Republicans***
Independents

	22	23	24
ALABAMA			
1 ***Callahan***	Y	Y	Y
2 ***Everett***	N	N	Y
3 ***Riley***	Y	Y	Y
4 ***Aderholt***	Y	Y	Y
5 Cramer	Y	Y	Y
6 ***Bachus***	Y	Y	Y
7 Hilliard	Y	Y	Y
ALASKA			
AL ***Young***	Y	Y	Y
ARIZONA			
1 ***Salmon***	Y	Y	Y
2 Pastor	Y	Y	Y
3 ***Stump***	N	N	Y
4 ***Shadegg***	Y	Y	Y
5 ***Kolbe***	Y	Y	Y
6 ***Hayworth***	Y	Y	Y
ARKANSAS			
1 Berry	Y	Y	Y
2 Snyder	Y	Y	Y
3 ***Hutchinson***	Y	Y	Y
4 ***Dickey***	Y	Y	Y
CALIFORNIA			
1 Thompson	Y	Y	Y
2 ***Herger***	Y	Y	Y
3 ***Ose***	Y	Y	Y
4 ***Doolittle***	Y	N	Y
5 Matsui	Y	Y	Y
6 Woolsey	Y	Y	Y
7 Miller, George	Y	Y	Y
8 Pelosi	Y	Y	Y
9 Lee	Y	Y	Y
10 Tauscher	Y	Y	Y
11 ***Pombo***	N	N	Y
12 Lantos	Y	Y	Y
13 Stark	Y	Y	Y
14 Eshoo	Y	Y	Y
15 ***Campbell***	Y	Y	Y
16 Lofgren	Y	Y	Y
17 Farr	Y	Y	Y
18 Condit	Y	Y	Y
19 ***Radanovich***	N	Y	Y
20 Dooley	Y	Y	Y
21 ***Thomas***	Y	Y	Y
22 Capps	+	+	+
23 ***Gallegly***	Y	Y	Y
24 Sherman	Y	Y	Y
25 ***McKeon***	Y	Y	Y
26 Berman	Y	Y	Y
27 ***Rogan***	Y	Y	Y
28 ***Dreier***	Y	Y	Y
29 Waxman	Y	Y	Y
30 Becerra	Y	Y	Y
31 Martinez	Y	Y	Y
32 Dixon	Y	Y	Y
33 Roybal-Allard	Y	Y	Y
34 Napolitano	Y	Y	Y
35 Waters	Y	Y	Y
36 ***Kuykendall***	Y	Y	Y
37 Millender-McD.	?	?	Y
38 ***Horn***	Y	Y	Y
39 ***Royce***	N	N	Y
40 ***Lewis***	Y	Y	Y
41 ***Miller, Gary***	Y	Y	Y
42 Brown	Y	Y	Y
43 ***Calvert***	Y	Y	Y
44 ***Bono***	Y	Y	Y
45 ***Rohrabacher***	N	N	Y
46 Sanchez	Y	Y	Y
47 ***Cox***	Y	Y	Y
48 ***Packard***	Y	Y	Y
49 ***Bilbray***	Y	Y	Y
50 Filner	Y	Y	Y
51 ***Cunningham***	Y	Y	Y
52 ***Hunter***	Y	Y	Y
COLORADO			
1 DeGette	Y	Y	Y
2 Udall	Y	Y	Y
3 ***McInnis***	Y	Y	+
4 ***Schaffer***	Y	Y	Y
5 ***Hefley***	Y	Y	Y
6 ***Tancredo***	Y	Y	Y
CONNECTICUT			
1 Larson	Y	Y	Y
2 Gejdenson	Y	Y	Y
3 DeLauro	Y	Y	Y
4 ***Shays***	Y	Y	Y
5 Maloney	Y	Y	Y
6 ***Johnson***	Y	Y	Y
DELAWARE			
AL ***Castle***	Y	Y	Y
FLORIDA			
1 ***Scarborough***	Y	Y	Y
2 Boyd	Y	Y	Y
3 Brown	Y	Y	Y
4 ***Fowler***	Y	Y	Y
5 Thurman	Y	Y	Y
6 ***Stearns***	N	N	Y
7 ***Mica***	Y	Y	Y
8 ***McCollum***	Y	Y	Y
9 ***Bilirakis***	Y	Y	Y
10 ***Young***	Y	Y	Y
11 Davis	Y	Y	Y
12 ***Canady***	Y	Y	Y
13 ***Miller***	Y	Y	Y
14 ***Goss***	Y	Y	Y
15 ***Weldon***	Y	Y	Y
16 ***Foley***	Y	Y	Y
17 Meek	Y	Y	Y
18 ***Ros-Lehtinen***	Y	Y	Y
19 Wexler	Y	Y	Y
20 Deutsch	Y	Y	Y
21 ***Diaz-Balart***	Y	Y	Y
22 ***Shaw***	Y	Y	Y
23 Hastings	Y	Y	Y
GEORGIA			
1 ***Kingston***	Y	Y	Y
2 Bishop	Y	Y	Y
3 ***Collins***	Y	Y	Y
4 McKinney	Y	Y	Y
5 Lewis	Y	Y	Y
6 Vacancy			
7 ***Barr***	N	Y	Y
8 ***Chambliss***	Y	Y	Y
9 ***Deal***	Y	Y	Y
10 ***Norwood***	Y	Y	Y
11 ***Linder***	Y	Y	Y
HAWAII			
1 Abercrombie	Y	Y	Y
2 Mink	Y	Y	Y
IDAHO			
1 ***Chenoweth***	N	N	N
2 ***Simpson***	Y	Y	Y
ILLINOIS			
1 Rush	?	?	?
2 Jackson	Y	Y	Y
3 Lipinski	?	?	Y
4 Gutierrez	?	?	Y
5 Blagojevich	Y	Y	Y
6 ***Hyde***	Y	Y	Y
7 Davis	+	+	+
8 ***Crane***	Y	Y	Y
9 Schakowsky	Y	Y	Y
10 ***Porter***	Y	Y	Y
11 ***Weller***	Y	Y	Y
12 Costello	Y	Y	Y
13 ***Biggert***	Y	Y	Y
14 ***Hastert***			

ND Northern Democrats SD Southern Democrats

	22	23	24
15 ***Ewing***	Y	Y	Y
16 ***Manzullo***	Y	Y	Y
17 Evans	Y	Y	Y
18 ***LaHood***	Y	Y	Y
19 Phelps	Y	Y	Y
20 ***Shimkus***	Y	Y	Y
INDIANA			
1 Visclosky	Y	Y	Y
2 ***McIntosh***	Y	Y	Y
3 Roemer	Y	Y	Y
4 ***Souder***	Y	Y	Y
5 ***Buyer***	Y	Y	Y
6 ***Burton***	N	N	Y
7 ***Pease***	Y	Y	Y
8 ***Hostettler***	N	N	Y
9 Hill	Y	Y	+
10 Carson	Y	Y	Y
IOWA			
1 ***Leach***	Y	Y	Y
2 ***Nussle***	Y	Y	Y
3 Boswell	Y	Y	Y
4 ***Ganske***	Y	Y	?
5 ***Latham***	Y	Y	Y
KANSAS			
1 ***Moran***	Y	Y	Y
2 ***Ryun***	Y	Y	Y
3 Moore	Y	Y	Y
4 ***Tiahrt***	N	N	Y
KENTUCKY			
1 ***Whitfield***	Y	Y	Y
2 ***Lewis***	Y	Y	Y
3 ***Northup***	Y	Y	Y
4 Lucas	Y	Y	Y
5 ***Rogers***	Y	Y	Y
6 ***Fletcher***	Y	Y	Y
LOUISIANA			
1 ***Livingston***	Y	Y	?
2 Jefferson	Y	Y	Y
3 ***Tauzin***	Y	Y	Y
4 ***McCrery***	Y	Y	Y
5 ***Cooksey***	Y	Y	Y
6 ***Baker***	Y	Y	Y
7 John	?	?	Y
MAINE			
1 Allen	Y	Y	Y
2 Baldacci	Y	Y	Y
MARYLAND			
1 ***Gilchrest***	Y	Y	Y
2 ***Ehrlich***	Y	Y	Y
3 Cardin	Y	Y	Y
4 Wynn	Y	Y	Y
5 Hoyer	Y	Y	Y
6 ***Bartlett***	Y	Y	Y
7 Cummings	Y	Y	Y
8 ***Morella***	Y	Y	Y
MASSACHUSETTS			
1 Olver	Y	Y	Y
2 Neal	Y	Y	?
3 McGovern	?	?	Y
4 Frank	Y	Y	Y
5 Meehan	Y	Y	Y
6 Tierney	Y	Y	Y
7 Markey	Y	Y	Y
8 Capuano	Y	Y	Y
9 Moakley	Y	Y	Y
10 Delahunt	Y	Y	Y
MICHIGAN			
1 Stupak	Y	Y	Y
2 ***Hoekstra***	Y	Y	Y
3 ***Ehlers***	Y	Y	Y
4 ***Camp***	Y	Y	Y
5 Barcia	Y	Y	Y
6 ***Upton***	Y	Y	Y
7 ***Smith***	Y	Y	Y
8 Stabenow	Y	Y	Y
9 Kildee	Y	Y	Y
10 Bonior	Y	Y	Y
11 ***Knollenberg***	Y	Y	Y
12 Levin	Y	Y	Y
13 Rivers	Y	Y	Y
14 Conyers	Y	Y	Y
15 Kilpatrick	Y	Y	Y
16 Dingell	Y	Y	Y
MINNESOTA			
1 ***Gutknecht***	Y	Y	Y
2 Minge	Y	Y	Y
3 ***Ramstad***	Y	Y	Y
4 Vento	Y	Y	Y
5 Sabo	Y	Y	Y
6 Luther	Y	Y	Y
7 Peterson	Y	Y	Y
8 Oberstar	Y	Y	Y
MISSISSIPPI			
1 ***Wicker***	Y	Y	Y
2 Thompson	Y	Y	Y
3 ***Pickering***	Y	Y	?
4 Shows	Y	Y	Y
5 Taylor	?	?	Y
MISSOURI			
1 Clay	Y	Y	Y
2 ***Talent***	Y	Y	Y
3 Gephardt	Y	Y	Y
4 Skelton	Y	Y	Y
5 McCarthy	+	+	Y
6 Danner	Y	Y	Y
7 ***Blunt***	?	?	Y
8 ***Emerson***	Y	Y	Y
9 ***Hulshof***	+	+	Y
MONTANA			
AL ***Hill***	Y	Y	Y
NEBRASKA			
1 ***Bereuter***	Y	Y	Y
2 ***Terry***	Y	Y	Y
3 ***Barrett***	Y	Y	Y
NEVADA			
1 Berkley	Y	Y	Y
2 ***Gibbons***	Y	N	Y
NEW HAMPSHIRE			
1 ***Sununu***	Y	Y	Y
2 ***Bass***	?	Y	Y
NEW JERSEY			
1 Andrews	Y	Y	Y
2 ***LoBiondo***	Y	Y	Y
3 ***Saxton***	Y	Y	Y
4 ***Smith***	Y	Y	Y
5 ***Roukema***	Y	Y	Y
6 Pallone	Y	Y	Y
7 ***Franks***	Y	Y	Y
8 Pascrell	Y	Y	Y
9 Rothman	Y	Y	Y
10 Payne	Y	Y	Y
11 ***Frelinghuysen***	Y	Y	Y
12 Holt	Y	Y	Y
13 Menendez	Y	Y	Y
NEW MEXICO			
1 ***Wilson***	Y	Y	Y
2 ***Skeen***	Y	Y	Y
3 Udall	Y	Y	Y
NEW YORK			
1 ***Forbes***	Y	Y	Y
2 ***Lazio***	Y	Y	Y
3 ***King***	Y	Y	Y
4 McCarthy	Y	Y	Y
5 Ackerman	Y	Y	Y
6 Meeks	Y	Y	Y
7 Crowley	Y	Y	Y
8 Nadler	Y	Y	Y
9 Weiner	Y	Y	Y
10 Towns	Y	Y	Y
11 Owens	Y	Y	?
12 Velázquez	Y	Y	Y
13 ***Fossella***	Y	Y	Y
14 Maloney	Y	Y	Y
15 Rangel	?	?	Y
16 Serrano	Y	Y	Y
17 Engel	Y	Y	?
18 Lowey	Y	Y	Y
19 ***Kelly***	Y	Y	Y
20 ***Gilman***	Y	Y	Y
21 McNulty	Y	Y	Y
22 ***Sweeney***	Y	Y	Y
23 ***Boehlert***	Y	Y	Y
24 ***McHugh***	Y	Y	Y
25 ***Walsh***	Y	Y	Y
26 Hinchey	Y	Y	?
27 ***Reynolds***	Y	Y	Y
28 Slaughter	Y	Y	Y
29 LaFalce	Y	Y	Y
30 ***Quinn***	Y	Y	Y
31 ***Houghton***	Y	Y	Y
NORTH CAROLINA			
1 Clayton	Y	Y	Y
2 Etheridge	Y	Y	Y
3 ***Jones***	N	N	Y
4 Price	Y	Y	Y
5 ***Burr***	Y	Y	Y
6 ***Coble***	N	N	Y
7 McIntyre	Y	Y	Y
8 ***Hayes***	Y	Y	Y
9 ***Myrick***	Y	Y	Y
10 ***Ballenger***	Y	Y	Y
11 ***Taylor***	N	N	Y
12 Watt	Y	Y	Y
NORTH DAKOTA			
AL Pomeroy	Y	Y	Y
OHIO			
1 ***Chabot***	N	Y	Y
2 ***Portman***	Y	Y	Y
3 Hall	Y	Y	Y
4 ***Oxley***	Y	Y	Y
5 ***Gillmor***	?	Y	Y
6 Strickland	Y	Y	Y
7 ***Hobson***	Y	Y	Y
8 ***Boehner***	Y	Y	Y
9 Kaptur	Y	Y	Y
10 Kucinich	Y	Y	Y
11 Jones	Y	Y	Y
12 ***Kasich***	Y	Y	Y
13 Brown	Y	Y	Y
14 Sawyer	Y	Y	Y
15 ***Pryce***	Y	Y	Y
16 ***Regula***	Y	Y	Y
17 Traficant	Y	Y	Y
18 ***Ney***	Y	Y	Y
19 ***LaTourette***	Y	Y	Y
OKLAHOMA			
1 ***Largent***	Y	Y	Y
2 ***Coburn***	N	N	Y
3 ***Watkins***	Y	Y	Y
4 ***Watts***	Y	Y	Y
5 ***Istook***	Y	Y	Y
6 ***Lucas***	Y	Y	Y
OREGON			
1 Wu	Y	Y	Y
2 ***Walden***	Y	Y	Y
3 Blumenauer	Y	Y	Y
4 DeFazio	Y	Y	Y
5 Hooley	Y	Y	Y
PENNSYLVANIA			
1 Brady	Y	Y	Y
2 Fattah	Y	Y	Y
3 Borski	Y	Y	Y
4 Klink	Y	Y	Y
5 ***Peterson***	Y	Y	Y
6 Holden	Y	Y	Y
7 ***Weldon***	Y	Y	Y
8 ***Greenwood***	Y	Y	Y
9 ***Shuster***	Y	Y	Y
10 ***Sherwood***	Y	Y	Y
11 Kanjorski	Y	Y	Y
12 Murtha	Y	Y	Y
13 Hoeffel	Y	Y	Y
14 Coyne	Y	Y	Y
15 ***Toomey***	Y	Y	Y
16 ***Pitts***	Y	Y	Y
17 ***Gekas***	Y	Y	Y
18 Doyle	Y	Y	Y
19 ***Goodling***	Y	Y	Y
20 Mascara	Y	Y	Y
21 ***English***	Y	Y	Y
RHODE ISLAND			
1 Kennedy	Y	Y	?
2 Weygand	Y	Y	Y
SOUTH CAROLINA			
1 ***Sanford***	N	N	Y
2 ***Spence***	Y	Y	Y
3 ***Graham***	Y	Y	Y
4 ***DeMint***	Y	Y	Y
5 Spratt	Y	Y	Y
6 Clyburn	Y	Y	Y
SOUTH DAKOTA			
AL ***Thune***	Y	Y	Y
TENNESSEE			
1 ***Jenkins***	Y	Y	Y
2 ***Duncan***	?	?	Y
3 ***Wamp***	Y	Y	Y
4 ***Hilleary***	?	?	Y
5 Clement	Y	Y	Y
6 Gordon	Y	Y	Y
7 ***Bryant***	Y	Y	Y
8 Tanner	Y	Y	Y
9 Ford	Y	Y	Y
TEXAS			
1 Sandlin	Y	Y	Y
2 Turner	Y	Y	Y
3 ***Johnson, Sam***	Y	Y	Y
4 Hall	Y	Y	Y
5 ***Sessions***	Y	Y	Y
6 ***Barton***	Y	Y	Y
7 ***Archer***	Y	Y	Y
8 ***Brady***	Y	Y	?
9 Lampson	Y	Y	Y
10 Doggett	?	?	Y
11 Edwards	Y	Y	Y
12 ***Granger***	Y	Y	Y
13 ***Thornberry***	Y	Y	Y
14 ***Paul***	N	N	N
15 Hinojosa	Y	Y	Y
16 Reyes	Y	Y	?
17 Stenholm	Y	Y	Y
18 Jackson-Lee	Y	Y	Y
19 ***Combest***	Y	Y	Y
20 Gonzalez	Y	Y	Y
21 ***Smith***	Y	Y	Y
22 ***DeLay***	Y	N	Y
23 ***Bonilla***	Y	Y	Y
24 Frost	Y	Y	Y
25 Bentsen	Y	Y	Y
26 ***Armey***	Y	Y	Y
27 Ortiz	Y	Y	Y
28 Rodriguez	Y	Y	Y
29 Green	Y	Y	Y
30 Johnson, E.B.	Y	Y	Y
UTAH			
1 ***Hansen***	Y	Y	Y
2 ***Cook***	Y	Y	Y
3 ***Cannon***	Y	N	Y
VERMONT			
AL *Sanders*	Y	Y	?
VIRGINIA			
1 ***Bateman***	Y	Y	Y
2 Pickett	Y	Y	Y
3 Scott	Y	Y	Y
4 Sisisky	Y	Y	Y
5 Goode	Y	Y	Y
6 ***Goodlatte***	Y	Y	Y
7 ***Bliley***	Y	Y	Y
8 Moran	Y	Y	Y
9 Boucher	Y	Y	Y
10 ***Wolf***	Y	Y	Y
11 ***Davis***	Y	Y	Y
WASHINGTON			
1 Inslee	Y	Y	Y
2 ***Metcalf***	Y	Y	Y
3 Baird	Y	Y	Y
4 ***Hastings***	Y	Y	Y
5 ***Nethercutt***	Y	Y	Y
6 Dicks	Y	Y	Y
7 McDermott	Y	Y	Y
8 ***Dunn***	Y	Y	Y
9 Smith	Y	Y	Y
WEST VIRGINIA			
1 Mollohan	Y	Y	Y
2 Wise	Y	Y	Y
3 Rahall	Y	Y	Y
WISCONSIN			
1 ***Ryan***	Y	Y	Y
2 Baldwin	Y	Y	Y
3 Kind	Y	Y	Y
4 Kleczka	Y	Y	Y
5 Barrett	Y	Y	Y
6 ***Petri***	N	N	Y
7 Obey	Y	Y	Y
8 ***Green***	Y	Y	Y
9 ***Sensenbrenner***	N	N	Y
WYOMING			
AL ***Cubin***	Y	Y	Y

Southern states - Ala., Ark., Fla., Ga., Ky., La., Miss., N.C., Okla., S.C., Tenn., Texas, Va.

25. HR 436. Federal Agencies' Debt Collection/Passage. Passage of the bill to provide federal agencies with a variety of additional procedures to collect delinquent non-tax debts, and to make technical corrections to the Debt Collection Improvement Act of 1996 (PL 104-134). Passed 419-1: R 214-1; D 204-0 (ND 150-0, SD 54-0); I 1-0. Feb. 24, 1999.

26. HR 409. Federal Financial Assistance Management/Passage. Passage of the bill to require federal agencies to develop plans within 18 months to streamline application, administrative and reporting requirements for federal financial assistance (or grant) programs. The bill also directs agencies to develop and expand use of electronic applications and reporting via the Internet. Passed 426-0: R 219-0; D 206-0 (ND 153-0, SD 53-0); I 1-0. Feb. 24, 1999.

27. Procedural Motion/Journal. Approval of the House Journal of Wednesday, Feb. 24, 1999. Approved 362-28: R 196-8; D 165-20 (ND 121-15, SD 44-5); I 1-0. Feb. 25, 1999.

28. HR 514. Wireless Communication Privacy/Passage. Passage of the bill to strengthen wireless communication privacy laws and to require the Federal Communications Commission to step up its enforcement actions against violations of such privacy laws. The bill would make illegal any modification of scanners to receive private wireless communications. Passed 403-3: R 212-1; D 190-2 (ND 136-2, SD 54-0); I 1-0. Feb. 25, 1999.

[1] *Johnny Isakson, R-Ga., was sworn in Feb. 25, 1999, replacing Newt Gingrich, R-Ga., who resigned effective Jan. 3, 1999. The first vote for which Isakson was eligible was vote 28.*

[2] *Robert L. Livingston, R-La., resigned effective Feb. 28, 1999.*

Key

- Y Voted for (yea).
- # Paired for.
- + Announced for.
- N Voted against (nay).
- X Paired against.
- – Announced against.
- P Voted "present."
- C Voted "present" to avoid possible conflict of interest.
- ? Did not vote or otherwise make a position known.

•

Democrats ***Republicans***
Independents

	25	26	27	28
ALABAMA				
1 ***Callahan***	Y	Y	Y	Y
2 ***Everett***	Y	Y	Y	Y
3 ***Riley***	Y	Y	Y	Y
4 ***Aderholt***	+	Y	Y	Y
5 Cramer	Y	Y	Y	Y
6 ***Bachus***	Y	Y	Y	Y
7 Hilliard	Y	Y	N	Y
ALASKA				
AL ***Young***	Y	Y	?	Y
ARIZONA				
1 ***Salmon***	Y	Y	?	Y
2 Pastor	Y	Y	?	?
3 ***Stump***	Y	Y	Y	Y
4 ***Shadegg***	Y	Y	Y	Y
5 ***Kolbe***	Y	Y	?	?
6 ***Hayworth***	Y	Y	Y	Y
ARKANSAS				
1 Berry	Y	Y	Y	Y
2 Snyder	Y	Y	Y	Y
3 ***Hutchinson***	Y	Y	Y	Y
4 ***Dickey***	Y	Y	Y	?
CALIFORNIA				
1 Thompson	Y	Y	Y	Y
2 ***Herger***	Y	Y	?	Y
3 ***Ose***	Y	Y	Y	Y
4 ***Doolittle***	Y	Y	Y	Y
5 Matsui	Y	Y	Y	Y
6 Woolsey	Y	Y	Y	?
7 Miller, George	Y	Y	Y	?
8 Pelosi	Y	Y	?	?
9 Lee	Y	Y	?	+
10 Tauscher	Y	Y	Y	Y
11 ***Pombo***	Y	Y	Y	Y
12 Lantos	Y	Y	Y	Y
13 Stark	Y	Y	Y	Y
14 Eshoo	Y	Y	Y	?
15 ***Campbell***	Y	Y	Y	Y
16 Lofgren	Y	Y	Y	Y
17 Farr	Y	Y	Y	Y
18 Condit	Y	Y	Y	Y
19 ***Radanovich***	Y	Y	Y	Y
20 Dooley	Y	Y	Y	Y
21 ***Thomas***	Y	Y	Y	Y
22 Capps	+	+	+	+
23 ***Gallegly***	Y	Y	Y	Y
24 Sherman	Y	Y	Y	Y
25 ***McKeon***	Y	Y	Y	Y
26 Berman	Y	Y	Y	Y
27 ***Rogan***	Y	Y	?	?
28 ***Dreier***	Y	Y	Y	Y
29 Waxman	Y	Y	?	Y
30 Becerra	Y	Y	?	Y
31 Martinez	?	Y	?	Y
32 Dixon	Y	Y	Y	Y
33 Roybal-Allard	Y	Y	?	Y
34 Napolitano	Y	Y	Y	Y
35 Waters	Y	Y	N	?
36 ***Kuykendall***	Y	Y	Y	Y
37 Millender-McD.	Y	Y	Y	Y
38 ***Horn***	Y	Y	Y	Y
39 ***Royce***	Y	Y	?	?
40 ***Lewis***	Y	Y	Y	Y
41 ***Miller, Gary***	Y	Y	Y	Y
42 Brown	Y	Y	N	Y
43 ***Calvert***	Y	Y	Y	Y
44 ***Bono***	Y	Y	Y	Y
45 ***Rohrabacher***	Y	Y	Y	Y
46 Sanchez	Y	Y	Y	Y
47 ***Cox***	Y	Y	?	Y
48 ***Packard***	Y	Y	Y	Y
49 ***Bilbray***	Y	Y	Y	Y
50 Filner	Y	Y	N	Y
51 ***Cunningham***	Y	Y	Y	Y
52 ***Hunter***	Y	Y	Y	Y
COLORADO				
1 DeGette	Y	Y	Y	Y
2 Udall	Y	Y	Y	Y
3 ***McInnis***	+	+	Y	Y
4 ***Schaffer***	Y	Y	N	Y
5 ***Hefley***	Y	Y	Y	Y
6 ***Tancredo***	Y	Y	Y	Y
CONNECTICUT				
1 Larson	Y	Y	Y	Y
2 Gejdenson	Y	Y	Y	Y
3 DeLauro	Y	Y	Y	Y
4 ***Shays***	Y	Y	Y	Y
5 Maloney	Y	Y	Y	Y
6 ***Johnson***	Y	Y	Y	Y
DELAWARE				
AL ***Castle***	Y	Y	Y	Y
FLORIDA				
1 ***Scarborough***	Y	Y	Y	Y
2 Boyd	Y	Y	Y	Y
3 Brown	Y	Y	?	Y
4 ***Fowler***	Y	Y	Y	Y
5 Thurman	Y	Y	Y	Y
6 ***Stearns***	Y	Y	Y	Y
7 ***Mica***	Y	Y	Y	Y
8 ***McCollum***	Y	Y	Y	Y
9 ***Bilirakis***	Y	Y	Y	Y
10 ***Young***	Y	Y	Y	Y
11 Davis	Y	Y	Y	Y
12 ***Canady***	Y	Y	?	Y
13 ***Miller***	Y	Y	Y	Y
14 ***Goss***	Y	Y	Y	Y
15 ***Weldon***	Y	Y	Y	Y
16 ***Foley***	Y	Y	Y	Y
17 Meek	Y	Y	Y	Y
18 ***Ros-Lehtinen***	Y	Y	Y	Y
19 Wexler	Y	Y	Y	Y
20 Deutsch	Y	Y	Y	Y
21 ***Diaz-Balart***	Y	Y	Y	Y
22 ***Shaw***	Y	Y	Y	Y
23 Hastings	Y	Y	?	Y
GEORGIA				
1 ***Kingston***	Y	Y	Y	Y
2 Bishop	Y	Y	?	Y
3 ***Collins***	Y	Y	Y	Y
4 McKinney	Y	Y	Y	Y
5 Lewis	Y	Y	Y	Y
6 ***Isakson*** [1]				Y
7 ***Barr***	Y	Y	Y	Y
8 ***Chambliss***	Y	Y	Y	Y
9 ***Deal***	Y	Y	Y	Y
10 ***Norwood***	Y	Y	Y	Y
11 ***Linder***	Y	Y	Y	Y
HAWAII				
1 Abercrombie	Y	Y	Y	Y
2 Mink	Y	Y	Y	Y
IDAHO				
1 ***Chenoweth***	Y	Y	Y	Y
2 ***Simpson***	Y	Y	Y	Y
ILLINOIS				
1 Rush	?	?	?	?
2 Jackson	Y	Y	Y	Y
3 Lipinski	Y	Y	Y	Y
4 Gutierrez	Y	Y	P	Y
5 Blagojevich	Y	Y	Y	Y
6 ***Hyde***	Y	Y	Y	Y
7 Davis	+	+	+	Y
8 ***Crane***	Y	Y	N	Y
9 Schakowsky	Y	Y	Y	Y
10 ***Porter***	Y	Y	Y	Y
11 ***Weller***	Y	Y	?	Y
12 Costello	Y	Y	N	Y
13 ***Biggert***	Y	Y	Y	Y
14 ***Hastert***				

ND Northern Democrats SD Southern Democrats

	25	26	27	28
15 ***Ewing***	Y	Y	Y	Y
16 ***Manzullo***	Y	Y	Y	Y
17 Evans	Y	Y	Y	Y
18 ***LaHood***	Y	Y	Y	Y
19 Phelps	Y	Y	Y	Y
20 ***Shimkus***	Y	Y	Y	Y
INDIANA				
1 Visclosky	Y	Y	N	Y
2 ***McIntosh***	Y	Y	?	Y
3 Roemer	Y	Y	Y	Y
4 ***Souder***	Y	Y	Y	Y
5 ***Buyer***	Y	Y	Y	Y
6 ***Burton***	Y	Y	Y	Y
7 ***Pease***	Y	Y	Y	Y
8 ***Hostettler***	Y	Y	Y	Y
9 Hill	Y	Y	Y	Y
10 Carson	Y	Y	Y	Y
IOWA				
1 ***Leach***	Y	Y	Y	Y
2 ***Nussle***	Y	Y	Y	Y
3 Boswell	Y	Y	Y	Y
4 ***Ganske***	Y	Y	Y	Y
5 ***Latham***	Y	Y	Y	Y
KANSAS				
1 ***Moran***	Y	Y	N	Y
2 ***Ryun***	Y	Y	Y	Y
3 Moore	Y	Y	Y	Y
4 ***Tiahrt***	Y	Y	Y	Y
KENTUCKY				
1 ***Whitfield***	Y	Y	Y	Y
2 ***Lewis***	Y	Y	Y	Y
3 ***Northup***	?	Y	Y	Y
4 Lucas	Y	Y	Y	Y
5 ***Rogers***	Y	Y	?	Y
6 ***Fletcher***	Y	Y	Y	Y
LOUISIANA				
1 ***Livingston*** [2]	?	?	Y	?
2 Jefferson	Y	Y	Y	Y
3 ***Tauzin***	Y	Y	Y	Y
4 ***McCrery***	Y	Y	Y	Y
5 ***Cooksey***	Y	Y	Y	Y
6 ***Baker***	Y	Y	Y	Y
7 John	Y	Y	Y	Y
MAINE				
1 Allen	Y	Y	Y	Y
2 Baldacci	Y	Y	Y	Y
MARYLAND				
1 ***Gilchrest***	Y	Y	Y	Y
2 ***Ehrlich***	Y	Y	Y	Y
3 Cardin	Y	Y	Y	Y
4 Wynn	Y	Y	Y	Y
5 Hoyer	Y	Y	Y	Y
6 ***Bartlett***	Y	Y	Y	Y
7 Cummings	Y	Y	Y	Y
8 ***Morella***	?	Y	Y	Y
MASSACHUSETTS				
1 Olver	Y	Y	Y	Y
2 Neal	Y	Y	Y	Y
3 McGovern	Y	Y	Y	Y
4 Frank	Y	Y	Y	?
5 Meehan	Y	Y	Y	Y
6 Tierney	Y	Y	Y	Y
7 Markey	Y	Y	Y	Y
8 Capuano	Y	Y	Y	Y
9 Moakley	Y	Y	?	?
10 Delahunt	Y	Y	Y	Y
MICHIGAN				
1 Stupak	Y	Y	N	Y
2 ***Hoekstra***	Y	Y	Y	Y
3 ***Ehlers***	Y	Y	Y	Y
4 ***Camp***	Y	Y	Y	Y
5 Barcia	Y	Y	Y	Y
6 ***Upton***	Y	Y	Y	Y
7 ***Smith***	Y	Y	Y	Y
8 Stabenow	Y	Y	Y	Y
9 Kildee	Y	Y	Y	Y
10 Bonior	Y	Y	Y	?
11 ***Knollenberg***	Y	Y	Y	Y
12 Levin	Y	Y	Y	Y
13 Rivers	Y	Y	Y	Y
14 Conyers	Y	Y	?	Y
15 Kilpatrick	Y	Y	Y	Y
16 Dingell	Y	Y	Y	Y

	25	26	27	28
MINNESOTA				
1 ***Gutknecht***	Y	Y	N	Y
2 Minge	Y	Y	Y	Y
3 ***Ramstad***	Y	Y	N	Y
4 Vento	Y	Y	Y	Y
5 Sabo	Y	Y	N	Y
6 Luther	Y	Y	Y	Y
7 Peterson	Y	Y	N	Y
8 Oberstar	Y	Y	N	Y
MISSISSIPPI				
1 ***Wicker***	Y	Y	Y	Y
2 Thompson	Y	Y	N	Y
3 ***Pickering***	+	Y	Y	Y
4 Shows	Y	Y	Y	Y
5 Taylor	Y	?	N	Y
MISSOURI				
1 Clay	Y	Y	N	Y
2 ***Talent***	Y	Y	Y	Y
3 Gephardt	Y	Y	Y	?
4 Skelton	Y	Y	Y	Y
5 McCarthy	Y	Y	Y	Y
6 Danner	Y	Y	Y	Y
7 ***Blunt***	Y	Y	Y	Y
8 ***Emerson***	Y	Y	Y	Y
9 ***Hulshof***	Y	Y	Y	Y
MONTANA				
AL ***Hill***	Y	Y	N	Y
NEBRASKA				
1 ***Bereuter***	Y	Y	Y	Y
2 ***Terry***	Y	Y	Y	Y
3 ***Barrett***	Y	Y	Y	Y
NEVADA				
1 Berkley	Y	Y	Y	Y
2 ***Gibbons***	Y	Y	Y	Y
NEW HAMPSHIRE				
1 ***Sununu***	Y	Y	Y	Y
2 ***Bass***	Y	Y	Y	Y
NEW JERSEY				
1 Andrews	Y	Y	Y	Y
2 ***LoBiondo***	Y	Y	N	Y
3 ***Saxton***	Y	Y	Y	Y
4 ***Smith***	Y	Y	Y	Y
5 ***Roukema***	Y	Y	Y	Y
6 Pallone	Y	Y	Y	Y
7 ***Franks***	Y	Y	Y	Y
8 Pascrell	Y	Y	Y	Y
9 Rothman	Y	Y	Y	Y
10 Payne	Y	Y	?	?
11 ***Frelinghuysen***	Y	Y	Y	Y
12 Holt	Y	Y	Y	Y
13 Menendez	?	Y	Y	Y
NEW MEXICO				
1 ***Wilson***	Y	Y	Y	Y
2 ***Skeen***	Y	Y	Y	Y
3 Udall	Y	Y	Y	Y
NEW YORK				
1 ***Forbes***	Y	Y	Y	Y
2 ***Lazio***	Y	Y	Y	Y
3 ***King***	Y	Y	Y	Y
4 McCarthy	Y	Y	Y	Y
5 Ackerman	Y	Y	?	?
6 Meeks	Y	Y	?	?
7 Crowley	Y	Y	Y	Y
8 Nadler	Y	Y	Y	Y
9 Weiner	Y	Y	Y	Y
10 Towns	Y	Y	?	?
11 Owens	Y	Y	Y	Y
12 Velázquez	Y	Y	Y	Y
13 ***Fossella***	Y	Y	Y	Y
14 Maloney	Y	Y	Y	Y
15 Rangel	Y	Y	?	Y
16 Serrano	Y	Y	Y	Y
17 Engel	Y	Y	Y	Y
18 Lowey	?	Y	Y	Y
19 ***Kelly***	Y	Y	Y	Y
20 ***Gilman***	Y	Y	Y	Y
21 McNulty	Y	Y	Y	Y
22 ***Sweeney***	Y	Y	Y	Y
23 ***Boehlert***	Y	Y	Y	Y
24 ***McHugh***	Y	Y	Y	Y
25 ***Walsh***	Y	Y	Y	Y
26 Hinchey	Y	Y	Y	N
27 ***Reynolds***	Y	Y	Y	Y
28 Slaughter	Y	Y	Y	Y
29 LaFalce	Y	Y	Y	Y

	25	26	27	28
30 ***Quinn***	Y	Y	Y	Y
31 ***Houghton***	Y	Y	Y	Y
NORTH CAROLINA				
1 Clayton	Y	Y	Y	Y
2 Etheridge	Y	Y	?	Y
3 ***Jones***	Y	Y	Y	Y
4 Price	Y	Y	Y	Y
5 ***Burr***	Y	Y	Y	Y
6 ***Coble***	Y	Y	Y	Y
7 McIntyre	Y	Y	Y	Y
8 ***Hayes***	Y	Y	Y	Y
9 ***Myrick***	Y	Y	Y	Y
10 ***Ballenger***	Y	Y	Y	Y
11 ***Taylor***	Y	Y	?	Y
12 Watt	Y	Y	Y	Y
NORTH DAKOTA				
AL Pomeroy	Y	Y	Y	Y
OHIO				
1 ***Chabot***	Y	Y	Y	Y
2 ***Portman***	Y	Y	Y	Y
3 Hall	Y	Y	Y	Y
4 ***Oxley***	Y	Y	Y	Y
5 ***Gillmor***	Y	Y	Y	Y
6 Strickland	Y	Y	Y	Y
7 ***Hobson***	Y	Y	Y	Y
8 ***Boehner***	Y	Y	Y	Y
9 Kaptur	Y	Y	Y	Y
10 Kucinich	Y	Y	N	Y
11 Jones	Y	Y	Y	Y
12 ***Kasich***	Y	Y	+	+
13 Brown	Y	Y	Y	Y
14 Sawyer	Y	Y	Y	Y
15 ***Pryce***	Y	Y	Y	Y
16 ***Regula***	Y	Y	Y	?
17 Traficant	Y	Y	Y	Y
18 ***Ney***	Y	Y	Y	Y
19 ***LaTourette***	Y	Y	Y	Y
OKLAHOMA				
1 ***Largent***	Y	Y	Y	Y
2 ***Coburn***	Y	Y	?	Y
3 ***Watkins***	Y	Y	?	Y
4 ***Watts***	Y	Y	Y	Y
5 ***Istook***	Y	Y	Y	Y
6 ***Lucas***	Y	Y	Y	Y
OREGON				
1 Wu	Y	Y	Y	Y
2 ***Walden***	Y	Y	Y	Y
3 Blumenauer	Y	Y	Y	Y
4 DeFazio	Y	Y	N	Y
5 Hooley	Y	Y	Y	Y
PENNSYLVANIA				
1 Brady	Y	Y	N	Y
2 Fattah	Y	Y	?	Y
3 Borski	Y	Y	N	Y
4 Klink	Y	Y	Y	Y
5 ***Peterson***	Y	Y	Y	Y
6 Holden	Y	Y	Y	Y
7 ***Weldon***	?	Y	Y	Y
8 ***Greenwood***	Y	Y	Y	Y
9 ***Shuster***	Y	Y	Y	Y
10 ***Sherwood***	Y	Y	Y	Y
11 Kanjorski	Y	Y	Y	Y
12 Murtha	Y	Y	Y	Y
13 Hoeffel	Y	Y	Y	Y
14 Coyne	Y	Y	Y	Y
15 ***Toomey***	Y	Y	Y	Y
16 ***Pitts***	Y	Y	Y	Y
17 ***Gekas***	Y	Y	Y	Y
18 Doyle	Y	Y	?	Y
19 ***Goodling***	Y	Y	?	+
20 Mascara	Y	Y	Y	Y
21 ***English***	Y	Y	N	Y
RHODE ISLAND				
1 Kennedy	Y	Y	Y	?
2 Weygand	Y	Y	Y	Y
SOUTH CAROLINA				
1 ***Sanford***	Y	Y	Y	Y
2 ***Spence***	Y	Y	Y	Y
3 ***Graham***	Y	Y	Y	Y
4 ***DeMint***	Y	Y	Y	Y
5 Spratt	Y	Y	Y	Y
6 Clyburn	Y	Y	Y	Y
SOUTH DAKOTA				
AL ***Thune***	Y	Y	Y	Y

	25	26	27	28
TENNESSEE				
1 ***Jenkins***	Y	Y	Y	Y
2 ***Duncan***	Y	Y	Y	Y
3 ***Wamp***	Y	Y	Y	Y
4 ***Hilleary***	Y	Y	Y	Y
5 Clement	Y	Y	Y	Y
6 Gordon	Y	Y	Y	Y
7 ***Bryant***	Y	Y	Y	Y
8 Tanner	Y	Y	Y	Y
9 Ford	Y	Y	N	Y
TEXAS				
1 Sandlin	Y	Y	Y	Y
2 Turner	Y	Y	Y	Y
3 ***Johnson, Sam***	Y	Y	Y	Y
4 Hall	Y	Y	Y	Y
5 ***Sessions***	Y	Y	Y	Y
6 ***Barton***	Y	Y	Y	Y
7 ***Archer***	Y	Y	?	Y
8 ***Brady***	Y	Y	Y	Y
9 Lampson	Y	Y	Y	Y
10 Doggett	Y	Y	Y	Y
11 Edwards	Y	Y	Y	Y
12 ***Granger***	Y	Y	Y	Y
13 ***Thornberry***	Y	Y	Y	Y
14 ***Paul***	N	Y	Y	N
15 Hinojosa	Y	Y	Y	Y
16 Reyes	?	?	?	?
17 Stenholm	Y	Y	P	Y
18 Jackson-Lee	Y	Y	Y	Y
19 ***Combest***	Y	Y	Y	Y
20 Gonzalez	Y	Y	Y	Y
21 ***Smith***	Y	Y	Y	Y
22 ***DeLay***	Y	Y	Y	Y
23 ***Bonilla***	Y	Y	Y	Y
24 Frost	Y	Y	Y	Y
25 Bentsen	Y	Y	Y	Y
26 ***Armey***	Y	Y	Y	Y
27 Ortiz	Y	Y	Y	Y
28 Rodriguez	Y	Y	Y	Y
29 Green	Y	Y	Y	Y
30 Johnson, E.B.	Y	Y	Y	Y
UTAH				
1 ***Hansen***	Y	Y	Y	Y
2 ***Cook***	Y	Y	Y	Y
3 ***Cannon***	Y	Y	Y	Y
VERMONT				
AL *Sanders*	Y	Y	Y	Y
VIRGINIA				
1 ***Bateman***	Y	Y	Y	Y
2 Pickett	Y	Y	N	Y
3 Scott	Y	Y	Y	Y
4 Sisisky	Y	Y	Y	Y
5 Goode	Y	Y	Y	Y
6 ***Goodlatte***	Y	Y	Y	Y
7 ***Bliley***	Y	Y	Y	Y
8 Moran	Y	Y	Y	Y
9 Boucher	Y	Y	Y	Y
10 ***Wolf***	Y	Y	Y	Y
11 ***Davis***	Y	Y	Y	?
WASHINGTON				
1 Inslee	Y	Y	Y	Y
2 ***Metcalf***	Y	Y	Y	Y
3 Baird	Y	Y	Y	Y
4 ***Hastings***	Y	Y	Y	Y
5 ***Nethercutt***	Y	Y	Y	Y
6 Dicks	Y	Y	Y	Y
7 McDermott	Y	Y	N	N
8 ***Dunn***	Y	Y	Y	Y
9 Smith	Y	Y	Y	Y
WEST VIRGINIA				
1 Mollohan	Y	Y	Y	Y
2 Wise	Y	Y	Y	Y
3 Rahall	Y	Y	Y	Y
WISCONSIN				
1 ***Ryan***	Y	Y	Y	Y
2 Baldwin	Y	Y	Y	Y
3 Kind	Y	Y	Y	Y
4 Kleczka	Y	Y	Y	Y
5 Barrett	Y	Y	Y	Y
6 ***Petri***	Y	Y	Y	Y
7 Obey	Y	Y	Y	Y
8 ***Green***	Y	Y	Y	Y
9 ***Sensenbrenner***	Y	Y	Y	Y
WYOMING				
AL ***Cubin***	Y	Y	Y	Y

Southern states - Ala., Ark., Fla., Ga., Ky., La., Miss., N.C., Okla., S.C., Tenn., Texas, Va.

29. **H J Res 32. Social Security/Passage.** Shaw, R-Fla., motion to suspend the rules and pass the joint resolution to express the sense of Congress that the president and Congress should join to strengthen and protect the retirement income security of all Americans through the creation of a fair and modern Social Security program that ensures equal treatment, provides a continuous benefit safety net for workers, protects guaranteed lifetime benefits and does not increase taxes. Motion agreed to 416-1: R 209-1; D 206-0 (ND 152-0, SD 54-0); I 1-0. March 2, 1999. A two-thirds majority of those present and voting (278 in this case) is required for passage under suspension of the rules.

30. **HR 609. Pear Exports/Passage.** Combest, R-Texas, motion to suspend the rules and pass the bill to amend the Export Apple and Pear Act of 1933 to exclude pears from the act's requirements. The bill would permit the export of any grade of U.S. pears. Motion agreed to 416-0: R 210-0; D 205-0 (ND 152-0, SD 53-0); I 1-0. March 2, 1999. A two-thirds majority of those present and voting (277 in this case) is required for passage under suspension of the rules.

31. **HR 669. Peace Corps Authorization/Passage.** Passage of the bill to authorize the Peace Corps in fiscal years 2000-03. The bill would authorize $270 million in fiscal 2000, equal to the president's request and $29 million more than the current level. Passed 326-90: R 128-86; D 197-4 (ND 148-0, SD 49-4); I 1-0. March 3, 1999.

32. **HR 603. Aviation Accidents/Passage.** Passage of the bill to specify that the Death on the High Seas Act does not apply to lawsuits involving aviation accidents — thereby treating airline crashes in the ocean the same as those on land, and allowing families of ocean plane crash victims to seek noneconomic and punitive damages. Passed 412-2: R 211-2; D 200-0 (ND 148-0, SD 52-0); I 1-0. March 3, 1999. A "yea" was a vote in support of the president's position.

33. **HR 707. Natural Disaster Mitigation Program/Passage.** Passage of the bill to authorize $25 million in fiscal 1999 and $80 million in fiscal 2000 for a federal predisaster hazard mitigation program, under which grants would be provided to state and local governments to try to substantially reduce the risk of future damages, hardships or suffering from future natural disasters. The bill also would streamline and modify existing federal disaster assistance programs administered by the Federal Emergency Management Agency (FEMA). Passed 415-2: R 212-2; D 202-0 (ND 147-0, SD 55-0); I 1-0. March 4, 1999.

Key

Y Voted for (yea).
\# Paired for.
\+ Announced for.
N Voted against (nay).
X Paired against.
– Announced against.
P Voted "present."
C Voted "present" to avoid possible conflict of interest.
? Did not vote or otherwise make a position known.

•

Democrats ***Republicans***
Independents

	29	30	31	32	33
ALABAMA					
1 ***Callahan***	?	?	?	?	Y
2 ***Everett***	?	?	?	?	?
3 ***Riley***	Y	Y	N	Y	Y
4 ***Aderholt***	Y	Y	Y	Y	Y
5 Cramer	Y	Y	N	Y	Y
6 ***Bachus***	Y	Y	Y	Y	Y
7 Hilliard	?	?	Y	Y	Y
ALASKA					
AL ***Young***	Y	Y	Y	Y	Y
ARIZONA					
1 ***Salmon***	Y	Y	Y	Y	Y
2 Pastor	Y	Y	Y	Y	Y
3 ***Stump***	Y	Y	N	Y	N
4 ***Shadegg***	Y	Y	N	Y	Y
5 ***Kolbe***	Y	Y	N	Y	Y
6 ***Hayworth***	Y	Y	N	Y	Y
ARKANSAS					
1 Berry	Y	Y	Y	Y	Y
2 Snyder	Y	Y	Y	Y	Y
3 ***Hutchinson***	Y	Y	Y	Y	Y
4 ***Dickey***	Y	Y	?	?	Y
CALIFORNIA					
1 Thompson	?	Y	Y	Y	Y
2 ***Herger***	Y	Y	Y	Y	Y
3 ***Ose***	Y	Y	Y	Y	Y
4 ***Doolittle***	Y	Y	N	Y	Y
5 Matsui	Y	Y	Y	Y	Y
6 Woolsey	Y	Y	Y	Y	Y
7 Miller, George	Y	Y	Y	Y	Y
8 Pelosi	Y	Y	Y	Y	Y
9 Lee	Y	Y	Y	Y	Y
10 Tauscher	Y	Y	Y	Y	Y
11 ***Pombo***	Y	Y	N	Y	Y
12 Lantos	Y	Y	Y	Y	Y
13 Stark	Y	Y	Y	Y	?
14 Eshoo	Y	Y	Y	Y	Y
15 ***Campbell***	Y	Y	Y	Y	Y
16 Lofgren	Y	Y	Y	Y	Y
17 Farr	Y	Y	Y	Y	Y
18 Condit	Y	Y	Y	Y	Y
19 ***Radanovich***	Y	Y	N	Y	Y
20 Dooley	Y	Y	Y	Y	Y
21 ***Thomas***	Y	Y	Y	Y	Y
22 Capps	+	+	+	+	+
23 ***Gallegly***	Y	Y	Y	Y	Y
24 Sherman	Y	Y	Y	Y	Y
25 ***McKeon***	Y	Y	Y	Y	Y
26 Berman	?	?	Y	Y	Y
27 ***Rogan***	Y	Y	Y	Y	Y
28 ***Dreier***	Y	Y	Y	Y	Y
29 Waxman	Y	Y	Y	Y	Y
30 Becerra	Y	Y	Y	Y	Y
31 Martinez	Y	Y	Y	Y	Y
32 Dixon	Y	Y	Y	Y	Y
33 Roybal-Allard	Y	Y	Y	Y	Y
34 Napolitano	Y	Y	Y	Y	Y
35 Waters	Y	Y	Y	Y	Y
36 ***Kuykendall***	Y	Y	Y	Y	Y
37 Millender-McD.	Y	Y	Y	Y	Y
38 ***Horn***	Y	Y	Y	Y	Y
39 ***Royce***	Y	Y	N	Y	Y
40 ***Lewis***	Y	Y	Y	Y	Y
41 ***Miller, Gary***	Y	Y	Y	Y	Y
42 Brown	Y	Y	Y	Y	Y
43 ***Calvert***	Y	Y	Y	Y	Y
44 ***Bono***	Y	Y	Y	Y	Y
45 ***Rohrabacher***	Y	Y	N	Y	Y
46 Sanchez	Y	Y	+	+	+
47 ***Cox***	Y	Y	N	Y	Y
48 ***Packard***	Y	Y	Y	Y	Y
49 ***Bilbray***	+	Y	N	Y	Y
50 Filner	Y	Y	Y	Y	Y
51 ***Cunningham***	Y	Y	N	Y	Y
52 ***Hunter***	?	?	Y	Y	Y
COLORADO					
1 DeGette	Y	Y	Y	Y	Y
2 Udall	Y	Y	Y	Y	Y
3 ***McInnis***	Y	Y	Y	Y	Y
4 ***Schaffer***	Y	Y	N	Y	Y
5 ***Hefley***	Y	Y	N	Y	Y
6 ***Tancredo***	Y	Y	N	Y	Y
CONNECTICUT					
1 Larson	Y	Y	Y	Y	Y
2 Gejdenson	Y	Y	Y	Y	Y
3 DeLauro	Y	Y	Y	Y	Y
4 ***Shays***	Y	Y	Y	Y	Y
5 Maloney	Y	Y	Y	Y	Y
6 ***Johnson***	Y	Y	Y	Y	Y
DELAWARE					
AL ***Castle***	Y	Y	Y	Y	Y
FLORIDA					
1 ***Scarborough***	Y	Y	N	Y	+
2 Boyd	Y	Y	Y	Y	Y
3 Brown	Y	Y	Y	Y	Y
4 ***Fowler***	Y	Y	N	Y	Y
5 Thurman	Y	Y	Y	Y	Y
6 ***Stearns***	Y	Y	N	Y	Y
7 ***Mica***	Y	Y	N	Y	Y
8 ***McCollum***	?	?	?	?	?
9 ***Bilirakis***	Y	Y	Y	Y	Y
10 ***Young***	Y	Y	Y	Y	Y
11 Davis	Y	Y	Y	?	Y
12 ***Canady***	Y	Y	Y	Y	Y
13 ***Miller***	Y	Y	Y	Y	Y
14 ***Goss***	Y	Y	Y	Y	Y
15 ***Weldon***	Y	Y	Y	Y	Y
16 ***Foley***	Y	Y	Y	Y	Y
17 Meek	Y	Y	?	?	Y
18 ***Ros-Lehtinen***	Y	Y	Y	Y	Y
19 Wexler	Y	Y	Y	Y	Y
20 Deutsch	Y	Y	Y	Y	Y
21 ***Diaz-Balart***	Y	Y	Y	Y	Y
22 ***Shaw***	Y	Y	Y	Y	Y
23 Hastings	Y	Y	Y	Y	Y
GEORGIA					
1 ***Kingston***	Y	Y	N	Y	Y
2 Bishop	Y	Y	Y	Y	Y
3 ***Collins***	Y	Y	N	Y	Y
4 McKinney	Y	?	Y	Y	Y
5 Lewis	Y	Y	Y	Y	Y
6 ***Isakson***	Y	Y	Y	Y	Y
7 ***Barr***	Y	Y	N	Y	Y
8 ***Chambliss***	Y	Y	Y	Y	Y
9 ***Deal***	Y	Y	Y	Y	Y
10 ***Norwood***	Y	Y	Y	Y	Y
11 ***Linder***	Y	Y	Y	Y	Y
HAWAII					
1 Abercrombie	Y	Y	Y	Y	Y
2 Mink	Y	Y	Y	Y	Y
IDAHO					
1 ***Chenoweth***	Y	Y	N	Y	?
2 ***Simpson***	Y	Y	N	Y	Y
ILLINOIS					
1 Rush	Y	?	Y	Y	Y
2 Jackson	Y	Y	Y	Y	Y
3 Lipinski	Y	Y	Y	Y	Y
4 Gutierrez	Y	Y	Y	Y	Y
5 Blagojevich	Y	Y	Y	Y	Y
6 ***Hyde***	Y	Y	Y	Y	Y
7 Davis	Y	Y	Y	Y	Y
8 ***Crane***	Y	Y	N	Y	Y
9 Schakowsky	Y	Y	Y	Y	Y
10 ***Porter***	Y	Y	Y	Y	Y
11 ***Weller***	Y	Y	Y	Y	Y
12 Costello	Y	Y	Y	Y	Y
13 ***Biggert***	Y	Y	Y	Y	Y
14 ***Hastert***	Y				

ND Northern Democrats SD Southern Democrats

	29	30	31	32	33
15 ***Ewing***	Y	Y	Y	Y	Y
16 ***Manzullo***	Y	Y	N	Y	Y
17 Evans	?	?	?	?	?
18 ***LaHood***	Y	Y	Y	Y	Y
19 Phelps	Y	Y	Y	Y	Y
20 ***Shimkus***	Y	Y	Y	Y	Y
INDIANA					
1 Visclosky	Y	Y	Y	Y	Y
2 ***McIntosh***	Y	Y	N	Y	Y
3 Roemer	Y	Y	Y	Y	Y
4 ***Souder***	Y	Y	Y	Y	Y
5 ***Buyer***	?	?	Y	Y	Y
6 ***Burton***	Y	Y	N	Y	Y
7 ***Pease***	Y	Y	Y	Y	Y
8 ***Hostettler***	Y	Y	N	N	Y
9 Hill	Y	Y	Y	Y	Y
10 Carson	Y	Y	+	+	Y
IOWA					
1 ***Leach***	Y	Y	Y	Y	Y
2 ***Nussle***	Y	Y	Y	Y	Y
3 Boswell	Y	Y	Y	Y	Y
4 ***Ganske***	Y	Y	Y	Y	Y
5 ***Latham***	Y	Y	N	Y	Y
KANSAS					
1 ***Moran***	Y	Y	N	Y	Y
2 ***Ryun***	Y	Y	N	Y	Y
3 Moore	Y	Y	Y	Y	Y
4 ***Tiahrt***	Y	Y	N	Y	Y
KENTUCKY					
1 ***Whitfield***	Y	Y	Y	Y	Y
2 ***Lewis***	Y	Y	N	Y	Y
3 ***Northup***	Y	Y	Y	Y	Y
4 Lucas	Y	Y	Y	Y	Y
5 ***Rogers***	+	+	Y	Y	Y
6 ***Fletcher***	Y	Y	Y	Y	Y
LOUISIANA					
1 Vacant					
2 Jefferson	Y	Y	Y	Y	Y
3 ***Tauzin***	Y	Y	Y	Y	Y
4 ***McCrery***	Y	Y	Y	Y	Y
5 ***Cooksey***	+	Y	Y	?	Y
6 ***Baker***	Y	Y	Y	Y	Y
7 John	Y	Y	Y	Y	Y
MAINE					
1 Allen	Y	Y	Y	Y	Y
2 Baldacci	Y	Y	Y	Y	Y
MARYLAND					
1 ***Gilchrest***	Y	Y	Y	Y	?
2 ***Ehrlich***	Y	Y	Y	Y	Y
3 Cardin	Y	Y	Y	Y	Y
4 Wynn	Y	Y	Y	Y	Y
5 Hoyer	Y	Y	Y	Y	Y
6 ***Bartlett***	Y	Y	N	Y	Y
7 Cummings	Y	Y	Y	Y	Y
8 ***Morella***	Y	Y	Y	Y	Y
MASSACHUSETTS					
1 Olver	Y	Y	Y	Y	Y
2 Neal	Y	Y	Y	Y	Y
3 McGovern	Y	Y	Y	Y	Y
4 Frank	Y	Y	Y	Y	Y
5 Meehan	Y	Y	Y	Y	Y
6 Tierney	Y	Y	Y	Y	Y
7 Markey	Y	Y	Y	Y	Y
8 Capuano	Y	Y	Y	Y	Y
9 Moakley	Y	Y	Y	Y	Y
10 Delahunt	Y	Y	?	Y	Y
MICHIGAN					
1 Stupak	Y	Y	Y	Y	Y
2 ***Hoekstra***	Y	Y	Y	Y	Y
3 ***Ehlers***	Y	Y	Y	Y	Y
4 ***Camp***	Y	Y	Y	Y	Y
5 Barcia	Y	Y	Y	Y	Y
6 ***Upton***	Y	Y	Y	Y	Y
7 ***Smith***	Y	Y	N	Y	Y
8 Stabenow	Y	Y	Y	Y	Y
9 Kildee	Y	Y	Y	Y	Y
10 Bonior	Y	Y	Y	Y	Y
11 ***Knollenberg***	Y	Y	Y	Y	Y
12 Levin	Y	Y	Y	Y	Y
13 Rivers	Y	Y	Y	Y	Y
14 Conyers	Y	Y	Y	Y	Y
15 Kilpatrick	Y	Y	Y	Y	Y
16 Dingell	Y	Y	Y	Y	Y

	29	30	31	32	33
MINNESOTA					
1 ***Gutknecht***	Y	Y	N	Y	Y
2 Minge	Y	Y	Y	Y	Y
3 ***Ramstad***	Y	Y	N	Y	Y
4 Vento	Y	Y	Y	Y	Y
5 Sabo	Y	Y	Y	Y	Y
6 Luther	Y	Y	Y	Y	Y
7 Peterson	Y	Y	Y	Y	Y
8 Oberstar	Y	Y	?	+	Y
MISSISSIPPI					
1 ***Wicker***	Y	Y	N	Y	Y
2 Thompson	Y	Y	Y	Y	Y
3 ***Pickering***	Y	Y	N	Y	Y
4 Shows	Y	Y	Y	Y	Y
5 Taylor	Y	Y	Y	Y	Y
MISSOURI					
1 Clay	Y	Y	Y	Y	Y
2 ***Talent***	Y	Y	Y	Y	Y
3 Gephardt	Y	Y	Y	Y	Y
4 Skelton	Y	Y	Y	Y	Y
5 McCarthy	Y	Y	Y	Y	Y
6 Danner	Y	Y	Y	Y	Y
7 ***Blunt***	Y	Y	N	N	Y
8 ***Emerson***	Y	Y	Y	Y	Y
9 ***Hulshof***	Y	Y	Y	Y	Y
MONTANA					
AL ***Hill***	Y	Y	N	Y	Y
NEBRASKA					
1 ***Bereuter***	Y	Y	Y	Y	Y
2 ***Terry***	Y	Y	?	Y	Y
3 ***Barrett***	Y	Y	N	Y	Y
NEVADA					
1 Berkley	Y	Y	Y	Y	Y
2 ***Gibbons***	Y	Y	Y	Y	Y
NEW HAMPSHIRE					
1 ***Sununu***	Y	Y	N	Y	Y
2 ***Bass***	Y	Y	Y	Y	Y
NEW JERSEY					
1 Andrews	Y	Y	Y	Y	Y
2 ***LoBiondo***	Y	Y	Y	Y	Y
3 ***Saxton***	Y	Y	Y	Y	Y
4 ***Smith***	Y	Y	Y	Y	Y
5 ***Roukema***	Y	Y	Y	Y	Y
6 Pallone	Y	Y	Y	Y	Y
7 ***Franks***	Y	Y	Y	Y	Y
8 Pascrell	Y	Y	?	?	Y
9 Rothman	Y	Y	Y	Y	Y
10 Payne	Y	Y	Y	Y	Y
11 ***Frelinghuysen***	Y	Y	Y	Y	Y
12 Holt	Y	Y	Y	Y	?
13 Menendez	Y	Y	Y	Y	Y
NEW MEXICO					
1 ***Wilson***	Y	Y	N	Y	Y
2 ***Skeen***	Y	Y	Y	Y	Y
3 Udall	Y	Y	Y	Y	Y
NEW YORK					
1 ***Forbes***	Y	Y	Y	Y	Y
2 ***Lazio***	Y	Y	Y	Y	Y
3 ***King***	Y	Y	Y	Y	Y
4 McCarthy	Y	Y	Y	Y	Y
5 Ackerman	Y	Y	?	?	Y
6 Meeks	Y	Y	Y	Y	Y
7 Crowley	Y	Y	Y	Y	Y
8 Nadler	Y	Y	Y	Y	Y
9 Weiner	Y	Y	Y	Y	Y
10 Towns	Y	Y	Y	Y	Y
11 Owens	Y	Y	Y	Y	Y
12 Velázquez	Y	Y	Y	Y	Y
13 ***Fossella***	Y	Y	Y	Y	Y
14 Maloney	Y	Y	Y	Y	Y
15 Rangel	Y	Y	Y	?	?
16 Serrano	Y	Y	Y	Y	Y
17 Engel	Y	Y	Y	Y	?
18 Lowey	Y	Y	Y	Y	Y
19 ***Kelly***	Y	Y	Y	Y	Y
20 ***Gilman***	Y	Y	Y	Y	Y
21 McNulty	Y	Y	Y	Y	Y
22 ***Sweeney***	Y	Y	N	Y	Y
23 ***Boehlert***	Y	Y	Y	Y	Y
24 ***McHugh***	Y	Y	Y	Y	Y
25 ***Walsh***	Y	Y	Y	Y	Y
26 Hinchey	Y	Y	Y	Y	Y
27 ***Reynolds***	Y	Y	Y	Y	Y
28 Slaughter	Y	Y	Y	Y	Y
29 LaFalce	Y	Y	Y	Y	Y

	29	30	31	32	33
30 ***Quinn***	Y	Y	Y	Y	Y
31 ***Houghton***	Y	Y	Y	Y	Y
NORTH CAROLINA					
1 Clayton	Y	Y	Y	Y	Y
2 Etheridge	Y	Y	Y	Y	Y
3 ***Jones***	Y	Y	N	Y	Y
4 Price	Y	Y	Y	Y	Y
5 ***Burr***	Y	Y	Y	Y	Y
6 ***Coble***	Y	Y	N	Y	Y
7 McIntyre	Y	Y	Y	Y	Y
8 ***Hayes***	Y	Y	N	Y	Y
9 ***Myrick***	Y	Y	Y	Y	Y
10 ***Ballenger***	Y	Y	N	Y	Y
11 ***Taylor***	Y	Y	N	Y	Y
12 Watt	Y	Y	Y	Y	Y
NORTH DAKOTA					
AL Pomeroy	Y	Y	Y	Y	Y
OHIO					
1 ***Chabot***	Y	Y	N	Y	Y
2 ***Portman***	Y	Y	Y	Y	Y
3 Hall	Y	Y	Y	Y	Y
4 ***Oxley***	Y	Y	Y	Y	Y
5 ***Gillmor***	Y	Y	Y	Y	Y
6 Strickland	Y	Y	Y	Y	Y
7 ***Hobson***	Y	Y	Y	Y	Y
8 ***Boehner***	Y	Y	N	Y	Y
9 Kaptur	Y	Y	Y	Y	Y
10 Kucinich	Y	Y	Y	Y	Y
11 Jones	Y	Y	Y	Y	Y
12 ***Kasich***	Y	Y	Y	+	Y
13 Brown	Y	Y	Y	Y	Y
14 Sawyer	Y	Y	Y	Y	Y
15 ***Pryce***	Y	Y	Y	Y	Y
16 ***Regula***	Y	Y	Y	Y	Y
17 Traficant	Y	Y	Y	Y	Y
18 ***Ney***	Y	Y	Y	Y	Y
19 ***LaTourette***	Y	Y	Y	Y	Y
OKLAHOMA					
1 ***Largent***	Y	Y	N	Y	Y
2 ***Coburn***	Y	Y	N	Y	Y
3 ***Watkins***	Y	?	N	Y	Y
4 ***Watts***	Y	Y	N	Y	Y
5 ***Istook***	Y	Y	N	Y	Y
6 ***Lucas***	Y	Y	N	Y	Y
OREGON					
1 Wu	Y	Y	Y	Y	Y
2 ***Walden***	Y	Y	N	Y	Y
3 Blumenauer	Y	Y	Y	Y	Y
4 DeFazio	Y	Y	Y	Y	Y
5 Hooley	Y	Y	Y	Y	Y
PENNSYLVANIA					
1 Brady	Y	Y	Y	Y	Y
2 Fattah	Y	Y	Y	Y	Y
3 Borski	Y	Y	Y	Y	Y
4 Klink	Y	Y	Y	Y	Y
5 ***Peterson***	Y	Y	Y	Y	Y
6 Holden	Y	Y	Y	Y	Y
7 ***Weldon***	Y	Y	?	?	Y
8 ***Greenwood***	Y	Y	Y	Y	Y
9 ***Shuster***	Y	Y	N	Y	Y
10 ***Sherwood***	Y	Y	Y	Y	Y
11 Kanjorski	Y	Y	Y	Y	Y
12 Murtha	Y	Y	Y	Y	Y
13 Hoeffel	Y	Y	Y	Y	Y
14 Coyne	Y	Y	Y	Y	Y
15 ***Toomey***	Y	Y	N	Y	Y
16 ***Pitts***	Y	Y	Y	Y	Y
17 ***Gekas***	Y	Y	Y	Y	+
18 Doyle	Y	Y	Y	Y	Y
19 ***Goodling***	Y	Y	N	Y	Y
20 Mascara	Y	Y	Y	Y	Y
21 ***English***	Y	Y	Y	Y	Y
RHODE ISLAND					
1 Kennedy	Y	Y	Y	Y	?
2 Weygand	Y	Y	Y	Y	Y
SOUTH CAROLINA					
1 ***Sanford***	Y	Y	N	Y	Y
2 ***Spence***	Y	?	N	Y	Y
3 ***Graham***	Y	Y	N	Y	Y
4 ***DeMint***	Y	Y	Y	Y	Y
5 Spratt	Y	Y	Y	Y	Y
6 Clyburn	Y	Y	Y	Y	Y
SOUTH DAKOTA					
AL ***Thune***	Y	Y	Y	Y	Y

	29	30	31	32	33
TENNESSEE					
1 ***Jenkins***	Y	Y	Y	Y	Y
2 ***Duncan***	Y	Y	N	Y	Y
3 ***Wamp***	Y	Y	N	Y	Y
4 ***Hilleary***	Y	Y	N	Y	Y
5 Clement	Y	Y	Y	Y	Y
6 Gordon	Y	Y	Y	Y	Y
7 ***Bryant***	Y	Y	Y	Y	Y
8 Tanner	Y	Y	Y	Y	Y
9 Ford	Y	Y	Y	Y	Y
TEXAS					
1 Sandlin	Y	Y	Y	Y	Y
2 Turner	Y	Y	Y	Y	Y
3 ***Johnson, Sam***	Y	Y	N	Y	Y
4 Hall	Y	Y	N	Y	Y
5 ***Sessions***	Y	Y	N	Y	Y
6 ***Barton***	Y	Y	Y	Y	Y
7 ***Archer***	Y	Y	N	Y	Y
8 ***Brady***	Y	Y	Y	Y	Y
9 Lampson	Y	Y	Y	Y	Y
10 Doggett	Y	Y	Y	Y	Y
11 Edwards	Y	Y	Y	Y	Y
12 ***Granger***	?	?	?	?	?
13 ***Thornberry***	Y	Y	Y	Y	Y
14 ***Paul***	N	Y	N	Y	N
15 Hinojosa	Y	Y	Y	Y	Y
16 Reyes	Y	Y	Y	Y	Y
17 Stenholm	Y	Y	N	Y	Y
18 Jackson-Lee	Y	Y	Y	Y	Y
19 ***Combest***	Y	Y	N	Y	Y
20 Gonzalez	Y	Y	Y	Y	Y
21 ***Smith***	Y	Y	Y	Y	Y
22 ***DeLay***	Y	Y	N	Y	Y
23 ***Bonilla***	Y	Y	N	Y	Y
24 Frost	Y	Y	Y	Y	Y
25 Bentsen	Y	Y	Y	Y	Y
26 ***Armey***	Y	Y	N	Y	Y
27 Ortiz	Y	Y	Y	Y	Y
28 Rodriguez	Y	Y	Y	Y	Y
29 Green	Y	Y	Y	Y	Y
30 Johnson, E.B.	Y	Y	Y	Y	Y
UTAH					
1 ***Hansen***	+	Y	Y	Y	Y
2 ***Cook***	Y	Y	Y	Y	Y
3 ***Cannon***	?	?	N	Y	Y
VERMONT					
AL *Sanders*	Y	Y	Y	Y	Y
VIRGINIA					
1 ***Bateman***	Y	Y	Y	Y	Y
2 Pickett	Y	Y	Y	Y	Y
3 Scott	Y	Y	Y	Y	Y
4 Sisisky	Y	Y	Y	Y	Y
5 Goode	Y	Y	N	Y	Y
6 ***Goodlatte***	Y	Y	N	Y	Y
7 ***Bliley***	Y	Y	Y	Y	Y
8 Moran	Y	Y	Y	Y	Y
9 Boucher	Y	Y	?	?	Y
10 ***Wolf***	Y	Y	Y	Y	Y
11 ***Davis***	Y	Y	Y	Y	Y
WASHINGTON					
1 Inslee	Y	Y	Y	Y	Y
2 ***Metcalf***	Y	Y	N	Y	Y
3 Baird	Y	Y	Y	Y	Y
4 ***Hastings***	Y	Y	N	Y	Y
5 ***Nethercutt***	Y	Y	Y	Y	Y
6 Dicks	Y	Y	Y	Y	Y
7 McDermott	Y	Y	Y	Y	Y
8 ***Dunn***	?	?	Y	Y	Y
9 Smith	Y	Y	Y	Y	Y
WEST VIRGINIA					
1 Mollohan	Y	Y	Y	Y	?
2 Wise	Y	Y	Y	Y	Y
3 Rahall	Y	Y	Y	Y	Y
WISCONSIN					
1 ***Ryan***	Y	Y	N	Y	Y
2 Baldwin	Y	Y	Y	Y	Y
3 Kind	Y	Y	Y	Y	Y
4 Kleczka	Y	Y	Y	Y	Y
5 Barrett	Y	Y	Y	Y	Y
6 ***Petri***	Y	Y	Y	Y	Y
7 Obey	Y	Y	Y	Y	Y
8 ***Green***	Y	Y	N	Y	Y
9 ***Sensenbrenner***	Y	Y	N	Y	Y
WYOMING					
AL ***Cubin***	Y	Y	N	Y	Y

Southern states - Ala., Ark., Fla., Ga., Ky., La., Miss., N.C., Okla., S.C., Tenn., Texas, Va.

34. Procedural Motion/Journal. Approval of House Journal of Tuesday, March 9, 1999. Approved 356-39: R 191-15; D 164-24 (ND 120-18, SD 44-6); I 1-0. March 10, 1999.

35. HR 540. Nursing Home Resident Protections/Passage. Bilirakis, R-Fla., motion to suspend the rules and pass the bill to prohibit the discharge or transfer of nursing home residents as a result of a nursing home's voluntary withdrawal from the Medicaid program. Motion agreed to 398-12: R 198-12; D 199-0 (ND 147-0, SD 52-0); I 1-0. March 10, 1999. A two-thirds majority of those present and voting (274 in this case) is required for passage under suspension of the rules. A "yea" was a vote in support of the president's position.

36. HR 800. Educational Flexibility/Previous Question. Pryce, R-Ohio, motion to order the previous question (thus ending debate and the possibility of amendment) on adoption of the rule (H Res 100) to provide for House floor consideration of the bill to expand the current Education Flexibility Partnership program. Motion agreed to 217-198: R 215-0; D 2-197 (ND 0-147, SD 2-50); I 0-1. March 10, 1999. (The rule was subsequently adopted by voice vote.)

37. HR 800. Educational Flexibility/Math and Science Professional Development Needs. Holt, D-N.J., amendment to the Ehlers, R-Mich., amendment to the bill to expand the current Education Flexibility Partnership. The Holt amendment would require that schools applying for a waiver of the math-science priority demonstrate how the professional development needs of their teachers in the areas of science and math will be met. Rejected 204-218: R 2-216; D 201-2 (ND 149-1, SD 52-1); I 1-0. March 10, 1999.

38. HR 800. Educational Flexibility/Underlying Purpose of Federal Programs. Ehlers, R-Mich., amendment to require that state agencies ensure that the underlying purposes of the federal programs being waived are met. The bill would expand the current Education Flexibility Partnership program by making all 50 states (plus the District of Columbia, Puerto Rico and other U.S. territories) eligible to participate. Adopted 406-13: R 207-10; D 198-3 (ND 145-3, SD 53-0); I 1-0. March 10, 1999.

39. HR 800. Educational Flexibility/Student Performance Assessments. Miller, D-Calif., amendment to require that in order to obtain waiver authority under the bill, states must have in place a plan for assessing students' performance, and must use the same plan throughout the five-year period for which they would be granted waiver authority. The amendment also would require states to have a goal of closing gaps in achievement between economically disadvantaged children and their peers. Rejected 196-228: R 0-219; D 195-9 (ND 148-4, SD 47-5); I 1-0. March 10, 1999.

40. HR 800. Educational Flexibility/Low-Income Families Waiver Restriction. Scott, D-Va., amendment to prohibit states or state education agencies from waiving the requirements for Title I funding unless 35 percent or more of the children in the school district come from low-income families. Rejected 195-223: R 1-216; D 193-7 (ND 145-3, SD 48-4); I 1-0. March 11, 1999.

41. HR 800. Educational Flexibility/Passage. Passage of the bill to expand the current Education Flexibility Partnership program by making all 50 states (plus the District of Columbia, Puerto Rico and other U.S. territories) eligible to participate in the program, instead of only the 12 states permitted under current law. Under the bill, participating states could waive certain federal statutory or regulatory requirements for education programs, as well as state requirements. The bill would remove the "ed flex" program from the Goals 2000 statute but would require states to have implemented content and performance standards and assessments required under the Title I program for disadvantaged students. Passed 330-90: R 217-0; D 112-90 (ND 75-75, SD 37-15); I 1-0. March 11, 1999.

Key

- Y Voted for (yea).
- # Paired for.
- + Announced for.
- N Voted against (nay).
- X Paired against.
- – Announced against.
- P Voted "present."
- C Voted "present" to avoid possible conflict of interest.
- ? Did not vote or otherwise make a position known.

•

Democrats ***Republicans***
Independents

	34	35	36	37	38	39	40	41
ALABAMA								
1 ***Callahan***	Y	Y	Y	N	Y	N	N	Y
2 ***Everett***	Y	Y	Y	N	Y	N	N	Y
3 ***Riley***	Y	Y	Y	N	Y	N	N	Y
4 ***Aderholt***	N	Y	Y	N	Y	N	N	Y
5 Cramer	Y	Y	N	Y	Y	Y	Y	Y
6 ***Bachus***	Y	Y	Y	N	Y	N	N	Y
7 Hilliard	N	Y	N	Y	Y	Y	Y	N
ALASKA								
AL ***Young***	?	Y	Y	N	Y	N	N	Y
ARIZONA								
1 ***Salmon***	Y	Y	Y	N	Y	N	N	Y
2 Pastor	Y	Y	N	Y	Y	Y	Y	N
3 ***Stump***	Y	N	Y	N	N	N	N	Y
4 ***Shadegg***	Y	N	Y	N	Y	N	N	Y
5 ***Kolbe***	Y	Y	Y	N	Y	N	N	Y
6 ***Hayworth***	Y	Y	Y	N	Y	N	N	Y
ARKANSAS								
1 Berry	Y	Y	N	Y	Y	Y	Y	Y
2 Snyder	Y	Y	N	Y	Y	N	Y	Y
3 ***Hutchinson***	Y	Y	Y	N	Y	N	N	Y
4 ***Dickey***	Y	Y	Y	N	Y	N	N	Y
CALIFORNIA								
1 Thompson	Y	Y	N	Y	Y	Y	Y	Y
2 ***Herger***	Y	Y	Y	N	Y	N	N	Y
3 ***Ose***	Y	Y	Y	N	Y	N	N	Y
4 ***Doolittle***	Y	Y	Y	N	Y	N	N	Y
5 Matsui	Y	Y	N	Y	Y	Y	Y	Y
6 Woolsey	Y	Y	N	Y	Y	Y	Y	N
7 Miller, George	Y	Y	N	Y	Y	Y	Y	N
8 Pelosi	Y	Y	N	Y	Y	Y	Y	N
9 Lee	Y	Y	N	Y	Y	Y	Y	N
10 Tauscher	Y	Y	N	Y	Y	Y	Y	Y
11 ***Pombo***	Y	Y	Y	N	Y	N	N	Y
12 Lantos	Y	Y	N	Y	Y	Y	Y	Y
13 Stark	Y	Y	N	Y	Y	Y	Y	N
14 Eshoo	Y	Y	N	Y	Y	Y	Y	Y
15 ***Campbell***	Y	N	Y	N	Y	N	N	Y
16 Lofgren	Y	Y	N	Y	Y	Y	Y	Y
17 Farr	Y	Y	N	Y	Y	Y	Y	Y
18 Condit	Y	Y	N	Y	Y	Y	Y	Y
19 ***Radanovich***	Y	Y	Y	N	Y	N	N	Y
20 Dooley	Y	Y	?	Y	Y	Y	Y	Y
21 ***Thomas***	Y	Y	Y	N	Y	N	N	Y
22 Capps	?	?	?	?	?	?	?	?
23 ***Gallegly***	Y	Y	Y	N	Y	N	N	Y
24 Sherman	?	?	?	?	?	Y	Y	Y
25 ***McKeon***	Y	Y	Y	N	Y	N	N	Y
26 Berman	Y	Y	N	Y	Y	Y	Y	N
27 ***Rogan***	N	Y	Y	N	Y	N	N	Y
28 ***Dreier***	Y	Y	Y	N	Y	N	N	Y
29 Waxman	Y	Y	N	Y	Y	Y	Y	N
30 Becerra	?	?	?	?	?	?	?	?
31 Martinez	Y	Y	N	Y	Y	Y	?	?
32 Dixon	?	?	N	Y	Y	Y	Y	N
33 Roybal-Allard	Y	Y	N	Y	Y	Y	Y	N
34 Napolitano	Y	Y	N	Y	Y	Y	Y	Y
35 Waters	N	Y	N	Y	Y	Y	Y	N
36 ***Kuykendall***	Y	Y	Y	N	Y	N	N	Y
37 Millender-McD.	+	Y	N	Y	Y	Y	Y	N
38 ***Horn***	Y	Y	Y	N	Y	N	N	Y
39 ***Royce***	Y	Y	Y	N	Y	N	N	Y
40 ***Lewis***	Y	Y	Y	N	Y	N	N	Y
41 ***Miller, Gary***	Y	Y	Y	N	Y	N	N	Y
42 Brown	N	Y	N	Y	Y	Y	Y	Y
43 ***Calvert***	Y	Y	Y	N	Y	N	N	Y
44 ***Bono***	Y	Y	Y	N	Y	N	N	Y
45 ***Rohrabacher***	Y	Y	Y	N	Y	N	N	Y
46 Sanchez	Y	Y	N	Y	Y	Y	Y	N
47 ***Cox***	Y	Y	Y	N	Y	N	?	Y
48 ***Packard***	Y	Y	Y	N	Y	N	N	Y
49 ***Bilbray***	?	?	?	?	?	?	?	?
50 Filner	N	Y	N	Y	Y	Y	Y	N
51 ***Cunningham***	Y	Y	Y	N	Y	N	N	Y
52 ***Hunter***	Y	Y	Y	N	Y	N	N	Y
COLORADO								
1 DeGette	Y	Y	N	Y	Y	Y	Y	Y
2 Udall	Y	Y	N	Y	Y	Y	Y	Y
3 ***McInnis***	Y	Y	Y	N	Y	N	N	Y
4 ***Schaffer***	N	Y	Y	N	N	N	N	Y
5 ***Hefley***	N	Y	Y	N	Y	N	N	Y
6 ***Tancredo***	N	Y	Y	N	Y	N	N	Y
CONNECTICUT								
1 Larson	Y	Y	N	Y	Y	Y	Y	Y
2 Gejdenson	Y	Y	N	Y	?	Y	Y	Y
3 DeLauro	Y	Y	N	Y	Y	Y	Y	Y
4 ***Shays***	Y	Y	Y	N	Y	N	N	Y
5 Maloney	Y	Y	N	Y	Y	Y	Y	Y
6 ***Johnson***	Y	Y	Y	N	Y	N	N	Y
DELAWARE								
AL ***Castle***	Y	Y	Y	N	Y	N	N	Y
FLORIDA								
1 ***Scarborough***	Y	Y	Y	N	Y	N	N	Y
2 Boyd	Y	Y	N	Y	Y	N	N	Y
3 Brown	Y	Y	N	Y	Y	Y	Y	N
4 ***Fowler***	Y	Y	Y	N	Y	N	N	Y
5 Thurman	Y	Y	N	Y	Y	Y	Y	N
6 ***Stearns***	Y	Y	Y	N	Y	N	N	Y
7 ***Mica***	Y	Y	Y	N	Y	N	N	Y
8 ***McCollum***	Y	Y	Y	N	Y	N	N	Y
9 ***Bilirakis***	Y	Y	Y	N	Y	N	N	Y
10 ***Young***	Y	Y	Y	N	Y	N	N	Y
11 Davis	Y	Y	N	Y	Y	Y	Y	Y
12 ***Canady***	Y	Y	Y	N	Y	N	N	Y
13 ***Miller***	Y	?	Y	N	Y	N	N	+
14 ***Goss***	Y	Y	Y	N	Y	N	N	Y
15 ***Weldon***	Y	Y	Y	N	Y	N	N	Y
16 ***Foley***	Y	Y	Y	N	Y	N	N	Y
17 Meek	Y	Y	N	Y	Y	Y	Y	N
18 ***Ros-Lehtinen***	Y	Y	Y	N	Y	N	N	Y
19 Wexler	Y	Y	N	Y	Y	Y	Y	Y
20 Deutsch	Y	Y	N	Y	Y	Y	Y	Y
21 ***Diaz-Balart***	Y	Y	Y	N	Y	N	N	Y
22 ***Shaw***	Y	Y	Y	N	Y	N	N	Y
23 Hastings	N	Y	N	Y	Y	Y	Y	N
GEORGIA								
1 ***Kingston***	Y	Y	Y	N	Y	N	N	Y
2 Bishop	Y	Y	N	Y	Y	Y	Y	Y
3 ***Collins***	Y	Y	Y	N	N	N	N	Y
4 McKinney	?	Y	N	Y	Y	Y	Y	N
5 Lewis	Y	Y	N	Y	Y	Y	Y	N
6 ***Isakson***	Y	Y	Y	N	Y	N	N	Y
7 ***Barr***	Y	N	Y	N	Y	N	N	Y
8 ***Chambliss***	Y	Y	Y	N	Y	N	N	Y
9 ***Deal***	Y	Y	Y	N	Y	N	N	Y
10 ***Norwood***	Y	Y	Y	N	Y	N	N	Y
11 ***Linder***	Y	Y	Y	N	Y	N	N	Y
HAWAII								
1 Abercrombie	Y	Y	N	Y	N	Y	Y	N
2 Mink	Y	Y	N	Y	N	Y	Y	N
IDAHO								
1 ***Chenoweth***	Y	N	Y	N	N	N	N	Y
2 ***Simpson***	Y	Y	Y	N	Y	N	N	Y
ILLINOIS								
1 Rush	Y	Y	N	Y	Y	Y	Y	N
2 Jackson	Y	Y	N	Y	Y	Y	Y	N
3 Lipinski	Y	Y	N	Y	Y	N	N	Y
4 Gutierrez	N	Y	N	Y	Y	Y	Y	Y
5 Blagojevich	Y	Y	N	Y	Y	Y	?	Y
6 ***Hyde***	Y	Y	Y	N	Y	N	N	Y
7 Davis	Y	Y	N	Y	Y	Y	Y	N
8 ***Crane***	N	Y	Y	N	Y	N	N	Y
9 Schakowsky	Y	Y	N	Y	Y	Y	Y	N
10 ***Porter***	Y	Y	Y	N	Y	N	N	Y
11 ***Weller***	N	Y	Y	N	Y	N	N	Y
12 Costello	N	Y	N	Y	Y	Y	Y	N
13 ***Biggert***	Y	Y	Y	N	Y	N	N	Y
14 ***Hastert***			Y					Y

ND Northern Democrats SD Southern Democrats

	34	35	36	37	38	39	40	41
15 ***Ewing***	Y	Y	Y	N	Y	N	N	Y
16 ***Manzullo***	Y	Y	Y	N	N	N	N	Y
17 Evans	Y	Y	N	Y	Y	Y	Y	Y
18 ***LaHood***	Y	Y	Y	N	Y	N	N	Y
19 Phelps	Y	Y	N	Y	Y	Y	Y	Y
20 ***Shimkus***	Y	Y	Y	N	Y	N	N	Y
INDIANA								
1 Visclosky	N	Y	N	Y	Y	Y	Y	N
2 ***McIntosh***	Y	Y	Y	N	Y	N	N	Y
3 Roemer	Y	Y	N	Y	Y	N	Y	Y
4 ***Souder***	Y	Y	Y	N	N	N	N	Y
5 ***Buyer***	Y	Y	Y	N	Y	N	N	Y
6 ***Burton***	Y	Y	Y	N	Y	N	N	Y
7 ***Pease***	Y	Y	Y	N	Y	N	N	Y
8 ***Hostettler***	+	+	Y	N	Y	N	N	Y
9 Hill	Y	Y	N	Y	Y	N	Y	Y
10 Carson	Y	Y	N	Y	Y	Y	Y	N
IOWA								
1 ***Leach***	Y	Y	Y	N	Y	N	N	Y
2 ***Nussle***	Y	Y	Y	N	Y	N	N	Y
3 Boswell	Y	Y	N	Y	Y	Y	Y	Y
4 ***Ganske***	Y	Y	Y	N	Y	N	N	Y
5 ***Latham***	Y	Y	Y	N	Y	N	N	Y
KANSAS								
1 ***Moran***	N	Y	Y	N	Y	N	N	Y
2 ***Ryun***	Y	Y	Y	N	Y	N	N	Y
3 Moore	Y	Y	N	Y	Y	Y	Y	Y
4 ***Tiahrt***	?	+	Y	N	Y	N	N	Y
KENTUCKY								
1 ***Whitfield***	Y	Y	Y	N	Y	N	N	Y
2 ***Lewis***	Y	Y	Y	N	Y	N	N	Y
3 ***Northup***	Y	Y	Y	N	Y	N	N	Y
4 Lucas	Y	Y	N	Y	Y	Y	Y	Y
5 ***Rogers***	Y	Y	Y	N	Y	N	N	Y
6 ***Fletcher***	Y	Y	Y	N	Y	N	N	Y
LOUISIANA								
1 Vacant								
2 Jefferson	Y	Y	?	Y	Y	Y	Y	N
3 ***Tauzin***	Y	Y	Y	N	Y	N	N	Y
4 ***McCrery***	?	?	?	?	?	?	?	?
5 ***Cooksey***	?	Y	Y	N	Y	N	N	Y
6 ***Baker***	Y	Y	Y	N	Y	N	N	Y
7 John	Y	Y	N	Y	Y	Y	?	?
MAINE								
1 Allen	Y	Y	N	Y	Y	Y	Y	Y
2 Baldacci	Y	Y	N	Y	Y	Y	Y	Y
MARYLAND								
1 ***Gilchrest***	?	Y	Y	N	Y	N	N	Y
2 ***Ehrlich***	Y	Y	Y	N	Y	N	N	Y
3 Cardin	Y	Y	N	Y	Y	Y	Y	Y
4 Wynn	Y	Y	N	Y	Y	Y	Y	Y
5 Hoyer	Y	Y	N	Y	Y	Y	Y	Y
6 ***Bartlett***	Y	Y	Y	N	Y	N	N	Y
7 Cummings	Y	Y	N	Y	Y	Y	Y	N
8 ***Morella***	Y	Y	Y	Y	Y	N	N	Y
MASSACHUSETTS								
1 Olver	Y	Y	N	Y	Y	Y	Y	N
2 Neal	Y	Y	N	Y	Y	Y	Y	N
3 McGovern	Y	Y	N	Y	Y	Y	Y	N
4 Frank	Y	Y	N	Y	Y	Y	Y	N
5 Meehan	Y	Y	N	Y	Y	Y	Y	N
6 Tierney	Y	Y	N	Y	Y	Y	Y	N
7 Markey	?	Y	N	Y	Y	Y	Y	N
8 Capuano	Y	Y	N	Y	Y	Y	Y	N
9 Moakley	Y	Y	N	Y	Y	Y	Y	N
10 Delahunt	Y	Y	N	Y	Y	Y	?	?
MICHIGAN								
1 Stupak	N	Y	N	Y	Y	Y	Y	N
2 ***Hoekstra***	Y	Y	Y	N	Y	N	N	Y
3 ***Ehlers***	Y	Y	Y	N	Y	N	N	Y
4 ***Camp***	Y	Y	Y	N	Y	N	N	Y
5 Barcia	Y	Y	N	Y	Y	Y	Y	Y
6 ***Upton***	Y	Y	Y	N	Y	N	N	Y
7 ***Smith***	Y	Y	Y	N	Y	N	N	Y
8 Stabenow	Y	Y	N	Y	Y	Y	Y	Y
9 Kildee	Y	Y	N	Y	Y	Y	Y	N
10 Bonior	Y	Y	N	Y	Y	Y	Y	N
11 ***Knollenberg***	Y	Y	Y	N	Y	N	N	Y
12 Levin	Y	Y	N	Y	Y	Y	Y	N
13 Rivers	Y	Y	N	Y	Y	Y	Y	N
14 Conyers	Y	Y	?	Y	?	?	Y	N
15 Kilpatrick	Y	Y	N	Y	Y	Y	Y	N
16 Dingell	Y	Y	N	Y	Y	Y	Y	N
MINNESOTA								
1 ***Gutknecht***	N	Y	Y	N	Y	N	N	Y
2 Minge	?	+	–	+	+	+	Y	+
3 ***Ramstad***	N	Y	Y	N	Y	N	N	Y
4 Vento	Y	Y	N	Y	Y	Y	Y	N
5 Sabo	N	Y	N	Y	Y	Y	Y	Y
6 Luther	Y	Y	N	Y	Y	Y	Y	Y
7 Peterson	N	Y	N	Y	Y	Y	Y	Y
8 Oberstar	N	Y	N	Y	Y	Y	Y	N
MISSISSIPPI								
1 ***Wicker***	N	Y	Y	N	Y	N	N	Y
2 Thompson	N	Y	N	Y	Y	Y	Y	N
3 ***Pickering***	Y	Y	Y	N	Y	N	N	Y
4 Shows	Y	Y	N	Y	Y	Y	Y	Y
5 Taylor	N	Y	N	Y	Y	Y	N	Y
MISSOURI								
1 Clay	N	Y	N	Y	Y	Y	Y	N
2 ***Talent***	Y	Y	Y	N	Y	N	N	Y
3 Gephardt	?	?	N	Y	Y	Y	Y	Y
4 Skelton	Y	Y	N	Y	?	Y	Y	Y
5 McCarthy	Y	Y	N	Y	Y	Y	Y	N
6 Danner	Y	Y	N	Y	Y	Y	Y	Y
7 ***Blunt***	Y	Y	Y	N	Y	N	N	Y
8 ***Emerson***	Y	Y	Y	N	Y	N	N	Y
9 ***Hulshof***	N	Y	Y	N	Y	N	N	Y
MONTANA								
AL ***Hill***	Y	Y	Y	N	Y	N	N	Y
NEBRASKA								
1 ***Bereuter***	Y	Y	Y	N	Y	N	Y	Y
2 ***Terry***	Y	Y	Y	N	Y	N	N	Y
3 ***Barrett***	Y	Y	Y	N	Y	N	–	Y
NEVADA								
1 Berkley	Y	Y	N	Y	Y	Y	Y	Y
2 ***Gibbons***	Y	Y	Y	N	Y	N	N	Y
NEW HAMPSHIRE								
1 ***Sununu***	Y	Y	Y	N	Y	N	N	Y
2 ***Bass***	Y	Y	Y	N	Y	N	N	Y
NEW JERSEY								
1 Andrews	Y	Y	N	Y	Y	Y	Y	Y
2 ***LoBiondo***	N	Y	Y	N	Y	N	N	Y
3 ***Saxton***	Y	Y	Y	N	Y	N	N	Y
4 ***Smith***	?	?	Y	N	Y	N	N	?
5 ***Roukema***	?	?	?	N	Y	N	N	Y
6 Pallone	Y	Y	N	Y	Y	Y	Y	N
7 ***Franks***	Y	Y	Y	N	Y	N	N	Y
8 Pascrell	Y	Y	N	Y	Y	Y	Y	Y
9 Rothman	Y	Y	N	Y	Y	Y	Y	Y
10 Payne	Y	Y	N	Y	Y	Y	Y	N
11 ***Frelinghuysen***	Y	Y	Y	N	Y	N	N	Y
12 Holt	Y	Y	N	Y	Y	Y	Y	N
13 Menendez	Y	Y	N	Y	Y	Y	Y	N
NEW MEXICO								
1 ***Wilson***	Y	Y	Y	N	Y	N	N	Y
2 ***Skeen***	Y	Y	Y	N	Y	N	N	Y
3 Udall	Y	Y	N	Y	Y	Y	Y	Y
NEW YORK								
1 ***Forbes***	Y	Y	Y	N	Y	N	N	Y
2 ***Lazio***	Y	Y	Y	N	Y	N	N	Y
3 ***King***	Y	Y	Y	N	Y	N	N	Y
4 McCarthy	Y	Y	N	Y	Y	Y	Y	Y
5 Ackerman	Y	Y	N	Y	Y	Y	Y	N
6 Meeks	Y	Y	N	Y	Y	Y	Y	N
7 Crowley	Y	Y	N	Y	Y	Y	Y	N
8 Nadler	Y	Y	N	Y	Y	Y	Y	N
9 Weiner	Y	Y	N	Y	Y	Y	Y	N
10 Towns	N	Y	N	Y	Y	Y	Y	N
11 Owens	?	Y	?	Y	Y	Y	Y	N
12 Velázquez	Y	Y	N	Y	Y	Y	Y	N
13 ***Fossella***	Y	Y	Y	N	Y	N	N	Y
14 Maloney	Y	Y	N	Y	Y	Y	Y	N
15 Rangel	Y	Y	N	?	?	Y	?	N
16 Serrano	Y	Y	N	Y	Y	Y	Y	N
17 Engel	+	Y	N	Y	Y	Y	Y	N
18 Lowey	Y	Y	N	Y	Y	Y	Y	N
19 ***Kelly***	Y	Y	Y	N	Y	N	N	Y
20 ***Gilman***	Y	Y	Y	N	Y	N	N	Y
21 McNulty	N	Y	N	Y	Y	Y	Y	N
22 ***Sweeney***	Y	Y	Y	N	Y	N	N	Y
23 ***Boehlert***	?	Y	Y	N	Y	N	N	Y
24 ***McHugh***	Y	Y	Y	N	Y	N	N	Y
25 ***Walsh***	Y	Y	Y	N	Y	N	N	Y
26 Hinchey	?	?	?	Y	Y	Y	Y	N
27 ***Reynolds***	Y	Y	Y	N	Y	N	N	Y
28 Slaughter	Y	Y	N	Y	Y	Y	Y	Y
29 LaFalce	Y	Y	N	Y	Y	Y	Y	N
30 ***Quinn***	Y	Y	Y	N	Y	N	N	Y
31 ***Houghton***	Y	Y	Y	N	Y	N	N	Y
NORTH CAROLINA								
1 Clayton	Y	Y	N	Y	Y	Y	Y	N
2 Etheridge	Y	Y	N	Y	Y	Y	Y	Y
3 ***Jones***	Y	Y	Y	N	Y	N	N	Y
4 Price	Y	Y	N	Y	Y	Y	Y	Y
5 ***Burr***	Y	N	Y	N	Y	N	N	Y
6 ***Coble***	?	?	?	?	?	N	N	Y
7 McIntyre	Y	Y	N	Y	Y	Y	Y	Y
8 ***Hayes***	N	Y	Y	N	Y	N	N	Y
9 ***Myrick***	Y	Y	Y	N	Y	N	N	Y
10 ***Ballenger***	Y	Y	Y	N	Y	N	N	Y
11 ***Taylor***	?	?	?	N	Y	N	N	Y
12 Watt	Y	Y	N	Y	Y	Y	Y	N
NORTH DAKOTA								
AL Pomeroy	N	Y	N	Y	Y	Y	Y	Y
OHIO								
1 ***Chabot***	Y	Y	Y	N	Y	N	N	Y
2 ***Portman***	Y	Y	Y	N	Y	N	N	Y
3 Hall	Y	Y	N	?	Y	Y	Y	Y
4 ***Oxley***	?	Y	Y	N	Y	N	N	Y
5 ***Gillmor***	Y	Y	Y	N	Y	N	N	Y
6 Strickland	Y	Y	N	Y	Y	Y	Y	Y
7 ***Hobson***	Y	Y	Y	N	Y	N	N	Y
8 ***Boehner***	Y	Y	Y	N	Y	N	N	Y
9 Kaptur	?	?	?	Y	Y	Y	?	N
10 Kucinich	N	Y	N	Y	Y	Y	Y	N
11 Jones	Y	Y	N	Y	Y	Y	Y	N
12 ***Kasich***	Y	Y	Y	N	Y	N	N	Y
13 Brown	Y	Y	N	Y	Y	Y	Y	N
14 Sawyer	Y	Y	N	Y	Y	Y	Y	N
15 ***Pryce***	Y	Y	Y	N	Y	N	N	Y
16 ***Regula***	Y	Y	Y	N	Y	N	N	Y
17 Traficant	Y	Y	N	Y	Y	Y	Y	Y
18 ***Ney***	?	?	?	N	Y	N	N	Y
19 ***LaTourette***	Y	Y	Y	N	Y	N	N	Y
OKLAHOMA								
1 ***Largent***	Y	Y	Y	N	Y	N	N	Y
2 ***Coburn***	Y	N	Y	N	Y	N	N	Y
3 ***Watkins***	Y	Y	Y	N	Y	N	N	Y
4 ***Watts***	Y	Y	Y	N	N	N	N	Y
5 ***Istook***	Y	Y	Y	N	Y	N	N	Y
6 ***Lucas***	Y	Y	Y	N	Y	N	N	Y
OREGON								
1 Wu	Y	Y	N	Y	Y	Y	Y	Y
2 ***Walden***	Y	Y	Y	N	Y	N	N	Y
3 Blumenauer	Y	Y	N	Y	Y	Y	Y	Y
4 DeFazio	N	Y	N	Y	Y	Y	Y	N
5 Hooley	Y	Y	N	Y	Y	Y	Y	Y
PENNSYLVANIA								
1 Brady	N	Y	N	Y	Y	Y	Y	N
2 Fattah	?	Y	N	Y	Y	Y	?	?
3 Borski	N	Y	N	Y	Y	Y	Y	N
4 Klink	?	?	N	Y	Y	Y	Y	Y
5 ***Peterson***	Y	Y	Y	N	Y	N	N	Y
6 Holden	Y	Y	N	Y	Y	Y	Y	Y
7 ***Weldon***	Y	Y	Y	N	Y	N	N	Y
8 ***Greenwood***	Y	Y	Y	N	Y	N	N	Y
9 ***Shuster***	Y	Y	Y	N	Y	N	N	Y
10 ***Sherwood***	Y	Y	Y	N	Y	N	N	Y
11 Kanjorski	Y	Y	N	Y	Y	Y	Y	Y
12 Murtha	Y	Y	N	Y	Y	Y	Y	Y
13 Hoeffel	Y	Y	N	Y	Y	Y	N	Y
14 Coyne	Y	Y	N	Y	Y	Y	Y	N
15 ***Toomey***	Y	Y	Y	N	Y	N	N	Y
16 ***Pitts***	Y	Y	Y	N	Y	N	N	Y
17 ***Gekas***	Y	Y	Y	N	?	N	N	Y
18 Doyle	?	Y	N	Y	Y	Y	Y	Y
19 ***Goodling***	Y	Y	Y	N	Y	N	N	Y
20 Mascara	Y	Y	N	Y	Y	Y	Y	Y
21 ***English***	N	Y	Y	N	Y	N	N	Y
RHODE ISLAND								
1 Kennedy	Y	Y	N	Y	Y	Y	Y	N
2 Weygand	Y	Y	N	Y	Y	Y	Y	Y
SOUTH CAROLINA								
1 ***Sanford***	Y	N	Y	N	Y	N	N	Y
2 ***Spence***	Y	Y	Y	N	Y	N	N	Y
3 ***Graham***	Y	Y	Y	N	Y	N	N	Y
4 ***DeMint***	?	+	Y	N	Y	N	N	Y
5 Spratt	Y	Y	N	Y	Y	Y	Y	Y
6 Clyburn	Y	Y	N	Y	Y	Y	Y	N
SOUTH DAKOTA								
AL ***Thune***	Y	Y	Y	N	Y	N	N	Y
TENNESSEE								
1 ***Jenkins***	Y	Y	Y	N	Y	N	N	Y
2 ***Duncan***	Y	Y	Y	N	Y	N	N	Y
3 ***Wamp***	Y	Y	Y	N	Y	N	N	Y
4 ***Hilleary***	Y	Y	Y	N	Y	N	N	Y
5 Clement	Y	Y	N	Y	Y	Y	Y	Y
6 Gordon	?	?	N	Y	Y	Y	Y	Y
7 ***Bryant***	Y	Y	Y	N	Y	N	N	Y
8 Tanner	Y	Y	N	Y	Y	N	Y	Y
9 Ford	N	Y	N	Y	Y	Y	Y	Y
TEXAS								
1 Sandlin	Y	Y	N	Y	Y	Y	Y	Y
2 Turner	Y	Y	N	Y	Y	Y	Y	Y
3 ***Johnson, Sam***	Y	Y	Y	N	Y	N	N	Y
4 Hall	Y	Y	Y	N	Y	N	N	Y
5 ***Sessions***	Y	Y	Y	N	N	N	N	Y
6 ***Barton***	Y	N	Y	N	Y	N	N	Y
7 ***Archer***	Y	Y	?	N	Y	N	N	Y
8 ***Brady***	Y	Y	Y	N	Y	N	N	Y
9 Lampson	Y	Y	N	Y	Y	Y	Y	Y
10 Doggett	Y	Y	N	Y	Y	Y	Y	Y
11 Edwards	Y	Y	N	Y	Y	Y	Y	Y
12 ***Granger***	Y	Y	Y	N	Y	N	N	Y
13 ***Thornberry***	Y	N	Y	N	Y	N	N	Y
14 ***Paul***	Y	N	Y	N	N	N	N	Y
15 Hinojosa	Y	Y	N	Y	Y	+	Y	Y
16 Reyes	?	?	?	?	?	?	?	?
17 Stenholm	Y	Y	N	Y	Y	Y	Y	Y
18 Jackson-Lee	Y	Y	N	Y	Y	Y	Y	N
19 ***Combest***	Y	Y	Y	N	Y	N	N	Y
20 Gonzalez	Y	Y	N	Y	Y	Y	Y	Y
21 ***Smith***	Y	Y	Y	N	Y	N	N	Y
22 ***DeLay***	Y	N	Y	N	Y	N	N	Y
23 ***Bonilla***	Y	Y	Y	N	Y	N	N	Y
24 Frost	?	?	?	?	?	?	?	?
25 Bentsen	Y	Y	N	Y	Y	Y	Y	Y
26 ***Armey***	Y	Y	Y	N	Y	N	N	Y
27 Ortiz	Y	Y	N	Y	Y	Y	Y	Y
28 Rodriguez	Y	Y	N	Y	Y	Y	Y	Y
29 Green	Y	Y	N	Y	Y	Y	Y	Y
30 Johnson, E.B.	Y	Y	N	Y	Y	Y	Y	N
UTAH								
1 ***Hansen***	Y	Y	Y	N	Y	N	N	Y
2 ***Cook***	Y	Y	Y	N	Y	N	N	Y
3 ***Cannon***	Y	Y	Y	N	Y	N	N	Y
VERMONT								
AL *Sanders*	Y	Y	N	Y	Y	Y	Y	Y
VIRGINIA								
1 ***Bateman***	Y	Y	Y	N	Y	N	N	Y
2 Pickett	N	Y	N	Y	Y	Y	Y	Y
3 Scott	Y	Y	N	Y	Y	Y	Y	N
4 Sisisky	Y	Y	N	Y	Y	Y	Y	Y
5 Goode	Y	Y	Y	Y	Y	N	N	Y
6 ***Goodlatte***	Y	Y	Y	N	Y	N	N	Y
7 ***Bliley***	Y	Y	Y	N	Y	N	N	Y
8 Moran	Y	Y	N	Y	Y	Y	Y	Y
9 Boucher	?	Y	N	Y	Y	Y	Y	Y
10 ***Wolf***	Y	Y	Y	N	Y	N	N	Y
11 ***Davis***	Y	Y	Y	N	Y	N	N	Y
WASHINGTON								
1 Inslee	Y	Y	N	Y	Y	Y	Y	Y
2 ***Metcalf***	Y	Y	Y	N	Y	N	N	Y
3 Baird	Y	Y	N	Y	Y	Y	Y	Y
4 ***Hastings***	Y	Y	Y	N	Y	N	N	+
5 ***Nethercutt***	Y	Y	Y	N	Y	N	N	Y
6 Dicks	Y	Y	N	Y	Y	Y	Y	Y
7 McDermott	?	Y	N	Y	Y	Y	Y	N
8 ***Dunn***	Y	Y	Y	N	Y	N	N	Y
9 Smith	Y	Y	N	N	N	N	N	Y
WEST VIRGINIA								
1 Mollohan	Y	Y	N	Y	Y	Y	Y	Y
2 Wise	?	Y	N	Y	Y	Y	Y	Y
3 Rahall	Y	Y	N	Y	Y	Y	Y	Y
WISCONSIN								
1 ***Ryan***	Y	Y	Y	N	Y	N	N	Y
2 Baldwin	Y	Y	N	Y	Y	Y	Y	Y
3 Kind	?	Y	N	Y	Y	Y	Y	Y
4 Kleczka	Y	Y	N	Y	Y	Y	Y	Y
5 Barrett	Y	Y	N	Y	Y	Y	Y	N
6 ***Petri***	Y	Y	Y	N	Y	N	N	Y
7 Obey	Y	Y	N	Y	Y	Y	Y	N
8 ***Green***	Y	Y	Y	N	Y	N	N	Y
9 ***Sensenbrenner***	Y	Y	Y	N	Y	N	N	Y
WYOMING								
AL ***Cubin***	Y	Y	Y	N	N	N	N	Y

Southern states - Ala., Ark., Fla., Ga., Ky., La., Miss., N.C., Okla., S.C., Tenn., Texas, Va.

42. HR 808. Farm Bankruptcy Extension/Passage. Gekas, R-Pa., motion to suspend the rules and pass the bill to extend until Oct. 1, 1999, Chapter 12 of the bankruptcy code, which deals with family farm bankruptcies. Motion agreed to 418-1: R 216-1; D 201-0 (ND 151-0, SD 50-0); I 1-0. March 11, 1999. A two-thirds majority of those present and voting (280 in this case) is required for passage under suspension of the rules.

43. H Res 32. Open Elections in Indonesia/Adoption. Bereuter, R-Neb., motion to suspend the rules and adopt the resolution to urge the Indonesian government to conduct its upcoming elections in a free and fair manner. Motion agreed to 413-6: R 212-6; D 200-0 (ND 150-0, SD 50-0); I 1-0. March 11, 1999. A two-thirds majority of those present and voting (280 in this case) is required for passage under suspension of the rules.

44. H Con Res 28. Human Rights Abuses in China/Adoption. Gilman, R-N.Y., motion to suspend the rules and adopt the resolution to express the sense of Congress that the United States should introduce and make all efforts necessary to pass a resolution at the annual meeting of the U.N. Commission on Human Rights criticizing the People's Republic of China for its human rights abuses in China and Tibet. Motion agreed to 421-0: R 218-0; D 202-0 (ND 151-0, SD 51-0); I 1-0. March 11, 1999. A two-thirds majority of those present and voting (281 in this case) is required for passage under suspension of the rules.

45. H Con Res 42. Peacekeeping Operations in Kosovo/Previous Question. Diaz-Balart, R-Fla., motion to order the previous question (thus ending debate and the possibility of amendment) on adoption of the rule (H Res 103) to provide for floor consideration of the resolution to authorize the deployment of U.S. armed forces to Kosovo as a part of a NATO peacekeeping operation implementing a Kosovo peace agreement. Motion agreed to 219-203: R 217-0; D 2-202 (ND 0-152, SD 2-50); I 0-1. March 11, 1999.

46. H Con Res 42. Peacekeeping Operations in Kosovo/Rule. Adoption of the rule (H Res 103) to provide for floor consideration of the resolution to authorize deployment of U.S. armed forces as a part of a NATO peacekeeping operation implementing a Kosovo peace agreement. Adopted 218-201: R 213-1; D 5-199 (ND 2-150, SD 3-49); I 0-1. March 11, 1999.

47. H Con Res 42. Peacekeeping Operations in Kosovo/Ruling of the Chair. Motion to sustain the ruling of the chair that upheld the Gilman, R-N.Y., point of order against the Gejdenson, D-Conn., amendment to urge the president to continue support for efforts to reach an interim agreement between the Serbian government and the Kosovar Albanians. The amendment would authorize the use of troops, but only if and when such an agreement is reached, and express support for the troops. Motion agreed to 218-205: R 218-0; D 0-204 (ND 0-152, SD 0-52); I 0-1. March 11, 1999.

48. H Con Res 42. Peacekeeping Operations in Kosovo/Prohibit Deployment. Fowler, R-Fla., substitute amendment to the Gejdenson, D-Conn., amendment to urge the president to continue support for efforts to reach an interim agreement between the Serbian government and the Kosovar Albanians. The Gejdenson amendment would authorize the use of troops, but only if and when such an agreement is reached and would limit U.S. deployment to 15 percent of the total peacekeeping force. The Fowler substitute would bar the deployment of troops but allow U.S. forces to act to protect the lives of U.S. citizens or for self-defense against an immediate threat. Rejected 178-237: R 169-48; D 9-188 (ND 6-140, SD 3-48); I 0-1. March 11, 1999. (Subsequently, the Gejdenson amendment was adopted by voice vote.)

49. H Con Res 42. Peacekeeping Operations in Kosovo/Adoption. Adoption of the resolution to authorize deployment of U.S. armed forces to Kosovo as a part of a NATO peacekeeping operation implementing a Kosovo peace agreement. Adopted 219-191: R 44-173; D 174-18 (ND 129-13, SD 45-5); I 1-0. March 11, 1999. A "yea" was a vote in support of the president's position.

Key

- Y Voted for (yea).
- # Paired for.
- \+ Announced for.
- N Voted against (nay).
- X Paired against.
- – Announced against.
- P Voted "present."
- C Voted "present" to avoid possible conflict of interest.
- ? Did not vote or otherwise make a position known.

•

Democrats ***Republicans***
Independents

	42	43	44	45	46	47	48	49
ALABAMA								
1 ***Callahan***	Y	Y	Y	Y	Y	Y	P	P
2 ***Everett***	Y	Y	Y	Y	Y	Y	Y	N
3 ***Riley***	Y	Y	Y	Y	Y	Y	Y	N
4 ***Aderholt***	Y	Y	Y	Y	Y	Y	Y	N
5 Cramer	Y	Y	Y	N	N	N	N	Y
6 ***Bachus***	Y	Y	Y	Y	Y	Y	Y	N
7 Hilliard	Y	Y	Y	N	N	N	N	Y
ALASKA								
AL ***Young***	Y	Y	Y	Y	Y	?	Y	N
ARIZONA								
1 ***Salmon***	Y	Y	Y	Y	Y	Y	Y	N
2 Pastor	Y	Y	Y	N	N	N	N	Y
3 ***Stump***	Y	Y	Y	Y	Y	Y	Y	N
4 ***Shadegg***	Y	Y	Y	Y	Y	Y	Y	N
5 ***Kolbe***	Y	Y	Y	Y	Y	Y	N	N
6 ***Hayworth***	Y	Y	Y	Y	Y	Y	Y	N
ARKANSAS								
1 Berry	Y	Y	Y	N	N	N	N	Y
2 Snyder	Y	Y	Y	N	N	N	N	Y
3 ***Hutchinson***	Y	Y	Y	Y	Y	Y	Y	N
4 ***Dickey***	Y	Y	Y	Y	Y	Y	Y	N
CALIFORNIA								
1 Thompson	Y	Y	Y	N	N	N	N	Y
2 ***Herger***	Y	Y	Y	Y	Y	Y	Y	N
3 ***Ose***	Y	Y	Y	Y	Y	Y	N	Y
4 ***Doolittle***	Y	Y	Y	Y	Y	Y	Y	N
5 Matsui	Y	Y	Y	N	N	N	N	Y
6 Woolsey	Y	Y	Y	N	N	N	N	Y
7 Miller, George	Y	Y	Y	N	N	N	N	Y
8 Pelosi	Y	Y	Y	N	N	N	N	Y
9 Lee	Y	Y	Y	N	N	N	N	Y
10 Tauscher	Y	Y	Y	N	N	N	N	Y
11 ***Pombo***	Y	N	Y	Y	Y	Y	Y	N
12 Lantos	Y	Y	Y	N	N	N	N	Y
13 Stark	Y	Y	Y	N	N	N	N	Y
14 Eshoo	Y	Y	Y	N	N	N	N	Y
15 ***Campbell***	Y	Y	Y	Y	Y	Y	Y	N
16 Lofgren	Y	Y	Y	N	N	N	N	P
17 Farr	Y	Y	Y	N	N	N	N	Y
18 Condit	Y	Y	Y	N	N	N	Y	N
19 ***Radanovich***	Y	Y	Y	Y	Y	Y	Y	Y
20 Dooley	Y	Y	Y	N	N	N	N	Y
21 ***Thomas***	Y	Y	Y	Y	Y	Y	Y	N
22 Capps	?	?	?	?	?	?	?	?
23 ***Gallegly***	Y	Y	Y	Y	Y	Y	Y	N
24 Sherman	Y	Y	Y	N	N	N	N	Y
25 ***McKeon***	Y	Y	Y	Y	Y	Y	Y	N
26 Berman	Y	Y	Y	N	N	N	N	Y
27 ***Rogan***	Y	Y	Y	Y	Y	Y	Y	N
28 ***Dreier***	Y	Y	Y	Y	Y	Y	N	Y
29 Waxman	Y	Y	?	N	N	N	N	Y
30 Becerra	?	?	?	?	?	?	?	?
31 Martinez	Y	Y	Y	N	N	N	N	Y
32 Dixon	Y	Y	Y	N	N	N	N	Y
33 Roybal-Allard	Y	Y	Y	N	N	N	N	Y
34 Napolitano	Y	Y	Y	N	N	N	N	Y
35 Waters	Y	Y	Y	N	N	N	N	Y
36 ***Kuykendall***	Y	Y	Y	Y	Y	Y	Y	N
37 Millender-McD.	Y	Y	Y	N	N	N	N	Y
38 ***Horn***	Y	Y	Y	Y	?	Y	Y	N
39 ***Royce***	Y	Y	Y	Y	Y	Y	Y	N

	42	43	44	45	46	47	48	49
40 ***Lewis***	Y	Y	Y	Y	Y	Y	N	Y
41 ***Miller, Gary***	Y	Y	Y	Y	Y	Y	Y	N
42 Brown	Y	Y	Y	N	N	N	?	?
43 ***Calvert***	Y	Y	Y	Y	Y	Y	N	Y
44 ***Bono***	Y	Y	Y	Y	Y	Y	N	Y
45 ***Rohrabacher***	Y	Y	Y	Y	Y	Y	Y	N
46 Sanchez	Y	Y	Y	N	N	N	N	Y
47 ***Cox***	?	Y	Y	Y	Y	Y	Y	N
48 ***Packard***	Y	Y	Y	Y	Y	Y	Y	N
49 ***Bilbray***	?	?	?	?	?	?	?	?
50 Filner	Y	Y	Y	N	N	N	N	Y
51 ***Cunningham***	Y	Y	Y	Y	Y	Y	Y	N
52 ***Hunter***	Y	Y	Y	Y	?	Y	N	Y
COLORADO								
1 DeGette	Y	Y	Y	N	N	N	N	Y
2 Udall	Y	Y	Y	N	N	N	N	Y
3 ***McInnis***	Y	Y	Y	Y	Y	Y	Y	N
4 ***Schaffer***	Y	Y	Y	Y	Y	Y	Y	N
5 ***Hefley***	Y	Y	Y	Y	Y	Y	Y	N
6 ***Tancredo***	Y	Y	Y	Y	Y	Y	Y	N
CONNECTICUT								
1 Larson	Y	Y	Y	N	N	N	N	Y
2 Gejdenson	Y	Y	Y	N	N	N	N	Y
3 DeLauro	Y	Y	Y	N	N	N	N	Y
4 ***Shays***	Y	Y	Y	Y	Y	Y	N	N
5 Maloney	Y	Y	Y	N	N	N	N	Y
6 ***Johnson***	Y	Y	Y	Y	Y	Y	N	Y
DELAWARE								
AL ***Castle***	Y	Y	Y	Y	Y	Y	N	Y
FLORIDA								
1 ***Scarborough***	Y	Y	Y	Y	Y	Y	Y	N
2 Boyd	Y	Y	Y	N	N	N	N	Y
3 Brown	Y	Y	Y	N	N	N	N	Y
4 ***Fowler***	Y	Y	Y	Y	Y	Y	Y	N
5 Thurman	Y	Y	Y	N	N	N	N	Y
6 ***Stearns***	Y	Y	Y	Y	Y	Y	Y	N
7 ***Mica***	Y	Y	Y	Y	Y	Y	Y	N
8 ***McCollum***	Y	Y	Y	Y	Y	Y	Y	N
9 ***Bilirakis***	Y	Y	Y	Y	Y	Y	Y	N
10 ***Young***	Y	Y	Y	Y	Y	Y	Y	N
11 Davis	Y	Y	Y	N	N	N	N	Y
12 ***Canady***	Y	Y	Y	Y	Y	Y	Y	N
13 ***Miller***	Y	Y	Y	Y	Y	Y	Y	N
14 ***Goss***	Y	Y	Y	Y	Y	Y	N	Y
15 ***Weldon***	Y	Y	Y	Y	Y	Y	Y	N
16 ***Foley***	Y	Y	Y	Y	Y	Y	Y	N
17 Meek	Y	Y	Y	N	N	N	N	Y
18 ***Ros-Lehtinen***	Y	Y	Y	Y	Y	Y	Y	N
19 Wexler	Y	Y	Y	N	N	N	N	Y
20 Deutsch	Y	Y	Y	N	N	N	N	Y
21 ***Diaz-Balart***	Y	Y	Y	Y	Y	Y	N	Y
22 ***Shaw***	Y	Y	Y	Y	Y	Y	N	Y
23 Hastings	Y	Y	Y	N	N	N	N	Y
GEORGIA								
1 ***Kingston***	Y	Y	Y	Y	Y	Y	Y	N
2 Bishop	Y	Y	Y	N	N	N	N	Y
3 ***Collins***	Y	Y	Y	Y	Y	Y	Y	N
4 McKinney	Y	Y	Y	N	N	N	N	N
5 Lewis	Y	Y	Y	N	N	N	N	Y
6 ***Isakson***	Y	Y	Y	Y	Y	Y	Y	N
7 ***Barr***	Y	Y	Y	Y	Y	Y	Y	N
8 ***Chambliss***	Y	Y	?	Y	Y	Y	Y	N
9 ***Deal***	Y	Y	Y	Y	Y	Y	Y	N
10 ***Norwood***	Y	Y	Y	Y	Y	Y	Y	N
11 ***Linder***	Y	Y	Y	Y	Y	Y	N	Y
HAWAII								
1 Abercrombie	Y	Y	Y	N	N	N	P	P
2 Mink	Y	Y	Y	N	N	N	N	P
IDAHO								
1 ***Chenoweth***	Y	N	Y	Y	Y	Y	Y	N
2 ***Simpson***	Y	Y	Y	Y	Y	Y	N	N
ILLINOIS								
1 Rush	Y	Y	Y	N	N	N	N	Y
2 Jackson	Y	Y	Y	N	N	N	N	Y
3 Lipinski	Y	Y	Y	N	N	N	?	?
4 Gutierrez	Y	Y	Y	N	N	N	N	Y
5 Blagojevich	Y	Y	Y	N	N	N	N	N
6 ***Hyde***	Y	Y	Y	Y	Y	Y	N	Y
7 Davis	Y	Y	Y	N	N	N	N	Y
8 ***Crane***	Y	Y	Y	Y	Y	Y	Y	N
9 Schakowsky	Y	Y	Y	N	N	N	N	Y
10 ***Porter***	Y	Y	Y	Y	Y	Y	N	Y
11 ***Weller***	Y	Y	Y	Y	Y	Y	Y	N
12 Costello	Y	Y	Y	N	N	N	N	N
13 ***Biggert***	Y	Y	Y	Y	Y	Y	N	Y
14 ***Hastert***				Y	Y			Y

ND Northern Democrats SD Southern Democrats

	42	43	44	45	46	47	48	49
15 ***Ewing***	Y	Y	Y	Y	Y	Y	Y	N
16 ***Manzullo***	Y	Y	Y	Y	Y	Y	Y	N
17 Evans	Y	Y	Y	N	N	N	N	Y
18 ***LaHood***	Y	Y	Y	Y	Y	Y	Y	N
19 Phelps	Y	Y	Y	N	N	N	N	N
20 ***Shimkus***	Y	Y	Y	Y	Y	Y	Y	N
INDIANA								
1 Visclosky	Y	Y	Y	N	N	N	N	N
2 ***McIntosh***	Y	Y	Y	Y	Y	Y	Y	N
3 Roemer	Y	Y	Y	N	Y	N	Y	N
4 ***Souder***	Y	Y	Y	Y	Y	Y	Y	N
5 ***Buyer***	Y	Y	Y	Y	Y	Y	N	Y
6 ***Burton***	Y	Y	Y	Y	Y	Y	Y	N
7 ***Pease***	Y	Y	Y	Y	Y	Y	Y	N
8 ***Hostettler***	Y	Y	Y	Y	Y	Y	Y	N
9 Hill	Y	Y	Y	N	N	N	N	Y
10 Carson	Y	Y	Y	N	N	N	N	Y
IOWA								
1 ***Leach***	Y	Y	Y	Y	Y	Y	Y	N
2 ***Nussle***	Y	Y	Y	Y	Y	Y	Y	N
3 Boswell	Y	Y	Y	N	N	N	N	Y
4 ***Ganske***	Y	Y	Y	Y	Y	Y	Y	N
5 ***Latham***	Y	Y	Y	Y	Y	Y	Y	N
KANSAS								
1 ***Moran***	Y	Y	Y	Y	Y	Y	Y	N
2 ***Ryun***	Y	Y	Y	Y	Y	Y	Y	N
3 Moore	Y	Y	Y	N	N	N	N	Y
4 ***Tiahrt***	Y	Y	Y	Y	Y	Y	Y	N
KENTUCKY								
1 ***Whitfield***	Y	Y	Y	Y	Y	Y	Y	N
2 ***Lewis***	Y	Y	Y	Y	Y	Y	Y	N
3 ***Northup***	Y	Y	Y	Y	Y	Y	N	N
4 Lucas	Y	Y	Y	N	N	N	N	Y
5 ***Rogers***	Y	Y	Y	Y	Y	Y	Y	N
6 ***Fletcher***	Y	Y	Y	Y	Y	Y	N	N
LOUISIANA								
1 Vacant								
2 Jefferson	?	Y	Y	N	N	N	N	Y
3 ***Tauzin***	Y	Y	Y	Y	Y	Y	Y	N
4 ***McCrery***	?	?	?	Y	Y	Y	Y	N
5 ***Cooksey***	Y	N	Y	Y	Y	Y	N	Y
6 ***Baker***	Y	Y	Y	Y	Y	Y	Y	N
7 John	?	?	?	?	?	?	?	?
MAINE								
1 Allen	Y	Y	Y	N	N	N	N	Y
2 Baldacci	Y	Y	Y	N	N	N	N	Y
MARYLAND								
1 ***Gilchrest***	Y	Y	Y	Y	Y	Y	N	Y
2 ***Ehrlich***	Y	Y	Y	Y	Y	Y	Y	N
3 Cardin	Y	Y	Y	N	N	N	N	Y
4 Wynn	Y	Y	Y	N	N	N	N	Y
5 Hoyer	Y	Y	Y	N	N	N	N	Y
6 ***Bartlett***	Y	Y	Y	Y	?	Y	Y	N
7 Cummings	Y	Y	Y	N	N	N	N	Y
8 ***Morella***	Y	Y	Y	?	?	Y	N	Y
MASSACHUSETTS								
1 Olver	Y	Y	Y	N	N	N	N	Y
2 Neal	Y	Y	Y	N	N	N	N	Y
3 McGovern	Y	Y	Y	N	N	N	N	Y
4 Frank	Y	Y	Y	N	Y	N	N	N
5 Meehan	Y	Y	Y	N	N	N	N	Y
6 Tierney	Y	Y	Y	N	N	N	N	Y
7 Markey	Y	Y	Y	N	N	N	N	Y
8 Capuano	Y	Y	Y	N	N	N	N	Y
9 Moakley	Y	Y	Y	N	N	N	N	Y
10 Delahunt	?	?	?	?	?	N	N	Y
MICHIGAN								
1 Stupak	Y	Y	Y	N	N	N	N	Y
2 ***Hoekstra***	Y	Y	Y	Y	Y	Y	Y	N
3 ***Ehlers***	Y	Y	Y	Y	Y	Y	Y	N
4 ***Camp***	Y	Y	Y	Y	Y	Y	Y	N
5 Barcia	Y	Y	Y	N	N	N	N	Y
6 ***Upton***	Y	Y	Y	Y	Y	Y	Y	N
7 ***Smith***	Y	Y	Y	Y	Y	Y	Y	N
8 Stabenow	Y	Y	+	N	N	N	N	Y
9 Kildee	Y	Y	Y	N	N	N	N	Y
10 Bonior	Y	Y	Y	N	N	N	N	Y
11 ***Knollenberg***	Y	Y	Y	Y	Y	Y	N	Y
12 Levin	Y	Y	Y	N	N	N	N	Y
13 Rivers	Y	Y	Y	N	N	N	N	Y
14 Conyers	Y	Y	Y	N	N	N	N	Y
15 Kilpatrick	Y	Y	Y	N	N	N	N	Y
16 Dingell	Y	Y	Y	N	N	N	N	Y
MINNESOTA								
1 ***Gutknecht***	Y	Y	Y	?	Y	Y	Y	N
2 Minge	Y	Y	Y	N	N	N	N	Y
3 ***Ramstad***	Y	Y	Y	Y	Y	Y	Y	N
4 Vento	Y	Y	Y	N	N	N	N	Y
5 Sabo	Y	Y	Y	N	N	N	N	Y
6 Luther	Y	Y	Y	N	N	N	N	Y
7 Peterson	Y	Y	Y	N	N	N	Y	N
8 Oberstar	Y	Y	Y	N	N	N	N	Y
MISSISSIPPI								
1 ***Wicker***	Y	Y	Y	Y	Y	Y	Y	N
2 Thompson	Y	Y	Y	N	N	N	?	?
3 ***Pickering***	Y	Y	Y	Y	Y	Y	Y	N
4 Shows	Y	Y	Y	N	N	N	N	Y
5 Taylor	Y	Y	Y	N	Y	N	N	N
MISSOURI								
1 Clay	Y	Y	Y	N	N	N	?	?
2 ***Talent***	Y	Y	Y	Y	Y	Y	Y	N
3 Gephardt	Y	Y	Y	N	N	N	N	Y
4 Skelton	Y	Y	Y	N	N	N	N	Y
5 McCarthy	Y	Y	Y	N	N	N	N	Y
6 Danner	Y	Y	Y	N	N	N	Y	N
7 ***Blunt***	Y	Y	Y	Y	Y	Y	Y	N
8 ***Emerson***	Y	Y	Y	Y	Y	Y	Y	N
9 ***Hulshof***	Y	Y	Y	Y	Y	Y	Y	N
MONTANA								
AL ***Hill***	Y	Y	Y	Y	Y	Y	Y	N
NEBRASKA								
1 ***Bereuter***	Y	Y	Y	Y	Y	Y	Y	N
2 ***Terry***	Y	Y	Y	Y	Y	Y	Y	N
3 ***Barrett***	Y	Y	Y	Y	Y	Y	Y	N
NEVADA								
1 Berkley	Y	Y	Y	N	N	N	N	Y
2 ***Gibbons***	Y	Y	Y	Y	Y	Y	Y	N
NEW HAMPSHIRE								
1 ***Sununu***	Y	Y	Y	Y	Y	Y	Y	N
2 ***Bass***	Y	Y	Y	Y	Y	Y	Y	N
NEW JERSEY								
1 Andrews	Y	Y	Y	N	N	N	Y	N
2 ***LoBiondo***	Y	Y	Y	Y	Y	Y	Y	N
3 ***Saxton***	Y	Y	Y	?	?	Y	Y	N
4 ***Smith***	Y	Y	Y	Y	Y	Y	N	Y
5 ***Roukema***	Y	Y	Y	Y	Y	Y	Y	N
6 Pallone	Y	Y	Y	N	N	N	N	Y
7 ***Franks***	Y	Y	Y	Y	Y	Y	Y	N
8 Pascrell	Y	Y	Y	N	N	N	N	Y
9 Rothman	Y	Y	Y	N	N	N	N	Y
10 Payne	Y	Y	Y	N	N	N	N	Y
11 ***Frelinghuysen***	Y	Y	Y	Y	Y	Y	Y	N
12 Holt	Y	Y	Y	N	N	N	N	Y
13 Menendez	Y	Y	Y	N	N	N	N	Y
NEW MEXICO								
1 ***Wilson***	Y	Y	Y	Y	Y	Y	Y	Y
2 ***Skeen***	Y	Y	Y	Y	Y	Y	Y	Y
3 Udall	Y	Y	Y	N	N	N	N	Y
NEW YORK								
1 ***Forbes***	Y	Y	Y	Y	Y	Y	N	Y
2 ***Lazio***	Y	Y	Y	Y	Y	Y	N	Y
3 ***King***	Y	Y	Y	Y	Y	Y	N	Y
4 McCarthy	Y	Y	Y	N	N	N	N	Y
5 Ackerman	Y	Y	Y	N	N	N	N	Y
6 Meeks	Y	Y	Y	N	N	N	N	Y
7 Crowley	Y	Y	Y	N	N	N	N	Y
8 Nadler	Y	Y	Y	N	N	N	N	Y
9 Weiner	+	+	Y	N	N	N	N	Y
10 Towns	Y	Y	Y	N	N	N	?	?
11 Owens	Y	Y	Y	N	N	N	N	Y
12 Velázquez	Y	Y	Y	N	N	N	?	Y
13 ***Fossella***	Y	Y	Y	Y	Y	Y	Y	N
14 Maloney	Y	Y	Y	N	N	N	N	Y
15 Rangel	Y	?	Y	N	N	N	N	Y
16 Serrano	Y	Y	Y	N	N	N	N	Y
17 Engel	Y	Y	Y	N	N	N	N	Y
18 Lowey	Y	Y	Y	N	N	N	N	Y
19 ***Kelly***	Y	Y	Y	Y	Y	Y	N	Y
20 ***Gilman***	Y	Y	Y	Y	Y	Y	N	Y
21 McNulty	Y	Y	Y	N	N	N	N	N
22 ***Sweeney***	Y	Y	Y	Y	Y	Y	Y	N
23 ***Boehlert***	Y	Y	Y	Y	Y	Y	N	Y
24 ***McHugh***	Y	Y	Y	Y	Y	Y	Y	N
25 ***Walsh***	Y	Y	Y	Y	Y	Y	Y	N
26 Hinchey	Y	Y	Y	N	N	N	N	Y
27 ***Reynolds***	Y	Y	Y	Y	Y	Y	Y	N
28 Slaughter	Y	Y	Y	N	N	N	N	P
29 LaFalce	Y	Y	Y	N	N	N	N	Y
30 ***Quinn***	Y	Y	Y	Y	N	?	?	?
31 ***Houghton***	Y	Y	Y	Y	Y	Y	N	Y
NORTH CAROLINA								
1 Clayton	Y	Y	Y	N	N	N	N	Y
2 Etheridge	Y	Y	Y	N	N	N	N	Y
3 ***Jones***	Y	N	Y	Y	Y	Y	Y	N
4 Price	Y	Y	Y	N	N	N	N	Y
5 ***Burr***	Y	Y	Y	Y	Y	Y	Y	N
6 ***Coble***	Y	Y	Y	Y	Y	Y	Y	N
7 McIntyre	Y	Y	Y	N	N	N	N	Y
8 ***Hayes***	Y	Y	Y	Y	Y	Y	Y	N
9 ***Myrick***	Y	Y	Y	Y	Y	Y	Y	N
10 ***Ballenger***	Y	Y	Y	Y	Y	Y	Y	N
11 ***Taylor***	Y	Y	Y	Y	Y	Y	Y	N
12 Watt	Y	Y	Y	N	N	N	N	Y
NORTH DAKOTA								
AL Pomeroy	Y	Y	Y	N	N	N	N	Y
OHIO								
1 ***Chabot***	Y	Y	Y	Y	Y	Y	Y	N
2 ***Portman***	Y	Y	Y	Y	Y	Y	N	Y
3 Hall	Y	Y	Y	N	N	N	N	Y
4 ***Oxley***	Y	Y	Y	Y	Y	Y	N	Y
5 ***Gillmor***	Y	Y	Y	Y	Y	Y	Y	N
6 Strickland	Y	Y	Y	N	N	N	?	?
7 ***Hobson***	Y	Y	Y	Y	Y	Y	N	Y
8 ***Boehner***	Y	Y	Y	Y	Y	Y	N	N
9 Kaptur	Y	Y	Y	N	N	N	N	Y
10 Kucinich	Y	Y	Y	N	N	N	N	Y
11 Jones	Y	Y	Y	N	N	N	N	Y
12 ***Kasich***	Y	Y	Y	Y	Y	Y	Y	N
13 Brown	Y	Y	Y	N	N	N	N	P
14 Sawyer	Y	Y	Y	N	N	N	N	Y
15 ***Pryce***	Y	Y	Y	Y	Y	Y	Y	N
16 ***Regula***	Y	Y	Y	Y	Y	Y	N	Y
17 Traficant	Y	Y	Y	N	N	N	Y	N
18 ***Ney***	Y	Y	Y	Y	Y	Y	Y	N
19 ***LaTourette***	Y	Y	Y	Y	Y	Y	N	Y
OKLAHOMA								
1 ***Largent***	Y	Y	Y	Y	Y	Y	Y	N
2 ***Coburn***	Y	Y	Y	Y	Y	Y	Y	P
3 ***Watkins***	Y	Y	Y	Y	Y	Y	Y	N
4 ***Watts***	Y	?	Y	Y	Y	Y	Y	N
5 ***Istook***	Y	Y	Y	Y	Y	Y	Y	N
6 ***Lucas***	Y	Y	Y	Y	Y	Y	Y	N
OREGON								
1 Wu	Y	+	Y	N	N	?	?	?
2 ***Walden***	Y	Y	Y	Y	Y	Y	Y	N
3 Blumenauer	Y	Y	Y	N	N	N	N	Y
4 DeFazio	Y	Y	Y	N	N	N	N	Y
5 Hooley	Y	Y	Y	N	N	N	N	Y
PENNSYLVANIA								
1 Brady	Y	Y	Y	N	N	N	N	Y
2 Fattah	?	Y	Y	N	N	N	N	Y
3 Borski	Y	Y	Y	N	N	N	N	Y
4 Klink	Y	Y	Y	N	N	N	N	N
5 ***Peterson***	Y	Y	Y	Y	Y	Y	Y	N
6 Holden	Y	Y	Y	N	N	N	N	Y
7 ***Weldon***	Y	Y	Y	Y	Y	Y	Y	N
8 ***Greenwood***	Y	Y	Y	Y	Y	Y	Y	N
9 ***Shuster***	Y	Y	Y	Y	Y	Y	?	–
10 ***Sherwood***	Y	Y	Y	Y	Y	Y	N	Y
11 Kanjorski	Y	Y	Y	N	N	N	N	Y
12 Murtha	Y	Y	Y	N	N	N	N	Y
13 Hoeffel	Y	Y	Y	N	N	N	N	Y
14 Coyne	Y	Y	Y	N	N	N	N	Y
15 ***Toomey***	Y	Y	Y	Y	Y	Y	Y	N
16 ***Pitts***	Y	Y	Y	Y	Y	Y	Y	N
17 ***Gekas***	Y	Y	Y	Y	Y	Y	N	Y
18 Doyle	Y	Y	Y	N	N	N	N	Y
19 ***Goodling***	Y	Y	Y	+	+	Y	Y	N
20 Mascara	Y	Y	Y	N	N	N	N	Y
21 ***English***	Y	Y	Y	Y	Y	Y	Y	N
RHODE ISLAND								
1 Kennedy	Y	Y	Y	N	N	N	N	Y
2 Weygand	Y	Y	Y	N	N	N	N	Y
SOUTH CAROLINA								
1 ***Sanford***	Y	Y	Y	Y	Y	Y	Y	N
2 ***Spence***	Y	Y	Y	Y	Y	Y	Y	N
3 ***Graham***	Y	Y	Y	Y	Y	Y	Y	N
4 ***DeMint***	Y	Y	Y	Y	Y	Y	Y	N
5 Spratt	Y	Y	Y	N	N	N	N	Y
6 Clyburn	Y	Y	Y	N	N	N	N	Y
SOUTH DAKOTA								
AL ***Thune***	Y	Y	Y	Y	Y	Y	Y	N
TENNESSEE								
1 ***Jenkins***	Y	Y	Y	Y	Y	Y	Y	N
2 ***Duncan***	Y	Y	Y	Y	Y	Y	Y	N
3 ***Wamp***	Y	Y	Y	Y	Y	Y	Y	N
4 ***Hilleary***	?	Y	Y	Y	Y	Y	Y	N
5 Clement	Y	Y	Y	N	N	N	N	Y
6 Gordon	Y	Y	Y	N	N	N	Y	N
7 ***Bryant***	Y	Y	Y	Y	Y	Y	Y	N
8 Tanner	Y	Y	Y	N	N	N	N	Y
9 Ford	?	?	Y	N	N	N	N	Y
TEXAS								
1 Sandlin	Y	Y	Y	N	N	N	N	Y
2 Turner	Y	Y	Y	N	N	N	N	Y
3 ***Johnson, Sam***	Y	Y	Y	Y	Y	Y	Y	N
4 Hall	Y	Y	Y	Y	Y	N	Y	N
5 ***Sessions***	Y	Y	Y	Y	Y	Y	Y	N
6 ***Barton***	Y	Y	Y	Y	Y	Y	Y	N
7 ***Archer***	Y	Y	Y	Y	?	Y	Y	N
8 ***Brady***	Y	Y	Y	Y	Y	Y	Y	N
9 Lampson	Y	?	Y	N	N	N	N	Y
10 Doggett	Y	Y	Y	N	N	N	N	Y
11 Edwards	Y	Y	Y	N	N	N	N	Y
12 ***Granger***	Y	Y	Y	Y	Y	Y	Y	N
13 ***Thornberry***	Y	Y	Y	Y	Y	Y	Y	N
14 ***Paul***	N	N	Y	Y	Y	Y	Y	N
15 Hinojosa	Y	Y	Y	N	N	N	N	Y
16 Reyes	?	?	?	?	?	?	?	?
17 Stenholm	Y	Y	Y	N	N	N	N	Y
18 Jackson-Lee	Y	Y	Y	N	N	N	N	Y
19 ***Combest***	Y	Y	Y	Y	Y	Y	Y	N
20 Gonzalez	Y	Y	Y	N	N	N	N	Y
21 ***Smith***	Y	Y	Y	Y	Y	Y	Y	N
22 ***DeLay***	Y	Y	Y	Y	Y	Y	Y	N
23 ***Bonilla***	Y	N	Y	Y	Y	Y	Y	N
24 Frost	?	?	?	?	?	?	?	?
25 Bentsen	Y	Y	Y	N	N	N	N	P
26 ***Armey***	Y	Y	Y	Y	Y	Y	Y	N
27 Ortiz	Y	Y	Y	N	N	N	N	Y
28 Rodriguez	Y	Y	Y	N	N	N	N	Y
29 Green	Y	Y	Y	N	N	N	N	Y
30 Johnson, E.B.	Y	Y	Y	N	N	N	N	Y
UTAH								
1 ***Hansen***	Y	Y	Y	Y	Y	Y	Y	N
2 ***Cook***	Y	Y	Y	Y	Y	Y	Y	N
3 ***Cannon***	Y	Y	Y	Y	Y	Y	Y	N
VERMONT								
AL *Sanders*	Y	Y	Y	N	N	N	N	Y
VIRGINIA								
1 ***Bateman***	Y	Y	Y	Y	Y	Y	N	N
2 Pickett	Y	Y	?	N	N	N	N	Y
3 Scott	Y	Y	Y	N	N	N	N	Y
4 Sisisky	Y	Y	Y	N	N	N	N	Y
5 Goode	Y	Y	Y	Y	Y	N	Y	N
6 ***Goodlatte***	Y	Y	Y	Y	Y	Y	Y	N
7 ***Bliley***	Y	Y	Y	Y	Y	Y	N	Y
8 Moran	Y	Y	Y	N	N	N	N	Y
9 Boucher	Y	Y	Y	N	N	N	N	Y
10 ***Wolf***	Y	Y	Y	Y	Y	Y	N	Y
11 ***Davis***	Y	Y	Y	Y	Y	Y	N	Y
WASHINGTON								
1 Inslee	Y	Y	Y	N	N	N	N	Y
2 ***Metcalf***	Y	Y	Y	Y	Y	Y	Y	N
3 Baird	Y	Y	Y	N	N	N	N	Y
4 ***Hastings***	Y	Y	Y	Y	Y	Y	Y	N
5 ***Nethercutt***	Y	Y	Y	Y	Y	Y	N	Y
6 Dicks	Y	Y	Y	N	N	N	N	Y
7 McDermott	Y	Y	Y	N	N	N	N	Y
8 ***Dunn***	Y	Y	Y	Y	Y	Y	N	Y
9 Smith	Y	Y	Y	N	N	N	N	Y
WEST VIRGINIA								
1 Mollohan	Y	Y	Y	?	?	?	N	Y
2 Wise	Y	Y	Y	N	N	N	N	Y
3 Rahall	Y	Y	Y	N	N	N	N	Y
WISCONSIN								
1 ***Ryan***	Y	Y	Y	Y	Y	Y	Y	N
2 Baldwin	Y	Y	Y	N	N	N	N	Y
3 Kind	Y	Y	Y	N	N	N	N	Y
4 Kleczka	Y	Y	Y	N	N	N	N	Y
5 Barrett	Y	Y	Y	N	N	N	N	Y
6 ***Petri***	Y	Y	Y	Y	Y	Y	Y	N
7 Obey	Y	Y	Y	N	N	N	N	P
8 ***Green***	Y	Y	Y	Y	Y	Y	N	N
9 ***Sensenbrenner***	Y	Y	Y	Y	Y	Y	Y	N
WYOMING								
AL ***Cubin***	Y	Y	Y	Y	Y	Y	Y	N

Southern states - Ala., Ark., Fla., Ga., Ky., La., Miss., N.C., Okla., S.C., Tenn., Texas, Va.

50. HR 819. Federal Maritime Commission Reauthorization/Passage. Passage of the bill to reauthorize activities of the Federal Maritime Commission for two years. The measure would authorize $15.7 million in fiscal 2000 and $16.3 million for fiscal 2001. Passed 403-3: R 201-3; D 201-0 (ND 150-0, SD 51-0); I 1-0. March 16, 1999.

51. HR 774. Women's Business Center Program Authorization/Passage. Kelly, R-N.Y., motion to suspend the rules and pass the bill to increase the authorization for the Women's Business Center Program from $8 million to $11 million in fiscal 2000. Motion agreed to 385-23: R 182-22; D 202-1 (ND 152-0, SD 50-1); I 1-0. March 16, 1999. A two-thirds majority of those present and voting (272 in this case) is required for passage under suspension of the rules.

52. H Con Res 24. Palestinian Statehood/Adoption. Gilman, R-N.Y., motion to suspend the rules and adopt the concurrent resolution to express the sense of Congress against unilateral Palestinian declaration of statehood and urge the president to assert clearly that the United States would not recognize such a state. Motion agreed to 380-24: R 196-6; D 183-18 (ND 136-14, SD 47-4); I 1-0. March 16, 1999. A two-thirds majority of those present and voting (270 in this case) is required for adoption under suspension of the rules.

53. HR 820. Coast Guard Authorization/Lighthouse Preservation. Upton, R-Mich., amendment to encourage the Coast Guard to continue working with Great Lakes lighthouse preservation groups and to publicly announce plans to dispose of "surplus" lighthouses so that such local groups can mobilize to acquire the lighthouse. Adopted 428-0: R 216-0; D 211-0 (ND 156-0, SD 55-0); I 1-0. March 17, 1999.

54. HR 820. Coast Guard Authorization/Coast Guard Patrol Vessels. LoBiondo, R-N.J., amendment to authorize an additional $210 million over two years for Coast Guard acquisition of patrol vessels for anti-drug activities, and $20 million for certain shoreside facilities. Adopted 424-4: R 212-4; D 211-0 (ND 156-0, SD 55-0); I 1-0. March 17, 1999.

55. HR 820. Coast Guard Authorization/Passage. Passage of the bill to reauthorize certain Coast Guard programs and activities for two years, authorizing approximately $4.6 billion in fiscal 2000 and $4.9 billion in fiscal 2001. Passed 424-7: R 212-7; D 211-0 (ND 156-0, SD 55-0); I 1-0. March 17, 1999.

56. HR 975. Steel Imports/Passage. Passage of the bill to direct the president, within 60 days of enactment, to take necessary steps — including imposing quotas, tariff surcharges or negotiated enforceable voluntary export restraints — to ensure that the volume of steel products imported into the United States (based on tonnage) during any month does not exceed the average of monthly import volumes during the three years preceding July 1997. The bill also requires the Commerce secretary to establish a steel import notification and monitoring program within 30 days after enactment that requires any person importing steel products to obtain an import notification certificate before such products can enter the United States. Passed 289-141: R 91-128; D 197-13 (ND 146-9, SD 51-4); I 1-0. March 17, 1999. A "nay" was a vote in support of the president's position.

Key

- Y Voted for (yea).
- # Paired for.
- + Announced for.
- N Voted against (nay).
- X Paired against.
- – Announced against.
- P Voted "present."
- C Voted "present" to avoid possible conflict of interest.
- ? Did not vote or otherwise make a position known.

•

Democrats ***Republicans***
Independents

	50	51	52	53	54	55	56
ALABAMA							
1 ***Callahan***	+	+	+	Y	Y	Y	Y
2 ***Everett***	Y	Y	Y	Y	Y	Y	Y
3 ***Riley***	Y	Y	Y	Y	Y	Y	Y
4 ***Aderholt***	Y	Y	Y	Y	Y	Y	Y
5 Cramer	?	?	?	Y	Y	Y	Y
6 ***Bachus***	Y	Y	Y	Y	Y	Y	Y
7 Hilliard	Y	Y	Y	Y	Y	Y	Y
ALASKA							
AL ***Young***	Y	Y	Y	Y	Y	Y	Y
ARIZONA							
1 ***Salmon***	Y	Y	Y	Y	Y	Y	N
2 Pastor	Y	Y	Y	Y	Y	Y	Y
3 ***Stump***	Y	N	Y	Y	Y	Y	N
4 ***Shadegg***	Y	Y	Y	Y	Y	Y	N
5 ***Kolbe***	Y	Y	Y	Y	Y	Y	N
6 ***Hayworth***	Y	Y	Y	Y	Y	Y	N
ARKANSAS							
1 Berry	Y	Y	Y	Y	Y	Y	Y
2 Snyder	Y	Y	Y	Y	Y	Y	Y
3 ***Hutchinson***	Y	Y	Y	Y	Y	Y	N
4 ***Dickey***	Y	Y	Y	Y	Y	Y	Y
CALIFORNIA							
1 Thompson	Y	Y	Y	Y	Y	Y	Y
2 ***Herger***	Y	N	Y	Y	Y	Y	N
3 ***Ose***	Y	Y	Y	Y	Y	Y	N
4 ***Doolittle***	Y	N	Y	Y	Y	N	N
5 Matsui	Y	Y	Y	Y	Y	Y	Y
6 Woolsey	Y	Y	Y	Y	Y	Y	Y
7 Miller, George	Y	Y	N	Y	Y	Y	Y
8 Pelosi	Y	Y	Y	Y	Y	Y	Y
9 Lee	Y	Y	N	Y	Y	Y	Y
10 Tauscher	Y	Y	Y	Y	Y	Y	Y
11 ***Pombo***	Y	Y	Y	Y	Y	N	Y
12 Lantos	Y	Y	Y	Y	Y	Y	Y
13 Stark	Y	Y	N	Y	Y	Y	Y
14 Eshoo	Y	Y	Y	Y	Y	Y	N
15 ***Campbell***	Y	N	N	Y	Y	Y	N
16 Lofgren	Y	Y	Y	Y	Y	Y	N
17 Farr	Y	Y	Y	Y	Y	Y	Y
18 Condit	Y	Y	Y	Y	Y	Y	Y
19 ***Radanovich***	Y	Y	P	Y	Y	Y	N
20 Dooley	?	Y	Y	Y	Y	Y	N
21 ***Thomas***	Y	Y	Y	Y	Y	Y	N
22 Capps	Y	Y	Y	Y	Y	Y	Y
23 ***Gallegly***	Y	Y	Y	Y	Y	Y	Y
24 Sherman	Y	Y	Y	Y	Y	Y	Y
25 ***McKeon***	Y	Y	Y	Y	Y	Y	N
26 Berman	Y	Y	Y	Y	Y	Y	N
27 ***Rogan***	Y	Y	Y	Y	Y	Y	Y
28 ***Dreier***	Y	Y	Y	Y	Y	Y	N
29 Waxman	Y	Y	Y	Y	Y	Y	Y
30 Becerra	Y	Y	Y	Y	Y	Y	Y
31 Martinez	Y	Y	Y	Y	Y	Y	Y
32 Dixon	Y	Y	Y	Y	Y	Y	Y
33 Roybal-Allard	Y	Y	Y	Y	Y	Y	Y
34 Napolitano	Y	Y	Y	Y	Y	Y	Y
35 Waters	Y	Y	N	Y	Y	Y	Y
36 ***Kuykendall***	Y	Y	Y	Y	Y	Y	N
37 Millender-McD.	?	?	?	Y	Y	Y	Y
38 ***Horn***	Y	Y	Y	Y	Y	Y	Y
39 ***Royce***	Y	N	Y	Y	N	N	N
40 ***Lewis***	Y	Y	Y	Y	Y	Y	N
41 ***Miller, Gary***	Y	N	Y	Y	Y	Y	N
42 Brown	Y	Y	Y	Y	Y	Y	Y
43 ***Calvert***	Y	Y	Y	Y	Y	Y	N
44 ***Bono***	Y	Y	Y	Y	Y	Y	N
45 ***Rohrabacher***	Y	N	N	Y	Y	Y	N
46 Sanchez	Y	Y	Y	Y	Y	Y	Y
47 ***Cox***	Y	N	Y	Y	Y	Y	N
48 ***Packard***	Y	Y	Y	Y	Y	Y	N
49 ***Bilbray***	Y	Y	Y	Y	Y	Y	N
50 Filner	Y	Y	Y	Y	Y	Y	Y
51 ***Cunningham***	Y	Y	Y	Y	Y	Y	N
52 ***Hunter***	Y	Y	?	Y	Y	Y	Y
COLORADO							
1 DeGette	Y	Y	Y	Y	Y	Y	Y
2 Udall	Y	Y	Y	Y	Y	Y	Y
3 ***McInnis***	Y	Y	Y	Y	Y	Y	Y
4 ***Schaffer***	?	?	?	Y	Y	Y	N
5 ***Hefley***	Y	N	Y	Y	Y	Y	Y
6 ***Tancredo***	Y	N	Y	Y	Y	Y	N
CONNECTICUT							
1 Larson	Y	Y	Y	Y	Y	Y	Y
2 Gejdenson	Y	Y	Y	Y	Y	Y	Y
3 DeLauro	Y	Y	Y	Y	Y	Y	Y
4 ***Shays***	Y	Y	Y	Y	Y	Y	N
5 Maloney	Y	Y	Y	Y	Y	Y	Y
6 ***Johnson***	Y	Y	Y	Y	Y	Y	N
DELAWARE							
AL ***Castle***	Y	Y	Y	Y	Y	Y	N
FLORIDA							
1 ***Scarborough***	?	?	?	Y	Y	Y	N
2 Boyd	?	?	?	Y	Y	Y	Y
3 Brown	Y	Y	Y	Y	Y	Y	Y
4 ***Fowler***	Y	Y	Y	Y	Y	Y	N
5 Thurman	Y	Y	Y	Y	Y	Y	Y
6 ***Stearns***	Y	Y	Y	Y	Y	Y	Y
7 ***Mica***	Y	Y	Y	Y	Y	Y	Y
8 ***McCollum***	Y	Y	Y	Y	Y	Y	N
9 ***Bilirakis***	+	Y	Y	Y	Y	Y	Y
10 ***Young***	Y	Y	Y	Y	Y	Y	Y
11 Davis	Y	Y	Y	Y	Y	Y	N
12 ***Canady***	Y	N	Y	Y	Y	Y	N
13 ***Miller***	Y	?	Y	Y	Y	Y	N
14 ***Goss***	Y	Y	Y	Y	Y	Y	N
15 ***Weldon***	Y	Y	Y	Y	Y	Y	N
16 ***Foley***	Y	Y	Y	Y	Y	Y	N
17 Meek	Y	Y	Y	Y	Y	Y	Y
18 ***Ros-Lehtinen***	Y	Y	Y	Y	Y	Y	Y
19 Wexler	Y	Y	Y	Y	Y	Y	Y
20 Deutsch	Y	Y	Y	Y	Y	Y	Y
21 ***Diaz-Balart***	Y	Y	Y	Y	Y	Y	Y
22 ***Shaw***	Y	Y	Y	Y	Y	Y	N
23 Hastings	?	?	?	Y	Y	Y	Y
GEORGIA							
1 ***Kingston***	Y	Y	Y	Y	Y	Y	N
2 Bishop	Y	Y	Y	Y	Y	Y	Y
3 ***Collins***	Y	Y	Y	Y	Y	Y	Y
4 McKinney	Y	Y	N	Y	Y	Y	Y
5 Lewis	Y	Y	Y	Y	Y	Y	Y
6 ***Isakson***	Y	Y	Y	Y	Y	Y	N
7 ***Barr***	Y	Y	Y	Y	Y	Y	Y
8 ***Chambliss***	Y	Y	Y	Y	Y	Y	N
9 ***Deal***	Y	Y	Y	Y	Y	Y	N
10 ***Norwood***	Y	Y	Y	Y	Y	Y	Y
11 ***Linder***	Y	Y	Y	Y	Y	Y	N
HAWAII							
1 Abercrombie	Y	Y	Y	Y	Y	Y	Y
2 Mink	Y	Y	Y	Y	Y	Y	Y
IDAHO							
1 ***Chenoweth***	N	N	Y	Y	Y	N	Y
2 ***Simpson***	Y	Y	Y	Y	Y	Y	N
ILLINOIS							
1 Rush	Y	Y	Y	Y	Y	Y	Y
2 Jackson	Y	Y	N	Y	Y	Y	Y
3 Lipinski	Y	Y	Y	Y	Y	Y	Y
4 Gutierrez	Y	Y	Y	Y	Y	Y	Y
5 Blagojevich	Y	Y	Y	Y	Y	Y	Y
6 ***Hyde***	Y	Y	Y	?	Y	Y	N
7 Davis	Y	Y	Y	Y	Y	Y	Y
8 ***Crane***	Y	N	Y	Y	Y	Y	N
9 Schakowsky	Y	Y	Y	Y	Y	Y	Y
10 ***Porter***	Y	Y	Y	Y	Y	Y	N
11 ***Weller***	Y	Y	Y	Y	Y	Y	Y
12 Costello	Y	Y	Y	Y	Y	Y	Y
13 ***Biggert***	Y	Y	Y	Y	Y	Y	N
14 ***Hastert***			Y				

ND Northern Democrats SD Southern Democrats

	50	51	52	53	54	55	56
15 ***Ewing***	Y	Y	Y	Y	Y	Y	Y
16 ***Manzullo***	Y	N	Y	Y	Y	Y	N
17 Evans	Y	Y	Y	Y	Y	Y	Y
18 ***LaHood***	Y	Y	Y	Y	Y	Y	N
19 Phelps	Y	Y	Y	Y	Y	Y	Y
20 ***Shimkus***	Y	Y	Y	Y	Y	Y	Y
INDIANA							
1 Visclosky	Y	Y	Y	Y	Y	Y	Y
2 ***McIntosh***	Y	Y	Y	Y	Y	Y	Y
3 Roemer	Y	Y	Y	Y	Y	Y	Y
4 ***Souder***	Y	Y	?	Y	Y	Y	Y
5 ***Buyer***	Y	Y	Y	Y	Y	Y	Y
6 ***Burton***	Y	Y	Y	Y	Y	Y	Y
7 ***Pease***	Y	Y	Y	Y	Y	Y	Y
8 ***Hostettler***	+	–	?	Y	Y	Y	Y
9 Hill	Y	Y	Y	Y	Y	Y	Y
10 Carson	Y	Y	Y	Y	Y	Y	Y
IOWA							
1 ***Leach***	Y	Y	Y	Y	Y	Y	N
2 ***Nussle***	Y	Y	Y	Y	Y	Y	Y
3 Boswell	Y	Y	Y	Y	Y	Y	Y
4 ***Ganske***	Y	Y	Y	Y	Y	Y	Y
5 ***Latham***	Y	Y	Y	Y	Y	Y	N
KANSAS							
1 ***Moran***	Y	Y	Y	Y	Y	Y	N
2 ***Ryun***	Y	Y	Y	Y	Y	Y	N
3 Moore	Y	Y	Y	Y	Y	Y	Y
4 ***Tiahrt***	Y	Y	Y	Y	Y	Y	N
KENTUCKY							
1 ***Whitfield***	Y	Y	Y	?	?	Y	Y
2 ***Lewis***	+	+	+	Y	Y	Y	Y
3 ***Northup***	Y	Y	Y	Y	Y	Y	N
4 Lucas	Y	Y	Y	Y	Y	Y	Y
5 ***Rogers***	Y	Y	Y	Y	Y	Y	Y
6 ***Fletcher***	Y	Y	Y	Y	Y	Y	N
LOUISIANA							
1 Vacant							
2 Jefferson	Y	Y	Y	Y	Y	Y	Y
3 ***Tauzin***	Y	Y	Y	Y	Y	Y	N
4 ***McCrery***	Y	Y	Y	Y	Y	Y	N
5 ***Cooksey***	Y	Y	?	Y	Y	Y	N
6 ***Baker***	Y	Y	Y	Y	Y	Y	N
7 John	Y	Y	N	Y	Y	Y	N
MAINE							
1 Allen	Y	Y	Y	Y	Y	Y	Y
2 Baldacci	Y	Y	Y	Y	Y	Y	Y
MARYLAND							
1 ***Gilchrest***	?	?	?	Y	Y	Y	Y
2 ***Ehrlich***	Y	Y	Y	Y	Y	Y	Y
3 Cardin	Y	Y	Y	Y	Y	Y	Y
4 Wynn	Y	Y	Y	Y	Y	Y	Y
5 Hoyer	Y	Y	Y	Y	Y	Y	Y
6 ***Bartlett***	?	?	?	Y	Y	Y	Y
7 Cummings	Y	Y	Y	Y	Y	Y	Y
8 ***Morella***	Y	Y	Y	Y	Y	Y	N
MASSACHUSETTS							
1 Olver	Y	Y	Y	Y	Y	Y	Y
2 Neal	Y	Y	Y	Y	Y	Y	Y
3 McGovern	Y	Y	Y	Y	Y	Y	Y
4 Frank	Y	Y	Y	Y	Y	Y	Y
5 Meehan	Y	Y	Y	Y	Y	Y	Y
6 Tierney	Y	Y	Y	Y	Y	Y	Y
7 Markey	Y	Y	Y	Y	Y	Y	Y
8 Capuano	Y	Y	Y	Y	Y	Y	Y
9 Moakley	?	Y	Y	Y	Y	Y	Y
10 Delahunt	Y	Y	Y	Y	Y	Y	Y
MICHIGAN							
1 Stupak	Y	Y	Y	Y	Y	Y	Y
2 ***Hoekstra***	Y	Y	Y	Y	Y	Y	N
3 ***Ehlers***	Y	Y	Y	Y	Y	Y	N
4 ***Camp***	Y	Y	Y	Y	Y	Y	N
5 Barcia	Y	Y	Y	Y	Y	Y	Y
6 ***Upton***	Y	Y	Y	Y	Y	Y	N
7 ***Smith***	Y	Y	Y	Y	Y	Y	N
8 Stabenow	Y	Y	Y	Y	Y	Y	Y
9 Kildee	Y	Y	Y	Y	Y	Y	Y
10 Bonior	Y	Y	N	Y	Y	Y	Y
11 ***Knollenberg***	Y	Y	Y	Y	Y	Y	N
12 Levin	Y	Y	Y	Y	Y	Y	N
13 Rivers	Y	Y	P	Y	Y	Y	Y
14 Conyers	Y	Y	N	Y	Y	Y	Y
15 Kilpatrick	Y	Y	Y	Y	Y	Y	Y
16 Dingell	Y	Y	N	Y	Y	Y	Y

	50	51	52	53	54	55	56
MINNESOTA							
1 ***Gutknecht***	Y	Y	Y	Y	Y	Y	Y
2 Minge	Y	Y	Y	Y	Y	Y	Y
3 ***Ramstad***	Y	Y	Y	Y	Y	Y	N
4 Vento	?	Y	Y	Y	Y	Y	+
5 Sabo	Y	Y	Y	Y	Y	Y	Y
6 Luther	Y	Y	Y	Y	Y	Y	Y
7 Peterson	Y	Y	+	Y	Y	Y	Y
8 Oberstar	Y	Y	Y	Y	Y	Y	Y
MISSISSIPPI							
1 ***Wicker***	?	?	?	Y	Y	Y	N
2 Thompson	Y	Y	Y	Y	Y	Y	Y
3 ***Pickering***	Y	Y	Y	Y	Y	Y	N
4 Shows	Y	Y	Y	Y	Y	Y	Y
5 Taylor	Y	N	Y	Y	Y	Y	Y
MISSOURI							
1 Clay	Y	Y	N	Y	Y	Y	Y
2 ***Talent***	Y	Y	Y	Y	Y	Y	N
3 Gephardt	Y	Y	Y	Y	Y	Y	Y
4 Skelton	Y	Y	Y	Y	Y	Y	Y
5 McCarthy	Y	Y	Y	Y	Y	Y	Y
6 Danner	Y	Y	Y	Y	Y	Y	Y
7 ***Blunt***	Y	Y	Y	Y	Y	Y	N
8 ***Emerson***	Y	Y	Y	Y	Y	Y	Y
9 ***Hulshof***	Y	Y	Y	Y	Y	Y	N
MONTANA							
AL ***Hill***	Y	Y	Y	Y	Y	Y	N
NEBRASKA							
1 ***Bereuter***	Y	Y	Y	Y	Y	Y	N
2 ***Terry***	Y	Y	Y	Y	Y	Y	N
3 ***Barrett***	Y	Y	Y	Y	Y	Y	N
NEVADA							
1 Berkley	Y	Y	Y	Y	Y	Y	Y
2 ***Gibbons***	Y	Y	Y	Y	Y	Y	Y
NEW HAMPSHIRE							
1 ***Sununu***	Y	Y	N	Y	Y	Y	N
2 ***Bass***	Y	Y	?	Y	Y	Y	N
NEW JERSEY							
1 Andrews	Y	Y	Y	Y	Y	Y	Y
2 ***LoBiondo***	Y	Y	Y	Y	Y	Y	Y
3 ***Saxton***	Y	Y	Y	Y	Y	Y	N
4 ***Smith***	Y	Y	Y	Y	Y	Y	Y
5 ***Roukema***	Y	Y	Y	Y	Y	Y	Y
6 Pallone	Y	Y	Y	Y	Y	Y	Y
7 ***Franks***	Y	Y	Y	Y	Y	Y	Y
8 Pascrell	Y	Y	Y	Y	Y	Y	Y
9 Rothman	Y	Y	?	Y	Y	Y	Y
10 Payne	Y	Y	N	Y	Y	Y	Y
11 ***Frelinghuysen***	Y	Y	Y	Y	Y	Y	N
12 Holt	Y	Y	Y	Y	Y	Y	Y
13 Menendez	Y	Y	Y	Y	Y	Y	Y
NEW MEXICO							
1 ***Wilson***	Y	Y	Y	Y	Y	Y	N
2 ***Skeen***	Y	Y	Y	Y	Y	Y	Y
3 Udall	Y	Y	Y	Y	Y	Y	Y
NEW YORK							
1 ***Forbes***	Y	Y	Y	Y	Y	Y	Y
2 ***Lazio***	Y	Y	Y	Y	Y	Y	Y
3 ***King***	?	?	?	Y	Y	Y	Y
4 McCarthy	Y	+	Y	Y	Y	Y	Y
5 Ackerman	Y	Y	Y	Y	Y	Y	Y
6 Meeks	Y	Y	Y	Y	Y	Y	Y
7 Crowley	Y	Y	Y	Y	Y	Y	Y
8 Nadler	Y	Y	Y	Y	Y	Y	Y
9 Weiner	Y	Y	Y	Y	Y	Y	Y
10 Towns	Y	Y	Y	Y	Y	Y	Y
11 Owens	Y	Y	Y	Y	Y	Y	Y
12 Velázquez	Y	Y	Y	Y	Y	Y	Y
13 ***Fossella***	Y	Y	Y	Y	Y	Y	N
14 Maloney	Y	Y	Y	Y	Y	Y	Y
15 Rangel	Y	Y	Y	Y	Y	Y	Y
16 Serrano	Y	Y	Y	Y	Y	Y	Y
17 Engel	Y	Y	Y	Y	Y	Y	Y
18 Lowey	Y	Y	Y	Y	Y	Y	Y
19 ***Kelly***	Y	Y	Y	Y	Y	Y	Y
20 ***Gilman***	Y	Y	Y	Y	Y	Y	Y
21 McNulty	Y	Y	Y	Y	Y	Y	Y
22 ***Sweeney***	Y	Y	Y	Y	Y	Y	Y
23 ***Boehlert***	Y	Y	Y	Y	Y	Y	Y
24 ***McHugh***	Y	Y	Y	Y	Y	Y	Y
25 ***Walsh***	Y	Y	Y	Y	Y	Y	Y
26 Hinchey	Y	Y	Y	Y	Y	Y	Y
27 ***Reynolds***	Y	Y	Y	Y	Y	Y	N
28 Slaughter	Y	+	Y	Y	Y	Y	Y
29 LaFalce	Y	Y	Y	Y	Y	Y	Y

	50	51	52	53	54	55	56
30 ***Quinn***	Y	Y	Y	Y	Y	Y	Y
31 ***Houghton***	Y	Y	N	Y	?	Y	N
NORTH CAROLINA							
1 Clayton	Y	Y	Y	Y	Y	Y	Y
2 Etheridge	Y	Y	Y	Y	Y	Y	Y
3 ***Jones***	Y	Y	?	Y	Y	Y	Y
4 Price	Y	Y	Y	Y	Y	Y	Y
5 ***Burr***	Y	Y	Y	Y	Y	Y	N
6 ***Coble***	Y	N	Y	Y	Y	Y	Y
7 McIntyre	Y	Y	Y	Y	Y	Y	Y
8 ***Hayes***	Y	Y	Y	Y	Y	Y	Y
9 ***Myrick***	Y	Y	Y	?	?	?	?
10 ***Ballenger***	Y	Y	Y	Y	Y	Y	N
11 ***Taylor***	Y	N	Y	Y	Y	Y	N
12 Watt	Y	Y	N	Y	Y	Y	Y
NORTH DAKOTA							
AL Pomeroy	Y	Y	Y	Y	Y	Y	Y
OHIO							
1 ***Chabot***	Y	Y	Y	Y	Y	Y	N
2 ***Portman***	Y	Y	Y	Y	Y	Y	N
3 Hall	?	Y	Y	Y	Y	Y	Y
4 ***Oxley***	?	Y	Y	Y	Y	Y	N
5 ***Gillmor***	Y	Y	Y	Y	Y	Y	Y
6 Strickland	Y	Y	Y	Y	Y	Y	Y
7 ***Hobson***	Y	Y	Y	Y	Y	Y	Y
8 ***Boehner***	Y	Y	Y	Y	Y	Y	N
9 Kaptur	Y	Y	Y	Y	Y	Y	Y
10 Kucinich	Y	Y	N	Y	Y	Y	Y
11 Jones	Y	Y	Y	Y	Y	Y	Y
12 ***Kasich***	Y	Y	Y	Y	Y	Y	Y
13 Brown	Y	Y	Y	Y	Y	Y	Y
14 Sawyer	Y	Y	Y	Y	Y	Y	Y
15 ***Pryce***	?	?	?	Y	Y	Y	N
16 ***Regula***	Y	Y	Y	Y	Y	Y	Y
17 Traficant	Y	Y	Y	Y	Y	Y	Y
18 ***Ney***	Y	Y	N	Y	Y	Y	Y
19 ***LaTourette***	Y	Y	Y	Y	Y	Y	Y
OKLAHOMA							
1 ***Largent***	Y	Y	Y	?	?	Y	Y
2 ***Coburn***	Y	N	Y	Y	Y	Y	Y
3 ***Watkins***	?	Y	Y	Y	Y	Y	N
4 ***Watts***	Y	Y	Y	Y	Y	Y	N
5 ***Istook***	Y	Y	Y	Y	Y	Y	N
6 ***Lucas***	Y	Y	Y	Y	Y	Y	N
OREGON							
1 Wu	Y	Y	Y	Y	Y	Y	Y
2 ***Walden***	Y	Y	Y	Y	Y	Y	N
3 Blumenauer	Y	Y	Y	Y	Y	Y	Y
4 DeFazio	?	?	?	Y	Y	Y	Y
5 Hooley	Y	Y	Y	Y	Y	Y	Y
PENNSYLVANIA							
1 Brady	Y	Y	Y	Y	Y	Y	Y
2 Fattah	Y	Y	Y	Y	Y	Y	Y
3 Borski	Y	Y	Y	Y	Y	Y	Y
4 Klink	Y	Y	Y	Y	Y	Y	Y
5 ***Peterson***	Y	Y	Y	Y	Y	Y	Y
6 Holden	Y	Y	Y	Y	Y	Y	Y
7 ***Weldon***	?	?	?	Y	Y	Y	Y
8 ***Greenwood***	Y	Y	Y	Y	Y	Y	Y
9 ***Shuster***	Y	Y	Y	Y	Y	Y	Y
10 ***Sherwood***	Y	Y	Y	Y	Y	Y	Y
11 Kanjorski	Y	Y	N	Y	Y	Y	Y
12 Murtha	Y	Y	N	Y	Y	Y	Y
13 Hoeffel	Y	Y	Y	Y	Y	Y	Y
14 Coyne	Y	Y	Y	Y	Y	Y	Y
15 ***Toomey***	Y	Y	Y	Y	Y	Y	Y
16 ***Pitts***	?	?	?	?	?	?	?
17 ***Gekas***	Y	Y	Y	Y	Y	Y	Y
18 Doyle	Y	Y	Y	Y	Y	Y	Y
19 ***Goodling***	Y	Y	Y	Y	Y	Y	Y
20 Mascara	Y	Y	Y	Y	Y	Y	Y
21 ***English***	Y	Y	Y	Y	Y	Y	Y
RHODE ISLAND							
1 Kennedy	Y	Y	Y	Y	Y	Y	Y
2 Weygand	Y	Y	Y	Y	Y	Y	Y
SOUTH CAROLINA							
1 ***Sanford***	Y	N	Y	Y	N	N	N
2 ***Spence***	Y	Y	Y	Y	Y	Y	N
3 ***Graham***	Y	Y	Y	Y	Y	Y	N
4 ***DeMint***	Y	Y	Y	Y	Y	Y	N
5 Spratt	Y	Y	Y	Y	Y	Y	Y
6 Clyburn	Y	Y	Y	Y	Y	Y	Y
SOUTH DAKOTA							
AL ***Thune***	Y	Y	Y	Y	Y	Y	N

	50	51	52	53	54	55	56
TENNESSEE							
1 ***Jenkins***	Y	Y	Y	Y	Y	Y	Y
2 ***Duncan***	?	?	?	Y	Y	Y	Y
3 ***Wamp***	Y	Y	Y	Y	Y	Y	Y
4 ***Hilleary***	Y	Y	Y	Y	Y	Y	Y
5 Clement	Y	Y	Y	Y	Y	Y	Y
6 Gordon	Y	Y	Y	Y	Y	Y	Y
7 ***Bryant***	Y	Y	Y	Y	Y	Y	Y
8 Tanner	Y	Y	Y	Y	Y	Y	Y
9 Ford	Y	Y	Y	Y	Y	Y	Y
TEXAS							
1 Sandlin	Y	Y	Y	Y	Y	Y	Y
2 Turner	?	?	?	Y	Y	Y	Y
3 ***Johnson, Sam***	Y	Y	Y	Y	Y	Y	N
4 Hall	Y	Y	Y	Y	Y	Y	N
5 ***Sessions***	Y	Y	Y	Y	Y	Y	N
6 ***Barton***	Y	Y	Y	Y	Y	Y	N
7 ***Archer***	Y	Y	Y	Y	Y	Y	N
8 ***Brady***	Y	Y	Y	Y	Y	Y	N
9 Lampson	Y	Y	Y	Y	Y	Y	Y
10 Doggett	Y	Y	Y	Y	Y	Y	Y
11 Edwards	Y	Y	Y	Y	Y	Y	Y
12 ***Granger***	Y	Y	Y	Y	Y	Y	N
13 ***Thornberry***	Y	Y	Y	Y	Y	Y	N
14 ***Paul***	N	N	N	Y	N	N	N
15 Hinojosa	Y	Y	Y	Y	Y	Y	Y
16 Reyes	Y	Y	Y	Y	Y	Y	Y
17 Stenholm	Y	Y	Y	Y	Y	Y	Y
18 Jackson-Lee	Y	Y	Y	Y	Y	Y	Y
19 ***Combest***	Y	Y	Y	Y	Y	Y	N
20 Gonzalez	Y	Y	Y	Y	Y	Y	Y
21 ***Smith***	Y	Y	Y	Y	Y	Y	N
22 ***DeLay***	Y	N	Y	Y	Y	Y	N
23 ***Bonilla***	Y	?	Y	Y	Y	Y	N
24 Frost	Y	Y	Y	Y	Y	Y	Y
25 Bentsen	Y	Y	Y	Y	Y	Y	Y
26 ***Armey***	Y	Y	Y	Y	Y	Y	N
27 Ortiz	Y	Y	Y	Y	Y	Y	Y
28 Rodriguez	Y	Y	Y	Y	Y	Y	Y
29 Green	Y	Y	Y	Y	Y	Y	Y
30 Johnson, E.B.	Y	Y	Y	Y	Y	Y	Y
UTAH							
1 ***Hansen***	Y	Y	Y	Y	Y	Y	Y
2 ***Cook***	Y	Y	Y	Y	Y	Y	Y
3 ***Cannon***	Y	N	Y	Y	Y	Y	Y
VERMONT							
AL *Sanders*	Y	Y	Y	Y	Y	Y	Y
VIRGINIA							
1 ***Bateman***	Y	Y	Y	Y	Y	Y	N
2 Pickett	Y	Y	Y	Y	Y	Y	Y
3 Scott	Y	Y	Y	Y	Y	Y	Y
4 Sisisky	Y	Y	Y	Y	Y	Y	Y
5 Goode	Y	Y	Y	Y	Y	Y	Y
6 ***Goodlatte***	Y	?	Y	Y	Y	Y	N
7 ***Bliley***	Y	Y	Y	Y	Y	Y	N
8 Moran	Y	Y	N	Y	Y	Y	N
9 Boucher	Y	Y	Y	Y	Y	Y	Y
10 ***Wolf***	Y	Y	Y	Y	Y	Y	N
11 ***Davis***	Y	Y	Y	Y	Y	Y	N
WASHINGTON							
1 Inslee	Y	Y	Y	Y	Y	Y	Y
2 ***Metcalf***	Y	Y	Y	Y	Y	Y	Y
3 Baird	Y	Y	Y	Y	Y	Y	Y
4 ***Hastings***	Y	Y	Y	Y	Y	Y	N
5 ***Nethercutt***	Y	Y	Y	Y	Y	Y	N
6 Dicks	Y	Y	Y	Y	Y	Y	N
7 McDermott	Y	Y	Y	Y	Y	Y	N
8 ***Dunn***	Y	Y	Y	Y	Y	Y	N
9 Smith	Y	Y	Y	Y	Y	Y	N
WEST VIRGINIA							
1 Mollohan	Y	Y	Y	Y	Y	Y	Y
2 Wise	Y	Y	Y	Y	Y	Y	Y
3 Rahall	Y	Y	N	Y	Y	Y	Y
WISCONSIN							
1 ***Ryan***	Y	Y	Y	Y	Y	Y	Y
2 Baldwin	Y	Y	Y	Y	Y	Y	Y
3 Kind	Y	Y	Y	Y	Y	Y	N
4 Kleczka	Y	Y	Y	Y	Y	Y	Y
5 Barrett	Y	Y	Y	Y	Y	Y	Y
6 ***Petri***	Y	Y	Y	Y	Y	Y	Y
7 Obey	Y	Y	?	Y	Y	Y	Y
8 ***Green***	Y	Y	Y	Y	Y	Y	N
9 ***Sensenbrenner***	N	N	Y	Y	N	N	N
WYOMING							
AL ***Cubin***	?	?	?	Y	Y	Y	N

Southern states - Ala., Ark., Fla., Ga., Ky., La., Miss., N.C., Okla., S.C., Tenn., Texas, Va.

57. HR 4. Anti-Missile Defense/Rule. Adoption of the rule (H Res 120) to provide for House floor consideration of the bill to declare that it is the policy of the United States to deploy a national missile defense system. The measure does not mandate the deployment of such a system or establish a schedule for development. Adopted 239-185: R 215-0; D 24-184 (ND 6-149, SD 18-35); I 0-1. March 18, 1999.

58. HR 4. Anti-Missile Defense/Recommit. Allen, D-Maine, motion to recommit the bill to the Armed Services Committee with instructions to report it back with an amendment that it is the policy of the United States to deploy a missile defense system that is demonstrated to be effective, does not diminish overall national security by jeopardizing other efforts to reduce threats to the United States, is affordable and does not compromise U.S. ability to provide for other military priorities. Motion rejected 152-269: R 2-212; D 150-56 (ND 125-28, SD 25-28); I 0-1. March 18, 1999.

59. HR 4. Anti-Missile Defense/Passage. Passage of the bill to declare that it is the policy of the United States to deploy a national missile defense system. The measure does not mandate the deployment of such a system or establish a schedule for development. Passed 317-105: R 214-2; D 103-102 (ND 58-94, SD 45-8); I 0-1. March 18, 1999.

Key

- Y Voted for (yea).
- # Paired for.
- \+ Announced for.
- N Voted against (nay).
- X Paired against.
- – Announced against.
- P Voted "present."
- C Voted "present" to avoid possible conflict of interest.
- ? Did not vote or otherwise make a position known.

Democrats ***Republicans*** *Independents*

	57	58	59
ALABAMA			
1 ***Callahan***	Y	N	Y
2 ***Everett***	Y	N	Y
3 ***Riley***	Y	N	Y
4 ***Aderholt***	Y	N	Y
5 Cramer	Y	N	Y
6 ***Bachus***	Y	N	Y
7 Hilliard	N	Y	N
ALASKA			
AL ***Young***	Y	N	Y
ARIZONA			
1 ***Salmon***	Y	N	Y
2 Pastor	N	Y	N
3 ***Stump***	Y	N	Y
4 ***Shadegg***	Y	N	Y
5 ***Kolbe***	Y	N	Y
6 ***Hayworth***	Y	N	Y
ARKANSAS			
1 Berry	Y	Y	Y
2 Snyder	N	N	Y
3 ***Hutchinson***	Y	N	Y
4 ***Dickey***	Y	N	Y
CALIFORNIA			
1 Thompson	N	Y	Y
2 ***Herger***	Y	N	Y
3 ***Ose***	Y	N	Y
4 ***Doolittle***	Y	?	Y
5 Matsui	N	Y	Y
6 Woolsey	N	Y	N
7 Miller, George	N	Y	N
8 Pelosi	N	Y	N
9 Lee	N	N	N
10 Tauscher	N	N	Y
11 ***Pombo***	Y	N	Y
12 Lantos	N	Y	N
13 Stark	N	+	–
14 Eshoo	N	Y	N
15 ***Campbell***	Y	N	Y
16 Lofgren	N	Y	N
17 Farr	N	Y	N
18 Condit	N	N	Y
19 ***Radanovich***	Y	N	Y
20 Dooley	N	Y	Y
21 ***Thomas***	Y	N	Y
22 Capps	N	Y	Y
23 ***Gallegly***	Y	N	Y
24 Sherman	N	Y	Y
25 ***McKeon***	Y	–	+
26 Berman	N	Y	Y
27 ***Rogan***	Y	N	Y
28 ***Dreier***	Y	N	Y
29 Waxman	N	Y	N
30 Becerra	N	Y	N
31 Martinez	N	Y	Y
32 Dixon	N	Y	Y
33 Roybal-Allard	N	Y	N
34 Napolitano	N	Y	N
35 Waters	N	Y	N
36 ***Kuykendall***	Y	N	Y
37 Millender-McD.	N	Y	Y
38 ***Horn***	Y	N	Y
39 ***Royce***	Y	N	Y
40 ***Lewis***	Y	N	Y
41 ***Miller, Gary***	Y	N	Y
42 Brown	N	Y	N
43 ***Calvert***	Y	N	Y
44 ***Bono***	Y	N	Y
45 ***Rohrabacher***	Y	N	Y
46 Sanchez	N	Y	Y
47 ***Cox***	Y	N	Y
48 ***Packard***	Y	N	Y
49 ***Bilbray***	Y	N	Y
50 Filner	N	Y	N
51 ***Cunningham***	Y	N	Y
52 ***Hunter***	Y	N	Y
COLORADO			
1 DeGette	N	Y	N
2 Udall	N	Y	N
3 ***McInnis***	Y	N	Y
4 ***Schaffer***	Y	N	Y
5 ***Hefley***	Y	N	Y
6 ***Tancredo***	Y	N	Y
CONNECTICUT			
1 Larson	N	N	Y
2 Gejdenson	N	Y	N
3 DeLauro	N	Y	N
4 ***Shays***	Y	N	Y
5 Maloney	N	N	Y
6 ***Johnson***	Y	N	Y
DELAWARE			
AL ***Castle***	Y	N	Y
FLORIDA			
1 ***Scarborough***	Y	N	Y
2 Boyd	Y	N	Y
3 Brown	N	Y	Y
4 ***Fowler***	Y	N	Y
5 Thurman	N	Y	Y
6 ***Stearns***	Y	N	Y
7 ***Mica***	Y	N	Y
8 ***McCollum***	Y	N	Y
9 ***Bilirakis***	Y	N	Y
10 ***Young***	Y	N	Y
11 Davis	N	N	Y
12 ***Canady***	Y	N	Y
13 ***Miller***	Y	N	Y
14 ***Goss***	Y	N	Y
15 ***Weldon***	Y	N	Y
16 ***Foley***	Y	N	Y
17 Meek	N	Y	N
18 ***Ros-Lehtinen***	Y	N	Y
19 Wexler	Y	N	Y
20 Deutsch	N	N	Y
21 ***Diaz-Balart***	Y	N	Y
22 ***Shaw***	Y	N	Y
23 Hastings	N	Y	Y
GEORGIA			
1 ***Kingston***	Y	N	Y
2 Bishop	N	N	Y
3 ***Collins***	Y	N	Y
4 McKinney	N	Y	N
5 Lewis	N	Y	N
6 ***Isakson***	Y	N	Y
7 ***Barr***	Y	N	Y
8 ***Chambliss***	Y	N	Y
9 ***Deal***	Y	N	Y
10 ***Norwood***	Y	N	Y
11 ***Linder***	Y	N	Y
HAWAII			
1 Abercrombie	N	N	Y
2 Mink	N	Y	N
IDAHO			
1 ***Chenoweth***	Y	N	Y
2 ***Simpson***	Y	N	Y
ILLINOIS			
1 Rush	N	Y	N
2 Jackson	N	Y	N
3 Lipinski	Y	N	Y
4 Gutierrez	N	Y	N
5 Blagojevich	N	Y	Y
6 ***Hyde***	Y	N	Y
7 Davis	N	Y	N
8 ***Crane***	Y	N	Y
9 Schakowsky	N	Y	N
10 ***Porter***	Y	N	Y
11 ***Weller***	Y	N	Y
12 Costello	N	Y	N
13 ***Biggert***	Y	N	Y
14 ***Hastert***			Y

ND Northern Democrats SD Southern Democrats

	57	58	59
15 *Ewing*	Y	N	Y
16 *Manzullo*	Y	N	Y
17 Evans	N	Y	N
18 *LaHood*	Y	N	Y
19 Phelps	N	N	N
20 *Shimkus*	Y	N	Y
INDIANA			
1 Visclosky	N	N	Y
2 *McIntosh*	Y	N	Y
3 Roemer	N	N	Y
4 *Souder*	Y	N	Y
5 *Buyer*	?	?	?
6 *Burton*	+	−	+
7 *Pease*	Y	N	Y
8 *Hostettler*	Y	N	Y
9 Hill	N	Y	Y
10 Carson	N	Y	N
IOWA			
1 *Leach*	Y	N	Y
2 *Nussle*	Y	N	Y
3 Boswell	N	N	Y
4 *Ganske*	Y	N	Y
5 *Latham*	Y	N	Y
KANSAS			
1 *Moran*	Y	N	Y
2 *Ryun*	Y	N	Y
3 Moore	N	N	Y
4 *Tiahrt*	Y	N	Y
KENTUCKY			
1 *Whitfield*	Y	N	Y
2 *Lewis*	Y	N	Y
3 *Northup*	Y	N	Y
4 Lucas	N	N	Y
5 *Rogers*	Y	N	Y
6 *Fletcher*	Y	N	Y
LOUISIANA			
1 Vacant			
2 Jefferson	N	Y	Y
3 *Tauzin*	Y	N	Y
4 *McCrery*	Y	N	Y
5 *Cooksey*	Y	Y	Y
6 *Baker*	Y	N	Y
7 John	N	N	Y
MAINE			
1 Allen	N	Y	N
2 Baldacci	N	Y	N
MARYLAND			
1 *Gilchrest*	Y	N	Y
2 *Ehrlich*	Y	N	Y
3 Cardin	N	Y	Y
4 Wynn	N	Y	N
5 Hoyer	N	N	Y
6 *Bartlett*	Y	N	Y
7 Cummings	N	Y	N
8 *Morella*	Y	Y	N
MASSACHUSETTS			
1 Olver	N	Y	N
2 Neal	N	Y	N
3 McGovern	N	Y	N
4 Frank	N	Y	N
5 Meehan	N	Y	?
6 Tierney	N	Y	N
7 Markey	N	Y	N
8 Capuano	N	Y	N
9 Moakley	N	Y	N
10 Delahunt	N	Y	N
MICHIGAN			
1 Stupak	N	?	?
2 *Hoekstra*	Y	N	Y
3 *Ehlers*	Y	N	N
4 *Camp*	Y	N	Y
5 Barcia	Y	N	Y
6 *Upton*	Y	N	Y
7 *Smith*	Y	N	Y
8 Stabenow	N	Y	Y
9 Kildee	N	Y	Y
10 Bonior	N	Y	N
11 *Knollenberg*	Y	N	Y
12 Levin	N	Y	N
13 Rivers	N	Y	N
14 Conyers	N	Y	N
15 Kilpatrick	N	Y	N
16 Dingell	N	Y	N

	57	58	59
MINNESOTA			
1 *Gutknecht*	Y	N	Y
2 Minge	N	Y	N
3 *Ramstad*	Y	N	Y
4 Vento	N	Y	N
5 Sabo	N	Y	N
6 Luther	N	Y	N
7 Peterson	N	N	Y
8 Oberstar	N	Y	N
MISSISSIPPI			
1 *Wicker*	Y	N	Y
2 Thompson	N	Y	Y
3 *Pickering*	Y	N	Y
4 Shows	Y	N	Y
5 Taylor	Y	N	Y
MISSOURI			
1 Clay	N	Y	N
2 *Talent*	Y	N	Y
3 Gephardt	N	Y	N
4 Skelton	Y	Y	Y
5 McCarthy	N	+	+
6 Danner	N	Y	Y
7 *Blunt*	Y	N	Y
8 *Emerson*	Y	N	Y
9 *Hulshof*	Y	N	Y
MONTANA			
AL *Hill*	Y	N	Y
NEBRASKA			
1 *Bereuter*	Y	N	Y
2 *Terry*	Y	N	Y
3 *Barrett*	Y	N	Y
NEVADA			
1 Berkley	N	Y	Y
2 *Gibbons*	Y	N	Y
NEW HAMPSHIRE			
1 *Sununu*	Y	N	Y
2 *Bass*	Y	N	Y
NEW JERSEY			
1 Andrews	Y	N	Y
2 *LoBiondo*	Y	N	Y
3 *Saxton*	Y	N	Y
4 *Smith*	Y	N	Y
5 *Roukema*	Y	N	Y
6 Pallone	N	Y	Y
7 *Franks*	Y	N	Y
8 Pascrell	N	N	Y
9 Rothman	N	Y	Y
10 Payne	?	Y	N
11 *Frelinghuysen*	Y	N	Y
12 Holt	N	Y	N
13 Menendez	N	Y	Y
NEW MEXICO			
1 *Wilson*	Y	N	Y
2 *Skeen*	Y	N	Y
3 Udall	N	Y	N
NEW YORK			
1 *Forbes*	Y	N	Y
2 *Lazio*	Y	N	Y
3 *King*	Y	N	Y
4 McCarthy	N	Y	Y
5 Ackerman	N	Y	N
6 Meeks	N	Y	N
7 Crowley	N	Y	N
8 Nadler	N	Y	N
9 Weiner	N	Y	N
10 Towns	N	Y	N
11 Owens	N	Y	N
12 Velázquez	N	Y	N
13 *Fossella*	Y	N	Y
14 Maloney	N	Y	Y
15 Rangel	N	Y	N
16 Serrano	N	Y	N
17 Engel	N	Y	N
18 Lowey	N	Y	N
19 *Kelly*	Y	N	Y
20 *Gilman*	Y	N	Y
21 McNulty	N	Y	N
22 *Sweeney*	Y	N	Y
23 *Boehlert*	Y	N	Y
24 *McHugh*	Y	N	Y
25 *Walsh*	Y	N	Y
26 Hinchey	N	Y	N
27 *Reynolds*	Y	N	Y
28 Slaughter	N	N	N
29 LaFalce	N	Y	Y

	57	58	59
30 *Quinn*	Y	N	Y
31 *Houghton*	Y	N	Y
NORTH CAROLINA			
1 Clayton	N	Y	N
2 Etheridge	N	N	Y
3 *Jones*	Y	N	Y
4 Price	N	Y	Y
5 *Burr*	Y	N	Y
6 *Coble*	Y	N	Y
7 McIntyre	Y	N	Y
8 *Hayes*	Y	N	Y
9 *Myrick*	?	?	?
10 *Ballenger*	Y	N	Y
11 *Taylor*	Y	N	Y
12 Watt	N	Y	N
NORTH DAKOTA			
AL Pomeroy	N	Y	Y
OHIO			
1 *Chabot*	Y	N	Y
2 *Portman*	Y	N	Y
3 Hall	N	Y	Y
4 *Oxley*	Y	N	Y
5 *Gillmor*	Y	N	Y
6 Strickland	N	Y	N
7 *Hobson*	Y	N	Y
8 *Boehner*	?	?	?
9 Kaptur	N	Y	N
10 Kucinich	N	N	N
11 Jones	N	Y	N
12 *Kasich*	Y	N	Y
13 Brown	N	Y	N
14 Sawyer	N	Y	N
15 *Pryce*	Y	N	Y
16 *Regula*	Y	N	Y
17 Traficant	N	N	Y
18 *Ney*	Y	N	Y
19 *LaTourette*	Y	N	Y
OKLAHOMA			
1 *Largent*	Y	N	Y
2 *Coburn*	?	?	?
3 *Watkins*	Y	N	Y
4 *Watts*	Y	N	Y
5 *Istook*	Y	N	Y
6 *Lucas*	Y	N	Y
OREGON			
1 Wu	N	Y	N
2 *Walden*	Y	N	Y
3 Blumenauer	N	Y	N
4 DeFazio	N	Y	N
5 Hooley	N	Y	N
PENNSYLVANIA			
1 Brady	N	N	N
2 Fattah	N	Y	N
3 Borski	N	Y	Y
4 Klink	N	Y	Y
5 *Peterson*	Y	N	Y
6 Holden	N	N	Y
7 *Weldon*	Y	N	Y
8 *Greenwood*	Y	N	Y
9 *Shuster*	Y	N	Y
10 *Sherwood*	Y	N	Y
11 Kanjorski	N	Y	Y
12 Murtha	Y	N	Y
13 Hoeffel	N	Y	Y
14 Coyne	N	Y	N
15 *Toomey*	Y	N	Y
16 *Pitts*	Y	N	Y
17 *Gekas*	Y	N	Y
18 Doyle	Y	N	Y
19 *Goodling*	Y	N	Y
20 Mascara	N	N	Y
21 *English*	Y	N	Y
RHODE ISLAND			
1 Kennedy	N	Y	Y
2 Weygand	N	Y	Y
SOUTH CAROLINA			
1 *Sanford*	Y	N	Y
2 *Spence*	Y	N	Y
3 *Graham*	Y	N	Y
4 *DeMint*	Y	N	Y
5 Spratt	Y	P	Y
6 Clyburn	?	?	?
SOUTH DAKOTA			
AL *Thune*	Y	N	Y

	57	58	59
TENNESSEE			
1 *Jenkins*	Y	N	Y
2 *Duncan*	Y	N	Y
3 *Wamp*	Y	N	Y
4 *Hilleary*	Y	N	Y
5 Clement	N	N	Y
6 Gordon	N	N	Y
7 *Bryant*	Y	N	Y
8 Tanner	N	N	Y
9 Ford	N	Y	Y
TEXAS			
1 Sandlin	N	Y	Y
2 Turner	Y	N	Y
3 *Johnson, Sam*	Y	N	Y
4 Hall	Y	N	Y
5 *Sessions*	Y	N	Y
6 *Barton*	Y	N	Y
7 *Archer*	?	N	Y
8 *Brady*	Y	N	Y
9 Lampson	N	Y	Y
10 Doggett	N	Y	N
11 Edwards	N	Y	Y
12 *Granger*	Y	N	Y
13 *Thornberry*	Y	N	Y
14 *Paul*	Y	N	Y
15 Hinojosa	N	Y	Y
16 Reyes	Y	N	Y
17 Stenholm	Y	N	Y
18 Jackson-Lee	N	Y	Y
19 *Combest*	Y	N	Y
20 Gonzalez	N	Y	Y
21 *Smith*	Y	N	Y
22 *DeLay*	Y	N	Y
23 *Bonilla*	Y	N	Y
24 Frost	?	Y	Y
25 Bentsen	N	Y	Y
26 *Armey*	Y	N	Y
27 Ortiz	Y	N	?
28 Rodriguez	Y	Y	Y
29 Green	N	N	Y
30 Johnson, E.B.	N	Y	N
UTAH			
1 *Hansen*	Y	N	Y
2 *Cook*	Y	N	Y
3 *Cannon*	Y	N	Y
VERMONT			
AL *Sanders*	N	N	N
VIRGINIA			
1 *Bateman*	Y	N	Y
2 Pickett	Y	N	Y
3 Scott	Y	N	Y
4 Sisisky	Y	N	Y
5 Goode	Y	N	Y
6 *Goodlatte*	Y	N	Y
7 *Bliley*	Y	N	Y
8 Moran	N	N	Y
9 Boucher	N	N	Y
10 *Wolf*	Y	N	Y
11 *Davis*	Y	N	Y
WASHINGTON			
1 Inslee	N	Y	Y
2 *Metcalf*	Y	N	Y
3 Baird	N	Y	N
4 *Hastings*	Y	N	Y
5 *Nethercutt*	Y	N	Y
6 Dicks	N	Y	Y
7 McDermott	N	Y	N
8 *Dunn*	Y	N	Y
9 Smith	N	N	Y
WEST VIRGINIA			
1 Mollohan	N	N	Y
2 Wise	N	N	Y
3 Rahall	N	Y	N
WISCONSIN			
1 *Ryan*	Y	N	Y
2 Baldwin	N	Y	N
3 Kind	N	Y	N
4 Kleczka	N	Y	Y
5 Barrett	N	Y	N
6 *Petri*	Y	N	Y
7 Obey	N	Y	N
8 *Green*	Y	N	Y
9 *Sensenbrenner*	Y	N	Y
WYOMING			
AL *Cubin*	Y	N	Y

Southern states - Ala., Ark., Fla., Ga., Ky., La., Miss., N.C., Okla., S.C., Tenn., Texas, Va.

House Votes 60, 61, 62, 63, 64, 65, 66, 67

60. H Res 121. Opposition to Racism/Adoption. Gekas, R-Pa., motion to suspend the rules and adopt the resolution to denounce all those individuals and groups that practice or promote racism, anti-Semitism, ethnic prejudice or religious intolerance. The bill was introduced as an alternative to a similar resolution (H Res 35) that specifically condemns the Council of Conservative Citizens. Motion rejected 254-152: R 218-1; D 36-150 (ND 20-120, SD 16-30); I 0-1. March 23, 1999. A two-thirds majority of those present and voting (271 in this case) is required for adoption under suspension of the rules.

61. HR 70. Arlington National Cemetery Burial Eligibility/Passage. Stump, R-Ariz., motion to suspend the rules and pass the bill to codify regulatory eligibility criteria for burial at Arlington National Cemetery. Motion agreed to 428-2: R 219-0; D 208-2 (ND 154-1, SD 54-1); I 1-0. March 23, 1999. A two-thirds majority of those present and voting (286 in this case) is required for passage under suspension of the rules.

62. H Con Res 56. Taiwan Relations Act Commemoration/Adoption. Gilman, R-N.Y., motion to suspend the rules and adopt the concurrent resolution to express the sense of Congress that the United States should reaffirm its commitment to the Taiwan Relations Act and the specific guarantees for the provision of legitimate defense articles to Taiwan contained in that law. Motion agreed to 429-1: R 219-1; D 209-0 (ND 155-0, SD 54-0); I 1-0. March 23, 1999. A two-thirds majority of those present and voting (286 in this case) is required for adoption under suspension of the rules.

63. H Con Res 37. Anti-Semitic Statements in Russian Duma/Adoption. Smith, R-N.J., motion to suspend the rules and adopt the concurrent resolution to express the sense of Congress condemning anti-Semitic statements made by members of the Russian Duma and commending President Boris Yeltsin and other members of the Duma and the Russian government for condemning the statements. Motion agreed to 421-0: R 212-0; D 208-0 (ND 153-0, SD 55-0); I 1-0. March 23, 1999. A two-thirds majority of those present and voting (280 in this case) is required for adoption under suspension of the rules.

64. HR 800. Educational Flexibility/Motion To Instruct. Clay, D-Mo., motion to instruct the House conferees to reject Senate provisions that would allow local education agencies to redirect all or part of $1.2 billion previously appropriated for new teachers to special education programs under the Individuals with Disabilities Act (IDEA). The motion would also instruct House conferees to insist that additional funding be authorized for IDEA, but not by reducing funds for class size reduction. Motion rejected 205-222: R 1-216; D 203-6 (ND 150-4, SD 53-2); I 1-0. March 23, 1999.

65. H Res 101. Committee Funding/Recommit. Hoyer, D-Md., motion to recommit the resolution to the House Administration Committee with instructions to report it back with an amendment to assure that the minority on each committee will receive at least one-third of the funds allocated to that committee, and that the minority would receive one-third of funds distributed from the reserve fund to a committee. Motion rejected 205-218: R 0-217; D 204-1 (ND 150-0, SD 54-1); I 1-0. March 23, 1999.

66. H Res 101. Committee Funding/Adoption. Adoption of the resolution to provide $183.3 million in the 106th Congress for 18 House standing committees and the Permanent Select Committee on Intelligence — $5.3 million (3 percent) more than they received in the 105th. The total funding includes $88.8 million for these 19 committees in 1999 and $91.5 million in 2000. The total also includes a $3.0 million reserve fund that would be allocated by the House Administration Committee to other committees to meet unaticipated needs. (The Appropriations Committee is not covered by this resolution because it receives its funding separately through the legislative branch appropriations bill.) Adopted 216-210: R 216-3; D 0-206 (ND 0-151, SD 0-55); I 0-1. March 23, 1999.

67. HR 1141. Fiscal 1999 Supplemental Spending/Emergency Funding Designation. Stenholm, D-Texas, amendment to remove the "emergency funding" designation from the section of the bill that provides funding for agricultural programs. Without the emergency designation, the funding would have to be offset. Rejected 77-345: R 6-210; D 71-134 (ND 49-101, SD 22-33); I 0-1. March 24, 1999.

Key

Y Voted for (yea).
\# Paired for.
\+ Announced for.
N Voted against (nay).
X Paired against.
– Announced against.
P Voted "present."
C Voted "present" to avoid possible conflict of interest.
? Did not vote or otherwise make a position known.

•

Democrats ***Republicans***
Independents

	60	61	62	63	64	65	66	67
ALABAMA								
1 ***Callahan***	Y	Y	Y	Y	N	N	Y	N
2 ***Everett***	Y	Y	Y	Y	N	N	Y	N
3 ***Riley***	Y	Y	Y	Y	N	N	Y	N
4 ***Aderholt***	Y	Y	Y	Y	N	N	Y	N
5 Cramer	P	Y	Y	Y	Y	Y	N	Y
6 ***Bachus***	Y	Y	Y	Y	N	N	Y	N
7 Hilliard	N	Y	Y	Y	Y	Y	N	N
ALASKA								
AL ***Young***	Y	Y	Y	Y	N	N	Y	N
ARIZONA								
1 ***Salmon***	Y	Y	Y	Y	N	N	Y	N
2 Pastor	N	Y	Y	Y	Y	Y	N	N
3 ***Stump***	Y	Y	Y	Y	N	N	Y	N
4 ***Shadegg***	Y	Y	Y	Y	N	N	Y	N
5 ***Kolbe***	Y	Y	Y	Y	N	N	Y	N
6 ***Hayworth***	Y	Y	Y	Y	N	N	Y	N
ARKANSAS								
1 Berry	Y	Y	Y	Y	Y	Y	N	N
2 Snyder	Y	N	Y	Y	Y	Y	N	N
3 ***Hutchinson***	Y	Y	Y	Y	N	N	Y	N
4 ***Dickey***	Y	Y	Y	Y	N	N	Y	N
CALIFORNIA								
1 Thompson	N	Y	Y	Y	Y	Y	N	Y
2 ***Herger***	Y	Y	Y	+	N	N	Y	N
3 ***Ose***	Y	Y	Y	Y	N	N	Y	N
4 ***Doolittle***	Y	Y	Y	Y	N	N	Y	N
5 Matsui	N	Y	Y	Y	Y	Y	N	N
6 Woolsey	N	Y	Y	Y	Y	Y	N	N
7 Miller, George	N	Y	Y	Y	Y	Y	N	N
8 Pelosi	N	Y	Y	Y	Y	Y	N	Y
9 Lee	N	Y	Y	Y	Y	Y	N	N
10 Tauscher	Y	Y	Y	Y	Y	Y	N	Y
11 ***Pombo***	Y	Y	Y	Y	N	N	Y	N
12 Lantos	?	Y	Y	Y	Y	Y	N	N
13 Stark	N	Y	Y	Y	Y	Y	N	N
14 Eshoo	P	Y	Y	Y	Y	Y	N	Y
15 ***Campbell***	Y	Y	Y	Y	N	N	Y	N
16 Lofgren	P	Y	Y	Y	Y	Y	N	Y
17 Farr	N	Y	Y	Y	Y	Y	N	N
18 Condit	N	Y	Y	Y	Y	Y	N	Y
19 ***Radanovich***	Y	Y	Y	Y	N	N	Y	N
20 Dooley	N	Y	Y	Y	Y	Y	N	Y
21 ***Thomas***	Y	Y	Y	?	N	N	Y	N
22 Capps	N	Y	Y	Y	Y	Y	N	Y
23 ***Gallegly***	Y	Y	Y	Y	N	N	Y	N
24 Sherman	Y	Y	Y	Y	Y	Y	N	N
25 ***McKeon***	Y	Y	Y	Y	N	N	Y	N
26 Berman	N	Y	Y	Y	Y	Y	N	N
27 ***Rogan***	Y	Y	Y	Y	N	N	Y	N
28 ***Dreier***	Y	Y	Y	Y	N	N	Y	N
29 Waxman	N	Y	Y	Y	Y	Y	N	N
30 Becerra	N	Y	Y	Y	Y	Y	N	N
31 Martinez	N	Y	Y	?	Y	Y	N	N
32 Dixon	N	Y	Y	Y	Y	Y	N	N
33 Roybal-Allard	N	Y	Y	Y	Y	Y	N	N
34 Napolitano	N	Y	Y	Y	Y	Y	N	N
35 Waters	N	Y	Y	Y	Y	Y	N	N
36 ***Kuykendall***	Y	Y	Y	Y	N	N	Y	N
37 Millender-McD.	N	Y	Y	Y	Y	Y	N	N
38 ***Horn***	Y	Y	Y	Y	N	N	Y	N
39 ***Royce***	Y	Y	Y	Y	N	N	Y	N
40 ***Lewis***	Y	Y	Y	Y	N	N	Y	N
41 ***Miller, Gary***	Y	Y	Y	Y	N	N	Y	N
42 Brown	N	Y	Y	Y	Y	?	?	?
43 ***Calvert***	Y	Y	Y	Y	N	N	Y	N
44 ***Bono***	Y	Y	Y	Y	N	N	Y	N
45 ***Rohrabacher***	Y	Y	Y	Y	N	N	Y	N
46 Sanchez	N	Y	Y	Y	Y	?	N	Y
47 ***Cox***	Y	Y	Y	Y	N	?	?	N
48 ***Packard***	Y	Y	Y	Y	N	N	Y	N
49 ***Bilbray***	Y	Y	Y	Y	N	N	Y	N
50 Filner	Y	N	Y	Y	Y	Y	N	N
51 ***Cunningham***	Y	Y	Y	Y	N	N	Y	N
52 ***Hunter***	Y	Y	Y	Y	N	N	Y	N
COLORADO								
1 DeGette	Y	Y	Y	Y	Y	Y	N	N
2 Udall	N	Y	Y	Y	Y	Y	N	Y
3 ***McInnis***	Y	Y	Y	Y	N	N	Y	N
4 ***Schaffer***	Y	Y	Y	Y	N	N	Y	Y
5 ***Hefley***	Y	Y	Y	Y	N	N	Y	N
6 ***Tancredo***	Y	Y	Y	Y	N	N	Y	N
CONNECTICUT								
1 Larson	N	Y	Y	Y	Y	Y	N	N
2 Gejdenson	N	Y	Y	Y	Y	Y	N	N
3 DeLauro	N	Y	Y	Y	Y	Y	N	N
4 ***Shays***	Y	Y	Y	Y	N	N	Y	N
5 Maloney	N	Y	Y	Y	Y	Y	N	N
6 ***Johnson***	Y	Y	Y	Y	N	N	Y	N
DELAWARE								
AL ***Castle***	Y	Y	Y	Y	N	N	Y	N
FLORIDA								
1 ***Scarborough***	Y	Y	Y	?	N	N	Y	N
2 Boyd	P	Y	Y	Y	Y	Y	N	Y
3 Brown	N	Y	Y	Y	Y	Y	N	N
4 ***Fowler***	Y	Y	Y	Y	N	N	Y	N
5 Thurman	N	Y	Y	Y	Y	Y	N	Y
6 ***Stearns***	Y	Y	Y	Y	N	N	Y	N
7 ***Mica***	Y	Y	Y	Y	N	N	Y	N
8 ***McCollum***	Y	Y	Y	Y	N	N	Y	N
9 ***Bilirakis***	Y	Y	Y	Y	N	N	Y	N
10 ***Young***	Y	Y	Y	Y	N	N	Y	N
11 Davis	N	Y	Y	Y	Y	Y	N	N
12 ***Canady***	Y	Y	Y	Y	N	N	Y	N
13 ***Miller***	Y	Y	Y	Y	N	N	Y	N
14 ***Goss***	Y	Y	Y	Y	N	N	Y	N
15 ***Weldon***	Y	Y	Y	Y	N	N	Y	N
16 ***Foley***	Y	Y	Y	Y	N	N	Y	N
17 Meek	N	Y	Y	Y	Y	Y	N	N
18 ***Ros-Lehtinen***	Y	Y	Y	Y	?	N	Y	N
19 Wexler	N	Y	Y	Y	Y	Y	N	N
20 Deutsch	N	Y	Y	Y	Y	Y	N	N
21 ***Diaz-Balart***	Y	Y	Y	Y	N	N	Y	N
22 ***Shaw***	Y	Y	Y	Y	N	N	Y	N
23 Hastings	N	Y	Y	Y	Y	Y	N	N
GEORGIA								
1 ***Kingston***	Y	Y	Y	Y	N	N	Y	N
2 Bishop	N	Y	Y	Y	Y	Y	N	N
3 ***Collins***	Y	Y	Y	Y	N	N	Y	N
4 McKinney	N	Y	Y	Y	Y	Y	N	N
5 Lewis	N	Y	Y	Y	Y	Y	N	Y
6 ***Isakson***	Y	Y	Y	Y	N	N	Y	N
7 ***Barr***	Y	Y	Y	Y	?	N	Y	N
8 ***Chambliss***	Y	Y	Y	Y	N	N	Y	N
9 ***Deal***	Y	Y	Y	Y	N	N	Y	N
10 ***Norwood***	Y	Y	Y	Y	N	N	Y	N
11 ***Linder***	Y	Y	Y	Y	N	N	Y	N
HAWAII								
1 Abercrombie	N	Y	Y	Y	Y	Y	N	N
2 Mink	N	Y	Y	Y	Y	Y	N	N
IDAHO								
1 ***Chenoweth***	Y	Y	Y	Y	N	N	Y	N
2 ***Simpson***	Y	Y	Y	Y	N	N	Y	N
ILLINOIS								
1 Rush	N	Y	Y	Y	Y	Y	N	Y
2 Jackson	N	Y	Y	Y	Y	Y	N	Y
3 Lipinski	N	Y	Y	Y	N	Y	N	N
4 Gutierrez	N	Y	Y	Y	Y	Y	N	N
5 Blagojevich	N	Y	Y	Y	Y	Y	N	Y
6 ***Hyde***	Y	Y	Y	Y	N	N	Y	N
7 Davis	N	Y	Y	Y	Y	Y	N	Y
8 ***Crane***	Y	Y	Y	Y	N	N	Y	N
9 Schakowsky	N	Y	Y	Y	Y	Y	N	N
10 ***Porter***	Y	Y	Y	Y	N	N	Y	N
11 ***Weller***	Y	Y	Y	Y	N	N	Y	N
12 Costello	Y	Y	Y	Y	Y	Y	N	N
13 ***Biggert***	Y	Y	Y	Y	N	N	Y	N
14 ***Hastert***	Y					N	Y	

ND Northern Democrats SD Southern Democrats

	60	61	62	63	64	65	66	67
15 ***Ewing***	Y	Y	Y	Y	N	N	Y	N
16 ***Manzullo***	Y	Y	Y	Y	N	N	Y	N
17 Evans	N	Y	Y	Y	Y	Y	N	N
18 ***LaHood***	Y	Y	Y	Y	N	N	Y	N
19 Phelps	N	Y	Y	Y	Y	Y	N	N
20 ***Shimkus***	Y	Y	Y	Y	N	N	Y	N
INDIANA								
1 Visclosky	N	Y	Y	Y	Y	Y	N	N
2 ***McIntosh***	Y	Y	Y	Y	N	N	Y	N
3 Roemer	N	Y	Y	Y	Y	Y	N	Y
4 ***Souder***	Y	Y	Y	Y	N	N	Y	N
5 ***Buyer***	Y	Y	Y	?	N	N	Y	N
6 ***Burton***	Y	Y	Y	Y	N	N	Y	N
7 ***Pease***	Y	Y	Y	Y	N	N	Y	N
8 ***Hostettler***	Y	Y	Y	Y	N	N	Y	N
9 Hill	N	Y	Y	Y	Y	Y	N	N
10 Carson	N	Y	Y	Y	Y	Y	N	N
IOWA								
1 ***Leach***	Y	Y	Y	Y	N	N	Y	N
2 ***Nussle***	Y	Y	Y	?	N	N	Y	N
3 Boswell	N	Y	Y	Y	Y	Y	N	N
4 ***Ganske***	Y	Y	Y	Y	N	?	Y	N
5 ***Latham***	Y	Y	Y	Y	N	N	Y	N
KANSAS								
1 ***Moran***	Y	Y	Y	Y	N	N	Y	N
2 ***Ryun***	Y	Y	Y	Y	N	N	Y	N
3 Moore	Y	Y	Y	Y	Y	Y	N	N
4 ***Tiahrt***	Y	Y	Y	Y	N	N	Y	N
KENTUCKY								
1 ***Whitfield***	Y	Y	Y	Y	N	N	Y	N
2 ***Lewis***	Y	Y	Y	Y	N	N	Y	N
3 ***Northup***	Y	Y	Y	Y	N	N	Y	N
4 Lucas	Y	Y	Y	Y	Y	Y	N	Y
5 ***Rogers***	Y	Y	Y	Y	N	N	Y	N
6 ***Fletcher***	Y	Y	Y	Y	N	N	Y	?
LOUISIANA								
1 Vacant								
2 Jefferson	N	Y	Y	Y	Y	Y	N	Y
3 ***Tauzin***	Y	Y	Y	Y	N	N	Y	N
4 ***McCrery***	Y	Y	Y	Y	N	N	Y	N
5 ***Cooksey***	Y	Y	Y	Y	N	N	Y	N
6 ***Baker***	Y	Y	Y	Y	N	N	Y	N
7 John	Y	Y	Y	Y	Y	Y	N	N
MAINE								
1 Allen	N	Y	Y	Y	Y	Y	N	N
2 Baldacci	N	Y	Y	Y	Y	Y	N	N
MARYLAND								
1 ***Gilchrest***	Y	Y	Y	Y	N	N	Y	N
2 ***Ehrlich***	Y	Y	Y	Y	N	N	Y	N
3 Cardin	Y	Y	Y	Y	Y	?	?	N
4 Wynn	N	Y	Y	Y	Y	Y	N	Y
5 Hoyer	Y	Y	Y	Y	Y	Y	N	N
6 ***Bartlett***	Y	Y	Y	Y	N	N	Y	Y
7 Cummings	N	Y	Y	Y	Y	Y	N	Y
8 ***Morella***	Y	Y	Y	Y	N	N	Y	N
MASSACHUSETTS								
1 Olver	N	Y	Y	Y	Y	Y	N	N
2 Neal	N	Y	Y	Y	Y	?	?	Y
3 McGovern	N	Y	Y	Y	Y	Y	N	Y
4 Frank	N	Y	Y	Y	Y	Y	N	P
5 Meehan	N	Y	Y	Y	Y	Y	N	Y
6 Tierney	N	Y	Y	Y	Y	Y	N	Y
7 Markey	N	Y	Y	Y	Y	Y	N	N
8 Capuano	N	Y	Y	Y	Y	Y	N	Y
9 Moakley	N	Y	Y	Y	Y	Y	N	Y
10 Delahunt	N	Y	Y	Y	Y	Y	N	Y
MICHIGAN								
1 Stupak	?	?	?	?	?	?	?	?
2 ***Hoekstra***	Y	Y	Y	Y	N	N	Y	N
3 ***Ehlers***	Y	Y	Y	Y	N	N	Y	N
4 ***Camp***	Y	Y	Y	Y	N	N	Y	N
5 Barcia	N	Y	Y	Y	Y	Y	N	N
6 ***Upton***	Y	Y	Y	Y	N	N	Y	N
7 ***Smith***	Y	Y	Y	Y	N	N	Y	Y
8 Stabenow	Y	Y	Y	Y	Y	Y	N	Y
9 Kildee	N	Y	Y	Y	Y	Y	N	N
10 Bonior	N	Y	Y	Y	Y	Y	N	N
11 ***Knollenberg***	Y	Y	Y	Y	N	N	Y	N
12 Levin	N	Y	Y	Y	Y	Y	N	N
13 Rivers	N	Y	Y	Y	Y	Y	N	N
14 Conyers	N	Y	Y	?	Y	Y	N	N
15 Kilpatrick	N	Y	Y	Y	Y	Y	N	N
16 Dingell	N	Y	Y	Y	Y	Y	N	N

	60	61	62	63	64	65	66	67
MINNESOTA								
1 ***Gutknecht***	Y	Y	Y	Y	N	N	Y	Y
2 Minge	N	Y	Y	Y	Y	Y	N	Y
3 ***Ramstad***	Y	Y	Y	Y	N	N	Y	N
4 Vento	N	Y	Y	Y	Y	Y	N	Y
5 Sabo	N	Y	Y	Y	N	Y	N	P
6 Luther	N	Y	Y	Y	Y	Y	N	Y
7 Peterson	N	Y	Y	Y	Y	Y	N	Y
8 Oberstar	N	Y	Y	Y	Y	Y	N	Y
MISSISSIPPI								
1 ***Wicker***	Y	Y	Y	Y	N	N	Y	N
2 Thompson	N	Y	Y	Y	Y	Y	N	N
3 ***Pickering***	Y	Y	Y	Y	N	N	Y	N
4 Shows	N	Y	Y	Y	Y	Y	N	Y
5 Taylor	Y	Y	Y	Y	Y	Y	N	Y
MISSOURI								
1 Clay	N	Y	Y	Y	Y	Y	N	N
2 ***Talent***	Y	Y	Y	Y	N	N	Y	N
3 Gephardt	N	Y	Y	Y	Y	Y	N	N
4 Skelton	N	Y	Y	Y	Y	Y	N	N
5 McCarthy	N	Y	Y	Y	Y	Y	N	Y
6 Danner	Y	Y	Y	Y	Y	Y	N	Y
7 ***Blunt***	Y	Y	Y	Y	N	N	Y	N
8 ***Emerson***	+	+	Y	Y	N	N	Y	Y
9 ***Hulshof***	Y	Y	Y	Y	N	N	N	N
MONTANA								
AL ***Hill***	Y	Y	Y	Y	N	N	Y	N
NEBRASKA								
1 ***Bereuter***	Y	Y	Y	Y	N	N	Y	Y
2 ***Terry***	Y	Y	Y	Y	N	N	Y	N
3 ***Barrett***	Y	Y	Y	Y	N	N	Y	?
NEVADA								
1 Berkley	Y	Y	Y	Y	Y	Y	N	N
2 ***Gibbons***	Y	Y	Y	Y	N	N	Y	N
NEW HAMPSHIRE								
1 ***Sununu***	Y	Y	Y	Y	N	N	Y	N
2 ***Bass***	Y	Y	Y	Y	N	N	Y	N
NEW JERSEY								
1 Andrews	N	Y	Y	Y	Y	Y	N	N
2 ***LoBiondo***	Y	Y	Y	Y	N	N	Y	N
3 ***Saxton***	Y	Y	Y	Y	N	?	?	N
4 ***Smith***	Y	Y	Y	Y	N	N	Y	N
5 ***Roukema***	Y	Y	Y	Y	Y	N	Y	N
6 Pallone	N	Y	Y	Y	Y	Y	N	N
7 ***Franks***	Y	Y	Y	Y	N	N	Y	N
8 Pascrell	Y	Y	Y	Y	Y	Y	N	N
9 Rothman	Y	Y	Y	Y	Y	Y	N	N
10 Payne	N	Y	Y	Y	Y	Y	N	N
11 ***Frelinghuysen***	Y	Y	Y	Y	N	N	Y	N
12 Holt	N	Y	Y	Y	Y	Y	N	N
13 Menendez	N	Y	Y	Y	Y	Y	N	N
NEW MEXICO								
1 ***Wilson***	Y	Y	Y	Y	N	N	Y	N
2 ***Skeen***	Y	Y	Y	Y	N	N	Y	N
3 Udall	N	Y	Y	Y	Y	Y	N	Y
NEW YORK								
1 ***Forbes***	P	Y	Y	Y	N	N	Y	N
2 ***Lazio***	Y	Y	Y	Y	N	N	Y	N
3 ***King***	Y	Y	Y	Y	N	N	Y	N
4 McCarthy	P	Y	Y	Y	Y	Y	N	N
5 Ackerman	N	Y	Y	Y	Y	?	?	N
6 Meeks	N	Y	Y	Y	Y	Y	N	N
7 Crowley	P	Y	Y	Y	Y	Y	N	Y
8 Nadler	P	Y	Y	Y	Y	Y	N	Y
9 Weiner	N	Y	Y	Y	Y	Y	N	Y
10 Towns	N	Y	Y	Y	Y	Y	N	N
11 Owens	N	Y	Y	Y	Y	Y	N	N
12 Velázquez	N	Y	Y	Y	Y	Y	N	N
13 ***Fossella***	Y	Y	Y	Y	N	N	Y	N
14 Maloney	P	Y	Y	Y	Y	Y	N	N
15 Rangel	N	Y	Y	Y	Y	Y	N	N
16 Serrano	N	Y	Y	Y	Y	Y	N	N
17 Engel	P	Y	Y	Y	Y	Y	N	N
18 Lowey	P	Y	Y	Y	Y	Y	N	?
19 ***Kelly***	Y	Y	Y	Y	N	N	Y	N
20 ***Gilman***	Y	Y	Y	Y	N	N	Y	N
21 McNulty	Y	Y	Y	Y	Y	Y	N	N
22 ***Sweeney***	Y	Y	Y	Y	N	N	Y	N
23 ***Boehlert***	Y	Y	Y	Y	N	N	Y	N
24 ***McHugh***	Y	Y	Y	Y	N	N	Y	N
25 ***Walsh***	Y	Y	Y	Y	N	N	Y	N
26 Hinchey	N	Y	Y	Y	Y	Y	N	Y
27 ***Reynolds***	Y	Y	Y	Y	N	N	Y	N
28 Slaughter	P	Y	Y	Y	Y	Y	N	–
29 LaFalce	N	Y	Y	Y	Y	Y	N	Y

	60	61	62	63	64	65	66	67
30 ***Quinn***	Y	Y	Y	Y	N	N	Y	N
31 ***Houghton***	Y	Y	Y	Y	N	N	Y	N
NORTH CAROLINA								
1 Clayton	P	Y	Y	Y	Y	Y	N	Y
2 Etheridge	P	Y	Y	Y	Y	Y	N	N
3 ***Jones***	Y	Y	Y	Y	N	N	Y	N
4 Price	P	Y	Y	Y	Y	Y	N	N
5 ***Burr***	Y	Y	Y	Y	N	N	Y	N
6 ***Coble***	Y	Y	Y	Y	N	N	Y	N
7 McIntyre	Y	Y	Y	Y	Y	Y	N	Y
8 ***Hayes***	Y	Y	Y	Y	N	N	Y	N
9 ***Myrick***	?	?	?	?	?	?	?	?
10 ***Ballenger***	Y	Y	Y	Y	N	N	Y	N
11 ***Taylor***	Y	Y	Y	Y	N	N	Y	N
12 Watt	P	Y	Y	Y	Y	Y	N	Y
NORTH DAKOTA								
AL Pomeroy	N	Y	Y	Y	N	Y	N	Y
OHIO								
1 ***Chabot***	Y	Y	Y	Y	N	N	Y	N
2 ***Portman***	Y	Y	Y	Y	N	N	Y	N
3 Hall	Y	Y	Y	Y	Y	Y	N	N
4 ***Oxley***	Y	Y	Y	Y	N	N	Y	N
5 ***Gillmor***	Y	Y	Y	Y	N	N	Y	N
6 Strickland	P	Y	Y	Y	Y	Y	N	N
7 ***Hobson***	Y	Y	Y	Y	N	N	Y	N
8 ***Boehner***	Y	Y	Y	Y	N	N	Y	N
9 Kaptur	N	Y	Y	Y	Y	Y	N	Y
10 Kucinich	N	Y	Y	Y	Y	Y	N	Y
11 Jones	N	Y	Y	Y	Y	Y	N	N
12 ***Kasich***	Y	Y	Y	Y	N	N	Y	N
13 Brown	N	Y	Y	Y	Y	Y	N	Y
14 Sawyer	N	Y	Y	Y	Y	Y	N	Y
15 ***Pryce***	Y	Y	Y	Y	N	N	Y	N
16 ***Regula***	Y	Y	Y	Y	N	N	Y	N
17 Traficant	Y	Y	Y	Y	Y	Y	N	N
18 ***Ney***	Y	Y	Y	Y	N	N	Y	N
19 ***LaTourette***	Y	Y	Y	Y	N	N	Y	N
OKLAHOMA								
1 ***Largent***	Y	Y	Y	Y	N	N	Y	N
2 ***Coburn***	Y	Y	Y	Y	N	N	Y	N
3 ***Watkins***	Y	Y	Y	Y	N	N	Y	N
4 ***Watts***	Y	Y	Y	Y	N	N	Y	N
5 ***Istook***	Y	Y	Y	Y	N	N	Y	N
6 ***Lucas***	Y	Y	Y	Y	N	N	Y	N
OREGON								
1 Wu	N	Y	Y	Y	Y	Y	N	Y
2 ***Walden***	Y	Y	Y	Y	N	N	Y	N
3 Blumenauer	P	Y	Y	Y	Y	Y	N	Y
4 DeFazio	P	Y	Y	Y	Y	Y	N	N
5 Hooley	Y	Y	Y	Y	?	Y	N	N
PENNSYLVANIA								
1 Brady	N	Y	Y	Y	Y	Y	N	N
2 Fattah	N	Y	Y	Y	Y	Y	N	N
3 Borski	N	Y	Y	Y	Y	Y	N	N
4 Klink	N	Y	Y	Y	Y	Y	N	N
5 ***Peterson***	Y	Y	Y	Y	N	N	Y	?
6 Holden	Y	Y	Y	Y	Y	Y	N	N
7 ***Weldon***	Y	Y	Y	Y	N	N	Y	?
8 ***Greenwood***	Y	Y	Y	Y	N	N	Y	N
9 ***Shuster***	Y	Y	Y	Y	N	N	Y	N
10 ***Sherwood***	Y	Y	Y	Y	N	N	Y	N
11 Kanjorski	N	Y	Y	Y	Y	Y	N	N
12 Murtha	N	Y	Y	Y	Y	Y	N	N
13 Hoeffel	N	Y	Y	Y	Y	Y	N	N
14 Coyne	N	Y	Y	Y	Y	Y	N	N
15 ***Toomey***	Y	Y	Y	Y	N	N	Y	N
16 ***Pitts***	Y	Y	Y	Y	N	N	Y	N
17 ***Gekas***	Y	Y	Y	Y	?	N	Y	N
18 Doyle	N	Y	Y	Y	Y	Y	N	N
19 ***Goodling***	Y	Y	Y	Y	N	?	Y	N
20 Mascara	N	Y	Y	Y	Y	Y	N	N
21 ***English***	Y	Y	Y	Y	N	N	Y	N
RHODE ISLAND								
1 Kennedy	N	Y	Y	Y	Y	Y	N	Y
2 Weygand	N	Y	Y	Y	Y	Y	N	N
SOUTH CAROLINA								
1 ***Sanford***	N	Y	Y	Y	N	N	Y	N
2 ***Spence***	Y	Y	Y	Y	N	N	Y	N
3 ***Graham***	Y	Y	Y	Y	N	N	Y	N
4 ***DeMint***	Y	Y	Y	Y	N	N	Y	N
5 Spratt	N	Y	Y	Y	Y	Y	N	N
6 Clyburn	N	Y	Y	Y	Y	Y	N	N
SOUTH DAKOTA								
AL ***Thune***	Y	Y	Y	+	N	N	Y	N

	60	61	62	63	64	65	66	67
TENNESSEE								
1 ***Jenkins***	Y	Y	Y	Y	N	N	Y	N
2 ***Duncan***	Y	Y	Y	Y	N	N	Y	N
3 ***Wamp***	Y	Y	Y	Y	N	N	Y	N
4 ***Hilleary***	Y	Y	Y	?	N	N	Y	N
5 Clement	P	Y	Y	Y	Y	Y	N	N
6 Gordon	Y	Y	Y	Y	Y	Y	N	N
7 ***Bryant***	Y	Y	Y	Y	N	N	Y	N
8 Tanner	P	Y	Y	Y	Y	Y	N	Y
9 Ford	N	Y	Y	Y	Y	Y	N	Y
TEXAS								
1 Sandlin	Y	Y	Y	Y	Y	Y	N	N
2 Turner	Y	Y	Y	Y	Y	Y	N	N
3 ***Johnson, Sam***	Y	Y	Y	Y	N	N	Y	N
4 Hall	Y	Y	Y	Y	N	Y	N	Y
5 ***Sessions***	Y	Y	Y	Y	N	N	Y	N
6 ***Barton***	Y	Y	Y	Y	N	N	Y	N
7 ***Archer***	Y	Y	Y	Y	N	N	Y	N
8 ***Brady***	Y	Y	Y	Y	N	N	Y	N
9 Lampson	N	Y	Y	Y	Y	Y	N	Y
10 Doggett	N	Y	Y	Y	Y	Y	N	Y
11 Edwards	Y	Y	Y	Y	Y	Y	N	N
12 ***Granger***	Y	Y	Y	Y	N	N	Y	N
13 ***Thornberry***	Y	Y	Y	Y	N	N	Y	N
14 ***Paul***	Y	Y	N	Y	N	N	N	N
15 Hinojosa	N	Y	Y	Y	Y	Y	N	N
16 Reyes	N	Y	Y	Y	Y	Y	N	N
17 Stenholm	Y	Y	Y	Y	Y	Y	N	Y
18 Jackson-Lee	N	Y	Y	Y	Y	Y	N	N
19 ***Combest***	Y	Y	Y	Y	N	N	Y	N
20 Gonzalez	N	Y	Y	Y	Y	Y	N	Y
21 ***Smith***	Y	Y	Y	Y	N	N	Y	N
22 ***DeLay***	Y	Y	Y	Y	N	N	Y	N
23 ***Bonilla***	Y	Y	Y	Y	N	N	Y	N
24 Frost	N	Y	Y	Y	Y	Y	N	N
25 Bentsen	N	Y	Y	Y	Y	Y	N	N
26 ***Armey***	Y	Y	Y	Y	N	N	Y	N
27 Ortiz	N	Y	Y	Y	Y	Y	N	N
28 Rodriguez	N	Y	Y	Y	Y	Y	N	N
29 Green	Y	Y	Y	Y	Y	Y	N	N
30 Johnson, E.B.	N	Y	Y	Y	Y	Y	N	N
UTAH								
1 ***Hansen***	Y	Y	Y	Y	N	N	Y	N
2 ***Cook***	Y	Y	Y	Y	N	N	Y	N
3 ***Cannon***	Y	Y	Y	Y	N	N	Y	N
VERMONT								
AL *Sanders*	N	Y	Y	Y	Y	Y	N	N
VIRGINIA								
1 ***Bateman***	Y	Y	Y	Y	N	N	Y	N
2 Pickett	Y	Y	?	Y	Y	Y	N	Y
3 Scott	P	Y	Y	Y	Y	Y	N	N
4 Sisisky	N	Y	Y	Y	Y	Y	N	Y
5 Goode	Y	Y	Y	Y	N	N	N	Y
6 ***Goodlatte***	Y	Y	Y	Y	N	N	Y	N
7 ***Bliley***	Y	Y	Y	Y	N	N	Y	N
8 Moran	N	Y	Y	Y	Y	Y	N	N
9 Boucher	Y	Y	Y	Y	Y	Y	N	Y
10 ***Wolf***	Y	Y	Y	Y	N	N	Y	N
11 ***Davis***	Y	Y	Y	Y	N	N	Y	N
WASHINGTON								
1 Inslee	Y	Y	Y	Y	Y	Y	N	N
2 ***Metcalf***	Y	Y	Y	Y	N	N	Y	N
3 Baird	N	Y	Y	Y	Y	Y	N	Y
4 ***Hastings***	Y	Y	Y	Y	N	N	Y	N
5 ***Nethercutt***	Y	Y	Y	Y	N	N	Y	N
6 Dicks	P	Y	Y	Y	Y	Y	N	N
7 McDermott	N	Y	Y	Y	Y	Y	N	N
8 ***Dunn***	Y	Y	Y	Y	N	N	Y	N
9 Smith	Y	Y	Y	Y	N	Y	N	Y
WEST VIRGINIA								
1 Mollohan	N	Y	Y	Y	Y	Y	N	N
2 Wise	P	Y	Y	Y	Y	Y	N	N
3 Rahall	N	Y	Y	Y	Y	Y	N	N
WISCONSIN								
1 ***Ryan***	Y	Y	Y	Y	N	N	N	N
2 Baldwin	N	Y	Y	Y	Y	Y	N	Y
3 Kind	N	Y	Y	Y	Y	Y	N	Y
4 Kleczka	N	Y	Y	Y	Y	Y	N	N
5 Barrett	N	Y	Y	Y	Y	Y	N	Y
6 ***Petri***	Y	Y	Y	Y	N	N	Y	N
7 Obey	N	Y	Y	Y	Y	Y	N	Y
8 ***Green***	Y	Y	Y	Y	N	N	Y	N
9 ***Sensenbrenner***	Y	Y	Y	Y	N	N	Y	N
WYOMING								
AL ***Cubin***	Y	Y	Y	?	N	N	Y	N

Southern states - Ala., Ark., Fla., Ga., Ky., La., Miss., N.C., Okla., S.C., Tenn., Texas, Va.

House Votes 68, 69, 70, 71, 72, 73, 74, 75

68. HR 1141. Fiscal 1999 Supplemental Spending/Rescissions Restoration. Obey, D-Wis., amendment to restore four of the bill's rescissions, including $648 million in "callable capital" for international financial institutions; $150 million from the U.S. program that aids in disarming Russian nuclear weapons; $30 million from the PL 480 (Food for Peace) foreign food aid and loan program; and $25 million from the U.S. Export-Import Bank. Rejected 201-228: R 2-217; D 198-11 (ND 149-5, SD 49-6); I 1-0. March 24, 1999. A "yea" was a vote in support of the president's position.

69. HR 1141. Fiscal 1999 Supplemental Spending/Emergency Defense Spending. Tiahrt, R-Kan., amendment to rescind a further $195 million in "callable capital" for international financial institutions. The funds would be used to offset the only "emergency spending" in the bill — $195 million to cover money the Defense Department spent on hurricane aid in Central America. Rejected 164-264: R 153-66; D 11-198 (ND 5-149, SD 6-49); I 0-0. March 24, 1999. A "nay" was a vote in support of the president's position.

70. HR 1141. Fiscal 1999 Supplemental Spending/Passage. Passage of the bill to appropriate a total of $1.3 billion in emergency and non-emergency supplemental funds for fiscal 1999, roughly equal to the president's request. The measure offsets $1.1 billion of the funding by rescinding a variety of previous appropriations, leaving $195 million in "emergency" spending that is not offset. Passed 220-211: R 210-11; D 10-199 (ND 8-146,SD 2-53); I 0-1. March 24, 1999. A "nay" was a vote in support of the president's position.

71. H Res 130. U.S. Troops in Kosovo/Adoption. Adoption of the resolution to express the support of the House for the members of the U.S. armed forces who are engaged in military operations against the Federal Republic of Yugoslavia. Adopted 424-1: R 215-0; D 208-1 (ND 153-1, SD 55-0); I 1-0. March 24, 1999.

72. H Con Res 68. Fiscal 2000 Budget Resolution/Previous Question. Linder, R-Ga., motion to order the previous question (thus ending debate and the possibility of amendment) on adoption of the rule (H Res 131) to provide for House floor consideration of the resolution to set broad spending and revenue targets for the next 10 years. The resolution calls for cutting taxes by $778.5 billion over 10 years, devotes Social Security surpluses for national debt reduction, and calls for increases in defense and education. Because the budget resolution proposes to stay within the existing caps on discretionary spending, it would require the Appropriations Committee to make significant cuts in non-defense discretionary spending from the fiscal 1999 funding levels. Motion agreed to 224-203: R 219-0; D 5-202 (ND 2-150, SD 3-52); I 0-1. March 25, 1999.

73. H Con Res 68. Fiscal 2000 Budget Resolution/Rule. Adoption of the rule (H Res 131) to provide for House floor consideration of the resolution to set broad spending and revenue targets for the next ten years. The resolution calls for cutting taxes by $778.5 billion over ten years, declares all Social Security revenues off-limits for other uses, and calls for increases in defense and education. Because the budget resolution proposes to stay within the existing caps on discretionary spending, it would require the Appropriations Committee to make significant cuts in non-defense discretionary spending from the fiscal 1999 funding levels. Adopted 228-194: R 214-0; D 14-193 (ND 4-149, SD 10-44); I 0-1. March 25, 1999.

74. H Con Res 68. Fiscal 2000 Budget Resolution/Coburn Substitute. Coburn, R-Okla., substitute amendment that the sponsors say reflects the Clinton budget proposals as re-estimated by the Congressional Budget Office (CBO). (The President's budget is prepared by the Office of Management and Budget (OMB), and OMB and CBO have different scorekeeping conventions.) According to the amendment's sponsor, the CBO re-estimate calls for revenue increases totalling $108 billion, and would exceed the spending caps by $30 billion in fiscal 2000. Sponsors also claim the amendment would take at least $116 billion of the Social Security surplus to use for new spending. Rejected 2-426: R 0-220; D 2-205 (ND 2-150, SD 0-55); I 0-1. March 25, 1999.

75. H Con Res 68. Fiscal 2000 Budget Resolution/Democratic Substitute. Minge, D-Minn., substitute amendment on behalf of the The Coalition, also known as the Blue Dogs, that calls for a smaller ($100.8 billion less than the resolution) over five years. The substitute amendment also uses debt reduction dividends to shore up Social Security and Medicare and allocates 25 percent of the on-budget surplus to fund defense, agriculture and veterans programs. Compared with the resolution, the amendment calls for $12.2 billion more in defense spending, $3.4 billion more in discretionary agricultural spending and $1.1 billion for veterans' health care. Rejected 134-295: R 26-193; D 108-101 (ND 65-89, SD 43-12); I 0-1. March 25, 1999.

Key

- Y Voted for (yea).
- # Paired for.
- + Announced for.
- N Voted against (nay).
- X Paired against.
- – Announced against.
- P Voted "present."
- C Voted "present" to avoid possible conflict of interest.
- ? Did not vote or otherwise make a position known.

•

Democrats ***Republicans***
Independents

	68	69	70	71	72	73	74	75
ALABAMA								
1 ***Callahan***	N	N	Y	Y	Y	Y	N	N
2 ***Everett***	N	Y	Y	Y	Y	Y	N	N
3 ***Riley***	N	Y	Y	Y	Y	Y	N	N
4 ***Aderholt***	N	Y	Y	Y	Y	Y	N	N
5 Cramer	Y	N	N	Y	N	Y	N	Y
6 ***Bachus***	N	Y	Y	Y	Y	Y	N	N
7 Hilliard	Y	N	N	Y	N	N	N	N
ALASKA								
AL ***Young***	N	Y	Y	Y	Y	Y	N	N
ARIZONA								
1 ***Salmon***	N	Y	N	Y	Y	Y	N	N
2 Pastor	Y	N	N	Y	N	N	N	N
3 ***Stump***	N	Y	Y	Y	Y	Y	N	N
4 ***Shadegg***	N	Y	Y	Y	Y	Y	N	N
5 ***Kolbe***	N	N	Y	Y	Y	Y	N	N
6 ***Hayworth***	N	Y	Y	Y	Y	Y	N	N
ARKANSAS								
1 Berry	Y	N	Y	Y	N	Y	N	Y
2 Snyder	Y	N	N	Y	N	N	N	Y
3 ***Hutchinson***	N	Y	Y	Y	Y	Y	N	N
4 ***Dickey***	N	Y	Y	Y	Y	Y	N	N
CALIFORNIA								
1 Thompson	Y	N	N	Y	N	Y	N	Y
2 ***Herger***	N	Y	Y	Y	Y	Y	N	N
3 ***Ose***	N	Y	Y	Y	Y	Y	N	Y
4 ***Doolittle***	N	Y	Y	Y	Y	Y	N	N
5 Matsui	Y	N	N	Y	N	N	N	Y
6 Woolsey	Y	N	N	Y	N	N	N	N
7 Miller, George	Y	N	N	Y	N	N	N	N
8 Pelosi	Y	N	N	Y	N	N	?	?
9 Lee	Y	N	N	N	N	N	N	N
10 Tauscher	Y	N	N	Y	N	N	N	Y
11 ***Pombo***	N	N	Y	Y	Y	Y	N	N
12 Lantos	Y	N	N	Y	N	N	N	N
13 Stark	Y	N	N	Y	N	N	N	N
14 Eshoo	Y	N	N	Y	N	N	N	N
15 ***Campbell***	N	Y	N	Y	Y	Y	N	N
16 Lofgren	Y	N	N	Y	N	N	N	N
17 Farr	Y	N	N	Y	N	N	N	Y
18 Condit	N	Y	N	Y	Y	Y	N	Y
19 ***Radanovich***	N	Y	Y	Y	Y	Y	N	N
20 Dooley	Y	N	N	Y	N	N	N	Y
21 ***Thomas***	N	N	Y	Y	Y	Y	N	N
22 Capps	Y	N	N	Y	N	N	N	Y
23 ***Gallegly***	N	Y	Y	Y	Y	Y	N	N
24 Sherman	Y	N	N	Y	N	N	N	Y
25 ***McKeon***	N	N	Y	Y	Y	Y	N	N
26 Berman	Y	N	N	Y	N	N	N	N
27 ***Rogan***	N	Y	Y	Y	Y	Y	N	N
28 ***Dreier***	N	N	Y	Y	Y	Y	N	N
29 Waxman	Y	N	N	Y	N	N	N	N
30 Becerra	Y	N	Y	Y	N	N	N	N
31 Martinez	Y	N	N	Y	N	N	N	Y
32 Dixon	Y	N	N	Y	N	N	N	N
33 Roybal-Allard	Y	N	N	Y	N	N	N	N
34 Napolitano	Y	N	N	Y	N	N	N	N
35 Waters	Y	N	N	Y	N	N	N	N
36 ***Kuykendall***	N	N	Y	Y	Y	Y	N	N
37 Millender-McD.	Y	N	N	Y	N	N	N	N
38 ***Horn***	N	Y	Y	Y	Y	Y	N	Y
39 ***Royce***	N	Y	Y	Y	Y	Y	N	N
40 ***Lewis***	N	N	Y	Y	Y	Y	N	N
41 ***Miller, Gary***	N	N	Y	Y	Y	Y	N	N
42 Brown	Y	N	N	Y	N	N	N	N
43 ***Calvert***	N	N	Y	?	Y	Y	N	N
44 ***Bono***	N	N	Y	Y	Y	Y	N	N
45 ***Rohrabacher***	N	Y	Y	Y	Y	Y	N	N
46 Sanchez	Y	N	N	Y	N	N	N	Y
47 ***Cox***	N	Y	Y	Y	Y	Y	N	N
48 ***Packard***	N	Y	Y	Y	Y	Y	N	N
49 ***Bilbray***	N	Y	Y	Y	Y	Y	N	Y
50 Filner	Y	N	N	Y	N	N	P	N
51 ***Cunningham***	N	Y	Y	Y	Y	Y	N	N
52 ***Hunter***	N	N	Y	Y	Y	Y	N	N
COLORADO								
1 DeGette	Y	N	N	Y	N	N	N	N
2 Udall	Y	N	N	Y	N	N	N	Y
3 ***McInnis***	N	Y	Y	Y	Y	Y	N	N
4 ***Schaffer***	N	Y	N	Y	Y	Y	N	N
5 ***Hefley***	N	Y	N	Y	Y	Y	N	N
6 ***Tancredo***	N	Y	N	Y	Y	Y	N	N
CONNECTICUT								
1 Larson	Y	N	N	Y	N	N	N	Y
2 Gejdenson	Y	N	N	Y	N	N	N	N
3 DeLauro	Y	N	N	Y	N	N	N	N
4 ***Shays***	N	Y	Y	Y	Y	Y	N	N
5 Maloney	Y	N	N	Y	N	N	N	N
6 ***Johnson***	N	N	Y	Y	Y	?	N	N
DELAWARE								
AL ***Castle***	N	Y	Y	Y	Y	Y	N	Y
FLORIDA								
1 ***Scarborough***	N	Y	Y	Y	Y	Y	N	Y
2 Boyd	Y	N	N	Y	N	Y	N	Y
3 Brown	Y	N	N	Y	N	N	N	N
4 ***Fowler***	N	N	Y	Y	Y	Y	N	N
5 Thurman	Y	N	N	Y	N	N	N	Y
6 ***Stearns***	N	Y	Y	Y	Y	Y	N	N
7 ***Mica***	N	Y	Y	Y	Y	Y	N	N
8 ***McCollum***	N	Y	Y	Y	Y	Y	N	N
9 ***Bilirakis***	N	N	Y	Y	Y	Y	N	N
10 ***Young***	N	N	Y	Y	Y	Y	N	N
11 Davis	Y	N	N	Y	N	N	N	Y
12 ***Canady***	N	N	Y	Y	Y	Y	N	N
13 ***Miller***	N	N	Y	Y	Y	Y	N	N
14 ***Goss***	N	N	Y	Y	Y	Y	N	N
15 ***Weldon***	N	Y	Y	Y	Y	Y	N	N
16 ***Foley***	N	Y	Y	Y	Y	Y	N	N
17 Meek	Y	N	N	Y	N	N	N	Y
18 ***Ros-Lehtinen***	N	N	Y	Y	Y	Y	N	N
19 Wexler	Y	N	N	Y	N	N	N	Y
20 Deutsch	Y	N	N	Y	N	N	N	Y
21 ***Diaz-Balart***	N	N	Y	Y	Y	Y	N	N
22 ***Shaw***	N	Y	Y	Y	Y	Y	N	N
23 Hastings	Y	N	N	Y	N	N	N	Y
GEORGIA								
1 ***Kingston***	N	Y	Y	Y	Y	Y	N	N
2 Bishop	Y	N	N	Y	N	Y	N	Y
3 ***Collins***	N	Y	N	Y	Y	Y	N	N
4 McKinney	Y	N	N	Y	N	N	N	N
5 Lewis	Y	N	N	Y	N	N	N	N
6 ***Isakson***	N	Y	Y	Y	Y	Y	N	N
7 ***Barr***	N	Y	N	Y	+	+	N	N
8 ***Chambliss***	N	Y	Y	Y	Y	Y	N	N
9 ***Deal***	N	Y	Y	Y	Y	Y	N	N
10 ***Norwood***	N	Y	Y	Y	Y	Y	N	N
11 ***Linder***	N	Y	Y	Y	Y	Y	N	N
HAWAII								
1 Abercrombie	Y	N	N	Y	N	N	N	Y
2 Mink	Y	N	N	Y	N	N	N	N
IDAHO								
1 ***Chenoweth***	N	Y	Y	Y	Y	Y	N	Y
2 ***Simpson***	N	N	Y	Y	Y	Y	N	N
ILLINOIS								
1 Rush	Y	N	N	Y	N	N	Y	N
2 Jackson	Y	N	N	Y	N	N	N	N
3 Lipinski	Y	N	N	Y	N	N	N	N
4 Gutierrez	Y	N	Y	Y	N	N	N	N
5 Blagojevich	Y	N	N	Y	N	N	N	N
6 ***Hyde***	N	N	Y	Y	Y	Y	N	N
7 Davis	Y	N	N	Y	N	N	N	N
8 ***Crane***	N	Y	Y	Y	Y	Y	N	N
9 Schakowsky	Y	N	N	Y	N	N	N	N
10 ***Porter***	N	N	Y	Y	Y	Y	N	N
11 ***Weller***	N	Y	Y	+	Y	Y	N	N
12 Costello	Y	N	N	Y	N	N	N	N
13 ***Biggert***	N	N	Y	Y	Y	Y	N	N
14 ***Hastert***			Y	Y	Y			

ND Northern Democrats SD Southern Democrats

	68	69	70	71	72	73	74	75
15 ***Ewing***	N	Y	Y	Y	Y	Y	N	N
16 ***Manzullo***	N	Y	Y	Y	Y	Y	N	N
17 Evans	Y	N	N	Y	N	N	N	N
18 ***LaHood***	N	Y	Y	Y	Y	Y	N	Y
19 Phelps	Y	N	N	Y	N	N	N	Y
20 ***Shimkus***	N	Y	Y	Y	Y	Y	N	Y
INDIANA								
1 Visclosky	Y	N	N	Y	N	N	N	Y
2 ***McIntosh***	N	Y	Y	Y	Y	Y	N	N
3 Roemer	Y	N	N	Y	N	N	N	Y
4 ***Souder***	N	Y	Y	Y	Y	Y	N	N
5 ***Buyer***	N	N	Y	Y	Y	+	N	N
6 ***Burton***	N	N	Y	Y	Y	Y	–	–
7 ***Pease***	N	Y	Y	Y	Y	Y	N	N
8 ***Hostettler***	N	Y	Y	Y	Y	Y	N	N
9 Hill	N	N	Y	Y	N	N	N	Y
10 Carson	Y	N	N	Y	N	N	N	N
IOWA								
1 ***Leach***	N	N	Y	Y	Y	Y	N	N
2 ***Nussle***	N	Y	Y	?	Y	Y	N	N
3 Boswell	Y	N	Y	Y	N	N	N	Y
4 ***Ganske***	N	Y	Y	Y	Y	Y	N	Y
5 ***Latham***	N	N	Y	Y	Y	Y	N	N
KANSAS								
1 ***Moran***	N	Y	Y	Y	Y	Y	N	Y
2 ***Ryun***	N	Y	Y	Y	Y	Y	N	N
3 Moore	Y	N	N	Y	N	N	N	Y
4 ***Tiahrt***	N	Y	Y	Y	Y	Y	N	N
KENTUCKY								
1 ***Whitfield***	N	N	Y	Y	Y	Y	N	N
2 ***Lewis***	N	Y	Y	Y	Y	Y	N	N
3 ***Northup***	N	Y	Y	Y	Y	Y	N	N
4 Lucas	Y	N	N	Y	N	N	N	Y
5 ***Rogers***	N	N	Y	Y	Y	Y	N	N
6 ***Fletcher***	N	Y	Y	Y	Y	Y	N	N
LOUISIANA								
1 Vacant								
2 Jefferson	Y	N	N	Y	N	N	N	Y
3 ***Tauzin***	N	N	Y	Y	Y	Y	N	N
4 ***McCrery***	N	N	Y	Y	Y	Y	N	N
5 ***Cooksey***	N	Y	Y	Y	Y	Y	N	N
6 ***Baker***	N	N	Y	Y	Y	Y	N	N
7 John	Y	N	N	Y	N	Y	N	Y
MAINE								
1 Allen	Y	N	N	Y	N	N	N	N
2 Baldacci	Y	N	N	Y	N	N	N	N
MARYLAND								
1 ***Gilchrest***	N	Y	Y	Y	Y	Y	N	N
2 ***Ehrlich***	N	Y	Y	Y	Y	Y	N	N
3 Cardin	Y	N	N	Y	N	N	N	Y
4 Wynn	Y	N	N	Y	N	N	N	Y
5 Hoyer	Y	N	N	Y	N	N	N	Y
6 ***Bartlett***	N	Y	Y	Y	Y	Y	N	N
7 Cummings	Y	N	N	Y	?	N	N	N
8 ***Morella***	N	Y	Y	Y	Y	Y	N	Y
MASSACHUSETTS								
1 Olver	Y	N	N	Y	N	N	N	N
2 Neal	Y	N	N	Y	N	N	N	Y
3 McGovern	Y	N	N	Y	N	N	N	N
4 Frank	Y	N	N	Y	N	N	N	N
5 Meehan	Y	N	N	Y	N	N	N	Y
6 Tierney	Y	N	N	Y	N	N	N	N
7 Markey	Y	N	N	Y	N	N	N	Y
8 Capuano	Y	N	N	Y	N	N	N	N
9 Moakley	Y	N	N	Y	N	N	N	N
10 Delahunt	Y	N	N	Y	N	N	N	N
MICHIGAN								
1 Stupak	?	?	?	?	?	?	?	?
2 ***Hoekstra***	N	Y	Y	Y	Y	Y	N	N
3 ***Ehlers***	N	Y	Y	Y	Y	Y	N	N
4 ***Camp***	N	Y	Y	Y	Y	Y	N	N
5 Barcia	Y	Y	N	Y	N	N	N	Y
6 ***Upton***	N	Y	Y	Y	Y	Y	N	Y
7 ***Smith***	N	Y	Y	Y	Y	Y	N	Y
8 Stabenow	Y	N	N	Y	N	N	N	Y
9 Kildee	Y	N	N	Y	N	N	N	N
10 Bonior	Y	N	N	Y	N	N	N	N
11 ***Knollenberg***	N	N	Y	Y	Y	Y	N	N
12 Levin	Y	N	N	Y	N	N	N	N
13 Rivers	N	N	N	Y	N	N	N	N
14 Conyers	Y	N	N	Y	N	N	N	N
15 Kilpatrick	Y	N	N	Y	N	N	N	N
16 Dingell	Y	N	N	Y	N	N	N	Y

	68	69	70	71	72	73	74	75
MINNESOTA								
1 ***Gutknecht***	N	Y	N	Y	Y	Y	N	N
2 Minge	Y	N	Y	Y	N	Y	N	Y
3 ***Ramstad***	N	Y	Y	Y	Y	Y	N	N
4 Vento	Y	N	N	Y	N	N	N	N
5 Sabo	Y	N	N	Y	N	N	Y	N
6 Luther	Y	N	N	Y	N	N	N	Y
7 Peterson	N	Y	N	Y	Y	N	Y	Y
8 Oberstar	Y	N	N	Y	N	N	N	Y
MISSISSIPPI								
1 ***Wicker***	N	N	Y	Y	Y	Y	N	N
2 Thompson	Y	N	N	Y	N	N	N	N
3 ***Pickering***	N	N	Y	+	Y	Y	N	Y
4 Shows	Y	N	N	Y	N	N	N	Y
5 Taylor	N	Y	N	Y	N	N	N	Y
MISSOURI								
1 Clay	Y	N	N	Y	N	N	N	N
2 ***Talent***	N	N	Y	Y	Y	Y	N	N
3 Gephardt	Y	N	N	Y	N	N	N	Y
4 Skelton	Y	N	N	Y	N	N	N	Y
5 McCarthy	Y	N	N	Y	N	N	N	Y
6 Danner	Y	N	Y	Y	N	N	N	Y
7 ***Blunt***	N	Y	Y	Y	Y	Y	N	N
8 ***Emerson***	N	N	Y	Y	+	+	N	Y
9 ***Hulshof***	N	Y	Y	Y	Y	Y	N	N
MONTANA								
AL ***Hill***	N	Y	Y	Y	Y	Y	N	N
NEBRASKA								
1 ***Bereuter***	Y	N	Y	Y	Y	Y	N	Y
2 ***Terry***	N	Y	Y	Y	Y	Y	N	N
3 ***Barrett***	N	N	Y	Y	Y	Y	N	Y
NEVADA								
1 Berkley	Y	N	N	Y	N	N	N	Y
2 ***Gibbons***	N	Y	Y	Y	Y	Y	N	N
NEW HAMPSHIRE								
1 ***Sununu***	N	Y	Y	Y	Y	Y	N	N
2 ***Bass***	N	Y	Y	Y	Y	Y	N	N
NEW JERSEY								
1 Andrews	Y	N	N	Y	N	N	N	Y
2 ***LoBiondo***	N	Y	Y	Y	Y	Y	N	N
3 ***Saxton***	N	N	Y	Y	Y	Y	N	N
4 ***Smith***	N	Y	Y	Y	Y	Y	N	N
5 ***Roukema***	N	N	Y	Y	Y	Y	N	Y
6 Pallone	Y	N	N	Y	N	N	N	Y
7 ***Franks***	N	Y	Y	Y	Y	?	N	N
8 Pascrell	Y	N	N	Y	N	N	N	Y
9 Rothman	Y	N	N	Y	N	N	N	N
10 Payne	Y	N	N	Y	N	N	N	N
11 ***Frelinghuysen***	N	N	Y	?	Y	Y	N	N
12 Holt	Y	N	N	Y	N	N	N	Y
13 Menendez	Y	N	N	Y	N	N	N	Y
NEW MEXICO								
1 ***Wilson***	N	N	Y	Y	Y	Y	N	N
2 ***Skeen***	N	N	Y	Y	Y	Y	N	N
3 Udall	Y	N	N	Y	N	N	N	Y
NEW YORK								
1 ***Forbes***	N	Y	Y	Y	Y	Y	N	N
2 ***Lazio***	N	Y	Y	Y	Y	Y	N	N
3 ***King***	N	N	Y	Y	Y	Y	N	N
4 McCarthy	Y	N	N	Y	N	N	N	Y
5 Ackerman	Y	N	N	Y	N	N	N	N
6 Meeks	Y	N	N	Y	N	N	N	N
7 Crowley	Y	N	N	Y	N	N	N	Y
8 Nadler	Y	N	N	Y	N	N	N	N
9 Weiner	Y	N	N	Y	N	N	N	N
10 Towns	Y	N	N	Y	N	N	N	N
11 Owens	Y	N	N	Y	N	N	?	N
12 Velázquez	Y	N	N	Y	N	N	N	N
13 ***Fossella***	?	Y	Y	Y	Y	Y	N	N
14 Maloney	Y	N	N	Y	N	N	N	N
15 Rangel	Y	N	N	Y	N	N	N	N
16 Serrano	Y	N	N	Y	N	N	N	N
17 Engel	Y	N	N	Y	?	?	N	Y
18 Lowey	Y	N	N	Y	?	?	N	N
19 ***Kelly***	N	N	Y	Y	Y	Y	N	N
20 ***Gilman***	N	N	Y	Y	Y	Y	N	N
21 McNulty	Y	N	N	Y	N	N	N	N
22 ***Sweeney***	N	Y	Y	Y	Y	Y	N	N
23 ***Boehlert***	N	Y	Y	Y	Y	Y	N	N
24 ***McHugh***	N	Y	Y	Y	Y	Y	N	N
25 ***Walsh***	N	N	Y	Y	Y	Y	N	N
26 Hinchey	Y	N	N	Y	N	N	N	N
27 ***Reynolds***	N	Y	Y	Y	Y	Y	N	N
28 Slaughter	+	–	–	+	N	N	N	N
29 LaFalce	Y	N	N	Y	N	N	N	Y

	68	69	70	71	72	73	74	75
30 ***Quinn***	N	Y	Y	Y	Y	Y	N	N
31 ***Houghton***	N	N	Y	Y	Y	Y	N	N
NORTH CAROLINA								
1 Clayton	Y	N	N	Y	N	N	N	Y
2 Etheridge	Y	N	N	Y	N	N	N	Y
3 ***Jones***	N	Y	Y	Y	Y	Y	N	N
4 Price	Y	N	N	Y	N	N	N	N
5 ***Burr***	N	Y	Y	Y	Y	Y	N	N
6 ***Coble***	N	Y	Y	Y	Y	Y	N	N
7 McIntyre	N	Y	N	Y	N	N	N	Y
8 ***Hayes***	N	Y	Y	Y	Y	Y	N	N
9 ***Myrick***	?	?	?	?	Y	Y	N	N
10 ***Ballenger***	N	Y	Y	Y	Y	Y	N	N
11 ***Taylor***	N	Y	Y	Y	Y	Y	N	N
12 Watt	Y	N	N	Y	N	N	N	Y
NORTH DAKOTA								
AL Pomeroy	Y	N	Y	Y	N	N	N	Y
OHIO								
1 ***Chabot***	N	Y	N	Y	Y	Y	N	N
2 ***Portman***	N	Y	Y	Y	Y	Y	N	N
3 Hall	Y	N	N	Y	N	N	N	N
4 ***Oxley***	N	N	Y	Y	Y	Y	N	N
5 ***Gillmor***	N	Y	Y	Y	Y	Y	N	N
6 Strickland	Y	N	N	Y	N	N	N	N
7 ***Hobson***	N	N	Y	Y	Y	Y	N	N
8 ***Boehner***	N	Y	Y	Y	Y	Y	N	N
9 Kaptur	Y	N	N	Y	N	N	N	Y
10 Kucinich	Y	Y	N	Y	N	N	N	Y
11 Jones	Y	N	N	Y	N	N	N	N
12 ***Kasich***	N	N	Y	Y	Y	Y	N	N
13 Brown	Y	N	N	Y	N	N	N	N
14 Sawyer	Y	N	N	Y	N	N	N	Y
15 ***Pryce***	N	N	Y	Y	Y	Y	N	N
16 ***Regula***	N	N	Y	Y	Y	Y	N	N
17 Traficant	N	N	Y	Y	N	N	N	N
18 ***Ney***	N	Y	Y	Y	Y	Y	N	N
19 ***LaTourette***	N	Y	Y	Y	Y	Y	N	Y
OKLAHOMA								
1 ***Largent***	N	Y	Y	Y	Y	Y	N	N
2 ***Coburn***	N	Y	Y	Y	Y	Y	N	Y
3 ***Watkins***	N	Y	Y	Y	Y	Y	N	N
4 ***Watts***	N	Y	Y	Y	Y	Y	N	N
5 ***Istook***	N	Y	Y	Y	Y	Y	N	N
6 ***Lucas***	N	Y	Y	Y	Y	Y	N	N
OREGON								
1 Wu	Y	N	N	Y	N	N	N	N
2 ***Walden***	N	N	Y	Y	Y	Y	N	N
3 Blumenauer	Y	N	N	Y	N	N	N	Y
4 DeFazio	Y	N	N	Y	N	N	N	N
5 Hooley	Y	N	N	Y	N	N	N	Y
PENNSYLVANIA								
1 Brady	Y	N	N	Y	N	N	N	N
2 Fattah	Y	N	N	Y	N	N	N	N
3 Borski	Y	N	N	Y	N	N	N	N
4 Klink	Y	N	N	Y	N	N	N	Y
5 ***Peterson***	N	?	Y	Y	Y	Y	N	N
6 Holden	Y	N	N	Y	N	N	N	Y
7 ***Weldon***	Y	N	Y	Y	Y	?	N	?
8 ***Greenwood***	N	Y	Y	Y	Y	Y	N	N
9 ***Shuster***	N	N	Y	Y	Y	Y	N	N
10 ***Sherwood***	N	Y	Y	Y	Y	Y	N	N
11 Kanjorski	Y	N	N	Y	N	N	N	N
12 Murtha	Y	N	N	Y	N	N	N	N
13 Hoeffel	Y	N	N	Y	N	N	N	Y
14 Coyne	Y	N	N	Y	N	N	N	N
15 ***Toomey***	N	Y	Y	Y	Y	Y	N	N
16 ***Pitts***	N	Y	Y	Y	Y	Y	N	N
17 ***Gekas***	N	Y	Y	Y	Y	Y	N	N
18 Doyle	Y	N	N	Y	N	N	N	Y
19 ***Goodling***	N	N	Y	Y	Y	Y	N	N
20 Mascara	Y	N	N	Y	N	N	N	Y
21 ***English***	N	Y	Y	?	Y	Y	N	N
RHODE ISLAND								
1 Kennedy	Y	N	N	Y	N	N	N	N
2 Weygand	Y	N	N	Y	N	N	N	N
SOUTH CAROLINA								
1 ***Sanford***	N	Y	N	Y	Y	Y	N	N
2 ***Spence***	N	N	Y	Y	Y	Y	N	N
3 ***Graham***	N	Y	Y	Y	Y	Y	N	N
4 ***DeMint***	N	Y	Y	Y	Y	Y	N	N
5 Spratt	Y	N	N	Y	N	N	N	N
6 Clyburn	Y	N	N	Y	N	N	N	N
SOUTH DAKOTA								
AL ***Thune***	N	Y	Y	Y	Y	Y	N	Y

	68	69	70	71	72	73	74	75
TENNESSEE								
1 ***Jenkins***	N	Y	Y	Y	Y	Y	N	N
2 ***Duncan***	N	Y	Y	Y	Y	Y	N	Y
3 ***Wamp***	N	Y	Y	Y	Y	Y	N	N
4 ***Hilleary***	N	Y	Y	Y	Y	Y	N	N
5 Clement	Y	N	N	Y	N	N	N	Y
6 Gordon	Y	N	N	Y	N	N	N	N
7 ***Bryant***	N	Y	Y	Y	Y	Y	N	N
8 Tanner	Y	N	N	Y	N	Y	N	Y
9 Ford	Y	N	N	Y	N	N	N	Y
TEXAS								
1 Sandlin	Y	N	N	Y	N	N	N	Y
2 Turner	Y	N	N	Y	N	N	N	Y
3 ***Johnson, Sam***	N	Y	Y	Y	Y	Y	N	N
4 Hall	N	Y	N	Y	Y	Y	N	Y
5 ***Sessions***	N	Y	Y	Y	Y	Y	N	N
6 ***Barton***	N	Y	Y	Y	Y	Y	N	Y
7 ***Archer***	N	Y	Y	Y	Y	Y	N	N
8 ***Brady***	N	Y	Y	Y	?	?	N	N
9 Lampson	Y	N	N	Y	N	N	N	Y
10 Doggett	N	Y	N	Y	N	N	N	Y
11 Edwards	Y	N	N	Y	N	N	N	Y
12 ***Granger***	N	Y	Y	Y	Y	Y	N	N
13 ***Thornberry***	N	Y	Y	Y	Y	Y	N	N
14 ***Paul***	N	Y	N	Y	Y	Y	N	N
15 Hinojosa	Y	N	Y	Y	N	N	N	N
16 Reyes	Y	N	N	Y	N	N	N	Y
17 Stenholm	N	N	N	Y	Y	Y	N	Y
18 Jackson-Lee	Y	N	N	Y	N	N	N	Y
19 ***Combest***	N	Y	Y	Y	Y	Y	N	N
20 Gonzalez	Y	N	N	Y	N	?	N	Y
21 ***Smith***	N	Y	Y	Y	Y	Y	N	N
22 ***DeLay***	N	Y	Y	Y	Y	Y	N	N
23 ***Bonilla***	N	N	Y	Y	Y	Y	N	N
24 Frost	Y	N	N	Y	N	N	N	Y
25 Bentsen	Y	N	N	Y	N	N	N	Y
26 ***Armey***	N	Y	Y	Y	Y	Y	N	N
27 Ortiz	Y	N	N	Y	N	N	N	Y
28 Rodriguez	Y	N	N	Y	N	N	N	Y
29 Green	Y	Y	N	Y	N	N	N	Y
30 Johnson, E.B.	Y	N	N	Y	N	N	N	Y
UTAH								
1 ***Hansen***	N	N	Y	Y	Y	Y	N	N
2 ***Cook***	N	Y	Y	Y	Y	Y	N	N
3 ***Cannon***	N	Y	Y	Y	Y	Y	N	N
VERMONT								
AL *Sanders*	Y	?	N	Y	N	N	N	N
VIRGINIA								
1 ***Bateman***	N	N	Y	Y	Y	Y	N	N
2 Pickett	Y	N	N	Y	N	N	N	N
3 Scott	Y	N	N	Y	N	N	N	Y
4 Sisisky	Y	N	N	Y	N	N	N	Y
5 Goode	N	N	Y	Y	Y	Y	N	Y
6 ***Goodlatte***	N	Y	Y	Y	Y	Y	N	Y
7 ***Bliley***	N	N	Y	Y	Y	Y	N	N
8 Moran	Y	N	N	Y	N	N	N	Y
9 Boucher	Y	N	N	Y	N	N	N	N
10 ***Wolf***	N	N	Y	Y	Y	Y	N	N
11 ***Davis***	N	Y	Y	Y	Y	Y	N	Y
WASHINGTON								
1 Inslee	Y	Y	N	Y	N	N	N	Y
2 ***Metcalf***	N	Y	Y	Y	Y	Y	N	Y
3 Baird	Y	N	N	Y	N	N	N	Y
4 ***Hastings***	N	Y	Y	Y	Y	Y	N	N
5 ***Nethercutt***	N	Y	Y	Y	Y	Y	N	N
6 Dicks	Y	N	N	Y	N	N	N	N
7 McDermott	Y	N	N	Y	N	N	N	Y
8 ***Dunn***	N	Y	Y	Y	Y	Y	N	N
9 Smith	Y	N	N	Y	N	N	N	Y
WEST VIRGINIA								
1 Mollohan	Y	N	N	Y	N	N	N	N
2 Wise	Y	N	N	Y	N	N	N	Y
3 Rahall	Y	N	N	Y	N	N	N	N
WISCONSIN								
1 ***Ryan***	N	Y	Y	Y	Y	Y	N	N
2 Baldwin	Y	N	N	Y	N	N	N	N
3 Kind	Y	N	N	Y	N	N	N	Y
4 Kleczka	Y	N	N	Y	N	N	N	N
5 Barrett	Y	N	N	Y	N	N	N	Y
6 ***Petri***	N	Y	Y	Y	Y	Y	N	N
7 Obey	Y	N	N	Y	N	N	N	N
8 ***Green***	N	Y	Y	Y	Y	Y	N	N
9 ***Sensenbrenner***	N	Y	Y	Y	Y	Y	N	N
WYOMING								
AL ***Cubin***	N	Y	Y	Y	Y	Y	N	N

Southern states - Ala., Ark., Fla., Ga., Ky., La., Miss., N.C., Okla., S.C., Tenn., Texas, Va.

76. H Con Res 68. Fiscal 2000 Budget Resolution/Democratic Substitute. Spratt, D-S.C., substitute amendment that provides for no new net tax cuts or net new spending until legislation is enacted that addresses the solvency of the Medicare and Social Security Trust Funds. The Spratt substitute calls for saving all of the surplus — the Social Security surplus and the non-Social Security surplus — until the issue of Medicare and Social Security solvency is addressed. After solvency for these programs is extended, the substitute calls for more discretionary funding for non-defense programs than the resolution, and provides for net tax cuts of $116 billion over 10 years. Rejected 173-250: R 0-216; D 173-33 (ND 128-23, SD 45-10); I 0-1. March 25, 1999.

77. H Con Res 68. Fiscal 2000 Budget Resolution/Adoption. Adoption of the resolution to set broad spending and revenue targets for the next 10 years. The resolution calls for cutting taxes by $778.5 billion over 10 years, declares all Social Security revenues off-limits for other uses, and calls for increases in defense and education. Because the budget resolution proposes to stay within the existing caps on discretionary spending, it would require the Appropriations Committee to make significant cuts in non-defense discretionary spending from the fiscal 1999 funding levels. Adopted 221-208: R 217-2; D 4-205 (ND 1-153, SD 3-52); I 0-1. March 25, 1999.

Key

- Y Voted for (yea).
- # Paired for.
- \+ Announced for.
- N Voted against (nay).
- X Paired against.
- – Announced against.
- P Voted "present."
- C Voted "present" to avoid possible conflict of interest.
- ? Did not vote or otherwise make a position known.

•

Democrats ***Republicans***
Independents

	76	77
ALABAMA		
1 ***Callahan***	N	Y
2 ***Everett***	N	Y
3 ***Riley***	N	Y
4 ***Aderholt***	N	Y
5 Cramer	Y	Y
6 ***Bachus***	N	Y
7 Hilliard	Y	N
ALASKA		
AL ***Young***	N	Y
ARIZONA		
1 ***Salmon***	N	Y
2 Pastor	N	N
3 ***Stump***	N	Y
4 ***Shadegg***	N	Y
5 ***Kolbe***	N	Y
6 ***Hayworth***	N	Y
ARKANSAS		
1 Berry	N	N
2 Snyder	Y	N
3 ***Hutchinson***	N	Y
4 ***Dickey***	N	Y
CALIFORNIA		
1 Thompson	Y	N
2 ***Herger***	N	Y
3 ***Ose***	N	Y
4 ***Doolittle***	N	Y
5 Matsui	Y	N
6 Woolsey	Y	N
7 Miller, George	N	N
8 Pelosi	?	?
9 Lee	N	N
10 Tauscher	Y	N
11 ***Pombo***	N	Y
12 Lantos	Y	N
13 Stark	N	N
14 Eshoo	Y	N
15 ***Campbell***	N	Y
16 Lofgren	Y	N
17 Farr	Y	N
18 Condit	Y	Y
19 ***Radanovich***	N	Y
20 Dooley	Y	N
21 ***Thomas***	N	Y
22 Capps	Y	N
23 ***Gallegly***	N	Y
24 Sherman	Y	N
25 ***McKeon***	N	Y
26 Berman	Y	N
27 ***Rogan***	N	Y
28 ***Dreier***	N	Y
29 Waxman	Y	N
30 Becerra	Y	N
31 Martinez	Y	N
32 Dixon	Y	N
33 Roybal-Allard	Y	N
34 Napolitano	Y	N
35 Waters	Y	N
36 ***Kuykendall***	N	Y
37 Millender-McD.	Y	N
38 ***Horn***	N	Y
39 ***Royce***	N	Y
40 ***Lewis***	N	Y
41 ***Miller, Gary***	N	Y
42 Brown	?	N
43 ***Calvert***	N	Y
44 ***Bono***	N	Y
45 ***Rohrabacher***	N	Y
46 Sanchez	Y	N
47 ***Cox***	N	Y
48 ***Packard***	N	Y
49 ***Bilbray***	N	Y
50 Filner	Y	N
51 ***Cunningham***	N	Y
52 ***Hunter***	N	Y
COLORADO		
1 DeGette	Y	N
2 Udall	Y	N
3 ***McInnis***	N	Y
4 ***Schaffer***	N	Y
5 ***Hefley***	N	Y
6 ***Tancredo***	N	Y
CONNECTICUT		
1 Larson	Y	N
2 Gejdenson	Y	N
3 DeLauro	Y	N
4 ***Shays***	N	Y
5 Maloney	Y	N
6 ***Johnson***	N	Y
DELAWARE		
AL ***Castle***	N	Y
FLORIDA		
1 ***Scarborough***	N	Y
2 Boyd	N	N
3 Brown	Y	N
4 ***Fowler***	N	Y
5 Thurman	Y	N
6 ***Stearns***	N	Y
7 ***Mica***	N	Y
8 ***McCollum***	N	Y
9 ***Bilirakis***	N	Y
10 ***Young***	N	Y
11 Davis	Y	N
12 ***Canady***	N	Y
13 ***Miller***	N	Y
14 ***Goss***	N	Y
15 ***Weldon***	N	Y
16 ***Foley***	N	Y
17 Meek	Y	N
18 ***Ros-Lehtinen***	N	Y
19 Wexler	Y	N
20 Deutsch	Y	N
21 ***Diaz-Balart***	N	Y
22 ***Shaw***	N	Y
23 Hastings	Y	N
GEORGIA		
1 ***Kingston***	N	Y
2 Bishop	N	N
3 ***Collins***	N	Y
4 McKinney	Y	N
5 Lewis	Y	N
6 ***Isakson***	N	Y
7 ***Barr***	N	Y
8 ***Chambliss***	N	Y
9 ***Deal***	N	Y
10 ***Norwood***	N	Y
11 ***Linder***	N	Y
HAWAII		
1 Abercrombie	Y	N
2 Mink	Y	N
IDAHO		
1 ***Chenoweth***	N	Y
2 ***Simpson***	N	Y
ILLINOIS		
1 Rush	Y	N
2 Jackson	Y	N
3 Lipinski	N	N
4 Gutierrez	Y	N
5 Blagojevich	Y	N
6 ***Hyde***	N	Y
7 Davis	Y	N
8 ***Crane***	N	Y
9 Schakowsky	N	N
10 ***Porter***	N	Y
11 ***Weller***	N	Y
12 Costello	N	N
13 ***Biggert***	N	Y
14 ***Hastert***		Y

ND Northern Democrats SD Southern Democrats

	76	77
15 ***Ewing***	N	Y
16 ***Manzullo***	N	Y
17 Evans	Y	N
18 ***LaHood***	N	Y
19 Phelps	N	N
20 ***Shimkus***	N	Y
INDIANA		
1 Visclosky	N	N
2 ***McIntosh***	N	Y
3 Roemer	Y	N
4 ***Souder***	N	Y
5 ***Buyer***	N	Y
6 ***Burton***	–	+
7 ***Pease***	N	Y
8 ***Hostettler***	?	Y
9 Hill	Y	N
10 Carson	Y	N
IOWA		
1 ***Leach***	N	Y
2 ***Nussle***	N	Y
3 Boswell	Y	N
4 ***Ganske***	N	Y
5 ***Latham***	N	Y
KANSAS		
1 ***Moran***	N	Y
2 ***Ryun***	N	Y
3 Moore	Y	N
4 ***Tiahrt***	N	Y
KENTUCKY		
1 ***Whitfield***	N	Y
2 ***Lewis***	N	Y
3 ***Northup***	N	Y
4 Lucas	N	N
5 ***Rogers***	N	Y
6 ***Fletcher***	N	Y
LOUISIANA		
1 Vacant		
2 Jefferson	Y	N
3 ***Tauzin***	N	Y
4 ***McCrery***	N	Y
5 ***Cooksey***	?	Y
6 ***Baker***	N	Y
7 John	Y	N
MAINE		
1 Allen	Y	N
2 Baldacci	Y	N
MARYLAND		
1 ***Gilchrest***	N	Y
2 ***Ehrlich***	N	Y
3 Cardin	Y	N
4 Wynn	Y	N
5 Hoyer	Y	N
6 ***Bartlett***	N	Y
7 Cummings	Y	N
8 ***Morella***	N	N
MASSACHUSETTS		
1 Olver	Y	N
2 Neal	Y	N
3 McGovern	Y	N
4 Frank	N	N
5 Meehan	Y	N
6 Tierney	N	N
7 Markey	Y	N
8 Capuano	Y	N
9 Moakley	Y	N
10 Delahunt	Y	N
MICHIGAN		
1 Stupak	?	?
2 ***Hoekstra***	N	Y
3 ***Ehlers***	N	Y
4 ***Camp***	N	Y
5 Barcia	?	N
6 ***Upton***	N	Y
7 ***Smith***	N	Y
8 Stabenow	Y	N
9 Kildee	Y	N
10 Bonior	Y	N
11 ***Knollenberg***	N	Y
12 Levin	Y	N
13 Rivers	N	N
14 Conyers	Y	N
15 Kilpatrick	Y	N
16 Dingell	?	N
MINNESOTA		
1 ***Gutknecht***	N	Y
2 Minge	N	N
3 ***Ramstad***	N	Y
4 Vento	Y	N
5 Sabo	Y	N
6 Luther	Y	N
7 Peterson	N	N
8 Oberstar	Y	N
MISSISSIPPI		
1 ***Wicker***	N	Y
2 Thompson	Y	N
3 ***Pickering***	N	Y
4 Shows	Y	N
5 Taylor	N	N
MISSOURI		
1 Clay	Y	N
2 ***Talent***	N	Y
3 Gephardt	Y	N
4 Skelton	Y	N
5 McCarthy	Y	N
6 Danner	Y	N
7 ***Blunt***	N	Y
8 ***Emerson***	N	Y
9 ***Hulshof***	N	Y
MONTANA		
AL ***Hill***	N	Y
NEBRASKA		
1 ***Bereuter***	N	Y
2 ***Terry***	N	Y
3 ***Barrett***	N	Y
NEVADA		
1 Berkley	Y	N
2 ***Gibbons***	N	Y
NEW HAMPSHIRE		
1 ***Sununu***	N	Y
2 ***Bass***	N	Y
NEW JERSEY		
1 Andrews	Y	N
2 ***LoBiondo***	N	Y
3 ***Saxton***	N	Y
4 ***Smith***	N	Y
5 ***Roukema***	N	Y
6 Pallone	Y	N
7 ***Franks***	N	Y
8 Pascrell	Y	N
9 Rothman	Y	N
10 Payne	Y	N
11 ***Frelinghuysen***	N	Y
12 Holt	Y	N
13 Menendez	Y	N
NEW MEXICO		
1 ***Wilson***	N	Y
2 ***Skeen***	N	Y
3 Udall	Y	N
NEW YORK		
1 ***Forbes***	N	Y
2 ***Lazio***	N	Y
3 ***King***	N	Y
4 McCarthy	N	N
5 Ackerman	Y	N
6 Meeks	Y	N
7 Crowley	Y	N
8 Nadler	Y	N
9 Weiner	Y	N
10 Towns	Y	N
11 Owens	N	N
12 Velázquez	Y	N
13 ***Fossella***	N	Y
14 Maloney	Y	N
15 Rangel	Y	N
16 Serrano	Y	N
17 Engel	Y	N
18 Lowey	Y	N
19 ***Kelly***	N	Y
20 ***Gilman***	N	Y
21 McNulty	Y	N
22 ***Sweeney***	N	Y
23 ***Boehlert***	N	Y
24 ***McHugh***	N	Y
25 ***Walsh***	N	Y
26 Hinchey	Y	N
27 ***Reynolds***	N	Y
28 Slaughter	Y	N
29 LaFalce	Y	N
30 ***Quinn***	N	N
31 ***Houghton***	N	Y
NORTH CAROLINA		
1 Clayton	Y	N
2 Etheridge	Y	N
3 ***Jones***	N	Y
4 Price	Y	N
5 ***Burr***	N	Y
6 ***Coble***	N	Y
7 McIntyre	N	N
8 ***Hayes***	N	Y
9 ***Myrick***	N	Y
10 ***Ballenger***	N	Y
11 ***Taylor***	N	Y
12 Watt	Y	N
NORTH DAKOTA		
AL Pomeroy	N	N
OHIO		
1 ***Chabot***	N	Y
2 ***Portman***	N	Y
3 Hall	Y	N
4 ***Oxley***	N	Y
5 ***Gillmor***	N	Y
6 Strickland	Y	N
7 ***Hobson***	N	Y
8 ***Boehner***	N	Y
9 Kaptur	Y	N
10 Kucinich	Y	N
11 Jones	Y	N
12 ***Kasich***	N	Y
13 Brown	Y	N
14 Sawyer	Y	N
15 ***Pryce***	N	Y
16 ***Regula***	N	Y
17 Traficant	N	N
18 ***Ney***	N	Y
19 ***LaTourette***	N	Y
OKLAHOMA		
1 ***Largent***	N	Y
2 ***Coburn***	N	Y
3 ***Watkins***	N	Y
4 ***Watts***	N	Y
5 ***Istook***	N	Y
6 ***Lucas***	N	Y
OREGON		
1 Wu	Y	N
2 ***Walden***	N	Y
3 Blumenauer	Y	N
4 DeFazio	N	N
5 Hooley	Y	N
PENNSYLVANIA		
1 Brady	Y	N
2 Fattah	Y	N
3 Borski	Y	N
4 Klink	Y	N
5 ***Peterson***	N	Y
6 Holden	N	N
7 ***Weldon***	N	Y
8 ***Greenwood***	N	Y
9 ***Shuster***	N	Y
10 ***Sherwood***	N	Y
11 Kanjorski	N	N
12 Murtha	N	N
13 Hoeffel	Y	N
14 Coyne	Y	N
15 ***Toomey***	N	Y
16 ***Pitts***	N	Y
17 ***Gekas***	N	Y
18 Doyle	Y	N
19 ***Goodling***	N	Y
20 Mascara	Y	N
21 ***English***	N	Y
RHODE ISLAND		
1 Kennedy	Y	N
2 Weygand	Y	N
SOUTH CAROLINA		
1 ***Sanford***	N	Y
2 ***Spence***	N	Y
3 ***Graham***	N	Y
4 ***DeMint***	N	Y
5 Spratt	Y	N
6 Clyburn	Y	N
SOUTH DAKOTA		
AL ***Thune***	N	Y
TENNESSEE		
1 ***Jenkins***	N	Y
2 ***Duncan***	N	Y
3 ***Wamp***	N	Y
4 ***Hilleary***	N	Y
5 Clement	Y	N
6 Gordon	Y	N
7 ***Bryant***	N	Y
8 Tanner	N	N
9 Ford	Y	N
TEXAS		
1 Sandlin	Y	N
2 Turner	Y	N
3 ***Johnson, Sam***	N	Y
4 Hall	Y	Y
5 ***Sessions***	N	Y
6 ***Barton***	N	Y
7 ***Archer***	N	Y
8 ***Brady***	N	Y
9 Lampson	Y	N
10 Doggett	Y	N
11 Edwards	Y	N
12 ***Granger***	N	Y
13 ***Thornberry***	N	Y
14 ***Paul***	N	?
15 Hinojosa	Y	N
16 Reyes	Y	N
17 Stenholm	N	N
18 Jackson-Lee	Y	N
19 ***Combest***	N	Y
20 Gonzalez	Y	N
21 ***Smith***	?	?
22 ***DeLay***	N	Y
23 ***Bonilla***	N	Y
24 Frost	Y	N
25 Bentsen	Y	N
26 ***Armey***	N	Y
27 Ortiz	Y	N
28 Rodriguez	Y	N
29 Green	Y	N
30 Johnson, E.B.	Y	N
UTAH		
1 ***Hansen***	N	Y
2 ***Cook***	N	Y
3 ***Cannon***	N	Y
VERMONT		
AL *Sanders*	N	N
VIRGINIA		
1 ***Bateman***	N	Y
2 Pickett	N	N
3 Scott	Y	N
4 Sisisky	Y	N
5 Goode	N	Y
6 ***Goodlatte***	N	Y
7 ***Bliley***	N	Y
8 Moran	Y	N
9 Boucher	Y	N
10 ***Wolf***	N	Y
11 ***Davis***	N	Y
WASHINGTON		
1 Inslee	Y	N
2 ***Metcalf***	?	Y
3 Baird	Y	N
4 ***Hastings***	N	Y
5 ***Nethercutt***	N	Y
6 Dicks	Y	N
7 McDermott	Y	N
8 ***Dunn***	N	Y
9 Smith	Y	N
WEST VIRGINIA		
1 Mollohan	N	N
2 Wise	Y	N
3 Rahall	Y	N
WISCONSIN		
1 ***Ryan***	N	Y
2 Baldwin	Y	N
3 Kind	Y	N
4 Kleczka	Y	N
5 Barrett	Y	N
6 ***Petri***	N	Y
7 Obey	Y	N
8 ***Green***	N	Y
9 ***Sensenbrenner***	N	Y
WYOMING		
AL ***Cubin***	N	Y

Southern states - Ala., Ark., Fla., Ga., Ky., La., Miss., N.C., Okla., S.C., Tenn., Texas, Va.

78. HR 98. Federal Aviation War Risk Insurance Program/Concur With Senate Amendments. Petri, R-Wis., motion to suspend the rules and adopt the resolution (H Res 135) to concur with Senate amendments, with an amendment, to the bill to reauthorize the federal aviation war risk insurance program through Dec. 31, 2003. The House amendment makes a minor change reflecting the fact that legislation was recently enacted to extend the program for two months. Motion agreed to 392-1: R 202-1; D 189-0 (ND 139-0, SD 50-0); I 1-0. April 12, 1999. A two-thirds majority of those present and voting (262 in this case) is required for passage under suspension of the rules.

79. HR 911. Terry Sanford Federal Building/Passage. Coble, R-N.C., motion to suspend the rules and pass the bill to designate a federal building in Raleigh, N.C., the "Terry Sanford Federal Building" to honor former Sen. Terry Sanford, D-N.C. (1986-93). Motion agreed to 394-0: R 205-0; D 188-0 (ND 139-0, SD 49-0); I 1-0. April 12, 1999. A two-thirds majority of those present and voting (263 in this case) is required for passage under suspension of the rules.

80. H Con Res 68. Fiscal 2000 Budget Resolution/Motion To Instruct. Spratt, D-S.C., motion to instruct the House conferees to insist that the reconciliation bills necessary to implement tax cuts outlined in the resolution be enacted as late as possible to give Congress time to enact bills to extend the solvency of Medicare and Social Security. Motion agreed to 349-44: R 161-44; D 187-0 (ND 137-0, SD 50-0); I 1-0. April 12, 1999.

81. HR 46. Medal of Valor for Public Safety Officers/Passage. McCollum, R-Fla., motion to suspend the rules and pass the bill to establish a national medal for public safety officers "who act with extraordinary valor above and beyond the call of duty." Motion agreed to 412-2: R 210-2; D 201-0 (ND 149-0, SD 52-0); I 1-0. April 13, 1999. A two-thirds majority of those present and voting (276 in this case) is required for passage under suspension of the rules.

82. H Con Res 35. Congratulations to Qatar/Adoption. Ros-Lehtinen, R-Fla., motion to suspend the rules and adopt the concurrent resolution to commend the emir and the citizens of Qatar for their commitment to democratic ideals and women's suffrage. Motion agreed to 418-0: R 217-0; D 200-0 (ND 149-0, SD 51-0); I 1-0. April 13, 1999. A two-thirds majority of those present and voting (279 in this case) is required for adoption under suspension of the rules.

Key

- Y Voted for (yea).
- # Paired for.
- + Announced for.
- N Voted against (nay).
- X Paired against.
- – Announced against.
- P Voted "present."
- C Voted "present" to avoid possible conflict of interest.
- ? Did not vote or otherwise make a position known.

•

Democrats ***Republicans***
Independents

	78	79	80	81	82
ALABAMA					
1 ***Callahan***	Y	Y	Y	Y	Y
2 ***Everett***	Y	Y	Y	Y	Y
3 ***Riley***	Y	Y	Y	Y	Y
4 ***Aderholt***	Y	Y	Y	+	+
5 Cramer	Y	Y	Y	Y	Y
6 ***Bachus***	Y	Y	Y	Y	Y
7 Hilliard	Y	Y	Y	Y	Y
ALASKA					
AL ***Young***	Y	Y	Y	Y	Y
ARIZONA					
1 ***Salmon***	Y	Y	N	Y	Y
2 Pastor	Y	Y	Y	Y	Y
3 ***Stump***	Y	Y	Y	Y	Y
4 ***Shadegg***	Y	Y	N	Y	Y
5 ***Kolbe***	Y	Y	Y	Y	Y
6 ***Hayworth***	Y	Y	N	Y	Y
ARKANSAS					
1 Berry	Y	Y	Y	Y	Y
2 Snyder	Y	Y	Y	Y	Y
3 ***Hutchinson***	Y	Y	Y	Y	Y
4 ***Dickey***	Y	Y	Y	Y	Y
CALIFORNIA					
1 Thompson	Y	Y	Y	Y	Y
2 ***Herger***	Y	Y	N	Y	Y
3 ***Ose***	Y	Y	Y	Y	Y
4 ***Doolittle***	?	Y	Y	Y	Y
5 Matsui	Y	Y	Y	Y	Y
6 Woolsey	+	+	+	Y	Y
7 Miller, George	Y	Y	Y	Y	Y
8 Pelosi	Y	Y	Y	Y	Y
9 Lee	+	+	+	Y	Y
10 Tauscher	Y	Y	Y	Y	Y
11 ***Pombo***	Y	Y	Y	Y	Y
12 Lantos	?	?	?	?	?
13 Stark	Y	Y	Y	Y	Y
14 Eshoo	Y	Y	Y	Y	Y
15 ***Campbell***	Y	Y	Y	Y	Y
16 Lofgren	Y	Y	Y	Y	Y
17 Farr	Y	Y	Y	Y	Y
18 Condit	Y	Y	Y	Y	Y
19 ***Radanovich***	?	?	?	Y	Y
20 Dooley	Y	Y	Y	Y	Y
21 ***Thomas***	Y	Y	N	Y	Y
22 Capps	Y	Y	Y	Y	Y
23 ***Gallegly***	Y	Y	Y	Y	Y
24 Sherman	Y	Y	Y	Y	Y
25 ***McKeon***	Y	Y	Y	Y	Y
26 Berman	?	?	?	Y	Y
27 ***Rogan***	Y	Y	Y	Y	Y
28 ***Dreier***	Y	Y	Y	Y	Y
29 Waxman	Y	Y	Y	Y	Y
30 Becerra	Y	Y	Y	Y	Y
31 Martinez	Y	Y	Y	Y	Y
32 Dixon	Y	Y	Y	Y	Y
33 Roybal-Allard	Y	Y	Y	Y	Y
34 Napolitano	Y	Y	Y	Y	Y
35 Waters	Y	Y	Y	Y	Y
36 ***Kuykendall***	Y	Y	Y	Y	Y
37 Millender-McD.	Y	Y	Y	Y	Y
38 ***Horn***	Y	Y	Y	Y	Y
39 ***Royce***	Y	Y	Y	Y	Y

	78	79	80	81	82
40 ***Lewis***	Y	Y	Y	Y	Y
41 ***Miller, Gary***	Y	Y	Y	Y	Y
42 Brown	Y	Y	Y	?	?
43 ***Calvert***	Y	Y	Y	Y	Y
44 ***Bono***	Y	Y	Y	Y	Y
45 ***Rohrabacher***	Y	Y	Y	Y	Y
46 Sanchez	Y	Y	Y	Y	Y
47 ***Cox***	?	Y	Y	Y	Y
48 ***Packard***	Y	Y	N	Y	Y
49 ***Bilbray***	Y	Y	Y	Y	Y
50 Filner	Y	Y	Y	Y	Y
51 ***Cunningham***	?	?	?	Y	Y
52 ***Hunter***	Y	Y	Y	Y	Y
COLORADO					
1 DeGette	Y	Y	Y	Y	Y
2 Udall	Y	Y	Y	Y	Y
3 ***McInnis***	Y	Y	Y	Y	Y
4 ***Schaffer***	Y	Y	N	Y	Y
5 ***Hefley***	Y	Y	N	Y	Y
6 ***Tancredo***	Y	Y	N	Y	Y
CONNECTICUT					
1 Larson	Y	Y	Y	Y	Y
2 Gejdenson	Y	Y	Y	Y	Y
3 DeLauro	Y	Y	Y	Y	Y
4 ***Shays***	Y	Y	Y	Y	Y
5 Maloney	Y	Y	Y	Y	Y
6 ***Johnson***	Y	Y	Y	Y	Y
DELAWARE					
AL ***Castle***	Y	Y	Y	Y	Y
FLORIDA					
1 ***Scarborough***	Y	Y	Y	Y	Y
2 Boyd	Y	Y	Y	Y	Y
3 Brown	?	?	?	?	?
4 ***Fowler***	Y	Y	Y	Y	Y
5 Thurman	Y	Y	Y	Y	Y
6 ***Stearns***	Y	Y	N	Y	Y
7 ***Mica***	Y	Y	Y	Y	Y
8 ***McCollum***	?	?	?	Y	Y
9 ***Bilirakis***	Y	Y	Y	Y	Y
10 ***Young***	Y	Y	Y	Y	Y
11 Davis	Y	Y	Y	Y	Y
12 ***Canady***	Y	Y	Y	Y	Y
13 ***Miller***	Y	Y	Y	Y	Y
14 ***Goss***	Y	Y	Y	+	Y
15 ***Weldon***	Y	Y	Y	Y	Y
16 ***Foley***	Y	Y	Y	Y	Y
17 Meek	Y	Y	Y	Y	Y
18 ***Ros-Lehtinen***	Y	Y	Y	Y	Y
19 Wexler	Y	Y	Y	?	?
20 Deutsch	Y	Y	Y	Y	Y
21 ***Diaz-Balart***	Y	Y	Y	Y	Y
22 ***Shaw***	Y	Y	Y	Y	Y
23 Hastings	?	?	?	?	?
GEORGIA					
1 ***Kingston***	Y	Y	N	Y	Y
2 Bishop	?	?	?	Y	Y
3 ***Collins***	Y	Y	Y	Y	Y
4 McKinney	Y	Y	Y	Y	Y
5 Lewis	Y	Y	Y	Y	Y
6 ***Isakson***	Y	Y	Y	Y	Y
7 ***Barr***	?	?	?	Y	Y
8 ***Chambliss***	Y	Y	Y	Y	Y
9 ***Deal***	Y	Y	N	Y	Y
10 ***Norwood***	Y	Y	Y	Y	Y
11 ***Linder***	Y	Y	N	Y	Y
HAWAII					
1 Abercrombie	Y	Y	Y	Y	Y
2 Mink	?	?	?	Y	Y
IDAHO					
1 ***Chenoweth***	Y	Y	Y	Y	Y
2 ***Simpson***	Y	Y	Y	Y	Y
ILLINOIS					
1 Rush	Y	Y	Y	Y	Y
2 Jackson	Y	Y	Y	Y	Y
3 Lipinski	Y	Y	Y	Y	Y
4 Gutierrez	Y	Y	Y	Y	Y
5 Blagojevich	Y	Y	Y	Y	Y
6 ***Hyde***	Y	Y	Y	Y	Y
7 Davis	+	+	+	+	+
8 ***Crane***	?	?	?	Y	Y
9 Schakowsky	Y	Y	Y	Y	Y
10 ***Porter***	Y	Y	Y	Y	Y
11 ***Weller***	Y	Y	Y	Y	Y
12 Costello	Y	Y	Y	Y	Y
13 ***Biggert***	Y	Y	Y	Y	Y
14 ***Hastert***					

ND Northern Democrats SD Southern Democrats

Member	78	79	80	81	82
15 ***Ewing***	Y	Y	Y	Y	Y
16 ***Manzullo***	Y	Y	Y	Y	Y
17 Evans	Y	Y	Y	Y	Y
18 ***LaHood***	Y	Y	Y	Y	Y
19 Phelps	Y	Y	Y	Y	Y
20 ***Shimkus***	Y	Y	Y	Y	Y
INDIANA					
1 Visclosky	Y	Y	Y	Y	Y
2 ***McIntosh***	Y	Y	N	Y	Y
3 Roemer	Y	Y	Y	Y	Y
4 ***Souder***	Y	Y	N	Y	Y
5 ***Buyer***	Y	Y	N	Y	Y
6 ***Burton***	Y	Y	N	Y	Y
7 ***Pease***	Y	Y	Y	Y	Y
8 ***Hostettler***	Y	Y	N	Y	Y
9 Hill	Y	Y	Y	Y	Y
10 Carson	+	+	+	+	+
IOWA					
1 ***Leach***	Y	Y	Y	Y	Y
2 ***Nussle***	Y	Y	Y	Y	Y
3 Boswell	Y	Y	Y	Y	Y
4 ***Ganske***	Y	Y	Y	Y	Y
5 ***Latham***	Y	Y	Y	Y	Y
KANSAS					
1 ***Moran***	Y	Y	Y	Y	Y
2 ***Ryun***	Y	Y	Y	Y	Y
3 Moore	Y	Y	Y	Y	Y
4 ***Tiahrt***	Y	Y	N	Y	Y
KENTUCKY					
1 ***Whitfield***	Y	Y	Y	Y	Y
2 ***Lewis***	Y	Y	Y	Y	Y
3 ***Northup***	Y	Y	Y	Y	Y
4 Lucas	Y	Y	Y	Y	Y
5 ***Rogers***	Y	Y	Y	Y	Y
6 ***Fletcher***	Y	Y	Y	Y	Y
LOUISIANA					
1 Vacant					
2 Jefferson	Y	?	Y	Y	Y
3 ***Tauzin***	Y	Y	Y	Y	Y
4 ***McCrery***	Y	Y	N	Y	Y
5 ***Cooksey***	?	?	?	?	?
6 ***Baker***	?	?	?	Y	Y
7 John	Y	Y	Y	Y	Y
MAINE					
1 Allen	Y	Y	Y	Y	Y
2 Baldacci	Y	Y	Y	Y	Y
MARYLAND					
1 ***Gilchrest***	Y	Y	Y	Y	Y
2 ***Ehrlich***	Y	Y	N	Y	Y
3 Cardin	Y	Y	Y	Y	Y
4 Wynn	Y	Y	Y	Y	Y
5 Hoyer	Y	Y	Y	Y	Y
6 ***Bartlett***	Y	Y	Y	Y	Y
7 Cummings	Y	Y	Y	Y	Y
8 ***Morella***	Y	Y	Y	Y	Y
MASSACHUSETTS					
1 Olver	Y	Y	Y	Y	Y
2 Neal	?	?	?	Y	Y
3 McGovern	Y	Y	Y	Y	Y
4 Frank	Y	Y	Y	Y	Y
5 Meehan	Y	Y	Y	Y	Y
6 Tierney	?	?	?	?	?
7 Markey	Y	Y	Y	Y	Y
8 Capuano	Y	Y	Y	Y	Y
9 Moakley	Y	Y	Y	Y	Y
10 Delahunt	Y	Y	Y	Y	Y
MICHIGAN					
1 Stupak	Y	Y	Y	Y	Y
2 ***Hoekstra***	?	?	?	?	?
3 ***Ehlers***	Y	Y	N	Y	Y
4 ***Camp***	Y	Y	N	Y	Y
5 Barcia	Y	Y	Y	Y	Y
6 ***Upton***	Y	Y	Y	Y	Y
7 ***Smith***	Y	Y	N	Y	Y
8 Stabenow	Y	Y	Y	Y	Y
9 Kildee	Y	Y	Y	Y	Y
10 Bonior	Y	Y	Y	Y	Y
11 ***Knollenberg***	Y	Y	Y	Y	Y
12 Levin	Y	Y	Y	Y	Y
13 Rivers	Y	Y	Y	Y	Y
14 Conyers	Y	Y	Y	Y	Y
15 Kilpatrick	+	+	+	Y	Y
16 Dingell	?	?	?	Y	Y
MINNESOTA					
1 ***Gutknecht***	Y	Y	Y	Y	Y
2 Minge	Y	Y	Y	Y	Y
3 ***Ramstad***	Y	Y	Y	Y	Y
4 Vento	Y	Y	Y	Y	Y
5 Sabo	Y	Y	Y	Y	Y
6 Luther	Y	Y	Y	Y	Y
7 Peterson	Y	Y	?	Y	Y
8 Oberstar	Y	Y	Y	?	?
MISSISSIPPI					
1 ***Wicker***	Y	Y	Y	Y	Y
2 Thompson	?	?	?	Y	Y
3 ***Pickering***	Y	Y	Y	Y	Y
4 Shows	Y	Y	Y	Y	Y
5 Taylor	Y	Y	Y	Y	Y
MISSOURI					
1 Clay	Y	Y	Y	Y	Y
2 ***Talent***	Y	Y	Y	Y	Y
3 Gephardt	Y	Y	Y	Y	Y
4 Skelton	Y	Y	Y	Y	Y
5 McCarthy	Y	Y	Y	Y	Y
6 Danner	?	?	?	Y	Y
7 ***Blunt***	Y	Y	Y	Y	Y
8 ***Emerson***	Y	Y	Y	Y	Y
9 ***Hulshof***	Y	Y	N	Y	Y
MONTANA					
AL ***Hill***	Y	Y	Y	Y	Y
NEBRASKA					
1 ***Bereuter***	Y	Y	Y	Y	Y
2 ***Terry***	Y	Y	Y	Y	Y
3 ***Barrett***	Y	Y	Y	Y	Y
NEVADA					
1 Berkley	Y	Y	Y	Y	Y
2 ***Gibbons***	Y	Y	Y	Y	Y
NEW HAMPSHIRE					
1 ***Sununu***	Y	Y	N	Y	Y
2 ***Bass***	Y	Y	Y	Y	Y
NEW JERSEY					
1 Andrews	Y	Y	Y	Y	Y
2 ***LoBiondo***	Y	Y	Y	Y	Y
3 ***Saxton***	Y	Y	Y	Y	Y
4 ***Smith***	Y	Y	Y	Y	Y
5 ***Roukema***	?	?	?	Y	Y
6 Pallone	Y	Y	Y	Y	Y
7 ***Franks***	Y	Y	Y	Y	Y
8 Pascrell	Y	Y	Y	Y	Y
9 Rothman	Y	Y	Y	Y	Y
10 Payne	Y	Y	Y	Y	Y
11 ***Frelinghuysen***	Y	Y	Y	Y	Y
12 Holt	Y	Y	Y	Y	Y
13 Menendez	Y	Y	Y	Y	Y
NEW MEXICO					
1 ***Wilson***	Y	Y	Y	Y	Y
2 ***Skeen***	Y	Y	Y	Y	Y
3 Udall	Y	Y	Y	Y	Y
NEW YORK					
1 ***Forbes***	Y	Y	Y	Y	Y
2 ***Lazio***	Y	Y	Y	Y	Y
3 ***King***	Y	Y	Y	Y	Y
4 McCarthy	Y	Y	Y	Y	Y
5 Ackerman	Y	Y	Y	Y	Y
6 Meeks	Y	Y	Y	Y	Y
7 Crowley	Y	Y	Y	Y	Y
8 Nadler	?	?	?	Y	Y
9 Weiner	Y	Y	Y	Y	Y
10 Towns	Y	Y	Y	Y	Y
11 Owens	Y	Y	Y	Y	Y
12 Velázquez	Y	Y	Y	Y	Y
13 ***Fossella***	Y	Y	Y	Y	Y
14 Maloney	Y	Y	Y	Y	Y
15 Rangel	Y	Y	?	?	?
16 Serrano	Y	Y	Y	Y	Y
17 Engel	?	?	?	Y	Y
18 Lowey	Y	Y	Y	Y	Y
19 ***Kelly***	Y	Y	Y	Y	Y
20 ***Gilman***	Y	Y	Y	Y	Y
21 McNulty	Y	Y	Y	Y	Y
22 ***Sweeney***	Y	Y	Y	Y	Y
23 ***Boehlert***	Y	Y	Y	Y	Y
24 ***McHugh***	Y	Y	Y	Y	Y
25 ***Walsh***	?	?	?	Y	Y
26 Hinchey	Y	Y	Y	Y	Y
27 ***Reynolds***	Y	Y	Y	Y	Y
28 Slaughter	Y	Y	Y	Y	Y
29 LaFalce	Y	Y	Y	Y	Y
30 ***Quinn***	Y	Y	Y	Y	Y
31 ***Houghton***	Y	Y	Y	Y	Y
NORTH CAROLINA					
1 Clayton	Y	Y	Y	Y	Y
2 Etheridge	Y	Y	Y	Y	Y
3 ***Jones***	Y	Y	N	Y	Y
4 Price	Y	Y	Y	Y	Y
5 ***Burr***	Y	Y	Y	Y	Y
6 ***Coble***	Y	Y	N	Y	Y
7 McIntyre	Y	Y	Y	Y	Y
8 ***Hayes***	Y	Y	N	Y	Y
9 ***Myrick***	Y	Y	Y	Y	Y
10 ***Ballenger***	Y	Y	Y	Y	Y
11 ***Taylor***	?	?	?	?	Y
12 Watt	Y	Y	Y	Y	Y
NORTH DAKOTA					
AL Pomeroy	Y	Y	Y	Y	Y
OHIO					
1 ***Chabot***	Y	Y	N	Y	Y
2 ***Portman***	Y	Y	Y	Y	Y
3 Hall	?	?	?	Y	Y
4 ***Oxley***	Y	Y	Y	Y	Y
5 ***Gillmor***	Y	Y	Y	Y	Y
6 Strickland	Y	Y	Y	Y	Y
7 ***Hobson***	Y	Y	Y	Y	Y
8 ***Boehner***	Y	Y	Y	Y	Y
9 Kaptur	Y	Y	Y	Y	Y
10 Kucinich	Y	Y	Y	Y	Y
11 Jones	Y	Y	Y	Y	Y
12 ***Kasich***	Y	Y	Y	Y	Y
13 Brown	Y	Y	Y	Y	Y
14 Sawyer	Y	Y	Y	Y	Y
15 ***Pryce***	?	?	?	Y	Y
16 ***Regula***	Y	Y	Y	Y	Y
17 Traficant	Y	Y	Y	Y	Y
18 ***Ney***	Y	Y	Y	Y	Y
19 ***LaTourette***	Y	Y	Y	Y	Y
OKLAHOMA					
1 ***Largent***	?	?	?	?	?
2 ***Coburn***	?	?	?	?	Y
3 ***Watkins***	Y	Y	Y	Y	Y
4 ***Watts***	Y	Y	Y	Y	Y
5 ***Istook***	Y	Y	Y	Y	Y
6 ***Lucas***	Y	Y	Y	Y	Y
OREGON					
1 Wu	Y	Y	Y	Y	Y
2 ***Walden***	Y	Y	Y	Y	Y
3 Blumenauer	Y	Y	Y	Y	Y
4 DeFazio	Y	Y	Y	Y	Y
5 Hooley	Y	Y	Y	Y	Y
PENNSYLVANIA					
1 Brady	Y	Y	Y	Y	Y
2 Fattah	Y	Y	Y	Y	Y
3 Borski	?	?	?	Y	Y
4 Klink	Y	Y	Y	Y	Y
5 ***Peterson***	Y	Y	Y	Y	Y
6 Holden	Y	Y	Y	Y	Y
7 ***Weldon***	Y	Y	Y	Y	Y
8 ***Greenwood***	Y	Y	Y	Y	Y
9 ***Shuster***	Y	Y	Y	Y	Y
10 ***Sherwood***	Y	Y	Y	Y	Y
11 Kanjorski	Y	Y	Y	Y	Y
12 Murtha	Y	Y	Y	Y	Y
13 Hoeffel	Y	Y	Y	Y	Y
14 Coyne	Y	Y	Y	Y	Y
15 ***Toomey***	Y	Y	Y	Y	Y
16 ***Pitts***	Y	Y	Y	Y	Y
17 ***Gekas***	Y	Y	Y	Y	Y
18 Doyle	Y	Y	Y	Y	Y
19 ***Goodling***	Y	Y	N	Y	Y
20 Mascara	Y	Y	Y	Y	Y
21 ***English***	Y	Y	N	Y	Y
RHODE ISLAND					
1 Kennedy	Y	Y	Y	Y	Y
2 Weygand	?	?	?	Y	Y
SOUTH CAROLINA					
1 ***Sanford***	Y	Y	Y	N	Y
2 ***Spence***	Y	Y	Y	Y	Y
3 ***Graham***	Y	Y	Y	Y	Y
4 ***DeMint***	?	?	?	?	?
5 Spratt	Y	Y	Y	Y	Y
6 Clyburn	Y	Y	Y	Y	Y
SOUTH DAKOTA					
AL ***Thune***	Y	Y	Y	Y	Y
TENNESSEE					
1 ***Jenkins***	Y	Y	Y	Y	Y
2 ***Duncan***	Y	Y	Y	Y	Y
3 ***Wamp***	Y	Y	Y	Y	Y
4 ***Hilleary***	Y	Y	Y	Y	Y
5 Clement	Y	Y	Y	Y	Y
6 Gordon	?	?	?	Y	Y
7 ***Bryant***	Y	Y	N	Y	Y
8 Tanner	Y	Y	Y	Y	Y
9 Ford	Y	Y	Y	Y	Y
TEXAS					
1 Sandlin	Y	Y	Y	Y	Y
2 Turner	Y	Y	Y	Y	Y
3 ***Johnson, Sam***	Y	Y	N	Y	Y
4 Hall	Y	Y	Y	Y	Y
5 ***Sessions***	Y	Y	N	Y	Y
6 ***Barton***	?	?	?	Y	Y
7 ***Archer***	Y	Y	N	Y	Y
8 ***Brady***	Y	Y	Y	Y	Y
9 Lampson	Y	Y	Y	Y	Y
10 Doggett	Y	Y	Y	Y	Y
11 Edwards	Y	Y	Y	Y	Y
12 ***Granger***	Y	Y	Y	Y	Y
13 ***Thornberry***	Y	Y	N	Y	Y
14 ***Paul***	N	Y	N	N	Y
15 Hinojosa	Y	Y	Y	Y	Y
16 Reyes	Y	Y	Y	Y	Y
17 Stenholm	Y	Y	Y	Y	Y
18 Jackson-Lee	Y	Y	Y	Y	Y
19 ***Combest***	Y	Y	Y	Y	Y
20 Gonzalez	Y	Y	Y	Y	Y
21 ***Smith***	Y	Y	Y	Y	Y
22 ***DeLay***	Y	Y	N	?	Y
23 ***Bonilla***	Y	Y	Y	Y	Y
24 Frost	Y	Y	Y	Y	Y
25 Bentsen	Y	Y	Y	Y	Y
26 ***Armey***	Y	Y	N	?	Y
27 Ortiz	Y	Y	Y	Y	Y
28 Rodriguez	Y	Y	Y	Y	Y
29 Green	Y	Y	Y	Y	Y
30 Johnson, E.B.	Y	Y	Y	Y	Y
UTAH					
1 ***Hansen***	Y	Y	N	Y	Y
2 ***Cook***	Y	Y	Y	Y	Y
3 ***Cannon***	Y	Y	N	Y	Y
VERMONT					
AL Sanders	Y	Y	Y	Y	Y
VIRGINIA					
1 ***Bateman***	Y	Y	Y	Y	Y
2 Pickett	Y	Y	Y	Y	Y
3 Scott	Y	Y	Y	Y	Y
4 Sisisky	Y	Y	Y	Y	Y
5 Goode	Y	Y	Y	Y	?
6 ***Goodlatte***	Y	Y	Y	Y	Y
7 ***Bliley***	Y	Y	Y	Y	Y
8 Moran	Y	Y	Y	Y	Y
9 Boucher	Y	Y	Y	Y	Y
10 ***Wolf***	Y	Y	Y	Y	Y
11 ***Davis***	Y	Y	Y	Y	Y
WASHINGTON					
1 Inslee	Y	Y	Y	Y	Y
2 ***Metcalf***	Y	Y	Y	Y	Y
3 Baird	Y	Y	Y	Y	Y
4 ***Hastings***	Y	Y	Y	Y	Y
5 ***Nethercutt***	Y	Y	Y	Y	Y
6 Dicks	Y	Y	Y	Y	Y
7 McDermott	Y	Y	Y	Y	Y
8 ***Dunn***	Y	Y	N	Y	Y
9 Smith	Y	Y	Y	Y	Y
WEST VIRGINIA					
1 Mollohan	Y	Y	Y	Y	Y
2 Wise	Y	Y	Y	Y	Y
3 Rahall	Y	Y	Y	Y	Y
WISCONSIN					
1 ***Ryan***	Y	Y	Y	Y	Y
2 Baldwin	Y	Y	Y	Y	Y
3 Kind	Y	Y	Y	Y	Y
4 Kleczka	Y	Y	Y	Y	Y
5 Barrett	Y	Y	Y	Y	Y
6 ***Petri***	Y	Y	Y	Y	Y
7 Obey	Y	Y	Y	Y	Y
8 ***Green***	Y	Y	Y	Y	Y
9 ***Sensenbrenner***	Y	Y	Y	Y	Y
WYOMING					
AL ***Cubin***	Y	Y	N	Y	Y

Southern states - Ala., Ark., Fla., Ga., Ky., La., Miss., N.C., Okla., S.C., Tenn., Texas, Va.

83. **Procedural Motion/Journal.** Approval of the House Journal of Wednesday, April 13, 1999. Approved 343-53: R 191-15; D 151-38 (ND 107-29, SD 44-9); I 1-0. April 14, 1999.

84. **H Con Res 68. Fiscal 2000 Budget Resolution/Conference Report Rule.** Adoption of the rule (H Res 137) to provide for House floor consideration of the conference report on the concurrent resolution to set broad spending and revenue targets for the next 10 years. Adopted 221-205: R 218-0; D 3-204 (ND 1-153, SD 2-51); I 0-1. April 14, 1999.

85. **H Con Res 68. Fiscal 2000 Budget Resolution/Conference Report.** Adoption of the conference report on the concurrent resolution to set broad spending and revenue targets for the next 10 years. For fiscal 2000, the resolution provides for $536.3 billion in discretionary spending, $290 billion of which would go to defense. It calls for $142 billion in tax cuts over five years and $778 billion over 10 years. The resolution recommends that Social Security surpluses be used only for retirement security purposes or to pay down the debt. Adopted 220-208: R 217-3; D 3-204 (ND 1-153, SD 2-51); I 0-1. April 14, 1999.

86. **HR 472. Local Government Census Review/Previous Question.** Sessions, R-Texas, motion to order the previous question (thus ending debate and the possibility of amendment) on adoption of the rule (H Res 138) to provide for House floor consideration of the bill to allow local government officials to review and challenge 2000 census data before the count is finalized. Motion agreed to 220-207: R 219-0; D 1-206 (ND 0-153, SD 1-53); I 0-1. April 14, 1999.

87. **HR 472. Local Government Census Review/Rule.** Adoption of the rule (H Res 138) to provide for House floor consideration of the bill to allow local government officials to review and challenge 2000 census data before the count is finalized. Under the bill, the data subject to local review would include numbers of housing units and vacancies in those units, but not necessarily a count of specific individuals. The localities would be able to challenge the preliminary census data. Adopted 219-205: R 217-0; D 2-204 (ND 1-153, SD 1-51); I 0-1. April 14, 1999.

Key

- Y Voted for (yea).
- # Paired for.
- + Announced for.
- N Voted against (nay).
- X Paired against.
- – Announced against.
- P Voted "present."
- C Voted "present" to avoid possible conflict of interest.
- ? Did not vote or otherwise make a position known.

•

Democrats ***Republicans***
Independents

	83	84	85	86	87
ALABAMA					
1 ***Callahan***	Y	Y	Y	Y	Y
2 ***Everett***	Y	Y	Y	Y	Y
3 ***Riley***	Y	Y	Y	Y	Y
4 ***Aderholt***	N	Y	Y	Y	Y
5 Cramer	Y	N	N	N	N
6 ***Bachus***	Y	Y	Y	Y	Y
7 Hilliard	N	N	N	N	N
ALASKA					
AL ***Young***	?	Y	Y	Y	Y
ARIZONA					
1 ***Salmon***	Y	Y	Y	Y	Y
2 Pastor	N	N	N	N	N
3 ***Stump***	Y	Y	Y	Y	Y
4 ***Shadegg***	Y	Y	Y	Y	Y
5 ***Kolbe***	Y	Y	Y	Y	Y
6 ***Hayworth***	Y	Y	Y	Y	Y
ARKANSAS					
1 Berry	Y	N	N	N	N
2 Snyder	Y	N	N	N	N
3 ***Hutchinson***	N	Y	Y	Y	Y
4 ***Dickey***	Y	Y	Y	Y	Y
CALIFORNIA					
1 Thompson	N	N	N	N	N
2 ***Herger***	Y	Y	Y	Y	Y
3 ***Ose***	Y	Y	Y	Y	Y
4 ***Doolittle***	Y	Y	Y	Y	Y
5 Matsui	Y	N	N	N	N
6 Woolsey	Y	N	N	N	N
7 Miller, George	Y	N	N	N	N
8 Pelosi	Y	N	N	N	N
9 Lee	N	N	N	N	N
10 Tauscher	Y	N	N	N	N
11 ***Pombo***	Y	Y	Y	Y	Y
12 Lantos	?	?	?	?	?
13 Stark	Y	N	N	N	N
14 Eshoo	Y	N	N	N	N
15 ***Campbell***	Y	Y	Y	Y	Y
16 Lofgren	Y	N	N	N	N
17 Farr	Y	N	N	N	N
18 Condit	Y	N	Y	N	N
19 ***Radanovich***	Y	Y	Y	Y	Y
20 Dooley	Y	N	N	N	N
21 ***Thomas***	Y	Y	+	Y	Y
22 Capps	Y	N	N	N	N
23 ***Gallegly***	Y	Y	Y	Y	Y
24 Sherman	Y	N	N	N	N
25 ***McKeon***	Y	Y	Y	Y	Y
26 Berman	Y	N	N	N	N
27 ***Rogan***	N	Y	Y	Y	Y
28 ***Dreier***	Y	Y	Y	Y	Y
29 Waxman	Y	N	N	N	N
30 Becerra	?	N	N	N	N
31 Martinez	Y	N	N	N	N
32 Dixon	?	N	N	N	N
33 Roybal-Allard	Y	N	N	N	N
34 Napolitano	Y	N	N	–	N
35 Waters	?	N	N	N	N
36 ***Kuykendall***	Y	Y	Y	Y	Y
37 Millender-McD.	Y	N	N	N	N
38 ***Horn***	Y	Y	Y	Y	Y
39 ***Royce***	Y	Y	Y	Y	Y
40 ***Lewis***	Y	Y	Y	Y	Y
41 ***Miller, Gary***	Y	Y	Y	Y	Y
42 Brown	N	N	N	?	?
43 ***Calvert***	Y	Y	Y	Y	Y
44 ***Bono***	Y	Y	Y	Y	Y
45 ***Rohrabacher***	?	Y	Y	Y	Y
46 Sanchez	Y	N	N	N	N
47 ***Cox***	?	Y	Y	Y	Y
48 ***Packard***	Y	Y	Y	Y	Y
49 ***Bilbray***	Y	Y	Y	Y	Y
50 Filner	N	N	N	N	N
51 ***Cunningham***	Y	Y	Y	Y	Y
52 ***Hunter***	Y	Y	Y	Y	Y
COLORADO					
1 DeGette	Y	N	N	N	N
2 Udall	Y	N	N	N	N
3 ***McInnis***	Y	Y	Y	Y	Y
4 ***Schaffer***	N	Y	Y	Y	Y
5 ***Hefley***	Y	Y	Y	Y	Y
6 ***Tancredo***	N	Y	Y	Y	Y
CONNECTICUT					
1 Larson	N	N	N	N	N
2 Gejdenson	Y	N	N	N	N
3 DeLauro	Y	N	N	N	N
4 ***Shays***	Y	Y	Y	Y	Y
5 Maloney	Y	N	N	N	N
6 ***Johnson***	Y	Y	Y	Y	Y
DELAWARE					
AL ***Castle***	Y	Y	Y	Y	Y
FLORIDA					
1 ***Scarborough***	?	?	Y	Y	Y
2 Boyd	Y	N	N	N	N
3 Brown	Y	N	N	N	N
4 ***Fowler***	Y	Y	Y	Y	Y
5 Thurman	Y	N	N	N	N
6 ***Stearns***	Y	Y	Y	Y	Y
7 ***Mica***	Y	Y	Y	Y	Y
8 ***McCollum***	Y	Y	Y	Y	Y
9 ***Bilirakis***	Y	Y	Y	Y	Y
10 ***Young***	Y	Y	Y	Y	Y
11 Davis	Y	N	N	N	N
12 ***Canady***	Y	Y	Y	Y	Y
13 ***Miller***	Y	Y	Y	Y	Y
14 ***Goss***	Y	Y	Y	Y	Y
15 ***Weldon***	Y	Y	Y	Y	Y
16 ***Foley***	Y	Y	Y	Y	Y
17 Meek	Y	N	N	N	?
18 ***Ros-Lehtinen***	Y	Y	Y	Y	Y
19 Wexler	Y	N	N	N	N
20 Deutsch	Y	N	N	N	N
21 ***Diaz-Balart***	Y	Y	Y	Y	Y
22 ***Shaw***	Y	Y	Y	Y	Y
23 Hastings	?	?	?	?	?
GEORGIA					
1 ***Kingston***	Y	Y	Y	Y	Y
2 Bishop	Y	N	N	N	N
3 ***Collins***	Y	Y	Y	Y	Y
4 McKinney	Y	N	N	N	N
5 Lewis	N	N	N	N	N
6 ***Isakson***	Y	Y	Y	Y	Y
7 ***Barr***	Y	Y	Y	Y	Y
8 ***Chambliss***	Y	Y	Y	Y	Y
9 ***Deal***	Y	Y	Y	Y	Y
10 ***Norwood***	Y	Y	Y	Y	Y
11 ***Linder***	Y	Y	Y	Y	Y
HAWAII					
1 Abercrombie	?	N	N	N	N
2 Mink	Y	N	N	N	N
IDAHO					
1 ***Chenoweth***	N	Y	Y	Y	Y
2 ***Simpson***	Y	Y	Y	Y	Y
ILLINOIS					
1 Rush	Y	N	N	N	N
2 Jackson	Y	N	N	N	N
3 Lipinski	Y	N	N	N	N
4 Gutierrez	N	N	N	N	N
5 Blagojevich	Y	N	N	N	N
6 ***Hyde***	Y	Y	Y	Y	Y
7 Davis	+	–	–	N	N
8 ***Crane***	?	Y	Y	Y	Y
9 Schakowsky	Y	N	N	N	N
10 ***Porter***	?	Y	Y	Y	Y
11 ***Weller***	N	Y	Y	?	Y
12 Costello	N	N	N	N	N
13 ***Biggert***	Y	Y	Y	Y	Y
14 ***Hastert***			Y		

ND Northern Democrats SD Southern Democrats

	83	84	85	86	87
15 ***Ewing***	Y	Y	Y	Y	?
16 ***Manzullo***	Y	Y	Y	Y	Y
17 Evans	Y	N	N	N	N
18 ***LaHood***	+	+	+	+	+
19 Phelps	Y	N	N	N	N
20 ***Shimkus***	Y	Y	Y	Y	Y
INDIANA					
1 Visclosky	N	N	N	N	N
2 ***McIntosh***	Y	Y	Y	Y	Y
3 Roemer	Y	N	N	N	N
4 ***Souder***	Y	Y	Y	Y	Y
5 ***Buyer***	Y	Y	Y	Y	Y
6 ***Burton***	Y	Y	Y	Y	Y
7 ***Pease***	Y	Y	Y	Y	Y
8 ***Hostettler***	Y	Y	Y	Y	Y
9 Hill	Y	N	N	N	N
10 Carson	P	N	N	N	N
IOWA					
1 ***Leach***	Y	Y	Y	Y	Y
2 ***Nussle***	Y	Y	Y	Y	Y
3 Boswell	Y	N	N	N	N
4 ***Ganske***	Y	Y	Y	Y	Y
5 ***Latham***	Y	Y	Y	Y	Y
KANSAS					
1 ***Moran***	N	Y	Y	Y	Y
2 ***Ryun***	Y	Y	Y	Y	?
3 Moore	Y	N	N	N	N
4 ***Tiahrt***	Y	Y	Y	Y	Y
KENTUCKY					
1 ***Whitfield***	Y	Y	Y	Y	Y
2 ***Lewis***	Y	Y	Y	Y	Y
3 ***Northup***	Y	Y	Y	Y	Y
4 Lucas	Y	N	N	N	N
5 ***Rogers***	Y	Y	Y	Y	Y
6 ***Fletcher***	Y	Y	Y	Y	Y
LOUISIANA					
1 Vacant					
2 Jefferson	Y	N	N	N	N
3 ***Tauzin***	?	Y	Y	Y	Y
4 ***McCrery***	?	Y	Y	Y	Y
5 ***Cooksey***	Y	Y	Y	Y	Y
6 ***Baker***	Y	Y	Y	Y	Y
7 John	Y	Y	N	N	N
MAINE					
1 Allen	Y	N	N	N	N
2 Baldacci	Y	N	N	N	N
MARYLAND					
1 ***Gilchrest***	Y	Y	Y	Y	Y
2 ***Ehrlich***	Y	Y	Y	Y	Y
3 Cardin	Y	N	N	N	N
4 Wynn	Y	N	N	N	N
5 Hoyer	Y	N	N	N	N
6 ***Bartlett***	Y	Y	Y	Y	Y
7 Cummings	Y	N	N	N	N
8 ***Morella***	Y	Y	N	Y	Y
MASSACHUSETTS					
1 Olver	?	N	N	N	N
2 Neal	?	N	N	N	N
3 McGovern	Y	N	N	N	N
4 Frank	Y	N	N	N	N
5 Meehan	Y	N	N	N	N
6 Tierney	Y	N	N	N	N
7 Markey	Y	N	N	N	N
8 Capuano	Y	N	N	N	N
9 Moakley	Y	N	N	N	N
10 Delahunt	Y	N	N	N	N
MICHIGAN					
1 Stupak	N	N	N	N	N
2 ***Hoekstra***	Y	Y	Y	Y	Y
3 ***Ehlers***	Y	Y	Y	Y	Y
4 ***Camp***	Y	Y	Y	Y	Y
5 Barcia	Y	N	N	N	N
6 ***Upton***	Y	Y	Y	Y	Y
7 ***Smith***	Y	Y	Y	Y	Y
8 Stabenow	Y	N	N	N	N
9 Kildee	Y	N	N	N	N
10 Bonior	N	N	N	N	N
11 ***Knollenberg***	Y	Y	Y	Y	Y
12 Levin	Y	N	N	N	N
13 Rivers	Y	N	N	N	N
14 Conyers	?	N	N	N	N
15 Kilpatrick	Y	N	N	N	N
16 Dingell	Y	N	N	N	N

	83	84	85	86	87
MINNESOTA					
1 ***Gutknecht***	N	Y	Y	Y	Y
2 Minge	Y	N	N	N	N
3 ***Ramstad***	N	Y	Y	Y	Y
4 Vento	Y	N	N	N	N
5 Sabo	N	N	N	N	N
6 Luther	Y	N	N	N	N
7 Peterson	N	N	N	N	N
8 Oberstar	N	N	N	N	N
MISSISSIPPI					
1 ***Wicker***	Y	Y	Y	Y	Y
2 Thompson	N	N	N	N	N
3 ***Pickering***	Y	Y	Y	Y	Y
4 Shows	Y	N	–	N	N
5 Taylor	N	N	N	N	N
MISSOURI					
1 Clay	N	N	N	N	N
2 ***Talent***	Y	Y	Y	Y	Y
3 Gephardt	N	N	N	N	N
4 Skelton	Y	N	N	N	N
5 McCarthy	Y	N	N	N	N
6 Danner	Y	N	N	N	N
7 ***Blunt***	Y	Y	Y	Y	Y
8 ***Emerson***	Y	Y	Y	Y	Y
9 ***Hulshof***	N	Y	Y	Y	Y
MONTANA					
AL ***Hill***	Y	Y	Y	Y	Y
NEBRASKA					
1 ***Bereuter***	Y	Y	Y	Y	Y
2 ***Terry***	Y	Y	Y	Y	Y
3 ***Barrett***	Y	Y	Y	Y	Y
NEVADA					
1 Berkley	Y	N	N	N	N
2 ***Gibbons***	N	Y	Y	Y	Y
NEW HAMPSHIRE					
1 ***Sununu***	Y	Y	Y	Y	Y
2 ***Bass***	Y	Y	Y	Y	Y
NEW JERSEY					
1 Andrews	Y	N	N	N	N
2 ***LoBiondo***	N	Y	Y	Y	Y
3 ***Saxton***	Y	Y	Y	Y	Y
4 ***Smith***	Y	Y	Y	Y	Y
5 ***Roukema***	Y	Y	Y	Y	Y
6 Pallone	N	N	N	N	N
7 ***Franks***	Y	Y	Y	Y	Y
8 Pascrell	N	N	N	N	N
9 Rothman	Y	N	N	N	N
10 Payne	Y	N	N	N	N
11 ***Frelinghuysen***	Y	Y	Y	Y	Y
12 Holt	Y	N	N	N	N
13 Menendez	N	N	N	N	N
NEW MEXICO					
1 ***Wilson***	Y	Y	Y	Y	Y
2 ***Skeen***	Y	Y	Y	Y	Y
3 Udall	Y	N	N	N	N
NEW YORK					
1 ***Forbes***	Y	Y	Y	Y	Y
2 ***Lazio***	Y	Y	Y	Y	Y
3 ***King***	Y	Y	Y	Y	Y
4 McCarthy	?	N	N	N	N
5 Ackerman	Y	N	N	N	N
6 Meeks	Y	N	N	N	N
7 Crowley	Y	N	N	N	N
8 Nadler	Y	N	N	N	N
9 Weiner	?	N	N	N	N
10 Towns	Y	N	N	N	N
11 Owens	Y	N	N	N	N
12 Velázquez	?	N	N	N	N
13 ***Fossella***	Y	Y	Y	Y	Y
14 Maloney	Y	N	N	N	N
15 Rangel	?	N	N	N	N
16 Serrano	N	N	N	N	N
17 Engel	N	N	N	N	N
18 Lowey	Y	N	N	N	N
19 ***Kelly***	Y	Y	Y	Y	Y
20 ***Gilman***	Y	Y	Y	Y	Y
21 McNulty	N	N	N	N	N
22 ***Sweeney***	N	Y	Y	Y	Y
23 ***Boehlert***	Y	Y	Y	Y	Y
24 ***McHugh***	Y	Y	Y	Y	Y
25 ***Walsh***	Y	Y	Y	Y	Y
26 Hinchey	?	N	N	N	N
27 ***Reynolds***	Y	Y	Y	Y	Y
28 Slaughter	Y	N	N	N	N
29 LaFalce	Y	N	N	N	N

	83	84	85	86	87
30 ***Quinn***	Y	Y	N	Y	Y
31 ***Houghton***	Y	Y	Y	Y	Y
NORTH CAROLINA					
1 Clayton	Y	N	N	N	?
2 Etheridge	Y	N	N	N	N
3 ***Jones***	Y	Y	Y	Y	Y
4 Price	Y	N	N	N	N
5 ***Burr***	Y	Y	Y	Y	Y
6 ***Coble***	Y	Y	Y	Y	Y
7 McIntyre	Y	N	N	N	N
8 ***Hayes***	Y	Y	Y	Y	Y
9 ***Myrick***	?	Y	Y	Y	Y
10 ***Ballenger***	Y	Y	Y	Y	Y
11 ***Taylor***	Y	Y	Y	Y	Y
12 Watt	Y	N	N	N	N
NORTH DAKOTA					
AL Pomeroy	Y	N	N	N	N
OHIO					
1 ***Chabot***	Y	Y	Y	Y	Y
2 ***Portman***	Y	Y	Y	Y	Y
3 Hall	Y	N	N	N	N
4 ***Oxley***	?	Y	Y	Y	Y
5 ***Gillmor***	Y	Y	Y	Y	Y
6 Strickland	N	N	N	N	N
7 ***Hobson***	Y	Y	Y	Y	Y
8 ***Boehner***	Y	Y	Y	Y	Y
9 Kaptur	Y	N	N	N	N
10 Kucinich	N	N	N	N	N
11 Jones	Y	N	N	N	N
12 ***Kasich***	Y	Y	Y	Y	Y
13 Brown	Y	N	N	N	N
14 Sawyer	Y	N	N	N	N
15 ***Pryce***	Y	Y	Y	Y	Y
16 ***Regula***	Y	Y	Y	Y	Y
17 Traficant	Y	Y	N	N	Y
18 ***Ney***	Y	Y	Y	Y	Y
19 ***LaTourette***	Y	Y	Y	Y	Y
OKLAHOMA					
1 ***Largent***	Y	Y	Y	Y	Y
2 ***Coburn***	Y	Y	Y	Y	Y
3 ***Watkins***	Y	Y	Y	Y	?
4 ***Watts***	Y	Y	Y	Y	Y
5 ***Istook***	Y	Y	Y	Y	Y
6 ***Lucas***	Y	Y	Y	Y	Y
OREGON					
1 Wu	Y	N	N	N	N
2 ***Walden***	Y	Y	Y	Y	Y
3 Blumenauer	Y	N	N	N	N
4 DeFazio	N	N	N	N	N
5 Hooley	Y	N	N	N	N
PENNSYLVANIA					
1 Brady	N	N	N	N	N
2 Fattah	?	N	N	N	N
3 Borski	N	N	N	N	N
4 Klink	N	N	N	N	N
5 ***Peterson***	Y	Y	Y	Y	Y
6 Holden	Y	N	N	N	N
7 ***Weldon***	Y	Y	Y	Y	Y
8 ***Greenwood***	Y	Y	Y	Y	Y
9 ***Shuster***	Y	Y	Y	Y	Y
10 ***Sherwood***	?	Y	Y	Y	Y
11 Kanjorski	Y	N	N	N	N
12 Murtha	Y	N	N	N	N
13 Hoeffel	Y	N	N	N	N
14 Coyne	Y	N	N	N	N
15 ***Toomey***	Y	Y	Y	Y	Y
16 ***Pitts***	Y	Y	Y	Y	Y
17 ***Gekas***	Y	Y	Y	Y	Y
18 Doyle	?	N	N	N	N
19 ***Goodling***	Y	Y	Y	Y	Y
20 Mascara	Y	N	N	N	N
21 ***English***	N	Y	Y	Y	Y
RHODE ISLAND					
1 Kennedy	Y	N	N	N	N
2 Weygand	Y	N	N	N	N
SOUTH CAROLINA					
1 ***Sanford***	Y	Y	Y	Y	Y
2 ***Spence***	Y	Y	Y	Y	Y
3 ***Graham***	Y	Y	Y	Y	Y
4 ***DeMint***	Y	Y	Y	Y	Y
5 Spratt	Y	N	N	N	N
6 Clyburn	N	N	N	N	N
SOUTH DAKOTA					
AL ***Thune***	Y	Y	Y	Y	Y

	83	84	85	86	87
TENNESSEE					
1 ***Jenkins***	Y	Y	Y	Y	Y
2 ***Duncan***	Y	Y	Y	Y	Y
3 ***Wamp***	Y	Y	Y	Y	Y
4 ***Hilleary***	Y	Y	Y	Y	Y
5 Clement	Y	N	N	N	N
6 Gordon	Y	N	N	N	N
7 ***Bryant***	Y	Y	Y	Y	Y
8 Tanner	Y	N	N	N	N
9 Ford	N	N	N	N	N
TEXAS					
1 Sandlin	Y	N	N	N	N
2 Turner	Y	N	N	N	N
3 ***Johnson, Sam***	Y	Y	Y	Y	Y
4 Hall	Y	Y	Y	N	N
5 ***Sessions***	Y	Y	Y	Y	Y
6 ***Barton***	Y	Y	Y	Y	Y
7 ***Archer***	Y	Y	Y	Y	Y
8 ***Brady***	Y	Y	Y	Y	Y
9 Lampson	Y	N	N	N	N
10 Doggett	Y	N	N	N	N
11 Edwards	Y	N	N	N	N
12 ***Granger***	Y	Y	Y	Y	Y
13 ***Thornberry***	Y	Y	Y	Y	Y
14 ***Paul***	Y	Y	N	Y	Y
15 Hinojosa	Y	N	N	N	N
16 Reyes	Y	N	N	N	N
17 Stenholm	Y	N	N	N	N
18 Jackson-Lee	Y	N	N	N	N
19 ***Combest***	Y	Y	Y	Y	Y
20 Gonzalez	Y	N	N	N	N
21 ***Smith***	Y	Y	Y	Y	Y
22 ***DeLay***	Y	Y	Y	Y	Y
23 ***Bonilla***	Y	Y	Y	Y	Y
24 Frost	Y	N	N	N	N
25 Bentsen	Y	N	N	N	N
26 ***Armey***	Y	Y	Y	Y	Y
27 Ortiz	Y	N	N	N	N
28 Rodriguez	?	N	N	N	N
29 Green	N	N	N	N	N
30 Johnson, E.B.	N	N	N	N	N
UTAH					
1 ***Hansen***	Y	Y	Y	Y	Y
2 ***Cook***	Y	Y	Y	Y	Y
3 ***Cannon***	Y	Y	Y	Y	Y
VERMONT					
AL *Sanders*	Y	N	N	N	N
VIRGINIA					
1 ***Bateman***	?	Y	Y	Y	Y
2 Pickett	N	?	N	N	N
3 Scott	Y	N	N	N	N
4 Sisisky	Y	N	N	N	N
5 Goode	Y	N	Y	Y	Y
6 ***Goodlatte***	Y	Y	Y	Y	Y
7 ***Bliley***	Y	Y	Y	Y	Y
8 Moran	Y	N	N	N	N
9 Boucher	Y	N	N	N	N
10 ***Wolf***	Y	Y	Y	Y	Y
11 ***Davis***	Y	Y	Y	Y	Y
WASHINGTON					
1 Inslee	Y	N	N	N	N
2 ***Metcalf***	?	Y	Y	Y	Y
3 Baird	Y	N	N	N	N
4 ***Hastings***	Y	Y	Y	Y	Y
5 ***Nethercutt***	Y	Y	Y	Y	Y
6 Dicks	?	N	N	N	N
7 McDermott	N	N	N	N	N
8 ***Dunn***	?	?	Y	Y	Y
9 Smith	Y	N	N	N	N
WEST VIRGINIA					
1 Mollohan	Y	N	N	N	N
2 Wise	?	N	N	N	N
3 Rahall	Y	N	N	N	N
WISCONSIN					
1 ***Ryan***	Y	Y	Y	Y	Y
2 Baldwin	Y	N	N	N	N
3 Kind	Y	N	N	N	N
4 Kleczka	?	N	N	N	N
5 Barrett	Y	N	N	N	N
6 ***Petri***	Y	Y	Y	Y	Y
7 Obey	Y	N	N	N	N
8 ***Green***	Y	Y	Y	Y	Y
9 ***Sensenbrenner***	Y	Y	Y	Y	Y
WYOMING					
AL ***Cubin***	Y	Y	Y	Y	Y

Southern states - Ala., Ark., Fla., Ga., Ky., La., Miss., N.C., Okla., S.C., Tenn., Texas, Va.

88. **HR 472. Local Government Census Review/Substitute.** Maloney, D-N.Y., substitute amendment to give local governments an opportunity to review housing unit counts, jurisdictional boundaries and such other data as the Commerce secretary considers appropriate before the census is conducted. Rejected 202-226: R 1-220; D 200-6 (ND 148-4, SD 52-2); I 1-0. April 14, 1999.

89. **HR 472. Local Government Census Review/Passage.** Passage of the bill to allow local government officials to review and challenge 2000 census data before the count is finalized. Under the bill, the data subject to local review would include numbers of housing units and vacancies in those units, but not necessarily a count of specific individuals. Passed 223-206: R 219-1; D 4-204 (ND 2-152, SD 2-52); I 0-1. April 14, 1999. A "nay" was a vote in support of the president's position.

90. **H J Res 37. Tax Limitation Constitutional Amendment/Passage.** Passage of the joint resolution to propose a constitutional amendment to require a two-thirds majority vote of the House and Senate to pass any legislation that increases federal revenues by more than a "de minimis," or insignificant, amount. The exact definition of "de minimis" would be left to Congress. Rejected 229-199: R 203-17; D 26-181 (ND 12-141, SD 14-40); I 0-1. April 15, 1999. A two-thirds majority of those present and voting (286 in this case) is required to pass a joint resolution proposing an amendment to the Constitution.

91. **HR 1376. Tax Benefits for Troops/Passage.** Passage of the bill to allow U.S. military personnel currently serving in Yugoslavia to receive hazard pay tax-free. The measure also would allow military personnel, reporters and relief workers a 180-day extension on the filing of their 1998 tax returns beginning when they return from Yugoslavia, and it would exempt personnel from the 3 percent excise tax on long-distance telephone calls. Passed 424-0: R 217-0; D 206-0 (ND 152-0, SD 54-0); I 1-0. April 15, 1999.

Key

- Y Voted for (yea).
- # Paired for.
- + Announced for.
- N Voted against (nay).
- X Paired against.
- – Announced against.
- P Voted "present."
- C Voted "present" to avoid possible conflict of interest.
- ? Did not vote or otherwise make a position known.

•

Democrats ***Republicans***
Independents

	88	89	90	91
ALABAMA				
1 ***Callahan***	N	Y	Y	Y
2 ***Everett***	N	Y	Y	Y
3 ***Riley***	N	Y	Y	Y
4 ***Aderholt***	N	Y	Y	Y
5 Cramer	Y	N	Y	Y
6 ***Bachus***	N	Y	Y	Y
7 Hilliard	Y	N	N	Y
ALASKA				
AL ***Young***	N	Y	Y	Y
ARIZONA				
1 ***Salmon***	N	Y	Y	Y
2 Pastor	Y	N	N	Y
3 ***Stump***	N	Y	Y	Y
4 ***Shadegg***	N	Y	Y	Y
5 ***Kolbe***	N	Y	Y	Y
6 ***Hayworth***	N	Y	Y	Y
ARKANSAS				
1 Berry	Y	N	Y	Y
2 Snyder	Y	N	N	Y
3 ***Hutchinson***	N	Y	Y	Y
4 ***Dickey***	N	Y	Y	Y
CALIFORNIA				
1 Thompson	Y	N	N	Y
2 ***Herger***	N	Y	Y	Y
3 ***Ose***	N	Y	Y	Y
4 ***Doolittle***	N	Y	Y	Y
5 Matsui	Y	N	N	Y
6 Woolsey	Y	N	N	Y
7 Miller, George	Y	N	N	Y
8 Pelosi	Y	N	N	Y
9 Lee	Y	N	N	Y
10 Tauscher	Y	N	N	Y
11 ***Pombo***	N	Y	Y	Y
12 Lantos	?	?	N	Y
13 Stark	Y	N	N	Y
14 Eshoo	Y	N	N	Y
15 ***Campbell***	N	Y	N	Y
16 Lofgren	Y	N	N	Y
17 Farr	Y	N	N	Y
18 Condit	Y	N	Y	Y
19 ***Radanovich***	N	Y	Y	Y
20 Dooley	Y	N	N	Y
21 ***Thomas***	N	Y	N	Y
22 Capps	Y	N	N	Y
23 ***Gallegly***	N	Y	Y	Y
24 Sherman	Y	N	Y	Y
25 ***McKeon***	N	Y	Y	Y
26 Berman	Y	N	N	Y
27 ***Rogan***	N	Y	Y	Y
28 ***Dreier***	N	Y	N	Y
29 Waxman	Y	N	?	?
30 Becerra	Y	N	N	Y
31 Martinez	Y	N	N	Y
32 Dixon	Y	N	N	Y
33 Roybal-Allard	Y	N	N	Y
34 Napolitano	Y	N	N	Y
35 Waters	Y	N	N	Y
36 ***Kuykendall***	N	Y	Y	Y
37 Millender-McD.	Y	N	N	Y
38 ***Horn***	N	Y	Y	Y
39 ***Royce***	N	Y	Y	Y
40 ***Lewis***	N	Y	N	Y
41 ***Miller, Gary***	N	Y	Y	Y
42 Brown	?	?	?	?
43 ***Calvert***	N	Y	Y	Y
44 ***Bono***	N	Y	Y	Y
45 ***Rohrabacher***	N	Y	Y	Y
46 Sanchez	Y	N	Y	Y
47 ***Cox***	N	Y	Y	Y
48 ***Packard***	N	Y	Y	Y
49 ***Bilbray***	N	Y	Y	Y
50 Filner	Y	N	N	Y
51 ***Cunningham***	N	Y	Y	Y
52 ***Hunter***	N	Y	Y	Y
COLORADO				
1 DeGette	Y	N	N	Y
2 Udall	Y	N	N	Y
3 ***McInnis***	N	Y	Y	Y
4 ***Schaffer***	N	Y	Y	Y
5 ***Hefley***	N	Y	Y	Y
6 ***Tancredo***	N	Y	Y	Y
CONNECTICUT				
1 Larson	Y	N	N	Y
2 Gejdenson	Y	N	N	Y
3 DeLauro	Y	N	N	Y
4 ***Shays***	N	Y	Y	Y
5 Maloney	Y	N	Y	Y
6 ***Johnson***	N	Y	N	Y
DELAWARE				
AL ***Castle***	N	Y	Y	Y
FLORIDA				
1 ***Scarborough***	N	Y	Y	Y
2 Boyd	Y	N	N	Y
3 Brown	Y	N	N	Y
4 ***Fowler***	N	Y	Y	Y
5 Thurman	Y	N	N	Y
6 ***Stearns***	N	Y	Y	Y
7 ***Mica***	N	Y	Y	Y
8 ***McCollum***	N	Y	Y	Y
9 ***Bilirakis***	N	Y	Y	Y
10 ***Young***	N	Y	Y	Y
11 Davis	Y	N	N	Y
12 ***Canady***	N	Y	Y	Y
13 ***Miller***	N	Y	Y	Y
14 ***Goss***	N	Y	Y	Y
15 ***Weldon***	N	Y	Y	Y
16 ***Foley***	N	Y	Y	Y
17 Meek	Y	N	N	Y
18 ***Ros-Lehtinen***	N	Y	+	+
19 Wexler	Y	N	N	Y
20 Deutsch	Y	N	N	Y
21 ***Diaz-Balart***	N	Y	Y	Y
22 ***Shaw***	N	Y	N	Y
23 Hastings	?	?	?	?
GEORGIA				
1 ***Kingston***	N	Y	Y	Y
2 Bishop	Y	N	Y	Y
3 ***Collins***	N	Y	Y	Y
4 McKinney	Y	N	N	Y
5 Lewis	Y	N	N	Y
6 ***Isakson***	N	Y	Y	Y
7 ***Barr***	N	Y	Y	Y
8 ***Chambliss***	N	Y	Y	Y
9 ***Deal***	N	Y	Y	Y
10 ***Norwood***	N	Y	Y	Y
11 ***Linder***	N	Y	N	Y
HAWAII				
1 Abercrombie	Y	N	N	Y
2 Mink	Y	N	N	Y
IDAHO				
1 ***Chenoweth***	N	Y	Y	Y
2 ***Simpson***	N	Y	Y	Y
ILLINOIS				
1 Rush	Y	N	N	Y
2 Jackson	Y	N	N	Y
3 Lipinski	Y	N	N	Y
4 Gutierrez	Y	N	N	Y
5 Blagojevich	Y	N	N	Y
6 ***Hyde***	N	Y	N	Y
7 Davis	Y	N	N	Y
8 ***Crane***	N	Y	Y	Y
9 Schakowsky	Y	N	N	Y
10 ***Porter***	N	Y	N	Y
11 ***Weller***	N	Y	Y	Y
12 Costello	Y	N	N	Y
13 ***Biggert***	N	Y	Y	Y
14 ***Hastert***	N	Y	Y	Y

ND Northern Democrats SD Southern Democrats

	88	89	90	91
15 ***Ewing***	N	Y	Y	Y
16 ***Manzullo***	N	Y	Y	Y
17 Evans	Y	N	N	Y
18 ***LaHood***	–	+	Y	Y
19 Phelps	Y	N	N	Y
20 ***Shimkus***	N	Y	Y	Y
INDIANA				
1 Visclosky	Y	N	N	Y
2 ***McIntosh***	N	Y	Y	Y
3 Roemer	Y	N	Y	Y
4 ***Souder***	N	Y	Y	Y
5 ***Buyer***	N	Y	Y	Y
6 ***Burton***	N	Y	Y	Y
7 ***Pease***	N	Y	Y	Y
8 ***Hostettler***	N	Y	N	Y
9 Hill	Y	N	N	Y
10 Carson	Y	N	N	Y
IOWA				
1 ***Leach***	N	Y	Y	Y
2 ***Nussle***	N	Y	Y	Y
3 Boswell	Y	Y	Y	Y
4 ***Ganske***	N	Y	Y	Y
5 ***Latham***	N	Y	Y	Y
KANSAS				
1 ***Moran***	N	Y	Y	Y
2 ***Ryun***	N	Y	Y	Y
3 Moore	Y	N	N	Y
4 ***Tiahrt***	N	Y	Y	Y
KENTUCKY				
1 ***Whitfield***	N	Y	Y	Y
2 ***Lewis***	N	Y	Y	Y
3 ***Northup***	N	Y	Y	Y
4 Lucas	Y	N	Y	Y
5 ***Rogers***	N	Y	Y	Y
6 ***Fletcher***	N	Y	Y	Y
LOUISIANA				
1 Vacant				
2 Jefferson	Y	N	N	Y
3 ***Tauzin***	N	Y	Y	Y
4 ***McCrery***	N	Y	Y	Y
5 ***Cooksey***	N	Y	Y	Y
6 ***Baker***	N	Y	Y	Y
7 John	Y	N	Y	Y
MAINE				
1 Allen	Y	N	N	Y
2 Baldacci	Y	N	N	Y
MARYLAND				
1 ***Gilchrest***	N	Y	Y	Y
2 ***Ehrlich***	N	Y	Y	Y
3 Cardin	Y	N	N	Y
4 Wynn	Y	N	N	Y
5 Hoyer	Y	N	N	Y
6 ***Bartlett***	N	Y	Y	Y
7 Cummings	Y	N	N	Y
8 ***Morella***	Y	N	N	Y
MASSACHUSETTS				
1 Olver	Y	N	N	Y
2 Neal	Y	N	N	Y
3 McGovern	Y	N	N	Y
4 Frank	Y	N	N	Y
5 Meehan	Y	N	N	Y
6 Tierney	Y	N	N	Y
7 Markey	Y	N	N	Y
8 Capuano	Y	N	N	Y
9 Moakley	Y	N	N	?
10 Delahunt	?	N	N	Y
MICHIGAN				
1 Stupak	Y	N	N	Y
2 ***Hoekstra***	N	Y	Y	Y
3 ***Ehlers***	N	Y	Y	Y
4 ***Camp***	N	Y	Y	Y
5 Barcia	Y	N	Y	Y
6 ***Upton***	N	Y	Y	Y
7 ***Smith***	N	Y	Y	Y
8 Stabenow	Y	N	N	Y
9 Kildee	Y	N	N	Y
10 Bonior	Y	N	N	Y
11 ***Knollenberg***	N	Y	Y	Y
12 Levin	Y	N	N	Y
13 Rivers	Y	N	N	Y
14 Conyers	Y	N	N	Y
15 Kilpatrick	Y	N	N	Y
16 Dingell	Y	N	N	Y

	88	89	90	91
MINNESOTA				
1 ***Gutknecht***	N	Y	Y	Y
2 Minge	Y	N	N	Y
3 ***Ramstad***	N	Y	Y	Y
4 Vento	Y	N	N	Y
5 Sabo	Y	N	N	Y
6 Luther	Y	N	N	Y
7 Peterson	Y	N	N	Y
8 Oberstar	Y	N	N	Y
MISSISSIPPI				
1 ***Wicker***	N	Y	Y	Y
2 Thompson	Y	N	N	Y
3 ***Pickering***	N	Y	Y	Y
4 Shows	Y	N	Y	Y
5 Taylor	N	Y	Y	Y
MISSOURI				
1 Clay	Y	N	N	Y
2 ***Talent***	N	Y	Y	Y
3 Gephardt	Y	N	N	Y
4 Skelton	Y	N	Y	Y
5 McCarthy	Y	N	N	Y
6 Danner	Y	N	N	Y
7 ***Blunt***	N	Y	Y	Y
8 ***Emerson***	N	Y	Y	Y
9 ***Hulshof***	N	Y	Y	Y
MONTANA				
AL ***Hill***	N	Y	N	Y
NEBRASKA				
1 ***Bereuter***	N	Y	N	Y
2 ***Terry***	N	Y	Y	Y
3 ***Barrett***	N	Y	Y	Y
NEVADA				
1 Berkley	Y	N	N	Y
2 ***Gibbons***	N	Y	Y	Y
NEW HAMPSHIRE				
1 ***Sununu***	N	Y	Y	Y
2 ***Bass***	N	Y	Y	Y
NEW JERSEY				
1 Andrews	Y	N	Y	Y
2 ***LoBiondo***	N	Y	Y	Y
3 ***Saxton***	N	Y	Y	Y
4 ***Smith***	N	Y	Y	Y
5 ***Roukema***	N	Y	Y	Y
6 Pallone	Y	N	Y	Y
7 ***Franks***	N	Y	Y	Y
8 Pascrell	Y	N	N	Y
9 Rothman	Y	N	N	Y
10 Payne	Y	N	N	Y
11 ***Frelinghuysen***	N	Y	Y	Y
12 Holt	Y	N	N	Y
13 Menendez	Y	N	N	Y
NEW MEXICO				
1 ***Wilson***	N	Y	Y	Y
2 ***Skeen***	N	Y	Y	Y
3 Udall	Y	N	N	Y
NEW YORK				
1 ***Forbes***	N	Y	Y	Y
2 ***Lazio***	N	Y	Y	Y
3 ***King***	N	Y	Y	Y
4 McCarthy	Y	N	Y	Y
5 Ackerman	Y	N	N	Y
6 Meeks	Y	N	N	Y
7 Crowley	Y	N	N	Y
8 Nadler	Y	N	N	Y
9 Weiner	Y	N	N	Y
10 Towns	Y	N	N	Y
11 Owens	Y	N	N	Y
12 Velázquez	Y	N	N	Y
13 ***Fossella***	N	Y	Y	Y
14 Maloney	Y	N	N	Y
15 Rangel	Y	N	N	Y
16 Serrano	Y	N	N	Y
17 Engel	Y	N	N	Y
18 Lowey	Y	N	N	Y
19 ***Kelly***	N	Y	Y	Y
20 ***Gilman***	N	Y	Y	Y
21 McNulty	Y	N	N	Y
22 ***Sweeney***	N	Y	Y	+
23 ***Boehlert***	N	Y	N	Y
24 ***McHugh***	N	Y	Y	Y
25 ***Walsh***	N	Y	N	Y
26 Hinchey	Y	N	N	Y
27 ***Reynolds***	N	?	Y	Y
28 Slaughter	Y	N	N	Y
29 LaFalce	Y	N	N	Y

	88	89	90	91
30 ***Quinn***	N	Y	Y	Y
31 ***Houghton***	N	Y	N	Y
NORTH CAROLINA				
1 Clayton	Y	N	N	Y
2 Etheridge	Y	N	Y	Y
3 ***Jones***	N	Y	Y	Y
4 Price	Y	N	N	Y
5 ***Burr***	N	Y	Y	Y
6 ***Coble***	N	Y	Y	Y
7 McIntyre	Y	N	Y	Y
8 ***Hayes***	N	Y	Y	Y
9 ***Myrick***	N	Y	Y	Y
10 ***Ballenger***	N	Y	Y	Y
11 ***Taylor***	N	Y	Y	Y
12 Watt	Y	N	N	Y
NORTH DAKOTA				
AL Pomeroy	Y	N	N	Y
OHIO				
1 ***Chabot***	N	Y	Y	Y
2 ***Portman***	N	Y	Y	Y
3 Hall	Y	N	N	Y
4 ***Oxley***	N	Y	Y	Y
5 ***Gillmor***	N	Y	Y	Y
6 Strickland	Y	N	N	Y
7 ***Hobson***	N	Y	Y	Y
8 ***Boehner***	N	Y	Y	Y
9 Kaptur	Y	N	N	Y
10 Kucinich	Y	N	N	Y
11 Jones	+	N	N	Y
12 ***Kasich***	N	Y	Y	Y
13 Brown	Y	N	N	Y
14 Sawyer	Y	N	N	Y
15 ***Pryce***	N	Y	Y	Y
16 ***Regula***	N	Y	Y	Y
17 Traficant	N	Y	Y	Y
18 ***Ney***	N	Y	Y	Y
19 ***LaTourette***	N	Y	Y	Y
OKLAHOMA				
1 ***Largent***	N	Y	Y	Y
2 ***Coburn***	N	Y	Y	Y
3 ***Watkins***	N	Y	Y	Y
4 ***Watts***	N	Y	Y	Y
5 ***Istook***	N	Y	Y	+
6 ***Lucas***	N	Y	Y	Y
OREGON				
1 Wu	Y	N	N	Y
2 ***Walden***	N	Y	Y	Y
3 Blumenauer	Y	N	N	Y
4 DeFazio	Y	N	N	Y
5 Hooley	Y	N	N	Y
PENNSYLVANIA				
1 Brady	Y	N	N	Y
2 Fattah	Y	N	N	Y
3 Borski	Y	N	N	Y
4 Klink	Y	N	N	Y
5 ***Peterson***	N	Y	Y	Y
6 Holden	Y	N	N	Y
7 ***Weldon***	N	Y	Y	Y
8 ***Greenwood***	N	Y	Y	Y
9 ***Shuster***	N	Y	+	+
10 ***Sherwood***	N	Y	Y	Y
11 Kanjorski	Y	N	N	Y
12 Murtha	Y	N	N	Y
13 Hoeffel	Y	N	N	Y
14 Coyne	Y	N	N	Y
15 ***Toomey***	N	Y	Y	Y
16 ***Pitts***	N	Y	Y	Y
17 ***Gekas***	N	Y	Y	Y
18 Doyle	Y	N	N	Y
19 ***Goodling***	N	Y	Y	Y
20 Mascara	Y	N	N	Y
21 ***English***	N	Y	Y	Y
RHODE ISLAND				
1 Kennedy	Y	N	N	Y
2 Weygand	Y	N	N	Y
SOUTH CAROLINA				
1 ***Sanford***	N	Y	Y	Y
2 ***Spence***	N	Y	Y	Y
3 ***Graham***	N	Y	Y	Y
4 ***DeMint***	N	Y	Y	Y
5 Spratt	Y	N	N	Y
6 Clyburn	Y	N	N	Y
SOUTH DAKOTA				
AL ***Thune***	N	Y	Y	Y

	88	89	90	91
TENNESSEE				
1 ***Jenkins***	N	Y	Y	Y
2 ***Duncan***	N	Y	Y	Y
3 ***Wamp***	N	Y	Y	Y
4 ***Hilleary***	N	Y	Y	Y
5 Clement	Y	N	N	Y
6 Gordon	Y	N	Y	Y
7 ***Bryant***	N	Y	Y	Y
8 Tanner	Y	N	N	Y
9 Ford	Y	N	N	Y
TEXAS				
1 Sandlin	Y	N	Y	Y
2 Turner	Y	N	N	Y
3 ***Johnson, Sam***	N	Y	Y	Y
4 Hall	Y	N	Y	Y
5 ***Sessions***	N	Y	Y	Y
6 ***Barton***	N	Y	Y	Y
7 ***Archer***	N	Y	Y	Y
8 ***Brady***	N	Y	Y	Y
9 Lampson	Y	N	N	Y
10 Doggett	Y	N	N	Y
11 Edwards	Y	N	N	Y
12 ***Granger***	N	Y	Y	Y
13 ***Thornberry***	N	Y	Y	Y
14 ***Paul***	N	Y	Y	Y
15 Hinojosa	Y	N	N	Y
16 Reyes	Y	N	N	Y
17 Stenholm	Y	N	N	Y
18 Jackson-Lee	Y	N	N	Y
19 ***Combest***	N	Y	Y	Y
20 Gonzalez	Y	N	N	Y
21 ***Smith***	N	Y	Y	Y
22 ***DeLay***	N	Y	Y	Y
23 ***Bonilla***	N	Y	Y	Y
24 Frost	Y	N	N	Y
25 Bentsen	Y	N	N	Y
26 ***Armey***	N	Y	Y	Y
27 Ortiz	Y	N	N	Y
28 Rodriguez	Y	N	N	Y
29 Green	Y	N	Y	Y
30 Johnson, E.B.	Y	N	N	Y
UTAH				
1 ***Hansen***	N	Y	Y	Y
2 ***Cook***	N	Y	Y	Y
3 ***Cannon***	N	Y	Y	Y
VERMONT				
AL *Sanders*	Y	N	N	Y
VIRGINIA				
1 ***Bateman***	N	Y	N	Y
2 Pickett	Y	N	N	Y
3 Scott	Y	N	N	Y
4 Sisisky	Y	N	N	Y
5 Goode	N	Y	Y	Y
6 ***Goodlatte***	N	Y	Y	Y
7 ***Bliley***	N	Y	Y	Y
8 Moran	Y	N	N	Y
9 Boucher	Y	N	N	Y
10 ***Wolf***	N	Y	Y	Y
11 ***Davis***	N	Y	Y	Y
WASHINGTON				
1 Inslee	Y	N	N	Y
2 ***Metcalf***	N	Y	Y	Y
3 Baird	Y	N	N	Y
4 ***Hastings***	N	Y	Y	?
5 ***Nethercutt***	N	Y	Y	Y
6 Dicks	Y	N	?	?
7 McDermott	Y	N	N	Y
8 ***Dunn***	N	Y	Y	Y
9 Smith	Y	N	N	Y
WEST VIRGINIA				
1 Mollohan	Y	N	N	Y
2 Wise	Y	N	N	Y
3 Rahall	Y	N	N	Y
WISCONSIN				
1 ***Ryan***	N	Y	Y	Y
2 Baldwin	Y	N	N	Y
3 Kind	N	N	N	Y
4 Kleczka	N	N	N	Y
5 Barrett	N	N	N	Y
6 ***Petri***	N	Y	Y	Y
7 Obey	Y	N	N	Y
8 ***Green***	N	Y	Y	Y
9 ***Sensenbrenner***	N	Y	Y	Y
WYOMING				
AL ***Cubin***	N	Y	Y	Y

Southern states - Ala., Ark., Fla., Ga., Ky., La., Miss., N.C., Okla., S.C., Tenn., Texas, Va.

92. HR 573. Rosa Parks Gold Medal/Passage. Bachus, R-Ala., motion to suspend the rules and pass the bill to authorize the president to award a gold medal honoring Rosa Parks on behalf of Congress in recognition of her contributions to the nation. Motion agreed to 424-1: R 213-1; D 210-0 (ND 155-0, SD 55-0); I 1-0. April 20, 1999. A two-thirds majority of those present and voting (284 in this case) is required for passage under suspension of the rules. (Subsequently, the House passed S 531, a similar Senate bill, thus clearing the measure for the president.)

93. H Res 128. Investigation of Rosemary Nelson's Death/Passage. Gilman, R-N.Y., motion to suspend the rules and pass the bill to call on the government of the United Kingdom to conduct an independent inquiry and issue a detailed and public report on the car bombing that killed prominent Northern Ireland defense attorney Rosemary Nelson. Motion agreed to 421-2: R 211-2; D 209-0 (ND 155-0, SD 54-0); I 1-0. April 20, 1999. A two-thirds majority of those present and voting (282 in this case) is required for passage under suspension of the rules.

94. HR 800. Educational Flexibility/Conference Report. Adoption of the conference report on the bill to expand the Education Flexibility Partnership Program by making all 50 states (plus the District of Columbia, Puerto Rico and other U.S. territories) eligible to participate in the program, instead of only the 12 states permitted under existing law. Under the bill, participating states could waive certain requirements of federal education programs. The agreement does not include a Senate provision that would have allowed states to use money appropriated for reducing class size for special education programs instead. Adopted (thus sent to the Senate) 368-57: R 218-0; D 149-57 (ND 105-46, SD 44-11); I 1-0. April 21, 1999.

95. HR 1184. Earthquake Preparedness/Passage. Passage of the bill to authorize funds for earthquake preparedness program under various agencies for fiscal 2000 and fiscal 2001. The measure would authorize $19.8 million in fiscal 2000 and $20.4 million in fiscal 2001 for the Federal Emergency Management Agency; $46 million in fiscal 2000 and $47.5 million in fiscal 2001 for the U.S. Geological Survey; and $30 million in fiscal 2000 and $32 million in fiscal 2001 for the National Science Foundation. Passed 414-3: R 206-3; D 207-0 (ND 153-0, SD 54-0); I 1-0. April 21, 1999.

96. HR 1141. Fiscal 1999 Supplemental Spending/Motion To Instruct. Obey, D-Wis., motion to instruct House conferees to reject Senate provisions that would offset part of the spending in the bill by cutting previous appropriations for anti-terrorism and anti-drug activities, year 2000 computer upgrades, embassy security improvements, and other programs. Motion agreed to 414-0: R 213-0; D 200-0 (ND 150-0, SD 50-0); I 1-0. April 22, 1999.

Key

Y Voted for (yea).
\# Paired for.
\+ Announced for.
N Voted against (nay).
X Paired against.
– Announced against.
P Voted "present."
C Voted "present" to avoid possible conflict of interest.
? Did not vote or otherwise make a position known.

•

Democrats ***Republicans***
Independents

	92	93	94	95	96
ALABAMA					
1 ***Callahan***	Y	Y	Y	Y	Y
2 ***Everett***	Y	Y	Y	Y	Y
3 ***Riley***	Y	Y	Y	Y	Y
4 ***Aderholt***	Y	Y	Y	Y	Y
5 Cramer	Y	Y	Y	Y	Y
6 ***Bachus***	Y	Y	Y	Y	Y
7 Hilliard	Y	Y	N	Y	Y
ALASKA					
AL ***Young***	Y	Y	Y	Y	Y
ARIZONA					
1 ***Salmon***	Y	Y	?	Y	Y
2 Pastor	Y	Y	N	Y	Y
3 ***Stump***	Y	Y	Y	Y	Y
4 ***Shadegg***	Y	Y	Y	Y	Y
5 ***Kolbe***	Y	Y	Y	Y	Y
6 ***Hayworth***	Y	Y	Y	Y	Y
ARKANSAS					
1 Berry	Y	Y	Y	Y	Y
2 Snyder	Y	Y	Y	Y	Y
3 ***Hutchinson***	Y	Y	Y	Y	Y
4 ***Dickey***	Y	Y	Y	Y	Y
CALIFORNIA					
1 Thompson	Y	Y	+	Y	Y
2 ***Herger***	Y	Y	Y	Y	Y
3 ***Ose***	Y	Y	Y	Y	Y
4 ***Doolittle***	Y	Y	Y	Y	Y
5 Matsui	Y	Y	Y	Y	Y
6 Woolsey	Y	Y	N	Y	Y
7 Miller, George	Y	Y	N	Y	Y
8 Pelosi	Y	Y	N	Y	Y
9 Lee	Y	Y	N	Y	Y
10 Tauscher	Y	Y	Y	Y	Y
11 ***Pombo***	Y	Y	Y	Y	Y
12 Lantos	Y	Y	?	?	Y
13 Stark	Y	Y	N	Y	Y
14 Eshoo	Y	Y	Y	Y	Y
15 ***Campbell***	Y	Y	Y	Y	Y
16 Lofgren	Y	Y	Y	Y	Y
17 Farr	Y	Y	Y	Y	Y
18 Condit	Y	Y	Y	Y	Y
19 ***Radanovich***	Y	Y	Y	?	?
20 Dooley	Y	Y	Y	Y	Y
21 ***Thomas***	Y	Y	Y	Y	Y
22 Capps	Y	Y	Y	Y	Y
23 ***Gallegly***	Y	Y	Y	Y	Y
24 Sherman	Y	Y	Y	Y	Y
25 ***McKeon***	Y	Y	Y	Y	?
26 Berman	Y	Y	Y	Y	Y
27 ***Rogan***	Y	Y	Y	Y	Y
28 ***Dreier***	Y	Y	Y	Y	Y
29 Waxman	Y	Y	Y	Y	Y
30 Becerra	Y	Y	N	Y	Y
31 Martinez	Y	Y	N	Y	Y
32 Dixon	Y	Y	Y	Y	Y
33 Roybal-Allard	Y	Y	N	Y	Y
34 Napolitano	Y	Y	Y	Y	Y
35 Waters	Y	Y	N	Y	Y
36 ***Kuykendall***	Y	Y	Y	Y	Y
37 Millender-McD.	Y	Y	Y	Y	Y
38 ***Horn***	Y	Y	Y	Y	Y
39 ***Royce***	Y	Y	Y	Y	Y
40 ***Lewis***	Y	Y	Y	Y	Y
41 ***Miller, Gary***	Y	Y	Y	+	Y
42 Brown	Y	Y	Y	Y	?
43 ***Calvert***	Y	Y	Y	Y	Y
44 ***Bono***	Y	Y	Y	Y	Y
45 ***Rohrabacher***	Y	Y	Y	Y	Y
46 Sanchez	Y	Y	Y	Y	Y
47 ***Cox***	Y	?	Y	Y	Y
48 ***Packard***	Y	Y	Y	Y	Y
49 ***Bilbray***	Y	Y	Y	Y	Y
50 Filner	Y	Y	N	Y	Y
51 ***Cunningham***	Y	Y	Y	Y	Y
52 ***Hunter***	Y	Y	Y	Y	Y
COLORADO					
1 DeGette	Y	Y	Y	Y	Y
2 Udall	Y	Y	?	Y	Y
3 ***McInnis***	Y	Y	Y	Y	Y
4 ***Schaffer***	Y	Y	Y	Y	Y
5 ***Hefley***	Y	Y	Y	Y	Y
6 ***Tancredo***	Y	Y	Y	Y	?
CONNECTICUT					
1 Larson	Y	Y	Y	Y	Y
2 Gejdenson	Y	Y	Y	Y	Y
3 DeLauro	Y	Y	Y	Y	Y
4 ***Shays***	Y	Y	Y	Y	Y
5 Maloney	Y	Y	Y	Y	Y
6 ***Johnson***	Y	Y	Y	Y	Y
DELAWARE					
AL ***Castle***	Y	Y	Y	Y	Y
FLORIDA					
1 ***Scarborough***	Y	Y	Y	Y	Y
2 Boyd	Y	Y	Y	Y	Y
3 Brown	Y	Y	N	Y	?
4 ***Fowler***	Y	Y	Y	Y	Y
5 Thurman	Y	Y	Y	Y	Y
6 ***Stearns***	Y	Y	Y	Y	Y
7 ***Mica***	Y	Y	Y	Y	Y
8 ***McCollum***	?	?	Y	Y	Y
9 ***Bilirakis***	Y	Y	Y	Y	Y
10 ***Young***	Y	Y	Y	?	Y
11 Davis	Y	Y	Y	Y	Y
12 ***Canady***	Y	Y	Y	Y	Y
13 ***Miller***	Y	Y	Y	Y	Y
14 ***Goss***	Y	Y	Y	Y	Y
15 ***Weldon***	Y	Y	Y	Y	Y
16 ***Foley***	Y	Y	Y	Y	Y
17 Meek	Y	Y	N	Y	Y
18 ***Ros-Lehtinen***	Y	Y	Y	Y	Y
19 Wexler	Y	Y	Y	Y	Y
20 Deutsch	Y	Y	Y	Y	Y
21 ***Diaz-Balart***	Y	Y	Y	Y	Y
22 ***Shaw***	Y	Y	Y	Y	Y
23 Hastings	Y	Y	N	?	?
GEORGIA					
1 ***Kingston***	Y	Y	Y	Y	Y
2 Bishop	Y	Y	Y	Y	Y
3 ***Collins***	Y	Y	Y	Y	Y
4 McKinney	Y	Y	N	Y	Y
5 Lewis	Y	Y	N	Y	?
6 ***Isakson***	Y	Y	Y	Y	Y
7 ***Barr***	Y	Y	Y	Y	Y
8 ***Chambliss***	Y	Y	Y	Y	Y
9 ***Deal***	Y	Y	Y	?	Y
10 ***Norwood***	Y	Y	Y	Y	Y
11 ***Linder***	Y	Y	Y	Y	?
HAWAII					
1 Abercrombie	Y	Y	Y	Y	Y
2 Mink	Y	Y	N	Y	Y
IDAHO					
1 ***Chenoweth***	Y	?	Y	?	Y
2 ***Simpson***	Y	Y	Y	Y	Y
ILLINOIS					
1 Rush	Y	Y	N	Y	Y
2 Jackson	Y	Y	N	Y	Y
3 Lipinski	Y	Y	Y	Y	Y
4 Gutierrez	Y	Y	N	Y	Y
5 Blagojevich	Y	Y	Y	Y	Y
6 ***Hyde***	Y	Y	Y	Y	Y
7 Davis	Y	Y	N	Y	Y
8 ***Crane***	Y	Y	Y	Y	Y
9 Schakowsky	Y	Y	?	Y	Y
10 ***Porter***	Y	Y	Y	Y	Y
11 ***Weller***	Y	Y	Y	Y	Y
12 Costello	Y	Y	Y	Y	Y
13 ***Biggert***	Y	Y	Y	Y	Y
14 ***Hastert***	Y		Y		

ND Northern Democrats SD Southern Democrats

Member	92	93	94	95	96
15 ***Ewing***	?	?	Y	Y	Y
16 ***Manzullo***	Y	Y	Y	Y	Y
17 Evans	Y	Y	Y	Y	Y
18 ***LaHood***	Y	Y	Y	Y	Y
19 Phelps	Y	Y	Y	Y	Y
20 ***Shimkus***	Y	Y	Y	Y	Y
INDIANA					
1 Visclosky	Y	Y	Y	Y	Y
2 ***McIntosh***	Y	Y	Y	Y	Y
3 Roemer	Y	Y	Y	Y	Y
4 ***Souder***	Y	Y	Y	?	Y
5 ***Buyer***	Y	Y	Y	Y	Y
6 ***Burton***	Y	Y	Y	Y	Y
7 ***Pease***	Y	Y	Y	Y	Y
8 ***Hostettler***	Y	N	Y	Y	Y
9 Hill	Y	Y	Y	Y	Y
10 Carson	Y	Y	N	Y	Y
IOWA					
1 ***Leach***	Y	Y	Y	Y	Y
2 ***Nussle***	+	+	+	+	+
3 Boswell	Y	Y	Y	Y	Y
4 ***Ganske***	Y	Y	Y	Y	Y
5 ***Latham***	Y	Y	Y	Y	Y
KANSAS					
1 ***Moran***	Y	Y	Y	Y	Y
2 ***Ryun***	Y	Y	Y	Y	Y
3 Moore	Y	Y	Y	Y	?
4 ***Tiahrt***	Y	Y	Y	Y	Y
KENTUCKY					
1 ***Whitfield***	Y	Y	Y	Y	Y
2 ***Lewis***	Y	Y	Y	Y	Y
3 ***Northup***	Y	Y	Y	Y	Y
4 Lucas	Y	Y	Y	Y	Y
5 ***Rogers***	Y	Y	Y	Y	Y
6 ***Fletcher***	Y	Y	Y	Y	Y
LOUISIANA					
1 Vacant					
2 Jefferson	Y	Y	Y	Y	Y
3 ***Tauzin***	Y	Y	Y	Y	Y
4 ***McCrery***	Y	Y	Y	Y	Y
5 ***Cooksey***	Y	Y	Y	Y	Y
6 ***Baker***	Y	Y	Y	Y	Y
7 John	Y	Y	Y	Y	Y
MAINE					
1 Allen	Y	Y	Y	Y	Y
2 Baldacci	Y	Y	Y	Y	Y
MARYLAND					
1 ***Gilchrest***	Y	Y	Y	Y	Y
2 ***Ehrlich***	Y	Y	Y	Y	Y
3 Cardin	Y	Y	Y	Y	Y
4 Wynn	Y	Y	Y	Y	Y
5 Hoyer	Y	Y	Y	Y	Y
6 ***Bartlett***	Y	Y	Y	Y	Y
7 Cummings	Y	Y	N	Y	Y
8 ***Morella***	Y	Y	Y	Y	Y
MASSACHUSETTS					
1 Olver	Y	Y	N	Y	Y
2 Neal	Y	Y	Y	Y	Y
3 McGovern	Y	Y	Y	Y	Y
4 Frank	Y	Y	Y	Y	Y
5 Meehan	Y	Y	Y	Y	Y
6 Tierney	Y	Y	N	Y	Y
7 Markey	Y	Y	N	Y	Y
8 Capuano	Y	Y	Y	Y	Y
9 Moakley	Y	Y	Y	Y	Y
10 Delahunt	Y	Y	Y	Y	Y
MICHIGAN					
1 Stupak	Y	Y	Y	Y	Y
2 ***Hoekstra***	Y	Y	Y	Y	Y
3 ***Ehlers***	Y	Y	Y	Y	Y
4 ***Camp***	Y	Y	Y	Y	Y
5 Barcia	Y	Y	Y	Y	Y
6 ***Upton***	Y	Y	Y	Y	Y
7 ***Smith***	Y	Y	+	Y	Y
8 Stabenow	Y	Y	Y	Y	Y
9 Kildee	Y	Y	Y	Y	Y
10 Bonior	Y	Y	N	Y	Y
11 ***Knollenberg***	Y	Y	Y	Y	Y
12 Levin	Y	Y	Y	Y	Y
13 Rivers	Y	Y	N	Y	Y
14 Conyers	Y	Y	N	Y	Y
15 Kilpatrick	Y	Y	N	Y	Y
16 Dingell	Y	Y	N	Y	Y
MINNESOTA					
1 ***Gutknecht***	Y	Y	Y	Y	Y
2 Minge	Y	Y	Y	Y	Y
3 ***Ramstad***	Y	Y	Y	Y	Y
4 Vento	Y	Y	N	Y	Y
5 Sabo	Y	Y	Y	Y	Y
6 Luther	Y	Y	Y	Y	Y
7 Peterson	Y	Y	Y	Y	Y
8 Oberstar	Y	Y	Y	Y	Y
MISSISSIPPI					
1 ***Wicker***	Y	Y	Y	Y	Y
2 Thompson	Y	Y	N	Y	Y
3 ***Pickering***	Y	Y	Y	Y	Y
4 Shows	Y	Y	Y	Y	Y
5 Taylor	Y	?	Y	Y	Y
MISSOURI					
1 Clay	Y	Y	N	Y	Y
2 ***Talent***	Y	Y	Y	Y	Y
3 Gephardt	Y	Y	Y	Y	Y
4 Skelton	Y	Y	Y	Y	Y
5 McCarthy	Y	Y	Y	Y	Y
6 Danner	Y	Y	Y	Y	Y
7 ***Blunt***	Y	Y	Y	Y	Y
8 ***Emerson***	Y	Y	Y	Y	Y
9 ***Hulshof***	Y	Y	Y	Y	Y
MONTANA					
AL ***Hill***	Y	Y	Y	Y	Y
NEBRASKA					
1 ***Bereuter***	Y	Y	Y	Y	Y
2 ***Terry***	Y	Y	Y	Y	Y
3 ***Barrett***	Y	Y	Y	Y	Y
NEVADA					
1 Berkley	Y	Y	Y	Y	Y
2 ***Gibbons***	Y	Y	Y	Y	Y
NEW HAMPSHIRE					
1 ***Sununu***	Y	Y	Y	Y	Y
2 ***Bass***	Y	Y	Y	Y	Y
NEW JERSEY					
1 Andrews	Y	Y	Y	Y	Y
2 ***LoBiondo***	Y	Y	Y	Y	Y
3 ***Saxton***	+	+	+	+	?
4 ***Smith***	Y	Y	Y	Y	Y
5 ***Roukema***	Y	Y	Y	Y	Y
6 Pallone	Y	Y	Y	Y	Y
7 ***Franks***	Y	Y	Y	Y	Y
8 Pascrell	Y	Y	Y	Y	Y
9 Rothman	Y	Y	Y	Y	Y
10 Payne	Y	Y	N	Y	Y
11 ***Frelinghuysen***	Y	Y	Y	Y	Y
12 Holt	Y	Y	Y	Y	Y
13 Menendez	Y	Y	N	Y	Y
NEW MEXICO					
1 ***Wilson***	Y	Y	Y	Y	Y
2 ***Skeen***	Y	Y	Y	Y	Y
3 Udall	Y	Y	Y	Y	Y
NEW YORK					
1 ***Forbes***	?	?	Y	Y	Y
2 ***Lazio***	Y	Y	Y	Y	Y
3 ***King***	Y	Y	Y	Y	Y
4 McCarthy	Y	Y	+	Y	Y
5 Ackerman	Y	Y	Y	Y	Y
6 Meeks	Y	Y	N	Y	Y
7 Crowley	Y	Y	N	Y	Y
8 Nadler	Y	Y	N	Y	Y
9 Weiner	Y	Y	Y	Y	?
10 Towns	Y	Y	Y	Y	?
11 Owens	Y	Y	N	?	Y
12 Velázquez	Y	Y	N	Y	Y
13 ***Fossella***	Y	Y	Y	Y	Y
14 Maloney	Y	Y	Y	Y	Y
15 Rangel	Y	Y	Y	Y	Y
16 Serrano	?	?	N	Y	Y
17 Engel	Y	Y	N	Y	?
18 Lowey	Y	Y	Y	Y	Y
19 ***Kelly***	Y	Y	Y	Y	Y
20 ***Gilman***	Y	Y	Y	Y	Y
21 McNulty	Y	Y	Y	Y	Y
22 ***Sweeney***	Y	Y	Y	Y	Y
23 ***Boehlert***	?	Y	Y	Y	Y
24 ***McHugh***	Y	Y	Y	Y	Y
25 ***Walsh***	Y	Y	Y	Y	Y
26 Hinchey	Y	Y	N	Y	Y
27 ***Reynolds***	Y	Y	Y	Y	Y
28 Slaughter	Y	Y	Y	Y	Y
29 LaFalce	Y	Y	Y	Y	Y
30 ***Quinn***	Y	Y	Y	Y	Y
31 ***Houghton***	Y	Y	Y	Y	Y
NORTH CAROLINA					
1 Clayton	Y	Y	N	Y	Y
2 Etheridge	Y	Y	Y	Y	Y
3 ***Jones***	Y	Y	Y	Y	Y
4 Price	Y	Y	Y	Y	Y
5 ***Burr***	Y	Y	Y	Y	Y
6 ***Coble***	Y	Y	Y	Y	Y
7 McIntyre	Y	Y	Y	Y	Y
8 ***Hayes***	Y	Y	Y	Y	Y
9 ***Myrick***	Y	Y	Y	Y	Y
10 ***Ballenger***	Y	Y	Y	Y	Y
11 ***Taylor***	Y	Y	Y	Y	Y
12 Watt	Y	Y	N	Y	Y
NORTH DAKOTA					
AL Pomeroy	Y	Y	Y	Y	Y
OHIO					
1 ***Chabot***	Y	Y	Y	Y	Y
2 ***Portman***	Y	Y	Y	Y	Y
3 Hall	Y	Y	Y	Y	Y
4 ***Oxley***	Y	Y	Y	?	Y
5 ***Gillmor***	Y	Y	Y	Y	Y
6 Strickland	Y	Y	Y	Y	Y
7 ***Hobson***	Y	Y	Y	Y	Y
8 ***Boehner***	Y	Y	Y	Y	Y
9 Kaptur	Y	Y	Y	Y	Y
10 Kucinich	Y	Y	N	Y	Y
11 Jones	Y	Y	Y	Y	Y
12 ***Kasich***	+	+	Y	Y	+
13 Brown	Y	Y	Y	Y	Y
14 Sawyer	Y	Y	Y	Y	Y
15 ***Pryce***	Y	Y	Y	Y	Y
16 ***Regula***	Y	Y	Y	Y	Y
17 Traficant	Y	Y	Y	Y	Y
18 ***Ney***	Y	Y	Y	Y	Y
19 ***LaTourette***	Y	Y	Y	Y	Y
OKLAHOMA					
1 ***Largent***	Y	Y	Y	Y	Y
2 ***Coburn***	Y	Y	Y	Y	Y
3 ***Watkins***	Y	Y	Y	Y	Y
4 ***Watts***	Y	Y	Y	Y	Y
5 ***Istook***	Y	Y	Y	Y	Y
6 ***Lucas***	Y	Y	Y	Y	Y
OREGON					
1 Wu	Y	Y	Y	Y	Y
2 ***Walden***	Y	Y	Y	Y	Y
3 Blumenauer	Y	Y	Y	Y	Y
4 DeFazio	Y	Y	Y	Y	Y
5 Hooley	Y	Y	Y	Y	Y
PENNSYLVANIA					
1 Brady	Y	Y	N	Y	Y
2 Fattah	Y	Y	N	Y	Y
3 Borski	Y	Y	N	Y	Y
4 Klink	Y	Y	Y	?	Y
5 ***Peterson***	Y	Y	Y	Y	Y
6 Holden	Y	Y	Y	Y	Y
7 ***Weldon***	Y	Y	Y	Y	Y
8 ***Greenwood***	Y	Y	Y	Y	Y
9 ***Shuster***	Y	Y	Y	Y	Y
10 ***Sherwood***	Y	Y	Y	Y	Y
11 Kanjorski	Y	Y	Y	Y	Y
12 Murtha	Y	Y	Y	Y	Y
13 Hoeffel	Y	Y	Y	Y	Y
14 Coyne	Y	Y	N	Y	Y
15 ***Toomey***	Y	Y	Y	Y	Y
16 ***Pitts***	Y	Y	Y	Y	Y
17 ***Gekas***	?	Y	Y	+	Y
18 Doyle	Y	Y	Y	Y	Y
19 ***Goodling***	Y	Y	Y	Y	Y
20 Mascara	Y	Y	Y	Y	Y
21 ***English***	Y	Y	Y	Y	Y
RHODE ISLAND					
1 Kennedy	Y	Y	N	Y	Y
2 Weygand	Y	Y	Y	Y	Y
SOUTH CAROLINA					
1 ***Sanford***	Y	Y	Y	N	Y
2 ***Spence***	Y	Y	Y	Y	Y
3 ***Graham***	Y	Y	Y	Y	Y
4 ***DeMint***	Y	Y	Y	Y	Y
5 Spratt	Y	Y	Y	Y	Y
6 Clyburn	Y	Y	N	Y	Y
SOUTH DAKOTA					
AL ***Thune***	Y	Y	Y	Y	Y
TENNESSEE					
1 ***Jenkins***	Y	Y	Y	Y	Y
2 ***Duncan***	Y	Y	Y	N	Y
3 ***Wamp***	Y	Y	Y	Y	Y
4 ***Hilleary***	Y	Y	Y	Y	Y
5 Clement	Y	Y	Y	Y	Y
6 Gordon	Y	Y	Y	Y	Y
7 ***Bryant***	Y	Y	Y	Y	Y
8 Tanner	Y	Y	Y	Y	?
9 Ford	Y	Y	Y	Y	?
TEXAS					
1 Sandlin	Y	Y	Y	Y	Y
2 Turner	Y	Y	Y	Y	Y
3 ***Johnson, Sam***	Y	Y	Y	Y	Y
4 Hall	Y	Y	Y	Y	Y
5 ***Sessions***	Y	Y	Y	Y	Y
6 ***Barton***	Y	Y	Y	Y	Y
7 ***Archer***	Y	Y	Y	Y	Y
8 ***Brady***	Y	Y	Y	Y	Y
9 Lampson	Y	Y	Y	Y	Y
10 Doggett	Y	Y	Y	Y	Y
11 Edwards	Y	Y	Y	Y	Y
12 ***Granger***	Y	Y	Y	Y	Y
13 ***Thornberry***	Y	Y	Y	Y	Y
14 ***Paul***	N	N	Y	N	Y
15 Hinojosa	Y	Y	Y	Y	Y
16 Reyes	Y	Y	Y	Y	Y
17 Stenholm	Y	Y	Y	Y	Y
18 Jackson-Lee	Y	Y	Y	Y	Y
19 ***Combest***	Y	Y	Y	Y	Y
20 Gonzalez	Y	Y	Y	Y	Y
21 ***Smith***	Y	Y	Y	Y	Y
22 ***DeLay***	Y	Y	Y	Y	Y
23 ***Bonilla***	Y	Y	Y	Y	?
24 Frost	Y	Y	Y	Y	Y
25 Bentsen	Y	Y	Y	Y	Y
26 ***Armey***	Y	Y	Y	Y	Y
27 Ortiz	Y	Y	Y	Y	Y
28 Rodriguez	Y	Y	Y	Y	Y
29 Green	Y	Y	Y	Y	Y
30 Johnson, E.B.	Y	Y	Y	Y	Y
UTAH					
1 ***Hansen***	Y	Y	Y	Y	Y
2 ***Cook***	Y	Y	Y	Y	Y
3 ***Cannon***	Y	Y	Y	Y	Y
VERMONT					
AL *Sanders*	Y	Y	Y	Y	Y
VIRGINIA					
1 ***Bateman***	Y	Y	Y	Y	Y
2 Pickett	Y	Y	Y	Y	Y
3 Scott	Y	Y	N	Y	Y
4 Sisisky	Y	Y	Y	Y	Y
5 Goode	Y	Y	Y	Y	Y
6 ***Goodlatte***	Y	Y	Y	Y	Y
7 ***Bliley***	Y	Y	Y	Y	Y
8 Moran	Y	Y	Y	Y	Y
9 Boucher	Y	Y	Y	Y	Y
10 ***Wolf***	Y	Y	Y	Y	Y
11 ***Davis***	Y	Y	Y	Y	Y
WASHINGTON					
1 Inslee	Y	Y	Y	Y	Y
2 ***Metcalf***	Y	Y	Y	?	Y
3 Baird	Y	Y	Y	Y	Y
4 ***Hastings***	Y	Y	Y	Y	Y
5 ***Nethercutt***	Y	Y	Y	?	Y
6 Dicks	Y	Y	Y	Y	Y
7 McDermott	Y	Y	N	Y	Y
8 ***Dunn***	Y	Y	Y	Y	Y
9 Smith	Y	Y	Y	Y	Y
WEST VIRGINIA					
1 Mollohan	Y	Y	Y	Y	Y
2 Wise	Y	Y	Y	Y	Y
3 Rahall	Y	Y	Y	Y	?
WISCONSIN					
1 ***Ryan***	Y	Y	Y	Y	Y
2 Baldwin	Y	Y	Y	Y	Y
3 Kind	Y	Y	Y	Y	Y
4 Kleczka	Y	Y	Y	Y	Y
5 Barrett	Y	Y	Y	Y	Y
6 ***Petri***	Y	Y	Y	Y	Y
7 Obey	Y	Y	N	Y	Y
8 ***Green***	Y	Y	Y	Y	Y
9 ***Sensenbrenner***	Y	Y	Y	Y	Y
WYOMING					
AL ***Cubin***	Y	Y	Y	Y	Y

Southern states - Ala., Ark., Fla., Ga., Ky., La., Miss., N.C., Okla., S.C., Tenn., Texas, Va.

***House Votes* 97, 98, 99, 100, 101, 102, 103, 104**

97. HR 1554. Satellite Copyright, Competition and Consumer Protection Act/Passage. Armey, R-Texas, motion to suspend the rules and pass the bill that would allow satellite television companies to provide local programming immediately and require those that do so to carry the signals of all broadcasters in the market by 2002. The bill would extend for five years the satellite industry's authority to retransmit superstation and distant network signals and reduce the copyright fees they pay for such signals. And it would establish new standards to determine eligibility of satellite subscribers to receive distant network signals. Motion agreed to 422-1: R 218-0; D 203-1 (ND 150-1, SD 53-0); I 1-0. April 27, 1999. A two-thirds majority of those present and voting (282 in this case) is required for passage under suspension of the rules.

98. Procedural Motion/Journal. Approval of the House Journal of Tuesday, April 27, 1999. Approved 348-46: R 191-12; D 156-34 (ND 115-27, SD 41-7); I 1-0. April 28, 1999.

99. H Res 151. Kosovo Conflict/Rule. Adoption of the rule (H Res 151) to provide for House floor consideration of four separate measures regarding policy options in the current conflict over Kosovo: HR 1569, H Con Res 82, H J Res 44 and S Con Res 21. Adopted 213-210: R 213-2; D 0-207 (ND 0-153, SD 0-54); I 0-1. April 28, 1999.

100. HR 1569. Kosovo Conflict/Ground Forces/Passage. Passage of the bill to prohibit funds for U.S. ground forces in Yugoslavia without prior authorization by Congress. Passed 249-180: R 203-16; D 45-164 (ND 38-116, SD 7-48); I 1-0. April 28, 1999.

101. H Con Res 82. Kosovo Conflict/Removal of U.S. Troops/Adoption. Adoption of the concurrent resolution to direct the removal of U.S. armed forces from the conflict in Yugoslavia. Rejected 139-290: R 127-92; D 12-197 (ND 9-145, SD 3-52); I 0-1. April 28, 1999.

102. H J Res 44. Kosovo Conflict/Declaration of War/Passage. Passage of the joint resolution to declare war against the Federal Republic of Yugoslavia. Rejected 2-427: R 1-219; D 1-207 (ND 0-153, SD 1-54); I 0-1. April 28, 1999.

103. S Con Res 21. Kosovo Conflict/Air Operation/Adoption. Adoption of the concurrent resolution to authorize military air operations and missile strikes against Yugoslavia. Rejected 213-213: R 31-187; D 181-26 (ND 131-21, SD 50-5); I 1-0. April 28, 1999.

104. HR 1480. Water Resource Development Projects/Passage. Passage of the bill to authorize construction of water resource development projects by the U.S. Army Corps of Engineers for flood control, navigation (primarily dredging), beach erosion control and environmental restoration. It is estimated that the total cost of the projects authorized by the bill would be about $4.3 billion, with a federal cost of $3 billion. Passed 418-5: R 212-5; D 205-0 (ND 150-0, SD 55-0); I 1-0. April 29, 1999.

Key

Y Voted for (yea).
\# Paired for.
\+ Announced for.
N Voted against (nay).
X Paired against.
– Announced against.
P Voted "present."
C Voted "present" to avoid possible conflict of interest.
? Did not vote or otherwise make a position known.

•

Democrats ***Republicans***
Independents

	97	98	99	100	101	102	103	104
ALABAMA								
1 ***Callahan***	Y	Y	+	Y	N	N	Y	Y
2 ***Everett***	Y	Y	Y	Y	Y	N	N	Y
3 ***Riley***	Y	Y	Y	Y	N	N	Y	Y
4 ***Aderholt***	?	?	?	?	?	?	?	?
5 Cramer	Y	Y	N	Y	N	N	Y	Y
6 ***Bachus***	Y	Y	Y	Y	Y	N	N	Y
7 Hilliard	Y	Y	N	N	N	N	Y	Y
ALASKA								
AL ***Young***	Y	?	Y	Y	Y	N	N	Y
ARIZONA								
1 ***Salmon***	Y	?	Y	Y	Y	N	N	Y
2 Pastor	Y	Y	N	N	N	N	Y	Y
3 ***Stump***	Y	Y	Y	Y	Y	N	N	Y
4 ***Shadegg***	Y	Y	Y	Y	Y	N	N	Y
5 ***Kolbe***	Y	Y	Y	Y	N	N	Y	Y
6 ***Hayworth***	Y	Y	Y	Y	Y	N	N	Y
ARKANSAS								
1 Berry	Y	Y	N	N	N	N	Y	Y
2 Snyder	Y	Y	N	N	N	N	Y	Y
3 ***Hutchinson***	Y	N	Y	Y	N	N	N	Y
4 ***Dickey***	Y	Y	Y	Y	Y	N	N	Y
CALIFORNIA								
1 Thompson	Y	N	N	Y	N	N	Y	Y
2 ***Herger***	Y	Y	Y	Y	Y	N	N	Y
3 ***Ose***	Y	Y	Y	Y	Y	N	N	Y
4 ***Doolittle***	Y	Y	Y	Y	Y	N	N	Y
5 Matsui	Y	Y	N	N	N	N	Y	Y
6 Woolsey	Y	Y	N	N	N	N	N	Y
7 Miller, George	Y	N	N	Y	N	N	Y	Y
8 Pelosi	Y	Y	N	N	N	N	Y	Y
9 Lee	Y	Y	N	Y	Y	N	N	Y
10 Tauscher	Y	Y	N	N	N	N	Y	Y
11 ***Pombo***	Y	Y	Y	Y	Y	N	N	Y
12 Lantos	Y	Y	N	N	N	N	Y	Y
13 Stark	Y	Y	N	Y	Y	N	N	Y
14 Eshoo	Y	Y	N	N	N	N	Y	Y
15 ***Campbell***	Y	Y	Y	Y	Y	N	N	Y
16 Lofgren	Y	Y	N	Y	N	N	N	Y
17 Farr	Y	Y	N	N	N	N	Y	Y
18 Condit	Y	Y	N	Y	N	N	N	Y
19 ***Radanovich***	Y	Y	Y	Y	Y	N	N	Y
20 Dooley	Y	Y	N	N	N	N	Y	Y
21 ***Thomas***	Y	Y	Y	Y	Y	N	N	Y
22 Capps	Y	Y	N	N	N	N	Y	Y
23 ***Gallegly***	Y	Y	Y	Y	Y	N	N	Y
24 Sherman	Y	Y	N	Y	N	N	Y	Y
25 ***McKeon***	Y	Y	Y	Y	Y	N	N	Y
26 Berman	Y	Y	N	N	N	N	Y	Y
27 ***Rogan***	Y	Y	Y	Y	Y	N	N	Y
28 ***Dreier***	Y	Y	Y	N	N	N	N	Y
29 Waxman	Y	Y	N	N	N	N	Y	Y
30 Becerra	Y	Y	N	N	N	N	Y	Y
31 Martinez	Y	?	N	N	N	N	Y	Y
32 Dixon	Y	?	N	N	N	N	Y	Y
33 Roybal-Allard	Y	Y	N	N	N	N	Y	Y
34 Napolitano	Y	Y	N	N	N	N	Y	Y
35 Waters	Y	N	N	N	N	N	Y	Y
36 ***Kuykendall***	Y	Y	Y	Y	Y	N	N	Y
37 Millender-McD.	Y	Y	N	N	N	N	Y	Y
38 ***Horn***	Y	Y	Y	Y	Y	N	N	Y
39 ***Royce***	Y	Y	Y	Y	Y	N	N	Y
40 ***Lewis***	Y	Y	N	N	N	N	N	Y
41 ***Miller, Gary***	Y	Y	Y	Y	N	N	N	Y
42 Brown	?	N	N	N	N	N	Y	?
43 ***Calvert***	Y	Y	Y	Y	N	N	N	Y
44 ***Bono***	Y	Y	Y	N	N	N	N	Y
45 ***Rohrabacher***	Y	Y	Y	Y	Y	N	N	Y
46 Sanchez	Y	Y	N	N	N	N	Y	Y
47 ***Cox***	Y	?	Y	Y	N	N	N	Y
48 ***Packard***	Y	Y	Y	Y	Y	N	N	Y
49 ***Bilbray***	Y	Y	Y	Y	Y	N	N	Y
50 Filner	Y	N	N	N	N	N	Y	Y
51 ***Cunningham***	Y	Y	Y	Y	Y	N	N	Y
52 ***Hunter***	Y	Y	Y	N	N	N	Y	Y
COLORADO								
1 DeGette	Y	?	N	N	N	N	N	Y
2 Udall	Y	Y	N	Y	N	N	Y	Y
3 ***McInnis***	Y	Y	Y	Y	Y	N	N	Y
4 ***Schaffer***	Y	N	Y	Y	Y	N	N	Y
5 ***Hefley***	Y	N	Y	Y	Y	N	N	N
6 ***Tancredo***	Y	Y	Y	Y	Y	N	N	Y
CONNECTICUT								
1 Larson	Y	Y	N	N	N	N	Y	Y
2 Gejdenson	Y	Y	N	N	N	N	Y	Y
3 DeLauro	Y	Y	N	N	N	N	Y	Y
4 ***Shays***	Y	Y	Y	Y	N	N	N	Y
5 Maloney	Y	Y	N	N	N	N	Y	Y
6 ***Johnson***	Y	Y	Y	Y	N	N	N	Y
DELAWARE								
AL ***Castle***	Y	Y	Y	Y	N	N	Y	Y
FLORIDA								
1 ***Scarborough***	Y	Y	Y	Y	Y	N	N	Y
2 Boyd	Y	Y	N	N	N	N	Y	Y
3 Brown	Y	Y	N	N	N	N	Y	Y
4 ***Fowler***	Y	Y	Y	Y	Y	N	N	Y
5 Thurman	Y	Y	N	N	N	N	Y	Y
6 ***Stearns***	Y	Y	Y	Y	Y	N	N	Y
7 ***Mica***	Y	Y	Y	Y	Y	N	N	Y
8 ***McCollum***	Y	Y	Y	Y	Y	N	N	Y
9 ***Bilirakis***	Y	Y	Y	Y	Y	N	N	Y
10 ***Young***	Y	?	Y	?	N	N	N	?
11 Davis	Y	Y	N	N	N	N	Y	Y
12 ***Canady***	Y	Y	Y	Y	Y	N	N	Y
13 ***Miller***	Y	Y	Y	Y	Y	N	N	Y
14 ***Goss***	Y	Y	Y	Y	N	N	N	Y
15 ***Weldon***	Y	Y	Y	N	Y	N	N	Y
16 ***Foley***	Y	Y	Y	Y	Y	N	N	Y
17 Meek	Y	N	N	N	N	N	Y	Y
18 ***Ros-Lehtinen***	Y	Y	Y	Y	Y	N	N	Y
19 Wexler	Y	Y	N	N	N	N	Y	Y
20 Deutsch	Y	?	N	Y	N	N	Y	Y
21 ***Diaz-Balart***	Y	Y	Y	Y	N	N	Y	Y
22 ***Shaw***	Y	Y	Y	Y	N	N	N	Y
23 Hastings	Y	N	N	N	N	N	Y	Y
GEORGIA								
1 ***Kingston***	Y	?	Y	Y	Y	N	N	Y
2 Bishop	Y	Y	N	N	N	N	Y	Y
3 ***Collins***	Y	Y	Y	Y	Y	N	N	Y
4 McKinney	Y	?	N	Y	Y	N	N	Y
5 Lewis	Y	Y	N	N	N	N	Y	Y
6 ***Isakson***	Y	Y	Y	Y	N	N	N	Y
7 ***Barr***	Y	Y	?	Y	Y	N	N	Y
8 ***Chambliss***	Y	Y	Y	Y	N	N	N	Y
9 ***Deal***	Y	Y	Y	Y	Y	N	N	Y
10 ***Norwood***	Y	?	N	Y	Y	N	N	Y
11 ***Linder***	Y	Y	Y	Y	Y	N	N	Y
HAWAII								
1 Abercrombie	Y	Y	N	Y	N	N	N	Y
2 Mink	Y	Y	N	Y	Y	N	N	Y
IDAHO								
1 ***Chenoweth***	Y	?	Y	Y	Y	N	N	Y
2 ***Simpson***	Y	Y	Y	Y	Y	N	N	Y
ILLINOIS								
1 Rush	Y	Y	N	N	N	N	Y	Y
2 Jackson	Y	Y	N	Y	N	N	N	Y
3 Lipinski	Y	Y	N	Y	N	N	N	Y
4 Gutierrez	Y	N	N	N	N	N	Y	Y
5 Blagojevich	Y	Y	N	Y	N	?	?	?
6 ***Hyde***	Y	?	Y	Y	N	N	Y	Y
7 Davis	Y	Y	N	N	N	N	Y	Y
8 ***Crane***	Y	?	Y	Y	Y	N	N	Y
9 Schakowsky	Y	Y	N	Y	N	N	Y	Y
10 ***Porter***	Y	Y	Y	N	N	N	Y	Y
11 ***Weller***	Y	N	Y	Y	N	N	N	Y
12 Costello	Y	N	N	Y	N	N	Y	Y
13 ***Biggert***	Y	Y	Y	Y	Y	N	N	Y
14 ***Hastert***			Y	Y		N	Y	Y

ND Northern Democrats SD Southern Democrats

	97	98	99	100	101	102	103	104
15 ***Ewing***	Y	Y	Y	Y	Y	N	N	Y
16 ***Manzullo***	Y	Y	Y	Y	Y	N	N	Y
17 Evans	Y	Y	N	N	N	N	Y	Y
18 ***LaHood***	Y	Y	Y	Y	Y	N	N	Y
19 Phelps	Y	Y	N	Y	N	N	Y	Y
20 ***Shimkus***	Y	Y	Y	Y	Y	N	N	Y
INDIANA								
1 Visclosky	Y	N	N	Y	N	N	N	Y
2 ***McIntosh***	Y	Y	Y	Y	N	N	N	Y
3 Roemer	Y	Y	N	N	N	N	Y	Y
4 ***Souder***	Y	Y	Y	Y	Y	N	N	Y
5 ***Buyer***	Y	Y	Y	Y	N	N	N	Y
6 ***Burton***	Y	?	Y	Y	Y	N	N	Y
7 ***Pease***	Y	Y	Y	Y	Y	N	N	Y
8 ***Hostettler***	Y	Y	Y	Y	Y	N	N	Y
9 Hill	Y	Y	N	Y	N	N	Y	Y
10 Carson	Y	Y	N	N	N	N	Y	Y
IOWA								
1 ***Leach***	Y	Y	Y	Y	Y	N	N	Y
2 ***Nussle***	Y	Y	Y	Y	Y	N	N	Y
3 Boswell	Y	Y	N	N	N	N	Y	Y
4 ***Ganske***	Y	?	Y	Y	Y	N	N	Y
5 ***Latham***	Y	Y	Y	Y	Y	N	N	Y
KANSAS								
1 ***Moran***	Y	N	Y	Y	Y	N	N	Y
2 ***Ryun***	Y	Y	Y	Y	N	N	N	Y
3 Moore	Y	Y	N	N	N	N	Y	Y
4 ***Tiahrt***	Y	Y	Y	Y	N	N	N	Y
KENTUCKY								
1 ***Whitfield***	Y	?	Y	Y	N	N	N	Y
2 ***Lewis***	Y	Y	Y	Y	Y	N	N	Y
3 ***Northup***	Y	Y	Y	Y	N	N	N	Y
4 Lucas	Y	Y	N	Y	N	N	Y	Y
5 ***Rogers***	Y	Y	Y	Y	Y	N	N	Y
6 ***Fletcher***	Y	Y	Y	Y	N	N	N	Y
LOUISIANA								
1 Vacant								
2 Jefferson	Y	Y	N	N	N	N	Y	Y
3 ***Tauzin***	Y	?	?	?	?	?	?	?
4 ***McCrery***	Y	Y	Y	Y	Y	N	N	Y
5 ***Cooksey***	Y	Y	?	Y	Y	N	N	?
6 ***Baker***	Y	Y	Y	Y	Y	N	N	Y
7 John	Y	Y	N	N	N	N	Y	Y
MAINE								
1 Allen	Y	Y	N	N	N	N	Y	Y
2 Baldacci	Y	Y	N	N	N	N	Y	Y
MARYLAND								
1 ***Gilchrest***	Y	Y	Y	Y	N	N	Y	Y
2 ***Ehrlich***	Y	Y	Y	Y	N	N	N	Y
3 Cardin	Y	Y	N	N	N	N	Y	Y
4 Wynn	?	?	?	?	?	?	?	?
5 Hoyer	Y	?	N	N	N	N	Y	Y
6 ***Bartlett***	Y	Y	Y	Y	Y	N	N	Y
7 Cummings	Y	Y	N	N	N	N	Y	Y
8 ***Morella***	Y	Y	Y	N	N	N	Y	Y
MASSACHUSETTS								
1 Olver	Y	N	N	N	N	N	Y	Y
2 Neal	Y	Y	N	N	N	N	Y	Y
3 McGovern	Y	N	N	Y	N	N	Y	Y
4 Frank	Y	Y	N	Y	N	N	Y	Y
5 Meehan	Y	Y	N	N	N	N	Y	Y
6 Tierney	Y	Y	N	Y	N	N	Y	Y
7 Markey	Y	?	N	Y	N	N	Y	Y
8 Capuano	Y	Y	N	N	N	N	Y	Y
9 Moakley	Y	Y	N	N	N	N	Y	Y
10 Delahunt	Y	Y	N	N	N	N	Y	Y
MICHIGAN								
1 Stupak	Y	N	N	N	N	N	Y	Y
2 ***Hoekstra***	Y	Y	Y	Y	N	N	N	Y
3 ***Ehlers***	Y	Y	Y	Y	N	N	N	Y
4 ***Camp***	Y	Y	Y	Y	Y	N	N	Y
5 Barcia	Y	Y	N	Y	N	N	Y	Y
6 ***Upton***	Y	Y	Y	Y	Y	N	N	Y
7 ***Smith***	Y	Y	Y	Y	N	N	N	+
8 Stabenow	Y	Y	N	N	N	N	Y	Y
9 Kildee	Y	Y	N	N	N	N	Y	Y
10 Bonior	Y	N	N	N	N	N	Y	Y
11 ***Knollenberg***	Y	Y	Y	Y	N	N	Y	Y
12 Levin	Y	Y	N	N	N	N	Y	Y
13 Rivers	Y	Y	N	Y	Y	N	N	Y
14 Conyers	Y	Y	N	N	N	N	Y	Y
15 Kilpatrick	Y	Y	N	N	N	N	Y	Y
16 Dingell	Y	Y	N	N	N	N	Y	Y

	97	98	99	100	101	102	103	104
MINNESOTA								
1 ***Gutknecht***	Y	N	Y	Y	Y	N	N	Y
2 Minge	Y	Y	N	N	N	N	Y	Y
3 ***Ramstad***	Y	N	Y	Y	Y	Y	N	Y
4 Vento	Y	Y	N	N	N	N	Y	Y
5 Sabo	Y	N	N	N	N	N	Y	Y
6 Luther	Y	Y	N	N	N	N	Y	Y
7 Peterson	Y	N	N	Y	Y	Y	N	Y
8 Oberstar	Y	N	N	N	N	N	Y	Y
MISSISSIPPI								
1 ***Wicker***	Y	Y	Y	Y	Y	N	N	Y
2 Thompson	Y	N	N	N	N	N	Y	Y
3 ***Pickering***	Y	Y	Y	Y	Y	N	N	Y
4 Shows	Y	Y	N	N	N	N	Y	Y
5 Taylor	Y	?	N	N	N	Y	N	Y
MISSOURI								
1 Clay	Y	N	N	N	N	N	Y	Y
2 ***Talent***	Y	N	Y	Y	Y	N	N	Y
3 Gephardt	Y	N	N	N	N	N	Y	Y
4 Skelton	Y	Y	N	N	N	N	Y	Y
5 McCarthy	Y	Y	N	N	N	N	Y	Y
6 Danner	Y	Y	N	Y	Y	N	N	Y
7 ***Blunt***	Y	Y	Y	Y	Y	N	N	Y
8 ***Emerson***	Y	Y	Y	Y	N	N	N	Y
9 ***Hulshof***	Y	N	Y	Y	Y	N	N	Y
MONTANA								
AL ***Hill***	Y	Y	Y	Y	Y	N	N	Y
NEBRASKA								
1 ***Bereuter***	Y	Y	Y	Y	N	N	N	Y
2 ***Terry***	Y	Y	Y	Y	Y	N	N	Y
3 ***Barrett***	Y	Y	Y	Y	N	N	N	Y
NEVADA								
1 Berkley	Y	Y	N	N	N	N	Y	Y
2 ***Gibbons***	Y	N	Y	Y	Y	N	N	Y
NEW HAMPSHIRE								
1 ***Sununu***	Y	Y	Y	Y	Y	N	N	N
2 ***Bass***	Y	Y	Y	Y	Y	N	N	Y
NEW JERSEY								
1 Andrews	Y	Y	N	N	N	N	Y	Y
2 ***LoBiondo***	Y	N	Y	Y	N	N	N	Y
3 ***Saxton***	Y	Y	Y	Y	N	N	N	Y
4 ***Smith***	Y	Y	Y	Y	N	N	N	Y
5 ***Roukema***	Y	Y	Y	Y	N	N	N	Y
6 Pallone	Y	N	N	N	N	N	Y	Y
7 ***Franks***	Y	Y	Y	Y	N	N	N	Y
8 Pascrell	Y	Y	N	N	N	N	Y	Y
9 Rothman	Y	N	N	N	N	N	Y	Y
10 Payne	Y	Y	N	N	N	N	Y	Y
11 ***Frelinghuysen***	Y	Y	Y	Y	N	N	N	Y
12 Holt	Y	Y	N	N	N	N	Y	Y
13 Menendez	Y	Y	N	N	N	N	Y	Y
NEW MEXICO								
1 ***Wilson***	Y	Y	Y	Y	Y	N	N	Y
2 ***Skeen***	Y	Y	Y	Y	Y	N	N	Y
3 Udall	Y	Y	N	Y	N	N	Y	Y
NEW YORK								
1 ***Forbes***	Y	Y	Y	N	N	N	Y	Y
2 ***Lazio***	Y	Y	Y	Y	N	N	N	Y
3 ***King***	Y	Y	Y	Y	N	N	N	Y
4 McCarthy	Y	Y	N	N	N	N	Y	Y
5 Ackerman	Y	Y	N	N	N	N	Y	Y
6 Meeks	Y	?	N	N	N	N	Y	Y
7 Crowley	Y	Y	N	N	N	N	Y	Y
8 Nadler	Y	Y	N	N	N	N	Y	Y
9 Weiner	Y	Y	N	N	N	N	Y	Y
10 Towns	Y	Y	N	N	N	N	N	Y
11 Owens	Y	?	N	N	N	N	Y	Y
12 Velazquez	Y	?	N	N	N	N	Y	Y
13 ***Fossella***	Y	Y	Y	Y	N	N	N	Y
14 Maloney	Y	Y	N	N	N	N	Y	Y
15 Rangel	?	?	N	N	N	N	Y	Y
16 Serrano	Y	Y	N	Y	Y	N	N	Y
17 Engel	?	?	?	N	N	N	Y	?
18 Lowey	Y	Y	N	N	N	N	Y	Y
19 ***Kelly***	Y	Y	Y	Y	N	N	N	Y
20 ***Gilman***	Y	Y	Y	Y	N	N	Y	Y
21 McNulty	Y	N	N	N	N	N	Y	Y
22 ***Sweeney***	Y	N	Y	Y	Y	N	N	Y
23 ***Boehlert***	Y	Y	Y	N	N	N	Y	Y
24 ***McHugh***	Y	Y	Y	Y	N	N	Y	Y
25 ***Walsh***	Y	Y	Y	Y	N	N	Y	Y
26 Hinchey	Y	N	N	N	N	N	Y	Y
27 ***Reynolds***	Y	Y	Y	Y	N	N	N	Y
28 Slaughter	+	+	–	–	–	–	+	+
29 LaFalce	Y	Y	N	N	N	N	Y	Y

	97	98	99	100	101	102	103	104
30 ***Quinn***	Y	Y	Y	Y	N	N	Y	Y
31 ***Houghton***	Y	Y	Y	N	N	N	Y	Y
NORTH CAROLINA								
1 Clayton	Y	Y	N	N	N	N	Y	Y
2 Etheridge	Y	Y	N	N	N	N	Y	Y
3 ***Jones***	Y	Y	Y	Y	Y	N	N	Y
4 Price	Y	Y	N	N	N	N	Y	Y
5 ***Burr***	Y	Y	Y	Y	Y	N	N	Y
6 ***Coble***	Y	Y	Y	Y	Y	N	N	Y
7 McIntyre	Y	Y	N	Y	N	N	Y	Y
8 ***Hayes***	Y	Y	Y	Y	N	N	Y	Y
9 ***Myrick***	Y	Y	Y	Y	Y	N	N	Y
10 ***Ballenger***	Y	Y	Y	Y	N	N	N	Y
11 ***Taylor***	Y	Y	Y	Y	N	N	N	Y
12 Watt	Y	Y	N	N	N	N	Y	Y
NORTH DAKOTA								
AL Pomeroy	Y	Y	N	N	N	N	Y	Y
OHIO								
1 ***Chabot***	Y	Y	Y	Y	Y	N	N	Y
2 ***Portman***	Y	Y	Y	Y	N	N	N	Y
3 Hall	Y	Y	N	N	N	N	Y	Y
4 ***Oxley***	Y	Y	Y	Y	N	N	Y	Y
5 ***Gillmor***	Y	Y	Y	N	N	N	N	Y
6 Strickland	Y	Y	N	N	N	N	Y	?
7 ***Hobson***	Y	Y	Y	Y	N	N	N	Y
8 ***Boehner***	Y	Y	Y	Y	N	N	N	Y
9 Kaptur	Y	Y	N	Y	N	N	Y	Y
10 Kucinich	Y	N	N	Y	Y	N	N	Y
11 Jones	Y	Y	N	N	N	N	Y	Y
12 ***Kasich***	Y	Y	Y	Y	N	N	N	Y
13 Brown	Y	N	N	N	N	N	Y	Y
14 Sawyer	Y	Y	N	N	N	N	Y	Y
15 ***Pryce***	?	Y	Y	Y	N	N	N	Y
16 ***Regula***	Y	Y	Y	Y	N	N	N	Y
17 Traficant	Y	Y	N	Y	N	N	Y	Y
18 ***Ney***	Y	Y	Y	Y	Y	N	N	Y
19 ***LaTourette***	Y	Y	Y	Y	N	N	N	Y
OKLAHOMA								
1 ***Largent***	Y	Y	Y	Y	Y	N	N	Y
2 ***Coburn***	Y	?	?	Y	Y	N	N	Y
3 ***Watkins***	Y	Y	Y	Y	N	N	N	Y
4 ***Watts***	Y	Y	Y	Y	Y	N	N	Y
5 ***Istook***	Y	Y	Y	Y	Y	N	N	Y
6 ***Lucas***	Y	Y	Y	Y	Y	N	N	Y
OREGON								
1 Wu	Y	Y	N	N	N	N	Y	Y
2 ***Walden***	Y	Y	Y	Y	Y	N	N	Y
3 Blumenauer	Y	Y	N	N	N	N	Y	Y
4 DeFazio	Y	N	N	Y	N	N	Y	Y
5 Hooley	Y	Y	N	N	N	N	Y	Y
PENNSYLVANIA								
1 Brady	N	Y	N	N	N	N	Y	Y
2 Fattah	Y	?	N	N	N	N	Y	Y
3 Borski	Y	N	N	N	N	N	Y	Y
4 Klink	Y	?	N	N	N	N	Y	Y
5 ***Peterson***	Y	Y	Y	Y	Y	N	N	Y
6 Holden	Y	Y	N	N	N	N	Y	Y
7 ***Weldon***	Y	Y	Y	Y	N	N	N	Y
8 ***Greenwood***	Y	Y	Y	Y	N	N	Y	Y
9 ***Shuster***	Y	Y	Y	Y	Y	N	?	Y
10 ***Sherwood***	Y	Y	Y	Y	N	N	N	Y
11 Kanjorski	Y	Y	N	N	N	N	Y	Y
12 Murtha	Y	Y	N	N	N	N	Y	Y
13 Hoeffel	Y	Y	N	N	N	N	Y	Y
14 Coyne	Y	Y	N	N	N	N	Y	Y
15 ***Toomey***	Y	Y	Y	Y	N	N	N	Y
16 ***Pitts***	Y	Y	Y	Y	Y	N	N	Y
17 ***Gekas***	Y	Y	Y	Y	N	N	N	Y
18 Doyle	Y	Y	N	Y	N	N	Y	Y
19 ***Goodling***	Y	Y	Y	Y	Y	N	N	Y
20 Mascara	Y	Y	N	N	N	N	Y	Y
21 ***English***	Y	?	Y	Y	Y	N	N	Y
RHODE ISLAND								
1 Kennedy	Y	N	N	N	N	N	Y	Y
2 Weygand	Y	Y	N	N	N	N	Y	Y
SOUTH CAROLINA								
1 ***Sanford***	Y	Y	Y	Y	Y	N	N	N
2 ***Spence***	Y	Y	Y	Y	N	N	N	Y
3 ***Graham***	Y	Y	Y	Y	N	N	N	Y
4 ***DeMint***	Y	Y	Y	Y	Y	N	N	Y
5 Spratt	Y	Y	N	N	N	N	Y	Y
6 Clyburn	?	N	N	N	N	N	Y	Y
SOUTH DAKOTA								
AL ***Thune***	Y	Y	Y	Y	Y	N	N	Y

	97	98	99	100	101	102	103	104
TENNESSEE								
1 ***Jenkins***	Y	Y	Y	Y	Y	N	N	Y
2 ***Duncan***	Y	Y	Y	Y	Y	N	N	Y
3 ***Wamp***	Y	Y	Y	Y	Y	N	N	Y
4 ***Hilleary***	Y	Y	Y	Y	Y	N	N	Y
5 Clement	Y	Y	N	N	N	N	Y	Y
6 Gordon	Y	?	N	N	N	N	Y	Y
7 ***Bryant***	Y	Y	Y	Y	Y	N	N	Y
8 Tanner	Y	Y	N	N	N	N	Y	Y
9 Ford	Y	N	N	N	N	N	Y	Y
TEXAS								
1 Sandlin	Y	?	N	N	N	N	Y	Y
2 Turner	Y	Y	N	N	N	N	Y	Y
3 ***Johnson, Sam***	Y	Y	Y	Y	Y	N	N	Y
4 Hall	Y	Y	N	Y	Y	N	N	Y
5 ***Sessions***	Y	Y	Y	Y	Y	N	N	Y
6 ***Barton***	Y	?	Y	Y	Y	Y	N	Y
7 ***Archer***	Y	?	?	Y	Y	N	N	Y
8 ***Brady***	Y	Y	Y	Y	Y	N	N	Y
9 Lampson	Y	Y	N	N	N	N	Y	Y
10 Doggett	Y	Y	N	N	N	N	N	Y
11 Edwards	Y	?	N	N	N	N	Y	Y
12 ***Granger***	Y	Y	Y	Y	N	N	N	Y
13 ***Thornberry***	Y	Y	Y	Y	N	N	N	Y
14 ***Paul***	P	Y	Y	Y	Y	N	N	N
15 Hinojosa	Y	Y	N	N	N	N	Y	Y
16 Reyes	Y	Y	N	N	N	N	Y	Y
17 Stenholm	Y	N	N	N	N	N	Y	Y
18 Jackson-Lee	Y	Y	N	N	N	N	Y	Y
19 ***Combest***	Y	Y	Y	Y	Y	N	N	Y
20 Gonzalez	Y	Y	N	N	N	N	Y	Y
21 ***Smith***	Y	Y	Y	Y	Y	N	N	Y
22 ***DeLay***	Y	Y	Y	Y	Y	N	N	Y
23 ***Bonilla***	Y	Y	Y	Y	Y	N	N	Y
24 Frost	Y	Y	N	N	N	N	Y	Y
25 Bentsen	Y	Y	N	N	N	N	Y	Y
26 ***Armey***	Y	Y	Y	Y	N	N	N	Y
27 Ortiz	Y	Y	N	N	N	N	Y	Y
28 Rodriguez	Y	Y	N	N	N	N	Y	Y
29 Green	Y	Y	N	N	N	N	Y	Y
30 Johnson, E.B.	Y	Y	N	N	N	N	Y	Y
UTAH								
1 ***Hansen***	Y	Y	Y	Y	Y	N	?	Y
2 ***Cook***	Y	Y	Y	Y	Y	N	N	Y
3 ***Cannon***	Y	Y	Y	Y	Y	N	N	Y
VERMONT								
AL *Sanders*	Y	Y	N	Y	N	N	Y	Y
VIRGINIA								
1 ***Bateman***	Y	Y	Y	N	N	N	N	Y
2 Pickett	Y	N	N	N	N	N	Y	Y
3 Scott	Y	Y	N	N	N	N	Y	Y
4 Sisisky	Y	Y	N	N	N	N	Y	Y
5 Goode	Y	Y	N	Y	Y	N	N	Y
6 ***Goodlatte***	Y	Y	Y	Y	Y	N	N	Y
7 ***Bliley***	Y	Y	Y	Y	N	N	Y	Y
8 Moran	?	?	?	N	N	N	Y	Y
9 Boucher	Y	Y	N	N	N	N	Y	Y
10 ***Wolf***	Y	Y	Y	N	N	N	Y	Y
11 ***Davis***	Y	Y	Y	Y	N	N	Y	Y
WASHINGTON								
1 Inslee	Y	Y	N	Y	N	N	Y	Y
2 ***Metcalf***	Y	Y	Y	Y	Y	N	N	Y
3 Baird	Y	Y	N	N	N	N	Y	Y
4 ***Hastings***	Y	Y	Y	Y	Y	N	N	Y
5 ***Nethercutt***	Y	Y	Y	Y	Y	N	N	Y
6 Dicks	Y	Y	N	N	N	N	Y	Y
7 McDermott	Y	N	N	Y	N	N	Y	Y
8 ***Dunn***	Y	Y	Y	Y	Y	N	N	Y
9 Smith	Y	Y	N	N	N	N	Y	Y
WEST VIRGINIA								
1 Mollohan	Y	Y	N	N	N	N	?	Y
2 Wise	Y	Y	N	N	N	N	Y	Y
3 Rahall	Y	Y	N	N	N	N	Y	Y
WISCONSIN								
1 ***Ryan***	Y	Y	Y	Y	Y	N	N	Y
2 Baldwin	Y	Y	N	Y	N	N	N	Y
3 Kind	Y	Y	N	N	N	N	Y	Y
4 Kleczka	Y	Y	N	Y	N	N	N	Y
5 Barrett	Y	Y	N	Y	N	N	Y	Y
6 ***Petri***	Y	Y	Y	Y	Y	N	N	Y
7 Obey	Y	Y	N	N	N	N	Y	Y
8 ***Green***	Y	Y	Y	Y	Y	N	N	Y
9 ***Sensenbrenner***	Y	Y	Y	Y	Y	N	N	N
WYOMING								
AL ***Cubin***	Y	Y	Y	Y	Y	N	N	Y

Southern states - Ala., Ark., Fla., Ga., Ky., La., Miss., N.C., Okla., S.C., Tenn., Texas, Va.

105. H Con Res 84. Full Funding for Education for Disabled Children/Adoption. Goodling, R-Pa., motion to suspend the rules and adopt the concurrent resolution to urge the Congress and the president to fully fund education programs for the disabled. Motion agreed to 413-2: R 209-1; D 203-1 (ND 148-1, SD 55-0); I 1-0. May 4, 1999. A two-thirds majority of those present and voting (277 in this case) is required for adoption under suspension of the rules.

106. H Con Res 88. Funding Pell Grant Program/Adoption. McKeon, R-Calif., motion to suspend the rules and adopt the concurrent resolution to urge the Congress and president to increase funding for the Pell grant student aid program. Motion agreed to 397-13: R 207-2; D 189-11 (ND 139-7, SD 50-4); I 1-0. May 4, 1999. A two-thirds majority of those present and voting (274 in this case) is required for adoption under suspension of the rules.

107. H Res 157. Support America's Teachers/Adoption. Isakson, R-Ga., motion to suspend the rules and adopt the resolution to express support for the country's teachers. Motion agreed to 408-1: R 204-1; D 203-0 (ND 149-0, SD 54-0); I 1-0. May 4, 1999. A two-thirds majority of those present and voting (273 in this case) is required for adoption under suspension of the rules.

108. Procedural Motion/Journal. Approval of the House Journal of Tuesday, May 4, 1999. Approved 359-41: R 192-11; D 167-30 (ND 123-21, SD 44-9); I 0-0. May 5, 1999.

109. HR 833. Bankruptcy Overhaul/Previous Question. Sessions, R-Texas, motion to order the previous question (thus ending debate and the possibility of amendment) on adoption of the rule (H Res 158) to provide for House floor consideration of the bill to overhaul U.S. bankruptcy regulations. Motion agreed to 227-190: R 214-0; D 13-189 (ND 7-141, SD 6-48); I 0-1. May 5, 1999. (Subsequently, the rule was adopted by voice vote.)

Key

- Y Voted for (yea).
- # Paired for.
- \+ Announced for.
- N Voted against (nay).
- X Paired against.
- – Announced against.
- P Voted "present."
- C Voted "present" to avoid possible conflict of interest.
- ? Did not vote or otherwise make a position known.

•

Democrats ***Republicans***
Independents

	105	106	107	108	109
ALABAMA					
1 ***Callahan***	Y	Y	Y	Y	Y
2 ***Everett***	Y	Y	Y	Y	Y
3 ***Riley***	Y	Y	Y	Y	Y
4 ***Aderholt***	Y	Y	Y	N	Y
5 Cramer	Y	Y	Y	Y	Y
6 ***Bachus***	Y	Y	Y	Y	Y
7 Hilliard	Y	N	Y	N	N
ALASKA					
AL ***Young***	Y	Y	Y	?	Y
ARIZONA					
1 ***Salmon***	Y	Y	N	Y	Y
2 Pastor	Y	Y	Y	Y	N
3 ***Stump***	Y	Y	Y	Y	Y
4 ***Shadegg***	Y	Y	Y	Y	Y
5 ***Kolbe***	Y	Y	Y	Y	Y
6 ***Hayworth***	Y	Y	Y	Y	Y
ARKANSAS					
1 Berry	Y	Y	Y	Y	N
2 Snyder	Y	Y	?	Y	N
3 ***Hutchinson***	Y	Y	Y	?	Y
4 ***Dickey***	Y	Y	Y	?	Y
CALIFORNIA					
1 Thompson	Y	Y	Y	N	N
2 ***Herger***	Y	Y	Y	Y	Y
3 ***Ose***	Y	Y	Y	Y	Y
4 ***Doolittle***	Y	Y	Y	Y	Y
5 Matsui	Y	Y	Y	Y	N
6 Woolsey	Y	Y	Y	Y	N
7 Miller, George	Y	Y	Y	N	N
8 Pelosi	Y	Y	Y	Y	N
9 Lee	Y	Y	Y	N	N
10 Tauscher	Y	Y	Y	Y	N
11 ***Pombo***	Y	Y	Y	Y	Y
12 Lantos	Y	Y	Y	Y	N
13 Stark	Y	Y	Y	Y	N
14 Eshoo	Y	Y	Y	Y	Y
15 ***Campbell***	Y	Y	Y	Y	Y
16 Lofgren	Y	Y	Y	Y	N
17 Farr	Y	Y	Y	?	N
18 Condit	Y	Y	Y	Y	N
19 ***Radanovich***	Y	Y	Y	Y	Y
20 Dooley	Y	Y	Y	Y	N
21 ***Thomas***	Y	Y	Y	Y	Y
22 Capps	Y	Y	Y	Y	N
23 ***Gallegly***	Y	Y	Y	Y	Y
24 Sherman	Y	Y	Y	Y	N
25 ***McKeon***	Y	Y	Y	Y	Y
26 Berman	?	?	?	?	?
27 ***Rogan***	Y	Y	Y	Y	Y
28 ***Dreier***	Y	Y	Y	Y	Y
29 Waxman	Y	Y	Y	Y	?
30 Becerra	Y	P	Y	+	–
31 Martinez	Y	P	Y	Y	N
32 Dixon	Y	Y	Y	Y	N
33 Roybal-Allard	Y	Y	Y	Y	N
34 Napolitano	Y	Y	Y	Y	N
35 Waters	Y	N	Y	N	N
36 ***Kuykendall***	Y	Y	Y	Y	Y
37 Millender-McD.	Y	Y	Y	Y	N
38 ***Horn***	Y	Y	Y	Y	Y
39 ***Royce***	Y	Y	Y	Y	Y
40 ***Lewis***	Y	Y	Y	Y	Y
41 ***Miller, Gary***	Y	Y	Y	Y	Y
42 Brown	?	?	?	?	?
43 ***Calvert***	Y	Y	Y	Y	Y
44 ***Bono***	Y	Y	Y	Y	Y
45 ***Rohrabacher***	Y	Y	Y	Y	Y
46 Sanchez	Y	Y	Y	Y	N
47 ***Cox***	Y	Y	?	Y	Y
48 ***Packard***	Y	Y	Y	Y	Y
49 ***Bilbray***	Y	Y	Y	Y	Y
50 Filner	Y	Y	Y	N	N
51 ***Cunningham***	Y	Y	Y	Y	Y
52 ***Hunter***	Y	Y	Y	Y	Y
COLORADO					
1 DeGette	Y	Y	Y	Y	N
2 Udall	Y	Y	Y	Y	N
3 ***McInnis***	Y	Y	Y	Y	Y
4 ***Schaffer***	Y	Y	Y	N	Y
5 ***Hefley***	Y	Y	Y	N	Y
6 ***Tancredo***	Y	Y	Y	Y	Y
CONNECTICUT					
1 Larson	Y	Y	Y	Y	N
2 Gejdenson	Y	Y	Y	Y	N
3 DeLauro	Y	Y	Y	Y	N
4 ***Shays***	Y	Y	Y	Y	Y
5 Maloney	Y	Y	Y	Y	N
6 ***Johnson***	?	?	?	Y	Y
DELAWARE					
AL ***Castle***	Y	Y	Y	Y	Y
FLORIDA					
1 ***Scarborough***	Y	Y	Y	?	Y
2 Boyd	Y	Y	Y	Y	Y
3 Brown	Y	Y	Y	Y	N
4 ***Fowler***	Y	Y	Y	Y	Y
5 Thurman	Y	Y	Y	Y	N
6 ***Stearns***	Y	Y	Y	Y	Y
7 ***Mica***	Y	Y	?	Y	Y
8 ***McCollum***	Y	Y	Y	Y	Y
9 ***Bilirakis***	Y	Y	Y	Y	Y
10 ***Young***	Y	Y	Y	?	?
11 Davis	Y	Y	Y	Y	?
12 ***Canady***	Y	Y	Y	Y	Y
13 ***Miller***	Y	Y	Y	Y	Y
14 ***Goss***	Y	Y	Y	Y	Y
15 ***Weldon***	Y	Y	Y	Y	Y
16 ***Foley***	Y	Y	Y	Y	Y
17 Meek	Y	Y	Y	Y	N
18 ***Ros-Lehtinen***	Y	Y	Y	Y	Y
19 Wexler	Y	Y	Y	Y	N
20 Deutsch	Y	Y	Y	Y	N
21 ***Diaz-Balart***	Y	Y	?	Y	Y
22 ***Shaw***	Y	Y	Y	Y	Y
23 Hastings	Y	Y	Y	N	N
GEORGIA					
1 ***Kingston***	Y	Y	Y	Y	Y
2 Bishop	Y	Y	Y	?	N
3 ***Collins***	Y	Y	Y	Y	Y
4 McKinney	Y	Y	Y	Y	N
5 Lewis	Y	Y	Y	N	N
6 ***Isakson***	Y	Y	Y	Y	Y
7 ***Barr***	Y	Y	Y	Y	Y
8 ***Chambliss***	Y	Y	Y	Y	Y
9 ***Deal***	Y	Y	Y	Y	Y
10 ***Norwood***	Y	Y	Y	Y	Y
11 ***Linder***	Y	Y	Y	Y	Y
HAWAII					
1 Abercrombie	Y	Y	Y	Y	N
2 Mink	Y	Y	Y	Y	N
IDAHO					
1 ***Chenoweth***	Y	Y	Y	Y	Y
2 ***Simpson***	?	?	?	?	?
ILLINOIS					
1 Rush	Y	Y	Y	N	N
2 Jackson	Y	Y	Y	Y	N
3 Lipinski	Y	Y	Y	Y	N
4 Gutierrez	Y	Y	Y	?	N
5 Blagojevich	Y	Y	Y	Y	N
6 ***Hyde***	Y	Y	Y	?	Y
7 Davis	Y	Y	Y	Y	N
8 ***Crane***	Y	Y	Y	Y	Y
9 Schakowsky	Y	Y	Y	Y	Y
10 ***Porter***	Y	Y	Y	Y	Y
11 ***Weller***	Y	Y	Y	N	Y
12 Costello	Y	Y	Y	N	N
13 ***Biggert***	Y	Y	Y	Y	Y
14 ***Hastert***					

ND Northern Democrats SD Southern Democrats

	105	106	107	108	109
15 ***Ewing***	Y	Y	Y	Y	Y
16 ***Manzullo***	Y	Y	Y	Y	Y
17 Evans	Y	Y	Y	Y	N
18 ***LaHood***	Y	Y	Y	Y	Y
19 Phelps	Y	Y	Y	Y	N
20 ***Shimkus***	Y	Y	Y	Y	Y
INDIANA					
1 Visclosky	Y	Y	Y	N	N
2 ***McIntosh***	Y	Y	Y	Y	Y
3 Roemer	Y	Y	Y	Y	N
4 ***Souder***	Y	Y	Y	Y	Y
5 ***Buyer***	Y	Y	Y	Y	Y
6 ***Burton***	Y	Y	Y	Y	Y
7 ***Pease***	Y	Y	Y	Y	Y
8 ***Hostettler***	Y	Y	Y	Y	Y
9 Hill	Y	Y	Y	Y	N
10 Carson	+	+	+	?	–
IOWA					
1 ***Leach***	Y	Y	Y	Y	Y
2 ***Nussle***	Y	Y	Y	Y	Y
3 Boswell	Y	Y	Y	Y	N
4 ***Ganske***	Y	Y	Y	Y	Y
5 ***Latham***	Y	Y	Y	Y	Y
KANSAS					
1 ***Moran***	Y	Y	Y	N	Y
2 ***Ryun***	Y	Y	Y	Y	Y
3 Moore	Y	Y	Y	Y	N
4 ***Tiahrt***	+	+	+	+	+
KENTUCKY					
1 ***Whitfield***	Y	Y	Y	Y	Y
2 ***Lewis***	Y	Y	Y	?	Y
3 ***Northup***	Y	Y	Y	Y	Y
4 Lucas	Y	Y	Y	Y	N
5 ***Rogers***	Y	Y	Y	Y	Y
6 ***Fletcher***	Y	Y	Y	Y	Y
LOUISIANA					
1 Vacant					
2 Jefferson	Y	Y	Y	Y	N
3 ***Tauzin***	Y	Y	Y	Y	Y
4 ***McCrery***	?	?	?	Y	Y
5 ***Cooksey***	Y	Y	Y	Y	Y
6 ***Baker***	Y	Y	Y	Y	Y
7 John	Y	Y	Y	Y	Y
MAINE					
1 Allen	Y	Y	Y	Y	N
2 Baldacci	Y	Y	Y	Y	N
MARYLAND					
1 ***Gilchrest***	Y	Y	Y	Y	Y
2 ***Ehrlich***	Y	Y	Y	Y	Y
3 Cardin	Y	Y	Y	Y	N
4 Wynn	?	?	?	?	?
5 Hoyer	Y	Y	Y	Y	N
6 ***Bartlett***	Y	Y	Y	Y	Y
7 Cummings	Y	Y	Y	Y	N
8 ***Morella***	Y	Y	Y	Y	Y
MASSACHUSETTS					
1 Olver	Y	Y	Y	Y	N
2 Neal	Y	Y	Y	Y	N
3 McGovern	Y	Y	Y	N	N
4 Frank	Y	Y	Y	Y	N
5 Meehan	Y	Y	Y	Y	N
6 Tierney	Y	Y	Y	?	N
7 Markey	Y	Y	Y	Y	N
8 Capuano	Y	Y	Y	Y	N
9 Moakley	Y	Y	Y	Y	N
10 Delahunt	Y	Y	Y	Y	N
MICHIGAN					
1 Stupak	Y	Y	Y	N	N
2 ***Hoekstra***	Y	Y	Y	Y	Y
3 ***Ehlers***	Y	Y	Y	Y	Y
4 ***Camp***	Y	Y	Y	Y	Y
5 Barcia	Y	Y	Y	Y	Y
6 ***Upton***	Y	Y	Y	Y	Y
7 ***Smith***	Y	Y	Y	Y	Y
8 Stabenow	Y	Y	Y	Y	N
9 Kildee	Y	Y	Y	Y	N
10 Bonior	Y	Y	Y	Y	N
11 ***Knollenberg***	Y	Y	Y	Y	Y
12 Levin	Y	Y	Y	Y	N
13 Rivers	Y	Y	Y	Y	N
14 Conyers	Y	N	Y	Y	N
15 Kilpatrick	Y	Y	Y	Y	N
16 Dingell	?	?	?	Y	N
MINNESOTA					
1 ***Gutknecht***	Y	Y	Y	N	Y
2 Minge	Y	Y	Y	Y	N
3 ***Ramstad***	Y	Y	Y	N	Y
4 Vento	Y	Y	Y	Y	N
5 Sabo	Y	Y	Y	N	N
6 Luther	Y	Y	Y	Y	N
7 Peterson	Y	Y	Y	Y	N
8 Oberstar	Y	Y	Y	N	N
MISSISSIPPI					
1 ***Wicker***	Y	Y	Y	Y	Y
2 Thompson	Y	N	Y	N	N
3 ***Pickering***	Y	Y	Y	Y	Y
4 Shows	Y	Y	Y	Y	N
5 Taylor	Y	Y	Y	N	N
MISSOURI					
1 Clay	Y	N	Y	N	N
2 ***Talent***	Y	Y	Y	Y	Y
3 Gephardt	Y	Y	Y	N	N
4 Skelton	Y	Y	Y	Y	N
5 McCarthy	Y	Y	Y	Y	N
6 Danner	Y	Y	Y	Y	N
7 ***Blunt***	Y	Y	Y	Y	Y
8 ***Emerson***	Y	Y	Y	Y	Y
9 ***Hulshof***	Y	Y	Y	Y	Y
MONTANA					
AL ***Hill***	Y	Y	Y	Y	Y
NEBRASKA					
1 ***Bereuter***	Y	Y	Y	Y	Y
2 ***Terry***	Y	Y	Y	Y	Y
3 ***Barrett***	Y	Y	Y	Y	Y
NEVADA					
1 Berkley	Y	Y	Y	Y	N
2 ***Gibbons***	Y	Y	Y	N	Y
NEW HAMPSHIRE					
1 ***Sununu***	Y	Y	Y	Y	Y
2 ***Bass***	Y	Y	Y	Y	Y
NEW JERSEY					
1 Andrews	Y	Y	Y	Y	N
2 ***LoBiondo***	Y	Y	Y	N	Y
3 ***Saxton***	Y	Y	Y	Y	Y
4 ***Smith***	Y	Y	Y	?	Y
5 ***Roukema***	Y	?	Y	Y	Y
6 Pallone	Y	Y	Y	Y	N
7 ***Franks***	Y	Y	Y	Y	Y
8 Pascrell	Y	Y	Y	Y	N
9 Rothman	Y	Y	Y	Y	Y
10 Payne	Y	N	Y	Y	N
11 ***Frelinghuysen***	Y	Y	Y	Y	Y
12 Holt	Y	Y	Y	N	N
13 Menendez	Y	Y	Y	Y	N
NEW MEXICO					
1 ***Wilson***	Y	Y	Y	Y	Y
2 ***Skeen***	Y	Y	Y	Y	Y
3 Udall	Y	Y	Y	Y	N
NEW YORK					
1 ***Forbes***	Y	Y	Y	Y	Y
2 ***Lazio***	Y	Y	Y	Y	Y
3 ***King***	Y	Y	Y	Y	Y
4 McCarthy	Y	Y	Y	Y	N
5 Ackerman	Y	Y	Y	Y	N
6 Meeks	Y	Y	Y	Y	N
7 Crowley	Y	Y	Y	Y	N
8 Nadler	Y	N	Y	Y	N
9 Weiner	Y	Y	Y	Y	N
10 Towns	Y	N	Y	Y	N
11 Owens	P	P	Y	Y	N
12 Velazquez	Y	Y	Y	Y	Y
13 ***Fossella***	Y	Y	Y	Y	Y
14 Maloney	Y	Y	Y	Y	N
15 Rangel	Y	Y	Y	?	N
16 Serrano	Y	Y	Y	Y	N
17 Engel	Y	Y	Y	?	N
18 Lowey	Y	Y	Y	Y	N
19 ***Kelly***	Y	Y	Y	Y	Y
20 ***Gilman***	Y	Y	Y	Y	Y
21 McNulty	Y	Y	Y	Y	N
22 ***Sweeney***	Y	Y	Y	N	Y
23 ***Boehlert***	Y	Y	Y	Y	Y
24 ***McHugh***	Y	Y	Y	Y	Y
25 ***Walsh***	Y	Y	Y	Y	Y
26 Hinchey	Y	Y	Y	Y	N
27 ***Reynolds***	Y	Y	Y	Y	Y
28 Slaughter	+	+	+	+	–
29 LaFalce	Y	Y	Y	Y	N
30 ***Quinn***	Y	Y	Y	Y	Y
31 ***Houghton***	?	?	?	Y	Y
NORTH CAROLINA					
1 Clayton	Y	P	Y	Y	N
2 Etheridge	Y	Y	Y	Y	N
3 ***Jones***	Y	Y	Y	Y	Y
4 Price	Y	Y	Y	Y	N
5 ***Burr***	Y	Y	Y	Y	Y
6 ***Coble***	Y	Y	Y	Y	Y
7 McIntyre	Y	Y	Y	Y	N
8 ***Hayes***	Y	Y	Y	Y	Y
9 ***Myrick***	Y	Y	?	Y	Y
10 ***Ballenger***	Y	Y	Y	Y	Y
11 ***Taylor***	Y	Y	Y	Y	Y
12 Watt	Y	Y	Y	Y	N
NORTH DAKOTA					
AL Pomeroy	Y	Y	Y	Y	N
OHIO					
1 ***Chabot***	Y	Y	Y	Y	Y
2 ***Portman***	Y	Y	Y	Y	Y
3 Hall	Y	Y	Y	Y	N
4 ***Oxley***	Y	Y	Y	Y	Y
5 ***Gillmor***	Y	Y	Y	Y	Y
6 Strickland	Y	Y	Y	Y	N
7 ***Hobson***	Y	Y	Y	Y	Y
8 ***Boehner***	Y	Y	Y	Y	Y
9 Kaptur	Y	Y	Y	Y	N
10 Kucinich	Y	Y	Y	N	N
11 Jones	Y	Y	Y	Y	N
12 ***Kasich***	Y	Y	Y	Y	Y
13 Brown	Y	Y	Y	Y	N
14 Sawyer	Y	Y	Y	Y	N
15 ***Pryce***	Y	Y	Y	Y	Y
16 ***Regula***	Y	Y	Y	Y	Y
17 Traficant	Y	Y	Y	Y	Y
18 ***Ney***	Y	Y	Y	Y	Y
19 ***LaTourette***	Y	Y	Y	Y	Y
OKLAHOMA					
1 ***Largent***	?	?	?	Y	Y
2 ***Coburn***	Y	Y	Y	Y	Y
3 ***Watkins***	?	?	?	?	?
4 ***Watts***	?	?	?	?	?
5 ***Istook***	?	?	?	?	?
6 ***Lucas***	?	?	?	Y	Y
OREGON					
1 Wu	Y	Y	Y	N	N
2 ***Walden***	Y	Y	Y	Y	Y
3 Blumenauer	Y	Y	Y	Y	N
4 DeFazio	Y	Y	Y	N	N
5 Hooley	Y	Y	Y	Y	N
PENNSYLVANIA					
1 Brady	Y	Y	Y	Y	N
2 Fattah	Y	?	?	?	N
3 Borski	Y	Y	Y	N	N
4 Klink	Y	Y	Y	N	N
5 ***Peterson***	Y	Y	Y	Y	Y
6 Holden	Y	Y	Y	Y	N
7 ***Weldon***	Y	Y	Y	Y	Y
8 ***Greenwood***	Y	Y	Y	?	Y
9 ***Shuster***	?	?	?	Y	Y
10 ***Sherwood***	Y	Y	Y	Y	Y
11 Kanjorski	Y	Y	Y	Y	N
12 Murtha	Y	Y	Y	Y	N
13 Hoeffel	Y	Y	Y	Y	N
14 Coyne	Y	Y	Y	Y	N
15 ***Toomey***	Y	Y	Y	Y	Y
16 ***Pitts***	Y	Y	Y	Y	Y
17 ***Gekas***	Y	Y	Y	Y	Y
18 Doyle	Y	Y	Y	Y	N
19 ***Goodling***	Y	Y	Y	Y	Y
20 Mascara	Y	Y	Y	Y	N
21 ***English***	Y	Y	Y	N	Y
RHODE ISLAND					
1 Kennedy	Y	Y	Y	Y	N
2 Weygand	Y	Y	Y	Y	N
SOUTH CAROLINA					
1 ***Sanford***	Y	N	Y	Y	Y
2 ***Spence***	Y	Y	Y	Y	Y
3 ***Graham***	Y	Y	Y	Y	Y
4 ***DeMint***	Y	Y	Y	Y	Y
5 Spratt	Y	Y	Y	Y	N
6 Clyburn	Y	N	Y	N	N
SOUTH DAKOTA					
AL ***Thune***	Y	Y	Y	Y	Y
TENNESSEE					
1 ***Jenkins***	Y	Y	+	Y	Y
2 ***Duncan***	Y	Y	Y	Y	Y
3 ***Wamp***	Y	Y	Y	Y	Y
4 ***Hilleary***	Y	Y	Y	Y	Y
5 Clement	Y	Y	Y	Y	N
6 Gordon	Y	Y	Y	Y	N
7 ***Bryant***	Y	Y	Y	Y	Y
8 Tanner	Y	Y	Y	Y	N
9 Ford	Y	Y	Y	N	N
TEXAS					
1 Sandlin	Y	Y	Y	Y	N
2 Turner	Y	Y	Y	Y	N
3 ***Johnson, Sam***	Y	Y	Y	Y	Y
4 Hall	Y	Y	Y	Y	N
5 ***Sessions***	Y	Y	Y	Y	Y
6 ***Barton***	Y	Y	Y	?	Y
7 ***Archer***	Y	Y	Y	Y	Y
8 ***Brady***	Y	Y	Y	Y	Y
9 Lampson	Y	Y	Y	Y	N
10 Doggett	Y	Y	Y	Y	N
11 Edwards	Y	Y	Y	Y	N
12 ***Granger***	Y	Y	Y	?	Y
13 ***Thornberry***	Y	Y	Y	Y	Y
14 ***Paul***	N	N	Y	Y	Y
15 Hinojosa	Y	Y	Y	Y	N
16 Reyes	Y	Y	Y	Y	N
17 Stenholm	Y	Y	Y	Y	N
18 Jackson-Lee	Y	Y	Y	Y	N
19 ***Combest***	Y	Y	Y	Y	Y
20 Gonzalez	Y	Y	Y	Y	N
21 ***Smith***	Y	Y	Y	Y	Y
22 ***DeLay***	Y	Y	Y	Y	Y
23 ***Bonilla***	Y	Y	Y	Y	Y
24 Frost	Y	Y	Y	Y	N
25 Bentsen	Y	Y	Y	Y	N
26 ***Armey***	Y	Y	Y	Y	Y
27 Ortiz	Y	Y	Y	Y	N
28 Rodriguez	Y	Y	Y	Y	N
29 Green	Y	Y	Y	Y	N
30 Johnson, E.B.	Y	Y	Y	N	N
UTAH					
1 ***Hansen***	Y	Y	Y	Y	Y
2 ***Cook***	Y	Y	Y	Y	Y
3 ***Cannon***	Y	Y	Y	Y	Y
VERMONT					
AL *Sanders*	Y	Y	Y	?	N
VIRGINIA					
1 ***Bateman***	Y	Y	Y	Y	Y
2 Pickett	Y	Y	Y	N	N
3 Scott	Y	N	Y	?	N
4 Sisisky	Y	Y	Y	Y	N
5 Goode	Y	Y	Y	Y	Y
6 ***Goodlatte***	Y	Y	Y	Y	Y
7 ***Bliley***	Y	Y	Y	Y	?
8 Moran	Y	Y	Y	Y	Y
9 Boucher	Y	Y	Y	Y	Y
10 ***Wolf***	Y	Y	Y	Y	Y
11 ***Davis***	Y	Y	Y	Y	Y
WASHINGTON					
1 Inslee	Y	Y	Y	Y	N
2 ***Metcalf***	Y	Y	Y	Y	Y
3 Baird	Y	Y	Y	Y	N
4 ***Hastings***	Y	Y	Y	Y	Y
5 ***Nethercutt***	Y	Y	Y	Y	Y
6 Dicks	Y	Y	Y	Y	N
7 McDermott	Y	Y	Y	N	N
8 ***Dunn***	Y	Y	Y	Y	Y
9 Smith	Y	Y	Y	Y	N
WEST VIRGINIA					
1 Mollohan	Y	Y	Y	Y	?
2 Wise	Y	Y	Y	Y	N
3 Rahall	Y	Y	Y	Y	N
WISCONSIN					
1 ***Ryan***	Y	Y	Y	Y	Y
2 Baldwin	Y	Y	Y	Y	N
3 Kind	Y	Y	Y	Y	N
4 Kleczka	Y	Y	Y	Y	Y
5 Barrett	Y	Y	Y	Y	N
6 ***Petri***	Y	Y	Y	Y	Y
7 Obey	N	N	Y	Y	N
8 ***Green***	Y	Y	Y	+	Y
9 ***Sensenbrenner***	Y	Y	Y	Y	Y
WYOMING					
AL ***Cubin***	Y	Y	Y	?	Y

Southern states - Ala., Ark., Fla., Ga., Ky., La., Miss., N.C., Okla., S.C., Tenn., Texas, Va.

110. HR 833. Bankruptcy Overhaul/Living Expenses. Hyde, R-Ill., amendment to ease the means testing requirements in the bill by dropping reliance on IRS living expense guidelines and instead allowing the courts to consider "reasonably necessary" living expenses. Rejected 184-238: R 26-192; D 157-46 (ND 123-25, SD 34-21); I 1-0. May 5, 1999.

111. HR 833. Bankruptcy Overhaul/Debt Relief Agency. Moran, D-Va., amendment to require debt-relief agencies to disclose the nature of the services they supply, the alternatives to filing bankruptcy, and the rights and responsibilities of a bankruptcy filer, and to give debtors a written contract specifying the costs and services provided to debtors. Adopted 373-47: R 198-17; D 174-30 (ND 123-26, SD 51-4); I 1-0. May 5, 1999.

112. HR 833. Bankruptcy Overhaul/Small-Business Exemptions. Conyers, D-Mich., amendment to waive the provisions of Chapter 11 relating to small-business debtors or single-asset real estate in cases where the application of those provisions could result in the loss of five or more jobs. Rejected 143-278: R 3-213; D 139-65 (ND 109-40, SD 30-25); I 1-0. May 5, 1999.

113. HR 833. Bankruptcy Overhaul/Tax Returns. Watt, D-N.C., amendment to require persons filing for bankruptcy to file income tax returns with the bankruptcy court only when requested to do so by an interested party of the case. Rejected 192-230: R 30-188; D 161-42 (ND 125-24, SD 36-18); I 1-0. May 5, 1999.

114. HR 833. Bankruptcy Overhaul/Substitute. Nadler, D-N.Y., substitute amendment to ease the bill's means test to allow the courts more discretion in determining whether a debtor can file under Chapter 7 of the bankruptcy code; strike a provision barring victims of illegal reaffirmation cases from filing lawsuits; ensure that proceeds from sale of farm equipment are used to keep the farm running; prohibit landlords from evicting tenants when they file; allow forgiveness of credit card debt; and grant judges leeway on small-business claims that would eliminate five or more jobs. Rejected 149-272: R 0-216; D 148-56 (ND 117-32, SD 31-24); I 1-0. May 5, 1999. A "yea" was a vote in support of the president's position.

Key

- Y Voted for (yea).
- # Paired for.
- + Announced for.
- N Voted against (nay).
- X Paired against.
- – Announced against.
- P Voted "present."
- C Voted "present" to avoid possible conflict of interest.
- ? Did not vote or otherwise make a position known.

•

Democrats ***Republicans***
Independents

	110	111	112	113	114
ALABAMA					
1 ***Callahan***	N	Y	N	N	N
2 ***Everett***	N	N	N	N	N
3 ***Riley***	N	Y	N	N	N
4 ***Aderholt***	N	Y	N	N	N
5 Cramer	N	Y	N	N	N
6 ***Bachus***	Y	Y	N	Y	N
7 Hilliard	Y	Y	Y	Y	Y
ALASKA					
AL ***Young***	N	Y	N	N	N
ARIZONA					
1 ***Salmon***	N	Y	N	Y	N
2 Pastor	N	Y	N	Y	N
3 ***Stump***	N	Y	N	N	N
4 ***Shadegg***	N	Y	N	N	N
5 ***Kolbe***	N	Y	N	N	N
6 ***Hayworth***	N	Y	N	N	N
ARKANSAS					
1 Berry	N	Y	N	N	N
2 Snyder	Y	Y	N	Y	N
3 ***Hutchinson***	N	Y	N	N	N
4 ***Dickey***	Y	Y	N	N	N
CALIFORNIA					
1 Thompson	N	Y	N	N	N
2 ***Herger***	N	Y	N	N	N
3 ***Ose***	N	Y	N	N	N
4 ***Doolittle***	N	Y	N	N	N
5 Matsui	Y	Y	N	Y	Y
6 Woolsey	Y	Y	Y	Y	Y
7 Miller, George	Y	Y	Y	Y	Y
8 Pelosi	Y	Y	Y	Y	Y
9 Lee	Y	N	Y	Y	Y
10 Tauscher	N	Y	N	N	N
11 ***Pombo***	N	N	N	N	N
12 Lantos	Y	Y	Y	Y	Y
13 Stark	Y	Y	Y	Y	Y
14 Eshoo	Y	Y	Y	Y	Y
15 ***Campbell***	N	Y	N	Y	N
16 Lofgren	Y	N	N	Y	Y
17 Farr	Y	Y	Y	Y	Y
18 Condit	N	Y	N	N	N
19 ***Radanovich***	N	Y	N	N	N
20 Dooley	N	Y	N	Y	N
21 ***Thomas***	N	Y	N	N	N
22 Capps	Y	Y	N	Y	Y
23 ***Gallegly***	N	Y	N	N	N
24 Sherman	Y	Y	N	N	N
25 ***McKeon***	N	Y	N	N	N
26 Berman	+	?	+	+	+
27 ***Rogan***	N	Y	N	N	N
28 ***Dreier***	N	Y	N	N	N
29 Waxman	+	+	+	+	–
30 Becerra	+	+	+	+	–
31 Martinez	Y	N	Y	Y	Y
32 Dixon	Y	Y	N	Y	Y
33 Roybal-Allard	Y	Y	Y	Y	Y
34 Napolitano	Y	Y	Y	Y	Y
35 Waters	Y	N	Y	Y	Y
36 ***Kuykendall***	N	Y	N	N	N
37 Millender-McD.	?	Y	Y	Y	Y
38 ***Horn***	N	Y	N	N	N
39 ***Royce***	N	Y	N	N	N
40 ***Lewis***	N	Y	N	N	N
41 ***Miller, Gary***	N	Y	N	N	N
42 Brown	?	?	?	?	?
43 ***Calvert***	N	Y	N	N	N
44 ***Bono***	N	N	N	N	N
45 ***Rohrabacher***	N	Y	N	N	N
46 Sanchez	Y	Y	N	Y	N
47 ***Cox***	N	?	N	N	N
48 ***Packard***	N	Y	N	N	N
49 ***Bilbray***	N	Y	N	N	N
50 Filner	Y	Y	Y	Y	Y
51 ***Cunningham***	N	Y	N	N	N
52 ***Hunter***	N	Y	N	N	N
COLORADO					
1 DeGette	Y	Y	Y	Y	Y
2 Udall	Y	Y	Y	Y	Y
3 ***McInnis***	N	N	N	N	N
4 ***Schaffer***	N	N	N	N	N
5 ***Hefley***	N	N	N	N	N
6 ***Tancredo***	N	Y	N	Y	N
CONNECTICUT					
1 Larson	Y	Y	Y	Y	Y
2 Gejdenson	Y	Y	Y	Y	Y
3 DeLauro	Y	N	Y	Y	Y
4 ***Shays***	N	Y	N	N	N
5 Maloney	N	Y	N	N	N
6 ***Johnson***	N	Y	N	N	N
DELAWARE					
AL ***Castle***	N	Y	N	N	N
FLORIDA					
1 ***Scarborough***	N	Y	N	N	?
2 Boyd	N	Y	N	Y	N
3 Brown	Y	Y	Y	Y	Y
4 ***Fowler***	N	Y	N	N	N
5 Thurman	Y	Y	Y	Y	Y
6 ***Stearns***	N	Y	N	N	N
7 ***Mica***	N	Y	N	N	N
8 ***McCollum***	N	Y	N	N	N
9 ***Bilirakis***	N	Y	–	N	N
10 ***Young***	?	?	?	?	?
11 Davis	N	Y	N	N	N
12 ***Canady***	N	N	N	Y	N
13 ***Miller***	N	Y	N	Y	N
14 ***Goss***	N	Y	N	N	N
15 ***Weldon***	N	Y	N	N	N
16 ***Foley***	N	Y	N	N	N
17 Meek	Y	Y	Y	Y	Y
18 ***Ros-Lehtinen***	Y	Y	N	N	N
19 Wexler	Y	Y	Y	Y	Y
20 Deutsch	Y	Y	N	N	N
21 ***Diaz-Balart***	Y	Y	N	Y	N
22 ***Shaw***	N	Y	N	N	N
23 Hastings	Y	Y	Y	Y	Y
GEORGIA					
1 ***Kingston***	N	Y	N	N	N
2 Bishop	Y	Y	Y	Y	Y
3 ***Collins***	N	Y	N	N	N
4 McKinney	Y	Y	Y	Y	Y
5 Lewis	Y	Y	Y	Y	Y
6 ***Isakson***	N	Y	N	N	N
7 ***Barr***	N	Y	N	N	N
8 ***Chambliss***	Y	Y	N	N	N
9 ***Deal***	N	Y	N	N	N
10 ***Norwood***	N	Y	N	N	N
11 ***Linder***	N	Y	Y	Y	N
HAWAII					
1 Abercrombie	Y	Y	Y	Y	Y
2 Mink	Y	Y	N	Y	Y
IDAHO					
1 ***Chenoweth***	N	N	N	Y	N
2 ***Simpson***	?	?	?	?	?
ILLINOIS					
1 Rush	Y	Y	Y	Y	Y
2 Jackson	Y	Y	Y	Y	Y
3 Lipinski	Y	N	N	Y	Y
4 Gutierrez	Y	Y	Y	Y	Y
5 Blagojevich	Y	Y	Y	Y	Y
6 ***Hyde***	Y	Y	N	Y	N
7 Davis	Y	Y	Y	Y	Y
8 ***Crane***	N	Y	N	N	N
9 Schakowsky	Y	Y	Y	Y	Y
10 ***Porter***	N	Y	N	N	N
11 ***Weller***	N	Y	N	N	N
12 Costello	Y	Y	N	Y	Y
13 ***Biggert***	N	Y	N	N	N
14 ***Hastert***					

ND Northern Democrats SD Southern Democrats

	110	111	112	113	114
15 ***Ewing***	N	Y	N	N	N
16 ***Manzullo***	Y	Y	N	Y	N
17 Evans	Y	N	Y	Y	Y
18 ***LaHood***	Y	Y	N	N	N
19 Phelps	Y	Y	Y	Y	Y
20 ***Shimkus***	N	Y	N	N	N
INDIANA					
1 Visclosky	Y	N	Y	Y	Y
2 ***McIntosh***	Y	Y	N	N	N
3 Roemer	N	Y	N	N	N
4 ***Souder***	N	N	N	N	N
5 ***Buyer***	N	Y	N	N	N
6 ***Burton***	N	Y	N	N	N
7 ***Pease***	N	Y	N	Y	N
8 ***Hostettler***	N	Y	N	N	N
9 Hill	Y	Y	N	Y	N
10 Carson	Y	Y	Y	Y	Y
IOWA					
1 ***Leach***	Y	Y	N	N	N
2 ***Nussle***	N	Y	N	N	N
3 Boswell	N	Y	N	N	N
4 ***Ganske***	Y	Y	N	N	N
5 ***Latham***	N	Y	N	N	N
KANSAS					
1 ***Moran***	N	Y	N	N	N
2 ***Ryun***	N	Y	N	N	N
3 Moore	N	Y	N	N	N
4 ***Tiahrt***	N	Y	N	N	N
KENTUCKY					
1 ***Whitfield***	N	Y	N	Y	N
2 ***Lewis***	N	Y	N	N	N
3 ***Northup***	N	Y	N	N	N
4 Lucas	N	Y	N	N	N
5 ***Rogers***	N	Y	N	N	N
6 ***Fletcher***	N	Y	N	N	N
LOUISIANA					
1 Vacant					
2 Jefferson	Y	Y	N	Y	Y
3 ***Tauzin***	N	Y	N	N	N
4 ***McCrery***	N	Y	N	Y	N
5 ***Cooksey***	N	Y	N	N	?
6 ***Baker***	N	Y	N	N	N
7 John	N	Y	N	Y	N
MAINE					
1 Allen	Y	Y	Y	Y	Y
2 Baldacci	Y	Y	Y	N	N
MARYLAND					
1 ***Gilchrest***	Y	Y	N	N	N
2 ***Ehrlich***	N	Y	N	N	N
3 Cardin	Y	Y	N	Y	Y
4 Wynn	?	?	?	?	?
5 Hoyer	Y	Y	N	N	N
6 ***Bartlett***	N	Y	N	N	N
7 Cummings	Y	Y	Y	Y	Y
8 ***Morella***	Y	Y	N	N	N
MASSACHUSETTS					
1 Olver	Y	Y	Y	Y	Y
2 Neal	Y	Y	Y	Y	N
3 McGovern	Y	Y	Y	Y	Y
4 Frank	Y	Y	Y	N	N
5 Meehan	Y	N	Y	Y	Y
6 Tierney	Y	Y	Y	Y	Y
7 Markey	Y	Y	Y	Y	Y
8 Capuano	Y	Y	Y	Y	Y
9 Moakley	Y	Y	Y	Y	Y
10 Delahunt	Y	N	Y	Y	Y
MICHIGAN					
1 Stupak	Y	Y	Y	Y	Y
2 ***Hoekstra***	N	Y	N	N	N
3 ***Ehlers***	N	N	N	N	N
4 ***Camp***	Y	Y	N	N	N
5 Barcia	N	Y	Y	Y	N
6 ***Upton***	N	Y	N	N	N
7 ***Smith***	N	Y	?	N	N
8 Stabenow	Y	Y	N	Y	Y
9 Kildee	Y	Y	Y	Y	Y
10 Bonior	Y	N	Y	Y	Y
11 ***Knollenberg***	N	Y	N	N	N
12 Levin	Y	Y	N	Y	Y
13 Rivers	N	Y	Y	Y	N
14 Conyers	Y	N	Y	Y	Y
15 Kilpatrick	Y	N	Y	Y	Y
16 Dingell	Y	Y	Y	Y	Y
MINNESOTA					
1 ***Gutknecht***	N	Y	N	N	N
2 Minge	Y	Y	Y	Y	Y
3 ***Ramstad***	N	Y	N	N	N
4 Vento	Y	Y	Y	Y	Y
5 Sabo	Y	Y	Y	Y	Y
6 Luther	?	?	?	?	?
7 Peterson	N	N	N	N	N
8 Oberstar	Y	Y	Y	Y	Y
MISSISSIPPI					
1 ***Wicker***	N	Y	N	N	N
2 Thompson	Y	Y	Y	Y	Y
3 ***Pickering***	N	Y	N	N	N
4 Shows	Y	Y	Y	N	Y
5 Taylor	N	Y	N	N	N
MISSOURI					
1 Clay	Y	Y	Y	Y	Y
2 ***Talent***	N	Y	N	N	N
3 Gephardt	?	?	?	?	?
4 Skelton	N	Y	N	N	N
5 McCarthy	Y	Y	Y	Y	Y
6 Danner	Y	Y	N	N	Y
7 ***Blunt***	N	Y	N	N	N
8 ***Emerson***	N	Y	N	N	N
9 ***Hulshof***	N	Y	N	N	N
MONTANA					
AL ***Hill***	N	Y	N	N	N
NEBRASKA					
1 ***Bereuter***	N	Y	N	Y	N
2 ***Terry***	N	Y	N	N	N
3 ***Barrett***	Y	Y	N	N	N
NEVADA					
1 Berkley	Y	Y	Y	Y	Y
2 ***Gibbons***	N	Y	N	N	N
NEW HAMPSHIRE					
1 ***Sununu***	N	Y	N	N	N
2 ***Bass***	N	Y	N	N	N
NEW JERSEY					
1 Andrews	N	Y	N	N	N
2 ***LoBiondo***	N	Y	N	N	N
3 ***Saxton***	N	?	Y	N	N
4 ***Smith***	N	Y	N	Y	N
5 ***Roukema***	N	Y	N	N	N
6 Pallone	Y	Y	Y	Y	Y
7 ***Franks***	N	?	N	N	N
8 Pascrell	N	Y	Y	N	Y
9 Rothman	N	Y	Y	Y	N
10 Payne	Y	N	Y	Y	Y
11 ***Frelinghuysen***	N	Y	N	N	N
12 Holt	Y	Y	Y	Y	Y
13 Menendez	N	Y	Y	Y	N
NEW MEXICO					
1 ***Wilson***	Y	N	N	N	N
2 ***Skeen***	N	Y	N	N	N
3 Udall	Y	Y	N	N	Y
NEW YORK					
1 ***Forbes***	Y	Y	N	N	N
2 ***Lazio***	N	Y	N	N	N
3 ***King***	Y	Y	N	Y	N
4 McCarthy	Y	Y	Y	Y	Y
5 Ackerman	Y	Y	Y	Y	Y
6 Meeks	Y	N	Y	Y	Y
7 Crowley	N	Y	Y	Y	Y
8 Nadler	Y	N	Y	Y	Y
9 Weiner	Y	Y	Y	Y	Y
10 Towns	Y	Y	Y	Y	Y
11 Owens	Y	N	Y	Y	Y
12 Velazquez	N	Y	Y	Y	Y
13 ***Fossella***	Y	Y	N	Y	N
14 Maloney	Y	Y	Y	Y	Y
15 Rangel	Y	Y	Y	Y	Y
16 Serrano	Y	Y	Y	Y	Y
17 Engel	Y	Y	Y	N	Y
18 Lowey	Y	N	Y	Y	Y
19 ***Kelly***	N	Y	N	N	N
20 ***Gilman***	Y	Y	N	N	N
21 McNulty	Y	Y	Y	Y	Y
22 ***Sweeney***	N	Y	N	N	N
23 ***Boehlert***	Y	Y	N	Y	N
24 ***McHugh***	Y	Y	N	Y	N
25 ***Walsh***	N	Y	N	N	N
26 Hinchey	Y	N	Y	Y	Y
27 ***Reynolds***	N	Y	N	Y	N
28 Slaughter	+	+	+	+	+
29 LaFalce	Y	Y	Y	Y	Y
30 ***Quinn***	N	Y	N	N	N
31 ***Houghton***	Y	Y	Y	N	N
NORTH CAROLINA					
1 Clayton	Y	Y	Y	Y	Y
2 Etheridge	N	Y	Y	Y	Y
3 ***Jones***	N	Y	N	N	N
4 Price	Y	Y	Y	Y	Y
5 ***Burr***	N	N	N	Y	N
6 ***Coble***	N	Y	N	Y	N
7 McIntyre	N	Y	Y	N	N
8 ***Hayes***	N	Y	N	N	N
9 ***Myrick***	N	Y	N	Y	N
10 ***Ballenger***	N	Y	N	N	N
11 ***Taylor***	N	N	N	N	N
12 Watt	Y	N	Y	Y	Y
NORTH DAKOTA					
AL Pomeroy	Y	Y	N	N	Y
OHIO					
1 ***Chabot***	N	Y	N	N	N
2 ***Portman***	N	Y	N	N	N
3 Hall	Y	Y	N	Y	Y
4 ***Oxley***	N	Y	N	N	N
5 ***Gillmor***	N	Y	N	N	N
6 Strickland	Y	Y	Y	Y	N
7 ***Hobson***	N	Y	N	N	N
8 ***Boehner***	N	Y	N	N	N
9 Kaptur	Y	Y	Y	Y	Y
10 Kucinich	Y	Y	Y	Y	Y
11 Jones	Y	Y	Y	Y	Y
12 ***Kasich***	N	Y	N	N	N
13 Brown	Y	Y	Y	Y	Y
14 Sawyer	Y	Y	Y	Y	Y
15 ***Pryce***	N	Y	N	N	N
16 ***Regula***	N	Y	N	N	N
17 Traficant	Y	Y	Y	Y	Y
18 ***Ney***	N	Y	N	N	N
19 ***LaTourette***	Y	Y	N	Y	N
OKLAHOMA					
1 ***Largent***	N	Y	N	N	N
2 ***Coburn***	N	Y	N	N	N
3 ***Watkins***	N	Y	N	N	N
4 ***Watts***	?	?	?	?	?
5 ***Istook***	N	Y	N	N	N
6 ***Lucas***	N	Y	N	N	N
OREGON					
1 Wu	Y	Y	Y	Y	Y
2 ***Walden***	N	Y	N	N	N
3 Blumenauer	Y	Y	N	Y	N
4 DeFazio	Y	N	Y	Y	Y
5 Hooley	N	Y	N	Y	N
PENNSYLVANIA					
1 Brady	Y	N	Y	Y	Y
2 Fattah	Y	N	Y	Y	Y
3 Borski	Y	N	Y	Y	Y
4 Klink	Y	Y	Y	Y	Y
5 ***Peterson***	N	Y	N	N	N
6 Holden	N	Y	Y	N	N
7 ***Weldon***	Y	Y	N	N	N
8 ***Greenwood***	N	Y	N	N	N
9 ***Shuster***	N	Y	N	N	N
10 ***Sherwood***	N	Y	N	Y	N
11 Kanjorski	Y	Y	Y	Y	Y
12 Murtha	Y	Y	Y	Y	N
13 Hoeffel	Y	Y	Y	Y	Y
14 Coyne	Y	Y	Y	Y	Y
15 ***Toomey***	N	Y	N	N	N
16 ***Pitts***	N	Y	N	N	N
17 ***Gekas***	N	Y	N	N	N
18 Doyle	Y	Y	Y	Y	Y
19 ***Goodling***	N	N	N	N	N
20 Mascara	Y	Y	Y	Y	Y
21 ***English***	N	Y	N	N	N
RHODE ISLAND					
1 Kennedy	N	Y	N	N	N
2 Weygand	N	Y	N	N	N
SOUTH CAROLINA					
1 ***Sanford***	N	Y	N	Y	N
2 ***Spence***	N	Y	N	N	N
3 ***Graham***	N	Y	N	N	N
4 ***DeMint***	N	Y	N	N	N
5 Spratt	Y	N	N	Y	Y
6 Clyburn	Y	Y	Y	Y	Y
SOUTH DAKOTA					
AL ***Thune***	N	Y	N	N	N
TENNESSEE					
1 ***Jenkins***	N	Y	N	N	N
2 ***Duncan***	N	Y	N	N	N
3 ***Wamp***	Y	Y	N	N	N
4 ***Hilleary***	N	Y	N	N	N
5 Clement	Y	Y	N	N	N
6 Gordon	N	Y	N	Y	N
7 ***Bryant***	N	Y	N	Y	N
8 Tanner	N	Y	N	N	N
9 Ford	Y	Y	Y	N	Y
TEXAS					
1 Sandlin	N	N	N	Y	N
2 Turner	N	Y	N	Y	N
3 ***Johnson, Sam***	N	Y	N	N	N
4 Hall	N	Y	N	N	N
5 ***Sessions***	N	Y	N	N	N
6 ***Barton***	N	Y	N	N	N
7 ***Archer***	N	Y	N	N	N
8 ***Brady***	N	Y	N	N	N
9 Lampson	Y	Y	Y	Y	Y
10 Doggett	Y	Y	N	Y	Y
11 Edwards	Y	Y	Y	Y	Y
12 ***Granger***	N	Y	N	N	N
13 ***Thornberry***	N	Y	N	N	N
14 ***Paul***	N	N	N	N	N
15 Hinojosa	Y	Y	Y	Y	Y
16 Reyes	Y	Y	Y	Y	Y
17 Stenholm	N	Y	N	N	N
18 Jackson-Lee	Y	N	Y	+	Y
19 ***Combest***	N	Y	N	N	N
20 Gonzalez	Y	Y	Y	Y	Y
21 ***Smith***	N	Y	N	N	N
22 ***DeLay***	N	Y	N	N	N
23 ***Bonilla***	N	Y	N	N	N
24 Frost	N	Y	Y	N	N
25 Bentsen	Y	Y	N	Y	N
26 ***Armey***	N	Y	N	N	N
27 Ortiz	Y	Y	Y	Y	Y
28 Rodriguez	Y	Y	Y	Y	Y
29 Green	Y	Y	Y	Y	Y
30 Johnson, E.B.	Y	Y	Y	Y	Y
UTAH					
1 ***Hansen***	N	Y	N	N	N
2 ***Cook***	N	Y	N	N	N
3 ***Cannon***	N	N	N	N	N
VERMONT					
AL *Sanders*	Y	Y	Y	Y	Y
VIRGINIA					
1 ***Bateman***	N	Y	N	N	N
2 Pickett	N	Y	N	N	N
3 Scott	Y	Y	Y	Y	Y
4 Sisisky	N	Y	N	N	N
5 Goode	N	Y	N	N	N
6 ***Goodlatte***	N	Y	N	N	N
7 ***Bliley***	N	Y	N	N	N
8 Moran	N	Y	N	Y	N
9 Boucher	N	Y	N	N	N
10 ***Wolf***	N	Y	N	Y	N
11 ***Davis***	N	Y	N	N	N
WASHINGTON					
1 Inslee	Y	Y	N	Y	Y
2 ***Metcalf***	N	Y	N	N	N
3 Baird	Y	Y	Y	Y	Y
4 ***Hastings***	N	Y	N	N	N
5 ***Nethercutt***	N	Y	N	N	N
6 Dicks	Y	Y	N	Y	Y
7 McDermott	Y	N	Y	Y	Y
8 ***Dunn***	N	Y	N	N	N
9 Smith	N	Y	N	N	N
WEST VIRGINIA					
1 Mollohan	N	Y	N	Y	N
2 Wise	Y	Y	N	Y	Y
3 Rahall	Y	Y	Y	Y	Y
WISCONSIN					
1 ***Ryan***	N	N	N	N	N
2 Baldwin	Y	N	Y	Y	Y
3 Kind	Y	Y	N	N	Y
4 Kleczka	Y	Y	Y	Y	Y
5 Barrett	Y	Y	Y	Y	Y
6 ***Petri***	N	Y	N	Y	N
7 Obey	Y	Y	Y	Y	Y
8 ***Green***	N	Y	N	N	N
9 ***Sensenbrenner***	N	Y	N	N	N
WYOMING					
AL ***Cubin***	N	Y	N	N	N

Southern states - Ala., Ark., Fla., Ga., Ky., La., Miss., N.C., Okla., S.C., Tenn., Texas, Va.

115. HR 833. Bankruptcy Overhaul/Passage. Passage of the bill to revise the nation's bankruptcy laws to require individuals with earnings above the regional median who can repay $6,000 of unsecured debt over five years to file for relief under Chapter 13, rather than Chapter 7, which is more forgiving; provide more information to consumers about bankruptcy and credit; increase judicial oversight of small-business bankruptcy cases; and create a separate chapter for international insolvencies. Passed 313-108: R 217-0; D 96-107 (ND 61-87, SD 35-20); I 0-1. May 5, 1999. A "nay" was a vote in support of the president's position.

116. HR 1664. Fiscal 1999 Defense Supplemental/Rule. Adoption of the rule (H Res 159) to provide for House floor consideration of the bill to provide funding for U.S. involvement in the NATO-led mission in Yugoslavia. Adopted 253-171: R 216-1; D 37-169 (ND 21-130, SD 16-39); I 0-1. May 6, 1999.

117. HR 1664. Fiscal 1999 Defense Supplemental/Offsets. Coburn, R-Okla., amendment to require across-the-board cuts in fiscal 2000 non-defense discretionary spending equal to the amount appropriated in the bill minus any reimbursements from NATO. Rejected 101-322: R 97-120; D 4-201 (ND 0-151, SD 4-50); I 0-1. May 6, 1999.

118. HR 1664. Fiscal 1999 Defense Supplemental/Substitute. Obey, D-Wis., substitute amendment to pare the defense portion of the bill to $10.2 billion and add $1.7 billion for items contained in a separate supplemental (HR 1141) for farm loans and disaster relief in Central America. Rejected 164-260: R 3-215; D 160-45 (ND 120-31, SD 40-14); I 1-0. May 6, 1999.

119. HR 1664. Fiscal 1999 Defense Supplemental/Ground Troops. Istook, R-Okla., amendment that would prohibit the use of funds authorized in the bill for a planned invasion of Yugoslavia by U.S. ground troops except in time of war. Rejected 117-301: R 97-116; D 19-185 (ND 16-135, SD 3-50); I 1-0. May 6, 1999.

120. HR 1664. Fiscal 1999 Defense Supplemental/Passage. Passage of the bill to provide $13.1 billion in emergency spending for U.S. military operations, refugee aid and economic assistance in Yugoslavia; and for military operations in southwest Asia. The bill would provide $3.1 billion for spare parts, depot maintenance, recruitment and training and base operations to cover shortfalls before the operation in Kosovo started; $1.8 billion for increases in military pay and retirement benefits; and funds for military construction, humanitarian aid and other purposes. Passed 311-105: R 174-38; D 137-66 (ND 90-60, SD 47-6); I 0-1. May 6, 1999.

Key

- Y Voted for (yea).
- # Paired for.
- + Announced for.
- N Voted against (nay).
- X Paired against.
- – Announced against.
- P Voted "present."
- C Voted "present" to avoid possible conflict of interest.
- ? Did not vote or otherwise make a position known.

•

Democrats ***Republicans***
Independents

	115	116	117	118	119	120
ALABAMA						
1 ***Callahan***	Y	Y	N	N	N	Y
2 ***Everett***	Y	Y	N	N	N	Y
3 ***Riley***	Y	Y	Y	N	N	Y
4 ***Aderholt***	Y	Y	Y	N	N	Y
5 Cramer	Y	Y	N	N	N	Y
6 ***Bachus***	Y	Y	Y	N	Y	Y
7 Hilliard	N	N	N	Y	N	Y
ALASKA						
AL ***Young***	Y	Y	N	N	Y	Y
ARIZONA						
1 ***Salmon***	Y	Y	Y	N	Y	N
2 Pastor	Y	N	N	Y	N	Y
3 ***Stump***	Y	Y	N	N	Y	Y
4 ***Shadegg***	Y	Y	Y	N	Y	Y
5 ***Kolbe***	Y	Y	N	N	N	Y
6 ***Hayworth***	Y	Y	Y	N	Y	Y
ARKANSAS						
1 Berry	Y	N	N	Y	N	Y
2 Snyder	Y	N	N	Y	N	Y
3 ***Hutchinson***	?	Y	Y	N	N	Y
4 ***Dickey***	Y	Y	N	N	N	Y
CALIFORNIA						
1 Thompson	Y	N	N	Y	N	N
2 ***Herger***	Y	Y	Y	N	Y	Y
3 ***Ose***	Y	Y	N	N	Y	Y
4 ***Doolittle***	Y	Y	Y	N	Y	Y
5 Matsui	N	N	N	Y	N	Y
6 Woolsey	N	N	N	Y	N	N
7 Miller, George	N	N	N	Y	Y	N
8 Pelosi	N	N	N	Y	N	N
9 Lee	N	N	N	N	Y	N
10 Tauscher	Y	N	N	Y	N	Y
11 ***Pombo***	Y	Y	N	N	Y	Y
12 Lantos	N	N	N	Y	N	Y
13 Stark	N	N	N	N	Y	N
14 Eshoo	N	N	N	Y	N	N
15 ***Campbell***	Y	Y	Y	Y	Y	N
16 Lofgren	N	N	N	Y	N	N
17 Farr	N	N	N	Y	N	Y
18 Condit	Y	Y	N	Y	N	Y
19 ***Radanovich***	Y	Y	Y	N	N	Y
20 Dooley	Y	N	N	N	N	Y
21 ***Thomas***	Y	Y	Y	N	N	Y
22 Capps	Y	N	N	Y	N	Y
23 ***Gallegly***	Y	Y	N	N	N	Y
24 Sherman	Y	N	N	Y	N	Y
25 ***McKeon***	Y	Y	N	N	N	Y
26 Berman	–	?	–	+	–	+
27 ***Rogan***	Y	Y	N	N	Y	Y
28 ***Dreier***	Y	Y	N	N	N	Y
29 Waxman	N	N	N	Y	N	N
30 Becerra	+	N	N	Y	N	N
31 Martinez	N	N	N	Y	N	Y
32 Dixon	N	N	N	Y	N	Y
33 Roybal-Allard	N	N	N	Y	N	Y
34 Napolitano	Y	N	N	Y	N	Y
35 Waters	N	N	N	Y	N	N
36 ***Kuykendall***	Y	+	–	–	–	+
37 Millender-McD.	N	N	N	Y	N	Y
38 ***Horn***	Y	Y	N	N	N	Y
39 ***Royce***	Y	Y	Y	N	Y	Y
40 ***Lewis***	Y	Y	N	N	N	Y
41 ***Miller, Gary***	Y	Y	N	N	N	Y
42 Brown	?	?	?	?	?	?
43 ***Calvert***	Y	Y	N	N	N	Y
44 ***Bono***	Y	Y	N	N	N	Y
45 ***Rohrabacher***	Y	Y	Y	N	Y	N
46 Sanchez	N	N	N	Y	N	Y
47 ***Cox***	Y	?	?	?	?	?
48 ***Packard***	Y	Y	N	N	?	?
49 ***Bilbray***	Y	Y	Y	N	Y	Y
50 Filner	N	N	N	Y	N	Y
51 ***Cunningham***	Y	Y	N	N	N	Y
52 ***Hunter***	Y	Y	N	N	N	Y
COLORADO						
1 DeGette	N	N	N	Y	N	N
2 Udall	N	N	N	Y	N	N
3 ***McInnis***	Y	Y	N	N	N	Y
4 ***Schaffer***	Y	Y	Y	N	Y	N
5 ***Hefley***	Y	Y	Y	N	Y	Y
6 ***Tancredo***	Y	Y	Y	N	Y	Y
CONNECTICUT						
1 Larson	Y	N	N	Y	N	Y
2 Gejdenson	N	N	N	Y	N	Y
3 DeLauro	N	N	N	Y	N	Y
4 ***Shays***	Y	Y	Y	N	N	Y
5 Maloney	Y	Y	N	N	N	Y
6 ***Johnson***	Y	Y	N	N	N	Y
DELAWARE						
AL ***Castle***	Y	Y	N	N	N	Y
FLORIDA						
1 ***Scarborough***	Y	Y	Y	N	Y	Y
2 Boyd	Y	N	N	Y	N	Y
3 Brown	N	Y	N	Y	N	Y
4 ***Fowler***	Y	Y	N	N	N	Y
5 Thurman	N	N	N	Y	N	Y
6 ***Stearns***	Y	Y	N	N	N	Y
7 ***Mica***	Y	Y	Y	N	N	Y
8 ***McCollum***	Y	Y	N	N	N	Y
9 ***Bilirakis***	Y	Y	N	N	Y	Y
10 ***Young***	?	Y	N	N	N	Y
11 Davis	N	N	N	Y	N	Y
12 ***Canady***	Y	Y	N	N	Y	Y
13 ***Miller***	Y	Y	N	N	N	Y
14 ***Goss***	Y	Y	Y	N	N	Y
15 ***Weldon***	Y	Y	Y	N	Y	Y
16 ***Foley***	Y	Y	Y	N	N	Y
17 Meek	N	Y	N	Y	N	Y
18 ***Ros-Lehtinen***	Y	Y	N	N	Y	N
19 Wexler	N	N	N	Y	N	Y
20 Deutsch	Y	N	N	Y	N	Y
21 ***Diaz-Balart***	Y	Y	N	N	N	Y
22 ***Shaw***	Y	Y	N	N	N	Y
23 Hastings	N	N	N	Y	N	Y
GEORGIA						
1 ***Kingston***	Y	Y	Y	N	N	Y
2 Bishop	Y	Y	N	Y	N	Y
3 ***Collins***	Y	Y	Y	N	N	Y
4 McKinney	N	N	N	N	Y	N
5 Lewis	N	N	N	Y	?	?
6 ***Isakson***	Y	Y	Y	N	N	Y
7 ***Barr***	Y	Y	Y	N	Y	N
8 ***Chambliss***	Y	Y	Y	N	N	Y
9 ***Deal***	Y	Y	Y	N	N	Y
10 ***Norwood***	Y	Y	Y	N	Y	Y
11 ***Linder***	Y	Y	Y	N	Y	Y
HAWAII						
1 Abercrombie	N	Y	N	N	N	Y
2 Mink	N	N	N	Y	Y	N
IDAHO						
1 ***Chenoweth***	Y	?	Y	N	Y	Y
2 ***Simpson***	?	Y	N	N	N	Y
ILLINOIS						
1 Rush	N	N	N	Y	N	N
2 Jackson	N	N	N	Y	Y	N
3 Lipinski	Y	N	N	Y	N	Y
4 Gutierrez	N	N	N	Y	N	Y
5 Blagojevich	Y	N	N	Y	N	Y
6 ***Hyde***	Y	Y	N	N	N	Y
7 Davis	Y	N	N	Y	N	N
8 ***Crane***	Y	Y	Y	N	Y	Y
9 Schakowsky	N	N	N	Y	N	N
10 ***Porter***	Y	Y	N	N	N	Y
11 ***Weller***	Y	Y	N	N	N	Y
12 Costello	Y	N	N	Y	N	Y
13 ***Biggert***	Y	Y	Y	N	N	Y
14 ***Hastert***	Y	Y			N	Y

ND Northern Democrats SD Southern Democrats

	115	116	117	118	119	120
15 ***Ewing***	Y	Y	N	N	N	N
16 ***Manzullo***	Y	Y	Y	N	Y	N
17 Evans	N	N	N	Y	N	Y
18 ***LaHood***	Y	Y	Y	N	N	N
19 Phelps	Y	N	N	Y	N	Y
20 ***Shimkus***	Y	Y	N	N	N	Y
INDIANA						
1 Visclosky	N	N	N	Y	N	Y
2 ***McIntosh***	Y	Y	Y	N	Y	Y
3 Roemer	Y	Y	N	N	N	Y
4 ***Souder***	Y	Y	Y	N	Y	N
5 ***Buyer***	Y	Y	N	N	N	Y
6 ***Burton***	Y	Y	Y	N	Y	Y
7 ***Pease***	Y	Y	Y	N	Y	Y
8 ***Hostettler***	Y	Y	Y	N	Y	Y
9 Hill	Y	N	N	N	N	N
10 Carson	N	N	N	Y	N	N
IOWA						
1 ***Leach***	Y	Y	N	N	N	N
2 ***Nussle***	Y	Y	N	N	N	N
3 Boswell	Y	N	N	Y	N	Y
4 ***Ganske***	Y	Y	N	N	Y	N
5 ***Latham***	Y	Y	N	N	N	Y
KANSAS						
1 ***Moran***	Y	Y	Y	N	Y	Y
2 ***Ryun***	Y	Y	Y	N	N	Y
3 Moore	Y	N	N	Y	N	Y
4 ***Tiahrt***	Y	?	?	?	?	?
KENTUCKY						
1 ***Whitfield***	Y	Y	N	N	N	Y
2 ***Lewis***	Y	Y	N	N	N	Y
3 ***Northup***	Y	Y	N	N	N	?
4 Lucas	Y	N	N	Y	N	Y
5 ***Rogers***	Y	Y	N	N	N	Y
6 ***Fletcher***	Y	Y	Y	N	N	Y
LOUISIANA						
1 Vacant						
2 Jefferson	Y	N	N	Y	N	Y
3 ***Tauzin***	Y	Y	N	N	Y	Y
4 ***McCrery***	Y	Y	N	N	N	Y
5 ***Cooksey***	Y	Y	Y	N	?	?
6 ***Baker***	Y	Y	?	N	Y	Y
7 John	Y	N	N	Y	N	Y
MAINE						
1 Allen	N	N	N	Y	N	Y
2 Baldacci	N	Y	N	N	N	Y
MARYLAND						
1 ***Gilchrest***	Y	Y	N	N	N	Y
2 ***Ehrlich***	Y	Y	N	N	N	Y
3 Cardin	Y	N	N	Y	N	Y
4 Wynn	?	?	?	?	?	?
5 Hoyer	Y	N	N	Y	N	Y
6 ***Bartlett***	Y	Y	Y	N	Y	Y
7 Cummings	N	N	N	Y	N	Y
8 ***Morella***	Y	Y	N	N	N	Y
MASSACHUSETTS						
1 Olver	N	N	N	Y	N	Y
2 Neal	Y	N	N	Y	N	Y
3 McGovern	N	N	N	Y	N	N
4 Frank	Y	N	N	Y	N	N
5 Meehan	N	N	N	Y	N	Y
6 Tierney	N	N	N	Y	N	N
7 Markey	N	N	N	Y	N	N
8 Capuano	N	N	N	Y	N	N
9 Moakley	N	N	N	Y	N	Y
10 Delahunt	N	N	N	Y	N	Y
MICHIGAN						
1 Stupak	N	N	N	Y	N	N
2 ***Hoekstra***	Y	Y	Y	N	Y	Y
3 ***Ehlers***	Y	Y	Y	N	Y	N
4 ***Camp***	Y	Y	N	N	N	Y
5 Barcia	Y	N	N	Y	N	Y
6 ***Upton***	Y	Y	N	N	Y	Y
7 ***Smith***	Y	Y	Y	N	Y	Y
8 Stabenow	Y	N	N	Y	N	Y
9 Kildee	N	N	N	N	N	Y
10 Bonior	N	N	N	Y	N	Y
11 ***Knollenberg***	Y	Y	N	N	N	Y
12 Levin	N	N	N	Y	N	Y
13 Rivers	Y	N	N	N	Y	N
14 Conyers	N	N	N	Y	Y	N
15 Kilpatrick	N	N	N	Y	N	N
16 Dingell	N	N	N	Y	N	Y

	115	116	117	118	119	120
MINNESOTA						
1 ***Gutknecht***	Y	N	N	N	Y	N
2 Minge	Y	N	N	Y	N	N
3 ***Ramstad***	Y	Y	Y	N	Y	Y
4 Vento	N	N	N	Y	N	N
5 Sabo	N	N	N	Y	N	N
6 Luther	?	N	N	Y	N	N
7 Peterson	Y	N	N	Y	Y	N
8 Oberstar	N	N	N	Y	N	N
MISSISSIPPI						
1 ***Wicker***	Y	Y	N	N	N	Y
2 Thompson	N	N	N	Y	N	Y
3 ***Pickering***	Y	Y	Y	N	N	Y
4 Shows	Y	Y	N	Y	N	Y
5 Taylor	Y	Y	Y	N	N	Y
MISSOURI						
1 Clay	N	N	N	Y	N	?
2 ***Talent***	Y	Y	N	N	Y	Y
3 Gephardt	?	N	N	Y	N	Y
4 Skelton	Y	Y	N	N	N	Y
5 McCarthy	Y	N	N	Y	N	N
6 Danner	Y	N	N	N	Y	N
7 ***Blunt***	Y	Y	N	N	N	Y
8 ***Emerson***	Y	Y	N	N	N	Y
9 ***Hulshof***	Y	Y	N	N	Y	N
MONTANA						
AL ***Hill***	Y	Y	Y	N	Y	Y
NEBRASKA						
1 ***Bereuter***	Y	Y	N	N	?	?
2 ***Terry***	Y	Y	Y	N	N	N
3 ***Barrett***	Y	Y	N	N	N	Y
NEVADA						
1 Berkley	Y	N	N	Y	N	Y
2 ***Gibbons***	Y	Y	N	N	Y	Y
NEW HAMPSHIRE						
1 ***Sununu***	Y	Y	Y	N	Y	Y
2 ***Bass***	Y	Y	N	N	Y	Y
NEW JERSEY						
1 Andrews	Y	N	N	N	N	Y
2 ***LoBiondo***	Y	Y	N	N	Y	Y
3 ***Saxton***	Y	Y	N	N	N	Y
4 ***Smith***	Y	Y	N	N	N	Y
5 ***Roukema***	Y	Y	N	N	N	Y
6 Pallone	Y	N	N	Y	N	Y
7 ***Franks***	Y	Y	N	N	Y	Y
8 Pascrell	Y	Y	N	Y	N	Y
9 Rothman	Y	N	N	Y	N	Y
10 Payne	N	N	N	Y	N	N
11 ***Frelinghuysen***	Y	Y	N	N	N	Y
12 Holt	Y	N	N	Y	N	Y
13 Menendez	Y	N	N	Y	N	Y
NEW MEXICO						
1 ***Wilson***	Y	?	N	N	N	Y
2 ***Skeen***	Y	Y	N	N	N	Y
3 Udall	N	N	N	Y	N	N
NEW YORK						
1 ***Forbes***	Y	Y	N	N	N	Y
2 ***Lazio***	Y	Y	N	N	N	Y
3 ***King***	Y	Y	N	N	?	?
4 McCarthy	Y	N	N	Y	N	Y
5 Ackerman	?	Y	N	Y	N	Y
6 Meeks	Y	N	N	Y	N	N
7 Crowley	Y	N	N	Y	N	Y
8 Nadler	N	N	N	Y	N	Y
9 Weiner	N	N	N	Y	N	Y
10 Towns	N	N	N	Y	Y	N
11 Owens	N	N	N	Y	N	N
12 Velazquez	Y	N	N	Y	N	N
13 ***Fossella***	Y	Y	Y	N	N	Y
14 Maloney	Y	N	N	Y	N	Y
15 Rangel	Y	N	N	Y	N	N
16 Serrano	N	N	N	N	Y	N
17 Engel	N	N	N	Y	N	Y
18 Lowey	N	N	N	Y	N	Y
19 ***Kelly***	Y	Y	N	N	N	Y
20 ***Gilman***	Y	Y	N	N	N	Y
21 McNulty	N	?	?	?	?	?
22 ***Sweeney***	Y	Y	Y	N	N	Y
23 ***Boehlert***	Y	Y	N	N	N	Y
24 ***McHugh***	Y	Y	N	N	N	Y
25 ***Walsh***	Y	Y	N	N	N	Y
26 Hinchey	N	N	N	Y	N	Y
27 ***Reynolds***	Y	Y	N	N	N	Y
28 Slaughter	–	–	–	+	–	+
29 LaFalce	N	N	N	Y	N	Y

	115	116	117	118	119	120
30 ***Quinn***	Y	Y	N	N	N	Y
31 ***Houghton***	Y	Y	N	N	N	Y
NORTH CAROLINA						
1 Clayton	N	N	N	Y	N	N
2 Etheridge	Y	N	N	Y	N	Y
3 ***Jones***	Y	Y	Y	N	Y	Y
4 Price	Y	N	N	Y	N	Y
5 ***Burr***	Y	Y	Y	N	N	Y
6 ***Coble***	Y	Y	Y	N	Y	N
7 McIntyre	Y	N	Y	Y	N	Y
8 ***Hayes***	Y	Y	Y	N	N	Y
9 ***Myrick***	Y	Y	Y	N	Y	N
10 ***Ballenger***	Y	Y	N	N	N	Y
11 ***Taylor***	Y	Y	N	N	Y	Y
12 Watt	N	Y	N	Y	N	N
NORTH DAKOTA						
AL Pomeroy	Y	N	N	Y	N	Y
OHIO						
1 ***Chabot***	Y	Y	Y	N	Y	N
2 ***Portman***	Y	Y	Y	N	N	N
3 Hall	N	N	N	Y	N	Y
4 ***Oxley***	Y	Y	N	N	N	Y
5 ***Gillmor***	Y	Y	N	N	N	Y
6 Strickland	Y	N	N	Y	N	Y
7 ***Hobson***	Y	Y	N	N	N	Y
8 ***Boehner***	Y	Y	Y	N	N	Y
9 Kaptur	Y	N	N	Y	N	Y
10 Kucinich	N	N	N	N	Y	N
11 Jones	N	N	N	Y	N	N
12 ***Kasich***	Y	Y	Y	N	Y	Y
13 Brown	N	N	N	Y	N	N
14 Sawyer	N	N	N	Y	N	Y
15 ***Pryce***	Y	Y	N	N	N	Y
16 ***Regula***	Y	Y	N	N	N	Y
17 Traficant	N	Y	N	N	N	Y
18 ***Ney***	Y	Y	N	N	Y	Y
19 ***LaTourette***	+	Y	N	N	N	N
OKLAHOMA						
1 ***Largent***	Y	Y	Y	N	Y	N
2 ***Coburn***	Y	Y	Y	N	Y	Y
3 ***Watkins***	Y	Y	N	N	Y	Y
4 ***Watts***	?	Y	Y	N	N	Y
5 ***Istook***	Y	Y	Y	N	Y	Y
6 ***Lucas***	Y	Y	N	N	Y	Y
OREGON						
1 Wu	Y	N	N	Y	N	N
2 ***Walden***	Y	Y	Y	N	N	Y
3 Blumenauer	Y	N	N	Y	N	N
4 DeFazio	N	N	N	N	Y	N
5 Hooley	Y	Y	N	Y	N	N
PENNSYLVANIA						
1 Brady	N	Y	N	N	N	Y
2 Fattah	N	N	N	Y	N	Y
3 Borski	N	Y	N	N	N	Y
4 Klink	N	Y	N	N	N	Y
5 ***Peterson***	Y	Y	N	N	N	Y
6 Holden	Y	Y	N	N	N	Y
7 ***Weldon***	Y	Y	N	N	Y	Y
8 ***Greenwood***	Y	Y	Y	N	?	?
9 ***Shuster***	Y	Y	N	N	Y	N
10 ***Sherwood***	Y	Y	Y	N	N	Y
11 Kanjorski	N	Y	N	N	N	Y
12 Murtha	N	Y	N	N	N	Y
13 Hoeffel	N	Y	N	N	N	Y
14 Coyne	N	N	N	Y	N	N
15 ***Toomey***	Y	Y	Y	N	N	N
16 ***Pitts***	Y	Y	Y	N	Y	Y
17 ***Gekas***	Y	Y	N	N	N	Y
18 Doyle	N	Y	N	N	N	Y
19 ***Goodling***	Y	Y	N	N	Y	Y
20 Mascara	N	Y	N	N	N	Y
21 ***English***	Y	Y	N	N	Y	Y
RHODE ISLAND						
1 Kennedy	Y	N	N	Y	N	Y
2 Weygand	Y	N	N	Y	N	Y
SOUTH CAROLINA						
1 ***Sanford***	Y	Y	Y	N	Y	N
2 ***Spence***	Y	Y	N	N	N	Y
3 ***Graham***	Y	Y	Y	N	Y	Y
4 ***DeMint***	Y	Y	Y	N	Y	Y
5 Spratt	Y	N	N	Y	N	Y
6 Clyburn	N	N	N	Y	N	Y
SOUTH DAKOTA						
AL ***Thune***	Y	Y	N	N	Y	Y

	115	116	117	118	119	120
TENNESSEE						
1 ***Jenkins***	Y	Y	N	N	N	Y
2 ***Duncan***	Y	Y	Y	N	Y	N
3 ***Wamp***	Y	Y	N	N	Y	Y
4 ***Hilleary***	Y	Y	Y	N	Y	Y
5 Clement	Y	Y	N	N	N	Y
6 Gordon	Y	N	N	N	N	Y
7 ***Bryant***	Y	Y	N	N	Y	Y
8 Tanner	Y	N	N	Y	N	Y
9 Ford	N	N	N	Y	N	Y
TEXAS						
1 Sandlin	Y	N	N	Y	N	Y
2 Turner	Y	N	N	N	N	Y
3 ***Johnson, Sam***	Y	Y	Y	N	Y	N
4 Hall	Y	Y	N	N	Y	N
5 ***Sessions***	Y	Y	Y	N	Y	N
6 ***Barton***	Y	Y	Y	N	Y	N
7 ***Archer***	Y	Y	N	N	Y	N
8 ***Brady***	Y	Y	N	N	Y	Y
9 Lampson	Y	N	N	Y	N	Y
10 Doggett	N	N	N	N	N	N
11 Edwards	N	N	N	N	N	Y
12 ***Granger***	Y	Y	N	N	N	Y
13 ***Thornberry***	Y	Y	Y	N	N	Y
14 ***Paul***	Y	Y	Y	Y	Y	N
15 Hinojosa	Y	N	N	Y	N	Y
16 Reyes	Y	N	N	Y	N	Y
17 Stenholm	Y	Y	Y	Y	N	Y
18 Jackson-Lee	N	N	N	Y	N	Y
19 ***Combest***	Y	Y	Y	N	Y	Y
20 Gonzalez	Y	N	N	Y	N	Y
21 ***Smith***	Y	Y	N	N	Y	Y
22 ***DeLay***	Y	Y	N	N	Y	Y
23 ***Bonilla***	Y	Y	N	N	Y	Y
24 Frost	Y	N	N	Y	N	Y
25 Bentsen	Y	N	N	Y	N	Y
26 ***Armey***	Y	Y	N	N	N	Y
27 Ortiz	Y	N	N	Y	N	Y
28 Rodriguez	N	N	N	N	N	Y
29 Green	N	Y	?	+	?	+
30 Johnson, E.B.	Y	Y	N	Y	N	Y
UTAH						
1 ***Hansen***	Y	Y	N	N	N	Y
2 ***Cook***	Y	Y	Y	N	Y	N
3 ***Cannon***	Y	Y	Y	N	Y	Y
VERMONT						
AL *Sanders*	N	N	N	Y	Y	N
VIRGINIA						
1 ***Bateman***	Y	Y	N	N	N	Y
2 Pickett	Y	Y	N	N	N	Y
3 Scott	N	N	N	Y	N	Y
4 Sisisky	Y	Y	N	N	N	Y
5 Goode	Y	Y	Y	N	Y	N
6 ***Goodlatte***	Y	Y	Y	N	Y	Y
7 ***Bliley***	Y	Y	N	N	?	?
8 Moran	Y	Y	N	N	N	Y
9 Boucher	Y	N	N	Y	N	Y
10 ***Wolf***	Y	Y	N	N	N	Y
11 ***Davis***	Y	Y	N	N	N	Y
WASHINGTON						
1 Inslee	Y	N	N	Y	N	N
2 ***Metcalf***	Y	Y	Y	N	Y	N
3 Baird	Y	N	N	N	N	N
4 ***Hastings***	Y	Y	Y	N	N	Y
5 ***Nethercutt***	Y	Y	N	N	N	Y
6 Dicks	Y	Y	N	N	N	Y
7 McDermott	N	N	N	Y	Y	N
8 ***Dunn***	Y	Y	Y	N	N	Y
9 Smith	Y	N	N	N	N	Y
WEST VIRGINIA						
1 Mollohan	Y	Y	N	N	N	Y
2 Wise	Y	N	N	Y	N	Y
3 Rahall	N	N	N	Y	N	N
WISCONSIN						
1 ***Ryan***	Y	Y	Y	N	Y	N
2 Baldwin	N	N	N	Y	N	N
3 Kind	Y	N	N	Y	N	Y
4 Kleczka	Y	N	N	N	Y	N
5 Barrett	N	N	N	Y	N	N
6 ***Petri***	Y	Y	Y	Y	Y	N
7 Obey	N	N	N	Y	N	Y
8 ***Green***	Y	Y	Y	N	N	N
9 ***Sensenbrenner***	Y	Y	Y	N	Y	N
WYOMING						
AL ***Cubin***	Y	Y	Y	N	Y	Y

Southern states - Ala., Ark., Fla., Ga., Ky., La., Miss., N.C., Okla., S.C., Tenn., Texas, Va.

121. HR 1550. Authorize Funds for U.S. Fire Administration/Passage. Sensenbrenner, R-Wis., motion to suspend the rules and pass the bill to authorize $46.1 million in fiscal 2000 for the U.S. Fire Administration. Motion agreed to 417-3: R 212-3; D 204-0 (ND 150-0, SD 54-0); I 1-0. May 11, 1999. A two-thirds majority of those present and voting (280 in this case) is required for passage under suspension of the rules.

122. H Res 165. Honor Slain Police Officers/Adoption. Chabot, R-Ohio, motion to suspend the rules and adopt the resolution to honor police officers who lost their lives in the line of duty. Motion agreed to 420-0: R 217-0; D 202-0 (ND 149-0, SD 53-0); I 1-0. May 11, 1999. A two-thirds majority of those present and voting (280 in this case) is required for adoption under suspension of the rules.

123. HR 775. Y2K Liability Limitations/Rule. Adoption of the rule (H Res 166) to provide for House floor consideration of the bill to limit lawsuits resulting from Year 2000 computer failures. Adopted 236-188: R 216-0; D 20-187 (ND 9-143, SD 11-44); I 0-1. May 12, 1999.

124. HR 775. Y2K Liability Limitations/Cap on Damages. Scott, D-Va., amendment to strike the section of the bill that caps punitive damages at $250,000 or three times the amount awarded for compensatory damages. Rejected 192-235: R 11-207; D 180-28 (ND 139-14, SD 41-14); I 1-0. May 12, 1999.

125. HR 775. Y2K Liability Limitations/Class Action Suits. Nadler, D-N.Y., amendment to strike the section of the bill that limits class action lawsuits, for example, by requiring the removal of state class action suits to federal court if the amount the defendant is being sued for is greater than $1 million. Rejected, 180-244: R 7-209; D 172-35 (ND 134-18, SD 38-17); I 1-0. May 12, 1999.

Key

- Y Voted for (yea).
- # Paired for.
- + Announced for.
- N Voted against (nay).
- X Paired against.
- – Announced against.
- P Voted "present."
- C Voted "present" to avoid possible conflict of interest.
- ? Did not vote or otherwise make a position known.

•

Democrats ***Republicans***
Independents

	121	122	123	124	125
ALABAMA					
1 ***Callahan***	Y	Y	Y	N	N
2 ***Everett***	Y	Y	Y	N	N
3 ***Riley***	Y	Y	Y	N	N
4 ***Aderholt***	Y	Y	Y	N	N
5 Cramer	Y	Y	Y	N	N
6 ***Bachus***	Y	Y	Y	N	N
7 Hilliard	Y	Y	N	Y	Y
ALASKA					
AL ***Young***	Y	Y	Y	N	N
ARIZONA					
1 ***Salmon***	Y	Y	Y	N	N
2 Pastor	Y	Y	N	Y	Y
3 ***Stump***	Y	Y	Y	N	N
4 ***Shadegg***	Y	Y	Y	N	N
5 ***Kolbe***	Y	Y	Y	N	N
6 ***Hayworth***	Y	Y	Y	N	N
ARKANSAS					
1 Berry	Y	Y	N	Y	Y
2 Snyder	Y	Y	N	Y	Y
3 ***Hutchinson***	Y	Y	Y	N	N
4 ***Dickey***	Y	Y	Y	N	N
CALIFORNIA					
1 Thompson	Y	Y	N	N	Y
2 ***Herger***	Y	Y	Y	N	?
3 ***Ose***	+	+	Y	N	N
4 ***Doolittle***	Y	Y	Y	N	N
5 Matsui	Y	Y	N	Y	Y
6 Woolsey	Y	Y	N	Y	Y
7 Miller, George	Y	Y	N	Y	Y
8 Pelosi	Y	Y	N	Y	Y
9 Lee	Y	Y	N	Y	Y
10 Tauscher	Y	Y	Y	N	N
11 ***Pombo***	Y	Y	Y	N	N
12 Lantos	Y	Y	N	Y	Y
13 Stark	Y	Y	N	Y	Y
14 Eshoo	Y	Y	N	N	N
15 ***Campbell***	Y	Y	Y	N	N
16 Lofgren	Y	Y	N	Y	Y
17 Farr	Y	Y	N	Y	Y
18 Condit	Y	Y	Y	N	N
19 ***Radanovich***	Y	Y	Y	N	N
20 Dooley	Y	Y	Y	N	N
21 ***Thomas***	Y	Y	Y	N	N
22 Capps	+	+	N	Y	N
23 ***Gallegly***	Y	Y	Y	N	N
24 Sherman	Y	Y	N	Y	Y
25 ***McKeon***	Y	Y	Y	N	N
26 Berman	Y	Y	N	Y	Y
27 ***Rogan***	Y	Y	Y	N	N
28 ***Dreier***	Y	Y	Y	N	N
29 Waxman	Y	Y	N	Y	Y
30 Becerra	Y	Y	N	Y	Y
31 Martinez	Y	Y	N	Y	Y
32 Dixon	Y	Y	N	Y	Y
33 Roybal-Allard	Y	?	N	Y	Y
34 Napolitano	?	?	?	?	?
35 Waters	Y	Y	N	Y	Y
36 ***Kuykendall***	Y	Y	Y	N	N
37 Millender-McD.	Y	Y	N	Y	Y
38 ***Horn***	Y	Y	Y	N	N
39 ***Royce***	Y	Y	Y	N	N
40 ***Lewis***	Y	Y	Y	N	N
41 ***Miller, Gary***	Y	Y	Y	N	N
42 Brown	?	?	?	?	?
43 ***Calvert***	Y	Y	Y	N	N
44 ***Bono***	Y	Y	Y	N	N
45 ***Rohrabacher***	Y	Y	Y	N	N
46 Sanchez	Y	Y	N	Y	Y
47 ***Cox***	Y	Y	Y	?	?
48 ***Packard***	Y	Y	Y	N	N
49 ***Bilbray***	Y	Y	Y	N	N
50 Filner	Y	Y	N	Y	Y
51 ***Cunningham***	Y	Y	Y	N	N
52 ***Hunter***	Y	Y	Y	N	N
COLORADO					
1 DeGette	Y	Y	N	Y	Y
2 Udall	Y	Y	N	Y	Y
3 ***McInnis***	Y	Y	Y	N	N
4 ***Schaffer***	Y	Y	Y	N	N
5 ***Hefley***	Y	Y	Y	N	N
6 ***Tancredo***	Y	Y	Y	N	N
CONNECTICUT					
1 Larson	Y	Y	N	Y	Y
2 Gejdenson	Y	Y	N	Y	Y
3 DeLauro	Y	Y	N	Y	Y
4 ***Shays***	Y	Y	Y	N	N
5 Maloney	Y	Y	N	Y	Y
6 ***Johnson***	Y	Y	Y	N	N
DELAWARE					
AL ***Castle***	Y	Y	Y	N	N
FLORIDA					
1 ***Scarborough***	?	?	?	N	N
2 Boyd	Y	Y	Y	N	N
3 Brown	Y	Y	N	Y	Y
4 ***Fowler***	Y	Y	Y	N	N
5 Thurman	Y	Y	N	Y	N
6 ***Stearns***	Y	Y	Y	N	N
7 ***Mica***	Y	Y	Y	N	N
8 ***McCollum***	Y	Y	Y	N	N
9 ***Bilirakis***	Y	Y	Y	N	N
10 ***Young***	Y	Y	Y	N	N
11 Davis	Y	Y	N	Y	N
12 ***Canady***	Y	Y	Y	N	N
13 ***Miller***	Y	Y	Y	N	N
14 ***Goss***	Y	Y	Y	N	N
15 ***Weldon***	Y	Y	Y	N	N
16 ***Foley***	Y	Y	Y	N	N
17 Meek	Y	Y	N	Y	Y
18 ***Ros-Lehtinen***	Y	Y	Y	N	N
19 Wexler	Y	Y	N	Y	Y
20 Deutsch	Y	Y	N	Y	Y
21 ***Diaz-Balart***	Y	Y	Y	Y	Y
22 ***Shaw***	Y	Y	Y	N	N
23 Hastings	Y	Y	N	Y	Y
GEORGIA					
1 ***Kingston***	Y	Y	Y	N	N
2 Bishop	Y	Y	N	Y	Y
3 ***Collins***	Y	Y	Y	N	N
4 McKinney	Y	Y	N	Y	Y
5 Lewis	Y	Y	N	Y	Y
6 ***Isakson***	Y	Y	Y	N	N
7 ***Barr***	Y	Y	Y	N	N
8 ***Chambliss***	Y	Y	Y	N	N
9 ***Deal***	Y	Y	Y	N	N
10 ***Norwood***	Y	Y	Y	N	N
11 ***Linder***	Y	Y	Y	N	N
HAWAII					
1 Abercrombie	Y	Y	N	Y	Y
2 Mink	Y	Y	N	Y	Y
IDAHO					
1 ***Chenoweth***	N	Y	Y	N	N
2 ***Simpson***	Y	Y	Y	N	N
ILLINOIS					
1 Rush	Y	Y	N	Y	Y
2 Jackson	Y	Y	N	Y	Y
3 Lipinski	Y	Y	N	Y	Y
4 Gutierrez	Y	Y	N	Y	Y
5 Blagojevich	Y	Y	N	Y	Y
6 ***Hyde***	Y	Y	Y	N	N
7 Davis	Y	Y	N	Y	Y
8 ***Crane***	Y	Y	Y	N	N
9 Schakowsky	Y	Y	N	Y	Y
10 ***Porter***	Y	Y	Y	N	N
11 ***Weller***	Y	Y	Y	N	N
12 Costello	Y	Y	N	Y	Y
13 ***Biggert***	Y	Y	Y	N	N
14 ***Hastert***					

ND Northern Democrats SD Southern Democrats

	121	122	123	124	125
15 ***Ewing***	Y	Y	Y	N	N
16 ***Manzullo***	Y	Y	Y	N	N
17 Evans	Y	Y	N	Y	Y
18 ***LaHood***	Y	Y	Y	N	N
19 Phelps	Y	Y	N	Y	Y
20 ***Shimkus***	Y	Y	Y	N	N
INDIANA					
1 Visclosky	Y	Y	N	Y	Y
2 ***McIntosh***	Y	Y	?	N	N
3 Roemer	Y	Y	Y	N	Y
4 ***Souder***	Y	Y	Y	N	N
5 ***Buyer***	Y	Y	Y	N	N
6 ***Burton***	Y	Y	Y	N	N
7 ***Pease***	Y	Y	Y	N	N
8 ***Hostettler***	Y	Y	Y	N	N
9 Hill	Y	Y	N	N	Y
10 Carson	Y	Y	N	Y	Y
IOWA					
1 ***Leach***	Y	Y	Y	N	N
2 ***Nussle***	Y	Y	Y	N	N
3 Boswell	Y	Y	N	Y	N
4 ***Ganske***	Y	Y	Y	Y	Y
5 ***Latham***	Y	Y	Y	N	N
KANSAS					
1 ***Moran***	Y	Y	Y	N	N
2 ***Ryun***	Y	Y	Y	N	N
3 Moore	Y	Y	N	Y	N
4 ***Tiahrt***	Y	Y	Y	N	N
KENTUCKY					
1 ***Whitfield***	Y	Y	Y	N	N
2 ***Lewis***	Y	Y	Y	N	N
3 ***Northup***	Y	Y	Y	N	N
4 Lucas	Y	Y	Y	N	N
5 ***Rogers***	Y	Y	Y	N	N
6 ***Fletcher***	Y	Y	Y	N	N
LOUISIANA					
1 Vacant					
2 Jefferson	Y	Y	N	Y	Y
3 ***Tauzin***	Y	Y	Y	N	N
4 ***McCrery***	Y	Y	Y	N	N
5 ***Cooksey***	Y	Y	Y	N	N
6 ***Baker***	Y	Y	Y	N	N
7 John	Y	Y	N	N	N
MAINE					
1 Allen	Y	Y	N	Y	Y
2 Baldacci	Y	Y	N	Y	Y
MARYLAND					
1 ***Gilchrest***	Y	Y	Y	N	N
2 ***Ehrlich***	Y	Y	Y	N	N
3 Cardin	Y	Y	N	Y	Y
4 Wynn	Y	Y	N	Y	Y
5 Hoyer	Y	Y	N	Y	Y
6 ***Bartlett***	Y	Y	Y	N	N
7 Cummings	Y	Y	N	Y	Y
8 ***Morella***	Y	Y	Y	N	N
MASSACHUSETTS					
1 Olver	Y	Y	N	Y	Y
2 Neal	Y	Y	N	Y	Y
3 McGovern	Y	Y	N	Y	Y
4 Frank	Y	Y	N	N	Y
5 Meehan	Y	Y	N	Y	Y
6 Tierney	Y	Y	N	Y	Y
7 Markey	Y	Y	N	Y	Y
8 Capuano	Y	Y	N	Y	Y
9 Moakley	Y	Y	N	Y	Y
10 Delahunt	Y	Y	N	Y	Y
MICHIGAN					
1 Stupak	Y	Y	N	Y	Y
2 ***Hoekstra***	Y	Y	Y	N	N
3 ***Ehlers***	Y	Y	Y	N	N
4 ***Camp***	Y	Y	Y	N	N
5 Barcia	Y	Y	N	N	N
6 ***Upton***	Y	Y	Y	N	N
7 ***Smith***	Y	Y	Y	N	N
8 Stabenow	Y	Y	N	Y	Y
9 Kildee	Y	Y	N	Y	Y
10 Bonior	Y	Y	N	Y	Y
11 ***Knollenberg***	Y	Y	Y	N	N
12 Levin	Y	Y	N	Y	Y
13 Rivers	Y	Y	N	Y	N
14 Conyers	Y	Y	N	Y	Y
15 Kilpatrick	Y	Y	N	Y	Y
16 Dingell	Y	Y	N	Y	Y
MINNESOTA					
1 ***Gutknecht***	Y	Y	Y	N	N
2 Minge	Y	Y	N	N	Y
3 ***Ramstad***	Y	Y	Y	N	N
4 Vento	Y	Y	N	Y	Y
5 Sabo	Y	Y	N	Y	Y
6 Luther	Y	Y	N	Y	Y
7 Peterson	Y	Y	Y	N	N
8 Oberstar	Y	Y	N	Y	Y
MISSISSIPPI					
1 ***Wicker***	Y	Y	Y	N	N
2 Thompson	Y	Y	N	Y	Y
3 ***Pickering***	Y	Y	Y	N	N
4 Shows	Y	Y	N	Y	Y
5 Taylor	Y	Y	Y	N	N
MISSOURI					
1 Clay	Y	Y	N	Y	Y
2 ***Talent***	Y	Y	Y	N	N
3 Gephardt	Y	?	N	Y	Y
4 Skelton	Y	Y	N	Y	N
5 McCarthy	Y	Y	N	Y	Y
6 Danner	Y	Y	N	N	N
7 ***Blunt***	Y	Y	Y	N	N
8 ***Emerson***	Y	Y	Y	N	N
9 ***Hulshof***	Y	Y	Y	N	Y
MONTANA					
AL ***Hill***	Y	Y	Y	N	N
NEBRASKA					
1 ***Bereuter***	Y	Y	Y	N	N
2 ***Terry***	Y	Y	Y	N	N
3 ***Barrett***	Y	Y	Y	N	N
NEVADA					
1 Berkley	Y	Y	N	Y	Y
2 ***Gibbons***	Y	Y	Y	Y	N
NEW HAMPSHIRE					
1 ***Sununu***	Y	Y	Y	N	N
2 ***Bass***	Y	Y	Y	N	N
NEW JERSEY					
1 Andrews	Y	Y	N	Y	Y
2 ***LoBiondo***	Y	Y	Y	N	N
3 ***Saxton***	Y	Y	Y	N	N
4 ***Smith***	Y	Y	Y	N	N
5 ***Roukema***	Y	Y	Y	N	N
6 Pallone	Y	Y	N	Y	Y
7 ***Franks***	Y	Y	Y	N	N
8 Pascrell	Y	Y	N	Y	Y
9 Rothman	Y	Y	N	Y	Y
10 Payne	Y	Y	N	Y	Y
11 ***Frelinghuysen***	Y	Y	Y	N	N
12 Holt	Y	Y	Y	Y	Y
13 Menendez	Y	Y	N	Y	Y
NEW MEXICO					
1 ***Wilson***	Y	Y	Y	N	N
2 ***Skeen***	Y	Y	Y	N	N
3 Udall	Y	Y	N	Y	Y
NEW YORK					
1 ***Forbes***	Y	Y	Y	N	N
2 ***Lazio***	Y	Y	Y	Y	N
3 ***King***	Y	Y	Y	Y	N
4 McCarthy	Y	Y	Y	Y	Y
5 Ackerman	Y	Y	N	Y	Y
6 Meeks	Y	Y	N	Y	Y
7 Crowley	Y	Y	N	Y	Y
8 Nadler	Y	Y	N	Y	Y
9 Weiner	Y	Y	N	Y	Y
10 Towns	Y	Y	N	Y	Y
11 Owens	Y	Y	N	Y	Y
12 Velázquez	Y	Y	N	Y	Y
13 ***Fossella***	Y	Y	Y	N	N
14 Maloney	Y	Y	N	Y	Y
15 Rangel	Y	Y	N	Y	Y
16 Serrano	Y	Y	N	Y	Y
17 Engel	Y	Y	?	Y	Y
18 Lowey	?	?	N	Y	Y
19 ***Kelly***	Y	Y	Y	N	N
20 ***Gilman***	Y	Y	Y	N	N
21 McNulty	Y	Y	N	Y	Y
22 ***Sweeney***	Y	Y	Y	N	N
23 ***Boehlert***	Y	Y	Y	N	N
24 ***McHugh***	Y	Y	Y	N	N
25 ***Walsh***	Y	Y	Y	N	?
26 Hinchey	Y	Y	N	Y	Y
27 ***Reynolds***	Y	Y	Y	N	N
28 Slaughter	+	+	−	+	+
29 LaFalce	Y	Y	N	Y	Y
30 ***Quinn***	Y	Y	Y	N	N
31 ***Houghton***	Y	Y	Y	N	N
NORTH CAROLINA					
1 Clayton	Y	Y	N	Y	Y
2 Etheridge	Y	Y	N	Y	Y
3 ***Jones***	Y	Y	Y	N	N
4 Price	Y	Y	N	Y	Y
5 ***Burr***	Y	Y	Y	N	N
6 ***Coble***	+	Y	Y	Y	N
7 McIntyre	Y	Y	N	Y	N
8 ***Hayes***	Y	Y	Y	N	N
9 ***Myrick***	Y	Y	Y	N	N
10 ***Ballenger***	Y	Y	Y	N	N
11 ***Taylor***	Y	Y	Y	N	N
12 Watt	Y	Y	N	Y	Y
NORTH DAKOTA					
AL Pomeroy	Y	Y	N	Y	N
OHIO					
1 ***Chabot***	Y	Y	Y	N	N
2 ***Portman***	Y	Y	Y	N	N
3 Hall	Y	Y	N	Y	N
4 ***Oxley***	Y	Y	Y	N	N
5 ***Gillmor***	Y	Y	Y	N	N
6 Strickland	Y	Y	N	Y	Y
7 ***Hobson***	Y	Y	Y	N	N
8 ***Boehner***	Y	Y	Y	N	N
9 Kaptur	Y	Y	N	Y	Y
10 Kucinich	Y	Y	N	Y	Y
11 Jones	?	Y	N	Y	Y
12 ***Kasich***	+	+	Y	N	N
13 Brown	Y	Y	N	Y	Y
14 Sawyer	Y	Y	N	Y	Y
15 ***Pryce***	Y	Y	Y	N	Y
16 ***Regula***	Y	Y	Y	N	N
17 Traficant	Y	Y	Y	Y	Y
18 ***Ney***	Y	Y	Y	N	N
19 ***LaTourette***	Y	Y	Y	N	N
OKLAHOMA					
1 ***Largent***	Y	Y	Y	N	N
2 ***Coburn***	Y	Y	Y	N	N
3 ***Watkins***	Y	Y	Y	N	N
4 ***Watts***	Y	Y	Y	N	N
5 ***Istook***	Y	Y	Y	N	N
6 ***Lucas***	Y	Y	Y	N	N
OREGON					
1 Wu	Y	Y	N	Y	Y
2 ***Walden***	Y	Y	Y	N	N
3 Blumenauer	Y	Y	N	Y	N
4 DeFazio	Y	Y	N	Y	Y
5 Hooley	Y	Y	N	Y	N
PENNSYLVANIA					
1 Brady	Y	Y	N	Y	Y
2 Fattah	Y	Y	N	Y	Y
3 Borski	Y	Y	N	Y	Y
4 Klink	Y	Y	N	Y	Y
5 ***Peterson***	?	Y	?	N	N
6 Holden	Y	Y	Y	N	N
7 ***Weldon***	Y	Y	Y	N	?
8 ***Greenwood***	?	?	Y	N	N
9 ***Shuster***	Y	Y	Y	N	N
10 ***Sherwood***	Y	Y	Y	N	N
11 Kanjorski	Y	Y	N	Y	Y
12 Murtha	Y	Y	N	Y	Y
13 Hoeffel	Y	Y	N	Y	Y
14 Coyne	Y	Y	N	Y	Y
15 ***Toomey***	Y	Y	Y	N	N
16 ***Pitts***	Y	Y	Y	N	N
17 ***Gekas***	Y	Y	Y	N	N
18 Doyle	Y	Y	N	Y	?
19 ***Goodling***	Y	Y	Y	N	N
20 Mascara	Y	Y	N	Y	Y
21 ***English***	Y	Y	Y	Y	N
RHODE ISLAND					
1 Kennedy	Y	Y	N	Y	Y
2 Weygand	Y	Y	N	Y	Y
SOUTH CAROLINA					
1 ***Sanford***	N	Y	Y	N	N
2 ***Spence***	Y	Y	Y	N	N
3 ***Graham***	Y	Y	Y	Y	N
4 ***DeMint***	Y	Y	Y	N	N
5 Spratt	Y	Y	N	Y	Y
6 Clyburn	Y	Y	N	Y	Y
SOUTH DAKOTA					
AL ***Thune***	Y	Y	Y	N	N
TENNESSEE					
1 ***Jenkins***	Y	Y	Y	Y	N
2 ***Duncan***	Y	Y	Y	Y	Y
3 ***Wamp***	Y	Y	Y	N	N
4 ***Hilleary***	Y	Y	Y	N	N
5 Clement	Y	Y	N	Y	Y
6 Gordon	Y	Y	N	Y	N
7 ***Bryant***	Y	Y	Y	N	N
8 Tanner	Y	Y	N	N	N
9 Ford	Y	Y	Y	Y	Y
TEXAS					
1 Sandlin	Y	Y	N	Y	Y
2 Turner	Y	Y	N	N	Y
3 ***Johnson, Sam***	Y	Y	Y	N	N
4 Hall	Y	Y	Y	N	N
5 ***Sessions***	Y	Y	Y	N	N
6 ***Barton***	Y	Y	?	?	?
7 ***Archer***	Y	Y	Y	N	N
8 ***Brady***	Y	Y	Y	N	N
9 Lampson	Y	Y	N	Y	Y
10 Doggett	Y	Y	N	Y	Y
11 Edwards	Y	Y	N	N	Y
12 ***Granger***	Y	Y	Y	N	N
13 ***Thornberry***	Y	Y	?	N	N
14 ***Paul***	N	Y	Y	Y	Y
15 Hinojosa	Y	Y	N	Y	Y
16 Reyes	Y	?	N	Y	Y
17 Stenholm	Y	Y	Y	N	N
18 Jackson-Lee	Y	Y	N	Y	Y
19 ***Combest***	Y	Y	Y	N	N
20 Gonzalez	Y	Y	N	Y	Y
21 ***Smith***	Y	Y	Y	N	N
22 ***DeLay***	Y	Y	Y	N	N
23 ***Bonilla***	Y	Y	Y	N	N
24 Frost	Y	Y	N	Y	Y
25 Bentsen	Y	Y	N	Y	Y
26 ***Armey***	Y	Y	Y	N	N
27 Ortiz	Y	Y	N	Y	Y
28 Rodriguez	Y	Y	N	Y	Y
29 Green	Y	Y	N	Y	Y
30 Johnson, E.B.	Y	Y	N	Y	Y
UTAH					
1 ***Hansen***	Y	Y	Y	N	N
2 ***Cook***	Y	Y	Y	N	N
3 ***Cannon***	Y	Y	Y	N	N
VERMONT					
AL *Sanders*	Y	Y	N	Y	Y
VIRGINIA					
1 ***Bateman***	Y	Y	Y	N	N
2 Pickett	Y	Y	N	N	N
3 Scott	Y	Y	N	Y	Y
4 Sisisky	?	?	Y	N	N
5 Goode	Y	Y	Y	N	N
6 ***Goodlatte***	Y	Y	Y	N	N
7 ***Bliley***	Y	Y	Y	N	N
8 Moran	Y	Y	Y	N	N
9 Boucher	Y	Y	Y	N	N
10 ***Wolf***	Y	Y	Y	N	N
11 ***Davis***	Y	Y	Y	N	N
WASHINGTON					
1 Inslee	Y	Y	N	Y	Y
2 ***Metcalf***	Y	Y	Y	N	N
3 Baird	Y	Y	N	Y	Y
4 ***Hastings***	Y	Y	Y	N	N
5 ***Nethercutt***	Y	Y	Y	N	N
6 Dicks	Y	Y	N	Y	Y
7 McDermott	Y	Y	N	Y	Y
8 ***Dunn***	Y	Y	Y	-	N
9 Smith	Y	Y	N	N	Y
WEST VIRGINIA					
1 Mollohan	Y	Y	N	Y	N
2 Wise	Y	Y	N	Y	Y
3 Rahall	Y	Y	N	Y	Y
WISCONSIN					
1 ***Ryan***	Y	Y	Y	N	N
2 Baldwin	Y	Y	N	Y	Y
3 Kind	Y	Y	N	Y	Y
4 Kleczka	Y	Y	N	Y	Y
5 Barrett	Y	Y	N	Y	Y
6 ***Petri***	Y	Y	Y	N	N
7 Obey	Y	Y	N	Y	Y
8 ***Green***	Y	Y	Y	N	N
9 ***Sensenbrenner***	Y	Y	Y	N	N
WYOMING					
AL ***Cubin***	Y	Y	Y	N	N

Southern states - Ala., Ark., Fla., Ga., Ky., La., Miss., N.C., Okla., S.C., Tenn., Texas, Va.

126. HR 775. Y2K Liability Limitations/Substitute. Conyers, D-Mich., substitute amendment to strike provisions including the $250,000 cap on punitive damages and requirements for attorneys fee disclosures and limitations on the liability of directors and officers of a defendant company. Rejected 190-236: R 7-212; D 182-24 (ND 144-8, SD 38-16); I 1-0. May 12, 1999.

127. HR 775. Y2K Liability Limitations/Recommit. Conyers, D-Mich., motion to recommit the bill to the Judiciary Committee with instructions to report it back with an amendment to provide for jurisdiction, service of process and discovery in Y2K actions brought against corporate defendants outside the United States. Rejected 184-246: R 1-220; D 182-26 (ND 142-11, SD 40-15); I 1-0. May 12, 1999.

128. HR 775. Y2K Liability Limitations/Passage. Passage of the bill to limit lawsuits resulting from Year 2000 computer failures. Damage awards would be capped at $250,000, or three times the actual damage, whichever was greater; for businesses with fewer than 25 employees, the cap would be the lesser of $250,000 or three times the actual damage. The bill would impose a 90 day waiting period before a lawsuit could be brought. Passed 236-190: R 208-9; D 28-180 (ND 14-139, SD 14-41); I 0-1. May 12, 1999.

129. HR 1555. Intelligence Authorization/Funding Limit. Sanders, I-Vt., amendment to limit the fiscal 2000 intelligence authorization to the fiscal 1998 level, and require the Director of Central Intelligence to report on recent errors, including the mapping failures that contributed to the bombing of the Chinese embassy in Belgrade, Yugoslavia. Rejected 68-343: R 6-213; D 61-130 (ND 58-84, SD 3-46); I 1-0. May 13, 1999. (Subsequently, the bill was passed by voice vote.)

130. HR 1141. Fiscal 1999 Supplemental Appropriations/Motion To Instruct. Upton, R-Mich., motion to instruct House conferees to reject any provisions not in the House-passed versions of HR 1141 or HR 1664, or in the Senate-passed version of HR 1664. Motion agreed to 381-46: R 201-17; D 179-29 (ND 131-23, SD 48-6); I 1-0. May 13, 1999.

Key

Y Voted for (yea).
\# Paired for.
\+ Announced for.
N Voted against (nay).
X Paired against.
– Announced against.
P Voted "present."
C Voted "present" to avoid possible conflict of interest.
? Did not vote or otherwise make a position known.

•

Democrats ***Republicans***
Independents

	126	127	128	129	130
ALABAMA					
1 ***Callahan***	N	N	Y	N	N
2 ***Everett***	N	N	Y	N	N
3 ***Riley***	N	N	?	N	N
4 ***Aderholt***	N	N	Y	N	N
5 Cramer	N	N	Y	N	N
6 ***Bachus***	N	N	Y	N	Y
7 Hilliard	Y	Y	N	Y	N
ALASKA					
AL ***Young***	N	N	Y	N	N
ARIZONA					
1 ***Salmon***	N	N	Y	N	Y
2 Pastor	Y	Y	N	Y	N
3 ***Stump***	N	N	Y	N	Y
4 ***Shadegg***	N	N	Y	N	Y
5 ***Kolbe***	N	N	Y	N	Y
6 ***Hayworth***	N	N	Y	N	Y
ARKANSAS					
1 Berry	Y	Y	N	N	Y
2 Snyder	Y	N	N	N	Y
3 ***Hutchinson***	N	N	Y	N	Y
4 ***Dickey***	N	N	Y	N	Y
CALIFORNIA					
1 Thompson	Y	Y	N	N	Y
2 ***Herger***	N	N	Y	N	Y
3 ***Ose***	N	N	Y	N	Y
4 ***Doolittle***	N	N	N	N	Y
5 Matsui	Y	Y	N	?	Y
6 Woolsey	Y	Y	N	Y	Y
7 Miller, George	Y	Y	N	?	Y
8 Pelosi	Y	Y	N	N	N
9 Lee	Y	Y	N	Y	Y
10 Tauscher	N	N	Y	N	Y
11 ***Pombo***	N	N	Y	N	N
12 Lantos	Y	Y	N	N	Y
13 Stark	Y	Y	N	Y	Y
14 Eshoo	N	Y	N	N	Y
15 ***Campbell***	N	N	Y	N	Y
16 Lofgren	Y	Y	N	N	Y
17 Farr	Y	Y	N	Y	N
18 Condit	N	N	Y	N	Y
19 ***Radanovich***	N	N	Y	N	Y
20 Dooley	N	N	Y	N	Y
21 ***Thomas***	N	N	Y	N	Y
22 Capps	Y	Y	Y	N	Y
23 ***Gallegly***	N	N	Y	N	N
24 Sherman	Y	Y	N	N	Y
25 ***McKeon***	N	N	Y	N	Y
26 Berman	Y	Y	N	N	N
27 ***Rogan***	N	N	Y	N	Y
28 ***Dreier***	N	N	Y	N	Y
29 Waxman	Y	Y	N	N	Y
30 Becerra	Y	Y	N	?	Y
31 Martinez	Y	Y	N	N	Y
32 Dixon	Y	Y	N	N	Y
33 Roybal-Allard	Y	Y	N	N	Y
34 Napolitano	?	?	?	N	Y
35 Waters	Y	Y	N	Y	N
36 ***Kuykendall***	N	N	Y	N	Y
37 Millender-McD.	Y	Y	N	N	Y
38 ***Horn***	N	N	Y	N	Y
39 ***Royce***	N	N	Y	N	Y
40 ***Lewis***	N	N	Y	N	N
41 ***Miller, Gary***	N	N	Y	N	Y
42 Brown	?	?	?	?	?
43 ***Calvert***	N	N	Y	N	Y
44 ***Bono***	N	N	Y	N	Y
45 ***Rohrabacher***	N	N	Y	Y	Y
46 Sanchez	Y	Y	N	N	Y
47 ***Cox***	?	N	?	N	Y
48 ***Packard***	N	N	Y	N	N
49 ***Bilbray***	N	N	Y	N	Y
50 Filner	Y	Y	N	Y	Y
51 ***Cunningham***	N	N	Y	N	Y
52 ***Hunter***	N	N	Y	N	Y
COLORADO					
1 DeGette	Y	Y	N	N	Y
2 Udall	Y	Y	Y	N	Y
3 ***McInnis***	N	N	Y	N	Y
4 ***Schaffer***	N	N	Y	N	Y
5 ***Hefley***	N	N	Y	N	Y
6 ***Tancredo***	N	N	Y	N	Y
CONNECTICUT					
1 Larson	Y	Y	N	N	Y
2 Gejdenson	Y	Y	N	Y	Y
3 DeLauro	Y	Y	N	Y	Y
4 ***Shays***	N	N	Y	N	Y
5 Maloney	Y	Y	N	N	Y
6 ***Johnson***	N	N	Y	N	Y
DELAWARE					
AL ***Castle***	N	N	Y	N	Y
FLORIDA					
1 ***Scarborough***	N	N	Y	N	Y
2 Boyd	N	N	Y	N	N
3 Brown	Y	Y	N	N	Y
4 ***Fowler***	N	N	Y	N	Y
5 Thurman	Y	Y	N	?	Y
6 ***Stearns***	N	N	Y	Y	Y
7 ***Mica***	N	N	Y	N	Y
8 ***McCollum***	N	N	Y	N	Y
9 ***Bilirakis***	N	N	Y	N	Y
10 ***Young***	N	N	Y	N	P
11 Davis	Y	Y	N	N	Y
12 ***Canady***	N	N	Y	N	Y
13 ***Miller***	N	N	Y	N	Y
14 ***Goss***	N	N	Y	N	Y
15 ***Weldon***	N	N	Y	N	Y
16 ***Foley***	N	N	Y	N	Y
17 Meek	Y	Y	N	N	N
18 ***Ros-Lehtinen***	N	N	Y	N	+
19 Wexler	Y	Y	N	N	Y
20 Deutsch	Y	Y	N	N	Y
21 ***Diaz-Balart***	N	N	N	N	Y
22 ***Shaw***	N	N	Y	N	Y
23 Hastings	Y	Y	N	N	Y
GEORGIA					
1 ***Kingston***	N	N	Y	N	Y
2 Bishop	Y	Y	N	N	Y
3 ***Collins***	N	N	Y	N	Y
4 McKinney	Y	Y	N	Y	Y
5 Lewis	Y	Y	N	?	Y
6 ***Isakson***	N	N	Y	N	Y
7 ***Barr***	N	N	Y	N	Y
8 ***Chambliss***	N	N	Y	N	Y
9 ***Deal***	N	N	Y	N	Y
10 ***Norwood***	N	N	Y	N	Y
11 ***Linder***	N	N	Y	N	Y
HAWAII					
1 Abercrombie	Y	Y	N	Y	Y
2 Mink	Y	Y	N	Y	Y
IDAHO					
1 ***Chenoweth***	N	N	Y	Y	N
2 ***Simpson***	N	N	Y	N	Y
ILLINOIS					
1 Rush	Y	Y	N	N	Y
2 Jackson	Y	Y	N	Y	Y
3 Lipinski	Y	Y	N	N	Y
4 Gutierrez	Y	Y	N	N	Y
5 Blagojevich	Y	Y	N	N	Y
6 ***Hyde***	N	N	Y	N	Y
7 Davis	Y	Y	N	Y	Y
8 ***Crane***	N	N	Y	N	Y
9 Schakowsky	N	Y	N	Y	Y
10 ***Porter***	N	N	Y	N	Y
11 ***Weller***	?	N	Y	N	Y
12 Costello	Y	Y	N	N	Y
13 ***Biggert***	N	N	Y	N	Y
14 ***Hastert***	N	N	Y		

ND Northern Democrats SD Southern Democrats

	126	127	128	129	130
15 ***Ewing***	N	N	Y	N	Y
16 ***Manzullo***	N	N	Y	N	Y
17 Evans	Y	Y	N	Y	Y
18 ***LaHood***	N	N	Y	N	Y
19 Phelps	Y	Y	N	N	Y
20 ***Shimkus***	N	N	Y	N	Y
INDIANA					
1 Visclosky	Y	Y	N	N	N
2 ***McIntosh***	N	N	Y	N	Y
3 Roemer	Y	N	Y	N	Y
4 ***Souder***	N	N	Y	N	Y
5 ***Buyer***	N	N	Y	N	Y
6 ***Burton***	N	N	Y	N	Y
7 ***Pease***	N	N	Y	N	Y
8 ***Hostettler***	N	N	Y	N	Y
9 Hill	Y	Y	N	N	Y
10 Carson	Y	Y	N	N	Y
IOWA					
1 ***Leach***	N	N	Y	N	Y
2 ***Nussle***	N	N	Y	N	Y
3 Boswell	Y	N	N	N	Y
4 ***Ganske***	Y	N	N	N	Y
5 ***Latham***	N	N	Y	N	Y
KANSAS					
1 ***Moran***	N	N	Y	N	N
2 ***Ryun***	N	N	Y	N	N
3 Moore	Y	Y	N	N	Y
4 ***Tiahrt***	N	N	Y	N	N
KENTUCKY					
1 ***Whitfield***	N	N	Y	N	Y
2 ***Lewis***	N	N	Y	N	N
3 ***Northup***	N	N	Y	N	Y
4 Lucas	N	N	Y	N	Y
5 ***Rogers***	N	N	Y	N	Y
6 ***Fletcher***	N	N	Y	N	Y
LOUISIANA					
1 Vacant					
2 Jefferson	?	Y	N	?	Y
3 ***Tauzin***	N	N	Y	N	Y
4 ***McCrery***	N	N	Y	N	N
5 ***Cooksey***	N	N	Y	N	Y
6 ***Baker***	N	N	Y	N	N
7 John	N	N	Y	N	Y
MAINE					
1 Allen	Y	Y	N	Y	Y
2 Baldacci	Y	Y	N	Y	Y
MARYLAND					
1 ***Gilchrest***	N	N	Y	N	Y
2 ***Ehrlich***	N	N	Y	N	Y
3 Cardin	Y	Y	N	–	Y
4 Wynn	Y	Y	N	N	Y
5 Hoyer	Y	Y	N	N	N
6 ***Bartlett***	N	N	Y	N	Y
7 Cummings	Y	Y	N	Y	Y
8 ***Morella***	N	N	Y	?	Y
MASSACHUSETTS					
1 Olver	Y	Y	N	Y	Y
2 Neal	Y	Y	N	?	Y
3 McGovern	Y	Y	N	Y	Y
4 Frank	Y	Y	N	Y	Y
5 Meehan	Y	Y	N	Y	Y
6 Tierney	Y	Y	N	Y	Y
7 Markey	Y	Y	N	Y	Y
8 Capuano	Y	Y	N	Y	Y
9 Moakley	Y	Y	N	N	Y
10 Delahunt	Y	Y	N	Y	Y
MICHIGAN					
1 Stupak	Y	Y	N	Y	N
2 ***Hoekstra***	N	N	Y	N	Y
3 ***Ehlers***	N	N	Y	N	Y
4 ***Camp***	N	N	Y	N	Y
5 Barcia	N	N	Y	N	Y
6 ***Upton***	N	N	Y	N	Y
7 ***Smith***	N	N	Y	N	Y
8 Stabenow	Y	Y	N	Y	Y
9 Kildee	Y	Y	N	N	Y
10 Bonior	Y	Y	N	Y	Y
11 ***Knollenberg***	N	N	Y	N	Y
12 Levin	Y	Y	N	?	Y
13 Rivers	Y	Y	N	Y	Y
14 Conyers	Y	Y	N	Y	Y
15 Kilpatrick	Y	Y	N	N	N
16 Dingell	Y	Y	N	N	Y

	126	127	128	129	130
MINNESOTA					
1 ***Gutknecht***	N	N	Y	N	Y
2 Minge	Y	Y	N	Y	Y
3 ***Ramstad***	N	N	Y	Y	Y
4 Vento	Y	Y	N	Y	N
5 Sabo	Y	Y	N	N	N
6 Luther	Y	Y	N	Y	Y
7 Peterson	N	N	Y	Y	Y
8 Oberstar	Y	Y	N	Y	N
MISSISSIPPI					
1 ***Wicker***	N	N	Y	N	Y
2 Thompson	Y	Y	N	N	Y
3 ***Pickering***	N	N	Y	N	Y
4 Shows	Y	Y	N	N	Y
5 Taylor	N	N	Y	N	Y
MISSOURI					
1 Clay	Y	Y	N	Y	Y
2 ***Talent***	N	N	Y	N	Y
3 Gephardt	Y	Y	N	?	?
4 Skelton	Y	Y	N	N	Y
5 McCarthy	Y	Y	N	Y	Y
6 Danner	Y	Y	Y	Y	Y
7 ***Blunt***	N	N	Y	N	Y
8 ***Emerson***	N	N	Y	N	Y
9 ***Hulshof***	N	N	Y	N	Y
MONTANA					
AL ***Hill***	N	N	Y	N	Y
NEBRASKA					
1 ***Bereuter***	N	N	Y	N	Y
2 ***Terry***	Y	N	Y	N	Y
3 ***Barrett***	N	N	Y	N	Y
NEVADA					
1 Berkley	Y	Y	N	N	Y
2 ***Gibbons***	N	N	N	N	Y
NEW HAMPSHIRE					
1 ***Sununu***	N	N	Y	N	Y
2 ***Bass***	N	N	Y	N	Y
NEW JERSEY					
1 Andrews	Y	Y	N	N	Y
2 ***LoBiondo***	N	N	Y	N	Y
3 ***Saxton***	N	N	Y	N	Y
4 ***Smith***	N	N	Y	N	Y
5 ***Roukema***	N	N	Y	N	Y
6 Pallone	Y	Y	N	N	Y
7 ***Franks***	N	N	Y	N	Y
8 Pascrell	Y	Y	N	N	Y
9 Rothman	Y	Y	N	N	Y
10 Payne	Y	Y	N	Y	N
11 ***Frelinghuysen***	N	N	Y	N	Y
12 Holt	Y	Y	N	Y	Y
13 Menendez	Y	Y	N	N	Y
NEW MEXICO					
1 ***Wilson***	N	N	Y	N	Y
2 ***Skeen***	N	N	?	N	Y
3 Udall	Y	Y	N	Y	Y
NEW YORK					
1 ***Forbes***	N	N	Y	N	Y
2 ***Lazio***	N	N	Y	N	Y
3 ***King***	Y	N	N	N	Y
4 McCarthy	Y	Y	N	Y	Y
5 Ackerman	Y	Y	N	N	Y
6 Meeks	Y	Y	N	Y	Y
7 Crowley	Y	Y	N	N	Y
8 Nadler	Y	Y	N	Y	Y
9 Weiner	Y	Y	N	N	Y
10 Towns	Y	Y	N	Y	Y
11 Owens	Y	Y	N	Y	Y
12 Velázquez	Y	Y	Y	Y	Y
13 ***Fossella***	N	N	Y	N	Y
14 Maloney	Y	Y	N	N	Y
15 Rangel	?	Y	N	?	Y
16 Serrano	Y	Y	N	Y	N
17 Engel	Y	Y	N	N	Y
18 Lowey	Y	Y	N	N	Y
19 ***Kelly***	N	N	Y	N	Y
20 ***Gilman***	Y	N	Y	N	Y
21 McNulty	Y	Y	N	N	Y
22 ***Sweeney***	N	N	Y	N	Y
23 ***Boehlert***	N	N	Y	N	Y
24 ***McHugh***	N	N	Y	N	Y
25 ***Walsh***	N	N	Y	N	Y
26 Hinchey	Y	Y	N	N	Y
27 ***Reynolds***	N	N	Y	N	Y
28 Slaughter	+	+	-	?	Y
29 LaFalce	Y	Y	N	N	Y

	126	127	128	129	130
30 ***Quinn***	N	N	Y	N	?
31 ***Houghton***	N	N	Y	N	Y
NORTH CAROLINA					
1 Clayton	Y	Y	N	N	Y
2 Etheridge	Y	Y	Y	N	Y
3 ***Jones***	N	N	Y	N	Y
4 Price	Y	Y	N	N	Y
5 ***Burr***	N	N	Y	N	Y
6 ***Coble***	N	N	Y	N	Y
7 McIntyre	N	N	N	N	Y
8 ***Hayes***	N	N	Y	N	Y
9 ***Myrick***	N	N	Y	N	Y
10 ***Ballenger***	N	N	Y	N	Y
11 ***Taylor***	N	N	Y	N	Y
12 Watt	Y	Y	N	N	Y
NORTH DAKOTA					
AL Pomeroy	Y	Y	N	N	Y
OHIO					
1 ***Chabot***	N	N	Y	N	Y
2 ***Portman***	N	N	Y	N	Y
3 Hall	Y	Y	Y	N	Y
4 ***Oxley***	N	N	Y	N	Y
5 ***Gillmor***	N	N	Y	N	Y
6 Strickland	Y	Y	N	N	Y
7 ***Hobson***	N	N	Y	N	Y
8 ***Boehner***	N	N	Y	N	Y
9 Kaptur	Y	Y	N	N	Y
10 Kucinich	Y	Y	N	Y	N
11 Jones	Y	Y	N	Y	N
12 ***Kasich***	N	N	Y	N	Y
13 Brown	Y	Y	N	Y	Y
14 Sawyer	Y	Y	N	N	Y
15 ***Pryce***	N	N	Y	N	Y
16 ***Regula***	N	N	Y	N	Y
17 Traficant	Y	Y	N	N	N
18 ***Ney***	N	N	Y	N	Y
19 ***LaTourette***	N	N	Y	N	Y
OKLAHOMA					
1 ***Largent***	N	N	Y	N	Y
2 ***Coburn***	N	N	Y	N	Y
3 ***Watkins***	N	N	Y	N	Y
4 ***Watts***	N	N	Y	N	Y
5 ***Istook***	N	N	N	N	Y
6 ***Lucas***	N	N	Y	N	Y
OREGON					
1 Wu	Y	Y	N	Y	Y
2 ***Walden***	N	N	Y	N	Y
3 Blumenauer	Y	Y	Y	Y	Y
4 DeFazio	Y	Y	N	Y	Y
5 Hooley	Y	Y	N	Y	Y
PENNSYLVANIA					
1 Brady	Y	Y	N	N	Y
2 Fattah	Y	Y	N	N	Y
3 Borski	Y	Y	N	N	Y
4 Klink	Y	Y	N	N	Y
5 ***Peterson***	N	N	Y	N	Y
6 Holden	N	N	Y	N	Y
7 ***Weldon***	N	N	Y	N	Y
8 ***Greenwood***	N	N	Y	?	Y
9 ***Shuster***	N	N	Y	N	Y
10 ***Sherwood***	N	N	Y	N	Y
11 Kanjorski	Y	Y	N	Y	Y
12 Murtha	Y	Y	N	N	N
13 Hoeffel	Y	Y	N	N	Y
14 Coyne	Y	Y	N	?	Y
15 ***Toomey***	N	N	Y	N	Y
16 ***Pitts***	N	N	Y	N	Y
17 ***Gekas***	N	N	Y	N	Y
18 Doyle	Y	Y	N	N	Y
19 ***Goodling***	N	N	Y	N	Y
20 Mascara	Y	Y	N	N	Y
21 ***English***	Y	N	Y	N	Y
RHODE ISLAND					
1 Kennedy	Y	Y	N	N	Y
2 Weygand	Y	Y	N	N	Y
SOUTH CAROLINA					
1 ***Sanford***	N	N	Y	N	Y
2 ***Spence***	N	N	Y	N	Y
3 ***Graham***	N	N	N	N	Y
4 ***DeMint***	N	N	+	N	Y
5 Spratt	Y	Y	N	N	Y
6 Clyburn	Y	Y	N	N	N
SOUTH DAKOTA					
AL ***Thune***	N	N	Y	N	Y

	126	127	128	129	130
TENNESSEE					
1 ***Jenkins***	N	N	Y	N	Y
2 ***Duncan***	Y	Y	N	Y	Y
3 ***Wamp***	N	N	Y	N	Y
4 ***Hilleary***	N	N	Y	N	Y
5 Clement	N	N	Y	N	Y
6 Gordon	N	Y	Y	N	Y
7 ***Bryant***	N	N	Y	N	Y
8 Tanner	N	N	Y	?	Y
9 Ford	Y	Y	N	N	Y
TEXAS					
1 Sandlin	Y	Y	N	N	Y
2 Turner	Y	Y	N	N	Y
3 ***Johnson, Sam***	N	N	Y	N	Y
4 Hall	N	N	Y	N	Y
5 ***Sessions***	N	N	Y	N	Y
6 ***Barton***	?	?	?	N	Y
7 ***Archer***	N	N	Y	N	Y
8 ***Brady***	N	N	Y	N	Y
9 Lampson	Y	Y	N	N	Y
10 Doggett	N	Y	N	?	Y
11 Edwards	Y	Y	N	N	Y
12 ***Granger***	N	N	Y	N	Y
13 ***Thornberry***	N	N	Y	N	Y
14 ***Paul***	Y	N	N	Y	Y
15 Hinojosa	Y	Y	N	N	Y
16 Reyes	Y	Y	N	N	Y
17 Stenholm	N	N	Y	N	Y
18 Jackson-Lee	Y	Y	N	Y	Y
19 ***Combest***	N	N	Y	N	Y
20 Gonzalez	Y	Y	N	N	Y
21 ***Smith***	N	N	Y	N	Y
22 ***DeLay***	N	N	Y	N	Y
23 ***Bonilla***	N	N	Y	N	Y
24 Frost	Y	Y	N	N	Y
25 Bentsen	Y	Y	N	N	Y
26 ***Armey***	N	N	Y	N	Y
27 Ortiz	Y	Y	N	N	Y
28 Rodriguez	Y	Y	N	N	Y
29 Green	Y	Y	N	N	Y
30 Johnson, E.B.	Y	Y	N	N	Y
UTAH					
1 ***Hansen***	N	N	Y	N	Y
2 ***Cook***	N	N	Y	N	Y
3 ***Cannon***	N	N	Y	N	Y
VERMONT					
AL *Sanders*	Y	Y	N	Y	Y
VIRGINIA					
1 ***Bateman***	N	N	Y	N	Y
2 Pickett	N	N	N	N	Y
3 Scott	Y	Y	N	N	Y
4 Sisisky	N	N	Y	N	Y
5 Goode	N	N	Y	N	Y
6 ***Goodlatte***	N	N	Y	N	Y
7 ***Bliley***	N	N	Y	N	Y
8 Moran	N	N	Y	?	N
9 Boucher	Y	Y	N	N	?
10 ***Wolf***	N	N	Y	N	Y
11 ***Davis***	N	N	Y	N	Y
WASHINGTON					
1 Inslee	Y	N	N	N	Y
2 ***Metcalf***	N	N	Y	N	Y
3 Baird	Y	Y	N	N	Y
4 ***Hastings***	N	N	Y	N	N
5 ***Nethercutt***	N	N	Y	N	Y
6 Dicks	Y	N	N	N	N
7 McDermott	Y	Y	N	–	Y
8 ***Dunn***	N	N	Y	N	Y
9 Smith	Y	N	Y	N	Y
WEST VIRGINIA					
1 Mollohan	Y	Y	N	N	N
2 Wise	Y	Y	N	N	N
3 Rahall	Y	Y	N	?	N
WISCONSIN					
1 ***Ryan***	N	N	Y	N	Y
2 Baldwin	Y	Y	N	Y	Y
3 Kind	Y	Y	N	N	Y
4 Kleczka	Y	Y	N	?	Y
5 Barrett	Y	Y	N	N	Y
6 ***Petri***	N	N	Y	N	Y
7 Obey	Y	Y	N	N	N
8 ***Green***	N	N	Y	N	Y
9 ***Sensenbrenner***	N	N	Y	N	Y
WYOMING					
AL ***Cubin***	N	N	Y	N	Y

Southern states - Ala., Ark., Fla., Ga., Ky., La., Miss., N.C., Okla., S.C., Tenn., Texas, Va.

House Votes 131, 132, 133, 134, 135, 136, 137

131. HR 1141. Fiscal 1999 Supplemental Appropriations/Rule. Adoption of the rule (H Res 173) to provide for House floor consideration of the conference report on the bill to provide emergency supplemental funding for fiscal 1999. Adopted 315-109: R 218-0; D 97-108 (ND 56-94, SD 41-14); I 0-1. May 18, 1999.

132. HR 1141. Fiscal 1999 Supplemental Appropriations/Recommit. Obey, D-Wis., motion to recommit to the House Appropriations Committee the conference report to provide emergency supplemental funds for fiscal 1999. Rejected 182-243: R 13-207; D 168-36 (ND 136-13, SD 32-23); I 1-0. May 18, 1999.

133. HR 1141. Fiscal 1999 Supplemental Appropriations/Conference Report. Adoption of the conference report on the $14.5 billion bill, which would provide $10.9 billion for the ongoing military operations in Kosovo and other defense needs, $1.8 billion for a pay raise for the military, and $1.1 billion for international refugee and economic assistance. Adopted (thus sent to the Senate) 269-158: R 152-68; D 117-89 (ND 70-81, SD 47-8); I 0-1. May 18, 1999.

134. HR 1654. NASA Authorization/Noise Reduction. Weiner, D-N.Y., amendment to increase funding by $10 million for fiscal years 2000 and 2001 and by $9.5 million for fiscal 2002 for aircraft noise reduction technology. Adopted 225-203: R 29-191; D 195-12 (ND 144-8, SD 51-4); I 1-0. May 19, 1999.

135. HR 1654. NASA Authorization/Space Station. Roemer, D-Ind., amendment to limit International Space Station costs through the assembly phase to $21.9 billion, and to limit space shuttle launch costs in connection to the station's assembly to $17.7 billion. Rejected 114-315: R 53-168; D 60-147 (ND 58-94, SD 2-53); I 1-0. May 19, 1999.

136. HR 1654. NASA Authorization/Russian Partnership. Roemer, D-Ind., amendment to remove Russia as a partner in the International Space Station program and to prohibit NASA from entering into a new partnership with Russia relating to the station. Rejected 117-313: R 95-126; D 22-186 (ND 20-133, SD 2-53); I 0-1. May 19, 1999.

137. HR 1654. NASA Authorization/Space Station. Roemer, D-Ind., amendment to eliminate the bill's authorization for the International Space Station. Rejected 92-337: R 43-177; D 48-160 (ND 46-107, SD 2-53); I 1-0. May 19, 1999. A "nay" was a vote in support of the president's position.

Key

Y Voted for (yea).
\# Paired for.
\+ Announced for.
N Voted against (nay).
X Paired against.
– Announced against.
P Voted "present."
C Voted "present" to avoid possible conflict of interest.
? Did not vote or otherwise make a position known.

•

Democrats ***Republicans***
Independents

	131	132	133	134	135	136	137
ALABAMA							
1 ***Callahan***	Y	N	Y	N	N	N	N
2 ***Everett***	Y	N	Y	N	N	N	N
3 ***Riley***	Y	N	Y	N	N	N	N
4 ***Aderholt***	Y	N	N	N	N	N	N
5 Cramer	Y	N	Y	Y	N	N	N
6 ***Bachus***	Y	N	Y	N	N	N	N
7 Hilliard	N	Y	Y	Y	N	N	N
ALASKA							
AL ***Young***	Y	N	Y	N	N	N	N
ARIZONA							
1 ***Salmon***	Y	N	N	N	N	Y	N
2 Pastor	N	Y	N	Y	N	N	N
3 ***Stump***	Y	N	Y	N	N	Y	N
4 ***Shadegg***	Y	Y	N	N	N	Y	N
5 ***Kolbe***	Y	N	Y	N	N	N	N
6 ***Hayworth***	Y	N	Y	N	N	N	N
ARKANSAS							
1 Berry	Y	N	Y	N	Y	N	Y
2 Snyder	Y	N	Y	Y	N	N	N
3 ***Hutchinson***	Y	N	Y	N	N	Y	N
4 ***Dickey***	Y	N	Y	N	N	Y	N
CALIFORNIA							
1 Thompson	N	Y	N	Y	N	N	N
2 ***Herger***	Y	N	Y	N	Y	Y	Y
3 ***Ose***	Y	Y	Y	N	N	N	N
4 ***Doolittle***	Y	N	N	N	N	Y	N
5 Matsui	Y	Y	Y	Y	N	N	N
6 Woolsey	N	Y	N	Y	Y	N	Y
7 Miller, George	N	Y	N	Y	Y	N	Y
8 Pelosi	Y	?	?	Y	Y	N	Y
9 Lee	N	Y	N	Y	Y	N	Y
10 Tauscher	Y	Y	Y	Y	N	N	N
11 ***Pombo***	Y	N	Y	N	N	Y	N
12 Lantos	Y	Y	N	Y	N	N	N
13 Stark	N	Y	N	Y	Y	N	Y
14 Eshoo	N	Y	N	Y	N	N	N
15 ***Campbell***	Y	Y	N	N	N	N	N
16 Lofgren	Y	Y	N	Y	N	N	N
17 Farr	Y	Y	Y	Y	N	N	N
18 Condit	?	Y	Y	N	N	Y	N
19 ***Radanovich***	Y	N	Y	N	N	N	N
20 Dooley	Y	Y	Y	Y	N	N	N
21 ***Thomas***	Y	N	Y	N	N	Y	N
22 Capps	Y	Y	Y	Y	N	N	N
23 ***Gallegly***	Y	N	Y	N	N	N	N
24 Sherman	N	Y	Y	Y	N	N	N
25 ***McKeon***	Y	N	Y	N	N	N	N
26 Berman	N	Y	Y	Y	N	N	N
27 ***Rogan***	Y	N	N	Y	N	N	N
28 ***Dreier***	Y	N	Y	N	N	N	N
29 Waxman	N	Y	N	Y	Y	N	N
30 Becerra	N	Y	N	Y	N	N	N
31 Martinez	N	Y	N	Y	N	N	N
32 Dixon	N	Y	Y	Y	N	N	N
33 Roybal-Allard	N	Y	Y	Y	N	N	N
34 Napolitano	N	Y	Y	?	?	?	?
35 Waters	N	Y	N	Y	N	N	N
36 ***Kuykendall***	Y	N	Y	Y	N	N	N
37 Millender-McD.	N	Y	Y	Y	N	N	N
38 ***Horn***	Y	N	Y	Y	N	N	N
39 ***Royce***	Y	N	N	N	N	Y	N
40 ***Lewis***	Y	N	Y	N	N	N	N
41 ***Miller, Gary***	Y	N	Y	N	N	N	N
42 Brown	?	?	?	?	?	?	?
43 ***Calvert***	Y	N	Y	N	N	N	N
44 ***Bono***	Y	N	Y	N	N	N	N
45 ***Rohrabacher***	Y	N	N	N	N	Y	N
46 Sanchez	N	Y	Y	Y	N	N	N
47 ***Cox***	Y	N	Y	?	N	N	?
48 ***Packard***	Y	N	Y	N	N	N	N
49 ***Bilbray***	Y	N	N	N	N	Y	N
50 Filner	N	Y	Y	Y	N	N	N
51 ***Cunningham***	Y	N	Y	N	N	Y	N
52 ***Hunter***	Y	N	Y	N	N	Y	N
COLORADO							
1 DeGette	N	Y	N	Y	N	N	N
2 Udall	Y	Y	N	Y	N	N	N
3 ***McInnis***	Y	N	Y	N	Y	Y	Y
4 ***Schaffer***	Y	N	N	N	Y	Y	N
5 ***Hefley***	Y	N	N	Y	Y	Y	Y
6 ***Tancredo***	Y	N	N	N	Y	Y	Y
CONNECTICUT							
1 Larson	Y	Y	Y	Y	N	N	N
2 Gejdenson	N	Y	Y	Y	N	N	N
3 DeLauro	N	Y	Y	Y	N	N	N
4 ***Shays***	Y	Y	N	Y	Y	Y	Y
5 Maloney	N	Y	Y	N	N	N	N
6 ***Johnson***	Y	N	Y	N	N	N	N
DELAWARE							
AL ***Castle***	Y	N	N	N	N	N	N
FLORIDA							
1 ***Scarborough***	Y	Y	Y	N	N	N	N
2 Boyd	Y	N	Y	Y	N	N	N
3 Brown	Y	Y	Y	Y	N	N	N
4 ***Fowler***	Y	N	Y	N	N	N	N
5 Thurman	N	Y	Y	Y	N	N	N
6 ***Stearns***	Y	N	Y	N	Y	Y	N
7 ***Mica***	Y	N	N	N	N	Y	N
8 ***McCollum***	Y	N	Y	N	N	N	N
9 ***Bilirakis***	Y	N	Y	N	N	N	N
10 ***Young***	Y	N	Y	N	N	N	N
11 Davis	Y	Y	Y	Y	N	N	N
12 ***Canady***	Y	N	Y	N	N	Y	N
13 ***Miller***	Y	N	Y	N	N	N	N
14 ***Goss***	Y	N	Y	N	N	N	N
15 ***Weldon***	Y	N	Y	N	N	N	N
16 ***Foley***	Y	N	Y	N	N	N	N
17 Meek	N	Y	Y	Y	N	N	N
18 ***Ros-Lehtinen***	Y	N	Y	N	N	Y	N
19 Wexler	Y	Y	Y	Y	N	N	N
20 Deutsch	N	Y	Y	Y	N	N	N
21 ***Diaz-Balart***	Y	N	Y	N	N	Y	N
22 ***Shaw***	Y	N	Y	N	N	N	N
23 Hastings	N	Y	Y	Y	N	N	N
GEORGIA							
1 ***Kingston***	Y	Y	N	N	Y	Y	Y
2 Bishop	Y	N	Y	Y	N	N	N
3 ***Collins***	Y	N	Y	N	Y	N	N
4 McKinney	N	Y	N	Y	N	N	N
5 Lewis	Y	Y	N	Y	N	N	N
6 ***Isakson***	Y	N	Y	N	N	Y	N
7 ***Barr***	Y	N	N	N	N	Y	N
8 ***Chambliss***	Y	N	Y	N	N	Y	N
9 ***Deal***	Y	N	N	N	Y	Y	N
10 ***Norwood***	Y	N	N	N	N	N	N
11 ***Linder***	Y	N	Y	N	N	Y	N
HAWAII							
1 Abercrombie	Y	Y	Y	Y	Y	N	N
2 Mink	N	Y	N	Y	Y	Y	Y
IDAHO							
1 ***Chenoweth***	Y	N	N	N	Y	Y	Y
2 ***Simpson***	Y	N	Y	N	N	N	N
ILLINOIS							
1 Rush	N	Y	N	Y	N	N	N
2 Jackson	N	Y	N	Y	N	N	N
3 Lipinski	N	Y	Y	Y	N	N	N
4 Gutierrez	?	Y	Y	Y	Y	N	Y
5 Blagojevich	Y	Y	Y	Y	Y	Y	Y
6 ***Hyde***	Y	N	Y	Y	N	Y	N
7 Davis	N	Y	N	Y	N	N	N
8 ***Crane***	Y	N	N	N	N	N	N
9 Schakowsky	N	Y	N	Y	N	N	N
10 ***Porter***	Y	N	Y	Y	N	N	Y
11 ***Weller***	Y	N	Y	Y	N	N	N
12 Costello	N	Y	N	Y	Y	Y	Y
13 ***Biggert***	Y	N	Y	N	N	Y	N
14 ***Hastert***			Y				

ND Northern Democrats SD Southern Democrats

	131	132	133	134	135	136	137
15 ***Ewing***	Y	N	N	N	N	N	N
16 ***Manzullo***	Y	N	N	N	Y	N	Y
17 Evans	N	Y	Y	Y	Y	N	Y
18 ***LaHood***	Y	N	N	N	N	Y	N
19 Phelps	N	Y	Y	N	N	N	N
20 ***Shimkus***	Y	N	Y	N	N	N	N
INDIANA							
1 Visclosky	N	Y	N	N	Y	Y	Y
2 ***McIntosh***	Y	N	Y	N	N	Y	N
3 Roemer	Y	N	Y	Y	Y	Y	Y
4 ***Souder***	Y	N	N	N	N	N	N
5 ***Buyer***	Y	N	Y	N	N	N	N
6 ***Burton***	Y	N	Y	N	N	N	N
7 ***Pease***	Y	N	Y	N	Y	N	N
8 ***Hostettler***	Y	N	Y	N	N	N	N
9 Hill	N	Y	N	Y	N	N	N
10 Carson	N	Y	N	Y	N	N	N
IOWA							
1 ***Leach***	Y	N	N	N	Y	N	Y
2 ***Nussle***	Y	Y	N	N	Y	N	Y
3 Boswell	Y	Y	Y	Y	N	N	N
4 ***Ganske***	Y	N	N	N	Y	Y	Y
5 ***Latham***	Y	N	Y	N	Y	Y	Y
KANSAS							
1 ***Moran***	Y	N	N	N	N	Y	N
2 ***Ryun***	Y	N	Y	N	N	Y	N
3 Moore	Y	Y	Y	Y	N	N	N
4 ***Tiahrt***	Y	N	Y	N	N	Y	N
KENTUCKY							
1 ***Whitfield***	Y	N	Y	N	N	Y	N
2 ***Lewis***	Y	N	Y	N	N	N	N
3 ***Northup***	Y	N	Y	N	N	N	N
4 Lucas	Y	N	Y	Y	N	N	N
5 ***Rogers***	Y	N	Y	N	N	N	N
6 ***Fletcher***	Y	N	Y	N	N	N	N
LOUISIANA							
1 Vacant							
2 Jefferson	N	Y	Y	Y	N	N	N
3 ***Tauzin***	Y	N	Y	N	N	N	N
4 ***McCrery***	Y	N	Y	N	N	N	N
5 ***Cooksey***	Y	N	Y	N	N	N	N
6 ***Baker***	Y	N	Y	N	N	Y	N
7 John	Y	N	Y	Y	N	N	N
MAINE							
1 Allen	Y	Y	Y	Y	N	N	N
2 Baldacci	Y	Y	Y	Y	N	N	N
MARYLAND							
1 ***Gilchrest***	Y	N	Y	N	N	Y	N
2 ***Ehrlich***	Y	N	Y	N	N	N	N
3 Cardin	Y	Y	Y	Y	N	N	N
4 Wynn	Y	Y	Y	Y	N	N	N
5 Hoyer	Y	Y	Y	Y	N	N	N
6 ***Bartlett***	Y	N	Y	N	N	N	N
7 Cummings	N	Y	N	Y	N	N	N
8 ***Morella***	Y	Y	Y	N	N	N	N
MASSACHUSETTS							
1 Olver	Y	Y	Y	Y	N	N	N
2 Neal	N	Y	N	Y	N	N	N
3 McGovern	N	Y	N	Y	N	N	N
4 Frank	N	Y	N	Y	Y	N	Y
5 Meehan	N	Y	N	Y	Y	Y	Y
6 Tierney	N	Y	N	Y	Y	Y	Y
7 Markey	N	Y	N	Y	Y	N	N
8 Capuano	N	Y	N	Y	N	N	N
9 Moakley	Y	Y	N	Y	N	N	N
10 Delahunt	N	Y	N	Y	Y	Y	Y
MICHIGAN							
1 Stupak	N	Y	N	Y	Y	N	N
2 ***Hoekstra***	Y	N	N	N	Y	Y	Y
3 ***Ehlers***	Y	N	N	N	N	Y	N
4 ***Camp***	Y	N	Y	N	Y	Y	Y
5 Barcia	Y	N	Y	Y	N	N	N
6 ***Upton***	Y	N	N	N	Y	Y	Y
7 ***Smith***	Y	N	N	N	Y	N	Y
8 Stabenow	N	Y	Y	Y	N	N	N
9 Kildee	Y	Y	Y	Y	Y	N	Y
10 Bonior	Y	Y	Y	Y	N	N	N
11 ***Knollenberg***	Y	N	Y	N	N	N	N
12 Levin	Y	Y	Y	Y	Y	N	Y
13 Rivers	Y	N	N	Y	Y	N	Y
14 Conyers	N	Y	N	Y	Y	N	Y
15 Kilpatrick	N	Y	N	Y	N	N	N
16 Dingell	Y	N	Y	Y	Y	Y	Y

	131	132	133	134	135	136	137
MINNESOTA							
1 ***Gutknecht***	Y	N	N	N	N	Y	N
2 Minge	Y	Y	N	Y	Y	N	Y
3 ***Ramstad***	Y	N	N	N	Y	Y	Y
4 Vento	N	Y	N	Y	Y	N	Y
5 Sabo	Y	N	Y	Y	N	N	N
6 Luther	N	Y	N	Y	Y	N	Y
7 Peterson	N	N	N	Y	Y	N	Y
8 Oberstar	N	Y	N	Y	Y	N	Y
MISSISSIPPI							
1 ***Wicker***	Y	N	Y	N	N	N	N
2 Thompson	N	Y	Y	Y	N	N	N
3 ***Pickering***	Y	N	Y	N	N	Y	N
4 Shows	Y	N	Y	Y	N	N	N
5 Taylor	Y	N	Y	Y	N	N	N
MISSOURI							
1 Clay	N	Y	N	Y	N	N	N
2 ***Talent***	Y	N	Y	Y	N	N	N
3 Gephardt	N	?	Y	Y	N	N	N
4 Skelton	Y	N	Y	Y	N	N	N
5 McCarthy	Y	Y	N	Y	Y	N	N
6 Danner	N	Y	N	N	Y	Y	Y
7 ***Blunt***	Y	N	Y	N	N	N	N
8 ***Emerson***	Y	N	Y	N	N	N	N
9 ***Hulshof***	Y	N	N	Y	N	N	N
MONTANA							
AL ***Hill***	Y	N	Y	N	N	N	N
NEBRASKA							
1 ***Bereuter***	Y	N	Y	N	Y	Y	Y
2 ***Terry***	Y	N	N	N	N	N	N
3 ***Barrett***	Y	N	Y	N	N	N	N
NEVADA							
1 Berkley	Y	Y	Y	Y	N	N	N
2 ***Gibbons***	Y	N	Y	N	N	N	N
NEW HAMPSHIRE							
1 ***Sununu***	Y	N	N	N	Y	Y	N
2 ***Bass***	Y	N	Y	N	Y	Y	Y
NEW JERSEY							
1 Andrews	Y	N	Y	Y	N	N	N
2 ***LoBiondo***	Y	N	Y	Y	Y	Y	Y
3 ***Saxton***	Y	N	Y	N	N	N	N
4 ***Smith***	Y	N	Y	Y	N	N	N
5 ***Roukema***	Y	N	Y	Y	Y	Y	Y
6 Pallone	N	Y	Y	Y	Y	N	Y
7 ***Franks***	Y	N	Y	Y	N	N	Y
8 Pascrell	N	Y	Y	Y	N	N	N
9 Rothman	N	Y	Y	Y	N	N	N
10 Payne	N	Y	N	Y	N	N	N
11 ***Frelinghuysen***	Y	N	Y	Y	N	N	N
12 Holt	N	Y	N	Y	Y	N	Y
13 Menendez	Y	Y	Y	Y	N	N	N
NEW MEXICO							
1 ***Wilson***	Y	N	Y	Y	N	N	N
2 ***Skeen***	Y	N	Y	N	N	N	N
3 Udall	Y	Y	Y	Y	Y	N	Y
NEW YORK							
1 ***Forbes***	Y	N	Y	Y	N	N	N
2 ***Lazio***	Y	N	Y	N	Y	Y	Y
3 ***King***	Y	N	Y	Y	N	N	N
4 McCarthy	Y	Y	Y	Y	N	N	N
5 Ackerman	Y	Y	Y	Y	N	N	N
6 Meeks	N	Y	N	Y	N	N	N
7 Crowley	N	Y	N	Y	Y	N	N
8 Nadler	N	Y	N	Y	Y	N	Y
9 Weiner	N	Y	N	Y	Y	N	N
10 Towns	N	Y	N	Y	N	N	N
11 Owens	N	Y	N	Y	N	N	N
12 Velázquez	Y	Y	N	Y	Y	N	Y
13 ***Fossella***	Y	N	Y	N	Y	Y	Y
14 Maloney	Y	Y	Y	Y	Y	N	Y
15 Rangel	N	Y	N	Y	N	N	N
16 Serrano	?	?	?	?	?	?	?
17 Engel	Y	Y	Y	Y	N	N	N
18 Lowey	Y	?	Y	Y	Y	N	Y
19 ***Kelly***	Y	Y	Y	Y	Y	Y	Y
20 ***Gilman***	Y	N	Y	Y	N	N	N
21 McNulty	N	Y	N	Y	N	N	N
22 ***Sweeney***	Y	N	N	N	N	Y	N
23 ***Boehlert***	Y	N	Y	Y	Y	N	N
24 ***McHugh***	Y	N	Y	N	Y	N	Y
25 ***Walsh***	Y	N	Y	Y	N	N	N
26 Hinchey	Y	Y	N	Y	N	N	N
27 ***Reynolds***	Y	N	Y	N	N	N	N
28 Slaughter	N	Y	Y	Y	N	N	Y
29 LaFalce	N	Y	N	Y	Y	N	N

	131	132	133	134	135	136	137
30 ***Quinn***	?	N	Y	Y	N	N	N
31 ***Houghton***	Y	N	Y	N	N	N	N
NORTH CAROLINA							
1 Clayton	N	Y	N	Y	N	N	N
2 Etheridge	Y	N	Y	Y	N	N	N
3 ***Jones***	Y	Y	N	N	N	Y	N
4 Price	Y	Y	Y	Y	N	N	N
5 ***Burr***	Y	N	N	N	N	N	N
6 ***Coble***	Y	N	N	N	Y	Y	Y
7 McIntyre	N	Y	Y	N	N	N	N
8 ***Hayes***	Y	N	Y	N	N	Y	N
9 ***Myrick***	Y	N	N	N	Y	Y	Y
10 ***Ballenger***	Y	N	Y	N	N	Y	N
11 ***Taylor***	Y	N	Y	N	N	N	N
12 Watt	Y	Y	N	Y	N	N	N
NORTH DAKOTA							
AL Pomeroy	Y	N	Y	Y	Y	N	Y
OHIO							
1 ***Chabot***	Y	Y	N	N	Y	Y	Y
2 ***Portman***	Y	N	N	N	Y	Y	Y
3 Hall	Y	N	Y	Y	N	N	N
4 ***Oxley***	Y	N	Y	N	N	N	N
5 ***Gillmor***	Y	N	Y	Y	N	Y	N
6 Strickland	N	Y	Y	Y	Y	Y	Y
7 ***Hobson***	Y	N	Y	N	N	N	N
8 ***Boehner***	Y	N	Y	N	N	N	N
9 Kaptur	N	Y	N	Y	Y	Y	Y
10 Kucinich	N	Y	N	Y	N	N	N
11 Jones	N	Y	N	Y	N	N	N
12 ***Kasich***	Y	N	Y	N	Y	N	N
13 Brown	N	Y	N	Y	Y	Y	Y
14 Sawyer	N	Y	Y	Y	N	N	N
15 ***Pryce***	Y	N	Y	N	N	N	N
16 ***Regula***	Y	N	Y	N	N	N	N
17 Traficant	Y	N	Y	N	N	N	N
18 ***Ney***	Y	N	Y	Y	N	N	N
19 ***LaTourette***	Y	N	N	Y	N	N	N
OKLAHOMA							
1 ***Largent***	Y	N	N	N	Y	Y	Y
2 ***Coburn***	Y	N	N	N	Y	Y	Y
3 ***Watkins***	Y	N	Y	N	Y	Y	N
4 ***Watts***	Y	N	Y	N	Y	Y	N
5 ***Istook***	Y	N	Y	N	N	N	N
6 ***Lucas***	Y	N	Y	N	N	Y	N
OREGON							
1 Wu	N	Y	N	Y	N	N	N
2 ***Walden***	Y	N	Y	N	N	N	N
3 Blumenauer	Y	Y	N	Y	Y	N	Y
4 DeFazio	N	Y	N	Y	Y	N	Y
5 Hooley	N	Y	N	Y	N	N	N
PENNSYLVANIA							
1 Brady	?	?	?	Y	Y	Y	Y
2 Fattah	N	Y	N	Y	Y	Y	Y
3 Borski	?	?	?	Y	N	N	N
4 Klink	N	Y	N	Y	N	N	N
5 ***Peterson***	Y	N	Y	N	N	N	N
6 Holden	Y	Y	Y	Y	Y	Y	Y
7 ***Weldon***	+	−	+	N	N	N	N
8 ***Greenwood***	Y	N	Y	Y	N	N	N
9 ***Shuster***	Y	N	N	N	Y	Y	Y
10 ***Sherwood***	Y	N	Y	N	Y	N	N
11 Kanjorski	N	Y	N	N	N	N	N
12 Murtha	Y	N	Y	Y	N	N	N
13 Hoeffel	Y	Y	Y	Y	N	N	N
14 Coyne	N	Y	N	Y	Y	N	Y
15 ***Toomey***	Y	N	N	N	Y	N	N
16 ***Pitts***	Y	N	N	N	N	N	N
17 ***Gekas***	Y	N	N	N	N	Y	N
18 Doyle	N	Y	Y	Y	Y	Y	Y
19 ***Goodling***	Y	N	Y	N	Y	Y	N
20 Mascara	N	Y	Y	Y	Y	N	N
21 ***English***	Y	N	Y	N	N	N	N
RHODE ISLAND							
1 Kennedy	N	Y	Y	Y	N	N	N
2 Weygand	N	Y	Y	Y	N	N	N
SOUTH CAROLINA							
1 ***Sanford***	Y	Y	N	N	Y	Y	Y
2 ***Spence***	Y	N	Y	N	N	Y	N
3 ***Graham***	Y	N	Y	N	N	N	N
4 ***DeMint***	Y	N	N	N	Y	Y	Y
5 Spratt	Y	Y	Y	Y	N	N	N
6 Clyburn	N	Y	Y	Y	N	N	N
SOUTH DAKOTA							
AL ***Thune***	Y	N	Y	N	N	N	N

	131	132	133	134	135	136	137
TENNESSEE							
1 ***Jenkins***	Y	N	Y	N	N	N	N
2 ***Duncan***	Y	N	N	N	Y	Y	Y
3 ***Wamp***	Y	N	Y	N	Y	Y	Y
4 ***Hilleary***	Y	N	N	N	Y	Y	Y
5 Clement	Y	Y	Y	Y	N	N	N
6 Gordon	Y	Y	Y	Y	N	N	N
7 ***Bryant***	Y	Y	Y	N	N	N	N
8 Tanner	Y	N	Y	N	N	N	N
9 Ford	Y	Y	Y	Y	N	N	N
TEXAS							
1 Sandlin	Y	N	Y	Y	N	N	N
2 Turner	Y	N	Y	Y	N	N	N
3 ***Johnson, Sam***	Y	N	N	N	N	N	N
4 Hall	Y	Y	Y	Y	N	N	N
5 ***Sessions***	?	N	N	N	N	N	N
6 ***Barton***	Y	N	N	N	N	N	N
7 ***Archer***	Y	N	N	N	N	N	N
8 ***Brady***	Y	N	N	N	N	N	N
9 Lampson	Y	Y	N	Y	N	N	N
10 Doggett	N	Y	N	Y	N	N	N
11 Edwards	Y	N	Y	Y	N	N	N
12 ***Granger***	Y	N	Y	N	N	N	N
13 ***Thornberry***	Y	N	Y	N	N	N	N
14 ***Paul***	Y	N	N	N	Y	Y	Y
15 Hinojosa	Y	N	Y	Y	N	N	N
16 Reyes	Y	N	Y	Y	N	N	N
17 Stenholm	Y	N	Y	Y	N	N	N
18 Jackson-Lee	N	Y	N	Y	N	N	N
19 ***Combest***	Y	N	Y	N	N	Y	N
20 Gonzalez	Y	Y	Y	Y	N	N	N
21 ***Smith***	Y	N	Y	N	N	Y	N
22 ***DeLay***	Y	N	Y	N	N	N	N
23 ***Bonilla***	Y	N	Y	N	N	Y	N
24 Frost	Y	N	Y	Y	N	N	N
25 Bentsen	Y	Y	Y	Y	N	N	N
26 ***Armey***	Y	N	Y	Y	N	Y	N
27 Ortiz	Y	N	Y	Y	N	N	N
28 Rodriguez	N	Y	Y	Y	N	N	N
29 Green	Y	Y	Y	Y	N	N	N
30 Johnson, E.B.	Y	Y	Y	Y	N	N	N
UTAH							
1 ***Hansen***	Y	N	Y	N	N	N	N
2 ***Cook***	Y	N	N	N	N	Y	N
3 ***Cannon***	Y	N	Y	N	N	Y	N
VERMONT							
AL *Sanders*	N	Y	N	Y	Y	N	Y
VIRGINIA							
1 ***Bateman***	Y	N	Y	N	N	N	N
2 Pickett	Y	N	Y	Y	N	N	N
3 Scott	Y	N	Y	Y	N	N	N
4 Sisisky	Y	N	Y	Y	N	N	N
5 Goode	Y	Y	N	N	Y	Y	Y
6 ***Goodlatte***	Y	N	Y	N	Y	Y	Y
7 ***Bliley***	Y	N	Y	N	N	Y	N
8 Moran	Y	N	Y	Y	N	Y	N
9 Boucher	Y	Y	Y	Y	N	N	N
10 ***Wolf***	Y	N	Y	Y	N	N	N
11 ***Davis***	Y	N	Y	Y	N	N	N
WASHINGTON							
1 Inslee	N	Y	N	Y	N	N	N
2 ***Metcalf***	Y	N	N	N	N	N	N
3 Baird	Y	Y	N	Y	N	N	N
4 ***Hastings***	Y	N	Y	N	N	N	N
5 ***Nethercutt***	Y	N	Y	N	N	N	N
6 Dicks	Y	Y	Y	Y	N	N	N
7 McDermott	N	Y	N	+	−	N	N
8 ***Dunn***	Y	N	?	N	N	N	N
9 Smith	Y	Y	N	Y	N	N	N
WEST VIRGINIA							
1 Mollohan	Y	N	Y	N	N	N	N
2 Wise	Y	Y	Y	Y	N	N	N
3 Rahall	N	Y	N	Y	N	N	N
WISCONSIN							
1 ***Ryan***	Y	N	N	N	Y	Y	Y
2 Baldwin	N	Y	N	Y	N	N	N
3 Kind	N	Y	N	Y	Y	Y	Y
4 Kleczka	N	Y	N	Y	N	N	N
5 Barrett	N	Y	N	Y	Y	N	Y
6 ***Petri***	Y	N	N	N	N	Y	N
7 Obey	Y	Y	N	Y	Y	N	N
8 ***Green***	Y	N	N	N	N	Y	N
9 ***Sensenbrenner***	Y	N	N	N	N	Y	N
WYOMING							
AL ***Cubin***	Y	N	Y	N	Y	N	Y

Southern states - Ala., Ark., Fla., Ga., Ky., La., Miss., N.C., Okla., S.C., Tenn., Texas, Va.

138. **HR 1654. NASA Authorization/Aeronautic Research.** Bateman, R-Va., amendment to transfer $300 million from funds designated for the International Space Station to aeronautic research. Rejected 140-286: R 65-154; D 74-132 (ND 64-87, SD 10-45); I 1-0. May 19, 1999.

139. **HR 1654. NASA Authorization/Passage.** Passage of the bill to authorize $41.2 billion for NASA through fiscal 2002. Passed 259-168: R 206-14; D 53-153 (ND 23-128, SD 30-25); I 0-1. May 19, 1999.

140. **HR 883. Land Sovereignty/Rule.** Adoption of the rule (H Res 180) to provide for House floor consideration of the bill to require congressional approval for U.S. participation in two U.N.-sponsored land initiatives. Adopted 240-178: R 214-0; D 26-177 (ND 13-135, SD 13-42); I 0-1. May 20, 1999.

141. **HR 883. Land Sovereignty/Commercial Use.** Vento, D-Minn., amendment to require congressional approval for federal lands to be used for commercial use or development through agreements with international or foreign entities or their U.S. subsidiaries. Adopted 262-158: R 63-153; D 198-5 (ND 147-2, SD 51-3); I 1-0. May 20, 1999.

142. **HR 883. Land Sovereignty/ Biosphere.** Udall, D-Colo., amendment to exempt all Biosphere Reserve projects in Colorado from the bill's provisions. Rejected 191-231: R 7-209; D 183-22 (ND 143-7, SD 40-15); I 1-0. May 20, 1999.

143. **HR 883. Land Sovereignty/Biosphere.** Sweeney, R-N.Y. amendment to require congressionally approved Biosphere Reserve plans to specifically ensure that the designation of reserves does not adversely affect local or state revenues. Adopted 407-15: R 211-5; D 195-10 (ND 142-9, SD 53-1); I 1-0. May 20, 1999. (Subsequently the bill was passed by voice vote.)

144. **HR 4. Missile Defense/Concur With Senate Amendments.** Spence, R-S.C., motion to concur in the Senate amendment to the bill that would declare it to be U.S. policy to deploy a national missile defense system as soon as it is technologically feasible. Motion agreed to (thus clearing the bill for the president) 345-71: R 213-1; D 132-69 (ND 84-64, SD 48-5); I 0-1. May 20, 1999.

Key

- Y Voted for (yea).
- \# Paired for.
- \+ Announced for.
- N Voted against (nay).
- X Paired against.
- – Announced against.
- P Voted "present."
- C Voted "present" to avoid possible conflict of interest.
- ? Did not vote or otherwise make a position known.

•

Democrats ***Republicans***
Independents

	138	139	140	141	142	143	144
ALABAMA							
1 ***Callahan***	N	Y	Y	N	N	Y	Y
2 ***Everett***	N	Y	Y	N	N	Y	Y
3 ***Riley***	N	Y	Y	N	N	Y	Y
4 ***Aderholt***	N	Y	Y	N	N	Y	Y
5 Cramer	N	Y	Y	Y	N	Y	Y
6 ***Bachus***	N	Y	Y	N	N	Y	Y
7 Hilliard	N	N	N	Y	Y	Y	Y
ALASKA							
AL ***Young***	N	Y	Y	N	N	Y	Y
ARIZONA							
1 ***Salmon***	N	Y	?	?	?	?	?
2 Pastor	N	+	N	Y	Y	Y	N
3 ***Stump***	Y	Y	Y	N	N	Y	Y
4 ***Shadegg***	N	Y	Y	N	N	Y	Y
5 ***Kolbe***	N	Y	Y	N	N	Y	Y
6 ***Hayworth***	N	Y	Y	N	N	Y	Y
ARKANSAS							
1 Berry	Y	N	Y	N	N	Y	Y
2 Snyder	N	N	N	Y	Y	Y	Y
3 ***Hutchinson***	Y	Y	Y	N	N	Y	Y
4 ***Dickey***	Y	Y	Y	N	N	Y	Y
CALIFORNIA							
1 Thompson	N	N	N	N	Y	N	Y
2 ***Herger***	Y	N	Y	N	N	Y	Y
3 ***Ose***	N	Y	?	N	N	Y	Y
4 ***Doolittle***	N	Y	?	N	N	Y	Y
5 Matsui	N	N	N	Y	Y	Y	Y
6 Woolsey	Y	N	N	Y	Y	Y	N
7 Miller, George	Y	N	Y	Y	Y	Y	N
8 Pelosi	Y	N	Y	Y	Y	Y	N
9 Lee	Y	N	N	Y	Y	Y	N
10 Tauscher	N	N	N	Y	Y	Y	Y
11 ***Pombo***	N	Y	Y	N	N	Y	Y
12 Lantos	N	N	N	Y	Y	Y	Y
13 Stark	Y	N	N	?	?	?	?
14 Eshoo	N	N	Y	Y	Y	Y	N
15 ***Campbell***	?	Y	Y	Y	N	Y	Y
16 Lofgren	N	N	N	Y	Y	Y	N
17 Farr	N	N	N	Y	Y	Y	N
18 Condit	N	Y	Y	Y	N	Y	Y
19 ***Radanovich***	N	Y	Y	N	N	Y	Y
20 Dooley	N	N	N	Y	Y	Y	Y
21 ***Thomas***	N	Y	Y	N	N	Y	+
22 Capps	Y	N	N	Y	Y	Y	Y
23 ***Gallegly***	N	Y	Y	N	N	Y	Y
24 Sherman	N	Y	N	Y	Y	Y	Y
25 ***McKeon***	N	Y	Y	N	N	Y	Y
26 Berman	N	N	N	Y	Y	Y	Y
27 ***Rogan***	N	Y	Y	N	N	Y	Y
28 ***Dreier***	N	Y	Y	N	N	Y	Y
29 Waxman	N	N	?	Y	Y	Y	?
30 Becerra	N	N	N	Y	Y	Y	Y
31 Martinez	N	N	N	Y	Y	Y	Y
32 Dixon	N	N	N	?	?	Y	Y
33 Roybal-Allard	N	N	N	Y	Y	Y	Y
34 Napolitano	?	?	?	?	?	?	?
35 Waters	N	N	N	Y	N	Y	N
36 ***Kuykendall***	N	Y	Y	N	N	Y	Y
37 Millender-McD.	N	N	N	Y	Y	Y	Y
38 ***Horn***	N	Y	Y	?	N	Y	Y
39 ***Royce***	N	Y	Y	Y	N	Y	Y
40 ***Lewis***	N	Y	Y	N	N	Y	Y
41 ***Miller, Gary***	N	Y	Y	N	N	Y	Y
42 Brown	?	?	?	?	?	?	?
43 ***Calvert***	N	Y	Y	N	N	Y	Y
44 ***Bono***	N	Y	Y	N	N	Y	Y
45 ***Rohrabacher***	N	Y	Y	Y	N	Y	Y
46 Sanchez	N	N	N	Y	Y	Y	Y
47 ***Cox***	N	Y	Y	N	N	?	Y
48 ***Packard***	N	Y	Y	N	N	Y	Y
49 ***Bilbray***	N	Y	Y	+	N	N	Y
50 Filner	N	N	N	Y	Y	N	N
51 ***Cunningham***	N	Y	Y	Y	N	Y	Y
52 ***Hunter***	Y	Y	Y	Y	N	Y	Y
COLORADO							
1 DeGette	N	Y	N	Y	Y	Y	N
2 Udall	N	N	N	Y	Y	Y	Y
3 ***McInnis***	Y	N	Y	N	N	Y	Y
4 ***Schaffer***	N	N	Y	N	N	Y	Y
5 ***Hefley***	Y	Y	Y	Y	N	Y	Y
6 ***Tancredo***	Y	N	Y	N	N	Y	Y
CONNECTICUT							
1 Larson	N	Y	N	Y	Y	Y	Y
2 Gejdenson	N	Y	N	Y	Y	Y	Y
3 DeLauro	Y	Y	N	Y	Y	Y	Y
4 ***Shays***	Y	Y	Y	N	N	N	Y
5 Maloney	N	Y	N	Y	Y	Y	Y
6 ***Johnson***	N	Y	Y	Y	N	Y	Y
DELAWARE							
AL ***Castle***	N	Y	Y	Y	Y	N	Y
FLORIDA							
1 ***Scarborough***	N	Y	Y	N	N	Y	Y
2 Boyd	N	N	N	Y	Y	Y	Y
3 Brown	N	Y	N	Y	Y	Y	Y
4 ***Fowler***	N	Y	Y	N	N	Y	Y
5 Thurman	N	N	N	Y	Y	Y	Y
6 ***Stearns***	N	Y	Y	Y	N	Y	Y
7 ***Mica***	N	Y	Y	N	N	Y	Y
8 ***McCollum***	N	Y	Y	N	N	Y	Y
9 ***Bilirakis***	N	Y	Y	Y	N	Y	?
10 ***Young***	N	Y	Y	Y	N	Y	Y
11 Davis	N	N	N	Y	Y	Y	Y
12 ***Canady***	N	Y	Y	N	N	Y	Y
13 ***Miller***	N	Y	Y	N	N	Y	Y
14 ***Goss***	N	Y	Y	N	N	Y	Y
15 ***Weldon***	N	Y	Y	N	N	Y	Y
16 ***Foley***	N	Y	?	?	?	?	?
17 Meek	N	N	N	Y	Y	Y	Y
18 ***Ros-Lehtinen***	N	Y	Y	N	N	Y	Y
19 Wexler	N	Y	N	Y	Y	Y	Y
20 Deutsch	N	Y	N	+	Y	Y	–
21 ***Diaz-Balart***	N	Y	Y	N	N	Y	Y
22 ***Shaw***	N	Y	Y	N	N	Y	Y
23 Hastings	N	Y	N	Y	Y	Y	Y
GEORGIA							
1 ***Kingston***	Y	Y	Y	Y	N	Y	Y
2 Bishop	N	Y	Y	Y	N	Y	Y
3 ***Collins***	N	Y	Y	N	N	Y	Y
4 McKinney	N	N	N	Y	Y	Y	N
5 Lewis	N	N	N	Y	Y	Y	N
6 ***Isakson***	N	Y	Y	N	N	Y	Y
7 ***Barr***	N	Y	Y	Y	N	Y	Y
8 ***Chambliss***	N	Y	Y	N	N	Y	Y
9 ***Deal***	N	Y	Y	Y	N	Y	Y
10 ***Norwood***	Y	Y	Y	N	N	Y	Y
11 ***Linder***	N	Y	Y	N	N	Y	Y
HAWAII							
1 Abercrombie	?	Y	N	Y	Y	Y	Y
2 Mink	Y	N	N	Y	Y	Y	Y
IDAHO							
1 ***Chenoweth***	Y	Y	Y	N	N	Y	Y
2 ***Simpson***	N	Y	Y	N	N	Y	Y
ILLINOIS							
1 Rush	N	N	N	Y	Y	Y	Y
2 Jackson	N	N	N	Y	Y	N	N
3 Lipinski	?	Y	N	Y	Y	Y	Y
4 Gutierrez	N	N	N	Y	Y	Y	N
5 Blagojevich	Y	N	?	Y	Y	Y	Y
6 ***Hyde***	N	Y	Y	N	N	Y	Y
7 Davis	N	N	N	Y	Y	Y	Y
8 ***Crane***	N	Y	Y	N	N	Y	Y
9 Schakowsky	Y	N	N	Y	Y	N	N
10 ***Porter***	Y	Y	Y	Y	Y	Y	Y
11 ***Weller***	N	Y	Y	Y	N	Y	Y
12 Costello	Y	N	N	Y	Y	Y	Y
13 ***Biggert***	N	Y	Y	N	N	Y	Y
14 ***Hastert***		Y					Y

ND Northern Democrats SD Southern Democrats

	138	139	140	141	142	143	144
15 ***Ewing***	N	Y	Y	Y	N	Y	Y
16 ***Manzullo***	Y	Y	Y	Y	N	Y	Y
17 Evans	Y	N	?	Y	Y	Y	N
18 ***LaHood***	N	Y	Y	Y	N	Y	Y
19 Phelps	N	N	N	Y	Y	Y	Y
20 ***Shimkus***	N	?	Y	Y	N	Y	Y
INDIANA							
1 Visclosky	Y	N	N	Y	Y	Y	Y
2 ***McIntosh***	Y	Y	Y	N	N	Y	Y
3 Roemer	Y	N	N	Y	Y	Y	Y
4 ***Souder***	N	Y	Y	N	N	Y	Y
5 ***Buyer***	N	Y	Y	N	N	Y	Y
6 ***Burton***	N	Y	+	N	N	Y	Y
7 ***Pease***	Y	Y	Y	Y	N	Y	Y
8 ***Hostettler***	Y	Y	Y	N	N	Y	Y
9 Hill	N	N	N	Y	Y	Y	Y
10 Carson	Y	N	N	Y	Y	Y	N
IOWA							
1 ***Leach***	Y	Y	Y	Y	Y	Y	Y
2 ***Nussle***	Y	Y	Y	N	N	Y	Y
3 Boswell	N	N	N	Y	N	Y	Y
4 ***Ganske***	?	N	Y	Y	N	Y	Y
5 ***Latham***	Y	Y	Y	N	N	Y	Y
KANSAS							
1 ***Moran***	N	Y	Y	N	N	Y	Y
2 ***Ryun***	N	Y	Y	N	N	Y	Y
3 Moore	Y	Y	N	Y	Y	Y	Y
4 ***Tiahrt***	N	Y	Y	N	N	Y	Y
KENTUCKY							
1 ***Whitfield***	N	Y	Y	N	N	Y	Y
2 ***Lewis***	N	Y	Y	N	N	Y	Y
3 ***Northup***	N	Y	Y	Y	N	Y	Y
4 Lucas	N	Y	N	Y	N	Y	Y
5 ***Rogers***	N	Y	Y	N	N	Y	+
6 ***Fletcher***	N	Y	Y	N	N	Y	Y
LOUISIANA							
1 Vacant							
2 Jefferson	N	N	N	Y	Y	Y	Y
3 ***Tauzin***	N	Y	Y	N	N	Y	Y
4 ***McCrery***	N	Y	Y	N	N	Y	Y
5 ***Cooksey***	N	Y	Y	N	N	Y	Y
6 ***Baker***	N	Y	Y	N	N	Y	Y
7 John	N	N	N	N	Y	Y	Y
MAINE							
1 Allen	N	N	N	Y	Y	Y	N
2 Baldacci	N	N	N	Y	Y	Y	N
MARYLAND							
1 ***Gilchrest***	Y	Y	Y	N	N	Y	Y
2 ***Ehrlich***	N	Y	Y	Y	N	Y	Y
3 Cardin	N	N	N	Y	Y	Y	Y
4 Wynn	N	N	N	Y	Y	Y	Y
5 Hoyer	N	N	N	Y	Y	Y	Y
6 ***Bartlett***	N	Y	Y	N	N	Y	Y
7 Cummings	N	N	N	Y	Y	Y	Y
8 ***Morella***	N	Y	Y	Y	Y	N	Y
MASSACHUSETTS							
1 Olver	Y	N	N	Y	Y	Y	N
2 Neal	N	N	N	Y	Y	Y	N
3 McGovern	N	N	N	Y	Y	Y	N
4 Frank	Y	N	N	Y	Y	Y	?
5 Meehan	Y	N	N	Y	Y	N	Y
6 Tierney	Y	N	N	Y	Y	Y	N
7 Markey	Y	Y	N	Y	Y	N	N
8 Capuano	Y	N	N	Y	Y	Y	N
9 Moakley	N	N	N	?	?	?	?
10 Delahunt	Y	N	N	Y	Y	Y	N
MICHIGAN							
1 Stupak	Y	N	N	Y	Y	Y	Y
2 ***Hoekstra***	Y	Y	Y	N	N	Y	Y
3 ***Ehlers***	N	Y	Y	Y	N	Y	N
4 ***Camp***	Y	Y	Y	Y	N	Y	Y
5 Barcia	N	N	N	N	Y	Y	Y
6 ***Upton***	Y	Y	Y	Y	N	Y	Y
7 ***Smith***	N	Y	Y	N	N	Y	Y
8 Stabenow	N	N	N	Y	Y	Y	Y
9 Kildee	Y	N	N	Y	Y	Y	Y
10 Bonior	N	N	N	Y	Y	Y	N
11 ***Knollenberg***	N	Y	Y	N	N	Y	Y
12 Levin	Y	N	N	Y	Y	Y	Y
13 Rivers	Y	N	N	Y	Y	Y	N
14 Conyers	Y	N	N	Y	Y	Y	N
15 Kilpatrick	N	N	N	Y	Y	Y	N
16 Dingell	Y	N	N	Y	Y	Y	Y
MINNESOTA							
1 ***Gutknecht***	N	Y	Y	Y	N	Y	Y
2 Minge	Y	N	N	Y	Y	Y	N
3 ***Ramstad***	Y	Y	Y	Y	Y	Y	Y
4 Vento	Y	N	N	Y	Y	Y	N
5 Sabo	N	N	N	Y	Y	Y	N
6 Luther	Y	N	N	Y	Y	Y	N
7 Peterson	Y	N	Y	Y	N	Y	Y
8 Oberstar	Y	N	N	Y	Y	Y	N
MISSISSIPPI							
1 ***Wicker***	N	Y	Y	N	N	Y	Y
2 Thompson	Y	N	N	Y	Y	Y	Y
3 ***Pickering***	N	Y	Y	N	N	Y	Y
4 Shows	N	Y	Y	Y	N	Y	Y
5 Taylor	N	Y	Y	Y	N	Y	Y
MISSOURI							
1 Clay	Y	N	N	Y	Y	Y	N
2 ***Talent***	N	Y	Y	N	N	Y	Y
3 Gephardt	N	N	?	Y	Y	Y	Y
4 Skelton	Y	Y	Y	Y	N	Y	Y
5 McCarthy	N	N	Y	Y	Y	Y	Y
6 Danner	Y	N	Y	Y	Y	Y	Y
7 ***Blunt***	N	Y	Y	N	N	Y	Y
8 ***Emerson***	N	Y	Y	N	N	Y	Y
9 ***Hulshof***	N	Y	Y	N	N	Y	Y
MONTANA							
AL ***Hill***	N	Y	Y	Y	N	Y	Y
NEBRASKA							
1 ***Bereuter***	Y	Y	Y	Y	N	Y	Y
2 ***Terry***	N	?	Y	N	N	Y	Y
3 ***Barrett***	N	Y	Y	N	N	Y	Y
NEVADA							
1 Berkley	N	N	N	Y	Y	Y	Y
2 ***Gibbons***	Y	Y	Y	N	N	Y	Y
NEW HAMPSHIRE							
1 ***Sununu***	Y	Y	Y	Y	N	Y	Y
2 ***Bass***	Y	Y	Y	Y	N	Y	Y
NEW JERSEY							
1 Andrews	N	N	N	Y	Y	Y	Y
2 ***LoBiondo***	Y	Y	Y	Y	N	Y	Y
3 ***Saxton***	N	Y	Y	Y	N	Y	Y
4 ***Smith***	N	Y	Y	Y	N	Y	Y
5 ***Roukema***	N	Y	Y	Y	Y	Y	Y
6 Pallone	Y	N	N	Y	Y	Y	Y
7 ***Franks***	Y	N	Y	Y	N	Y	Y
8 Pascrell	Y	N	N	Y	Y	Y	Y
9 Rothman	N	N	N	Y	Y	Y	Y
10 Payne	N	N	N	Y	Y	Y	N
11 ***Frelinghuysen***	N	Y	Y	Y	N	Y	Y
12 Holt	Y	N	N	Y	Y	Y	N
13 Menendez	N	N	N	Y	Y	Y	Y
NEW MEXICO							
1 ***Wilson***	Y	Y	Y	N	N	Y	Y
2 ***Skeen***	N	Y	Y	N	N	Y	Y
3 Udall	Y	N	N	Y	Y	Y	N
NEW YORK							
1 ***Forbes***	N	Y	Y	Y	N	Y	Y
2 ***Lazio***	Y	Y	Y	N	N	Y	Y
3 ***King***	N	Y	Y	N	N	Y	Y
4 McCarthy	N	N	N	Y	Y	Y	Y
5 Ackerman	N	N	N	Y	Y	Y	Y
6 Meeks	N	N	N	Y	Y	Y	N
7 Crowley	Y	N	N	Y	Y	Y	Y
8 Nadler	Y	N	N	Y	Y	Y	N
9 Weiner	N	Y	N	N	Y	Y	N
10 Towns	N	N	?	?	?	?	?
11 Owens	Y	N	N	Y	Y	Y	N
12 Velázquez	N	N	N	Y	Y	Y	N
13 ***Fossella***	Y	Y	Y	N	N	Y	Y
14 Maloney	N	N	N	Y	Y	Y	Y
15 Rangel	Y	N	N	Y	Y	Y	N
16 Serrano	?	?	N	Y	Y	Y	Y
17 Engel	N	N	N	Y	Y	Y	Y
18 Lowey	Y	N	N	Y	Y	Y	Y
19 ***Kelly***	Y	Y	Y	Y	N	Y	Y
20 ***Gilman***	N	Y	?	N	Y	Y	Y
21 McNulty	N	N	N	Y	Y	Y	?
22 ***Sweeney***	N	Y	Y	N	N	Y	Y
23 ***Boehlert***	N	Y	Y	Y	N	Y	Y
24 ***McHugh***	Y	Y	Y	N	N	Y	Y
25 ***Walsh***	N	Y	Y	Y	N	Y	?
26 Hinchey	Y	N	N	Y	Y	Y	N
27 ***Reynolds***	N	Y	Y	N	N	Y	Y
28 Slaughter	N	N	N	Y	Y	Y	N
29 LaFalce	Y	N	N	Y	Y	Y	Y
30 ***Quinn***	N	Y	Y	Y	N	Y	Y
31 ***Houghton***	N	Y	Y	Y	N	Y	Y
NORTH CAROLINA							
1 Clayton	N	N	N	Y	Y	Y	N
2 Etheridge	N	Y	N	Y	Y	Y	Y
3 ***Jones***	Y	Y	Y	N	N	Y	Y
4 Price	N	Y	N	Y	Y	Y	Y
5 ***Burr***	N	Y	Y	N	N	Y	Y
6 ***Coble***	Y	N	Y	Y	N	Y	Y
7 McIntyre	N	Y	Y	Y	N	Y	Y
8 ***Hayes***	N	Y	Y	N	N	Y	Y
9 ***Myrick***	Y	Y	Y	N	N	Y	Y
10 ***Ballenger***	N	Y	Y	N	N	Y	Y
11 ***Taylor***	Y	Y	Y	N	N	Y	Y
12 Watt	N	N	N	Y	Y	Y	N
NORTH DAKOTA							
AL Pomeroy	Y	N	N	Y	Y	Y	Y
OHIO							
1 ***Chabot***	Y	Y	Y	N	N	Y	Y
2 ***Portman***	Y	Y	Y	N	N	Y	Y
3 Hall	N	N	Y	Y	Y	Y	Y
4 ***Oxley***	Y	Y	Y	N	N	Y	Y
5 ***Gillmor***	N	Y	Y	N	N	Y	Y
6 Strickland	Y	Y	N	Y	Y	Y	N
7 ***Hobson***	N	Y	Y	Y	N	Y	Y
8 ***Boehner***	N	Y	Y	N	N	Y	Y
9 Kaptur	Y	N	N	Y	Y	Y	N
10 Kucinich	Y	Y	?	Y	Y	N	N
11 Jones	Y	N	N	Y	Y	Y	N
12 ***Kasich***	N	Y	Y	Y	N	Y	Y
13 Brown	Y	N	N	Y	Y	Y	N
14 Sawyer	Y	N	N	Y	Y	Y	N
15 ***Pryce***	N	Y	Y	Y	N	Y	Y
16 ***Regula***	Y	Y	Y	Y	N	Y	Y
17 Traficant	Y	Y	Y	Y	N	Y	Y
18 ***Ney***	N	Y	Y	Y	N	Y	Y
19 ***LaTourette***	Y	Y	Y	N	N	Y	Y
OKLAHOMA							
1 ***Largent***	Y	Y	Y	?	?	?	?
2 ***Coburn***	Y	N	Y	N	N	Y	Y
3 ***Watkins***	N	Y	Y	N	N	Y	Y
4 ***Watts***	N	Y	Y	N	N	Y	Y
5 ***Istook***	N	Y	Y	N	N	Y	Y
6 ***Lucas***	N	Y	Y	N	N	Y	Y
OREGON							
1 Wu	N	Y	N	Y	Y	Y	N
2 ***Walden***	N	Y	Y	N	N	Y	Y
3 Blumenauer	Y	N	Y	Y	Y	N	N
4 DeFazio	Y	N	N	Y	Y	Y	N
5 Hooley	N	?	Y	Y	Y	Y	N
PENNSYLVANIA							
1 Brady	N	N	N	Y	Y	Y	N
2 Fattah	N	N	N	Y	Y	Y	N
3 Borski	N	N	N	?	Y	Y	Y
4 Klink	N	Y	N	Y	Y	N	Y
5 ***Peterson***	N	Y	Y	N	N	Y	Y
6 Holden	Y	N	N	Y	Y	Y	Y
7 ***Weldon***	N	Y	Y	Y	N	Y	Y
8 ***Greenwood***	N	Y	Y	Y	N	Y	Y
9 ***Shuster***	Y	N	Y	N	N	Y	Y
10 ***Sherwood***	Y	Y	Y	N	Y	Y	Y
11 Kanjorski	N	N	N	Y	Y	Y	Y
12 Murtha	N	Y	N	Y	Y	Y	Y
13 Hoeffel	N	Y	N	Y	Y	Y	Y
14 Coyne	Y	N	N	Y	Y	Y	N
15 ***Toomey***	N	Y	Y	N	N	Y	Y
16 ***Pitts***	N	Y	Y	N	N	Y	Y
17 ***Gekas***	N	Y	Y	N	N	Y	Y
18 Doyle	N	Y	N	Y	Y	Y	Y
19 ***Goodling***	Y	Y	Y	N	N	Y	Y
20 Mascara	N	N	N	Y	Y	Y	Y
21 ***English***	N	Y	Y	Y	N	Y	Y
RHODE ISLAND							
1 Kennedy	N	N	N	Y	Y	Y	Y
2 Weygand	N	Y	N	Y	Y	Y	Y
SOUTH CAROLINA							
1 ***Sanford***	Y	N	Y	N	N	Y	Y
2 ***Spence***	Y	Y	Y	Y	N	Y	Y
3 ***Graham***	Y	Y	Y	N	?	Y	Y
4 ***DeMint***	N	Y	Y	N	N	Y	?
5 Spratt	Y	Y	N	Y	Y	Y	Y
6 Clyburn	Y	N	N	Y	Y	Y	Y
SOUTH DAKOTA							
AL ***Thune***	N	Y	Y	N	N	Y	Y
TENNESSEE							
1 ***Jenkins***	N	Y	Y	N	N	Y	Y
2 ***Duncan***	Y	N	Y	Y	N	Y	Y
3 ***Wamp***	Y	Y	Y	Y	N	Y	Y
4 ***Hilleary***	Y	Y	Y	N	N	Y	Y
5 Clement	N	N	N	Y	Y	Y	Y
6 Gordon	N	N	N	Y	Y	Y	Y
7 ***Bryant***	Y	Y	Y	N	N	Y	Y
8 Tanner	N	N	N	Y	Y	Y	Y
9 Ford	Y	N	N	Y	Y	Y	Y
TEXAS							
1 Sandlin	N	Y	N	Y	N	Y	Y
2 Turner	N	Y	Y	Y	N	Y	Y
3 ***Johnson, Sam***	N	Y	Y	N	N	Y	Y
4 Hall	N	Y	Y	Y	N	Y	Y
5 ***Sessions***	N	Y	Y	N	N	Y	Y
6 ***Barton***	N	Y	Y	N	N	Y	Y
7 ***Archer***	N	Y	Y	N	N	Y	Y
8 ***Brady***	N	Y	Y	N	N	Y	Y
9 Lampson	N	Y	N	Y	Y	Y	Y
10 Doggett	Y	N	N	Y	Y	Y	N
11 Edwards	N	Y	N	Y	N	Y	Y
12 ***Granger***	N	Y	Y	N	N	?	Y
13 ***Thornberry***	N	Y	Y	N	?	Y	Y
14 ***Paul***	Y	N	Y	Y	N	Y	Y
15 Hinojosa	N	Y	N	Y	Y	Y	Y
16 Reyes	N	Y	N	Y	Y	Y	Y
17 Stenholm	N	Y	N	Y	N	Y	Y
18 Jackson-Lee	N	Y	N	Y	Y	Y	Y
19 ***Combest***	N	Y	Y	N	N	Y	Y
20 Gonzalez	N	Y	N	Y	Y	?	Y
21 ***Smith***	N	Y	Y	N	N	Y	Y
22 ***DeLay***	N	Y	Y	N	N	Y	Y
23 ***Bonilla***	N	Y	Y	N	N	Y	Y
24 Frost	N	Y	N	Y	Y	Y	Y
25 Bentsen	N	Y	N	Y	Y	Y	Y
26 ***Armey***	N	Y	Y	N	N	Y	Y
27 Ortiz	N	Y	N	Y	Y	Y	Y
28 Rodriguez	N	Y	N	Y	Y	Y	Y
29 Green	N	Y	Y	Y	Y	Y	Y
30 Johnson, E.B.	N	Y	N	Y	Y	Y	Y
UTAH							
1 ***Hansen***	N	Y	Y	N	N	Y	Y
2 ***Cook***	N	Y	Y	Y	N	Y	Y
3 ***Cannon***	N	Y	Y	N	N	Y	Y
VERMONT							
AL *Sanders*	Y	N	N	Y	Y	Y	N
VIRGINIA							
1 ***Bateman***	Y	Y	Y	N	N	Y	Y
2 Pickett	N	Y	Y	N	N	Y	?
3 Scott	Y	N	Y	Y	Y	N	Y
4 Sisisky	Y	N	Y	Y	N	Y	Y
5 Goode	Y	N	Y	Y	N	Y	Y
6 ***Goodlatte***	Y	N	Y	N	N	Y	Y
7 ***Bliley***	Y	Y	Y	N	N	Y	Y
8 Moran	N	N	N	Y	Y	Y	Y
9 Boucher	Y	N	N	Y	Y	Y	Y
10 ***Wolf***	Y	Y	Y	Y	N	Y	Y
11 ***Davis***	Y	Y	Y	N	N	Y	Y
WASHINGTON							
1 Inslee	N	N	N	Y	Y	Y	Y
2 ***Metcalf***	N	Y	Y	Y	N	Y	Y
3 Baird	N	N	N	Y	Y	Y	N
4 ***Hastings***	N	Y	Y	N	N	Y	Y
5 ***Nethercutt***	N	Y	Y	N	N	Y	Y
6 Dicks	N	N	N	Y	Y	Y	Y
7 McDermott	N	N	N	Y	Y	Y	N
8 ***Dunn***	N	Y	?	Y	N	Y	Y
9 Smith	N	N	N	Y	N	Y	Y
WEST VIRGINIA							
1 Mollohan	N	N	N	Y	Y	Y	Y
2 Wise	N	N	N	Y	Y	Y	Y
3 Rahall	N	N	N	Y	Y	Y	Y
WISCONSIN							
1 ***Ryan***	Y	Y	Y	N	N	Y	Y
2 Baldwin	Y	N	N	Y	Y	Y	N
3 Kind	Y	N	N	Y	Y	Y	Y
4 Kleczka	N	Y	N	Y	Y	Y	Y
5 Barrett	Y	N	N	Y	Y	Y	N
6 ***Petri***	Y	Y	Y	N	N	Y	Y
7 Obey	Y	N	N	Y	Y	Y	N
8 ***Green***	N	Y	Y	N	N	Y	Y
9 ***Sensenbrenner***	N	Y	Y	N	N	Y	Y
WYOMING							
AL ***Cubin***	N	N	Y	N	N	N	Y

Southern states - Ala., Ark., Fla., Ga., Ky., La., Miss., N.C., Okla., S.C., Tenn., Texas, Va.

House Votes 145, 146, 147, 148, 149, 150, 152, 153*

145. HR 1251. Noal Cushing Bateman Post Office/Concur with Senate Amendments. Davis, R-Va., motion to suspend the rules and pass the bill to name the post office building in Sandy, Utah, the "Noal Cushing Bateman Post Office Building." Motion agreed to 362-0: R 198-0; D 164-0 (ND 118-0, SD 46-0); I 0-0. May 24, 1999. A two-thirds majority of those present and voting (242 in this case) is required for passage under suspension of the rules.

146. HR 100. Rename Philadelphia Post Offices/Passage. Davis, R-Va., motion to suspend the rules and pass the bill to rename post office buildings in Philadelphia, Pa., as the "Roxanne H. Jones Post Office Building," the "Freeman Hankins Post Office Building" and the "Max Weiner Post Office Building." Motion agreed to 368-0: R 201-0; D 167-0 (ND 120-0, SD 47-0); I 0-0. May 24, 1999. A two-thirds majority of those present and voting (246 in this case) is required for passage under suspension of the rules.

147. HR 1906. Fiscal 2000 Agriculture Appropriations/Rule. Adoption of the rule (H Res 185) to provide for House floor consideration of the bill to provide funding for agriculture, rural development, Food and Drug Administration, and related agencies for fiscal 2000. Adopted 402-10: R 208-4; D 193-6 (ND 149-2, SD 44-4); I 1-0. May 25, 1999.

148. S 249. Missing Children Protection Act/Passage. Castle, R-Del., motion to suspend the rules and pass the bill to reauthorize programs for missing, runaway and exploited children for fiscal 2000 through 2003, and to authorize a grant of $10 million in each of those years to the National Center for Missing and Exploited Children. Motion agreed to 414-1: R 213-1; D 200-0 (ND 152-0, SD 48-0); I 1-0. May 25, 1999. A two-thirds majority of those present and voting (277 in this case) is required for passage under suspension of the rules.

149. HR 1833. Trade Agency Authorization/Passage. Crane, R-Ill., motion to suspend the rules and pass the bill to reauthorize funding for fiscal 2000-01 for the U.S. Customs Service, Office of the U.S. Trade Representative, and the International Trade Commission. Motion agreed to 410-2: R 208-2; D 201-0 (ND 151-0, SD 50-0); I 1-0. May 25, 1999. A two-thirds majority of those present and voting (275 in this case) is required for passage under suspension of the rules.

150. H Res 178. Condemn Chinese Human Rights Abuse/Adoption. Gilman, R-N.Y., motion to suspend the rules and adopt the resolution to express the House's sympathy to the families of those killed in the 1989 protests in Tiananmen Square and to condemn ongoing human rights abuses in China. Motion agreed to 418-0: R 215-0; D 202-0 (ND 152-0, SD 50-0); I 1-0. May 25, 1999. A two-thirds majority of those present and voting (242 in this case) is required for adoption under suspension of the rules.

151. Quorum Call.* 399 responded. May 25, 1999.

152. HR 1906. Fiscal 2000 Agriculture Appropriations/Budget Office. Coburn, R-Okla., amendment to eliminate the proposed $463,000 increase for the Agriculture Department's Office of Budget and Program Analysis. Rejected 133-285: R 120-94; D 13-190 (ND 9-143, SD 4-47); I 0-1. May 25, 1999.

153. HR 1906. Fiscal 2000 Agriculture Appropriations/Budget Office. Coburn, R-Okla., amendment to reduce the proposed budget increase for the Agriculture Department's Office of Budget and Program Analysis by $231,000. Rejected 146-267: R 132-81; D 14-185 (ND 9-140, SD 5-45); I 0-1. May 25, 1999.

CQ does not include quorum calls in its vote charts.

Key

- Y Voted for (yea).
- # Paired for.
- + Announced for.
- N Voted against (nay).
- X Paired against.
- – Announced against.
- P Voted "present."
- C Voted "present" to avoid possible conflict of interest.
- ? Did not vote or otherwise make a position known.

•

Democrats ***Republicans***
Independents

	145	146	147	148	149	150	152	153
ALABAMA								
1 ***Callahan***	Y	Y	Y	Y	Y	Y	N	N
2 ***Everett***	Y	Y	Y	Y	Y	Y	N	N
3 ***Riley***	Y	Y	Y	Y	Y	Y	Y	?
4 ***Aderholt***	Y	Y	Y	Y	Y	Y	Y	Y
5 Cramer	Y	Y	Y	Y	Y	Y	N	N
6 ***Bachus***	Y	Y	Y	?	Y	Y	Y	Y
7 Hilliard	Y	Y	N	Y	Y	Y	N	N
ALASKA								
AL ***Young***	Y	Y	?	Y	Y	Y	N	?
ARIZONA								
1 ***Salmon***	Y	Y	Y	Y	Y	Y	Y	Y
2 Pastor	Y	Y	Y	Y	Y	Y	N	N
3 ***Stump***	Y	Y	Y	Y	Y	Y	Y	Y
4 ***Shadegg***	Y	Y	Y	Y	Y	Y	Y	Y
5 ***Kolbe***	Y	Y	Y	Y	Y	Y	N	N
6 ***Hayworth***	Y	Y	Y	Y	Y	Y	Y	Y
ARKANSAS								
1 Berry	+	+	Y	Y	Y	Y	N	N
2 Snyder	Y	Y	Y	Y	Y	Y	N	N
3 ***Hutchinson***	Y	Y	Y	Y	Y	Y	Y	Y
4 ***Dickey***	Y	Y	Y	Y	Y	Y	N	N
CALIFORNIA								
1 Thompson	Y	Y	Y	Y	Y	Y	N	N
2 ***Herger***	Y	Y	Y	Y	?	Y	Y	Y
3 ***Ose***	Y	Y	Y	Y	Y	Y	N	Y
4 ***Doolittle***	Y	Y	Y	Y	Y	Y	Y	Y
5 Matsui	Y	Y	Y	Y	Y	Y	N	N
6 Woolsey	Y	Y	Y	Y	?	Y	N	N
7 Miller, George	Y	Y	N	Y	Y	Y	N	Y
8 Pelosi	?	?	Y	Y	Y	Y	N	N
9 Lee	Y	Y	Y	Y	Y	Y	N	N
10 Tauscher	Y	Y	Y	Y	Y	Y	N	N
11 ***Pombo***	Y	Y	Y	Y	Y	Y	Y	Y
12 Lantos	?	?	Y	Y	Y	Y	N	N
13 Stark	Y	Y	Y	Y	Y	Y	N	N
14 Eshoo	Y	Y	Y	Y	Y	Y	N	N
15 ***Campbell***	Y	Y	Y	Y	Y	Y	Y	Y
16 Lofgren	Y	Y	Y	Y	Y	Y	Y	Y
17 Farr	Y	Y	Y	Y	Y	Y	N	N
18 Condit	Y	Y	Y	Y	Y	Y	N	N
19 ***Radanovich***	Y	Y	Y	Y	Y	Y	N	N
20 Dooley	Y	Y	Y	Y	Y	Y	N	N
21 ***Thomas***	Y	Y	Y	Y	Y	Y	N	N
22 Capps	Y	Y	Y	Y	Y	Y	N	N
23 ***Gallegly***	Y	Y	Y	Y	Y	Y	N	N
24 Sherman	Y	Y	Y	Y	Y	Y	N	N
25 ***McKeon***	Y	Y	Y	Y	Y	Y	N	N
26 Berman	Y	Y	Y	Y	Y	Y	N	N
27 ***Rogan***	Y	Y	Y	Y	Y	Y	Y	Y
28 ***Dreier***	Y	Y	Y	Y	Y	Y	Y	Y
29 Waxman	Y	Y	?	?	Y	Y	N	N
30 Becerra	+	+	Y	Y	Y	Y	N	N
31 Martinez	Y	Y	Y	Y	Y	?	Y	?
32 Dixon	Y	Y	Y	Y	Y	Y	N	?
33 Roybal-Allard	Y	Y	Y	Y	Y	Y	N	N
34 Napolitano	Y	Y	+	+	+	Y	N	N
35 Waters	Y	Y	Y	Y	Y	Y	N	N
36 ***Kuykendall***	Y	Y	Y	Y	Y	Y	N	N
37 Millender-McD.	Y	Y	?	?	?	?	?	?
38 ***Horn***	Y	Y	Y	Y	Y	Y	N	N
39 ***Royce***	Y	Y	Y	Y	Y	Y	Y	Y
40 ***Lewis***	Y	Y	Y	Y	Y	Y	N	N
41 ***Miller, Gary***	Y	Y	Y	Y	Y	Y	Y	Y
42 Brown	?	?	?	?	?	?	?	?
43 ***Calvert***	Y	Y	Y	Y	Y	Y	N	N
44 ***Bono***	Y	Y	Y	Y	Y	Y	N	N
45 ***Rohrabacher***	Y	Y	Y	Y	Y	Y	Y	Y
46 Sanchez	?	?	Y	Y	Y	Y	N	N
47 ***Cox***	Y	Y	?	Y	Y	Y	Y	Y
48 ***Packard***	Y	Y	?	Y	Y	Y	N	N
49 ***Bilbray***	Y	Y	Y	Y	?	Y	N	N
50 Filner	Y	Y	Y	Y	Y	Y	N	N
51 ***Cunningham***	Y	Y	Y	Y	Y	Y	N	Y
52 ***Hunter***	Y	Y	Y	Y	Y	Y	Y	Y
COLORADO								
1 DeGette	Y	Y	Y	Y	Y	Y	N	N
2 Udall	Y	Y	Y	Y	Y	Y	N	N
3 ***McInnis***	Y	Y	Y	Y	Y	Y	Y	Y
4 ***Schaffer***	?	?	Y	Y	Y	Y	Y	Y
5 ***Hefley***	?	?	Y	Y	Y	Y	Y	Y
6 ***Tancredo***	Y	Y	Y	Y	Y	Y	Y	Y
CONNECTICUT								
1 Larson	Y	Y	Y	Y	Y	Y	N	N
2 Gejdenson	?	?	Y	Y	Y	Y	N	N
3 DeLauro	+	+	Y	Y	Y	Y	N	N
4 ***Shays***	Y	Y	Y	Y	Y	Y	Y	Y
5 Maloney	Y	Y	Y	Y	Y	Y	Y	Y
6 ***Johnson***	Y	Y	Y	Y	Y	Y	Y	Y
DELAWARE								
AL ***Castle***	Y	Y	Y	Y	Y	Y	Y	Y
FLORIDA								
1 ***Scarborough***	?	Y	Y	Y	Y	Y	Y	Y
2 Boyd	Y	Y	Y	Y	Y	Y	N	N
3 Brown	?	?	Y	Y	Y	Y	N	?
4 ***Fowler***	Y	Y	Y	Y	Y	Y	Y	Y
5 Thurman	Y	Y	Y	Y	Y	Y	N	N
6 ***Stearns***	Y	Y	Y	Y	Y	Y	Y	Y
7 ***Mica***	Y	Y	Y	Y	Y	Y	Y	Y
8 ***McCollum***	Y	Y	Y	Y	Y	Y	Y	Y
9 ***Bilirakis***	Y	Y	Y	Y	Y	Y	N	Y
10 ***Young***	?	?	Y	Y	Y	Y	N	N
11 Davis	Y	Y	Y	?	Y	Y	N	N
12 ***Canady***	Y	Y	Y	Y	Y	Y	N	N
13 ***Miller***	Y	Y	Y	Y	Y	Y	Y	Y
14 ***Goss***	Y	Y	Y	Y	Y	Y	Y	Y
15 ***Weldon***	Y	Y	Y	Y	Y	Y	Y	Y
16 ***Foley***	Y	Y	Y	Y	Y	Y	Y	Y
17 Meek	Y	Y	Y	Y	Y	Y	N	N
18 ***Ros-Lehtinen***	Y	Y	Y	Y	Y	Y	N	Y
19 Wexler	Y	Y	Y	Y	Y	Y	N	N
20 Deutsch	Y	Y	Y	Y	Y	Y	N	N
21 ***Diaz-Balart***	Y	Y	Y	Y	Y	Y	Y	Y
22 ***Shaw***	Y	Y	Y	Y	Y	Y	Y	Y
23 Hastings	Y	Y	Y	Y	Y	Y	N	N
GEORGIA								
1 ***Kingston***	Y	Y	Y	Y	Y	Y	N	N
2 Bishop	Y	Y	N	Y	Y	Y	N	N
3 ***Collins***	Y	Y	Y	Y	Y	Y	Y	Y
4 McKinney	?	Y	N	Y	Y	Y	N	N
5 Lewis	Y	Y	Y	Y	Y	Y	N	N
6 ***Isakson***	Y	Y	Y	Y	Y	Y	Y	N
7 ***Barr***	Y	Y	Y	Y	Y	Y	Y	Y
8 ***Chambliss***	Y	Y	Y	Y	Y	Y	N	N
9 ***Deal***	Y	Y	Y	Y	Y	Y	Y	Y
10 ***Norwood***	?	?	Y	Y	Y	Y	Y	Y
11 ***Linder***	Y	Y	Y	Y	Y	Y	Y	Y
HAWAII								
1 Abercrombie	?	Y	Y	Y	Y	Y	N	N
2 Mink	Y	Y	Y	Y	Y	Y	N	N
IDAHO								
1 ***Chenoweth***	?	?	Y	Y	Y	Y	Y	Y
2 ***Simpson***	Y	Y	Y	Y	Y	Y	N	N
ILLINOIS								
1 Rush	Y	Y	Y	Y	Y	Y	N	N
2 Jackson	Y	Y	Y	Y	Y	Y	N	N
3 Lipinski	?	?	Y	Y	Y	Y	N	N
4 Gutierrez	?	?	Y	Y	Y	Y	N	?
5 Blagojevich	Y	Y	Y	Y	Y	Y	N	N
6 ***Hyde***	Y	Y	Y	Y	Y	Y	N	Y
7 Davis	Y	Y	Y	Y	Y	Y	N	N
8 ***Crane***	Y	Y	Y	Y	Y	Y	Y	Y
9 Schakowsky	Y	Y	Y	Y	Y	Y	N	N
10 ***Porter***	?	?	Y	Y	Y	Y	N	N
11 ***Weller***	Y	Y	Y	Y	Y	Y	Y	Y
12 Costello	Y	Y	Y	Y	Y	Y	N	N
13 ***Biggert***	Y	Y	Y	Y	Y	Y	N	Y
14 ***Hastert***								

ND Northern Democrats SD Southern Democrats

	145	146	147	148	149	150	152	153
15 ***Ewing***	Y	Y	?	?	?	?	N	N
16 ***Manzullo***	?	?	Y	Y	Y	Y	Y	Y
17 Evans	Y	Y	Y	Y	Y	Y	N	N
18 ***LaHood***	Y	Y	Y	Y	Y	Y	N	N
19 Phelps	Y	Y	Y	Y	Y	Y	N	N
20 ***Shimkus***	Y	Y	Y	Y	Y	Y	N	N
INDIANA								
1 Visclosky	Y	Y	Y	Y	Y	Y	N	N
2 ***McIntosh***	Y	Y	N	Y	Y	Y	Y	Y
3 Roemer	Y	Y	Y	Y	Y	Y	N	N
4 ***Souder***	Y	Y	Y	Y	Y	Y	Y	Y
5 ***Buyer***	?	?	?	?	?	?	Y	Y
6 ***Burton***	Y	Y	Y	Y	Y	Y	Y	Y
7 ***Pease***	Y	Y	Y	Y	Y	Y	Y	Y
8 ***Hostettler***	Y	Y	N	Y	Y	Y	Y	Y
9 Hill	Y	Y	Y	Y	Y	Y	N	N
10 Carson	+	+	Y	Y	Y	Y	N	N
IOWA								
1 ***Leach***	Y	Y	Y	Y	Y	Y	Y	Y
2 ***Nussle***	Y	Y	Y	Y	Y	Y	N	N
3 Boswell	Y	Y	Y	Y	Y	Y	N	N
4 ***Ganske***	?	Y	Y	Y	Y	Y	Y	Y
5 ***Latham***	Y	Y	Y	Y	Y	Y	N	N
KANSAS								
1 ***Moran***	Y	Y	Y	Y	Y	Y	N	N
2 ***Ryun***	Y	Y	Y	Y	Y	Y	Y	Y
3 Moore	Y	Y	Y	Y	Y	Y	N	N
4 ***Tiahrt***	Y	Y	Y	Y	Y	Y	Y	Y
KENTUCKY								
1 ***Whitfield***	Y	Y	?	Y	Y	Y	?	N
2 ***Lewis***	Y	Y	Y	Y	Y	Y	N	N
3 ***Northup***	Y	Y	Y	Y	Y	Y	Y	Y
4 Lucas	Y	Y	?	?	Y	Y	N	N
5 ***Rogers***	Y	Y	Y	Y	Y	Y	N	N
6 ***Fletcher***	Y	Y	Y	Y	Y	Y	N	?
LOUISIANA								
1 Vacant								
2 Jefferson	Y	Y	Y	Y	Y	Y	N	N
3 ***Tauzin***	?	?	Y	Y	Y	Y	N	N
4 ***McCrery***	Y	Y	Y	Y	Y	Y	N	N
5 ***Cooksey***	?	?	Y	Y	Y	Y	N	N
6 ***Baker***	?	?	Y	Y	Y	Y	?	N
7 John	Y	Y	?	Y	Y	Y	N	N
MAINE								
1 Allen	Y	Y	Y	Y	Y	Y	N	N
2 Baldacci	Y	Y	Y	Y	Y	Y	N	N
MARYLAND								
1 ***Gilchrest***	Y	Y	Y	Y	Y	Y	N	N
2 ***Ehrlich***	Y	Y	Y	Y	Y	Y	Y	Y
3 Cardin	Y	Y	Y	Y	Y	Y	N	N
4 Wynn	Y	Y	Y	Y	Y	Y	N	N
5 Hoyer	Y	Y	Y	Y	Y	Y	N	N
6 ***Bartlett***	Y	Y	Y	Y	Y	Y	Y	Y
7 Cummings	Y	Y	Y	Y	Y	Y	N	N
8 ***Morella***	?	Y	Y	Y	Y	Y	N	N
MASSACHUSETTS								
1 Olver	Y	Y	Y	Y	Y	Y	N	N
2 Neal	?	?	Y	Y	Y	Y	N	N
3 McGovern	?	?	Y	Y	Y	Y	N	N
4 Frank	?	?	Y	Y	Y	Y	Y	Y
5 Meehan	?	?	Y	Y	Y	Y	Y	Y
6 Tierney	?	?	Y	Y	Y	Y	N	N
7 Markey	Y	Y	Y	Y	Y	Y	N	N
8 Capuano	+	+	Y	Y	Y	Y	N	N
9 Moakley	?	?	Y	Y	?	Y	N	N
10 Delahunt	?	?	Y	Y	Y	Y	N	N
MICHIGAN								
1 Stupak	Y	Y	Y	Y	Y	Y	Y	Y
2 ***Hoekstra***	Y	Y	Y	Y	Y	Y	Y	Y
3 ***Ehlers***	Y	Y	Y	Y	Y	Y	N	Y
4 ***Camp***	Y	Y	Y	Y	Y	Y	Y	Y
5 Barcia	Y	Y	Y	Y	Y	Y	N	N
6 ***Upton***	Y	Y	Y	Y	Y	Y	Y	Y
7 ***Smith***	Y	Y	Y	Y	Y	Y	Y	Y
8 Stabenow	?	?	Y	Y	Y	Y	N	N
9 Kildee	Y	Y	Y	Y	Y	Y	N	N
10 Bonior	Y	Y	Y	Y	Y	Y	N	N
11 ***Knollenberg***	Y	Y	Y	Y	Y	Y	N	N
12 Levin	Y	Y	Y	Y	Y	Y	N	N
13 Rivers	Y	Y	Y	Y	Y	Y	N	N
14 Conyers	Y	Y	Y	Y	Y	Y	N	N
15 Kilpatrick	Y	Y	Y	Y	Y	Y	N	N
16 Dingell	Y	Y	Y	Y	Y	Y	N	N

	145	146	147	148	149	150	152	153
MINNESOTA								
1 ***Gutknecht***	Y	Y	Y	Y	Y	Y	Y	Y
2 Minge	Y	Y	Y	Y	Y	Y	N	N
3 ***Ramstad***	Y	Y	Y	Y	Y	Y	Y	Y
4 Vento	Y	Y	Y	Y	Y	Y	N	N
5 Sabo	Y	Y	Y	Y	Y	Y	N	N
6 Luther	Y	Y	Y	Y	Y	Y	Y	Y
7 Peterson	Y	Y	?	Y	Y	Y	N	N
8 Oberstar	Y	Y	Y	Y	Y	Y	N	N
MISSISSIPPI								
1 ***Wicker***	Y	Y	Y	Y	Y	Y	N	N
2 Thompson	Y	Y	Y	Y	Y	Y	N	N
3 ***Pickering***	Y	Y	Y	Y	Y	Y	N	Y
4 Shows	?	?	Y	Y	Y	Y	N	N
5 Taylor	Y	Y	Y	Y	Y	Y	Y	Y
MISSOURI								
1 Clay	?	?	Y	Y	Y	Y	N	N
2 ***Talent***	Y	Y	Y	Y	Y	Y	N	N
3 Gephardt	Y	Y	Y	Y	Y	Y	N	N
4 Skelton	Y	Y	Y	Y	Y	Y	N	N
5 McCarthy	Y	Y	Y	Y	Y	Y	N	N
6 Danner	Y	Y	Y	Y	Y	Y	N	N
7 ***Blunt***	Y	Y	Y	Y	Y	Y	Y	Y
8 ***Emerson***	Y	Y	Y	Y	Y	Y	N	N
9 ***Hulshof***	Y	Y	Y	Y	Y	Y	N	N
MONTANA								
AL ***Hill***	Y	Y	Y	Y	Y	Y	N	Y
NEBRASKA								
1 ***Bereuter***	Y	Y	Y	Y	?	Y	N	N
2 ***Terry***	Y	Y	Y	Y	Y	Y	Y	N
3 ***Barrett***	Y	Y	Y	Y	Y	Y	N	N
NEVADA								
1 Berkley	Y	Y	Y	Y	Y	Y	N	N
2 ***Gibbons***	Y	Y	Y	Y	Y	Y	Y	Y
NEW HAMPSHIRE								
1 ***Sununu***	Y	Y	Y	Y	Y	Y	Y	Y
2 ***Bass***	?	?	Y	Y	Y	Y	Y	Y
NEW JERSEY								
1 Andrews	Y	Y	Y	Y	Y	Y	N	N
2 ***LoBiondo***	Y	Y	Y	Y	Y	Y	N	N
3 ***Saxton***	Y	Y	Y	Y	Y	Y	N	N
4 ***Smith***	Y	Y	Y	Y	Y	Y	N	N
5 ***Roukema***	Y	Y	Y	Y	Y	Y	Y	Y
6 Pallone	?	?	Y	Y	Y	Y	N	N
7 ***Franks***	Y	Y	Y	Y	Y	Y	Y	Y
8 Pascrell	?	?	Y	Y	Y	Y	N	N
9 Rothman	?	?	Y	Y	Y	Y	?	?
10 Payne	?	?	Y	Y	Y	Y	N	N
11 ***Frelinghuysen***	Y	Y	Y	Y	Y	Y	N	N
12 Holt	Y	Y	Y	Y	Y	Y	N	N
13 Menendez	?	?	Y	Y	Y	Y	N	N
NEW MEXICO								
1 ***Wilson***	Y	Y	Y	Y	Y	Y	N	N
2 ***Skeen***	Y	Y	Y	Y	Y	Y	N	N
3 Udall	Y	Y	Y	Y	Y	Y	N	N
NEW YORK								
1 ***Forbes***	Y	Y	Y	Y	Y	Y	N	N
2 ***Lazio***	?	?	Y	Y	Y	Y	Y	Y
3 ***King***	Y	Y	Y	Y	Y	Y	N	N
4 McCarthy	Y	Y	Y	Y	Y	?	N	N
5 Ackerman	?	?	Y	Y	Y	Y	N	N
6 Meeks	?	?	Y	Y	Y	Y	N	N
7 Crowley	+	+	Y	Y	Y	Y	N	N
8 Nadler	Y	Y	Y	Y	Y	Y	?	?
9 Weiner	?	?	Y	Y	Y	Y	N	N
10 Towns	Y	Y	Y	Y	Y	Y	N	N
11 Owens	?	?	Y	Y	Y	Y	N	N
12 Velázquez	?	?	Y	Y	Y	Y	N	N
13 ***Fossella***	Y	Y	Y	Y	Y	Y	Y	Y
14 Maloney	?	?	Y	Y	Y	Y	N	N
15 Rangel	?	Y	Y	Y	Y	Y	N	N
16 Serrano	Y	Y	Y	Y	Y	Y	N	N
17 Engel	Y	Y	Y	Y	Y	Y	N	N
18 Lowey	?	?	Y	Y	Y	Y	N	N
19 ***Kelly***	Y	Y	Y	Y	Y	Y	Y	Y
20 ***Gilman***	Y	Y	Y	Y	Y	Y	N	N
21 McNulty	Y	Y	Y	Y	Y	Y	N	N
22 ***Sweeney***	Y	Y	Y	Y	Y	Y	Y	Y
23 ***Boehlert***	Y	Y	Y	Y	Y	Y	N	N
24 ***McHugh***	Y	Y	Y	Y	N	Y	N	N
25 ***Walsh***	Y	Y	Y	Y	Y	Y	N	N
26 Hinchey	?	?	Y	Y	Y	Y	N	N
27 ***Reynolds***	Y	Y	Y	Y	Y	Y	N	N
28 Slaughter	Y	Y	Y	Y	Y	Y	N	N
29 LaFalce	Y	Y	Y	Y	Y	Y	N	N

	145	146	147	148	149	150	152	153
30 ***Quinn***	Y	Y	Y	Y	Y	Y	N	N
31 ***Houghton***	Y	Y	Y	Y	Y	Y	N	N
NORTH CAROLINA								
1 Clayton	Y	Y	Y	Y	Y	Y	N	N
2 Etheridge	Y	Y	Y	Y	Y	Y	N	N
3 ***Jones***	Y	Y	Y	Y	Y	Y	Y	Y
4 Price	Y	Y	Y	Y	Y	Y	N	N
5 ***Burr***	?	?	Y	Y	Y	Y	Y	Y
6 ***Coble***	Y	Y	Y	Y	Y	Y	Y	Y
7 McIntyre	Y	Y	Y	Y	Y	Y	N	N
8 ***Hayes***	Y	Y	Y	Y	Y	Y	Y	Y
9 ***Myrick***	Y	Y	Y	Y	Y	Y	Y	Y
10 ***Ballenger***	Y	Y	Y	Y	Y	Y	Y	Y
11 ***Taylor***	Y	Y	Y	Y	Y	Y	Y	Y
12 Watt	Y	Y	Y	Y	Y	Y	N	N
NORTH DAKOTA								
AL Pomeroy	Y	Y	Y	Y	Y	Y	N	N
OHIO								
1 ***Chabot***	Y	Y	Y	Y	Y	Y	Y	Y
2 ***Portman***	Y	Y	Y	Y	Y	Y	Y	+
3 Hall	Y	Y	Y	Y	Y	Y	N	N
4 ***Oxley***	Y	Y	Y	Y	Y	Y	N	N
5 ***Gillmor***	Y	Y	Y	Y	Y	Y	N	N
6 Strickland	Y	Y	Y	Y	Y	Y	N	N
7 ***Hobson***	Y	Y	Y	Y	Y	Y	N	N
8 ***Boehner***	Y	Y	Y	Y	Y	Y	Y	Y
9 Kaptur	Y	Y	Y	Y	Y	Y	N	N
10 Kucinich	Y	Y	Y	Y	Y	Y	N	N
11 Jones	Y	Y	Y	Y	Y	Y	N	N
12 ***Kasich***	?	?	?	?	?	?	?	?
13 Brown	Y	Y	Y	Y	Y	Y	N	N
14 Sawyer	Y	Y	Y	Y	Y	Y	N	N
15 ***Pryce***	Y	Y	Y	Y	Y	Y	N	Y
16 ***Regula***	Y	Y	Y	Y	Y	Y	N	N
17 Traficant	Y	Y	Y	Y	Y	Y	N	N
18 ***Ney***	Y	Y	Y	Y	Y	Y	N	N
19 ***LaTourette***	Y	Y	Y	Y	Y	Y	N	N
OKLAHOMA								
1 ***Largent***	Y	Y	Y	Y	Y	Y	?	Y
2 ***Coburn***	?	?	N	Y	Y	Y	Y	Y
3 ***Watkins***	Y	Y	Y	Y	Y	Y	N	N
4 ***Watts***	Y	Y	Y	Y	Y	Y	Y	Y
5 ***Istook***	Y	Y	Y	Y	Y	Y	Y	Y
6 ***Lucas***	Y	Y	Y	?	?	Y	N	N
OREGON								
1 Wu	Y	Y	N	Y	Y	Y	N	N
2 ***Walden***	Y	Y	Y	Y	Y	Y	Y	Y
3 Blumenauer	Y	Y	Y	Y	Y	Y	N	N
4 DeFazio	Y	Y	Y	Y	Y	Y	N	N
5 Hooley	Y	Y	Y	Y	Y	Y	N	N
PENNSYLVANIA								
1 Brady	Y	Y	Y	Y	Y	Y	N	N
2 Fattah	Y	Y	Y	Y	Y	Y	N	N
3 Borski	?	?	Y	Y	Y	Y	N	N
4 Klink	Y	Y	Y	Y	Y	Y	N	Y
5 ***Peterson***	Y	Y	Y	Y	Y	Y	N	N
6 Holden	Y	Y	Y	Y	Y	Y	N	N
7 ***Weldon***	Y	Y	Y	Y	Y	Y	N	N
8 ***Greenwood***	Y	Y	Y	Y	Y	Y	Y	Y
9 ***Shuster***	Y	Y	Y	Y	Y	Y	N	N
10 ***Sherwood***	Y	Y	Y	Y	?	Y	N	Y
11 Kanjorski	Y	Y	Y	Y	Y	Y	N	N
12 Murtha	Y	Y	Y	Y	Y	Y	N	N
13 Hoeffel	Y	Y	Y	Y	Y	Y	N	N
14 Coyne	Y	Y	Y	Y	Y	Y	N	N
15 ***Toomey***	Y	Y	Y	Y	Y	Y	Y	Y
16 ***Pitts***	Y	Y	Y	Y	Y	Y	Y	Y
17 ***Gekas***	Y	Y	Y	Y	?	?	N	?
18 Doyle	Y	Y	Y	Y	Y	Y	N	N
19 ***Goodling***	Y	Y	Y	Y	Y	Y	Y	Y
20 Mascara	Y	Y	Y	Y	Y	Y	N	N
21 ***English***	Y	Y	Y	Y	Y	Y	Y	Y
RHODE ISLAND								
1 Kennedy	Y	Y	Y	Y	Y	Y	N	N
2 Weygand	+	+	Y	Y	Y	Y	N	N
SOUTH CAROLINA								
1 ***Sanford***	Y	Y	N	Y	Y	Y	Y	Y
2 ***Spence***	Y	Y	Y	Y	Y	Y	Y	Y
3 ***Graham***	Y	Y	?	?	?	?	?	?
4 ***DeMint***	Y	Y	Y	Y	Y	Y	Y	Y
5 Spratt	Y	Y	Y	Y	Y	Y	N	N
6 Clyburn	Y	Y	Y	Y	Y	Y	N	N
SOUTH DAKOTA								
AL ***Thune***	Y	Y	Y	Y	Y	Y	N	N

	145	146	147	148	149	150	152	153
TENNESSEE								
1 ***Jenkins***	Y	Y	Y	Y	Y	Y	N	N
2 ***Duncan***	Y	Y	Y	Y	Y	Y	Y	Y
3 ***Wamp***	Y	Y	Y	Y	Y	Y	Y	Y
4 ***Hilleary***	Y	Y	Y	Y	Y	Y	Y	Y
5 Clement	+	+	Y	Y	Y	Y	N	N
6 Gordon	Y	Y	Y	Y	Y	Y	N	N
7 ***Bryant***	Y	Y	Y	Y	Y	Y	Y	Y
8 Tanner	Y	Y	Y	Y	Y	Y	N	N
9 Ford	Y	Y	Y	Y	Y	Y	N	N
TEXAS								
1 Sandlin	Y	Y	Y	Y	Y	Y	N	N
2 Turner	Y	Y	Y	Y	Y	Y	N	N
3 ***Johnson, Sam***	Y	Y	Y	Y	Y	Y	Y	Y
4 Hall	Y	Y	Y	Y	Y	Y	Y	Y
5 ***Sessions***	Y	Y	Y	Y	Y	Y	Y	Y
6 ***Barton***	Y	Y	Y	Y	Y	Y	Y	Y
7 ***Archer***	Y	Y	Y	Y	Y	Y	Y	Y
8 ***Brady***	Y	Y	Y	Y	Y	Y	Y	Y
9 Lampson	Y	Y	Y	Y	Y	Y	N	N
10 Doggett	Y	Y	Y	Y	Y	Y	Y	Y
11 Edwards	Y	Y	N	Y	Y	Y	N	N
12 ***Granger***	Y	Y	Y	Y	Y	Y	?	Y
13 ***Thornberry***	Y	Y	Y	Y	Y	Y	Y	Y
14 ***Paul***	Y	Y	Y	N	N	Y	Y	Y
15 Hinojosa	?	?	?	?	?	?	?	?
16 Reyes	Y	Y	?	?	?	?	?	?
17 Stenholm	Y	Y	Y	Y	Y	Y	N	N
18 Jackson-Lee	Y	Y	?	+	+	+	–	–
19 ***Combest***	Y	Y	Y	Y	Y	Y	N	N
20 Gonzalez	?	?	Y	Y	Y	Y	N	N
21 ***Smith***	?	?	?	?	?	?	?	?
22 ***DeLay***	Y	Y	Y	Y	Y	Y	Y	Y
23 ***Bonilla***	Y	Y	Y	Y	Y	Y	N	N
24 Frost	Y	Y	Y	Y	Y	Y	N	N
25 Bentsen	Y	Y	Y	Y	Y	Y	N	N
26 ***Armey***	Y	Y	Y	Y	Y	Y	N	Y
27 Ortiz	+	+	+	+	+	+	–	–
28 Rodriguez	?	?	Y	Y	Y	Y	N	N
29 Green	Y	Y	Y	Y	Y	Y	N	N
30 Johnson, E.B.	Y	Y	Y	Y	Y	Y	N	N
UTAH								
1 ***Hansen***	?	?	Y	Y	Y	Y	N	N
2 ***Cook***	Y	Y	Y	Y	Y	Y	N	N
3 ***Cannon***	Y	Y	Y	Y	Y	Y	Y	Y
VERMONT								
AL *Sanders*	?	?	Y	Y	Y	Y	N	N
VIRGINIA								
1 ***Bateman***	Y	Y	Y	Y	Y	Y	N	N
2 Pickett	Y	Y	Y	Y	Y	Y	N	N
3 Scott	Y	Y	Y	Y	Y	Y	N	N
4 Sisisky	Y	Y	Y	Y	Y	Y	N	N
5 Goode	Y	Y	Y	Y	Y	Y	Y	Y
6 ***Goodlatte***	Y	Y	Y	Y	Y	Y	Y	Y
7 ***Bliley***	Y	Y	Y	Y	Y	Y	N	N
8 Moran	Y	Y	Y	Y	Y	Y	N	Y
9 Boucher	Y	Y	?	?	?	?	N	N
10 ***Wolf***	Y	Y	Y	Y	Y	Y	N	N
11 ***Davis***	Y	Y	Y	Y	Y	Y	N	Y
WASHINGTON								
1 Inslee	Y	Y	Y	Y	Y	Y	Y	N
2 ***Metcalf***	Y	Y	Y	Y	Y	Y	Y	Y
3 Baird	Y	Y	Y	Y	Y	Y	N	N
4 ***Hastings***	Y	Y	Y	Y	Y	Y	Y	Y
5 ***Nethercutt***	Y	Y	Y	Y	Y	Y	N	N
6 Dicks	Y	Y	Y	Y	Y	Y	N	N
7 McDermott	Y	Y	Y	Y	Y	Y	N	N
8 ***Dunn***	Y	Y	Y	Y	Y	Y	N	Y
9 Smith	Y	Y	Y	Y	Y	Y	Y	Y
WEST VIRGINIA								
1 Mollohan	Y	Y	Y	Y	Y	Y	N	N
2 Wise	Y	Y	Y	Y	Y	Y	N	N
3 Rahall	Y	Y	Y	Y	Y	Y	N	N
WISCONSIN								
1 ***Ryan***	+	+	Y	Y	Y	Y	Y	Y
2 Baldwin	Y	Y	Y	Y	Y	Y	N	N
3 Kind	Y	Y	Y	Y	Y	Y	N	N
4 Kleczka	Y	Y	Y	Y	Y	Y	N	N
5 Barrett	Y	Y	Y	Y	Y	Y	N	N
6 ***Petri***	Y	Y	Y	Y	Y	Y	Y	Y
7 Obey	Y	Y	Y	Y	Y	Y	N	N
8 ***Green***	Y	Y	Y	Y	Y	Y	Y	Y
9 ***Sensenbrenner***	Y	Y	Y	Y	Y	Y	Y	Y
WYOMING								
AL ***Cubin***	Y	Y	Y	Y	Y	Y	Y	Y

Southern states - Ala., Ark., Fla., Ga., Ky., La., Miss., N.C., Okla., S.C., Tenn., Texas, Va.

154. HR 1906. Fiscal 2000 Agriculture Appropriations/Information Office. Coburn, R-Okla., amendment to eliminate the proposed $500,000 increase for the Agriculture Department's Chief Information Officer. Adopted 239-177: R 144-74; D 95-102 (ND 83-63, SD 12-39); I 0-1. May 25, 1999.

155. HR 1906. Fiscal 2000 Agriculture Appropriations/Building Planning. Sanford, R-S.C., amendment to reduce proposed spending for the Agriculture Department's building lease program by $22 million. Rejected 143-274: R 107-107; D 36-166 (ND 26-124, SD 10-42); I 0-1. May 25, 1999.

156. HR 1906. Fiscal 2000 Agriculture Appropriations/Administration. Coburn, R-Okla., amendment to reduce proposed spending for Agriculture Department administration by $3 million. Rejected 129-289: R 121-93; D 8-195 (ND 5-146, SD 3-49); I 0-1. May 25, 1999.

157. HR 1906. Fiscal 2000 Agriculture Appropriations/Research. Coburn, R-Okla., amendment to reduce proposed spending for the Agriculture Department's Office of Research, Education and Economics by $400,000. Rejected 139-278: R 104-110; D 35-167 (ND 27-123, SD 8-44); I 0-1. May 25, 1999.

158. HR 1906. Fiscal 2000 Agriculture Appropriations/Research. Coburn, R-Okla., amendment to reduce the funding for the Agricultural Research Service by $50.8 million. Rejected 35-390: R 30-185; D 5-204 (ND 3-151, SD 2-53); I 0-1. May 26, 1999.

159. HR 1906. Fiscal 2000 Agriculture Appropriations/Climate Change Research. Coburn, R-Okla., amendment to reduce the funding for the Agriculture Department's climate change research program by $1 million. Rejected 93-330: R 85-128; D 8-201 (ND 3-151, SD 5-50); I 0-1. May 26, 1999.

160. HR 1906. Fiscal 2000 Agriculture Appropriations/Wood Research. Sanford, R-S.C., amendment to reduce funding for Agriculture Department wood-utilization research programs by $5.1 million. Rejected 79-348: R 65-152; D 14-195 (ND 11-143, SD 3-52); I 0-1. May 26, 1999.

161. HR 1906. Fiscal 2000 Agriculture Appropriations/Peanuts Research. Coburn, R-Okla., amendment to reduce funding for the Agriculture Department's peanut research by $300,000. Rejected 119-308: R 85-131; D 34-176 (ND 30-125, SD 4-51); I 0-1. May 26, 1999.

Key

Y Voted for (yea).
Paired for.
+ Announced for.
N Voted against (nay).
X Paired against.
– Announced against.
P Voted "present."
C Voted "present" to avoid possible conflict of interest.
? Did not vote or otherwise make a position known.

•

Democrats ***Republicans***
Independents

	154	155	156	157	158	159	160	161
ALABAMA								
1 ***Callahan***	N	N	N	N	N	N	N	N
2 ***Everett***	N	N	N	N	N	N	N	N
3 ***Riley***	Y	Y	Y	Y	N	Y	N	N
4 ***Aderholt***	Y	Y	Y	N	N	N	N	N
5 Cramer	N	N	N	N	N	N	N	N
6 ***Bachus***	Y	Y	N	N	N	Y	N	N
7 Hilliard	N	N	N	N	N	N	N	N
ALASKA								
AL ***Young***	N	N	N	N	?	?	?	?
ARIZONA								
1 ***Salmon***	Y	Y	Y	Y	Y	Y	Y	Y
2 Pastor	Y	N	N	N	N	N	N	N
3 ***Stump***	Y	Y	Y	Y	N	N	N	N
4 ***Shadegg***	Y	Y	Y	Y	Y	Y	Y	Y
5 ***Kolbe***	N	N	N	N	N	N	N	N
6 ***Hayworth***	Y	Y	Y	Y	Y	Y	Y	Y
ARKANSAS								
1 Berry	N	N	N	N	N	N	N	N
2 Snyder	Y	N	N	N	N	N	N	N
3 ***Hutchinson***	Y	Y	N	N	N	?	N	N
4 ***Dickey***	N	N	N	N	N	N	N	N
CALIFORNIA								
1 Thompson	N	N	N	N	N	N	N	N
2 ***Herger***	Y	Y	Y	Y	N	Y	Y	Y
3 ***Ose***	N	N	N	N	N	N	N	N
4 ***Doolittle***	Y	Y	Y	Y	N	Y	N	Y
5 Matsui	Y	N	N	N	N	N	N	N
6 Woolsey	Y	N	N	N	N	N	N	N
7 Miller, George	Y	Y	N	Y	N	N	N	Y
8 Pelosi	Y	N	N	N	N	N	N	N
9 Lee	Y	N	N	N	N	N	N	Y
10 Tauscher	N	Y	N	Y	N	N	N	N
11 ***Pombo***	Y	Y	Y	Y	N	Y	N	N
12 Lantos	Y	N	N	N	N	N	N	N
13 Stark	Y	?	?	?	N	N	Y	Y
14 Eshoo	Y	Y	N	Y	N	N	N	Y
15 ***Campbell***	Y	Y	Y	Y	N	Y	Y	Y
16 Lofgren	N	Y	N	N	N	N	Y	Y
17 Farr	N	N	N	N	N	N	N	N
18 Condit	N	N	Y	N	N	N	N	N
19 ***Radanovich***	N	N	N	N	N	N	N	N
20 Dooley	N	N	N	N	N	N	N	N
21 ***Thomas***	N	N	N	N	N	N	N	N
22 Capps	N	N	N	N	N	N	N	N
23 ***Gallegly***	Y	N	N	N	N	N	N	N
24 Sherman	Y	N	N	N	N	N	N	N
25 ***McKeon***	N	N	N	N	N	N	N	N
26 Berman	Y	N	N	N	N	N	N	N
27 ***Rogan***	Y	N	Y	Y	Y	Y	N	Y
28 ***Dreier***	Y	N	Y	N	N	N	N	N
29 Waxman	Y	N	N	N	N	N	N	N
30 Becerra	Y	N	N	N	N	N	N	N
31 Martinez	Y	N	N	N	N	N	N	N
32 Dixon	N	N	N	N	N	N	N	N
33 Roybal-Allard	N	N	N	N	N	N	N	N
34 Napolitano	N	Y	N	N	N	N	N	N
35 Waters	Y	N	N	N	N	N	N	N
36 ***Kuykendall***	N	N	N	N	N	N	N	N
37 Millender-McD.	?	?	?	?	N	N	N	N
38 ***Horn***	N	N	N	N	N	N	N	N
39 ***Royce***	Y	Y	Y	Y	Y	Y	Y	Y
40 ***Lewis***	N	N	N	N	N	N	N	N
41 ***Miller, Gary***	Y	Y	Y	Y	Y	Y	N	Y
42 Brown	?	?	?	?	?	?	?	?
43 ***Calvert***	Y	N	N	N	N	N	N	N
44 ***Bono***	N	N	N	N	N	Y	N	N
45 ***Rohrabacher***	Y	Y	Y	Y	Y	Y	Y	Y
46 Sanchez	Y	N	N	N	N	N	N	N
47 ***Cox***	Y	Y	Y	?	Y	Y	Y	Y
48 ***Packard***	N	N	N	N	N	?	N	N
49 ***Bilbray***	Y	N	N	N	Y	N	Y	Y
50 Filner	Y	N	N	N	N	N	N	N
51 ***Cunningham***	Y	Y	Y	Y	N	N	N	N
52 ***Hunter***	N	Y	Y	Y	N	N	N	N
COLORADO								
1 DeGette	N	N	N	N	N	N	N	N
2 Udall	N	N	N	N	N	N	N	N
3 ***McInnis***	Y	Y	Y	Y	Y	Y	Y	Y
4 ***Schaffer***	Y	N	Y	Y	N	N	N	N
5 ***Hefley***	Y	Y	Y	Y	N	Y	Y	Y
6 ***Tancredo***	Y	Y	Y	Y	Y	Y	Y	Y
CONNECTICUT								
1 Larson	Y	Y	N	N	N	N	N	N
2 Gejdenson	Y	N	N	N	N	N	?	N
3 DeLauro	N	N	N	N	N	N	N	N
4 ***Shays***	Y	Y	Y	Y	Y	Y	Y	Y
5 Maloney	Y	N	N	Y	N	N	Y	Y
6 ***Johnson***	Y	N	Y	Y	N	N	N	Y
DELAWARE								
AL ***Castle***	Y	Y	Y	Y	N	N	Y	Y
FLORIDA								
1 ***Scarborough***	Y	Y	Y	Y	N	Y	Y	N
2 Boyd	N	N	N	N	N	N	N	N
3 Brown	N	N	N	N	N	N	N	N
4 ***Fowler***	Y	Y	Y	Y	N	Y	N	N
5 Thurman	N	N	N	N	N	N	N	N
6 ***Stearns***	Y	Y	Y	Y	N	N	Y	N
7 ***Mica***	Y	Y	Y	Y	N	N	N	N
8 ***McCollum***	Y	Y	Y	?	?	?	?	?
9 ***Bilirakis***	N	Y	N	N	N	N	N	N
10 ***Young***	N	N	N	N	N	N	N	N
11 Davis	N	N	N	N	N	N	N	N
12 ***Canady***	N	N	N	N	N	N	N	N
13 ***Miller***	N	Y	Y	N	Y	Y	Y	Y
14 ***Goss***	Y	Y	Y	Y	N	N	N	N
15 ***Weldon***	Y	Y	Y	Y	N	Y	Y	Y
16 ***Foley***	Y	N	Y	Y	N	N	Y	N
17 Meek	N	N	N	N	N	N	N	N
18 ***Ros-Lehtinen***	Y	Y	Y	N	N	N	N	N
19 Wexler	N	N	N	N	N	N	N	N
20 Deutsch	Y	N	N	N	N	N	N	N
21 ***Diaz-Balart***	N	N	Y	Y	N	N	N	N
22 ***Shaw***	Y	Y	Y	N	N	N	N	N
23 Hastings	N	N	N	N	N	N	N	N
GEORGIA								
1 ***Kingston***	N	N	N	N	N	N	N	N
2 Bishop	N	N	N	N	N	N	N	N
3 ***Collins***	Y	Y	Y	Y	Y	Y	Y	Y
4 McKinney	N	Y	N	Y	N	N	N	N
5 Lewis	N	N	N	N	N	N	N	N
6 ***Isakson***	N	N	N	N	N	N	N	N
7 ***Barr***	Y	Y	Y	Y	Y	Y	Y	N
8 ***Chambliss***	N	N	N	N	N	N	N	N
9 ***Deal***	Y	Y	Y	Y	N	N	N	N
10 ***Norwood***	Y	Y	N	N	N	N	N	N
11 ***Linder***	Y	Y	Y	Y	N	Y	N	N
HAWAII								
1 Abercrombie	N	N	N	N	N	N	N	N
2 Mink	Y	Y	N	Y	N	N	N	N
IDAHO								
1 ***Chenoweth***	Y	Y	Y	Y	N	Y	N	N
2 ***Simpson***	N	N	N	N	N	?	N	N
ILLINOIS								
1 Rush	N	N	N	N	N	N	N	N
2 Jackson	N	N	N	N	N	N	N	N
3 Lipinski	Y	N	N	N	N	N	N	N
4 Gutierrez	Y	N	N	N	N	N	N	Y
5 Blagojevich	Y	Y	N	N	N	N	N	N
6 ***Hyde***	N	N	N	N	N	N	N	N
7 Davis	N	N	N	N	N	N	N	N
8 ***Crane***	Y	Y	Y	Y	Y	Y	Y	Y
9 Schakowsky	N	N	N	N	N	N	N	N
10 ***Porter***	N	N	N	N	N	N	N	Y
11 ***Weller***	Y	Y	Y	Y	N	N	N	N
12 Costello	Y	N	N	N	N	N	N	N
13 ***Biggert***	Y	Y	Y	Y	Y	Y	Y	Y
14 ***Hastert***								

ND Northern Democrats SD Southern Democrats

	154	155	156	157	158	159	160	161
15 ***Ewing***	N	N	N	N	N	N	N	N
16 ***Manzullo***	Y	Y	Y	Y	N	Y	Y	Y
17 Evans	Y	N	N	N	N	N	N	N
18 ***LaHood***	Y	N	N	N	N	N	N	N
19 Phelps	Y	Y	N	N	N	N	N	N
20 ***Shimkus***	Y	N	N	N	N	N	N	N
INDIANA								
1 Visclosky	N	N	N	N	N	N	N	N
2 ***McIntosh***	Y	Y	Y	Y	N	Y	Y	Y
3 Roemer	N	N	N	N	N	N	N	Y
4 ***Souder***	Y	N	Y	Y	N	N	N	Y
5 ***Buyer***	Y	Y	Y	Y	N	N	Y	Y
6 ***Burton***	Y	Y	Y	Y	N	Y	Y	Y
7 ***Pease***	Y	Y	Y	N	N	N	N	N
8 ***Hostettler***	Y	Y	Y	Y	Y	Y	Y	Y
9 Hill	N	N	N	N	N	N	N	N
10 Carson	N	N	N	N	N	N	N	N
IOWA								
1 ***Leach***	Y	N	N	N	N	N	N	N
2 ***Nussle***	N	N	N	N	N	N	N	N
3 Boswell	N	N	N	N	N	N	N	N
4 ***Ganske***	Y	N	N	N	N	N	Y	Y
5 ***Latham***	N	N	N	N	N	N	N	N
KANSAS								
1 ***Moran***	N	N	N	N	N	N	N	N
2 ***Ryun***	Y	N	Y	Y	N	Y	Y	Y
3 Moore	Y	Y	N	N	N	N	N	N
4 ***Tiahrt***	Y	Y	Y	Y	N	Y	Y	Y
KENTUCKY								
1 ***Whitfield***	Y	N	N	N	N	N	N	N
2 ***Lewis***	N	N	N	N	N	N	N	N
3 ***Northup***	Y	Y	Y	Y	N	N	N	N
4 Lucas	N	N	N	N	N	N	N	N
5 ***Rogers***	N	N	N	N	N	N	N	N
6 ***Fletcher***	N	N	N	N	N	N	N	N
LOUISIANA								
1 Vacant								
2 Jefferson	Y	N	N	N	N	N	N	N
3 ***Tauzin***	N	N	N	N	N	N	N	N
4 ***McCrery***	N	N	N	N	N	N	N	N
5 ***Cooksey***	N	N	N	N	N	N	N	N
6 ***Baker***	Y	N	N	N	N	N	Y	N
7 John	N	N	N	N	N	N	N	N
MAINE								
1 Allen	N	N	N	N	N	N	N	N
2 Baldacci	N	N	N	N	N	N	N	N
MARYLAND								
1 ***Gilchrest***	N	N	N	N	N	N	N	N
2 ***Ehrlich***	Y	Y	Y	Y	N	N	Y	Y
3 Cardin	Y	N	N	N	N	N	N	N
4 Wynn	N	N	N	N	N	N	N	N
5 Hoyer	N	N	N	N	N	N	N	N
6 ***Bartlett***	Y	Y	Y	Y	N	Y	Y	Y
7 Cummings	N	N	N	N	N	N	N	N
8 ***Morella***	N	?	?	N	?	?	N	N
MASSACHUSETTS								
1 Olver	N	N	N	N	N	N	N	Y
2 Neal	Y	N	N	N	N	N	N	Y
3 McGovern	Y	N	N	N	N	N	N	Y
4 Frank	Y	Y	N	Y	N	N	Y	Y
5 Meehan	Y	Y	N	Y	N	N	N	Y
6 Tierney	Y	N	N	Y	N	N	Y	Y
7 Markey	N	Y	N	Y	N	N	N	N
8 Capuano	Y	Y	N	Y	N	N	N	N
9 Moakley	Y	N	N	N	N	N	N	N
10 Delahunt	Y	N	N	Y	Y	Y	Y	Y
MICHIGAN								
1 Stupak	Y	N	N	N	N	N	N	N
2 ***Hoekstra***	Y	Y	Y	Y	N	Y	Y	Y
3 ***Ehlers***	Y	N	N	N	N	N	N	N
4 ***Camp***	Y	N	Y	N	N	N	N	N
5 Barcia	N	N	N	N	N	N	N	N
6 ***Upton***	Y	Y	Y	Y	N	Y	Y	Y
7 ***Smith***	Y	Y	Y	Y	N	Y	Y	Y
8 Stabenow	N	N	N	N	N	N	N	N
9 Kildee	N	N	N	N	N	N	N	N
10 Bonior	N	N	N	N	N	N	N	N
11 ***Knollenberg***	N	N	N	N	N	N	N	N
12 Levin	Y	N	N	N	N	N	N	N
13 Rivers	Y	Y	N	Y	N	N	N	N
14 Conyers	Y	N	N	Y	N	N	N	N
15 Kilpatrick	N	N	N	N	N	N	N	N
16 Dingell	N	N	N	N	N	N	N	N

	154	155	156	157	158	159	160	161
MINNESOTA								
1 ***Gutknecht***	Y	Y	Y	Y	N	Y	N	N
2 Minge	N	N	N	N	N	N	N	N
3 ***Ramstad***	Y	Y	Y	Y	Y	Y	N	Y
4 Vento	N	N	N	N	N	N	N	N
5 Sabo	N	N	N	Y	N	N	N	N
6 Luther	Y	Y	Y	Y	Y	Y	Y	Y
7 Peterson	N	N	N	N	N	N	N	N
8 Oberstar	N	N	N	N	N	N	N	N
MISSISSIPPI								
1 ***Wicker***	Y	N	N	N	N	N	N	N
2 Thompson	N	N	N	N	N	N	N	N
3 ***Pickering***	Y	N	N	N	N	N	N	N
4 Shows	N	Y	N	Y	N	N	N	N
5 Taylor	Y	Y	Y	Y	Y	Y	N	Y
MISSOURI								
1 Clay	?	N	N	N	N	N	N	N
2 ***Talent***	N	N	N	N	N	N	N	Y
3 Gephardt	Y	N	N	N	N	N	N	N
4 Skelton	N	N	N	N	N	N	N	N
5 McCarthy	N	Y	N	N	N	N	N	N
6 Danner	N	N	N	N	N	N	N	N
7 ***Blunt***	Y	Y	?	N	N	Y	N	N
8 ***Emerson***	N	N	N	N	N	N	N	N
9 ***Hulshof***	N	N	N	N	N	N	N	N
MONTANA								
AL ***Hill***	Y	N	Y	Y	N	N	N	N
NEBRASKA								
1 ***Bereuter***	Y	N	N	N	N	N	N	N
2 ***Terry***	Y	N	N	N	N	Y	Y	Y
3 ***Barrett***	N	N	N	N	N	N	N	N
NEVADA								
1 Berkley	Y	N	N	N	N	N	N	Y
2 ***Gibbons***	Y	Y	Y	Y	N	Y	N	N
NEW HAMPSHIRE								
1 ***Sununu***	Y	Y	Y	Y	Y	Y	Y	Y
2 ***Bass***	Y	Y	Y	Y	Y	Y	Y	Y
NEW JERSEY								
1 Andrews	Y	Y	Y	Y	N	N	N	N
2 ***LoBiondo***	Y	Y	Y	Y	N	N	Y	Y
3 ***Saxton***	N	N	N	N	N	N	N	N
4 ***Smith***	Y	N	N	Y	N	N	N	Y
5 ***Roukema***	Y	Y	Y	Y	N	Y	Y	Y
6 Pallone	?	?	?	?	N	N	N	N
7 ***Franks***	Y	Y	Y	Y	Y	Y	Y	Y
8 Pascrell	Y	N	N	N	N	N	N	N
9 Rothman	?	?	?	?	N	N	N	Y
10 Payne	N	N	N	N	N	N	N	N
11 ***Frelinghuysen***	N	N	N	N	N	N	N	Y
12 Holt	Y	N	N	N	N	N	N	N
13 Menendez	P	N	N	N	N	N	N	N
NEW MEXICO								
1 ***Wilson***	N	N	N	N	N	N	N	N
2 ***Skeen***	N	N	N	N	N	N	N	N
3 Udall	Y	N	N	N	N	N	N	N
NEW YORK								
1 ***Forbes***	N	N	N	N	N	N	N	N
2 ***Lazio***	Y	Y	Y	Y	N	N	N	Y
3 ***King***	N	N	N	N	N	N	N	N
4 McCarthy	Y	N	N	N	N	N	N	N
5 Ackerman	N	N	N	N	?	?	N	N
6 Meeks	Y	N	N	N	N	N	N	N
7 Crowley	Y	N	N	N	N	N	N	Y
8 Nadler	?	N	Y	N	N	N	N	Y
9 Weiner	Y	N	N	N	N	N	N	N
10 Towns	Y	N	N	N	N	N	N	N
11 Owens	N	N	N	N	N	N	N	N
12 Velázquez	Y	N	N	N	N	N	N	N
13 ***Fossella***	Y	Y	Y	Y	N	Y	Y	Y
14 Maloney	Y	Y	N	Y	N	N	N	N
15 Rangel	Y	N	N	N	N	N	N	N
16 Serrano	N	N	N	N	N	N	N	N
17 Engel	N	N	N	N	N	N	N	N
18 Lowey	Y	N	N	N	N	N	N	N
19 ***Kelly***	Y	Y	Y	Y	N	N	Y	Y
20 ***Gilman***	N	N	N	N	N	N	N	N
21 McNulty	Y	Y	N	Y	N	N	N	N
22 ***Sweeney***	Y	N	N	N	N	N	N	Y
23 ***Boehlert***	N	N	N	N	N	N	N	N
24 ***McHugh***	N	N	N	N	N	N	N	Y
25 ***Walsh***	N	N	N	N	N	N	N	N
26 Hinchey	N	N	N	N	N	N	N	N
27 ***Reynolds***	Y	N	N	N	N	Y	Y	Y
28 Slaughter	Y	N	N	N	N	N	N	N
29 LaFalce	N	N	N	N	N	N	N	N

	154	155	156	157	158	159	160	161
30 ***Quinn***	N	N	N	N	N	N	N	N
31 ***Houghton***	N	N	N	N	N	N	N	N
NORTH CAROLINA								
1 Clayton	N	N	N	N	N	N	N	N
2 Etheridge	N	N	N	N	N	N	N	N
3 ***Jones***	Y	Y	Y	Y	N	Y	N	N
4 Price	N	N	N	N	N	N	N	N
5 ***Burr***	Y	Y	Y	Y	N	N	N	N
6 ***Coble***	Y	Y	Y	Y	N	N	N	Y
7 McIntyre	N	N	N	N	N	N	N	N
8 ***Hayes***	Y	N	N	N	N	N	N	N
9 ***Myrick***	Y	Y	Y	Y	?	Y	Y	Y
10 ***Ballenger***	Y	Y	Y	Y	N	Y	Y	Y
11 ***Taylor***	N	Y	Y	Y	N	Y	N	Y
12 Watt	N	N	N	N	N	N	N	N
NORTH DAKOTA								
AL Pomeroy	N	N	N	N	N	N	N	N
OHIO								
1 ***Chabot***	Y	Y	Y	Y	Y	Y	Y	Y
2 ***Portman***	Y	Y	Y	Y	N	N	N	Y
3 Hall	Y	N	N	N	N	N	N	N
4 ***Oxley***	N	?	?	?	?	?	?	?
5 ***Gillmor***	Y	N	Y	N	N	N	N	Y
6 Strickland	N	N	N	N	N	N	N	N
7 ***Hobson***	N	N	N	N	N	N	N	N
8 ***Boehner***	Y	N	Y	Y	N	Y	N	N
9 Kaptur	P	N	N	N	N	N	N	N
10 Kucinich	P	N	N	N	N	N	N	N
11 Jones	N	N	N	N	N	N	N	N
12 ***Kasich***	?	?	?	?	?	?	?	?
13 Brown	Y	Y	N	Y	N	N	N	Y
14 Sawyer	Y	N	N	N	N	N	N	Y
15 ***Pryce***	Y	Y	Y	N	N	N	N	N
16 ***Regula***	N	N	Y	N	N	N	N	N
17 Traficant	N	N	N	N	N	N	N	N
18 ***Ney***	N	N	N	N	N	N	N	N
19 ***LaTourette***	N	N	N	N	N	N	N	N
OKLAHOMA								
1 ***Largent***	Y	Y	Y	?	N	Y	Y	Y
2 ***Coburn***	Y	Y	Y	Y	N	Y	Y	Y
3 ***Watkins***	N	N	N	N	N	N	N	N
4 ***Watts***	Y	Y	Y	Y	N	Y	Y	N
5 ***Istook***	Y	Y	Y	Y	N	Y	Y	N
6 ***Lucas***	N	N	N	N	N	N	N	N
OREGON								
1 Wu	Y	N	N	Y	N	N	N	N
2 ***Walden***	Y	N	Y	N	N	N	N	N
3 Blumenauer	Y	N	N	N	N	N	N	N
4 DeFazio	Y	Y	N	Y	N	N	N	Y
5 Hooley	N	N	N	N	N	N	N	N
PENNSYLVANIA								
1 Brady	Y	N	N	N	N	N	N	N
2 Fattah	Y	N	N	N	N	N	N	N
3 Borski	Y	N	N	N	N	N	N	N
4 Klink	Y	N	N	N	N	N	N	N
5 ***Peterson***	N	N	N	N	N	N	N	N
6 Holden	?	N	N	N	N	N	N	N
7 ***Weldon***	Y	N	?	Y	N	N	N	Y
8 ***Greenwood***	Y	Y	Y	Y	N	N	N	Y
9 ***Shuster***	N	N	N	N	N	N	N	N
10 ***Sherwood***	Y	Y	Y	N	N	Y	N	N
11 Kanjorski	N	N	N	N	N	N	N	N
12 Murtha	Y	N	N	N	N	N	N	N
13 Hoeffel	Y	N	N	N	N	N	N	N
14 Coyne	Y	N	N	N	N	N	N	N
15 ***Toomey***	Y	Y	Y	Y	Y	Y	Y	Y
16 ***Pitts***	Y	Y	Y	Y	N	N	N	N
17 ***Gekas***	N	N	N	N	N	N	N	N
18 Doyle	Y	N	N	N	N	N	N	N
19 ***Goodling***	Y	N	Y	N	N	N	N	N
20 Mascara	N	N	N	N	N	N	N	N
21 ***English***	Y	N	Y	Y	N	N	N	Y
RHODE ISLAND								
1 Kennedy	Y	N	N	N	N	N	N	N
2 Weygand	Y	N	N	N	N	N	N	N
SOUTH CAROLINA								
1 ***Sanford***	Y	Y	Y	Y	Y	Y	Y	Y
2 ***Spence***	N	Y	N	N	N	Y	N	Y
3 ***Graham***	?	?	?	?	N	Y	Y	Y
4 ***DeMint***	Y	Y	Y	Y	N	Y	Y	Y
5 Spratt	Y	N	N	N	N	N	N	N
6 Clyburn	N	N	N	N	N	N	N	N
SOUTH DAKOTA								
AL ***Thune***	Y	N	N	N	N	N	N	N

	154	155	156	157	158	159	160	161
TENNESSEE								
1 ***Jenkins***	N	N	N	N	N	Y	N	N
2 ***Duncan***	Y	Y	Y	Y	Y	Y	N	Y
3 ***Wamp***	Y	Y	Y	Y	N	Y	N	Y
4 ***Hilleary***	Y	Y	Y	Y	N	Y	N	Y
5 Clement	Y	N	N	N	N	N	N	N
6 Gordon	Y	Y	N	Y	N	Y	N	Y
7 ***Bryant***	Y	N	Y	N	N	N	N	N
8 Tanner	N	N	N	N	N	N	N	N
9 Ford	N	N	N	N	N	N	N	N
TEXAS								
1 Sandlin	N	N	N	N	N	N	N	N
2 Turner	N	N	N	N	N	N	N	N
3 ***Johnson, Sam***	Y	Y	Y	Y	N	Y	Y	Y
4 Hall	Y	Y	Y	Y	N	Y	Y	N
5 ***Sessions***	Y	Y	Y	Y	N	Y	N	Y
6 ***Barton***	Y	Y	Y	Y	N	Y	Y	Y
7 ***Archer***	Y	Y	Y	Y	N	Y	Y	?
8 ***Brady***	Y	+	N	Y	N	N	N	N
9 Lampson	N	N	N	N	N	N	N	N
10 Doggett	Y	Y	N	Y	Y	N	Y	Y
11 Edwards	N	N	N	N	N	N	N	N
12 ***Granger***	Y	?	Y	Y	N	Y	Y	Y
13 ***Thornberry***	Y	N	Y	N	N	Y	N	N
14 ***Paul***	Y	Y	Y	Y	Y	Y	Y	Y
15 Hinojosa	?	?	?	?	N	N	N	N
16 Reyes	?	?	?	?	N	N	N	N
17 Stenholm	N	N	N	N	N	N	N	N
18 Jackson-Lee	–	–	–	–	N	N	N	N
19 ***Combest***	N	N	N	N	N	N	N	N
20 Gonzalez	N	N	N	N	N	N	N	N
21 ***Smith***	?	?	?	?	N	N	N	N
22 ***DeLay***	Y	Y	Y	Y	N	Y	N	N
23 ***Bonilla***	N	N	N	N	N	N	N	N
24 Frost	N	N	N	N	N	N	N	N
25 Bentsen	Y	N	N	N	N	N	N	N
26 ***Armey***	Y	Y	Y	Y	N	N	N	N
27 Ortiz	–	N	N	N	N	N	N	N
28 Rodriguez	N	N	N	N	N	N	N	N
29 Green	Y	Y	N	Y	N	Y	Y	Y
30 Johnson, E.B.	N	Y	N	N	N	N	N	N
UTAH								
1 ***Hansen***	N	N	N	N	N	N	N	N
2 ***Cook***	Y	N	Y	Y	N	N	N	N
3 ***Cannon***	Y	Y	Y	Y	Y	Y	Y	Y
VERMONT								
AL *Sanders*	N	N	N	N	N	N	N	N
VIRGINIA								
1 ***Bateman***	N	N	N	N	N	N	N	N
2 Pickett	N	N	N	N	N	N	N	N
3 Scott	N	N	N	N	N	N	N	N
4 Sisisky	N	N	N	N	N	N	N	N
5 Goode	Y	Y	Y	Y	N	Y	N	N
6 ***Goodlatte***	Y	Y	Y	Y	N	Y	N	N
7 ***Bliley***	Y	N	N	N	N	N	N	N
8 Moran	N	Y	N	N	N	N	N	N
9 Boucher	N	N	N	N	N	N	N	N
10 ***Wolf***	N	N	N	N	N	N	N	N
11 ***Davis***	Y	N	N	N	N	N	N	Y
WASHINGTON								
1 Inslee	Y	N	N	Y	N	N	N	Y
2 ***Metcalf***	Y	Y	N	Y	N	Y	N	N
3 Baird	Y	Y	N	Y	N	N	N	Y
4 ***Hastings***	Y	Y	Y	N	N	N	N	N
5 ***Nethercutt***	N	N	N	N	N	N	N	N
6 Dicks	N	N	N	?	N	N	N	N
7 McDermott	Y	Y	N	Y	N	N	N	N
8 ***Dunn***	Y	Y	Y	Y	N	Y	N	N
9 Smith	N	Y	Y	Y	Y	N	Y	Y
WEST VIRGINIA								
1 Mollohan	N	N	N	N	N	N	N	N
2 Wise	Y	N	N	N	N	N	N	N
3 Rahall	Y	N	N	N	N	N	N	N
WISCONSIN								
1 ***Ryan***	Y	Y	Y	Y	N	N	Y	Y
2 Baldwin	Y	N	N	N	N	N	N	N
3 Kind	Y	N	N	N	N	N	Y	Y
4 Kleczka	Y	?	N	Y	N	N	Y	Y
5 Barrett	Y	Y	N	Y	N	Y	Y	Y
6 ***Petri***	Y	Y	Y	Y	Y	Y	Y	Y
7 Obey	N	N	N	N	N	N	N	Y
8 ***Green***	Y	Y	Y	N	N	Y	N	Y
9 ***Sensenbrenner***	Y	Y	Y	Y	Y	Y	Y	Y
WYOMING								
AL ***Cubin***	Y	N	Y	N	N	N	N	N

Southern states - Ala., Ark., Fla., Ga., Ky., La., Miss., N.C., Okla., S.C., Tenn., Texas, Va.

162. HR 1259. Social Security Lockbox/Rule. Adoption of the rule (H Res 186) to provide for House floor consideration of the bill to reserve surplus funds collected for Social Security and only permit the funds to be used for ensuring the solvency of the Social Security and Medicare programs. Adopted 223-205: R 218-0; D 5-204 (ND 4-150, SD 1-54); I 0-1. May 26, 1999.

163. HR 1259. Social Security Lockbox/Recommit. Rangel, D-N.Y., motion to recommit the bill to the Ways and Means Committee with instructions to report it back with an amendment requiring that all federal budget surpluses be reserved until the solvency of Social Security and Medicare are ensured. Motion rejected 205-222: R 1-217; D 203-5 (ND 148-5, SD 55-0); I 1-0. May 26, 1999.

164. HR 1259. Social Security Lockbox/Passage. Passage of the bill to reserve all of the Social Security surplus to be used only to guarantee the solvency of the Social Security and Medicare system. Passed 416-12: R 217-1; D 198-11 (ND 143-11, SD 55-0); I 1-0. May 26, 1999.

165. S Con Res 35. Adjournment/Adoption. Adoption of the concurrent resolution to adjourn after the end of business May 27 and reconvene June 7 at 12:30 p.m. in the House. Adopted 249-178: R 218-1; D 31-176 (ND 13-139, SD 18-37); I 0-1. May 26, 1999.

166. Procedural Motion/Journal. Approval of the House Journal of Wednesday, May 26, 1999. Approved 309-76: R 187-18; D 122-58 (ND 88-48, SD 34-10); I 0-0. May 27, 1999.

Key

Y Voted for (yea).
\# Paired for.
\+ Announced for.
N Voted against (nay).
X Paired against.
– Announced against.
P Voted "present."
C Voted "present" to avoid possible conflict of interest.
? Did not vote or otherwise make a position known.

•

Democrats ***Republicans***
Independents

	162	163	164	165	166
ALABAMA					
1 ***Callahan***	Y	N	Y	Y	?
2 ***Everett***	Y	N	Y	Y	Y
3 ***Riley***	Y	N	Y	Y	Y
4 ***Aderholt***	Y	N	Y	Y	N
5 Cramer	N	Y	Y	Y	Y
6 ***Bachus***	Y	N	Y	Y	Y
7 Hilliard	N	Y	Y	N	?
ALASKA					
AL ***Young***	?	?	?	?	?
ARIZONA					
1 ***Salmon***	Y	N	Y	Y	Y
2 Pastor	N	Y	Y	N	N
3 ***Stump***	Y	N	Y	Y	Y
4 ***Shadegg***	Y	N	Y	Y	Y
5 ***Kolbe***	Y	N	Y	Y	Y
6 ***Hayworth***	Y	N	Y	Y	Y
ARKANSAS					
1 Berry	N	Y	Y	N	N
2 Snyder	N	Y	Y	N	Y
3 ***Hutchinson***	Y	N	Y	Y	Y
4 ***Dickey***	Y	N	Y	Y	Y
CALIFORNIA					
1 Thompson	N	Y	Y	N	N
2 ***Herger***	Y	N	Y	Y	Y
3 ***Ose***	Y	N	Y	Y	Y
4 ***Doolittle***	Y	N	Y	Y	Y
5 Matsui	N	Y	Y	N	Y
6 Woolsey	N	Y	Y	N	?
7 Miller, George	N	Y	Y	N	N
8 Pelosi	?	?	?	?	?
9 Lee	N	Y	Y	N	?
10 Tauscher	N	Y	Y	N	N
11 ***Pombo***	Y	N	Y	Y	?
12 Lantos	N	Y	Y	N	N
13 Stark	N	Y	Y	N	N
14 Eshoo	Y	Y	Y	N	Y
15 ***Campbell***	Y	N	Y	Y	Y
16 Lofgren	N	N	Y	N	Y
17 Farr	N	Y	Y	N	Y
18 Condit	N	Y	Y	N	N
19 ***Radanovich***	Y	N	Y	?	Y
20 Dooley	N	Y	Y	N	Y
21 ***Thomas***	Y	N	Y	Y	Y
22 Capps	N	Y	Y	N	Y
23 ***Gallegly***	Y	N	Y	Y	Y
24 Sherman	N	Y	Y	N	Y
25 ***McKeon***	Y	N	Y	Y	Y
26 Berman	N	Y	Y	N	Y
27 ***Rogan***	Y	N	Y	Y	Y
28 ***Dreier***	Y	N	Y	Y	Y
29 Waxman	N	Y	Y	N	Y
30 Becerra	N	Y	Y	N	Y
31 Martinez	N	Y	Y	N	Y
32 Dixon	N	Y	Y	N	Y
33 Roybal-Allard	N	Y	Y	N	N
34 Napolitano	N	Y	Y	N	Y
35 Waters	N	Y	Y	N	Y
36 ***Kuykendall***	Y	N	Y	Y	Y
37 Millender-McD.	N	Y	Y	N	?
38 ***Horn***	Y	N	Y	Y	Y
39 ***Royce***	Y	N	Y	Y	?
40 ***Lewis***	Y	N	Y	Y	Y
41 ***Miller, Gary***	Y	N	Y	Y	Y
42 Brown	?	?	?	?	?
43 ***Calvert***	Y	N	Y	Y	Y
44 ***Bono***	Y	N	Y	Y	?
45 ***Rohrabacher***	Y	N	Y	Y	Y
46 Sanchez	N	Y	Y	N	Y
47 ***Cox***	?	N	Y	Y	Y
48 ***Packard***	Y	N	Y	Y	Y
49 ***Bilbray***	Y	N	Y	Y	N
50 Filner	N	Y	N	N	N
51 ***Cunningham***	Y	N	Y	Y	Y
52 ***Hunter***	Y	N	Y	Y	?
COLORADO					
1 DeGette	N	Y	Y	N	Y
2 Udall	N	Y	Y	N	N
3 ***McInnis***	Y	N	Y	Y	Y
4 ***Schaffer***	Y	N	Y	N	N
5 ***Hefley***	Y	N	Y	Y	N
6 ***Tancredo***	Y	N	Y	Y	N
CONNECTICUT					
1 Larson	N	Y	Y	?	Y
2 Gejdenson	N	Y	Y	N	Y
3 DeLauro	N	Y	Y	N	Y
4 ***Shays***	Y	N	Y	Y	Y
5 Maloney	N	Y	Y	N	Y
6 ***Johnson***	Y	N	Y	Y	Y
DELAWARE					
AL ***Castle***	Y	N	Y	Y	Y
FLORIDA					
1 ***Scarborough***	Y	?	?	?	?
2 Boyd	N	Y	Y	Y	Y
3 Brown	N	Y	Y	N	?
4 ***Fowler***	Y	N	Y	Y	Y
5 Thurman	N	Y	Y	N	Y
6 ***Stearns***	Y	N	Y	Y	Y
7 ***Mica***	Y	N	Y	Y	Y
8 ***McCollum***	Y	N	Y	Y	Y
9 ***Bilirakis***	Y	N	Y	Y	Y
10 ***Young***	Y	N	Y	Y	Y
11 Davis	N	Y	Y	N	Y
12 ***Canady***	Y	N	Y	Y	Y
13 ***Miller***	Y	N	Y	Y	Y
14 ***Goss***	Y	N	Y	Y	Y
15 ***Weldon***	Y	N	Y	Y	Y
16 ***Foley***	Y	N	Y	Y	Y
17 Meek	N	Y	Y	N	Y
18 ***Ros-Lehtinen***	Y	N	Y	Y	Y
19 Wexler	N	Y	Y	N	?
20 Deutsch	N	Y	Y	N	N
21 ***Diaz-Balart***	Y	N	Y	Y	Y
22 ***Shaw***	Y	N	Y	Y	Y
23 Hastings	N	Y	Y	N	?
GEORGIA					
1 ***Kingston***	Y	N	Y	Y	N
2 Bishop	N	Y	Y	N	Y
3 ***Collins***	Y	N	Y	Y	Y
4 McKinney	N	Y	Y	N	?
5 Lewis	N	Y	Y	N	Y
6 ***Isakson***	Y	N	Y	Y	Y
7 ***Barr***	Y	N	Y	Y	Y
8 ***Chambliss***	Y	N	Y	Y	Y
9 ***Deal***	Y	N	Y	Y	Y
10 ***Norwood***	Y	N	Y	Y	?
11 ***Linder***	Y	N	Y	Y	Y
HAWAII					
1 Abercrombie	N	Y	Y	N	Y
2 Mink	N	Y	Y	N	Y
IDAHO					
1 ***Chenoweth***	Y	N	Y	Y	Y
2 ***Simpson***	Y	N	Y	Y	Y
ILLINOIS					
1 Rush	N	Y	Y	N	Y
2 Jackson	N	Y	Y	N	Y
3 Lipinski	N	Y	Y	Y	Y
4 Gutierrez	N	Y	Y	N	N
5 Blagojevich	N	Y	Y	N	?
6 ***Hyde***	Y	N	Y	Y	Y
7 Davis	N	Y	Y	N	?
8 ***Crane***	Y	N	Y	Y	N
9 Schakowsky	N	Y	Y	N	N
10 ***Porter***	Y	N	Y	Y	Y
11 ***Weller***	Y	N	Y	Y	N
12 Costello	N	Y	Y	Y	N
13 ***Biggert***	Y	N	Y	Y	Y
14 ***Hastert***	Y		Y	Y	Y

ND Northern Democrats SD Southern Democrats

	162	163	164	165	166
15 ***Ewing***	Y	N	Y	Y	Y
16 ***Manzullo***	Y	N	Y	Y	Y
17 Evans	N	Y	Y	N	?
18 ***LaHood***	Y	N	Y	Y	Y
19 Phelps	N	Y	Y	Y	Y
20 ***Shimkus***	Y	N	Y	Y	Y
INDIANA					
1 Visclosky	N	Y	Y	N	N
2 ***McIntosh***	Y	Y	Y	Y	Y
3 Roemer	N	Y	Y	N	Y
4 ***Souder***	Y	N	Y	Y	Y
5 ***Buyer***	Y	N	Y	Y	Y
6 ***Burton***	Y	N	Y	Y	Y
7 ***Pease***	Y	N	Y	Y	Y
8 ***Hostettler***	Y	N	Y	Y	Y
9 Hill	N	Y	Y	N	Y
10 Carson	N	Y	Y	N	?
IOWA					
1 ***Leach***	Y	N	Y	Y	?
2 ***Nussle***	Y	N	Y	Y	Y
3 Boswell	N	Y	Y	Y	N
4 ***Ganske***	Y	N	Y	Y	Y
5 ***Latham***	Y	N	Y	Y	Y
KANSAS					
1 ***Moran***	Y	N	Y	Y	N
2 ***Ryun***	Y	N	Y	Y	Y
3 Moore	N	Y	Y	N	Y
4 ***Tiahrt***	Y	N	Y	Y	Y
KENTUCKY					
1 ***Whitfield***	?	N	Y	Y	Y
2 ***Lewis***	Y	N	Y	Y	Y
3 ***Northup***	Y	N	Y	Y	Y
4 Lucas	N	Y	Y	Y	Y
5 ***Rogers***	Y	N	Y	Y	Y
6 ***Fletcher***	Y	N	Y	Y	Y
LOUISIANA					
1 Vacant					
2 Jefferson	N	Y	Y	N	?
3 ***Tauzin***	Y	N	Y	Y	Y
4 ***McCrery***	Y	N	Y	Y	Y
5 ***Cooksey***	Y	N	Y	Y	Y
6 ***Baker***	Y	N	Y	Y	Y
7 John	N	Y	Y	N	Y
MAINE					
1 Allen	N	Y	Y	N	Y
2 Baldacci	N	Y	Y	N	N
MARYLAND					
1 ***Gilchrest***	Y	N	Y	Y	Y
2 ***Ehrlich***	Y	N	Y	Y	Y
3 Cardin	N	Y	Y	N	Y
4 Wynn	N	Y	Y	N	?
5 Hoyer	N	Y	Y	N	Y
6 ***Bartlett***	Y	N	Y	Y	Y
7 Cummings	N	Y	Y	N	?
8 ***Morella***	Y	N	Y	Y	Y
MASSACHUSETTS					
1 Olver	N	Y	N	N	N
2 Neal	N	Y	Y	N	N
3 McGovern	N	Y	Y	N	N
4 Frank	N	Y	N	N	N
5 Meehan	N	Y	Y	N	Y
6 Tierney	N	Y	Y	N	Y
7 Markey	N	Y	Y	N	Y
8 Capuano	N	Y	Y	N	Y
9 Moakley	N	Y	Y	N	Y
10 Delahunt	N	Y	Y	N	Y
MICHIGAN					
1 Stupak	N	Y	Y	N	N
2 ***Hoekstra***	Y	N	Y	Y	N
3 ***Ehlers***	Y	N	Y	Y	Y
4 ***Camp***	Y	N	Y	Y	Y
5 Barcia	N	Y	Y	N	Y
6 ***Upton***	Y	N	Y	Y	Y
7 ***Smith***	Y	N	Y	Y	Y
8 Stabenow	N	Y	Y	N	Y
9 Kildee	N	Y	Y	N	Y
10 Bonior	N	Y	Y	N	N
11 ***Knollenberg***	Y	N	Y	Y	Y
12 Levin	N	Y	Y	N	N
13 Rivers	N	Y	Y	N	Y
14 Conyers	N	Y	Y	N	?
15 Kilpatrick	N	Y	Y	N	N
16 Dingell	N	Y	N	Y	Y
MINNESOTA					
1 ***Gutknecht***	Y	N	Y	Y	N
2 Minge	Y	Y	Y	N	Y
3 ***Ramstad***	Y	N	Y	Y	N
4 Vento	N	Y	Y	N	Y
5 Sabo	N	N	N	N	N
6 Luther	N	Y	Y	N	Y
7 Peterson	Y	Y	Y	Y	N
8 Oberstar	N	Y	Y	N	N
MISSISSIPPI					
1 ***Wicker***	Y	N	Y	Y	Y
2 Thompson	N	Y	Y	N	N
3 ***Pickering***	Y	N	Y	Y	Y
4 Shows	N	Y	Y	Y	Y
5 Taylor	N	Y	Y	Y	N
MISSOURI					
1 Clay	N	Y	Y	N	?
2 ***Talent***	Y	N	Y	Y	Y
3 Gephardt	N	Y	Y	N	N
4 Skelton	N	Y	Y	Y	Y
5 McCarthy	N	Y	Y	N	Y
6 Danner	N	Y	Y	Y	Y
7 ***Blunt***	Y	N	Y	Y	Y
8 ***Emerson***	Y	N	Y	Y	Y
9 ***Hulshof***	Y	N	Y	Y	N
MONTANA					
AL ***Hill***	Y	N	Y	Y	N
NEBRASKA					
1 ***Bereuter***	Y	N	Y	Y	Y
2 ***Terry***	Y	N	Y	Y	Y
3 ***Barrett***	Y	N	Y	Y	Y
NEVADA					
1 Berkley	N	Y	Y	N	Y
2 ***Gibbons***	Y	N	Y	Y	N
NEW HAMPSHIRE					
1 ***Sununu***	Y	N	Y	Y	Y
2 ***Bass***	Y	N	Y	Y	Y
NEW JERSEY					
1 Andrews	N	Y	Y	N	Y
2 ***LoBiondo***	Y	N	Y	Y	N
3 ***Saxton***	Y	N	Y	Y	Y
4 ***Smith***	Y	N	Y	Y	?
5 ***Roukema***	Y	N	Y	Y	?
6 Pallone	N	Y	Y	N	N
7 ***Franks***	Y	N	Y	Y	Y
8 Pascrell	N	Y	Y	N	Y
9 Rothman	N	Y	Y	N	?
10 Payne	N	Y	Y	N	Y
11 ***Frelinghuysen***	Y	N	Y	Y	Y
12 Holt	N	Y	Y	N	?
13 Menendez	N	Y	Y	N	N
NEW MEXICO					
1 ***Wilson***	Y	N	Y	Y	Y
2 ***Skeen***	Y	N	Y	Y	Y
3 Udall	N	Y	Y	N	N
NEW YORK					
1 ***Forbes***	Y	N	Y	Y	Y
2 ***Lazio***	Y	N	Y	Y	Y
3 ***King***	Y	N	Y	Y	Y
4 McCarthy	N	Y	Y	N	Y
5 Ackerman	N	Y	Y	N	Y
6 Meeks	N	Y	Y	N	?
7 Crowley	N	Y	Y	N	Y
8 Nadler	N	Y	N	N	Y
9 Weiner	N	Y	Y	N	Y
10 Towns	N	Y	Y	N	Y
11 Owens	N	Y	Y	N	?
12 Velázquez	N	Y	Y	N	N
13 ***Fossella***	Y	N	Y	Y	Y
14 Maloney	Y	Y	Y	N	Y
15 Rangel	N	Y	Y	N	Y
16 Serrano	N	Y	Y	N	Y
17 Engel	N	Y	Y	N	N
18 Lowey	N	Y	Y	N	Y
19 ***Kelly***	Y	N	Y	Y	Y
20 ***Gilman***	Y	N	Y	Y	Y
21 McNulty	N	Y	Y	N	N
22 ***Sweeney***	Y	N	Y	Y	Y
23 ***Boehlert***	Y	N	Y	Y	Y
24 ***McHugh***	Y	N	Y	Y	Y
25 ***Walsh***	Y	N	Y	Y	Y
26 Hinchey	N	Y	Y	N	Y
27 ***Reynolds***	Y	N	Y	Y	Y
28 Slaughter	N	Y	Y	N	N
29 LaFalce	N	Y	Y	N	N
30 ***Quinn***	Y	N	Y	Y	Y
31 ***Houghton***	Y	N	N	Y	Y
NORTH CAROLINA					
1 Clayton	N	Y	Y	N	?
2 Etheridge	N	Y	Y	N	Y
3 ***Jones***	Y	N	Y	Y	Y
4 Price	N	Y	Y	N	Y
5 ***Burr***	Y	N	Y	Y	Y
6 ***Coble***	Y	N	Y	Y	Y
7 McIntyre	N	Y	Y	Y	Y
8 ***Hayes***	Y	N	Y	Y	Y
9 ***Myrick***	Y	N	Y	Y	Y
10 ***Ballenger***	Y	N	Y	Y	Y
11 ***Taylor***	Y	N	Y	Y	Y
12 Watt	N	Y	Y	N	?
NORTH DAKOTA					
AL Pomeroy	N	Y	Y	N	N
OHIO					
1 ***Chabot***	Y	N	Y	Y	Y
2 ***Portman***	Y	N	Y	Y	Y
3 Hall	N	Y	Y	Y	Y
4 ***Oxley***	Y	N	Y	Y	Y
5 ***Gillmor***	Y	N	Y	Y	Y
6 Strickland	N	Y	Y	N	N
7 ***Hobson***	Y	N	Y	Y	Y
8 ***Boehner***	Y	N	Y	Y	Y
9 Kaptur	N	Y	Y	N	Y
10 Kucinich	N	Y	Y	N	N
11 Jones	N	Y	Y	N	?
12 ***Kasich***	?	?	?	Y	?
13 Brown	N	Y	Y	N	N
14 Sawyer	N	?	Y	N	Y
15 ***Pryce***	Y	N	Y	Y	Y
16 ***Regula***	Y	N	Y	Y	Y
17 Traficant	N	Y	Y	Y	Y
18 ***Ney***	Y	N	Y	Y	Y
19 ***LaTourette***	Y	N	Y	Y	Y
OKLAHOMA					
1 ***Largent***	Y	N	Y	Y	Y
2 ***Coburn***	Y	N	Y	Y	Y
3 ***Watkins***	Y	N	Y	Y	Y
4 ***Watts***	Y	N	Y	Y	Y
5 ***Istook***	Y	N	Y	Y	Y
6 ***Lucas***	Y	N	Y	Y	Y
OREGON					
1 Wu	N	Y	Y	N	N
2 ***Walden***	Y	N	Y	Y	?
3 Blumenauer	N	Y	Y	N	Y
4 DeFazio	N	Y	Y	N	N
5 Hooley	N	Y	Y	N	N
PENNSYLVANIA					
1 Brady	N	Y	Y	N	Y
2 Fattah	N	Y	Y	N	?
3 Borski	N	Y	Y	N	N
4 Klink	N	Y	Y	N	Y
5 ***Peterson***	Y	N	Y	Y	Y
6 Holden	N	Y	Y	N	Y
7 ***Weldon***	Y	N	+	Y	Y
8 ***Greenwood***	Y	N	Y	Y	Y
9 ***Shuster***	Y	N	Y	Y	Y
10 ***Sherwood***	Y	N	Y	Y	Y
11 Kanjorski	N	Y	Y	N	?
12 Murtha	N	Y	N	Y	Y
13 Hoeffel	N	Y	Y	N	Y
14 Coyne	N	Y	Y	N	Y
15 ***Toomey***	Y	N	Y	Y	Y
16 ***Pitts***	Y	N	Y	Y	Y
17 ***Gekas***	Y	N	Y	Y	Y
18 Doyle	N	Y	Y	N	Y
19 ***Goodling***	Y	N	Y	Y	Y
20 Mascara	N	Y	Y	N	Y
21 ***English***	Y	N	Y	Y	N
RHODE ISLAND					
1 Kennedy	N	Y	Y	N	N
2 Weygand	N	Y	Y	N	Y
SOUTH CAROLINA					
1 ***Sanford***	Y	N	Y	Y	Y
2 ***Spence***	Y	N	Y	Y	Y
3 ***Graham***	Y	N	Y	Y	Y
4 ***DeMint***	Y	N	Y	Y	Y
5 Spratt	N	Y	Y	N	N
6 Clyburn	N	Y	Y	N	?
SOUTH DAKOTA					
AL ***Thune***	Y	N	Y	Y	Y
TENNESSEE					
1 ***Jenkins***	Y	N	Y	Y	Y
2 ***Duncan***	Y	N	Y	Y	Y
3 ***Wamp***	Y	N	Y	Y	Y
4 ***Hilleary***	Y	N	Y	Y	N
5 Clement	N	Y	Y	N	Y
6 Gordon	Y	Y	Y	Y	Y
7 ***Bryant***	Y	N	Y	Y	Y
8 Tanner	N	Y	Y	N	N
9 Ford	N	Y	Y	N	N
TEXAS					
1 Sandlin	N	Y	Y	Y	Y
2 Turner	N	Y	Y	Y	Y
3 ***Johnson, Sam***	Y	N	Y	Y	Y
4 Hall	N	Y	Y	Y	Y
5 ***Sessions***	Y	N	Y	Y	Y
6 ***Barton***	Y	N	Y	Y	?
7 ***Archer***	Y	N	Y	Y	Y
8 ***Brady***	Y	N	Y	Y	Y
9 Lampson	N	Y	Y	Y	Y
10 Doggett	N	Y	Y	N	?
11 Edwards	N	Y	Y	?	Y
12 ***Granger***	Y	N	Y	Y	Y
13 ***Thornberry***	Y	N	Y	Y	Y
14 ***Paul***	Y	N	Y	Y	Y
15 Hinojosa	N	Y	Y	N	Y
16 Reyes	N	Y	Y	N	Y
17 Stenholm	N	Y	Y	Y	N
18 Jackson-Lee	N	Y	Y	N	N
19 ***Combest***	Y	N	Y	Y	Y
20 Gonzalez	N	Y	Y	N	Y
21 ***Smith***	Y	N	Y	Y	?
22 ***DeLay***	Y	N	Y	Y	Y
23 ***Bonilla***	Y	N	Y	Y	?
24 Frost	N	Y	Y	N	Y
25 Bentsen	N	Y	Y	N	Y
26 ***Armey***	Y	N	Y	Y	?
27 Ortiz	N	Y	Y	N	Y
28 Rodriguez	N	Y	Y	N	Y
29 Green	N	Y	Y	Y	Y
30 Johnson, E.B.	N	Y	Y	N	?
UTAH					
1 ***Hansen***	Y	N	Y	Y	Y
2 ***Cook***	Y	N	Y	Y	Y
3 ***Cannon***	Y	N	Y	Y	Y
VERMONT					
AL *Sanders*	N	Y	Y	N	?
VIRGINIA					
1 ***Bateman***	Y	N	Y	Y	Y
2 Pickett	N	Y	Y	Y	N
3 Scott	N	Y	Y	N	Y
4 Sisisky	N	Y	Y	Y	Y
5 Goode	N	Y	Y	Y	Y
6 ***Goodlatte***	Y	N	Y	Y	Y
7 ***Bliley***	Y	N	Y	Y	Y
8 Moran	N	Y	Y	N	Y
9 Boucher	N	Y	Y	Y	Y
10 ***Wolf***	Y	N	Y	Y	Y
11 ***Davis***	Y	N	Y	Y	Y
WASHINGTON					
1 Inslee	N	Y	Y	N	Y
2 ***Metcalf***	Y	N	Y	Y	Y
3 Baird	N	Y	Y	N	N
4 ***Hastings***	Y	N	Y	Y	Y
5 ***Nethercutt***	Y	N	Y	Y	Y
6 Dicks	N	Y	Y	N	N
7 McDermott	N	N	N	N	N
8 ***Dunn***	Y	N	Y	Y	Y
9 Smith	N	Y	Y	Y	Y
WEST VIRGINIA					
1 Mollohan	N	N	N	N	Y
2 Wise	N	Y	Y	N	Y
3 Rahall	N	N	N	N	Y
WISCONSIN					
1 ***Ryan***	Y	N	Y	Y	Y
2 Baldwin	N	Y	Y	N	Y
3 Kind	N	Y	Y	Y	Y
4 Kleczka	N	Y	Y	N	Y
5 Barrett	N	Y	Y	N	Y
6 ***Petri***	Y	N	Y	Y	Y
7 Obey	N	Y	Y	Y	Y
8 ***Green***	Y	N	Y	Y	Y
9 ***Sensenbrenner***	Y	N	Y	Y	Y
WYOMING					
AL ***Cubin***	Y	N	Y	Y	Y

Southern states - Ala., Ark., Fla., Ga., Ky., La., Miss., N.C., Okla., S.C., Tenn., Texas, Va.

House Votes 167, 168, 169, 170, 171, 172, 173, 174

167. Procedural Motion/Journal. Approval of the House Journal of Thursday, May 27, 1999. Approved 325-42: R 177-16; D 148-26 (ND 104-19, SD 44-7); I 0-0. June 7, 1999.

168. HR 435. Miscellaneous Trade and Technical Corrections Act/Concur with Senate Amendments. Dunn, R-Wash., motion to suspend the rules and concur in the Senate amendment to the bill that would authorize 50 new Customs Service inspectors to process passengers entering the United States on planes and cruise ships. Passengers would be charged $1.75 to pay for the new officers. The measure would also clarify the tax treatment of certain transfers of assets and liabilities to a corporation. Motion agreed to (thus clearing the bill for the president) 375-1: R 194-1; D 181-0 (ND 130-0, SD 51-0); I 0-0. June 7, 1999. A two-thirds majority of those present and voting (251 in this case) is required for passage under suspension of the rules.

169. HR 1915. Missing Persons/Passage. Lazio, R-N.Y., motion to suspend the rules and pass the bill to authorize a total of $6 million in fiscal 2000-2002 for grants to help state and local law enforcement agencies register unidentified crime victims with the FBI's National Crime Information Center. Passed 370-4: R 191-4; D 179-0 (ND 128-0, SD 51-0); I 0-0. June 7, 1999. A two-thirds majority of those present and voting (250 in this case) is required for passage under suspension of the rules.

170. Procedural Motion/Journal. Approval of the House Journal of Monday, June 7, 1999. Approved 355-46: R 192-16; D 163-30 (ND 121-21, SD 42-9); I 0-0. June 8, 1999.

171. HR 150. Education Land Grants/Passage. Passage of the bill to authorize the Agriculture Department to convey up to 80 acres of National Forest Service land to publicly funded schools for a nominal payment, provided the transfer would benefit the public interest, would involve lands not needed by the National Forest System and would serve education purposes. The transfer would not include mineral rights. Passed 420-0: R 215-0; D 204-0 (ND 151-0, SD 53-0); I 1-0. June 8, 1999.

172. HR 1906. Fiscal 2000 Agriculture Appropriations/Wild Predator Control. DeFazio, D-Ore., amendment to prohibit the use of funds under the bill to destroy wild animals for the purpose of protecting livestock. Rejected 193-230: R 63-153; D 129-77 (ND 114-39, SD 15-38); I 1-0, June 8, 1999.

173. HR 1906. Fiscal 2000 Agriculture Appropriations/Abortion. Coburn, R-Okla., amendment to prohibit the use of any funding for the Food and Drug Administration to test, develop or approve any drug for the chemical inducement of abortion. Adopted 217-214: R 181-40; D 36-173 (ND 26-128, SD 10-45); I 0-1. June 8, 1999.

174. HR 1906. Fiscal 2000 Agriculture Appropriations/Market Access Program. Chabot, R-Ohio, amendment to prohibit the use of funds in the bill for the U.S. Department of Agriculture's Market Access Program, which provides grants to businesses and trade associations to promote exports of agricultural products. Rejected 72-355: R 55-163; D 17-191 (ND 15-139, SD 2-52); I 0-1. June 8, 1999.

[1] *David Vitter, R-La., was sworn in June 8, 1999, replacing Robert L. Livingston, R-La., who resigned effective Feb. 28, 1999. The first vote for which Vitter was eligible was vote 171.*

Key

- Y Voted for (yea).
- # Paired for.
- + Announced for.
- N Voted against (nay).
- X Paired against.
- – Announced against.
- P Voted "present."
- C Voted "present" to avoid possible conflict of interest.
- ? Did not vote or otherwise make a position known.

•

Democrats ***Republicans***
Independents

	167	168	169	170	171	172	173	174
ALABAMA								
1 ***Callahan***	Y	Y	Y	Y	Y	N	Y	N
2 ***Everett***	Y	Y	Y	Y	Y	N	Y	N
3 ***Riley***	Y	Y	Y	N	Y	N	Y	N
4 ***Aderholt***	N	Y	Y	N	Y	N	Y	N
5 Cramer	Y	Y	Y	Y	Y	N	N	N
6 ***Bachus***	Y	Y	Y	Y	Y	N	Y	Y
7 Hilliard	N	Y	Y	N	Y	N	N	N
ALASKA								
AL ***Young***	?	?	?	?	Y	N	Y	N
ARIZONA								
1 ***Salmon***	Y	Y	Y	Y	Y	N	Y	Y
2 Pastor	Y	Y	Y	N	Y	N	N	N
3 ***Stump***	Y	Y	Y	Y	Y	N	Y	N
4 ***Shadegg***	Y	Y	Y	Y	Y	N	Y	Y
5 ***Kolbe***	Y	Y	Y	Y	Y	N	N	N
6 ***Hayworth***	Y	Y	Y	Y	Y	N	Y	Y
ARKANSAS								
1 Berry	Y	Y	Y	Y	Y	N	Y	N
2 Snyder	Y	Y	Y	Y	Y	Y	N	N
3 ***Hutchinson***	Y	Y	Y	N	Y	N	Y	N
4 ***Dickey***	Y	Y	Y	Y	Y	N	Y	N
CALIFORNIA								
1 Thompson	N	Y	Y	N	Y	N	N	N
2 ***Herger***	Y	Y	Y	Y	Y	N	Y	N
3 ***Ose***	Y	Y	Y	Y	Y	N	N	N
4 ***Doolittle***	Y	Y	Y	Y	Y	N	Y	N
5 Matsui	Y	Y	Y	Y	Y	N	N	N
6 Woolsey	Y	Y	Y	Y	Y	Y	N	N
7 Miller, George	?	?	?	Y	Y	Y	N	N
8 Pelosi	?	Y	Y	Y	Y	Y	N	N
9 Lee	Y	Y	Y	+	+	Y	N	N
10 Tauscher	Y	Y	Y	Y	Y	Y	N	N
11 ***Pombo***	N	Y	Y	N	Y	N	Y	N
12 Lantos	Y	Y	Y	Y	Y	?	N	N
13 Stark	Y	Y	Y	Y	Y	Y	N	N
14 Eshoo	Y	Y	Y	Y	Y	Y	N	N
15 ***Campbell***	Y	Y	Y	Y	Y	Y	N	Y
16 Lofgren	Y	Y	Y	Y	Y	Y	N	N
17 Farr	Y	Y	Y	Y	Y	N	N	N
18 Condit	Y	Y	Y	Y	Y	N	N	N
19 ***Radanovich***	Y	Y	Y	Y	Y	N	Y	N
20 Dooley	Y	Y	?	Y	Y	N	N	N
21 ***Thomas***	?	+	+	Y	Y	N	N	N
22 Capps	Y	Y	Y	Y	Y	N	N	N
23 ***Gallegly***	Y	Y	Y	Y	Y	N	Y	N
24 Sherman	Y	Y	Y	Y	Y	Y	N	N
25 ***McKeon***	Y	Y	Y	Y	Y	N	Y	N
26 Berman	?	?	?	Y	Y	Y	N	N
27 ***Rogan***	Y	Y	Y	Y	Y	N	Y	Y
28 ***Dreier***	Y	Y	Y	Y	Y	N	Y	N
29 Waxman	?	?	?	Y	Y	Y	N	N
30 Becerra	+	+	+	Y	Y	Y	N	N
31 Martinez	?	?	?	N	Y	N	N	N
32 Dixon	Y	Y	Y	Y	Y	Y	N	N
33 Roybal-Allard	Y	Y	Y	Y	Y	Y	N	N
34 Napolitano	Y	Y	Y	Y	Y	N	N	N
35 Waters	?	?	?	?	?	?	?	?
36 ***Kuykendall***	Y	Y	Y	Y	Y	N	N	N
37 Millender-McD.	Y	Y	Y	Y	Y	Y	N	N
38 ***Horn***	Y	Y	Y	Y	Y	Y	N	Y
39 ***Royce***	Y	Y	N	Y	Y	Y	Y	Y
40 ***Lewis***	Y	Y	Y	Y	Y	N	Y	N
41 ***Miller, Gary***	Y	Y	Y	Y	Y	N	Y	N
42 Brown	?	?	?	?	?	?	?	?
43 ***Calvert***	Y	Y	Y	Y	Y	N	Y	N
44 ***Bono***	?	+	+	Y	Y	N	Y	N
45 ***Rohrabacher***	Y	Y	Y	?	Y	N	Y	Y
46 Sanchez	Y	Y	Y	Y	Y	Y	N	N
47 ***Cox***	Y	Y	?	Y	Y	N	Y	Y
48 ***Packard***	Y	Y	Y	Y	Y	N	Y	N
49 ***Bilbray***	N	Y	Y	N	Y	Y	N	Y
50 Filner	N	Y	Y	N	Y	Y	N	N
51 ***Cunningham***	Y	Y	Y	Y	Y	N	Y	N
52 ***Hunter***	?	?	Y	Y	Y	N	Y	N
COLORADO								
1 DeGette	?	?	?	Y	Y	Y	N	N
2 Udall	Y	Y	Y	Y	Y	Y	N	N
3 ***McInnis***	Y	Y	Y	Y	Y	N	Y	N
4 ***Schaffer***	N	Y	Y	?	Y	N	Y	N
5 ***Hefley***	N	Y	Y	N	Y	Y	Y	N
6 ***Tancredo***	N	Y	Y	N	Y	Y	Y	N
CONNECTICUT								
1 Larson	Y	Y	Y	Y	Y	Y	N	N
2 Gejdenson	?	?	?	Y	Y	Y	N	N
3 DeLauro	Y	Y	Y	Y	Y	Y	N	N
4 ***Shays***	Y	Y	Y	Y	Y	Y	N	Y
5 Maloney	Y	Y	Y	Y	Y	Y	N	Y
6 ***Johnson***	Y	Y	Y	Y	Y	Y	N	N
DELAWARE								
AL ***Castle***	Y	Y	Y	Y	Y	Y	N	N
FLORIDA								
1 ***Scarborough***	?	?	?	P	Y	Y	Y	Y
2 Boyd	Y	Y	Y	Y	Y	N	N	N
3 Brown	?	?	?	N	Y	N	N	N
4 ***Fowler***	Y	Y	Y	Y	Y	N	N	N
5 Thurman	Y	Y	Y	Y	Y	N	N	N
6 ***Stearns***	Y	Y	Y	Y	Y	N	Y	N
7 ***Mica***	Y	Y	Y	Y	Y	N	Y	N
8 ***McCollum***	?	?	?	?	?	?	?	?
9 ***Bilirakis***	Y	Y	Y	Y	Y	N	Y	N
10 ***Young***	Y	Y	Y	Y	Y	N	Y	N
11 Davis	Y	Y	Y	Y	Y	N	N	N
12 ***Canady***	Y	Y	Y	Y	Y	N	Y	N
13 ***Miller***	Y	Y	Y	Y	Y	Y	N	Y
14 ***Goss***	Y	Y	Y	Y	Y	Y	Y	N
15 ***Weldon***	Y	Y	Y	Y	Y	N	Y	N
16 ***Foley***	Y	Y	Y	Y	Y	N	N	N
17 Meek	Y	Y	Y	Y	Y	N	N	N
18 ***Ros-Lehtinen***	Y	Y	Y	Y	Y	Y	Y	N
19 Wexler	Y	Y	Y	Y	Y	Y	N	N
20 Deutsch	Y	Y	Y	Y	Y	Y	N	N
21 ***Diaz-Balart***	Y	Y	Y	?	Y	Y	Y	N
22 ***Shaw***	Y	Y	Y	Y	Y	N	Y	N
23 Hastings	N	Y	Y	N	Y	Y	N	N
GEORGIA								
1 ***Kingston***	?	?	?	?	?	N	Y	N
2 Bishop	Y	Y	Y	Y	Y	N	N	N
3 ***Collins***	Y	Y	Y	Y	Y	Y	Y	Y
4 McKinney	Y	Y	Y	Y	Y	Y	N	N
5 Lewis	Y	Y	Y	N	Y	Y	N	N
6 ***Isakson***	Y	Y	Y	Y	Y	N	N	N
7 ***Barr***	Y	N	Y	Y	Y	Y	Y	Y
8 ***Chambliss***	Y	Y	Y	Y	Y	N	Y	N
9 ***Deal***	Y	Y	Y	Y	Y	N	Y	N
10 ***Norwood***	Y	Y	Y	Y	Y	N	Y	N
11 ***Linder***	Y	Y	Y	?	Y	Y	Y	Y
HAWAII								
1 Abercrombie	Y	Y	Y	Y	Y	N	N	N
2 Mink	Y	Y	Y	Y	Y	N	N	N
IDAHO								
1 ***Chenoweth***	?	?	?	?	?	?	?	?
2 ***Simpson***	Y	Y	Y	Y	Y	N	Y	N
ILLINOIS								
1 Rush	?	?	?	?	?	Y	N	N
2 Jackson	Y	Y	Y	Y	Y	Y	N	N
3 Lipinski	?	?	?	?	Y	Y	Y	N
4 Gutierrez	Y	Y	Y	N	Y	Y	N	N
5 Blagojevich	Y	Y	Y	Y	Y	Y	N	N
6 ***Hyde***	Y	Y	Y	Y	Y	N	Y	N
7 Davis	Y	Y	Y	Y	Y	Y	N	N
8 ***Crane***	N	Y	Y	N	?	N	Y	Y
9 Schakowsky	Y	Y	Y	?	Y	Y	N	N
10 ***Porter***	Y	Y	Y	Y	Y	Y	N	N
11 ***Weller***	N	Y	Y	N	Y	Y	Y	N
12 Costello	N	Y	Y	N	Y	Y	Y	N
13 ***Biggert***	Y	Y	Y	Y	Y	Y	N	N
14 ***Hastert***							Y	

ND Northern Democrats SD Southern Democrats

	167	168	169	170	171	172	173	174
15 ***Ewing***	Y	Y	Y	Y	Y	N	Y	N
16 ***Manzullo***	Y	Y	Y	Y	Y	N	Y	Y
17 Evans	Y	Y	Y	Y	Y	Y	N	N
18 ***LaHood***	Y	Y	Y	Y	Y	N	Y	N
19 Phelps	Y	Y	Y	Y	Y	N	Y	N
20 ***Shimkus***	Y	Y	Y	Y	Y	N	Y	N
INDIANA								
1 Visclosky	N	Y	Y	N	Y	Y	N	N
2 ***McIntosh***	Y	Y	Y	Y	Y	N	Y	N
3 Roemer	Y	Y	Y	Y	Y	Y	Y	N
4 ***Souder***	Y	Y	Y	Y	Y	N	Y	N
5 ***Buyer***	?	?	?	Y	Y	N	Y	?
6 ***Burton***	?	+	+	Y	Y	N	Y	N
7 ***Pease***	Y	Y	Y	Y	Y	Y	Y	N
8 ***Hostettler***	Y	Y	Y	Y	Y	N	Y	Y
9 Hill	Y	Y	Y	Y	Y	Y	N	N
10 Carson	P	Y	Y	Y	Y	Y	N	N
IOWA								
1 ***Leach***	Y	Y	Y	Y	Y	Y	N	N
2 ***Nussle***	Y	Y	Y	Y	Y	N	Y	N
3 Boswell	Y	Y	Y	Y	Y	N	N	N
4 ***Ganske***	Y	Y	Y	Y	Y	N	N	N
5 ***Latham***	Y	Y	Y	Y	Y	N	Y	N
KANSAS								
1 ***Moran***	N	Y	Y	N	Y	N	Y	N
2 ***Ryun***	Y	Y	Y	Y	Y	N	Y	N
3 Moore	?	?	+	Y	Y	Y	N	N
4 ***Tiahrt***	Y	Y	Y	?	Y	N	Y	N
KENTUCKY								
1 ***Whitfield***	Y	Y	Y	Y	Y	Y	Y	N
2 ***Lewis***	Y	Y	Y	Y	Y	N	Y	N
3 ***Northup***	Y	Y	Y	Y	Y	N	Y	N
4 Lucas	Y	Y	Y	Y	Y	N	Y	N
5 ***Rogers***	?	?	?	Y	Y	N	Y	N
6 ***Fletcher***	?	?	?	Y	Y	N	Y	N
LOUISIANA								
1 ***Vitter*** [1]					Y	N	Y	N
2 Jefferson	Y	Y	Y	Y	Y	N	N	N
3 ***Tauzin***	Y	Y	Y	Y	Y	N	Y	N
4 ***McCrery***	Y	Y	Y	Y	Y	N	Y	N
5 ***Cooksey***	?	?	?	Y	Y	N	Y	N
6 ***Baker***	Y	Y	Y	Y	Y	N	Y	N
7 John	?	?	?	?	Y	N	Y	N
MAINE								
1 Allen	Y	Y	Y	Y	Y	Y	N	N
2 Baldacci	Y	Y	Y	Y	Y	Y	N	N
MARYLAND								
1 ***Gilchrest***	?	?	?	Y	Y	Y	N	N
2 ***Ehrlich***	?	+	+	Y	Y	N	N	Y
3 Cardin	Y	Y	Y	Y	Y	Y	N	N
4 Wynn	Y	Y	Y	Y	Y	Y	N	N
5 Hoyer	Y	Y	Y	Y	Y	Y	N	N
6 ***Bartlett***	Y	Y	Y	Y	Y	N	Y	N
7 Cummings	Y	Y	Y	Y	Y	Y	N	N
8 ***Morella***	Y	Y	Y	Y	Y	Y	N	Y
MASSACHUSETTS								
1 Olver	Y	Y	Y	Y	Y	Y	N	N
2 Neal	Y	Y	Y	Y	Y	Y	N	N
3 McGovern	Y	Y	Y	Y	Y	Y	N	N
4 Frank	Y	Y	?	Y	Y	Y	N	N
5 Meehan	Y	Y	Y	Y	Y	Y	N	Y
6 Tierney	Y	Y	Y	Y	Y	Y	N	Y
7 Markey	Y	Y	Y	Y	Y	Y	N	N
8 Capuano	Y	Y	Y	Y	Y	Y	N	N
9 Moakley	Y	Y	?	Y	Y	Y	N	N
10 Delahunt	Y	Y	Y	Y	Y	Y	N	N
MICHIGAN								
1 Stupak	N	Y	Y	N	Y	Y	N	N
2 ***Hoekstra***	Y	Y	Y	Y	Y	N	Y	Y
3 ***Ehlers***	Y	Y	Y	Y	Y	Y	Y	Y
4 ***Camp***	Y	Y	Y	Y	Y	N	Y	N
5 Barcia	Y	Y	Y	Y	Y	N	Y	N
6 ***Upton***	Y	Y	Y	Y	Y	Y	N	N
7 ***Smith***	P	Y	Y	?	+	N	Y	N
8 Stabenow	Y	Y	Y	Y	Y	N	N	N
9 Kildee	Y	Y	Y	Y	Y	Y	Y	N
10 Bonior	N	Y	Y	Y	Y	Y	N	N
11 ***Knollenberg***	Y	Y	Y	Y	Y	N	Y	N
12 Levin	Y	Y	Y	Y	Y	Y	N	N
13 Rivers	Y	Y	Y	Y	Y	Y	N	Y
14 Conyers	P	Y	Y	Y	Y	Y	N	Y
15 Kilpatrick	?	+	+	+	+	Y	N	N
16 Dingell	N	Y	Y	?	Y	N	N	N
MINNESOTA								
1 ***Gutknecht***	N	Y	Y	N	Y	–	Y	N
2 Minge	Y	Y	Y	Y	Y	N	N	N
3 ***Ramstad***	N	Y	Y	N	Y	Y	N	Y
4 Vento	Y	Y	Y	N	Y	Y	N	N
5 Sabo	?	?	?	N	Y	Y	N	N
6 Luther	Y	Y	Y	Y	Y	Y	N	Y
7 Peterson	N	Y	Y	N	Y	N	Y	N
8 Oberstar	N	Y	Y	N	Y	N	Y	N
MISSISSIPPI								
1 ***Wicker***	Y	Y	Y	Y	Y	N	Y	N
2 Thompson	N	Y	Y	N	Y	N	N	N
3 ***Pickering***	Y	Y	Y	Y	Y	N	Y	N
4 Shows	Y	Y	Y	Y	Y	N	Y	N
5 Taylor	N	Y	Y	N	Y	Y	Y	N
MISSOURI								
1 Clay	?	?	?	N	Y	Y	N	N
2 ***Talent***	Y	Y	Y	Y	Y	N	Y	N
3 Gephardt	N	Y	Y	N	Y	Y	N	N
4 Skelton	Y	Y	Y	Y	Y	N	Y	N
5 McCarthy	Y	Y	Y	Y	Y	Y	N	N
6 Danner	?	?	?	?	Y	N	N	N
7 ***Blunt***	Y	Y	Y	Y	Y	N	Y	N
8 ***Emerson***	Y	Y	Y	Y	Y	N	Y	N
9 ***Hulshof***	–	+	+	Y	Y	Y	Y	N
MONTANA								
AL ***Hill***	Y	Y	Y	Y	Y	N	Y	N
NEBRASKA								
1 ***Bereuter***	Y	Y	Y	Y	Y	N	Y	N
2 ***Terry***	Y	Y	Y	Y	Y	N	Y	N
3 ***Barrett***	Y	Y	Y	Y	Y	N	Y	N
NEVADA								
1 Berkley	Y	Y	Y	Y	Y	Y	N	Y
2 ***Gibbons***	N	Y	Y	N	Y	N	N	N
NEW HAMPSHIRE								
1 ***Sununu***	Y	Y	Y	Y	Y	Y	Y	Y
2 ***Bass***	Y	Y	Y	Y	Y	Y	N	Y
NEW JERSEY								
1 Andrews	+	+	+	Y	Y	Y	N	N
2 ***LoBiondo***	N	Y	Y	N	Y	Y	Y	Y
3 ***Saxton***	Y	Y	Y	Y	Y	Y	Y	N
4 ***Smith***	Y	Y	Y	Y	Y	Y	Y	N
5 ***Roukema***	Y	Y	Y	Y	Y	Y	N	Y
6 Pallone	N	Y	Y	N	Y	Y	N	N
7 ***Franks***	Y	Y	Y	Y	Y	Y	N	Y
8 Pascrell	Y	Y	Y	Y	Y	Y	N	N
9 Rothman	Y	Y	Y	Y	Y	Y	N	Y
10 Payne	Y	Y	Y	Y	Y	Y	N	N
11 ***Frelinghuysen***	Y	Y	Y	Y	Y	Y	N	Y
12 Holt	Y	Y	Y	Y	Y	Y	N	Y
13 Menendez	Y	Y	Y	Y	Y	Y	N	N
NEW MEXICO								
1 ***Wilson***	Y	Y	Y	Y	Y	N	N	N
2 ***Skeen***	Y	Y	Y	Y	Y	N	Y	N
3 Udall	N	Y	Y	N	Y	N	N	N
NEW YORK								
1 ***Forbes***	Y	Y	Y	Y	Y	Y	Y	N
2 ***Lazio***	Y	Y	Y	Y	Y	Y	N	Y
3 ***King***	Y	Y	Y	Y	Y	Y	Y	N
4 McCarthy	Y	Y	Y	Y	Y	Y	N	N
5 Ackerman	?	?	?	Y	Y	Y	N	N
6 Meeks	?	Y	Y	Y	Y	N	N	N
7 Crowley	Y	Y	Y	Y	Y	Y	Y	N
8 Nadler	Y	Y	Y	Y	Y	Y	N	N
9 Weiner	?	+	+	Y	Y	Y	N	Y
10 Towns	?	?	?	Y	Y	Y	N	N
11 Owens	?	?	?	Y	Y	Y	N	N
12 Velázquez	N	Y	Y	Y	Y	Y	N	N
13 ***Fossella***	Y	Y	Y	Y	Y	Y	Y	Y
14 Maloney	?	?	?	Y	Y	Y	N	N
15 Rangel	?	Y	Y	?	Y	Y	N	N
16 Serrano	?	?	Y	Y	Y	Y	N	N
17 Engel	?	Y	Y	Y	Y	N	N	N
18 Lowey	?	Y	Y	Y	Y	Y	N	N
19 ***Kelly***	Y	Y	Y	Y	Y	Y	N	Y
20 ***Gilman***	Y	Y	Y	Y	Y	Y	Y	N
21 McNulty	N	Y	Y	Y	Y	Y	N	N
22 ***Sweeney***	?	Y	?	N	Y	N	N	N
23 ***Boehlert***	Y	Y	Y	Y	Y	Y	N	N
24 ***McHugh***	Y	Y	Y	Y	Y	Y	N	N
25 ***Walsh***	Y	Y	Y	Y	Y	Y	Y	N
26 Hinchey	Y	Y	Y	Y	Y	N	N	N
27 ***Reynolds***	Y	Y	Y	Y	Y	?	Y	N
28 Slaughter	N	Y	Y	Y	Y	Y	N	N
29 LaFalce	?	?	?	N	Y	N	Y	N
30 ***Quinn***	Y	Y	Y	Y	Y	N	Y	N
31 ***Houghton***	Y	Y	Y	Y	Y	Y	N	N
NORTH CAROLINA								
1 Clayton	Y	Y	Y	Y	Y	N	N	N
2 Etheridge	Y	Y	Y	N	Y	Y	N	N
3 ***Jones***	Y	Y	Y	Y	Y	Y	Y	N
4 Price	Y	Y	Y	Y	Y	Y	N	N
5 ***Burr***	Y	?	Y	Y	Y	N	Y	N
6 ***Coble***	Y	Y	Y	Y	Y	N	Y	Y
7 McIntyre	Y	Y	Y	Y	Y	N	Y	N
8 ***Hayes***	Y	Y	Y	Y	Y	N	Y	N
9 ***Myrick***	Y	Y	Y	Y	Y	N	Y	Y
10 ***Ballenger***	Y	Y	Y	Y	Y	N	Y	N
11 ***Taylor***	?	?	?	Y	Y	N	Y	N
12 Watt	Y	Y	Y	Y	Y	N	N	N
NORTH DAKOTA								
AL Pomeroy	Y	Y	Y	Y	Y	N	N	N
OHIO								
1 ***Chabot***	Y	Y	Y	Y	Y	Y	Y	Y
2 ***Portman***	Y	Y	Y	Y	Y	N	Y	Y
3 Hall	?	?	?	Y	Y	Y	Y	N
4 ***Oxley***	?	+	+	Y	Y	N	Y	N
5 ***Gillmor***	?	?	?	Y	Y	N	Y	N
6 Strickland	Y	Y	Y	Y	Y	Y	N	N
7 ***Hobson***	Y	Y	Y	Y	Y	N	Y	N
8 ***Boehner***	Y	Y	Y	Y	Y	N	Y	N
9 Kaptur	Y	Y	Y	Y	Y	N	N	N
10 Kucinich	N	Y	Y	N	Y	Y	Y	N
11 Jones	Y	Y	Y	Y	Y	Y	N	N
12 ***Kasich***	?	?	?	Y	Y	N	Y	N
13 Brown	N	Y	Y	N	Y	Y	N	N
14 Sawyer	Y	Y	Y	Y	Y	Y	N	N
15 ***Pryce***	Y	Y	Y	Y	Y	N	N	Y
16 ***Regula***	Y	Y	Y	Y	Y	N	Y	N
17 Traficant	Y	Y	Y	Y	Y	Y	Y	N
18 ***Ney***	Y	Y	Y	Y	Y	N	Y	?
19 ***LaTourette***	Y	Y	Y	Y	Y	Y	Y	N
OKLAHOMA								
1 ***Largent***	?	?	?	Y	Y	Y	Y	Y
2 ***Coburn***	?	?	?	?	Y	Y	Y	Y
3 ***Watkins***	Y	Y	Y	Y	Y	N	Y	N
4 ***Watts***	Y	Y	Y	Y	Y	N	Y	N
5 ***Istook***	Y	Y	Y	Y	Y	N	Y	Y
6 ***Lucas***	Y	Y	Y	Y	Y	N	Y	N
OREGON								
1 Wu	?	Y	Y	Y	Y	Y	N	Y
2 ***Walden***	Y	Y	Y	Y	Y	N	Y	N
3 Blumenauer	Y	Y	Y	Y	Y	Y	N	N
4 DeFazio	N	Y	Y	N	Y	Y	N	N
5 Hooley	Y	Y	Y	Y	Y	N	N	N
PENNSYLVANIA								
1 Brady	Y	Y	Y	Y	Y	Y	N	N
2 Fattah	Y	Y	Y	Y	Y	Y	N	N
3 Borski	?	?	?	N	Y	Y	Y	N
4 Klink	Y	Y	Y	Y	Y	Y	Y	N
5 ***Peterson***	Y	Y	Y	Y	Y	N	Y	N
6 Holden	Y	Y	Y	Y	Y	Y	Y	N
7 ***Weldon***	Y	Y	Y	Y	?	N	Y	N
8 ***Greenwood***	Y	Y	Y	Y	Y	Y	N	N
9 ***Shuster***	Y	Y	Y	Y	Y	N	Y	N
10 ***Sherwood***	Y	Y	Y	Y	Y	N	Y	N
11 Kanjorski	Y	Y	Y	Y	Y	Y	Y	N
12 Murtha	Y	Y	Y	Y	Y	N	Y	N
13 Hoeffel	Y	Y	Y	Y	Y	Y	N	N
14 Coyne	Y	Y	Y	?	Y	Y	N	N
15 ***Toomey***	Y	Y	Y	Y	Y	N	Y	Y
16 ***Pitts***	Y	Y	Y	Y	Y	N	Y	N
17 ***Gekas***	Y	Y	Y	Y	Y	N	Y	N
18 Doyle	Y	Y	Y	Y	Y	Y	Y	Y
19 ***Goodling***	Y	Y	Y	Y	Y	N	Y	N
20 Mascara	Y	Y	Y	Y	Y	N	Y	N
21 ***English***	N	Y	Y	N	Y	Y	Y	N
RHODE ISLAND								
1 Kennedy	Y	Y	Y	Y	Y	Y	N	N
2 Weygand	Y	Y	Y	Y	Y	Y	Y	N
SOUTH CAROLINA								
1 ***Sanford***	Y	Y	N	Y	Y	Y	Y	Y
2 ***Spence***	Y	Y	Y	Y	Y	N	Y	N
3 ***Graham***	Y	Y	Y	Y	Y	N	Y	Y
4 ***DeMint***	Y	Y	Y	Y	Y	N	Y	Y
5 Spratt	Y	Y	Y	Y	Y	N	N	N
6 Clyburn	N	Y	Y	Y	Y	N	N	N
SOUTH DAKOTA								
AL ***Thune***	Y	Y	Y	Y	Y	N	Y	N
TENNESSEE								
1 ***Jenkins***	Y	Y	Y	Y	Y	?	Y	N
2 ***Duncan***	Y	Y	Y	Y	Y	Y	Y	Y
3 ***Wamp***	Y	Y	Y	Y	Y	N	Y	Y
4 ***Hilleary***	N	Y	Y	Y	Y	N	Y	N
5 Clement	Y	Y	Y	Y	Y	N	N	N
6 Gordon	Y	Y	Y	Y	Y	N	N	N
7 ***Bryant***	Y	Y	Y	Y	Y	N	Y	N
8 Tanner	?	?	?	N	Y	N	N	N
9 Ford	Y	Y	Y	Y	Y	N	N	–
TEXAS								
1 Sandlin	Y	Y	Y	Y	Y	N	N	N
2 Turner	Y	Y	Y	Y	Y	N	N	N
3 ***Johnson, Sam***	Y	Y	Y	Y	Y	N	Y	N
4 Hall	Y	Y	Y	Y	Y	N	Y	N
5 ***Sessions***	Y	Y	Y	Y	Y	N	Y	Y
6 ***Barton***	Y	Y	Y	Y	Y	N	Y	N
7 ***Archer***	?	Y	Y	Y	Y	N	Y	Y
8 ***Brady***	Y	Y	Y	Y	Y	?	Y	N
9 Lampson	Y	Y	Y	Y	Y	N	N	N
10 Doggett	Y	Y	Y	Y	Y	Y	N	Y
11 Edwards	Y	Y	Y	Y	Y	N	N	N
12 ***Granger***	Y	Y	Y	Y	Y	N	N	N
13 ***Thornberry***	Y	Y	Y	Y	Y	N	Y	N
14 ***Paul***	Y	Y	N	Y	Y	Y	Y	Y
15 Hinojosa	Y	Y	Y	Y	Y	N	N	N
16 Reyes	Y	Y	Y	Y	Y	N	N	N
17 Stenholm	Y	Y	Y	Y	Y	N	Y	N
18 Jackson-Lee	N	Y	Y	Y	Y	Y	N	N
19 ***Combest***	Y	Y	Y	Y	Y	N	Y	N
20 Gonzalez	Y	Y	Y	Y	Y	Y	N	N
21 ***Smith***	Y	Y	Y	Y	Y	N	Y	N
22 ***DeLay***	Y	Y	Y	Y	Y	N	Y	Y
23 ***Bonilla***	Y	Y	Y	Y	Y	N	Y	N
24 Frost	Y	Y	Y	?	Y	N	N	N
25 Bentsen	Y	Y	Y	Y	Y	N	N	N
26 ***Armey***	Y	Y	Y	Y	Y	N	Y	Y
27 Ortiz	Y	Y	Y	Y	Y	N	Y	N
28 Rodriguez	Y	Y	Y	Y	Y	N	N	N
29 Green	N	Y	Y	N	Y	Y	N	N
30 Johnson, E.B.	Y	Y	Y	Y	Y	N	N	N
UTAH								
1 ***Hansen***	Y	Y	Y	Y	Y	N	Y	N
2 ***Cook***	Y	Y	Y	Y	Y	N	Y	N
3 ***Cannon***	?	?	?	?	Y	N	Y	N
VERMONT								
AL *Sanders*	?	?	?	?	Y	Y	N	N
VIRGINIA								
1 ***Bateman***	?	+	+	Y	Y	N	Y	N
2 Pickett	?	?	?	?	?	?	N	N
3 Scott	Y	Y	Y	Y	Y	N	N	N
4 Sisisky	Y	Y	Y	Y	Y	Y	N	N
5 Goode	Y	Y	Y	Y	Y	N	Y	N
6 ***Goodlatte***	Y	Y	Y	Y	Y	N	Y	N
7 ***Bliley***	?	?	?	Y	?	N	Y	N
8 Moran	Y	Y	Y	Y	Y	N	N	Y
9 Boucher	Y	Y	Y	?	?	?	N	N
10 ***Wolf***	N	Y	Y	Y	Y	N	Y	N
11 ***Davis***	Y	Y	Y	Y	Y	Y	N	N
WASHINGTON								
1 Inslee	Y	Y	Y	Y	Y	Y	N	N
2 ***Metcalf***	Y	Y	N	Y	Y	Y	Y	N
3 Baird	Y	Y	Y	Y	Y	Y	N	N
4 ***Hastings***	Y	Y	Y	Y	Y	N	Y	N
5 ***Nethercutt***	Y	Y	Y	Y	Y	N	Y	N
6 Dicks	Y	Y	Y	Y	Y	N	N	N
7 McDermott	N	Y	Y	Y	Y	Y	N	N
8 ***Dunn***	Y	Y	Y	Y	Y	N	Y	N
9 Smith	Y	Y	Y	Y	Y	Y	N	N
WEST VIRGINIA								
1 Mollohan	Y	Y	Y	Y	Y	N	Y	N
2 Wise	?	?	?	?	Y	N	N	N
3 Rahall	Y	Y	Y	Y	Y	N	Y	N
WISCONSIN								
1 ***Ryan***	Y	Y	Y	Y	Y	Y	Y	N
2 Baldwin	Y	Y	Y	Y	Y	Y	N	N
3 Kind	Y	Y	Y	Y	Y	Y	N	Y
4 Kleczka	Y	Y	Y	?	Y	Y	N	Y
5 Barrett	Y	Y	Y	Y	Y	Y	N	Y
6 ***Petri***	Y	Y	Y	Y	Y	Y	Y	Y
7 Obey	Y	Y	Y	?	Y	Y	N	N
8 ***Green***	Y	Y	Y	Y	Y	Y	Y	N
9 ***Sensenbrenner***	Y	Y	Y	Y	Y	Y	Y	Y
WYOMING								
AL ***Cubin***	Y	Y	Y	Y	Y	N	Y	N

Southern states - Ala., Ark., Fla., Ga., Ky., La., Miss., N.C., Okla., S.C., Tenn., Texas, Va.

175. HR 1906. Fiscal 2000 Agriculture Appropriations/Spending Reductions. Young, R-Fla., amendment to reduce funding in the bill by a total of $103 million, largely by delaying certain Agriculture Department (USDA) construction projects. Cuts included $26 million for USDA buildings, facilities and rental payments; $10 million for the Cooperative State Research Education and Extension Service (bringing it to zero); $44.5 million for buildings and facilities for the Agricultural Research Service (bringing it to zero); $2 million for administrative expenses for the Rural Housing Insurance Fund Program; and $20 million for salaries and expenses of the Food and Drug Administration. Adopted 234-195: R 217-4; D 17-190 (ND 12-141, SD 5-49); I 0-1. June 8, 1999.

176. HR 1906. Fiscal 2000 Agriculture Appropriations/Motion To Recommit. Obey, D-Wis., motion to recommit the bill to the Appropriations Committee with instructions to report it back with an amendment to restore $20 million in funding for salaries and expenses at the Food and Drug Administration. Motion rejected, 207-220: R 0-218; D 206-2 (ND 153-1, SD 53-1); I 1-0. June 8, 1999.

177. HR 1906. Fiscal 2000 Agriculture Appropriations/Passage. Passage of the bill that would appropriate $60.7 billion in funds for agricultural and conservation programs in fiscal 2000, including $20.1 billion for agricultural programs, $800 million for conservation programs, $2.1 billion for rural economic and community development programs, $21.6 billion for food stamps, $1.1 billion for the Food and Drug Administration, $9.5 billion for child nutrition programs, $997 million for the Federal Crop Insurance Corporation, and $4 billion for the Women, Infants and Children supplemental nutrition program. Passed 246-183: R 213-8; D 33-174 (ND 19-135, SD 14-39); I 0-1. June 8, 1999.

178. Procedural Motion/Journal. Approval of the House Journal of Tuesday, June 8, 1999. Approved 355-62: R 197-19; D 157-43 (ND 114-33, SD 43-10); I 1-0. June 9, 1999.

179. HR 1401. Defense Authorization/Rule. Adoption of the rule (H Res 200) to provide for House floor consideration of the bill to authorize funding for defense programs for fiscal 2000-01. Adopted 354-75: R 221-0; D 133-74 (ND 88-65, SD 45-9); I 0-1. June 9, 1999.

180. HR 1401. Defense Authorization/Nuclear Spying Counterintelligence. Cox, R-Calif., amendment to implement the recommendations of the Cox-Dicks report on nuclear security breaches at U.S. sites. Adopted 428-0: R 220-0; D 207-0 (ND 152-0, SD 55-0); I 1-0. June 9, 1999.

181. HR 1401. Defense Authorization/Visitors to National Labs. Ryun, R-Kan., amendment to institute a two-year moratorium on foreign visitors to national laboratories. Rejected 159-266: R 152-65; D 7-200 (ND 4-148, SD 3-52); I 0-1. June 9, 1999.

182. HR 1401. Defense Authorization/Joint Training Exercises With China. DeLay, R-Texas, amendment to prohibit all military-to-military exchange or joint training exercises with the military of China; permit joint training in search and rescue operations. Adopted 284-143: R 214-6; D 69-137 (ND 49-102, SD 20-35); I 1-0. June 9, 1999.

Key

- Y Voted for (yea).
- # Paired for.
- + Announced for.
- N Voted against (nay).
- X Paired against.
- – Announced against.
- P Voted "present."
- C Voted "present" to avoid possible conflict of interest.
- ? Did not vote or otherwise make a position known.

•

Democrats ***Republicans***
Independents

	175	176	177	178	179	180	181	182
ALABAMA								
1 ***Callahan***	Y	N	Y	Y	Y	Y	Y	Y
2 ***Everett***	Y	N	Y	Y	Y	Y	Y	Y
3 ***Riley***	Y	N	Y	N	Y	Y	Y	Y
4 ***Aderholt***	Y	N	Y	N	Y	Y	Y	Y
5 Cramer	N	Y	Y	Y	Y	Y	N	Y
6 ***Bachus***	Y	N	Y	Y	Y	Y	Y	Y
7 Hilliard	N	Y	N	N	N	Y	N	N
ALASKA								
AL ***Young***	Y	N	Y	?	Y	Y	Y	Y
ARIZONA								
1 ***Salmon***	Y	N	Y	Y	Y	Y	N	Y
2 Pastor	N	Y	N	Y	Y	Y	N	N
3 ***Stump***	Y	N	Y	Y	Y	Y	N	Y
4 ***Shadegg***	Y	N	Y	Y	Y	Y	Y	Y
5 ***Kolbe***	Y	N	Y	Y	Y	Y	N	N
6 ***Hayworth***	Y	N	Y	Y	Y	Y	Y	Y
ARKANSAS								
1 Berry	N	Y	N	Y	Y	Y	N	Y
2 Snyder	N	Y	N	Y	Y	Y	N	N
3 ***Hutchinson***	Y	N	Y	N	Y	Y	Y	Y
4 ***Dickey***	Y	N	Y	Y	Y	Y	Y	Y
CALIFORNIA								
1 Thompson	N	Y	N	N	Y	Y	N	N
2 ***Herger***	Y	N	Y	Y	Y	Y	Y	Y
3 ***Ose***	Y	N	Y	Y	Y	Y	N	N
4 ***Doolittle***	Y	N	Y	Y	Y	Y	Y	Y
5 Matsui	N	Y	N	Y	Y	Y	N	N
6 Woolsey	N	Y	N	Y	Y	Y	N	N
7 Miller, George	N	Y	N	N	N	Y	N	N
8 Pelosi	N	Y	N	Y	N	Y	N	Y
9 Lee	N	Y	N	Y	N	Y	N	N
10 Tauscher	N	Y	N	Y	Y	Y	N	N
11 ***Pombo***	Y	N	Y	N	Y	Y	Y	Y
12 Lantos	N	Y	N	Y	Y	Y	N	N
13 Stark	N	Y	N	?	N	Y	N	?
14 Eshoo	N	Y	N	Y	N	Y	N	N
15 ***Campbell***	Y	N	Y	Y	Y	Y	Y	Y
16 Lofgren	N	Y	N	Y	N	Y	N	Y
17 Farr	N	Y	N	Y	Y	Y	N	N
18 Condit	N	Y	Y	Y	Y	Y	N	Y
19 ***Radanovich***	Y	N	Y	Y	Y	Y	Y	Y
20 Dooley	N	Y	Y	Y	Y	Y	N	N
21 ***Thomas***	Y	N	Y	Y	Y	Y	N	Y
22 Capps	N	Y	N	Y	Y	Y	N	N
23 ***Gallegly***	Y	N	Y	Y	Y	Y	N	Y
24 Sherman	N	Y	N	Y	N	Y	N	Y
25 ***McKeon***	Y	N	Y	Y	Y	Y	Y	Y
26 Berman	N	Y	N	Y	Y	Y	N	N
27 ***Rogan***	Y	N	Y	?	Y	Y	Y	Y
28 ***Dreier***	Y	N	Y	Y	Y	Y	N	Y
29 Waxman	N	Y	N	Y	Y	Y	N	N
30 Becerra	N	Y	N	Y	N	Y	N	N
31 Martinez	N	Y	N	N	N	Y	N	N
32 Dixon	N	Y	N	Y	Y	Y	N	N
33 Roybal-Allard	N	Y	N	Y	Y	Y	N	N
34 Napolitano	N	Y	N	Y	Y	Y	N	N
35 Waters	?	?	?	?	?	?	?	N
36 ***Kuykendall***	Y	N	Y	Y	Y	Y	N	Y
37 Millender-McD.	N	Y	N	Y	Y	Y	N	N
38 ***Horn***	Y	N	Y	Y	Y	Y	N	N
39 ***Royce***	Y	N	N	Y	Y	Y	Y	Y
40 ***Lewis***	Y	N	Y	Y	Y	Y	N	N
41 ***Miller, Gary***	Y	N	Y	Y	Y	Y	Y	Y
42 Brown	?	?	?	?	?	?	?	?
43 ***Calvert***	Y	N	Y	Y	Y	Y	N	Y
44 ***Bono***	Y	N	Y	Y	Y	Y	Y	Y
45 ***Rohrabacher***	Y	N	Y	Y	Y	Y	Y	Y
46 Sanchez	N	Y	N	Y	Y	Y	N	N
47 ***Cox***	Y	N	Y	Y	Y	Y	Y	Y
48 ***Packard***	Y	N	Y	Y	Y	Y	Y	Y
49 ***Bilbray***	Y	N	Y	N	Y	Y	Y	Y
50 Filner	N	Y	N	N	N	Y	N	N
51 ***Cunningham***	Y	N	Y	Y	Y	Y	Y	Y
52 ***Hunter***	Y	N	Y	Y	Y	Y	Y	Y
COLORADO								
1 DeGette	N	Y	N	Y	N	Y	N	Y
2 Udall	N	Y	N	N	N	Y	N	N
3 ***McInnis***	Y	N	Y	Y	Y	Y	Y	Y
4 ***Schaffer***	Y	N	Y	N	Y	Y	N	Y
5 ***Hefley***	Y	N	N	N	Y	Y	Y	Y
6 ***Tancredo***	Y	N	N	N	Y	Y	Y	Y
CONNECTICUT								
1 Larson	N	Y	N	Y	Y	Y	N	N
2 Gejdenson	N	Y	N	Y	N	Y	N	N
3 DeLauro	N	Y	N	Y	N	Y	N	N
4 ***Shays***	Y	N	N	Y	Y	Y	Y	Y
5 Maloney	N	Y	N	Y	Y	Y	N	Y
6 ***Johnson***	Y	N	Y	Y	Y	Y	Y	Y
DELAWARE								
AL ***Castle***	Y	N	Y	Y	Y	Y	N	Y
FLORIDA								
1 ***Scarborough***	Y	N	N	Y	Y	Y	Y	Y
2 Boyd	N	Y	N	Y	Y	Y	N	N
3 Brown	N	Y	N	Y	Y	Y	N	N
4 ***Fowler***	Y	N	Y	Y	Y	Y	N	Y
5 Thurman	N	Y	N	Y	Y	Y	N	N
6 ***Stearns***	Y	N	N	Y	Y	Y	Y	Y
7 ***Mica***	Y	–	Y	Y	Y	Y	Y	Y
8 ***McCollum***	?	?	?	Y	Y	Y	Y	Y
9 ***Bilirakis***	Y	N	Y	Y	Y	Y	Y	Y
10 ***Young***	Y	N	Y	Y	Y	Y	Y	Y
11 Davis	N	Y	N	Y	Y	Y	N	N
12 ***Canady***	Y	N	Y	Y	Y	Y	N	Y
13 ***Miller***	Y	N	Y	Y	Y	Y	Y	Y
14 ***Goss***	Y	N	Y	Y	Y	Y	N	Y
15 ***Weldon***	Y	N	Y	Y	Y	Y	Y	Y
16 ***Foley***	Y	N	Y	Y	Y	Y	N	Y
17 Meek	N	Y	N	?	N	Y	N	N
18 ***Ros-Lehtinen***	Y	N	Y	Y	Y	Y	Y	Y
19 Wexler	N	Y	?	Y	Y	Y	N	N
20 Deutsch	N	Y	N	Y	Y	Y	N	N
21 ***Diaz-Balart***	Y	N	Y	Y	Y	Y	Y	Y
22 ***Shaw***	Y	N	Y	Y	Y	Y	Y	Y
23 Hastings	N	Y	N	N	N	Y	N	N
GEORGIA								
1 ***Kingston***	Y	N	Y	Y	Y	Y	Y	Y
2 Bishop	N	Y	Y	Y	Y	Y	N	Y
3 ***Collins***	Y	N	Y	Y	Y	Y	Y	Y
4 McKinney	N	Y	N	Y	Y	Y	N	N
5 Lewis	N	Y	N	N	N	Y	N	N
6 ***Isakson***	Y	N	Y	Y	Y	Y	Y	Y
7 ***Barr***	Y	N	Y	Y	Y	Y	Y	Y
8 ***Chambliss***	Y	N	Y	Y	Y	Y	Y	Y
9 ***Deal***	Y	N	Y	Y	Y	Y	Y	Y
10 ***Norwood***	Y	N	Y	Y	Y	Y	Y	Y
11 ***Linder***	Y	N	Y	Y	Y	Y	Y	Y
HAWAII								
1 Abercrombie	N	Y	Y	Y	Y	Y	N	N
2 Mink	N	Y	N	Y	Y	Y	N	N
IDAHO								
1 ***Chenoweth***	?	?	?	Y	+	Y	Y	Y
2 ***Simpson***	Y	N	Y	Y	Y	Y	N	Y
ILLINOIS								
1 Rush	N	Y	N	Y	N	Y	N	N
2 Jackson	N	Y	N	Y	N	Y	N	N
3 Lipinski	Y	Y	Y	Y	Y	Y	N	Y
4 Gutierrez	N	Y	N	?	Y	Y	N	N
5 Blagojevich	N	Y	N	Y	Y	Y	N	N
6 ***Hyde***	Y	N	Y	Y	Y	Y	Y	Y
7 Davis	N	Y	N	Y	Y	Y	N	N
8 ***Crane***	Y	N	Y	N	Y	Y	Y	Y
9 Schakowsky	N	Y	N	Y	N	Y	N	N
10 ***Porter***	Y	N	Y	Y	Y	Y	N	Y
11 ***Weller***	Y	N	Y	N	Y	Y	Y	Y
12 Costello	N	Y	N	N	Y	Y	N	Y
13 ***Biggert***	Y	N	Y	Y	Y	Y	N	Y
14 ***Hastert***	Y	N	Y		Y			

ND Northern Democrats SD Southern Democrats

	175	176	177	178	179	180	181	182
15 ***Ewing***	Y	N	Y	Y	Y	Y	?	Y
16 ***Manzullo***	Y	N	Y	Y	Y	Y	Y	Y
17 Evans	N	Y	Y	Y	N	Y	N	N
18 ***LaHood***	Y	N	Y	Y	Y	Y	Y	Y
19 Phelps	N	Y	N	Y	Y	Y	N	N
20 ***Shimkus***	Y	N	Y	Y	Y	Y	Y	Y
INDIANA								
1 Visclosky	N	Y	N	N	N	Y	N	?
2 ***McIntosh***	Y	N	Y	Y	Y	Y	N	Y
3 Roemer	N	Y	Y	Y	Y	Y	N	Y
4 ***Souder***	Y	N	Y	Y	Y	Y	Y	Y
5 ***Buyer***	Y	?	Y	Y	Y	Y	Y	Y
6 ***Burton***	Y	N	Y	Y	Y	Y	Y	Y
7 ***Pease***	Y	N	Y	Y	Y	Y	Y	Y
8 ***Hostettler***	Y	N	Y	Y	Y	Y	Y	Y
9 Hill	N	Y	N	Y	Y	Y	N	N
10 Carson	N	Y	N	Y	Y	Y	N	N
IOWA								
1 ***Leach***	Y	N	Y	Y	Y	Y	Y	Y
2 ***Nussle***	Y	N	Y	Y	Y	Y	Y	Y
3 Boswell	N	Y	Y	Y	Y	Y	N	N
4 ***Ganske***	Y	N	Y	Y	Y	Y	Y	Y
5 ***Latham***	Y	N	Y	Y	Y	Y	Y	Y
KANSAS								
1 ***Moran***	Y	N	Y	N	Y	Y	Y	Y
2 ***Ryun***	Y	N	Y	Y	Y	Y	Y	Y
3 Moore	N	Y	Y	Y	Y	Y	N	Y
4 ***Tiahrt***	Y	N	Y	Y	Y	Y	Y	Y
KENTUCKY								
1 ***Whitfield***	Y	N	Y	Y	Y	Y	Y	Y
2 ***Lewis***	Y	N	Y	Y	Y	Y	Y	Y
3 ***Northup***	Y	N	Y	Y	Y	Y	Y	Y
4 Lucas	N	Y	N	Y	Y	Y	N	Y
5 ***Rogers***	Y	N	Y	Y	Y	Y	Y	Y
6 ***Fletcher***	Y	N	Y	Y	Y	Y	Y	Y
LOUISIANA								
1 ***Vitter***	Y	N	Y	Y	Y	Y	N	Y
2 Jefferson	N	Y	N	Y	Y	Y	N	N
3 ***Tauzin***	Y	N	Y	Y	Y	Y	Y	Y
4 ***McCrery***	Y	N	Y	?	Y	Y	N	Y
5 ***Cooksey***	Y	N	Y	Y	Y	Y	Y	Y
6 ***Baker***	Y	N	Y	Y	Y	Y	N	Y
7 John	N	Y	Y	Y	Y	Y	N	N
MAINE								
1 Allen	N	Y	N	Y	Y	Y	N	N
2 Baldacci	N	Y	N	N	Y	Y	N	Y
MARYLAND								
1 ***Gilchrest***	Y	N	Y	Y	Y	Y	Y	Y
2 ***Ehrlich***	Y	N	Y	Y	Y	Y	N	Y
3 Cardin	N	Y	N	Y	N	Y	N	N
4 Wynn	N	Y	N	Y	N	Y	N	N
5 Hoyer	N	Y	N	Y	Y	Y	N	N
6 ***Bartlett***	Y	N	Y	Y	Y	Y	Y	Y
7 Cummings	N	Y	N	?	Y	Y	N	N
8 ***Morella***	N	N	Y	Y	Y	Y	N	Y
MASSACHUSETTS								
1 Olver	N	Y	N	Y	N	Y	N	N
2 Neal	N	Y	N	Y	Y	Y	N	N
3 McGovern	N	Y	N	N	Y	Y	N	N
4 Frank	Y	Y	N	Y	Y	Y	N	N
5 Meehan	Y	Y	N	Y	Y	Y	N	N
6 Tierney	Y	Y	N	Y	N	Y	N	Y
7 Markey	Y	Y	N	N	Y	Y	N	N
8 Capuano	N	Y	N	Y	N	Y	N	Y
9 Moakley	N	Y	N	Y	Y	Y	N	Y
10 Delahunt	Y	Y	N	Y	N	Y	N	N
MICHIGAN								
1 Stupak	N	Y	N	N	N	Y	N	Y
2 ***Hoekstra***	Y	N	Y	Y	Y	Y	Y	Y
3 ***Ehlers***	Y	N	Y	Y	Y	Y	N	Y
4 ***Camp***	Y	N	Y	Y	Y	Y	Y	Y
5 Barcia	N	Y	Y	Y	Y	Y	Y	Y
6 ***Upton***	Y	N	Y	Y	Y	Y	Y	Y
7 ***Smith***	Y	N	Y	Y	Y	Y	N	Y
8 Stabenow	N	Y	Y	Y	N	Y	N	Y
9 Kildee	N	Y	N	Y	Y	Y	N	Y
10 Bonior	N	Y	Y	N	N	Y	N	Y
11 ***Knollenberg***	Y	N	Y	Y	Y	Y	N	Y
12 Levin	N	Y	N	Y	Y	Y	N	Y
13 Rivers	N	Y	N	Y	Y	Y	N	Y
14 Conyers	N	Y	N	Y	N	Y	N	N
15 Kilpatrick	N	Y	N	Y	N	Y	N	N
16 Dingell	N	Y	N	Y	N	Y	N	Y

	175	176	177	178	179	180	181	182
MINNESOTA								
1 ***Gutknecht***	Y	N	Y	N	Y	Y	Y	Y
2 Minge	N	Y	N	Y	N	Y	N	Y
3 ***Ramstad***	Y	N	Y	N	Y	Y	Y	Y
4 Vento	N	Y	N	N	N	Y	N	N
5 Sabo	N	Y	N	N	N	Y	N	N
6 Luther	Y	Y	N	?	?	?	?	N
7 Peterson	N	Y	N	N	N	Y	Y	Y
8 Oberstar	N	Y	N	N	N	Y	N	N
MISSISSIPPI								
1 ***Wicker***	Y	N	Y	N	Y	Y	Y	Y
2 Thompson	N	Y	N	N	N	Y	N	N
3 ***Pickering***	Y	N	Y	Y	Y	Y	Y	Y
4 Shows	N	Y	Y	Y	Y	Y	N	Y
5 Taylor	Y	Y	Y	N	Y	Y	Y	Y
MISSOURI								
1 Clay	N	Y	N	N	N	Y	N	N
2 ***Talent***	Y	N	Y	Y	Y	Y	Y	Y
3 Gephardt	N	Y	N	N	N	Y	N	Y
4 Skelton	N	Y	Y	Y	Y	Y	N	N
5 McCarthy	–	Y	N	Y	Y	Y	N	N
6 Danner	N	Y	Y	Y	Y	Y	N	N
7 ***Blunt***	Y	N	Y	Y	Y	Y	Y	Y
8 ***Emerson***	Y	N	Y	Y	Y	Y	N	Y
9 ***Hulshof***	Y	N	Y	N	Y	Y	Y	Y
MONTANA								
AL ***Hill***	Y	N	Y	N	Y	Y	Y	Y
NEBRASKA								
1 ***Bereuter***	Y	N	Y	Y	Y	Y	N	N
2 ***Terry***	Y	N	Y	Y	Y	Y	Y	Y
3 ***Barrett***	Y	N	Y	Y	Y	Y	N	Y
NEVADA								
1 Berkley	N	Y	N	Y	Y	Y	N	Y
2 ***Gibbons***	Y	N	Y	Y	Y	Y	Y	Y
NEW HAMPSHIRE								
1 ***Sununu***	Y	N	Y	Y	Y	Y	Y	Y
2 ***Bass***	Y	N	Y	Y	Y	Y	N	Y
NEW JERSEY								
1 Andrews	N	Y	N	Y	Y	Y	N	N
2 ***LoBiondo***	Y	N	Y	N	Y	Y	Y	Y
3 ***Saxton***	Y	N	Y	Y	Y	Y	Y	Y
4 ***Smith***	Y	N	Y	Y	Y	Y	Y	Y
5 ***Roukema***	Y	N	Y	Y	Y	Y	Y	Y
6 Pallone	N	Y	N	N	N	Y	N	Y
7 ***Franks***	Y	N	Y	Y	Y	Y	Y	Y
8 Pascrell	N	Y	N	?	Y	Y	N	Y
9 Rothman	N	Y	N	Y	Y	Y	N	N
10 Payne	N	Y	N	Y	N	Y	N	N
11 ***Frelinghuysen***	Y	N	Y	Y	Y	Y	N	Y
12 Holt	N	Y	N	Y	N	Y	N	Y
13 Menendez	N	Y	N	Y	N	Y	N	Y
NEW MEXICO								
1 ***Wilson***	Y	N	Y	Y	Y	Y	N	Y
2 ***Skeen***	Y	N	Y	Y	Y	Y	N	Y
3 Udall	N	Y	N	N	N	Y	N	N
NEW YORK								
1 ***Forbes***	N	N	Y	Y	Y	Y	N	Y
2 ***Lazio***	Y	N	Y	Y	Y	Y	Y	Y
3 ***King***	Y	N	Y	Y	Y	Y	Y	Y
4 McCarthy	N	Y	N	Y	Y	Y	N	N
5 Ackerman	N	Y	N	Y	Y	Y	N	N
6 Meeks	N	Y	N	Y	N	Y	N	N
7 Crowley	N	Y	N	N	Y	Y	N	N
8 Nadler	N	Y	N	Y	N	Y	N	N
9 Weiner	N	Y	N	Y	Y	Y	N	N
10 Towns	N	Y	N	Y	N	Y	N	N
11 Owens	N	Y	N	Y	N	Y	N	N
12 Velázquez	N	Y	N	N	N	Y	N	N
13 ***Fossella***	Y	N	Y	Y	Y	Y	Y	Y
14 Maloney	N	Y	N	Y	Y	Y	N	Y
15 Rangel	N	Y	N	Y	N	Y	N	N
16 Serrano	N	Y	N	Y	Y	Y	N	N
17 Engel	N	Y	N	Y	Y	Y	N	N
18 Lowey	N	Y	N	Y	Y	Y	N	N
19 ***Kelly***	Y	N	Y	Y	Y	Y	Y	Y
20 ***Gilman***	Y	N	Y	Y	Y	Y	Y	Y
21 McNulty	N	Y	N	N	Y	Y	N	Y
22 ***Sweeney***	Y	N	Y	Y	Y	Y	Y	Y
23 ***Boehlert***	Y	N	Y	Y	Y	Y	Y	Y
24 ***McHugh***	Y	N	Y	?	?	?	?	Y
25 ***Walsh***	Y	N	Y	Y	Y	Y	N	Y
26 Hinchey	N	Y	N	N	N	?	?	?
27 ***Reynolds***	Y	N	Y	Y	Y	Y	Y	Y
28 Slaughter	N	Y	N	N	Y	Y	N	Y
29 LaFalce	N	Y	Y	Y	N	Y	N	N

	175	176	177	178	179	180	181	182
30 ***Quinn***	Y	N	Y	Y	Y	Y	?	Y
31 ***Houghton***	Y	N	Y	Y	Y	Y	N	Y
NORTH CAROLINA								
1 Clayton	N	Y	N	Y	Y	Y	N	N
2 Etheridge	N	Y	N	Y	Y	Y	N	Y
3 ***Jones***	Y	N	Y	Y	Y	Y	Y	Y
4 Price	N	Y	N	Y	Y	Y	N	N
5 ***Burr***	Y	N	Y	Y	Y	Y	N	Y
6 ***Coble***	Y	N	Y	Y	Y	Y	Y	Y
7 McIntyre	N	Y	Y	Y	Y	Y	N	Y
8 ***Hayes***	Y	N	Y	Y	Y	Y	Y	Y
9 ***Myrick***	Y	N	Y	Y	Y	Y	Y	Y
10 ***Ballenger***	Y	N	Y	Y	Y	Y	Y	Y
11 ***Taylor***	Y	N	Y	Y	Y	Y	Y	Y
12 Watt	N	Y	N	Y	N	Y	N	N
NORTH DAKOTA								
AL Pomeroy	N	Y	N	N	Y	Y	N	N
OHIO								
1 ***Chabot***	Y	N	Y	Y	Y	Y	Y	Y
2 ***Portman***	Y	N	Y	Y	Y	Y	Y	Y
3 Hall	N	Y	Y	Y	Y	Y	N	Y
4 ***Oxley***	Y	N	Y	Y	Y	Y	N	Y
5 ***Gillmor***	Y	N	Y	Y	Y	Y	Y	Y
6 Strickland	N	Y	Y	N	Y	Y	N	Y
7 ***Hobson***	Y	N	Y	Y	Y	Y	N	Y
8 ***Boehner***	Y	N	Y	Y	Y	Y	N	Y
9 Kaptur	N	Y	N	Y	Y	Y	N	N
10 Kucinich	N	Y	N	N	N	Y	N	Y
11 Jones	N	Y	N	Y	N	Y	N	?
12 ***Kasich***	Y	N	Y	Y	Y	Y	?	?
13 Brown	N	Y	N	N	Y	Y	N	Y
14 Sawyer	N	Y	N	Y	Y	Y	N	N
15 ***Pryce***	Y	N	Y	Y	Y	Y	N	Y
16 ***Regula***	Y	N	Y	Y	Y	Y	N	Y
17 Traficant	Y	N	Y	Y	Y	Y	Y	Y
18 ***Ney***	Y	N	Y	Y	Y	Y	Y	Y
19 ***LaTourette***	Y	N	Y	Y	Y	Y	N	Y
OKLAHOMA								
1 ***Largent***	Y	N	Y	Y	Y	Y	N	Y
2 ***Coburn***	Y	N	Y	Y	Y	Y	Y	Y
3 ***Watkins***	N	N	Y	Y	Y	Y	Y	Y
4 ***Watts***	Y	N	Y	Y	Y	Y	Y	Y
5 ***Istook***	Y	N	Y	Y	Y	Y	Y	Y
6 ***Lucas***	Y	N	Y	Y	Y	?	Y	Y
OREGON								
1 Wu	N	Y	N	Y	N	Y	Y	Y
2 ***Walden***	Y	N	Y	Y	Y	Y	Y	Y
3 Blumenauer	N	Y	N	Y	Y	Y	N	N
4 DeFazio	N	Y	N	N	N	Y	N	Y
5 Hooley	N	Y	N	Y	N	Y	N	Y
PENNSYLVANIA								
1 Brady	N	Y	N	Y	Y	Y	N	N
2 Fattah	N	Y	N	Y	N	Y	N	N
3 Borski	N	Y	N	N	Y	Y	N	N
4 Klink	N	Y	N	Y	N	Y	N	N
5 ***Peterson***	Y	N	Y	Y	Y	Y	N	Y
6 Holden	N	Y	N	Y	Y	Y	N	Y
7 ***Weldon***	Y	N	Y	Y	Y	Y	N	N
8 ***Greenwood***	Y	N	Y	Y	Y	Y	Y	Y
9 ***Shuster***	Y	N	Y	Y	Y	Y	Y	Y
10 ***Sherwood***	Y	N	Y	Y	Y	Y	?	?
11 Kanjorski	N	Y	N	?	N	Y	N	N
12 Murtha	N	Y	N	Y	Y	Y	N	N
13 Hoeffel	N	Y	N	Y	Y	Y	N	N
14 Coyne	N	Y	N	Y	Y	Y	N	N
15 ***Toomey***	Y	N	Y	Y	Y	Y	Y	Y
16 ***Pitts***	Y	N	Y	Y	Y	Y	Y	Y
17 ***Gekas***	Y	N	Y	Y	Y	Y	Y	Y
18 Doyle	Y	Y	Y	?	Y	Y	N	Y
19 ***Goodling***	Y	N	Y	Y	Y	Y	Y	Y
20 Mascara	N	Y	N	Y	Y	Y	N	Y
21 ***English***	Y	N	Y	N	Y	Y	N	Y
RHODE ISLAND								
1 Kennedy	N	Y	N	Y	Y	Y	N	N
2 Weygand	N	Y	N	Y	Y	Y	N	Y
SOUTH CAROLINA								
1 ***Sanford***	Y	N	Y	Y	Y	Y	Y	Y
2 ***Spence***	Y	N	Y	Y	Y	Y	Y	Y
3 ***Graham***	Y	N	Y	Y	Y	Y	N	Y
4 ***DeMint***	Y	N	Y	Y	Y	Y	Y	Y
5 Spratt	N	Y	N	Y	Y	Y	N	N
6 Clyburn	N	Y	N	N	N	Y	N	N
SOUTH DAKOTA								
AL ***Thune***	Y	N	Y	Y	Y	Y	Y	Y

	175	176	177	178	179	180	181	182
TENNESSEE								
1 ***Jenkins***	Y	N	Y	Y	Y	Y	Y	Y
2 ***Duncan***	Y	N	Y	Y	Y	Y	Y	Y
3 ***Wamp***	Y	N	Y	Y	Y	Y	Y	Y
4 ***Hilleary***	Y	?	Y	N	Y	Y	Y	Y
5 Clement	N	Y	N	Y	Y	Y	N	Y
6 Gordon	N	Y	N	Y	Y	Y	N	Y
7 ***Bryant***	Y	N	Y	Y	Y	Y	Y	Y
8 Tanner	N	Y	N	N	Y	Y	N	Y
9 Ford	–	+	–	Y	Y	Y	N	N
TEXAS								
1 Sandlin	N	Y	N	Y	Y	Y	N	N
2 Turner	N	Y	N	Y	Y	Y	N	Y
3 ***Johnson, Sam***	Y	N	Y	Y	Y	Y	Y	Y
4 Hall	Y	Y	Y	Y	Y	Y	Y	Y
5 ***Sessions***	Y	N	Y	Y	Y	Y	Y	Y
6 ***Barton***	Y	N	Y	Y	Y	Y	Y	Y
7 ***Archer***	Y	N	Y	Y	Y	Y	Y	Y
8 ***Brady***	Y	N	Y	?	Y	Y	N	Y
9 Lampson	N	Y	N	Y	Y	Y	N	N
10 Doggett	Y	Y	N	Y	N	Y	N	N
11 Edwards	N	Y	Y	Y	Y	Y	N	Y
12 ***Granger***	Y	N	Y	Y	Y	Y	Y	Y
13 ***Thornberry***	Y	N	Y	Y	Y	Y	N	Y
14 ***Paul***	Y	N	N	?	Y	Y	Y	Y
15 Hinojosa	N	Y	N	Y	N	Y	N	N
16 Reyes	N	Y	Y	Y	Y	Y	N	N
17 Stenholm	N	Y	N	N	Y	Y	N	Y
18 Jackson-Lee	N	Y	N	Y	Y	Y	N	Y
19 ***Combest***	Y	N	Y	Y	Y	Y	N	Y
20 Gonzalez	N	Y	N	Y	Y	Y	N	N
21 ***Smith***	N	N	Y	Y	Y	Y	Y	Y
22 ***DeLay***	Y	N	Y	Y	Y	Y	Y	Y
23 ***Bonilla***	Y	N	Y	Y	Y	Y	Y	Y
24 Frost	N	Y	N	Y	Y	Y	N	Y
25 Bentsen	N	Y	Y	Y	Y	Y	N	Y
26 ***Armey***	Y	N	Y	Y	Y	Y	Y	Y
27 Ortiz	N	Y	Y	Y	Y	Y	N	N
28 Rodriguez	N	Y	N	Y	Y	Y	N	N
29 Green	N	Y	N	Y	Y	Y	N	Y
30 Johnson, E.B.	N	Y	N	N	Y	Y	N	N
UTAH								
1 ***Hansen***	Y	N	Y	Y	Y	Y	Y	Y
2 ***Cook***	Y	N	Y	Y	Y	Y	N	Y
3 ***Cannon***	Y	N	Y	Y	Y	Y	Y	Y
VERMONT								
AL *Sanders*	N	Y	N	Y	N	Y	N	Y
VIRGINIA								
1 ***Bateman***	Y	N	Y	Y	Y	Y	N	Y
2 Pickett	N	Y	Y	N	Y	Y	N	N
3 Scott	N	Y	N	Y	Y	Y	N	N
4 Sisisky	N	Y	Y	Y	Y	Y	N	N
5 Goode	Y	N	Y	Y	Y	Y	Y	Y
6 ***Goodlatte***	Y	N	Y	Y	Y	Y	Y	Y
7 ***Bliley***	Y	N	Y	Y	Y	Y	N	Y
8 Moran	Y	Y	N	Y	?	Y	N	N
9 Boucher	N	Y	N	?	Y	Y	N	N
10 ***Wolf***	Y	N	Y	Y	Y	Y	Y	Y
11 ***Davis***	Y	N	Y	Y	Y	Y	N	Y
WASHINGTON								
1 Inslee	N	Y	N	Y	Y	Y	N	Y
2 ***Metcalf***	Y	N	Y	Y	Y	Y	Y	Y
3 Baird	N	Y	N	N	Y	Y	N	N
4 ***Hastings***	Y	N	Y	Y	Y	Y	N	Y
5 ***Nethercutt***	Y	N	Y	Y	Y	Y	N	Y
6 Dicks	N	Y	N	Y	Y	Y	N	N
7 McDermott	N	Y	N	N	N	Y	N	N
8 ***Dunn***	Y	N	Y	Y	Y	Y	N	Y
9 Smith	Y	Y	N	Y	Y	Y	N	N
WEST VIRGINIA								
1 Mollohan	N	Y	Y	Y	Y	Y	N	N
2 Wise	N	Y	N	Y	Y	Y	N	Y
3 Rahall	N	Y	N	Y	Y	Y	N	N
WISCONSIN								
1 ***Ryan***	Y	N	Y	Y	Y	Y	Y	Y
2 Baldwin	N	Y	N	Y	N	Y	N	N
3 Kind	N	Y	N	Y	N	Y	N	N
4 Kleczka	Y	Y	N	Y	N	Y	N	N
5 Barrett	Y	Y	N	Y	N	Y	N	N
6 ***Petri***	Y	N	Y	Y	Y	Y	N	Y
7 Obey	N	Y	N	Y	N	Y	N	N
8 ***Green***	Y	N	Y	Y	Y	Y	N	Y
9 ***Sensenbrenner***	Y	N	N	Y	Y	Y	N	Y
WYOMING								
AL ***Cubin***	Y	N	Y	Y	Y	Y	Y	Y

Southern states - Ala., Ark., Fla., Ga., Ky., La., Miss., N.C., Okla., S.C., Tenn., Texas, Va.

183. HR 1401. Defense Authorization/End U.S. Military Presence in Haiti. Goss, R-Fla., amendment to prohibit use of Department of Defense funds to maintain a permanent U.S. military presence in Haiti beyond Dec. 31, 1999. Adopted 227-198: R 212-6; D 15-191 (ND 9-142, SD 6-49); I 0-1. June 9, 1999.

184. HR 1401. Defense Authorization/Permit Abortions in Military Hospitals. Meek, D-Fla., amendment to permit privately funded abortions in overseas military hospitals. Rejected 203-225: R 34-186; D 168-39 (ND 123-29, SD 45-10); I 1-0. June 9, 1999.

185. HR 1401. Defense Authorization/Thrift Savings Plan. Buyer, R-Ind., amendment to permit members of the armed services to deposit up to 5 percent of their monthly salary into a tax-deferred savings account. Adopted 425-0: R 218-0; D 206-0 (ND 151-0, SD 55-0); I 1-0. June 10, 1999.

186. HR 1401. Defense Authorization/Border Control. Traficant, D-Ohio, amendment to allow the Defense Department to assign military personnel to assist the border patrol and U.S. Customs Service in drug interdiction and counterterrorism activities along U.S. borders. Adopted 242-181: R 179-38; D 63-142 (ND 45-105, SD 18-37); I 0-1. June 10, 1999.

187. HR 1401. Defense Authorization/Operations in Yugoslavia. Souder, R-Ind., amendment to prohibit the Department of Defense from using any fiscal 2000 funds for military operations in Yugoslavia. The amendment would remove a provision of the bill that would allow the president to request supplemental funding for operations in Yugoslavia if he deems them necessary. Rejected 97-328: R 91-128; D 6-199 (ND 4-147, SD 2-52); I 0-1. June 10, 1999.

188. HR 1401. Defense Authorization/Space Launch Facilities. Weldon, R-Fla., amendment to authorize an additional $7.3 million for Air Force space launch facilities. Adopted 303-118: R 168-49; D 134-69 (ND 91-58, SD 43-11); I 1-0. June 10, 1999.

189. HR 1401. Defense Authorization/Operations in Yugoslavia. Skelton, D-Mo., amendment to strike bill language that would prohibit the use of funds authorized in the bill for air combat or peacekeeping operations in Yugoslavia. Adopted 270-155: R 77-142; D 192-13 (ND 141-10, SD 51-3); I 1-0. June 10, 1999.

190. HR 1401. Defense Authorization/Reduce U.S. Troops in Europe. Shays, R-Conn., amendment to reduce the number of U.S. troops in Europe from 100,000 to 25,000 over three fiscal years; the reductions would not apply if war were declared or a NATO member were attacked. Rejected 116-307: R 51-166; D 64-141 (ND 58-93, SD 6-48); I 1-0. June 10, 1999.

Key

- Y Voted for (yea).
- # Paired for.
- + Announced for.
- N Voted against (nay).
- X Paired against.
- – Announced against.
- P Voted "present."
- C Voted "present" to avoid possible conflict of interest.
- ? Did not vote or otherwise make a position known.

•

Democrats ***Republicans***
Independents

	183	184	185	186	187	188	189	190
ALABAMA								
1 ***Callahan***	Y	N	Y	N	N	Y	Y	N
2 ***Everett***	Y	N	Y	Y	N	Y	N	N
3 ***Riley***	Y	N	Y	Y	N	Y	N	N
4 ***Aderholt***	Y	N	Y	Y	Y	Y	N	N
5 Cramer	N	Y	Y	Y	N	Y	Y	N
6 ***Bachus***	Y	N	Y	Y	Y	Y	N	N
7 Hilliard	N	Y	Y	N	N	Y	Y	N
ALASKA								
AL ***Young***	Y	N	Y	N	N	Y	Y	N
ARIZONA								
1 ***Salmon***	Y	N	Y	Y	Y	Y	N	Y
2 Pastor	N	Y	Y	N	N	Y	Y	N
3 ***Stump***	Y	N	Y	N	Y	N	N	N
4 ***Shadegg***	Y	N	Y	Y	Y	Y	N	Y
5 ***Kolbe***	Y	Y	Y	N	N	Y	Y	N
6 ***Hayworth***	Y	N	Y	N	Y	Y	N	N
ARKANSAS								
1 Berry	N	N	Y	N	N	Y	Y	N
2 Snyder	N	Y	Y	N	N	Y	Y	N
3 ***Hutchinson***	Y	N	Y	Y	N	Y	N	N
4 ***Dickey***	Y	N	Y	Y	?	N	N	N
CALIFORNIA								
1 Thompson	N	Y	Y	N	N	Y	Y	Y
2 ***Herger***	Y	N	Y	Y	Y	Y	N	N
3 ***Ose***	Y	Y	Y	N	N	Y	Y	N
4 ***Doolittle***	Y	N	Y	N	Y	Y	N	N
5 Matsui	N	Y	Y	N	N	N	Y	N
6 Woolsey	N	Y	Y	N	N	N	Y	Y
7 Miller, George	N	Y	Y	N	N	N	Y	Y
8 Pelosi	N	Y	Y	N	N	Y	Y	Y
9 Lee	N	Y	Y	N	N	N	N	Y
10 Tauscher	N	Y	Y	Y	N	N	Y	N
11 ***Pombo***	Y	N	Y	N	Y	Y	N	N
12 Lantos	N	Y	Y	Y	N	Y	Y	N
13 Stark	?	?	Y	N	N	N	N	Y
14 Eshoo	N	Y	Y	Y	N	Y	Y	Y
15 ***Campbell***	N	Y	Y	Y	Y	Y	N	Y
16 Lofgren	N	Y	?	?	?	?	?	?
17 Farr	N	Y	Y	N	N	Y	Y	Y
18 Condit	Y	Y	Y	N	N	N	Y	Y
19 ***Radanovich***	Y	N	Y	Y	Y	Y	N	N
20 Dooley	N	Y	Y	N	N	Y	Y	N
21 ***Thomas***	Y	Y	Y	Y	N	Y	Y	N
22 Capps	N	Y	Y	N	N	Y	Y	N
23 ***Gallegly***	Y	N	Y	Y	N	Y	N	N
24 Sherman	N	Y	Y	Y	N	Y	Y	N
25 ***McKeon***	Y	N	Y	Y	N	Y	Y	N
26 Berman	N	Y	Y	N	N	Y	Y	N
27 ***Rogan***	Y	N	Y	Y	Y	N	N	N
28 ***Dreier***	Y	N	Y	N	N	N	Y	N
29 Waxman	N	Y	Y	N	N	Y	Y	Y
30 Becerra	N	Y	Y	N	N	Y	Y	N
31 Martinez	N	Y	Y	N	N	Y	Y	N
32 Dixon	N	Y	Y	N	N	Y	Y	N
33 Roybal-Allard	N	Y	Y	N	N	Y	Y	N
34 Napolitano	N	Y	Y	N	N	Y	Y	N
35 Waters	N	Y	Y	N	N	Y	Y	N
36 ***Kuykendall***	Y	Y	Y	Y	N	N	Y	N
37 Millender-McD.	N	Y	Y	N	N	Y	Y	N
38 ***Horn***	Y	Y	Y	Y	Y	N	N	N
39 ***Royce***	Y	N	Y	Y	Y	Y	N	Y
40 ***Lewis***	?	N	Y	Y	N	Y	Y	N
41 ***Miller, Gary***	Y	N	Y	Y	Y	N	N	N
42 Brown	?	?	?	?	?	?	?	?
43 ***Calvert***	Y	N	Y	Y	N	Y	Y	N
44 ***Bono***	Y	Y	+	+	–	+	–	+
45 ***Rohrabacher***	Y	N	Y	Y	Y	Y	N	Y
46 Sanchez	N	Y	Y	N	N	N	Y	N
47 ***Cox***	Y	N	Y	N	N	Y	Y	N
48 ***Packard***	Y	N	Y	Y	N	Y	Y	N
49 ***Bilbray***	Y	N	Y	Y	Y	N	N	Y
50 Filner	N	Y	Y	N	N	Y	Y	N
51 ***Cunningham***	Y	N	Y	Y	N	Y	Y	N
52 ***Hunter***	Y	N	Y	Y	N	Y	Y	N
COLORADO								
1 DeGette	N	Y	Y	N	N	N	Y	N
2 Udall	N	Y	Y	N	N	Y	Y	N
3 ***McInnis***	Y	N	Y	Y	N	N	N	N
4 ***Schaffer***	Y	N	Y	Y	Y	Y	N	N
5 ***Hefley***	Y	N	Y	Y	Y	Y	N	N
6 ***Tancredo***	Y	N	Y	Y	Y	Y	Y	Y
CONNECTICUT								
1 Larson	N	Y	Y	N	N	Y	Y	N
2 Gejdenson	N	Y	Y	N	N	Y	Y	N
3 DeLauro	N	Y	Y	N	N	Y	Y	N
4 ***Shays***	Y	Y	Y	Y	Y	N	N	Y
5 Maloney	N	Y	Y	Y	N	N	Y	N
6 ***Johnson***	Y	Y	Y	Y	N	N	Y	N
DELAWARE								
AL ***Castle***	Y	Y	Y	Y	N	Y	Y	N
FLORIDA								
1 ***Scarborough***	Y	N	Y	Y	Y	Y	N	N
2 Boyd	N	Y	Y	Y	N	Y	Y	N
3 Brown	N	Y	Y	Y	N	Y	Y	N
4 ***Fowler***	Y	Y	Y	Y	N	Y	Y	N
5 Thurman	N	Y	Y	Y	N	Y	Y	N
6 ***Stearns***	Y	N	Y	Y	N	Y	N	N
7 ***Mica***	Y	N	Y	Y	Y	Y	N	N
8 ***McCollum***	Y	N	Y	Y	N	Y	N	N
9 ***Bilirakis***	Y	N	Y	Y	Y	Y	N	N
10 ***Young***	Y	N	Y	Y	N	Y	Y	N
11 Davis	N	Y	Y	N	N	Y	Y	N
12 ***Canady***	Y	N	Y	Y	Y	Y	N	N
13 ***Miller***	Y	Y	Y	Y	N	Y	N	N
14 ***Goss***	Y	N	Y	Y	N	Y	Y	N
15 ***Weldon***	Y	N	Y	Y	Y	Y	N	N
16 ***Foley***	Y	Y	Y	Y	N	Y	N	Y
17 Meek	N	Y	Y	N	N	Y	Y	N
18 ***Ros-Lehtinen***	N	N	Y	Y	Y	Y	N	Y
19 Wexler	N	Y	Y	N	N	Y	Y	N
20 Deutsch	N	Y	Y	Y	N	Y	Y	N
21 ***Diaz-Balart***	N	N	Y	Y	N	Y	Y	N
22 ***Shaw***	Y	Y	Y	Y	N	Y	Y	N
23 Hastings	N	Y	Y	N	N	Y	Y	N
GEORGIA								
1 ***Kingston***	Y	N	Y	Y	Y	Y	N	Y
2 Bishop	N	Y	Y	N	N	Y	Y	N
3 ***Collins***	Y	N	Y	Y	Y	Y	N	N
4 McKinney	N	Y	Y	N	Y	Y	N	Y
5 Lewis	N	Y	Y	N	N	Y	Y	Y
6 ***Isakson***	Y	Y	Y	Y	N	Y	Y	N
7 ***Barr***	Y	N	Y	Y	Y	Y	N	Y
8 ***Chambliss***	Y	N	Y	Y	N	Y	Y	N
9 ***Deal***	Y	N	Y	Y	N	Y	N	Y
10 ***Norwood***	Y	N	Y	Y	N	Y	N	Y
11 ***Linder***	Y	N	Y	Y	N	Y	N	Y
HAWAII								
1 Abercrombie	N	Y	Y	N	N	Y	Y	N
2 Mink	N	Y	Y	N	N	N	N	Y
IDAHO								
1 ***Chenoweth***	Y	N	Y	N	Y	Y	N	Y
2 ***Simpson***	Y	N	Y	Y	N	N	Y	N
ILLINOIS								
1 Rush	?	Y	Y	N	N	Y	Y	Y
2 Jackson	N	Y	Y	N	N	Y	N	Y
3 Lipinski	N	N	Y	Y	N	N	Y	N
4 Gutierrez	N	Y	Y	N	N	N	Y	N
5 Blagojevich	N	Y	Y	N	N	N	Y	Y
6 ***Hyde***	Y	N	Y	N	N	Y	Y	N
7 Davis	N	Y	Y	N	N	Y	Y	Y
8 ***Crane***	Y	N	Y	Y	Y	Y	N	Y
9 Schakowsky	N	Y	Y	N	N	Y	Y	Y
10 ***Porter***	Y	Y	Y	N	N	N	Y	N
11 ***Weller***	Y	N	Y	Y	N	Y	Y	N
12 Costello	N	N	Y	Y	N	N	Y	Y
13 ***Biggert***	Y	Y	Y	N	N	Y	Y	N
14 ***Hastert***							Y	

ND Northern Democrats SD Southern Democrats

	183	184	185	186	187	188	189	190
15 *Ewing*	Y	N	Y	Y	Y	N	N	N
16 *Manzullo*	Y	N	Y	+	Y	Y	N	N
17 Evans	N	Y	Y	N	N	Y	Y	Y
18 *LaHood*	Y	N	Y	Y	Y	Y	N	N
19 Phelps	N	N	Y	Y	N	N	Y	Y
20 *Shimkus*	Y	N	Y	Y	N	N	N	Y
INDIANA								
1 Visclosky	?	?	Y	N	N	Y	Y	N
2 *McIntosh*	Y	N	Y	Y	N	Y	N	N
3 Roemer	Y	N	Y	Y	N	N	Y	N
4 *Souder*	Y	N	Y	Y	Y	Y	N	Y
5 *Buyer*	Y	N	Y	N	N	Y	Y	N
6 *Burton*	Y	N	Y	Y	Y	Y	N	N
7 *Pease*	Y	N	Y	Y	Y	Y	N	N
8 *Hostettler*	Y	N	Y	Y	Y	Y	N	N
9 Hill	N	Y	Y	N	N	Y	Y	N
10 Carson	N	Y	Y	N	N	Y	Y	N
IOWA								
1 *Leach*	Y	Y	Y	N	N	Y	N	N
2 *Nussle*	Y	N	Y	Y	N	N	N	Y
3 Boswell	N	Y	Y	Y	N	N	Y	N
4 *Ganske*	Y	N	Y	Y	Y	Y	N	Y
5 *Latham*	Y	N	Y	Y	N	N	N	N
KANSAS								
1 *Moran*	Y	N	Y	Y	N	N	N	N
2 *Ryun*	Y	N	Y	Y	N	Y	N	N
3 Moore	N	Y	Y	N	N	Y	Y	N
4 *Tiahrt*	Y	N	Y	Y	N	Y	N	Y
KENTUCKY								
1 *Whitfield*	Y	N	Y	N	N	N	N	N
2 *Lewis*	Y	N	Y	Y	Y	Y	N	N
3 *Northup*	Y	N	Y	Y	N	Y	Y	N
4 Lucas	N	N	Y	Y	N	N	Y	N
5 *Rogers*	Y	N	Y	Y	N	Y	N	N
6 *Fletcher*	Y	N	Y	Y	N	Y	N	N
LOUISIANA								
1 *Vitter*	Y	N	Y	Y	Y	Y	N	N
2 Jefferson	N	Y	Y	N	N	Y	Y	Y
3 *Tauzin*	Y	N	Y	Y	Y	Y	N	Y
4 *McCrery*	Y	N	Y	Y	N	Y	N	N
5 *Cooksey*	Y	N	?	Y	N	Y	Y	N
6 *Baker*	Y	N	Y	Y	Y	N	N	N
7 John	N	N	Y	Y	N	Y	Y	N
MAINE								
1 Allen	N	Y	Y	N	N	Y	Y	N
2 Baldacci	N	Y	Y	N	N	Y	Y	N
MARYLAND								
1 *Gilchrest*	Y	Y	Y	Y	N	Y	Y	N
2 *Ehrlich*	Y	Y	Y	N	N	Y	N	N
3 Cardin	N	Y	Y	N	N	Y	Y	N
4 Wynn	N	Y	?	?	N	Y	Y	N
5 Hoyer	N	Y	Y	N	N	Y	Y	N
6 *Bartlett*	Y	N	Y	Y	Y	Y	N	Y
7 Cummings	N	Y	Y	N	N	N	Y	N
8 *Morella*	Y	Y	Y	N	N	Y	Y	Y
MASSACHUSETTS								
1 Olver	N	Y	?	?	?	?	?	?
2 Neal	N	Y	Y	N	N	N	Y	Y
3 McGovern	N	Y	Y	N	N	Y	Y	Y
4 Frank	N	Y	Y	N	N	N	Y	Y
5 Meehan	N	Y	Y	N	N	Y	Y	Y
6 Tierney	N	Y	Y	N	N	N	Y	Y
7 Markey	N	Y	Y	N	N	N	Y	Y
8 Capuano	N	Y	Y	N	N	N	Y	Y
9 Moakley	N	N	Y	Y	N	?	Y	Y
10 Delahunt	N	Y	Y	N	N	Y	Y	Y
MICHIGAN								
1 Stupak	N	N	Y	N	N	Y	Y	N
2 *Hoekstra*	Y	N	Y	Y	Y	Y	N	Y
3 *Ehlers*	Y	N	Y	N	N	Y	N	N
4 *Camp*	Y	N	Y	Y	N	N	Y	N
5 Barcia	Y	N	Y	Y	N	Y	Y	Y
6 *Upton*	Y	N	Y	Y	N	N	Y	Y
7 *Smith*	Y	N	Y	Y	Y	Y	Y	N
8 Stabenow	N	Y	Y	Y	N	Y	Y	Y
9 Kildee	N	N	Y	Y	N	Y	Y	N
10 Bonior	N	Y	Y	N	N	N	Y	Y
11 *Knollenberg*	Y	N	Y	N	N	N	Y	N
12 Levin	N	Y	Y	Y	N	Y	Y	N
13 Rivers	N	Y	Y	Y	N	N	N	Y
14 Conyers	N	Y	Y	?	N	N	Y	Y
15 Kilpatrick	N	Y	Y	N	N	N	Y	N
16 Dingell	N	Y	Y	N	N	N	Y	N

	183	184	185	186	187	188	189	190
MINNESOTA								
1 *Gutknecht*	Y	N	Y	Y	N	Y	N	Y
2 Minge	Y	Y	Y	N	N	N	Y	Y
3 *Ramstad*	Y	Y	Y	Y	Y	N	N	Y
4 Vento	N	Y	Y	N	N	N	Y	Y
5 Sabo	N	Y	Y	N	N	N	Y	N
6 Luther	N	Y	Y	Y	N	?	?	?
7 Peterson	Y	N	Y	Y	Y	N	N	Y
8 Oberstar	N	N	Y	N	N	Y	Y	N
MISSISSIPPI								
1 *Wicker*	Y	N	Y	Y	N	Y	N	N
2 Thompson	N	Y	Y	N	N	Y	Y	N
3 *Pickering*	Y	N	Y	Y	N	Y	N	N
4 Shows	N	N	Y	Y	N	Y	Y	N
5 Taylor	Y	N	Y	Y	N	Y	Y	N
MISSOURI								
1 Clay	N	Y	Y	Y	N	?	?	?
2 *Talent*	Y	N	Y	Y	N	N	N	N
3 Gephardt	N	Y	Y	Y	N	N	Y	Y
4 Skelton	N	N	Y	N	N	N	Y	N
5 McCarthy	N	Y	Y	N	N	Y	Y	N
6 Danner	Y	N	Y	Y	Y	N	N	Y
7 *Blunt*	Y	N	Y	Y	N	?	N	N
8 *Emerson*	Y	N	Y	Y	N	Y	N	Y
9 *Hulshof*	Y	N	Y	Y	Y	Y	N	N
MONTANA								
AL *Hill*	Y	N	Y	Y	Y	Y	N	Y
NEBRASKA								
1 *Bereuter*	Y	N	Y	Y	N	Y	Y	N
2 *Terry*	Y	N	Y	N	Y	Y	Y	N
3 *Barrett*	Y	N	Y	Y	N	Y	N	N
NEVADA								
1 Berkley	N	Y	Y	N	N	Y	Y	N
2 *Gibbons*	Y	N	Y	Y	Y	Y	N	N
NEW HAMPSHIRE								
1 *Sununu*	Y	N	Y	Y	Y	Y	N	N
2 *Bass*	Y	Y	Y	Y	N	Y	N	N
NEW JERSEY								
1 Andrews	N	Y	Y	Y	N	N	Y	N
2 *LoBiondo*	Y	N	Y	Y	Y	Y	N	N
3 *Saxton*	Y	N	Y	Y	N	Y	Y	N
4 *Smith*	Y	N	Y	Y	N	Y	Y	N
5 *Roukema*	Y	Y	Y	Y	N	N	N	N
6 Pallone	N	Y	Y	Y	N	Y	Y	N
7 *Franks*	Y	Y	Y	Y	N	N	Y	Y
8 Pascrell	N	Y	Y	Y	N	Y	Y	N
9 Rothman	N	Y	Y	N	N	Y	Y	N
10 Payne	N	Y	Y	N	N	Y	Y	N
11 *Frelinghuysen*	Y	Y	Y	Y	N	Y	N	N
12 Holt	N	Y	+	–	–	Y	Y	N
13 Menendez	N	Y	Y	N	N	Y	Y	N
NEW MEXICO								
1 *Wilson*	Y	N	Y	Y	N	Y	N	N
2 *Skeen*	Y	N	Y	Y	N	Y	Y	N
3 Udall	N	Y	Y	N	N	N	Y	Y
NEW YORK								
1 *Forbes*	N	N	Y	Y	N	Y	Y	N
2 *Lazio*	Y	N	Y	Y	N	Y	N	N
3 *King*	N	N	Y	N	N	Y	Y	N
4 McCarthy	N	Y	Y	Y	N	Y	Y	N
5 Ackerman	N	Y	Y	N	N	N	Y	N
6 Meeks	N	Y	Y	N	N	Y	Y	Y
7 Crowley	N	N	Y	N	N	N	Y	N
8 Nadler	N	Y	Y	N	N	?	Y	Y
9 Weiner	N	Y	Y	N	N	N	Y	Y
10 Towns	N	Y	Y	N	N	N	Y	Y
11 Owens	N	Y	Y	N	N	N	Y	Y
12 Velázquez	N	Y	Y	N	N	N	Y	Y
13 *Fossella*	Y	N	Y	Y	N	N	N	N
14 Maloney	N	Y	Y	N	N	N	Y	N
15 Rangel	N	Y	Y	N	N	N	Y	N
16 Serrano	N	Y	Y	N	N	N	N	Y
17 Engel	N	Y	Y	Y	?	Y	Y	N
18 Lowey	N	Y	Y	Y	N	Y	Y	N
19 *Kelly*	Y	Y	Y	Y	N	Y	Y	N
20 *Gilman*	Y	Y	Y	Y	N	Y	Y	N
21 McNulty	Y	N	Y	Y	N	N	Y	N
22 *Sweeney*	Y	N	Y	Y	N	Y	N	N
23 *Boehlert*	Y	Y	Y	Y	N	Y	Y	N
24 *McHugh*	N	N	Y	Y	N	Y	Y	N
25 *Walsh*	Y	N	Y	N	N	Y	Y	Y
26 Hinchey	?	?	Y	N	N	N	Y	N
27 *Reynolds*	Y	N	Y	Y	N	Y	N	N
28 Slaughter	N	Y	Y	N	N	N	Y	Y
29 LaFalce	N	N	Y	Y	N	Y	Y	N

	183	184	185	186	187	188	189	190
30 *Quinn*	Y	N	Y	Y	N	Y	N	N
31 *Houghton*	Y	Y	Y	N	N	Y	Y	N
NORTH CAROLINA								
1 Clayton	N	Y	Y	N	–	+	+	–
2 Etheridge	N	Y	Y	Y	N	Y	Y	N
3 *Jones*	Y	N	Y	Y	Y	N	N	Y
4 Price	N	Y	Y	Y	N	Y	Y	N
5 *Burr*	Y	N	Y	N	N	Y	N	N
6 *Coble*	Y	N	Y	Y	Y	N	N	Y
7 McIntyre	Y	N	Y	Y	N	Y	Y	N
8 *Hayes*	Y	N	Y	N	Y	Y	N	Y
9 *Myrick*	Y	N	Y	Y	Y	Y	N	Y
10 *Ballenger*	Y	N	Y	Y	N	Y	Y	Y
11 *Taylor*	Y	N	Y	Y	Y	N	N	N
12 Watt	N	Y	Y	N	N	N	Y	N
NORTH DAKOTA								
AL Pomeroy	N	Y	Y	N	N	Y	Y	N
OHIO								
1 *Chabot*	Y	N	Y	Y	Y	N	N	Y
2 *Portman*	Y	N	Y	Y	N	Y	N	N
3 Hall	N	N	Y	Y	N	Y	Y	N
4 *Oxley*	Y	N	Y	Y	N	Y	N	N
5 *Gillmor*	Y	N	Y	Y	N	Y	Y	N
6 Strickland	N	Y	Y	N	N	Y	Y	N
7 *Hobson*	Y	N	Y	Y	N	Y	Y	N
8 *Boehner*	Y	N	Y	Y	N	Y	Y	N
9 Kaptur	N	N	Y	Y	N	Y	Y	N
10 Kucinich	N	N	Y	Y	Y	Y	N	Y
11 Jones	N	Y	Y	N	N	Y	Y	N
12 *Kasich*	?	?	?	?	Y	?	?	?
13 Brown	N	Y	Y	N	N	N	Y	Y
14 Sawyer	N	Y	Y	N	N	Y	Y	N
15 *Pryce*	Y	Y	Y	Y	N	Y	Y	N
16 *Regula*	Y	N	Y	Y	N	Y	Y	N
17 Traficant	Y	N	Y	Y	N	Y	Y	Y
18 *Ney*	Y	N	Y	Y	N	Y	N	Y
19 *LaTourette*	Y	N	Y	Y	N	Y	Y	N
OKLAHOMA								
1 *Largent*	Y	N	Y	Y	Y	Y	Y	N
2 *Coburn*	?	N	Y	Y	Y	Y	N	N
3 *Watkins*	Y	N	Y	Y	Y	Y	N	N
4 *Watts*	Y	N	Y	Y	Y	Y	Y	N
5 *Istook*	Y	N	Y	Y	Y	Y	N	N
6 *Lucas*	Y	N	Y	Y	Y	Y	N	N
OREGON								
1 Wu	N	Y	Y	N	N	Y	Y	Y
2 *Walden*	Y	Y	Y	Y	N	Y	N	N
3 Blumenauer	N	Y	Y	N	N	Y	Y	Y
4 DeFazio	Y	Y	Y	N	N	Y	Y	Y
5 Hooley	N	Y	Y	N	N	Y	Y	Y
PENNSYLVANIA								
1 Brady	N	Y	Y	N	N	Y	Y	N
2 Fattah	N	Y	Y	N	N	Y	Y	N
3 Borski	N	N	Y	N	N	N	Y	N
4 Klink	N	N	Y	N	N	Y	Y	N
5 *Peterson*	Y	N	Y	Y	N	Y	N	?
6 Holden	N	N	Y	Y	N	Y	Y	N
7 *Weldon*	Y	N	Y	Y	N	Y	Y	N
8 *Greenwood*	Y	Y	Y	Y	N	N	Y	N
9 *Shuster*	Y	N	Y	Y	Y	N	N	N
10 *Sherwood*	?	?	Y	Y	N	N	Y	N
11 Kanjorski	N	N	Y	N	N	Y	Y	N
12 Murtha	N	N	Y	Y	N	Y	Y	N
13 Hoeffel	N	Y	Y	N	N	Y	Y	N
14 Coyne	N	Y	Y	N	N	N	Y	N
15 *Toomey*	Y	N	Y	N	N	Y	N	N
16 *Pitts*	Y	N	Y	Y	Y	N	N	N
17 *Gekas*	Y	N	Y	Y	N	Y	Y	N
18 Doyle	N	N	Y	Y	N	Y	Y	N
19 *Goodling*	Y	N	Y	N	Y	N	N	N
20 Mascara	N	N	Y	Y	N	Y	Y	N
21 *English*	Y	N	Y	Y	N	Y	Y	Y
RHODE ISLAND								
1 Kennedy	N	Y	Y	N	N	Y	Y	N
2 Weygand	N	N	Y	N	N	Y	Y	N
SOUTH CAROLINA								
1 *Sanford*	Y	N	Y	N	Y	N	N	Y
2 *Spence*	Y	N	Y	Y	N	Y	Y	N
3 *Graham*	Y	N	Y	N	Y	?	?	?
4 *DeMint*	Y	N	Y	Y	Y	Y	N	Y
5 Spratt	N	Y	Y	Y	N	Y	Y	N
6 Clyburn	N	Y	Y	N	N	Y	Y	N
SOUTH DAKOTA								
AL *Thune*	Y	N	Y	Y	N	N	N	N

	183	184	185	186	187	188	189	190
TENNESSEE								
1 *Jenkins*	Y	N	Y	N	Y	N	N	N
2 *Duncan*	Y	N	Y	Y	Y	N	N	Y
3 *Wamp*	Y	N	Y	Y	Y	N	N	Y
4 *Hilleary*	Y	N	+	+	+	+	–	+
5 Clement	N	Y	Y	N	N	Y	Y	N
6 Gordon	N	Y	Y	Y	N	N	Y	N
7 *Bryant*	Y	N	Y	Y	Y	Y	N	N
8 Tanner	Y	Y	Y	N	N	Y	Y	N
9 Ford	N	Y	Y	N	N	Y	Y	N
TEXAS								
1 Sandlin	N	Y	Y	Y	N	Y	Y	N
2 Turner	N	Y	Y	N	N	N	Y	N
3 *Johnson, Sam*	Y	N	Y	Y	N	N	N	N
4 Hall	Y	N	Y	Y	Y	Y	N	Y
5 *Sessions*	Y	N	Y	Y	Y	Y	N	N
6 *Barton*	Y	N	Y	Y	N	Y	N	N
7 *Archer*	Y	N	Y	Y	Y	N	N	N
8 *Brady*	Y	N	Y	Y	Y	Y	N	N
9 Lampson	N	Y	Y	N	N	Y	Y	N
10 Doggett	N	Y	Y	N	N	N	Y	N
11 Edwards	N	Y	Y	N	N	Y	Y	N
12 *Granger*	Y	N	Y	Y	N	Y	Y	N
13 *Thornberry*	Y	N	Y	N	N	Y	N	N
14 *Paul*	Y	N	Y	N	Y	N	N	Y
15 Hinojosa	N	Y	Y	N	N	Y	Y	N
16 Reyes	N	Y	Y	N	N	Y	Y	N
17 Stenholm	Y	N	Y	N	N	Y	Y	N
18 Jackson-Lee	N	Y	Y	N	N	Y	Y	N
19 *Combest*	Y	N	Y	Y	Y	Y	N	N
20 Gonzalez	N	Y	Y	N	N	Y	Y	N
21 *Smith*	Y	N	Y	Y	N	Y	N	Y
22 *DeLay*	Y	N	Y	Y	N	Y	Y	N
23 *Bonilla*	Y	N	Y	N	Y	Y	N	N
24 Frost	N	Y	Y	N	N	Y	Y	N
25 Bentsen	N	Y	Y	N	N	Y	Y	N
26 *Armey*	Y	N	Y	N	N	Y	Y	N
27 Ortiz	N	N	Y	N	N	Y	Y	N
28 Rodriguez	N	Y	Y	N	N	Y	Y	N
29 Green	N	Y	Y	N	N	Y	Y	Y
30 Johnson, E.B.	N	Y	Y	N	N	Y	Y	N
UTAH								
1 *Hansen*	Y	N	Y	N	N	Y	Y	N
2 *Cook*	Y	N	Y	Y	Y	Y	N	Y
3 *Cannon*	Y	N	Y	Y	Y	Y	N	Y
VERMONT								
AL Sanders	N	Y	Y	N	N	Y	Y	Y
VIRGINIA								
1 *Bateman*	Y	N	Y	N	N	N	N	N
2 Pickett	N	Y	Y	N	N	N	Y	N
3 Scott	N	Y	Y	N	N	N	Y	N
4 Sisisky	N	Y	Y	Y	N	N	Y	N
5 Goode	Y	N	Y	Y	Y	N	N	Y
6 *Goodlatte*	Y	N	Y	Y	Y	Y	N	N
7 *Bliley*	Y	N	Y	?	N	N	N	N
8 Moran	N	Y	Y	N	N	N	Y	N
9 Boucher	N	Y	Y	N	N	N	Y	N
10 *Wolf*	Y	N	Y	Y	N	Y	Y	N
11 *Davis*	Y	N	Y	Y	N	N	Y	N
WASHINGTON								
1 Inslee	N	Y	Y	Y	N	Y	Y	Y
2 *Metcalf*	Y	N	Y	Y	Y	Y	N	Y
3 Baird	N	Y	Y	Y	N	Y	Y	N
4 *Hastings*	Y	N	Y	Y	Y	Y	N	N
5 *Nethercutt*	Y	N	Y	Y	Y	Y	N	N
6 Dicks	N	Y	Y	Y	N	Y	Y	N
7 McDermott	N	Y	Y	N	N	N	Y	Y
8 *Dunn*	Y	Y	Y	Y	N	N	N	N
9 Smith	N	Y	Y	Y	N	N	Y	N
WEST VIRGINIA								
1 Mollohan	N	N	Y	N	N	Y	Y	N
2 Wise	N	Y	Y	Y	N	Y	Y	N
3 Rahall	N	N	Y	Y	N	N	Y	N
WISCONSIN								
1 *Ryan*	Y	N	Y	Y	N	Y	Y	N
2 Baldwin	N	Y	Y	N	N	Y	N	Y
3 Kind	N	Y	Y	Y	N	Y	Y	N
4 Kleczka	N	Y	Y	N	N	Y	Y	N
5 Barrett	N	Y	Y	N	N	N	Y	Y
6 *Petri*	Y	N	Y	Y	Y	N	N	N
7 Obey	N	Y	Y	N	N	N	Y	N
8 *Green*	Y	N	Y	Y	N	Y	Y	N
9 *Sensenbrenner*	Y	N	Y	Y	Y	Y	N	Y
WYOMING								
AL *Cubin*	Y	N	Y	Y	Y	Y	Y	N

Southern states - Ala., Ark., Fla., Ga., Ky., La., Miss., N.C., Okla., S.C., Tenn., Texas, Va.

House Votes 191, 192, 193, 194, 195, 196, 197, 198

191. HR 1401. Defense Authorization/Passage. Passage of the bill to provide $288.8 billion in new budget authority for defense activities in fiscal 2000 including $74 billion for military personnel; $106.5 billion for operations and maintenance; $55.6 billion for weapons procurement; $35.8 for research and development; $8.6 billion for military construction and family housing; and $12.3 billion for defense-related programs at the Department of Energy; and a 4.8 percent military pay raise and increased retirement benefits. Passed 365-58: R 214-4; D 151-53 (ND 101-50, SD 50-3); I 0-1. June 10, 1999.

192. Procedural Motion/Adjourn. Obey, D-Wis., motion to adjourn. Rejected 104-302: R 0-210; D 103-92 (ND 86-58, SD 17-34); I 1-0. June 10, 1999.

193. Procedural Motion/Adjourn. Obey, D-Wis., motion to adjourn. Rejected 96-298: R 1-202; D 95-96 (ND 80-64, SD 15-32); I 0-0. June 10, 1999.

194. HR 1905. Fiscal 2000 Legislative Branch Appropriations/Previous Question. Pryce, R-Ohio, motion to order the previous question (thus ending debate and the possibility of amendment) on adoption of the rule (H Res 190), with an amendment, to allow for House floor consideration of the legislative branch appropriations bill. Motion agreed to 213-198: R 209-0; D 4-197 (ND 2-146, SD 2-51); I 0-1. June 10, 1999.

195. HR 1905. Fiscal 2000 Legislative Branch Appropriations/Motion To Table. Pryce, R-Ohio, motion to table (kill) Obey, D-Wis., motion to reconsider the previous vote. Motion agreed to 218-194: R 212-0; D 6-193 (ND 3-144, SD 3-49); I 0-1. June 10, 1999.

196. HR 1905. Fiscal 2000 Legislative Branch Appropriations/Rule. Pryce, R-Ohio, amendment to the rule (H Res 190) for floor consideration of the legislative branch appropriations bill. The amendment would make in order an amendment by Young, R-Fla., to cut $54.8 million from the bill. Adopted 232-182: R 212-1; D 20-180 (ND 9-138, SD 11-42); I 0-1. June 10, 1999.

197. HR 1905. Fiscal 2000 Legislative Branch Appropriations/Motion To Table. Pryce, R-Ohio, motion to table Obey, D-Wis., motion to reconsider the previous vote. Motion agreed to 230-180: R 213-1; D 17-178 (ND 8-134, SD 9-44); I 0-1. June 10, 1999.

198. HR 1905. Legislative Branch Appropriations/Rule. Adoption of the rule (H Res 190), as amended, to provide for House floor consideration of the bill to provide $1.9 billion in fiscal 2000 appropriations for the House of Representatives and other legislative branch operations. Adopted 216-194: R 213-0; D 3-193 (ND 3-140, SD 0-53); I 0-1. June 10, 1999.

Key

Y Voted for (yea).
\# Paired for.
\+ Announced for.
N Voted against (nay).
X Paired against.
– Announced against.
P Voted "present."
C Voted "present" to avoid possible conflict of interest.
? Did not vote or otherwise make a position known.

•

Democrats ***Republicans***
Independents

	191	192	193	194	195	196	197	198
ALABAMA								
1 ***Callahan***	Y	N	N	Y	Y	Y	Y	Y
2 ***Everett***	Y	N	N	Y	Y	Y	Y	Y
3 ***Riley***	Y	N	N	Y	Y	Y	Y	Y
4 ***Aderholt***	Y	N	N	Y	Y	Y	Y	Y
5 Cramer	Y	N	N	N	N	Y	Y	N
6 ***Bachus***	Y	N	N	Y	Y	Y	Y	Y
7 Hilliard	Y	N	N	N	N	N	N	N
ALASKA								
AL ***Young***	Y	N	N	Y	Y	Y	Y	Y
ARIZONA								
1 ***Salmon***	Y	N	N	Y	Y	Y	Y	Y
2 Pastor	Y	Y	Y	N	N	N	N	N
3 ***Stump***	Y	N	N	Y	Y	Y	Y	Y
4 ***Shadegg***	Y	N	N	Y	Y	Y	Y	Y
5 ***Kolbe***	Y	N	N	Y	Y	Y	Y	Y
6 ***Hayworth***	Y	N	N	Y	Y	Y	Y	Y
ARKANSAS								
1 Berry	Y	N	N	N	N	Y	N	N
2 Snyder	Y	N	N	N	N	N	N	N
3 ***Hutchinson***	Y	N	N	Y	Y	Y	Y	Y
4 ***Dickey***	Y	N	N	Y	Y	Y	Y	Y
CALIFORNIA								
1 Thompson	Y	N	N	N	N	N	N	N
2 ***Herger***	Y	N	N	Y	Y	Y	Y	Y
3 ***Ose***	Y	N	N	Y	Y	Y	Y	Y
4 ***Doolittle***	Y	N	N	Y	Y	Y	Y	Y
5 Matsui	Y	Y	Y	N	N	N	N	N
6 Woolsey	N	Y	Y	N	N	N	?	N
7 Miller, George	N	Y	Y	N	N	N	N	N
8 Pelosi	N	Y	Y	N	N	N	N	N
9 Lee	N	Y	Y	N	N	N	N	N
10 Tauscher	Y	Y	Y	N	N	N	N	N
11 ***Pombo***	Y	N	N	Y	Y	Y	Y	Y
12 Lantos	Y	Y	Y	N	N	N	N	N
13 Stark	N	Y	Y	N	?	N	N	N
14 Eshoo	N	Y	Y	N	N	N	N	N
15 ***Campbell***	N	N	N	Y	Y	Y	Y	Y
16 Lofgren	?	?	?	?	?	?	?	?
17 Farr	Y	Y	Y	N	N	N	N	N
18 Condit	Y	N	N	N	N	Y	Y	N
19 ***Radanovich***	Y	N	N	Y	Y	Y	Y	Y
20 Dooley	Y	N	Y	N	N	N	N	N
21 ***Thomas***	Y	N	N	Y	Y	Y	Y	Y
22 Capps	Y	N	N	N	N	N	N	N
23 ***Gallegly***	Y	N	N	Y	Y	Y	Y	Y
24 Sherman	Y	N	N	N	N	N	N	N
25 ***McKeon***	Y	N	N	Y	Y	Y	Y	Y
26 Berman	Y	N	N	N	N	N	?	N
27 ***Rogan***	Y	N	N	Y	Y	Y	Y	Y
28 ***Dreier***	Y	N	N	Y	Y	Y	Y	Y
29 Waxman	Y	Y	Y	N	N	N	N	N
30 Becerra	N	Y	Y	N	N	N	N	N
31 Martinez	Y	?	N	N	N	N	N	N
32 Dixon	Y	Y	Y	N	N	N	N	N
33 Roybal-Allard	Y	Y	Y	N	N	N	N	N
34 Napolitano	Y	Y	Y	N	N	N	N	N
35 Waters	N	Y	Y	N	N	N	N	N
36 ***Kuykendall***	Y	?	N	Y	Y	Y	Y	Y
37 Millender-McD.	Y	Y	Y	N	N	N	N	N
38 ***Horn***	Y	N	N	Y	Y	Y	Y	Y
39 ***Royce***	Y	N	N	Y	Y	Y	Y	Y
40 ***Lewis***	Y	N	N	Y	Y	Y	Y	Y
41 ***Miller, Gary***	Y	?	N	Y	Y	Y	Y	Y
42 Brown	?	?	?	?	?	?	?	?
43 ***Calvert***	Y	N	N	Y	Y	Y	Y	Y
44 ***Bono***	+	?	?	?	?	?	?	?
45 ***Rohrabacher***	Y	N	N	Y	Y	Y	Y	Y
46 Sanchez	Y	N	N	N	N	N	N	N
47 ***Cox***	Y	N	N	Y	Y	Y	Y	Y
48 ***Packard***	Y	N	N	Y	Y	Y	Y	Y
49 ***Bilbray***	Y	N	N	Y	Y	Y	Y	Y
50 Filner	N	Y	Y	N	N	N	N	N
51 ***Cunningham***	Y	N	N	Y	Y	Y	Y	Y
52 ***Hunter***	Y	N	?	?	?	Y	Y	Y
COLORADO								
1 DeGette	N	N	N	N	N	N	N	N
2 Udall	Y	N	N	N	N	N	N	N
3 ***McInnis***	Y	N	N	Y	Y	Y	Y	Y
4 ***Schaffer***	Y	N	N	Y	Y	Y	Y	Y
5 ***Hefley***	Y	N	N	Y	Y	Y	Y	Y
6 ***Tancredo***	Y	N	Y	Y	Y	Y	Y	Y
CONNECTICUT								
1 Larson	Y	Y	Y	N	N	N	N	N
2 Gejdenson	Y	Y	Y	N	N	N	N	N
3 DeLauro	Y	Y	Y	N	N	N	N	N
4 ***Shays***	N	N	N	Y	Y	Y	Y	Y
5 Maloney	Y	N	N	N	N	Y	N	N
6 ***Johnson***	Y	N	N	Y	Y	Y	Y	?
DELAWARE								
AL ***Castle***	Y	N	N	Y	Y	Y	Y	Y
FLORIDA								
1 ***Scarborough***	Y	N	N	Y	?	Y	Y	Y
2 Boyd	Y	N	N	N	N	Y	N	N
3 Brown	Y	Y	Y	N	N	N	N	N
4 ***Fowler***	Y	N	N	Y	Y	Y	Y	Y
5 Thurman	Y	Y	Y	N	N	N	N	N
6 ***Stearns***	Y	N	?	Y	Y	Y	Y	Y
7 ***Mica***	Y	N	N	Y	Y	Y	Y	Y
8 ***McCollum***	Y	N	N	Y	Y	Y	Y	Y
9 ***Bilirakis***	Y	N	N	Y	Y	Y	Y	Y
10 ***Young***	Y	?	N	Y	Y	Y	Y	Y
11 Davis	Y	Y	N	N	N	N	N	N
12 ***Canady***	Y	N	N	Y	Y	Y	Y	Y
13 ***Miller***	Y	N	N	Y	Y	Y	Y	Y
14 ***Goss***	Y	?	?	Y	Y	Y	Y	Y
15 ***Weldon***	Y	N	N	Y	Y	Y	Y	Y
16 ***Foley***	Y	N	N	Y	Y	Y	Y	Y
17 Meek	Y	Y	Y	N	N	N	N	N
18 ***Ros-Lehtinen***	Y	N	N	Y	Y	Y	Y	Y
19 Wexler	Y	N	Y	N	?	N	N	N
20 Deutsch	Y	N	N	N	N	N	N	N
21 ***Diaz-Balart***	Y	N	N	Y	Y	Y	Y	Y
22 ***Shaw***	Y	?	?	Y	Y	Y	Y	Y
23 Hastings	Y	Y	Y	N	N	N	N	N
GEORGIA								
1 ***Kingston***	Y	N	N	Y	Y	Y	Y	Y
2 Bishop	Y	N	Y	N	N	N	N	N
3 ***Collins***	Y	N	N	Y	Y	Y	Y	Y
4 McKinney	N	N	N	N	N	N	N	N
5 Lewis	N	Y	Y	N	N	N	N	N
6 ***Isakson***	Y	N	N	Y	Y	Y	Y	Y
7 ***Barr***	Y	N	N	Y	Y	Y	Y	Y
8 ***Chambliss***	Y	N	N	Y	Y	Y	Y	Y
9 ***Deal***	Y	N	N	Y	Y	Y	Y	Y
10 ***Norwood***	?	N	N	Y	Y	Y	Y	Y
11 ***Linder***	Y	N	N	Y	Y	Y	Y	Y
HAWAII								
1 Abercrombie	Y	Y	Y	N	N	N	N	N
2 Mink	Y	Y	Y	N	N	N	N	N
IDAHO								
1 ***Chenoweth***	Y	N	N	Y	Y	Y	Y	Y
2 ***Simpson***	Y	N	N	Y	Y	Y	Y	Y
ILLINOIS								
1 Rush	N	Y	Y	N	N	N	N	N
2 Jackson	N	Y	Y	N	N	N	N	N
3 Lipinski	Y	Y	Y	N	N	N	N	N
4 Gutierrez	N	N	?	N	N	N	N	N
5 Blagojevich	Y	N	N	N	N	N	N	N
6 ***Hyde***	Y	N	N	Y	?	Y	Y	Y
7 Davis	N	Y	Y	N	N	N	N	N
8 ***Crane***	Y	N	N	Y	Y	Y	Y	Y
9 Schakowsky	N	N	N	N	N	N	N	N
10 ***Porter***	Y	N	N	Y	Y	N	N	?
11 ***Weller***	Y	N	N	Y	Y	Y	Y	Y
12 Costello	Y	N	N	N	N	N	N	N
13 ***Biggert***	Y	N	N	Y	Y	Y	Y	Y
14 ***Hastert***	Y				Y			Y

ND Northern Democrats SD Southern Democrats

	191	192	193	194	195	196	197	198
15 ***Ewing***	Y	N	N	Y	Y	Y	Y	Y
16 ***Manzullo***	Y	N	N	Y	Y	Y	Y	Y
17 Evans	Y	Y	Y	N	N	N	N	N
18 ***LaHood***	Y	N	N	Y	Y	Y	Y	Y
19 Phelps	Y	N	N	N	N	N	N	N
20 ***Shimkus***	Y	N	N	Y	Y	Y	Y	Y
INDIANA								
1 Visclosky	Y	Y	Y	N	N	N	N	N
2 ***McIntosh***	Y	N	N	Y	Y	Y	Y	Y
3 Roemer	Y	N	N	N	N	Y	Y	N
4 ***Souder***	Y	N	N	Y	Y	Y	Y	Y
5 ***Buyer***	Y	N	N	Y	Y	Y	Y	Y
6 ***Burton***	Y	N	N	Y	Y	Y	Y	Y
7 ***Pease***	Y	N	N	Y	Y	Y	Y	Y
8 ***Hostettler***	Y	N	N	Y	Y	Y	Y	Y
9 Hill	Y	Y	N	N	N	N	N	N
10 Carson	Y	N	N	N	N	N	N	N
IOWA								
1 ***Leach***	Y	N	?	Y	Y	Y	Y	Y
2 ***Nussle***	Y	N	N	Y	Y	Y	Y	Y
3 Boswell	Y	N	N	N	N	Y	Y	N
4 ***Ganske***	Y	N	N	Y	Y	Y	Y	Y
5 ***Latham***	Y	N	N	Y	Y	Y	Y	Y
KANSAS								
1 ***Moran***	Y	N	N	Y	Y	Y	Y	Y
2 ***Ryun***	Y	N	N	Y	Y	Y	Y	Y
3 Moore	Y	N	N	N	N	N	N	N
4 ***Tiahrt***	Y	N	N	Y	Y	Y	Y	Y
KENTUCKY								
1 ***Whitfield***	Y	N	?	Y	Y	Y	Y	Y
2 ***Lewis***	Y	N	N	Y	Y	Y	Y	Y
3 ***Northup***	Y	N	N	Y	Y	Y	Y	Y
4 Lucas	Y	N	N	N	N	N	N	N
5 ***Rogers***	Y	N	N	Y	Y	Y	Y	Y
6 ***Fletcher***	Y	N	N	Y	Y	Y	Y	Y
LOUISIANA								
1 ***Vitter***	Y	N	N	Y	Y	Y	Y	Y
2 Jefferson	Y	Y	Y	N	N	N	N	N
3 ***Tauzin***	Y	N	N	Y	Y	Y	Y	Y
4 ***McCrery***	Y	N	N	Y	Y	Y	Y	Y
5 ***Cooksey***	Y	?	?	?	?	?	?	?
6 ***Baker***	Y	N	N	Y	Y	Y	Y	Y
7 John	Y	N	N	N	N	Y	Y	N
MAINE								
1 Allen	Y	Y	Y	N	N	N	N	N
2 Baldacci	Y	N	N	N	N	N	N	N
MARYLAND								
1 ***Gilchrest***	Y	N	N	Y	Y	Y	Y	Y
2 ***Ehrlich***	Y	N	N	Y	Y	Y	Y	Y
3 Cardin	Y	Y	Y	N	N	N	N	N
4 Wynn	Y	N	N	N	N	N	N	N
5 Hoyer	Y	Y	Y	N	N	N	N	N
6 ***Bartlett***	Y	N	N	Y	Y	Y	Y	Y
7 Cummings	N	Y	Y	N	N	N	N	N
8 ***Morella***	Y	N	N	Y	Y	Y	Y	Y
MASSACHUSETTS								
1 Olver	?	?	?	N	N	N	N	N
2 Neal	Y	N	N	N	N	?	?	?
3 McGovern	N	Y	Y	N	N	N	N	N
4 Frank	N	Y	Y	N	N	N	N	N
5 Meehan	Y	N	N	N	N	N	N	N
6 Tierney	N	Y	Y	N	N	N	N	N
7 Markey	N	Y	Y	N	N	N	N	N
8 Capuano	N	Y	Y	N	N	N	N	N
9 Moakley	Y	Y	Y	N	N	N	N	N
10 Delahunt	Y	N	Y	N	N	N	N	N
MICHIGAN								
1 Stupak	Y	Y	Y	N	N	N	N	N
2 ***Hoekstra***	Y	N	N	Y	Y	Y	Y	Y
3 ***Ehlers***	Y	N	N	Y	Y	Y	Y	Y
4 ***Camp***	Y	N	N	Y	Y	Y	Y	Y
5 Barcia	Y	Y	N	N	N	N	N	N
6 ***Upton***	Y	N	N	Y	Y	Y	Y	Y
7 ***Smith***	Y	N	N	Y	Y	Y	Y	Y
8 Stabenow	Y	Y	N	N	N	N	N	N
9 Kildee	Y	N	N	N	N	N	N	N
10 Bonior	Y	Y	?	N	N	N	N	N
11 ***Knollenberg***	Y	N	N	Y	Y	Y	Y	Y
12 Levin	Y	N	N	N	N	N	N	N
13 Rivers	N	Y	N	N	N	N	N	N
14 Conyers	N	Y	Y	?	?	?	?	?
15 Kilpatrick	Y	Y	Y	N	N	N	N	N
16 Dingell	Y	Y	Y	N	N	N	N	N
MINNESOTA								
1 ***Gutknecht***	Y	N	N	Y	Y	Y	Y	Y
2 Minge	N	N	N	N	N	N	N	N
3 ***Ramstad***	Y	N	N	Y	Y	Y	Y	Y
4 Vento	N	Y	Y	N	N	N	N	N
5 Sabo	N	Y	Y	N	N	N	N	N
6 Luther	?	?	?	?	?	?	?	?
7 Peterson	N	Y	Y	N	N	Y	Y	N
8 Oberstar	N	Y	Y	N	N	N	N	N
MISSISSIPPI								
1 ***Wicker***	Y	?	?	Y	Y	Y	Y	Y
2 Thompson	Y	N	N	N	N	N	N	N
3 ***Pickering***	Y	N	N	Y	Y	Y	Y	Y
4 Shows	Y	N	N	Y	Y	Y	Y	N
5 Taylor	Y	Y	Y	Y	Y	Y	Y	N
MISSOURI								
1 Clay	?	?	?	?	?	?	?	?
2 ***Talent***	Y	N	N	Y	Y	Y	Y	Y
3 Gephardt	Y	Y	?	N	?	?	?	N
4 Skelton	Y	Y	Y	N	N	N	N	N
5 McCarthy	Y	N	N	N	N	N	N	N
6 Danner	Y	Y	Y	N	N	N	N	N
7 ***Blunt***	Y	N	N	Y	Y	Y	Y	Y
8 ***Emerson***	Y	N	N	Y	Y	Y	Y	Y
9 ***Hulshof***	Y	N	N	Y	Y	Y	Y	Y
MONTANA								
AL ***Hill***	Y	N	N	Y	Y	Y	Y	Y
NEBRASKA								
1 ***Bereuter***	Y	N	N	Y	Y	Y	Y	Y
2 ***Terry***	Y	N	N	Y	Y	Y	Y	Y
3 ***Barrett***	Y	N	N	Y	Y	Y	Y	Y
NEVADA								
1 Berkley	Y	N	N	N	N	N	N	N
2 ***Gibbons***	Y	N	N	Y	Y	Y	Y	Y
NEW HAMPSHIRE								
1 ***Sununu***	Y	N	N	Y	Y	Y	Y	Y
2 ***Bass***	Y	N	N	?	Y	Y	Y	Y
NEW JERSEY								
1 Andrews	Y	Y	Y	N	N	N	N	N
2 ***LoBiondo***	Y	N	N	Y	Y	Y	Y	Y
3 ***Saxton***	Y	N	N	Y	Y	Y	Y	Y
4 ***Smith***	Y	N	N	?	Y	Y	Y	Y
5 ***Roukema***	Y	N	?	Y	Y	Y	Y	Y
6 Pallone	Y	Y	Y	N	N	N	N	N
7 ***Franks***	Y	N	N	Y	Y	Y	Y	Y
8 Pascrell	Y	N	N	N	N	N	N	N
9 Rothman	Y	N	N	N	N	N	Y	N
10 Payne	N	Y	Y	?	N	N	N	N
11 ***Frelinghuysen***	Y	N	N	?	Y	Y	Y	Y
12 Holt	N	N	N	N	N	Y	Y	N
13 Menendez	Y	N	?	N	N	N	N	N
NEW MEXICO								
1 ***Wilson***	Y	N	N	Y	Y	Y	Y	Y
2 ***Skeen***	Y	N	N	Y	Y	Y	Y	Y
3 Udall	Y	N	N	N	N	N	N	N
NEW YORK								
1 ***Forbes***	Y	N	N	Y	Y	Y	Y	Y
2 ***Lazio***	Y	N	N	Y	Y	Y	Y	Y
3 ***King***	Y	N	N	Y	Y	Y	Y	Y
4 McCarthy	Y	N	N	N	N	N	N	N
5 Ackerman	Y	Y	Y	N	N	N	N	N
6 Meeks	Y	Y	Y	N	N	N	N	N
7 Crowley	N	Y	Y	N	N	N	?	N
8 Nadler	N	Y	Y	N	N	N	N	N
9 Weiner	N	Y	Y	N	N	N	N	N
10 Towns	N	Y	Y	N	N	N	N	N
11 Owens	N	Y	Y	N	N	N	N	N
12 Velázquez	N	Y	Y	N	N	N	N	N
13 ***Fossella***	Y	N	N	Y	Y	Y	Y	Y
14 Maloney	Y	N	N	N	N	N	N	?
15 Rangel	Y	?	?	?	?	?	?	?
16 Serrano	N	N	N	N	N	N	N	N
17 Engel	Y	Y	Y	?	?	?	?	?
18 Lowey	N	Y	Y	N	N	N	N	N
19 ***Kelly***	Y	N	N	Y	Y	Y	Y	Y
20 ***Gilman***	Y	N	N	Y	Y	Y	Y	Y
21 McNulty	Y	Y	Y	N	N	N	N	N
22 ***Sweeney***	Y	N	?	Y	Y	Y	Y	Y
23 ***Boehlert***	Y	N	N	Y	Y	Y	Y	Y
24 ***McHugh***	Y	N	N	Y	Y	Y	Y	Y
25 ***Walsh***	Y	N	N	Y	Y	Y	Y	Y
26 Hinchey	Y	Y	Y	N	N	N	N	N
27 ***Reynolds***	Y	N	N	Y	Y	Y	Y	Y
28 Slaughter	Y	Y	N	N	N	N	N	N
29 LaFalce	Y	N	N	N	N	N	N	N
30 ***Quinn***	Y	N	N	Y	Y	Y	Y	Y
31 ***Houghton***	Y	N	N	Y	Y	?	Y	Y
NORTH CAROLINA								
1 Clayton	+	?	?	N	N	N	N	N
2 Etheridge	Y	N	N	N	N	N	N	N
3 ***Jones***	Y	N	N	Y	Y	Y	Y	Y
4 Price	Y	N	N	N	N	N	N	N
5 ***Burr***	Y	N	N	Y	Y	Y	Y	Y
6 ***Coble***	Y	N	N	Y	Y	Y	Y	Y
7 McIntyre	Y	N	N	N	N	N	N	N
8 ***Hayes***	Y	N	N	Y	Y	Y	Y	Y
9 ***Myrick***	Y	N	N	Y	Y	Y	Y	Y
10 ***Ballenger***	Y	N	N	Y	Y	Y	Y	Y
11 ***Taylor***	Y	N	N	Y	Y	Y	Y	Y
12 Watt	Y	N	N	N	N	N	N	N
NORTH DAKOTA								
AL Pomeroy	Y	Y	Y	N	Y	N	N	N
OHIO								
1 ***Chabot***	Y	N	N	Y	Y	Y	Y	Y
2 ***Portman***	Y	N	N	Y	Y	Y	Y	Y
3 Hall	Y	N	N	N	N	N	N	N
4 ***Oxley***	Y	N	?	?	?	?	?	?
5 ***Gillmor***	Y	N	N	Y	Y	Y	Y	Y
6 Strickland	Y	N	N	N	N	N	N	N
7 ***Hobson***	Y	N	N	Y	Y	Y	Y	Y
8 ***Boehner***	Y	N	?	Y	Y	Y	Y	Y
9 Kaptur	Y	Y	Y	N	N	N	N	N
10 Kucinich	N	N	N	N	N	N	N	N
11 Jones	N	?	Y	N	N	N	N	N
12 ***Kasich***	?	?	?	?	?	?	?	?
13 Brown	N	N	N	N	N	N	N	N
14 Sawyer	Y	Y	Y	N	N	N	N	N
15 ***Pryce***	Y	N	N	Y	Y	Y	Y	Y
16 ***Regula***	Y	N	N	Y	Y	Y	Y	Y
17 Traficant	Y	N	N	Y	Y	Y	Y	Y
18 ***Ney***	Y	N	N	Y	Y	Y	Y	Y
19 ***LaTourette***	Y	N	N	Y	Y	Y	Y	Y
OKLAHOMA								
1 ***Largent***	Y	N	N	?	?	?	?	?
2 ***Coburn***	Y	N	N	Y	Y	Y	Y	Y
3 ***Watkins***	Y	N	N	Y	Y	Y	Y	Y
4 ***Watts***	Y	N	N	Y	Y	Y	Y	Y
5 ***Istook***	Y	N	N	Y	Y	Y	Y	Y
6 ***Lucas***	Y	N	?	Y	Y	Y	Y	Y
OREGON								
1 Wu	N	N	N	N	N	N	N	N
2 ***Walden***	Y	N	N	Y	Y	Y	Y	Y
3 Blumenauer	Y	N	N	N	N	N	N	?
4 DeFazio	N	P	P	N	N	N	N	N
5 Hooley	N	N	N	N	N	N	N	N
PENNSYLVANIA								
1 Brady	Y	N	N	N	N	N	N	N
2 Fattah	N	Y	Y	N	N	N	N	N
3 Borski	Y	N	N	N	N	N	N	N
4 Klink	Y	N	N	N	N	N	N	N
5 ***Peterson***	Y	N	N	Y	Y	Y	Y	Y
6 Holden	Y	N	N	N	N	N	N	N
7 ***Weldon***	Y	N	N	Y	Y	Y	Y	Y
8 ***Greenwood***	Y	N	N	Y	Y	Y	Y	Y
9 ***Shuster***	Y	N	N	Y	Y	Y	Y	Y
10 ***Sherwood***	Y	N	N	Y	Y	Y	Y	Y
11 Kanjorski	Y	?	N	N	N	N	N	N
12 Murtha	Y	N	N	N	N	N	N	N
13 Hoeffel	Y	N	N	N	N	N	N	N
14 Coyne	Y	Y	Y	N	N	N	N	N
15 ***Toomey***	Y	N	N	Y	Y	Y	Y	Y
16 ***Pitts***	Y	N	N	Y	Y	Y	Y	Y
17 ***Gekas***	Y	N	N	Y	Y	Y	Y	Y
18 Doyle	Y	?	N	N	N	N	N	N
19 ***Goodling***	Y	N	N	Y	Y	Y	Y	Y
20 Mascara	Y	N	N	N	N	N	N	N
21 ***English***	Y	N	N	Y	Y	Y	Y	Y
RHODE ISLAND								
1 Kennedy	Y	Y	?	N	N	N	N	N
2 Weygand	Y	Y	Y	N	N	N	?	?
SOUTH CAROLINA								
1 ***Sanford***	Y	N	N	Y	Y	Y	Y	Y
2 ***Spence***	Y	N	N	Y	Y	Y	Y	Y
3 ***Graham***	?	?	?	?	?	?	?	?
4 ***DeMint***	Y	N	N	Y	Y	Y	Y	Y
5 Spratt	Y	Y	Y	N	N	N	N	N
6 Clyburn	Y	Y	Y	N	N	N	N	N
SOUTH DAKOTA								
AL ***Thune***	Y	N	N	Y	Y	Y	Y	Y
TENNESSEE								
1 ***Jenkins***	Y	N	N	Y	Y	Y	Y	Y
2 ***Duncan***	Y	N	N	Y	Y	Y	Y	Y
3 ***Wamp***	Y	N	N	Y	Y	Y	Y	Y
4 ***Hilleary***	+	−	−	+	+	+	+	+
5 Clement	Y	Y	Y	N	N	N	N	N
6 Gordon	Y	N	N	N	N	N	N	N
7 ***Bryant***	Y	N	N	Y	Y	Y	Y	Y
8 Tanner	Y	N	N	N	N	N	N	N
9 Ford	Y	Y	N	N	N	N	N	N
TEXAS								
1 Sandlin	Y	N	N	N	N	N	N	N
2 Turner	Y	N	N	N	N	Y	Y	N
3 ***Johnson, Sam***	Y	N	?	Y	Y	Y	Y	Y
4 Hall	?	N	N	N	N	Y	Y	N
5 ***Sessions***	Y	N	N	Y	Y	Y	Y	Y
6 ***Barton***	Y	N	N	Y	Y	Y	Y	Y
7 ***Archer***	Y	N	N	Y	Y	Y	Y	Y
8 ***Brady***	Y	N	N	Y	Y	Y	Y	Y
9 Lampson	Y	N	N	N	N	N	N	N
10 Doggett	N	Y	N	N	N	N	N	N
11 Edwards	Y	N	N	N	N	N	N	N
12 ***Granger***	Y	N	N	Y	Y	Y	Y	Y
13 ***Thornberry***	Y	N	N	Y	Y	Y	Y	Y
14 ***Paul***	N	N	N	Y	Y	Y	Y	Y
15 Hinojosa	Y	N	?	N	N	N	N	N
16 Reyes	Y	N	?	N	N	N	N	N
17 Stenholm	Y	N	N	N	N	Y	Y	N
18 Jackson-Lee	Y	Y	Y	N	N	N	N	N
19 ***Combest***	Y	N	N	Y	Y	Y	Y	Y
20 Gonzalez	Y	N	N	N	N	N	N	N
21 ***Smith***	Y	N	N	Y	Y	Y	Y	Y
22 ***DeLay***	Y	N	N	Y	Y	Y	Y	Y
23 ***Bonilla***	Y	N	N	Y	Y	Y	Y	Y
24 Frost	Y	?	?	N	N	N	N	N
25 Bentsen	Y	?	?	?	?	?	?	?
26 ***Armey***	Y	N	N	Y	Y	Y	Y	Y
27 Ortiz	Y	N	?	N	N	N	N	N
28 Rodriguez	Y	N	N	N	N	N	N	N
29 Green	Y	−	−	−	−	−	−	−
30 Johnson, E.B.	Y	Y	N	N	N	N	N	N
UTAH								
1 ***Hansen***	Y	N	N	Y	Y	Y	Y	Y
2 ***Cook***	Y	N	N	Y	Y	Y	Y	Y
3 ***Cannon***	Y	N	N	Y	Y	Y	Y	Y
VERMONT								
AL *Sanders*	N	Y	?	N	N	N	N	N
VIRGINIA								
1 ***Bateman***	Y	N	N	Y	Y	Y	Y	Y
2 Pickett	Y	N	N	N	N	N	N	N
3 Scott	Y	N	?	N	N	N	N	N
4 Sisisky	Y	N	N	N	N	Y	Y	N
5 Goode	Y	N	N	N	Y	Y	Y	N
6 ***Goodlatte***	Y	N	N	Y	Y	Y	Y	Y
7 ***Bliley***	Y	N	N	Y	Y	Y	Y	Y
8 Moran	Y	Y	Y	N	N	N	N	N
9 Boucher	Y	Y	Y	N	N	N	N	N
10 ***Wolf***	Y	N	N	Y	Y	Y	Y	Y
11 ***Davis***	Y	N	N	Y	Y	Y	Y	Y
WASHINGTON								
1 Inslee	Y	N	N	N	N	N	N	N
2 ***Metcalf***	Y	N	N	Y	Y	Y	Y	Y
3 Baird	Y	N	N	N	N	N	N	N
4 ***Hastings***	Y	N	N	Y	Y	Y	Y	Y
5 ***Nethercutt***	Y	−	−	+	+	+	+	+
6 Dicks	Y	N	N	N	N	N	N	N
7 McDermott	N	Y	Y	N	N	N	N	?
8 ***Dunn***	Y	N	N	Y	Y	Y	Y	Y
9 Smith	Y	N	N	N	N	N	N	N
WEST VIRGINIA								
1 Mollohan	Y	?	N	N	N	N	N	N
2 Wise	Y	N	N	N	N	N	N	N
3 Rahall	Y	N	N	N	N	N	?	?
WISCONSIN								
1 ***Ryan***	Y	N	N	Y	Y	Y	Y	Y
2 Baldwin	N	Y	Y	N	N	N	N	N
3 Kind	Y	N	N	N	Y	Y	Y	Y
4 Kleczka	N	Y	Y	N	N	N	N	N
5 Barrett	N	Y	Y	N	N	N	N	N
6 ***Petri***	Y	N	N	?	Y	Y	Y	Y
7 Obey	N	Y	Y	N	N	Y	N	Y
8 ***Green***	Y	N	N	Y	Y	Y	Y	Y
9 ***Sensenbrenner***	N	N	N	Y	Y	Y	Y	Y
WYOMING								
AL ***Cubin***	Y	N	N	Y	Y	Y	Y	Y

Southern states - Ala., Ark., Fla., Ga., Ky., La., Miss., N.C., Okla., S.C., Tenn., Texas, Va.

199. HR 1905. Fiscal 2000 Legislative Branch Appropriations/Motion To Table. Pryce, R-Ohio, motion to table (kill) the Obey, D-Wis., motion to reconsider the vote for the adoption of the rule. Motion agreed to 218-197: R 213-1; D 5-195 (ND 4-143, SD 1-52); I 0-1. June 10, 1999.

200. Procedural Motion/Adjourn. Obey, D-Wis., motion to adjourn. Motion rejected 90-325: R 0-215; D 90-109 (ND 73-73, SD 17-36); I 0-1. June 10, 1999.

201. Procedural Motion/Motion to Rise. Obey, D-Wis., motion for the Committee of the Whole House to rise. Motion rejected 130-263: R 0-202; D 129-61 (ND 102-41, SD 27-20); I 1-0. June 10, 1999.

202. HR 1905. Fiscal 2000 Legislative Branch Appropriations/Recommit. Obey, D-Wis., motion to recommit with instructions that the bill not be reported back unless spending reductions in the bill are in line with the average reduction in all the domestic spending bills. Motion rejected 198-214: R 0-212; D 197-2 (ND 146-0, SD 51-2); I 1-0. June 10, 1999.

203. HR 1905. Fiscal 2000 Legislative Branch Appropriations/Passage. Passage of the bill to appropriate $1.9 billion for the House of Representatives and other legislative branch operations, including $769 million for the House of Representatives; $98.8 million for joint functions of the House and Senate; and $738.9 million for related agencies including the Library of Congress and the non-congressional work of the Government Printing Office. Passed 214-197: R 206-6; D 8-190 (ND 5-140, SD 3-50); I 0-1. June 10, 1999.

Key

- Y Voted for (yea).
- # Paired for.
- \+ Announced for.
- N Voted against (nay).
- X Paired against.
- – Announced against.
- P Voted "present."
- C Voted "present" to avoid possible conflict of interest.
- ? Did not vote or otherwise make a position known.

•

Democrats ***Republicans***
Independents

	199	200	201	202	203
ALABAMA					
1 ***Callahan***	Y	N	N	N	Y
2 ***Everett***	Y	N	N	N	Y
3 ***Riley***	Y	N	N	N	Y
4 ***Aderholt***	Y	N	N	N	Y
5 Cramer	N	N	N	Y	Y
6 ***Bachus***	Y	N	N	N	Y
7 Hilliard	N	N	Y	Y	N
ALASKA					
AL ***Young***	Y	N	N	N	Y
ARIZONA					
1 ***Salmon***	Y	N	?	N	Y
2 Pastor	N	Y	Y	Y	N
3 ***Stump***	Y	N	N	N	Y
4 ***Shadegg***	Y	N	N	N	Y
5 ***Kolbe***	Y	N	N	N	Y
6 ***Hayworth***	Y	N	N	N	Y
ARKANSAS					
1 Berry	N	Y	Y	Y	N
2 Snyder	N	N	N	Y	N
3 ***Hutchinson***	Y	N	N	N	Y
4 ***Dickey***	Y	N	N	N	Y
CALIFORNIA					
1 Thompson	N	N	N	Y	N
2 ***Herger***	Y	N	N	N	Y
3 ***Ose***	Y	N	N	N	Y
4 ***Doolittle***	Y	N	N	N	Y
5 Matsui	N	Y	Y	Y	N
6 Woolsey	N	N	Y	Y	N
7 Miller, George	N	Y	Y	Y	N
8 Pelosi	N	Y	Y	Y	N
9 Lee	N	Y	Y	Y	N
10 Tauscher	N	Y	Y	Y	N
11 ***Pombo***	Y	N	?	N	Y
12 Lantos	N	Y	Y	Y	N
13 Stark	N	N	Y	Y	N
14 Eshoo	N	Y	Y	Y	N
15 ***Campbell***	Y	N	N	N	Y
16 Lofgren	?	?	?	?	?
17 Farr	N	Y	Y	Y	N
18 Condit	N	N	N	Y	N
19 ***Radanovich***	Y	N	N	N	Y
20 Dooley	N	Y	Y	Y	N
21 ***Thomas***	Y	N	N	N	Y
22 Capps	N	Y	Y	Y	N
23 ***Gallegly***	Y	N	N	N	Y
24 Sherman	N	N	N	Y	N
25 ***McKeon***	Y	N	N	N	Y
26 Berman	N	N	N	Y	N
27 ***Rogan***	Y	N	N	N	Y
28 ***Dreier***	Y	N	N	N	Y
29 Waxman	N	Y	Y	Y	N
30 Becerra	N	Y	Y	Y	N
31 Martinez	N	Y	Y	?	?
32 Dixon	N	Y	?	Y	N
33 Roybal-Allard	N	Y	Y	Y	N
34 Napolitano	N	N	Y	Y	N
35 Waters	N	Y	N	Y	N
36 ***Kuykendall***	Y	N	N	N	Y
37 Millender-McD.	N	Y	Y	?	N
38 ***Horn***	Y	N	N	N	Y
39 ***Royce***	Y	N	N	N	Y

	199	200	201	202	203
40 ***Lewis***	Y	N	N	N	Y
41 ***Miller, Gary***	Y	N	N	N	Y
42 Brown	?	?	?	?	?
43 ***Calvert***	Y	N	N	N	Y
44 ***Bono***	?	?	?	?	?
45 ***Rohrabacher***	Y	N	N	N	Y
46 Sanchez	N	N	N	Y	N
47 ***Cox***	?	N	?	N	Y
48 ***Packard***	Y	N	N	N	Y
49 ***Bilbray***	Y	N	N	N	Y
50 Filner	N	Y	Y	Y	N
51 ***Cunningham***	Y	N	N	N	Y
52 ***Hunter***	Y	N	N	N	Y
COLORADO					
1 DeGette	N	N	N	Y	N
2 Udall	N	N	Y	Y	N
3 ***McInnis***	Y	N	N	N	Y
4 ***Schaffer***	Y	N	N	N	N
5 ***Hefley***	Y	N	N	N	Y
6 ***Tancredo***	Y	N	N	N	Y
CONNECTICUT					
1 Larson	N	N	Y	Y	N
2 Gejdenson	N	Y	Y	Y	N
3 DeLauro	N	Y	Y	Y	N
4 ***Shays***	Y	N	N	N	N
5 Maloney	N	N	Y	Y	N
6 ***Johnson***	Y	N	N	N	Y
DELAWARE					
AL ***Castle***	Y	N	N	N	Y
FLORIDA					
1 ***Scarborough***	Y	N	N	N	Y
2 Boyd	N	N	N	Y	N
3 Brown	N	Y	Y	Y	N
4 ***Fowler***	Y	N	N	N	Y
5 Thurman	N	Y	N	Y	N
6 ***Stearns***	Y	N	?	N	Y
7 ***Mica***	Y	N	N	N	Y
8 ***McCollum***	Y	N	N	N	Y
9 ***Bilirakis***	Y	N	N	N	Y
10 ***Young***	Y	N	N	N	Y
11 Davis	N	N	N	Y	N
12 ***Canady***	Y	N	N	N	Y
13 ***Miller***	Y	N	N	N	Y
14 ***Goss***	Y	N	N	N	Y
15 ***Weldon***	Y	N	N	N	Y
16 ***Foley***	Y	N	N	N	Y
17 Meek	N	Y	Y	Y	N
18 ***Ros-Lehtinen***	Y	N	N	N	Y
19 Wexler	N	N	Y	Y	N
20 Deutsch	N	N	N	Y	Y
21 ***Diaz-Balart***	Y	N	N	N	Y
22 ***Shaw***	Y	N	N	N	Y
23 Hastings	N	Y	Y	Y	N
GEORGIA					
1 ***Kingston***	Y	N	N	N	Y
2 Bishop	N	N	?	Y	N
3 ***Collins***	Y	N	N	N	Y
4 McKinney	N	N	?	N	N
5 Lewis	N	Y	Y	Y	N
6 ***Isakson***	Y	N	N	N	Y
7 ***Barr***	Y	N	N	N	Y
8 ***Chambliss***	Y	N	N	N	Y
9 ***Deal***	Y	N	N	N	Y
10 ***Norwood***	Y	N	N	N	Y
11 ***Linder***	Y	N	N	N	Y
HAWAII					
1 Abercrombie	N	Y	Y	Y	Y
2 Mink	N	Y	Y	Y	N
IDAHO					
1 ***Chenoweth***	Y	N	N	N	Y
2 ***Simpson***	Y	N	N	N	Y
ILLINOIS					
1 Rush	N	N	N	Y	N
2 Jackson	N	Y	Y	Y	N
3 Lipinski	N	N	Y	Y	N
4 Gutierrez	N	N	N	Y	N
5 Blagojevich	N	N	N	Y	N
6 ***Hyde***	Y	N	N	N	Y
7 Davis	N	Y	N	Y	N
8 ***Crane***	Y	N	N	N	Y
9 Schakowsky	N	N	Y	Y	N
10 ***Porter***	N	N	N	N	Y
11 ***Weller***	Y	N	N	N	Y
12 Costello	N	N	N	Y	N
13 ***Biggert***	Y	N	N	N	Y
14 ***Hastert***	Y	N	N	N	Y

ND Northern Democrats SD Southern Democrats

	199	200	201	202	203
15 ***Ewing***	Y	N	N	N	Y
16 ***Manzullo***	Y	N	N	N	Y
17 Evans	N	Y	Y	Y	N
18 ***LaHood***	Y	N	N	N	Y
19 Phelps	N	N	Y	Y	N
20 ***Shimkus***	Y	N	N	N	Y
INDIANA					
1 Visclosky	N	N	Y	Y	N
2 ***McIntosh***	Y	N	N	N	Y
3 Roemer	N	N	N	Y	N
4 ***Souder***	Y	N	N	N	Y
5 ***Buyer***	Y	N	?	?	?
6 ***Burton***	Y	N	N	N	Y
7 ***Pease***	Y	N	N	N	Y
8 ***Hostettler***	Y	N	N	N	Y
9 Hill	N	N	Y	Y	N
10 Carson	N	N	Y	Y	N
IOWA					
1 ***Leach***	Y	N	N	N	Y
2 ***Nussle***	Y	N	N	N	Y
3 Boswell	N	N	N	Y	N
4 ***Ganske***	Y	N	?	N	Y
5 ***Latham***	Y	N	N	N	Y
KANSAS					
1 ***Moran***	Y	N	N	N	Y
2 ***Ryun***	Y	N	N	N	Y
3 Moore	N	N	N	Y	N
4 ***Tiahrt***	Y	N	N	N	Y
KENTUCKY					
1 ***Whitfield***	Y	N	N	N	Y
2 ***Lewis***	Y	N	N	N	Y
3 ***Northup***	Y	N	N	N	Y
4 Lucas	N	N	N	Y	N
5 ***Rogers***	Y	N	N	N	Y
6 ***Fletcher***	Y	N	N	N	Y
LOUISIANA					
1 ***Vitter***	Y	N	N	N	Y
2 Jefferson	N	Y	?	Y	N
3 ***Tauzin***	Y	N	N	N	Y
4 ***McCrery***	Y	N	N	N	Y
5 ***Cooksey***	?	?	?	?	?
6 ***Baker***	Y	N	N	N	Y
7 John	N	N	Y	Y	N
MAINE					
1 Allen	N	Y	Y	Y	N
2 Baldacci	N	N	N	Y	N
MARYLAND					
1 ***Gilchrest***	Y	N	?	N	Y
2 ***Ehrlich***	Y	N	N	N	Y
3 Cardin	N	Y	Y	Y	N
4 Wynn	N	N	Y	Y	N
5 Hoyer	N	Y	Y	Y	N
6 ***Bartlett***	Y	N	N	N	Y
7 Cummings	N	N	Y	Y	N
8 ***Morella***	Y	N	N	N	Y
MASSACHUSETTS					
1 Olver	N	Y	?	Y	N
2 Neal	?	?	?	?	?
3 McGovern	N	Y	Y	Y	N
4 Frank	N	?	?	Y	N
5 Meehan	N	N	Y	Y	N
6 Tierney	N	Y	Y	Y	N
7 Markey	N	Y	N	Y	N
8 Capuano	N	Y	Y	Y	N
9 Moakley	N	Y	Y	Y	N
10 Delahunt	N	Y	N	Y	N
MICHIGAN					
1 Stupak	N	Y	Y	Y	N
2 ***Hoekstra***	Y	N	N	N	Y
3 ***Ehlers***	Y	N	N	N	Y
4 ***Camp***	Y	N	N	N	Y
5 Barcia	N	N	N	Y	N
6 ***Upton***	Y	N	N	N	Y
7 ***Smith***	Y	N	N	N	Y
8 Stabenow	N	N	N	Y	N
9 Kildee	N	N	Y	Y	N
10 Bonior	N	Y	?	Y	N
11 ***Knollenberg***	Y	N	N	N	Y
12 Levin	N	Y	Y	Y	N
13 Rivers	N	N	Y	Y	N
14 Conyers	?	?	?	?	?
15 Kilpatrick	N	Y	Y	Y	N
16 Dingell	N	Y	Y	Y	N

	199	200	201	202	203
MINNESOTA					
1 ***Gutknecht***	Y	N	N	N	Y
2 Minge	N	N	N	Y	N
3 ***Ramstad***	Y	N	N	N	Y
4 Vento	N	Y	Y	Y	N
5 Sabo	N	Y	Y	Y	N
6 Luther	?	?	?	?	?
7 Peterson	N	Y	Y	Y	N
8 Oberstar	N	Y	Y	Y	N
MISSISSIPPI					
1 ***Wicker***	Y	N	N	N	Y
2 Thompson	N	N	Y	Y	N
3 ***Pickering***	Y	N	N	N	Y
4 Shows	Y	N	N	Y	N
5 Taylor	N	Y	N	Y	N
MISSOURI					
1 Clay	?	?	?	?	?
2 ***Talent***	Y	N	N	N	Y
3 Gephardt	N	Y	Y	Y	N
4 Skelton	N	Y	N	Y	N
5 McCarthy	N	N	Y	Y	N
6 Danner	N	Y	Y	Y	N
7 ***Blunt***	Y	N	N	N	Y
8 ***Emerson***	Y	N	N	N	Y
9 ***Hulshof***	Y	N	N	N	N
MONTANA					
AL ***Hill***	Y	N	N	N	Y
NEBRASKA					
1 ***Bereuter***	Y	N	N	N	Y
2 ***Terry***	Y	N	N	N	Y
3 ***Barrett***	Y	N	N	N	Y
NEVADA					
1 Berkley	N	N	Y	Y	N
2 ***Gibbons***	Y	N	N	N	Y
NEW HAMPSHIRE					
1 ***Sununu***	Y	N	N	N	Y
2 ***Bass***	Y	N	N	N	Y
NEW JERSEY					
1 Andrews	N	Y	Y	Y	N
2 ***LoBiondo***	Y	N	N	N	Y
3 ***Saxton***	Y	N	N	N	Y
4 ***Smith***	Y	N	N	N	Y
5 ***Roukema***	Y	N	N	?	?
6 Pallone	N	Y	Y	Y	N
7 ***Franks***	Y	N	N	N	Y
8 Pascrell	N	N	Y	Y	N
9 Rothman	N	N	N	Y	N
10 Payne	N	N	Y	Y	N
11 ***Frelinghuysen***	Y	N	N	N	Y
12 Holt	N	N	Y	Y	N
13 Menendez	N	N	Y	Y	N
NEW MEXICO					
1 ***Wilson***	Y	N	N	N	Y
2 ***Skeen***	Y	N	N	N	Y
3 Udall	N	N	Y	Y	N
NEW YORK					
1 ***Forbes***	Y	N	N	N	Y
2 ***Lazio***	Y	N	N	N	Y
3 ***King***	Y	N	N	N	Y
4 McCarthy	N	N	Y	Y	N
5 Ackerman	N	Y	Y	Y	N
6 Meeks	N	Y	Y	Y	N
7 Crowley	N	Y	Y	Y	N
8 Nadler	N	Y	Y	Y	N
9 Weiner	N	Y	Y	Y	N
10 Towns	N	Y	Y	Y	?
11 Owens	N	Y	Y	Y	N
12 Velázquez	N	Y	Y	Y	N
13 ***Fossella***	Y	N	N	N	Y
14 Maloney	N	N	Y	Y	N
15 Rangel	?	?	?	?	?
16 Serrano	N	N	Y	Y	N
17 Engel	?	?	N	Y	N
18 Lowey	N	Y	Y	Y	N
19 ***Kelly***	Y	N	N	N	Y
20 ***Gilman***	Y	N	N	N	Y
21 McNulty	N	Y	Y	Y	N
22 ***Sweeney***	Y	N	N	N	Y
23 ***Boehlert***	Y	N	N	N	Y
24 ***McHugh***	Y	N	N	N	Y
25 ***Walsh***	Y	N	N	N	Y
26 Hinchey	N	Y	Y	Y	N
27 ***Reynolds***	Y	N	N	N	Y
28 Slaughter	N	Y	Y	Y	N
29 LaFalce	N	N	N	Y	N

	199	200	201	202	203
30 ***Quinn***	Y	N	N	N	Y
31 ***Houghton***	Y	N	N	N	Y
NORTH CAROLINA					
1 Clayton	N	N	N	Y	N
2 Etheridge	N	N	Y	Y	N
3 ***Jones***	Y	N	N	N	Y
4 Price	N	N	Y	Y	N
5 ***Burr***	Y	N	N	N	Y
6 ***Coble***	Y	N	N	N	Y
7 McIntyre	N	N	N	Y	Y
8 ***Hayes***	Y	N	N	N	Y
9 ***Myrick***	Y	N	N	N	Y
10 ***Ballenger***	Y	N	N	N	Y
11 ***Taylor***	Y	N	N	N	Y
12 Watt	N	N	?	Y	N
NORTH DAKOTA					
AL Pomeroy	N	Y	Y	Y	N
OHIO					
1 ***Chabot***	Y	N	N	N	Y
2 ***Portman***	Y	N	N	N	Y
3 Hall	N	Y	Y	Y	N
4 ***Oxley***	?	?	?	?	?
5 ***Gillmor***	Y	N	N	N	Y
6 Strickland	N	N	Y	Y	N
7 ***Hobson***	Y	N	N	N	Y
8 ***Boehner***	Y	N	N	N	Y
9 Kaptur	Y	Y	Y	Y	N
10 Kucinich	N	N	N	Y	N
11 Jones	N	N	Y	Y	N
12 ***Kasich***	?	?	?	?	?
13 Brown	N	N	Y	Y	N
14 Sawyer	N	Y	Y	Y	N
15 ***Pryce***	Y	N	N	N	Y
16 ***Regula***	Y	N	N	N	Y
17 Traficant	Y	N	N	Y	Y
18 ***Ney***	Y	N	N	N	Y
19 ***LaTourette***	Y	N	N	N	Y
OKLAHOMA					
1 ***Largent***	?	?	?	?	?
2 ***Coburn***	Y	N	N	N	Y
3 ***Watkins***	Y	N	N	N	Y
4 ***Watts***	Y	N	?	N	Y
5 ***Istook***	Y	N	N	N	Y
6 ***Lucas***	Y	N	?	N	Y
OREGON					
1 Wu	N	N	N	Y	N
2 ***Walden***	Y	N	N	N	Y
3 Blumenauer	N	N	N	Y	N
4 DeFazio	N	P	P	Y	N
5 Hooley	N	N	Y	Y	N
PENNSYLVANIA					
1 Brady	N	N	N	Y	N
2 Fattah	N	N	Y	Y	N
3 Borski	N	N	N	Y	N
4 Klink	N	N	N	Y	N
5 ***Peterson***	Y	N	N	N	Y
6 Holden	N	N	N	Y	N
7 ***Weldon***	Y	N	?	N	Y
8 ***Greenwood***	Y	N	N	N	Y
9 ***Shuster***	Y	N	?	?	?
10 ***Sherwood***	Y	N	N	N	Y
11 Kanjorski	N	N	Y	Y	N
12 Murtha	N	N	N	Y	N
13 Hoeffel	N	N	Y	Y	Y
14 Coyne	N	Y	Y	Y	N
15 ***Toomey***	Y	N	N	N	Y
16 ***Pitts***	Y	N	N	N	Y
17 ***Gekas***	Y	N	N	N	Y
18 Doyle	N	N	N	Y	Y
19 ***Goodling***	Y	N	N	N	Y
20 Mascara	N	N	N	Y	Y
21 ***English***	Y	N	N	N	Y
RHODE ISLAND					
1 Kennedy	N	N	Y	+	?
2 Weygand	N	N	Y	Y	N
SOUTH CAROLINA					
1 ***Sanford***	Y	N	N	N	Y
2 ***Spence***	Y	N	N	N	Y
3 ***Graham***	?	?	?	?	?
4 ***DeMint***	Y	N	N	N	Y
5 Spratt	N	Y	Y	Y	N
6 Clyburn	N	Y	Y	Y	N
SOUTH DAKOTA					
AL ***Thune***	Y	N	N	N	N

	199	200	201	202	203
TENNESSEE					
1 ***Jenkins***	Y	N	N	N	Y
2 ***Duncan***	Y	N	N	N	Y
3 ***Wamp***	Y	N	N	N	Y
4 ***Hilleary***	+	–	–	–	?
5 Clement	N	Y	Y	Y	N
6 Gordon	N	N	N	Y	N
7 ***Bryant***	Y	N	N	N	Y
8 Tanner	N	N	Y	Y	N
9 Ford	N	N	Y	Y	N
TEXAS					
1 Sandlin	N	N	N	Y	N
2 Turner	N	N	N	Y	N
3 ***Johnson, Sam***	Y	N	N	N	Y
4 Hall	N	N	N	Y	N
5 ***Sessions***	Y	N	N	N	Y
6 ***Barton***	Y	N	N	N	Y
7 ***Archer***	Y	N	?	N	Y
8 ***Brady***	Y	N	N	N	Y
9 Lampson	N	N	N	Y	N
10 Doggett	N	Y	Y	N	N
11 Edwards	N	N	Y	Y	N
12 ***Granger***	Y	N	N	N	Y
13 ***Thornberry***	Y	N	N	N	Y
14 ***Paul***	Y	N	N	N	N
15 Hinojosa	N	N	Y	Y	N
16 Reyes	N	N	Y	Y	N
17 Stenholm	N	N	N	Y	N
18 Jackson-Lee	N	Y	Y	Y	N
19 ***Combest***	Y	N	N	N	Y
20 Gonzalez	N	N	Y	Y	N
21 ***Smith***	Y	N	N	N	Y
22 ***DeLay***	Y	N	?	N	Y
23 ***Bonilla***	Y	N	N	N	Y
24 Frost	N	Y	Y	Y	N
25 Bentsen	?	?	?	?	?
26 ***Armey***	Y	N	N	N	Y
27 Ortiz	N	N	Y	Y	N
28 Rodriguez	N	N	N	Y	N
29 Green	–	–	–	+	?
30 Johnson, E.B.	N	Y	Y	Y	N
UTAH					
1 ***Hansen***	Y	N	N	N	Y
2 ***Cook***	Y	N	N	N	Y
3 ***Cannon***	Y	N	N	N	Y
VERMONT					
AL *Sanders*	N	N	Y	Y	N
VIRGINIA					
1 ***Bateman***	Y	N	N	N	Y
2 Pickett	N	N	Y	Y	N
3 Scott	N	N	?	Y	N
4 Sisisky	N	N	Y	Y	N
5 Goode	N	N	N	Y	N
6 ***Goodlatte***	Y	N	N	N	Y
7 ***Bliley***	Y	N	N	N	Y
8 Moran	N	Y	N	Y	N
9 Boucher	N	Y	?	Y	N
10 ***Wolf***	Y	N	N	N	Y
11 ***Davis***	Y	N	N	N	Y
WASHINGTON					
1 Inslee	N	N	Y	Y	N
2 ***Metcalf***	Y	N	N	N	Y
3 Baird	N	N	N	Y	N
4 ***Hastings***	Y	N	N	N	Y
5 ***Nethercutt***	+	–	–	–	?
6 Dicks	N	Y	Y	Y	?
7 McDermott	N	Y	Y	Y	N
8 ***Dunn***	Y	N	N	N	Y
9 Smith	N	N	?	Y	N
WEST VIRGINIA					
1 Mollohan	N	N	N	Y	N
2 Wise	N	N	N	Y	N
3 Rahall	?	N	N	Y	N
WISCONSIN					
1 ***Ryan***	Y	N	N	N	Y
2 Baldwin	N	Y	Y	Y	N
3 Kind	Y	N	N	Y	N
4 Kleczka	Y	Y	Y	Y	N
5 Barrett	N	Y	Y	Y	N
6 ***Petri***	Y	N	N	N	Y
7 Obey	N	Y	Y	Y	N
8 ***Green***	Y	N	N	N	Y
9 ***Sensenbrenner***	Y	N	N	N	Y
WYOMING					
AL ***Cubin***	Y	N	N	N	Y

Southern states - Ala., Ark., Fla., Ga., Ky., La., Miss., N.C., Okla., S.C., Tenn., Texas, Va.

204. HR 1400. Bond Price Transparency/Passage. Bliley, R-Va., motion to suspend the rules and pass the bill to direct the Securities and Exchange Commission to adopt rules to ensure that information about bond transactions, including price, volume and yield, is provided to the public on a timely basis. Motion agreed to 332-1: R 172-1; D 160-0 (ND 116-0, SD 44-0); I 0-0. June 14, 1999. A two-thirds majority of those present and voting (222 in this case) is required for passage under suspension of the rules.

205. H Res 62. Violence in Sierra Leone/Adoption. Royce, R-Calif., motion to suspend the rules and adopt the resolution to express concern over the escalating violence, violations of human rights and ongoing attempts to overthrow the democratically elected government in Sierra Leone. Adopted 414-1: R 212-1; D 201-0 (ND 147-0, SD 54-0); I 1-0. June 15, 1999. A two-thirds majority of those present and voting (277 in this case) is required for passage under suspension of the rules.

206. H Con Res 75. Condemn National Islamic Front of Sudan/Adoption. Royce, R-Calif., motion to suspend the rules and adopt the concurrent resolution to condemn the National Islamic Front government of Sudan for its genocidal war in southern Sudan, support for terrorism and continued human rights violations. Motion agreed to 416-1: R 214-1; D 201-0 (ND 147-0, SD 54-0); I 1-0. June 15, 1999. A two-thirds majority of those present and voting (278 in this case) is required for passage under suspension of the rules.

207. HR 1000. FAA Reauthorization/Off-Budget Funds. Young, R-Fla., amendment to strike the provisions of the bill that would take the Airport and Airway Trust Fund off budget and thereby permit all aviation tax revenue to be spent on aviation programs, exempt from budgetary restrictions but still subject to annual appropriations. Rejected 179-248: R 111-108; D 68-139 (ND 49-106, SD 19-33); I 0-1. June 15, 1999.

208. HR 1000. FAA Reauthorization/Passenger Fees. Graham, R-S.C., amendment to strike provisions of the bill that would allow airports to increase passenger facility charges from a maximum of $3 to $6. Rejected 183-245: R 137-82; D 46-162 (ND 28-127, SD 18-35); I 0-1. June 15, 1999.

209. HR 1000. FAA Reauthorization/Passage. Passage of the bill to authorize $59.3 billion for the Federal Aviation Administration (FAA) over five years; take the aviation trust fund off budget, permit airports to double their passenger fees to $6; eliminate restrictions on the number of flights permitted at O'Hare, Kennedy and LaGuardia airports; allow six more flights a day at Reagan National Airport. Passed 316-110: R 146-71; D 169-39 (ND 130-25, SD 39-14); I 1-0. June 15, 1999. A "nay" was a vote in support of the president's position.

Key

- Y Voted for (yea).
- \# Paired for.
- \+ Announced for.
- N Voted against (nay).
- X Paired against.
- – Announced against.
- P Voted "present."
- C Voted "present" to avoid possible conflict of interest.
- ? Did not vote or otherwise make a position known.

Democrats ***Republicans*** *Independents*

	204	205	206	207	208	209
ALABAMA						
1 ***Callahan***	Y	Y	Y	Y	N	N
2 ***Everett***	Y	Y	Y	Y	Y	N
3 ***Riley***	Y	Y	Y	Y	Y	N
4 ***Aderholt***	Y	Y	Y	Y	Y	N
5 Cramer	Y	Y	Y	Y	N	Y
6 ***Bachus***	Y	Y	Y	N	N	Y
7 Hilliard	Y	Y	Y	N	N	Y
ALASKA						
AL ***Young***	Y	Y	Y	N	N	Y
ARIZONA						
1 ***Salmon***	Y	Y	Y	Y	Y	N
2 Pastor	Y	Y	Y	Y	N	N
3 ***Stump***	Y	Y	Y	Y	Y	N
4 ***Shadegg***	Y	Y	Y	Y	Y	N
5 ***Kolbe***	Y	Y	Y	Y	Y	N
6 ***Hayworth***	+	Y	Y	Y	Y	N
ARKANSAS						
1 Berry	Y	Y	Y	N	N	Y
2 Snyder	Y	Y	Y	Y	N	N
3 ***Hutchinson***	Y	Y	Y	N	Y	Y
4 ***Dickey***	Y	Y	Y	Y	N	Y
CALIFORNIA						
1 Thompson	Y	Y	Y	N	N	Y
2 ***Herger***	Y	Y	Y	Y	Y	N
3 ***Ose***	Y	Y	Y	Y	Y	Y
4 ***Doolittle***	Y	Y	Y	N	N	Y
5 Matsui	?	Y	Y	N	N	Y
6 Woolsey	+	Y	Y	N	N	Y
7 Miller, George	?	Y	?	Y	N	N
8 Pelosi	?	Y	Y	Y	N	N
9 Lee	+	Y	Y	N	N	Y
10 Tauscher	Y	Y	Y	N	N	Y
11 ***Pombo***	Y	Y	Y	N	N	Y
12 Lantos	?	Y	Y	N	N	Y
13 Stark	Y	Y	Y	N	N	N
14 Eshoo	Y	Y	Y	Y	N	Y
15 ***Campbell***	Y	Y	Y	N	N	Y
16 Lofgren	Y	Y	Y	Y	N	Y
17 Farr	Y	Y	Y	Y	N	N
18 Condit	?	Y	Y	Y	Y	Y
19 ***Radanovich***	Y	Y	Y	N	N	?
20 Dooley	Y	?	Y	Y	N	Y
21 ***Thomas***	Y	Y	Y	Y	Y	Y
22 Capps	Y	Y	Y	N	N	Y
23 ***Gallegly***	?	Y	Y	N	Y	Y
24 Sherman	Y	Y	Y	N	N	Y
25 ***McKeon***	Y	Y	Y	Y	Y	Y
26 Berman	Y	Y	Y	Y	N	Y
27 ***Rogan***	Y	Y	Y	Y	Y	Y
28 ***Dreier***	Y	Y	Y	Y	N	Y
29 Waxman	Y	Y	Y	Y	N	Y
30 Becerra	Y	Y	Y	Y	N	Y
31 Martinez	Y	Y	Y	N	N	Y
32 Dixon	Y	Y	Y	Y	N	Y
33 Roybal-Allard	Y	Y	Y	Y	N	N
34 Napolitano	Y	?	?	N	N	Y
35 Waters	Y	Y	Y	N	Y	N
36 ***Kuykendall***	+	Y	Y	N	Y	Y
37 Millender-McD.	Y	Y	Y	N	N	Y
38 ***Horn***	Y	Y	Y	N	N	Y
39 ***Royce***	Y	Y	Y	Y	Y	N
40 ***Lewis***	?	Y	Y	Y	N	Y
41 ***Miller, Gary***	?	Y	Y	N	Y	Y
42 Brown	?	?	?	?	?	?
43 ***Calvert***	+	Y	Y	Y	Y	Y
44 ***Bono***	?	Y	Y	N	Y	Y
45 ***Rohrabacher***	Y	Y	Y	Y	Y	N
46 Sanchez	Y	Y	Y	N	Y	Y
47 ***Cox***	Y	Y	Y	Y	Y	N
48 ***Packard***	+	Y	Y	Y	Y	N
49 ***Bilbray***	Y	Y	Y	N	N	Y
50 Filner	Y	Y	Y	N	N	Y
51 ***Cunningham***	Y	Y	Y	Y	Y	Y
52 ***Hunter***	Y	Y	Y	Y	N	Y
COLORADO						
1 DeGette	Y	Y	Y	N	N	Y
2 Udall	Y	Y	Y	N	N	Y
3 ***McInnis***	Y	Y	Y	Y	Y	N
4 ***Schaffer***	Y	Y	Y	Y	Y	Y
5 ***Hefley***	Y	Y	Y	Y	Y	Y
6 ***Tancredo***	Y	Y	Y	Y	Y	Y
CONNECTICUT						
1 Larson	Y	Y	Y	N	N	Y
2 Gejdenson	Y	Y	Y	N	N	Y
3 DeLauro	Y	Y	Y	Y	N	Y
4 ***Shays***	Y	Y	Y	Y	N	N
5 Maloney	+	Y	Y	N	Y	Y
6 ***Johnson***	Y	Y	Y	Y	N	N
DELAWARE						
AL ***Castle***	Y	Y	Y	Y	Y	N
FLORIDA						
1 ***Scarborough***	Y	Y	Y	Y	Y	N
2 Boyd	Y	Y	Y	Y	N	N
3 Brown	?	Y	Y	N	N	Y
4 ***Fowler***	Y	Y	Y	N	N	Y
5 Thurman	Y	Y	Y	Y	N	N
6 ***Stearns***	Y	Y	Y	Y	Y	N
7 ***Mica***	Y	Y	Y	N	N	Y
8 ***McCollum***	Y	Y	Y	N	Y	Y
9 ***Bilirakis***	Y	Y	Y	Y	N	Y
10 ***Young***	?	Y	Y	Y	Y	?
11 Davis	Y	Y	Y	Y	N	N
12 ***Canady***	Y	Y	Y	Y	N	Y
13 ***Miller***	Y	Y	Y	Y	Y	N
14 ***Goss***	Y	Y	Y	Y	Y	N
15 ***Weldon***	Y	Y	Y	N	N	Y
16 ***Foley***	?	Y	Y	Y	Y	N
17 Meek	Y	Y	Y	N	N	Y
18 ***Ros-Lehtinen***	Y	Y	Y	N	N	Y
19 Wexler	Y	Y	Y	N	Y	N
20 Deutsch	Y	Y	Y	N	N	Y
21 ***Diaz-Balart***	Y	Y	Y	N	N	Y
22 ***Shaw***	Y	Y	Y	Y	N	Y
23 Hastings	Y	Y	Y	N	N	Y
GEORGIA						
1 ***Kingston***	?	Y	Y	Y	Y	N
2 Bishop	Y	Y	Y	N	N	Y
3 ***Collins***	Y	Y	Y	N	Y	Y
4 McKinney	?	Y	Y	N	N	Y
5 Lewis	Y	?	?	?	?	?
6 ***Isakson***	Y	Y	Y	N	N	Y
7 ***Barr***	Y	P	P	N	N	Y
8 ***Chambliss***	Y	Y	Y	Y	Y	Y
9 ***Deal***	?	Y	Y	N	Y	Y
10 ***Norwood***	Y	Y	Y	N	Y	Y
11 ***Linder***	Y	Y	Y	Y	Y	Y
HAWAII						
1 Abercrombie	Y	Y	Y	N	N	Y
2 Mink	Y	Y	Y	N	Y	Y
IDAHO						
1 ***Chenoweth***	?	Y	Y	N	N	N
2 ***Simpson***	Y	Y	Y	N	Y	Y
ILLINOIS						
1 Rush	?	?	?	N	N	Y
2 Jackson	Y	Y	Y	Y	Y	N
3 Lipinski	?	Y	Y	N	N	Y
4 Gutierrez	?	Y	Y	N	N	Y
5 Blagojevich	?	Y	Y	N	N	Y
6 ***Hyde***	Y	Y	Y	Y	Y	N
7 Davis	?	Y	Y	N	N	Y
8 ***Crane***	Y	Y	Y	N	Y	N
9 Schakowsky	?	Y	Y	N	N	Y
10 ***Porter***	Y	Y	Y	Y	N	N
11 ***Weller***	Y	Y	Y	Y	Y	N
12 Costello	?	Y	Y	N	N	Y
13 ***Biggert***	Y	Y	Y	Y	Y	Y
14 ***Hastert***						Y

ND Northern Democrats SD Southern Democrats

	204	205	206	207	208	209
15 ***Ewing***	Y	Y	Y	N	N	Y
16 ***Manzullo***	Y	Y	Y	N	N	Y
17 Evans	Y	Y	Y	N	N	Y
18 ***LaHood***	Y	Y	Y	N	N	Y
19 Phelps	?	Y	Y	N	N	Y
20 ***Shimkus***	?	Y	Y	N	Y	Y
INDIANA						
1 Visclosky	?	Y	Y	Y	N	N
2 ***McIntosh***	?	Y	Y	Y	Y	N
3 Roemer	Y	Y	Y	Y	Y	Y
4 ***Souder***	?	Y	Y	N	Y	Y
5 ***Buyer***	?	?	Y	N	N	Y
6 ***Burton***	Y	Y	Y	N	Y	Y
7 ***Pease***	Y	Y	Y	N	N	Y
8 ***Hostettler***	Y	Y	Y	?	?	?
9 Hill	Y	Y	Y	N	Y	Y
10 Carson	Y	Y	Y	N	N	Y
IOWA						
1 ***Leach***	Y	Y	Y	N	N	Y
2 ***Nussle***	Y	Y	Y	N	Y	Y
3 Boswell	?	Y	Y	N	N	Y
4 ***Ganske***	Y	Y	Y	N	N	Y
5 ***Latham***	Y	Y	Y	Y	N	Y
KANSAS						
1 ***Moran***	Y	Y	Y	N	N	Y
2 ***Ryun***	?	?	?	Y	Y	N
3 Moore	+	Y	Y	N	Y	Y
4 ***Tiahrt***	?	Y	Y	Y	Y	N
KENTUCKY						
1 ***Whitfield***	Y	Y	Y	N	Y	Y
2 ***Lewis***	Y	Y	Y	N	Y	Y
3 ***Northup***	Y	Y	Y	N	Y	Y
4 Lucas	Y	Y	Y	N	Y	Y
5 ***Rogers***	?	Y	Y	Y	N	Y
6 ***Fletcher***	Y	Y	Y	N	Y	Y
LOUISIANA						
1 ***Vitter***	Y	Y	Y	N	N	Y
2 Jefferson	?	Y	Y	?	N	Y
3 ***Tauzin***	Y	Y	Y	N	N	Y
4 ***McCrery***	Y	Y	Y	Y	Y	Y
5 ***Cooksey***	Y	Y	Y	N	N	Y
6 ***Baker***	?	Y	Y	N	N	Y
7 John	Y	Y	Y	N	N	Y
MAINE						
1 Allen	Y	Y	Y	N	N	Y
2 Baldacci	Y	Y	Y	N	N	Y
MARYLAND						
1 ***Gilchrest***	Y	Y	Y	N	N	Y
2 ***Ehrlich***	Y	Y	Y	Y	N	Y
3 Cardin	Y	?	?	Y	Y	Y
4 Wynn	Y	Y	Y	N	N	N
5 Hoyer	Y	Y	Y	Y	Y	N
6 ***Bartlett***	Y	Y	Y	N	Y	Y
7 Cummings	Y	Y	Y	N	N	Y
8 ***Morella***	Y	Y	Y	Y	Y	N
MASSACHUSETTS						
1 Olver	Y	Y	Y	Y	N	N
2 Neal	?	Y	Y	N	N	Y
3 McGovern	Y	Y	Y	N	N	Y
4 Frank	Y	Y	Y	N	N	Y
5 Meehan	Y	Y	Y	Y	N	N
6 Tierney	Y	Y	Y	N	N	Y
7 Markey	Y	Y	Y	N	N	Y
8 Capuano	?	Y	Y	N	Y	Y
9 Moakley	Y	Y	Y	N	N	Y
10 Delahunt	Y	Y	Y	N	N	Y
MICHIGAN						
1 Stupak	?	Y	Y	N	N	Y
2 ***Hoekstra***	Y	Y	Y	Y	N	Y
3 ***Ehlers***	Y	Y	Y	N	N	Y
4 ***Camp***	Y	Y	Y	N	Y	Y
5 Barcia	Y	Y	Y	N	N	Y
6 ***Upton***	Y	Y	Y	N	N	Y
7 ***Smith***	+	Y	Y	Y	Y	Y
8 Stabenow	Y	Y	Y	N	N	Y
9 Kildee	Y	Y	Y	N	N	Y
10 Bonior	?	Y	Y	N	N	Y
11 ***Knollenberg***	Y	Y	Y	Y	Y	N
12 Levin	Y	Y	Y	Y	Y	Y
13 Rivers	Y	Y	Y	N	N	Y
14 Conyers	Y	Y	Y	Y	N	Y
15 Kilpatrick	Y	Y	Y	Y	N	N
16 Dingell	Y	Y	Y	N	N	Y

	204	205	206	207	208	209
MINNESOTA						
1 ***Gutknecht***	Y	Y	Y	N	Y	Y
2 Minge	Y	Y	Y	Y	N	N
3 ***Ramstad***	+	Y	Y	Y	Y	N
4 Vento	Y	Y	Y	Y	N	Y
5 Sabo	?	Y	Y	Y	N	N
6 Luther	Y	Y	Y	Y	N	N
7 Peterson	Y	Y	Y	N	N	Y
8 Oberstar	?	Y	Y	N	N	Y
MISSISSIPPI						
1 ***Wicker***	Y	Y	Y	Y	N	Y
2 Thompson	Y	Y	Y	Y	N	Y
3 ***Pickering***	Y	?	Y	Y	Y	Y
4 Shows	+	Y	Y	N	Y	Y
5 Taylor	?	Y	Y	N	Y	Y
MISSOURI						
1 Clay	?	Y	Y	N	N	Y
2 ***Talent***	Y	Y	Y	N	Y	Y
3 Gephardt	Y	Y	?	N	N	Y
4 Skelton	Y	Y	Y	Y	Y	Y
5 McCarthy	+	Y	Y	N	N	Y
6 Danner	?	?	?	N	Y	Y
7 ***Blunt***	Y	Y	Y	Y	Y	Y
8 ***Emerson***	+	Y	Y	Y	Y	N
9 ***Hulshof***	?	Y	Y	Y	Y	N
MONTANA						
AL ***Hill***	Y	Y	Y	N	Y	Y
NEBRASKA						
1 ***Bereuter***	Y	Y	Y	N	N	Y
2 ***Terry***	Y	Y	Y	N	Y	Y
3 ***Barrett***	Y	Y	Y	Y	N	N
NEVADA						
1 Berkley	Y	Y	Y	N	N	Y
2 ***Gibbons***	Y	Y	Y	Y	Y	N
NEW HAMPSHIRE						
1 ***Sununu***	Y	Y	Y	Y	Y	N
2 ***Bass***	?	Y	Y	N	N	Y
NEW JERSEY						
1 Andrews	Y	Y	Y	N	Y	Y
2 ***LoBiondo***	Y	Y	Y	N	Y	Y
3 ***Saxton***	Y	Y	Y	N	N	Y
4 ***Smith***	Y	Y	Y	N	N	Y
5 ***Roukema***	Y	Y	Y	Y	Y	N
6 Pallone	Y	Y	Y	N	Y	Y
7 ***Franks***	Y	Y	Y	N	Y	Y
8 Pascrell	Y	Y	Y	N	Y	Y
9 Rothman	Y	Y	Y	N	Y	Y
10 Payne	Y	Y	Y	N	N	Y
11 ***Frelinghuysen***	Y	Y	Y	Y	Y	N
12 Holt	Y	Y	Y	Y	Y	Y
13 Menendez	Y	Y	Y	N	N	Y
NEW MEXICO						
1 ***Wilson***	Y	Y	Y	N	Y	Y
2 ***Skeen***	Y	Y	Y	Y	Y	Y
3 Udall	Y	Y	Y	N	N	Y
NEW YORK						
1 ***Forbes***	?	Y	Y	N	N	Y
2 ***Lazio***	Y	Y	Y	N	Y	Y
3 ***King***	?	Y	Y	N	Y	Y
4 McCarthy	Y	?	?	N	N	Y
5 Ackerman	Y	Y	Y	N	N	Y
6 Meeks	Y	Y	Y	N	N	Y
7 Crowley	Y	Y	Y	N	N	Y
8 Nadler	Y	Y	Y	N	N	Y
9 Weiner	Y	Y	Y	N	N	Y
10 Towns	Y	Y	Y	N	N	Y
11 Owens	Y	Y	Y	N	N	Y
12 Velázquez	Y	Y	Y	N	N	Y
13 ***Fossella***	+	Y	Y	Y	Y	Y
14 Maloney	Y	Y	Y	N	N	Y
15 Rangel	?	Y	Y	N	N	Y
16 Serrano	Y	Y	Y	Y	N	Y
17 Engel	?	Y	Y	N	N	Y
18 Lowey	Y	Y	Y	Y	N	N
19 ***Kelly***	Y	Y	Y	N	N	Y
20 ***Gilman***	+	Y	Y	N	Y	Y
21 McNulty	Y	Y	Y	N	N	Y
22 ***Sweeney***	Y	Y	Y	N	N	Y
23 ***Boehlert***	Y	Y	Y	N	N	Y
24 ***McHugh***	Y	Y	Y	N	N	Y
25 ***Walsh***	Y	Y	Y	Y	N	Y
26 Hinchey	Y	Y	Y	Y	N	Y
27 ***Reynolds***	Y	Y	Y	N	Y	Y
28 Slaughter	Y	Y	Y	N	N	Y
29 LaFalce	Y	Y	Y	Y	N	Y

	204	205	206	207	208	209
30 ***Quinn***	Y	Y	Y	N	N	Y
31 ***Houghton***	?	?	?	?	?	?
NORTH CAROLINA						
1 Clayton	?	Y	Y	Y	N	Y
2 Etheridge	Y	Y	Y	Y	Y	Y
3 ***Jones***	Y	Y	Y	Y	Y	N
4 Price	Y	Y	Y	Y	Y	Y
5 ***Burr***	Y	Y	Y	Y	Y	N
6 ***Coble***	Y	Y	Y	N	Y	Y
7 McIntyre	Y	Y	Y	N	Y	Y
8 ***Hayes***	Y	Y	Y	N	Y	Y
9 ***Myrick***	Y	Y	Y	Y	Y	N
10 ***Ballenger***	Y	Y	Y	Y	Y	N
11 ***Taylor***	?	Y	Y	Y	Y	N
12 Watt	Y	Y	Y	Y	N	N
NORTH DAKOTA						
AL Pomeroy	Y	Y	Y	N	N	Y
OHIO						
1 ***Chabot***	Y	Y	Y	Y	Y	N
2 ***Portman***	Y	Y	Y	Y	Y	N
3 Hall	Y	Y	Y	Y	Y	Y
4 ***Oxley***	Y	Y	Y	Y	N	Y
5 ***Gillmor***	?	Y	Y	Y	N	Y
6 Strickland	Y	Y	Y	N	Y	Y
7 ***Hobson***	?	Y	Y	Y	Y	N
8 ***Boehner***	?	Y	Y	Y	Y	N
9 Kaptur	?	Y	Y	Y	N	Y
10 Kucinich	Y	Y	Y	N	N	Y
11 Jones	Y	Y	Y	N	N	Y
12 ***Kasich***	?	Y	Y	Y	Y	N
13 Brown	Y	Y	Y	Y	N	N
14 Sawyer	Y	Y	Y	Y	N	Y
15 ***Pryce***	?	?	?	?	?	?
16 ***Regula***	Y	Y	Y	Y	Y	N
17 Traficant	Y	Y	Y	N	N	Y
18 ***Ney***	Y	Y	Y	N	N	Y
19 ***LaTourette***	Y	Y	Y	N	Y	Y
OKLAHOMA						
1 ***Largent***	Y	Y	Y	N	Y	N
2 ***Coburn***	?	Y	Y	Y	Y	N
3 ***Watkins***	Y	Y	Y	Y	Y	Y
4 ***Watts***	Y	Y	Y	N	Y	Y
5 ***Istook***	Y	Y	Y	Y	Y	N
6 ***Lucas***	Y	Y	Y	N	Y	Y
OREGON						
1 Wu	Y	Y	Y	Y	Y	Y
2 ***Walden***	+	Y	Y	N	N	Y
3 Blumenauer	Y	Y	Y	N	N	Y
4 DeFazio	Y	Y	Y	N	N	Y
5 Hooley	Y	Y	Y	N	N	Y
PENNSYLVANIA						
1 Brady	Y	Y	Y	N	N	Y
2 Fattah	Y	Y	Y	N	N	Y
3 Borski	Y	Y	Y	N	N	Y
4 Klink	?	Y	Y	N	N	Y
5 ***Peterson***	Y	Y	Y	N	N	Y
6 Holden	Y	Y	Y	N	N	Y
7 ***Weldon***	?	?	Y	N	Y	Y
8 ***Greenwood***	Y	Y	?	N	Y	Y
9 ***Shuster***	Y	Y	Y	N	N	Y
10 ***Sherwood***	Y	Y	Y	N	N	Y
11 Kanjorski	Y	Y	Y	N	N	Y
12 Murtha	?	Y	Y	N	N	Y
13 Hoeffel	Y	Y	Y	Y	Y	N
14 Coyne	?	?	?	N	N	Y
15 ***Toomey***	?	Y	Y	Y	Y	N
16 ***Pitts***	Y	Y	Y	Y	Y	N
17 ***Gekas***	Y	Y	Y	N	N	Y
18 Doyle	Y	Y	Y	N	N	Y
19 ***Goodling***	Y	Y	Y	N	N	Y
20 Mascara	Y	Y	Y	N	N	Y
21 ***English***	Y	Y	Y	N	N	Y
RHODE ISLAND						
1 Kennedy	Y	Y	Y	N	N	Y
2 Weygand	Y	Y	Y	Y	N	Y
SOUTH CAROLINA						
1 ***Sanford***	Y	Y	Y	Y	Y	N
2 ***Spence***	Y	Y	Y	N	Y	Y
3 ***Graham***	Y	Y	Y	Y	Y	N
4 ***DeMint***	Y	Y	Y	N	Y	Y
5 Spratt	Y	Y	Y	Y	Y	N
6 Clyburn	Y	Y	Y	Y	N	N
SOUTH DAKOTA						
AL ***Thune***	Y	Y	Y	N	Y	Y

	204	205	206	207	208	209
TENNESSEE						
1 ***Jenkins***	Y	Y	Y	N	N	Y
2 ***Duncan***	Y	Y	Y	N	N	Y
3 ***Wamp***	Y	Y	Y	Y	Y	N
4 ***Hilleary***	+	Y	Y	N	N	Y
5 Clement	Y	Y	Y	N	N	Y
6 Gordon	Y	Y	Y	N	?	?
7 ***Bryant***	Y	Y	Y	N	Y	Y
8 Tanner	Y	Y	Y	N	N	Y
9 Ford	Y	Y	Y	N	Y	Y
TEXAS						
1 Sandlin	Y	Y	Y	N	N	Y
2 Turner	Y	Y	Y	N	Y	Y
3 ***Johnson, Sam***	Y	Y	Y	Y	Y	N
4 Hall	Y	Y	Y	Y	Y	N
5 ***Sessions***	Y	Y	Y	Y	Y	N
6 ***Barton***	Y	Y	Y	Y	Y	Y
7 ***Archer***	Y	Y	Y	Y	Y	N
8 ***Brady***	+	?	?	N	Y	+
9 Lampson	Y	Y	Y	N	N	Y
10 Doggett	Y	Y	Y	Y	Y	N
11 Edwards	Y	Y	Y	Y	Y	N
12 ***Granger***	?	Y	Y	Y	N	Y
13 ***Thornberry***	Y	Y	Y	Y	Y	N
14 ***Paul***	N	N	N	N	Y	N
15 Hinojosa	Y	Y	Y	N	N	Y
16 Reyes	Y	Y	Y	N	N	Y
17 Stenholm	?	Y	Y	Y	Y	N
18 Jackson-Lee	Y	Y	Y	N	N	Y
19 ***Combest***	Y	Y	Y	N	Y	Y
20 Gonzalez	Y	Y	Y	N	N	Y
21 ***Smith***	Y	Y	Y	Y	Y	Y
22 ***DeLay***	?	Y	Y	Y	Y	N
23 ***Bonilla***	Y	Y	Y	Y	N	N
24 Frost	Y	Y	Y	N	N	Y
25 Bentsen	Y	Y	Y	Y	Y	N
26 ***Armey***	Y	Y	Y	Y	Y	Y
27 Ortiz	Y	Y	Y	N	N	Y
28 Rodriguez	Y	Y	Y	Y	N	Y
29 Green	+	Y	Y	N	N	Y
30 Johnson, E.B.	Y	Y	Y	N	N	Y
UTAH						
1 ***Hansen***	?	Y	Y	N	Y	Y
2 ***Cook***	Y	Y	Y	N	Y	Y
3 ***Cannon***	Y	Y	Y	N	Y	Y
VERMONT						
AL *Sanders*	?	Y	Y	N	N	Y
VIRGINIA						
1 ***Bateman***	Y	Y	Y	N	N	Y
2 Pickett	Y	Y	Y	N	Y	Y
3 Scott	Y	Y	Y	N	N	Y
4 Sisisky	Y	Y	Y	N	Y	Y
5 Goode	?	Y	Y	N	Y	Y
6 ***Goodlatte***	Y	Y	Y	Y	Y	Y
7 ***Bliley***	Y	Y	Y	Y	Y	Y
8 Moran	?	Y	Y	Y	N	N
9 Boucher	?	Y	Y	?	N	Y
10 ***Wolf***	Y	Y	Y	Y	Y	N
11 ***Davis***	Y	Y	Y	N	N	Y
WASHINGTON						
1 Inslee	Y	Y	Y	N	Y	N
2 ***Metcalf***	?	?	?	N	N	Y
3 Baird	Y	Y	Y	N	N	Y
4 ***Hastings***	Y	Y	Y	N	N	Y
5 ***Nethercutt***	Y	Y	Y	Y	Y	N
6 Dicks	Y	Y	Y	Y	N	Y
7 McDermott	Y	Y	Y	N	N	Y
8 ***Dunn***	Y	Y	Y	Y	N	Y
9 Smith	Y	Y	Y	Y	Y	N
WEST VIRGINIA						
1 Mollohan	?	Y	Y	Y	N	Y
2 Wise	Y	Y	Y	N	N	Y
3 Rahall	?	Y	Y	N	N	Y
WISCONSIN						
1 ***Ryan***	+	Y	Y	Y	Y	Y
2 Baldwin	Y	Y	Y	Y	N	N
3 Kind	+	Y	Y	Y	Y	Y
4 Kleczka	?	?	Y	N	N	Y
5 Barrett	?	Y	Y	Y	N	N
6 ***Petri***	Y	Y	Y	N	N	Y
7 Obey	Y	Y	Y	Y	Y	N
8 ***Green***	?	Y	Y	Y	N	Y
9 ***Sensenbrenner***	Y	Y	Y	Y	Y	N
WYOMING						
AL ***Cubin***	Y	Y	Y	N	N	Y

Southern states - Ala., Ark., Fla., Ga., Ky., La., Miss., N.C., Okla., S.C., Tenn., Texas, Va.

210. HR 1501, HR 2122. Juvenile Justice, Gun Show Checks/Rule. Adoption of the rule (H Res 209) to provide for House floor consideration of two bills: HR 1501, to provide legal consequences for juvenile offenders, and HR 2122, to require background checks for firearms purchases at gun shows. Adopted 240-189: R 222-0; D 18-188 (ND 9-143, SD 9-45); I 0-1. June 16, 1999.

211. HR 1501. Juvenile Justice/Increased Penalties. McCollum, R-Fla., amendment to increase penalties for juveniles who are convicted of possession of a firearm and for those who provide a firearm to a juvenile, including a mandatory minimum of three years for an adult who gives or sells a firearm to a child if the adult knows the child intends to bring the firearm to school; not less than 10 years if the child intends to commit a violent felony; and up to one year for a minor who illegally possesses a firearm. The amendment would also allow the prosecutor rather than the courts to decide whether to charge certain juveniles as adults. Adopted 249-181: R 186-34; D 63-146 (ND 40-114, SD 23-32); I 0-1. June 16, 1999.

212. HR 1501. Juvenile Justice/'Truth in Sentencing.' Salmon, R-Ariz., amendment to provide additional funding to states that convict a murderer, rapist or child molester, if that criminal had previously been convicted of one of those crimes in a different state. The cost of incarcerating the criminal would be deducted from the federal crime funds intended to go to the first state, and instead be sent to the state that obtained the second conviction. The amendment would not require the funds if the criminal had served 85 percent of the original sentence, and if the first state was a "truth-in-sentencing" state with a higher-than-average typical sentence for the crime. Adopted 412-15: R 218-0; D 193-15 (ND 141-12, SD 52-3); I 1-0. June 16, 1999.

213. HR 1501. Juvenile Justice/Media Violence. Hyde, R-Ill., amendment to prohibit the sale, loan or exhibition to juveniles of any material that contains sexual or violent depictions or detailed verbal descriptions, including any picture, drawing, sculpture, video game, motion picture, book, magazine or sound recording. Anyone convicted of providing such materials to a juvenile would be subject to a fine and/or up to five years' imprisonment for a first offense and a fine and/or up to 10 years' imprisonment for a second offense. The amendment would encourage all retail establishments to make the lyrics available for review by a customer before purchase, and would require the National Institute of Health to study the effects of violence on children. Rejected 146-282: R 127-92; D 19-189 (ND 10-143, SD 9-46); I 0-1. June 16, 1999.

214. HR 1501. Juvenile Justice/Crimes Against Children. Cunningham, R-Calif., amendment to direct the U.S. Sentencing Commission to amend the federal sentencing guidelines to increase a sentence by no less than five levels for a violent crime, if the crime is against a child under age 13. The FBI would be authorized to assist state and local authorities in murder cases where the victim is less than 13 years of age. Adopted 401-27: R 214-4; D 186-23 (ND 138-16, SD 48-7); I 1-0. June 16, 1999.

215. HR 1501. Juvenile Justice/Prison Condition Orders. DeLay, R-Texas, amendment to prohibit federal courts in civil cases from ordering the release from prison, or the non-admission to prison, of a convicted felon on the basis of prison overcrowding. Adopted 296-133: R 215-4; D 81-128 (ND 48-106, SD 33-22); I 0-1. June 16, 1999.

Key

- Y Voted for (yea).
- # Paired for.
- + Announced for.
- N Voted against (nay).
- X Paired against.
- – Announced against.
- P Voted "present."
- C Voted "present" to avoid possible conflict of interest.
- ? Did not vote or otherwise make a position known.

•

Democrats ***Republicans***
Independents

	210	211	212	213	214	215
ALABAMA						
1 ***Callahan***	Y	Y	Y	Y	Y	Y
2 ***Everett***	Y	Y	Y	Y	Y	Y
3 ***Riley***	Y	Y	Y	Y	Y	Y
4 ***Aderholt***	Y	Y	Y	Y	Y	Y
5 Cramer	N	Y	Y	N	Y	Y
6 ***Bachus***	Y	Y	Y	Y	Y	Y
7 Hilliard	Y	N	Y	N	N	N
ALASKA						
AL ***Young***	Y	Y	Y	N	Y	Y
ARIZONA						
1 ***Salmon***	Y	Y	Y	N	Y	Y
2 Pastor	N	N	Y	N	Y	N
3 ***Stump***	Y	Y	Y	Y	Y	Y
4 ***Shadegg***	Y	Y	Y	Y	N	Y
5 ***Kolbe***	Y	Y	Y	N	Y	Y
6 ***Hayworth***	Y	Y	Y	N	Y	Y
ARKANSAS						
1 Berry	N	Y	Y	N	Y	Y
2 Snyder	N	N	Y	N	Y	N
3 ***Hutchinson***	Y	Y	Y	N	Y	Y
4 ***Dickey***	Y	Y	Y	N	Y	Y
CALIFORNIA						
1 Thompson	N	Y	Y	N	Y	N
2 ***Herger***	Y	Y	Y	Y	Y	Y
3 ***Ose***	Y	Y	Y	N	Y	Y
4 ***Doolittle***	Y	N	Y	N	Y	Y
5 Matsui	N	N	Y	N	Y	N
6 Woolsey	N	N	Y	N	Y	N
7 Miller, George	N	N	Y	N	Y	N
8 Pelosi	N	N	Y	N	N	N
9 Lee	N	N	N	N	N	N
10 Tauscher	N	Y	Y	N	Y	N
11 ***Pombo***	Y	N	Y	N	Y	Y
12 Lantos	?	N	Y	N	Y	N
13 Stark	N	N	Y	N	Y	N
14 Eshoo	N	N	Y	N	Y	Y
15 ***Campbell***	Y	N	Y	N	N	N
16 Lofgren	N	N	Y	N	Y	Y
17 Farr	N	N	Y	N	Y	N
18 Condit	N	Y	Y	N	Y	Y
19 ***Radanovich***	Y	Y	Y	Y	Y	Y
20 Dooley	N	N	Y	N	Y	N
21 ***Thomas***	Y	Y	?	?	?	?
22 Capps	N	Y	Y	N	Y	Y
23 ***Gallegly***	Y	Y	Y	Y	Y	Y
24 Sherman	N	N	Y	N	Y	Y
25 ***McKeon***	Y	Y	Y	Y	Y	Y
26 Berman	N	N	Y	N	Y	N
27 ***Rogan***	Y	Y	Y	N	Y	Y
28 ***Dreier***	Y	Y	Y	N	Y	Y
29 Waxman	N	N	Y	N	Y	N
30 Becerra	N	N	Y	N	Y	N
31 Martinez	N	N	N	N	Y	N
32 Dixon	N	N	Y	N	Y	N
33 Roybal-Allard	N	N	N	N	Y	N
34 Napolitano	N	N	Y	N	Y	N
35 Waters	N	N	N	N	N	N
36 ***Kuykendall***	Y	Y	Y	N	Y	Y
37 Millender-McD.	N	N	Y	N	Y	N
38 ***Horn***	Y	Y	Y	Y	Y	Y
39 ***Royce***	Y	Y	Y	N	Y	Y
40 ***Lewis***	Y	Y	Y	N	Y	Y
41 ***Miller, Gary***	Y	Y	Y	Y	Y	Y
42 Brown	?	?	?	?	?	?
43 ***Calvert***	Y	Y	Y	Y	Y	Y
44 ***Bono***	Y	Y	Y	N	Y	Y
45 ***Rohrabacher***	Y	Y	Y	N	Y	Y
46 Sanchez	N	Y	Y	N	Y	N
47 ***Cox***	Y	Y	Y	N	Y	Y
48 ***Packard***	Y	Y	Y	Y	Y	Y
49 ***Bilbray***	Y	Y	Y	Y	Y	Y
50 Filner	N	N	Y	N	Y	N
51 ***Cunningham***	Y	Y	Y	Y	Y	Y
52 ***Hunter***	Y	Y	Y	Y	Y	Y
COLORADO						
1 DeGette	N	N	Y	N	Y	N
2 Udall	N	N	Y	N	Y	N
3 ***McInnis***	Y	Y	Y	N	Y	Y
4 ***Schaffer***	Y	Y	Y	N	Y	Y
5 ***Hefley***	Y	Y	Y	Y	Y	Y
6 ***Tancredo***	Y	Y	Y	Y	Y	Y
CONNECTICUT						
1 Larson	N	N	Y	N	Y	N
2 Gejdenson	N	N	Y	N	Y	N
3 DeLauro	N	N	Y	N	Y	N
4 ***Shays***	Y	Y	Y	Y	Y	Y
5 Maloney	N	Y	Y	Y	Y	Y
6 ***Johnson***	Y	Y	Y	Y	Y	Y
DELAWARE						
AL ***Castle***	Y	Y	Y	N	Y	Y
FLORIDA						
1 ***Scarborough***	Y	N	Y	N	Y	Y
2 Boyd	N	Y	Y	N	Y	Y
3 Brown	N	N	Y	N	Y	N
4 ***Fowler***	Y	Y	Y	N	Y	Y
5 Thurman	N	N	Y	N	Y	Y
6 ***Stearns***	Y	Y	Y	Y	Y	Y
7 ***Mica***	Y	Y	Y	Y	Y	Y
8 ***McCollum***	Y	Y	Y	N	Y	Y
9 ***Bilirakis***	Y	Y	Y	Y	Y	Y
10 ***Young***	Y	Y	Y	Y	Y	Y
11 Davis	N	Y	Y	N	Y	Y
12 ***Canady***	Y	Y	Y	Y	Y	Y
13 ***Miller***	Y	Y	Y	N	Y	Y
14 ***Goss***	Y	Y	Y	N	Y	Y
15 ***Weldon***	Y	Y	Y	Y	Y	Y
16 ***Foley***	Y	N	Y	N	Y	Y
17 Meek	N	N	N	N	N	N
18 ***Ros-Lehtinen***	Y	Y	Y	N	Y	Y
19 Wexler	N	Y	Y	N	Y	Y
20 Deutsch	N	Y	Y	N	Y	Y
21 ***Diaz-Balart***	Y	Y	Y	N	Y	Y
22 ***Shaw***	Y	Y	Y	N	Y	Y
23 Hastings	N	N	Y	N	N	N
GEORGIA						
1 ***Kingston***	Y	Y	Y	Y	Y	Y
2 Bishop	Y	Y	Y	N	Y	Y
3 ***Collins***	Y	Y	Y	Y	Y	Y
4 McKinney	N	N	Y	N	Y	N
5 Lewis	N	N	Y	N	Y	N
6 ***Isakson***	Y	Y	Y	Y	Y	Y
7 ***Barr***	Y	Y	Y	N	Y	Y
8 ***Chambliss***	Y	Y	Y	Y	Y	Y
9 ***Deal***	Y	Y	Y	Y	Y	Y
10 ***Norwood***	Y	Y	Y	Y	Y	Y
11 ***Linder***	Y	Y	Y	N	Y	Y
HAWAII						
1 Abercrombie	N	N	Y	N	Y	N
2 Mink	N	N	Y	N	N	N
IDAHO						
1 ***Chenoweth***	Y	N	Y	Y	Y	Y
2 ***Simpson***	Y	Y	Y	Y	Y	Y
ILLINOIS						
1 Rush	N	N	Y	N	N	N
2 Jackson	N	N	N	N	N	N
3 Lipinski	N	N	Y	Y	Y	Y
4 Gutierrez	N	N	Y	N	Y	N
5 Blagojevich	N	N	Y	N	Y	Y
6 ***Hyde***	Y	N	Y	Y	Y	Y
7 Davis	–	–	+	–	Y	N
8 ***Crane***	Y	Y	Y	N	Y	Y
9 Schakowsky	N	N	Y	N	Y	N
10 ***Porter***	Y	Y	Y	N	Y	Y
11 ***Weller***	Y	Y	Y	N	Y	Y
12 Costello	N	Y	Y	N	Y	Y
13 ***Biggert***	Y	Y	Y	N	Y	Y
14 ***Hastert***	Y					

ND Northern Democrats SD Southern Democrats

	210	211	212	213	214	215
15 ***Ewing***	Y	Y	Y	Y	+	Y
16 ***Manzullo***	Y	N	Y	N	Y	Y
17 Evans	N	Y	Y	N	Y	N
18 ***LaHood***	Y	Y	Y	Y	Y	Y
19 Phelps	N	Y	Y	N	Y	Y
20 ***Shimkus***	Y	Y	Y	Y	Y	Y
INDIANA						
1 Visclosky	N	N	Y	N	Y	Y
2 ***McIntosh***	Y	Y	Y	Y	Y	Y
3 Roemer	N	Y	Y	N	Y	Y
4 ***Souder***	Y	N	Y	Y	Y	Y
5 ***Buyer***	Y	Y	Y	Y	Y	Y
6 ***Burton***	Y	Y	Y	N	Y	Y
7 ***Pease***	Y	N	Y	N	Y	Y
8 ***Hostettler***	Y	N	Y	Y	Y	Y
9 Hill	N	Y	Y	N	Y	Y
10 Carson	N	N	Y	N	Y	N
IOWA						
1 ***Leach***	Y	Y	Y	N	Y	Y
2 ***Nussle***	Y	Y	Y	N	Y	Y
3 Boswell	N	Y	Y	N	Y	Y
4 ***Ganske***	Y	Y	Y	N	Y	Y
5 ***Latham***	Y	Y	Y	N	Y	Y
KANSAS						
1 ***Moran***	Y	Y	Y	N	Y	Y
2 ***Ryun***	Y	Y	Y	Y	Y	Y
3 Moore	N	Y	Y	N	Y	N
4 ***Tiahrt***	Y	N	Y	Y	Y	Y
KENTUCKY						
1 ***Whitfield***	Y	Y	Y	Y	Y	Y
2 ***Lewis***	Y	Y	Y	Y	Y	Y
3 ***Northup***	Y	Y	Y	N	Y	Y
4 Lucas	Y	Y	Y	Y	Y	Y
5 ***Rogers***	Y	Y	Y	Y	Y	Y
6 ***Fletcher***	Y	Y	Y	N	Y	Y
LOUISIANA						
1 ***Vitter***	Y	Y	Y	Y	Y	Y
2 Jefferson	N	N	Y	N	Y	N
3 ***Tauzin***	Y	Y	Y	N	Y	Y
4 ***McCrery***	Y	Y	Y	Y	Y	Y
5 ***Cooksey***	Y	N	Y	N	Y	Y
6 ***Baker***	Y	Y	Y	Y	Y	Y
7 John	Y	Y	Y	N	Y	Y
MAINE						
1 Allen	N	N	Y	N	Y	N
2 Baldacci	N	N	Y	N	Y	N
MARYLAND						
1 ***Gilchrest***	Y	Y	Y	Y	Y	Y
2 ***Ehrlich***	Y	Y	Y	N	Y	Y
3 Cardin	N	N	Y	N	Y	N
4 Wynn	N	N	Y	N	Y	N
5 Hoyer	N	N	Y	N	Y	N
6 ***Bartlett***	Y	Y	Y	Y	Y	Y
7 Cummings	N	N	Y	N	N	N
8 ***Morella***	Y	N	Y	N	Y	N
MASSACHUSETTS						
1 Olver	N	N	Y	N	Y	N
2 Neal	N	N	Y	N	Y	N
3 McGovern	N	N	Y	N	Y	N
4 Frank	N	N	N	N	Y	N
5 Meehan	N	N	Y	N	Y	N
6 Tierney	N	N	Y	N	Y	N
7 Markey	N	N	Y	N	Y	N
8 Capuano	N	N	Y	N	Y	N
9 Moakley	N	N	Y	N	Y	N
10 Delahunt	N	N	Y	N	Y	N
MICHIGAN						
1 Stupak	Y	N	Y	N	Y	N
2 ***Hoekstra***	Y	N	Y	N	Y	Y
3 ***Ehlers***	Y	N	+	Y	Y	Y
4 ***Camp***	Y	Y	Y	N	Y	Y
5 Barcia	Y	Y	Y	N	Y	Y
6 ***Upton***	Y	Y	Y	Y	Y	Y
7 ***Smith***	Y	Y	Y	Y	Y	Y
8 Stabenow	N	Y	Y	N	Y	Y
9 Kildee	N	N	Y	N	Y	Y
10 Bonior	N	N	Y	N	Y	Y
11 ***Knollenberg***	Y	Y	Y	N	Y	Y
12 Levin	N	N	Y	N	Y	Y
13 Rivers	N	N	Y	N	Y	Y
14 Conyers	N	N	N	N	N	N
15 Kilpatrick	N	N	N	N	N	N
16 Dingell	Y	N	Y	N	Y	N

	210	211	212	213	214	215
MINNESOTA						
1 ***Gutknecht***	Y	Y	Y	Y	Y	Y
2 Minge	N	Y	Y	N	Y	N
3 ***Ramstad***	Y	Y	Y	Y	Y	Y
4 Vento	N	N	Y	N	Y	N
5 Sabo	N	N	Y	N	Y	N
6 Luther	N	Y	Y	N	Y	Y
7 Peterson	N	Y	Y	Y	Y	Y
8 Oberstar	N	N	Y	N	Y	N
MISSISSIPPI						
1 ***Wicker***	Y	Y	Y	Y	Y	Y
2 Thompson	N	N	Y	N	Y	N
3 ***Pickering***	Y	Y	Y	Y	Y	Y
4 Shows	Y	Y	Y	Y	Y	Y
5 Taylor	Y	Y	Y	Y	Y	Y
MISSOURI						
1 Clay	N	N	N	N	N	N
2 ***Talent***	Y	Y	Y	Y	Y	Y
3 Gephardt	N	N	Y	N	Y	N
4 Skelton	N	Y	Y	Y	Y	Y
5 McCarthy	N	N	Y	N	Y	N
6 Danner	Y	N	Y	Y	Y	Y
7 ***Blunt***	Y	Y	Y	Y	Y	Y
8 ***Emerson***	Y	Y	Y	Y	Y	Y
9 ***Hulshof***	Y	Y	Y	N	Y	Y
MONTANA						
AL ***Hill***	Y	N	Y	Y	Y	Y
NEBRASKA						
1 ***Bereuter***	Y	Y	Y	Y	Y	Y
2 ***Terry***	Y	Y	Y	N	Y	Y
3 ***Barrett***	Y	Y	Y	N	Y	Y
NEVADA						
1 Berkley	N	Y	Y	N	Y	N
2 ***Gibbons***	Y	Y	Y	N	Y	Y
NEW HAMPSHIRE						
1 ***Sununu***	Y	Y	Y	N	Y	Y
2 ***Bass***	Y	Y	Y	N	Y	Y
NEW JERSEY						
1 Andrews	N	Y	Y	N	Y	Y
2 ***LoBiondo***	Y	Y	Y	Y	Y	Y
3 ***Saxton***	Y	Y	Y	Y	Y	Y
4 ***Smith***	Y	N	Y	Y	Y	Y
5 ***Roukema***	Y	Y	Y	Y	Y	Y
6 Pallone	N	Y	Y	N	Y	Y
7 ***Franks***	Y	Y	Y	Y	Y	Y
8 Pascrell	N	Y	Y	N	Y	Y
9 Rothman	N	Y	Y	N	Y	Y
10 Payne	N	N	N	N	N	N
11 ***Frelinghuysen***	Y	Y	Y	Y	Y	Y
12 Holt	N	Y	Y	N	Y	Y
13 Menendez	N	N	Y	N	Y	Y
NEW MEXICO						
1 ***Wilson***	Y	N	Y	Y	Y	Y
2 ***Skeen***	Y	N	Y	N	Y	Y
3 Udall	N	Y	Y	N	Y	N
NEW YORK						
1 ***Forbes***	Y	Y	Y	N	Y	Y
2 ***Lazio***	Y	Y	Y	Y	Y	Y
3 ***King***	Y	Y	Y	Y	Y	Y
4 McCarthy	N	Y	Y	N	Y	N
5 Ackerman	N	N	Y	N	Y	N
6 Meeks	N	N	N	N	N	N
7 Crowley	N	N	Y	N	Y	N
8 Nadler	N	N	Y	N	Y	N
9 Weiner	N	Y	+	–	+	+
10 Towns	N	N	Y	N	Y	N
11 Owens	?	N	Y	N	N	N
12 Velázquez	N	N	Y	N	Y	N
13 ***Fossella***	Y	N	Y	Y	Y	Y
14 Maloney	N	N	Y	N	Y	Y
15 Rangel	N	N	Y	N	Y	N
16 Serrano	N	N	Y	N	Y	N
17 Engel	N	N	Y	N	N	N
18 Lowey	N	Y	Y	N	Y	Y
19 ***Kelly***	Y	Y	Y	Y	Y	Y
20 ***Gilman***	Y	Y	Y	N	Y	Y
21 McNulty	N	N	Y	N	Y	N
22 ***Sweeney***	Y	N	Y	Y	Y	Y
23 ***Boehlert***	Y	Y	Y	N	Y	Y
24 ***McHugh***	Y	Y	Y	Y	Y	Y
25 ***Walsh***	Y	Y	Y	N	Y	Y
26 Hinchey	N	N	Y	N	Y	N
27 ***Reynolds***	Y	Y	Y	Y	Y	Y
28 Slaughter	N	N	Y	N	Y	N
29 LaFalce	N	N	Y	N	Y	N

	210	211	212	213	214	215
30 ***Quinn***	Y	Y	Y	N	Y	Y
31 ***Houghton***	?	?	?	?	?	?
NORTH CAROLINA						
1 Clayton	N	N	Y	N	N	N
2 Etheridge	N	Y	Y	N	Y	Y
3 ***Jones***	Y	Y	Y	Y	Y	Y
4 Price	N	N	Y	N	Y	Y
5 ***Burr***	Y	Y	Y	N	Y	Y
6 ***Coble***	Y	N	Y	N	Y	Y
7 McIntyre	N	Y	Y	Y	Y	Y
8 ***Hayes***	Y	Y	Y	Y	Y	Y
9 ***Myrick***	Y	Y	Y	N	Y	Y
10 ***Ballenger***	Y	Y	Y	N	Y	Y
11 ***Taylor***	Y	Y	Y	Y	Y	Y
12 Watt	N	N	N	N	N	N
NORTH DAKOTA						
AL Pomeroy	N	Y	Y	N	Y	N
OHIO						
1 ***Chabot***	Y	Y	Y	Y	Y	Y
2 ***Portman***	Y	Y	Y	Y	Y	Y
3 Hall	N	Y	Y	Y	Y	N
4 ***Oxley***	Y	Y	Y	Y	Y	Y
5 ***Gillmor***	Y	Y	Y	Y	Y	Y
6 Strickland	N	N	Y	N	Y	N
7 ***Hobson***	Y	Y	Y	Y	Y	Y
8 ***Boehner***	Y	Y	Y	N	Y	Y
9 Kaptur	N	N	Y	N	Y	N
10 Kucinich	Y	N	Y	N	Y	N
11 Jones	N	N	N	N	N	N
12 ***Kasich***	Y	?	?	?	?	?
13 Brown	N	N	Y	N	Y	N
14 Sawyer	N	N	Y	N	Y	N
15 ***Pryce***	Y	N	Y	N	Y	Y
16 ***Regula***	Y	Y	Y	Y	Y	Y
17 Traficant	Y	Y	Y	Y	Y	Y
18 ***Ney***	Y	N	Y	N	Y	Y
19 ***LaTourette***	Y	N	Y	N	Y	Y
OKLAHOMA						
1 ***Largent***	Y	Y	Y	Y	Y	Y
2 ***Coburn***	Y	N	Y	Y	Y	Y
3 ***Watkins***	Y	Y	Y	Y	Y	Y
4 ***Watts***	Y	Y	Y	Y	Y	Y
5 ***Istook***	Y	Y	Y	Y	Y	Y
6 ***Lucas***	Y	Y	Y	Y	Y	Y
OREGON						
1 Wu	N	Y	Y	N	Y	Y
2 ***Walden***	Y	Y	Y	Y	Y	Y
3 Blumenauer	N	N	Y	N	Y	N
4 DeFazio	N	N	Y	N	Y	N
5 Hooley	N	Y	Y	N	Y	Y
PENNSYLVANIA						
1 Brady	N	N	Y	N	Y	N
2 Fattah	N	N	Y	N	Y	N
3 Borski	N	Y	Y	N	Y	Y
4 Klink	N	N	Y	N	Y	N
5 ***Peterson***	Y	Y	Y	Y	Y	Y
6 Holden	N	Y	Y	Y	Y	Y
7 ***Weldon***	Y	Y	Y	Y	Y	Y
8 ***Greenwood***	Y	Y	Y	Y	Y	N
9 ***Shuster***	Y	Y	Y	Y	Y	Y
10 ***Sherwood***	Y	Y	Y	Y	Y	Y
11 Kanjorski	N	N	Y	N	Y	N
12 Murtha	Y	N	Y	N	Y	Y
13 Hoeffel	N	N	Y	N	Y	N
14 Coyne	N	N	Y	N	Y	N
15 ***Toomey***	Y	Y	Y	Y	Y	Y
16 ***Pitts***	Y	Y	Y	Y	Y	Y
17 ***Gekas***	Y	Y	Y	N	Y	Y
18 Doyle	N	Y	Y	N	Y	Y
19 ***Goodling***	Y	Y	Y	Y	Y	Y
20 Mascara	N	Y	Y	N	Y	Y
21 ***English***	Y	Y	Y	Y	Y	N
RHODE ISLAND						
1 Kennedy	N	N	Y	N	Y	N
2 Weygand	N	N	Y	N	Y	Y
SOUTH CAROLINA						
1 ***Sanford***	Y	N	Y	N	N	Y
2 ***Spence***	Y	Y	Y	Y	Y	Y
3 ***Graham***	Y	Y	Y	Y	Y	Y
4 ***DeMint***	Y	Y	Y	Y	Y	Y
5 Spratt	N	N	Y	N	Y	Y
6 Clyburn	N	N	Y	N	Y	N
SOUTH DAKOTA						
AL ***Thune***	Y	Y	Y	N	Y	Y

	210	211	212	213	214	215
TENNESSEE						
1 ***Jenkins***	Y	Y	Y	Y	Y	Y
2 ***Duncan***	Y	Y	Y	Y	Y	Y
3 ***Wamp***	Y	N	Y	N	Y	Y
4 ***Hilleary***	Y	Y	Y	Y	Y	Y
5 Clement	N	Y	Y	Y	Y	Y
6 Gordon	?	Y	Y	N	Y	Y
7 ***Bryant***	Y	Y	Y	Y	Y	Y
8 Tanner	N	N	Y	N	Y	Y
9 Ford	N	N	Y	N	Y	N
TEXAS						
1 Sandlin	N	N	Y	N	Y	Y
2 Turner	N	Y	Y	Y	Y	Y
3 ***Johnson, Sam***	Y	Y	Y	Y	Y	Y
4 Hall	Y	N	Y	Y	Y	Y
5 ***Sessions***	Y	Y	Y	Y	Y	Y
6 ***Barton***	Y	Y	Y	Y	Y	Y
7 ***Archer***	Y	Y	Y	Y	Y	Y
8 ***Brady***	Y	Y	Y	Y	Y	Y
9 Lampson	N	Y	Y	N	Y	Y
10 Doggett	N	N	Y	N	Y	N
11 Edwards	N	Y	Y	N	Y	Y
12 ***Granger***	Y	Y	Y	Y	Y	Y
13 ***Thornberry***	Y	N	Y	N	Y	Y
14 ***Paul***	Y	N	Y	N	N	Y
15 Hinojosa	N	N	Y	N	Y	Y
16 Reyes	N	Y	Y	N	Y	Y
17 Stenholm	N	N	Y	Y	Y	Y
18 Jackson-Lee	N	N	Y	N	Y	N
19 ***Combest***	Y	Y	Y	Y	Y	Y
20 Gonzalez	N	N	Y	N	Y	N
21 ***Smith***	Y	Y	Y	Y	Y	Y
22 ***DeLay***	Y	Y	Y	Y	Y	Y
23 ***Bonilla***	Y	N	Y	N	Y	Y
24 Frost	N	Y	Y	N	Y	N
25 Bentsen	N	N	Y	N	Y	Y
26 ***Armey***	Y	Y	Y	Y	Y	Y
27 Ortiz	N	Y	Y	N	Y	Y
28 Rodriguez	N	N	Y	N	Y	N
29 Green	N	Y	Y	N	Y	Y
30 Johnson, E.B.	N	N	Y	N	N	N
UTAH						
1 ***Hansen***	Y	Y	Y	Y	Y	Y
2 ***Cook***	Y	Y	Y	Y	Y	Y
3 ***Cannon***	Y	N	Y	N	Y	Y
VERMONT						
AL *Sanders*	N	N	Y	N	Y	N
VIRGINIA						
1 ***Bateman***	Y	Y	Y	N	Y	Y
2 Pickett	N	N	Y	N	Y	Y
3 Scott	N	N	N	N	N	N
4 Sisisky	N	N	Y	N	Y	Y
5 Goode	Y	N	Y	Y	Y	Y
6 ***Goodlatte***	Y	Y	Y	Y	Y	Y
7 ***Bliley***	Y	Y	Y	Y	Y	Y
8 Moran	N	N	Y	N	Y	N
9 Boucher	Y	Y	Y	N	Y	N
10 ***Wolf***	Y	Y	Y	Y	Y	Y
11 ***Davis***	Y	Y	Y	N	Y	Y
WASHINGTON						
1 Inslee	N	N	Y	N	Y	Y
2 ***Metcalf***	Y	N	Y	Y	Y	Y
3 Baird	N	Y	Y	N	Y	Y
4 ***Hastings***	Y	Y	Y	Y	Y	Y
5 ***Nethercutt***	Y	Y	Y	N	Y	Y
6 Dicks	N	N	Y	N	Y	N
7 McDermott	N	N	Y	N	N	N
8 ***Dunn***	Y	Y	Y	N	Y	Y
9 Smith	N	Y	Y	N	Y	Y
WEST VIRGINIA						
1 Mollohan	N	N	Y	Y	Y	Y
2 Wise	Y	N	Y	N	Y	Y
3 Rahall	Y	N	Y	N	Y	N
WISCONSIN						
1 ***Ryan***	Y	Y	Y	N	Y	Y
2 Baldwin	N	N	Y	N	Y	N
3 Kind	N	N	Y	N	Y	N
4 Kleczka	N	N	Y	N	Y	Y
5 Barrett	N	N	Y	N	Y	N
6 ***Petri***	Y	Y	Y	N	Y	Y
7 Obey	N	N	Y	N	Y	N
8 ***Green***	Y	Y	Y	N	Y	Y
9 ***Sensenbrenner***	Y	Y	Y	N	Y	Y
WYOMING						
AL ***Cubin***	Y	Y	Y	Y	Y	Y

Southern states - Ala., Ark., Fla., Ga., Ky., La., Miss., N.C., Okla., S.C., Tenn., Texas, Va.

216. HR 1501. Juvenile Justice/Enforcement of Firearms Laws. Stearns, R-Fla., amendment to establish a set of congressional findings that enhanced punishment and aggressive prosecution under firearms laws are key to deter gun violence. Adopted 293-134: R 218-2; D 75-131 (ND 42-109, SD 33-22); I 0-1. June 16, 1999.

217. HR 1501. Juvenile Justice/Drug Dealer Liability. Latham, R-Iowa, amendment to make drug dealers liable for certain crimes and provide a civil remedy for victims of illegal drugs; to specifically make controlled substance manufacturers liable for any person harmed directly or indirectly by the use of the drug; users filing liability suits would be required to disclose all information to narcotics agents. Adopted 424-3: R 218-2; D 205-1 (ND 151-0, SD 54-1); I 1-0. June 16, 1999.

218. HR 1501. Juvenile Justice/'Zero Tolerance' in Schools. Rogan, R-Calif., amendment to require any school accepting federal education funds to adopt a "zero tolerance" policy regarding possession of felonious quantities of drugs, or drugs determined to be for the purpose of distribution; students caught in possession of such quantities of drugs would be expelled for one year. Rejected 184-243: R 136-84; D 48-158 (ND 31-120, SD 17-38); I 0-1. June 16, 1999.

219. HR 1501. Juvenile Justice/School Memorials. Tancredo, R-Colo., amendment to declare that a memorial or memorial service on public school campuses to honor the memory of a person slain on that campus may contain religious speech without violating the U.S. Constitution. Adopted 300-127: R 214-6; D 86-120; I 0-1. June 16, 1999.

220. HR 1501. Juvenile Justice/Religion in Public Schools. DeMint, R-S.C., amendment to require each side in a court action against a public school based on a claim that permitting or accommodating a student's religious expression violates the First Amendment to pay its own attorneys' fees. Adopted 238-189: R 206-14; D 32-174 (ND 15-136, SD 17-38); I 0-1. June 17, 1999 (in the session that began and the Congressional Record dated June 16).

221. HR 1501. Juvenile Justice/Ten Commandments Display. Aderholt, R-Ala., amendment to declare that states and municipalities may display the Ten Commandments on or within property owned or administered by the state or municipality; also state that federal courts must exercise their judicial power in a manner consistent with these declarations. Adopted 248-180: R 203-15; D 45-164 (ND 24-130, SD 21-34); I 0-1. June 17, 1999.

Key

- Y Voted for (yea).
- # Paired for.
- + Announced for.
- N Voted against (nay).
- X Paired against.
- – Announced against.
- P Voted "present."
- C Voted "present" to avoid possible conflict of interest.
- ? Did not vote or otherwise make a position known.

•

Democrats ***Republicans***
Independents

	216	217	218	219	220	221
ALABAMA						
1 ***Callahan***	Y	Y	Y	Y	Y	Y
2 ***Everett***	Y	Y	Y	Y	Y	Y
3 ***Riley***	Y	Y	Y	Y	Y	Y
4 ***Aderholt***	Y	Y	Y	Y	Y	Y
5 Cramer	Y	Y	Y	Y	Y	Y
6 ***Bachus***	Y	Y	Y	Y	Y	Y
7 Hilliard	N	Y	N	N	N	N
ALASKA						
AL ***Young***	Y	Y	Y	Y	Y	Y
ARIZONA						
1 ***Salmon***	Y	Y	Y	Y	Y	Y
2 Pastor	N	Y	N	Y	N	N
3 ***Stump***	Y	Y	Y	Y	Y	Y
4 ***Shadegg***	Y	Y	Y	Y	Y	Y
5 ***Kolbe***	Y	Y	N	Y	Y	Y
6 ***Hayworth***	Y	Y	Y	Y	Y	Y
ARKANSAS						
1 Berry	Y	Y	N	Y	Y	Y
2 Snyder	Y	Y	N	N	N	N
3 ***Hutchinson***	Y	Y	N	Y	Y	Y
4 ***Dickey***	Y	Y	N	Y	Y	Y
CALIFORNIA						
1 Thompson	N	Y	N	Y	N	N
2 ***Herger***	Y	Y	Y	Y	Y	Y
3 ***Ose***	Y	Y	Y	Y	Y	Y
4 ***Doolittle***	Y	Y	N	Y	Y	Y
5 Matsui	N	Y	N	Y	N	N
6 Woolsey	N	Y	N	N	N	N
7 Miller, George	N	Y	N	N	N	N
8 Pelosi	N	Y	N	N	N	N
9 Lee	N	Y	N	N	N	N
10 Tauscher	N	Y	N	N	N	N
11 ***Pombo***	Y	Y	N	Y	Y	Y
12 Lantos	N	Y	N	N	N	N
13 Stark	N	Y	N	N	N	N
14 Eshoo	N	Y	N	N	N	N
15 ***Campbell***	Y	Y	N	N	N	N
16 Lofgren	N	Y	Y	Y	N	N
17 Farr	N	Y	N	N	N	N
18 Condit	Y	Y	Y	Y	Y	Y
19 ***Radanovich***	Y	Y	Y	Y	Y	Y
20 Dooley	N	Y	N	Y	N	Y
21 ***Thomas***	?	?	?	?	?	?
22 Capps	N	Y	N	N	N	N
23 ***Gallegly***	Y	Y	Y	Y	Y	Y
24 Sherman	N	Y	N	N	N	N
25 ***McKeon***	Y	Y	N	Y	Y	+
26 Berman	N	Y	N	N	N	N
27 ***Rogan***	Y	Y	Y	Y	Y	Y
28 ***Dreier***	Y	Y	Y	Y	Y	Y
29 Waxman	N	Y	N	Y	N	N
30 Becerra	N	Y	N	N	N	N
31 Martinez	?	?	?	?	?	N
32 Dixon	N	Y	N	N	N	N
33 Roybal-Allard	N	Y	N	N	N	N
34 Napolitano	N	Y	N	Y	N	N
35 Waters	N	Y	N	N	N	N
36 ***Kuykendall***	Y	Y	N	Y	Y	N
37 Millender-McD.	N	Y	N	N	N	N
38 ***Horn***	Y	Y	Y	Y	Y	N
39 ***Royce***	Y	Y	Y	Y	Y	Y

	216	217	218	219	220	221
40 ***Lewis***	Y	Y	N	Y	Y	Y
41 ***Miller, Gary***	Y	Y	Y	Y	Y	Y
42 Brown	?	?	?	?	?	?
43 ***Calvert***	Y	Y	Y	Y	Y	Y
44 ***Bono***	Y	Y	Y	Y	Y	Y
45 ***Rohrabacher***	Y	Y	Y	Y	Y	Y
46 Sanchez	Y	Y	N	N	N	N
47 ***Cox***	Y	Y	Y	Y	Y	Y
48 ***Packard***	Y	Y	Y	Y	Y	Y
49 ***Bilbray***	Y	Y	Y	Y	Y	Y
50 Filner	N	Y	N	N	N	N
51 ***Cunningham***	Y	Y	Y	Y	Y	Y
52 ***Hunter***	Y	Y	Y	Y	Y	Y
COLORADO						
1 DeGette	N	Y	N	N	N	N
2 Udall	N	Y	Y	N	N	N
3 ***McInnis***	Y	Y	Y	Y	Y	Y
4 ***Schaffer***	Y	Y	Y	Y	Y	Y
5 ***Hefley***	Y	Y	N	Y	Y	Y
6 ***Tancredo***	Y	Y	Y	Y	Y	Y
CONNECTICUT						
1 Larson	N	Y	N	N	N	N
2 Gejdenson	N	Y	N	N	N	N
3 DeLauro	N	Y	N	N	N	N
4 ***Shays***	Y	Y	Y	Y	N	Y
5 Maloney	Y	Y	Y	N	N	N
6 ***Johnson***	Y	Y	Y	Y	N	Y
DELAWARE						
AL ***Castle***	Y	Y	N	Y	N	N
FLORIDA						
1 ***Scarborough***	Y	Y	N	Y	Y	Y
2 Boyd	Y	Y	N	Y	N	Y
3 Brown	N	Y	N	N	N	N
4 ***Fowler***	Y	Y	Y	Y	Y	Y
5 Thurman	Y	Y	N	Y	N	N
6 ***Stearns***	Y	Y	Y	Y	Y	Y
7 ***Mica***	Y	Y	Y	Y	Y	Y
8 ***McCollum***	Y	Y	Y	Y	Y	Y
9 ***Bilirakis***	Y	Y	Y	Y	Y	Y
10 ***Young***	Y	Y	Y	Y	Y	Y
11 Davis	Y	Y	N	Y	N	N
12 ***Canady***	Y	Y	Y	Y	Y	Y
13 ***Miller***	Y	Y	N	Y	Y	Y
14 ***Goss***	Y	Y	Y	Y	Y	Y
15 ***Weldon***	Y	Y	Y	Y	Y	Y
16 ***Foley***	Y	Y	Y	Y	Y	Y
17 Meek	N	Y	N	N	N	N
18 ***Ros-Lehtinen***	Y	Y	Y	Y	Y	Y
19 Wexler	N	Y	N	N	N	N
20 Deutsch	Y	Y	Y	Y	N	N
21 ***Diaz-Balart***	Y	Y	Y	Y	Y	Y
22 ***Shaw***	Y	Y	N	Y	Y	Y
23 Hastings	N	Y	N	N	N	N
GEORGIA						
1 ***Kingston***	Y	Y	N	Y	Y	Y
2 Bishop	Y	Y	Y	Y	Y	Y
3 ***Collins***	Y	Y	Y	Y	Y	Y
4 McKinney	N	Y	N	N	N	N
5 Lewis	N	Y	N	Y	N	N
6 ***Isakson***	Y	Y	N	Y	Y	Y
7 ***Barr***	Y	Y	Y	Y	Y	Y
8 ***Chambliss***	Y	Y	Y	Y	Y	Y
9 ***Deal***	Y	Y	Y	N	Y	Y
10 ***Norwood***	Y	Y	Y	Y	Y	Y
11 ***Linder***	Y	Y	Y	Y	Y	Y
HAWAII						
1 Abercrombie	N	Y	N	N	N	N
2 Mink	N	Y	N	N	N	N
IDAHO						
1 ***Chenoweth***	Y	Y	Y	Y	Y	Y
2 ***Simpson***	Y	Y	Y	Y	Y	Y
ILLINOIS						
1 Rush	N	Y	N	N	N	N
2 Jackson	N	Y	N	N	N	N
3 Lipinski	Y	Y	N	Y	N	Y
4 Gutierrez	Y	Y	N	N	N	N
5 Blagojevich	N	Y	N	Y	N	Y
6 ***Hyde***	Y	Y	Y	Y	Y	Y
7 Davis	N	Y	N	N	N	N
8 ***Crane***	Y	Y	Y	Y	Y	Y
9 Schakowsky	N	Y	N	N	N	N
10 ***Porter***	Y	Y	N	N	N	N
11 ***Weller***	Y	Y	Y	Y	Y	Y
12 Costello	Y	Y	N	Y	N	Y
13 ***Biggert***	Y	Y	N	Y	Y	Y
14 ***Hastert***						

ND Northern Democrats SD Southern Democrats

	216	217	218	219	220	221
15 ***Ewing***	Y	Y	N	Y	Y	Y
16 ***Manzullo***	Y	Y	N	Y	Y	Y
17 Evans	N	Y	N	N	N	N
18 ***LaHood***	Y	Y	N	Y	Y	Y
19 Phelps	Y	Y	N	Y	N	Y
20 ***Shimkus***	Y	Y	N	Y	Y	Y
INDIANA						
1 Visclosky	Y	Y	N	Y	N	N
2 ***McIntosh***	Y	Y	Y	Y	Y	Y
3 Roemer	Y	Y	Y	Y	Y	Y
4 ***Souder***	Y	Y	N	Y	Y	Y
5 ***Buyer***	Y	Y	Y	Y	Y	Y
6 ***Burton***	Y	Y	Y	Y	Y	Y
7 ***Pease***	Y	Y	Y	Y	Y	Y
8 ***Hostettler***	Y	Y	N	Y	Y	Y
9 Hill	Y	Y	Y	Y	Y	N
10 Carson	N	Y	N	N	N	–
IOWA						
1 ***Leach***	Y	Y	Y	Y	Y	Y
2 ***Nussle***	Y	Y	N	Y	Y	Y
3 Boswell	Y	Y	Y	Y	Y	Y
4 ***Ganske***	Y	Y	N	Y	Y	Y
5 ***Latham***	Y	Y	Y	Y	Y	Y
KANSAS						
1 ***Moran***	Y	Y	N	Y	Y	Y
2 ***Ryun***	Y	Y	Y	Y	Y	Y
3 Moore	Y	Y	Y	Y	N	N
4 ***Tiahrt***	Y	Y	Y	Y	Y	Y
KENTUCKY						
1 ***Whitfield***	Y	Y	N	Y	Y	Y
2 ***Lewis***	Y	Y	Y	Y	Y	Y
3 ***Northup***	Y	Y	N	Y	Y	Y
4 Lucas	Y	Y	Y	Y	Y	Y
5 ***Rogers***	Y	Y	Y	Y	Y	Y
6 ***Fletcher***	Y	Y	Y	Y	Y	Y
LOUISIANA						
1 ***Vitter***	Y	Y	Y	Y	Y	Y
2 Jefferson	N	Y	N	N	N	N
3 ***Tauzin***	Y	Y	Y	Y	Y	Y
4 ***McCrery***	Y	Y	N	Y	Y	Y
5 ***Cooksey***	N	Y	Y	N	N	N
6 ***Baker***	Y	Y	Y	Y	Y	Y
7 John	Y	Y	Y	Y	Y	Y
MAINE						
1 Allen	N	Y	N	N	N	N
2 Baldacci	Y	Y	N	N	N	N
MARYLAND						
1 ***Gilchrest***	Y	Y	Y	Y	Y	Y
2 ***Ehrlich***	Y	N	N	Y	Y	N
3 Cardin	N	Y	N	N	N	N
4 Wynn	N	Y	N	Y	N	N
5 Hoyer	N	Y	N	N	N	N
6 ***Bartlett***	Y	Y	Y	Y	Y	Y
7 Cummings	N	Y	N	N	N	N
8 ***Morella***	Y	Y	Y	N	N	N
MASSACHUSETTS						
1 Olver	N	Y	N	N	N	N
2 Neal	N	Y	N	N	N	N
3 McGovern	N	Y	N	N	N	N
4 Frank	N	Y	N	N	N	N
5 Meehan	N	Y	N	N	N	N
6 Tierney	N	Y	N	N	N	N
7 Markey	N	Y	N	N	N	N
8 Capuano	N	Y	N	N	N	N
9 Moakley	N	Y	N	N	N	N
10 Delahunt	N	Y	N	N	N	N
MICHIGAN						
1 Stupak	N	Y	N	Y	N	Y
2 ***Hoekstra***	Y	Y	N	Y	Y	Y
3 ***Ehlers***	Y	Y	N	Y	Y	Y
4 ***Camp***	Y	Y	N	Y	Y	Y
5 Barcia	Y	Y	Y	Y	Y	Y
6 ***Upton***	Y	Y	Y	Y	Y	Y
7 ***Smith***	Y	Y	N	Y	Y	Y
8 Stabenow	Y	Y	Y	Y	N	Y
9 Kildee	N	Y	N	N	N	N
10 Bonior	N	Y	N	N	N	N
11 ***Knollenberg***	Y	Y	Y	Y	Y	Y
12 Levin	N	Y	N	N	N	N
13 Rivers	N	Y	N	N	N	N
14 Conyers	N	Y	N	N	N	N
15 Kilpatrick	N	Y	N	N	N	N
16 Dingell	N	Y	N	N	N	N
MINNESOTA						
1 ***Gutknecht***	Y	Y	Y	Y	Y	Y
2 Minge	N	Y	N	N	N	N
3 ***Ramstad***	Y	Y	Y	Y	Y	Y
4 Vento	N	Y	N	N	N	N
5 Sabo	N	Y	N	N	N	N
6 Luther	N	Y	Y	N	N	N
7 Peterson	Y	Y	Y	Y	Y	Y
8 Oberstar	N	Y	N	N	N	N
MISSISSIPPI						
1 ***Wicker***	Y	Y	N	Y	Y	Y
2 Thompson	N	Y	N	N	N	N
3 ***Pickering***	Y	Y	Y	Y	Y	Y
4 Shows	Y	Y	Y	Y	Y	Y
5 Taylor	Y	Y	Y	Y	Y	Y
MISSOURI						
1 Clay	N	Y	N	N	N	N
2 ***Talent***	Y	Y	N	Y	Y	Y
3 Gephardt	?	?	?	?	?	N
4 Skelton	Y	Y	Y	Y	Y	Y
5 McCarthy	N	Y	N	N	N	N
6 Danner	Y	Y	Y	Y	Y	Y
7 ***Blunt***	Y	Y	N	Y	Y	Y
8 ***Emerson***	Y	Y	N	Y	Y	Y
9 ***Hulshof***	Y	Y	N	Y	Y	Y
MONTANA						
AL ***Hill***	Y	Y	N	Y	Y	Y
NEBRASKA						
1 ***Bereuter***	Y	Y	Y	N	N	Y
2 ***Terry***	Y	Y	N	Y	Y	Y
3 ***Barrett***	Y	Y	Y	Y	Y	Y
NEVADA						
1 Berkley	Y	Y	N	N	N	N
2 ***Gibbons***	Y	Y	Y	Y	Y	Y
NEW HAMPSHIRE						
1 ***Sununu***	Y	Y	N	Y	Y	Y
2 ***Bass***	Y	Y	Y	Y	Y	Y
NEW JERSEY						
1 Andrews	N	Y	Y	N	N	N
2 ***LoBiondo***	Y	Y	Y	Y	Y	Y
3 ***Saxton***	Y	Y	Y	Y	Y	Y
4 ***Smith***	Y	Y	Y	Y	Y	?
5 ***Roukema***	Y	Y	Y	Y	Y	Y
6 Pallone	N	Y	Y	Y	N	N
7 ***Franks***	Y	Y	Y	Y	N	N
8 Pascrell	Y	Y	Y	Y	N	N
9 Rothman	N	Y	Y	Y	N	N
10 Payne	N	Y	N	N	N	N
11 ***Frelinghuysen***	Y	Y	Y	N	Y	N
12 Holt	N	Y	N	N	N	N
13 Menendez	N	Y	Y	Y	N	N
NEW MEXICO						
1 ***Wilson***	Y	Y	N	Y	Y	N
2 ***Skeen***	Y	Y	N	Y	Y	Y
3 Udall	Y	Y	Y	N	N	N
NEW YORK						
1 ***Forbes***	Y	Y	N	Y	Y	Y
2 ***Lazio***	Y	Y	N	Y	Y	N
3 ***King***	Y	Y	N	Y	N	Y
4 McCarthy	Y	Y	N	Y	N	N
5 Ackerman	N	Y	N	N	N	N
6 Meeks	N	Y	N	N	N	N
7 Crowley	N	Y	N	Y	N	N
8 Nadler	N	Y	N	N	N	N
9 Weiner	+	+	–	+	–	N
10 Towns	N	Y	N	N	N	N
11 Owens	N	Y	N	N	N	N
12 Velázquez	N	Y	N	N	N	N
13 ***Fossella***	Y	Y	N	Y	Y	Y
14 Maloney	N	Y	N	N	N	N
15 Rangel	N	Y	N	N	N	N
16 Serrano	N	Y	N	N	N	N
17 Engel	N	Y	N	N	N	N
18 Lowey	Y	Y	N	N	N	N
19 ***Kelly***	Y	Y	N	Y	Y	Y
20 ***Gilman***	Y	Y	N	Y	Y	Y
21 McNulty	Y	Y	N	Y	N	N
22 ***Sweeney***	Y	Y	N	Y	Y	Y
23 ***Boehlert***	Y	Y	N	Y	N	N
24 ***McHugh***	Y	Y	N	Y	Y	Y
25 ***Walsh***	Y	Y	N	Y	Y	Y
26 Hinchey	N	Y	N	N	N	N
27 ***Reynolds***	Y	Y	N	Y	Y	Y
28 Slaughter	N	Y	N	N	N	N
29 LaFalce	N	Y	N	Y	N	Y
30 ***Quinn***	Y	Y	N	Y	Y	Y
31 ***Houghton***	?	?	?	?	?	?
NORTH CAROLINA						
1 Clayton	N	Y	N	N	N	N
2 Etheridge	Y	Y	N	Y	Y	Y
3 ***Jones***	Y	Y	Y	Y	Y	Y
4 Price	Y	Y	N	Y	N	N
5 ***Burr***	Y	Y	Y	Y	Y	Y
6 ***Coble***	Y	Y	Y	Y	Y	Y
7 McIntyre	Y	Y	Y	Y	Y	Y
8 ***Hayes***	Y	Y	Y	Y	Y	Y
9 ***Myrick***	Y	Y	Y	Y	Y	Y
10 ***Ballenger***	Y	Y	Y	Y	Y	Y
11 ***Taylor***	Y	Y	Y	Y	Y	Y
12 Watt	N	Y	N	N	N	N
NORTH DAKOTA						
AL Pomeroy	Y	Y	Y	Y	N	N
OHIO						
1 ***Chabot***	Y	Y	Y	Y	Y	Y
2 ***Portman***	Y	Y	N	Y	Y	Y
3 Hall	Y	Y	Y	Y	Y	Y
4 ***Oxley***	Y	Y	Y	Y	Y	Y
5 ***Gillmor***	Y	Y	Y	Y	Y	Y
6 Strickland	N	Y	N	Y	N	N
7 ***Hobson***	Y	Y	Y	Y	Y	Y
8 ***Boehner***	Y	Y	Y	Y	Y	Y
9 Kaptur	Y	Y	N	Y	N	N
10 Kucinich	Y	Y	Y	N	N	N
11 Jones	N	Y	N	Y	N	N
12 ***Kasich***	Y	Y	Y	Y	N	Y
13 Brown	N	Y	N	Y	N	N
14 Sawyer	N	Y	N	Y	N	N
15 ***Pryce***	Y	Y	N	Y	Y	Y
16 ***Regula***	Y	Y	Y	Y	Y	Y
17 Traficant	Y	Y	Y	Y	Y	Y
18 ***Ney***	Y	Y	Y	Y	Y	Y
19 ***LaTourette***	Y	Y	N	Y	Y	Y
OKLAHOMA						
1 ***Largent***	Y	Y	N	Y	Y	Y
2 ***Coburn***	Y	Y	N	Y	Y	Y
3 ***Watkins***	Y	Y	Y	Y	Y	Y
4 ***Watts***	Y	Y	Y	Y	Y	Y
5 ***Istook***	Y	Y	Y	Y	Y	Y
6 ***Lucas***	Y	Y	N	Y	Y	Y
OREGON						
1 Wu	N	Y	Y	Y	N	N
2 ***Walden***	Y	Y	N	Y	Y	Y
3 Blumenauer	N	Y	N	N	N	N
4 DeFazio	Y	Y	N	Y	N	N
5 Hooley	Y	Y	N	Y	N	N
PENNSYLVANIA						
1 Brady	N	Y	N	N	N	N
2 Fattah	N	Y	N	N	N	N
3 Borski	N	Y	N	Y	N	N
4 Klink	N	Y	Y	Y	N	Y
5 ***Peterson***	Y	Y	Y	Y	Y	Y
6 Holden	Y	Y	Y	Y	Y	N
7 ***Weldon***	Y	Y	Y	Y	Y	Y
8 ***Greenwood***	Y	Y	N	Y	N	N
9 ***Shuster***	Y	Y	Y	Y	Y	Y
10 ***Sherwood***	Y	Y	Y	Y	Y	Y
11 Kanjorski	N	Y	N	Y	N	N
12 Murtha	Y	Y	N	Y	N	Y
13 Hoeffel	Y	Y	N	Y	N	N
14 Coyne	N	Y	N	N	N	N
15 ***Toomey***	Y	Y	N	Y	Y	N
16 ***Pitts***	Y	Y	Y	Y	Y	Y
17 ***Gekas***	Y	Y	Y	Y	Y	Y
18 Doyle	Y	Y	Y	Y	Y	Y
19 ***Goodling***	Y	Y	N	Y	Y	Y
20 Mascara	Y	Y	Y	Y	Y	Y
21 ***English***	Y	Y	Y	Y	N	Y
RHODE ISLAND						
1 Kennedy	N	Y	N	N	N	N
2 Weygand	Y	Y	N	N	N	N
SOUTH CAROLINA						
1 ***Sanford***	Y	Y	N	Y	Y	Y
2 ***Spence***	Y	Y	Y	Y	Y	Y
3 ***Graham***	Y	Y	Y	Y	Y	Y
4 ***DeMint***	Y	Y	Y	Y	Y	Y
5 Spratt	Y	Y	Y	Y	Y	N
6 Clyburn	N	Y	N	N	N	N
SOUTH DAKOTA						
AL ***Thune***	Y	Y	N	Y	Y	Y
TENNESSEE						
1 ***Jenkins***	Y	Y	Y	Y	Y	Y
2 ***Duncan***	Y	Y	Y	Y	Y	Y
3 ***Wamp***	Y	Y	N	Y	Y	Y
4 ***Hilleary***	Y	Y	Y	Y	Y	Y
5 Clement	Y	Y	N	Y	Y	Y
6 Gordon	N	Y	Y	Y	Y	Y
7 ***Bryant***	Y	Y	Y	Y	Y	Y
8 Tanner	Y	Y	N	N	N	Y
9 Ford	Y	Y	N	Y	N	Y
TEXAS						
1 Sandlin	Y	Y	Y	Y	N	Y
2 Turner	Y	Y	Y	Y	N	Y
3 ***Johnson, Sam***	Y	Y	N	Y	Y	Y
4 Hall	Y	Y	Y	Y	Y	Y
5 ***Sessions***	Y	Y	Y	Y	Y	Y
6 ***Barton***	Y	Y	Y	Y	Y	Y
7 ***Archer***	Y	Y	N	Y	Y	Y
8 ***Brady***	Y	Y	Y	Y	Y	Y
9 Lampson	Y	Y	Y	Y	N	N
10 Doggett	N	Y	N	N	N	N
11 Edwards	Y	Y	N	N	N	N
12 ***Granger***	Y	Y	Y	Y	Y	Y
13 ***Thornberry***	Y	Y	N	Y	Y	Y
14 ***Paul***	N	N	N	Y	Y	Y
15 Hinojosa	N	Y	N	N	N	N
16 Reyes	Y	Y	N	N	N	N
17 Stenholm	Y	Y	Y	Y	Y	Y
18 Jackson-Lee	N	Y	N	N	N	N
19 ***Combest***	Y	Y	Y	Y	Y	Y
20 Gonzalez	N	N	N	N	N	N
21 ***Smith***	Y	Y	Y	Y	Y	Y
22 ***DeLay***	Y	Y	N	Y	Y	Y
23 ***Bonilla***	Y	Y	N	Y	Y	Y
24 Frost	N	Y	N	N	N	N
25 Bentsen	N	Y	N	N	N	N
26 ***Armey***	Y	Y	Y	Y	Y	Y
27 Ortiz	Y	Y	N	Y	Y	Y
28 Rodriguez	N	Y	N	N	N	N
29 Green	Y	Y	Y	Y	N	Y
30 Johnson, E.B.	N	Y	N	N	N	N
UTAH						
1 ***Hansen***	Y	Y	N	Y	Y	Y
2 ***Cook***	Y	Y	Y	Y	Y	Y
3 ***Cannon***	Y	Y	Y	Y	Y	Y
VERMONT						
AL *Sanders*	N	Y	N	N	N	N
VIRGINIA						
1 ***Bateman***	Y	Y	N	Y	Y	Y
2 Pickett	Y	Y	N	N	N	N
3 Scott	N	Y	N	N	N	N
4 Sisisky	Y	Y	N	Y	N	N
5 Goode	Y	Y	Y	Y	Y	Y
6 ***Goodlatte***	Y	Y	Y	Y	Y	Y
7 ***Bliley***	Y	Y	Y	Y	Y	Y
8 Moran	Y	Y	N	Y	N	N
9 Boucher	Y	Y	N	Y	Y	N
10 ***Wolf***	Y	Y	Y	Y	Y	Y
11 ***Davis***	Y	Y	Y	Y	Y	Y
WASHINGTON						
1 Inslee	N	Y	N	Y	N	N
2 ***Metcalf***	Y	Y	Y	Y	Y	Y
3 Baird	N	Y	N	Y	N	N
4 ***Hastings***	Y	Y	N	Y	Y	Y
5 ***Nethercutt***	Y	Y	N	Y	Y	Y
6 Dicks	?	?	?	?	?	N
7 McDermott	N	Y	N	N	N	N
8 ***Dunn***	Y	Y	Y	Y	Y	Y
9 Smith	Y	Y	N	Y	N	N
WEST VIRGINIA						
1 Mollohan	Y	Y	Y	Y	Y	Y
2 Wise	Y	Y	Y	Y	N	N
3 Rahall	Y	Y	N	Y	Y	Y
WISCONSIN						
1 ***Ryan***	Y	Y	N	Y	Y	Y
2 Baldwin	N	Y	N	N	N	N
3 Kind	N	Y	N	N	N	N
4 Kleczka	N	Y	N	N	N	N
5 Barrett	N	Y	N	Y	N	N
6 ***Petri***	Y	Y	N	Y	Y	Y
7 Obey	Y	Y	N	Y	N	Y
8 ***Green***	Y	Y	N	Y	Y	Y
9 ***Sensenbrenner***	Y	Y	Y	Y	Y	Y
WYOMING						
AL ***Cubin***	Y	Y	N	Y	Y	Y

Southern states - Ala., Ark., Fla., Ga., Ky., La., Miss., N.C., Okla., S.C., Tenn., Texas, Va.

222. HR 1501. Juvenile Justice/Permit Religious Juvenile Justice Programs. Souder, R-Ind., amendment to ensure that religious organizations that desire to provide services relating to juvenile justice programs are not discriminated against when they compete for grants or contracts. Adopted 346-83: R 216-3; D 130-79 (ND 89-65, SD 41-14); I 0-1. June 17, 1999.

223. HR 1501. Juvenile Justice/Religious Discrimination. Souder, R-Ind., amendment to prohibit the Office of Juvenile Justice from discriminating against, denigrating or undermining the religious beliefs of any juvenile or adult participating in programs authorized by the bill. Rejected 210-216: R 174-43; D 36-172 (ND 16-138, SD 20-34); I 0-1. June 17, 1999.

224. HR 1501. Juvenile Justice/Violent Content Labels. Wamp, R-Tenn., amendment to create a comprehensive system for labeling violent content in audio and visual media products, including specifying a minimum age for purchasing, viewing or listening to the product; the system would be developed by producers of media products and subject to modification and final approval by the Federal Trade Commission. Rejected 161-266: R 114-105; D 47-160 (ND 33-119, SD 14-41); I 0-1. June 17, 1999.

225. HR 1501. Juvenile Justice/Violence in Media. Markey, D-Mass., amendment to require the surgeon general to review existing research and analysis and prepare a report to Congress on the impact on the health and welfare of children from violent messages delivered through television, radio, recordings, video games, advertisements and the Internet. Adopted 417-9: R 212-6; D 204-3 (ND 150-2, SD 54-1); I 1-0. June 17, 1999.

226. HR 1501. Juvenile Justice/Prevention Programs. Goodling, R-Pa., amendment to revise the current Juvenile Justice and Delinquency Prevention Act to give states and localities greater flexibility to address juvenile justice issues and combine several discretionary grant programs into a state block grant program; funds would be distributed to states based on the number of youths under age 18 in the state. Adopted 424-2: R 216-2; D 207-0 (ND 152-0, SD 55-0); I 1-0. June 17, 1999.

227. HR 1501. Juvenile Justice/Discipline of Disabled Students. Norwood, R-Ga., amendment to allow schools to discipline students with disabilities who bring weapons to school, in the same manner as they would students without disabilities, including suspending them or expelling them from school. Adopted 300-128: R 208-10; D 92-117 (ND 61-93, SD 31-24); I 0-1. June 17, 1999.

228. HR 1501. Juvenile Justice/Character Education Programs. Fletcher, R-Ky., amendment to allow state and local education agencies to form partnerships designed to implement character education programs. Adopted 422-1: R 215-0; D 206-1 (ND 151-1, SD 55-0); I 1-0. June 17, 1999.

Key

- Y Voted for (yea).
- # Paired for.
- \+ Announced for.
- N Voted against (nay).
- X Paired against.
- – Announced against.
- P Voted "present."
- C Voted "present" to avoid possible conflict of interest.
- ? Did not vote or otherwise make a position known.

•

Democrats ***Republicans***
Independents

	222	223	224	225	226	227	228
ALABAMA							
1 ***Callahan***	Y	Y	Y	Y	Y	Y	Y
2 ***Everett***	Y	Y	Y	Y	Y	Y	Y
3 ***Riley***	Y	Y	Y	Y	Y	Y	Y
4 ***Aderholt***	Y	Y	Y	Y	Y	Y	Y
5 Cramer	Y	Y	N	Y	Y	Y	Y
6 ***Bachus***	Y	Y	Y	Y	Y	Y	Y
7 Hilliard	N	N	N	Y	Y	N	Y
ALASKA							
AL ***Young***	Y	N	Y	Y	Y	Y	Y
ARIZONA							
1 ***Salmon***	Y	Y	Y	Y	Y	?	?
2 Pastor	Y	N	N	Y	Y	N	Y
3 ***Stump***	Y	Y	N	N	Y	Y	Y
4 ***Shadegg***	Y	Y	Y	N	Y	Y	Y
5 ***Kolbe***	Y	–	N	Y	Y	Y	Y
6 ***Hayworth***	Y	Y	Y	Y	Y	Y	Y
ARKANSAS							
1 Berry	Y	Y	Y	Y	Y	Y	Y
2 Snyder	Y	N	N	Y	Y	Y	Y
3 ***Hutchinson***	Y	Y	N	Y	Y	Y	Y
4 ***Dickey***	Y	Y	Y	Y	Y	Y	Y
CALIFORNIA							
1 Thompson	Y	N	Y	Y	Y	N	Y
2 ***Herger***	Y	Y	N	Y	Y	Y	Y
3 ***Ose***	Y	N	N	Y	Y	Y	Y
4 ***Doolittle***	Y	Y	N	Y	Y	Y	Y
5 Matsui	Y	N	N	Y	Y	N	Y
6 Woolsey	N	N	Y	Y	Y	N	Y
7 Miller, George	N	N	N	Y	Y	N	Y
8 Pelosi	N	N	N	Y	Y	N	Y
9 Lee	N	N	N	Y	Y	N	Y
10 Tauscher	Y	N	N	Y	Y	Y	Y
11 ***Pombo***	Y	Y	N	Y	Y	Y	Y
12 Lantos	N	N	N	Y	Y	N	Y
13 Stark	N	N	N	Y	Y	N	Y
14 Eshoo	N	N	N	Y	Y	N	Y
15 ***Campbell***	Y	Y	N	Y	Y	Y	Y
16 Lofgren	Y	N	N	Y	Y	Y	Y
17 Farr	Y	N	N	Y	Y	N	Y
18 Condit	Y	Y	N	Y	Y	Y	Y
19 ***Radanovich***	Y	Y	Y	Y	Y	Y	?
20 Dooley	Y	N	N	Y	Y	Y	Y
21 ***Thomas***	?	?	?	?	?	?	?
22 Capps	Y	N	N	Y	Y	N	Y
23 ***Gallegly***	Y	Y	N	Y	Y	Y	Y
24 Sherman	Y	N	N	Y	Y	Y	Y
25 ***McKeon***	Y	N	N	Y	Y	Y	Y
26 Berman	Y	N	N	Y	Y	N	Y
27 ***Rogan***	Y	Y	N	Y	Y	Y	Y
28 ***Dreier***	Y	N	N	Y	Y	Y	Y
29 Waxman	N	N	N	Y	?	N	Y
30 Becerra	Y	N	N	Y	Y	N	Y
31 Martinez	N	N	N	Y	Y	N	Y
32 Dixon	N	N	N	Y	Y	N	Y
33 Roybal-Allard	N	N	N	Y	Y	N	Y
34 Napolitano	N	N	N	Y	Y	N	Y
35 Waters	N	N	N	Y	Y	N	Y
36 ***Kuykendall***	Y	N	N	Y	Y	Y	Y
37 Millender-McD.	N	N	N	Y	Y	N	Y
38 ***Horn***	N	N	Y	Y	Y	Y	Y
39 ***Royce***	Y	Y	N	Y	Y	Y	Y
40 ***Lewis***	Y	N	N	Y	Y	Y	Y
41 ***Miller, Gary***	Y	Y	Y	Y	?	Y	Y
42 Brown	?	?	?	?	?	?	?
43 ***Calvert***	Y	Y	N	Y	Y	Y	Y
44 ***Bono***	Y	Y	N	Y	Y	Y	Y
45 ***Rohrabacher***	Y	Y	N	Y	Y	Y	Y
46 Sanchez	Y	N	N	Y	Y	N	Y
47 ***Cox***	Y	Y	N	Y	Y	Y	Y
48 ***Packard***	Y	Y	N	Y	Y	Y	Y
49 ***Bilbray***	Y	N	Y	Y	Y	Y	Y
50 Filner	N	N	N	Y	Y	N	Y
51 ***Cunningham***	Y	Y	N	Y	Y	Y	Y
52 ***Hunter***	Y	Y	Y	Y	Y	Y	Y
COLORADO							
1 DeGette	N	N	N	Y	Y	N	Y
2 Udall	N	N	N	Y	Y	Y	Y
3 ***McInnis***	Y	Y	N	Y	Y	Y	Y
4 ***Schaffer***	Y	Y	N	Y	Y	Y	Y
5 ***Hefley***	Y	Y	Y	Y	Y	Y	Y
6 ***Tancredo***	Y	Y	Y	Y	Y	Y	Y
CONNECTICUT							
1 Larson	Y	N	N	Y	Y	Y	Y
2 Gejdenson	N	N	N	Y	Y	N	Y
3 DeLauro	Y	N	N	Y	Y	N	Y
4 ***Shays***	Y	N	Y	Y	+	+	+
5 Maloney	Y	Y	Y	Y	Y	Y	Y
6 ***Johnson***	Y	N	N	Y	Y	Y	Y
DELAWARE							
AL ***Castle***	Y	N	Y	Y	Y	Y	Y
FLORIDA							
1 ***Scarborough***	Y	Y	N	Y	Y	Y	Y
2 Boyd	Y	Y	N	Y	Y	Y	Y
3 Brown	Y	N	N	Y	Y	N	Y
4 ***Fowler***	Y	Y	N	Y	Y	Y	Y
5 Thurman	Y	N	N	Y	Y	Y	Y
6 ***Stearns***	Y	Y	Y	Y	Y	Y	Y
7 ***Mica***	Y	Y	Y	Y	Y	Y	Y
8 ***McCollum***	Y	Y	N	Y	Y	Y	Y
9 ***Bilirakis***	Y	Y	Y	Y	Y	Y	Y
10 ***Young***	Y	Y	Y	Y	Y	Y	Y
11 Davis	Y	N	N	Y	Y	N	Y
12 ***Canady***	Y	Y	N	Y	Y	Y	Y
13 ***Miller***	Y	N	N	Y	Y	Y	Y
14 ***Goss***	Y	N	N	Y	Y	Y	Y
15 ***Weldon***	Y	Y	Y	Y	Y	Y	Y
16 ***Foley***	Y	N	N	Y	Y	Y	Y
17 Meek	N	N	N	Y	Y	N	Y
18 ***Ros-Lehtinen***	Y	Y	N	Y	Y	N	Y
19 Wexler	Y	N	N	Y	Y	N	Y
20 Deutsch	Y	N	N	Y	Y	N	Y
21 ***Diaz-Balart***	Y	Y	N	Y	Y	N	Y
22 ***Shaw***	Y	N	N	Y	Y	Y	Y
23 Hastings	N	N	N	Y	Y	N	Y
GEORGIA							
1 ***Kingston***	Y	Y	N	Y	Y	Y	Y
2 Bishop	Y	N	N	Y	Y	Y	Y
3 ***Collins***	Y	Y	Y	Y	Y	Y	Y
4 McKinney	Y	N	N	Y	Y	N	Y
5 Lewis	N	N	N	Y	Y	N	Y
6 ***Isakson***	Y	N	N	Y	Y	Y	Y
7 ***Barr***	Y	Y	N	N	Y	Y	Y
8 ***Chambliss***	Y	Y	Y	Y	Y	Y	Y
9 ***Deal***	Y	N	Y	Y	Y	Y	Y
10 ***Norwood***	Y	Y	Y	Y	Y	Y	Y
11 ***Linder***	Y	?	N	Y	Y	Y	Y
HAWAII							
1 Abercrombie	Y	N	N	Y	Y	N	Y
2 Mink	N	N	N	Y	Y	N	Y
IDAHO							
1 ***Chenoweth***	Y	Y	Y	Y	Y	Y	Y
2 ***Simpson***	Y	Y	N	Y	Y	Y	Y
ILLINOIS							
1 Rush	N	N	N	Y	Y	N	Y
2 Jackson	N	N	N	Y	Y	N	Y
3 Lipinski	Y	Y	Y	Y	Y	Y	Y
4 Gutierrez	N	N	N	Y	Y	N	Y
5 Blagojevich	N	N	Y	Y	Y	N	Y
6 ***Hyde***	Y	Y	Y	Y	Y	Y	Y
7 Davis	N	N	N	Y	Y	N	Y
8 ***Crane***	Y	Y	Y	Y	Y	Y	Y
9 Schakowsky	N	N	N	Y	Y	N	Y
10 ***Porter***	Y	Y	Y	Y	Y	Y	Y
11 ***Weller***	Y	Y	N	Y	Y	Y	Y
12 Costello	Y	Y	Y	Y	Y	Y	Y
13 ***Biggert***	Y	N	N	Y	Y	Y	Y
14 ***Hastert***							

ND Northern Democrats SD Southern Democrats

	222	223	224	225	226	227	228
15 ***Ewing***	Y	N	Y	Y	Y	Y	Y
16 ***Manzullo***	Y	Y	N	Y	Y	Y	Y
17 Evans	N	N	N	Y	?	N	Y
18 ***LaHood***	Y	Y	Y	Y	Y	Y	Y
19 Phelps	Y	N	N	Y	Y	Y	Y
20 ***Shimkus***	Y	Y	Y	Y	Y	Y	Y
INDIANA							
1 Visclosky	Y	N	Y	Y	Y	Y	Y
2 ***McIntosh***	Y	Y	Y	Y	Y	Y	Y
3 Roemer	Y	Y	Y	Y	Y	Y	Y
4 ***Souder***	Y	Y	Y	Y	Y	N	Y
5 ***Buyer***	Y	Y	N	Y	Y	Y	Y
6 ***Burton***	Y	Y	N	Y	Y	Y	Y
7 ***Pease***	Y	N	N	Y	Y	Y	Y
8 ***Hostettler***	Y	Y	N	Y	Y	Y	Y
9 Hill	Y	N	Y	Y	Y	Y	Y
10 Carson	+	−	−	+	+	−	+
IOWA							
1 ***Leach***	Y	N	Y	Y	Y	Y	Y
2 ***Nussle***	Y	Y	Y	?	Y	Y	Y
3 Boswell	Y	Y	N	Y	Y	Y	Y
4 ***Ganske***	Y	N	N	Y	Y	Y	Y
5 ***Latham***	Y	Y	N	Y	Y	Y	Y
KANSAS							
1 ***Moran***	Y	Y	N	Y	Y	Y	Y
2 ***Ryun***	Y	Y	Y	Y	Y	Y	Y
3 Moore	Y	N	N	Y	Y	Y	Y
4 ***Tiahrt***	Y	Y	Y	Y	Y	Y	Y
KENTUCKY							
1 ***Whitfield***	Y	Y	N	Y	Y	Y	Y
2 ***Lewis***	Y	Y	Y	Y	Y	Y	Y
3 ***Northup***	Y	N	N	Y	Y	Y	?
4 Lucas	Y	Y	Y	Y	Y	Y	Y
5 ***Rogers***	Y	Y	Y	Y	Y	Y	Y
6 ***Fletcher***	Y	Y	Y	Y	Y	Y	Y
LOUISIANA							
1 ***Vitter***	Y	Y	Y	Y	Y	Y	Y
2 Jefferson	Y	N	N	Y	Y	Y	Y
3 ***Tauzin***	Y	Y	N	Y	Y	Y	Y
4 ***McCrery***	Y	Y	N	Y	Y	Y	Y
5 ***Cooksey***	Y	N	N	Y	Y	Y	Y
6 ***Baker***	Y	Y	N	Y	Y	Y	Y
7 John	Y	Y	N	Y	Y	Y	Y
MAINE							
1 Allen	N	N	N	Y	Y	Y	Y
2 Baldacci	Y	N	N	Y	Y	Y	Y
MARYLAND							
1 ***Gilchrest***	Y	N	Y	Y	Y	Y	Y
2 ***Ehrlich***	Y	Y	N	Y	Y	Y	Y
3 Cardin	N	N	N	Y	Y	N	Y
4 Wynn	Y	N	N	Y	Y	Y	Y
5 Hoyer	Y	N	N	Y	Y	N	Y
6 ***Bartlett***	Y	Y	Y	Y	Y	Y	Y
7 Cummings	N	N	N	Y	Y	N	Y
8 ***Morella***	N	N	N	Y	Y	N	Y
MASSACHUSETTS							
1 Olver	N	N	N	Y	Y	N	Y
2 Neal	Y	N	N	Y	Y	N	Y
3 McGovern	Y	N	N	Y	Y	N	Y
4 Frank	Y	N	N	Y	Y	N	Y
5 Meehan	Y	N	N	Y	Y	N	Y
6 Tierney	N	N	N	Y	Y	N	Y
7 Markey	Y	N	N	Y	Y	N	Y
8 Capuano	Y	N	N	Y	Y	Y	N
9 Moakley	Y	N	N	Y	Y	N	Y
10 Delahunt	Y	N	N	Y	Y	N	Y
MICHIGAN							
1 Stupak	Y	N	Y	Y	Y	N	Y
2 ***Hoekstra***	Y	Y	N	Y	Y	Y	Y
3 ***Ehlers***	Y	Y	Y	Y	Y	Y	Y
4 ***Camp***	Y	Y	N	Y	Y	Y	Y
5 Barcia	Y	Y	Y	Y	Y	Y	?
6 ***Upton***	Y	Y	N	Y	Y	Y	Y
7 ***Smith***	Y	N	Y	Y	Y	Y	Y
8 Stabenow	Y	N	Y	Y	Y	N	Y
9 Kildee	Y	N	N	Y	Y	Y	Y
10 Bonior	Y	N	N	Y	Y	Y	Y
11 ***Knollenberg***	Y	Y	N	Y	Y	N	Y
12 Levin	Y	N	N	Y	Y	Y	Y
13 Rivers	Y	N	N	Y	Y	N	Y
14 Conyers	N	N	N	Y	Y	N	Y
15 Kilpatrick	N	N	N	Y	Y	N	Y
16 Dingell	Y	Y	N	Y	Y	Y	Y

	222	223	224	225	226	227	228
MINNESOTA							
1 ***Gutknecht***	Y	Y	Y	Y	Y	Y	Y
2 Minge	Y	N	Y	Y	Y	Y	?
3 ***Ramstad***	Y	Y	Y	Y	Y	Y	Y
4 Vento	N	N	N	Y	Y	Y	Y
5 Sabo	Y	N	N	Y	Y	Y	Y
6 Luther	Y	N	Y	Y	Y	N	Y
7 Peterson	Y	Y	Y	N	Y	Y	Y
8 Oberstar	N	N	N	Y	Y	Y	Y
MISSISSIPPI							
1 ***Wicker***	Y	Y	Y	Y	Y	Y	Y
2 Thompson	Y	N	N	Y	Y	N	Y
3 ***Pickering***	Y	Y	Y	Y	Y	Y	Y
4 Shows	Y	Y	Y	Y	Y	Y	Y
5 Taylor	Y	Y	Y	Y	Y	Y	Y
MISSOURI							
1 Clay	N	N	N	Y	Y	N	Y
2 ***Talent***	Y	Y	Y	Y	Y	Y	Y
3 Gephardt	Y	N	N	Y	Y	N	Y
4 Skelton	Y	Y	Y	Y	Y	Y	Y
5 McCarthy	Y	N	N	Y	Y	N	Y
6 Danner	Y	Y	Y	Y	Y	Y	Y
7 ***Blunt***	Y	Y	Y	Y	Y	Y	Y
8 ***Emerson***	Y	Y	Y	Y	Y	Y	Y
9 ***Hulshof***	Y	Y	N	N	Y	Y	Y
MONTANA							
AL ***Hill***	Y	Y	Y	Y	Y	Y	Y
NEBRASKA							
1 ***Bereuter***	Y	Y	Y	Y	N	Y	Y
2 ***Terry***	Y	Y	N	Y	Y	Y	Y
3 ***Barrett***	Y	Y	N	Y	Y	Y	Y
NEVADA							
1 Berkley	N	N	N	N	Y	Y	Y
2 ***Gibbons***	Y	Y	N	Y	Y	Y	Y
NEW HAMPSHIRE							
1 ***Sununu***	Y	Y	N	Y	Y	Y	Y
2 ***Bass***	Y	Y	Y	Y	Y	Y	Y
NEW JERSEY							
1 Andrews	Y	N	N	Y	Y	Y	Y
2 ***LoBiondo***	Y	Y	Y	Y	Y	Y	Y
3 ***Saxton***	Y	Y	Y	Y	Y	Y	Y
4 ***Smith***	?	?	?	?	Y	Y	Y
5 ***Roukema***	Y	Y	Y	Y	Y	Y	Y
6 Pallone	N	N	N	Y	Y	N	Y
7 ***Franks***	Y	Y	Y	Y	Y	Y	Y
8 Pascrell	Y	N	Y	Y	Y	N	Y
9 Rothman	N	N	Y	Y	Y	Y	Y
10 Payne	N	N	N	Y	Y	N	Y
11 ***Frelinghuysen***	Y	N	Y	Y	Y	N	Y
12 Holt	Y	N	Y	Y	Y	Y	Y
13 Menendez	N	N	N	Y	Y	Y	Y
NEW MEXICO							
1 ***Wilson***	Y	N	Y	Y	Y	Y	Y
2 ***Skeen***	Y	Y	Y	Y	Y	Y	Y
3 Udall	Y	N	N	Y	Y	N	Y
NEW YORK							
1 ***Forbes***	Y	N	Y	Y	Y	Y	Y
2 ***Lazio***	Y	Y	N	Y	Y	Y	Y
3 ***King***	Y	Y	Y	Y	Y	Y	Y
4 McCarthy	N	N	Y	Y	Y	N	Y
5 Ackerman	N	N	N	Y	Y	N	Y
6 Meeks	Y	N	N	Y	Y	N	Y
7 Crowley	Y	N	N	Y	Y	N	Y
8 Nadler	N	N	N	Y	Y	N	Y
9 Weiner	Y	N	N	Y	Y	N	Y
10 Towns	Y	N	N	Y	Y	N	Y
11 Owens	Y	N	N	Y	Y	N	Y
12 Velazquez	N	N	N	Y	Y	N	Y
13 ***Fossella***	Y	Y	N	Y	Y	Y	Y
14 Maloney	N	N	N	Y	Y	N	Y
15 Rangel	N	N	N	Y	Y	N	Y
16 Serrano	N	N	N	Y	Y	N	Y
17 Engel	N	N	N	Y	Y	N	Y
18 Lowey	N	N	N	Y	Y	N	Y
19 ***Kelly***	Y	N	Y	Y	Y	N	Y
20 ***Gilman***	Y	N	N	Y	Y	N	Y
21 McNulty	N	N	N	Y	Y	N	Y
22 ***Sweeney***	Y	Y	N	Y	Y	Y	Y
23 ***Boehlert***	Y	N	Y	Y	Y	N	Y
24 ***McHugh***	Y	Y	Y	Y	Y	Y	Y
25 ***Walsh***	Y	Y	Y	Y	Y	N	Y
26 Hinchey	N	N	N	Y	Y	N	Y
27 ***Reynolds***	Y	Y	N	Y	Y	Y	Y
28 Slaughter	N	N	N	Y	Y	N	Y
29 LaFalce	Y	N	N	Y	Y	Y	Y

	222	223	224	225	226	227	228
30 ***Quinn***	Y	Y	N	Y	Y	Y	Y
31 ***Houghton***	?	?	?	?	?	?	?
NORTH CAROLINA							
1 Clayton	N	N	N	Y	Y	N	Y
2 Etheridge	Y	N	Y	Y	Y	Y	Y
3 ***Jones***	Y	Y	Y	Y	Y	Y	Y
4 Price	Y	N	Y	Y	Y	Y	Y
5 ***Burr***	Y	Y	Y	Y	Y	Y	Y
6 ***Coble***	Y	Y	N	Y	Y	Y	Y
7 McIntyre	Y	Y	Y	Y	Y	Y	Y
8 ***Hayes***	Y	Y	Y	Y	Y	Y	Y
9 ***Myrick***	Y	Y	Y	Y	Y	Y	Y
10 ***Ballenger***	Y	N	N	Y	Y	Y	Y
11 ***Taylor***	Y	Y	Y	Y	Y	Y	Y
12 Watt	N	N	N	Y	Y	N	Y
NORTH DAKOTA							
AL Pomeroy	Y	Y	Y	Y	Y	Y	Y
OHIO							
1 ***Chabot***	Y	Y	N	Y	Y	Y	Y
2 ***Portman***	Y	Y	N	Y	Y	Y	Y
3 Hall	Y	N	Y	Y	Y	Y	Y
4 ***Oxley***	Y	Y	N	Y	Y	Y	Y
5 ***Gillmor***	Y	Y	N	Y	Y	Y	Y
6 Strickland	Y	N	N	Y	Y	N	Y
7 ***Hobson***	Y	Y	N	Y	Y	Y	Y
8 ***Boehner***	Y	Y	N	Y	Y	Y	Y
9 Kaptur	Y	N	Y	Y	Y	Y	Y
10 Kucinich	N	N	N	Y	Y	Y	Y
11 Jones	N	N	N	Y	Y	N	Y
12 ***Kasich***	Y	Y	N	Y	Y	Y	Y
13 Brown	N	N	N	Y	Y	N	Y
14 Sawyer	Y	N	N	Y	Y	N	Y
15 ***Pryce***	Y	N	Y	Y	Y	Y	Y
16 ***Regula***	Y	N	Y	Y	Y	Y	Y
17 Traficant	Y	Y	Y	Y	Y	Y	Y
18 ***Ney***	Y	Y	N	Y	Y	Y	Y
19 ***LaTourette***	Y	N	Y	Y	Y	Y	Y
OKLAHOMA							
1 ***Largent***	Y	Y	Y	Y	Y	Y	Y
2 ***Coburn***	Y	Y	Y	Y	Y	Y	Y
3 ***Watkins***	Y	Y	Y	Y	Y	Y	Y
4 ***Watts***	Y	Y	Y	Y	Y	Y	Y
5 ***Istook***	Y	Y	N	Y	Y	Y	Y
6 ***Lucas***	Y	Y	Y	Y	Y	Y	Y
OREGON							
1 Wu	N	N	N	Y	Y	Y	Y
2 ***Walden***	Y	Y	N	Y	Y	Y	Y
3 Blumenauer	N	N	N	Y	Y	Y	Y
4 DeFazio	Y	N	Y	Y	Y	N	Y
5 Hooley	Y	N	N	Y	Y	Y	Y
PENNSYLVANIA							
1 Brady	N	N	N	Y	Y	N	Y
2 Fattah	N	N	N	Y	Y	N	Y
3 Borski	Y	N	N	Y	Y	Y	Y
4 Klink	Y	N	N	Y	Y	Y	Y
5 ***Peterson***	Y	Y	Y	Y	Y	Y	Y
6 Holden	Y	N	Y	Y	Y	Y	Y
7 ***Weldon***	Y	Y	Y	Y	Y	Y	Y
8 ***Greenwood***	Y	N	Y	Y	Y	Y	Y
9 ***Shuster***	Y	N	Y	Y	Y	Y	Y
10 ***Sherwood***	Y	Y	N	Y	Y	Y	Y
11 Kanjorski	Y	N	N	Y	Y	Y	Y
12 Murtha	Y	N	N	Y	Y	N	Y
13 Hoeffel	N	N	N	Y	Y	N	Y
14 Coyne	Y	N	N	Y	Y	N	Y
15 ***Toomey***	Y	Y	N	Y	Y	Y	Y
16 ***Pitts***	Y	Y	Y	Y	Y	Y	Y
17 ***Gekas***	Y	Y	Y	Y	Y	Y	Y
18 Doyle	Y	N	Y	Y	Y	Y	Y
19 ***Goodling***	Y	N	Y	Y	Y	N	Y
20 Mascara	Y	N	Y	Y	Y	Y	Y
21 ***English***	Y	Y	N	Y	Y	Y	Y
RHODE ISLAND							
1 Kennedy	N	N	N	Y	Y	N	Y
2 Weygand	Y	N	N	Y	Y	N	Y
SOUTH CAROLINA							
1 ***Sanford***	Y	Y	N	Y	Y	Y	Y
2 ***Spence***	Y	Y	Y	Y	Y	Y	Y
3 ***Graham***	Y	Y	Y	Y	Y	Y	Y
4 ***DeMint***	Y	Y	Y	Y	Y	Y	Y
5 Spratt	Y	Y	N	Y	Y	Y	Y
6 Clyburn	Y	N	N	Y	Y	N	Y
SOUTH DAKOTA							
AL ***Thune***	Y	Y	N	Y	Y	Y	Y

	222	223	224	225	226	227	228
TENNESSEE							
1 ***Jenkins***	Y	Y	Y	Y	Y	Y	Y
2 ***Duncan***	Y	Y	Y	Y	Y	Y	Y
3 ***Wamp***	Y	Y	Y	Y	Y	Y	Y
4 ***Hilleary***	Y	Y	Y	Y	Y	Y	Y
5 Clement	Y	Y	N	Y	Y	Y	Y
6 Gordon	Y	Y	N	Y	Y	Y	Y
7 ***Bryant***	Y	Y	Y	Y	Y	Y	Y
8 Tanner	Y	Y	N	Y	Y	Y	Y
9 Ford	Y	Y	N	Y	Y	N	Y
TEXAS							
1 Sandlin	Y	N	N	Y	Y	N	Y
2 Turner	Y	Y	Y	Y	Y	Y	Y
3 ***Johnson, Sam***	Y	Y	N	Y	Y	Y	?
4 Hall	Y	Y	Y	Y	Y	Y	Y
5 ***Sessions***	Y	Y	Y	Y	Y	N	Y
6 ***Barton***	Y	Y	N	Y	Y	Y	Y
7 ***Archer***	Y	Y	N	Y	Y	Y	Y
8 ***Brady***	Y	Y	Y	Y	Y	Y	Y
9 Lampson	N	N	N	Y	Y	N	Y
10 Doggett	N	N	N	Y	Y	N	Y
11 Edwards	N	N	N	Y	Y	Y	Y
12 ***Granger***	Y	Y	Y	Y	Y	Y	Y
13 ***Thornberry***	Y	Y	Y	Y	Y	Y	Y
14 ***Paul***	N	Y	N	N	N	Y	Y
15 Hinojosa	Y	N	N	Y	Y	N	Y
16 Reyes	Y	Y	N	Y	Y	N	Y
17 Stenholm	Y	Y	Y	Y	Y	Y	Y
18 Jackson-Lee	Y	N	N	Y	Y	N	Y
19 ***Combest***	Y	Y	Y	Y	Y	Y	Y
20 Gonzalez	N	N	N	Y	Y	N	Y
21 ***Smith***	Y	N	Y	Y	Y	Y	Y
22 ***DeLay***	Y	Y	Y	Y	Y	Y	Y
23 ***Bonilla***	Y	Y	N	N	Y	Y	Y
24 Frost	Y	N	N	Y	Y	Y	Y
25 Bentsen	Y	N	N	Y	Y	Y	Y
26 ***Armey***	Y	Y	N	Y	Y	Y	Y
27 Ortiz	Y	Y	Y	Y	Y	Y	Y
28 Rodriguez	Y	Y	Y	Y	Y	N	Y
29 Green	Y	N	N	Y	Y	N	Y
30 Johnson, E.B.	N	N	N	Y	Y	Y	Y
UTAH							
1 ***Hansen***	Y	Y	Y	Y	Y	Y	Y
2 ***Cook***	Y	Y	Y	Y	Y	Y	Y
3 ***Cannon***	Y	Y	Y	Y	Y	Y	Y
VERMONT							
AL *Sanders*	N	N	N	Y	Y	N	Y
VIRGINIA							
1 ***Bateman***	Y	Y	Y	Y	Y	Y	Y
2 Pickett	N	N	N	Y	Y	Y	Y
3 Scott	N	N	N	Y	Y	N	Y
4 Sisisky	N	N	Y	Y	Y	Y	Y
5 Goode	Y	Y	Y	N	Y	Y	Y
6 ***Goodlatte***	Y	Y	N	Y	Y	Y	Y
7 ***Bliley***	Y	Y	N	Y	Y	Y	Y
8 Moran	Y	N	N	Y	Y	Y	Y
9 Boucher	Y	?	N	Y	Y	Y	Y
10 ***Wolf***	Y	Y	Y	Y	Y	Y	Y
11 ***Davis***	Y	Y	N	Y	Y	Y	Y
WASHINGTON							
1 Inslee	Y	N	N	Y	Y	Y	Y
2 ***Metcalf***	Y	Y	N	Y	Y	Y	Y
3 Baird	Y	N	N	Y	Y	Y	Y
4 ***Hastings***	Y	Y	N	Y	Y	Y	Y
5 ***Nethercutt***	Y	Y	N	Y	Y	Y	Y
6 Dicks	Y	N	N	Y	Y	Y	Y
7 McDermott	N	N	N	Y	Y	N	Y
8 ***Dunn***	Y	Y	N	Y	Y	Y	Y
9 Smith	Y	N	N	Y	Y	Y	Y
WEST VIRGINIA							
1 Mollohan	Y	Y	?	?	Y	Y	Y
2 Wise	Y	Y	Y	Y	Y	Y	Y
3 Rahall	Y	Y	?	?	Y	N	Y
WISCONSIN							
1 ***Ryan***	Y	Y	N	Y	Y	Y	Y
2 Baldwin	N	N	N	Y	Y	N	Y
3 Kind	N	N	N	Y	Y	Y	Y
4 Kleczka	Y	N	Y	Y	Y	Y	Y
5 Barrett	Y	N	N	Y	Y	N	Y
6 ***Petri***	Y	N	N	Y	Y	Y	Y
7 Obey	Y	N	Y	Y	Y	Y	Y
8 ***Green***	Y	Y	Y	Y	Y	Y	Y
9 ***Sensenbrenner***	Y	Y	N	Y	Y	Y	Y
WYOMING							
AL ***Cubin***	Y	N	Y	Y	Y	Y	Y

Southern states - Ala., Ark., Fla., Ga., Ky., La., Miss., N.C., Okla., S.C., Tenn., Texas, Va.

229. HR 1501. Juvenile Justice/Civil Immunity For Teachers. McIntosh, R-Ind., amendment to provide limited civil immunity for teachers, principals, local school board members and other education professionals who engage in reasonable actions to maintain order, discipline and an appropriate educational environment in schools and classrooms. Adopted 300-126: R 200-17; D 100-108; I 0-1. June 17, 1999.

230. HR 1501. Juvenile Justice/GAO Study. Schaffer, R-Colo., amendment to require a comprehensive General Accounting Office (GAO) study of the effectiveness of current juvenile justice prevention programs, with legislative recommendations to improve their effectiveness. Adopted 364-60: R 210-6; D 153-54 (ND 107-45, SD 46-9); I 1-0. June 17, 1999.

231. HR 1501. Juvenile Justice/Entertainment Industry. Emerson, R-Mo., amendment to express the sense of Congress condemning the entertainment industry for the use of pointless acts of brutality in movies, television, music and video games. Adopted 355-68: R 207-7; D 147-61 (ND 102-51, SD 45-10); I 1-0. June 17, 1999.

232. HR 1501. Juvenile Justice/Recommit. Conyers, D-Mich., motion to recommit the bill to the Judiciary Committee with instructions to report it back with provisions to reauthorize the "COPS" program; authorize funds for school resource officers and counselors, school safety programs and after-school programs; and require a study on the impact of violence in the media on children. Rejected 191-233: R 1-215; D 189-18 (ND 144-9, SD 45-9); I 1-0. June 17, 1999. A "yea" was a vote in support of the president's position.

233. HR 1501. Juvenile Justice/Passage. Passage of the bill to authorize a $1.5 billion five-year juvenile crime grant program; to increase sentences on juveniles for gun crimes; to impose mandatory sentences for those providing guns to minors; to permit prosecutors to try as adults minors charged with serious felonies; and to revise juvenile crime prevention programs. Passed 287-139: R 206-11; D 81-127 (ND 49-104, SD 32-23); I 0-1. June 17, 1999.

234. HR 2122. Gun Shows/24-Hour Background Checks. Dingell, D-Mich., amendment to require all gun show sales to complete a background check on purchases within 24 hours, and to require mandatory minimum prison sentence of 15 years for people who use gun clips with 10 rounds or more during the commission of a crime. Adopted 218-211: R 173-47; D 45-163 (ND 20-133, SD 25-30); I 0-1. June 18, 1999 (in the session that began and the Congressional Record dated June 17). A "nay" was a vote in support of the president's position.

235. HR 2122. Gun Shows/Three-Day Background Check. McCarthy, D-N.Y., amendment to require background checks for purchases at any event in which two or more vendors sell more than 50 guns and at least one gun is shipped across state lines; the amendment would give authorities up to three business days to complete the check. Rejected 193-235: R 33-186; D 159-49 (ND 129-24, SD 30-25); I 1-0. June 18, 1999 (in the session that began and the Congressional Record dated June 17). A "yea" was a vote in support of the president's position.

Key

- Y Voted for (yea).
- # Paired for.
- + Announced for.
- N Voted against (nay).
- X Paired against.
- – Announced against.
- P Voted "present."
- C Voted "present" to avoid possible conflict of interest.
- ? Did not vote or otherwise make a position known.

•

Democrats ***Republicans***
Independents

	229	230	231	232	233	234	235
ALABAMA							
1 ***Callahan***	Y	Y	Y	N	Y	Y	N
2 ***Everett***	Y	Y	Y	N	Y	Y	N
3 ***Riley***	Y	Y	Y	N	Y	Y	N
4 ***Aderholt***	Y	Y	Y	N	Y	Y	N
5 Cramer	Y	Y	Y	N	Y	Y	N
6 ***Bachus***	Y	Y	Y	N	Y	Y	N
7 Hilliard	Y	Y	Y	Y	N	Y	N
ALASKA							
AL ***Young***	Y	Y	Y	N	Y	Y	N
ARIZONA							
1 ***Salmon***	?	?	?	?	?	?	?
2 Pastor	N	Y	Y	Y	N	N	Y
3 ***Stump***	Y	Y	Y	N	Y	Y	N
4 ***Shadegg***	Y	Y	Y	N	Y	Y	N
5 ***Kolbe***	Y	Y	Y	N	Y	Y	N
6 ***Hayworth***	Y	Y	Y	N	Y	Y	N
ARKANSAS							
1 Berry	Y	Y	Y	Y	Y	N	Y
2 Snyder	N	Y	Y	Y	Y	N	Y
3 ***Hutchinson***	Y	Y	?	N	Y	Y	N
4 ***Dickey***	Y	Y	Y	N	Y	Y	N
CALIFORNIA							
1 Thompson	N	Y	N	Y	Y	N	Y
2 ***Herger***	Y	Y	Y	N	Y	Y	N
3 ***Ose***	Y	Y	N	N	Y	N	Y
4 ***Doolittle***	N	Y	Y	N	Y	N	N
5 Matsui	Y	Y	Y	Y	N	N	Y
6 Woolsey	N	Y	Y	Y	N	N	Y
7 Miller, George	N	N	N	Y	N	N	Y
8 Pelosi	N	N	N	Y	N	N	Y
9 Lee	N	N	N	Y	N	N	Y
10 Tauscher	Y	Y	Y	Y	Y	N	Y
11 ***Pombo***	Y	Y	Y	N	Y	Y	N
12 Lantos	Y	Y	Y	Y	N	N	Y
13 Stark	N	N	Y	Y	N	N	Y
14 Eshoo	N	N	N	Y	N	N	Y
15 ***Campbell***	N	Y	Y	N	N	N	Y
16 Lofgren	N	Y	Y	Y	N	N	Y
17 Farr	N	N	N	Y	N	N	Y
18 Condit	Y	Y	Y	Y	Y	N	Y
19 ***Radanovich***	Y	Y	Y	N	Y	Y	N
20 Dooley	Y	Y	N	Y	Y	N	Y
21 ***Thomas***	?	?	?	?	?	?	?
22 Capps	N	Y	Y	Y	Y	N	Y
23 ***Gallegly***	Y	Y	Y	N	Y	Y	N
24 Sherman	N	Y	N	Y	Y	N	Y
25 ***McKeon***	Y	Y	Y	N	Y	Y	N
26 Berman	N	N	N	Y	N	N	Y
27 ***Rogan***	Y	Y	N	N	Y	N	Y
28 ***Dreier***	Y	Y	Y	N	Y	Y	N
29 Waxman	N	N	N	Y	N	N	Y
30 Becerra	N	N	N	Y	N	N	Y
31 Martinez	Y	Y	N	Y	N	Y	Y
32 Dixon	N	Y	N	Y	N	N	Y
33 Roybal-Allard	N	N	N	Y	N	N	Y
34 Napolitano	N	Y	N	Y	N	N	Y
35 Waters	N	N	N	Y	N	N	Y
36 ***Kuykendall***	Y	Y	Y	N	Y	N	Y
37 Millender-McD.	N	N	N	Y	N	N	Y
38 ***Horn***	Y	Y	Y	N	Y	N	Y
39 ***Royce***	Y	Y	Y	N	Y	Y	N
40 ***Lewis***	Y	Y	N	N	Y	Y	N
41 ***Miller, Gary***	Y	Y	Y	N	Y	Y	N
42 Brown	?	?	?	?	?	?	?
43 ***Calvert***	Y	Y	Y	N	Y	Y	N
44 ***Bono***	N	Y	N	N	Y	N	N
45 ***Rohrabacher***	Y	Y	Y	N	Y	Y	N
46 Sanchez	Y	N	Y	Y	Y	N	Y
47 ***Cox***	Y	Y	?	N	Y	Y	N
48 ***Packard***	Y	Y	Y	N	Y	Y	N
49 ***Bilbray***	Y	Y	Y	N	Y	N	Y
50 Filner	N	N	N	Y	N	N	Y
51 ***Cunningham***	Y	Y	Y	N	Y	Y	N
52 ***Hunter***	Y	Y	Y	N	Y	Y	N
COLORADO							
1 DeGette	N	Y	Y	Y	N	N	Y
2 Udall	N	Y	Y	Y	Y	N	Y
3 ***McInnis***	Y	Y	Y	N	Y	Y	N
4 ***Schaffer***	Y	Y	Y	N	Y	Y	N
5 ***Hefley***	Y	Y	Y	N	Y	Y	N
6 ***Tancredo***	Y	Y	Y	N	Y	Y	N
CONNECTICUT							
1 Larson	Y	Y	Y	Y	Y	N	Y
2 Gejdenson	N	Y	Y	Y	N	N	Y
3 DeLauro	N	Y	Y	Y	N	N	Y
4 ***Shays***	+	+	+	–	+	N	Y
5 Maloney	N	N	Y	Y	Y	N	Y
6 ***Johnson***	Y	Y	Y	N	Y	N	Y
DELAWARE							
AL ***Castle***	Y	N	Y	N	Y	N	Y
FLORIDA							
1 ***Scarborough***	N	Y	Y	N	Y	N	N
2 Boyd	Y	Y	Y	Y	Y	Y	N
3 Brown	N	Y	Y	Y	N	N	Y
4 ***Fowler***	Y	Y	Y	N	Y	Y	N
5 Thurman	Y	Y	Y	Y	N	N	N
6 ***Stearns***	Y	Y	Y	N	Y	Y	N
7 ***Mica***	Y	Y	Y	N	Y	Y	N
8 ***McCollum***	Y	Y	Y	N	Y	N	N
9 ***Bilirakis***	Y	Y	Y	N	Y	Y	N
10 ***Young***	Y	Y	Y	N	Y	N	N
11 Davis	N	Y	Y	Y	Y	N	Y
12 ***Canady***	Y	Y	Y	N	Y	Y	N
13 ***Miller***	Y	Y	Y	N	Y	N	N
14 ***Goss***	Y	Y	Y	N	Y	Y	N
15 ***Weldon***	Y	Y	Y	N	Y	Y	N
16 ***Foley***	N	Y	N	N	Y	Y	N
17 Meek	N	N	N	Y	N	N	Y
18 ***Ros-Lehtinen***	Y	Y	Y	N	Y	N	Y
19 Wexler	N	N	Y	Y	N	N	Y
20 Deutsch	N	N	Y	Y	Y	N	Y
21 ***Diaz-Balart***	N	Y	Y	N	Y	N	Y
22 ***Shaw***	Y	Y	Y	N	Y	N	Y
23 Hastings	N	N	N	Y	N	N	Y
GEORGIA							
1 ***Kingston***	Y	Y	Y	N	Y	Y	N
2 Bishop	Y	Y	Y	Y	Y	Y	N
3 ***Collins***	Y	Y	Y	N	Y	Y	N
4 McKinney	Y	Y	N	Y	N	N	Y
5 Lewis	N	N	N	Y	N	N	Y
6 ***Isakson***	Y	Y	Y	N	Y	Y	N
7 ***Barr***	Y	Y	Y	N	Y	Y	N
8 ***Chambliss***	Y	Y	Y	N	Y	Y	N
9 ***Deal***	Y	Y	Y	N	Y	Y	N
10 ***Norwood***	Y	Y	Y	N	Y	Y	N
11 ***Linder***	Y	Y	Y	N	Y	Y	N
HAWAII							
1 Abercrombie	N	Y	Y	Y	N	N	Y
2 Mink	N	N	Y	Y	N	N	Y
IDAHO							
1 ***Chenoweth***	Y	Y	?	N	Y	Y	N
2 ***Simpson***	Y	Y	Y	N	Y	Y	N
ILLINOIS							
1 Rush	N	N	N	Y	N	N	Y
2 Jackson	N	N	N	Y	N	N	Y
3 Lipinski	Y	Y	Y	N	Y	N	Y
4 Gutierrez	N	Y	Y	Y	N	N	Y
5 Blagojevich	N	Y	Y	Y	N	N	Y
6 ***Hyde***	Y	Y	Y	N	Y	N	N
7 Davis	N	N	Y	Y	N	N	Y
8 ***Crane***	Y	Y	Y	N	Y	Y	N
9 Schakowsky	N	Y	N	Y	N	N	Y
10 ***Porter***	N	N	Y	N	Y	N	Y
11 ***Weller***	Y	Y	Y	N	Y	Y	N
12 Costello	Y	Y	Y	Y	N	Y	N
13 ***Biggert***	N	Y	Y	N	Y	Y	N
14 ***Hastert***					Y	Y	

ND Northern Democrats SD Southern Democrats

	229	230	231	232	233	234	235
15 ***Ewing***	Y	Y	Y	?	Y	Y	N
16 ***Manzullo***	N	Y	Y	N	Y	Y	N
17 Evans	Y	Y	Y	Y	Y	N	Y
18 ***LaHood***	N	Y	Y	N	Y	Y	N
19 Phelps	Y	Y	Y	N	Y	Y	N
20 ***Shimkus***	Y	Y	Y	N	Y	Y	N
INDIANA							
1 Visclosky	Y	Y	Y	Y	N	N	Y
2 ***McIntosh***	Y	Y	Y	N	Y	Y	N
3 Roemer	Y	Y	Y	Y	Y	N	N
4 ***Souder***	Y	Y	Y	N	Y	Y	N
5 ***Buyer***	Y	Y	Y	N	Y	Y	N
6 ***Burton***	Y	Y	Y	N	Y	Y	N
7 ***Pease***	Y	Y	Y	N	N	Y	N
8 ***Hostettler***	Y	Y	Y	N	N	Y	N
9 Hill	Y	Y	Y	N	Y	Y	N
10 Carson	+	+	−	+	−	?	?
IOWA							
1 ***Leach***	Y	Y	Y	N	Y	N	Y
2 ***Nussle***	Y	Y	Y	N	Y	Y	N
3 Boswell	Y	Y	Y	Y	Y	Y	N
4 ***Ganske***	Y	Y	Y	N	Y	N	Y
5 ***Latham***	Y	Y	Y	N	Y	Y	N
KANSAS							
1 ***Moran***	Y	Y	Y	N	N	Y	N
2 ***Ryun***	Y	Y	Y	N	Y	Y	N
3 Moore	Y	Y	Y	Y	Y	N	Y
4 ***Tiahrt***	Y	Y	Y	N	N	Y	N
KENTUCKY							
1 ***Whitfield***	Y	Y	Y	N	Y	Y	N
2 ***Lewis***	Y	Y	Y	N	Y	Y	N
3 ***Northup***	Y	Y	Y	N	Y	N	N
4 Lucas	Y	Y	Y	N	Y	Y	N
5 ***Rogers***	Y	Y	Y	N	Y	Y	N
6 ***Fletcher***	Y	Y	Y	?	Y	Y	N
LOUISIANA							
1 ***Vitter***	N	Y	Y	N	Y	Y	N
2 Jefferson	Y	Y	Y	Y	N	N	Y
3 ***Tauzin***	Y	Y	Y	N	Y	Y	N
4 ***McCrery***	N	Y	Y	N	Y	Y	N
5 ***Cooksey***	Y	Y	Y	N	Y	Y	N
6 ***Baker***	Y	Y	Y	N	Y	Y	N
7 John	Y	Y	Y	Y	Y	Y	N
MAINE							
1 Allen	N	N	Y	Y	N	N	Y
2 Baldacci	N	Y	Y	Y	N	N	Y
MARYLAND							
1 ***Gilchrest***	Y	Y	Y	N	Y	N	Y
2 ***Ehrlich***	N	Y	Y	N	Y	Y	N
3 Cardin	Y	Y	N	Y	N	N	Y
4 Wynn	Y	Y	N	Y	N	N	Y
5 Hoyer	N	Y	Y	Y	N	N	Y
6 ***Bartlett***	Y	Y	Y	N	Y	Y	N
7 Cummings	N	N	N	Y	N	N	Y
8 ***Morella***	N	N	Y	Y	N	N	Y
MASSACHUSETTS							
1 Olver	N	N	N	Y	N	N	Y
2 Neal	N	Y	Y	Y	N	N	Y
3 McGovern	N	Y	N	Y	N	N	Y
4 Frank	N	N	N	Y	N	N	Y
5 Meehan	N	Y	Y	Y	N	N	Y
6 Tierney	N	Y	Y	Y	N	N	Y
7 Markey	N	Y	Y	Y	N	N	Y
8 Capuano	N	Y	N	Y	N	N	Y
9 Moakley	N	Y	Y	Y	N	N	Y
10 Delahunt	N	Y	N	Y	N	N	Y
MICHIGAN							
1 Stupak	Y	Y	N	Y	N	N	Y
2 ***Hoekstra***	Y	Y	Y	N	Y	Y	N
3 ***Ehlers***	Y	Y	Y	N	Y	N	N
4 ***Camp***	Y	Y	Y	N	Y	Y	N
5 Barcia	Y	Y	Y	Y	Y	Y	N
6 ***Upton***	Y	Y	Y	N	Y	N	Y
7 ***Smith***	Y	Y	Y	N	Y	Y	N
8 Stabenow	Y	N	Y	Y	Y	N	Y
9 Kildee	Y	Y	Y	Y	Y	N	Y
10 Bonior	N	Y	Y	Y	Y	N	Y
11 ***Knollenberg***	Y	Y	Y	N	Y	Y	N
12 Levin	N	N	Y	Y	N	N	Y
13 Rivers	N	Y	Y	Y	N	N	Y
14 Conyers	N	N	N	Y	N	N	Y
15 Kilpatrick	N	N	N	Y	N	N	Y
16 Dingell	N	N	N	N	N	Y	N

	229	230	231	232	233	234	235
MINNESOTA							
1 ***Gutknecht***	Y	Y	Y	N	Y	Y	N
2 Minge	?	?	?	?	?	?	?
3 ***Ramstad***	Y	Y	Y	N	Y	N	Y
4 Vento	N	Y	Y	Y	N	N	Y
5 Sabo	Y	Y	Y	Y	N	N	Y
6 Luther	Y	Y	Y	Y	Y	N	Y
7 Peterson	Y	Y	Y	N	Y	N	N
8 Oberstar	Y	Y	Y	Y	N	Y	N
MISSISSIPPI							
1 ***Wicker***	Y	Y	Y	N	Y	Y	N
2 Thompson	Y	Y	N	Y	N	N	Y
3 ***Pickering***	Y	Y	Y	N	Y	Y	N
4 Shows	Y	Y	Y	N	Y	Y	N
5 Taylor	Y	Y	Y	N	Y	Y	N
MISSOURI							
1 Clay	N	N	N	Y	N	N	Y
2 ***Talent***	Y	Y	Y	N	Y	Y	N
3 Gephardt	Y	Y	N	Y	N	N	Y
4 Skelton	Y	Y	Y	N	Y	Y	N
5 McCarthy	Y	Y	N	Y	N	N	Y
6 Danner	Y	Y	Y	N	N	Y	N
7 ***Blunt***	Y	Y	Y	N	Y	Y	N
8 ***Emerson***	Y	Y	Y	N	Y	Y	N
9 ***Hulshof***	Y	Y	N	N	Y	Y	N
MONTANA							
AL ***Hill***	Y	Y	Y	N	Y	Y	N
NEBRASKA							
1 ***Bereuter***	Y	Y	Y	N	Y	N	Y
2 ***Terry***	Y	Y	Y	N	Y	Y	N
3 ***Barrett***	Y	Y	Y	N	Y	Y	N
NEVADA							
1 Berkley	N	Y	N	Y	Y	N	Y
2 ***Gibbons***	Y	Y	Y	N	Y	Y	N
NEW HAMPSHIRE							
1 ***Sununu***	Y	Y	Y	N	Y	Y	N
2 ***Bass***	Y	Y	Y	N	Y	Y	N
NEW JERSEY							
1 Andrews	N	Y	Y	Y	N	N	Y
2 ***LoBiondo***	Y	Y	Y	N	Y	Y	N
3 ***Saxton***	Y	Y	Y	N	?	Y	N
4 ***Smith***	Y	Y	Y	N	Y	N	Y
5 ***Roukema***	Y	Y	Y	N	Y	N	Y
6 Pallone	N	N	Y	Y	N	N	Y
7 ***Franks***	Y	Y	Y	N	Y	N	Y
8 Pascrell	Y	Y	Y	Y	Y	N	Y
9 Rothman	N	Y	Y	Y	Y	N	Y
10 Payne	N	N	N	Y	N	N	Y
11 ***Frelinghuysen***	Y	Y	Y	N	Y	N	Y
12 Holt	N	Y	Y	Y	N	N	Y
13 Menendez	N	+	Y	Y	N	N	Y
NEW MEXICO							
1 ***Wilson***	Y	Y	Y	N	Y	Y	N
2 ***Skeen***	Y	Y	Y	N	Y	Y	N
3 Udall	N	Y	Y	Y	Y	N	Y
NEW YORK							
1 ***Forbes***	Y	Y	Y	N	Y	N	Y
2 ***Lazio***	Y	Y	Y	N	Y	N	Y
3 ***King***	Y	Y	Y	N	Y	N	Y
4 McCarthy	Y	Y	Y	Y	Y	N	Y
5 Ackerman	N	N	Y	Y	N	N	Y
6 Meeks	N	N	N	Y	N	N	Y
7 Crowley	N	Y	Y	Y	N	N	Y
8 Nadler	N	N	Y	Y	N	N	Y
9 Weiner	N	N	Y	Y	N	N	Y
10 Towns	Y	N	N	Y	N	N	Y
11 Owens	N	N	N	Y	N	N	Y
12 Velazquez	N	Y	Y	Y	N	N	Y
13 ***Fossella***	Y	Y	Y	N	Y	N	N
14 Maloney	Y	Y	Y	Y	N	N	Y
15 Rangel	N	Y	N	Y	N	N	Y
16 Serrano	N	Y	N	Y	N	N	Y
17 Engel	Y	Y	Y	Y	N	N	Y
18 Lowey	N	N	Y	Y	Y	N	Y
19 ***Kelly***	Y	Y	Y	N	Y	N	Y
20 ***Gilman***	N	N	Y	N	Y	N	Y
21 McNulty	Y	Y	Y	Y	N	N	Y
22 ***Sweeney***	Y	Y	Y	N	Y	Y	N
23 ***Boehlert***	Y	N	Y	N	Y	N	Y
24 ***McHugh***	Y	Y	Y	N	Y	N	Y
25 ***Walsh***	Y	Y	Y	N	Y	Y	N
26 Hinchey	Y	N	Y	Y	N	N	Y
27 ***Reynolds***	Y	Y	Y	N	Y	Y	N
28 Slaughter	N	Y	Y	Y	N	N	Y
29 LaFalce	N	Y	Y	Y	N	N	Y

	229	230	231	232	233	234	235
30 ***Quinn***	Y	Y	Y	N	Y	N	Y
31 ***Houghton***	?	?	?	?	?	?	?
NORTH CAROLINA							
1 Clayton	N	Y	Y	Y	N	N	Y
2 Etheridge	Y	Y	Y	Y	Y	N	N
3 ***Jones***	Y	Y	Y	N	Y	Y	N
4 Price	Y	Y	Y	Y	Y	N	Y
5 ***Burr***	Y	Y	Y	N	Y	Y	N
6 ***Coble***	Y	Y	Y	N	Y	Y	N
7 McIntyre	Y	Y	Y	Y	Y	Y	N
8 ***Hayes***	Y	Y	Y	N	Y	Y	N
9 ***Myrick***	Y	Y	Y	N	Y	Y	N
10 ***Ballenger***	Y	Y	Y	N	Y	Y	N
11 ***Taylor***	Y	Y	Y	N	Y	Y	N
12 Watt	N	N	N	Y	N	N	Y
NORTH DAKOTA							
AL Pomeroy	Y	Y	Y	Y	Y	N	Y
OHIO							
1 ***Chabot***	Y	Y	Y	N	Y	Y	N
2 ***Portman***	Y	Y	Y	N	Y	Y	N
3 Hall	Y	Y	Y	Y	Y	N	Y
4 ***Oxley***	Y	Y	Y	N	Y	Y	N
5 ***Gillmor***	Y	Y	Y	N	Y	Y	N
6 Strickland	N	Y	Y	Y	Y	Y	N
7 ***Hobson***	Y	Y	Y	N	Y	Y	N
8 ***Boehner***	Y	Y	Y	N	Y	Y	N
9 Kaptur	Y	Y	Y	Y	Y	N	Y
10 Kucinich	N	N	N	Y	N	N	Y
11 Jones	N	N	N	Y	N	N	Y
12 ***Kasich***	Y	Y	Y	N	Y	Y	N
13 Brown	N	Y	Y	Y	N	N	Y
14 Sawyer	Y	Y	Y	Y	N	N	Y
15 ***Pryce***	Y	Y	Y	N	Y	N	N
16 ***Regula***	Y	Y	Y	N	Y	Y	N
17 Traficant	Y	Y	Y	N	Y	Y	N
18 ***Ney***	Y	Y	Y	N	Y	Y	N
19 ***LaTourette***	Y	Y	Y	N	Y	Y	N
OKLAHOMA							
1 ***Largent***	Y	Y	Y	N	Y	Y	N
2 ***Coburn***	Y	Y	Y	N	N	Y	N
3 ***Watkins***	Y	Y	Y	N	Y	Y	N
4 ***Watts***	Y	Y	Y	N	Y	Y	N
5 ***Istook***	Y	Y	Y	N	Y	Y	N
6 ***Lucas***	Y	?	Y	N	Y	Y	N
OREGON							
1 Wu	Y	Y	Y	Y	Y	N	Y
2 ***Walden***	Y	Y	Y	N	Y	Y	N
3 Blumenauer	Y	Y	N	Y	N	N	Y
4 DeFazio	Y	Y	Y	Y	N	N	Y
5 Hooley	Y	Y	Y	Y	Y	N	Y
PENNSYLVANIA							
1 Brady	N	Y	Y	Y	N	N	Y
2 Fattah	N	N	N	Y	N	N	Y
3 Borski	Y	Y	Y	Y	N	N	Y
4 Klink	Y	N	N	Y	N	N	Y
5 ***Peterson***	Y	Y	Y	N	Y	Y	N
6 Holden	Y	Y	Y	Y	Y	Y	N
7 ***Weldon***	Y	Y	Y	N	Y	Y	N
8 ***Greenwood***	Y	N	Y	N	Y	N	Y
9 ***Shuster***	Y	Y	Y	N	Y	Y	N
10 ***Sherwood***	Y	Y	Y	N	Y	Y	N
11 Kanjorski	Y	Y	Y	Y	N	Y	N
12 Murtha	Y	Y	Y	Y	N	Y	N
13 Hoeffel	N	Y	Y	Y	N	N	Y
14 Coyne	N	N	Y	Y	N	N	Y
15 ***Toomey***	Y	Y	Y	N	Y	Y	N
16 ***Pitts***	Y	Y	Y	N	Y	Y	N
17 ***Gekas***	Y	Y	Y	N	Y	Y	N
18 Doyle	Y	Y	Y	Y	Y	N	Y
19 ***Goodling***	Y	Y	Y	N	Y	Y	Y
20 Mascara	Y	Y	Y	Y	Y	Y	N
21 ***English***	Y	Y	Y	N	Y	Y	N
RHODE ISLAND							
1 Kennedy	N	N	N	Y	N	N	Y
2 Weygand	N	Y	Y	Y	Y	N	Y
SOUTH CAROLINA							
1 ***Sanford***	Y	Y	Y	N	N	Y	N
2 ***Spence***	Y	Y	?	N	Y	Y	N
3 ***Graham***	Y	Y	Y	N	Y	Y	N
4 ***DeMint***	Y	Y	Y	N	Y	Y	N
5 Spratt	Y	Y	Y	Y	Y	N	Y
6 Clyburn	Y	Y	N	Y	N	N	Y
SOUTH DAKOTA							
AL ***Thune***	Y	Y	Y	N	Y	Y	N

	229	230	231	232	233	234	235
TENNESSEE							
1 ***Jenkins***	Y	Y	Y	N	Y	Y	N
2 ***Duncan***	Y	Y	Y	N	Y	Y	N
3 ***Wamp***	Y	Y	Y	N	Y	Y	N
4 ***Hilleary***	Y	Y	Y	N	Y	Y	N
5 Clement	Y	Y	Y	Y	Y	Y	N
6 Gordon	Y	Y	Y	N	Y	Y	N
7 ***Bryant***	Y	Y	Y	N	Y	Y	N
8 Tanner	Y	Y	Y	Y	Y	Y	N
9 Ford	N	Y	Y	Y	N	N	Y
TEXAS							
1 Sandlin	Y	Y	Y	Y	Y	Y	N
2 Turner	Y	Y	Y	N	Y	Y	N
3 ***Johnson, Sam***	?	?	Y	N	Y	Y	N
4 Hall	Y	Y	Y	N	Y	Y	N
5 ***Sessions***	Y	Y	Y	N	Y	Y	N
6 ***Barton***	Y	Y	Y	N	Y	Y	N
7 ***Archer***	Y	Y	Y	N	Y	Y	N
8 ***Brady***	Y	Y	Y	N	Y	Y	N
9 Lampson	Y	Y	Y	Y	Y	Y	N
10 Doggett	N	Y	Y	Y	N	N	Y
11 Edwards	Y	Y	Y	Y	N	N	Y
12 ***Granger***	Y	Y	Y	N	Y	Y	N
13 ***Thornberry***	Y	Y	Y	N	Y	Y	N
14 ***Paul***	N	Y	N	N	N	Y	N
15 Hinojosa	Y	Y	Y	Y	Y	N	Y
16 Reyes	Y	Y	Y	Y	Y	Y	Y
17 Stenholm	Y	Y	Y	N	Y	Y	N
18 Jackson-Lee	N	N	N	Y	N	N	Y
19 ***Combest***	Y	Y	Y	N	Y	Y	N
20 Gonzalez	N	N	Y	Y	N	N	Y
21 ***Smith***	Y	Y	Y	N	Y	Y	N
22 ***DeLay***	Y	Y	Y	N	Y	Y	N
23 ***Bonilla***	Y	Y	Y	N	Y	Y	N
24 Frost	Y	Y	N	Y	Y	N	Y
25 Bentsen	Y	Y	Y	Y	Y	N	Y
26 ***Armey***	Y	Y	Y	N	Y	Y	N
27 Ortiz	Y	Y	Y	Y	Y	Y	N
28 Rodriguez	Y	Y	Y	Y	N	Y	Y
29 Green	Y	Y	Y	Y	Y	Y	N
30 Johnson, E.B.	N	Y	Y	Y	N	N	Y
UTAH							
1 ***Hansen***	Y	Y	Y	N	Y	Y	N
2 ***Cook***	Y	Y	Y	N	Y	Y	N
3 ***Cannon***	Y	Y	Y	N	N	Y	N
VERMONT							
AL *Sanders*	N	Y	Y	Y	N	N	Y
VIRGINIA							
1 ***Bateman***	N	Y	Y	N	Y	N	Y
2 Pickett	N	Y	Y	Y	N	Y	N
3 Scott	N	N	N	Y	N	N	Y
4 Sisisky	Y	Y	Y	Y	Y	Y	N
5 Goode	Y	Y	Y	N	Y	Y	N
6 ***Goodlatte***	Y	Y	Y	N	Y	Y	N
7 ***Bliley***	Y	Y	Y	N	Y	Y	N
8 Moran	Y	Y	Y	Y	Y	N	Y
9 Boucher	Y	Y	Y	?	N	Y	N
10 ***Wolf***	Y	Y	Y	N	Y	Y	N
11 ***Davis***	Y	Y	Y	N	Y	N	Y
WASHINGTON							
1 Inslee	Y	Y	Y	N	Y	N	Y
2 ***Metcalf***	Y	Y	Y	N	N	Y	N
3 Baird	Y	Y	Y	Y	Y	N	N
4 ***Hastings***	Y	Y	Y	N	Y	Y	N
5 ***Nethercutt***	Y	Y	Y	N	Y	Y	N
6 Dicks	Y	Y	Y	Y	Y	N	Y
7 McDermott	N	Y	N	Y	N	N	Y
8 ***Dunn***	Y	Y	Y	N	Y	N	N
9 Smith	Y	Y	Y	Y	Y	N	N
WEST VIRGINIA							
1 Mollohan	Y	Y	Y	Y	N	Y	N
2 Wise	Y	Y	Y	Y	N	Y	N
3 Rahall	Y	Y	Y	Y	N	Y	N
WISCONSIN							
1 ***Ryan***	Y	Y	Y	N	Y	Y	N
2 Baldwin	N	Y	N	Y	N	N	Y
3 Kind	Y	Y	Y	Y	N	N	N
4 Kleczka	N	Y	Y	Y	N	N	Y
5 Barrett	N	Y	Y	Y	N	N	Y
6 ***Petri***	Y	Y	Y	N	Y	Y	N
7 Obey	Y	Y	Y	Y	N	Y	N
8 ***Green***	Y	Y	Y	N	Y	Y	N
9 ***Sensenbrenner***	Y	Y	Y	N	Y	Y	N
WYOMING							
AL ***Cubin***	Y	Y	Y	N	+	Y	N

Southern states - Ala., Ark., Fla., Ga., Ky., La., Miss., N.C., Okla., S.C., Tenn., Texas, Va.

236. HR 2122. Gun Shows/Gun Safety Devices. Davis, R-Va., amendment to prohibit the sale of a handgun without a secure gun storage or safety device, defined to include any part that could render the gun inoperable if removed. The amendment would grant limited immunity from civil liability for a lawful gun owner who uses such a device and whose gun is used by others without permission. Adopted 311-115: R 120-98; D 190-17 (ND 148-5, SD 42-12); I 1-0. June 18, 1999.

237. HR 2122. Gun Shows/Concealed Weapons for Police. Cunningham, R-Calif., amendment to allow qualified current and former law enforcement officers to carry a concealed weapon. Adopted 372-53: R 205-12; D 166-41 (ND 120-33, SD 46-8); I 1-0. June 18, 1999.

238. HR 2122. Gun Shows/Semi-Automatic Weapons. McCollum, R-Fla., amendment to prohibit anyone under the age of 18 from possessing a semi-automatic assault weapon or large-capacity ammunition feeding device. Adopted 354-69: R 156-60; D 197-9 (ND 146-6, SD 51-3); I 1-0. June 18, 1999.

239. HR 2122. Gun Shows/Pawn Shop Checks. Sessions, R-Texas, amendment to require background checks for gun owners before they can retrieve guns they have left in a pawn shop for more than one year. Adopted 247-181: R 179-40; D 68-140 (ND 37-116, SD 31-24); I 0-1. June 18, 1999.

240. HR 2122. Gun Shows/D.C. Gun Law. Goode, D-Va., amendment to repeal the District of Columbia law that prohibits D.C. residents from possessing a firearm. Rejected 175-250: R 145-73; D 30-176 (ND 8-143, SD 22-33); I 0-1. June 18, 1999.

241. HR 2122. Gun Shows/D.C. Guns. Hunter, R-Calif., amendment to permit citizens of the District of Columbia who have not been jailed for any crime and who have not been convicted of a violent crime to own a handgun and keep it in their homes. Adopted 213-208: R 174-41; D 39-166 (ND 17-133, SD 22-33); I 0-1. June 18, 1999.

242. HR 2122. Gun Shows/Juvenile Delinquents. Rogan, R-Calif., amendment to prohibit individuals who are convicted of violent acts of juvenile delinquency from owning a gun after they turn 18. Adopted 395-27: R 188-25; D 206-2 (ND 151-2, SD 55-0); I 1-0. June 18, 1999.

243. HR 2122. Gun Shows/Conyers Substitute. Conyers, D-Mich., substitute amendment to require background checks at any event where 50 or more guns are for sale and at least one of those guns is shipped across state lines; require checks for any part of a firearm transaction, including a customer expressing interest in buying a gun; ban the importation of any weapon with capacity for more than 10 rounds of ammunition; continue current law permitting up to three business days to complete a background check. Rejected 184-242: R 25-193; D 158-49 (ND 129-24, SD 29-25); I 1-0. June 18, 1999.

Key

Y Voted for (yea).
\# Paired for.
\+ Announced for.
N Voted against (nay).
X Paired against.
– Announced against.
P Voted "present."
C Voted "present" to avoid possible conflict of interest.
? Did not vote or otherwise make a position known.

•

Democrats ***Republicans***
Independents

	236	237	238	239	240	241	242	243
ALABAMA								
1 *Callahan*	N	Y	N	Y	Y	Y	Y	N
2 *Everett*	N	Y	N	Y	Y	Y	?	N
3 *Riley*	N	Y	N	Y	Y	Y	N	N
4 *Aderholt*	N	Y	N	Y	Y	Y	N	N
5 Cramer	N	Y	Y	Y	Y	Y	Y	N
6 *Bachus*	N	Y	Y	Y	Y	Y	Y	N
7 Hilliard	N	Y	Y	Y	N	N	Y	?
ALASKA								
AL *Young*	N	Y	N	Y	Y	Y	Y	N
ARIZONA								
1 *Salmon*	?	?	?	?	?	?	?	?
2 Pastor	Y	Y	Y	N	N	N	Y	Y
3 *Stump*	N	Y	N	Y	Y	Y	N	N
4 *Shadegg*	N	Y	N	N	Y	Y	N	N
5 *Kolbe*	Y	N	Y	N	N	N	Y	N
6 *Hayworth*	N	Y	N	Y	Y	Y	Y	N
ARKANSAS								
1 Berry	Y	Y	Y	Y	Y	Y	Y	N
2 Snyder	Y	Y	Y	N	N	N	Y	Y
3 *Hutchinson*	Y	Y	Y	Y	N	Y	Y	N
4 *Dickey*	Y	Y	Y	Y	Y	Y	N	N
CALIFORNIA								
1 Thompson	N	Y	Y	Y	N	Y	Y	Y
2 *Herger*	N	Y	N	Y	Y	Y	Y	N
3 *Ose*	Y	Y	Y	Y	N	Y	Y	Y
4 *Doolittle*	N	Y	N	Y	Y	Y	N	N
5 Matsui	Y	Y	Y	N	N	N	Y	Y
6 Woolsey	Y	N	Y	N	N	N	Y	Y
7 Miller, George	Y	N	Y	N	N	N	Y	Y
8 Pelosi	Y	N	Y	N	N	N	Y	Y
9 Lee	Y	N	Y	N	N	N	Y	Y
10 Tauscher	Y	N	Y	N	N	N	Y	Y
11 *Pombo*	Y	Y	N	Y	Y	Y	Y	N
12 Lantos	Y	Y	Y	N	N	N	Y	Y
13 Stark	Y	N	Y	N	N	N	Y	Y
14 Eshoo	Y	N	Y	N	N	N	Y	Y
15 *Campbell*	Y	N	N	N	N	Y	Y	Y
16 Lofgren	Y	Y	N	N	N	N	Y	Y
17 Farr	Y	Y	Y	N	N	?	Y	Y
18 Condit	N	Y	Y	Y	N	Y	Y	Y
19 *Radanovich*	N	Y	?	Y	Y	Y	Y	N
20 Dooley	Y	Y	Y	N	N	N	Y	Y
21 *Thomas*	?	?	?	?	?	?	?	?
22 Capps	Y	Y	Y	Y	N	N	Y	Y
23 *Gallegly*	Y	Y	Y	Y	N	Y	Y	N
24 Sherman	Y	Y	Y	N	N	N	Y	Y
25 *McKeon*	Y	Y	Y	Y	Y	Y	Y	N
26 Berman	Y	Y	Y	N	N	N	Y	Y
27 *Rogan*	Y	Y	Y	N	Y	Y	?	Y
28 *Dreier*	Y	Y	Y	Y	Y	Y	Y	N
29 Waxman	Y	N	Y	N	N	N	Y	Y
30 Becerra	Y	Y	Y	N	N	N	Y	Y
31 Martinez	Y	Y	Y	N	N	Y	Y	Y
32 Dixon	Y	Y	Y	N	N	N	Y	Y
33 Roybal-Allard	Y	Y	Y	N	N	N	Y	Y
34 Napolitano	Y	N	Y	N	N	N	Y	Y
35 Waters	Y	N	Y	N	N	N	Y	Y
36 *Kuykendall*	Y	Y	Y	Y	N	Y	Y	Y
37 Millender-McD.	Y	Y	Y	N	N	N	Y	Y
38 *Horn*	Y	Y	Y	N	N	N	Y	Y
39 *Royce*	Y	Y	Y	Y	Y	Y	Y	N
40 *Lewis*	?	?	?	?	?	?	?	?
41 *Miller, Gary*	Y	Y	Y	Y	Y	Y	Y	N
42 Brown	?	?	?	?	?	?	?	?
43 *Calvert*	Y	Y	Y	Y	Y	Y	Y	N
44 *Bono*	Y	Y	Y	Y	N	Y	Y	N
45 *Rohrabacher*	Y	N	Y	Y	Y	Y	Y	N
46 Sanchez	Y	Y	Y	Y	N	N	Y	Y
47 *Cox*	Y	Y	Y	Y	Y	?	Y	N
48 *Packard*	N	Y	N	Y	Y	Y	Y	N
49 *Bilbray*	Y	Y	Y	N	Y	Y	Y	Y
50 Filner	Y	Y	Y	N	N	N	Y	Y
51 *Cunningham*	Y	Y	Y	Y	Y	Y	Y	N
52 *Hunter*	N	Y	N	Y	Y	Y	Y	N
COLORADO								
1 DeGette	Y	Y	Y	N	N	N	Y	Y
2 Udall	Y	Y	Y	N	N	N	Y	Y
3 *McInnis*	Y	Y	Y	Y	Y	Y	Y	N
4 *Schaffer*	N	N	N	Y	Y	Y	Y	N
5 *Hefley*	Y	Y	Y	Y	Y	Y	Y	N
6 *Tancredo*	Y	Y	Y	Y	Y	Y	Y	N
CONNECTICUT								
1 Larson	Y	Y	Y	N	N	N	Y	Y
2 Gejdenson	Y	Y	Y	N	N	N	Y	Y
3 DeLauro	Y	Y	Y	N	N	N	Y	Y
4 *Shays*	Y	Y	Y	N	N	N	Y	Y
5 Maloney	Y	Y	Y	N	N	N	Y	N
6 *Johnson*	Y	Y	Y	N	N	N	Y	Y
DELAWARE								
AL *Castle*	Y	Y	Y	N	N	N	Y	Y
FLORIDA								
1 *Scarborough*	N	Y	N	N	Y	Y	N	N
2 Boyd	Y	Y	Y	N	N	N	Y	N
3 Brown	Y	Y	Y	N	N	N	Y	Y
4 *Fowler*	Y	Y	Y	Y	N	N	Y	N
5 Thurman	Y	Y	Y	N	N	N	Y	N
6 *Stearns*	Y	Y	Y	Y	Y	Y	Y	N
7 *Mica*	N	Y	Y	N	Y	Y	Y	N
8 *McCollum*	Y	Y	Y	Y	N	Y	Y	N
9 *Bilirakis*	Y	Y	Y	Y	N	Y	Y	N
10 *Young*	Y	Y	Y	Y	N	Y	Y	N
11 Davis	Y	Y	Y	N	N	N	Y	Y
12 *Canady*	Y	Y	Y	Y	Y	Y	Y	N
13 *Miller*	Y	N	Y	Y	N	N	Y	N
14 *Goss*	Y	Y	Y	Y	Y	Y	Y	N
15 *Weldon*	Y	Y	Y	Y	Y	Y	Y	N
16 *Foley*	Y	Y	Y	Y	N	N	Y	N
17 Meek	Y	N	Y	N	N	N	Y	Y
18 *Ros-Lehtinen*	Y	Y	Y	Y	N	Y	Y	Y
19 Wexler	Y	N	Y	N	N	N	Y	Y
20 Deutsch	Y	Y	Y	N	N	N	Y	Y
21 *Diaz-Balart*	Y	Y	Y	Y	Y	Y	Y	Y
22 *Shaw*	Y	Y	Y	Y	N	N	Y	N
23 Hastings	Y	Y	Y	N	N	N	Y	Y
GEORGIA								
1 *Kingston*	N	Y	Y	Y	Y	Y	N	N
2 Bishop	Y	Y	Y	Y	Y	Y	Y	N
3 *Collins*	N	Y	Y	Y	Y	Y	Y	N
4 McKinney	Y	N	Y	N	N	N	Y	Y
5 Lewis	Y	N	Y	N	N	N	Y	Y
6 *Isakson*	Y	Y	Y	Y	Y	Y	Y	N
7 *Barr*	N	Y	N	Y	Y	Y	Y	N
8 *Chambliss*	N	Y	Y	Y	Y	Y	N	N
9 *Deal*	N	Y	Y	Y	Y	Y	Y	N
10 *Norwood*	N	Y	Y	Y	Y	Y	Y	N
11 *Linder*	N	Y	Y	Y	N	Y	N	N
HAWAII								
1 Abercrombie	Y	Y	Y	N	N	N	Y	Y
2 Mink	Y	N	Y	N	N	N	Y	Y
IDAHO								
1 *Chenoweth*	N	N	N	Y	Y	Y	Y	N
2 *Simpson*	Y	Y	Y	Y	Y	Y	Y	N
ILLINOIS								
1 Rush	Y	N	Y	Y	N	N	Y	Y
2 Jackson	Y	N	Y	Y	N	N	Y	Y
3 Lipinski	Y	Y	Y	N	N	N	Y	Y
4 Gutierrez	Y	Y	Y	Y	N	N	Y	Y
5 Blagojevich	Y	Y	Y	N	N	N	Y	Y
6 *Hyde*	Y	Y	Y	Y	N	Y	Y	N
7 Davis	Y	N	Y	N	N	N	Y	Y
8 *Crane*	N	Y	N	Y	Y	Y	Y	N
9 Schakowsky	Y	N	Y	N	N	N	Y	Y
10 *Porter*	Y	Y	Y	N	N	N	Y	Y
11 *Weller*	Y	Y	Y	N	N	N	Y	N
12 Costello	Y	Y	Y	Y	N	N	Y	N
13 *Biggert*	Y	Y	Y	N	N	N	Y	N
14 *Hastert*								

ND Northern Democrats SD Southern Democrats

	236	237	238	239	240	241	242	243
15 *Ewing*	Y	Y	Y	Y	N	N	Y	N
16 *Manzullo*	N	Y	Y	Y	Y	Y	Y	N
17 Evans	Y	Y	Y	N	N	N	Y	Y
18 *LaHood*	Y	Y	Y	Y	N	N	Y	N
19 Phelps	Y	Y	Y	Y	Y	Y	Y	N
20 *Shimkus*	N	Y	Y	Y	Y	Y	Y	N
INDIANA								
1 Visclosky	Y	N	Y	N	N	N	Y	Y
2 *McIntosh*	Y	Y	Y	Y	Y	Y	Y	N
3 Roemer	Y	Y	Y	N	N	N	Y	Y
4 *Souder*	N	Y	Y	Y	Y	Y	Y	N
5 *Buyer*	N	Y	Y	Y	Y	Y	Y	N
6 *Burton*	N	Y	N	Y	Y	Y	N	N
7 *Pease*	N	Y	Y	Y	Y	Y	Y	N
8 *Hostettler*	N	Y	N	Y	Y	Y	N	N
9 Hill	Y	Y	Y	Y	N	N	Y	N
10 Carson	Y	Y	Y	Y	N	N	Y	Y
IOWA								
1 *Leach*	Y	Y	Y	N	N	N	Y	Y
2 *Nussle*	Y	Y	Y	Y	N	Y	Y	N
3 Boswell	Y	Y	Y	Y	N	Y	Y	N
4 *Ganske*	N	Y	Y	N	N	N	Y	Y
5 *Latham*	Y	Y	Y	Y	N	Y	Y	N
KANSAS								
1 *Moran*	N	Y	Y	N	N	Y	Y	N
2 *Ryun*	N	Y	Y	Y	Y	Y	Y	N
3 Moore	Y	Y	Y	Y	N	N	Y	Y
4 *Tiahrt*	N	Y	N	N	Y	Y	N	N
KENTUCKY								
1 *Whitfield*	N	Y	Y	Y	Y	Y	Y	N
2 *Lewis*	N	Y	N	Y	Y	Y	Y	N
3 *Northup*	Y	Y	Y	Y	N	Y	Y	N
4 Lucas	N	Y	N	Y	Y	Y	Y	N
5 *Rogers*	N	Y	Y	Y	Y	Y	Y	N
6 *Fletcher*	Y	Y	Y	Y	Y	Y	Y	N
LOUISIANA								
1 *Vitter*	N	Y	N	Y	Y	Y	Y	N
2 Jefferson	Y	Y	Y	N	N	N	Y	Y
3 *Tauzin*	Y	Y	Y	Y	Y	Y	Y	N
4 *McCrery*	N	N	N	Y	Y	Y	Y	N
5 *Cooksey*	N	Y	Y	Y	N	N	?	N
6 *Baker*	Y	Y	Y	Y	Y	Y	Y	N
7 John	Y	Y	Y	Y	Y	Y	Y	N
MAINE								
1 Allen	Y	N	Y	N	N	N	Y	Y
2 Baldacci	Y	Y	Y	N	N	N	Y	Y
MARYLAND								
1 *Gilchrest*	Y	Y	Y	N	N	Y	Y	Y
2 *Ehrlich*	Y	Y	Y	Y	Y	Y	Y	N
3 Cardin	Y	Y	Y	N	N	N	Y	Y
4 Wynn	Y	Y	Y	N	N	N	Y	Y
5 Hoyer	Y	Y	Y	N	N	N	Y	Y
6 *Bartlett*	Y	Y	Y	Y	Y	Y	Y	N
7 Cummings	Y	Y	Y	N	N	N	Y	Y
8 *Morella*	Y	Y	Y	N	N	N	Y	Y
MASSACHUSETTS								
1 Olver	Y	Y	Y	N	N	N	Y	Y
2 Neal	Y	Y	Y	N	N	N	Y	Y
3 McGovern	Y	Y	Y	N	N	N	Y	Y
4 Frank	Y	Y	Y	N	N	N	Y	Y
5 Meehan	Y	Y	Y	N	N	N	Y	Y
6 Tierney	Y	N	Y	N	N	N	Y	Y
7 Markey	Y	Y	Y	N	N	N	Y	Y
8 Capuano	Y	N	Y	N	N	N	Y	Y
9 Moakley	Y	Y	Y	N	N	N	Y	Y
10 Delahunt	Y	Y	Y	N	N	N	Y	Y
MICHIGAN								
1 Stupak	Y	Y	Y	Y	N	Y	Y	Y
2 *Hoekstra*	Y	Y	Y	Y	N	N	Y	N
3 *Ehlers*	Y	Y	Y	Y	N	N	Y	N
4 *Camp*	Y	Y	Y	Y	Y	Y	Y	N
5 Barcia	Y	Y	N	Y	Y	Y	Y	Y
6 *Upton*	Y	Y	Y	N	Y	Y	Y	N
7 *Smith*	Y	N	Y	Y	N	N	Y	N
8 Stabenow	Y	Y	Y	N	N	N	Y	Y
9 Kildee	Y	Y	Y	N	N	N	Y	Y
10 Bonior	Y	Y	Y	N	N	N	Y	Y
11 *Knollenberg*	Y	Y	Y	Y	Y	Y	Y	N
12 Levin	Y	Y	Y	N	N	N	Y	Y
13 Rivers	Y	Y	Y	N	N	N	Y	Y
14 Conyers	Y	N	Y	N	N	N	Y	Y
15 Kilpatrick	Y	N	Y	N	N	N	Y	Y
16 Dingell	Y	Y	N	Y	Y	Y	Y	N

	236	237	238	239	240	241	242	243
MINNESOTA								
1 *Gutknecht*	N	Y	Y	Y	Y	Y	Y	N
2 Minge	?	?	?	?	?	?	?	?
3 *Ramstad*	Y	Y	Y	N	Y	Y	Y	Y
4 Vento	Y	Y	Y	N	N	N	Y	Y
5 Sabo	Y	Y	Y	N	N	N	Y	Y
6 Luther	Y	Y	Y	N	N	N	Y	Y
7 Peterson	N	Y	N	Y	Y	Y	Y	N
8 Oberstar	Y	Y	Y	Y	N	N	Y	N
MISSISSIPPI								
1 *Wicker*	N	Y	N	Y	Y	Y	Y	N
2 Thompson	Y	Y	Y	N	N	N	Y	Y
3 *Pickering*	N	Y	N	Y	Y	Y	Y	N
4 Shows	N	Y	Y	Y	Y	Y	Y	N
5 Taylor	Y	Y	Y	Y	Y	Y	Y	N
MISSOURI								
1 Clay	Y	N	N	N	N	N	Y	Y
2 *Talent*	Y	Y	Y	Y	Y	Y	Y	N
3 Gephardt	Y	Y	Y	N	N	N	Y	Y
4 Skelton	N	Y	Y	Y	Y	Y	Y	N
5 McCarthy	Y	Y	Y	N	N	N	Y	Y
6 Danner	N	Y	Y	Y	Y	Y	Y	N
7 *Blunt*	N	Y	?	Y	Y	Y	N	N
8 *Emerson*	N	Y	N	Y	Y	Y	Y	N
9 *Hulshof*	N	Y	Y	Y	Y	Y	Y	N
MONTANA								
AL *Hill*	N	Y	N	Y	Y	Y	N	N
NEBRASKA								
1 *Bereuter*	Y	Y	Y	Y	N	Y	Y	N
2 *Terry*	N	Y	Y	Y	Y	Y	Y	N
3 *Barrett*	Y	Y	Y	Y	N	Y	Y	N
NEVADA								
1 Berkley	Y	Y	Y	N	N	N	Y	Y
2 *Gibbons*	N	Y	N	Y	Y	Y	Y	N
NEW HAMPSHIRE								
1 *Sununu*	Y	Y	Y	Y	Y	Y	Y	N
2 *Bass*	Y	Y	Y	Y	Y	Y	Y	N
NEW JERSEY								
1 Andrews	Y	Y	Y	N	N	N	Y	Y
2 *LoBiondo*	Y	Y	Y	N	N	N	Y	N
3 *Saxton*	Y	Y	Y	N	N	N	Y	N
4 *Smith*	Y	Y	Y	Y	Y	Y	Y	N
5 *Roukema*	Y	Y	Y	N	Y	Y	Y	Y
6 Pallone	Y	Y	Y	N	N	N	Y	Y
7 *Franks*	Y	Y	Y	N	N	Y	Y	Y
8 Pascrell	Y	Y	Y	?	?	?	?	?
9 Rothman	Y	N	Y	N	N	N	Y	Y
10 Payne	Y	N	Y	N	N	N	Y	Y
11 *Frelinghuysen*	Y	Y	Y	N	N	N	Y	Y
12 Holt	Y	Y	Y	N	N	N	Y	Y
13 Menendez	Y	Y	Y	Y	N	N	Y	Y
NEW MEXICO								
1 *Wilson*	Y	Y	Y	Y	Y	Y	Y	N
2 *Skeen*	N	Y	N	Y	Y	Y	Y	N
3 Udall	Y	Y	Y	Y	N	N	Y	Y
NEW YORK								
1 *Forbes*	Y	Y	Y	N	N	N	?	Y
2 *Lazio*	Y	Y	Y	Y	Y	Y	Y	N
3 *King*	Y	Y	Y	N	N	N	Y	N
4 McCarthy	Y	Y	Y	N	N	N	Y	Y
5 Ackerman	Y	Y	Y	N	N	N	Y	Y
6 Meeks	Y	N	Y	N	N	N	Y	Y
7 Crowley	Y	Y	Y	N	N	N	Y	Y
8 Nadler	Y	Y	Y	N	N	N	Y	Y
9 Weiner	Y	Y	Y	N	N	N	Y	Y
10 Towns	Y	N	Y	N	N	N	Y	Y
11 Owens	Y	N	Y	N	N	N	Y	Y
12 Velázquez	Y	N	Y	N	N	N	Y	Y
13 *Fossella*	Y	Y	Y	Y	N	N	Y	N
14 Maloney	Y	Y	Y	N	N	N	Y	Y
15 Rangel	Y	Y	Y	N	N	N	Y	Y
16 Serrano	Y	N	Y	N	N	N	Y	Y
17 Engel	Y	N	Y	N	N	N	Y	Y
18 Lowey	Y	Y	Y	N	N	N	Y	Y
19 *Kelly*	Y	Y	Y	N	N	N	Y	Y
20 *Gilman*	Y	Y	Y	N	N	N	Y	N
21 McNulty	Y	Y	Y	N	N	N	Y	Y
22 *Sweeney*	Y	Y	Y	Y	Y	Y	Y	N
23 *Boehlert*	Y	Y	Y	N	N	N	Y	Y
24 *McHugh*	Y	Y	Y	Y	Y	Y	Y	N
25 *Walsh*	Y	Y	Y	Y	Y	Y	Y	N
26 Hinchey	Y	Y	Y	N	Y	N	Y	Y
27 *Reynolds*	Y	Y	Y	Y	Y	Y	Y	N
28 Slaughter	Y	Y	Y	N	N	N	Y	Y
29 LaFalce	Y	N	Y	N	N	N	Y	Y

	236	237	238	239	240	241	242	243
30 *Quinn*	Y	Y	Y	Y	N	N	Y	Y
31 *Houghton*	?	?	?	Y	N	N	Y	N
NORTH CAROLINA								
1 Clayton	Y	N	Y	N	N	N	Y	Y
2 Etheridge	Y	Y	Y	N	N	N	Y	N
3 *Jones*	N	Y	N	Y	Y	Y	Y	N
4 Price	Y	Y	Y	N	N	N	Y	Y
5 *Burr*	N	Y	N	Y	Y	Y	Y	N
6 *Coble*	N	Y	N	Y	Y	Y	N	N
7 McIntyre	N	Y	Y	Y	Y	Y	Y	N
8 *Hayes*	N	Y	Y	Y	Y	Y	Y	N
9 *Myrick*	Y	Y	Y	Y	Y	Y	Y	N
10 *Ballenger*	N	Y	Y	Y	Y	Y	Y	N
11 *Taylor*	N	Y	N	Y	Y	Y	N	N
12 Watt	Y	N	Y	N	N	N	Y	Y
NORTH DAKOTA								
AL Pomeroy	Y	Y	?	N	N	Y	Y	Y
OHIO								
1 *Chabot*	N	Y	Y	Y	Y	Y	Y	N
2 *Portman*	Y	Y	Y	Y	N	Y	Y	N
3 Hall	Y	Y	Y	Y	N	N	Y	Y
4 *Oxley*	Y	N	Y	Y	N	N	Y	N
5 *Gillmor*	Y	Y	Y	Y	N	Y	Y	N
6 Strickland	Y	Y	Y	Y	P	P	Y	N
7 *Hobson*	Y	Y	Y	Y	N	Y	Y	N
8 *Boehner*	N	Y	Y	Y	N	Y	Y	N
9 Kaptur	?	?	?	N	N	N	Y	Y
10 Kucinich	Y	Y	Y	N	N	N	Y	Y
11 Jones	Y	Y	Y	N	N	N	Y	Y
12 *Kasich*	Y	Y	Y	Y	N	Y	Y	N
13 Brown	Y	Y	Y	N	N	N	Y	Y
14 Sawyer	Y	Y	Y	N	N	N	Y	Y
15 *Pryce*	Y	Y	Y	Y	N	Y	Y	N
16 *Regula*	Y	Y	Y	Y	N	Y	Y	N
17 Traficant	Y	Y	Y	Y	N	Y	Y	N
18 *Ney*	N	Y	N	Y	Y	Y	Y	N
19 *LaTourette*	Y	Y	Y	Y	N	N	Y	N
OKLAHOMA								
1 *Largent*	N	Y	N	Y	Y	Y	Y	N
2 *Coburn*	N	Y	N	N	Y	Y	Y	N
3 *Watkins*	N	Y	N	Y	Y	Y	Y	N
4 *Watts*	N	Y	N	Y	Y	Y	Y	N
5 *Istook*	N	Y	N	Y	Y	Y	Y	N
6 *Lucas*	N	Y	N	N	Y	Y	Y	N
OREGON								
1 Wu	Y	Y	Y	Y	N	N	Y	Y
2 *Walden*	Y	Y	Y	Y	N	Y	Y	N
3 Blumenauer	Y	Y	Y	N	N	N	Y	Y
4 DeFazio	Y	Y	Y	N	N	N	Y	Y
5 Hooley	Y	Y	Y	N	N	N	Y	Y
PENNSYLVANIA								
1 Brady	Y	Y	Y	N	N	N	Y	Y
2 Fattah	Y	N	Y	N	N	N	Y	Y
3 Borski	Y	Y	Y	N	N	N	Y	Y
4 Klink	Y	Y	Y	Y	N	N	Y	Y
5 *Peterson*	N	Y	N	Y	Y	Y	Y	N
6 Holden	Y	Y	Y	Y	N	Y	Y	N
7 *Weldon*	Y	Y	Y	Y	N	N	Y	N
8 *Greenwood*	Y	Y	Y	N	N	N	Y	Y
9 *Shuster*	N	Y	Y	Y	Y	Y	Y	N
10 *Sherwood*	N	Y	Y	Y	N	Y	Y	N
11 Kanjorski	Y	Y	Y	Y	N	N	Y	Y
12 Murtha	Y	Y	Y	Y	N	Y	Y	N
13 Hoeffel	Y	Y	Y	N	N	N	Y	Y
14 Coyne	Y	Y	Y	N	N	N	Y	Y
15 *Toomey*	Y	Y	Y	Y	Y	Y	Y	N
16 *Pitts*	N	Y	Y	Y	Y	Y	Y	N
17 *Gekas*	Y	Y	Y	Y	Y	Y	Y	N
18 Doyle	Y	Y	Y	Y	N	N	Y	Y
19 *Goodling*	Y	Y	Y	Y	Y	Y	Y	N
20 Mascara	Y	Y	Y	Y	N	N	Y	N
21 *English*	Y	Y	Y	Y	N	Y	Y	N
RHODE ISLAND								
1 Kennedy	Y	Y	Y	N	N	N	Y	Y
2 Weygand	Y	Y	Y	N	N	N	Y	Y
SOUTH CAROLINA								
1 *Sanford*	N	Y	N	Y	Y	Y	Y	N
2 *Spence*	Y	Y	N	Y	Y	Y	Y	N
3 *Graham*	Y	Y	Y	Y	Y	Y	?	N
4 *DeMint*	N	Y	Y	Y	Y	Y	Y	N
5 Spratt	Y	Y	Y	Y	N	N	Y	Y
6 Clyburn	Y	Y	Y	N	N	N	Y	Y
SOUTH DAKOTA								
AL *Thune*	N	Y	Y	Y	Y	Y	Y	N

	236	237	238	239	240	241	242	243
TENNESSEE								
1 *Jenkins*	N	Y	Y	Y	Y	Y	Y	N
2 *Duncan*	N	Y	Y	Y	Y	Y	Y	N
3 *Wamp*	N	Y	N	Y	Y	Y	N	N
4 *Hilleary*	N	Y	Y	Y	Y	Y	Y	N
5 Clement	Y	Y	Y	N	N	N	Y	N
6 Gordon	Y	Y	Y	Y	Y	Y	Y	N
7 *Bryant*	N	Y	Y	Y	Y	Y	Y	N
8 Tanner	Y	Y	Y	Y	Y	Y	Y	N
9 Ford	Y	Y	Y	Y	N	N	Y	Y
TEXAS								
1 Sandlin	N	Y	N	Y	Y	Y	Y	N
2 Turner	N	Y	Y	Y	Y	Y	Y	N
3 *Johnson, Sam*	N	Y	N	Y	Y	Y	Y	N
4 Hall	Y	Y	Y	Y	Y	Y	Y	N
5 *Sessions*	N	Y	N	Y	Y	Y	N	N
6 *Barton*	N	Y	N	Y	Y	Y	Y	N
7 *Archer*	Y	Y	Y	Y	Y	?	N	N
8 *Brady*	Y	N	Y	N	N	N	Y	N
9 Lampson	Y	Y	Y	Y	Y	Y	Y	N
10 Doggett	Y	Y	Y	Y	N	N	Y	Y
11 Edwards	Y	Y	Y	Y	Y	Y	Y	Y
12 *Granger*	Y	Y	Y	Y	Y	Y	Y	N
13 *Thornberry*	N	Y	N	Y	Y	Y	Y	N
14 *Paul*	N	N	N	Y	Y	Y	N	N
15 Hinojosa	Y	Y	Y	Y	N	N	Y	Y
16 Reyes	Y	Y	Y	Y	Y	Y	Y	Y
17 Stenholm	N	Y	Y	Y	Y	Y	Y	N
18 Jackson-Lee	Y	Y	Y	N	N	N	Y	Y
19 *Combest*	N	Y	N	Y	Y	Y	Y	N
20 Gonzalez	Y	Y	Y	Y	N	N	Y	Y
21 *Smith*	N	Y	Y	Y	Y	Y	Y	N
22 *DeLay*	N	Y	N	Y	Y	Y	N	N
23 *Bonilla*	N	Y	N	Y	?	?	?	?
24 Frost	?	?	?	Y	N	N	Y	Y
25 Bentsen	N	Y	Y	Y	N	N	Y	Y
26 *Armey*	N	Y	Y	Y	Y	Y	Y	N
27 Ortiz	Y	Y	Y	Y	Y	Y	Y	N
28 Rodriguez	Y	Y	Y	Y	N	N	Y	Y
29 Green	N	Y	Y	Y	Y	Y	Y	N
30 Johnson, E.B.	Y	N	Y	N	N	N	Y	Y
UTAH								
1 *Hansen*	N	Y	N	Y	Y	Y	N	N
2 *Cook*	Y	Y	Y	Y	Y	Y	Y	N
3 *Cannon*	N	Y	N	Y	Y	Y	Y	N
VERMONT								
AL Sanders	Y	Y	Y	N	N	N	Y	Y
VIRGINIA								
1 *Bateman*	Y	Y	Y	Y	Y	Y	Y	N
2 Pickett	Y	Y	Y	Y	Y	Y	Y	N
3 Scott	Y	N	Y	N	N	N	Y	Y
4 Sisisky	Y	Y	Y	Y	N	N	Y	N
5 Goode	N	Y	N	Y	Y	Y	Y	N
6 *Goodlatte*	N	Y	Y	Y	Y	Y	Y	N
7 *Bliley*	Y	Y	Y	Y	Y	Y	Y	N
8 Moran	Y	Y	Y	N	N	N	Y	Y
9 Boucher	N	Y	N	Y	Y	Y	Y	N
10 *Wolf*	Y	Y	Y	Y	N	N	Y	N
11 *Davis*	Y	Y	Y	Y	N	N	Y	Y
WASHINGTON								
1 Inslee	Y	Y	Y	N	N	N	Y	Y
2 *Metcalf*	N	Y	N	N	Y	Y	Y	N
3 Baird	Y	Y	Y	N	N	N	Y	N
4 *Hastings*	N	Y	N	Y	Y	Y	Y	N
5 *Nethercutt*	N	Y	Y	Y	Y	Y	Y	N
6 Dicks	Y	Y	Y	N	N	N	Y	Y
7 McDermott	Y	N	Y	N	N	N	Y	Y
8 *Dunn*	Y	?	Y	N	Y	Y	Y	N
9 Smith	Y	Y	Y	N	N	N	Y	N
WEST VIRGINIA								
1 Mollohan	Y	Y	N	Y	Y	Y	Y	N
2 Wise	Y	Y	Y	Y	N	N	Y	N
3 Rahall	Y	Y	Y	Y	Y	Y	Y	N
WISCONSIN								
1 *Ryan*	Y	Y	Y	Y	N	Y	Y	N
2 Baldwin	Y	Y	Y	N	N	N	Y	Y
3 Kind	Y	Y	Y	Y	N	N	Y	N
4 Kleczka	Y	Y	Y	N	N	N	Y	Y
5 Barrett	Y	Y	Y	N	N	N	Y	Y
6 *Petri*	Y	Y	Y	Y	N	N	Y	N
7 Obey	Y	Y	Y	Y	P	P	N	N
8 *Green*	Y	Y	Y	Y	N	P	Y	N
9 *Sensenbrenner*	N	N	Y	Y	Y	Y	Y	N
WYOMING								
AL *Cubin*	N	Y	N	Y	Y	Y	N	N

Southern states - Ala., Ark., Fla., Ga., Ky., La., Miss., N.C., Okla., S.C., Tenn., Texas, Va.

244. HR 2122. Gun Shows/Passage. Passage of the bill to require background checks for purchasers at gun shows, defined as any event with 10 or more vendors and where 50 or more guns are offered for sale; background checks would have to be completed in 24 hours; gun show organizers would be required to destroy purchase records of those who pass background checks. Rejected 147-280: R 137-82; D 10-197 (ND 6-146, SD 4-51); I 0-1. June 18, 1999.

245. HR 659. Revolutionary War Battlefields/Passage. Passage of the bill to authorize $4.3 million for the National Park Service to purchase the Paoli and Brandywine Revolutionary War battlefields in Pennsylvania. The bill would also authorize construction of a museum at the Valley Forge National Historical Park. Passed 418-4: R 211-4; D 206-0 (ND 151-0, SD 55-0); I 1-0. June 22, 1999.

246. HR 1175. Missing Israeli Soldier/Passage. Gilman, R-N.Y., motion to suspend the rules and pass the bill to direct the State Department to investigate the case of three Israeli soldiers, including Zachary Baumel, a U.S. citizen serving in the Israeli army, who have been missing in action since 1982. The bill would make the cooperation of the governments of Syria, Lebanon and the Palestine Authority a factor in decisions about U.S. policy and economic aid to those nations. Motion agreed to 415-5: R 211-4; D 203-1 (ND 149-1, SD 54-0); I 1-0. June 22, 1999.

247. HR 2084. Fiscal 2000 Transportation Appropriations/Rule. Adoption of the rule (H Res 218) to provide for House floor consideration of the bill to provide fiscal 2000 appropriations for federal transportation programs. Adopted 416-3: R 212-1; D 203-2 (ND 148-2, SD 55-0); I 1-0. June 23, 1999.

Key

- Y Voted for (yea).
- # Paired for.
- \+ Announced for.
- N Voted against (nay).
- X Paired against.
- – Announced against.
- P Voted "present."
- C Voted "present" to avoid possible conflict of interest.
- ? Did not vote or otherwise make a position known.

•

Democrats ***Republicans***
Independents

	244	245	246	247
ALABAMA				
1 ***Callahan***	N	Y	Y	Y
2 ***Everett***	N	Y	Y	Y
3 ***Riley***	N	Y	Y	Y
4 ***Aderholt***	N	Y	Y	Y
5 Cramer	N	Y	Y	Y
6 ***Bachus***	N	Y	Y	Y
7 Hilliard	N	Y	Y	Y
ALASKA				
AL ***Young***	N	Y	Y	Y
ARIZONA				
1 ***Salmon***	?	Y	Y	Y
2 Pastor	N	Y	Y	Y
3 ***Stump***	N	Y	Y	Y
4 ***Shadegg***	N	Y	Y	Y
5 ***Kolbe***	Y	Y	Y	N
6 ***Hayworth***	N	Y	Y	Y
ARKANSAS				
1 Berry	N	Y	Y	Y
2 Snyder	N	Y	Y	Y
3 ***Hutchinson***	Y	Y	Y	Y
4 ***Dickey***	N	Y	Y	Y
CALIFORNIA				
1 Thompson	N	Y	Y	Y
2 ***Herger***	N	Y	Y	Y
3 ***Ose***	N	Y	Y	Y
4 ***Doolittle***	N	Y	Y	Y
5 Matsui	N	Y	Y	Y
6 Woolsey	N	Y	Y	Y
7 Miller, George	N	Y	Y	Y
8 Pelosi	N	Y	Y	Y
9 Lee	N	Y	Y	Y
10 Tauscher	N	Y	Y	Y
11 ***Pombo***	N	Y	Y	Y
12 Lantos	N	Y	Y	Y
13 Stark	N	Y	Y	Y
14 Eshoo	N	Y	Y	Y
15 ***Campbell***	N	Y	Y	Y
16 Lofgren	N	Y	Y	Y
17 Farr	N	Y	Y	Y
18 Condit	N	Y	Y	Y
19 ***Radanovich***	Y	Y	Y	Y
20 Dooley	N	Y	Y	Y
21 ***Thomas***	?	+	Y	Y
22 Capps	N	Y	Y	Y
23 ***Gallegly***	Y	Y	Y	Y
24 Sherman	N	Y	Y	Y
25 ***McKeon***	Y	Y	Y	Y
26 Berman	–	Y	Y	Y
27 ***Rogan***	Y	Y	Y	Y
28 ***Dreier***	Y	Y	Y	Y
29 Waxman	N	Y	Y	Y
30 Becerra	N	Y	Y	Y
31 Martinez	N	Y	Y	Y
32 Dixon	N	Y	Y	Y
33 Roybal-Allard	N	Y	Y	Y
34 Napolitano	N	Y	Y	Y
35 Waters	N	Y	Y	Y
36 ***Kuykendall***	Y	Y	Y	+
37 Millender-McD.	N	Y	Y	Y
38 ***Horn***	Y	Y	Y	Y
39 ***Royce***	Y	Y	Y	Y
40 ***Lewis***	?	Y	Y	Y
41 ***Miller, Gary***	Y	Y	Y	Y
42 Brown	?	?	?	?
43 ***Calvert***	Y	Y	Y	Y
44 ***Bono***	Y	Y	Y	Y
45 ***Rohrabacher***	Y	Y	Y	Y
46 Sanchez	N	Y	Y	Y
47 ***Cox***	Y	Y	Y	Y
48 ***Packard***	Y	Y	Y	Y
49 ***Bilbray***	N	?	Y	Y
50 Filner	N	Y	Y	Y
51 ***Cunningham***	Y	Y	Y	Y
52 ***Hunter***	Y	Y	Y	Y
COLORADO				
1 DeGette	N	Y	Y	Y
2 Udall	N	Y	Y	Y
3 ***McInnis***	N	Y	Y	Y
4 ***Schaffer***	N	Y	Y	Y
5 ***Hefley***	N	Y	Y	Y
6 ***Tancredo***	Y	Y	Y	Y
CONNECTICUT				
1 Larson	N	Y	Y	Y
2 Gejdenson	N	Y	Y	Y
3 DeLauro	N	Y	Y	Y
4 ***Shays***	N	Y	Y	Y
5 Maloney	N	Y	Y	Y
6 ***Johnson***	N	Y	Y	Y
DELAWARE				
AL ***Castle***	N	Y	Y	Y
FLORIDA				
1 ***Scarborough***	N	Y	Y	Y
2 Boyd	N	Y	Y	Y
3 Brown	N	Y	Y	Y
4 ***Fowler***	Y	Y	Y	Y
5 Thurman	N	Y	Y	Y
6 ***Stearns***	Y	Y	Y	Y
7 ***Mica***	N	Y	Y	Y
8 ***McCollum***	Y	Y	Y	Y
9 ***Bilirakis***	Y	Y	Y	Y
10 ***Young***	Y	Y	Y	Y
11 Davis	N	Y	Y	Y
12 ***Canady***	Y	Y	Y	Y
13 ***Miller***	Y	Y	Y	Y
14 ***Goss***	Y	Y	Y	Y
15 ***Weldon***	Y	Y	Y	Y
16 ***Foley***	Y	Y	Y	Y
17 Meek	N	Y	Y	Y
18 ***Ros-Lehtinen***	Y	Y	Y	Y
19 Wexler	N	Y	Y	Y
20 Deutsch	N	Y	Y	Y
21 ***Diaz-Balart***	Y	Y	Y	?
22 ***Shaw***	Y	Y	Y	Y
23 Hastings	N	Y	Y	Y
GEORGIA				
1 ***Kingston***	Y	Y	Y	Y
2 Bishop	N	Y	Y	Y
3 ***Collins***	N	Y	N	Y
4 McKinney	N	Y	Y	Y
5 Lewis	N	Y	Y	Y
6 ***Isakson***	Y	Y	Y	Y
7 ***Barr***	Y	Y	P	Y
8 ***Chambliss***	N	Y	Y	Y
9 ***Deal***	N	Y	N	Y
10 ***Norwood***	Y	Y	Y	Y
11 ***Linder***	Y	Y	Y	Y
HAWAII				
1 Abercrombie	N	Y	Y	Y
2 Mink	N	Y	Y	Y
IDAHO				
1 ***Chenoweth***	N	N	Y	Y
2 ***Simpson***	Y	Y	Y	Y
ILLINOIS				
1 Rush	N	Y	Y	Y
2 Jackson	N	Y	Y	Y
3 Lipinski	Y	Y	Y	Y
4 Gutierrez	N	Y	Y	Y
5 Blagojevich	N	Y	Y	Y
6 ***Hyde***	Y	Y	Y	Y
7 Davis	N	Y	Y	Y
8 ***Crane***	Y	Y	Y	Y
9 Schakowsky	N	Y	Y	Y
10 ***Porter***	N	Y	Y	Y
11 ***Weller***	Y	Y	Y	Y
12 Costello	N	Y	Y	Y
13 ***Biggert***	Y	Y	Y	Y
14 ***Hastert***	Y			

ND Northern Democrats SD Southern Democrats

	244	245	246	247
15 *Ewing*	Y	Y	Y	Y
16 *Manzullo*	Y	Y	Y	Y
17 Evans	N	Y	Y	Y
18 *LaHood*	Y	Y	Y	Y
19 Phelps	Y	Y	?	Y
20 *Shimkus*	N	Y	Y	Y
INDIANA				
1 Visclosky	N	Y	Y	Y
2 *McIntosh*	N	Y	Y	Y
3 Roemer	N	Y	Y	Y
4 *Souder*	N	Y	Y	Y
5 *Buyer*	N	Y	Y	Y
6 *Burton*	Y	Y	Y	Y
7 *Pease*	N	Y	Y	Y
8 *Hostettler*	N	Y	Y	Y
9 Hill	N	Y	Y	Y
10 Carson	N	Y	Y	Y
IOWA				
1 *Leach*	N	Y	Y	?
2 *Nussle*	Y	Y	Y	Y
3 Boswell	N	Y	Y	Y
4 *Ganske*	N	Y	Y	Y
5 *Latham*	Y	Y	Y	Y
KANSAS				
1 *Moran*	N	Y	Y	Y
2 *Ryun*	N	Y	Y	Y
3 Moore	N	Y	Y	Y
4 *Tiahrt*	N	?	?	Y
KENTUCKY				
1 *Whitfield*	N	Y	Y	Y
2 *Lewis*	N	Y	Y	Y
3 *Northup*	Y	Y	Y	Y
4 Lucas	N	Y	Y	Y
5 *Rogers*	Y	Y	Y	?
6 *Fletcher*	Y	?	?	?
LOUISIANA				
1 *Vitter*	N	Y	Y	Y
2 Jefferson	N	Y	Y	Y
3 *Tauzin*	Y	Y	Y	Y
4 *McCrery*	Y	Y	Y	Y
5 *Cooksey*	N	?	?	Y
6 *Baker*	Y	Y	Y	Y
7 John	N	Y	Y	Y
MAINE				
1 Allen	N	Y	Y	Y
2 Baldacci	N	Y	Y	Y
MARYLAND				
1 *Gilchrest*	Y	?	?	?
2 *Ehrlich*	Y	Y	Y	Y
3 Cardin	N	Y	Y	Y
4 Wynn	N	Y	Y	Y
5 Hoyer	N	Y	Y	Y
6 *Bartlett*	Y	Y	Y	Y
7 Cummings	N	Y	Y	Y
8 *Morella*	N	Y	Y	Y
MASSACHUSETTS				
1 Olver	N	?	?	?
2 Neal	N	Y	Y	Y
3 McGovern	N	Y	Y	Y
4 Frank	N	Y	Y	Y
5 Meehan	N	Y	Y	Y
6 Tierney	N	Y	Y	Y
7 Markey	N	Y	Y	Y
8 Capuano	N	Y	Y	Y
9 Moakley	N	Y	Y	Y
10 Delahunt	N	Y	Y	Y
MICHIGAN				
1 Stupak	N	Y	Y	Y
2 *Hoekstra*	Y	Y	Y	Y
3 *Ehlers*	Y	Y	Y	Y
4 *Camp*	Y	Y	Y	Y
5 Barcia	N	Y	Y	Y
6 *Upton*	N	Y	Y	Y
7 *Smith*	Y	Y	Y	Y
8 Stabenow	N	Y	Y	Y
9 Kildee	N	Y	Y	Y
10 Bonior	N	Y	Y	Y
11 *Knollenberg*	Y	Y	Y	Y
12 Levin	N	Y	Y	Y
13 Rivers	N	Y	Y	Y
14 Conyers	N	Y	Y	Y
15 Kilpatrick	N	Y	Y	Y
16 Dingell	N	Y	Y	Y
MINNESOTA				
1 *Gutknecht*	Y	Y	Y	Y
2 Minge	?	Y	Y	Y
3 *Ramstad*	N	Y	Y	Y
4 Vento	N	Y	Y	Y
5 Sabo	N	Y	Y	Y
6 Luther	N	Y	Y	Y
7 Peterson	N	Y	Y	Y
8 Oberstar	N	Y	Y	Y
MISSISSIPPI				
1 *Wicker*	Y	Y	Y	Y
2 Thompson	N	Y	Y	Y
3 *Pickering*	Y	Y	Y	Y
4 Shows	N	Y	Y	Y
5 Taylor	Y	Y	Y	Y
MISSOURI				
1 Clay	N	Y	Y	Y
2 *Talent*	Y	Y	Y	Y
3 Gephardt	N	Y	Y	Y
4 Skelton	N	Y	Y	Y
5 McCarthy	N	Y	Y	Y
6 Danner	N	?	?	Y
7 *Blunt*	Y	Y	Y	Y
8 *Emerson*	N	Y	Y	Y
9 *Hulshof*	N	Y	Y	Y
MONTANA				
AL *Hill*	N	Y	Y	Y
NEBRASKA				
1 *Bereuter*	Y	Y	Y	Y
2 *Terry*	Y	Y	Y	Y
3 *Barrett*	Y	Y	Y	Y
NEVADA				
1 Berkley	N	Y	Y	Y
2 *Gibbons*	N	Y	Y	Y
NEW HAMPSHIRE				
1 *Sununu*	Y	Y	N	Y
2 *Bass*	Y	Y	Y	Y
NEW JERSEY				
1 Andrews	N	Y	Y	Y
2 *LoBiondo*	Y	Y	Y	Y
3 *Saxton*	Y	Y	Y	Y
4 *Smith*	N	Y	Y	Y
5 *Roukema*	N	Y	Y	Y
6 Pallone	N	Y	Y	Y
7 *Franks*	Y	Y	Y	Y
8 Pascrell	–	Y	Y	Y
9 Rothman	N	Y	Y	Y
10 Payne	N	Y	Y	Y
11 *Frelinghuysen*	N	Y	Y	Y
12 Holt	N	Y	Y	Y
13 Menendez	N	Y	Y	Y
NEW MEXICO				
1 *Wilson*	Y	Y	Y	Y
2 *Skeen*	Y	Y	Y	Y
3 Udall	N	Y	Y	Y
NEW YORK				
1 *Forbes*	N	Y	Y	Y
2 *Lazio*	Y	Y	Y	Y
3 *King*	Y	Y	Y	Y
4 McCarthy	N	Y	Y	Y
5 Ackerman	N	Y	Y	Y
6 Meeks	N	Y	Y	Y
7 Crowley	N	Y	Y	Y
8 Nadler	N	Y	Y	Y
9 Weiner	N	Y	Y	Y
10 Towns	N	Y	Y	?
11 Owens	N	Y	Y	Y
12 Velázquez	N	Y	Y	Y
13 *Fossella*	Y	Y	Y	Y
14 Maloney	N	Y	Y	Y
15 Rangel	N	Y	Y	Y
16 Serrano	N	Y	Y	Y
17 Engel	N	Y	Y	?
18 Lowey	N	Y	Y	Y
19 *Kelly*	Y	Y	Y	Y
20 *Gilman*	N	Y	Y	Y
21 McNulty	N	Y	Y	Y
22 *Sweeney*	Y	Y	Y	Y
23 *Boehlert*	N	Y	Y	Y
24 *McHugh*	N	Y	Y	Y
25 *Walsh*	Y	Y	Y	Y
26 Hinchey	N	Y	Y	Y
27 *Reynolds*	Y	Y	Y	Y
28 Slaughter	N	Y	Y	Y
29 LaFalce	N	Y	Y	Y
30 *Quinn*	Y	Y	Y	Y
31 *Houghton*	Y	Y	Y	Y
NORTH CAROLINA				
1 Clayton	N	Y	Y	Y
2 Etheridge	N	Y	Y	Y
3 *Jones*	N	Y	Y	Y
4 Price	N	Y	Y	Y
5 *Burr*	N	Y	Y	Y
6 *Coble*	Y	Y	Y	Y
7 McIntyre	N	Y	Y	Y
8 *Hayes*	N	Y	Y	Y
9 *Myrick*	Y	Y	Y	Y
10 *Ballenger*	Y	Y	Y	Y
11 *Taylor*	Y	Y	Y	Y
12 Watt	N	Y	Y	Y
NORTH DAKOTA				
AL Pomeroy	N	Y	Y	Y
OHIO				
1 *Chabot*	N	Y	Y	Y
2 *Portman*	Y	Y	Y	?
3 Hall	N	Y	Y	Y
4 *Oxley*	Y	Y	Y	Y
5 *Gillmor*	Y	Y	Y	Y
6 Strickland	N	Y	Y	Y
7 *Hobson*	Y	Y	Y	Y
8 *Boehner*	Y	Y	Y	Y
9 Kaptur	N	Y	Y	?
10 Kucinich	N	Y	Y	Y
11 Jones	N	Y	Y	Y
12 *Kasich*	Y	?	?	Y
13 Brown	N	Y	Y	Y
14 Sawyer	N	Y	Y	Y
15 *Pryce*	Y	Y	Y	Y
16 *Regula*	Y	Y	Y	Y
17 Traficant	Y	Y	Y	Y
18 *Ney*	N	Y	Y	Y
19 *LaTourette*	Y	Y	Y	Y
OKLAHOMA				
1 *Largent*	Y	Y	Y	Y
2 *Coburn*	N	N	Y	Y
3 *Watkins*	Y	Y	Y	Y
4 *Watts*	Y	Y	Y	Y
5 *Istook*	N	Y	Y	Y
6 *Lucas*	N	Y	Y	Y
OREGON				
1 Wu	N	Y	Y	N
2 *Walden*	Y	Y	Y	Y
3 Blumenauer	N	Y	Y	Y
4 DeFazio	N	?	?	?
5 Hooley	N	?	?	Y
PENNSYLVANIA				
1 Brady	N	Y	Y	Y
2 Fattah	N	Y	Y	Y
3 Borski	N	Y	Y	Y
4 Klink	N	Y	Y	Y
5 *Peterson*	N	Y	Y	Y
6 Holden	N	Y	Y	Y
7 *Weldon*	Y	Y	Y	Y
8 *Greenwood*	Y	Y	Y	Y
9 *Shuster*	Y	Y	Y	Y
10 *Sherwood*	Y	Y	Y	Y
11 Kanjorski	N	Y	Y	Y
12 Murtha	N	Y	Y	Y
13 Hoeffel	N	Y	Y	Y
14 Coyne	N	Y	Y	Y
15 *Toomey*	Y	Y	Y	Y
16 *Pitts*	Y	Y	Y	Y
17 *Gekas*	Y	Y	Y	Y
18 Doyle	N	Y	Y	Y
19 *Goodling*	Y	Y	Y	Y
20 Mascara	N	Y	Y	Y
21 *English*	Y	Y	Y	Y
RHODE ISLAND				
1 Kennedy	N	Y	Y	Y
2 Weygand	N	Y	Y	Y
SOUTH CAROLINA				
1 *Sanford*	N	N	Y	Y
2 *Spence*	Y	Y	Y	Y
3 *Graham*	Y	Y	Y	Y
4 *DeMint*	Y	Y	Y	Y
5 Spratt	N	Y	Y	Y
6 Clyburn	N	Y	Y	Y
SOUTH DAKOTA				
AL *Thune*	N	Y	Y	Y
TENNESSEE				
1 *Jenkins*	N	Y	Y	Y
2 *Duncan*	Y	Y	Y	Y
3 *Wamp*	N	Y	Y	Y
4 *Hilleary*	N	Y	Y	Y
5 Clement	Y	Y	Y	Y
6 Gordon	N	Y	Y	Y
7 *Bryant*	Y	Y	Y	Y
8 Tanner	Y	Y	Y	Y
9 Ford	N	Y	Y	Y
TEXAS				
1 Sandlin	N	Y	Y	Y
2 Turner	N	Y	Y	Y
3 *Johnson, Sam*	N	Y	Y	Y
4 Hall	N	Y	Y	Y
5 *Sessions*	Y	Y	Y	Y
6 *Barton*	N	Y	Y	?
7 *Archer*	Y	Y	?	Y
8 *Brady*	N	Y	Y	Y
9 Lampson	N	Y	Y	Y
10 Doggett	N	Y	Y	Y
11 Edwards	N	Y	Y	Y
12 *Granger*	Y	Y	Y	?
13 *Thornberry*	N	Y	Y	Y
14 *Paul*	N	N	N	Y
15 Hinojosa	N	Y	Y	Y
16 Reyes	N	Y	Y	Y
17 Stenholm	N	Y	Y	Y
18 Jackson-Lee	N	Y	Y	Y
19 *Combest*	N	Y	Y	Y
20 Gonzalez	N	Y	Y	Y
21 *Smith*	Y	Y	Y	Y
22 *DeLay*	Y	Y	Y	Y
23 *Bonilla*	?	Y	Y	Y
24 Frost	N	Y	Y	Y
25 Bentsen	N	Y	Y	Y
26 *Armey*	Y	Y	Y	Y
27 Ortiz	N	Y	Y	Y
28 Rodriguez	N	Y	Y	Y
29 Green	N	Y	Y	Y
30 Johnson, E.B.	N	Y	Y	Y
UTAH				
1 *Hansen*	Y	Y	Y	Y
2 *Cook*	Y	Y	Y	Y
3 *Cannon*	Y	Y	Y	Y
VERMONT				
AL *Sanders*	N	Y	Y	Y
VIRGINIA				
1 *Bateman*	Y	Y	Y	Y
2 Pickett	N	Y	?	Y
3 Scott	N	Y	Y	Y
4 Sisisky	Y	Y	Y	Y
5 Goode	N	Y	Y	Y
6 *Goodlatte*	Y	Y	Y	Y
7 *Bliley*	Y	Y	Y	Y
8 Moran	N	Y	Y	Y
9 Boucher	N	Y	Y	Y
10 *Wolf*	Y	Y	Y	Y
11 *Davis*	Y	Y	Y	Y
WASHINGTON				
1 Inslee	N	Y	Y	Y
2 *Metcalf*	N	Y	Y	Y
3 Baird	N	Y	Y	Y
4 *Hastings*	N	Y	Y	Y
5 *Nethercutt*	N	Y	Y	Y
6 Dicks	N	Y	Y	Y
7 McDermott	N	Y	Y	Y
8 *Dunn*	Y	Y	Y	Y
9 Smith	Y	Y	Y	Y
WEST VIRGINIA				
1 Mollohan	N	Y	Y	Y
2 Wise	Y	Y	Y	Y
3 Rahall	Y	Y	N	Y
WISCONSIN				
1 *Ryan*	Y	Y	Y	Y
2 Baldwin	N	Y	Y	N
3 Kind	N	Y	Y	Y
4 Kleczka	N	Y	Y	Y
5 Barrett	N	Y	Y	Y
6 *Petri*	Y	Y	Y	Y
7 Obey	N	Y	Y	Y
8 *Green*	Y	Y	Y	Y
9 *Sensenbrenner*	Y	Y	Y	Y
WYOMING				
AL *Cubin*	N	Y	Y	Y

Southern states - Ala., Ark., Fla., Ga., Ky., La., Miss., N.C., Okla., S.C., Tenn., Texas, Va.

248. HR 2084. Fiscal 2000 Transportation Appropriations/Amtrak Board. Andrews, D-N.J., amendment to reduce funding for the Amtrak Reform Council by $300,000, bringing funding down to the fiscal 1999 level of $450,000. Adopted 289-141: R 84-136; D 204-5 (ND 153-1, SD 51-4); I 1-0. June 23, 1999.

249. HR 2084. Fiscal 2000 Transportation Appropriations/Pasadena Freeway. Rogan, R-Calif., amendment to prohibit funds in the bill from being used in planning or construction of the State Route 710 Freeway project in Pasadena, Calif. Adopted 241-190: R 221-0; D 20-189 (ND 11-143, SD 9-46); I 0-1. June 23, 1999.

250. HR 2084. Fiscal 2000 Transportation Appropriations/Passage. Passage of the bill to appropriate $44.5 billion in funding for transportation programs for fiscal 2000, including $27.7 billion in highway construction and repair programs; $5.8 billion for transit programs; $2.4 billion for the Federal Aviation Administration; $4 billion for the U.S. Coast Guard; and $571 million for Amtrak. Passed 429-3: R 219-3; D 209-0 (ND 154-0, SD 55-0); I 1-0. June 23, 1999.

251. H J Res 33. Flag Desecration/Watt Substitute. Watt, D-N.C., substitute amendment to state that Congress shall have the power to prohibit the physical desecration of the U.S. flag, but adding that it must be in a manner consistent with the First Amendment of the Constitution. Rejected 115-310: R 6-211; D 108-99 (ND 89-63, SD 19-36); I 1-0. June 24, 1999.

252. H J Res 33. Flag Desecration/Passage. Passage of the joint resolution to propose a constitutional amendment to state that Congress shall have the power to prohibit the physical desecration of the U.S. flag. Passed 305-124: R 210-10; D 95-113 (ND 57-96, SD 38-17); I 0-1. June 24, 1999. A two-thirds majority of those present and voting (286 in this case) is required to pass a joint resolution proposing an amendment to the Constitution.

Key

- Y Voted for (yea).
- # Paired for.
- + Announced for.
- N Voted against (nay).
- X Paired against.
- – Announced against.
- P Voted "present."
- C Voted "present" to avoid possible conflict of interest.
- ? Did not vote or otherwise make a position known.

•

Democrats ***Republicans***
Independents

	248	249	250	251	252
ALABAMA					
1 *Callahan*	N	Y	Y	N	Y
2 *Everett*	N	Y	Y	N	Y
3 *Riley*	N	Y	Y	N	Y
4 *Aderholt*	N	Y	Y	N	Y
5 Cramer	Y	N	Y	N	Y
6 *Bachus*	Y	Y	Y	N	Y
7 Hilliard	Y	N	Y	N	Y
ALASKA					
AL *Young*	Y	Y	Y	N	Y
ARIZONA					
1 *Salmon*	Y	Y	Y	N	Y
2 Pastor	Y	N	Y	Y	N
3 *Stump*	N	Y	Y	N	Y
4 *Shadegg*	N	Y	Y	N	N
5 *Kolbe*	N	Y	Y	Y	N
6 *Hayworth*	N	Y	Y	N	Y
ARKANSAS					
1 Berry	Y	N	Y	N	Y
2 Snyder	Y	Y	Y	N	N
3 *Hutchinson*	Y	Y	Y	N	Y
4 *Dickey*	Y	Y	Y	N	Y
CALIFORNIA					
1 Thompson	Y	Y	Y	N	N
2 *Herger*	N	Y	Y	N	Y
3 *Ose*	Y	Y	Y	N	Y
4 *Doolittle*	N	Y	Y	N	Y
5 Matsui	Y	N	Y	N	N
6 Woolsey	Y	N	Y	Y	N
7 Miller, George	Y	N	Y	Y	N
8 Pelosi	Y	N	Y	Y	N
9 Lee	Y	N	Y	Y	N
10 Tauscher	Y	N	Y	Y	N
11 *Pombo*	N	Y	Y	N	Y
12 Lantos	Y	N	Y	Y	Y
13 Stark	Y	N	Y	Y	N
14 Eshoo	Y	N	Y	Y	N
15 *Campbell*	Y	Y	Y	N	Y
16 Lofgren	Y	N	Y	N	N
17 Farr	Y	N	Y	Y	N
18 Condit	Y	N	Y	N	Y
19 *Radanovich*	Y	Y	Y	N	Y
20 Dooley	Y	N	Y	N	Y
21 *Thomas*	N	Y	Y	N	Y
22 Capps	Y	N	Y	N	Y
23 *Gallegly*	N	Y	Y	N	Y
24 Sherman	Y	N	Y	N	Y
25 *McKeon*	Y	Y	Y	N	Y
26 Berman	Y	N	Y	Y	N
27 *Rogan*	N	Y	Y	N	Y
28 *Dreier*	N	Y	Y	N	Y
29 Waxman	N	N	Y	Y	N
30 Becerra	Y	N	Y	Y	N
31 Martinez	Y	N	Y	Y	Y
32 Dixon	Y	N	Y	Y	N
33 Roybal-Allard	Y	N	Y	Y	N
34 Napolitano	Y	N	Y	N	Y
35 Waters	Y	N	Y	Y	N
36 *Kuykendall*	N	Y	Y	N	Y
37 Millender-McD.	Y	N	Y	+	–
38 *Horn*	N	Y	Y	N	Y
39 *Royce*	N	Y	N	N	Y
40 *Lewis*	Y	Y	Y	N	Y
41 *Miller, Gary*	N	Y	Y	N	Y
42 Brown	?	?	?	?	?
43 *Calvert*	N	Y	Y	N	Y
44 *Bono*	N	Y	Y	N	Y
45 *Rohrabacher*	N	Y	Y	N	Y
46 Sanchez	Y	N	Y	Y	Y
47 *Cox*	N	Y	Y	N	Y
48 *Packard*	N	Y	Y	N	Y
49 *Bilbray*	N	Y	Y	N	Y
50 Filner	Y	N	Y	N	N
51 *Cunningham*	N	Y	Y	N	Y
52 *Hunter*	N	Y	Y	N	Y
COLORADO					
1 DeGette	Y	N	Y	N	N
2 Udall	Y	N	Y	Y	N
3 *McInnis*	Y	Y	Y	N	Y
4 *Schaffer*	Y	Y	Y	N	Y
5 *Hefley*	Y	Y	Y	?	Y
6 *Tancredo*	Y	Y	Y	N	Y
CONNECTICUT					
1 Larson	Y	N	Y	Y	Y
2 Gejdenson	Y	N	Y	Y	N
3 DeLauro	Y	N	Y	N	N
4 *Shays*	N	Y	Y	N	N
5 Maloney	Y	N	Y	Y	Y
6 *Johnson*	N	Y	Y	N	Y
DELAWARE					
AL *Castle*	N	Y	Y	N	Y
FLORIDA					
1 *Scarborough*	N	Y	Y	N	Y
2 Boyd	Y	N	Y	N	Y
3 Brown	Y	N	Y	N	Y
4 *Fowler*	N	Y	Y	N	Y
5 Thurman	Y	N	Y	N	Y
6 *Stearns*	Y	Y	Y	N	Y
7 *Mica*	N	Y	Y	N	Y
8 *McCollum*	N	Y	Y	N	Y
9 *Bilirakis*	Y	Y	Y	N	Y
10 *Young*	N	Y	Y	N	Y
11 Davis	Y	N	Y	N	Y
12 *Canady*	N	Y	Y	N	Y
13 *Miller*	N	Y	Y	N	Y
14 *Goss*	N	Y	Y	N	Y
15 *Weldon*	N	Y	Y	N	Y
16 *Foley*	Y	Y	Y	N	Y
17 Meek	Y	N	Y	Y	N
18 *Ros-Lehtinen*	Y	Y	Y	N	Y
19 Wexler	Y	N	Y	Y	N
20 Deutsch	Y	N	Y	N	Y
21 *Diaz-Balart*	Y	Y	Y	N	Y
22 *Shaw*	N	Y	Y	N	Y
23 Hastings	Y	N	Y	Y	N
GEORGIA					
1 *Kingston*	N	Y	Y	N	Y
2 Bishop	Y	N	Y	N	Y
3 *Collins*	N	Y	Y	N	Y
4 McKinney	Y	N	Y	Y	N
5 Lewis	Y	N	Y	N	N
6 *Isakson*	N	Y	Y	N	Y
7 *Barr*	N	Y	Y	N	Y
8 *Chambliss*	N	Y	Y	N	Y
9 *Deal*	Y	Y	Y	N	Y
10 *Norwood*	Y	Y	Y	N	Y
11 *Linder*	Y	Y	Y	N	Y
HAWAII					
1 Abercrombie	Y	N	Y	Y	N
2 Mink	Y	N	Y	Y	N
IDAHO					
1 *Chenoweth*	Y	Y	N	N	Y
2 *Simpson*	N	Y	Y	N	Y
ILLINOIS					
1 Rush	Y	N	Y	Y	N
2 Jackson	Y	N	Y	Y	N
3 Lipinski	Y	N	Y	N	Y
4 Gutierrez	Y	N	Y	N	Y
5 Blagojevich	Y	N	Y	Y	Y
6 *Hyde*	N	Y	Y	N	Y
7 Davis	Y	N	Y	Y	N
8 *Crane*	N	Y	Y	N	Y
9 Schakowsky	Y	N	Y	Y	N
10 *Porter*	N	Y	Y	Y	N
11 *Weller*	Y	Y	Y	N	Y
12 Costello	Y	N	Y	N	Y
13 *Biggert*	N	Y	Y	N	Y
14 *Hastert*			Y		

ND Northern Democrats SD Southern Democrats

	248	249	250	251	252
15 *Ewing*	Y	Y	Y	N	Y
16 *Manzullo*	N	Y	Y	N	Y
17 Evans	Y	N	Y	Y	N
18 *LaHood*	Y	Y	Y	N	Y
19 Phelps	Y	N	Y	N	Y
20 *Shimkus*	Y	Y	Y	N	Y
INDIANA					
1 Visclosky	Y	N	Y	N	N
2 *McIntosh*	N	Y	Y	Y	Y
3 Roemer	Y	N	Y	N	Y
4 *Souder*	N	Y	Y	N	Y
5 *Buyer*	N	Y	Y	N	Y
6 *Burton*	N	Y	Y	N	Y
7 *Pease*	N	Y	Y	N	Y
8 *Hostettler*	Y	Y	Y	N	Y
9 Hill	Y	N	Y	N	N
10 Carson	Y	Y	Y	Y	N
IOWA					
1 *Leach*	Y	Y	Y	Y	N
2 *Nussle*	Y	Y	Y	N	Y
3 Boswell	Y	N	Y	N	Y
4 *Ganske*	Y	Y	Y	N	Y
5 *Latham*	Y	Y	Y	N	Y
KANSAS					
1 *Moran*	Y	Y	Y	N	Y
2 *Ryun*	N	Y	Y	N	Y
3 Moore	Y	Y	Y	Y	N
4 *Tiahrt*	N	Y	Y	N	Y
KENTUCKY					
1 *Whitfield*	Y	Y	Y	N	Y
2 *Lewis*	N	Y	Y	N	Y
3 *Northup*	N	Y	Y	N	Y
4 Lucas	Y	N	Y	N	Y
5 *Rogers*	N	Y	Y	N	Y
6 *Fletcher*	?	Y	Y	N	Y
LOUISIANA					
1 *Vitter*	Y	Y	Y	N	Y
2 Jefferson	Y	N	Y	N	Y
3 *Tauzin*	Y	Y	Y	N	Y
4 *McCrery*	N	Y	Y	N	Y
5 *Cooksey*	N	Y	Y	N	Y
6 *Baker*	N	Y	Y	N	Y
7 John	Y	N	Y	N	Y
MAINE					
1 Allen	Y	N	Y	Y	N
2 Baldacci	Y	N	Y	N	Y
MARYLAND					
1 *Gilchrest*	?	?	?	?	?
2 *Ehrlich*	N	Y	Y	N	Y
3 Cardin	Y	N	Y	Y	N
4 Wynn	Y	N	Y	N	Y
5 Hoyer	Y	N	Y	N	N
6 *Bartlett*	N	Y	Y	N	Y
7 Cummings	Y	N	Y	Y	N
8 *Morella*	N	Y	Y	N	Y
MASSACHUSETTS					
1 Olver	Y	N	Y	Y	N
2 Neal	Y	N	Y	Y	Y
3 McGovern	Y	N	Y	N	Y
4 Frank	Y	N	Y	Y	N
5 Meehan	Y	N	Y	Y	N
6 Tierney	Y	N	Y	Y	N
7 Markey	Y	N	Y	Y	N
8 Capuano	Y	N	Y	N	N
9 Moakley	Y	N	Y	N	Y
10 Delahunt	Y	N	Y	N	Y
MICHIGAN					
1 Stupak	Y	N	Y	N	Y
2 *Hoekstra*	N	Y	Y	Y	N
3 *Ehlers*	N	Y	Y	N	N
4 *Camp*	Y	Y	Y	N	N
5 Barcia	Y	N	Y	N	Y
6 *Upton*	Y	Y	Y	N	Y
7 *Smith*	N	Y	Y	N	Y
8 Stabenow	Y	N	Y	N	Y
9 Kildee	Y	N	Y	N	Y
10 Bonior	Y	N	Y	Y	N
11 *Knollenberg*	N	Y	Y	N	Y
12 Levin	Y	N	Y	Y	N
13 Rivers	Y	N	Y	Y	N
14 Conyers	Y	N	Y	Y	N
15 Kilpatrick	Y	N	Y	Y	N
16 Dingell	Y	N	Y	N	N

	248	249	250	251	252
MINNESOTA					
1 *Gutknecht*	N	Y	Y	N	Y
2 Minge	Y	N	Y	Y	N
3 *Ramstad*	N	Y	Y	N	Y
4 Vento	Y	N	Y	Y	N
5 Sabo	Y	N	Y	Y	N
6 Luther	Y	N	Y	N	Y
7 Peterson	Y	Y	Y	N	Y
8 Oberstar	Y	N	Y	Y	N
MISSISSIPPI					
1 *Wicker*	N	Y	Y	N	Y
2 Thompson	Y	N	Y	Y	Y
3 *Pickering*	N	Y	Y	N	Y
4 Shows	Y	N	Y	N	Y
5 Taylor	Y	Y	Y	N	Y
MISSOURI					
1 Clay	Y	N	Y	Y	N
2 *Talent*	N	Y	Y	N	Y
3 Gephardt	Y	N	Y	N	Y
4 Skelton	Y	N	Y	N	Y
5 McCarthy	Y	Y	Y	Y	N
6 Danner	Y	Y	Y	N	Y
7 *Blunt*	Y	Y	Y	N	Y
8 *Emerson*	Y	Y	Y	N	Y
9 *Hulshof*	Y	Y	Y	N	Y
MONTANA					
AL *Hill*	Y	Y	Y	N	Y
NEBRASKA					
1 *Bereuter*	N	Y	Y	N	Y
2 *Terry*	N	Y	Y	N	Y
3 *Barrett*	N	Y	Y	N	Y
NEVADA					
1 Berkley	Y	N	Y	N	Y
2 *Gibbons*	N	Y	Y	N	Y
NEW HAMPSHIRE					
1 *Sununu*	N	Y	Y	N	Y
2 *Bass*	Y	Y	Y	N	Y
NEW JERSEY					
1 Andrews	Y	N	Y	N	Y
2 *LoBiondo*	Y	Y	Y	N	Y
3 *Saxton*	N	Y	Y	N	Y
4 *Smith*	Y	Y	Y	N	Y
5 *Roukema*	N	Y	Y	N	Y
6 Pallone	Y	N	Y	N	Y
7 *Franks*	N	Y	Y	N	Y
8 Pascrell	Y	N	Y	N	Y
9 Rothman	Y	N	Y	N	Y
10 Payne	Y	N	Y	Y	N
11 *Frelinghuysen*	N	Y	Y	N	Y
12 Holt	Y	N	Y	N	N
13 Menendez	Y	N	Y	N	Y
NEW MEXICO					
1 *Wilson*	Y	Y	Y	N	Y
2 *Skeen*	N	Y	Y	N	Y
3 Udall	Y	N	Y	Y	N
NEW YORK					
1 *Forbes*	Y	Y	Y	N	Y
2 *Lazio*	Y	Y	Y	N	Y
3 *King*	Y	Y	Y	N	Y
4 McCarthy	Y	N	Y	N	Y
5 Ackerman	Y	N	Y	Y	N
6 Meeks	Y	N	Y	Y	N
7 Crowley	Y	N	Y	N	Y
8 Nadler	Y	N	Y	Y	N
9 Weiner	Y	N	Y	Y	N
10 Towns	Y	N	Y	?	?
11 Owens	Y	N	Y	Y	N
12 Velázquez	Y	N	Y	Y	N
13 *Fossella*	Y	Y	Y	N	Y
14 Maloney	Y	N	Y	Y	N
15 Rangel	Y	N	Y	?	N
16 Serrano	Y	N	Y	Y	N
17 Engel	Y	N	Y	Y	N
18 Lowey	Y	N	Y	Y	N
19 *Kelly*	Y	Y	Y	N	Y
20 *Gilman*	Y	Y	Y	N	Y
21 McNulty	Y	N	Y	Y	Y
22 *Sweeney*	Y	Y	Y	N	Y
23 *Boehlert*	Y	Y	Y	N	Y
24 *McHugh*	N	Y	Y	N	Y
25 *Walsh*	Y	Y	Y	N	Y
26 Hinchey	Y	N	Y	Y	N
27 *Reynolds*	Y	Y	Y	N	Y
28 Slaughter	Y	N	Y	Y	N
29 LaFalce	Y	N	Y	Y	N

	248	249	250	251	252
30 *Quinn*	Y	Y	Y	N	Y
31 *Houghton*	N	Y	Y	N	Y
NORTH CAROLINA					
1 Clayton	Y	Y	Y	Y	N
2 Etheridge	Y	N	Y	Y	Y
3 *Jones*	Y	Y	Y	N	Y
4 Price	Y	N	Y	Y	N
5 *Burr*	N	Y	Y	N	Y
6 *Coble*	N	Y	Y	N	Y
7 McIntyre	Y	Y	Y	N	Y
8 *Hayes*	N	Y	Y	N	Y
9 *Myrick*	Y	Y	Y	N	Y
10 *Ballenger*	Y	Y	Y	N	Y
11 *Taylor*	N	Y	Y	N	Y
12 Watt	Y	N	Y	Y	N
NORTH DAKOTA					
AL Pomeroy	Y	N	Y	N	Y
OHIO					
1 *Chabot*	N	Y	Y	N	Y
2 *Portman*	Y	Y	Y	N	Y
3 Hall	Y	N	Y	N	N
4 *Oxley*	Y	Y	Y	N	Y
5 *Gillmor*	Y	Y	Y	N	Y
6 Strickland	Y	N	Y	N	Y
7 *Hobson*	N	Y	Y	N	Y
8 *Boehner*	Y	Y	Y	N	Y
9 Kaptur	Y	N	Y	Y	Y
10 Kucinich	Y	Y	Y	Y	Y
11 Jones	Y	N	Y	Y	N
12 *Kasich*	N	Y	Y	?	?
13 Brown	Y	N	Y	Y	Y
14 Sawyer	Y	N	Y	Y	N
15 *Pryce*	N	Y	Y	N	Y
16 *Regula*	N	Y	Y	N	Y
17 Traficant	Y	Y	Y	N	Y
18 *Ney*	Y	Y	Y	N	Y
19 *LaTourette*	Y	Y	Y	N	Y
OKLAHOMA					
1 *Largent*	N	Y	Y	N	Y
2 *Coburn*	N	Y	Y	N	Y
3 *Watkins*	N	Y	Y	N	Y
4 *Watts*	N	Y	Y	N	Y
5 *Istook*	N	Y	Y	N	Y
6 *Lucas*	N	Y	Y	N	Y
OREGON					
1 Wu	Y	N	Y	N	N
2 *Walden*	Y	Y	Y	N	Y
3 Blumenauer	Y	Y	Y	Y	N
4 DeFazio	?	?	?	Y	N
5 Hooley	Y	Y	Y	Y	N
PENNSYLVANIA					
1 Brady	Y	N	Y	Y	N
2 Fattah	Y	N	Y	Y	N
3 Borski	Y	N	Y	Y	N
4 Klink	Y	N	Y	N	N
5 *Peterson*	N	Y	Y	N	Y
6 Holden	Y	N	Y	N	Y
7 *Weldon*	Y	Y	Y	N	Y
8 *Greenwood*	Y	Y	Y	Y	N
9 *Shuster*	N	Y	Y	N	Y
10 *Sherwood*	N	Y	Y	N	Y
11 Kanjorski	Y	N	Y	N	Y
12 Murtha	Y	N	Y	N	Y
13 Hoeffel	Y	N	Y	Y	N
14 Coyne	Y	N	Y	Y	N
15 *Toomey*	N	Y	Y	N	Y
16 *Pitts*	N	Y	Y	N	Y
17 *Gekas*	N	Y	Y	N	Y
18 Doyle	Y	N	Y	N	Y
19 *Goodling*	Y	Y	Y	N	Y
20 Mascara	Y	N	Y	N	Y
21 *English*	Y	Y	Y	N	Y
RHODE ISLAND					
1 Kennedy	Y	N	Y	Y	N
2 Weygand	Y	N	Y	N	N
SOUTH CAROLINA					
1 *Sanford*	N	Y	Y	N	Y
2 *Spence*	N	Y	Y	N	Y
3 *Graham*	Y	Y	Y	N	Y
4 *DeMint*	Y	Y	Y	N	Y
5 Spratt	Y	N	Y	N	Y
6 Clyburn	Y	N	Y	Y	Y
SOUTH DAKOTA					
AL *Thune*	Y	Y	Y	N	Y

	248	249	250	251	252
TENNESSEE					
1 *Jenkins*	Y	Y	Y	N	Y
2 *Duncan*	Y	Y	Y	N	Y
3 *Wamp*	N	Y	Y	N	Y
4 *Hilleary*	Y	Y	Y	N	Y
5 Clement	Y	N	Y	N	Y
6 Gordon	Y	N	Y	N	Y
7 *Bryant*	N	Y	Y	N	Y
8 Tanner	Y	N	Y	N	N
9 Ford	Y	N	Y	Y	Y
TEXAS					
1 Sandlin	Y	N	Y	N	Y
2 Turner	Y	N	Y	N	Y
3 *Johnson, Sam*	Y	Y	Y	N	Y
4 Hall	N	N	Y	N	Y
5 *Sessions*	Y	Y	Y	N	Y
6 *Barton*	N	Y	Y	?	Y
7 *Archer*	N	Y	Y	N	Y
8 *Brady*	N	Y	Y	N	Y
9 Lampson	Y	N	Y	Y	Y
10 Doggett	Y	Y	Y	N	N
11 Edwards	Y	Y	Y	N	Y
12 *Granger*	N	Y	Y	N	Y
13 *Thornberry*	N	Y	Y	N	Y
14 *Paul*	Y	Y	N	N	N
15 Hinojosa	Y	N	Y	N	Y
16 Reyes	Y	N	Y	N	Y
17 Stenholm	N	N	Y	N	Y
18 Jackson-Lee	Y	N	Y	Y	N
19 *Combest*	N	Y	Y	N	Y
20 Gonzalez	Y	N	Y	Y	N
21 *Smith*	N	Y	Y	N	Y
22 *DeLay*	N	Y	Y	N	Y
23 *Bonilla*	N	Y	Y	N	Y
24 Frost	Y	N	Y	Y	Y
25 Bentsen	Y	N	Y	Y	Y
26 *Armey*	N	Y	Y	N	Y
27 Ortiz	Y	N	Y	N	Y
28 Rodriguez	Y	N	Y	N	Y
29 Green	Y	N	Y	N	Y
30 Johnson, E.B.	Y	N	Y	Y	N
UTAH					
1 *Hansen*	N	Y	Y	N	Y
2 *Cook*	N	Y	Y	N	Y
3 *Cannon*	Y	Y	Y	N	Y
VERMONT					
AL *Sanders*	Y	N	Y	Y	N
VIRGINIA					
1 *Bateman*	N	Y	Y	N	Y
2 Pickett	N	Y	Y	N	Y
3 Scott	Y	N	Y	Y	N
4 Sisisky	Y	N	Y	N	Y
5 Goode	N	Y	Y	N	Y
6 *Goodlatte*	N	Y	Y	N	Y
7 *Bliley*	N	Y	Y	N	Y
8 Moran	Y	Y	Y	N	N
9 Boucher	Y	N	Y	Y	N
10 *Wolf*	N	Y	Y	N	Y
11 *Davis*	N	Y	Y	?	Y
WASHINGTON					
1 Inslee	Y	N	Y	Y	N
2 *Metcalf*	Y	Y	Y	N	Y
3 Baird	Y	N	Y	N	Y
4 *Hastings*	N	Y	Y	N	Y
5 *Nethercutt*	N	Y	Y	N	Y
6 Dicks	Y	Y	Y	Y	N
7 McDermott	Y	N	Y	Y	N
8 *Dunn*	N	Y	Y	N	Y
9 Smith	Y	N	Y	N	Y
WEST VIRGINIA					
1 Mollohan	Y	N	Y	N	Y
2 Wise	Y	N	Y	N	Y
3 Rahall	Y	N	Y	N	Y
WISCONSIN					
1 *Ryan*	Y	Y	Y	N	Y
2 Baldwin	Y	N	Y	Y	N
3 Kind	Y	N	Y	Y	N
4 Kleczka	Y	N	Y	N	N
5 Barrett	Y	N	Y	Y	N
6 *Petri*	N	Y	Y	N	N
7 Obey	Y	N	Y	Y	N
8 *Green*	Y	Y	Y	N	Y
9 *Sensenbrenner*	Y	Y	Y	N	Y
WYOMING					
AL *Cubin*	N	Y	Y	N	Y

Southern states - Ala., Ark., Fla., Ga., Ky., La., Miss., N.C., Okla., S.C., Tenn., Texas, Va.

253. HR 775. Y2K Liability Limits/Motion To Instruct. Conyers, D-Mich., motion to instruct House conferees on the Y2K liability bill to ensure that the final conference report reflects the "substantive inputs" of the administration and the bipartisan leadership in the House and Senate. Motion agreed to 426-0: R 217-0; D 208-0 (ND 154-0, SD 54-0); I 1-0. June 24, 1999.

254. HR 1658. Civil Asset Forfeiture/Hutchinson Substitute. Hutchinson, R-Ark., substitute amendment to require the government to prove "by a preponderance of the evidence" that seized property was used in the commission of a crime, rather than establishing the more stringent standard of "clear and convincing evidence" proposed in the underlying bill. (Rejected 155-268: R 85-131; D 70-136 (ND 54-97, SD 16-39); I 0-1. June 24, 1999.

255. HR 1658. Civil Asset Forfeiture/Passage. Passage of the bill to increase safeguards for persons whose property is seized under federal civil forfeiture proceedings. The bill would shift the main burden of proof in such proceedings by requiring the government to show "clear and convincing evidence" that the property was used illegally. Owners would not be required to forfeit property if they had taken reasonable steps to prevent its illegal use. The bill also would allow courts to appoint counsel to property owners who could not afford representation while challenging a seizure, and would allow owners to sue the government for negligence if the property was damaged or lost while in the government's possession. Passed 375-48: R 191-26; D 183-22 (ND 135-15, SD 48-7); I 1-0. June 24, 1999.

Key

Y Voted for (yea).
\# Paired for.
\+ Announced for.
N Voted against (nay).
X Paired against.
– Announced against.
P Voted "present."
C Voted "present" to avoid possible conflict of interest.
? Did not vote or otherwise make a position known.

•

Democrats ***Republicans***
Independents

	253	254	255
ALABAMA			
1 ***Callahan***	Y	N	Y
2 ***Everett***	Y	N	Y
3 ***Riley***	Y	N	Y
4 ***Aderholt***	Y	N	Y
5 Cramer	Y	Y	Y
6 ***Bachus***	Y	Y	N
7 Hilliard	Y	N	Y
ALASKA			
AL ***Young***	Y	N	Y
ARIZONA			
1 ***Salmon***	Y	Y	Y
2 Pastor	Y	N	Y
3 ***Stump***	Y	N	Y
4 ***Shadegg***	Y	N	Y
5 ***Kolbe***	Y	N	Y
6 ***Hayworth***	Y	N	Y
ARKANSAS			
1 Berry	Y	N	Y
2 Snyder	Y	N	Y
3 ***Hutchinson***	Y	Y	N
4 ***Dickey***	Y	Y	Y
CALIFORNIA			
1 Thompson	Y	Y	N
2 ***Herger***	Y	Y	Y
3 ***Ose***	Y	Y	Y
4 ***Doolittle***	Y	N	Y
5 Matsui	Y	N	Y
6 Woolsey	Y	N	Y
7 Miller, George	Y	N	Y
8 Pelosi	Y	N	Y
9 Lee	Y	N	Y
10 Tauscher	Y	N	Y
11 ***Pombo***	Y	N	Y
12 Lantos	Y	N	Y
13 Stark	Y	N	Y
14 Eshoo	Y	N	Y
15 ***Campbell***	Y	N	Y
16 Lofgren	Y	N	Y
17 Farr	Y	N	Y
18 Condit	Y	Y	N
19 ***Radanovich***	Y	N	Y
20 Dooley	Y	Y	Y
21 ***Thomas***	Y	Y	Y
22 Capps	Y	Y	Y
23 ***Gallegly***	Y	N	Y
24 Sherman	Y	Y	Y
25 ***McKeon***	Y	N	Y
26 Berman	Y	?	+
27 ***Rogan***	?	N	Y
28 ***Dreier***	Y	N	Y
29 Waxman	Y	Y	Y
30 Becerra	Y	N	Y
31 Martinez	Y	N	Y
32 Dixon	Y	Y	Y
33 Roybal-Allard	Y	N	Y
34 Napolitano	Y	N	Y
35 Waters	Y	N	?
36 ***Kuykendall***	Y	Y	Y
37 Millender-McD.	Y	N	Y
38 ***Horn***	Y	Y	Y
39 ***Royce***	Y	N	Y
40 ***Lewis***	Y	N	Y
41 ***Miller, Gary***	Y	N	Y
42 Brown	?	?	?
43 ***Calvert***	Y	Y	Y
44 ***Bono***	Y	N	Y
45 ***Rohrabacher***	Y	N	Y
46 Sanchez	Y	Y	Y
47 ***Cox***	Y	N	Y
48 ***Packard***	Y	?	+
49 ***Bilbray***	Y	Y	N
50 Filner	Y	N	Y
51 ***Cunningham***	Y	N	Y
52 ***Hunter***	Y	N	Y
COLORADO			
1 DeGette	Y	N	Y
2 Udall	Y	N	Y
3 ***McInnis***	Y	?	?
4 ***Schaffer***	Y	N	Y
5 ***Hefley***	Y	N	Y
6 ***Tancredo***	Y	N	Y
CONNECTICUT			
1 Larson	Y	Y	Y
2 Gejdenson	Y	N	Y
3 DeLauro	Y	N	Y
4 ***Shays***	Y	Y	N
5 Maloney	Y	Y	N
6 ***Johnson***	Y	Y	N
DELAWARE			
AL ***Castle***	Y	Y	Y
FLORIDA			
1 ***Scarborough***	Y	N	Y
2 Boyd	Y	Y	N
3 Brown	Y	N	Y
4 ***Fowler***	Y	Y	Y
5 Thurman	Y	Y	Y
6 ***Stearns***	Y	Y	Y
7 ***Mica***	Y	Y	N
8 ***McCollum***	Y	Y	Y
9 ***Bilirakis***	Y	N	Y
10 ***Young***	Y	Y	Y
11 Davis	Y	N	Y
12 ***Canady***	Y	N	Y
13 ***Miller***	Y	Y	Y
14 ***Goss***	Y	Y	Y
15 ***Weldon***	Y	Y	N
16 ***Foley***	Y	N	Y
17 Meek	Y	N	Y
18 ***Ros-Lehtinen***	Y	Y	Y
19 Wexler	Y	N	Y
20 Deutsch	Y	Y	N
21 ***Diaz-Balart***	Y	N	Y
22 ***Shaw***	Y	Y	Y
23 Hastings	Y	N	Y
GEORGIA			
1 ***Kingston***	Y	N	Y
2 Bishop	Y	N	Y
3 ***Collins***	Y	Y	N
4 McKinney	Y	N	Y
5 Lewis	Y	N	Y
6 ***Isakson***	Y	Y	Y
7 ***Barr***	Y	N	Y
8 ***Chambliss***	Y	Y	N
9 ***Deal***	Y	Y	Y
10 ***Norwood***	Y	Y	Y
11 ***Linder***	Y	N	Y
HAWAII			
1 Abercrombie	Y	N	Y
2 Mink	Y	N	Y
IDAHO			
1 ***Chenoweth***	Y	N	Y
2 ***Simpson***	Y	N	Y
ILLINOIS			
1 Rush	Y	N	Y
2 Jackson	Y	N	Y
3 Lipinski	Y	N	Y
4 Gutierrez	Y	Y	Y
5 Blagojevich	Y	Y	Y
6 ***Hyde***	Y	N	Y
7 Davis	Y	N	Y
8 ***Crane***	Y	N	Y
9 Schakowsky	Y	N	Y
10 ***Porter***	Y	Y	Y
11 ***Weller***	Y	N	Y
12 Costello	Y	?	?
13 ***Biggert***	Y	N	Y
14 ***Hastert***			

ND Northern Democrats SD Southern Democrats

	253	254	255
15 ***Ewing***	Y	N	Y
16 ***Manzullo***	Y	N	Y
17 Evans	Y	N	Y
18 ***LaHood***	Y	N	Y
19 Phelps	Y	N	Y
20 ***Shimkus***	Y	N	Y
INDIANA			
1 Visclosky	Y	Y	N
2 ***McIntosh***	Y	N	Y
3 Roemer	Y	N	Y
4 ***Souder***	Y	Y	N
5 ***Buyer***	Y	Y	Y
6 ***Burton***	Y	N	Y
7 ***Pease***	Y	N	Y
8 ***Hostettler***	Y	N	Y
9 Hill	Y	Y	N
10 Carson	Y	N	Y
IOWA			
1 ***Leach***	Y	Y	Y
2 ***Nussle***	Y	Y	Y
3 Boswell	Y	Y	N
4 ***Ganske***	Y	N	Y
5 ***Latham***	Y	Y	N
KANSAS			
1 ***Moran***	Y	Y	Y
2 ***Ryun***	Y	N	Y
3 Moore	Y	Y	N
4 ***Tiahrt***	Y	N	Y
KENTUCKY			
1 ***Whitfield***	Y	Y	Y
2 ***Lewis***	Y	N	Y
3 ***Northup***	Y	N	Y
4 Lucas	Y	N	Y
5 ***Rogers***	Y	Y	Y
6 ***Fletcher***	Y	N	Y
LOUISIANA			
1 ***Vitter***	Y	Y	Y
2 Jefferson	Y	N	Y
3 ***Tauzin***	Y	N	Y
4 ***McCrery***	Y	Y	N
5 ***Cooksey***	Y	Y	Y
6 ***Baker***	Y	N	Y
7 John	Y	Y	N
MAINE			
1 Allen	Y	Y	Y
2 Baldacci	Y	N	Y
MARYLAND			
1 ***Gilchrest***	?	?	?
2 ***Ehrlich***	?	Y	Y
3 Cardin	Y	Y	Y
4 Wynn	Y	N	Y
5 Hoyer	Y	Y	Y
6 ***Bartlett***	Y	N	Y
7 Cummings	Y	N	Y
8 ***Morella***	Y	Y	Y
MASSACHUSETTS			
1 Olver	Y	N	Y
2 Neal	Y	N	Y
3 McGovern	Y	N	Y
4 Frank	Y	N	Y
5 Meehan	Y	N	Y
6 Tierney	Y	N	Y
7 Markey	Y	N	Y
8 Capuano	Y	N	Y
9 Moakley	Y	N	Y
10 Delahunt	Y	N	Y
MICHIGAN			
1 Stupak	Y	Y	Y
2 ***Hoekstra***	Y	N	Y
3 ***Ehlers***	Y	Y	Y
4 ***Camp***	Y	N	Y
5 Barcia	Y	Y	Y
6 ***Upton***	Y	N	Y
7 ***Smith***	Y	N	Y
8 Stabenow	Y	Y	Y
9 Kildee	Y	Y	Y
10 Bonior	Y	Y	Y
11 ***Knollenberg***	Y	Y	Y
12 Levin	Y	Y	Y
13 Rivers	Y	N	Y
14 Conyers	Y	N	Y
15 Kilpatrick	Y	N	Y
16 Dingell	Y	N	Y

	253	254	255
MINNESOTA			
1 ***Gutknecht***	Y	N	Y
2 Minge	Y	N	Y
3 ***Ramstad***	Y	Y	N
4 Vento	Y	N	Y
5 Sabo	Y	N	Y
6 Luther	Y	Y	Y
7 Peterson	Y	Y	N
8 Oberstar	Y	N	Y
MISSISSIPPI			
1 ***Wicker***	Y	N	Y
2 Thompson	Y	N	Y
3 ***Pickering***	Y	Y	N
4 Shows	Y	Y	N
5 Taylor	Y	Y	N
MISSOURI			
1 Clay	Y	N	Y
2 ***Talent***	Y	N	Y
3 Gephardt	Y	N	Y
4 Skelton	Y	N	Y
5 McCarthy	Y	N	Y
6 Danner	Y	N	Y
7 ***Blunt***	Y	Y	Y
8 ***Emerson***	Y	N	Y
9 ***Hulshof***	Y	Y	Y
MONTANA			
AL ***Hill***	Y	N	Y
NEBRASKA			
1 ***Bereuter***	Y	N	Y
2 ***Terry***	Y	Y	Y
3 ***Barrett***	Y	N	Y
NEVADA			
1 Berkley	Y	N	Y
2 ***Gibbons***	Y	N	Y
NEW HAMPSHIRE			
1 ***Sununu***	Y	N	Y
2 ***Bass***	Y	N	Y
NEW JERSEY			
1 Andrews	Y	Y	N
2 ***LoBiondo***	Y	N	Y
3 ***Saxton***	Y	Y	Y
4 ***Smith***	Y	N	Y
5 ***Roukema***	Y	Y	N
6 Pallone	Y	Y	Y
7 ***Franks***	Y	N	Y
8 Pascrell	Y	Y	N
9 Rothman	Y	Y	Y
10 Payne	Y	N	Y
11 ***Frelinghuysen***	Y	Y	Y
12 Holt	Y	Y	Y
13 Menendez	Y	N	Y
NEW MEXICO			
1 ***Wilson***	Y	N	Y
2 ***Skeen***	Y	N	Y
3 Udall	Y	N	Y
NEW YORK			
1 ***Forbes***	Y	N	Y
2 ***Lazio***	Y	?	?
3 ***King***	Y	N	Y
4 McCarthy	Y	Y	Y
5 Ackerman	Y	N	Y
6 Meeks	Y	N	Y
7 Crowley	Y	Y	N
8 Nadler	Y	N	Y
9 Weiner	Y	Y	N
10 Towns	?	N	Y
11 Owens	Y	N	Y
12 Velázquez	Y	N	Y
13 ***Fossella***	Y	N	Y
14 Maloney	Y	Y	Y
15 Rangel	Y	N	Y
16 Serrano	Y	N	Y
17 Engel	Y	N	Y
18 Lowey	Y	Y	Y
19 ***Kelly***	Y	N	Y
20 ***Gilman***	Y	Y	N
21 McNulty	Y	Y	Y
22 ***Sweeney***	Y	Y	N
23 ***Boehlert***	Y	Y	Y
24 ***McHugh***	Y	Y	Y
25 ***Walsh***	Y	Y	Y
26 Hinchey	Y	N	Y
27 ***Reynolds***	Y	Y	N
28 Slaughter	Y	Y	Y
29 LaFalce	Y	N	Y

	253	254	255
30 ***Quinn***	Y	Y	Y
31 ***Houghton***	Y	Y	N
NORTH CAROLINA			
1 Clayton	Y	N	Y
2 Etheridge	Y	Y	Y
3 ***Jones***	Y	Y	N
4 Price	Y	N	Y
5 ***Burr***	Y	N	Y
6 ***Coble***	Y	N	Y
7 McIntyre	Y	Y	Y
8 ***Hayes***	Y	Y	N
9 ***Myrick***	Y	Y	N
10 ***Ballenger***	Y	Y	Y
11 ***Taylor***	Y	N	Y
12 Watt	Y	N	Y
NORTH DAKOTA			
AL Pomeroy	Y	Y	Y
OHIO			
1 ***Chabot***	Y	N	Y
2 ***Portman***	Y	Y	N
3 Hall	Y	N	Y
4 ***Oxley***	Y	Y	Y
5 ***Gillmor***	Y	N	Y
6 Strickland	Y	N	Y
7 ***Hobson***	Y	N	Y
8 ***Boehner***	Y	N	Y
9 Kaptur	Y	N	Y
10 Kucinich	Y	N	Y
11 Jones	Y	Y	Y
12 ***Kasich***	?	?	?
13 Brown	Y	N	Y
14 Sawyer	Y	N	Y
15 ***Pryce***	Y	Y	Y
16 ***Regula***	Y	Y	Y
17 Traficant	Y	N	Y
18 ***Ney***	Y	N	Y
19 ***LaTourette***	Y	N	Y
OKLAHOMA			
1 ***Largent***	Y	?	Y
2 ***Coburn***	Y	Y	Y
3 ***Watkins***	Y	N	Y
4 ***Watts***	Y	N	Y
5 ***Istook***	Y	N	Y
6 ***Lucas***	Y	N	Y
OREGON			
1 Wu	Y	Y	Y
2 ***Walden***	Y	Y	Y
3 Blumenauer	Y	Y	N
4 DeFazio	Y	N	Y
5 Hooley	Y	Y	Y
PENNSYLVANIA			
1 Brady	Y	N	Y
2 Fattah	Y	N	Y
3 Borski	Y	N	Y
4 Klink	Y	N	Y
5 ***Peterson***	Y	N	Y
6 Holden	Y	Y	Y
7 ***Weldon***	Y	Y	Y
8 ***Greenwood***	Y	Y	Y
9 ***Shuster***	Y	N	Y
10 ***Sherwood***	Y	N	Y
11 Kanjorski	Y	N	Y
12 Murtha	Y	N	Y
13 Hoeffel	Y	Y	Y
14 Coyne	Y	N	Y
15 ***Toomey***	Y	N	Y
16 ***Pitts***	Y	N	Y
17 ***Gekas***	Y	Y	N
18 Doyle	Y	N	Y
19 ***Goodling***	Y	N	Y
20 Mascara	Y	N	Y
21 ***English***	Y	N	Y
RHODE ISLAND			
1 Kennedy	Y	N	Y
2 Weygand	Y	Y	Y
SOUTH CAROLINA			
1 ***Sanford***	Y	N	Y
2 ***Spence***	Y	N	Y
3 ***Graham***	Y	N	Y
4 ***DeMint***	Y	N	Y
5 Spratt	Y	N	Y
6 Clyburn	Y	N	Y
SOUTH DAKOTA			
AL ***Thune***	Y	Y	Y

	253	254	255
TENNESSEE			
1 ***Jenkins***	Y	N	Y
2 ***Duncan***	Y	N	Y
3 ***Wamp***	Y	N	Y
4 ***Hilleary***	Y	Y	Y
5 Clement	?	N	Y
6 Gordon	Y	Y	Y
7 ***Bryant***	Y	Y	N
8 Tanner	Y	N	Y
9 Ford	Y	N	Y
TEXAS			
1 Sandlin	Y	N	Y
2 Turner	Y	Y	N
3 ***Johnson, Sam***	Y	N	Y
4 Hall	Y	N	Y
5 ***Sessions***	Y	N	Y
6 ***Barton***	Y	Y	Y
7 ***Archer***	Y	N	Y
8 ***Brady***	Y	Y	Y
9 Lampson	Y	N	Y
10 Doggett	Y	Y	Y
11 Edwards	Y	Y	Y
12 ***Granger***	Y	N	Y
13 ***Thornberry***	Y	Y	Y
14 ***Paul***	Y	N	Y
15 Hinojosa	Y	N	Y
16 Reyes	Y	Y	N
17 Stenholm	Y	N	Y
18 Jackson-Lee	Y	N	Y
19 ***Combest***	Y	N	Y
20 Gonzalez	Y	N	Y
21 ***Smith***	Y	N	Y
22 ***DeLay***	?	N	Y
23 ***Bonilla***	Y	N	Y
24 Frost	Y	N	Y
25 Bentsen	Y	N	Y
26 ***Armey***	Y	N	Y
27 Ortiz	Y	N	Y
28 Rodriguez	Y	N	Y
29 Green	Y	N	Y
30 Johnson, E.B.	Y	N	Y
UTAH			
1 ***Hansen***	Y	N	Y
2 ***Cook***	Y	N	Y
3 ***Cannon***	Y	N	Y
VERMONT			
AL *Sanders*	Y	N	Y
VIRGINIA			
1 ***Bateman***	Y	Y	Y
2 Pickett	Y	N	Y
3 Scott	Y	N	Y
4 Sisisky	Y	Y	Y
5 Goode	Y	N	Y
6 ***Goodlatte***	Y	N	Y
7 ***Bliley***	Y	N	Y
8 Moran	Y	Y	Y
9 Boucher	Y	N	Y
10 ***Wolf***	Y	Y	Y
11 ***Davis***	Y	N	Y
WASHINGTON			
1 Inslee	Y	Y	Y
2 ***Metcalf***	Y	N	Y
3 Baird	Y	Y	Y
4 ***Hastings***	Y	N	Y
5 ***Nethercutt***	Y	N	Y
6 Dicks	Y	N	Y
7 McDermott	Y	Y	Y
8 ***Dunn***	Y	Y	Y
9 Smith	Y	Y	Y
WEST VIRGINIA			
1 Mollohan	Y	?	?
2 Wise	Y	?	?
3 Rahall	Y	N	Y
WISCONSIN			
1 ***Ryan***	Y	N	Y
2 Baldwin	Y	N	Y
3 Kind	Y	Y	N
4 Kleczka	Y	Y	Y
5 Barrett	Y	Y	N
6 ***Petri***	Y	N	Y
7 Obey	Y	N	Y
8 ***Green***	Y	Y	Y
9 ***Sensenbrenner***	Y	N	Y
WYOMING			
AL ***Cubin***	Y	Y	N

Southern states - Ala., Ark., Fla., Ga., Ky., La., Miss., N.C., Okla., S.C., Tenn., Texas, Va.

256. HR 1802. Foster Care Assistance/Passage. Passage of the bill to increase from $70 million to $140 million the funding for programs to help teenagers in foster care programs prepare to leave the system at age 18 and to provide assistance to former foster care recipients between the ages of 18 and 21. Passed 380-6: R 194-6; D 185-0 (ND 133-0, SD 52-0); I 1-0. June 25, 1999. A "yea" was a vote in support of the president's position.

257. HR 2280. Veterans Benefits/Passage. Stump, R-Ariz., motion to suspend the rules and pass the bill to authorize a cost-of-living adjustment for veterans receiving disability compensation and their surviving family members; restore eligibility for certain medical care, education, and housing loans to surviving spouses who have remarried; authorize a $65 million loan for the American Battle Monuments Commission to hasten construction of the World War II Memorial; and authorize $100 million for fiscal 2000-2004 for the Labor Department's Homeless Veterans Reintegration Program. The bill would also direct the Secretary of Veterans Affairs to build four new national cemeteries and begin a comprehensive assessment of national cemeteries. Motion agreed to 424-0: R 218-0; D 205-0 (ND 151-0, SD 54-0); I 1-0. June 29, 1999. A two-thirds majority of those present and voting (283 in this case) is required for passage under suspension of the rules.

258. H Res 226. Condemning Arson/Adoption. Ose, R-Calif., motion to suspend the rules and adopt the resolution to condemn the arsons that occurred at Congregation B'Nai Israel, Congregation Beth Shalom, and Knesset Israel Torah Center in Sacramento, Calif. on the evening of June 18, 1999. Motion agreed to 425-0: R 216-0; D 208-0 (ND 153-0, SD 55-0); I 1-0. June 29, 1999. A two-thirds majority of those present and voting (284 in this case) is required for passage under suspension of the rules.

259. H Con Res 94. Need for Prayer/Passage. Chenoweth, R-Idaho, motion to suspend the rules and adopt the concurrent resolution to call for a national day of prayer and fasting before God and recognize the public need for repentance, reconciliation, and healing. Motion rejected, 275-140: R 211-7; D 64-132 (ND 34-111, SD 30-21); I 0-1. June 29, 1999. A two-thirds majority of those present and voting (277 in this case) is required for passage under suspension of the rules.

260. HR 1218. Abortion Assistance for Minors/Recommit. Jackson-Lee, D-Texas, motion to recommit the bill to the Judiciary Committee with instructions to report it back with an amendment that declares the proposed prohibitions on transporting minors across state lines to circumvent parental consent laws would not apply to adult siblings, grandparents, ministers, rabbis, pastors, priests, or any other religious leader of the minor. Motion rejected 164-268: R 12-210; D 151-58 (ND 116-38, SD 35-20);I 1-0. June 30, 1999.

261. HR 1218. Abortion Assistance for Minors/Passage. Passage of the bill to make it a federal crime for anyone other than a parent to transport a minor across state lines to seek an abortion, thus circumventing state parental-consent laws. Passed 270-159: R 206-14; D 64-144 (ND 40-114, SD 24-30); I 0-1. June 30, 1999. A "nay" was a vote in support of the president's position.

262. Procedural Motion/Journal. Approval of the House Journal of Wednesday, June 30, 1999. Approved 358-56: R 200-13; D 157-43 (ND 111-36, SD 46-7); I 1-0, July 1, 1999.

Key

- Y Voted for (yea).
- # Paired for.
- + Announced for.
- N Voted against (nay).
- X Paired against.
- – Announced against.
- P Voted "present."
- C Voted "present" to avoid possible conflict of interest.
- ? Did not vote or otherwise make a position known.

Democrats ***Republicans*** *Independents*

	256	257	258	259	260	261	262
ALABAMA							
1 ***Callahan***	?	Y	Y	Y	N	Y	Y
2 ***Everett***	?	Y	Y	Y	N	Y	Y
3 ***Riley***	Y	Y	Y	Y	N	Y	N
4 ***Aderholt***	Y	Y	Y	Y	N	Y	N
5 Cramer	Y	Y	Y	Y	N	Y	Y
6 ***Bachus***	Y	Y	Y	Y	N	Y	Y
7 Hilliard	Y	Y	Y	Y	Y	Y	N
ALASKA							
AL ***Young***	Y	Y	Y	Y	N	Y	?
ARIZONA							
1 ***Salmon***	Y	Y	Y	Y	N	Y	Y
2 Pastor	Y	Y	Y	Y	Y	N	N
3 ***Stump***	Y	Y	Y	Y	N	Y	Y
4 ***Shadegg***	Y	Y	Y	Y	N	Y	Y
5 ***Kolbe***	Y	Y	Y	N	N	Y	Y
6 ***Hayworth***	Y	Y	Y	Y	N	Y	Y
ARKANSAS							
1 Berry	Y	Y	Y	Y	N	Y	Y
2 Snyder	Y	Y	Y	Y	N	Y	Y
3 ***Hutchinson***	Y	Y	Y	Y	N	Y	?
4 ***Dickey***	Y	Y	Y	Y	N	Y	Y
CALIFORNIA							
1 Thompson	Y	Y	Y	N	Y	N	N
2 ***Herger***	Y	Y	Y	Y	N	Y	Y
3 ***Ose***	Y	Y	Y	Y	N	Y	Y
4 ***Doolittle***	Y	Y	Y	Y	N	Y	Y
5 Matsui	Y	Y	Y	N	Y	N	Y
6 Woolsey	Y	Y	Y	N	Y	N	Y
7 Miller, George	Y	Y	Y	N	Y	N	N
8 Pelosi	Y	Y	Y	N	Y	N	Y
9 Lee	Y	Y	Y	N	Y	N	N
10 Tauscher	Y	Y	Y	N	Y	N	N
11 ***Pombo***	Y	Y	Y	Y	N	Y	Y
12 Lantos	Y	Y	Y	N	Y	N	Y
13 Stark	Y	Y	Y	N	Y	N	Y
14 Eshoo	Y	Y	Y	N	Y	N	Y
15 ***Campbell***	Y	Y	Y	N	Y	N	Y
16 Lofgren	Y	Y	Y	N	Y	N	Y
17 Farr	Y	Y	Y	N	Y	N	Y
18 Condit	Y	Y	Y	Y	N	Y	Y
19 ***Radanovich***	Y	Y	Y	Y	N	Y	Y
20 Dooley	Y	Y	Y	N	Y	N	Y
21 ***Thomas***	Y	Y	Y	Y	N	Y	Y
22 Capps	Y	Y	Y	Y	Y	N	Y
23 ***Gallegly***	?	Y	Y	Y	N	Y	Y
24 Sherman	Y	Y	Y	N	Y	N	Y
25 ***McKeon***	?	Y	Y	Y	N	Y	Y
26 Berman	?	Y	Y	N	Y	N	Y
27 ***Rogan***	?	Y	Y	Y	N	Y	Y
28 ***Dreier***	Y	Y	Y	Y	N	Y	Y
29 Waxman	Y	Y	Y	N	Y	N	Y
30 Becerra	Y	Y	Y	N	Y	N	Y
31 Martinez	Y	Y	Y	N	?	?	Y
32 Dixon	Y	Y	Y	N	Y	N	Y
33 Roybal-Allard	Y	Y	Y	N	Y	N	Y
34 Napolitano	Y	Y	Y	Y	Y	N	Y
35 Waters	Y	Y	Y	N	Y	N	N
36 ***Kuykendall***	Y	Y	Y	N	N	Y	Y
37 Millender-McD.	Y	Y	Y	N	Y	N	Y
38 ***Horn***	Y	Y	Y	Y	Y	Y	Y
39 ***Royce***	Y	Y	Y	Y	N	Y	Y
40 ***Lewis***	Y	Y	Y	Y	N	?	Y
41 ***Miller, Gary***	?	Y	Y	Y	N	Y	Y
42 Brown	?	?	?	?	?	?	?
43 ***Calvert***	Y	Y	Y	Y	N	Y	Y
44 ***Bono***	Y	Y	Y	Y	N	Y	Y
45 ***Rohrabacher***	Y	Y	Y	Y	N	Y	Y
46 Sanchez	Y	Y	Y	N	Y	N	Y
47 ***Cox***	Y	Y	Y	Y	N	Y	?
48 ***Packard***	+	Y	Y	Y	N	Y	Y
49 ***Bilbray***	Y	Y	Y	N	N	Y	N
50 Filner	Y	Y	Y	N	Y	N	N
51 ***Cunningham***	?	?	?	?	N	Y	Y
52 ***Hunter***	Y	Y	Y	Y	N	Y	Y
COLORADO							
1 DeGette	Y	Y	Y	N	Y	N	Y
2 Udall	Y	Y	Y	P	Y	N	N
3 ***McInnis***	?	Y	Y	Y	N	Y	Y
4 ***Schaffer***	Y	Y	Y	Y	N	Y	N
5 ***Hefley***	N	Y	Y	Y	N	Y	N
6 ***Tancredo***	Y	Y	Y	Y	N	Y	Y
CONNECTICUT							
1 Larson	Y	Y	Y	N	Y	N	Y
2 Gejdenson	Y	Y	Y	N	Y	N	Y
3 DeLauro	Y	Y	Y	N	Y	N	Y
4 ***Shays***	Y	Y	Y	Y	Y	N	Y
5 Maloney	Y	Y	Y	Y	Y	N	Y
6 ***Johnson***	Y	Y	Y	N	Y	N	Y
DELAWARE							
AL ***Castle***	Y	Y	Y	Y	Y	N	Y
FLORIDA							
1 ***Scarborough***	?	Y	Y	Y	N	Y	Y
2 Boyd	Y	Y	Y	P	N	Y	Y
3 Brown	Y	Y	Y	Y	Y	N	Y
4 ***Fowler***	Y	Y	Y	Y	N	Y	Y
5 Thurman	Y	Y	Y	P	Y	N	Y
6 ***Stearns***	Y	Y	Y	Y	N	Y	Y
7 ***Mica***	Y	Y	Y	Y	N	Y	Y
8 ***McCollum***	Y	Y	Y	Y	N	Y	Y
9 ***Bilirakis***	Y	Y	Y	Y	N	Y	Y
10 ***Young***	Y	Y	Y	Y	N	Y	Y
11 Davis	Y	Y	Y	Y	N	Y	Y
12 ***Canady***	Y	Y	Y	Y	N	Y	Y
13 ***Miller***	Y	Y	Y	Y	N	Y	Y
14 ***Goss***	Y	Y	Y	Y	N	Y	Y
15 ***Weldon***	Y	Y	Y	Y	N	Y	Y
16 ***Foley***	Y	Y	Y	Y	N	Y	Y
17 Meek	Y	Y	Y	N	Y	N	N
18 ***Ros-Lehtinen***	Y	+	+	Y	N	Y	Y
19 Wexler	Y	Y	Y	N	Y	N	Y
20 Deutsch	Y	Y	Y	N	Y	N	Y
21 ***Diaz-Balart***	Y	Y	?	?	N	Y	Y
22 ***Shaw***	Y	Y	Y	Y	N	Y	Y
23 Hastings	Y	Y	Y	N	Y	N	N
GEORGIA							
1 ***Kingston***	Y	Y	Y	Y	N	Y	Y
2 Bishop	Y	Y	Y	Y	Y	Y	Y
3 ***Collins***	Y	Y	Y	Y	N	Y	Y
4 McKinney	Y	?	Y	N	Y	N	Y
5 Lewis	Y	Y	Y	N	Y	N	Y
6 ***Isakson***	Y	Y	Y	Y	N	Y	Y
7 ***Barr***	Y	Y	Y	Y	N	Y	Y
8 ***Chambliss***	Y	Y	Y	Y	N	Y	Y
9 ***Deal***	Y	Y	Y	Y	N	Y	Y
10 ***Norwood***	Y	Y	Y	Y	N	Y	Y
11 ***Linder***	Y	Y	Y	Y	N	Y	Y
HAWAII							
1 Abercrombie	Y	Y	Y	N	Y	N	Y
2 Mink	?	Y	Y	N	Y	N	Y
IDAHO							
1 ***Chenoweth***	N	Y	Y	Y	N	Y	Y
2 ***Simpson***	Y	Y	Y	Y	N	Y	Y
ILLINOIS							
1 Rush	Y	Y	Y	N	Y	N	Y
2 Jackson	Y	Y	Y	N	Y	N	Y
3 Lipinski	?	Y	Y	Y	N	Y	Y
4 Gutierrez	?	Y	Y	N	Y	N	Y
5 Blagojevich	Y	?	?	?	Y	N	Y
6 ***Hyde***	Y	Y	Y	Y	N	Y	?
7 Davis	Y	Y	Y	N	Y	N	Y
8 ***Crane***	Y	Y	Y	Y	N	Y	N
9 Schakowsky	Y	Y	Y	N	Y	N	N
10 ***Porter***	Y	Y	Y	Y	Y	N	Y
11 ***Weller***	Y	Y	Y	Y	N	Y	N
12 Costello	?	Y	Y	Y	N	Y	N
13 ***Biggert***	Y	Y	Y	Y	Y	N	Y
14 ***Hastert***							

ND Northern Democrats SD Southern Democrats

	256	257	258	259	260	261	262
15 ***Ewing***	Y	Y	Y	Y	N	Y	Y
16 ***Manzullo***	Y	Y	Y	Y	N	Y	Y
17 Evans	Y	Y	Y	N	Y	N	?
18 ***LaHood***	Y	Y	Y	Y	N	Y	Y
19 Phelps	Y	Y	Y	Y	N	Y	Y
20 ***Shimkus***	Y	Y	Y	Y	N	Y	Y
INDIANA							
1 Visclosky	Y	Y	Y	Y	Y	N	N
2 ***McIntosh***	?	Y	Y	Y	N	Y	Y
3 Roemer	Y	Y	Y	Y	N	Y	Y
4 ***Souder***	Y	Y	Y	Y	N	Y	Y
5 ***Buyer***	Y	Y	Y	Y	N	Y	Y
6 ***Burton***	Y	Y	Y	Y	N	Y	Y
7 ***Pease***	Y	Y	Y	Y	N	Y	Y
8 ***Hostettler***	N	Y	Y	Y	N	Y	Y
9 Hill	Y	Y	Y	Y	N	Y	Y
10 Carson	Y	Y	Y	N	Y	N	P
IOWA							
1 ***Leach***	Y	Y	Y	Y	N	Y	Y
2 ***Nussle***	Y	Y	Y	Y	N	Y	Y
3 Boswell	Y	Y	Y	Y	N	Y	Y
4 ***Ganske***	Y	Y	Y	Y	N	Y	Y
5 ***Latham***	Y	Y	Y	Y	N	Y	Y
KANSAS							
1 ***Moran***	Y	Y	Y	Y	N	Y	N
2 ***Ryun***	Y	Y	Y	Y	N	Y	Y
3 Moore	Y	Y	Y	N	Y	N	Y
4 ***Tiahrt***	Y	Y	Y	Y	N	Y	Y
KENTUCKY							
1 ***Whitfield***	Y	Y	Y	Y	N	Y	Y
2 ***Lewis***	Y	Y	Y	Y	N	Y	Y
3 ***Northup***	Y	Y	Y	Y	N	Y	Y
4 Lucas	Y	Y	Y	Y	N	Y	Y
5 ***Rogers***	Y	Y	Y	Y	N	Y	Y
6 ***Fletcher***	?	Y	Y	Y	N	Y	Y
LOUISIANA							
1 ***Vitter***	Y	Y	Y	Y	N	Y	Y
2 Jefferson	?	Y	Y	Y	Y	N	Y
3 ***Tauzin***	?	Y	Y	Y	N	Y	Y
4 ***McCrery***	Y	Y	Y	Y	N	Y	Y
5 ***Cooksey***	Y	Y	Y	Y	N	Y	Y
6 ***Baker***	Y	Y	Y	Y	N	Y	Y
7 John	Y	Y	Y	Y	N	Y	Y
MAINE							
1 Allen	Y	?	Y	N	Y	N	Y
2 Baldacci	Y	Y	Y	N	Y	N	Y
MARYLAND							
1 ***Gilchrest***	?	Y	Y	Y	Y	N	Y
2 ***Ehrlich***	Y	Y	Y	Y	N	Y	?
3 Cardin	Y	Y	Y	N	Y	N	Y
4 Wynn	Y	Y	Y	P	Y	N	Y
5 Hoyer	Y	?	Y	N	Y	N	Y
6 ***Bartlett***	Y	Y	Y	Y	N	Y	Y
7 Cummings	Y	Y	Y	N	Y	N	?
8 ***Morella***	Y	Y	Y	Y	Y	N	Y
MASSACHUSETTS							
1 Olver	?	Y	Y	N	Y	N	Y
2 Neal	Y	Y	Y	N	N	Y	N
3 McGovern	Y	Y	Y	N	Y	N	N
4 Frank	Y	Y	Y	N	Y	N	N
5 Meehan	Y	?	?	?	Y	N	Y
6 Tierney	Y	Y	Y	N	Y	N	?
7 Markey	Y	Y	Y	N	Y	N	N
8 Capuano	+	Y	Y	N	Y	N	Y
9 Moakley	Y	Y	Y	N	N	Y	Y
10 Delahunt	?	Y	Y	N	Y	N	Y
MICHIGAN							
1 Stupak	Y	Y	Y	N	N	Y	N
2 ***Hoekstra***	Y	Y	Y	Y	N	Y	Y
3 ***Ehlers***	Y	Y	Y	Y	N	Y	Y
4 ***Camp***	Y	Y	Y	Y	N	Y	Y
5 Barcia	Y	Y	Y	Y	N	Y	Y
6 ***Upton***	Y	Y	Y	Y	N	Y	Y
7 ***Smith***	Y	Y	Y	Y	N	Y	Y
8 Stabenow	Y	Y	Y	Y	Y	N	Y
9 Kildee	Y	Y	Y	Y	Y	N	Y
10 Bonior	Y	Y	Y	N	N	Y	N
11 ***Knollenberg***	Y	Y	Y	Y	N	Y	Y
12 Levin	Y	Y	Y	N	Y	N	Y
13 Rivers	Y	Y	Y	N	N	N	Y
14 Conyers	?	Y	Y	N	Y	N	?
15 Kilpatrick	Y	Y	Y	N	Y	N	Y
16 Dingell	Y	Y	Y	N	Y	Y	Y
MINNESOTA							
1 ***Gutknecht***	Y	Y	Y	Y	N	Y	Y
2 Minge	Y	Y	Y	N	Y	Y	Y
3 ***Ramstad***	Y	Y	Y	Y	N	Y	N
4 Vento	Y	Y	Y	N	Y	Y	Y
5 Sabo	Y	Y	Y	N	Y	N	N
6 Luther	Y	Y	Y	N	Y	N	Y
7 Peterson	Y	Y	Y	Y	N	Y	N
8 Oberstar	Y	Y	Y	N	N	Y	N
MISSISSIPPI							
1 ***Wicker***	Y	Y	Y	Y	N	Y	Y
2 Thompson	Y	Y	Y	Y	Y	N	N
3 ***Pickering***	Y	Y	Y	Y	N	Y	Y
4 Shows	Y	Y	Y	Y	N	Y	Y
5 Taylor	?	Y	Y	Y	N	Y	N
MISSOURI							
1 Clay	?	Y	Y	N	Y	N	N
2 ***Talent***	Y	Y	Y	Y	N	Y	Y
3 Gephardt	Y	Y	Y	N	Y	N	N
4 Skelton	Y	Y	Y	Y	N	Y	Y
5 McCarthy	Y	Y	Y	N	Y	N	Y
6 Danner	?	Y	Y	Y	N	Y	Y
7 ***Blunt***	Y	Y	Y	Y	N	Y	?
8 ***Emerson***	Y	Y	Y	Y	N	Y	Y
9 ***Hulshof***	?	Y	Y	Y	N	Y	Y
MONTANA							
AL ***Hill***	Y	Y	Y	Y	N	Y	Y
NEBRASKA							
1 ***Bereuter***	Y	Y	Y	Y	N	Y	Y
2 ***Terry***	Y	Y	Y	Y	N	Y	Y
3 ***Barrett***	Y	Y	Y	Y	N	Y	Y
NEVADA							
1 Berkley	Y	Y	Y	N	Y	N	Y
2 ***Gibbons***	Y	Y	Y	Y	N	Y	Y
NEW HAMPSHIRE							
1 ***Sununu***	Y	Y	Y	Y	N	Y	Y
2 ***Bass***	Y	Y	Y	Y	N	N	Y
NEW JERSEY							
1 Andrews	Y	Y	Y	N	Y	N	Y
2 ***LoBiondo***	Y	Y	Y	Y	N	Y	N
3 ***Saxton***	Y	Y	Y	Y	N	Y	Y
4 ***Smith***	Y	Y	Y	Y	N	Y	Y
5 ***Roukema***	Y	Y	Y	Y	N	Y	Y
6 Pallone	Y	Y	Y	N	Y	N	N
7 ***Franks***	Y	Y	Y	Y	N	Y	Y
8 Pascrell	Y	Y	Y	P	N	Y	Y
9 Rothman	Y	Y	Y	N	Y	N	Y
10 Payne	Y	Y	Y	N	Y	N	Y
11 ***Frelinghuysen***	Y	Y	Y	Y	N	Y	Y
12 Holt	Y	Y	Y	N	Y	N	Y
13 Menendez	?	Y	Y	N	Y	N	Y
NEW MEXICO							
1 ***Wilson***	Y	Y	Y	Y	N	Y	Y
2 ***Skeen***	Y	Y	Y	Y	N	Y	Y
3 Udall	Y	Y	Y	N	Y	N	N
NEW YORK							
1 ***Forbes***	?	Y	Y	Y	N	Y	Y
2 ***Lazio***	Y	Y	Y	Y	N	Y	Y
3 ***King***	Y	Y	Y	Y	N	Y	Y
4 McCarthy	+	Y	Y	N	Y	N	Y
5 Ackerman	Y	Y	Y	N	Y	N	Y
6 Meeks	Y	Y	Y	N	Y	N	N
7 Crowley	Y	Y	Y	N	Y	N	Y
8 Nadler	Y	Y	Y	N	Y	N	?
9 Weiner	?	Y	Y	N	Y	N	Y
10 Towns	?	Y	Y	Y	Y	N	Y
11 Owens	Y	Y	Y	N	Y	N	Y
12 Velázquez	Y	Y	Y	N	Y	N	N
13 ***Fossella***	Y	Y	Y	Y	N	Y	?
14 Maloney	Y	Y	Y	P	Y	N	Y
15 Rangel	Y	Y	Y	N	Y	N	?
16 Serrano	Y	Y	Y	N	Y	N	Y
17 Engel	?	Y	Y	N	Y	N	Y
18 Lowey	?	Y	Y	N	Y	N	Y
19 ***Kelly***	Y	Y	Y	Y	N	Y	Y
20 ***Gilman***	Y	Y	Y	Y	Y	N	Y
21 McNulty	Y	Y	Y	N	N	Y	N
22 ***Sweeney***	Y	Y	Y	Y	N	Y	Y
23 ***Boehlert***	?	Y	Y	Y	Y	N	Y
24 ***McHugh***	Y	Y	Y	Y	N	Y	Y
25 ***Walsh***	Y	Y	Y	Y	N	Y	Y
26 Hinchey	Y	Y	Y	Y	Y	N	N
27 ***Reynolds***	Y	Y	Y	Y	N	Y	Y
28 Slaughter	+	Y	Y	N	Y	N	Y
29 LaFalce	Y	Y	Y	Y	N	Y	N
30 ***Quinn***	Y	Y	Y	Y	N	Y	Y
31 ***Houghton***	Y	Y	Y	Y	N	N	Y
NORTH CAROLINA							
1 Clayton	Y	Y	Y	P	Y	N	Y
2 Etheridge	Y	Y	Y	Y	Y	Y	Y
3 ***Jones***	Y	Y	Y	Y	N	Y	Y
4 Price	Y	Y	Y	Y	Y	N	Y
5 ***Burr***	Y	Y	Y	Y	N	Y	Y
6 ***Coble***	Y	Y	Y	Y	N	Y	Y
7 McIntyre	Y	Y	Y	Y	N	Y	Y
8 ***Hayes***	Y	Y	Y	Y	N	Y	Y
9 ***Myrick***	Y	Y	Y	Y	N	Y	Y
10 ***Ballenger***	Y	Y	Y	Y	N	Y	Y
11 ***Taylor***	?	Y	Y	Y	N	Y	Y
12 Watt	Y	Y	Y	P	Y	N	Y
NORTH DAKOTA							
AL Pomeroy	Y	Y	Y	P	N	Y	N
OHIO							
1 ***Chabot***	Y	Y	Y	Y	N	Y	Y
2 ***Portman***	Y	Y	Y	Y	N	Y	Y
3 Hall	Y	Y	Y	Y	N	Y	N
4 ***Oxley***	Y	Y	Y	Y	N	Y	Y
5 ***Gillmor***	Y	Y	Y	Y	N	Y	N
6 Strickland	Y	Y	Y	P	Y	Y	Y
7 ***Hobson***	+	Y	Y	Y	N	Y	Y
8 ***Boehner***	Y	Y	Y	Y	N	Y	Y
9 Kaptur	Y	Y	Y	P	N	N	Y
10 Kucinich	Y	Y	Y	N	N	Y	N
11 Jones	Y	Y	Y	N	Y	N	Y
12 ***Kasich***	?	Y	Y	Y	N	Y	Y
13 Brown	Y	Y	Y	N	Y	N	Y
14 Sawyer	Y	Y	Y	N	Y	N	Y
15 ***Pryce***	Y	Y	Y	Y	N	Y	Y
16 ***Regula***	Y	Y	Y	Y	N	Y	Y
17 Traficant	Y	Y	Y	Y	N	Y	Y
18 ***Ney***	Y	Y	Y	Y	N	Y	Y
19 ***LaTourette***	Y	Y	Y	Y	N	Y	Y
OKLAHOMA							
1 ***Largent***	Y	Y	Y	Y	N	Y	Y
2 ***Coburn***	N	Y	Y	Y	N	Y	Y
3 ***Watkins***	Y	Y	Y	Y	N	Y	Y
4 ***Watts***	Y	?	?	?	N	Y	Y
5 ***Istook***	Y	Y	Y	Y	N	Y	Y
6 ***Lucas***	Y	Y	Y	Y	N	?	Y
OREGON							
1 Wu	Y	Y	Y	N	Y	N	Y
2 ***Walden***	Y	Y	Y	Y	N	Y	Y
3 Blumenauer	Y	Y	Y	N	Y	N	Y
4 DeFazio	?	Y	Y	N	Y	N	N
5 Hooley	Y	Y	Y	N	Y	N	Y
PENNSYLVANIA							
1 Brady	Y	Y	Y	N	Y	N	Y
2 Fattah	Y	Y	Y	N	Y	N	Y
3 Borski	Y	Y	Y	Y	N	Y	N
4 Klink	Y	Y	Y	Y	N	Y	Y
5 ***Peterson***	Y	Y	Y	Y	N	Y	Y
6 Holden	Y	Y	Y	Y	N	Y	Y
7 ***Weldon***	Y	Y	Y	Y	N	Y	Y
8 ***Greenwood***	Y	Y	Y	Y	Y	N	Y
9 ***Shuster***	Y	Y	Y	Y	N	Y	Y
10 ***Sherwood***	Y	Y	Y	Y	N	Y	Y
11 Kanjorski	Y	Y	Y	N	N	Y	Y
12 Murtha	Y	Y	Y	Y	N	Y	Y
13 Hoeffel	Y	Y	Y	Y	Y	N	Y
14 Coyne	Y	Y	Y	N	Y	N	Y
15 ***Toomey***	Y	Y	Y	Y	N	Y	Y
16 ***Pitts***	Y	Y	Y	Y	N	Y	Y
17 ***Gekas***	Y	Y	Y	Y	N	Y	Y
18 Doyle	Y	Y	Y	Y	N	Y	Y
19 ***Goodling***	Y	Y	Y	Y	N	Y	Y
20 Mascara	Y	Y	Y	Y	N	Y	Y
21 ***English***	Y	Y	Y	Y	N	Y	N
RHODE ISLAND							
1 Kennedy	Y	Y	Y	N	Y	N	Y
2 Weygand	Y	Y	Y	N	N	Y	Y
SOUTH CAROLINA							
1 ***Sanford***	?	Y	Y	N	N	Y	Y
2 ***Spence***	Y	Y	Y	Y	N	Y	Y
3 ***Graham***	Y	Y	Y	Y	N	Y	Y
4 ***DeMint***	Y	Y	Y	Y	N	Y	Y
5 Spratt	Y	Y	Y	Y	N	Y	Y
6 Clyburn	Y	Y	Y	N	Y	N	Y
SOUTH DAKOTA							
AL ***Thune***	Y	Y	Y	Y	N	Y	Y
TENNESSEE							
1 ***Jenkins***	Y	Y	Y	Y	N	Y	Y
2 ***Duncan***	Y	Y	Y	Y	N	Y	Y
3 ***Wamp***	Y	Y	Y	Y	N	Y	Y
4 ***Hilleary***	Y	Y	Y	Y	N	Y	Y
5 Clement	Y	Y	Y	Y	N	Y	Y
6 Gordon	Y	Y	Y	Y	N	Y	Y
7 ***Bryant***	Y	Y	Y	Y	N	Y	Y
8 Tanner	Y	Y	Y	Y	N	Y	Y
9 Ford	Y	Y	Y	N	Y	+	N
TEXAS							
1 Sandlin	Y	Y	Y	Y	Y	Y	Y
2 Turner	Y	Y	Y	Y	N	Y	Y
3 ***Johnson, Sam***	Y	Y	Y	Y	N	Y	Y
4 Hall	?	Y	Y	Y	N	Y	Y
5 ***Sessions***	Y	Y	Y	Y	N	Y	Y
6 ***Barton***	Y	Y	Y	Y	N	Y	Y
7 ***Archer***	Y	Y	Y	Y	N	Y	?
8 ***Brady***	Y	Y	Y	Y	N	Y	Y
9 Lampson	Y	Y	Y	Y	Y	N	Y
10 Doggett	Y	Y	Y	N	Y	N	Y
11 Edwards	Y	Y	Y	N	Y	N	Y
12 ***Granger***	?	Y	Y	Y	N	Y	Y
13 ***Thornberry***	Y	Y	Y	Y	N	Y	Y
14 ***Paul***	N	Y	P	N	N	N	Y
15 Hinojosa	Y	Y	Y	N	Y	N	Y
16 Reyes	Y	Y	Y	N	N	Y	Y
17 Stenholm	Y	Y	Y	Y	N	Y	Y
18 Jackson-Lee	Y	Y	Y	N	Y	N	Y
19 ***Combest***	Y	Y	Y	Y	N	Y	Y
20 Gonzalez	Y	Y	Y	N	Y	N	Y
21 ***Smith***	Y	Y	Y	Y	N	Y	Y
22 ***DeLay***	Y	Y	Y	Y	N	Y	Y
23 ***Bonilla***	Y	Y	Y	Y	N	Y	Y
24 Frost	Y	Y	Y	N	Y	N	Y
25 Bentsen	Y	Y	Y	Y	Y	N	Y
26 ***Armey***	Y	Y	Y	Y	N	Y	Y
27 Ortiz	Y	Y	Y	Y	N	Y	Y
28 Rodriguez	Y	Y	Y	N	Y	N	Y
29 Green	Y	Y	Y	Y	Y	N	?
30 Johnson, E.B.	Y	Y	Y	N	Y	N	Y
UTAH							
1 ***Hansen***	Y	Y	Y	Y	N	Y	Y
2 ***Cook***	Y	Y	Y	Y	N	Y	Y
3 ***Cannon***	N	?	?	?	N	Y	Y
VERMONT							
AL *Sanders*	Y	Y	Y	N	Y	N	Y
VIRGINIA							
1 ***Bateman***	Y	Y	Y	Y	N	Y	Y
2 Pickett	Y	Y	Y	N	Y	N	N
3 Scott	Y	Y	Y	N	Y	N	?
4 Sisisky	Y	Y	Y	Y	N	Y	Y
5 Goode	Y	Y	Y	Y	N	Y	Y
6 ***Goodlatte***	Y	Y	Y	Y	N	Y	Y
7 ***Bliley***	Y	Y	Y	Y	N	Y	Y
8 Moran	Y	Y	Y	N	Y	N	Y
9 Boucher	Y	Y	Y	N	Y	N	Y
10 ***Wolf***	Y	Y	Y	Y	N	Y	Y
11 ***Davis***	Y	Y	Y	Y	N	Y	Y
WASHINGTON							
1 Inslee	Y	Y	Y	N	Y	N	Y
2 ***Metcalf***	Y	Y	Y	Y	N	Y	Y
3 Baird	Y	Y	Y	N	Y	N	N
4 ***Hastings***	Y	Y	Y	Y	N	Y	Y
5 ***Nethercutt***	Y	Y	Y	Y	N	Y	Y
6 Dicks	Y	Y	Y	N	Y	N	Y
7 McDermott	Y	Y	Y	N	Y	N	N
8 ***Dunn***	Y	Y	Y	Y	N	Y	Y
9 Smith	?	Y	Y	N	Y	N	Y
WEST VIRGINIA							
1 Mollohan	?	Y	Y	Y	N	Y	Y
2 Wise	Y	Y	Y	Y	Y	N	?
3 Rahall	Y	Y	Y	Y	N	Y	Y
WISCONSIN							
1 ***Ryan***	Y	Y	Y	Y	N	Y	Y
2 Baldwin	Y	Y	Y	N	Y	N	Y
3 Kind	Y	Y	Y	N	Y	N	Y
4 Kleczka	Y	Y	Y	Y	N	Y	Y
5 Barrett	Y	Y	Y	N	Y	N	Y
6 ***Petri***	Y	Y	Y	Y	N	Y	Y
7 Obey	?	Y	Y	?	N	Y	Y
8 ***Green***	Y	Y	Y	Y	N	Y	Y
9 ***Sensenbrenner***	Y	Y	Y	Y	N	Y	Y
WYOMING							
AL ***Cubin***	Y	Y	Y	Y	N	Y	?

Southern states - Ala., Ark., Fla., Ga., Ky., La., Miss., N.C., Okla., S.C., Tenn., Texas, Va.

263. HR 775. Y2K Liability Limits/Rule. Adoption of the rule (H Res 234) to provide for House floor consideration of the conference report on the bill to limit lawsuits resulting from Year 2000 computer failures. Adopted 423-1: R 217-0; D 205-1 (ND 153-1, SD 52-0); I 1-0, July 1, 1999.

264. HR 10. Financial Services Overhaul/Rule. Adoption of the rule (H Res 235) to provide for House floor consideration of the bill to eliminate barriers against cross ownership between banks, securities firms, insurance companies and other firms. Adopted 227-203: R 221-0; D 6-202 (ND 1-153, SD 5-49); I 0-1, July 1, 1999.

265. HR 775. Y2K Liability Limits/Conference Report. Adoption of the conference report on the bill that would limit liability from so-called Year 2000 computer problems, which will occur if computers mistake a two-digit code of "00" for 1900 instead of 2000. The agreement would cap punitive damages for business with 50 or fewer employees at $250,000, or three times the amount of compensatory damages, whichever is less, would require a plaintiff to wait at least 30 days and up to 90 days before suing and would establish "proportional liability" to link defendants' share of liability to their degree of responsibility. Adopted, 404-24: R 219-2; D 185-21 (ND 134-18, SD 51-3); I 0-1, July 1, 1999.

266. S 1059. Fiscal 2000 Defense Authorization/Motion to Instruct. Skelton, D-Mo., motion to instruct the House conferees to insist upon a provision to recognize the achievement of goals in Yugoslavia by the U.S. armed forces, President Clinton and other top officials, the forces of the NATO allies, and the front- line states of Albania, Macedonia, Bulgaria and Romania. Motion agreed to 261-162: R 66-150; D 194-12 (ND 144-8, SD 50-4); I 1-0, July 1, 1999.

267. S 1059. Fiscal 2000 Defense Authorization/Closed Conference. Spence, R-S.C., motion to close portions of the conference to the public during consideration of national security issues. Motion agreed to 413-9: R 215-0; D 197-9 (ND 145-7, SD 52-2); I 1-0, July 1, 1999.

268. HR 10. Financial Services Overhaul/Communications. Burr, R-N.C., amendment to permit a company that has owned broadcasting stations since Jan. 1, 1998, to reorganize as a financial holding company and affiliate with an insured bank, while being allowed to expand its commercial activities. The provision would only apply to the Jefferson Pilot Corp. of Greensboro, N.C. Adopted 238-189: R 181-39; D 57-149 (ND 28-124, SD 29-25); I 0-1, July 1, 1999.

269. HR 10. Financial Services Overhaul/Suspicious Activity. Barr, R-Ga., amendment to prohibit federal banking regulators from requiring banks to identify their customers and their sources of income and financial patterns in order to identify suspicious behavior. The amendment would replace current "suspicious activity reports" with a legal liability "safe harbor" for financial institutions to report transactions relevant to a possible violation of law, and would increase from $10,000 to $25,000 the threshold at which commercial businesses must submit to the government currency transaction reports which detail large transactions. Rejected 129-299: R 117-104; D 12-194 (ND 6-146, SD 6-48); I 0-1, July 1, 1999.

Key

- Y Voted for (yea).
- # Paired for.
- + Announced for.
- N Voted against (nay).
- X Paired against.
- – Announced against.
- P Voted "present."
- C Voted "present" to avoid possible conflict of interest.
- ? Did not vote or otherwise make a position known.

•

Democrats ***Republicans***
Independents

	263	264	265	266	267	268	269
ALABAMA							
1 ***Callahan***	Y	Y	Y	Y	Y	Y	Y
2 ***Everett***	Y	Y	Y	N	Y	Y	Y
3 ***Riley***	Y	Y	Y	N	Y	N	Y
4 ***Aderholt***	Y	Y	Y	N	Y	Y	Y
5 Cramer	Y	N	Y	Y	Y	Y	N
6 ***Bachus***	Y	Y	Y	N	Y	Y	N
7 Hilliard	Y	N	Y	Y	Y	Y	N
ALASKA							
AL ***Young***	Y	Y	Y	N	Y	Y	Y
ARIZONA							
1 ***Salmon***	Y	Y	Y	N	?	Y	N
2 Pastor	Y	N	Y	Y	Y	N	N
3 ***Stump***	Y	Y	Y	N	Y	Y	Y
4 ***Shadegg***	Y	Y	Y	N	Y	Y	N
5 ***Kolbe***	Y	Y	Y	Y	Y	N	N
6 ***Hayworth***	Y	Y	Y	N	Y	Y	Y
ARKANSAS							
1 Berry	Y	N	Y	Y	Y	N	N
2 Snyder	Y	N	Y	Y	Y	N	N
3 ***Hutchinson***	Y	Y	Y	Y	Y	N	N
4 ***Dickey***	Y	Y	Y	Y	Y	Y	N
CALIFORNIA							
1 Thompson	Y	N	Y	Y	Y	Y	N
2 ***Herger***	Y	Y	Y	N	Y	Y	Y
3 ***Ose***	Y	Y	Y	N	Y	Y	Y
4 ***Doolittle***	+	Y	Y	N	Y	Y	Y
5 Matsui	Y	N	Y	Y	Y	N	N
6 Woolsey	Y	N	Y	Y	Y	N	Y
7 Miller, George	Y	N	Y	Y	Y	N	Y
8 Pelosi	Y	N	Y	Y	Y	?	?
9 Lee	Y	N	N	N	N	N	N
10 Tauscher	Y	N	Y	Y	Y	Y	N
11 ***Pombo***	Y	Y	Y	N	Y	Y	Y
12 Lantos	Y	N	Y	Y	Y	N	N
13 Stark	Y	N	N	N	N	N	N
14 Eshoo	Y	N	Y	Y	Y	N	N
15 ***Campbell***	Y	Y	Y	N	Y	N	Y
16 Lofgren	Y	N	Y	Y	Y	N	N
17 Farr	Y	N	Y	Y	Y	N	N
18 Condit	Y	N	Y	N	Y	N	N
19 ***Radanovich***	Y	Y	Y	N	Y	Y	Y
20 Dooley	Y	N	Y	Y	Y	N	N
21 ***Thomas***	Y	Y	Y	N	Y	Y	N
22 Capps	Y	N	Y	Y	Y	N	N
23 ***Gallegly***	Y	Y	Y	N	Y	Y	Y
24 Sherman	Y	N	Y	Y	Y	N	N
25 ***McKeon***	Y	Y	Y	N	Y	Y	Y
26 Berman	Y	N	Y	Y	Y	N	N
27 ***Rogan***	Y	Y	Y	P	Y	Y	N
28 ***Dreier***	Y	Y	Y	Y	Y	Y	Y
29 Waxman	Y	N	N	Y	Y	N	N
30 Becerra	?	N	Y	Y	Y	N	N
31 Martinez	Y	N	Y	Y	Y	N	N
32 Dixon	Y	N	Y	Y	Y	Y	N
33 Roybal-Allard	Y	N	Y	Y	Y	N	N
34 Napolitano	Y	N	Y	Y	Y	N	N
35 Waters	Y	N	Y	Y	Y	N	N
36 ***Kuykendall***	Y	Y	Y	N	Y	N	N
37 Millender-McD.	Y	N	Y	Y	Y	N	N
38 ***Horn***	Y	Y	Y	Y	Y	Y	N
39 ***Royce***	Y	Y	Y	N	Y	N	Y
40 ***Lewis***	?	Y	Y	Y	Y	Y	Y
41 ***Miller, Gary***	Y	Y	Y	Y	Y	N	Y
42 Brown	?	?	?	?	?	?	?
43 ***Calvert***	Y	Y	Y	Y	Y	Y	N
44 ***Bono***	Y	Y	Y	Y	Y	N	Y
45 ***Rohrabacher***	Y	Y	Y	N	Y	Y	Y
46 Sanchez	Y	N	Y	Y	Y	N	N
47 ***Cox***	?	Y	Y	?	Y	Y	N
48 ***Packard***	Y	Y	Y	N	Y	Y	Y
49 ***Bilbray***	Y	Y	Y	Y	Y	Y	N
50 Filner	Y	N	N	Y	Y	N	N
51 ***Cunningham***	Y	Y	Y	N	Y	Y	N
52 ***Hunter***	Y	Y	Y	N	Y	Y	Y
COLORADO							
1 DeGette	Y	N	Y	Y	Y	N	N
2 Udall	Y	N	Y	Y	Y	Y	N
3 ***McInnis***	Y	Y	Y	N	Y	Y	Y
4 ***Schaffer***	Y	Y	Y	N	Y	Y	Y
5 ***Hefley***	Y	Y	Y	N	Y	N	Y
6 ***Tancredo***	Y	Y	Y	N	Y	Y	Y
CONNECTICUT							
1 Larson	Y	N	Y	Y	+	N	N
2 Gejdenson	Y	N	Y	Y	Y	N	N
3 DeLauro	Y	N	Y	Y	Y	N	N
4 ***Shays***	Y	Y	Y	Y	Y	Y	N
5 Maloney	Y	N	Y	Y	Y	N	N
6 ***Johnson***	Y	Y	Y	Y	Y	Y	N
DELAWARE							
AL ***Castle***	Y	Y	Y	Y	Y	Y	N
FLORIDA							
1 ***Scarborough***	Y	Y	Y	N	Y	N	Y
2 Boyd	Y	N	Y	Y	Y	N	N
3 Brown	?	N	Y	Y	Y	Y	N
4 ***Fowler***	Y	Y	Y	N	Y	Y	N
5 Thurman	Y	N	Y	Y	Y	Y	N
6 ***Stearns***	Y	Y	Y	N	Y	N	Y
7 ***Mica***	Y	Y	Y	Y	Y	N	N
8 ***McCollum***	Y	Y	Y	Y	Y	Y	N
9 ***Bilirakis***	Y	Y	Y	N	Y	Y	N
10 ***Young***	Y	Y	Y	Y	Y	Y	N
11 Davis	Y	N	Y	Y	Y	Y	N
12 ***Canady***	Y	Y	Y	N	Y	Y	N
13 ***Miller***	Y	Y	Y	Y	Y	Y	N
14 ***Goss***	Y	Y	Y	N	Y	Y	Y
15 ***Weldon***	Y	Y	Y	N	Y	Y	Y
16 ***Foley***	Y	Y	Y	Y	Y	N	N
17 Meek	Y	N	Y	Y	Y	Y	N
18 ***Ros-Lehtinen***	Y	Y	Y	N	Y	Y	N
19 Wexler	Y	N	Y	Y	Y	N	N
20 Deutsch	Y	N	Y	Y	Y	N	N
21 ***Diaz-Balart***	Y	Y	Y	N	Y	Y	N
22 ***Shaw***	Y	Y	Y	Y	Y	Y	N
23 Hastings	Y	N	Y	Y	Y	Y	N
GEORGIA							
1 ***Kingston***	Y	Y	Y	N	Y	Y	Y
2 Bishop	Y	N	Y	Y	Y	Y	N
3 ***Collins***	Y	Y	Y	N	Y	Y	Y
4 McKinney	Y	N	N	N	N	N	N
5 Lewis	Y	N	N	Y	Y	Y	N
6 ***Isakson***	Y	Y	Y	Y	Y	Y	N
7 ***Barr***	Y	Y	Y	N	Y	Y	Y
8 ***Chambliss***	Y	Y	Y	N	Y	Y	N
9 ***Deal***	Y	Y	Y	N	Y	Y	Y
10 ***Norwood***	Y	Y	Y	N	Y	Y	Y
11 ***Linder***	Y	Y	Y	N	Y	Y	Y
HAWAII							
1 Abercrombie	Y	N	Y	N	?	Y	N
2 Mink	Y	N	Y	Y	Y	N	Y
IDAHO							
1 ***Chenoweth***	Y	Y	Y	N	Y	Y	Y
2 ***Simpson***	Y	Y	Y	N	Y	Y	N
ILLINOIS							
1 Rush	Y	N	Y	Y	Y	Y	N
2 Jackson	Y	N	Y	N	Y	N	N
3 Lipinski	Y	Y	?	?	?	?	?
4 Gutierrez	Y	N	Y	Y	Y	N	N
5 Blagojevich	Y	N	Y	P	Y	N	N
6 ***Hyde***	Y	Y	Y	Y	Y	Y	N
7 Davis	Y	N	Y	Y	Y	N	N
8 ***Crane***	Y	Y	Y	N	Y	Y	Y
9 Schakowsky	Y	N	N	Y	Y	N	N
10 ***Porter***	Y	Y	Y	Y	Y	N	N
11 ***Weller***	Y	Y	Y	Y	Y	Y	Y
12 Costello	Y	N	Y	Y	Y	N	N
13 ***Biggert***	Y	Y	Y	N	Y	Y	N
14 ***Hastert***		Y	Y	Y			

ND Northern Democrats SD Southern Democrats

	263	264	265	266	267	268	269
15 ***Ewing***	Y	Y	Y	N	Y	Y	N
16 ***Manzullo***	Y	Y	Y	N	Y	Y	Y
17 Evans	Y	N	Y	Y	Y	N	N
18 ***LaHood***	Y	Y	Y	Y	Y	Y	N
19 Phelps	Y	N	Y	Y	Y	N	N
20 ***Shimkus***	Y	Y	Y	N	Y	Y	N
INDIANA							
1 Visclosky	Y	N	Y	Y	Y	N	N
2 ***McIntosh***	Y	Y	Y	N	Y	Y	N
3 Roemer	Y	N	Y	Y	Y	N	N
4 ***Souder***	Y	Y	Y	N	?	Y	N
5 ***Buyer***	Y	Y	Y	N	Y	Y	Y
6 ***Burton***	Y	Y	Y	N	Y	Y	N
7 ***Pease***	Y	Y	Y	N	Y	Y	Y
8 ***Hostettler***	Y	Y	Y	N	Y	N	Y
9 Hill	Y	N	Y	Y	Y	N	N
10 Carson	Y	N	Y	Y	Y	N	N
IOWA							
1 ***Leach***	Y	Y	Y	Y	Y	N	N
2 ***Nussle***	Y	Y	Y	Y	Y	Y	N
3 Boswell	Y	N	Y	Y	Y	Y	N
4 ***Ganske***	Y	Y	Y	Y	Y	?	N
5 ***Latham***	Y	Y	Y	Y	Y	Y	N
KANSAS							
1 ***Moran***	Y	Y	Y	Y	Y	N	Y
2 ***Ryun***	Y	Y	Y	N	Y	N	Y
3 Moore	Y	N	Y	Y	Y	N	N
4 ***Tiahrt***	Y	Y	Y	N	Y	N	Y
KENTUCKY							
1 ***Whitfield***	Y	Y	Y	N	Y	Y	N
2 ***Lewis***	Y	Y	Y	N	Y	Y	Y
3 ***Northup***	Y	Y	Y	Y	Y	Y	N
4 Lucas	Y	Y	Y	Y	Y	Y	N
5 ***Rogers***	Y	Y	Y	N	Y	Y	N
6 ***Fletcher***	Y	Y	Y	N	Y	Y	Y
LOUISIANA							
1 ***Vitter***	Y	Y	Y	N	Y	Y	N
2 Jefferson	Y	N	Y	Y	Y	Y	N
3 ***Tauzin***	Y	Y	Y	N	Y	Y	N
4 ***McCrery***	Y	Y	Y	N	Y	Y	N
5 ***Cooksey***	Y	Y	Y	N	Y	Y	N
6 ***Baker***	Y	Y	Y	N	Y	Y	N
7 John	Y	N	Y	Y	Y	Y	N
MAINE							
1 Allen	Y	N	Y	Y	Y	N	N
2 Baldacci	Y	N	Y	Y	Y	N	N
MARYLAND							
1 ***Gilchrest***	Y	Y	Y	Y	Y	N	N
2 ***Ehrlich***	?	Y	Y	N	Y	Y	Y
3 Cardin	Y	N	Y	Y	Y	N	N
4 Wynn	Y	N	Y	Y	Y	Y	N
5 Hoyer	Y	N	Y	Y	Y	Y	N
6 ***Bartlett***	Y	Y	Y	N	Y	Y	Y
7 Cummings	Y	N	Y	Y	Y	N	N
8 ***Morella***	Y	Y	Y	Y	Y	Y	N
MASSACHUSETTS							
1 Olver	Y	N	Y	Y	Y	N	N
2 Neal	Y	N	Y	Y	Y	N	N
3 McGovern	Y	N	Y	Y	Y	N	N
4 Frank	Y	N	Y	Y	Y	N	N
5 Meehan	Y	N	Y	Y	Y	N	N
6 Tierney	Y	N	N	Y	Y	N	N
7 Markey	Y	N	Y	Y	Y	N	N
8 Capuano	Y	N	N	Y	Y	N	N
9 Moakley	Y	N	Y	Y	Y	N	N
10 Delahunt	Y	N	N	Y	Y	Y	N
MICHIGAN							
1 Stupak	Y	N	Y	Y	Y	Y	N
2 ***Hoekstra***	Y	Y	Y	N	Y	N	Y
3 ***Ehlers***	Y	Y	Y	Y	Y	N	N
4 ***Camp***	Y	Y	Y	Y	Y	Y	Y
5 Barcia	Y	N	Y	Y	Y	Y	Y
6 ***Upton***	Y	Y	Y	Y	Y	Y	N
7 ***Smith***	Y	Y	Y	N	?	N	Y
8 Stabenow	Y	N	Y	Y	Y	N	N
9 Kildee	Y	N	Y	Y	Y	Y	N
10 Bonior	Y	N	N	Y	Y	N	N
11 ***Knollenberg***	Y	Y	Y	N	Y	Y	N
12 Levin	Y	N	Y	Y	Y	N	N
13 Rivers	Y	N	Y	P	Y	N	Y
14 Conyers	Y	N	Y	N	Y	N	N
15 Kilpatrick	Y	N	Y	Y	Y	N	N
16 Dingell	Y	N	?	Y	Y	N	N

	263	264	265	266	267	268	269
MINNESOTA							
1 ***Gutknecht***	Y	Y	Y	N	Y	Y	Y
2 Minge	Y	N	Y	Y	Y	Y	N
3 ***Ramstad***	Y	Y	Y	Y	Y	Y	N
4 Vento	Y	N	Y	Y	Y	N	N
5 Sabo	Y	N	Y	Y	Y	N	N
6 Luther	Y	N	Y	Y	Y	N	N
7 Peterson	Y	N	Y	N	Y	Y	Y
8 Oberstar	Y	N	Y	Y	N	N	N
MISSISSIPPI							
1 ***Wicker***	Y	Y	Y	N	Y	Y	Y
2 Thompson	Y	N	Y	Y	Y	Y	N
3 ***Pickering***	Y	Y	Y	N	Y	Y	Y
4 Shows	Y	N	Y	Y	Y	Y	N
5 Taylor	Y	N	Y	Y	Y	Y	Y
MISSOURI							
1 Clay	Y	N	Y	Y	Y	Y	N
2 ***Talent***	Y	Y	Y	N	Y	Y	N
3 Gephardt	Y	N	Y	Y	Y	N	N
4 Skelton	Y	N	Y	Y	Y	Y	N
5 McCarthy	Y	N	Y	Y	Y	N	N
6 Danner	Y	N	Y	Y	Y	N	N
7 ***Blunt***	Y	Y	Y	N	Y	Y	Y
8 ***Emerson***	Y	Y	Y	Y	?	Y	N
9 ***Hulshof***	Y	Y	Y	Y	Y	Y	Y
MONTANA							
AL ***Hill***	Y	Y	Y	N	Y	N	Y
NEBRASKA							
1 ***Bereuter***	Y	Y	Y	P	Y	N	N
2 ***Terry***	Y	Y	Y	N	Y	Y	N
3 ***Barrett***	Y	Y	Y	N	Y	Y	N
NEVADA							
1 Berkley	Y	N	Y	Y	Y	N	N
2 ***Gibbons***	Y	Y	Y	?	?	Y	Y
NEW HAMPSHIRE							
1 ***Sununu***	Y	Y	Y	N	Y	Y	Y
2 ***Bass***	Y	Y	Y	N	Y	Y	N
NEW JERSEY							
1 Andrews	Y	N	Y	Y	Y	N	N
2 ***LoBiondo***	Y	Y	Y	N	Y	Y	N
3 ***Saxton***	Y	Y	Y	N	Y	Y	N
4 ***Smith***	Y	Y	Y	?	Y	N	Y
5 ***Roukema***	Y	Y	Y	N	Y	N	N
6 Pallone	Y	N	Y	Y	Y	N	N
7 ***Franks***	Y	Y	Y	Y	?	Y	N
8 Pascrell	Y	N	Y	Y	Y	N	N
9 Rothman	Y	N	N	Y	Y	Y	N
10 Payne	Y	N	Y	Y	Y	Y	N
11 ***Frelinghuysen***	Y	Y	Y	Y	Y	N	N
12 Holt	Y	N	Y	Y	Y	N	N
13 Menendez	Y	N	Y	Y	Y	N	N
NEW MEXICO							
1 ***Wilson***	Y	Y	Y	N	Y	Y	N
2 ***Skeen***	Y	Y	Y	N	Y	N	Y
3 Udall	Y	N	Y	Y	Y	N	N
NEW YORK							
1 ***Forbes***	Y	Y	Y	Y	Y	N	N
2 ***Lazio***	Y	Y	Y	N	Y	Y	N
3 ***King***	Y	Y	Y	Y	Y	Y	N
4 McCarthy	Y	N	Y	Y	Y	N	N
5 Ackerman	Y	N	Y	Y	Y	N	N
6 Meeks	Y	N	N	Y	Y	N	N
7 Crowley	Y	N	N	Y	Y	N	N
8 Nadler	Y	N	Y	Y	Y	N	N
9 Weiner	Y	N	N	Y	Y	Y	N
10 Towns	Y	N	Y	Y	Y	N	N
11 Owens	Y	N	Y	Y	N	N	N
12 Velázquez	Y	N	Y	Y	Y	N	N
13 ***Fossella***	?	?	?	?	?	?	?
14 Maloney	Y	N	Y	Y	Y	N	N
15 Rangel	Y	N	Y	Y	Y	N	N
16 Serrano	Y	?	Y	Y	Y	N	N
17 Engel	Y	N	Y	Y	Y	N	N
18 Lowey	Y	N	Y	Y	Y	N	N
19 ***Kelly***	Y	Y	Y	N	Y	Y	N
20 ***Gilman***	Y	Y	Y	Y	Y	Y	N
21 McNulty	Y	N	Y	Y	Y	N	N
22 ***Sweeney***	Y	Y	Y	N	Y	Y	N
23 ***Boehlert***	Y	Y	Y	Y	Y	Y	N
24 ***McHugh***	Y	Y	Y	Y	Y	Y	N
25 ***Walsh***	Y	Y	Y	Y	Y	Y	N
26 Hinchey	Y	N	N	Y	Y	N	N
27 ***Reynolds***	Y	Y	Y	N	Y	Y	Y
28 Slaughter	Y	N	Y	Y	Y	N	N
29 LaFalce	Y	N	Y	Y	Y	N	N

	263	264	265	266	267	268	269
30 ***Quinn***	Y	Y	Y	Y	Y	Y	N
31 ***Houghton***	Y	Y	Y	Y	Y	Y	N
NORTH CAROLINA							
1 Clayton	Y	N	Y	Y	Y	Y	N
2 Etheridge	Y	N	Y	Y	Y	Y	N
3 ***Jones***	Y	Y	Y	N	Y	Y	Y
4 Price	Y	N	Y	Y	Y	Y	N
5 ***Burr***	Y	Y	Y	N	Y	Y	Y
6 ***Coble***	Y	Y	Y	N	Y	Y	Y
7 McIntyre	Y	N	Y	Y	Y	Y	Y
8 ***Hayes***	Y	Y	Y	N	Y	Y	Y
9 ***Myrick***	Y	Y	Y	N	Y	Y	Y
10 ***Ballenger***	Y	Y	Y	N	Y	Y	N
11 ***Taylor***	Y	Y	Y	N	Y	Y	Y
12 Watt	Y	N	Y	Y	N	Y	N
NORTH DAKOTA							
AL Pomeroy	Y	N	Y	Y	Y	N	N
OHIO							
1 ***Chabot***	Y	Y	Y	N	Y	Y	Y
2 ***Portman***	Y	Y	Y	Y	Y	Y	N
3 Hall	Y	N	?	Y	Y	N	N
4 ***Oxley***	Y	Y	Y	N	Y	Y	N
5 ***Gillmor***	Y	Y	Y	Y	Y	Y	Y
6 Strickland	Y	N	Y	Y	Y	Y	N
7 ***Hobson***	Y	Y	Y	Y	Y	Y	N
8 ***Boehner***	Y	Y	Y	N	Y	Y	Y
9 Kaptur	Y	N	Y	Y	Y	N	N
10 Kucinich	N	N	N	N	N	N	N
11 Jones	Y	N	Y	Y	Y	N	N
12 ***Kasich***	Y	Y	Y	N	Y	Y	N
13 Brown	Y	N	Y	Y	Y	N	N
14 Sawyer	Y	N	Y	Y	Y	Y	N
15 ***Pryce***	Y	Y	Y	Y	Y	Y	N
16 ***Regula***	Y	Y	Y	Y	Y	N	N
17 Traficant	Y	N	Y	Y	Y	Y	N
18 ***Ney***	Y	Y	Y	N	Y	Y	Y
19 ***LaTourette***	Y	Y	Y	Y	Y	Y	Y
OKLAHOMA							
1 ***Largent***	Y	Y	Y	N	Y	Y	Y
2 ***Coburn***	Y	Y	Y	N	Y	Y	Y
3 ***Watkins***	Y	Y	Y	N	Y	Y	Y
4 ***Watts***	Y	Y	Y	N	Y	Y	Y
5 ***Istook***	Y	Y	Y	N	Y	Y	Y
6 ***Lucas***	Y	Y	Y	N	Y	Y	Y
OREGON							
1 Wu	Y	N	Y	Y	Y	N	N
2 ***Walden***	Y	Y	Y	N	Y	Y	Y
3 Blumenauer	Y	N	Y	Y	N	N	N
4 DeFazio	Y	N	Y	Y	N	N	N
5 Hooley	Y	N	Y	Y	Y	N	N
PENNSYLVANIA							
1 Brady	Y	N	Y	Y	Y	N	N
2 Fattah	Y	N	Y	Y	Y	N	N
3 Borski	Y	N	Y	Y	Y	?	?
4 Klink	Y	N	Y	Y	Y	N	N
5 ***Peterson***	Y	Y	Y	N	Y	Y	N
6 Holden	Y	N	Y	Y	Y	N	N
7 ***Weldon***	Y	Y	Y	N	Y	Y	N
8 ***Greenwood***	Y	Y	Y	Y	Y	Y	N
9 ***Shuster***	Y	Y	Y	N	Y	Y	Y
10 ***Sherwood***	Y	Y	Y	Y	Y	Y	Y
11 Kanjorski	Y	N	Y	Y	Y	N	N
12 Murtha	Y	N	Y	Y	Y	N	N
13 Hoeffel	Y	N	Y	Y	Y	N	N
14 Coyne	Y	N	Y	Y	Y	N	N
15 ***Toomey***	Y	Y	Y	N	Y	Y	Y
16 ***Pitts***	Y	Y	Y	N	Y	Y	Y
17 ***Gekas***	Y	Y	Y	Y	Y	Y	Y
18 Doyle	Y	N	Y	Y	Y	N	N
19 ***Goodling***	Y	Y	?	N	Y	Y	Y
20 Mascara	Y	N	Y	Y	Y	N	N
21 ***English***	Y	Y	Y	Y	Y	N	Y
RHODE ISLAND							
1 Kennedy	Y	N	N	Y	Y	N	N
2 Weygand	Y	N	N	Y	Y	N	N
SOUTH CAROLINA							
1 ***Sanford***	Y	Y	Y	N	Y	Y	Y
2 ***Spence***	Y	Y	Y	Y	Y	Y	Y
3 ***Graham***	Y	?	Y	N	Y	Y	Y
4 ***DeMint***	Y	Y	Y	N	Y	Y	Y
5 Spratt	Y	N	Y	Y	Y	Y	N
6 Clyburn	Y	N	Y	Y	Y	Y	N
SOUTH DAKOTA							
AL ***Thune***	Y	Y	Y	N	Y	Y	N

	263	264	265	266	267	268	269
TENNESSEE							
1 ***Jenkins***	Y	Y	Y	N	Y	Y	Y
2 ***Duncan***	Y	Y	N	N	Y	Y	Y
3 ***Wamp***	Y	Y	Y	N	Y	Y	Y
4 ***Hilleary***	Y	Y	Y	N	Y	Y	Y
5 Clement	Y	N	Y	Y	Y	N	Y
6 Gordon	Y	Y	Y	Y	Y	N	N
7 ***Bryant***	Y	Y	Y	N	Y	Y	N
8 Tanner	Y	Y	Y	Y	Y	N	N
9 Ford	Y	N	Y	Y	Y	N	N
TEXAS							
1 Sandlin	Y	N	Y	Y	Y	N	N
2 Turner	Y	N	Y	Y	Y	N	N
3 ***Johnson, Sam***	Y	Y	Y	N	Y	N	Y
4 Hall	Y	N	Y	N	Y	Y	Y
5 ***Sessions***	Y	Y	Y	N	Y	Y	Y
6 ***Barton***	Y	Y	Y	N	Y	Y	Y
7 ***Archer***	Y	Y	Y	N	Y	Y	Y
8 ***Brady***	Y	Y	Y	N	Y	Y	Y
9 Lampson	Y	N	Y	Y	Y	N	N
10 Doggett	Y	N	Y	Y	Y	N	N
11 Edwards	Y	N	Y	Y	Y	Y	N
12 ***Granger***	Y	Y	Y	N	Y	Y	N
13 ***Thornberry***	Y	Y	Y	Y	Y	Y	Y
14 ***Paul***	Y	Y	N	N	Y	Y	Y
15 Hinojosa	Y	N	Y	Y	Y	N	N
16 Reyes	Y	N	Y	Y	Y	N	N
17 Stenholm	Y	N	Y	Y	Y	Y	N
18 Jackson-Lee	Y	N	Y	Y	Y	N	N
19 ***Combest***	Y	Y	Y	N	Y	Y	Y
20 Gonzalez	Y	N	Y	Y	Y	N	N
21 ***Smith***	Y	Y	Y	N	Y	Y	N
22 ***DeLay***	Y	Y	Y	N	Y	Y	N
23 ***Bonilla***	Y	Y	Y	N	Y	Y	Y
24 Frost	Y	N	Y	Y	Y	N	N
25 Bentsen	Y	N	Y	Y	Y	N	N
26 ***Armey***	Y	Y	Y	N	Y	Y	Y
27 Ortiz	Y	N	Y	Y	Y	N	N
28 Rodriguez	Y	N	Y	Y	Y	N	N
29 Green	?	?	?	?	?	?	?
30 Johnson, E.B.	Y	N	Y	Y	Y	Y	N
UTAH							
1 ***Hansen***	Y	Y	Y	N	Y	Y	N
2 ***Cook***	Y	Y	Y	N	Y	Y	Y
3 ***Cannon***	Y	Y	Y	N	Y	Y	N
VERMONT							
AL *Sanders*	Y	N	N	Y	Y	N	N
VIRGINIA							
1 ***Bateman***	Y	Y	Y	P	Y	Y	N
2 Pickett	?	N	Y	N	Y	N	Y
3 Scott	Y	N	N	Y	Y	Y	N
4 Sisisky	Y	N	Y	Y	Y	N	N
5 Goode	Y	Y	Y	N	Y	Y	Y
6 ***Goodlatte***	Y	Y	Y	N	Y	Y	Y
7 ***Bliley***	Y	Y	Y	Y	Y	Y	N
8 Moran	Y	N	Y	Y	Y	N	N
9 Boucher	Y	Y	Y	Y	Y	Y	N
10 ***Wolf***	Y	Y	Y	Y	Y	Y	N
11 ***Davis***	Y	Y	Y	Y	Y	Y	N
WASHINGTON							
1 Inslee	Y	N	Y	Y	Y	N	N
2 ***Metcalf***	Y	Y	Y	N	Y	Y	Y
3 Baird	Y	N	Y	Y	Y	Y	N
4 ***Hastings***	Y	Y	Y	N	Y	Y	Y
5 ***Nethercutt***	Y	Y	Y	N	Y	Y	Y
6 Dicks	Y	N	Y	Y	Y	N	N
7 McDermott	Y	N	Y	Y	Y	N	N
8 ***Dunn***	Y	Y	Y	Y	Y	Y	N
9 Smith	Y	N	Y	Y	Y	N	N
WEST VIRGINIA							
1 Mollohan	Y	N	Y	Y	Y	N	N
2 Wise	Y	N	Y	Y	Y	Y	N
3 Rahall	Y	N	N	Y	Y	N	N
WISCONSIN							
1 ***Ryan***	Y	Y	Y	N	Y	N	Y
2 Baldwin	Y	N	Y	Y	Y	N	N
3 Kind	Y	N	Y	Y	Y	N	N
4 Kleczka	Y	N	Y	Y	Y	Y	N
5 Barrett	Y	N	Y	Y	Y	Y	N
6 ***Petri***	Y	Y	Y	N	Y	N	N
7 Obey	Y	N	Y	Y	Y	N	N
8 ***Green***	Y	Y	Y	N	Y	N	Y
9 ***Sensenbrenner***	Y	Y	Y	N	Y	Y	Y
WYOMING							
AL ***Cubin***	Y	Y	Y	N	Y	Y	Y

Southern states - Ala., Ark., Fla., Ga., Ky., La., Miss., N.C., Okla., S.C., Tenn., Texas, Va.

House Votes 270, 271, 272, 273, 274, 275, 276

270. HR 10. Financial Services Overhaul/Fee Disclosure. Cook, R-Utah, amendment to strike provisions of the bill that would require federal financial regulators to prescribe or revise rules to improve the accuracy and understandability of fee disclosures to customers for financial products. Rejected 114-313: R 103-117; D11-195 (ND 8-144, SD 3-51); I 0-1, July 1, 1999.

271. HR 10. Financial Services Overhaul/Loan Loss Reserves. Roukema, R-N.J., amendment to require the Securities and Exchange Commission to consult with federal banking regulators and coordinate its comments with theirs before taking any actions or rendering any opinion regarding how a bank has reported loan loss reserves in its financial statements. Adopted 407-20: R 219-1; D 187-19 (ND 135-17, SD 52-2); I 1-0, July 1, 1999.

272. HR 10. Financial Services Overhaul/Motion To Rise. LaFalce, D-N.Y., motion to rise from the Committee of the Whole. Motion rejected 179-232: R 0-213; D 178-19 (ND 129-14, SD 49-5); I 1-0, July 1, 1999.

273. HR 10. Financial Services Overhaul/State Transfers. Bliley, R-Va., amendment to allow mutual insurance companies to move to another state and reorganize into a mutual holding company or stock company, and to prohibit banks from discriminating against victims of domestic violence when providing insurance. Adopted 226-203: R 200-21; D 26-181 (ND 14-139, SD 12-42); I 0-1, July 1, 1999.

274. HR 10. Financial Services Overhaul/Information Privacy. Oxley, R-Ohio, amendment to limit the ability of financial institutions to provide confidential customer information to unaffiliated third parties. The amendment would require financial institutions to inform consumers that they have the right to "opt out" of disclosure of non-public personal information. Adopted 427-1: R 219-1; D 207-0 (ND 153-0, SD 54-0); I 1-0, July 1, 1999.

275. HR 10. Financial Services Overhaul/Recommit. Markey, D-Mass., motion to recommit the bill to the Banking Committee with instructions to report it back with an amendment to prohibit insurance "redlining," in which companies refuse to sell policies in certain neighborhoods, and to strengthen privacy protections concerning customers' medical and financial information. Motion rejected 198-232: R 1-221; D 196-11 (ND 148-5, SD 48-6); I 1-0. July 1, 1999.

276. HR10. Financial Services Overhaul/Passage. Passage of the bill to eliminate barriers against cross ownership among banks, securities firms, insurance companies and other firms. The bill would prohibit banks from selling private customer financial information to telemarketing firms and would allow customers to "opt out"of information-sharing by financial firms with other companies. The bill would allow mutual insurance companies to move their businesses to a different state when reorganizing into a stock company. The bill would prohibit financial companies from conditioning the sale of products on the purchase of other financial products. Passed 343-86: R 205-16; D 138-69 (ND 95-58, SD 43-11); I 0-1, July 1, 1999.

Key

Y Voted for (yea).
\# Paired for.
\+ Announced for.
N Voted against (nay).
X Paired against.
– Announced against.
P Voted "present."
C Voted "present" to avoid possible conflict of interest.
? Did not vote or otherwise make a position known.

•

Democrats ***Republicans***
Independents

	270	271	272	273	274	275	276
ALABAMA							
1 ***Callahan***	Y	Y	N	Y	Y	N	Y
2 ***Everett***	Y	Y	N	Y	Y	N	Y
3 ***Riley***	Y	Y	N	Y	Y	N	Y
4 ***Aderholt***	Y	Y	N	Y	Y	N	Y
5 Cramer	Y	Y	Y	Y	Y	N	Y
6 ***Bachus***	Y	Y	N	Y	Y	N	Y
7 Hilliard	N	Y	Y	N	Y	Y	N
ALASKA							
AL ***Young***	N	Y	N	Y	Y	N	Y
ARIZONA							
1 ***Salmon***	Y	Y	N	Y	Y	N	Y
2 Pastor	N	N	N	N	Y	Y	Y
3 ***Stump***	Y	Y	N	Y	Y	N	Y
4 ***Shadegg***	Y	Y	N	Y	Y	N	Y
5 ***Kolbe***	N	Y	N	N	Y	N	Y
6 ***Hayworth***	Y	Y	N	Y	Y	N	Y
ARKANSAS							
1 Berry	N	Y	Y	N	Y	Y	Y
2 Snyder	N	Y	Y	N	Y	Y	Y
3 ***Hutchinson***	Y	Y	N	Y	Y	N	Y
4 ***Dickey***	N	Y	N	Y	Y	N	Y
CALIFORNIA							
1 Thompson	N	Y	Y	N	Y	Y	Y
2 ***Herger***	Y	Y	N	Y	Y	N	Y
3 ***Ose***	Y	Y	N	Y	Y	N	Y
4 ***Doolittle***	N	Y	N	Y	Y	N	Y
5 Matsui	N	Y	Y	N	Y	Y	Y
6 Woolsey	N	Y	Y	N	Y	Y	N
7 Miller, George	N	Y	N	N	Y	Y	N
8 Pelosi	?	?	?	?	?	?	?
9 Lee	N	Y	Y	N	Y	Y	N
10 Tauscher	N	Y	Y	N	Y	Y	Y
11 ***Pombo***	N	Y	?	Y	Y	N	Y
12 Lantos	N	Y	Y	N	Y	Y	N
13 Stark	N	N	Y	N	Y	Y	N
14 Eshoo	N	Y	Y	N	Y	Y	N
15 ***Campbell***	N	Y	N	Y	Y	N	N
16 Lofgren	N	Y	Y	N	Y	Y	N
17 Farr	N	Y	Y	N	Y	Y	N
18 Condit	N	Y	Y	N	Y	Y	N
19 ***Radanovich***	N	Y	?	Y	Y	N	Y
20 Dooley	N	Y	?	N	Y	N	Y
21 ***Thomas***	N	Y	N	Y	Y	N	Y
22 Capps	N	Y	Y	Y	Y	Y	N
23 ***Gallegly***	N	Y	N	Y	Y	N	Y
24 Sherman	N	Y	Y	Y	Y	Y	Y
25 ***McKeon***	Y	Y	N	Y	Y	N	Y
26 Berman	N	Y	Y	N	Y	Y	Y
27 ***Rogan***	N	Y	?	Y	Y	Y	Y
28 ***Dreier***	Y	Y	N	Y	Y	N	Y
29 Waxman	N	Y	Y	N	Y	Y	N
30 Becerra	N	Y	Y	N	Y	Y	Y
31 Martinez	N	N	Y	N	Y	Y	N
32 Dixon	N	Y	Y	N	Y	Y	Y
33 Roybal-Allard	N	Y	Y	N	Y	Y	N
34 Napolitano	N	Y	Y	N	Y	Y	Y
35 Waters	N	Y	Y	N	Y	Y	N
36 ***Kuykendall***	Y	Y	N	Y	Y	N	Y
37 Millender-McD.	N	Y	Y	N	Y	Y	Y
38 ***Horn***	Y	Y	N	Y	Y	N	Y
39 ***Royce***	Y	Y	N	Y	Y	N	Y
40 ***Lewis***	N	Y	N	Y	Y	N	Y
41 ***Miller, Gary***	Y	Y	?	Y	Y	N	Y
42 Brown	?	?	?	?	?	?	?
43 ***Calvert***	N	Y	N	Y	Y	N	Y
44 ***Bono***	N	Y	N	Y	Y	N	Y
45 ***Rohrabacher***	N	Y	N	Y	Y	N	Y
46 Sanchez	N	N	Y	N	Y	Y	Y
47 ***Cox***	N	Y	N	Y	Y	N	Y
48 ***Packard***	Y	Y	N	Y	Y	N	Y
49 ***Bilbray***	N	Y	N	Y	Y	N	Y
50 Filner	N	Y	Y	N	Y	Y	N
51 ***Cunningham***	Y	Y	N	Y	Y	N	Y
52 ***Hunter***	N	Y	N	Y	Y	N	Y
COLORADO							
1 DeGette	N	N	Y	Y	Y	Y	N
2 Udall	N	Y	Y	N	Y	Y	Y
3 ***McInnis***	Y	Y	N	Y	Y	N	Y
4 ***Schaffer***	N	Y	N	Y	Y	N	Y
5 ***Hefley***	Y	Y	N	Y	Y	N	N
6 ***Tancredo***	Y	Y	N	Y	Y	N	N
CONNECTICUT							
1 Larson	N	N	Y	N	Y	Y	Y
2 Gejdenson	N	Y	Y	N	Y	Y	N
3 DeLauro	N	Y	Y	N	Y	Y	N
4 ***Shays***	N	Y	N	Y	Y	N	Y
5 Maloney	N	Y	Y	Y	Y	N	Y
6 ***Johnson***	N	Y	N	Y	Y	N	Y
DELAWARE							
AL ***Castle***	N	Y	N	Y	Y	N	Y
FLORIDA							
1 ***Scarborough***	Y	Y	N	Y	Y	N	Y
2 Boyd	N	Y	Y	N	Y	Y	Y
3 Brown	N	Y	Y	N	Y	Y	Y
4 ***Fowler***	N	Y	N	Y	Y	N	Y
5 Thurman	N	Y	Y	N	Y	Y	N
6 ***Stearns***	Y	Y	N	Y	Y	N	Y
7 ***Mica***	N	Y	N	N	Y	N	N
8 ***McCollum***	Y	Y	N	Y	Y	N	Y
9 ***Bilirakis***	N	Y	N	Y	Y	N	Y
10 ***Young***	N	Y	N	Y	Y	N	Y
11 Davis	N	Y	Y	Y	Y	Y	Y
12 ***Canady***	N	Y	N	Y	Y	N	Y
13 ***Miller***	N	Y	N	Y	Y	N	Y
14 ***Goss***	Y	Y	N	Y	Y	N	Y
15 ***Weldon***	Y	Y	N	N	Y	N	Y
16 ***Foley***	N	Y	N	N	Y	N	Y
17 Meek	N	Y	Y	N	Y	Y	Y
18 ***Ros-Lehtinen***	N	Y	N	Y	Y	N	Y
19 Wexler	N	Y	Y	N	Y	Y	Y
20 Deutsch	N	N	Y	Y	Y	Y	Y
21 ***Diaz-Balart***	Y	?	N	Y	Y	N	Y
22 ***Shaw***	N	Y	N	Y	Y	N	Y
23 Hastings	N	Y	Y	N	Y	Y	Y
GEORGIA							
1 ***Kingston***	Y	Y	N	Y	Y	N	Y
2 Bishop	N	Y	Y	N	Y	Y	Y
3 ***Collins***	Y	Y	N	Y	Y	N	Y
4 McKinney	N	N	Y	N	Y	Y	N
5 Lewis	N	Y	Y	N	Y	Y	Y
6 ***Isakson***	Y	Y	N	Y	Y	N	Y
7 ***Barr***	Y	Y	N	Y	Y	N	Y
8 ***Chambliss***	Y	Y	N	Y	Y	N	Y
9 ***Deal***	N	Y	N	Y	Y	N	Y
10 ***Norwood***	Y	Y	N	Y	Y	N	Y
11 ***Linder***	Y	Y	N	Y	Y	N	Y
HAWAII							
1 Abercrombie	N	Y	Y	N	Y	Y	N
2 Mink	N	Y	Y	N	Y	Y	N
IDAHO							
1 ***Chenoweth***	?	Y	N	N	Y	N	N
2 ***Simpson***	Y	Y	N	Y	Y	N	Y
ILLINOIS							
1 Rush	N	N	Y	N	Y	Y	Y
2 Jackson	N	Y	Y	N	Y	Y	Y
3 Lipinski	?	?	?	?	?	?	?
4 Gutierrez	N	Y	?	N	Y	Y	Y
5 Blagojevich	N	Y	Y	N	Y	Y	Y
6 ***Hyde***	N	Y	N	Y	Y	N	Y
7 Davis	N	Y	Y	N	Y	Y	Y
8 ***Crane***	Y	Y	N	Y	Y	N	Y
9 Schakowsky	N	Y	Y	N	Y	Y	N
10 ***Porter***	N	Y	?	Y	Y	N	Y
11 ***Weller***	Y	Y	N	Y	Y	N	Y
12 Costello	N	Y	N	N	Y	Y	N
13 ***Biggert***	Y	Y	N	N	Y	N	Y
14 ***Hastert***						N	Y

ND Northern Democrats SD Southern Democrats

	270	271	272	273	274	275	276
15 ***Ewing***	N	Y	N	Y	Y	N	Y
16 ***Manzullo***	N	Y	N	N	Y	N	Y
17 Evans	N	Y	Y	N	Y	Y	N
18 ***LaHood***	N	Y	N	Y	Y	N	N
19 Phelps	N	Y	N	N	Y	Y	N
20 ***Shimkus***	N	Y	N	Y	Y	N	Y
INDIANA							
1 Visclosky	N	Y	Y	N	Y	Y	Y
2 ***McIntosh***	Y	Y	N	Y	Y	N	Y
3 Roemer	N	Y	Y	N	Y	Y	Y
4 ***Souder***	N	Y	N	Y	Y	N	Y
5 ***Buyer***	Y	Y	N	Y	Y	N	Y
6 ***Burton***	Y	Y	N	Y	Y	N	Y
7 ***Pease***	N	Y	N	Y	Y	N	Y
8 ***Hostettler***	Y	Y	N	Y	Y	N	Y
9 Hill	N	Y	Y	N	Y	Y	Y
10 Carson	N	Y	Y	N	Y	Y	Y
IOWA							
1 ***Leach***	Y	Y	N	N	Y	N	Y
2 ***Nussle***	Y	Y	?	N	Y	N	Y
3 Boswell	Y	Y	N	N	Y	Y	Y
4 ***Ganske***	N	Y	N	Y	Y	N	Y
5 ***Latham***	Y	Y	N	Y	Y	N	Y
KANSAS							
1 ***Moran***	N	Y	N	Y	Y	N	N
2 ***Ryun***	Y	Y	N	N	Y	N	Y
3 Moore	N	Y	Y	N	Y	Y	Y
4 ***Tiahrt***	Y	Y	N	Y	Y	N	Y
KENTUCKY							
1 ***Whitfield***	N	Y	N	Y	Y	N	Y
2 ***Lewis***	Y	Y	N	Y	Y	N	Y
3 ***Northup***	N	Y	N	Y	Y	N	Y
4 Lucas	N	Y	Y	Y	Y	N	Y
5 ***Rogers***	Y	Y	N	Y	Y	N	Y
6 ***Fletcher***	Y	Y	N	Y	Y	N	Y
LOUISIANA							
1 ***Vitter***	N	Y	N	Y	Y	N	Y
2 Jefferson	N	Y	Y	N	Y	Y	Y
3 ***Tauzin***	N	Y	N	Y	Y	N	Y
4 ***McCrery***	Y	Y	N	Y	Y	N	Y
5 ***Cooksey***	N	Y	N	Y	Y	N	Y
6 ***Baker***	Y	Y	N	Y	Y	N	Y
7 John	N	Y	Y	Y	Y	Y	Y
MAINE							
1 Allen	N	Y	Y	N	Y	Y	Y
2 Baldacci	N	Y	?	N	Y	Y	Y
MARYLAND							
1 ***Gilchrest***	Y	Y	N	N	Y	N	Y
2 ***Ehrlich***	N	Y	N	Y	Y	N	Y
3 Cardin	N	Y	Y	N	Y	Y	Y
4 Wynn	N	N	N	N	Y	Y	Y
5 Hoyer	N	Y	Y	N	Y	Y	Y
6 ***Bartlett***	Y	Y	N	Y	Y	N	Y
7 Cummings	N	Y	Y	N	Y	Y	N
8 ***Morella***	Y	Y	N	N	Y	N	Y
MASSACHUSETTS							
1 Olver	N	Y	Y	N	Y	Y	N
2 Neal	N	Y	Y	N	Y	Y	Y
3 McGovern	Y	Y	Y	N	Y	Y	Y
4 Frank	N	Y	Y	N	Y	Y	N
5 Meehan	N	Y	Y	N	Y	Y	N
6 Tierney	N	Y	Y	N	Y	Y	N
7 Markey	N	N	Y	N	Y	Y	N
8 Capuano	N	Y	Y	N	Y	Y	N
9 Moakley	N	Y	Y	N	Y	Y	Y
10 Delahunt	N	Y	Y	N	Y	Y	N
MICHIGAN							
1 Stupak	N	Y	Y	N	Y	Y	N
2 ***Hoekstra***	Y	Y	N	Y	Y	N	N
3 ***Ehlers***	N	Y	N	Y	Y	N	Y
4 ***Camp***	N	Y	N	Y	Y	N	Y
5 Barcia	N	Y	Y	N	Y	Y	Y
6 ***Upton***	Y	Y	N	Y	Y	N	Y
7 ***Smith***	Y	Y	N	Y	Y	N	Y
8 Stabenow	N	Y	Y	N	Y	Y	Y
9 Kildee	N	Y	Y	Y	Y	Y	Y
10 Bonior	N	Y	Y	N	Y	Y	Y
11 ***Knollenberg***	N	Y	N	Y	Y	N	Y
12 Levin	N	N	Y	N	Y	Y	Y
13 Rivers	N	N	Y	N	Y	Y	N
14 Conyers	N	Y	Y	N	Y	Y	N
15 Kilpatrick	N	Y	Y	N	Y	Y	Y
16 Dingell	N	N	N	Y	Y	Y	N
MINNESOTA							
1 ***Gutknecht***	Y	Y	N	Y	Y	N	Y
2 Minge	N	Y	N	N	Y	Y	Y
3 ***Ramstad***	N	Y	N	Y	Y	N	Y
4 Vento	N	Y	Y	N	Y	Y	Y
5 Sabo	N	Y	Y	N	Y	Y	Y
6 Luther	N	N	Y	N	Y	Y	N
7 Peterson	Y	Y	Y	N	Y	N	N
8 Oberstar	N	Y	Y	N	Y	Y	Y
MISSISSIPPI							
1 ***Wicker***	Y	Y	N	Y	Y	N	Y
2 Thompson	N	Y	Y	N	Y	Y	Y
3 ***Pickering***	N	Y	N	Y	Y	N	Y
4 Shows	N	Y	Y	Y	Y	Y	Y
5 Taylor	N	Y	Y	N	Y	Y	N
MISSOURI							
1 Clay	N	Y	?	N	Y	Y	N
2 ***Talent***	N	Y	N	Y	Y	N	Y
3 Gephardt	N	Y	Y	N	Y	Y	Y
4 Skelton	N	Y	N	N	Y	Y	Y
5 McCarthy	N	N	Y	N	Y	Y	N
6 Danner	N	Y	Y	Y	Y	Y	Y
7 ***Blunt***	Y	Y	N	Y	Y	N	Y
8 ***Emerson***	N	Y	N	Y	Y	N	Y
9 ***Hulshof***	N	Y	N	Y	Y	N	Y
MONTANA							
AL ***Hill***	Y	N	N	Y	Y	N	Y
NEBRASKA							
1 ***Bereuter***	N	Y	N	N	Y	N	Y
2 ***Terry***	Y	Y	N	Y	Y	N	Y
3 ***Barrett***	N	Y	N	Y	Y	N	Y
NEVADA							
1 Berkley	N	Y	Y	N	Y	Y	Y
2 ***Gibbons***	Y	Y	N	N	Y	N	Y
NEW HAMPSHIRE							
1 ***Sununu***	Y	Y	N	Y	Y	N	Y
2 ***Bass***	N	Y	N	Y	Y	N	Y
NEW JERSEY							
1 Andrews	N	Y	Y	N	Y	Y	Y
2 ***LoBiondo***	N	Y	N	Y	Y	N	Y
3 ***Saxton***	N	Y	N	Y	Y	N	Y
4 ***Smith***	N	Y	N	Y	Y	N	Y
5 ***Roukema***	N	Y	N	Y	Y	N	Y
6 Pallone	N	N	Y	Y	Y	Y	Y
7 ***Franks***	N	Y	N	Y	Y	N	Y
8 Pascrell	N	Y	Y	N	Y	Y	Y
9 Rothman	N	Y	N	N	Y	Y	Y
10 Payne	N	Y	Y	N	Y	Y	N
11 ***Frelinghuysen***	N	Y	N	Y	Y	N	Y
12 Holt	N	Y	Y	N	Y	Y	Y
13 Menendez	N	Y	?	N	Y	Y	Y
NEW MEXICO							
1 ***Wilson***	N	Y	N	Y	Y	N	Y
2 ***Skeen***	N	Y	N	Y	Y	N	Y
3 Udall	N	Y	Y	N	Y	Y	Y
NEW YORK							
1 ***Forbes***	N	Y	N	Y	Y	N	Y
2 ***Lazio***	N	Y	N	Y	Y	N	Y
3 ***King***	N	Y	N	Y	Y	N	Y
4 McCarthy	N	Y	Y	N	Y	Y	Y
5 Ackerman	N	Y	Y	N	Y	Y	Y
6 Meeks	N	Y	Y	N	Y	Y	Y
7 Crowley	N	Y	Y	N	Y	Y	Y
8 Nadler	Y	Y	Y	N	Y	Y	N
9 Weiner	N	Y	Y	N	Y	Y	Y
10 Towns	N	N	Y	Y	Y	Y	Y
11 Owens	N	Y	Y	N	Y	Y	Y
12 Velázquez	N	Y	Y	N	Y	Y	Y
13 ***Fossella***	?	?	?	?	?	?	?
14 Maloney	Y	Y	Y	N	Y	Y	Y
15 Rangel	N	N	Y	N	Y	Y	Y
16 Serrano	N	Y	Y	N	Y	Y	N
17 Engel	Y	N	Y	N	Y	Y	Y
18 Lowey	N	Y	Y	N	Y	Y	Y
19 ***Kelly***	N	Y	N	Y	Y	N	Y
20 ***Gilman***	N	Y	N	N	Y	N	Y
21 McNulty	Y	Y	Y	N	Y	Y	Y
22 ***Sweeney***	Y	Y	N	N	Y	N	Y
23 ***Boehlert***	N	Y	N	N	Y	N	Y
24 ***McHugh***	N	Y	N	N	Y	N	Y
25 ***Walsh***	N	Y	N	N	?	N	Y
26 Hinchey	N	Y	Y	N	Y	Y	N
27 ***Reynolds***	N	Y	N	Y	Y	N	Y
28 Slaughter	Y	Y	Y	N	Y	Y	Y
29 LaFalce	N	Y	Y	N	Y	Y	Y
30 ***Quinn***	N	Y	N	Y	Y	N	Y
31 ***Houghton***	N	Y	N	Y	Y	N	Y
NORTH CAROLINA							
1 Clayton	N	Y	Y	N	Y	Y	Y
2 Etheridge	N	Y	Y	N	Y	Y	Y
3 ***Jones***	N	Y	N	N	Y	N	Y
4 Price	N	Y	Y	N	Y	Y	Y
5 ***Burr***	N	Y	N	Y	Y	N	Y
6 ***Coble***	N	Y	N	Y	Y	N	Y
7 McIntyre	N	Y	Y	Y	Y	Y	Y
8 ***Hayes***	Y	Y	N	Y	Y	N	Y
9 ***Myrick***	Y	Y	N	Y	Y	N	Y
10 ***Ballenger***	N	Y	N	Y	Y	N	Y
11 ***Taylor***	Y	Y	N	Y	Y	N	Y
12 Watt	N	Y	Y	N	Y	Y	Y
NORTH DAKOTA							
AL Pomeroy	N	Y	Y	N	Y	Y	Y
OHIO							
1 ***Chabot***	N	Y	N	Y	Y	N	Y
2 ***Portman***	N	Y	N	Y	Y	N	Y
3 Hall	N	Y	Y	Y	Y	Y	Y
4 ***Oxley***	N	Y	N	Y	Y	N	Y
5 ***Gillmor***	N	Y	N	Y	Y	N	Y
6 Strickland	N	Y	Y	Y	Y	Y	Y
7 ***Hobson***	N	Y	N	Y	Y	N	Y
8 ***Boehner***	Y	Y	N	Y	Y	N	Y
9 Kaptur	N	Y	Y	N	Y	Y	N
10 Kucinich	N	Y	Y	N	Y	Y	N
11 Jones	N	Y	Y	N	Y	Y	Y
12 ***Kasich***	N	Y	N	Y	Y	N	Y
13 Brown	N	Y	Y	Y	Y	Y	N
14 Sawyer	N	Y	?	N	Y	Y	Y
15 ***Pryce***	N	Y	N	Y	Y	N	Y
16 ***Regula***	N	Y	N	Y	Y	N	Y
17 Traficant	N	Y	N	Y	Y	Y	Y
18 ***Ney***	N	Y	N	Y	Y	N	Y
19 ***LaTourette***	N	Y	N	Y	Y	N	Y
OKLAHOMA							
1 ***Largent***	N	Y	N	Y	Y	N	Y
2 ***Coburn***	Y	Y	N	Y	Y	N	N
3 ***Watkins***	N	Y	N	Y	Y	N	Y
4 ***Watts***	N	Y	N	Y	Y	N	Y
5 ***Istook***	N	Y	N	Y	Y	N	Y
6 ***Lucas***	N	Y	N	Y	Y	N	Y
OREGON							
1 Wu	N	Y	Y	N	Y	Y	Y
2 ***Walden***	Y	Y	N	Y	Y	N	Y
3 Blumenauer	N	Y	Y	N	Y	Y	Y
4 DeFazio	N	Y	Y	N	Y	Y	N
5 Hooley	N	Y	Y	N	Y	Y	Y
PENNSYLVANIA							
1 Brady	N	Y	Y	N	Y	Y	N
2 Fattah	N	Y	Y	N	Y	Y	N
3 Borski	?	?	?	N	Y	Y	Y
4 Klink	N	Y	Y	N	Y	Y	Y
5 ***Peterson***	N	Y	N	Y	Y	N	Y
6 Holden	N	Y	?	N	Y	Y	Y
7 ***Weldon***	N	Y	N	Y	Y	N	Y
8 ***Greenwood***	Y	Y	N	Y	Y	N	Y
9 ***Shuster***	Y	Y	N	Y	Y	N	Y
10 ***Sherwood***	N	Y	N	Y	Y	N	Y
11 Kanjorski	N	Y	Y	N	Y	Y	Y
12 Murtha	N	Y	Y	N	Y	Y	Y
13 Hoeffel	N	Y	Y	N	Y	Y	Y
14 Coyne	N	Y	Y	N	Y	Y	N
15 ***Toomey***	Y	Y	N	Y	Y	N	Y
16 ***Pitts***	N	Y	N	Y	Y	N	Y
17 ***Gekas***	N	Y	N	Y	Y	N	Y
18 Doyle	N	Y	?	N	Y	Y	Y
19 ***Goodling***	Y	Y	N	Y	Y	N	Y
20 Mascara	N	Y	Y	N	Y	Y	Y
21 ***English***	Y	Y	N	Y	Y	N	Y
RHODE ISLAND							
1 Kennedy	N	Y	Y	N	Y	Y	Y
2 Weygand	N	Y	Y	N	Y	Y	Y
SOUTH CAROLINA							
1 ***Sanford***	Y	Y	N	Y	Y	N	Y
2 ***Spence***	Y	Y	N	Y	Y	N	Y
3 ***Graham***	N	Y	N	Y	Y	N	Y
4 ***DeMint***	Y	Y	N	Y	Y	N	Y
5 Spratt	N	Y	Y	N	Y	Y	Y
6 Clyburn	N	Y	Y	N	Y	Y	Y
SOUTH DAKOTA							
AL ***Thune***	Y	Y	N	Y	Y	N	Y
TENNESSEE							
1 ***Jenkins***	Y	Y	N	Y	Y	N	Y
2 ***Duncan***	Y	Y	N	Y	Y	N	Y
3 ***Wamp***	N	Y	N	Y	Y	N	Y
4 ***Hilleary***	Y	Y	N	Y	Y	N	Y
5 Clement	N	Y	Y	N	Y	Y	Y
6 Gordon	N	Y	Y	N	Y	Y	Y
7 ***Bryant***	N	Y	N	Y	Y	N	Y
8 Tanner	N	Y	Y	N	Y	Y	Y
9 Ford	N	Y	N	N	Y	Y	Y
TEXAS							
1 Sandlin	N	Y	Y	N	Y	Y	Y
2 Turner	N	Y	Y	N	Y	Y	N
3 ***Johnson, Sam***	N	Y	N	Y	Y	N	Y
4 Hall	Y	Y	N	Y	Y	N	Y
5 ***Sessions***	Y	Y	N	Y	Y	N	Y
6 ***Barton***	N	Y	?	Y	Y	N	N
7 ***Archer***	Y	Y	N	Y	Y	N	?
8 ***Brady***	N	Y	N	Y	Y	N	N
9 Lampson	N	Y	Y	N	Y	Y	N
10 Doggett	N	Y	Y	N	Y	Y	Y
11 Edwards	N	Y	Y	N	Y	Y	N
12 ***Granger***	N	Y	N	Y	Y	N	N
13 ***Thornberry***	Y	Y	N	Y	Y	N	N
14 ***Paul***	Y	Y	N	N	N	N	N
15 Hinojosa	N	Y	Y	N	Y	Y	Y
16 Reyes	N	Y	Y	N	Y	Y	Y
17 Stenholm	N	Y	Y	N	Y	Y	N
18 Jackson-Lee	N	Y	Y	N	Y	Y	Y
19 ***Combest***	N	Y	?	Y	Y	N	N
20 Gonzalez	N	Y	Y	N	Y	Y	Y
21 ***Smith***	N	Y	N	Y	Y	N	Y
22 ***DeLay***	Y	Y	N	Y	Y	N	Y
23 ***Bonilla***	Y	Y	N	Y	Y	N	N
24 Frost	N	Y	Y	N	Y	Y	Y
25 Bentsen	Y	Y	Y	N	Y	Y	Y
26 ***Armey***	Y	Y	N	Y	Y	N	Y
27 Ortiz	N	Y	Y	N	Y	Y	N
28 Rodriguez	N	Y	Y	N	Y	Y	N
29 Green	?	?	?	?	?	?	?
30 Johnson, E.B.	N	Y	Y	N	Y	Y	Y
UTAH							
1 ***Hansen***	Y	Y	N	Y	Y	N	Y
2 ***Cook***	Y	Y	N	Y	Y	N	Y
3 ***Cannon***	Y	Y	N	Y	Y	N	Y
VERMONT							
AL *Sanders*	N	Y	Y	N	Y	Y	N
VIRGINIA							
1 ***Bateman***	N	Y	N	Y	Y	N	Y
2 Pickett	N	Y	Y	N	Y	N	Y
3 Scott	N	Y	Y	N	Y	Y	Y
4 Sisisky	N	Y	N	Y	Y	Y	Y
5 Goode	N	Y	N	Y	Y	N	Y
6 ***Goodlatte***	N	Y	N	Y	Y	N	Y
7 ***Bliley***	N	Y	N	Y	Y	N	Y
8 Moran	N	Y	Y	N	Y	Y	Y
9 Boucher	N	Y	Y	Y	Y	Y	Y
10 ***Wolf***	N	Y	N	Y	Y	N	Y
11 ***Davis***	Y	Y	N	Y	Y	N	Y
WASHINGTON							
1 Inslee	N	Y	Y	Y	Y	Y	N
2 ***Metcalf***	Y	Y	N	Y	Y	N	Y
3 Baird	N	Y	Y	N	Y	Y	Y
4 ***Hastings***	Y	Y	N	Y	Y	N	Y
5 ***Nethercutt***	Y	Y	N	Y	Y	N	Y
6 Dicks	N	Y	?	N	Y	Y	Y
7 McDermott	N	Y	Y	N	Y	Y	N
8 ***Dunn***	Y	Y	N	Y	Y	N	Y
9 Smith	N	Y	Y	N	Y	Y	Y
WEST VIRGINIA							
1 Mollohan	N	Y	Y	N	Y	N	Y
2 Wise	N	Y	N	N	Y	N	Y
3 Rahall	N	Y	N	N	Y	Y	Y
WISCONSIN							
1 ***Ryan***	Y	Y	N	Y	Y	N	Y
2 Baldwin	N	Y	Y	N	Y	Y	N
3 Kind	N	Y	Y	N	Y	Y	Y
4 Kleczka	N	Y	N	N	Y	Y	N
5 Barrett	N	Y	Y	N	Y	Y	N
6 ***Petri***	N	Y	N	Y	Y	N	Y
7 Obey	N	Y	Y	N	Y	Y	N
8 ***Green***	N	Y	N	Y	Y	N	Y
9 ***Sensenbrenner***	N	Y	N	Y	Y	N	Y
WYOMING							
AL ***Cubin***	Y	Y	N	Y	Y	N	Y

Southern states - Ala., Ark., Fla., Ga., Ky., La., Miss., N.C., Okla., S.C., Tenn., Texas, Va.

277. Procedural Motion/Journal. Approval of the House Journal of Thursday, July 1, 1999. Approved 329-36: R 182-11; D 146-25 (ND 108-19, SD 38-6); I 1-0. July 12, 1999.

278. H Con Res 107. Child Sexuality Report/Adoption. Salmon, R-Ariz., motion to suspend the rules and adopt the concurrent resolution to express the sense of Congress rejecting the conclusions of a recent article published by the American Psychological Association suggesting that sexual relationships between adults and children might be positive for children. Motion agreed to 355-0: R 192-0; D 162-0 (ND 121-0, SD 41-0); I 1-0. July 12, 1999. A two-thirds majority of those present and voting (237 in this case) is required for adoption under suspension of the rules.

279. H Con Res 117. U.N. Resolution/Adoption. Salmon, R-Ariz., motion to suspend the rules and adopt the concurrent resolution criticizing U.N. Resolution ES10/6, adopted Feb. 9, which called for the convening on July 15 of the Fourth Geneva Convention for protecting civilians in time of war to condemn Israeli housing construction in East Jerusalem. Motion agreed to 365-5: R 194-1; D 170-4 (ND 126-4, SD 44-0); I 1-0. July 12, 1999. A two-thirds majority of those present and voting (247 in this case) is required for adoption under suspension of the rules.

280. HR 2465. Fiscal 2000 Military Construction Appropriations/Passage. Passage of the bill to provide $8.5 billion in fiscal 2000 for military construction spending. The bill includes $4.6 billion for military construction, $3.6 billion for family housing and $706 million for base closing costs. Passed 418-4: R 215-3; D 202-1 (ND 150-1, SD 52-0); I 1-0. July 13, 1999.)

281. HR 2466. Fiscal 2000 Interior Appropriations/Conservation Fund. McGovern, D-Mass., amendment to appropriate $30 million for the state-side matching grant program of the Land and Water Conservation Fund. The increase would be offset by reducing funding for Energy Department fossil energy research and development and for the Bureau of Land Management transportation facilities and management. Adopted 213-202: R 55-157; D 157-45 (ND 124-26, SD 33-19); I 1-0. July 13, 1999.

282. HR 2466. Fiscal 2000 Interior Appropriations/Payments in Lieu of Taxes. Sanders, I-Vt., amendment to increase funding for payments to localities in lieu of taxes on federal lands by $20 million, to $145 million; to reduce the debt by $30 million; and to reduce funding for fossil energy research and development programs by $50 million. Adopted 248-169: R 119-94; D 128-75 (ND 103-48, SD 25-27); I 1-0. July 13, 1999.

283. HR 2466. Fiscal 2000 Interior Appropriations/Wildlife Service. Coburn, R-Okla., amendment to reduce funding for the U.S. Fish and Wildlife Service by $2 million to $708 million. Rejected 131-287: R 118-96; D 13-190 (ND 7-144, SD 6-46); I 0-1. July 13, 1999.

284. HR 2466. Fiscal 2000 Interior Appropriations/Weatherization. Sanders, I-Vt., amendment to increase funding by $13 million, to $113 million, for the low-income weatherization program, and reduce funding for the Strategic Petroleum Reserve by a like amount. Adopted 243-180: R 55-165; D 187-15 (ND 144-4, SD 43-11); I 1-0. July 14, 1999.

Key

- Y Voted for (yea).
- # Paired for.
- + Announced for.
- N Voted against (nay).
- X Paired against.
- – Announced against.
- P Voted "present."
- C Voted "present" to avoid possible conflict of interest.
- ? Did not vote or otherwise make a position known.

•

Democrats ***Republicans***
Independents

	277	278	279	280	281	282	283	284
ALABAMA								
1 ***Callahan***	Y	Y	Y	Y	N	N	Y	N
2 ***Everett***	Y	Y	Y	Y	N	Y	Y	N
3 ***Riley***	Y	Y	Y	Y	N	N	Y	N
4 ***Aderholt***	N	Y	Y	Y	N	N	Y	N
5 Cramer	Y	Y	Y	Y	N	N	N	N
6 ***Bachus***	Y	Y	Y	Y	N	N	Y	N
7 Hilliard	N	Y	Y	Y	N	N	N	Y
ALASKA								
AL ***Young***	Y	Y	Y	Y	N	Y	Y	N
ARIZONA								
1 ***Salmon***	Y	Y	Y	Y	N	Y	Y	N
2 Pastor	Y	Y	Y	Y	Y	Y	N	Y
3 ***Stump***	Y	Y	Y	Y	N	Y	Y	N
4 ***Shadegg***	Y	Y	Y	Y	N	Y	Y	N
5 ***Kolbe***	+	+	+	Y	N	Y	N	N
6 ***Hayworth***	Y	Y	Y	Y	Y	Y	Y	N
ARKANSAS								
1 Berry	Y	Y	Y	Y	N	Y	Y	Y
2 Snyder	Y	Y	Y	Y	Y	Y	N	Y
3 ***Hutchinson***	Y	Y	Y	Y	N	Y	Y	N
4 ***Dickey***	Y	Y	?	Y	N	N	Y	N
CALIFORNIA								
1 Thompson	N	Y	Y	Y	?	Y	N	Y
2 ***Herger***	Y	Y	Y	Y	N	Y	Y	N
3 ***Ose***	Y	Y	Y	Y	N	N	N	N
4 ***Doolittle***	?	?	Y	Y	N	Y	Y	N
5 Matsui	Y	Y	Y	Y	Y	Y	N	Y
6 Woolsey	Y	Y	Y	Y	Y	Y	N	Y
7 Miller, George	N	Y	?	Y	Y	N	N	Y
8 Pelosi	Y	Y	Y	Y	Y	N	N	Y
9 Lee	Y	Y	Y	Y	Y	N	N	Y
10 Tauscher	Y	Y	Y	Y	Y	N	N	Y
11 ***Pombo***	Y	Y	Y	Y	N	Y	Y	N
12 Lantos	?	?	?	Y	Y	N	N	Y
13 Stark	?	P	Y	N	Y	N	N	Y
14 Eshoo	Y	Y	Y	Y	Y	N	N	Y
15 ***Campbell***	Y	Y	Y	Y	Y	Y	Y	N
16 Lofgren	Y	Y	Y	Y	Y	N	N	Y
17 Farr	Y	Y	Y	Y	Y	Y	N	Y
18 Condit	Y	Y	Y	Y	Y	Y	N	Y
19 ***Radanovich***	Y	Y	Y	Y	N	Y	Y	N
20 Dooley	Y	Y	Y	Y	N	Y	N	Y
21 ***Thomas***	Y	Y	Y	Y	N	N	N	N
22 Capps	Y	Y	Y	Y	Y	Y	N	Y
23 ***Gallegly***	Y	Y	Y	Y	Y	N	N	Y
24 Sherman	Y	Y	Y	Y	Y	Y	N	Y
25 ***McKeon***	Y	Y	Y	Y	N	Y	N	N
26 Berman	Y	Y	Y	Y	Y	Y	N	Y
27 ***Rogan***	Y	Y	Y	Y	Y	N	Y	N
28 ***Dreier***	Y	Y	Y	Y	N	Y	N	N
29 Waxman	Y	Y	Y	Y	Y	Y	N	Y
30 Becerra	Y	Y	Y	Y	Y	Y	N	Y
31 Martinez	Y	Y	Y	Y	N	Y	N	Y
32 Dixon	Y	Y	Y	Y	Y	Y	N	Y
33 Roybal-Allard	Y	Y	Y	Y	Y	Y	N	Y
34 Napolitano	Y	Y	Y	Y	Y	Y	N	Y
35 Waters	?	?	Y	Y	Y	Y	N	Y
36 ***Kuykendall***	Y	Y	Y	Y	Y	+	–	Y
37 Millender-McD.	+	?	+	Y	Y	Y	N	Y
38 ***Horn***	Y	Y	Y	Y	N	N	N	N
39 ***Royce***	?	?	?	N	N	Y	Y	N
40 ***Lewis***	Y	Y	Y	Y	N	N	N	?
41 ***Miller, Gary***	+	+	+	Y	N	N	Y	N
42 Brown	?	?	?	?	?	?	?	?
43 ***Calvert***	Y	Y	Y	Y	N	N	N	N
44 ***Bono***	?	?	?	Y	N	N	N	N
45 ***Rohrabacher***	Y	Y	Y	Y	N	Y	Y	N
46 Sanchez	Y	Y	Y	Y	Y	N	N	Y
47 ***Cox***	Y	Y	Y	Y	?	Y	Y	N
48 ***Packard***	Y	Y	Y	Y	N	N	N	N
49 ***Bilbray***	?	?	?	Y	Y	Y	Y	N
50 Filner	N	P	Y	Y	Y	Y	N	Y
51 ***Cunningham***	Y	Y	Y	Y	N	Y	Y	N
52 ***Hunter***	Y	Y	Y	Y	N	N	Y	N
COLORADO								
1 DeGette	?	?	?	Y	Y	Y	N	Y
2 Udall	Y	Y	Y	Y	Y	Y	N	Y
3 ***McInnis***	Y	Y	Y	Y	Y	Y	N	N
4 ***Schaffer***	N	Y	Y	Y	N	Y	Y	N
5 ***Hefley***	N	Y	Y	Y	N	Y	Y	N
6 ***Tancredo***	P	Y	Y	Y	N	Y	Y	N
CONNECTICUT								
1 Larson	Y	Y	Y	Y	Y	N	N	Y
2 Gejdenson	Y	Y	Y	?	Y	N	N	Y
3 DeLauro	Y	Y	Y	Y	Y	Y	N	Y
4 ***Shays***	Y	Y	Y	Y	Y	Y	N	Y
5 Maloney	Y	Y	Y	Y	N	N	N	Y
6 ***Johnson***	Y	Y	Y	Y	N	Y	N	Y
DELAWARE								
AL ***Castle***	Y	Y	Y	Y	Y	Y	N	N
FLORIDA								
1 ***Scarborough***	Y	Y	Y	?	?	?	?	N
2 Boyd	Y	Y	Y	Y	N	Y	N	Y
3 Brown	Y	Y	Y	Y	Y	Y	N	Y
4 ***Fowler***	Y	Y	Y	Y	Y	N	N	N
5 Thurman	?	?	?	?	?	?	?	?
6 ***Stearns***	Y	Y	Y	Y	N	Y	Y	N
7 ***Mica***	Y	Y	Y	Y	N	N	Y	Y
8 ***McCollum***	Y	Y	Y	Y	N	Y	N	N
9 ***Bilirakis***	Y	Y	Y	Y	N	N	N	N
10 ***Young***	Y	Y	Y	Y	N	N	N	N
11 Davis	Y	Y	Y	Y	Y	Y	N	Y
12 ***Canady***	Y	Y	Y	Y	N	Y	N	N
13 ***Miller***	Y	Y	Y	Y	N	Y	N	N
14 ***Goss***	Y	Y	Y	Y	Y	Y	N	N
15 ***Weldon***	Y	?	Y	Y	N	Y	Y	N
16 ***Foley***	Y	Y	Y	Y	Y	Y	Y	Y
17 Meek	Y	Y	Y	?	?	?	?	Y
18 ***Ros-Lehtinen***	Y	Y	Y	Y	N	N	N	N
19 Wexler	Y	Y	Y	Y	Y	Y	N	Y
20 Deutsch	Y	Y	Y	Y	Y	Y	N	Y
21 ***Diaz-Balart***	Y	Y	Y	Y	N	N	N	N
22 ***Shaw***	Y	Y	Y	Y	N	N	N	N
23 Hastings	N	P	Y	?	?	?	?	Y
GEORGIA								
1 ***Kingston***	Y	Y	Y	Y	N	N	N	N
2 Bishop	?	?	?	Y	Y	Y	N	Y
3 ***Collins***	Y	Y	Y	Y	Y	Y	Y	N
4 McKinney	Y	Y	Y	Y	Y	Y	N	Y
5 Lewis	Y	Y	Y	Y	Y	Y	N	Y
6 ***Isakson***	?	+	+	Y	N	Y	Y	N
7 ***Barr***	?	?	?	Y	N	Y	Y	N
8 ***Chambliss***	Y	Y	Y	Y	N	Y	Y	N
9 ***Deal***	Y	Y	Y	Y	N	Y	Y	N
10 ***Norwood***	Y	Y	Y	N	N	Y	Y	N
11 ***Linder***	Y	Y	Y	Y	N	Y	Y	N
HAWAII								
1 Abercrombie	Y	P	Y	Y	Y	Y	N	Y
2 Mink	Y	P	Y	Y	Y	Y	N	Y
IDAHO								
1 ***Chenoweth***	?	?	?	?	?	Y	Y	N
2 ***Simpson***	?	?	?	Y	–	+	N	N
ILLINOIS								
1 Rush	?	?	?	Y	Y	Y	N	Y
2 Jackson	Y	Y	Y	Y	Y	Y	N	Y
3 Lipinski	Y	Y	Y	Y	N	Y	N	Y
4 Gutierrez	N	Y	Y	Y	Y	Y	N	Y
5 Blagojevich	?	Y	Y	Y	Y	N	N	Y
6 ***Hyde***	Y	Y	Y	Y	N	N	N	N
7 Davis	Y	Y	Y	Y	Y	Y	N	Y
8 ***Crane***	Y	Y	Y	Y	N	Y	Y	N
9 Schakowsky	P	Y	Y	Y	Y	N	N	Y
10 ***Porter***	Y	Y	Y	Y	Y	N	N	N
11 ***Weller***	N	Y	Y	Y	N	N	Y	Y
12 Costello	N	Y	Y	Y	N	N	N	Y
13 ***Biggert***	Y	Y	Y	Y	Y	N	Y	N
14 ***Hastert***				Y				

ND Northern Democrats SD Southern Democrats

	277	278	279	280	281	282	283	284
15 ***Ewing***	Y	Y	Y	Y	N	N	N	N
16 ***Manzullo***	Y	Y	Y	Y	N	Y	Y	N
17 Evans	N	Y	Y	Y	Y	Y	N	Y
18 ***LaHood***	Y	Y	Y	Y	N	N	Y	Y
19 Phelps	Y	Y	Y	Y	N	N	N	Y
20 ***Shimkus***	Y	Y	Y	Y	N	N	N	Y
INDIANA								
1 Visclosky	N	Y	Y	Y	Y	Y	N	Y
2 ***McIntosh***	?	?	?	Y	N	Y	Y	N
3 Roemer	Y	Y	Y	Y	Y	Y	N	Y
4 ***Souder***	Y	Y	Y	Y	N	N	Y	N
5 ***Buyer***	Y	Y	Y	Y	N	Y	Y	N
6 ***Burton***	Y	Y	Y	Y	N	N	Y	N
7 ***Pease***	Y	Y	Y	Y	Y	N	N	N
8 ***Hostettler***	Y	Y	Y	Y	N	Y	Y	N
9 Hill	Y	Y	Y	Y	N	N	N	Y
10 Carson	Y	Y	Y	Y	Y	Y	N	Y
IOWA								
1 ***Leach***	Y	Y	Y	Y	Y	N	N	Y
2 ***Nussle***	Y	Y	Y	Y	N	N	N	N
3 Boswell	Y	Y	Y	Y	N	N	N	Y
4 ***Ganske***	Y	Y	Y	Y	N	N	N	N
5 ***Latham***	Y	Y	Y	Y	N	N	N	N
KANSAS								
1 ***Moran***	N	Y	Y	Y	Y	N	Y	N
2 ***Ryun***	Y	Y	Y	Y	N	N	Y	N
3 Moore	Y	Y	Y	Y	Y	Y	N	N
4 ***Tiahrt***	Y	Y	Y	Y	N	N	Y	N
KENTUCKY								
1 ***Whitfield***	Y	Y	Y	Y	N	N	N	Y
2 ***Lewis***	Y	Y	Y	Y	N	Y	N	N
3 ***Northup***	Y	+	Y	Y	N	N	N	N
4 Lucas	Y	Y	Y	Y	N	N	Y	Y
5 ***Rogers***	+	+	+	Y	N	Y	N	N
6 ***Fletcher***	Y	+	Y	Y	N	Y	N	N
LOUISIANA								
1 ***Vitter***	Y	Y	Y	Y	N	N	N	N
2 Jefferson	?	?	?	Y	N	N	N	N
3 ***Tauzin***	Y	Y	Y	Y	?	?	?	N
4 ***McCrery***	Y	Y	Y	Y	N	N	N	N
5 ***Cooksey***	Y	Y	Y	Y	N	N	N	N
6 ***Baker***	?	?	?	Y	N	N	Y	N
7 John	Y	Y	Y	Y	N	N	N	N
MAINE								
1 Allen	Y	P	Y	Y	?	?	?	Y
2 Baldacci	Y	Y	Y	Y	Y	Y	Y	Y
MARYLAND								
1 ***Gilchrest***	Y	Y	Y	Y	Y	Y	N	N
2 ***Ehrlich***	Y	Y	Y	Y	Y	Y	Y	N
3 Cardin	Y	Y	Y	Y	Y	N	N	Y
4 Wynn	Y	Y	Y	Y	Y	Y	N	?
5 Hoyer	Y	Y	Y	Y	Y	N	N	N
6 ***Bartlett***	?	?	Y	Y	N	N	Y	Y
7 Cummings	Y	Y	Y	Y	Y	Y	N	Y
8 ***Morella***	Y	Y	Y	Y	Y	Y	N	Y
MASSACHUSETTS								
1 Olver	Y	Y	Y	Y	Y	Y	N	Y
2 Neal	Y	Y	Y	Y	Y	Y	N	Y
3 McGovern	Y	Y	Y	Y	Y	Y	N	Y
4 Frank	Y	P	Y	Y	Y	N	N	Y
5 Meehan	Y	Y	Y	Y	Y	Y	N	Y
6 Tierney	Y	Y	Y	Y	Y	N	N	Y
7 Markey	?	?	?	Y	Y	Y	N	Y
8 Capuano	Y	Y	Y	Y	Y	Y	N	Y
9 Moakley	Y	Y	Y	Y	Y	N	N	Y
10 Delahunt	Y	P	Y	Y	Y	Y	N	Y
MICHIGAN								
1 Stupak	N	Y	Y	Y	Y	Y	N	Y
2 ***Hoekstra***	Y	Y	Y	Y	N	Y	Y	N
3 ***Ehlers***	Y	Y	Y	Y	Y	N	N	Y
4 ***Camp***	Y	Y	Y	Y	N	N	N	N
5 Barcia	Y	Y	?	Y	N	Y	N	Y
6 ***Upton***	Y	Y	Y	Y	Y	N	Y	Y
7 ***Smith***	Y	Y	Y	Y	N	Y	Y	N
8 Stabenow	Y	Y	Y	Y	Y	Y	N	Y
9 Kildee	Y	Y	Y	Y	Y	Y	N	Y
10 Bonior	?	Y	N	Y	Y	Y	N	Y
11 ***Knollenberg***	Y	Y	Y	Y	N	N	N	N
12 Levin	Y	Y	Y	Y	Y	Y	N	Y
13 Rivers	Y	Y	Y	Y	?	?	?	?
14 Conyers	Y	P	N	Y	Y	Y	Y	Y
15 Kilpatrick	+	+	+	Y	Y	Y	N	Y
16 Dingell	Y	Y	N	Y	Y	Y	N	Y

	277	278	279	280	281	282	283	284
MINNESOTA								
1 ***Gutknecht***	N	Y	Y	Y	N	Y	Y	Y
2 Minge	Y	Y	Y	Y	Y	Y	N	Y
3 ***Ramstad***	Y	Y	Y	Y	Y	Y	Y	Y
4 Vento	Y	Y	Y	Y	Y	Y	N	Y
5 Sabo	N	Y	Y	Y	Y	N	N	Y
6 Luther	Y	Y	Y	Y	Y	Y	Y	Y
7 Peterson	N	Y	Y	Y	N	Y	N	Y
8 Oberstar	N	Y	Y	Y	N	Y	N	Y
MISSISSIPPI								
1 ***Wicker***	N	Y	Y	Y	N	N	N	N
2 Thompson	N	Y	Y	Y	Y	Y	N	Y
3 ***Pickering***	Y	Y	Y	Y	N	Y	Y	N
4 Shows	+	+	+	Y	Y	Y	N	N
5 Taylor	N	Y	Y	Y	Y	N	N	N
MISSOURI								
1 Clay	?	?	?	Y	Y	Y	N	Y
2 ***Talent***	Y	Y	Y	Y	Y	N	Y	Y
3 Gephardt	?	?	?	Y	Y	N	N	Y
4 Skelton	Y	Y	Y	Y	Y	Y	Y	Y
5 McCarthy	Y	Y	Y	Y	Y	Y	N	Y
6 Danner	?	?	?	Y	Y	Y	N	Y
7 ***Blunt***	Y	Y	Y	Y	N	N	N	N
8 ***Emerson***	Y	Y	Y	Y	N	Y	Y	Y
9 ***Hulshof***	?	?	?	Y	Y	Y	Y	Y
MONTANA								
AL ***Hill***	Y	Y	Y	Y	N	Y	Y	Y
NEBRASKA								
1 ***Bereuter***	Y	Y	Y	Y	Y	Y	N	N
2 ***Terry***	Y	Y	Y	Y	N	Y	Y	N
3 ***Barrett***	Y	Y	Y	Y	N	N	N	N
NEVADA								
1 Berkley	?	?	?	Y	Y	Y	N	Y
2 ***Gibbons***	N	Y	Y	Y	N	Y	Y	N
NEW HAMPSHIRE								
1 ***Sununu***	Y	Y	N	Y	?	?	?	Y
2 ***Bass***	Y	Y	Y	Y	Y	Y	Y	Y
NEW JERSEY								
1 Andrews	Y	Y	Y	Y	Y	Y	N	Y
2 ***LoBiondo***	N	Y	Y	Y	Y	Y	N	Y
3 ***Saxton***	Y	Y	Y	Y	Y	Y	N	Y
4 ***Smith***	Y	Y	Y	Y	Y	Y	N	Y
5 ***Roukema***	Y	Y	Y	Y	Y	Y	N	Y
6 Pallone	N	Y	Y	Y	Y	Y	N	Y
7 ***Franks***	Y	Y	Y	Y	Y	Y	N	Y
8 Pascrell	Y	Y	Y	Y	Y	Y	N	Y
9 Rothman	Y	Y	Y	Y	Y	Y	N	Y
10 Payne	?	?	?	Y	Y	Y	N	Y
11 ***Frelinghuysen***	Y	Y	Y	Y	Y	Y	N	Y
12 Holt	Y	Y	Y	Y	Y	Y	N	Y
13 Menendez	Y	Y	Y	Y	Y	Y	N	Y
NEW MEXICO								
1 ***Wilson***	Y	Y	Y	Y	N	N	N	N
2 ***Skeen***	Y	Y	Y	Y	N	Y	N	N
3 Udall	Y	Y	Y	Y	Y	Y	N	Y
NEW YORK								
1 ***Forbes***	Y	Y	Y	Y	Y	N	N	Y
2 ***Lazio***	Y	Y	Y	Y	Y	N	Y	Y
3 ***King***	Y	Y	Y	Y	Y	Y	N	N
4 McCarthy	Y	Y	Y	Y	Y	Y	N	?
5 Ackerman	Y	Y	Y	Y	Y	Y	N	Y
6 Meeks	Y	Y	Y	Y	Y	N	N	Y
7 Crowley	Y	Y	Y	Y	Y	Y	N	Y
8 Nadler	Y	Y	Y	Y	Y	Y	N	Y
9 Weiner	Y	Y	Y	Y	Y	Y	N	Y
10 Towns	?	?	?	Y	Y	Y	N	Y
11 Owens	Y	Y	Y	Y	Y	Y	N	Y
12 Velázquez	Y	Y	Y	Y	Y	Y	N	Y
13 ***Fossella***	Y	Y	Y	Y	Y	Y	Y	Y
14 Maloney	Y	Y	Y	Y	Y	Y	N	Y
15 Rangel	Y	Y	?	Y	Y	Y	N	Y
16 Serrano	?	?	?	Y	Y	Y	N	Y
17 Engel	?	?	?	Y	Y	Y	N	Y
18 Lowey	Y	Y	Y	Y	Y	N	N	Y
19 ***Kelly***	Y	Y	Y	Y	Y	Y	N	Y
20 ***Gilman***	Y	Y	Y	Y	Y	N	N	Y
21 McNulty	Y	Y	Y	Y	Y	Y	N	?
22 ***Sweeney***	Y	Y	Y	?	?	?	?	?
23 ***Boehlert***	?	?	?	Y	Y	Y	N	Y
24 ***McHugh***	Y	Y	Y	Y	Y	Y	Y	Y
25 ***Walsh***	Y	Y	Y	Y	Y	N	N	Y
26 Hinchey	N	Y	Y	Y	Y	N	N	Y
27 ***Reynolds***	Y	Y	Y	Y	Y	Y	N	Y
28 Slaughter	N	Y	Y	Y	Y	N	N	Y
29 LaFalce	N	Y	Y	Y	Y	Y	N	Y

	277	278	279	280	281	282	283	284
30 ***Quinn***	Y	Y	Y	Y	Y	Y	N	Y
31 ***Houghton***	Y	Y	Y	Y	Y	Y	N	Y
NORTH CAROLINA								
1 Clayton	Y	Y	Y	Y	Y	Y	N	Y
2 Etheridge	Y	Y	Y	Y	Y	Y	N	Y
3 ***Jones***	Y	Y	Y	Y	N	Y	Y	N
4 Price	Y	Y	Y	Y	Y	Y	N	Y
5 ***Burr***	Y	Y	Y	Y	N	N	Y	N
6 ***Coble***	Y	Y	Y	Y	N	Y	Y	N
7 McIntyre	Y	Y	Y	Y	Y	Y	N	Y
8 ***Hayes***	Y	Y	Y	Y	N	Y	Y	N
9 ***Myrick***	Y	Y	Y	Y	N	Y	Y	N
10 ***Ballenger***	Y	Y	Y	Y	N	Y	Y	N
11 ***Taylor***	?	?	?	Y	N	Y	Y	N
12 Watt	?	?	?	Y	Y	Y	N	Y
NORTH DAKOTA								
AL Pomeroy	?	?	?	Y	N	N	N	N
OHIO								
1 ***Chabot***	Y	Y	Y	Y	N	Y	Y	N
2 ***Portman***	Y	Y	Y	Y	N	Y	Y	N
3 Hall	Y	Y	Y	Y	Y	N	N	Y
4 ***Oxley***	Y	Y	Y	Y	N	N	N	N
5 ***Gillmor***	?	?	?	Y	N	N	N	Y
6 Strickland	Y	P	Y	Y	N	Y	N	Y
7 ***Hobson***	Y	Y	Y	Y	N	N	N	N
8 ***Boehner***	Y	Y	Y	Y	N	N	Y	N
9 Kaptur	?	?	?	Y	Y	Y	N	Y
10 Kucinich	N	Y	Y	Y	Y	N	N	Y
11 Jones	+	+	+	Y	Y	Y	N	Y
12 ***Kasich***	?	?	?	?	?	?	?	?
13 Brown	Y	Y	Y	Y	Y	Y	N	Y
14 Sawyer	Y	Y	Y	Y	Y	Y	N	Y
15 ***Pryce***	?	?	?	Y	N	N	N	N
16 ***Regula***	Y	Y	Y	Y	N	N	N	N
17 Traficant	Y	Y	Y	Y	N	N	N	Y
18 ***Ney***	Y	Y	Y	Y	N	N	N	Y
19 ***LaTourette***	Y	Y	Y	Y	N	Y	N	Y
OKLAHOMA								
1 ***Largent***	Y	Y	Y	Y	N	N	Y	N
2 ***Coburn***	?	?	?	Y	N	Y	Y	N
3 ***Watkins***	Y	Y	?	Y	N	N	N	N
4 ***Watts***	Y	Y	Y	Y	N	N	N	N
5 ***Istook***	Y	Y	Y	Y	N	N	Y	N
6 ***Lucas***	Y	Y	Y	Y	N	N	N	N
OREGON								
1 Wu	Y	Y	Y	Y	Y	Y	N	Y
2 ***Walden***	Y	Y	Y	Y	N	Y	N	N
3 Blumenauer	Y	Y	Y	Y	Y	Y	N	Y
4 DeFazio	N	Y	Y	Y	Y	Y	N	Y
5 Hooley	Y	Y	Y	Y	Y	Y	N	Y
PENNSYLVANIA								
1 Brady	Y	Y	Y	Y	N	N	N	Y
2 Fattah	Y	Y	Y	Y	N	N	N	Y
3 Borski	N	Y	Y	Y	N	N	N	Y
4 Klink	Y	Y	Y	Y	N	N	N	Y
5 ***Peterson***	Y	Y	Y	Y	N	N	N	N
6 Holden	Y	Y	Y	Y	N	N	N	Y
7 ***Weldon***	?	Y	?	Y	N	N	N	N
8 ***Greenwood***	Y	Y	Y	Y	Y	N	N	N
9 ***Shuster***	Y	Y	Y	Y	N	N	N	N
10 ***Sherwood***	Y	Y	Y	Y	N	N	N	Y
11 Kanjorski	Y	Y	Y	Y	N	N	N	Y
12 Murtha	Y	Y	Y	Y	N	N	N	N
13 Hoeffel	Y	Y	Y	Y	Y	N	N	Y
14 Coyne	Y	Y	Y	Y	Y	N	N	Y
15 ***Toomey***	Y	Y	Y	Y	N	Y	Y	N
16 ***Pitts***	Y	Y	Y	Y	N	Y	Y	N
17 ***Gekas***	Y	+	Y	Y	N	N	Y	N
18 Doyle	Y	Y	Y	Y	N	N	Y	Y
19 ***Goodling***	?	Y	Y	Y	N	N	Y	N
20 Mascara	Y	Y	Y	Y	N	N	Y	Y
21 ***English***	N	Y	Y	Y	N	N	N	Y
RHODE ISLAND								
1 Kennedy	Y	Y	Y	Y	Y	Y	N	Y
2 Weygand	?	+	+	+	Y	Y	N	Y
SOUTH CAROLINA								
1 ***Sanford***	Y	Y	Y	Y	Y	Y	Y	N
2 ***Spence***	Y	Y	Y	Y	Y	N	N	N
3 ***Graham***	Y	Y	Y	Y	N	Y	Y	N
4 ***DeMint***	Y	Y	Y	Y	N	Y	Y	N
5 Spratt	?	?	?	Y	Y	Y	N	Y
6 Clyburn	?	?	?	Y	Y	Y	N	Y
SOUTH DAKOTA								
AL ***Thune***	Y	Y	Y	Y	N	Y	Y	N

	277	278	279	280	281	282	283	284
TENNESSEE								
1 ***Jenkins***	Y	Y	Y	Y	Y	Y	Y	Y
2 ***Duncan***	Y	Y	Y	Y	N	Y	Y	Y
3 ***Wamp***	Y	Y	Y	Y	N	N	N	N
4 ***Hilleary***	N	Y	Y	Y	Y	Y	Y	Y
5 Clement	Y	Y	Y	Y	Y	N	N	Y
6 Gordon	Y	Y	Y	Y	Y	N	N	Y
7 ***Bryant***	Y	Y	Y	Y	N	Y	Y	Y
8 Tanner	Y	Y	Y	Y	Y	Y	N	Y
9 Ford	Y	Y	Y	Y	Y	Y	N	Y
TEXAS								
1 Sandlin	Y	Y	Y	Y	N	N	N	N
2 Turner	Y	Y	Y	Y	Y	Y	Y	Y
3 ***Johnson, Sam***	Y	Y	Y	Y	N	Y	Y	N
4 Hall	Y	Y	Y	Y	N	N	Y	N
5 ***Sessions***	Y	Y	Y	Y	N	Y	Y	N
6 ***Barton***	Y	Y	Y	Y	N	N	Y	N
7 ***Archer***	Y	Y	Y	Y	N	Y	Y	N
8 ***Brady***	?	?	?	Y	N	N	Y	N
9 Lampson	?	?	?	Y	Y	N	N	N
10 Doggett	Y	Y	Y	Y	Y	N	N	Y
11 Edwards	?	?	Y	Y	N	N	N	Y
12 ***Granger***	Y	Y	Y	Y	N	N	N	N
13 ***Thornberry***	Y	Y	Y	Y	N	N	Y	N
14 ***Paul***	Y	Y	Y	N	N	Y	Y	N
15 Hinojosa	Y	Y	Y	Y	Y	N	N	Y
16 Reyes	Y	Y	Y	Y	Y	N	N	Y
17 Stenholm	Y	Y	Y	Y	N	N	Y	N
18 Jackson-Lee	?	?	?	Y	Y	N	N	Y
19 ***Combest***	?	?	?	?	?	?	?	N
20 Gonzalez	Y	Y	Y	Y	Y	N	N	Y
21 ***Smith***	Y	Y	Y	Y	N	N	N	N
22 ***DeLay***	?	?	?	Y	N	Y	Y	N
23 ***Bonilla***	Y	Y	Y	Y	N	N	N	N
24 Frost	Y	Y	Y	Y	N	Y	N	Y
25 Bentsen	Y	Y	Y	Y	Y	N	N	N
26 ***Armey***	?	?	?	Y	N	Y	Y	N
27 Ortiz	Y	Y	Y	Y	N	N	N	Y
28 Rodriguez	Y	Y	Y	Y	Y	N	N	Y
29 Green	N	Y	Y	Y	N	N	N	N
30 Johnson, E.B.	Y	P	Y	Y	Y	N	N	Y
UTAH								
1 ***Hansen***	Y	Y	Y	Y	Y	Y	Y	N
2 ***Cook***	Y	Y	Y	Y	Y	Y	Y	Y
3 ***Cannon***	Y	Y	Y	Y	N	Y	Y	N
VERMONT								
AL *Sanders*	Y	Y	Y	Y	Y	Y	N	Y
VIRGINIA								
1 ***Bateman***	+	+	+	Y	N	N	N	N
2 Pickett	N	Y	?	Y	N	N	N	Y
3 Scott	?	?	?	Y	N	N	N	Y
4 Sisisky	Y	Y	Y	Y	N	N	Y	Y
5 Goode	Y	Y	Y	Y	Y	Y	Y	Y
6 ***Goodlatte***	Y	Y	Y	Y	N	Y	Y	N
7 ***Bliley***	Y	Y	Y	Y	N	N	Y	N
8 Moran	Y	P	Y	Y	N	N	N	Y
9 Boucher	Y	Y	Y	Y	N	N	N	Y
10 ***Wolf***	Y	Y	Y	Y	N	N	N	N
11 ***Davis***	Y	Y	Y	Y	?	?	?	N
WASHINGTON								
1 Inslee	Y	Y	Y	Y	Y	Y	N	Y
2 ***Metcalf***	Y	Y	Y	Y	Y	N	Y	N
3 Baird	N	P	Y	Y	Y	Y	N	Y
4 ***Hastings***	Y	Y	Y	Y	N	N	Y	N
5 ***Nethercutt***	Y	Y	Y	Y	Y	Y	N	N
6 Dicks	Y	Y	Y	Y	Y	Y	N	Y
7 McDermott	?	?	?	?	?	?	?	?
8 ***Dunn***	Y	Y	Y	Y	N	Y	N	N
9 Smith	Y	Y	Y	Y	Y	Y	N	Y
WEST VIRGINIA								
1 Mollohan	?	?	?	Y	N	N	N	Y
2 Wise	?	+	+	?	N	N	N	Y
3 Rahall	Y	Y	N	Y	Y	Y	N	?
WISCONSIN								
1 ***Ryan***	Y	Y	Y	Y	N	Y	Y	Y
2 Baldwin	?	?	?	?	?	?	?	?
3 Kind	+	+	+	Y	Y	Y	N	Y
4 Kleczka	Y	Y	Y	Y	Y	Y	N	Y
5 Barrett	Y	Y	Y	Y	Y	Y	N	Y
6 ***Petri***	Y	Y	Y	Y	N	Y	Y	Y
7 Obey	Y	Y	Y	Y	Y	Y	N	Y
8 ***Green***	Y	Y	Y	Y	N	N	N	Y
9 ***Sensenbrenner***	Y	Y	Y	Y	N	Y	Y	N
WYOMING								
AL ***Cubin***	Y	Y	Y	Y	N	Y	Y	N

Southern states - Ala., Ark., Fla., Ga., Ky., La., Miss., N.C., Okla., S.C., Tenn., Texas, Va.

285. HR 2466. Fiscal 2000 Interior Appropriations/Matching Funds. Sanders, I-Vt., amendment to strike bill language that would require states to match 25 percent of the federal grant funding they receive from the low-income weatherization program. Rejected 198-225: R 25-195; D 172-30 (ND 132-16, SD 40-14); I 1-0. July 14, 1999.

286. HR 2466. Fiscal 2000 Interior Appropriations/NEA Funding Increase. Slaughter, D-N.Y., amendment to increase the bill's funding by $10 million each for the National Endowment for the Arts (NEA) and the National Endowment for the Humanities (NEH), bringing the totals to $108 million for the NEA and $121 million for the NEH. The increase would be offset with a $20 million reduction in funding for the Strategic Petroleum Reserve. Rejected 207-217: R 32-188; D 174-29 (ND 140-10, SD 34-19); I 1-0. July 14, 1999.

287. HR 2466. Fiscal 2000 Interior Appropriations/NEA Funding Reduction. Stearns, R-Fla., amendment to reduce funding for the National Endowment for the Arts by $2.1 million. Rejected 124-300: R 118-101; D 6-198 (ND 2-148, SD 4-50); I 0-1. July 14, 1999.

288. HR 2466. Fiscal 2000 Interior Appropriations/Mining Waste. Rahall, D-W.Va., amendment to prohibit use of funds in the bill to process applications for mining plans or operations that would use more than five acres to dispose of mining waste. Adopted 273-151: R 78-143; D 194-8 (ND 146-2, SD 48-6); I 1-0. July 14, 1999.

289. HR 2466. Fiscal 2000 Interior Appropriations/Casino Gambling. Weldon, R-Fla., amendment to prohibit use of funds in the bill to approve Class III (or "casino-style") gambling on Indian lands by any means other than through a tribal-state compact. Adopted 205-217: R 169-48; D 36-168 (ND 20-130, SD 16-38); I 0-1. July 14, 1999.

290. HR 2466. Fiscal 2000 Interior Appropriations/Gettysburg Visitors Center. Klink, D-Pa., amendment to prohibit the U.S. Park Service from using funds in the bill to construct a visitors center at the Gettysburg National Battlefield in Gettysburg, Pa. Adopted 227-199: R 25-196; D 201-3 (ND 150-0, SD 51-3); I 1-0. July 14, 1999.

291. HR 2466. Fiscal 2000 Interior Appropriations/Leghold Traps. Farr, D-Calif., amendment to prohibit the use of funds in the bill to authorize the use of jawed leghold traps or neck snares in the National Wildlife Refuge System, except for use in research, conservation or facilities protection. Adopted 259-166: R 89-131; D 169-35 (ND 131-19, SD 38-16); I 1-0. July 14, 1999.

292. HR 2466. Fiscal 2000 Interior Appropriations/Forest Research. Tancredo, R-Colo., amendment to reduce funding for the U.S. Forest Service's forest and rangeland research by $16.9 million to $187.4 million. Rejected 135-291: R 128-93; D 7-197 (ND 4-146, SD 3-51); I 0-1. July 14, 1999.

Key

- Y Voted for (yea).
- # Paired for.
- \+ Announced for.
- N Voted against (nay).
- X Paired against.
- – Announced against.
- P Voted "present."
- C Voted "present" to avoid possible conflict of interest.
- ? Did not vote or otherwise make a position known.

•

Democrats ***Republicans***
Independents

	285	286	287	288	289	290	291	292
ALABAMA								
1 ***Callahan***	N	N	Y	N	Y	N	N	Y
2 ***Everett***	N	N	Y	N	Y	N	N	Y
3 ***Riley***	N	N	Y	N	Y	N	N	Y
4 ***Aderholt***	N	N	Y	N	Y	N	N	Y
5 Cramer	N	N	N	N	Y	Y	N	N
6 ***Bachus***	N	N	Y	N	Y	Y	N	Y
7 Hilliard	Y	Y	N	Y	N	Y	Y	N
ALASKA								
AL ***Young***	N	N	N	N	N	N	N	Y
ARIZONA								
1 ***Salmon***	N	N	Y	N	Y	N	N	Y
2 Pastor	Y	Y	N	N	N	Y	Y	N
3 ***Stump***	N	N	Y	N	Y	N	N	Y
4 ***Shadegg***	N	N	Y	N	Y	N	N	Y
5 ***Kolbe***	N	N	N	N	N	N	Y	N
6 ***Hayworth***	N	N	Y	N	N	N	N	Y
ARKANSAS								
1 Berry	Y	N	N	Y	N	Y	N	N
2 Snyder	N	Y	N	Y	N	N	Y	N
3 ***Hutchinson***	N	N	N	N	Y	N	Y	Y
4 ***Dickey***	N	N	Y	N	Y	N	N	N
CALIFORNIA								
1 Thompson	Y	Y	N	Y	N	Y	Y	N
2 ***Herger***	N	N	Y	N	Y	N	N	N
3 ***Ose***	N	N	N	N	Y	N	Y	N
4 ***Doolittle***	N	N	Y	N	Y	N	N	Y
5 Matsui	Y	Y	N	Y	N	Y	Y	N
6 Woolsey	Y	Y	N	Y	N	Y	Y	N
7 Miller, George	Y	Y	N	Y	N	Y	Y	N
8 Pelosi	Y	Y	N	Y	N	Y	Y	N
9 Lee	Y	Y	N	Y	N	Y	Y	N
10 Tauscher	N	Y	N	Y	N	Y	Y	N
11 ***Pombo***	N	N	Y	N	N	N	N	Y
12 Lantos	Y	Y	N	Y	N	Y	Y	N
13 Stark	Y	Y	N	Y	N	Y	Y	N
14 Eshoo	Y	Y	N	Y	N	Y	Y	N
15 ***Campbell***	N	N	Y	Y	Y	Y	Y	Y
16 Lofgren	N	Y	N	Y	Y	Y	Y	N
17 Farr	Y	Y	N	Y	N	Y	Y	N
18 Condit	Y	N	Y	Y	N	Y	Y	N
19 ***Radanovich***	N	N	N	N	Y	N	N	N
20 Dooley	N	N	N	Y	N	Y	Y	N
21 ***Thomas***	N	N	N	N	?	N	N	Y
22 Capps	Y	Y	N	Y	N	Y	Y	N
23 ***Gallegly***	N	N	N	Y	N	N	Y	N
24 Sherman	N	Y	N	Y	N	Y	Y	N
25 ***McKeon***	N	N	N	N	N	N	N	N
26 Berman	N	Y	N	Y	N	Y	Y	N
27 ***Rogan***	N	N	Y	N	N	N	N	N
28 ***Dreier***	N	N	Y	N	Y	N	?	N
29 Waxman	Y	Y	N	Y	N	Y	Y	N
30 Becerra	N	Y	N	Y	N	Y	Y	N
31 Martinez	Y	Y	N	Y	N	Y	N	N
32 Dixon	Y	Y	N	Y	N	Y	Y	N
33 Roybal-Allard	N	Y	N	Y	N	Y	Y	N
34 Napolitano	Y	Y	N	Y	N	Y	Y	N
35 Waters	Y	Y	N	Y	N	Y	Y	N
36 ***Kuykendall***	N	Y	N	Y	N	N	Y	Y
37 Millender-McD.	Y	Y	N	Y	N	Y	Y	N
38 ***Horn***	N	Y	N	Y	Y	Y	Y	N
39 ***Royce***	N	N	Y	N	?	Y	Y	Y
40 ***Lewis***	?	N	N	N	N	N	N	Y
41 ***Miller, Gary***	N	N	Y	N	N	N	N	Y
42 Brown	?	?	?	?	?	?	?	?
43 ***Calvert***	N	N	N	N	N	N	N	N
44 ***Bono***	N	N	N	N	N	N	Y	N
45 ***Rohrabacher***	N	N	Y	Y	N	N	Y	Y
46 Sanchez	Y	Y	N	Y	N	Y	Y	Y
47 ***Cox***	N	N	Y	N	Y	N	Y	Y
48 ***Packard***	N	N	Y	N	Y	N	N	N
49 ***Bilbray***	N	Y	N	Y	N	Y	Y	Y
50 Filner	Y	Y	N	Y	N	Y	Y	N
51 ***Cunningham***	N	N	Y	N	N	N	N	Y
52 ***Hunter***	N	N	N	N	N	N	N	Y
COLORADO								
1 DeGette	Y	Y	N	Y	N	Y	Y	N
2 Udall	Y	Y	N	Y	N	Y	Y	N
3 ***McInnis***	N	N	Y	N	Y	N	N	Y
4 ***Schaffer***	Y	N	Y	N	Y	N	N	Y
5 ***Hefley***	N	N	Y	N	Y	Y	N	Y
6 ***Tancredo***	N	N	Y	N	Y	N	N	Y
CONNECTICUT								
1 Larson	Y	Y	N	Y	N	Y	Y	N
2 Gejdenson	Y	Y	N	Y	N	Y	Y	N
3 DeLauro	Y	Y	N	Y	N	Y	Y	N
4 ***Shays***	N	Y	N	Y	Y	N	Y	Y
5 Maloney	Y	Y	N	Y	N	Y	Y	N
6 ***Johnson***	N	Y	N	Y	Y	N	Y	N
DELAWARE								
AL ***Castle***	N	Y	N	Y	Y	N	Y	N
FLORIDA								
1 ***Scarborough***	N	N	N	Y	Y	N	Y	Y
2 Boyd	Y	Y	N	Y	N	Y	N	N
3 Brown	Y	Y	N	Y	N	Y	Y	N
4 ***Fowler***	N	Y	N	N	Y	N	N	N
5 Thurman	?	?	?	?	?	?	?	?
6 ***Stearns***	N	N	Y	N	Y	N	N	Y
7 ***Mica***	N	Y	N	N	Y	Y	Y	Y
8 ***McCollum***	N	Y	N	Y	Y	N	Y	N
9 ***Bilirakis***	N	N	N	N	Y	Y	Y	N
10 ***Young***	N	N	N	N	Y	N	Y	N
11 Davis	Y	?	N	Y	N	Y	Y	N
12 ***Canady***	N	N	Y	N	Y	N	Y	Y
13 ***Miller***	N	N	N	Y	Y	N	Y	Y
14 ***Goss***	N	N	N	Y	N	N	Y	Y
15 ***Weldon***	N	N	Y	N	Y	N	N	Y
16 ***Foley***	N	Y	N	Y	N	N	Y	Y
17 Meek	Y	Y	N	Y	N	Y	Y	N
18 ***Ros-Lehtinen***	N	N	N	Y	?	N	Y	N
19 Wexler	Y	Y	N	Y	Y	Y	Y	N
20 Deutsch	Y	Y	N	Y	N	Y	Y	N
21 ***Diaz-Balart***	N	N	N	Y	N	N	Y	N
22 ***Shaw***	N	N	N	Y	Y	N	Y	Y
23 Hastings	Y	Y	N	Y	N	Y	Y	N
GEORGIA								
1 ***Kingston***	N	N	Y	Y	Y	N	Y	N
2 Bishop	Y	Y	N	Y	N	Y	N	N
3 ***Collins***	N	N	Y	N	Y	N	N	Y
4 McKinney	Y	Y	N	Y	Y	Y	Y	N
5 Lewis	Y	Y	N	Y	N	Y	Y	N
6 ***Isakson***	N	N	N	N	Y	N	Y	Y
7 ***Barr***	N	N	Y	N	Y	N	N	Y
8 ***Chambliss***	N	N	Y	N	Y	N	N	Y
9 ***Deal***	N	N	Y	Y	Y	N	N	Y
10 ***Norwood***	N	N	Y	N	Y	N	N	Y
11 ***Linder***	N	N	Y	N	Y	N	N	Y
HAWAII								
1 Abercrombie	Y	Y	N	Y	N	Y	Y	N
2 Mink	Y	Y	N	Y	N	Y	Y	N
IDAHO								
1 ***Chenoweth***	N	N	Y	N	Y	N	N	Y
2 ***Simpson***	N	N	N	N	N	N	N	Y
ILLINOIS								
1 Rush	Y	Y	N	Y	N	Y	Y	N
2 Jackson	Y	Y	N	Y	N	Y	Y	N
3 Lipinski	N	Y	N	Y	Y	Y	Y	N
4 Gutierrez	Y	Y	N	Y	N	Y	Y	N
5 Blagojevich	Y	Y	N	Y	N	Y	Y	N
6 ***Hyde***	N	N	Y	N	Y	N	Y	Y
7 Davis	Y	Y	N	Y	N	Y	Y	N
8 ***Crane***	N	N	Y	N	Y	N	Y	Y
9 Schakowsky	Y	Y	N	Y	N	Y	Y	N
10 ***Porter***	N	Y	N	Y	Y	N	Y	N
11 ***Weller***	N	N	Y	Y	N	N	Y	N
12 Costello	Y	Y	N	Y	N	Y	Y	N
13 ***Biggert***	N	Y	N	Y	Y	N	Y	N
14 ***Hastert***						N		

ND Northern Democrats SD Southern Democrats

	285	286	287	288	289	290	291	292
15 *Ewing*	N	N	N	Y	Y	N	Y	N
16 *Manzullo*	N	N	Y	N	Y	N	N	Y
17 Evans	Y	Y	N	Y	N	Y	Y	N
18 *LaHood*	N	Y	N	Y	Y	N	Y	N
19 Phelps	Y	N	N	Y	Y	Y	Y	N
20 *Shimkus*	N	N	N	N	Y	N	N	Y
INDIANA								
1 Visclosky	Y	Y	N	Y	N	Y	Y	N
2 *McIntosh*	Y	N	Y	N	?	N	N	Y
3 Roemer	Y	Y	N	Y	Y	Y	Y	N
4 *Souder*	N	N	N	N	Y	N	N	Y
5 *Buyer*	N	N	Y	N	N	N	N	N
6 *Burton*	N	N	Y	N	Y	N	Y	Y
7 *Pease*	N	N	N	Y	Y	N	Y	Y
8 *Hostettler*	Y	N	Y	N	Y	N	N	Y
9 Hill	Y	N	N	Y	Y	Y	N	N
10 Carson	Y	Y	N	Y	N	Y	Y	N
IOWA								
1 *Leach*	Y	Y	N	Y	Y	N	Y	N
2 *Nussle*	N	N	Y	N	Y	Y	N	N
3 Boswell	Y	Y	N	Y	Y	Y	N	N
4 *Ganske*	N	N	N	Y	Y	N	N	N
5 *Latham*	N	N	Y	N	Y	N	N	N
KANSAS								
1 *Moran*	N	N	N	Y	Y	N	N	Y
2 *Ryun*	N	N	Y	N	Y	N	N	Y
3 Moore	N	Y	N	Y	N	Y	Y	N
4 *Tiahrt*	N	N	Y	N	Y	N	N	Y
KENTUCKY								
1 *Whitfield*	N	N	N	Y	Y	N	Y	N
2 *Lewis*	N	N	Y	N	Y	N	N	Y
3 *Northup*	N	N	N	N	Y	N	Y	N
4 Lucas	Y	N	Y	Y	Y	Y	N	N
5 *Rogers*	N	N	N	N	Y	N	N	Y
6 *Fletcher*	Y	N	Y	N	Y	N	N	Y
LOUISIANA								
1 *Vitter*	N	N	Y	N	Y	N	N	Y
2 Jefferson	Y	Y	N	Y	N	Y	Y	N
3 *Tauzin*	N	N	N	N	Y	N	N	N
4 *McCrery*	N	N	N	N	Y	N	N	N
5 *Cooksey*	N	N	Y	N	N	N	Y	N
6 *Baker*	N	N	N	N	Y	N	N	Y
7 John	N	N	N	N	N	Y	N	N
MAINE								
1 Allen	Y	Y	N	Y	N	Y	Y	N
2 Baldacci	Y	Y	N	Y	N	Y	N	N
MARYLAND								
1 *Gilchrest*	N	N	N	Y	Y	N	N	N
2 *Ehrlich*	N	?	?	Y	N	N	Y	N
3 Cardin	Y	Y	N	Y	N	Y	Y	N
4 Wynn	?	?	?	?	?	?	?	?
5 Hoyer	Y	Y	N	?	N	Y	Y	N
6 *Bartlett*	N	N	Y	Y	Y	N	Y	Y
7 Cummings	Y	Y	N	Y	N	Y	Y	N
8 *Morella*	Y	Y	N	Y	N	N	Y	N
MASSACHUSETTS								
1 Olver	Y	Y	N	Y	N	Y	Y	N
2 Neal	Y	Y	N	Y	N	Y	Y	N
3 McGovern	Y	Y	N	Y	N	Y	Y	N
4 Frank	Y	Y	N	Y	N	Y	Y	N
5 Meehan	Y	Y	N	Y	N	Y	Y	N
6 Tierney	Y	Y	N	Y	N	Y	Y	N
7 Markey	Y	Y	N	Y	N	Y	Y	N
8 Capuano	Y	Y	N	Y	N	Y	Y	N
9 Moakley	Y	Y	N	Y	Y	Y	Y	N
10 Delahunt	Y	Y	N	Y	N	Y	Y	N
MICHIGAN								
1 Stupak	Y	Y	N	Y	N	Y	Y	N
2 *Hoekstra*	N	N	N	N	Y	N	N	Y
3 *Ehlers*	N	Y	N	Y	Y	N	Y	N
4 *Camp*	Y	N	N	N	N	N	N	N
5 Barcia	Y	Y	N	Y	Y	N	Y	N
6 *Upton*	N	N	N	Y	Y	N	Y	N
7 *Smith*	N	N	N	Y	Y	N	N	Y
8 Stabenow	Y	Y	N	Y	N	Y	Y	N
9 Kildee	Y	Y	N	Y	N	Y	Y	N
10 Bonior	Y	Y	N	Y	N	Y	Y	N
11 *Knollenberg*	N	N	N	N	N	N	N	N
12 Levin	Y	Y	N	Y	N	Y	Y	N
13 Rivers	?	?	?	?	?	?	?	?
14 Conyers	Y	Y	N	Y	N	Y	Y	N
15 Kilpatrick	Y	Y	N	Y	N	Y	Y	N
16 Dingell	N	Y	N	Y	N	Y	N	N

	285	286	287	288	289	290	291	292
MINNESOTA								
1 *Gutknecht*	Y	N	N	N	N	N	N	Y
2 Minge	Y	Y	N	Y	N	Y	Y	N
3 *Ramstad*	N	Y	N	Y	N	N	Y	Y
4 Vento	Y	Y	N	Y	N	Y	Y	N
5 Sabo	N	Y	N	Y	N	Y	Y	N
6 Luther	N	Y	N	Y	N	Y	Y	Y
7 Peterson	Y	Y	N	Y	N	Y	N	N
8 Oberstar	Y	Y	N	Y	N	Y	N	N
MISSISSIPPI								
1 *Wicker*	N	N	Y	N	Y	N	N	N
2 Thompson	Y	Y	N	Y	N	Y	Y	N
3 *Pickering*	N	N	Y	N	Y	N	N	N
4 Shows	Y	N	Y	Y	N	Y	N	N
5 Taylor	N	N	Y	Y	N	Y	Y	Y
MISSOURI								
1 Clay	Y	Y	N	Y	N	Y	Y	N
2 *Talent*	N	N	Y	Y	Y	N	Y	N
3 Gephardt	Y	Y	N	Y	N	Y	Y	N
4 Skelton	Y	N	Y	Y	Y	Y	N	N
5 McCarthy	N	Y	N	Y	N	Y	Y	N
6 Danner	Y	Y	N	Y	Y	Y	N	N
7 *Blunt*	N	N	N	N	Y	N	N	N
8 *Emerson*	Y	N	Y	N	Y	N	N	N
9 *Hulshof*	Y	N	Y	Y	Y	N	Y	Y
MONTANA								
AL *Hill*	N	N	Y	N	Y	N	N	Y
NEBRASKA								
1 *Bereuter*	N	N	N	Y	Y	N	Y	N
2 *Terry*	N	N	Y	Y	Y	N	N	Y
3 *Barrett*	N	N	Y	N	N	N	N	N
NEVADA								
1 Berkley	Y	Y	N	N	Y	Y	Y	N
2 *Gibbons*	N	N	Y	N	Y	N	N	N
NEW HAMPSHIRE								
1 *Sununu*	N	N	Y	Y	Y	N	N	Y
2 *Bass*	N	N	N	Y	Y	N	N	Y
NEW JERSEY								
1 Andrews	Y	Y	N	Y	Y	Y	Y	N
2 *LoBiondo*	N	Y	N	Y	Y	N	Y	Y
3 *Saxton*	N	N	N	Y	Y	N	N	N
4 *Smith*	N	N	Y	Y	Y	Y	Y	Y
5 *Roukema*	N	Y	N	Y	Y	N	Y	Y
6 Pallone	Y	Y	N	Y	N	Y	Y	N
7 *Franks*	N	N	Y	Y	Y	N	Y	Y
8 Pascrell	Y	Y	N	Y	N	Y	Y	N
9 Rothman	Y	Y	N	Y	N	Y	Y	N
10 Payne	Y	Y	N	Y	N	Y	Y	N
11 *Frelinghuysen*	N	Y	N	Y	Y	N	Y	Y
12 Holt	Y	Y	N	Y	Y	Y	Y	N
13 Menendez	N	Y	N	Y	Y	Y	Y	N
NEW MEXICO								
1 *Wilson*	Y	N	N	N	Y	N	Y	N
2 *Skeen*	N	N	N	N	N	Y	N	N
3 Udall	Y	Y	N	Y	N	Y	Y	N
NEW YORK								
1 *Forbes*	Y	Y	N	Y	N	Y	Y	N
2 *Lazio*	N	Y	N	Y	Y	N	Y	N
3 *King*	Y	N	N	Y	Y	N	Y	N
4 McCarthy	?	Y	N	Y	N	Y	Y	N
5 Ackerman	Y	Y	N	Y	N	Y	Y	N
6 Meeks	Y	Y	N	Y	N	Y	Y	N
7 Crowley	Y	Y	N	Y	N	Y	Y	N
8 Nadler	Y	Y	N	Y	N	Y	Y	N
9 Weiner	Y	Y	N	Y	N	Y	Y	N
10 Towns	Y	Y	N	Y	N	Y	Y	N
11 Owens	Y	Y	N	Y	N	Y	Y	N
12 Velázquez	Y	Y	N	Y	N	Y	Y	N
13 *Fossella*	Y	Y	Y	Y	Y	N	Y	Y
14 Maloney	Y	Y	N	Y	N	Y	Y	N
15 Rangel	Y	Y	N	Y	N	Y	Y	N
16 Serrano	Y	Y	N	Y	N	Y	Y	N
17 Engel	Y	Y	N	Y	N	Y	Y	N
18 Lowey	Y	Y	N	Y	N	Y	Y	N
19 *Kelly*	Y	Y	N	Y	Y	Y	Y	N
20 *Gilman*	Y	Y	N	Y	Y	N	Y	N
21 McNulty	?	?	?	?	?	?	?	?
22 *Sweeney*	Y	N	N	Y	Y	N	N	N
23 *Boehlert*	Y	Y	N	Y	Y	Y	Y	N
24 *McHugh*	Y	Y	N	Y	Y	N	N	N
25 *Walsh*	N	N	N	Y	Y	N	N	N
26 Hinchey	Y	Y	N	Y	N	Y	Y	N
27 *Reynolds*	N	N	N	Y	Y	N	N	N
28 Slaughter	Y	Y	N	Y	N	Y	Y	N
29 LaFalce	Y	Y	N	Y	Y	Y	Y	N

	285	286	287	288	289	290	291	292
30 *Quinn*	Y	N	N	Y	Y	N	N	N
31 *Houghton*	Y	Y	N	N	N	N	Y	N
NORTH CAROLINA								
1 Clayton	Y	Y	N	Y	N	Y	Y	N
2 Etheridge	Y	Y	N	Y	Y	Y	Y	N
3 *Jones*	N	N	Y	N	Y	Y	Y	Y
4 Price	Y	Y	N	Y	Y	Y	Y	N
5 *Burr*	N	N	N	N	Y	N	N	Y
6 *Coble*	N	N	Y	N	Y	N	N	Y
7 McIntyre	Y	N	N	Y	Y	N	Y	N
8 *Hayes*	N	N	Y	Y	Y	N	N	Y
9 *Myrick*	N	N	Y	N	Y	N	Y	Y
10 *Ballenger*	N	N	N	N	Y	N	N	N
11 *Taylor*	N	N	Y	N	Y	N	N	Y
12 Watt	Y	Y	N	Y	N	Y	Y	N
NORTH DAKOTA								
AL Pomeroy	Y	N	N	Y	N	Y	N	N
OHIO								
1 *Chabot*	N	N	Y	Y	Y	Y	Y	Y
2 *Portman*	N	N	Y	Y	Y	N	Y	N
3 Hall	Y	Y	N	Y	Y	Y	Y	N
4 *Oxley*	N	N	N	N	N	N	N	N
5 *Gillmor*	N	N	N	N	Y	N	Y	N
6 Strickland	Y	Y	N	Y	N	Y	Y	N
7 *Hobson*	N	N	N	N	Y	N	Y	N
8 *Boehner*	N	N	Y	N	N	N	N	N
9 Kaptur	Y	Y	N	Y	N	Y	Y	N
10 Kucinich	Y	Y	N	Y	Y	Y	Y	N
11 Jones	Y	Y	N	Y	N	Y	Y	N
12 *Kasich*	?	?	?	Y	Y	N	N	Y
13 Brown	Y	Y	N	?	N	Y	Y	N
14 Sawyer	Y	Y	N	Y	N	Y	Y	N
15 *Pryce*	N	N	N	N	N	N	Y	N
16 *Regula*	N	N	N	N	N	N	Y	N
17 Traficant	Y	N	N	Y	Y	Y	Y	N
18 *Ney*	N	N	Y	N	N	N	N	N
19 *LaTourette*	N	N	N	N	N	Y	Y	N
OKLAHOMA								
1 *Largent*	N	N	Y	N	Y	N	N	Y
2 *Coburn*	N	N	Y	N	Y	N	N	Y
3 *Watkins*	N	N	Y	N	Y	N	N	N
4 *Watts*	N	N	Y	N	Y	N	N	Y
5 *Istook*	N	N	Y	N	Y	N	N	Y
6 *Lucas*	N	N	Y	N	Y	N	N	N
OREGON								
1 Wu	Y	Y	N	Y	N	Y	Y	N
2 *Walden*	N	N	N	N	N	N	N	N
3 Blumenauer	N	Y	N	Y	N	Y	Y	N
4 DeFazio	Y	Y	N	Y	N	Y	Y	N
5 Hooley	Y	Y	N	Y	N	Y	Y	N
PENNSYLVANIA								
1 Brady	Y	Y	N	Y	N	Y	Y	N
2 Fattah	Y	Y	N	Y	N	Y	Y	N
3 Borski	Y	Y	N	Y	N	Y	Y	N
4 Klink	Y	Y	N	Y	N	Y	N	N
5 *Peterson*	N	N	Y	N	Y	N	N	N
6 Holden	Y	N	N	Y	N	Y	N	Y
7 *Weldon*	N	N	N	Y	N	N	Y	N
8 *Greenwood*	N	Y	N	Y	Y	N	Y	N
9 *Shuster*	N	N	N	N	Y	N	N	Y
10 *Sherwood*	Y	N	N	Y	Y	N	N	N
11 Kanjorski	Y	Y	N	Y	N	Y	Y	N
12 Murtha	N	N	N	Y	N	Y	N	N
13 Hoeffel	Y	Y	N	Y	N	Y	Y	N
14 Coyne	Y	Y	N	Y	N	Y	Y	N
15 *Toomey*	N	N	Y	Y	Y	N	N	Y
16 *Pitts*	N	N	Y	N	Y	N	N	Y
17 *Gekas*	N	N	N	N	Y	N	N	Y
18 Doyle	Y	Y	N	Y	N	Y	Y	N
19 *Goodling*	N	N	Y	N	Y	N	N	N
20 Mascara	Y	Y	N	Y	N	Y	N	N
21 *English*	Y	N	N	Y	N	N	N	N
RHODE ISLAND								
1 Kennedy	Y	Y	N	Y	N	Y	Y	N
2 Weygand	Y	Y	N	Y	Y	Y	Y	N
SOUTH CAROLINA								
1 *Sanford*	N	N	Y	Y	N	N	Y	Y
2 *Spence*	N	N	N	N	Y	N	N	Y
3 *Graham*	N	N	Y	N	Y	N	N	Y
4 *DeMint*	N	N	Y	N	Y	N	N	Y
5 Spratt	Y	Y	N	Y	N	Y	Y	N
6 Clyburn	Y	Y	N	Y	N	Y	Y	N
SOUTH DAKOTA								
AL *Thune*	N	N	N	N	Y	N	N	Y

	285	286	287	288	289	290	291	292
TENNESSEE								
1 *Jenkins*	N	N	Y	N	N	N	N	Y
2 *Duncan*	Y	N	Y	N	Y	Y	N	Y
3 *Wamp*	N	N	Y	Y	Y	N	Y	Y
4 *Hilleary*	N	N	Y	N	N	N	N	Y
5 Clement	Y	Y	N	Y	N	Y	Y	N
6 Gordon	Y	N	N	Y	N	Y	Y	N
7 *Bryant*	N	N	Y	N	Y	N	N	Y
8 Tanner	Y	N	N	Y	Y	Y	N	N
9 Ford	Y	Y	N	Y	N	Y	Y	N
TEXAS								
1 Sandlin	Y	N	N	Y	N	Y	N	N
2 Turner	N	N	N	Y	Y	Y	N	N
3 *Johnson, Sam*	N	N	Y	N	Y	N	N	Y
4 Hall	N	N	Y	N	Y	Y	Y	N
5 *Sessions*	N	N	Y	N	Y	N	Y	Y
6 *Barton*	N	N	Y	N	Y	N	N	Y
7 *Archer*	N	N	N	N	Y	?	N	Y
8 *Brady*	N	N	Y	N	Y	N	N	N
9 Lampson	N	Y	N	Y	N	Y	Y	N
10 Doggett	N	Y	N	Y	N	Y	Y	N
11 Edwards	Y	N	N	Y	Y	N	Y	N
12 *Granger*	N	N	–	N	Y	N	Y	N
13 *Thornberry*	N	N	Y	N	Y	N	N	N
14 *Paul*	N	N	Y	N	N	Y	Y	Y
15 Hinojosa	Y	Y	N	Y	N	Y	Y	N
16 Reyes	Y	Y	N	N	N	Y	Y	N
17 Stenholm	N	N	N	N	Y	Y	N	N
18 Jackson-Lee	N	Y	N	Y	N	Y	Y	N
19 *Combest*	N	N	Y	?	?	?	?	?
20 Gonzalez	Y	N	N	Y	N	Y	Y	N
21 *Smith*	N	N	Y	N	Y	N	N	Y
22 *DeLay*	N	N	Y	N	Y	N	N	Y
23 *Bonilla*	N	N	N	N	Y	N	N	N
24 Frost	Y	Y	N	Y	N	Y	Y	N
25 Bentsen	Y	Y	N	Y	N	Y	Y	N
26 *Armey*	N	N	Y	N	Y	N	N	Y
27 Ortiz	Y	Y	N	N	N	Y	Y	N
28 Rodriguez	N	Y	N	Y	N	Y	Y	N
29 Green	Y	N	N	Y	Y	Y	Y	N
30 Johnson, E.B.	Y	Y	N	Y	N	Y	Y	N
UTAH								
1 *Hansen*	N	N	Y	N	Y	Y	N	Y
2 *Cook*	N	Y	N	N	Y	Y	N	Y
3 *Cannon*	N	N	Y	N	Y	N	N	Y
VERMONT								
AL *Sanders*	Y	Y	N	Y	N	Y	Y	N
VIRGINIA								
1 *Bateman*	N	N	Y	N	Y	N	N	Y
2 Pickett	N	N	N	Y	Y	Y	N	N
3 Scott	Y	Y	N	Y	N	Y	Y	N
4 Sisisky	Y	N	N	Y	Y	Y	N	Y
5 Goode	Y	N	N	Y	Y	Y	N	Y
6 *Goodlatte*	N	N	Y	N	Y	N	N	N
7 *Bliley*	N	N	N	N	N	N	N	Y
8 Moran	N	Y	N	Y	N	Y	Y	N
9 Boucher	Y	Y	N	Y	Y	Y	Y	N
10 *Wolf*	N	N	Y	Y	Y	N	Y	N
11 *Davis*	N	Y	N	Y	Y	N	Y	N
WASHINGTON								
1 Inslee	Y	Y	N	Y	N	Y	Y	Y
2 *Metcalf*	N	N	Y	N	Y	Y	Y	Y
3 Baird	Y	Y	N	Y	N	Y	Y	N
4 *Hastings*	N	N	Y	N	Y	N	N	Y
5 *Nethercutt*	N	N	Y	N	N	N	N	Y
6 Dicks	Y	Y	N	Y	N	Y	Y	N
7 McDermott	?	?	?	?	?	?	?	?
8 *Dunn*	N	N	Y	N	Y	N	Y	Y
9 Smith	Y	Y	N	Y	N	Y	Y	N
WEST VIRGINIA								
1 Mollohan	Y	N	N	Y	N	Y	N	N
2 Wise	Y	Y	N	Y	N	Y	N	N
3 Rahall	?	Y	N	Y	N	Y	N	N
WISCONSIN								
1 *Ryan*	N	N	Y	Y	Y	N	Y	Y
2 Baldwin	?	?	?	?	?	?	?	?
3 Kind	Y	Y	N	Y	N	Y	Y	N
4 Kleczka	Y	Y	N	Y	N	Y	Y	N
5 Barrett	Y	Y	N	Y	N	Y	Y	N
6 *Petri*	Y	N	Y	Y	Y	Y	Y	Y
7 Obey	Y	Y	N	Y	N	Y	Y	N
8 *Green*	N	N	Y	Y	Y	N	Y	Y
9 *Sensenbrenner*	N	N	Y	Y	Y	Y	Y	Y
WYOMING								
AL *Cubin*	N	N	Y	N	Y	N	N	Y

Southern states - Ala., Ark., Fla., Ga., Ky., La., Miss., N.C., Okla., S.C., Tenn., Texas, Va.

House Votes 293, 294, 295, 296, 297, 298, 299, 300

293. HR 2466. Fiscal 2000 Interior Appropriations/Fisheries Management. Wu, D-Ore., amendment to reduce funding for National Forest System timber sales management by $24 million and reallocate the funds to wildlife and fisheries habitat management, and to watershed improvements. Rejected 174-250: R 25-195; D 148-55 (ND 121-29, SD 27-26); I 1-0. July 14, 1999.

294. HR 2466. Fiscal 2000 Interior Appropriations/Gettysburg Visitors Center. Separate vote at the request of Goodling, R-Pa., on the Klink, D-Pa., amendment to prohibit the U.S. Park Service from using funds to construct a visitors center at the Gettysburg National Battlefield in Gettysburg, Pa. Adopted 220-206: R 16-205; D 203-1 (ND 150-0, SD 53-1); I 1-0. July 14, 1999.

295. HR 2466. Fiscal 2000 Interior Appropriations/Recommit. Obey, D-Wis., motion to send the bill back to the Appropriations Committee with instructions to restore $87 million to Land Legacy programs, $13 million to the Strategic Petroleum Reserve, $20 million to the National Endowment for the Arts, and $4 million to the Urban Parks Initiative. Motion rejected 187-239: R 2-220; D 184-19 (ND 144-5, SD 40-14); I 1-0. July 14, 1999.

296. HR 2466. Fiscal 2000 Interior Appropriations/Passage. Passage of the bill to appropriate $13.9 billion in fiscal 2000 for the Interior Department and related agencies, including $7.1 billion for Interior Department programs, $2.6 billion for the Agriculture Department's Forest Service, and $2.4 billion for the Indian Health Service. Passed 377-47: R 204-16; D 172-31 (ND 121-28, SD 51-3); I 1-0. July 14, 1999.

297. Procedural Motion/Journal. Approval of the House Journal of Wednesday, July 14, 1999. Approved 346-53: R 188-19; D 157-34 (ND 112-27, SD 45-7); I 1-0. July 15, 1999.

298. HR 1691. Religious Expression/Nadler Substitute. Nadler, D-N.Y., substitute amendment to limit the right to make a claim regarding infringement on religious liberty to individuals. Under the amendment, the claim could not be used as a defense in a housing, employment, or public accommodation suit, unless the defendant had fewer than four housing units or was a religious corporation, associations or educational institution employing people whose duties were religious in nature. Rejected 190-234: R 15-204; D 174-30 (ND 142-9, SD 32-21); I 1-0. July 15, 1999.

299. HR 1691. Religious Expression/Passage. Passage of the bill to prohibit the government from interfering with an individual's religious practices unless the government can prove the action is the least restrictive means of furthering a "compelling state interest." The bill would alter court procedures involving religious matters by requiring the government to prove that the individual's rights were not violated, instead of the current standard where the individual must prove his rights were violated. Passed 306-118: R 199-20; D 107-97 (ND 69-82, SD 38-15); I 0-1. July 15, 1999.

300. HR 2490. Fiscal 2000 Treasury-Postal Appropriations/Previous Question. Sessions, R-Texas, motion to order the previous question on adoption of the rule (H Res 246) to provide for House floor consideration of the bill to appropriate $28 billion for the Treasury Department, Postal Service and general government operations. Motion agreed to 276-147: R 142-78; D 134-68 (ND 100-49, SD 34-19); I 0-1. July 15, 1999. (Subsequently, the rule was adopted by voice vote.)

[1] *George E. Brown Jr., D-Calif., died July 15.*

Key

- Y Voted for (yea).
- # Paired for.
- \+ Announced for.
- N Voted against (nay).
- X Paired against.
- – Announced against.
- P Voted "present."
- C Voted "present" to avoid possible conflict of interest.
- ? Did not vote or otherwise make a position known.

•

Democrats ***Republicans***
Independents

	293	294	295	296	297	298	299	300
ALABAMA								
1 ***Callahan***	N	N	N	Y	Y	N	Y	Y
2 ***Everett***	N	N	N	Y	Y	N	Y	Y
3 ***Riley***	N	N	N	Y	Y	N	Y	N
4 ***Aderholt***	N	N	N	Y	N	N	Y	N
5 Cramer	N	Y	N	Y	Y	N	Y	N
6 ***Bachus***	N	N	N	Y	Y	N	Y	Y
7 Hilliard	N	Y	Y	Y	N	Y	N	Y
ALASKA								
AL ***Young***	N	N	N	Y	Y	N	Y	Y
ARIZONA								
1 ***Salmon***	N	N	N	Y	Y	N	Y	N
2 Pastor	Y	Y	Y	Y	N	Y	N	Y
3 ***Stump***	N	N	N	Y	Y	N	Y	N
4 ***Shadegg***	N	N	N	Y	Y	N	Y	Y
5 ***Kolbe***	N	N	N	Y	Y	Y	N	Y
6 ***Hayworth***	N	N	N	Y	Y	N	Y	N
ARKANSAS								
1 Berry	N	Y	N	N	Y	N	Y	N
2 Snyder	Y	N	Y	Y	Y	Y	N	Y
3 ***Hutchinson***	N	N	N	Y	N	N	Y	N
4 ***Dickey***	N	N	N	Y	Y	N	Y	Y
CALIFORNIA								
1 Thompson	N	Y	Y	Y	N	Y	N	Y
2 ***Herger***	N	N	N	Y	Y	N	Y	N
3 ***Ose***	N	N	N	Y	Y	N	Y	N
4 ***Doolittle***	N	N	N	Y	Y	N	Y	Y
5 Matsui	Y	Y	Y	Y	Y	Y	N	Y
6 Woolsey	Y	Y	Y	N	Y	Y	N	Y
7 Miller, George	Y	Y	Y	N	?	Y	N	Y
8 Pelosi	Y	Y	Y	Y	Y	Y	N	Y
9 Lee	Y	Y	Y	N	Y	Y	N	Y
10 Tauscher	Y	Y	Y	Y	Y	Y	N	Y
11 ***Pombo***	N	N	N	Y	N	N	N	Y
12 Lantos	Y	Y	Y	Y	Y	Y	N	Y
13 Stark	Y	Y	Y	N	Y	Y	N	Y
14 Eshoo	Y	Y	Y	Y	Y	Y	N	Y
15 ***Campbell***	Y	N	N	Y	Y	N	N	Y
16 Lofgren	Y	Y	Y	Y	Y	Y	N	N
17 Farr	Y	Y	Y	Y	Y	Y	N	Y
18 Condit	N	Y	N	Y	Y	Y	Y	Y
19 ***Radanovich***	N	N	N	Y	Y	N	Y	Y
20 Dooley	N	Y	Y	Y	Y	Y	Y	Y
21 ***Thomas***	N	N	N	Y	Y	N	Y	Y
22 Capps	Y	Y	Y	Y	Y	Y	Y	N
23 ***Gallegly***	N	N	N	Y	Y	N	Y	N
24 Sherman	Y	Y	Y	Y	Y	Y	N	N
25 ***McKeon***	N	N	N	Y	Y	N	Y	Y
26 Berman	Y	Y	Y	Y	Y	Y	N	Y
27 ***Rogan***	N	N	N	Y	N	N	Y	N
28 ***Dreier***	N	N	N	Y	Y	N	Y	Y
29 Waxman	Y	Y	Y	Y	Y	Y	N	Y
30 Becerra	Y	Y	Y	Y	Y	Y	N	N
31 Martinez	Y	Y	Y	Y	Y	Y	Y	Y
32 Dixon	Y	Y	Y	Y	?	Y	N	Y
33 Roybal-Allard	Y	Y	Y	Y	Y	Y	N	Y
34 Napolitano	Y	Y	Y	Y	Y	Y	Y	Y
35 Waters	Y	Y	Y	Y	N	Y	N	Y
36 ***Kuykendall***	N	N	N	Y	Y	N	N	Y
37 Millender-McD.	Y	Y	Y	Y	Y	Y	N	Y
38 ***Horn***	Y	Y	N	Y	Y	Y	Y	Y
39 ***Royce***	N	N	N	N	Y	N	Y	N
40 ***Lewis***	N	N	N	Y	?	N	Y	Y
41 ***Miller, Gary***	N	N	N	Y	Y	N	Y	Y
42 Brown [1]	?	?	?	?	?	?	?	?
43 ***Calvert***	N	N	N	Y	Y	N	Y	Y
44 ***Bono***	N	N	N	Y	Y	N	Y	Y
45 ***Rohrabacher***	N	N	N	N	Y	N	Y	Y
46 Sanchez	Y	Y	Y	Y	Y	Y	Y	N
47 ***Cox***	N	N	N	Y	Y	N	Y	Y
48 ***Packard***	N	N	N	Y	Y	N	Y	Y
49 ***Bilbray***	N	Y	N	Y	N	Y	Y	Y
50 Filner	Y	Y	Y	N	N	Y	N	Y
51 ***Cunningham***	N	N	N	Y	Y	N	Y	Y
52 ***Hunter***	N	N	N	Y	?	N	Y	Y
COLORADO								
1 DeGette	Y	Y	Y	Y	Y	Y	N	Y
2 Udall	Y	Y	Y	Y	N	Y	N	N
3 ***McInnis***	N	N	N	Y	Y	N	Y	Y
4 ***Schaffer***	N	N	N	Y	N	N	N	N
5 ***Hefley***	N	Y	N	N	Y	N	Y	Y
6 ***Tancredo***	N	N	N	N	P	N	N	N
CONNECTICUT								
1 Larson	Y	Y	Y	N	Y	Y	Y	Y
2 Gejdenson	Y	Y	Y	N	Y	Y	N	Y
3 DeLauro	Y	Y	Y	Y	Y	Y	N	Y
4 ***Shays***	Y	N	N	Y	Y	Y	Y	Y
5 Maloney	Y	Y	Y	Y	Y	Y	Y	N
6 ***Johnson***	N	N	Y	Y	?	Y	Y	N
DELAWARE								
AL ***Castle***	Y	N	N	Y	Y	Y	Y	Y
FLORIDA								
1 ***Scarborough***	Y	N	N	N	Y	N	N	N
2 Boyd	N	Y	Y	Y	Y	N	Y	Y
3 Brown	Y	Y	Y	Y	Y	Y	Y	Y
4 ***Fowler***	N	N	N	Y	Y	N	Y	Y
5 Thurman	?	?	?	?	?	?	?	?
6 ***Stearns***	N	N	N	N	Y	N	Y	N
7 ***Mica***	N	Y	N	Y	Y	N	Y	N
8 ***McCollum***	N	N	N	Y	Y	N	Y	Y
9 ***Bilirakis***	N	N	N	Y	N	N	Y	Y
10 ***Young***	N	N	N	Y	Y	N	Y	Y
11 Davis	?	Y	Y	Y	Y	N	Y	Y
12 ***Canady***	N	N	N	Y	Y	N	Y	Y
13 ***Miller***	N	N	N	Y	Y	N	Y	Y
14 ***Goss***	N	N	N	Y	Y	N	Y	Y
15 ***Weldon***	N	N	N	Y	Y	N	Y	Y
16 ***Foley***	Y	N	N	Y	Y	Y	Y	Y
17 Meek	Y	Y	Y	Y	?	Y	Y	Y
18 ***Ros-Lehtinen***	N	N	N	Y	Y	N	Y	Y
19 Wexler	Y	Y	Y	Y	Y	Y	N	Y
20 Deutsch	Y	Y	Y	Y	Y	Y	N	N
21 ***Diaz-Balart***	N	N	N	Y	Y	N	Y	Y
22 ***Shaw***	N	N	N	Y	Y	N	Y	Y
23 Hastings	Y	Y	Y	Y	Y	Y	N	Y
GEORGIA								
1 ***Kingston***	N	N	N	Y	Y	N	Y	Y
2 Bishop	N	Y	N	Y	Y	Y	Y	Y
3 ***Collins***	N	N	N	Y	Y	N	N	Y
4 McKinney	Y	Y	Y	N	N	Y	N	N
5 Lewis	Y	Y	Y	Y	Y	Y	N	Y
6 ***Isakson***	N	N	N	Y	Y	N	Y	Y
7 ***Barr***	N	N	N	Y	Y	N	N	Y
8 ***Chambliss***	N	N	N	Y	Y	N	Y	N
9 ***Deal***	N	N	N	Y	Y	N	N	Y
10 ***Norwood***	N	N	N	Y	Y	N	Y	N
11 ***Linder***	N	N	N	Y	Y	N	Y	Y
HAWAII								
1 Abercrombie	Y	Y	Y	Y	Y	Y	N	Y
2 Mink	Y	Y	Y	Y	Y	Y	N	Y
IDAHO								
1 ***Chenoweth***	N	N	N	Y	?	?	?	?
2 ***Simpson***	N	N	N	N	Y	N	Y	Y
ILLINOIS								
1 Rush	Y	Y	Y	Y	?	Y	N	Y
2 Jackson	Y	Y	Y	N	Y	Y	N	Y
3 Lipinski	Y	Y	Y	Y	Y	N	Y	Y
4 Gutierrez	Y	Y	Y	?	?	Y	N	Y
5 Blagojevich	Y	Y	Y	N	Y	Y	N	Y
6 ***Hyde***	N	N	N	Y	Y	N	Y	Y
7 Davis	Y	Y	Y	N	Y	Y	N	Y
8 ***Crane***	N	N	N	Y	N	N	N	Y
9 Schakowsky	Y	Y	Y	N	Y	Y	N	Y
10 ***Porter***	Y	N	N	Y	?	N	Y	Y
11 ***Weller***	N	N	N	Y	N	N	Y	N
12 Costello	Y	Y	Y	Y	N	N	Y	N
13 ***Biggert***	N	N	N	Y	Y	N	Y	Y
14 ***Hastert***		N	N	Y				Y

ND Northern Democrats SD Southern Democrats

	293	294	295	296	297	298	299	300
15 **Ewing**	N	N	N	Y	Y	N	Y	Y
16 **Manzullo**	N	N	N	Y	Y	N	N	N
17 Evans	N	Y	Y	N	Y	Y	N	N
18 **LaHood**	N	N	N	Y	Y	N	Y	N
19 Phelps	Y	Y	N	Y	N	N	Y	N
20 **Shimkus**	N	N	N	Y	Y	N	Y	N
INDIANA								
1 Visclosky	N	Y	Y	Y	N	Y	Y	N
2 **McIntosh**	N	N	N	Y	Y	N	Y	Y
3 Roemer	Y	Y	N	Y	Y	Y	Y	Y
4 **Souder**	N	N	N	N	Y	N	Y	N
5 **Buyer**	N	N	N	Y	Y	N	Y	Y
6 **Burton**	N	N	N	Y	Y	N	Y	Y
7 **Pease**	N	N	N	Y	Y	N	Y	Y
8 **Hostettler**	N	N	N	N	Y	N	N	N
9 Hill	Y	Y	Y	Y	Y	Y	Y	N
10 Carson	Y	Y	Y	Y	P	Y	N	N
IOWA								
1 **Leach**	Y	N	N	Y	Y	Y	Y	Y
2 **Nussle**	N	N	N	+	Y	N	Y	Y
3 Boswell	N	Y	Y	Y	Y	Y	Y	N
4 **Ganske**	N	N	N	Y	Y	N	Y	Y
5 **Latham**	N	N	N	Y	?	?	?	?
KANSAS								
1 **Moran**	N	N	N	Y	N	N	Y	N
2 **Ryun**	N	N	N	Y	?	N	Y	Y
3 Moore	Y	Y	Y	Y	Y	Y	Y	N
4 **Tiahrt**	N	N	N	N	Y	N	Y	Y
KENTUCKY								
1 **Whitfield**	N	N	N	Y	Y	N	Y	N
2 **Lewis**	N	N	N	Y	Y	N	Y	Y
3 **Northup**	N	N	N	Y	Y	N	Y	Y
4 Lucas	N	Y	N	Y	Y	N	Y	N
5 **Rogers**	N	N	N	Y	Y	N	Y	Y
6 **Fletcher**	N	N	N	Y	Y	N	Y	N
LOUISIANA								
1 **Vitter**	N	N	N	Y	Y	N	Y	N
2 Jefferson	Y	Y	Y	Y	Y	Y	Y	Y
3 **Tauzin**	N	N	N	Y	Y	N	Y	Y
4 **McCrery**	N	N	N	Y	Y	N	Y	Y
5 **Cooksey**	N	N	N	Y	Y	N	Y	Y
6 **Baker**	N	N	N	Y	Y	N	Y	N
7 John	N	Y	Y	Y	Y	N	Y	Y
MAINE								
1 Allen	Y	Y	Y	Y	Y	Y	Y	N
2 Baldacci	N	Y	Y	Y	Y	Y	Y	N
MARYLAND								
1 **Gilchrest**	N	N	N	Y	Y	?	?	?
2 **Ehrlich**	N	N	N	Y	Y	N	Y	Y
3 Cardin	Y	Y	Y	Y	Y	Y	Y	Y
4 Wynn	?	?	?	?	Y	Y	Y	?
5 Hoyer	N	Y	Y	Y	Y	Y	Y	Y
6 **Bartlett**	N	N	N	Y	Y	N	N	N
7 Cummings	Y	Y	Y	Y	?	Y	N	Y
8 **Morella**	Y	N	Y	Y	Y	Y	Y	Y
MASSACHUSETTS								
1 Olver	Y	Y	Y	N	Y	Y	N	Y
2 Neal	Y	Y	Y	Y	N	Y	N	Y
3 McGovern	Y	Y	Y	Y	N	Y	N	N
4 Frank	Y	Y	Y	Y	Y	Y	N	Y
5 Meehan	Y	Y	Y	Y	Y	Y	N	N
6 Tierney	Y	Y	Y	Y	Y	Y	N	N
7 Markey	Y	Y	Y	N	Y	Y	N	Y
8 Capuano	Y	Y	Y	Y	?	Y	N	Y
9 Moakley	Y	Y	Y	Y	Y	Y	N	Y
10 Delahunt	Y	Y	Y	N	?	Y	N	Y
MICHIGAN								
1 Stupak	N	Y	Y	Y	Y	Y	Y	Y
2 **Hoekstra**	N	N	N	Y	Y	N	Y	Y
3 **Ehlers**	N	N	N	Y	Y	N	Y	Y
4 **Camp**	N	N	N	Y	Y	N	Y	Y
5 Barcia	N	Y	Y	Y	Y	N	Y	N
6 **Upton**	N	N	N	Y	Y	N	Y	Y
7 **Smith**	N	N	N	Y	Y	N	Y	Y
8 Stabenow	Y	Y	Y	Y	?	Y	Y	N
9 Kildee	Y	Y	Y	Y	Y	Y	Y	N
10 Bonior	Y	Y	Y	N	N	Y	Y	Y
11 **Knollenberg**	N	N	N	Y	Y	N	Y	Y
12 Levin	Y	Y	Y	Y	Y	Y	N	Y
13 Rivers	?	?	?	?	?	?	?	?
14 Conyers	Y	Y	Y	N	Y	Y	N	Y
15 Kilpatrick	Y	Y	Y	Y	Y	Y	N	Y
16 Dingell	Y	Y	Y	Y	?	Y	N	Y
MINNESOTA								
1 **Gutknecht**	N	N	N	Y	N	N	Y	Y
2 Minge	N	Y	Y	Y	Y	Y	N	N
3 **Ramstad**	Y	N	N	Y	N	N	Y	N
4 Vento	Y	Y	Y	Y	Y	Y	N	Y
5 Sabo	Y	Y	Y	Y	N	Y	N	Y
6 Luther	Y	Y	Y	Y	Y	Y	Y	N
7 Peterson	N	Y	?	Y	N	N	Y	N
8 Oberstar	N	Y	Y	Y	N	Y	N	Y
MISSISSIPPI								
1 **Wicker**	N	N	N	Y	Y	N	Y	Y
2 Thompson	N	Y	Y	Y	N	Y	N	Y
3 **Pickering**	N	N	N	?	Y	N	Y	Y
4 Shows	N	Y	N	Y	Y	N	Y	N
5 Taylor	N	Y	N	Y	N	N	Y	N
MISSOURI								
1 Clay	Y	Y	Y	Y	N	Y	N	Y
2 **Talent**	N	N	N	Y	Y	N	Y	N
3 Gephardt	Y	Y	Y	N	N	Y	Y	Y
4 Skelton	N	Y	N	Y	Y	N	Y	Y
5 McCarthy	Y	Y	Y	Y	Y	Y	Y	Y
6 Danner	N	Y	Y	Y	Y	N	Y	N
7 **Blunt**	N	N	N	Y	Y	N	Y	Y
8 **Emerson**	N	N	N	Y	Y	N	Y	N
9 **Hulshof**	Y	N	N	Y	N	N	Y	N
MONTANA								
AL **Hill**	N	N	N	Y	N	N	Y	N
NEBRASKA								
1 **Bereuter**	?	N	N	Y	Y	N	Y	Y
2 **Terry**	N	N	N	Y	Y	N	Y	N
3 **Barrett**	N	N	N	Y	Y	N	Y	N
NEVADA								
1 Berkley	Y	Y	Y	Y	Y	Y	Y	N
2 **Gibbons**	N	N	N	N	N	N	Y	N
NEW HAMPSHIRE								
1 **Sununu**	N	N	N	Y	Y	N	N	Y
2 **Bass**	N	N	N	Y	Y	N	N	Y
NEW JERSEY								
1 Andrews	Y	Y	Y	Y	Y	Y	Y	Y
2 **LoBiondo**	Y	N	N	Y	N	N	Y	N
3 **Saxton**	Y	N	N	Y	Y	N	Y	Y
4 **Smith**	Y	Y	N	Y	Y	N	Y	Y
5 **Roukema**	N	N	N	Y	Y	N	Y	N
6 Pallone	Y	Y	Y	Y	N	Y	Y	Y
7 **Franks**	Y	N	N	Y	Y	N	Y	N
8 Pascrell	Y	Y	Y	Y	Y	Y	Y	N
9 Rothman	Y	Y	Y	N	Y	Y	Y	N
10 Payne	Y	Y	Y	N	Y	Y	N	Y
11 **Frelinghuysen**	N	N	N	Y	Y	N	Y	N
12 Holt	Y	Y	Y	Y	Y	Y	Y	N
13 Menendez	Y	Y	Y	N	Y	Y	Y	Y
NEW MEXICO								
1 **Wilson**	N	N	N	Y	Y	N	Y	N
2 **Skeen**	N	N	N	Y	Y	N	Y	Y
3 Udall	Y	Y	Y	Y	N	Y	Y	N
NEW YORK								
1 **Forbes**	Y	Y	N	N	Y	Y	N	Y
2 **Lazio**	Y	N	N	Y	Y	N	Y	N
3 **King**	N	N	N	Y	Y	N	Y	Y
4 McCarthy	Y	Y	Y	Y	Y	Y	Y	Y
5 Ackerman	Y	Y	Y	Y	Y	Y	N	?
6 Meeks	Y	Y	Y	Y	Y	Y	N	Y
7 Crowley	Y	Y	Y	Y	Y	Y	Y	Y
8 Nadler	Y	Y	Y	Y	Y	Y	N	Y
9 Weiner	Y	Y	Y	N	Y	Y	Y	Y
10 Towns	Y	Y	Y	Y	Y	Y	N	Y
11 Owens	Y	Y	Y	Y	Y	Y	N	Y
12 Velázquez	Y	Y	Y	Y	Y	Y	N	Y
13 **Fossella**	Y	N	N	Y	Y	N	Y	N
14 Maloney	Y	Y	Y	Y	Y	Y	N	Y
15 Rangel	Y	Y	Y	Y	Y	Y	N	Y
16 Serrano	Y	Y	Y	Y	Y	Y	N	Y
17 Engel	Y	Y	Y	Y	Y	Y	N	Y
18 Lowey	Y	Y	Y	Y	Y	Y	Y	Y
19 **Kelly**	Y	Y	N	Y	Y	Y	Y	N
20 **Gilman**	Y	N	N	Y	Y	Y	Y	Y
21 McNulty	?	?	?	?	?	?	?	?
22 **Sweeney**	N	N	N	Y	N	N	Y	Y
23 **Boehlert**	N	Y	N	Y	Y	Y	Y	Y
24 **McHugh**	N	N	N	Y	Y	N	Y	Y
25 **Walsh**	Y	N	N	Y	Y	N	Y	Y
26 Hinchey	Y	Y	Y	Y	N	Y	N	Y
27 **Reynolds**	N	N	N	Y	Y	N	Y	N
28 Slaughter	Y	Y	Y	N	N	Y	Y	Y
29 LaFalce	Y	Y	Y	Y	N	Y	Y	Y
30 **Quinn**	N	N	N	Y	Y	N	Y	Y
31 **Houghton**	N	N	N	Y	Y	Y	Y	Y
NORTH CAROLINA								
1 Clayton	N	Y	Y	Y	Y	Y	Y	Y
2 Etheridge	Y	Y	Y	Y	Y	Y	Y	N
3 **Jones**	Y	Y	N	Y	Y	N	Y	N
4 Price	Y	Y	Y	Y	Y	Y	Y	N
5 **Burr**	N	N	N	Y	?	N	Y	N
6 **Coble**	N	N	N	Y	Y	N	Y	N
7 McIntyre	N	Y	N	Y	Y	N	Y	N
8 **Hayes**	N	N	N	Y	Y	N	Y	N
9 **Myrick**	N	N	N	Y	Y	N	Y	Y
10 **Ballenger**	N	N	N	Y	Y	N	Y	Y
11 **Taylor**	N	N	N	Y	Y	N	Y	N
12 Watt	Y	Y	Y	Y	Y	Y	N	Y
NORTH DAKOTA								
AL Pomeroy	Y	Y	Y	Y	Y	Y	Y	N
OHIO								
1 **Chabot**	Y	Y	N	Y	Y	N	Y	N
2 **Portman**	Y	N	N	Y	Y	N	Y	N
3 Hall	Y	Y	Y	Y	Y	N	Y	Y
4 **Oxley**	N	N	N	Y	Y	N	Y	Y
5 **Gillmor**	N	N	N	Y	N	N	Y	Y
6 Strickland	N	Y	Y	Y	N	Y	Y	N
7 **Hobson**	N	N	N	Y	Y	N	Y	Y
8 **Boehner**	N	N	N	Y	Y	N	Y	Y
9 Kaptur	Y	Y	Y	Y	Y	Y	Y	N
10 Kucinich	Y	Y	Y	Y	N	Y	N	N
11 Jones	Y	Y	Y	Y	?	Y	N	Y
12 **Kasich**	N	N	N	Y	?	N	Y	N
13 Brown	Y	Y	Y	Y	Y	Y	N	N
14 Sawyer	Y	Y	Y	Y	Y	Y	Y	Y
15 **Pryce**	N	N	N	Y	Y	N	Y	Y
16 **Regula**	N	N	N	Y	?	N	Y	Y
17 Traficant	N	Y	N	Y	Y	N	Y	N
18 **Ney**	N	N	N	Y	Y	N	Y	Y
19 **LaTourette**	N	Y	N	Y	Y	N	Y	Y
OKLAHOMA								
1 **Largent**	N	N	N	Y	Y	N	Y	Y
2 **Coburn**	N	N	N	Y	Y	N	Y	Y
3 **Watkins**	N	N	N	Y	Y	N	Y	Y
4 **Watts**	N	N	N	Y	?	N	Y	Y
5 **Istook**	N	N	N	Y	Y	N	Y	Y
6 **Lucas**	N	N	N	Y	Y	N	Y	Y
OREGON								
1 Wu	Y	Y	Y	Y	N	Y	N	N
2 **Walden**	N	N	N	Y	Y	N	Y	N
3 Blumenauer	Y	Y	Y	Y	Y	Y	Y	N
4 DeFazio	N	Y	Y	Y	N	Y	N	N
5 Hooley	Y	Y	Y	Y	Y	Y	Y	N
PENNSYLVANIA								
1 Brady	N	Y	Y	Y	Y	Y	N	Y
2 Fattah	Y	Y	Y	N	N	Y	N	Y
3 Borski	Y	Y	Y	Y	N	Y	Y	Y
4 Klink	N	Y	Y	Y	Y	Y	Y	Y
5 **Peterson**	N	N	N	Y	Y	N	Y	N
6 Holden	N	Y	Y	N	Y	Y	Y	Y
7 **Weldon**	N	N	N	Y	?	N	Y	Y
8 **Greenwood**	N	N	N	Y	Y	Y	Y	Y
9 **Shuster**	N	Y	N	Y	Y	N	Y	Y
10 **Sherwood**	N	N	N	Y	Y	N	Y	N
11 Kanjorski	Y	Y	Y	N	Y	Y	Y	Y
12 Murtha	N	Y	Y	Y	Y	Y	Y	Y
13 Hoeffel	Y	Y	Y	Y	Y	Y	Y	N
14 Coyne	Y	Y	Y	Y	Y	Y	N	Y
15 **Toomey**	N	N	N	Y	Y	N	Y	N
16 **Pitts**	N	N	N	Y	Y	N	Y	Y
17 **Gekas**	N	N	N	Y	Y	N	Y	Y
18 Doyle	N	Y	Y	Y	Y	Y	Y	Y
19 **Goodling**	N	N	N	N	Y	N	Y	Y
20 Mascara	N	Y	Y	Y	Y	Y	Y	N
21 **English**	N	N	N	Y	?	N	Y	N
RHODE ISLAND								
1 Kennedy	Y	Y	Y	N	?	Y	N	Y
2 Weygand	Y	Y	Y	Y	Y	Y	N	N
SOUTH CAROLINA								
1 **Sanford**	N	N	N	N	Y	N	N	N
2 **Spence**	N	N	N	Y	Y	N	Y	Y
3 **Graham**	N	N	N	Y	Y	N	Y	Y
4 **DeMint**	N	N	N	Y	Y	N	Y	N
5 Spratt	Y	Y	Y	Y	Y	N	Y	Y
6 Clyburn	Y	Y	Y	Y	N	Y	N	Y
SOUTH DAKOTA								
AL **Thune**	N	N	N	Y	Y	N	Y	N
TENNESSEE								
1 **Jenkins**	N	N	N	Y	Y	N	Y	N
2 **Duncan**	N	Y	N	Y	Y	N	Y	N
3 **Wamp**	N	N	N	Y	Y	N	Y	N
4 **Hilleary**	N	N	N	Y	N	N	Y	N
5 Clement	N	Y	Y	Y	Y	N	Y	Y
6 Gordon	Y	Y	N	Y	Y	N	Y	N
7 **Bryant**	N	N	N	Y	Y	N	Y	N
8 Tanner	N	Y	N	Y	N	N	Y	Y
9 Ford	Y	Y	Y	Y	Y	Y	Y	Y
TEXAS								
1 Sandlin	N	Y	Y	Y	Y	Y	Y	N
2 Turner	N	Y	Y	Y	Y	N	Y	N
3 **Johnson, Sam**	N	N	N	Y	Y	N	Y	Y
4 Hall	N	Y	N	Y	Y	N	Y	N
5 **Sessions**	N	N	N	Y	Y	N	Y	Y
6 **Barton**	N	N	N	Y	Y	N	Y	Y
7 **Archer**	N	N	N	Y	?	N	Y	Y
8 **Brady**	N	N	N	Y	Y	N	Y	N
9 Lampson	Y	Y	Y	Y	Y	Y	Y	Y
10 Doggett	Y	Y	Y	N	Y	Y	N	N
11 Edwards	N	Y	Y	Y	Y	N	Y	N
12 **Granger**	N	N	N	Y	Y	N	Y	Y
13 **Thornberry**	N	N	N	Y	Y	N	Y	Y
14 **Paul**	N	?	N	N	Y	N	N	N
15 Hinojosa	N	Y	Y	Y	Y	Y	Y	N
16 Reyes	Y	Y	Y	Y	Y	Y	Y	Y
17 Stenholm	N	Y	N	Y	Y	N	Y	Y
18 Jackson-Lee	Y	Y	Y	Y	Y	Y	Y	Y
19 **Combest**	?	?	?	?	Y	N	Y	Y
20 Gonzalez	Y	Y	Y	Y	Y	Y	Y	Y
21 **Smith**	N	N	N	Y	Y	N	Y	Y
22 **DeLay**	N	N	N	Y	Y	N	Y	Y
23 **Bonilla**	N	N	N	Y	Y	N	Y	Y
24 Frost	N	Y	Y	Y	?	?	?	?
25 Bentsen	N	Y	Y	Y	Y	Y	Y	Y
26 **Armey**	N	N	N	Y	Y	N	Y	Y
27 Ortiz	N	Y	Y	Y	Y	N	Y	Y
28 Rodriguez	Y	Y	Y	Y	Y	Y	Y	N
29 Green	Y	Y	Y	Y	Y	N	Y	Y
30 Johnson, E.B.	Y	Y	Y	Y	Y	Y	N	Y
UTAH								
1 **Hansen**	N	Y	N	Y	Y	N	Y	Y
2 **Cook**	N	Y	N	Y	Y	N	Y	N
3 **Cannon**	N	N	N	Y	Y	N	Y	Y
VERMONT								
AL Sanders	Y	Y	Y	Y	Y	Y	N	N
VIRGINIA								
1 **Bateman**	N	N	N	Y	Y	N	Y	Y
2 Pickett	N	Y	N	Y	N	N	N	Y
3 Scott	Y	Y	Y	Y	Y	Y	N	Y
4 Sisisky	N	Y	N	Y	Y	Y	Y	Y
5 Goode	N	Y	N	Y	Y	N	Y	N
6 **Goodlatte**	N	N	N	Y	Y	N	Y	Y
7 **Bliley**	N	N	N	Y	Y	N	Y	Y
8 Moran	Y	Y	Y	Y	Y	Y	Y	Y
9 Boucher	Y	Y	Y	Y	Y	Y	N	Y
10 **Wolf**	N	N	N	Y	Y	N	Y	Y
11 **Davis**	N	N	N	Y	Y	N	Y	Y
WASHINGTON								
1 Inslee	Y	Y	Y	Y	Y	Y	Y	N
2 **Metcalf**	N	N	N	Y	Y	N	N	Y
3 Baird	N	Y	Y	Y	Y	Y	N	N
4 **Hastings**	N	N	N	Y	Y	N	Y	Y
5 **Nethercutt**	N	N	N	Y	Y	N	Y	N
6 Dicks	N	Y	Y	Y	Y	Y	Y	Y
7 McDermott	?	?	?	?	?	?	?	?
8 **Dunn**	N	N	N	Y	Y	N	Y	N
9 Smith	Y	Y	Y	Y	Y	Y	N	N
WEST VIRGINIA								
1 Mollohan	N	Y	Y	Y	Y	Y	Y	Y
2 Wise	N	Y	Y	Y	Y	Y	Y	N
3 Rahall	Y	Y	Y	Y	Y	Y	Y	Y
WISCONSIN								
1 **Ryan**	Y	N	N	Y	Y	N	Y	N
2 Baldwin	?	?	?	?	?	?	?	?
3 Kind	Y	Y	Y	Y	Y	Y	Y	N
4 Kleczka	Y	Y	Y	Y	Y	Y	Y	Y
5 Barrett	Y	Y	Y	Y	Y	Y	N	Y
6 **Petri**	N	Y	N	Y	Y	N	Y	N
7 Obey	N	Y	Y	N	Y	Y	Y	Y
8 **Green**	N	N	N	Y	Y	N	Y	N
9 **Sensenbrenner**	N	N	N	N	Y	N	Y	N
WYOMING								
AL **Cubin**	N	N	N	Y	Y	N	Y	Y

Southern states - Ala., Ark., Fla., Ga., Ky., La., Miss., N.C., Okla., S.C., Tenn., Texas, Va.

301. HR 2490. Fiscal 2000 Treasury-Postal Appropriations/Abortion Coverage. DeLauro, D-Conn., amendment to strike provisions of the bill that would prohibit federal employee health plans from providing coverage for abortions. Rejected 188-230: R 28-186; D 159-44 (ND 120-31, SD 39-13); I 1-0. July 15, 1999.

302. HR 2490. Fiscal 2000 Treasury-Postal Appropriations/Presidential Salary. Sessions, R-Texas, amendment to strike language from the bill that would raise the president's annual salary from $200,000 to $400,000. Rejected 82-334: R 64-149; D 17-185 (ND 10-139, SD 7-46); I 1-0. July 15, 1999.

303. HR 2490. Fiscal 2000 Treasury-Postal Appropriations/Contraceptive Coverage. Lowey, D-N.Y., amendment to the Smith, R-N.J., amendment. The Smith amendment would exempt health plans from requirements to offer contraceptive coverage if doing so would violate the plan's religious beliefs or moral convictions. The Lowey amendment would remove the exemption for moral convictions. Adopted 217-200: R 42-171; D 174-29 (ND 132-19, SD 42-10); I 1-0. July 15, 1999. (Subsequently, the Smith amendment, as amended, was adopted by voice vote.)

304. HR 2490. Fiscal 2000 Treasury-Postal Appropriations/Exchange Stabilization Fund. Sanders, I-Vt., amendment to prohibit the use of funds in the bill to make any loan or credit in excess of $1 billion to foreign countries through the Exchange Stabilization Fund of the Treasury Department, unless Congress specifically approves the action by statute. The amendment would not require congressional approval for Treasury action to use the fund for exchange stabilization. Rejected 192-228: R 147-68; D 44-160 (ND 36-115, SD 8-45); I 1-0. July 15, 1999.

305. HR 2490. Fiscal 2000 Treasury-Postal Appropriations/Passage. Passage of the bill to appropriate $28 billion in funds for the Treasury Department, U.S. Postal Service, the Executive Office of the President, and certain independent agencies. The bill would increase the annual salary of the president from $200,000 to $400,000, ban the use of funds in the bill to pay for most abortions under federal employee health benefit plans, require federal employee health plans to include contraceptives in any prescription drug coverage. Passed 210-209: R 202-13; D 8-195 (ND 7-143, SD 1-52); I 0-1. July 15, 1999.

[1] George E. Brown Jr., D-Calif., died July 15.

Key

- Y Voted for (yea).
- # Paired for.
- \+ Announced for.
- N Voted against (nay).
- X Paired against.
- – Announced against.
- P Voted "present."
- C Voted "present" to avoid possible conflict of interest.
- ? Did not vote or otherwise make a position known.

•

Democrats ***Republicans***
Independents

	301	302	303	304	305
ALABAMA					
1 ***Callahan***	N	N	N	N	Y
2 ***Everett***	N	Y	N	Y	Y
3 ***Riley***	N	Y	N	Y	Y
4 ***Aderholt***	N	Y	N	Y	Y
5 Cramer	Y	N	Y	N	N
6 ***Bachus***	N	N	N	Y	Y
7 Hilliard	?	N	Y	N	N
ALASKA					
AL ***Young***	N	N	N	N	Y
ARIZONA					
1 ***Salmon***	N	Y	N	Y	N
2 Pastor	Y	N	Y	N	N
3 ***Stump***	N	Y	N	Y	Y
4 ***Shadegg***	N	N	N	Y	Y
5 ***Kolbe***	N	N	Y	N	Y
6 ***Hayworth***	N	Y	N	Y	Y
ARKANSAS					
1 Berry	N	Y	Y	N	N
2 Snyder	Y	N	Y	N	N
3 ***Hutchinson***	N	N	N	Y	Y
4 ***Dickey***	N	N	N	N	Y
CALIFORNIA					
1 Thompson	Y	N	Y	N	N
2 ***Herger***	N	N	N	N	Y
3 ***Ose***	Y	N	Y	N	Y
4 ***Doolittle***	N	N	N	Y	Y
5 Matsui	Y	N	Y	N	Y
6 Woolsey	Y	N	Y	Y	N
7 Miller, George	Y	N	Y	Y	N
8 Pelosi	Y	N	Y	N	N
9 Lee	Y	N	Y	Y	N
10 Tauscher	Y	N	Y	N	N
11 ***Pombo***	N	N	N	Y	Y
12 Lantos	Y	N	Y	N	N
13 Stark	Y	N	Y	Y	N
14 Eshoo	Y	N	Y	N	N
15 ***Campbell***	Y	N	Y	Y	Y
16 Lofgren	Y	N	Y	N	N
17 Farr	Y	N	Y	N	N
18 Condit	Y	N	Y	Y	Y
19 ***Radanovich***	N	Y	N	N	Y
20 Dooley	Y	N	Y	N	N
21 ***Thomas***	N	N	N	N	Y
22 Capps	Y	N	Y	N	N
23 ***Gallegly***	N	N	Y	N	Y
24 Sherman	Y	N	Y	N	N
25 ***McKeon***	N	N	N	Y	Y
26 Berman	Y	N	Y	N	N
27 ***Rogan***	N	Y	N	Y	Y
28 ***Dreier***	N	N	N	N	Y
29 Waxman	Y	N	Y	N	Y
30 Becerra	Y	N	Y	N	N
31 Martinez	Y	N	Y	N	N
32 Dixon	Y	N	Y	N	N
33 Roybal-Allard	Y	N	Y	N	N
34 Napolitano	Y	N	Y	N	N
35 Waters	Y	N	Y	N	N
36 ***Kuykendall***	Y	N	Y	N	Y
37 Millender-McD.	Y	N	Y	N	N
38 ***Horn***	Y	N	Y	N	Y
39 ***Royce***	N	?	?	Y	Y
40 ***Lewis***	N	N	N	N	Y
41 ***Miller, Gary***	N	N	N	N	Y
42 Brown [1]	?	?	?	?	?
43 ***Calvert***	N	N	N	N	Y
44 ***Bono***	N	Y	Y	N	Y
45 ***Rohrabacher***	N	N	N	Y	Y
46 Sanchez	Y	N	Y	N	N
47 ***Cox***	?	N	N	Y	Y
48 ***Packard***	N	N	N	Y	Y
49 ***Bilbray***	N	N	Y	Y	Y
50 Filner	Y	N	Y	N	N
51 ***Cunningham***	N	N	N	Y	Y
52 ***Hunter***	N	N	N	Y	Y
COLORADO					
1 DeGette	Y	N	Y	N	N
2 Udall	Y	Y	Y	N	N
3 ***McInnis***	N	N	N	Y	Y
4 ***Schaffer***	N	Y	–	Y	N
5 ***Hefley***	N	Y	N	Y	Y
6 ***Tancredo***	N	Y	N	Y	Y
CONNECTICUT					
1 Larson	Y	N	Y	N	N
2 Gejdenson	Y	?	Y	N	N
3 DeLauro	Y	N	Y	N	N
4 ***Shays***	Y	N	N	N	Y
5 Maloney	Y	N	Y	N	N
6 ***Johnson***	Y	N	Y	N	Y
DELAWARE					
AL ***Castle***	Y	N	Y	N	Y
FLORIDA					
1 ***Scarborough***	N	N	N	Y	N
2 Boyd	Y	N	Y	N	N
3 Brown	Y	N	Y	N	N
4 ***Fowler***	N	N	Y	Y	Y
5 Thurman	?	?	?	?	?
6 ***Stearns***	N	Y	N	Y	Y
7 ***Mica***	N	Y	N	Y	Y
8 ***McCollum***	N	Y	N	Y	Y
9 ***Bilirakis***	N	N	N	Y	Y
10 ***Young***	N	N	N	N	Y
11 Davis	Y	N	Y	N	N
12 ***Canady***	N	N	N	Y	Y
13 ***Miller***	Y	N	Y	N	Y
14 ***Goss***	N	N	N	N	Y
15 ***Weldon***	N	N	N	Y	Y
16 ***Foley***	Y	N	Y	Y	Y
17 Meek	Y	N	Y	N	N
18 ***Ros-Lehtinen***	N	N	N	Y	Y
19 Wexler	Y	N	Y	N	N
20 Deutsch	Y	N	Y	N	N
21 ***Diaz-Balart***	N	N	N	Y	Y
22 ***Shaw***	N	N	Y	N	Y
23 Hastings	Y	N	Y	N	N
GEORGIA					
1 ***Kingston***	N	N	N	Y	Y
2 Bishop	Y	N	Y	N	N
3 ***Collins***	N	N	N	Y	Y
4 McKinney	Y	N	Y	Y	N
5 Lewis	Y	N	Y	N	N
6 ***Isakson***	N	N	Y	N	Y
7 ***Barr***	N	N	N	Y	N
8 ***Chambliss***	N	N	N	N	Y
9 ***Deal***	N	N	N	Y	Y
10 ***Norwood***	N	N	N	Y	Y
11 ***Linder***	N	N	N	Y	Y
HAWAII					
1 Abercrombie	Y	N	Y	Y	Y
2 Mink	Y	N	Y	Y	N
IDAHO					
1 ***Chenoweth***	?	?	?	?	?
2 ***Simpson***	N	N	Y	Y	Y
ILLINOIS					
1 Rush	Y	N	Y	N	N
2 Jackson	Y	N	Y	N	N
3 Lipinski	N	N	N	Y	N
4 Gutierrez	Y	N	Y	Y	N
5 Blagojevich	Y	N	Y	N	N
6 ***Hyde***	N	N	N	Y	Y
7 Davis	Y	N	Y	Y	N
8 ***Crane***	N	Y	N	Y	Y
9 Schakowsky	Y	N	Y	N	N
10 ***Porter***	Y	N	Y	N	Y
11 ***Weller***	N	N	N	Y	Y
12 Costello	N	N	N	Y	N
13 ***Biggert***	Y	N	Y	N	Y
14 ***Hastert***					Y

ND Northern Democrats SD Southern Democrats

	301	302	303	304	305
15 ***Ewing***	N	N	N	N	Y
16 ***Manzullo***	N	Y	N	Y	Y
17 Evans	Y	N	Y	Y	N
18 ***LaHood***	N	N	N	N	Y
19 Phelps	N	N	N	Y	N
20 ***Shimkus***	N	Y	N	Y	Y
INDIANA					
1 Visclosky	Y	N	Y	Y	N
2 ***McIntosh***	N	N	N	Y	Y
3 Roemer	N	N	Y	N	N
4 ***Souder***	N	N	N	Y	Y
5 ***Buyer***	N	N	N	Y	Y
6 ***Burton***	N	?	?	?	?
7 ***Pease***	N	N	N	Y	Y
8 ***Hostettler***	N	N	N	Y	Y
9 Hill	Y	Y	Y	N	N
10 Carson	Y	N	Y	N	N
IOWA					
1 ***Leach***	N	N	N	N	Y
2 ***Nussle***	N	N	N	N	Y
3 Boswell	Y	Y	Y	N	N
4 ***Ganske***	N	N	Y	Y	Y
5 ***Latham***	?	?	?	?	?
KANSAS					
1 ***Moran***	N	Y	N	Y	Y
2 ***Ryun***	N	Y	N	Y	Y
3 Moore	Y	N	Y	N	N
4 ***Tiahrt***	N	Y	N	Y	N
KENTUCKY					
1 ***Whitfield***	N	N	N	Y	Y
2 ***Lewis***	N	Y	N	Y	Y
3 ***Northup***	N	N	N	N	Y
4 Lucas	N	Y	N	Y	N
5 ***Rogers***	N	N	N	Y	Y
6 ***Fletcher***	N	Y	N	Y	Y
LOUISIANA					
1 ***Vitter***	N	Y	N	Y	Y
2 Jefferson	Y	N	Y	N	N
3 ***Tauzin***	N	N	N	N	Y
4 ***McCrery***	N	N	N	N	Y
5 ***Cooksey***	?	?	?	?	?
6 ***Baker***	N	N	N	Y	N
7 John	N	N	N	N	N
MAINE					
1 Allen	Y	N	Y	N	N
2 Baldacci	Y	N	Y	N	N
MARYLAND					
1 ***Gilchrest***	?	?	?	?	?
2 ***Ehrlich***	Y	N	Y	Y	Y
3 Cardin	Y	N	Y	N	N
4 Wynn	Y	N	Y	N	N
5 Hoyer	Y	N	Y	N	N
6 ***Bartlett***	N	Y	N	Y	Y
7 Cummings	Y	N	Y	N	N
8 ***Morella***	Y	N	Y	N	Y
MASSACHUSETTS					
1 Olver	Y	N	Y	N	N
2 Neal	N	N	Y	N	N
3 McGovern	Y	N	Y	N	N
4 Frank	Y	N	Y	N	?
5 Meehan	Y	N	Y	N	N
6 Tierney	Y	N	Y	N	N
7 Markey	Y	N	Y	N	N
8 Capuano	Y	N	Y	N	N
9 Moakley	N	N	Y	N	N
10 Delahunt	Y	N	Y	N	N
MICHIGAN					
1 Stupak	N	N	N	Y	N
2 ***Hoekstra***	N	N	N	Y	Y
3 ***Ehlers***	N	N	N	N	Y
4 ***Camp***	N	N	N	Y	Y
5 Barcia	N	Y	N	N	N
6 ***Upton***	N	N	N	Y	Y
7 ***Smith***	N	N	N	Y	Y
8 Stabenow	Y	Y	Y	N	N
9 Kildee	N	N	N	N	N
10 Bonior	N	N	Y	N	N
11 ***Knollenberg***	N	N	N	N	Y
12 Levin	Y	N	Y	N	N
13 Rivers	Y	N	Y	Y	N
14 Conyers	Y	N	Y	Y	N
15 Kilpatrick	Y	N	Y	N	N
16 Dingell	Y	N	Y	N	N

	301	302	303	304	305
MINNESOTA					
1 ***Gutknecht***	N	N	N	Y	Y
2 Minge	Y	N	Y	N	N
3 ***Ramstad***	Y	Y	Y	Y	N
4 Vento	Y	N	Y	N	N
5 Sabo	Y	N	Y	N	N
6 Luther	?	?	?	?	?
7 Peterson	N	N	N	Y	N
8 Oberstar	N	N	N	N	N
MISSISSIPPI					
1 ***Wicker***	N	N	N	Y	Y
2 Thompson	Y	N	Y	N	N
3 ***Pickering***	N	N	N	Y	Y
4 Shows	N	Y	N	Y	N
5 Taylor	N	Y	N	Y	N
MISSOURI					
1 Clay	Y	N	Y	Y	N
2 ***Talent***	N	N	N	Y	Y
3 Gephardt	Y	N	Y	N	N
4 Skelton	N	N	N	N	N
5 McCarthy	Y	N	Y	N	N
6 Danner	N	Y	Y	Y	N
7 ***Blunt***	N	N	N	Y	Y
8 ***Emerson***	N	Y	N	Y	Y
9 ***Hulshof***	N	N	N	Y	Y
MONTANA					
AL ***Hill***	N	N	N	Y	Y
NEBRASKA					
1 ***Bereuter***	N	N	Y	N	Y
2 ***Terry***	N	N	N	Y	Y
3 ***Barrett***	N	N	N	N	Y
NEVADA					
1 Berkley	Y	Y	Y	N	N
2 ***Gibbons***	N	Y	Y	Y	Y
NEW HAMPSHIRE					
1 ***Sununu***	N	N	N	Y	Y
2 ***Bass***	Y	N	Y	Y	Y
NEW JERSEY					
1 Andrews	Y	N	Y	Y	N
2 ***LoBiondo***	N	Y	N	Y	Y
3 ***Saxton***	N	N	N	Y	Y
4 ***Smith***	N	N	N	Y	Y
5 ***Roukema***	Y	N	Y	N	Y
6 Pallone	Y	N	Y	N	N
7 ***Franks***	Y	N	Y	Y	Y
8 Pascrell	Y	N	Y	Y	N
9 Rothman	Y	N	Y	N	N
10 Payne	Y	N	Y	N	N
11 ***Frelinghuysen***	Y	N	Y	N	Y
12 Holt	Y	N	Y	N	N
13 Menendez	Y	N	Y	N	N
NEW MEXICO					
1 ***Wilson***	N	N	N	N	Y
2 ***Skeen***	N	Y	N	Y	Y
3 Udall	Y	N	Y	N	N
NEW YORK					
1 ***Forbes***	N	N	N	N	Y
2 ***Lazio***	Y	N	Y	N	Y
3 ***King***	N	N	N	N	Y
4 McCarthy	Y	N	Y	N	N
5 Ackerman	Y	N	Y	N	N
6 Meeks	Y	N	Y	N	N
7 Crowley	N	N	Y	N	N
8 Nadler	Y	N	Y	N	N
9 Weiner	Y	N	Y	N	N
10 Towns	Y	N	Y	N	N
11 Owens	Y	N	Y	N	N
12 Velázquez	Y	N	Y	Y	N
13 ***Fossella***	N	Y	N	Y	Y
14 Maloney	Y	N	Y	N	N
15 Rangel	Y	N	Y	N	N
16 Serrano	Y	N	Y	Y	N
17 Engel	Y	N	Y	N	Y
18 Lowey	Y	N	Y	N	N
19 ***Kelly***	Y	Y	Y	N	Y
20 ***Gilman***	Y	N	Y	N	Y
21 McNulty	?	?	?	?	?
22 ***Sweeney***	Y	N	N	Y	Y
23 ***Boehlert***	Y	N	Y	N	Y
24 ***McHugh***	N	N	N	Y	Y
25 ***Walsh***	N	N	N	N	Y
26 Hinchey	Y	N	Y	N	N
27 ***Reynolds***	N	N	N	Y	Y
28 Slaughter	Y	N	Y	Y	N
29 LaFalce	N	N	N	N	Y

	301	302	303	304	305
30 ***Quinn***	?	?	N	Y	Y
31 ***Houghton***	Y	N	Y	N	Y
NORTH CAROLINA					
1 Clayton	Y	N	Y	N	N
2 Etheridge	Y	N	Y	N	N
3 ***Jones***	N	Y	N	Y	Y
4 Price	Y	N	Y	N	N
5 ***Burr***	N	N	N	Y	Y
6 ***Coble***	?	?	?	?	?
7 McIntyre	N	N	N	Y	N
8 ***Hayes***	N	N	N	Y	Y
9 ***Myrick***	N	Y	N	Y	Y
10 ***Ballenger***	N	N	N	N	Y
11 ***Taylor***	N	N	N	N	Y
12 Watt	Y	N	Y	N	N
NORTH DAKOTA					
AL Pomeroy	Y	N	Y	N	N
OHIO					
1 ***Chabot***	N	Y	N	Y	N
2 ***Portman***	N	N	N	N	Y
3 Hall	N	N	N	N	N
4 ***Oxley***	N	N	N	N	Y
5 ***Gillmor***	N	N	N	Y	Y
6 Strickland	Y	N	Y	Y	N
7 ***Hobson***	N	N	Y	N	Y
8 ***Boehner***	N	N	N	N	Y
9 Kaptur	N	N	Y	Y	N
10 Kucinich	N	Y	N	Y	N
11 Jones	Y	N	Y	N	N
12 ***Kasich***	N	Y	N	Y	Y
13 Brown	Y	N	Y	Y	N
14 Sawyer	Y	N	Y	N	N
15 ***Pryce***	Y	Y	Y	Y	Y
16 ***Regula***	N	N	N	Y	Y
17 Traficant	N	N	N	Y	N
18 ***Ney***	N	N	N	Y	Y
19 ***LaTourette***	N	N	Y	N	Y
OKLAHOMA					
1 ***Largent***	N	Y	N	Y	Y
2 ***Coburn***	N	N	N	Y	Y
3 ***Watkins***	N	Y	N	N	Y
4 ***Watts***	N	N	N	Y	Y
5 ***Istook***	N	N	N	Y	Y
6 ***Lucas***	N	N	N	Y	Y
OREGON					
1 Wu	Y	Y	Y	N	N
2 ***Walden***	N	N	Y	Y	Y
3 Blumenauer	Y	N	Y	N	Y
4 DeFazio	Y	N	Y	Y	N
5 Hooley	Y	N	Y	N	N
PENNSYLVANIA					
1 Brady	Y	N	Y	N	N
2 Fattah	Y	?	Y	N	N
3 Borski	N	N	Y	N	N
4 Klink	N	N	Y	N	N
5 ***Peterson***	N	?	?	?	?
6 Holden	N	N	N	Y	N
7 ***Weldon***	N	N	N	Y	Y
8 ***Greenwood***	Y	N	Y	Y	Y
9 ***Shuster***	N	N	N	Y	Y
10 ***Sherwood***	N	N	N	Y	Y
11 Kanjorski	N	N	Y	N	N
12 Murtha	N	N	N	N	N
13 Hoeffel	Y	N	Y	N	N
14 Coyne	Y	N	Y	N	N
15 ***Toomey***	N	Y	N	Y	N
16 ***Pitts***	N	N	N	Y	N
17 ***Gekas***	N	N	N	N	Y
18 Doyle	N	N	N	N	N
19 ***Goodling***	N	N	N	Y	Y
20 Mascara	N	N	N	N	N
21 ***English***	N	N	N	Y	Y
RHODE ISLAND					
1 Kennedy	Y	N	Y	N	N
2 Weygand	N	N	Y	N	N
SOUTH CAROLINA					
1 ***Sanford***	N	Y	N	Y	?
2 ***Spence***	N	N	N	Y	Y
3 ***Graham***	N	Y	N	Y	Y
4 ***DeMint***	N	Y	N	Y	Y
5 Spratt	Y	N	Y	N	N
6 Clyburn	Y	N	Y	N	N
SOUTH DAKOTA					
AL ***Thune***	N	Y	N	Y	Y

	301	302	303	304	305
TENNESSEE					
1 ***Jenkins***	N	Y	N	Y	Y
2 ***Duncan***	N	Y	N	Y	N
3 ***Wamp***	N	Y	N	Y	Y
4 ***Hilleary***	N	Y	N	Y	N
5 Clement	Y	N	Y	N	N
6 Gordon	Y	N	?	N	N
7 ***Bryant***	N	Y	N	Y	Y
8 Tanner	Y	N	Y	N	N
9 Ford	Y	N	Y	N	N
TEXAS					
1 Sandlin	Y	N	Y	N	N
2 Turner	N	Y	N	Y	N
3 ***Johnson, Sam***	N	Y	N	Y	Y
4 Hall	N	Y	N	Y	N
5 ***Sessions***	N	Y	N	Y	Y
6 ***Barton***	?	N	N	N	Y
7 ***Archer***	N	N	N	N	Y
8 ***Brady***	N	Y	N	N	Y
9 Lampson	N	N	Y	N	N
10 Doggett	Y	N	Y	N	N
11 Edwards	N	N	Y	N	N
12 ***Granger***	N	N	Y	Y	Y
13 ***Thornberry***	N	Y	N	Y	Y
14 ***Paul***	N	Y	N	Y	N
15 Hinojosa	Y	N	Y	N	N
16 Reyes	Y	N	Y	N	N
17 Stenholm	N	N	N	N	N
18 Jackson-Lee	Y	N	Y	N	N
19 ***Combest***	N	Y	N	N	Y
20 Gonzalez	Y	N	Y	N	N
21 ***Smith***	N	N	N	Y	Y
22 ***DeLay***	N	N	N	N	Y
23 ***Bonilla***	Y	N	N	Y	Y
24 Frost	?	?	?	?	?
25 Bentsen	Y	N	Y	N	N
26 ***Armey***	N	N	N	Y	Y
27 Ortiz	N	N	N	N	N
28 Rodriguez	Y	N	Y	N	N
29 Green	Y	N	Y	N	N
30 Johnson, E.B.	Y	N	Y	N	N
UTAH					
1 ***Hansen***	N	Y	N	N	Y
2 ***Cook***	N	Y	Y	Y	Y
3 ***Cannon***	N	N	N	Y	Y
VERMONT					
AL *Sanders*	Y	Y	Y	Y	N
VIRGINIA					
1 ***Bateman***	N	N	N	Y	Y
2 Pickett	Y	N	Y	N	Y
3 Scott	Y	N	Y	N	N
4 Sisisky	Y	N	Y	N	N
5 Goode	N	Y	N	Y	N
6 ***Goodlatte***	N	N	N	Y	N
7 ***Bliley***	N	N	N	Y	Y
8 Moran	Y	N	Y	N	N
9 Boucher	Y	N	Y	N	N
10 ***Wolf***	N	N	N	Y	Y
11 ***Davis***	Y	N	N	N	Y
WASHINGTON					
1 Inslee	Y	N	Y	N	N
2 ***Metcalf***	N	Y	N	Y	Y
3 Baird	Y	N	Y	N	N
4 ***Hastings***	N	Y	N	Y	Y
5 ***Nethercutt***	N	Y	N	Y	Y
6 Dicks	Y	N	Y	N	N
7 McDermott	?	?	?	?	?
8 ***Dunn***	N	Y	Y	N	Y
9 Smith	Y	N	Y	N	N
WEST VIRGINIA					
1 Mollohan	N	N	N	N	N
2 Wise	Y	N	Y	Y	N
3 Rahall	N	N	N	Y	N
WISCONSIN					
1 ***Ryan***	N	N	N	Y	Y
2 Baldwin	?	?	?	?	?
3 Kind	Y	Y	Y	N	N
4 Kleczka	N	N	Y	N	N
5 Barrett	Y	N	Y	N	N
6 ***Petri***	N	N	N	Y	Y
7 Obey	Y	N	Y	N	N
8 ***Green***	N	Y	N	Y	Y
9 ***Sensenbrenner***	N	Y	N	Y	Y
WYOMING					
AL ***Cubin***	N	N	N	Y	Y

Southern states - Ala., Ark., Fla., Ga., Ky., La., Miss., N.C., Okla., S.C., Tenn., Texas, Va.

House Votes 306, 307, 308, 309, 310, 311, 312, 313

306. HR 434. Trade with Sub-Saharan Africa/Rule. Adoption of the rule (H Res 250) to provide for House floor consideration of the bill to extend certain trade preferences to the nations of sub-Saharan Africa. Adopted 263-141: R 184-25; D 79-115 (ND 58-86, SD 21-29); I 0-1. July 16, 1999.

307. HR 434. Trade with Sub-Saharan Africa/Passage. Passage of the bill to extend certain trade preferences to the nations of sub-Saharan Africa. The bill would grant duty-free status to many products, with a particular focus on textiles and apparel, and would seek to promote private investment in the region. Passed 234-163: R 136-63; D 98-99 (ND 73-76, SD 25-23); I 0-1. July 16, 1999. A "yea" was a vote in support of the president's position.

308. HR 1033. Lewis and Clark/Passage. Bereuter, R-Neb., motion to suspend the rules and pass the bill to require the Treasury Department to mint 500,000 one-dollar coins to commemorate the bicentennial of the Lewis and Clark expedition. Motion agreed to 381-1: R 197-1; D 184-0 (ND 134-0, SD 50-0); I 0-0. July 19, 1999. A two-thirds majority of those present and voting (255 in this case) is required for passage under suspension of the rules.

309. H Con Res 121. Cold War Victory/Passage. Gilman, R-N.Y., motion to suspend the rules and adopt the concurrent resolution to call for a celebration of the U.S. victory in the Cold War and the 10th anniversary of the fall of the Berlin Wall. Motion agreed to 381-0: R 197-0; D 184-0 (ND 134-0, SD 50-0); I 0-0. July 19, 1999. A two-thirds majority of those present and voting (254 in this case) is required for passage under suspension of the rules.

310. HR 1477. Iran Nuclear Proliferation/Passage. Gilman, R-N.Y., motion to suspend the rules and pass the bill to authorize the U.S. to withhold assistance for programs of the International Atomic Energy Agency relating to the development and completion of the Bushehr nuclear power plant in Iran. Motion agreed to 383-1: R 197-0; D 186-1 (ND 136-1, SD 50-0); I 0-0. July 19, 1999. A two-thirds majority of those present and voting (256 in this case) is required for passage under suspension of the rules. A "nay" was a vote in support of the president's position.

311. H Con Res 158. Memorial Door for Fallen Officers/Passage. Franks, R-N.J., motion to suspend the rules and adopt the concurrent resolution to designate the Document Door of the U.S. Capitol as the "Memorial Door" in honor of officers Jacob Chestnut and John Gibson, who were killed in the line of duty on July 24, 1998, near the door. Motion agreed to 417-0: R 217-0; D 199-0 (ND 147-0, SD 52-0); I 1-0. July 20, 1999. A two-thirds majority of those present and voting (278 in this case) is required for passage under suspension of the rules.

312. HR 2415. State Department Reauthorization/U.N. Population Fund. Campbell, R-Calif., amendment to the Smith, R-N.J., amendment. The Campbell amendment would authorize a $25 million U.S. contribution to the United Nations Fund for Population Activities (UNFPA) but prohibit use of any of the money in China, and reduce the U.S. contribution by the amount the UNFPA plans to spend in that country. The Smith amendment would eliminate the $25 million contribution unless the UNFPA halts all activities in China or the president certifies that there are no forced abortions in that country. Adopted 221-198: R 46-170; D 174-28 (ND 131-19, SD 43-9); I 1-0. July 20, 1999. (Subsequently, the Smith amendment, as amended, was adopted by voice vote.)

313. HR 2415. State Department Reauthorization/East-West Center. Sanford, R-S.C., amendment to reduce funding for the East-West Center for the study of Asian affairs to its fiscal 1998 level of $12 million, cap funding for the North-South Center at $1.5 million, and cap funding for the Asia Foundation at $8 million. Rejected 180-237: R 153-61; D 27-175 (ND 17-133, SD 10-42); I 0-1. July 20, 1999.

Key

- Y Voted for (yea).
- \# Paired for.
- \+ Announced for.
- N Voted against (nay).
- X Paired against.
- – Announced against.
- P Voted "present."
- C Voted "present" to avoid possible conflict of interest.
- ? Did not vote or otherwise make a position known.

•

Democrats ***Republicans***
Independents

	306	307	308	309	310	311	312	313
ALABAMA								
1 ***Callahan***	Y	N	Y	Y	Y	Y	N	Y
2 ***Everett***	N	N	Y	Y	Y	Y	N	Y
3 ***Riley***	N	N	Y	Y	Y	Y	N	Y
4 ***Aderholt***	N	N	Y	Y	Y	Y	N	Y
5 Cramer	N	N	Y	Y	Y	Y	Y	Y
6 ***Bachus***	N	N	Y	Y	Y	Y	N	Y
7 Hilliard	Y	Y	Y	Y	Y	Y	Y	N
ALASKA								
AL ***Young***	?	N	Y	Y	Y	Y	N	Y
ARIZONA								
1 ***Salmon***	Y	Y	Y	Y	Y	Y	N	Y
2 Pastor	Y	N	Y	Y	Y	Y	Y	N
3 ***Stump***	Y	N	Y	Y	Y	Y	N	Y
4 ***Shadegg***	Y	?	Y	Y	Y	Y	N	Y
5 ***Kolbe***	Y	Y	Y	Y	Y	Y	Y	N
6 ***Hayworth***	Y	Y	Y	Y	Y	Y	N	Y
ARKANSAS								
1 Berry	N	N	Y	Y	Y	Y	Y	Y
2 Snyder	Y	Y	Y	Y	Y	Y	Y	N
3 ***Hutchinson***	Y	Y	Y	Y	?	Y	N	Y
4 ***Dickey***	Y	Y	Y	Y	Y	Y	N	Y
CALIFORNIA								
1 Thompson	Y	N	Y	Y	Y	Y	Y	N
2 ***Herger***	Y	Y	Y	Y	Y	Y	N	Y
3 ***Ose***	Y	Y	Y	Y	Y	Y	Y	N
4 ***Doolittle***	Y	Y	Y	Y	Y	Y	N	Y
5 Matsui	Y	Y	Y	Y	Y	Y	Y	N
6 Woolsey	N	N	Y	Y	Y	Y	Y	N
7 Miller, George	N	N	Y	Y	Y	Y	Y	N
8 Pelosi	N	Y	Y	Y	Y	Y	Y	N
9 Lee	N	N	Y	P	Y	Y	Y	N
10 Tauscher	Y	Y	Y	Y	Y	Y	Y	N
11 ***Pombo***	Y	Y	Y	Y	Y	Y	N	Y
12 Lantos	N	N	Y	Y	Y	Y	Y	N
13 Stark	?	?	Y	Y	Y	?	?	?
14 Eshoo	Y	Y	Y	Y	Y	Y	Y	N
15 ***Campbell***	Y	Y	Y	Y	Y	Y	Y	P
16 Lofgren	Y	Y	Y	Y	Y	Y	Y	N
17 Farr	N	Y	Y	Y	Y	Y	Y	N
18 Condit	N	N	Y	Y	Y	Y	Y	N
19 ***Radanovich***	Y	Y	Y	Y	Y	Y	N	Y
20 Dooley	Y	Y	Y	Y	Y	Y	Y	N
21 ***Thomas***	Y	Y	Y	Y	Y	Y	Y	N
22 Capps	N	Y	Y	Y	Y	Y	Y	N
23 ***Gallegly***	Y	Y	Y	Y	Y	Y	N	Y
24 Sherman	N	N	Y	Y	Y	Y	Y	N
25 ***McKeon***	Y	Y	Y	Y	Y	Y	N	N
26 Berman	Y	Y	?	?	?	Y	Y	N
27 ***Rogan***	Y	Y	Y	Y	Y	Y	N	Y
28 ***Dreier***	Y	Y	Y	Y	Y	Y	N	N
29 Waxman	N	Y	Y	Y	Y	Y	Y	N
30 Becerra	Y	Y	Y	Y	Y	Y	Y	N
31 Martinez	Y	Y	Y	Y	Y	Y	Y	N
32 Dixon	Y	Y	Y	Y	Y	Y	Y	N
33 Roybal-Allard	N	N	Y	Y	Y	Y	Y	N
34 Napolitano	Y	N	Y	Y	Y	Y	Y	N
35 Waters	N	N	Y	Y	Y	Y	Y	N
36 ***Kuykendall***	Y	Y	Y	Y	Y	Y	Y	N
37 Millender-McD.	Y	Y	Y	Y	Y	Y	Y	N
38 ***Horn***	Y	Y	Y	Y	Y	Y	Y	N
39 ***Royce***	Y	Y	Y	Y	Y	Y	N	Y
40 ***Lewis***	Y	Y	Y	Y	Y	Y	Y	N
41 ***Miller, Gary***	Y	Y	Y	Y	Y	Y	N	Y
42 Vacant								
43 ***Calvert***	Y	Y	Y	Y	Y	Y	N	N
44 ***Bono***	Y	Y	Y	Y	Y	Y	N	N
45 ***Rohrabacher***	Y	N	Y	Y	Y	Y	N	Y
46 Sanchez	N	Y	+	+	+	Y	Y	N
47 ***Cox***	Y	Y	Y	Y	Y	Y	N	Y
48 ***Packard***	Y	Y	Y	Y	Y	Y	N	N
49 ***Bilbray***	Y	Y	Y	Y	Y	Y	Y	N
50 Filner	N	N	Y	Y	Y	Y	Y	N
51 ***Cunningham***	Y	Y	Y	Y	Y	Y	N	Y
52 ***Hunter***	N	N	Y	Y	?	Y	N	Y
COLORADO								
1 DeGette	N	Y	Y	Y	Y	Y	Y	N
2 Udall	Y	N	Y	Y	Y	Y	Y	N
3 ***McInnis***	Y	?	Y	Y	Y	Y	N	Y
4 ***Schaffer***	Y	Y	Y	Y	Y	Y	N	Y
5 ***Hefley***	?	?	Y	Y	Y	Y	N	Y
6 ***Tancredo***	Y	Y	Y	Y	Y	Y	N	Y
CONNECTICUT								
1 Larson	Y	Y	+	+	+	Y	Y	N
2 Gejdenson	Y	Y	Y	Y	Y	Y	Y	N
3 DeLauro	Y	N	Y	Y	Y	Y	Y	N
4 ***Shays***	Y	Y	Y	Y	Y	Y	Y	Y
5 Maloney	Y	N	Y	Y	Y	Y	Y	N
6 ***Johnson***	Y	Y	?	?	?	Y	Y	N
DELAWARE								
AL ***Castle***	Y	Y	Y	Y	Y	Y	Y	N
FLORIDA								
1 ***Scarborough***	Y	Y	Y	Y	Y	Y	N	Y
2 Boyd	N	N	Y	Y	Y	Y	Y	N
3 Brown	Y	Y	?	?	?	Y	Y	N
4 ***Fowler***	Y	N	?	?	?	Y	Y	N
5 Thurman	?	?	?	?	?	Y	Y	N
6 ***Stearns***	Y	N	Y	Y	Y	Y	N	Y
7 ***Mica***	Y	N	Y	Y	Y	Y	N	Y
8 ***McCollum***	Y	Y	Y	Y	Y	Y	N	N
9 ***Bilirakis***	Y	?	Y	Y	Y	Y	N	Y
10 ***Young***	Y	?	Y	Y	Y	Y	N	Y
11 Davis	Y	Y	Y	Y	Y	Y	Y	N
12 ***Canady***	Y	Y	Y	Y	Y	Y	N	N
13 ***Miller***	Y	?	Y	Y	Y	Y	Y	N
14 ***Goss***	Y	Y	Y	Y	Y	Y	N	N
15 ***Weldon***	Y	Y	Y	Y	Y	Y	N	Y
16 ***Foley***	Y	Y	Y	Y	Y	Y	Y	N
17 Meek	Y	Y	Y	Y	Y	Y	Y	N
18 ***Ros-Lehtinen***	Y	Y	Y	Y	Y	Y	N	N
19 Wexler	Y	Y	Y	Y	Y	Y	Y	N
20 Deutsch	Y	Y	Y	Y	Y	Y	Y	N
21 ***Diaz-Balart***	Y	N	Y	Y	Y	Y	N	N
22 ***Shaw***	Y	Y	Y	Y	Y	Y	Y	N
23 Hastings	?	?	Y	Y	Y	Y	Y	N
GEORGIA								
1 ***Kingston***	Y	N	Y	Y	Y	Y	N	Y
2 Bishop	N	N	Y	Y	Y	Y	Y	N
3 ***Collins***	N	N	?	?	?	Y	N	Y
4 McKinney	N	N	Y	Y	Y	Y	Y	N
5 Lewis	Y	N	?	?	?	?	?	?
6 ***Isakson***	N	N	Y	Y	Y	Y	Y	Y
7 ***Barr***	Y	N	Y	Y	Y	Y	N	Y
8 ***Chambliss***	N	N	Y	Y	Y	Y	N	Y
9 ***Deal***	N	N	Y	Y	Y	Y	N	Y
10 ***Norwood***	N	N	?	?	?	Y	N	Y
11 ***Linder***	Y	Y	Y	Y	Y	Y	N	Y
HAWAII								
1 Abercrombie	Y	N	Y	Y	Y	?	Y	N
2 Mink	N	Y	Y	Y	Y	Y	Y	N
IDAHO								
1 ***Chenoweth***	?	?	?	?	?	Y	N	Y
2 ***Simpson***	Y	Y	Y	Y	Y	Y	N	Y
ILLINOIS								
1 Rush	N	N	?	Y	Y	Y	Y	N
2 Jackson	N	N	Y	Y	Y	Y	Y	N
3 Lipinski	N	N	Y	Y	Y	Y	N	N
4 Gutierrez	Y	N	+	+	+	Y	Y	N
5 Blagojevich	N	N	Y	Y	Y	Y	Y	N
6 ***Hyde***	Y	Y	Y	Y	Y	Y	N	Y
7 Davis	N	N	Y	Y	Y	Y	Y	N
8 ***Crane***	Y	Y	Y	Y	Y	Y	N	Y
9 Schakowsky	N	N	Y	Y	Y	Y	Y	N
10 ***Porter***	?	Y	?	?	?	Y	Y	N
11 ***Weller***	Y	Y	Y	Y	Y	Y	N	N
12 Costello	N	N	Y	Y	Y	Y	N	Y
13 ***Biggert***	Y	Y	Y	Y	Y	Y	Y	N
14 ***Hastert***	Y	Y				Y		

ND Northern Democrats SD Southern Democrats

	306	307	308	309	310	311	312	313
15 ***Ewing***	Y	Y	Y	Y	Y	Y	N	N
16 ***Manzullo***	Y	Y	Y	Y	Y	Y	N	Y
17 Evans	N	N	Y	Y	Y	Y	Y	N
18 ***LaHood***	Y	Y	Y	Y	Y	Y	N	N
19 Phelps	N	N	Y	Y	Y	Y	N	Y
20 ***Shimkus***	Y	Y	Y	Y	Y	Y	N	Y
INDIANA								
1 Visclosky	N	N	Y	Y	Y	Y	Y	N
2 ***McIntosh***	Y	Y	?	?	?	Y	N	Y
3 Roemer	Y	Y	Y	Y	Y	Y	N	N
4 ***Souder***	Y	N	Y	Y	Y	Y	N	Y
5 ***Buyer***	Y	N	Y	Y	Y	Y	N	Y
6 ***Burton***	+	–	Y	Y	Y	Y	N	Y
7 ***Pease***	Y	Y	Y	Y	Y	Y	N	Y
8 ***Hostettler***	Y	N	Y	Y	Y	Y	N	Y
9 Hill	N	Y	Y	Y	Y	Y	Y	N
10 Carson	N	N	Y	Y	N	Y	Y	N
IOWA								
1 ***Leach***	Y	Y	Y	Y	Y	Y	Y	N
2 ***Nussle***	Y	Y	Y	Y	Y	Y	N	N
3 Boswell	N	?	Y	Y	Y	Y	Y	N
4 ***Ganske***	?	Y	Y	Y	Y	Y	Y	Y
5 ***Latham***	?	?	Y	Y	Y	Y	N	N
KANSAS								
1 ***Moran***	N	N	Y	Y	Y	Y	N	Y
2 ***Ryun***	Y	Y	+	+	+	Y	N	Y
3 Moore	Y	Y	+	+	+	Y	Y	N
4 ***Tiahrt***	Y	Y	Y	Y	Y	Y	N	Y
KENTUCKY								
1 ***Whitfield***	?	Y	Y	Y	Y	Y	N	Y
2 ***Lewis***	Y	Y	Y	Y	Y	Y	N	Y
3 ***Northup***	Y	Y	Y	Y	Y	Y	N	Y
4 Lucas	N	Y	Y	Y	Y	Y	N	Y
5 ***Rogers***	N	N	Y	Y	Y	Y	N	Y
6 ***Fletcher***	Y	Y	Y	Y	Y	Y	N	Y
LOUISIANA								
1 ***Vitter***	Y	Y	Y	Y	Y	Y	N	Y
2 Jefferson	Y	Y	?	?	?	?	?	?
3 ***Tauzin***	?	?	?	?	?	Y	N	Y
4 ***McCrery***	Y	Y	Y	Y	Y	Y	N	Y
5 ***Cooksey***	?	?	?	?	?	Y	Y	Y
6 ***Baker***	Y	?	?	?	?	?	?	?
7 John	?	?	Y	Y	Y	Y	N	N
MAINE								
1 Allen	N	Y	?	?	?	Y	Y	N
2 Baldacci	N	N	Y	Y	Y	Y	Y	N
MARYLAND								
1 ***Gilchrest***	Y	Y	Y	Y	Y	Y	Y	N
2 ***Ehrlich***	Y	Y	Y	Y	Y	Y	Y	Y
3 Cardin	Y	Y	Y	Y	Y	Y	Y	N
4 Wynn	Y	Y	Y	Y	Y	Y	Y	N
5 Hoyer	Y	Y	Y	Y	Y	Y	Y	N
6 ***Bartlett***	Y	N	Y	Y	Y	Y	N	Y
7 Cummings	N	Y	Y	Y	Y	Y	Y	N
8 ***Morella***	Y	Y	Y	Y	Y	Y	Y	N
MASSACHUSETTS								
1 Olver	Y	Y	?	?	?	Y	Y	N
2 Neal	Y	Y	?	?	?	Y	Y	N
3 McGovern	N	N	Y	Y	Y	Y	Y	N
4 Frank	N	N	Y	Y	Y	Y	Y	N
5 Meehan	Y	Y	Y	Y	Y	Y	Y	N
6 Tierney	N	N	Y	Y	Y	Y	Y	N
7 Markey	Y	N	Y	Y	Y	Y	Y	N
8 Capuano	N	N	Y	Y	Y	Y	Y	N
9 Moakley	N	N	Y	Y	Y	Y	Y	N
10 Delahunt	N	N	Y	Y	Y	Y	Y	N
MICHIGAN								
1 Stupak	N	N	Y	Y	Y	Y	N	N
2 ***Hoekstra***	Y	Y	Y	Y	Y	Y	N	Y
3 ***Ehlers***	Y	Y	Y	Y	Y	Y	N	Y
4 ***Camp***	Y	Y	Y	Y	Y	Y	N	Y
5 Barcia	N	N	Y	Y	Y	Y	N	N
6 ***Upton***	Y	Y	Y	Y	Y	Y	Y	Y
7 ***Smith***	Y	Y	Y	Y	Y	Y	N	Y
8 Stabenow	N	Y	Y	Y	Y	Y	Y	N
9 Kildee	N	N	Y	Y	Y	Y	N	N
10 Bonior	N	N	Y	Y	Y	Y	Y	N
11 ***Knollenberg***	Y	Y	Y	Y	Y	Y	N	N
12 Levin	Y	Y	Y	Y	Y	Y	Y	N
13 Rivers	N	Y	Y	Y	Y	Y	Y	Y
14 Conyers	N	N	Y	Y	Y	Y	Y	N
15 Kilpatrick	Y	Y	Y	Y	Y	Y	Y	N
16 Dingell	N	N	Y	Y	Y	Y	Y	N

	306	307	308	309	310	311	312	313
MINNESOTA								
1 ***Gutknecht***	Y	Y	Y	Y	Y	Y	N	Y
2 Minge	N	Y	Y	Y	Y	Y	Y	N
3 ***Ramstad***	Y	Y	Y	Y	Y	Y	Y	Y
4 Vento	N	N	Y	Y	Y	Y	Y	N
5 Sabo	Y	Y	Y	Y	Y	Y	Y	N
6 Luther	?	Y	Y	Y	Y	Y	Y	Y
7 Peterson	N	N	Y	Y	Y	Y	N	Y
8 Oberstar	Y	Y	Y	Y	Y	Y	Y	N
MISSISSIPPI								
1 ***Wicker***	Y	?	Y	Y	Y	Y	N	Y
2 Thompson	N	N	Y	Y	Y	Y	Y	N
3 ***Pickering***	N	N	Y	Y	Y	Y	N	Y
4 Shows	N	N	Y	Y	Y	Y	N	Y
5 Taylor	N	N	Y	Y	Y	Y	N	N
MISSOURI								
1 Clay	Y	Y	Y	Y	Y	Y	Y	N
2 ***Talent***	Y	N	Y	Y	Y	Y	N	Y
3 Gephardt	?	Y	Y	Y	Y	Y	Y	N
4 Skelton	Y	Y	Y	Y	Y	Y	N	Y
5 McCarthy	Y	Y	Y	Y	Y	Y	Y	N
6 Danner	N	N	?	?	?	?	N	Y
7 ***Blunt***	Y	?	Y	Y	Y	Y	N	Y
8 ***Emerson***	N	N	Y	Y	Y	Y	N	Y
9 ***Hulshof***	Y	Y	Y	Y	Y	Y	N	Y
MONTANA								
AL ***Hill***	Y	Y	Y	Y	Y	Y	N	Y
NEBRASKA								
1 ***Bereuter***	Y	Y	Y	Y	Y	Y	Y	N
2 ***Terry***	Y	Y	Y	Y	Y	Y	N	Y
3 ***Barrett***	Y	Y	?	?	?	Y	N	Y
NEVADA								
1 Berkley	N	Y	Y	Y	Y	Y	Y	N
2 ***Gibbons***	Y	N	Y	Y	Y	Y	Y	Y
NEW HAMPSHIRE								
1 ***Sununu***	Y	Y	Y	Y	Y	Y	N	Y
2 ***Bass***	Y	Y	Y	Y	Y	Y	Y	Y
NEW JERSEY								
1 Andrews	N	N	+	+	+	Y	Y	N
2 ***LoBiondo***	Y	N	Y	Y	Y	Y	N	Y
3 ***Saxton***	Y	Y	Y	Y	Y	Y	N	N
4 ***Smith***	Y	N	Y	Y	Y	Y	N	N
5 ***Roukema***	Y	Y	Y	Y	Y	Y	Y	Y
6 Pallone	N	N	Y	Y	Y	Y	Y	N
7 ***Franks***	Y	Y	Y	Y	Y	Y	Y	Y
8 Pascrell	N	N	Y	Y	Y	Y	Y	N
9 Rothman	?	Y	Y	Y	Y	Y	Y	N
10 Payne	Y	Y	Y	Y	Y	Y	Y	N
11 ***Frelinghuysen***	Y	Y	Y	Y	Y	Y	Y	N
12 Holt	N	N	Y	Y	Y	Y	Y	N
13 Menendez	N	N	Y	Y	Y	Y	Y	N
NEW MEXICO								
1 ***Wilson***	Y	Y	Y	Y	Y	Y	Y	Y
2 ***Skeen***	Y	N	Y	Y	Y	Y	N	Y
3 Udall	?	N	Y	Y	Y	Y	Y	N
NEW YORK								
1 Forbes	?	N	Y	Y	Y	Y	N	Y
2 ***Lazio***	Y	Y	Y	Y	Y	Y	Y	N
3 ***King***	Y	Y	Y	Y	Y	Y	N	N
4 McCarthy	N	Y	Y	Y	Y	Y	Y	N
5 Ackerman	Y	Y	Y	Y	Y	Y	Y	N
6 Meeks	Y	Y	?	?	?	Y	Y	N
7 Crowley	Y	N	+	+	+	Y	Y	N
8 Nadler	N	N	Y	Y	Y	Y	Y	N
9 Weiner	Y	Y	?	Y	Y	Y	Y	N
10 Towns	Y	Y	?	?	?	?	?	?
11 Owens	N	Y	?	?	Y	Y	Y	N
12 Velázquez	N	N	Y	Y	Y	Y	Y	N
13 ***Fossella***	Y	Y	+	+	+	Y	N	Y
14 Maloney	Y	Y	Y	Y	Y	Y	Y	N
15 Rangel	Y	Y	Y	Y	Y	Y	Y	N
16 Serrano	?	N	Y	Y	Y	Y	Y	N
17 Engel	?	Y	Y	Y	Y	Y	Y	N
18 Lowey	Y	Y	Y	Y	Y	Y	Y	N
19 ***Kelly***	Y	Y	Y	Y	Y	Y	Y	Y
20 ***Gilman***	Y	Y	Y	Y	Y	Y	Y	N
21 McNulty	?	?	Y	Y	Y	Y	Y	N
22 ***Sweeney***	Y	N	?	?	?	Y	Y	Y
23 ***Boehlert***	Y	Y	Y	Y	Y	Y	Y	Y
24 ***McHugh***	Y	N	Y	Y	Y	Y	N	N
25 ***Walsh***	Y	Y	Y	Y	Y	Y	N	N
26 Hinchey	N	Y	?	?	?	?	?	?
27 ***Reynolds***	Y	Y	Y	Y	Y	Y	N	N
28 Slaughter	Y	N	Y	Y	Y	Y	Y	N
29 LaFalce	N	Y	Y	Y	Y	Y	N	N

	306	307	308	309	310	311	312	313
30 ***Quinn***	Y	Y	Y	Y	Y	Y	N	N
31 ***Houghton***	Y	Y	?	?	?	Y	Y	N
NORTH CAROLINA								
1 Clayton	N	N	Y	Y	Y	Y	Y	N
2 Etheridge	N	N	Y	Y	Y	Y	Y	N
3 ***Jones***	N	N	Y	Y	Y	Y	N	Y
4 Price	N	N	Y	Y	Y	Y	Y	N
5 ***Burr***	N	N	Y	Y	Y	Y	N	Y
6 ***Coble***	–	–	+	+	+	+	–	+
7 McIntyre	N	N	Y	Y	Y	Y	N	Y
8 ***Hayes***	N	N	+	+	+	Y	N	Y
9 ***Myrick***	N	N	Y	Y	Y	Y	N	Y
10 ***Ballenger***	N	N	Y	Y	Y	Y	N	N
11 ***Taylor***	N	N	?	?	?	Y	N	Y
12 Watt	N	N	Y	Y	Y	Y	Y	N
NORTH DAKOTA								
AL Pomeroy	Y	Y	Y	Y	Y	Y	Y	N
OHIO								
1 ***Chabot***	Y	Y	Y	Y	Y	Y	N	Y
2 ***Portman***	Y	Y	Y	Y	Y	Y	N	Y
3 Hall	N	Y	Y	Y	Y	Y	N	N
4 ***Oxley***	Y	Y	Y	Y	Y	Y	N	N
5 ***Gillmor***	Y	Y	Y	Y	Y	Y	N	Y
6 Strickland	N	N	Y	Y	Y	Y	Y	N
7 ***Hobson***	Y	?	Y	Y	Y	Y	Y	N
8 ***Boehner***	Y	?	Y	Y	Y	Y	N	Y
9 Kaptur	N	N	Y	Y	Y	Y	Y	N
10 Kucinich	N	N	Y	P	Y	Y	N	N
11 Jones	Y	Y	Y	Y	Y	Y	Y	N
12 ***Kasich***	Y	Y	Y	Y	Y	Y	N	Y
13 Brown	N	N	Y	Y	Y	Y	Y	N
14 Sawyer	Y	Y	Y	Y	Y	Y	Y	N
15 ***Pryce***	Y	Y	?	?	?	Y	Y	N
16 ***Regula***	Y	Y	Y	Y	Y	Y	Y	N
17 Traficant	N	N	Y	Y	Y	Y	N	Y
18 ***Ney***	Y	N	Y	Y	Y	Y	N	N
19 ***LaTourette***	Y	Y	Y	Y	Y	Y	Y	Y
OKLAHOMA								
1 ***Largent***	N	?	Y	Y	Y	Y	N	Y
2 ***Coburn***	Y	?	Y	Y	Y	Y	N	Y
3 ***Watkins***	Y	Y	Y	Y	Y	Y	N	N
4 ***Watts***	Y	Y	Y	Y	Y	Y	N	Y
5 ***Istook***	Y	?	Y	Y	Y	Y	N	Y
6 ***Lucas***	Y	N	Y	Y	Y	Y	N	Y
OREGON								
1 Wu	–	Y	Y	Y	Y	Y	Y	N
2 ***Walden***	Y	N	Y	Y	Y	Y	N	Y
3 Blumenauer	Y	Y	Y	Y	Y	Y	Y	N
4 DeFazio	N	N	Y	Y	Y	Y	Y	N
5 Hooley	N	Y	Y	Y	Y	Y	Y	N
PENNSYLVANIA								
1 Brady	N	N	Y	Y	Y	Y	Y	N
2 Fattah	Y	Y	Y	Y	Y	?	Y	N
3 Borski	Y	Y	Y	Y	Y	Y	Y	N
4 Klink	N	N	?	?	?	?	Y	Y
5 ***Peterson***	?	?	?	?	?	?	?	?
6 Holden	N	N	Y	Y	Y	?	?	?
7 ***Weldon***	Y	N	Y	Y	Y	Y	N	N
8 ***Greenwood***	Y	Y	Y	Y	Y	Y	Y	N
9 ***Shuster***	Y	Y	Y	Y	Y	Y	N	Y
10 ***Sherwood***	Y	N	Y	Y	Y	Y	N	Y
11 Kanjorski	Y	N	Y	Y	Y	Y	Y	Y
12 Murtha	Y	Y	Y	Y	Y	Y	Y	N
13 Hoeffel	N	Y	Y	Y	Y	Y	Y	N
14 Coyne	Y	Y	Y	Y	Y	Y	Y	N
15 ***Toomey***	Y	Y	?	?	?	Y	N	Y
16 ***Pitts***	Y	Y	Y	Y	Y	Y	N	Y
17 ***Gekas***	Y	Y	Y	Y	Y	Y	N	?
18 Doyle	N	N	Y	Y	Y	Y	Y	Y
19 ***Goodling***	Y	Y	Y	Y	Y	Y	N	Y
20 Mascara	N	N	Y	Y	Y	Y	N	Y
21 ***English***	Y	Y	Y	Y	Y	?	?	?
RHODE ISLAND								
1 Kennedy	N	N	?	?	?	?	?	?
2 Weygand	N	N	Y	Y	Y	Y	N	N
SOUTH CAROLINA								
1 ***Sanford***	N	N	Y	Y	Y	Y	N	Y
2 ***Spence***	Y	N	Y	Y	Y	Y	N	Y
3 ***Graham***	N	N	Y	Y	Y	Y	N	Y
4 ***DeMint***	N	N	Y	Y	Y	Y	N	Y
5 Spratt	N	N	Y	Y	Y	Y	Y	N
6 Clyburn	N	N	Y	Y	Y	Y	Y	N
SOUTH DAKOTA								
AL ***Thune***	Y	Y	Y	Y	Y	Y	N	Y

	306	307	308	309	310	311	312	313
TENNESSEE								
1 ***Jenkins***	Y	N	Y	Y	Y	Y	N	Y
2 ***Duncan***	Y	N	Y	Y	Y	Y	N	Y
3 ***Wamp***	Y	N	Y	Y	Y	Y	N	Y
4 ***Hilleary***	Y	N	Y	Y	Y	Y	N	Y
5 Clement	N	Y	Y	Y	Y	Y	Y	N
6 Gordon	?	?	Y	Y	Y	Y	Y	Y
7 ***Bryant***	Y	N	Y	Y	Y	Y	N	Y
8 Tanner	N	N	Y	Y	Y	Y	N	Y
9 Ford	Y	Y	Y	Y	Y	Y	Y	N
TEXAS								
1 Sandlin	N	Y	Y	Y	Y	Y	Y	N
2 Turner	N	Y	Y	Y	Y	Y	Y	Y
3 ***Johnson, Sam***	Y	Y	Y	Y	Y	Y	N	Y
4 Hall	N	N	Y	Y	Y	Y	N	Y
5 ***Sessions***	Y	Y	?	?	Y	Y	N	Y
6 ***Barton***	Y	Y	Y	Y	Y	Y	N	N
7 ***Archer***	Y	Y	Y	Y	Y	Y	N	Y
8 ***Brady***	Y	Y	Y	Y	Y	Y	N	Y
9 Lampson	Y	Y	Y	Y	Y	Y	Y	N
10 Doggett	N	Y	Y	Y	Y	Y	Y	N
11 Edwards	Y	Y	?	?	?	Y	Y	N
12 ***Granger***	Y	Y	Y	?	Y	Y	Y	Y
13 ***Thornberry***	Y	N	Y	Y	Y	Y	N	Y
14 ***Paul***	Y	N	N	Y	Y	Y	N	Y
15 Hinojosa	N	Y	Y	Y	Y	Y	Y	N
16 Reyes	Y	Y	Y	Y	Y	Y	Y	N
17 Stenholm	N	N	Y	Y	Y	Y	N	Y
18 Jackson-Lee	Y	Y	Y	Y	Y	Y	Y	N
19 ***Combest***	Y	N	Y	Y	Y	+	–	+
20 Gonzalez	Y	Y	Y	Y	Y	Y	Y	N
21 ***Smith***	N	Y	?	?	?	Y	N	Y
22 ***DeLay***	Y	Y	Y	Y	Y	Y	N	Y
23 ***Bonilla***	Y	N	Y	Y	Y	Y	N	Y
24 Frost	?	?	Y	Y	Y	Y	Y	N
25 Bentsen	Y	Y	Y	Y	Y	Y	Y	N
26 ***Armey***	Y	Y	Y	Y	Y	Y	N	Y
27 Ortiz	Y	–	Y	Y	Y	+	–	–
28 Rodriguez	N	N	Y	Y	Y	Y	Y	N
29 Green	N	N	Y	Y	Y	Y	Y	N
30 Johnson, E.B.	Y	Y	Y	Y	Y	Y	Y	N
UTAH								
1 ***Hansen***	?	?	Y	Y	Y	Y	N	Y
2 ***Cook***	Y	Y	Y	Y	Y	Y	N	Y
3 ***Cannon***	Y	Y	Y	Y	Y	Y	N	Y
VERMONT								
AL *Sanders*	N	N	?	?	?	Y	Y	N
VIRGINIA								
1 ***Bateman***	Y	Y	Y	Y	Y	Y	N	N
2 Pickett	N	Y	Y	Y	Y	Y	N	N
3 Scott	Y	Y	Y	Y	Y	Y	Y	N
4 Sisisky	N	N	Y	Y	Y	Y	Y	N
5 Goode	N	N	Y	Y	Y	Y	N	Y
6 ***Goodlatte***	Y	N	Y	Y	Y	Y	N	Y
7 ***Bliley***	Y	Y	Y	Y	Y	Y	N	Y
8 Moran	Y	Y	Y	Y	Y	Y	Y	N
9 Boucher	Y	?	Y	Y	Y	Y	Y	N
10 ***Wolf***	Y	Y	Y	Y	Y	Y	N	N
11 ***Davis***	Y	Y	Y	Y	Y	Y	Y	N
WASHINGTON								
1 Inslee	N	Y	Y	Y	Y	Y	Y	Y
2 ***Metcalf***	Y	N	Y	Y	Y	Y	N	Y
3 Baird	Y	+	Y	Y	Y	Y	Y	N
4 ***Hastings***	Y	Y	Y	Y	Y	Y	N	Y
5 ***Nethercutt***	Y	?	Y	Y	Y	Y	N	Y
6 Dicks	N	Y	Y	Y	Y	Y	Y	N
7 McDermott	+	+	+	+	+	+	+	–
8 ***Dunn***	Y	Y	Y	Y	Y	Y	N	N
9 Smith	Y	Y	Y	Y	Y	Y	Y	Y
WEST VIRGINIA								
1 Mollohan	N	N	?	?	?	Y	N	N
2 Wise	N	N	?	?	?	Y	Y	N
3 Rahall	N	N	Y	Y	Y	Y	N	N
WISCONSIN								
1 ***Ryan***	Y	Y	Y	Y	Y	Y	N	Y
2 Baldwin	?	?	Y	Y	Y	Y	Y	N
3 Kind	Y	Y	Y	Y	Y	Y	Y	N
4 Kleczka	N	N	Y	Y	Y	Y	Y	N
5 Barrett	N	Y	Y	Y	Y	Y	Y	Y
6 ***Petri***	Y	Y	Y	Y	Y	Y	N	Y
7 Obey	N	N	Y	Y	Y	Y	Y	N
8 ***Green***	Y	Y	Y	Y	Y	Y	N	Y
9 ***Sensenbrenner***	Y	Y	Y	Y	Y	Y	N	Y
WYOMING								
AL ***Cubin***	Y	N	Y	Y	Y	Y	N	Y

Southern states - Ala., Ark., Fla., Ga., Ky., La., Miss., N.C., Okla., S.C., Tenn., Texas, Va.

314. HR 2415. State Department Reauthorization/U.N. Peacekeeping Activities. Paul, R-Texas, amendment to eliminate all U.N.-related authorizations in the bill. Rejected 74-342: R 70-145; D 4-196 (ND 2-148, SD 2-48); I 0-1. July 20, 1999. A "nay" was a vote in support of the president's position.

315. HR 1995. New Teachers and Training Programs/Rule. Adoption of the rule (H Res 253) to provide for House floor consideration of the bill to authorize $2 billion a year for five years for teachers' professional development, hiring of new teachers and class-size reduction. Adopted 227-187: R 216-0; 11-186 (ND 7-138, SD 4-48); I 0-1. July 20, 1999.

316. HR 1995. New Teachers and Training Programs/Qualified Teachers. Goodling, R-Pa., amendment to replace bill language on teacher accountability with language that would require states to report publicly on their progress in improving student achievement and reducing the disparities in achievement by low-income and minority students. The amendment also would require that participating states have a plan to ensure that all their teachers are fully qualified by Dec. 31, 2003, and that they establish programs to hold school districts and schools accountable for making annual gains in performance. Adopted 424-1: R 218-1; D 205-0 (ND 151-0, SD 54-0); I 1-0. July 20, 1999.

317. HR 1995. New Teachers and Training Programs/Sabbatical Programs. Mink, D-Hawaii, amendment to authorize $200 million in fiscal 2000 and such sums as may be necessary for fiscal 2001 through 2004 for matching grants to states for a sabbatical program for public school teachers who take leave to pursue professional development. Rejected 181-242: R 0-217; D 180-25 (ND 135-16, SD 45-9); I 1-0. July 20, 1999.

318. HR 1995. New Teachers and Training Programs/Importance of Teachers. Crowley, D-N.Y., amendment to express the sense of Congress that it is essential to ensure that American teachers are of the highest quality possible. Adopted 425-0: R 219-0; D 205-0 (ND 151-0, SD 54-0); I 1-0. July 20, 1999.

319. HR 1995. New Teachers and Training Programs/Funding Increases. Martinez, D-Calif., substitute amendment to increase funding for professional development and class-size reduction activities, with a separate authorization for the class-size reduction program. The amendment would authorize $1.5 billion in fiscal 2000 for the class-size reduction program, increasing to $3 billion by fiscal 2005; it would authorize $1.5 billion for teachers' professional development increasing to $3 billion by fiscal 2004. Rejected 207-217: R 3-215; D 203-2 (ND 151-0, SD 52-2); I 1-0. July 20, 1999. A "yea" was a vote in support of the president's position.

320. HR 1995. New Teachers and Training Programs/Passage. Passage of the bill to establish a new block grant that would combine three existing education programs — a teacher performance program, the Goals 2000 program and a program to reduce class size by hiring 100,000 teachers. The new grant would be authorized at $2 billion per year for five years, and states would be given greater flexibility in deciding how to spend the funds. Passed 239-185: R 215-4; D 24-180 (ND 17-133, SD 7-47); I 0-1. July 20, 1999. A "nay" was a vote in support of the president's position.

321. HR 2415. State Department Reauthorization/North Korea Nuclear Program. Gilman, R-N.Y., amendment to restrict all nuclear cooperation with North Korea until the president certifies — and Congress passes a concurrent resolution agreeing — that North Korea is in compliance with all international agreements regarding nuclear proliferation, that it has terminated its nuclear weapons program, and that it has permitted the International Atomic Energy Agency full access to verify nuclear sites and material. Adopted 305-120: R 217-0; D 87-120 (ND 62-90, SD 25-30); I 1-0. July 21, 1999. A "nay" was a vote in support of the president's position.

Key

- Y Voted for (yea).
- # Paired for.
- \+ Announced for.
- N Voted against (nay).
- X Paired against.
- – Announced against.
- P Voted "present."
- C Voted "present" to avoid possible conflict of interest.
- ? Did not vote or otherwise make a position known.

•

Democrats ***Republicans***
Independents

	314	315	316	317	318	319	320	321
ALABAMA								
1 ***Callahan***	N	Y	Y	N	Y	N	Y	Y
2 ***Everett***	Y	Y	Y	N	Y	N	Y	Y
3 ***Riley***	Y	Y	Y	N	Y	N	Y	Y
4 ***Aderholt***	Y	Y	Y	N	Y	N	Y	Y
5 Cramer	N	N	Y	Y	Y	Y	N	Y
6 ***Bachus***	Y	Y	Y	N	Y	N	Y	Y
7 Hilliard	N	N	Y	Y	Y	Y	N	N
ALASKA								
AL ***Young***	Y	Y	Y	N	Y	N	Y	Y
ARIZONA								
1 ***Salmon***	Y	Y	Y	N	Y	N	Y	Y
2 Pastor	N	N	Y	Y	Y	Y	N	N
3 ***Stump***	Y	Y	Y	N	Y	N	Y	Y
4 ***Shadegg***	Y	Y	Y	N	Y	N	Y	Y
5 ***Kolbe***	N	Y	Y	N	Y	N	Y	Y
6 ***Hayworth***	N	Y	Y	N	Y	N	Y	Y
ARKANSAS								
1 Berry	N	N	Y	Y	Y	Y	N	Y
2 Snyder	N	N	Y	Y	Y	Y	N	N
3 ***Hutchinson***	N	Y	Y	N	Y	N	Y	Y
4 ***Dickey***	Y	Y	Y	N	Y	N	Y	Y
CALIFORNIA								
1 Thompson	N	N	Y	Y	Y	Y	Y	N
2 ***Herger***	N	Y	Y	N	Y	N	Y	Y
3 ***Ose***	N	Y	Y	N	Y	N	Y	Y
4 ***Doolittle***	Y	Y	Y	N	Y	N	Y	Y
5 Matsui	N	N	Y	Y	Y	Y	N	N
6 Woolsey	N	N	Y	Y	Y	Y	N	N
7 Miller, George	N	N	Y	Y	Y	Y	Y	N
8 Pelosi	N	N	Y	Y	Y	Y	N	N
9 Lee	N	N	Y	Y	Y	Y	N	Y
10 Tauscher	N	N	Y	Y	Y	Y	Y	N
11 ***Pombo***	Y	Y	Y	N	Y	N	Y	Y
12 Lantos	N	?	Y	Y	Y	Y	N	N
13 Stark	?	?	?	?	?	?	?	N
14 Eshoo	N	Y	Y	Y	Y	Y	Y	Y
15 ***Campbell***	N	Y	Y	N	Y	N	Y	Y
16 Lofgren	N	N	Y	Y	Y	Y	N	N
17 Farr	N	N	Y	Y	Y	Y	N	N
18 Condit	N	N	Y	Y	Y	Y	Y	Y
19 ***Radanovich***	?	Y	Y	N	Y	N	Y	Y
20 Dooley	N	N	Y	N	Y	Y	Y	N
21 ***Thomas***	N	Y	Y	N	Y	N	Y	Y
22 Capps	N	N	Y	Y	Y	Y	N	Y
23 ***Gallegly***	N	Y	Y	N	Y	N	Y	Y
24 Sherman	N	N	Y	Y	Y	Y	N	Y
25 ***McKeon***	N	Y	Y	N	Y	N	Y	Y
26 Berman	N	?	Y	Y	Y	Y	N	N
27 ***Rogan***	N	Y	Y	N	Y	N	Y	Y
28 ***Dreier***	N	Y	Y	N	Y	N	Y	Y
29 Waxman	N	N	Y	Y	Y	Y	?	N
30 Becerra	N	N	Y	Y	Y	Y	N	N
31 Martinez	Y	N	Y	Y	Y	Y	N	N
32 Dixon	N	N	Y	Y	Y	Y	N	N
33 Roybal-Allard	N	N	Y	Y	Y	Y	N	N
34 Napolitano	N	N	Y	Y	Y	Y	N	N
35 Waters	N	N	Y	Y	Y	Y	N	N
36 ***Kuykendall***	N	Y	Y	N	Y	N	Y	Y
37 Millender-McD.	N	N	Y	Y	Y	Y	N	N
38 ***Horn***	N	Y	Y	N	Y	N	Y	Y
39 ***Royce***	Y	Y	Y	N	Y	N	Y	Y
40 ***Lewis***	N	Y	Y	N	Y	N	Y	Y
41 ***Miller, Gary***	N	Y	Y	N	Y	N	Y	Y
42 Vacant								
43 ***Calvert***	N	?	Y	N	Y	N	Y	Y
44 ***Bono***	N	Y	Y	N	Y	N	Y	Y
45 ***Rohrabacher***	Y	Y	Y	N	Y	N	Y	Y
46 Sanchez	N	N	Y	Y	Y	Y	N	Y
47 ***Cox***	N	Y	Y	N	Y	N	Y	Y
48 ***Packard***	Y	Y	Y	N	Y	N	Y	Y
49 ***Bilbray***	N	Y	Y	N	Y	Y	N	Y
50 Filner	N	N	Y	Y	Y	Y	N	N
51 ***Cunningham***	Y	Y	Y	N	Y	N	Y	Y
52 ***Hunter***	Y	Y	Y	N	Y	N	Y	Y
COLORADO								
1 DeGette	N	N	Y	Y	Y	Y	N	N
2 Udall	N	N	Y	Y	Y	Y	N	N
3 ***McInnis***	Y	Y	Y	N	Y	N	Y	Y
4 ***Schaffer***	Y	Y	Y	N	Y	N	Y	Y
5 ***Hefley***	Y	Y	Y	N	Y	N	Y	Y
6 ***Tancredo***	Y	Y	Y	N	Y	N	Y	Y
CONNECTICUT								
1 Larson	N	N	Y	Y	Y	Y	N	N
2 Gejdenson	N	N	Y	Y	Y	Y	N	N
3 DeLauro	N	N	Y	Y	Y	Y	N	N
4 ***Shays***	N	Y	Y	N	Y	N	Y	Y
5 Maloney	N	N	Y	Y	Y	Y	N	Y
6 ***Johnson***	N	Y	Y	N	Y	N	N	Y
DELAWARE								
AL ***Castle***	N	Y	Y	N	Y	N	Y	Y
FLORIDA								
1 ***Scarborough***	Y	Y	Y	N	Y	N	Y	Y
2 Boyd	N	N	Y	Y	Y	Y	Y	N
3 Brown	N	N	Y	Y	Y	Y	N	Y
4 ***Fowler***	N	Y	Y	N	Y	N	Y	Y
5 Thurman	N	N	Y	Y	Y	Y	N	Y
6 ***Stearns***	N	Y	Y	N	Y	N	Y	Y
7 ***Mica***	N	Y	Y	N	Y	N	Y	Y
8 ***McCollum***	N	Y	Y	N	Y	N	Y	Y
9 ***Bilirakis***	Y	Y	Y	N	Y	N	Y	Y
10 ***Young***	N	Y	Y	N	Y	?	Y	Y
11 Davis	N	Y	Y	Y	Y	Y	Y	N
12 ***Canady***	N	Y	Y	N	Y	N	Y	Y
13 ***Miller***	N	Y	Y	N	Y	N	Y	Y
14 ***Goss***	N	Y	Y	N	Y	N	Y	Y
15 ***Weldon***	Y	Y	Y	N	Y	N	Y	Y
16 ***Foley***	Y	Y	Y	N	Y	N	Y	Y
17 Meek	?	N	Y	Y	Y	Y	N	N
18 ***Ros-Lehtinen***	N	Y	Y	N	Y	N	Y	Y
19 Wexler	N	N	Y	Y	Y	Y	N	N
20 Deutsch	N	N	Y	Y	Y	Y	N	N
21 ***Diaz-Balart***	N	Y	Y	N	Y	N	Y	Y
22 ***Shaw***	N	Y	Y	N	Y	N	Y	Y
23 Hastings	N	N	Y	Y	Y	Y	N	N
GEORGIA								
1 ***Kingston***	Y	Y	Y	N	Y	N	Y	Y
2 Bishop	N	N	Y	Y	Y	Y	N	N
3 ***Collins***	Y	Y	Y	N	Y	N	Y	Y
4 McKinney	N	N	Y	Y	Y	Y	N	Y
5 Lewis	?	?	?	?	?	?	?	N
6 ***Isakson***	N	Y	Y	N	Y	N	Y	Y
7 ***Barr***	Y	Y	Y	N	Y	N	Y	Y
8 ***Chambliss***	N	Y	Y	N	Y	N	Y	Y
9 ***Deal***	N	Y	Y	N	Y	N	Y	Y
10 ***Norwood***	Y	Y	Y	N	Y	N	Y	Y
11 ***Linder***	N	Y	Y	N	Y	N	Y	Y
HAWAII								
1 Abercrombie	N	N	Y	Y	Y	Y	N	Y
2 Mink	N	N	Y	Y	Y	Y	N	N
IDAHO								
1 ***Chenoweth***	Y	Y	Y	N	Y	N	Y	?
2 ***Simpson***	Y	Y	Y	N	Y	N	Y	Y
ILLINOIS								
1 Rush	N	N	Y	Y	Y	Y	N	N
2 Jackson	N	N	Y	Y	Y	Y	N	N
3 Lipinski	N	N	Y	N	Y	Y	Y	Y
4 Gutierrez	N	N	Y	Y	Y	Y	N	Y
5 Blagojevich	N	N	Y	Y	Y	Y	N	Y
6 ***Hyde***	N	Y	Y	N	Y	N	Y	Y
7 Davis	N	N	Y	Y	Y	Y	N	N
8 ***Crane***	Y	Y	Y	N	Y	N	Y	Y
9 Schakowsky	N	N	Y	Y	Y	Y	N	Y
10 ***Porter***	N	Y	Y	?	Y	N	Y	Y
11 ***Weller***	N	Y	Y	N	Y	N	Y	Y
12 Costello	N	N	Y	Y	Y	Y	N	Y
13 ***Biggert***	N	Y	Y	N	Y	N	Y	Y
14 ***Hastert***							Y	

ND Northern Democrats SD Southern Democrats

	314	315	316	317	318	319	320	321
15 ***Ewing***	N	Y	Y	N	Y	N	Y	Y
16 ***Manzullo***	Y	Y	Y	N	Y	N	Y	Y
17 Evans	N	N	Y	Y	Y	Y	N	Y
18 ***LaHood***	N	Y	Y	N	Y	N	Y	Y
19 Phelps	N	N	Y	Y	Y	Y	N	Y
20 ***Shimkus***	N	Y	Y	N	Y	N	Y	Y
INDIANA								
1 Visclosky	N	N	Y	Y	Y	Y	N	N
2 ***McIntosh***	Y	Y	Y	N	Y	N	Y	Y
3 Roemer	N	Y	Y	N	Y	Y	Y	N
4 ***Souder***	N	Y	Y	N	Y	N	Y	Y
5 ***Buyer***	N	Y	Y	N	Y	N	Y	Y
6 ***Burton***	Y	Y	Y	N	Y	N	Y	Y
7 ***Pease***	Y	Y	Y	N	Y	N	Y	Y
8 ***Hostettler***	Y	Y	Y	N	Y	N	Y	Y
9 Hill	N	N	Y	Y	Y	Y	N	N
10 Carson	N	N	Y	Y	Y	Y	N	Y
IOWA								
1 ***Leach***	N	Y	Y	N	Y	N	Y	Y
2 ***Nussle***	N	Y	Y	N	Y	N	Y	Y
3 Boswell	N	N	Y	Y	Y	Y	N	Y
4 ***Ganske***	N	Y	Y	N	Y	N	Y	Y
5 ***Latham***	N	Y	Y	N	Y	N	Y	Y
KANSAS								
1 ***Moran***	Y	Y	Y	N	Y	N	Y	Y
2 ***Ryun***	Y	Y	Y	N	Y	N	Y	Y
3 Moore	N	N	Y	Y	Y	Y	N	Y
4 ***Tiahrt***	Y	Y	Y	N	Y	N	Y	Y
KENTUCKY								
1 ***Whitfield***	N	Y	Y	N	Y	N	Y	Y
2 ***Lewis***	Y	Y	Y	N	Y	N	Y	Y
3 ***Northup***	N	Y	Y	N	Y	N	Y	Y
4 Lucas	N	N	Y	N	Y	Y	N	Y
5 ***Rogers***	N	Y	Y	N	Y	N	Y	Y
6 ***Fletcher***	N	Y	Y	N	Y	N	Y	Y
LOUISIANA								
1 ***Vitter***	N	Y	Y	N	Y	N	Y	Y
2 Jefferson	?	N	Y	Y	Y	Y	N	N
3 ***Tauzin***	N	Y	Y	N	Y	N	Y	Y
4 ***McCrery***	N	Y	Y	N	Y	N	Y	Y
5 ***Cooksey***	Y	?	Y	N	Y	N	Y	Y
6 ***Baker***	?	Y	Y	N	Y	N	Y	Y
7 John	N	N	Y	N	Y	Y	N	N
MAINE								
1 Allen	N	N	Y	Y	Y	Y	N	N
2 Baldacci	N	N	Y	Y	Y	Y	N	N
MARYLAND								
1 ***Gilchrest***	N	Y	Y	N	Y	N	Y	Y
2 ***Ehrlich***	N	Y	Y	N	Y	N	Y	Y
3 Cardin	N	?	Y	N	Y	Y	N	N
4 Wynn	N	N	Y	Y	Y	Y	N	Y
5 Hoyer	N	N	Y	Y	Y	Y	N	N
6 ***Bartlett***	Y	Y	Y	N	Y	N	Y	Y
7 Cummings	N	N	Y	Y	Y	Y	N	N
8 ***Morella***	N	Y	Y	N	Y	Y	N	Y
MASSACHUSETTS								
1 Olver	N	N	Y	Y	Y	Y	N	N
2 Neal	N	N	Y	Y	Y	Y	N	Y
3 McGovern	N	N	Y	Y	Y	Y	N	Y
4 Frank	N	N	Y	Y	Y	Y	N	N
5 Meehan	N	N	Y	Y	Y	Y	N	Y
6 Tierney	N	N	Y	Y	Y	Y	Y	Y
7 Markey	N	N	Y	Y	Y	Y	N	Y
8 Capuano	N	N	Y	Y	Y	Y	N	N
9 Moakley	N	N	Y	Y	Y	Y	N	Y
10 Delahunt	N	N	Y	Y	Y	Y	N	N
MICHIGAN								
1 Stupak	N	N	Y	Y	Y	Y	N	N
2 ***Hoekstra***	N	Y	Y	N	Y	N	Y	Y
3 ***Ehlers***	N	Y	Y	N	Y	N	Y	Y
4 ***Camp***	N	Y	Y	N	Y	N	Y	Y
5 Barcia	N	N	Y	Y	Y	Y	N	Y
6 ***Upton***	N	Y	Y	N	Y	N	Y	Y
7 ***Smith***	N	Y	Y	N	Y	N	Y	Y
8 Stabenow	N	N	Y	Y	Y	Y	N	Y
9 Kildee	N	N	Y	Y	Y	Y	N	Y
10 Bonior	N	N	Y	Y	Y	Y	N	N
11 ***Knollenberg***	N	Y	Y	N	Y	N	Y	Y
12 Levin	N	?	Y	Y	Y	Y	N	N
13 Rivers	N	N	Y	N	Y	Y	Y	Y
14 Conyers	N	N	Y	Y	Y	Y	N	N
15 Kilpatrick	N	N	Y	Y	Y	Y	N	N
16 Dingell	N	N	Y	Y	Y	Y	N	N

	314	315	316	317	318	319	320	321
MINNESOTA								
1 ***Gutknecht***	N	Y	Y	N	Y	N	Y	Y
2 Minge	N	N	Y	Y	Y	Y	N	N
3 ***Ramstad***	N	Y	Y	N	Y	N	Y	Y
4 Vento	N	N	Y	Y	Y	Y	N	Y
5 Sabo	N	N	Y	Y	Y	Y	Y	N
6 Luther	N	N	Y	Y	Y	Y	N	N
7 Peterson	Y	N	Y	Y	Y	Y	Y	Y
8 Oberstar	N	N	Y	Y	Y	Y	N	N
MISSISSIPPI								
1 ***Wicker***	N	Y	Y	N	Y	N	Y	Y
2 Thompson	N	N	Y	Y	Y	Y	N	N
3 ***Pickering***	N	Y	Y	N	Y	N	Y	Y
4 Shows	N	N	Y	Y	Y	Y	N	Y
5 Taylor	Y	N	Y	N	Y	Y	Y	Y
MISSOURI								
1 Clay	N	N	Y	Y	Y	Y	N	N
2 ***Talent***	N	Y	Y	N	Y	N	Y	+
3 Gephardt	N	N	Y	Y	Y	Y	N	N
4 Skelton	N	N	Y	Y	Y	Y	N	N
5 McCarthy	N	N	Y	Y	Y	Y	N	N
6 Danner	N	N	Y	Y	Y	Y	N	Y
7 ***Blunt***	N	Y	Y	N	Y	N	Y	Y
8 ***Emerson***	N	Y	Y	N	Y	N	Y	Y
9 ***Hulshof***	N	Y	Y	N	Y	N	Y	Y
MONTANA								
AL ***Hill***	Y	Y	Y	N	Y	N	Y	Y
NEBRASKA								
1 ***Bereuter***	N	Y	Y	N	Y	N	Y	Y
2 ***Terry***	N	Y	Y	N	Y	N	Y	Y
3 ***Barrett***	N	Y	Y	N	Y	N	Y	Y
NEVADA								
1 Berkley	N	N	Y	Y	Y	Y	N	Y
2 ***Gibbons***	Y	Y	Y	N	Y	N	Y	Y
NEW HAMPSHIRE								
1 ***Sununu***	N	Y	Y	N	Y	N	Y	Y
2 ***Bass***	N	Y	Y	N	Y	N	Y	Y
NEW JERSEY								
1 Andrews	N	N	Y	Y	Y	Y	N	Y
2 ***LoBiondo***	N	Y	Y	N	Y	N	Y	Y
3 ***Saxton***	N	Y	Y	N	Y	N	Y	Y
4 ***Smith***	N	Y	Y	N	Y	N	Y	Y
5 ***Roukema***	N	Y	Y	N	Y	N	Y	Y
6 Pallone	N	N	Y	Y	Y	Y	N	Y
7 ***Franks***	N	Y	Y	N	Y	N	Y	Y
8 Pascrell	N	N	Y	Y	Y	Y	N	Y
9 Rothman	N	N	Y	Y	Y	Y	N	Y
10 Payne	N	N	Y	Y	Y	Y	N	N
11 ***Frelinghuysen***	N	Y	Y	N	Y	N	Y	Y
12 Holt	N	N	Y	Y	Y	Y	Y	Y
13 Menendez	N	N	Y	Y	Y	Y	N	Y
NEW MEXICO								
1 ***Wilson***	N	Y	Y	N	Y	N	Y	Y
2 ***Skeen***	N	Y	Y	N	Y	N	Y	Y
3 Udall	N	N	Y	Y	Y	Y	N	Y
NEW YORK								
1 Forbes	N	N	Y	N	Y	Y	Y	Y
2 ***Lazio***	N	Y	Y	N	Y	N	?	Y
3 ***King***	N	Y	Y	N	Y	N	Y	Y
4 McCarthy	N	N	Y	Y	Y	Y	N	Y
5 Ackerman	N	N	Y	Y	Y	Y	N	N
6 Meeks	N	N	Y	Y	Y	Y	N	N
7 Crowley	N	Y	Y	Y	Y	Y	N	N
8 Nadler	N	N	Y	Y	Y	Y	N	N
9 Weiner	N	N	Y	Y	Y	Y	N	N
10 Towns	?	?	Y	Y	Y	Y	N	N
11 Owens	N	N	Y	Y	Y	Y	N	N
12 Velázquez	N	N	Y	Y	Y	Y	N	Y
13 ***Fossella***	N	Y	Y	N	Y	N	Y	Y
14 Maloney	N	N	Y	Y	Y	Y	N	N
15 Rangel	N	N	Y	Y	Y	Y	N	N
16 Serrano	N	N	Y	Y	Y	Y	N	Y
17 Engel	N	?	Y	Y	Y	Y	N	N
18 Lowey	N	N	Y	Y	Y	Y	N	Y
19 ***Kelly***	N	Y	Y	N	Y	N	Y	Y
20 ***Gilman***	N	Y	Y	N	Y	N	Y	Y
21 McNulty	N	N	Y	Y	Y	Y	N	Y
22 ***Sweeney***	Y	Y	Y	N	Y	N	Y	Y
23 ***Boehlert***	N	Y	Y	N	Y	N	Y	Y
24 ***McHugh***	N	Y	Y	N	Y	Y	Y	Y
25 ***Walsh***	N	Y	Y	N	Y	N	Y	Y
26 Hinchey	?	?	?	?	?	?	?	?
27 ***Reynolds***	N	Y	Y	N	Y	N	Y	Y
28 Slaughter	N	N	Y	Y	Y	Y	N	N
29 LaFalce	N	N	Y	Y	Y	Y	N	N

	314	315	316	317	318	319	320	321
30 ***Quinn***	N	Y	Y	N	Y	N	Y	Y
31 ***Houghton***	N	Y	Y	N	Y	N	Y	Y
NORTH CAROLINA								
1 Clayton	N	N	Y	Y	Y	Y	N	N
2 Etheridge	N	N	Y	Y	Y	Y	N	Y
3 ***Jones***	Y	Y	Y	N	Y	N	Y	Y
4 Price	N	N	Y	Y	Y	Y	N	Y
5 ***Burr***	N	Y	Y	N	Y	N	Y	Y
6 ***Coble***	+	+	Y	N	Y	N	Y	Y
7 McIntyre	N	N	Y	N	Y	Y	N	Y
8 ***Hayes***	N	Y	Y	N	Y	N	Y	Y
9 ***Myrick***	Y	Y	Y	N	Y	N	Y	Y
10 ***Ballenger***	N	Y	Y	N	Y	N	Y	Y
11 ***Taylor***	Y	Y	Y	N	Y	N	Y	Y
12 Watt	N	?	Y	Y	Y	Y	N	Y
NORTH DAKOTA								
AL Pomeroy	N	N	Y	Y	Y	Y	N	N
OHIO								
1 ***Chabot***	N	Y	Y	N	Y	N	Y	Y
2 ***Portman***	N	Y	Y	N	Y	N	Y	Y
3 Hall	N	N	Y	Y	Y	Y	N	N
4 ***Oxley***	N	Y	Y	N	Y	N	Y	Y
5 ***Gillmor***	N	Y	Y	N	Y	N	Y	Y
6 Strickland	N	N	Y	Y	Y	Y	N	Y
7 ***Hobson***	N	Y	Y	N	Y	N	Y	Y
8 ***Boehner***	N	Y	Y	N	Y	N	Y	Y
9 Kaptur	N	N	Y	Y	Y	Y	N	Y
10 Kucinich	N	Y	Y	Y	Y	Y	N	Y
11 Jones	N	N	Y	Y	Y	Y	N	N
12 ***Kasich***	N	Y	Y	N	Y	N	Y	Y
13 Brown	N	N	Y	Y	Y	Y	N	Y
14 Sawyer	N	N	Y	Y	Y	Y	N	N
15 ***Pryce***	N	Y	Y	N	Y	N	Y	Y
16 ***Regula***	N	Y	Y	N	Y	N	Y	Y
17 Traficant	N	Y	Y	Y	Y	Y	N	Y
18 ***Ney***	Y	Y	Y	N	Y	N	Y	Y
19 ***LaTourette***	N	Y	Y	N	Y	N	Y	Y
OKLAHOMA								
1 ***Largent***	N	Y	Y	N	Y	N	Y	?
2 ***Coburn***	Y	Y	Y	N	Y	N	Y	Y
3 ***Watkins***	N	Y	Y	N	Y	N	Y	Y
4 ***Watts***	N	Y	Y	N	Y	N	Y	Y
5 ***Istook***	Y	Y	Y	N	Y	N	Y	Y
6 ***Lucas***	Y	Y	Y	N	Y	N	Y	Y
OREGON								
1 Wu	N	N	Y	Y	Y	Y	N	Y
2 ***Walden***	N	Y	Y	N	Y	N	Y	Y
3 Blumenauer	N	N	Y	N	Y	Y	N	N
4 DeFazio	N	N	Y	Y	Y	Y	N	Y
5 Hooley	N	N	Y	Y	Y	Y	N	Y
PENNSYLVANIA								
1 Brady	N	N	Y	Y	Y	Y	N	N
2 Fattah	N	N	Y	Y	Y	Y	N	N
3 Borski	N	N	Y	Y	Y	Y	N	N
4 Klink	N	N	Y	N	Y	Y	N	N
5 ***Peterson***	?	?	?	?	?	?	?	?
6 Holden	?	?	?	?	?	?	?	N
7 ***Weldon***	N	Y	Y	N	Y	N	Y	Y
8 ***Greenwood***	N	Y	Y	N	Y	N	Y	Y
9 ***Shuster***	Y	Y	Y	N	Y	N	Y	Y
10 ***Sherwood***	N	Y	Y	N	Y	N	Y	Y
11 Kanjorski	N	N	Y	Y	Y	Y	N	N
12 Murtha	N	N	Y	N	Y	Y	N	N
13 Hoeffel	N	N	Y	Y	Y	Y	N	N
14 Coyne	N	N	Y	Y	Y	Y	N	N
15 ***Toomey***	N	Y	Y	N	Y	N	Y	Y
16 ***Pitts***	N	Y	Y	N	Y	N	Y	Y
17 ***Gekas***	N	Y	Y	N	Y	N	Y	Y
18 Doyle	N	N	Y	N	Y	Y	N	N
19 ***Goodling***	N	Y	Y	N	Y	N	Y	Y
20 Mascara	N	N	Y	Y	Y	Y	N	N
21 ***English***	?	?	?	?	?	?	?	Y
RHODE ISLAND								
1 Kennedy	?	?	?	?	?	?	?	?
2 Weygand	N	N	Y	Y	Y	Y	N	Y
SOUTH CAROLINA								
1 ***Sanford***	Y	Y	Y	N	Y	N	Y	Y
2 ***Spence***	N	Y	Y	N	Y	N	Y	Y
3 ***Graham***	N	Y	Y	N	Y	N	Y	Y
4 ***DeMint***	Y	Y	Y	N	Y	N	Y	Y
5 Spratt	N	N	Y	Y	Y	Y	N	Y
6 Clyburn	N	N	Y	Y	Y	Y	N	N
SOUTH DAKOTA								
AL ***Thune***	N	Y	Y	N	Y	N	Y	Y

	314	315	316	317	318	319	320	321
TENNESSEE								
1 ***Jenkins***	Y	Y	Y	N	Y	N	Y	Y
2 ***Duncan***	Y	Y	Y	N	Y	N	Y	Y
3 ***Wamp***	Y	Y	Y	N	Y	N	Y	Y
4 ***Hilleary***	Y	Y	Y	?	Y	N	Y	Y
5 Clement	N	N	Y	Y	Y	Y	N	N
6 Gordon	N	N	Y	Y	Y	Y	N	Y
7 ***Bryant***	N	Y	Y	N	Y	N	Y	Y
8 Tanner	N	N	Y	N	Y	Y	N	Y
9 Ford	N	N	Y	Y	Y	Y	N	Y
TEXAS								
1 Sandlin	N	N	Y	Y	Y	Y	N	N
2 Turner	N	N	Y	N	Y	Y	N	Y
3 ***Johnson, Sam***	Y	Y	Y	N	Y	N	Y	Y
4 Hall	N	Y	Y	N	Y	N	Y	Y
5 ***Sessions***	Y	Y	Y	N	Y	N	Y	Y
6 ***Barton***	Y	Y	Y	N	Y	N	Y	Y
7 ***Archer***	N	Y	Y	N	Y	N	Y	Y
8 ***Brady***	N	Y	Y	N	Y	N	Y	Y
9 Lampson	N	N	Y	Y	Y	Y	N	N
10 Doggett	N	N	Y	Y	Y	Y	Y	N
11 Edwards	?	N	Y	Y	Y	Y	N	N
12 ***Granger***	N	Y	Y	N	Y	N	Y	Y
13 ***Thornberry***	N	Y	Y	N	Y	N	Y	Y
14 ***Paul***	Y	Y	N	N	Y	N	N	Y
15 Hinojosa	N	N	Y	Y	Y	Y	N	N
16 Reyes	N	N	Y	Y	Y	Y	N	N
17 Stenholm	N	N	Y	N	Y	Y	Y	Y
18 Jackson-Lee	N	N	Y	Y	Y	Y	N	Y
19 ***Combest***	+	Y	Y	N	Y	N	Y	Y
20 Gonzalez	N	N	Y	Y	Y	Y	N	N
21 ***Smith***	N	Y	Y	N	Y	N	Y	Y
22 ***DeLay***	Y	Y	Y	N	Y	N	Y	Y
23 ***Bonilla***	Y	Y	Y	N	Y	N	Y	Y
24 Frost	N	N	Y	Y	Y	Y	N	Y
25 Bentsen	N	N	Y	Y	Y	Y	N	N
26 ***Armey***	N	Y	Y	N	Y	N	Y	Y
27 Ortiz	–	–	Y	Y	Y	Y	N	Y
28 Rodriguez	N	N	Y	Y	Y	Y	N	N
29 Green	N	N	Y	Y	Y	Y	N	N
30 Johnson, E.B.	N	N	Y	Y	Y	Y	N	N
UTAH								
1 ***Hansen***	N	Y	Y	N	Y	N	Y	Y
2 ***Cook***	N	Y	Y	N	Y	N	Y	Y
3 ***Cannon***	Y	Y	Y	N	Y	N	Y	Y
VERMONT								
AL *Sanders*	N	N	Y	Y	Y	Y	N	Y
VIRGINIA								
1 ***Bateman***	N	Y	Y	N	Y	N	Y	Y
2 Pickett	N	N	Y	Y	Y	Y	N	N
3 Scott	N	N	Y	Y	Y	Y	N	N
4 Sisisky	N	N	Y	Y	Y	Y	N	N
5 Goode	Y	Y	Y	N	Y	N	Y	Y
6 ***Goodlatte***	N	Y	Y	N	Y	N	Y	Y
7 ***Bliley***	N	Y	Y	N	Y	N	Y	Y
8 Moran	N	Y	Y	Y	Y	Y	N	Y
9 Boucher	N	N	Y	Y	Y	Y	N	Y
10 ***Wolf***	N	Y	Y	N	Y	N	Y	Y
11 ***Davis***	N	Y	Y	N	Y	N	Y	Y
WASHINGTON								
1 Inslee	N	N	Y	Y	Y	Y	N	Y
2 ***Metcalf***	Y	Y	Y	N	Y	N	Y	Y
3 Baird	N	N	Y	N	Y	Y	N	Y
4 ***Hastings***	Y	Y	Y	N	Y	N	Y	Y
5 ***Nethercutt***	Y	Y	Y	N	Y	N	Y	Y
6 Dicks	N	N	Y	Y	Y	Y	N	?
7 McDermott	–	–	+	+	+	+	–	–
8 ***Dunn***	N	Y	Y	N	Y	N	Y	Y
9 Smith	N	Y	Y	N	Y	Y	Y	N
WEST VIRGINIA								
1 Mollohan	N	N	Y	N	Y	Y	Y	N
2 Wise	N	N	Y	N	Y	Y	N	Y
3 Rahall	N	N	Y	Y	Y	Y	N	N
WISCONSIN								
1 ***Ryan***	N	Y	Y	N	Y	N	Y	Y
2 Baldwin	N	N	Y	Y	Y	Y	N	N
3 Kind	N	Y	Y	Y	Y	Y	Y	Y
4 Kleczka	N	N	Y	Y	Y	Y	N	N
5 Barrett	N	N	Y	N	Y	Y	N	Y
6 ***Petri***	N	Y	Y	N	Y	N	Y	Y
7 Obey	N	N	Y	Y	Y	Y	N	N
8 ***Green***	N	Y	Y	N	Y	N	Y	Y
9 ***Sensenbrenner***	Y	Y	Y	N	Y	N	Y	Y
WYOMING								
AL ***Cubin***	N	Y	Y	N	Y	N	Y	Y

Southern states - Ala., Ark., Fla., Ga., Ky., La., Miss., N.C., Okla., S.C., Tenn., Texas, Va.

322. HR 2415. State Department Reauthorization/AIDS Medications. Sanders, I-Vt., amendment to prohibit the State Department from imposing restrictions on Israel or any Asian or African nation that seeks to make prescription drugs more affordable by allowing their purchase from sources other than pharmaceutical companies, as long as the action complies with World Trade Organization intellectual property rights agreements. Rejected 117-307: R 19-197; D 97-110 (ND 80-72, SD 17-38); I 1-0. July 21, 1999. A "nay" was a vote in support of the president's position.

323. HR 2415. State Department Reauthorization/Children's Passports. Gibbons, R-Nev., amendment to attempt to stop the abduction of children out of the United States by instituting safeguards during the issuance of passports to children under the age of 14. Adopted 418-3: R 214-2; D 203-1 (ND 150-0, SD 53-1); I 1-0. July 21, 1999.

324. HR 2415. State Department Reauthorization/Military Assistance to U.S.-Supporting Nations. Goodling, R-Pa., amendment to prohibit foreign military assistance (but not humanitarian aid or developmental assistance) to countries that fail to support the United States at least 25 percent of the time in the U.N. General Assembly. Rejected 169-256: R 161-54; D 8-201 (ND 4-150, SD 4-51); I 0-1. July 21, 1999. A "nay" was a vote in support of the president's position.

325. HR 2415. State Department Reauthorization/Whistleblower Protections. Stearns, R-Fla., amendment to express the sense of Congress that State Department employees should not be demoted or removed from federal employment because they have, in the performance of their duties, informed Congress of facts regarding their job responsibilities. Adopted 287-136: R 214-1; D 72-135 (ND 44-108, SD 28-27); I 1-0. July 21, 1999.

326. HR 2415. State Department Reauthorization/Human Rights in Peru. Waters, D-Calif., amendment to express the sense of Congress that the United States should increase support to democracy and human rights activists in Peru, and that it should use all diplomatic means to get the government of Peru to release Lori Berenson, a U.S. citizen sentenced to life in prison by a military judge in 1996 for alleged terrorist acts. Rejected 189-234: R 14-204; D 174-30 (ND 130-21, SD 44-9); I 1-0. July 21, 1999.

327. HR 2415. State Department Reauthorization/U.S.-Mexico Sewage Agreement. Bilbray, R-Calif., amendment to call for the United States and Mexico to enter into an agreement to provide for a long-term and comprehensive solution to eliminate sewage pollution of the San Diego and Tijuana border region. Adopted 427-0: R 218-0; D 208-0 (ND 153-0, SD 55-0); I 1-0. July 21, 1999.

328. HR 2415. State Department Reauthorization/Claims Against Iraq. Doggett, D-Texas, amendment to authorize the Foreign Claims Settlement Commission to determine the validity of claims by U.S. nationals against the Iraqi government, giving priority to claims registered by members of the U.S. armed forces and other claims arising from the 1990 Iraqi invasion of Kuwait or from the 1987 attack on the USS *Stark*. The amendment would authorize the Treasury Department to establish a fund for the payment of claims, to be financed by the liquidation of Iraqi government assets in the United States. Adopted 427-0: R 219-0; D 207-0 (ND 152-0, SD 55-0); I 1-0. July 21, 1999.

329. HR 2415. State Department Reauthorization/Red Cross Access to Kosovar Prisoners. Engel, D-N.Y., amendment to call for immediate Red Cross access to, and the release of, Kosovar Albanians detained in prisons in Kosovo before and during the withdrawal of Serbian forces. Adopted 424-0: R 216-0; D 207-0 (ND 152-0, SD 55-0); I 1-0. July 21, 1999. (Subsequently, the bill to authorize $2.4 billion in funding for the State Department was passed by voice vote.)

Key

- Y Voted for (yea).
- # Paired for.
- \+ Announced for.
- N Voted against (nay).
- X Paired against.
- – Announced against.
- P Voted "present."
- C Voted "present" to avoid possible conflict of interest.
- ? Did not vote or otherwise make a position known.

•

Democrats ***Republicans***
Independents

	322	323	324	325	326	327	328	329
ALABAMA								
1 ***Callahan***	N	Y	N	Y	Y	Y	Y	Y
2 ***Everett***	N	Y	Y	Y	N	Y	Y	Y
3 ***Riley***	N	Y	Y	Y	N	Y	Y	Y
4 ***Aderholt***	N	Y	Y	Y	N	Y	Y	Y
5 Cramer	N	Y	N	Y	N	Y	Y	Y
6 ***Bachus***	Y	Y	Y	Y	N	Y	Y	Y
7 Hilliard	Y	Y	N	N	Y	Y	Y	Y
ALASKA								
AL ***Young***	N	Y	Y	Y	N	Y	Y	Y
ARIZONA								
1 ***Salmon***	N	Y	N	Y	Y	Y	Y	Y
2 Pastor	N	Y	N	N	Y	Y	Y	Y
3 ***Stump***	N	Y	Y	Y	N	Y	Y	Y
4 ***Shadegg***	N	Y	Y	Y	N	Y	Y	Y
5 ***Kolbe***	N	Y	N	Y	N	Y	Y	Y
6 ***Hayworth***	Y	Y	Y	Y	N	Y	Y	Y
ARKANSAS								
1 Berry	Y	Y	N	Y	Y	Y	Y	Y
2 Snyder	Y	Y	N	N	P	Y	Y	Y
3 ***Hutchinson***	N	Y	Y	Y	N	Y	Y	Y
4 ***Dickey***	N	Y	Y	Y	N	Y	Y	Y
CALIFORNIA								
1 Thompson	Y	Y	N	N	Y	Y	Y	Y
2 ***Herger***	N	Y	Y	Y	N	Y	Y	Y
3 ***Ose***	N	Y	N	Y	Y	Y	Y	Y
4 ***Doolittle***	N	Y	Y	Y	N	Y	Y	Y
5 Matsui	N	Y	N	N	Y	Y	Y	Y
6 Woolsey	Y	Y	N	N	Y	Y	Y	Y
7 Miller, George	Y	Y	N	N	Y	Y	Y	Y
8 Pelosi	Y	Y	N	N	Y	Y	Y	Y
9 Lee	Y	Y	N	N	Y	Y	Y	Y
10 Tauscher	N	Y	N	N	Y	Y	Y	Y
11 ***Pombo***	N	Y	Y	Y	N	Y	Y	Y
12 Lantos	Y	Y	N	N	Y	Y	Y	Y
13 Stark	Y	Y	N	Y	Y	Y	Y	Y
14 Eshoo	N	Y	N	Y	Y	Y	Y	Y
15 ***Campbell***	Y	Y	N	Y	Y	Y	Y	Y
16 Lofgren	N	Y	N	N	Y	Y	Y	Y
17 Farr	Y	Y	N	N	Y	Y	Y	Y
18 Condit	Y	Y	N	Y	N	Y	Y	Y
19 ***Radanovich***	N	Y	Y	Y	N	Y	Y	Y
20 Dooley	N	Y	N	N	Y	Y	Y	Y
21 ***Thomas***	N	Y	Y	Y	N	Y	Y	Y
22 Capps	N	Y	N	N	Y	Y	Y	Y
23 ***Gallegly***	N	Y	Y	Y	N	Y	Y	Y
24 Sherman	N	Y	N	Y	Y	Y	Y	Y
25 ***McKeon***	N	Y	Y	Y	N	Y	Y	Y
26 Berman	N	Y	N	N	Y	Y	Y	Y
27 ***Rogan***	N	Y	Y	Y	N	Y	Y	Y
28 ***Dreier***	N	Y	Y	Y	N	Y	Y	Y
29 Waxman	Y	Y	N	N	Y	Y	Y	Y
30 Becerra	Y	?	N	N	Y	Y	Y	Y
31 Martinez	N	Y	N	N	Y	Y	Y	Y
32 Dixon	Y	Y	N	N	Y	Y	Y	Y
33 Roybal-Allard	Y	Y	N	N	Y	Y	Y	Y
34 Napolitano	N	Y	N	N	Y	Y	Y	Y
35 Waters	Y	Y	N	N	Y	Y	Y	Y
36 ***Kuykendall***	N	Y	N	Y	N	Y	Y	Y
37 Millender-McD.	N	Y	N	N	Y	Y	Y	Y
38 ***Horn***	N	Y	N	Y	Y	Y	Y	Y
39 ***Royce***	N	Y	N	Y	N	Y	Y	Y
40 ***Lewis***	?	Y	N	Y	N	Y	Y	Y
41 ***Miller, Gary***	N	Y	Y	Y	N	Y	Y	Y
42 Vacant								
43 ***Calvert***	N	Y	N	Y	N	Y	Y	Y
44 ***Bono***	N	Y	Y	Y	N	Y	Y	Y
45 ***Rohrabacher***	Y	Y	Y	Y	N	Y	Y	Y
46 Sanchez	N	Y	N	N	Y	Y	Y	Y
47 ***Cox***	Y	Y	Y	Y	N	Y	Y	Y
48 ***Packard***	N	Y	Y	Y	N	Y	Y	Y
49 ***Bilbray***	N	Y	Y	Y	N	Y	Y	Y
50 Filner	Y	Y	N	N	Y	Y	Y	Y
51 ***Cunningham***	N	Y	Y	Y	N	Y	Y	Y
52 ***Hunter***	N	Y	Y	Y	N	Y	Y	Y
COLORADO								
1 DeGette	N	Y	N	N	Y	Y	Y	Y
2 Udall	N	+	N	N	Y	Y	Y	Y
3 ***McInnis***	N	Y	Y	Y	N	Y	Y	Y
4 ***Schaffer***	N	Y	Y	Y	N	Y	Y	Y
5 ***Hefley***	N	Y	Y	Y	N	Y	Y	Y
6 ***Tancredo***	N	Y	Y	Y	N	Y	Y	Y
CONNECTICUT								
1 Larson	N	Y	N	N	Y	Y	Y	Y
2 Gejdenson	N	Y	N	N	Y	Y	Y	Y
3 DeLauro	Y	Y	N	N	N	Y	Y	Y
4 ***Shays***	Y	Y	N	Y	N	Y	Y	Y
5 Maloney	N	Y	N	Y	Y	Y	Y	Y
6 ***Johnson***	N	Y	N	Y	Y	Y	Y	Y
DELAWARE								
AL ***Castle***	Y	Y	Y	Y	N	Y	Y	Y
FLORIDA								
1 ***Scarborough***	Y	Y	Y	Y	Y	Y	Y	Y
2 Boyd	N	Y	N	N	Y	Y	Y	Y
3 Brown	Y	Y	N	Y	Y	Y	Y	Y
4 ***Fowler***	N	Y	Y	Y	N	Y	Y	Y
5 Thurman	N	Y	N	Y	Y	Y	Y	Y
6 ***Stearns***	N	Y	Y	Y	N	Y	Y	Y
7 ***Mica***	–	Y	N	Y	N	Y	Y	Y
8 ***McCollum***	N	Y	N	Y	N	Y	Y	Y
9 ***Bilirakis***	N	Y	Y	Y	N	Y	Y	Y
10 ***Young***	N	Y	Y	?	N	Y	Y	Y
11 Davis	N	Y	N	N	Y	Y	Y	Y
12 ***Canady***	N	Y	Y	Y	N	Y	Y	Y
13 ***Miller***	N	Y	Y	Y	N	Y	Y	Y
14 ***Goss***	N	Y	N	Y	N	Y	Y	Y
15 ***Weldon***	Y	Y	Y	Y	N	Y	Y	Y
16 ***Foley***	N	Y	Y	Y	N	Y	Y	Y
17 Meek	Y	Y	N	Y	Y	Y	Y	Y
18 ***Ros-Lehtinen***	Y	Y	Y	Y	N	Y	Y	Y
19 Wexler	Y	Y	N	N	Y	Y	Y	Y
20 Deutsch	N	Y	N	N	Y	Y	Y	Y
21 ***Diaz-Balart***	N	Y	Y	Y	N	Y	Y	Y
22 ***Shaw***	N	Y	N	Y	N	Y	Y	Y
23 Hastings	Y	Y	N	N	Y	Y	Y	Y
GEORGIA								
1 ***Kingston***	N	Y	N	Y	N	Y	Y	Y
2 Bishop	N	?	N	N	Y	Y	Y	Y
3 ***Collins***	N	Y	Y	Y	N	Y	Y	Y
4 McKinney	Y	N	N	Y	Y	Y	Y	Y
5 Lewis	Y	Y	N	Y	Y	Y	Y	Y
6 ***Isakson***	N	Y	Y	Y	N	Y	Y	Y
7 ***Barr***	N	N	Y	Y	N	Y	Y	Y
8 ***Chambliss***	N	Y	Y	Y	N	Y	Y	Y
9 ***Deal***	N	Y	Y	Y	N	Y	Y	Y
10 ***Norwood***	N	Y	Y	Y	N	Y	Y	Y
11 ***Linder***	N	Y	Y	Y	N	Y	Y	Y
HAWAII								
1 Abercrombie	Y	Y	N	Y	Y	Y	?	Y
2 Mink	Y	Y	N	Y	Y	Y	Y	Y
IDAHO								
1 ***Chenoweth***	?	?	?	?	?	?	?	?
2 ***Simpson***	N	Y	Y	Y	N	Y	Y	Y
ILLINOIS								
1 Rush	Y	Y	N	N	Y	Y	Y	Y
2 Jackson	Y	Y	N	N	Y	Y	Y	Y
3 Lipinski	N	Y	N	Y	Y	Y	Y	Y
4 Gutierrez	Y	Y	N	N	Y	Y	Y	Y
5 Blagojevich	Y	Y	N	N	Y	Y	Y	Y
6 ***Hyde***	N	Y	?	?	N	Y	Y	Y
7 Davis	Y	Y	N	N	Y	Y	Y	Y
8 ***Crane***	N	Y	Y	Y	N	Y	Y	Y
9 Schakowsky	Y	Y	N	N	Y	Y	Y	Y
10 ***Porter***	N	Y	N	Y	N	Y	Y	Y
11 ***Weller***	N	Y	Y	Y	N	Y	Y	Y
12 Costello	N	Y	N	Y	Y	Y	Y	Y
13 ***Biggert***	N	Y	N	Y	N	Y	Y	Y
14 ***Hastert***								

ND Northern Democrats SD Southern Democrats

	322	323	324	325	326	327	328	329
15 ***Ewing***	N	Y	N	Y	N	Y	Y	Y
16 ***Manzullo***	N	Y	Y	Y	N	Y	Y	Y
17 Evans	Y	Y	N	Y	Y	Y	Y	Y
18 ***LaHood***	N	Y	N	Y	N	Y	Y	Y
19 Phelps	N	Y	N	Y	Y	Y	Y	Y
20 ***Shimkus***	Y	Y	Y	Y	N	Y	Y	Y
INDIANA								
1 Visclosky	N	Y	N	Y	N	Y	Y	Y
2 ***McIntosh***	N	Y	Y	Y	N	Y	Y	Y
3 Roemer	N	Y	Y	Y	N	Y	Y	Y
4 ***Souder***	N	Y	N	Y	N	Y	Y	Y
5 ***Buyer***	N	Y	Y	Y	N	Y	Y	Y
6 ***Burton***	N	Y	Y	Y	N	Y	Y	Y
7 ***Pease***	N	Y	Y	Y	N	Y	Y	Y
8 ***Hostettler***	N	Y	Y	Y	N	Y	Y	Y
9 Hill	N	Y	N	N	P	Y	Y	Y
10 Carson	Y	Y	N	N	Y	Y	Y	Y
IOWA								
1 ***Leach***	N	Y	N	Y	N	Y	Y	Y
2 ***Nussle***	N	Y	Y	Y	N	Y	Y	Y
3 Boswell	N	Y	N	Y	Y	Y	Y	Y
4 ***Ganske***	N	Y	N	Y	N	Y	Y	Y
5 ***Latham***	N	Y	Y	Y	N	Y	Y	Y
KANSAS								
1 ***Moran***	N	Y	Y	Y	N	Y	Y	Y
2 ***Ryun***	N	Y	Y	Y	N	Y	Y	Y
3 Moore	N	Y	N	N	Y	Y	Y	Y
4 ***Tiahrt***	N	Y	Y	Y	N	Y	Y	Y
KENTUCKY								
1 ***Whitfield***	N	Y	N	Y	Y	Y	Y	Y
2 ***Lewis***	N	Y	Y	Y	N	Y	Y	Y
3 ***Northup***	N	Y	Y	Y	N	Y	Y	Y
4 Lucas	N	Y	Y	Y	Y	Y	Y	Y
5 ***Rogers***	N	Y	Y	Y	N	Y	Y	Y
6 ***Fletcher***	N	Y	Y	Y	N	Y	Y	Y
LOUISIANA								
1 ***Vitter***	N	Y	Y	Y	N	Y	Y	Y
2 Jefferson	N	Y	N	N	Y	Y	Y	Y
3 ***Tauzin***	N	Y	Y	Y	N	Y	Y	Y
4 ***McCrery***	N	Y	Y	Y	N	Y	Y	Y
5 ***Cooksey***	N	Y	N	Y	N	Y	Y	Y
6 ***Baker***	N	Y	Y	Y	N	Y	Y	Y
7 John	N	Y	N	Y	N	Y	Y	Y
MAINE								
1 Allen	Y	Y	N	N	Y	Y	Y	Y
2 Baldacci	Y	Y	N	N	Y	Y	Y	Y
MARYLAND								
1 ***Gilchrest***	N	Y	Y	Y	N	Y	Y	Y
2 ***Ehrlich***	N	Y	Y	Y	N	Y	Y	Y
3 Cardin	N	Y	N	N	Y	Y	Y	Y
4 Wynn	Y	Y	N	Y	Y	Y	Y	Y
5 Hoyer	N	Y	N	?	Y	Y	Y	Y
6 ***Bartlett***	Y	Y	Y	Y	N	Y	Y	Y
7 Cummings	Y	Y	N	N	Y	Y	Y	Y
8 ***Morella***	N	Y	N	Y	Y	Y	Y	Y
MASSACHUSETTS								
1 Olver	Y	Y	N	N	Y	Y	Y	Y
2 Neal	Y	Y	N	N	Y	Y	Y	Y
3 McGovern	Y	Y	N	N	Y	Y	Y	Y
4 Frank	Y	Y	N	N	N	Y	Y	Y
5 Meehan	Y	Y	N	N	Y	Y	Y	Y
6 Tierney	Y	Y	N	Y	Y	Y	Y	Y
7 Markey	Y	Y	N	Y	Y	Y	Y	Y
8 Capuano	Y	Y	N	N	Y	Y	Y	Y
9 Moakley	Y	Y	N	N	Y	Y	Y	Y
10 Delahunt	Y	Y	N	N	Y	Y	Y	Y
MICHIGAN								
1 Stupak	N	Y	N	N	N	Y	Y	Y
2 ***Hoekstra***	N	Y	Y	Y	N	Y	Y	Y
3 ***Ehlers***	N	Y	N	Y	N	Y	Y	Y
4 ***Camp***	N	Y	Y	Y	N	Y	Y	Y
5 Barcia	N	Y	N	Y	N	Y	Y	Y
6 ***Upton***	N	Y	Y	Y	N	Y	Y	Y
7 ***Smith***	N	Y	Y	Y	N	Y	Y	Y
8 Stabenow	Y	Y	N	N	Y	Y	Y	Y
9 Kildee	Y	Y	N	N	Y	Y	Y	Y
10 Bonior	Y	Y	N	N	Y	Y	Y	Y
11 ***Knollenberg***	N	Y	N	Y	N	Y	Y	Y
12 Levin	N	Y	N	N	Y	Y	Y	Y
13 Rivers	Y	Y	N	N	Y	Y	Y	Y
14 Conyers	Y	Y	N	N	Y	Y	Y	Y
15 Kilpatrick	Y	Y	N	N	Y	Y	Y	Y
16 Dingell	N	Y	N	N	N	Y	Y	Y
MINNESOTA								
1 ***Gutknecht***	N	Y	Y	Y	N	Y	Y	Y
2 Minge	N	Y	N	Y	N	Y	Y	Y
3 ***Ramstad***	N	Y	Y	Y	N	Y	Y	Y
4 Vento	Y	Y	N	N	Y	Y	Y	Y
5 Sabo	Y	Y	N	N	Y	Y	Y	Y
6 Luther	Y	Y	N	Y	Y	Y	Y	Y
7 Peterson	Y	Y	Y	Y	N	Y	Y	Y
8 Oberstar	Y	Y	N	N	Y	Y	Y	Y
MISSISSIPPI								
1 ***Wicker***	N	Y	Y	Y	N	Y	Y	Y
2 Thompson	Y	Y	N	N	Y	Y	Y	Y
3 ***Pickering***	N	Y	Y	Y	N	Y	Y	Y
4 Shows	Y	Y	N	Y	N	Y	Y	Y
5 Taylor	Y	Y	Y	Y	N	Y	Y	Y
MISSOURI								
1 Clay	Y	Y	N	Y	Y	Y	Y	Y
2 ***Talent***	+	+	N	Y	N	Y	Y	Y
3 Gephardt	N	Y	N	N	Y	Y	Y	Y
4 Skelton	N	Y	N	Y	Y	Y	Y	Y
5 McCarthy	N	Y	N	N	Y	Y	Y	Y
6 Danner	N	Y	N	Y	Y	Y	Y	Y
7 ***Blunt***	N	Y	Y	Y	N	Y	Y	Y
8 ***Emerson***	Y	Y	Y	Y	N	Y	Y	Y
9 ***Hulshof***	N	Y	Y	Y	N	Y	Y	Y
MONTANA								
AL ***Hill***	N	Y	Y	Y	N	Y	Y	Y
NEBRASKA								
1 ***Bereuter***	N	Y	N	Y	N	Y	Y	Y
2 ***Terry***	N	Y	Y	Y	N	Y	Y	Y
3 ***Barrett***	N	Y	Y	Y	N	Y	Y	Y
NEVADA								
1 Berkley	N	Y	N	Y	Y	Y	Y	Y
2 ***Gibbons***	N	Y	Y	Y	N	Y	Y	Y
NEW HAMPSHIRE								
1 ***Sununu***	N	Y	Y	Y	N	Y	Y	Y
2 ***Bass***	N	Y	Y	Y	N	Y	Y	Y
NEW JERSEY								
1 Andrews	N	Y	Y	Y	Y	Y	Y	Y
2 ***LoBiondo***	N	Y	Y	Y	N	Y	Y	Y
3 ***Saxton***	N	Y	N	Y	N	Y	Y	Y
4 ***Smith***	Y	Y	Y	Y	N	Y	Y	Y
5 ***Roukema***	N	Y	?	Y	N	Y	Y	Y
6 Pallone	N	Y	N	N	Y	Y	Y	Y
7 ***Franks***	N	Y	Y	Y	N	Y	Y	Y
8 Pascrell	N	Y	N	N	Y	Y	Y	Y
9 Rothman	N	Y	N	N	Y	Y	Y	Y
10 Payne	Y	Y	N	N	Y	Y	Y	Y
11 ***Frelinghuysen***	N	Y	N	Y	N	Y	Y	Y
12 Holt	N	Y	N	N	Y	Y	Y	Y
13 Menendez	N	Y	N	N	N	Y	Y	Y
NEW MEXICO								
1 ***Wilson***	N	Y	N	N	P	Y	Y	Y
2 ***Skeen***	N	Y	Y	Y	N	Y	Y	Y
3 Udall	Y	Y	N	Y	Y	Y	Y	Y
NEW YORK								
1 Forbes	N	Y	N	Y	N	Y	Y	?
2 ***Lazio***	N	Y	N	Y	N	Y	Y	Y
3 ***King***	N	Y	Y	Y	N	Y	Y	Y
4 McCarthy	N	Y	N	N	Y	Y	Y	Y
5 Ackerman	N	Y	N	N	N	Y	Y	Y
6 Meeks	Y	Y	N	N	Y	Y	Y	Y
7 Crowley	N	Y	N	N	Y	Y	Y	Y
8 Nadler	Y	Y	N	N	Y	Y	Y	Y
9 Weiner	Y	Y	N	N	Y	Y	Y	Y
10 Towns	Y	Y	N	N	?	?	?	?
11 Owens	Y	Y	N	N	Y	Y	Y	Y
12 Velázquez	Y	Y	N	N	Y	Y	Y	Y
13 ***Fossella***	N	Y	N	Y	N	Y	Y	Y
14 Maloney	Y	Y	N	N	Y	Y	Y	Y
15 Rangel	Y	Y	N	N	Y	Y	Y	Y
16 Serrano	Y	Y	N	N	Y	Y	Y	Y
17 Engel	N	Y	N	N	Y	Y	Y	Y
18 Lowey	N	Y	N	N	Y	Y	Y	Y
19 ***Kelly***	N	Y	N	Y	N	Y	Y	Y
20 ***Gilman***	N	Y	N	Y	N	Y	Y	Y
21 McNulty	Y	Y	N	N	Y	Y	Y	Y
22 ***Sweeney***	N	Y	Y	Y	N	Y	Y	Y
23 ***Boehlert***	N	Y	N	Y	N	Y	Y	Y
24 ***McHugh***	N	Y	Y	Y	N	Y	Y	Y
25 ***Walsh***	N	Y	N	Y	N	Y	Y	Y
26 Hinchey	?	?	N	N	Y	Y	Y	Y
27 ***Reynolds***	N	Y	Y	Y	N	Y	Y	Y
28 Slaughter	Y	Y	N	N	Y	Y	Y	Y
29 LaFalce	N	?	N	N	Y	Y	Y	Y
30 ***Quinn***	N	Y	N	Y	N	Y	Y	Y
31 ***Houghton***	N	Y	N	Y	N	Y	Y	Y
NORTH CAROLINA								
1 Clayton	N	Y	N	N	Y	Y	Y	Y
2 Etheridge	N	Y	N	Y	Y	Y	Y	Y
3 ***Jones***	N	Y	Y	Y	N	Y	Y	Y
4 Price	N	Y	N	N	Y	Y	Y	Y
5 ***Burr***	N	Y	Y	Y	N	Y	Y	Y
6 ***Coble***	N	Y	Y	Y	N	Y	Y	Y
7 McIntyre	N	Y	N	Y	Y	Y	Y	Y
8 ***Hayes***	N	Y	Y	Y	N	Y	Y	Y
9 ***Myrick***	N	Y	Y	Y	N	Y	Y	Y
10 ***Ballenger***	N	Y	?	Y	N	Y	Y	Y
11 ***Taylor***	N	Y	Y	Y	N	Y	Y	Y
12 Watt	N	Y	N	N	Y	Y	Y	Y
NORTH DAKOTA								
AL Pomeroy	N	Y	N	N	Y	Y	Y	Y
OHIO								
1 ***Chabot***	N	Y	Y	Y	N	Y	Y	Y
2 ***Portman***	N	Y	N	Y	N	Y	Y	Y
3 Hall	Y	Y	N	N	Y	Y	Y	Y
4 ***Oxley***	N	Y	N	Y	N	Y	Y	Y
5 ***Gillmor***	N	Y	Y	Y	N	Y	Y	Y
6 Strickland	Y	Y	N	N	Y	Y	Y	Y
7 ***Hobson***	N	Y	N	Y	Y	Y	Y	Y
8 ***Boehner***	N	Y	Y	Y	N	Y	Y	Y
9 Kaptur	Y	Y	N	N	Y	Y	Y	Y
10 Kucinich	Y	Y	N	Y	Y	Y	Y	Y
11 Jones	Y	Y	N	N	Y	Y	Y	Y
12 ***Kasich***	N	Y	Y	Y	N	Y	Y	Y
13 Brown	Y	Y	N	N	Y	Y	Y	Y
14 Sawyer	N	Y	N	N	Y	Y	Y	Y
15 ***Pryce***	N	Y	Y	Y	Y	Y	Y	Y
16 ***Regula***	N	Y	Y	Y	N	Y	Y	Y
17 Traficant	N	Y	Y	Y	N	Y	Y	Y
18 ***Ney***	N	Y	N	Y	N	Y	Y	Y
19 ***LaTourette***	N	Y	N	Y	N	Y	Y	Y
OKLAHOMA								
1 ***Largent***	N	Y	Y	Y	N	Y	Y	Y
2 ***Coburn***	Y	Y	Y	Y	N	Y	Y	?
3 ***Watkins***	N	Y	Y	Y	N	Y	Y	Y
4 ***Watts***	N	Y	Y	Y	N	Y	Y	?
5 ***Istook***	N	Y	Y	Y	N	Y	Y	Y
6 ***Lucas***	N	Y	Y	Y	N	Y	Y	Y
OREGON								
1 Wu	Y	Y	N	Y	Y	Y	Y	Y
2 ***Walden***	N	Y	Y	Y	N	Y	Y	Y
3 Blumenauer	N	Y	N	N	Y	Y	Y	Y
4 DeFazio	Y	Y	N	Y	Y	Y	Y	Y
5 Hooley	N	Y	N	N	Y	Y	Y	Y
PENNSYLVANIA								
1 Brady	Y	Y	N	N	Y	Y	Y	Y
2 Fattah	Y	Y	N	N	Y	Y	Y	Y
3 Borski	N	Y	N	N	Y	Y	Y	Y
4 Klink	N	Y	N	Y	N	Y	Y	Y
5 ***Peterson***	?	?	?	?	?	?	?	?
6 Holden	N	Y	N	Y	Y	Y	Y	Y
7 ***Weldon***	N	Y	N	Y	N	Y	Y	Y
8 ***Greenwood***	N	Y	N	Y	N	Y	Y	Y
9 ***Shuster***	N	Y	Y	Y	N	Y	Y	Y
10 ***Sherwood***	N	Y	Y	Y	Y	Y	Y	Y
11 Kanjorski	N	Y	N	Y	N	Y	Y	Y
12 Murtha	N	Y	N	Y	N	Y	Y	Y
13 Hoeffel	N	Y	N	Y	Y	Y	Y	Y
14 Coyne	N	Y	N	N	Y	Y	Y	Y
15 ***Toomey***	N	Y	Y	Y	N	Y	Y	Y
16 ***Pitts***	N	Y	Y	Y	N	Y	Y	Y
17 ***Gekas***	N	Y	Y	Y	N	Y	Y	Y
18 Doyle	N	Y	N	Y	Y	Y	Y	Y
19 ***Goodling***	N	Y	Y	Y	N	Y	Y	Y
20 Mascara	N	Y	N	Y	Y	Y	Y	Y
21 ***English***	N	Y	N	Y	Y	Y	Y	Y
RHODE ISLAND								
1 Kennedy	?	?	?	?	?	?	?	?
2 Weygand	Y	Y	N	N	Y	Y	Y	Y
SOUTH CAROLINA								
1 ***Sanford***	Y	Y	Y	Y	N	Y	Y	Y
2 ***Spence***	N	Y	Y	Y	N	Y	Y	Y
3 ***Graham***	N	Y	Y	Y	N	Y	Y	Y
4 ***DeMint***	N	Y	Y	Y	N	Y	Y	Y
5 Spratt	N	Y	N	Y	Y	Y	Y	Y
6 Clyburn	Y	Y	N	N	Y	Y	Y	Y
SOUTH DAKOTA								
AL ***Thune***	N	Y	Y	Y	N	Y	Y	Y
TENNESSEE								
1 ***Jenkins***	N	Y	Y	Y	N	Y	Y	Y
2 ***Duncan***	Y	Y	Y	Y	N	Y	Y	Y
3 ***Wamp***	Y	Y	Y	Y	N	Y	Y	Y
4 ***Hilleary***	N	Y	Y	?	N	Y	Y	Y
5 Clement	N	Y	N	Y	Y	Y	Y	Y
6 Gordon	N	Y	N	N	Y	Y	Y	Y
7 ***Bryant***	N	Y	Y	Y	N	Y	Y	Y
8 Tanner	N	Y	Y	Y	Y	Y	Y	Y
9 Ford	N	Y	N	N	Y	Y	Y	Y
TEXAS								
1 Sandlin	N	Y	N	Y	Y	Y	Y	Y
2 Turner	N	Y	N	N	Y	Y	Y	Y
3 ***Johnson, Sam***	N	?	Y	Y	N	Y	Y	Y
4 Hall	N	Y	N	Y	N	Y	Y	Y
5 ***Sessions***	N	Y	Y	Y	N	Y	Y	Y
6 ***Barton***	N	Y	Y	Y	N	Y	Y	Y
7 ***Archer***	N	Y	?	?	N	Y	Y	Y
8 ***Brady***	N	Y	Y	Y	N	Y	Y	Y
9 Lampson	N	Y	N	N	Y	Y	Y	Y
10 Doggett	N	Y	N	Y	Y	Y	Y	Y
11 Edwards	N	Y	N	N	Y	Y	Y	Y
12 ***Granger***	N	Y	Y	Y	N	Y	Y	Y
13 ***Thornberry***	N	Y	Y	Y	N	Y	Y	Y
14 ***Paul***	Y	N	Y	Y	N	Y	Y	Y
15 Hinojosa	Y	Y	N	Y	Y	Y	Y	Y
16 Reyes	N	Y	N	Y	P	Y	Y	Y
17 Stenholm	N	Y	N	Y	N	Y	Y	Y
18 Jackson-Lee	N	Y	N	N	Y	Y	Y	Y
19 ***Combest***	N	Y	Y	Y	N	Y	Y	Y
20 Gonzalez	N	Y	N	N	Y	Y	Y	Y
21 ***Smith***	N	Y	Y	Y	N	Y	Y	Y
22 ***DeLay***	N	+	Y	Y	N	Y	Y	+
23 ***Bonilla***	N	Y	Y	Y	N	Y	Y	Y
24 Frost	N	Y	N	N	Y	Y	Y	Y
25 Bentsen	N	Y	N	N	N	Y	Y	Y
26 ***Armey***	N	Y	Y	Y	N	Y	Y	Y
27 Ortiz	N	Y	N	Y	Y	Y	Y	Y
28 Rodriguez	N	Y	N	N	Y	Y	Y	Y
29 Green	Y	Y	N	Y	Y	Y	Y	Y
30 Johnson, E.B.	Y	Y	N	N	Y	Y	Y	Y
UTAH								
1 ***Hansen***	N	Y	Y	Y	N	Y	Y	Y
2 ***Cook***	N	Y	N	Y	N	Y	Y	Y
3 ***Cannon***	N	Y	Y	Y	N	Y	Y	Y
VERMONT								
AL *Sanders*	Y	Y	N	Y	Y	Y	Y	Y
VIRGINIA								
1 ***Bateman***	N	Y	Y	Y	N	+	Y	Y
2 Pickett	N	Y	N	N	Y	Y	Y	Y
3 Scott	Y	Y	N	Y	Y	Y	Y	Y
4 Sisisky	N	Y	N	Y	N	Y	Y	Y
5 Goode	N	Y	Y	Y	N	Y	Y	Y
6 ***Goodlatte***	N	Y	Y	Y	N	Y	Y	Y
7 ***Bliley***	N	Y	Y	Y	N	Y	Y	Y
8 Moran	N	Y	N	N	Y	Y	Y	Y
9 Boucher	N	Y	N	Y	Y	Y	Y	Y
10 ***Wolf***	N	Y	N	Y	N	Y	Y	Y
11 ***Davis***	N	Y	N	Y	N	Y	Y	Y
WASHINGTON								
1 Inslee	N	Y	N	Y	Y	Y	Y	Y
2 ***Metcalf***	N	Y	Y	Y	N	Y	Y	Y
3 Baird	Y	Y	N	N	Y	Y	Y	Y
4 ***Hastings***	N	Y	Y	Y	N	Y	Y	Y
5 ***Nethercutt***	N	Y	Y	Y	N	Y	Y	Y
6 Dicks	?	Y	N	N	Y	Y	Y	Y
7 McDermott	–	+	–	–	+	+	+	+
8 ***Dunn***	N	Y	N	Y	N	Y	Y	Y
9 Smith	N	Y	N	Y	N	Y	Y	Y
WEST VIRGINIA								
1 Mollohan	N	Y	N	N	N	Y	Y	Y
2 Wise	N	Y	N	N	N	Y	Y	Y
3 Rahall	N	Y	N	Y	Y	Y	Y	Y
WISCONSIN								
1 ***Ryan***	N	Y	Y	Y	N	Y	Y	Y
2 Baldwin	Y	Y	N	N	Y	Y	Y	Y
3 Kind	N	Y	N	Y	N	Y	Y	Y
4 Kleczka	N	Y	N	N	Y	Y	Y	Y
5 Barrett	Y	Y	N	N	P	Y	Y	Y
6 ***Petri***	N	Y	Y	Y	N	Y	Y	Y
7 Obey	Y	Y	N	?	Y	Y	Y	Y
8 ***Green***	N	Y	Y	Y	N	Y	Y	Y
9 ***Sensenbrenner***	N	Y	Y	Y	N	Y	Y	Y
WYOMING								
AL ***Cubin***	N	Y	Y	Y	N	Y	Y	Y

Southern states - Ala., Ark., Fla., Ga., Ky., La., Miss., N.C., Okla., S.C., Tenn., Texas, Va.

330. HR 2488. Tax Reconciliation/Rule. Adoption of the rule (H Res 256) to provide for House floor consideration of the 10-year tax cut package. The rule reduced the cost of the bill to $792 billion by slowing the phase-in period for several provisions, and it linked the bill's cuts in individual income tax rates to reductions in interest on the federal debt starting in 2004. Adopted 219-208: R 219-2; D 0-205 (ND 0-151, SD 0-54); I 0-1. July 21, 1999.

331. HR 2488. Tax Reconciliation/Democratic Substitute. Rangel, D-N.Y., substitute amendment to reduce taxes by $250 billion over 10 years, but not allow most of the tax cuts to take effect until there is a certification of Medicare and Social Security solvency. The amendment would accelerate the estate tax exclusion to $1 million beginning Jan. 1, 2000; increase the family child tax credit by $250 for each child under age 5; provide about $25 billion for public school construction and modernization; provide a non-refundable $1,000 income tax credit for individuals with long-term health care needs, as well as 100 percent deductibility for health insurance purchased by the self-employed. Rejected 173-258: R 1-220; D 171-38 (ND 131-23, SD 40-15); I 1-0. July 22, 1999.

332. HR 2488. Tax Reconciliation/Recommit. Tanner, D-Tenn., motion to recommit the bill to the Ways and Means Committee and report it back with an amendment to provide a net 10-year tax reduction of not more than 25 percent of the currently projected non-Social Security surpluses, and a provision to make the tax reductions contingent on a certification by the director of the Office of Management and Budget that 100 percent of the Social Security surpluses and 50 percent of the non-Social Security surpluses are dedicated to reducing the national debt. Motion rejected 211-220: R 1-220; D 209-0 (ND 154-0, SD 55-0); I 1-0. July 22, 1999.

333. HR 2488. Tax Reconciliation/Passage. Passage of the bill to reduce federal taxes by $792 billion over 10 years. The measure would reduce individual income tax rates by 10 percent over a 10-year period, contingent upon annual progress in reducing interest on the nation's debt. It would reduce the "marriage penalty" by increasing the standard deduction for married couples to double that for singles; cut the capital gains tax rate for individuals from 20 percent to 15 percent for property held for more than one year; gradually lower the corporate capital gains tax rate from 35 percent to 30 percent by 2005; reduce the estate and gift tax rates until they are completely eliminated in 2009; accelerate the phase-in of a 100 percent deduction for health insurance premiums for the self-employed, and allow all taxpayers to deduct health care and long-term care insurance if employers pay 50 percent or less of the premium; increase the annual contribution limit for Education Savings Accounts from $500 to $2,000 and permit tax-free withdrawals to pay for public and private elementary and secondary tuition and expenses. Passed 223-208: R 217-4; D 6-203 (ND 2-152, SD 4-51); I 0-1. July 22, 1999. A "nay" was a vote in support of the president's position.

334. HR 2561. Fiscal 2000 Defense Appropriations/Passage. Passage of the bill to appropriate $268.7 billion in defense spending for fiscal 2000. The bill would not include $1.8 billion in procurement funds for the new F-22 Raptor combat aircraft. The measure would fund a 4.8 percent pay increase for military personnel, and appropriate $93.7 billion for operations and maintenance. It would not provide funds for peacekeeping efforts or reconstruction in Kosovo, but it would not bar additional supplemental spending bills from funding those activities. Passed 379-45: R 210-6; D 169-38 (ND 116-36, SD 53-2); I 0-1. July 22, 1999.

Key

- Y Voted for (yea).
- # Paired for.
- + Announced for.
- N Voted against (nay).
- X Paired against.
- – Announced against.
- P Voted "present."
- C Voted "present" to avoid possible conflict of interest.
- ? Did not vote or otherwise make a position known.

•

Democrats ***Republicans***
Independents

	330	331	332	333	334
ALABAMA					
1 ***Callahan***	Y	N	N	Y	Y
2 ***Everett***	Y	N	N	Y	Y
3 ***Riley***	Y	N	N	Y	Y
4 ***Aderholt***	Y	N	N	Y	Y
5 Cramer	N	N	Y	N	Y
6 ***Bachus***	Y	N	N	Y	Y
7 Hilliard	N	Y	Y	N	Y
ALASKA					
AL ***Young***	Y	N	N	Y	Y
ARIZONA					
1 ***Salmon***	Y	N	N	Y	Y
2 Pastor	N	Y	Y	N	Y
3 ***Stump***	Y	N	N	Y	Y
4 ***Shadegg***	Y	N	N	Y	Y
5 ***Kolbe***	Y	N	N	Y	Y
6 ***Hayworth***	Y	N	N	Y	Y
ARKANSAS					
1 Berry	N	N	Y	N	Y
2 Snyder	N	N	Y	N	Y
3 ***Hutchinson***	Y	N	N	Y	Y
4 ***Dickey***	Y	N	N	Y	Y
CALIFORNIA					
1 Thompson	N	Y	Y	N	Y
2 ***Herger***	Y	N	N	Y	Y
3 ***Ose***	Y	N	N	Y	Y
4 ***Doolittle***	Y	N	N	Y	Y
5 Matsui	N	Y	Y	N	Y
6 Woolsey	N	Y	Y	N	Y
7 Miller, George	N	N	Y	N	N
8 Pelosi	N	Y	Y	N	Y
9 Lee	N	N	Y	N	N
10 Tauscher	N	Y	Y	N	Y
11 ***Pombo***	Y	N	N	Y	Y
12 Lantos	N	Y	Y	N	Y
13 Stark	N	Y	Y	N	N
14 Eshoo	N	Y	Y	N	N
15 ***Campbell***	Y	N	N	Y	Y
16 Lofgren	N	Y	Y	N	N
17 Farr	N	Y	Y	N	Y
18 Condit	N	Y	Y	Y	Y
19 ***Radanovich***	Y	N	N	Y	Y
20 Dooley	N	Y	Y	N	Y
21 ***Thomas***	Y	N	N	Y	Y
22 Capps	N	Y	Y	N	Y
23 ***Gallegly***	Y	N	N	Y	Y
24 Sherman	N	Y	Y	N	Y
25 ***McKeon***	Y	N	N	Y	Y
26 Berman	N	Y	Y	N	Y
27 ***Rogan***	Y	N	N	Y	Y
28 ***Dreier***	Y	N	N	Y	Y
29 Waxman	N	Y	Y	N	N
30 Becerra	N	Y	Y	N	–
31 Martinez	N	Y	Y	N	Y
32 Dixon	N	Y	Y	N	Y
33 Roybal-Allard	N	Y	Y	N	Y
34 Napolitano	N	Y	Y	N	Y
35 Waters	N	Y	Y	N	N
36 ***Kuykendall***	Y	N	N	Y	Y
37 Millender-McD.	N	Y	Y	N	Y
38 ***Horn***	Y	N	N	Y	Y
39 ***Royce***	Y	N	N	Y	Y
40 ***Lewis***	Y	N	N	Y	Y
41 ***Miller, Gary***	Y	N	N	Y	Y
42 Vacant					
43 ***Calvert***	Y	N	N	Y	Y
44 ***Bono***	Y	N	N	Y	Y
45 ***Rohrabacher***	Y	N	N	Y	Y
46 Sanchez	N	Y	Y	N	Y
47 ***Cox***	Y	N	N	Y	Y
48 ***Packard***	Y	N	N	Y	Y
49 ***Bilbray***	Y	N	N	Y	Y
50 Filner	N	Y	Y	N	N
51 ***Cunningham***	Y	N	N	Y	Y
52 ***Hunter***	Y	N	N	Y	Y
COLORADO					
1 DeGette	N	Y	Y	N	Y
2 Udall	N	Y	Y	N	Y
3 ***McInnis***	Y	N	N	Y	?
4 ***Schaffer***	Y	N	N	Y	Y
5 ***Hefley***	Y	N	N	Y	Y
6 ***Tancredo***	Y	N	N	Y	Y
CONNECTICUT					
1 Larson	N	Y	Y	N	N
2 Gejdenson	N	Y	Y	N	N
3 DeLauro	N	Y	Y	N	Y
4 ***Shays***	Y	N	N	Y	Y
5 Maloney	N	Y	Y	N	Y
6 ***Johnson***	Y	N	N	Y	Y
DELAWARE					
AL ***Castle***	Y	N	N	N	Y
FLORIDA					
1 ***Scarborough***	Y	N	N	Y	Y
2 Boyd	N	N	Y	N	Y
3 Brown	N	Y	Y	N	Y
4 ***Fowler***	Y	N	N	Y	Y
5 Thurman	N	Y	Y	N	Y
6 ***Stearns***	Y	N	N	Y	Y
7 ***Mica***	Y	N	N	Y	Y
8 ***McCollum***	Y	N	N	Y	Y
9 ***Bilirakis***	Y	N	N	Y	Y
10 ***Young***	Y	N	N	Y	Y
11 Davis	N	Y	Y	N	Y
12 ***Canady***	Y	N	N	Y	Y
13 ***Miller***	Y	N	N	Y	Y
14 ***Goss***	Y	N	N	Y	Y
15 ***Weldon***	Y	N	N	Y	Y
16 ***Foley***	Y	N	N	Y	Y
17 Meek	N	Y	Y	N	Y
18 ***Ros-Lehtinen***	Y	N	N	Y	Y
19 Wexler	N	Y	Y	N	Y
20 Deutsch	N	Y	Y	N	Y
21 ***Diaz-Balart***	Y	N	N	Y	Y
22 ***Shaw***	Y	N	N	Y	Y
23 Hastings	N	Y	Y	N	Y
GEORGIA					
1 ***Kingston***	Y	N	N	Y	Y
2 Bishop	N	Y	Y	Y	Y
3 ***Collins***	Y	N	N	Y	Y
4 McKinney	N	Y	Y	N	N
5 Lewis	N	Y	Y	N	Y
6 ***Isakson***	Y	N	N	Y	Y
7 ***Barr***	Y	N	N	Y	Y
8 ***Chambliss***	Y	N	N	Y	Y
9 ***Deal***	Y	N	N	Y	Y
10 ***Norwood***	Y	N	N	Y	Y
11 ***Linder***	Y	N	N	Y	Y
HAWAII					
1 Abercrombie	N	Y	Y	N	Y
2 Mink	N	Y	Y	N	Y
IDAHO					
1 ***Chenoweth***	Y	N	N	Y	Y
2 ***Simpson***	Y	N	N	Y	Y
ILLINOIS					
1 Rush	N	Y	Y	N	N
2 Jackson	N	Y	Y	N	N
3 Lipinski	N	N	Y	N	Y
4 Gutierrez	N	Y	Y	N	N
5 Blagojevich	N	Y	Y	N	Y
6 ***Hyde***	Y	N	N	Y	Y
7 Davis	N	Y	Y	N	N
8 ***Crane***	Y	N	N	Y	Y
9 Schakowsky	N	Y	Y	N	N
10 ***Porter***	Y	N	N	Y	Y
11 ***Weller***	Y	N	N	Y	Y
12 Costello	N	N	Y	N	Y
13 ***Biggert***	Y	N	N	Y	Y
14 ***Hastert***	Y	N	N	Y	Y

ND Northern Democrats SD Southern Democrats

	330	331	332	333	334
15 ***Ewing***	Y	N	N	Y	Y
16 ***Manzullo***	Y	N	N	Y	Y
17 Evans	N	Y	Y	N	Y
18 ***LaHood***	Y	N	N	Y	Y
19 Phelps	N	N	Y	N	Y
20 ***Shimkus***	Y	N	N	Y	Y
INDIANA					
1 Visclosky	N	N	Y	N	Y
2 ***McIntosh***	Y	N	N	Y	Y
3 Roemer	N	Y	Y	N	Y
4 ***Souder***	Y	N	N	Y	Y
5 ***Buyer***	Y	N	N	Y	Y
6 ***Burton***	Y	N	N	Y	Y
7 ***Pease***	Y	N	N	Y	Y
8 ***Hostettler***	Y	N	N	Y	Y
9 Hill	N	Y	Y	N	Y
10 Carson	N	Y	Y	N	Y
IOWA					
1 ***Leach***	Y	N	N	Y	Y
2 ***Nussle***	Y	N	N	Y	Y
3 Boswell	N	Y	Y	N	Y
4 ***Ganske***	N	Y	Y	N	N
5 ***Latham***	Y	N	N	Y	Y
KANSAS					
1 ***Moran***	Y	N	N	Y	Y
2 ***Ryun***	Y	N	N	Y	Y
3 Moore	N	Y	Y	N	Y
4 ***Tiahrt***	Y	N	N	Y	Y
KENTUCKY					
1 ***Whitfield***	Y	N	N	Y	?
2 ***Lewis***	Y	N	N	Y	Y
3 ***Northup***	Y	N	N	Y	Y
4 Lucas	N	N	Y	Y	Y
5 ***Rogers***	Y	N	N	Y	Y
6 ***Fletcher***	Y	N	N	Y	Y
LOUISIANA					
1 ***Vitter***	Y	N	N	Y	Y
2 Jefferson	N	Y	Y	N	Y
3 ***Tauzin***	Y	N	N	Y	Y
4 ***McCrery***	Y	N	N	Y	Y
5 ***Cooksey***	Y	N	N	Y	Y
6 ***Baker***	Y	N	N	Y	Y
7 John	N	N	Y	N	Y
MAINE					
1 Allen	N	Y	Y	N	Y
2 Baldacci	N	Y	Y	N	Y
MARYLAND					
1 ***Gilchrest***	Y	N	N	Y	Y
2 ***Ehrlich***	Y	N	N	Y	Y
3 Cardin	N	Y	Y	N	Y
4 Wynn	N	Y	Y	N	Y
5 Hoyer	N	Y	Y	N	Y
6 ***Bartlett***	Y	N	N	Y	Y
7 Cummings	N	Y	Y	N	Y
8 ***Morella***	N	N	N	N	Y
MASSACHUSETTS					
1 Olver	N	N	Y	N	Y
2 Neal	N	Y	Y	N	Y
3 McGovern	N	Y	Y	N	N
4 Frank	N	Y	Y	N	Y
5 Meehan	N	Y	Y	N	Y
6 Tierney	N	Y	Y	N	Y
7 Markey	N	Y	Y	N	Y
8 Capuano	N	Y	Y	N	N
9 Moakley	N	Y	Y	N	Y
10 Delahunt	N	N	Y	N	Y
MICHIGAN					
1 Stupak	N	Y	Y	N	Y
2 ***Hoekstra***	Y	N	N	Y	Y
3 ***Ehlers***	Y	N	N	Y	Y
4 ***Camp***	Y	N	N	Y	Y
5 Barcia	N	Y	Y	N	Y
6 ***Upton***	Y	N	N	Y	Y
7 ***Smith***	Y	N	N	Y	Y
8 Stabenow	N	Y	Y	N	Y
9 Kildee	N	Y	Y	N	Y
10 Bonior	N	Y	Y	N	Y
11 ***Knollenberg***	Y	N	N	Y	Y
12 Levin	N	Y	Y	N	Y
13 Rivers	N	N	Y	N	N
14 Conyers	N	Y	Y	N	N
15 Kilpatrick	N	Y	Y	N	Y
16 Dingell	N	Y	Y	N	Y

	330	331	332	333	334
MINNESOTA					
1 ***Gutknecht***	Y	N	N	Y	Y
2 Minge	N	Y	Y	N	Y
3 ***Ramstad***	Y	N	N	Y	Y
4 Vento	N	Y	Y	N	N
5 Sabo	?	Y	Y	N	Y
6 Luther	N	Y	Y	N	N
7 Peterson	N	N	Y	N	Y
8 Oberstar	N	Y	Y	N	N
MISSISSIPPI					
1 ***Wicker***	Y	N	N	Y	Y
2 Thompson	N	Y	Y	N	Y
3 ***Pickering***	Y	N	N	Y	Y
4 Shows	N	N	Y	N	Y
5 Taylor	N	N	Y	N	Y
MISSOURI					
1 Clay	N	Y	Y	N	Y
2 ***Talent***	Y	N	N	Y	Y
3 Gephardt	N	Y	Y	N	Y
4 Skelton	N	N	Y	N	Y
5 McCarthy	N	Y	Y	N	Y
6 Danner	N	Y	Y	Y	Y
7 ***Blunt***	Y	N	N	Y	Y
8 ***Emerson***	Y	N	N	Y	Y
9 ***Hulshof***	Y	N	N	Y	Y
MONTANA					
AL ***Hill***	Y	N	N	Y	Y
NEBRASKA					
1 ***Bereuter***	Y	N	N	Y	Y
2 ***Terry***	Y	N	N	Y	Y
3 ***Barrett***	Y	N	N	Y	Y
NEVADA					
1 Berkley	N	Y	Y	N	Y
2 ***Gibbons***	Y	N	N	Y	Y
NEW HAMPSHIRE					
1 ***Sununu***	Y	N	N	Y	Y
2 ***Bass***	Y	N	N	Y	Y
NEW JERSEY					
1 Andrews	N	Y	Y	N	Y
2 ***LoBiondo***	Y	N	N	Y	Y
3 ***Saxton***	Y	N	N	Y	Y
4 ***Smith***	Y	N	N	Y	Y
5 ***Roukema***	Y	N	N	Y	Y
6 Pallone	N	Y	Y	N	Y
7 ***Franks***	Y	N	N	Y	Y
8 Pascrell	N	Y	Y	N	Y
9 Rothman	N	Y	Y	N	Y
10 Payne	N	Y	Y	N	N
11 ***Frelinghuysen***	Y	N	N	Y	Y
12 Holt	N	Y	Y	N	Y
13 Menendez	N	Y	Y	N	Y
NEW MEXICO					
1 ***Wilson***	Y	N	N	Y	Y
2 ***Skeen***	Y	N	N	Y	Y
3 Udall	N	Y	Y	N	Y
NEW YORK					
1 Forbes	N	Y	Y	N	Y
2 ***Lazio***	Y	N	N	Y	N
3 ***King***	Y	N	N	Y	Y
4 McCarthy	N	Y	Y	N	Y
5 Ackerman	N	Y	Y	N	Y
6 Meeks	N	Y	Y	N	N
7 Crowley	N	Y	Y	N	Y
8 Nadler	N	Y	Y	N	N
9 Weiner	N	Y	Y	N	Y
10 Towns	N	Y	Y	N	?
11 Owens	N	Y	Y	N	N
12 Velázquez	N	Y	Y	N	N
13 ***Fossella***	Y	N	N	Y	Y
14 Maloney	N	Y	Y	N	Y
15 Rangel	N	Y	Y	N	N
16 Serrano	N	Y	Y	N	Y
17 Engel	?	Y	Y	N	Y
18 Lowey	N	Y	Y	N	Y
19 ***Kelly***	Y	N	N	Y	Y
20 ***Gilman***	Y	N	N	Y	Y
21 McNulty	N	Y	Y	N	Y
22 ***Sweeney***	Y	N	N	Y	Y
23 ***Boehlert***	Y	N	N	Y	Y
24 ***McHugh***	Y	N	N	Y	Y
25 ***Walsh***	Y	N	N	Y	Y
26 Hinchey	N	Y	Y	N	Y
27 ***Reynolds***	Y	N	N	Y	Y
28 Slaughter	N	Y	Y	N	Y
29 LaFalce	N	Y	Y	N	Y

	330	331	332	333	334
30 ***Quinn***	Y	N	N	N	Y
31 ***Houghton***	Y	N	N	Y	Y
NORTH CAROLINA					
1 Clayton	N	Y	Y	N	Y
2 Etheridge	N	Y	Y	N	Y
3 ***Jones***	Y	N	N	Y	Y
4 Price	N	Y	Y	N	Y
5 ***Burr***	Y	N	N	Y	Y
6 ***Coble***	Y	N	N	Y	Y
7 McIntyre	N	N	Y	N	Y
8 ***Hayes***	Y	N	N	Y	Y
9 ***Myrick***	Y	N	N	Y	Y
10 ***Ballenger***	Y	N	N	Y	Y
11 ***Taylor***	Y	N	N	Y	Y
12 Watt	N	Y	Y	N	Y
NORTH DAKOTA					
AL Pomeroy	N	Y	Y	N	Y
OHIO					
1 ***Chabot***	Y	N	N	Y	Y
2 ***Portman***	Y	N	N	Y	+
3 Hall	N	Y	Y	N	Y
4 ***Oxley***	Y	N	N	Y	Y
5 ***Gillmor***	Y	N	N	Y	Y
6 Strickland	N	Y	Y	N	Y
7 ***Hobson***	Y	N	N	Y	Y
8 ***Boehner***	Y	N	N	Y	Y
9 Kaptur	N	Y	Y	N	Y
10 Kucinich	N	Y	Y	N	N
11 Jones	N	Y	Y	N	N
12 ***Kasich***	Y	N	N	Y	?
13 Brown	N	Y	Y	N	N
14 Sawyer	N	Y	Y	N	Y
15 ***Pryce***	Y	N	N	Y	Y
16 ***Regula***	Y	N	N	Y	Y
17 Traficant	N	N	Y	N	Y
18 ***Ney***	Y	N	N	Y	Y
19 ***LaTourette***	Y	N	N	Y	Y
OKLAHOMA					
1 ***Largent***	Y	N	N	Y	Y
2 ***Coburn***	Y	N	N	Y	N
3 ***Watkins***	Y	N	N	Y	Y
4 ***Watts***	Y	N	N	Y	Y
5 ***Istook***	Y	N	N	Y	Y
6 ***Lucas***	Y	N	N	Y	Y
OREGON					
1 Wu	N	Y	Y	N	Y
2 ***Walden***	Y	N	N	Y	Y
3 Blumenauer	N	Y	Y	N	Y
4 DeFazio	N	N	Y	N	N
5 Hooley	N	Y	Y	N	N
PENNSYLVANIA					
1 Brady	N	Y	Y	N	Y
2 Fattah	N	Y	Y	N	Y
3 Borski	N	N	Y	N	Y
4 Klink	N	N	Y	N	Y
5 ***Peterson***	?	?	?	?	?
6 Holden	N	N	Y	N	Y
7 ***Weldon***	Y	N	N	Y	Y
8 ***Greenwood***	Y	N	N	Y	Y
9 ***Shuster***	Y	N	N	Y	Y
10 ***Sherwood***	Y	N	N	Y	Y
11 Kanjorski	N	N	Y	N	Y
12 Murtha	N	N	Y	N	Y
13 Hoeffel	N	Y	Y	N	Y
14 Coyne	N	Y	Y	N	Y
15 ***Toomey***	Y	N	N	Y	Y
16 ***Pitts***	Y	N	N	Y	Y
17 ***Gekas***	Y	N	N	Y	Y
18 Doyle	N	N	Y	N	Y
19 ***Goodling***	Y	N	N	Y	Y
20 Mascara	N	N	Y	N	Y
21 ***English***	Y	N	N	Y	Y
RHODE ISLAND					
1 Kennedy	?	?	?	?	?
2 Weygand	N	Y	Y	N	Y
SOUTH CAROLINA					
1 ***Sanford***	Y	N	N	Y	Y
2 ***Spence***	Y	N	N	Y	Y
3 ***Graham***	Y	N	N	Y	Y
4 ***DeMint***	Y	N	N	Y	Y
5 Spratt	N	Y	Y	N	Y
6 Clyburn	N	Y	Y	N	Y
SOUTH DAKOTA					
AL ***Thune***	Y	N	N	Y	Y

	330	331	332	333	334
TENNESSEE					
1 ***Jenkins***	Y	N	N	Y	Y
2 ***Duncan***	Y	N	N	Y	N
3 ***Wamp***	Y	N	N	Y	Y
4 ***Hilleary***	Y	N	N	Y	Y
5 Clement	N	Y	Y	N	Y
6 Gordon	N	Y	Y	N	Y
7 ***Bryant***	Y	N	N	Y	Y
8 Tanner	N	Y	Y	N	Y
9 Ford	N	Y	Y	N	Y
TEXAS					
1 Sandlin	N	Y	Y	N	Y
2 Turner	N	Y	Y	N	Y
3 ***Johnson, Sam***	Y	N	N	Y	Y
4 Hall	N	Y	Y	Y	Y
5 ***Sessions***	Y	N	N	Y	Y
6 ***Barton***	Y	N	N	Y	Y
7 ***Archer***	Y	N	N	Y	Y
8 ***Brady***	Y	N	N	Y	Y
9 Lampson	N	Y	Y	N	Y
10 Doggett	N	Y	Y	N	N
11 Edwards	N	N	Y	N	Y
12 ***Granger***	Y	N	N	Y	Y
13 ***Thornberry***	Y	N	N	Y	Y
14 ***Paul***	Y	N	N	Y	N
15 Hinojosa	N	Y	Y	N	Y
16 Reyes	N	Y	Y	N	Y
17 Stenholm	N	N	Y	N	Y
18 Jackson-Lee	N	Y	Y	N	Y
19 ***Combest***	Y	N	N	Y	Y
20 Gonzalez	N	Y	Y	N	Y
21 ***Smith***	Y	N	N	Y	Y
22 ***DeLay***	Y	N	N	Y	Y
23 ***Bonilla***	Y	N	N	Y	Y
24 Frost	N	Y	Y	N	Y
25 Bentsen	N	Y	Y	N	Y
26 ***Armey***	Y	N	N	Y	Y
27 Ortiz	N	Y	Y	N	Y
28 Rodriguez	N	Y	Y	N	Y
29 Green	N	Y	Y	N	Y
30 Johnson, E.B.	N	Y	Y	N	Y
UTAH					
1 ***Hansen***	Y	N	N	Y	Y
2 ***Cook***	Y	N	N	Y	Y
3 ***Cannon***	Y	N	N	Y	Y
VERMONT					
AL *Sanders*	N	Y	Y	N	N
VIRGINIA					
1 ***Bateman***	Y	N	N	Y	Y
2 Pickett	?	N	Y	N	Y
3 Scott	N	N	Y	N	Y
4 Sisisky	N	N	Y	N	Y
5 Goode	N	N	Y	Y	Y
6 ***Goodlatte***	Y	N	N	Y	Y
7 ***Bliley***	Y	N	N	Y	Y
8 Moran	N	Y	Y	N	Y
9 Boucher	N	Y	Y	N	Y
10 ***Wolf***	Y	N	N	Y	Y
11 ***Davis***	Y	N	N	Y	Y
WASHINGTON					
1 Inslee	N	Y	Y	N	Y
2 ***Metcalf***	Y	N	N	Y	Y
3 Baird	N	Y	Y	N	Y
4 ***Hastings***	Y	N	N	Y	Y
5 ***Nethercutt***	Y	N	N	Y	Y
6 Dicks	N	Y	Y	N	Y
7 McDermott	–	+	+	–	–
8 ***Dunn***	Y	N	N	Y	?
9 Smith	N	Y	Y	N	Y
WEST VIRGINIA					
1 Mollohan	?	Y	Y	N	Y
2 Wise	N	Y	Y	N	Y
3 Rahall	N	N	Y	N	Y
WISCONSIN					
1 ***Ryan***	Y	N	N	Y	Y
2 Baldwin	N	Y	Y	N	N
3 Kind	N	N	Y	N	Y
4 Kleczka	N	Y	Y	N	Y
5 Barrett	N	N	Y	N	N
6 ***Petri***	Y	N	N	Y	Y
7 Obey	N	Y	Y	N	N
8 ***Green***	Y	N	N	Y	Y
9 ***Sensenbrenner***	Y	N	N	Y	N
WYOMING					
AL ***Cubin***	Y	N	N	Y	Y

Southern states - Ala., Ark., Fla., Ga., Ky., La., Miss., N.C., Okla., S.C., Tenn., Texas, Va.

335. HR 1074. Regulatory Cost-Benefit Analysis/Funding Limit. Hoeffel, D-Pa., amendment to require an analysis of the degree to which the costs of regulations imposed on corporations are offset by federal government subsidies, including grants, preferential tax treatment and federally funded research. The amendment would also limit the amount the government could spend to implement the bill to $1 million a year, and end the regulation analysis program after four years. Rejected 192-217: R 20-186; D 171-31 (ND 139-10, SD 32-21); I 1-0. July 26, 1999.

336. HR 1074. Regulatory Cost-Benefit Analysis/Passage. Passage of the bill to require the Office of Management and Budget to make annual cost-benefit analysis reports to Congress on federal regulations. The reports would also assess the impact of federal regulations on areas such as state and local government, the private sector, wages, public health and the environment. Passed 254-157: R 202-6; D 52-150 (ND 23-126, SD 29-24); I 0-1. July 26, 1999. A "nay" was a vote in support of the president's position.

337. Procedural Motion/Journal. Approval of the House Journal of Monday, July 26, 1999. Approved 352-53: R 188-19; D 163-34 (ND 123-27, SD 40-7); I 1-0. July 27, 1999.

338. H J Res 57. Disapprove Normal Trade Relations with China/Passage. Passage of the Joint Resolution to reject the President's decision to extend normal trade relations to China for another year. Rejected 170-260: R 71-150; D 98-110 (ND 81-72, SD 17-38); I 1-0. July 27, 1999.

339. HR 2587. Fiscal 2000 District of Columbia Appropriations/Rule. Adoption of the rule (H Res 260) to provide for House floor consideration of the bill to appropriate $453 million in federal funds to the District of Columbia for fiscal 2000. Adopted 227-201: R 219-0; D 8-200 (ND 3-150, SD 5-50); I 0-1. July 27, 1999.

340. HR 2605. Fiscal 2000 Energy and Water Appropriations/Wetlands Permits. Boehlert, R-N.Y., amendment to require the U.S. Army Corps of Engineers to submit studies and analyses by Dec. 30, 1999, on the costs of implementing a revised permit program for developing wetlands of less than three acres. Adopted 426-1: R 218-0; D 207-1 (ND 152-1, SD 55-0); I 1-0. July 27, 1999.

341. HR 2605. Fiscal 2000 Energy and Water Appropriations/Wetlands Permits. Visclosky, D-Ind., amendment to remove provisions that would require the U.S. Army Corps of Engineers to undertake studies and issue a report to Congress before it revises its permit program for developing wetlands areas of less than three acres. The amendment also would remove provisions that would authorize the federal appeal of certain wetlands designations prior to completion of the Corps permit process. Rejected 183-245: R 6-214; D 176-31 (ND 141-11, SD 35-20); I 1-0. July 27, 1999.

342. HR 2605. Fiscal 2000 Energy and Water Appropriations/Passage. Passage of the bill to appropriate $20.2 billion in fiscal 2000 for the Department of Energy and related agencies, including $15.6 billion for the Energy Department and just under $5 billion for water projects. The bill would withhold $1 billion for the Energy Department until June 30, 2000, pending improvements in the agency's national security programs. Passed 420-8: R 215-6; D 204-2 (ND 150-2, SD 54-0); I 1-0. July 27, 1999.

Key

- Y Voted for (yea).
- # Paired for.
- + Announced for.
- N Voted against (nay).
- X Paired against.
- – Announced against.
- P Voted "present."
- C Voted "present" to avoid possible conflict of interest.
- ? Did not vote or otherwise make a position known.

•

Democrats ***Republicans***
Independents

	335	336	337	338	339	340	341	342
ALABAMA								
1 ***Callahan***	N	Y	Y	N	Y	Y	N	Y
2 ***Everett***	N	Y	Y	Y	Y	Y	N	Y
3 ***Riley***	N	Y	N	Y	Y	Y	N	Y
4 ***Aderholt***	N	Y	N	Y	Y	Y	N	Y
5 Cramer	N	Y	?	N	N	Y	N	Y
6 ***Bachus***	N	Y	Y	N	Y	Y	N	Y
7 Hilliard	Y	N	N	Y	N	Y	Y	Y
ALASKA								
AL ***Young***	N	Y	?	Y	Y	Y	N	Y
ARIZONA								
1 ***Salmon***	N	Y	Y	N	Y	Y	N	Y
2 Pastor	Y	N	N	N	N	Y	N	Y
3 ***Stump***	N	Y	Y	N	Y	Y	N	Y
4 ***Shadegg***	N	Y	Y	N	Y	Y	N	Y
5 ***Kolbe***	N	Y	Y	N	Y	Y	N	Y
6 ***Hayworth***	N	Y	Y	Y	Y	Y	N	Y
ARKANSAS								
1 Berry	N	Y	Y	N	N	Y	N	Y
2 Snyder	Y	N	?	N	N	Y	Y	Y
3 ***Hutchinson***	N	Y	N	N	Y	Y	N	Y
4 ***Dickey***	N	Y	Y	Y	Y	Y	N	Y
CALIFORNIA								
1 Thompson	Y	N	N	N	N	Y	Y	Y
2 ***Herger***	N	Y	Y	N	Y	Y	N	Y
3 ***Ose***	N	Y	Y	N	Y	Y	N	Y
4 ***Doolittle***	N	Y	Y	Y	Y	Y	N	Y
5 Matsui	Y	N	Y	N	N	Y	Y	Y
6 Woolsey	Y	N	Y	Y	N	Y	Y	Y
7 Miller, George	Y	N	N	Y	N	Y	Y	Y
8 Pelosi	Y	N	Y	Y	N	Y	Y	Y
9 Lee	Y	N	Y	Y	N	Y	Y	Y
10 Tauscher	N	Y	Y	N	N	Y	Y	Y
11 ***Pombo***	N	Y	Y	Y	Y	Y	N	Y
12 Lantos	Y	N	Y	Y	N	Y	Y	Y
13 Stark	Y	N	N	Y	N	Y	Y	Y
14 Eshoo	Y	N	Y	N	N	Y	Y	Y
15 ***Campbell***	Y	Y	?	N	Y	Y	N	Y
16 Lofgren	N	N	Y	N	N	Y	Y	Y
17 Farr	?	?	Y	N	N	Y	Y	Y
18 Condit	N	Y	Y	Y	N	Y	N	Y
19 ***Radanovich***	N	Y	Y	N	Y	Y	N	Y
20 Dooley	N	Y	Y	N	N	Y	N	Y
21 ***Thomas***	N	Y	Y	N	Y	Y	N	Y
22 Capps	Y	N	Y	N	N	Y	Y	Y
23 ***Gallegly***	N	Y	Y	Y	Y	Y	N	Y
24 Sherman	Y	N	Y	N	N	Y	Y	Y
25 ***McKeon***	N	Y	Y	N	Y	Y	N	Y
26 Berman	Y	N	Y	N	N	Y	Y	Y
27 ***Rogan***	N	Y	Y	N	Y	Y	N	Y
28 ***Dreier***	N	Y	Y	N	Y	Y	N	Y
29 Waxman	Y	N	Y	Y	N	Y	Y	Y
30 Becerra	Y	N	Y	N	N	Y	Y	Y
31 Martinez	?	?	Y	Y	N	?	?	?
32 Dixon	?	?	Y	N	N	Y	Y	Y
33 Roybal-Allard	Y	N	Y	N	N	Y	?	Y
34 Napolitano	Y	Y	Y	N	N	Y	Y	Y
35 Waters	Y	N	N	Y	N	Y	Y	Y
36 ***Kuykendall***	N	Y	Y	N	Y	Y	N	Y
37 Millender-McD.	Y	N	Y	N	N	Y	Y	Y
38 ***Horn***	N	Y	Y	Y	Y	Y	N	Y
39 ***Royce***	Y	Y	Y	Y	Y	Y	N	N
40 ***Lewis***	N	Y	Y	N	Y	Y	N	Y
41 ***Miller, Gary***	N	Y	Y	N	Y	Y	N	Y
42 Vacant								
43 ***Calvert***	N	Y	Y	N	Y	Y	N	Y
44 ***Bono***	N	Y	Y	Y	Y	Y	N	Y
45 ***Rohrabacher***	N	Y	Y	Y	Y	Y	N	Y
46 Sanchez	Y	Y	Y	Y	N	Y	Y	Y
47 ***Cox***	?	Y	Y	Y	Y	Y	N	Y
48 ***Packard***	N	Y	Y	N	Y	Y	N	Y
49 ***Bilbray***	Y	N	N	N	Y	Y	N	Y
50 Filner	Y	N	N	N	N	Y	Y	Y
51 ***Cunningham***	N	Y	Y	N	Y	Y	N	Y
52 ***Hunter***	?	?	Y	Y	Y	Y	N	Y
COLORADO								
1 DeGette	Y	N	Y	N	N	Y	Y	Y
2 Udall	Y	N	Y	Y	N	Y	Y	Y
3 ***McInnis***	N	Y	Y	N	Y	Y	N	Y
4 ***Schaffer***	N	Y	N	Y	Y	Y	N	Y
5 ***Hefley***	N	Y	N	Y	Y	Y	N	Y
6 ***Tancredo***	N	Y	P	Y	Y	Y	N	Y
CONNECTICUT								
1 Larson	Y	N	Y	N	N	Y	Y	Y
2 Gejdenson	Y	N	Y	Y	N	Y	Y	Y
3 DeLauro	Y	N	Y	Y	N	Y	Y	Y
4 ***Shays***	Y	Y	Y	N	Y	Y	Y	Y
5 Maloney	Y	N	Y	N	N	Y	Y	Y
6 ***Johnson***	N	Y	Y	N	Y	?	Y	Y
DELAWARE								
AL ***Castle***	N	Y	Y	N	Y	Y	N	Y
FLORIDA								
1 ***Scarborough***	N	Y	Y	Y	Y	Y	N	Y
2 Boyd	N	Y	Y	N	N	Y	N	Y
3 Brown	Y	N	N	Y	N	Y	Y	Y
4 ***Fowler***	N	Y	?	Y	Y	Y	N	Y
5 Thurman	Y	Y	Y	N	N	Y	Y	Y
6 ***Stearns***	N	Y	Y	Y	Y	Y	N	Y
7 ***Mica***	N	Y	Y	N	Y	Y	N	Y
8 ***McCollum***	?	?	Y	N	Y	Y	N	Y
9 ***Bilirakis***	N	Y	Y	N	Y	Y	N	Y
10 ***Young***	N	Y	Y	N	Y	Y	N	Y
11 Davis	Y	N	?	N	N	Y	Y	Y
12 ***Canady***	N	Y	Y	N	Y	Y	N	Y
13 ***Miller***	N	Y	Y	N	Y	Y	N	Y
14 ***Goss***	N	Y	Y	N	Y	Y	N	Y
15 ***Weldon***	N	Y	Y	Y	Y	Y	N	Y
16 ***Foley***	Y	Y	Y	N	Y	Y	N	Y
17 Meek	Y	N	?	Y	N	Y	Y	Y
18 ***Ros-Lehtinen***	N	Y	Y	Y	Y	Y	N	Y
19 Wexler	Y	N	Y	Y	N	Y	Y	Y
20 Deutsch	Y	N	?	N	N	Y	Y	Y
21 ***Diaz-Balart***	N	Y	Y	Y	Y	Y	N	Y
22 ***Shaw***	N	Y	Y	N	Y	Y	N	Y
23 Hastings	Y	N	Y	Y	N	Y	Y	Y
GEORGIA								
1 ***Kingston***	N	Y	Y	Y	Y	Y	N	Y
2 Bishop	N	Y	Y	Y	N	Y	N	Y
3 ***Collins***	N	Y	?	Y	Y	Y	N	Y
4 McKinney	Y	N	Y	Y	N	Y	Y	Y
5 Lewis	Y	N	Y	Y	N	Y	Y	Y
6 ***Isakson***	N	Y	Y	N	Y	Y	N	Y
7 ***Barr***	N	Y	Y	Y	Y	Y	N	Y
8 ***Chambliss***	N	Y	Y	Y	Y	Y	N	Y
9 ***Deal***	N	Y	Y	Y	Y	Y	N	Y
10 ***Norwood***	N	Y	Y	Y	Y	Y	N	Y
11 ***Linder***	N	Y	Y	N	Y	Y	N	Y
HAWAII								
1 Abercrombie	Y	N	?	Y	N	Y	Y	Y
2 Mink	Y	N	Y	Y	N	Y	Y	Y
IDAHO								
1 ***Chenoweth***	?	?	?	Y	?	Y	N	N
2 ***Simpson***	N	Y	Y	N	Y	Y	N	Y
ILLINOIS								
1 Rush	Y	N	Y	N	N	Y	Y	Y
2 Jackson	Y	N	Y	Y	N	Y	Y	Y
3 Lipinski	Y	N	Y	Y	N	Y	Y	Y
4 Gutierrez	Y	N	N	Y	N	Y	Y	Y
5 Blagojevich	?	?	Y	N	N	Y	Y	Y
6 ***Hyde***	N	Y	Y	Y	Y	Y	N	Y
7 Davis	Y	N	Y	Y	N	Y	Y	Y
8 ***Crane***	?	?	N	N	Y	Y	N	Y
9 Schakowsky	Y	N	Y	Y	N	Y	Y	Y
10 ***Porter***	N	Y	Y	N	Y	Y	N	Y
11 ***Weller***	N	Y	N	N	Y	Y	N	Y
12 Costello	Y	N	N	Y	N	Y	Y	Y
13 ***Biggert***	N	Y	Y	N	Y	Y	N	Y
14 ***Hastert***				N				Y

ND Northern Democrats SD Southern Democrats

	335	336	337	338	339	340	341	342
15 ***Ewing***	N	Y	Y	N	Y	Y	N	Y
16 ***Manzullo***	N	Y	Y	N	Y	Y	N	Y
17 Evans	Y	N	Y	Y	N	Y	Y	Y
18 ***LaHood***	N	Y	Y	N	Y	Y	N	Y
19 Phelps	Y	N	Y	N	N	Y	N	?
20 ***Shimkus***	N	Y	Y	N	Y	Y	N	Y
INDIANA								
1 Visclosky	Y	N	N	Y	N	Y	Y	Y
2 ***McIntosh***	N	Y	Y	N	Y	Y	N	Y
3 Roemer	Y	Y	Y	N	N	Y	Y	Y
4 ***Souder***	N	Y	Y	Y	Y	Y	N	Y
5 ***Buyer***	N	Y	Y	N	Y	Y	N	Y
6 ***Burton***	N	Y	+	Y	Y	Y	N	Y
7 ***Pease***	N	Y	Y	N	Y	Y	N	Y
8 ***Hostettler***	N	Y	Y	Y	Y	Y	N	Y
9 Hill	Y	Y	Y	N	N	Y	Y	Y
10 Carson	Y	N	Y	Y	N	Y	Y	Y
IOWA								
1 ***Leach***	Y	Y	Y	N	Y	Y	N	Y
2 ***Nussle***	N	Y	Y	N	Y	Y	N	Y
3 Boswell	Y	Y	Y	N	N	Y	N	Y
4 ***Ganske***	?	?	Y	Y	Y	Y	N	Y
5 ***Latham***	N	Y	Y	N	Y	Y	N	Y
KANSAS								
1 ***Moran***	N	Y	N	N	Y	Y	N	Y
2 ***Ryun***	N	Y	Y	N	Y	Y	N	Y
3 Moore	Y	Y	Y	N	N	Y	Y	Y
4 ***Tiahrt***	N	Y	Y	Y	Y	Y	N	Y
KENTUCKY								
1 ***Whitfield***	N	Y	Y	N	Y	Y	N	Y
2 ***Lewis***	N	Y	Y	N	Y	Y	N	Y
3 ***Northup***	N	Y	Y	N	Y	+	N	Y
4 Lucas	N	Y	Y	N	Y	Y	N	Y
5 ***Rogers***	N	Y	Y	Y	Y	Y	N	Y
6 ***Fletcher***	N	Y	Y	N	Y	Y	N	Y
LOUISIANA								
1 ***Vitter***	N	Y	Y	N	Y	Y	N	Y
2 Jefferson	Y	Y	Y	N	N	Y	N	Y
3 ***Tauzin***	N	Y	Y	N	Y	Y	N	Y
4 ***McCrery***	N	Y	Y	N	Y	Y	N	Y
5 ***Cooksey***	N	Y	Y	N	Y	Y	N	Y
6 ***Baker***	N	Y	Y	N	Y	Y	N	Y
7 John	N	Y	Y	N	N	Y	N	Y
MAINE								
1 Allen	Y	N	Y	N	N	Y	Y	Y
2 Baldacci	Y	N	Y	N	N	Y	Y	Y
MARYLAND								
1 ***Gilchrest***	N	N	Y	N	Y	Y	N	Y
2 ***Ehrlich***	–	+	Y	Y	Y	Y	N	Y
3 Cardin	Y	N	Y	Y	N	Y	Y	Y
4 Wynn	Y	N	Y	Y	N	Y	N	Y
5 Hoyer	Y	N	Y	Y	N	Y	N	Y
6 ***Bartlett***	N	Y	Y	Y	Y	Y	N	Y
7 Cummings	Y	N	Y	Y	?	Y	Y	Y
8 ***Morella***	Y	N	Y	N	Y	Y	Y	Y
MASSACHUSETTS								
1 Olver	Y	N	Y	Y	N	Y	Y	Y
2 Neal	Y	N	N	N	N	Y	Y	Y
3 McGovern	Y	N	N	N	N	Y	Y	Y
4 Frank	Y	N	Y	Y	N	Y	Y	Y
5 Meehan	Y	N	Y	N	N	Y	Y	Y
6 Tierney	Y	N	Y	Y	N	Y	Y	Y
7 Markey	Y	N	N	Y	N	Y	Y	Y
8 Capuano	Y	N	Y	Y	N	Y	Y	Y
9 Moakley	Y	N	Y	N	N	Y	Y	Y
10 Delahunt	Y	N	Y	Y	N	Y	Y	Y
MICHIGAN								
1 Stupak	Y	N	N	Y	N	Y	Y	Y
2 ***Hoekstra***	N	Y	Y	N	Y	Y	N	Y
3 ***Ehlers***	N	Y	Y	N	Y	Y	N	Y
4 ***Camp***	N	Y	Y	N	Y	Y	N	Y
5 Barcia	Y	N	Y	Y	N	Y	Y	Y
6 ***Upton***	N	Y	Y	N	Y	Y	N	Y
7 ***Smith***	N	Y	Y	N	Y	Y	N	Y
8 Stabenow	Y	N	Y	N	N	Y	Y	Y
9 Kildee	Y	N	Y	Y	N	Y	Y	Y
10 Bonior	Y	N	Y	Y	N	Y	Y	Y
11 ***Knollenberg***	N	Y	Y	N	Y	Y	N	Y
12 Levin	Y	N	Y	N	N	Y	Y	Y
13 Rivers	Y	N	Y	Y	N	Y	Y	Y
14 Conyers	Y	N	Y	N	N	Y	Y	Y
15 Kilpatrick	Y	N	?	Y	N	Y	Y	Y
16 Dingell	Y	N	Y	N	N	N	Y	Y

	335	336	337	338	339	340	341	342
MINNESOTA								
1 ***Gutknecht***	N	Y	N	N	Y	Y	N	Y
2 Minge	Y	N	Y	N	N	Y	Y	Y
3 ***Ramstad***	N	Y	N	N	Y	Y	Y	Y
4 Vento	Y	N	Y	Y	N	Y	Y	Y
5 Sabo	Y	N	N	Y	N	Y	Y	Y
6 Luther	Y	Y	Y	N	N	Y	Y	Y
7 Peterson	N	Y	N	N	N	Y	N	Y
8 Oberstar	?	?	?	?	?	?	?	?
MISSISSIPPI								
1 ***Wicker***	N	Y	N	N	Y	Y	N	Y
2 Thompson	Y	N	N	Y	N	Y	Y	Y
3 ***Pickering***	N	Y	Y	Y	Y	Y	N	Y
4 Shows	N	Y	Y	N	N	Y	N	Y
5 Taylor	N	Y	N	Y	Y	Y	Y	Y
MISSOURI								
1 Clay	Y	N	N	Y	N	Y	Y	Y
2 ***Talent***	N	Y	Y	N	Y	Y	N	Y
3 Gephardt	Y	N	N	Y	N	Y	Y	Y
4 Skelton	Y	Y	Y	N	N	Y	N	Y
5 McCarthy	Y	Y	Y	N	N	Y	Y	Y
6 Danner	N	Y	Y	Y	N	Y	N	Y
7 ***Blunt***	N	Y	Y	N	Y	Y	N	Y
8 ***Emerson***	N	Y	Y	N	Y	Y	N	Y
9 ***Hulshof***	N	Y	Y	N	Y	Y	N	Y
MONTANA								
AL ***Hill***	N	Y	N	N	Y	Y	N	Y
NEBRASKA								
1 ***Bereuter***	N	Y	?	N	Y	Y	N	Y
2 ***Terry***	N	Y	Y	N	Y	Y	N	Y
3 ***Barrett***	N	Y	Y	N	Y	Y	N	Y
NEVADA								
1 Berkley	Y	N	Y	N	N	Y	Y	Y
2 ***Gibbons***	N	Y	Y	Y	Y	Y	N	N
NEW HAMPSHIRE								
1 ***Sununu***	N	Y	Y	N	Y	Y	N	Y
2 ***Bass***	N	Y	Y	N	Y	Y	N	Y
NEW JERSEY								
1 Andrews	Y	N	Y	N	N	Y	Y	Y
2 ***LoBiondo***	N	Y	N	Y	Y	Y	N	Y
3 ***Saxton***	Y	N	Y	N	Y	Y	N	Y
4 ***Smith***	Y	Y	Y	Y	Y	Y	Y	Y
5 ***Roukema***	Y	Y	Y	N	Y	Y	N	Y
6 Pallone	Y	N	N	Y	N	Y	Y	Y
7 ***Franks***	Y	Y	Y	N	Y	Y	N	Y
8 Pascrell	Y	N	Y	Y	N	Y	Y	Y
9 Rothman	Y	N	Y	Y	N	Y	Y	Y
10 Payne	Y	N	Y	Y	N	Y	Y	Y
11 ***Frelinghuysen***	Y	Y	Y	N	Y	Y	N	Y
12 Holt	Y	N	Y	N	N	Y	Y	Y
13 Menendez	Y	N	Y	Y	N	Y	Y	Y
NEW MEXICO								
1 ***Wilson***	N	Y	Y	N	Y	Y	N	N
2 ***Skeen***	N	Y	Y	N	Y	Y	N	Y
3 Udall	Y	N	N	Y	N	Y	Y	Y
NEW YORK								
1 Forbes	Y	N	Y	Y	N	Y	Y	Y
2 ***Lazio***	Y	Y	Y	N	Y	Y	Y	Y
3 ***King***	Y	Y	Y	Y	Y	Y	Y	Y
4 McCarthy	Y	N	Y	N	N	Y	Y	Y
5 Ackerman	Y	N	Y	N	N	Y	Y	Y
6 Meeks	Y	N	Y	Y	N	Y	Y	Y
7 Crowley	Y	N	Y	N	N	Y	Y	Y
8 Nadler	Y	N	Y	Y	N	Y	Y	Y
9 Weiner	Y	N	Y	Y	N	Y	Y	Y
10 Towns	N	N	Y	Y	N	Y	Y	Y
11 Owens	Y	N	Y	Y	N	Y	Y	Y
12 Velázquez	Y	N	Y	Y	N	Y	Y	Y
13 ***Fossella***	–	+	Y	N	Y	Y	N	Y
14 Maloney	Y	N	Y	N	N	Y	Y	Y
15 Rangel	Y	N	Y	Y	N	Y	Y	Y
16 Serrano	Y	N	Y	N	N	Y	Y	Y
17 Engel	Y	N	Y	Y	N	Y	Y	Y
18 Lowey	Y	N	Y	N	N	Y	Y	Y
19 ***Kelly***	N	Y	Y	N	Y	Y	N	Y
20 ***Gilman***	Y	N	Y	Y	Y	Y	N	Y
21 McNulty	Y	N	N	N	N	Y	Y	Y
22 ***Sweeney***	N	Y	N	Y	Y	Y	N	Y
23 ***Boehlert***	Y	N	Y	N	Y	Y	N	Y
24 ***McHugh***	N	Y	Y	N	Y	Y	N	Y
25 ***Walsh***	Y	Y	Y	Y	Y	Y	N	Y
26 Hinchey	Y	N	?	Y	N	Y	Y	Y
27 ***Reynolds***	N	Y	Y	N	Y	Y	N	Y
28 Slaughter	Y	N	Y	P	N	Y	Y	Y
29 LaFalce	Y	N	Y	N	N	Y	Y	Y

	335	336	337	338	339	340	341	342
30 ***Quinn***	N	Y	Y	N	Y	Y	N	Y
31 ***Houghton***	N	Y	Y	N	Y	Y	N	Y
NORTH CAROLINA								
1 Clayton	Y	Y	Y	N	N	Y	Y	Y
2 Etheridge	Y	Y	Y	N	N	Y	Y	Y
3 ***Jones***	N	Y	Y	Y	Y	Y	N	Y
4 Price	Y	Y	Y	N	N	Y	Y	Y
5 ***Burr***	N	Y	Y	Y	Y	Y	N	Y
6 ***Coble***	N	Y	Y	Y	Y	Y	N	Y
7 McIntyre	N	Y	Y	Y	Y	Y	N	Y
8 ***Hayes***	N	Y	Y	Y	Y	Y	N	Y
9 ***Myrick***	N	Y	Y	N	Y	Y	N	Y
10 ***Ballenger***	N	Y	Y	Y	Y	Y	N	Y
11 ***Taylor***	–	+	Y	Y	Y	Y	N	Y
12 Watt	Y	N	Y	Y	N	Y	Y	Y
NORTH DAKOTA								
AL Pomeroy	Y	Y	Y	N	N	Y	N	Y
OHIO								
1 ***Chabot***	N	Y	Y	N	Y	Y	N	Y
2 ***Portman***	N	Y	Y	N	Y	Y	N	Y
3 Hall	Y	N	Y	Y	Y	Y	Y	Y
4 ***Oxley***	N	Y	Y	N	Y	Y	N	Y
5 ***Gillmor***	N	Y	Y	N	Y	Y	N	Y
6 Strickland	Y	N	N	Y	N	Y	Y	Y
7 ***Hobson***	N	Y	Y	Y	Y	Y	N	Y
8 ***Boehner***	N	Y	Y	N	Y	Y	N	Y
9 Kaptur	Y	Y	Y	Y	N	Y	Y	Y
10 Kucinich	Y	N	N	Y	N	Y	Y	Y
11 Jones	Y	N	Y	Y	N	Y	Y	Y
12 ***Kasich***	Y	Y	Y	Y	Y	Y	N	Y
13 Brown	Y	N	N	Y	N	Y	Y	Y
14 Sawyer	Y	N	Y	N	N	Y	Y	Y
15 ***Pryce***	?	?	?	N	Y	Y	N	Y
16 ***Regula***	N	Y	Y	N	Y	Y	N	Y
17 Traficant	Y	Y	Y	Y	Y	Y	Y	Y
18 ***Ney***	N	Y	Y	Y	Y	Y	N	Y
19 ***LaTourette***	N	Y	Y	N	Y	Y	N	Y
OKLAHOMA								
1 ***Largent***	N	Y	Y	N	Y	Y	N	Y
2 ***Coburn***	?	?	Y	Y	Y	Y	N	Y
3 ***Watkins***	N	Y	?	N	Y	Y	N	Y
4 ***Watts***	N	Y	Y	N	Y	Y	N	Y
5 ***Istook***	N	Y	Y	N	Y	Y	N	Y
6 ***Lucas***	N	Y	Y	N	Y	Y	N	Y
OREGON								
1 Wu	Y	N	Y	Y	N	Y	Y	Y
2 ***Walden***	N	Y	Y	N	Y	Y	N	Y
3 Blumenauer	Y	N	Y	N	N	Y	Y	Y
4 DeFazio	Y	N	N	Y	N	Y	Y	N
5 Hooley	Y	N	Y	N	Y	Y	Y	Y
PENNSYLVANIA								
1 Brady	Y	N	Y	Y	N	Y	Y	Y
2 Fattah	Y	N	N	N	N	Y	Y	Y
3 Borski	Y	N	Y	N	N	Y	Y	Y
4 Klink	Y	N	Y	Y	N	Y	Y	Y
5 ***Peterson***	?	?	?	?	?	?	?	?
6 Holden	N	Y	Y	N	N	Y	Y	Y
7 ***Weldon***	Y	Y	?	N	Y	Y	N	Y
8 ***Greenwood***	N	Y	?	N	Y	Y	N	Y
9 ***Shuster***	N	Y	Y	N	Y	Y	N	Y
10 ***Sherwood***	N	Y	Y	N	Y	Y	N	Y
11 Kanjorski	Y	Y	Y	N	N	Y	Y	Y
12 Murtha	?	?	Y	N	N	Y	Y	Y
13 Hoeffel	Y	N	Y	N	N	Y	Y	Y
14 Coyne	Y	N	Y	Y	N	Y	Y	Y
15 ***Toomey***	N	Y	Y	N	Y	Y	N	Y
16 ***Pitts***	N	Y	Y	N	Y	Y	N	Y
17 ***Gekas***	N	Y	Y	N	Y	Y	N	Y
18 Doyle	Y	Y	Y	Y	N	Y	Y	Y
19 ***Goodling***	N	Y	Y	Y	Y	Y	N	Y
20 Mascara	Y	N	Y	Y	N	Y	Y	Y
21 ***English***	N	Y	N	N	Y	Y	N	Y
RHODE ISLAND								
1 Kennedy	Y	N	Y	Y	N	Y	Y	Y
2 Weygand	Y	Y	Y	Y	N	Y	Y	Y
SOUTH CAROLINA								
1 ***Sanford***	N	Y	N	Y	Y	Y	N	N
2 ***Spence***	N	Y	Y	Y	Y	Y	N	Y
3 ***Graham***	N	Y	Y	Y	Y	Y	N	Y
4 ***DeMint***	N	Y	Y	N	Y	Y	N	Y
5 Spratt	Y	Y	Y	Y	N	Y	Y	Y
6 Clyburn	Y	N	N	Y	N	Y	Y	Y
SOUTH DAKOTA								
AL ***Thune***	N	Y	Y	N	Y	Y	N	Y

	335	336	337	338	339	340	341	342
TENNESSEE								
1 ***Jenkins***	N	Y	Y	N	Y	Y	N	Y
2 ***Duncan***	N	Y	Y	Y	Y	Y	N	Y
3 ***Wamp***	N	Y	Y	Y	Y	Y	N	Y
4 ***Hilleary***	N	Y	N	Y	Y	Y	N	Y
5 Clement	N	Y	Y	N	N	Y	N	?
6 Gordon	?	?	?	N	N	Y	Y	Y
7 ***Bryant***	N	Y	Y	N	Y	Y	N	Y
8 Tanner	N	Y	Y	N	N	Y	N	Y
9 Ford	Y	Y	N	N	N	Y	Y	Y
TEXAS								
1 Sandlin	N	Y	Y	N	N	Y	N	Y
2 Turner	N	Y	Y	N	N	Y	N	Y
3 ***Johnson, Sam***	N	Y	Y	N	Y	Y	N	Y
4 Hall	N	Y	Y	N	N	Y	N	Y
5 ***Sessions***	N	Y	Y	N	Y	Y	N	Y
6 ***Barton***	N	Y	Y	Y	Y	Y	N	Y
7 ***Archer***	N	Y	Y	N	Y	Y	N	Y
8 ***Brady***	N	Y	Y	N	Y	Y	N	Y
9 Lampson	Y	N	Y	N	N	Y	Y	Y
10 Doggett	Y	N	Y	N	N	Y	Y	Y
11 Edwards	N	Y	?	N	N	Y	N	Y
12 ***Granger***	?	?	Y	N	Y	Y	N	Y
13 ***Thornberry***	N	Y	Y	N	Y	Y	N	Y
14 ***Paul***	N	Y	Y	N	Y	Y	N	N
15 Hinojosa	Y	N	Y	N	N	Y	Y	Y
16 Reyes	Y	N	Y	N	N	Y	Y	Y
17 Stenholm	N	Y	Y	N	N	Y	N	Y
18 Jackson-Lee	Y	N	Y	N	N	Y	Y	Y
19 ***Combest***	N	Y	Y	N	Y	Y	N	Y
20 Gonzalez	Y	N	Y	N	N	Y	Y	Y
21 ***Smith***	N	Y	Y	Y	Y	Y	N	Y
22 ***DeLay***	N	Y	Y	N	Y	Y	N	Y
23 ***Bonilla***	N	Y	Y	N	Y	Y	N	Y
24 Frost	Y	N	Y	N	N	Y	N	Y
25 Bentsen	N	Y	Y	N	N	Y	Y	Y
26 ***Armey***	N	Y	?	N	Y	Y	N	Y
27 Ortiz	Y	N	Y	N	N	Y	Y	Y
28 Rodriguez	Y	N	Y	N	N	Y	Y	Y
29 Green	Y	N	Y	N	Y	Y	Y	Y
30 Johnson, E.B.	–	–	N	N	N	Y	Y	Y
UTAH								
1 ***Hansen***	N	Y	Y	N	Y	Y	N	Y
2 ***Cook***	N	Y	Y	Y	Y	Y	N	Y
3 ***Cannon***	?	Y	Y	N	Y	Y	N	Y
VERMONT								
AL *Sanders*	Y	N	Y	Y	N	Y	Y	Y
VIRGINIA								
1 ***Bateman***	N	Y	Y	N	Y	Y	N	Y
2 Pickett	N	Y	?	N	N	Y	N	Y
3 Scott	Y	N	Y	Y	N	Y	Y	Y
4 Sisisky	N	Y	Y	Y	N	Y	N	Y
5 Goode	N	Y	Y	Y	Y	Y	N	Y
6 ***Goodlatte***	N	Y	Y	N	Y	Y	N	Y
7 ***Bliley***	N	Y	Y	N	Y	Y	N	Y
8 Moran	Y	Y	Y	N	N	Y	Y	Y
9 Boucher	N	Y	Y	N	N	Y	Y	Y
10 ***Wolf***	N	Y	N	Y	Y	Y	N	Y
11 ***Davis***	N	Y	Y	N	Y	Y	N	Y
WASHINGTON								
1 Inslee	Y	N	Y	N	N	Y	Y	Y
2 ***Metcalf***	N	Y	Y	N	Y	Y	N	Y
3 Baird	Y	N	N	N	N	Y	Y	Y
4 ***Hastings***	N	Y	Y	N	Y	Y	N	Y
5 ***Nethercutt***	N	Y	Y	N	Y	Y	N	Y
6 Dicks	Y	N	Y	N	N	Y	Y	Y
7 McDermott	?	?	?	?	?	?	?	?
8 ***Dunn***	N	Y	Y	N	Y	Y	N	Y
9 Smith	N	N	Y	N	N	Y	Y	N
WEST VIRGINIA								
1 Mollohan	N	N	Y	Y	N	Y	Y	Y
2 Wise	Y	N	?	Y	N	Y	Y	Y
3 Rahall	Y	N	Y	Y	N	Y	Y	Y
WISCONSIN								
1 ***Ryan***	N	Y	Y	N	Y	Y	N	Y
2 Baldwin	Y	N	Y	N	N	Y	Y	Y
3 Kind	Y	Y	Y	N	N	Y	Y	Y
4 Kleczka	Y	N	Y	N	N	Y	Y	Y
5 Barrett	Y	N	Y	N	N	Y	Y	Y
6 ***Petri***	N	Y	Y	N	Y	Y	N	Y
7 Obey	Y	N	Y	Y	N	Y	Y	Y
8 ***Green***	N	Y	Y	N	Y	Y	N	Y
9 ***Sensenbrenner***	N	Y	Y	Y	Y	Y	N	Y
WYOMING								
AL ***Cubin***	?	?	Y	Y	Y	Y	N	Y

Southern states - Ala., Ark., Fla., Ga., Ky., La., Miss., N.C., Okla., S.C., Tenn., Texas, Va.

343. HR 2465. Fiscal 2000 Military Construction Appropriations/Conference Report. Adoption of the conference report on the bill to appropriate $8.4 billion in fiscal 2000 for military construction. The conference report would appropriate $3.6 billion for family housing, $672 million for environmental cleanup, $695 million for the National Guard and reserves and $643 million for military barracks. Adopted (thus sent to the Senate) 412-8: R 212-4; D 199-4 (ND 144-4, SD 55-0); I 1-0. July 29, 1999.

344. HR 2587. Fiscal 2000 District of Columbia Appropriations/Needle Exchange Programs. Tiahrt, R-Kan., amendment to prohibit the District of Columbia from using any federal, local or other funds for a needle exchange program. Adopted 241-187: R 201-18; D 40-168 (ND 24-129, SD 16-39); I 0-1. July 29, 1999.

345. HR 2587. Fiscal 2000 District of Columbia Appropriations/District Representation in Congress. Norton, D-D.C., amendment to strike language in the bill that would bar the use of federal or local funds to seek a court ruling on District of Columbia voting representation in Congress. Rejected 214-214: R 15-204; D 198-10 (ND 148-5, SD 50-5); I 1-0. July 29, 1999.

346. HR 2587. Fiscal 2000 District of Columbia Appropriations/Adoption. Largent, R-Okla., amendment to bar joint adoptions in the District of Columbia by gays or other people who are not related by blood or marriage. Rejected 213-215: R 183-36; D 30-178 (ND 9-144, SD 21-34); I 0-1. July 29, 1999.

347. HR 2587. Fiscal 2000 District of Columbia Appropriations/Passage. Passage of the bill to appropriate $453 million in fiscal 2000 funds for the District of Columbia. The bill also would approve the District's own $6.8 billion fiscal 2000 budget. Passed 333-92: R 176-41; D 156-51 (ND 113-39, SD 43-12); I 1-0. July 29, 1999.

348. HR 2606. Fiscal 2000 Foreign Operations Appropriations/Rule. Adoption of the rule (H Res 263) to provide for House floor consideration of the bill to appropriate $12.7 billion in fiscal 2000 for foreign operations. Adopted 256-172: R 220-1; D 36-170 (ND 26-125, SD 10-45); I 0-1. July 29, 1999.

Key

Y Voted for (yea).
\# Paired for.
\+ Announced for.
N Voted against (nay).
X Paired against.
– Announced against.
P Voted "present."
C Voted "present" to avoid possible conflict of interest.
? Did not vote or otherwise make a position known.

•

Democrats ***Republicans***
Independents

	343	344	345	346	347	348
ALABAMA						
1 ***Callahan***	Y	Y	N	Y	Y	Y
2 ***Everett***	Y	Y	N	Y	N	Y
3 ***Riley***	Y	Y	N	Y	N	Y
4 ***Aderholt***	Y	Y	N	Y	Y	Y
5 Cramer	Y	Y	Y	Y	Y	Y
6 ***Bachus***	Y	Y	N	Y	Y	Y
7 Hilliard	Y	N	Y	N	Y	N
ALASKA						
AL ***Young***	Y	Y	N	Y	Y	Y
ARIZONA						
1 ***Salmon***	Y	Y	N	Y	N	Y
2 Pastor	Y	N	Y	N	N	N
3 ***Stump***	Y	Y	N	Y	N	Y
4 ***Shadegg***	Y	Y	N	Y	Y	Y
5 ***Kolbe***	Y	N	N	N	Y	Y
6 ***Hayworth***	Y	Y	N	Y	N	Y
ARKANSAS						
1 Berry	Y	N	Y	Y	Y	N
2 Snyder	Y	N	Y	N	Y	N
3 ***Hutchinson***	Y	Y	N	Y	Y	Y
4 ***Dickey***	?	Y	N	Y	Y	Y
CALIFORNIA						
1 Thompson	N	N	Y	N	Y	N
2 ***Herger***	Y	Y	N	Y	N	Y
3 ***Ose***	Y	Y	N	N	Y	Y
4 ***Doolittle***	Y	Y	N	Y	Y	Y
5 Matsui	Y	N	Y	N	Y	N
6 Woolsey	Y	N	Y	N	Y	N
7 Miller, George	Y	Y	Y	N	Y	N
8 Pelosi	Y	N	Y	N	Y	N
9 Lee	Y	N	Y	N	N	N
10 Tauscher	Y	N	Y	N	Y	N
11 ***Pombo***	Y	Y	N	Y	Y	Y
12 Lantos	Y	N	Y	N	Y	N
13 Stark	N	N	Y	N	Y	N
14 Eshoo	Y	N	Y	N	Y	N
15 ***Campbell***	Y	N	Y	N	N	Y
16 Lofgren	Y	N	Y	N	N	N
17 Farr	Y	N	Y	N	Y	N
18 Condit	Y	N	N	N	N	Y
19 ***Radanovich***	Y	Y	N	Y	Y	Y
20 Dooley	Y	N	Y	N	Y	Y
21 ***Thomas***	Y	Y	N	N	Y	Y
22 Capps	Y	N	Y	N	Y	N
23 ***Gallegly***	Y	Y	N	Y	Y	Y
24 Sherman	Y	N	Y	N	N	N
25 ***McKeon***	Y	Y	N	Y	Y	Y
26 Berman	Y	N	Y	N	Y	Y
27 ***Rogan***	Y	Y	N	Y	Y	Y
28 ***Dreier***	Y	Y	N	Y	?	Y
29 Waxman	Y	N	Y	N	Y	N
30 Becerra	+	N	Y	N	Y	N
31 Martinez	Y	N	Y	N	Y	?
32 Dixon	Y	N	Y	N	N	N
33 Roybal-Allard	Y	N	Y	N	Y	N
34 Napolitano	Y	N	Y	N	Y	N
35 Waters	Y	N	Y	N	N	N
36 ***Kuykendall***	Y	Y	N	N	Y	Y
37 Millender-McD.	Y	N	Y	N	N	N
38 ***Horn***	Y	N	Y	N	Y	Y
39 ***Royce***	Y	Y	N	Y	N	Y
40 ***Lewis***	Y	Y	N	N	Y	Y
41 ***Miller, Gary***	Y	Y	N	Y	Y	Y
42 Vacant						
43 ***Calvert***	Y	Y	N	Y	Y	Y
44 ***Bono***	Y	Y	N	Y	Y	Y
45 ***Rohrabacher***	Y	Y	N	Y	Y	Y
46 Sanchez	Y	N	Y	N	Y	N
47 ***Cox***	Y	Y	N	Y	Y	Y
48 ***Packard***	Y	Y	N	Y	Y	Y
49 ***Bilbray***	Y	Y	N	N	Y	Y
50 Filner	Y	N	Y	N	N	N
51 ***Cunningham***	Y	Y	N	Y	Y	Y
52 ***Hunter***	Y	Y	N	Y	Y	Y
COLORADO						
1 DeGette	Y	N	Y	N	Y	N
2 Udall	Y	N	Y	N	Y	N
3 ***McInnis***	Y	Y	N	Y	N	Y
4 ***Schaffer***	Y	Y	N	Y	N	Y
5 ***Hefley***	N	Y	N	Y	N	Y
6 ***Tancredo***	Y	Y	N	Y	N	Y
CONNECTICUT						
1 Larson	Y	N	Y	N	Y	N
2 Gejdenson	Y	N	Y	N	Y	N
3 DeLauro	Y	N	Y	N	Y	N
4 ***Shays***	Y	N	N	N	Y	Y
5 Maloney	Y	N	Y	N	N	N
6 ***Johnson***	Y	N	N	N	Y	Y
DELAWARE						
AL ***Castle***	Y	N	N	Y	Y	Y
FLORIDA						
1 ***Scarborough***	Y	Y	Y	Y	Y	Y
2 Boyd	Y	N	Y	N	Y	N
3 Brown	Y	N	Y	N	Y	Y
4 ***Fowler***	Y	Y	N	Y	Y	Y
5 Thurman	Y	N	Y	N	Y	N
6 ***Stearns***	Y	Y	N	Y	N	Y
7 ***Mica***	Y	Y	N	Y	N	Y
8 ***McCollum***	Y	Y	N	Y	Y	Y
9 ***Bilirakis***	Y	Y	N	Y	Y	Y
10 ***Young***	Y	Y	N	Y	Y	Y
11 Davis	Y	N	Y	N	Y	N
12 ***Canady***	Y	Y	N	Y	Y	Y
13 ***Miller***	Y	N	N	N	Y	Y
14 ***Goss***	Y	Y	N	Y	Y	Y
15 ***Weldon***	Y	Y	N	Y	Y	Y
16 ***Foley***	Y	N	N	N	Y	Y
17 Meek	Y	N	Y	N	Y	N
18 ***Ros-Lehtinen***	Y	Y	N	Y	Y	Y
19 Wexler	Y	N	Y	N	Y	N
20 Deutsch	Y	N	Y	N	Y	N
21 ***Diaz-Balart***	Y	Y	N	Y	Y	Y
22 ***Shaw***	Y	Y	N	Y	Y	Y
23 Hastings	Y	N	Y	N	Y	N
GEORGIA						
1 ***Kingston***	Y	Y	N	Y	Y	Y
2 Bishop	Y	N	Y	Y	Y	N
3 ***Collins***	Y	Y	N	Y	Y	Y
4 McKinney	Y	N	Y	N	N	N
5 Lewis	Y	N	Y	N	N	N
6 ***Isakson***	Y	Y	N	Y	Y	Y
7 ***Barr***	Y	Y	N	Y	N	Y
8 ***Chambliss***	Y	Y	N	Y	Y	Y
9 ***Deal***	Y	Y	N	Y	Y	Y
10 ***Norwood***	N	Y	N	Y	Y	Y
11 ***Linder***	Y	Y	N	Y	Y	Y
HAWAII						
1 Abercrombie	Y	N	Y	N	Y	N
2 Mink	Y	N	Y	N	Y	N
IDAHO						
1 ***Chenoweth***	Y	Y	N	Y	Y	Y
2 ***Simpson***	Y	Y	N	Y	Y	Y
ILLINOIS						
1 Rush	Y	N	Y	N	N	N
2 Jackson	Y	N	Y	N	N	N
3 Lipinski	?	Y	N	Y	N	Y
4 Gutierrez	Y	N	Y	N	Y	N
5 Blagojevich	Y	N	Y	N	N	N
6 ***Hyde***	Y	Y	N	Y	Y	Y
7 Davis	Y	N	Y	N	N	N
8 ***Crane***	Y	Y	N	Y	Y	Y
9 Schakowsky	Y	N	Y	N	Y	N
10 ***Porter***	Y	Y	N	N	Y	Y
11 ***Weller***	Y	Y	N	Y	Y	Y
12 Costello	Y	Y	Y	Y	N	N
13 ***Biggert***	Y	Y	N	N	Y	Y
14 ***Hastert***		Y			Y	Y

ND Northern Democrats SD Southern Democrats

	343	344	345	346	347	348
15 ***Ewing***	Y	Y	N	N	Y	Y
16 ***Manzullo***	Y	Y	N	Y	Y	Y
17 Evans	Y	N	Y	N	Y	N
18 ***LaHood***	Y	Y	N	Y	N	Y
19 Phelps	Y	Y	Y	Y	N	Y
20 ***Shimkus***	Y	Y	N	Y	Y	Y
INDIANA						
1 Visclosky	Y	Y	Y	N	Y	N
2 ***McIntosh***	Y	Y	N	Y	Y	Y
3 Roemer	Y	Y	Y	N	N	N
4 ***Souder***	Y	Y	N	Y	Y	Y
5 ***Buyer***	Y	Y	N	Y	N	Y
6 ***Burton***	Y	Y	N	Y	N	Y
7 ***Pease***	Y	Y	N	Y	Y	Y
8 ***Hostettler***	Y	Y	N	Y	Y	Y
9 Hill	Y	Y	Y	Y	Y	N
10 Carson	Y	N	Y	N	Y	N
IOWA						
1 ***Leach***	Y	Y	N	N	Y	Y
2 ***Nussle***	Y	Y	N	Y	Y	Y
3 Boswell	Y	Y	Y	N	Y	Y
4 ***Ganske***	Y	N	N	Y	Y	Y
5 ***Latham***	Y	Y	N	Y	Y	Y
KANSAS						
1 ***Moran***	Y	Y	N	Y	N	Y
2 ***Ryun***	Y	Y	N	Y	Y	Y
3 Moore	Y	Y	Y	Y	Y	Y
4 ***Tiahrt***	Y	Y	N	Y	Y	Y
KENTUCKY						
1 ***Whitfield***	Y	Y	N	N	Y	Y
2 ***Lewis***	Y	Y	N	Y	Y	Y
3 ***Northup***	Y	Y	N	Y	Y	Y
4 Lucas	Y	Y	Y	Y	Y	Y
5 ***Rogers***	Y	Y	N	Y	Y	Y
6 ***Fletcher***	Y	Y	N	Y	Y	Y
LOUISIANA						
1 ***Vitter***	Y	Y	N	Y	Y	Y
2 Jefferson	Y	N	Y	N	Y	N
3 ***Tauzin***	Y	Y	N	Y	Y	Y
4 ***McCrery***	Y	Y	N	Y	Y	Y
5 ***Cooksey***	Y	N	Y	N	Y	Y
6 ***Baker***	Y	Y	N	Y	Y	Y
7 John	Y	Y	Y	Y	Y	Y
MAINE						
1 Allen	Y	N	Y	N	Y	N
2 Baldacci	Y	N	Y	N	Y	N
MARYLAND						
1 ***Gilchrest***	Y	N	Y	N	Y	Y
2 ***Ehrlich***	Y	Y	N	Y	Y	Y
3 Cardin	Y	N	Y	N	Y	N
4 Wynn	Y	N	Y	N	Y	N
5 Hoyer	Y	N	Y	N	Y	N
6 ***Bartlett***	Y	Y	N	Y	N	Y
7 Cummings	Y	N	Y	N	N	N
8 ***Morella***	Y	N	Y	N	Y	Y
MASSACHUSETTS						
1 Olver	Y	N	Y	N	N	N
2 Neal	?	N	Y	N	Y	N
3 McGovern	Y	N	Y	N	Y	N
4 Frank	Y	N	Y	N	Y	N
5 Meehan	Y	N	Y	N	Y	N
6 Tierney	Y	N	Y	N	Y	N
7 Markey	Y	N	Y	N	Y	N
8 Capuano	Y	N	Y	N	Y	N
9 Moakley	Y	N	Y	N	Y	N
10 Delahunt	Y	N	Y	N	Y	N
MICHIGAN						
1 Stupak	Y	N	Y	N	Y	Y
2 ***Hoekstra***	Y	Y	N	Y	Y	Y
3 ***Ehlers***	Y	Y	N	Y	Y	Y
4 ***Camp***	Y	Y	N	N	Y	Y
5 Barcia	Y	Y	Y	N	Y	Y
6 ***Upton***	Y	Y	N	Y	Y	Y
7 ***Smith***	Y	Y	N	Y	Y	Y
8 Stabenow	Y	N	Y	N	Y	N
9 Kildee	Y	N	Y	N	Y	N
10 Bonior	Y	N	Y	N	Y	N
11 ***Knollenberg***	Y	Y	N	Y	Y	Y
12 Levin	Y	N	Y	N	Y	N
13 Rivers	Y	N	Y	N	Y	N
14 Conyers	Y	N	Y	N	N	N
15 Kilpatrick	Y	N	Y	N	N	N
16 Dingell	Y	N	Y	N	N	N
MINNESOTA						
1 ***Gutknecht***	Y	Y	N	Y	Y	Y
2 Minge	Y	N	Y	N	Y	N
3 ***Ramstad***	Y	Y	N	Y	Y	Y
4 Vento	Y	N	Y	N	Y	N
5 Sabo	?	N	Y	N	Y	N
6 Luther	Y	Y	Y	N	Y	N
7 Peterson	Y	Y	N	Y	N	Y
8 Oberstar	Y	N	Y	N	Y	N
MISSISSIPPI						
1 ***Wicker***	?	Y	N	Y	Y	Y
2 Thompson	Y	N	Y	N	N	N
3 ***Pickering***	Y	Y	N	Y	N	Y
4 Shows	Y	Y	Y	Y	Y	Y
5 Taylor	Y	Y	N	Y	N	Y
MISSOURI						
1 Clay	Y	N	Y	N	?	N
2 ***Talent***	Y	Y	N	Y	Y	Y
3 Gephardt	Y	N	Y	N	N	N
4 Skelton	?	?	?	?	?	?
5 McCarthy	Y	N	Y	N	Y	N
6 Danner	Y	Y	N	N	Y	Y
7 ***Blunt***	Y	Y	N	Y	Y	Y
8 ***Emerson***	Y	Y	N	Y	Y	Y
9 ***Hulshof***	Y	Y	N	Y	Y	Y
MONTANA						
AL ***Hill***	Y	Y	N	Y	N	Y
NEBRASKA						
1 ***Bereuter***	Y	Y	Y	Y	Y	Y
2 ***Terry***	Y	Y	N	Y	Y	Y
3 ***Barrett***	Y	Y	N	Y	Y	Y
NEVADA						
1 Berkley	Y	N	Y	N	Y	N
2 ***Gibbons***	Y	Y	N	Y	Y	Y
NEW HAMPSHIRE						
1 ***Sununu***	Y	?	?	?	Y	Y
2 ***Bass***	Y	Y	N	N	Y	Y
NEW JERSEY						
1 Andrews	Y	N	Y	N	Y	N
2 ***LoBiondo***	Y	Y	N	Y	Y	Y
3 ***Saxton***	Y	Y	N	Y	Y	Y
4 ***Smith***	Y	Y	N	Y	Y	Y
5 ***Roukema***	Y	Y	N	Y	N	Y
6 Pallone	Y	N	Y	N	Y	N
7 ***Franks***	Y	Y	N	N	Y	Y
8 Pascrell	Y	Y	Y	N	Y	N
9 Rothman	Y	N	Y	N	Y	N
10 Payne	Y	N	Y	N	N	N
11 ***Frelinghuysen***	Y	N	N	N	Y	Y
12 Holt	Y	N	Y	N	Y	N
13 Menendez	Y	N	Y	N	Y	N
NEW MEXICO						
1 ***Wilson***	Y	Y	N	N	Y	Y
2 ***Skeen***	Y	Y	N	Y	Y	Y
3 Udall	Y	N	Y	N	Y	N
NEW YORK						
1 Forbes	Y	Y	Y	N	Y	N
2 ***Lazio***	Y	Y	N	Y	Y	Y
3 ***King***	Y	Y	N	Y	Y	Y
4 McCarthy	Y	N	Y	N	Y	N
5 Ackerman	Y	N	Y	N	Y	N
6 Meeks	Y	N	Y	N	N	N
7 Crowley	Y	N	Y	N	Y	N
8 Nadler	Y	N	Y	N	N	N
9 Weiner	?	N	Y	N	Y	N
10 Towns	Y	N	Y	N	N	N
11 Owens	Y	N	Y	N	Y	N
12 Velázquez	Y	N	Y	N	Y	N
13 ***Fossella***	Y	Y	N	Y	N	Y
14 Maloney	Y	N	Y	N	Y	N
15 Rangel	Y	N	Y	N	Y	N
16 Serrano	Y	N	Y	N	Y	Y
17 Engel	Y	N	Y	N	Y	N
18 Lowey	Y	N	Y	N	Y	N
19 ***Kelly***	Y	Y	N	N	Y	Y
20 ***Gilman***	Y	Y	N	N	Y	Y
21 McNulty	Y	Y	Y	N	Y	N
22 ***Sweeney***	Y	Y	Y	Y	Y	Y
23 ***Boehlert***	Y	N	N	N	Y	Y
24 ***McHugh***	Y	Y	N	Y	Y	Y
25 ***Walsh***	Y	Y	N	Y	Y	Y
26 Hinchey	Y	N	Y	N	N	Y
27 ***Reynolds***	Y	Y	N	Y	Y	Y
28 Slaughter	Y	N	Y	N	N	N
29 LaFalce	Y	N	Y	N	Y	N
30 ***Quinn***	Y	Y	N	Y	Y	Y
31 ***Houghton***	Y	N	Y	N	Y	Y
NORTH CAROLINA						
1 Clayton	Y	N	Y	N	Y	N
2 Etheridge	Y	Y	Y	Y	Y	N
3 ***Jones***	Y	Y	N	Y	Y	Y
4 Price	Y	N	Y	N	Y	N
5 ***Burr***	Y	Y	N	Y	Y	Y
6 ***Coble***	Y	Y	N	Y	N	Y
7 McIntyre	Y	Y	Y	Y	N	Y
8 ***Hayes***	Y	Y	N	Y	Y	Y
9 ***Myrick***	Y	Y	N	Y	Y	Y
10 ***Ballenger***	Y	Y	N	Y	?	Y
11 ***Taylor***	Y	Y	N	Y	N	Y
12 Watt	Y	N	Y	N	Y	N
NORTH DAKOTA						
AL Pomeroy	Y	Y	Y	N	Y	N
OHIO						
1 ***Chabot***	Y	Y	N	Y	N	Y
2 ***Portman***	Y	Y	N	Y	Y	Y
3 Hall	Y	Y	Y	Y	Y	N
4 ***Oxley***	Y	Y	N	N	Y	Y
5 ***Gillmor***	Y	Y	N	Y	Y	Y
6 Strickland	Y	Y	Y	N	N	N
7 ***Hobson***	Y	Y	N	N	Y	Y
8 ***Boehner***	Y	Y	N	Y	Y	Y
9 Kaptur	Y	N	Y	N	Y	N
10 Kucinich	Y	N	Y	N	N	Y
11 Jones	?	?	?	?	?	?
12 ***Kasich***	Y	Y	N	Y	Y	Y
13 Brown	Y	N	Y	N	N	N
14 Sawyer	Y	N	Y	N	Y	N
15 ***Pryce***	Y	Y	N	N	Y	Y
16 ***Regula***	Y	Y	N	N	Y	Y
17 Traficant	Y	Y	Y	N	Y	Y
18 ***Ney***	Y	Y	N	Y	Y	Y
19 ***LaTourette***	Y	N	Y	N	Y	Y
OKLAHOMA						
1 ***Largent***	Y	Y	Y	Y	N	Y
2 ***Coburn***	Y	Y	N	Y	Y	N
3 ***Watkins***	Y	Y	N	Y	N	Y
4 ***Watts***	Y	Y	N	Y	Y	Y
5 ***Istook***	Y	Y	N	Y	Y	Y
6 ***Lucas***	Y	Y	N	Y	N	Y
OREGON						
1 Wu	Y	N	Y	N	Y	Y
2 ***Walden***	Y	Y	N	Y	Y	Y
3 Blumenauer	Y	N	Y	N	Y	N
4 DeFazio	Y	N	Y	N	N	N
5 Hooley	Y	N	Y	N	Y	N
PENNSYLVANIA						
1 Brady	Y	N	Y	N	Y	N
2 Fattah	Y	N	Y	N	Y	N
3 Borski	Y	N	Y	N	Y	N
4 Klink	Y	N	Y	N	Y	Y
5 ***Peterson***	?	?	?	?	?	?
6 Holden	Y	Y	Y	Y	Y	Y
7 ***Weldon***	Y	Y	N	Y	Y	Y
8 ***Greenwood***	Y	N	Y	N	?	Y
9 ***Shuster***	Y	Y	N	Y	Y	Y
10 ***Sherwood***	?	Y	N	Y	Y	Y
11 Kanjorski	Y	N	Y	N	Y	Y
12 Murtha	Y	Y	Y	N	Y	Y
13 Hoeffel	Y	N	Y	N	Y	N
14 Coyne	Y	N	Y	N	Y	N
15 ***Toomey***	Y	Y	N	Y	Y	Y
16 ***Pitts***	Y	Y	N	Y	Y	Y
17 ***Gekas***	Y	Y	N	Y	Y	Y
18 Doyle	Y	N	Y	N	Y	Y
19 ***Goodling***	Y	Y	N	Y	N	Y
20 Mascara	Y	Y	Y	Y	Y	Y
21 ***English***	Y	Y	N	Y	Y	Y
RHODE ISLAND						
1 Kennedy	Y	N	Y	N	Y	N
2 Weygand	Y	N	Y	N	Y	Y
SOUTH CAROLINA						
1 ***Sanford***	Y	Y	N	Y	N	Y
2 ***Spence***	Y	Y	N	Y	Y	Y
3 ***Graham***	Y	Y	N	Y	?	Y
4 ***DeMint***	Y	Y	N	Y	Y	Y
5 Spratt	Y	N	Y	Y	Y	N
6 Clyburn	Y	N	Y	N	N	N
SOUTH DAKOTA						
AL ***Thune***	Y	Y	N	Y	Y	Y
TENNESSEE						
1 ***Jenkins***	Y	Y	N	Y	Y	Y
2 ***Duncan***	Y	Y	N	Y	N	Y
3 ***Wamp***	Y	Y	N	Y	Y	Y
4 ***Hilleary***	Y	Y	N	Y	Y	Y
5 Clement	Y	Y	Y	Y	Y	N
6 Gordon	Y	N	Y	Y	Y	N
7 ***Bryant***	Y	Y	N	Y	Y	Y
8 Tanner	Y	Y	Y	Y	Y	N
9 Ford	Y	N	Y	N	Y	N
TEXAS						
1 Sandlin	Y	Y	Y	Y	Y	N
2 Turner	Y	Y	Y	Y	Y	N
3 ***Johnson, Sam***	Y	?	N	Y	Y	Y
4 Hall	Y	Y	Y	Y	N	Y
5 ***Sessions***	Y	Y	N	Y	N	Y
6 ***Barton***	Y	Y	N	Y	Y	Y
7 ***Archer***	Y	Y	N	Y	N	Y
8 ***Brady***	Y	Y	N	Y	Y	Y
9 Lampson	Y	N	Y	N	Y	N
10 Doggett	Y	N	Y	N	N	N
11 Edwards	Y	N	Y	N	Y	N
12 ***Granger***	Y	Y	N	Y	Y	Y
13 ***Thornberry***	Y	Y	N	Y	Y	Y
14 ***Paul***	N	Y	N	Y	N	Y
15 Hinojosa	Y	N	Y	N	Y	N
16 Reyes	Y	N	Y	N	Y	N
17 Stenholm	Y	Y	N	Y	N	N
18 Jackson-Lee	Y	N	Y	N	Y	N
19 ***Combest***	Y	Y	N	Y	N	Y
20 Gonzalez	Y	N	Y	N	Y	N
21 ***Smith***	Y	Y	N	Y	Y	Y
22 ***DeLay***	Y	Y	N	Y	Y	Y
23 ***Bonilla***	Y	N	N	N	Y	Y
24 Frost	Y	N	Y	N	Y	N
25 Bentsen	Y	N	Y	N	Y	N
26 ***Armey***	Y	Y	N	Y	Y	Y
27 Ortiz	Y	Y	Y	Y	Y	Y
28 Rodriguez	Y	N	Y	N	Y	N
29 Green	Y	Y	Y	N	N	N
30 Johnson, E.B.	Y	N	Y	N	Y	N
UTAH						
1 ***Hansen***	Y	Y	N	Y	Y	Y
2 ***Cook***	Y	Y	N	Y	Y	Y
3 ***Cannon***	Y	Y	N	Y	Y	Y
VERMONT						
AL *Sanders*	Y	N	Y	N	Y	N
VIRGINIA						
1 ***Bateman***	Y	Y	N	Y	Y	Y
2 Pickett	Y	N	N	Y	N	N
3 Scott	Y	N	Y	N	Y	N
4 Sisisky	Y	N	Y	Y	Y	N
5 Goode	Y	Y	N	Y	N	Y
6 ***Goodlatte***	Y	Y	N	Y	N	Y
7 ***Bliley***	Y	Y	N	Y	Y	Y
8 Moran	Y	N	Y	N	Y	N
9 Boucher	Y	N	N	N	Y	N
10 ***Wolf***	Y	Y	Y	Y	Y	Y
11 ***Davis***	Y	Y	Y	Y	Y	Y
WASHINGTON						
1 Inslee	Y	N	Y	N	Y	N
2 ***Metcalf***	Y	Y	N	Y	N	Y
3 Baird	Y	N	Y	N	Y	N
4 ***Hastings***	Y	Y	N	Y	Y	Y
5 ***Nethercutt***	Y	Y	N	Y	Y	Y
6 Dicks	Y	N	Y	N	N	?
7 McDermott	?	?	?	?	?	?
8 ***Dunn***	Y	Y	N	Y	Y	Y
9 Smith	Y	N	N	N	Y	N
WEST VIRGINIA						
1 Mollohan	Y	N	Y	N	Y	Y
2 Wise	Y	Y	Y	N	Y	Y
3 Rahall	Y	N	Y	N	Y	Y
WISCONSIN						
1 ***Ryan***	Y	Y	N	Y	Y	Y
2 Baldwin	Y	N	Y	N	Y	N
3 Kind	Y	N	Y	N	Y	N
4 Kleczka	N	N	Y	N	N	N
5 Barrett	N	N	Y	N	N	N
6 ***Petri***	Y	Y	N	Y	N	Y
7 Obey	Y	N	Y	N	N	N
8 ***Green***	Y	Y	N	Y	Y	Y
9 ***Sensenbrenner***	N	Y	N	Y	N	Y
WYOMING						
AL ***Cubin***	?	Y	Y	Y	Y	Y

Southern states - Ala., Ark., Fla., Ga., Ky., La., Miss., N.C., Okla., S.C., Tenn., Texas, Va.

349. **HR 2606. Fiscal 2000 Foreign Operations Appropriations/Abortion.** Smith, R-N.J., amendment to bar U.S. population control funds to foreign organizations that perform abortions, except when the life of the mother is in danger, or in cases of rape or incest. The amendment also would bar funds to organizations which violate the abortion laws of foreign countries or that lobby to change the laws of foreign countries. Adopted 228-200: R 189-31; D 39-168 (ND 28-124, SD 11-44); I 0-1. July 29, 1999.

350. **HR 2606. Fiscal 2000 Foreign Operations Appropriations/Foreign Abortion Laws.** Greenwood, R-Pa., amendment to ensure that no U.S. population control funds are used to lobby for or against abortion in foreign countries, and that no funds are used to promote abortion as a method of family planning. The amendment also would make clear that organizations that receive U.S. funds for family planning must be committed to using those funds to reduce the incidence of abortion, and that they must not violate foreign abortion laws or governmental policies. Adopted 221-208: R 46-173; D 174-35 (ND 129-25, SD 45-10); I 1-0. July 29, 1999.

351. **HR 2606. Fiscal 2000 Foreign Operations Appropriations/Israel/Egypt.** Campbell, R-Calif., amendment to reduce economic aid to Israel from $960 million to $930 million and to reduce economic aid to Egypt from $735 million to $715 million in fiscal 2000. Rejected 13-414: R 6-212; D 7-201 (ND 2-151, SD 5-50); I 0-1. July 29, 1999.

352. **HR 2606. Fiscal 2000 Foreign Operations Appropriations/School of the Americas.** Moakley, D-Mass., amendment to prohibit any funding in the bill from being used to recruit and send students to the U.S. Army School of the Americas at Fort Benning in Columbus, Ga. Adopted 230-197: R 58-160; D 171-37 (ND 140-13, SD 31-24); I 1-0. July 29, 1999.

353. **HR 2606. Fiscal 2000 Foreign Operations Appropriations/Child Survival Account.** Pitts, R-Pa., amendment to state that no funds from the Child Survival and Disease Account may be used for population control. Rejected 187-237: R 162-55; D 25-181 (ND 16-136, SD 9-45); I 0-1. July 29, 1999.

Key

Y Voted for (yea).
\# Paired for.
\+ Announced for.
N Voted against (nay).
X Paired against.
– Announced against.
P Voted "present."
C Voted "present" to avoid possible conflict of interest.
? Did not vote or otherwise make a position known.

•

Democrats ***Republicans***
Independents

	349	350	351	352	353
ALABAMA					
1 ***Callahan***	Y	N	N	N	Y
2 ***Everett***	Y	N	N	N	Y
3 ***Riley***	Y	N	N	N	Y
4 ***Aderholt***	Y	N	N	N	Y
5 Cramer	N	Y	N	N	N
6 ***Bachus***	Y	N	N	N	Y
7 Hilliard	N	Y	N	Y	N
ALASKA					
AL ***Young***	Y	N	N	N	Y
ARIZONA					
1 ***Salmon***	Y	N	N	Y	Y
2 Pastor	N	Y	N	Y	N
3 ***Stump***	Y	N	N	N	Y
4 ***Shadegg***	Y	N	N	N	Y
5 ***Kolbe***	N	Y	N	N	N
6 ***Hayworth***	Y	N	N	Y	Y
ARKANSAS					
1 Berry	Y	N	N	N	N
2 Snyder	N	Y	N	N	N
3 ***Hutchinson***	Y	N	N	N	Y
4 ***Dickey***	Y	N	N	N	Y
CALIFORNIA					
1 Thompson	N	Y	N	Y	N
2 ***Herger***	Y	N	N	N	Y
3 ***Ose***	N	Y	N	N	N
4 ***Doolittle***	Y	N	N	N	Y
5 Matsui	N	Y	N	Y	N
6 Woolsey	N	Y	N	Y	N
7 Miller, George	N	Y	N	Y	N
8 Pelosi	N	Y	N	Y	N
9 Lee	N	Y	N	Y	N
10 Tauscher	N	Y	N	Y	N
11 ***Pombo***	Y	N	N	N	Y
12 Lantos	N	Y	N	Y	N
13 Stark	N	Y	N	Y	N
14 Eshoo	N	Y	N	Y	N
15 ***Campbell***	N	Y	Y	Y	N
16 Lofgren	N	Y	N	Y	N
17 Farr	N	Y	N	Y	N
18 Condit	N	Y	N	N	N
19 ***Radanovich***	Y	N	N	N	Y
20 Dooley	N	Y	N	Y	N
21 ***Thomas***	Y	Y	N	N	N
22 Capps	N	Y	N	Y	N
23 ***Gallegly***	Y	N	N	N	N
24 Sherman	N	Y	N	Y	N
25 ***McKeon***	Y	N	N	N	Y
26 Berman	N	Y	N	Y	N
27 ***Rogan***	Y	N	N	N	Y
28 ***Dreier***	Y	N	N	N	Y
29 Waxman	N	Y	N	Y	N
30 Becerra	N	Y	N	Y	N
31 Martinez	N	Y	N	N	N
32 Dixon	N	Y	N	Y	N
33 Roybal-Allard	N	Y	N	N	N
34 Napolitano	N	Y	N	N	N
35 Waters	N	Y	N	Y	N
36 ***Kuykendall***	N	Y	N	N	N
37 Millender-McD.	N	Y	N	Y	N
38 ***Horn***	N	Y	N	N	N
39 ***Royce***	Y	N	N	N	Y
40 ***Lewis***	N	Y	N	N	N
41 ***Miller, Gary***	Y	N	N	N	Y
42 Vacant					
43 ***Calvert***	Y	N	N	N	Y
44 ***Bono***	Y	N	N	Y	Y
45 ***Rohrabacher***	Y	N	Y	N	Y
46 Sanchez	N	Y	N	Y	N
47 ***Cox***	Y	N	N	N	Y
48 ***Packard***	Y	N	N	N	Y
49 ***Bilbray***	N	Y	N	N	N
50 Filner	N	Y	N	Y	N
51 ***Cunningham***	Y	N	N	N	Y
52 ***Hunter***	Y	N	N	N	Y
COLORADO					
1 DeGette	N	Y	N	Y	N
2 Udall	N	Y	N	Y	N
3 ***McInnis***	Y	N	N	Y	N
4 ***Schaffer***	Y	N	N	Y	Y
5 ***Hefley***	Y	N	N	Y	Y
6 ***Tancredo***	Y	N	N	Y	Y
CONNECTICUT					
1 Larson	N	Y	N	Y	N
2 Gejdenson	N	Y	N	Y	N
3 DeLauro	N	Y	N	Y	N
4 ***Shays***	N	Y	N	Y	N
5 Maloney	N	Y	N	Y	N
6 ***Johnson***	N	Y	N	Y	N
DELAWARE					
AL ***Castle***	N	Y	N	N	N
FLORIDA					
1 ***Scarborough***	Y	N	N	Y	Y
2 Boyd	N	Y	N	N	N
3 Brown	N	Y	N	Y	N
4 ***Fowler***	Y	Y	N	N	N
5 Thurman	N	Y	N	Y	N
6 ***Stearns***	Y	N	N	N	Y
7 ***Mica***	Y	N	N	N	Y
8 ***McCollum***	Y	N	N	N	Y
9 ***Bilirakis***	Y	N	N	N	Y
10 ***Young***	Y	N	N	N	Y
11 Davis	N	Y	N	N	N
12 ***Canady***	Y	N	N	N	Y
13 ***Miller***	Y	Y	N	Y	Y
14 ***Goss***	Y	N	N	N	Y
15 ***Weldon***	Y	N	N	N	Y
16 ***Foley***	Y	Y	N	Y	N
17 Meek	N	Y	N	Y	N
18 ***Ros-Lehtinen***	Y	N	N	N	N
19 Wexler	N	Y	N	Y	N
20 Deutsch	N	Y	N	N	N
21 ***Diaz-Balart***	Y	N	N	N	N
22 ***Shaw***	Y	Y	N	N	N
23 Hastings	N	Y	N	Y	N
GEORGIA					
1 ***Kingston***	Y	N	N	N	Y
2 Bishop	N	Y	N	N	N
3 ***Collins***	Y	N	N	N	Y
4 McKinney	N	Y	Y	Y	N
5 Lewis	N	Y	N	Y	N
6 ***Isakson***	N	Y	N	N	N
7 ***Barr***	Y	N	N	N	Y
8 ***Chambliss***	Y	N	N	N	Y
9 ***Deal***	Y	N	N	N	Y
10 ***Norwood***	Y	N	N	N	Y
11 ***Linder***	Y	N	N	N	Y
HAWAII					
1 Abercrombie	N	Y	N	Y	N
2 Mink	N	Y	N	Y	N
IDAHO					
1 ***Chenoweth***	?	?	N	N	Y
2 ***Simpson***	Y	N	N	N	N
ILLINOIS					
1 Rush	N	Y	N	Y	?
2 Jackson	N	Y	N	Y	N
3 Lipinski	Y	N	N	Y	Y
4 Gutierrez	N	Y	?	?	?
5 Blagojevich	N	Y	N	Y	N
6 ***Hyde***	Y	N	N	N	Y
7 Davis	N	Y	N	Y	N
8 ***Crane***	Y	N	N	N	Y
9 Schakowsky	N	Y	N	Y	N
10 ***Porter***	N	Y	N	Y	N
11 ***Weller***	Y	N	N	Y	Y
12 Costello	Y	N	N	Y	Y
13 ***Biggert***	N	Y	N	Y	N
14 ***Hastert***	Y				

ND Northern Democrats SD Southern Democrats

	349	350	351	352	353
15 ***Ewing***	Y	N	N	Y	Y
16 ***Manzullo***	Y	N	N	Y	Y
17 Evans	N	Y	N	Y	N
18 ***LaHood***	Y	N	N	Y	Y
19 Phelps	Y	N	N	Y	Y
20 ***Shimkus***	Y	N	N	N	Y
INDIANA					
1 Visclosky	N	Y	N	N	N
2 ***McIntosh***	Y	N	N	N	Y
3 Roemer	Y	N	N	Y	N
4 ***Souder***	Y	N	N	N	Y
5 ***Buyer***	Y	N	N	N	Y
6 ***Burton***	Y	N	N	N	Y
7 ***Pease***	Y	N	N	N	Y
8 ***Hostettler***	Y	N	Y	N	Y
9 Hill	N	Y	N	Y	N
10 Carson	N	Y	N	Y	N
IOWA					
1 ***Leach***	N	Y	N	Y	N
2 ***Nussle***	Y	N	N	Y	Y
3 Boswell	N	Y	N	N	N
4 ***Ganske***	Y	N	N	N	N
5 ***Latham***	Y	N	N	N	Y
KANSAS					
1 ***Moran***	Y	N	N	Y	Y
2 ***Ryun***	Y	N	N	N	Y
3 Moore	N	Y	N	Y	N
4 ***Tiahrt***	Y	N	N	N	Y
KENTUCKY					
1 ***Whitfield***	Y	N	N	N	Y
2 ***Lewis***	Y	N	N	N	Y
3 ***Northup***	Y	N	N	N	Y
4 Lucas	Y	N	N	Y	Y
5 ***Rogers***	Y	N	N	N	Y
6 ***Fletcher***	Y	N	N	N	Y
LOUISIANA					
1 ***Vitter***	Y	N	N	N	Y
2 Jefferson	N	Y	N	Y	N
3 ***Tauzin***	Y	N	N	N	Y
4 ***McCrery***	Y	N	N	N	Y
5 ***Cooksey***	Y	Y	N	N	N
6 ***Baker***	Y	N	N	N	Y
7 John	Y	N	N	N	Y
MAINE					
1 Allen	N	Y	N	Y	N
2 Baldacci	N	Y	N	Y	N
MARYLAND					
1 ***Gilchrest***	N	Y	N	Y	N
2 ***Ehrlich***	N	Y	N	N	N
3 Cardin	N	Y	N	Y	N
4 Wynn	N	Y	N	Y	N
5 Hoyer	N	Y	N	N	N
6 ***Bartlett***	Y	N	N	N	Y
7 Cummings	N	Y	N	Y	N
8 ***Morella***	N	Y	N	Y	N
MASSACHUSETTS					
1 Olver	N	Y	N	Y	N
2 Neal	N	Y	N	Y	N
3 McGovern	N	Y	N	Y	N
4 Frank	N	Y	N	Y	N
5 Meehan	N	Y	N	Y	N
6 Tierney	N	Y	N	Y	N
7 Markey	N	Y	N	Y	N
8 Capuano	N	Y	N	Y	N
9 Moakley	Y	Y	N	Y	N
10 Delahunt	N	Y	N	Y	N
MICHIGAN					
1 Stupak	Y	N	N	Y	Y
2 ***Hoekstra***	Y	N	N	N	Y
3 ***Ehlers***	Y	N	N	Y	Y
4 ***Camp***	Y	N	N	Y	Y
5 Barcia	Y	N	N	Y	Y
6 ***Upton***	Y	Y	N	Y	N
7 ***Smith***	Y	N	N	Y	N
8 Stabenow	N	Y	N	Y	N
9 Kildee	Y	N	N	Y	Y
10 Bonior	Y	Y	N	Y	N
11 ***Knollenberg***	Y	N	N	N	Y
12 Levin	N	Y	N	Y	N
13 Rivers	N	Y	N	Y	N
14 Conyers	N	Y	Y	Y	N
15 Kilpatrick	N	Y	N	Y	N
16 Dingell	N	N	N	N	N

	349	350	351	352	353
MINNESOTA					
1 ***Gutknecht***	Y	N	N	Y	Y
2 Minge	N	Y	N	Y	N
3 ***Ramstad***	N	Y	N	Y	N
4 Vento	N	Y	N	Y	N
5 Sabo	N	Y	N	Y	N
6 Luther	N	Y	N	Y	N
7 Peterson	Y	N	N	Y	Y
8 Oberstar	Y	N	N	Y	N
MISSISSIPPI					
1 ***Wicker***	Y	N	N	N	Y
2 Thompson	N	Y	Y	Y	N
3 ***Pickering***	Y	N	N	N	Y
4 Shows	Y	N	N	N	Y
5 Taylor	Y	N	Y	N	Y
MISSOURI					
1 Clay	N	Y	N	Y	N
2 ***Talent***	Y	N	N	Y	Y
3 Gephardt	N	Y	N	Y	N
4 Skelton	?	?	?	?	?
5 McCarthy	N	Y	N	Y	N
6 Danner	Y	N	N	Y	N
7 ***Blunt***	Y	N	N	N	Y
8 ***Emerson***	Y	N	N	N	Y
9 ***Hulshof***	Y	N	N	Y	Y
MONTANA					
AL ***Hill***	Y	N	N	N	Y
NEBRASKA					
1 ***Bereuter***	Y	Y	N	N	N
2 ***Terry***	Y	N	N	N	Y
3 ***Barrett***	Y	N	N	N	Y
NEVADA					
1 Berkley	N	Y	N	Y	N
2 ***Gibbons***	Y	Y	N	Y	N
NEW HAMPSHIRE					
1 ***Sununu***	Y	N	N	N	Y
2 ***Bass***	N	Y	N	N	N
NEW JERSEY					
1 Andrews	N	Y	N	Y	N
2 ***LoBiondo***	Y	N	N	Y	Y
3 ***Saxton***	Y	N	N	N	Y
4 ***Smith***	Y	N	N	Y	Y
5 ***Roukema***	N	Y	N	Y	N
6 Pallone	N	Y	N	Y	N
7 ***Franks***	N	Y	N	Y	Y
8 Pascrell	N	Y	N	Y	N
9 Rothman	N	Y	N	Y	N
10 Payne	N	Y	Y	Y	N
11 ***Frelinghuysen***	N	Y	N	N	N
12 Holt	N	Y	N	Y	N
13 Menendez	N	Y	N	Y	N
NEW MEXICO					
1 ***Wilson***	Y	Y	N	N	N
2 ***Skeen***	Y	Y	N	N	N
3 Udall	N	Y	N	Y	N
NEW YORK					
1 Forbes	Y	N	N	Y	Y
2 ***Lazio***	N	Y	N	Y	N
3 ***King***	Y	N	N	N	Y
4 McCarthy	N	Y	N	Y	N
5 Ackerman	N	Y	N	Y	N
6 Meeks	N	Y	N	Y	N
7 Crowley	Y	Y	N	Y	N
8 Nadler	N	Y	N	Y	N
9 Weiner	N	Y	N	Y	N
10 Towns	N	Y	N	Y	N
11 Owens	N	Y	N	Y	N
12 Velázquez	N	Y	N	Y	N
13 ***Fossella***	Y	N	N	N	Y
14 Maloney	N	Y	N	Y	N
15 Rangel	N	Y	N	Y	N
16 Serrano	N	Y	N	Y	N
17 Engel	N	Y	N	Y	N
18 Lowey	N	Y	N	Y	N
19 ***Kelly***	N	Y	N	Y	N
20 ***Gilman***	N	Y	N	N	N
21 McNulty	N	Y	N	Y	N
22 ***Sweeney***	Y	Y	N	N	N
23 ***Boehlert***	N	Y	N	Y	N
24 ***McHugh***	Y	N	N	N	Y
25 ***Walsh***	Y	N	N	Y	Y
26 Hinchey	N	Y	N	Y	N
27 ***Reynolds***	Y	N	N	N	Y
28 Slaughter	N	Y	N	Y	N
29 LaFalce	Y	N	N	N	Y

	349	350	351	352	353
30 ***Quinn***	Y	N	N	Y	Y
31 ***Houghton***	N	Y	N	N	N
NORTH CAROLINA					
1 Clayton	N	Y	N	Y	N
2 Etheridge	N	Y	N	Y	N
3 ***Jones***	Y	N	N	N	Y
4 Price	N	Y	N	Y	N
5 ***Burr***	Y	N	N	N	Y
6 ***Coble***	Y	N	N	Y	Y
7 McIntyre	Y	N	N	N	Y
8 ***Hayes***	Y	N	N	N	Y
9 ***Myrick***	Y	N	N	N	Y
10 ***Ballenger***	Y	N	N	N	Y
11 ***Taylor***	Y	N	N	Y	Y
12 Watt	N	Y	Y	Y	N
NORTH DAKOTA					
AL Pomeroy	N	Y	N	Y	N
OHIO					
1 ***Chabot***	Y	N	N	Y	Y
2 ***Portman***	Y	N	N	N	Y
3 Hall	Y	N	N	Y	Y
4 ***Oxley***	Y	N	N	N	Y
5 ***Gillmor***	Y	N	N	N	N
6 Strickland	N	Y	N	Y	N
7 ***Hobson***	N	Y	N	N	N
8 ***Boehner***	Y	N	N	Y	Y
9 Kaptur	Y	Y	N	Y	N
10 Kucinich	Y	N	N	Y	N
11 Jones	?	Y	N	Y	N
12 ***Kasich***	Y	N	N	N	Y
13 Brown	N	Y	N	Y	N
14 Sawyer	N	Y	N	Y	N
15 ***Pryce***	N	Y	N	Y	N
16 ***Regula***	Y	Y	N	Y	N
17 Traficant	Y	N	N	Y	Y
18 ***Ney***	Y	N	N	N	Y
19 ***LaTourette***	Y	N	N	Y	N
OKLAHOMA					
1 ***Largent***	Y	N	N	Y	Y
2 ***Coburn***	Y	N	N	N	Y
3 ***Watkins***	Y	N	N	N	Y
4 ***Watts***	Y	N	N	N	Y
5 ***Istook***	Y	N	N	N	Y
6 ***Lucas***	Y	N	N	N	Y
OREGON					
1 Wu	N	Y	N	Y	N
2 ***Walden***	Y	N	N	N	N
3 Blumenauer	N	Y	N	Y	N
4 DeFazio	N	Y	N	Y	N
5 Hooley	N	Y	N	Y	N
PENNSYLVANIA					
1 Brady	N	Y	N	Y	N
2 Fattah	N	Y	N	Y	N
3 Borski	Y	Y	N	Y	N
4 Klink	Y	N	N	Y	N
5 ***Peterson***	?	?	?	?	?
6 Holden	Y	N	N	Y	Y
7 ***Weldon***	Y	N	N	N	Y
8 ***Greenwood***	N	Y	N	Y	N
9 ***Shuster***	Y	N	?	?	?
10 ***Sherwood***	Y	N	N	N	Y
11 Kanjorski	Y	N	N	Y	N
12 Murtha	Y	N	N	N	Y
13 Hoeffel	N	Y	N	Y	N
14 Coyne	N	Y	N	Y	N
15 ***Toomey***	Y	Y	N	N	Y
16 ***Pitts***	Y	N	N	N	Y
17 ***Gekas***	Y	N	N	N	Y
18 Doyle	Y	N	N	Y	N
19 ***Goodling***	Y	N	N	N	Y
20 Mascara	Y	N	N	Y	Y
21 ***English***	Y	N	N	Y	Y
RHODE ISLAND					
1 Kennedy	N	Y	N	Y	N
2 Weygand	Y	N	N	Y	N
SOUTH CAROLINA					
1 ***Sanford***	Y	N	Y	Y	Y
2 ***Spence***	Y	N	N	N	Y
3 ***Graham***	Y	N	N	N	Y
4 ***DeMint***	Y	N	N	N	Y
5 Spratt	N	Y	N	N	N
6 Clyburn	N	Y	N	N	N
SOUTH DAKOTA					
AL ***Thune***	Y	N	N	N	Y

	349	350	351	352	353
TENNESSEE					
1 ***Jenkins***	Y	N	N	N	Y
2 ***Duncan***	Y	N	N	Y	Y
3 ***Wamp***	Y	N	N	Y	Y
4 ***Hilleary***	Y	N	N	N	Y
5 Clement	N	Y	N	Y	N
6 Gordon	N	Y	N	Y	N
7 ***Bryant***	Y	N	N	N	Y
8 Tanner	N	Y	N	N	N
9 Ford	N	Y	N	Y	?
TEXAS					
1 Sandlin	N	Y	N	N	N
2 Turner	N	Y	N	N	N
3 ***Johnson, Sam***	Y	N	N	N	Y
4 Hall	Y	N	N	N	Y
5 ***Sessions***	Y	N	N	N	Y
6 ***Barton***	Y	N	?	?	?
7 ***Archer***	Y	N	N	N	Y
8 ***Brady***	Y	N	N	N	Y
9 Lampson	N	Y	N	Y	N
10 Doggett	N	Y	N	Y	N
11 Edwards	N	Y	N	N	N
12 ***Granger***	Y	N	N	N	N
13 ***Thornberry***	Y	N	N	N	Y
14 ***Paul***	Y	N	Y	Y	Y
15 Hinojosa	N	Y	N	Y	N
16 Reyes	N	Y	N	N	N
17 Stenholm	Y	N	N	N	Y
18 Jackson-Lee	N	Y	N	Y	N
19 ***Combest***	Y	N	N	N	Y
20 Gonzalez	N	Y	N	Y	N
21 ***Smith***	Y	N	N	N	Y
22 ***DeLay***	Y	N	N	N	Y
23 ***Bonilla***	Y	N	N	N	Y
24 Frost	N	Y	N	N	N
25 Bentsen	N	Y	N	Y	N
26 ***Armey***	Y	N	N	N	Y
27 Ortiz	Y	N	N	N	Y
28 Rodriguez	N	Y	N	Y	N
29 Green	N	Y	N	Y	N
30 Johnson, E.B.	Y	Y	N	Y	N
UTAH					
1 ***Hansen***	Y	N	N	N	Y
2 ***Cook***	Y	N	N	N	Y
3 ***Cannon***	Y	N	N	N	Y
VERMONT					
AL *Sanders*	N	Y	N	Y	N
VIRGINIA					
1 ***Bateman***	Y	N	N	N	N
2 Pickett	N	Y	N	N	N
3 Scott	N	Y	N	Y	N
4 Sisisky	N	Y	N	N	N
5 Goode	Y	N	N	Y	Y
6 ***Goodlatte***	Y	N	N	N	Y
7 ***Bliley***	Y	N	N	N	Y
8 Moran	N	Y	N	Y	N
9 Boucher	N	Y	Y	Y	N
10 ***Wolf***	Y	N	N	N	Y
11 ***Davis***	N	N	N	N	N
WASHINGTON					
1 Inslee	N	Y	N	Y	N
2 ***Metcalf***	Y	N	N	Y	Y
3 Baird	N	Y	N	Y	N
4 ***Hastings***	Y	N	N	N	Y
5 ***Nethercutt***	Y	Y	N	N	Y
6 Dicks	N	Y	N	Y	N
7 McDermott	?	?	?	?	?
8 ***Dunn***	Y	Y	N	N	N
9 Smith	N	Y	N	Y	N
WEST VIRGINIA					
1 Mollohan	Y	N	N	N	Y
2 Wise	N	Y	N	N	N
3 Rahall	?	N	N	N	Y
WISCONSIN					
1 ***Ryan***	Y	N	N	N	Y
2 Baldwin	N	Y	N	Y	N
3 Kind	N	Y	N	Y	N
4 Kleczka	N	Y	N	Y	N
5 Barrett	N	Y	N	Y	N
6 ***Petri***	Y	N	N	Y	Y
7 Obey	N	Y	N	Y	N
8 ***Green***	Y	N	N	N	Y
9 ***Sensenbrenner***	Y	N	Y	Y	Y
WYOMING					
AL ***Cubin***	Y	N	N	N	?

Southern states - Ala., Ark., Fla., Ga., Ky., La., Miss., N.C., Okla., S.C., Tenn., Texas, Va.

354. HR 1501. Juvenile Justice/Motion To Instruct. Conyers, D-Mich., motion to instruct the House conferees on the juvenile crime bill to support provisions that require background checks at gun shows, to reject provisions that would weaken background checks or firearm regulations, and to include violence prevention measures in schools. Motion agreed to 305-84: R 129-71; D 175-13 (ND 133-4, SD 42-9); I 1-0. July 30, 1999.

355. S 900. Financial Services Overhaul/Motion to Instruct. LaFalce, D-N.Y., motion to instruct the House conferees to insist on the strongest possible provisions on financial and medical privacy for consumers. Motion agreed to 241-132: R 58-131; D 182-1 (ND 135-0, SD 47-1); I 1-0. July 30, 1999.

356. HR 2488. Tax Reconciliation/Motion to Instruct. Rangel, D-N.Y., motion to instruct the House conferees on the tax-reconciliation bill to limit the 10-year tax reduction in the bill to not more than 25 percent of the currently projected non-Social Security budget surplus. Motion rejected 205-213: R 0-212; D 204-1 (ND 152-0, SD 52-1); I 1-0. Aug. 2, 1999.

357. HR 747. Arizona Land Trust Investment/Passage. Saxton, R-N.J., motion to suspend the rules and pass the bill to allow the state of Arizona to reinvest interest and dividends generated from state trust funds rather than using all of the revenue for public schools, universities and other institutions. Motion agreed to 416-0: R 211-0; D 204-0 (ND 151-0, SD 53-0); I 1-0. Aug. 2, 1999. A two-thirds majority of those present and voting (278 in this case) is required for passage under suspension of the rules.

358. HR 1219. Construction Industry Subcontractor Protection/Passage. Horn, R-Calif., motion to suspend the rules and pass the bill to increase protection for subcontractors on federal construction projects by requiring that the general contractor obtain payment bonds equal to the total value of the contract. Motion agreed to 416-0: R 212-0; D 203-0 (ND 151-0, SD 52-0); I 1-0. Aug. 2, 1999. A two-thirds majority of those present and voting (278 in this case) is required for passage under suspension of the rules. A "yea" was a vote in support of the president's position.

359. HR 2606. Fiscal 2000 Foreign Operations Appropriations/OPIC. Andrews, D-N.J., amendment to prohibit the use of any funds in the bill for new projects by the Overseas Private Investment Corporation (OPIC). Rejected 103-315: R 68-146; D 34-169 (ND 31-118, SD 3-51); I 1-0. Aug. 2, 1999.

360. HR 2606. Fiscal 2000 Foreign Operations Appropriations/Family Planning Activities. Paul, R-Texas, amendment to prohibit the use of funds in the bill for international population control or family planning activities or for abortion procedures. Rejected 145-272: R 133-79; D 12-192 (ND 7-143, SD 5-49); I 0-1. Aug. 3, 1999.

361. HR 2606. Fiscal 2000 Foreign Operations Appropriations/Export-Import Bank and Trade Organizations. Paul, R-Texas, amendment to prohibit the use of funds in the bill for new obligations or commitments by the Export-Import Bank, the Overseas Private Investment Corporation or the Trade and Development Agency. Rejected 58-360: R 50-165; D 7-195 (ND 4-144, SD 3-51); I 1-0. Aug. 3, 1999.

Key

- Y Voted for (yea).
- \# Paired for.
- \+ Announced for.
- N Voted against (nay).
- X Paired against.
- – Announced against.
- P Voted "present."
- C Voted "present" to avoid possible conflict of interest.
- ? Did not vote or otherwise make a position known.

•

Democrats ***Republicans***
Independents

	354	355	356	357	358	359	360	361
ALABAMA								
1 ***Callahan***	N	N	N	Y	Y	N	N	N
2 ***Everett***	N	N	N	Y	Y	N	Y	N
3 ***Riley***	N	N	N	Y	Y	N	Y	N
4 ***Aderholt***	N	N	N	Y	Y	N	Y	N
5 Cramer	Y	Y	Y	Y	Y	N	N	N
6 ***Bachus***	N	N	N	Y	Y	Y	Y	N
7 Hilliard	Y	Y	Y	Y	Y	N	N	N
ALASKA								
AL ***Young***	?	N	N	Y	Y	N	?	?
ARIZONA								
1 ***Salmon***	N	?	N	Y	Y	Y	Y	N
2 Pastor	Y	Y	Y	Y	Y	N	N	N
3 ***Stump***	N	N	N	Y	Y	N	Y	N
4 ***Shadegg***	N	N	N	Y	Y	Y	Y	Y
5 ***Kolbe***	Y	N	N	Y	Y	N	N	N
6 ***Hayworth***	N	N	N	Y	Y	Y	Y	Y
ARKANSAS								
1 Berry	Y	Y	Y	Y	Y	N	N	N
2 Snyder	Y	Y	Y	Y	Y	N	N	N
3 ***Hutchinson***	+	+	N	Y	Y	N	Y	N
4 ***Dickey***	Y	Y	N	Y	Y	Y	Y	N
CALIFORNIA								
1 Thompson	Y	Y	Y	Y	Y	N	N	N
2 ***Herger***	Y	N	N	Y	Y	Y	Y	N
3 ***Ose***	Y	Y	N	Y	Y	N	N	N
4 ***Doolittle***	N	N	N	Y	Y	Y	Y	Y
5 Matsui	Y	Y	Y	Y	Y	N	N	N
6 Woolsey	Y	Y	Y	Y	Y	Y	N	N
7 Miller, George	Y	?	Y	Y	Y	Y	N	N
8 Pelosi	Y	Y	Y	Y	Y	N	N	N
9 Lee	Y	Y	Y	Y	Y	N	N	N
10 Tauscher	Y	Y	Y	Y	Y	N	N	N
11 ***Pombo***	N	N	N	Y	Y	Y	Y	Y
12 Lantos	?	Y	?	?	?	?	?	?
13 Stark	?	Y	Y	Y	Y	Y	N	N
14 Eshoo	Y	Y	Y	Y	Y	N	N	N
15 ***Campbell***	Y	Y	N	Y	Y	Y	N	Y
16 Lofgren	Y	Y	Y	Y	Y	N	N	N
17 Farr	Y	Y	Y	Y	Y	Y	N	N
18 Condit	Y	Y	Y	Y	Y	Y	N	Y
19 ***Radanovich***	Y	N	N	Y	Y	N	Y	Y
20 Dooley	Y	Y	Y	Y	Y	N	N	N
21 ***Thomas***	Y	N	N	Y	Y	N	N	N
22 Capps	Y	Y	Y	Y	Y	N	N	N
23 ***Gallegly***	?	?	N	Y	Y	N	N	N
24 Sherman	Y	Y	Y	Y	Y	N	N	N
25 ***McKeon***	Y	N	N	Y	Y	N	N	N
26 Berman	Y	?	Y	Y	Y	N	N	N
27 ***Rogan***	Y	Y	N	Y	Y	Y	Y	Y
28 ***Dreier***	Y	N	N	Y	Y	N	N	N
29 Waxman	Y	Y	Y	Y	Y	?	N	N
30 Becerra	Y	Y	Y	Y	Y	N	N	N
31 Martinez	Y	Y	Y	Y	Y	N	N	N
32 Dixon	Y	Y	Y	Y	Y	N	N	N
33 Roybal-Allard	Y	Y	Y	Y	Y	N	N	N
34 Napolitano	Y	Y	Y	Y	Y	N	N	N
35 Waters	?	Y	Y	Y	Y	N	N	N
36 ***Kuykendall***	Y	N	N	Y	Y	N	N	N
37 Millender-McD.	Y	Y	Y	Y	Y	N	N	N
38 ***Horn***	Y	Y	N	Y	Y	N	N	N
39 ***Royce***	Y	Y	N	Y	Y	Y	N	Y
40 ***Lewis***	Y	N	N	Y	Y	N	N	N
41 ***Miller, Gary***	Y	?	N	Y	Y	N	Y	N
42 Vacant								
43 ***Calvert***	Y	N	N	Y	Y	N	Y	N
44 ***Bono***	Y	N	N	Y	Y	Y	Y	Y
45 ***Rohrabacher***	Y	N	N	Y	Y	Y	N	Y
46 Sanchez	Y	Y	Y	Y	Y	N	N	N
47 ***Cox***	?	?	?	?	?	Y	N	Y
48 ***Packard***	Y	N	N	Y	Y	N	Y	N
49 ***Bilbray***	Y	Y	?	?	?	?	?	?
50 Filner	Y	Y	Y	Y	Y	N	N	N
51 ***Cunningham***	Y	N	N	Y	Y	N	?	N
52 ***Hunter***	N	N	N	Y	Y	Y	Y	Y
COLORADO								
1 DeGette	Y	Y	Y	Y	Y	N	N	N
2 Udall	Y	Y	Y	Y	Y	N	N	N
3 ***McInnis***	Y	Y	N	Y	Y	Y	Y	Y
4 ***Schaffer***	N	N	N	Y	Y	Y	Y	Y
5 ***Hefley***	Y	?	N	Y	Y	Y	Y	Y
6 ***Tancredo***	Y	N	N	Y	Y	Y	Y	Y
CONNECTICUT								
1 Larson	Y	Y	Y	Y	Y	N	N	N
2 Gejdenson	Y	Y	Y	Y	Y	N	N	N
3 DeLauro	Y	Y	Y	Y	Y	N	N	N
4 ***Shays***	Y	N	N	Y	Y	N	N	N
5 Maloney	Y	Y	Y	Y	Y	N	N	N
6 ***Johnson***	?	N	N	Y	Y	N	?	?
DELAWARE								
AL ***Castle***	Y	Y	N	Y	Y	N	N	N
FLORIDA								
1 ***Scarborough***	N	Y	?	?	?	?	Y	Y
2 Boyd	Y	Y	Y	Y	Y	N	N	N
3 Brown	?	Y	Y	Y	Y	N	N	N
4 ***Fowler***	?	?	N	Y	Y	N	N	N
5 Thurman	Y	Y	Y	Y	Y	N	N	N
6 ***Stearns***	?	Y	N	Y	Y	Y	Y	N
7 ***Mica***	Y	?	N	Y	Y	Y	Y	N
8 ***McCollum***	Y	Y	N	Y	Y	N	Y	N
9 ***Bilirakis***	N	?	N	Y	Y	N	Y	N
10 ***Young***	Y	N	N	Y	Y	N	N	N
11 Davis	?	Y	Y	Y	Y	N	N	N
12 ***Canady***	Y	N	N	Y	Y	N	Y	N
13 ***Miller***	Y	N	N	Y	Y	Y	N	Y
14 ***Goss***	Y	N	N	Y	Y	N	N	N
15 ***Weldon***	Y	Y	N	?	Y	N	Y	N
16 ***Foley***	Y	N	N	Y	Y	N	N	N
17 Meek	Y	Y	Y	Y	Y	N	N	N
18 ***Ros-Lehtinen***	Y	?	N	Y	Y	N	N	N
19 Wexler	Y	Y	Y	Y	Y	N	N	N
20 Deutsch	+	Y	Y	Y	Y	N	N	N
21 ***Diaz-Balart***	Y	?	N	Y	Y	N	N	N
22 ***Shaw***	Y	?	N	Y	Y	N	N	N
23 Hastings	Y	?	Y	Y	Y	N	N	N
GEORGIA								
1 ***Kingston***	N	Y	N	Y	Y	Y	Y	Y
2 Bishop	Y	Y	Y	Y	Y	N	N	N
3 ***Collins***	N	N	N	Y	Y	Y	Y	Y
4 McKinney	Y	Y	Y	Y	Y	Y	N	Y
5 Lewis	Y	Y	Y	Y	Y	N	N	N
6 ***Isakson***	Y	N	N	Y	Y	N	N	N
7 ***Barr***	N	N	N	Y	Y	Y	Y	Y
8 ***Chambliss***	Y	N	N	Y	Y	N	Y	N
9 ***Deal***	N	?	N	Y	Y	N	Y	N
10 ***Norwood***	Y	N	N	Y	Y	Y	Y	N
11 ***Linder***	Y	N	N	Y	Y	Y	Y	Y
HAWAII								
1 Abercrombie	Y	Y	?	?	?	?	N	N
2 Mink	Y	Y	Y	Y	Y	N	N	N
IDAHO								
1 ***Chenoweth***	N	N	N	Y	Y	Y	Y	Y
2 ***Simpson***	Y	N	N	Y	Y	N	N	N
ILLINOIS								
1 Rush	Y	Y	Y	Y	Y	N	N	N
2 Jackson	Y	Y	Y	Y	Y	N	N	N
3 Lipinski	Y	Y	Y	Y	Y	Y	Y	N
4 Gutierrez	+	+	Y	Y	Y	N	N	N
5 Blagojevich	?	Y	Y	Y	Y	N	N	N
6 ***Hyde***	Y	N	N	Y	Y	N	Y	N
7 Davis	Y	Y	Y	Y	Y	N	N	N
8 ***Crane***	?	N	N	Y	Y	Y	Y	N
9 Schakowsky	Y	Y	Y	Y	Y	N	N	N
10 ***Porter***	Y	Y	N	Y	Y	N	N	N
11 ***Weller***	+	Y	N	Y	Y	N	Y	N
12 Costello	Y	?	Y	Y	Y	N	Y	N
13 ***Biggert***	Y	Y	N	Y	Y	N	N	N
14 ***Hastert***		N						

ND Northern Democrats SD Southern Democrats

	354	355	356	357	358	359	360	361
15 ***Ewing***	Y	N	N	Y	Y	N	N	N
16 ***Manzullo***	?	?	N	Y	Y	N	Y	N
17 Evans	Y	Y	Y	Y	Y	Y	N	N
18 ***LaHood***	Y	?	N	Y	Y	N	Y	N
19 Phelps	Y	Y	Y	Y	Y	N	Y	N
20 ***Shimkus***	N	N	N	Y	Y	N	Y	N
INDIANA								
1 Visclosky	Y	Y	Y	Y	Y	Y	N	Y
2 ***McIntosh***	N	?	–	Y	Y	Y	Y	Y
3 Roemer	Y	+	Y	Y	Y	N	N	N
4 ***Souder***	N	?	N	Y	Y	Y	Y	N
5 ***Buyer***	Y	?	N	Y	Y	N	Y	N
6 ***Burton***	+	N	N	Y	Y	Y	Y	Y
7 ***Pease***	Y	N	N	Y	Y	Y	Y	Y
8 ***Hostettler***	N	N	N	Y	Y	Y	Y	Y
9 Hill	Y	Y	Y	Y	Y	N	N	N
10 Carson	Y	+	Y	Y	Y	N	N	N
IOWA								
1 ***Leach***	Y	Y	N	Y	Y	N	N	N
2 ***Nussle***	Y	N	N	Y	Y	N	Y	N
3 Boswell	Y	Y	Y	Y	Y	N	N	N
4 ***Ganske***	Y	Y	?	Y	Y	N	N	N
5 ***Latham***	Y	Y	N	Y	Y	N	Y	N
KANSAS								
1 ***Moran***	Y	N	N	Y	Y	N	Y	N
2 ***Ryun***	N	N	N	Y	Y	Y	Y	Y
3 Moore	Y	Y	Y	Y	Y	N	N	N
4 ***Tiahrt***	N	?	N	Y	Y	N	Y	N
KENTUCKY								
1 ***Whitfield***	N	N	N	Y	Y	N	Y	N
2 ***Lewis***	N	N	N	Y	Y	N	Y	N
3 ***Northup***	Y	Y	N	Y	Y	N	N	N
4 Lucas	N	Y	Y	Y	Y	N	Y	N
5 ***Rogers***	N	N	N	Y	Y	N	Y	N
6 ***Fletcher***	N	Y	N	Y	Y	Y	Y	N
LOUISIANA								
1 ***Vitter***	N	N	N	Y	Y	N	Y	N
2 Jefferson	Y	?	Y	Y	Y	N	N	N
3 ***Tauzin***	?	?	N	Y	Y	N	N	N
4 ***McCrery***	?	N	N	Y	Y	N	Y	N
5 ***Cooksey***	Y	Y	?	?	?	?	N	N
6 ***Baker***	Y	?	N	Y	Y	N	Y	N
7 John	Y	?	Y	Y	Y	N	N	N
MAINE								
1 Allen	Y	Y	Y	Y	Y	N	N	N
2 Baldacci	Y	Y	Y	Y	Y	N	N	N
MARYLAND								
1 ***Gilchrest***	Y	Y	N	Y	Y	N	N	N
2 ***Ehrlich***	Y	N	N	Y	Y	Y	N	N
3 Cardin	Y	Y	Y	Y	Y	N	N	N
4 Wynn	Y	Y	Y	Y	Y	N	N	N
5 Hoyer	Y	Y	Y	Y	Y	N	N	N
6 ***Bartlett***	N	N	N	Y	Y	Y	Y	Y
7 Cummings	?	Y	Y	Y	Y	N	N	N
8 ***Morella***	Y	Y	N	Y	Y	N	N	N
MASSACHUSETTS								
1 Olver	Y	Y	Y	Y	Y	N	N	N
2 Neal	Y	Y	Y	Y	Y	N	N	N
3 McGovern	Y	Y	Y	Y	Y	N	N	N
4 Frank	?	?	?	?	?	?	?	?
5 Meehan	Y	?	Y	Y	Y	N	N	N
6 Tierney	?	Y	Y	Y	Y	Y	N	N
7 Markey	?	Y	Y	Y	Y	N	N	N
8 Capuano	Y	Y	Y	Y	Y	N	N	N
9 Moakley	Y	Y	Y	Y	Y	N	N	N
10 Delahunt	Y	Y	Y	Y	Y	N	N	N
MICHIGAN								
1 Stupak	Y	Y	Y	Y	Y	Y	N	Y
2 ***Hoekstra***	Y	?	N	Y	Y	Y	Y	Y
3 ***Ehlers***	+	N	N	Y	Y	N	N	N
4 ***Camp***	Y	?	N	Y	Y	N	Y	N
5 Barcia	Y	Y	Y	Y	Y	Y	N	N
6 ***Upton***	Y	Y	N	Y	Y	N	N	N
7 ***Smith***	Y	?	N	Y	Y	Y	N	Y
8 Stabenow	Y	Y	Y	Y	Y	N	N	N
9 Kildee	Y	Y	Y	Y	Y	N	N	N
10 Bonior	Y	?	Y	Y	Y	N	N	N
11 ***Knollenberg***	Y	N	N	Y	Y	N	N	N
12 Levin	Y	Y	Y	Y	Y	N	N	N
13 Rivers	Y	Y	Y	Y	Y	Y	N	N
14 Conyers	Y	Y	Y	Y	Y	N	N	N
15 Kilpatrick	Y	Y	Y	Y	Y	N	N	N
16 Dingell	Y	Y	Y	Y	Y	N	N	N
MINNESOTA								
1 ***Gutknecht***	Y	N	N	Y	Y	N	Y	N
2 Minge	Y	Y	Y	Y	Y	N	N	N
3 ***Ramstad***	Y	N	N	Y	Y	Y	N	N
4 Vento	Y	Y	Y	Y	Y	N	N	N
5 Sabo	Y	Y	Y	Y	Y	N	N	N
6 Luther	?	?	Y	Y	Y	Y	N	N
7 Peterson	Y	Y	Y	Y	Y	Y	Y	N
8 Oberstar	Y	Y	Y	Y	Y	N	N	N
MISSISSIPPI								
1 ***Wicker***	N	N	N	Y	Y	N	Y	N
2 Thompson	Y	Y	Y	Y	Y	N	?	?
3 ***Pickering***	N	N	N	Y	Y	N	+	–
4 Shows	N	Y	Y	Y	Y	N	Y	N
5 Taylor	N	Y	Y	Y	Y	N	Y	N
MISSOURI								
1 Clay	Y	?	Y	Y	Y	N	N	N
2 ***Talent***	N	N	N	Y	Y	N	Y	N
3 Gephardt	Y	Y	Y	?	?	?	N	N
4 Skelton	?	?	Y	Y	Y	N	N	N
5 McCarthy	Y	Y	Y	Y	Y	N	N	N
6 Danner	Y	?	Y	Y	Y	N	Y	N
7 ***Blunt***	Y	N	N	Y	Y	N	Y	N
8 ***Emerson***	N	Y	N	Y	Y	N	Y	N
9 ***Hulshof***	N	Y	N	Y	Y	N	N	N
MONTANA								
AL ***Hill***	N	Y	N	Y	Y	N	Y	N
NEBRASKA								
1 ***Bereuter***	Y	Y	N	Y	Y	N	N	N
2 ***Terry***	Y	Y	N	Y	Y	Y	Y	Y
3 ***Barrett***	Y	N	N	Y	Y	N	Y	N
NEVADA								
1 Berkley	Y	Y	Y	Y	Y	Y	N	N
2 ***Gibbons***	N	Y	N	Y	Y	N	N	N
NEW HAMPSHIRE								
1 ***Sununu***	N	N	N	Y	Y	Y	N	N
2 ***Bass***	N	N	N	Y	Y	Y	N	N
NEW JERSEY								
1 Andrews	Y	Y	Y	Y	Y	Y	N	N
2 ***LoBiondo***	Y	N	N	Y	Y	Y	Y	N
3 ***Saxton***	Y	N	N	Y	Y	N	Y	N
4 ***Smith***	Y	Y	N	Y	Y	N	?	N
5 ***Roukema***	Y	?	N	Y	Y	N	N	N
6 Pallone	Y	Y	Y	Y	Y	N	N	N
7 ***Franks***	Y	Y	N	Y	Y	N	N	N
8 Pascrell	Y	Y	Y	Y	Y	Y	N	N
9 Rothman	Y	Y	Y	Y	Y	N	N	N
10 Payne	Y	Y	Y	Y	Y	N	N	N
11 ***Frelinghuysen***	Y	Y	N	Y	Y	N	N	N
12 Holt	Y	Y	Y	Y	Y	N	N	N
13 Menendez	Y	Y	Y	Y	Y	N	N	N
NEW MEXICO								
1 ***Wilson***	Y	N	N	Y	Y	N	N	N
2 ***Skeen***	Y	N	N	Y	Y	N	N	N
3 Udall	Y	Y	Y	Y	Y	N	N	N
NEW YORK								
1 Forbes	Y	Y	Y	Y	Y	N	Y	N
2 ***Lazio***	Y	Y	N	Y	Y	N	N	N
3 ***King***	Y	N	N	Y	Y	N	Y	N
4 McCarthy	Y	Y	Y	Y	Y	N	N	N
5 Ackerman	Y	Y	Y	Y	Y	N	N	N
6 Meeks	Y	Y	Y	Y	Y	N	N	N
7 Crowley	Y	Y	Y	Y	Y	N	N	N
8 Nadler	?	Y	Y	Y	Y	Y	N	N
9 Weiner	Y	Y	Y	Y	Y	N	N	N
10 Towns	?	Y	Y	Y	Y	N	N	N
11 Owens	?	Y	Y	Y	Y	N	–	–
12 Velázquez	Y	Y	Y	Y	Y	N	N	N
13 ***Fossella***	Y	N	N	Y	Y	N	Y	N
14 Maloney	Y	Y	Y	Y	Y	N	N	N
15 Rangel	Y	Y	Y	Y	Y	Y	N	N
16 Serrano	Y	Y	Y	Y	Y	N	N	?
17 Engel	?	Y	Y	Y	Y	N	N	N
18 Lowey	Y	Y	Y	Y	Y	N	N	N
19 ***Kelly***	Y	Y	N	Y	Y	N	N	N
20 ***Gilman***	Y	Y	N	Y	Y	N	N	N
21 McNulty	Y	Y	Y	Y	Y	N	N	N
22 ***Sweeney***	Y	N	N	Y	Y	N	N	N
23 ***Boehlert***	Y	Y	N	Y	Y	N	N	N
24 ***McHugh***	Y	N	N	Y	Y	N	N	N
25 ***Walsh***	Y	Y	N	Y	Y	N	N	N
26 Hinchey	Y	Y	Y	Y	Y	Y	?	?
27 ***Reynolds***	Y	N	N	Y	Y	N	Y	N
28 Slaughter	Y	Y	Y	Y	Y	N	N	N
29 LaFalce	Y	Y	Y	Y	Y	N	N	N
30 ***Quinn***	Y	?	N	Y	Y	N	Y	N
31 ***Houghton***	Y	Y	N	Y	Y	N	N	N
NORTH CAROLINA								
1 Clayton	Y	Y	?	?	?	N	N	N
2 Etheridge	Y	Y	Y	Y	Y	N	N	N
3 ***Jones***	N	Y	N	Y	Y	Y	Y	Y
4 Price	Y	Y	Y	Y	Y	N	N	N
5 ***Burr***	?	?	N	Y	Y	N	Y	N
6 ***Coble***	N	N	N	Y	Y	Y	Y	Y
7 McIntyre	N	Y	Y	Y	Y	Y	N	Y
8 ***Hayes***	N	N	N	Y	Y	N	Y	Y
9 ***Myrick***	Y	N	N	Y	Y	Y	Y	Y
10 ***Ballenger***	Y	?	N	Y	Y	N	N	N
11 ***Taylor***	N	N	?	?	?	N	Y	N
12 Watt	Y	Y	Y	Y	Y	N	N	N
NORTH DAKOTA								
AL Pomeroy	Y	?	Y	Y	Y	N	N	N
OHIO								
1 ***Chabot***	N	?	N	Y	Y	Y	Y	Y
2 ***Portman***	Y	N	N	Y	Y	N	Y	N
3 Hall	?	Y	Y	Y	Y	?	N	N
4 ***Oxley***	Y	?	N	Y	Y	N	N	N
5 ***Gillmor***	Y	N	N	Y	Y	N	N	N
6 Strickland	Y	Y	Y	Y	Y	Y	N	N
7 ***Hobson***	Y	N	N	Y	Y	Y	N	N
8 ***Boehner***	Y	?	N	Y	Y	N	Y	N
9 Kaptur	Y	Y	Y	Y	Y	Y	N	N
10 Kucinich	Y	Y	Y	Y	Y	Y	N	N
11 Jones	Y	Y	Y	Y	Y	N	N	N
12 ***Kasich***	Y	N	N	Y	Y	Y	Y	Y
13 Brown	Y	Y	Y	Y	Y	Y	N	N
14 Sawyer	Y	Y	Y	Y	Y	N	N	N
15 ***Pryce***	Y	N	?	?	?	?	?	?
16 ***Regula***	Y	Y	N	Y	Y	N	N	N
17 Traficant	Y	Y	Y	Y	Y	Y	N	N
18 ***Ney***	N	N	N	Y	?	N	Y	N
19 ***LaTourette***	Y	Y	N	Y	Y	N	N	N
OKLAHOMA								
1 ***Largent***	N	Y	N	Y	Y	Y	Y	N
2 ***Coburn***	N	N	N	Y	Y	Y	Y	Y
3 ***Watkins***	N	?	N	Y	Y	N	Y	N
4 ***Watts***	N	Y	N	Y	Y	N	Y	N
5 ***Istook***	Y	N	N	Y	Y	N	Y	Y
6 ***Lucas***	N	N	N	Y	Y	N	Y	N
OREGON								
1 Wu	Y	?	Y	Y	Y	N	N	N
2 ***Walden***	Y	N	N	Y	Y	N	N	N
3 Blumenauer	Y	Y	Y	Y	Y	N	N	N
4 DeFazio	Y	?	Y	Y	Y	Y	N	Y
5 Hooley	Y	Y	Y	Y	Y	N	N	N
PENNSYLVANIA								
1 Brady	Y	Y	Y	Y	Y	N	N	N
2 Fattah	Y	Y	Y	Y	Y	N	N	N
3 Borski	Y	Y	Y	Y	Y	N	N	N
4 Klink	Y	Y	Y	Y	Y	N	N	?
5 ***Peterson***	?	?	?	?	?	?	?	?
6 Holden	Y	Y	Y	Y	Y	Y	N	N
7 ***Weldon***	Y	Y	N	Y	Y	N	N	N
8 ***Greenwood***	Y	N	N	Y	Y	N	N	N
9 ***Shuster***	Y	N	N	Y	Y	?	Y	N
10 ***Sherwood***	Y	N	N	Y	Y	–	Y	N
11 Kanjorski	Y	Y	Y	Y	Y	Y	N	N
12 Murtha	N	Y	Y	Y	Y	N	N	N
13 Hoeffel	Y	Y	Y	Y	Y	N	N	N
14 Coyne	Y	?	Y	Y	Y	N	N	N
15 ***Toomey***	Y	N	N	Y	Y	Y	N	N
16 ***Pitts***	N	N	N	Y	Y	N	Y	N
17 ***Gekas***	?	N	N	Y	Y	N	N	N
18 Doyle	Y	Y	Y	Y	Y	N	N	N
19 ***Goodling***	Y	N	N	Y	Y	N	Y	N
20 Mascara	Y	Y	Y	Y	Y	N	N	N
21 ***English***	?	N	N	Y	Y	N	Y	N
RHODE ISLAND								
1 Kennedy	Y	Y	Y	Y	Y	N	N	N
2 Weygand	Y	Y	Y	Y	Y	N	N	N
SOUTH CAROLINA								
1 ***Sanford***	N	N	N	Y	Y	Y	Y	Y
2 ***Spence***	N	N	N	Y	Y	N	Y	N
3 ***Graham***	N	Y	N	Y	Y	Y	Y	N
4 ***DeMint***	Y	N	N	Y	Y	Y	Y	Y
5 Spratt	Y	Y	Y	Y	Y	N	N	N
6 Clyburn	Y	Y	Y	Y	Y	N	N	N
SOUTH DAKOTA								
AL ***Thune***	N	N	N	Y	Y	N	Y	Y
TENNESSEE								
1 ***Jenkins***	N	N	N	Y	Y	N	Y	N
2 ***Duncan***	Y	Y	N	Y	Y	Y	Y	Y
3 ***Wamp***	N	N	N	Y	Y	Y	Y	Y
4 ***Hilleary***	N	Y	N	Y	Y	Y	Y	Y
5 Clement	Y	Y	Y	Y	Y	N	N	N
6 Gordon	Y	Y	Y	Y	Y	N	N	N
7 ***Bryant***	Y	N	N	Y	Y	N	Y	N
8 Tanner	Y	Y	Y	Y	Y	N	N	N
9 Ford	Y	Y	Y	Y	Y	N	N	N
TEXAS								
1 Sandlin	Y	Y	Y	Y	Y	N	N	N
2 Turner	Y	Y	Y	Y	Y	N	N	N
3 ***Johnson, Sam***	?	N	N	Y	Y	N	Y	N
4 Hall	N	N	Y	Y	Y	N	Y	N
5 ***Sessions***	N	N	N	Y	Y	N	Y	Y
6 ***Barton***	?	Y	N	Y	Y	N	Y	N
7 ***Archer***	N	N	N	Y	Y	Y	Y	N
8 ***Brady***	N	N	N	Y	Y	N	N	N
9 Lampson	Y	Y	Y	Y	Y	N	N	N
10 Doggett	Y	Y	Y	Y	Y	N	N	N
11 Edwards	Y	Y	Y	Y	Y	N	N	N
12 ***Granger***	Y	N	N	Y	Y	N	N	N
13 ***Thornberry***	N	N	N	Y	Y	N	N	N
14 ***Paul***	N	N	N	Y	Y	Y	Y	Y
15 Hinojosa	Y	Y	Y	Y	Y	N	N	N
16 Reyes	Y	Y	?	?	?	?	N	N
17 Stenholm	Y	Y	Y	Y	Y	N	N	N
18 Jackson-Lee	Y	Y	Y	Y	Y	N	N	N
19 ***Combest***	Y	N	N	Y	Y	N	Y	N
20 Gonzalez	Y	Y	Y	Y	Y	N	N	N
21 ***Smith***	Y	N	N	?	Y	N	N	N
22 ***DeLay***	N	N	N	Y	Y	N	Y	N
23 ***Bonilla***	N	N	N	Y	Y	N	Y	N
24 Frost	Y	Y	Y	Y	Y	N	N	N
25 Bentsen	Y	Y	Y	Y	Y	N	N	N
26 ***Armey***	N	N	N	Y	Y	Y	Y	Y
27 Ortiz	+	+	Y	Y	Y	N	N	N
28 Rodriguez	Y	Y	Y	Y	Y	N	N	N
29 Green	Y	Y	Y	Y	Y	N	N	N
30 Johnson, E.B.	Y	Y	Y	Y	Y	N	N	N
UTAH								
1 ***Hansen***	N	N	N	Y	Y	N	Y	N
2 ***Cook***	Y	Y	N	Y	Y	N	Y	N
3 ***Cannon***	N	N	N	Y	Y	Y	Y	Y
VERMONT								
AL *Sanders*	Y	Y	Y	Y	Y	Y	N	Y
VIRGINIA								
1 ***Bateman***	Y	N	N	Y	Y	N	N	N
2 Pickett	N	?	Y	Y	Y	N	N	N
3 Scott	Y	Y	Y	Y	Y	N	N	N
4 Sisisky	N	Y	Y	Y	Y	N	N	N
5 Goode	N	?	N	Y	Y	Y	Y	Y
6 ***Goodlatte***	N	N	N	Y	Y	Y	Y	N
7 ***Bliley***	Y	N	N	Y	Y	N	Y	N
8 Moran	Y	Y	Y	Y	?	N	N	N
9 Boucher	N	?	Y	Y	Y	N	N	N
10 ***Wolf***	Y	Y	N	Y	Y	N	?	N
11 ***Davis***	Y	Y	N	Y	Y	N	N	N
WASHINGTON								
1 Inslee	Y	Y	Y	Y	Y	N	N	N
2 ***Metcalf***	Y	N	N	?	Y	Y	Y	N
3 Baird	Y	Y	Y	Y	Y	N	N	N
4 ***Hastings***	Y	N	N	Y	?	N	Y	N
5 ***Nethercutt***	Y	N	N	Y	Y	N	N	N
6 Dicks	?	?	Y	Y	Y	N	N	N
7 McDermott	?	?	+	+	+	–	–	–
8 ***Dunn***	Y	N	N	Y	Y	N	N	N
9 Smith	Y	?	Y	Y	Y	N	N	N
WEST VIRGINIA								
1 Mollohan	N	Y	Y	Y	Y	N	?	?
2 Wise	N	?	Y	Y	Y	N	N	N
3 Rahall	N	Y	Y	Y	Y	N	Y	N
WISCONSIN								
1 ***Ryan***	Y	Y	N	Y	Y	N	Y	N
2 Baldwin	Y	Y	Y	Y	Y	Y	N	N
3 Kind	Y	Y	Y	Y	Y	N	N	N
4 Kleczka	?	Y	Y	Y	Y	N	N	N
5 Barrett	Y	Y	Y	Y	Y	Y	N	N
6 ***Petri***	Y	Y	N	Y	Y	Y	Y	N
7 Obey	Y	Y	Y	Y	Y	Y	N	N
8 ***Green***	Y	Y	N	Y	Y	N	Y	N
9 ***Sensenbrenner***	Y	N	N	Y	Y	Y	Y	N
WYOMING								
AL ***Cubin***	?	Y	N	Y	Y	N	Y	N

Southern states - Ala., Ark., Fla., Ga., Ky., La., Miss., N.C., Okla., S.C., Tenn., Texas, Va.

House Votes 362, 363, 364, 365, 366, 367, 368, 369

362. HR 2606. Fiscal 2000 Foreign Operations Appropriations/Passage. Passage of the bill to appropriate $12.7 billion for foreign operations in fiscal 2000. Passed 385-35: R 190-24; D 194-11 (ND 145-6, SD 49-5); I 1-0. Aug. 3, 1999. A "nay" was a vote in support of the president's position.

363. HR 2031. Internet Alcohol Sales/Engrossment and Third Reading. Engrossment and third reading of the bill to assist states in restricting alcohol sales over the Internet and allow state attorneys general to prosecute in federal court out-of-state companies that ship alcohol in violation of state law via the Internet, mail-order catalogs and telephone sales. Agreed to 325-99: R 194-24; D 130-75 (ND 82-68, SD 48-7); I 1-0. Aug. 3, 1999.

364. HR 2031. Internet Alcohol Sales/Passage. Passage of the bill to assist states in restricting alcohol sales over the Internet and allow state attorneys general to prosecute in federal court out-of-state companies that ship alcohol in violation of state law via the Internet, mail-order catalogs and telephone sales. Passed 310-112: R 176-41; D 133-71 (ND 85-65, SD 48-6); I 1-0. Aug. 3, 1999.

365. H J Res 58. Trade Ties With Vietnam/Passage. Passage of the joint resolution to disapprove the presidential waiver that allows U.S. trade credits and guarantees for companies that do business with Vietnam. Rejected 130-297: R 95-123; D 34-174 (ND 27-126, SD 7-48); I 1-0. Aug. 3, 1999. A "nay" was a vote in support of the president's position.

366. HR 987. OSHA Ergonomics Regulations/Passage. Passage of the bill to prevent the Occupational Safety and Health Administration (OSHA) from issuing new ergonomics rules until the National Academy of Sciences has completed a congressionally mandated study on the issue. Passed 217-209: R 202-17; D 15-191 (ND 1-152, SD 14-39); I 0-1. Aug. 3, 1999. A "nay" was a vote in suppot of the president's position.

367. Procedural Motion/Journal. Approval of the House Journal of Tuesday, August 3, 1999. Approved 366-56: R 199-18; D 166-38 (ND 120-31, SD 46-7); I 1-0. Aug. 4, 1999.

368. HR 1907. Modernize Patent Process/Passage. Coble, R-N.C., motion to suspend the rules and pass the bill to require that applications be published at the same time and to the same extent that they are published in foreign countries. The bill would waive the publication requirement if a patent application is subject to a secrecy order, or if the application is no longer pending and the patent has been granted. The requirements also would be waived if a similar application has not been filed in a foreign country. The measure would also reorganize the U.S. Patent and Trademark Office as an agency within the Commerce Department, but allow it to retain control over its own budget. Motion agreed to 376-43: R 206-8; D 170-34 (ND 120-31, SD 50-3); I 0-1. Aug. 4, 1999. A two-thirds majority of those present and voting (280 in this case) is required for passage under suspension of the rules.

369. HR 2670. Fiscal 2000 Commerce-Justice-State Appropriations/Rule. Adoption of the rule (H Res 273) to provide for House floor consideration of the fiscal 2000 appropriations bill for the departments of Commerce, Justice, and State and the federal judiciary. Adopted 221-205: R 217-1; D 4-203 (ND 3-151, SD 1-52); I 0-1. Aug. 4, 1999.

Key

- Y Voted for (yea).
- # Paired for.
- + Announced for.
- N Voted against (nay).
- X Paired against.
- – Announced against.
- P Voted "present."
- C Voted "present" to avoid possible conflict of interest.
- ? Did not vote or otherwise make a position known.

•

Democrats ***Republicans***
Independents

	362	363	364	365	366	367	368	369
ALABAMA								
1 ***Callahan***	Y	Y	Y	N	Y	Y	Y	Y
2 ***Everett***	Y	Y	Y	Y	Y	Y	Y	Y
3 ***Riley***	Y	Y	Y	Y	Y	N	Y	Y
4 ***Aderholt***	Y	Y	Y	Y	Y	N	Y	Y
5 Cramer	Y	Y	Y	N	N	Y	Y	N
6 ***Bachus***	Y	Y	Y	N	Y	Y	N	Y
7 Hilliard	Y	Y	Y	N	N	N	Y	N
ALASKA								
AL ***Young***	Y	Y	N	Y	Y	Y	Y	Y
ARIZONA								
1 ***Salmon***	Y	Y	Y	N	Y	Y	Y	Y
2 Pastor	Y	N	Y	N	N	Y	Y	N
3 ***Stump***	N	Y	Y	Y	Y	Y	Y	Y
4 ***Shadegg***	Y	Y	Y	Y	Y	Y	Y	Y
5 ***Kolbe***	Y	Y	N	N	Y	Y	Y	Y
6 ***Hayworth***	Y	Y	N	Y	Y	Y	Y	Y
ARKANSAS								
1 Berry	Y	Y	Y	N	Y	Y	Y	N
2 Snyder	Y	Y	Y	N	N	Y	Y	N
3 ***Hutchinson***	Y	Y	Y	Y	Y	N	Y	Y
4 ***Dickey***	Y	Y	Y	N	Y	N	Y	Y
CALIFORNIA								
1 Thompson	Y	N	N	N	N	N	Y	N
2 ***Herger***	N	Y	Y	N	Y	Y	Y	Y
3 ***Ose***	Y	Y	Y	N	Y	Y	Y	Y
4 ***Doolittle***	N	Y	N	Y	Y	Y	Y	Y
5 Matsui	Y	N	N	N	N	Y	Y	N
6 Woolsey	Y	N	N	N	N	Y	Y	N
7 Miller, George	Y	N	N	N	N	?	?	N
8 Pelosi	Y	N	N	Y	N	Y	Y	N
9 Lee	Y	N	N	N	N	Y	N	N
10 Tauscher	Y	N	N	N	N	Y	Y	N
11 ***Pombo***	N	N	N	Y	Y	Y	Y	Y
12 Lantos	?	?	?	?	?	?	?	?
13 Stark	N	N	N	N	N	N	N	N
14 Eshoo	Y	N	N	N	N	Y	Y	N
15 ***Campbell***	Y	Y	Y	N	N	Y	Y	Y
16 Lofgren	Y	N	N	Y	N	Y	Y	N
17 Farr	Y	N	N	N	N	Y	Y	N
18 Condit	N	Y	Y	N	N	N	Y	N
19 ***Radanovich***	?	N	N	Y	Y	Y	?	Y
20 Dooley	Y	N	N	N	Y	Y	Y	N
21 ***Thomas***	Y	N	N	N	Y	Y	Y	Y
22 Capps	Y	N	N	N	N	Y	Y	N
23 ***Gallegly***	Y	N	N	N	Y	Y	Y	Y
24 Sherman	Y	N	N	N	N	Y	Y	N
25 ***McKeon***	Y	Y	N	N	Y	Y	Y	Y
26 Berman	Y	N	N	N	N	Y	Y	N
27 ***Rogan***	Y	Y	Y	Y	Y	N	Y	Y
28 ***Dreier***	Y	Y	N	N	Y	Y	Y	Y
29 Waxman	Y	N	N	N	N	Y	Y	N
30 Becerra	Y	Y	Y	N	N	Y	Y	N
31 Martinez	Y	N	N	Y	N	Y	Y	N
32 Dixon	Y	Y	N	N	N	Y	Y	N
33 Roybal-Allard	Y	N	N	N	N	Y	Y	N
34 Napolitano	Y	N	N	N	N	Y	Y	N
35 Waters	Y	N	N	N	N	Y	N	N
36 ***Kuykendall***	Y	N	N	N	Y	Y	Y	Y
37 Millender-McD.	Y	N	N	N	N	Y	Y	N
38 ***Horn***	Y	N	N	N	N	Y	Y	Y
39 ***Royce***	Y	Y	Y	Y	Y	Y	Y	Y
40 ***Lewis***	Y	N	N	N	Y	Y	Y	Y
41 ***Miller, Gary***	Y	Y	Y	Y	Y	Y	Y	Y
42 Vacant								
43 ***Calvert***	Y	N	N	N	Y	Y	Y	Y
44 ***Bono***	Y	Y	Y	Y	Y	Y	Y	Y
45 ***Rohrabacher***	N	N	N	Y	Y	Y	Y	Y
46 Sanchez	Y	Y	Y	Y	N	Y	Y	N
47 ***Cox***	Y	N	N	Y	Y	Y	?	Y
48 ***Packard***	Y	N	N	N	Y	Y	Y	Y
49 ***Bilbray***	?	?	?	?	?	?	?	?
50 Filner	Y	Y	Y	N	N	N	N	N
51 ***Cunningham***	Y	Y	Y	Y	Y	Y	Y	Y
52 ***Hunter***	Y	N	N	Y	Y	Y	N	Y
COLORADO								
1 DeGette	Y	N	N	N	N	Y	Y	N
2 Udall	Y	Y	Y	N	N	N	Y	N
3 ***McInnis***	N	Y	Y	N	Y	Y	Y	Y
4 ***Schaffer***	Y	Y	Y	Y	Y	N	Y	Y
5 ***Hefley***	N	Y	Y	Y	Y	Y	Y	Y
6 ***Tancredo***	Y	Y	Y	N	Y	P	Y	Y
CONNECTICUT								
1 Larson	Y	Y	Y	N	N	Y	Y	N
2 Gejdenson	Y	N	N	N	N	Y	Y	N
3 DeLauro	Y	N	N	N	N	Y	Y	N
4 ***Shays***	Y	N	N	N	Y	Y	Y	Y
5 Maloney	Y	Y	Y	N	N	Y	Y	N
6 ***Johnson***	?	Y	Y	N	Y	Y	Y	Y
DELAWARE								
AL ***Castle***	Y	Y	Y	N	Y	Y	Y	Y
FLORIDA								
1 ***Scarborough***	Y	Y	Y	Y	Y	Y	Y	Y
2 Boyd	Y	Y	Y	N	Y	Y	Y	N
3 Brown	Y	Y	Y	N	N	Y	Y	N
4 ***Fowler***	Y	Y	Y	N	Y	Y	Y	Y
5 Thurman	Y	Y	Y	N	N	Y	Y	N
6 ***Stearns***	N	Y	Y	Y	Y	Y	Y	Y
7 ***Mica***	Y	Y	Y	Y	Y	Y	Y	Y
8 ***McCollum***	Y	Y	Y	Y	Y	Y	Y	Y
9 ***Bilirakis***	Y	Y	Y	Y	Y	Y	Y	Y
10 ***Young***	Y	Y	Y	N	Y	Y	Y	Y
11 Davis	Y	Y	Y	N	N	Y	Y	N
12 ***Canady***	Y	Y	Y	Y	Y	Y	Y	Y
13 ***Miller***	Y	Y	N	Y	Y	Y	Y	Y
14 ***Goss***	Y	Y	N	N	Y	Y	Y	Y
15 ***Weldon***	Y	Y	Y	Y	Y	Y	Y	Y
16 ***Foley***	Y	Y	Y	N	Y	Y	Y	Y
17 Meek	Y	N	?	N	N	Y	Y	N
18 ***Ros-Lehtinen***	Y	Y	Y	Y	Y	Y	Y	Y
19 Wexler	Y	Y	Y	N	N	Y	Y	N
20 Deutsch	Y	Y	Y	N	N	Y	Y	N
21 ***Diaz-Balart***	Y	Y	Y	Y	Y	Y	Y	Y
22 ***Shaw***	Y	Y	N	N	Y	Y	Y	Y
23 Hastings	Y	N	Y	N	N	Y	Y	N
GEORGIA								
1 ***Kingston***	Y	Y	Y	Y	Y	Y	Y	Y
2 Bishop	Y	Y	Y	N	N	Y	Y	N
3 ***Collins***	Y	Y	Y	Y	Y	Y	Y	Y
4 McKinney	Y	N	N	Y	N	N	Y	N
5 Lewis	Y	Y	Y	N	N	N	Y	N
6 ***Isakson***	Y	Y	Y	N	Y	Y	Y	Y
7 ***Barr***	N	Y	Y	Y	Y	Y	Y	Y
8 ***Chambliss***	Y	Y	Y	N	Y	Y	Y	Y
9 ***Deal***	Y	Y	Y	Y	Y	Y	Y	?
10 ***Norwood***	Y	Y	Y	Y	Y	Y	Y	Y
11 ***Linder***	Y	Y	Y	N	Y	Y	Y	Y
HAWAII								
1 Abercrombie	Y	Y	Y	N	N	N	N	N
2 Mink	Y	Y	Y	N	N	N	N	N
IDAHO								
1 ***Chenoweth***	N	Y	Y	Y	Y	N	N	Y
2 ***Simpson***	Y	Y	Y	N	Y	Y	Y	Y
ILLINOIS								
1 Rush	Y	N	N	N	N	Y	Y	N
2 Jackson	Y	N	N	N	N	Y	Y	N
3 Lipinski	Y	Y	Y	N	N	Y	Y	N
4 Gutierrez	Y	N	N	N	N	N	Y	N
5 Blagojevich	Y	Y	Y	N	N	Y	Y	N
6 ***Hyde***	Y	Y	Y	Y	Y	Y	Y	Y
7 Davis	Y	N	N	N	N	Y	N	N
8 ***Crane***	Y	Y	Y	N	Y	N	Y	Y
9 Schakowsky	Y	N	N	N	N	Y	N	N
10 ***Porter***	Y	Y	Y	Y	Y	Y	Y	Y
11 ***Weller***	Y	Y	Y	N	N	N	Y	Y
12 Costello	Y	Y	Y	Y	N	N	Y	N
13 ***Biggert***	Y	Y	Y	N	Y	Y	Y	Y
14 ***Hastert***	Y				Y			Y

ND Northern Democrats SD Southern Democrats

	362	363	364	365	366	367	368	369
15 ***Ewing***	Y	Y	Y	N	Y	Y	Y	Y
16 ***Manzullo***	Y	Y	Y	N	Y	Y	Y	Y
17 Evans	Y	Y	Y	N	N	N	Y	N
18 ***LaHood***	Y	Y	Y	Y	N	Y	Y	Y
19 Phelps	Y	N	N	N	N	Y	Y	N
20 ***Shimkus***	Y	Y	Y	N	Y	Y	Y	Y
INDIANA								
1 Visclosky	Y	Y	Y	Y	N	N	N	N
2 ***McIntosh***	Y	Y	Y	N	Y	Y	Y	Y
3 Roemer	N	Y	Y	N	N	Y	Y	N
4 ***Souder***	Y	Y	Y	Y	Y	Y	Y	Y
5 ***Buyer***	?	N	N	Y	Y	Y	Y	Y
6 ***Burton***	Y	Y	Y	Y	Y	Y	Y	Y
7 ***Pease***	Y	Y	Y	N	Y	Y	Y	Y
8 ***Hostettler***	Y	Y	N	Y	Y	Y	Y	Y
9 Hill	Y	N	N	N	N	Y	Y	N
10 Carson	Y	N	N	Y	N	Y	Y	N
IOWA								
1 ***Leach***	Y	Y	Y	N	Y	Y	Y	Y
2 ***Nussle***	Y	Y	Y	N	Y	Y	Y	Y
3 Boswell	Y	Y	Y	N	N	Y	Y	N
4 ***Ganske***	Y	Y	Y	N	Y	Y	Y	Y
5 ***Latham***	Y	Y	Y	N	Y	Y	Y	Y
KANSAS								
1 ***Moran***	Y	Y	Y	N	Y	N	Y	Y
2 ***Ryun***	Y	Y	Y	Y	Y	Y	Y	Y
3 Moore	Y	Y	Y	N	N	Y	Y	N
4 ***Tiahrt***	Y	Y	Y	N	Y	Y	Y	Y
KENTUCKY								
1 ***Whitfield***	Y	Y	Y	N	Y	Y	Y	Y
2 ***Lewis***	Y	Y	Y	N	Y	Y	Y	Y
3 ***Northup***	Y	Y	Y	N	Y	Y	Y	Y
4 Lucas	Y	Y	Y	N	N	Y	Y	N
5 ***Rogers***	N	Y	Y	N	Y	Y	Y	Y
6 ***Fletcher***	Y	Y	Y	N	Y	Y	Y	Y
LOUISIANA								
1 ***Vitter***	Y	?	?	N	Y	Y	Y	Y
2 Jefferson	Y	Y	Y	N	?	?	?	?
3 ***Tauzin***	Y	N	N	N	Y	Y	Y	Y
4 ***McCrery***	Y	Y	N	N	Y	Y	Y	Y
5 ***Cooksey***	Y	Y	N	N	Y	Y	Y	Y
6 ***Baker***	Y	Y	Y	N	Y	Y	Y	Y
7 John	Y	Y	Y	N	Y	Y	Y	N
MAINE								
1 Allen	Y	Y	Y	N	N	Y	Y	N
2 Baldacci	Y	Y	Y	N	N	Y	Y	N
MARYLAND								
1 ***Gilchrest***	?	Y	Y	N	Y	Y	Y	Y
2 ***Ehrlich***	Y	Y	Y	Y	Y	Y	Y	?
3 Cardin	Y	Y	Y	N	N	Y	Y	N
4 Wynn	Y	?	?	N	N	Y	Y	N
5 Hoyer	Y	N	N	N	N	N	N	N
6 ***Bartlett***	Y	Y	Y	Y	Y	Y	N	Y
7 Cummings	Y	N	Y	N	N	Y	Y	N
8 ***Morella***	Y	Y	Y	N	Y	Y	Y	Y
MASSACHUSETTS								
1 Olver	Y	Y	Y	N	N	N	Y	N
2 Neal	Y	Y	Y	N	N	Y	Y	N
3 McGovern	Y	Y	N	N	N	Y	N	N
4 Frank	?	?	Y	N	N	Y	Y	N
5 Meehan	Y	Y	N	N	N	Y	Y	N
6 Tierney	Y	Y	Y	N	N	Y	N	N
7 Markey	Y	Y	Y	N	N	Y	Y	N
8 Capuano	Y	Y	Y	N	N	Y	Y	N
9 Moakley	Y	Y	Y	N	N	Y	N	N
10 Delahunt	Y	Y	Y	N	N	Y	Y	N
MICHIGAN								
1 Stupak	Y	Y	Y	Y	N	N	Y	N
2 ***Hoekstra***	Y	Y	Y	Y	Y	Y	Y	Y
3 ***Ehlers***	Y	Y	Y	N	Y	Y	Y	Y
4 ***Camp***	Y	Y	Y	N	Y	Y	Y	Y
5 Barcia	Y	Y	?	Y	N	Y	N	N
6 ***Upton***	Y	Y	Y	N	Y	Y	Y	Y
7 ***Smith***	Y	Y	Y	N	Y	Y	Y	Y
8 Stabenow	Y	Y	Y	N	N	Y	N	N
9 Kildee	Y	N	Y	N	N	Y	Y	N
10 Bonior	Y	Y	Y	N	N	Y	N	N
11 ***Knollenberg***	Y	Y	Y	N	Y	Y	Y	Y
12 Levin	Y	Y	Y	N	N	Y	Y	N
13 Rivers	Y	Y	Y	Y	N	Y	Y	N
14 Conyers	Y	N	N	N	N	Y	Y	N
15 Kilpatrick	Y	N	N	N	N	Y	Y	N
16 Dingell	Y	Y	Y	N	N	Y	N	N
MINNESOTA								
1 ***Gutknecht***	Y	Y	Y	Y	Y	N	Y	Y
2 Minge	Y	N	N	N	N	Y	Y	N
3 ***Ramstad***	Y	Y	Y	N	Y	N	Y	Y
4 Vento	Y	N	N	Y	N	N	Y	N
5 Sabo	Y	Y	Y	N	N	N	Y	N
6 Luther	Y	Y	Y	N	N	Y	Y	N
7 Peterson	Y	Y	Y	N	N	N	Y	N
8 Oberstar	Y	Y	Y	N	N	N	Y	N
MISSISSIPPI								
1 ***Wicker***	Y	Y	Y	N	Y	Y	Y	Y
2 Thompson	?	Y	Y	N	?	?	?	?
3 ***Pickering***	+	Y	Y	N	Y	Y	Y	Y
4 Shows	Y	Y	Y	N	Y	Y	N	N
5 Taylor	N	Y	Y	N	Y	N	Y	N
MISSOURI								
1 Clay	Y	N	N	N	N	N	Y	N
2 ***Talent***	Y	Y	Y	Y	Y	Y	Y	Y
3 Gephardt	Y	?	Y	N	N	Y	Y	N
4 Skelton	Y	N	Y	N	N	Y	Y	N
5 McCarthy	Y	N	N	N	N	Y	Y	N
6 Danner	Y	Y	Y	N	N	Y	Y	N
7 ***Blunt***	Y	Y	Y	N	Y	Y	Y	Y
8 ***Emerson***	Y	Y	Y	Y	Y	Y	Y	Y
9 ***Hulshof***	Y	N	N	N	Y	Y	Y	Y
MONTANA								
AL ***Hill***	Y	Y	Y	Y	Y	N	Y	Y
NEBRASKA								
1 ***Bereuter***	Y	Y	Y	N	Y	Y	Y	Y
2 ***Terry***	Y	Y	Y	N	Y	Y	Y	Y
3 ***Barrett***	Y	Y	Y	N	Y	Y	Y	Y
NEVADA								
1 Berkley	Y	Y	Y	N	N	Y	Y	N
2 ***Gibbons***	Y	Y	N	Y	Y	Y	Y	Y
NEW HAMPSHIRE								
1 ***Sununu***	Y	Y	Y	N	Y	Y	Y	Y
2 ***Bass***	Y	Y	Y	N	Y	Y	Y	Y
NEW JERSEY								
1 Andrews	Y	N	N	Y	N	Y	N	N
2 ***LoBiondo***	Y	Y	Y	Y	N	N	Y	Y
3 ***Saxton***	Y	Y	Y	Y	Y	Y	N	Y
4 ***Smith***	Y	Y	Y	Y	N	Y	Y	Y
5 ***Roukema***	Y	Y	Y	N	Y	Y	+	Y
6 Pallone	Y	N	N	N	N	N	Y	N
7 ***Franks***	Y	Y	Y	N	Y	Y	Y	Y
8 Pascrell	Y	Y	Y	N	N	Y	Y	N
9 Rothman	Y	Y	Y	Y	N	Y	?	N
10 Payne	Y	Y	N	N	N	Y	Y	N
11 ***Frelinghuysen***	Y	Y	Y	Y	Y	Y	Y	Y
12 Holt	Y	Y	Y	N	N	Y	Y	N
13 Menendez	Y	Y	Y	Y	N	Y	Y	N
NEW MEXICO								
1 ***Wilson***	Y	Y	Y	N	Y	Y	Y	Y
2 ***Skeen***	Y	Y	N	N	Y	Y	Y	Y
3 Udall	Y	N	Y	N	N	N	Y	N
NEW YORK								
1 Forbes	Y	N	N	Y	N	Y	N	N
2 ***Lazio***	Y	Y	Y	Y	N	Y	Y	Y
3 ***King***	Y	Y	Y	Y	N	Y	Y	Y
4 McCarthy	Y	N	N	N	N	Y	Y	N
5 Ackerman	Y	N	N	N	N	Y	Y	N
6 Meeks	Y	N	N	N	N	Y	Y	N
7 Crowley	Y	Y	Y	N	N	N	Y	N
8 Nadler	Y	N	N	N	N	Y	Y	N
9 Weiner	Y	N	N	N	N	Y	Y	N
10 Towns	Y	Y	Y	Y	N	Y	Y	N
11 Owens	+	N	N	N	N	Y	N	N
12 Velázquez	Y	N	N	Y	N	N	Y	N
13 ***Fossella***	Y	Y	Y	N	Y	Y	Y	Y
14 Maloney	Y	N	N	N	N	?	Y	N
15 Rangel	Y	N	N	N	N	Y	N	N
16 Serrano	Y	N	N	Y	N	Y	Y	N
17 Engel	Y	N	N	N	N	Y	Y	N
18 Lowey	Y	N	N	N	N	Y	Y	N
19 ***Kelly***	Y	Y	Y	Y	Y	Y	Y	Y
20 ***Gilman***	Y	Y	Y	Y	N	Y	Y	Y
21 McNulty	Y	Y	Y	Y	N	N	Y	N
22 ***Sweeney***	Y	Y	Y	Y	N	N	Y	Y
23 ***Boehlert***	Y	Y	Y	N	N	Y	Y	Y
24 ***McHugh***	Y	Y	Y	N	N	Y	Y	Y
25 ***Walsh***	Y	Y	Y	N	Y	Y	Y	Y
26 Hinchey	Y	N	N	N	N	N	N	N
27 ***Reynolds***	Y	Y	Y	N	Y	Y	Y	Y
28 Slaughter	Y	N	N	Y	N	N	N	N
29 LaFalce	N	Y	N	N	N	Y	Y	N
30 ***Quinn***	Y	Y	Y	N	N	Y	Y	Y
31 ***Houghton***	Y	N	N	N	Y	Y	Y	Y
NORTH CAROLINA								
1 Clayton	Y	Y	Y	N	N	Y	Y	N
2 Etheridge	Y	Y	Y	N	N	Y	Y	N
3 ***Jones***	N	N	N	Y	Y	Y	Y	Y
4 Price	Y	Y	Y	N	N	Y	Y	N
5 ***Burr***	Y	Y	Y	N	Y	Y	Y	Y
6 ***Coble***	Y	Y	Y	Y	Y	Y	Y	Y
7 McIntyre	Y	Y	Y	Y	Y	Y	Y	N
8 ***Hayes***	Y	Y	Y	Y	Y	Y	Y	Y
9 ***Myrick***	Y	Y	Y	N	Y	Y	Y	Y
10 ***Ballenger***	Y	Y	Y	N	Y	Y	Y	Y
11 ***Taylor***	Y	Y	Y	Y	Y	Y	Y	Y
12 Watt	Y	Y	Y	N	N	Y	Y	N
NORTH DAKOTA								
AL Pomeroy	Y	Y	Y	N	N	Y	Y	N
OHIO								
1 ***Chabot***	N	Y	Y	Y	Y	Y	Y	Y
2 ***Portman***	Y	Y	+	N	Y	Y	Y	Y
3 Hall	Y	Y	Y	N	N	Y	Y	N
4 ***Oxley***	Y	N	N	N	Y	Y	Y	Y
5 ***Gillmor***	Y	Y	Y	Y	Y	Y	Y	Y
6 Strickland	Y	Y	Y	Y	N	Y	Y	N
7 ***Hobson***	Y	Y	Y	N	Y	Y	Y	Y
8 ***Boehner***	Y	Y	Y	N	Y	Y	Y	Y
9 Kaptur	Y	Y	Y	N	N	Y	N	N
10 Kucinich	Y	Y	Y	N	N	N	N	Y
11 Jones	Y	N	N	N	N	Y	Y	N
12 ***Kasich***	Y	N	N	Y	Y	Y	Y	Y
13 Brown	Y	Y	Y	Y	N	N	N	N
14 Sawyer	Y	Y	Y	N	N	Y	Y	N
15 ***Pryce***	?	Y	Y	N	Y	Y	Y	Y
16 ***Regula***	Y	Y	Y	Y	Y	Y	Y	Y
17 Traficant	N	Y	Y	Y	N	Y	Y	Y
18 ***Ney***	Y	Y	Y	N	Y	Y	Y	Y
19 ***LaTourette***	Y	N	N	N	Y	Y	Y	Y
OKLAHOMA								
1 ***Largent***	N	Y	Y	N	Y	Y	Y	Y
2 ***Coburn***	N	Y	Y	Y	Y	Y	Y	N
3 ***Watkins***	Y	Y	Y	N	Y	Y	?	Y
4 ***Watts***	Y	Y	Y	N	Y	Y	Y	Y
5 ***Istook***	Y	Y	Y	N	Y	Y	Y	Y
6 ***Lucas***	N	Y	Y	N	Y	Y	Y	Y
OREGON								
1 Wu	Y	Y	N	Y	N	Y	N	N
2 ***Walden***	Y	Y	Y	N	Y	Y	Y	Y
3 Blumenauer	Y	N	N	N	N	Y	Y	N
4 DeFazio	Y	N	N	N	N	N	N	N
5 Hooley	Y	Y	Y	N	N	Y	Y	N
PENNSYLVANIA								
1 Brady	Y	Y	Y	N	N	Y	Y	N
2 Fattah	Y	N	Y	N	N	?	?	N
3 Borski	Y	N	Y	N	N	N	Y	N
4 Klink	Y	Y	Y	N	N	Y	Y	N
5 ***Peterson***	?	?	?	?	?	?	?	?
6 Holden	Y	Y	Y	Y	N	Y	Y	N
7 ***Weldon***	Y	Y	Y	Y	N	Y	Y	Y
8 ***Greenwood***	Y	Y	Y	N	Y	Y	Y	Y
9 ***Shuster***	Y	Y	Y	Y	Y	Y	Y	Y
10 ***Sherwood***	Y	Y	Y	Y	Y	Y	Y	Y
11 Kanjorski	Y	Y	Y	N	N	Y	N	N
12 Murtha	Y	Y	Y	N	N	Y	Y	N
13 Hoeffel	Y	Y	Y	N	N	Y	Y	N
14 Coyne	Y	Y	Y	N	N	Y	Y	N
15 ***Toomey***	Y	Y	Y	Y	Y	Y	Y	Y
16 ***Pitts***	Y	Y	Y	N	Y	Y	Y	Y
17 ***Gekas***	Y	Y	Y	N	Y	Y	Y	Y
18 Doyle	Y	Y	Y	N	N	Y	Y	N
19 ***Goodling***	N	Y	Y	Y	Y	Y	Y	Y
20 Mascara	Y	Y	Y	N	N	Y	Y	N
21 ***English***	Y	Y	Y	Y	N	N	Y	Y
RHODE ISLAND								
1 Kennedy	Y	Y	+	Y	N	Y	Y	N
2 Weygand	Y	Y	Y	N	N	Y	Y	N
SOUTH CAROLINA								
1 ***Sanford***	N	Y	Y	N	Y	Y	Y	Y
2 ***Spence***	Y	Y	Y	Y	Y	Y	Y	Y
3 ***Graham***	Y	Y	Y	Y	Y	Y	Y	Y
4 ***DeMint***	Y	Y	Y	N	Y	Y	Y	Y
5 Spratt	Y	Y	Y	N	N	Y	Y	N
6 Clyburn	Y	Y	Y	N	N	Y	Y	N
SOUTH DAKOTA								
AL ***Thune***	Y	Y	Y	Y	Y	Y	Y	Y
TENNESSEE								
1 ***Jenkins***	Y	Y	Y	Y	Y	Y	Y	Y
2 ***Duncan***	N	Y	Y	Y	Y	Y	N	Y
3 ***Wamp***	Y	Y	Y	Y	Y	Y	N	Y
4 ***Hilleary***	Y	Y	Y	Y	Y	N	Y	Y
5 Clement	Y	Y	Y	N	Y	Y	Y	N
6 Gordon	Y	N	N	N	N	Y	Y	N
7 ***Bryant***	Y	Y	Y	Y	Y	Y	Y	Y
8 Tanner	N	Y	Y	N	Y	Y	Y	N
9 Ford	Y	Y	Y	N	N	Y	Y	N
TEXAS								
1 Sandlin	Y	Y	Y	N	N	Y	Y	N
2 Turner	Y	Y	Y	Y	Y	Y	Y	N
3 ***Johnson, Sam***	Y	Y	Y	Y	Y	Y	Y	Y
4 Hall	N	Y	Y	Y	Y	Y	Y	N
5 ***Sessions***	Y	Y	Y	N	Y	Y	Y	Y
6 ***Barton***	Y	Y	N	Y	Y	Y	Y	Y
7 ***Archer***	Y	Y	Y	N	Y	Y	?	Y
8 ***Brady***	Y	Y	Y	N	Y	Y	Y	Y
9 Lampson	Y	Y	Y	N	N	Y	Y	N
10 Doggett	Y	N	N	N	N	Y	Y	N
11 Edwards	Y	Y	Y	N	N	Y	Y	N
12 ***Granger***	Y	Y	Y	N	Y	Y	Y	Y
13 ***Thornberry***	Y	Y	Y	Y	Y	Y	Y	Y
14 ***Paul***	N	N	N	Y	Y	Y	N	Y
15 Hinojosa	Y	Y	Y	N	N	Y	Y	N
16 Reyes	Y	Y	Y	N	N	Y	Y	N
17 Stenholm	N	Y	Y	N	Y	Y	Y	N
18 Jackson-Lee	Y	N	N	Y	N	Y	Y	N
19 ***Combest***	N	Y	Y	Y	Y	Y	Y	Y
20 Gonzalez	Y	Y	Y	N	N	Y	Y	N
21 ***Smith***	Y	Y	Y	Y	Y	Y	Y	Y
22 ***DeLay***	Y	Y	Y	N	Y	Y	Y	Y
23 ***Bonilla***	Y	Y	Y	Y	Y	Y	Y	Y
24 Frost	Y	Y	Y	N	N	Y	Y	N
25 Bentsen	Y	Y	Y	N	N	Y	Y	N
26 ***Armey***	Y	Y	Y	N	Y	?	Y	Y
27 Ortiz	Y	Y	Y	N	N	Y	Y	N
28 Rodriguez	Y	Y	Y	N	N	Y	Y	N
29 Green	Y	Y	Y	Y	N	N	N	N
30 Johnson, E.B.	Y	Y	Y	N	N	N	Y	N
UTAH								
1 ***Hansen***	N	Y	Y	Y	Y	Y	Y	Y
2 ***Cook***	Y	Y	Y	Y	Y	Y	Y	Y
3 ***Cannon***	Y	Y	Y	N	Y	Y	Y	Y
VERMONT								
AL *Sanders*	Y	Y	Y	Y	N	Y	N	N
VIRGINIA								
1 ***Bateman***	Y	Y	Y	N	Y	Y	Y	Y
2 Pickett	Y	Y	Y	N	Y	N	Y	N
3 Scott	Y	Y	Y	N	N	Y	Y	N
4 Sisisky	Y	Y	Y	N	Y	Y	Y	N
5 Goode	N	Y	Y	Y	Y	Y	N	Y
6 ***Goodlatte***	Y	Y	Y	N	Y	Y	Y	Y
7 ***Bliley***	Y	Y	Y	N	Y	Y	Y	Y
8 Moran	Y	Y	N	N	N	Y	Y	N
9 Boucher	Y	N	N	N	N	Y	Y	N
10 ***Wolf***	Y	Y	Y	Y	Y	N	Y	Y
11 ***Davis***	Y	Y	N	Y	Y	Y	Y	Y
WASHINGTON								
1 Inslee	Y	N	N	N	N	Y	Y	N
2 ***Metcalf***	Y	Y	N	?	?	Y	Y	Y
3 Baird	Y	Y	Y	N	N	N	Y	N
4 ***Hastings***	Y	N	N	N	Y	Y	Y	Y
5 ***Nethercutt***	Y	N	N	N	Y	Y	Y	Y
6 Dicks	Y	N	Y	N	N	Y	Y	N
7 McDermott	+	+	+	–	–	+	+	–
8 ***Dunn***	Y	Y	Y	N	Y	Y	Y	Y
9 Smith	Y	Y	Y	N	N	Y	Y	N
WEST VIRGINIA								
1 Mollohan	?	?	?	?	?	Y	Y	Y
2 Wise	Y	Y	Y	N	N	Y	Y	N
3 Rahall	N	Y	Y	N	N	Y	Y	N
WISCONSIN								
1 ***Ryan***	Y	Y	Y	N	N	Y	Y	Y
2 Baldwin	Y	Y	Y	N	N	Y	N	N
3 Kind	Y	Y	Y	N	N	Y	Y	N
4 Kleczka	Y	Y	Y	N	N	Y	Y	N
5 Barrett	Y	Y	Y	N	N	Y	Y	N
6 ***Petri***	N	Y	Y	N	N	Y	Y	Y
7 Obey	Y	Y	Y	N	N	Y	Y	N
8 ***Green***	Y	Y	Y	Y	Y	Y	Y	Y
9 ***Sensenbrenner***	N	Y	Y	N	Y	Y	Y	Y
WYOMING								
AL ***Cubin***	Y	Y	Y	N	Y	Y	Y	Y

Southern states - Ala., Ark., Fla., Ga., Ky., La., Miss., N.C., Okla., S.C., Tenn., Texas, Va.

House Votes 370, 371, 372, 373, 374, 375, 376, 377

370. HR 2670. Fiscal 2000 Commerce-Justice-State Appropriations/ Legal Services Corporation. Serrano, D-N.Y., amendment to increase funding for the Legal Services Corporation by $109 million to $250 million, offset by cuts including reducing funding for the Department of Justice Assets Forfeiture Fund, FBI salaries, and salaries and expenses of the Federal Prison System and the federal judiciary system. The amendment would also increase funding for the Immigration and Naturalization Services' violent crime reduction programs by $44 million, offset by an equal reduction for Immigration and Naturalization Service detention facilities. Adopted 242-178: R 43-173; D 198-5 (ND 151-2, SD 47-3); I 1-0. Aug. 4, 1999. A "yea" was a vote in support of the president's position.

371. HR 2670. Fiscal 2000 Commerce-Justice-State Appropriations/ Motion to Rise. Obey, D-Wis., motion to rise from the Committee of the Whole, thus prohibiting the possibility of further amendments being offered for the day. Motion rejected 166-249: R 0-208; D 165-41 (ND 126-26, SD 39-15); I 1-0. Aug. 4, 1999.

372. HR 2670. Fiscal 2000 Commerce-Justice-State Appropriations/ Crime Prevention. Scott, D-Va., amendment to increase funding for crime prevention and treatment programs by $137.3 million, and reduce funding for violent offender incarceration and truth in sentencing block grants by an equal amount. Rejected 164-263: R 18-200; D 145-63 (ND 105-49, SD 40-14); I 1-0. Aug. 4, 1999.

373. HR 2670. Fiscal 2000 Commerce-Justice-State Appropriations/ Abortion Services in Federal Prisons. DeGette, D-Colo., amendment to strike language in the bill that would ban the use of federal funds for abortion services for women in federal prisons except in cases of rape, incest or danger to the woman's life. Rejected 160-268: R 15-204; D 144-64 (ND 113-41, SD 31-23); I 1-0. Aug. 4, 1999.

374. HR 2670. Fiscal 2000 Commerce-Justice-State Appropriations/ 2000 Census Funding Reduction. Coburn, R-Okla., amendment to reduce funding for the 2000 census by $2.8 billion dollars to $1.7 billion. Rejected 171-257: R 95-124; D 76-132 (ND 52-102, SD 24-30); I 0-1. Aug. 4, 1999.

375. HR 1664. Steel, Oil and Gas Industries Loan Program/Senate Amendments. Regula, R-Ohio, motion to agree to the Senate amendments to the bill to establish a $1 billion loan program for the steel industry, and a $500 million loan program for the oil and gas industries. The bill would appropriate $270 million to cover potential loan defaults. To offset the coverage, the bill would reduce executive branch travel accounts by the same amount. Motion agreed to, thus clearing the bill for the president 246-176: R 68-147; D 177-29 (ND 130-22, SD 47-7); I 1-0. Aug. 4, 1999.

376. Procedural Motion/Journal. Approval of the House Journal of Wednesday, August 4, 1999. Approved 356-50: R 194-14; D 162-36 (ND 119-26, SD 43-10); I 0-0. Aug. 5, 1999.

377. HR 2488. Tax Reconciliation/Rule. Adoption of the rule (H Res 274) to provide for House floor consideration of the conference report on the bill to reduce taxes by $792 billion over 10 years. Adopted 224-203: R 220-0; D 4-202 (ND 2-151, SD 2-51); I 0-1. Aug. 5, 1999.

Key

- Y Voted for (yea).
- # Paired for.
- + Announced for.
- N Voted against (nay).
- X Paired against.
- – Announced against.
- P Voted "present."
- C Voted "present" to avoid possible conflict of interest.
- ? Did not vote or otherwise make a position known.

•

Democrats ***Republicans***
Independents

	370	371	372	373	374	375	376	377
ALABAMA								
1 ***Callahan***	N	N	N	N	N	Y	Y	Y
2 ***Everett***	N	N	N	N	Y	Y	Y	Y
3 ***Riley***	N	N	N	N	Y	Y	Y	Y
4 ***Aderholt***	N	N	N	N	Y	Y	Y	Y
5 Cramer	?	N	N	N	Y	Y	Y	N
6 ***Bachus***	Y	N	N	N	N	Y	Y	Y
7 Hilliard	Y	Y	Y	Y	N	Y	N	N
ALASKA								
AL ***Young***	N	N	N	N	N	Y	?	Y
ARIZONA								
1 ***Salmon***	Y	N	N	N	Y	N	Y	Y
2 Pastor	Y	Y	Y	Y	N	Y	Y	N
3 ***Stump***	N	N	N	N	N	N	Y	Y
4 ***Shadegg***	N	N	N	N	N	N	Y	Y
5 ***Kolbe***	N	N	N	N	N	N	Y	Y
6 ***Hayworth***	N	N	N	N	Y	Y	Y	Y
ARKANSAS								
1 Berry	Y	Y	N	N	Y	Y	Y	N
2 Snyder	Y	Y	Y	N	N	Y	Y	N
3 ***Hutchinson***	Y	N	Y	N	Y	N	N	Y
4 ***Dickey***	N	N	N	N	N	Y	Y	Y
CALIFORNIA								
1 Thompson	Y	Y	N	Y	Y	N	N	N
2 ***Herger***	N	N	N	N	Y	N	Y	Y
3 ***Ose***	N	N	N	N	N	Y	Y	Y
4 ***Doolittle***	N	N	N	N	N	N	Y	Y
5 Matsui	Y	Y	N	Y	N	Y	Y	N
6 Woolsey	Y	Y	Y	Y	N	Y	Y	N
7 Miller, George	Y	N	Y	Y	Y	N	?	N
8 Pelosi	Y	Y	Y	Y	N	Y	Y	N
9 Lee	Y	Y	Y	Y	N	N	Y	N
10 Tauscher	Y	Y	N	Y	Y	Y	Y	N
11 ***Pombo***	N	N	N	N	N	N	Y	Y
12 Lantos	?	?	?	?	?	?	?	?
13 Stark	Y	Y	Y	Y	Y	Y	Y	N
14 Eshoo	Y	Y	Y	Y	Y	N	Y	N
15 ***Campbell***	N	N	N	Y	Y	N	Y	Y
16 Lofgren	Y	N	Y	Y	Y	N	Y	N
17 Farr	Y	Y	Y	Y	N	N	Y	N
18 Condit	Y	Y	N	Y	Y	N	N	Y
19 ***Radanovich***	N	N	N	N	N	N	?	Y
20 Dooley	Y	N	N	Y	Y	Y	Y	N
21 ***Thomas***	N	N	N	N	N	Y	Y	Y
22 Capps	Y	Y	Y	Y	Y	N	Y	N
23 ***Gallegly***	N	N	N	N	N	N	Y	Y
24 Sherman	Y	Y	N	Y	Y	N	Y	N
25 ***McKeon***	N	N	N	N	N	N	Y	Y
26 Berman	Y	Y	Y	Y	Y	?	Y	N
27 ***Rogan***	N	N	N	N	Y	N	N	Y
28 ***Dreier***	N	N	N	N	N	N	Y	Y
29 Waxman	Y	Y	Y	Y	N	Y	Y	N
30 Becerra	Y	Y	Y	Y	N	Y	Y	N
31 Martinez	Y	N	Y	Y	N	Y	Y	N
32 Dixon	Y	Y	Y	Y	N	Y	?	N
33 Roybal-Allard	Y	Y	Y	Y	N	Y	Y	N
34 Napolitano	Y	Y	N	Y	N	Y	Y	N
35 Waters	Y	Y	Y	Y	N	N	N	N
36 ***Kuykendall***	Y	N	N	Y	N	Y	Y	Y
37 Millender-McD.	Y	Y	Y	Y	N	Y	Y	N
38 ***Horn***	Y	N	N	Y	N	Y	Y	Y
39 ***Royce***	N	N	N	N	Y	N	Y	Y
40 ***Lewis***	N	N	N	N	N	N	Y	Y
41 ***Miller, Gary***	N	N	N	N	Y	N	Y	Y
42 Vacant								
43 ***Calvert***	N	N	N	N	N	N	Y	Y
44 ***Bono***	N	N	N	N	N	N	Y	Y
45 ***Rohrabacher***	N	N	N	N	N	N	Y	Y
46 Sanchez	Y	Y	Y	Y	N	Y	Y	N
47 ***Cox***	?	N	N	N	Y	N	?	Y
48 ***Packard***	N	N	N	N	N	N	Y	Y
49 ***Bilbray***	?	?	?	?	?	?	?	?
50 Filner	Y	Y	Y	Y	Y	Y	N	N
51 ***Cunningham***	N	N	N	N	Y	N	Y	Y
52 ***Hunter***	N	N	N	N	N	N	Y	Y
COLORADO								
1 DeGette	Y	Y	Y	Y	Y	Y	Y	N
2 Udall	Y	Y	Y	Y	N	Y	Y	N
3 ***McInnis***	N	N	N	N	N	Y	Y	Y
4 ***Schaffer***	N	N	N	N	Y	N	N	Y
5 ***Hefley***	N	N	N	N	Y	Y	N	Y
6 ***Tancredo***	N	N	N	N	Y	N	P	Y
CONNECTICUT								
1 Larson	Y	N	Y	Y	Y	Y	Y	N
2 Gejdenson	Y	Y	Y	Y	Y	Y	Y	N
3 DeLauro	Y	Y	Y	Y	N	Y	Y	N
4 ***Shays***	Y	N	Y	Y	Y	N	Y	Y
5 Maloney	N	Y	N	Y	N	Y	Y	N
6 ***Johnson***	Y	N	Y	Y	N	N	Y	Y
DELAWARE								
AL ***Castle***	Y	N	N	N	Y	N	Y	Y
FLORIDA								
1 ***Scarborough***	N	N	N	N	Y	N	Y	Y
2 Boyd	Y	N	N	N	Y	Y	Y	N
3 Brown	Y	Y	Y	Y	N	Y	Y	N
4 ***Fowler***	Y	?	N	N	N	N	Y	Y
5 Thurman	Y	N	Y	N	N	Y	Y	N
6 ***Stearns***	N	N	N	N	Y	N	Y	Y
7 ***Mica***	N	N	N	N	Y	N	Y	Y
8 ***McCollum***	Y	N	N	N	N	N	Y	Y
9 ***Bilirakis***	N	N	N	N	Y	Y	Y	Y
10 ***Young***	N	N	N	N	N	N	Y	Y
11 Davis	Y	Y	Y	Y	Y	Y	Y	N
12 ***Canady***	Y	N	N	N	Y	N	?	Y
13 ***Miller***	N	N	N	N	N	N	Y	Y
14 ***Goss***	N	N	N	N	N	N	Y	Y
15 ***Weldon***	N	N	N	N	Y	N	Y	Y
16 ***Foley***	N	N	Y	N	N	N	Y	Y
17 Meek	Y	Y	Y	Y	N	N	Y	N
18 ***Ros-Lehtinen***	Y	N	N	N	N	Y	Y	Y
19 Wexler	Y	Y	Y	Y	N	Y	?	N
20 Deutsch	Y	Y	N	Y	Y	N	Y	N
21 ***Diaz-Balart***	Y	?	N	N	N	Y	Y	Y
22 ***Shaw***	?	N	N	N	N	N	Y	Y
23 Hastings	Y	Y	Y	Y	N	Y	Y	N
GEORGIA								
1 ***Kingston***	N	N	N	N	N	N	Y	Y
2 Bishop	Y	Y	Y	Y	N	Y	Y	N
3 ***Collins***	N	N	N	N	Y	N	Y	Y
4 McKinney	Y	Y	Y	Y	N	Y	Y	N
5 Lewis	Y	Y	Y	Y	N	Y	Y	N
6 ***Isakson***	N	N	N	N	N	N	Y	Y
7 ***Barr***	N	N	N	N	Y	N	Y	Y
8 ***Chambliss***	Y	N	N	N	N	N	Y	Y
9 ***Deal***	N	N	N	N	N	N	Y	Y
10 ***Norwood***	N	N	N	N	N	N	Y	Y
11 ***Linder***	N	N	N	N	Y	N	Y	Y
HAWAII								
1 Abercrombie	Y	N	Y	Y	N	Y	Y	N
2 Mink	Y	N	Y	Y	Y	Y	Y	N
IDAHO								
1 ***Chenoweth***	N	N	N	N	Y	N	?	Y
2 ***Simpson***	N	N	N	N	N	N	Y	Y
ILLINOIS								
1 Rush	Y	Y	Y	Y	N	Y	Y	N
2 Jackson	Y	Y	Y	Y	N	Y	Y	N
3 Lipinski	Y	N	N	N	N	Y	Y	N
4 Gutierrez	Y	N	Y	Y	N	Y	N	N
5 Blagojevich	Y	?	N	Y	N	Y	Y	N
6 ***Hyde***	N	N	N	N	Y	N	Y	Y
7 Davis	Y	Y	Y	Y	N	Y	Y	N
8 ***Crane***	N	N	N	N	Y	N	?	Y
9 Schakowsky	Y	Y	Y	Y	N	Y	Y	N
10 ***Porter***	Y	N	N	Y	N	N	Y	Y
11 ***Weller***	N	N	N	N	Y	Y	N	Y
12 Costello	Y	N	N	N	Y	Y	N	N
13 ***Biggert***	Y	N	N	Y	N	N	Y	Y
14 ***Hastert***						N	Y	Y

ND Northern Democrats SD Southern Democrats

	370	371	372	373	374	375	376	377
15 ***Ewing***	N	N	N	N	Y	N	Y	Y
16 ***Manzullo***	N	N	Y	N	Y	N	Y	Y
17 Evans	Y	Y	N	Y	N	Y	N	N
18 ***LaHood***	Y	N	Y	N	Y	Y	Y	Y
19 Phelps	Y	N	N	N	Y	Y	Y	N
20 ***Shimkus***	N	N	Y	N	Y	Y	Y	Y
INDIANA								
1 Visclosky	Y	N	N	N	N	Y	N	N
2 ***McIntosh***	N	N	N	N	Y	Y	Y	Y
3 Roemer	Y	N	N	N	Y	Y	Y	N
4 ***Souder***	N	N	N	N	N	P	Y	Y
5 ***Buyer***	N	N	N	N	N	Y	Y	Y
6 ***Burton***	N	N	N	N	Y	Y	Y	Y
7 ***Pease***	N	N	N	N	Y	Y	Y	Y
8 ***Hostettler***	N	N	N	N	Y	N	Y	Y
9 Hill	Y	Y	Y	N	Y	Y	Y	N
10 Carson	Y	Y	Y	Y	N	Y	Y	N
IOWA								
1 ***Leach***	Y	N	Y	N	N	N	Y	Y
2 ***Nussle***	N	N	N	N	Y	N	Y	Y
3 Boswell	Y	N	N	Y	Y	Y	Y	N
4 ***Ganske***	Y	N	N	N	Y	N	?	Y
5 ***Latham***	N	N	N	N	N	N	Y	Y
KANSAS								
1 ***Moran***	Y	N	N	N	Y	Y	N	Y
2 ***Ryun***	N	N	N	N	Y	N	Y	Y
3 Moore	Y	Y	Y	N	Y	Y	Y	N
4 ***Tiahrt***	N	N	N	N	Y	Y	Y	Y
KENTUCKY								
1 ***Whitfield***	N	N	N	N	N	N	Y	Y
2 ***Lewis***	N	N	N	N	N	Y	Y	Y
3 ***Northup***	N	N	N	N	N	N	Y	Y
4 Lucas	Y	Y	N	N	N	Y	Y	Y
5 ***Rogers***	N	N	N	N	N	Y	Y	Y
6 ***Fletcher***	N	?	N	N	N	N	Y	Y
LOUISIANA								
1 ***Vitter***	N	N	N	N	Y	Y	Y	Y
2 Jefferson	?	Y	Y	N	N	Y	Y	N
3 ***Tauzin***	N	N	N	N	N	Y	?	Y
4 ***McCrery***	N	?	N	N	N	Y	Y	Y
5 ***Cooksey***	N	N	N	N	N	Y	Y	Y
6 ***Baker***	N	N	N	N	N	N	Y	Y
7 John	?	N	N	N	N	Y	Y	N
MAINE								
1 Allen	Y	Y	Y	Y	Y	Y	Y	N
2 Baldacci	Y	Y	Y	Y	N	Y	Y	N
MARYLAND								
1 ***Gilchrest***	N	N	Y	Y	N	N	Y	Y
2 ***Ehrlich***	N	N	N	N	Y	Y	Y	Y
3 Cardin	Y	Y	Y	Y	N	Y	Y	N
4 Wynn	Y	Y	Y	Y	N	Y	Y	N
5 Hoyer	Y	Y	N	Y	N	Y	Y	N
6 ***Bartlett***	N	N	N	N	N	N	Y	Y
7 Cummings	Y	Y	Y	Y	N	Y	Y	N
8 ***Morella***	Y	N	Y	Y	N	N	Y	Y
MASSACHUSETTS								
1 Olver	Y	Y	Y	Y	Y	Y	?	N
2 Neal	Y	Y	Y	N	N	Y	N	N
3 McGovern	Y	Y	Y	Y	N	Y	Y	N
4 Frank	Y	Y	Y	Y	Y	?	Y	N
5 Meehan	Y	Y	Y	Y	Y	Y	Y	N
6 Tierney	Y	Y	Y	Y	Y	N	Y	N
7 Markey	Y	Y	Y	Y	N	N	Y	N
8 Capuano	Y	Y	Y	Y	N	Y	Y	N
9 Moakley	Y	Y	Y	N	Y	Y	Y	N
10 Delahunt	Y	Y	Y	Y	N	Y	Y	N
MICHIGAN								
1 Stupak	Y	N	Y	N	Y	Y	N	N
2 ***Hoekstra***	N	N	N	N	Y	N	Y	Y
3 ***Ehlers***	Y	N	N	N	N	N	Y	Y
4 ***Camp***	Y	N	N	N	Y	N	Y	Y
5 Barcia	Y	Y	Y	N	N	Y	Y	N
6 ***Upton***	Y	N	Y	N	N	Y	Y	Y
7 ***Smith***	N	N	N	N	N	N	Y	Y
8 Stabenow	Y	Y	Y	Y	Y	Y	Y	N
9 Kildee	Y	Y	N	N	Y	Y	Y	N
10 Bonior	Y	Y	N	N	N	Y	Y	N
11 ***Knollenberg***	N	N	N	N	N	N	Y	Y
12 Levin	Y	Y	N	Y	Y	Y	Y	N
13 Rivers	Y	Y	Y	N	Y	Y	Y	N
14 Conyers	Y	Y	Y	Y	Y	Y	Y	N
15 Kilpatrick	Y	Y	Y	Y	N	Y	Y	N
16 Dingell	Y	Y	Y	N	N	Y	Y	N
MINNESOTA								
1 ***Gutknecht***	N	N	N	N	Y	N	N	Y
2 Minge	Y	N	Y	Y	Y	Y	Y	N
3 ***Ramstad***	Y	N	N	N	Y	N	N	Y
4 Vento	Y	N	Y	Y	N	N	N	N
5 Sabo	Y	Y	Y	Y	N	Y	N	N
6 Luther	Y	N	Y	Y	Y	N	Y	N
7 Peterson	Y	Y	Y	N	Y	Y	N	N
8 Oberstar	Y	Y	Y	N	N	Y	N	N
MISSISSIPPI								
1 ***Wicker***	N	N	N	N	N	N	Y	Y
2 Thompson	Y	Y	Y	Y	N	Y	N	N
3 ***Pickering***	N	N	N	N	Y	Y	Y	Y
4 Shows	Y	N	N	N	N	Y	Y	Y
5 Taylor	N	N	N	N	Y	Y	N	N
MISSOURI								
1 Clay	Y	Y	Y	Y	N	Y	N	N
2 ***Talent***	N	N	N	N	N	Y	Y	Y
3 Gephardt	Y	Y	N	Y	N	Y	N	N
4 Skelton	Y	N	Y	N	Y	Y	Y	N
5 McCarthy	Y	Y	N	Y	N	Y	Y	N
6 Danner	Y	Y	N	N	N	Y	Y	N
7 ***Blunt***	N	N	N	N	N	Y	Y	Y
8 ***Emerson***	N	N	N	N	N	Y	Y	Y
9 ***Hulshof***	Y	N	N	N	Y	N	N	Y
MONTANA								
AL ***Hill***	N	N	N	N	Y	Y	Y	Y
NEBRASKA								
1 ***Bereuter***	N	N	N	N	N	N	Y	Y
2 ***Terry***	N	N	N	N	Y	N	Y	Y
3 ***Barrett***	N	N	N	N	N	N	Y	Y
NEVADA								
1 Berkley	Y	Y	Y	Y	N	Y	Y	N
2 ***Gibbons***	N	N	N	N	Y	Y	N	Y
NEW HAMPSHIRE								
1 ***Sununu***	N	N	N	N	Y	N	Y	Y
2 ***Bass***	N	N	N	N	N	N	Y	Y
NEW JERSEY								
1 Andrews	Y	Y	N	Y	N	Y	Y	N
2 ***LoBiondo***	N	N	N	N	N	N	N	Y
3 ***Saxton***	N	N	N	N	N	N	Y	Y
4 ***Smith***	N	N	N	N	N	Y	Y	Y
5 ***Roukema***	N	N	N	N	Y	N	Y	Y
6 Pallone	Y	Y	N	Y	N	Y	N	N
7 ***Franks***	Y	N	N	N	N	N	Y	Y
8 Pascrell	Y	Y	N	N	N	Y	Y	N
9 Rothman	Y	Y	N	Y	N	Y	Y	N
10 Payne	Y	Y	Y	Y	N	Y	?	N
11 ***Frelinghuysen***	Y	N	N	Y	N	N	Y	Y
12 Holt	Y	Y	N	Y	N	Y	N	N
13 Menendez	Y	Y	Y	Y	N	Y	Y	N
NEW MEXICO								
1 ***Wilson***	Y	N	Y	N	N	Y	Y	Y
2 ***Skeen***	N	N	N	N	N	Y	Y	Y
3 Udall	Y	Y	Y	N	Y	Y	N	N
NEW YORK								
1 Forbes	Y	Y	N	N	N	Y	Y	N
2 ***Lazio***	N	N	N	N	Y	N	Y	Y
3 ***King***	N	N	N	N	N	Y	Y	Y
4 McCarthy	Y	Y	N	Y	N	Y	Y	N
5 Ackerman	Y	Y	Y	Y	N	Y	Y	N
6 Meeks	Y	Y	Y	Y	N	N	Y	N
7 Crowley	Y	Y	N	N	N	Y	Y	N
8 Nadler	Y	Y	Y	Y	N	N	Y	N
9 Weiner	Y	Y	Y	Y	N	Y	Y	N
10 Towns	Y	Y	Y	Y	N	Y	Y	N
11 Owens	Y	Y	Y	Y	N	Y	Y	N
12 Velázquez	Y	N	Y	Y	N	Y	Y	N
13 ***Fossella***	N	N	N	N	N	Y	Y	Y
14 Maloney	Y	Y	Y	Y	N	Y	N	N
15 Rangel	Y	Y	Y	Y	N	Y	Y	N
16 Serrano	Y	Y	Y	Y	N	Y	Y	N
17 Engel	Y	Y	Y	Y	N	Y	?	N
18 Lowey	Y	Y	N	Y	N	Y	Y	N
19 ***Kelly***	Y	N	N	N	N	Y	Y	Y
20 ***Gilman***	Y	N	N	N	Y	N	Y	Y
21 McNulty	Y	Y	Y	N	N	Y	?	N
22 ***Sweeney***	N	N	N	N	N	N	N	Y
23 ***Boehlert***	Y	N	N	Y	N	Y	Y	Y
24 ***McHugh***	N	N	N	N	N	Y	Y	Y
25 ***Walsh***	Y	N	N	N	N	Y	Y	Y
26 Hinchey	Y	Y	Y	Y	N	Y	N	N
27 ***Reynolds***	N	N	N	N	N	N	Y	Y
28 Slaughter	+	Y	Y	Y	N	Y	?	N
29 LaFalce	N	Y	Y	N	N	N	Y	N
30 ***Quinn***	N	N	N	N	N	Y	Y	Y
31 ***Houghton***	Y	N	N	Y	N	?	Y	Y
NORTH CAROLINA								
1 Clayton	Y	Y	Y	Y	N	N	Y	N
2 Etheridge	Y	Y	N	N	Y	Y	Y	N
3 ***Jones***	N	N	N	N	Y	N	Y	Y
4 Price	Y	Y	Y	Y	Y	Y	Y	N
5 ***Burr***	N	?	N	N	Y	N	Y	Y
6 ***Coble***	N	N	N	N	Y	N	Y	Y
7 McIntyre	Y	Y	N	N	Y	Y	Y	N
8 ***Hayes***	N	N	N	N	N	N	Y	Y
9 ***Myrick***	N	N	N	N	Y	N	Y	Y
10 ***Ballenger***	N	?	N	N	N	N	Y	Y
11 ***Taylor***	N	N	N	N	N	N	Y	Y
12 Watt	Y	Y	Y	Y	N	N	Y	N
NORTH DAKOTA								
AL Pomeroy	Y	Y	N	N	Y	Y	Y	N
OHIO								
1 ***Chabot***	N	N	N	N	Y	N	Y	Y
2 ***Portman***	Y	N	N	N	N	N	Y	Y
3 Hall	Y	Y	N	N	N	Y	Y	N
4 ***Oxley***	N	?	N	N	N	?	Y	Y
5 ***Gillmor***	N	N	Y	N	N	Y	Y	Y
6 Strickland	Y	Y	Y	Y	N	Y	Y	N
7 ***Hobson***	N	N	N	N	N	N	Y	Y
8 ***Boehner***	N	?	N	N	N	N	Y	Y
9 Kaptur	Y	N	N	N	N	Y	Y	N
10 Kucinich	Y	Y	Y	N	N	Y	N	N
11 Jones	Y	Y	Y	Y	N	Y	Y	N
12 ***Kasich***	N	N	N	N	N	N	Y	Y
13 Brown	Y	Y	Y	Y	N	Y	Y	N
14 Sawyer	Y	?	Y	Y	N	Y	Y	N
15 ***Pryce***	Y	N	N	N	N	N	Y	Y
16 ***Regula***	Y	N	N	N	N	Y	Y	Y
17 Traficant	Y	N	N	N	N	Y	Y	Y
18 ***Ney***	N	N	N	N	N	Y	Y	Y
19 ***LaTourette***	Y	N	N	N	Y	Y	Y	Y
OKLAHOMA								
1 ***Largent***	?	N	N	N	Y	N	Y	Y
2 ***Coburn***	N	N	Y	N	Y	N	Y	Y
3 ***Watkins***	N	N	N	N	N	Y	Y	Y
4 ***Watts***	N	?	N	N	N	Y	Y	Y
5 ***Istook***	N	N	N	N	Y	N	Y	Y
6 ***Lucas***	N	N	N	N	N	Y	Y	Y
OREGON								
1 Wu	Y	Y	N	Y	Y	Y	Y	N
2 ***Walden***	N	N	N	N	Y	N	Y	Y
3 Blumenauer	Y	Y	Y	Y	Y	Y	Y	N
4 DeFazio	Y	Y	Y	Y	Y	Y	N	N
5 Hooley	Y	Y	Y	Y	Y	Y	N	N
PENNSYLVANIA								
1 Brady	Y	Y	Y	Y	N	Y	Y	N
2 Fattah	Y	Y	Y	Y	N	Y	N	N
3 Borski	Y	Y	N	N	Y	Y	N	N
4 Klink	Y	Y	N	N	Y	Y	Y	N
5 ***Peterson***	?	?	?	?	?	?	?	?
6 Holden	Y	Y	N	N	Y	Y	Y	N
7 ***Weldon***	Y	N	N	N	Y	?	Y	Y
8 ***Greenwood***	Y	N	N	Y	N	N	Y	Y
9 ***Shuster***	N	?	N	N	N	?	Y	Y
10 ***Sherwood***	N	N	N	N	N	N	Y	Y
11 Kanjorski	Y	Y	N	N	Y	Y	Y	N
12 Murtha	Y	Y	N	N	N	Y	?	N
13 Hoeffel	Y	Y	N	Y	N	Y	Y	N
14 Coyne	Y	Y	Y	Y	N	Y	Y	N
15 ***Toomey***	N	N	N	N	Y	N	Y	Y
16 ***Pitts***	N	N	N	N	Y	N	Y	Y
17 ***Gekas***	Y	N	N	N	N	Y	Y	Y
18 Doyle	Y	Y	N	N	Y	Y	Y	N
19 ***Goodling***	N	N	Y	N	Y	N	Y	Y
20 Mascara	Y	Y	N	N	N	Y	Y	N
21 ***English***	N	N	N	N	N	Y	N	Y
RHODE ISLAND								
1 Kennedy	Y	Y	Y	Y	N	Y	Y	N
2 Weygand	Y	Y	Y	N	Y	Y	Y	N
SOUTH CAROLINA								
1 ***Sanford***	N	N	N	N	Y	N	N	Y
2 ***Spence***	N	N	N	N	N	N	Y	Y
3 ***Graham***	N	N	N	N	Y	N	Y	Y
4 ***DeMint***	N	N	N	N	Y	N	Y	Y
5 Spratt	Y	Y	N	Y	Y	Y	N	N
6 Clyburn	Y	Y	Y	Y	N	Y	N	N
SOUTH DAKOTA								
AL ***Thune***	N	N	N	N	Y	N	Y	Y
TENNESSEE								
1 ***Jenkins***	N	N	N	N	Y	N	Y	Y
2 ***Duncan***	N	N	Y	N	Y	N	Y	Y
3 ***Wamp***	N	N	N	N	N	N	Y	Y
4 ***Hilleary***	N	N	N	N	Y	N	Y	Y
5 Clement	Y	N	Y	N	Y	Y	Y	N
6 Gordon	Y	N	Y	N	Y	Y	Y	N
7 ***Bryant***	N	N	N	N	Y	N	Y	Y
8 Tanner	?	Y	N	N	Y	Y	Y	N
9 Ford	Y	N	Y	Y	Y	Y	Y	N
TEXAS								
1 Sandlin	Y	Y	Y	Y	Y	Y	Y	N
2 Turner	Y	Y	Y	N	Y	Y	Y	N
3 ***Johnson, Sam***	N	N	N	N	N	N	Y	Y
4 Hall	N	N	Y	N	Y	Y	Y	N
5 ***Sessions***	N	N	N	N	Y	N	Y	Y
6 ***Barton***	N	?	N	N	N	Y	?	Y
7 ***Archer***	N	N	N	N	N	N	Y	Y
8 ***Brady***	N	N	?	N	Y	N	Y	Y
9 Lampson	Y	Y	Y	N	Y	Y	Y	N
10 Doggett	Y	Y	Y	Y	Y	N	N	N
11 Edwards	Y	N	Y	N	Y	Y	Y	N
12 ***Granger***	N	N	N	N	N	N	Y	Y
13 ***Thornberry***	N	N	N	N	Y	Y	Y	Y
14 ***Paul***	N	N	Y	N	Y	N	Y	Y
15 Hinojosa	Y	Y	Y	Y	N	Y	Y	N
16 Reyes	Y	?	?	?	?	?	?	?
17 Stenholm	?	Y	Y	N	Y	Y	Y	N
18 Jackson-Lee	Y	Y	Y	Y	N	Y	N	N
19 ***Combest***	N	N	N	N	N	Y	Y	Y
20 Gonzalez	Y	Y	Y	Y	N	Y	N	N
21 ***Smith***	N	N	N	N	N	Y	Y	Y
22 ***DeLay***	N	N	N	N	N	N	Y	Y
23 ***Bonilla***	N	N	N	N	N	Y	Y	Y
24 Frost	Y	Y	Y	N	N	Y	Y	N
25 Bentsen	Y	Y	Y	Y	N	N	Y	N
26 ***Armey***	N	N	N	N	N	N	Y	Y
27 Ortiz	Y	N	Y	N	N	Y	Y	N
28 Rodriguez	Y	Y	Y	Y	N	Y	Y	?
29 Green	Y	N	Y	Y	N	Y	Y	N
30 Johnson, E.B.	Y	Y	Y	Y	N	Y	Y	N
UTAH								
1 ***Hansen***	N	N	N	N	N	Y	Y	Y
2 ***Cook***	N	N	N	N	N	Y	Y	Y
3 ***Cannon***	N	N	N	N	N	Y	?	Y
VERMONT								
AL *Sanders*	Y	Y	Y	Y	N	Y	?	N
VIRGINIA								
1 ***Bateman***	N	N	N	N	N	N	Y	Y
2 Pickett	Y	Y	N	Y	N	Y	N	N
3 Scott	Y	Y	Y	Y	Y	Y	N	N
4 Sisisky	Y	Y	Y	Y	Y	Y	Y	N
5 Goode	N	N	Y	N	Y	Y	Y	Y
6 ***Goodlatte***	N	N	N	N	Y	N	Y	Y
7 ***Bliley***	N	N	N	N	Y	N	Y	Y
8 Moran	Y	Y	Y	Y	N	N	Y	N
9 Boucher	Y	N	N	Y	N	Y	Y	N
10 ***Wolf***	N	N	N	N	N	N	Y	Y
11 ***Davis***	Y	N	Y	N	N	N	Y	Y
WASHINGTON								
1 Inslee	Y	Y	N	Y	Y	Y	Y	N
2 ***Metcalf***	N	N	N	N	N	N	?	Y
3 Baird	Y	Y	Y	Y	Y	Y	N	N
4 ***Hastings***	N	N	N	N	N	N	Y	Y
5 ***Nethercutt***	Y	N	N	N	N	N	Y	Y
6 Dicks	Y	Y	N	Y	N	Y	Y	N
7 McDermott	+	+	+	+	+	+	+	−
8 ***Dunn***	N	N	N	N	Y	N	Y	Y
9 Smith	Y	Y	N	Y	Y	Y	Y	N
WEST VIRGINIA								
1 Mollohan	Y	Y	Y	N	N	Y	?	?
2 Wise	Y	N	Y	Y	N	Y	Y	N
3 Rahall	Y	N	Y	N	N	Y	Y	N
WISCONSIN								
1 ***Ryan***	N	N	N	N	Y	N	Y	Y
2 Baldwin	Y	Y	Y	Y	Y	Y	Y	N
3 Kind	Y	N	Y	Y	Y	N	Y	N
4 Kleczka	Y	N	Y	N	Y	Y	Y	N
5 Barrett	Y	Y	Y	Y	N	N	Y	N
6 ***Petri***	N	N	N	N	Y	N	Y	Y
7 Obey	Y	Y	Y	N	N	N	Y	N
8 ***Green***	N	N	N	N	Y	N	Y	Y
9 ***Sensenbrenner***	N	N	N	N	Y	N	Y	Y
WYOMING								
AL ***Cubin***	N	N	N	N	Y	Y	Y	Y

Southern states - Ala., Ark., Fla., Ga., Ky., La., Miss., N.C., Okla., S.C., Tenn., Texas, Va.

378. HR 2488. Tax Reconciliation/Motion To Recommit. Rangel, D-N.Y., motion to recommit the conference report to the conference committee with instructions to the House conferees to insist on preserving 100 percent of the Social Security surpluses for Social Security and devoting 50 percent of the non-Social Security surpluses to debt reduction by limiting the net tax reduction to no more than 25 percent of the currently projected non-Social Security surpluses and removing limited tax benefits as defined under the Line-Item Veto Act. Motion rejected 205-221: R 0-218; D 204-3 (ND 152-1, SD 52-2); I 1-0. Aug. 5, 1999.

379. HR 2488. Tax Reconciliation/Conference Report. Adoption of the conference report on the bill to reduce taxes by $792 billion over 10 years. The conference report would reduce each of the five income tax rates by 1 percentage point, phase out the estate tax, and raise the standard deduction available to taxpayers filing jointly from $7,200 to $8,600 gradually over five years. The conference report would reduce the capital gains tax rate from 10 percent and 20 percent to 8 percent and 18 percent effective Jan. 1, 1999. Adopted (thus sent to the Senate) 221-206: R 216-4; D 5-201 (ND 2-150, SD 3-51); I 0-1. Aug. 5, 1999. A "nay" was a vote in support of the president's position.

380. HR 2670. Fiscal 2000 Commerce-Justice-State Appropriations/Back Payments to the United Nations. Hall, D-Ohio, amendment to strike language from the bill that would make the release of $244 million in back payments to the United Nations contingent on the enactment of an authorization bill that ties the payments to U.N. reforms. Rejected 206-221: R 15-205; D 190-16 (ND 145-8, SD 45-8); I 1-0. Aug. 5, 1999.

381. HR 2670. Fiscal 2000 Commerce-Justice-State Appropriations/Area Code Shortage Plan. Bass, R-N.H., amendment to give the Federal Communications Commission (FCC) until March 31, 2000 to develop and implement a plan to address the manner in which central office codes, the first three digits of a seven-digit phone number, are distributed. States would be allowed to implement phone number conservation plans if the FCC does not take action in a timely manner. Rejected 169-256: R 68-150; D 100-106 (ND 85-67, SD 15-39); I 1-0. Aug. 5, 1999.

382. HR 2670. Fiscal 2000 Commerce-Justice-State Appropriations/Inter-American Tropical Tuna Commission. Miller, D-Calif., amendment to reduce funding for the Inter-American Tropical Tuna Commission from $4.7 million to $2.4 million in fiscal 2000. Rejected 211-215: R 20-199; D 190-16 (ND 145-7, SD 45-9); I 1-0. Aug. 5, 1999.

383. HR 2670. Fiscal 2000 Commerce-Justice-State Appropriations/World Heritage Sites. Hayworth, R-Ariz., amendment to prohibit any funds in the bill from being used to add any natural site or cultural monument currently recognized as a World Heritage Site by the United Nations' World Heritage Committee to the committee's list of endangered world heritage sites. Adopted 217-209: R 199-20; D 18-188 (ND 7-145, SD 11-43); I 0-1. Aug. 5, 1999.

384. HR 2670. Fiscal 2000 Commerce-Justice-State Appropriations/FCC Uniform System of Accounts. Tauzin, R-La., amendment to prevent any funds in the bill from being used to administer or fund the Uniform System of Accounts for telecommunications companies of the Federal Communications Commission. Adopted 374-49: R 212-7; D 162-41 (ND 114-36, SD 48-5); I 0-1. Aug. 5, 1999.

Key

Y	Voted for (yea).
#	Paired for.
+	Announced for.
N	Voted against (nay).
X	Paired against.
–	Announced against.
P	Voted "present."
C	Voted "present" to avoid possible conflict of interest.
?	Did not vote or otherwise make a position known.

•

Democrats ***Republicans***
Independents

	378	379	380	381	382	383	384
ALABAMA							
1 ***Callahan***	N	Y	N	N	N	Y	Y
2 ***Everett***	N	Y	N	N	N	Y	Y
3 ***Riley***	N	Y	N	N	N	Y	Y
4 ***Aderholt***	N	Y	N	N	N	Y	Y
5 Cramer	Y	N	Y	N	Y	N	Y
6 ***Bachus***	N	Y	N	N	N	Y	Y
7 Hilliard	Y	N	Y	N	Y	N	Y
ALASKA							
AL ***Young***	N	Y	N	N	N	Y	Y
ARIZONA							
1 ***Salmon***	N	Y	N	N	N	Y	Y
2 Pastor	Y	N	Y	Y	Y	N	Y
3 ***Stump***	N	Y	N	N	N	Y	Y
4 ***Shadegg***	N	Y	N	N	N	Y	Y
5 ***Kolbe***	N	Y	N	N	N	Y	Y
6 ***Hayworth***	N	Y	N	N	N	Y	Y
ARKANSAS							
1 Berry	Y	N	Y	N	Y	Y	Y
2 Snyder	Y	N	Y	N	Y	N	Y
3 ***Hutchinson***	N	Y	N	N	N	Y	Y
4 ***Dickey***	N	Y	N	N	N	Y	Y
CALIFORNIA							
1 Thompson	Y	N	Y	N	Y	N	Y
2 ***Herger***	N	Y	N	Y	N	Y	Y
3 ***Ose***	N	Y	Y	N	N	Y	Y
4 ***Doolittle***	N	Y	N	N	N	Y	Y
5 Matsui	Y	N	Y	Y	Y	N	Y
6 Woolsey	Y	N	Y	Y	Y	N	Y
7 Miller, George	Y	N	Y	Y	Y	N	N
8 Pelosi	Y	N	Y	Y	Y	N	Y
9 Lee	Y	N	Y	Y	Y	N	N
10 Tauscher	Y	N	Y	Y	Y	N	Y
11 ***Pombo***	N	Y	N	N	N	Y	Y
12 Lantos	?	?	?	?	?	?	?
13 Stark	Y	N	Y	Y	Y	N	N
14 Eshoo	Y	N	Y	Y	Y	N	N
15 ***Campbell***	N	Y	N	Y	Y	Y	Y
16 Lofgren	Y	N	Y	Y	Y	N	N
17 Farr	Y	N	Y	Y	Y	N	N
18 Condit	Y	Y	Y	N	Y	N	Y
19 ***Radanovich***	N	Y	N	Y	N	Y	Y
20 Dooley	Y	N	Y	N	Y	N	Y
21 ***Thomas***	N	Y	N	N	N	Y	Y
22 Capps	Y	N	Y	Y	Y	N	Y
23 ***Gallegly***	N	Y	N	N	N	Y	Y
24 Sherman	Y	N	Y	Y	Y	N	Y
25 ***McKeon***	N	Y	N	N	N	Y	Y
26 Berman	Y	N	Y	Y	Y	N	Y
27 ***Rogan***	N	Y	N	N	N	Y	Y
28 ***Dreier***	N	Y	N	Y	N	Y	Y
29 Waxman	Y	N	Y	Y	Y	N	N
30 Becerra	Y	N	Y	Y	Y	N	Y
31 Martinez	Y	N	Y	Y	Y	N	N
32 Dixon	Y	N	Y	Y	Y	N	Y
33 Roybal-Allard	Y	N	Y	Y	Y	N	Y
34 Napolitano	Y	N	Y	Y	Y	N	Y
35 Waters	Y	N	Y	Y	Y	N	N
36 ***Kuykendall***	N	Y	N	N	N	Y	Y
37 Millender-McD.	Y	N	Y	Y	Y	N	Y
38 ***Horn***	N	Y	N	Y	Y	N	Y
39 ***Royce***	N	Y	N	Y	N	Y	N
40 ***Lewis***	N	Y	N	N	N	Y	Y
41 ***Miller, Gary***	N	Y	N	Y	N	Y	Y
42 Vacant							
43 ***Calvert***	N	Y	N	N	N	Y	Y
44 ***Bono***	N	Y	N	Y	N	Y	Y
45 ***Rohrabacher***	N	Y	N	Y	N	Y	Y
46 Sanchez	Y	N	Y	Y	Y	N	Y
47 ***Cox***	N	Y	N	N	N	Y	Y
48 ***Packard***	N	Y	N	N	N	Y	Y
49 ***Bilbray***	?	?	?	?	?	?	?
50 Filner	Y	N	Y	Y	Y	N	N
51 ***Cunningham***	N	Y	N	N	N	Y	Y
52 ***Hunter***	N	Y	N	Y	N	Y	Y
COLORADO							
1 DeGette	Y	N	Y	Y	Y	N	N
2 Udall	Y	N	Y	Y	Y	N	Y
3 ***McInnis***	N	Y	N	Y	N	Y	Y
4 ***Schaffer***	N	Y	N	N	N	Y	Y
5 ***Hefley***	N	Y	N	N	N	Y	Y
6 ***Tancredo***	N	Y	N	Y	N	Y	Y
CONNECTICUT							
1 Larson	Y	N	Y	Y	Y	N	Y
2 Gejdenson	Y	N	Y	Y	Y	N	N
3 DeLauro	Y	N	Y	Y	Y	N	N
4 ***Shays***	N	Y	Y	Y	Y	N	Y
5 Maloney	Y	N	Y	Y	Y	N	N
6 ***Johnson***	N	Y	Y	Y	N	N	Y
DELAWARE							
AL ***Castle***	N	N	N	Y	N	N	Y
FLORIDA							
1 ***Scarborough***	N	Y	N	N	Y	Y	Y
2 Boyd	Y	N	Y	N	N	N	Y
3 Brown	Y	N	Y	N	Y	N	Y
4 ***Fowler***	N	Y	N	Y	N	Y	Y
5 Thurman	Y	N	Y	N	Y	N	Y
6 ***Stearns***	N	Y	N	N	N	Y	Y
7 ***Mica***	N	Y	N	N	N	Y	Y
8 ***McCollum***	N	Y	N	N	N	Y	Y
9 ***Bilirakis***	N	Y	N	N	Y	Y	Y
10 ***Young***	N	Y	N	N	N	Y	Y
11 Davis	Y	N	Y	N	Y	N	Y
12 ***Canady***	N	Y	N	N	N	Y	Y
13 ***Miller***	N	Y	N	N	N	Y	Y
14 ***Goss***	N	Y	N	N	N	Y	Y
15 ***Weldon***	N	Y	N	N	N	Y	Y
16 ***Foley***	N	Y	N	N	N	Y	Y
17 Meek	Y	N	?	N	Y	N	Y
18 ***Ros-Lehtinen***	N	Y	N	N	N	Y	Y
19 Wexler	Y	N	Y	N	Y	N	Y
20 Deutsch	Y	N	Y	N	Y	N	N
21 ***Diaz-Balart***	N	Y	N	N	N	Y	Y
22 ***Shaw***	N	Y	N	N	N	Y	Y
23 Hastings	Y	N	Y	N	Y	N	Y
GEORGIA							
1 ***Kingston***	N	Y	N	Y	N	Y	Y
2 Bishop	Y	N	Y	Y	N	N	Y
3 ***Collins***	N	Y	N	N	N	Y	Y
4 McKinney	Y	N	Y	Y	Y	N	N
5 Lewis	Y	N	Y	Y	Y	N	N
6 ***Isakson***	N	Y	N	N	N	Y	Y
7 ***Barr***	N	Y	N	Y	N	Y	Y
8 ***Chambliss***	N	Y	N	N	N	Y	Y
9 ***Deal***	N	Y	N	N	N	Y	Y
10 ***Norwood***	N	Y	N	N	N	Y	Y
11 ***Linder***	N	Y	N	N	N	Y	Y
HAWAII							
1 Abercrombie	Y	N	Y	Y	Y	N	Y
2 Mink	Y	N	Y	Y	Y	N	N
IDAHO							
1 ***Chenoweth***	N	Y	N	N	N	Y	Y
2 ***Simpson***	N	Y	N	Y	N	Y	Y
ILLINOIS							
1 Rush	Y	N	Y	Y	Y	N	Y
2 Jackson	Y	N	Y	Y	Y	N	Y
3 Lipinski	Y	N	N	Y	Y	N	Y
4 Gutierrez	Y	?	Y	Y	Y	N	?
5 Blagojevich	Y	N	Y	Y	Y	N	Y
6 ***Hyde***	N	Y	N	Y	N	Y	Y
7 Davis	Y	N	Y	Y	Y	N	Y
8 ***Crane***	N	Y	N	N	Y	Y	Y
9 Schakowsky	Y	N	Y	Y	Y	N	N
10 ***Porter***	N	Y	Y	N	N	N	Y
11 ***Weller***	N	Y	N	N	N	Y	Y
12 Costello	Y	N	N	Y	Y	N	Y
13 ***Biggert***	N	Y	N	Y	N	Y	Y
14 ***Hastert***	N	Y	N				

ND Northern Democrats SD Southern Democrats

	378	379	380	381	382	383	384
15 ***Ewing***	N	Y	N	N	N	Y	Y
16 ***Manzullo***	N	Y	N	Y	N	Y	Y
17 Evans	Y	N	Y	Y	Y	N	Y
18 ***LaHood***	N	Y	N	N	N	Y	Y
19 Phelps	Y	N	N	N	Y	N	Y
20 ***Shimkus***	N	Y	N	N	N	Y	Y
INDIANA							
1 Visclosky	Y	N	Y	N	Y	N	Y
2 ***McIntosh***	N	Y	N	Y	N	Y	Y
3 Roemer	Y	N	Y	N	Y	Y	Y
4 ***Souder***	N	Y	N	N	N	Y	Y
5 ***Buyer***	N	Y	N	N	N	Y	Y
6 ***Burton***	N	Y	N	N	N	Y	Y
7 ***Pease***	N	Y	N	N	N	Y	Y
8 ***Hostettler***	N	Y	N	Y	N	Y	Y
9 Hill	Y	N	Y	N	Y	Y	Y
10 Carson	Y	N	Y	Y	Y	N	Y
IOWA							
1 ***Leach***	N	Y	Y	?	N	N	Y
2 ***Nussle***	N	Y	N	N	N	Y	Y
3 Boswell	Y	N	Y	N	N	N	Y
4 ***Ganske***	?	N	N	N	N	N	Y
5 ***Latham***	N	Y	N	N	N	Y	Y
KANSAS							
1 ***Moran***	N	Y	N	N	N	Y	Y
2 ***Ryun***	N	Y	N	Y	N	Y	Y
3 Moore	Y	N	Y	N	Y	N	Y
4 ***Tiahrt***	N	Y	N	Y	N	Y	Y
KENTUCKY							
1 ***Whitfield***	N	Y	N	Y	N	Y	Y
2 ***Lewis***	N	Y	N	N	N	Y	Y
3 ***Northup***	N	Y	N	N	N	Y	Y
4 Lucas	Y	Y	N	N	Y	Y	Y
5 ***Rogers***	N	Y	N	N	N	Y	N
6 ***Fletcher***	N	Y	N	N	N	Y	Y
LOUISIANA							
1 ***Vitter***	N	Y	N	N	N	Y	Y
2 Jefferson	Y	N	Y	N	Y	N	Y
3 ***Tauzin***	N	Y	N	N	N	Y	Y
4 ***McCrery***	N	Y	N	N	N	Y	Y
5 ***Cooksey***	N	Y	Y	N	N	Y	Y
6 ***Baker***	N	Y	N	N	N	Y	Y
7 John	Y	N	N	N	N	Y	Y
MAINE							
1 Allen	Y	N	Y	Y	Y	N	Y
2 Baldacci	Y	N	Y	Y	Y	N	Y
MARYLAND							
1 ***Gilchrest***	N	Y	N	Y	N	N	Y
2 ***Ehrlich***	N	Y	N	N	N	Y	Y
3 Cardin	Y	N	Y	Y	Y	N	Y
4 Wynn	Y	N	Y	N	Y	N	Y
5 Hoyer	Y	N	Y	N	Y	N	Y
6 ***Bartlett***	N	Y	N	Y	N	Y	Y
7 Cummings	Y	N	Y	N	Y	N	Y
8 ***Morella***	N	N	Y	N	N	N	Y
MASSACHUSETTS							
1 Olver	Y	N	Y	N	Y	N	Y
2 Neal	Y	N	Y	N	Y	N	Y
3 McGovern	Y	N	Y	Y	Y	N	Y
4 Frank	Y	N	Y	?	?	?	Y
5 Meehan	Y	N	Y	Y	Y	N	Y
6 Tierney	Y	N	Y	N	Y	N	Y
7 Markey	Y	N	Y	N	Y	N	N
8 Capuano	Y	N	Y	Y	Y	N	Y
9 Moakley	Y	N	Y	Y	Y	N	Y
10 Delahunt	Y	N	Y	Y	Y	N	Y
MICHIGAN							
1 Stupak	Y	N	Y	N	Y	N	N
2 ***Hoekstra***	N	Y	N	N	N	Y	Y
3 ***Ehlers***	N	Y	Y	Y	N	N	Y
4 ***Camp***	N	Y	N	N	N	Y	Y
5 Barcia	Y	N	N	Y	Y	Y	Y
6 ***Upton***	N	Y	N	N	N	Y	Y
7 ***Smith***	N	Y	N	N	N	Y	Y
8 Stabenow	Y	N	Y	N	Y	N	Y
9 Kildee	Y	N	Y	N	Y	N	Y
10 Bonior	Y	N	Y	N	Y	N	Y
11 ***Knollenberg***	N	Y	N	N	N	Y	Y
12 Levin	Y	N	Y	Y	N	N	?
13 Rivers	Y	N	Y	N	Y	N	Y
14 Conyers	Y	N	Y	Y	Y	N	N
15 Kilpatrick	Y	N	Y	N	Y	N	Y
16 Dingell	Y	N	Y	N	Y	N	Y
MINNESOTA							
1 ***Gutknecht***	N	Y	N	Y	N	Y	Y
2 Minge	Y	N	Y	N	Y	N	Y
3 ***Ramstad***	N	Y	N	Y	Y	Y	Y
4 Vento	Y	N	Y	N	Y	N	Y
5 Sabo	Y	N	Y	N	Y	N	Y
6 Luther	Y	N	Y	N	Y	N	N
7 Peterson	Y	N	N	N	Y	Y	Y
8 Oberstar	Y	N	Y	N	N	N	N
MISSISSIPPI							
1 ***Wicker***	N	Y	N	N	N	Y	Y
2 Thompson	Y	N	Y	Y	Y	N	Y
3 ***Pickering***	N	Y	N	N	N	Y	Y
4 Shows	Y	N	N	N	Y	Y	Y
5 Taylor	Y	N	N	Y	Y	Y	Y
MISSOURI							
1 Clay	Y	N	Y	Y	Y	N	Y
2 ***Talent***	N	Y	N	N	N	Y	Y
3 Gephardt	Y	N	Y	N	Y	N	Y
4 Skelton	Y	N	Y	N	N	Y	Y
5 McCarthy	Y	N	Y	N	Y	N	N
6 Danner	N	Y	N	N	N	Y	Y
7 ***Blunt***	N	Y	N	Y	N	Y	Y
8 ***Emerson***	N	Y	N	N	N	Y	Y
9 ***Hulshof***	N	Y	N	Y	N	Y	Y
MONTANA							
AL ***Hill***	N	Y	N	N	N	Y	Y
NEBRASKA							
1 ***Bereuter***	N	Y	N	Y	N	N	Y
2 ***Terry***	N	Y	N	Y	N	Y	Y
3 ***Barrett***	N	Y	N	N	N	Y	Y
NEVADA							
1 Berkley	Y	N	Y	N	Y	N	Y
2 ***Gibbons***	N	Y	N	N	N	Y	Y
NEW HAMPSHIRE							
1 ***Sununu***	N	Y	N	Y	N	Y	Y
2 ***Bass***	N	Y	Y	Y	N	Y	Y
NEW JERSEY							
1 Andrews	Y	N	Y	Y	Y	N	Y
2 ***LoBiondo***	N	Y	N	Y	N	Y	Y
3 ***Saxton***	N	Y	N	N	N	N	Y
4 ***Smith***	N	Y	N	N	N	Y	Y
5 ***Roukema***	N	Y	Y	N	N	N	Y
6 Pallone	Y	N	Y	Y	Y	N	N
7 ***Franks***	N	Y	N	Y	N	N	Y
8 Pascrell	Y	N	Y	Y	Y	N	Y
9 Rothman	Y	N	Y	Y	Y	N	Y
10 Payne	Y	N	Y	Y	Y	N	Y
11 ***Frelinghuysen***	N	Y	N	Y	N	N	N
12 Holt	Y	N	Y	Y	Y	N	Y
13 Menendez	Y	N	Y	Y	N	N	Y
NEW MEXICO							
1 ***Wilson***	N	Y	N	N	N	Y	N
2 ***Skeen***	N	Y	N	N	N	Y	Y
3 Udall	Y	N	Y	N	Y	N	Y
NEW YORK							
1 Forbes	Y	N	Y	Y	Y	N	N
2 ***Lazio***	N	Y	N	N	N	Y	Y
3 ***King***	N	Y	N	N	N	Y	Y
4 McCarthy	Y	N	Y	N	Y	N	Y
5 Ackerman	Y	N	Y	Y	Y	N	Y
6 Meeks	Y	N	Y	N	Y	N	Y
7 Crowley	Y	N	Y	N	Y	N	Y
8 Nadler	Y	N	Y	Y	Y	N	N
9 Weiner	Y	N	Y	N	Y	N	Y
10 Towns	Y	N	Y	Y	Y	N	Y
11 Owens	Y	N	Y	Y	Y	N	N
12 Velázquez	Y	N	Y	Y	Y	N	Y
13 ***Fossella***	N	Y	N	N	N	Y	Y
14 Maloney	Y	N	Y	N	Y	N	Y
15 Rangel	Y	N	Y	N	Y	N	Y
16 Serrano	Y	N	Y	Y	Y	N	Y
17 Engel	Y	N	Y	Y	Y	N	Y
18 Lowey	Y	N	Y	Y	Y	N	N
19 ***Kelly***	N	Y	N	N	Y	Y	Y
20 ***Gilman***	N	Y	N	Y	Y	Y	Y
21 McNulty	Y	N	Y	Y	Y	N	Y
22 ***Sweeney***	N	Y	N	N	N	Y	Y
23 ***Boehlert***	N	Y	Y	Y	N	N	Y
24 ***McHugh***	N	Y	N	Y	N	Y	N
25 ***Walsh***	N	Y	N	N	N	N	Y
26 Hinchey	Y	N	Y	Y	Y	N	N
27 ***Reynolds***	N	Y	N	Y	N	Y	Y
28 Slaughter	Y	N	Y	Y	Y	N	Y
29 LaFalce	Y	N	Y	Y	Y	N	N
30 ***Quinn***	N	N	N	Y	N	Y	Y
31 ***Houghton***	N	Y	Y	N	N	N	Y
NORTH CAROLINA							
1 Clayton	Y	N	Y	N	Y	N	Y
2 Etheridge	Y	N	Y	N	Y	N	Y
3 ***Jones***	N	Y	N	N	Y	Y	Y
4 Price	Y	N	Y	N	Y	N	Y
5 ***Burr***	N	Y	N	N	Y	Y	Y
6 ***Coble***	N	Y	N	N	N	Y	Y
7 McIntyre	Y	N	N	Y	N	Y	Y
8 ***Hayes***	N	Y	N	N	N	Y	Y
9 ***Myrick***	N	Y	N	Y	Y	Y	Y
10 ***Ballenger***	N	Y	N	N	N	Y	Y
11 ***Taylor***	N	Y	N	N	N	Y	Y
12 Watt	Y	N	Y	N	Y	N	Y
NORTH DAKOTA							
AL Pomeroy	Y	N	Y	N	Y	N	N
OHIO							
1 ***Chabot***	N	Y	N	Y	Y	Y	Y
2 ***Portman***	N	Y	N	Y	Y	Y	Y
3 Hall	Y	N	Y	Y	Y	N	Y
4 ***Oxley***	N	Y	N	N	N	Y	Y
5 ***Gillmor***	N	Y	N	N	N	Y	Y
6 Strickland	Y	N	Y	N	Y	N	Y
7 ***Hobson***	N	Y	N	N	N	Y	Y
8 ***Boehner***	N	Y	N	N	N	Y	Y
9 Kaptur	Y	N	Y	Y	Y	N	Y
10 Kucinich	Y	N	Y	Y	Y	N	N
11 Jones	Y	N	Y	Y	Y	N	Y
12 ***Kasich***	N	Y	N	Y	N	Y	Y
13 Brown	Y	N	Y	Y	Y	N	N
14 Sawyer	Y	N	Y	Y	Y	N	Y
15 ***Pryce***	N	Y	Y	N	N	Y	Y
16 ***Regula***	N	Y	N	N	N	Y	Y
17 Traficant	Y	N	N	N	N	Y	Y
18 ***Ney***	N	Y	N	N	N	Y	Y
19 ***LaTourette***	N	Y	N	N	N	Y	Y
OKLAHOMA							
1 ***Largent***	?	Y	N	N	N	Y	N
2 ***Coburn***	N	Y	N	N	N	Y	Y
3 ***Watkins***	N	Y	N	N	N	Y	Y
4 ***Watts***	N	Y	N	N	N	Y	Y
5 ***Istook***	N	Y	N	N	N	Y	Y
6 ***Lucas***	N	Y	N	N	N	Y	Y
OREGON							
1 Wu	Y	N	Y	N	Y	N	Y
2 ***Walden***	N	Y	N	Y	N	Y	Y
3 Blumenauer	Y	N	Y	N	Y	N	Y
4 DeFazio	Y	N	Y	Y	Y	N	?
5 Hooley	Y	N	Y	N	Y	N	Y
PENNSYLVANIA							
1 Brady	Y	N	Y	N	Y	N	Y
2 Fattah	Y	N	Y	N	Y	N	Y
3 Borski	Y	N	Y	N	Y	N	Y
4 Klink	Y	N	Y	N	Y	N	Y
5 ***Peterson***	?	?	?	?	?	?	?
6 Holden	Y	N	Y	Y	Y	N	Y
7 ***Weldon***	N	Y	N	Y	N	Y	Y
8 ***Greenwood***	N	Y	Y	N	N	N	Y
9 ***Shuster***	N	Y	N	N	N	Y	Y
10 ***Sherwood***	N	Y	N	Y	N	Y	Y
11 Kanjorski	Y	N	Y	N	Y	N	Y
12 Murtha	Y	N	Y	N	Y	N	Y
13 Hoeffel	Y	N	Y	N	Y	N	Y
14 Coyne	Y	N	Y	Y	Y	N	N
15 ***Toomey***	N	Y	N	Y	N	Y	Y
16 ***Pitts***	N	Y	N	N	N	Y	Y
17 ***Gekas***	N	Y	N	N	N	Y	Y
18 Doyle	Y	N	Y	N	Y	N	Y
19 ***Goodling***	N	Y	N	Y	N	Y	Y
20 Mascara	Y	N	N	N	Y	N	Y
21 ***English***	N	Y	N	Y	N	N	Y
RHODE ISLAND							
1 Kennedy	Y	N	Y	Y	Y	N	Y
2 Weygand	Y	N	Y	N	Y	N	Y
SOUTH CAROLINA							
1 ***Sanford***	N	Y	N	N	Y	Y	Y
2 ***Spence***	N	Y	N	N	N	Y	Y
3 ***Graham***	N	Y	N	N	N	Y	Y
4 ***DeMint***	N	Y	N	N	N	Y	Y
5 Spratt	Y	N	Y	N	Y	N	Y
6 Clyburn	Y	N	Y	Y	Y	N	Y
SOUTH DAKOTA							
AL ***Thune***	N	Y	N	N	N	Y	Y
TENNESSEE							
1 ***Jenkins***	N	Y	N	Y	N	Y	Y
2 ***Duncan***	N	Y	N	Y	N	Y	Y
3 ***Wamp***	N	Y	N	Y	N	Y	Y
4 ***Hilleary***	N	Y	N	N	N	Y	Y
5 Clement	Y	N	Y	N	Y	N	N
6 Gordon	Y	N	Y	N	Y	N	Y
7 ***Bryant***	N	Y	N	N	N	Y	Y
8 Tanner	Y	N	Y	N	N	Y	Y
9 Ford	Y	N	Y	N	Y	N	Y
TEXAS							
1 Sandlin	Y	N	Y	N	Y	Y	Y
2 Turner	Y	N	Y	N	Y	N	Y
3 ***Johnson, Sam***	N	Y	N	N	N	Y	Y
4 Hall	N	Y	N	Y	Y	Y	Y
5 ***Sessions***	N	Y	N	N	N	Y	Y
6 ***Barton***	N	Y	N	N	N	Y	Y
7 ***Archer***	N	Y	N	N	N	Y	Y
8 ***Brady***	N	Y	N	N	N	Y	Y
9 Lampson	Y	N	Y	Y	Y	N	Y
10 Doggett	Y	N	Y	N	Y	N	N
11 Edwards	Y	N	Y	Y	Y	N	?
12 ***Granger***	N	Y	N	N	N	Y	Y
13 ***Thornberry***	N	Y	N	Y	N	Y	Y
14 ***Paul***	N	Y	N	Y	Y	Y	Y
15 Hinojosa	Y	N	Y	N	N	N	Y
16 Reyes	?	?	?	?	?	?	?
17 Stenholm	Y	N	Y	N	N	Y	Y
18 Jackson-Lee	Y	N	Y	Y	Y	N	Y
19 ***Combest***	N	Y	N	N	N	Y	Y
20 Gonzalez	Y	N	Y	N	Y	N	Y
21 ***Smith***	N	Y	N	N	N	Y	Y
22 ***DeLay***	N	Y	N	N	N	Y	Y
23 ***Bonilla***	N	Y	N	N	N	Y	Y
24 Frost	Y	N	Y	N	Y	N	Y
25 Bentsen	Y	N	Y	Y	Y	N	Y
26 ***Armey***	N	Y	N	N	N	Y	Y
27 Ortiz	Y	N	N	N	Y	N	Y
28 Rodriguez	Y	N	Y	Y	N	N	Y
29 Green	Y	N	Y	Y	Y	N	Y
30 Johnson, E.B.	Y	N	Y	N	Y	N	Y
UTAH							
1 ***Hansen***	N	Y	N	N	N	Y	Y
2 ***Cook***	N	Y	N	Y	N	Y	Y
3 ***Cannon***	N	Y	N	N	N	Y	Y
VERMONT							
AL *Sanders*	Y	N	Y	Y	Y	N	N
VIRGINIA							
1 ***Bateman***	N	Y	N	N	N	Y	Y
2 Pickett	Y	N	Y	N	Y	N	Y
3 Scott	Y	N	Y	N	Y	N	Y
4 Sisisky	Y	N	Y	N	Y	N	Y
5 Goode	N	Y	N	Y	Y	Y	Y
6 ***Goodlatte***	N	Y	N	Y	Y	Y	Y
7 ***Bliley***	N	Y	N	N	N	Y	Y
8 Moran	Y	N	Y	N	Y	N	Y
9 Boucher	Y	N	Y	N	Y	N	Y
10 ***Wolf***	N	Y	N	N	N	Y	Y
11 ***Davis***	N	Y	N	N	N	Y	Y
WASHINGTON							
1 Inslee	Y	N	Y	N	Y	N	Y
2 ***Metcalf***	N	Y	N	N	Y	Y	Y
3 Baird	Y	N	Y	N	Y	N	N
4 ***Hastings***	N	Y	N	Y	N	Y	Y
5 ***Nethercutt***	N	Y	N	N	N	Y	Y
6 Dicks	Y	N	Y	N	Y	N	Y
7 McDermott	+	–	?	?	?	?	?
8 ***Dunn***	N	Y	N	N	N	Y	Y
9 Smith	Y	N	Y	N	Y	N	Y
WEST VIRGINIA							
1 Mollohan	?	?	?	?	?	?	?
2 Wise	Y	N	Y	Y	Y	N	Y
3 Rahall	Y	N	Y	N	Y	N	Y
WISCONSIN							
1 ***Ryan***	N	Y	N	N	N	Y	Y
2 Baldwin	Y	N	Y	N	Y	N	Y
3 Kind	Y	N	Y	N	Y	N	Y
4 Kleczka	Y	N	Y	Y	Y	N	Y
5 Barrett	Y	N	Y	N	Y	N	N
6 ***Petri***	N	Y	N	Y	Y	Y	Y
7 Obey	Y	N	Y	N	Y	N	N
8 ***Green***	N	Y	N	N	N	Y	Y
9 ***Sensenbrenner***	N	Y	N	Y	Y	Y	Y
WYOMING							
AL ***Cubin***	N	Y	N	N	N	Y	Y

Southern states - Ala., Ark., Fla., Ga., Ky., La., Miss., N.C., Okla., S.C., Tenn., Texas, Va.

385. HR 2670. Fiscal 2000 Commerce-Justice-State Appropriations/ Federal Challenges to State Trade Laws. Kucinich, D-Ohio, amendment to prohibit any funds in the bill from being used to file a federal challenge to any state, local or tribal law on the grounds that the law is inconsistent with the North American Free Trade Agreement Implementation Act or policies of the World Trade Organization. Rejected 196-226: R 57-157; D 138-69 (ND 111-42, SD 27-27); I 1-0. Aug. 5, 1999.

386. HR 2670. Fiscal 2000 Commerce-Justice-State Appropriations/ Motion to Recommit. Bonior, D-Mich., motion to recommit the bill back to the Appropriations Committee with instructions to increase the amount of funding for the Community Oriented Policing Services (COPS) program by $1 billion to the President's requested level of $1.3 billion. Motion rejected 208-219: R 0-219; D 207-0 (ND 153-0, SD 54-0); I 1-0. Aug. 5, 1999. A "yea" was a vote in support of the president's position.

387. HR 2670. Fiscal 2000 Commerce-Justice State Appropriations/ Passage. Passage of the bill to appropriate $35.8 billion for the Departments of Commerce, Justice, and State and the federal judiciary for fiscal 2000. Passed 217-210: R 202-18; D 15-191 (ND 9-143, SD 6-48); I 0-1. Aug. 5, 1999. A "nay" was a vote in support of the president's position.

388. HR 2684. Fiscal 2000 VA-HUD Appropriations/Previous Question. Moakley, D-Mass., motion to order the previous question (thus ending debate and possibility of amendment on adoption of the rule (H Res 275) to provide for House floor consideration of the bill to appropriate $92 billion for the Departments of Veterans Affairs and Housing and Urban Development. Motion agreed to 217-208: R 217-0; D 0-207 (ND 0-152, SD 0-55); I 0-1. Aug. 5, 1999. (Subsequently, the rule was adopted by voice vote.)

389. HR 1905. Fiscal 2000 Legislative Branch Appropriations/ Conference Report. Adoption of the conference report on the bill to appropriate $2.5 billion for legislative branch operations in fiscal 2000. Adopted 367-49: R 187-28; D 179-21 (ND 135-12, SD 44-9); I 1-0. Aug. 5, 1999.

Key

- Y Voted for (yea).
- # Paired for.
- + Announced for.
- N Voted against (nay).
- X Paired against.
- – Announced against.
- P Voted "present."
- C Voted "present" to avoid possible conflict of interest.
- ? Did not vote or otherwise make a position known.

•

Democrats ***Republicans***
Independents

	385	386	387	388	389
ALABAMA					
1 ***Callahan***	N	N	Y	Y	Y
2 ***Everett***	Y	N	Y	Y	Y
3 ***Riley***	Y	N	Y	Y	Y
4 ***Aderholt***	Y	N	Y	Y	N
5 Cramer	Y	Y	Y	N	Y
6 ***Bachus***	N	N	Y	Y	Y
7 Hilliard	Y	Y	N	N	Y
ALASKA					
AL ***Young***	N	N	Y	Y	Y
ARIZONA					
1 ***Salmon***	N	N	N	Y	Y
2 Pastor	N	Y	N	N	Y
3 ***Stump***	N	N	Y	Y	N
4 ***Shadegg***	N	N	Y	Y	N
5 ***Kolbe***	N	N	Y	Y	Y
6 ***Hayworth***	N	N	Y	Y	Y
ARKANSAS					
1 Berry	N	Y	N	N	N
2 Snyder	N	Y	N	N	Y
3 ***Hutchinson***	N	N	Y	Y	Y
4 ***Dickey***	N	N	Y	Y	Y
CALIFORNIA					
1 Thompson	N	Y	N	N	Y
2 ***Herger***	N	N	Y	Y	Y
3 ***Ose***	N	N	Y	Y	Y
4 ***Doolittle***	N	N	Y	Y	Y
5 Matsui	N	Y	N	N	Y
6 Woolsey	Y	Y	N	N	Y
7 Miller, George	Y	Y	N	N	Y
8 Pelosi	Y	Y	N	N	Y
9 Lee	Y	Y	N	N	Y
10 Tauscher	N	Y	N	N	Y
11 ***Pombo***	Y	N	Y	Y	Y
12 Lantos	?	?	?	?	?
13 Stark	Y	Y	N	N	?
14 Eshoo	N	Y	N	N	Y
15 ***Campbell***	N	N	Y	Y	Y
16 Lofgren	N	Y	N	N	Y
17 Farr	Y	Y	N	N	Y
18 Condit	Y	Y	N	N	Y
19 ***Radanovich***	N	N	Y	Y	?
20 Dooley	N	Y	N	N	Y
21 ***Thomas***	N	N	Y	Y	Y
22 Capps	Y	Y	N	N	Y
23 ***Gallegly***	N	N	Y	Y	Y
24 Sherman	Y	Y	N	N	Y
25 ***McKeon***	N	N	Y	Y	Y
26 Berman	N	Y	N	N	Y
27 ***Rogan***	N	N	Y	Y	Y
28 ***Dreier***	N	N	Y	Y	Y
29 Waxman	Y	Y	N	N	?
30 Becerra	N	Y	N	N	Y
31 Martinez	Y	Y	N	N	Y
32 Dixon	Y	Y	N	N	Y
33 Roybal-Allard	Y	Y	N	N	Y
34 Napolitano	N	Y	N	N	Y
35 Waters	Y	Y	N	N	Y
36 ***Kuykendall***	N	N	Y	Y	Y
37 Millender-McD.	Y	Y	N	N	Y
38 ***Horn***	N	N	Y	Y	Y
39 ***Royce***	N	N	Y	Y	N
40 ***Lewis***	N	N	Y	Y	Y
41 ***Miller, Gary***	N	N	Y	Y	Y
42 Vacant					
43 ***Calvert***	N	N	Y	Y	Y
44 ***Bono***	N	N	Y	Y	Y
45 ***Rohrabacher***	Y	N	Y	Y	Y
46 Sanchez	N	Y	N	N	Y
47 ***Cox***	N	N	Y	Y	Y
48 ***Packard***	N	N	Y	Y	Y
49 ***Bilbray***	?	?	?	?	?
50 Filner	Y	Y	N	N	Y
51 ***Cunningham***	N	N	Y	Y	Y
52 ***Hunter***	Y	N	Y	Y	Y
COLORADO					
1 DeGette	Y	Y	N	N	Y
2 Udall	N	Y	N	N	Y
3 ***McInnis***	N	N	Y	Y	Y
4 ***Schaffer***	N	N	N	Y	N
5 ***Hefley***	N	N	N	Y	Y
6 ***Tancredo***	Y	N	N	Y	Y
CONNECTICUT					
1 Larson	N	Y	N	N	Y
2 Gejdenson	N	Y	N	N	Y
3 DeLauro	Y	Y	N	N	Y
4 ***Shays***	N	N	Y	Y	N
5 Maloney	N	Y	N	N	Y
6 ***Johnson***	N	N	Y	Y	Y
DELAWARE					
AL ***Castle***	N	N	N	Y	Y
FLORIDA					
1 ***Scarborough***	Y	N	Y	Y	Y
2 Boyd	Y	Y	N	N	Y
3 Brown	Y	Y	N	N	Y
4 ***Fowler***	Y	N	Y	Y	Y
5 Thurman	Y	Y	N	N	Y
6 ***Stearns***	?	N	Y	Y	Y
7 ***Mica***	Y	N	Y	Y	Y
8 ***McCollum***	N	N	Y	Y	Y
9 ***Bilirakis***	Y	N	Y	Y	Y
10 ***Young***	Y	N	Y	Y	?
11 Davis	N	Y	N	N	Y
12 ***Canady***	N	N	Y	Y	Y
13 ***Miller***	N	N	Y	Y	Y
14 ***Goss***	N	N	Y	Y	Y
15 ***Weldon***	N	N	Y	Y	Y
16 ***Foley***	N	N	Y	Y	Y
17 Meek	Y	Y	N	N	Y
18 ***Ros-Lehtinen***	Y	N	Y	Y	Y
19 Wexler	N	Y	N	N	Y
20 Deutsch	Y	Y	N	N	N
21 ***Diaz-Balart***	Y	N	Y	Y	Y
22 ***Shaw***	N	N	Y	Y	Y
23 Hastings	Y	Y	N	N	Y
GEORGIA					
1 ***Kingston***	N	N	Y	Y	Y
2 Bishop	Y	Y	N	N	Y
3 ***Collins***	N	N	Y	Y	Y
4 McKinney	Y	Y	N	N	Y
5 Lewis	Y	Y	N	N	Y
6 ***Isakson***	N	N	Y	Y	Y
7 ***Barr***	Y	N	N	Y	N
8 ***Chambliss***	N	N	Y	Y	Y
9 ***Deal***	Y	N	Y	Y	Y
10 ***Norwood***	N	N	Y	Y	Y
11 ***Linder***	N	N	Y	?	?
HAWAII					
1 Abercrombie	Y	Y	Y	N	Y
2 Mink	Y	Y	N	N	Y
IDAHO					
1 ***Chenoweth***	Y	N	N	Y	N
2 ***Simpson***	N	N	Y	Y	Y
ILLINOIS					
1 Rush	Y	Y	N	N	Y
2 Jackson	Y	Y	N	N	Y
3 Lipinski	Y	Y	N	N	Y
4 Gutierrez	Y	Y	N	N	Y
5 Blagojevich	Y	Y	N	N	Y
6 ***Hyde***	N	N	Y	Y	Y
7 Davis	Y	Y	N	N	Y
8 ***Crane***	N	N	Y	Y	Y
9 Schakowsky	Y	Y	N	N	Y
10 ***Porter***	N	N	Y	Y	Y
11 ***Weller***	N	N	Y	Y	Y
12 Costello	Y	Y	N	N	Y
13 ***Biggert***	N	N	Y	Y	Y
14 ***Hastert***			Y		

ND Northern Democrats SD Southern Democrats

	385	386	387	388	389
15 ***Ewing***	?	N	Y	Y	Y
16 ***Manzullo***	N	N	Y	Y	N
17 Evans	Y	Y	N	N	Y
18 ***LaHood***	N	N	Y	Y	Y
19 Phelps	Y	Y	N	N	Y
20 ***Shimkus***	N	N	Y	Y	Y
INDIANA					
1 Visclosky	Y	Y	N	N	Y
2 ***McIntosh***	Y	N	Y	Y	Y
3 Roemer	Y	Y	N	N	Y
4 ***Souder***	N	N	Y	Y	N
5 ***Buyer***	N	N	Y	Y	Y
6 ***Burton***	Y	N	Y	Y	Y
7 ***Pease***	N	N	Y	Y	Y
8 ***Hostettler***	Y	N	N	Y	Y
9 Hill	N	Y	N	N	Y
10 Carson	Y	Y	N	N	N
IOWA					
1 ***Leach***	N	N	Y	?	?
2 ***Nussle***	N	N	Y	Y	Y
3 Boswell	N	Y	N	N	Y
4 ***Ganske***	N	N	N	Y	Y
5 ***Latham***	N	N	Y	Y	Y
KANSAS					
1 ***Moran***	N	N	Y	Y	N
2 ***Ryun***	Y	N	Y	Y	N
3 Moore	N	Y	N	N	Y
4 ***Tiahrt***	Y	N	Y	Y	Y
KENTUCKY					
1 ***Whitfield***	N	N	Y	Y	Y
2 ***Lewis***	N	N	Y	Y	Y
3 ***Northup***	N	N	Y	Y	Y
4 Lucas	N	Y	Y	N	N
5 ***Rogers***	N	N	Y	Y	Y
6 ***Fletcher***	N	N	Y	Y	Y
LOUISIANA					
1 ***Vitter***	N	N	Y	Y	N
2 Jefferson	N	Y	N	N	Y
3 ***Tauzin***	N	N	Y	Y	Y
4 ***McCrery***	N	N	Y	Y	Y
5 ***Cooksey***	N	N	Y	Y	Y
6 ***Baker***	N	N	Y	Y	Y
7 John	N	Y	N	N	Y
MAINE					
1 Allen	N	Y	N	N	Y
2 Baldacci	Y	Y	N	N	Y
MARYLAND					
1 ***Gilchrest***	N	N	Y	Y	Y
2 ***Ehrlich***	N	N	Y	Y	Y
3 Cardin	N	Y	N	N	Y
4 Wynn	Y	Y	N	N	Y
5 Hoyer	N	Y	N	N	Y
6 ***Bartlett***	Y	N	Y	Y	Y
7 Cummings	Y	Y	N	N	Y
8 ***Morella***	N	N	Y	Y	Y
MASSACHUSETTS					
1 Olver	Y	Y	N	N	Y
2 Neal	N	Y	N	N	Y
3 McGovern	Y	Y	N	N	Y
4 Frank	Y	Y	N	N	Y
5 Meehan	Y	Y	N	N	Y
6 Tierney	Y	Y	N	N	Y
7 Markey	Y	Y	N	N	Y
8 Capuano	Y	Y	N	N	Y
9 Moakley	Y	Y	N	N	Y
10 Delahunt	Y	Y	N	N	Y
MICHIGAN					
1 Stupak	Y	Y	N	N	Y
2 ***Hoekstra***	N	N	Y	Y	Y
3 ***Ehlers***	N	N	Y	Y	Y
4 ***Camp***	N	N	Y	Y	Y
5 Barcia	Y	Y	Y	N	Y
6 ***Upton***	N	N	N	Y	Y
7 ***Smith***	N	N	Y	Y	Y
8 Stabenow	Y	Y	N	N	Y
9 Kildee	Y	Y	N	N	N
10 Bonior	Y	Y	N	N	Y
11 ***Knollenberg***	N	N	Y	Y	Y
12 Levin	N	Y	N	N	Y
13 Rivers	Y	Y	N	N	Y
14 Conyers	Y	Y	N	N	Y
15 Kilpatrick	Y	Y	N	N	Y
16 Dingell	N	Y	N	N	Y

	385	386	387	388	389
MINNESOTA					
1 ***Gutknecht***	N	N	Y	Y	Y
2 Minge	Y	Y	N	N	Y
3 ***Ramstad***	N	N	Y	Y	Y
4 Vento	Y	Y	N	N	Y
5 Sabo	N	Y	N	N	Y
6 Luther	Y	Y	N	N	N
7 Peterson	Y	Y	N	N	N
8 Oberstar	Y	Y	N	N	Y
MISSISSIPPI					
1 ***Wicker***	Y	N	Y	Y	Y
2 Thompson	Y	Y	N	N	Y
3 ***Pickering***	Y	N	Y	Y	Y
4 Shows	Y	Y	Y	N	N
5 Taylor	Y	Y	N	N	N
MISSOURI					
1 Clay	Y	Y	N	?	?
2 ***Talent***	N	N	Y	Y	Y
3 Gephardt	Y	Y	N	N	?
4 Skelton	N	Y	N	N	Y
5 McCarthy	N	Y	N	N	Y
6 Danner	Y	Y	N	N	Y
7 ***Blunt***	N	N	Y	Y	Y
8 ***Emerson***	Y	N	Y	Y	Y
9 ***Hulshof***	N	N	Y	Y	N
MONTANA					
AL ***Hill***	N	N	N	Y	Y
NEBRASKA					
1 ***Bereuter***	N	N	Y	Y	Y
2 ***Terry***	N	N	Y	Y	Y
3 ***Barrett***	N	N	Y	Y	Y
NEVADA					
1 Berkley	Y	Y	N	N	N
2 ***Gibbons***	Y	N	Y	Y	Y
NEW HAMPSHIRE					
1 ***Sununu***	N	N	Y	Y	Y
2 ***Bass***	N	N	Y	Y	Y
NEW JERSEY					
1 Andrews	Y	Y	N	N	Y
2 ***LoBiondo***	Y	N	Y	Y	Y
3 ***Saxton***	Y	N	Y	Y	Y
4 ***Smith***	Y	N	Y	Y	Y
5 ***Roukema***	N	N	Y	Y	Y
6 Pallone	Y	Y	N	N	Y
7 ***Franks***	Y	N	Y	Y	Y
8 Pascrell	Y	Y	N	N	N
9 Rothman	Y	Y	N	N	Y
10 Payne	N	Y	N	N	Y
11 ***Frelinghuysen***	N	N	Y	Y	Y
12 Holt	Y	Y	N	N	Y
13 Menendez	N	Y	N	N	Y
NEW MEXICO					
1 ***Wilson***	N	N	Y	Y	Y
2 ***Skeen***	N	N	Y	Y	Y
3 Udall	Y	Y	N	N	Y
NEW YORK					
1 Forbes	Y	Y	N	N	Y
2 ***Lazio***	N	N	Y	Y	Y
3 ***King***	Y	N	Y	Y	Y
4 McCarthy	Y	Y	Y	N	Y
5 Ackerman	Y	Y	N	N	Y
6 Meeks	Y	Y	N	N	Y
7 Crowley	Y	Y	N	N	Y
8 Nadler	Y	Y	N	N	Y
9 Weiner	Y	Y	N	N	Y
10 Towns	Y	Y	N	N	Y
11 Owens	Y	Y	N	N	Y
12 Velázquez	Y	Y	N	N	Y
13 ***Fossella***	N	N	Y	Y	Y
14 Maloney	N	Y	Y	N	N
15 Rangel	N	Y	N	N	?
16 Serrano	Y	Y	N	N	Y
17 Engel	Y	Y	N	N	Y
18 Lowey	N	Y	N	N	Y
19 ***Kelly***	Y	N	Y	Y	Y
20 ***Gilman***	Y	N	Y	Y	Y
21 McNulty	Y	Y	N	N	Y
22 ***Sweeney***	Y	N	Y	Y	Y
23 ***Boehlert***	N	N	Y	Y	Y
24 ***McHugh***	Y	N	Y	Y	Y
25 ***Walsh***	Y	N	Y	Y	Y
26 Hinchey	Y	Y	N	N	Y
27 ***Reynolds***	N	N	Y	Y	Y
28 Slaughter	Y	Y	N	N	Y
29 LaFalce	N	Y	N	N	Y

	385	386	387	388	389
30 ***Quinn***	Y	N	Y	Y	Y
31 ***Houghton***	N	N	Y	Y	Y
NORTH CAROLINA					
1 Clayton	Y	Y	N	N	Y
2 Etheridge	N	Y	N	N	Y
3 ***Jones***	Y	N	N	Y	N
4 Price	N	Y	N	N	Y
5 ***Burr***	N	N	Y	Y	Y
6 ***Coble***	N	N	Y	Y	N
7 McIntyre	Y	Y	N	N	Y
8 ***Hayes***	Y	N	Y	Y	Y
9 ***Myrick***	N	N	Y	Y	Y
10 ***Ballenger***	N	N	Y	Y	Y
11 ***Taylor***	Y	N	Y	Y	Y
12 Watt	Y	Y	N	N	Y
NORTH DAKOTA					
AL Pomeroy	Y	Y	N	N	Y
OHIO					
1 ***Chabot***	Y	N	N	Y	N
2 ***Portman***	N	N	Y	Y	Y
3 Hall	Y	Y	N	N	Y
4 ***Oxley***	N	N	Y	Y	Y
5 ***Gillmor***	N	N	Y	Y	Y
6 Strickland	Y	Y	N	N	N
7 ***Hobson***	N	N	Y	Y	Y
8 ***Boehner***	N	N	Y	Y	Y
9 Kaptur	Y	Y	N	N	Y
10 Kucinich	Y	Y	N	N	Y
11 Jones	Y	Y	N	N	Y
12 ***Kasich***	N	N	Y	Y	Y
13 Brown	Y	Y	N	N	Y
14 Sawyer	N	Y	N	N	Y
15 ***Pryce***	N	N	Y	Y	Y
16 ***Regula***	N	N	Y	Y	Y
17 Traficant	Y	Y	Y	N	Y
18 ***Ney***	Y	N	Y	Y	Y
19 ***LaTourette***	N	N	Y	Y	Y
OKLAHOMA					
1 ***Largent***	N	N	Y	Y	Y
2 ***Coburn***	Y	N	N	Y	N
3 ***Watkins***	N	N	Y	Y	Y
4 ***Watts***	N	N	Y	Y	Y
5 ***Istook***	?	N	Y	Y	Y
6 ***Lucas***	Y	N	Y	Y	Y
OREGON					
1 Wu	N	Y	N	N	N
2 ***Walden***	N	N	Y	Y	Y
3 Blumenauer	N	Y	N	N	Y
4 DeFazio	Y	Y	N	N	Y
5 Hooley	N	Y	N	N	Y
PENNSYLVANIA					
1 Brady	Y	Y	N	N	Y
2 Fattah	Y	Y	N	N	Y
3 Borski	Y	Y	N	N	Y
4 Klink	Y	Y	N	N	Y
5 ***Peterson***	?	?	?	?	?
6 Holden	Y	Y	N	N	Y
7 ***Weldon***	Y	N	Y	Y	Y
8 ***Greenwood***	N	N	Y	Y	Y
9 ***Shuster***	Y	N	Y	Y	Y
10 ***Sherwood***	N	N	Y	Y	Y
11 Kanjorski	Y	Y	N	N	Y
12 Murtha	Y	Y	Y	N	?
13 Hoeffel	Y	Y	N	N	Y
14 Coyne	Y	Y	N	N	Y
15 ***Toomey***	N	N	N	Y	N
16 ***Pitts***	Y	N	Y	Y	Y
17 ***Gekas***	N	N	Y	Y	Y
18 Doyle	Y	Y	N	N	Y
19 ***Goodling***	Y	N	Y	Y	Y
20 Mascara	Y	Y	N	N	Y
21 ***English***	N	N	Y	Y	Y
RHODE ISLAND					
1 Kennedy	Y	Y	N	N	Y
2 Weygand	N	Y	N	N	Y
SOUTH CAROLINA					
1 ***Sanford***	N	N	N	Y	N
2 ***Spence***	N	N	Y	Y	Y
3 ***Graham***	N	N	Y	Y	N
4 ***DeMint***	N	N	Y	Y	N
5 Spratt	Y	Y	N	N	?
6 Clyburn	Y	Y	N	N	Y
SOUTH DAKOTA					
AL ***Thune***	N	N	Y	Y	N

	385	386	387	388	389
TENNESSEE					
1 ***Jenkins***	Y	N	Y	Y	Y
2 ***Duncan***	Y	N	Y	Y	Y
3 ***Wamp***	Y	N	Y	Y	Y
4 ***Hilleary***	Y	N	Y	Y	Y
5 Clement	N	Y	N	N	Y
6 Gordon	Y	Y	N	N	Y
7 ***Bryant***	N	N	Y	Y	Y
8 Tanner	N	Y	N	N	Y
9 Ford	Y	Y	N	N	Y
TEXAS					
1 Sandlin	N	Y	N	N	Y
2 Turner	N	Y	N	N	Y
3 ***Johnson, Sam***	N	N	Y	Y	Y
4 Hall	N	Y	N	N	Y
5 ***Sessions***	N	N	Y	Y	Y
6 ***Barton***	N	N	Y	Y	Y
7 ***Archer***	N	N	Y	Y	Y
8 ***Brady***	N	N	Y	Y	Y
9 Lampson	N	Y	N	N	Y
10 Doggett	Y	Y	N	N	N
11 Edwards	N	Y	N	N	Y
12 ***Granger***	N	N	Y	Y	Y
13 ***Thornberry***	N	N	Y	Y	Y
14 ***Paul***	Y	N	N	Y	N
15 Hinojosa	N	Y	N	N	Y
16 Reyes	?	?	?	N	Y
17 Stenholm	N	Y	N	N	N
18 Jackson-Lee	Y	Y	N	N	Y
19 ***Combest***	N	N	Y	Y	Y
20 Gonzalez	N	Y	N	N	Y
21 ***Smith***	N	N	Y	Y	Y
22 ***DeLay***	N	N	Y	Y	Y
23 ***Bonilla***	N	N	Y	Y	Y
24 Frost	N	Y	N	N	Y
25 Bentsen	N	Y	N	N	Y
26 ***Armey***	N	N	Y	Y	Y
27 Ortiz	N	Y	Y	N	?
28 Rodriguez	N	Y	Y	N	Y
29 Green	Y	Y	N	N	N
30 Johnson, E.B.	N	Y	N	N	Y
UTAH					
1 ***Hansen***	N	N	Y	Y	Y
2 ***Cook***	Y	N	Y	Y	Y
3 ***Cannon***	N	N	Y	Y	Y
VERMONT					
AL *Sanders*	Y	Y	N	N	Y
VIRGINIA					
1 ***Bateman***	N	N	Y	Y	Y
2 Pickett	N	Y	N	N	Y
3 Scott	Y	Y	N	N	Y
4 Sisisky	Y	Y	N	N	Y
5 Goode	Y	Y	N	N	N
6 ***Goodlatte***	N	N	Y	Y	Y
7 ***Bliley***	?	N	Y	Y	Y
8 Moran	N	Y	N	N	Y
9 Boucher	N	Y	Y	N	Y
10 ***Wolf***	Y	N	Y	Y	Y
11 ***Davis***	N	N	Y	Y	Y
WASHINGTON					
1 Inslee	N	Y	N	N	N
2 ***Metcalf***	Y	N	Y	Y	Y
3 Baird	Y	Y	N	N	N
4 ***Hastings***	N	N	Y	Y	Y
5 ***Nethercutt***	N	N	Y	Y	Y
6 Dicks	N	Y	Y	N	Y
7 McDermott	?	?	?	?	?
8 ***Dunn***	N	N	Y	Y	Y
9 Smith	N	Y	N	N	N
WEST VIRGINIA					
1 Mollohan	?	?	?	?	?
2 Wise	Y	Y	N	N	Y
3 Rahall	Y	Y	N	N	Y
WISCONSIN					
1 ***Ryan***	N	N	Y	Y	N
2 Baldwin	Y	Y	N	N	Y
3 Kind	N	Y	N	N	Y
4 Kleczka	Y	Y	?	N	Y
5 Barrett	Y	Y	N	N	Y
6 ***Petri***	N	N	Y	Y	N
7 Obey	Y	Y	N	N	Y
8 ***Green***	N	N	Y	Y	N
9 ***Sensenbrenner***	N	N	N	Y	N
WYOMING					
AL ***Cubin***	?	N	Y	Y	Y

Southern states - Ala., Ark., Fla., Ga., Ky., La., Miss., N.C., Okla., S.C., Tenn., Texas, Va.

House Votes 390, 391, 392, 393, 394, 395, 396, 397

390. HR 2684. Fiscal 2000 VA-HUD Appropriations/Ruling of the Chair. Judgment of the House to affirm the ruling of the chair that the Filner, D-Calif., amendment was out of order because it would violate the 1974 budget act. The Filner amendment would increase funding for veterans' medical care by $1.1 billion and designate the amount "emergency spending." Ruling of the chair upheld. 219-198: R 214-0; D 5-197 (ND 4-147, SD 1-50); I 0-1. Sept. 8, 1999.

391. HR 2684. Fiscal 2000 VA-HUD Appropriations/Selective Service System. Cunningham, R-Calif., amendment to strike bill language terminating the Selective Service System and provide $24.5 million for draft registration activities. The increase would be offset by reducing funding for the Federal Emergency Management Agency, the Environmental Protection Agency, the Chemical Safety and Hazard Investigation Board and housing programs. Rejected 187-232: R 130-83; D 57-148 (ND 30-123, SD 27-25); I 0-1. Sept. 8, 1999.

392. HR 2684. Fiscal 2000 VA-HUD Appropriations/International Space Station. Roemer, D-Ind., amendment to eliminate $2.1 billion in the bill for the international space station, leaving $300 million for termination costs. The funds would be reallocated to veterans medical care, housing programs, and NASA's science, aeronautics, technology program and debt reduction. Rejected 121-298: R 58-157; D 62-141 (ND 60-91, SD 2-50); I 1-0. Sept. 8, 1999.

393. HR 2684. Fiscal 2000 VA-HUD Appropriations/Rental Housing Subsidies. Nadler, D-N.Y., amendment to increase funding for Section 8 rental housing subsidies and for maintenance of public housing by a total of $305 million, offset by cutting $305 million from funding for the space station. Rejected 154-267: R 27-188; D 126-79 (ND 115-38, SD 11-41); I 1-0. Sept. 8, 1999.

394. HR 2684. Fiscal 2000 VA-HUD Appropriations/Housing for AIDS Patients. Nadler, D-N.Y., amendment to increase funding for the Opportunities for Persons with AIDS housing program by $10 million, offset by cuts in funding for the National Science Foundation. Adopted 212-207: R 49-166; D 162-41 (ND 133-18, SD 29-23); I 1-0. Sept. 8, 1999.

395. HR 2684. Fiscal 2000 VA-HUD Appropriations/NASA Science and Technology. Rogan, R-Calif., amendment to increase funding for NASA science, aeronautics and technology activities by $95 million, offset by reducing funding for the Environmental Protection Agency. Rejected 185-235: R 151-64; D 34-170 (ND 12-141, SD 22-29); I 0-1. Sept. 8, 1999.

396. HR 2684. Fiscal 2000 VA-HUD Appropriations/Brownfields Redevelopment. Gutierrez, D-Ill., amendment to increase funding for HUD brownfields redevelopment activities and for housing programs by a total of $5 million, offset by cuts in funding for NASA. Rejected 152-269: R 35-180; D 116-89 (ND 105-48, SD 11-41); I 1-0. Sept. 8, 1999.

397. H Con Res 180. Opposing Clemency for Puerto Rican Nationalists/Rule. Adoption of the rule (H Res 281) to provide for House floor consideration of the concurrent resolution to express the sense of Congress that the president should not have offered clemency to 16 Puerto Rican nationalists with ties to terrorist activities. Adopted 253-172: R 216-0; D 37-171 (ND 19-135, SD 18-36); I 0-1. Sept. 9, 1999.

Key

Y	Voted for (yea).
#	Paired for.
+	Announced for.
N	Voted against (nay).
X	Paired against.
–	Announced against.
P	Voted "present."
C	Voted "present" to avoid possible conflict of interest.
?	Did not vote or otherwise make a position known.

•

Democrats ***Republicans***
Independents

	390	391	392	393	394	395	396	397
ALABAMA								
1 ***Callahan***	Y	Y	N	N	N	Y	N	Y
2 ***Everett***	Y	Y	N	N	N	Y	N	Y
3 ***Riley***	Y	Y	N	N	N	Y	N	Y
4 ***Aderholt***	Y	Y	N	N	N	Y	N	Y
5 Cramer	N	Y	N	N	N	Y	N	N
6 ***Bachus***	Y	Y	N	N	Y	Y	N	Y
7 Hilliard	N	N	N	N	N	N	N	N
ALASKA								
AL ***Young***	?	?	?	?	?	?	?	?
ARIZONA								
1 ***Salmon***	Y	Y	N	N	N	Y	N	Y
2 Pastor	N	Y	N	Y	Y	N	Y	N
3 ***Stump***	Y	Y	N	N	N	Y	N	Y
4 ***Shadegg***	Y	Y	N	N	N	Y	N	Y
5 ***Kolbe***	Y	Y	Y	Y	Y	Y	N	Y
6 ***Hayworth***	Y	N	N	N	N	Y	N	Y
ARKANSAS								
1 Berry	+	+	–	+	+	+	–	+
2 Snyder	N	N	N	N	N	N	N	N
3 ***Hutchinson***	Y	N	N	N	N	Y	N	Y
4 ***Dickey***	Y	Y	Y	N	N	N	N	Y
CALIFORNIA								
1 Thompson	N	N	N	Y	Y	N	Y	N
2 ***Herger***	Y	Y	Y	N	N	Y	N	Y
3 ***Ose***	Y	N	N	N	Y	N	N	Y
4 ***Doolittle***	Y	Y	N	N	N	N	N	Y
5 Matsui	N	N	N	N	Y	N	N	N
6 Woolsey	N	N	Y	Y	?	N	Y	N
7 Miller, George	N	N	Y	Y	Y	N	Y	N
8 Pelosi	N	N	Y	Y	Y	N	Y	N
9 Lee	N	N	Y	Y	Y	N	Y	N
10 Tauscher	N	Y	N	N	Y	N	N	N
11 ***Pombo***	Y	Y	N	N	N	Y	N	Y
12 Lantos	?	?	?	?	?	?	?	N
13 Stark	N	N	Y	Y	Y	N	Y	N
14 Eshoo	N	N	N	Y	Y	N	Y	N
15 ***Campbell***	Y	N	N	Y	Y	N	N	Y
16 Lofgren	N	N	N	N	Y	Y	N	N
17 Farr	N	N	N	Y	Y	N	N	N
18 Condit	N	N	N	N	N	Y	N	N
19 ***Radanovich***	Y	Y	N	N	N	Y	N	Y
20 Dooley	N	N	N	N	N	N	N	N
21 ***Thomas***	Y	N	N	N	N	N	N	Y
22 Capps	N	N	N	Y	Y	Y	N	N
23 ***Gallegly***	Y	Y	N	N	N	N	N	Y
24 Sherman	N	N	N	N	Y	N	N	N
25 ***McKeon***	Y	Y	N	N	N	Y	N	Y
26 Berman	N	Y	N	N	Y	N	N	N
27 ***Rogan***	Y	Y	N	N	Y	Y	N	?
28 ***Dreier***	Y	Y	N	N	N	Y	N	Y
29 Waxman	N	N	Y	Y	Y	N	Y	N
30 Becerra	N	Y	N	Y	Y	N	Y	N
31 Martinez	N	N	?	Y	Y	Y	Y	N
32 Dixon	N	N	N	Y	Y	Y	Y	N
33 Roybal-Allard	N	N	N	Y	Y	N	Y	N
34 Napolitano	N	N	N	Y	Y	N	Y	N
35 Waters	N	N	N	Y	Y	N	Y	N
36 ***Kuykendall***	Y	Y	N	N	Y	Y	N	Y
37 Millender-McD.	N	N	N	Y	Y	N	Y	N
38 ***Horn***	Y	N	N	N	Y	Y	N	Y
39 ***Royce***	Y	N	N	N	Y	Y	N	Y

	390	391	392	393	394	395	396	397
40 ***Lewis***	Y	N	N	N	N	N	N	Y
41 ***Miller, Gary***	Y	Y	N	N	N	Y	N	Y
42 Vacant								
43 ***Calvert***	Y	Y	N	N	N	Y	N	Y
44 ***Bono***	Y	Y	N	N	N	Y	N	Y
45 ***Rohrabacher***	Y	N	N	N	N	Y	N	Y
46 Sanchez	N	Y	N	Y	Y	N	Y	N
47 ***Cox***	Y	N	N	N	N	Y	N	Y
48 ***Packard***	Y	Y	N	N	N	Y	N	Y
49 ***Bilbray***	Y	Y	Y	Y	Y	N	N	Y
50 Filner	N	N	Y	Y	Y	N	Y	N
51 ***Cunningham***	Y	Y	N	N	Y	Y	N	Y
52 ***Hunter***	Y	Y	N	N	N	Y	N	Y
COLORADO								
1 DeGette	N	N	N	Y	Y	N	Y	N
2 Udall	N	Y	N	N	Y	Y	N	N
3 ***McInnis***	Y	Y	Y	N	N	Y	N	Y
4 ***Schaffer***	Y	N	Y	N	N	Y	N	Y
5 ***Hefley***	Y	N	Y	N	N	N	N	Y
6 ***Tancredo***	Y	Y	Y	N	N	Y	N	Y
CONNECTICUT								
1 Larson	N	N	N	Y	Y	N	Y	N
2 Gejdenson	N	N	N	Y	Y	N	Y	N
3 DeLauro	N	N	Y	Y	Y	N	Y	N
4 ***Shays***	Y	N	Y	Y	Y	N	Y	Y
5 Maloney	N	Y	N	Y	Y	N	Y	N
6 ***Johnson***	Y	N	N	N	Y	N	N	Y
DELAWARE								
AL ***Castle***	Y	Y	N	N	Y	N	Y	Y
FLORIDA								
1 ***Scarborough***	?	Y	N	N	Y	Y	N	Y
2 Boyd	N	Y	N	N	N	Y	N	N
3 Brown	N	N	N	Y	Y	N	Y	N
4 ***Fowler***	Y	Y	N	N	Y	Y	N	Y
5 Thurman	N	Y	N	N	Y	N	N	N
6 ***Stearns***	Y	Y	N	N	N	Y	N	Y
7 ***Mica***	Y	Y	N	N	N	Y	N	Y
8 ***McCollum***	Y	Y	N	N	N	Y	N	Y
9 ***Bilirakis***	Y	Y	N	N	N	N	N	Y
10 ***Young***	Y	Y	N	N	N	N	N	Y
11 Davis	?	Y	N	N	Y	N	N	N
12 ***Canady***	Y	Y	N	N	N	Y	N	Y
13 ***Miller***	Y	Y	Y	N	N	Y	N	Y
14 ***Goss***	Y	Y	N	N	N	Y	N	Y
15 ***Weldon***	Y	N	N	N	N	Y	N	Y
16 ***Foley***	Y	Y	N	N	Y	Y	N	Y
17 Meek	N	Y	N	N	Y	N	N	N
18 ***Ros-Lehtinen***	Y	Y	N	Y	Y	N	Y	Y
19 Wexler	N	N	N	N	Y	N	N	N
20 Deutsch	N	N	N	N	Y	N	N	N
21 ***Diaz-Balart***	Y	Y	N	Y	Y	N	N	Y
22 ***Shaw***	Y	Y	N	N	N	Y	N	Y
23 Hastings	N	N	N	N	Y	N	N	N
GEORGIA								
1 ***Kingston***	Y	Y	Y	Y	N	Y	N	Y
2 Bishop	N	Y	Y	Y	Y	Y	Y	N
3 ***Collins***	Y	Y	N	N	N	Y	N	Y
4 McKinney	N	N	N	Y	Y	N	Y	N
5 Lewis	N	N	N	Y	Y	N	Y	N
6 ***Isakson***	Y	Y	N	N	N	Y	N	Y
7 ***Barr***	Y	Y	N	N	N	Y	N	Y
8 ***Chambliss***	Y	Y	N	N	N	Y	N	Y
9 ***Deal***	Y	Y	N	N	N	Y	N	Y
10 ***Norwood***	Y	Y	N	N	N	Y	N	Y
11 ***Linder***	Y	Y	N	N	N	Y	N	Y
HAWAII								
1 Abercrombie	N	Y	N	Y	Y	Y	N	N
2 Mink	N	N	Y	Y	Y	N	Y	N
IDAHO								
1 ***Chenoweth***	Y	Y	N	N	N	Y	N	Y
2 ***Simpson***	Y	Y	N	N	N	Y	N	Y
ILLINOIS								
1 Rush	N	N	Y	Y	Y	N	Y	N
2 Jackson	N	N	N	Y	Y	N	Y	N
3 Lipinski	N	N	N	N	N	N	Y	Y
4 Gutierrez	N	Y	Y	Y	Y	N	Y	N
5 Blagojevich	N	Y	Y	Y	Y	N	Y	Y
6 ***Hyde***	Y	?	N	N	N	N	N	Y
7 Davis	N	N	N	Y	Y	N	Y	N
8 ***Crane***	Y	N	N	N	N	Y	N	Y
9 Schakowsky	N	N	N	Y	Y	N	Y	N
10 ***Porter***	Y	Y	Y	N	Y	Y	Y	Y
11 ***Weller***	Y	?	Y	N	N	Y	Y	Y
12 Costello	N	N	Y	Y	Y	N	Y	N
13 ***Biggert***	Y	N	N	N	N	N	N	Y
14 ***Hastert***								

ND Northern Democrats SD Southern Democrats

	390	391	392	393	394	395	396	397
15 ***Ewing***	Y	Y	N	N	N	N	N	Y
16 ***Manzullo***	Y	N	Y	N	N	Y	N	Y
17 Evans	N	N	Y	Y	Y	N	Y	N
18 ***LaHood***	Y	Y	N	N	Y	Y	Y	Y
19 Phelps	N	N	Y	Y	N	N	Y	Y
20 ***Shimkus***	Y	Y	N	N	N	Y	N	Y
INDIANA								
1 Visclosky	N	N	Y	Y	Y	N	Y	N
2 ***McIntosh***	?	?	?	?	?	?	?	?
3 Roemer	N	N	Y	Y	Y	N	N	Y
4 ***Souder***	Y	Y	N	N	N	Y	N	Y
5 ***Buyer***	?	?	?	?	?	?	?	Y
6 ***Burton***	Y	Y	N	N	N	Y	N	Y
7 ***Pease***	Y	N	N	N	Y	N	Y	Y
8 ***Hostettler***	Y	Y	N	N	N	N	N	Y
9 Hill	Y	N	N	N	N	N	N	N
10 Carson	N	N	Y	Y	Y	N	Y	N
IOWA								
1 ***Leach***	Y	N	Y	Y	Y	N	Y	Y
2 ***Nussle***	Y	N	Y	Y	Y	N	Y	Y
3 Boswell	N	Y	N	N	N	N	N	N
4 ***Ganske***	Y	Y	Y	Y	N	N	Y	Y
5 ***Latham***	Y	Y	Y	N	N	N	Y	Y
KANSAS								
1 ***Moran***	Y	N	Y	Y	N	Y	Y	Y
2 ***Ryun***	Y	Y	Y	N	N	Y	N	Y
3 Moore	N	N	Y	Y	Y	N	Y	Y
4 ***Tiahrt***	Y	N	Y	N	Y	Y	N	Y
KENTUCKY								
1 ***Whitfield***	Y	Y	Y	Y	N	Y	N	Y
2 ***Lewis***	Y	Y	N	N	N	Y	N	Y
3 ***Northup***	Y	N	N	N	N	N	N	Y
4 Lucas	N	Y	N	N	N	Y	Y	Y
5 ***Rogers***	Y	Y	N	N	N	N	N	Y
6 ***Fletcher***	Y	Y	N	N	N	Y	N	Y
LOUISIANA								
1 ***Vitter***	Y	N	N	N	N	Y	N	Y
2 Jefferson	?	?	?	?	?	?	?	N
3 ***Tauzin***	Y	N	N	N	N	Y	N	Y
4 ***McCrery***	Y	N	N	N	N	N	N	Y
5 ***Cooksey***	Y	Y	N	N	N	Y	N	Y
6 ***Baker***	Y	N	N	N	N	Y	N	Y
7 John	N	N	N	N	N	Y	N	Y
MAINE								
1 Allen	N	N	N	Y	Y	N	Y	N
2 Baldacci	N	Y	N	Y	Y	N	Y	N
MARYLAND								
1 ***Gilchrest***	Y	Y	Y	N	N	Y	N	Y
2 ***Ehrlich***	Y	N	N	N	N	Y	Y	Y
3 Cardin	N	N	N	N	Y	N	N	N
4 Wynn	N	N	N	N	Y	N	N	N
5 Hoyer	N	Y	N	N	N	N	N	N
6 ***Bartlett***	Y	Y	N	N	N	Y	N	Y
7 Cummings	N	N	N	Y	Y	N	N	N
8 ***Morella***	Y	Y	N	N	Y	N	Y	Y
MASSACHUSETTS								
1 Olver	N	N	N	Y	N	N	Y	N
2 Neal	N	N	N	N	Y	N	N	N
3 McGovern	N	N	N	N	Y	N	N	N
4 Frank	Y	N	Y	Y	Y	N	Y	N
5 Meehan	N	N	N	Y	Y	N	N	N
6 Tierney	N	N	Y	Y	Y	N	Y	N
7 Markey	N	N	N	Y	Y	N	Y	N
8 Capuano	N	N	N	N	Y	N	N	N
9 Moakley	N	N	N	Y	Y	N	N	N
10 Delahunt	N	N	Y	Y	Y	N	Y	N
MICHIGAN								
1 Stupak	N	N	N	Y	Y	N	Y	Y
2 ***Hoekstra***	Y	N	Y	N	N	Y	Y	Y
3 ***Ehlers***	Y	N	N	N	N	Y	N	Y
4 ***Camp***	Y	N	Y	Y	Y	N	Y	Y
5 Barcia	N	N	N	N	Y	N	N	Y
6 ***Upton***	Y	N	Y	Y	N	N	Y	Y
7 ***Smith***	Y	Y	Y	N	N	Y	Y	Y
8 Stabenow	N	Y	N	Y	Y	Y	N	N
9 Kildee	N	N	Y	Y	Y	N	Y	N
10 Bonior	N	N	Y	Y	Y	N	Y	N
11 ***Knollenberg***	Y	N	N	N	N	N	N	Y
12 Levin	N	N	Y	Y	Y	N	Y	N
13 Rivers	N	N	Y	Y	Y	Y	N	N
14 Conyers	N	N	N	Y	Y	N	Y	N
15 Kilpatrick	N	N	N	Y	Y	N	Y	N
16 Dingell	N	N	N	Y	N	N	N	N
MINNESOTA								
1 ***Gutknecht***	Y	N	N	N	N	Y	N	Y
2 Minge	N	N	Y	Y	Y	N	Y	N
3 ***Ramstad***	Y	N	Y	Y	Y	N	Y	Y
4 Vento	N	N	Y	Y	Y	N	Y	N
5 Sabo	N	N	N	Y	Y	N	Y	N
6 Luther	N	N	Y	Y	Y	N	Y	Y
7 Peterson	N	N	N	N	N	N	Y	N
8 Oberstar	N	N	Y	Y	Y	N	Y	N
MISSISSIPPI								
1 ***Wicker***	Y	Y	N	N	N	Y	N	Y
2 Thompson	N	N	N	Y	Y	N	N	N
3 ***Pickering***	Y	Y	N	N	N	Y	N	Y
4 Shows	N	Y	N	Y	N	Y	Y	Y
5 Taylor	N	Y	N	N	N	Y	N	Y
MISSOURI								
1 Clay	N	N	N	N	Y	N	N	N
2 ***Talent***	Y	Y	N	N	Y	Y	N	Y
3 Gephardt	Y	N	N	N	Y	N	Y	N
4 Skelton	N	Y	N	N	N	Y	N	Y
5 McCarthy	–	N	N	Y	Y	N	Y	N
6 Danner	?	N	Y	Y	Y	Y	Y	Y
7 ***Blunt***	Y	N	N	N	N	Y	N	Y
8 ***Emerson***	Y	Y	Y	N	N	Y	N	Y
9 ***Hulshof***	Y	Y	N	N	Y	Y	N	Y
MONTANA								
AL ***Hill***	Y	N	N	N	N	Y	N	Y
NEBRASKA								
1 ***Bereuter***	Y	N	N	N	N	Y	Y	Y
2 ***Terry***	Y	Y	N	N	N	N	N	Y
3 ***Barrett***	Y	N	N	N	N	N	N	Y
NEVADA								
1 Berkley	N	Y	N	Y	Y	N	N	Y
2 ***Gibbons***	Y	Y	N	N	N	Y	N	Y
NEW HAMPSHIRE								
1 ***Sununu***	?	?	?	?	?	?	?	?
2 ***Bass***	Y	Y	Y	Y	N	N	N	Y
NEW JERSEY								
1 Andrews	N	Y	N	N	Y	N	N	N
2 ***LoBiondo***	Y	N	Y	Y	Y	N	Y	Y
3 ***Saxton***	Y	Y	N	N	N	N	N	Y
4 ***Smith***	Y	N	N	N	Y	N	Y	Y
5 ***Roukema***	Y	N	Y	N	N	N	N	Y
6 Pallone	N	N	Y	Y	Y	N	Y	N
7 ***Franks***	Y	N	Y	Y	Y	N	Y	Y
8 Pascrell	N	Y	Y	Y	Y	N	Y	N
9 Rothman	N	Y	N	Y	Y	N	Y	N
10 Payne	N	N	Y	Y	Y	N	Y	N
11 ***Frelinghuysen***	Y	Y	N	N	Y	N	N	Y
12 Holt	N	N	Y	Y	N	N	Y	N
13 Menendez	N	N	Y	Y	Y	N	Y	N
NEW MEXICO								
1 ***Wilson***	Y	N	N	Y	Y	Y	Y	Y
2 ***Skeen***	Y	Y	N	N	N	Y	N	Y
3 Udall	N	N	Y	Y	N	N	Y	N
NEW YORK								
1 Forbes	N	Y	N	N	Y	N	N	Y
2 ***Lazio***	Y	Y	Y	Y	Y	N	Y	Y
3 ***King***	Y	Y	N	N	Y	N	N	Y
4 McCarthy	N	Y	Y	Y	Y	N	N	N
5 Ackerman	N	N	?	Y	Y	N	Y	N
6 Meeks	N	N	N	Y	Y	Y	Y	N
7 Crowley	N	N	N	Y	Y	N	Y	N
8 Nadler	N	N	Y	Y	Y	N	Y	N
9 Weiner	N	N	N	Y	Y	N	Y	N
10 Towns	?	?	?	?	?	?	?	?
11 Owens	N	N	N	Y	Y	N	Y	N
12 Velázquez	N	N	Y	Y	Y	N	Y	N
13 ***Fossella***	Y	Y	Y	N	Y	N	N	Y
14 Maloney	N	N	Y	Y	Y	N	Y	N
15 Rangel	?	?	?	?	?	?	?	?
16 Serrano	Y	N	Y	Y	?	N	Y	N
17 Engel	N	N	N	Y	Y	N	Y	N
18 Lowey	N	N	Y	Y	Y	N	Y	N
19 ***Kelly***	Y	N	Y	Y	Y	N	Y	Y
20 ***Gilman***	Y	N	N	Y	Y	N	N	Y
21 McNulty	N	N	N	Y	Y	N	Y	N
22 ***Sweeney***	Y	Y	N	N	Y	Y	N	Y
23 ***Boehlert***	Y	N	N	N	N	N	N	Y
24 ***McHugh***	?	?	?	?	?	?	?	Y
25 ***Walsh***	Y	N	N	N	N	N	N	Y
26 Hinchey	N	N	N	N	Y	N	Y	N
27 ***Reynolds***	Y	N	N	N	N	N	Y	Y
28 Slaughter	N	N	N	Y	Y	N	N	N
29 LaFalce	N	N	N	Y	Y	N	Y	N
30 ***Quinn***	Y	Y	N	N	Y	N	Y	Y
31 ***Houghton***	Y	Y	N	N	N	N	N	Y
NORTH CAROLINA								
1 Clayton	N	N	N	Y	Y	N	N	N
2 Etheridge	N	Y	N	N	N	N	N	Y
3 ***Jones***	Y	Y	N	N	N	Y	N	Y
4 Price	N	N	N	N	N	N	N	N
5 ***Burr***	Y	Y	N	N	N	N	Y	Y
6 ***Coble***	Y	N	Y	N	N	Y	N	Y
7 McIntyre	N	Y	N	N	N	Y	N	Y
8 ***Hayes***	Y	Y	Y	N	N	Y	N	Y
9 ***Myrick***	Y	Y	Y	Y	Y	N	Y	Y
10 ***Ballenger***	Y	Y	N	N	N	Y	N	Y
11 ***Taylor***	Y	Y	N	N	N	Y	N	Y
12 Watt	N	N	N	Y	Y	N	Y	N
NORTH DAKOTA								
AL Pomeroy	N	N	Y	Y	Y	N	Y	N
OHIO								
1 ***Chabot***	Y	N	Y	N	Y	N	Y	Y
2 ***Portman***	Y	N	Y	N	N	N	N	Y
3 Hall	N	N	N	Y	Y	N	Y	N
4 ***Oxley***	Y	Y	N	N	N	Y	N	Y
5 ***Gillmor***	Y	Y	N	N	N	N	Y	Y
6 Strickland	N	N	Y	Y	Y	N	Y	N
7 ***Hobson***	Y	N	N	N	N	N	N	Y
8 ***Boehner***	Y	N	N	N	Y	Y	N	Y
9 Kaptur	N	N	Y	Y	Y	N	N	N
10 Kucinich	N	N	N	N	Y	N	N	N
11 Jones	N	N	N	N	Y	N	N	N
12 ***Kasich***	Y	N	N	N	N	N	N	Y
13 Brown	N	N	Y	Y	Y	N	N	N
14 Sawyer	N	N	N	Y	Y	N	N	N
15 ***Pryce***	?	?	?	?	?	?	?	?
16 ***Regula***	Y	Y	N	N	N	N	Y	Y
17 Traficant	N	Y	N	Y	Y	N	Y	Y
18 ***Ney***	Y	Y	N	N	N	Y	N	Y
19 ***LaTourette***	Y	N	N	N	N	Y	N	Y
OKLAHOMA								
1 ***Largent***	Y	N	N	N	N	Y	N	Y
2 ***Coburn***	Y	Y	Y	N	N	Y	N	Y
3 ***Watkins***	Y	Y	Y	N	N	Y	N	Y
4 ***Watts***	Y	N	N	N	N	Y	N	Y
5 ***Istook***	Y	Y	N	N	N	Y	N	Y
6 ***Lucas***	Y	Y	N	N	N	Y	N	Y
OREGON								
1 Wu	N	N	N	Y	Y	N	N	N
2 ***Walden***	Y	Y	N	N	N	Y	N	Y
3 Blumenauer	N	N	Y	Y	Y	N	Y	N
4 DeFazio	N	N	Y	Y	Y	N	Y	N
5 Hooley	N	Y	N	Y	Y	N	Y	N
PENNSYLVANIA								
1 Brady	N	N	Y	Y	Y	N	Y	N
2 Fattah	N	N	Y	Y	Y	N	Y	N
3 Borski	N	N	N	N	Y	N	Y	N
4 Klink	N	Y	Y	Y	Y	N	Y	N
5 ***Peterson***	Y	N	N	N	N	Y	Y	Y
6 Holden	N	Y	Y	N	N	N	N	N
7 ***Weldon***	Y	Y	N	N	N	Y	N	Y
8 ***Greenwood***	Y	Y	N	N	Y	Y	N	Y
9 ***Shuster***	Y	N	Y	N	N	Y	N	Y
10 ***Sherwood***	Y	Y	N	N	N	Y	N	Y
11 Kanjorski	N	Y	Y	Y	N	N	Y	N
12 Murtha	N	Y	N	N	N	N	N	N
13 Hoeffel	N	N	N	Y	Y	N	Y	N
14 Coyne	N	N	Y	Y	Y	N	Y	N
15 ***Toomey***	Y	N	N	N	N	Y	N	Y
16 ***Pitts***	Y	N	N	N	N	N	N	Y
17 ***Gekas***	Y	N	N	N	N	Y	N	Y
18 Doyle	N	Y	N	N	Y	N	Y	N
19 ***Goodling***	Y	N	Y	N	N	Y	N	Y
20 Mascara	N	Y	N	N	N	N	Y	N
21 ***English***	Y	N	N	N	Y	Y	N	Y
RHODE ISLAND								
1 Kennedy	N	N	N	Y	Y	N	Y	Y
2 Weygand	N	N	N	Y	Y	N	Y	N
SOUTH CAROLINA								
1 ***Sanford***	Y	Y	Y	N	N	Y	N	Y
2 ***Spence***	Y	Y	N	N	N	Y	N	Y
3 ***Graham***	Y	Y	N	N	N	Y	N	Y
4 ***DeMint***	Y	N	Y	N	N	Y	N	Y
5 Spratt	N	N	N	N	N	N	N	N
6 Clyburn	N	N	N	N	N	N	Y	N
SOUTH DAKOTA								
AL ***Thune***	Y	N	Y	N	N	Y	Y	Y
TENNESSEE								
1 ***Jenkins***	Y	Y	N	N	N	Y	N	Y
2 ***Duncan***	Y	N	Y	Y	N	Y	N	Y
3 ***Wamp***	Y	N	Y	Y	N	Y	N	Y
4 ***Hilleary***	Y	Y	Y	Y	N	Y	N	Y
5 Clement	N	Y	N	N	Y	N	N	Y
6 Gordon	N	Y	N	N	N	Y	N	N
7 ***Bryant***	Y	Y	N	N	N	Y	N	Y
8 Tanner	N	Y	N	N	N	Y	N	N
9 Ford	N	N	N	Y	Y	N	Y	N
TEXAS								
1 Sandlin	?	?	?	?	?	?	?	Y
2 Turner	N	Y	N	N	Y	Y	N	Y
3 ***Johnson, Sam***	Y	Y	N	N	N	Y	N	Y
4 Hall	N	Y	N	N	N	Y	N	Y
5 ***Sessions***	Y	N	N	N	N	Y	N	Y
6 ***Barton***	Y	N	N	N	N	Y	N	Y
7 ***Archer***	Y	Y	N	N	N	Y	N	Y
8 ***Brady***	Y	N	N	N	Y	Y	N	Y
9 Lampson	N	N	N	N	Y	Y	N	N
10 Doggett	Y	N	N	N	Y	N	N	Y
11 Edwards	N	Y	N	N	Y	N	N	N
12 ***Granger***	Y	Y	N	N	N	Y	N	Y
13 ***Thornberry***	Y	Y	N	N	N	Y	N	Y
14 ***Paul***	Y	N	Y	N	N	Y	N	Y
15 Hinojosa	N	Y	N	N	Y	N	N	N
16 Reyes	N	Y	N	N	Y	Y	N	N
17 Stenholm	N	Y	N	N	N	Y	N	Y
18 Jackson-Lee	N	N	N	N	Y	N	N	N
19 ***Combest***	Y	Y	N	N	N	Y	N	Y
20 Gonzalez	N	N	N	Y	Y	N	Y	N
21 ***Smith***	Y	Y	N	N	N	Y	N	Y
22 ***DeLay***	Y	N	N	N	N	Y	N	Y
23 ***Bonilla***	Y	Y	Y	N	N	Y	N	Y
24 Frost	N	Y	N	N	Y	N	N	Y
25 Bentsen	N	N	N	N	N	N	N	Y
26 ***Armey***	Y	Y	N	N	N	Y	N	Y
27 Ortiz	N	Y	N	N	Y	Y	N	N
28 Rodriguez	N	Y	N	N	Y	N	Y	N
29 Green	N	N	N	N	Y	Y	N	N
30 Johnson, E.B.	N	N	N	N	N	N	N	N
UTAH								
1 ***Hansen***	Y	Y	N	N	N	Y	N	Y
2 ***Cook***	Y	N	N	N	N	Y	N	Y
3 ***Cannon***	Y	Y	N	N	N	Y	N	Y
VERMONT								
AL *Sanders*	N	N	Y	Y	Y	N	Y	N
VIRGINIA								
1 ***Bateman***	Y	Y	N	N	N	Y	N	Y
2 Pickett	N	Y	N	N	N	Y	N	Y
3 Scott	N	N	N	N	Y	Y	N	N
4 Sisisky	N	Y	N	N	N	Y	N	Y
5 Goode	N	Y	Y	N	N	Y	N	Y
6 ***Goodlatte***	Y	N	Y	N	N	Y	N	Y
7 ***Bliley***	Y	Y	N	N	N	Y	N	Y
8 Moran	N	Y	N	Y	Y	Y	N	N
9 Boucher	N	N	N	N	N	?	N	Y
10 ***Wolf***	Y	Y	N	N	N	Y	N	Y
11 ***Davis***	Y	N	N	N	Y	Y	N	Y
WASHINGTON								
1 Inslee	N	N	N	N	Y	N	N	Y
2 ***Metcalf***	Y	N	N	N	N	Y	N	Y
3 Baird	N	N	N	N	Y	N	N	N
4 ***Hastings***	Y	Y	N	N	N	Y	N	Y
5 ***Nethercutt***	Y	Y	N	N	N	Y	N	Y
6 Dicks	N	N	N	N	Y	N	N	N
7 McDermott	N	N	N	Y	Y	N	Y	N
8 ***Dunn***	Y	N	N	N	Y	Y	N	Y
9 Smith	N	N	N	N	Y	N	N	N
WEST VIRGINIA								
1 Mollohan	N	N	N	N	Y	N	N	Y
2 Wise	N	N	N	N	Y	N	N	Y
3 Rahall	N	Y	Y	Y	N	N	N	N
WISCONSIN								
1 ***Ryan***	Y	Y	Y	N	N	N	N	Y
2 Baldwin	N	N	Y	Y	Y	N	Y	N
3 Kind	N	N	Y	Y	Y	N	Y	Y
4 Kleczka	N	N	N	Y	Y	N	Y	Y
5 Barrett	N	N	Y	Y	Y	N	Y	N
6 ***Petri***	Y	N	Y	N	N	N	N	Y
7 Obey	N	N	Y	Y	Y	N	Y	N
8 ***Green***	Y	Y	Y	N	N	N	N	Y
9 ***Sensenbrenner***	Y	N	N	N	N	Y	N	Y
WYOMING								
AL ***Cubin***	Y	N	Y	Y	N	Y	N	Y

Southern states - Ala., Ark., Fla., Ga., Ky., La., Miss., N.C., Okla., S.C., Tenn., Texas, Va.

Key

Y	Voted for (yea).
#	Paired for.
+	Announced for.
N	Voted against (nay).
X	Paired against.
–	Announced against.
P	Voted "present."
C	Voted "present" to avoid possible conflict of interest.
?	Did not vote or otherwise make a position known.

•

Democrats ***Republicans***
Independents

398. H Con Res 180. Opposing Clemency for 16 Puerto Rico Nationals/Adoption. Pease, R-Ind., motion to suspend the rules and adopt the concurrent resolution to express the sense of Congress that the president should not have offered or granted clemency to 16 members of a Puerto Rico independence group convicted of seditious conspiracy against the United States. Motion agreed to 311-41: R 218-0; D 93-41 (ND 63-33, SD 30-8); I 0-0. Sept. 9, 1999. A two-thirds majority of those present and voting (283 in this case) is required for passage under suspension of the rules.

399. HR 2684. Fiscal 2000 VA-HUD Appropriations/U.S. Fire Administration. Smith, R-Mich., amendment to increase funding for the U.S. Fire Administration, a division of the Federal Emergency Management Agency, by $5 million, offset by $5 million in funding cuts for the Environmental Protection Agency by $5 million. Rejected 69-354: R 56-159; D 13-194 (ND 12-141, SD 1-53); I 0-1. Sept. 9, 1999.

400. HR 2684. Fiscal 2000 VA-HUD Appropriations/Veterans Health Care Funding Formula. Hinchey, D-N.Y., amendment to prohibit the use of funds in the bill to implement the Veterans Equitable Resource Allocation system, which is intended to distribute funding to regional VA health care networks in a way that accounts for shifting populations of veterans. Rejected 158-266: R 67-149; D 90-117 (ND 90-63, SD 0-54); I 1-0. Sept. 9, 1999.

401. HR 2684. Fiscal 2000 VA-HUD Appropriations/VA Construction Grants. Tancredo, R-Colo., amendment to increase funding for the VA's state extended care facilities construction grant program by $10 million, offset by reductions in funding for the Chemical Safety Hazard Investigation Board and the Environmental Protection Agency's Office of Inspector General. Adopted 366-54: R 196-17; D 169-37 (ND 122-29, SD 47-8); I 1-0. Sept. 9, 1999.

402. HR 2684. Fiscal 2000 VA-HUD Appropriations/Recommit. Obey, D-Wis., motion to recommit the bill to the committee with instructions to find new offsets to replace a $3 billion reduction in borrowing authority for the TVA in the bill. Motion rejected 207-215: R 0-213; D 206-2 (ND 153-0, SD 53-2); I 1-0. Sept. 9, 1999.

403. HR 2684. Fiscal 2000 VA-HUD Appropriations/Passage. Passage of the bill to appropriate $92 billion for the departments of Veteran's Affairs, and Housing and Urban Development, NASA, the Federal Emergency Management Agency, and related agencies. The measure would appropriate $26.1 billion for HUD, $12.7 billion for NASA, $3.6 billion for the National Science Foundation and $7.3 billion for the Environmental Protection Agency. Passed 235-187: R 196-18; D 39-168 (ND 26-126, SD 13-42); I 0-1. Sept. 9, 1999. A "nay" was a vote in support of the president's position.

404. HR 2587. Fiscal 2000 District of Columbia Appropriations/Conference Report. Adoption of the conference report on the bill to appropriate $429.1 million in federal payments to the District of Columbia and approve the districts $6.8 billion budget. Adopted (thus sent to the Senate) 208-206: R 203-8; D 5-197 (ND 2-145, SD 3-52); I 0-1. Sept. 9, 1999.

	398	399	400	401	402	403	404
ALABAMA							
1 ***Callahan***	Y	N	N	Y	N	Y	Y
2 ***Everett***	Y	Y	N	Y	N	Y	Y
3 ***Riley***	Y	N	Y	Y	N	Y	Y
4 ***Aderholt***	Y	N	N	Y	N	Y	Y
5 Cramer	Y	N	N	Y	Y	N	N
6 ***Bachus***	Y	N	Y	Y	N	Y	Y
7 Hilliard	N	N	N	N	Y	N	N
ALASKA							
AL ***Young***	?	?	?	?	?	?	?
ARIZONA							
1 ***Salmon***	Y	Y	N	Y	N	N	Y
2 Pastor	P	N	N	Y	Y	N	N
3 ***Stump***	Y	N	N	N	N	Y	Y
4 ***Shadegg***	Y	Y	N	Y	N	N	Y
5 ***Kolbe***	Y	N	N	Y	N	Y	Y
6 ***Hayworth***	Y	Y	N	Y	N	Y	Y
ARKANSAS							
1 Berry	+	+	–	Y	Y	N	N
2 Snyder	P	N	N	Y	Y	N	N
3 ***Hutchinson***	Y	?	N	Y	N	Y	Y
4 ***Dickey***	Y	N	N	Y	N	Y	Y
CALIFORNIA							
1 Thompson	Y	N	N	Y	Y	N	N
2 ***Herger***	Y	Y	N	Y	N	Y	Y
3 ***Ose***	Y	N	N	N	N	Y	Y
4 ***Doolittle***	Y	N	N	Y	N	Y	Y
5 Matsui	Y	N	Y	Y	Y	N	N
6 Woolsey	P	N	N	Y	Y	N	N
7 Miller, George	P	N	N	N	Y	?	?
8 Pelosi	?	N	N	Y	Y	N	N
9 Lee	N	N	N	N	Y	N	N
10 Tauscher	P	N	N	Y	Y	N	N
11 ***Pombo***	Y	Y	Y	Y	N	Y	Y
12 Lantos	P	N	N	Y	Y	N	N
13 Stark	P	N	N	N	Y	N	?
14 Eshoo	P	N	N	Y	Y	N	N
15 ***Campbell***	Y	N	N	N	N	Y	N
16 Lofgren	P	N	N	Y	Y	N	N
17 Farr	P	N	N	Y	Y	N	N
18 Condit	Y	N	N	Y	Y	Y	N
19 ***Radanovich***	Y	Y	N	Y	N	Y	Y
20 Dooley	Y	N	N	N	Y	N	N
21 ***Thomas***	Y	N	N	Y	N	Y	Y
22 Capps	Y	N	N	Y	Y	N	N
23 ***Gallegly***	Y	N	N	Y	N	Y	Y
24 Sherman	Y	N	N	N	Y	N	N
25 ***McKeon***	Y	N	N	Y	N	Y	Y
26 Berman	P	N	Y	N	Y	N	N
27 ***Rogan***	?	?	?	?	?	?	?
28 ***Dreier***	Y	N	N	Y	N	Y	Y
29 Waxman	P	N	Y	N	Y	N	N
30 Becerra	N	N	N	Y	Y	N	N
31 Martinez	P	Y	Y	Y	Y	N	N
32 Dixon	P	N	N	N	Y	N	N
33 Roybal-Allard	N	N	N	Y	Y	N	N
34 Napolitano	N	N	N	Y	Y	Y	N
35 Waters	N	N	Y	N	Y	N	N
36 ***Kuykendall***	Y	N	N	N	N	Y	Y
37 Millender-McD.	P	N	N	N	Y	N	N
38 ***Horn***	Y	N	N	Y	N	Y	Y
39 ***Royce***	Y	N	N	Y	N	Y	Y
40 ***Lewis***	Y	N	N	N	N	Y	Y
41 ***Miller, Gary***	Y	N	N	Y	N	Y	Y
42 Vacant							
43 ***Calvert***	Y	N	N	Y	N	Y	Y
44 ***Bono***	Y	N	N	Y	N	Y	Y
45 ***Rohrabacher***	Y	Y	N	Y	N	Y	Y
46 Sanchez	P	N	N	Y	Y	N	N
47 ***Cox***	Y	N	N	N	N	Y	Y
48 ***Packard***	Y	N	N	N	N	Y	Y
49 ***Bilbray***	Y	N	N	N	N	Y	Y
50 Filner	P	N	N	Y	Y	N	N
51 ***Cunningham***	Y	N	N	Y	N	Y	Y
52 ***Hunter***	Y	Y	N	Y	N	Y	Y
COLORADO							
1 DeGette	P	N	N	Y	Y	N	N
2 Udall	P	N	N	Y	Y	N	N
3 ***McInnis***	Y	N	N	Y	N	N	N
4 ***Schaffer***	Y	Y	N	Y	N	N	N
5 ***Hefley***	Y	Y	N	Y	N	Y	Y
6 ***Tancredo***	Y	Y	N	Y	N	Y	Y
CONNECTICUT							
1 Larson	Y	Y	Y	Y	Y	N	N
2 Gejdenson	P	N	Y	Y	Y	N	N
3 DeLauro	Y	N	Y	Y	Y	N	N
4 ***Shays***	Y	N	Y	Y	N	Y	Y
5 Maloney	Y	N	Y	Y	Y	Y	N
6 ***Johnson***	Y	N	Y	Y	N	Y	Y
DELAWARE							
AL ***Castle***	Y	N	Y	Y	N	Y	Y
FLORIDA							
1 ***Scarborough***	Y	N	N	Y	N	Y	Y
2 Boyd	Y	N	N	Y	Y	Y	N
3 Brown	P	N	N	Y	Y	N	N
4 ***Fowler***	Y	Y	N	Y	N	Y	Y
5 Thurman	Y	N	N	Y	Y	Y	N
6 ***Stearns***	Y	N	N	Y	N	Y	Y
7 ***Mica***	Y	Y	N	Y	N	Y	Y
8 ***McCollum***	Y	N	N	Y	N	N	Y
9 ***Bilirakis***	Y	N	N	Y	N	Y	Y
10 ***Young***	Y	N	N	N	N	Y	Y
11 Davis	Y	N	N	Y	Y	N	N
12 ***Canady***	Y	N	N	Y	N	Y	Y
13 ***Miller***	Y	N	N	Y	N	Y	Y
14 ***Goss***	Y	N	N	Y	N	Y	Y
15 ***Weldon***	Y	N	N	?	N	N	Y
16 ***Foley***	Y	N	N	Y	N	Y	Y
17 Meek	N	N	N	N	Y	N	N
18 ***Ros-Lehtinen***	Y	N	N	Y	N	Y	Y
19 Wexler	P	N	N	Y	Y	N	N
20 Deutsch	P	N	N	Y	Y	N	N
21 ***Diaz-Balart***	Y	N	N	Y	N	Y	?
22 ***Shaw***	Y	N	N	Y	N	Y	Y
23 Hastings	N	N	N	N	Y	N	N
GEORGIA							
1 ***Kingston***	Y	Y	N	Y	N	Y	Y
2 Bishop	P	N	N	Y	Y	N	N
3 ***Collins***	Y	N	N	Y	N	Y	Y
4 McKinney	N	N	N	N	Y	N	N
5 Lewis	P	N	N	Y	Y	N	N
6 ***Isakson***	Y	N	N	Y	N	Y	Y
7 ***Barr***	Y	Y	N	Y	N	Y	Y
8 ***Chambliss***	Y	N	N	Y	N	Y	Y
9 ***Deal***	Y	N	N	Y	N	Y	Y
10 ***Norwood***	Y	N	N	Y	N	Y	Y
11 ***Linder***	Y	N	N	Y	?	Y	Y
HAWAII							
1 Abercrombie	N	N	N	Y	Y	Y	N
2 Mink	N	N	N	Y	Y	N	N
IDAHO							
1 ***Chenoweth***	Y	N	N	Y	N	Y	Y
2 ***Simpson***	Y	N	N	Y	N	Y	Y
ILLINOIS							
1 Rush	N	N	Y	N	Y	N	N
2 Jackson	N	N	Y	N	Y	N	N
3 Lipinski	Y	N	Y	Y	Y	Y	?
4 Gutierrez	N	N	Y	Y	Y	N	N
5 Blagojevich	Y	N	Y	Y	Y	N	N
6 ***Hyde***	Y	N	N	Y	N	Y	Y
7 Davis	N	N	Y	N	Y	N	N
8 ***Crane***	Y	Y	Y	Y	N	Y	Y
9 Schakowsky	N	N	Y	N	Y	N	N
10 ***Porter***	Y	N	Y	Y	N	Y	Y
11 ***Weller***	Y	N	Y	Y	N	Y	Y
12 Costello	Y	N	Y	Y	Y	N	N
13 ***Biggert***	Y	N	Y	Y	N	Y	Y
14 ***Hastert***	Y				N	Y	Y

ND Northern Democrats SD Southern Democrats

	398	399	400	401	402	403	404
15 ***Ewing***	Y	N	Y	Y	N	Y	Y
16 ***Manzullo***	Y	N	Y	Y	N	Y	Y
17 Evans	Y	N	Y	Y	Y	N	N
18 ***LaHood***	Y	N	Y	Y	N	Y	Y
19 Phelps	Y	N	Y	Y	Y	Y	Y
20 ***Shimkus***	Y	Y	Y	Y	N	Y	Y
INDIANA							
1 Visclosky	Y	N	Y	Y	Y	Y	N
2 ***McIntosh***	Y	Y	N	Y	N	Y	Y
3 Roemer	Y	N	Y	Y	Y	N	N
4 ***Souder***	Y	N	N	Y	N	Y	Y
5 ***Buyer***	Y	N	N	Y	N	Y	Y
6 ***Burton***	Y	Y	N	Y	N	Y	Y
7 ***Pease***	Y	N	N	Y	N	Y	Y
8 ***Hostettler***	Y	Y	N	Y	N	N	Y
9 Hill	Y	N	N	Y	Y	N	N
10 Carson	N	N	N	Y	Y	N	N
IOWA							
1 ***Leach***	Y	N	Y	Y	N	Y	Y
2 ***Nussle***	Y	Y	Y	Y	N	Y	Y
3 Boswell	Y	N	Y	Y	Y	N	N
4 ***Ganske***	Y	N	Y	Y	N	N	Y
5 ***Latham***	Y	Y	Y	?	?	?	?
KANSAS							
1 ***Moran***	Y	N	N	Y	N	Y	Y
2 ***Ryun***	Y	Y	N	Y	N	Y	Y
3 Moore	Y	N	N	Y	Y	N	N
4 ***Tiahrt***	Y	Y	N	Y	N	Y	Y
KENTUCKY							
1 ***Whitfield***	Y	N	N	Y	N	Y	Y
2 ***Lewis***	Y	N	N	Y	N	Y	Y
3 ***Northup***	Y	N	N	Y	N	Y	Y
4 Lucas	Y	N	N	Y	Y	Y	Y
5 ***Rogers***	Y	N	N	Y	N	Y	Y
6 ***Fletcher***	Y	N	N	Y	N	Y	Y
LOUISIANA							
1 ***Vitter***	Y	N	N	Y	N	Y	Y
2 Jefferson	?	N	N	Y	Y	N	N
3 ***Tauzin***	Y	N	N	Y	N	Y	Y
4 ***McCrery***	Y	N	N	Y	N	Y	Y
5 ***Cooksey***	Y	?	?	?	?	?	?
6 ***Baker***	Y	N	N	Y	N	Y	Y
7 John	Y	N	N	Y	Y	N	N
MAINE							
1 Allen	Y	N	Y	Y	Y	N	N
2 Baldacci	Y	N	Y	Y	Y	N	N
MARYLAND							
1 ***Gilchrest***	Y	N	N	Y	N	Y	Y
2 ***Ehrlich***	Y	N	N	Y	N	N	Y
3 Cardin	Y	N	N	Y	Y	N	N
4 Wynn	N	N	N	Y	Y	N	N
5 Hoyer	P	Y	N	Y	Y	N	N
6 ***Bartlett***	Y	Y	N	Y	N	N	Y
7 Cummings	Y	N	N	Y	Y	N	N
8 ***Morella***	Y	N	N	N	N	N	N
MASSACHUSETTS							
1 Olver	N	N	Y	N	Y	N	N
2 Neal	P	N	Y	Y	Y	Y	N
3 McGovern	P	N	Y	Y	Y	N	N
4 Frank	P	N	Y	N	Y	N	N
5 Meehan	P	N	Y	Y	Y	N	N
6 Tierney	P	N	Y	Y	Y	N	N
7 Markey	P	N	Y	N	Y	N	N
8 Capuano	P	N	Y	Y	Y	N	N
9 Moakley	P	N	Y	Y	Y	N	?
10 Delahunt	P	N	Y	N	Y	N	N
MICHIGAN							
1 Stupak	Y	N	Y	Y	Y	Y	N
2 ***Hoekstra***	Y	N	Y	Y	N	Y	Y
3 ***Ehlers***	Y	N	Y	N	N	Y	Y
4 ***Camp***	Y	N	Y	Y	N	Y	Y
5 Barcia	Y	Y	Y	Y	Y	Y	Y
6 ***Upton***	Y	N	Y	Y	N	Y	Y
7 ***Smith***	Y	Y	Y	Y	N	N	Y
8 Stabenow	P	N	Y	Y	Y	N	N
9 Kildee	Y	N	Y	Y	Y	N	N
10 Bonior	P	N	Y	?	Y	N	N
11 ***Knollenberg***	Y	N	N	N	N	Y	Y
12 Levin	Y	N	Y	Y	Y	N	N
13 Rivers	P	N	Y	Y	Y	N	N
14 Conyers	N	N	Y	N	Y	N	N
15 Kilpatrick	N	N	Y	N	Y	N	N
16 Dingell	N	Y	N	Y	Y	N	N

	398	399	400	401	402	403	404
MINNESOTA							
1 ***Gutknecht***	Y	N	N	Y	N	Y	Y
2 Minge	Y	N	N	Y	Y	N	N
3 ***Ramstad***	Y	N	Y	Y	N	Y	Y
4 Vento	P	N	N	N	Y	N	N
5 Sabo	P	Y	N	N	Y	N	N
6 Luther	Y	N	Y	Y	Y	N	N
7 Peterson	P	Y	N	Y	Y	N	N
8 Oberstar	P	Y	Y	Y	Y	N	N
MISSISSIPPI							
1 ***Wicker***	Y	N	N	Y	N	Y	Y
2 Thompson	N	N	N	Y	Y	N	N
3 ***Pickering***	Y	Y	N	Y	N	Y	Y
4 Shows	Y	N	N	Y	Y	Y	N
5 Taylor	Y	N	N	Y	Y	Y	N
MISSOURI							
1 Clay	N	N	N	N	Y	N	N
2 ***Talent***	Y	N	N	Y	N	Y	Y
3 Gephardt	P	N	N	Y	Y	N	N
4 Skelton	Y	N	Y	Y	Y	N	N
5 McCarthy	P	N	N	Y	Y	Y	N
6 Danner	Y	Y	N	Y	Y	Y	N
7 ***Blunt***	Y	N	N	Y	N	Y	Y
8 ***Emerson***	Y	Y	N	Y	N	Y	Y
9 ***Hulshof***	Y	N	Y	Y	N	Y	Y
MONTANA							
AL ***Hill***	Y	N	N	Y	N	Y	Y
NEBRASKA							
1 ***Bereuter***	Y	N	Y	Y	N	Y	Y
2 ***Terry***	Y	N	Y	Y	N	Y	Y
3 ***Barrett***	Y	N	Y	Y	N	Y	Y
NEVADA							
1 Berkley	Y	N	N	Y	Y	N	N
2 ***Gibbons***	Y	Y	N	Y	N	Y	Y
NEW HAMPSHIRE							
1 ***Sununu***	?	?	?	?	?	?	?
2 ***Bass***	Y	N	Y	Y	N	Y	Y
NEW JERSEY							
1 Andrews	Y	N	Y	Y	Y	N	N
2 ***LoBiondo***	Y	N	Y	Y	N	Y	Y
3 ***Saxton***	Y	N	Y	Y	N	Y	Y
4 ***Smith***	Y	N	Y	Y	N	Y	Y
5 ***Roukema***	Y	N	Y	Y	N	Y	?
6 Pallone	P	N	Y	Y	Y	N	N
7 ***Franks***	Y	N	Y	Y	N	Y	Y
8 Pascrell	P	Y	Y	Y	Y	N	N
9 Rothman	Y	N	Y	Y	Y	N	N
10 Payne	N	N	Y	Y	Y	N	N
11 ***Frelinghuysen***	Y	N	Y	N	N	Y	Y
12 Holt	N	N	Y	Y	Y	N	N
13 Menendez	N	N	Y	Y	Y	N	N
NEW MEXICO							
1 ***Wilson***	Y	N	N	Y	N	Y	Y
2 ***Skeen***	Y	N	N	Y	N	Y	Y
3 Udall	Y	N	N	Y	Y	N	N
NEW YORK							
1 Forbes	Y	N	Y	Y	Y	Y	N
2 ***Lazio***	Y	N	Y	Y	N	Y	Y
3 ***King***	Y	N	Y	Y	N	Y	Y
4 McCarthy	Y	Y	Y	Y	Y	N	N
5 Ackerman	P	N	Y	Y	Y	N	?
6 Meeks	N	N	Y	Y	Y	N	N
7 Crowley	P	?	?	?	?	?	?
8 Nadler	P	N	Y	Y	Y	N	N
9 Weiner	P	N	Y	Y	Y	N	N
10 Towns	?	?	?	?	?	?	?
11 Owens	N	N	Y	N	Y	N	N
12 Velázquez	N	N	Y	N	Y	N	N
13 ***Fossella***	Y	N	Y	Y	N	Y	N
14 Maloney	Y	N	Y	Y	Y	N	N
15 Rangel	?	?	?	?	?	?	?
16 Serrano	N	N	Y	Y	Y	N	N
17 Engel	N	N	Y	Y	Y	N	N
18 Lowey	Y	N	Y	Y	Y	N	N
19 ***Kelly***	Y	N	Y	Y	N	Y	Y
20 ***Gilman***	Y	N	Y	Y	N	Y	Y
21 McNulty	Y	N	Y	Y	Y	N	N
22 ***Sweeney***	Y	Y	Y	Y	N	Y	Y
23 ***Boehlert***	Y	N	Y	N	N	Y	Y
24 ***McHugh***	Y	N	Y	N	N	Y	Y
25 ***Walsh***	Y	N	Y	N	N	Y	Y
26 Hinchey	N	N	Y	Y	Y	N	N
27 ***Reynolds***	Y	N	Y	Y	N	Y	Y
28 Slaughter	P	N	Y	Y	Y	N	N
29 LaFalce	P	N	Y	N	Y	N	N

	398	399	400	401	402	403	404
30 ***Quinn***	Y	N	Y	Y	N	Y	Y
31 ***Houghton***	Y	N	Y	?	?	?	?
NORTH CAROLINA							
1 Clayton	P	N	N	N	Y	N	N
2 Etheridge	Y	N	N	Y	Y	N	N
3 ***Jones***	Y	N	N	Y	N	Y	Y
4 Price	Y	N	N	Y	Y	Y	N
5 ***Burr***	Y	N	N	Y	N	Y	Y
6 ***Coble***	Y	Y	N	Y	N	Y	Y
7 McIntyre	Y	N	N	Y	Y	N	Y
8 ***Hayes***	Y	Y	N	Y	N	Y	Y
9 ***Myrick***	Y	N	N	Y	N	Y	Y
10 ***Ballenger***	Y	N	N	N	N	Y	Y
11 ***Taylor***	Y	N	N	Y	N	Y	Y
12 Watt	P	N	N	N	Y	Y	N
NORTH DAKOTA							
AL Pomeroy	Y	N	N	Y	Y	N	N
OHIO							
1 ***Chabot***	Y	N	Y	Y	N	Y	Y
2 ***Portman***	Y	N	N	Y	N	Y	Y
3 Hall	Y	N	N	Y	Y	N	N
4 ***Oxley***	Y	N	N	Y	N	Y	?
5 ***Gillmor***	Y	N	N	Y	N	Y	Y
6 Strickland	Y	N	N	Y	Y	Y	N
7 ***Hobson***	Y	N	N	N	N	Y	Y
8 ***Boehner***	Y	N	N	Y	N	Y	Y
9 Kaptur	Y	N	N	Y	Y	Y	N
10 Kucinich	N	N	Y	N	Y	N	N
11 Jones	N	N	Y	+	Y	N	N
12 ***Kasich***	Y	N	N	Y	N	Y	Y
13 Brown	P	N	N	Y	Y	N	N
14 Sawyer	P	N	Y	Y	Y	N	N
15 ***Pryce***	?	?	?	?	?	?	?
16 ***Regula***	Y	N	N	Y	N	Y	Y
17 Traficant	Y	N	Y	Y	Y	N	N
18 ***Ney***	Y	Y	Y	Y	N	Y	Y
19 ***LaTourette***	Y	N	Y	Y	N	Y	Y
OKLAHOMA							
1 ***Largent***	Y	N	N	Y	N	Y	Y
2 ***Coburn***	Y	N	N	Y	N	N	Y
3 ***Watkins***	Y	N	N	Y	N	Y	Y
4 ***Watts***	Y	N	N	Y	N	Y	Y
5 ***Istook***	Y	N	N	Y	N	Y	Y
6 ***Lucas***	Y	Y	N	Y	N	Y	Y
OREGON							
1 Wu	Y	N	N	Y	Y	N	N
2 ***Walden***	Y	Y	N	Y	N	Y	Y
3 Blumenauer	P	N	N	Y	Y	N	N
4 DeFazio	P	N	N	Y	Y	N	N
5 Hooley	P	N	N	Y	Y	Y	N
PENNSYLVANIA							
1 Brady	N	N	Y	Y	Y	N	N
2 Fattah	N	N	Y	Y	Y	N	N
3 Borski	P	N	Y	N	Y	N	N
4 Klink	Y	N	Y	Y	Y	N	N
5 ***Peterson***	Y	Y	Y	Y	N	Y	Y
6 Holden	Y	Y	Y	Y	Y	Y	N
7 ***Weldon***	Y	Y	Y	Y	?	?	?
8 ***Greenwood***	Y	N	Y	Y	N	Y	Y
9 ***Shuster***	Y	N	Y	Y	N	Y	Y
10 ***Sherwood***	Y	Y	Y	Y	N	Y	Y
11 Kanjorski	P	N	Y	Y	Y	N	N
12 Murtha	Y	N	Y	Y	Y	Y	?
13 Hoeffel	N	N	Y	Y	Y	N	N
14 Coyne	P	N	Y	Y	Y	N	N
15 ***Toomey***	Y	N	Y	Y	N	N	Y
16 ***Pitts***	Y	Y	Y	Y	N	Y	Y
17 ***Gekas***	Y	Y	Y	Y	N	Y	Y
18 Doyle	Y	N	Y	Y	Y	Y	N
19 ***Goodling***	Y	Y	Y	Y	N	Y	Y
20 Mascara	Y	N	Y	Y	Y	Y	N
21 ***English***	Y	Y	Y	Y	N	Y	Y
RHODE ISLAND							
1 Kennedy	Y	N	Y	Y	Y	N	N
2 Weygand	Y	N	Y	Y	Y	N	N
SOUTH CAROLINA							
1 ***Sanford***	Y	N	N	Y	N	N	Y
2 ***Spence***	Y	N	Y	Y	N	Y	Y
3 ***Graham***	Y	N	Y	Y	N	Y	Y
4 ***DeMint***	Y	Y	N	Y	N	Y	Y
5 Spratt	Y	N	N	Y	Y	Y	N
6 Clyburn	N	N	N	Y	Y	N	N
SOUTH DAKOTA							
AL ***Thune***	Y	N	N	Y	N	Y	Y

	398	399	400	401	402	403	404
TENNESSEE							
1 ***Jenkins***	Y	Y	N	Y	N	Y	Y
2 ***Duncan***	Y	Y	N	Y	N	Y	N
3 ***Wamp***	Y	N	N	Y	N	Y	Y
4 ***Hilleary***	Y	Y	N	Y	N	Y	Y
5 Clement	Y	N	N	Y	Y	N	N
6 Gordon	Y	N	N	Y	Y	Y	N
7 ***Bryant***	Y	N	N	Y	N	Y	Y
8 Tanner	Y	N	N	Y	Y	N	N
9 Ford	P	N	N	Y	Y	N	N
TEXAS							
1 Sandlin	Y	N	N	Y	Y	N	N
2 Turner	Y	N	N	Y	Y	N	N
3 ***Johnson, Sam***	Y	Y	N	Y	N	Y	Y
4 Hall	Y	N	N	Y	Y	N	N
5 ***Sessions***	Y	Y	N	Y	N	Y	Y
6 ***Barton***	Y	N	Y	Y	N	N	Y
7 ***Archer***	Y	N	N	Y	N	Y	Y
8 ***Brady***	Y	Y	N	Y	N	Y	Y
9 Lampson	Y	N	N	Y	Y	N	N
10 Doggett	Y	N	N	Y	Y	N	N
11 Edwards	Y	N	N	Y	Y	N	N
12 ***Granger***	Y	N	N	Y	N	Y	Y
13 ***Thornberry***	Y	Y	N	Y	N	Y	Y
14 ***Paul***	Y	Y	N	Y	N	N	N
15 Hinojosa	?	N	N	Y	Y	N	N
16 Reyes	P	N	N	Y	Y	N	N
17 Stenholm	Y	N	N	Y	Y	N	N
18 Jackson-Lee	P	N	N	Y	Y	N	N
19 ***Combest***	Y	N	N	Y	N	Y	Y
20 Gonzalez	Y	N	N	Y	Y	N	N
21 ***Smith***	Y	N	N	Y	N	Y	Y
22 ***DeLay***	Y	N	N	Y	N	Y	Y
23 ***Bonilla***	Y	Y	N	Y	N	Y	Y
24 Frost	Y	N	N	Y	Y	N	N
25 Bentsen	Y	N	N	Y	Y	N	N
26 ***Armey***	Y	Y	N	Y	N	Y	Y
27 Ortiz	P	N	N	Y	Y	N	N
28 Rodriguez	N	N	N	Y	Y	N	N
29 Green	Y	N	N	Y	Y	N	N
30 Johnson, E.B.	P	N	N	N	Y	N	N
UTAH							
1 ***Hansen***	Y	N	N	Y	N	Y	Y
2 ***Cook***	Y	N	N	Y	N	Y	Y
3 ***Cannon***	Y	N	N	Y	N	Y	Y
VERMONT							
AL *Sanders*	P	N	Y	Y	Y	N	N
VIRGINIA							
1 ***Bateman***	Y	N	N	Y	N	Y	Y
2 Pickett	Y	N	N	Y	Y	N	N
3 Scott	N	N	N	N	Y	N	N
4 Sisisky	Y	N	N	Y	Y	N	N
5 Goode	Y	Y	N	Y	N	Y	Y
6 ***Goodlatte***	Y	Y	N	Y	N	Y	N
7 ***Bliley***	Y	N	N	Y	N	Y	Y
8 Moran	P	N	N	Y	Y	Y	N
9 Boucher	Y	N	N	Y	Y	Y	N
10 ***Wolf***	Y	N	N	Y	N	Y	Y
11 ***Davis***	Y	N	N	Y	N	Y	Y
WASHINGTON							
1 Inslee	Y	N	N	Y	Y	N	N
2 ***Metcalf***	Y	N	N	Y	N	Y	Y
3 Baird	Y	N	N	Y	Y	N	N
4 ***Hastings***	Y	N	N	Y	N	Y	Y
5 ***Nethercutt***	Y	N	N	Y	N	Y	Y
6 Dicks	Y	N	N	Y	Y	N	N
7 McDermott	P	N	N	Y	Y	N	N
8 ***Dunn***	Y	N	N	Y	N	Y	Y
9 Smith	Y	N	N	Y	Y	N	N
WEST VIRGINIA							
1 Mollohan	Y	N	Y	N	Y	Y	N
2 Wise	Y	N	N	Y	Y	Y	N
3 Rahall	P	N	N	Y	Y	Y	N
WISCONSIN							
1 ***Ryan***	Y	N	Y	Y	N	Y	Y
2 Baldwin	N	N	N	Y	Y	N	N
3 Kind	Y	N	Y	Y	Y	N	N
4 Kleczka	Y	N	Y	Y	Y	N	N
5 Barrett	Y	N	N	Y	Y	N	N
6 ***Petri***	Y	N	Y	Y	N	Y	Y
7 Obey	P	N	Y	Y	Y	N	N
8 ***Green***	Y	N	Y	Y	N	Y	Y
9 ***Sensenbrenner***	Y	Y	Y	Y	N	N	Y
WYOMING							
AL ***Cubin***	Y	N	N	Y	N	Y	Y

Southern states - Ala., Ark., Fla., Ga., Ky., La., Miss., N.C., Okla., S.C., Tenn., Texas, Va.

405. HR 2561. Fiscal 2000 Defense Appropriations/Closed Conference. Lewis, R-Calif., motion to close portions of the conference to the public during consideration of national security issues. Motion agreed to 388-7: R 198-0; D 189-7 (ND 139-5, SD 50-2); I 1-0. Sept. 13, 1999.

406. HR 658. Thomas Cole National Historic Site/Passage. Sherwood, R-Pa., motion to suspend the rules and pass the bill to establish the Thomas Cole National Historic Site in the state of New York as an affiliated area of the National Park System. Motion agreed to 396-6: R 197-6; D 198-0 (ND 146-0, SD 52-0); I 1-0. Sept. 13, 1999. A two-thirds majority of those present and voting (268 in this case) is required for passage under suspension of the rules.

407. H Con Res 184. 'Family Friendly' Television/Adoption. Upton, R-Mich., motion to suspend the rules and adopt the concurrent resolution to express the sense of Congress that it is important to encourage television networks, studios and the production community to produce more quality programs. Motion agreed to 396-0: R 203-0; D 192-0 (ND 142-0, SD 50-0); I 1-0. Sept. 13, 1999. A two-thirds majority of those present and voting (264 in this case) is required for adoption under suspension of the rules.

408. Procedural Motion/Journal. Approval of the House Journal of Monday, Sept. 13, 1999. Approved 360-41: R 189-15; D 170-26 (ND 125-20, SD 45-6); I 1-0. Sept. 14, 1999.

409. HR 1883. Iran Non-proliferation/Passage. Gilman, R-N.Y., motion to suspend the rules and pass the bill to require the president to submit a report to Congress identifying countries or persons that have transferred, or allowed the transfer of, missile components or technology to Iran since January 1999. The bill would mandate sanctions against those countries, including denying arms export licenses. The United States would be prohibited from making payments to the Russian Space Agency for the international space station, unless the president determines that Russia is acting to prevent weapons proliferation in Iran. Motion agreed to 419-0: R 213-0; D 205-0 (ND 152-0, SD 53-0); I 1-0. Sept. 14, 1999. A two-thirds majority of those present and voting (280 in this case) is required for passage under suspension of the rules. A "nay" was a vote in support of the president's position.

410. HR 2606. Fiscal 2000 Foreign Operations Appropriations/Motion To Instruct. Pelosi, D-Calif., motion to instruct conferees to insist upon House provisions with respect to limiting Indonesian participation in International Military Education and Training to "expanded military and training only." Motion agreed to 419-0: R 211-0; D 207-0 (ND 154-0, SD 53-0); I 1-0. Sept. 14, 1999.

411. HR 417. Campaign Finance Overhaul/Individual Contribution Limit. Whitfield, R-Ky., amendment to increase the limit on individual campaign contributions per election from $1,000 to $3,000. Rejected 127-300: R 125-91; D 2-208 (ND 1-155, SD 1-53); I 0-1. Sept. 14, 1999.

412. HR 417. Campaign Finance Overhaul/Aggregate Individual Contribution Limit. Doolittle, R-Calif., amendment to increase the aggregate annual individual contribution level from $30,000 to $75,000. Rejected 123-302: R 122-93; D 1-208 (ND 1-154, SD 0-54); I 0-1. Sept. 14, 1999.

Key

- Y Voted for (yea).
- # Paired for.
- + Announced for.
- N Voted against (nay).
- X Paired against.
- – Announced against.
- P Voted "present."
- C Voted "present" to avoid possible conflict of interest.
- ? Did not vote or otherwise make a position known.

•

Democrats ***Republicans***
Independents

	405	406	407	408	409	410	411	412
ALABAMA								
1 ***Callahan***	Y	Y	Y	Y	Y	Y	Y	Y
2 ***Everett***	Y	Y	Y	Y	Y	Y	Y	Y
3 ***Riley***	Y	Y	Y	N	Y	Y	Y	Y
4 ***Aderholt***	Y	Y	Y	N	Y	Y	N	N
5 Cramer	Y	Y	Y	Y	Y	Y	N	N
6 ***Bachus***	Y	Y	Y	Y	Y	Y	N	N
7 Hilliard	N	Y	Y	N	Y	Y	N	N
ALASKA								
AL ***Young***	Y	Y	Y	?	Y	Y	Y	Y
ARIZONA								
1 ***Salmon***	Y	Y	Y	Y	Y	Y	Y	?
2 Pastor	Y	Y	Y	Y	Y	Y	N	N
3 ***Stump***	Y	Y	Y	Y	Y	Y	Y	Y
4 ***Shadegg***	Y	Y	Y	Y	Y	Y	Y	Y
5 ***Kolbe***	Y	Y	Y	Y	Y	Y	Y	N
6 ***Hayworth***	Y	Y	Y	Y	Y	Y	Y	Y
ARKANSAS								
1 Berry	Y	Y	Y	Y	Y	Y	N	N
2 Snyder	Y	Y	Y	Y	Y	Y	N	N
3 ***Hutchinson***	Y	Y	Y	N	Y	Y	Y	Y
4 ***Dickey***	Y	Y	Y	Y	Y	Y	Y	Y
CALIFORNIA								
1 Thompson	Y	Y	Y	N	Y	Y	N	N
2 ***Herger***	Y	Y	Y	Y	Y	Y	Y	Y
3 ***Ose***	Y	Y	Y	Y	Y	Y	N	N
4 ***Doolittle***	Y	Y	Y	Y	Y	Y	Y	Y
5 Matsui	Y	Y	Y	Y	Y	Y	N	N
6 Woolsey	Y	Y	Y	Y	Y	Y	N	N
7 Miller, George	Y	Y	Y	Y	Y	Y	N	N
8 Pelosi	Y	Y	Y	Y	Y	Y	N	N
9 Lee	N	Y	Y	Y	Y	Y	N	N
10 Tauscher	Y	Y	Y	Y	Y	Y	N	N
11 ***Pombo***	Y	Y	Y	Y	Y	Y	Y	Y
12 Lantos	?	?	?	Y	Y	Y	N	N
13 Stark	N	Y	Y	Y	Y	Y	N	N
14 Eshoo	Y	Y	Y	Y	Y	Y	N	N
15 ***Campbell***	Y	Y	Y	Y	Y	Y	N	N
16 Lofgren	Y	Y	Y	Y	Y	Y	N	N
17 Farr	Y	Y	Y	Y	Y	Y	N	N
18 Condit	Y	Y	Y	Y	Y	Y	N	N
19 ***Radanovich***	Y	Y	Y	Y	Y	Y	Y	Y
20 Dooley	?	?	?	Y	Y	Y	N	N
21 ***Thomas***	Y	Y	Y	Y	Y	Y	Y	Y
22 Capps	Y	Y	Y	Y	Y	Y	N	N
23 ***Gallegly***	Y	Y	Y	Y	Y	Y	N	N
24 Sherman	Y	Y	Y	Y	Y	Y	N	N
25 ***McKeon***	Y	Y	Y	Y	Y	Y	Y	Y
26 Berman	Y	Y	Y	Y	Y	Y	N	N
27 ***Rogan***	?	?	?	N	Y	Y	Y	Y
28 ***Dreier***	Y	Y	Y	?	Y	Y	Y	Y
29 Waxman	Y	Y	Y	Y	Y	Y	N	N
30 Becerra	Y	Y	Y	Y	+	Y	N	N
31 Martinez	Y	Y	Y	Y	Y	Y	N	N
32 Dixon	Y	Y	Y	?	Y	Y	N	N
33 Roybal-Allard	Y	Y	?	Y	Y	Y	N	N
34 Napolitano	Y	Y	Y	Y	Y	Y	N	N
35 Waters	Y	Y	Y	N	Y	Y	N	N
36 ***Kuykendall***	Y	Y	Y	Y	Y	Y	N	N
37 Millender-McD.	Y	Y	Y	Y	Y	Y	N	N
38 ***Horn***	Y	Y	Y	Y	Y	Y	N	N
39 ***Royce***	Y	N	Y	Y	Y	Y	Y	Y
40 ***Lewis***	Y	Y	Y	Y	Y	Y	N	Y
41 ***Miller***	Y	Y	Y	Y	Y	Y	Y	Y
42 Vacant								
43 ***Calvert***	Y	Y	Y	Y	Y	Y	Y	Y
44 ***Bono***	Y	Y	Y	Y	Y	Y	Y	Y
45 ***Rohrabacher***	Y	Y	Y	Y	Y	Y	Y	Y
46 Sanchez	Y	Y	Y	Y	Y	Y	N	N
47 ***Cox***	Y	Y	Y	Y	Y	Y	Y	Y
48 ***Packard***	Y	Y	Y	Y	Y	Y	Y	Y
49 ***Bilbray***	Y	Y	Y	N	Y	Y	N	N
50 Filner	Y	Y	Y	N	Y	Y	N	N
51 ***Cunningham***	Y	Y	Y	Y	Y	Y	N	N
52 ***Hunter***	Y	Y	Y	?	Y	Y	N	N
COLORADO								
1 DeGette	Y	Y	Y	Y	Y	Y	N	N
2 Udall	Y	Y	Y	Y	Y	Y	N	N
3 ***McInnis***	Y	Y	Y	Y	Y	Y	Y	Y
4 ***Schaffer***	Y	Y	Y	N	Y	Y	Y	Y
5 ***Hefley***	Y	Y	Y	N	Y	Y	N	Y
6 ***Tancredo***	Y	Y	Y	Y	Y	Y	Y	Y
CONNECTICUT								
1 Larson	Y	Y	Y	Y	Y	Y	N	N
2 Gejdenson	Y	Y	Y	Y	Y	Y	N	N
3 DeLauro	Y	Y	Y	Y	Y	Y	N	N
4 ***Shays***	Y	Y	Y	Y	Y	Y	N	N
5 Maloney	Y	Y	Y	Y	Y	Y	N	N
6 ***Johnson***	Y	Y	Y	Y	Y	Y	N	N
DELAWARE								
AL ***Castle***	Y	Y	Y	Y	Y	Y	N	N
FLORIDA								
1 ***Scarborough***	?	?	?	Y	Y	Y	Y	Y
2 Boyd	Y	Y	Y	Y	Y	Y	N	N
3 Brown	?	?	?	?	Y	Y	N	N
4 ***Fowler***	Y	Y	Y	Y	Y	Y	Y	Y
5 Thurman	Y	Y	Y	Y	Y	Y	N	N
6 ***Stearns***	Y	Y	Y	Y	Y	Y	Y	N
7 ***Mica***	Y	Y	Y	Y	Y	Y	N	N
8 ***McCollum***	Y	Y	Y	Y	Y	Y	Y	Y
9 ***Bilirakis***	Y	Y	Y	Y	Y	Y	N	N
10 ***Young***	Y	Y	Y	Y	Y	Y	N	N
11 Davis	Y	Y	Y	Y	Y	Y	N	N
12 ***Canady***	Y	Y	Y	Y	Y	Y	Y	Y
13 ***Miller***	Y	Y	Y	Y	Y	Y	Y	Y
14 ***Goss***	Y	Y	Y	Y	Y	Y	N	N
15 ***Weldon***	Y	Y	Y	Y	Y	Y	Y	Y
16 ***Foley***	Y	Y	Y	Y	Y	Y	N	N
17 Meek	Y	Y	Y	Y	Y	Y	N	N
18 ***Ros-Lehtinen***	+	+	+	?	?	?	?	?
19 Wexler	Y	Y	Y	Y	Y	Y	N	N
20 Deutsch	Y	Y	Y	Y	Y	Y	N	N
21 ***Diaz-Balart***	Y	Y	Y	Y	Y	Y	N	N
22 ***Shaw***	?	?	?	?	?	?	?	?
23 Hastings	?	?	?	?	?	?	?	?
GEORGIA								
1 ***Kingston***	?	?	?	?	?	?	?	?
2 Bishop	Y	Y	Y	Y	Y	Y	N	N
3 ***Collins***	Y	Y	Y	Y	Y	Y	Y	Y
4 McKinney	N	Y	Y	Y	Y	Y	N	N
5 Lewis	Y	Y	Y	Y	Y	Y	N	N
6 ***Isakson***	Y	Y	Y	Y	Y	Y	N	N
7 ***Barr***	Y	Y	Y	Y	Y	Y	Y	Y
8 ***Chambliss***	Y	Y	Y	Y	Y	Y	Y	Y
9 ***Deal***	Y	Y	Y	Y	?	?	N	N
10 ***Norwood***	Y	Y	Y	Y	Y	Y	Y	Y
11 ***Linder***	?	Y	Y	Y	Y	Y	Y	Y
HAWAII								
1 Abercrombie	Y	Y	Y	Y	Y	Y	N	N
2 Mink	Y	Y	Y	Y	Y	Y	N	N
IDAHO								
1 ***Chenoweth***	Y	N	Y	Y	Y	Y	Y	Y
2 ***Simpson***	Y	Y	Y	Y	Y	Y	Y	Y
ILLINOIS								
1 Rush	Y	Y	Y	Y	Y	Y	N	N
2 Jackson	Y	Y	Y	Y	Y	Y	N	N
3 Lipinski	Y	Y	Y	Y	Y	Y	N	N
4 Gutierrez	N	Y	Y	N	Y	Y	N	N
5 Blagojevich	Y	Y	Y	Y	Y	Y	N	N
6 ***Hyde***	Y	Y	Y	Y	Y	Y	Y	N
7 Davis	Y	Y	Y	Y	Y	Y	N	N
8 ***Crane***	Y	Y	Y	N	Y	Y	Y	Y
9 Schakowsky	Y	Y	Y	Y	Y	Y	N	N
10 ***Porter***	?	?	?	+	+	+	–	–
11 ***Weller***	Y	Y	Y	N	Y	Y	N	N
12 Costello	Y	Y	Y	N	Y	Y	N	N
13 ***Biggert***	Y	Y	Y	Y	Y	Y	Y	Y
14 ***Hastert***								

ND Northern Democrats SD Southern Democrats

	405	406	407	408	409	410	411	412
15 ***Ewing***	Y	Y	Y	Y	Y	Y	N	N
16 ***Manzullo***	?	?	?	Y	Y	Y	N	N
17 Evans	Y	Y	Y	Y	Y	Y	N	N
18 ***LaHood***	Y	Y	Y	Y	Y	Y	N	N
19 Phelps	Y	Y	Y	Y	Y	Y	N	N
20 ***Shimkus***	Y	Y	Y	Y	Y	Y	Y	Y
INDIANA								
1 Visclosky	Y	Y	Y	N	Y	Y	N	N
2 ***McIntosh***	?	?	Y	?	Y	Y	Y	Y
3 Roemer	Y	Y	Y	Y	Y	Y	N	N
4 ***Souder***	Y	Y	Y	Y	Y	Y	N	Y
5 ***Buyer***	?	Y	Y	Y	Y	?	Y	Y
6 ***Burton***	Y	Y	Y	?	Y	Y	Y	Y
7 ***Pease***	Y	Y	Y	Y	Y	Y	Y	Y
8 ***Hostettler***	Y	Y	Y	Y	Y	Y	Y	Y
9 Hill	Y	Y	Y	Y	Y	Y	Y	Y
10 Carson	+	+	+	P	Y	Y	N	N
IOWA								
1 ***Leach***	Y	Y	Y	?	Y	Y	N	N
2 ***Nussle***	Y	Y	Y	Y	Y	Y	N	N
3 Boswell	Y	Y	Y	Y	Y	Y	N	N
4 ***Ganske***	Y	Y	Y	Y	Y	Y	N	N
5 ***Latham***	Y	Y	Y	Y	Y	Y	N	Y
KANSAS								
1 ***Moran***	Y	Y	Y	N	Y	Y	N	N
2 ***Ryun***	Y	Y	Y	Y	Y	Y	Y	Y
3 Moore	Y	Y	Y	Y	Y	Y	N	N
4 ***Tiahrt***	Y	Y	Y	Y	Y	Y	Y	Y
KENTUCKY								
1 ***Whitfield***	?	Y	Y	Y	Y	Y	Y	Y
2 ***Lewis***	Y	Y	Y	Y	Y	Y	Y	Y
3 ***Northup***	Y	Y	Y	Y	Y	Y	N	N
4 Lucas	Y	Y	Y	Y	Y	Y	N	N
5 ***Rogers***	Y	Y	Y	Y	Y	Y	N	Y
6 ***Fletcher***	Y	Y	Y	Y	Y	Y	N	N
LOUISIANA								
1 ***Vitter***	Y	Y	Y	Y	Y	Y	Y	Y
2 Jefferson	?	?	?	?	?	?	N	N
3 ***Tauzin***	?	Y	Y	Y	Y	Y	Y	Y
4 ***McCrery***	?	?	?	Y	Y	Y	Y	Y
5 ***Cooksey***	Y	Y	Y	Y	Y	Y	N	Y
6 ***Baker***	Y	Y	Y	Y	Y	Y	Y	Y
7 John	Y	Y	Y	Y	Y	Y	N	N
MAINE								
1 Allen	Y	Y	Y	Y	Y	Y	N	N
2 Baldacci	Y	Y	Y	Y	Y	Y	N	N
MARYLAND								
1 ***Gilchrest***	Y	Y	Y	Y	Y	Y	N	N
2 ***Ehrlich***	Y	Y	Y	Y	Y	Y	Y	Y
3 Cardin	Y	Y	Y	Y	Y	Y	N	N
4 Wynn	Y	Y	?	Y	Y	Y	N	N
5 Hoyer	Y	Y	Y	Y	Y	Y	N	N
6 ***Bartlett***	Y	Y	Y	Y	Y	Y	N	N
7 Cummings	Y	Y	Y	Y	Y	Y	N	N
8 ***Morella***	Y	Y	Y	Y	Y	Y	N	N
MASSACHUSETTS								
1 Olver	Y	Y	Y	Y	Y	Y	N	N
2 Neal	?	?	?	Y	Y	Y	N	N
3 McGovern	Y	Y	Y	N	Y	Y	N	N
4 Frank	Y	Y	Y	Y	Y	Y	N	N
5 Meehan	Y	Y	?	?	Y	Y	N	N
6 Tierney	Y	Y	Y	Y	Y	Y	N	N
7 Markey	Y	Y	Y	N	Y	Y	N	N
8 Capuano	Y	Y	Y	Y	Y	Y	N	N
9 Moakley	?	?	?	Y	Y	Y	N	N
10 Delahunt	Y	Y	Y	Y	Y	Y	N	?
MICHIGAN								
1 Stupak	Y	Y	Y	N	Y	Y	N	N
2 ***Hoekstra***	Y	Y	Y	Y	Y	Y	Y	Y
3 ***Ehlers***	+	Y	Y	Y	Y	Y	N	Y
4 ***Camp***	Y	Y	Y	Y	Y	Y	N	N
5 Barcia	?	?	?	?	Y	Y	N	N
6 ***Upton***	Y	Y	Y	Y	Y	Y	N	N
7 ***Smith***	Y	Y	Y	Y	Y	Y	Y	Y
8 Stabenow	Y	Y	Y	Y	Y	Y	N	N
9 Kildee	Y	Y	Y	Y	Y	Y	N	N
10 Bonior	Y	Y	Y	?	Y	Y	N	N
11 ***Knollenberg***	Y	Y	Y	Y	Y	Y	Y	Y
12 Levin	Y	Y	Y	Y	Y	Y	N	N
13 Rivers	Y	Y	Y	Y	Y	Y	N	N
14 Conyers	Y	Y	Y	Y	Y	Y	N	N
15 Kilpatrick	Y	Y	Y	Y	Y	Y	N	N
16 Dingell	Y	Y	Y	Y	Y	Y	N	N
MINNESOTA								
1 ***Gutknecht***	Y	Y	Y	N	Y	Y	Y	Y
2 Minge	Y	Y	Y	Y	Y	Y	N	N
3 ***Ramstad***	Y	Y	Y	N	Y	Y	N	N
4 Vento	Y	Y	Y	Y	Y	Y	N	N
5 Sabo	Y	Y	Y	N	Y	Y	N	N
6 Luther	Y	Y	Y	Y	Y	Y	N	N
7 Peterson	Y	Y	Y	Y	Y	Y	N	N
8 Oberstar	Y	Y	Y	N	Y	Y	N	N
MISSISSIPPI								
1 ***Wicker***	?	?	?	Y	Y	Y	Y	Y
2 Thompson	Y	Y	Y	N	Y	Y	N	N
3 ***Pickering***	Y	Y	Y	Y	Y	Y	Y	Y
4 Shows	Y	Y	Y	Y	Y	Y	N	N
5 Taylor	Y	Y	Y	N	Y	Y	N	N
MISSOURI								
1 Clay	?	?	?	N	Y	Y	N	N
2 ***Talent***	Y	Y	Y	Y	Y	Y	Y	N
3 Gephardt	?	?	?	N	Y	Y	N	N
4 Skelton	Y	Y	Y	Y	Y	Y	N	N
5 McCarthy	+	Y	Y	Y	Y	Y	N	N
6 Danner	Y	Y	Y	Y	Y	Y	N	N
7 ***Blunt***	Y	Y	Y	Y	Y	Y	Y	Y
8 ***Emerson***	Y	Y	Y	Y	Y	Y	N	N
9 ***Hulshof***	+	+	+	Y	Y	Y	Y	Y
MONTANA								
AL ***Hill***	Y	Y	Y	N	Y	Y	Y	Y
NEBRASKA								
1 ***Bereuter***	Y	Y	Y	Y	Y	Y	Y	Y
2 ***Terry***	Y	Y	Y	Y	Y	Y	Y	Y
3 ***Barrett***	Y	Y	Y	Y	Y	Y	N	N
NEVADA								
1 Berkley	Y	Y	Y	Y	Y	Y	N	N
2 ***Gibbons***	Y	Y	Y	N	Y	Y	Y	Y
NEW HAMPSHIRE								
1 ***Sununu***	Y	Y	Y	Y	Y	Y	Y	Y
2 ***Bass***	Y	Y	Y	Y	Y	Y	N	N
NEW JERSEY								
1 Andrews	Y	Y	Y	Y	Y	Y	N	N
2 ***LoBiondo***	Y	Y	Y	N	Y	Y	N	N
3 ***Saxton***	Y	Y	Y	Y	Y	Y	N	N
4 ***Smith***	Y	Y	Y	Y	Y	Y	N	N
5 ***Roukema***	Y	Y	?	Y	Y	Y	N	N
6 Pallone	Y	Y	Y	Y	Y	Y	N	N
7 ***Franks***	Y	Y	Y	Y	Y	Y	N	N
8 Pascrell	Y	Y	Y	Y	Y	Y	N	N
9 Rothman	Y	Y	Y	Y	Y	Y	N	N
10 Payne	Y	Y	Y	Y	Y	Y	N	N
11 ***Frelinghuysen***	Y	Y	Y	Y	Y	Y	N	N
12 Holt	Y	Y	Y	Y	Y	Y	N	N
13 Menendez	Y	Y	Y	Y	Y	Y	N	N
NEW MEXICO								
1 ***Wilson***	Y	Y	Y	Y	Y	Y	Y	Y
2 ***Skeen***	Y	Y	Y	Y	Y	Y	N	N
3 Udall	Y	Y	Y	N	Y	Y	N	N
NEW YORK								
1 Forbes	Y	Y	Y	Y	Y	Y	N	N
2 ***Lazio***	Y	Y	Y	Y	Y	Y	N	N
3 ***King***	Y	Y	Y	Y	Y	Y	Y	Y
4 McCarthy	Y	Y	Y	Y	Y	Y	N	N
5 Ackerman	Y	Y	Y	Y	Y	Y	N	N
6 Meeks	?	Y	Y	Y	Y	Y	N	N
7 Crowley	Y	Y	Y	Y	Y	Y	N	N
8 Nadler	Y	Y	Y	Y	Y	Y	N	N
9 Weiner	Y	Y	?	Y	Y	Y	N	N
10 Towns	Y	Y	Y	Y	Y	Y	N	N
11 Owens	Y	Y	Y	Y	Y	Y	N	N
12 Velázquez	Y	Y	Y	Y	Y	Y	N	N
13 ***Fossella***	Y	Y	Y	?	Y	Y	Y	Y
14 Maloney	Y	Y	Y	Y	Y	Y	N	N
15 Rangel	Y	Y	Y	N	Y	Y	N	N
16 Serrano	?	?	?	?	Y	Y	N	N
17 Engel	Y	Y	Y	Y	Y	Y	N	N
18 Lowey	Y	Y	Y	Y	Y	Y	N	N
19 ***Kelly***	Y	Y	Y	Y	Y	Y	N	N
20 ***Gilman***	Y	Y	Y	Y	Y	Y	N	N
21 McNulty	Y	Y	Y	Y	Y	Y	N	N
22 ***Sweeney***	Y	Y	Y	Y	Y	Y	Y	N
23 ***Boehlert***	Y	Y	Y	Y	Y	Y	N	N
24 ***McHugh***	Y	Y	Y	Y	Y	Y	N	N
25 ***Walsh***	Y	Y	Y	Y	Y	Y	N	N
26 Hinchey	Y	Y	Y	?	Y	Y	N	N
27 ***Reynolds***	Y	Y	Y	Y	Y	Y	Y	Y
28 Slaughter	Y	Y	Y	Y	Y	Y	N	N
29 LaFalce	Y	Y	Y	Y	Y	Y	N	N
30 ***Quinn***	Y	Y	Y	Y	Y	Y	N	N
31 ***Houghton***	Y	Y	Y	Y	Y	Y	Y	N
NORTH CAROLINA								
1 Clayton	Y	Y	Y	Y	Y	Y	N	N
2 Etheridge	Y	Y	Y	Y	Y	Y	N	N
3 ***Jones***	Y	Y	Y	Y	+	+	Y	Y
4 Price	Y	Y	Y	Y	Y	Y	N	N
5 ***Burr***	Y	Y	Y	Y	Y	Y	Y	N
6 ***Coble***	Y	N	Y	Y	Y	Y	N	N
7 McIntyre	Y	Y	Y	Y	Y	Y	N	N
8 ***Hayes***	Y	Y	Y	Y	Y	Y	Y	N
9 ***Myrick***	Y	Y	Y	Y	Y	Y	Y	N
10 ***Ballenger***	Y	Y	Y	Y	Y	Y	Y	Y
11 ***Taylor***	?	?	?	?	Y	Y	Y	Y
12 Watt	Y	Y	Y	Y	Y	Y	N	N
NORTH DAKOTA								
AL Pomeroy	Y	Y	Y	Y	Y	Y	N	N
OHIO								
1 ***Chabot***	Y	Y	Y	Y	Y	Y	N	N
2 ***Portman***	Y	Y	Y	Y	Y	Y	N	N
3 Hall	Y	Y	Y	Y	Y	Y	N	N
4 ***Oxley***	Y	Y	Y	Y	Y	Y	Y	Y
5 ***Gillmor***	Y	Y	Y	Y	Y	Y	N	N
6 Strickland	Y	Y	Y	Y	Y	Y	N	N
7 ***Hobson***	Y	Y	Y	Y	Y	Y	Y	Y
8 ***Boehner***	Y	Y	Y	Y	Y	Y	Y	Y
9 Kaptur	Y	Y	Y	?	?	?	N	N
10 Kucinich	N	Y	Y	N	Y	Y	N	N
11 Jones	Y	Y	Y	+	Y	Y	N	N
12 ***Kasich***	?	Y	Y	Y	Y	Y	Y	Y
13 Brown	Y	Y	Y	Y	Y	Y	N	N
14 Sawyer	Y	Y	Y	Y	Y	Y	N	N
15 ***Pryce***	?	?	?	?	?	?	?	?
16 ***Regula***	Y	Y	Y	Y	Y	Y	N	N
17 Traficant	Y	Y	Y	Y	Y	Y	N	N
18 ***Ney***	Y	Y	Y	Y	Y	Y	N	N
19 ***LaTourette***	Y	Y	Y	Y	Y	Y	N	N
OKLAHOMA								
1 ***Largent***	?	?	?	?	Y	Y	Y	Y
2 ***Coburn***	Y	Y	Y	Y	Y	Y	Y	Y
3 ***Watkins***	Y	Y	Y	Y	Y	Y	N	N
4 ***Watts***	Y	Y	Y	Y	Y	Y	N	N
5 ***Istook***	Y	Y	Y	Y	Y	Y	Y	Y
6 ***Lucas***	Y	Y	Y	Y	Y	Y	N	N
OREGON								
1 Wu	?	?	?	Y	Y	Y	N	N
2 ***Walden***	Y	Y	Y	Y	Y	Y	N	N
3 Blumenauer	Y	Y	Y	Y	Y	Y	N	N
4 DeFazio	N	Y	Y	N	Y	Y	N	N
5 Hooley	Y	Y	Y	Y	Y	Y	N	N
PENNSYLVANIA								
1 Brady	Y	Y	Y	Y	Y	Y	N	N
2 Fattah	Y	Y	Y	?	?	?	N	N
3 Borski	Y	Y	Y	N	Y	Y	N	N
4 Klink	Y	Y	Y	Y	Y	Y	N	N
5 ***Peterson***	Y	Y	Y	Y	Y	Y	Y	Y
6 Holden	Y	Y	Y	Y	Y	Y	N	N
7 ***Weldon***	Y	Y	Y	Y	Y	Y	Y	Y
8 ***Greenwood***	Y	Y	Y	Y	Y	Y	N	N
9 ***Shuster***	?	?	?	Y	Y	Y	Y	Y
10 ***Sherwood***	Y	Y	Y	Y	Y	Y	N	N
11 Kanjorski	Y	Y	Y	Y	Y	Y	N	N
12 Murtha	Y	Y	Y	Y	Y	Y	N	N
13 Hoeffel	Y	Y	Y	Y	Y	Y	N	N
14 Coyne	Y	Y	Y	Y	Y	Y	N	N
15 ***Toomey***	Y	Y	Y	Y	Y	Y	Y	Y
16 ***Pitts***	Y	Y	Y	Y	Y	Y	Y	N
17 ***Gekas***	Y	Y	Y	Y	Y	Y	N	Y
18 Doyle	Y	Y	Y	Y	Y	Y	N	N
19 ***Goodling***	Y	Y	Y	Y	Y	?	N	N
20 Mascara	Y	Y	Y	Y	Y	Y	N	N
21 ***English***	Y	Y	Y	?	Y	Y	N	Y
RHODE ISLAND								
1 Kennedy	Y	Y	Y	Y	Y	Y	N	N
2 Weygand	Y	Y	Y	Y	Y	Y	N	N
SOUTH CAROLINA								
1 ***Sanford***	Y	N	Y	Y	Y	Y	Y	N
2 ***Spence***	Y	Y	Y	?	Y	Y	N	Y
3 ***Graham***	Y	Y	Y	Y	Y	Y	N	N
4 ***DeMint***	Y	Y	Y	Y	Y	Y	Y	Y
5 Spratt	Y	Y	?	Y	Y	Y	N	N
6 Clyburn	Y	Y	Y	N	Y	Y	N	N
SOUTH DAKOTA								
AL ***Thune***	Y	Y	Y	Y	Y	Y	N	N
TENNESSEE								
1 ***Jenkins***	Y	Y	Y	Y	Y	Y	Y	N
2 ***Duncan***	Y	Y	Y	Y	Y	Y	Y	N
3 ***Wamp***	Y	Y	Y	Y	Y	Y	N	N
4 ***Hilleary***	Y	Y	Y	Y	Y	+	N	N
5 Clement	Y	Y	Y	?	Y	Y	N	N
6 Gordon	Y	Y	Y	Y	Y	Y	N	N
7 ***Bryant***	Y	Y	Y	Y	Y	Y	Y	N
8 Tanner	Y	Y	Y	Y	Y	Y	N	N
9 Ford	Y	Y	Y	Y	Y	Y	N	N
TEXAS								
1 Sandlin	Y	Y	Y	Y	Y	Y	N	N
2 Turner	Y	Y	Y	Y	Y	Y	N	N
3 ***Johnson, Sam***	?	?	?	Y	Y	Y	Y	Y
4 Hall	Y	Y	Y	Y	Y	Y	N	N
5 ***Sessions***	Y	Y	Y	Y	Y	Y	Y	Y
6 ***Barton***	Y	Y	Y	Y	Y	Y	Y	Y
7 ***Archer***	Y	Y	Y	?	Y	Y	N	N
8 ***Brady***	Y	Y	Y	Y	Y	Y	Y	Y
9 Lampson	Y	Y	Y	Y	Y	Y	N	N
10 Doggett	Y	Y	Y	N	Y	Y	N	N
11 Edwards	Y	Y	Y	Y	Y	Y	N	N
12 ***Granger***	Y	Y	Y	Y	Y	Y	N	N
13 ***Thornberry***	Y	Y	Y	Y	Y	Y	Y	N
14 ***Paul***	Y	N	Y	Y	Y	Y	Y	Y
15 Hinojosa	Y	Y	Y	Y	Y	Y	N	N
16 Reyes	Y	Y	Y	Y	Y	Y	N	N
17 Stenholm	Y	Y	Y	Y	Y	Y	N	N
18 Jackson-Lee	Y	Y	Y	Y	Y	Y	N	N
19 ***Combest***	Y	Y	Y	Y	Y	Y	Y	Y
20 Gonzalez	Y	Y	Y	Y	Y	Y	N	N
21 ***Smith***	Y	Y	Y	Y	Y	Y	Y	Y
22 ***DeLay***	Y	Y	Y	Y	Y	Y	Y	Y
23 ***Bonilla***	Y	Y	Y	Y	?	Y	Y	Y
24 Frost	Y	Y	Y	Y	Y	Y	N	N
25 Bentsen	Y	Y	Y	Y	Y	Y	N	N
26 ***Armey***	Y	Y	Y	Y	Y	Y	Y	Y
27 Ortiz	Y	Y	?	Y	Y	Y	N	N
28 Rodriguez	Y	Y	Y	Y	Y	Y	N	N
29 Green	Y	Y	Y	Y	Y	Y	N	N
30 Johnson, E.B.	Y	Y	Y	Y	Y	Y	N	N
UTAH								
1 ***Hansen***	?	?	?	Y	Y	Y	Y	Y
2 ***Cook***	Y	Y	Y	Y	Y	Y	N	N
3 ***Cannon***	Y	Y	Y	Y	Y	Y	Y	Y
VERMONT								
AL *Sanders*	Y	Y	Y	Y	Y	Y	N	N
VIRGINIA								
1 ***Bateman***	Y	Y	Y	Y	Y	Y	Y	Y
2 Pickett	Y	Y	Y	N	Y	Y	N	N
3 Scott	Y	Y	Y	Y	Y	Y	N	N
4 Sisisky	Y	Y	Y	Y	Y	Y	Y	N
5 Goode	Y	Y	Y	Y	Y	Y	N	N
6 ***Goodlatte***	Y	Y	Y	Y	Y	Y	N	Y
7 ***Bliley***	Y	?	?	Y	Y	Y	Y	Y
8 Moran	Y	Y	Y	Y	Y	Y	N	N
9 Boucher	Y	Y	Y	Y	Y	Y	N	N
10 ***Wolf***	Y	Y	Y	Y	Y	Y	N	N
11 ***Davis***	Y	Y	Y	Y	Y	Y	Y	Y
WASHINGTON								
1 Inslee	Y	Y	Y	Y	Y	Y	N	N
2 ***Metcalf***	Y	Y	Y	Y	Y	Y	N	Y
3 Baird	Y	Y	Y	N	Y	Y	N	N
4 ***Hastings***	Y	Y	Y	Y	Y	Y	Y	Y
5 ***Nethercutt***	Y	Y	Y	Y	Y	Y	Y	Y
6 Dicks	Y	Y	Y	Y	Y	Y	N	N
7 McDermott	Y	Y	Y	N	?	Y	N	N
8 ***Dunn***	Y	Y	Y	Y	Y	Y	Y	Y
9 Smith	Y	Y	Y	Y	Y	Y	N	N
WEST VIRGINIA								
1 Mollohan	Y	Y	Y	Y	Y	Y	N	N
2 Wise	Y	Y	Y	Y	Y	Y	N	N
3 Rahall	Y	Y	Y	Y	Y	Y	N	N
WISCONSIN								
1 ***Ryan***	Y	Y	Y	Y	Y	Y	Y	Y
2 Baldwin	Y	Y	Y	Y	Y	Y	N	N
3 Kind	Y	Y	Y	Y	Y	Y	N	N
4 Kleczka	Y	Y	Y	Y	Y	Y	N	N
5 Barrett	Y	Y	Y	Y	Y	Y	N	N
6 ***Petri***	Y	Y	Y	Y	Y	Y	N	Y
7 Obey	Y	Y	Y	?	Y	Y	N	N
8 ***Green***	Y	Y	Y	Y	Y	Y	N	N
9 ***Sensenbrenner***	Y	N	Y	Y	Y	Y	Y	Y
WYOMING								
AL ***Cubin***	Y	Y	Y	Y	Y	Y	Y	Y

Southern states - Ala., Ark., Fla., Ga., Ky., La., Miss., N.C., Okla., S.C., Tenn., Texas, Va.

413. HR 417. Campaign Finance Overhaul/Voter Guide Exemption. Doolittle, R-Calif., amendment to exempt voter guides from the bill's "issue advocacy" regulations. Rejected 189-238: R 174-42; D 15-195 (ND 9-147, SD 6-48); I 0-1. Sept. 14, 1999.

414. HR 417. Campaign Finance Overhaul/Contributions From Non-U.S. Citizens. Bereuter, R-Neb., amendment to clarify current law to prohibit individual contributions to federal campaigns from non-U.S. citizens, including permanent U.S. residents. Adopted 242-181: R 188-26; D 54-154 (ND 34-121, SD 20-33); I 0-1. Sept. 14, 1999.

415. HR 417. Campaign Finance Overhaul/In-State Funding Requirements. Calvert, R-Calif., amendment to require that candidates running for the House or Senate collect at least 50 percent of their total contributions from people living within their states, unless their opponent uses more than $250,000 of personal funds. Rejected 179-248: R 166-51; D 13-196 (ND 7-148, SD 6-48); I 0-1. Sept. 14, 1999.

416. HR 417. Campaign Finance Overhaul/Use of Government Vehicles. Sweeney, R-N.Y., amendment to require candidates for federal office who do not already hold a federal office and who use government vehicles, such as cars or Air Force One, for campaign purposes to reimburse the government for all costs associated with the vehicle's use. Adopted 261-167: R 215-2; D 46-164 (ND 27-129, SD 19-35); I 0-1. Sept. 14, 1999.

417. HR 417. Campaign Finance Overhaul/Internet Communications Exemption. DeLay, R-Texas, amendment to exempt Internet communication from all regulations under the measure. Rejected 160-268: R 155-62; D 5-205 (ND 3-153, SD 2-52); I 0-1. Sept. 14, 1999.

418. HR 417. Campaign Finance Overhaul/Constitutionality. Ewing, R-Ill., amendment to revise the bill to state that if any provision of the legislation is held unconstitutional, the entire act would be considered invalid. Rejected 167-259: R 159-56; D 8-202 (ND 6-150, SD 2-52); I 0-1. Sept. 14, 1999.

419. HR 417. Campaign Finance Overhaul/Doolittle Substitute. Doolittle, R-Calif., substitute amendment to eliminate all federal contribution limits, and end public financing of presidential campaigns. National political parties would be required to disclose transfers of funds to state and local parties, and to distinguish between federal and non-federal funds. State and local parties would be required to file with the Federal Election Commission (FEC) all disclosure reports required by state law. The measure would also require electronic filing of all disclosure reports and FEC notification within 24 hours of every donation received in the last 90 days of a campaign. Rejected 117-306: R 115-100; D 2-205 (ND 1-152, SD 1-53); I 0-1. Sept. 14, 1999.

Key

Y Voted for (yea).
Paired for.
+ Announced for.
N Voted against (nay).
X Paired against.
– Announced against.
P Voted "present."
C Voted "present" to avoid possible conflict of interest.
? Did not vote or otherwise make a position known.

•

Democrats ***Republicans***
Independents

	413	414	415	416	417	418	419
ALABAMA							
1 ***Callahan***	Y	Y	Y	Y	Y	Y	Y
2 ***Everett***	Y	Y	Y	Y	Y	Y	Y
3 ***Riley***	Y	Y	Y	Y	Y	Y	Y
4 ***Aderholt***	Y	Y	Y	Y	Y	Y	N
5 Cramer	N	Y	Y	Y	N	N	N
6 ***Bachus***	Y	Y	Y	Y	N	N	N
7 Hilliard	N	N	N	N	N	N	N
ALASKA							
AL ***Young***	Y	Y	N	Y	Y	Y	Y
ARIZONA							
1 ***Salmon***	Y	Y	Y	Y	Y	Y	Y
2 Pastor	N	N	N	N	N	N	N
3 ***Stump***	Y	Y	Y	Y	Y	Y	Y
4 ***Shadegg***	Y	Y	Y	Y	Y	Y	Y
5 ***Kolbe***	Y	Y	Y	Y	Y	Y	Y
6 ***Hayworth***	Y	Y	Y	Y	Y	Y	Y
ARKANSAS							
1 Berry	N	N	N	Y	N	N	N
2 Snyder	N	N	N	N	N	N	N
3 ***Hutchinson***	Y	N	Y	Y	Y	Y	N
4 ***Dickey***	Y	Y	Y	Y	Y	Y	Y
CALIFORNIA							
1 Thompson	N	N	N	N	N	N	N
2 ***Herger***	Y	Y	Y	Y	Y	Y	Y
3 ***Ose***	N	N	Y	Y	N	N	N
4 ***Doolittle***	Y	N	Y	Y	Y	Y	Y
5 Matsui	N	N	N	N	N	N	N
6 Woolsey	N	N	N	N	N	N	N
7 Miller, George	N	N	N	Y	N	N	N
8 Pelosi	N	N	N	N	N	N	N
9 Lee	N	N	N	N	N	N	N
10 Tauscher	N	N	N	N	N	N	N
11 ***Pombo***	Y	N	Y	Y	Y	Y	Y
12 Lantos	N	N	N	N	N	N	N
13 Stark	N	N	N	N	N	N	N
14 Eshoo	N	N	N	N	N	N	N
15 ***Campbell***	N	Y	N	N	N	N	N
16 Lofgren	N	N	N	N	N	N	N
17 Farr	N	N	N	N	N	N	N
18 Condit	N	Y	Y	N	N	N	N
19 ***Radanovich***	Y	Y	Y	Y	Y	Y	Y
20 Dooley	N	N	N	N	N	N	N
21 ***Thomas***	Y	Y	Y	Y	Y	Y	Y
22 Capps	N	N	N	N	N	N	N
23 ***Gallegly***	N	Y	Y	Y	N	N	N
24 Sherman	N	Y	N	N	N	N	N
25 ***McKeon***	Y	Y	Y	Y	Y	?	Y
26 Berman	N	N	N	N	N	N	N
27 ***Rogan***	Y	Y	Y	Y	Y	N	Y
28 ***Dreier***	Y	N	N	Y	Y	Y	Y
29 Waxman	N	N	N	N	N	N	N
30 Becerra	N	N	N	N	N	N	N
31 Martinez	N	N	N	N	N	N	?
32 Dixon	N	N	N	Y	N	N	N
33 Roybal-Allard	N	N	N	N	N	N	N
34 Napolitano	N	N	N	N	N	N	N
35 Waters	N	N	N	N	N	N	N
36 ***Kuykendall***	N	Y	Y	Y	N	N	N
37 Millender-McD.	N	N	N	N	N	N	N
38 ***Horn***	N	N	N	Y	N	N	N
39 ***Royce***	Y	Y	Y	Y	Y	Y	N
40 ***Lewis***	Y	Y	Y	Y	Y	Y	?
41 ***Miller***	Y	Y	Y	Y	Y	Y	Y
42 Vacant							
43 ***Calvert***	Y	Y	Y	Y	Y	Y	Y
44 ***Bono***	Y	Y	Y	Y	Y	Y	N
45 ***Rohrabacher***	Y	Y	Y	Y	Y	Y	Y
46 Sanchez	N	N	N	N	N	N	N
47 ***Cox***	Y	Y	N	Y	N	Y	Y
48 ***Packard***	Y	Y	N	Y	Y	Y	Y
49 ***Bilbray***	N	Y	Y	Y	N	N	N
50 Filner	N	N	N	N	N	N	N
51 ***Cunningham***	Y	Y	Y	Y	Y	Y	Y
52 ***Hunter***	Y	Y	Y	Y	N	Y	Y
COLORADO							
1 DeGette	N	N	N	N	N	N	N
2 Udall	N	N	N	Y	N	N	N
3 ***McInnis***	Y	Y	N	Y	Y	Y	Y
4 ***Schaffer***	Y	Y	Y	Y	Y	Y	Y
5 ***Hefley***	Y	Y	N	Y	Y	N	Y
6 ***Tancredo***	Y	Y	Y	Y	Y	Y	Y
CONNECTICUT							
1 Larson	N	N	N	N	N	N	N
2 Gejdenson	N	N	N	N	N	N	N
3 DeLauro	N	N	N	N	N	N	N
4 ***Shays***	N	N	N	Y	N	N	N
5 Maloney	N	Y	Y	N	N	N	N
6 ***Johnson***	N	N	Y	Y	N	N	N
DELAWARE							
AL ***Castle***	N	N	N	Y	N	N	N
FLORIDA							
1 ***Scarborough***	Y	Y	Y	Y	Y	Y	Y
2 Boyd	N	N	N	N	N	N	N
3 Brown	N	N	N	N	N	N	N
4 ***Fowler***	Y	Y	Y	Y	Y	Y	Y
5 Thurman	N	Y	N	N	N	N	N
6 ***Stearns***	Y	Y	Y	Y	Y	Y	N
7 ***Mica***	Y	Y	Y	Y	Y	Y	N
8 ***McCollum***	Y	Y	Y	Y	N	Y	N
9 ***Bilirakis***	Y	Y	Y	Y	N	N	Y
10 ***Young***	Y	?	Y	Y	Y	Y	?
11 Davis	N	N	N	N	N	N	N
12 ***Canady***	Y	Y	Y	Y	Y	Y	N
13 ***Miller***	Y	Y	Y	Y	Y	Y	Y
14 ***Goss***	N	Y	Y	Y	Y	Y	Y
15 ***Weldon***	Y	Y	Y	Y	Y	Y	Y
16 ***Foley***	N	N	Y	Y	N	N	N
17 Meek	N	N	N	N	N	N	N
18 ***Ros-Lehtinen***	?	?	?	?	?	?	?
19 Wexler	N	N	N	N	N	N	N
20 Deutsch	N	N	N	Y	N	N	N
21 ***Diaz-Balart***	Y	N	Y	Y	Y	Y	N
22 ***Shaw***	?	?	?	?	?	?	?
23 Hastings	?	?	?	?	?	?	?
GEORGIA							
1 ***Kingston***	?	?	?	?	?	?	?
2 Bishop	Y	N	N	N	N	N	N
3 ***Collins***	Y	Y	Y	Y	Y	Y	Y
4 McKinney	N	N	N	N	N	N	N
5 Lewis	N	N	N	N	N	N	N
6 ***Isakson***	Y	Y	Y	Y	N	N	N
7 ***Barr***	Y	Y	N	Y	Y	Y	Y
8 ***Chambliss***	Y	Y	Y	Y	Y	Y	Y
9 ***Deal***	N	N	Y	Y	N	N	N
10 ***Norwood***	Y	Y	Y	Y	Y	Y	Y
11 ***Linder***	Y	Y	Y	Y	Y	Y	Y
HAWAII							
1 Abercrombie	N	N	N	N	N	N	N
2 Mink	N	N	N	N	N	N	N
IDAHO							
1 ***Chenoweth***	Y	Y	Y	Y	Y	Y	Y
2 ***Simpson***	Y	Y	N	Y	Y	Y	Y
ILLINOIS							
1 Rush	N	N	N	N	N	N	N
2 Jackson	N	N	N	N	N	N	N
3 Lipinski	Y	Y	N	Y	N	N	N
4 Gutierrez	N	N	N	N	N	N	N
5 Blagojevich	N	N	N	N	N	N	N
6 ***Hyde***	Y	Y	N	Y	N	Y	N
7 Davis	N	N	N	N	N	N	N
8 ***Crane***	Y	Y	Y	Y	Y	Y	Y
9 Schakowsky	N	N	N	N	N	N	N
10 ***Porter***	–	+	N	Y	N	N	N
11 ***Weller***	Y	Y	Y	Y	N	Y	N
12 Costello	Y	Y	Y	N	N	N	N
13 ***Biggert***	Y	Y	N	Y	Y	Y	Y
14 ***Hastert***							

ND Northern Democrats SD Southern Democrats

	413	414	415	416	417	418	419
15 ***Ewing***	Y	Y	Y	Y	Y	Y	N
16 ***Manzullo***	Y	Y	Y	Y	Y	Y	N
17 Evans	N	Y	N	N	N	N	N
18 ***LaHood***	Y	Y	Y	Y	N	Y	N
19 Phelps	N	Y	N	Y	N	N	N
20 ***Shimkus***	Y	Y	Y	Y	Y	Y	Y
INDIANA							
1 Visclosky	N	Y	N	N	N	N	?
2 ***McIntosh***	Y	Y	Y	Y	Y	Y	Y
3 Roemer	N	Y	N	Y	N	N	N
4 ***Souder***	Y	Y	Y	Y	Y	Y	N
5 ***Buyer***	Y	Y	Y	Y	Y	Y	Y
6 ***Burton***	Y	N	Y	Y	Y	Y	Y
7 ***Pease***	Y	Y	Y	Y	Y	Y	Y
8 ***Hostettler***	Y	Y	Y	Y	Y	Y	Y
9 Hill	N	N	N	Y	N	N	N
10 Carson	N	N	N	N	N	N	N
IOWA							
1 ***Leach***	N	Y	Y	Y	N	N	N
2 ***Nussle***	Y	Y	Y	Y	Y	N	N
3 Boswell	N	Y	N	Y	N	N	N
4 ***Ganske***	N	Y	N	Y	N	N	N
5 ***Latham***	Y	Y	Y	Y	Y	Y	Y
KANSAS							
1 ***Moran***	Y	Y	Y	Y	Y	N	N
2 ***Ryun***	Y	Y	N	Y	Y	Y	Y
3 Moore	N	N	N	Y	N	N	N
4 ***Tiahrt***	Y	Y	Y	Y	Y	Y	Y
KENTUCKY							
1 ***Whitfield***	Y	Y	N	Y	Y	Y	Y
2 ***Lewis***	Y	Y	Y	Y	Y	Y	Y
3 ***Northup***	Y	Y	Y	Y	Y	Y	N
4 Lucas	Y	Y	Y	Y	N	N	N
5 ***Rogers***	Y	Y	N	Y	Y	Y	Y
6 ***Fletcher***	Y	Y	N	Y	Y	Y	N
LOUISIANA							
1 ***Vitter***	Y	Y	Y	Y	Y	Y	N
2 Jefferson	N	N	N	Y	N	N	N
3 ***Tauzin***	Y	Y	Y	Y	Y	Y	Y
4 ***McCrery***	Y	Y	Y	Y	Y	Y	Y
5 ***Cooksey***	Y	Y	Y	Y	Y	Y	Y
6 ***Baker***	Y	Y	Y	Y	Y	N	N
7 John	N	Y	N	Y	N	N	N
MAINE							
1 Allen	N	N	N	N	N	N	N
2 Baldacci	N	Y	N	N	N	N	N
MARYLAND							
1 ***Gilchrest***	N	N	N	Y	N	N	N
2 ***Ehrlich***	Y	N	Y	Y	Y	Y	Y
3 Cardin	N	N	N	N	N	N	N
4 Wynn	N	N	N	N	N	N	N
5 Hoyer	N	N	N	N	N	N	N
6 ***Bartlett***	Y	Y	Y	Y	Y	Y	N
7 Cummings	N	N	N	N	N	N	N
8 ***Morella***	N	N	N	Y	N	N	N
MASSACHUSETTS							
1 Olver	N	N	N	N	N	N	N
2 Neal	N	N	N	N	N	N	N
3 McGovern	N	N	N	N	N	N	N
4 Frank	N	N	N	N	N	N	N
5 Meehan	N	N	N	N	N	N	N
6 Tierney	N	N	N	N	N	N	N
7 Markey	N	Y	N	N	N	N	N
8 Capuano	N	N	N	N	N	N	N
9 Moakley	N	N	N	N	N	N	N
10 Delahunt	N	N	N	N	N	N	N
MICHIGAN							
1 Stupak	Y	Y	N	N	N	N	N
2 ***Hoekstra***	Y	Y	Y	Y	Y	Y	Y
3 ***Ehlers***	Y	N	Y	Y	Y	N	N
4 ***Camp***	Y	Y	Y	Y	Y	Y	Y
5 Barcia	Y	Y	Y	N	N	Y	N
6 ***Upton***	N	Y	Y	Y	N	N	N
7 ***Smith***	N	Y	Y	Y	Y	N	N
8 Stabenow	N	Y	N	N	N	N	N
9 Kildee	N	Y	N	Y	N	N	N
10 Bonior	N	N	N	N	N	N	N
11 ***Knollenberg***	Y	Y	Y	Y	Y	Y	Y
12 Levin	N	N	N	N	N	N	N
13 Rivers	N	N	N	N	N	N	N
14 Conyers	N	N	N	N	N	N	N
15 Kilpatrick	N	N	N	N	N	N	N
16 Dingell	N	N	N	N	N	N	N
MINNESOTA							
1 ***Gutknecht***	Y	Y	Y	Y	Y	Y	Y
2 Minge	N	N	N	Y	N	N	N
3 ***Ramstad***	N	Y	N	Y	N	N	N
4 Vento	N	N	N	N	N	N	N
5 Sabo	N	N	N	N	N	Y	N
6 Luther	N	Y	Y	Y	N	N	N
7 Peterson	Y	Y	Y	Y	Y	Y	N
8 Oberstar	Y	N	N	N	N	N	N
MISSISSIPPI							
1 ***Wicker***	Y	Y	Y	Y	Y	Y	Y
2 Thompson	N	N	N	N	N	N	N
3 ***Pickering***	Y	Y	N	Y	Y	Y	Y
4 Shows	N	Y	N	Y	N	N	N
5 Taylor	N	Y	Y	Y	N	N	N
MISSOURI							
1 Clay	N	N	N	N	N	N	N
2 ***Talent***	Y	N	Y	Y	Y	Y	N
3 Gephardt	N	N	N	N	N	N	N
4 Skelton	N	N	N	Y	N	N	N
5 McCarthy	N	Y	N	N	N	N	N
6 Danner	N	Y	N	Y	N	N	N
7 ***Blunt***	Y	Y	Y	Y	Y	Y	Y
8 ***Emerson***	N	Y	Y	Y	N	Y	N
9 ***Hulshof***	Y	Y	Y	Y	Y	Y	N
MONTANA							
AL ***Hill***	Y	Y	Y	Y	Y	Y	N
NEBRASKA							
1 ***Bereuter***	N	Y	Y	Y	N	N	N
2 ***Terry***	Y	Y	Y	Y	Y	Y	N
3 ***Barrett***	N	Y	Y	Y	N	N	N
NEVADA							
1 Berkley	N	Y	N	Y	N	N	N
2 ***Gibbons***	Y	Y	Y	Y	Y	Y	Y
NEW HAMPSHIRE							
1 ***Sununu***	Y	Y	N	Y	Y	Y	Y
2 ***Bass***	N	Y	N	Y	N	N	N
NEW JERSEY							
1 Andrews	N	N	N	N	N	N	N
2 ***LoBiondo***	N	Y	N	Y	N	N	N
3 ***Saxton***	N	Y	Y	Y	N	N	N
4 ***Smith***	Y	Y	Y	Y	Y	Y	N
5 ***Roukema***	N	Y	N	Y	N	N	N
6 Pallone	N	N	N	N	N	N	N
7 ***Franks***	N	Y	N	Y	N	N	N
8 Pascrell	N	N	N	N	N	N	N
9 Rothman	N	Y	N	N	N	N	N
10 Payne	N	N	?	N	N	N	N
11 ***Frelinghuysen***	N	N	N	Y	N	N	N
12 Holt	N	N	N	N	N	N	N
13 Menendez	N	N	N	N	N	N	N
NEW MEXICO							
1 ***Wilson***	Y	N	N	Y	Y	Y	N
2 ***Skeen***	N	Y	Y	Y	Y	Y	Y
3 Udall	N	N	N	Y	N	N	N
NEW YORK							
1 Forbes	N	?	N	Y	N	N	N
2 ***Lazio***	N	+	Y	Y	N	N	N
3 ***King***	Y	N	N	N	Y	Y	Y
4 McCarthy	N	N	N	N	N	N	N
5 Ackerman	N	N	N	N	N	N	N
6 Meeks	N	N	N	N	N	N	N
7 Crowley	N	N	N	N	N	N	N
8 Nadler	N	N	N	N	N	N	N
9 Weiner	N	N	N	N	N	N	N
10 Towns	N	N	N	N	N	N	N
11 Owens	N	N	N	N	N	N	N
12 Velázquez	N	N	N	N	N	N	N
13 ***Fossella***	Y	Y	N	Y	Y	Y	Y
14 Maloney	N	N	N	N	N	N	N
15 Rangel	N	N	N	N	N	N	N
16 Serrano	N	N	N	N	N	N	N
17 Engel	N	N	N	N	N	N	N
18 Lowey	N	N	N	N	N	N	N
19 ***Kelly***	N	Y	Y	Y	N	N	N
20 ***Gilman***	N	Y	N	Y	N	N	N
21 McNulty	N	N	N	Y	N	N	N
22 ***Sweeney***	Y	Y	Y	Y	Y	Y	Y
23 ***Boehlert***	N	N	N	Y	N	N	N
24 ***McHugh***	Y	Y	Y	Y	N	N	N
25 ***Walsh***	N	N	Y	Y	N	Y	N
26 Hinchey	N	N	N	N	N	N	N
27 ***Reynolds***	Y	Y	N	Y	Y	Y	N
28 Slaughter	N	N	N	N	N	N	–
29 LaFalce	N	Y	N	N	N	N	N
30 ***Quinn***	N	N	N	Y	N	N	N
31 ***Houghton***	N	N	N	Y	N	N	N
NORTH CAROLINA							
1 Clayton	N	N	N	N	N	N	N
2 Etheridge	N	N	N	N	N	N	N
3 ***Jones***	Y	Y	Y	Y	Y	Y	Y
4 Price	N	N	N	N	N	N	N
5 ***Burr***	Y	Y	Y	Y	Y	Y	Y
6 ***Coble***	Y	Y	N	Y	Y	N	Y
7 McIntyre	N	Y	N	Y	N	N	N
8 ***Hayes***	Y	Y	N	Y	Y	Y	Y
9 ***Myrick***	Y	Y	N	Y	N	N	N
10 ***Ballenger***	Y	Y	Y	Y	Y	Y	Y
11 ***Taylor***	Y	Y	Y	Y	Y	Y	Y
12 Watt	N	N	N	N	N	N	N
NORTH DAKOTA							
AL Pomeroy	N	Y	N	Y	N	N	N
OHIO							
1 ***Chabot***	Y	Y	Y	Y	N	N	N
2 ***Portman***	Y	Y	Y	Y	N	N	N
3 Hall	N	N	N	N	N	N	N
4 ***Oxley***	Y	Y	Y	Y	Y	Y	Y
5 ***Gillmor***	N	Y	Y	Y	N	Y	N
6 Strickland	N	Y	N	Y	N	N	N
7 ***Hobson***	Y	Y	Y	Y	Y	Y	Y
8 ***Boehner***	Y	Y	Y	Y	Y	Y	Y
9 Kaptur	N	Y	N	Y	N	N	N
10 Kucinich	N	Y	N	N	N	N	N
11 Jones	N	N	N	N	N	N	N
12 ***Kasich***	Y	Y	N	Y	Y	Y	Y
13 Brown	N	N	N	Y	N	N	N
14 Sawyer	N	N	N	N	N	N	N
15 ***Pryce***	?	?	?	?	?	?	?
16 ***Regula***	N	Y	Y	Y	N	N	N
17 Traficant	Y	Y	Y	Y	Y	Y	Y
18 ***Ney***	Y	Y	Y	Y	Y	Y	N
19 ***LaTourette***	Y	Y	Y	Y	N	Y	N
OKLAHOMA							
1 ***Largent***	Y	Y	Y	Y	Y	Y	Y
2 ***Coburn***	Y	Y	Y	Y	Y	Y	Y
3 ***Watkins***	Y	Y	Y	Y	Y	Y	Y
4 ***Watts***	Y	Y	Y	N	Y	Y	N
5 ***Istook***	Y	Y	Y	Y	Y	Y	N
6 ***Lucas***	Y	Y	Y	Y	Y	Y	Y
OREGON							
1 Wu	N	N	N	Y	Y	N	N
2 ***Walden***	Y	Y	Y	Y	Y	Y	N
3 Blumenauer	N	N	N	N	N	N	N
4 DeFazio	N	N	N	N	N	N	N
5 Hooley	N	N	N	N	N	N	N
PENNSYLVANIA							
1 Brady	N	N	N	N	N	N	N
2 Fattah	N	N	N	N	N	N	N
3 Borski	N	N	N	N	N	N	N
4 Klink	N	N	N	N	N	N	N
5 ***Peterson***	Y	Y	Y	Y	Y	Y	Y
6 Holden	N	Y	N	Y	N	N	N
7 ***Weldon***	Y	Y	N	Y	Y	Y	N
8 ***Greenwood***	N	Y	N	Y	N	N	N
9 ***Shuster***	Y	Y	Y	Y	Y	Y	Y
10 ***Sherwood***	Y	Y	Y	Y	Y	Y	N
11 Kanjorski	N	N	N	N	N	N	N
12 Murtha	N	N	N	N	N	N	N
13 Hoeffel	N	N	N	N	N	N	N
14 Coyne	N	N	N	N	N	N	N
15 ***Toomey***	Y	Y	N	Y	Y	Y	Y
16 ***Pitts***	Y	Y	Y	Y	Y	Y	Y
17 ***Gekas***	Y	Y	Y	Y	N	Y	Y
18 Doyle	N	N	N	N	N	N	N
19 ***Goodling***	Y	Y	Y	Y	Y	N	N
20 Mascara	N	Y	N	N	N	N	N
21 ***English***	Y	Y	Y	Y	Y	Y	N
RHODE ISLAND							
1 Kennedy	N	N	N	N	N	N	N
2 Weygand	N	N	N	N	N	N	N
SOUTH CAROLINA							
1 ***Sanford***	N	Y	Y	Y	N	N	N
2 ***Spence***	Y	Y	N	Y	Y	Y	Y
3 ***Graham***	N	Y	Y	Y	N	N	N
4 ***DeMint***	Y	Y	Y	Y	Y	Y	N
5 Spratt	N	N	N	N	N	N	N
6 Clyburn	N	N	N	N	N	N	N
SOUTH DAKOTA							
AL ***Thune***	Y	Y	Y	Y	N	Y	N
TENNESSEE							
1 ***Jenkins***	Y	Y	Y	Y	Y	Y	Y
2 ***Duncan***	Y	Y	Y	Y	N	Y	N
3 ***Wamp***	N	Y	Y	Y	N	N	N
4 ***Hilleary***	Y	Y	Y	Y	Y	Y	N
5 Clement	N	Y	N	N	N	N	N
6 Gordon	N	Y	N	Y	N	N	N
7 ***Bryant***	Y	Y	Y	Y	Y	Y	Y
8 Tanner	N	N	N	N	N	N	N
9 Ford	N	?	N	Y	N	N	N
TEXAS							
1 Sandlin	N	Y	N	Y	N	N	N
2 Turner	N	Y	N	Y	N	N	N
3 ***Johnson, Sam***	Y	Y	Y	Y	Y	Y	Y
4 Hall	Y	Y	Y	Y	Y	Y	Y
5 ***Sessions***	Y	Y	Y	Y	Y	Y	Y
6 ***Barton***	Y	Y	Y	Y	Y	Y	Y
7 ***Archer***	Y	Y	Y	Y	Y	Y	N
8 ***Brady***	Y	Y	Y	Y	Y	Y	Y
9 Lampson	N	N	N	N	N	N	N
10 Doggett	N	N	N	N	N	N	N
11 Edwards	N	Y	N	N	N	N	N
12 ***Granger***	Y	Y	Y	Y	Y	Y	N
13 ***Thornberry***	Y	Y	Y	Y	Y	Y	Y
14 ***Paul***	Y	Y	N	Y	Y	Y	Y
15 Hinojosa	N	N	N	N	N	N	N
16 Reyes	N	N	N	N	N	N	N
17 Stenholm	N	Y	N	Y	N	N	N
18 Jackson-Lee	N	N	N	N	N	N	N
19 ***Combest***	Y	Y	Y	Y	Y	Y	Y
20 Gonzalez	N	N	N	Y	N	N	N
21 ***Smith***	Y	Y	Y	Y	Y	Y	Y
22 ***DeLay***	Y	Y	Y	Y	Y	Y	Y
23 ***Bonilla***	Y	Y	N	Y	Y	Y	Y
24 Frost	N	N	N	N	N	Y	N
25 Bentsen	N	Y	N	N	N	N	N
26 ***Armey***	Y	Y	Y	Y	Y	Y	Y
27 Ortiz	Y	N	N	N	N	N	N
28 Rodriguez	N	N	N	N	N	N	N
29 Green	N	Y	N	N	N	N	N
30 Johnson, E.B.	N	N	N	N	N	N	N
UTAH							
1 ***Hansen***	Y	Y	Y	Y	Y	Y	Y
2 ***Cook***	Y	Y	Y	Y	Y	N	N
3 ***Cannon***	Y	Y	Y	Y	Y	Y	Y
VERMONT							
AL *Sanders*	N	N	N	N	N	N	N
VIRGINIA							
1 ***Bateman***	Y	Y	N	Y	Y	Y	Y
2 Pickett	N	Y	N	N	N	N	N
3 Scott	Y	N	N	N	N	N	N
4 Sisisky	N	Y	N	Y	N	N	N
5 Goode	Y	Y	Y	Y	Y	N	N
6 ***Goodlatte***	Y	Y	Y	Y	Y	Y	Y
7 ***Bliley***	Y	Y	N	Y	Y	Y	Y
8 Moran	N	N	Y	N	N	N	N
9 Boucher	N	Y	N	Y	N	N	N
10 ***Wolf***	Y	Y	Y	Y	Y	Y	Y
11 ***Davis***	Y	N	Y	Y	Y	N	N
WASHINGTON							
1 Inslee	N	Y	N	N	N	N	N
2 ***Metcalf***	Y	Y	Y	Y	N	N	N
3 Baird	N	N	N	N	N	N	N
4 ***Hastings***	Y	Y	Y	Y	Y	Y	Y
5 ***Nethercutt***	Y	Y	Y	Y	Y	Y	Y
6 Dicks	N	N	N	N	N	N	N
7 McDermott	N	N	N	N	N	N	N
8 ***Dunn***	Y	Y	Y	Y	Y	Y	Y
9 Smith	N	Y	N	Y	N	N	N
WEST VIRGINIA							
1 Mollohan	Y	N	N	N	N	Y	N
2 Wise	N	Y	N	N	N	N	N
3 Rahall	Y	N	N	N	N	N	N
WISCONSIN							
1 ***Ryan***	Y	Y	Y	Y	Y	Y	N
2 Baldwin	N	N	N	N	N	N	N
3 Kind	N	N	N	N	N	N	N
4 Kleczka	N	N	N	N	N	N	N
5 Barrett	N	N	N	N	N	N	N
6 ***Petri***	Y	Y	Y	Y	N	Y	N
7 Obey	N	Y	N	N	N	Y	N
8 ***Green***	Y	Y	Y	Y	N	Y	N
9 ***Sensenbrenner***	Y	Y	Y	Y	Y	Y	N
WYOMING							
AL ***Cubin***	Y	Y	Y	Y	Y	?	Y

Southern states - Ala., Ark., Fla., Ga., Ky., La., Miss., N.C., Okla., S.C., Tenn., Texas, Va.

420. HR 417. Campaign Finance Overhaul/Hutchinson Substitute. Hutchinson, R-Ark., substitute amendment to index federal individual, political action committee and party contribution limits for inflation. The amendment also would forbid federal officeholders and federal candidates from raising soft money or directing it to state parties. State political party committees could continue to raise and spend soft money, including activities designed to influence federal elections. Candidates for federal office would be required to disclose expenditures to the Federal Election Commission, on a monthly, rather than a quarterly, basis. Rejected 99-327: R 93-123; D 6-203 (ND 2-153, SD 4-50); I 0-1. Sept. 14, 1999.

421. HR 417. Campaign Finance Overhaul/Thomas Substitute. Thomas, R-Calif., substitute amendment to require electronic filing of reports to the Federal Election Commission detailing contributions and expenditures by individuals, political party committees or political action committees raising or spending at least $50,000 in an election cycle. Rejected 173-256: R 168-50; D 5-205 (ND 1-155, SD 4-50); I 0-1. Sept. 14, 1999.

422. HR 417. Campaign Finance Overhaul/Passage. Passage of the bill to ban all contributions of soft money — money used for party-building activities as opposed to supporting a specific candidate — and impose restrictions on issue advocacy communications. The measure would raise the individual aggregate contribution limit from $25,000 to $30,000 per year and raise the amount that individuals could give to state political parties from $5,000 to $10,000. House candidates who receive coordinated party contributions would be barred from spending more than $50,000 in personal funds. The measure would require labor unions to notify dues-paying non-members of any portion of their dues used for political purposes. Passed 252-177: R 54-164; D 197-13 (ND 148-8, SD 49-5); I 1-0. Sept. 14, 1999. A "yea" was a vote in support of the president's position.

423. S 1059. Fiscal 2000 Defense Authorization/Recommit. Dingell, D-Mich., motion to recommit the bill to the conference committee with instructions to House conferees to insist on striking provisions that would limit the authority of the secretary of Defense to manage, supervise and direct a new agency that would control Energy Department defense programs. Motion rejected 139-281: R 5-211; D 133-70 (ND 112-41, SD 21-29); I 1-0. Sept. 15, 1999.

424. S 1059. Fiscal 2000 Defense Authorization/Conference Report. Adoption of the conference report on the bill to authorize $288.8 billion in funds for the Department of Defense. The conference report would establish a semi-autonomous agency within the Energy Department that would be responsible for nuclear weapons development, naval nuclear propulsion, defense nuclear non-proliferation and fissile material disposition and would establish security, intelligence and counterintelligence offices. The conference report includes $1.9 billion for six F-22 fighters. Adopted (thus sent to the Senate) 375-45: R 206-8; D 169-36 (ND 119-35, SD 50-1); I 0-1. Sept. 15, 1999.

425. HR 2490. Fiscal 2000 Treasury-Postal Appropriations/Recommit. Murtha, D-Pa., motion to recommit to the conference committee the appropriations bill for the Treasury Department, Postal Service and general government expenditures. Motion rejected 61-359: R 32-183; D 29-175 (ND 17-137, SD 12-38); I 0-1. Sept. 15, 1999.

426. HR 2490. Fiscal 2000 Treasury-Postal Appropriations/Conference Report. Adoption of the conference report on the bill to provide $28.2 billion for the Treasury Department, Postal Service, Executive Office of the President and other federal agencies. The conference report would increase pay for federal civilian employees by 4.8 percent, and would increase the president's salary to $400,000 when the new president takes office in 2001. Adopted (thus sent to the Senate) 292-126: R 139-76; D 153-49 (ND 117-36, SD 36-13); I 0-1. Sept. 15, 1999.

Key

- Y Voted for (yea).
- # Paired for.
- + Announced for.
- N Voted against (nay).
- X Paired against.
- – Announced against.
- P Voted "present."
- C Voted "present" to avoid possible conflict of interest.
- ? Did not vote or otherwise make a position known.

•

Democrats ***Republicans***
Independents

	420	421	422	423	424	425	426
ALABAMA							
1 ***Callahan***	Y	Y	N	N	Y	N	Y
2 ***Everett***	Y	Y	N	N	Y	N	Y
3 ***Riley***	Y	Y	N	N	Y	N	N
4 ***Aderholt***	Y	Y	N	N	Y	N	Y
5 Cramer	N	N	Y	N	Y	Y	Y
6 ***Bachus***	Y	Y	Y	N	Y	N	Y
7 Hilliard	N	N	Y	N	Y	N	Y
ALASKA							
AL ***Young***	Y	Y	N	N	Y	N	Y
ARIZONA							
1 ***Salmon***	Y	Y	N	N	Y	Y	N
2 Pastor	N	N	Y	Y	Y	N	Y
3 ***Stump***	Y	Y	N	N	Y	N	N
4 ***Shadegg***	N	Y	N	N	Y	Y	N
5 ***Kolbe***	Y	Y	N	N	Y	N	Y
6 ***Hayworth***	N	Y	N	N	Y	Y	N
ARKANSAS							
1 Berry	N	N	Y	Y	Y	N	N
2 Snyder	N	N	Y	N	Y	N	Y
3 ***Hutchinson***	Y	Y	N	N	Y	N	N
4 ***Dickey***	Y	N	N	N	Y	N	Y
CALIFORNIA							
1 Thompson	N	N	Y	Y	Y	N	Y
2 ***Herger***	N	Y	N	N	Y	N	N
3 ***Ose***	N	N	Y	N	Y	N	Y
4 ***Doolittle***	N	Y	N	N	Y	N	N
5 Matsui	N	N	Y	Y	Y	N	Y
6 Woolsey	N	N	Y	Y	Y	N	Y
7 Miller, George	N	N	Y	Y	Y	N	Y
8 Pelosi	N	N	Y	?	N	Y	Y
9 Lee	N	N	Y	Y	N	N	Y
10 Tauscher	N	N	Y	N	Y	N	Y
11 ***Pombo***	N	Y	N	N	Y	N	N
12 Lantos	N	N	Y	Y	Y	N	Y
13 Stark	N	N	Y	Y	N	N	Y
14 Eshoo	N	N	Y	Y	Y	N	Y
15 ***Campbell***	N	N	Y	N	Y	N	Y
16 Lofgren	N	N	Y	Y	Y	N	Y
17 Farr	N	N	Y	Y	Y	N	Y
18 Condit	N	N	Y	N	Y	Y	N
19 ***Radanovich***	Y	Y	N	N	Y	N	N
20 Dooley	N	N	Y	N	Y	N	Y
21 ***Thomas***	Y	Y	N	N	Y	N	Y
22 Capps	N	N	Y	Y	Y	N	Y
23 ***Gallegly***	N	Y	Y	N	Y	N	Y
24 Sherman	N	N	Y	N	Y	N	Y
25 ***McKeon***	Y	Y	N	N	Y	N	Y
26 Berman	N	N	Y	Y	Y	N	Y
27 ***Rogan***	N	Y	N	N	Y	N	N
28 ***Dreier***	N	Y	N	N	Y	N	Y
29 Waxman	N	N	Y	Y	N	N	Y
30 Becerra	N	N	Y	Y	Y	N	Y
31 Martinez	N	N	Y	Y	Y	N	Y
32 Dixon	N	N	Y	Y	Y	N	Y
33 Roybal-Allard	N	N	Y	Y	?	N	Y
34 Napolitano	N	N	Y	Y	Y	N	Y
35 Waters	N	N	Y	?	Y	N	Y
36 ***Kuykendall***	N	N	Y	N	Y	N	Y
37 Millender-McD.	N	N	Y	?	?	N	Y
38 ***Horn***	N	N	Y	N	Y	N	Y
39 ***Royce***	Y	Y	N	N	Y	N	N
40 ***Lewis***	N	Y	N	N	Y	N	Y
41 ***Miller***	N	Y	N	N	Y	N	N
42 Vacant							
43 ***Calvert***	N	Y	N	N	Y	N	Y
44 ***Bono***	Y	Y	N	N	Y	N	Y
45 ***Rohrabacher***	Y	Y	N	N	Y	N	N
46 Sanchez	N	N	Y	N	Y	N	Y
47 ***Cox***	N	Y	N	N	Y	N	Y
48 ***Packard***	N	Y	N	N	Y	N	Y
49 ***Bilbray***	N	N	Y	N	Y	N	Y
50 Filner	N	N	Y	Y	N	N	Y
51 ***Cunningham***	Y	Y	N	N	Y	N	N
52 ***Hunter***	N	Y	N	N	Y	N	Y
COLORADO							
1 DeGette	N	N	Y	Y	N	N	Y
2 Udall	N	N	Y	Y	N	N	N
3 ***McInnis***	N	Y	N	N	Y	N	N
4 ***Schaffer***	N	Y	N	N	Y	N	N
5 ***Hefley***	N	Y	N	N	Y	N	N
6 ***Tancredo***	N	Y	N	N	Y	Y	N
CONNECTICUT							
1 Larson	N	N	Y	N	Y	N	Y
2 Gejdenson	N	N	Y	N	Y	N	Y
3 DeLauro	N	N	Y	Y	Y	N	Y
4 ***Shays***	N	N	Y	N	N	N	N
5 Maloney	N	N	Y	Y	Y	N	Y
6 ***Johnson***	N	N	Y	N	Y	N	Y
DELAWARE							
AL ***Castle***	N	N	Y	N	Y	N	Y
FLORIDA							
1 ***Scarborough***	Y	Y	N	N	Y	Y	Y
2 Boyd	N	N	Y	Y	Y	N	Y
3 Brown	N	N	Y	Y	Y	N	Y
4 ***Fowler***	Y	Y	N	N	Y	N	Y
5 Thurman	N	N	Y	Y	Y	N	N
6 ***Stearns***	Y	Y	N	N	Y	N	N
7 ***Mica***	N	Y	N	N	Y	N	Y
8 ***McCollum***	Y	Y	N	N	Y	N	Y
9 ***Bilirakis***	N	Y	N	N	Y	N	Y
10 ***Young***	N	Y	N	N	Y	N	Y
11 Davis	N	N	Y	Y	Y	N	Y
12 ***Canady***	N	Y	N	N	Y	N	N
13 ***Miller***	Y	Y	N	N	Y	Y	N
14 ***Goss***	Y	Y	N	N	Y	N	N
15 ***Weldon***	Y	Y	N	N	Y	N	N
16 ***Foley***	N	N	Y	N	Y	N	Y
17 Meek	N	N	Y	Y	Y	N	Y
18 ***Ros-Lehtinen***	?	?	?	?	?	?	?
19 Wexler	N	N	Y	N	Y	N	Y
20 Deutsch	N	N	Y	Y	Y	Y	N
21 ***Diaz-Balart***	Y	Y	N	N	Y	N	Y
22 ***Shaw***	?	?	?	?	?	N	Y
23 Hastings	?	?	?	?	?	?	?
GEORGIA							
1 ***Kingston***	?	?	?	?	?	?	?
2 Bishop	N	Y	N	Y	Y	N	Y
3 ***Collins***	Y	Y	Y	N	Y	N	N
4 McKinney	N	N	Y	?	N	N	Y
5 Lewis	N	N	Y	Y	Y	N	Y
6 ***Isakson***	N	Y	N	N	Y	N	Y
7 ***Barr***	N	Y	N	N	Y	N	N
8 ***Chambliss***	N	Y	N	N	Y	N	Y
9 ***Deal***	N	N	Y	N	Y	Y	N
10 ***Norwood***	N	Y	N	N	Y	N	Y
11 ***Linder***	Y	Y	N	N	Y	N	Y
HAWAII							
1 Abercrombie	N	N	Y	N	Y	N	Y
2 Mink	N	N	N	N	Y	N	Y
IDAHO							
1 ***Chenoweth***	N	Y	N	N	Y	N	N
2 ***Simpson***	N	Y	N	N	Y	N	Y
ILLINOIS							
1 Rush	N	N	Y	Y	Y	N	Y
2 Jackson	N	N	Y	N	N	N	Y
3 Lipinski	N	N	Y	N	Y	N	Y
4 Gutierrez	?	N	Y	Y	N	N	Y
5 Blagojevich	N	N	Y	N	Y	N	Y
6 ***Hyde***	N	Y	N	N	Y	N	Y
7 Davis	N	N	Y	Y	N	N	Y
8 ***Crane***	N	Y	N	N	Y	Y	N
9 Schakowsky	N	N	Y	Y	N	N	Y
10 ***Porter***	N	N	Y	Y	Y	N	Y
11 ***Weller***	N	Y	N	N	Y	N	Y
12 Costello	N	N	Y	Y	Y	Y	Y
13 ***Biggert***	N	Y	N	N	Y	N	Y
14 ***Hastert***		Y	N				

ND Northern Democrats SD Southern Democrats

	420	421	422	423	424	425	426
15 ***Ewing***	Y	Y	N	N	Y	N	Y
16 ***Manzullo***	N	Y	N	N	Y	Y	N
17 Evans	N	N	Y	Y	Y	N	N
18 ***LaHood***	Y	N	N	N	Y	N	Y
19 Phelps	N	N	Y	Y	Y	Y	N
20 ***Shimkus***	Y	Y	Y	N	Y	N	Y
INDIANA							
1 Visclosky	N	N	Y	Y	N	N	Y
2 ***McIntosh***	N	Y	N	N	Y	Y	N
3 Roemer	N	N	Y	N	Y	N	N
4 ***Souder***	N	Y	N	N	Y	Y	N
5 ***Buyer***	Y	Y	N	N	Y	N	Y
6 ***Burton***	Y	Y	N	N	Y	N	Y
7 ***Pease***	N	Y	N	N	Y	Y	Y
8 ***Hostettler***	N	Y	N	N	Y	Y	N
9 Hill	N	N	Y	Y	Y	N	N
10 Carson	N	N	Y	Y	Y	Y	N
IOWA							
1 ***Leach***	N	N	Y	N	Y	N	Y
2 ***Nussle***	Y	N	N	N	Y	N	Y
3 Boswell	N	N	Y	N	Y	Y	N
4 ***Ganske***	N	N	Y	N	Y	N	Y
5 ***Latham***	N	Y	N	N	Y	N	Y
KANSAS							
1 ***Moran***	Y	Y	N	N	Y	N	N
2 ***Ryun***	N	Y	N	N	Y	N	N
3 Moore	N	N	Y	Y	Y	N	Y
4 ***Tiahrt***	N	Y	N	N	Y	Y	N
KENTUCKY							
1 ***Whitfield***	Y	Y	N	N	Y	N	Y
2 ***Lewis***	N	Y	N	N	Y	N	Y
3 ***Northup***	N	Y	N	N	Y	N	Y
4 Lucas	N	N	Y	N	Y	Y	N
5 ***Rogers***	N	Y	N	N	Y	N	Y
6 ***Fletcher***	N	Y	N	N	Y	Y	N
LOUISIANA							
1 ***Vitter***	Y	Y	N	?	Y	N	Y
2 Jefferson	N	N	Y	?	?	?	?
3 ***Tauzin***	Y	Y	N	N	Y	N	Y
4 ***McCrery***	Y	Y	N	N	Y	N	Y
5 ***Cooksey***	N	Y	N	N	Y	N	Y
6 ***Baker***	Y	Y	N	N	Y	N	N
7 John	Y	Y	N	Y	Y	Y	Y
MAINE							
1 Allen	N	N	Y	N	Y	N	Y
2 Baldacci	N	N	Y	N	Y	N	N
MARYLAND							
1 ***Gilchrest***	N	N	Y	N	Y	N	Y
2 ***Ehrlich***	N	Y	N	N	Y	N	Y
3 Cardin	N	N	Y	Y	Y	N	Y
4 Wynn	N	N	Y	Y	Y	N	Y
5 Hoyer	N	N	Y	N	Y	N	Y
6 ***Bartlett***	N	Y	N	N	Y	Y	N
7 Cummings	N	N	Y	Y	Y	N	Y
8 ***Morella***	N	N	Y	N	Y	N	Y
MASSACHUSETTS							
1 Olver	N	N	Y	Y	Y	N	Y
2 Neal	N	N	Y	Y	Y	N	Y
3 McGovern	N	N	Y	Y	Y	N	Y
4 Frank	N	N	Y	Y	N	N	Y
5 Meehan	N	N	Y	Y	Y	N	Y
6 Tierney	N	N	Y	Y	Y	Y	Y
7 Markey	N	N	Y	Y	N	N	Y
8 Capuano	N	N	Y	Y	N	N	Y
9 Moakley	N	N	Y	Y	Y	N	Y
10 Delahunt	N	N	Y	Y	Y	N	Y
MICHIGAN							
1 Stupak	N	N	N	Y	Y	N	Y
2 ***Hoekstra***	Y	Y	N	N	Y	N	N
3 ***Ehlers***	Y	Y	N	N	N	N	N
4 ***Camp***	N	Y	N	N	Y	N	Y
5 Barcia	Y	N	N	N	Y	N	N
6 ***Upton***	N	N	Y	N	Y	N	Y
7 ***Smith***	N	Y	Y	N	Y	Y	Y
8 Stabenow	N	N	Y	Y	Y	Y	N
9 Kildee	N	N	Y	Y	Y	N	Y
10 Bonior	N	N	Y	Y	Y	N	Y
11 ***Knollenberg***	N	Y	N	N	Y	N	Y
12 Levin	N	N	Y	Y	Y	N	Y
13 Rivers	N	N	Y	Y	N	N	N
14 Conyers	N	N	Y	Y	N	N	Y
15 Kilpatrick	N	N	Y	Y	Y	N	Y
16 Dingell	N	N	Y	Y	N	N	Y

	420	421	422	423	424	425	426
MINNESOTA							
1 ***Gutknecht***	Y	Y	N	N	Y	Y	N
2 Minge	N	N	Y	Y	N	N	N
3 ***Ramstad***	N	N	Y	N	Y	N	N
4 Vento	N	N	Y	Y	N	N	Y
5 Sabo	N	N	Y	Y	N	N	Y
6 Luther	N	N	Y	Y	Y	Y	N
7 Peterson	Y	Y	N	N	Y	N	N
8 Oberstar	N	N	Y	Y	N	N	Y
MISSISSIPPI							
1 ***Wicker***	Y	Y	N	N	Y	N	Y
2 Thompson	N	N	Y	N	Y	N	Y
3 ***Pickering***	Y	Y	N	N	Y	Y	N
4 Shows	N	N	Y	N	Y	Y	N
5 Taylor	N	N	Y	N	Y	Y	N
MISSOURI							
1 Clay	N	N	Y	N	Y	?	?
2 ***Talent***	Y	Y	N	N	Y	N	Y
3 Gephardt	N	N	Y	Y	Y	N	Y
4 Skelton	N	N	Y	N	Y	N	Y
5 McCarthy	N	N	Y	Y	Y	N	Y
6 Danner	N	N	Y	N	Y	Y	N
7 ***Blunt***	Y	Y	N	N	Y	N	Y
8 ***Emerson***	Y	Y	N	N	Y	N	Y
9 ***Hulshof***	Y	Y	Y	N	?	N	N
MONTANA							
AL ***Hill***	Y	Y	Y	N	Y	N	N
NEBRASKA							
1 ***Bereuter***	N	N	Y	N	Y	N	Y
2 ***Terry***	N	Y	N	N	Y	N	Y
3 ***Barrett***	N	N	Y	N	Y	N	Y
NEVADA							
1 Berkley	N	N	Y	Y	Y	Y	N
2 ***Gibbons***	Y	Y	N	N	Y	N	N
NEW HAMPSHIRE							
1 ***Sununu***	Y	Y	N	N	Y	N	Y
2 ***Bass***	N	N	Y	N	Y	N	Y
NEW JERSEY							
1 Andrews	N	N	Y	N	Y	N	Y
2 ***LoBiondo***	N	N	Y	N	Y	N	N
3 ***Saxton***	N	N	Y	N	Y	N	Y
4 ***Smith***	Y	Y	N	N	Y	N	N
5 ***Roukema***	N	N	Y	N	Y	N	Y
6 Pallone	N	N	Y	Y	Y	N	Y
7 ***Franks***	N	N	Y	N	Y	N	N
8 Pascrell	N	N	Y	N	Y	Y	N
9 Rothman	N	N	Y	Y	Y	N	Y
10 Payne	N	N	Y	Y	N	N	Y
11 ***Frelinghuysen***	N	N	Y	N	Y	N	Y
12 Holt	N	N	Y	N	N	N	N
13 Menendez	N	N	Y	Y	Y	N	Y
NEW MEXICO							
1 ***Wilson***	Y	Y	N	N	Y	N	Y
2 ***Skeen***	N	N	N	N	Y	N	Y
3 Udall	N	N	Y	Y	Y	Y	N
NEW YORK							
1 Forbes	N	N	Y	N	Y	N	Y
2 ***Lazio***	N	N	Y	N	N	N	Y
3 ***King***	N	N	N	N	Y	N	Y
4 McCarthy	N	N	Y	Y	Y	N	Y
5 Ackerman	N	N	Y	Y	Y	N	Y
6 Meeks	N	N	Y	Y	Y	N	Y
7 Crowley	N	N	Y	Y	Y	N	Y
8 Nadler	N	N	Y	Y	N	Y	Y
9 Weiner	N	N	Y	Y	Y	N	Y
10 Towns	N	N	Y	Y	N	N	Y
11 Owens	N	N	Y	Y	Y	N	Y
12 Velázquez	N	N	Y	Y	Y	N	Y
13 ***Fossella***	N	Y	N	N	Y	N	Y
14 Maloney	N	N	Y	Y	N	N	N
15 Rangel	N	N	Y	Y	N	N	Y
16 Serrano	N	N	Y	Y	Y	N	Y
17 Engel	N	N	Y	Y	Y	N	Y
18 Lowey	N	N	Y	Y	N	N	Y
19 ***Kelly***	N	N	Y	N	Y	N	Y
20 ***Gilman***	N	N	Y	N	Y	N	Y
21 McNulty	N	N	Y	Y	Y	?	?
22 ***Sweeney***	Y	Y	N	N	Y	N	Y
23 ***Boehlert***	N	N	Y	N	Y	N	Y
24 ***McHugh***	N	N	Y	N	Y	N	Y
25 ***Walsh***	N	N	Y	N	Y	N	Y
26 Hinchey	N	N	Y	Y	Y	N	Y
27 ***Reynolds***	N	Y	N	N	Y	N	Y
28 Slaughter	N	N	Y	Y	Y	N	?
29 LaFalce	N	N	Y	Y	Y	N	Y

	420	421	422	423	424	425	426
30 ***Quinn***	N	N	Y	N	Y	N	Y
31 ***Houghton***	N	N	Y	N	Y	?	?
NORTH CAROLINA							
1 Clayton	N	N	Y	?	Y	N	?
2 Etheridge	N	N	Y	N	Y	?	?
3 ***Jones***	Y	Y	N	N	Y	Y	N
4 Price	N	N	Y	?	?	?	?
5 ***Burr***	Y	Y	N	N	Y	N	Y
6 ***Coble***	Y	Y	N	N	Y	N	N
7 McIntyre	N	N	Y	N	Y	?	?
8 ***Hayes***	N	Y	N	N	Y	N	Y
9 ***Myrick***	Y	Y	N	N	Y	N	Y
10 ***Ballenger***	Y	Y	N	N	Y	N	Y
11 ***Taylor***	Y	Y	N	N	Y	N	Y
12 Watt	N	N	Y	Y	Y	N	Y
NORTH DAKOTA							
AL Pomeroy	N	N	Y	N	Y	N	Y
OHIO							
1 ***Chabot***	Y	Y	N	N	Y	Y	N
2 ***Portman***	N	Y	N	N	Y	N	Y
3 Hall	N	N	Y	Y	Y	N	Y
4 ***Oxley***	Y	Y	N	N	Y	N	Y
5 ***Gillmor***	N	N	Y	N	Y	N	Y
6 Strickland	N	N	Y	Y	Y	N	N
7 ***Hobson***	Y	Y	N	N	Y	N	Y
8 ***Boehner***	N	Y	N	N	Y	N	Y
9 Kaptur	N	N	Y	N	Y	N	N
10 Kucinich	N	N	Y	Y	N	N	N
11 Jones	N	N	Y	Y	Y	N	Y
12 ***Kasich***	N	Y	N	N	Y	Y	N
13 Brown	N	N	Y	Y	Y	N	Y
14 Sawyer	N	N	Y	Y	Y	N	Y
15 ***Pryce***	?	?	?	?	?	?	?
16 ***Regula***	N	N	Y	N	Y	N	Y
17 Traficant	N	N	N	N	Y	N	Y
18 ***Ney***	Y	Y	N	N	Y	N	Y
19 ***LaTourette***	N	N	Y	N	Y	N	Y
OKLAHOMA							
1 ***Largent***	Y	Y	N	N	Y	Y	N
2 ***Coburn***	Y	Y	N	N	Y	Y	N
3 ***Watkins***	Y	Y	N	N	Y	N	N
4 ***Watts***	N	Y	N	N	Y	N	Y
5 ***Istook***	N	Y	N	N	Y	?	N
6 ***Lucas***	N	Y	N	N	Y	N	Y
OREGON							
1 Wu	N	N	Y	Y	N	N	N
2 ***Walden***	Y	Y	N	N	Y	N	Y
3 Blumenauer	N	N	Y	Y	Y	N	Y
4 DeFazio	N	N	Y	Y	N	N	N
5 Hooley	N	N	Y	Y	Y	N	N
PENNSYLVANIA							
1 Brady	N	N	Y	N	Y	N	Y
2 Fattah	N	N	Y	N	Y	N	Y
3 Borski	N	N	Y	Y	Y	N	Y
4 Klink	N	N	Y	Y	Y	N	Y
5 ***Peterson***	?	Y	N	N	Y	N	Y
6 Holden	N	N	Y	N	Y	N	Y
7 ***Weldon***	N	Y	Y	N	Y	N	Y
8 ***Greenwood***	N	N	Y	N	Y	N	Y
9 ***Shuster***	Y	Y	N	N	Y	N	Y
10 ***Sherwood***	Y	N	Y	N	Y	N	Y
11 Kanjorski	N	N	Y	Y	Y	N	Y
12 Murtha	N	N	N	N	Y	Y	Y
13 Hoeffel	N	N	Y	N	Y	N	Y
14 Coyne	N	N	Y	Y	Y	N	Y
15 ***Toomey***	N	Y	N	N	Y	Y	N
16 ***Pitts***	N	Y	N	N	Y	N	N
17 ***Gekas***	Y	Y	N	N	Y	N	Y
18 Doyle	N	N	Y	Y	Y	N	Y
19 ***Goodling***	N	N	N	N	Y	N	Y
20 Mascara	N	N	Y	N	Y	N	N
21 ***English***	Y	Y	N	N	Y	N	Y
RHODE ISLAND							
1 Kennedy	N	N	Y	N	Y	N	Y
2 Weygand	N	N	Y	N	Y	N	N
SOUTH CAROLINA							
1 ***Sanford***	N	N	Y	N	Y	?	?
2 ***Spence***	Y	Y	N	N	Y	N	Y
3 ***Graham***	N	N	Y	N	Y	Y	N
4 ***DeMint***	N	Y	N	N	Y	N	Y
5 Spratt	N	N	Y	Y	Y	N	N
6 Clyburn	N	N	Y	Y	Y	N	Y
SOUTH DAKOTA							
AL ***Thune***	Y	Y	Y	N	Y	N	N

	420	421	422	423	424	425	426
TENNESSEE							
1 ***Jenkins***	Y	N	N	N	Y	N	N
2 ***Duncan***	Y	N	Y	N	Y	Y	N
3 ***Wamp***	N	N	Y	N	Y	N	Y
4 ***Hilleary***	N	Y	N	N	Y	Y	N
5 Clement	N	N	Y	N	Y	N	Y
6 Gordon	N	N	Y	Y	Y	Y	N
7 ***Bryant***	N	Y	N	N	Y	N	Y
8 Tanner	N	N	Y	N	Y	Y	N
9 Ford	N	N	Y	N	Y	N	N
TEXAS							
1 Sandlin	N	N	Y	N	Y	N	Y
2 Turner	N	N	Y	N	Y	Y	N
3 ***Johnson, Sam***	N	Y	N	N	Y	Y	N
4 Hall	Y	Y	N	Y	Y	N	N
5 ***Sessions***	N	Y	N	N	Y	N	Y
6 ***Barton***	Y	Y	N	Y	N	N	N
7 ***Archer***	Y	Y	N	N	Y	N	Y
8 ***Brady***	Y	Y	N	N	Y	N	?
9 Lampson	N	N	Y	N	Y	N	Y
10 Doggett	N	N	Y	Y	Y	N	Y
11 Edwards	N	N	Y	N	?	Y	Y
12 ***Granger***	Y	Y	N	N	Y	N	Y
13 ***Thornberry***	Y	Y	N	N	Y	N	N
14 ***Paul***	Y	Y	N	N	N	N	N
15 Hinojosa	N	N	Y	N	Y	N	Y
16 Reyes	N	N	Y	N	Y	N	Y
17 Stenholm	N	N	Y	N	Y	N	Y
18 Jackson-Lee	N	N	Y	Y	Y	N	Y
19 ***Combest***	Y	Y	N	N	Y	N	Y
20 Gonzalez	N	N	Y	Y	Y	N	Y
21 ***Smith***	N	Y	N	N	Y	N	Y
22 ***DeLay***	N	Y	N	N	Y	N	Y
23 ***Bonilla***	N	Y	N	N	Y	N	Y
24 Frost	N	N	Y	N	Y	N	Y
25 Bentsen	N	N	Y	Y	Y	N	Y
26 ***Armey***	N	Y	N	N	Y	N	Y
27 Ortiz	N	N	Y	N	Y	N	Y
28 Rodriguez	N	N	Y	N	Y	N	Y
29 Green	N	N	Y	N	Y	Y	Y
30 Johnson, E.B.	N	N	Y	N	Y	N	Y
UTAH							
1 ***Hansen***	Y	Y	N	N	Y	N	Y
2 ***Cook***	Y	Y	Y	N	Y	N	Y
3 ***Cannon***	N	Y	N	N	Y	Y	Y
VERMONT							
AL *Sanders*	N	N	Y	Y	N	N	N
VIRGINIA							
1 ***Bateman***	Y	Y	N	N	Y	N	Y
2 Pickett	Y	N	N	N	Y	N	Y
3 Scott	Y	N	N	N	Y	N	Y
4 Sisisky	N	N	Y	N	Y	N	Y
5 Goode	Y	Y	N	N	Y	Y	N
6 ***Goodlatte***	Y	Y	N	N	Y	Y	N
7 ***Bliley***	N	Y	N	N	Y	N	Y
8 Moran	N	N	Y	Y	Y	N	Y
9 Boucher	N	N	Y	Y	Y	N	Y
10 ***Wolf***	Y	N	Y	N	Y	N	Y
11 ***Davis***	Y	Y	N	N	Y	N	Y
WASHINGTON							
1 Inslee	N	N	Y	Y	Y	Y	N
2 ***Metcalf***	N	N	Y	N	Y	N	Y
3 Baird	N	N	Y	Y	Y	N	N
4 ***Hastings***	N	Y	N	N	Y	N	Y
5 ***Nethercutt***	N	Y	N	N	Y	N	Y
6 Dicks	N	N	Y	N	Y	N	Y
7 McDermott	N	N	Y	Y	Y	N	Y
8 ***Dunn***	N	Y	N	N	?	N	Y
9 Smith	N	N	Y	N	Y	Y	N
WEST VIRGINIA							
1 Mollohan	N	N	N	N	Y	N	Y
2 Wise	N	N	Y	N	Y	N	N
3 Rahall	N	N	N	Y	Y	N	Y
WISCONSIN							
1 ***Ryan***	Y	Y	N	N	Y	N	N
2 Baldwin	N	N	Y	Y	N	N	N
3 Kind	N	N	Y	Y	Y	N	N
4 Kleczka	N	N	Y	Y	Y	N	Y
5 Barrett	N	N	Y	Y	N	N	N
6 ***Petri***	Y	Y	Y	Y	N	N	N
7 Obey	N	N	Y	Y	N	N	Y
8 ***Green***	Y	Y	N	N	+	N	N
9 ***Sensenbrenner***	Y	Y	N	Y	N	N	N
WYOMING							
AL ***Cubin***	N	Y	N	N	Y	N	Y

Southern states - Ala., Ark., Fla., Ga., Ky., La., Miss., N.C., Okla., S.C., Tenn., Texas, Va.

427. HR 2116. Veterans' Benefits Expansion/Passage. Stump, R-Ariz., motion to suspend the rules and pass the bill to authorize the Department of Veterans Affairs (VA) to expand long-term care services for veterans and allow the VA to generate increased revenue to help pay for health care costs. The measure also would extend the length of time the VA could lease facilities, space or land to private companies from 35 years to 75 years. Motion agreed to 369-46: R 201-13; D 168-32 (ND 119-32, SD 49-0); I 0-1. Sept. 21, 1999. A two-thirds majority of those present and voting (277 in this case) is required for passage under suspension of the rules.

428. HR 1431. Coastal Barrier Resources/Passage. Saxton, R-N.J., motion to suspend the rules and pass the bill to renew the 1982 Coastal Barrier Resources Act and correct maps of protected areas in Delaware, Florida and North Carolina. The measure would bar most federal funding, including flood insurance, for any development projects on coastal barriers. Motion agreed to 309-106: R 202-11; D 107-94 (ND 66-86, SD 41-8); I 0-1. Sept. 21, 1999. A two-thirds majority of those present and voting (278 in this case) is required for passage under suspension of the rules.

429. HR 468. Saint Helena Island/Passage. Sherwood, R-Pa., motion to suspend the rules and pass the bill to designate Lake Michigan's Saint Helena Island a national scenic area as part of the Hiawatha National Forest. Motion agreed to 410-2: R 210-2; D 199-0 (ND 151-0, SD 48-0); I 1-0. Sept. 21, 1999. A two-thirds majority of those present and voting (275 in this case) is required for passage under suspension of the rules.

430. HR 1402. Milk Marketing Orders/Producers Referendum. Green, R-Wis., amendment to require the Department of Agriculture (USDA) to hold a new national milk producers referendum on the department's proposed milk marketing reforms as soon as possible. The referendum would ask producers whether they would prefer the USDA to price fluid milk under the orders using the Class 1 price differentials of USDA Option 1-A or Option 1-B. The amendment specifies that cooperative associations would not be permitted to vote in the referendum on behalf of their members. Rejected 102-323: R 52-162; D 50-160 (ND 49-106, SD 1-54); I 0-1. Sept. 22, 1999.

431. HR 1402. Milk Marketing Orders/Forward Pricing. Dooley, D-Calif., amendment to the Stenholm-Pombo amendment. The Stenholm-Pombo amendment would permit milk producers and cooperatives to voluntarily enter into forward pricing contracts with milk handlers, locking in the current price for milk to be delivered at a later date. The program would sunset at the end of 2004 and would apply only to milk that is not intended for Class 1, or beverage, purposes. The Dooley amendment would allow the forward pricing contract program to be used for all classes of milk. Rejected 155-270: R 89-124; D 66-145 (ND 62-94, SD 4-51); I 0-1. Sept. 22, 1999. (Subsequently, the Stenholm-Pombo amendment was adopted by voice vote.)

Key

- Y Voted for (yea).
- # Paired for.
- + Announced for.
- N Voted against (nay).
- X Paired against.
- – Announced against.
- P Voted "present."
- C Voted "present" to avoid possible conflict of interest.
- ? Did not vote or otherwise make a position known.

•

Democrats ***Republicans***
Independents

	427	428	429	430	431
ALABAMA					
1 ***Callahan***	Y	Y	Y	N	Y
2 ***Everett***	Y	Y	Y	N	N
3 ***Riley***	Y	Y	Y	N	N
4 ***Aderholt***	Y	Y	Y	N	N
5 Cramer	Y	Y	Y	N	N
6 ***Bachus***	Y	Y	Y	N	N
7 Hilliard	Y	N	Y	N	N
ALASKA					
AL ***Young***	Y	Y	Y	N	Y
ARIZONA					
1 ***Salmon***	Y	Y	Y	N	Y
2 Pastor	Y	Y	Y	N	N
3 ***Stump***	Y	Y	Y	N	N
4 ***Shadegg***	Y	Y	Y	N	N
5 ***Kolbe***	Y	Y	Y	Y	Y
6 ***Hayworth***	Y	Y	Y	N	N
ARKANSAS					
1 Berry	Y	Y	Y	N	N
2 Snyder	Y	N	Y	N	N
3 ***Hutchinson***	Y	Y	Y	N	N
4 ***Dickey***	Y	Y	Y	?	?
CALIFORNIA					
1 Thompson	Y	Y	Y	N	N
2 ***Herger***	Y	Y	Y	N	N
3 ***Ose***	Y	Y	Y	–	Y
4 ***Doolittle***	Y	Y	Y	?	?
5 Matsui	Y	N	Y	Y	Y
6 Woolsey	Y	Y	Y	N	N
7 Miller, George	Y	Y	Y	N	N
8 Pelosi	Y	N	Y	N	N
9 Lee	Y	N	Y	N	N
10 Tauscher	Y	Y	Y	N	N
11 ***Pombo***	Y	N	Y	N	N
12 Lantos	Y	Y	Y	N	N
13 Stark	Y	N	Y	N	N
14 Eshoo	Y	Y	Y	N	N
15 ***Campbell***	Y	Y	Y	N	Y
16 Lofgren	Y	Y	Y	N	N
17 Farr	Y	Y	Y	N	N
18 Condit	Y	Y	Y	N	N
19 ***Radanovich***	Y	Y	Y	N	N
20 Dooley	Y	Y	Y	Y	Y
21 ***Thomas***	Y	Y	Y	N	N
22 Capps	Y	Y	Y	N	Y
23 ***Gallegly***	Y	Y	Y	N	Y
24 Sherman	Y	Y	Y	N	Y
25 ***McKeon***	Y	Y	Y	N	Y
26 Berman	Y	Y	Y	N	Y
27 ***Rogan***	Y	Y	Y	Y	Y
28 ***Dreier***	Y	Y	Y	Y	Y
29 Waxman	Y	Y	Y	N	Y
30 Becerra	Y	Y	Y	Y	Y
31 Martinez	Y	Y	Y	N	Y
32 Dixon	Y	Y	Y	N	Y
33 Roybal-Allard	Y	Y	Y	Y	Y
34 Napolitano	Y	N	Y	Y	N
35 Waters	N	N	Y	N	Y
36 ***Kuykendall***	Y	Y	Y	N	N
37 Millender-McD.	Y	Y	Y	N	N
38 ***Horn***	Y	Y	Y	N	N
39 ***Royce***	Y	Y	Y	Y	Y
40 ***Lewis***	Y	Y	Y	N	N
41 ***Miller***	Y	Y	Y	N	N
42 Vacant					
43 ***Calvert***	Y	Y	Y	Y	Y
44 ***Bono***	Y	Y	Y	N	N
45 ***Rohrabacher***	Y	Y	Y	Y	Y
46 Sanchez	Y	Y	Y	Y	Y
47 ***Cox***	Y	Y	Y	Y	Y
48 ***Packard***	Y	Y	Y	N	N
49 ***Bilbray***	Y	Y	Y	N	Y
50 Filner	Y	N	Y	N	N
51 ***Cunningham***	Y	Y	Y	N	N
52 ***Hunter***	?	?	?	N	N
COLORADO					
1 DeGette	Y	N	Y	N	Y
2 Udall	Y	N	Y	N	N
3 ***McInnis***	Y	Y	Y	N	Y
4 ***Schaffer***	Y	Y	Y	N	Y
5 ***Hefley***	Y	Y	Y	N	Y
6 ***Tancredo***	Y	Y	Y	Y	Y
CONNECTICUT					
1 Larson	Y	N	Y	N	N
2 Gejdenson	Y	N	Y	N	N
3 DeLauro	Y	N	Y	N	N
4 ***Shays***	Y	N	Y	Y	Y
5 Maloney	Y	N	Y	N	N
6 ***Johnson***	Y	Y	Y	N	N
DELAWARE					
AL ***Castle***	Y	Y	Y	N	N
FLORIDA					
1 ***Scarborough***	?	?	?	?	?
2 Boyd	Y	Y	Y	N	N
3 Brown	Y	Y	Y	N	N
4 ***Fowler***	?	?	?	?	?
5 Thurman	Y	Y	Y	N	N
6 ***Stearns***	Y	N	Y	N	N
7 ***Mica***	Y	Y	Y	N	N
8 ***McCollum***	Y	Y	Y	N	N
9 ***Bilirakis***	Y	Y	Y	N	N
10 ***Young***	Y	Y	Y	N	N
11 Davis	Y	Y	Y	N	N
12 ***Canady***	Y	Y	Y	N	Y
13 ***Miller***	Y	Y	Y	Y	Y
14 ***Goss***	Y	Y	Y	Y	Y
15 ***Weldon***	Y	Y	Y	N	N
16 ***Foley***	Y	Y	Y	N	N
17 Meek	Y	Y	Y	N	N
18 ***Ros-Lehtinen***	Y	Y	Y	N	N
19 Wexler	Y	Y	Y	N	N
20 Deutsch	Y	Y	Y	N	N
21 ***Diaz-Balart***	Y	Y	Y	N	N
22 ***Shaw***	Y	Y	Y	N	Y
23 Hastings	Y	Y	Y	N	N
GEORGIA					
1 ***Kingston***	Y	Y	Y	N	N
2 Bishop	Y	Y	Y	N	N
3 ***Collins***	Y	Y	Y	N	N
4 McKinney	?	?	?	N	N
5 Lewis	Y	N	Y	N	N
6 ***Isakson***	Y	Y	Y	N	N
7 ***Barr***	Y	Y	Y	N	N
8 ***Chambliss***	Y	Y	Y	N	N
9 ***Deal***	Y	Y	Y	N	N
10 ***Norwood***	Y	Y	Y	N	N
11 ***Linder***	Y	Y	Y	Y	Y
HAWAII					
1 Abercrombie	Y	Y	Y	N	N
2 Mink	Y	Y	Y	N	N
IDAHO					
1 ***Chenoweth***	Y	N	?	N	N
2 ***Simpson***	Y	Y	Y	N	N
ILLINOIS					
1 Rush	?	?	?	Y	Y
2 Jackson	Y	N	Y	Y	Y
3 Lipinski	Y	Y	Y	Y	Y
4 Gutierrez	Y	Y	Y	N	Y
5 Blagojevich	Y	Y	Y	Y	Y
6 ***Hyde***	Y	Y	Y	Y	Y
7 Davis	Y	N	Y	Y	Y
8 ***Crane***	Y	Y	Y	Y	Y
9 Schakowsky	Y	N	Y	Y	Y
10 ***Porter***	Y	Y	Y	N	Y
11 ***Weller***	Y	Y	Y	Y	Y
12 Costello	Y	N	Y	N	Y
13 ***Biggert***	Y	Y	Y	Y	Y
14 ***Hastert***					

ND Northern Democrats SD Southern Democrats

	427	428	429	430	431
15 ***Ewing***	Y	Y	Y	Y	Y
16 ***Manzullo***	Y	Y	Y	Y	Y
17 Evans	Y	N	Y	Y	Y
18 ***LaHood***	Y	Y	Y	Y	Y
19 Phelps	Y	N	Y	N	N
20 ***Shimkus***	Y	Y	Y	Y	Y
INDIANA					
1 Visclosky	Y	Y	Y	Y	Y
2 ***McIntosh***	Y	Y	Y	Y	Y
3 Roemer	Y	N	Y	N	N
4 ***Souder***	Y	Y	Y	Y	Y
5 ***Buyer***	?	?	?	N	Y
6 ***Burton***	Y	Y	Y	N	N
7 ***Pease***	Y	Y	Y	N	Y
8 ***Hostettler***	Y	Y	N	Y	Y
9 Hill	Y	Y	Y	N	N
10 Carson	Y	N	Y	Y	Y
IOWA					
1 ***Leach***	Y	?	Y	Y	Y
2 ***Nussle***	Y	Y	Y	Y	Y
3 Boswell	Y	Y	Y	Y	Y
4 ***Ganske***	Y	Y	Y	Y	Y
5 ***Latham***	Y	Y	Y	Y	+
KANSAS					
1 ***Moran***	Y	Y	Y	N	Y
2 ***Ryun***	Y	Y	Y	N	Y
3 Moore	Y	Y	Y	N	Y
4 ***Tiahrt***	Y	Y	Y	N	N
KENTUCKY					
1 ***Whitfield***	Y	Y	Y	N	N
2 ***Lewis***	Y	Y	Y	N	N
3 ***Northup***	Y	Y	Y	N	Y
4 Lucas	Y	Y	Y	N	N
5 ***Rogers***	Y	Y	Y	N	N
6 ***Fletcher***	Y	N	Y	N	N
LOUISIANA					
1 ***Vitter***	Y	Y	Y	N	N
2 Jefferson	?	?	?	N	N
3 ***Tauzin***	Y	Y	Y	?	?
4 ***McCrery***	Y	Y	Y	N	N
5 ***Cooksey***	Y	Y	Y	N	N
6 ***Baker***	Y	Y	Y	N	N
7 John	Y	Y	Y	N	N
MAINE					
1 Allen	Y	N	Y	N	N
2 Baldacci	Y	N	Y	N	N
MARYLAND					
1 ***Gilchrest***	Y	Y	Y	N	N
2 ***Ehrlich***	Y	Y	Y	N	N
3 Cardin	Y	N	Y	N	N
4 Wynn	Y	Y	Y	N	Y
5 Hoyer	N	N	Y	N	N
6 ***Bartlett***	Y	Y	Y	N	N
7 Cummings	Y	Y	Y	N	Y
8 ***Morella***	Y	Y	Y	N	N
MASSACHUSETTS					
1 Olver	N	N	Y	N	N
2 Neal	Y	N	Y	N	N
3 McGovern	N	N	Y	N	N
4 Frank	Y	Y	Y	Y	Y
5 Meehan	Y	N	Y	Y	Y
6 Tierney	N	N	Y	N	Y
7 Markey	Y	N	Y	Y	Y
8 Capuano	Y	N	Y	N	N
9 Moakley	?	N	Y	Y	Y
10 Delahunt	N	N	Y	Y	Y
MICHIGAN					
1 Stupak	Y	N	Y	Y	Y
2 ***Hoekstra***	Y	Y	Y	N	N
3 ***Ehlers***	Y	Y	Y	N	Y
4 ***Camp***	Y	Y	Y	N	N
5 Barcia	Y	Y	Y	N	N
6 ***Upton***	Y	Y	Y	N	N
7 ***Smith***	Y	Y	Y	N	N
8 Stabenow	Y	Y	Y	N	N
9 Kildee	Y	Y	Y	N	N
10 Bonior	Y	N	Y	N	N
11 ***Knollenberg***	Y	Y	Y	N	N
12 Levin	Y	Y	Y	N	N
13 Rivers	Y	N	Y	N	N
14 Conyers	N	N	Y	N	Y
15 Kilpatrick	Y	Y	?	N	N
16 Dingell	?	?	?	N	N

	427	428	429	430	431
MINNESOTA					
1 ***Gutknecht***	Y	Y	Y	Y	Y
2 Minge	Y	N	Y	Y	Y
3 ***Ramstad***	Y	Y	Y	Y	Y
4 Vento	Y	N	Y	Y	Y
5 Sabo	Y	N	Y	Y	Y
6 Luther	Y	N	Y	Y	Y
7 Peterson	Y	N	Y	Y	Y
8 Oberstar	Y	N	Y	Y	Y
MISSISSIPPI					
1 ***Wicker***	Y	Y	Y	N	N
2 Thompson	?	?	?	N	N
3 ***Pickering***	Y	Y	Y	N	N
4 Shows	Y	Y	Y	N	N
5 Taylor	Y	Y	Y	N	N
MISSOURI					
1 Clay	?	?	?	N	Y
2 ***Talent***	Y	Y	Y	N	N
3 Gephardt	Y	Y	Y	N	N
4 Skelton	Y	Y	Y	N	N
5 McCarthy	Y	N	Y	N	N
6 Danner	Y	Y	Y	N	N
7 ***Blunt***	Y	Y	Y	N	N
8 ***Emerson***	Y	Y	Y	N	N
9 ***Hulshof***	Y	Y	Y	N	N
MONTANA					
AL ***Hill***	Y	Y	Y	N	N
NEBRASKA					
1 ***Bereuter***	Y	N	Y	Y	Y
2 ***Terry***	Y	Y	Y	N	Y
3 ***Barrett***	Y	Y	Y	Y	Y
NEVADA					
1 Berkley	Y	N	Y	Y	N
2 ***Gibbons***	Y	Y	Y	N	N
NEW HAMPSHIRE					
1 ***Sununu***	Y	Y	Y	Y	Y
2 ***Bass***	+	+	+	N	N
NEW JERSEY					
1 Andrews	N	Y	Y	N	N
2 ***LoBiondo***	N	Y	Y	N	N
3 ***Saxton***	N	Y	Y	N	N
4 ***Smith***	Y	Y	Y	N	Y
5 ***Roukema***	N	Y	Y	N	N
6 Pallone	N	N	Y	Y	Y
7 ***Franks***	N	Y	Y	N	N
8 Pascrell	N	N	Y	Y	Y
9 Rothman	N	N	Y	N	Y
10 Payne	N	N	Y	Y	Y
11 ***Frelinghuysen***	N	Y	Y	N	N
12 Holt	N	N	Y	N	N
13 Menendez	N	N	Y	Y	Y
NEW MEXICO					
1 ***Wilson***	Y	Y	Y	N	Y
2 ***Skeen***	Y	Y	Y	N	N
3 Udall	Y	N	Y	N	N
NEW YORK					
1 Forbes	N	Y	Y	N	N
2 ***Lazio***	N	Y	Y	N	N
3 ***King***	N	Y	Y	N	N
4 McCarthy	N	N	Y	N	N
5 Ackerman	N	N	Y	N	N
6 Meeks	N	N	Y	N	N
7 Crowley	N	N	Y	N	N
8 Nadler	N	N	Y	N	N
9 Weiner	N	N	Y	N	N
10 Towns	N	N	Y	N	N
11 Owens	Y	Y	Y	N	N
12 Velázquez	+	+	+	N	N
13 ***Fossella***	N	Y	Y	N	N
14 Maloney	N	Y	Y	Y	Y
15 Rangel	Y	Y	Y	N	N
16 Serrano	N	Y	Y	N	N
17 Engel	N	N	Y	N	N
18 Lowey	N	N	Y	N	N
19 ***Kelly***	N	Y	Y	N	N
20 ***Gilman***	N	Y	Y	N	N
21 McNulty	N	Y	Y	N	N
22 ***Sweeney***	N	Y	Y	N	N
23 ***Boehlert***	Y	Y	Y	N	N
24 ***McHugh***	Y	Y	Y	N	Y
25 ***Walsh***	Y	Y	Y	N	N
26 Hinchey	N	N	Y	N	N
27 ***Reynolds***	Y	Y	Y	N	N
28 Slaughter	N	N	Y	N	N
29 LaFalce	Y	Y	Y	N	N

	427	428	429	430	431
30 ***Quinn***	Y	Y	Y	N	N
31 ***Houghton***	N	Y	Y	N	N
NORTH CAROLINA					
1 Clayton	+	+	+	N	N
2 Etheridge	Y	Y	Y	N	N
3 ***Jones***	Y	Y	Y	N	N
4 Price	Y	Y	Y	N	N
5 ***Burr***	Y	Y	Y	N	N
6 ***Coble***	Y	Y	Y	?	?
7 McIntyre	Y	Y	Y	N	N
8 ***Hayes***	Y	Y	Y	N	N
9 ***Myrick***	Y	Y	Y	N	N
10 ***Ballenger***	Y	Y	Y	N	N
11 ***Taylor***	Y	Y	Y	N	N
12 Watt	Y	Y	Y	N	N
NORTH DAKOTA					
AL Pomeroy	Y	N	Y	Y	N
OHIO					
1 ***Chabot***	Y	Y	Y	Y	Y
2 ***Portman***	Y	Y	?	Y	Y
3 Hall	Y	Y	Y	Y	N
4 ***Oxley***	Y	Y	Y	N	Y
5 ***Gillmor***	Y	Y	Y	N	N
6 Strickland	Y	Y	Y	Y	N
7 ***Hobson***	Y	Y	Y	Y	Y
8 ***Boehner***	Y	Y	Y	Y	Y
9 Kaptur	Y	Y	Y	Y	Y
10 Kucinich	N	Y	Y	Y	Y
11 Jones	Y	Y	Y	N	Y
12 ***Kasich***	Y	Y	Y	Y	Y
13 Brown	Y	N	Y	Y	N
14 Sawyer	Y	Y	Y	Y	N
15 ***Pryce***	Y	Y	Y	Y	Y
16 ***Regula***	Y	Y	Y	N	Y
17 Traficant	Y	Y	Y	N	Y
18 ***Ney***	Y	Y	Y	N	Y
19 ***LaTourette***	Y	Y	Y	Y	Y
OKLAHOMA					
1 ***Largent***	Y	Y	Y	Y	Y
2 ***Coburn***	Y	Y	Y	N	N
3 ***Watkins***	Y	Y	Y	N	N
4 ***Watts***	Y	Y	Y	N	N
5 ***Istook***	Y	Y	Y	N	Y
6 ***Lucas***	Y	Y	Y	N	N
OREGON					
1 Wu	Y	N	Y	Y	Y
2 ***Walden***	Y	Y	Y	N	N
3 Blumenauer	Y	N	Y	Y	Y
4 DeFazio	Y	N	Y	N	N
5 Hooley	Y	N	Y	N	N
PENNSYLVANIA					
1 Brady	Y	N	Y	N	N
2 Fattah	Y	N	Y	N	N
3 Borski	Y	N	Y	N	N
4 Klink	Y	N	Y	N	N
5 ***Peterson***	Y	Y	Y	N	N
6 Holden	Y	N	Y	N	N
7 ***Weldon***	Y	Y	Y	N	N
8 ***Greenwood***	Y	Y	Y	N	N
9 ***Shuster***	Y	Y	Y	N	N
10 ***Sherwood***	Y	Y	Y	N	N
11 Kanjorski	Y	N	Y	N	N
12 Murtha	Y	Y	Y	N	N
13 Hoeffel	Y	N	Y	N	N
14 Coyne	Y	Y	Y	N	N
15 ***Toomey***	Y	Y	Y	N	N
16 ***Pitts***	Y	Y	Y	N	N
17 ***Gekas***	Y	Y	Y	N	N
18 Doyle	Y	Y	Y	N	N
19 ***Goodling***	Y	Y	Y	N	N
20 Mascara	Y	Y	Y	N	N
21 ***English***	Y	Y	Y	N	N
RHODE ISLAND					
1 Kennedy	N	N	Y	N	N
2 Weygand	N	N	Y	?	N
SOUTH CAROLINA					
1 ***Sanford***	N	N	N	Y	Y
2 ***Spence***	Y	Y	Y	N	N
3 ***Graham***	Y	Y	Y	N	N
4 ***DeMint***	Y	Y	Y	Y	Y
5 Spratt	Y	Y	Y	Y	N
6 Clyburn	Y	N	Y	N	N
SOUTH DAKOTA					
AL ***Thune***	Y	Y	Y	Y	Y

	427	428	429	430	431
TENNESSEE					
1 ***Jenkins***	Y	Y	Y	N	N
2 ***Duncan***	Y	Y	Y	N	Y
3 ***Wamp***	?	?	?	N	Y
4 ***Hilleary***	Y	N	Y	N	Y
5 Clement	?	?	?	N	Y
6 Gordon	Y	Y	Y	N	N
7 ***Bryant***	Y	Y	Y	N	N
8 Tanner	Y	Y	Y	N	N
9 Ford	Y	N	Y	N	N
TEXAS					
1 Sandlin	Y	Y	Y	N	N
2 Turner	Y	Y	Y	N	N
3 ***Johnson, Sam***	Y	Y	Y	Y	Y
4 Hall	?	Y	Y	N	N
5 ***Sessions***	Y	Y	Y	Y	Y
6 ***Barton***	Y	Y	Y	N	Y
7 ***Archer***	Y	Y	Y	N	Y
8 ***Brady***	Y	Y	Y	N	N
9 Lampson	Y	Y	Y	N	N
10 Doggett	Y	N	Y	N	Y
11 Edwards	Y	Y	Y	N	N
12 ***Granger***	Y	Y	Y	N	Y
13 ***Thornberry***	Y	N	Y	N	N
14 ***Paul***	?	?	?	N	Y
15 Hinojosa	Y	Y	Y	N	N
16 Reyes	Y	Y	Y	N	N
17 Stenholm	Y	Y	Y	N	N
18 Jackson-Lee	Y	Y	Y	N	N
19 ***Combest***	Y	Y	Y	N	Y
20 Gonzalez	Y	N	Y	N	N
21 ***Smith***	Y	Y	Y	N	N
22 ***DeLay***	Y	Y	Y	N	Y
23 ***Bonilla***	Y	N	Y	N	N
24 Frost	Y	Y	Y	N	N
25 Bentsen	Y	Y	Y	N	N
26 ***Armey***	Y	Y	Y	Y	Y
27 Ortiz	Y	Y	Y	N	N
28 Rodriguez	Y	Y	Y	N	N
29 Green	Y	Y	Y	N	N
30 Johnson, E.B.	Y	P	Y	N	Y
UTAH					
1 ***Hansen***	Y	Y	Y	N	N
2 ***Cook***	Y	Y	Y	N	N
3 ***Cannon***	Y	Y	Y	N	N
VERMONT					
AL *Sanders*	N	N	Y	N	N
VIRGINIA					
1 ***Bateman***	Y	Y	Y	N	N
2 Pickett	Y	Y	?	N	N
3 Scott	Y	Y	Y	N	N
4 Sisisky	Y	Y	?	N	N
5 Goode	Y	Y	Y	N	N
6 ***Goodlatte***	Y	Y	Y	N	Y
7 ***Bliley***	Y	Y	Y	N	N
8 Moran	Y	Y	Y	N	Y
9 Boucher	Y	N	Y	N	N
10 ***Wolf***	Y	Y	Y	N	N
11 ***Davis***	Y	Y	Y	Y	Y
WASHINGTON					
1 Inslee	Y	N	Y	N	Y
2 ***Metcalf***	Y	Y	Y	N	?
3 Baird	Y	N	Y	N	N
4 ***Hastings***	Y	Y	Y	N	N
5 ***Nethercutt***	Y	Y	Y	Y	Y
6 Dicks	Y	Y	Y	N	N
7 McDermott	Y	N	Y	N	N
8 ***Dunn***	Y	Y	Y	N	N
9 Smith	Y	Y	Y	N	Y
WEST VIRGINIA					
1 Mollohan	Y	Y	Y	N	N
2 Wise	Y	Y	Y	N	N
3 Rahall	Y	Y	Y	N	N
WISCONSIN					
1 ***Ryan***	Y	N	Y	Y	Y
2 Baldwin	Y	N	Y	Y	Y
3 Kind	Y	N	Y	Y	Y
4 Kleczka	Y	N	Y	Y	Y
5 Barrett	Y	N	Y	Y	Y
6 ***Petri***	Y	Y	Y	Y	Y
7 Obey	Y	Y	Y	Y	Y
8 ***Green***	Y	Y	Y	Y	Y
9 ***Sensenbrenner***	Y	Y	Y	Y	Y
WYOMING					
AL ***Cubin***	Y	Y	Y	N	N

Southern states - Ala., Ark., Fla., Ga., Ky., La., Miss., N.C., Okla., S.C., Tenn., Texas, Va.

432. HR 1402. Milk Marketing Orders/Minimum Price for Cooperative Associations. Gutknecht, R-Minn., amendment to eliminate a technicality in current law that prevents certain dairy producers in cooperative associations from receiving the federal minimum price for their milk. Rejected 112-313: R 57-157; D 55-155 (ND 54-101, SD 1-54); I 0-1. Sept. 22, 1999.

433. HR 1402. Milk Marketing Orders/Class 1 Price Differential. Ryan, R-Wis., amendment to cap Class 1, or fluid, milk price differentials at $2.27 per hundredweight for any milk marketing order region in the country. Rejected 109-318: R 59-156; D 50-161 (ND 49-107, SD 1-54); I 0-1. Sept. 22, 1999.

434. HR 1402. Milk Marketing Orders/International Negotiations. Manzullo, R-Ill., amendment to specify that the bill could be implemented only if the U.S. Trade Representative found that it would not interfere with any U.S. international trade negotiations, or with achieving any U.S. trade policy objectives. Rejected 113-315: R 61-155; D 52-159 (ND 51-105, SD 1-54); I 0-1. Sept. 22, 1999.

435. HR 1402. Milk Marketing Orders/Termination. Boehner, R-Ohio, amendment to terminate the federal milk marketing orders program by Jan. 1, 2001. Rejected 124-302: R 71-144; D 53-157 (ND 48-108, SD 5-49); I 0-1. Sept. 22, 1999.

Key

Y Voted for (yea).
\# Paired for.
\+ Announced for.
N Voted against (nay).
X Paired against.
– Announced against.
P Voted "present."
C Voted "present" to avoid possible conflict of interest.
? Did not vote or otherwise make a position known.

•

Democrats ***Republicans***
Independents

	432	433	434	435
ALABAMA				
1 ***Callahan***	N	N	N	N
2 ***Everett***	N	N	N	N
3 ***Riley***	N	N	N	N
4 ***Aderholt***	N	N	N	N
5 Cramer	N	N	N	N
6 ***Bachus***	N	N	N	N
7 Hilliard	N	N	N	N
ALASKA				
AL ***Young***	N	N	N	N
ARIZONA				
1 ***Salmon***	N	Y	Y	Y
2 Pastor	N	N	N	N
3 ***Stump***	N	N	N	N
4 ***Shadegg***	N	N	N	N
5 ***Kolbe***	Y	Y	Y	Y
6 ***Hayworth***	N	N	N	N
ARKANSAS				
1 Berry	N	N	N	N
2 Snyder	N	N	N	N
3 ***Hutchinson***	N	N	N	N
4 ***Dickey***	?	?	?	?
CALIFORNIA				
1 Thompson	N	N	N	N
2 ***Herger***	?	Y	Y	Y
3 ***Ose***	Y	N	N	Y
4 ***Doolittle***	N	N	N	Y
5 Matsui	Y	Y	Y	N
6 Woolsey	N	N	N	N
7 Miller, George	N	N	N	N
8 Pelosi	N	N	N	N
9 Lee	N	N	N	Y
10 Tauscher	N	N	Y	N
11 ***Pombo***	N	N	N	N
12 Lantos	N	N	N	N
13 Stark	N	N	N	Y
14 Eshoo	N	Y	Y	N
15 ***Campbell***	N	Y	Y	Y
16 Lofgren	N	Y	Y	N
17 Farr	N	N	N	N
18 Condit	N	N	N	N
19 ***Radanovich***	N	N	N	N
20 Dooley	Y	Y	Y	N
21 ***Thomas***	N	N	N	–
22 Capps	Y	N	Y	Y
23 ***Gallegly***	N	N	N	N
24 Sherman	N	Y	Y	Y
25 ***McKeon***	N	N	N	N
26 Berman	N	N	Y	N
27 ***Rogan***	Y	Y	Y	Y
28 ***Dreier***	Y	Y	Y	Y
29 Waxman	Y	Y	Y	Y
30 Becerra	Y	Y	N	N
31 Martinez	N	N	N	Y
32 Dixon	Y	Y	Y	N
33 Roybal-Allard	Y	Y	Y	N
34 Napolitano	N	N	N	N
35 Waters	N	N	N	N
36 ***Kuykendall***	N	N	N	N
37 Millender-McD.	N	N	N	N
38 ***Horn***	N	N	N	N
39 ***Royce***	Y	Y	Y	Y
40 ***Lewis***	N	N	N	N
41 ***Miller***	N	N	N	N
42 Vacant				
43 ***Calvert***	Y	Y	Y	Y
44 ***Bono***	N	N	N	?
45 ***Rohrabacher***	Y	Y	Y	Y
46 Sanchez	Y	Y	Y	N
47 ***Cox***	Y	Y	Y	Y
48 ***Packard***	N	N	N	N
49 ***Bilbray***	Y	Y	Y	Y
50 Filner	N	N	N	N
51 ***Cunningham***	N	N	N	N
52 ***Hunter***	N	N	N	N
COLORADO				
1 DeGette	N	N	Y	N
2 Udall	N	N	N	N
3 ***McInnis***	N	N	Y	N
4 ***Schaffer***	N	N	N	N
5 ***Hefley***	Y	Y	Y	N
6 ***Tancredo***	Y	Y	Y	Y
CONNECTICUT				
1 Larson	N	N	N	N
2 Gejdenson	N	N	N	N
3 DeLauro	N	N	N	N
4 ***Shays***	Y	Y	Y	Y
5 Maloney	N	N	N	N
6 ***Johnson***	N	N	N	N
DELAWARE				
AL ***Castle***	N	N	N	N
FLORIDA				
1 ***Scarborough***	?	?	?	?
2 Boyd	N	N	N	N
3 Brown	N	N	N	Y
4 ***Fowler***	?	?	?	?
5 Thurman	N	N	N	N
6 ***Stearns***	N	N	N	N
7 ***Mica***	N	N	N	N
8 ***McCollum***	N	N	N	N
9 ***Bilirakis***	N	N	N	N
10 ***Young***	N	N	N	N
11 Davis	N	N	N	N
12 ***Canady***	N	N	N	N
13 ***Miller***	Y	Y	Y	Y
14 ***Goss***	Y	Y	Y	Y
15 ***Weldon***	N	N	N	N
16 ***Foley***	N	N	N	N
17 Meek	N	N	N	Y
18 ***Ros-Lehtinen***	N	N	N	N
19 Wexler	N	N	N	N
20 Deutsch	N	N	N	N
21 ***Diaz-Balart***	?	N	N	N
22 ***Shaw***	Y	Y	Y	Y
23 Hastings	N	N	N	N
GEORGIA				
1 ***Kingston***	Y	N	N	N
2 Bishop	N	N	N	N
3 ***Collins***	N	N	N	N
4 McKinney	N	N	N	N
5 Lewis	N	N	N	N
6 ***Isakson***	N	N	?	N
7 ***Barr***	N	N	N	N
8 ***Chambliss***	N	N	N	N
9 ***Deal***	N	N	N	N
10 ***Norwood***	N	N	N	N
11 ***Linder***	Y	N	Y	N
HAWAII				
1 Abercrombie	N	N	N	N
2 Mink	N	N	N	N
IDAHO				
1 ***Chenoweth***	N	N	N	N
2 ***Simpson***	N	N	N	N
ILLINOIS				
1 Rush	Y	Y	Y	Y
2 Jackson	Y	Y	Y	Y
3 Lipinski	Y	Y	Y	Y
4 Gutierrez	Y	Y	Y	Y
5 Blagojevich	Y	Y	Y	Y
6 ***Hyde***	Y	Y	Y	Y
7 Davis	Y	Y	Y	Y
8 ***Crane***	Y	Y	Y	Y
9 Schakowsky	Y	Y	Y	Y
10 ***Porter***	Y	N	N	Y
11 ***Weller***	Y	Y	Y	Y
12 Costello	N	N	N	N
13 ***Biggert***	Y	Y	Y	Y
14 ***Hastert***				

ND Northern Democrats SD Southern Democrats

	432	433	434	435
15 ***Ewing***	Y	Y	Y	Y
16 ***Manzullo***	Y	Y	Y	Y
17 Evans	Y	Y	Y	Y
18 ***LaHood***	Y	Y	Y	Y
19 Phelps	N	N	N	N
20 ***Shimkus***	N	N	Y	N
INDIANA				
1 Visclosky	Y	Y	Y	Y
2 ***McIntosh***	N	Y	Y	Y
3 Roemer	N	N	N	N
4 ***Souder***	Y	Y	Y	Y
5 ***Buyer***	Y	Y	Y	Y
6 ***Burton***	N	N	N	N
7 ***Pease***	N	Y	N	N
8 ***Hostettler***	Y	Y	Y	Y
9 Hill	Y	N	N	N
10 Carson	Y	Y	Y	N
IOWA				
1 ***Leach***	Y	Y	Y	Y
2 ***Nussle***	Y	Y	Y	Y
3 Boswell	Y	Y	Y	Y
4 ***Ganske***	Y	Y	N	Y
5 ***Latham***	Y	Y	Y	Y
KANSAS				
1 ***Moran***	N	N	N	N
2 ***Ryun***	N	N	N	N
3 Moore	?	N	N	N
4 ***Tiahrt***	N	N	N	Y
KENTUCKY				
1 ***Whitfield***	N	N	N	N
2 ***Lewis***	N	N	N	N
3 ***Northup***	N	N	Y	Y
4 Lucas	N	N	N	N
5 ***Rogers***	N	N	N	N
6 ***Fletcher***	N	N	N	N
LOUISIANA				
1 ***Vitter***	N	N	N	N
2 Jefferson	N	N	N	?
3 ***Tauzin***	N	?	N	N
4 ***McCrery***	N	N	N	N
5 ***Cooksey***	N	N	N	N
6 ***Baker***	N	N	N	N
7 John	N	N	N	N
MAINE				
1 Allen	N	N	N	N
2 Baldacci	N	N	N	N
MARYLAND				
1 ***Gilchrest***	N	N	N	N
2 ***Ehrlich***	N	N	N	N
3 Cardin	N	N	N	N
4 Wynn	N	N	N	N
5 Hoyer	N	N	N	N
6 ***Bartlett***	N	N	N	N
7 Cummings	N	N	N	N
8 ***Morella***	N	N	N	N
MASSACHUSETTS				
1 Olver	N	N	N	N
2 Neal	N	N	N	N
3 McGovern	N	N	N	N
4 Frank	Y	Y	Y	Y
5 Meehan	Y	Y	Y	Y
6 Tierney	Y	Y	Y	Y
7 Markey	Y	Y	N	Y
8 Capuano	N	N	N	N
9 Moakley	N	N	N	N
10 Delahunt	Y	Y	Y	Y
MICHIGAN				
1 Stupak	Y	Y	Y	Y
2 ***Hoekstra***	Y	Y	N	N
3 ***Ehlers***	Y	N	N	N
4 ***Camp***	N	N	N	N
5 Barcia	N	N	N	N
6 ***Upton***	N	Y	N	N
7 ***Smith***	N	N	N	N
8 Stabenow	N	N	N	N
9 Kildee	N	N	N	N
10 Bonior	N	N	N	N
11 ***Knollenberg***	N	N	N	N
12 Levin	N	N	N	N
13 Rivers	N	N	N	N
14 Conyers	Y	N	N	N
15 Kilpatrick	Y	N	N	N
16 Dingell	N	N	N	N

	432	433	434	435
MINNESOTA				
1 ***Gutknecht***	Y	Y	Y	Y
2 Minge	Y	Y	Y	Y
3 ***Ramstad***	Y	Y	Y	Y
4 Vento	Y	Y	Y	Y
5 Sabo	Y	Y	Y	Y
6 Luther	Y	Y	Y	Y
7 Peterson	Y	Y	Y	Y
8 Oberstar	Y	Y	Y	Y
MISSISSIPPI				
1 ***Wicker***	N	N	N	N
2 Thompson	N	N	N	N
3 ***Pickering***	N	N	N	N
4 Shows	N	N	N	N
5 Taylor	N	N	N	N
MISSOURI				
1 Clay	N	N	N	N
2 ***Talent***	N	N	N	N
3 Gephardt	N	N	N	N
4 Skelton	N	N	N	N
5 McCarthy	N	N	N	N
6 Danner	N	N	N	N
7 ***Blunt***	N	N	N	N
8 ***Emerson***	N	N	N	N
9 ***Hulshof***	N	N	N	N
MONTANA				
AL ***Hill***	N	N	N	N
NEBRASKA				
1 ***Bereuter***	N	Y	N	N
2 ***Terry***	Y	Y	Y	Y
3 ***Barrett***	N	Y	Y	Y
NEVADA				
1 Berkley	N	N	N	Y
2 ***Gibbons***	N	N	N	N
NEW HAMPSHIRE				
1 ***Sununu***	Y	N	Y	Y
2 ***Bass***	N	N	N	N
NEW JERSEY				
1 Andrews	N	N	N	N
2 ***LoBiondo***	N	N	N	N
3 ***Saxton***	N	N	N	N
4 ***Smith***	N	N	N	N
5 ***Roukema***	N	N	N	N
6 Pallone	Y	Y	Y	Y
7 ***Franks***	N	N	N	N
8 Pascrell	Y	Y	Y	Y
9 Rothman	Y	Y	Y	Y
10 Payne	Y	Y	Y	Y
11 ***Frelinghuysen***	N	N	N	N
12 Holt	N	N	N	N
13 Menendez	Y	Y	Y	Y
NEW MEXICO				
1 ***Wilson***	N	N	N	N
2 ***Skeen***	N	N	N	N
3 Udall	N	N	N	N
NEW YORK				
1 Forbes	N	N	N	N
2 ***Lazio***	N	N	N	N
3 ***King***	N	N	N	N
4 McCarthy	N	N	N	N
5 Ackerman	N	N	N	N
6 Meeks	N	N	N	N
7 Crowley	N	N	N	N
8 Nadler	N	N	N	N
9 Weiner	N	N	N	N
10 Towns	N	N	N	N
11 Owens	N	N	N	N
12 Velázquez	N	N	N	N
13 ***Fossella***	N	N	N	N
14 Maloney	N	Y	Y	Y
15 Rangel	N	N	N	N
16 Serrano	N	N	N	N
17 Engel	N	N	N	N
18 Lowey	N	N	N	N
19 ***Kelly***	N	N	N	N
20 ***Gilman***	N	N	N	N
21 McNulty	N	N	N	N
22 ***Sweeney***	N	N	N	N
23 ***Boehlert***	N	N	N	N
24 ***McHugh***	N	N	N	N
25 ***Walsh***	N	N	N	N
26 Hinchey	N	N	N	N
27 ***Reynolds***	N	N	N	N
28 Slaughter	N	N	N	N
29 LaFalce	N	N	N	N

	432	433	434	435
30 ***Quinn***	N	N	N	N
31 ***Houghton***	N	N	N	N
NORTH CAROLINA				
1 Clayton	N	N	N	N
2 Etheridge	N	N	N	N
3 ***Jones***	N	N	N	N
4 Price	N	N	N	N
5 ***Burr***	N	N	N	N
6 ***Coble***	?	?	?	?
7 McIntyre	N	N	N	N
8 ***Hayes***	N	N	N	N
9 ***Myrick***	N	N	N	N
10 ***Ballenger***	N	N	N	N
11 ***Taylor***	N	N	N	N
12 Watt	N	N	N	N
NORTH DAKOTA				
AL Pomeroy	Y	Y	Y	Y
OHIO				
1 ***Chabot***	Y	Y	Y	Y
2 ***Portman***	Y	Y	Y	Y
3 Hall	Y	N	N	Y
4 ***Oxley***	N	N	Y	Y
5 ***Gillmor***	N	N	N	N
6 Strickland	Y	N	N	N
7 ***Hobson***	Y	Y	N	Y
8 ***Boehner***	Y	Y	Y	Y
9 Kaptur	Y	Y	Y	Y
10 Kucinich	N	N	N	Y
11 Jones	Y	N	N	Y
12 ***Kasich***	Y	Y	Y	Y
13 Brown	N	N	N	N
14 Sawyer	Y	N	N	N
15 ***Pryce***	Y	Y	Y	Y
16 ***Regula***	Y	N	N	N
17 Traficant	N	N	N	N
18 ***Ney***	N	N	N	N
19 ***LaTourette***	Y	Y	Y	Y
OKLAHOMA				
1 ***Largent***	Y	Y	Y	Y
2 ***Coburn***	N	N	N	Y
3 ***Watkins***	N	N	N	N
4 ***Watts***	N	N	N	N
5 ***Istook***	?	?	Y	Y
6 ***Lucas***	N	N	N	N
OREGON				
1 Wu	Y	Y	Y	Y
2 ***Walden***	N	N	N	N
3 Blumenauer	Y	Y	Y	Y
4 DeFazio	N	N	N	N
5 Hooley	N	N	N	N
PENNSYLVANIA				
1 Brady	N	N	N	N
2 Fattah	N	N	N	N
3 Borski	N	N	N	N
4 Klink	N	N	N	N
5 ***Peterson***	N	N	N	N
6 Holden	N	N	N	N
7 ***Weldon***	N	N	N	N
8 ***Greenwood***	N	N	N	N
9 ***Shuster***	N	N	N	N
10 ***Sherwood***	N	N	N	N
11 Kanjorski	N	N	N	N
12 Murtha	N	N	N	N
13 Hoeffel	N	N	N	N
14 Coyne	N	N	N	N
15 ***Toomey***	N	N	Y	Y
16 ***Pitts***	N	N	N	N
17 ***Gekas***	N	N	N	N
18 Doyle	N	N	N	N
19 ***Goodling***	N	N	N	N
20 Mascara	N	N	N	N
21 ***English***	N	N	N	N
RHODE ISLAND				
1 Kennedy	N	N	N	N
2 Weygand	N	N	N	N
SOUTH CAROLINA				
1 ***Sanford***	Y	N	Y	Y
2 ***Spence***	N	N	N	N
3 ***Graham***	N	N	N	N
4 ***DeMint***	Y	Y	Y	Y
5 Spratt	N	N	N	N
6 Clyburn	N	N	N	N
SOUTH DAKOTA				
AL ***Thune***	Y	Y	Y	Y

	432	433	434	435
TENNESSEE				
1 ***Jenkins***	N	N	N	N
2 ***Duncan***	N	N	N	Y
3 ***Wamp***	N	N	N	Y
4 ***Hilleary***	N	N	N	N
5 Clement	N	N	N	N
6 Gordon	N	N	N	N
7 ***Bryant***	N	N	N	N
8 Tanner	N	N	N	N
9 Ford	N	N	N	N
TEXAS				
1 Sandlin	N	N	N	N
2 Turner	N	N	N	N
3 ***Johnson, Sam***	Y	Y	Y	Y
4 Hall	N	N	N	N
5 ***Sessions***	Y	Y	Y	Y
6 ***Barton***	N	N	N	Y
7 ***Archer***	N	N	Y	Y
8 ***Brady***	N	N	N	N
9 Lampson	N	N	N	N
10 Doggett	N	N	N	Y
11 Edwards	N	N	N	N
12 ***Granger***	N	N	N	N
13 ***Thornberry***	N	N	N	N
14 ***Paul***	N	Y	N	Y
15 Hinojosa	N	N	N	N
16 Reyes	N	N	N	N
17 Stenholm	N	N	N	N
18 Jackson-Lee	N	N	N	N
19 ***Combest***	N	N	N	N
20 Gonzalez	N	N	N	N
21 ***Smith***	N	N	N	N
22 ***DeLay***	N	N	N	Y
23 ***Bonilla***	N	N	N	N
24 Frost	N	N	N	N
25 Bentsen	N	N	N	N
26 ***Armey***	Y	Y	Y	Y
27 Ortiz	N	N	N	N
28 Rodriguez	N	N	N	N
29 Green	N	N	N	N
30 Johnson, E.B.	Y	Y	Y	Y
UTAH				
1 ***Hansen***	N	N	N	N
2 ***Cook***	N	N	N	N
3 ***Cannon***	N	N	N	N
VERMONT				
AL *Sanders*	N	N	N	N
VIRGINIA				
1 ***Bateman***	N	N	N	N
2 Pickett	N	N	N	N
3 Scott	N	N	N	N
4 Sisisky	N	N	N	N
5 Goode	N	N	N	N
6 ***Goodlatte***	N	N	N	Y
7 ***Bliley***	N	N	N	N
8 Moran	N	N	N	Y
9 Boucher	N	N	N	N
10 ***Wolf***	N	N	N	N
11 ***Davis***	N	Y	N	Y
WASHINGTON				
1 Inslee	N	N	N	N
2 ***Metcalf***	N	N	N	N
3 Baird	N	N	N	N
4 ***Hastings***	N	N	N	N
5 ***Nethercutt***	N	N	N	N
6 Dicks	N	N	N	N
7 McDermott	Y	Y	Y	Y
8 ***Dunn***	N	N	N	N
9 Smith	Y	N	N	N
WEST VIRGINIA				
1 Mollohan	N	N	N	N
2 Wise	N	N	N	N
3 Rahall	N	N	N	N
WISCONSIN				
1 ***Ryan***	Y	Y	Y	Y
2 Baldwin	Y	Y	Y	Y
3 Kind	Y	Y	Y	Y
4 Kleczka	Y	Y	Y	Y
5 Barrett	Y	Y	Y	Y
6 ***Petri***	Y	Y	Y	Y
7 Obey	Y	Y	Y	Y
8 ***Green***	Y	Y	Y	Y
9 ***Sensenbrenner***	Y	Y	Y	Y
WYOMING				
AL ***Cubin***	N	N	N	N

Southern states - Ala., Ark., Fla., Ga., Ky., La., Miss., N.C., Okla., S.C., Tenn., Texas, Va.

436. HR 1402. Milk Marketing Orders/Passage. Passage of the bill to implement the Department of Agriculture's Option 1-A Class 1 differential milk pricing structure. The bill would extend the current federal milk price support program for one year and repeal the existing authorization to begin a new recourse loan program for commercial processors of dairy products. The bill would direct the department to develop new pricing formulas for Class 3 and Class 4 products (cheese, butter and dry milk), and would allow milk producers and cooperatives to voluntarily enter into forward pricing contracts with milk handlers for Class 1, or fluid, milk. Passed 285-140: R 148-68; D 136-72 (ND 87-68, SD 49-4); I 1-0. Sept. 22, 1999. A "nay" was a vote in support of the president's position.

437. HR 1875. Class Action Lawsuits/Rule. Adoption of the rule (H Res 295) to provide for House floor consideration of the bill to amend the federal judicial code to give federal courts jurisdiction over certain class action lawsuits. Under the measure, a suit could be moved from state to federal court if any plaintiff or defendant resides in a different state and petitions for the transfer. Adopted 241-181: R 216-0; D 25-180 (ND 15-136, SD 10-44); I 0-1. Sept. 23, 1999.

438. HR 1501. Juvenile Justice/Motion to Instruct. Lofgren, D-Calif., motion to instruct House conferees to insist upon a conference substitute that assures that no criminals or other prohibited purchasers obtain firearms at gun shows; omits provisions that weaken current gun safety law; and include provisions that aid in the enforcement of current laws against criminals who use guns. Motion agreed to 305-117: R 130-85; D 174-32 (ND 140-12, SD 34-20); I 1-0. Sept. 23, 1999.

439. HR 1875. Class Action Lawsuits/Firearms. Nadler, D-N.Y., amendment to specify that no provisions in the bill would affect any class action lawsuit dealing with harm caused by a firearm or ammunition. Rejected 152-277: R 3-216; D 148-61 (ND 125-30, SD 23-31); I 1-0. Sept. 23, 1999.

Key

- Y Voted for (yea).
- # Paired for.
- \+ Announced for.
- N Voted against (nay).
- X Paired against.
- – Announced against.
- P Voted "present."
- C Voted "present" to avoid possible conflict of interest.
- ? Did not vote or otherwise make a position known.

Democrats ***Republicans*** *Independents*

	436	437	438	439
ALABAMA				
1 ***Callahan***	Y	Y	N	N
2 ***Everett***	Y	Y	N	N
3 ***Riley***	Y	Y	N	N
4 ***Aderholt***	Y	Y	N	N
5 Cramer	Y	Y	N	N
6 ***Bachus***	Y	Y	N	N
7 Hilliard	Y	N	N	N
ALASKA				
AL ***Young***	Y	Y	Y	N
ARIZONA				
1 ***Salmon***	N	Y	Y	N
2 Pastor	Y	N	Y	Y
3 ***Stump***	Y	Y	N	N
4 ***Shadegg***	Y	Y	N	N
5 ***Kolbe***	N	Y	Y	N
6 ***Hayworth***	Y	Y	N	N
ARKANSAS				
1 Berry	Y	N	N	N
2 Snyder	Y	N	Y	N
3 ***Hutchinson***	Y	Y	Y	N
4 ***Dickey***	?	Y	Y	N
CALIFORNIA				
1 Thompson	Y	N	Y	N
2 ***Herger***	N	Y	Y	N
3 ***Ose***	N	Y	Y	N
4 ***Doolittle***	N	Y	Y	N
5 Matsui	N	N	Y	Y
6 Woolsey	Y	N	Y	Y
7 Miller, George	Y	N	Y	Y
8 Pelosi	Y	N	Y	Y
9 Lee	N	N	Y	Y
10 Tauscher	N	N	Y	Y
11 ***Pombo***	Y	Y	N	N
12 Lantos	N	N	Y	Y
13 Stark	N	N	Y	Y
14 Eshoo	N	N	Y	Y
15 ***Campbell***	N	Y	Y	N
16 Lofgren	N	N	Y	Y
17 Farr	Y	N	Y	Y
18 Condit	Y	Y	Y	N
19 ***Radanovich***	Y	Y	Y	N
20 Dooley	N	Y	Y	N
21 ***Thomas***	Y	Y	Y	N
22 Capps	N	N	Y	Y
23 ***Gallegly***	N	Y	Y	N
24 Sherman	N	N	Y	Y
25 ***McKeon***	Y	Y	Y	N
26 Berman	?	N	Y	Y
27 ***Rogan***	N	Y	Y	N
28 ***Dreier***	N	Y	Y	N
29 Waxman	N	N	Y	Y
30 Becerra	N	N	Y	Y
31 Martinez	Y	Y	Y	Y
32 Dixon	N	N	Y	Y
33 Roybal-Allard	N	N	Y	Y
34 Napolitano	Y	N	Y	Y
35 Waters	N	?	Y	Y
36 ***Kuykendall***	Y	Y	Y	N
37 Millender-McD.	N	N	Y	Y
38 ***Horn***	Y	Y	Y	N
39 ***Royce***	N	?	?	N

	436	437	438	439
40 ***Lewis***	Y	Y	Y	N
41 ***Miller***	Y	Y	Y	N
42 Vacant				
43 ***Calvert***	N	Y	Y	N
44 ***Bono***	?	Y	Y	N
45 ***Rohrabacher***	N	Y	Y	N
46 Sanchez	N	N	Y	Y
47 ***Cox***	N	Y	?	N
48 ***Packard***	Y	Y	Y	N
49 ***Bilbray***	N	Y	Y	N
50 Filner	Y	N	Y	Y
51 ***Cunningham***	Y	Y	Y	N
52 ***Hunter***	Y	Y	Y	N
COLORADO				
1 DeGette	N	N	Y	Y
2 Udall	N	N	Y	Y
3 ***McInnis***	Y	Y	Y	N
4 ***Schaffer***	Y	Y	Y	N
5 ***Hefley***	N	Y	Y	N
6 ***Tancredo***	N	Y	Y	N
CONNECTICUT				
1 Larson	Y	N	Y	Y
2 Gejdenson	Y	N	Y	Y
3 DeLauro	Y	N	Y	Y
4 ***Shays***	N	Y	Y	N
5 Maloney	Y	N	Y	Y
6 ***Johnson***	Y	Y	Y	N
DELAWARE				
AL ***Castle***	Y	Y	Y	N
FLORIDA				
1 ***Scarborough***	?	?	?	?
2 Boyd	Y	Y	Y	N
3 Brown	Y	N	Y	Y
4 ***Fowler***	?	Y	Y	N
5 Thurman	Y	N	Y	N
6 ***Stearns***	Y	Y	Y	N
7 ***Mica***	Y	Y	Y	N
8 ***McCollum***	Y	Y	Y	N
9 ***Bilirakis***	Y	Y	Y	N
10 ***Young***	N	Y	Y	N
11 Davis	Y	N	Y	N
12 ***Canady***	Y	Y	Y	N
13 ***Miller***	N	Y	Y	N
14 ***Goss***	N	Y	Y	N
15 ***Weldon***	Y	Y	Y	N
16 ***Foley***	Y	Y	Y	N
17 Meek	N	N	Y	Y
18 ***Ros-Lehtinen***	Y	Y	Y	N
19 Wexler	Y	N	Y	Y
20 Deutsch	Y	N	Y	Y
21 ***Diaz-Balart***	Y	?	Y	N
22 ***Shaw***	N	Y	Y	N
23 Hastings	Y	N	Y	Y
GEORGIA				
1 ***Kingston***	Y	Y	N	N
2 Bishop	Y	N	N	N
3 ***Collins***	Y	Y	N	N
4 McKinney	Y	N	Y	Y
5 Lewis	Y	N	Y	Y
6 ***Isakson***	Y	Y	Y	N
7 ***Barr***	Y	Y	N	N
8 ***Chambliss***	Y	Y	Y	N
9 ***Deal***	Y	Y	Y	N
10 ***Norwood***	Y	Y	N	N
11 ***Linder***	Y	Y	Y	N
HAWAII				
1 Abercrombie	Y	N	Y	Y
2 Mink	Y	N	Y	Y
IDAHO				
1 ***Chenoweth***	N	Y	N	N
2 ***Simpson***	Y	Y	Y	N
ILLINOIS				
1 Rush	N	N	Y	Y
2 Jackson	N	N	Y	Y
3 Lipinski	N	N	Y	Y
4 Gutierrez	N	N	Y	Y
5 Blagojevich	N	N	Y	Y
6 ***Hyde***	N	Y	Y	N
7 Davis	N	N	Y	Y
8 ***Crane***	N	Y	Y	N
9 Schakowsky	N	N	Y	Y
10 ***Porter***	N	Y	Y	Y
11 ***Weller***	N	Y	Y	N
12 Costello	Y	N	N	N
13 ***Biggert***	N	Y	Y	N
14 ***Hastert***				?

ND Northern Democrats SD Southern Democrats

	436	437	438	439
15 ***Ewing***	N	Y	Y	N
16 ***Manzullo***	N	Y	Y	N
17 Evans	N	N	Y	Y
18 ***LaHood***	N	Y	N	N
19 Phelps	Y	Y	N	N
20 ***Shimkus***	Y	Y	N	N
INDIANA				
1 Visclosky	N	N	Y	N
2 ***McIntosh***	Y	Y	N	N
3 Roemer	Y	N	Y	N
4 ***Souder***	N	Y	N	N
5 ***Buyer***	N	Y	Y	N
6 ***Burton***	Y	Y	N	N
7 ***Pease***	Y	Y	N	N
8 ***Hostettler***	N	Y	N	N
9 Hill	Y	N	N	N
10 Carson	N	N	Y	Y
IOWA				
1 ***Leach***	N	Y	Y	N
2 ***Nussle***	N	Y	Y	N
3 Boswell	N	N	Y	N
4 ***Ganske***	N	Y	Y	Y
5 ***Latham***	N	Y	Y	N
KANSAS				
1 ***Moran***	Y	Y	N	N
2 ***Ryun***	Y	Y	N	N
3 Moore	N	Y	Y	N
4 ***Tiahrt***	Y	Y	N	N
KENTUCKY				
1 ***Whitfield***	Y	Y	N	N
2 ***Lewis***	Y	Y	N	N
3 ***Northup***	N	Y	Y	N
4 Lucas	Y	Y	N	N
5 ***Rogers***	Y	Y	N	N
6 ***Fletcher***	Y	Y	N	N
LOUISIANA				
1 ***Vitter***	Y	Y	N	N
2 Jefferson	?	?	?	?
3 ***Tauzin***	Y	Y	Y	N
4 ***McCrery***	Y	Y	N	N
5 ***Cooksey***	Y	Y	N	N
6 ***Baker***	Y	Y	N	N
7 John	Y	Y	Y	N
MAINE				
1 Allen	Y	N	Y	Y
2 Baldacci	Y	N	Y	Y
MARYLAND				
1 ***Gilchrest***	Y	Y	Y	N
2 ***Ehrlich***	Y	Y	Y	N
3 Cardin	Y	N	Y	Y
4 Wynn	Y	N	Y	Y
5 Hoyer	Y	N	Y	Y
6 ***Bartlett***	Y	Y	Y	N
7 Cummings	Y	N	Y	Y
8 ***Morella***	Y	Y	Y	N
MASSACHUSETTS				
1 Olver	Y	N	Y	Y
2 Neal	Y	N	Y	Y
3 McGovern	Y	N	Y	Y
4 Frank	N	Y	Y	Y
5 Meehan	N	N	Y	Y
6 Tierney	N	N	Y	Y
7 Markey	N	N	Y	Y
8 Capuano	Y	N	Y	Y
9 Moakley	Y	N	Y	Y
10 Delahunt	N	N	Y	Y
MICHIGAN				
1 Stupak	N	N	Y	Y
2 ***Hoekstra***	Y	Y	Y	N
3 ***Ehlers***	N	Y	Y	N
4 ***Camp***	Y	Y	Y	N
5 Barcia	Y	N	N	N
6 ***Upton***	Y	Y	Y	N
7 ***Smith***	Y	Y	N	N
8 Stabenow	Y	N	Y	Y
9 Kildee	Y	N	Y	Y
10 Bonior	Y	N	Y	Y
11 ***Knollenberg***	Y	Y	Y	N
12 Levin	Y	N	Y	Y
13 Rivers	Y	N	Y	Y
14 Conyers	N	N	Y	Y
15 Kilpatrick	Y	N	Y	Y
16 Dingell	Y	N	N	N
MINNESOTA				
1 ***Gutknecht***	N	Y	Y	N
2 Minge	N	N	Y	Y
3 ***Ramstad***	N	Y	Y	N
4 Vento	N	N	Y	Y
5 Sabo	N	N	Y	N
6 Luther	N	N	Y	Y
7 Peterson	N	Y	N	N
8 Oberstar	N	N	N	Y
MISSISSIPPI				
1 ***Wicker***	Y	Y	N	N
2 Thompson	Y	N	Y	Y
3 ***Pickering***	Y	Y	N	N
4 Shows	Y	N	N	N
5 Taylor	Y	N	Y	N
MISSOURI				
1 Clay	N	N	Y	Y
2 ***Talent***	Y	Y	N	N
3 Gephardt	Y	N	Y	Y
4 Skelton	Y	N	N	N
5 McCarthy	Y	N	Y	Y
6 Danner	Y	N	N	N
7 ***Blunt***	Y	Y	Y	N
8 ***Emerson***	Y	Y	N	N
9 ***Hulshof***	Y	Y	N	N
MONTANA				
AL ***Hill***	Y	Y	N	N
NEBRASKA				
1 ***Bereuter***	Y	Y	Y	N
2 ***Terry***	N	Y	Y	N
3 ***Barrett***	N	Y	N	N
NEVADA				
1 Berkley	Y	N	Y	Y
2 ***Gibbons***	Y	Y	N	N
NEW HAMPSHIRE				
1 ***Sununu***	Y	Y	N	N
2 ***Bass***	Y	Y	N	N
NEW JERSEY				
1 Andrews	Y	N	Y	Y
2 ***LoBiondo***	Y	Y	Y	N
3 ***Saxton***	Y	Y	Y	N
4 ***Smith***	Y	Y	Y	N
5 ***Roukema***	Y	Y	Y	N
6 Pallone	N	N	Y	Y
7 ***Franks***	Y	Y	Y	N
8 Pascrell	N	N	Y	Y
9 Rothman	N	N	Y	Y
10 Payne	N	N	Y	Y
11 ***Frelinghuysen***	Y	Y	Y	N
12 Holt	Y	N	Y	Y
13 Menendez	N	N	Y	Y
NEW MEXICO				
1 ***Wilson***	Y	Y	Y	N
2 ***Skeen***	Y	Y	Y	N
3 Udall	Y	N	Y	Y
NEW YORK				
1 Forbes	Y	Y	Y	N
2 ***Lazio***	Y	Y	Y	N
3 ***King***	Y	Y	Y	N
4 McCarthy	Y	N	Y	Y
5 Ackerman	Y	N	Y	Y
6 Meeks	Y	N	Y	Y
7 Crowley	Y	N	Y	Y
8 Nadler	Y	N	Y	Y
9 Weiner	Y	N	Y	Y
10 Towns	Y	N	Y	Y
11 Owens	N	N	Y	Y
12 Velázquez	N	N	Y	Y
13 ***Fossella***	Y	Y	Y	N
14 Maloney	N	N	Y	Y
15 Rangel	Y	?	?	Y
16 Serrano	Y	N	Y	Y
17 Engel	Y	?	?	Y
18 Lowey	Y	N	Y	Y
19 ***Kelly***	Y	Y	Y	N
20 ***Gilman***	Y	Y	Y	N
21 McNulty	Y	N	Y	Y
22 ***Sweeney***	Y	?	Y	N
23 ***Boehlert***	Y	Y	Y	N
24 ***McHugh***	Y	Y	Y	N
25 ***Walsh***	Y	Y	Y	N
26 Hinchey	Y	N	Y	Y
27 ***Reynolds***	Y	Y	Y	N
28 Slaughter	Y	N	Y	Y
29 LaFalce	Y	N	Y	N
30 ***Quinn***	Y	Y	Y	N
31 ***Houghton***	Y	Y	Y	N
NORTH CAROLINA				
1 Clayton	Y	N	Y	Y
2 Etheridge	Y	N	Y	N
3 ***Jones***	Y	Y	N	N
4 Price	Y	N	Y	Y
5 ***Burr***	Y	Y	N	N
6 ***Coble***	?	?	?	?
7 McIntyre	Y	N	N	N
8 ***Hayes***	Y	Y	N	N
9 ***Myrick***	Y	Y	N	N
10 ***Ballenger***	Y	Y	Y	N
11 ***Taylor***	Y	Y	N	N
12 Watt	Y	N	Y	N
NORTH DAKOTA				
AL Pomeroy	N	Y	Y	N
OHIO				
1 ***Chabot***	N	Y	N	N
2 ***Portman***	N	Y	Y	N
3 Hall	N	?	?	Y
4 ***Oxley***	N	Y	Y	N
5 ***Gillmor***	Y	Y	Y	N
6 Strickland	Y	Y	N	N
7 ***Hobson***	N	Y	Y	N
8 ***Boehner***	N	Y	N	N
9 Kaptur	N	N	Y	Y
10 Kucinich	N	N	Y	Y
11 Jones	N	N	Y	Y
12 ***Kasich***	N	Y	Y	N
13 Brown	N	N	Y	Y
14 Sawyer	N	N	Y	Y
15 ***Pryce***	N	Y	Y	N
16 ***Regula***	Y	Y	Y	N
17 Traficant	Y	Y	Y	N
18 ***Ney***	N	Y	N	N
19 ***LaTourette***	N	Y	Y	N
OKLAHOMA				
1 ***Largent***	N	Y	N	N
2 ***Coburn***	Y	Y	N	N
3 ***Watkins***	Y	Y	N	N
4 ***Watts***	Y	Y	N	N
5 ***Istook***	N	Y	?	N
6 ***Lucas***	Y	Y	N	N
OREGON				
1 Wu	N	N	Y	Y
2 ***Walden***	Y	Y	Y	N
3 Blumenauer	N	Y	Y	Y
4 DeFazio	Y	N	Y	Y
5 Hooley	Y	N	Y	N
PENNSYLVANIA				
1 Brady	Y	N	Y	Y
2 Fattah	Y	N	Y	Y
3 Borski	Y	N	Y	Y
4 Klink	Y	N	Y	Y
5 ***Peterson***	Y	Y	N	N
6 Holden	Y	?	?	?
7 ***Weldon***	Y	Y	Y	N
8 ***Greenwood***	Y	Y	Y	N
9 ***Shuster***	Y	Y	N	N
10 ***Sherwood***	Y	Y	N	N
11 Kanjorski	Y	N	Y	Y
12 Murtha	Y	Y	N	N
13 Hoeffel	Y	N	Y	Y
14 Coyne	Y	N	Y	Y
15 ***Toomey***	N	Y	N	N
16 ***Pitts***	Y	Y	N	N
17 ***Gekas***	Y	Y	N	N
18 Doyle	Y	Y	Y	Y
19 ***Goodling***	Y	Y	N	N
20 Mascara	Y	N	Y	N
21 ***English***	Y	Y	Y	N
RHODE ISLAND				
1 Kennedy	Y	N	Y	Y
2 Weygand	Y	N	Y	Y
SOUTH CAROLINA				
1 ***Sanford***	N	Y	N	N
2 ***Spence***	Y	Y	N	N
3 ***Graham***	Y	Y	N	N
4 ***DeMint***	Y	Y	N	N
5 Spratt	Y	N	Y	N
6 Clyburn	Y	N	Y	Y
SOUTH DAKOTA				
AL ***Thune***	N	Y	N	N
TENNESSEE				
1 ***Jenkins***	Y	Y	N	N
2 ***Duncan***	Y	Y	Y	N
3 ***Wamp***	Y	Y	N	N
4 ***Hilleary***	Y	Y	Y	N
5 Clement	Y	N	Y	Y
6 Gordon	Y	N	N	N
7 ***Bryant***	Y	Y	N	N
8 Tanner	Y	N	N	N
9 Ford	?	N	Y	Y
TEXAS				
1 Sandlin	Y	N	N	N
2 Turner	Y	N	N	N
3 ***Johnson, Sam***	N	Y	N	N
4 Hall	Y	Y	N	Y
5 ***Sessions***	N	Y	N	N
6 ***Barton***	Y	Y	Y	N
7 ***Archer***	N	Y	N	N
8 ***Brady***	Y	Y	Y	N
9 Lampson	Y	N	N	N
10 Doggett	N	N	Y	Y
11 Edwards	Y	N	Y	N
12 ***Granger***	Y	Y	Y	N
13 ***Thornberry***	Y	Y	N	N
14 ***Paul***	N	Y	N	Y
15 Hinojosa	Y	N	Y	Y
16 Reyes	Y	N	Y	Y
17 Stenholm	Y	Y	N	N
18 Jackson-Lee	Y	N	Y	Y
19 ***Combest***	Y	Y	Y	N
20 Gonzalez	Y	N	Y	Y
21 ***Smith***	Y	Y	N	N
22 ***DeLay***	N	Y	N	N
23 ***Bonilla***	Y	Y	N	N
24 Frost	Y	N	Y	N
25 Bentsen	Y	N	Y	N
26 ***Armey***	N	Y	N	N
27 Ortiz	Y	N	N	N
28 Rodriguez	Y	N	Y	Y
29 Green	Y	N	N	Y
30 Johnson, E.B.	N	N	Y	Y
UTAH				
1 ***Hansen***	Y	Y	N	N
2 ***Cook***	Y	Y	Y	N
3 ***Cannon***	Y	Y	?	N
VERMONT				
AL *Sanders*	Y	N	Y	Y
VIRGINIA				
1 ***Bateman***	Y	Y	Y	N
2 Pickett	Y	N	Y	N
3 Scott	Y	N	Y	N
4 Sisisky	Y	Y	N	N
5 Goode	Y	Y	N	N
6 ***Goodlatte***	Y	Y	N	N
7 ***Bliley***	Y	Y	N	N
8 Moran	N	Y	Y	Y
9 Boucher	Y	Y	N	N
10 ***Wolf***	Y	Y	Y	N
11 ***Davis***	N	Y	Y	N
WASHINGTON				
1 Inslee	Y	N	Y	Y
2 ***Metcalf***	Y	Y	Y	N
3 Baird	Y	N	Y	Y
4 ***Hastings***	Y	Y	N	N
5 ***Nethercutt***	Y	Y	Y	N
6 Dicks	Y	N	Y	Y
7 McDermott	N	N	Y	Y
8 ***Dunn***	Y	Y	Y	N
9 Smith	Y	N	Y	Y
WEST VIRGINIA				
1 Mollohan	Y	N	Y	N
2 Wise	Y	N	Y	N
3 Rahall	Y	N	N	N
WISCONSIN				
1 ***Ryan***	N	Y	Y	N
2 Baldwin	N	N	Y	Y
3 Kind	N	N	Y	N
4 Kleczka	N	N	Y	N
5 Barrett	N	N	Y	Y
6 ***Petri***	N	Y	Y	N
7 Obey	N	N	Y	N
8 ***Green***	N	Y	Y	N
9 ***Sensenbrenner***	N	Y	Y	N
WYOMING				
AL ***Cubin***	Y	Y	N	N

Southern states - Ala., Ark., Fla., Ga., Ky., La., Miss., N.C., Okla., S.C., Tenn., Texas, Va.

440. HR 1875. Class Action Lawsuits/Tobacco Products. Jackson-Lee, D-Texas, amendment to specify that no provisions in the bill would affect any class action lawsuit dealing with harm caused by a tobacco product. Rejected 162-266: R 6-212; D 155-54 (ND 133-22, SD 22-32); I 1-0. Sept. 23, 1999.

441. HR 1875. Class Action Lawsuits/Federal Court Dismissal. Frank, D-Mass., amendment to require that once a class action lawsuit is dismissed by the federal court, it be sent back to the state court for all further actions. Under the amendment, the suit could not be sent to the federal court again. Rejected 202-225: R 12-207; D 189-18 (ND 146-7, SD 43-11); I 1-0. Sept. 23, 1999.

442. HR 1875. Class Action Lawsuits/Judicial Vacancies. Waters, D-Calif., amendment to prohibit the bill's provisions from taking effect until certification from the U.S. Judicial Conference that the number of federal judicial vacancies is no more than 3 percent of the total number of judgeships available. Rejected 185-241: R 0-217; D 184-24 (ND 143-11, SD 41-13); I 1-0. Sept. 23, 1999.

443. HR 1875. Class Action Lawsuits/Passage. Passage of the bill to amend the federal judicial code to give federal courts jurisdiction over certain class action lawsuits. Under the measure, a suit could be moved from state to federal court if any plaintiff or defendant resides in a different state and petitions for the transfer. Passed 222-207: R 204-15; D 18-191 (ND 5-150, SD 13-41); I 0-1. Sept. 23, 1999. A "nay" was a vote in support of the president's position.

Key

Y	Voted for (yea).
#	Paired for.
+	Announced for.
N	Voted against (nay).
X	Paired against.
–	Announced against.
P	Voted "present."
C	Voted "present" to avoid possible conflict of interest.
?	Did not vote or otherwise make a position known.

•

Democrats ***Republicans***
Independents

	440	441	442	443
ALABAMA				
1 ***Callahan***	N	N	N	Y
2 ***Everett***	N	N	N	Y
3 ***Riley***	N	N	N	Y
4 ***Aderholt***	N	N	N	Y
5 Cramer	N	N	N	Y
6 ***Bachus***	N	N	N	Y
7 Hilliard	N	Y	Y	N
ALASKA				
AL ***Young***	N	N	N	Y
ARIZONA				
1 ***Salmon***	N	N	N	Y
2 Pastor	Y	Y	Y	N
3 ***Stump***	N	N	N	Y
4 ***Shadegg***	N	N	N	Y
5 ***Kolbe***	N	N	N	Y
6 ***Hayworth***	N	N	N	Y
ARKANSAS				
1 Berry	N	Y	Y	N
2 Snyder	N	Y	Y	N
3 ***Hutchinson***	N	N	N	Y
4 ***Dickey***	N	N	N	Y
CALIFORNIA				
1 Thompson	N	N	N	N
2 ***Herger***	N	N	N	Y
3 ***Ose***	N	N	N	Y
4 ***Doolittle***	N	N	N	N
5 Matsui	Y	Y	Y	N
6 Woolsey	Y	Y	Y	N
7 Miller, George	Y	?	Y	N
8 Pelosi	Y	Y	Y	N
9 Lee	Y	Y	Y	N
10 Tauscher	Y	N	Y	N
11 ***Pombo***	N	N	N	Y
12 Lantos	Y	Y	Y	N
13 Stark	Y	Y	Y	N
14 Eshoo	Y	Y	Y	N
15 ***Campbell***	N	Y	N	N
16 Lofgren	Y	Y	Y	N
17 Farr	Y	Y	Y	N
18 Condit	N	N	N	Y
19 ***Radanovich***	N	N	?	Y
20 Dooley	N	Y	N	Y
21 ***Thomas***	N	N	N	Y
22 Capps	Y	Y	Y	N
23 ***Gallegly***	N	N	N	Y
24 Sherman	Y	Y	Y	N
25 ***McKeon***	N	N	N	Y
26 Berman	Y	Y	Y	N
27 ***Rogan***	N	N	N	Y
28 ***Dreier***	N	N	N	Y
29 Waxman	Y	Y	Y	N
30 Becerra	Y	Y	Y	N
31 Martinez	Y	Y	Y	N
32 Dixon	Y	Y	Y	N
33 Roybal-Allard	Y	Y	Y	N
34 Napolitano	Y	Y	Y	N
35 Waters	Y	Y	Y	N
36 ***Kuykendall***	N	N	N	Y
37 Millender-McD.	Y	Y	Y	N
38 ***Horn***	N	N	N	Y
39 ***Royce***	N	N	N	Y
40 ***Lewis***	N	N	N	Y
41 ***Miller***	N	N	N	Y
42 Vacant				
43 ***Calvert***	N	N	N	Y
44 ***Bono***	N	N	N	Y
45 ***Rohrabacher***	N	N	N	Y
46 Sanchez	Y	Y	Y	N
47 ***Cox***	N	N	N	Y
48 ***Packard***	N	N	N	Y
49 ***Bilbray***	Y	N	N	Y
50 Filner	Y	Y	Y	N
51 ***Cunningham***	N	N	N	Y
52 ***Hunter***	N	N	N	Y
COLORADO				
1 DeGette	Y	Y	Y	N
2 Udall	Y	Y	Y	N
3 ***McInnis***	N	N	N	Y
4 ***Schaffer***	N	N	N	Y
5 ***Hefley***	N	N	N	Y
6 ***Tancredo***	N	N	N	Y
CONNECTICUT				
1 Larson	Y	Y	Y	N
2 Gejdenson	Y	Y	Y	N
3 DeLauro	Y	Y	Y	N
4 ***Shays***	N	N	N	Y
5 Maloney	Y	Y	Y	N
6 ***Johnson***	N	N	N	Y
DELAWARE				
AL ***Castle***	N	N	N	Y
FLORIDA				
1 ***Scarborough***	?	?	?	?
2 Boyd	N	N	N	Y
3 Brown	Y	Y	Y	N
4 ***Fowler***	N	N	N	Y
5 Thurman	N	Y	Y	N
6 ***Stearns***	N	N	N	Y
7 ***Mica***	N	N	N	Y
8 ***McCollum***	N	N	N	Y
9 ***Bilirakis***	N	N	N	Y
10 ***Young***	N	N	N	Y
11 Davis	N	Y	Y	N
12 ***Canady***	N	N	N	Y
13 ***Miller***	N	N	N	Y
14 ***Goss***	N	N	N	Y
15 ***Weldon***	N	N	N	Y
16 ***Foley***	N	N	N	N
17 Meek	Y	Y	Y	N
18 ***Ros-Lehtinen***	N	N	N	Y
19 Wexler	Y	Y	Y	N
20 Deutsch	Y	Y	Y	N
21 ***Diaz-Balart***	N	Y	N	N
22 ***Shaw***	N	N	N	Y
23 Hastings	Y	Y	Y	N
GEORGIA				
1 ***Kingston***	N	N	N	Y
2 Bishop	N	Y	Y	N
3 ***Collins***	N	N	N	Y
4 McKinney	Y	Y	Y	N
5 Lewis	Y	Y	Y	N
6 ***Isakson***	N	Y	N	Y
7 ***Barr***	N	N	N	Y
8 ***Chambliss***	N	N	N	Y
9 ***Deal***	N	N	N	Y
10 ***Norwood***	N	N	N	Y
11 ***Linder***	N	N	N	Y
HAWAII				
1 Abercrombie	Y	Y	Y	N
2 Mink	Y	Y	Y	N
IDAHO				
1 ***Chenoweth***	N	N	N	N
2 ***Simpson***	N	N	N	Y
ILLINOIS				
1 Rush	Y	Y	Y	N
2 Jackson	Y	Y	Y	N
3 Lipinski	Y	Y	Y	N
4 Gutierrez	Y	Y	?	N
5 Blagojevich	Y	Y	Y	N
6 ***Hyde***	N	N	N	Y
7 Davis	Y	Y	Y	N
8 ***Crane***	N	N	N	Y
9 Schakowsky	Y	Y	Y	N
10 ***Porter***	Y	Y	N	Y
11 ***Weller***	N	N	N	Y
12 Costello	N	Y	Y	N
13 ***Biggert***	N	N	N	Y
14 ***Hastert***				

ND Northern Democrats SD Southern Democrats

	440	441	442	443
15 ***Ewing***	N	N	N	Y
16 ***Manzullo***	N	N	N	Y
17 Evans	Y	Y	Y	N
18 ***LaHood***	N	N	N	Y
19 Phelps	N	Y	Y	N
20 ***Shimkus***	N	N	N	Y
INDIANA				
1 Visclosky	Y	Y	Y	N
2 ***McIntosh***	N	N	N	Y
3 Roemer	Y	Y	N	N
4 ***Souder***	N	N	N	Y
5 ***Buyer***	N	N	N	Y
6 ***Burton***	N	N	N	Y
7 ***Pease***	N	Y	N	Y
8 ***Hostettler***	N	N	N	Y
9 Hill	N	N	Y	N
10 Carson	Y	Y	Y	N
IOWA				
1 ***Leach***	N	N	N	Y
2 ***Nussle***	N	N	N	Y
3 Boswell	Y	Y	Y	N
4 ***Ganske***	Y	Y	N	N
5 ***Latham***	N	N	N	Y
KANSAS				
1 ***Moran***	N	N	N	Y
2 ***Ryun***	N	N	N	Y
3 Moore	N	Y	Y	N
4 ***Tiahrt***	N	N	N	Y
KENTUCKY				
1 ***Whitfield***	N	N	N	Y
2 ***Lewis***	N	N	N	Y
3 ***Northup***	N	N	N	Y
4 Lucas	N	N	N	Y
5 ***Rogers***	N	N	N	Y
6 ***Fletcher***	N	N	N	Y
LOUISIANA				
1 ***Vitter***	N	N	N	Y
2 Jefferson	?	?	?	?
3 ***Tauzin***	N	N	N	Y
4 ***McCrery***	N	N	N	Y
5 ***Cooksey***	N	N	N	Y
6 ***Baker***	N	N	N	Y
7 John	N	N	N	Y
MAINE				
1 Allen	Y	Y	Y	N
2 Baldacci	Y	Y	Y	N
MARYLAND				
1 ***Gilchrest***	N	N	N	Y
2 ***Ehrlich***	N	Y	N	Y
3 Cardin	Y	Y	N	N
4 Wynn	Y	Y	Y	N
5 Hoyer	Y	Y	Y	N
6 ***Bartlett***	N	N	N	Y
7 Cummings	Y	Y	Y	N
8 ***Morella***	N	N	N	N
MASSACHUSETTS				
1 Olver	Y	Y	Y	N
2 Neal	Y	Y	Y	N
3 McGovern	Y	Y	Y	N
4 Frank	Y	Y	Y	N
5 Meehan	Y	Y	Y	N
6 Tierney	Y	Y	Y	N
7 Markey	Y	Y	Y	N
8 Capuano	Y	Y	Y	N
9 Moakley	Y	Y	Y	N
10 Delahunt	Y	Y	Y	N
MICHIGAN				
1 Stupak	Y	Y	Y	N
2 ***Hoekstra***	N	N	N	Y
3 ***Ehlers***	N	N	N	Y
4 ***Camp***	N	N	N	Y
5 Barcia	Y	Y	Y	Y
6 ***Upton***	N	N	N	Y
7 ***Smith***	N	N	N	Y
8 Stabenow	Y	Y	Y	N
9 Kildee	Y	Y	Y	N
10 Bonior	Y	Y	Y	N
11 ***Knollenberg***	N	N	N	Y
12 Levin	Y	Y	Y	N
13 Rivers	Y	Y	Y	N
14 Conyers	Y	Y	Y	N
15 Kilpatrick	Y	Y	Y	N
16 Dingell	Y	Y	Y	N
MINNESOTA				
1 ***Gutknecht***	N	N	N	Y
2 Minge	Y	Y	Y	N
3 ***Ramstad***	N	N	N	Y
4 Vento	Y	Y	Y	N
5 Sabo	N	Y	Y	N
6 Luther	Y	Y	Y	N
7 Peterson	N	N	N	Y
8 Oberstar	Y	Y	Y	N
MISSISSIPPI				
1 ***Wicker***	N	N	N	Y
2 Thompson	N	Y	Y	N
3 ***Pickering***	N	N	N	Y
4 Shows	Y	Y	Y	N
5 Taylor	Y	Y	N	Y
MISSOURI				
1 Clay	Y	Y	Y	N
2 ***Talent***	N	N	N	Y
3 Gephardt	Y	Y	Y	N
4 Skelton	N	Y	Y	N
5 McCarthy	Y	Y	Y	N
6 Danner	N	Y	N	Y
7 ***Blunt***	N	N	N	Y
8 ***Emerson***	N	N	?	Y
9 ***Hulshof***	N	N	N	Y
MONTANA				
AL ***Hill***	N	N	N	Y
NEBRASKA				
1 ***Bereuter***	N	N	N	Y
2 ***Terry***	N	N	N	N
3 ***Barrett***	N	N	N	Y
NEVADA				
1 Berkley	Y	Y	Y	N
2 ***Gibbons***	N	N	N	Y
NEW HAMPSHIRE				
1 ***Sununu***	N	N	N	Y
2 ***Bass***	N	N	N	Y
NEW JERSEY				
1 Andrews	Y	Y	Y	N
2 ***LoBiondo***	N	N	N	Y
3 ***Saxton***	N	N	N	Y
4 ***Smith***	N	N	N	Y
5 ***Roukema***	?	N	N	Y
6 Pallone	Y	Y	Y	N
7 ***Franks***	Y	N	N	Y
8 Pascrell	Y	Y	Y	N
9 Rothman	Y	Y	Y	N
10 Payne	Y	Y	Y	N
11 ***Frelinghuysen***	N	N	N	Y
12 Holt	Y	Y	Y	N
13 Menendez	Y	Y	Y	N
NEW MEXICO				
1 ***Wilson***	N	N	N	Y
2 ***Skeen***	N	N	N	Y
3 Udall	Y	Y	Y	N
NEW YORK				
1 Forbes	N	N	N	N
2 ***Lazio***	N	N	N	Y
3 ***King***	N	N	N	N
4 McCarthy	Y	Y	Y	N
5 Ackerman	Y	Y	Y	N
6 Meeks	Y	Y	Y	N
7 Crowley	Y	Y	Y	N
8 Nadler	Y	Y	Y	N
9 Weiner	Y	Y	Y	N
10 Towns	Y	Y	Y	N
11 Owens	Y	Y	Y	N
12 Velázquez	Y	Y	Y	N
13 ***Fossella***	N	N	N	Y
14 Maloney	Y	Y	Y	N
15 Rangel	Y	Y	Y	N
16 Serrano	Y	Y	Y	N
17 Engel	Y	Y	Y	N
18 Lowey	Y	Y	Y	N
19 ***Kelly***	N	N	N	Y
20 ***Gilman***	N	N	N	N
21 McNulty	Y	Y	Y	N
22 ***Sweeney***	N	N	N	Y
23 ***Boehlert***	N	N	N	Y
24 ***McHugh***	N	N	N	Y
25 ***Walsh***	N	N	N	Y
26 Hinchey	Y	Y	Y	N
27 ***Reynolds***	N	N	N	Y
28 Slaughter	Y	Y	Y	N
29 LaFalce	N	Y	Y	N
30 ***Quinn***	N	N	N	Y
31 ***Houghton***	N	N	N	Y
NORTH CAROLINA				
1 Clayton	N	Y	Y	N
2 Etheridge	N	Y	Y	N
3 ***Jones***	N	N	N	Y
4 Price	N	Y	Y	N
5 ***Burr***	N	N	N	Y
6 ***Coble***	?	?	?	?
7 McIntyre	N	Y	Y	N
8 ***Hayes***	N	N	N	Y
9 ***Myrick***	N	N	N	Y
10 ***Ballenger***	N	N	N	Y
11 ***Taylor***	N	N	N	Y
12 Watt	N	Y	Y	N
NORTH DAKOTA				
AL Pomeroy	Y	N	Y	N
OHIO				
1 ***Chabot***	N	N	N	Y
2 ***Portman***	N	N	N	Y
3 Hall	Y	Y	Y	N
4 ***Oxley***	N	N	N	Y
5 ***Gillmor***	N	N	N	Y
6 Strickland	N	Y	Y	N
7 ***Hobson***	N	N	N	Y
8 ***Boehner***	N	N	N	Y
9 Kaptur	Y	Y	Y	N
10 Kucinich	Y	Y	Y	N
11 Jones	Y	Y	Y	N
12 ***Kasich***	N	N	N	Y
13 Brown	Y	Y	Y	N
14 Sawyer	Y	Y	Y	N
15 ***Pryce***	N	Y	N	Y
16 ***Regula***	N	N	N	Y
17 Traficant	Y	Y	Y	N
18 ***Ney***	N	N	N	Y
19 ***LaTourette***	N	N	N	Y
OKLAHOMA				
1 ***Largent***	N	N	N	Y
2 ***Coburn***	N	N	N	Y
3 ***Watkins***	N	N	N	Y
4 ***Watts***	N	N	N	Y
5 ***Istook***	N	Y	N	Y
6 ***Lucas***	N	N	N	Y
OREGON				
1 Wu	Y	Y	Y	N
2 ***Walden***	N	N	N	Y
3 Blumenauer	Y	Y	Y	N
4 DeFazio	Y	Y	Y	N
5 Hooley	N	Y	Y	N
PENNSYLVANIA				
1 Brady	Y	Y	Y	N
2 Fattah	Y	Y	Y	N
3 Borski	Y	Y	Y	N
4 Klink	Y	Y	Y	N
5 ***Peterson***	N	N	N	Y
6 Holden	?	?	?	?
7 ***Weldon***	N	N	N	Y
8 ***Greenwood***	N	Y	N	N
9 ***Shuster***	N	N	N	Y
10 ***Sherwood***	N	N	N	Y
11 Kanjorski	Y	Y	Y	N
12 Murtha	N	?	N	N
13 Hoeffel	Y	Y	Y	N
14 Coyne	Y	Y	Y	N
15 ***Toomey***	N	N	N	Y
16 ***Pitts***	N	N	N	Y
17 ***Gekas***	N	N	N	Y
18 Doyle	Y	Y	Y	N
19 ***Goodling***	N	N	N	Y
20 Mascara	Y	Y	Y	N
21 ***English***	N	N	N	N
RHODE ISLAND				
1 Kennedy	Y	Y	Y	N
2 Weygand	Y	Y	Y	N
SOUTH CAROLINA				
1 ***Sanford***	N	N	N	Y
2 ***Spence***	N	N	N	Y
3 ***Graham***	N	N	N	N
4 ***DeMint***	N	N	N	Y
5 Spratt	N	Y	Y	N
6 Clyburn	N	Y	Y	N
SOUTH DAKOTA				
AL ***Thune***	N	N	N	Y
TENNESSEE				
1 ***Jenkins***	N	N	N	Y
2 ***Duncan***	N	Y	N	Y
3 ***Wamp***	N	N	N	Y
4 ***Hilleary***	N	N	N	Y
5 Clement	Y	Y	Y	N
6 Gordon	N	Y	N	Y
7 ***Bryant***	N	N	N	Y
8 Tanner	N	N	N	Y
9 Ford	Y	Y	Y	N
TEXAS				
1 Sandlin	N	Y	Y	N
2 Turner	N	Y	Y	N
3 ***Johnson, Sam***	N	N	N	Y
4 Hall	Y	Y	Y	Y
5 ***Sessions***	N	N	N	Y
6 ***Barton***	N	N	N	Y
7 ***Archer***	N	N	N	Y
8 ***Brady***	N	N	N	Y
9 Lampson	N	Y	Y	N
10 Doggett	Y	Y	Y	N
11 Edwards	N	Y	Y	N
12 ***Granger***	N	N	N	Y
13 ***Thornberry***	N	N	N	Y
14 ***Paul***	Y	Y	N	N
15 Hinojosa	Y	Y	Y	N
16 Reyes	Y	Y	Y	N
17 Stenholm	N	N	N	Y
18 Jackson-Lee	Y	Y	Y	N
19 ***Combest***	N	N	N	Y
20 Gonzalez	Y	Y	Y	N
21 ***Smith***	N	N	N	Y
22 ***DeLay***	N	N	N	Y
23 ***Bonilla***	N	N	N	Y
24 Frost	Y	Y	Y	N
25 Bentsen	N	Y	Y	N
26 ***Armey***	N	N	N	Y
27 Ortiz	N	Y	Y	N
28 Rodriguez	Y	Y	Y	N
29 Green	Y	Y	Y	N
30 Johnson, E.B.	Y	Y	Y	N
UTAH				
1 ***Hansen***	Y	N	N	Y
2 ***Cook***	N	N	N	Y
3 ***Cannon***	N	N	N	Y
VERMONT				
AL *Sanders*	Y	Y	Y	N
VIRGINIA				
1 ***Bateman***	N	N	N	Y
2 Pickett	N	N	N	N
3 Scott	N	Y	Y	N
4 Sisisky	N	N	N	Y
5 Goode	N	N	N	Y
6 ***Goodlatte***	N	N	N	Y
7 ***Bliley***	N	N	N	Y
8 Moran	Y	N	N	Y
9 Boucher	N	N	N	Y
10 ***Wolf***	N	N	N	Y
11 ***Davis***	N	N	N	Y
WASHINGTON				
1 Inslee	Y	Y	Y	N
2 ***Metcalf***	N	N	N	Y
3 Baird	Y	Y	Y	N
4 ***Hastings***	N	N	N	Y
5 ***Nethercutt***	N	N	N	N
6 Dicks	Y	Y	Y	N
7 McDermott	Y	Y	Y	N
8 ***Dunn***	N	N	N	Y
9 Smith	Y	Y	Y	N
WEST VIRGINIA				
1 Mollohan	N	Y	N	N
2 Wise	N	Y	Y	N
3 Rahall	N	Y	N	N
WISCONSIN				
1 ***Ryan***	N	N	N	Y
2 Baldwin	Y	Y	Y	N
3 Kind	N	Y	Y	N
4 Kleczka	N	Y	Y	N
5 Barrett	Y	Y	Y	N
6 ***Petri***	N	N	N	Y
7 Obey	N	Y	Y	N
8 ***Green***	N	N	N	Y
9 ***Sensenbrenner***	N	N	N	Y
WYOMING				
AL ***Cubin***	N	N	N	Y

Southern states - Ala., Ark., Fla., Ga., Ky., La., Miss., N.C., Okla., S.C., Tenn., Texas, Va.

House Votes 444, 445, 446, 447, 448, 449, 450, 451

444. HR 1487. National Monuments/Passage. Passage of the bill to require the president to solicit public participation and comments when considering and preparing a proposal to declare a national monument. The bill also requires the president to consult with the governor and congressional delegation of the state in which the lands are located. The measure includes an amendment stating that nothing in the bill should be construed as enlarging, diminishing or modifying the authority of the president to protect public lands and resources. Passed 408-2: R 210-0; D 197-2 (ND 146-2, SD 51-0); I 1-0, Sept. 24, 1999. A "nay" was a vote in support of the president's position.

445. HR 1501. Juvenile Justice/Motion to Instruct. McCarthy, D-N.Y., motion to instruct House conferees to insist that the conference this week [of September 27] has its first substantive meeting to offer amendments, including gun safety amendments; and that the conference meet every weekday in public session until it is finished. Motion rejected 190-218: R 32-177; D 157-41 (ND 129-18, SD 28-23); I 1-0, Sept. 24, 1999.

446. HR 1501. Juvenile Justice/Motion to Instruct. Doolittle, R-Calif., motion to instruct House conferees to accept only a conference agreement that recognizes that the Second Amendment to the U.S. Constitution protects the individual rights of U.S. citizens to keep and bear arms, and that would not impose unconstitutional restrictions on individuals' Second Amendment rights. Motion agreed to 337-73: R 201-8; D 135-65 (ND 93-55, SD 42-10); I 1-0, Sept. 24, 1999.

447. HR 1501. Juvenile Justice/Motion to Instruct. Lofgren, D-Calif., motion to instruct House conferees to recognize that certain provisions, including requiring unlicensed dealers at gun shows to perform background checks on all sales, banning juveniles from possessing assault weapons, requiring safety locks to be sold with all handguns, and prohibiting anyone, including those who committed crimes as juveniles, from purchasing a gun do not violate the Second Amendment. Motion agreed to 241-167: R 79-129; D 161-38 (ND 129-18, SD 32-20); I 1-0, Sept. 24, 1999.

448. H Con Res 187. European Aircraft Regulations/Adoption. Duncan, R-Tenn., motion to suspend the rules and adopt the concurrent resolution expressing the sense of Congress that the European Union should rescind a regulation that bans U.S. aircraft from flying in Europe if the planes have engines that have been modified with a "hushkit" or a new engine to reduce air noise. Motion agreed to 402-2: R 207-2; D 194-0 (ND 142-0, SD 52-0); I 1-0. Sept. 27, 1999. A two-thirds majority of those present and voting (270 in this case) is required for adoption under suspension of the rules.

449. H Con Res 140. Haitian Elections/Adoption. Gilman, R-N.Y., motion to suspend the rules and adopt the concurrent resolution to express the sense of Congress that Haiti should conduct free, fair, transparent and peaceful elections. Motion agreed to 400-1: R 205-1; D 194-0 (ND 142-0, SD 52-0); I 1-0. Sept. 27, 1999. A two-thirds majority of those present and voting (268 in this case) is required for adoption under suspension of the rules.

450. S 293. San Juan County Land Transfer/Passage. Saxton, R-N.J., motion to suspend the rules and pass the bill to direct the secretaries of Agriculture and Interior to transfer up to 20 acres of land in San Juan County, New Mexico, to San Juan College. Motion agreed to 406-1: R 208-1; D 197-0 (ND 145-0, SD 52-0); I 1-0. Sept. 27, 1999. A two-thirds majority of those present and voting (272 in this case) is required for passage under suspension of the rules.

451. HR 202. Senior Citizen Housing Program/Passage. Bereuter, R-Neb., motion to suspend the rules and pass the bill to preserve and increase the availability of low-income housing for the elderly, including allowing the use of Section 8 rental vouchers for assisted living facilities. Motion agreed to 405-5: R 205-5; D 199-0 (ND 145-0, SD 54-0); I 1-0. Sept. 27, 1999. A two-thirds majority of those present and voting (274 in this case) is required for passage under suspension of the rules.

Key

- Y Voted for (yea).
- \# Paired for.
- \+ Announced for.
- N Voted against (nay).
- X Paired against.
- – Announced against.
- P Voted "present."
- C Voted "present" to avoid possible conflict of interest.
- ? Did not vote or otherwise make a position known.

•

Democrats ***Republicans***
Independents

	444	445	446	447	448	449	450	451
ALABAMA								
1 ***Callahan***	Y	N	Y	N	Y	Y	Y	Y
2 ***Everett***	Y	N	Y	N	Y	Y	Y	Y
3 ***Riley***	Y	N	Y	N	?	?	?	?
4 ***Aderholt***	Y	N	Y	N	Y	Y	Y	Y
5 Cramer	Y	N	Y	N	Y	Y	Y	Y
6 ***Bachus***	Y	N	Y	N	Y	Y	Y	Y
7 Hilliard	Y	N	Y	N	Y	Y	Y	Y
ALASKA								
AL ***Young***	Y	N	Y	N	Y	Y	Y	Y
ARIZONA								
1 ***Salmon***	Y	N	Y	N	Y	Y	Y	Y
2 Pastor	Y	Y	N	Y	Y	Y	Y	Y
3 ***Stump***	Y	N	Y	N	Y	Y	Y	Y
4 ***Shadegg***	?	?	?	?	Y	Y	Y	Y
5 ***Kolbe***	Y	N	Y	Y	Y	Y	Y	Y
6 ***Hayworth***	Y	N	Y	N	Y	Y	Y	Y
ARKANSAS								
1 Berry	Y	Y	Y	Y	Y	Y	Y	Y
2 Snyder	Y	Y	Y	Y	Y	Y	Y	Y
3 ***Hutchinson***	Y	N	Y	N	?	?	Y	?
4 ***Dickey***	Y	N	Y	N	Y	Y	Y	Y
CALIFORNIA								
1 Thompson	Y	Y	Y	Y	Y	Y	Y	Y
2 ***Herger***	Y	N	Y	N	Y	Y	Y	Y
3 ***Ose***	Y	Y	Y	Y	Y	Y	Y	Y
4 ***Doolittle***	Y	N	Y	N	Y	Y	Y	Y
5 Matsui	Y	Y	Y	Y	Y	Y	Y	Y
6 Woolsey	Y	Y	N	Y	Y	Y	Y	Y
7 Miller, George	?	?	?	?	?	?	?	?
8 Pelosi	Y	Y	N	Y	Y	Y	Y	Y
9 Lee	Y	Y	N	Y	Y	Y	Y	Y
10 Tauscher	Y	Y	Y	Y	Y	Y	Y	Y
11 ***Pombo***	Y	N	Y	N	Y	Y	Y	Y
12 Lantos	Y	Y	Y	Y	Y	Y	Y	Y
13 Stark	Y	Y	N	Y	Y	Y	Y	Y
14 Eshoo	Y	Y	N	Y	Y	Y	Y	Y
15 ***Campbell***	Y	Y	N	N	Y	Y	Y	Y
16 Lofgren	Y	Y	N	Y	Y	Y	Y	Y
17 Farr	Y	Y	N	Y	Y	Y	Y	Y
18 Condit	Y	Y	Y	Y	Y	Y	Y	Y
19 ***Radanovich***	Y	N	Y	N	Y	Y	Y	Y
20 Dooley	Y	Y	Y	Y	Y	Y	Y	Y
21 ***Thomas***	Y	N	Y	N	Y	Y	Y	Y
22 Capps	Y	Y	Y	Y	Y	Y	Y	Y
23 ***Gallegly***	?	?	?	?	Y	Y	Y	Y
24 Sherman	Y	Y	Y	Y	Y	Y	Y	Y
25 ***McKeon***	Y	N	Y	N	Y	Y	Y	Y
26 Berman	Y	Y	Y	Y	?	?	?	?
27 ***Rogan***	Y	N	Y	Y	Y	Y	Y	Y
28 ***Dreier***	Y	N	Y	Y	Y	Y	Y	Y
29 Waxman	Y	Y	Y	Y	Y	Y	Y	Y
30 Becerra	Y	Y	N	Y	Y	Y	Y	Y
31 Martinez	Y	Y	N	Y	Y	Y	Y	Y
32 Dixon	Y	Y	N	Y	Y	Y	Y	Y
33 Roybal-Allard	Y	Y	N	Y	Y	Y	Y	Y
34 Napolitano	Y	Y	N	Y	Y	Y	Y	Y
35 Waters	Y	Y	N	Y	Y	Y	Y	Y
36 ***Kuykendall***	Y	Y	Y	Y	Y	Y	Y	Y
37 Millender-McD.	Y	Y	N	Y	Y	Y	Y	Y
38 ***Horn***	Y	Y	N	Y	Y	Y	Y	Y
39 ***Royce***	Y	N	Y	Y	Y	Y	Y	N
40 ***Lewis***	Y	N	N	N	Y	?	Y	Y
41 ***Miller***	Y	N	Y	N	Y	Y	Y	Y
42 Vacant								
43 ***Calvert***	?	?	?	?	Y	Y	Y	Y
44 ***Bono***	Y	N	Y	Y	Y	Y	Y	Y
45 ***Rohrabacher***	Y	N	Y	N	Y	Y	Y	Y
46 Sanchez	Y	Y	Y	Y	Y	Y	Y	Y
47 ***Cox***	Y	N	Y	Y	Y	Y	Y	Y
48 ***Packard***	Y	N	Y	N	Y	Y	Y	Y
49 ***Bilbray***	Y	Y	Y	Y	Y	Y	Y	Y
50 Filner	Y	Y	Y	Y	Y	Y	Y	Y
51 ***Cunningham***	?	?	?	?	Y	Y	Y	Y
52 ***Hunter***	Y	?	Y	N	Y	Y	Y	Y
COLORADO								
1 DeGette	Y	Y	N	Y	Y	Y	Y	Y
2 Udall	Y	Y	Y	Y	Y	Y	Y	Y
3 ***McInnis***	Y	N	Y	N	Y	Y	Y	Y
4 ***Schaffer***	Y	N	Y	N	Y	Y	Y	Y
5 ***Hefley***	Y	N	Y	N	Y	Y	Y	Y
6 ***Tancredo***	Y	N	Y	Y	Y	Y	Y	Y
CONNECTICUT								
1 Larson	Y	Y	Y	Y	+	+	+	+
2 Gejdenson	Y	Y	Y	Y	Y	Y	Y	Y
3 DeLauro	Y	Y	Y	Y	Y	Y	Y	Y
4 ***Shays***	Y	Y	Y	Y	Y	Y	Y	Y
5 Maloney	Y	Y	Y	Y	+	+	Y	Y
6 ***Johnson***	Y	Y	Y	Y	?	?	?	?
DELAWARE								
AL ***Castle***	Y	Y	Y	Y	Y	Y	Y	Y
FLORIDA								
1 ***Scarborough***	?	?	?	?	?	?	?	?
2 Boyd	Y	N	Y	Y	Y	Y	Y	Y
3 Brown	Y	Y	Y	Y	?	?	?	Y
4 ***Fowler***	Y	N	Y	Y	Y	Y	Y	Y
5 Thurman	Y	Y	Y	Y	Y	Y	Y	Y
6 ***Stearns***	Y	N	Y	Y	Y	Y	Y	Y
7 ***Mica***	Y	N	Y	N	Y	Y	Y	Y
8 ***McCollum***	Y	N	Y	Y	Y	Y	Y	Y
9 ***Bilirakis***	Y	N	Y	N	Y	Y	Y	Y
10 ***Young***	Y	N	Y	Y	Y	Y	Y	Y
11 Davis	Y	Y	Y	Y	Y	Y	Y	Y
12 ***Canady***	Y	N	Y	Y	Y	Y	Y	Y
13 ***Miller***	Y	N	Y	Y	Y	Y	Y	Y
14 ***Goss***	Y	N	Y	Y	Y	Y	Y	Y
15 ***Weldon***	Y	N	Y	Y	Y	Y	Y	Y
16 ***Foley***	Y	Y	Y	Y	Y	Y	Y	Y
17 Meek	Y	Y	N	Y	Y	Y	Y	Y
18 ***Ros-Lehtinen***	Y	N	Y	Y	Y	Y	Y	Y
19 Wexler	Y	Y	N	Y	Y	Y	Y	Y
20 Deutsch	Y	Y	Y	Y	Y	Y	Y	Y
21 ***Diaz-Balart***	Y	N	?	Y	Y	Y	Y	Y
22 ***Shaw***	Y	N	Y	Y	Y	Y	Y	Y
23 Hastings	Y	Y	N	Y	Y	Y	Y	Y
GEORGIA								
1 ***Kingston***	Y	N	Y	N	Y	Y	Y	Y
2 Bishop	Y	N	Y	N	?	?	?	Y
3 ***Collins***	Y	N	Y	N	Y	Y	Y	Y
4 McKinney	Y	Y	N	Y	Y	Y	Y	Y
5 Lewis	Y	Y	N	Y	Y	Y	Y	Y
6 ***Isakson***	Y	N	Y	Y	Y	Y	Y	Y
7 ***Barr***	Y	N	Y	N	Y	P	Y	Y
8 ***Chambliss***	Y	N	Y	N	Y	Y	Y	Y
9 ***Deal***	Y	N	Y	N	Y	Y	Y	Y
10 ***Norwood***	Y	N	Y	N	?	?	?	?
11 ***Linder***	Y	N	Y	Y	Y	Y	Y	Y
HAWAII								
1 Abercrombie	Y	Y	N	Y	Y	Y	Y	Y
2 Mink	Y	Y	N	Y	Y	Y	Y	Y
IDAHO								
1 ***Chenoweth***	Y	N	Y	?	N	Y	Y	N
2 ***Simpson***	Y	N	Y	N	Y	Y	Y	Y
ILLINOIS								
1 Rush	Y	Y	N	Y	Y	Y	Y	Y
2 Jackson	Y	Y	N	Y	Y	Y	Y	Y
3 Lipinski	Y	Y	Y	Y	Y	Y	Y	Y
4 Gutierrez	Y	Y	N	Y	Y	Y	Y	Y
5 Blagojevich	Y	Y	N	Y	Y	Y	Y	Y
6 ***Hyde***	Y	N	Y	Y	Y	Y	Y	Y
7 Davis	Y	Y	N	Y	Y	Y	Y	Y
8 ***Crane***	Y	N	Y	N	Y	Y	Y	Y
9 Schakowsky	Y	Y	N	Y	Y	Y	Y	Y
10 ***Porter***	Y	Y	N	Y	Y	Y	Y	Y
11 ***Weller***	Y	Y	Y	Y	Y	Y	Y	Y
12 Costello	Y	N	Y	N	Y	Y	Y	Y
13 ***Biggert***	Y	N	Y	Y	Y	Y	Y	Y
14 ***Hastert***								

ND Northern Democrats SD Southern Democrats

	444	445	446	447	448	449	450	451
15 ***Ewing***	Y	N	Y	Y	Y	Y	Y	Y
16 ***Manzullo***	Y	N	Y	N	Y	Y	Y	Y
17 Evans	Y	Y	Y	Y	Y	Y	Y	Y
18 ***LaHood***	Y	N	Y	Y	Y	Y	Y	Y
19 Phelps	Y	N	Y	N	Y	Y	Y	Y
20 ***Shimkus***	Y	N	Y	N	Y	Y	Y	Y
INDIANA								
1 Visclosky	Y	Y	Y	?	Y	Y	Y	Y
2 ***McIntosh***	Y	N	Y	N	?	?	?	?
3 Roemer	Y	Y	Y	Y	Y	Y	Y	Y
4 ***Souder***	Y	N	Y	N	Y	Y	Y	Y
5 ***Buyer***	Y	N	Y	N	Y	Y	Y	Y
6 ***Burton***	+	−	+	?	Y	Y	Y	Y
7 ***Pease***	Y	N	Y	N	Y	Y	Y	Y
8 ***Hostettler***	Y	N	Y	N	Y	Y	Y	N
9 Hill	Y	N	Y	N	Y	Y	Y	Y
10 Carson	?	?	?	?	?	?	?	?
IOWA								
1 ***Leach***	Y	Y	Y	Y	Y	Y	Y	Y
2 ***Nussle***	Y	Y	Y	Y	Y	Y	Y	Y
3 Boswell	Y	Y	Y	Y	Y	Y	Y	Y
4 ***Ganske***	Y	Y	Y	Y	Y	Y	Y	Y
5 ***Latham***	Y	Y	Y	Y	Y	Y	Y	Y
KANSAS								
1 ***Moran***	Y	N	Y	N	Y	Y	Y	Y
2 ***Ryun***	Y	N	Y	N	Y	Y	Y	Y
3 Moore	Y	Y	Y	Y	Y	Y	Y	Y
4 ***Tiahrt***	Y	N	Y	N	Y	Y	?	Y
KENTUCKY								
1 ***Whitfield***	Y	N	Y	N	Y	Y	Y	Y
2 ***Lewis***	Y	N	Y	N	Y	Y	Y	Y
3 ***Northup***	Y	N	Y	Y	Y	Y	Y	Y
4 Lucas	Y	N	Y	N	Y	Y	Y	Y
5 ***Rogers***	Y	N	Y	N	Y	Y	Y	Y
6 ***Fletcher***	Y	N	Y	N	Y	Y	Y	Y
LOUISIANA								
1 ***Vitter***	Y	N	Y	N	Y	Y	Y	Y
2 Jefferson	?	?	?	?	?	?	?	?
3 ***Tauzin***	Y	N	Y	N	Y	Y	Y	Y
4 ***McCrery***	Y	N	Y	N	Y	Y	Y	Y
5 ***Cooksey***	Y	N	Y	N	Y	Y	Y	Y
6 ***Baker***	?	?	?	?	Y	Y	Y	Y
7 John	Y	N	Y	N	Y	Y	Y	Y
MAINE								
1 Allen	Y	Y	Y	Y	Y	Y	Y	Y
2 Baldacci	Y	Y	Y	Y	Y	Y	Y	Y
MARYLAND								
1 ***Gilchrest***	Y	Y	Y	Y	Y	Y	?	Y
2 ***Ehrlich***	Y	N	Y	Y	Y	Y	Y	Y
3 Cardin	Y	Y	Y	Y	Y	Y	Y	Y
4 Wynn	Y	Y	N	Y	Y	Y	Y	Y
5 Hoyer	Y	Y	Y	Y	Y	Y	Y	Y
6 ***Bartlett***	Y	N	Y	N	Y	Y	Y	Y
7 Cummings	Y	Y	Y	Y	Y	Y	Y	Y
8 ***Morella***	Y	Y	N	Y	Y	Y	Y	Y
MASSACHUSETTS								
1 Olver	Y	Y	N	Y	Y	Y	Y	Y
2 Neal	Y	Y	N	Y	?	?	?	?
3 McGovern	Y	Y	N	Y	Y	Y	Y	Y
4 Frank	Y	Y	N	Y	Y	Y	Y	Y
5 Meehan	Y	Y	N	Y	Y	Y	Y	Y
6 Tierney	Y	Y	N	Y	Y	Y	Y	Y
7 Markey	Y	Y	N	Y	Y	Y	Y	Y
8 Capuano	Y	Y	N	Y	Y	Y	Y	Y
9 Moakley	?	?	?	?	Y	Y	Y	Y
10 Delahunt	Y	Y	N	Y	Y	Y	Y	Y
MICHIGAN								
1 Stupak	Y	Y	Y	Y	Y	Y	Y	Y
2 ***Hoekstra***	Y	N	Y	N	Y	Y	Y	Y
3 ***Ehlers***	Y	N	Y	Y	Y	Y	Y	Y
4 ***Camp***	Y	Y	Y	Y	Y	Y	Y	Y
5 Barcia	Y	N	Y	N	Y	Y	Y	Y
6 ***Upton***	Y	Y	Y	Y	Y	Y	Y	Y
7 ***Smith***	Y	N	Y	Y	Y	Y	Y	Y
8 Stabenow	Y	Y	Y	Y	Y	Y	Y	Y
9 Kildee	Y	Y	Y	Y	Y	Y	Y	Y
10 Bonior	Y	Y	Y	Y	?	?	?	?
11 ***Knollenberg***	Y	N	Y	N	Y	Y	Y	Y
12 Levin	Y	Y	Y	Y	Y	Y	Y	Y
13 Rivers	Y	Y	Y	Y	Y	Y	Y	Y
14 Conyers	Y	Y	N	Y	Y	Y	Y	Y
15 Kilpatrick	Y	Y	N	Y	Y	Y	Y	Y
16 Dingell	Y	N	Y	N	Y	Y	Y	Y
MINNESOTA								
1 ***Gutknecht***	Y	N	Y	Y	Y	Y	Y	Y
2 Minge	Y	Y	Y	Y	Y	Y	Y	Y
3 ***Ramstad***	Y	Y	Y	Y	Y	Y	Y	Y
4 Vento	Y	Y	N	Y	Y	Y	Y	Y
5 Sabo	Y	Y	Y	Y	Y	Y	Y	Y
6 Luther	Y	Y	Y	Y	Y	Y	Y	Y
7 Peterson	Y	N	Y	N	Y	Y	Y	Y
8 Oberstar	Y	N	Y	N	Y	Y	Y	Y
MISSISSIPPI								
1 ***Wicker***	Y	N	Y	N	Y	Y	Y	Y
2 Thompson	Y	Y	Y	Y	Y	Y	Y	Y
3 ***Pickering***	Y	N	Y	N	Y	Y	Y	Y
4 Shows	Y	N	Y	N	Y	Y	Y	Y
5 Taylor	Y	N	Y	N	Y	Y	Y	Y
MISSOURI								
1 Clay	Y	Y	N	Y	Y	Y	Y	Y
2 ***Talent***	Y	N	Y	N	Y	Y	Y	Y
3 Gephardt	Y	Y	Y	Y	Y	Y	Y	Y
4 Skelton	Y	N	Y	N	Y	Y	Y	Y
5 McCarthy	Y	Y	Y	Y	Y	Y	Y	Y
6 Danner	Y	N	Y	N	Y	Y	Y	Y
7 ***Blunt***	Y	N	Y	N	Y	Y	Y	Y
8 ***Emerson***	Y	N	Y	N	Y	Y	Y	Y
9 ***Hulshof***	Y	N	Y	N	Y	Y	Y	Y
MONTANA								
AL ***Hill***	Y	N	Y	N	Y	Y	Y	Y
NEBRASKA								
1 ***Bereuter***	Y	N	Y	Y	Y	Y	Y	Y
2 ***Terry***	Y	N	Y	N	Y	Y	Y	Y
3 ***Barrett***	Y	N	Y	N	Y	Y	Y	Y
NEVADA								
1 Berkley	Y	Y	Y	Y	Y	Y	Y	Y
2 ***Gibbons***	Y	N	Y	N	Y	Y	Y	Y
NEW HAMPSHIRE								
1 ***Sununu***	Y	N	Y	N	Y	Y	Y	Y
2 ***Bass***	Y	N	Y	N	Y	Y	Y	Y
NEW JERSEY								
1 Andrews	Y	Y	Y	Y	Y	Y	Y	Y
2 ***LoBiondo***	Y	N	Y	Y	Y	Y	Y	Y
3 ***Saxton***	Y	Y	Y	Y	Y	Y	Y	Y
4 ***Smith***	Y	N	Y	Y	?	?	?	?
5 ***Roukema***	Y	Y	Y	Y	Y	Y	Y	Y
6 Pallone	Y	Y	Y	Y	Y	Y	Y	Y
7 ***Franks***	Y	Y	N	Y	Y	Y	Y	Y
8 Pascrell	Y	Y	Y	Y	Y	Y	Y	Y
9 Rothman	Y	Y	Y	Y	Y	Y	Y	Y
10 Payne	Y	Y	N	Y	Y	Y	Y	Y
11 ***Frelinghuysen***	Y	Y	N	Y	Y	Y	Y	Y
12 Holt	Y	Y	Y	Y	Y	Y	Y	Y
13 Menendez	Y	Y	Y	Y	Y	Y	Y	Y
NEW MEXICO								
1 ***Wilson***	Y	Y	Y	N	Y	Y	Y	Y
2 ***Skeen***	Y	N	Y	N	Y	Y	Y	Y
3 Udall	Y	Y	Y	Y	Y	Y	Y	Y
NEW YORK								
1 Forbes	Y	Y	Y	Y	Y	Y	Y	Y
2 ***Lazio***	Y	N	Y	Y	Y	Y	Y	Y
3 ***King***	Y	N	Y	N	Y	Y	Y	Y
4 McCarthy	Y	Y	Y	Y	Y	Y	Y	Y
5 Ackerman	Y	Y	N	Y	Y	Y	Y	Y
6 Meeks	Y	Y	N	Y	?	?	?	?
7 Crowley	Y	Y	Y	Y	Y	Y	Y	Y
8 Nadler	N	Y	N	Y	Y	Y	Y	Y
9 Weiner	Y	Y	Y	Y	Y	Y	Y	Y
10 Towns	Y	Y	N	Y	?	?	Y	Y
11 Owens	Y	Y	N	Y	?	?	Y	Y
12 Velázquez	Y	Y	N	Y	Y	Y	Y	Y
13 ***Fossella***	Y	N	Y	Y	Y	Y	Y	Y
14 Maloney	Y	Y	Y	Y	Y	Y	Y	Y
15 Rangel	Y	Y	N	Y	Y	Y	Y	Y
16 Serrano	Y	Y	N	Y	Y	Y	Y	Y
17 Engel	Y	Y	N	Y	Y	Y	Y	Y
18 Lowey	Y	Y	N	Y	Y	Y	Y	Y
19 ***Kelly***	Y	Y	Y	Y	Y	Y	Y	Y
20 ***Gilman***	Y	Y	Y	Y	Y	Y	Y	Y
21 McNulty	Y	Y	Y	Y	Y	Y	Y	Y
22 ***Sweeney***	Y	N	Y	N	?	?	?	?
23 ***Boehlert***	Y	Y	Y	Y	Y	Y	Y	Y
24 ***McHugh***	Y	N	Y	N	Y	Y	Y	Y
25 ***Walsh***	Y	N	Y	Y	?	?	?	?
26 Hinchey	Y	Y	Y	Y	Y	Y	Y	Y
27 ***Reynolds***	Y	N	Y	Y	Y	Y	Y	Y
28 Slaughter	Y	Y	N	Y	Y	Y	Y	Y
29 LaFalce	Y	Y	Y	Y	Y	Y	Y	Y
30 ***Quinn***	Y	Y	Y	Y	Y	Y	Y	Y
31 ***Houghton***	Y	N	Y	Y	Y	Y	Y	Y
NORTH CAROLINA								
1 Clayton	+	+	−	+	Y	Y	Y	Y
2 Etheridge	Y	N	Y	Y	Y	Y	Y	Y
3 ***Jones***	Y	N	Y	N	Y	Y	Y	Y
4 Price	Y	Y	Y	Y	Y	Y	Y	Y
5 ***Burr***	?	?	?	?	Y	Y	Y	Y
6 ***Coble***	?	?	?	?	Y	Y	Y	Y
7 McIntyre	Y	N	Y	N	Y	Y	Y	Y
8 ***Hayes***	Y	N	Y	N	Y	Y	Y	Y
9 ***Myrick***	Y	N	Y	Y	Y	Y	Y	Y
10 ***Ballenger***	Y	N	Y	N	Y	Y	Y	Y
11 ***Taylor***	Y	N	Y	N	Y	Y	Y	Y
12 Watt	Y	Y	N	Y	Y	Y	Y	Y
NORTH DAKOTA								
AL Pomeroy	Y	Y	Y	Y	Y	Y	Y	Y
OHIO								
1 ***Chabot***	Y	N	Y	N	Y	Y	Y	Y
2 ***Portman***	Y	N	Y	Y	Y	Y	Y	Y
3 Hall	Y	Y	Y	Y	Y	Y	Y	Y
4 ***Oxley***	Y	N	Y	N	Y	Y	Y	Y
5 ***Gillmor***	Y	N	Y	N	Y	Y	Y	Y
6 Strickland	Y	N	Y	N	Y	Y	Y	Y
7 ***Hobson***	Y	N	Y	Y	Y	Y	Y	Y
8 ***Boehner***	Y	N	Y	N	Y	Y	Y	Y
9 Kaptur	Y	?	Y	Y	Y	Y	Y	Y
10 Kucinich	Y	Y	Y	Y	Y	Y	Y	Y
11 Jones	?	?	?	?	Y	Y	Y	Y
12 ***Kasich***	Y	N	Y	Y	Y	Y	Y	Y
13 Brown	Y	Y	Y	Y	Y	Y	Y	Y
14 Sawyer	Y	Y	Y	Y	Y	Y	Y	Y
15 ***Pryce***	?	?	?	?	?	?	?	?
16 ***Regula***	Y	N	Y	Y	Y	Y	Y	Y
17 Traficant	Y	N	Y	N	Y	Y	Y	Y
18 ***Ney***	Y	N	Y	N	Y	Y	Y	Y
19 ***LaTourette***	Y	N	Y	Y	Y	Y	Y	Y
OKLAHOMA								
1 ***Largent***	?	?	?	?	Y	Y	N	Y
2 ***Coburn***	Y	N	Y	N	Y	Y	Y	Y
3 ***Watkins***	Y	N	Y	N	Y	Y	Y	Y
4 ***Watts***	Y	N	Y	N	Y	Y	Y	Y
5 ***Istook***	Y	N	Y	N	?	?	Y	Y
6 ***Lucas***	Y	N	Y	N	Y	Y	Y	Y
OREGON								
1 Wu	?	?	?	?	?	?	?	?
2 ***Walden***	Y	N	Y	N	Y	Y	Y	Y
3 Blumenauer	Y	Y	N	Y	Y	Y	Y	Y
4 DeFazio	Y	Y	Y	Y	Y	Y	Y	Y
5 Hooley	Y	Y	Y	Y	Y	Y	Y	Y
PENNSYLVANIA								
1 Brady	Y	Y	Y	Y	Y	Y	Y	Y
2 Fattah	Y	Y	Y	Y	?	?	?	?
3 Borski	Y	Y	Y	Y	Y	Y	Y	Y
4 Klink	Y	Y	Y	Y	Y	Y	Y	Y
5 ***Peterson***	Y	N	Y	N	Y	Y	Y	Y
6 Holden	?	?	?	?	Y	Y	Y	Y
7 ***Weldon***	Y	N	Y	Y	Y	Y	Y	Y
8 ***Greenwood***	Y	Y	Y	?	Y	Y	Y	Y
9 ***Shuster***	Y	N	Y	N	Y	Y	Y	Y
10 ***Sherwood***	Y	N	Y	N	Y	Y	Y	Y
11 Kanjorski	Y	N	Y	N	Y	Y	Y	Y
12 Murtha	Y	N	Y	N	Y	Y	Y	Y
13 Hoeffel	Y	Y	N	Y	Y	Y	Y	Y
14 Coyne	Y	Y	N	Y	Y	Y	Y	Y
15 ***Toomey***	Y	N	Y	N	Y	Y	Y	Y
16 ***Pitts***	Y	N	Y	N	Y	Y	Y	Y
17 ***Gekas***	Y	N	Y	N	Y	Y	Y	Y
18 Doyle	Y	Y	Y	Y	Y	Y	Y	Y
19 ***Goodling***	Y	N	N	Y	Y	Y	Y	Y
20 Mascara	Y	N	Y	N	?	?	?	?
21 ***English***	Y	N	Y	Y	Y	Y	Y	Y
RHODE ISLAND								
1 Kennedy	Y	Y	N	Y	Y	Y	Y	Y
2 Weygand	+	−	+	+	Y	Y	Y	Y
SOUTH CAROLINA								
1 ***Sanford***	Y	N	Y	N	Y	Y	Y	N
2 ***Spence***	Y	N	Y	N	Y	Y	Y	Y
3 ***Graham***	Y	N	Y	N	Y	Y	Y	Y
4 ***DeMint***	Y	N	Y	N	Y	Y	Y	Y
5 Spratt	Y	Y	Y	Y	Y	Y	Y	Y
6 Clyburn	Y	Y	Y	Y	Y	Y	Y	Y
SOUTH DAKOTA								
AL ***Thune***	Y	N	Y	N	Y	Y	Y	Y
TENNESSEE								
1 ***Jenkins***	Y	N	Y	N	Y	Y	Y	Y
2 ***Duncan***	Y	N	Y	N	Y	Y	Y	Y
3 ***Wamp***	Y	N	Y	N	Y	Y	Y	Y
4 ***Hilleary***	Y	N	Y	N	Y	Y	Y	Y
5 Clement	Y	N	Y	Y	Y	Y	Y	Y
6 Gordon	Y	N	Y	N	Y	Y	Y	Y
7 ***Bryant***	Y	N	Y	N	Y	Y	Y	Y
8 Tanner	?	?	?	?	Y	Y	Y	Y
9 Ford	Y	Y	Y	Y	Y	Y	Y	Y
TEXAS								
1 Sandlin	Y	N	Y	N	Y	Y	Y	Y
2 Turner	Y	N	Y	N	Y	Y	Y	Y
3 ***Johnson, Sam***	Y	N	Y	N	Y	?	Y	Y
4 Hall	Y	N	Y	N	Y	Y	Y	Y
5 ***Sessions***	Y	N	Y	N	Y	Y	Y	Y
6 ***Barton***	Y	N	Y	N	Y	Y	Y	Y
7 ***Archer***	Y	N	Y	N	Y	Y	Y	Y
8 ***Brady***	Y	N	Y	N	Y	Y	Y	Y
9 Lampson	Y	N	Y	N	Y	Y	Y	Y
10 Doggett	Y	Y	Y	Y	Y	Y	Y	Y
11 Edwards	Y	Y	Y	Y	Y	Y	Y	Y
12 ***Granger***	Y	N	Y	N	Y	Y	Y	Y
13 ***Thornberry***	Y	N	Y	N	Y	Y	Y	Y
14 ***Paul***	Y	N	Y	N	N	N	Y	N
15 Hinojosa	Y	Y	Y	Y	Y	Y	Y	Y
16 Reyes	Y	Y	Y	Y	Y	Y	Y	Y
17 Stenholm	Y	N	Y	N	Y	Y	Y	Y
18 Jackson-Lee	Y	Y	N	Y	Y	Y	Y	Y
19 ***Combest***	Y	N	Y	N	Y	Y	Y	Y
20 Gonzalez	Y	Y	Y	Y	Y	Y	Y	Y
21 ***Smith***	Y	N	Y	N	Y	Y	Y	Y
22 ***DeLay***	Y	N	Y	N	Y	Y	Y	Y
23 ***Bonilla***	Y	N	Y	N	Y	Y	Y	Y
24 Frost	?	?	Y	Y	Y	Y	Y	Y
25 Bentsen	Y	Y	Y	Y	Y	Y	Y	Y
26 ***Armey***	Y	N	Y	N	Y	Y	Y	Y
27 Ortiz	Y	N	Y	N	Y	Y	Y	Y
28 Rodriguez	Y	Y	Y	Y	Y	Y	Y	Y
29 Green	Y	N	Y	N	Y	Y	Y	Y
30 Johnson, E.B.	Y	Y	N	Y	Y	Y	Y	Y
UTAH								
1 ***Hansen***	Y	N	Y	N	Y	Y	Y	Y
2 ***Cook***	Y	N	Y	N	Y	Y	Y	Y
3 ***Cannon***	Y	N	Y	N	?	?	?	?
VERMONT								
AL *Sanders*	Y	Y	Y	Y	Y	Y	Y	Y
VIRGINIA								
1 ***Bateman***	Y	N	Y	Y	Y	Y	Y	Y
2 Pickett	Y	N	Y	N	Y	Y	Y	Y
3 Scott	Y	Y	N	Y	Y	Y	Y	Y
4 Sisisky	Y	N	Y	N	Y	Y	Y	Y
5 Goode	Y	N	Y	N	Y	Y	Y	Y
6 ***Goodlatte***	Y	N	Y	N	Y	Y	Y	Y
7 ***Bliley***	Y	N	Y	N	Y	Y	Y	Y
8 Moran	Y	Y	N	Y	Y	Y	Y	Y
9 Boucher	Y	N	Y	N	Y	Y	Y	Y
10 ***Wolf***	Y	N	Y	Y	Y	Y	Y	Y
11 ***Davis***	Y	Y	Y	Y	Y	Y	Y	Y
WASHINGTON								
1 Inslee	Y	Y	Y	Y	Y	Y	Y	Y
2 ***Metcalf***	Y	N	Y	N	Y	Y	Y	Y
3 Baird	Y	Y	Y	Y	Y	Y	Y	Y
4 ***Hastings***	Y	N	Y	N	Y	Y	Y	Y
5 ***Nethercutt***	Y	N	Y	N	Y	Y	Y	Y
6 Dicks	Y	Y	Y	Y	Y	Y	Y	Y
7 McDermott	Y	Y	N	Y	Y	Y	Y	Y
8 ***Dunn***	Y	Y	Y	Y	Y	Y	Y	Y
9 Smith	?	?	?	?	Y	Y	Y	Y
WEST VIRGINIA								
1 Mollohan	N	N	Y	N	Y	Y	Y	Y
2 Wise	Y	N	Y	N	Y	Y	Y	Y
3 Rahall	Y	N	Y	N	Y	Y	Y	Y
WISCONSIN								
1 ***Ryan***	Y	N	Y	Y	Y	Y	Y	Y
2 Baldwin	Y	Y	Y	Y	Y	Y	Y	Y
3 Kind	Y	N	Y	Y	Y	Y	Y	Y
4 Kleczka	Y	Y	Y	Y	+	+	+	+
5 Barrett	Y	Y	Y	Y	Y	Y	Y	Y
6 ***Petri***	Y	N	Y	N	Y	Y	Y	Y
7 Obey	Y	Y	Y	N	Y	Y	Y	Y
8 ***Green***	Y	N	Y	Y	Y	Y	Y	Y
9 ***Sensenbrenner***	Y	N	Y	N	Y	Y	Y	Y
WYOMING								
AL ***Cubin***	Y	N	Y	N	Y	Y	Y	Y

Southern states - Ala., Ark., Fla., Ga., Ky., La., Miss., N.C., Okla., S.C., Tenn., Texas, Va.

452. HR 2605. Fiscal 2000 Energy and Water Appropriations/Conference Report. Adoption of the conference report on the bill to provide $21.3 billion in funding for the Energy Department, U.S. Army Corps of Engineers, the Interior Department's Bureau of Reclamation, and other independent agencies. Adopted (thus sent to the Senate) 327-87: R 147-66; D 179-21 (ND 136-10, SD 43-11); I 1-0. Sept. 27, 1999.

453. H J Res 68. Fiscal 2000 Continuing Appropriations/Passage. Passage of the joint resolution to provide appropriations through Oct. 21 for agencies covered by the 12 fiscal 2000 spending bills not yet enacted. The resolution would set spending levels at the fiscal 1999 level; it would also provide for additional spending on the census and year 2000 computer preparations. Passed 421-2: R 217-1; D 203-1 (ND 150-1, SD 53-0); I 1-0. Sept. 28, 1999.

454. H Res 292. East Timor/Adoption. Gilman, R-N.Y., motion to suspend the rules and adopt the resolution to commend the East Timorese on their participation in the recent referendum and condemn the violent paramilitary assaults on the East Timorese people, local clergy and humanitarian workers. Motion agreed to 390-38: R 182-36; D 207-2 (ND 154-0, SD 53-2); I 1-0. Sept. 28, 1999. A two-thirds majority of those present and voting (286 in this case) is required for adoption under suspension of the rules.

455. H Res 297. Taiwan Earthquake Victims/Adoption. Gilman, R-N.Y., motion to suspend the rules and adopt the resolution to express the House's sympathies to the citizens of Taiwan for the losses suffered as a result of the Sept. 21 earthquake. Motion agreed to 424-0: R 216-0; D 207-0 (ND 153-0, SD 54-0); I 1-0. Sept. 28, 1999. A two-thirds majority of those present and voting (283 in this case) is required for adoption under suspension of the rules.

456. H Res 306. Social Security Surplus/Adoption. Herger, R-Calif., motion to suspend the rules and adopt the resolution expressing the desire of the House not to spend any of the budget surplus created by Social Security receipts and to continue to retire the debt held by the public. Motion agreed to 417-2: R 216-0; D 200-2 (ND 146-2, SD 54-0); I 1-0. Sept. 28, 1999. A two-thirds majority of those present and voting (280 in this case) is required for adoption under suspension of the rules.

Key

- Y Voted for (yea).
- \# Paired for.
- \+ Announced for.
- N Voted against (nay).
- X Paired against.
- – Announced against.
- P Voted "present."
- C Voted "present" to avoid possible conflict of interest.
- ? Did not vote or otherwise make a position known.

•

Democrats ***Republicans***
Independents

	452	453	454	455	456
ALABAMA					
1 ***Callahan***	Y	Y	Y	Y	Y
2 ***Everett***	Y	Y	N	Y	Y
3 ***Riley***	?	?	?	?	?
4 ***Aderholt***	Y	Y	Y	Y	Y
5 Cramer	Y	Y	Y	Y	Y
6 ***Bachus***	Y	Y	Y	Y	Y
7 Hilliard	N	Y	Y	Y	Y
ALASKA					
AL ***Young***	N	Y	Y	Y	Y
ARIZONA					
1 ***Salmon***	Y	Y	Y	Y	Y
2 Pastor	Y	Y	Y	Y	Y
3 ***Stump***	Y	Y	N	Y	Y
4 ***Shadegg***	N	Y	Y	Y	Y
5 ***Kolbe***	Y	Y	Y	Y	Y
6 ***Hayworth***	Y	Y	Y	Y	Y
ARKANSAS					
1 Berry	Y	Y	Y	Y	Y
2 Snyder	Y	Y	Y	Y	Y
3 ***Hutchinson***	N	Y	Y	Y	Y
4 ***Dickey***	Y	Y	N	Y	Y
CALIFORNIA					
1 Thompson	Y	Y	Y	Y	Y
2 ***Herger***	Y	Y	Y	Y	Y
3 ***Ose***	Y	Y	Y	Y	Y
4 ***Doolittle***	N	Y	N	Y	Y
5 Matsui	Y	Y	Y	Y	Y
6 Woolsey	Y	Y	Y	Y	Y
7 Miller, George	?	?	Y	Y	Y
8 Pelosi	Y	Y	Y	Y	Y
9 Lee	Y	Y	Y	Y	Y
10 Tauscher	Y	Y	Y	Y	Y
11 ***Pombo***	Y	Y	Y	Y	Y
12 Lantos	Y	Y	Y	Y	Y
13 Stark	Y	Y	Y	Y	Y
14 Eshoo	Y	Y	Y	Y	Y
15 ***Campbell***	Y	Y	Y	Y	Y
16 Lofgren	Y	Y	Y	Y	Y
17 Farr	Y	Y	Y	Y	Y
18 Condit	N	Y	Y	Y	Y
19 ***Radanovich***	Y	Y	Y	Y	Y
20 Dooley	Y	Y	Y	Y	Y
21 ***Thomas***	Y	Y	Y	+	+
22 Capps	Y	Y	Y	Y	Y
23 ***Gallegly***	Y	Y	Y	Y	Y
24 Sherman	Y	Y	Y	Y	Y
25 ***McKeon***	Y	Y	Y	Y	Y
26 Berman	?	Y	Y	Y	Y
27 ***Rogan***	Y	Y	Y	Y	Y
28 ***Dreier***	Y	Y	Y	Y	Y
29 Waxman	Y	Y	Y	Y	Y
30 Becerra	Y	Y	Y	Y	Y
31 Martinez	Y	Y	Y	Y	Y
32 Dixon	Y	Y	Y	Y	Y
33 Roybal-Allard	Y	Y	Y	Y	Y
34 Napolitano	Y	Y	Y	Y	Y
35 Waters	Y	Y	Y	Y	Y
36 ***Kuykendall***	Y	Y	Y	Y	Y
37 Millender-McD.	Y	Y	Y	Y	Y
38 ***Horn***	Y	Y	Y	Y	Y
39 ***Royce***	Y	Y	Y	Y	Y
40 ***Lewis***	Y	Y	Y	Y	Y
41 ***Miller***	Y	Y	Y	Y	Y
42 Vacant					
43 ***Calvert***	Y	Y	Y	Y	Y
44 ***Bono***	Y	Y	Y	Y	Y
45 ***Rohrabacher***	Y	Y	Y	Y	Y
46 Sanchez	Y	Y	Y	Y	Y
47 ***Cox***	Y	?	Y	Y	Y
48 ***Packard***	Y	Y	Y	Y	Y
49 ***Bilbray***	N	Y	Y	Y	Y
50 Filner	N	Y	Y	Y	Y
51 ***Cunningham***	Y	Y	Y	Y	Y
52 ***Hunter***	Y	Y	Y	Y	Y
COLORADO					
1 DeGette	Y	Y	Y	Y	Y
2 Udall	Y	Y	Y	Y	Y
3 ***McInnis***	N	Y	Y	Y	Y
4 ***Schaffer***	N	Y	N	Y	Y
5 ***Hefley***	N	Y	N	Y	Y
6 ***Tancredo***	N	Y	N	Y	+
CONNECTICUT					
1 Larson	Y	Y	Y	Y	Y
2 Gejdenson	Y	Y	Y	Y	Y
3 DeLauro	Y	Y	Y	Y	Y
4 ***Shays***	N	Y	Y	Y	Y
5 Maloney	Y	Y	Y	Y	Y
6 ***Johnson***	?	Y	Y	Y	Y
DELAWARE					
AL ***Castle***	Y	Y	Y	Y	Y
FLORIDA					
1 ***Scarborough***	?	?	?	?	?
2 Boyd	Y	Y	Y	Y	Y
3 Brown	Y	Y	Y	Y	Y
4 ***Fowler***	Y	Y	Y	Y	Y
5 Thurman	Y	Y	Y	Y	Y
6 ***Stearns***	N	Y	Y	Y	Y
7 ***Mica***	Y	Y	Y	Y	Y
8 ***McCollum***	Y	Y	Y	Y	Y
9 ***Bilirakis***	Y	Y	Y	Y	Y
10 ***Young***	Y	Y	Y	Y	Y
11 Davis	Y	Y	Y	Y	Y
12 ***Canady***	Y	Y	Y	Y	Y
13 ***Miller***	Y	Y	Y	Y	Y
14 ***Goss***	Y	Y	Y	Y	Y
15 ***Weldon***	Y	Y	Y	Y	Y
16 ***Foley***	Y	Y	Y	Y	Y
17 Meek	Y	Y	Y	Y	Y
18 ***Ros-Lehtinen***	Y	Y	Y	Y	Y
19 Wexler	Y	Y	Y	Y	Y
20 Deutsch	Y	Y	Y	Y	Y
21 ***Diaz-Balart***	Y	Y	Y	Y	Y
22 ***Shaw***	Y	Y	Y	Y	Y
23 Hastings	Y	Y	Y	Y	Y
GEORGIA					
1 ***Kingston***	Y	Y	Y	Y	Y
2 Bishop	Y	?	Y	Y	Y
3 ***Collins***	N	Y	N	Y	Y
4 McKinney	Y	Y	Y	Y	Y
5 Lewis	Y	Y	Y	Y	Y
6 ***Isakson***	N	Y	Y	Y	Y
7 ***Barr***	N	Y	P	Y	Y
8 ***Chambliss***	N	Y	Y	Y	Y
9 ***Deal***	N	Y	Y	Y	Y
10 ***Norwood***	?	Y	Y	Y	Y
11 ***Linder***	Y	Y	Y	Y	Y
HAWAII					
1 Abercrombie	Y	Y	Y	Y	Y
2 Mink	Y	Y	Y	Y	Y
IDAHO					
1 ***Chenoweth***	N	Y	N	Y	Y
2 ***Simpson***	Y	Y	Y	Y	Y
ILLINOIS					
1 Rush	Y	?	Y	Y	Y
2 Jackson	Y	Y	Y	Y	Y
3 Lipinski	N	Y	Y	Y	Y
4 Gutierrez	Y	Y	Y	Y	?
5 Blagojevich	Y	Y	Y	Y	Y
6 ***Hyde***	Y	Y	Y	Y	Y
7 Davis	Y	Y	Y	Y	Y
8 ***Crane***	Y	Y	Y	Y	Y
9 Schakowsky	Y	Y	Y	Y	P
10 ***Porter***	Y	Y	Y	Y	Y
11 ***Weller***	Y	Y	Y	Y	Y
12 Costello	Y	Y	Y	Y	Y
13 ***Biggert***	Y	Y	Y	Y	Y
14 ***Hastert***					

ND Northern Democrats SD Southern Democrats

	452	453	454	455	456
15 ***Ewing***	Y	Y	Y	Y	Y
16 ***Manzullo***	Y	Y	N	Y	Y
17 Evans	Y	Y	Y	Y	Y
18 ***LaHood***	Y	Y	Y	Y	Y
19 Phelps	Y	Y	Y	Y	Y
20 ***Shimkus***	N	Y	Y	Y	Y
INDIANA					
1 Visclosky	Y	Y	Y	Y	Y
2 ***McIntosh***	Y	Y	Y	Y	Y
3 Roemer	Y	Y	Y	Y	Y
4 ***Souder***	Y	Y	N	Y	Y
5 ***Buyer***	Y	Y	Y	Y	Y
6 ***Burton***	Y	Y	N	Y	Y
7 ***Pease***	N	Y	Y	Y	Y
8 ***Hostettler***	N	Y	Y	Y	Y
9 Hill	Y	Y	Y	Y	Y
10 Carson	?	Y	Y	Y	Y
IOWA					
1 ***Leach***	Y	Y	Y	Y	Y
2 ***Nussle***	Y	Y	Y	Y	Y
3 Boswell	Y	Y	Y	Y	Y
4 ***Ganske***	Y	Y	Y	Y	Y
5 ***Latham***	Y	Y	Y	Y	Y
KANSAS					
1 ***Moran***	N	Y	N	Y	Y
2 ***Ryun***	N	Y	Y	Y	Y
3 Moore	Y	Y	Y	Y	Y
4 ***Tiahrt***	Y	Y	Y	Y	Y
KENTUCKY					
1 ***Whitfield***	Y	Y	Y	Y	Y
2 ***Lewis***	Y	Y	Y	Y	Y
3 ***Northup***	Y	Y	Y	Y	Y
4 Lucas	Y	Y	Y	Y	Y
5 ***Rogers***	Y	Y	Y	Y	Y
6 ***Fletcher***	Y	Y	Y	Y	Y
LOUISIANA					
1 ***Vitter***	Y	Y	Y	Y	Y
2 Jefferson	?	Y	Y	?	Y
3 ***Tauzin***	Y	Y	Y	Y	Y
4 ***McCrery***	Y	Y	Y	Y	Y
5 ***Cooksey***	Y	Y	Y	Y	Y
6 ***Baker***	N	Y	Y	Y	Y
7 John	Y	Y	Y	Y	Y
MAINE					
1 Allen	Y	Y	Y	Y	Y
2 Baldacci	Y	Y	Y	Y	Y
MARYLAND					
1 ***Gilchrest***	Y	Y	Y	Y	Y
2 ***Ehrlich***	Y	Y	Y	Y	Y
3 Cardin	Y	Y	Y	Y	Y
4 Wynn	Y	Y	Y	Y	Y
5 Hoyer	Y	?	?	?	?
6 ***Bartlett***	N	Y	N	Y	Y
7 Cummings	Y	Y	Y	Y	Y
8 ***Morella***	Y	Y	Y	Y	Y
MASSACHUSETTS					
1 Olver	Y	Y	Y	Y	Y
2 Neal	?	Y	Y	Y	Y
3 McGovern	Y	Y	Y	Y	Y
4 Frank	Y	Y	Y	Y	P
5 Meehan	Y	Y	Y	Y	Y
6 Tierney	Y	Y	Y	Y	Y
7 Markey	Y	Y	Y	Y	Y
8 Capuano	Y	Y	Y	Y	P
9 Moakley	Y	Y	Y	Y	Y
10 Delahunt	Y	Y	Y	Y	Y
MICHIGAN					
1 Stupak	Y	Y	Y	Y	Y
2 ***Hoekstra***	Y	Y	N	Y	Y
3 ***Ehlers***	N	Y	Y	Y	Y
4 ***Camp***	Y	Y	Y	Y	Y
5 Barcia	Y	Y	Y	Y	Y
6 ***Upton***	Y	Y	Y	Y	Y
7 ***Smith***	N	Y	Y	Y	Y
8 Stabenow	Y	Y	Y	Y	Y
9 Kildee	Y	Y	Y	Y	Y
10 Bonior	?	Y	Y	Y	Y
11 ***Knollenberg***	Y	Y	Y	Y	Y
12 Levin	Y	Y	Y	Y	Y
13 Rivers	Y	Y	Y	Y	Y
14 Conyers	Y	Y	Y	Y	Y
15 Kilpatrick	Y	Y	Y	Y	Y
16 Dingell	Y	Y	Y	Y	Y

	452	453	454	455	456
MINNESOTA					
1 ***Gutknecht***	Y	Y	N	Y	Y
2 Minge	N	Y	Y	Y	Y
3 ***Ramstad***	N	Y	Y	Y	Y
4 Vento	Y	Y	Y	Y	Y
5 Sabo	Y	Y	Y	Y	N
6 Luther	N	Y	Y	Y	Y
7 Peterson	N	Y	Y	Y	Y
8 Oberstar	N	Y	Y	Y	Y
MISSISSIPPI					
1 ***Wicker***	Y	Y	Y	Y	Y
2 Thompson	Y	Y	Y	Y	Y
3 ***Pickering***	Y	Y	Y	Y	Y
4 Shows	Y	Y	Y	Y	Y
5 Taylor	Y	Y	Y	Y	Y
MISSOURI					
1 Clay	Y	Y	Y	Y	Y
2 ***Talent***	Y	Y	Y	Y	Y
3 Gephardt	Y	Y	Y	Y	Y
4 Skelton	Y	Y	Y	Y	Y
5 McCarthy	Y	Y	Y	Y	Y
6 Danner	Y	Y	Y	Y	Y
7 ***Blunt***	Y	Y	Y	Y	Y
8 ***Emerson***	Y	Y	Y	Y	Y
9 ***Hulshof***	Y	Y	Y	Y	Y
MONTANA					
AL ***Hill***	N	Y	Y	Y	Y
NEBRASKA					
1 ***Bereuter***	N	Y	Y	Y	Y
2 ***Terry***	N	Y	Y	Y	Y
3 ***Barrett***	Y	Y	Y	Y	Y
NEVADA					
1 Berkley	Y	Y	Y	Y	Y
2 ***Gibbons***	N	Y	Y	Y	Y
NEW HAMPSHIRE					
1 ***Sununu***	N	Y	Y	Y	Y
2 ***Bass***	N	Y	Y	Y	Y
NEW JERSEY					
1 Andrews	Y	Y	Y	Y	Y
2 ***LoBiondo***	Y	Y	Y	Y	Y
3 ***Saxton***	Y	Y	Y	Y	Y
4 ***Smith***	Y	Y	Y	Y	Y
5 ***Roukema***	Y	Y	Y	Y	Y
6 Pallone	Y	Y	Y	Y	Y
7 ***Franks***	Y	Y	Y	Y	Y
8 Pascrell	Y	Y	Y	Y	Y
9 Rothman	Y	Y	Y	Y	Y
10 Payne	Y	Y	Y	Y	Y
11 ***Frelinghuysen***	Y	Y	Y	Y	Y
12 Holt	Y	Y	Y	Y	Y
13 Menendez	Y	Y	Y	Y	Y
NEW MEXICO					
1 ***Wilson***	Y	Y	Y	Y	Y
2 ***Skeen***	Y	Y	Y	Y	Y
3 Udall	Y	Y	Y	Y	Y
NEW YORK					
1 Forbes	Y	Y	Y	Y	Y
2 ***Lazio***	Y	Y	Y	Y	Y
3 ***King***	Y	Y	Y	Y	Y
4 McCarthy	Y	Y	Y	Y	Y
5 Ackerman	Y	Y	Y	Y	Y
6 Meeks	?	Y	Y	Y	Y
7 Crowley	Y	Y	Y	Y	Y
8 Nadler	Y	Y	Y	Y	N
9 Weiner	Y	Y	Y	Y	Y
10 Towns	Y	Y	Y	Y	Y
11 Owens	Y	Y	Y	Y	Y
12 Velázquez	N	Y	Y	Y	Y
13 ***Fossella***	Y	Y	Y	Y	Y
14 Maloney	Y	Y	Y	Y	Y
15 Rangel	Y	Y	Y	Y	Y
16 Serrano	Y	Y	Y	Y	Y
17 Engel	Y	Y	Y	Y	Y
18 Lowey	Y	Y	Y	Y	Y
19 ***Kelly***	Y	Y	Y	Y	Y
20 ***Gilman***	Y	Y	Y	Y	Y
21 McNulty	Y	Y	Y	Y	Y
22 ***Sweeney***	?	Y	Y	Y	Y
23 ***Boehlert***	N	Y	Y	Y	Y
24 ***McHugh***	Y	Y	Y	Y	Y
25 ***Walsh***	?	Y	Y	?	Y
26 Hinchey	Y	Y	Y	Y	Y
27 ***Reynolds***	Y	Y	Y	Y	Y
28 Slaughter	Y	Y	Y	Y	Y
29 LaFalce	Y	Y	Y	Y	Y

	452	453	454	455	456
30 ***Quinn***	Y	Y	Y	Y	Y
31 ***Houghton***	Y	Y	Y	Y	P
NORTH CAROLINA					
1 Clayton	Y	Y	Y	Y	Y
2 Etheridge	Y	Y	Y	Y	Y
3 ***Jones***	N	Y	N	Y	Y
4 Price	Y	Y	Y	Y	Y
5 ***Burr***	N	Y	Y	Y	Y
6 ***Coble***	N	Y	N	Y	Y
7 McIntyre	Y	Y	Y	Y	Y
8 ***Hayes***	N	Y	N	Y	Y
9 ***Myrick***	N	Y	Y	Y	Y
10 ***Ballenger***	Y	Y	Y	Y	Y
11 ***Taylor***	N	Y	N	Y	Y
12 Watt	Y	Y	Y	Y	P
NORTH DAKOTA					
AL Pomeroy	Y	Y	Y	Y	Y
OHIO					
1 ***Chabot***	Y	Y	Y	Y	Y
2 ***Portman***	Y	Y	Y	Y	Y
3 Hall	Y	Y	Y	Y	Y
4 ***Oxley***	Y	Y	Y	Y	Y
5 ***Gillmor***	Y	Y	Y	Y	Y
6 Strickland	Y	Y	Y	Y	Y
7 ***Hobson***	Y	Y	Y	Y	Y
8 ***Boehner***	Y	Y	Y	Y	Y
9 Kaptur	Y	P	Y	Y	Y
10 Kucinich	Y	Y	Y	Y	Y
11 Jones	Y	Y	Y	Y	Y
12 ***Kasich***	N	Y	Y	Y	Y
13 Brown	Y	Y	Y	Y	Y
14 Sawyer	Y	Y	Y	Y	Y
15 ***Pryce***	?	Y	Y	Y	Y
16 ***Regula***	Y	Y	Y	Y	Y
17 Traficant	Y	Y	Y	Y	Y
18 ***Ney***	Y	Y	N	Y	Y
19 ***LaTourette***	N	Y	Y	Y	Y
OKLAHOMA					
1 ***Largent***	N	Y	Y	Y	Y
2 ***Coburn***	N	Y	Y	Y	Y
3 ***Watkins***	Y	Y	Y	Y	Y
4 ***Watts***	Y	Y	Y	Y	Y
5 ***Istook***	Y	Y	Y	Y	Y
6 ***Lucas***	Y	Y	Y	Y	Y
OREGON					
1 Wu	?	?	?	?	?
2 ***Walden***	Y	Y	Y	Y	Y
3 Blumenauer	Y	Y	Y	Y	P
4 DeFazio	N	N	Y	Y	Y
5 Hooley	Y	Y	Y	Y	Y
PENNSYLVANIA					
1 Brady	Y	Y	Y	Y	Y
2 Fattah	?	Y	Y	Y	Y
3 Borski	Y	Y	Y	Y	Y
4 Klink	Y	Y	Y	Y	Y
5 ***Peterson***	Y	Y	Y	Y	Y
6 Holden	N	Y	Y	Y	Y
7 ***Weldon***	Y	Y	Y	Y	Y
8 ***Greenwood***	Y	Y	Y	Y	Y
9 ***Shuster***	N	Y	N	Y	Y
10 ***Sherwood***	Y	Y	Y	Y	Y
11 Kanjorski	Y	Y	Y	Y	Y
12 Murtha	Y	Y	Y	Y	Y
13 Hoeffel	Y	Y	Y	Y	Y
14 Coyne	Y	Y	Y	Y	Y
15 ***Toomey***	N	Y	Y	Y	Y
16 ***Pitts***	Y	Y	Y	Y	Y
17 ***Gekas***	Y	Y	Y	Y	Y
18 Doyle	Y	Y	Y	Y	Y
19 ***Goodling***	Y	Y	Y	Y	Y
20 Mascara	?	Y	Y	Y	Y
21 ***English***	N	Y	Y	Y	Y
RHODE ISLAND					
1 Kennedy	Y	Y	Y	Y	Y
2 Weygand	Y	Y	Y	Y	Y
SOUTH CAROLINA					
1 ***Sanford***	N	Y	Y	Y	Y
2 ***Spence***	Y	Y	Y	Y	Y
3 ***Graham***	N	Y	Y	Y	Y
4 ***DeMint***	N	Y	Y	Y	Y
5 Spratt	N	Y	Y	Y	Y
6 Clyburn	N	Y	Y	Y	Y
SOUTH DAKOTA					
AL ***Thune***	Y	Y	N	Y	Y

	452	453	454	455	456
TENNESSEE					
1 ***Jenkins***	N	Y	Y	Y	Y
2 ***Duncan***	N	Y	N	Y	Y
3 ***Wamp***	N	Y	Y	Y	Y
4 ***Hilleary***	N	Y	Y	Y	Y
5 Clement	N	Y	Y	Y	Y
6 Gordon	N	Y	Y	Y	Y
7 ***Bryant***	N	Y	Y	Y	Y
8 Tanner	N	Y	Y	Y	Y
9 Ford	N	Y	Y	Y	Y
TEXAS					
1 Sandlin	N	Y	Y	Y	Y
2 Turner	Y	Y	Y	Y	Y
3 ***Johnson, Sam***	N	Y	N	Y	Y
4 Hall	N	Y	N	Y	Y
5 ***Sessions***	N	Y	N	Y	Y
6 ***Barton***	N	Y	Y	?	Y
7 ***Archer***	Y	Y	N	Y	Y
8 ***Brady***	N	Y	N	Y	Y
9 Lampson	Y	Y	Y	Y	Y
10 Doggett	Y	Y	Y	Y	Y
11 Edwards	Y	Y	Y	Y	Y
12 ***Granger***	Y	Y	Y	Y	Y
13 ***Thornberry***	Y	Y	Y	Y	Y
14 ***Paul***	N	N	N	Y	Y
15 Hinojosa	Y	Y	Y	Y	Y
16 Reyes	Y	Y	Y	Y	Y
17 Stenholm	Y	Y	Y	Y	Y
18 Jackson-Lee	Y	Y	Y	Y	Y
19 ***Combest***	Y	Y	N	Y	Y
20 Gonzalez	Y	Y	Y	Y	Y
21 ***Smith***	Y	Y	Y	Y	Y
22 ***DeLay***	Y	Y	Y	Y	Y
23 ***Bonilla***	Y	Y	N	Y	Y
24 Frost	Y	Y	Y	Y	Y
25 Bentsen	Y	Y	Y	Y	Y
26 ***Armey***	Y	Y	Y	Y	Y
27 Ortiz	N	Y	Y	Y	Y
28 Rodriguez	Y	Y	Y	Y	Y
29 Green	Y	Y	Y	Y	Y
30 Johnson, E.B.	Y	Y	Y	Y	Y
UTAH					
1 ***Hansen***	Y	Y	N	Y	Y
2 ***Cook***	Y	Y	Y	Y	Y
3 ***Cannon***	?	Y	Y	Y	Y
VERMONT					
AL *Sanders*	Y	Y	Y	Y	Y
VIRGINIA					
1 ***Bateman***	Y	Y	Y	Y	Y
2 Pickett	Y	Y	Y	Y	Y
3 Scott	Y	Y	Y	Y	Y
4 Sisisky	Y	Y	Y	Y	Y
5 Goode	N	Y	N	Y	Y
6 ***Goodlatte***	N	Y	Y	Y	Y
7 ***Bliley***	Y	Y	Y	Y	Y
8 Moran	Y	+	Y	Y	Y
9 Boucher	Y	Y	Y	Y	Y
10 ***Wolf***	Y	Y	Y	Y	Y
11 ***Davis***	N	Y	Y	Y	Y
WASHINGTON					
1 Inslee	Y	Y	Y	Y	Y
2 ***Metcalf***	Y	Y	N	Y	Y
3 Baird	Y	Y	Y	Y	Y
4 ***Hastings***	Y	Y	Y	Y	Y
5 ***Nethercutt***	Y	Y	Y	Y	Y
6 Dicks	Y	Y	Y	Y	Y
7 McDermott	Y	Y	Y	Y	Y
8 ***Dunn***	Y	Y	Y	Y	Y
9 Smith	Y	Y	Y	Y	Y
WEST VIRGINIA					
1 Mollohan	Y	Y	Y	Y	Y
2 Wise	Y	Y	Y	Y	Y
3 Rahall	Y	Y	Y	Y	Y
WISCONSIN					
1 ***Ryan***	N	Y	Y	Y	Y
2 Baldwin	Y	Y	Y	Y	Y
3 Kind	Y	Y	Y	Y	Y
4 Kleczka	+	Y	Y	Y	Y
5 Barrett	Y	Y	Y	Y	Y
6 ***Petri***	N	Y	N	Y	Y
7 Obey	Y	Y	Y	?	?
8 ***Green***	N	Y	Y	Y	Y
9 ***Sensenbrenner***	N	Y	N	Y	Y
WYOMING					
AL ***Cubin***	Y	Y	N	Y	Y

Southern states - Ala., Ark., Fla., Ga., Ky., La., Miss., N.C., Okla., S.C., Tenn., Texas, Va.

457. HR 2506. Agency for Health Research and Quality/Passage. Passage of the bill to reauthorize and rename the Agency for Health Research and Quality (formerly the Agency for Health Care Policy and Research) and to redefine its mission to focus on supporting private sector initiatives. Passed 417-7: R 208-7; D 208-0 (ND 154-0, SD 54-0); I 1-0. Sept. 28, 1999.

458. HR 2559. Expand Federal Crop Insurance/Rule. Adoption of the rule (H Res 308) for the bill revising the federal crop insurance program to provide more affordable risk management tools and improved protection from production and income loss. Adopted 422-1: R 217-0; D 204-1 (ND 151-1, SD 53-0); I 1-0. Sept. 29, 1999. (Subsequently, the bill as amended was passed by voice vote.)

459. Procedural Motion/Journal. Approval of the House Journal of Sept. 28, 1999. Approved 375-43: R 202-13; D 172-30 (ND 124-25, SD 48-5); I 1-0. Sept. 29, 1999.

460. HR 2910. NTSB Authorization/Rule. Adoption of the rule (H Res 312) for the bill to authorize $194 million over three years for the National Transportation Safety Board (NTSB). Adopted 420-0: R 215-0; D 204-0 (ND 150-0, SD 54-0); I 1-0. Sept. 30, 1999.

461. Procedural Motion/Journal. Approval of the House Journal of Sept. 29, 1999. Approved 362-52: R 196-15; D 165-37 (ND 119-29, SD 46-8); I 1-0. Sept. 30, 1999.

Key

Y Voted for (yea).
\# Paired for.
\+ Announced for.
N Voted against (nay).
X Paired against.
– Announced against.
P Voted "present."
C Voted "present" to avoid possible conflict of interest.
? Did not vote or otherwise make a position known.

•

Democrats ***Republicans***
Independents

	457	458	459	460	461
ALABAMA					
1 ***Callahan***	Y	Y	Y	Y	Y
2 ***Everett***	Y	Y	Y	Y	Y
3 ***Riley***	?	Y	N	Y	Y
4 ***Aderholt***	Y	Y	N	Y	N
5 Cramer	Y	Y	Y	Y	Y
6 ***Bachus***	Y	Y	Y	Y	Y
7 Hilliard	Y	Y	N	Y	N
ALASKA					
AL ***Young***	Y	Y	Y	Y	Y
ARIZONA					
1 ***Salmon***	Y	Y	Y	Y	Y
2 Pastor	Y	Y	N	Y	Y
3 ***Stump***	Y	Y	Y	Y	Y
4 ***Shadegg***	Y	Y	Y	Y	Y
5 ***Kolbe***	Y	Y	Y	Y	Y
6 ***Hayworth***	Y	Y	Y	Y	Y
ARKANSAS					
1 Berry	Y	Y	Y	Y	Y
2 Snyder	Y	Y	Y	Y	Y
3 ***Hutchinson***	Y	Y	Y	Y	Y
4 ***Dickey***	Y	Y	Y	Y	N
CALIFORNIA					
1 Thompson	Y	Y	N	Y	N
2 ***Herger***	Y	Y	Y	Y	Y
3 ***Ose***	Y	Y	Y	Y	Y
4 ***Doolittle***	Y	Y	Y	Y	Y
5 Matsui	Y	Y	Y	Y	Y
6 Woolsey	Y	Y	Y	Y	Y
7 Miller, George	Y	Y	N	Y	N
8 Pelosi	Y	Y	Y	Y	Y
9 Lee	Y	Y	Y	Y	Y
10 Tauscher	Y	Y	Y	Y	Y
11 ***Pombo***	Y	Y	Y	Y	Y
12 Lantos	Y	Y	Y	Y	Y
13 Stark	Y	Y	Y	Y	N
14 Eshoo	Y	Y	Y	Y	Y
15 ***Campbell***	Y	Y	Y	Y	Y
16 Lofgren	Y	Y	Y	Y	Y
17 Farr	Y	Y	Y	Y	Y
18 Condit	Y	Y	Y	Y	Y
19 ***Radanovich***	Y	Y	Y	Y	Y
20 Dooley	Y	Y	Y	Y	Y
21 ***Thomas***	+	+	+	Y	Y
22 Capps	Y	Y	Y	Y	Y
23 ***Gallegly***	Y	Y	Y	Y	Y
24 Sherman	Y	Y	Y	Y	Y
25 ***McKeon***	Y	Y	Y	?	?
26 Berman	Y	Y	Y	Y	Y
27 ***Rogan***	Y	Y	Y	Y	Y
28 ***Dreier***	Y	Y	Y	Y	Y
29 Waxman	Y	Y	Y	Y	Y
30 Becerra	Y	Y	Y	?	?
31 Martinez	Y	Y	Y	Y	Y
32 Dixon	Y	?	?	Y	Y
33 Roybal-Allard	Y	Y	Y	Y	Y
34 Napolitano	Y	Y	Y	Y	Y
35 Waters	Y	Y	N	Y	N
36 ***Kuykendall***	Y	Y	Y	Y	Y
37 Millender-McD.	Y	Y	Y	Y	Y
38 ***Horn***	Y	Y	Y	Y	Y
39 ***Royce***	N	Y	Y	Y	Y
40 ***Lewis***	Y	Y	Y	Y	Y
41 ***Miller***	Y	Y	Y	Y	Y
42 Vacant					
43 ***Calvert***	Y	Y	Y	Y	Y
44 ***Bono***	Y	Y	Y	Y	Y
45 ***Rohrabacher***	Y	Y	Y	Y	Y
46 Sanchez	Y	Y	Y	Y	Y
47 ***Cox***	Y	Y	Y	Y	Y
48 ***Packard***	Y	Y	Y	Y	Y
49 ***Bilbray***	Y	Y	Y	Y	N
50 Filner	Y	Y	N	Y	N
51 ***Cunningham***	Y	Y	Y	Y	Y
52 ***Hunter***	Y	Y	Y	Y	Y
COLORADO					
1 DeGette	Y	Y	Y	Y	Y
2 Udall	Y	Y	Y	Y	N
3 ***McInnis***	Y	Y	Y	Y	Y
4 ***Schaffer***	Y	Y	N	Y	N
5 ***Hefley***	Y	Y	Y	Y	N
6 ***Tancredo***	Y	Y	Y	Y	P
CONNECTICUT					
1 Larson	Y	Y	Y	Y	Y
2 Gejdenson	Y	Y	Y	Y	Y
3 DeLauro	Y	Y	Y	Y	Y
4 ***Shays***	Y	Y	Y	Y	Y
5 Maloney	Y	Y	Y	Y	Y
6 ***Johnson***	Y	Y	Y	Y	Y
DELAWARE					
AL ***Castle***	Y	Y	Y	Y	Y
FLORIDA					
1 ***Scarborough***	?	?	?	?	?
2 Boyd	Y	Y	Y	Y	Y
3 Brown	Y	Y	Y	Y	Y
4 ***Fowler***	Y	Y	Y	Y	Y
5 Thurman	Y	Y	Y	Y	N
6 ***Stearns***	Y	Y	Y	Y	Y
7 ***Mica***	Y	Y	Y	Y	Y
8 ***McCollum***	Y	Y	Y	Y	Y
9 ***Bilirakis***	Y	Y	Y	Y	Y
10 ***Young***	Y	Y	Y	Y	Y
11 Davis	Y	Y	Y	Y	Y
12 ***Canady***	Y	Y	Y	Y	Y
13 ***Miller***	Y	Y	Y	Y	Y
14 ***Goss***	Y	Y	Y	Y	Y
15 ***Weldon***	Y	Y	Y	Y	Y
16 ***Foley***	Y	Y	Y	Y	Y
17 Meek	Y	Y	Y	Y	Y
18 ***Ros-Lehtinen***	Y	Y	Y	Y	Y
19 Wexler	Y	Y	Y	Y	Y
20 Deutsch	Y	Y	Y	Y	Y
21 ***Diaz-Balart***	Y	Y	Y	Y	Y
22 ***Shaw***	Y	Y	Y	Y	Y
23 Hastings	Y	Y	Y	Y	N
GEORGIA					
1 ***Kingston***	Y	Y	Y	Y	Y
2 Bishop	Y	Y	Y	Y	Y
3 ***Collins***	Y	Y	Y	Y	?
4 McKinney	?	Y	Y	Y	Y
5 Lewis	Y	Y	Y	Y	Y
6 ***Isakson***	Y	Y	Y	Y	Y
7 ***Barr***	Y	Y	Y	Y	Y
8 ***Chambliss***	Y	Y	Y	Y	Y
9 ***Deal***	Y	Y	Y	Y	Y
10 ***Norwood***	Y	Y	Y	Y	Y
11 ***Linder***	Y	Y	Y	Y	Y
HAWAII					
1 Abercrombie	Y	Y	Y	Y	Y
2 Mink	Y	Y	Y	Y	Y
IDAHO					
1 ***Chenoweth***	N	Y	Y	?	?
2 ***Simpson***	Y	Y	Y	Y	Y
ILLINOIS					
1 Rush	Y	Y	Y	Y	Y
2 Jackson	Y	Y	Y	Y	Y
3 Lipinski	Y	Y	Y	Y	Y
4 Gutierrez	Y	Y	N	Y	Y
5 Blagojevich	Y	Y	Y	Y	Y
6 ***Hyde***	Y	Y	Y	Y	Y
7 Davis	Y	Y	Y	Y	Y
8 ***Crane***	Y	Y	N	Y	N
9 Schakowsky	Y	Y	Y	Y	Y
10 ***Porter***	Y	Y	Y	Y	Y
11 ***Weller***	Y	Y	N	Y	N
12 Costello	Y	Y	N	Y	N
13 ***Biggert***	Y	Y	Y	Y	Y
14 ***Hastert***					

ND Northern Democrats SD Southern Democrats

	457	458	459	460	461
15 ***Ewing***	Y	Y	Y	Y	Y
16 ***Manzullo***	Y	Y	Y	Y	Y
17 Evans	Y	Y	Y	Y	Y
18 ***LaHood***	Y	Y	Y	Y	Y
19 Phelps	Y	Y	?	Y	Y
20 ***Shimkus***	Y	Y	Y	Y	Y
INDIANA					
1 Visclosky	Y	Y	N	Y	N
2 ***McIntosh***	Y	Y	Y	Y	Y
3 Roemer	Y	Y	Y	Y	Y
4 ***Souder***	Y	Y	Y	Y	Y
5 ***Buyer***	Y	Y	Y	Y	Y
6 ***Burton***	Y	Y	Y	Y	Y
7 ***Pease***	Y	Y	Y	Y	Y
8 ***Hostettler***	N	Y	Y	Y	Y
9 Hill	Y	?	Y	Y	Y
10 Carson	Y	Y	Y	Y	Y
IOWA					
1 ***Leach***	Y	Y	Y	Y	Y
2 ***Nussle***	Y	Y	Y	Y	Y
3 Boswell	Y	Y	?	Y	Y
4 ***Ganske***	Y	Y	Y	Y	Y
5 ***Latham***	Y	Y	Y	Y	Y
KANSAS					
1 ***Moran***	Y	Y	N	Y	N
2 ***Ryun***	Y	Y	Y	Y	Y
3 Moore	Y	Y	Y	Y	N
4 ***Tiahrt***	Y	Y	Y	Y	Y
KENTUCKY					
1 ***Whitfield***	Y	Y	Y	Y	Y
2 ***Lewis***	Y	Y	Y	Y	Y
3 ***Northup***	Y	Y	Y	Y	Y
4 Lucas	Y	Y	Y	Y	Y
5 ***Rogers***	Y	Y	Y	Y	Y
6 ***Fletcher***	Y	Y	Y	Y	Y
LOUISIANA					
1 ***Vitter***	Y	Y	Y	Y	Y
2 Jefferson	Y	?	?	?	?
3 ***Tauzin***	Y	Y	Y	Y	Y
4 ***McCrery***	Y	Y	Y	Y	Y
5 ***Cooksey***	Y	Y	Y	Y	Y
6 ***Baker***	Y	Y	Y	Y	Y
7 John	Y	Y	Y	Y	Y
MAINE					
1 Allen	Y	Y	Y	Y	Y
2 Baldacci	Y	Y	Y	Y	Y
MARYLAND					
1 ***Gilchrest***	Y	Y	Y	Y	Y
2 ***Ehrlich***	Y	Y	Y	Y	Y
3 Cardin	Y	Y	Y	Y	Y
4 Wynn	Y	Y	Y	Y	Y
5 Hoyer	Y	Y	Y	Y	N
6 ***Bartlett***	Y	Y	Y	Y	Y
7 Cummings	Y	Y	Y	Y	Y
8 ***Morella***	Y	Y	Y	Y	Y
MASSACHUSETTS					
1 Olver	Y	Y	Y	Y	Y
2 Neal	Y	Y	Y	Y	Y
3 McGovern	Y	Y	Y	Y	Y
4 Frank	Y	Y	Y	Y	Y
5 Meehan	Y	Y	Y	Y	Y
6 Tierney	Y	Y	Y	Y	Y
7 Markey	Y	Y	N	Y	Y
8 Capuano	Y	Y	N	Y	N
9 Moakley	Y	Y	Y	Y	Y
10 Delahunt	Y	Y	Y	Y	Y
MICHIGAN					
1 Stupak	Y	Y	Y	Y	N
2 ***Hoekstra***	Y	Y	Y	Y	Y
3 ***Ehlers***	Y	Y	Y	Y	Y
4 ***Camp***	Y	Y	Y	Y	Y
5 Barcia	Y	Y	Y	Y	Y
6 ***Upton***	Y	Y	Y	Y	Y
7 ***Smith***	Y	Y	Y	Y	Y
8 Stabenow	Y	Y	Y	Y	Y
9 Kildee	Y	Y	Y	Y	Y
10 Bonior	Y	Y	Y	Y	?
11 ***Knollenberg***	Y	Y	Y	Y	Y
12 Levin	Y	Y	Y	Y	Y
13 Rivers	Y	Y	Y	Y	Y
14 Conyers	Y	Y	Y	Y	Y
15 Kilpatrick	Y	Y	Y	Y	Y
16 Dingell	Y	Y	Y	Y	Y

	457	458	459	460	461
MINNESOTA					
1 ***Gutknecht***	Y	Y	N	Y	N
2 Minge	Y	Y	Y	Y	Y
3 ***Ramstad***	Y	Y	N	Y	N
4 Vento	Y	N	Y	Y	N
5 Sabo	Y	Y	N	Y	N
6 Luther	Y	Y	Y	Y	Y
7 Peterson	Y	Y	?	Y	N
8 Oberstar	Y	Y	N	Y	N
MISSISSIPPI					
1 ***Wicker***	Y	Y	Y	Y	Y
2 Thompson	Y	Y	N	Y	N
3 ***Pickering***	Y	Y	Y	Y	Y
4 Shows	Y	Y	Y	Y	Y
5 Taylor	Y	Y	N	Y	N
MISSOURI					
1 Clay	Y	Y	N	Y	N
2 ***Talent***	Y	Y	Y	Y	Y
3 Gephardt	Y	Y	Y	Y	?
4 Skelton	Y	Y	Y	Y	Y
5 McCarthy	Y	Y	Y	Y	Y
6 Danner	Y	Y	Y	?	?
7 ***Blunt***	Y	Y	Y	Y	Y
8 ***Emerson***	Y	Y	Y	Y	Y
9 ***Hulshof***	Y	Y	N	Y	Y
MONTANA					
AL ***Hill***	Y	Y	Y	Y	Y
NEBRASKA					
1 ***Bereuter***	Y	Y	Y	Y	Y
2 ***Terry***	Y	Y	Y	Y	Y
3 ***Barrett***	Y	Y	Y	Y	Y
NEVADA					
1 Berkley	Y	Y	Y	Y	Y
2 ***Gibbons***	Y	Y	N	Y	N
NEW HAMPSHIRE					
1 ***Sununu***	Y	Y	Y	Y	Y
2 ***Bass***	Y	Y	Y	Y	Y
NEW JERSEY					
1 Andrews	Y	Y	Y	Y	Y
2 ***LoBiondo***	Y	Y	N	Y	N
3 ***Saxton***	Y	Y	Y	Y	Y
4 ***Smith***	Y	Y	Y	Y	Y
5 ***Roukema***	Y	Y	Y	Y	Y
6 Pallone	Y	Y	Y	Y	Y
7 ***Franks***	Y	Y	Y	Y	Y
8 Pascrell	Y	Y	Y	Y	Y
9 Rothman	Y	Y	Y	Y	Y
10 Payne	Y	Y	Y	Y	Y
11 ***Frelinghuysen***	Y	Y	Y	Y	Y
12 Holt	Y	Y	Y	Y	Y
13 Menendez	Y	Y	Y	Y	Y
NEW MEXICO					
1 ***Wilson***	Y	Y	Y	Y	Y
2 ***Skeen***	Y	Y	Y	Y	Y
3 Udall	Y	Y	Y	Y	N
NEW YORK					
1 Forbes	Y	Y	Y	Y	Y
2 ***Lazio***	Y	Y	Y	Y	Y
3 ***King***	Y	Y	Y	Y	Y
4 McCarthy	?	Y	Y	Y	Y
5 Ackerman	Y	Y	Y	Y	Y
6 Meeks	Y	Y	Y	?	?
7 Crowley	Y	Y	Y	Y	Y
8 Nadler	Y	?	?	Y	Y
9 Weiner	Y	Y	Y	Y	Y
10 Towns	Y	Y	Y	Y	Y
11 Owens	Y	Y	Y	Y	Y
12 Velázquez	Y	Y	Y	Y	N
13 ***Fossella***	Y	Y	Y	Y	Y
14 Maloney	Y	Y	Y	Y	Y
15 Rangel	Y	Y	Y	Y	Y
16 Serrano	Y	Y	Y	Y	Y
17 Engel	Y	Y	Y	?	Y
18 Lowey	Y	Y	Y	Y	Y
19 ***Kelly***	Y	Y	Y	Y	Y
20 ***Gilman***	Y	Y	Y	Y	Y
21 McNulty	Y	Y	N	Y	N
22 ***Sweeney***	Y	Y	Y	Y	N
23 ***Boehlert***	Y	Y	Y	Y	Y
24 ***McHugh***	Y	Y	Y	Y	Y
25 ***Walsh***	Y	Y	Y	Y	Y
26 Hinchey	Y	Y	N	Y	N
27 ***Reynolds***	Y	Y	Y	Y	Y
28 Slaughter	Y	Y	N	Y	Y
29 LaFalce	Y	Y	Y	Y	Y

	457	458	459	460	461
30 ***Quinn***	Y	Y	Y	Y	Y
31 ***Houghton***	Y	Y	Y	?	?
NORTH CAROLINA					
1 Clayton	Y	Y	Y	Y	Y
2 Etheridge	Y	Y	Y	Y	Y
3 ***Jones***	Y	Y	Y	Y	Y
4 Price	Y	Y	Y	Y	Y
5 ***Burr***	Y	Y	Y	Y	Y
6 ***Coble***	Y	Y	Y	Y	Y
7 McIntyre	Y	Y	Y	Y	Y
8 ***Hayes***	Y	Y	Y	Y	Y
9 ***Myrick***	Y	Y	Y	Y	Y
10 ***Ballenger***	Y	Y	Y	Y	Y
11 ***Taylor***	Y	Y	Y	Y	Y
12 Watt	Y	Y	Y	Y	Y
NORTH DAKOTA					
AL Pomeroy	Y	Y	Y	Y	Y
OHIO					
1 ***Chabot***	Y	Y	Y	Y	Y
2 ***Portman***	Y	Y	Y	Y	Y
3 Hall	Y	Y	Y	Y	Y
4 ***Oxley***	Y	Y	Y	Y	Y
5 ***Gillmor***	Y	Y	Y	Y	N
6 Strickland	Y	Y	N	Y	Y
7 ***Hobson***	Y	Y	Y	Y	Y
8 ***Boehner***	Y	Y	Y	Y	Y
9 Kaptur	Y	Y	Y	Y	Y
10 Kucinich	Y	Y	N	Y	N
11 Jones	Y	Y	Y	Y	Y
12 ***Kasich***	Y	Y	Y	Y	Y
13 Brown	Y	Y	N	Y	Y
14 Sawyer	Y	Y	Y	Y	N
15 ***Pryce***	Y	Y	Y	Y	Y
16 ***Regula***	Y	Y	Y	Y	Y
17 Traficant	Y	Y	Y	Y	Y
18 ***Ney***	Y	Y	Y	Y	Y
19 ***LaTourette***	Y	Y	Y	Y	Y
OKLAHOMA					
1 ***Largent***	Y	Y	Y	Y	Y
2 ***Coburn***	N	Y	Y	Y	Y
3 ***Watkins***	Y	Y	Y	Y	Y
4 ***Watts***	Y	?	Y	Y	Y
5 ***Istook***	Y	?	?	Y	Y
6 ***Lucas***	Y	Y	Y	Y	Y
OREGON					
1 Wu	?	?	?	?	?
2 ***Walden***	Y	Y	Y	Y	Y
3 Blumenauer	Y	Y	Y	Y	Y
4 DeFazio	Y	Y	N	Y	?
5 Hooley	Y	Y	N	+	+
PENNSYLVANIA					
1 Brady	Y	Y	N	Y	N
2 Fattah	Y	Y	Y	Y	N
3 Borski	Y	Y	N	Y	N
4 Klink	Y	Y	Y	Y	N
5 ***Peterson***	Y	Y	Y	Y	Y
6 Holden	Y	Y	Y	Y	Y
7 ***Weldon***	Y	Y	Y	?	?
8 ***Greenwood***	Y	Y	Y	Y	Y
9 ***Shuster***	Y	Y	Y	Y	Y
10 ***Sherwood***	Y	Y	Y	Y	Y
11 Kanjorski	Y	Y	Y	Y	Y
12 Murtha	Y	Y	Y	Y	Y
13 Hoeffel	Y	Y	Y	Y	Y
14 Coyne	Y	Y	Y	Y	Y
15 ***Toomey***	Y	Y	Y	Y	Y
16 ***Pitts***	Y	Y	Y	Y	Y
17 ***Gekas***	Y	Y	Y	Y	Y
18 Doyle	Y	Y	Y	Y	Y
19 ***Goodling***	Y	Y	Y	Y	Y
20 Mascara	Y	Y	Y	Y	Y
21 ***English***	Y	Y	N	Y	N
RHODE ISLAND					
1 Kennedy	Y	Y	Y	Y	Y
2 Weygand	Y	Y	Y	Y	Y
SOUTH CAROLINA					
1 ***Sanford***	?	Y	Y	Y	Y
2 ***Spence***	Y	Y	Y	Y	Y
3 ***Graham***	Y	Y	Y	Y	Y
4 ***DeMint***	Y	Y	Y	Y	Y
5 Spratt	Y	?	Y	Y	Y
6 Clyburn	Y	Y	Y	Y	Y
SOUTH DAKOTA					
AL ***Thune***	Y	Y	Y	Y	Y

	457	458	459	460	461
TENNESSEE					
1 ***Jenkins***	Y	Y	Y	Y	Y
2 ***Duncan***	N	Y	Y	Y	Y
3 ***Wamp***	Y	Y	Y	Y	Y
4 ***Hilleary***	Y	Y	N	Y	Y
5 Clement	Y	Y	Y	Y	Y
6 Gordon	Y	Y	?	Y	Y
7 ***Bryant***	Y	Y	Y	Y	Y
8 Tanner	Y	Y	Y	Y	Y
9 Ford	Y	Y	Y	Y	N
TEXAS					
1 Sandlin	Y	Y	Y	Y	Y
2 Turner	Y	Y	Y	Y	Y
3 ***Johnson, Sam***	N	Y	Y	Y	Y
4 Hall	Y	Y	Y	Y	Y
5 ***Sessions***	?	Y	Y	Y	Y
6 ***Barton***	Y	Y	Y	Y	Y
7 ***Archer***	?	Y	Y	Y	Y
8 ***Brady***	Y	Y	Y	Y	Y
9 Lampson	Y	Y	Y	Y	Y
10 Doggett	Y	Y	Y	Y	Y
11 Edwards	Y	Y	Y	Y	Y
12 ***Granger***	Y	Y	Y	Y	Y
13 ***Thornberry***	Y	Y	Y	Y	Y
14 ***Paul***	N	Y	Y	Y	?
15 Hinojosa	Y	Y	Y	Y	Y
16 Reyes	Y	Y	Y	Y	Y
17 Stenholm	Y	Y	N	Y	Y
18 Jackson-Lee	Y	Y	Y	Y	Y
19 ***Combest***	Y	Y	Y	Y	Y
20 Gonzalez	Y	Y	Y	Y	Y
21 ***Smith***	Y	Y	Y	Y	Y
22 ***DeLay***	Y	Y	?	Y	?
23 ***Bonilla***	Y	Y	Y	Y	Y
24 Frost	Y	Y	Y	Y	Y
25 Bentsen	Y	Y	Y	Y	Y
26 ***Armey***	Y	Y	Y	Y	Y
27 Ortiz	Y	Y	Y	Y	Y
28 Rodriguez	Y	Y	Y	Y	Y
29 Green	Y	Y	Y	Y	Y
30 Johnson, E.B.	Y	Y	Y	Y	N
UTAH					
1 ***Hansen***	Y	Y	Y	Y	Y
2 ***Cook***	Y	Y	Y	Y	Y
3 ***Cannon***	Y	Y	Y	Y	Y
VERMONT					
AL *Sanders*	Y	Y	Y	Y	Y
VIRGINIA					
1 ***Bateman***	Y	Y	Y	Y	Y
2 Pickett	Y	Y	N	Y	N
3 Scott	Y	Y	Y	Y	Y
4 Sisisky	Y	Y	Y	Y	Y
5 Goode	Y	Y	Y	Y	Y
6 ***Goodlatte***	Y	Y	Y	Y	Y
7 ***Bliley***	Y	Y	Y	Y	Y
8 Moran	Y	Y	Y	Y	Y
9 Boucher	Y	Y	Y	Y	Y
10 ***Wolf***	Y	Y	Y	Y	Y
11 ***Davis***	Y	Y	Y	Y	Y
WASHINGTON					
1 Inslee	Y	Y	Y	Y	Y
2 ***Metcalf***	Y	Y	Y	Y	Y
3 Baird	Y	Y	N	Y	N
4 ***Hastings***	Y	Y	Y	Y	Y
5 ***Nethercutt***	Y	Y	Y	Y	Y
6 Dicks	Y	Y	Y	Y	Y
7 McDermott	Y	Y	N	Y	N
8 ***Dunn***	Y	Y	Y	Y	Y
9 Smith	Y	Y	Y	Y	Y
WEST VIRGINIA					
1 Mollohan	Y	Y	Y	Y	Y
2 Wise	Y	Y	Y	Y	Y
3 Rahall	Y	Y	Y	Y	Y
WISCONSIN					
1 ***Ryan***	Y	Y	Y	Y	Y
2 Baldwin	Y	Y	Y	Y	Y
3 Kind	Y	Y	?	Y	Y
4 Kleczka	Y	Y	Y	Y	Y
5 Barrett	Y	Y	Y	Y	Y
6 ***Petri***	Y	Y	Y	Y	Y
7 Obey	Y	Y	Y	Y	Y
8 ***Green***	Y	Y	?	Y	Y
9 ***Sensenbrenner***	Y	Y	Y	Y	Y
WYOMING					
AL ***Cubin***	Y	Y	?	?	?

Southern states - Ala., Ark., Fla., Ga., Ky., La., Miss., N.C., Okla., S.C., Tenn., Texas, Va.

Key

- Y Voted for (yea).
- # Paired for.
- + Announced for.
- N Voted against (nay).
- X Paired against.
- – Announced against.
- P Voted "present."
- C Voted "present" to avoid possible conflict of interest.
- ? Did not vote or otherwise make a position known.

•

Democrats ***Republicans***
Independents

462. HR 2910. NTSB Authorization/Passage. Passage of the bill to authorize $194 million over three years for the National Transportation Safety Board (NTSB). The bill would require the NTSB to allow the FBI to lead any investigation of an accident that appeared to involve criminal activity. Passed 420-4: R 215-4; D 204-0 (ND 151-0, SD 53-0); I 1-0. Sept. 30, 1999.

463. HR 2436. Criminal Penalties for Harming a Fetus/Surrogate Decision. Canady, R-Fla., amendment to clarify that the punishment under the bill is for intentionally killing or attempting to kill an unborn child in lieu of — not in addition to — the punishment otherwise provided in the bill. The amendment also would clarify that the exemption for abortion-related conduct includes situations in which a surrogate decision-maker acts on behalf of the pregnant woman. Adopted 269-158: R 206-13; D 63-144 (ND 42-111, SD 21-33); I 0-1. Sept. 30, 1999.

464. HR 2436. Criminal Penalties for Harming a Fetus/Assault on Pregnant Women. Lofgren, D-Calif., substitute amendment to make assault on a pregnant woman a federal crime. Under the substitute, if the assault causes prenatal injury, the perpetrator could be subject to up to 20 years' imprisonment. If the assault causes termination of the pregnancy, the perpetrator could be sentenced to up to life in prison. Rejected 201-224: R 36-181; D 164-43 (ND 125-28, SD 39-15); I 1-0. Sept. 30, 1999.

465. HR 2436. Criminal Penalties for Harming a Fetus/Passage. Passage of the bill to make it a criminal offense to injure or kill a fetus during the commission of a violent crime. The measure would establish criminal penalties for those who harm a fetus, regardless of the perpetrator's knowledge of the pregnancy or intent to harm the fetus. The bill states that its provisions should not be interpreted to apply to consensual abortion or to a woman's actions with respect to her pregnancy. Passed 254-172: R 198-21; D 56-150 (ND 40-113, SD 16-37); I 0-1. Sept. 30, 1999. A "nay" was a vote in support of the president's position.

	462	463	464	465
ALABAMA				
1 ***Callahan***	Y	Y	N	Y
2 ***Everett***	Y	Y	N	Y
3 ***Riley***	Y	Y	N	Y
4 ***Aderholt***	Y	Y	N	Y
5 Cramer	Y	Y	N	Y
6 ***Bachus***	Y	Y	N	Y
7 Hilliard	Y	N	Y	N
ALASKA				
AL ***Young***	Y	Y	N	Y
ARIZONA				
1 ***Salmon***	Y	Y	N	Y
2 Pastor	Y	N	Y	N
3 ***Stump***	Y	Y	N	Y
4 ***Shadegg***	Y	Y	N	Y
5 ***Kolbe***	Y	Y	Y	N
6 ***Hayworth***	Y	Y	N	Y
ARKANSAS				
1 Berry	Y	Y	N	Y
2 Snyder	Y	Y	Y	N
3 ***Hutchinson***	Y	Y	N	Y
4 ***Dickey***	Y	Y	N	Y
CALIFORNIA				
1 Thompson	Y	N	Y	N
2 ***Herger***	Y	Y	?	Y
3 ***Ose***	Y	Y	Y	N
4 ***Doolittle***	Y	Y	N	Y
5 Matsui	Y	N	Y	N
6 Woolsey	Y	N	Y	N
7 Miller, George	Y	N	Y	N
8 Pelosi	Y	N	Y	N
9 Lee	Y	N	Y	N
10 Tauscher	Y	N	Y	N
11 ***Pombo***	Y	Y	N	Y
12 Lantos	Y	N	Y	N
13 Stark	Y	N	Y	N
14 Eshoo	Y	N	Y	N
15 ***Campbell***	Y	Y	Y	N
16 Lofgren	Y	N	Y	N
17 Farr	Y	N	Y	N
18 Condit	Y	N	Y	N
19 ***Radanovich***	Y	Y	N	Y
20 Dooley	Y	N	Y	N
21 ***Thomas***	Y	Y	Y	Y
22 Capps	Y	N	Y	N
23 ***Gallegly***	Y	Y	N	Y
24 Sherman	Y	N	Y	N
25 ***McKeon***	Y	Y	N	Y
26 Berman	Y	N	Y	N
27 ***Rogan***	Y	Y	N	Y
28 ***Dreier***	Y	Y	N	Y
29 Waxman	Y	N	Y	N
30 Becerra	?	N	Y	N
31 Martinez	Y	N	Y	N
32 Dixon	Y	N	Y	N
33 Roybal-Allard	Y	N	Y	N
34 Napolitano	Y	N	Y	N
35 Waters	Y	N	Y	N
36 ***Kuykendall***	Y	N	Y	N
37 Millender-McD.	Y	N	Y	N
38 ***Horn***	Y	N	Y	N
39 ***Royce***	Y	Y	N	Y

	462	463	464	465
40 ***Lewis***	Y	Y	N	Y
41 ***Miller***	Y	Y	N	Y
42 Vacant				
43 ***Calvert***	Y	Y	N	Y
44 ***Bono***	Y	N	Y	N
45 ***Rohrabacher***	Y	Y	N	Y
46 Sanchez	Y	N	Y	N
47 ***Cox***	Y	Y	N	Y
48 ***Packard***	Y	Y	N	Y
49 ***Bilbray***	Y	Y	Y	Y
50 Filner	Y	N	Y	N
51 ***Cunningham***	Y	Y	N	Y
52 ***Hunter***	Y	Y	N	Y
COLORADO				
1 DeGette	Y	N	Y	N
2 Udall	Y	N	Y	N
3 ***McInnis***	Y	Y	Y	Y
4 ***Schaffer***	Y	Y	N	Y
5 ***Hefley***	Y	Y	N	Y
6 ***Tancredo***	Y	Y	N	Y
CONNECTICUT				
1 Larson	Y	N	Y	N
2 Gejdenson	Y	N	Y	N
3 DeLauro	Y	N	Y	N
4 ***Shays***	Y	N	Y	N
5 Maloney	Y	Y	Y	N
6 ***Johnson***	Y	Y	Y	N
DELAWARE				
AL ***Castle***	Y	Y	Y	Y
FLORIDA				
1 ***Scarborough***	?	?	?	?
2 Boyd	?	N	Y	N
3 Brown	Y	N	Y	N
4 ***Fowler***	Y	Y	N	Y
5 Thurman	Y	N	Y	N
6 ***Stearns***	Y	Y	N	Y
7 ***Mica***	Y	Y	N	Y
8 ***McCollum***	Y	Y	N	Y
9 ***Bilirakis***	Y	Y	N	Y
10 ***Young***	Y	Y	N	Y
11 Davis	Y	Y	Y	N
12 ***Canady***	Y	Y	N	Y
13 ***Miller***	Y	Y	N	Y
14 ***Goss***	Y	Y	N	Y
15 ***Weldon***	Y	Y	N	Y
16 ***Foley***	Y	Y	Y	N
17 Meek	Y	N	Y	N
18 ***Ros-Lehtinen***	Y	Y	N	Y
19 Wexler	Y	N	Y	N
20 Deutsch	Y	N	Y	N
21 ***Diaz-Balart***	Y	Y	N	Y
22 ***Shaw***	Y	Y	N	Y
23 Hastings	Y	N	Y	N
GEORGIA				
1 ***Kingston***	Y	Y	N	Y
2 Bishop	Y	Y	Y	N
3 ***Collins***	Y	Y	N	Y
4 McKinney	Y	N	Y	N
5 Lewis	Y	N	Y	N
6 ***Isakson***	Y	Y	N	Y
7 ***Barr***	Y	Y	N	Y
8 ***Chambliss***	Y	Y	N	Y
9 ***Deal***	Y	Y	N	Y
10 ***Norwood***	Y	Y	N	Y
11 ***Linder***	Y	Y	N	Y
HAWAII				
1 Abercrombie	Y	N	Y	N
2 Mink	Y	N	Y	N
IDAHO				
1 ***Chenoweth***	N	+	–	+
2 ***Simpson***	Y	Y	N	Y
ILLINOIS				
1 Rush	Y	N	Y	N
2 Jackson	Y	N	Y	N
3 Lipinski	Y	Y	N	Y
4 Gutierrez	Y	N	Y	N
5 Blagojevich	Y	N	Y	N
6 ***Hyde***	Y	Y	N	Y
7 Davis	Y	N	Y	N
8 ***Crane***	Y	Y	N	Y
9 Schakowsky	Y	N	Y	N
10 ***Porter***	Y	N	Y	N
11 ***Weller***	Y	Y	?	Y
12 Costello	Y	Y	N	Y
13 ***Biggert***	Y	N	Y	N
14 ***Hastert***				

ND Northern Democrats SD Southern Democrats

	462	463	464	465
15 ***Ewing***	Y	Y	N	Y
16 ***Manzullo***	Y	Y	N	Y
17 Evans	Y	N	Y	N
18 ***LaHood***	Y	Y	N	Y
19 Phelps	Y	Y	N	Y
20 ***Shimkus***	Y	Y	N	Y
INDIANA				
1 Visclosky	Y	N	N	N
2 ***McIntosh***	Y	Y	N	Y
3 Roemer	Y	Y	N	Y
4 ***Souder***	Y	Y	N	Y
5 ***Buyer***	Y	Y	N	Y
6 ***Burton***	?	Y	N	Y
7 ***Pease***	Y	Y	N	Y
8 ***Hostettler***	Y	Y	N	Y
9 Hill	Y	Y	Y	Y
10 Carson	Y	N	Y	N
IOWA				
1 ***Leach***	Y	Y	Y	Y
2 ***Nussle***	Y	Y	N	Y
3 Boswell	Y	N	Y	N
4 ***Ganske***	Y	Y	N	Y
5 ***Latham***	Y	Y	N	Y
KANSAS				
1 ***Moran***	Y	Y	N	Y
2 ***Ryun***	Y	Y	N	Y
3 Moore	Y	N	Y	N
4 ***Tiahrt***	Y	Y	N	Y
KENTUCKY				
1 ***Whitfield***	Y	Y	N	Y
2 ***Lewis***	Y	Y	N	Y
3 ***Northup***	Y	Y	N	Y
4 Lucas	Y	Y	N	Y
5 ***Rogers***	Y	Y	N	Y
6 ***Fletcher***	Y	Y	N	Y
LOUISIANA				
1 ***Vitter***	Y	Y	N	Y
2 Jefferson	?	?	?	?
3 ***Tauzin***	Y	Y	N	Y
4 ***McCrery***	Y	Y	N	Y
5 ***Cooksey***	Y	Y	N	Y
6 ***Baker***	Y	Y	N	Y
7 John	Y	Y	N	Y
MAINE				
1 Allen	Y	N	Y	N
2 Baldacci	Y	N	Y	N
MARYLAND				
1 ***Gilchrest***	Y	Y	Y	Y
2 ***Ehrlich***	Y	Y	N	Y
3 Cardin	Y	N	Y	N
4 Wynn	Y	N	Y	N
5 Hoyer	Y	N	Y	N
6 ***Bartlett***	Y	Y	N	Y
7 Cummings	Y	N	Y	N
8 ***Morella***	Y	N	Y	N
MASSACHUSETTS				
1 Olver	Y	N	Y	N
2 Neal	Y	Y	N	Y
3 McGovern	Y	N	Y	N
4 Frank	Y	N	Y	N
5 Meehan	Y	N	Y	N
6 Tierney	Y	N	Y	N
7 Markey	Y	N	Y	N
8 Capuano	Y	N	Y	N
9 Moakley	Y	Y	N	Y
10 Delahunt	Y	N	Y	N
MICHIGAN				
1 Stupak	Y	Y	N	Y
2 ***Hoekstra***	Y	Y	N	Y
3 ***Ehlers***	Y	Y	N	Y
4 ***Camp***	Y	Y	N	Y
5 Barcia	Y	Y	N	Y
6 ***Upton***	Y	Y	Y	Y
7 ***Smith***	Y	Y	N	Y
8 Stabenow	Y	N	Y	N
9 Kildee	Y	Y	N	Y
10 Bonior	Y	Y	Y	Y
11 ***Knollenberg***	Y	Y	N	Y
12 Levin	Y	N	Y	N
13 Rivers	Y	N	Y	N
14 Conyers	Y	N	Y	N
15 Kilpatrick	Y	N	Y	N
16 Dingell	Y	Y	Y	Y

	462	463	464	465
MINNESOTA				
1 ***Gutknecht***	Y	Y	N	Y
2 Minge	Y	Y	Y	Y
3 ***Ramstad***	Y	Y	Y	Y
4 Vento	Y	N	Y	N
5 Sabo	Y	N	Y	N
6 Luther	Y	N	Y	Y
7 Peterson	Y	Y	N	Y
8 Oberstar	Y	Y	N	Y
MISSISSIPPI				
1 ***Wicker***	Y	Y	N	Y
2 Thompson	Y	N	Y	N
3 ***Pickering***	Y	Y	N	Y
4 Shows	Y	Y	N	Y
5 Taylor	Y	Y	N	Y
MISSOURI				
1 Clay	Y	N	Y	N
2 ***Talent***	Y	Y	N	Y
3 Gephardt	Y	N	Y	N
4 Skelton	Y	Y	N	Y
5 McCarthy	Y	N	Y	N
6 Danner	Y	Y	Y	Y
7 ***Blunt***	Y	Y	N	Y
8 ***Emerson***	Y	Y	N	Y
9 ***Hulshof***	Y	Y	N	Y
MONTANA				
AL ***Hill***	Y	Y	N	Y
NEBRASKA				
1 ***Bereuter***	Y	Y	N	Y
2 ***Terry***	Y	Y	N	Y
3 ***Barrett***	Y	Y	N	Y
NEVADA				
1 Berkley	Y	N	Y	N
2 ***Gibbons***	Y	Y	Y	Y
NEW HAMPSHIRE				
1 ***Sununu***	Y	Y	N	Y
2 ***Bass***	Y	Y	Y	N
NEW JERSEY				
1 Andrews	Y	N	Y	N
2 ***LoBiondo***	Y	Y	N	Y
3 ***Saxton***	Y	Y	N	Y
4 ***Smith***	Y	Y	N	Y
5 ***Roukema***	Y	Y	Y	N
6 Pallone	Y	N	Y	N
7 ***Franks***	Y	Y	N	Y
8 Pascrell	Y	N	Y	N
9 Rothman	Y	N	Y	N
10 Payne	Y	N	Y	N
11 ***Frelinghuysen***	Y	N	Y	N
12 Holt	Y	N	Y	N
13 Menendez	Y	N	Y	N
NEW MEXICO				
1 ***Wilson***	Y	Y	N	Y
2 ***Skeen***	Y	Y	N	Y
3 Udall	Y	N	Y	N
NEW YORK				
1 Forbes	Y	Y	N	Y
2 ***Lazio***	Y	Y	Y	Y
3 ***King***	Y	Y	N	Y
4 McCarthy	Y	N	Y	N
5 Ackerman	Y	N	Y	N
6 Meeks	?	?	?	?
7 Crowley	Y	Y	Y	Y
8 Nadler	Y	N	Y	N
9 Weiner	Y	N	Y	N
10 Towns	Y	N	Y	N
11 Owens	Y	N	Y	N
12 Velázquez	Y	N	Y	N
13 ***Fossella***	Y	Y	N	Y
14 Maloney	Y	N	Y	N
15 Rangel	Y	N	Y	N
16 Serrano	Y	N	Y	N
17 Engel	Y	N	Y	N
18 Lowey	Y	N	Y	N
19 ***Kelly***	Y	N	Y	N
20 ***Gilman***	Y	N	Y	N
21 McNulty	Y	Y	Y	Y
22 ***Sweeney***	Y	Y	Y	Y
23 ***Boehlert***	Y	N	Y	N
24 ***McHugh***	Y	Y	N	Y
25 ***Walsh***	Y	Y	N	Y
26 Hinchey	Y	N	Y	N
27 ***Reynolds***	Y	Y	N	Y
28 Slaughter	Y	N	Y	N
29 LaFalce	Y	Y	N	Y

	462	463	464	465
30 ***Quinn***	Y	Y	N	Y
31 ***Houghton***	Y	Y	Y	N
NORTH CAROLINA				
1 Clayton	Y	N	Y	N
2 Etheridge	Y	N	Y	N
3 ***Jones***	Y	Y	N	Y
4 Price	Y	N	Y	N
5 ***Burr***	Y	Y	N	Y
6 ***Coble***	Y	Y	N	Y
7 McIntyre	Y	Y	N	Y
8 ***Hayes***	Y	Y	N	Y
9 ***Myrick***	Y	Y	N	Y
10 ***Ballenger***	Y	Y	N	Y
11 ***Taylor***	Y	Y	N	Y
12 Watt	Y	N	N	N
NORTH DAKOTA				
AL Pomeroy	Y	Y	Y	Y
OHIO				
1 ***Chabot***	Y	Y	N	Y
2 ***Portman***	Y	Y	N	Y
3 Hall	Y	Y	N	Y
4 ***Oxley***	Y	Y	N	Y
5 ***Gillmor***	Y	Y	N	Y
6 Strickland	Y	Y	Y	N
7 ***Hobson***	Y	Y	Y	Y
8 ***Boehner***	Y	Y	N	Y
9 Kaptur	Y	Y	Y	Y
10 Kucinich	Y	Y	N	Y
11 Jones	Y	N	Y	N
12 ***Kasich***	Y	Y	N	Y
13 Brown	Y	N	Y	N
14 Sawyer	Y	N	Y	N
15 ***Pryce***	Y	Y	Y	Y
16 ***Regula***	Y	Y	N	Y
17 Traficant	Y	Y	N	Y
18 ***Ney***	Y	Y	N	Y
19 ***LaTourette***	Y	Y	N	Y
OKLAHOMA				
1 ***Largent***	Y	Y	N	Y
2 ***Coburn***	N	Y	N	Y
3 ***Watkins***	Y	Y	N	Y
4 ***Watts***	Y	Y	N	Y
5 ***Istook***	Y	Y	N	Y
6 ***Lucas***	Y	Y	N	Y
OREGON				
1 Wu	?	?	?	?
2 ***Walden***	Y	Y	N	Y
3 Blumenauer	Y	N	Y	N
4 DeFazio	Y	N	Y	N
5 Hooley	+	−	+	−
PENNSYLVANIA				
1 Brady	Y	N	Y	N
2 Fattah	Y	N	Y	N
3 Borski	Y	Y	N	Y
4 Klink	Y	Y	N	Y
5 ***Peterson***	Y	Y	N	Y
6 Holden	Y	Y	N	Y
7 ***Weldon***	Y	Y	N	Y
8 ***Greenwood***	Y	N	Y	N
9 ***Shuster***	Y	Y	N	Y
10 ***Sherwood***	Y	Y	N	Y
11 Kanjorski	Y	Y	N	Y
12 Murtha	Y	Y	N	Y
13 Hoeffel	Y	N	Y	N
14 Coyne	Y	N	Y	N
15 ***Toomey***	Y	Y	N	Y
16 ***Pitts***	Y	Y	N	Y
17 ***Gekas***	Y	Y	N	Y
18 Doyle	Y	Y	N	Y
19 ***Goodling***	Y	Y	N	Y
20 Mascara	Y	Y	N	Y
21 ***English***	Y	Y	N	Y
RHODE ISLAND				
1 Kennedy	Y	N	Y	N
2 Weygand	Y	Y	Y	Y
SOUTH CAROLINA				
1 ***Sanford***	N	Y	N	Y
2 ***Spence***	Y	Y	N	Y
3 ***Graham***	Y	Y	N	Y
4 ***DeMint***	Y	Y	N	Y
5 Spratt	Y	Y	Y	Y
6 Clyburn	Y	N	Y	N
SOUTH DAKOTA				
AL ***Thune***	Y	Y	N	Y

	462	463	464	465
TENNESSEE				
1 ***Jenkins***	Y	Y	N	Y
2 ***Duncan***	Y	Y	N	Y
3 ***Wamp***	Y	Y	N	Y
4 ***Hilleary***	Y	Y	N	Y
5 Clement	Y	Y	N	Y
6 Gordon	Y	Y	Y	Y
7 ***Bryant***	Y	Y	N	Y
8 Tanner	Y	Y	Y	Y
9 Ford	Y	N	Y	?
TEXAS				
1 Sandlin	Y	Y	Y	N
2 Turner	Y	Y	Y	Y
3 ***Johnson, Sam***	Y	Y	N	Y
4 Hall	Y	Y	N	Y
5 ***Sessions***	Y	Y	N	Y
6 ***Barton***	Y	Y	N	Y
7 ***Archer***	Y	Y	N	Y
8 ***Brady***	Y	Y	N	Y
9 Lampson	Y	N	Y	N
10 Doggett	Y	N	Y	N
11 Edwards	Y	N	Y	N
12 ***Granger***	Y	Y	Y	Y
13 ***Thornberry***	Y	Y	N	Y
14 ***Paul***	N	N	N	N
15 Hinojosa	Y	N	Y	N
16 Reyes	Y	N	Y	N
17 Stenholm	Y	Y	N	Y
18 Jackson-Lee	Y	N	Y	N
19 ***Combest***	Y	Y	N	Y
20 Gonzalez	Y	N	Y	N
21 ***Smith***	Y	Y	N	Y
22 ***DeLay***	Y	Y	N	Y
23 ***Bonilla***	Y	Y	N	Y
24 Frost	Y	N	Y	N
25 Bentsen	Y	N	Y	N
26 ***Armey***	Y	Y	N	Y
27 Ortiz	Y	Y	N	Y
28 Rodriguez	Y	N	Y	N
29 Green	Y	N	Y	N
30 Johnson, E.B.	Y	N	Y	N
UTAH				
1 ***Hansen***	Y	Y	N	Y
2 ***Cook***	Y	Y	N	Y
3 ***Cannon***	Y	Y	N	Y
VERMONT				
AL *Sanders*	Y	N	Y	N
VIRGINIA				
1 ***Bateman***	Y	Y	N	Y
2 Pickett	Y	N	N	N
3 Scott	Y	N	N	N
4 Sisisky	Y	N	Y	N
5 Goode	Y	Y	N	Y
6 ***Goodlatte***	Y	Y	N	Y
7 ***Bliley***	Y	Y	N	Y
8 Moran	Y	Y	Y	N
9 Boucher	Y	N	Y	N
10 ***Wolf***	Y	Y	N	Y
11 ***Davis***	Y	Y	Y	Y
WASHINGTON				
1 Inslee	Y	N	Y	N
2 ***Metcalf***	Y	Y	N	Y
3 Baird	Y	N	Y	N
4 ***Hastings***	Y	Y	N	Y
5 ***Nethercutt***	Y	Y	N	Y
6 Dicks	Y	N	Y	N
7 McDermott	Y	N	N	N
8 ***Dunn***	Y	Y	Y	Y
9 Smith	Y	Y	Y	N
WEST VIRGINIA				
1 Mollohan	Y	Y	N	Y
2 Wise	?	N	Y	N
3 Rahall	Y	Y	N	Y
WISCONSIN				
1 ***Ryan***	Y	Y	N	Y
2 Baldwin	Y	N	Y	N
3 Kind	Y	Y	Y	Y
4 Kleczka	Y	Y	Y	Y
5 Barrett	Y	N	Y	N
6 ***Petri***	Y	Y	N	Y
7 Obey	Y	Y	Y	Y
8 ***Green***	Y	Y	N	Y
9 ***Sensenbrenner***	Y	Y	N	Y
WYOMING				
AL ***Cubin***	Y	Y	N	Y

Southern states - Ala., Ark., Fla., Ga., Ky., La., Miss., N.C., Okla., S.C., Tenn., Texas, Va.

466. HR 2084. Fiscal 2000 Transportation Appropriations/Conference Report. Adoption of the conference report on the bill to appropriate $50.2 billion for the Transportation programs in fiscal 2000. The report would provide $27.7 billion for highways, $5.8 billion for mass transit, $10.1 billion for the Federal Aviation Administration (FAA), $4 billion for the Coast Guard and $571 million for Amtrak. The conference report includes Senate-passed language to fund the FAA entirely out of the Airport and Airway Trust Fund, which would eliminate the general fund contribution to the agency. Adopted (thus sent to the Senate) 304-91: R 168-37; D 135-54 (ND 96-42, SD 39-12); I 1-0. Oct. 1, 1999.

467. HR 1906. Fiscal 2000 Agricultural Appropriations/Rule. Adoption of the rule (H Res 317) to provide for House floor consideration of the conference report to appropriate $69 billion for the Agriculture Department, the Food and Drug Administration, and rural development programs in fiscal 2000. Adopted 230-188: R 188-30; D 42-157 (ND 23-124, SD 19-33); I 0-1. Oct. 1, 1999.

468. HR 1906. Fiscal 2000 Agricultural Appropriations/Motion to Recommit. Kaptur, D-Ohio, motion to recommit to the conference committee the bill to provide $69 billion in spending. Motion rejected 187-228: R 21-196; D 165-32 (ND 130-16, SD 35-16); I 1-0. Oct. 1, 1999.

469. HR 1906. Fiscal 2000 Agricultural Appropriations/Conference Report. Adoption of the conference report on the bill to appropriate $69 billion for the Agriculture Department, the Food and Drug Administration, and rural development programs in fiscal 2000. The bill includes $8.7 billion in emergency spending for farmers. Adopted (thus sent to the Senate) 240-175: R 154-63; D 86-111 (ND 46-100, SD 40-11); I 0. Oct. 1, 1999.

470. H Res 181. Condemning Colombia Kidnapping/Adoption. Bereuter, R-Neb., motion to suspend the rules and adopt the resolution condemning the kidnapping and murder of three U.S. citizens by the Revolutionary Armed Forces of Colombia. Motion agreed to 413-0: R 213-0; D 199-0 (ND 147-0, SD 52-0); I 1-0. Oct. 4, 1999. A two-thirds majority of those present and voting (276 in this case) is required for adoption under suspension of the rules.

471. HR 1451. Lincoln Bicentennial Commission/Passage. Biggert, R-Ill., motion to suspend the rules and pass the bill to create a commission to study the best way to honor the 200th anniversary, in 2009, of the birth of Abraham Lincoln. Motion agreed to 411-2: R 212-2; D 198-0 (ND 146-0, SD 52-0); I 1-0. Oct. 4, 1999. A two-thirds majority of those present and voting (276 in this case) is required for passage under suspension of the rules.

472. HR 2684. Fiscal 2000 VA-HUD Appropriations/Motion to Instruct. Mollohan, D-W.Va., motion to instruct the managers on the part of the House to agree with the higher funding levels recommended in the Senate amendment for the Department of Housing and Urban Development; for the Science, Aeronautics and Technology and Mission Support accounts of the National Aeronautics and Space Administration; and for the National Science Foundation. Motion agreed to 306-113: R 110-107; D 195-6 (ND 145-4, SD 50-2); I 1-0. Oct. 4, 1999.

473. HR 2466. Fiscal 2000 Interior Appropriations/Motion to Instruct. Dicks, D-Wash., motion to instruct House conferees to agree with the higher funding levels recommended in the Senate amendment for the National Endowment for the Arts and the National Endowment for the Humanities and to disagree with the Senate-passed provisions that would nullify a ruling that limits mining waste disposal to one five-acre site per mine on federal land. Motion agreed to 218-199: R 31-185; D 186-14 (ND 145-3, SD 41-11); I 1-0. Oct. 4, 1999.

Key

- Y Voted for (yea).
- # Paired for.
- + Announced for.
- N Voted against (nay).
- X Paired against.
- – Announced against.
- P Voted "present."
- C Voted "present" to avoid possible conflict of interest.
- ? Did not vote or otherwise make a position known.

•

Democrats ***Republicans***
Independents

	466	467	468	469	470	471	472	473
ALABAMA								
1 ***Callahan***	Y	Y	N	Y	Y	Y	Y	N
2 ***Everett***	Y	Y	N	Y	Y	Y	Y	N
3 ***Riley***	Y	Y	N	Y	Y	Y	Y	N
4 ***Aderholt***	Y	Y	N	Y	Y	Y	Y	N
5 Cramer	Y	Y	Y	Y	Y	Y	Y	Y
6 ***Bachus***	Y	N	N	Y	Y	Y	Y	N
7 Hilliard	Y	Y	Y	Y	Y	Y	Y	Y
ALASKA								
AL ***Young***	?	Y	N	Y	Y	Y	Y	N
ARIZONA								
1 ***Salmon***	N	N	N	N	Y	Y	Y	N
2 Pastor	Y	Y	Y	Y	Y	Y	Y	Y
3 ***Stump***	Y	Y	N	Y	Y	Y	Y	N
4 ***Shadegg***	Y	Y	N	Y	Y	Y	N	N
5 ***Kolbe***	Y	Y	N	Y	Y	Y	Y	N
6 ***Hayworth***	Y	Y	N	Y	Y	Y	Y	N
ARKANSAS								
1 Berry	N	Y	N	Y	Y	Y	Y	N
2 Snyder	N	N	N	Y	Y	Y	Y	Y
3 ***Hutchinson***	N	N	N	Y	Y	Y	N	N
4 ***Dickey***	Y	Y	N	Y	Y	Y	N	N
CALIFORNIA								
1 Thompson	Y	N	N	Y	Y	Y	Y	Y
2 ***Herger***	N	Y	N	Y	Y	Y	Y	N
3 ***Ose***	Y	Y	N	Y	Y	Y	N	N
4 ***Doolittle***	N	Y	N	Y	Y	Y	N	N
5 Matsui	Y	N	Y	N	Y	Y	Y	Y
6 Woolsey	Y	N	Y	N	Y	Y	Y	Y
7 Miller, George	N	N	Y	N	Y	Y	Y	Y
8 Pelosi	Y	N	Y	N	Y	Y	Y	Y
9 Lee	Y	N	Y	N	Y	Y	Y	Y
10 Tauscher	Y	N	Y	N	Y	Y	Y	Y
11 ***Pombo***	Y	Y	N	Y	Y	Y	N	N
12 Lantos	Y	N	Y	N	Y	Y	Y	Y
13 Stark	Y	N	Y	N	Y	Y	Y	Y
14 Eshoo	Y	N	Y	N	Y	Y	Y	Y
15 ***Campbell***	Y	Y	N	N	Y	Y	N	N
16 Lofgren	Y	N	Y	N	Y	Y	Y	Y
17 Farr	Y	N	Y	Y	?	?	?	?
18 Condit	N	N	Y	Y	Y	Y	N	N
19 ***Radanovich***	Y	Y	N	Y	Y	Y	N	N
20 Dooley	Y	Y	N	Y	Y	Y	Y	Y
21 ***Thomas***	Y	Y	N	Y	Y	Y	Y	N
22 Capps	Y	Y	Y	Y	Y	Y	Y	Y
23 ***Gallegly***	Y	Y	N	Y	Y	Y	Y	N
24 Sherman	Y	N	Y	N	Y	Y	Y	Y
25 ***McKeon***	Y	Y	N	Y	Y	Y	N	N
26 Berman	?	?	?	–	?	?	?	?
27 ***Rogan***	Y	Y	N	Y	Y	Y	Y	N
28 ***Dreier***	Y	Y	N	Y	Y	Y	Y	N
29 Waxman	?	?	?	?	Y	Y	Y	Y
30 Becerra	Y	N	Y	N	Y	Y	Y	Y
31 Martinez	Y	N	Y	N	Y	Y	Y	Y
32 Dixon	Y	N	Y	N	Y	Y	Y	Y
33 Roybal-Allard	Y	N	Y	N	Y	Y	Y	Y
34 Napolitano	Y	N	Y	N	Y	Y	Y	Y
35 Waters	N	N	Y	N	Y	Y	Y	Y
36 ***Kuykendall***	Y	Y	N	Y	Y	Y	Y	Y
37 Millender-McD.	N	Y	Y	N	Y	Y	Y	Y
38 ***Horn***	N	Y	N	Y	Y	Y	Y	Y
39 ***Royce***	N	Y	N	N	Y	Y	N	N
40 ***Lewis***	Y	Y	N	Y	Y	Y	Y	N
41 ***Miller***	Y	Y	N	Y	Y	Y	Y	N
42 Vacant								
43 ***Calvert***	Y	Y	N	Y	Y	?	Y	N
44 ***Bono***	Y	Y	N	Y	Y	Y	Y	N
45 ***Rohrabacher***	Y	Y	N	N	Y	Y	N	N
46 Sanchez	N	Y	Y	Y	Y	?	Y	Y
47 ***Cox***	Y	Y	N	N	Y	Y	N	N
48 ***Packard***	Y	Y	N	Y	Y	Y	N	N
49 ***Bilbray***	Y	Y	N	Y	Y	Y	Y	Y
50 Filner	N	N	Y	N	Y	Y	Y	Y
51 ***Cunningham***	Y	Y	N	Y	Y	Y	N	N
52 ***Hunter***	Y	Y	N	Y	Y	Y	N	N
COLORADO								
1 DeGette	Y	N	Y	N	Y	Y	Y	Y
2 Udall	Y	N	Y	N	Y	Y	Y	Y
3 ***McInnis***	Y	Y	N	Y	Y	Y	N	N
4 ***Schaffer***	N	Y	N	Y	Y	Y	N	N
5 ***Hefley***	N	Y	N	N	Y	Y	N	N
6 ***Tancredo***	Y	Y	N	N	Y	Y	N	N
CONNECTICUT								
1 Larson	Y	N	Y	N	Y	Y	Y	Y
2 Gejdenson	?	N	Y	N	Y	Y	Y	Y
3 DeLauro	Y	N	Y	N	Y	Y	Y	Y
4 ***Shays***	Y	Y	N	N	Y	Y	N	Y
5 Maloney	Y	N	Y	N	Y	Y	Y	Y
6 ***Johnson***	?	N	N	N	Y	Y	Y	Y
DELAWARE								
AL ***Castle***	Y	Y	N	N	Y	Y	N	Y
FLORIDA								
1 ***Scarborough***	?	?	?	?	?	?	?	?
2 Boyd	Y	N	Y	Y	Y	Y	Y	Y
3 Brown	?	N	Y	N	?	?	?	?
4 ***Fowler***	Y	Y	N	Y	+	+	Y	Y
5 Thurman	Y	N	Y	N	Y	Y	Y	Y
6 ***Stearns***	N	Y	N	N	Y	Y	N	N
7 ***Mica***	Y	Y	N	Y	Y	Y	N	N
8 ***McCollum***	Y	Y	N	Y	Y	Y	Y	N
9 ***Bilirakis***	Y	Y	N	Y	Y	Y	N	N
10 ***Young***	Y	Y	N	Y	Y	Y	N	N
11 Davis	Y	N	Y	Y	Y	Y	Y	Y
12 ***Canady***	Y	Y	N	Y	Y	Y	Y	N
13 ***Miller***	Y	N	N	N	Y	Y	N	N
14 ***Goss***	Y	Y	N	Y	Y	Y	Y	N
15 ***Weldon***	Y	Y	?	?	Y	Y	Y	N
16 ***Foley***	Y	Y	Y	Y	Y	Y	Y	Y
17 Meek	Y	N	Y	N	Y	Y	Y	Y
18 ***Ros-Lehtinen***	Y	Y	N	Y	Y	Y	Y	N
19 Wexler	Y	N	N	Y	Y	Y	Y	Y
20 Deutsch	Y	N	Y	N	Y	Y	Y	Y
21 ***Diaz-Balart***	Y	Y	N	Y	Y	Y	Y	N
22 ***Shaw***	Y	Y	N	N	Y	Y	Y	N
23 Hastings	N	N	Y	Y	Y	Y	Y	Y
GEORGIA								
1 ***Kingston***	Y	Y	N	Y	Y	Y	N	N
2 Bishop	Y	Y	Y	Y	Y	Y	Y	Y
3 ***Collins***	Y	Y	N	N	Y	Y	N	N
4 McKinney	Y	N	Y	N	?	?	?	?
5 Lewis	Y	N	Y	N	Y	Y	Y	Y
6 ***Isakson***	Y	Y	N	Y	Y	Y	Y	N
7 ***Barr***	Y	Y	N	N	Y	Y	N	N
8 ***Chambliss***	Y	Y	N	Y	Y	Y	N	N
9 ***Deal***	Y	Y	N	N	Y	Y	Y	N
10 ***Norwood***	Y	Y	Y	N	Y	Y	Y	N
11 ***Linder***	Y	Y	N	Y	Y	Y	N	N
HAWAII								
1 Abercrombie	Y	N	Y	Y	Y	Y	Y	Y
2 Mink	Y	N	N	Y	Y	Y	Y	Y
IDAHO								
1 ***Chenoweth***	?	?	?	?	?	?	?	?
2 ***Simpson***	Y	Y	N	Y	Y	Y	N	N
ILLINOIS								
1 Rush	?	?	?	?	Y	Y	Y	Y
2 Jackson	Y	N	Y	Y	Y	Y	Y	Y
3 Lipinski	N	N	Y	N	Y	Y	Y	Y
4 Gutierrez	N	N	Y	N	Y	Y	Y	Y
5 Blagojevich	N	N	Y	Y	Y	Y	Y	Y
6 ***Hyde***	Y	Y	N	Y	Y	Y	N	N
7 Davis	N	N	Y	N	Y	Y	Y	Y
8 ***Crane***	Y	Y	N	N	Y	Y	N	N
9 Schakowsky	N	N	Y	Y	Y	Y	Y	Y
10 ***Porter***	?	Y	N	Y	Y	Y	Y	Y
11 ***Weller***	Y	Y	N	Y	Y	Y	Y	N
12 Costello	Y	N	Y	Y	Y	Y	Y	Y
13 ***Biggert***	Y	Y	N	Y	Y	Y	Y	Y
14 ***Hastert***		Y						

ND Northern Democrats SD Southern Democrats

	466	467	468	469	470	471	472	473
15 ***Ewing***	Y	Y	N	Y	Y	Y	Y	N
16 ***Manzullo***	N	Y	N	Y	Y	Y	N	N
17 Evans	Y	Y	Y	Y	Y	Y	Y	Y
18 ***LaHood***	N	Y	N	Y	Y	Y	N	Y
19 Phelps	N	Y	Y	Y	Y	Y	Y	Y
20 ***Shimkus***	Y	Y	N	Y	Y	Y	N	N
INDIANA								
1 Visclosky	Y	N	Y	N	Y	Y	Y	Y
2 ***McIntosh***	Y	Y	N	Y	Y	Y	N	N
3 Roemer	Y	N	Y	Y	Y	Y	N	Y
4 ***Souder***	Y	Y	N	Y	Y	Y	N	N
5 ***Buyer***	Y	Y	N	Y	Y	Y	N	N
6 ***Burton***	+	Y	N	Y	Y	Y	N	N
7 ***Pease***	N	Y	N	Y	Y	Y	N	N
8 ***Hostettler***	N	Y	N	N	Y	Y	N	N
9 Hill	Y	Y	Y	Y	Y	Y	N	Y
10 Carson	Y	N	+	–	Y	Y	Y	Y
IOWA								
1 ***Leach***	Y	Y	N	Y	Y	Y	Y	Y
2 ***Nussle***	Y	Y	N	Y	Y	Y	N	N
3 Boswell	N	Y	N	Y	Y	Y	Y	Y
4 ***Ganske***	Y	Y	N	Y	Y	Y	Y	N
5 ***Latham***	Y	Y	N	Y	Y	Y	N	N
KANSAS								
1 ***Moran***	N	Y	N	Y	Y	Y	N	N
2 ***Ryun***	Y	Y	N	Y	Y	Y	N	N
3 Moore	Y	N	Y	Y	Y	Y	Y	Y
4 ***Tiahrt***	Y	Y	N	Y	Y	Y	N	N
KENTUCKY								
1 ***Whitfield***	Y	Y	N	Y	Y	Y	Y	N
2 ***Lewis***	Y	Y	N	Y	Y	Y	Y	N
3 ***Northup***	+	Y	N	Y	Y	Y	Y	N
4 Lucas	Y	Y	N	Y	Y	Y	Y	N
5 ***Rogers***	Y	Y	N	Y	Y	Y	Y	N
6 ***Fletcher***	Y	Y	N	Y	Y	Y	Y	N
LOUISIANA								
1 ***Vitter***	Y	N	Y	N	Y	Y	N	N
2 Jefferson	?	?	?	?	Y	Y	Y	Y
3 ***Tauzin***	Y	Y	N	Y	?	Y	N	N
4 ***McCrery***	Y	N	N	Y	Y	Y	Y	N
5 ***Cooksey***	N	N	N	Y	Y	Y	Y	N
6 ***Baker***	N	Y	N	Y	Y	Y	Y	N
7 John	N	N	Y	Y	Y	Y	Y	N
MAINE								
1 Allen	Y	N	Y	N	Y	Y	Y	Y
2 Baldacci	N	N	Y	N	Y	Y	Y	Y
MARYLAND								
1 ***Gilchrest***	N	Y	N	N	Y	Y	Y	N
2 ***Ehrlich***	?	Y	Y	N	Y	Y	N	N
3 Cardin	N	N	Y	N	Y	Y	Y	Y
4 Wynn	Y	N	Y	N	Y	Y	Y	Y
5 Hoyer	Y	N	Y	N	Y	Y	Y	Y
6 ***Bartlett***	Y	N	Y	N	Y	Y	Y	N
7 Cummings	–	N	Y	N	Y	Y	Y	Y
8 ***Morella***	Y	Y	N	Y	Y	Y	Y	Y
MASSACHUSETTS								
1 Olver	Y	N	Y	N	Y	Y	Y	Y
2 Neal	Y	N	Y	N	?	?	?	?
3 McGovern	Y	N	Y	N	Y	Y	Y	Y
4 Frank	Y	N	Y	Y	Y	Y	Y	Y
5 Meehan	Y	N	Y	N	Y	Y	Y	Y
6 Tierney	Y	N	Y	N	Y	Y	Y	Y
7 Markey	Y	N	Y	N	Y	Y	Y	Y
8 Capuano	Y	Y	N	Y	Y	Y	Y	Y
9 Moakley	Y	N	Y	N	Y	Y	Y	Y
10 Delahunt	?	N	Y	N	Y	Y	Y	Y
MICHIGAN								
1 Stupak	Y	Y	?	?	Y	Y	Y	Y
2 ***Hoekstra***	Y	Y	N	N	Y	Y	N	N
3 ***Ehlers***	Y	Y	N	N	Y	Y	Y	N
4 ***Camp***	Y	N	N	Y	Y	Y	N	N
5 Barcia	N	N	Y	Y	Y	Y	Y	Y
6 ***Upton***	Y	Y	N	N	Y	Y	N	Y
7 ***Smith***	Y	Y	N	Y	Y	Y	Y	N
8 Stabenow	Y	N	N	Y	Y	Y	Y	Y
9 Kildee	N	N	Y	N	Y	Y	Y	Y
10 Bonior	Y	N	Y	N	Y	Y	Y	Y
11 ***Knollenberg***	Y	Y	N	Y	Y	Y	Y	N
12 Levin	+	–	+	–	Y	Y	Y	Y
13 Rivers	Y	N	Y	N	Y	Y	Y	Y
14 Conyers	N	N	Y	N	Y	Y	Y	Y
15 Kilpatrick	Y	N	Y	N	Y	Y	Y	Y
16 Dingell	N	Y	Y	N	Y	Y	Y	?

	466	467	468	469	470	471	472	473
MINNESOTA								
1 ***Gutknecht***	Y	Y	N	Y	Y	Y	N	N
2 Minge	Y	Y	Y	Y	Y	Y	Y	Y
3 ***Ramstad***	Y	Y	N	Y	Y	Y	N	Y
4 Vento	Y	N	Y	N	Y	Y	Y	Y
5 Sabo	Y	N	Y	Y	Y	Y	Y	Y
6 Luther	Y	N	Y	N	Y	Y	Y	Y
7 Peterson	N	N	Y	N	Y	Y	N	Y
8 Oberstar	N	N	Y	N	Y	Y	Y	Y
MISSISSIPPI								
1 ***Wicker***	Y	Y	N	Y	Y	Y	Y	N
2 Thompson	Y	Y	Y	Y	Y	Y	Y	Y
3 ***Pickering***	+	N	N	Y	Y	Y	Y	N
4 Shows	N	N	Y	Y	Y	Y	Y	N
5 Taylor	Y	Y	Y	N	Y	Y	Y	N
MISSOURI								
1 Clay	?	?	?	?	Y	Y	Y	Y
2 ***Talent***	Y	Y	N	Y	?	?	Y	N
3 Gephardt	Y	N	Y	N	Y	Y	Y	Y
4 Skelton	Y	Y	Y	Y	Y	Y	Y	N
5 McCarthy	Y	N	Y	Y	Y	Y	Y	Y
6 Danner	Y	Y	Y	Y	Y	Y	Y	Y
7 ***Blunt***	Y	Y	N	Y	Y	Y	Y	N
8 ***Emerson***	Y	Y	N	Y	Y	Y	Y	N
9 ***Hulshof***	Y	Y	N	Y	Y	Y	N	N
MONTANA								
AL ***Hill***	Y	Y	N	Y	Y	Y	N	N
NEBRASKA								
1 ***Bereuter***	N	Y	N	Y	Y	Y	Y	N
2 ***Terry***	N	Y	N	Y	Y	Y	N	N
3 ***Barrett***	Y	Y	N	Y	Y	Y	N	N
NEVADA								
1 Berkley	N	N	Y	Y	?	?	Y	Y
2 ***Gibbons***	Y	Y	N	Y	Y	Y	Y	N
NEW HAMPSHIRE								
1 ***Sununu***	Y	Y	N	N	Y	Y	N	N
2 ***Bass***	N	?	N	N	Y	Y	Y	Y
NEW JERSEY								
1 Andrews	Y	N	Y	N	Y	Y	Y	Y
2 ***LoBiondo***	Y	N	Y	N	Y	Y	Y	Y
3 ***Saxton***	Y	N	Y	N	Y	Y	Y	N
4 ***Smith***	Y	N	Y	N	Y	Y	Y	Y
5 ***Roukema***	Y	N	Y	N	Y	Y	Y	Y
6 Pallone	Y	N	Y	N	Y	Y	Y	Y
7 ***Franks***	Y	N	Y	N	Y	Y	Y	Y
8 Pascrell	Y	N	Y	N	Y	Y	Y	Y
9 Rothman	Y	N	Y	N	Y	Y	Y	Y
10 Payne	Y	N	Y	N	Y	Y	Y	Y
11 ***Frelinghuysen***	Y	Y	N	N	Y	Y	Y	Y
12 Holt	Y	N	Y	N	Y	Y	Y	Y
13 Menendez	Y	N	Y	Y	Y	Y	Y	Y
NEW MEXICO								
1 ***Wilson***	Y	Y	N	Y	Y	Y	Y	N
2 ***Skeen***	Y	Y	N	Y	Y	Y	Y	N
3 Udall	Y	N	Y	Y	Y	Y	Y	Y
NEW YORK								
1 Forbes	Y	N	Y	N	Y	Y	Y	Y
2 ***Lazio***	Y	N	N	N	Y	Y	Y	Y
3 ***King***	Y	N	Y	N	Y	Y	N	N
4 McCarthy	Y	N	Y	N	Y	Y	Y	Y
5 Ackerman	?	N	Y	N	Y	Y	Y	Y
6 Meeks	?	?	?	?	?	?	?	?
7 Crowley	Y	N	Y	Y	Y	Y	Y	Y
8 Nadler	N	N	Y	N	Y	Y	Y	Y
9 Weiner	N	N	Y	N	Y	Y	Y	Y
10 Towns	Y	N	Y	Y	?	?	?	?
11 Owens	Y	N	Y	N	Y	Y	Y	Y
12 Velázquez	+	N	Y	N	Y	Y	Y	Y
13 ***Fossella***	+	N	N	N	Y	Y	N	N
14 Maloney	N	N	Y	N	Y	Y	Y	Y
15 Rangel	Y	N	Y	N	Y	Y	Y	Y
16 Serrano	Y	Y	Y	N	Y	Y	Y	Y
17 Engel	Y	N	Y	N	Y	Y	Y	Y
18 Lowey	Y	N	Y	N	Y	Y	Y	Y
19 ***Kelly***	N	N	N	N	Y	Y	Y	Y
20 ***Gilman***	Y	N	Y	N	Y	Y	Y	Y
21 McNulty	Y	N	Y	N	Y	Y	Y	Y
22 ***Sweeney***	N	N	Y	N	Y	Y	N	N
23 ***Boehlert***	N	N	Y	N	Y	Y	Y	Y
24 ***McHugh***	?	N	Y	N	Y	Y	Y	Y
25 ***Walsh***	Y	N	N	N	Y	Y	Y	N
26 Hinchey	?	N	Y	N	Y	Y	Y	Y
27 ***Reynolds***	Y	Y	N	N	Y	Y	Y	N
28 Slaughter	N	N	Y	N	Y	Y	Y	Y
29 LaFalce	Y	N	Y	N	Y	Y	Y	Y

	466	467	468	469	470	471	472	473
30 ***Quinn***	?	N	N	N	Y	Y	Y	Y
31 ***Houghton***	Y	Y	N	N	Y	Y	Y	Y
NORTH CAROLINA								
1 Clayton	Y	N	Y	Y	Y	Y	Y	Y
2 Etheridge	Y	N	Y	Y	+	+	+	+
3 ***Jones***	N	Y	N	Y	Y	Y	N	N
4 Price	Y	N	Y	Y	Y	Y	Y	Y
5 ***Burr***	Y	Y	N	N	Y	Y	N	N
6 ***Coble***	N	Y	N	Y	Y	Y	N	N
7 McIntyre	Y	Y	Y	Y	Y	Y	Y	Y
8 ***Hayes***	Y	Y	N	Y	Y	Y	N	N
9 ***Myrick***	Y	Y	N	Y	Y	Y	N	N
10 ***Ballenger***	Y	Y	N	N	Y	Y	Y	N
11 ***Taylor***	Y	Y	?	?	?	?	?	?
12 Watt	Y	N	Y	Y	Y	Y	Y	Y
NORTH DAKOTA								
AL Pomeroy	Y	?	Y	Y	Y	Y	Y	Y
OHIO								
1 ***Chabot***	Y	Y	N	N	Y	Y	N	N
2 ***Portman***	Y	Y	N	Y	Y	Y	Y	N
3 Hall	Y	Y	N	Y	Y	Y	Y	Y
4 ***Oxley***	Y	Y	N	Y	Y	Y	N	?
5 ***Gillmor***	Y	Y	N	Y	Y	Y	Y	N
6 Strickland	Y	N	Y	Y	Y	Y	Y	Y
7 ***Hobson***	Y	Y	N	Y	Y	Y	Y	N
8 ***Boehner***	Y	Y	N	Y	Y	Y	N	N
9 Kaptur	Y	N	Y	N	Y	Y	Y	Y
10 Kucinich	N	N	Y	N	Y	Y	Y	Y
11 Jones	?	N	Y	N	Y	Y	Y	Y
12 ***Kasich***	N	Y	N	Y	Y	Y	N	N
13 Brown	Y	N	Y	N	Y	Y	Y	Y
14 Sawyer	Y	N	Y	N	Y	Y	Y	Y
15 ***Pryce***	Y	Y	N	Y	Y	Y	N	N
16 ***Regula***	Y	Y	N	Y	Y	Y	Y	N
17 Traficant	N	Y	N	Y	Y	Y	Y	N
18 ***Ney***	Y	Y	N	Y	Y	Y	Y	N
19 ***LaTourette***	N	Y	N	Y	Y	Y	Y	N
OKLAHOMA								
1 ***Largent***	Y	Y	N	Y	Y	Y	N	N
2 ***Coburn***	Y	Y	N	Y	Y	Y	N	N
3 ***Watkins***	Y	Y	N	Y	Y	Y	Y	N
4 ***Watts***	Y	Y	N	Y	Y	Y	Y	N
5 ***Istook***	Y	Y	Y	N	Y	Y	N	N
6 ***Lucas***	Y	Y	N	Y	Y	Y	Y	N
OREGON								
1 Wu	?	?	?	?	Y	Y	Y	Y
2 ***Walden***	Y	Y	N	Y	Y	Y	N	N
3 Blumenauer	N	N	Y	N	?	?	?	?
4 DeFazio	N	N	Y	N	Y	Y	Y	Y
5 Hooley	+	–	+	+	Y	Y	Y	Y
PENNSYLVANIA								
1 Brady	N	N	Y	N	Y	Y	Y	Y
2 Fattah	?	N	Y	N	Y	Y	Y	Y
3 Borski	N	N	Y	N	Y	Y	Y	Y
4 Klink	N	N	Y	N	Y	Y	Y	Y
5 ***Peterson***	Y	N	N	N	Y	Y	Y	N
6 Holden	N	N	Y	N	Y	Y	Y	Y
7 ***Weldon***	Y	Y	N	N	Y	Y	Y	N
8 ***Greenwood***	Y	Y	N	Y	Y	Y	Y	Y
9 ***Shuster***	N	N	Y	N	Y	Y	N	N
10 ***Sherwood***	Y	N	Y	N	Y	Y	N	N
11 Kanjorski	Y	N	Y	N	Y	Y	Y	Y
12 Murtha	Y	N	Y	N	Y	Y	Y	Y
13 Hoeffel	N	N	Y	N	Y	Y	Y	Y
14 Coyne	Y	N	Y	N	Y	Y	Y	Y
15 ***Toomey***	Y	Y	Y	N	Y	Y	N	N
16 ***Pitts***	Y	Y	N	N	Y	Y	N	N
17 ***Gekas***	Y	Y	N	N	Y	Y	Y	N
18 Doyle	Y	N	Y	N	+	+	+	+
19 ***Goodling***	+	–	Y	N	Y	Y	N	N
20 Mascara	Y	N	Y	N	Y	Y	Y	Y
21 ***English***	Y	N	Y	N	Y	Y	Y	N
RHODE ISLAND								
1 Kennedy	Y	N	Y	N	+	+	Y	Y
2 Weygand	Y	N	Y	N	Y	Y	Y	Y
SOUTH CAROLINA								
1 ***Sanford***	N	Y	N	N	Y	N	N	N
2 ***Spence***	Y	Y	N	Y	Y	Y	Y	N
3 ***Graham***	Y	Y	N	Y	Y	Y	Y	N
4 ***DeMint***	Y	Y	N	Y	Y	Y	N	N
5 Spratt	Y	Y	Y	Y	Y	Y	Y	Y
6 Clyburn	Y	Y	Y	Y	Y	Y	Y	Y
SOUTH DAKOTA								
AL ***Thune***	N	Y	N	Y	Y	Y	N	N

	466	467	468	469	470	471	472	473
TENNESSEE								
1 ***Jenkins***	Y	Y	N	Y	Y	Y	Y	N
2 ***Duncan***	N	Y	N	N	Y	Y	N	N
3 ***Wamp***	Y	Y	N	Y	Y	Y	Y	N
4 ***Hilleary***	Y	Y	N	Y	Y	Y	N	N
5 Clement	Y	N	Y	Y	Y	Y	Y	Y
6 Gordon	Y	N	Y	Y	Y	Y	Y	Y
7 ***Bryant***	Y	Y	N	Y	Y	Y	N	N
8 Tanner	Y	Y	N	Y	Y	Y	Y	N
9 Ford	?	?	?	?	Y	Y	Y	Y
TEXAS								
1 Sandlin	N	Y	N	Y	Y	Y	Y	N
2 Turner	Y	N	Y	Y	Y	Y	N	N
3 ***Johnson, Sam***	?	Y	N	Y	Y	Y	N	N
4 Hall	N	Y	N	Y	Y	Y	Y	N
5 ***Sessions***	Y	Y	N	Y	Y	Y	N	N
6 ***Barton***	?	Y	N	Y	Y	Y	N	N
7 ***Archer***	Y	Y	N	Y	Y	Y	N	N
8 ***Brady***	Y	Y	N	Y	Y	Y	Y	N
9 Lampson	N	N	Y	Y	Y	Y	Y	Y
10 Doggett	N	N	Y	N	Y	Y	Y	Y
11 Edwards	Y	Y	N	Y	Y	Y	Y	Y
12 ***Granger***	Y	Y	N	Y	Y	Y	Y	N
13 ***Thornberry***	Y	Y	N	Y	Y	Y	N	N
14 ***Paul***	N	Y	N	N	Y	N	N	N
15 Hinojosa	+	–	+	+	Y	Y	Y	Y
16 Reyes	Y	Y	N	Y	Y	Y	Y	Y
17 Stenholm	Y	Y	N	Y	Y	Y	Y	N
18 Jackson-Lee	Y	N	Y	N	Y	Y	Y	Y
19 ***Combest***	Y	Y	N	Y	Y	Y	N	N
20 Gonzalez	Y	N	Y	Y	Y	Y	Y	Y
21 ***Smith***	Y	Y	N	Y	Y	Y	Y	N
22 ***DeLay***	Y	Y	N	Y	Y	Y	N	N
23 ***Bonilla***	Y	Y	N	Y	Y	Y	N	N
24 Frost	N	N	N	Y	Y	Y	Y	Y
25 Bentsen	Y	N	Y	Y	Y	Y	Y	Y
26 ***Armey***	Y	Y	N	Y	Y	Y	N	N
27 Ortiz	Y	N	Y	Y	Y	Y	Y	Y
28 Rodriguez	Y	N	N	Y	Y	Y	Y	Y
29 Green	N	N	Y	N	Y	Y	Y	Y
30 Johnson, E.B.	N	N	Y	Y	Y	Y	Y	Y
UTAH								
1 ***Hansen***	Y	Y	N	Y	Y	Y	Y	N
2 ***Cook***	N	Y	N	Y	Y	Y	Y	N
3 ***Cannon***	Y	Y	N	Y	Y	Y	N	N
VERMONT								
AL *Sanders*	Y	N	Y	N	Y	Y	Y	Y
VIRGINIA								
1 ***Bateman***	P	Y	N	Y	Y	Y	Y	N
2 Pickett	Y	Y	N	Y	Y	Y	Y	Y
3 Scott	Y	N	N	Y	Y	Y	Y	Y
4 Sisisky	Y	Y	N	Y	Y	Y	Y	Y
5 Goode	Y	Y	N	Y	Y	Y	N	N
6 ***Goodlatte***	Y	Y	N	Y	?	Y	N	N
7 ***Bliley***	Y	Y	N	Y	?	?	?	?
8 Moran	Y	N	Y	N	Y	Y	Y	Y
9 Boucher	Y	N	?	?	Y	Y	Y	Y
10 ***Wolf***	Y	Y	N	Y	Y	Y	Y	Y
11 ***Davis***	Y	Y	N	Y	Y	Y	Y	Y
WASHINGTON								
1 Inslee	Y	N	Y	N	Y	Y	Y	Y
2 ***Metcalf***	N	Y	N	Y	Y	Y	N	N
3 Baird	N	N	Y	N	Y	Y	Y	Y
4 ***Hastings***	Y	Y	N	Y	Y	Y	Y	N
5 ***Nethercutt***	Y	Y	N	Y	Y	Y	Y	N
6 Dicks	Y	N	Y	N	Y	Y	Y	Y
7 McDermott	N	N	Y	N	Y	Y	Y	Y
8 ***Dunn***	Y	Y	N	Y	Y	Y	N	N
9 Smith	Y	N	Y	Y	Y	Y	Y	Y
WEST VIRGINIA								
1 Mollohan	?	Y	N	Y	Y	Y	Y	Y
2 Wise	N	Y	N	Y	Y	Y	Y	Y
3 Rahall	N	Y	N	Y	Y	Y	Y	Y
WISCONSIN								
1 ***Ryan***	Y	Y	N	Y	Y	Y	N	N
2 Baldwin	N	N	N	Y	Y	Y	Y	Y
3 Kind	N	N	N	Y	Y	Y	Y	Y
4 Kleczka	–	Y	N	Y	Y	Y	Y	Y
5 Barrett	N	N	N	Y	Y	Y	Y	Y
6 ***Petri***	N	Y	N	Y	Y	Y	N	N
7 Obey	Y	Y	N	Y	Y	Y	Y	Y
8 ***Green***	Y	Y	N	Y	Y	Y	N	N
9 ***Sensenbrenner***	N	Y	N	N	Y	Y	Y	N
WYOMING								
AL ***Cubin***	N	Y	N	Y	Y	Y	N	N

Southern states - Ala., Ark., Fla., Ga., Ky., La., Miss., N.C., Okla., S.C., Tenn., Texas, Va.

474. HR 1663. National Medal of Honor Memorial/Passage. Stump, R-Ariz., motion to suspend the rules and pass the bill to recognize three sites as National Medal of Honor memorials. The sites are in Riverside, Calif.; Indianapolis, Ind.; and Mount Pleasant, S.C. Motion agreed to 424-0: R 217-0; D 206-0 (ND 153-0, SD 53-0); I 1-0. Oct. 5, 1999. A two-thirds majority of those present and voting (283 in this case) is required for passage under suspension of the rules.

475. H J Res 65. Honor Veterans of Battle of the Bulge/Passage. Stump, R-Ariz., motion to suspend the rules and pass the joint resolution to honor U.S. Army veterans who fought in the Battle of the Bulge during World War II. Motion agreed to 422-0: R 216-0; D 205-0 (ND 153-0, SD 52-0); I 1-0. Oct. 5, 1999. A two-thirds majority of those present and voting (282 in this case) is required for passage under suspension of the rules.

476. H Res 322. Sympathy for Victims of Hurricane Floyd/Adoption. Franks, R-N.J., motion to suspend the rules and adopt the resolution expressing the sympathy of the House of Representatives for those affected by Hurricane Floyd, which struck the Eastern seaboard from Sept. 14 to Sept. 17, 1999. Motion agreed to 417-0: R 211-0; D 205-0 (ND 151-0, SD 54-0); I 1-0. Oct. 5, 1999. A two-thirds majority of those present and voting (278 in this case) is required for adoption under suspension of the rules.

477. HR 764. Child Abuse Prevention/Abuse Definition. Jackson-Lee, D-Texas, amendment to clarify that child abuse includes child sexual abuse. Adopted 424-0: R 220-0; D 203-0 (ND 151-0, SD 52-0); I 1-0 . Oct. 5, 1999.

478. HR 764. Child Abuse Prevention/Crime Victims Fund Limitations. Jones, D-Ohio, amendment to direct that any increase in funding provided for prevention of child abuse under the measure would not be affected by any dollar limitation on the Crime Victims' Fund. Adopted 389-32: R 183-31; D 205-1 (ND 153-0, SD 52-1); I 1-0. Oct. 5, 1999.

479. HR 764. Child Abuse Prevention/Passage. Passage of the bill to prevent child abuse by increasing funds for victims' assistance and giving social workers access to conviction records. The measure would double the designation for child abuse victims within the Crime Victims' Fund to $20 million. Passed 425-2: R 217-2; D 207-0 (ND 154-0, SD 53-0); I 1-0. Oct. 5, 1999.

480. HR 2606. Fiscal 2000 Foreign Operations Appropriations/Conference Report. Adoption of the conference report on the bill to provide $12.7 billion for foreign aid programs in fiscal 2000. The measure is $1.9 billion less than the President's request. The measure does not include language that would reduce funding for abortions in international family planning programs. Adopted (thus sent to the Senate) 214-211: R 212-6; D 2-204 (ND 1-152, SD 1-52); I 0-1. Oct. 5, 1999. A "nay" was a vote in support of the president's position.

481. Procedural Motion/Journal. Approval of the House Journal of Oct. 5, 1999. Approved 340-68: R 190-17; D 149-51 (ND 106-41, SD 43-10); I 1-0. Oct. 6, 1999.

Key

- Y Voted for (yea).
- \# Paired for.
- \+ Announced for.
- N Voted against (nay).
- X Paired against.
- – Announced against.
- P Voted "present."
- C Voted "present" to avoid possible conflict of interest.
- ? Did not vote or otherwise make a position known.

•

Democrats ***Republicans***
Independents

	474	475	476	477	478	479	480	481
ALABAMA								
1 ***Callahan***	Y	Y	Y	Y	Y	Y	Y	Y
2 ***Everett***	Y	Y	Y	Y	N	Y	Y	Y
3 ***Riley***	Y	Y	Y	Y	N	Y	Y	N
4 ***Aderholt***	Y	Y	Y	Y	Y	Y	Y	N
5 Cramer	Y	Y	Y	Y	Y	Y	N	Y
6 ***Bachus***	Y	Y	Y	Y	Y	Y	Y	Y
7 Hilliard	Y	Y	Y	Y	Y	Y	N	N
ALASKA								
AL ***Young***	Y	Y	Y	Y	Y	Y	Y	?
ARIZONA								
1 ***Salmon***	Y	Y	Y	Y	Y	Y	Y	?
2 Pastor	Y	Y	Y	Y	Y	Y	N	N
3 ***Stump***	Y	Y	Y	Y	N	Y	Y	Y
4 ***Shadegg***	Y	Y	Y	Y	N	Y	Y	Y
5 ***Kolbe***	Y	Y	Y	Y	Y	Y	Y	Y
6 ***Hayworth***	Y	Y	Y	Y	Y	Y	Y	Y
ARKANSAS								
1 Berry	+	+	Y	Y	Y	Y	N	Y
2 Snyder	Y	Y	Y	Y	Y	Y	N	Y
3 ***Hutchinson***	Y	Y	Y	Y	?	Y	Y	?
4 ***Dickey***	Y	Y	Y	Y	Y	Y	Y	N
CALIFORNIA								
1 Thompson	Y	Y	Y	Y	Y	Y	N	N
2 ***Herger***	Y	Y	Y	Y	N	Y	Y	Y
3 ***Ose***	Y	Y	Y	Y	Y	Y	Y	Y
4 ***Doolittle***	Y	Y	Y	Y	N	Y	Y	Y
5 Matsui	Y	Y	Y	Y	Y	Y	N	Y
6 Woolsey	Y	Y	Y	Y	Y	Y	N	Y
7 Miller, George	Y	Y	Y	Y	Y	Y	N	Y
8 Pelosi	Y	Y	Y	Y	Y	Y	N	Y
9 Lee	Y	Y	Y	Y	Y	Y	N	Y
10 Tauscher	Y	Y	Y	Y	Y	Y	N	Y
11 ***Pombo***	Y	Y	Y	Y	Y	Y	Y	N
12 Lantos	Y	Y	Y	Y	Y	Y	N	Y
13 Stark	Y	Y	Y	Y	Y	Y	N	Y
14 Eshoo	Y	Y	Y	Y	Y	Y	N	Y
15 ***Campbell***	Y	Y	Y	Y	N	Y	Y	Y
16 Lofgren	Y	Y	Y	Y	Y	Y	N	Y
17 Farr	Y	Y	Y	Y	Y	Y	N	Y
18 Condit	Y	Y	Y	Y	Y	Y	N	Y
19 ***Radanovich***	Y	Y	Y	Y	Y	Y	Y	Y
20 Dooley	Y	Y	Y	Y	Y	Y	N	Y
21 ***Thomas***	Y	Y	Y	Y	Y	Y	Y	Y
22 Capps	Y	Y	Y	Y	Y	Y	N	Y
23 ***Gallegly***	Y	Y	Y	Y	Y	Y	Y	Y
24 Sherman	Y	Y	Y	Y	Y	Y	N	Y
25 ***McKeon***	Y	Y	Y	Y	Y	Y	Y	Y
26 Berman	Y	Y	Y	Y	Y	Y	N	Y
27 ***Rogan***	Y	Y	Y	Y	Y	Y	Y	?
28 ***Dreier***	Y	Y	Y	Y	Y	Y	Y	Y
29 Waxman	Y	Y	Y	Y	Y	Y	N	?
30 Becerra	Y	Y	Y	Y	Y	Y	N	N
31 Martinez	Y	Y	Y	Y	Y	Y	N	Y
32 Dixon	Y	Y	Y	Y	Y	Y	N	?
33 Roybal-Allard	Y	Y	Y	Y	Y	Y	N	Y
34 Napolitano	Y	Y	Y	Y	Y	Y	N	Y
35 Waters	Y	Y	Y	?	Y	Y	N	N
36 ***Kuykendall***	Y	Y	Y	Y	Y	Y	Y	Y
37 Millender-McD.	Y	Y	Y	Y	Y	Y	N	Y
38 ***Horn***	Y	Y	Y	Y	Y	Y	Y	Y
39 ***Royce***	Y	Y	?	Y	Y	Y	Y	Y
40 ***Lewis***	Y	Y	Y	Y	Y	Y	Y	Y
41 ***Miller***	Y	Y	Y	Y	Y	Y	Y	Y
42 Vacant								
43 ***Calvert***	Y	Y	Y	Y	Y	Y	Y	Y
44 ***Bono***	Y	Y	Y	Y	Y	Y	Y	Y
45 ***Rohrabacher***	Y	Y	Y	Y	Y	Y	Y	Y
46 Sanchez	Y	Y	Y	Y	Y	Y	N	Y
47 ***Cox***	Y	Y	Y	Y	Y	Y	Y	?
48 ***Packard***	Y	Y	Y	Y	Y	Y	Y	Y
49 ***Bilbray***	Y	?	Y	Y	Y	Y	Y	N
50 Filner	Y	Y	Y	Y	Y	Y	N	N
51 ***Cunningham***	Y	Y	Y	Y	Y	Y	Y	Y
52 ***Hunter***	Y	Y	Y	Y	N	Y	Y	Y
COLORADO								
1 DeGette	Y	Y	Y	Y	Y	Y	N	Y
2 Udall	Y	Y	Y	Y	Y	Y	N	N
3 ***McInnis***	Y	Y	Y	Y	Y	Y	Y	Y
4 ***Schaffer***	Y	Y	Y	Y	N	Y	N	N
5 ***Hefley***	Y	Y	Y	Y	N	Y	Y	N
6 ***Tancredo***	Y	Y	Y	Y	N	Y	Y	P
CONNECTICUT								
1 Larson	Y	Y	Y	Y	Y	Y	N	Y
2 Gejdenson	Y	Y	Y	Y	Y	Y	N	Y
3 DeLauro	Y	Y	Y	Y	Y	Y	N	N
4 ***Shays***	Y	Y	Y	Y	Y	Y	Y	Y
5 Maloney	Y	Y	Y	Y	Y	Y	N	Y
6 ***Johnson***	Y	Y	Y	Y	Y	Y	Y	Y
DELAWARE								
AL ***Castle***	Y	Y	Y	Y	Y	Y	Y	Y
FLORIDA								
1 ***Scarborough***	?	?	?	?	?	?	?	?
2 Boyd	Y	Y	Y	Y	Y	Y	N	Y
3 Brown	Y	Y	Y	Y	Y	Y	N	Y
4 ***Fowler***	Y	Y	Y	Y	Y	Y	Y	Y
5 Thurman	Y	Y	Y	Y	Y	Y	N	Y
6 ***Stearns***	Y	Y	Y	Y	N	Y	Y	Y
7 ***Mica***	Y	Y	Y	Y	Y	Y	Y	Y
8 ***McCollum***	Y	Y	Y	Y	Y	Y	Y	Y
9 ***Bilirakis***	Y	Y	Y	Y	Y	Y	Y	Y
10 ***Young***	Y	Y	Y	Y	Y	Y	Y	Y
11 Davis	Y	Y	Y	Y	Y	Y	N	Y
12 ***Canady***	Y	Y	Y	Y	Y	Y	Y	Y
13 ***Miller***	Y	Y	Y	Y	Y	Y	Y	Y
14 ***Goss***	Y	Y	Y	Y	Y	Y	Y	Y
15 ***Weldon***	Y	Y	Y	Y	Y	Y	Y	Y
16 ***Foley***	Y	Y	Y	Y	Y	Y	Y	Y
17 Meek	Y	Y	Y	Y	Y	Y	N	Y
18 ***Ros-Lehtinen***	Y	Y	Y	Y	Y	Y	Y	Y
19 Wexler	Y	Y	Y	Y	Y	Y	N	Y
20 Deutsch	Y	Y	Y	Y	Y	Y	N	Y
21 ***Diaz-Balart***	Y	Y	Y	Y	Y	Y	Y	Y
22 ***Shaw***	Y	Y	Y	Y	Y	Y	Y	Y
23 Hastings	Y	Y	Y	Y	Y	Y	N	N
GEORGIA								
1 ***Kingston***	Y	Y	Y	Y	N	Y	Y	Y
2 Bishop	Y	Y	Y	Y	Y	Y	Y	Y
3 ***Collins***	Y	Y	Y	Y	N	Y	Y	Y
4 McKinney	?	?	?	?	?	?	?	?
5 Lewis	Y	Y	Y	Y	Y	Y	N	Y
6 ***Isakson***	Y	Y	Y	Y	Y	Y	Y	Y
7 ***Barr***	Y	Y	Y	Y	N	Y	N	Y
8 ***Chambliss***	Y	Y	Y	Y	Y	Y	Y	Y
9 ***Deal***	Y	Y	Y	Y	N	Y	Y	Y
10 ***Norwood***	Y	Y	Y	Y	Y	Y	Y	?
11 ***Linder***	Y	Y	Y	Y	N	Y	Y	Y
HAWAII								
1 Abercrombie	Y	Y	?	Y	Y	Y	N	?
2 Mink	Y	Y	Y	Y	Y	Y	N	Y
IDAHO								
1 ***Chenoweth***	Y	Y	Y	Y	N	N	N	?
2 ***Simpson***	Y	Y	Y	Y	Y	Y	Y	Y
ILLINOIS								
1 Rush	Y	Y	Y	Y	Y	Y	N	Y
2 Jackson	Y	Y	Y	Y	Y	Y	N	Y
3 Lipinski	Y	Y	Y	Y	Y	Y	N	Y
4 Gutierrez	Y	Y	Y	Y	Y	Y	N	N
5 Blagojevich	Y	Y	Y	Y	Y	Y	N	N
6 ***Hyde***	Y	Y	Y	Y	Y	Y	Y	Y
7 Davis	Y	Y	Y	Y	Y	Y	N	Y
8 ***Crane***	Y	Y	Y	Y	Y	Y	Y	N
9 Schakowsky	Y	Y	Y	Y	Y	Y	N	N
10 ***Porter***	Y	Y	Y	Y	N	Y	Y	Y
11 ***Weller***	Y	Y	Y	Y	Y	Y	Y	N
12 Costello	Y	Y	Y	Y	Y	Y	N	N
13 ***Biggert***	Y	Y	Y	Y	Y	Y	Y	Y
14 ***Hastert***				Y		Y	Y	

ND Northern Democrats SD Southern Democrats

	474	475	476	477	478	479	480	481
15 ***Ewing***	Y	Y	Y	Y	Y	Y	Y	Y
16 ***Manzullo***	Y	Y	?	Y	N	Y	N	Y
17 Evans	Y	Y	Y	Y	Y	Y	N	Y
18 ***LaHood***	?	?	?	?	?	?	?	Y
19 Phelps	Y	Y	Y	Y	Y	Y	N	Y
20 ***Shimkus***	Y	Y	Y	Y	Y	Y	Y	Y
INDIANA								
1 Visclosky	Y	Y	Y	Y	Y	Y	N	N
2 ***McIntosh***	Y	Y	Y	Y	Y	Y	Y	Y
3 Roemer	Y	Y	Y	Y	Y	Y	N	Y
4 ***Souder***	Y	Y	Y	Y	N	Y	Y	Y
5 ***Buyer***	Y	Y	Y	Y	Y	Y	Y	Y
6 ***Burton***	Y	Y	Y	Y	N	Y	Y	Y
7 ***Pease***	Y	Y	Y	Y	Y	Y	Y	Y
8 ***Hostettler***	Y	Y	Y	Y	N	Y	Y	Y
9 Hill	Y	Y	Y	Y	Y	Y	N	Y
10 Carson	Y	Y	Y	Y	Y	Y	N	Y
IOWA								
1 ***Leach***	Y	Y	Y	Y	Y	Y	Y	Y
2 ***Nussle***	Y	Y	Y	Y	Y	Y	Y	Y
3 Boswell	Y	Y	Y	Y	Y	Y	N	Y
4 ***Ganske***	Y	Y	Y	Y	?	Y	Y	Y
5 ***Latham***	Y	Y	Y	Y	Y	Y	Y	Y
KANSAS								
1 ***Moran***	Y	Y	Y	Y	Y	Y	Y	N
2 ***Ryun***	Y	Y	Y	Y	Y	Y	Y	Y
3 Moore	Y	Y	Y	?	Y	Y	N	N
4 ***Tiahrt***	Y	Y	Y	Y	Y	Y	Y	Y
KENTUCKY								
1 ***Whitfield***	Y	Y	Y	Y	Y	Y	Y	Y
2 ***Lewis***	Y	Y	Y	Y	N	Y	Y	Y
3 ***Northup***	Y	Y	Y	Y	Y	Y	Y	Y
4 Lucas	Y	Y	Y	Y	Y	Y	N	Y
5 ***Rogers***	Y	Y	Y	Y	Y	Y	Y	Y
6 ***Fletcher***	Y	Y	Y	Y	Y	?	Y	Y
LOUISIANA								
1 ***Vitter***	Y	Y	Y	Y	Y	Y	Y	Y
2 Jefferson	Y	?	Y	?	?	?	?	Y
3 ***Tauzin***	Y	Y	Y	Y	Y	Y	Y	Y
4 ***McCrery***	Y	Y	Y	Y	Y	Y	Y	?
5 ***Cooksey***	Y	Y	Y	Y	Y	Y	Y	Y
6 ***Baker***	Y	Y	Y	Y	Y	Y	Y	Y
7 John	Y	Y	Y	Y	Y	Y	N	Y
MAINE								
1 Allen	Y	Y	Y	Y	Y	Y	N	Y
2 Baldacci	Y	Y	Y	Y	Y	Y	N	Y
MARYLAND								
1 ***Gilchrest***	Y	Y	Y	Y	Y	Y	Y	Y
2 ***Ehrlich***	Y	Y	Y	Y	Y	Y	Y	Y
3 Cardin	Y	Y	Y	Y	Y	Y	N	Y
4 Wynn	Y	Y	Y	Y	Y	Y	N	Y
5 Hoyer	Y	Y	Y	Y	Y	Y	N	Y
6 ***Bartlett***	Y	Y	Y	Y	Y	Y	Y	Y
7 Cummings	Y	Y	Y	Y	Y	Y	N	Y
8 ***Morella***	Y	Y	Y	Y	Y	Y	Y	Y
MASSACHUSETTS								
1 Olver	Y	Y	Y	Y	Y	Y	N	Y
2 Neal	Y	Y	Y	Y	Y	Y	N	Y
3 McGovern	Y	Y	Y	Y	Y	Y	N	Y
4 Frank	Y	Y	Y	Y	Y	Y	N	Y
5 Meehan	Y	Y	Y	Y	Y	Y	N	Y
6 Tierney	Y	Y	Y	Y	Y	Y	N	Y
7 Markey	Y	Y	Y	Y	Y	Y	N	?
8 Capuano	Y	Y	Y	Y	Y	Y	N	N
9 Moakley	Y	Y	Y	Y	Y	Y	N	Y
10 Delahunt	Y	Y	Y	Y	Y	Y	N	?
MICHIGAN								
1 Stupak	Y	Y	Y	Y	Y	Y	N	N
2 ***Hoekstra***	Y	Y	Y	Y	Y	Y	Y	Y
3 ***Ehlers***	Y	Y	Y	Y	Y	Y	Y	Y
4 ***Camp***	Y	Y	Y	Y	Y	Y	Y	Y
5 Barcia	Y	Y	Y	Y	Y	Y	N	Y
6 ***Upton***	Y	Y	Y	Y	Y	Y	Y	Y
7 ***Smith***	Y	Y	Y	Y	Y	Y	Y	Y
8 Stabenow	Y	Y	Y	Y	Y	Y	Y	Y
9 Kildee	Y	Y	Y	Y	Y	Y	N	Y
10 Bonior	Y	Y	Y	Y	Y	Y	N	Y
11 ***Knollenberg***	Y	Y	Y	Y	Y	Y	Y	Y
12 Levin	Y	Y	Y	Y	Y	Y	N	N
13 Rivers	Y	Y	Y	Y	Y	Y	N	Y
14 Conyers	Y	Y	Y	Y	Y	Y	N	?
15 Kilpatrick	Y	Y	Y	Y	Y	Y	N	Y
16 Dingell	Y	Y	Y	Y	Y	Y	N	N

	474	475	476	477	478	479	480	481
MINNESOTA								
1 ***Gutknecht***	Y	Y	Y	Y	Y	Y	Y	N
2 Minge	Y	Y	Y	Y	Y	Y	N	Y
3 ***Ramstad***	Y	Y	Y	Y	Y	Y	Y	N
4 Vento	Y	Y	Y	Y	Y	Y	N	N
5 Sabo	Y	Y	Y	Y	Y	Y	N	N
6 Luther	Y	Y	Y	Y	Y	Y	N	Y
7 Peterson	Y	Y	Y	Y	Y	Y	N	Y
8 Oberstar	Y	Y	Y	Y	Y	Y	N	N
MISSISSIPPI								
1 ***Wicker***	Y	Y	Y	Y	Y	Y	Y	?
2 Thompson	Y	Y	Y	Y	Y	Y	N	N
3 ***Pickering***	Y	Y	Y	Y	Y	Y	Y	Y
4 Shows	Y	Y	Y	Y	Y	Y	N	Y
5 Taylor	Y	Y	Y	Y	Y	Y	N	N
MISSOURI								
1 Clay	Y	Y	Y	Y	Y	Y	N	N
2 ***Talent***	Y	Y	Y	Y	Y	Y	Y	Y
3 Gephardt	Y	Y	Y	Y	Y	Y	N	?
4 Skelton	Y	Y	Y	Y	Y	Y	N	Y
5 McCarthy	Y	Y	Y	Y	Y	Y	N	Y
6 Danner	Y	Y	Y	Y	Y	Y	N	Y
7 ***Blunt***	Y	Y	Y	Y	Y	Y	Y	Y
8 ***Emerson***	Y	Y	Y	Y	Y	Y	Y	Y
9 ***Hulshof***	Y	Y	Y	Y	Y	Y	Y	Y
MONTANA								
AL ***Hill***	?	?	?	Y	Y	Y	Y	N
NEBRASKA								
1 ***Bereuter***	Y	Y	?	Y	Y	Y	Y	Y
2 ***Terry***	Y	Y	Y	Y	Y	Y	Y	Y
3 ***Barrett***	Y	Y	Y	Y	Y	Y	Y	Y
NEVADA								
1 Berkley	Y	Y	Y	Y	Y	Y	N	Y
2 ***Gibbons***	Y	Y	Y	Y	Y	Y	Y	N
NEW HAMPSHIRE								
1 ***Sununu***	Y	Y	Y	Y	Y	Y	Y	Y
2 ***Bass***	Y	Y	Y	Y	Y	Y	Y	Y
NEW JERSEY								
1 Andrews	Y	Y	Y	Y	Y	Y	N	Y
2 ***LoBiondo***	Y	Y	Y	Y	Y	Y	Y	N
3 ***Saxton***	Y	Y	Y	Y	Y	Y	Y	Y
4 ***Smith***	Y	Y	Y	Y	Y	Y	N	Y
5 ***Roukema***	Y	Y	Y	Y	Y	Y	Y	Y
6 Pallone	Y	Y	Y	Y	Y	Y	N	N
7 ***Franks***	Y	Y	Y	Y	Y	Y	Y	Y
8 Pascrell	Y	Y	Y	Y	Y	Y	N	Y
9 Rothman	Y	Y	Y	Y	Y	Y	N	Y
10 Payne	Y	Y	Y	Y	Y	Y	N	N
11 ***Frelinghuysen***	Y	Y	Y	Y	Y	Y	Y	Y
12 Holt	Y	Y	Y	Y	Y	Y	N	N
13 Menendez	Y	Y	Y	Y	Y	Y	N	Y
NEW MEXICO								
1 ***Wilson***	Y	Y	Y	Y	Y	Y	Y	Y
2 ***Skeen***	Y	Y	Y	Y	Y	Y	Y	Y
3 Udall	Y	Y	Y	Y	Y	Y	N	N
NEW YORK								
1 Forbes	Y	Y	Y	Y	Y	Y	N	Y
2 ***Lazio***	Y	Y	Y	Y	Y	Y	Y	Y
3 ***King***	Y	Y	Y	Y	Y	Y	Y	Y
4 McCarthy	Y	Y	Y	Y	Y	Y	N	Y
5 Ackerman	Y	Y	Y	Y	Y	Y	N	Y
6 Meeks	?	?	?	?	?	?	?	?
7 Crowley	Y	Y	Y	Y	Y	Y	N	N
8 Nadler	Y	Y	Y	Y	Y	Y	N	Y
9 Weiner	Y	Y	Y	Y	Y	Y	N	Y
10 Towns	Y	Y	Y	Y	Y	Y	N	N
11 Owens	Y	Y	Y	Y	Y	Y	N	Y
12 Velázquez	Y	Y	Y	Y	Y	Y	N	Y
13 ***Fossella***	Y	Y	Y	Y	Y	Y	Y	Y
14 Maloney	Y	Y	Y	Y	Y	Y	N	Y
15 Rangel	Y	Y	?	Y	Y	Y	N	Y
16 Serrano	Y	Y	Y	Y	Y	Y	N	Y
17 Engel	Y	Y	Y	Y	Y	Y	N	Y
18 Lowey	Y	Y	Y	Y	Y	Y	N	Y
19 ***Kelly***	Y	Y	Y	Y	Y	Y	Y	Y
20 ***Gilman***	Y	Y	Y	Y	Y	Y	Y	Y
21 McNulty	Y	Y	Y	Y	Y	Y	N	N
22 ***Sweeney***	Y	Y	Y	Y	Y	Y	Y	N
23 ***Boehlert***	Y	Y	Y	Y	Y	Y	Y	Y
24 ***McHugh***	Y	Y	Y	Y	Y	Y	Y	Y
25 ***Walsh***	Y	Y	Y	Y	Y	Y	Y	Y
26 Hinchey	Y	Y	Y	Y	Y	Y	N	N
27 ***Reynolds***	Y	Y	Y	Y	Y	Y	Y	Y
28 Slaughter	Y	Y	Y	Y	Y	Y	N	Y
29 LaFalce	Y	Y	Y	Y	Y	Y	N	N

	474	475	476	477	478	479	480	481
30 ***Quinn***	Y	Y	Y	Y	Y	Y	Y	Y
31 ***Houghton***	Y	Y	Y	Y	Y	Y	Y	Y
NORTH CAROLINA								
1 Clayton	Y	Y	Y	Y	Y	Y	N	Y
2 Etheridge	Y	Y	Y	Y	Y	Y	N	N
3 ***Jones***	Y	Y	Y	Y	?	Y	N	Y
4 Price	Y	Y	Y	Y	Y	Y	N	Y
5 ***Burr***	Y	Y	Y	Y	Y	Y	Y	Y
6 ***Coble***	Y	Y	Y	Y	N	Y	Y	Y
7 McIntyre	Y	Y	Y	Y	Y	Y	N	Y
8 ***Hayes***	Y	Y	Y	Y	Y	Y	Y	Y
9 ***Myrick***	Y	Y	Y	Y	Y	Y	Y	Y
10 ***Ballenger***	Y	Y	Y	Y	Y	Y	Y	Y
11 ***Taylor***	Y	Y	Y	Y	?	Y	Y	Y
12 Watt	Y	Y	Y	Y	Y	Y	N	Y
NORTH DAKOTA								
AL Pomeroy	Y	Y	Y	Y	Y	Y	–	Y
OHIO								
1 ***Chabot***	Y	Y	Y	Y	N	Y	Y	Y
2 ***Portman***	Y	Y	Y	Y	Y	Y	Y	Y
3 Hall	Y	Y	Y	Y	Y	Y	N	Y
4 ***Oxley***	Y	Y	Y	Y	Y	Y	Y	Y
5 ***Gillmor***	Y	Y	Y	Y	Y	Y	Y	Y
6 Strickland	Y	Y	Y	Y	Y	Y	N	N
7 ***Hobson***	Y	Y	Y	Y	Y	Y	Y	Y
8 ***Boehner***	Y	Y	Y	Y	Y	Y	Y	Y
9 Kaptur	Y	Y	Y	Y	Y	Y	N	Y
10 Kucinich	Y	Y	Y	Y	Y	Y	N	N
11 Jones	Y	Y	Y	Y	Y	Y	N	N
12 ***Kasich***	Y	Y	Y	Y	Y	Y	Y	Y
13 Brown	Y	Y	Y	Y	Y	Y	N	?
14 Sawyer	Y	Y	Y	Y	Y	Y	N	Y
15 ***Pryce***	Y	Y	Y	Y	Y	Y	Y	Y
16 ***Regula***	Y	Y	Y	Y	Y	Y	Y	Y
17 Traficant	Y	Y	Y	Y	Y	Y	N	Y
18 ***Ney***	Y	Y	Y	Y	Y	Y	Y	Y
19 ***LaTourette***	Y	Y	Y	Y	Y	Y	Y	?
OKLAHOMA								
1 ***Largent***	Y	Y	Y	Y	N	Y	Y	Y
2 ***Coburn***	Y	Y	Y	Y	Y	Y	Y	Y
3 ***Watkins***	Y	Y	Y	Y	Y	Y	Y	Y
4 ***Watts***	Y	Y	Y	Y	N	Y	Y	Y
5 ***Istook***	Y	Y	Y	Y	Y	Y	Y	Y
6 ***Lucas***	Y	Y	Y	Y	Y	Y	Y	Y
OREGON								
1 Wu	Y	Y	Y	Y	Y	Y	N	Y
2 ***Walden***	Y	Y	Y	Y	Y	Y	Y	Y
3 Blumenauer	?	?	?	?	?	?	?	?
4 DeFazio	Y	Y	Y	Y	Y	Y	N	N
5 Hooley	Y	Y	Y	Y	Y	Y	N	N
PENNSYLVANIA								
1 Brady	Y	Y	Y	Y	Y	Y	N	N
2 Fattah	Y	Y	Y	Y	Y	Y	N	Y
3 Borski	Y	Y	Y	Y	Y	Y	N	N
4 Klink	Y	Y	Y	Y	Y	Y	N	N
5 ***Peterson***	Y	Y	Y	Y	Y	Y	?	Y
6 Holden	Y	Y	Y	Y	Y	Y	N	Y
7 ***Weldon***	Y	Y	Y	Y	Y	Y	Y	Y
8 ***Greenwood***	Y	Y	Y	Y	Y	Y	Y	Y
9 ***Shuster***	Y	Y	Y	Y	Y	Y	Y	Y
10 ***Sherwood***	Y	Y	Y	Y	Y	Y	Y	Y
11 Kanjorski	Y	Y	Y	Y	Y	Y	N	Y
12 Murtha	Y	Y	Y	Y	Y	Y	N	Y
13 Hoeffel	Y	Y	Y	Y	Y	Y	N	Y
14 Coyne	Y	Y	Y	Y	Y	Y	N	Y
15 ***Toomey***	Y	Y	Y	Y	Y	Y	Y	Y
16 ***Pitts***	Y	Y	Y	Y	Y	Y	Y	Y
17 ***Gekas***	Y	Y	Y	Y	Y	Y	Y	Y
18 Doyle	Y	Y	Y	Y	Y	Y	N	Y
19 ***Goodling***	Y	Y	Y	Y	?	Y	Y	Y
20 Mascara	+	+	+	+	+	Y	N	Y
21 ***English***	Y	Y	Y	Y	Y	Y	Y	?
RHODE ISLAND								
1 Kennedy	Y	Y	Y	Y	Y	Y	N	Y
2 Weygand	Y	Y	Y	Y	Y	Y	N	Y
SOUTH CAROLINA								
1 ***Sanford***	Y	Y	Y	Y	N	Y	Y	Y
2 ***Spence***	Y	Y	Y	Y	Y	Y	Y	Y
3 ***Graham***	Y	Y	Y	Y	Y	Y	Y	Y
4 ***DeMint***	Y	Y	Y	Y	Y	Y	Y	Y
5 Spratt	Y	Y	Y	Y	Y	Y	N	Y
6 Clyburn	Y	Y	Y	Y	Y	Y	N	N
SOUTH DAKOTA								
AL ***Thune***	Y	Y	Y	Y	Y	Y	Y	Y

	474	475	476	477	478	479	480	481
TENNESSEE								
1 ***Jenkins***	Y	Y	Y	Y	Y	Y	Y	Y
2 ***Duncan***	Y	Y	Y	Y	Y	Y	Y	Y
3 ***Wamp***	Y	Y	Y	Y	Y	Y	Y	Y
4 ***Hilleary***	Y	Y	?	Y	Y	Y	Y	N
5 Clement	Y	Y	Y	Y	Y	Y	N	Y
6 Gordon	Y	Y	Y	Y	Y	Y	N	Y
7 ***Bryant***	Y	Y	Y	Y	Y	Y	Y	Y
8 Tanner	Y	Y	Y	Y	Y	Y	N	Y
9 Ford	Y	Y	Y	Y	Y	Y	N	N
TEXAS								
1 Sandlin	Y	Y	Y	Y	Y	Y	N	Y
2 Turner	Y	Y	Y	Y	Y	Y	N	Y
3 ***Johnson, Sam***	Y	Y	Y	Y	Y	Y	Y	Y
4 Hall	Y	Y	Y	Y	Y	Y	N	Y
5 ***Sessions***	Y	Y	Y	Y	Y	Y	Y	Y
6 ***Barton***	Y	Y	Y	Y	Y	Y	Y	Y
7 ***Archer***	Y	Y	Y	Y	N	Y	Y	Y
8 ***Brady***	Y	Y	Y	Y	Y	Y	Y	Y
9 Lampson	Y	Y	Y	Y	Y	Y	N	Y
10 Doggett	Y	Y	Y	Y	Y	Y	N	N
11 Edwards	Y	Y	Y	Y	Y	Y	N	Y
12 ***Granger***	Y	Y	Y	Y	Y	Y	Y	Y
13 ***Thornberry***	Y	Y	Y	Y	Y	Y	Y	Y
14 ***Paul***	Y	Y	P	Y	N	N	?	Y
15 Hinojosa	Y	Y	Y	Y	Y	Y	N	Y
16 Reyes	Y	Y	Y	Y	Y	Y	N	Y
17 Stenholm	Y	Y	Y	Y	Y	Y	N	Y
18 Jackson-Lee	Y	Y	Y	Y	Y	Y	N	Y
19 ***Combest***	Y	Y	Y	Y	Y	Y	Y	Y
20 Gonzalez	Y	Y	Y	Y	Y	Y	N	Y
21 ***Smith***	Y	Y	Y	Y	Y	Y	Y	Y
22 ***DeLay***	Y	Y	?	Y	Y	Y	Y	Y
23 ***Bonilla***	Y	Y	Y	Y	Y	Y	Y	Y
24 Frost	Y	Y	Y	Y	Y	Y	N	N
25 Bentsen	Y	Y	Y	Y	Y	Y	N	Y
26 ***Armey***	Y	Y	Y	Y	Y	Y	Y	Y
27 Ortiz	Y	Y	Y	Y	Y	Y	N	Y
28 Rodriguez	Y	Y	Y	Y	Y	Y	N	Y
29 Green	Y	Y	Y	Y	Y	Y	N	Y
30 Johnson, E.B.	Y	Y	Y	Y	Y	Y	N	Y
UTAH								
1 ***Hansen***	Y	Y	Y	Y	Y	Y	Y	?
2 ***Cook***	Y	Y	Y	Y	Y	Y	Y	Y
3 ***Cannon***	Y	Y	Y	Y	Y	Y	Y	Y
VERMONT								
AL *Sanders*	Y	Y	Y	Y	Y	Y	N	Y
VIRGINIA								
1 ***Bateman***	Y	Y	Y	Y	Y	Y	Y	Y
2 Pickett	Y	Y	Y	Y	Y	Y	N	N
3 Scott	Y	Y	Y	Y	Y	Y	N	Y
4 Sisisky	Y	Y	Y	Y	Y	Y	N	Y
5 Goode	Y	Y	Y	Y	N	Y	N	Y
6 ***Goodlatte***	Y	Y	Y	Y	Y	Y	Y	Y
7 ***Bliley***	Y	Y	Y	Y	Y	Y	Y	Y
8 Moran	Y	Y	Y	Y	Y	Y	N	Y
9 Boucher	Y	Y	Y	?	Y	Y	N	?
10 ***Wolf***	Y	Y	Y	Y	Y	Y	Y	Y
11 ***Davis***	Y	Y	Y	Y	Y	Y	Y	Y
WASHINGTON								
1 Inslee	Y	Y	Y	Y	Y	Y	N	Y
2 ***Metcalf***	?	?	?	Y	Y	Y	Y	Y
3 Baird	Y	Y	Y	Y	Y	Y	N	N
4 ***Hastings***	Y	Y	Y	Y	Y	Y	Y	Y
5 ***Nethercutt***	Y	Y	Y	Y	Y	Y	Y	Y
6 Dicks	Y	Y	Y	Y	Y	Y	N	Y
7 McDermott	Y	Y	Y	Y	Y	Y	N	N
8 ***Dunn***	Y	Y	Y	Y	Y	Y	Y	Y
9 Smith	Y	Y	Y	Y	Y	Y	N	Y
WEST VIRGINIA								
1 Mollohan	Y	Y	Y	Y	Y	Y	N	Y
2 Wise	Y	Y	Y	Y	Y	Y	N	Y
3 Rahall	Y	Y	Y	Y	Y	Y	N	Y
WISCONSIN								
1 ***Ryan***	Y	Y	Y	Y	Y	Y	Y	Y
2 Baldwin	Y	Y	Y	Y	Y	Y	N	Y
3 Kind	Y	Y	Y	Y	Y	Y	N	Y
4 Kleczka	Y	Y	Y	Y	Y	Y	N	Y
5 Barrett	Y	Y	Y	Y	Y	Y	N	Y
6 ***Petri***	Y	Y	Y	Y	Y	Y	Y	Y
7 Obey	Y	Y	Y	Y	Y	Y	N	Y
8 ***Green***	Y	Y	Y	Y	Y	Y	Y	Y
9 ***Sensenbrenner***	Y	Y	Y	Y	Y	Y	Y	Y
WYOMING								
AL ***Cubin***	Y	Y	Y	Y	Y	Y	Y	Y

Southern states - Ala., Ark., Fla., Ga., Ky., La., Miss., N.C., Okla., S.C., Tenn., Texas, Va.

482. **Procedural Motion/Adjourn.** Frost, D-Texas, motion to adjourn. Motion rejected 3-423: R 0-218; D 3-204 (ND 3-150, SD 0-54); I 0-1. Oct. 6, 1999.

483. **HR 2990, HR 2723. Access to Care for the Uninsured and Managed Care Patient Protections/Rule.** Adoption of the rule (H Res 323) to provide for House floor consideration of the bill to enact tax provisions designed to improve access to health care, as well as a second bill (HR 2723) to impose new federal regulations on managed care companies, including allowing patients to sue their health plans in state courts. Adopted 221-209: R 220-0; D 1-208 (ND 1-154, SD 0-54); I 0-1. Oct. 6, 1999.

484. **HR 2990. Access to Care for the Uninsured/Recommit.** Rangel, D-N.Y., motion to recommit the bill to the Ways and Means Committee with instructions to report it back with a substitute amendment that would preserve the budget surplus until there is action on Medicare and Social Security solvency. Motion rejected 211-220: R 0-220; D 210-0; (ND 156-0, SD 54-0); I 1-0. Oct. 6, 1999.

485. **HR 2990. Access to Care for the Uninsured/Passage.** Passage of the bill to make medical savings accounts available to all Americans, provide tax deductions for health insurance premiums and establish association health plans and HealthMarts, intended to make health insurance more accessible to small business and the self-employed through enhanced purchasing power. Passed 227-205: R 216-5; D 11-199 (ND 6-150, SD 5-49); I 0-1. Oct. 6, 1999. A "nay" is a vote in support of the president's position.

Key

- Y Voted for (yea).
- # Paired for.
- + Announced for.
- N Voted against (nay).
- X Paired against.
- – Announced against.
- P Voted "present."
- C Voted "present" to avoid possible conflict of interest.
- ? Did not vote or otherwise make a position known.

•

Democrats ***Republicans***
Independents

	482	483	484	485
ALABAMA				
1 ***Callahan***	N	Y	N	Y
2 ***Everett***	N	Y	N	Y
3 ***Riley***	N	Y	N	Y
4 ***Aderholt***	N	Y	N	Y
5 Cramer	N	N	Y	Y
6 ***Bachus***	N	Y	N	Y
7 Hilliard	N	N	Y	N
ALASKA				
AL ***Young***	N	Y	N	Y
ARIZONA				
1 ***Salmon***	N	Y	N	Y
2 Pastor	N	N	Y	N
3 ***Stump***	N	Y	N	Y
4 ***Shadegg***	N	Y	N	Y
5 ***Kolbe***	N	Y	N	Y
6 ***Hayworth***	N	Y	N	Y
ARKANSAS				
1 Berry	N	N	Y	N
2 Snyder	N	N	Y	N
3 ***Hutchinson***	N	Y	N	Y
4 ***Dickey***	N	Y	N	Y
CALIFORNIA				
1 Thompson	N	N	Y	N
2 ***Herger***	N	Y	N	Y
3 ***Ose***	N	Y	N	Y
4 ***Doolittle***	N	Y	N	Y
5 Matsui	N	N	Y	N
6 Woolsey	N	N	Y	N
7 Miller, George	N	N	Y	N
8 Pelosi	N	N	Y	N
9 Lee	N	N	Y	N
10 Tauscher	N	N	Y	N
11 ***Pombo***	N	Y	N	Y
12 Lantos	N	N	Y	N
13 Stark	N	N	Y	N
14 Eshoo	N	N	Y	N
15 ***Campbell***	N	Y	N	N
16 Lofgren	N	N	Y	N
17 Farr	N	N	Y	N
18 Condit	N	N	Y	N
19 ***Radanovich***	N	Y	N	Y
20 Dooley	N	N	Y	Y
21 ***Thomas***	N	Y	N	Y
22 Capps	N	N	Y	N
23 ***Gallegly***	N	Y	N	Y
24 Sherman	N	N	Y	N
25 ***McKeon***	N	Y	N	Y
26 Berman	N	N	Y	N
27 ***Rogan***	N	Y	N	Y
28 ***Dreier***	N	Y	N	Y
29 Waxman	N	N	Y	N
30 Becerra	N	N	Y	N
31 Martinez	N	N	Y	N
32 Dixon	N	N	Y	N
33 Roybal-Allard	N	N	Y	N
34 Napolitano	N	N	Y	N
35 Waters	N	N	Y	N
36 ***Kuykendall***	N	Y	N	Y
37 Millender-McD.	N	N	Y	N
38 ***Horn***	N	Y	N	Y
39 ***Royce***	N	Y	N	Y
40 ***Lewis***	N	Y	N	Y
41 ***Miller***	N	Y	N	Y
42 Vacant				
43 ***Calvert***	N	Y	N	Y
44 ***Bono***	N	Y	N	Y
45 ***Rohrabacher***	N	Y	N	Y
46 Sanchez	N	N	Y	N
47 ***Cox***	N	Y	N	Y
48 ***Packard***	N	Y	N	Y
49 ***Bilbray***	N	Y	N	Y
50 Filner	N	N	Y	N
51 ***Cunningham***	N	Y	N	Y
52 ***Hunter***	?	Y	N	Y
COLORADO				
1 DeGette	N	N	Y	N
2 Udall	N	N	Y	N
3 ***McInnis***	N	Y	N	Y
4 ***Schaffer***	N	Y	N	Y
5 ***Hefley***	N	Y	N	Y
6 ***Tancredo***	N	Y	N	Y
CONNECTICUT				
1 Larson	N	N	Y	N
2 Gejdenson	N	N	Y	N
3 DeLauro	N	N	Y	N
4 ***Shays***	N	Y	N	Y
5 Maloney	N	N	Y	Y
6 ***Johnson***	N	Y	N	Y
DELAWARE				
AL ***Castle***	N	Y	N	Y
FLORIDA				
1 ***Scarborough***	?	?	?	?
2 Boyd	N	N	Y	N
3 Brown	N	N	Y	N
4 ***Fowler***	N	Y	N	Y
5 Thurman	N	N	Y	N
6 ***Stearns***	N	Y	N	Y
7 ***Mica***	N	Y	N	Y
8 ***McCollum***	N	Y	N	Y
9 ***Bilirakis***	N	Y	N	Y
10 ***Young***	N	Y	N	Y
11 Davis	N	N	Y	N
12 ***Canady***	N	Y	N	Y
13 ***Miller***	N	Y	N	Y
14 ***Goss***	N	Y	N	Y
15 ***Weldon***	N	Y	N	Y
16 ***Foley***	N	Y	N	Y
17 Meek	N	N	Y	N
18 ***Ros-Lehtinen***	N	Y	N	Y
19 Wexler	N	N	Y	N
20 Deutsch	N	N	Y	N
21 ***Diaz-Balart***	N	Y	N	Y
22 ***Shaw***	N	Y	N	Y
23 Hastings	N	N	Y	N
GEORGIA				
1 ***Kingston***	N	Y	N	Y
2 Bishop	N	N	Y	N
3 ***Collins***	N	Y	N	Y
4 McKinney	?	?	?	?
5 Lewis	N	N	Y	N
6 ***Isakson***	N	Y	N	Y
7 ***Barr***	N	Y	N	Y
8 ***Chambliss***	N	Y	N	Y
9 ***Deal***	N	Y	N	Y
10 ***Norwood***	N	Y	N	N
11 ***Linder***	N	Y	N	Y
HAWAII				
1 Abercrombie	N	N	Y	N
2 Mink	N	N	Y	N
IDAHO				
1 ***Chenoweth***	N	Y	N	Y
2 ***Simpson***	N	Y	N	Y
ILLINOIS				
1 Rush	N	N	Y	N
2 Jackson	N	N	Y	N
3 Lipinski	N	N	Y	Y
4 Gutierrez	N	N	Y	N
5 Blagojevich	N	N	Y	N
6 ***Hyde***	N	Y	N	Y
7 Davis	N	N	Y	N
8 ***Crane***	N	Y	N	Y
9 Schakowsky	N	N	Y	N
10 ***Porter***	N	Y	N	Y
11 ***Weller***	N	Y	N	Y
12 Costello	N	N	Y	N
13 ***Biggert***	N	Y	N	Y
14 ***Hastert***		Y		Y

ND Northern Democrats SD Southern Democrats

	482	483	484	485
15 **Ewing**	N	Y	N	Y
16 **Manzullo**	N	Y	N	Y
17 Evans	N	N	Y	N
18 **LaHood**	N	Y	N	Y
19 Phelps	N	N	Y	N
20 **Shimkus**	N	Y	N	Y
INDIANA				
1 Visclosky	N	N	Y	N
2 **McIntosh**	N	Y	N	Y
3 Roemer	N	N	Y	N
4 **Souder**	N	Y	N	Y
5 **Buyer**	N	Y	N	Y
6 **Burton**	N	Y	N	Y
7 **Pease**	N	Y	N	Y
8 **Hostettler**	N	Y	N	Y
9 Hill	N	N	Y	N
10 Carson	N	N	Y	N
IOWA				
1 **Leach**	N	Y	N	Y
2 **Nussle**	N	Y	N	Y
3 Boswell	N	N	Y	N
4 **Ganske**	N	Y	N	N
5 **Latham**	N	Y	N	Y
KANSAS				
1 **Moran**	N	Y	N	Y
2 **Ryun**	N	Y	N	Y
3 Moore	N	N	Y	N
4 **Tiahrt**	N	Y	N	Y
KENTUCKY				
1 **Whitfield**	N	Y	N	Y
2 **Lewis**	N	Y	N	Y
3 **Northup**	N	Y	N	Y
4 Lucas	N	N	Y	Y
5 **Rogers**	N	Y	N	Y
6 **Fletcher**	N	Y	N	Y
LOUISIANA				
1 **Vitter**	N	Y	N	Y
2 Jefferson	N	N	Y	N
3 **Tauzin**	N	Y	N	Y
4 **McCrery**	N	Y	N	Y
5 **Cooksey**	N	Y	N	Y
6 **Baker**	N	Y	N	Y
7 John	N	N	Y	N
MAINE				
1 Allen	N	N	Y	N
2 Baldacci	N	N	Y	N
MARYLAND				
1 **Gilchrest**	N	Y	N	Y
2 **Ehrlich**	N	Y	N	Y
3 Cardin	N	N	Y	N
4 Wynn	N	N	Y	N
5 Hoyer	N	N	Y	N
6 **Bartlett**	N	Y	N	Y
7 Cummings	N	N	Y	N
8 **Morella**	N	Y	N	N
MASSACHUSETTS				
1 Olver	N	N	Y	N
2 Neal	N	N	Y	N
3 McGovern	N	N	Y	N
4 Frank	N	N	Y	N
5 Meehan	N	N	Y	N
6 Tierney	N	N	Y	N
7 Markey	N	N	Y	N
8 Capuano	N	N	Y	N
9 Moakley	N	N	Y	N
10 Delahunt	?	?	Y	N
MICHIGAN				
1 Stupak	N	N	Y	N
2 **Hoekstra**	N	Y	N	Y
3 **Ehlers**	N	Y	N	Y
4 **Camp**	N	Y	N	Y
5 Barcia	N	N	Y	N
6 **Upton**	N	Y	N	Y
7 **Smith**	N	Y	N	Y
8 Stabenow	N	N	Y	N
9 Kildee	N	N	Y	N
10 Bonior	N	N	Y	N
11 **Knollenberg**	N	Y	N	Y
12 Levin	N	N	Y	N
13 Rivers	N	N	Y	N
14 Conyers	N	N	Y	N
15 Kilpatrick	N	N	Y	N
16 Dingell	Y	N	Y	N

	482	483	484	485
MINNESOTA				
1 **Gutknecht**	N	Y	N	Y
2 Minge	N	N	Y	N
3 **Ramstad**	N	Y	N	Y
4 Vento	N	N	Y	N
5 Sabo	N	N	Y	N
6 Luther	N	N	Y	N
7 Peterson	N	Y	Y	N
8 Oberstar	N	N	Y	N
MISSISSIPPI				
1 **Wicker**	N	Y	N	Y
2 Thompson	N	N	Y	N
3 **Pickering**	N	Y	N	Y
4 Shows	N	N	Y	N
5 Taylor	N	N	Y	N
MISSOURI				
1 Clay	N	N	Y	N
2 **Talent**	N	Y	N	Y
3 Gephardt	N	N	Y	N
4 Skelton	N	N	Y	N
5 McCarthy	N	N	Y	N
6 Danner	N	N	Y	Y
7 **Blunt**	N	Y	N	Y
8 **Emerson**	N	Y	N	Y
9 **Hulshof**	N	Y	N	Y
MONTANA				
AL **Hill**	N	Y	N	Y
NEBRASKA				
1 **Bereuter**	N	Y	N	Y
2 **Terry**	N	Y	N	Y
3 **Barrett**	N	Y	N	Y
NEVADA				
1 Berkley	N	N	Y	N
2 **Gibbons**	N	Y	N	Y
NEW HAMPSHIRE				
1 **Sununu**	N	Y	N	Y
2 **Bass**	N	Y	N	Y
NEW JERSEY				
1 Andrews	N	N	Y	N
2 **LoBiondo**	N	Y	N	Y
3 **Saxton**	N	Y	N	Y
4 **Smith**	N	Y	N	Y
5 **Roukema**	N	Y	N	Y
6 Pallone	N	N	Y	N
7 **Franks**	N	Y	N	Y
8 Pascrell	N	N	Y	N
9 Rothman	N	N	Y	N
10 Payne	N	N	Y	N
11 **Frelinghuysen**	N	Y	N	Y
12 Holt	N	N	Y	N
13 Menendez	N	N	Y	N
NEW MEXICO				
1 **Wilson**	N	Y	N	Y
2 **Skeen**	N	Y	N	Y
3 Udall	N	N	Y	N
NEW YORK				
1 Forbes	N	N	Y	Y
2 **Lazio**	N	Y	N	Y
3 **King**	N	Y	N	Y
4 McCarthy	N	N	Y	N
5 Ackerman	N	N	Y	N
6 Meeks	N	N	Y	N
7 Crowley	N	N	Y	N
8 Nadler	N	N	Y	N
9 Weiner	N	N	Y	N
10 Towns	N	N	Y	N
11 Owens	N	N	Y	N
12 Velázquez	N	N	Y	N
13 **Fossella**	N	Y	N	Y
14 Maloney	N	N	Y	N
15 Rangel	N	N	Y	N
16 Serrano	N	N	Y	N
17 Engel	N	N	Y	N
18 Lowey	N	N	Y	N
19 **Kelly**	N	Y	N	Y
20 **Gilman**	N	Y	N	N
21 McNulty	N	N	Y	N
22 **Sweeney**	N	Y	N	Y
23 **Boehlert**	N	Y	N	Y
24 **McHugh**	N	Y	N	Y
25 **Walsh**	N	Y	N	Y
26 Hinchey	N	N	Y	N
27 **Reynolds**	N	Y	N	Y
28 Slaughter	N	N	Y	N
29 LaFalce	N	N	Y	N

	482	483	484	485
30 **Quinn**	N	Y	N	Y
31 **Houghton**	N	Y	N	Y
NORTH CAROLINA				
1 Clayton	N	N	Y	N
2 Etheridge	N	N	Y	N
3 **Jones**	N	Y	N	Y
4 Price	N	N	Y	N
5 **Burr**	N	Y	N	Y
6 **Coble**	N	Y	N	Y
7 McIntyre	N	N	Y	N
8 **Hayes**	N	Y	N	Y
9 **Myrick**	N	Y	N	Y
10 **Ballenger**	N	Y	N	Y
11 **Taylor**	N	Y	N	Y
12 Watt	N	N	Y	N
NORTH DAKOTA				
AL Pomeroy	N	N	Y	N
OHIO				
1 **Chabot**	N	Y	N	Y
2 **Portman**	N	Y	N	Y
3 Hall	N	N	Y	N
4 **Oxley**	N	Y	N	Y
5 **Gillmor**	N	Y	N	Y
6 Strickland	N	N	Y	N
7 **Hobson**	N	Y	N	Y
8 **Boehner**	N	Y	N	Y
9 Kaptur	N	N	Y	N
10 Kucinich	N	N	Y	N
11 Jones	N	N	Y	N
12 **Kasich**	N	Y	N	Y
13 Brown	?	N	Y	N
14 Sawyer	N	N	Y	N
15 **Pryce**	N	Y	N	Y
16 **Regula**	N	Y	N	Y
17 Traficant	N	N	Y	N
18 **Ney**	N	Y	N	Y
19 **LaTourette**	N	Y	N	Y
OKLAHOMA				
1 **Largent**	N	Y	N	Y
2 **Coburn**	N	Y	N	Y
3 **Watkins**	N	Y	N	Y
4 **Watts**	N	+	N	Y
5 **Istook**	?	Y	N	Y
6 **Lucas**	N	Y	N	Y
OREGON				
1 Wu	N	N	Y	N
2 **Walden**	N	Y	N	Y
3 Blumenauer	N	N	Y	N
4 DeFazio	N	N	Y	N
5 Hooley	N	N	Y	N
PENNSYLVANIA				
1 Brady	N	N	Y	N
2 Fattah	N	N	Y	N
3 Borski	N	N	Y	N
4 Klink	N	N	Y	N
5 **Peterson**	N	Y	N	Y
6 Holden	N	N	Y	N
7 **Weldon**	N	Y	N	Y
8 **Greenwood**	N	Y	N	Y
9 **Shuster**	N	Y	N	Y
10 **Sherwood**	N	Y	N	Y
11 Kanjorski	N	N	Y	N
12 Murtha	N	N	Y	N
13 Hoeffel	N	N	Y	N
14 Coyne	N	N	Y	N
15 **Toomey**	N	Y	N	Y
16 **Pitts**	N	Y	N	Y
17 **Gekas**	N	Y	N	Y
18 Doyle	N	N	Y	N
19 **Goodling**	N	Y	N	Y
20 Mascara	N	N	Y	N
21 **English**	N	Y	N	Y
RHODE ISLAND				
1 Kennedy	Y	N	Y	N
2 Weygand	N	N	Y	N
SOUTH CAROLINA				
1 **Sanford**	N	Y	N	Y
2 **Spence**	N	Y	N	Y
3 **Graham**	N	Y	N	Y
4 **DeMint**	N	Y	N	Y
5 Spratt	N	N	Y	N
6 Clyburn	N	N	Y	N
SOUTH DAKOTA				
AL **Thune**	N	Y	N	Y

	482	483	484	485
TENNESSEE				
1 **Jenkins**	N	Y	N	Y
2 **Duncan**	N	Y	N	Y
3 **Wamp**	N	Y	N	Y
4 **Hilleary**	N	Y	N	Y
5 Clement	N	N	Y	N
6 Gordon	N	N	Y	Y
7 **Bryant**	N	Y	N	Y
8 Tanner	N	N	Y	N
9 Ford	N	N	Y	N
TEXAS				
1 Sandlin	N	N	Y	N
2 Turner	N	N	Y	N
3 **Johnson, Sam**	N	Y	N	Y
4 Hall	N	N	Y	N
5 **Sessions**	N	Y	N	Y
6 **Barton**	N	Y	N	Y
7 **Archer**	N	Y	N	Y
8 **Brady**	N	Y	N	Y
9 Lampson	N	N	Y	N
10 Doggett	N	N	Y	N
11 Edwards	N	N	Y	N
12 **Granger**	N	Y	N	Y
13 **Thornberry**	N	Y	N	Y
14 **Paul**	N	Y	N	Y
15 Hinojosa	N	N	Y	N
16 Reyes	N	N	Y	N
17 Stenholm	N	N	Y	N
18 Jackson-Lee	N	N	Y	N
19 **Combest**	N	Y	N	Y
20 Gonzalez	N	N	Y	N
21 **Smith**	N	Y	N	Y
22 **DeLay**	N	Y	N	Y
23 **Bonilla**	N	Y	N	Y
24 Frost	N	N	Y	N
25 Bentsen	N	N	Y	N
26 **Armey**	N	Y	N	Y
27 Ortiz	N	N	Y	N
28 Rodriguez	N	N	Y	N
29 Green	N	N	Y	N
30 Johnson, E.B.	N	N	Y	N
UTAH				
1 **Hansen**	N	Y	N	Y
2 **Cook**	N	Y	N	Y
3 **Cannon**	N	Y	N	Y
VERMONT				
AL Sanders	N	N	Y	N
VIRGINIA				
1 **Bateman**	N	Y	N	Y
2 Pickett	N	N	Y	N
3 Scott	N	N	Y	N
4 Sisisky	N	N	Y	N
5 Goode	N	N	Y	Y
6 **Goodlatte**	N	Y	N	Y
7 **Bliley**	N	Y	N	Y
8 Moran	N	N	Y	Y
9 Boucher	N	N	Y	N
10 **Wolf**	N	Y	N	Y
11 **Davis**	N	Y	N	Y
WASHINGTON				
1 Inslee	N	N	Y	N
2 **Metcalf**	N	Y	N	Y
3 Baird	N	N	Y	N
4 **Hastings**	N	Y	N	Y
5 **Nethercutt**	N	Y	N	Y
6 Dicks	N	N	Y	N
7 McDermott	N	N	Y	N
8 **Dunn**	N	Y	N	Y
9 Smith	N	N	Y	Y
WEST VIRGINIA				
1 Mollohan	N	N	Y	N
2 Wise	?	N	Y	N
3 Rahall	N	N	Y	N
WISCONSIN				
1 **Ryan**	N	Y	N	Y
2 Baldwin	N	N	Y	N
3 Kind	N	N	Y	N
4 Kleczka	N	N	Y	N
5 Barrett	N	N	Y	N
6 **Petri**	N	Y	N	Y
7 Obey	Y	N	Y	N
8 **Green**	N	Y	N	Y
9 **Sensenbrenner**	N	Y	N	Y
WYOMING				
AL **Cubin**	N	Y	N	Y

Southern states - Ala., Ark., Fla., Ga., Ky., La., Miss., N.C., Okla., S.C., Tenn., Texas, Va.

486. Procedural Motion/Journal. Approval of the House Journal of Oct. 6, 1999. Approved 341-73: R 194-19; D 146-54 (ND 109-39, SD 37-15); I 1-0. Oct. 7, 1999.

487. HR 2723. Managed Care Patient Protections/Boehner Substitute. Boehner, R-Ohio, substitute amendment to prohibit health plans from limiting the advice physicians can give to patients, guarantee patients' access to emergency care and allow direct access to gynecological and pediatric care. It would create an external process to review a health plans' denial of care, but would not include the right to sue in court. The substitute also includes malpractice law revisions that would limit non-economic damages to $250,000, but would permit states to set higher or lower limits. Rejected 145-284: R 143-76; D 2-207 (ND 0-154, SD 2-53); I 0-1. Oct. 7, 1999.

488. HR 2723. Managed Care Patient Protections/Goss-Coburn-Shadegg Substitute. Goss, R-Fla., substitute amendment to prohibit health plans from limiting the advice physicians can give to patients, guarantee patients' access to emergency care and allow direct access to gynecological and pediatric care. Patients would have the right to sue a health plan in federal court if all internal and external appeals have been exhausted. Non-economic damages would be capped at $500,000 or two times the economic loss, whichever is less. In some cases, punitive damages would be allowed. Patients and plans would be allowed to resolve disputes by binding arbitration. Rejected 193-238: R 191-29; D 2-208 (ND 0-155, SD 2-53); I 0-1. Oct. 7, 1999.

489. HR 2723. Managed Care Patient Protections/Houghton Substitute. Houghton, R-N.Y., substitute amendment to prohibit health plans from limiting the advice physicians can give to patients, guarantee patients' access to emergency care and allow direct access to gynecological and pediatric care. The substitute would permit suits against health plans in federal courts only and with capped damages. Patients would have to complete all internal and external reviews before filing a suit. The substitute would cap non-economic damages at $250,000 or two times the economic damages, up to $500,000. Patients could submit to binding arbitration instead of going to court. Rejected 160-269: R 158-61; D 2-207 (ND 0-154, SD 2-53); I 0-1. Oct. 7, 1999.

490. HR 2723. Managed Care Patient Protection/Passage. Passage of the bill to require health plans to cover emergency care when a "prudent layperson" could reasonably believe such care was required. Health plans would have to allow direct access to gynecological and pediatric care. The bill would establish an internal and external appeals process to review denial of care. Patients or their estates would have the right to sue their health plan in state courts when they make negligent decisions that result in injury or death of patients. Passed 275-151: R 68-149; D 206-2 (ND 153-1, SD 53-1); I 1-0. Oct. 7, 1999. A "yea" was a vote in support of the president's position.

Key

- Y Voted for (yea).
- # Paired for.
- \+ Announced for.
- N Voted against (nay).
- X Paired against.
- – Announced against.
- P Voted "present."
- C Voted "present" to avoid possible conflict of interest.
- ? Did not vote or otherwise make a position known.

•

Democrats ***Republicans***
Independents

	486	487	488	489	490
ALABAMA					
1 ***Callahan***	Y	Y	Y	Y	Y
2 ***Everett***	Y	Y	Y	Y	N
3 ***Riley***	N	Y	Y	Y	N
4 ***Aderholt***	N	Y	Y	Y	N
5 Cramer	Y	N	N	N	Y
6 ***Bachus***	Y	N	N	N	Y
7 Hilliard	N	N	N	N	Y
ALASKA					
AL ***Young***	?	Y	Y	Y	N
ARIZONA					
1 ***Salmon***	Y	Y	Y	Y	N
2 Pastor	Y	N	N	N	Y
3 ***Stump***	Y	Y	Y	Y	N
4 ***Shadegg***	Y	N	Y	Y	N
5 ***Kolbe***	Y	Y	Y	Y	N
6 ***Hayworth***	Y	Y	Y	Y	N
ARKANSAS					
1 Berry	Y	N	N	N	Y
2 Snyder	Y	N	N	N	Y
3 ***Hutchinson***	N	N	Y	Y	N
4 ***Dickey***	N	Y	Y	Y	N
CALIFORNIA					
1 Thompson	N	N	N	N	Y
2 ***Herger***	Y	Y	Y	N	N
3 ***Ose***	Y	Y	Y	Y	N
4 ***Doolittle***	Y	Y	Y	N	N
5 Matsui	Y	N	N	N	Y
6 Woolsey	Y	N	N	N	Y
7 Miller, George	N	N	N	N	Y
8 Pelosi	?	N	N	N	Y
9 Lee	N	N	N	N	Y
10 Tauscher	Y	N	N	N	Y
11 ***Pombo***	Y	Y	Y	N	N
12 Lantos	Y	N	N	N	Y
13 Stark	N	N	N	N	Y
14 Eshoo	Y	N	N	N	Y
15 ***Campbell***	Y	N	N	N	N
16 Lofgren	Y	N	N	N	Y
17 Farr	Y	N	N	N	Y
18 Condit	Y	N	N	N	Y
19 ***Radanovich***	Y	Y	Y	Y	N
20 Dooley	Y	N	N	N	Y
21 ***Thomas***	Y	Y	Y	Y	N
22 Capps	Y	N	N	N	Y
23 ***Gallegly***	Y	N	Y	Y	Y
24 Sherman	Y	N	N	N	Y
25 ***McKeon***	Y	Y	Y	Y	N
26 Berman	Y	N	N	N	Y
27 ***Rogan***	Y	N	Y	Y	N
28 ***Dreier***	Y	Y	Y	Y	N
29 Waxman	Y	N	N	N	Y
30 Becerra	Y	N	N	N	Y
31 Martinez	Y	N	N	N	Y
32 Dixon	Y	N	N	N	Y
33 Roybal-Allard	Y	N	N	N	Y
34 Napolitano	Y	N	N	N	Y
35 Waters	N	N	N	N	Y
36 ***Kuykendall***	Y	N	Y	Y	N
37 Millender-McD.	Y	N	N	N	Y
38 ***Horn***	Y	N	N	N	Y
39 ***Royce***	Y	Y	Y	N	N
40 ***Lewis***	Y	N	Y	Y	N
41 ***Miller***	Y	Y	Y	Y	N
42 Vacant					
43 ***Calvert***	Y	Y	Y	Y	N
44 ***Bono***	Y	N	Y	Y	Y
45 ***Rohrabacher***	Y	Y	Y	Y	N
46 Sanchez	Y	N	N	N	Y
47 ***Cox***	Y	Y	?	N	N
48 ***Packard***	Y	Y	Y	Y	N
49 ***Bilbray***	N	N	N	N	Y
50 Filner	N	N	N	N	Y
51 ***Cunningham***	Y	Y	Y	Y	N
52 ***Hunter***	Y	N	Y	Y	Y
COLORADO					
1 DeGette	Y	N	N	N	Y
2 Udall	N	N	N	N	Y
3 ***McInnis***	Y	Y	Y	Y	N
4 ***Schaffer***	N	N	Y	N	N
5 ***Hefley***	N	Y	Y	Y	Y
6 ***Tancredo***	Y	Y	Y	Y	N
CONNECTICUT					
1 Larson	Y	–	N	N	Y
2 Gejdenson	Y	N	N	N	Y
3 DeLauro	Y	N	N	N	Y
4 ***Shays***	Y	N	Y	Y	Y
5 Maloney	Y	N	N	N	Y
6 ***Johnson***	Y	?	Y	Y	N
DELAWARE					
AL ***Castle***	Y	N	Y	Y	Y
FLORIDA					
1 ***Scarborough***	?	?	?	?	?
2 Boyd	Y	N	N	N	Y
3 Brown	Y	N	N	N	Y
4 ***Fowler***	Y	Y	Y	Y	N
5 Thurman	N	N	N	N	Y
6 ***Stearns***	Y	N	Y	Y	N
7 ***Mica***	Y	Y	Y	Y	N
8 ***McCollum***	?	N	N	N	Y
9 ***Bilirakis***	Y	Y	Y	Y	Y
10 ***Young***	Y	N	Y	Y	Y
11 Davis	Y	N	N	N	Y
12 ***Canady***	Y	N	Y	Y	Y
13 ***Miller***	Y	Y	Y	Y	N
14 ***Goss***	Y	Y	Y	Y	N
15 ***Weldon***	Y	Y	Y	Y	Y
16 ***Foley***	Y	N	N	N	Y
17 Meek	N	N	N	N	Y
18 ***Ros-Lehtinen***	Y	N	Y	N	Y
19 Wexler	Y	N	N	N	Y
20 Deutsch	Y	N	N	N	Y
21 ***Diaz-Balart***	Y	N	Y	N	Y
22 ***Shaw***	Y	N	Y	Y	Y
23 Hastings	N	N	N	N	Y
GEORGIA					
1 ***Kingston***	Y	Y	Y	Y	N
2 Bishop	Y	N	N	N	Y
3 ***Collins***	Y	Y	Y	Y	N
4 McKinney	Y	N	N	N	Y
5 Lewis	N	N	N	N	Y
6 ***Isakson***	Y	N	Y	Y	N
7 ***Barr***	?	N	N	N	Y
8 ***Chambliss***	Y	Y	Y	Y	Y
9 ***Deal***	Y	Y	Y	Y	N
10 ***Norwood***	Y	N	N	N	Y
11 ***Linder***	?	Y	Y	Y	N
HAWAII					
1 Abercrombie	?	N	N	N	Y
2 Mink	Y	N	N	N	Y
IDAHO					
1 ***Chenoweth***	N	N	Y	Y	N
2 ***Simpson***	Y	Y	Y	Y	N
ILLINOIS					
1 Rush	Y	N	N	N	Y
2 Jackson	Y	N	N	N	Y
3 Lipinski	N	N	N	N	Y
4 Gutierrez	N	N	N	N	Y
5 Blagojevich	Y	N	N	N	Y
6 ***Hyde***	Y	Y	Y	Y	Y
7 Davis	?	N	N	N	Y
8 ***Crane***	N	Y	Y	Y	N
9 Schakowsky	Y	N	N	N	Y
10 ***Porter***	Y	N	Y	Y	Y
11 ***Weller***	N	Y	Y	Y	N
12 Costello	N	N	N	N	Y
13 ***Biggert***	Y	Y	Y	N	N
14 ***Hastert***		Y	Y	Y	

ND Northern Democrats SD Southern Democrats

	486	487	488	489	490
15 ***Ewing***	Y	Y	Y	Y	N
16 ***Manzullo***	Y	Y	Y	N	N
17 Evans	N	N	N	N	Y
18 ***LaHood***	Y	Y	Y	N	N
19 Phelps	Y	N	N	N	Y
20 ***Shimkus***	Y	Y	Y	Y	N
INDIANA					
1 Visclosky	N	N	N	N	Y
2 ***McIntosh***	Y	Y	N	N	N
3 Roemer	Y	N	N	N	Y
4 ***Souder***	Y	N	Y	Y	N
5 ***Buyer***	Y	N	Y	N	N
6 ***Burton***	Y	N	Y	N	N
7 ***Pease***	Y	Y	Y	Y	N
8 ***Hostettler***	Y	Y	N	N	N
9 Hill	Y	N	N	N	Y
10 Carson	Y	N	N	N	Y
IOWA					
1 ***Leach***	Y	N	N	N	Y
2 ***Nussle***	Y	Y	Y	Y	N
3 Boswell	Y	N	N	N	Y
4 ***Ganske***	Y	N	N	N	Y
5 ***Latham***	Y	Y	Y	Y	N
KANSAS					
1 ***Moran***	N	N	Y	N	Y
2 ***Ryun***	Y	Y	Y	Y	N
3 Moore	Y	N	N	N	Y
4 ***Tiahrt***	Y	Y	Y	Y	N
KENTUCKY					
1 ***Whitfield***	Y	Y	Y	N	N
2 ***Lewis***	Y	Y	Y	Y	N
3 ***Northup***	Y	Y	Y	Y	N
4 Lucas	Y	Y	Y	Y	Y
5 ***Rogers***	Y	Y	Y	Y	N
6 ***Fletcher***	Y	Y	Y	+	N
LOUISIANA					
1 ***Vitter***	Y	N	Y	Y	Y
2 Jefferson	?	N	N	N	Y
3 ***Tauzin***	Y	Y	Y	Y	N
4 ***McCrery***	Y	Y	Y	Y	N
5 ***Cooksey***	Y	N	Y	Y	Y
6 ***Baker***	Y	Y	Y	Y	N
7 John	Y	N	N	N	Y
MAINE					
1 Allen	N	N	N	N	Y
2 Baldacci	N	N	N	N	Y
MARYLAND					
1 ***Gilchrest***	Y	N	Y	N	Y
2 ***Ehrlich***	?	Y	Y	Y	N
3 Cardin	Y	N	N	N	Y
4 Wynn	Y	N	N	N	Y
5 Hoyer	Y	N	N	N	Y
6 ***Bartlett***	Y	Y	Y	Y	N
7 Cummings	Y	N	N	N	Y
8 ***Morella***	Y	N	N	N	Y
MASSACHUSETTS					
1 Olver	Y	N	N	N	Y
2 Neal	N	N	N	N	Y
3 McGovern	?	N	N	N	Y
4 Frank	Y	N	N	N	Y
5 Meehan	Y	N	N	N	Y
6 Tierney	Y	N	N	N	Y
7 Markey	Y	N	N	N	Y
8 Capuano	N	N	N	N	Y
9 Moakley	?	N	N	N	Y
10 Delahunt	Y	N	N	N	Y
MICHIGAN					
1 Stupak	N	N	N	N	Y
2 ***Hoekstra***	Y	Y	Y	Y	N
3 ***Ehlers***	Y	Y	Y	Y	N
4 ***Camp***	Y	Y	Y	Y	N
5 Barcia	Y	N	N	N	Y
6 ***Upton***	Y	Y	Y	Y	N
7 ***Smith***	Y	Y	Y	Y	N
8 Stabenow	Y	N	N	N	Y
9 Kildee	Y	N	N	N	Y
10 Bonior	Y	N	N	N	Y
11 ***Knollenberg***	Y	Y	Y	Y	N
12 Levin	Y	N	N	N	Y
13 Rivers	Y	N	N	N	Y
14 Conyers	Y	N	N	N	Y
15 Kilpatrick	Y	N	N	N	Y
16 Dingell	Y	N	N	N	Y

	486	487	488	489	490
MINNESOTA					
1 ***Gutknecht***	N	Y	Y	Y	N
2 Minge	Y	N	N	N	Y
3 ***Ramstad***	N	Y	Y	Y	N
4 Vento	N	N	N	N	Y
5 Sabo	N	N	N	N	+
6 Luther	N	N	N	N	Y
7 Peterson	N	N	N	N	N
8 Oberstar	N	N	N	N	Y
MISSISSIPPI					
1 ***Wicker***	Y	Y	Y	Y	N
2 Thompson	N	N	N	N	Y
3 ***Pickering***	Y	Y	Y	Y	N
4 Shows	Y	N	N	N	Y
5 Taylor	N	N	N	N	Y
MISSOURI					
1 Clay	N	N	N	N	Y
2 ***Talent***	Y	Y	Y	Y	N
3 Gephardt	Y	N	N	N	Y
4 Skelton	Y	N	N	N	Y
5 McCarthy	Y	N	N	N	Y
6 Danner	Y	N	N	N	Y
7 ***Blunt***	Y	Y	Y	Y	N
8 ***Emerson***	Y	N	Y	Y	N
9 ***Hulshof***	N	Y	Y	Y	–
MONTANA					
AL ***Hill***	Y	Y	Y	Y	N
NEBRASKA					
1 ***Bereuter***	Y	Y	Y	Y	N
2 ***Terry***	Y	Y	N	N	N
3 ***Barrett***	Y	Y	Y	N	N
NEVADA					
1 Berkley	Y	N	N	N	Y
2 ***Gibbons***	N	Y	Y	Y	Y
NEW HAMPSHIRE					
1 ***Sununu***	Y	Y	Y	N	N
2 ***Bass***	Y	N	Y	N	N
NEW JERSEY					
1 Andrews	Y	N	N	N	Y
2 ***LoBiondo***	N	N	N	N	Y
3 ***Saxton***	Y	N	N	N	Y
4 ***Smith***	Y	N	N	N	Y
5 ***Roukema***	Y	N	N	N	Y
6 Pallone	N	N	N	N	Y
7 ***Franks***	Y	N	N	N	Y
8 Pascrell	Y	N	N	N	Y
9 Rothman	Y	N	N	N	Y
10 Payne	Y	N	N	N	Y
11 ***Frelinghuysen***	Y	N	N	N	Y
12 Holt	Y	N	N	N	Y
13 Menendez	Y	N	N	N	Y
NEW MEXICO					
1 ***Wilson***	Y	N	Y	Y	Y
2 ***Skeen***	Y	N	Y	Y	N
3 Udall	N	N	N	N	Y
NEW YORK					
1 Forbes	Y	N	N	N	Y
2 ***Lazio***	Y	N	Y	Y	N
3 ***King***	Y	N	N	N	Y
4 McCarthy	Y	N	N	N	Y
5 Ackerman	Y	N	N	N	Y
6 Meeks	Y	N	N	N	Y
7 Crowley	N	N	N	N	Y
8 Nadler	Y	N	N	N	Y
9 Weiner	Y	N	N	N	Y
10 Towns	Y	N	N	N	Y
11 Owens	?	N	N	N	Y
12 Velázquez	N	N	N	N	Y
13 ***Fossella***	Y	Y	Y	Y	N
14 Maloney	Y	N	N	N	Y
15 Rangel	Y	N	N	N	Y
16 Serrano	Y	N	N	N	Y
17 Engel	Y	N	N	N	Y
18 Lowey	N	N	N	N	Y
19 ***Kelly***	Y	N	Y	Y	Y
20 ***Gilman***	Y	N	N	N	Y
21 McNulty	N	N	N	N	Y
22 ***Sweeney***	Y	N	Y	Y	Y
23 ***Boehlert***	Y	N	N	N	Y
24 ***McHugh***	Y	N	Y	Y	Y
25 ***Walsh***	Y	N	Y	Y	Y
26 Hinchey	Y	N	N	N	Y
27 ***Reynolds***	Y	N	Y	Y	Y
28 Slaughter	N	N	N	N	Y
29 LaFalce	N	N	N	N	Y

	486	487	488	489	490
30 ***Quinn***	Y	N	N	N	Y
31 ***Houghton***	Y	Y	Y	Y	N
NORTH CAROLINA					
1 Clayton	Y	N	N	N	Y
2 Etheridge	N	N	N	N	Y
3 ***Jones***	Y	Y	Y	N	Y
4 Price	Y	N	N	N	Y
5 ***Burr***	Y	Y	Y	N	N
6 ***Coble***	Y	Y	Y	Y	Y
7 McIntyre	Y	N	N	N	Y
8 ***Hayes***	Y	Y	Y	Y	N
9 ***Myrick***	Y	Y	Y	Y	N
10 ***Ballenger***	Y	Y	Y	Y	N
11 ***Taylor***	Y	Y	Y	Y	N
12 Watt	Y	N	N	N	Y
NORTH DAKOTA					
AL Pomeroy	Y	N	N	N	Y
OHIO					
1 ***Chabot***	Y	Y	Y	Y	N
2 ***Portman***	Y	Y	Y	Y	–
3 Hall	Y	N	N	N	Y
4 ***Oxley***	Y	Y	Y	N	N
5 ***Gillmor***	Y	Y	Y	Y	N
6 Strickland	N	N	N	N	Y
7 ***Hobson***	Y	Y	Y	Y	N
8 ***Boehner***	Y	Y	N	N	N
9 Kaptur	?	?	?	?	?
10 Kucinich	N	N	N	N	Y
11 Jones	N	N	N	N	Y
12 ***Kasich***	Y	Y	Y	N	N
13 Brown	Y	N	N	N	Y
14 Sawyer	?	N	N	N	Y
15 ***Pryce***	Y	Y	Y	Y	N
16 ***Regula***	Y	Y	Y	Y	N
17 Traficant	Y	N	N	?	Y
18 ***Ney***	Y	Y	Y	N	N
19 ***LaTourette***	Y	N	Y	Y	Y
OKLAHOMA					
1 ***Largent***	?	N	Y	Y	N
2 ***Coburn***	Y	N	Y	Y	Y
3 ***Watkins***	Y	Y	Y	Y	N
4 ***Watts***	Y	Y	Y	Y	N
5 ***Istook***	Y	N	Y	Y	N
6 ***Lucas***	Y	Y	Y	Y	N
OREGON					
1 Wu	Y	N	N	N	Y
2 ***Walden***	Y	Y	Y	Y	N
3 Blumenauer	Y	N	N	N	Y
4 DeFazio	N	N	N	N	Y
5 Hooley	N	N	N	N	Y
PENNSYLVANIA					
1 Brady	N	N	N	N	Y
2 Fattah	Y	N	N	N	Y
3 Borski	N	N	N	N	Y
4 Klink	Y	N	N	N	Y
5 ***Peterson***	Y	Y	Y	N	N
6 Holden	Y	N	N	N	Y
7 ***Weldon***	?	Y	Y	Y	Y
8 ***Greenwood***	Y	N	Y	Y	Y
9 ***Shuster***	Y	Y	Y	Y	?
10 ***Sherwood***	Y	Y	Y	Y	Y
11 Kanjorski	Y	N	N	N	Y
12 Murtha	Y	N	N	N	Y
13 Hoeffel	Y	N	N	N	Y
14 Coyne	Y	N	N	N	Y
15 ***Toomey***	Y	Y	Y	N	N
16 ***Pitts***	Y	Y	Y	Y	N
17 ***Gekas***	Y	Y	Y	Y	N
18 Doyle	Y	N	N	N	Y
19 ***Goodling***	Y	Y	Y	Y	N
20 Mascara	Y	N	N	N	Y
21 ***English***	N	N	Y	Y	N
RHODE ISLAND					
1 Kennedy	Y	N	N	N	Y
2 Weygand	Y	N	N	N	Y
SOUTH CAROLINA					
1 ***Sanford***	Y	N	Y	N	N
2 ***Spence***	Y	N	N	Y	Y
3 ***Graham***	Y	N	Y	Y	Y
4 ***DeMint***	Y	Y	Y	Y	N
5 Spratt	Y	N	N	N	Y
6 Clyburn	N	N	N	N	+
SOUTH DAKOTA					
AL ***Thune***	Y	Y	Y	Y	N

	486	487	488	489	490
TENNESSEE					
1 ***Jenkins***	Y	Y	Y	Y	Y
2 ***Duncan***	Y	N	Y	Y	Y
3 ***Wamp***	N	N	Y	Y	Y
4 ***Hilleary***	N	Y	Y	Y	N
5 Clement	?	N	N	N	Y
6 Gordon	Y	N	N	N	Y
7 ***Bryant***	Y	Y	Y	Y	N
8 Tanner	N	N	N	N	Y
9 Ford	?	N	N	N	Y
TEXAS					
1 Sandlin	Y	N	N	N	Y
2 Turner	Y	N	N	N	Y
3 ***Johnson, Sam***	Y	Y	Y	Y	N
4 Hall	Y	N	N	N	Y
5 ***Sessions***	Y	N	Y	N	Y
6 ***Barton***	Y	Y	Y	Y	N
7 ***Archer***	Y	Y	Y	Y	N
8 ***Brady***	Y	Y	Y	Y	Y
9 Lampson	Y	N	N	N	Y
10 Doggett	Y	N	N	N	Y
11 Edwards	Y	N	N	N	Y
12 ***Granger***	Y	Y	Y	?	?
13 ***Thornberry***	Y	N	Y	Y	Y
14 ***Paul***	Y	Y	N	N	N
15 Hinojosa	Y	N	N	N	Y
16 Reyes	Y	N	N	N	Y
17 Stenholm	N	N	N	N	Y
18 Jackson-Lee	N	N	N	N	Y
19 ***Combest***	Y	N	Y	Y	N
20 Gonzalez	Y	N	N	N	Y
21 ***Smith***	Y	Y	Y	Y	N
22 ***DeLay***	Y	Y	Y	Y	N
23 ***Bonilla***	Y	Y	N	N	N
24 Frost	N	N	N	N	Y
25 Bentsen	Y	N	N	N	Y
26 ***Armey***	Y	Y	Y	Y	N
27 Ortiz	Y	N	N	N	Y
28 Rodriguez	Y	N	N	N	Y
29 Green	Y	N	N	N	Y
30 Johnson, E.B.	N	N	N	N	Y
UTAH					
1 ***Hansen***	Y	Y	Y	Y	N
2 ***Cook***	Y	N	N	N	Y
3 ***Cannon***	Y	Y	Y	Y	Y
VERMONT					
AL *Sanders*	Y	N	N	N	Y
VIRGINIA					
1 ***Bateman***	Y	N	Y	Y	Y
2 Pickett	N	N	N	N	Y
3 Scott	Y	N	N	N	Y
4 Sisisky	Y	N	N	N	Y
5 Goode	Y	Y	Y	Y	N
6 ***Goodlatte***	Y	Y	Y	N	N
7 ***Bliley***	Y	Y	Y	Y	N
8 Moran	Y	N	N	N	Y
9 Boucher	Y	N	N	N	Y
10 ***Wolf***	Y	N	Y	Y	Y
11 ***Davis***	Y	N	Y	Y	Y
WASHINGTON					
1 Inslee	Y	N	N	N	Y
2 ***Metcalf***	Y	?	Y	Y	N
3 Baird	Y	N	N	N	Y
4 ***Hastings***	Y	Y	Y	Y	N
5 ***Nethercutt***	Y	Y	Y	Y	N
6 Dicks	Y	N	N	N	Y
7 McDermott	N	N	N	N	Y
8 ***Dunn***	Y	Y	Y	Y	N
9 Smith	Y	N	N	N	Y
WEST VIRGINIA					
1 Mollohan	Y	N	N	N	Y
2 Wise	Y	N	N	N	Y
3 Rahall	Y	N	N	N	Y
WISCONSIN					
1 ***Ryan***	Y	Y	Y	N	N
2 Baldwin	Y	N	N	N	Y
3 Kind	Y	N	N	N	Y
4 Kleczka	Y	N	N	N	Y
5 Barrett	Y	N	N	N	Y
6 ***Petri***	Y	Y	Y	Y	N
7 Obey	Y	N	N	N	Y
8 ***Green***	Y	Y	Y	Y	N
9 ***Sensenbrenner***	Y	Y	Y	Y	N
WYOMING					
AL ***Cubin***	Y	Y	Y	Y	N

Southern states - Ala., Ark., Fla., Ga., Ky., La., Miss., N.C., Okla., S.C., Tenn., Texas, Va.

491. H Res 303. Federal Education Assistance/Adoption. Goodling, R-Pa., motion to suspend the rules and adopt the resolution to express the sense of the House that 95 percent of federal education dollars should be spent on improving the performance of students in the classroom. Motion agreed to 421-5: R 219-0; D 201-5 (ND 149-4, SD 52-1); I 1-0. Oct. 12, 1999. A two-thirds majority of those present and voting (284 in this case) is required for passage under suspension of the rules.

492. S 800. Universal 911/Passage. Tauzin, R-La., motion to suspend the rules and pass the bill to direct the Federal Communications Commission to designate 911 as the universal emergency phone number, and to provide technical support to states to implement comprehensive emergency communications systems. Motion agreed to 424-2: R 216-2; D 207-0 (ND 154-0, SD 53-0); I 1-0. Oct. 12, 1999. A two-thirds majority of those present and voting (284 in this case) is required for passage under suspension of the rules.

493. HR 2130. 'Date Rape' Drugs/Passage. Upton, R-Mich., motion to suspend the rules and pass the bill to tighten regulations and increase criminal penalties for possession of three so-called date-rape drugs — gamma hydroxybutyric acid, also known as "Liquid Ecstasy"; ketamine; and gamma butyrolactone. Motion agreed to 423-1: R 216-1; D 206-0 (ND 153-0, SD 53-0); I 1-0. Oct. 12, 1999. A two-thirds majority of those present and voting (283 in this case) is required for passage under suspension of the rules.

494. HR 2561. Fiscal 2000 Defense Appropriations/Conference Report. Adoption of the conference report on the bill to appropriate $267.7 billion in defense spending for fiscal 2000. The conference report includes $1 billion of the $1.9 billion requested by the administration for the F-22 jet fighter program and would designate $7.2 billion of the bill's total budget authority as emergency spending. Adopted (thus sent to the Senate) 372-55: R 214-7; D 158-47 (ND 108-43, SD 50-4); I 0-1. Oct. 13, 1999.

495. HR 1993. OPIC Reauthorization/Foreign Manufacturing Enterprises. Manzullo, R-Ill., amendment to the Rohrabacher, R-Calif., amendment. The Rohrabacher amendment would prohibit the Overseas Private Investment Corporation (OPIC) from financing manufacturing enterprises in foreign countries. The Manzullo amendment would prohibit OPIC from financing such enterprises if OPIC determines that the investment would cause a reduction in manufacturing in the United States. Adopted 379-49: R 189-29; D 190-19 (ND 138-17, SD 52-2); I 0-1. Oct. 13, 1999. (Subsequently, the Rohrabacher amendment as amended by the Manzullo amendment was adopted by voice vote.)

496. HR 1993. OPIC Reauthorization/One-Year Authorization. Sanford, R-S.C., amendment to limit the authorization for the Overseas Private Investment Corporation (OPIC) to one year instead of four years. Rejected 104-323: R 76-141; D 27-182 (ND 21-134, SD 6-48); I 1-0. Oct. 13, 1999.

497. HR 1993. OPIC Reauthorization/GAO Claim Review. Menendez, D-N.J., amendment to the Terry, R-Neb., amendment. The Terry amendment would state that the Overseas Private Investment Corporation (OPIC) should settle claims within 90 days, allow a 60-day extension for receipt of supplemental information, and pay interest at the prime rate for each day after the specified time limit. The Menendez amendment would substitute a request that the General Accounting Office review OPIC's claims processing and report to Congress. Adopted 259-169: R 62-156; D 196-13 (ND 148-7, SD 48-6); I 1-0. Oct. 13, 1999. (Subsequently, the Terry amendment, as amended, was adopted by voice vote.)

Key

Y Voted for (yea).
\# Paired for.
\+ Announced for.
N Voted against (nay).
X Paired against.
– Announced against.
P Voted "present."
C Voted "present" to avoid possible conflict of interest.
? Did not vote or otherwise make a position known.

•

Democrats ***Republicans***
Independents

	491	492	493	494	495	496	497
ALABAMA							
1 ***Callahan***	Y	Y	Y	Y	Y	N	N
2 ***Everett***	Y	Y	Y	Y	Y	N	N
3 ***Riley***	Y	Y	Y	Y	Y	N	N
4 ***Aderholt***	Y	Y	Y	Y	Y	N	N
5 Cramer	Y	Y	Y	Y	Y	N	Y
6 ***Bachus***	Y	Y	Y	Y	N	Y	N
7 Hilliard	Y	Y	Y	Y	Y	N	Y
ALASKA							
AL ***Young***	Y	Y	Y	Y	?	?	?
ARIZONA							
1 ***Salmon***	Y	Y	Y	Y	Y	Y	N
2 Pastor	Y	Y	Y	Y	Y	N	Y
3 ***Stump***	Y	Y	Y	Y	Y	Y	N
4 ***Shadegg***	Y	Y	Y	Y	N	Y	N
5 ***Kolbe***	Y	Y	Y	Y	Y	N	N
6 ***Hayworth***	Y	Y	Y	Y	N	Y	N
ARKANSAS							
1 Berry	Y	Y	Y	Y	Y	N	Y
2 Snyder	Y	Y	Y	Y	Y	N	Y
3 ***Hutchinson***	Y	Y	Y	Y	Y	N	Y
4 ***Dickey***	Y	Y	Y	Y	Y	N	N
CALIFORNIA							
1 Thompson	Y	Y	Y	Y	Y	N	Y
2 ***Herger***	Y	Y	Y	Y	Y	Y	N
3 ***Ose***	Y	Y	Y	Y	Y	N	N
4 ***Doolittle***	Y	Y	Y	Y	Y	Y	Y
5 Matsui	Y	Y	Y	Y	Y	N	Y
6 Woolsey	Y	Y	Y	Y	Y	N	Y
7 Miller, George	Y	Y	Y	N	Y	N	Y
8 Pelosi	Y	Y	Y	Y	Y	N	Y
9 Lee	Y	Y	Y	N	Y	N	Y
10 Tauscher	Y	Y	Y	Y	Y	N	Y
11 ***Pombo***	Y	Y	Y	Y	Y	Y	Y
12 Lantos	Y	Y	Y	Y	Y	N	Y
13 Stark	Y	Y	Y	N	N	Y	Y
14 Eshoo	Y	Y	Y	N	Y	N	Y
15 ***Campbell***	Y	Y	Y	Y	Y	Y	N
16 Lofgren	Y	Y	Y	N	Y	N	Y
17 Farr	Y	Y	Y	Y	Y	N	Y
18 Condit	Y	Y	Y	Y	Y	Y	N
19 ***Radanovich***	Y	Y	Y	Y	N	N	N
20 Dooley	Y	Y	Y	Y	Y	N	Y
21 ***Thomas***	Y	Y	Y	Y	Y	N	N
22 Capps	Y	Y	Y	Y	Y	N	Y
23 ***Gallegly***	Y	Y	Y	Y	Y	N	N
24 Sherman	Y	Y	Y	Y	Y	N	Y
25 ***McKeon***	Y	Y	Y	Y	Y	N	N
26 Berman	Y	Y	Y	Y	Y	N	Y
27 ***Rogan***	Y	Y	Y	Y	Y	Y	N
28 ***Dreier***	Y	Y	Y	Y	Y	N	N
29 Waxman	Y	Y	Y	N	Y	N	Y
30 Becerra	Y	Y	Y	Y	Y	N	Y
31 Martinez	Y	Y	Y	Y	Y	N	Y
32 Dixon	Y	Y	Y	Y	Y	N	Y
33 Roybal-Allard	Y	Y	Y	Y	Y	N	Y
34 Napolitano	Y	Y	Y	Y	Y	N	Y
35 Waters	N	Y	Y	N	Y	N	Y
36 ***Kuykendall***	Y	Y	Y	Y	Y	N	Y
37 Millender-McD.	Y	Y	?	Y	Y	N	Y
38 ***Horn***	Y	Y	Y	Y	Y	N	N
39 ***Royce***	Y	Y	Y	Y	N	Y	N
40 ***Lewis***	Y	Y	Y	Y	Y	N	N
41 ***Miller***	Y	Y	Y	Y	Y	N	N
42 Vacant							
43 ***Calvert***	Y	Y	Y	Y	Y	N	N
44 ***Bono***	Y	Y	Y	Y	Y	N	Y
45 ***Rohrabacher***	Y	Y	Y	Y	N	Y	N
46 Sanchez	Y	Y	Y	Y	Y	N	Y
47 ***Cox***	Y	Y	Y	Y	N	Y	N
48 ***Packard***	Y	Y	Y	Y	Y	N	N
49 ***Bilbray***	Y	Y	Y	Y	Y	N	N
50 Filner	Y	Y	Y	N	Y	N	Y
51 ***Cunningham***	Y	Y	Y	Y	Y	N	N
52 ***Hunter***	Y	Y	Y	Y	N	Y	Y
COLORADO							
1 DeGette	Y	Y	Y	N	Y	N	Y
2 Udall	Y	Y	Y	Y	Y	N	Y
3 ***McInnis***	Y	Y	Y	Y	Y	N	N
4 ***Schaffer***	Y	Y	Y	Y	Y	Y	N
5 ***Hefley***	Y	Y	Y	N	Y	Y	Y
6 ***Tancredo***	Y	Y	Y	Y	Y	Y	N
CONNECTICUT							
1 Larson	Y	Y	Y	Y	Y	N	Y
2 Gejdenson	Y	Y	Y	Y	Y	N	Y
3 DeLauro	Y	Y	Y	Y	Y	N	Y
4 ***Shays***	Y	Y	Y	N	Y	Y	Y
5 Maloney	Y	Y	Y	Y	Y	N	Y
6 ***Johnson***	Y	Y	Y	Y	Y	N	Y
DELAWARE							
AL ***Castle***	Y	Y	Y	Y	Y	N	N
FLORIDA							
1 ***Scarborough***	?	?	?	?	?	?	?
2 Boyd	Y	Y	Y	Y	Y	N	Y
3 Brown	Y	Y	Y	Y	Y	N	Y
4 ***Fowler***	Y	Y	Y	Y	Y	N	Y
5 Thurman	Y	Y	Y	Y	Y	N	Y
6 ***Stearns***	Y	Y	Y	Y	N	Y	N
7 ***Mica***	Y	Y	Y	Y	Y	N	Y
8 ***McCollum***	Y	Y	Y	Y	Y	N	Y
9 ***Bilirakis***	Y	Y	Y	Y	Y	Y	N
10 ***Young***	Y	Y	Y	Y	Y	N	N
11 Davis	Y	Y	Y	Y	Y	N	Y
12 ***Canady***	Y	Y	Y	Y	Y	N	Y
13 ***Miller***	Y	Y	Y	Y	Y	N	N
14 ***Goss***	Y	Y	Y	Y	Y	Y	N
15 ***Weldon***	Y	Y	Y	Y	Y	N	N
16 ***Foley***	Y	Y	Y	Y	Y	N	N
17 Meek	?	?	?	Y	Y	N	Y
18 ***Ros-Lehtinen***	Y	Y	Y	Y	Y	N	Y
19 Wexler	Y	Y	Y	Y	Y	N	Y
20 Deutsch	Y	Y	Y	N	Y	N	Y
21 ***Diaz-Balart***	Y	Y	Y	Y	Y	N	Y
22 ***Shaw***	Y	Y	Y	Y	Y	N	N
23 Hastings	Y	Y	Y	Y	Y	N	Y
GEORGIA							
1 ***Kingston***	Y	Y	Y	Y	Y	Y	N
2 Bishop	Y	Y	Y	Y	Y	N	Y
3 ***Collins***	Y	Y	Y	Y	N	Y	N
4 McKinney	Y	Y	Y	N	N	Y	N
5 Lewis	Y	Y	Y	Y	Y	N	Y
6 ***Isakson***	Y	Y	Y	Y	Y	N	N
7 ***Barr***	Y	Y	Y	Y	N	Y	Y
8 ***Chambliss***	Y	Y	Y	Y	Y	N	N
9 ***Deal***	Y	Y	Y	Y	Y	N	N
10 ***Norwood***	Y	Y	Y	Y	Y	Y	N
11 ***Linder***	Y	Y	Y	Y	Y	Y	N
HAWAII							
1 Abercrombie	N	Y	Y	Y	N	Y	Y
2 Mink	N	Y	Y	Y	Y	N	Y
IDAHO							
1 ***Chenoweth***	Y	N	Y	Y	N	Y	N
2 ***Simpson***	Y	Y	Y	Y	Y	N	N
ILLINOIS							
1 Rush	Y	Y	Y	Y	Y	N	Y
2 Jackson	Y	Y	Y	N	N	Y	Y
3 Lipinski	Y	Y	Y	Y	Y	Y	N
4 Gutierrez	Y	Y	Y	Y	Y	N	Y
5 Blagojevich	Y	Y	Y	Y	Y	N	Y
6 ***Hyde***	Y	Y	Y	Y	Y	N	N
7 Davis	Y	Y	Y	N	Y	N	Y
8 ***Crane***	Y	Y	Y	Y	Y	Y	Y
9 Schakowsky	Y	Y	Y	N	Y	N	Y
10 ***Porter***	Y	Y	Y	Y	Y	N	N
11 ***Weller***	Y	Y	Y	Y	Y	N	N
12 Costello	Y	Y	Y	Y	Y	N	Y
13 ***Biggert***	Y	Y	Y	Y	Y	N	Y
14 ***Hastert***				Y			

ND Northern Democrats SD Southern Democrats

	491	492	493	494	495	496	497
15 ***Ewing***	Y	Y	Y	Y	Y	N	N
16 ***Manzullo***	Y	Y	Y	Y	Y	N	N
17 Evans	Y	Y	Y	Y	Y	N	Y
18 ***LaHood***	Y	Y	Y	Y	Y	N	Y
19 Phelps	Y	Y	Y	Y	Y	N	Y
20 ***Shimkus***	Y	Y	Y	Y	Y	N	Y
INDIANA							
1 Visclosky	Y	Y	Y	Y	Y	Y	Y
2 ***McIntosh***	Y	Y	Y	Y	N	Y	N
3 Roemer	Y	Y	Y	Y	Y	N	Y
4 ***Souder***	Y	Y	Y	Y	Y	N	Y
5 ***Buyer***	Y	Y	Y	Y	Y	Y	Y
6 ***Burton***	Y	Y	Y	Y	N	Y	Y
7 ***Pease***	Y	Y	Y	Y	Y	Y	Y
8 ***Hostettler***	Y	Y	Y	Y	N	Y	Y
9 Hill	Y	Y	Y	Y	Y	N	Y
10 Carson	Y	Y	Y	+	Y	Y	Y
IOWA							
1 ***Leach***	Y	Y	Y	Y	Y	N	N
2 ***Nussle***	Y	Y	Y	Y	Y	N	N
3 Boswell	Y	Y	Y	N	Y	N	N
4 ***Ganske***	Y	Y	Y	N	Y	N	N
5 ***Latham***	Y	Y	Y	Y	Y	Y	N
KANSAS							
1 ***Moran***	Y	Y	Y	Y	Y	N	N
2 ***Ryun***	Y	Y	Y	Y	Y	N	N
3 Moore	Y	Y	Y	Y	Y	N	Y
4 ***Tiahrt***	Y	Y	Y	Y	Y	N	N
KENTUCKY							
1 ***Whitfield***	Y	Y	Y	Y	Y	N	Y
2 ***Lewis***	Y	Y	Y	Y	Y	N	Y
3 ***Northup***	Y	Y	Y	Y	Y	N	N
4 Lucas	Y	Y	Y	Y	Y	N	Y
5 ***Rogers***	Y	Y	Y	Y	Y	N	Y
6 ***Fletcher***	Y	Y	Y	Y	Y	N	N
LOUISIANA							
1 ***Vitter***	Y	Y	Y	Y	Y	N	N
2 Jefferson	?	?	?	?	?	?	?
3 ***Tauzin***	Y	Y	Y	Y	Y	Y	N
4 ***McCrery***	Y	Y	Y	Y	Y	N	N
5 ***Cooksey***	Y	Y	Y	Y	Y	N	N
6 ***Baker***	Y	Y	Y	Y	Y	N	N
7 John	Y	Y	Y	Y	Y	N	N
MAINE							
1 Allen	Y	Y	Y	Y	Y	N	Y
2 Baldacci	Y	Y	Y	Y	Y	N	Y
MARYLAND							
1 ***Gilchrest***	Y	Y	Y	Y	Y	N	Y
2 ***Ehrlich***	Y	Y	Y	Y	Y	Y	N
3 Cardin	Y	Y	Y	Y	Y	N	Y
4 Wynn	Y	Y	Y	Y	Y	N	Y
5 Hoyer	Y	Y	Y	Y	Y	N	Y
6 ***Bartlett***	Y	Y	Y	Y	N	Y	N
7 Cummings	Y	Y	Y	Y	Y	N	Y
8 ***Morella***	Y	Y	Y	Y	Y	N	Y
MASSACHUSETTS							
1 Olver	Y	Y	Y	N	Y	N	Y
2 Neal	Y	Y	Y	Y	Y	N	Y
3 McGovern	Y	Y	Y	N	Y	N	Y
4 Frank	Y	Y	Y	Y	N	N	Y
5 Meehan	Y	Y	Y	Y	Y	Y	Y
6 Tierney	Y	Y	Y	Y	N	Y	Y
7 Markey	Y	Y	Y	N	Y	N	Y
8 Capuano	Y	Y	Y	N	Y	N	Y
9 Moakley	Y	Y	Y	Y	Y	N	Y
10 Delahunt	Y	Y	Y	N	Y	N	Y
MICHIGAN							
1 Stupak	Y	Y	Y	Y	Y	N	Y
2 ***Hoekstra***	Y	Y	Y	Y	Y	Y	N
3 ***Ehlers***	Y	Y	Y	N	Y	N	Y
4 ***Camp***	Y	Y	Y	Y	Y	N	N
5 Barcia	Y	Y	Y	Y	Y	N	Y
6 ***Upton***	Y	Y	Y	N	Y	N	Y
7 ***Smith***	Y	Y	Y	Y	N	Y	N
8 Stabenow	Y	Y	Y	Y	Y	N	Y
9 Kildee	Y	Y	Y	Y	Y	N	Y
10 Bonior	Y	Y	Y	Y	Y	Y	Y
11 ***Knollenberg***	Y	Y	Y	Y	Y	N	N
12 Levin	Y	Y	Y	Y	Y	N	Y
13 Rivers	Y	Y	Y	N	Y	Y	Y
14 Conyers	Y	Y	Y	N	N	N	Y
15 Kilpatrick	–	+	+	Y	Y	N	Y
16 Dingell	Y	Y	Y	Y	Y	N	Y
MINNESOTA							
1 ***Gutknecht***	Y	Y	Y	Y	Y	Y	N
2 Minge	Y	Y	Y	N	Y	N	Y
3 ***Ramstad***	Y	Y	Y	Y	Y	N	Y
4 Vento	Y	Y	Y	N	N	N	Y
5 Sabo	Y	Y	Y	Y	Y	N	Y
6 Luther	Y	Y	Y	N	Y	Y	Y
7 Peterson	Y	Y	Y	N	N	Y	N
8 Oberstar	Y	Y	Y	N	Y	N	Y
MISSISSIPPI							
1 ***Wicker***	Y	Y	Y	Y	Y	N	N
2 Thompson	Y	Y	Y	Y	Y	Y	Y
3 ***Pickering***	Y	Y	Y	Y	Y	N	N
4 Shows	Y	Y	Y	Y	Y	N	Y
5 Taylor	Y	Y	Y	Y	N	Y	Y
MISSOURI							
1 Clay	Y	Y	Y	Y	Y	N	Y
2 ***Talent***	Y	Y	Y	Y	Y	N	Y
3 Gephardt	Y	Y	Y	Y	Y	N	Y
4 Skelton	Y	Y	Y	Y	Y	N	Y
5 McCarthy	Y	Y	Y	N	Y	N	Y
6 Danner	Y	Y	Y	?	Y	N	Y
7 ***Blunt***	Y	Y	Y	Y	Y	N	Y
8 ***Emerson***	Y	Y	Y	Y	Y	N	N
9 ***Hulshof***	Y	Y	Y	Y	Y	N	N
MONTANA							
AL ***Hill***	Y	Y	Y	Y	Y	N	Y
NEBRASKA							
1 ***Bereuter***	Y	Y	Y	Y	Y	N	N
2 ***Terry***	Y	Y	Y	Y	Y	Y	N
3 ***Barrett***	Y	Y	Y	Y	Y	N	N
NEVADA							
1 Berkley	Y	Y	Y	Y	Y	N	Y
2 ***Gibbons***	Y	Y	Y	Y	Y	N	N
NEW HAMPSHIRE							
1 ***Sununu***	Y	Y	Y	Y	N	Y	N
2 ***Bass***	Y	Y	Y	Y	Y	?	Y
NEW JERSEY							
1 Andrews	Y	Y	Y	Y	N	Y	N
2 ***LoBiondo***	Y	Y	Y	Y	N	Y	Y
3 ***Saxton***	Y	Y	Y	Y	Y	N	N
4 ***Smith***	Y	Y	Y	Y	N	Y	Y
5 ***Roukema***	Y	?	?	?	Y	N	N
6 Pallone	Y	Y	Y	Y	Y	N	Y
7 ***Franks***	Y	Y	Y	Y	Y	N	N
8 Pascrell	+	+	+	Y	N	Y	N
9 Rothman	Y	Y	Y	Y	Y	N	Y
10 Payne	Y	Y	Y	N	Y	N	Y
11 ***Frelinghuysen***	Y	Y	Y	Y	Y	N	N
12 Holt	Y	Y	Y	Y	Y	N	Y
13 Menendez	Y	Y	Y	Y	Y	N	Y
NEW MEXICO							
1 ***Wilson***	Y	Y	Y	Y	Y	N	N
2 ***Skeen***	Y	Y	Y	Y	Y	N	N
3 Udall	Y	Y	Y	Y	Y	N	Y
NEW YORK							
1 Forbes	Y	Y	Y	Y	Y	N	Y
2 ***Lazio***	Y	Y	?	Y	Y	N	N
3 ***King***	Y	Y	Y	Y	Y	N	N
4 McCarthy	Y	Y	Y	+	Y	N	Y
5 Ackerman	Y	Y	Y	N	Y	N	Y
6 Meeks	Y	Y	Y	Y	Y	N	Y
7 Crowley	Y	Y	Y	Y	Y	N	Y
8 Nadler	N	Y	Y	N	N	N	Y
9 Weiner	Y	Y	Y	Y	Y	N	Y
10 Towns	Y	Y	Y	Y	N	N	Y
11 Owens	Y	Y	Y	N	Y	N	Y
12 Velázquez	Y	Y	Y	N	Y	N	Y
13 ***Fossella***	Y	Y	Y	Y	N	Y	N
14 Maloney	Y	Y	Y	Y	Y	N	Y
15 Rangel	Y	Y	Y	N	Y	N	Y
16 Serrano	Y	Y	Y	Y	Y	N	Y
17 Engel	Y	Y	Y	Y	Y	N	Y
18 Lowey	Y	Y	Y	Y	Y	N	Y
19 ***Kelly***	Y	Y	Y	Y	Y	Y	Y
20 ***Gilman***	Y	Y	Y	Y	Y	N	N
21 McNulty	Y	Y	Y	Y	Y	N	Y
22 ***Sweeney***	Y	Y	Y	Y	Y	N	N
23 ***Boehlert***	Y	Y	Y	Y	Y	N	Y
24 ***McHugh***	Y	Y	Y	Y	Y	N	Y
25 ***Walsh***	Y	Y	Y	Y	Y	N	N
26 Hinchey	Y	Y	Y	Y	N	Y	Y
27 ***Reynolds***	Y	Y	Y	Y	Y	N	N
28 Slaughter	Y	Y	Y	Y	N	Y	Y
29 LaFalce	Y	Y	Y	Y	Y	N	Y
30 ***Quinn***	Y	Y	Y	Y	Y	N	N
31 ***Houghton***	Y	Y	Y	Y	Y	N	N
NORTH CAROLINA							
1 Clayton	Y	Y	Y	Y	Y	N	Y
2 Etheridge	Y	Y	Y	Y	Y	N	Y
3 ***Jones***	Y	Y	Y	Y	N	Y	Y
4 Price	Y	Y	Y	Y	Y	N	Y
5 ***Burr***	Y	Y	Y	Y	?	?	?
6 ***Coble***	Y	Y	Y	Y	Y	Y	Y
7 McIntyre	Y	Y	Y	Y	Y	Y	Y
8 ***Hayes***	Y	Y	Y	Y	Y	Y	N
9 ***Myrick***	Y	Y	Y	Y	N	Y	N
10 ***Ballenger***	Y	Y	Y	Y	Y	N	N
11 ***Taylor***	Y	Y	Y	Y	Y	Y	Y
12 Watt	Y	Y	Y	N	Y	N	Y
NORTH DAKOTA							
AL Pomeroy	Y	Y	Y	Y	Y	N	Y
OHIO							
1 ***Chabot***	Y	Y	Y	Y	Y	Y	N
2 ***Portman***	Y	Y	Y	Y	Y	N	N
3 Hall	Y	Y	Y	Y	Y	N	Y
4 ***Oxley***	Y	Y	Y	Y	Y	N	N
5 ***Gillmor***	Y	Y	Y	Y	Y	Y	N
6 Strickland	Y	Y	Y	Y	N	Y	Y
7 ***Hobson***	Y	Y	Y	Y	Y	N	Y
8 ***Boehner***	Y	Y	Y	Y	Y	N	N
9 Kaptur	Y	Y	Y	Y	Y	Y	Y
10 Kucinich	Y	Y	Y	N	N	Y	Y
11 Jones	Y	Y	Y	Y	Y	N	Y
12 ***Kasich***	Y	Y	Y	Y	N	Y	N
13 Brown	Y	Y	Y	N	?	?	?
14 Sawyer	Y	Y	Y	Y	Y	N	Y
15 ***Pryce***	Y	Y	Y	Y	Y	N	N
16 ***Regula***	Y	Y	Y	Y	Y	N	N
17 Traficant	Y	Y	Y	Y	Y	N	N
18 ***Ney***	Y	Y	Y	Y	Y	N	Y
19 ***LaTourette***	Y	Y	Y	Y	Y	N	N
OKLAHOMA							
1 ***Largent***	Y	Y	Y	Y	Y	Y	N
2 ***Coburn***	?	?	?	Y	N	Y	Y
3 ***Watkins***	Y	Y	Y	Y	Y	Y	N
4 ***Watts***	Y	Y	Y	Y	Y	Y	Y
5 ***Istook***	Y	Y	Y	Y	Y	Y	Y
6 ***Lucas***	Y	Y	Y	Y	Y	Y	N
OREGON							
1 Wu	Y	Y	Y	Y	Y	N	Y
2 ***Walden***	Y	Y	Y	Y	Y	N	Y
3 Blumenauer	Y	Y	Y	N	Y	N	Y
4 DeFazio	Y	Y	Y	N	N	Y	Y
5 Hooley	Y	Y	Y	N	Y	N	Y
PENNSYLVANIA							
1 Brady	Y	Y	Y	Y	Y	N	Y
2 Fattah	?	Y	Y	N	Y	N	Y
3 Borski	Y	Y	Y	Y	Y	N	Y
4 Klink	Y	Y	Y	Y	Y	N	Y
5 ***Peterson***	Y	Y	Y	Y	Y	N	Y
6 Holden	Y	Y	Y	Y	Y	N	Y
7 ***Weldon***	Y	Y	Y	Y	Y	N	N
8 ***Greenwood***	Y	Y	Y	Y	Y	N	N
9 ***Shuster***	Y	Y	Y	Y	Y	N	N
10 ***Sherwood***	Y	Y	Y	Y	Y	N	N
11 Kanjorski	Y	Y	Y	Y	Y	N	Y
12 Murtha	Y	Y	Y	Y	Y	N	Y
13 Hoeffel	Y	Y	Y	Y	Y	N	Y
14 Coyne	Y	Y	Y	Y	Y	N	Y
15 ***Toomey***	Y	Y	Y	Y	Y	Y	N
16 ***Pitts***	Y	Y	Y	Y	Y	N	N
17 ***Gekas***	Y	Y	Y	Y	Y	N	N
18 Doyle	Y	Y	Y	Y	Y	N	Y
19 ***Goodling***	Y	Y	Y	Y	Y	Y	Y
20 Mascara	Y	Y	Y	Y	Y	N	Y
21 ***English***	Y	Y	Y	Y	Y	N	N
RHODE ISLAND							
1 Kennedy	Y	Y	Y	+	Y	N	Y
2 Weygand	Y	Y	Y	Y	Y	N	Y
SOUTH CAROLINA							
1 ***Sanford***	Y	Y	Y	Y	N	Y	N
2 ***Spence***	Y	Y	Y	Y	Y	Y	N
3 ***Graham***	Y	Y	Y	Y	Y	Y	Y
4 ***DeMint***	Y	Y	Y	Y	Y	Y	N
5 Spratt	Y	Y	Y	Y	Y	N	Y
6 Clyburn	Y	Y	Y	Y	Y	N	Y
SOUTH DAKOTA							
AL ***Thune***	Y	Y	Y	Y	Y	Y	N
TENNESSEE							
1 ***Jenkins***	Y	Y	Y	Y	Y	Y	Y
2 ***Duncan***	Y	Y	Y	Y	N	Y	N
3 ***Wamp***	Y	Y	Y	Y	N	Y	N
4 ***Hilleary***	Y	Y	Y	Y	Y	Y	N
5 Clement	Y	Y	Y	Y	Y	N	Y
6 Gordon	Y	Y	Y	Y	Y	N	Y
7 ***Bryant***	Y	Y	Y	Y	Y	N	N
8 Tanner	Y	Y	Y	Y	Y	N	Y
9 Ford	Y	Y	Y	Y	Y	N	Y
TEXAS							
1 Sandlin	Y	Y	Y	Y	Y	N	Y
2 Turner	Y	Y	Y	Y	Y	N	Y
3 ***Johnson, Sam***	Y	Y	Y	Y	Y	N	N
4 Hall	Y	Y	Y	Y	Y	Y	N
5 ***Sessions***	Y	Y	Y	Y	Y	Y	N
6 ***Barton***	Y	Y	Y	Y	Y	N	N
7 ***Archer***	Y	Y	Y	Y	Y	N	N
8 ***Brady***	Y	Y	Y	Y	Y	N	N
9 Lampson	Y	Y	Y	Y	Y	N	Y
10 Doggett	Y	Y	Y	N	Y	N	Y
11 Edwards	Y	Y	Y	Y	Y	N	Y
12 ***Granger***	Y	Y	Y	Y	Y	N	Y
13 ***Thornberry***	Y	Y	Y	Y	Y	N	N
14 ***Paul***	Y	N	N	N	N	Y	Y
15 Hinojosa	Y	Y	Y	Y	Y	N	Y
16 Reyes	Y	Y	Y	Y	Y	N	Y
17 Stenholm	Y	Y	Y	Y	Y	N	N
18 Jackson-Lee	Y	Y	Y	Y	Y	N	Y
19 ***Combest***	Y	Y	Y	Y	Y	N	N
20 Gonzalez	Y	Y	Y	Y	Y	N	Y
21 ***Smith***	Y	Y	Y	Y	Y	N	N
22 ***DeLay***	Y	Y	Y	Y	Y	N	N
23 ***Bonilla***	Y	Y	Y	Y	Y	N	Y
24 Frost	Y	Y	Y	Y	Y	N	Y
25 Bentsen	Y	Y	Y	Y	Y	N	Y
26 ***Armey***	Y	Y	Y	Y	Y	Y	N
27 Ortiz	Y	Y	Y	Y	Y	N	Y
28 Rodriguez	Y	Y	Y	Y	Y	N	Y
29 Green	Y	Y	Y	Y	Y	N	Y
30 Johnson, E.B.	Y	Y	Y	Y	Y	N	Y
UTAH							
1 ***Hansen***	Y	Y	Y	Y	Y	N	N
2 ***Cook***	Y	Y	Y	Y	Y	N	N
3 ***Cannon***	Y	Y	Y	Y	Y	N	Y
VERMONT							
AL *Sanders*	Y	Y	Y	N	N	Y	Y
VIRGINIA							
1 ***Bateman***	Y	Y	Y	Y	Y	N	N
2 Pickett	Y	Y	Y	Y	Y	N	Y
3 Scott	N	Y	Y	Y	Y	N	Y
4 Sisisky	Y	Y	Y	Y	Y	N	Y
5 Goode	Y	Y	Y	Y	Y	Y	N
6 ***Goodlatte***	Y	Y	Y	Y	Y	Y	N
7 ***Bliley***	Y	Y	Y	Y	Y	N	N
8 Moran	Y	Y	Y	Y	Y	N	N
9 Boucher	Y	Y	Y	Y	Y	N	Y
10 ***Wolf***	Y	Y	Y	Y	Y	N	N
11 ***Davis***	Y	Y	Y	Y	Y	N	N
WASHINGTON							
1 Inslee	Y	Y	Y	Y	Y	N	Y
2 ***Metcalf***	Y	Y	Y	Y	Y	N	Y
3 Baird	Y	Y	Y	Y	Y	N	Y
4 ***Hastings***	Y	Y	Y	Y	Y	N	N
5 ***Nethercutt***	Y	Y	Y	Y	Y	N	N
6 Dicks	Y	Y	Y	Y	Y	N	Y
7 McDermott	Y	Y	Y	N	Y	N	Y
8 ***Dunn***	Y	Y	Y	Y	Y	N	Y
9 Smith	Y	Y	Y	Y	Y	N	Y
WEST VIRGINIA							
1 Mollohan	Y	Y	Y	Y	Y	N	Y
2 Wise	Y	Y	Y	?	Y	N	Y
3 Rahall	Y	Y	Y	Y	Y	N	Y
WISCONSIN							
1 ***Ryan***	Y	Y	Y	Y	Y	N	N
2 Baldwin	Y	Y	Y	N	Y	N	Y
3 Kind	Y	Y	Y	N	Y	N	Y
4 Kleczka	Y	Y	Y	Y	Y	N	Y
5 Barrett	Y	Y	Y	N	Y	N	Y
6 ***Petri***	Y	Y	Y	Y	Y	N	N
7 Obey	Y	Y	Y	N	Y	N	Y
8 ***Green***	Y	Y	Y	N	Y	N	N
9 ***Sensenbrenner***	Y	Y	Y	Y	Y	N	N
WYOMING							
AL ***Cubin***	Y	Y	Y	Y	Y	Y	Y

Southern states - Ala., Ark., Fla., Ga., Ky., La., Miss., N.C., Okla., S.C., Tenn., Texas, Va.

498. HR 1993. OPIC Reauthorization/Claim Settlement Disclosure. Menendez, D-N.J., amendment to the Terry, R-Neb., amendment. The Terry amendment would require the Overseas Private Investment Corporation (OPIC) to publish and report to Congress any intervention by other U.S. government departments or agencies regarding the timing or settlement of claims. The Menendez amendment would declare that such intervention would be subject to public disclosure only if it is intended to impede or delay. Adopted 253-173: R 54-162; D 198-11 (ND 148-7, SD 50-4); I 1-0. Oct. 13, 1999. (Subsequently, the Terry amendment, as amended, was adopted by voice vote.)

499. HR 1993. OPIC Reauthorization/Passage. Passage of the bill to reauthorize the Overseas Private Investment Corporation (OPIC) through fiscal 2003. The measure would set OPIC fees at a level sufficient to cover operating costs, require the agency to double its support for small businesses and direct OPIC to encourage private sector financing and participation. Passed 357-71: R 165-53; D 192-17 (ND 141-14, SD 51-3); I 0-1. Oct. 13, 1999.

500. HR 2684. Fiscal 2000 VA-HUD Appropriations/Conference Report. Adoption of the conference report on the bill to provide $99.5 billion for the departments of Veterans Affairs (VA), Housing and Urban Development (HUD) and 17 independent agencies. The bill would provide $44.3 billion in VA funding and $26 billion for HUD. The conference report total includes $4.2 billion in advance funding for HUD's Section 8 rental subsidy program for 2001, and $2.5 billion in emergency funding for the Federal Emergency Management Agency. Adopted 406-18: R 204-14; D 201-4 (ND 149-4, SD 52-0); I 1-0. Oct. 14, 1999.

501. HR 2679. National Motor Carrier Safety Administration/Passage. Passage of the bill to transfer oversight for truck and bus safety programs from the Federal Highway Administration to a new agency, the National Motor Carrier Safety Administration, that would be established within the Transportation Department. The measure would direct the agency to increase the number of inspections and compliance reviews of motor vehicles, operators, and carriers, to improve state reports of safety information, and to eliminate backlogs of rule-making and penalties for violations. Passed 415-5: R 210-5; D 204-0 (ND 152-0, SD 52-0); I 1-0. Oct. 14, 1999.

502. HR 1501. Juvenile Justice/Motion to Instruct. Jackson-Lee, D-Texas, motion to instruct House conferees to insist that the conference on the juvenile justice bill immediately hold its first substantive meeting to offer amendments and motions, including provisions on gun safety, and that the conference report a substitute by Oct. 20, the six-month anniversary of the shooting at Columbine High School. Motion rejected 174-249: R 19-198; D 154-51 (ND 127-27, SD 27-24); I 1-0. Oct. 14, 1999.

503. HR 3064. Fiscal 2000 District of Columbia Appropriations/Rule. Adoption of the rule (H Res 330) to provide for House floor consideration of the bill to provide $429.1 million in federal payments to the District of Columbia and approve the District's $6.8 billion budget. Adopted 217-202: R 216-0; D 1-201 (ND 0-151, SD 1-50); I 0-1. Oct. 14, 1999.

504. HR 3064. Fiscal 2000 District of Columbia Appropriations/Passage. Passage of the bill to appropriate $429.1 million in federal payments to the District of Columbia and approve the District's $6.8 billion budget. The bill would prevent the District from spending any funds on needle-exchange programs or legalizing marijuana for medical use and bar it from using any of its own funds to seek voting rights in Congress. It would bar the use of funds to permit domestic partners to receive health insurance benefits or to fund abortion, except in cases of rape or incest or to save the life of the woman. Passed 211-205: R 203-10; D 8-195 (ND 4-147, SD 4-48); I 0-0. Oct. 14, 1999. A "nay" was a vote in support of the president's position.

Key

- Y Voted for (yea).
- # Paired for.
- + Announced for.
- N Voted against (nay).
- X Paired against.
- – Announced against.
- P Voted "present."
- C Voted "present" to avoid possible conflict of interest.
- ? Did not vote or otherwise make a position known.

•

Democrats ***Republicans***
Independents

	498	499	500	501	502	503	504
ALABAMA							
1 ***Callahan***	Y	Y	Y	Y	N	Y	Y
2 ***Everett***	N	Y	Y	Y	N	Y	Y
3 ***Riley***	N	Y	Y	Y	N	Y	Y
4 ***Aderholt***	N	Y	Y	Y	N	Y	Y
5 Cramer	Y	Y	Y	Y	N	N	N
6 ***Bachus***	N	N	Y	Y	N	Y	Y
7 Hilliard	Y	Y	Y	Y	N	N	N
ALASKA							
AL ***Young***	?	?	?	?	?	?	?
ARIZONA							
1 ***Salmon***	N	N	N	Y	N	Y	N
2 Pastor	Y	Y	Y	Y	Y	N	N
3 ***Stump***	N	Y	Y	Y	N	Y	Y
4 ***Shadegg***	N	N	N	Y	N	Y	N
5 ***Kolbe***	Y	Y	Y	Y	N	Y	Y
6 ***Hayworth***	N	N	Y	Y	N	Y	Y
ARKANSAS							
1 Berry	Y	Y	Y	Y	N	N	N
2 Snyder	Y	Y	Y	Y	Y	N	N
3 ***Hutchinson***	N	Y	Y	Y	N	Y	Y
4 ***Dickey***	N	Y	Y	Y	N	Y	Y
CALIFORNIA							
1 Thompson	Y	Y	Y	Y	Y	N	N
2 ***Herger***	N	Y	Y	Y	N	Y	Y
3 ***Ose***	N	Y	Y	Y	N	Y	Y
4 ***Doolittle***	N	N	Y	Y	N	Y	Y
5 Matsui	Y	Y	Y	Y	Y	N	N
6 Woolsey	Y	Y	Y	Y	Y	N	N
7 Miller, George	Y	Y	Y	Y	Y	N	N
8 Pelosi	Y	Y	Y	Y	Y	N	N
9 Lee	Y	Y	Y	Y	Y	N	N
10 Tauscher	Y	Y	Y	?	Y	N	N
11 ***Pombo***	N	N	Y	Y	N	Y	Y
12 Lantos	Y	Y	Y	Y	Y	N	N
13 Stark	Y	N	Y	Y	Y	N	N
14 Eshoo	Y	Y	Y	Y	Y	N	N
15 ***Campbell***	N	N	Y	Y	Y	Y	N
16 Lofgren	Y	Y	Y	Y	Y	N	?
17 Farr	Y	Y	Y	Y	Y	N	N
18 Condit	N	N	Y	Y	N	N	N
19 ***Radanovich***	?	Y	Y	Y	N	Y	Y
20 Dooley	Y	Y	Y	Y	Y	?	N
21 ***Thomas***	N	Y	Y	Y	N	Y	Y
22 Capps	Y	Y	Y	Y	Y	N	N
23 ***Gallegly***	Y	Y	Y	Y	N	Y	Y
24 Sherman	Y	Y	Y	Y	Y	N	N
25 ***McKeon***	N	Y	Y	Y	N	Y	Y
26 Berman	Y	Y	Y	Y	Y	N	N
27 ***Rogan***	N	N	Y	Y	Y	Y	Y
28 ***Dreier***	N	Y	Y	Y	N	Y	Y
29 Waxman	Y	Y	Y	Y	Y	N	N
30 Becerra	Y	Y	Y	Y	Y	N	N
31 Martinez	Y	Y	Y	Y	Y	N	N
32 Dixon	Y	Y	Y	Y	Y	N	N
33 Roybal-Allard	Y	Y	Y	Y	Y	N	N
34 Napolitano	Y	Y	Y	Y	Y	N	N
35 Waters	Y	Y	Y	Y	Y	N	N
36 ***Kuykendall***	Y	Y	Y	Y	Y	Y	Y
37 Millender-McD.	Y	Y	Y	Y	Y	N	N
38 ***Horn***	N	Y	Y	Y	Y	Y	Y
39 ***Royce***	N	N	Y	N	N	Y	Y
40 ***Lewis***	N	Y	Y	Y	N	Y	Y
41 ***Miller***	N	Y	Y	Y	N	Y	Y
42 Vacant							
43 ***Calvert***	N	Y	Y	Y	N	Y	Y
44 ***Bono***	Y	Y	Y	Y	N	Y	Y
45 ***Rohrabacher***	N	N	Y	Y	N	Y	Y
46 Sanchez	Y	Y	Y	Y	Y	N	N
47 ***Cox***	N	N	Y	?	N	Y	?
48 ***Packard***	N	Y	Y	Y	N	Y	Y
49 ***Bilbray***	Y	Y	Y	Y	Y	Y	Y
50 Filner	Y	Y	N	Y	Y	N	N
51 ***Cunningham***	N	Y	Y	Y	N	Y	Y
52 ***Hunter***	N	Y	Y	Y	N	Y	Y
COLORADO							
1 DeGette	Y	Y	Y	Y	Y	N	N
2 Udall	Y	Y	Y	Y	Y	N	N
3 ***McInnis***	N	N	N	Y	N	Y	Y
4 ***Schaffer***	N	N	N	Y	N	Y	N
5 ***Hefley***	N	N	N	Y	N	Y	N
6 ***Tancredo***	N	N	Y	Y	Y	Y	Y
CONNECTICUT							
1 Larson	Y	Y	Y	Y	Y	N	N
2 Gejdenson	Y	Y	Y	Y	Y	N	N
3 DeLauro	Y	Y	Y	Y	Y	N	N
4 ***Shays***	Y	Y	Y	Y	Y	Y	Y
5 Maloney	Y	Y	Y	Y	Y	N	N
6 ***Johnson***	Y	Y	+	Y	N	Y	Y
DELAWARE							
AL ***Castle***	N	Y	Y	Y	N	Y	Y
FLORIDA							
1 ***Scarborough***	?	?	?	?	?	?	?
2 Boyd	Y	Y	Y	Y	N	N	N
3 Brown	Y	Y	Y	Y	Y	N	N
4 ***Fowler***	Y	Y	Y	Y	N	Y	Y
5 Thurman	Y	Y	Y	Y	N	N	N
6 ***Stearns***	Y	N	Y	Y	N	Y	Y
7 ***Mica***	Y	Y	Y	Y	N	Y	Y
8 ***McCollum***	N	Y	Y	Y	N	Y	Y
9 ***Bilirakis***	N	Y	Y	Y	N	Y	Y
10 ***Young***	Y	Y	Y	Y	N	Y	Y
11 Davis	Y	Y	Y	Y	Y	N	N
12 ***Canady***	N	Y	Y	Y	N	Y	Y
13 ***Miller***	N	N	Y	Y	N	Y	Y
14 ***Goss***	N	Y	Y	Y	N	Y	Y
15 ***Weldon***	N	Y	Y	Y	N	Y	Y
16 ***Foley***	Y	Y	Y	Y	N	Y	Y
17 Meek	Y	Y	Y	Y	Y	N	N
18 ***Ros-Lehtinen***	Y	Y	Y	Y	N	Y	Y
19 Wexler	Y	Y	Y	Y	Y	N	N
20 Deutsch	Y	Y	Y	Y	Y	N	N
21 ***Diaz-Balart***	Y	Y	Y	Y	N	Y	Y
22 ***Shaw***	N	Y	Y	Y	N	Y	Y
23 Hastings	Y	Y	Y	Y	Y	N	N
GEORGIA							
1 ***Kingston***	N	N	?	?	?	?	?
2 Bishop	Y	Y	Y	Y	N	N	N
3 ***Collins***	N	Y	Y	Y	N	Y	Y
4 McKinney	Y	N	Y	Y	?	N	N
5 Lewis	Y	Y	Y	Y	Y	N	N
6 ***Isakson***	N	Y	Y	Y	N	Y	Y
7 ***Barr***	N	N	Y	Y	N	Y	Y
8 ***Chambliss***	N	Y	Y	Y	N	Y	Y
9 ***Deal***	N	Y	Y	Y	N	Y	Y
10 ***Norwood***	N	Y	Y	Y	N	Y	Y
11 ***Linder***	N	Y	Y	Y	N	Y	Y
HAWAII							
1 Abercrombie	Y	Y	Y	Y	Y	N	N
2 Mink	Y	Y	Y	Y	Y	N	N
IDAHO							
1 ***Chenoweth***	N	N	N	N	N	Y	N
2 ***Simpson***	N	Y	Y	Y	N	Y	Y
ILLINOIS							
1 Rush	Y	Y	Y	Y	Y	N	N
2 Jackson	Y	N	Y	Y	Y	N	N
3 Lipinski	N	N	Y	Y	Y	N	N
4 Gutierrez	Y	Y	Y	Y	Y	N	N
5 Blagojevich	Y	Y	Y	Y	Y	N	N
6 ***Hyde***	N	Y	Y	Y	N	Y	Y
7 Davis	Y	Y	Y	Y	Y	N	N
8 ***Crane***	Y	N	N	Y	N	Y	Y
9 Schakowsky	Y	Y	Y	Y	Y	N	N
10 ***Porter***	N	Y	Y	Y	Y	Y	Y
11 ***Weller***	N	Y	Y	Y	N	Y	Y
12 Costello	Y	Y	Y	Y	N	N	N
13 ***Biggert***	Y	Y	Y	Y	N	Y	Y
14 ***Hastert***			Y				Y

ND Northern Democrats SD Southern Democrats

	498	499	500	501	502	503	504
15 ***Ewing***	N	Y	Y	Y	N	Y	Y
16 ***Manzullo***	N	Y	Y	Y	N	Y	Y
17 Evans	Y	Y	N	Y	Y	N	N
18 ***LaHood***	Y	Y	Y	Y	N	Y	Y
19 Phelps	Y	Y	Y	Y	N	N	Y
20 ***Shimkus***	Y	Y	Y	Y	N	Y	Y
INDIANA							
1 Visclosky	Y	Y	Y	Y	Y	N	N
2 ***McIntosh***	N	N	Y	Y	N	Y	?
3 Roemer	Y	Y	Y	Y	N	N	N
4 ***Souder***	Y	Y	Y	Y	N	Y	Y
5 ***Buyer***	Y	N	Y	?	?	?	?
6 ***Burton***	Y	N	Y	Y	N	Y	Y
7 ***Pease***	N	N	Y	Y	N	Y	Y
8 ***Hostettler***	N	N	N	Y	N	Y	Y
9 Hill	Y	Y	Y	Y	N	N	N
10 Carson	Y	Y	?	?	?	?	?
IOWA							
1 ***Leach***	N	Y	Y	Y	Y	Y	Y
2 ***Nussle***	N	Y	Y	Y	N	Y	Y
3 Boswell	Y	Y	N	Y	N	N	N
4 ***Ganske***	N	Y	Y	Y	N	Y	Y
5 ***Latham***	N	Y	Y	Y	N	Y	Y
KANSAS							
1 ***Moran***	N	Y	Y	Y	N	Y	Y
2 ***Ryun***	N	N	Y	Y	N	Y	Y
3 Moore	Y	Y	Y	Y	Y	N	N
4 ***Tiahrt***	N	Y	Y	Y	N	Y	Y
KENTUCKY							
1 ***Whitfield***	?	Y	Y	Y	N	Y	Y
2 ***Lewis***	Y	Y	Y	Y	N	Y	Y
3 ***Northup***	Y	Y	Y	Y	N	Y	Y
4 Lucas	Y	Y	Y	Y	N	N	Y
5 ***Rogers***	Y	Y	Y	Y	N	Y	Y
6 ***Fletcher***	Y	Y	Y	Y	N	Y	Y
LOUISIANA							
1 ***Vitter***	N	Y	Y	Y	N	Y	Y
2 Jefferson	?	?	?	?	?	?	?
3 ***Tauzin***	N	Y	Y	Y	N	Y	Y
4 ***McCrery***	N	Y	Y	Y	N	Y	Y
5 ***Cooksey***	N	Y	Y	Y	N	?	Y
6 ***Baker***	N	Y	Y	Y	N	Y	Y
7 John	N	Y	?	?	?	?	?
MAINE							
1 Allen	Y	Y	Y	Y	Y	N	N
2 Baldacci	Y	Y	Y	Y	Y	N	N
MARYLAND							
1 ***Gilchrest***	N	Y	Y	Y	N	Y	Y
2 ***Ehrlich***	N	N	Y	Y	N	Y	Y
3 Cardin	Y	Y	Y	Y	Y	N	N
4 Wynn	Y	Y	Y	Y	Y	N	N
5 Hoyer	Y	Y	Y	Y	Y	N	N
6 ***Bartlett***	N	N	Y	Y	N	Y	Y
7 Cummings	Y	Y	Y	Y	Y	N	N
8 ***Morella***	Y	Y	Y	Y	Y	Y	N
MASSACHUSETTS							
1 Olver	Y	Y	Y	Y	Y	N	N
2 Neal	Y	Y	Y	Y	Y	N	N
3 McGovern	Y	Y	Y	Y	Y	N	N
4 Frank	N	Y	Y	Y	Y	N	N
5 Meehan	Y	Y	Y	Y	Y	N	N
6 Tierney	Y	N	Y	Y	Y	N	N
7 Markey	Y	Y	Y	Y	Y	N	N
8 Capuano	Y	Y	Y	Y	Y	N	N
9 Moakley	Y	Y	Y	Y	Y	N	N
10 Delahunt	Y	Y	Y	Y	Y	N	N
MICHIGAN							
1 Stupak	Y	Y	Y	Y	Y	N	N
2 ***Hoekstra***	N	N	N	Y	N	Y	Y
3 ***Ehlers***	Y	Y	Y	Y	N	Y	Y
4 ***Camp***	N	Y	Y	Y	N	Y	Y
5 Barcia	Y	Y	Y	Y	N	N	Y
6 ***Upton***	Y	Y	Y	Y	N	Y	Y
7 ***Smith***	N	N	Y	Y	N	Y	Y
8 Stabenow	Y	Y	Y	Y	Y	N	N
9 Kildee	Y	Y	Y	Y	Y	N	N
10 Bonior	Y	Y	Y	Y	Y	N	N
11 ***Knollenberg***	N	Y	Y	Y	N	Y	Y
12 Levin	Y	Y	Y	Y	Y	N	N
13 Rivers	Y	Y	Y	Y	Y	N	N
14 Conyers	Y	N	?	?	?	?	N
15 Kilpatrick	Y	Y	Y	Y	Y	N	N
16 Dingell	Y	Y	Y	Y	N	N	N

	498	499	500	501	502	503	504
MINNESOTA							
1 ***Gutknecht***	N	Y	Y	Y	N	Y	Y
2 Minge	Y	Y	Y	Y	N	N	N
3 ***Ramstad***	Y	Y	Y	Y	Y	Y	Y
4 Vento	Y	Y	Y	Y	Y	N	N
5 Sabo	Y	Y	Y	Y	Y	N	N
6 Luther	Y	Y	Y	Y	Y	N	N
7 Peterson	N	N	Y	Y	N	N	N
8 Oberstar	Y	Y	Y	Y	Y	N	N
MISSISSIPPI							
1 ***Wicker***	N	Y	Y	Y	N	Y	Y
2 Thompson	Y	Y	Y	Y	Y	N	N
3 ***Pickering***	N	Y	Y	Y	N	Y	Y
4 Shows	N	Y	Y	Y	N	N	Y
5 Taylor	Y	Y	Y	Y	N	N	N
MISSOURI							
1 Clay	Y	Y	Y	Y	Y	?	?
2 ***Talent***	N	Y	Y	Y	N	Y	Y
3 Gephardt	Y	Y	Y	Y	Y	N	N
4 Skelton	Y	Y	Y	Y	N	N	N
5 McCarthy	Y	Y	Y	Y	Y	N	N
6 Danner	Y	Y	Y	Y	N	N	N
7 ***Blunt***	N	Y	Y	Y	N	Y	Y
8 ***Emerson***	N	Y	Y	Y	N	Y	Y
9 ***Hulshof***	N	Y	Y	Y	N	Y	Y
MONTANA							
AL ***Hill***	Y	Y	Y	Y	N	Y	Y
NEBRASKA							
1 ***Bereuter***	N	Y	Y	Y	N	Y	Y
2 ***Terry***	N	Y	Y	Y	N	Y	Y
3 ***Barrett***	N	Y	Y	Y	N	Y	Y
NEVADA							
1 Berkley	Y	Y	Y	Y	Y	N	N
2 ***Gibbons***	N	Y	Y	Y	N	Y	Y
NEW HAMPSHIRE							
1 ***Sununu***	N	N	Y	Y	N	Y	Y
2 ***Bass***	Y	Y	Y	Y	N	Y	Y
NEW JERSEY							
1 Andrews	N	N	+	+	Y	N	N
2 ***LoBiondo***	Y	N	Y	Y	N	Y	Y
3 ***Saxton***	N	Y	Y	Y	N	Y	Y
4 ***Smith***	Y	Y	Y	Y	N	Y	Y
5 ***Roukema***	N	Y	Y	Y	Y	Y	N
6 Pallone	Y	Y	Y	Y	Y	N	N
7 ***Franks***	Y	Y	Y	Y	Y	Y	Y
8 Pascrell	N	N	Y	Y	Y	N	N
9 Rothman	Y	Y	Y	Y	Y	N	N
10 Payne	Y	Y	Y	Y	Y	N	N
11 ***Frelinghuysen***	Y	Y	Y	Y	Y	Y	Y
12 Holt	Y	Y	N	Y	Y	N	N
13 Menendez	Y	Y	Y	Y	Y	N	N
NEW MEXICO							
1 ***Wilson***	N	Y	Y	Y	N	Y	Y
2 ***Skeen***	N	Y	Y	Y	N	Y	Y
3 Udall	Y	Y	Y	Y	Y	N	N
NEW YORK							
1 Forbes	Y	Y	Y	Y	Y	N	N
2 ***Lazio***	N	Y	Y	Y	Y	Y	Y
3 ***King***	N	Y	Y	Y	N	Y	Y
4 McCarthy	Y	Y	Y	Y	Y	N	N
5 Ackerman	Y	Y	Y	Y	Y	N	?
6 Meeks	Y	Y	Y	Y	Y	N	N
7 Crowley	Y	Y	Y	Y	Y	N	N
8 Nadler	Y	Y	Y	Y	Y	N	N
9 Weiner	Y	Y	Y	Y	Y	N	N
10 Towns	Y	Y	Y	Y	Y	N	N
11 Owens	Y	Y	Y	Y	Y	N	N
12 Velázquez	Y	Y	Y	Y	Y	N	N
13 ***Fossella***	N	Y	Y	Y	N	Y	N
14 Maloney	Y	Y	Y	Y	Y	N	N
15 Rangel	Y	Y	Y	Y	Y	N	N
16 Serrano	Y	Y	Y	Y	Y	N	N
17 Engel	Y	Y	Y	Y	Y	N	N
18 Lowey	Y	Y	Y	Y	Y	N	N
19 ***Kelly***	Y	Y	Y	Y	N	Y	Y
20 ***Gilman***	N	Y	Y	Y	N	Y	Y
21 McNulty	Y	Y	Y	Y	Y	?	?
22 ***Sweeney***	N	Y	Y	Y	N	Y	Y
23 ***Boehlert***	N	Y	Y	Y	Y	Y	Y
24 ***McHugh***	N	Y	Y	Y	N	Y	Y
25 ***Walsh***	Y	Y	Y	Y	N	Y	Y
26 Hinchey	Y	Y	Y	Y	N	N	N
27 ***Reynolds***	N	Y	Y	Y	N	Y	Y
28 Slaughter	Y	Y	Y	Y	Y	N	N
29 LaFalce	Y	Y	Y	Y	Y	N	Y

	498	499	500	501	502	503	504
30 ***Quinn***	N	Y	Y	Y	N	Y	Y
31 ***Houghton***	Y	Y	Y	Y	N	Y	Y
NORTH CAROLINA							
1 Clayton	Y	Y	Y	Y	Y	N	N
2 Etheridge	Y	Y	Y	Y	N	N	N
3 ***Jones***	Y	N	Y	Y	N	Y	Y
4 Price	Y	Y	Y	Y	Y	N	N
5 ***Burr***	?	?	Y	Y	N	Y	Y
6 ***Coble***	N	N	Y	Y	N	Y	Y
7 McIntyre	Y	N	Y	Y	N	N	Y
8 ***Hayes***	N	N	Y	Y	N	Y	Y
9 ***Myrick***	N	N	Y	Y	N	Y	Y
10 ***Ballenger***	N	Y	Y	Y	N	Y	Y
11 ***Taylor***	N	N	Y	Y	N	Y	Y
12 Watt	Y	Y	Y	Y	Y	N	N
NORTH DAKOTA							
AL Pomeroy	Y	Y	Y	Y	Y	N	N
OHIO							
1 ***Chabot***	N	N	N	Y	N	Y	Y
2 ***Portman***	Y	Y	Y	Y	N	Y	Y
3 Hall	Y	Y	Y	Y	N	N	N
4 ***Oxley***	Y	Y	Y	Y	N	Y	Y
5 ***Gillmor***	N	Y	Y	Y	N	Y	Y
6 Strickland	Y	N	Y	Y	N	N	N
7 ***Hobson***	Y	Y	Y	Y	N	Y	Y
8 ***Boehner***	N	Y	Y	Y	N	Y	Y
9 Kaptur	Y	N	Y	Y	N	N	N
10 Kucinich	Y	N	Y	Y	Y	N	N
11 Jones	Y	Y	Y	Y	Y	N	N
12 ***Kasich***	N	N	Y	Y	N	Y	Y
13 Brown	?	?	Y	Y	Y	N	N
14 Sawyer	Y	Y	Y	Y	Y	N	N
15 ***Pryce***	N	Y	Y	Y	N	Y	Y
16 ***Regula***	N	Y	Y	?	N	Y	Y
17 Traficant	N	Y	Y	Y	N	N	Y
18 ***Ney***	N	Y	Y	Y	N	Y	Y
19 ***LaTourette***	Y	Y	Y	Y	N	Y	Y
OKLAHOMA							
1 ***Largent***	N	Y	Y	Y	N	Y	Y
2 ***Coburn***	Y	N	N	Y	N	Y	Y
3 ***Watkins***	N	Y	Y	Y	N	Y	Y
4 ***Watts***	N	N	Y	Y	N	Y	Y
5 ***Istook***	N	N	Y	Y	N	Y	Y
6 ***Lucas***	N	Y	Y	Y	N	Y	Y
OREGON							
1 Wu	Y	Y	Y	Y	Y	N	N
2 ***Walden***	N	Y	Y	Y	N	Y	Y
3 Blumenauer	Y	Y	Y	Y	Y	N	N
4 DeFazio	Y	N	Y	Y	Y	N	N
5 Hooley	Y	Y	Y	Y	Y	N	N
PENNSYLVANIA							
1 Brady	Y	Y	Y	Y	Y	N	N
2 Fattah	Y	Y	Y	Y	Y	N	N
3 Borski	Y	Y	Y	Y	Y	N	N
4 Klink	Y	Y	Y	Y	N	N	N
5 ***Peterson***	Y	Y	Y	Y	N	Y	Y
6 Holden	Y	Y	Y	Y	N	N	N
7 ***Weldon***	N	Y	Y	Y	N	Y	?
8 ***Greenwood***	Y	Y	Y	Y	N	Y	Y
9 ***Shuster***	N	Y	Y	Y	N	Y	Y
10 ***Sherwood***	N	Y	Y	Y	N	Y	Y
11 Kanjorski	Y	Y	Y	Y	N	N	N
12 Murtha	Y	Y	Y	Y	N	N	N
13 Hoeffel	Y	Y	Y	Y	Y	N	N
14 Coyne	Y	Y	Y	Y	Y	N	N
15 ***Toomey***	N	N	Y	Y	N	Y	Y
16 ***Pitts***	N	Y	Y	Y	N	Y	Y
17 ***Gekas***	Y	Y	Y	Y	N	Y	Y
18 Doyle	Y	Y	Y	Y	Y	N	N
19 ***Goodling***	Y	Y	Y	Y	N	Y	Y
20 Mascara	Y	Y	Y	Y	N	N	N
21 ***English***	N	Y	Y	Y	N	Y	Y
RHODE ISLAND							
1 Kennedy	Y	Y	Y	Y	Y	N	N
2 Weygand	Y	Y	Y	Y	Y	N	N
SOUTH CAROLINA							
1 ***Sanford***	N	N	N	N	N	Y	Y
2 ***Spence***	N	Y	Y	Y	N	Y	Y
3 ***Graham***	Y	Y	Y	Y	N	Y	Y
4 ***DeMint***	N	N	Y	Y	N	Y	Y
5 Spratt	Y	Y	Y	Y	Y	N	N
6 Clyburn	Y	Y	Y	Y	Y	N	N
SOUTH DAKOTA							
AL ***Thune***	N	Y	Y	Y	N	Y	Y

	498	499	500	501	502	503	504
TENNESSEE							
1 ***Jenkins***	N	Y	Y	Y	N	Y	Y
2 ***Duncan***	N	N	Y	Y	N	Y	N
3 ***Wamp***	N	N	Y	Y	N	Y	Y
4 ***Hilleary***	N	N	Y	Y	N	Y	Y
5 Clement	Y	Y	Y	Y	N	N	N
6 Gordon	Y	Y	Y	Y	N	N	N
7 ***Bryant***	N	Y	Y	Y	N	Y	Y
8 Tanner	Y	Y	Y	Y	N	N	N
9 Ford	Y	Y	Y	Y	Y	N	N
TEXAS							
1 Sandlin	Y	Y	Y	Y	N	N	N
2 Turner	Y	Y	Y	Y	N	N	N
3 ***Johnson, Sam***	N	Y	Y	Y	N	Y	Y
4 Hall	Y	Y	Y	Y	N	N	N
5 ***Sessions***	N	Y	Y	Y	N	Y	Y
6 ***Barton***	N	Y	Y	Y	N	Y	Y
7 ***Archer***	N	Y	Y	Y	N	Y	Y
8 ***Brady***	N	Y	Y	Y	N	Y	Y
9 Lampson	Y	Y	Y	Y	N	N	N
10 Doggett	Y	Y	Y	Y	Y	N	N
11 Edwards	Y	Y	Y	Y	Y	N	N
12 ***Granger***	Y	Y	Y	Y	N	Y	Y
13 ***Thornberry***	N	Y	Y	Y	N	Y	Y
14 ***Paul***	Y	N	N	N	N	Y	?
15 Hinojosa	Y	Y	Y	Y	Y	N	N
16 Reyes	Y	Y	Y	Y	Y	N	N
17 Stenholm	N	Y	Y	Y	N	N	N
18 Jackson-Lee	Y	Y	Y	Y	Y	N	N
19 ***Combest***	N	Y	Y	Y	N	Y	Y
20 Gonzalez	Y	Y	Y	Y	Y	N	N
21 ***Smith***	N	Y	Y	Y	N	Y	Y
22 ***DeLay***	N	Y	Y	Y	N	Y	Y
23 ***Bonilla***	N	Y	Y	Y	N	Y	Y
24 Frost	Y	Y	Y	Y	Y	N	N
25 Bentsen	Y	Y	Y	Y	Y	N	N
26 ***Armey***	N	N	Y	Y	N	Y	Y
27 Ortiz	Y	Y	Y	Y	N	N	N
28 Rodriguez	Y	Y	Y	Y	Y	N	N
29 Green	Y	Y	?	?	?	?	?
30 Johnson, E.B.	Y	Y	Y	Y	Y	N	N
UTAH							
1 ***Hansen***	N	Y	Y	Y	N	Y	Y
2 ***Cook***	N	Y	Y	Y	N	Y	?
3 ***Cannon***	N	Y	Y	Y	N	Y	Y
VERMONT							
AL *Sanders*	Y	N	Y	Y	Y	N	?
VIRGINIA							
1 ***Bateman***	N	Y	Y	Y	N	Y	Y
2 Pickett	Y	Y	Y	Y	N	N	N
3 Scott	Y	Y	Y	Y	Y	N	N
4 Sisisky	Y	Y	Y	Y	N	N	N
5 Goode	N	N	Y	Y	N	Y	Y
6 ***Goodlatte***	N	Y	Y	Y	N	Y	Y
7 ***Bliley***	N	Y	Y	Y	N	Y	Y
8 Moran	Y	Y	Y	Y	Y	N	N
9 Boucher	Y	Y	Y	Y	N	?	N
10 ***Wolf***	N	Y	Y	Y	N	Y	Y
11 ***Davis***	N	Y	Y	Y	Y	Y	Y
WASHINGTON							
1 Inslee	Y	Y	Y	Y	Y	N	N
2 ***Metcalf***	Y	Y	Y	N	N	Y	Y
3 Baird	Y	Y	Y	Y	N	N	N
4 ***Hastings***	N	Y	Y	Y	N	Y	Y
5 ***Nethercutt***	N	Y	Y	Y	N	Y	Y
6 Dicks	Y	Y	Y	Y	Y	N	N
7 McDermott	Y	Y	Y	Y	Y	N	N
8 ***Dunn***	Y	Y	Y	Y	Y	Y	Y
9 Smith	Y	Y	Y	Y	Y	N	N
WEST VIRGINIA							
1 Mollohan	Y	Y	Y	Y	N	N	N
2 Wise	Y	Y	Y	Y	N	N	N
3 Rahall	Y	Y	Y	Y	N	N	N
WISCONSIN							
1 ***Ryan***	N	Y	Y	Y	N	Y	Y
2 Baldwin	Y	Y	Y	Y	Y	N	N
3 Kind	Y	Y	Y	Y	N	N	N
4 Kleczka	Y	Y	Y	Y	Y	N	N
5 Barrett	Y	N	Y	Y	Y	N	N
6 ***Petri***	N	N	Y	Y	N	Y	Y
7 Obey	Y	Y	Y	Y	Y	N	N
8 ***Green***	N	Y	Y	Y	N	Y	Y
9 ***Sensenbrenner***	N	N	N	Y	N	Y	Y
WYOMING							
AL ***Cubin***	N	Y	Y	Y	N	Y	Y

Southern states - Ala., Ark., Fla., Ga., Ky., La., Miss., N.C., Okla., S.C., Tenn., Texas, Va.

505. Procedural Motion/Journal. Approval of the House Journal of Thursday, Oct. 14, 1999. Approved 357-49: R 193-15; D 163-34 (ND 119-25, SD 44-9); I 1-0. Oct. 18, 1999.

506. HR 2140. Chattahoochee River National Recreation Area/Passage. Doolittle, R-Calif., motion to suspend the rules and pass the bill to expand the maximum size of the Chattahoochee River National Recreation Area from 6,800 acres to 10,000 acres and increase the authorization for the area from $79 million to $115 million to fund costs of the expansion. Motion agreed to 394-9: R 199-7; D 194-2 (ND 141-2, SD 53-0); I 1-0. Oct. 18, 1999. A two-thirds majority of those present and voting (269 in this case) is required for passage under suspension of the rules.

507. HR 2886. Adoption of Immigrant Children/Passage. Smith, R-Texas, motion to suspend the rules and pass the bill to allow orphaned immigrant siblings to stay together when adopted by U.S. families. Under the bill, an immigrant child age 16 or 17 would be allowed to qualify for adoption if a younger sibling had already been adopted or was being adopted by the same U.S. family. Motion agreed to 404-0: R 208-0; D 195-0 (ND 142-0, SD 53-0); I 1-0. Oct. 18, 1999. A two-thirds majority of those present and voting (270 in this case) is required for passage under suspension of the rules.

508. H Con Res 196. Use of Rotunda for Honoring President Ford/Adoption. Thomas, R-Calif., motion to suspend the rules and adopt the concurrent resolution to permit the use of the rotunda of the Capitol on Oct. 27, for the presentation of the Congressional Gold Medal to former President and Mrs. Gerald R. Ford. Motion agreed to 402-0: R 208-0; D 193-0 (ND 140-0, SD 53-0); I 1-0. Oct. 18, 1999. A two-thirds majority of those present and voting (268 in this case) is required for adoption under suspension of the rules.

509. Procedural Motion/Journal. Approval of the House Journal of Monday, Oct. 18, 1999. Approved 337-56: R 185-18; D 151-38 (ND 110-30, SD 41-8); I 1-0. Oct. 19, 1999.

510. H J Res 71. Fiscal 2000 Continuing Appropriations/Passage. Passage of the joint resolution to provide continuing appropriations through Oct. 29 for agencies covered by the fiscal 2000 spending bills not yet enacted. The continuing resolution would set spending levels at the fiscal 1999 level. Passed 421-2: R 216-1; D 204-1 (ND 152-1, SD 52-0); I 1-0. Oct. 19, 1999.

511. HR 3085. Discretionary Spending Offsets/Passage. Lewis, R-Ky., motion to suspend the rules and pass the bill to adopt President Clinton's proposals to increase taxes and user fees by $19.2 billion to offset discretionary spending increases for fiscal 2000. The bill would increase the tobacco excise tax by about $8 billion, almost tripling the tax from 24 cents per pack to 94 cents per pack; increase food inspection fees on poultry, livestock, and eggs by $504 million and forest service fees by $20 million; and increase a number of fees related to transportation, including the Federal Aviation Administration user fee and rail safety user fees by about $3 billion. Motion rejected 0-419: R 0-216; D 0-202 (ND 0-149, SD 0-53); I 0-1. Oct. 19, 1999. A two-thirds majority of those present and voting (280 in this case) is required for passage under suspension of the rules.

512. HR 2488. Tax Reconciliation/Table Discharge Motion. Terry, R-Neb., motion to table the Cardin, D-Md., motion to discharge from the Ways and Means Committee the $792 billion, 10-year tax cut bill (HR 2488) that was vetoed by President Clinton on Sept. 23. Motion agreed to 215-203: R 213-0; D 2-202 (ND 0-151, SD 2-51); I 0-1. Oct. 19, 1999.

Key

- Y Voted for (yea).
- \# Paired for.
- \+ Announced for.
- N Voted against (nay).
- X Paired against.
- – Announced against.
- P Voted "present."
- C Voted "present" to avoid possible conflict of interest.
- ? Did not vote or otherwise make a position known.

•

Democrats ***Republicans***
Independents

	505	506	507	508	509	510	511	512
ALABAMA								
1 ***Callahan***	Y	Y	Y	Y	Y	Y	N	Y
2 ***Everett***	Y	Y	Y	Y	Y	Y	N	Y
3 ***Riley***	Y	Y	Y	Y	Y	Y	N	Y
4 ***Aderholt***	Y	Y	Y	Y	N	Y	N	Y
5 Cramer	Y	Y	Y	Y	Y	Y	N	N
6 ***Bachus***	Y	Y	Y	Y	Y	Y	N	Y
7 Hilliard	N	Y	Y	Y	N	Y	N	N
ALASKA								
AL ***Young***	Y	Y	Y	Y	?	Y	N	Y
ARIZONA								
1 ***Salmon***	Y	Y	Y	Y	Y	Y	N	Y
2 Pastor	N	Y	Y	Y	N	Y	N	N
3 ***Stump***	Y	Y	Y	Y	Y	Y	N	Y
4 ***Shadegg***	Y	Y	Y	Y	Y	Y	N	Y
5 ***Kolbe***	Y	Y	Y	Y	Y	Y	N	Y
6 ***Hayworth***	Y	Y	Y	Y	Y	Y	N	Y
ARKANSAS								
1 Berry	Y	Y	Y	Y	Y	Y	N	N
2 Snyder	Y	Y	Y	Y	Y	Y	N	N
3 ***Hutchinson***	N	Y	Y	Y	Y	Y	N	Y
4 ***Dickey***	N	Y	Y	Y	N	Y	N	Y
CALIFORNIA								
1 Thompson	N	Y	Y	Y	N	Y	N	N
2 ***Herger***	Y	N	Y	Y	Y	Y	N	Y
3 ***Ose***	Y	Y	Y	Y	Y	Y	N	Y
4 ***Doolittle***	Y	Y	Y	Y	Y	Y	N	Y
5 Matsui	Y	Y	Y	Y	Y	Y	N	N
6 Woolsey	Y	Y	Y	Y	Y	Y	N	N
7 Miller, George	Y	Y	Y	Y	N	Y	N	N
8 Pelosi	Y	Y	Y	Y	Y	Y	N	N
9 Lee	Y	Y	Y	Y	Y	Y	N	N
10 Tauscher	Y	Y	Y	Y	N	Y	N	N
11 ***Pombo***	Y	N	Y	Y	Y	Y	N	Y
12 Lantos	Y	Y	Y	Y	Y	Y	N	N
13 Stark	Y	Y	Y	Y	Y	Y	N	N
14 Eshoo	Y	Y	Y	Y	Y	Y	N	N
15 ***Campbell***	Y	Y	Y	Y	Y	Y	N	Y
16 Lofgren	Y	Y	Y	Y	Y	Y	N	N
17 Farr	?	?	?	?	Y	Y	N	N
18 Condit	Y	Y	Y	Y	Y	Y	N	N
19 ***Radanovich***	Y	Y	Y	Y	Y	Y	N	?
20 Dooley	Y	Y	Y	Y	Y	Y	N	N
21 ***Thomas***	Y	Y	Y	Y	Y	Y	N	Y
22 Capps	Y	Y	Y	Y	Y	Y	N	N
23 ***Gallegly***	Y	Y	Y	Y	Y	Y	N	Y
24 Sherman	Y	Y	Y	Y	Y	Y	N	N
25 ***McKeon***	Y	Y	Y	Y	Y	Y	N	Y
26 Berman	Y	Y	Y	Y	Y	Y	P	N
27 ***Rogan***	Y	Y	Y	Y	Y	Y	N	Y
28 ***Dreier***	Y	Y	Y	Y	Y	Y	N	Y
29 Waxman	Y	Y	Y	Y	Y	Y	N	N
30 Becerra	Y	Y	Y	Y	Y	Y	N	N
31 Martinez	?	?	?	?	?	?	?	?
32 Dixon	Y	Y	Y	Y	?	Y	N	N
33 Roybal-Allard	Y	Y	Y	Y	Y	Y	N	N
34 Napolitano	Y	Y	Y	Y	Y	Y	N	N
35 Waters	Y	Y	Y	Y	N	Y	N	N
36 ***Kuykendall***	Y	Y	Y	Y	Y	Y	N	Y
37 Millender-McD.	Y	Y	Y	Y	Y	Y	N	N
38 ***Horn***	Y	Y	Y	Y	Y	Y	N	Y
39 ***Royce***	Y	Y	Y	Y	Y	Y	N	Y
40 ***Lewis***	Y	Y	Y	Y	Y	Y	N	Y
41 ***Miller***	Y	Y	Y	Y	Y	Y	N	Y
42 Vacant								
43 ***Calvert***	Y	Y	Y	Y	Y	Y	N	Y
44 ***Bono***	Y	Y	Y	Y	Y	Y	N	Y
45 ***Rohrabacher***	Y	Y	Y	Y	Y	Y	N	Y
46 Sanchez	Y	Y	Y	Y	Y	Y	N	N
47 ***Cox***	Y	Y	Y	Y	?	Y	N	Y
48 ***Packard***	Y	Y	Y	Y	Y	Y	N	Y
49 ***Bilbray***	Y	Y	Y	Y	N	Y	N	Y
50 Filner	N	Y	Y	Y	N	Y	N	N
51 ***Cunningham***	Y	Y	Y	Y	Y	Y	N	Y
52 ***Hunter***	Y	Y	Y	Y	Y	Y	N	Y
COLORADO								
1 DeGette	Y	Y	Y	Y	Y	Y	N	N
2 Udall	Y	Y	Y	Y	N	Y	N	N
3 ***McInnis***	Y	Y	Y	Y	Y	Y	N	Y
4 ***Schaffer***	N	N	Y	Y	N	Y	N	Y
5 ***Hefley***	Y	Y	Y	Y	N	Y	N	Y
6 ***Tancredo***	P	Y	Y	Y	P	Y	N	Y
CONNECTICUT								
1 Larson	Y	Y	Y	Y	Y	Y	N	N
2 Gejdenson	Y	Y	Y	Y	Y	Y	N	N
3 DeLauro	Y	Y	Y	Y	?	Y	N	N
4 ***Shays***	Y	Y	Y	Y	Y	Y	N	Y
5 Maloney	Y	Y	Y	Y	Y	Y	N	N
6 ***Johnson***	?	?	?	?	?	?	?	?
DELAWARE								
AL ***Castle***	Y	?	Y	Y	Y	Y	N	Y
FLORIDA								
1 ***Scarborough***	?	?	?	?	?	?	?	?
2 Boyd	Y	Y	Y	Y	Y	Y	N	N
3 Brown	N	Y	Y	Y	Y	Y	N	N
4 ***Fowler***	Y	Y	Y	Y	Y	Y	N	Y
5 Thurman	Y	Y	Y	Y	Y	Y	N	N
6 ***Stearns***	Y	Y	Y	Y	Y	Y	N	Y
7 ***Mica***	Y	Y	Y	Y	Y	Y	N	Y
8 ***McCollum***	Y	Y	Y	Y	Y	Y	N	Y
9 ***Bilirakis***	Y	Y	Y	Y	Y	Y	N	Y
10 ***Young***	Y	Y	Y	Y	Y	Y	N	Y
11 Davis	Y	Y	Y	Y	Y	Y	N	N
12 ***Canady***	Y	Y	Y	Y	Y	Y	N	Y
13 ***Miller***	Y	Y	Y	Y	Y	Y	N	Y
14 ***Goss***	Y	Y	Y	Y	Y	Y	N	Y
15 ***Weldon***	Y	Y	Y	Y	Y	Y	N	Y
16 ***Foley***	Y	Y	Y	Y	Y	Y	N	Y
17 Meek	N	Y	Y	Y	Y	Y	N	N
18 ***Ros-Lehtinen***	Y	Y	Y	Y	+	+	–	+
19 Wexler	Y	Y	Y	Y	Y	Y	N	N
20 Deutsch	Y	Y	Y	Y	Y	Y	N	N
21 ***Diaz-Balart***	Y	Y	Y	Y	Y	Y	N	Y
22 ***Shaw***	Y	Y	Y	Y	Y	Y	N	Y
23 Hastings	N	Y	Y	Y	Y	Y	N	N
GEORGIA								
1 ***Kingston***	Y	Y	Y	Y	Y	Y	N	Y
2 Bishop	Y	Y	Y	Y	Y	Y	N	N
3 ***Collins***	?	?	?	?	Y	Y	N	Y
4 McKinney	Y	Y	Y	Y	Y	Y	N	N
5 Lewis	+	+	+	+	?	?	?	?
6 ***Isakson***	Y	Y	Y	Y	Y	Y	N	Y
7 ***Barr***	Y	Y	Y	Y	Y	Y	N	Y
8 ***Chambliss***	Y	Y	Y	Y	Y	Y	N	Y
9 ***Deal***	Y	Y	Y	Y	Y	Y	N	Y
10 ***Norwood***	Y	Y	Y	Y	?	Y	N	Y
11 ***Linder***	Y	Y	Y	Y	Y	Y	N	Y
HAWAII								
1 Abercrombie	Y	Y	Y	Y	Y	Y	N	N
2 Mink	Y	Y	Y	Y	Y	Y	N	N
IDAHO								
1 ***Chenoweth***	Y	?	Y	Y	Y	Y	N	Y
2 ***Simpson***	Y	Y	Y	Y	Y	Y	N	Y
ILLINOIS								
1 Rush	?	?	?	?	?	?	?	?
2 Jackson	Y	Y	Y	Y	Y	Y	N	N
3 Lipinski	Y	Y	Y	Y	N	Y	N	N
4 Gutierrez	N	Y	Y	?	N	Y	N	?
5 Blagojevich	Y	Y	Y	Y	Y	Y	N	N
6 ***Hyde***	Y	Y	Y	Y	Y	Y	N	Y
7 Davis	Y	Y	Y	Y	Y	Y	N	N
8 ***Crane***	N	Y	Y	Y	N	Y	N	Y
9 Schakowsky	Y	Y	Y	Y	Y	Y	N	N
10 ***Porter***	Y	Y	Y	Y	?	Y	N	?
11 ***Weller***	N	Y	Y	Y	N	Y	N	Y
12 Costello	N	Y	Y	Y	N	Y	N	N
13 ***Biggert***	Y	Y	Y	Y	Y	Y	N	Y
14 ***Hastert***						Y		

ND Northern Democrats SD Southern Democrats

	505	506	507	508	509	510	511	512
15 **Ewing**	Y	Y	Y	Y	Y	Y	N	Y
16 **Manzullo**	Y	Y	Y	Y	Y	Y	N	Y
17 Evans	N	Y	Y	Y	N	Y	N	N
18 **LaHood**	Y	Y	Y	Y	Y	Y	N	Y
19 Phelps	Y	Y	Y	Y	N	Y	N	N
20 **Shimkus**	Y	Y	Y	Y	Y	Y	N	Y
INDIANA								
1 Visclosky	N	Y	Y	Y	N	Y	N	N
2 **McIntosh**	?	?	?	?	?	Y	N	Y
3 Roemer	Y	Y	Y	Y	Y	Y	N	N
4 **Souder**	Y	Y	Y	Y	Y	Y	N	Y
5 **Buyer**	?	?	?	?	?	?	?	?
6 **Burton**	Y	Y	Y	Y	?	Y	N	Y
7 **Pease**	Y	Y	Y	Y	Y	Y	N	Y
8 **Hostettler**	Y	N	Y	Y	Y	Y	N	Y
9 Hill	Y	Y	Y	Y	Y	Y	N	N
10 Carson	?	+	+	+	Y	Y	N	N
IOWA								
1 **Leach**	Y	Y	Y	?	Y	Y	N	Y
2 **Nussle**	Y	Y	Y	Y	Y	Y	N	Y
3 Boswell	Y	Y	Y	Y	Y	Y	N	N
4 **Ganske**	Y	Y	Y	Y	Y	Y	N	Y
5 **Latham**	Y	Y	Y	Y	Y	Y	N	Y
KANSAS								
1 **Moran**	N	Y	Y	Y	N	Y	N	Y
2 **Ryun**	Y	Y	Y	Y	Y	Y	N	Y
3 Moore	Y	Y	Y	Y	Y	Y	N	N
4 **Tiahrt**	Y	N	Y	Y	Y	Y	N	Y
KENTUCKY								
1 **Whitfield**	Y	Y	Y	Y	?	Y	N	Y
2 **Lewis**	Y	Y	Y	Y	Y	Y	N	Y
3 **Northup**	Y	Y	Y	Y	Y	Y	N	Y
4 Lucas	Y	Y	Y	Y	Y	Y	N	N
5 **Rogers**	Y	Y	Y	Y	Y	Y	N	Y
6 **Fletcher**	Y	Y	Y	Y	Y	Y	N	Y
LOUISIANA								
1 **Vitter**	Y	Y	Y	Y	Y	Y	N	Y
2 Jefferson	?	?	?	?	?	?	?	?
3 **Tauzin**	Y	Y	Y	Y	Y	Y	N	Y
4 **McCrery**	Y	Y	Y	Y	Y	Y	N	Y
5 **Cooksey**	?	?	?	?	Y	Y	N	Y
6 **Baker**	Y	Y	Y	Y	Y	Y	N	Y
7 John	Y	Y	Y	Y	Y	Y	N	N
MAINE								
1 Allen	Y	Y	Y	Y	Y	Y	N	N
2 Baldacci	Y	Y	Y	Y	Y	Y	N	N
MARYLAND								
1 **Gilchrest**	Y	Y	Y	Y	Y	Y	N	Y
2 **Ehrlich**	Y	Y	Y	Y	Y	Y	N	Y
3 Cardin	Y	Y	Y	Y	Y	Y	N	N
4 Wynn	Y	Y	Y	Y	Y	Y	N	N
5 Hoyer	Y	Y	Y	Y	Y	Y	N	N
6 **Bartlett**	Y	Y	Y	Y	Y	Y	N	Y
7 Cummings	Y	Y	Y	Y	?	Y	N	N
8 **Morella**	Y	Y	Y	Y	Y	Y	N	Y
MASSACHUSETTS								
1 Olver	N	Y	Y	Y	Y	Y	N	N
2 Neal	?	?	?	?	?	Y	N	N
3 McGovern	Y	Y	Y	Y	Y	Y	N	N
4 Frank	Y	Y	Y	Y	Y	Y	P	N
5 Meehan	Y	Y	Y	Y	Y	Y	P	N
6 Tierney	Y	Y	Y	Y	Y	Y	N	N
7 Markey	N	Y	Y	Y	Y	Y	N	N
8 Capuano	Y	Y	Y	Y	Y	Y	P	N
9 Moakley	Y	Y	Y	Y	Y	Y	N	N
10 Delahunt	Y	Y	Y	Y	Y	Y	N	N
MICHIGAN								
1 Stupak	N	Y	Y	Y	N	Y	N	N
2 **Hoekstra**	Y	Y	Y	Y	Y	Y	N	Y
3 **Ehlers**	Y	Y	Y	Y	Y	Y	N	Y
4 **Camp**	?	?	?	?	?	?	?	?
5 Barcia	Y	Y	Y	Y	Y	Y	N	N
6 **Upton**	Y	Y	Y	Y	Y	Y	N	Y
7 **Smith**	Y	Y	Y	Y	Y	Y	N	Y
8 Stabenow	Y	Y	Y	Y	Y	Y	N	N
9 Kildee	Y	Y	Y	Y	Y	Y	N	N
10 Bonior	Y	Y	Y	Y	?	Y	N	N
11 **Knollenberg**	?	?	?	?	?	Y	N	Y
12 Levin	Y	Y	Y	Y	Y	Y	N	N
13 Rivers	Y	Y	Y	Y	Y	Y	N	N
14 Conyers	Y	Y	?	Y	Y	Y	N	N
15 Kilpatrick	Y	Y	Y	Y	Y	Y	N	N
16 Dingell	Y	Y	Y	Y	Y	Y	N	N
MINNESOTA								
1 **Gutknecht**	N	Y	Y	Y	N	Y	N	Y
2 Minge	Y	Y	Y	Y	Y	Y	N	N
3 **Ramstad**	N	Y	Y	Y	N	Y	N	Y
4 Vento	N	Y	Y	Y	N	Y	N	N
5 Sabo	N	Y	Y	Y	N	Y	N	N
6 Luther	Y	Y	Y	Y	Y	Y	N	N
7 Peterson	N	N	Y	Y	N	Y	N	N
8 Oberstar	N	Y	Y	Y	?	Y	N	N
MISSISSIPPI								
1 **Wicker**	Y	Y	Y	Y	Y	Y	N	Y
2 Thompson	N	Y	Y	Y	N	Y	N	N
3 **Pickering**	Y	Y	Y	Y	Y	Y	N	Y
4 Shows	Y	Y	Y	Y	Y	Y	N	N
5 Taylor	N	Y	Y	Y	N	Y	N	N
MISSOURI								
1 Clay	N	Y	Y	Y	?	Y	N	N
2 **Talent**	Y	Y	Y	Y	Y	Y	N	Y
3 Gephardt	Y	Y	Y	Y	?	Y	N	N
4 Skelton	Y	Y	Y	Y	Y	Y	N	N
5 McCarthy	Y	Y	Y	Y	Y	Y	N	N
6 Danner	Y	Y	Y	Y	Y	Y	N	N
7 **Blunt**	Y	?	Y	Y	Y	Y	N	Y
8 **Emerson**	Y	Y	Y	Y	Y	Y	N	Y
9 **Hulshof**	Y	Y	Y	Y	Y	Y	N	Y
MONTANA								
AL **Hill**	N	Y	Y	Y	Y	Y	N	Y
NEBRASKA								
1 **Bereuter**	Y	Y	Y	Y	Y	Y	N	Y
2 **Terry**	Y	Y	Y	Y	Y	Y	N	Y
3 **Barrett**	Y	Y	Y	Y	Y	Y	N	Y
NEVADA								
1 Berkley	Y	Y	Y	Y	Y	Y	N	N
2 **Gibbons**	N	Y	Y	Y	Y	Y	N	Y
NEW HAMPSHIRE								
1 **Sununu**	Y	Y	Y	Y	Y	Y	N	Y
2 **Bass**	Y	Y	Y	Y	Y	Y	N	Y
NEW JERSEY								
1 Andrews	Y	Y	Y	Y	Y	Y	N	N
2 **LoBiondo**	N	Y	Y	Y	N	Y	N	Y
3 **Saxton**	Y	Y	Y	Y	Y	Y	N	Y
4 **Smith**	Y	Y	Y	Y	Y	Y	N	Y
5 **Roukema**	Y	Y	Y	Y	Y	Y	N	Y
6 Pallone	?	?	?	?	N	Y	N	N
7 **Franks**	Y	Y	Y	Y	Y	Y	N	Y
8 Pascrell	N	Y	Y	Y	Y	Y	N	N
9 Rothman	Y	Y	Y	Y	Y	Y	N	N
10 Payne	N	?	?	?	Y	Y	N	N
11 **Frelinghuysen**	+	+	+	+	Y	Y	N	Y
12 Holt	Y	Y	Y	Y	Y	Y	N	N
13 Menendez	?	?	?	?	?	Y	N	N
NEW MEXICO								
1 **Wilson**	Y	Y	Y	Y	Y	Y	N	Y
2 **Skeen**	Y	Y	Y	Y	Y	Y	N	Y
3 Udall	N	Y	Y	Y	N	Y	N	N
NEW YORK								
1 Forbes	Y	Y	Y	Y	Y	Y	N	N
2 **Lazio**	Y	Y	Y	Y	Y	Y	N	Y
3 **King**	Y	Y	Y	Y	Y	Y	N	Y
4 McCarthy	Y	Y	Y	Y	Y	Y	N	N
5 Ackerman	Y	Y	Y	Y	Y	Y	N	N
6 Meeks	Y	Y	Y	Y	Y	Y	N	N
7 Crowley	Y	Y	Y	Y	N	Y	N	N
8 Nadler	Y	Y	Y	Y	Y	Y	N	N
9 Weiner	Y	Y	Y	Y	Y	Y	N	N
10 Towns	?	?	?	?	Y	Y	N	N
11 Owens	Y	Y	Y	Y	Y	Y	N	N
12 Velázquez	N	Y	Y	Y	Y	Y	N	N
13 **Fossella**	Y	Y	Y	Y	Y	Y	N	Y
14 Maloney	Y	Y	Y	Y	Y	Y	N	N
15 Rangel	Y	Y	Y	Y	?	Y	N	N
16 Serrano	Y	Y	Y	?	Y	Y	N	N
17 Engel	Y	Y	Y	Y	?	Y	N	N
18 Lowey	Y	Y	Y	Y	Y	Y	N	N
19 **Kelly**	Y	Y	Y	Y	Y	Y	N	Y
20 **Gilman**	Y	Y	Y	Y	Y	Y	N	Y
21 McNulty	N	Y	Y	Y	N	Y	N	N
22 **Sweeney**	N	Y	Y	Y	N	Y	N	Y
23 **Boehlert**	Y	Y	Y	Y	Y	Y	N	Y
24 **McHugh**	Y	Y	Y	Y	Y	Y	N	Y
25 **Walsh**	Y	Y	Y	Y	Y	Y	N	Y
26 Hinchey	Y	Y	Y	Y	Y	Y	N	N
27 **Reynolds**	Y	Y	Y	Y	Y	Y	N	Y
28 Slaughter	Y	Y	Y	Y	?	Y	N	N
29 LaFalce	Y	Y	Y	Y	Y	?	N	N
30 **Quinn**	Y	Y	Y	Y	Y	Y	N	Y
31 **Houghton**	Y	Y	Y	Y	Y	Y	N	Y
NORTH CAROLINA								
1 Clayton	Y	Y	Y	Y	?	Y	N	N
2 Etheridge	Y	Y	Y	Y	Y	Y	N	N
3 **Jones**	Y	Y	Y	Y	Y	Y	N	Y
4 Price	Y	Y	Y	Y	Y	Y	N	N
5 **Burr**	Y	Y	Y	Y	Y	Y	N	Y
6 **Coble**	Y	Y	Y	Y	Y	Y	N	Y
7 McIntyre	Y	Y	Y	Y	Y	Y	N	N
8 **Hayes**	Y	Y	Y	Y	Y	Y	N	Y
9 **Myrick**	Y	Y	Y	Y	Y	Y	N	Y
10 **Ballenger**	Y	Y	Y	Y	Y	Y	N	Y
11 **Taylor**	Y	Y	Y	Y	Y	Y	N	Y
12 Watt	Y	Y	Y	Y	Y	Y	N	N
NORTH DAKOTA								
AL Pomeroy	Y	Y	Y	Y	N	Y	N	N
OHIO								
1 **Chabot**	Y	Y	Y	Y	Y	Y	N	Y
2 **Portman**	Y	Y	Y	Y	Y	Y	N	Y
3 Hall	Y	Y	Y	Y	Y	Y	N	N
4 **Oxley**	Y	Y	Y	Y	Y	Y	N	Y
5 **Gillmor**	Y	Y	Y	Y	N	Y	N	Y
6 Strickland	Y	Y	Y	Y	?	Y	N	N
7 **Hobson**	Y	Y	Y	Y	Y	Y	N	Y
8 **Boehner**	Y	Y	Y	Y	Y	Y	N	Y
9 Kaptur	Y	Y	Y	Y	Y	Y	N	N
10 Kucinich	N	Y	Y	Y	N	Y	N	N
11 Jones	?	?	?	?	Y	Y	N	N
12 **Kasich**	Y	Y	Y	Y	Y	Y	N	Y
13 Brown	Y	Y	Y	Y	N	Y	N	N
14 Sawyer	Y	Y	Y	Y	Y	Y	N	N
15 **Pryce**	?	?	?	?	?	Y	N	Y
16 **Regula**	Y	Y	Y	Y	Y	Y	N	Y
17 Traficant	Y	Y	Y	Y	Y	Y	N	N
18 **Ney**	Y	Y	Y	Y	Y	Y	N	Y
19 **LaTourette**	Y	Y	Y	Y	Y	Y	N	?
OKLAHOMA								
1 **Largent**	Y	Y	Y	Y	Y	Y	N	Y
2 **Coburn**	N	Y	Y	Y	N	Y	N	Y
3 **Watkins**	Y	Y	Y	Y	Y	Y	N	Y
4 **Watts**	Y	Y	Y	Y	Y	Y	N	Y
5 **Istook**	Y	Y	Y	Y	Y	Y	N	Y
6 **Lucas**	Y	Y	Y	Y	Y	Y	N	Y
OREGON								
1 Wu	Y	Y	Y	Y	Y	Y	N	N
2 **Walden**	Y	Y	Y	Y	Y	Y	N	Y
3 Blumenauer	Y	Y	Y	Y	Y	Y	P	N
4 DeFazio	N	Y	Y	Y	N	N	N	N
5 Hooley	Y	Y	Y	Y	Y	Y	N	N
PENNSYLVANIA								
1 Brady	?	?	?	?	N	Y	N	N
2 Fattah	?	?	?	?	?	Y	N	N
3 Borski	N	Y	Y	Y	N	Y	N	N
4 Klink	?	?	?	?	N	Y	N	N
5 **Peterson**	Y	Y	Y	Y	Y	Y	N	Y
6 Holden	Y	N	Y	Y	Y	Y	N	N
7 **Weldon**	Y	Y	Y	Y	Y	Y	N	Y
8 **Greenwood**	Y	Y	Y	Y	Y	Y	N	Y
9 **Shuster**	Y	Y	Y	Y	Y	Y	N	Y
10 **Sherwood**	Y	Y	Y	Y	Y	Y	N	Y
11 Kanjorski	Y	Y	Y	Y	Y	Y	N	N
12 Murtha	Y	Y	Y	Y	Y	Y	N	N
13 Hoeffel	Y	Y	Y	Y	Y	Y	N	N
14 Coyne	Y	Y	Y	Y	Y	Y	N	N
15 **Toomey**	Y	Y	Y	Y	Y	Y	N	Y
16 **Pitts**	Y	Y	Y	Y	Y	Y	N	Y
17 **Gekas**	Y	Y	Y	Y	Y	Y	N	Y
18 Doyle	Y	Y	Y	Y	Y	Y	N	N
19 **Goodling**	Y	Y	Y	Y	Y	Y	N	Y
20 Mascara	Y	Y	Y	Y	Y	Y	N	N
21 **English**	N	Y	Y	Y	N	Y	N	Y
RHODE ISLAND								
1 Kennedy	Y	Y	Y	Y	Y	Y	N	–
2 Weygand	Y	Y	Y	Y	Y	Y	N	N
SOUTH CAROLINA								
1 **Sanford**	?	?	?	?	N	Y	N	Y
2 **Spence**	Y	Y	Y	Y	Y	Y	N	Y
3 **Graham**	Y	Y	Y	Y	Y	Y	N	Y
4 **DeMint**	Y	Y	Y	Y	Y	Y	N	Y
5 Spratt	Y	Y	Y	Y	Y	Y	N	N
6 Clyburn	N	Y	Y	Y	N	Y	N	N
SOUTH DAKOTA								
AL **Thune**	Y	Y	Y	Y	Y	Y	N	Y
TENNESSEE								
1 **Jenkins**	Y	Y	Y	Y	Y	Y	N	Y
2 **Duncan**	Y	Y	Y	Y	Y	Y	N	Y
3 **Wamp**	Y	Y	Y	Y	N	Y	N	Y
4 **Hilleary**	N	Y	Y	Y	N	Y	N	Y
5 Clement	Y	Y	Y	Y	?	Y	N	N
6 Gordon	Y	Y	Y	Y	Y	Y	N	N
7 **Bryant**	Y	Y	Y	Y	Y	Y	N	Y
8 Tanner	Y	Y	Y	Y	Y	Y	N	N
9 Ford	Y	Y	Y	Y	N	Y	N	N
TEXAS								
1 Sandlin	Y	Y	Y	Y	Y	Y	N	N
2 Turner	Y	Y	Y	Y	Y	Y	N	N
3 **Johnson, Sam**	?	?	?	?	?	Y	N	Y
4 Hall	Y	Y	Y	Y	Y	Y	N	Y
5 **Sessions**	Y	Y	Y	Y	?	Y	N	Y
6 **Barton**	Y	Y	Y	Y	Y	Y	N	Y
7 **Archer**	Y	Y	Y	Y	Y	Y	N	Y
8 **Brady**	Y	Y	Y	Y	Y	Y	N	Y
9 Lampson	Y	Y	Y	Y	?	Y	N	N
10 Doggett	Y	Y	Y	Y	Y	Y	N	N
11 Edwards	Y	Y	Y	Y	Y	Y	N	N
12 **Granger**	Y	Y	Y	Y	Y	Y	N	Y
13 **Thornberry**	Y	Y	Y	Y	Y	Y	N	Y
14 **Paul**	Y	N	Y	Y	Y	N	N	Y
15 Hinojosa	Y	Y	Y	Y	Y	Y	N	N
16 Reyes	Y	Y	Y	Y	Y	Y	N	N
17 Stenholm	Y	Y	Y	Y	Y	Y	N	N
18 Jackson-Lee	Y	Y	Y	Y	N	Y	N	N
19 **Combest**	Y	Y	Y	Y	Y	Y	N	Y
20 Gonzalez	Y	Y	Y	Y	Y	Y	N	N
21 **Smith**	Y	Y	Y	Y	Y	Y	N	Y
22 **DeLay**	Y	Y	Y	Y	?	Y	N	Y
23 **Bonilla**	Y	Y	Y	Y	Y	Y	N	Y
24 Frost	Y	Y	Y	Y	?	Y	N	N
25 Bentsen	Y	Y	Y	Y	Y	Y	N	N
26 **Armey**	Y	Y	Y	Y	Y	Y	N	Y
27 Ortiz	Y	Y	Y	Y	Y	Y	N	N
28 Rodriguez	Y	Y	Y	Y	Y	Y	N	N
29 Green	N	Y	Y	Y	N	?	N	N
30 Johnson, E.B.	Y	Y	Y	Y	Y	Y	N	N
UTAH								
1 **Hansen**	Y	Y	Y	Y	Y	Y	N	Y
2 **Cook**	Y	Y	Y	Y	Y	Y	N	Y
3 **Cannon**	Y	Y	Y	Y	Y	Y	N	Y
VERMONT								
AL Sanders	Y	Y	Y	Y	Y	Y	N	N
VIRGINIA								
1 **Bateman**	Y	Y	Y	Y	Y	Y	N	Y
2 Pickett	N	Y	Y	Y	N	Y	N	N
3 Scott	Y	Y	Y	Y	Y	Y	N	N
4 Sisisky	Y	Y	Y	Y	Y	Y	N	N
5 Goode	Y	Y	Y	Y	Y	Y	N	Y
6 **Goodlatte**	Y	Y	Y	Y	Y	Y	N	Y
7 **Bliley**	Y	Y	Y	Y	Y	Y	N	Y
8 Moran	Y	Y	Y	Y	Y	Y	N	N
9 Boucher	Y	Y	Y	Y	Y	Y	N	N
10 **Wolf**	Y	Y	Y	Y	Y	Y	N	Y
11 **Davis**	Y	Y	Y	Y	Y	Y	N	Y
WASHINGTON								
1 Inslee	Y	Y	Y	Y	Y	Y	N	N
2 **Metcalf**	Y	Y	Y	Y	Y	Y	N	Y
3 Baird	N	Y	Y	Y	N	Y	N	N
4 **Hastings**	Y	Y	Y	Y	Y	Y	N	Y
5 **Nethercutt**	Y	Y	Y	Y	Y	Y	N	Y
6 Dicks	Y	Y	Y	?	Y	Y	N	N
7 McDermott	N	Y	Y	Y	N	Y	N	?
8 **Dunn**	Y	Y	Y	Y	Y	Y	N	Y
9 Smith	Y	Y	Y	Y	Y	Y	N	N
WEST VIRGINIA								
1 Mollohan	Y	Y	Y	Y	Y	Y	N	N
2 Wise	Y	Y	Y	Y	?	Y	N	N
3 Rahall	Y	Y	Y	Y	Y	Y	N	N
WISCONSIN								
1 **Ryan**	Y	Y	Y	Y	Y	Y	N	Y
2 Baldwin	Y	Y	Y	Y	Y	Y	N	N
3 Kind	Y	Y	Y	Y	Y	Y	N	N
4 Kleczka	Y	Y	Y	Y	Y	Y	N	N
5 Barrett	Y	Y	Y	Y	Y	Y	N	N
6 **Petri**	Y	Y	Y	Y	Y	Y	N	Y
7 Obey	Y	Y	Y	Y	Y	Y	N	N
8 **Green**	Y	Y	Y	Y	Y	Y	N	Y
9 **Sensenbrenner**	Y	N	Y	Y	Y	Y	N	Y
WYOMING								
AL **Cubin**	Y	Y	?	Y	?	Y	N	Y

Southern states - Ala., Ark., Fla., Ga., Ky., La., Miss., N.C., Okla., S.C., Tenn., Texas, Va.

513. HR 1180. Extended Benefits for the Disabled/Passage. Archer, R-Texas, motion to suspend the rules and pass the bill to allow disabled individuals receiving Social Security and Supplemental Security Income payments to retain their Medicare or Medicaid insurance for 10 years after returning to work. The bill would also establish a voucherlike program to help working disabled persons to purchase job training and rehabilitation services. Motion agreed to 412-9: R 206-9; D 205-0 (ND 152-0, SD 53-0); I 1-0. Oct. 19, 1999. A two-thirds majority of those present and voting (281 in this case) is required for passage under suspension of the rules.

514. HR 1887. Animal Cruelty/Passage. McCollum, R-Fla., motion to suspend the rules and pass the bill to make it a federal crime to depict animal cruelty for commercial purposes. Motion agreed to 372-42: R 177-35; D 194-7 (ND 146-3, SD 48-4); I 1-0. Oct. 19, 1999. A two-thirds majority of those present and voting (276 in this case) is required for passage under suspension of the rules.

515. Procedural Motion/Journal. Approval of the House Journal of Tuesday, Oct. 19, 1999. Approved 349-57: R 186-18; D 163-39 (ND 120-28, SD 43-11); I 0-0. Oct. 20, 1999.

516. HR 2670. Fiscal 2000 Commerce-Justice-State Appropriations/ Previous Question. Linder, R-Ga., motion to order the previous question (thus ending debate and possibility of amendment) on adoption of the rule (H Res 335) to provide for House floor consideration of the conference report on the bill to appropriate $37.8 billion to the departments of Commerce, Justice and State and the federal judiciary. Motion agreed to 221-204: R 218-0; D 3-203 (ND 1-151, SD 2-52); I 0-1. Oct. 20, 1999.

517. HR 2670. Fiscal 2000 Commerce-Justice-State Appropriations/ Rule. Adoption of the rule (H Res 335) to provide for House floor consideration of the conference report on the bill to appropriate $37.8 billion to the departments of Commerce, Justice and State and the federal judiciary. Adopted 221-204: R 217-0; D 4-203 (ND 2-151, SD 2-52); I 0-1. Oct. 20, 1999.

518. HR 2670. Fiscal 2000 Commerce-Justice-State Appropriations/ Conference Report. Adoption of the conference report on the bill to provide $37.8 billion for the departments of Commerce, Justice, and State, and the federal judiciary system. The measure includes $4.5 billion in "emergency" funding for the 2000 census. Adopted (thus sent to the Senate) 215-213: R 202-17; D 13-195 (ND 8-146, SD 5-49); I 0-1 Oct. 20, 1999.

519. HR 2. Title I Reauthorization/Women's Educational Equity Act. Mink, D-Hawaii, amendment to authorize $5 million for the Women's Educational Equity Act program. The amendment would reinsert provisions related to gender equity throughout the bill. Adopted 311-111: R 105-110; D 205-1 (ND 153-0, SD 52-1); I 1-0. Oct. 20, 1999.

520. Procedural Motion/Journal. Approval of the House Journal of Wednesday, Oct. 20, 1999. Approved 352-62: R 192-19; D 160-43 (ND 115-34, SD 45-9); I 0-0. Oct. 21, 1999.

Key

- Y Voted for (yea).
- # Paired for.
- + Announced for.
- N Voted against (nay).
- X Paired against.
- – Announced against.
- P Voted "present."
- C Voted "present" to avoid possible conflict of interest.
- ? Did not vote or otherwise make a position known.

•

Democrats ***Republicans***
Independents

	513	514	515	516	517	518	519	520
ALABAMA								
1 ***Callahan***	Y	Y	Y	Y	Y	Y	N	Y
2 ***Everett***	Y	Y	Y	Y	Y	Y	N	Y
3 ***Riley***	Y	Y	N	Y	Y	Y	N	Y
4 ***Aderholt***	Y	Y	N	Y	Y	Y	Y	N
5 Cramer	Y	Y	Y	N	N	Y	Y	Y
6 ***Bachus***	Y	Y	Y	Y	Y	Y	N	?
7 Hilliard	Y	Y	N	N	N	N	Y	N
ALASKA								
AL ***Young***	Y	Y	?	Y	Y	Y	Y	?
ARIZONA								
1 ***Salmon***	Y	Y	?	Y	Y	Y	N	Y
2 Pastor	Y	Y	Y	N	N	N	Y	N
3 ***Stump***	Y	Y	Y	Y	Y	Y	N	Y
4 ***Shadegg***	Y	N	Y	Y	Y	Y	N	Y
5 ***Kolbe***	Y	Y	Y	Y	Y	Y	N	Y
6 ***Hayworth***	Y	Y	Y	Y	Y	Y	Y	Y
ARKANSAS								
1 Berry	Y	Y	Y	N	N	N	Y	Y
2 Snyder	Y	Y	Y	N	N	N	Y	Y
3 ***Hutchinson***	Y	Y	?	Y	Y	Y	Y	Y
4 ***Dickey***	Y	Y	N	Y	Y	Y	Y	N
CALIFORNIA								
1 Thompson	Y	Y	N	N	N	N	Y	N
2 ***Herger***	Y	Y	Y	Y	Y	Y	N	Y
3 ***Ose***	Y	Y	Y	Y	Y	Y	Y	Y
4 ***Doolittle***	N	N	Y	Y	Y	Y	N	Y
5 Matsui	Y	Y	Y	N	N	N	Y	?
6 Woolsey	Y	Y	Y	N	N	N	Y	Y
7 Miller, George	Y	Y	N	N	N	N	Y	N
8 Pelosi	Y	Y	Y	N	N	N	Y	Y
9 Lee	Y	Y	Y	N	N	N	Y	Y
10 Tauscher	Y	Y	Y	N	N	N	Y	Y
11 ***Pombo***	Y	Y	Y	Y	Y	Y	N	Y
12 Lantos	Y	Y	Y	N	N	N	Y	Y
13 Stark	Y	Y	Y	N	N	N	Y	Y
14 Eshoo	Y	Y	Y	N	N	N	Y	Y
15 ***Campbell***	Y	Y	Y	Y	Y	Y	N	Y
16 Lofgren	Y	Y	Y	N	N	N	Y	Y
17 Farr	Y	Y	Y	N	N	N	Y	Y
18 Condit	Y	Y	Y	N	N	N	Y	Y
19 ***Radanovich***	Y	Y	Y	Y	Y	Y	N	Y
20 Dooley	Y	Y	Y	N	N	N	Y	Y
21 ***Thomas***	Y	Y	Y	Y	Y	Y	Y	Y
22 Capps	Y	Y	Y	N	N	N	Y	Y
23 ***Gallegly***	Y	Y	Y	Y	Y	Y	Y	Y
24 Sherman	Y	Y	Y	N	N	N	Y	Y
25 ***McKeon***	Y	Y	Y	Y	Y	Y	N	Y
26 Berman	Y	Y	Y	N	N	N	Y	Y
27 ***Rogan***	Y	Y	N	Y	Y	Y	N	N
28 ***Dreier***	Y	N	Y	Y	Y	Y	Y	Y
29 Waxman	Y	Y	Y	N	N	N	Y	Y
30 Becerra	Y	Y	Y	N	N	N	Y	N
31 Martinez	?	?	Y	N	N	N	Y	Y
32 Dixon	Y	Y	Y	N	N	Y	Y	Y
33 Roybal-Allard	Y	Y	Y	N	N	Y	Y	Y
34 Napolitano	Y	Y	Y	N	N	N	Y	Y
35 Waters	Y	N	N	N	N	N	Y	N
36 ***Kuykendall***	Y	Y	Y	Y	Y	Y	Y	Y
37 Millender-McD.	Y	Y	Y	N	N	N	Y	Y
38 ***Horn***	Y	Y	Y	Y	Y	Y	Y	Y
39 ***Royce***	Y	Y	Y	Y	Y	Y	Y	Y
40 ***Lewis***	Y	Y	?	Y	Y	Y	N	Y
41 ***Miller***	Y	Y	Y	Y	Y	Y	Y	Y
42 Vacant								
43 ***Calvert***	Y	Y	Y	Y	Y	Y	?	Y
44 ***Bono***	Y	Y	Y	Y	Y	Y	Y	Y
45 ***Rohrabacher***	Y	Y	Y	Y	Y	Y	N	Y
46 Sanchez	Y	Y	Y	N	N	N	Y	Y
47 ***Cox***	Y	Y	?	Y	Y	?	Y	Y
48 ***Packard***	Y	Y	Y	Y	Y	Y	N	Y
49 ***Bilbray***	Y	Y	N	Y	Y	Y	Y	N
50 Filner	Y	Y	N	N	N	N	Y	N
51 ***Cunningham***	Y	Y	Y	Y	Y	Y	N	Y
52 ***Hunter***	Y	N	Y	Y	Y	Y	N	Y
COLORADO								
1 DeGette	Y	N	Y	N	N	N	Y	Y
2 Udall	Y	Y	Y	N	N	N	Y	N
3 ***McInnis***	Y	Y	Y	Y	Y	Y	Y	Y
4 ***Schaffer***	Y	N	N	Y	Y	N	N	N
5 ***Hefley***	Y	Y	N	Y	Y	N	N	N
6 ***Tancredo***	Y	Y	P	Y	Y	Y	N	N
CONNECTICUT								
1 Larson	Y	Y	?	N	N	N	Y	Y
2 Gejdenson	Y	Y	Y	N	N	N	Y	Y
3 DeLauro	Y	Y	Y	N	N	N	Y	Y
4 ***Shays***	Y	Y	Y	Y	Y	N	Y	Y
5 Maloney	Y	Y	Y	N	N	N	Y	Y
6 ***Johnson***	Y	Y	Y	Y	Y	Y	Y	Y
DELAWARE								
AL ***Castle***	Y	Y	Y	Y	Y	Y	Y	Y
FLORIDA								
1 ***Scarborough***	?	?	?	?	?	?	?	?
2 Boyd	Y	Y	Y	N	N	N	Y	Y
3 Brown	Y	Y	Y	N	N	N	Y	Y
4 ***Fowler***	?	?	?	Y	Y	Y	Y	Y
5 Thurman	Y	Y	N	N	N	N	Y	Y
6 ***Stearns***	Y	Y	Y	Y	Y	Y	N	Y
7 ***Mica***	Y	Y	Y	Y	Y	Y	Y	Y
8 ***McCollum***	Y	Y	Y	Y	Y	Y	Y	Y
9 ***Bilirakis***	Y	Y	Y	Y	Y	Y	Y	Y
10 ***Young***	Y	Y	Y	Y	Y	Y	Y	Y
11 Davis	Y	Y	Y	N	N	N	Y	Y
12 ***Canady***	Y	Y	Y	Y	Y	Y	N	Y
13 ***Miller***	Y	Y	Y	Y	Y	Y	N	Y
14 ***Goss***	Y	Y	Y	Y	Y	Y	N	Y
15 ***Weldon***	Y	Y	Y	Y	Y	Y	Y	Y
16 ***Foley***	Y	Y	Y	Y	Y	Y	Y	Y
17 Meek	Y	N	N	N	N	N	Y	N
18 ***Ros-Lehtinen***	+	+	Y	Y	Y	Y	Y	Y
19 Wexler	Y	Y	Y	N	N	N	Y	Y
20. Deutsch	Y	Y	Y	N	N	N	Y	Y
21 ***Diaz-Balart***	Y	Y	Y	Y	Y	Y	Y	Y
22 ***Shaw***	Y	Y	Y	Y	Y	Y	Y	Y
23 Hastings	Y	Y	N	N	N	N	Y	Y
GEORGIA								
1 ***Kingston***	Y	N	Y	Y	Y	Y	N	Y
2 Bishop	Y	Y	Y	N	N	N	Y	Y
3 ***Collins***	Y	N	Y	Y	Y	Y	N	Y
4 McKinney	Y	Y	Y	N	N	N	Y	Y
5 Lewis	?	?	N	N	N	N	?	Y
6 ***Isakson***	Y	Y	Y	Y	Y	Y	N	+
7 ***Barr***	Y	N	Y	Y	Y	N	N	Y
8 ***Chambliss***	Y	Y	Y	Y	Y	Y	N	Y
9 ***Deal***	Y	Y	Y	Y	Y	Y	N	Y
10 ***Norwood***	Y	N	Y	Y	Y	Y	N	Y
11 ***Linder***	Y	N	Y	Y	Y	Y	N	?
HAWAII								
1 Abercrombie	Y	N	Y	N	N	N	Y	Y
2 Mink	Y	Y	Y	N	N	N	Y	Y
IDAHO								
1 ***Chenoweth***	Y	N	Y	Y	Y	N	N	Y
2 ***Simpson***	Y	Y	Y	Y	Y	Y	Y	Y
ILLINOIS								
1 Rush	?	?	?	?	?	?	Y	Y
2 Jackson	Y	Y	Y	N	N	N	Y	Y
3 Lipinski	Y	Y	N	N	N	N	?	N
4 Gutierrez	Y	Y	?	?	?	?	?	N
5 Blagojevich	Y	Y	Y	N	N	N	Y	Y
6 ***Hyde***	Y	Y	Y	Y	Y	Y	N	Y
7 Davis	Y	Y	?	N	N	N	Y	Y
8 ***Crane***	Y	Y	N	Y	Y	Y	N	N
9 Schakowsky	Y	Y	Y	N	N	N	Y	Y
10 ***Porter***	Y	Y	Y	Y	Y	Y	Y	Y
11 ***Weller***	Y	Y	N	Y	Y	Y	Y	N
12 Costello	Y	Y	N	N	N	N	Y	N
13 ***Biggert***	Y	Y	Y	Y	Y	Y	Y	Y
14 ***Hastert***						Y		

ND Northern Democrats SD Southern Democrats

	513	514	515	516	517	518	519	520
15 **Ewing**	Y	Y	Y	Y	Y	Y	N	Y
16 **Manzullo**	Y	N	Y	Y	Y	Y	N	Y
17 Evans	Y	Y	N	N	N	N	Y	N
18 **LaHood**	Y	Y	Y	Y	Y	Y	Y	Y
19 Phelps	Y	Y	N	N	N	N	Y	Y
20 **Shimkus**	Y	Y	Y	Y	Y	Y	Y	Y
INDIANA								
1 Visclosky	Y	Y	N	N	N	N	Y	N
2 **McIntosh**	N	Y	Y	Y	Y	N	?	Y
3 Roemer	Y	Y	Y	N	N	N	Y	Y
4 **Souder**	Y	Y	Y	Y	Y	Y	N	Y
5 **Buyer**	?	?	Y	Y	Y	Y	N	Y
6 **Burton**	Y	N	?	Y	Y	Y	N	?
7 **Pease**	Y	Y	Y	Y	Y	Y	Y	Y
8 **Hostettler**	Y	N	Y	Y	Y	N	N	Y
9 Hill	Y	Y	Y	N	N	N	Y	Y
10 Carson	Y	Y	Y	N	N	N	Y	Y
IOWA								
1 **Leach**	Y	Y	Y	Y	Y	Y	Y	Y
2 **Nussle**	Y	N	Y	Y	Y	Y	N	Y
3 Boswell	Y	Y	Y	N	N	N	Y	Y
4 **Ganske**	Y	Y	Y	Y	Y	Y	N	Y
5 **Latham**	Y	Y	Y	Y	Y	Y	N	Y
KANSAS								
1 **Moran**	N	Y	N	Y	Y	Y	Y	N
2 **Ryun**	Y	N	Y	Y	Y	Y	N	Y
3 Moore	Y	Y	N	N	N	N	Y	Y
4 **Tiahrt**	Y	N	Y	Y	Y	Y	N	Y
KENTUCKY								
1 **Whitfield**	Y	Y	?	Y	Y	Y	Y	Y
2 **Lewis**	Y	Y	Y	Y	Y	Y	N	Y
3 **Northup**	Y	Y	Y	Y	Y	Y	Y	Y
4 Lucas	Y	Y	Y	N	N	Y	Y	Y
5 **Rogers**	Y	Y	Y	Y	Y	Y	N	Y
6 **Fletcher**	Y	Y	Y	Y	Y	Y	Y	Y
LOUISIANA								
1 **Vitter**	Y	Y	Y	Y	Y	Y	N	Y
2 Jefferson	?	?	?	?	?	?	?	?
3 **Tauzin**	Y	N	Y	Y	Y	Y	N	Y
4 **McCrery**	Y	Y	Y	Y	Y	Y	N	Y
5 **Cooksey**	Y	N	Y	Y	Y	Y	Y	Y
6 **Baker**	Y	Y	Y	Y	Y	Y	N	Y
7 John	Y	+	Y	N	N	N	Y	Y
MAINE								
1 Allen	Y	Y	Y	N	N	N	Y	Y
2 Baldacci	Y	Y	Y	N	N	N	Y	Y
MARYLAND								
1 **Gilchrest**	Y	Y	Y	Y	Y	Y	Y	Y
2 **Ehrlich**	Y	Y	Y	Y	Y	Y	Y	Y
3 Cardin	Y	Y	Y	N	N	N	Y	Y
4 Wynn	Y	Y	Y	N	N	N	Y	Y
5 Hoyer	Y	Y	?	N	N	N	Y	Y
6 **Bartlett**	Y	Y	Y	Y	Y	Y	Y	Y
7 Cummings	Y	Y	Y	N	N	N	Y	?
8 **Morella**	Y	Y	Y	Y	Y	Y	Y	Y
MASSACHUSETTS								
1 Olver	Y	Y	Y	N	N	N	Y	Y
2 Neal	Y	Y	Y	N	N	N	Y	Y
3 McGovern	Y	Y	Y	N	N	N	Y	Y
4 Frank	Y	Y	Y	N	N	N	Y	Y
5 Meehan	Y	Y	Y	N	N	N	Y	Y
6 Tierney	Y	Y	Y	N	N	N	Y	Y
7 Markey	Y	Y	Y	N	N	N	Y	N
8 Capuano	Y	Y	Y	N	N	N	Y	N
9 Moakley	Y	Y	Y	N	N	N	Y	Y
10 Delahunt	Y	Y	Y	N	N	N	Y	Y
MICHIGAN								
1 Stupak	Y	?	N	N	N	N	Y	N
2 **Hoekstra**	Y	N	Y	Y	Y	Y	N	N
3 **Ehlers**	Y	Y	Y	Y	Y	Y	Y	Y
4 **Camp**	?	?	?	?	?	?	?	?
5 Barcia	Y	Y	Y	N	N	N	Y	Y
6 **Upton**	Y	Y	Y	Y	Y	Y	N	Y
7 **Smith**	Y	Y	Y	Y	Y	Y	Y	Y
8 Stabenow	Y	Y	Y	N	N	N	Y	Y
9 Kildee	Y	Y	Y	N	N	N	Y	Y
10 Bonior	Y	Y	Y	N	N	N	Y	Y
11 **Knollenberg**	Y	Y	Y	Y	Y	Y	N	Y
12 Levin	Y	Y	Y	N	N	N	Y	Y
13 Rivers	Y	Y	Y	N	N	N	Y	Y
14 Conyers	Y	Y	Y	N	N	N	Y	Y
15 Kilpatrick	Y	Y	Y	N	N	N	Y	Y
16 Dingell	Y	Y	Y	N	N	N	Y	Y

	513	514	515	516	517	518	519	520
MINNESOTA								
1 **Gutknecht**	Y	Y	N	Y	Y	Y	N	?
2 Minge	Y	Y	Y	N	N	N	Y	Y
3 **Ramstad**	Y	Y	N	Y	Y	Y	Y	N
4 Vento	Y	Y	N	N	N	N	Y	Y
5 Sabo	Y	Y	N	N	N	N	Y	N
6 Luther	Y	Y	Y	N	N	N	Y	Y
7 Peterson	Y	Y	N	N	N	N	Y	N
8 Oberstar	Y	Y	N	N	N	N	Y	N
MISSISSIPPI								
1 **Wicker**	Y	N	Y	Y	Y	Y	N	Y
2 Thompson	Y	Y	N	N	N	N	Y	N
3 **Pickering**	Y	Y	Y	Y	Y	Y	Y	Y
4 Shows	Y	Y	Y	N	N	N	Y	Y
5 Taylor	Y	Y	N	N	N	N	Y	N
MISSOURI								
1 Clay	Y	Y	N	N	N	N	Y	N
2 **Talent**	Y	Y	Y	Y	Y	Y	N	Y
3 Gephardt	?	?	Y	N	N	N	Y	?
4 Skelton	Y	Y	Y	N	N	N	Y	Y
5 McCarthy	Y	Y	Y	N	N	N	Y	+
6 Danner	Y	Y	?	?	N	Y	Y	Y
7 **Blunt**	Y	Y	Y	Y	Y	Y	?	Y
8 **Emerson**	Y	Y	Y	Y	Y	Y	Y	Y
9 **Hulshof**	Y	Y	Y	Y	Y	Y	Y	Y
MONTANA								
AL **Hill**	Y	N	N	Y	Y	N	Y	N
NEBRASKA								
1 **Bereuter**	Y	Y	Y	Y	Y	Y	Y	Y
2 **Terry**	Y	Y	Y	Y	Y	Y	Y	Y
3 **Barrett**	Y	Y	Y	Y	Y	Y	N	Y
NEVADA								
1 Berkley	Y	Y	Y	N	N	N	Y	Y
2 **Gibbons**	Y	Y	Y	Y	Y	Y	Y	N
NEW HAMPSHIRE								
1 **Sununu**	Y	N	Y	Y	Y	Y	N	Y
2 **Bass**	Y	Y	Y	Y	Y	Y	Y	Y
NEW JERSEY								
1 Andrews	Y	Y	Y	N	N	N	Y	Y
2 **LoBiondo**	Y	Y	N	Y	Y	Y	Y	N
3 **Saxton**	Y	Y	Y	Y	Y	Y	Y	Y
4 **Smith**	Y	Y	Y	Y	Y	Y	Y	Y
5 **Roukema**	Y	Y	Y	Y	Y	Y	N	Y
6 Pallone	Y	Y	N	N	N	N	Y	N
7 **Franks**	Y	Y	Y	Y	Y	Y	Y	Y
8 Pascrell	Y	Y	Y	N	N	N	Y	N
9 Rothman	Y	Y	Y	N	N	N	Y	Y
10 Payne	Y	Y	Y	N	N	N	Y	Y
11 **Frelinghuysen**	Y	Y	Y	Y	Y	Y	Y	Y
12 Holt	Y	Y	Y	N	N	N	Y	Y
13 Menendez	Y	Y	Y	N	N	N	Y	Y
NEW MEXICO								
1 **Wilson**	Y	Y	Y	Y	Y	Y	Y	Y
2 **Skeen**	Y	Y	Y	Y	Y	Y	N	Y
3 Udall	Y	Y	N	N	N	N	Y	N
NEW YORK								
1 Forbes	Y	Y	Y	N	N	N	Y	?
2 **Lazio**	Y	Y	Y	Y	Y	Y	Y	Y
3 **King**	Y	Y	Y	Y	Y	Y	N	Y
4 McCarthy	Y	Y	Y	N	N	N	?	?
5 Ackerman	Y	Y	Y	N	N	N	Y	Y
6 Meeks	Y	Y	Y	N	N	N	Y	Y
7 Crowley	Y	Y	N	N	N	N	Y	Y
8 Nadler	Y	Y	Y	N	N	N	Y	Y
9 Weiner	Y	Y	?	N	N	N	Y	Y
10 Towns	Y	Y	Y	N	N	N	Y	Y
11 Owens	Y	Y	Y	N	N	N	Y	Y
12 Velázquez	Y	Y	Y	N	N	N	Y	?
13 **Fossella**	Y	Y	?	Y	Y	Y	N	Y
14 Maloney	Y	Y	Y	N	N	N	Y	Y
15 Rangel	Y	Y	Y	N	N	N	Y	Y
16 Serrano	Y	Y	Y	N	N	N	Y	Y
17 Engel	Y	Y	Y	N	N	N	Y	Y
18 Lowey	Y	Y	Y	N	N	N	Y	Y
19 **Kelly**	Y	Y	Y	Y	Y	Y	Y	Y
20 **Gilman**	Y	Y	Y	Y	Y	Y	Y	Y
21 McNulty	Y	Y	N	N	N	N	Y	N
22 **Sweeney**	Y	Y	Y	Y	Y	Y	Y	N
23 **Boehlert**	Y	Y	Y	Y	Y	Y	Y	Y
24 **McHugh**	Y	Y	Y	Y	Y	Y	Y	Y
25 **Walsh**	Y	Y	Y	?	?	Y	Y	Y
26 Hinchey	Y	Y	Y	N	N	N	Y	Y
27 **Reynolds**	Y	Y	Y	Y	Y	Y	Y	Y
28 Slaughter	Y	Y	Y	N	N	N	Y	Y
29 LaFalce	Y	Y	Y	N	N	N	Y	Y

	513	514	515	516	517	518	519	520
30 **Quinn**	Y	Y	Y	Y	Y	N	Y	Y
31 **Houghton**	Y	Y	Y	Y	Y	Y	Y	Y
NORTH CAROLINA								
1 Clayton	Y	N	Y	N	N	N	Y	Y
2 Etheridge	Y	Y	Y	N	N	N	Y	N
3 **Jones**	Y	Y	Y	Y	Y	Y	N	Y
4 Price	Y	Y	Y	N	N	N	Y	Y
5 **Burr**	Y	N	Y	Y	Y	Y	N	Y
6 **Coble**	Y	Y	Y	Y	Y	Y	N	Y
7 McIntyre	Y	Y	Y	N	N	N	Y	Y
8 **Hayes**	Y	Y	Y	Y	Y	Y	N	Y
9 **Myrick**	Y	Y	Y	Y	Y	Y	Y	Y
10 **Ballenger**	Y	Y	Y	Y	Y	Y	N	Y
11 **Taylor**	Y	N	?	Y	Y	Y	N	Y
12 Watt	Y	N	Y	N	N	N	Y	Y
NORTH DAKOTA								
AL Pomeroy	Y	Y	Y	N	N	N	Y	Y
OHIO								
1 **Chabot**	Y	Y	Y	Y	Y	N	N	Y
2 **Portman**	Y	Y	Y	Y	Y	Y	N	Y
3 Hall	Y	Y	Y	N	Y	N	Y	Y
4 **Oxley**	Y	Y	?	Y	Y	Y	N	Y
5 **Gillmor**	Y	Y	N	Y	Y	Y	Y	N
6 Strickland	Y	Y	N	N	N	N	Y	N
7 **Hobson**	Y	Y	Y	Y	Y	Y	Y	Y
8 **Boehner**	Y	Y	Y	Y	Y	Y	N	Y
9 Kaptur	Y	Y	Y	N	N	N	Y	Y
10 Kucinich	Y	Y	N	N	N	N	Y	N
11 Jones	Y	Y	Y	N	N	N	Y	Y
12 **Kasich**	Y	Y	Y	Y	Y	Y	N	Y
13 Brown	Y	Y	Y	N	N	N	Y	Y
14 Sawyer	Y	Y	Y	N	N	N	Y	Y
15 **Pryce**	Y	Y	Y	Y	Y	Y	Y	Y
16 **Regula**	Y	Y	Y	Y	Y	Y	Y	Y
17 Traficant	Y	Y	Y	Y	Y	Y	Y	Y
18 **Ney**	Y	Y	Y	Y	Y	Y	Y	Y
19 **LaTourette**	Y	Y	Y	Y	Y	Y	Y	Y
OKLAHOMA								
1 **Largent**	Y	Y	Y	Y	Y	Y	N	?
2 **Coburn**	N	N	N	Y	Y	Y	N	Y
3 **Watkins**	Y	?	Y	Y	?	Y	Y	Y
4 **Watts**	Y	N	?	Y	Y	Y	Y	Y
5 **Istook**	Y	Y	Y	Y	Y	Y	N	Y
6 **Lucas**	Y	Y	Y	Y	Y	Y	Y	Y
OREGON								
1 Wu	Y	Y	Y	N	N	N	Y	N
2 **Walden**	Y	Y	Y	Y	Y	Y	Y	Y
3 Blumenauer	Y	Y	Y	N	N	N	Y	Y
4 DeFazio	Y	Y	N	N	N	N	Y	N
5 Hooley	Y	Y	Y	N	N	N	Y	N
PENNSYLVANIA								
1 Brady	Y	Y	N	N	N	N	Y	N
2 Fattah	Y	Y	?	N	N	N	Y	N
3 Borski	Y	?	N	N	N	N	Y	N
4 Klink	Y	Y	N	N	N	N	Y	N
5 **Peterson**	Y	Y	Y	Y	Y	Y	N	Y
6 Holden	Y	Y	Y	N	N	N	Y	Y
7 **Weldon**	Y	Y	Y	Y	Y	Y	Y	Y
8 **Greenwood**	Y	Y	Y	Y	Y	Y	Y	Y
9 **Shuster**	Y	Y	Y	Y	Y	Y	?	Y
10 **Sherwood**	Y	Y	Y	Y	Y	Y	Y	Y
11 Kanjorski	Y	Y	Y	N	N	N	Y	Y
12 Murtha	Y	?	Y	N	N	Y	Y	Y
13 Hoeffel	Y	Y	Y	N	N	N	Y	Y
14 Coyne	Y	Y	Y	N	N	N	Y	Y
15 **Toomey**	Y	Y	Y	Y	Y	Y	N	Y
16 **Pitts**	Y	Y	Y	Y	Y	Y	N	Y
17 **Gekas**	Y	Y	Y	Y	Y	Y	N	Y
18 Doyle	Y	Y	Y	N	N	N	Y	Y
19 **Goodling**	Y	Y	Y	Y	Y	Y	N	Y
20 Mascara	Y	Y	Y	N	N	N	Y	Y
21 **English**	Y	Y	N	Y	Y	N	Y	N
RHODE ISLAND								
1 Kennedy	Y	Y	Y	N	N	N	Y	Y
2 Weygand	Y	Y	Y	N	N	N	Y	Y
SOUTH CAROLINA								
1 **Sanford**	Y	N	Y	Y	Y	N	N	Y
2 **Spence**	Y	Y	Y	Y	Y	Y	Y	Y
3 **Graham**	Y	N	Y	Y	Y	Y	N	Y
4 **DeMint**	Y	Y	Y	Y	Y	Y	N	Y
5 Spratt	Y	Y	Y	N	N	N	Y	Y
6 Clyburn	Y	Y	N	N	N	N	Y	N
SOUTH DAKOTA								
AL **Thune**	Y	Y	Y	Y	Y	Y	N	Y

	513	514	515	516	517	518	519	520
TENNESSEE								
1 **Jenkins**	Y	+	Y	Y	Y	Y	Y	Y
2 **Duncan**	Y	+	Y	Y	Y	Y	Y	Y
3 **Wamp**	Y	Y	Y	Y	Y	Y	Y	Y
4 **Hilleary**	Y	Y	N	Y	Y	Y	Y	N
5 Clement	Y	Y	Y	N	N	N	Y	Y
6 Gordon	Y	Y	Y	N	N	N	Y	Y
7 **Bryant**	Y	Y	Y	Y	Y	Y	Y	Y
8 Tanner	Y	Y	Y	N	N	N	Y	Y
9 Ford	Y	Y	N	N	N	N	Y	Y
TEXAS								
1 Sandlin	Y	Y	Y	N	N	N	Y	Y
2 Turner	Y	Y	Y	N	N	N	Y	Y
3 **Johnson, Sam**	N	N	Y	Y	Y	Y	N	Y
4 Hall	Y	Y	Y	Y	Y	Y	Y	Y
5 **Sessions**	Y	N	Y	Y	Y	Y	Y	Y
6 **Barton**	Y	Y	Y	Y	Y	Y	N	Y
7 **Archer**	Y	Y	Y	Y	Y	Y	N	Y
8 **Brady**	Y	Y	Y	Y	Y	Y	N	Y
9 Lampson	Y	Y	Y	N	N	N	Y	Y
10 Doggett	Y	Y	Y	N	N	N	Y	Y
11 Edwards	Y	Y	Y	N	N	N	Y	Y
12 **Granger**	Y	Y	Y	Y	Y	Y	Y	Y
13 **Thornberry**	Y	N	Y	Y	Y	Y	N	Y
14 **Paul**	N	N	Y	Y	Y	N	N	Y
15 Hinojosa	Y	Y	Y	N	N	N	Y	Y
16 Reyes	Y	Y	Y	N	N	N	Y	Y
17 Stenholm	Y	Y	Y	N	N	N	Y	Y
18 Jackson-Lee	Y	Y	Y	N	N	N	Y	Y
19 **Combest**	Y	Y	Y	Y	Y	Y	N	?
20 Gonzalez	Y	Y	Y	N	N	N	Y	Y
21 **Smith**	Y	Y	Y	Y	Y	Y	N	Y
22 **DeLay**	Y	Y	Y	Y	Y	Y	N	Y
23 **Bonilla**	Y	Y	Y	Y	Y	Y	N	Y
24 Frost	Y	Y	Y	N	N	N	Y	Y
25 Bentsen	Y	Y	Y	N	N	N	Y	Y
26 **Armey**	?	?	Y	Y	Y	Y	N	Y
27 Ortiz	Y	Y	Y	N	N	N	Y	Y
28 Rodriguez	Y	Y	Y	N	N	N	Y	Y
29 Green	Y	Y	Y	N	N	N	Y	N
30 Johnson, E.B.	Y	Y	Y	N	N	N	Y	N
UTAH								
1 **Hansen**	N	Y	Y	Y	Y	Y	N	Y
2 **Cook**	N	Y	Y	Y	Y	Y	Y	Y
3 **Cannon**	N	N	Y	Y	Y	Y	N	Y
VERMONT								
AL *Sanders*	Y	Y	?	N	N	N	Y	?
VIRGINIA								
1 **Bateman**	Y	N	?	Y	Y	Y	N	Y
2 Pickett	Y	N	Y	N	N	N	Y	N
3 Scott	Y	N	Y	N	N	N	Y	Y
4 Sisisky	Y	Y	Y	N	N	N	Y	Y
5 Goode	Y	Y	Y	Y	Y	Y	N	Y
6 **Goodlatte**	Y	Y	Y	Y	Y	Y	N	Y
7 **Bliley**	Y	Y	Y	Y	Y	Y	N	Y
8 Moran	Y	Y	Y	N	N	N	Y	Y
9 Boucher	Y	Y	Y	N	N	N	Y	Y
10 **Wolf**	Y	Y	Y	Y	Y	Y	Y	Y
11 **Davis**	Y	Y	Y	Y	Y	Y	Y	Y
WASHINGTON								
1 Inslee	Y	Y	Y	N	N	N	Y	Y
2 **Metcalf**	Y	Y	Y	Y	Y	Y	N	Y
3 Baird	Y	Y	N	N	N	N	Y	N
4 **Hastings**	Y	Y	Y	Y	Y	Y	Y	Y
5 **Nethercutt**	Y	Y	Y	Y	Y	Y	N	Y
6 Dicks	Y	Y	Y	N	N	N	Y	Y
7 McDermott	Y	Y	N	N	N	N	Y	N
8 **Dunn**	Y	Y	?	Y	Y	Y	N	Y
9 Smith	Y	Y	Y	N	N	N	Y	Y
WEST VIRGINIA								
1 Mollohan	Y	Y	Y	?	?	Y	Y	Y
2 Wise	?	?	Y	N	N	N	Y	Y
3 Rahall	Y	Y	Y	N	N	N	Y	Y
WISCONSIN								
1 **Ryan**	Y	Y	Y	Y	Y	Y	Y	Y
2 Baldwin	Y	Y	Y	N	N	N	Y	Y
3 Kind	Y	Y	Y	N	N	N	Y	Y
4 Kleczka	Y	Y	Y	N	N	N	Y	Y
5 Barrett	Y	Y	Y	N	N	N	Y	Y
6 **Petri**	Y	Y	Y	Y	Y	Y	N	Y
7 Obey	Y	Y	Y	N	N	N	Y	Y
8 **Green**	Y	Y	Y	Y	Y	Y	Y	Y
9 **Sensenbrenner**	Y	Y	Y	Y	Y	Y	N	Y
WYOMING								
AL **Cubin**	Y	Y	Y	Y	Y	Y	N	Y

Southern states - Ala., Ark., Fla., Ga., Ky., La., Miss., N.C., Okla., S.C., Tenn., Texas, Va.

521. HR 2. Title I Reauthorization/Early Grade Vouchers. Armey, R-Texas, amendment to authorize $100 million in fiscal 2000 and each of the four following fiscal years for a program to offer certain students in grades 1 through 5 scholarships of $3,500 for tuition and fees at public or private schools if their governor has declared their school an "academic emergency." Students in grades K through 12 would be eligible for the scholarships if they were victims of a violent crime at school. Rejected 166-257: R 163-52; D 3-204 (ND 1-153, SD 2-51); I 0-1. Oct. 21, 1999.

522. HR 2. Title I Reauthorization/Schoolwide Program Eligibility. Payne, D-N.J., amendment to strike a provision that would permit Title I funds to be used for schoolwide programs if 40 percent of the school's student body comes from poor families. The amendment would retain the existing 50 percent threshold for schoolwide programs. Rejected 208-215: R 9-208; D 198-7 (ND 149-3, SD 49-4); I 1-0. Oct. 21, 1999.

523. HR 2. Title I Reauthorization/Total Funding Increase. Roemer, D-Ind., amendment to increase the authorization for Title I funding from $8.4 billion to $9.9 billion. Adopted 243-181: R 39-178; D 203-3 (ND 152-1, SD 51-2); I 1-0. Oct. 21, 1999.

524. HR 2. Title I Reauthorization/Portability Vouchers. Petri, R-Wis., amendment to permit 10 states to use Title I funding to provide "portability" vouchers to children to attend other schools, including public, private and parochial schools. Rejected 153-271: R 151-66; D 2-204 (ND 1-152, SD 1-52); I 0-1. Oct. 21, 1999.

525. HR 2. Title I Reauthorization/Science Standards and Assessments. Ehlers, R-Mich., amendment to add science as one of the subjects for which states would be required to develop standards and assessments. Adopted 360-62: R 158-58; D 201-4 (ND 148-4, SD 53-0); I 1-0. Oct. 21, 1999.

526. HR 2. Title I Reauthorization/Passage. Passage of the bill to authorize $9.9 billion for Title I school district grants. The measure would require states and Title I school districts to report annually to parents and the public on their academic performance and give parents the option of switching their children out of low-performing Title I schools. The measure would authorize $5 million in fiscal 2000 to reinstate the Women's Equity Act. Passed 358-67: R 157-60; D 200-7 (ND 149-5, SD 51-2); I 1-0. Oct. 21, 1999.

Key

- Y Voted for (yea).
- # Paired for.
- + Announced for.
- N Voted against (nay).
- X Paired against.
- – Announced against.
- P Voted "present."
- C Voted "present" to avoid possible conflict of interest.
- ? Did not vote or otherwise make a position known.

•

Democrats ***Republicans***
Independents

	521	522	523	524	525	526
ALABAMA						
1 ***Callahan***	Y	N	N	Y	Y	Y
2 ***Everett***	Y	N	N	Y	Y	Y
3 ***Riley***	Y	N	N	Y	Y	Y
4 ***Aderholt***	Y	N	N	Y	Y	Y
5 Cramer	N	Y	Y	N	Y	Y
6 ***Bachus***	Y	N	N	Y	Y	Y
7 Hilliard	N	Y	Y	N	Y	Y
ALASKA						
AL ***Young***	Y	N	N	Y	N	Y
ARIZONA						
1 ***Salmon***	Y	N	N	Y	Y	N
2 Pastor	N	Y	Y	N	Y	Y
3 ***Stump***	Y	N	N	Y	N	N
4 ***Shadegg***	Y	N	N	Y	N	N
5 ***Kolbe***	Y	N	N	Y	Y	Y
6 ***Hayworth***	Y	N	N	Y	Y	N
ARKANSAS						
1 Berry	N	Y	Y	N	Y	Y
2 Snyder	N	Y	Y	N	Y	Y
3 ***Hutchinson***	N	N	N	N	N	Y
4 ***Dickey***	Y	N	Y	Y	Y	Y
CALIFORNIA						
1 Thompson	N	N	Y	N	Y	Y
2 ***Herger***	Y	N	N	Y	N	N
3 ***Ose***	Y	N	N	N	Y	Y
4 ***Doolittle***	Y	N	N	Y	N	N
5 Matsui	N	Y	Y	N	Y	Y
6 Woolsey	N	Y	Y	N	Y	Y
7 Miller, George	N	Y	Y	N	Y	Y
8 Pelosi	N	Y	Y	N	Y	Y
9 Lee	N	Y	Y	N	Y	N
10 Tauscher	N	Y	Y	N	Y	Y
11 ***Pombo***	Y	N	N	N	N	N
12 Lantos	N	Y	Y	N	Y	Y
13 Stark	N	Y	Y	N	Y	Y
14 Eshoo	N	Y	Y	N	Y	Y
15 ***Campbell***	Y	N	N	Y	N	N
16 Lofgren	N	N	Y	N	Y	Y
17 Farr	N	Y	Y	N	Y	Y
18 Condit	N	Y	Y	N	Y	Y
19 ***Radanovich***	Y	N	N	Y	Y	N
20 Dooley	N	Y	Y	N	Y	Y
21 ***Thomas***	Y	N	N	Y	Y	Y
22 Capps	N	Y	Y	N	Y	Y
23 ***Gallegly***	Y	N	Y	N	Y	Y
24 Sherman	N	Y	Y	N	Y	Y
25 ***McKeon***	Y	N	N	Y	Y	Y
26 Berman	N	Y	Y	N	Y	Y
27 ***Rogan***	Y	N	N	Y	Y	Y
28 ***Dreier***	Y	N	N	Y	N	Y
29 Waxman	N	Y	Y	N	Y	Y
30 Becerra	N	Y	Y	N	Y	N
31 Martinez	N	Y	Y	N	Y	Y
32 Dixon	N	Y	Y	N	Y	Y
33 Roybal-Allard	N	Y	Y	N	Y	N
34 Napolitano	N	Y	Y	N	Y	Y
35 Waters	N	Y	Y	N	Y	N
36 ***Kuykendall***	N	N	Y	Y	Y	Y
37 Millender-McD.	N	Y	Y	N	Y	Y
38 ***Horn***	N	Y	Y	Y	Y	Y
39 ***Royce***	Y	N	N	Y	N	N
40 ***Lewis***	N	N	N	N	Y	Y
41 ***Miller***	Y	N	N	Y	Y	Y
42 Vacant						
43 ***Calvert***	Y	N	N	Y	Y	Y
44 ***Bono***	Y	N	N	Y	Y	Y
45 ***Rohrabacher***	Y	N	N	Y	N	N
46 Sanchez	N	Y	Y	N	Y	Y
47 ***Cox***	Y	N	N	Y	N	N
48 ***Packard***	Y	N	N	Y	Y	Y
49 ***Bilbray***	N	Y	Y	N	Y	Y
50 Filner	N	Y	Y	N	Y	Y
51 ***Cunningham***	Y	N	N	N	Y	Y
52 ***Hunter***	Y	N	N	Y	Y	N
COLORADO						
1 DeGette	N	Y	Y	N	Y	Y
2 Udall	N	?	?	?	?	Y
3 ***McInnis***	Y	?	?	?	?	N
4 ***Schaffer***	Y	N	N	Y	N	N
5 ***Hefley***	Y	N	N	Y	Y	N
6 ***Tancredo***	Y	N	N	Y	Y	N
CONNECTICUT						
1 Larson	N	+	Y	N	Y	Y
2 Gejdenson	N	Y	Y	N	Y	Y
3 DeLauro	N	Y	Y	N	Y	Y
4 ***Shays***	Y	N	Y	Y	Y	Y
5 Maloney	N	Y	Y	N	Y	Y
6 ***Johnson***	N	Y	Y	N	Y	Y
DELAWARE						
AL ***Castle***	N	N	N	N	N	Y
FLORIDA						
1 ***Scarborough***	?	?	?	?	?	?
2 Boyd	N	Y	Y	N	Y	Y
3 Brown	N	Y	Y	N	Y	Y
4 ***Fowler***	Y	N	N	Y	Y	Y
5 Thurman	N	Y	Y	N	Y	Y
6 ***Stearns***	Y	N	N	Y	Y	N
7 ***Mica***	Y	N	N	Y	Y	Y
8 ***McCollum***	Y	N	N	Y	Y	Y
9 ***Bilirakis***	N	N	N	Y	Y	Y
10 ***Young***	N	N	N	Y	Y	Y
11 Davis	N	Y	Y	N	Y	Y
12 ***Canady***	Y	N	N	Y	N	Y
13 ***Miller***	N	N	N	Y	N	N
14 ***Goss***	Y	N	N	Y	Y	Y
15 ***Weldon***	Y	N	N	Y	Y	Y
16 ***Foley***	Y	N	Y	N	Y	Y
17 Meek	N	Y	Y	N	Y	Y
18 ***Ros-Lehtinen***	Y	N	N	Y	Y	Y
19 Wexler	N	Y	Y	N	Y	Y
20 Deutsch	N	Y	Y	N	Y	Y
21 ***Diaz-Balart***	Y	N	N	Y	Y	Y
22 ***Shaw***	Y	N	N	Y	Y	Y
23 Hastings	N	Y	Y	N	Y	Y
GEORGIA						
1 ***Kingston***	Y	N	N	Y	Y	Y
2 Bishop	N	Y	Y	N	Y	Y
3 ***Collins***	Y	N	N	Y	N	Y
4 McKinney	N	Y	Y	N	Y	Y
5 Lewis	N	Y	Y	N	Y	Y
6 ***Isakson***	+	N	N	Y	N	Y
7 ***Barr***	Y	N	N	Y	N	N
8 ***Chambliss***	Y	N	N	Y	Y	Y
9 ***Deal***	Y	N	N	Y	Y	Y
10 ***Norwood***	Y	N	N	Y	Y	Y
11 ***Linder***	Y	N	N	Y	Y	Y
HAWAII						
1 Abercrombie	N	Y	Y	N	Y	Y
2 Mink	N	Y	Y	N	Y	Y
IDAHO						
1 ***Chenoweth***	N	N	N	Y	N	N
2 ***Simpson***	N	N	N	N	N	Y
ILLINOIS						
1 Rush	N	Y	Y	N	Y	Y
2 Jackson	N	Y	Y	N	Y	Y
3 Lipinski	Y	Y	N	Y	Y	Y
4 Gutierrez	N	Y	Y	N	Y	Y
5 Blagojevich	N	Y	Y	N	Y	Y
6 ***Hyde***	Y	N	N	Y	N	N
7 Davis	N	Y	Y	N	Y	Y
8 ***Crane***	Y	N	N	Y	N	N
9 Schakowsky	N	Y	Y	N	Y	Y
10 ***Porter***	N	N	N	N	Y	Y
11 ***Weller***	Y	N	Y	Y	Y	Y
12 Costello	N	Y	Y	N	Y	Y
13 ***Biggert***	N	N	N	N	Y	Y
14 ***Hastert***						

ND Northern Democrats SD Southern Democrats

	521	522	523	524	525	526
15 ***Ewing***	Y	N	N	N	N	N
16 ***Manzullo***	Y	N	N	Y	N	N
17 Evans	N	Y	Y	N	Y	Y
18 ***LaHood***	N	Y	Y	N	N	N
19 Phelps	N	Y	Y	N	Y	Y
20 ***Shimkus***	N	N	N	Y	Y	Y
INDIANA						
1 Visclosky	N	Y	Y	N	Y	Y
2 ***McIntosh***	Y	N	N	Y	Y	Y
3 Roemer	N	Y	Y	N	Y	Y
4 ***Souder***	Y	N	N	Y	N	N
5 ***Buyer***	Y	N	N	Y	Y	Y
6 ***Burton***	+	N	N	Y	Y	N
7 ***Pease***	N	N	Y	Y	Y	Y
8 ***Hostettler***	N	N	Y	N	Y	Y
9 Hill	N	Y	Y	N	Y	Y
10 Carson	N	Y	Y	N	Y	Y
IOWA						
1 ***Leach***	N	Y	Y	N	Y	Y
2 ***Nussle***	Y	N	N	N	Y	Y
3 Boswell	N	Y	Y	N	Y	Y
4 ***Ganske***	N	N	N	N	Y	Y
5 ***Latham***	Y	N	N	N	Y	Y
KANSAS						
1 ***Moran***	N	N	N	N	Y	N
2 ***Ryun***	Y	N	N	Y	Y	N
3 Moore	N	Y	Y	N	Y	Y
4 ***Tiahrt***	Y	N	N	Y	N	N
KENTUCKY						
1 ***Whitfield***	N	N	N	Y	N	Y
2 ***Lewis***	Y	N	N	Y	Y	Y
3 ***Northup***	Y	N	N	Y	Y	Y
4 Lucas	?	Y	Y	N	Y	Y
5 ***Rogers***	Y	N	N	Y	Y	Y
6 ***Fletcher***	Y	N	N	Y	Y	Y
LOUISIANA						
1 ***Vitter***	Y	?	?	Y	Y	Y
2 Jefferson	?	?	?	?	?	?
3 ***Tauzin***	Y	N	N	Y	Y	Y
4 ***McCrery***	Y	N	N	Y	Y	Y
5 ***Cooksey***	Y	N	N	N	Y	Y
6 ***Baker***	Y	N	N	Y	Y	N
7 John	N	Y	Y	N	Y	Y
MAINE						
1 Allen	N	Y	Y	N	Y	Y
2 Baldacci	N	Y	Y	N	Y	Y
MARYLAND						
1 ***Gilchrest***	Y	N	N	N	Y	Y
2 ***Ehrlich***	Y	N	N	Y	N	Y
3 Cardin	N	Y	Y	N	Y	Y
4 Wynn	N	Y	Y	N	Y	Y
5 Hoyer	N	Y	Y	N	?	Y
6 ***Bartlett***	Y	N	N	Y	Y	N
7 Cummings	N	Y	Y	N	Y	Y
8 ***Morella***	N	Y	Y	N	Y	Y
MASSACHUSETTS						
1 Olver	N	Y	Y	N	Y	Y
2 Neal	N	Y	Y	N	Y	Y
3 McGovern	N	Y	Y	N	Y	Y
4 Frank	N	Y	Y	N	N	Y
5 Meehan	N	Y	Y	N	Y	Y
6 Tierney	N	Y	Y	N	Y	Y
7 Markey	N	Y	Y	N	Y	Y
8 Capuano	N	Y	Y	N	Y	Y
9 Moakley	N	Y	Y	N	Y	Y
10 Delahunt	N	Y	Y	N	Y	Y
MICHIGAN						
1 Stupak	N	Y	Y	N	Y	Y
2 ***Hoekstra***	Y	N	N	Y	N	N
3 ***Ehlers***	Y	N	N	Y	Y	Y
4 ***Camp***	?	?	?	?	?	?
5 Barcia	N	Y	Y	N	Y	Y
6 ***Upton***	Y	N	Y	N	Y	Y
7 ***Smith***	Y	N	N	Y	Y	N
8 Stabenow	N	Y	Y	N	Y	Y
9 Kildee	N	Y	Y	N	Y	Y
10 Bonior	N	Y	Y	N	Y	Y
11 ***Knollenberg***	Y	N	N	Y	Y	Y
12 Levin	N	Y	Y	N	Y	Y
13 Rivers	N	Y	Y	N	Y	Y
14 Conyers	N	Y	Y	N	Y	Y
15 Kilpatrick	N	Y	Y	N	Y	Y
16 Dingell	N	Y	Y	N	Y	Y
MINNESOTA						
1 ***Gutknecht***	Y	N	N	Y	Y	N
2 Minge	N	Y	Y	N	Y	Y
3 ***Ramstad***	N	N	Y	N	Y	Y
4 Vento	N	Y	Y	N	Y	Y
5 Sabo	N	Y	Y	N	N	Y
6 Luther	N	Y	Y	N	Y	Y
7 Peterson	N	Y	Y	N	Y	Y
8 Oberstar	N	Y	Y	N	Y	Y
MISSISSIPPI						
1 ***Wicker***	Y	N	N	Y	Y	N
2 Thompson	N	Y	Y	N	Y	Y
3 ***Pickering***	Y	N	N	Y	Y	Y
4 Shows	N	Y	Y	N	Y	Y
5 Taylor	Y	N	Y	N	Y	Y
MISSOURI						
1 Clay	N	Y	Y	N	Y	Y
2 ***Talent***	Y	N	N	Y	N	Y
3 Gephardt	N	Y	Y	N	Y	Y
4 Skelton	N	Y	Y	N	Y	Y
5 McCarthy	–	+	+	–	+	+
6 Danner	N	Y	Y	N	Y	Y
7 ***Blunt***	N	N	N	N	N	N
8 ***Emerson***	N	N	Y	N	Y	Y
9 ***Hulshof***	N	N	Y	N	Y	Y
MONTANA						
AL ***Hill***	Y	N	N	Y	Y	Y
NEBRASKA						
1 ***Bereuter***	N	N	Y	Y	Y	Y
2 ***Terry***	Y	N	N	N	Y	Y
3 ***Barrett***	N	N	N	N	Y	Y
NEVADA						
1 Berkley	N	Y	Y	N	Y	Y
2 ***Gibbons***	Y	N	Y	Y	Y	Y
NEW HAMPSHIRE						
1 ***Sununu***	Y	N	N	Y	N	N
2 ***Bass***	Y	N	N	Y	Y	Y
NEW JERSEY						
1 Andrews	N	Y	Y	N	Y	Y
2 ***LoBiondo***	N	N	Y	N	Y	Y
3 ***Saxton***	N	N	N	N	Y	Y
4 ***Smith***	Y	N	Y	N	Y	Y
5 ***Roukema***	N	N	N	N	Y	Y
6 Pallone	N	Y	Y	N	Y	Y
7 ***Franks***	Y	N	Y	Y	Y	Y
8 Pascrell	N	Y	Y	N	Y	Y
9 Rothman	N	Y	Y	N	Y	Y
10 Payne	N	Y	Y	N	Y	N
11 ***Frelinghuysen***	Y	N	N	N	Y	Y
12 Holt	N	Y	Y	N	Y	Y
13 Menendez	N	Y	Y	N	Y	Y
NEW MEXICO						
1 ***Wilson***	Y	N	Y	N	Y	Y
2 ***Skeen***	Y	N	N	Y	Y	Y
3 Udall	N	Y	Y	N	Y	Y
NEW YORK						
1 Forbes	N	Y	Y	N	Y	Y
2 ***Lazio***	Y	N	N	N	Y	Y
3 ***King***	Y	N	Y	Y	N	Y
4 McCarthy	?	?	?	?	?	?
5 Ackerman	N	Y	Y	N	Y	Y
6 Meeks	N	Y	Y	N	N	Y
7 Crowley	N	Y	Y	N	Y	Y
8 Nadler	N	Y	Y	N	Y	Y
9 Weiner	N	Y	Y	N	Y	Y
10 Towns	N	Y	Y	N	Y	Y
11 Owens	N	Y	Y	N	Y	Y
12 Velázquez	N	Y	Y	N	Y	Y
13 ***Fossella***	Y	N	Y	Y	N	Y
14 Maloney	N	Y	Y	N	Y	Y
15 Rangel	N	Y	Y	N	Y	Y
16 Serrano	N	Y	Y	N	Y	Y
17 Engel	N	Y	Y	N	Y	Y
18 Lowey	N	Y	Y	N	Y	Y
19 ***Kelly***	N	N	Y	N	Y	Y
20 ***Gilman***	N	N	Y	N	Y	Y
21 McNulty	N	Y	Y	N	Y	Y
22 ***Sweeney***	Y	N	Y	N	Y	Y
23 ***Boehlert***	N	N	Y	N	Y	Y
24 ***McHugh***	N	N	Y	N	Y	Y
25 ***Walsh***	Y	N	Y	Y	Y	Y
26 Hinchey	N	Y	Y	N	Y	Y
27 ***Reynolds***	Y	N	N	Y	Y	Y
28 Slaughter	N	Y	Y	N	Y	Y
29 LaFalce	N	Y	Y	N	Y	Y
30 ***Quinn***	N	N	Y	N	Y	Y
31 ***Houghton***	N	Y	Y	N	Y	Y
NORTH CAROLINA						
1 Clayton	N	Y	Y	N	Y	Y
2 Etheridge	N	Y	Y	N	Y	Y
3 ***Jones***	?	N	N	Y	N	N
4 Price	N	Y	Y	N	Y	Y
5 ***Burr***	N	N	N	N	N	Y
6 ***Coble***	Y	N	N	Y	N	N
7 McIntyre	N	Y	Y	N	Y	Y
8 ***Hayes***	Y	N	N	Y	N	Y
9 ***Myrick***	Y	Y	N	Y	N	N
10 ***Ballenger***	Y	N	N	Y	Y	Y
11 ***Taylor***	Y	N	N	Y	Y	N
12 Watt	N	Y	Y	N	Y	Y
NORTH DAKOTA						
AL Pomeroy	N	Y	Y	N	Y	Y
OHIO						
1 ***Chabot***	Y	N	N	Y	Y	Y
2 ***Portman***	Y	N	N	N	Y	Y
3 Hall	N	Y	Y	N	Y	Y
4 ***Oxley***	Y	N	N	Y	Y	Y
5 ***Gillmor***	Y	N	N	N	Y	Y
6 Strickland	N	Y	Y	N	Y	Y
7 ***Hobson***	N	N	N	N	Y	Y
8 ***Boehner***	Y	N	N	Y	Y	Y
9 Kaptur	N	Y	Y	N	Y	Y
10 Kucinich	N	Y	Y	N	Y	Y
11 Jones	N	Y	Y	N	Y	Y
12 ***Kasich***	Y	N	N	Y	N	Y
13 Brown	N	Y	Y	N	Y	Y
14 Sawyer	N	Y	Y	N	Y	Y
15 ***Pryce***	Y	N	N	Y	Y	Y
16 ***Regula***	N	N	N	N	Y	Y
17 Traficant	N	Y	Y	N	Y	Y
18 ***Ney***	N	N	Y	N	Y	Y
19 ***LaTourette***	N	N	N	N	Y	Y
OKLAHOMA						
1 ***Largent***	Y	N	N	Y	N	N
2 ***Coburn***	Y	N	N	Y	N	N
3 ***Watkins***	Y	N	N	Y	Y	Y
4 ***Watts***	Y	N	N	Y	Y	Y
5 ***Istook***	Y	N	N	Y	Y	N
6 ***Lucas***	Y	N	N	Y	Y	Y
OREGON						
1 Wu	N	Y	Y	N	Y	Y
2 ***Walden***	N	N	N	N	N	Y
3 Blumenauer	N	Y	Y	N	Y	Y
4 DeFazio	N	Y	Y	N	Y	Y
5 Hooley	N	Y	Y	N	Y	Y
PENNSYLVANIA						
1 Brady	N	Y	Y	N	Y	Y
2 Fattah	N	Y	Y	N	Y	Y
3 Borski	N	Y	Y	N	Y	Y
4 Klink	N	Y	Y	N	Y	Y
5 ***Peterson***	Y	N	N	Y	Y	Y
6 Holden	N	Y	Y	N	Y	Y
7 ***Weldon***	Y	N	Y	N	Y	Y
8 ***Greenwood***	N	N	N	N	N	Y
9 ***Shuster***	Y	N	N	Y	N	Y
10 ***Sherwood***	Y	N	Y	Y	Y	Y
11 Kanjorski	N	Y	Y	N	Y	Y
12 Murtha	N	Y	Y	N	Y	Y
13 Hoeffel	N	Y	Y	N	Y	Y
14 Coyne	N	Y	Y	N	N	Y
15 ***Toomey***	Y	N	N	Y	N	N
16 ***Pitts***	Y	N	N	Y	Y	N
17 ***Gekas***	Y	N	N	N	N	Y
18 Doyle	N	Y	Y	N	Y	Y
19 ***Goodling***	N	N	N	N	N	Y
20 Mascara	N	Y	Y	N	Y	Y
21 ***English***	N	N	Y	Y	Y	Y
RHODE ISLAND						
1 Kennedy	N	Y	Y	N	Y	Y
2 Weygand	N	Y	Y	N	Y	Y
SOUTH CAROLINA						
1 ***Sanford***	Y	N	N	Y	N	N
2 ***Spence***	Y	N	N	Y	Y	Y
3 ***Graham***	N	N	N	Y	Y	Y
4 ***DeMint***	Y	N	N	Y	N	N
5 Spratt	N	Y	Y	N	Y	Y
6 Clyburn	N	Y	Y	N	Y	Y
SOUTH DAKOTA						
AL ***Thune***	N	N	N	N	N	Y
TENNESSEE						
1 ***Jenkins***	Y	N	N	?	Y	+
2 ***Duncan***	Y	N	N	Y	Y	N
3 ***Wamp***	Y	N	N	Y	Y	N
4 ***Hilleary***	Y	N	N	Y	Y	Y
5 Clement	N	Y	Y	N	Y	Y
6 Gordon	N	Y	Y	N	Y	Y
7 ***Bryant***	Y	N	N	Y	Y	Y
8 Tanner	N	N	Y	N	Y	Y
9 Ford	N	Y	Y	N	Y	Y
TEXAS						
1 Sandlin	N	Y	Y	N	Y	Y
2 Turner	N	Y	Y	N	Y	Y
3 ***Johnson, Sam***	+	N	N	Y	N	Y
4 Hall	Y	N	Y	Y	Y	Y
5 ***Sessions***	Y	N	N	Y	Y	N
6 ***Barton***	Y	N	N	Y	Y	N
7 ***Archer***	Y	N	N	Y	Y	N
8 ***Brady***	Y	N	N	Y	Y	Y
9 Lampson	N	Y	Y	N	Y	Y
10 Doggett	N	Y	Y	N	Y	Y
11 Edwards	N	Y	Y	N	Y	Y
12 ***Granger***	Y	N	N	N	Y	Y
13 ***Thornberry***	Y	N	N	N	Y	Y
14 ***Paul***	N	N	N	Y	N	N
15 Hinojosa	N	Y	Y	N	Y	Y
16 Reyes	N	Y	Y	N	Y	Y
17 Stenholm	N	Y	Y	N	Y	Y
18 Jackson-Lee	N	?	?	?	?	?
19 ***Combest***	Y	N	N	Y	Y	Y
20 Gonzalez	N	Y	Y	N	Y	N
21 ***Smith***	Y	N	N	Y	Y	Y
22 ***DeLay***	Y	N	N	Y	N	Y
23 ***Bonilla***	Y	Y	N	Y	Y	Y
24 Frost	N	Y	Y	N	Y	Y
25 Bentsen	N	Y	Y	N	Y	Y
26 ***Armey***	Y	N	N	Y	N	Y
27 Ortiz	N	Y	Y	N	Y	Y
28 Rodriguez	N	Y	Y	N	Y	N
29 Green	N	Y	Y	N	Y	Y
30 Johnson, E.B.	N	Y	Y	N	Y	Y
UTAH						
1 ***Hansen***	Y	N	N	Y	Y	Y
2 ***Cook***	Y	N	N	Y	Y	Y
3 ***Cannon***	Y	N	N	Y	Y	N
VERMONT						
AL *Sanders*	N	Y	Y	N	Y	Y
VIRGINIA						
1 ***Bateman***	Y	N	N	N	+	Y
2 Pickett	N	Y	N	N	Y	Y
3 Scott	N	Y	Y	N	Y	Y
4 Sisisky	N	Y	Y	N	Y	Y
5 Goode	N	N	N	N	Y	Y
6 ***Goodlatte***	N	N	N	N	Y	Y
7 ***Bliley***	Y	N	N	Y	Y	Y
8 Moran	N	Y	Y	N	Y	Y
9 Boucher	N	Y	Y	N	Y	Y
10 ***Wolf***	Y	N	N	N	Y	Y
11 ***Davis***	N	N	Y	N	Y	+
WASHINGTON						
1 Inslee	N	Y	Y	N	Y	Y
2 ***Metcalf***	Y	N	N	Y	Y	N
3 Baird	N	Y	Y	N	Y	Y
4 ***Hastings***	Y	N	N	Y	N	Y
5 ***Nethercutt***	Y	N	N	N	Y	Y
6 Dicks	N	Y	Y	N	Y	Y
7 McDermott	N	Y	Y	N	Y	Y
8 ***Dunn***	Y	N	N	Y	Y	Y
9 Smith	N	N	Y	N	Y	Y
WEST VIRGINIA						
1 Mollohan	N	Y	Y	N	Y	Y
2 Wise	N	Y	Y	N	Y	Y
3 Rahall	N	Y	Y	N	Y	Y
WISCONSIN						
1 ***Ryan***	Y	N	N	Y	–	Y
2 Baldwin	N	Y	Y	N	Y	Y
3 Kind	N	Y	Y	N	Y	Y
4 Kleczka	N	Y	Y	N	Y	Y
5 Barrett	N	Y	Y	N	Y	Y
6 ***Petri***	Y	N	N	Y	Y	Y
7 Obey	N	Y	Y	N	Y	Y
8 ***Green***	Y	N	N	N	N	Y
9 ***Sensenbrenner***	Y	N	N	Y	Y	N
WYOMING						
AL ***Cubin***	Y	N	N	Y	Y	N

Southern states - Ala., Ark., Fla., Ga., Ky., La., Miss., N.C., Okla., S.C., Tenn., Texas, Va.

House Votes 527, 528, 529, 530, 531, 532

527. HR 2466. Fiscal 2000 Interior Appropriations/Rule. Adoption of the rule (H Res 337) to provide for House floor consideration of the conference report on the bill to provide $14.5 billion for the Department of Interior, a portion of the Forest Service and the nation's primary land management agencies. Adopted 228-196: R 216-1; D 12-194 (ND 4-149, SD 8-45); I 0-1. Oct. 21, 1999.

528. HR 2466. Fiscal 2000 Interior Appropriations/Conference Report. Adoption of the conference report on the bill to provide $14.5 billion for the Department of Interior, a portion of the Forest Service and the nation's primary land management agencies. Adopted (thus sent to the Senate) 225-200: R 198-20; D 27-179 (ND 10-143, SD 17-36); I 0-1. Oct. 21, 1999.

529. HR 2300. 'Straight A's' Education Overhaul/Rule. Adoption of the rule (H Res 338) to provide for House floor consideration of the bill to give states flexibility to spend federal education funds in exchange for new accountability requirements and pledges to improve student performance. Adopted 214-201: R 211-3; D 3-197 (ND 1-147, SD 2-50); I 0-1. Oct. 21, 1999.

530. HR 2300. 'Straight A's' Education Overhaul/Equal Expenditure Per Pupil. Fattah, D-Pa., amendment to limit federal funding for school districts unless the state certifies annually to the Education Department that per-pupil expenditures are "substantially equal" across the state, or that student achievement levels in math and reading, graduation rates, and rates of college-bound students in the school districts with the lowest per-pupil expenditures are "substantially equal" to those of the school districts with the highest per-pupil expenditures. The Education Department, in consultation with the National Academy of Sciences, would be required to publish guidelines that define "substantially equal" and "per-pupil expenditures." Rejected 183-235: R 3-212; D 179-23 (ND 139-10, SD 40-13); I 1-0. Oct. 21, 1999.

531. HR 2300. 'Straight A's' Education Overhaul/Recommit. Clay, D-Mo., motion to recommit the bill to the Education and the Workforce Committee with instructions to report the bill back with an amendment to reduce school class sizes, ensure that teachers are highly qualified, and repair schools. Motion rejected 201-217: R 0-215; D 200-2 (ND 149-0, SD 51-2); I 1-0. Oct. 21, 1999.

532. HR 2300. 'Straight A's' Education Overhaul/Passage. Passage of the bill to establish a pilot program that would allow 10 states that develop student performance goals to participate in a flexible grant program under which they would receive a block grant of federal education funding to be used at their discretion. If a participating state could not meet its objectives within five years, it would have to revert back to the current allocation system. Passed 213-208: R 208-9; D 5-198 (ND 2-148, SD 3-50); I 0-1. Oct. 21, 1999. A "nay" was a vote in support of the president's position.

Key

- Y Voted for (yea).
- # Paired for.
- + Announced for.
- N Voted against (nay).
- X Paired against.
- – Announced against.
- P Voted "present."
- C Voted "present" to avoid possible conflict of interest.
- ? Did not vote or otherwise make a position known.

•

Democrats ***Republicans***
Independents

	527	528	529	530	531	532
ALABAMA						
1 ***Callahan***	Y	Y	Y	N	N	Y
2 ***Everett***	Y	Y	Y	N	N	Y
3 ***Riley***	Y	Y	Y	N	N	Y
4 ***Aderholt***	Y	Y	Y	N	N	Y
5 Cramer	N	N	N	Y	Y	N
6 ***Bachus***	Y	Y	Y	N	N	Y
7 Hilliard	N	N	N	Y	Y	N
ALASKA						
AL ***Young***	Y	Y	Y	N	N	Y
ARIZONA						
1 ***Salmon***	Y	Y	Y	N	N	Y
2 Pastor	N	N	N	Y	Y	N
3 ***Stump***	Y	Y	Y	N	N	Y
4 ***Shadegg***	Y	Y	N	N	N	Y
5 ***Kolbe***	Y	Y	Y	N	N	Y
6 ***Hayworth***	Y	Y	Y	N	N	Y
ARKANSAS						
1 Berry	N	N	N	N	Y	N
2 Snyder	N	N	N	N	Y	N
3 ***Hutchinson***	Y	Y	Y	N	N	Y
4 ***Dickey***	Y	Y	Y	N	N	Y
CALIFORNIA						
1 Thompson	N	N	N	Y	Y	N
2 ***Herger***	Y	Y	Y	N	N	Y
3 ***Ose***	Y	Y	Y	N	N	Y
4 ***Doolittle***	Y	Y	Y	N	N	Y
5 Matsui	N	N	N	Y	Y	N
6 Woolsey	N	N	N	Y	Y	N
7 Miller, George	N	N	N	Y	Y	N
8 Pelosi	N	N	N	Y	Y	N
9 Lee	N	N	N	Y	Y	N
10 Tauscher	N	N	N	Y	Y	N
11 ***Pombo***	Y	Y	Y	N	N	Y
12 Lantos	N	N	N	Y	Y	N
13 Stark	N	N	N	Y	Y	N
14 Eshoo	N	N	N	Y	Y	N
15 ***Campbell***	Y	N	Y	N	N	Y
16 Lofgren	N	N	N	Y	Y	N
17 Farr	N	N	N	Y	Y	N
18 Condit	N	N	N	Y	Y	Y
19 ***Radanovich***	Y	Y	Y	N	N	Y
20 Dooley	N	N	?	Y	Y	N
21 ***Thomas***	Y	Y	Y	N	N	Y
22 Capps	N	N	N	Y	Y	N
23 ***Gallegly***	Y	Y	Y	N	N	Y
24 Sherman	N	N	N	Y	Y	N
25 ***McKeon***	Y	Y	Y	N	N	Y
26 Berman	N	N	N	Y	Y	N
27 ***Rogan***	Y	Y	Y	N	N	Y
28 ***Dreier***	Y	Y	Y	N	N	Y
29 Waxman	N	N	N	Y	Y	N
30 Becerra	N	N	N	Y	Y	N
31 Martinez	N	N	N	Y	Y	N
32 Dixon	N	N	N	Y	Y	N
33 Roybal-Allard	N	N	N	Y	Y	N
34 Napolitano	N	N	N	Y	Y	N
35 Waters	N	N	N	Y	Y	N
36 ***Kuykendall***	Y	Y	Y	N	N	Y
37 Millender-McD.	N	N	N	Y	Y	N
38 ***Horn***	Y	Y	Y	N	N	Y
39 ***Royce***	Y	Y	?	N	N	Y
40 ***Lewis***	Y	Y	Y	N	N	Y
41 ***Miller***	Y	Y	Y	N	N	Y
42 Vacant						
43 ***Calvert***	Y	Y	Y	N	N	Y
44 ***Bono***	Y	Y	Y	N	N	Y
45 ***Rohrabacher***	Y	Y	Y	N	N	Y
46 Sanchez	N	N	N	Y	Y	N
47 ***Cox***	Y	Y	Y	N	N	Y
48 ***Packard***	Y	Y	Y	N	N	Y
49 ***Bilbray***	Y	N	Y	N	N	Y
50 Filner	N	N	N	Y	Y	N
51 ***Cunningham***	Y	Y	Y	N	N	Y
52 ***Hunter***	Y	Y	Y	N	N	Y
COLORADO						
1 DeGette	N	N	N	Y	Y	N
2 Udall	N	N	N	Y	Y	N
3 ***McInnis***	Y	Y	Y	N	N	Y
4 ***Schaffer***	Y	Y	Y	N	N	Y
5 ***Hefley***	Y	Y	Y	N	N	Y
6 ***Tancredo***	Y	Y	Y	N	N	Y
CONNECTICUT						
1 Larson	N	N	N	Y	Y	N
2 Gejdenson	N	N	N	Y	Y	N
3 DeLauro	N	N	N	Y	Y	N
4 ***Shays***	Y	N	Y	N	N	Y
5 Maloney	N	N	N	N	Y	N
6 ***Johnson***	Y	N	Y	N	N	N
DELAWARE						
AL ***Castle***	Y	N	Y	N	N	Y
FLORIDA						
1 ***Scarborough***	?	?	?	?	?	?
2 Boyd	N	N	N	N	Y	N
3 Brown	N	N	N	Y	Y	N
4 ***Fowler***	Y	Y	Y	N	N	Y
5 Thurman	N	N	N	N	Y	N
6 ***Stearns***	N	Y	Y	N	N	Y
7 ***Mica***	Y	Y	Y	N	N	Y
8 ***McCollum***	Y	Y	Y	N	N	Y
9 ***Bilirakis***	Y	Y	Y	N	N	Y
10 ***Young***	Y	?	?	?	?	?
11 Davis	N	N	N	N	Y	N
12 ***Canady***	Y	Y	Y	N	N	Y
13 ***Miller***	Y	Y	Y	N	N	Y
14 ***Goss***	Y	Y	Y	N	N	Y
15 ***Weldon***	Y	Y	Y	N	N	Y
16 ***Foley***	Y	Y	Y	Y	N	Y
17 Meek	N	N	N	Y	Y	N
18 ***Ros-Lehtinen***	Y	Y	Y	N	N	Y
19 Wexler	N	N	N	Y	Y	N
20 Deutsch	N	N	N	Y	Y	N
21 ***Diaz-Balart***	Y	Y	Y	N	N	Y
22 ***Shaw***	Y	Y	Y	N	N	Y
23 Hastings	N	N	N	Y	Y	N
GEORGIA						
1 ***Kingston***	Y	Y	Y	N	N	Y
2 Bishop	N	Y	N	Y	Y	N
3 ***Collins***	Y	Y	Y	N	N	Y
4 McKinney	N	N	N	Y	Y	N
5 Lewis	N	N	N	Y	Y	N
6 ***Isakson***	Y	Y	Y	N	N	Y
7 ***Barr***	Y	N	Y	N	N	Y
8 ***Chambliss***	Y	Y	Y	N	N	Y
9 ***Deal***	Y	Y	Y	N	N	Y
10 ***Norwood***	Y	Y	Y	N	N	Y
11 ***Linder***	?	Y	Y	N	N	Y
HAWAII						
1 Abercrombie	N	N	N	Y	Y	N
2 Mink	N	N	N	Y	Y	N
IDAHO						
1 ***Chenoweth***	Y	Y	Y	N	N	Y
2 ***Simpson***	Y	Y	Y	N	N	Y
ILLINOIS						
1 Rush	N	N	N	Y	Y	N
2 Jackson	N	N	N	Y	Y	N
3 Lipinski	N	N	?	?	?	?
4 Gutierrez	N	N	N	Y	Y	N
5 Blagojevich	N	N	N	Y	Y	N
6 ***Hyde***	Y	Y	Y	N	N	Y
7 Davis	N	N	N	Y	Y	N
8 ***Crane***	Y	Y	Y	N	N	Y
9 Schakowsky	N	N	N	Y	Y	N
10 ***Porter***	Y	Y	Y	N	N	Y
11 ***Weller***	Y	Y	Y	N	N	Y
12 Costello	N	N	N	Y	Y	N
13 ***Biggert***	Y	Y	Y	N	N	Y
14 ***Hastert***			Y		N	Y

ND Northern Democrats SD Southern Democrats

	527	528	529	530	531	532
15 ***Ewing***	Y	Y	Y	N	N	Y
16 ***Manzullo***	Y	Y	Y	N	N	Y
17 Evans	N	N	N	Y	Y	N
18 ***LaHood***	Y	Y	Y	N	N	Y
19 Phelps	N	N	N	Y	Y	N
20 ***Shimkus***	Y	Y	Y	N	N	Y
INDIANA						
1 Visclosky	N	N	N	Y	Y	N
2 ***McIntosh***	Y	Y	Y	N	N	Y
3 Roemer	N	N	N	Y	Y	N
4 ***Souder***	Y	Y	Y	N	N	Y
5 ***Buyer***	Y	Y	Y	N	N	Y
6 ***Burton***	Y	Y	Y	N	N	Y
7 ***Pease***	Y	Y	Y	N	N	Y
8 ***Hostettler***	Y	N	Y	N	N	Y
9 Hill	Y	Y	N	Y	Y	N
10 Carson	N	N	N	Y	Y	N
IOWA						
1 ***Leach***	Y	Y	Y	N	N	Y
2 ***Nussle***	Y	Y	Y	N	N	Y
3 Boswell	N	N	N	Y	Y	N
4 ***Ganske***	Y	Y	Y	N	N	Y
5 ***Latham***	Y	Y	Y	N	N	Y
KANSAS						
1 ***Moran***	Y	Y	Y	N	N	Y
2 ***Ryun***	Y	Y	Y	N	N	Y
3 Moore	N	N	N	N	Y	N
4 ***Tiahrt***	Y	Y	Y	N	N	Y
KENTUCKY						
1 ***Whitfield***	Y	Y	Y	N	N	Y
2 ***Lewis***	Y	Y	Y	N	N	Y
3 ***Northup***	Y	Y	Y	N	N	Y
4 Lucas	N	Y	N	Y	Y	N
5 ***Rogers***	Y	Y	Y	N	N	Y
6 ***Fletcher***	Y	Y	Y	N	N	Y
LOUISIANA						
1 ***Vitter***	Y	Y	Y	N	N	Y
2 Jefferson	?	?	?	?	?	?
3 ***Tauzin***	Y	Y	Y	N	N	Y
4 ***McCrery***	Y	Y	Y	N	N	Y
5 ***Cooksey***	Y	Y	Y	N	N	Y
6 ***Baker***	Y	Y	Y	N	N	Y
7 John	N	Y	N	Y	Y	N
MAINE						
1 Allen	N	N	N	Y	Y	N
2 Baldacci	N	N	N	Y	Y	N
MARYLAND						
1 ***Gilchrest***	Y	Y	Y	N	N	Y
2 ***Ehrlich***	Y	Y	Y	N	N	Y
3 Cardin	N	N	N	Y	Y	N
4 Wynn	N	N	N	Y	Y	N
5 Hoyer	N	N	N	Y	Y	N
6 ***Bartlett***	Y	Y	Y	N	N	Y
7 Cummings	N	N	?	Y	Y	N
8 ***Morella***	Y	Y	Y	Y	N	N
MASSACHUSETTS						
1 Olver	N	N	N	Y	Y	N
2 Neal	N	N	N	Y	Y	N
3 McGovern	N	N	N	Y	Y	N
4 Frank	N	N	N	Y	Y	N
5 Meehan	N	N	N	?	?	?
6 Tierney	N	N	N	Y	Y	N
7 Markey	N	N	N	?	Y	N
8 Capuano	N	N	N	Y	Y	N
9 Moakley	N	N	N	Y	Y	N
10 Delahunt	N	N	N	Y	Y	N
MICHIGAN						
1 Stupak	N	N	N	Y	Y	N
2 ***Hoekstra***	Y	Y	Y	N	N	Y
3 ***Ehlers***	Y	Y	Y	N	N	Y
4 ***Camp***	?	?	?	?	?	?
5 Barcia	N	N	N	Y	Y	N
6 ***Upton***	Y	Y	Y	N	N	Y
7 ***Smith***	Y	Y	Y	N	N	Y
8 Stabenow	N	N	N	Y	Y	N
9 Kildee	N	N	N	Y	Y	N
10 Bonior	N	N	N	Y	Y	N
11 ***Knollenberg***	Y	Y	Y	N	N	Y
12 Levin	N	N	N	Y	Y	N
13 Rivers	N	N	N	Y	Y	N
14 Conyers	N	N	N	Y	Y	N
15 Kilpatrick	N	N	N	Y	Y	N
16 Dingell	N	N	N	Y	Y	N
MINNESOTA						
1 ***Gutknecht***	Y	Y	Y	N	N	Y
2 Minge	N	N	N	Y	–	N
3 ***Ramstad***	Y	N	Y	N	N	Y
4 Vento	N	?	N	N	Y	N
5 Sabo	N	N	N	N	Y	N
6 Luther	N	N	N	Y	Y	N
7 Peterson	N	N	N	Y	Y	N
8 Oberstar	N	N	N	N	Y	N
MISSISSIPPI						
1 ***Wicker***	Y	Y	Y	N	N	Y
2 Thompson	N	N	N	Y	Y	N
3 ***Pickering***	Y	Y	Y	N	N	Y
4 Shows	Y	Y	N	Y	Y	Y
5 Taylor	Y	Y	N	Y	Y	N
MISSOURI						
1 Clay	N	N	N	Y	Y	N
2 ***Talent***	Y	Y	Y	N	N	Y
3 Gephardt	N	N	N	Y	Y	N
4 Skelton	N	N	N	N	Y	N
5 McCarthy	–	–	–	+	+	–
6 Danner	N	N	N	Y	Y	N
7 ***Blunt***	Y	Y	Y	N	N	Y
8 ***Emerson***	Y	Y	Y	N	N	Y
9 ***Hulshof***	Y	Y	Y	N	N	Y
MONTANA						
AL ***Hill***	Y	Y	Y	N	N	Y
NEBRASKA						
1 ***Bereuter***	Y	Y	Y	N	N	Y
2 ***Terry***	Y	Y	Y	N	N	Y
3 ***Barrett***	Y	Y	Y	N	N	Y
NEVADA						
1 Berkley	Y	Y	N	N	Y	N
2 ***Gibbons***	Y	Y	Y	N	N	Y
NEW HAMPSHIRE						
1 ***Sununu***	Y	Y	Y	N	N	Y
2 ***Bass***	Y	Y	Y	N	N	Y
NEW JERSEY						
1 Andrews	N	N	N	Y	Y	N
2 ***LoBiondo***	Y	Y	Y	N	N	Y
3 ***Saxton***	Y	Y	Y	N	N	Y
4 ***Smith***	Y	N	Y	N	N	Y
5 ***Roukema***	Y	Y	Y	N	N	Y
6 Pallone	N	N	N	Y	Y	N
7 ***Franks***	Y	N	Y	N	N	Y
8 Pascrell	N	N	N	Y	Y	N
9 Rothman	N	N	N	Y	Y	N
10 Payne	N	N	N	Y	Y	N
11 ***Frelinghuysen***	Y	Y	Y	N	N	Y
12 Holt	N	N	N	Y	Y	N
13 Menendez	N	N	N	Y	Y	N
NEW MEXICO						
1 ***Wilson***	Y	Y	Y	N	N	Y
2 ***Skeen***	Y	Y	Y	N	N	Y
3 Udall	N	N	N	Y	Y	N
NEW YORK						
1 Forbes	N	N	Y	N	Y	Y
2 ***Lazio***	Y	N	Y	N	N	Y
3 ***King***	Y	Y	Y	N	N	Y
4 McCarthy	?	?	?	?	?	?
5 Ackerman	N	N	N	Y	Y	N
6 Meeks	N	N	N	Y	Y	N
7 Crowley	N	N	N	Y	Y	N
8 Nadler	N	N	?	Y	Y	N
9 Weiner	N	N	N	Y	Y	N
10 Towns	?	N	N	Y	Y	N
11 Owens	N	N	N	Y	Y	N
12 Velázquez	N	N	N	Y	Y	N
13 ***Fossella***	Y	Y	Y	N	N	Y
14 Maloney	N	N	N	Y	Y	N
15 Rangel	N	N	N	Y	Y	N
16 Serrano	N	N	N	Y	Y	N
17 Engel	N	N	N	Y	Y	N
18 Lowey	N	N	N	Y	Y	N
19 ***Kelly***	Y	N	Y	N	N	Y
20 ***Gilman***	Y	N	Y	N	N	N
21 McNulty	N	N	N	Y	Y	N
22 ***Sweeney***	Y	Y	Y	N	N	N
23 ***Boehlert***	Y	Y	Y	N	N	N
24 ***McHugh***	Y	Y	Y	N	N	N
25 ***Walsh***	Y	Y	Y	N	N	Y
26 Hinchey	N	N	N	Y	Y	N
27 ***Reynolds***	Y	Y	Y	N	N	Y
28 Slaughter	N	N	N	Y	Y	N
29 LaFalce	N	N	N	Y	Y	N
30 ***Quinn***	Y	Y	Y	N	N	N
31 ***Houghton***	Y	Y	Y	N	N	Y
NORTH CAROLINA						
1 Clayton	N	N	N	Y	Y	N
2 Etheridge	N	N	N	Y	Y	N
3 ***Jones***	Y	N	Y	N	N	Y
4 Price	N	N	N	Y	Y	N
5 ***Burr***	Y	Y	Y	N	N	Y
6 ***Coble***	Y	Y	Y	N	N	Y
7 McIntyre	N	N	N	Y	Y	N
8 ***Hayes***	Y	Y	Y	N	N	Y
9 ***Myrick***	Y	Y	Y	N	N	Y
10 ***Ballenger***	Y	Y	Y	N	N	Y
11 ***Taylor***	Y	Y	Y	N	N	Y
12 Watt	N	N	N	Y	Y	N
NORTH DAKOTA						
AL Pomeroy	N	N	N	Y	Y	N
OHIO						
1 ***Chabot***	Y	N	Y	N	N	Y
2 ***Portman***	Y	Y	Y	N	N	Y
3 Hall	N	N	N	?	?	?
4 ***Oxley***	Y	Y	?	N	N	Y
5 ***Gillmor***	Y	Y	Y	N	N	Y
6 Strickland	N	Y	N	Y	Y	N
7 ***Hobson***	Y	Y	Y	N	N	Y
8 ***Boehner***	Y	Y	?	N	N	Y
9 Kaptur	N	Y	N	N	Y	N
10 Kucinich	N	N	N	Y	Y	N
11 Jones	N	N	N	Y	Y	N
12 ***Kasich***	Y	Y	Y	N	N	Y
13 Brown	N	N	N	Y	Y	N
14 Sawyer	N	N	N	Y	Y	N
15 ***Pryce***	Y	Y	Y	N	N	Y
16 ***Regula***	Y	Y	Y	N	N	Y
17 Traficant	Y	Y	N	Y	Y	N
18 ***Ney***	Y	Y	Y	Y	N	N
19 ***LaTourette***	Y	Y	Y	N	N	Y
OKLAHOMA						
1 ***Largent***	Y	Y	Y	N	N	Y
2 ***Coburn***	?	N	N	N	N	Y
3 ***Watkins***	Y	Y	Y	N	N	Y
4 ***Watts***	Y	Y	Y	N	N	Y
5 ***Istook***	Y	Y	Y	N	?	Y
6 ***Lucas***	Y	Y	Y	N	N	Y
OREGON						
1 Wu	N	N	N	Y	Y	N
2 ***Walden***	Y	Y	Y	N	N	Y
3 Blumenauer	N	N	N	Y	Y	N
4 DeFazio	N	N	N	Y	Y	N
5 Hooley	N	N	N	Y	Y	N
PENNSYLVANIA						
1 Brady	N	N	N	Y	Y	N
2 Fattah	N	N	?	Y	Y	N
3 Borski	N	N	N	Y	Y	N
4 Klink	N	N	N	Y	Y	N
5 ***Peterson***	Y	Y	Y	N	N	Y
6 Holden	N	N	N	Y	Y	N
7 ***Weldon***	Y	Y	?	?	?	?
8 ***Greenwood***	Y	Y	Y	N	N	Y
9 ***Shuster***	Y	Y	?	?	?	?
10 ***Sherwood***	Y	Y	Y	N	N	Y
11 Kanjorski	N	N	N	Y	Y	N
12 Murtha	N	Y	N	Y	Y	N
13 Hoeffel	N	N	N	Y	Y	N
14 Coyne	N	N	N	Y	Y	N
15 ***Toomey***	Y	N	Y	N	N	Y
16 ***Pitts***	Y	Y	Y	N	N	Y
17 ***Gekas***	Y	Y	Y	N	N	Y
18 Doyle	N	N	N	Y	Y	N
19 ***Goodling***	Y	Y	Y	N	N	Y
20 Mascara	N	Y	N	?	?	?
21 ***English***	Y	Y	Y	N	N	N
RHODE ISLAND						
1 Kennedy	N	N	?	Y	Y	N
2 Weygand	N	N	N	Y	Y	N
SOUTH CAROLINA						
1 ***Sanford***	Y	N	Y	N	N	Y
2 ***Spence***	Y	Y	Y	N	N	Y
3 ***Graham***	Y	Y	Y	N	N	Y
4 ***DeMint***	Y	Y	Y	N	N	Y
5 Spratt	N	N	N	N	Y	N
6 Clyburn	N	N	N	Y	Y	N
SOUTH DAKOTA						
AL ***Thune***	Y	Y	Y	N	N	Y
TENNESSEE						
1 ***Jenkins***	Y	Y	Y	N	N	Y
2 ***Duncan***	Y	Y	Y	N	N	Y
3 ***Wamp***	Y	Y	Y	N	N	Y
4 ***Hilleary***	Y	Y	Y	N	N	Y
5 Clement	N	N	N	Y	Y	N
6 Gordon	N	N	N	Y	Y	N
7 ***Bryant***	Y	Y	Y	N	N	Y
8 Tanner	N	Y	N	N	Y	N
9 Ford	N	N	N	Y	Y	N
TEXAS						
1 Sandlin	N	Y	N	Y	Y	N
2 Turner	Y	Y	N	N	Y	N
3 ***Johnson, Sam***	Y	Y	Y	N	N	Y
4 Hall	Y	Y	Y	Y	N	Y
5 ***Sessions***	Y	Y	Y	N	N	Y
6 ***Barton***	Y	Y	Y	N	N	Y
7 ***Archer***	Y	Y	Y	N	N	Y
8 ***Brady***	Y	Y	Y	–	N	Y
9 Lampson	N	Y	N	Y	Y	N
10 Doggett	N	N	N	Y	Y	N
11 Edwards	N	N	N	N	Y	N
12 ***Granger***	Y	Y	Y	N	N	Y
13 ***Thornberry***	Y	Y	Y	N	N	Y
14 ***Paul***	Y	N	Y	N	N	Y
15 Hinojosa	N	N	?	Y	Y	N
16 Reyes	N	N	N	Y	Y	N
17 Stenholm	Y	Y	N	Y	Y	N
18 Jackson-Lee	?	?	?	?	?	?
19 ***Combest***	Y	Y	Y	N	N	Y
20 Gonzalez	N	N	N	Y	Y	N
21 ***Smith***	Y	Y	Y	N	N	Y
22 ***DeLay***	Y	Y	Y	N	N	Y
23 ***Bonilla***	Y	Y	Y	N	N	Y
24 Frost	N	N	N	Y	Y	N
25 Bentsen	N	Y	N	Y	Y	N
26 ***Armey***	Y	Y	Y	N	N	Y
27 Ortiz	Y	Y	N	Y	Y	N
28 Rodriguez	N	N	N	Y	Y	N
29 Green	N	N	N	Y	Y	N
30 Johnson, E.B.	N	N	N	Y	Y	N
UTAH						
1 ***Hansen***	Y	Y	Y	N	N	Y
2 ***Cook***	Y	Y	Y	N	N	Y
3 ***Cannon***	Y	Y	Y	N	?	Y
VERMONT						
AL *Sanders*	N	N	N	Y	Y	N
VIRGINIA						
1 ***Bateman***	Y	Y	Y	N	N	Y
2 Pickett	N	Y	N	N	Y	N
3 Scott	N	N	N	Y	Y	N
4 Sisisky	N	Y	N	N	Y	N
5 Goode	Y	Y	Y	N	N	Y
6 ***Goodlatte***	Y	Y	Y	N	N	Y
7 ***Bliley***	Y	Y	Y	N	N	Y
8 Moran	N	N	N	N	Y	N
9 Boucher	Y	Y	N	Y	Y	N
10 ***Wolf***	Y	Y	Y	N	N	Y
11 ***Davis***	Y	Y	Y	N	N	Y
WASHINGTON						
1 Inslee	N	N	N	Y	Y	N
2 ***Metcalf***	Y	Y	Y	N	N	Y
3 Baird	N	N	N	N	Y	N
4 ***Hastings***	Y	Y	Y	N	N	Y
5 ***Nethercutt***	Y	Y	Y	N	N	Y
6 Dicks	N	N	N	Y	Y	N
7 McDermott	N	N	N	Y	Y	N
8 ***Dunn***	Y	Y	Y	N	N	Y
9 Smith	N	N	N	Y	Y	N
WEST VIRGINIA						
1 Mollohan	N	Y	N	Y	Y	N
2 Wise	Y	Y	N	Y	Y	N
3 Rahall	N	Y	N	Y	Y	N
WISCONSIN						
1 ***Ryan***	Y	N	Y	N	N	Y
2 Baldwin	N	N	N	Y	Y	N
3 Kind	N	N	N	Y	Y	N
4 Kleczka	N	N	N	Y	Y	N
5 Barrett	N	N	N	Y	Y	N
6 ***Petri***	Y	Y	Y	N	N	Y
7 Obey	N	N	N	Y	Y	N
8 ***Green***	Y	Y	Y	N	N	Y
9 ***Sensenbrenner***	Y	Y	Y	N	N	Y
WYOMING						
AL ***Cubin***	Y	Y	Y	N	N	Y

Southern states - Ala., Ark., Fla., Ga., Ky., La., Miss., N.C., Okla., S.C., Tenn., Texas, Va.

533. Procedural Motion/Journal. Approval of the House Journal of Thursday, Oct. 21, 1999. Approved 341-49: R 187-14; D 153-35 (ND 110-27, SD 43-8); I 1-0. Oct. 25, 1999.

534. HR 754. 'Made in America' Products/Passage. Bliley, R-Va., motion to suspend the rules and pass the bill to direct the Commerce Department to establish a toll-free phone number to confirm that a product is "Made in America." Motion agreed to 390-2: R 201-2; D 188-0 (ND 137-0, SD 51-0); I 1-0. Oct. 25, 1999. A two-thirds majority of those present and voting (262 in this case) is required for passage under suspension of the rules.

535. HR 2303. History of the House/Passage. Thomas, R-Calif., motion to suspend the rules and pass the bill to direct the librarian of Congress to prepare the complete written history of the House of Representatives. Motion agreed to 388-7: R 200-6; D 187-1 (ND 136-1, SD 51-0); I 1-0. Oct. 25, 1999. A two-thirds majority of those present and voting (264 in this case) is required for passage under suspension of the rules.

536. H Con Res 194. 4-H Club Contributions/Adoption. Deal, R-Ga., motion to suspend the rules and adopt the concurrent resolution to commend 4-H Clubs and their members for their contributions to voluntary community service. Motion agreed to 391-0: R 203-0; D 187-0 (ND 136-0, SD 51-0); I 1-0. Oct. 25, 1999. A two-thirds majority of those present and voting (261 in this case) is required for adoption under suspension of the rules.

537. H Con Res 190. Internet Tax Moratorium/Adoption. Crane, R-Ill., motion to suspend the rules and adopt the concurrent resolution urging the United States to seek a global consensus supporting a moratorium on tariffs and on special, multiple and discriminatory taxation of electronic commerce. Motion agreed to 423-1: R 218-0; D 204-1 (ND 151-1, SD 53-0); I 1-0. Oct. 26, 1999. A two-thirds majority of those present and voting (283 in this case) is required for adoption under suspension of the rules.

538. H Con Res 208. Federal Tax Increases/Adoption. Hayworth, R-Ariz., motion to suspend the rules and adopt the concurrent resolution to express the sense of Congress that there should be no increase in federal taxes to fund additional government spending. Motion agreed to 371-48: R 217-0; D 154-47 (ND 107-42, SD 47-5); I 0-1. Oct. 26, 1999. A two-thirds majority of those present and voting (280 in this case) is required for adoption under suspension of the rules.

Key

- Y Voted for (yea).
- # Paired for.
- \+ Announced for.
- N Voted against (nay).
- X Paired against.
- – Announced against.
- P Voted "present."
- C Voted "present" to avoid possible conflict of interest.
- ? Did not vote or otherwise make a position known.

•

Democrats ***Republicans***
Independents

	533	534	535	536	537	538
ALABAMA						
1 ***Callahan***	Y	Y	Y	Y	Y	Y
2 ***Everett***	Y	Y	Y	Y	Y	Y
3 ***Riley***	Y	Y	Y	Y	Y	Y
4 ***Aderholt***	N	Y	Y	Y	Y	Y
5 Cramer	?	?	?	?	Y	Y
6 ***Bachus***	Y	Y	Y	Y	Y	Y
7 Hilliard	N	Y	Y	Y	Y	Y
ALASKA						
AL ***Young***	Y	Y	Y	Y	Y	Y
ARIZONA						
1 ***Salmon***	Y	Y	Y	Y	Y	Y
2 Pastor	N	Y	Y	Y	Y	Y
3 ***Stump***	Y	Y	Y	Y	Y	Y
4 ***Shadegg***	Y	Y	Y	Y	Y	Y
5 ***Kolbe***	Y	Y	Y	Y	Y	Y
6 ***Hayworth***	Y	Y	Y	Y	Y	Y
ARKANSAS						
1 Berry	Y	Y	Y	Y	Y	Y
2 Snyder	N	Y	Y	Y	Y	Y
3 ***Hutchinson***	Y	Y	Y	Y	Y	Y
4 ***Dickey***	N	Y	Y	Y	Y	Y
CALIFORNIA						
1 Thompson	N	Y	Y	Y	Y	Y
2 ***Herger***	Y	Y	Y	Y	Y	Y
3 ***Ose***	Y	Y	N	Y	Y	Y
4 ***Doolittle***	Y	Y	Y	Y	Y	Y
5 Matsui	Y	Y	Y	Y	Y	Y
6 Woolsey	Y	Y	Y	Y	Y	Y
7 Miller, George	N	Y	Y	Y	Y	Y
8 Pelosi	?	?	?	?	Y	N
9 Lee	Y	Y	Y	Y	Y	N
10 Tauscher	Y	Y	Y	Y	Y	Y
11 ***Pombo***	Y	Y	Y	Y	Y	Y
12 Lantos	?	?	?	?	Y	Y
13 Stark	Y	Y	Y	Y	Y	N
14 Eshoo	Y	Y	Y	Y	Y	Y
15 ***Campbell***	Y	Y	N	Y	Y	Y
16 Lofgren	Y	Y	Y	Y	Y	N
17 Farr	Y	Y	Y	Y	Y	Y
18 Condit	Y	Y	Y	Y	Y	Y
19 ***Radanovich***	Y	Y	Y	Y	Y	Y
20 Dooley	?	?	?	?	Y	Y
21 ***Thomas***	Y	Y	Y	?	Y	Y
22 Capps	Y	Y	Y	Y	Y	Y
23 ***Gallegly***	Y	Y	Y	Y	Y	Y
24 Sherman	Y	Y	Y	Y	Y	Y
25 ***McKeon***	Y	Y	Y	Y	Y	Y
26 Berman	Y	Y	Y	Y	Y	N
27 ***Rogan***	Y	Y	Y	Y	Y	Y
28 ***Dreier***	Y	Y	Y	Y	Y	Y
29 Waxman	Y	Y	Y	Y	Y	N
30 Becerra	+	+	+	+	Y	Y
31 Martinez	Y	Y	Y	Y	Y	Y
32 Dixon	Y	Y	Y	Y	Y	N
33 Roybal-Allard	Y	Y	Y	Y	Y	Y
34 Napolitano	Y	Y	Y	Y	Y	Y
35 Waters	N	Y	Y	Y	Y	N
36 ***Kuykendall***	Y	Y	Y	Y	Y	Y
37 Millender-McD.	Y	Y	Y	Y	Y	Y
38 ***Horn***	Y	Y	Y	Y	Y	Y
39 ***Royce***	Y	Y	Y	Y	Y	Y

	533	534	535	536	537	538
40 ***Lewis***	Y	Y	Y	?	Y	Y
41 ***Miller***	Y	Y	Y	Y	Y	Y
42 Vacant						
43 ***Calvert***	Y	Y	Y	Y	Y	Y
44 ***Bono***	?	?	?	?	Y	Y
45 ***Rohrabacher***	Y	Y	Y	Y	Y	Y
46 Sanchez	Y	Y	Y	Y	Y	Y
47 ***Cox***	Y	Y	Y	Y	Y	Y
48 ***Packard***	Y	Y	Y	Y	Y	Y
49 ***Bilbray***	N	Y	Y	Y	Y	Y
50 Filner	N	Y	Y	Y	Y	Y
51 ***Cunningham***	Y	Y	Y	Y	Y	Y
52 ***Hunter***	Y	Y	Y	Y	Y	Y
COLORADO						
1 DeGette	Y	Y	Y	Y	Y	Y
2 Udall	Y	Y	Y	Y	Y	Y
3 ***McInnis***	Y	Y	Y	Y	Y	Y
4 ***Schaffer***	N	Y	Y	Y	Y	Y
5 ***Hefley***	N	Y	Y	Y	Y	Y
6 ***Tancredo***	P	Y	Y	Y	Y	Y
CONNECTICUT						
1 Larson	Y	Y	Y	Y	Y	Y
2 Gejdenson	Y	Y	Y	Y	Y	Y
3 DeLauro	Y	Y	Y	Y	Y	Y
4 ***Shays***	Y	Y	Y	Y	Y	Y
5 Maloney	Y	Y	Y	Y	Y	Y
6 ***Johnson***	Y	Y	Y	Y	Y	Y
DELAWARE						
AL ***Castle***	Y	Y	Y	Y	Y	Y
FLORIDA						
1 ***Scarborough***	?	?	?	?	?	?
2 Boyd	Y	Y	Y	Y	Y	Y
3 Brown	Y	Y	Y	Y	Y	Y
4 ***Fowler***	Y	Y	Y	Y	Y	Y
5 Thurman	Y	Y	Y	Y	Y	Y
6 ***Stearns***	Y	Y	Y	Y	Y	Y
7 ***Mica***	Y	Y	Y	Y	Y	Y
8 ***McCollum***	?	?	?	?	Y	Y
9 ***Bilirakis***	Y	Y	Y	Y	Y	Y
10 ***Young***	Y	Y	Y	Y	Y	Y
11 Davis	Y	Y	Y	Y	Y	Y
12 ***Canady***	Y	Y	Y	Y	Y	Y
13 ***Miller***	Y	Y	Y	Y	Y	Y
14 ***Goss***	Y	Y	Y	Y	Y	Y
15 ***Weldon***	Y	Y	Y	Y	Y	Y
16 ***Foley***	Y	Y	Y	Y	Y	Y
17 Meek	Y	Y	Y	Y	Y	N
18 ***Ros-Lehtinen***	Y	Y	Y	Y	Y	Y
19 Wexler	Y	Y	Y	Y	Y	Y
20 Deutsch	Y	Y	Y	Y	Y	Y
21 ***Diaz-Balart***	Y	Y	Y	Y	Y	Y
22 ***Shaw***	?	Y	Y	Y	Y	Y
23 Hastings	N	Y	Y	Y	Y	N
GEORGIA						
1 ***Kingston***	Y	Y	Y	Y	Y	Y
2 Bishop	Y	Y	Y	Y	Y	Y
3 ***Collins***	Y	Y	Y	Y	Y	Y
4 McKinney	Y	Y	Y	Y	Y	Y
5 Lewis	?	?	?	?	Y	Y
6 ***Isakson***	Y	Y	Y	Y	Y	Y
7 ***Barr***	Y	Y	Y	Y	Y	Y
8 ***Chambliss***	Y	Y	Y	Y	Y	Y
9 ***Deal***	Y	Y	Y	Y	Y	Y
10 ***Norwood***	Y	Y	Y	Y	Y	Y
11 ***Linder***	Y	Y	Y	Y	Y	Y
HAWAII						
1 Abercrombie	Y	Y	Y	Y	N	Y
2 Mink	Y	Y	Y	Y	Y	Y
IDAHO						
1 ***Chenoweth-Hage***	Y	Y	Y	Y	Y	Y
2 ***Simpson***	Y	Y	Y	Y	Y	Y
ILLINOIS						
1 Rush	?	?	?	?	?	?
2 Jackson	Y	Y	Y	Y	Y	N
3 Lipinski	?	?	?	?	Y	Y
4 Gutierrez	Y	Y	Y	Y	Y	Y
5 Blagojevich	Y	Y	Y	Y	Y	Y
6 ***Hyde***	Y	Y	Y	Y	Y	Y
7 Davis	Y	Y	Y	Y	Y	N
8 ***Crane***	N	Y	Y	Y	Y	Y
9 Schakowsky	Y	Y	Y	Y	Y	N
10 ***Porter***	Y	Y	Y	Y	Y	Y
11 ***Weller***	N	Y	Y	Y	Y	Y
12 Costello	N	Y	Y	Y	Y	Y
13 ***Biggert***	Y	Y	Y	Y	Y	Y
14 ***Hastert***						

ND Northern Democrats SD Southern Democrats

	533	534	535	536	537	538
15 ***Ewing***	Y	Y	Y	Y	Y	Y
16 ***Manzullo***	Y	Y	Y	Y	Y	Y
17 Evans	N	Y	Y	Y	Y	Y
18 ***LaHood***	Y	Y	Y	Y	Y	Y
19 Phelps	Y	Y	Y	Y	Y	Y
20 ***Shimkus***	Y	Y	Y	Y	Y	Y
INDIANA						
1 Visclosky	N	?	?	?	Y	Y
2 ***McIntosh***	?	?	?	?	Y	Y
3 Roemer	Y	Y	Y	Y	Y	Y
4 ***Souder***	Y	Y	Y	Y	Y	Y
5 ***Buyer***	Y	Y	Y	Y	Y	Y
6 ***Burton***	Y	Y	Y	Y	Y	Y
7 ***Pease***	Y	Y	Y	Y	Y	Y
8 ***Hostettler***	Y	Y	Y	Y	Y	Y
9 Hill	Y	Y	Y	Y	Y	Y
10 Carson	+	+	+	+	Y	Y
IOWA						
1 ***Leach***	Y	Y	Y	Y	Y	Y
2 ***Nussle***	?	?	?	?	Y	Y
3 Boswell	Y	Y	Y	Y	Y	Y
4 ***Ganske***	Y	Y	Y	Y	Y	?
5 ***Latham***	Y	Y	Y	Y	?	?
KANSAS						
1 ***Moran***	Y	Y	Y	Y	Y	Y
2 ***Ryun***	Y	Y	Y	Y	Y	Y
3 Moore	N	Y	Y	Y	Y	Y
4 ***Tiahrt***	Y	Y	Y	Y	Y	Y
KENTUCKY						
1 ***Whitfield***	Y	Y	Y	Y	Y	Y
2 ***Lewis***	Y	Y	Y	Y	Y	Y
3 ***Northup***	Y	Y	Y	Y	Y	Y
4 Lucas	Y	Y	Y	Y	Y	Y
5 ***Rogers***	?	?	?	?	Y	Y
6 ***Fletcher***	Y	Y	Y	Y	Y	Y
LOUISIANA						
1 ***Vitter***	Y	Y	Y	Y	Y	Y
2 Jefferson	?	?	?	?	Y	Y
3 ***Tauzin***	Y	Y	Y	Y	Y	Y
4 ***McCrery***	Y	Y	Y	Y	Y	Y
5 ***Cooksey***	Y	Y	Y	?	Y	Y
6 ***Baker***	Y	Y	Y	Y	Y	Y
7 John	Y	Y	Y	Y	Y	Y
MAINE						
1 Allen	Y	Y	Y	Y	Y	Y
2 Baldacci	?	Y	Y	Y	Y	Y
MARYLAND						
1 ***Gilchrest***	Y	Y	Y	Y	Y	Y
2 ***Ehrlich***	Y	Y	Y	Y	Y	Y
3 Cardin	Y	Y	Y	Y	Y	Y
4 Wynn	Y	Y	Y	Y	Y	N
5 Hoyer	Y	Y	Y	Y	Y	Y
6 ***Bartlett***	Y	Y	Y	Y	Y	Y
7 Cummings	Y	Y	Y	Y	Y	Y
8 ***Morella***	Y	Y	Y	Y	Y	Y
MASSACHUSETTS						
1 Olver	Y	Y	Y	Y	Y	N
2 Neal	?	?	?	?	Y	N
3 McGovern	Y	Y	Y	Y	Y	N
4 Frank	Y	Y	N	Y	Y	N
5 Meehan	Y	Y	Y	Y	Y	N
6 Tierney	Y	Y	Y	Y	Y	N
7 Markey	Y	Y	Y	Y	Y	N
8 Capuano	?	?	?	?	Y	P
9 Moakley	?	?	?	?	Y	N
10 Delahunt	Y	Y	Y	Y	Y	N
MICHIGAN						
1 Stupak	?	?	?	?	Y	Y
2 ***Hoekstra***	Y	Y	Y	Y	Y	Y
3 ***Ehlers***	Y	Y	Y	Y	Y	Y
4 ***Camp***	Y	Y	Y	Y	Y	Y
5 Barcia	Y	Y	Y	Y	Y	Y
6 ***Upton***	Y	Y	Y	Y	Y	Y
7 ***Smith***	Y	Y	N	Y	Y	Y
8 Stabenow	Y	Y	Y	Y	Y	Y
9 Kildee	Y	Y	Y	Y	Y	Y
10 Bonior	Y	Y	Y	Y	Y	Y
11 ***Knollenberg***	Y	Y	Y	Y	Y	Y
12 Levin	Y	Y	Y	Y	Y	Y
13 Rivers	Y	Y	Y	Y	Y	Y
14 Conyers	Y	Y	Y	Y	Y	Y
15 Kilpatrick	+	+	+	+	Y	Y
16 Dingell	Y	Y	Y	Y	Y	Y
MINNESOTA						
1 ***Gutknecht***	N	Y	Y	Y	Y	Y
2 Minge	Y	Y	Y	Y	Y	Y
3 ***Ramstad***	N	Y	Y	Y	Y	Y
4 Vento	Y	Y	Y	Y	Y	N
5 Sabo	N	Y	Y	Y	Y	N
6 Luther	Y	Y	Y	Y	Y	Y
7 Peterson	N	Y	Y	Y	Y	Y
8 Oberstar	N	Y	Y	Y	Y	N
MISSISSIPPI						
1 ***Wicker***	Y	Y	Y	Y	Y	Y
2 Thompson	N	Y	Y	Y	Y	Y
3 ***Pickering***	?	?	?	?	Y	Y
4 Shows	Y	Y	Y	Y	Y	Y
5 Taylor	N	Y	Y	Y	Y	Y
MISSOURI						
1 Clay	N	Y	Y	Y	Y	Y
2 ***Talent***	Y	Y	Y	Y	Y	Y
3 Gephardt	Y	Y	Y	Y	Y	Y
4 Skelton	Y	Y	Y	Y	Y	Y
5 McCarthy	Y	Y	Y	Y	Y	Y
6 Danner	Y	Y	Y	Y	Y	Y
7 ***Blunt***	Y	Y	Y	Y	Y	Y
8 ***Emerson***	?	Y	Y	Y	Y	Y
9 ***Hulshof***	Y	Y	Y	Y	Y	Y
MONTANA						
AL ***Hill***	N	Y	Y	Y	Y	Y
NEBRASKA						
1 ***Bereuter***	Y	Y	Y	Y	Y	Y
2 ***Terry***	Y	Y	Y	Y	Y	Y
3 ***Barrett***	Y	Y	Y	Y	Y	Y
NEVADA						
1 Berkley	Y	Y	Y	Y	Y	Y
2 ***Gibbons***	N	Y	Y	Y	Y	Y
NEW HAMPSHIRE						
1 ***Sununu***	Y	Y	Y	Y	Y	Y
2 ***Bass***	Y	Y	Y	Y	Y	Y
NEW JERSEY						
1 Andrews	Y	Y	Y	Y	Y	Y
2 ***LoBiondo***	N	Y	Y	Y	Y	Y
3 ***Saxton***	Y	Y	Y	Y	Y	Y
4 ***Smith***	Y	Y	Y	Y	Y	Y
5 ***Roukema***	Y	?	Y	Y	Y	Y
6 Pallone	N	Y	Y	Y	Y	Y
7 ***Franks***	Y	Y	Y	Y	Y	Y
8 Pascrell	Y	Y	Y	Y	Y	Y
9 Rothman	Y	Y	Y	Y	Y	Y
10 Payne	Y	Y	Y	Y	Y	N
11 ***Frelinghuysen***	Y	Y	Y	Y	Y	Y
12 Holt	Y	Y	Y	Y	Y	Y
13 Menendez	Y	Y	Y	Y	?	?
NEW MEXICO						
1 ***Wilson***	Y	Y	Y	Y	Y	Y
2 ***Skeen***	Y	Y	Y	Y	Y	Y
3 Udall	N	Y	Y	Y	Y	Y
NEW YORK						
1 Forbes	Y	Y	Y	Y	Y	Y
2 ***Lazio***	Y	Y	Y	Y	Y	Y
3 ***King***	Y	Y	Y	Y	Y	Y
4 McCarthy	?	?	?	?	Y	Y
5 Ackerman	?	?	?	?	Y	Y
6 Meeks	Y	Y	Y	Y	Y	Y
7 Crowley	N	Y	Y	Y	Y	Y
8 Nadler	Y	Y	Y	Y	Y	N
9 Weiner	Y	Y	Y	Y	Y	N
10 Towns	?	?	?	?	Y	Y
11 Owens	Y	Y	Y	Y	Y	P
12 Velázquez	Y	Y	Y	Y	Y	Y
13 ***Fossella***	Y	Y	Y	Y	Y	Y
14 Maloney	Y	Y	Y	Y	Y	Y
15 Rangel	Y	Y	Y	Y	Y	Y
16 Serrano	Y	Y	Y	Y	Y	N
17 Engel	Y	Y	Y	Y	Y	Y
18 Lowey	?	?	?	?	Y	Y
19 ***Kelly***	Y	Y	Y	Y	Y	Y
20 ***Gilman***	Y	Y	Y	Y	Y	Y
21 McNulty	N	Y	Y	Y	?	?
22 ***Sweeney***	Y	Y	Y	Y	Y	Y
23 ***Boehlert***	Y	Y	Y	Y	Y	Y
24 ***McHugh***	Y	Y	Y	Y	Y	Y
25 ***Walsh***	Y	Y	Y	Y	Y	Y
26 Hinchey	Y	Y	Y	Y	Y	N
27 ***Reynolds***	Y	Y	Y	Y	Y	Y
28 Slaughter	N	Y	Y	Y	Y	Y
29 LaFalce	Y	Y	Y	Y	Y	Y
30 ***Quinn***	Y	Y	Y	Y	Y	Y
31 ***Houghton***	Y	Y	Y	Y	Y	Y
NORTH CAROLINA						
1 Clayton	Y	Y	Y	Y	Y	Y
2 Etheridge	Y	Y	Y	Y	Y	Y
3 ***Jones***	Y	Y	Y	Y	Y	Y
4 Price	Y	Y	Y	Y	Y	Y
5 ***Burr***	Y	Y	Y	Y	Y	Y
6 ***Coble***	Y	Y	Y	Y	Y	Y
7 McIntyre	Y	Y	Y	Y	Y	Y
8 ***Hayes***	Y	+	Y	Y	Y	Y
9 ***Myrick***	?	?	?	?	Y	Y
10 ***Ballenger***	+	+	+	+	Y	Y
11 ***Taylor***	?	?	?	?	Y	Y
12 Watt	Y	Y	Y	Y	Y	N
NORTH DAKOTA						
AL Pomeroy	Y	Y	Y	Y	Y	Y
OHIO						
1 ***Chabot***	Y	Y	Y	Y	Y	Y
2 ***Portman***	Y	Y	Y	Y	Y	Y
3 Hall	Y	Y	Y	Y	Y	Y
4 ***Oxley***	Y	Y	Y	Y	Y	Y
5 ***Gillmor***	Y	Y	Y	Y	Y	Y
6 Strickland	N	Y	Y	Y	Y	Y
7 ***Hobson***	Y	Y	Y	Y	Y	Y
8 ***Boehner***	?	Y	Y	Y	Y	Y
9 Kaptur	Y	Y	Y	Y	Y	Y
10 Kucinich	N	Y	Y	Y	Y	Y
11 Jones	Y	Y	Y	?	Y	Y
12 ***Kasich***	?	Y	Y	Y	Y	Y
13 Brown	Y	Y	Y	Y	Y	Y
14 Sawyer	Y	Y	Y	Y	Y	Y
15 ***Pryce***	?	?	?	?	Y	Y
16 ***Regula***	Y	Y	Y	Y	Y	Y
17 Traficant	Y	Y	Y	Y	Y	Y
18 ***Ney***	Y	Y	Y	Y	Y	Y
19 ***LaTourette***	Y	Y	Y	Y	Y	Y
OKLAHOMA						
1 ***Largent***	?	?	?	?	Y	Y
2 ***Coburn***	Y	Y	Y	Y	Y	Y
3 ***Watkins***	Y	Y	Y	Y	Y	Y
4 ***Watts***	Y	Y	Y	Y	Y	Y
5 ***Istook***	Y	Y	Y	Y	Y	Y
6 ***Lucas***	Y	Y	Y	Y	Y	Y
OREGON						
1 Wu	N	Y	Y	Y	Y	Y
2 ***Walden***	Y	Y	Y	Y	Y	Y
3 Blumenauer	Y	Y	Y	Y	Y	Y
4 DeFazio	N	Y	Y	Y	Y	N
5 Hooley	N	Y	Y	Y	Y	N
PENNSYLVANIA						
1 Brady	?	?	?	?	Y	N
2 Fattah	Y	Y	Y	Y	Y	N
3 Borski	N	Y	Y	Y	Y	N
4 Klink	N	Y	Y	Y	Y	N
5 ***Peterson***	Y	Y	Y	Y	Y	Y
6 Holden	Y	Y	Y	Y	Y	Y
7 ***Weldon***	Y	Y	Y	Y	Y	Y
8 ***Greenwood***	Y	Y	Y	Y	Y	Y
9 ***Shuster***	Y	Y	Y	Y	Y	Y
10 ***Sherwood***	Y	Y	Y	Y	Y	Y
11 Kanjorski	Y	Y	Y	Y	Y	N
12 Murtha	Y	Y	Y	Y	Y	N
13 Hoeffel	Y	Y	Y	Y	Y	Y
14 Coyne	Y	Y	Y	Y	Y	N
15 ***Toomey***	Y	Y	Y	Y	Y	Y
16 ***Pitts***	Y	Y	Y	Y	Y	Y
17 ***Gekas***	Y	Y	Y	Y	Y	Y
18 Doyle	Y	Y	Y	Y	Y	Y
19 ***Goodling***	Y	Y	Y	Y	Y	Y
20 Mascara	?	?	?	?	?	?
21 ***English***	N	Y	N	Y	Y	Y
RHODE ISLAND						
1 Kennedy	Y	Y	Y	Y	Y	Y
2 Weygand	Y	Y	Y	Y	Y	Y
SOUTH CAROLINA						
1 ***Sanford***	Y	N	N	Y	Y	Y
2 ***Spence***	Y	Y	Y	Y	Y	Y
3 ***Graham***	Y	Y	Y	Y	Y	Y
4 ***DeMint***	Y	Y	Y	Y	Y	Y
5 Spratt	Y	Y	Y	Y	Y	Y
6 Clyburn	N	Y	Y	Y	Y	Y
SOUTH DAKOTA						
AL ***Thune***	Y	Y	Y	Y	Y	Y
TENNESSEE						
1 ***Jenkins***	Y	Y	Y	Y	Y	Y
2 ***Duncan***	Y	Y	Y	Y	Y	Y
3 ***Wamp***	Y	Y	Y	Y	Y	Y
4 ***Hilleary***	N	Y	Y	Y	Y	Y
5 Clement	Y	Y	Y	Y	Y	Y
6 Gordon	Y	Y	Y	Y	Y	Y
7 ***Bryant***	Y	Y	Y	Y	Y	Y
8 Tanner	Y	Y	Y	Y	Y	Y
9 Ford	Y	Y	Y	Y	Y	Y
TEXAS						
1 Sandlin	Y	Y	Y	Y	Y	Y
2 Turner	Y	Y	Y	Y	Y	Y
3 ***Johnson, Sam***	Y	?	Y	Y	Y	Y
4 Hall	Y	Y	Y	Y	Y	Y
5 ***Sessions***	Y	Y	Y	Y	Y	Y
6 ***Barton***	Y	Y	Y	Y	Y	Y
7 ***Archer***	Y	Y	Y	Y	Y	Y
8 ***Brady***	Y	Y	Y	Y	Y	Y
9 Lampson	Y	Y	Y	Y	Y	Y
10 Doggett	Y	Y	Y	Y	Y	Y
11 Edwards	Y	Y	Y	Y	Y	Y
12 ***Granger***	?	?	?	?	?	?
13 ***Thornberry***	Y	Y	Y	Y	Y	Y
14 ***Paul***	Y	N	N	Y	Y	Y
15 Hinojosa	?	?	?	?	?	?
16 Reyes	Y	Y	Y	Y	Y	Y
17 Stenholm	Y	Y	Y	Y	Y	Y
18 Jackson-Lee	Y	Y	Y	Y	?	?
19 ***Combest***	Y	Y	Y	Y	Y	Y
20 Gonzalez	Y	Y	Y	Y	Y	Y
21 ***Smith***	Y	Y	Y	Y	Y	Y
22 ***DeLay***	Y	Y	Y	Y	Y	Y
23 ***Bonilla***	?	?	?	?	Y	Y
24 Frost	Y	Y	Y	Y	Y	Y
25 Bentsen	Y	Y	Y	Y	Y	Y
26 ***Armey***	Y	Y	Y	Y	Y	Y
27 Ortiz	Y	Y	Y	Y	Y	Y
28 Rodriguez	Y	Y	Y	Y	Y	Y
29 Green	Y	Y	Y	Y	Y	Y
30 Johnson, E.B.	N	Y	Y	Y	Y	P
UTAH						
1 ***Hansen***	Y	Y	Y	Y	Y	Y
2 ***Cook***	?	?	?	?	Y	Y
3 ***Cannon***	Y	Y	Y	Y	Y	Y
VERMONT						
AL *Sanders*	Y	Y	Y	Y	Y	N
VIRGINIA						
1 ***Bateman***	Y	Y	Y	Y	Y	Y
2 Pickett	N	Y	Y	Y	Y	Y
3 Scott	Y	Y	Y	Y	Y	N
4 Sisisky	Y	Y	Y	Y	Y	Y
5 Goode	Y	Y	Y	Y	Y	Y
6 ***Goodlatte***	Y	Y	Y	Y	Y	Y
7 ***Bliley***	Y	Y	Y	Y	Y	Y
8 Moran	Y	Y	Y	Y	Y	N
9 Boucher	Y	Y	Y	Y	Y	Y
10 ***Wolf***	Y	Y	Y	Y	Y	Y
11 ***Davis***	Y	Y	Y	Y	Y	Y
WASHINGTON						
1 Inslee	Y	Y	Y	Y	Y	Y
2 ***Metcalf***	Y	Y	Y	Y	Y	Y
3 Baird	N	Y	Y	Y	Y	Y
4 ***Hastings***	Y	Y	Y	Y	Y	Y
5 ***Nethercutt***	Y	Y	Y	Y	Y	Y
6 Dicks	Y	Y	Y	Y	Y	N
7 McDermott	N	Y	Y	Y	Y	N
8 ***Dunn***	Y	Y	Y	Y	Y	Y
9 Smith	Y	Y	Y	Y	Y	Y
WEST VIRGINIA						
1 Mollohan	Y	Y	Y	Y	Y	N
2 Wise	Y	Y	Y	Y	Y	Y
3 Rahall	Y	Y	Y	Y	Y	N
WISCONSIN						
1 ***Ryan***	Y	Y	Y	Y	Y	Y
2 Baldwin	Y	Y	Y	Y	Y	Y
3 Kind	Y	Y	Y	Y	Y	Y
4 Kleczka	Y	Y	Y	Y	Y	Y
5 Barrett	Y	Y	Y	Y	Y	Y
6 ***Petri***	Y	Y	Y	Y	Y	Y
7 Obey	Y	Y	Y	Y	Y	?
8 ***Green***	Y	Y	Y	Y	Y	Y
9 ***Sensenbrenner***	Y	Y	Y	Y	Y	Y
WYOMING						
AL ***Cubin***	Y	Y	Y	Y	Y	Y

Southern states - Ala., Ark., Fla., Ga., Ky., La., Miss., N.C., Okla., S.C., Tenn., Texas, Va.

539. H Con Res 102. 50th Anniversary of the Geneva Convention/Adoption. Gilman, R-N.Y., motion to suspend the rules and adopt the concurrent resolution to celebrate the 50th anniversary of the Geneva Convention of 1949 and recognize the humanitarian safeguards the treaties provide in times of armed conflict. Motion agreed to 423-0: R 218-0; D 204-0 (ND 151-0, SD 53-0); I 1-0. Oct. 26, 1999. A two-thirds majority of those present and voting (282 in this case) is required for adoption under suspension of the rules.

540. H Con Res 188. Commending Greece and Turkey/Adoption. Gilman, R-N.Y., motion to suspend the rules and adopt the concurrent resolution to commend Greece and Turkey for their mutual and swift response to the recent earthquakes in both countries. Motion agreed to 424-0: R 218-0; D 205-0 (ND 152-0, SD 53-0); I 1-0. Oct. 26, 1999. A two-thirds majority of those present and voting (283 in this case) is required for adoption under suspension of the rules.

541. HR 1175. Missing Israeli Soldiers/Concur with Senate Amendments. Campbell, R-Calif., motion to suspend the rules and concur with Senate amendments to the bill to direct the State Department to investigate the case of three Israeli soldiers, including Zachary Baumel, an American citizen serving in the Israeli army, who have been missing in action since June 1982. The bill would make the cooperation of the governments of Syria and Lebanon, and the Palestinian Authority a factor in deciding on U.S. aid. Motion agreed to (thus cleared for the president) 421-0: R 216-0; D 204-0 (ND 152-0, SD 52-0); I 1-0. Oct. 26, 1999. A two-thirds majority of those present and voting (281 in this case) is required for passage under suspension of the rules.

542. HR 2260. Physician-Assisted Suicide/Preserve State Laws. Scott, D-Va., amendment to strike a section of the measure that would allow doctors to use controlled substances aggressively to alleviate pain, while barring them from using such drugs for the purpose of assisted suicide. Rejected 160-268: R 15-205; D 144-63 (ND 112-41, SD 32-22); I 1-0. Oct. 27, 1999.

543. HR 2260. Physician-Assisted Suicide/Pain Management. Johnson, R-Conn., substitute amendment to authorize $18 million over three years for the Department of Health and Human Services to set up a Web site to provide information on treatment for pain, and to provide funds to help carry out education projects to train medical caregivers on how to relieve pain and manage symptoms for the terminally ill. Rejected 188-239: R 28-191; D 159-48 (ND 119-34, SD 40-14); I 1-0. Oct. 27, 1999.

544. HR 2260. Physician-Assisted Suicide/Passage. Passage of the bill to allow doctors to use controlled substances aggressively to alleviate pain, while barring them from using such drugs for the purpose of assisted suicide. The measure would supersede state law, effectively overturning an Oregon law that allows lethal prescriptions to be issued to the terminally ill, and preventing such laws from going into effect in other states. Passed 271-156: R 200-20; D 71-135 (ND 48-104, SD 23-31); I 0-1. Oct. 27, 1999.

Key

Y Voted for (yea).
\# Paired for.
\+ Announced for.
N Voted against (nay).
X Paired against.
– Announced against.
P Voted "present."
C Voted "present" to avoid possible conflict of interest.
? Did not vote or otherwise make a position known.

•

Democrats ***Republicans***
Independents

	539	540	541	542	543	544
ALABAMA						
1 ***Callahan***	Y	Y	Y	N	N	Y
2 ***Everett***	Y	Y	Y	N	N	Y
3 ***Riley***	Y	Y	Y	N	N	Y
4 ***Aderholt***	Y	Y	Y	N	N	Y
5 Cramer	Y	Y	Y	N	Y	Y
6 ***Bachus***	Y	Y	Y	N	N	Y
7 Hilliard	Y	Y	Y	Y	Y	N
ALASKA						
AL ***Young***	Y	Y	Y	N	N	Y
ARIZONA						
1 ***Salmon***	Y	Y	Y	N	N	Y
2 Pastor	Y	Y	Y	Y	Y	N
3 ***Stump***	Y	Y	Y	N	N	N
4 ***Shadegg***	Y	Y	Y	N	N	Y
5 ***Kolbe***	Y	Y	Y	Y	Y	N
6 ***Hayworth***	Y	Y	Y	N	N	Y
ARKANSAS						
1 Berry	Y	Y	Y	N	N	Y
2 Snyder	Y	Y	Y	Y	Y	N
3 ***Hutchinson***	Y	Y	Y	N	N	Y
4 ***Dickey***	Y	Y	Y	N	N	Y
CALIFORNIA						
1 Thompson	Y	Y	Y	Y	Y	N
2 ***Herger***	Y	Y	Y	N	N	Y
3 ***Ose***	Y	Y	Y	N	N	Y
4 ***Doolittle***	Y	Y	Y	N	N	Y
5 Matsui	Y	Y	Y	Y	Y	N
6 Woolsey	Y	Y	Y	Y	Y	N
7 Miller, George	Y	Y	Y	Y	Y	N
8 Pelosi	Y	Y	Y	Y	Y	N
9 Lee	Y	Y	Y	Y	Y	N
10 Tauscher	Y	Y	Y	Y	Y	N
11 ***Pombo***	Y	Y	Y	N	N	Y
12 Lantos	Y	Y	Y	Y	Y	N
13 Stark	Y	Y	Y	Y	Y	N
14 Eshoo	Y	Y	Y	Y	Y	N
15 ***Campbell***	Y	Y	Y	Y	Y	N
16 Lofgren	Y	Y	Y	Y	Y	N
17 Farr	Y	Y	Y	Y	Y	N
18 Condit	Y	Y	Y	N	Y	N
19 ***Radanovich***	Y	Y	Y	N	N	Y
20 Dooley	Y	Y	Y	Y	Y	N
21 ***Thomas***	Y	Y	Y	N	Y	Y
22 Capps	Y	Y	Y	Y	Y	N
23 ***Gallegly***	Y	Y	Y	N	N	Y
24 Sherman	Y	Y	Y	Y	Y	N
25 ***McKeon***	Y	Y	Y	N	N	Y
26 Berman	Y	Y	Y	Y	Y	N
27 ***Rogan***	Y	Y	Y	N	N	Y
28 ***Dreier***	Y	Y	Y	N	N	Y
29 Waxman	Y	Y	Y	Y	Y	N
30 Becerra	Y	Y	Y	Y	Y	N
31 Martinez	Y	Y	Y	N	N	Y
32 Dixon	Y	Y	Y	Y	Y	N
33 Roybal-Allard	Y	Y	Y	Y	Y	N
34 Napolitano	Y	Y	Y	Y	Y	N
35 Waters	Y	Y	Y	Y	Y	N
36 ***Kuykendall***	Y	Y	Y	N	Y	Y
37 Millender-McD.	Y	Y	Y	Y	Y	N
38 ***Horn***	Y	Y	Y	Y	Y	N
39 ***Royce***	Y	Y	Y	N	N	Y
40 ***Lewis***	Y	Y	Y	N	N	Y
41 ***Miller***	Y	Y	Y	N	N	Y
42 Vacant						
43 ***Calvert***	Y	Y	Y	N	N	Y
44 ***Bono***	Y	Y	Y	N	N	Y
45 ***Rohrabacher***	Y	Y	Y	Y	Y	N
46 Sanchez	Y	Y	Y	Y	Y	N
47 ***Cox***	Y	Y	Y	N	N	Y
48 ***Packard***	Y	Y	Y	N	N	Y
49 ***Bilbray***	Y	Y	Y	N	N	Y
50 Filner	Y	Y	Y	Y	Y	N
51 ***Cunningham***	Y	Y	Y	N	N	Y
52 ***Hunter***	Y	Y	Y	N	N	Y
COLORADO						
1 DeGette	Y	Y	Y	Y	Y	N
2 Udall	Y	Y	Y	Y	Y	N
3 ***McInnis***	Y	Y	Y	N	N	Y
4 ***Schaffer***	Y	Y	Y	N	N	Y
5 ***Hefley***	Y	Y	Y	N	N	Y
6 ***Tancredo***	Y	Y	Y	N	N	Y
CONNECTICUT						
1 Larson	Y	Y	Y	Y	Y	N
2 Gejdenson	Y	Y	Y	Y	Y	N
3 DeLauro	Y	Y	Y	Y	Y	N
4 ***Shays***	Y	Y	Y	Y	Y	N
5 Maloney	Y	Y	Y	N	Y	Y
6 ***Johnson***	Y	Y	Y	Y	Y	N
DELAWARE						
AL ***Castle***	Y	Y	Y	Y	Y	N
FLORIDA						
1 ***Scarborough***	?	?	?	?	?	?
2 Boyd	Y	Y	Y	Y	Y	N
3 Brown	Y	Y	Y	Y	Y	N
4 ***Fowler***	Y	Y	Y	N	N	Y
5 Thurman	Y	Y	Y	Y	Y	N
6 ***Stearns***	Y	Y	Y	N	N	Y
7 ***Mica***	Y	Y	Y	N	N	Y
8 ***McCollum***	Y	Y	Y	N	N	Y
9 ***Bilirakis***	Y	Y	Y	N	N	Y
10 ***Young***	Y	Y	Y	N	N	Y
11 Davis	Y	Y	Y	N	N	Y
12 ***Canady***	Y	Y	Y	N	N	Y
13 ***Miller***	Y	Y	Y	N	N	Y
14 ***Goss***	Y	Y	Y	N	N	Y
15 ***Weldon***	Y	Y	Y	N	N	Y
16 ***Foley***	Y	Y	Y	N	N	Y
17 Meek	Y	Y	Y	Y	Y	N
18 ***Ros-Lehtinen***	Y	Y	Y	N	N	Y
19 Wexler	Y	Y	Y	Y	Y	N
20 Deutsch	Y	Y	Y	Y	Y	N
21 ***Diaz-Balart***	Y	Y	Y	N	N	Y
22 ***Shaw***	Y	Y	Y	N	Y	Y
23 Hastings	Y	Y	Y	Y	Y	N
GEORGIA						
1 ***Kingston***	Y	Y	Y	N	N	Y
2 Bishop	Y	Y	Y	Y	Y	Y
3 ***Collins***	Y	Y	Y	N	N	Y
4 McKinney	Y	Y	Y	Y	Y	N
5 Lewis	Y	Y	Y	Y	Y	N
6 ***Isakson***	Y	Y	Y	N	N	Y
7 ***Barr***	Y	Y	Y	N	N	Y
8 ***Chambliss***	Y	Y	Y	N	N	Y
9 ***Deal***	Y	Y	Y	N	N	Y
10 ***Norwood***	Y	Y	Y	N	N	Y
11 ***Linder***	Y	Y	Y	N	N	Y
HAWAII						
1 Abercrombie	Y	Y	Y	Y	Y	N
2 Mink	Y	Y	Y	Y	Y	N
IDAHO						
1 ***Chenoweth-Hage***	Y	Y	Y	Y	N	Y
2 ***Simpson***	Y	Y	Y	N	N	Y
ILLINOIS						
1 Rush	?	?	?	?	?	?
2 Jackson	Y	Y	Y	Y	Y	N
3 Lipinski	Y	Y	Y	N	N	Y
4 Gutierrez	Y	Y	Y	Y	Y	N
5 Blagojevich	Y	Y	Y	Y	Y	N
6 ***Hyde***	Y	Y	Y	N	N	Y
7 Davis	Y	Y	Y	Y	Y	N
8 ***Crane***	Y	Y	Y	N	N	Y
9 Schakowsky	Y	Y	Y	N	N	Y
10 ***Porter***	Y	Y	Y	Y	Y	N
11 ***Weller***	Y	Y	Y	N	N	Y
12 Costello	Y	Y	Y	N	N	Y
13 ***Biggert***	Y	Y	Y	N	Y	N
14 ***Hastert***						

ND Northern Democrats SD Southern Democrats

	539	540	541	542	543	544
15 ***Ewing***	Y	Y	Y	N	N	Y
16 ***Manzullo***	Y	Y	Y	N	N	Y
17 Evans	Y	Y	Y	Y	Y	N
18 ***LaHood***	Y	Y	Y	N	N	Y
19 Phelps	Y	Y	Y	N	N	Y
20 ***Shimkus***	Y	Y	Y	N	N	Y
INDIANA						
1 Visclosky	Y	Y	Y	Y	Y	Y
2 ***McIntosh***	Y	Y	Y	N	N	Y
3 Roemer	Y	Y	Y	N	N	Y
4 ***Souder***	Y	Y	Y	N	N	Y
5 ***Buyer***	Y	Y	Y	N	N	Y
6 ***Burton***	Y	Y	Y	N	N	Y
7 ***Pease***	Y	Y	Y	N	N	Y
8 ***Hostettler***	Y	Y	Y	N	N	Y
9 Hill	Y	Y	Y	N	N	Y
10 Carson	Y	Y	Y	Y	Y	N
IOWA						
1 ***Leach***	Y	Y	Y	N	N	Y
2 ***Nussle***	Y	Y	Y	N	N	Y
3 Boswell	Y	Y	Y	N	N	Y
4 ***Ganske***	Y	Y	Y	N	N	Y
5 ***Latham***	?	?	?	N	N	Y
KANSAS						
1 ***Moran***	Y	Y	Y	N	N	Y
2 ***Ryun***	Y	Y	Y	N	N	Y
3 Moore	Y	Y	Y	Y	Y	Y
4 ***Tiahrt***	Y	Y	Y	N	N	Y
KENTUCKY						
1 ***Whitfield***	Y	Y	Y	N	N	Y
2 ***Lewis***	Y	Y	Y	N	N	Y
3 ***Northup***	Y	Y	Y	N	N	Y
4 Lucas	Y	Y	Y	N	N	Y
5 ***Rogers***	Y	Y	Y	N	N	Y
6 ***Fletcher***	Y	Y	Y	N	N	Y
LOUISIANA						
1 ***Vitter***	Y	Y	Y	N	N	Y
2 Jefferson	Y	Y	Y	Y	Y	Y
3 ***Tauzin***	Y	Y	Y	N	N	Y
4 ***McCrery***	Y	Y	Y	N	N	Y
5 ***Cooksey***	Y	Y	Y	N	Y	N
6 ***Baker***	Y	Y	Y	N	N	Y
7 John	Y	Y	Y	N	N	Y
MAINE						
1 Allen	Y	Y	Y	Y	Y	N
2 Baldacci	Y	Y	Y	Y	Y	Y
MARYLAND						
1 ***Gilchrest***	Y	Y	Y	N	Y	N
2 ***Ehrlich***	Y	Y	Y	N	Y	N
3 Cardin	Y	Y	Y	Y	Y	N
4 Wynn	Y	Y	Y	Y	Y	Y
5 Hoyer	Y	Y	Y	Y	Y	Y
6 ***Bartlett***	Y	Y	Y	N	N	Y
7 Cummings	Y	Y	Y	Y	Y	N
8 ***Morella***	Y	Y	Y	Y	Y	N
MASSACHUSETTS						
1 Olver	Y	Y	Y	Y	Y	N
2 Neal	Y	Y	Y	N	Y	Y
3 McGovern	Y	Y	Y	Y	Y	N
4 Frank	Y	Y	Y	Y	Y	N
5 Meehan	Y	Y	Y	Y	Y	N
6 Tierney	Y	Y	Y	Y	Y	N
7 Markey	Y	Y	Y	Y	Y	N
8 Capuano	Y	Y	Y	Y	Y	N
9 Moakley	Y	Y	Y	N	Y	Y
10 Delahunt	Y	Y	Y	?	?	?
MICHIGAN						
1 Stupak	Y	Y	Y	N	N	Y
2 ***Hoekstra***	Y	Y	Y	N	N	Y
3 ***Ehlers***	Y	Y	Y	N	N	Y
4 ***Camp***	Y	Y	Y	N	N	Y
5 Barcia	Y	Y	Y	N	N	Y
6 ***Upton***	Y	Y	Y	N	N	Y
7 ***Smith***	Y	Y	Y	N	N	Y
8 Stabenow	Y	Y	Y	Y	Y	N
9 Kildee	Y	Y	Y	N	N	Y
10 Bonior	Y	Y	Y	Y	Y	N
11 ***Knollenberg***	Y	Y	Y	N	N	Y
12 Levin	Y	Y	Y	Y	Y	N
13 Rivers	Y	Y	Y	Y	Y	N
14 Conyers	Y	Y	Y	Y	Y	N
15 Kilpatrick	Y	Y	Y	Y	Y	N
16 Dingell	Y	Y	Y	N	N	N

	539	540	541	542	543	544
MINNESOTA						
1 ***Gutknecht***	Y	Y	Y	N	N	Y
2 Minge	Y	Y	Y	Y	Y	N
3 ***Ramstad***	Y	Y	Y	N	N	Y
4 Vento	Y	Y	Y	Y	Y	N
5 Sabo	Y	Y	Y	Y	Y	N
6 Luther	Y	Y	Y	Y	Y	N
7 Peterson	Y	Y	Y	N	N	Y
8 Oberstar	Y	Y	Y	N	N	Y
MISSISSIPPI						
1 ***Wicker***	Y	Y	Y	N	N	Y
2 Thompson	Y	Y	Y	Y	Y	N
3 ***Pickering***	Y	Y	Y	N	–	Y
4 Shows	Y	Y	Y	N	N	Y
5 Taylor	Y	Y	Y	N	N	Y
MISSOURI						
1 Clay	Y	Y	Y	Y	Y	N
2 ***Talent***	Y	Y	Y	N	N	Y
3 Gephardt	Y	Y	Y	Y	Y	N
4 Skelton	Y	Y	Y	N	N	Y
5 McCarthy	Y	Y	Y	Y	Y	N
6 Danner	Y	Y	Y	N	N	Y
7 ***Blunt***	Y	Y	Y	N	N	Y
8 ***Emerson***	Y	Y	Y	N	N	Y
9 ***Hulshof***	Y	Y	Y	N	N	Y
MONTANA						
AL ***Hill***	Y	Y	Y	N	N	Y
NEBRASKA						
1 ***Bereuter***	Y	Y	Y	N	N	Y
2 ***Terry***	Y	Y	Y	N	N	Y
3 ***Barrett***	Y	Y	Y	N	N	Y
NEVADA						
1 Berkley	Y	Y	Y	Y	Y	N
2 ***Gibbons***	Y	Y	Y	N	N	Y
NEW HAMPSHIRE						
1 ***Sununu***	Y	Y	Y	N	N	Y
2 ***Bass***	Y	Y	Y	N	Y	N
NEW JERSEY						
1 Andrews	Y	Y	Y	Y	Y	Y
2 ***LoBiondo***	Y	Y	Y	N	N	Y
3 ***Saxton***	Y	Y	Y	N	N	Y
4 ***Smith***	Y	Y	Y	N	N	Y
5 ***Roukema***	Y	Y	Y	N	N	Y
6 Pallone	Y	Y	Y	Y	Y	N
7 ***Franks***	Y	Y	Y	N	N	Y
8 Pascrell	Y	Y	Y	N	Y	Y
9 Rothman	Y	Y	Y	Y	Y	N
10 Payne	Y	Y	Y	Y	Y	N
11 ***Frelinghuysen***	Y	Y	Y	N	Y	Y
12 Holt	Y	Y	Y	Y	Y	N
13 Menendez	?	?	?	Y	Y	N
NEW MEXICO						
1 ***Wilson***	Y	Y	Y	N	N	Y
2 ***Skeen***	Y	Y	Y	N	N	Y
3 Udall	Y	Y	Y	Y	Y	N
NEW YORK						
1 Forbes	Y	Y	Y	N	N	Y
2 ***Lazio***	Y	Y	Y	N	N	Y
3 ***King***	Y	Y	Y	N	N	Y
4 McCarthy	Y	Y	Y	N	Y	Y
5 Ackerman	Y	Y	Y	Y	Y	N
6 Meeks	Y	Y	Y	Y	Y	N
7 Crowley	Y	Y	Y	Y	Y	Y
8 Nadler	Y	Y	Y	Y	Y	N
9 Weiner	Y	Y	Y	Y	Y	N
10 Towns	Y	Y	Y	Y	Y	N
11 Owens	Y	Y	Y	Y	Y	N
12 Velázquez	Y	Y	Y	Y	Y	N
13 ***Fossella***	Y	Y	Y	N	N	Y
14 Maloney	Y	Y	Y	Y	Y	N
15 Rangel	Y	Y	Y	Y	Y	N
16 Serrano	Y	Y	Y	Y	Y	N
17 Engel	Y	Y	Y	Y	Y	N
18 Lowey	Y	Y	Y	Y	Y	N
19 ***Kelly***	Y	Y	Y	N	N	Y
20 ***Gilman***	Y	Y	Y	Y	Y	Y
21 McNulty	?	?	?	N	N	Y
22 ***Sweeney***	Y	Y	Y	N	N	Y
23 ***Boehlert***	Y	Y	Y	N	Y	Y
24 ***McHugh***	Y	Y	Y	N	N	Y
25 ***Walsh***	Y	Y	Y	N	N	Y
26 Hinchey	Y	Y	Y	Y	Y	N
27 ***Reynolds***	Y	Y	Y	N	N	Y
28 Slaughter	Y	Y	Y	Y	Y	N
29 LaFalce	Y	Y	Y	N	N	Y

	539	540	541	542	543	544
30 ***Quinn***	Y	Y	Y	N	N	Y
31 ***Houghton***	Y	Y	?	N	Y	Y
NORTH CAROLINA						
1 Clayton	Y	Y	Y	Y	Y	N
2 Etheridge	Y	Y	Y	N	Y	Y
3 ***Jones***	Y	Y	Y	N	N	Y
4 Price	Y	Y	Y	N	Y	N
5 ***Burr***	Y	Y	Y	N	N	Y
6 ***Coble***	Y	Y	Y	N	N	Y
7 McIntyre	Y	Y	Y	N	N	Y
8 ***Hayes***	Y	Y	Y	N	N	Y
9 ***Myrick***	Y	Y	Y	N	N	Y
10 ***Ballenger***	Y	Y	Y	N	N	Y
11 ***Taylor***	Y	Y	Y	N	N	Y
12 Watt	Y	Y	Y	Y	Y	N
NORTH DAKOTA						
AL Pomeroy	Y	Y	Y	N	N	Y
OHIO						
1 ***Chabot***	Y	Y	Y	N	N	Y
2 ***Portman***	Y	Y	Y	N	N	Y
3 Hall	Y	Y	Y	N	N	Y
4 ***Oxley***	Y	Y	Y	N	N	Y
5 ***Gillmor***	Y	Y	Y	N	N	Y
6 Strickland	Y	Y	Y	N	Y	Y
7 ***Hobson***	Y	Y	Y	N	N	Y
8 ***Boehner***	Y	Y	Y	N	N	Y
9 Kaptur	Y	Y	Y	Y	Y	N
10 Kucinich	Y	Y	Y	N	N	Y
11 Jones	Y	Y	Y	Y	Y	N
12 ***Kasich***	Y	Y	Y	N	N	Y
13 Brown	Y	Y	Y	Y	Y	N
14 Sawyer	Y	Y	Y	Y	Y	N
15 ***Pryce***	Y	Y	Y	N	N	Y
16 ***Regula***	Y	Y	Y	N	N	Y
17 Traficant	Y	Y	Y	N	N	Y
18 ***Ney***	Y	Y	Y	N	N	Y
19 ***LaTourette***	Y	Y	Y	N	N	Y
OKLAHOMA						
1 ***Largent***	Y	Y	Y	N	N	Y
2 ***Coburn***	Y	Y	Y	N	N	Y
3 ***Watkins***	Y	Y	Y	N	N	Y
4 ***Watts***	Y	Y	Y	N	N	Y
5 ***Istook***	Y	Y	Y	N	N	Y
6 ***Lucas***	Y	Y	Y	N	N	Y
OREGON						
1 Wu	Y	Y	Y	Y	Y	N
2 ***Walden***	Y	Y	Y	Y	Y	N
3 Blumenauer	Y	Y	Y	Y	Y	N
4 DeFazio	Y	Y	Y	Y	Y	N
5 Hooley	Y	Y	Y	Y	Y	N
PENNSYLVANIA						
1 Brady	Y	Y	Y	Y	Y	Y
2 Fattah	Y	Y	Y	Y	Y	N
3 Borski	Y	Y	Y	N	N	Y
4 Klink	Y	Y	Y	N	N	Y
5 ***Peterson***	Y	Y	Y	N	N	Y
6 Holden	Y	Y	Y	N	N	Y
7 ***Weldon***	Y	Y	Y	N	N	Y
8 ***Greenwood***	Y	Y	Y	Y	Y	Y
9 ***Shuster***	Y	Y	Y	N	Y	N
10 ***Sherwood***	Y	Y	Y	N	N	Y
11 Kanjorski	Y	Y	Y	N	N	Y
12 Murtha	Y	Y	Y	N	N	Y
13 Hoeffel	Y	Y	Y	N	N	Y
14 Coyne	Y	Y	Y	Y	Y	N
15 ***Toomey***	Y	Y	Y	N	N	Y
16 ***Pitts***	Y	Y	Y	N	N	Y
17 ***Gekas***	Y	Y	Y	N	N	Y
18 Doyle	Y	Y	Y	N	N	Y
19 ***Goodling***	Y	Y	Y	N	N	Y
20 Mascara	?	?	?	?	?	?
21 ***English***	Y	Y	Y	N	N	Y
RHODE ISLAND						
1 Kennedy	Y	Y	Y	Y	Y	?
2 Weygand	Y	Y	Y	N	N	Y
SOUTH CAROLINA						
1 ***Sanford***	Y	Y	Y	N	Y	N
2 ***Spence***	Y	Y	?	N	N	Y
3 ***Graham***	Y	Y	Y	N	N	Y
4 ***DeMint***	Y	Y	Y	N	N	Y
5 Spratt	Y	Y	Y	N	Y	Y
6 Clyburn	Y	Y	Y	Y	Y	N
SOUTH DAKOTA						
AL ***Thune***	Y	Y	Y	N	N	Y

	539	540	541	542	543	544
TENNESSEE						
1 ***Jenkins***	Y	Y	Y	N	N	Y
2 ***Duncan***	Y	Y	Y	N	N	Y
3 ***Wamp***	Y	Y	Y	N	N	Y
4 ***Hilleary***	Y	Y	Y	N	N	Y
5 Clement	Y	Y	Y	N	N	Y
6 Gordon	Y	Y	Y	N	Y	Y
7 ***Bryant***	Y	Y	Y	N	N	Y
8 Tanner	Y	Y	Y	Y	Y	N
9 Ford	Y	Y	Y	Y	Y	N
TEXAS						
1 Sandlin	Y	Y	Y	Y	Y	N
2 Turner	Y	Y	Y	N	N	Y
3 ***Johnson, Sam***	Y	Y	Y	N	N	Y
4 Hall	Y	Y	Y	N	N	Y
5 ***Sessions***	Y	Y	Y	N	N	Y
6 ***Barton***	Y	Y	Y	N	N	Y
7 ***Archer***	Y	Y	Y	N	N	Y
8 ***Brady***	Y	Y	Y	N	N	Y
9 Lampson	Y	Y	Y	Y	Y	Y
10 Doggett	Y	Y	Y	Y	Y	N
11 Edwards	Y	Y	Y	N	Y	N
12 ***Granger***	?	?	?	N	N	Y
13 ***Thornberry***	Y	Y	Y	N	N	Y
14 ***Paul***	Y	Y	Y	Y	Y	N
15 Hinojosa	?	?	?	?	?	?
16 Reyes	Y	Y	Y	Y	Y	Y
17 Stenholm	Y	Y	Y	N	N	Y
18 Jackson-Lee	+	+	+	Y	Y	N
19 ***Combest***	Y	Y	Y	N	N	Y
20 Gonzalez	Y	Y	Y	Y	Y	N
21 ***Smith***	Y	Y	Y	N	N	Y
22 ***DeLay***	Y	Y	Y	N	N	Y
23 ***Bonilla***	Y	Y	Y	N	N	Y
24 Frost	Y	Y	Y	Y	Y	N
25 Bentsen	Y	Y	Y	N	Y	N
26 ***Armey***	Y	Y	Y	N	N	Y
27 Ortiz	Y	Y	Y	N	N	Y
28 Rodriguez	Y	Y	Y	Y	Y	N
29 Green	Y	Y	Y	N	Y	Y
30 Johnson, E.B.	Y	Y	Y	Y	Y	N
UTAH						
1 ***Hansen***	Y	Y	Y	N	N	Y
2 ***Cook***	Y	Y	Y	N	N	Y
3 ***Cannon***	Y	Y	Y	N	N	Y
VERMONT						
AL *Sanders*	Y	Y	Y	Y	Y	N
VIRGINIA						
1 ***Bateman***	Y	Y	Y	N	N	Y
2 Pickett	Y	Y	?	Y	N	N
3 Scott	Y	Y	Y	Y	Y	N
4 Sisisky	Y	Y	Y	N	Y	Y
5 Goode	Y	Y	Y	N	N	Y
6 ***Goodlatte***	Y	Y	Y	N	N	Y
7 ***Bliley***	Y	Y	Y	N	N	Y
8 Moran	Y	Y	Y	Y	Y	N
9 Boucher	Y	Y	Y	Y	Y	N
10 ***Wolf***	Y	Y	Y	N	N	Y
11 ***Davis***	Y	Y	Y	N	Y	Y
WASHINGTON						
1 Inslee	Y	Y	Y	Y	Y	N
2 ***Metcalf***	Y	Y	Y	Y	Y	N
3 Baird	Y	Y	Y	Y	Y	N
4 ***Hastings***	Y	Y	Y	N	N	Y
5 ***Nethercutt***	Y	Y	Y	N	N	Y
6 Dicks	Y	Y	Y	Y	Y	N
7 McDermott	Y	Y	Y	Y	Y	N
8 ***Dunn***	Y	Y	Y	N	N	Y
9 Smith	Y	Y	Y	Y	Y	N
WEST VIRGINIA						
1 Mollohan	Y	Y	Y	N	N	Y
2 Wise	Y	Y	Y	Y	Y	Y
3 Rahall	Y	Y	Y	N	N	Y
WISCONSIN						
1 ***Ryan***	Y	Y	Y	N	N	Y
2 Baldwin	Y	Y	Y	Y	Y	N
3 Kind	Y	Y	Y	Y	Y	N
4 Kleczka	Y	Y	Y	N	N	Y
5 Barrett	Y	Y	Y	Y	Y	N
6 ***Petri***	Y	Y	Y	N	N	Y
7 Obey	?	Y	Y	Y	Y	N
8 ***Green***	Y	Y	Y	N	N	Y
9 ***Sensenbrenner***	Y	Y	Y	N	N	Y
WYOMING						
AL ***Cubin***	Y	Y	Y	N	N	Y

Southern states - Ala., Ark., Fla., Ga., Ky., La., Miss., N.C., Okla., S.C., Tenn., Texas, Va.

545. **Procedural Motion/Journal.** Approval of the House Journal of Wednesday, Oct. 27, 1999. Approved 370-49: R 198-16; D 172-33 (ND 126-26, SD 46-7); I 0-0. Oct. 28, 1999.

546. **H J Res 73. Fiscal 2000 Continuing Appropriations/Passage.** Passage of the joint resolution to provide continuing appropriations through Nov. 5 for agencies covered by the fiscal 2000 spending bills not yet enacted. The continuing resolution would set spending levels at the fiscal 1999 level. Passed 424-2: R 218-1; D 205-1 (ND 151-1, SD 54-0); I 1-0. Oct. 28, 1999.

547. **HR 3064. Fiscal 2000 District of Columbia/Labor-HHS-Education Appropriations/Rule.** Adoption of the rule (H Res 345) to provide for House floor consideration of the conference report on the bill to provide $317.1 billion in budget authority for the departments of Labor, Health and Human Services (HHS) and Education and for related agencies, and $429.1 million in federal funds for the District of Columbia. Adopted 221-206: R 219-1; D 2-204 (ND 1-152, SD 1-52); I 0-1. Oct. 28, 1999.

548. **HR 3064. Fiscal 2000 District of Columbia/Labor-HHS-Education Appropriations/Recommit.** Hoyer, D-Md., motion to recommit the measure back to the conference committee with instructions to the House conferees to insist on striking provisions that would reduce congressional pay rates by 0.97 percent. Motion rejected 11-417: R 3-218; D 8-198 (ND 6-146, SD 2-52); I 0-1. Oct. 28, 1999.

549. **HR 3064. Fiscal 2000 District of Columbia/Labor-HHS-Education Appropriations/Conference Report.** Adoption of the conference report on the bill to provide $317.1 billion in budget authority for the departments of Labor, Health and Human Services (HHS) and Education, and for related agencies. The conference report would provide $429.1 million in federal funds for the District of Columbia. The conference report also includes a 0.97 percent across-the-board budget cut that would reduce fiscal 2000 outlays by $3.5 billion. Adopted (thus sent to the Senate) 218-211: R 214-7; D 4-203 (ND 2-151, SD 2-52); I 0-1. Oct. 28, 1999. A "nay" was a vote in support of the president's position.

Key

- Y Voted for (yea).
- # Paired for.
- + Announced for.
- N Voted against (nay).
- X Paired against.
- – Announced against.
- P Voted "present."
- C Voted "present" to avoid possible conflict of interest.
- ? Did not vote or otherwise make a position known.

•

Democrats ***Republicans*** *Independents*

	545	546	547	548	549
ALABAMA					
1 ***Callahan***	Y	Y	Y	N	Y
2 ***Everett***	Y	Y	Y	N	Y
3 ***Riley***	Y	Y	Y	N	Y
4 ***Aderholt***	N	Y	Y	N	Y
5 Cramer	Y	Y	N	N	N
6 ***Bachus***	Y	Y	Y	N	Y
7 Hilliard	N	Y	N	N	N
ALASKA					
AL ***Young***	Y	Y	Y	N	Y
ARIZONA					
1 ***Salmon***	Y	Y	Y	N	Y
2 Pastor	Y	Y	N	N	N
3 ***Stump***	Y	Y	Y	N	Y
4 ***Shadegg***	Y	Y	Y	N	Y
5 ***Kolbe***	Y	Y	Y	N	Y
6 ***Hayworth***	Y	Y	Y	N	Y
ARKANSAS					
1 Berry	Y	Y	N	N	N
2 Snyder	Y	Y	N	N	N
3 ***Hutchinson***	Y	Y	Y	N	Y
4 ***Dickey***	N	Y	Y	N	Y
CALIFORNIA					
1 Thompson	N	Y	N	N	N
2 ***Herger***	Y	Y	Y	N	Y
3 ***Ose***	Y	Y	Y	N	Y
4 ***Doolittle***	Y	Y	Y	Y	Y
5 Matsui	Y	Y	N	N	N
6 Woolsey	Y	Y	N	N	N
7 Miller, George	N	Y	N	N	N
8 Pelosi	Y	Y	N	N	N
9 Lee	Y	Y	N	N	N
10 Tauscher	Y	Y	N	N	N
11 ***Pombo***	Y	Y	Y	N	Y
12 Lantos	Y	Y	N	N	N
13 Stark	Y	Y	N	N	N
14 Eshoo	Y	Y	N	N	N
15 ***Campbell***	Y	Y	Y	N	Y
16 Lofgren	Y	Y	N	N	N
17 Farr	Y	Y	N	N	N
18 Condit	Y	Y	N	N	N
19 ***Radanovich***	Y	Y	Y	N	Y
20 Dooley	Y	Y	N	N	N
21 ***Thomas***	Y	Y	Y	N	Y
22 Capps	Y	Y	N	N	N
23 ***Gallegly***	Y	Y	Y	N	Y
24 Sherman	Y	Y	N	N	N
25 ***McKeon***	Y	Y	Y	N	Y
26 Berman	Y	Y	N	N	N
27 ***Rogan***	N	Y	Y	N	Y
28 ***Dreier***	Y	Y	Y	N	Y
29 Waxman	Y	Y	N	N	N
30 Becerra	Y	Y	N	N	N
31 Martinez	Y	Y	N	N	N
32 Dixon	Y	Y	N	N	N
33 Roybal-Allard	Y	Y	N	N	N
34 Napolitano	Y	Y	N	N	N
35 Waters	?	?	?	?	?
36 ***Kuykendall***	Y	Y	Y	N	Y
37 Millender-McD.	Y	Y	N	N	N
38 ***Horn***	Y	Y	Y	N	Y
39 ***Royce***	Y	Y	Y	N	Y
40 ***Lewis***	Y	Y	Y	Y	Y
41 ***Miller***	Y	Y	Y	N	Y
42 Vacant					
43 ***Calvert***	Y	Y	Y	N	Y
44 ***Bono***	Y	Y	Y	N	Y
45 ***Rohrabacher***	Y	Y	Y	N	Y
46 Sanchez	Y	Y	N	N	N
47 ***Cox***	Y	Y	Y	N	Y
48 ***Packard***	Y	Y	Y	N	Y
49 ***Bilbray***	N	Y	Y	N	Y
50 Filner	N	Y	N	N	N
51 ***Cunningham***	Y	Y	Y	N	Y
52 ***Hunter***	Y	Y	Y	N	Y
COLORADO					
1 DeGette	Y	Y	N	N	N
2 Udall	Y	Y	N	N	N
3 ***McInnis***	Y	Y	Y	N	Y
4 ***Schaffer***	N	Y	Y	N	N
5 ***Hefley***	N	Y	Y	N	N
6 ***Tancredo***	P	Y	Y	N	Y
CONNECTICUT					
1 Larson	Y	Y	N	N	N
2 Gejdenson	Y	Y	N	N	N
3 DeLauro	Y	Y	N	N	N
4 ***Shays***	Y	Y	Y	N	Y
5 Maloney	Y	Y	N	N	N
6 ***Johnson***	?	Y	Y	N	Y
DELAWARE					
AL ***Castle***	Y	Y	Y	N	Y
FLORIDA					
1 ***Scarborough***	?	?	?	?	?
2 Boyd	Y	Y	N	N	N
3 Brown	Y	Y	N	N	N
4 ***Fowler***	Y	Y	Y	N	Y
5 Thurman	Y	Y	N	N	N
6 ***Stearns***	Y	Y	Y	N	Y
7 ***Mica***	Y	Y	Y	N	Y
8 ***McCollum***	Y	Y	Y	N	Y
9 ***Bilirakis***	Y	Y	Y	N	Y
10 ***Young***	Y	Y	Y	N	Y
11 Davis	Y	Y	N	N	N
12 ***Canady***	Y	Y	Y	N	Y
13 ***Miller***	Y	Y	Y	N	Y
14 ***Goss***	Y	Y	Y	N	Y
15 ***Weldon***	Y	Y	Y	N	Y
16 ***Foley***	Y	Y	Y	N	Y
17 Meek	Y	Y	N	N	N
18 ***Ros-Lehtinen***	Y	Y	Y	N	Y
19 Wexler	?	Y	N	N	N
20 Deutsch	Y	Y	N	N	N
21 ***Diaz-Balart***	Y	Y	Y	N	Y
22 ***Shaw***	Y	Y	Y	N	Y
23 Hastings	N	Y	N	N	N
GEORGIA					
1 ***Kingston***	Y	Y	Y	N	Y
2 Bishop	Y	Y	N	N	N
3 ***Collins***	Y	Y	Y	N	Y
4 McKinney	Y	Y	N	N	N
5 Lewis	Y	Y	N	N	N
6 ***Isakson***	Y	Y	Y	N	Y
7 ***Barr***	Y	Y	Y	N	Y
8 ***Chambliss***	Y	Y	Y	N	Y
9 ***Deal***	Y	Y	Y	N	Y
10 ***Norwood***	Y	Y	Y	N	Y
11 ***Linder***	Y	Y	Y	N	Y
HAWAII					
1 Abercrombie	Y	Y	N	N	N
2 Mink	Y	Y	N	N	N
IDAHO					
1 ***Chenoweth-Hage***	Y	Y	Y	N	N
2 ***Simpson***	Y	Y	Y	N	Y
ILLINOIS					
1 Rush	?	?	?	?	?
2 Jackson	Y	Y	N	Y	N
3 Lipinski	N	Y	N	N	N
4 Gutierrez	Y	Y	N	N	N
5 Blagojevich	Y	Y	N	N	N
6 ***Hyde***	Y	Y	Y	N	Y
7 Davis	Y	Y	N	N	N
8 ***Crane***	N	Y	Y	N	Y
9 Schakowsky	Y	Y	N	N	N
10 ***Porter***	Y	Y	Y	N	Y
11 ***Weller***	N	Y	Y	N	Y
12 Costello	N	Y	N	N	N
13 ***Biggert***	Y	Y	Y	N	Y
14 ***Hastert***			Y	N	Y

ND Northern Democrats SD Southern Democrats

	545	546	547	548	549
15 ***Ewing***	Y	Y	Y	N	Y
16 ***Manzullo***	Y	Y	Y	N	Y
17 Evans	N	Y	N	N	N
18 ***LaHood***	Y	Y	Y	N	Y
19 Phelps	Y	Y	N	N	N
20 ***Shimkus***	Y	Y	Y	N	Y
INDIANA					
1 Visclosky	N	Y	N	N	N
2 ***McIntosh***	Y	Y	Y	N	Y
3 Roemer	Y	Y	N	N	N
4 ***Souder***	Y	Y	Y	N	Y
5 ***Buyer***	?	Y	Y	N	Y
6 ***Burton***	Y	Y	Y	N	Y
7 ***Pease***	Y	Y	Y	N	Y
8 ***Hostettler***	Y	Y	Y	N	Y
9 Hill	Y	Y	N	N	N
10 Carson	Y	Y	N	N	N
IOWA					
1 ***Leach***	Y	Y	Y	N	Y
2 ***Nussle***	Y	Y	Y	N	Y
3 Boswell	Y	Y	N	N	N
4 ***Ganske***	Y	Y	Y	N	Y
5 ***Latham***	Y	Y	Y	N	Y
KANSAS					
1 ***Moran***	Y	Y	Y	N	Y
2 ***Ryun***	Y	Y	Y	N	Y
3 Moore	N	Y	N	N	N
4 ***Tiahrt***	Y	Y	Y	N	Y
KENTUCKY					
1 ***Whitfield***	?	Y	Y	N	Y
2 ***Lewis***	Y	Y	Y	N	Y
3 ***Northup***	Y	Y	Y	N	Y
4 Lucas	Y	Y	N	N	Y
5 ***Rogers***	Y	Y	Y	N	Y
6 ***Fletcher***	Y	Y	Y	N	Y
LOUISIANA					
1 ***Vitter***	Y	Y	Y	N	Y
2 Jefferson	Y	Y	N	N	N
3 ***Tauzin***	Y	Y	Y	N	Y
4 ***McCrery***	Y	Y	Y	N	Y
5 ***Cooksey***	Y	Y	Y	N	Y
6 ***Baker***	Y	Y	Y	N	Y
7 John	Y	Y	N	N	N
MAINE					
1 Allen	Y	Y	N	N	N
2 Baldacci	Y	Y	N	N	N
MARYLAND					
1 ***Gilchrest***	Y	Y	Y	N	Y
2 ***Ehrlich***	Y	Y	Y	N	Y
3 Cardin	Y	Y	N	N	N
4 Wynn	Y	Y	N	N	N
5 Hoyer	Y	Y	N	Y	N
6 ***Bartlett***	Y	Y	Y	N	Y
7 Cummings	Y	Y	N	N	N
8 ***Morella***	Y	Y	Y	N	Y
MASSACHUSETTS					
1 Olver	Y	Y	N	N	N
2 Neal	Y	Y	N	N	N
3 McGovern	Y	Y	N	N	N
4 Frank	Y	Y	N	N	N
5 Meehan	Y	Y	N	N	N
6 Tierney	Y	Y	N	N	N
7 Markey	N	Y	N	N	N
8 Capuano	Y	Y	N	N	N
9 Moakley	Y	Y	N	N	N
10 Delahunt	Y	Y	N	N	N
MICHIGAN					
1 Stupak	N	Y	N	N	N
2 ***Hoekstra***	Y	Y	Y	N	Y
3 ***Ehlers***	Y	Y	Y	N	Y
4 ***Camp***	Y	Y	Y	N	Y
5 Barcia	Y	Y	N	N	N
6 ***Upton***	Y	Y	Y	N	Y
7 ***Smith***	Y	Y	Y	N	Y
8 Stabenow	Y	Y	N	N	N
9 Kildee	Y	Y	N	N	N
10 Bonior	Y	Y	N	N	N
11 ***Knollenberg***	Y	Y	Y	N	Y
12 Levin	Y	Y	N	N	N
13 Rivers	Y	Y	N	N	N
14 Conyers	Y	Y	N	N	N
15 Kilpatrick	Y	Y	N	N	N
16 Dingell	Y	Y	N	N	N
MINNESOTA					
1 ***Gutknecht***	Y	Y	Y	N	Y
2 Minge	Y	Y	N	N	N
3 ***Ramstad***	N	Y	Y	N	Y
4 Vento	Y	Y	N	N	N
5 Sabo	N	Y	N	N	N
6 Luther	Y	Y	N	N	N
7 Peterson	N	Y	N	N	N
8 Oberstar	N	Y	N	N	N
MISSISSIPPI					
1 ***Wicker***	Y	Y	Y	N	Y
2 Thompson	N	Y	N	N	N
3 ***Pickering***	Y	Y	Y	N	Y
4 Shows	Y	Y	N	N	N
5 Taylor	N	Y	N	N	N
MISSOURI					
1 Clay	N	Y	N	N	N
2 ***Talent***	Y	Y	Y	N	Y
3 Gephardt	Y	Y	N	N	N
4 Skelton	Y	Y	N	N	N
5 McCarthy	Y	Y	N	N	N
6 Danner	Y	Y	N	N	Y
7 ***Blunt***	Y	Y	Y	N	Y
8 ***Emerson***	Y	Y	Y	N	Y
9 ***Hulshof***	N	Y	Y	N	Y
MONTANA					
AL ***Hill***	N	Y	Y	N	Y
NEBRASKA					
1 ***Bereuter***	Y	Y	N	N	Y
2 ***Terry***	Y	Y	Y	N	Y
3 ***Barrett***	Y	Y	Y	N	Y
NEVADA					
1 Berkley	Y	Y	N	N	N
2 ***Gibbons***	N	Y	Y	N	Y
NEW HAMPSHIRE					
1 ***Sununu***	Y	Y	Y	N	Y
2 ***Bass***	Y	Y	Y	N	Y
NEW JERSEY					
1 Andrews	Y	Y	N	N	N
2 ***LoBiondo***	N	Y	Y	N	Y
3 ***Saxton***	Y	Y	Y	N	Y
4 ***Smith***	Y	Y	Y	N	Y
5 ***Roukema***	Y	Y	Y	N	Y
6 Pallone	N	Y	N	N	N
7 ***Franks***	Y	Y	Y	N	Y
8 Pascrell	Y	Y	N	N	N
9 Rothman	Y	Y	N	N	N
10 Payne	Y	Y	N	N	N
11 ***Frelinghuysen***	Y	Y	Y	N	Y
12 Holt	N	Y	N	N	N
13 Menendez	Y	Y	N	N	N
NEW MEXICO					
1 ***Wilson***	Y	Y	Y	N	Y
2 ***Skeen***	Y	Y	Y	N	Y
3 Udall	N	Y	N	N	N
NEW YORK					
1 Forbes	Y	Y	N	N	N
2 ***Lazio***	Y	Y	Y	N	Y
3 ***King***	Y	Y	Y	Y	Y
4 McCarthy	Y	Y	N	N	N
5 Ackerman	Y	Y	N	N	N
6 Meeks	Y	Y	N	Y	N
7 Crowley	Y	Y	N	N	N
8 Nadler	Y	Y	N	N	N
9 Weiner	Y	Y	N	N	N
10 Towns	Y	Y	N	N	N
11 Owens	Y	Y	N	N	N
12 Velázquez	Y	Y	N	N	N
13 ***Fossella***	Y	Y	Y	N	Y
14 Maloney	Y	Y	N	N	N
15 Rangel	Y	Y	N	N	N
16 Serrano	Y	Y	N	N	N
17 Engel	Y	Y	N	P	N
18 Lowey	Y	Y	N	N	N
19 ***Kelly***	Y	Y	Y	N	Y
20 ***Gilman***	Y	Y	+	N	Y
21 McNulty	N	Y	N	N	N
22 ***Sweeney***	?	Y	Y	N	Y
23 ***Boehlert***	Y	Y	Y	N	Y
24 ***McHugh***	Y	Y	Y	N	Y
25 ***Walsh***	?	Y	Y	N	Y
26 Hinchey	N	Y	N	N	N
27 ***Reynolds***	Y	Y	Y	N	Y
28 Slaughter	Y	Y	N	N	N
29 LaFalce	Y	Y	N	N	N
30 ***Quinn***	Y	Y	Y	N	Y
31 ***Houghton***	Y	Y	Y	N	Y
NORTH CAROLINA					
1 Clayton	Y	Y	N	N	N
2 Etheridge	Y	Y	N	N	N
3 ***Jones***	Y	Y	Y	N	N
4 Price	Y	Y	N	N	N
5 ***Burr***	Y	Y	Y	N	Y
6 ***Coble***	Y	Y	Y	N	Y
7 McIntyre	Y	Y	N	N	N
8 ***Hayes***	Y	Y	Y	N	Y
9 ***Myrick***	Y	Y	Y	N	Y
10 ***Ballenger***	Y	Y	Y	N	Y
11 ***Taylor***	Y	Y	Y	N	Y
12 Watt	Y	Y	N	Y	N
NORTH DAKOTA					
AL Pomeroy	Y	Y	N	N	N
OHIO					
1 ***Chabot***	Y	Y	Y	N	Y
2 ***Portman***	Y	Y	Y	N	Y
3 Hall	Y	Y	N	N	N
4 ***Oxley***	Y	Y	Y	N	Y
5 ***Gillmor***	Y	Y	Y	N	Y
6 Strickland	Y	Y	N	N	N
7 ***Hobson***	Y	Y	Y	N	Y
8 ***Boehner***	Y	Y	Y	N	Y
9 Kaptur	Y	Y	N	N	N
10 Kucinich	N	Y	N	N	N
11 Jones	Y	Y	N	N	N
12 ***Kasich***	Y	Y	Y	N	Y
13 Brown	Y	Y	N	N	N
14 Sawyer	Y	Y	N	N	N
15 ***Pryce***	Y	Y	Y	N	Y
16 ***Regula***	Y	Y	Y	N	Y
17 Traficant	Y	Y	Y	N	N
18 ***Ney***	Y	Y	Y	N	Y
19 ***LaTourette***	Y	Y	Y	N	Y
OKLAHOMA					
1 ***Largent***	Y	Y	Y	N	Y
2 ***Coburn***	Y	?	Y	N	Y
3 ***Watkins***	Y	Y	Y	N	Y
4 ***Watts***	Y	Y	Y	N	Y
5 ***Istook***	Y	Y	Y	N	Y
6 ***Lucas***	Y	Y	Y	N	Y
OREGON					
1 Wu	N	Y	N	N	N
2 ***Walden***	Y	Y	Y	N	Y
3 Blumenauer	Y	Y	N	N	N
4 DeFazio	N	N	N	N	N
5 Hooley	Y	Y	N	N	N
PENNSYLVANIA					
1 Brady	?	?	N	N	N
2 Fattah	N	Y	N	N	N
3 Borski	N	Y	N	N	N
4 Klink	Y	Y	N	N	N
5 ***Peterson***	Y	Y	Y	N	Y
6 Holden	Y	Y	N	N	N
7 ***Weldon***	Y	Y	Y	N	Y
8 ***Greenwood***	Y	Y	Y	N	Y
9 ***Shuster***	Y	Y	Y	N	Y
10 ***Sherwood***	Y	Y	Y	N	Y
11 Kanjorski	Y	Y	N	N	N
12 Murtha	Y	Y	N	Y	N
13 Hoeffel	Y	Y	N	N	N
14 Coyne	Y	Y	N	N	N
15 ***Toomey***	Y	Y	Y	N	Y
16 ***Pitts***	Y	Y	Y	N	Y
17 ***Gekas***	Y	Y	Y	N	Y
18 Doyle	Y	Y	N	N	N
19 ***Goodling***	Y	Y	Y	N	Y
20 Mascara	?	?	?	?	?
21 ***English***	N	Y	Y	N	Y
RHODE ISLAND					
1 Kennedy	Y	Y	N	N	N
2 Weygand	Y	Y	N	N	N
SOUTH CAROLINA					
1 ***Sanford***	Y	Y	Y	N	N
2 ***Spence***	Y	Y	Y	N	N
3 ***Graham***	Y	Y	Y	N	Y
4 ***DeMint***	Y	Y	Y	N	Y
5 Spratt	Y	Y	N	N	N
6 Clyburn	N	Y	N	N	N
SOUTH DAKOTA					
AL ***Thune***	Y	Y	Y	N	Y
TENNESSEE					
1 ***Jenkins***	Y	Y	Y	N	Y
2 ***Duncan***	Y	Y	Y	N	Y
3 ***Wamp***	N	Y	Y	N	Y
4 ***Hilleary***	N	Y	Y	N	Y
5 Clement	Y	Y	N	N	N
6 Gordon	Y	Y	N	N	N
7 ***Bryant***	Y	Y	Y	N	Y
8 Tanner	Y	Y	N	N	N
9 Ford	Y	Y	N	N	N
TEXAS					
1 Sandlin	Y	Y	N	N	N
2 Turner	Y	Y	N	N	N
3 ***Johnson, Sam***	Y	Y	Y	N	Y
4 Hall	Y	Y	N	N	N
5 ***Sessions***	Y	Y	Y	N	Y
6 ***Barton***	Y	Y	Y	N	Y
7 ***Archer***	Y	Y	Y	N	Y
8 ***Brady***	Y	Y	Y	N	Y
9 Lampson	Y	Y	N	N	N
10 Doggett	Y	Y	N	N	N
11 Edwards	Y	Y	N	N	N
12 ***Granger***	Y	Y	Y	N	Y
13 ***Thornberry***	Y	Y	Y	N	Y
14 ***Paul***	Y	N	Y	N	N
15 Hinojosa	?	?	?	?	?
16 Reyes	Y	Y	N	N	N
17 Stenholm	Y	Y	N	N	N
18 Jackson-Lee	Y	Y	N	N	N
19 ***Combest***	Y	Y	Y	N	Y
20 Gonzalez	Y	Y	N	N	N
21 ***Smith***	Y	Y	Y	N	Y
22 ***DeLay***	Y	Y	Y	N	Y
23 ***Bonilla***	Y	Y	Y	N	Y
24 Frost	Y	Y	N	N	N
25 Bentsen	Y	Y	N	N	N
26 ***Armey***	Y	Y	Y	N	Y
27 Ortiz	Y	Y	N	N	N
28 Rodriguez	Y	Y	-	N	N
29 Green	Y	Y	N	N	N
30 Johnson, E.B.	N	Y	N	N	N
UTAH					
1 ***Hansen***	Y	Y	Y	N	Y
2 ***Cook***	Y	Y	Y	N	Y
3 ***Cannon***	Y	Y	Y	N	Y
VERMONT					
AL *Sanders*	?	Y	N	N	N
VIRGINIA					
1 ***Bateman***	Y	Y	Y	N	Y
2 Pickett	N	Y	N	N	N
3 Scott	Y	Y	N	N	N
4 Sisisky	Y	Y	N	N	N
5 Goode	Y	Y	Y	N	Y
6 ***Goodlatte***	Y	Y	Y	N	Y
7 ***Bliley***	Y	Y	Y	N	Y
8 Moran	Y	Y	N	Y	N
9 Boucher	Y	Y	N	N	N
10 ***Wolf***	Y	Y	Y	N	Y
11 ***Davis***	Y	Y	Y	N	Y
WASHINGTON					
1 Inslee	Y	Y	N	N	N
2 ***Metcalf***	Y	Y	Y	N	Y
3 Baird	N	Y	N	N	N
4 ***Hastings***	Y	Y	Y	N	Y
5 ***Nethercutt***	Y	Y	Y	N	Y
6 Dicks	Y	Y	N	N	N
7 McDermott	Y	Y	N	N	N
8 ***Dunn***	Y	Y	Y	N	Y
9 Smith	Y	Y	N	N	Y
WEST VIRGINIA					
1 Mollohan	Y	Y	N	Y	N
2 Wise	Y	Y	N	N	N
3 Rahall	Y	Y	N	Y	N
WISCONSIN					
1 ***Ryan***	Y	Y	Y	N	Y
2 Baldwin	N	Y	N	N	N
3 Kind	Y	Y	N	N	N
4 Kleczka	Y	Y	N	N	N
5 Barrett	Y	Y	N	N	N
6 ***Petri***	Y	Y	Y	N	Y
7 Obey	Y	Y	N	N	N
8 ***Green***	Y	Y	Y	N	Y
9 ***Sensenbrenner***	Y	Y	Y	N	Y
WYOMING					
AL ***Cubin***	Y	Y	Y	N	Y

Southern states - Ala., Ark., Fla., Ga., Ky., La., Miss., N.C., Okla., S.C., Tenn., Texas, Va.

House Votes 550, 551, 552, 553, 554, 555, 556

550. HR 348. Civil Defense Worker Monument/Passage. Hansen, R-Utah, motion to suspend the rules and pass the bill to authorize the construction of a monument to honor U.S. civil defense and emergency management workers. Motion agreed to 349-4: R 182-4; D 167-0 (ND 123-0, SD 44-0); I 0-0. Nov. 1, 1999. A two-thirds majority of those present and voting (236 in this case) is required for passage under suspension of the rules.

551. HR 2737. Lewis and Clark Land Transfer/Passage. Hansen, R-Utah, motion to suspend the rules and pass the bill to authorize the Interior secretary to give the state of Illinois a 39-acre parcel of land in Madison County at the beginning of the Lewis and Clark historic trail. The land would be used to build an interpretive center at the site where the explorers set off for the West in 1803. Motion agreed to 355-0: R 184-0; D 171-0 (ND 128-0, SD 43-0); I 0-0. Nov. 1, 1999. A two-thirds majority of those present and voting (237 in this case) is required for passage under suspension of the rules.

552. HR 1714. Electronic Signature Authorization/Passage. Bliley, R-Va., motion to suspend the rules and pass the bill to promote electronic commerce and establish a minimum federal standard for the use and recognition of electronic signatures. The bill would ensure that electronic signatures be given the same legal validity and enforceability as written ones. Motion rejected 234-122: R 183-3; D 51-119 (ND 31-95, SD 20-24); I 0-0. Nov. 1, 1999. A two-thirds majority of those present and voting (238 in this case) is required for passage under suspension of the rules. A "nay" was a vote in support of the president's position.

553. H Con Res 213. Financial Literacy Training/Adoption. Petri, R-Wis., motion to suspend the rules and adopt the concurrent resolution to express the sense of the Congress that the Education Department should use funds to promote financial literacy programs in schools. Motion agreed to 411-3: R 210-3; D 200-0 (ND 146-0, SD 54-0); I 1-0. Nov. 2, 1999. A two-thirds majority of those present and voting (276 in this case) is required for adoption under suspension of the rules.

554. H Res 59. Affirm U.S. Commitment to NATO/Adoption. Gilman, R-N.Y., motion to suspend the rules and adopt the resolution to express the sense of the House that the North Atlantic Treaty Organization (NATO) should be commended for its pivotal role in preserving trans-Atlantic peace and stability. Motion agreed to 278-133: R 110-100; D 168-32 (ND 117-29, SD 51-3); I 0-1. Nov. 2, 1999. A two-thirds majority of those present and voting (274 in this case) is required for adoption under suspension of the rules.

555. HR 3164. Narcotics Traffickers/Passage. Gilman, R-N.Y., motion to suspend the rules and pass the bill to freeze the U.S. assets of major narcotics trafficking organizations as well as any organizations that deal with drug traffickers. The measure would deny visas to any known traffickers, their families and their business associates. Motion agreed to 385-26: R 203-8; D 182-17 (ND 134-11, SD 48-6); I 0-1. Nov. 2, 1999. A two-thirds majority of those present and voting (274 in this case) is required for passage under suspension of the rules.

556. H Res 349. Presidential Response to Hurricane Floyd/Adoption. Fowler, R-Fla., motion to suspend the rules and adopt the resolution to express the sense of the Congress that President Clinton should immediately recommend actions to Congress to provide relief to victims of Hurricane Floyd, including appropriations offsets. Motion agreed to 409-0: R 209-0; D 199-0 (ND 145-0, SD 54-0); I 1-0. Nov. 2, 1999. A two-thirds majority of those present and voting (273 in this case) is required for adoption under suspension of the rules.

Key

- Y Voted for (yea).
- # Paired for.
- + Announced for.
- N Voted against (nay).
- X Paired against.
- – Announced against.
- P Voted "present."
- C Voted "present" to avoid possible conflict of interest.
- ? Did not vote or otherwise make a position known.

•

Democrats ***Republicans***
Independents

	550	551	552	553	554	555	556
ALABAMA							
1 ***Callahan***	Y	Y	Y	Y	N	Y	Y
2 ***Everett***	?	?	?	Y	N	Y	Y
3 ***Riley***	Y	Y	Y	Y	N	Y	Y
4 ***Aderholt***	Y	Y	Y	Y	N	Y	Y
5 Cramer	Y	Y	Y	Y	Y	Y	Y
6 ***Bachus***	Y	Y	Y	Y	Y	Y	Y
7 Hilliard	?	?	?	Y	Y	Y	Y
ALASKA							
AL ***Young***	Y	Y	Y	Y	N	Y	Y
ARIZONA							
1 ***Salmon***	?	?	?	Y	N	Y	Y
2 Pastor	Y	Y	N	Y	Y	Y	Y
3 ***Stump***	Y	Y	Y	Y	N	Y	Y
4 ***Shadegg***	Y	Y	Y	Y	N	Y	Y
5 ***Kolbe***	Y	Y	Y	Y	Y	Y	Y
6 ***Hayworth***	?	?	?	Y	N	Y	Y
ARKANSAS							
1 Berry	Y	Y	N	Y	Y	Y	Y
2 Snyder	Y	Y	Y	Y	Y	Y	Y
3 ***Hutchinson***	Y	Y	Y	Y	N	Y	Y
4 ***Dickey***	Y	Y	Y	Y	N	Y	Y
CALIFORNIA							
1 Thompson	Y	Y	Y	Y	Y	Y	Y
2 ***Herger***	Y	Y	Y	Y	N	Y	Y
3 ***Ose***	Y	Y	Y	Y	Y	Y	Y
4 ***Doolittle***	Y	Y	Y	Y	N	Y	Y
5 Matsui	Y	Y	N	Y	Y	Y	Y
6 Woolsey	Y	Y	N	Y	N	Y	Y
7 Miller, George	Y	Y	N	Y	N	N	Y
8 Pelosi	Y	Y	Y	Y	Y	Y	Y
9 Lee	Y	Y	N	Y	N	N	Y
10 Tauscher	Y	Y	Y	Y	Y	Y	Y
11 ***Pombo***	Y	Y	Y	N	N	N	Y
12 Lantos	Y	Y	N	Y	Y	Y	Y
13 Stark	Y	Y	N	Y	N	N	Y
14 Eshoo	Y	Y	Y	Y	Y	Y	Y
15 ***Campbell***	Y	Y	Y	Y	N	N	Y
16 Lofgren	Y	Y	Y	Y	Y	Y	Y
17 Farr	Y	Y	N	Y	Y	Y	Y
18 Condit	Y	Y	Y	Y	N	Y	Y
19 ***Radanovich***	Y	Y	Y	Y	Y	Y	Y
20 Dooley	Y	Y	Y	Y	Y	Y	Y
21 ***Thomas***	Y	Y	Y	Y	Y	Y	Y
22 Capps	Y	Y	Y	Y	Y	Y	Y
23 ***Gallegly***	Y	Y	Y	Y	Y	Y	Y
24 Sherman	Y	Y	Y	Y	Y	Y	Y
25 ***McKeon***	Y	Y	Y	Y	N	Y	Y
26 Berman	Y	Y	N	Y	Y	N	Y
27 ***Rogan***	Y	Y	Y	Y	P	Y	Y
28 ***Dreier***	Y	Y	Y	Y	Y	Y	Y
29 Waxman	Y	Y	N	Y	Y	Y	Y
30 Becerra	Y	Y	N	Y	Y	Y	Y
31 Martinez	Y	Y	N	Y	Y	Y	Y
32 Dixon	Y	Y	N	Y	Y	Y	Y
33 Roybal-Allard	Y	Y	N	Y	Y	Y	Y
34 Napolitano	Y	Y	Y	Y	Y	Y	Y
35 Waters	Y	Y	N	Y	Y	Y	Y
36 ***Kuykendall***	Y	Y	Y	Y	Y	Y	Y
37 Millender-McD.	Y	Y	N	Y	Y	Y	Y
38 ***Horn***	Y	Y	Y	Y	Y	Y	Y
39 ***Royce***	Y	Y	Y	Y	N	Y	Y
40 ***Lewis***	Y	Y	Y	Y	Y	Y	Y
41 ***Miller***	Y	Y	Y	Y	Y	Y	Y
42 Vacant							
43 ***Calvert***	Y	Y	Y	Y	Y	Y	Y
44 ***Bono***	Y	Y	Y	Y	Y	Y	Y
45 ***Rohrabacher***	Y	Y	Y	Y	N	Y	Y
46 Sanchez	Y	Y	Y	Y	Y	Y	Y
47 ***Cox***	Y	Y	Y	Y	Y	Y	Y
48 ***Packard***	Y	Y	Y	Y	Y	Y	Y
49 ***Bilbray***	Y	Y	Y	Y	N	Y	Y
50 Filner	Y	Y	N	Y	N	Y	Y
51 ***Cunningham***	Y	Y	Y	Y	N	Y	Y
52 ***Hunter***	Y	Y	Y	Y	Y	Y	?
COLORADO							
1 DeGette	Y	Y	N	Y	Y	Y	Y
2 Udall	Y	Y	Y	Y	Y	Y	Y
3 ***McInnis***	Y	Y	Y	Y	Y	Y	Y
4 ***Schaffer***	?	?	Y	Y	N	Y	Y
5 ***Hefley***	Y	Y	Y	Y	Y	Y	Y
6 ***Tancredo***	Y	Y	Y	Y	N	Y	Y
CONNECTICUT							
1 Larson	Y	Y	Y	Y	Y	Y	Y
2 Gejdenson	?	?	?	Y	Y	Y	Y
3 DeLauro	Y	Y	N	Y	Y	Y	Y
4 ***Shays***	Y	Y	Y	Y	Y	Y	Y
5 Maloney	Y	Y	Y	Y	Y	Y	Y
6 ***Johnson***	Y	Y	Y	Y	Y	Y	Y
DELAWARE							
AL ***Castle***	Y	Y	Y	Y	Y	Y	Y
FLORIDA							
1 ***Scarborough***	?	?	?	?	?	?	?
2 Boyd	Y	Y	Y	Y	Y	Y	Y
3 Brown	Y	Y	N	Y	Y	Y	Y
4 ***Fowler***	Y	Y	Y	Y	Y	Y	Y
5 Thurman	Y	Y	N	Y	Y	Y	Y
6 ***Stearns***	Y	Y	Y	Y	N	Y	Y
7 ***Mica***	+	+	+	Y	Y	Y	Y
8 ***McCollum***	Y	Y	Y	Y	Y	Y	Y
9 ***Bilirakis***	Y	Y	Y	Y	N	Y	Y
10 ***Young***	Y	Y	Y	Y	?	?	?
11 Davis	Y	?	Y	Y	Y	Y	Y
12 ***Canady***	Y	Y	Y	Y	N	Y	Y
13 ***Miller***	Y	Y	Y	Y	Y	Y	Y
14 ***Goss***	Y	Y	Y	Y	Y	Y	Y
15 ***Weldon***	Y	Y	Y	Y	N	Y	Y
16 ***Foley***	Y	Y	Y	Y	Y	Y	Y
17 Meek	Y	Y	N	Y	Y	Y	Y
18 ***Ros-Lehtinen***	Y	Y	Y	Y	Y	Y	Y
19 Wexler	Y	Y	N	Y	Y	Y	Y
20 Deutsch	Y	Y	N	Y	Y	Y	Y
21 ***Diaz-Balart***	Y	Y	Y	?	?	?	?
22 ***Shaw***	Y	Y	Y	Y	Y	Y	Y
23 Hastings	Y	Y	N	Y	Y	N	Y
GEORGIA							
1 ***Kingston***	Y	Y	Y	Y	N	Y	Y
2 Bishop	?	?	?	Y	Y	Y	Y
3 ***Collins***	?	?	?	Y	N	Y	Y
4 McKinney	?	?	?	Y	N	N	Y
5 Lewis	Y	Y	N	Y	Y	Y	Y
6 ***Isakson***	Y	Y	Y	Y	Y	Y	Y
7 ***Barr***	?	?	?	Y	N	N	Y
8 ***Chambliss***	?	?	?	Y	N	Y	Y
9 ***Deal***	?	?	?	Y	N	Y	Y
10 ***Norwood***	Y	Y	Y	Y	N	Y	Y
11 ***Linder***	Y	Y	Y	Y	N	Y	Y
HAWAII							
1 Abercrombie	Y	Y	N	Y	N	Y	Y
2 Mink	?	?	?	Y	N	Y	Y
IDAHO							
1 ***Chenoweth-Hage***	N	Y	N	N	N	N	Y
2 ***Simpson***	Y	Y	Y	Y	N	Y	Y
ILLINOIS							
1 Rush	?	Y	N	Y	Y	Y	Y
2 Jackson	Y	Y	N	Y	N	N	Y
3 Lipinski	?	?	?	Y	Y	Y	Y
4 Gutierrez	+	+	–	Y	Y	Y	Y
5 Blagojevich	?	?	?	Y	N	Y	Y
6 ***Hyde***	Y	Y	Y	Y	Y	Y	Y
7 Davis	?	Y	N	Y	N	Y	Y
8 ***Crane***	Y	Y	Y	Y	N	Y	Y
9 Schakowsky	Y	Y	N	Y	Y	Y	Y
10 ***Porter***	Y	Y	Y	Y	Y	Y	Y
11 ***Weller***	Y	Y	Y	Y	Y	Y	Y
12 Costello	?	?	?	Y	Y	Y	Y
13 ***Biggert***	Y	Y	Y	Y	Y	Y	Y
14 ***Hastert***							

ND Northern Democrats SD Southern Democrats

	550	551	552	553	554	555	556
15 ***Ewing***	Y	Y	Y	Y	Y	Y	Y
16 ***Manzullo***	Y	Y	Y	Y	N	Y	Y
17 Evans	Y	Y	N	Y	Y	Y	Y
18 ***LaHood***	Y	Y	Y	Y	Y	Y	Y
19 Phelps	Y	Y	N	Y	Y	Y	Y
20 ***Shimkus***	Y	Y	Y	Y	N	Y	Y
INDIANA							
1 Visclosky	Y	Y	N	Y	Y	Y	Y
2 ***McIntosh***	Y	Y	Y	Y	N	Y	Y
3 Roemer	Y	Y	Y	Y	Y	Y	Y
4 ***Souder***	Y	Y	Y	Y	N	Y	Y
5 ***Buyer***	Y	?	Y	Y	Y	Y	Y
6 ***Burton***	Y	Y	Y	Y	N	Y	Y
7 ***Pease***	Y	Y	Y	Y	N	Y	Y
8 ***Hostettler***	Y	Y	Y	Y	N	Y	Y
9 Hill	Y	Y	N	Y	Y	Y	Y
10 Carson	?	?	?	?	?	?	?
IOWA							
1 ***Leach***	Y	Y	Y	Y	Y	Y	Y
2 ***Nussle***	Y	Y	Y	Y	Y	Y	Y
3 Boswell	Y	Y	Y	Y	Y	Y	Y
4 ***Ganske***	?	?	?	Y	Y	Y	Y
5 ***Latham***	Y	Y	Y	Y	Y	Y	Y
KANSAS							
1 ***Moran***	Y	Y	Y	Y	N	Y	Y
2 ***Ryun***	Y	Y	Y	Y	N	Y	Y
3 Moore	Y	Y	Y	Y	Y	Y	Y
4 ***Tiahrt***	Y	Y	Y	Y	Y	Y	Y
KENTUCKY							
1 ***Whitfield***	Y	Y	Y	Y	N	Y	Y
2 ***Lewis***	Y	Y	Y	Y	N	Y	Y
3 ***Northup***	Y	Y	Y	Y	Y	Y	Y
4 Lucas	Y	Y	Y	Y	Y	Y	Y
5 ***Rogers***	Y	Y	Y	Y	Y	Y	Y
6 ***Fletcher***	Y	Y	Y	Y	Y	Y	Y
LOUISIANA							
1 ***Vitter***	Y	Y	Y	Y	N	Y	Y
2 Jefferson	?	?	?	Y	Y	Y	Y
3 ***Tauzin***	Y	Y	Y	Y	Y	Y	Y
4 ***McCrery***	Y	Y	Y	Y	Y	Y	Y
5 ***Cooksey***	?	?	?	Y	Y	Y	Y
6 ***Baker***	?	?	?	Y	N	Y	Y
7 John	Y	Y	N	Y	Y	Y	Y
MAINE							
1 Allen	Y	Y	N	Y	Y	Y	Y
2 Baldacci	Y	Y	N	Y	Y	Y	Y
MARYLAND							
1 ***Gilchrest***	Y	Y	Y	Y	Y	Y	Y
2 ***Ehrlich***	Y	Y	Y	?	?	?	?
3 Cardin	Y	Y	N	Y	Y	Y	Y
4 Wynn	+	+	−	Y	Y	Y	Y
5 Hoyer	Y	Y	N	Y	Y	Y	Y
6 ***Bartlett***	Y	Y	Y	Y	N	N	Y
7 Cummings	Y	Y	N	Y	Y	Y	Y
8 ***Morella***	Y	Y	Y	Y	Y	Y	Y
MASSACHUSETTS							
1 Olver	Y	Y	N	Y	Y	Y	Y
2 Neal	?	?	?	Y	Y	Y	Y
3 McGovern	Y	Y	N	Y	Y	Y	Y
4 Frank	Y	Y	N	Y	N	N	Y
5 Meehan	Y	Y	N	Y	Y	Y	Y
6 Tierney	Y	Y	N	Y	N	Y	Y
7 Markey	Y	Y	N	Y	Y	Y	Y
8 Capuano	Y	Y	N	Y	Y	Y	Y
9 Moakley	?	?	?	Y	Y	Y	Y
10 Delahunt	?	?	?	Y	Y	N	Y
MICHIGAN							
1 Stupak	?	?	?	Y	Y	Y	Y
2 ***Hoekstra***	Y	Y	Y	Y	N	Y	Y
3 ***Ehlers***	Y	Y	Y	Y	Y	Y	Y
4 ***Camp***	Y	Y	Y	Y	Y	Y	Y
5 Barcia	Y	Y	Y	Y	N	Y	Y
6 ***Upton***	Y	Y	Y	Y	Y	Y	Y
7 ***Smith***	Y	Y	Y	Y	N	Y	Y
8 Stabenow	Y	Y	+	Y	Y	Y	Y
9 Kildee	Y	Y	N	Y	Y	Y	Y
10 Bonior	Y	Y	N	Y	Y	Y	Y
11 ***Knollenberg***	Y	Y	Y	Y	Y	Y	Y
12 Levin	Y	Y	N	Y	Y	Y	Y
13 Rivers	Y	Y	N	Y	N	Y	Y
14 Conyers	Y	Y	N	Y	N	N	Y
15 Kilpatrick	Y	Y	N	Y	Y	Y	Y
16 Dingell	Y	Y	N	Y	Y	Y	Y
MINNESOTA							
1 ***Gutknecht***	Y	Y	Y	Y	N	Y	Y
2 Minge	Y	Y	Y	Y	N	Y	Y
3 ***Ramstad***	Y	Y	Y	Y	N	Y	Y
4 Vento	Y	Y	N	Y	Y	Y	Y
5 Sabo	?	?	?	?	?	?	?
6 Luther	Y	Y	N	Y	Y	Y	Y
7 Peterson	Y	Y	Y	Y	N	Y	Y
8 Oberstar	Y	Y	N	Y	Y	Y	Y
MISSISSIPPI							
1 ***Wicker***	Y	Y	Y	Y	Y	Y	Y
2 Thompson	?	?	?	Y	Y	Y	Y
3 ***Pickering***	Y	Y	Y	Y	Y	Y	Y
4 Shows	+	+	−	+	+	+	?
5 Taylor	?	?	?	Y	Y	Y	Y
MISSOURI							
1 Clay	?	?	?	Y	N	Y	Y
2 ***Talent***	?	?	?	Y	Y	Y	Y
3 Gephardt	Y	Y	N	Y	Y	Y	Y
4 Skelton	Y	Y	N	Y	Y	Y	Y
5 McCarthy	Y	Y	N	Y	Y	Y	Y
6 Danner	?	?	?	Y	N	Y	Y
7 ***Blunt***	Y	Y	Y	Y	Y	Y	Y
8 ***Emerson***	Y	Y	Y	Y	Y	Y	Y
9 ***Hulshof***	+	+	+	+	+	+	+
MONTANA							
AL ***Hill***	Y	Y	Y	Y	N	N	Y
NEBRASKA							
1 ***Bereuter***	Y	Y	Y	Y	Y	Y	Y
2 ***Terry***	Y	Y	Y	Y	Y	Y	Y
3 ***Barrett***	Y	Y	Y	Y	Y	Y	Y
NEVADA							
1 Berkley	?	?	?	Y	Y	Y	Y
2 ***Gibbons***	Y	Y	Y	Y	N	Y	Y
NEW HAMPSHIRE							
1 ***Sununu***	Y	Y	Y	Y	N	Y	Y
2 ***Bass***	Y	Y	Y	Y	Y	Y	Y
NEW JERSEY							
1 Andrews	Y	Y	N	Y	Y	Y	Y
2 ***LoBiondo***	Y	Y	Y	Y	N	Y	Y
3 ***Saxton***	Y	Y	Y	Y	N	Y	Y
4 ***Smith***	Y	Y	Y	Y	Y	Y	Y
5 ***Roukema***	Y	Y	Y	Y	Y	Y	Y
6 Pallone	Y	Y	N	Y	Y	Y	Y
7 ***Franks***	Y	Y	Y	Y	Y	Y	Y
8 Pascrell	Y	Y	N	Y	Y	Y	Y
9 Rothman	Y	Y	N	Y	Y	Y	Y
10 Payne	Y	Y	N	Y	Y	N	Y
11 ***Frelinghuysen***	Y	Y	Y	Y	Y	Y	Y
12 Holt	Y	Y	Y	Y	Y	Y	Y
13 Menendez	Y	Y	N	Y	Y	Y	Y
NEW MEXICO							
1 ***Wilson***	Y	Y	Y	Y	Y	Y	Y
2 ***Skeen***	Y	Y	Y	Y	Y	Y	Y
3 Udall	Y	Y	N	Y	Y	Y	Y
NEW YORK							
1 Forbes	?	?	?	Y	Y	Y	Y
2 ***Lazio***	Y	Y	Y	Y	Y	Y	Y
3 ***King***	Y	Y	Y	Y	Y	Y	Y
4 McCarthy	Y	Y	Y	Y	Y	Y	Y
5 Ackerman	Y	Y	N	?	?	?	?
6 Meeks	Y	Y	N	+	+	+	+
7 Crowley	Y	Y	Y	Y	Y	Y	Y
8 Nadler	Y	Y	N	Y	N	N	Y
9 Weiner	?	?	?	Y	Y	Y	Y
10 Towns	Y	Y	Y	Y	Y	Y	Y
11 Owens	?	?	?	Y	Y	Y	Y
12 Velázquez	Y	Y	N	Y	Y	Y	Y
13 ***Fossella***	?	?	?	Y	Y	Y	Y
14 Maloney	Y	Y	N	Y	Y	Y	Y
15 Rangel	Y	Y	N	Y	Y	Y	Y
16 Serrano	?	?	?	?	?	?	?
17 Engel	?	Y	N	Y	Y	Y	Y
18 Lowey	?	?	?	?	?	?	?
19 ***Kelly***	Y	Y	Y	Y	Y	Y	Y
20 ***Gilman***	Y	Y	Y	Y	Y	Y	Y
21 McNulty	?	?	?	?	?	?	?
22 ***Sweeney***	?	?	?	?	?	?	?
23 ***Boehlert***	Y	Y	Y	Y	Y	Y	Y
24 ***McHugh***	Y	Y	Y	Y	N	Y	Y
25 ***Walsh***	Y	Y	Y	Y	Y	Y	Y
26 Hinchey	?	Y	N	Y	Y	Y	Y
27 ***Reynolds***	Y	Y	Y	Y	?	?	?
28 Slaughter	Y	Y	N	Y	N	Y	Y
29 LaFalce	Y	Y	N	Y	Y	Y	Y
30 ***Quinn***	Y	Y	Y	Y	Y	Y	Y
31 ***Houghton***	?	?	?	Y	Y	Y	Y
NORTH CAROLINA							
1 Clayton	Y	Y	N	Y	Y	Y	Y
2 Etheridge	Y	Y	Y	Y	Y	Y	Y
3 ***Jones***	Y	Y	Y	Y	N	Y	Y
4 Price	Y	Y	Y	Y	Y	Y	Y
5 ***Burr***	Y	Y	Y	Y	N	Y	Y
6 ***Coble***	Y	Y	Y	Y	N	Y	Y
7 McIntyre	+	+	+	Y	Y	Y	Y
8 ***Hayes***	Y	Y	Y	Y	Y	Y	Y
9 ***Myrick***	?	?	?	Y	N	Y	Y
10 ***Ballenger***	Y	Y	Y	Y	N	Y	Y
11 ***Taylor***	?	?	?	Y	N	Y	Y
12 Watt	Y	Y	N	Y	Y	N	Y
NORTH DAKOTA							
AL Pomeroy	Y	Y	N	Y	Y	Y	Y
OHIO							
1 ***Chabot***	Y	Y	Y	Y	Y	Y	Y
2 ***Portman***	Y	Y	Y	Y	Y	Y	Y
3 Hall	Y	Y	N	Y	Y	Y	Y
4 ***Oxley***	Y	Y	Y	Y	Y	Y	Y
5 ***Gillmor***	Y	Y	Y	Y	Y	Y	Y
6 Strickland	Y	Y	N	Y	Y	Y	Y
7 ***Hobson***	Y	Y	Y	Y	Y	Y	Y
8 ***Boehner***	?	?	?	Y	Y	Y	Y
9 Kaptur	Y	Y	N	Y	Y	Y	Y
10 Kucinich	Y	Y	N	Y	N	Y	Y
11 Jones	+	+	+	Y	Y	Y	Y
12 ***Kasich***	Y	Y	Y	Y	Y	Y	Y
13 Brown	?	Y	N	Y	Y	Y	Y
14 Sawyer	Y	Y	N	Y	Y	?	?
15 ***Pryce***	?	?	?	Y	Y	Y	Y
16 ***Regula***	Y	Y	Y	Y	Y	Y	Y
17 Traficant	Y	Y	Y	Y	N	Y	Y
18 ***Ney***	Y	Y	Y	Y	Y	Y	Y
19 ***LaTourette***	Y	Y	Y	Y	Y	Y	Y
OKLAHOMA							
1 ***Largent***	Y	Y	?	Y	N	Y	Y
2 ***Coburn***	?	?	?	Y	N	Y	Y
3 ***Watkins***	?	?	?	Y	N	Y	?
4 ***Watts***	+	+	+	Y	N	Y	Y
5 ***Istook***	Y	Y	Y	Y	N	Y	Y
6 ***Lucas***	Y	Y	Y	Y	N	Y	Y
OREGON							
1 Wu	Y	Y	Y	Y	Y	Y	Y
2 ***Walden***	Y	Y	Y	Y	Y	Y	Y
3 Blumenauer	Y	Y	Y	Y	N	Y	Y
4 DeFazio	Y	Y	N	Y	N	Y	Y
5 Hooley	Y	Y	Y	Y	Y	Y	Y
PENNSYLVANIA							
1 Brady	Y	Y	N	?	?	?	?
2 Fattah	Y	Y	N	?	?	?	?
3 Borski	Y	Y	N	?	?	?	?
4 Klink	?	?	?	Y	Y	Y	Y
5 ***Peterson***	Y	Y	Y	Y	Y	Y	Y
6 Holden	?	?	?	Y	Y	Y	Y
7 ***Weldon***	?	?	?	?	?	?	?
8 ***Greenwood***	?	?	?	Y	Y	Y	Y
9 ***Shuster***	Y	Y	Y	Y	N	Y	Y
10 ***Sherwood***	Y	Y	Y	Y	N	Y	Y
11 Kanjorski	Y	Y	N	Y	Y	Y	Y
12 Murtha	Y	Y	N	Y	Y	Y	Y
13 Hoeffel	Y	Y	N	Y	Y	Y	Y
14 Coyne	?	?	?	Y	Y	Y	Y
15 ***Toomey***	?	?	?	Y	N	Y	Y
16 ***Pitts***	Y	Y	Y	Y	N	Y	Y
17 ***Gekas***	Y	Y	Y	Y	Y	Y	Y
18 Doyle	?	?	?	Y	Y	Y	Y
19 ***Goodling***	?	?	?	Y	Y	Y	Y
20 Mascara	Y	Y	N	Y	Y	Y	Y
21 ***English***	Y	Y	Y	Y	Y	Y	Y
RHODE ISLAND							
1 Kennedy	Y	Y	?	Y	Y	Y	Y
2 Weygand	Y	Y	Y	Y	Y	Y	Y
SOUTH CAROLINA							
1 ***Sanford***	N	Y	Y	Y	N	N	Y
2 ***Spence***	Y	Y	Y	Y	N	Y	Y
3 ***Graham***	Y	Y	Y	Y	N	Y	Y
4 ***DeMint***	Y	Y	Y	Y	N	Y	Y
5 Spratt	Y	Y	N	Y	Y	Y	Y
6 Clyburn	Y	Y	N	Y	Y	Y	Y
SOUTH DAKOTA							
AL ***Thune***	Y	Y	Y	Y	N	Y	Y
TENNESSEE							
1 ***Jenkins***	Y	Y	Y	Y	N	Y	Y
2 ***Duncan***	Y	Y	N	Y	N	Y	Y
3 ***Wamp***	?	?	?	Y	N	Y	Y
4 ***Hilleary***	Y	Y	Y	Y	N	Y	Y
5 Clement	Y	Y	Y	Y	Y	Y	Y
6 Gordon	Y	Y	Y	Y	Y	Y	Y
7 ***Bryant***	Y	Y	Y	Y	N	Y	Y
8 Tanner	Y	Y	N	Y	Y	Y	Y
9 Ford	Y	Y	N	Y	Y	Y	Y
TEXAS							
1 Sandlin	+	+	+	Y	Y	Y	Y
2 Turner	Y	Y	Y	Y	Y	Y	Y
3 ***Johnson, Sam***	Y	Y	Y	Y	N	Y	Y
4 Hall	Y	Y	Y	Y	N	Y	Y
5 ***Sessions***	?	?	?	Y	N	Y	Y
6 ***Barton***	Y	Y	Y	Y	N	Y	Y
7 ***Archer***	?	?	?	Y	N	Y	Y
8 ***Brady***	Y	Y	Y	Y	Y	Y	Y
9 Lampson	Y	Y	N	Y	Y	Y	Y
10 Doggett	Y	Y	Y	Y	Y	Y	Y
11 Edwards	Y	Y	N	Y	Y	Y	Y
12 ***Granger***	Y	Y	Y	Y	Y	Y	Y
13 ***Thornberry***	Y	Y	Y	Y	Y	Y	Y
14 ***Paul***	N	Y	N	N	N	N	Y
15 Hinojosa	+	+	−	Y	Y	Y	Y
16 Reyes	Y	Y	N	Y	Y	Y	Y
17 Stenholm	Y	Y	Y	Y	Y	Y	Y
18 Jackson-Lee	+	+	−	Y	Y	Y	Y
19 ***Combest***	Y	Y	Y	Y	N	Y	Y
20 Gonzalez	Y	Y	N	Y	Y	N	Y
21 ***Smith***	Y	Y	Y	Y	Y	Y	Y
22 ***DeLay***	?	?	?	Y	N	Y	Y
23 ***Bonilla***	Y	?	Y	Y	N	Y	Y
24 Frost	Y	Y	Y	Y	Y	Y	Y
25 Bentsen	Y	Y	N	Y	Y	Y	Y
26 ***Armey***	Y	Y	Y	Y	Y	Y	Y
27 Ortiz	Y	Y	N	Y	Y	Y	Y
28 Rodriguez	Y	Y	N	Y	Y	N	Y
29 Green	Y	Y	Y	Y	Y	Y	Y
30 Johnson, E.B.	Y	Y	N	Y	Y	Y	Y
UTAH							
1 ***Hansen***	Y	Y	Y	Y	N	Y	Y
2 ***Cook***	?	?	?	Y	N	Y	Y
3 ***Cannon***	Y	Y	Y	?	?	?	?
VERMONT							
AL *Sanders*	+	+	−	Y	N	N	Y
VIRGINIA							
1 ***Bateman***	Y	Y	Y	Y	Y	Y	Y
2 Pickett	Y	Y	Y	Y	Y	Y	Y
3 Scott	Y	Y	N	Y	Y	N	Y
4 Sisisky	Y	Y	Y	Y	Y	Y	Y
5 Goode	Y	Y	Y	Y	N	Y	Y
6 ***Goodlatte***	Y	Y	Y	Y	Y	Y	Y
7 ***Bliley***	Y	Y	Y	?	?	?	?
8 Moran	Y	Y	Y	Y	Y	Y	Y
9 Boucher	Y	Y	Y	Y	Y	Y	Y
10 ***Wolf***	Y	Y	Y	Y	Y	Y	Y
11 ***Davis***	Y	Y	Y	Y	Y	Y	Y
WASHINGTON							
1 Inslee	Y	Y	Y	Y	Y	Y	Y
2 ***Metcalf***	N	Y	Y	Y	N	Y	Y
3 Baird	Y	Y	N	Y	Y	Y	Y
4 ***Hastings***	Y	Y	Y	Y	Y	Y	Y
5 ***Nethercutt***	Y	Y	Y	Y	Y	Y	Y
6 Dicks	Y	Y	N	Y	Y	Y	Y
7 McDermott	Y	Y	N	Y	N	N	Y
8 ***Dunn***	Y	Y	Y	Y	Y	Y	Y
9 Smith	?	?	?	Y	Y	Y	Y
WEST VIRGINIA							
1 Mollohan	Y	Y	N	Y	Y	Y	Y
2 Wise	Y	Y	N	Y	Y	Y	Y
3 Rahall	Y	Y	N	Y	Y	Y	Y
WISCONSIN							
1 ***Ryan***	Y	Y	Y	Y	Y	Y	Y
2 Baldwin	Y	Y	N	Y	N	Y	Y
3 Kind	Y	Y	Y	Y	Y	Y	Y
4 Kleczka	Y	Y	N	Y	Y	Y	Y
5 Barrett	Y	Y	N	Y	Y	Y	Y
6 ***Petri***	Y	Y	Y	Y	N	Y	Y
7 Obey	Y	Y	N	Y	N	Y	Y
8 ***Green***	Y	Y	Y	Y	Y	Y	Y
9 ***Sensenbrenner***	Y	Y	Y	Y	N	Y	Y
WYOMING							
AL ***Cubin***	?	?	?	Y	N	Y	Y

Southern states - Ala., Ark., Fla., Ga., Ky., La., Miss., N.C., Okla., S.C., Tenn., Texas, Va.

557. Procedural Motion/Journal. Approval of the House Journal of Tuesday, Nov. 2, 1999. Approved 336-59: R 185-19; D 150-40 (ND 114-31, SD 36-9); I 1-0. Nov. 3, 1999.

558. HR 2990. Access to Care for the Uninsured/Motion to Instruct. Dingell, D-Mich., motion to instruct House conferees to insist upon the provisions of HR 2990 as passed by the House and to insist that the provisions be paid for. Motion agreed to 257-167: R 52-165; D 204-2 (ND 151-1, SD 53-1); I 1-0. Nov. 3, 1999.

559. HR 2389. Timber Revenues for Rural Communities/Optional Use of Forest Land Payment. Udall, D-Colo., amendment to allow, but not require, counties to use 20 percent of their forest lands payments for projects on federal land. Under the bill, counties receiving an annual payment of more than $100,000 would be required to devote 20 percent of the funds to projects on federal land. Rejected 186-241: R 27-189; D 158-52 (ND 135-20, SD 23-32); I 1-0. Nov. 3, 1999.

560. HR 2389. Timber Revenues for Rural Communities/Passage. Passage of the bill to stabilize federal revenue-sharing payments over seven years to rural counties adjacent to National Forest Service lands and Bureau of Land Management lands. The annual payments, to make up for property taxes the county loses because it cannot tax federal land, would have to equal the average federal payment of the highest three years since Oct. 1, 1983. Counties receiving more than $100,000 in payments would be required to use 20 percent of the payments for projects on federal land, with the rest available for roads and schools. Passed 274-153: R 187-29; D 87-123 (ND 46-109, SD 41-14); I 0-1. Nov. 3, 1999. A "nay" was a vote in support of the president's position.

561. H Res 353. Expedited Floor Procedures/Adoption. Adoption of the resolution to allow legislation to be considered under suspension of the rules at any time on or before Nov. 10, 1999. Adopted 222-200: R 215-1; D 7-198 (ND 6-145, SD 1-53); I 0-1. Nov. 3, 1999.

562. HR 3194. Fiscal 2000 District of Columbia Appropriations/Passage. Passage of the bill to provide $429.1 million in federal funds for the District of Columbia and approve the District's $6.8 billion budget. The measure would prohibit the use of federal or local funds for public or private needle-exchange programs for drug addicts. Passed 216-210: R 210-8; D 6-201 (ND 3-149, SD 3-52); I 0-1. Nov. 3, 1999.

563. Procedural Motion/Journal. Approval of the House Journal of Wednesday, Nov. 3, 1999. Approved 346-65: R 187-22; D 158-43 (ND 113-35, SD 45-8); I 1-0. Nov. 4, 1999.

Key

Y Voted for (yea).
\# Paired for.
\+ Announced for.
N Voted against (nay).
X Paired against.
– Announced against.
P Voted "present."
C Voted "present" to avoid possible conflict of interest.
? Did not vote or otherwise make a position known.

•

Democrats ***Republicans***
Independents

	557	558	559	560	561	562	563
ALABAMA							
1 ***Callahan***	?	N	N	Y	Y	Y	Y
2 ***Everett***	N	N	N	Y	Y	Y	Y
3 ***Riley***	N	N	N	Y	Y	Y	N
4 ***Aderholt***	N	N	N	Y	Y	Y	N
5 Cramer	Y	Y	N	Y	N	N	Y
6 ***Bachus***	Y	Y	N	Y	Y	Y	Y
7 Hilliard	N	Y	Y	Y	N	N	N
ALASKA							
AL ***Young***	?	Y	N	Y	Y	Y	?
ARIZONA							
1 ***Salmon***	Y	N	N	Y	Y	Y	Y
2 Pastor	N	Y	Y	N	N	N	N
3 ***Stump***	Y	N	N	Y	Y	Y	Y
4 ***Shadegg***	Y	N	N	Y	Y	Y	Y
5 ***Kolbe***	?	N	N	N	Y	Y	Y
6 ***Hayworth***	Y	N	N	Y	Y	Y	Y
ARKANSAS							
1 Berry	N	Y	Y	Y	N	N	N
2 Snyder	Y	Y	Y	Y	N	N	Y
3 ***Hutchinson***	N	N	Y	Y	Y	Y	N
4 ***Dickey***	N	N	Y	Y	N	Y	N
CALIFORNIA							
1 Thompson	N	Y	Y	Y	N	N	N
2 ***Herger***	Y	N	N	Y	Y	Y	Y
3 ***Ose***	Y	N	N	Y	Y	Y	Y
4 ***Doolittle***	Y	N	N	Y	Y	Y	Y
5 Matsui	Y	Y	Y	N	N	N	Y
6 Woolsey	Y	Y	Y	N	N	N	Y
7 Miller, George	N	Y	Y	N	N	N	Y
8 Pelosi	Y	Y	Y	N	N	N	Y
9 Lee	Y	Y	Y	N	N	N	Y
10 Tauscher	Y	Y	N	N	N	N	Y
11 ***Pombo***	Y	N	N	Y	Y	Y	Y
12 Lantos	Y	Y	Y	N	N	N	Y
13 Stark	N	Y	Y	N	N	N	N
14 Eshoo	Y	Y	Y	N	Y	N	Y
15 ***Campbell***	Y	N	Y	Y	Y	N	Y
16 Lofgren	Y	Y	N	N	N	N	Y
17 Farr	Y	Y	Y	N	P	N	Y
18 Condit	Y	Y	Y	Y	N	N	Y
19 ***Radanovich***	Y	N	N	Y	Y	Y	Y
20 Dooley	Y	Y	Y	Y	Y	N	Y
21 ***Thomas***	Y	N	N	Y	Y	Y	Y
22 Capps	Y	Y	Y	N	N	N	Y
23 ***Gallegly***	Y	N	N	Y	Y	Y	Y
24 Sherman	Y	Y	Y	N	Y	N	Y
25 ***McKeon***	Y	N	N	Y	Y	Y	Y
26 Berman	?	?	Y	N	N	N	Y
27 ***Rogan***	N	N	N	Y	Y	Y	N
28 ***Dreier***	Y	N	N	Y	Y	Y	Y
29 Waxman	Y	Y	Y	N	N	N	Y
30 Becerra	Y	Y	Y	N	N	N	Y
31 Martinez	Y	Y	Y	Y	N	N	Y
32 Dixon	Y	Y	Y	N	N	N	Y
33 Roybal-Allard	Y	Y	Y	N	N	N	Y
34 Napolitano	Y	Y	Y	Y	N	N	Y
35 Waters	N	Y	Y	N	N	N	N
36 ***Kuykendall***	Y	N	N	Y	Y	Y	Y
37 Millender-McD.	Y	Y	Y	N	–	N	Y
38 ***Horn***	Y	Y	Y	Y	Y	Y	Y
39 ***Royce***	Y	N	Y	Y	Y	Y	Y
40 ***Lewis***	Y	N	N	Y	Y	Y	Y
41 ***Miller***	Y	N	N	Y	Y	Y	Y
42 Vacant							
43 ***Calvert***	Y	N	N	Y	Y	Y	Y
44 ***Bono***	Y	Y	N	Y	Y	Y	Y
45 ***Rohrabacher***	Y	N	Y	Y	Y	Y	Y
46 Sanchez	Y	Y	Y	Y	N	N	Y
47 ***Cox***	Y	N	N	Y	Y	Y	Y
48 ***Packard***	Y	N	N	Y	Y	Y	Y
49 ***Bilbray***	N	Y	N	N	Y	Y	N
50 Filner	N	Y	Y	N	N	N	N
51 ***Cunningham***	Y	N	N	Y	Y	Y	Y
52 ***Hunter***	?	Y	N	Y	Y	Y	?
COLORADO							
1 DeGette	Y	Y	Y	N	N	N	Y
2 Udall	N	Y	Y	N	N	N	Y
3 ***McInnis***	Y	N	Y	Y	Y	Y	Y
4 ***Schaffer***	N	N	N	Y	Y	N	N
5 ***Hefley***	N	N	N	Y	Y	Y	N
6 ***Tancredo***	P	N	N	Y	Y	N	N
CONNECTICUT							
1 Larson	Y	Y	Y	N	N	N	?
2 Gejdenson	Y	Y	Y	N	N	N	Y
3 DeLauro	Y	Y	Y	N	N	N	Y
4 ***Shays***	Y	Y	Y	N	Y	Y	Y
5 Maloney	Y	Y	Y	N	N	N	Y
6 ***Johnson***	Y	Y	Y	Y	Y	Y	Y
DELAWARE							
AL ***Castle***	Y	Y	Y	N	Y	Y	Y
FLORIDA							
1 ***Scarborough***	?	?	?	?	?	?	?
2 Boyd	Y	Y	N	Y	N	N	Y
3 Brown	Y	Y	N	N	N	N	Y
4 ***Fowler***	Y	N	N	Y	Y	Y	Y
5 Thurman	Y	Y	N	Y	N	N	Y
6 ***Stearns***	Y	N	Y	N	Y	Y	Y
7 ***Mica***	Y	N	N	Y	Y	Y	Y
8 ***McCollum***	Y	Y	N	Y	Y	Y	Y
9 ***Bilirakis***	Y	N	N	Y	Y	Y	Y
10 ***Young***	Y	Y	N	Y	Y	Y	Y
11 Davis	Y	Y	N	Y	N	N	?
12 ***Canady***	Y	N	N	Y	Y	Y	Y
13 ***Miller***	Y	N	N	N	Y	Y	Y
14 ***Goss***	Y	N	N	Y	Y	Y	Y
15 ***Weldon***	Y	Y	N	Y	Y	Y	Y
16 ***Foley***	Y	Y	N	Y	Y	Y	Y
17 Meek	?	Y	Y	N	N	N	?
18 ***Ros-Lehtinen***	Y	Y	N	Y	Y	Y	Y
19 Wexler	Y	Y	Y	N	N	N	Y
20 Deutsch	Y	Y	Y	N	N	N	Y
21 ***Diaz-Balart***	Y	Y	N	Y	Y	Y	Y
22 ***Shaw***	Y	Y	N	Y	Y	Y	Y
23 Hastings	N	Y	Y	N	N	N	Y
GEORGIA							
1 ***Kingston***	Y	N	N	Y	Y	Y	Y
2 Bishop	Y	Y	N	Y	N	N	Y
3 ***Collins***	Y	N	N	Y	Y	Y	Y
4 McKinney	Y	Y	Y	N	N	N	Y
5 Lewis	N	Y	Y	N	N	N	N
6 ***Isakson***	?	N	N	Y	Y	Y	Y
7 ***Barr***	Y	Y	N	Y	Y	Y	Y
8 ***Chambliss***	Y	Y	N	Y	Y	Y	Y
9 ***Deal***	Y	N	N	Y	Y	Y	Y
10 ***Norwood***	Y	Y	N	Y	Y	Y	Y
11 ***Linder***	Y	N	N	Y	Y	Y	Y
HAWAII							
1 Abercrombie	Y	Y	Y	N	N	N	Y
2 Mink	Y	Y	Y	N	N	N	Y
IDAHO							
1 ***Chenoweth-Hage***	Y	N	N	Y	Y	N	N
2 ***Simpson***	Y	N	N	Y	Y	Y	Y
ILLINOIS							
1 Rush	Y	?	Y	N	N	N	Y
2 Jackson	Y	Y	Y	N	N	N	Y
3 Lipinski	N	Y	N	Y	N	N	N
4 Gutierrez	N	Y	Y	Y	N	N	Y
5 Blagojevich	Y	Y	Y	N	N	N	Y
6 ***Hyde***	Y	Y	N	Y	Y	Y	Y
7 Davis	Y	Y	Y	N	N	N	Y
8 ***Crane***	?	N	N	N	Y	Y	N
9 Schakowsky	Y	Y	Y	N	N	N	Y
10 ***Porter***	Y	Y	Y	N	Y	Y	Y
11 ***Weller***	N	Y	N	Y	Y	Y	N
12 Costello	N	Y	Y	Y	N	N	N
13 ***Biggert***	Y	N	N	Y	Y	Y	Y
14 ***Hastert***						Y	

ND Northern Democrats SD Southern Democrats

	557	558	559	560	561	562	563
15 ***Ewing***	Y	N	N	Y	Y	Y	Y
16 ***Manzullo***	Y	N	N	Y	Y	Y	Y
17 Evans	Y	Y	Y	N	N	N	N
18 ***LaHood***	Y	N	N	Y	Y	Y	Y
19 Phelps	Y	Y	N	Y	N	N	N
20 ***Shimkus***	Y	N	N	Y	Y	Y	Y
INDIANA							
1 Visclosky	N	Y	Y	Y	N	N	N
2 ***McIntosh***	Y	N	N	Y	Y	Y	Y
3 Roemer	Y	Y	Y	Y	N	N	Y
4 ***Souder***	Y	N	?	Y	Y	Y	Y
5 ***Buyer***	Y	N	N	Y	Y	Y	Y
6 ***Burton***	?	N	N	Y	Y	Y	Y
7 ***Pease***	Y	N	N	Y	Y	Y	Y
8 ***Hostettler***	Y	N	N	Y	Y	Y	Y
9 Hill	Y	Y	Y	Y	N	N	Y
10 Carson	P	Y	Y	N	N	N	Y
IOWA							
1 ***Leach***	Y	Y	Y	Y	Y	Y	Y
2 ***Nussle***	Y	N	N	Y	Y	Y	Y
3 Boswell	Y	Y	N	Y	N	N	Y
4 ***Ganske***	Y	Y	Y	Y	Y	Y	Y
5 ***Latham***	Y	N	N	Y	Y	Y	N
KANSAS							
1 ***Moran***	Y	N	N	Y	Y	Y	Y
2 ***Ryun***	Y	N	N	Y	Y	Y	Y
3 Moore	N	Y	Y	Y	N	N	N
4 ***Tiahrt***	Y	N	N	Y	Y	Y	Y
KENTUCKY							
1 ***Whitfield***	Y	N	N	Y	Y	Y	Y
2 ***Lewis***	Y	N	N	Y	Y	Y	Y
3 ***Northup***	Y	N	N	Y	Y	Y	Y
4 Lucas	Y	Y	N	Y	N	Y	Y
5 ***Rogers***	Y	N	N	Y	Y	Y	Y
6 ***Fletcher***	Y	N	N	Y	Y	Y	Y
LOUISIANA							
1 ***Vitter***	Y	N	N	Y	Y	Y	Y
2 Jefferson	Y	Y	Y	N	N	N	Y
3 ***Tauzin***	Y	N	N	Y	Y	Y	Y
4 ***McCrery***	?	N	N	Y	Y	Y	Y
5 ***Cooksey***	Y	Y	N	Y	Y	Y	?
6 ***Baker***	Y	N	N	Y	Y	Y	Y
7 John	Y	Y	N	Y	N	N	Y
MAINE							
1 Allen	Y	Y	Y	Y	N	N	N
2 Baldacci	Y	Y	Y	Y	N	N	Y
MARYLAND							
1 ***Gilchrest***	Y	Y	N	Y	Y	Y	Y
2 ***Ehrlich***	Y	N	N	Y	Y	Y	Y
3 Cardin	Y	Y	Y	N	N	N	Y
4 Wynn	Y	Y	N	N	N	N	Y
5 Hoyer	Y	Y	N	Y	N	N	Y
6 ***Bartlett***	Y	N	N	Y	Y	Y	Y
7 Cummings	Y	Y	Y	N	N	N	Y
8 ***Morella***	Y	Y	Y	Y	Y	N	Y
MASSACHUSETTS							
1 Olver	Y	Y	Y	N	N	N	Y
2 Neal	Y	Y	Y	N	N	N	Y
3 McGovern	Y	Y	Y	N	N	N	Y
4 Frank	Y	Y	Y	N	N	N	Y
5 Meehan	Y	Y	Y	N	N	N	Y
6 Tierney	Y	Y	Y	N	N	N	Y
7 Markey	N	Y	Y	N	N	N	N
8 Capuano	Y	Y	Y	N	N	N	Y
9 Moakley	Y	Y	Y	N	N	N	Y
10 Delahunt	Y	Y	Y	N	N	N	Y
MICHIGAN							
1 Stupak	N	Y	Y	Y	N	N	N
2 ***Hoekstra***	Y	N	N	Y	Y	Y	Y
3 ***Ehlers***	Y	N	N	Y	Y	Y	Y
4 ***Camp***	Y	N	N	Y	Y	Y	Y
5 Barcia	Y	Y	Y	Y	N	Y	N
6 ***Upton***	Y	N	N	N	Y	Y	Y
7 ***Smith***	Y	N	N	Y	Y	Y	Y
8 Stabenow	Y	Y	Y	N	N	N	Y
9 Kildee	Y	Y	Y	N	N	N	Y
10 Bonior	?	Y	Y	N	N	N	Y
11 ***Knollenberg***	Y	N	N	Y	Y	Y	Y
12 Levin	Y	Y	Y	N	N	N	Y
13 Rivers	Y	Y	Y	N	N	N	Y
14 Conyers	Y	Y	Y	N	N	N	Y
15 Kilpatrick	Y	Y	+	–	–	–	Y
16 Dingell	Y	Y	N	Y	N	N	Y
MINNESOTA							
1 ***Gutknecht***	?	N	N	Y	Y	Y	N
2 Minge	Y	Y	Y	N	N	N	Y
3 ***Ramstad***	N	N	Y	N	Y	Y	N
4 Vento	Y	Y	Y	N	N	N	Y
5 Sabo	N	Y	Y	N	N	N	N
6 Luther	Y	Y	Y	N	N	N	Y
7 Peterson	N	N	N	Y	N	N	N
8 Oberstar	N	Y	N	N	N	N	N
MISSISSIPPI							
1 ***Wicker***	N	N	N	Y	Y	Y	N
2 Thompson	N	Y	Y	N	N	N	N
3 ***Pickering***	Y	N	N	Y	Y	Y	Y
4 Shows	?	Y	N	Y	N	N	Y
5 Taylor	N	Y	N	Y	N	N	N
MISSOURI							
1 Clay	N	Y	Y	N	N	N	N
2 ***Talent***	Y	N	N	Y	Y	Y	Y
3 Gephardt	Y	Y	Y	N	N	N	Y
4 Skelton	?	Y	N	Y	N	N	Y
5 McCarthy	Y	Y	Y	N	N	N	Y
6 Danner	Y	Y	N	Y	N	N	Y
7 ***Blunt***	Y	N	N	Y	Y	Y	Y
8 ***Emerson***	Y	Y	N	Y	Y	Y	?
9 ***Hulshof***	+	–	–	+	+	+	+
MONTANA							
AL ***Hill***	N	N	N	Y	Y	Y	N
NEBRASKA							
1 ***Bereuter***	Y	?	?	?	?	?	?
2 ***Terry***	Y	N	N	Y	Y	Y	Y
3 ***Barrett***	Y	N	N	Y	Y	Y	Y
NEVADA							
1 Berkley	Y	Y	Y	N	N	N	Y
2 ***Gibbons***	N	Y	N	Y	Y	Y	N
NEW HAMPSHIRE							
1 ***Sununu***	Y	N	N	N	Y	Y	Y
2 ***Bass***	Y	N	N	Y	Y	Y	Y
NEW JERSEY							
1 Andrews	Y	Y	Y	N	N	N	Y
2 ***LoBiondo***	N	Y	Y	N	Y	Y	N
3 ***Saxton***	Y	Y	N	N	Y	Y	Y
4 ***Smith***	Y	Y	Y	N	Y	Y	Y
5 ***Roukema***	Y	Y	N	N	Y	Y	Y
6 Pallone	N	Y	Y	N	N	N	N
7 ***Franks***	Y	Y	N	N	Y	Y	Y
8 Pascrell	Y	Y	Y	N	N	N	Y
9 Rothman	Y	Y	Y	Y	Y	N	Y
10 Payne	Y	Y	Y	N	N	N	?
11 ***Frelinghuysen***	Y	Y	N	N	Y	Y	Y
12 Holt	Y	Y	Y	N	N	N	Y
13 Menendez	Y	Y	Y	N	N	N	Y
NEW MEXICO							
1 ***Wilson***	Y	N	N	Y	Y	Y	Y
2 ***Skeen***	Y	N	N	Y	Y	Y	Y
3 Udall	N	Y	Y	Y	N	N	N
NEW YORK							
1 Forbes	Y	Y	Y	N	N	N	Y
2 ***Lazio***	Y	N	N	Y	Y	Y	Y
3 ***King***	Y	Y	N	Y	Y	Y	Y
4 McCarthy	Y	Y	Y	N	N	N	Y
5 Ackerman	Y	Y	Y	N	?	N	Y
6 Meeks	Y	Y	Y	N	N	N	N
7 Crowley	Y	Y	Y	N	N	N	Y
8 Nadler	Y	Y	Y	N	N	N	Y
9 Weiner	Y	Y	Y	N	N	N	Y
10 Towns	Y	Y	Y	N	N	N	Y
11 Owens	Y	Y	Y	N	N	N	Y
12 Velázquez	Y	Y	Y	Y	N	N	Y
13 ***Fossella***	Y	N	N	Y	Y	Y	Y
14 Maloney	Y	Y	N	N	N	?	Y
15 Rangel	Y	Y	Y	N	N	N	Y
16 Serrano	Y	Y	Y	N	N	N	Y
17 Engel	?	Y	Y	N	N	N	Y
18 Lowey	Y	Y	Y	N	N	N	Y
19 ***Kelly***	Y	N	N	Y	Y	Y	Y
20 ***Gilman***	Y	Y	Y	N	Y	Y	Y
21 McNulty	N	Y	Y	N	Y	N	N
22 ***Sweeney***	Y	N	Y	Y	Y	Y	Y
23 ***Boehlert***	Y	Y	N	Y	Y	Y	Y
24 ***McHugh***	Y	Y	Y	Y	Y	Y	Y
25 ***Walsh***	Y	Y	Y	Y	Y	Y	Y
26 Hinchey	N	Y	Y	N	N	N	Y
27 ***Reynolds***	?	Y	N	Y	Y	Y	Y
28 Slaughter	?	Y	Y	N	N	N	N
29 LaFalce	Y	Y	Y	N	N	N	Y
30 ***Quinn***	Y	Y	N	Y	Y	Y	Y
31 ***Houghton***	Y	N	N	Y	Y	Y	Y
NORTH CAROLINA							
1 Clayton	Y	Y	N	Y	N	N	Y
2 Etheridge	Y	Y	N	Y	N	N	Y
3 ***Jones***	Y	Y	N	Y	Y	Y	Y
4 Price	Y	Y	Y	Y	N	N	Y
5 ***Burr***	Y	N	N	Y	Y	Y	?
6 ***Coble***	Y	Y	N	Y	Y	Y	Y
7 McIntyre	Y	Y	N	Y	N	Y	Y
8 ***Hayes***	Y	N	N	Y	Y	Y	Y
9 ***Myrick***	Y	N	N	Y	Y	Y	?
10 ***Ballenger***	Y	N	N	Y	Y	Y	Y
11 ***Taylor***	Y	N	N	Y	Y	Y	Y
12 Watt	Y	Y	Y	Y	N	N	Y
NORTH DAKOTA							
AL Pomeroy	Y	Y	N	Y	N	N	Y
OHIO							
1 ***Chabot***	Y	N	N	Y	Y	Y	Y
2 ***Portman***	Y	N	N	N	Y	Y	Y
3 Hall	Y	Y	Y	Y	N	N	Y
4 ***Oxley***	Y	N	N	Y	Y	Y	Y
5 ***Gillmor***	Y	N	N	Y	Y	Y	Y
6 Strickland	N	Y	Y	Y	N	N	N
7 ***Hobson***	Y	N	N	Y	Y	Y	Y
8 ***Boehner***	Y	N	N	Y	Y	Y	Y
9 Kaptur	Y	Y	Y	N	N	N	Y
10 Kucinich	N	Y	Y	N	N	N	N
11 Jones	Y	Y	Y	N	N	N	Y
12 ***Kasich***	?	N	Y	Y	Y	Y	?
13 Brown	Y	Y	Y	N	N	N	N
14 Sawyer	?	?	Y	N	N	N	Y
15 ***Pryce***	Y	N	N	Y	Y	Y	Y
16 ***Regula***	Y	N	N	N	Y	Y	Y
17 Traficant	Y	Y	N	Y	Y	Y	Y
18 ***Ney***	Y	N	N	Y	Y	Y	Y
19 ***LaTourette***	Y	Y	N	Y	Y	Y	Y
OKLAHOMA							
1 ***Largent***	Y	N	N	N	Y	Y	Y
2 ***Coburn***	N	N	N	N	Y	Y	Y
3 ***Watkins***	Y	N	N	Y	Y	Y	?
4 ***Watts***	?	N	N	Y	Y	Y	Y
5 ***Istook***	Y	N	N	Y	Y	Y	Y
6 ***Lucas***	Y	N	N	Y	Y	Y	Y
OREGON							
1 Wu	N	Y	Y	Y	N	N	N
2 ***Walden***	Y	N	N	Y	Y	Y	Y
3 Blumenauer	Y	Y	Y	Y	N	N	Y
4 DeFazio	N	Y	N	Y	N	N	N
5 Hooley	N	Y	N	Y	N	N	Y
PENNSYLVANIA							
1 Brady	?	Y	Y	N	N	N	N
2 Fattah	Y	Y	Y	N	N	N	N
3 Borski	N	Y	Y	N	N	N	N
4 Klink	N	Y	N	Y	N	N	N
5 ***Peterson***	Y	N	N	Y	Y	Y	Y
6 Holden	Y	Y	Y	N	N	N	Y
7 ***Weldon***	?	?	?	?	?	?	Y
8 ***Greenwood***	Y	N	N	Y	Y	Y	Y
9 ***Shuster***	Y	N	N	Y	Y	Y	Y
10 ***Sherwood***	Y	N	N	Y	Y	Y	Y
11 Kanjorski	Y	Y	Y	N	N	N	?
12 Murtha	Y	?	N	Y	N	?	?
13 Hoeffel	Y	Y	Y	N	N	N	Y
14 Coyne	Y	Y	Y	N	N	N	Y
15 ***Toomey***	Y	N	N	N	Y	Y	Y
16 ***Pitts***	Y	N	N	Y	Y	Y	Y
17 ***Gekas***	Y	N	N	Y	Y	Y	Y
18 Doyle	Y	Y	Y	Y	N	N	?
19 ***Goodling***	Y	N	N	Y	Y	Y	Y
20 Mascara	Y	Y	N	Y	N	N	Y
21 ***English***	N	N	N	Y	Y	Y	N
RHODE ISLAND							
1 Kennedy	Y	Y	Y	N	N	N	Y
2 Weygand	Y	Y	Y	N	N	N	Y
SOUTH CAROLINA							
1 ***Sanford***	Y	N	N	N	Y	Y	Y
2 ***Spence***	Y	N	N	Y	Y	Y	Y
3 ***Graham***	Y	Y	N	Y	Y	Y	Y
4 ***DeMint***	Y	N	N	Y	Y	Y	Y
5 Spratt	Y	Y	Y	Y	N	N	Y
6 Clyburn	N	Y	Y	N	N	N	Y
SOUTH DAKOTA							
AL ***Thune***	Y	N	N	Y	Y	Y	Y
TENNESSEE							
1 ***Jenkins***	Y	Y	N	Y	Y	Y	Y
2 ***Duncan***	Y	Y	N	Y	Y	N	Y
3 ***Wamp***	N	N	N	N	Y	Y	Y
4 ***Hilleary***	N	N	N	Y	Y	Y	N
5 Clement	Y	Y	N	Y	N	N	Y
6 Gordon	?	Y	N	Y	N	N	Y
7 ***Bryant***	Y	N	N	Y	Y	Y	Y
8 Tanner	Y	Y	N	Y	N	N	Y
9 Ford	Y	Y	N	Y	N	N	Y
TEXAS							
1 Sandlin	Y	Y	N	Y	N	N	Y
2 Turner	Y	Y	N	Y	N	N	Y
3 ***Johnson, Sam***	Y	N	N	Y	Y	Y	Y
4 Hall	Y	Y	N	Y	Y	N	Y
5 ***Sessions***	Y	N	N	Y	Y	Y	?
6 ***Barton***	Y	N	N	Y	Y	Y	Y
7 ***Archer***	Y	N	N	Y	Y	N	Y
8 ***Brady***	Y	Y	N	Y	Y	Y	Y
9 Lampson	Y	Y	N	Y	N	N	Y
10 Doggett	Y	Y	Y	N	N	N	Y
11 Edwards	Y	Y	N	Y	N	N	Y
12 ***Granger***	Y	N	N	Y	Y	Y	Y
13 ***Thornberry***	?	N	N	Y	Y	Y	Y
14 ***Paul***	Y	N	Y	N	Y	N	Y
15 Hinojosa	+	Y	Y	Y	N	N	Y
16 Reyes	?	Y	N	Y	N	N	Y
17 Stenholm	Y	Y	N	Y	N	N	Y
18 Jackson-Lee	+	+	Y	Y	N	N	N
19 ***Combest***	Y	N	N	Y	Y	Y	Y
20 Gonzalez	?	Y	N	N	N	N	Y
21 ***Smith***	Y	N	N	Y	Y	Y	Y
22 ***DeLay***	Y	N	N	Y	Y	Y	Y
23 ***Bonilla***	Y	N	N	Y	Y	Y	Y
24 Frost	Y	Y	N	Y	N	N	Y
25 Bentsen	Y	Y	N	Y	N	N	Y
26 ***Armey***	Y	N	N	Y	Y	Y	Y
27 Ortiz	?	Y	N	Y	N	N	Y
28 Rodriguez	?	Y	Y	Y	N	N	Y
29 Green	Y	Y	N	Y	N	N	Y
30 Johnson, E.B.	Y	Y	Y	Y	N	N	N
UTAH							
1 ***Hansen***	Y	N	N	Y	Y	Y	Y
2 ***Cook***	Y	Y	N	Y	Y	Y	Y
3 ***Cannon***	Y	N	N	Y	Y	Y	Y
VERMONT							
AL *Sanders*	Y	Y	Y	N	N	N	Y
VIRGINIA							
1 ***Bateman***	Y	N	N	Y	Y	Y	Y
2 Pickett	N	Y	N	Y	N	N	N
3 Scott	N	Y	Y	N	?	N	Y
4 Sisisky	Y	Y	N	Y	N	N	Y
5 Goode	Y	N	N	Y	N	Y	Y
6 ***Goodlatte***	Y	N	N	Y	Y	Y	Y
7 ***Bliley***	Y	N	N	Y	Y	Y	Y
8 Moran	?	Y	Y	N	N	N	Y
9 Boucher	Y	Y	Y	Y	N	N	Y
10 ***Wolf***	Y	Y	N	Y	Y	Y	Y
11 ***Davis***	Y	Y	N	Y	Y	Y	Y
WASHINGTON							
1 Inslee	Y	Y	Y	N	N	N	Y
2 ***Metcalf***	Y	N	N	Y	Y	Y	Y
3 Baird	N	Y	Y	Y	N	N	N
4 ***Hastings***	Y	N	N	Y	Y	Y	Y
5 ***Nethercutt***	Y	N	N	Y	Y	Y	Y
6 Dicks	Y	Y	Y	Y	N	N	Y
7 McDermott	N	Y	Y	N	N	N	N
8 ***Dunn***	Y	N	N	Y	?	Y	Y
9 Smith	Y	Y	Y	N	N	N	Y
WEST VIRGINIA							
1 Mollohan	?	Y	Y	Y	N	N	?
2 Wise	?	Y	Y	Y	N	Y	?
3 Rahall	?	Y	Y	Y	?	?	?
WISCONSIN							
1 ***Ryan***	Y	N	N	+	Y	Y	Y
2 Baldwin	Y	Y	Y	N	N	N	Y
3 Kind	Y	Y	Y	Y	N	N	Y
4 Kleczka	Y	Y	Y	N	N	N	Y
5 Barrett	Y	Y	Y	N	N	N	Y
6 ***Petri***	Y	N	N	Y	Y	Y	Y
7 Obey	Y	Y	Y	N	N	N	Y
8 ***Green***	Y	N	N	Y	Y	Y	N
9 ***Sensenbrenner***	Y	N	N	Y	Y	Y	Y
WYOMING							
AL ***Cubin***	Y	N	N	Y	Y	Y	Y

Southern states - Ala., Ark., Fla., Ga., Ky., La., Miss., N.C., Okla., S.C., Tenn., Texas, Va.

564. H Con Res 214. Support for Teaching Phonics/Adoption. McIntosh, R-Ind., motion to suspend the rules and adopt the concurrent resolution to express Congress' support for teaching phonics in schools. The resolution would also state that reading instruction in "far too many" schools is still based on the whole language philosophy "often to the detriment of the students." Motion rejected 224-193: R 201-11; D 23-181 (ND 16-135, SD 7-46); I 0-1. A two-thirds majority of those present and voting (278 in this case) is required for adoption under suspension of the rules. Nov. 4, 1999.

565. H J Res 75. Fiscal 2000 Continuing Appropriations/Passage. Passage of the joint resolution to provide continuing appropriations through Nov. 10 for agencies covered by the fiscal 2000 spending bills not yet enacted. The continuing resolution would set spending levels at the fiscal 1999 level. Passed 417-6: R 214-2; D 202-4 (ND 149-3, SD 53-1); I 1-0. Nov. 4, 1999.

566. Anti-Dumping Trade Laws/Privileged Resolution. LaHood, R-Ill., motion to table (kill) the Visclosky, D-Ind., motion to appeal of the ruling of the chair that his resolution calling on the president to abstain from renegotiating international agreements governing anti-dumping and countervailing measures did not constitute a question of the privileges of the House. Motion agreed to 218-204: R 216-0; D 2-203 (ND 0-150, SD 2-53); I 0-1. Nov. 4, 1999.

567. Anti-Dumping Trade Laws/Privileged Resolution. Kolbe, R-Ariz., motion to table (kill) the Wise, D-W.Va., motion to appeal the ruling of the chair that his resolution calling on the president to abstain from renegotiating international agreements governing anti-dumping and countervailing measures did not constitute a question of the privileges of the House. Motion agreed to 216-201: R 213-0; D 3-200 (ND 1-148, SD 2-52); I 0-1. Nov. 4, 1999.

568. Anti-Dumping Trade Laws/Privileged Resolution. Kolbe, R-Ariz., motion to table (kill) the Kucinich, D-Ohio, motion to appeal the ruling of the chair that his resolution calling on the president to abstain from renegotiating international agreements governing anti-dumping and countervailing measures did not constitute a question of the privileges of the House. Motion agreed to 214-204: R 213-0; D 1-203 (ND 0-150, SD 1-53); I 0-1. Nov. 4, 1999.

569. S 900. Financial Services Overhaul/Rule. Adoption of the rule (H Res 355) to provide for House floor consideration of the conference report to accompany the bill to remove restrictions on cross-ownership among banks, brokerages and insurance companies. Adopted 335-79: R 210-0; D 125-78 (ND 81-67, SD 44-11); I 0-1. Nov. 4, 1999.

570. S 900. Financial Services Overhaul/Conference Report. Adoption of the conference report on the bill that would eliminate current barriers erected by the 1933 Glass-Steagall Act and other laws that impede affiliations between banking, securities, insurance and other firms. The bill also would require that owners of automated teller machines (ATMs) provide notice on the ATM and on-screen of any charges imposed for the use of the terminal. Adopted (thus cleared for the president) 362-57: R 207-5; D 155-51 (ND 108-43, SD 47-8); I 0-1. Nov. 4, 1999.

Key

- Y Voted for (yea).
- # Paired for.
- \+ Announced for.
- N Voted against (nay).
- X Paired against.
- – Announced against.
- P Voted "present."
- C Voted "present" to avoid possible conflict of interest.
- ? Did not vote or otherwise make a position known.

•

Democrats ***Republicans***
Independents

	564	565	566	567	568	569	570
ALABAMA							
1 ***Callahan***	Y	Y	Y	Y	Y	Y	Y
2 ***Everett***	Y	Y	Y	Y	Y	Y	Y
3 ***Riley***	Y	Y	Y	Y	Y	Y	Y
4 ***Aderholt***	Y	Y	Y	Y	Y	Y	Y
5 Cramer	N	Y	N	N	N	Y	Y
6 ***Bachus***	?	Y	Y	Y	Y	Y	Y
7 Hilliard	N	Y	N	N	N	Y	Y
ALASKA							
AL ***Young***	Y	Y	Y	Y	Y	Y	Y
ARIZONA							
1 ***Salmon***	Y	Y	Y	Y	Y	?	Y
2 Pastor	N	Y	N	N	N	Y	Y
3 ***Stump***	Y	Y	Y	Y	Y	Y	Y
4 ***Shadegg***	Y	Y	Y	Y	Y	Y	Y
5 ***Kolbe***	Y	Y	Y	Y	Y	Y	Y
6 ***Hayworth***	Y	Y	Y	Y	Y	Y	Y
ARKANSAS							
1 Berry	N	Y	N	N	N	Y	Y
2 Snyder	N	Y	N	N	N	Y	Y
3 ***Hutchinson***	Y	Y	Y	Y	Y	Y	Y
4 ***Dickey***	Y	N	Y	Y	Y	?	?
CALIFORNIA							
1 Thompson	N	Y	N	N	N	Y	Y
2 ***Herger***	Y	Y	Y	Y	Y	Y	Y
3 ***Ose***	Y	Y	Y	Y	Y	Y	Y
4 ***Doolittle***	Y	Y	Y	Y	Y	Y	Y
5 Matsui	N	Y	N	N	N	Y	Y
6 Woolsey	N	Y	N	N	N	N	N
7 Miller, George	N	N	N	N	N	N	N
8 Pelosi	N	Y	N	N	N	N	Y
9 Lee	N	Y	N	N	N	N	N
10 Tauscher	N	Y	N	N	N	Y	Y
11 ***Pombo***	Y	Y	Y	Y	Y	Y	Y
12 Lantos	N	Y	N	N	N	N	Y
13 Stark	N	Y	?	?	N	?	?
14 Eshoo	N	Y	N	N	N	Y	Y
15 ***Campbell***	Y	Y	Y	Y	Y	Y	N
16 Lofgren	N	Y	N	Y	N	N	Y
17 Farr	N	Y	N	N	N	N	Y
18 Condit	N	Y	N	N	N	N	N
19 ***Radanovich***	Y	Y	Y	Y	?	Y	?
20 Dooley	N	Y	N	N	N	Y	Y
21 ***Thomas***	Y	Y	Y	Y	Y	Y	Y
22 Capps	N	Y	N	N	N	Y	Y
23 ***Gallegly***	Y	Y	Y	Y	Y	Y	Y
24 Sherman	N	Y	N	N	N	Y	Y
25 ***McKeon***	Y	Y	Y	Y	Y	Y	Y
26 Berman	N	Y	N	N	N	Y	Y
27 ***Rogan***	Y	Y	Y	Y	Y	?	Y
28 ***Dreier***	Y	Y	Y	Y	Y	Y	Y
29 Waxman	Y	Y	N	N	N	N	N
30 Becerra	N	Y	N	N	N	N	Y
31 Martinez	N	Y	N	N	N	Y	?
32 Dixon	N	Y	N	N	?	N	N
33 Roybal-Allard	N	Y	N	N	N	N	N
34 Napolitano	N	Y	N	N	N	Y	Y
35 Waters	N	Y	N	N	N	N	N
36 ***Kuykendall***	Y	Y	Y	Y	Y	Y	Y
37 Millender-McD.	N	Y	N	N	N	N	Y
38 ***Horn***	Y	Y	Y	Y	Y	Y	Y
39 ***Royce***	Y	Y	Y	Y	Y	Y	Y
40 ***Lewis***	Y	Y	Y	Y	Y	Y	Y
41 ***Miller***	Y	Y	Y	Y	Y	Y	Y
42 Vacant							
43 ***Calvert***	Y	Y	Y	Y	Y	Y	Y
44 ***Bono***	Y	Y	Y	Y	Y	Y	Y
45 ***Rohrabacher***	Y	Y	Y	Y	Y	Y	Y
46 Sanchez	N	Y	N	N	N	N	Y
47 ***Cox***	Y	Y	Y	Y	Y	Y	Y
48 ***Packard***	Y	Y	Y	Y	Y	Y	Y
49 ***Bilbray***	Y	Y	Y	Y	Y	Y	Y
50 Filner	N	Y	N	N	N	N	N
51 ***Cunningham***	Y	Y	Y	Y	Y	Y	Y
52 ***Hunter***	Y	Y	Y	Y	?	Y	Y
COLORADO							
1 DeGette	N	Y	N	N	N	Y	Y
2 Udall	N	Y	N	N	?	?	Y
3 ***McInnis***	Y	Y	Y	Y	Y	?	?
4 ***Schaffer***	Y	Y	Y	Y	Y	Y	Y
5 ***Hefley***	Y	Y	Y	Y	Y	Y	N
6 ***Tancredo***	Y	Y	Y	Y	Y	Y	Y
CONNECTICUT							
1 Larson	?	?	?	?	?	?	?
2 Gejdenson	N	Y	N	N	N	N	N
3 DeLauro	N	Y	N	N	N	Y	N
4 ***Shays***	Y	Y	Y	?	Y	Y	Y
5 Maloney	Y	Y	N	?	N	Y	Y
6 ***Johnson***	Y	Y	Y	Y	Y	Y	Y
DELAWARE							
AL ***Castle***	Y	Y	Y	Y	Y	Y	Y
FLORIDA							
1 ***Scarborough***	?	?	?	?	?	?	?
2 Boyd	N	Y	N	N	N	Y	Y
3 Brown	N	Y	N	N	N	N	Y
4 ***Fowler***	Y	Y	Y	Y	Y	Y	Y
5 Thurman	N	Y	N	N	N	N	N
6 ***Stearns***	Y	Y	Y	Y	Y	?	Y
7 ***Mica***	Y	Y	Y	Y	Y	Y	N
8 ***McCollum***	Y	Y	Y	Y	Y	Y	Y
9 ***Bilirakis***	Y	Y	Y	Y	Y	Y	Y
10 ***Young***	Y	Y	Y	Y	Y	Y	Y
11 Davis	N	Y	N	N	N	Y	Y
12 ***Canady***	Y	Y	Y	Y	Y	Y	Y
13 ***Miller***	Y	Y	Y	Y	Y	Y	Y
14 ***Goss***	Y	Y	Y	Y	?	Y	Y
15 ***Weldon***	Y	Y	Y	Y	Y	Y	Y
16 ***Foley***	Y	Y	Y	Y	Y	Y	Y
17 Meek	?	Y	N	?	N	N	N
18 ***Ros-Lehtinen***	Y	Y	Y	Y	Y	Y	Y
19 Wexler	N	Y	N	N	N	Y	Y
20 Deutsch	N	Y	N	N	N	Y	Y
21 ***Diaz-Balart***	Y	Y	Y	Y	Y	Y	Y
22 ***Shaw***	Y	Y	Y	Y	Y	Y	Y
23 Hastings	N	N	N	N	N	N	N
GEORGIA							
1 ***Kingston***	Y	Y	Y	Y	Y	Y	Y
2 Bishop	?	Y	N	N	N	Y	Y
3 ***Collins***	Y	Y	Y	Y	Y	Y	Y
4 McKinney	N	Y	N	N	N	N	N
5 Lewis	N	Y	N	N	N	N	N
6 ***Isakson***	Y	Y	Y	Y	Y	Y	Y
7 ***Barr***	Y	Y	Y	Y	Y	Y	Y
8 ***Chambliss***	Y	Y	Y	Y	Y	Y	Y
9 ***Deal***	Y	Y	Y	Y	Y	Y	Y
10 ***Norwood***	Y	?	?	?	?	?	?
11 ***Linder***	?	Y	Y	Y	Y	Y	Y
HAWAII							
1 Abercrombie	P	Y	N	N	N	N	Y
2 Mink	N	Y	N	N	N	N	Y
IDAHO							
1 ***Chenoweth-Hage***	Y	Y	Y	?	Y	Y	Y
2 ***Simpson***	Y	Y	Y	Y	Y	Y	Y
ILLINOIS							
1 Rush	N	Y	N	N	N	N	N
2 Jackson	N	Y	N	N	N	N	N
3 Lipinski	Y	Y	N	N	N	N	N
4 Gutierrez	N	Y	N	N	N	N	N
5 Blagojevich	N	Y	N	N	N	N	Y
6 ***Hyde***	Y	Y	Y	Y	Y	Y	Y
7 Davis	N	Y	N	N	N	N	N
8 ***Crane***	Y	Y	Y	Y	Y	?	Y
9 Schakowsky	N	Y	N	N	N	N	N
10 ***Porter***	Y	Y	Y	?	Y	Y	Y
11 ***Weller***	Y	Y	Y	Y	Y	Y	Y
12 Costello	Y	Y	N	N	N	N	N
13 ***Biggert***	Y	Y	Y	Y	Y	Y	Y
14 ***Hastert***						Y	Y

ND Northern Democrats SD Southern Democrats

	564	565	566	567	568	569	570
15 ***Ewing***	Y	Y	Y	Y	Y	Y	Y
16 ***Manzullo***	Y	Y	Y	Y	Y	Y	Y
17 Evans	N	Y	N	N	N	N	N
18 ***LaHood***	Y	Y	Y	Y	Y	Y	Y
19 Phelps	Y	Y	N	N	N	N	N
20 ***Shimkus***	Y	Y	Y	Y	Y	Y	Y
INDIANA							
1 Visclosky	N	Y	N	N	N	N	Y
2 ***McIntosh***	Y	Y	Y	Y	Y	Y	Y
3 Roemer	N	Y	N	N	N	Y	Y
4 ***Souder***	Y	Y	Y	Y	Y	Y	Y
5 ***Buyer***	Y	Y	Y	Y	Y	Y	Y
6 ***Burton***	Y	Y	Y	Y	Y	Y	Y
7 ***Pease***	Y	Y	Y	Y	Y	Y	Y
8 ***Hostettler***	Y	Y	Y	Y	Y	Y	Y
9 Hill	N	Y	N	N	N	Y	Y
10 Carson	N	Y	N	N	N	N	Y
IOWA							
1 ***Leach***	?	Y	Y	Y	Y	Y	Y
2 ***Nussle***	Y	Y	Y	Y	Y	Y	Y
3 Boswell	Y	Y	N	N	N	Y	Y
4 ***Ganske***	Y	Y	Y	Y	Y	Y	Y
5 ***Latham***	Y	Y	Y	Y	Y	Y	Y
KANSAS							
1 ***Moran***	Y	Y	Y	Y	Y	Y	Y
2 ***Ryun***	Y	Y	Y	Y	Y	Y	Y
3 Moore	N	Y	N	N	N	Y	Y
4 ***Tiahrt***	Y	Y	Y	Y	Y	Y	Y
KENTUCKY							
1 ***Whitfield***	Y	Y	Y	Y	Y	Y	Y
2 ***Lewis***	Y	Y	Y	Y	Y	Y	Y
3 ***Northup***	Y	Y	Y	Y	Y	Y	Y
4 Lucas	N	Y	N	N	N	Y	Y
5 ***Rogers***	Y	Y	Y	Y	Y	Y	Y
6 ***Fletcher***	Y	Y	Y	Y	Y	Y	Y
LOUISIANA							
1 ***Vitter***	Y	Y	Y	Y	Y	Y	Y
2 Jefferson	N	Y	N	N	N	N	Y
3 ***Tauzin***	Y	?	Y	Y	Y	Y	Y
4 ***McCrery***	Y	Y	Y	Y	Y	Y	Y
5 ***Cooksey***	Y	Y	Y	Y	Y	Y	Y
6 ***Baker***	Y	Y	Y	Y	Y	Y	Y
7 John	Y	Y	N	N	N	Y	Y
MAINE							
1 Allen	N	Y	N	N	N	Y	Y
2 Baldacci	N	Y	N	N	N	Y	Y
MARYLAND							
1 ***Gilchrest***	Y	Y	Y	Y	Y	Y	Y
2 ***Ehrlich***	Y	Y	Y	Y	Y	Y	Y
3 Cardin	N	Y	N	N	N	Y	Y
4 Wynn	N	Y	N	N	N	Y	Y
5 Hoyer	N	Y	N	N	N	Y	Y
6 ***Bartlett***	Y	Y	Y	Y	Y	Y	Y
7 Cummings	N	Y	N	N	N	N	Y
8 ***Morella***	Y	Y	Y	Y	Y	Y	Y
MASSACHUSETTS							
1 Olver	N	Y	N	N	N	Y	Y
2 Neal	N	Y	N	N	N	Y	Y
3 McGovern	N	Y	N	N	N	Y	Y
4 Frank	N	Y	N	N	N	?	N
5 Meehan	N	Y	N	N	N	Y	Y
6 Tierney	N	Y	N	N	N	N	N
7 Markey	N	Y	N	N	N	N	N
8 Capuano	N	Y	N	N	N	N	N
9 Moakley	N	Y	N	N	N	Y	Y
10 Delahunt	N	Y	N	N	N	N	Y
MICHIGAN							
1 Stupak	N	Y	N	?	N	Y	Y
2 ***Hoekstra***	N	Y	Y	Y	Y	Y	Y
3 ***Ehlers***	+	+	Y	Y	Y	Y	Y
4 ***Camp***	Y	Y	Y	Y	Y	Y	Y
5 Barcia	N	Y	N	N	N	Y	Y
6 ***Upton***	Y	Y	Y	Y	Y	Y	Y
7 ***Smith***	Y	Y	Y	Y	Y	Y	Y
8 Stabenow	N	Y	N	N	N	Y	Y
9 Kildee	N	Y	N	N	N	N	N
10 Bonior	N	Y	?	N	N	Y	Y
11 ***Knollenberg***	Y	Y	Y	Y	Y	Y	Y
12 Levin	N	Y	N	N	N	Y	Y
13 Rivers	N	Y	N	N	N	N	N
14 Conyers	N	Y	N	?	N	N	N
15 Kilpatrick	N	Y	?	N	N	N	Y
16 Dingell	N	Y	N	N	N	N	N

	564	565	566	567	568	569	570
MINNESOTA							
1 ***Gutknecht***	N	Y	Y	Y	Y	Y	Y
2 Minge	N	Y	N	N	N	Y	Y
3 ***Ramstad***	N	Y	Y	Y	Y	Y	Y
4 Vento	N	Y	N	N	N	Y	Y
5 Sabo	N	Y	N	N	?	Y	Y
6 Luther	N	Y	N	N	N	N	N
7 Peterson	Y	Y	N	N	N	Y	Y
8 Oberstar	N	?	N	N	N	N	Y
MISSISSIPPI							
1 ***Wicker***	Y	Y	Y	Y	Y	Y	Y
2 Thompson	N	Y	N	N	N	Y	Y
3 ***Pickering***	Y	Y	Y	Y	Y	Y	Y
4 Shows	Y	Y	N	N	N	Y	Y
5 Taylor	Y	Y	N	N	N	N	N
MISSOURI							
1 Clay	N	Y	N	N	N	N	N
2 ***Talent***	Y	Y	Y	Y	Y	Y	Y
3 Gephardt	N	Y	N	N	N	?	Y
4 Skelton	N	Y	N	N	N	Y	Y
5 McCarthy	N	Y	N	N	N	Y	Y
6 Danner	N	Y	N	N	N	N	Y
7 ***Blunt***	Y	Y	Y	Y	Y	Y	Y
8 ***Emerson***	Y	Y	Y	Y	Y	Y	Y
9 ***Hulshof***	Y	Y	Y	Y	Y	Y	Y
MONTANA							
AL ***Hill***	Y	Y	Y	Y	Y	Y	Y
NEBRASKA							
1 ***Bereuter***	?	?	?	?	?	?	+
2 ***Terry***	Y	Y	Y	Y	Y	Y	Y
3 ***Barrett***	Y	Y	Y	Y	?	Y	Y
NEVADA							
1 Berkley	N	Y	N	N	N	Y	Y
2 ***Gibbons***	Y	Y	Y	Y	Y	Y	Y
NEW HAMPSHIRE							
1 ***Sununu***	Y	Y	Y	Y	Y	Y	Y
2 ***Bass***	Y	Y	Y	Y	Y	Y	Y
NEW JERSEY							
1 Andrews	N	Y	N	N	N	N	Y
2 ***LoBiondo***	N	Y	Y	Y	Y	Y	Y
3 ***Saxton***	Y	Y	Y	Y	Y	Y	Y
4 ***Smith***	Y	Y	Y	Y	Y	Y	Y
5 ***Roukema***	Y	Y	Y	Y	Y	Y	Y
6 Pallone	N	Y	N	N	N	Y	Y
7 ***Franks***	N	Y	Y	Y	Y	Y	Y
8 Pascrell	N	Y	N	N	N	Y	Y
9 Rothman	N	Y	N	N	N	Y	Y
10 Payne	?	?	?	?	?	N	Y
11 ***Frelinghuysen***	N	Y	Y	Y	Y	Y	Y
12 Holt	N	Y	N	N	N	Y	Y
13 Menendez	N	Y	N	N	N	Y	Y
NEW MEXICO							
1 ***Wilson***	Y	Y	Y	Y	Y	Y	Y
2 ***Skeen***	Y	Y	Y	Y	Y	Y	Y
3 Udall	N	Y	N	N	N	N	Y
NEW YORK							
1 Forbes	Y	N	N	N	N	Y	Y
2 ***Lazio***	Y	Y	Y	Y	Y	Y	Y
3 ***King***	Y	Y	Y	Y	Y	Y	Y
4 McCarthy	N	Y	N	N	N	Y	Y
5 Ackerman	N	Y	N	N	N	N	Y
6 Meeks	N	Y	N	N	N	Y	Y
7 Crowley	N	Y	N	N	N	Y	Y
8 Nadler	N	Y	N	N	N	Y	Y
9 Weiner	N	Y	N	N	N	Y	Y
10 Towns	N	Y	N	N	N	N	Y
11 Owens	N	Y	N	N	N	N	Y
12 Velázquez	N	Y	N	N	N	N	Y
13 ***Fossella***	Y	Y	Y	Y	Y	Y	Y
14 Maloney	N	Y	N	N	N	Y	Y
15 Rangel	N	Y	N	N	N	Y	Y
16 Serrano	N	Y	N	N	N	N	N
17 Engel	N	Y	N	N	N	Y	Y
18 Lowey	N	Y	N	N	N	Y	Y
19 ***Kelly***	Y	Y	Y	Y	Y	Y	Y
20 ***Gilman***	N	Y	Y	Y	Y	Y	Y
21 McNulty	N	Y	N	N	N	Y	Y
22 ***Sweeney***	Y	Y	Y	Y	Y	Y	Y
23 ***Boehlert***	N	Y	Y	Y	Y	Y	Y
24 ***McHugh***	Y	Y	Y	Y	Y	Y	Y
25 ***Walsh***	Y	Y	Y	Y	Y	Y	Y
26 Hinchey	Y	Y	N	N	N	N	N
27 ***Reynolds***	N	Y	Y	Y	Y	Y	Y
28 Slaughter	N	Y	N	N	N	Y	Y
29 LaFalce	N	Y	N	N	N	Y	Y

	564	565	566	567	568	569	570
30 ***Quinn***	Y	Y	Y	Y	Y	Y	Y
31 ***Houghton***	?	Y	Y	Y	Y	Y	Y
NORTH CAROLINA							
1 Clayton	N	Y	N	N	N	Y	Y
2 Etheridge	N	Y	N	N	N	Y	Y
3 ***Jones***	Y	Y	Y	Y	Y	Y	Y
4 Price	N	Y	N	N	N	Y	Y
5 ***Burr***	Y	Y	Y	Y	Y	Y	Y
6 ***Coble***	Y	Y	Y	Y	Y	Y	Y
7 McIntyre	Y	Y	N	N	N	Y	Y
8 ***Hayes***	Y	Y	Y	Y	Y	Y	Y
9 ***Myrick***	Y	Y	Y	Y	Y	Y	Y
10 ***Ballenger***	Y	Y	Y	Y	Y	Y	Y
11 ***Taylor***	Y	Y	Y	Y	Y	?	?
12 Watt	N	Y	N	N	N	N	Y
NORTH DAKOTA							
AL Pomeroy	N	Y	N	N	N	Y	Y
OHIO							
1 ***Chabot***	Y	Y	Y	Y	Y	Y	Y
2 ***Portman***	Y	Y	Y	Y	Y	Y	Y
3 Hall	N	Y	N	N	N	Y	Y
4 ***Oxley***	?	Y	Y	Y	Y	Y	Y
5 ***Gillmor***	Y	Y	Y	Y	Y	Y	Y
6 Strickland	N	Y	N	N	N	Y	Y
7 ***Hobson***	Y	Y	Y	Y	Y	Y	Y
8 ***Boehner***	Y	Y	Y	Y	Y	Y	Y
9 Kaptur	Y	Y	N	N	N	N	N
10 Kucinich	N	Y	N	N	N	N	N
11 Jones	N	Y	N	N	N	N	Y
12 ***Kasich***	Y	Y	Y	?	Y	Y	Y
13 Brown	N	Y	N	N	N	Y	Y
14 Sawyer	N	Y	N	N	N	Y	Y
15 ***Pryce***	Y	Y	Y	Y	Y	Y	Y
16 ***Regula***	Y	Y	Y	Y	Y	Y	Y
17 Traficant	Y	Y	N	N	N	Y	Y
18 ***Ney***	Y	Y	Y	Y	Y	Y	?
19 ***LaTourette***	Y	Y	Y	Y	Y	Y	Y
OKLAHOMA							
1 ***Largent***	Y	Y	Y	Y	Y	Y	Y
2 ***Coburn***	Y	Y	Y	Y	Y	Y	Y
3 ***Watkins***	Y	Y	Y	Y	Y	Y	Y
4 ***Watts***	Y	Y	Y	Y	Y	Y	Y
5 ***Istook***	Y	Y	Y	?	Y	Y	Y
6 ***Lucas***	Y	Y	Y	Y	Y	Y	Y
OREGON							
1 Wu	N	Y	N	N	N	N	Y
2 ***Walden***	Y	Y	Y	Y	Y	Y	Y
3 Blumenauer	N	Y	N	N	N	Y	Y
4 DeFazio	N	N	N	N	N	N	N
5 Hooley	N	Y	N	N	N	Y	Y
PENNSYLVANIA							
1 Brady	N	Y	N	N	N	N	N
2 Fattah	N	Y	N	N	N	N	N
3 Borski	Y	Y	N	N	N	Y	Y
4 Klink	N	Y	N	N	N	Y	Y
5 ***Peterson***	Y	Y	Y	Y	Y	Y	Y
6 Holden	Y	Y	N	N	N	Y	Y
7 ***Weldon***	Y	Y	Y	Y	Y	Y	Y
8 ***Greenwood***	Y	Y	Y	Y	Y	Y	Y
9 ***Shuster***	Y	Y	Y	Y	Y	?	?
10 ***Sherwood***	Y	Y	Y	Y	Y	Y	Y
11 Kanjorski	?	?	?	?	?	?	+
12 Murtha	N	Y	N	N	N	Y	Y
13 Hoeffel	N	Y	N	N	N	Y	Y
14 Coyne	N	Y	N	N	N	N	N
15 ***Toomey***	N	Y	Y	Y	Y	Y	Y
16 ***Pitts***	Y	Y	Y	Y	Y	Y	Y
17 ***Gekas***	Y	Y	Y	Y	Y	Y	Y
18 Doyle	N	Y	N	N	N	Y	Y
19 ***Goodling***	Y	Y	Y	Y	Y	Y	Y
20 Mascara	N	Y	N	N	N	Y	Y
21 ***English***	Y	Y	Y	Y	Y	Y	Y
RHODE ISLAND							
1 Kennedy	N	Y	N	N	N	?	Y
2 Weygand	N	Y	N	N	N	Y	Y
SOUTH CAROLINA							
1 ***Sanford***	Y	Y	Y	Y	Y	Y	N
2 ***Spence***	Y	Y	Y	Y	Y	Y	Y
3 ***Graham***	Y	Y	Y	Y	Y	Y	Y
4 ***DeMint***	Y	Y	Y	Y	Y	Y	Y
5 Spratt	N	Y	N	N	N	Y	Y
6 Clyburn	N	Y	N	N	N	Y	Y
SOUTH DAKOTA							
AL ***Thune***	Y	Y	Y	Y	Y	Y	Y

	564	565	566	567	568	569	570
TENNESSEE							
1 ***Jenkins***	Y	Y	Y	Y	Y	Y	Y
2 ***Duncan***	Y	Y	Y	Y	Y	Y	Y
3 ***Wamp***	Y	Y	Y	Y	Y	Y	Y
4 ***Hilleary***	Y	Y	Y	Y	Y	Y	Y
5 Clement	N	Y	N	N	N	Y	Y
6 Gordon	N	Y	N	N	N	Y	Y
7 ***Bryant***	Y	Y	Y	Y	Y	Y	Y
8 Tanner	N	Y	N	N	N	Y	Y
9 Ford	N	Y	N	N	N	Y	Y
TEXAS							
1 Sandlin	N	Y	N	N	N	Y	Y
2 Turner	N	Y	N	N	N	Y	Y
3 ***Johnson, Sam***	Y	Y	Y	Y	Y	Y	Y
4 Hall	N	Y	Y	Y	Y	Y	Y
5 ***Sessions***	?	Y	Y	Y	Y	Y	Y
6 ***Barton***	Y	Y	?	Y	Y	Y	N
7 ***Archer***	Y	Y	Y	Y	Y	Y	Y
8 ***Brady***	Y	Y	?	Y	Y	Y	Y
9 Lampson	N	Y	N	N	N	Y	Y
10 Doggett	N	Y	N	N	N	Y	Y
11 Edwards	N	Y	N	N	N	N	N
12 ***Granger***	Y	Y	Y	Y	Y	Y	Y
13 ***Thornberry***	Y	Y	Y	Y	Y	Y	Y
14 ***Paul***	N	N	Y	Y	Y	?	?
15 Hinojosa	N	Y	N	N	N	Y	Y
16 Reyes	N	Y	N	N	N	Y	Y
17 Stenholm	Y	Y	N	N	N	Y	Y
18 Jackson-Lee	N	Y	N	N	N	Y	Y
19 ***Combest***	Y	Y	Y	Y	Y	Y	Y
20 Gonzalez	N	Y	N	N	N	Y	Y
21 ***Smith***	Y	Y	Y	Y	Y	Y	Y
22 ***DeLay***	Y	Y	Y	Y	Y	Y	Y
23 ***Bonilla***	Y	Y	Y	Y	Y	Y	Y
24 Frost	N	Y	N	N	N	Y	Y
25 Bentsen	N	?	N	N	N	Y	Y
26 ***Armey***	Y	Y	Y	Y	Y	Y	Y
27 Ortiz	N	Y	N	N	N	Y	Y
28 Rodriguez	N	Y	N	N	N	Y	N
29 Green	Y	Y	N	N	N	Y	Y
30 Johnson, E.B.	N	Y	N	N	N	Y	Y
UTAH							
1 ***Hansen***	Y	Y	Y	Y	Y	Y	Y
2 ***Cook***	Y	Y	Y	Y	Y	Y	Y
3 ***Cannon***	Y	Y	Y	Y	Y	Y	Y
VERMONT							
AL *Sanders*	N	Y	N	N	N	N	N
VIRGINIA							
1 ***Bateman***	Y	Y	Y	Y	Y	Y	Y
2 Pickett	N	Y	N	N	N	Y	Y
3 Scott	N	Y	N	N	N	N	Y
4 Sisisky	N	Y	N	N	N	Y	Y
5 Goode	Y	Y	N	N	N	Y	Y
6 ***Goodlatte***	Y	Y	Y	Y	Y	Y	Y
7 ***Bliley***	Y	Y	Y	Y	Y	Y	Y
8 Moran	N	Y	Y	N	N	Y	Y
9 Boucher	N	Y	N	N	?	Y	Y
10 ***Wolf***	Y	Y	Y	Y	Y	Y	Y
11 ***Davis***	Y	Y	Y	Y	Y	Y	Y
WASHINGTON							
1 Inslee	N	Y	N	N	N	N	N
2 ***Metcalf***	Y	Y	Y	Y	?	Y	Y
3 Baird	N	Y	N	N	N	Y	Y
4 ***Hastings***	Y	Y	Y	Y	Y	Y	Y
5 ***Nethercutt***	Y	Y	Y	Y	Y	Y	Y
6 Dicks	N	Y	N	N	N	Y	Y
7 McDermott	N	Y	N	N	N	N	N
8 ***Dunn***	Y	Y	Y	Y	Y	Y	Y
9 Smith	N	Y	N	N	N	Y	Y
WEST VIRGINIA							
1 Mollohan	Y	Y	N	N	N	?	?
2 Wise	Y	Y	N	N	N	Y	Y
3 Rahall	Y	Y	N	N	N	Y	Y
WISCONSIN							
1 ***Ryan***	Y	Y	Y	Y	Y	Y	Y
2 Baldwin	N	Y	N	N	N	N	N
3 Kind	N	Y	N	N	N	Y	Y
4 Kleczka	N	Y	N	N	N	Y	Y
5 Barrett	N	Y	N	N	N	N	N
6 ***Petri***	Y	Y	Y	Y	Y	Y	Y
7 Obey	P	Y	N	N	N	N	N
8 ***Green***	Y	Y	Y	Y	Y	Y	Y
9 ***Sensenbrenner***	Y	Y	Y	Y	Y	Y	Y
WYOMING							
AL ***Cubin***	Y	Y	Y	Y	Y	Y	Y

Southern states - Ala., Ark., Fla., Ga., Ky., La., Miss., N.C., Okla., S.C., Tenn., Texas, Va.

571. HR 3196. Fiscal 2000 Foreign Operations Appropriations/Wye River Accords. Young, R-Fla., amendment to provide $1.8 billion to implement the Wye River peace agreement between Israel and the Palestinian Authority. The amendment also would provide $799 million more to other administration foreign operations priorities. Adopted 351-58: R 153-56; D 197-2 (ND 146-1, SD 51-1); I 1-0. Nov. 5, 1999.

572. HR 3196. Fiscal 2000 Foreign Operations Appropriations/Passage. Passage of the bill to provide $15.2 billion in foreign operations spending for fiscal 2000. The measure would provide $1.8 billion to implement the Wye River peace agreement between Israel and the Palestinian Authority, as well as $133 million for multilateral debt relief. Passed 316-100: R 127-84; D 188-16 (ND 142-9, SD 46-7); I 1-0. Nov. 5, 1999.

573. HR 3075. Medicare Adjustments to the Balanced Budget Act/Passage. Archer, R-Texas, motion to suspend the rules and pass the bill to make adjustments to Medicare payments set in the 1997 Balanced Budget Act (PL 105-33). The bill would increase Medicare payments to hospitals, managed care insurers and skilled nursing facilities; postpone a 15 percent across-the-board cut in payments to home health care agencies; and create new caps for therapy services. Motion agreed to 388-25: R 208-2; D 179-23 (ND 128-22, SD 51-1); I 1-0. Nov. 5, 1999. A two-thirds majority of those present and voting (276 in this case) is required for passage under suspension of the rules.

574. H Res 94. Kidney Donors/Adoption. Bliley, R-Va., motion to suspend the rules and adopt the resolution to recognize the contribution made by those who have donated kidneys to save lives. Motion agreed to 382-0: R 193-0; D 188-0 (ND 140-0, SD 48-0); I 1-0 . Nov. 8, 1999. A two-thirds majority of those present and voting (254 in this case) is required for adoption under suspension of the rules.

575. HR 2904. Office of Government Ethics/Passage. McHugh, R-N.Y., motion to suspend the rules and pass the bill to reauthorize the Office of Government Ethics, which oversees the executive branch's compliance with ethics laws and regulations, for four years. The measure would expand the definition of "special government employee" to include any paid or unpaid adviser who gives "regular advice, counsel, or recommendations" to the president, vice president or other federal officials. Motion agreed to 386-1: R 194-1; D 191-0 (ND 141-0, SD 50-0); I 1-0. Nov. 8, 1999. A two-thirds majority of those present and voting (258 in this case) is required for passage under suspension of the rules.

Key

- Y Voted for (yea).
- # Paired for.
- + Announced for.
- N Voted against (nay).
- X Paired against.
- – Announced against.
- P Voted "present."
- C Voted "present" to avoid possible conflict of interest.
- ? Did not vote or otherwise make a position known.

•

Democrats ***Republicans***
Independents

	571	572	573	574	575
ALABAMA					
1 ***Callahan***	N	N	Y	?	?
2 ***Everett***	N	N	Y	?	?
3 ***Riley***	Y	Y	Y	?	?
4 ***Aderholt***	Y	Y	Y	?	?
5 Cramer	?	?	?	Y	Y
6 ***Bachus***	Y	Y	Y	Y	Y
7 Hilliard	Y	Y	Y	Y	Y
ALASKA					
AL ***Young***	?	?	Y	Y	Y
ARIZONA					
1 ***Salmon***	Y	Y	Y	Y	Y
2 Pastor	Y	Y	Y	Y	Y
3 ***Stump***	N	N	Y	Y	Y
4 ***Shadegg***	Y	Y	Y	Y	Y
5 ***Kolbe***	Y	Y	Y	Y	Y
6 ***Hayworth***	Y	Y	Y	Y	Y
ARKANSAS					
1 Berry	Y	N	Y	Y	Y
2 Snyder	Y	Y	Y	Y	Y
3 ***Hutchinson***	Y	N	Y	Y	Y
4 ***Dickey***	?	?	?	Y	Y
CALIFORNIA					
1 Thompson	Y	Y	Y	Y	Y
2 ***Herger***	N	N	Y	?	Y
3 ***Ose***	Y	Y	Y	Y	Y
4 ***Doolittle***	N	N	Y	Y	Y
5 Matsui	Y	Y	Y	Y	Y
6 Woolsey	Y	Y	Y	Y	Y
7 Miller, George	Y	Y	N	Y	Y
8 Pelosi	Y	Y	Y	Y	Y
9 Lee	Y	Y	Y	Y	Y
10 Tauscher	Y	Y	Y	Y	Y
11 ***Pombo***	Y	N	Y	Y	Y
12 Lantos	Y	Y	Y	Y	Y
13 Stark	Y	N	N	Y	Y
14 Eshoo	Y	Y	Y	Y	Y
15 ***Campbell***	Y	Y	Y	Y	Y
16 Lofgren	Y	Y	Y	Y	Y
17 Farr	Y	Y	Y	Y	Y
18 Condit	Y	N	Y	Y	Y
19 ***Radanovich***	Y	Y	Y	Y	Y
20 Dooley	Y	Y	Y	Y	Y
21 ***Thomas***	Y	Y	Y	+	+
22 Capps	Y	Y	Y	Y	Y
23 ***Gallegly***	Y	Y	Y	Y	Y
24 Sherman	Y	Y	Y	Y	Y
25 ***McKeon***	Y	Y	Y	Y	Y
26 Berman	Y	Y	Y	?	?
27 ***Rogan***	Y	Y	Y	Y	Y
28 ***Dreier***	Y	Y	Y	Y	Y
29 Waxman	Y	Y	Y	Y	Y
30 Becerra	Y	Y	Y	Y	Y
31 Martinez	?	?	?	Y	Y
32 Dixon	Y	Y	Y	Y	Y
33 Roybal-Allard	Y	Y	Y	Y	Y
34 Napolitano	Y	Y	Y	Y	Y
35 Waters	Y	Y	Y	Y	Y
36 ***Kuykendall***	Y	Y	Y	Y	Y
37 Millender-McD.	Y	Y	Y	Y	Y
38 ***Horn***	Y	Y	Y	Y	Y
39 ***Royce***	N	N	Y	Y	Y
40 ***Lewis***	Y	Y	Y	Y	Y
41 ***Miller***	Y	Y	Y	+	+
42 Vacant					
43 ***Calvert***	Y	Y	?	?	?
44 ***Bono***	Y	Y	Y	?	?
45 ***Rohrabacher***	N	N	Y	Y	Y
46 Sanchez	Y	Y	Y	Y	Y
47 ***Cox***	?	Y	Y	?	?
48 ***Packard***	Y	Y	Y	Y	Y
49 ***Bilbray***	N	N	Y	Y	Y
50 Filner	Y	Y	Y	Y	Y
51 ***Cunningham***	+	N	Y	Y	Y
52 ***Hunter***	N	N	Y	Y	Y
COLORADO					
1 DeGette	Y	Y	Y	Y	Y
2 Udall	Y	Y	Y	Y	Y
3 ***McInnis***	?	?	?	Y	Y
4 ***Schaffer***	N	N	Y	Y	Y
5 ***Hefley***	Y	N	Y	Y	Y
6 ***Tancredo***	N	N	Y	Y	Y
CONNECTICUT					
1 Larson	Y	Y	Y	Y	Y
2 Gejdenson	Y	Y	Y	Y	Y
3 DeLauro	Y	Y	Y	Y	Y
4 ***Shays***	Y	Y	Y	Y	Y
5 Maloney	Y	Y	Y	Y	Y
6 ***Johnson***	Y	Y	Y	Y	Y
DELAWARE					
AL ***Castle***	Y	Y	Y	Y	Y
FLORIDA					
1 ***Scarborough***	?	?	?	?	?
2 Boyd	Y	Y	Y	Y	Y
3 Brown	Y	Y	Y	Y	Y
4 ***Fowler***	Y	Y	Y	+	+
5 Thurman	Y	Y	Y	Y	Y
6 ***Stearns***	Y	N	Y	Y	Y
7 ***Mica***	Y	Y	+	Y	Y
8 ***McCollum***	Y	Y	Y	Y	Y
9 ***Bilirakis***	Y	Y	Y	Y	Y
10 ***Young***	Y	Y	Y	Y	Y
11 Davis	Y	Y	Y	Y	Y
12 ***Canady***	Y	Y	Y	Y	Y
13 ***Miller***	N	N	Y	Y	Y
14 ***Goss***	N	N	Y	Y	Y
15 ***Weldon***	Y	N	Y	Y	Y
16 ***Foley***	Y	Y	Y	Y	Y
17 Meek	Y	Y	Y	Y	Y
18 ***Ros-Lehtinen***	Y	Y	Y	Y	Y
19 Wexler	Y	Y	Y	Y	Y
20 Deutsch	Y	Y	Y	Y	Y
21 ***Diaz-Balart***	Y	Y	Y	Y	Y
22 ***Shaw***	Y	Y	Y	Y	Y
23 Hastings	Y	Y	Y	Y	Y
GEORGIA					
1 ***Kingston***	Y	N	Y	Y	Y
2 Bishop	Y	Y	Y	?	Y
3 ***Collins***	N	N	Y	Y	Y
4 McKinney	Y	Y	Y	Y	Y
5 Lewis	Y	Y	Y	?	?
6 ***Isakson***	Y	Y	Y	Y	Y
7 ***Barr***	N	N	Y	Y	Y
8 ***Chambliss***	N	N	Y	Y	Y
9 ***Deal***	N	N	Y	Y	Y
10 ***Norwood***	?	?	?	Y	Y
11 ***Linder***	Y	Y	?	Y	Y
HAWAII					
1 Abercrombie	Y	Y	Y	Y	Y
2 Mink	Y	Y	Y	Y	Y
IDAHO					
1 ***Chenoweth-Hage***	N	N	Y	+	+
2 ***Simpson***	Y	Y	Y	Y	Y
ILLINOIS					
1 Rush	Y	Y	Y	?	?
2 Jackson	Y	Y	Y	Y	Y
3 Lipinski	Y	Y	Y	Y	Y
4 Gutierrez	Y	Y	Y	Y	Y
5 Blagojevich	Y	Y	Y	?	?
6 ***Hyde***	Y	Y	Y	Y	Y
7 Davis	Y	Y	Y	Y	Y
8 ***Crane***	Y	N	Y	?	?
9 Schakowsky	Y	Y	Y	Y	Y
10 ***Porter***	Y	Y	Y	Y	Y
11 ***Weller***	Y	Y	Y	Y	Y
12 Costello	Y	Y	Y	Y	Y
13 ***Biggert***	Y	Y	Y	Y	Y
14 ***Hastert***					

ND Northern Democrats SD Southern Democrats

	571	572	573	574	575
15 ***Ewing***	Y	Y	Y	Y	Y
16 ***Manzullo***	Y	N	Y	Y	Y
17 Evans	Y	Y	Y	Y	Y
18 ***LaHood***	Y	Y	Y	Y	Y
19 Phelps	Y	Y	Y	Y	Y
20 ***Shimkus***	Y	Y	Y	Y	Y
INDIANA					
1 Visclosky	Y	Y	Y	Y	Y
2 ***McIntosh***	Y	Y	Y	Y	Y
3 Roemer	N	N	Y	Y	Y
4 ***Souder***	Y	Y	Y	Y	Y
5 ***Buyer***	N	N	Y	Y	Y
6 ***Burton***	N	N	Y	Y	Y
7 ***Pease***	Y	N	Y	Y	Y
8 ***Hostettler***	N	N	Y	Y	Y
9 Hill	Y	Y	Y	Y	Y
10 Carson	Y	Y	Y	+	+
IOWA					
1 ***Leach***	Y	Y	Y	Y	Y
2 ***Nussle***	Y	Y	Y	Y	Y
3 Boswell	Y	Y	Y	Y	Y
4 ***Ganske***	Y	Y	Y	Y	Y
5 ***Latham***	Y	Y	Y	Y	Y
KANSAS					
1 ***Moran***	Y	N	Y	Y	Y
2 ***Ryun***	N	N	Y	Y	Y
3 Moore	Y	Y	Y	Y	Y
4 ***Tiahrt***	Y	N	Y	+	+
KENTUCKY					
1 ***Whitfield***	Y	Y	Y	Y	Y
2 ***Lewis***	N	N	Y	Y	Y
3 ***Northup***	+	Y	Y	Y	Y
4 Lucas	Y	N	Y	Y	Y
5 ***Rogers***	N	N	Y	Y	Y
6 ***Fletcher***	Y	Y	Y	Y	Y
LOUISIANA					
1 ***Vitter***	Y	Y	Y	Y	Y
2 Jefferson	Y	Y	Y	?	?
3 ***Tauzin***	Y	Y	Y	Y	Y
4 ***McCrery***	Y	Y	Y	Y	Y
5 ***Cooksey***	Y	Y	Y	Y	Y
6 ***Baker***	N	Y	Y	Y	Y
7 John	Y	Y	Y	Y	Y
MAINE					
1 Allen	Y	Y	Y	Y	Y
2 Baldacci	Y	Y	Y	Y	Y
MARYLAND					
1 ***Gilchrest***	Y	?	Y	Y	Y
2 ***Ehrlich***	Y	Y	Y	Y	Y
3 Cardin	Y	Y	Y	Y	Y
4 Wynn	Y	Y	Y	Y	Y
5 Hoyer	Y	Y	Y	Y	Y
6 ***Bartlett***	N	N	Y	Y	Y
7 Cummings	Y	Y	Y	Y	Y
8 ***Morella***	Y	Y	Y	Y	Y
MASSACHUSETTS					
1 Olver	Y	Y	Y	?	Y
2 Neal	Y	Y	Y	?	?
3 McGovern	Y	Y	Y	Y	Y
4 Frank	Y	Y	Y	Y	Y
5 Meehan	?	?	?	Y	Y
6 Tierney	Y	Y	Y	?	?
7 Markey	?	Y	N	Y	Y
8 Capuano	Y	Y	Y	Y	Y
9 Moakley	Y	Y	Y	?	?
10 Delahunt	Y	Y	Y	Y	Y
MICHIGAN					
1 Stupak	Y	Y	Y	Y	Y
2 ***Hoekstra***	N	N	Y	?	?
3 ***Ehlers***	Y	Y	Y	Y	Y
4 ***Camp***	Y	Y	Y	Y	Y
5 Barcia	Y	Y	Y	Y	Y
6 ***Upton***	N	N	Y	Y	Y
7 ***Smith***	Y	N	Y	Y	Y
8 Stabenow	Y	Y	Y	Y	Y
9 Kildee	Y	Y	Y	Y	Y
10 Bonior	Y	Y	Y	Y	Y
11 ***Knollenberg***	Y	Y	Y	Y	Y
12 Levin	Y	Y	Y	Y	Y
13 Rivers	Y	Y	Y	Y	Y
14 Conyers	Y	Y	Y	Y	Y
15 Kilpatrick	Y	Y	Y	+	+
16 Dingell	Y	Y	Y	Y	Y

	571	572	573	574	575
MINNESOTA					
1 ***Gutknecht***	Y	Y	Y	Y	Y
2 Minge	Y	Y	Y	Y	Y
3 ***Ramstad***	Y	Y	Y	?	?
4 Vento	Y	Y	Y	Y	Y
5 Sabo	Y	Y	Y	Y	Y
6 Luther	Y	Y	Y	Y	Y
7 Peterson	Y	N	Y	Y	Y
8 Oberstar	Y	Y	Y	Y	Y
MISSISSIPPI					
1 ***Wicker***	Y	Y	Y	Y	Y
2 Thompson	Y	Y	Y	Y	Y
3 ***Pickering***	Y	Y	Y	Y	Y
4 Shows	Y	Y	Y	Y	Y
5 Taylor	N	N	Y	Y	Y
MISSOURI					
1 Clay	?	?	?	Y	Y
2 ***Talent***	Y	Y	Y	Y	Y
3 Gephardt	?	Y	Y	Y	Y
4 Skelton	Y	Y	Y	Y	Y
5 McCarthy	Y	Y	+	Y	Y
6 Danner	Y	N	Y	Y	Y
7 ***Blunt***	Y	Y	Y	?	?
8 ***Emerson***	N	N	Y	Y	Y
9 ***Hulshof***	Y	Y	Y	Y	Y
MONTANA					
AL ***Hill***	N	N	Y	Y	Y
NEBRASKA					
1 ***Bereuter***	?	?	?	Y	Y
2 ***Terry***	Y	Y	Y	Y	Y
3 ***Barrett***	Y	Y	Y	Y	Y
NEVADA					
1 Berkley	Y	Y	Y	Y	Y
2 ***Gibbons***	Y	N	Y	Y	Y
NEW HAMPSHIRE					
1 ***Sununu***	Y	Y	Y	Y	Y
2 ***Bass***	Y	Y	Y	Y	Y
NEW JERSEY					
1 Andrews	Y	Y	Y	Y	Y
2 ***LoBiondo***	Y	Y	Y	Y	Y
3 ***Saxton***	Y	Y	Y	Y	Y
4 ***Smith***	Y	N	Y	Y	Y
5 ***Roukema***	Y	N	Y	Y	Y
6 Pallone	Y	Y	Y	Y	Y
7 ***Franks***	Y	Y	Y	Y	Y
8 Pascrell	Y	Y	Y	+	+
9 Rothman	Y	Y	Y	Y	Y
10 Payne	Y	Y	N	Y	Y
11 ***Frelinghuysen***	Y	Y	Y	Y	Y
12 Holt	Y	Y	Y	Y	Y
13 Menendez	Y	Y	Y	?	?
NEW MEXICO					
1 ***Wilson***	Y	Y	Y	Y	Y
2 ***Skeen***	Y	Y	Y	Y	Y
3 Udall	Y	Y	Y	Y	Y
NEW YORK					
1 Forbes	Y	Y	N	Y	Y
2 ***Lazio***	Y	Y	Y	Y	Y
3 ***King***	Y	Y	Y	Y	Y
4 McCarthy	Y	Y	Y	Y	Y
5 Ackerman	Y	Y	N	Y	Y
6 Meeks	Y	Y	Y	?	?
7 Crowley	Y	Y	N	Y	Y
8 Nadler	Y	Y	N	?	?
9 Weiner	Y	Y	N	Y	Y
10 Towns	?	Y	N	Y	Y
11 Owens	Y	Y	N	?	?
12 Velázquez	Y	Y	Y	Y	Y
13 ***Fossella***	Y	Y	Y	Y	Y
14 Maloney	Y	Y	N	Y	Y
15 Rangel	Y	Y	Y	Y	Y
16 Serrano	Y	Y	N	Y	Y
17 Engel	Y	Y	N	Y	Y
18 Lowey	Y	Y	N	Y	Y
19 ***Kelly***	Y	Y	Y	Y	Y
20 ***Gilman***	Y	Y	Y	Y	Y
21 McNulty	Y	Y	Y	Y	Y
22 ***Sweeney***	Y	Y	Y	Y	Y
23 ***Boehlert***	Y	Y	Y	Y	Y
24 ***McHugh***	Y	Y	Y	Y	Y
25 ***Walsh***	Y	Y	Y	?	?
26 Hinchey	Y	Y	N	?	?
27 ***Reynolds***	Y	Y	Y	Y	Y
28 Slaughter	Y	Y	N	Y	Y
29 LaFalce	Y	Y	Y	Y	Y

	571	572	573	574	575
30 ***Quinn***	Y	Y	Y	Y	Y
31 ***Houghton***	Y	Y	Y	Y	Y
NORTH CAROLINA					
1 Clayton	Y	Y	Y	Y	Y
2 Etheridge	Y	Y	Y	Y	Y
3 ***Jones***	N	N	Y	Y	Y
4 Price	Y	Y	Y	?	?
5 ***Burr***	Y	N	Y	Y	Y
6 ***Coble***	N	N	Y	Y	Y
7 McIntyre	Y	N	Y	Y	Y
8 ***Hayes***	N	N	Y	Y	Y
9 ***Myrick***	Y	Y	Y	Y	Y
10 ***Ballenger***	N	N	Y	Y	Y
11 ***Taylor***	?	?	?	Y	Y
12 Watt	Y	Y	Y	Y	Y
NORTH DAKOTA					
AL Pomeroy	?	N	Y	Y	Y
OHIO					
1 ***Chabot***	Y	Y	Y	Y	Y
2 ***Portman***	Y	Y	Y	Y	Y
3 Hall	Y	Y	Y	Y	Y
4 ***Oxley***	Y	Y	Y	Y	Y
5 ***Gillmor***	N	Y	Y	?	Y
6 Strickland	Y	Y	Y	Y	Y
7 ***Hobson***	Y	Y	Y	Y	Y
8 ***Boehner***	Y	Y	Y	Y	Y
9 Kaptur	Y	Y	Y	Y	Y
10 Kucinich	Y	Y	N	Y	Y
11 Jones	Y	Y	Y	Y	Y
12 ***Kasich***	Y	Y	Y	Y	Y
13 Brown	Y	Y	Y	Y	Y
14 Sawyer	Y	Y	Y	Y	Y
15 ***Pryce***	Y	Y	Y	Y	Y
16 ***Regula***	Y	Y	Y	Y	Y
17 Traficant	Y	N	Y	Y	Y
18 ***Ney***	Y	Y	Y	Y	Y
19 ***LaTourette***	Y	Y	Y	Y	Y
OKLAHOMA					
1 ***Largent***	N	N	Y	?	?
2 ***Coburn***	N	N	Y	Y	Y
3 ***Watkins***	N	N	Y	Y	Y
4 ***Watts***	Y	Y	Y	?	?
5 ***Istook***	N	N	Y	Y	Y
6 ***Lucas***	Y	N	Y	Y	Y
OREGON					
1 Wu	Y	Y	Y	Y	Y
2 ***Walden***	Y	Y	Y	Y	Y
3 Blumenauer	Y	Y	Y	Y	Y
4 DeFazio	Y	N	Y	Y	Y
5 Hooley	Y	Y	Y	Y	Y
PENNSYLVANIA					
1 Brady	Y	Y	Y	Y	Y
2 Fattah	Y	Y	Y	Y	Y
3 Borski	Y	Y	Y	Y	Y
4 Klink	Y	Y	N	Y	Y
5 ***Peterson***	Y	N	Y	Y	Y
6 Holden	Y	Y	Y	Y	Y
7 ***Weldon***	Y	Y	Y	Y	Y
8 ***Greenwood***	Y	Y	Y	Y	Y
9 ***Shuster***	Y	Y	Y	Y	Y
10 ***Sherwood***	Y	N	Y	Y	Y
11 Kanjorski	+	+	+	Y	Y
12 Murtha	Y	Y	Y	Y	Y
13 Hoeffel	Y	Y	Y	Y	Y
14 Coyne	Y	Y	N	Y	Y
15 ***Toomey***	N	N	Y	Y	Y
16 ***Pitts***	Y	N	Y	Y	Y
17 ***Gekas***	Y	Y	Y	Y	Y
18 Doyle	Y	Y	Y	Y	Y
19 ***Goodling***	N	N	Y	Y	Y
20 Mascara	Y	Y	Y	Y	Y
21 ***English***	Y	Y	Y	Y	Y
RHODE ISLAND					
1 Kennedy	Y	Y	N	Y	Y
2 Weygand	Y	Y	Y	Y	Y
SOUTH CAROLINA					
1 ***Sanford***	N	N	N	?	?
2 ***Spence***	N	N	Y	Y	Y
3 ***Graham***	N	N	Y	Y	Y
4 ***DeMint***	N	N	Y	Y	Y
5 Spratt	Y	Y	Y	Y	Y
6 Clyburn	Y	Y	Y	Y	Y
SOUTH DAKOTA					
AL ***Thune***	Y	N	Y	Y	Y

	571	572	573	574	575
TENNESSEE					
1 ***Jenkins***	N	N	Y	Y	Y
2 ***Duncan***	N	N	Y	Y	Y
3 ***Wamp***	N	N	Y	Y	Y
4 ***Hilleary***	N	N	Y	Y	Y
5 Clement	Y	Y	Y	Y	Y
6 Gordon	Y	Y	Y	Y	Y
7 ***Bryant***	Y	Y	Y	Y	Y
8 Tanner	Y	N	Y	Y	Y
9 Ford	Y	Y	Y	Y	Y
TEXAS					
1 Sandlin	Y	Y	Y	Y	Y
2 Turner	Y	Y	Y	Y	Y
3 ***Johnson, Sam***	?	?	?	Y	Y
4 Hall	Y	N	Y	Y	Y
5 ***Sessions***	N	N	Y	?	?
6 ***Barton***	Y	N	Y	Y	Y
7 ***Archer***	Y	N	Y	Y	Y
8 ***Brady***	Y	N	Y	Y	Y
9 Lampson	Y	Y	Y	Y	Y
10 Doggett	Y	Y	N	Y	Y
11 Edwards	Y	Y	Y	Y	Y
12 ***Granger***	Y	Y	Y	?	?
13 ***Thornberry***	N	N	Y	Y	Y
14 ***Paul***	N	N	N	Y	N
15 Hinojosa	Y	Y	Y	Y	Y
16 Reyes	+	+	+	Y	Y
17 Stenholm	Y	Y	Y	?	?
18 Jackson-Lee	Y	Y	Y	Y	Y
19 ***Combest***	N	N	Y	Y	Y
20 Gonzalez	Y	Y	Y	Y	Y
21 ***Smith***	Y	Y	Y	Y	Y
22 ***DeLay***	Y	Y	Y	Y	Y
23 ***Bonilla***	Y	Y	Y	Y	Y
24 Frost	Y	Y	Y	?	Y
25 Bentsen	Y	Y	Y	Y	Y
26 ***Armey***	Y	Y	Y	?	?
27 Ortiz	Y	Y	Y	Y	Y
28 Rodriguez	Y	Y	?	?	?
29 Green	Y	Y	Y	Y	Y
30 Johnson, E.B.	Y	Y	Y	Y	Y
UTAH					
1 ***Hansen***	N	N	Y	?	?
2 ***Cook***	Y	N	Y	?	?
3 ***Cannon***	Y	Y	Y	Y	Y
VERMONT					
AL *Sanders*	Y	Y	Y	Y	Y
VIRGINIA					
1 ***Bateman***	Y	Y	Y	Y	Y
2 Pickett	Y	Y	Y	Y	Y
3 Scott	Y	Y	Y	Y	Y
4 Sisisky	Y	Y	Y	Y	Y
5 Goode	Y	N	Y	Y	Y
6 ***Goodlatte***	Y	Y	Y	Y	Y
7 ***Bliley***	Y	Y	Y	Y	Y
8 Moran	?	Y	Y	Y	Y
9 Boucher	Y	Y	Y	Y	Y
10 ***Wolf***	Y	Y	Y	Y	Y
11 ***Davis***	Y	Y	Y	Y	Y
WASHINGTON					
1 Inslee	Y	Y	Y	Y	Y
2 ***Metcalf***	Y	Y	Y	Y	Y
3 Baird	Y	Y	Y	Y	Y
4 ***Hastings***	?	?	?	Y	Y
5 ***Nethercutt***	Y	N	Y	Y	Y
6 Dicks	Y	Y	Y	Y	Y
7 McDermott	Y	Y	N	Y	Y
8 ***Dunn***	Y	Y	Y	Y	Y
9 Smith	Y	Y	Y	Y	Y
WEST VIRGINIA					
1 Mollohan	?	?	?	Y	Y
2 Wise	Y	Y	Y	?	?
3 Rahall	Y	N	Y	Y	Y
WISCONSIN					
1 ***Ryan***	Y	N	Y	Y	Y
2 Baldwin	Y	Y	Y	Y	Y
3 Kind	Y	Y	Y	Y	Y
4 Kleczka	Y	Y	Y	Y	Y
5 Barrett	Y	Y	Y	Y	Y
6 ***Petri***	N	N	Y	Y	Y
7 Obey	Y	Y	Y	Y	Y
8 ***Green***	Y	N	Y	Y	Y
9 ***Sensenbrenner***	N	N	Y	Y	Y
WYOMING					
AL ***Cubin***	Y	N	Y	Y	Y

Southern states - Ala., Ark., Fla., Ga., Ky., La., Miss., N.C., Okla., S.C., Tenn., Texas, Va.

576. H Res 344. Mourning Payne Stewart/Adoption. Miller, R-Fla., motion to suspend the rules and adopt the resolution to express the condolences of the House of Representatives to the family of Payne Stewart and to the families of those who died with him. Motion agreed to 389-0: R 198-0; D 190-0 (ND 140-0, SD 50-0); I 1-0. Nov. 8, 1999. A two-thirds majority of those present and voting (260 in this case) is required for adoption under suspension of the rules.

577. HR 1714. Electronic Signatures/Consumer Consent. Inslee, D-Wash., amendment to give consumers the right to decide whether they want to receive information electronically. Consumers would have to affirm their consent and be informed of the hardware and software necessary to access the electronic records. Adopted 418-2: R 212-1; D 205-1 (ND 151-1, SD 54-0); I 1-0. Nov. 9, 1999.

578. HR 1714. Electronic Signatures/Dingell Substitute. Dingell, D-Mich., substitute amendment to provide federal recognition of the validity of electronic signatures in commercial transactions affecting interstate commerce. The substitute would strike provisions that would pre-empt state laws that require written notices be provided to consumers or written records maintained. Rejected 126-278: R 3-209; D 122-69 (ND 105-39, SD 17-30); I 1-0. Nov. 9, 1999.

579. HR 1714. Electronic Signatures/Passage. Passage of the bill to promote electronic commerce and establish a minimum federal standard for the use and recognition of electronic signatures. The bill would ensure that electronic signatures are given the same legal validity and enforceability as written ones. Consumers would have to consent to the use of electronic records and be provided with information on how to access those records. Passed 356-66: R 213-2; D 143-63 (ND 94-59, SD 49-4); I 0-1. Nov. 9, 1999. A "nay" was a vote in support of the president's position.

580. H Con Res 223. Anniversary of Fall of Berlin Wall/Adoption. Gilman, R-N.Y., motion to suspend the rules and adopt the concurrent resolution to commemorate the 10-year anniversary of the fall of the Berlin Wall. Motion agreed to 417-0: R 215-0; D 201-0 (ND 150-0, SD 51-0); I 1-0. Nov. 9, 1999. A two-thirds majority of those present and voting (278 in this case) is required for adoption under suspension of the rules.

Key

- Y Voted for (yea).
- # Paired for.
- + Announced for.
- N Voted against (nay).
- X Paired against.
- – Announced against.
- P Voted "present."
- C Voted "present" to avoid possible conflict of interest.
- ? Did not vote or otherwise make a position known.

•

Democrats ***Republicans***
Independents

	576	577	578	579	580
ALABAMA					
1 ***Callahan***	Y	Y	N	Y	Y
2 ***Everett***	Y	Y	N	Y	Y
3 ***Riley***	Y	Y	N	Y	Y
4 ***Aderholt***	Y	Y	N	Y	Y
5 Cramer	Y	Y	N	Y	Y
6 ***Bachus***	Y	Y	N	Y	Y
7 Hilliard	Y	Y	Y	Y	Y
ALASKA					
AL ***Young***	Y	Y	N	Y	Y
ARIZONA					
1 ***Salmon***	Y	Y	N	Y	Y
2 Pastor	Y	Y	Y	Y	Y
3 ***Stump***	Y	Y	N	Y	Y
4 ***Shadegg***	Y	Y	N	Y	Y
5 ***Kolbe***	Y	Y	N	Y	Y
6 ***Hayworth***	Y	Y	N	Y	Y
ARKANSAS					
1 Berry	Y	Y	+	Y	Y
2 Snyder	Y	Y	?	Y	Y
3 ***Hutchinson***	Y	?	?	Y	Y
4 ***Dickey***	Y	?	?	?	Y
CALIFORNIA					
1 Thompson	Y	Y	N	Y	Y
2 ***Herger***	Y	Y	N	Y	Y
3 ***Ose***	Y	Y	N	Y	Y
4 ***Doolittle***	Y	Y	N	Y	Y
5 Matsui	Y	?	?	?	?
6 Woolsey	Y	Y	Y	N	Y
7 Miller, George	Y	Y	Y	Y	Y
8 Pelosi	Y	Y	N	Y	Y
9 Lee	Y	Y	Y	N	Y
10 Tauscher	Y	Y	N	Y	Y
11 ***Pombo***	Y	Y	N	Y	Y
12 Lantos	Y	Y	Y	Y	Y
13 Stark	Y	Y	Y	N	Y
14 Eshoo	Y	Y	Y	Y	Y
15 ***Campbell***	Y	Y	N	Y	Y
16 Lofgren	Y	Y	N	Y	Y
17 Farr	Y	Y	Y	Y	Y
18 Condit	Y	?	N	Y	Y
19 ***Radanovich***	Y	Y	N	Y	Y
20 Dooley	Y	Y	N	Y	Y
21 ***Thomas***	+	Y	N	Y	Y
22 Capps	Y	Y	Y	Y	Y
23 ***Gallegly***	Y	Y	N	Y	Y
24 Sherman	Y	Y	N	Y	Y
25 ***McKeon***	Y	Y	N	Y	Y
26 Berman	?	Y	Y	N	Y
27 ***Rogan***	Y	Y	–	Y	Y
28 ***Dreier***	Y	Y	N	Y	Y
29 Waxman	Y	Y	Y	N	Y
30 Becerra	?	Y	Y	Y	Y
31 Martinez	Y	Y	Y	Y	?
32 Dixon	Y	Y	Y	N	Y
33 Roybal-Allard	Y	Y	Y	N	Y
34 Napolitano	Y	Y	N	Y	Y
35 Waters	Y	Y	Y	N	Y
36 ***Kuykendall***	Y	Y	N	Y	Y
37 Millender-McD.	Y	Y	?	Y	Y
38 ***Horn***	Y	Y	N	Y	Y
39 ***Royce***	Y	Y	N	Y	Y
40 ***Lewis***	Y	Y	N	Y	Y
41 ***Miller***	+	Y	N	Y	Y
42 Vacant					
43 ***Calvert***	?	Y	N	Y	Y
44 ***Bono***	?	Y	N	Y	Y
45 ***Rohrabacher***	Y	Y	N	Y	Y
46 Sanchez	Y	Y	N	Y	Y
47 ***Cox***	?	Y	N	Y	Y
48 ***Packard***	Y	Y	N	Y	Y
49 ***Bilbray***	Y	Y	N	Y	Y
50 Filner	Y	Y	Y	N	Y
51 ***Cunningham***	Y	Y	N	Y	Y
52 ***Hunter***	Y	Y	N	Y	Y
COLORADO					
1 DeGette	Y	Y	Y	Y	Y
2 Udall	Y	Y	N	Y	Y
3 ***McInnis***	Y	Y	N	Y	Y
4 ***Schaffer***	Y	Y	N	Y	Y
5 ***Hefley***	Y	Y	N	Y	Y
6 ***Tancredo***	Y	Y	N	Y	Y
CONNECTICUT					
1 Larson	Y	Y	N	Y	Y
2 Gejdenson	Y	Y	N	Y	Y
3 DeLauro	Y	Y	Y	Y	Y
4 ***Shays***	Y	Y	N	Y	Y
5 Maloney	Y	Y	N	Y	Y
6 ***Johnson***	?	Y	N	Y	Y
DELAWARE					
AL ***Castle***	Y	Y	N	Y	Y
FLORIDA					
1 ***Scarborough***	?	?	?	?	?
2 Boyd	Y	Y	N	Y	Y
3 Brown	Y	Y	N	Y	Y
4 ***Fowler***	Y	Y	N	Y	Y
5 Thurman	Y	Y	N	Y	Y
6 ***Stearns***	Y	Y	N	Y	Y
7 ***Mica***	Y	Y	N	Y	Y
8 ***McCollum***	Y	Y	N	Y	Y
9 ***Bilirakis***	Y	Y	N	Y	Y
10 ***Young***	Y	Y	N	Y	?
11 Davis	Y	Y	N	Y	Y
12 ***Canady***	Y	Y	N	Y	Y
13 ***Miller***	Y	Y	N	Y	Y
14 ***Goss***	Y	Y	N	Y	Y
15 ***Weldon***	Y	Y	N	Y	Y
16 ***Foley***	Y	Y	N	Y	Y
17 Meek	Y	?	?	Y	Y
18 ***Ros-Lehtinen***	Y	Y	N	Y	Y
19 Wexler	Y	Y	Y	?	?
20 Deutsch	Y	Y	N	Y	Y
21 ***Diaz-Balart***	Y	Y	N	Y	Y
22 ***Shaw***	Y	Y	N	Y	Y
23 Hastings	Y	Y	Y	Y	?
GEORGIA					
1 ***Kingston***	Y	Y	N	Y	Y
2 Bishop	Y	Y	N	Y	Y
3 ***Collins***	Y	Y	N	Y	Y
4 McKinney	Y	Y	Y	N	Y
5 Lewis	?	Y	Y	Y	Y
6 ***Isakson***	Y	Y	N	Y	Y
7 ***Barr***	Y	Y	N	Y	Y
8 ***Chambliss***	Y	Y	N	Y	Y
9 ***Deal***	Y	Y	N	?	?
10 ***Norwood***	Y	Y	N	Y	Y
11 ***Linder***	Y	Y	N	Y	Y
HAWAII					
1 Abercrombie	Y	Y	Y	Y	Y
2 Mink	Y	Y	Y	N	Y
IDAHO					
1 ***Chenoweth-Hage***	+	Y	N	N	+
2 ***Simpson***	Y	Y	N	Y	Y
ILLINOIS					
1 Rush	?	Y	Y	Y	Y
2 Jackson	Y	Y	Y	N	Y
3 Lipinski	Y	Y	Y	Y	Y
4 Gutierrez	Y	Y	Y	Y	Y
5 Blagojevich	?	Y	Y	N	Y
6 ***Hyde***	Y	Y	N	Y	Y
7 Davis	Y	Y	?	N	Y
8 ***Crane***	?	Y	N	Y	Y
9 Schakowsky	Y	Y	Y	N	Y
10 ***Porter***	Y	Y	N	Y	Y
11 ***Weller***	Y	Y	N	Y	Y
12 Costello	Y	Y	Y	N	Y
13 ***Biggert***	Y	Y	N	Y	Y
14 ***Hastert***					

ND Northern Democrats SD Southern Democrats

	576	577	578	579	580
15 ***Ewing***	Y	Y	N	Y	Y
16 ***Manzullo***	Y	Y	N	Y	Y
17 Evans	Y	Y	Y	N	Y
18 ***LaHood***	Y	Y	N	Y	Y
19 Phelps	Y	Y	Y	N	Y
20 ***Shimkus***	Y	Y	N	Y	Y
INDIANA					
1 Visclosky	Y	Y	Y	N	Y
2 ***McIntosh***	Y	Y	N	Y	Y
3 Roemer	Y	Y	N	Y	Y
4 ***Souder***	Y	Y	N	Y	Y
5 ***Buyer***	Y	Y	N	Y	Y
6 ***Burton***	Y	Y	N	Y	Y
7 ***Pease***	Y	Y	N	Y	Y
8 ***Hostettler***	Y	Y	N	Y	Y
9 Hill	Y	Y	N	Y	Y
10 Carson	+	Y	+	Y	Y
IOWA					
1 ***Leach***	Y	Y	N	Y	Y
2 ***Nussle***	Y	Y	N	Y	Y
3 Boswell	Y	Y	N	Y	Y
4 ***Ganske***	Y	Y	N	Y	Y
5 ***Latham***	Y	Y	N	Y	Y
KANSAS					
1 ***Moran***	Y	Y	N	Y	Y
2 ***Ryun***	Y	Y	N	Y	Y
3 Moore	Y	Y	N	Y	Y
4 ***Tiahrt***	+	?	N	Y	Y
KENTUCKY					
1 ***Whitfield***	Y	Y	N	Y	Y
2 ***Lewis***	Y	Y	N	Y	Y
3 ***Northup***	Y	Y	N	Y	Y
4 Lucas	Y	Y	N	Y	Y
5 ***Rogers***	Y	Y	N	Y	Y
6 ***Fletcher***	Y	Y	N	Y	Y
LOUISIANA					
1 ***Vitter***	Y	Y	N	Y	Y
2 Jefferson	?	Y	?	Y	Y
3 ***Tauzin***	Y	Y	N	Y	Y
4 ***McCrery***	Y	Y	N	Y	Y
5 ***Cooksey***	Y	Y	N	Y	Y
6 ***Baker***	Y	Y	N	Y	Y
7 John	Y	Y	N	Y	Y
MAINE					
1 Allen	Y	Y	Y	Y	Y
2 Baldacci	Y	Y	Y	Y	Y
MARYLAND					
1 ***Gilchrest***	Y	Y	N	Y	Y
2 ***Ehrlich***	Y	Y	N	Y	Y
3 Cardin	Y	Y	Y	Y	Y
4 Wynn	Y	Y	Y	Y	Y
5 Hoyer	Y	Y	Y	Y	?
6 ***Bartlett***	Y	Y	N	Y	Y
7 Cummings	Y	Y	?	Y	Y
8 ***Morella***	Y	Y	?	Y	Y
MASSACHUSETTS					
1 Olver	Y	Y	Y	N	Y
2 Neal	?	Y	Y	Y	Y
3 McGovern	Y	Y	Y	Y	Y
4 Frank	Y	Y	Y	Y	Y
5 Meehan	Y	Y	Y	Y	Y
6 Tierney	?	Y	Y	N	Y
7 Markey	Y	Y	Y	Y	Y
8 Capuano	Y	Y	Y	Y	Y
9 Moakley	?	Y	Y	Y	Y
10 Delahunt	Y	Y	Y	N	Y
MICHIGAN					
1 Stupak	Y	Y	Y	N	Y
2 ***Hoekstra***	?	Y	N	Y	Y
3 ***Ehlers***	Y	Y	N	Y	Y
4 ***Camp***	Y	Y	N	Y	Y
5 Barcia	Y	Y	N	Y	Y
6 ***Upton***	Y	Y	N	Y	Y
7 ***Smith***	Y	Y	Y	Y	Y
8 Stabenow	Y	Y	N	Y	Y
9 Kildee	Y	Y	Y	N	Y
10 Bonior	Y	Y	Y	N	Y
11 ***Knollenberg***	Y	Y	N	Y	Y
12 Levin	Y	Y	Y	N	Y
13 Rivers	Y	Y	Y	N	Y
14 Conyers	Y	Y	Y	N	Y
15 Kilpatrick	+	Y	Y	N	Y
16 Dingell	Y	Y	Y	N	Y
MINNESOTA					
1 ***Gutknecht***	Y	Y	N	Y	Y
2 Minge	Y	Y	N	Y	Y
3 ***Ramstad***	?	Y	N	Y	Y
4 Vento	Y	N	Y	N	Y
5 Sabo	Y	Y	Y	N	Y
6 Luther	Y	Y	Y	N	Y
7 Peterson	Y	Y	N	Y	Y
8 Oberstar	Y	Y	Y	N	Y
MISSISSIPPI					
1 ***Wicker***	Y	Y	N	Y	Y
2 Thompson	Y	Y	?	Y	Y
3 ***Pickering***	Y	Y	N	Y	Y
4 Shows	Y	Y	N	Y	Y
5 Taylor	Y	Y	N	N	Y
MISSOURI					
1 Clay	Y	Y	?	Y	Y
2 ***Talent***	Y	Y	N	Y	Y
3 Gephardt	Y	?	?	?	?
4 Skelton	Y	Y	N	Y	Y
5 McCarthy	Y	Y	Y	Y	Y
6 Danner	Y	Y	Y	Y	Y
7 ***Blunt***	?	Y	N	Y	Y
8 ***Emerson***	Y	Y	N	Y	Y
9 ***Hulshof***	Y	Y	N	Y	Y
MONTANA					
AL ***Hill***	Y	Y	N	Y	Y
NEBRASKA					
1 ***Bereuter***	Y	Y	N	Y	Y
2 ***Terry***	Y	Y	N	Y	Y
3 ***Barrett***	Y	Y	N	Y	Y
NEVADA					
1 Berkley	Y	Y	N	Y	Y
2 ***Gibbons***	Y	Y	N	Y	Y
NEW HAMPSHIRE					
1 ***Sununu***	Y	Y	N	Y	Y
2 ***Bass***	Y	Y	N	Y	Y
NEW JERSEY					
1 Andrews	Y	Y	Y	Y	Y
2 ***LoBiondo***	Y	Y	N	Y	Y
3 ***Saxton***	Y	Y	N	Y	Y
4 ***Smith***	Y	Y	N	Y	Y
5 ***Roukema***	Y	Y	N	Y	Y
6 Pallone	Y	Y	Y	Y	Y
7 ***Franks***	Y	Y	N	Y	Y
8 Pascrell	+	+	–	+	+
9 Rothman	Y	Y	Y	N	Y
10 Payne	Y	Y	?	N	Y
11 ***Frelinghuysen***	Y	Y	N	Y	Y
12 Holt	Y	Y	N	Y	Y
13 Menendez	?	Y	Y	N	Y
NEW MEXICO					
1 ***Wilson***	Y	Y	N	Y	Y
2 ***Skeen***	Y	Y	N	Y	Y
3 Udall	Y	Y	N	Y	Y
NEW YORK					
1 Forbes	Y	Y	N	Y	Y
2 ***Lazio***	Y	Y	N	Y	Y
3 ***King***	Y	Y	?	Y	Y
4 McCarthy	Y	Y	N	Y	Y
5 Ackerman	Y	Y	Y	N	Y
6 Meeks	?	Y	?	N	Y
7 Crowley	Y	Y	N	Y	Y
8 Nadler	?	Y	Y	N	Y
9 Weiner	Y	Y	Y	N	Y
10 Towns	Y	Y	Y	Y	Y
11 Owens	?	Y	+	Y	Y
12 Velázquez	Y	Y	Y	Y	Y
13 ***Fossella***	Y	Y	N	Y	Y
14 Maloney	Y	Y	Y	Y	Y
15 Rangel	Y	Y	Y	Y	Y
16 Serrano	Y	Y	Y	N	Y
17 Engel	Y	Y	Y	N	Y
18 Lowey	Y	Y	Y	N	Y
19 ***Kelly***	Y	Y	N	Y	Y
20 ***Gilman***	Y	Y	N	Y	Y
21 McNulty	Y	Y	Y	Y	Y
22 ***Sweeney***	Y	Y	N	Y	Y
23 ***Boehlert***	Y	Y	N	Y	Y
24 ***McHugh***	Y	Y	N	Y	Y
25 ***Walsh***	?	Y	N	Y	Y
26 Hinchey	Y	Y	Y	N	Y
27 ***Reynolds***	Y	Y	N	Y	Y
28 Slaughter	Y	Y	Y	N	Y
29 LaFalce	Y	Y	Y	N	Y
30 ***Quinn***	Y	Y	N	Y	Y
31 ***Houghton***	Y	Y	N	Y	Y
NORTH CAROLINA					
1 Clayton	Y	Y	Y	Y	Y
2 Etheridge	Y	Y	N	Y	Y
3 ***Jones***	Y	Y	N	Y	Y
4 Price	?	Y	N	Y	Y
5 ***Burr***	Y	Y	N	Y	Y
6 ***Coble***	Y	Y	N	Y	Y
7 McIntyre	Y	Y	N	Y	Y
8 ***Hayes***	Y	Y	N	Y	Y
9 ***Myrick***	Y	Y	N	Y	Y
10 ***Ballenger***	Y	Y	N	Y	Y
11 ***Taylor***	Y	Y	N	Y	Y
12 Watt	Y	Y	Y	N	Y
NORTH DAKOTA					
AL Pomeroy	Y	Y	Y	Y	Y
OHIO					
1 ***Chabot***	Y	Y	N	Y	Y
2 ***Portman***	Y	Y	N	Y	Y
3 Hall	Y	Y	Y	Y	Y
4 ***Oxley***	Y	Y	N	Y	Y
5 ***Gillmor***	Y	Y	N	Y	Y
6 Strickland	Y	Y	Y	Y	Y
7 ***Hobson***	Y	Y	N	Y	Y
8 ***Boehner***	Y	Y	N	Y	Y
9 Kaptur	Y	Y	Y	Y	Y
10 Kucinich	Y	Y	Y	N	Y
11 Jones	Y	Y	?	N	Y
12 ***Kasich***	Y	Y	N	Y	Y
13 Brown	Y	Y	Y	N	Y
14 Sawyer	Y	Y	Y	Y	Y
15 ***Pryce***	Y	Y	N	Y	Y
16 ***Regula***	Y	Y	N	Y	Y
17 Traficant	Y	Y	N	Y	Y
18 ***Ney***	Y	Y	N	Y	Y
19 ***LaTourette***	Y	Y	N	Y	Y
OKLAHOMA					
1 ***Largent***	?	?	?	?	Y
2 ***Coburn***	Y	?	?	?	Y
3 ***Watkins***	Y	Y	N	Y	Y
4 ***Watts***	?	Y	N	Y	Y
5 ***Istook***	Y	Y	N	Y	Y
6 ***Lucas***	Y	Y	N	Y	Y
OREGON					
1 Wu	Y	Y	N	Y	Y
2 ***Walden***	Y	Y	N	Y	Y
3 Blumenauer	Y	Y	N	Y	Y
4 DeFazio	Y	Y	Y	N	Y
5 Hooley	Y	Y	N	Y	Y
PENNSYLVANIA					
1 Brady	Y	Y	Y	N	Y
2 Fattah	Y	Y	Y	N	Y
3 Borski	Y	Y	Y	Y	Y
4 Klink	Y	Y	Y	N	Y
5 ***Peterson***	Y	Y	N	Y	Y
6 Holden	Y	Y	N	Y	Y
7 ***Weldon***	Y	Y	N	Y	Y
8 ***Greenwood***	Y	Y	N	Y	Y
9 ***Shuster***	Y	Y	N	Y	+
10 ***Sherwood***	Y	Y	N	Y	Y
11 Kanjorski	Y	Y	Y	N	Y
12 Murtha	Y	Y	N	Y	Y
13 Hoeffel	Y	Y	Y	N	Y
14 Coyne	Y	Y	Y	Y	Y
15 ***Toomey***	Y	Y	N	Y	Y
16 ***Pitts***	Y	Y	N	Y	Y
17 ***Gekas***	Y	Y	N	Y	Y
18 Doyle	Y	Y	Y	Y	Y
19 ***Goodling***	Y	Y	N	Y	Y
20 Mascara	Y	Y	Y	Y	Y
21 ***English***	Y	Y	N	Y	Y
RHODE ISLAND					
1 Kennedy	Y	Y	Y	Y	Y
2 Weygand	Y	Y	N	Y	Y
SOUTH CAROLINA					
1 ***Sanford***	?	Y	N	Y	Y
2 ***Spence***	Y	?	N	Y	Y
3 ***Graham***	Y	Y	N	Y	Y
4 ***DeMint***	Y	Y	N	Y	Y
5 Spratt	Y	Y	Y	Y	?
6 Clyburn	Y	Y	Y	Y	Y
SOUTH DAKOTA					
AL ***Thune***	Y	Y	N	Y	Y
TENNESSEE					
1 ***Jenkins***	Y	Y	N	Y	Y
2 ***Duncan***	Y	Y	Y	Y	Y
3 ***Wamp***	Y	Y	N	Y	Y
4 ***Hilleary***	Y	Y	N	Y	Y
5 Clement	Y	Y	N	Y	Y
6 Gordon	Y	Y	N	Y	Y
7 ***Bryant***	Y	Y	N	Y	Y
8 Tanner	Y	Y	N	Y	Y
9 Ford	Y	Y	N	Y	Y
TEXAS					
1 Sandlin	Y	Y	N	Y	Y
2 Turner	Y	Y	Y	Y	Y
3 ***Johnson, Sam***	Y	Y	N	Y	Y
4 Hall	Y	Y	N	Y	Y
5 ***Sessions***	?	Y	N	Y	Y
6 ***Barton***	Y	Y	N	Y	Y
7 ***Archer***	Y	Y	N	Y	Y
8 ***Brady***	Y	Y	N	Y	Y
9 Lampson	Y	Y	Y	Y	Y
10 Doggett	Y	Y	N	Y	Y
11 Edwards	Y	Y	Y	?	?
12 ***Granger***	?	Y	N	Y	Y
13 ***Thornberry***	Y	Y	N	Y	Y
14 ***Paul***	Y	N	Y	N	Y
15 Hinojosa	Y	Y	Y	Y	Y
16 Reyes	Y	Y	Y	Y	Y
17 Stenholm	?	Y	N	Y	Y
18 Jackson-Lee	Y	Y	+	Y	Y
19 ***Combest***	Y	Y	N	Y	Y
20 Gonzalez	Y	Y	N	Y	Y
21 ***Smith***	Y	?	?	?	?
22 ***DeLay***	Y	Y	N	Y	Y
23 ***Bonilla***	Y	Y	N	Y	Y
24 Frost	Y	Y	N	Y	Y
25 Bentsen	Y	Y	N	Y	Y
26 ***Armey***	?	Y	N	Y	Y
27 Ortiz	Y	Y	Y	Y	Y
28 Rodriguez	?	Y	?	Y	Y
29 Green	Y	Y	Y	Y	Y
30 Johnson, E.B.	Y	Y	–	Y	Y
UTAH					
1 ***Hansen***	?	Y	N	Y	Y
2 ***Cook***	?	Y	N	Y	Y
3 ***Cannon***	Y	Y	N	Y	Y
VERMONT					
AL *Sanders*	Y	Y	Y	N	Y
VIRGINIA					
1 ***Bateman***	Y	Y	N	Y	Y
2 Pickett	Y	Y	N	Y	Y
3 Scott	Y	Y	Y	N	Y
4 Sisisky	Y	Y	N	Y	Y
5 Goode	Y	Y	N	Y	Y
6 ***Goodlatte***	Y	Y	N	Y	Y
7 ***Bliley***	Y	Y	N	Y	Y
8 Moran	Y	Y	N	Y	Y
9 Boucher	Y	Y	N	Y	Y
10 ***Wolf***	Y	Y	N	Y	Y
11 ***Davis***	Y	Y	N	Y	Y
WASHINGTON					
1 Inslee	Y	Y	N	Y	Y
2 ***Metcalf***	Y	Y	N	Y	Y
3 Baird	Y	Y	N	Y	Y
4 ***Hastings***	Y	Y	N	Y	Y
5 ***Nethercutt***	Y	Y	N	Y	Y
6 Dicks	Y	Y	Y	Y	Y
7 McDermott	Y	Y	Y	Y	?
8 ***Dunn***	Y	Y	N	Y	Y
9 Smith	Y	Y	N	Y	Y
WEST VIRGINIA					
1 Mollohan	Y	Y	Y	Y	Y
2 Wise	?	Y	Y	Y	Y
3 Rahall	Y	Y	Y	N	Y
WISCONSIN					
1 ***Ryan***	Y	Y	N	Y	Y
2 Baldwin	Y	Y	Y	N	Y
3 Kind	Y	Y	N	Y	Y
4 Kleczka	?	Y	Y	Y	Y
5 Barrett	Y	Y	Y	N	Y
6 ***Petri***	Y	Y	N	Y	Y
7 Obey	Y	Y	Y	N	Y
8 ***Green***	?	Y	N	Y	Y
9 ***Sensenbrenner***	Y	Y	N	Y	Y
WYOMING					
AL ***Cubin***	Y	Y	N	Y	Y

Southern states - Ala., Ark., Fla., Ga., Ky., La., Miss., N.C., Okla., S.C., Tenn., Texas, Va.

581. **HR 1554. Satellite Copyright, Competition and Consumer Protection Act/Conference Report.** Armey, R-Texas, motion to suspend the rules and adopt the conference report on the bill to permit satellite television providers to deliver local broadcast stations to customers. The measure would require satellite providers to carry all local stations in all towns and cities they serve by 2002. Motion agreed to (thus sent to the Senate) 411-8: R 212-3; D 198-5 (ND 146-5, SD 52-0); I 1-0. Nov. 9, 1999. A two-thirds majority of those present and voting (280 in this case) is required for adoption under suspension of the rules. A "yea" was a vote in support of the presiden't position.

582. **HR 3073. Responsible Fatherhood/Rule.** Adoption of the rule (H Res 367) to provide for House floor consideration of the bill to establish a grant program to cover educational, economic and employment initiatives to promote responsible fatherhood. Adopted 278-144: R 211-4; D 67-139 (ND 43-108, SD 24-31); I 0-1. Nov. 10, 1999.

583. **HR 3073. Responsible Fatherhood/Parents.** Mink, D-Hawaii, amendment to replace the word "father" with the word "parent" and to make several other changes. Rejected 172-253: R 2-212; D 169-41 (ND 135-20, SD 34-21); I 1-0. Nov. 10, 1999.

584. **HR 3073. Responsible Fatherhood/Sectarian Organizations.** Edwards, D-Texas, amendment to prohibit funding under the bill to any faith-based organization that is "pervasively sectarian." Rejected 184-238: R 7-204; D 176-34 (ND 138-17, SD 38-17); I 1-0. Nov. 10, 1999.

585. **HR 3073. Responsible Fatherhood/Recommit.** Scott, D-Va., motion to recommit the bill to the Ways and Means Committee with instructions to report it back to the House with an amendment to prohibit employment discrimination by religious institutions that receive federal funding. Motion rejected 176-246: R 2-212; D 173-34 (ND 133-19, SD 40-15); I 1-0. Nov. 10, 1999.

586. **HR 3073. Responsible Fatherhood/Passage.** Passage of the bill to authorize $150 million over six years for grants to nonprofit groups and state agencies that create programs to promote responsible fatherhood and create educational, economic and employment opportunities. The measure includes offsets that would crack down on student loan defaults and would repeal a bonus to states that achieve high performance on welfare-to-work programs. Passed 328-93: R 172-42; D 156-50 (ND 112-39, SD 44-11); I 0-1. Nov. 10, 1999. A "yea" was a vote in support of the president's position.

Key

- Y Voted for (yea).
- # Paired for.
- \+ Announced for.
- N Voted against (nay).
- X Paired against.
- – Announced against.
- P Voted "present."
- C Voted "present" to avoid possible conflict of interest.
- ? Did not vote or otherwise make a position known.

•

Democrats ***Republicans***
Independents

	581	582	583	584	585	586
ALABAMA						
1 ***Callahan***	Y	Y	N	N	N	?
2 ***Everett***	Y	Y	N	N	N	Y
3 ***Riley***	Y	Y	N	N	N	Y
4 ***Aderholt***	Y	Y	N	N	N	Y
5 Cramer	Y	Y	N	N	N	Y
6 ***Bachus***	Y	Y	N	N	N	Y
7 Hilliard	Y	N	Y	Y	Y	Y
ALASKA						
AL ***Young***	Y	Y	N	N	N	Y
ARIZONA						
1 ***Salmon***	Y	Y	N	?	N	N
2 Pastor	Y	Y	Y	N	Y	Y
3 ***Stump***	Y	Y	N	N	N	N
4 ***Shadegg***	Y	N	N	N	N	N
5 ***Kolbe***	Y	Y	N	N	N	Y
6 ***Hayworth***	Y	Y	N	N	N	Y
ARKANSAS						
1 Berry	Y	Y	N	N	N	Y
2 Snyder	Y	N	N	Y	Y	Y
3 ***Hutchinson***	Y	Y	N	N	N	N
4 ***Dickey***	Y	N	N	N	Y	N
CALIFORNIA						
1 Thompson	Y	N	Y	Y	Y	Y
2 ***Herger***	Y	Y	N	N	N	Y
3 ***Ose***	Y	Y	N	Y	N	Y
4 ***Doolittle***	Y	Y	N	N	N	N
5 Matsui	?	?	?	?	?	?
6 Woolsey	Y	N	Y	Y	Y	N
7 Miller, George	Y	N	Y	Y	Y	Y
8 Pelosi	Y	N	Y	Y	Y	N
9 Lee	Y	N	Y	Y	Y	Y
10 Tauscher	Y	N	N	N	N	Y
11 ***Pombo***	Y	Y	N	N	N	N
12 Lantos	Y	N	Y	Y	Y	N
13 Stark	Y	N	Y	Y	Y	N
14 Eshoo	Y	Y	Y	Y	Y	Y
15 ***Campbell***	Y	Y	Y	N	N	N
16 Lofgren	Y	N	Y	Y	?	?
17 Farr	Y	N	Y	Y	Y	Y
18 Condit	Y	N	N	N	Y	Y
19 ***Radanovich***	Y	Y	N	N	N	Y
20 Dooley	Y	N	Y	Y	Y	Y
21 ***Thomas***	Y	Y	N	N	N	Y
22 Capps	Y	N	Y	Y	Y	Y
23 ***Gallegly***	Y	Y	N	N	N	Y
24 Sherman	Y	Y	Y	Y	Y	N
25 ***McKeon***	Y	Y	N	N	N	Y
26 Berman	Y	N	Y	Y	Y	N
27 ***Rogan***	Y	Y	–	–	–	Y
28 ***Dreier***	Y	Y	N	N	N	Y
29 Waxman	Y	N	Y	Y	Y	N
30 Becerra	Y	N	Y	Y	Y	Y
31 Martinez	?	N	Y	Y	Y	Y
32 Dixon	Y	N	Y	Y	Y	Y
33 Roybal-Allard	Y	N	Y	Y	Y	Y
34 Napolitano	Y	Y	Y	Y	Y	Y
35 Waters	N	N	Y	Y	Y	N
36 ***Kuykendall***	Y	Y	N	N	N	Y
37 Millender-McD.	Y	N	Y	Y	Y	Y
38 ***Horn***	Y	Y	N	N	N	Y
39 ***Royce***	Y	Y	N	N	N	N
40 ***Lewis***	Y	Y	N	N	N	Y
41 ***Miller***	Y	Y	N	N	N	Y
42 Vacant						
43 ***Calvert***	Y	Y	N	N	N	Y
44 ***Bono***	Y	Y	N	N	N	Y
45 ***Rohrabacher***	Y	Y	N	N	N	N
46 Sanchez	Y	N	Y	Y	Y	Y
47 ***Cox***	Y	Y	N	N	N	N
48 ***Packard***	Y	Y	N	N	N	Y
49 ***Bilbray***	Y	Y	N	N	N	Y
50 Filner	Y	N	Y	Y	Y	N
51 ***Cunningham***	Y	Y	N	N	N	Y
52 ***Hunter***	Y	Y	N	N	N	Y
COLORADO						
1 DeGette	Y	Y	Y	Y	?	?
2 Udall	Y	N	Y	Y	Y	Y
3 ***McInnis***	Y	Y	N	N	N	Y
4 ***Schaffer***	Y	Y	N	N	N	N
5 ***Hefley***	Y	Y	N	N	N	Y
6 ***Tancredo***	N	Y	N	N	N	Y
CONNECTICUT						
1 Larson	Y	N	Y	Y	Y	Y
2 Gejdenson	Y	N	Y	Y	Y	N
3 DeLauro	Y	Y	Y	Y	Y	Y
4 ***Shays***	Y	Y	N	N	N	Y
5 Maloney	Y	Y	Y	Y	Y	Y
6 ***Johnson***	Y	Y	N	N	N	Y
DELAWARE						
AL ***Castle***	Y	Y	N	N	N	Y
FLORIDA						
1 ***Scarborough***	?	?	N	N	N	N
2 Boyd	Y	N	N	Y	N	Y
3 Brown	Y	N	Y	Y	Y	Y
4 ***Fowler***	Y	Y	N	N	N	Y
5 Thurman	Y	N	Y	Y	Y	Y
6 ***Stearns***	Y	Y	N	N	N	Y
7 ***Mica***	Y	Y	N	N	N	Y
8 ***McCollum***	Y	Y	N	N	N	Y
9 ***Bilirakis***	Y	Y	N	N	N	Y
10 ***Young***	Y	Y	N	N	N	Y
11 Davis	Y	Y	N	Y	N	Y
12 ***Canady***	Y	Y	N	N	N	Y
13 ***Miller***	Y	Y	N	N	N	Y
14 ***Goss***	Y	Y	N	N	N	Y
15 ***Weldon***	Y	Y	N	N	N	Y
16 ***Foley***	Y	Y	N	N	N	Y
17 Meek	Y	N	Y	Y	Y	N
18 ***Ros-Lehtinen***	Y	Y	N	N	N	Y
19 Wexler	?	N	Y	Y	Y	N
20 Deutsch	Y	N	Y	Y	Y	N
21 ***Diaz-Balart***	Y	Y	N	N	N	Y
22 ***Shaw***	Y	Y	N	N	N	Y
23 Hastings	Y	N	Y	Y	Y	N
GEORGIA						
1 ***Kingston***	Y	Y	N	N	N	N
2 Bishop	Y	Y	N	N	Y	Y
3 ***Collins***	Y	Y	N	N	N	N
4 McKinney	Y	N	Y	Y	Y	N
5 Lewis	Y	N	Y	Y	Y	Y
6 ***Isakson***	Y	Y	N	N	N	Y
7 ***Barr***	Y	Y	N	N	N	N
8 ***Chambliss***	Y	Y	N	N	N	Y
9 ***Deal***	?	?	N	N	N	Y
10 ***Norwood***	Y	Y	N	N	N	Y
11 ***Linder***	Y	Y	N	N	N	Y
HAWAII						
1 Abercrombie	Y	N	Y	Y	Y	N
2 Mink	Y	N	Y	Y	Y	N
IDAHO						
1 ***Chenoweth-Hage***	+	Y	N	N	N	N
2 ***Simpson***	Y	Y	–	N	N	Y
ILLINOIS						
1 Rush	Y	N	Y	Y	Y	Y
2 Jackson	Y	N	Y	Y	Y	Y
3 Lipinski	?	Y	N	N	N	Y
4 Gutierrez	Y	N	Y	Y	Y	Y
5 Blagojevich	Y	Y	Y	Y	Y	Y
6 ***Hyde***	Y	Y	N	N	N	Y
7 Davis	Y	N	Y	Y	Y	Y
8 ***Crane***	Y	Y	N	N	?	Y
9 Schakowsky	Y	N	Y	Y	Y	N
10 ***Porter***	Y	Y	N	Y	N	Y
11 ***Weller***	Y	Y	N	N	N	Y
12 Costello	Y	N	N	Y	Y	Y
13 ***Biggert***	Y	Y	N	N	N	Y
14 ***Hastert***						

ND Northern Democrats SD Southern Democrats

	581	582	583	584	585	586
15 ***Ewing***	Y	Y	N	N	N	Y
16 ***Manzullo***	Y	Y	N	N	N	N
17 Evans	Y	N	Y	Y	Y	Y
18 ***LaHood***	Y	Y	N	N	N	N
19 Phelps	Y	Y	N	N	N	Y
20 ***Shimkus***	Y	Y	N	N	N	Y
INDIANA						
1 Visclosky	Y	N	N	N	N	Y
2 ***McIntosh***	Y	Y	N	N	N	Y
3 Roemer	Y	Y	N	N	N	Y
4 ***Souder***	Y	Y	N	N	N	Y
5 ***Buyer***	Y	Y	N	N	N	Y
6 ***Burton***	Y	Y	N	N	N	N
7 ***Pease***	Y	Y	N	N	N	Y
8 ***Hostettler***	Y	Y	N	N	N	N
9 Hill	Y	?	N	N	N	Y
10 Carson	Y	N	Y	Y	Y	Y
IOWA						
1 ***Leach***	Y	Y	N	N	N	Y
2 ***Nussle***	Y	Y	N	N	N	Y
3 Boswell	Y	Y	Y	Y	N	Y
4 ***Ganske***	Y	Y	N	N	N	Y
5 ***Latham***	Y	Y	N	N	N	Y
KANSAS						
1 ***Moran***	Y	Y	N	N	N	N
2 ***Ryun***	Y	Y	N	N	N	N
3 Moore	Y	N	Y	Y	Y	Y
4 ***Tiahrt***	Y	Y	N	N	N	Y
KENTUCKY						
1 ***Whitfield***	Y	Y	N	N	N	Y
2 ***Lewis***	Y	Y	N	N	N	Y
3 ***Northup***	Y	Y	N	N	N	Y
4 Lucas	Y	Y	N	N	N	Y
5 ***Rogers***	Y	Y	N	N	N	Y
6 ***Fletcher***	Y	Y	N	N	N	Y
LOUISIANA						
1 ***Vitter***	Y	Y	N	N	N	Y
2 Jefferson	Y	N	N	Y	Y	Y
3 ***Tauzin***	Y	Y	N	N	N	Y
4 ***McCrery***	Y	Y	N	N	N	Y
5 ***Cooksey***	Y	Y	N	N	N	N
6 ***Baker***	Y	Y	N	N	N	?
7 John	Y	Y	N	N	Y	Y
MAINE						
1 Allen	Y	Y	Y	Y	Y	Y
2 Baldacci	Y	Y	Y	Y	Y	Y
MARYLAND						
1 ***Gilchrest***	Y	Y	N	N	N	Y
2 ***Ehrlich***	Y	Y	N	N	N	Y
3 Cardin	Y	Y	N	Y	Y	Y
4 Wynn	Y	Y	N	Y	Y	Y
5 Hoyer	Y	N	N	Y	Y	Y
6 ***Bartlett***	Y	Y	N	N	N	N
7 Cummings	Y	N	Y	Y	Y	Y
8 ***Morella***	Y	Y	Y	Y	Y	Y
MASSACHUSETTS						
1 Olver	Y	N	Y	Y	Y	N
2 Neal	Y	N	Y	Y	Y	Y
3 McGovern	Y	N	Y	Y	Y	Y
4 Frank	Y	N	Y	Y	Y	N
5 Meehan	Y	N	Y	Y	Y	Y
6 Tierney	Y	?	Y	Y	Y	N
7 Markey	Y	N	Y	Y	Y	N
8 Capuano	Y	N	Y	Y	Y	N
9 Moakley	Y	N	Y	Y	Y	Y
10 Delahunt	Y	N	Y	Y	Y	Y
MICHIGAN						
1 Stupak	Y	N	Y	Y	Y	Y
2 ***Hoekstra***	Y	Y	N	N	N	N
3 ***Ehlers***	Y	Y	N	N	N	Y
4 ***Camp***	Y	Y	N	N	N	Y
5 Barcia	Y	Y	Y	N	N	Y
6 ***Upton***	Y	Y	N	N	N	Y
7 ***Smith***	Y	Y	N	N	N	N
8 Stabenow	Y	N	Y	Y	Y	Y
9 Kildee	Y	N	Y	Y	Y	Y
10 Bonior	Y	N	Y	Y	Y	Y
11 ***Knollenberg***	Y	Y	N	N	N	Y
12 Levin	Y	N	Y	Y	Y	Y
13 Rivers	Y	Y	Y	Y	Y	N
14 Conyers	Y	N	Y	Y	Y	N
15 Kilpatrick	Y	N	Y	Y	Y	N
16 Dingell	Y	N	Y	Y	Y	Y
MINNESOTA						
1 ***Gutknecht***	Y	?	N	N	N	Y
2 Minge	Y	N	Y	Y	Y	Y
3 ***Ramstad***	Y	Y	N	N	N	Y
4 Vento	N	N	Y	Y	Y	Y
5 Sabo	Y	Y	N	Y	Y	Y
6 Luther	Y	N	Y	Y	Y	Y
7 Peterson	Y	Y	N	N	N	N
8 Oberstar	Y	N	Y	Y	Y	Y
MISSISSIPPI						
1 ***Wicker***	Y	Y	N	N	N	Y
2 Thompson	Y	N	Y	Y	Y	Y
3 ***Pickering***	Y	Y	N	N	N	Y
4 Shows	Y	Y	N	N	N	Y
5 Taylor	Y	Y	N	N	N	Y
MISSOURI						
1 Clay	Y	N	Y	Y	Y	N
2 ***Talent***	Y	Y	N	N	N	Y
3 Gephardt	?	Y	Y	Y	Y	Y
4 Skelton	Y	Y	N	N	N	Y
5 McCarthy	Y	N	Y	Y	Y	Y
6 Danner	Y	Y	Y	Y	Y	Y
7 ***Blunt***	Y	Y	N	N	N	Y
8 ***Emerson***	Y	Y	N	N	N	Y
9 ***Hulshof***	Y	Y	N	N	N	Y
MONTANA						
AL ***Hill***	Y	Y	N	N	N	Y
NEBRASKA						
1 ***Bereuter***	Y	Y	N	Y	N	Y
2 ***Terry***	Y	Y	N	N	N	Y
3 ***Barrett***	Y	Y	N	N	N	Y
NEVADA						
1 Berkley	Y	Y	Y	Y	Y	Y
2 ***Gibbons***	Y	Y	N	N	N	Y
NEW HAMPSHIRE						
1 ***Sununu***	Y	Y	N	N	N	N
2 ***Bass***	Y	Y	N	N	N	Y
NEW JERSEY						
1 Andrews	Y	N	Y	Y	Y	Y
2 ***LoBiondo***	Y	Y	N	N	N	Y
3 ***Saxton***	Y	Y	N	N	N	Y
4 ***Smith***	Y	Y	N	N	N	Y
5 ***Roukema***	Y	Y	N	N	N	Y
6 Pallone	Y	N	Y	Y	Y	Y
7 ***Franks***	Y	Y	N	N	N	Y
8 Pascrell	+	Y	Y	Y	N	?
9 Rothman	Y	Y	Y	Y	Y	Y
10 Payne	Y	N	Y	Y	Y	N
11 ***Frelinghuysen***	Y	Y	N	N	N	Y
12 Holt	Y	N	Y	Y	Y	Y
13 Menendez	Y	Y	Y	Y	N	Y
NEW MEXICO						
1 ***Wilson***	Y	Y	N	N	N	Y
2 ***Skeen***	Y	Y	N	N	N	Y
3 Udall	Y	N	Y	Y	Y	Y
NEW YORK						
1 Forbes	Y	Y	N	N	N	Y
2 ***Lazio***	Y	Y	N	N	N	Y
3 ***King***	Y	Y	N	N	N	Y
4 McCarthy	Y	Y	Y	Y	Y	Y
5 Ackerman	Y	N	Y	Y	Y	N
6 Meeks	Y	N	Y	Y	Y	Y
7 Crowley	Y	N	Y	Y	Y	Y
8 Nadler	Y	N	Y	Y	Y	Y
9 Weiner	Y	N	Y	Y	Y	N
10 Towns	Y	?	Y	Y	Y	N
11 Owens	Y	N	Y	Y	Y	N
12 Velázquez	Y	N	Y	Y	Y	N
13 ***Fossella***	Y	Y	N	N	N	Y
14 Maloney	Y	N	Y	Y	Y	N
15 Rangel	Y	Y	Y	Y	Y	Y
16 Serrano	Y	N	Y	Y	Y	N
17 Engel	Y	Y	Y	Y	Y	Y
18 Lowey	Y	N	Y	Y	Y	Y
19 ***Kelly***	Y	Y	N	N	N	Y
20 ***Gilman***	Y	Y	N	N	N	Y
21 McNulty	Y	N	Y	Y	Y	Y
22 ***Sweeney***	Y	Y	N	N	N	Y
23 ***Boehlert***	Y	?	N	Y	N	Y
24 ***McHugh***	Y	Y	N	N	N	Y
25 ***Walsh***	Y	Y	N	N	N	Y
26 Hinchey	Y	N	Y	Y	Y	N
27 ***Reynolds***	Y	Y	N	N	N	Y
28 Slaughter	Y	N	Y	Y	Y	N
29 LaFalce	N	N	N	N	N	Y
30 ***Quinn***	Y	Y	?	?	?	?
31 ***Houghton***	Y	Y	N	?	?	?
NORTH CAROLINA						
1 Clayton	Y	N	Y	Y	Y	Y
2 Etheridge	Y	Y	Y	Y	Y	Y
3 ***Jones***	Y	Y	N	N	N	N
4 Price	Y	Y	Y	Y	Y	Y
5 ***Burr***	Y	Y	N	N	N	Y
6 ***Coble***	Y	Y	N	N	N	Y
7 McIntyre	Y	Y	N	Y	N	Y
8 ***Hayes***	Y	Y	N	N	N	Y
9 ***Myrick***	Y	Y	N	N	N	Y
10 ***Ballenger***	Y	Y	N	N	N	Y
11 ***Taylor***	Y	Y	N	N	N	Y
12 Watt	Y	N	Y	Y	Y	N
NORTH DAKOTA						
AL Pomeroy	Y	N	Y	Y	Y	Y
OHIO						
1 ***Chabot***	Y	Y	N	N	N	N
2 ***Portman***	Y	Y	N	N	N	Y
3 Hall	Y	Y	N	N	N	Y
4 ***Oxley***	Y	Y	N	N	N	Y
5 ***Gillmor***	?	Y	N	N	N	Y
6 Strickland	Y	N	N	Y	Y	Y
7 ***Hobson***	Y	Y	N	N	N	Y
8 ***Boehner***	Y	Y	N	N	N	Y
9 Kaptur	N	N	Y	Y	Y	Y
10 Kucinich	N	Y	Y	Y	Y	Y
11 Jones	Y	N	Y	Y	Y	N
12 ***Kasich***	Y	Y	N	N	N	Y
13 Brown	Y	N	Y	Y	Y	Y
14 Sawyer	Y	N	Y	Y	Y	Y
15 ***Pryce***	Y	Y	N	N	N	Y
16 ***Regula***	Y	Y	N	N	N	Y
17 Traficant	Y	Y	N	N	N	Y
18 ***Ney***	Y	Y	N	N	N	Y
19 ***LaTourette***	Y	?	?	?	N	Y
OKLAHOMA						
1 ***Largent***	Y	N	N	N	N	N
2 ***Coburn***	Y	N	N	N	N	N
3 ***Watkins***	Y	Y	N	N	N	N
4 ***Watts***	Y	Y	N	N	N	Y
5 ***Istook***	Y	Y	N	N	N	Y
6 ***Lucas***	Y	Y	N	N	N	Y
OREGON						
1 Wu	Y	N	Y	Y	Y	Y
2 ***Walden***	Y	Y	N	N	N	Y
3 Blumenauer	Y	Y	Y	Y	Y	Y
4 DeFazio	Y	N	Y	Y	Y	N
5 Hooley	Y	N	Y	Y	?	?
PENNSYLVANIA						
1 Brady	Y	Y	Y	Y	Y	Y
2 Fattah	Y	N	Y	Y	Y	Y
3 Borski	Y	Y	Y	Y	Y	Y
4 Klink	Y	N	Y	Y	Y	Y
5 ***Peterson***	Y	Y	N	N	N	Y
6 Holden	Y	Y	Y	Y	Y	Y
7 ***Weldon***	Y	Y	N	N	N	Y
8 ***Greenwood***	Y	Y	N	N	N	Y
9 ***Shuster***	+	Y	N	N	N	Y
10 ***Sherwood***	Y	Y	N	N	N	Y
11 Kanjorski	Y	N	Y	Y	Y	Y
12 Murtha	Y	?	Y	Y	Y	Y
13 Hoeffel	Y	Y	Y	Y	Y	N
14 Coyne	Y	N	Y	Y	Y	Y
15 ***Toomey***	Y	Y	N	N	N	N
16 ***Pitts***	Y	Y	N	N	N	Y
17 ***Gekas***	Y	Y	N	?	N	Y
18 Doyle	Y	Y	Y	Y	Y	Y
19 ***Goodling***	Y	Y	N	N	N	Y
20 Mascara	Y	Y	Y	Y	Y	Y
21 ***English***	Y	Y	N	N	N	Y
RHODE ISLAND						
1 Kennedy	Y	N	Y	Y	Y	Y
2 Weygand	Y	N	Y	Y	Y	Y
SOUTH CAROLINA						
1 ***Sanford***	N	Y	N	Y	N	N
2 ***Spence***	Y	Y	N	N	N	N
3 ***Graham***	Y	Y	N	N	N	N
4 ***DeMint***	Y	Y	N	N	N	N
5 Spratt	?	N	Y	Y	N	Y
6 Clyburn	Y	N	Y	Y	Y	Y
SOUTH DAKOTA						
AL ***Thune***	Y	Y	N	N	N	Y
TENNESSEE						
1 ***Jenkins***	Y	Y	N	N	N	Y
2 ***Duncan***	Y	Y	N	N	N	Y
3 ***Wamp***	Y	Y	N	N	N	Y
4 ***Hilleary***	Y	Y	N	N	N	Y
5 Clement	Y	Y	N	N	N	Y
6 Gordon	Y	N	N	N	N	Y
7 ***Bryant***	Y	Y	N	N	N	Y
8 Tanner	Y	Y	N	Y	Y	Y
9 Ford	Y	Y	Y	N	Y	Y
TEXAS						
1 Sandlin	Y	Y	Y	Y	Y	Y
2 Turner	Y	Y	N	Y	N	Y
3 ***Johnson, Sam***	Y	Y	N	N	N	N
4 Hall	Y	Y	N	N	N	Y
5 ***Sessions***	Y	Y	N	N	N	N
6 ***Barton***	Y	Y	?	?	?	?
7 ***Archer***	Y	Y	N	?	N	Y
8 ***Brady***	Y	Y	N	N	N	Y
9 Lampson	Y	N	Y	Y	Y	Y
10 Doggett	Y	N	Y	Y	Y	N
11 Edwards	?	N	Y	Y	Y	N
12 ***Granger***	Y	Y	N	N	N	Y
13 ***Thornberry***	Y	Y	?	?	?	?
14 ***Paul***	N	Y	N	Y	N	N
15 Hinojosa	Y	N	Y	N	Y	Y
16 Reyes	Y	Y	Y	N	Y	Y
17 Stenholm	Y	Y	N	N	N	Y
18 Jackson-Lee	Y	N	Y	Y	Y	Y
19 ***Combest***	Y	Y	N	N	N	Y
20 Gonzalez	Y	N	Y	Y	Y	Y
21 ***Smith***	?	?	?	?	?	?
22 ***DeLay***	Y	Y	N	N	N	Y
23 ***Bonilla***	Y	Y	N	N	N	Y
24 Frost	Y	N	Y	Y	Y	Y
25 Bentsen	Y	N	Y	Y	Y	Y
26 ***Armey***	Y	Y	N	N	N	Y
27 Ortiz	Y	Y	Y	N	Y	Y
28 Rodriguez	Y	Y	Y	Y	Y	Y
29 Green	Y	N	Y	Y	Y	Y
30 Johnson, E.B.	Y	N	Y	Y	Y	Y
UTAH						
1 ***Hansen***	Y	Y	N	N	N	Y
2 ***Cook***	Y	Y	N	N	N	Y
3 ***Cannon***	Y	Y	N	N	N	Y
VERMONT						
AL *Sanders*	Y	N	Y	Y	Y	N
VIRGINIA						
1 ***Bateman***	Y	Y	N	N	N	Y
2 Pickett	Y	N	N	N	Y	Y
3 Scott	Y	N	Y	Y	Y	N
4 Sisisky	Y	Y	N	Y	Y	N
5 Goode	Y	Y	N	N	N	N
6 ***Goodlatte***	Y	Y	N	N	N	Y
7 ***Bliley***	Y	Y	N	N	N	Y
8 Moran	Y	Y	Y	Y	Y	Y
9 Boucher	Y	N	Y	Y	Y	Y
10 ***Wolf***	Y	Y	N	N	N	Y
11 ***Davis***	Y	Y	N	N	N	Y
WASHINGTON						
1 Inslee	Y	N	Y	Y	Y	Y
2 ***Metcalf***	Y	Y	N	N	N	Y
3 Baird	Y	Y	Y	Y	Y	N
4 ***Hastings***	Y	Y	N	N	N	Y
5 ***Nethercutt***	Y	Y	N	N	N	Y
6 Dicks	Y	N	Y	Y	Y	Y
7 McDermott	Y	N	Y	Y	Y	N
8 ***Dunn***	Y	Y	N	N	N	Y
9 Smith	Y	N	N	Y	N	Y
WEST VIRGINIA						
1 Mollohan	Y	N	Y	N	N	Y
2 Wise	Y	Y	Y	N	N	Y
3 Rahall	Y	N	Y	Y	Y	Y
WISCONSIN						
1 ***Ryan***	Y	Y	N	N	N	Y
2 Baldwin	Y	N	Y	Y	Y	N
3 Kind	Y	N	Y	Y	Y	Y
4 Kleczka	Y	N	Y	Y	Y	Y
5 Barrett	Y	N	Y	Y	Y	Y
6 ***Petri***	Y	Y	N	N	N	Y
7 Obey	Y	N	Y	Y	Y	Y
8 ***Green***	Y	Y	N	N	N	Y
9 ***Sensenbrenner***	Y	Y	N	N	N	N
WYOMING						
AL ***Cubin***	Y	Y	N	N	N	Y

Southern states - Ala., Ark., Fla., Ga., Ky., La., Miss., N.C., Okla., S.C., Tenn., Texas, Va.

587. HR 3257. Unfunded Mandates/Passage. Reynolds, R-N.Y., motion to suspend the rules and pass the bill to expand the Congressional Budget Office's definition of unfunded federal mandates on state and local governments. Motion agreed to 401-0: R 202-0; D 198-0 (ND 147-0, SD 51-0); I 1-0. Nov. 16, 1999. A two-thirds majority of those present and voting (268 in this case) is required for passage under suspension of the rules.

588. H Con Res 222. Armenian Political Assassinations/Adoption. Gilman, R-N.Y., motion to suspend the rules and adopt the concurrent resolution to express the sense of Congress deploring the slaying of Prime Minister Vazgen Sargsian and other members of the Armenian government, who were killed in an attack in the nation's parliament Oct. 27, 1999. Motion agreed to 399-0: R 202-0; D 196-0 (ND 145-0, SD 51-0); I 1-0. Nov. 16, 1999. A two-thirds majority of those present and voting (266 in this case) is required for adoption under suspension of the rules.

589. H Con Res 211. Indian Elections/Adoption. Campbell, R-Calif., motion to suspend the rules and adopt the concurrent resolution to express the support of Congress for the recently concluded elections in India and congratulate the winner, Prime Minister Atal Bihari Vajpayee. Motion agreed to 396-4: R 200-2; D 195-2 (ND 144-2, SD 51-0); I 1-0. Nov. 16, 1999. A two-thirds majority of those present and voting (267 in this case) is required for adoption under suspension of the rules.

590. H Res 374. Consideration of Suspensions/Adoption. Adoption of the resolution to allow the House to consider bills under suspension of the rules with one hours notice at any time through the legislative day of Nov. 17. Adopted 214-202: R 211-2; D 3-199 (ND 3-146, SD 0-53); I 0-1. Nov. 16, 1999.

591. H Res 169. Democracy in Laos/Adoption. Gilman, R-N.Y., motion to suspend the rules and adopt the resolution to express the sense of the House that the government of Laos should fully institute a process of democracy, human rights, free and fair elections, and ensure that national assembly elections scheduled in 2002 are openly contested. Motion agreed to 412-1: R 209-1; D 202-0 (ND 149-0, SD 53-0); I 1-0. Nov. 16, 1999. A two-thirds majority of those present and voting (276 in this case) is required for adoption under suspension of the rules.

592. H Con Res 165. Democracy in Slovakia/Adoption. Gilman, R-N.Y., motion to suspend the rules and adopt the concurrent resolution to state that it is U.S. policy to promote the development of a market-based economy and a democratic government in the Slovak Republic, and to support the eventual integration of the Slovak Republic into pan-European and trans-Atlantic economic and security institutions. Motion agreed to 404-12: R 202-11; D 201-1 (ND 149-0, SD 52-1); I 1-0. Nov. 16, 1999. A two-thirds majority of those present and voting (278 in this case) is required for adoption under suspension of the rules.

593. H Con Res 206. Russian Aggression in Chechnya/Adoption. Gilman, R-N.Y., motion to suspend the rules and adopt the concurrent resolution to express the grave concern of Congress about the armed conflict in the North Caucasus region of the Russian Federation, and to urge all sides to pursue dialogue for peaceful resolution. Motion agreed to 407-4: R 205-3; D 201-1 (ND 148-1, SD 53-0); I 1-0. Nov. 16, 1999. A two-thirds majority of those present and voting (274 in this case) is required for adoption under suspension of the rules.

594. H Res 325. Diabetes Funding and Research/Adoption. Bilirakis, R-Fla., motion to suspend the rules and adopt the resolution to express the sense of the House regarding the importance of increased support and funding to combat diabetes. Motion agreed to 414-0: R 212-0; D 201-0 (ND 148-0, SD 53-0); I 1-0. Nov. 16, 1999. A two-thirds majority of those present and voting (276 in this case) is required for adoption under suspension of the rules.

Key

- Y Voted for (yea).
- # Paired for.
- \+ Announced for.
- N Voted against (nay).
- X Paired against.
- – Announced against.
- P Voted "present."
- C Voted "present" to avoid possible conflict of interest.
- ? Did not vote or otherwise make a position known.

•

Democrats ***Republicans***
Independents

	587	588	589	590	591	592	593	594
ALABAMA								
1 ***Callahan***	Y	Y	Y	Y	Y	Y	Y	Y
2 ***Everett***	Y	Y	Y	Y	Y	Y	Y	Y
3 ***Riley***	Y	Y	Y	Y	Y	Y	Y	Y
4 ***Aderholt***	Y	Y	Y	Y	Y	Y	Y	Y
5 Cramer	Y	Y	Y	N	Y	Y	Y	Y
6 ***Bachus***	Y	Y	Y	Y	Y	Y	Y	?
7 Hilliard	?	?	?	N	Y	Y	Y	Y
ALASKA								
AL ***Young***	Y	Y	Y	Y	Y	Y	Y	Y
ARIZONA								
1 ***Salmon***	Y	?	Y	Y	Y	Y	Y	Y
2 Pastor	Y	Y	Y	N	Y	Y	Y	Y
3 ***Stump***	Y	Y	Y	Y	Y	Y	Y	Y
4 ***Shadegg***	?	?	?	Y	Y	Y	Y	Y
5 ***Kolbe***	Y	Y	Y	Y	Y	Y	Y	Y
6 ***Hayworth***	Y	Y	Y	Y	Y	N	Y	Y
ARKANSAS								
1 Berry	Y	Y	Y	N	Y	Y	Y	Y
2 Snyder	Y	Y	Y	N	Y	Y	Y	Y
3 ***Hutchinson***	Y	Y	Y	Y	Y	Y	Y	Y
4 ***Dickey***	Y	Y	Y	Y	Y	Y	?	Y
CALIFORNIA								
1 Thompson	Y	Y	Y	N	Y	Y	Y	Y
2 ***Herger***	Y	Y	Y	Y	Y	Y	?	Y
3 ***Ose***	Y	Y	Y	Y	Y	Y	Y	Y
4 ***Doolittle***	Y	Y	Y	Y	Y	Y	?	Y
5 Matsui	Y	Y	Y	N	Y	Y	Y	Y
6 Woolsey	Y	Y	Y	Y	Y	Y	Y	Y
7 Miller, George	Y	Y	Y	N	Y	Y	Y	Y
8 Pelosi	Y	Y	Y	N	Y	Y	Y	Y
9 Lee	Y	Y	?	N	Y	Y	Y	Y
10 Tauscher	Y	Y	Y	N	Y	Y	Y	Y
11 ***Pombo***	Y	Y	Y	Y	Y	Y	?	Y
12 Lantos	Y	Y	Y	N	Y	Y	Y	Y
13 Stark	Y	Y	Y	N	Y	Y	Y	Y
14 Eshoo	Y	Y	Y	N	Y	Y	Y	Y
15 ***Campbell***	Y	Y	Y	Y	Y	Y	Y	Y
16 Lofgren	Y	Y	Y	N	Y	Y	Y	Y
17 Farr	Y	Y	Y	N	Y	Y	Y	Y
18 Condit	Y	Y	Y	N	Y	Y	Y	Y
19 ***Radanovich***	?	?	?	Y	Y	Y	Y	Y
20 Dooley	Y	Y	Y	N	Y	Y	Y	Y
21 ***Thomas***	Y	Y	Y	Y	?	Y	Y	Y
22 Capps	Y	Y	Y	N	Y	Y	Y	Y
23 ***Gallegly***	Y	Y	Y	Y	Y	Y	Y	Y
24 Sherman	Y	Y	Y	Y	Y	Y	N	Y
25 ***McKeon***	Y	Y	Y	Y	Y	Y	Y	Y
26 Berman	?	?	?	?	?	?	?	?
27 ***Rogan***	Y	Y	Y	Y	Y	Y	Y	Y
28 ***Dreier***	Y	Y	Y	Y	Y	Y	Y	Y
29 Waxman	?	?	?	?	?	?	?	?
30 Becerra	Y	Y	Y	N	Y	Y	Y	Y
31 Martinez	Y	Y	Y	N	Y	Y	Y	Y
32 Dixon	Y	Y	Y	N	Y	Y	Y	Y
33 Roybal-Allard	Y	Y	Y	N	Y	Y	Y	Y
34 Napolitano	Y	Y	Y	N	Y	Y	Y	Y
35 Waters	?	?	?	N	Y	Y	Y	Y
36 ***Kuykendall***	Y	Y	Y	Y	Y	Y	Y	Y
37 Millender-McD.	Y	Y	Y	N	Y	Y	Y	Y
38 ***Horn***	Y	Y	Y	Y	Y	Y	Y	Y
39 ***Royce***	Y	Y	Y	Y	Y	Y	Y	Y
40 ***Lewis***	Y	Y	Y	Y	Y	Y	Y	Y
41 ***Miller***	?	?	?	Y	Y	Y	Y	Y
42 Vacant								
43 ***Calvert***	Y	Y	Y	Y	Y	Y	Y	Y
44 ***Bono***	Y	Y	Y	Y	Y	Y	Y	Y
45 ***Rohrabacher***	Y	Y	Y	Y	Y	Y	Y	Y
46 Sanchez	Y	Y	Y	N	Y	Y	Y	Y
47 ***Cox***	Y	Y	Y	Y	Y	Y	Y	Y
48 ***Packard***	Y	Y	Y	Y	Y	Y	Y	Y
49 ***Bilbray***	Y	Y	Y	Y	Y	Y	Y	Y
50 Filner	Y	Y	Y	N	Y	Y	Y	Y
51 ***Cunningham***	Y	Y	Y	Y	Y	Y	Y	Y
52 ***Hunter***	Y	Y	Y	Y	Y	Y	Y	Y
COLORADO								
1 DeGette	Y	Y	Y	N	Y	Y	Y	Y
2 Udall	Y	Y	Y	N	Y	Y	Y	Y
3 ***McInnis***	Y	Y	Y	Y	Y	Y	Y	Y
4 ***Schaffer***	Y	Y	Y	Y	Y	Y	Y	Y
5 ***Hefley***	Y	Y	Y	Y	Y	Y	Y	Y
6 ***Tancredo***	Y	Y	Y	Y	Y	Y	Y	Y
CONNECTICUT								
1 Larson	Y	Y	Y	N	Y	Y	Y	Y
2 Gejdenson	Y	Y	Y	N	Y	Y	Y	Y
3 DeLauro	Y	Y	Y	N	Y	Y	Y	Y
4 ***Shays***	Y	Y	Y	Y	Y	Y	Y	Y
5 Maloney	Y	+	Y	N	Y	Y	Y	Y
6 ***Johnson***	Y	Y	Y	Y	Y	Y	Y	Y
DELAWARE								
AL ***Castle***	Y	Y	Y	Y	Y	Y	Y	Y
FLORIDA								
1 ***Scarborough***	Y	Y	Y	Y	Y	N	Y	Y
2 Boyd	Y	Y	Y	N	Y	Y	Y	Y
3 Brown	Y	Y	Y	N	Y	Y	Y	Y
4 ***Fowler***	Y	Y	Y	Y	Y	Y	Y	Y
5 Thurman	Y	Y	Y	N	Y	Y	Y	Y
6 ***Stearns***	Y	Y	Y	Y	Y	Y	Y	Y
7 ***Mica***	Y	Y	Y	Y	Y	Y	Y	Y
8 ***McCollum***	Y	Y	Y	Y	?	Y	Y	Y
9 ***Bilirakis***	Y	Y	Y	Y	Y	Y	Y	Y
10 ***Young***	Y	Y	Y	Y	Y	Y	Y	Y
11 Davis	Y	Y	Y	N	Y	Y	Y	Y
12 ***Canady***	Y	Y	Y	Y	Y	Y	Y	Y
13 ***Miller***	Y	Y	Y	Y	Y	Y	Y	Y
14 ***Goss***	Y	Y	Y	Y	Y	Y	Y	Y
15 ***Weldon***	Y	Y	Y	Y	Y	Y	Y	Y
16 ***Foley***	Y	Y	Y	Y	Y	Y	Y	Y
17 Meek	Y	Y	Y	N	Y	Y	Y	Y
18 ***Ros-Lehtinen***	Y	Y	Y	Y	Y	Y	Y	Y
19 Wexler	Y	Y	Y	N	Y	Y	Y	Y
20 Deutsch	Y	Y	Y	N	Y	Y	Y	Y
21 ***Diaz-Balart***	Y	Y	Y	Y	Y	Y	Y	Y
22 ***Shaw***	Y	Y	Y	Y	Y	Y	Y	Y
23 Hastings	Y	Y	Y	N	Y	Y	Y	Y
GEORGIA								
1 ***Kingston***	Y	Y	Y	Y	Y	Y	Y	Y
2 Bishop	Y	Y	Y	N	Y	Y	Y	Y
3 ***Collins***	?	?	?	Y	Y	N	Y	Y
4 McKinney	Y	Y	Y	N	Y	N	Y	Y
5 Lewis	Y	Y	Y	N	Y	Y	Y	Y
6 ***Isakson***	Y	Y	Y	Y	Y	Y	Y	Y
7 ***Barr***	Y	Y	Y	Y	Y	N	Y	Y
8 ***Chambliss***	Y	Y	Y	Y	Y	Y	Y	Y
9 ***Deal***	Y	Y	Y	Y	Y	Y	Y	Y
10 ***Norwood***	Y	Y	Y	Y	Y	Y	Y	Y
11 ***Linder***	Y	Y	Y	Y	Y	Y	Y	Y
HAWAII								
1 Abercrombie	Y	Y	Y	N	Y	Y	Y	Y
2 Mink	Y	Y	Y	N	Y	Y	Y	Y
IDAHO								
1 ***Chenoweth-Hage***	Y	Y	N	Y	Y	N	N	Y
2 ***Simpson***	Y	Y	Y	Y	Y	Y	Y	Y
ILLINOIS								
1 Rush	Y	?	Y	N	Y	Y	Y	Y
2 Jackson	Y	Y	Y	N	Y	Y	Y	Y
3 Lipinski	Y	Y	Y	N	Y	Y	Y	Y
4 Gutierrez	Y	Y	Y	N	Y	Y	Y	Y
5 Blagojevich	Y	Y	Y	N	Y	Y	Y	Y
6 ***Hyde***	Y	Y	Y	Y	Y	Y	Y	Y
7 Davis	Y	Y	Y	N	Y	Y	Y	Y
8 ***Crane***	Y	Y	Y	Y	Y	Y	Y	Y
9 Schakowsky	Y	Y	Y	N	Y	Y	Y	Y
10 ***Porter***	Y	Y	Y	Y	Y	Y	Y	Y
11 ***Weller***	Y	Y	Y	Y	Y	Y	Y	Y
12 Costello	Y	Y	Y	N	Y	Y	Y	Y
13 ***Biggert***	Y	Y	Y	Y	Y	Y	Y	Y
14 ***Hastert***								

ND Northern Democrats SD Southern Democrats

	587	588	589	590	591	592	593	594
15 ***Ewing***	?	?	?	?	?	?	?	?
16 ***Manzullo***	Y	Y	Y	Y	Y	N	Y	Y
17 Evans	Y	Y	Y	N	Y	Y	Y	Y
18 ***LaHood***	?	?	?	Y	Y	Y	Y	Y
19 Phelps	Y	Y	Y	N	Y	Y	Y	Y
20 ***Shimkus***	Y	Y	Y	Y	Y	Y	Y	Y
INDIANA								
1 Visclosky	Y	Y	Y	N	Y	Y	Y	Y
2 ***McIntosh***	Y	Y	Y	Y	Y	Y	Y	Y
3 Roemer	Y	Y	Y	N	Y	Y	Y	Y
4 ***Souder***	Y	Y	Y	Y	Y	N	Y	Y
5 ***Buyer***	Y	Y	Y	Y	Y	Y	Y	Y
6 ***Burton***	Y	Y	Y	Y	Y	Y	N	Y
7 ***Pease***	Y	Y	Y	Y	Y	Y	Y	Y
8 ***Hostettler***	Y	Y	Y	Y	Y	Y	?	Y
9 Hill	Y	Y	Y	N	Y	Y	Y	Y
10 Carson	Y	Y	Y	N	Y	Y	Y	Y
IOWA								
1 ***Leach***	Y	Y	Y	Y	Y	Y	Y	Y
2 ***Nussle***	Y	Y	Y	Y	Y	Y	Y	Y
3 Boswell	Y	Y	Y	N	Y	Y	Y	Y
4 ***Ganske***	Y	Y	Y	Y	Y	Y	Y	Y
5 ***Latham***	Y	Y	Y	Y	Y	Y	Y	Y
KANSAS								
1 ***Moran***	Y	Y	Y	Y	Y	Y	Y	Y
2 ***Ryun***	Y	Y	Y	Y	Y	Y	Y	Y
3 Moore	Y	Y	Y	N	Y	Y	Y	Y
4 ***Tiahrt***	Y	Y	Y	Y	Y	Y	Y	Y
KENTUCKY								
1 ***Whitfield***	Y	Y	Y	Y	Y	Y	Y	Y
2 ***Lewis***	Y	Y	Y	Y	Y	Y	Y	Y
3 ***Northup***	Y	Y	Y	Y	Y	Y	Y	Y
4 Lucas	Y	Y	Y	N	Y	Y	Y	Y
5 ***Rogers***	Y	Y	Y	Y	Y	Y	Y	Y
6 ***Fletcher***	Y	Y	Y	Y	Y	Y	Y	Y
LOUISIANA								
1 ***Vitter***	Y	Y	Y	Y	Y	Y	Y	Y
2 Jefferson	Y	Y	Y	N	Y	Y	Y	Y
3 ***Tauzin***	Y	Y	Y	Y	Y	Y	Y	Y
4 ***McCrery***	?	?	?	Y	Y	Y	Y	Y
5 ***Cooksey***	Y	Y	Y	Y	Y	Y	Y	Y
6 ***Baker***	Y	Y	Y	Y	Y	Y	Y	Y
7 John	Y	Y	Y	N	Y	Y	Y	Y
MAINE								
1 Allen	Y	+	Y	N	Y	Y	Y	Y
2 Baldacci	Y	Y	Y	N	Y	Y	Y	Y
MARYLAND								
1 ***Gilchrest***	Y	Y	Y	Y	Y	Y	Y	Y
2 ***Ehrlich***	?	?	?	Y	Y	Y	Y	Y
3 Cardin	Y	Y	Y	N	Y	Y	Y	Y
4 Wynn	Y	Y	Y	N	Y	Y	Y	Y
5 Hoyer	Y	Y	Y	N	Y	Y	Y	Y
6 ***Bartlett***	Y	Y	Y	Y	Y	Y	Y	Y
7 Cummings	Y	Y	Y	N	Y	Y	Y	Y
8 ***Morella***	Y	Y	Y	Y	Y	Y	Y	Y
MASSACHUSETTS								
1 Olver	Y	Y	Y	N	Y	Y	Y	Y
2 Neal	Y	Y	Y	N	Y	Y	Y	Y
3 McGovern	Y	Y	Y	N	Y	Y	Y	Y
4 Frank	Y	Y	Y	N	Y	Y	Y	Y
5 Meehan	?	?	?	?	?	?	?	?
6 Tierney	Y	Y	Y	N	Y	Y	Y	Y
7 Markey	Y	Y	N	N	Y	Y	Y	Y
8 Capuano	Y	Y	Y	N	Y	Y	Y	Y
9 Moakley	Y	Y	Y	N	Y	Y	Y	Y
10 Delahunt	Y	Y	Y	N	Y	Y	Y	Y
MICHIGAN								
1 Stupak	Y	Y	Y	N	Y	Y	Y	Y
2 ***Hoekstra***	Y	Y	Y	Y	Y	Y	Y	Y
3 ***Ehlers***	Y	Y	Y	Y	Y	Y	Y	Y
4 ***Camp***	Y	Y	Y	Y	Y	Y	Y	Y
5 Barcia	?	?	?	N	Y	Y	Y	Y
6 ***Upton***	Y	Y	Y	Y	Y	Y	Y	Y
7 ***Smith***	?	?	?	?	?	?	?	?
8 Stabenow	Y	Y	Y	N	Y	Y	Y	Y
9 Kildee	Y	Y	Y	N	Y	Y	Y	Y
10 Bonior	Y	Y	N	N	Y	Y	Y	Y
11 ***Knollenberg***	Y	Y	Y	Y	Y	Y	Y	Y
12 Levin	Y	Y	Y	N	Y	Y	Y	Y
13 Rivers	Y	Y	Y	N	Y	Y	Y	Y
14 Conyers	Y	Y	Y	N	Y	Y	Y	Y
15 Kilpatrick	Y	Y	Y	N	Y	Y	Y	Y
16 Dingell	Y	Y	Y	N	Y	Y	Y	Y

	587	588	589	590	591	592	593	594
MINNESOTA								
1 ***Gutknecht***	?	Y	Y	Y	Y	Y	Y	Y
2 Minge	Y	Y	Y	N	Y	Y	Y	Y
3 ***Ramstad***	Y	Y	Y	Y	Y	Y	Y	Y
4 Vento	Y	Y	Y	N	Y	Y	Y	Y
5 Sabo	Y	Y	Y	N	Y	Y	Y	Y
6 Luther	Y	Y	Y	N	Y	Y	Y	Y
7 Peterson	Y	Y	Y	N	Y	Y	Y	Y
8 Oberstar	Y	Y	Y	N	Y	Y	Y	Y
MISSISSIPPI								
1 ***Wicker***	Y	Y	Y	Y	Y	Y	Y	Y
2 Thompson	Y	Y	Y	N	Y	Y	Y	Y
3 ***Pickering***	Y	Y	Y	Y	Y	Y	Y	Y
4 Shows	Y	Y	Y	N	Y	Y	Y	Y
5 Taylor	Y	Y	Y	N	Y	Y	Y	Y
MISSOURI								
1 Clay	Y	Y	Y	N	Y	Y	Y	Y
2 ***Talent***	Y	Y	Y	Y	Y	Y	Y	Y
3 Gephardt	Y	Y	Y	?	?	?	?	?
4 Skelton	Y	Y	Y	N	Y	Y	Y	Y
5 McCarthy	Y	Y	Y	N	Y	Y	Y	Y
6 Danner	Y	Y	Y	N	Y	Y	Y	Y
7 ***Blunt***	Y	Y	Y	Y	Y	Y	Y	Y
8 ***Emerson***	Y	Y	Y	Y	Y	Y	Y	Y
9 ***Hulshof***	Y	Y	Y	Y	Y	Y	Y	Y
MONTANA								
AL ***Hill***	+	+	+	+	+	+	+	+
NEBRASKA								
1 ***Bereuter***	Y	Y	Y	Y	Y	Y	Y	Y
2 ***Terry***	Y	Y	Y	Y	Y	Y	Y	Y
3 ***Barrett***	Y	Y	Y	Y	Y	Y	Y	Y
NEVADA								
1 Berkley	Y	Y	Y	N	Y	Y	Y	Y
2 ***Gibbons***	Y	Y	Y	Y	Y	Y	Y	Y
NEW HAMPSHIRE								
1 ***Sununu***	Y	Y	Y	Y	Y	Y	Y	Y
2 ***Bass***	Y	Y	?	Y	Y	Y	Y	Y
NEW JERSEY								
1 Andrews	Y	Y	Y	N	Y	Y	Y	Y
2 ***LoBiondo***	Y	Y	Y	Y	Y	Y	Y	Y
3 ***Saxton***	Y	Y	Y	Y	Y	Y	Y	Y
4 ***Smith***	Y	Y	Y	Y	Y	Y	Y	Y
5 ***Roukema***	Y	Y	Y	Y	Y	Y	Y	Y
6 Pallone	Y	Y	Y	N	Y	Y	Y	Y
7 ***Franks***	Y	Y	Y	Y	Y	Y	Y	Y
8 Pascrell	Y	Y	Y	N	Y	Y	Y	Y
9 Rothman	Y	Y	Y	N	Y	Y	Y	Y
10 Payne	?	?	?	?	?	?	?	?
11 ***Frelinghuysen***	Y	Y	Y	Y	Y	Y	Y	Y
12 Holt	Y	Y	Y	N	Y	Y	Y	Y
13 Menendez	Y	Y	Y	N	Y	Y	Y	Y
NEW MEXICO								
1 ***Wilson***	Y	Y	Y	Y	Y	Y	Y	Y
2 ***Skeen***	Y	Y	Y	Y	Y	Y	Y	Y
3 Udall	Y	Y	Y	N	Y	Y	Y	Y
NEW YORK								
1 Forbes	Y	Y	Y	N	Y	Y	Y	Y
2 ***Lazio***	Y	Y	Y	Y	Y	Y	Y	Y
3 ***King***	Y	Y	Y	Y	Y	Y	Y	Y
4 McCarthy	Y	Y	Y	N	Y	Y	Y	Y
5 Ackerman	?	?	?	?	?	?	?	?
6 Meeks	Y	Y	Y	N	Y	Y	Y	Y
7 Crowley	Y	Y	Y	N	Y	Y	Y	Y
8 Nadler	Y	Y	Y	N	Y	Y	Y	Y
9 Weiner	Y	Y	Y	N	Y	Y	Y	Y
10 Towns	Y	Y	Y	N	Y	Y	Y	Y
11 Owens	Y	Y	Y	N	Y	Y	Y	Y
12 Velázquez	Y	Y	Y	N	Y	Y	Y	Y
13 ***Fossella***	?	?	?	?	?	?	?	?
14 Maloney	Y	Y	Y	N	Y	Y	Y	?
15 Rangel	Y	Y	?	N	Y	Y	Y	Y
16 Serrano	Y	Y	Y	N	Y	Y	Y	Y
17 Engel	?	Y	Y	N	Y	Y	Y	Y
18 Lowey	Y	Y	Y	N	Y	Y	Y	Y
19 ***Kelly***	Y	Y	Y	Y	Y	Y	Y	Y
20 ***Gilman***	Y	Y	Y	Y	Y	Y	Y	Y
21 McNulty	Y	Y	Y	N	Y	Y	Y	Y
22 ***Sweeney***	Y	Y	Y	Y	Y	Y	Y	Y
23 ***Boehlert***	Y	Y	Y	Y	Y	Y	Y	Y
24 ***McHugh***	Y	Y	Y	Y	Y	Y	Y	Y
25 ***Walsh***	Y	Y	Y	Y	Y	Y	Y	Y
26 Hinchey	Y	Y	Y	N	Y	Y	Y	Y
27 ***Reynolds***	Y	Y	Y	Y	Y	Y	Y	Y
28 Slaughter	Y	Y	Y	N	Y	Y	Y	Y
29 LaFalce	Y	Y	Y	N	Y	Y	Y	Y

	587	588	589	590	591	592	593	594
30 ***Quinn***	Y	Y	Y	?	?	?	?	?
31 ***Houghton***	Y	Y	Y	Y	Y	Y	Y	Y
NORTH CAROLINA								
1 Clayton	Y	Y	Y	N	Y	Y	Y	Y
2 Etheridge	Y	Y	Y	N	Y	Y	Y	Y
3 ***Jones***	?	?	?	Y	Y	Y	Y	Y
4 Price	Y	Y	Y	N	Y	Y	Y	Y
5 ***Burr***	Y	Y	Y	Y	Y	Y	Y	Y
6 ***Coble***	Y	Y	Y	Y	Y	N	Y	Y
7 McIntyre	?	?	?	?	?	?	?	?
8 ***Hayes***	Y	Y	Y	Y	Y	Y	Y	Y
9 ***Myrick***	Y	Y	Y	Y	Y	Y	Y	Y
10 ***Ballenger***	Y	Y	Y	Y	Y	Y	Y	Y
11 ***Taylor***	Y	Y	Y	Y	Y	Y	Y	Y
12 Watt	Y	Y	Y	N	Y	Y	Y	Y
NORTH DAKOTA								
AL Pomeroy	Y	Y	Y	N	Y	Y	Y	Y
OHIO								
1 ***Chabot***	Y	Y	Y	Y	Y	Y	Y	Y
2 ***Portman***	Y	Y	Y	Y	Y	Y	Y	Y
3 Hall	Y	Y	Y	N	Y	Y	Y	Y
4 ***Oxley***	?	?	?	Y	Y	Y	Y	Y
5 ***Gillmor***	Y	Y	Y	Y	Y	Y	Y	Y
6 Strickland	Y	Y	Y	N	Y	Y	Y	Y
7 ***Hobson***	Y	Y	Y	Y	Y	Y	Y	Y
8 ***Boehner***	Y	Y	Y	Y	Y	Y	Y	Y
9 Kaptur	Y	Y	Y	N	Y	Y	Y	Y
10 Kucinich	Y	Y	Y	N	Y	Y	Y	Y
11 Jones	Y	Y	Y	N	Y	Y	Y	Y
12 ***Kasich***	Y	Y	Y	Y	Y	Y	Y	Y
13 Brown	Y	Y	Y	N	Y	Y	Y	Y
14 Sawyer	Y	Y	Y	N	Y	Y	Y	Y
15 ***Pryce***	Y	Y	Y	Y	Y	Y	Y	Y
16 ***Regula***	Y	Y	Y	Y	Y	Y	Y	Y
17 Traficant	Y	Y	Y	Y	Y	Y	Y	Y
18 ***Ney***	Y	Y	Y	Y	Y	Y	Y	Y
19 ***LaTourette***	Y	Y	Y	Y	Y	Y	Y	Y
OKLAHOMA								
1 ***Largent***	Y	Y	Y	Y	Y	Y	Y	Y
2 ***Coburn***	Y	Y	Y	N	Y	Y	Y	Y
3 ***Watkins***	?	?	?	?	?	?	?	?
4 ***Watts***	Y	Y	Y	Y	Y	Y	Y	Y
5 ***Istook***	Y	Y	Y	?	Y	Y	Y	Y
6 ***Lucas***	Y	Y	Y	Y	Y	Y	?	Y
OREGON								
1 Wu	Y	Y	Y	N	Y	Y	Y	Y
2 ***Walden***	Y	Y	Y	Y	Y	Y	Y	Y
3 Blumenauer	Y	Y	Y	N	Y	Y	Y	Y
4 DeFazio	Y	Y	Y	N	Y	Y	Y	Y
5 Hooley	Y	Y	Y	N	Y	Y	Y	Y
PENNSYLVANIA								
1 Brady	Y	Y	Y	N	Y	Y	Y	Y
2 Fattah	Y	Y	Y	N	Y	Y	Y	Y
3 Borski	Y	Y	Y	N	Y	Y	Y	Y
4 Klink	Y	Y	Y	N	Y	Y	Y	Y
5 ***Peterson***	Y	Y	Y	Y	Y	Y	Y	Y
6 Holden	Y	Y	Y	N	Y	Y	Y	Y
7 ***Weldon***	Y	Y	Y	Y	Y	Y	Y	Y
8 ***Greenwood***	Y	Y	Y	Y	Y	Y	Y	Y
9 ***Shuster***	?	?	?	Y	Y	Y	Y	Y
10 ***Sherwood***	Y	Y	Y	Y	Y	Y	Y	Y
11 Kanjorski	Y	Y	Y	N	Y	Y	Y	Y
12 Murtha	Y	Y	Y	N	Y	Y	Y	Y
13 Hoeffel	Y	Y	Y	N	Y	Y	Y	Y
14 Coyne	Y	Y	Y	N	Y	Y	Y	Y
15 ***Toomey***	Y	Y	Y	Y	Y	Y	Y	Y
16 ***Pitts***	Y	Y	Y	Y	Y	Y	Y	Y
17 ***Gekas***	Y	Y	Y	Y	Y	Y	Y	Y
18 Doyle	Y	Y	Y	N	Y	Y	Y	Y
19 ***Goodling***	Y	Y	Y	Y	Y	Y	Y	Y
20 Mascara	Y	Y	Y	N	Y	Y	Y	Y
21 ***English***	Y	Y	Y	Y	Y	Y	Y	Y
RHODE ISLAND								
1 Kennedy	Y	Y	Y	N	Y	Y	Y	Y
2 Weygand	Y	Y	Y	N	Y	Y	Y	Y
SOUTH CAROLINA								
1 ***Sanford***	Y	Y	Y	Y	Y	N	Y	Y
2 ***Spence***	Y	Y	Y	Y	Y	Y	Y	Y
3 ***Graham***	Y	Y	Y	Y	Y	Y	Y	Y
4 ***DeMint***	Y	Y	Y	Y	Y	Y	Y	Y
5 Spratt	Y	Y	Y	N	Y	Y	Y	Y
6 Clyburn	Y	Y	Y	N	Y	Y	Y	Y
SOUTH DAKOTA								
AL ***Thune***	Y	Y	Y	Y	Y	Y	Y	Y

	587	588	589	590	591	592	593	594
TENNESSEE								
1 ***Jenkins***	Y	Y	Y	Y	Y	Y	Y	Y
2 ***Duncan***	Y	Y	Y	Y	Y	Y	Y	Y
3 ***Wamp***	Y	Y	Y	Y	Y	Y	Y	Y
4 ***Hilleary***	Y	Y	Y	Y	Y	Y	Y	Y
5 Clement	Y	Y	Y	N	Y	Y	Y	Y
6 Gordon	Y	Y	Y	N	Y	Y	Y	Y
7 ***Bryant***	Y	Y	Y	Y	Y	Y	Y	Y
8 Tanner	Y	Y	Y	N	Y	Y	Y	Y
9 Ford	Y	Y	Y	N	Y	Y	Y	Y
TEXAS								
1 Sandlin	Y	Y	Y	N	Y	Y	Y	Y
2 Turner	Y	Y	Y	N	Y	Y	Y	Y
3 ***Johnson, Sam***	Y	Y	Y	N	Y	Y	Y	Y
4 Hall	Y	Y	Y	N	Y	Y	Y	Y
5 ***Sessions***	Y	Y	Y	Y	Y	Y	Y	Y
6 ***Barton***	Y	Y	Y	Y	Y	Y	Y	Y
7 ***Archer***	Y	Y	Y	Y	?	Y	Y	Y
8 ***Brady***	Y	Y	Y	Y	Y	Y	Y	Y
9 Lampson	Y	Y	Y	N	Y	Y	Y	Y
10 Doggett	Y	Y	Y	N	Y	Y	Y	Y
11 Edwards	Y	Y	Y	N	Y	Y	Y	Y
12 ***Granger***	Y	Y	Y	Y	Y	Y	Y	Y
13 ***Thornberry***	Y	Y	Y	Y	Y	Y	Y	Y
14 ***Paul***	Y	Y	N	Y	N	N	N	?
15 Hinojosa	Y	Y	Y	N	Y	Y	Y	Y
16 Reyes	?	?	?	N	Y	Y	Y	Y
17 Stenholm	Y	Y	Y	N	Y	Y	Y	Y
18 Jackson-Lee	Y	Y	Y	N	Y	Y	Y	Y
19 ***Combest***	Y	Y	Y	Y	Y	Y	Y	Y
20 Gonzalez	Y	Y	Y	N	Y	Y	Y	Y
21 ***Smith***	Y	Y	Y	Y	Y	Y	Y	Y
22 ***DeLay***	Y	Y	Y	Y	Y	Y	Y	Y
23 ***Bonilla***	Y	Y	Y	Y	Y	Y	Y	Y
24 Frost	Y	Y	Y	N	Y	Y	Y	Y
25 Bentsen	Y	Y	Y	N	Y	Y	Y	Y
26 ***Armey***	Y	Y	Y	Y	Y	Y	Y	Y
27 Ortiz	+	+	+	–	+	+	+	+
28 Rodriguez	Y	Y	Y	N	Y	Y	Y	Y
29 Green	Y	Y	Y	N	Y	Y	Y	Y
30 Johnson, E.B.	Y	Y	Y	N	Y	Y	Y	Y
UTAH								
1 ***Hansen***	Y	Y	Y	Y	Y	Y	Y	Y
2 ***Cook***	Y	Y	Y	Y	Y	N	Y	Y
3 ***Cannon***	Y	Y	Y	Y	Y	Y	Y	Y
VERMONT								
AL *Sanders*	Y	Y	Y	N	Y	Y	Y	Y
VIRGINIA								
1 ***Bateman***	Y	Y	Y	Y	Y	Y	Y	Y
2 Pickett	Y	Y	Y	N	Y	Y	Y	Y
3 Scott	Y	Y	Y	N	Y	Y	Y	Y
4 Sisisky	Y	Y	Y	N	Y	Y	Y	Y
5 Goode	Y	Y	Y	N	Y	Y	Y	Y
6 ***Goodlatte***	Y	Y	Y	Y	Y	+	Y	Y
7 ***Bliley***	Y	Y	Y	Y	Y	Y	Y	Y
8 Moran	Y	Y	Y	N	Y	Y	Y	Y
9 Boucher	Y	Y	Y	N	Y	Y	Y	Y
10 ***Wolf***	Y	Y	Y	Y	Y	Y	Y	Y
11 ***Davis***	?	?	?	Y	Y	Y	Y	Y
WASHINGTON								
1 Inslee	Y	Y	Y	N	Y	Y	Y	Y
2 ***Metcalf***	?	?	?	Y	?	Y	Y	Y
3 Baird	Y	Y	Y	N	Y	Y	Y	Y
4 ***Hastings***	Y	Y	Y	Y	Y	Y	Y	Y
5 ***Nethercutt***	Y	Y	Y	Y	Y	Y	Y	Y
6 Dicks	Y	Y	Y	N	Y	Y	Y	Y
7 McDermott	Y	Y	Y	N	Y	Y	Y	Y
8 ***Dunn***	?	?	?	?	?	?	?	?
9 Smith	Y	Y	Y	N	Y	Y	Y	Y
WEST VIRGINIA								
1 Mollohan	Y	Y	Y	N	Y	Y	Y	Y
2 Wise	?	?	?	?	?	?	?	?
3 Rahall	Y	Y	Y	N	Y	Y	Y	Y
WISCONSIN								
1 ***Ryan***	Y	Y	Y	Y	Y	Y	Y	Y
2 Baldwin	Y	Y	Y	N	Y	Y	Y	Y
3 Kind	Y	Y	Y	N	Y	Y	Y	Y
4 Kleczka	Y	Y	Y	N	Y	Y	Y	Y
5 Barrett	Y	Y	Y	N	Y	Y	Y	Y
6 ***Petri***	Y	Y	Y	Y	Y	Y	Y	Y
7 Obey	Y	Y	Y	N	Y	Y	Y	Y
8 ***Green***	Y	Y	Y	Y	Y	Y	Y	Y
9 ***Sensenbrenner***	Y	Y	Y	Y	Y	Y	Y	Y
WYOMING								
AL ***Cubin***	Y	Y	Y	Y	Y	Y	Y	Y

Southern states - Ala., Ark., Fla., Ga., Ky., La., Miss., N.C., Okla., S.C., Tenn., Texas, Va.

House Votes 595, 596, 597, 598, 599, 600

595. HR 2336. U.S. Marshals Service Overhaul/Passage. Bachus, R-Ala., motion to suspend the rules and pass the bill to permit the attorney general, instead of the president, to appoint marshals to the U.S. Marshals Service. The measure would also require the attorney general to report to Congress the number of marshals appointed who are women or minorities. Motion rejected 183-231: R 100-113; D 82-118 (ND 71-76, SD 11-42); I 1-0. Nov. 16, 1999. A two-thirds majority of those present and voting (276 in this case) is required for passage under suspension of the rules.

596. H J Res 80. Fiscal Year 2000 Continuing Appropriations/Passage. Passage of the joint resolution to provide continuing appropriations through Nov. 18 for agencies covered by the fiscal year 2000 spending bills not yet enacted. The continuing resolution would set spending levels at the fiscal 1999 level. Passed 403-8: R 207-7; D 195-1 (ND 144-1, SD 51-0); I 1-0. Nov. 17, 1999.

597. S 440. Authorizing Funds of Institutes and Schools/Passage. Hilleary, R-Tenn., motion to suspend the rules and pass the bill to authorize funding for grants to establish the Howard Baker School of Government at the University of Tennessee, the John Glenn Institute for Public Service and Public Policy at Ohio State University, the Mark O. Hatfield School of Government at Portland State University, the Robert T. Stafford Public Policy Institute in Vermont, and to establish an endowment fund for the Paul Simon Public Policy Institute at Southern Illinois University. Motion rejected 128-291: R 50-164; D 77-127 (ND 66-86, SD 11-41); I 1-0. Nov. 17, 1999. A two-thirds majority of those present and voting (280 in this case) is required for passage under suspension of the rules.

598. Procedural Motion/Adjourn. Obey, D-Wis., motion to adjourn. Motion rejected 14-375: R 6-196; D 8-178 (ND 6-128, SD 2-50); I 0-1. Nov. 18, 1999.

599. H Res 385. Fiscal 2000 Continuing Appropriations/Previous Question. Goss, R-Fla., motion to order the previous question (thus ending debate and possibility of amendment) on adoption of the rule (H Res 385) to provide for House floor consideration of the joint resolution (H J Res 82) making further continuing appropriations for fiscal 2000 until Nov. 23, and for consideration of the joint resolution (H J Res 83) making further continuing appropriations for the fiscal year 2000 until Dec. 2. Motion agreed to 375-45: R 215-0; D 159-45 (ND 112-38, SD 47-7); I 1-0. Nov. 18, 1999.

600. H Res 385. Fiscal 2000 Continuing Appropriations/Motion to Reconsider. Goss, R-Fla. motion to table the Obey, D-Wis., motion to reconsider the vote on ordering the previous question. Motion agreed to 316-101: R 208-6; D 107-95 (ND 74-74, SD 33-21); I 1-0. Nov. 18, 1999.

Key

Y Voted for (yea).
\# Paired for.
\+ Announced for.
N Voted against (nay).
X Paired against.
– Announced against.
P Voted "present."
C Voted "present" to avoid possible conflict of interest.
? Did not vote or otherwise make a position known.

•

Democrats ***Republicans***
Independents

	595	596	597	598	599	600
ALABAMA						
1 ***Callahan***	N	Y	N	N	Y	Y
2 ***Everett***	N	Y	N	N	Y	Y
3 ***Riley***	Y	Y	N	N	Y	Y
4 ***Aderholt***	N	Y	N	N	Y	Y
5 Cramer	N	Y	N	N	Y	Y
6 ***Bachus***	Y	Y	N	N	Y	Y
7 Hilliard	N	Y	N	N	Y	Y
ALASKA						
AL ***Young***	Y	?	N	?	Y	Y
ARIZONA						
1 ***Salmon***	Y	N	N	N	Y	Y
2 Pastor	N	Y	N	?	N	Y
3 ***Stump***	N	Y	N	N	Y	Y
4 ***Shadegg***	N	N	N	N	Y	Y
5 ***Kolbe***	Y	Y	N	N	Y	Y
6 ***Hayworth***	N	Y	N	N	Y	Y
ARKANSAS						
1 Berry	N	Y	N	N	Y	N
2 Snyder	Y	Y	N	N	Y	Y
3 ***Hutchinson***	Y	Y	N	?	Y	Y
4 ***Dickey***	N	Y	Y	N	Y	Y
CALIFORNIA						
1 Thompson	N	Y	N	N	Y	N
2 ***Herger***	N	Y	N	?	Y	Y
3 ***Ose***	N	Y	N	N	Y	Y
4 ***Doolittle***	N	Y	N	N	Y	Y
5 Matsui	Y	Y	Y	N	Y	Y
6 Woolsey	N	Y	N	N	Y	N
7 Miller, George	Y	Y	N	N	N	N
8 Pelosi	Y	Y	N	N	Y	Y
9 Lee	N	Y	N	N	N	N
10 Tauscher	N	Y	Y	?	Y	Y
11 ***Pombo***	N	Y	N	N	Y	Y
12 Lantos	Y	Y	Y	N	Y	N
13 Stark	Y	Y	N	N	N	N
14 Eshoo	Y	Y	Y	N	Y	Y
15 ***Campbell***	Y	Y	N	N	Y	Y
16 Lofgren	N	Y	N	N	Y	Y
17 Farr	Y	Y	?	N	Y	Y
18 Condit	N	Y	N	N	N	N
19 ***Radanovich***	N	Y	Y	?	Y	Y
20 Dooley	N	Y	Y	?	Y	Y
21 ***Thomas***	Y	Y	N	N	Y	Y
22 Capps	N	Y	N	?	?	?
23 ***Gallegly***	Y	Y	N	N	Y	Y
24 Sherman	N	Y	N	N	Y	Y
25 ***McKeon***	Y	Y	N	N	Y	Y
26 Berman	?	Y	Y	N	Y	Y
27 ***Rogan***	Y	Y	N	N	Y	Y
28 ***Dreier***	N	Y	N	N	Y	Y
29 Waxman	?	?	Y	N	Y	Y
30 Becerra	N	Y	N	N	N	N
31 Martinez	Y	Y	Y	?	Y	N
32 Dixon	N	?	Y	N	Y	Y
33 Roybal-Allard	N	Y	N	N	Y	Y
34 Napolitano	N	Y	N	N	N	N
35 Waters	N	Y	N	N	N	N
36 ***Kuykendall***	Y	Y	N	N	Y	Y
37 Millender-McD.	N	Y	Y	?	Y	Y
38 ***Horn***	Y	Y	Y	N	Y	Y
39 ***Royce***	N	Y	N	N	Y	Y
40 ***Lewis***	Y	Y	Y	N	Y	Y
41 ***Miller***	Y	Y	N	N	Y	Y
42 Vacant						
43 ***Calvert***	Y	Y	N	N	Y	Y
44 ***Bono***	Y	Y	Y	N	Y	Y
45 ***Rohrabacher***	N	Y	N	N	Y	Y
46 Sanchez	N	Y	N	N	Y	N
47 ***Cox***	Y	Y	N	?	Y	Y
48 ***Packard***	Y	Y	Y	N	Y	Y
49 ***Bilbray***	Y	Y	N	?	Y	Y
50 Filner	N	Y	Y	Y	N	N
51 ***Cunningham***	N	Y	N	N	Y	Y
52 ***Hunter***	Y	Y	N	?	Y	Y
COLORADO						
1 DeGette	Y	Y	Y	N	Y	N
2 Udall	N	Y	N	N	Y	N
3 ***McInnis***	N	Y	N	N	Y	Y
4 ***Schaffer***	N	Y	N	N	Y	Y
5 ***Hefley***	N	Y	N	N	Y	Y
6 ***Tancredo***	N	Y	N	N	Y	Y
CONNECTICUT						
1 Larson	Y	Y	Y	N	Y	N
2 Gejdenson	Y	Y	Y	N	Y	N
3 DeLauro	Y	Y	Y	N	Y	N
4 ***Shays***	N	Y	N	N	Y	Y
5 Maloney	Y	Y	Y	N	N	N
6 ***Johnson***	Y	Y	Y	N	Y	Y
DELAWARE						
AL ***Castle***	?	Y	Y	N	Y	Y
FLORIDA						
1 ***Scarborough***	N	?	?	?	?	?
2 Boyd	N	Y	N	N	Y	Y
3 Brown	N	Y	N	N	Y	N
4 ***Fowler***	Y	Y	N	N	Y	Y
5 Thurman	N	Y	N	N	N	Y
6 ***Stearns***	N	Y	N	N	Y	Y
7 ***Mica***	N	Y	N	N	Y	Y
8 ***McCollum***	Y	Y	N	N	Y	Y
9 ***Bilirakis***	Y	Y	N	N	Y	Y
10 ***Young***	Y	Y	N	N	Y	Y
11 Davis	N	Y	?	N	Y	Y
12 ***Canady***	Y	Y	N	N	Y	Y
13 ***Miller***	Y	Y	N	N	Y	Y
14 ***Goss***	Y	Y	Y	N	Y	Y
15 ***Weldon***	Y	Y	N	N	Y	Y
16 ***Foley***	Y	Y	N	N	Y	Y
17 Meek	N	Y	N	?	Y	N
18 ***Ros-Lehtinen***	Y	Y	N	?	?	?
19 Wexler	Y	Y	?	?	?	?
20 Deutsch	Y	Y	N	N	Y	Y
21 ***Diaz-Balart***	Y	?	N	N	Y	Y
22 ***Shaw***	Y	N	N	N	Y	Y
23 Hastings	N	Y	Y	N	Y	N
GEORGIA						
1 ***Kingston***	N	Y	N	N	Y	Y
2 Bishop	N	Y	N	N	Y	Y
3 ***Collins***	N	Y	N	N	Y	Y
4 McKinney	N	?	N	N	Y	Y
5 Lewis	N	Y	N	N	N	N
6 ***Isakson***	N	Y	N	N	Y	Y
7 ***Barr***	N	Y	N	N	Y	Y
8 ***Chambliss***	N	Y	N	N	Y	Y
9 ***Deal***	N	N	N	N	Y	Y
10 ***Norwood***	N	?	N	N	Y	Y
11 ***Linder***	Y	Y	N	N	Y	Y
HAWAII						
1 Abercrombie	N	+	Y	N	Y	Y
2 Mink	N	Y	N	N	Y	Y
IDAHO						
1 ***Chenoweth-Hage***	N	N	N	N	Y	?
2 ***Simpson***	Y	Y	N	N	Y	Y
ILLINOIS						
1 Rush	N	Y	Y	N	Y	Y
2 Jackson	Y	Y	Y	N	Y	Y
3 Lipinski	Y	Y	N	N	Y	Y
4 Gutierrez	N	Y	N	?	N	Y
5 Blagojevich	Y	Y	Y	N	Y	Y
6 ***Hyde***	Y	Y	Y	N	Y	Y
7 Davis	N	Y	Y	N	Y	Y
8 ***Crane***	Y	Y	N	N	Y	Y
9 Schakowsky	Y	Y	Y	N	Y	Y
10 ***Porter***	Y	Y	?	N	Y	Y
11 ***Weller***	Y	Y	Y	N	Y	Y
12 Costello	N	Y	Y	N	Y	N
13 ***Biggert***	Y	Y	Y	N	Y	Y
14 ***Hastert***		Y				

ND Northern Democrats SD Southern Democrats

	595	596	597	598	599	600
15 ***Ewing***	?	Y	N	N	Y	Y
16 ***Manzullo***	N	Y	N	Y	Y	N
17 Evans	Y	Y	Y	N	N	N
18 ***LaHood***	N	Y	N	N	Y	Y
19 Phelps	N	Y	Y	N	Y	Y
20 ***Shimkus***	N	Y	Y	N	Y	Y
INDIANA						
1 Visclosky	N	Y	N	N	Y	N
2 ***McIntosh***	N	Y	?	?	?	?
3 Roemer	N	Y	N	N	Y	Y
4 ***Souder***	Y	Y	N	N	Y	Y
5 ***Buyer***	N	Y	N	N	Y	Y
6 ***Burton***	N	Y	N	?	Y	Y
7 ***Pease***	N	Y	N	N	Y	Y
8 ***Hostettler***	N	Y	N	N	Y	Y
9 Hill	N	Y	N	N	N	N
10 Carson	N	Y	N	?	N	N
IOWA						
1 ***Leach***	N	Y	Y	N	Y	Y
2 ***Nussle***	N	Y	N	N	Y	Y
3 Boswell	N	Y	N	N	Y	Y
4 ***Ganske***	Y	Y	N	N	Y	Y
5 ***Latham***	N	Y	N	N	Y	Y
KANSAS						
1 ***Moran***	N	Y	N	N	Y	Y
2 ***Ryun***	N	Y	N	N	Y	Y
3 Moore	N	Y	N	N	Y	Y
4 ***Tiahrt***	N	Y	Y	N	Y	Y
KENTUCKY						
1 ***Whitfield***	N	Y	N	N	Y	Y
2 ***Lewis***	N	Y	N	N	Y	Y
3 ***Northup***	Y	Y	N	N	Y	Y
4 Lucas	N	Y	N	N	Y	Y
5 ***Rogers***	N	Y	N	N	Y	Y
6 ***Fletcher***	N	Y	N	N	Y	Y
LOUISIANA						
1 ***Vitter***	Y	Y	N	N	Y	Y
2 Jefferson	Y	?	N	N	Y	Y
3 ***Tauzin***	N	Y	N	N	Y	Y
4 ***McCrery***	N	Y	N	Y	Y	Y
5 ***Cooksey***	Y	Y	N	N	Y	Y
6 ***Baker***	N	Y	N	N	Y	Y
7 John	N	Y	N	N	Y	Y
MAINE						
1 Allen	Y	Y	Y	N	Y	N
2 Baldacci	Y	Y	N	N	Y	Y
MARYLAND						
1 ***Gilchrest***	Y	Y	N	N	Y	Y
2 ***Ehrlich***	N	Y	N	N	Y	Y
3 Cardin	Y	Y	N	N	Y	Y
4 Wynn	N	Y	Y	N	Y	Y
5 Hoyer	Y	Y	Y	N	Y	Y
6 ***Bartlett***	Y	Y	N	N	Y	Y
7 Cummings	Y	Y	N	N	Y	Y
8 ***Morella***	Y	Y	?	N	Y	Y
MASSACHUSETTS						
1 Olver	N	Y	Y	N	Y	N
2 Neal	N	Y	Y	N	Y	Y
3 McGovern	N	Y	Y	N	Y	N
4 Frank	Y	Y	N	N	Y	Y
5 Meehan	?	?	Y	?	?	?
6 Tierney	N	Y	N	N	Y	N
7 Markey	Y	Y	Y	N	Y	N
8 Capuano	N	Y	Y	N	Y	N
9 Moakley	Y	Y	Y	N	Y	N
10 Delahunt	N	Y	Y	N	Y	Y
MICHIGAN						
1 Stupak	N	Y	Y	N	Y	Y
2 ***Hoekstra***	Y	Y	Y	?	?	?
3 ***Ehlers***	Y	Y	N	N	Y	Y
4 ***Camp***	N	Y	Y	N	Y	Y
5 Barcia	Y	Y	N	N	Y	Y
6 ***Upton***	N	Y	N	N	Y	Y
7 ***Smith***	?	Y	N	N	Y	Y
8 Stabenow	Y	Y	N	N	N	N
9 Kildee	N	Y	N	N	N	N
10 Bonior	Y	Y	Y	N	N	N
11 ***Knollenberg***	Y	Y	N	N	Y	Y
12 Levin	N	Y	N	N	Y	Y
13 Rivers	Y	Y	N	N	Y	N
14 Conyers	N	?	N	?	?	?
15 Kilpatrick	N	Y	N	N	Y	Y
16 Dingell	N	Y	N	?	Y	Y

	595	596	597	598	599	600
MINNESOTA						
1 ***Gutknecht***	Y	Y	N	N	Y	N
2 Minge	Y	Y	N	N	N	N
3 ***Ramstad***	N	Y	N	N	Y	Y
4 Vento	Y	Y	N	?	Y	Y
5 Sabo	N	Y	Y	?	Y	Y
6 Luther	Y	Y	N	N	N	N
7 Peterson	Y	Y	N	Y	Y	?
8 Oberstar	Y	Y	Y	?	Y	N
MISSISSIPPI						
1 ***Wicker***	Y	Y	Y	N	Y	Y
2 Thompson	N	Y	N	N	Y	Y
3 ***Pickering***	N	Y	Y	N	Y	Y
4 Shows	N	Y	N	N	N	Y
5 Taylor	N	Y	N	?	N	N
MISSOURI						
1 Clay	N	?	Y	N	Y	Y
2 ***Talent***	N	Y	N	N	Y	Y
3 Gephardt	?	Y	Y	N	Y	Y
4 Skelton	N	Y	Y	N	Y	Y
5 McCarthy	N	Y	N	N	Y	N
6 Danner	Y	Y	N	N	Y	Y
7 ***Blunt***	N	Y	N	N	Y	Y
8 ***Emerson***	N	Y	N	N	Y	Y
9 ***Hulshof***	N	Y	N	N	Y	Y
MONTANA						
AL ***Hill***	–	Y	N	?	Y	Y
NEBRASKA						
1 ***Bereuter***	Y	Y	N	N	Y	Y
2 ***Terry***	Y	Y	N	N	Y	Y
3 ***Barrett***	Y	Y	N	N	Y	Y
NEVADA						
1 Berkley	Y	Y	N	N	Y	Y
2 ***Gibbons***	N	Y	N	N	Y	Y
NEW HAMPSHIRE						
1 ***Sununu***	N	Y	N	N	Y	Y
2 ***Bass***	Y	Y	N	N	Y	Y
NEW JERSEY						
1 Andrews	N	Y	N	N	Y	N
2 ***LoBiondo***	N	Y	N	N	Y	Y
3 ***Saxton***	N	Y	N	N	Y	Y
4 ***Smith***	N	Y	N	N	Y	Y
5 ***Roukema***	N	Y	N	N	Y	Y
6 Pallone	Y	Y	N	N	Y	N
7 ***Franks***	N	Y	N	?	?	?
8 Pascrell	Y	Y	N	N	Y	N
9 Rothman	Y	?	N	N	Y	N
10 Payne	?	Y	N	N	Y	N
11 ***Frelinghuysen***	N	Y	Y	N	Y	Y
12 Holt	Y	Y	Y	N	Y	N
13 Menendez	N	Y	N	N	Y	Y
NEW MEXICO						
1 ***Wilson***	Y	Y	N	N	Y	Y
2 ***Skeen***	Y	Y	N	N	Y	Y
3 Udall	N	Y	N	N	N	N
NEW YORK						
1 Forbes	N	N	N	N	N	N
2 ***Lazio***	Y	Y	Y	N	Y	Y
3 ***King***	N	Y	Y	N	Y	Y
4 McCarthy	Y	Y	Y	N	Y	Y
5 Ackerman	?	?	?	?	?	?
6 Meeks	N	Y	N	?	Y	Y
7 Crowley	N	Y	N	N	Y	Y
8 Nadler	Y	Y	N	N	Y	Y
9 Weiner	Y	Y	N	N	Y	Y
10 Towns	Y	?	N	Y	Y	Y
11 Owens	Y	Y	N	N	Y	N
12 Velázquez	Y	Y	N	N	N	N
13 ***Fossella***	?	Y	N	N	Y	Y
14 Maloney	Y	Y	N	N	Y	Y
15 Rangel	N	Y	Y	N	N	Y
16 Serrano	Y	Y	N	N	Y	Y
17 Engel	Y	?	N	N	Y	Y
18 Lowey	Y	Y	N	N	Y	Y
19 ***Kelly***	N	Y	N	N	Y	Y
20 ***Gilman***	Y	Y	Y	N	Y	Y
21 McNulty	N	Y	Y	N	Y	N
22 ***Sweeney***	N	Y	N	N	Y	Y
23 ***Boehlert***	Y	Y	N	N	Y	Y
24 ***McHugh***	Y	Y	Y	N	Y	Y
25 ***Walsh***	N	Y	Y	N	Y	Y
26 Hinchey	Y	Y	N	?	N	N
27 ***Reynolds***	N	Y	N	N	Y	Y
28 Slaughter	Y	Y	N	N	Y	N
29 LaFalce	Y	Y	N	N	Y	Y

	595	596	597	598	599	600
30 ***Quinn***	?	Y	Y	N	Y	Y
31 ***Houghton***	Y	Y	Y	N	Y	Y
NORTH CAROLINA						
1 Clayton	N	Y	N	N	Y	N
2 Etheridge	N	Y	N	Y	Y	N
3 ***Jones***	N	Y	N	N	Y	Y
4 Price	N	Y	N	N	Y	Y
5 ***Burr***	N	Y	N	N	Y	Y
6 ***Coble***	N	Y	N	N	Y	Y
7 McIntyre	?	Y	N	N	Y	Y
8 ***Hayes***	N	Y	N	N	Y	Y
9 ***Myrick***	N	Y	N	N	Y	Y
10 ***Ballenger***	N	Y	N	N	Y	Y
11 ***Taylor***	N	Y	Y	N	Y	Y
12 Watt	Y	Y	N	N	Y	N
NORTH DAKOTA						
AL Pomeroy	N	Y	N	N	Y	N
OHIO						
1 ***Chabot***	Y	Y	N	N	Y	Y
2 ***Portman***	N	Y	N	N	Y	Y
3 Hall	Y	Y	Y	N	Y	Y
4 ***Oxley***	Y	Y	Y	N	Y	Y
5 ***Gillmor***	Y	Y	Y	N	Y	Y
6 Strickland	Y	Y	Y	N	N	?
7 ***Hobson***	Y	Y	Y	N	Y	Y
8 ***Boehner***	N	Y	Y	N	Y	Y
9 Kaptur	N	Y	Y	N	Y	Y
10 Kucinich	N	Y	Y	N	N	N
11 Jones	N	Y	N	N	Y	Y
12 ***Kasich***	Y	Y	Y	?	Y	Y
13 Brown	N	Y	Y	N	N	N
14 Sawyer	Y	Y	Y	N	Y	Y
15 ***Pryce***	Y	Y	Y	N	Y	Y
16 ***Regula***	Y	Y	Y	N	Y	Y
17 Traficant	Y	Y	Y	N	Y	Y
18 ***Ney***	Y	Y	Y	N	Y	Y
19 ***LaTourette***	N	Y	Y	N	Y	Y
OKLAHOMA						
1 ***Largent***	Y	?	?	N	Y	Y
2 ***Coburn***	Y	Y	N	N	Y	Y
3 ***Watkins***	?	N	N	N	Y	Y
4 ***Watts***	N	Y	N	?	Y	Y
5 ***Istook***	N	Y	N	N	Y	Y
6 ***Lucas***	N	Y	N	N	Y	Y
OREGON						
1 Wu	N	Y	Y	N	Y	N
2 ***Walden***	Y	Y	Y	N	Y	Y
3 Blumenauer	N	Y	Y	N	N	N
4 DeFazio	?	Y	Y	N	N	Y
5 Hooley	Y	Y	Y	N	Y	N
PENNSYLVANIA						
1 Brady	Y	Y	Y	N	Y	Y
2 Fattah	Y	Y	N	?	?	N
3 Borski	Y	Y	Y	N	Y	Y
4 Klink	N	Y	N	?	N	Y
5 ***Peterson***	N	Y	N	N	Y	Y
6 Holden	N	Y	N	N	Y	Y
7 ***Weldon***	Y	Y	N	N	Y	Y
8 ***Greenwood***	Y	Y	N	N	Y	Y
9 ***Shuster***	Y	Y	N	N	Y	Y
10 ***Sherwood***	N	Y	N	N	Y	Y
11 Kanjorski	N	Y	N	?	N	N
12 Murtha	?	Y	Y	N	Y	Y
13 Hoeffel	Y	Y	N	N	Y	N
14 Coyne	Y	Y	Y	N	Y	N
15 ***Toomey***	N	Y	N	N	Y	Y
16 ***Pitts***	Y	Y	N	N	Y	Y
17 ***Gekas***	N	Y	N	N	Y	Y
18 Doyle	Y	Y	N	N	Y	N
19 ***Goodling***	Y	Y	N	N	Y	Y
20 Mascara	Y	Y	N	N	Y	N
21 ***English***	Y	Y	Y	N	Y	Y
RHODE ISLAND						
1 Kennedy	N	Y	N	N	N	N
2 Weygand	Y	Y	N	?	?	?
SOUTH CAROLINA						
1 ***Sanford***	Y	Y	N	N	Y	Y
2 ***Spence***	Y	?	?	N	Y	Y
3 ***Graham***	N	Y	N	N	Y	Y
4 ***DeMint***	N	Y	N	N	Y	Y
5 Spratt	N	Y	N	Y	Y	N
6 Clyburn	N	Y	Y	N	Y	Y
SOUTH DAKOTA						
AL ***Thune***	N	Y	N	N	Y	Y

	595	596	597	598	599	600
TENNESSEE						
1 ***Jenkins***	Y	Y	Y	N	Y	Y
2 ***Duncan***	N	Y	Y	N	Y	Y
3 ***Wamp***	N	Y	Y	N	Y	Y
4 ***Hilleary***	N	Y	Y	N	Y	Y
5 Clement	Y	Y	Y	N	Y	N
6 Gordon	N	Y	Y	N	Y	N
7 ***Bryant***	Y	Y	Y	N	Y	Y
8 Tanner	Y	Y	Y	N	Y	Y
9 Ford	N	Y	Y	N	Y	N
TEXAS						
1 Sandlin	N	Y	N	N	Y	Y
2 Turner	N	Y	N	N	Y	Y
3 ***Johnson, Sam***	N	?	N	N	Y	Y
4 Hall	N	Y	Y	N	Y	Y
5 ***Sessions***	N	Y	N	N	Y	Y
6 ***Barton***	N	Y	N	N	Y	Y
7 ***Archer***	N	Y	N	N	Y	Y
8 ***Brady***	N	Y	Y	N	Y	Y
9 Lampson	N	?	?	N	Y	Y
10 Doggett	N	Y	N	N	N	Y
11 Edwards	N	Y	N	N	Y	N
12 ***Granger***	Y	Y	N	N	Y	Y
13 ***Thornberry***	Y	Y	N	N	Y	Y
14 ***Paul***	N	N	N	N	Y	Y
15 Hinojosa	N	Y	N	N	Y	Y
16 Reyes	N	Y	N	N	Y	Y
17 Stenholm	N	Y	N	N	Y	N
18 Jackson-Lee	N	Y	N	N	N	N
19 ***Combest***	Y	Y	N	N	Y	Y
20 Gonzalez	Y	Y	N	N	Y	Y
21 ***Smith***	Y	Y	N	N	Y	Y
22 ***DeLay***	N	Y	Y	N	Y	Y
23 ***Bonilla***	Y	Y	N	N	Y	Y
24 Frost	N	Y	N	N	Y	N
25 Bentsen	N	Y	N	N	Y	N
26 ***Armey***	N	Y	N	N	Y	Y
27 Ortiz	–	Y	Y	N	Y	Y
28 Rodriguez	N	Y	N	N	Y	Y
29 Green	N	Y	N	N	Y	N
30 Johnson, E.B.	N	Y	N	N	Y	N
UTAH						
1 ***Hansen***	Y	Y	N	N	Y	Y
2 ***Cook***	N	Y	N	N	Y	Y
3 ***Cannon***	Y	Y	N	N	Y	Y
VERMONT						
AL *Sanders*	Y	Y	Y	N	Y	Y
VIRGINIA						
1 ***Bateman***	Y	Y	Y	?	Y	Y
2 Pickett	Y	?	N	N	Y	Y
3 Scott	Y	Y	Y	N	N	N
4 Sisisky	Y	Y	N	N	Y	Y
5 Goode	N	Y	N	N	Y	Y
6 ***Goodlatte***	N	Y	N	N	Y	Y
7 ***Bliley***	Y	Y	Y	N	Y	Y
8 Moran	N	Y	Y	N	Y	Y
9 Boucher	N	Y	Y	N	Y	Y
10 ***Wolf***	Y	Y	N	N	Y	Y
11 ***Davis***	Y	Y	?	N	Y	Y
WASHINGTON						
1 Inslee	N	Y	N	N	N	N
2 ***Metcalf***	Y	Y	Y	N	Y	Y
3 Baird	N	Y	Y	N	N	Y
4 ***Hastings***	Y	Y	N	N	Y	Y
5 ***Nethercutt***	Y	Y	N	N	Y	Y
6 Dicks	Y	Y	Y	N	Y	Y
7 McDermott	N	Y	Y	N	N	N
8 ***Dunn***	?	?	Y	?	?	?
9 Smith	Y	Y	N	N	Y	Y
WEST VIRGINIA						
1 Mollohan	N	Y	N	N	N	N
2 Wise	?	?	?	?	N	N
3 Rahall	N	Y	Y	Y	N	N
WISCONSIN						
1 ***Ryan***	N	Y	N	Y	Y	N
2 Baldwin	N	Y	N	N	Y	N
3 Kind	Y	Y	N	Y	Y	N
4 Kleczka	N	Y	N	N	Y	?
5 Barrett	Y	Y	N	N	Y	N
6 ***Petri***	N	Y	N	Y	Y	N
7 Obey	N	Y	?	Y	Y	N
8 ***Green***	N	Y	N	Y	Y	N
9 ***Sensenbrenner***	N	Y	N	Y	Y	N
WYOMING						
AL ***Cubin***	N	Y	N	?	Y	Y

Southern states - Ala., Ark., Fla., Ga., Ky., La., Miss., N.C., Okla., S.C., Tenn., Texas, Va.

Key

- Y Voted for (yea).
- # Paired for.
- + Announced for.
- N Voted against (nay).
- X Paired against.
- – Announced against.
- P Voted "present."
- C Voted "present" to avoid possible conflict of interest.
- ? Did not vote or otherwise make a position known.

•

Democrats ***Republicans***
Independents

601. H Res 385. Fiscal 2000 Continuing Appropriations/Rule. Adoption of the rule (H Res 385) to provide for House floor consideration of the joint resolution (H J Res 82) making further continuing appropriations for fiscal 2000 until Nov. 23, and for consideration of the joint resolution (H J Res 83) making further continuing appropriations for fiscal 2000 until Dec. 2. Adopted 352-63: R 207-5; D 144-58 (ND 99-49, SD 45-9); I 1-0. Nov. 18, 1999.

602. H Res 385. Fiscal 2000 Continuing Appropriations/Motion to Reconsider. Goss, R-Fla., motion to table the Obey, D-Wis., motion to reconsider the vote on adoption of the rule to provide for House floor consideration of the resolutions to provide continuing appropriations for fiscal 2000. Motion agreed to 294-123: R 206-6; D 87-117 (ND 61-89, SD 26-28); I 1-0. Nov. 18, 1999.

603. Procedural Motion/Adjourn. Kind, D-Wis., motion to adjourn. Motion rejected 25-395: R 6-210; D 19-184 (ND 15-136, SD 4-48); I 0-1. Nov. 18, 1999.

604. Procedural Motion/Adjourn. Obey, D-Wis., motion to adjourn. Motion rejected 24-378: R 5-201; D 19-176 (ND 17-128, SD 2-48); I 0-1. Nov. 18, 1999.

605. Procedural Motion/Adjourn. Obey, D-Wis., motion to adjourn. Motion rejected 24-379: R 6-202; D 18-176 (ND 14-131, SD 4-45); I 0-1. Nov. 18, 1999.

606. H J Res 82. Fiscal 2000 Continuing Appropriations/Recommit. Obey, D-Wis., motion to recommit the joint resolution back to the Appropriations Committee. Motion rejected 1-420: R 0-216; D 1-203 (ND 1-150, SD 0-53); I 0-1. Nov. 18, 1999.

607. H J Res 82. Fiscal 2000 Continuing Appropriations/Passage. Passage of the joint resolution to provide continuing appropriations through Nov. 23 for agencies covered by the fiscal 2000 spending bills not yet enacted. The continuing resolution would set spending levels at the fiscal 1999 level. Passed 403-16: R 210-8; D 192-8 (ND 140-8, SD 52-0); I 1-0. Nov. 18, 1999.

[1] *Joe Baca, D-Calif., was sworn in Nov. 18, replacing George E. Brown Jr., D-Calif., who died July 15. The first vote for which Baca was eligible was 605.*

	601	602	603	604	605	606	607
ALABAMA							
1 ***Callahan***	Y	Y	N	N	N	N	Y
2 ***Everett***	Y	Y	N	N	N	N	Y
3 ***Riley***	?	?	N	?	N	N	Y
4 ***Aderholt***	Y	Y	N	N	N	N	Y
5 Cramer	Y	Y	N	N	N	N	Y
6 ***Bachus***	Y	Y	N	N	N	?	Y
7 Hilliard	N	Y	?	N	N	N	Y
ALASKA							
AL ***Young***	Y	Y	N	N	N	N	Y
ARIZONA							
1 ***Salmon***	Y	Y	N	?	N	N	Y
2 Pastor	Y	Y	N	N	N	N	Y
3 ***Stump***	Y	Y	N	N	N	N	Y
4 ***Shadegg***	Y	Y	N	?	N	N	Y
5 ***Kolbe***	Y	Y	N	N	N	N	Y
6 ***Hayworth***	Y	Y	N	N	N	N	Y
ARKANSAS							
1 Berry	Y	N	Y	Y	Y	N	Y
2 Snyder	Y	Y	N	N	N	N	Y
3 ***Hutchinson***	Y	Y	N	N	?	?	Y
4 ***Dickey***	Y	Y	N	N	N	N	Y
CALIFORNIA							
1 Thompson	Y	Y	N	N	N	N	Y
2 ***Herger***	Y	Y	N	N	N	N	?
3 ***Ose***	Y	Y	N	N	N	N	Y
4 ***Doolittle***	Y	Y	N	N	?	N	Y
5 Matsui	Y	Y	N	N	N	N	Y
6 Woolsey	Y	N	N	N	N	N	?
7 Miller, George	N	N	N	N	N	N	N
8 Pelosi	N	N	N	N	N	N	Y
9 Lee	N	N	N	N	N	N	Y
10 Tauscher	Y	Y	N	N	N	N	Y
11 ***Pombo***	Y	Y	N	N	?	N	Y
12 Lantos	Y	Y	N	N	N	N	Y
13 Stark	N	N	N	N	N	N	Y
14 Eshoo	Y	Y	N	N	N	N	Y
15 ***Campbell***	Y	Y	N	N	N	N	Y
16 Lofgren	Y	N	N	N	N	N	Y
17 Farr	Y	N	N	N	N	N	Y
18 Condit	N	N	N	N	N	N	Y
19 ***Radanovich***	Y	Y	N	N	N	N	Y
20 Dooley	Y	N	N	N	N	N	Y
21 ***Thomas***	Y	Y	N	N	N	N	Y
22 Capps	?	?	?	?	?	?	?
23 ***Gallegly***	Y	Y	N	N	N	N	Y
24 Sherman	Y	Y	N	N	N	N	Y
25 ***McKeon***	Y	Y	N	N	N	N	Y
26 Berman	?	N	N	N	?	N	Y
27 ***Rogan***	Y	Y	N	N	N	N	Y
28 ***Dreier***	Y	Y	N	N	N	N	Y
29 Waxman	Y	N	N	N	N	N	Y
30 Becerra	N	N	N	N	N	N	Y
31 Martinez	Y	N	N	N	N	N	Y
32 Dixon	Y	Y	N	N	N	N	Y
33 Roybal-Allard	Y	N	N	N	N	N	Y
34 Napolitano	Y	N	N	N	N	N	Y
35 Waters	N	N	N	Y	N	N	Y
36 ***Kuykendall***	Y	Y	N	N	N	N	Y
37 Millender-McD.	Y	N	N	N	N	N	Y
38 ***Horn***	Y	Y	N	N	N	N	Y
39 ***Royce***	Y	Y	N	N	N	N	Y
40 ***Lewis***	Y	Y	N	N	N	N	Y
41 ***Miller***	Y	Y	N	N	N	N	Y
42 Baca [1]					N	N	Y
43 ***Calvert***	Y	Y	N	N	N	N	Y
44 ***Bono***	Y	Y	N	N	N	N	Y
45 ***Rohrabacher***	Y	Y	N	N	N	N	Y
46 Sanchez	N	N	N	N	N	N	Y
47 ***Cox***	Y	Y	N	N	N	N	Y
48 ***Packard***	Y	Y	N	N	N	N	Y
49 ***Bilbray***	Y	Y	N	N	N	N	Y
50 Filner	N	N	Y	Y	Y	N	Y
51 ***Cunningham***	Y	Y	N	N	N	N	Y
52 ***Hunter***	Y	Y	N	N	N	N	Y
COLORADO							
1 DeGette	Y	Y	N	N	N	N	Y
2 Udall	Y	Y	Y	Y	N	N	Y
3 ***McInnis***	Y	Y	N	N	N	N	Y
4 ***Schaffer***	Y	Y	N	N	N	N	Y
5 ***Hefley***	Y	Y	N	N	N	N	Y
6 ***Tancredo***	Y	Y	N	N	N	N	Y
CONNECTICUT							
1 Larson	Y	N	N	N	N	N	Y
2 Gejdenson	Y	N	N	N	N	N	Y
3 DeLauro	Y	N	N	N	N	N	Y
4 ***Shays***	Y	Y	N	N	N	N	Y
5 Maloney	N	N	N	N	?	N	Y
6 ***Johnson***	Y	Y	N	N	N	N	Y
DELAWARE							
AL ***Castle***	Y	Y	N	N	N	N	Y
FLORIDA							
1 ***Scarborough***	?	?	?	?	?	N	Y
2 Boyd	Y	Y	N	N	N	N	Y
3 Brown	Y	N	N	N	Y	N	Y
4 ***Fowler***	Y	Y	N	N	?	N	Y
5 Thurman	Y	Y	N	N	N	N	Y
6 ***Stearns***	Y	Y	N	N	N	N	Y
7 ***Mica***	Y	Y	N	N	?	N	Y
8 ***McCollum***	Y	Y	N	N	N	N	Y
9 ***Bilirakis***	Y	Y	N	N	N	N	Y
10 ***Young***	Y	Y	N	N	N	N	Y
11 Davis	Y	Y	N	N	N	N	Y
12 ***Canady***	Y	Y	N	N	N	N	Y
13 ***Miller***	Y	Y	N	N	N	N	Y
14 ***Goss***	Y	Y	N	N	N	N	Y
15 ***Weldon***	Y	Y	N	?	N	N	Y
16 ***Foley***	Y	Y	N	N	N	N	Y
17 Meek	Y	Y	Y	N	N	N	Y
18 ***Ros-Lehtinen***	?	?	?	?	?	N	Y
19 Wexler	?	?	?	?	?	?	?
20 Deutsch	Y	Y	?	N	N	N	Y
21 ***Diaz-Balart***	Y	Y	N	N	N	N	Y
22 ***Shaw***	Y	Y	N	N	N	N	Y
23 Hastings	N	Y	N	N	N	N	Y
GEORGIA							
1 ***Kingston***	Y	Y	N	N	N	N	Y
2 Bishop	Y	Y	N	N	N	N	Y
3 ***Collins***	Y	Y	N	N	N	N	Y
4 McKinney	Y	Y	Y	N	Y	N	Y
5 Lewis	Y	N	N	N	N	N	Y
6 ***Isakson***	Y	Y	N	N	N	N	Y
7 ***Barr***	Y	Y	N	?	N	N	Y
8 ***Chambliss***	Y	Y	N	N	N	N	Y
9 ***Deal***	Y	Y	N	N	N	N	Y
10 ***Norwood***	Y	Y	N	N	N	N	Y
11 ***Linder***	Y	Y	N	N	N	N	Y
HAWAII							
1 Abercrombie	Y	Y	N	N	?	N	Y
2 Mink	Y	Y	N	N	N	N	?
IDAHO							
1 ***Chenoweth-Hage***	Y	Y	N	N	N	N	Y
2 ***Simpson***	Y	Y	N	N	N	N	Y
ILLINOIS							
1 Rush	Y	Y	N	N	N	N	Y
2 Jackson	Y	Y	N	N	N	N	Y
3 Lipinski	Y	Y	N	N	N	N	Y
4 Gutierrez	N	N	N	N	?	N	Y
5 Blagojevich	Y	Y	N	N	N	N	Y
6 ***Hyde***	Y	Y	N	N	N	N	Y
7 Davis	Y	Y	N	N	N	N	Y
8 ***Crane***	Y	Y	N	N	N	N	Y
9 Schakowsky	Y	N	N	N	N	N	Y
10 ***Porter***	Y	Y	N	N	N	N	?
11 ***Weller***	Y	Y	N	N	N	N	Y
12 Costello	N	N	N	N	N	N	Y
13 ***Biggert***	Y	Y	N	N	N	N	Y
14 ***Hastert***							

ND Northern Democrats SD Southern Democrats

	601	602	603	604	605	606	607
15 ***Ewing***	Y	Y	N	N	N	N	Y
16 ***Manzullo***	N	N	Y	Y	Y	N	N
17 Evans	Y	N	N	N	N	N	Y
18 ***LaHood***	Y	Y	N	N	N	N	Y
19 Phelps	Y	Y	N	N	N	N	Y
20 ***Shimkus***	Y	Y	N	N	N	N	Y
INDIANA							
1 Visclosky	N	N	N	Y	N	?	?
2 ***McIntosh***	?	?	?	N	N	N	Y
3 Roemer	Y	Y	N	N	N	N	Y
4 ***Souder***	Y	Y	N	N	N	N	N
5 ***Buyer***	Y	Y	N	N	N	N	Y
6 ***Burton***	Y	Y	N	N	N	?	Y
7 ***Pease***	Y	Y	N	N	N	N	Y
8 ***Hostettler***	Y	Y	N	N	N	N	Y
9 Hill	N	N	N	N	N	N	Y
10 Carson	Y	N	N	N	N	N	Y
IOWA							
1 ***Leach***	Y	Y	N	N	N	N	Y
2 ***Nussle***	Y	Y	N	?	N	N	Y
3 Boswell	Y	Y	N	N	N	N	Y
4 ***Ganske***	Y	Y	N	N	N	N	Y
5 ***Latham***	Y	Y	N	N	N	N	Y
KANSAS							
1 ***Moran***	Y	Y	N	N	N	N	Y
2 ***Ryun***	Y	Y	N	N	?	N	Y
3 Moore	?	Y	N	N	N	N	Y
4 ***Tiahrt***	Y	Y	N	N	N	N	Y
KENTUCKY							
1 ***Whitfield***	Y	Y	N	N	N	N	Y
2 ***Lewis***	Y	Y	N	N	N	N	Y
3 ***Northup***	Y	Y	N	N	N	N	Y
4 Lucas	Y	Y	N	N	N	N	Y
5 ***Rogers***	Y	Y	N	N	N	N	Y
6 ***Fletcher***	Y	Y	N	N	N	N	Y
LOUISIANA							
1 ***Vitter***	Y	Y	N	N	N	N	Y
2 Jefferson	Y	N	N	N	?	?	Y
3 ***Tauzin***	Y	Y	N	N	N	N	Y
4 ***McCrery***	Y	Y	N	N	N	N	Y
5 ***Cooksey***	Y	Y	N	N	N	N	Y
6 ***Baker***	Y	Y	N	N	N	N	Y
7 John	Y	Y	N	N	N	N	Y
MAINE							
1 Allen	Y	N	N	N	N	N	Y
2 Baldacci	Y	N	N	N	N	N	Y
MARYLAND							
1 ***Gilchrest***	Y	Y	N	N	N	N	Y
2 ***Ehrlich***	Y	Y	N	?	?	N	Y
3 Cardin	Y	Y	N	N	N	N	Y
4 Wynn	Y	Y	N	N	N	N	Y
5 Hoyer	Y	Y	N	N	N	N	Y
6 ***Bartlett***	Y	Y	N	N	N	N	Y
7 Cummings	Y	Y	N	N	N	N	Y
8 ***Morella***	Y	Y	N	N	N	N	Y
MASSACHUSETTS							
1 Olver	Y	N	Y	?	N	N	Y
2 Neal	Y	N	N	N	N	N	Y
3 McGovern	Y	N	N	N	N	N	Y
4 Frank	Y	N	N	N	N	N	Y
5 Meehan	?	?	?	?	?	?	?
6 Tierney	N	N	N	N	N	N	Y
7 Markey	Y	N	N	N	N	N	Y
8 Capuano	Y	N	N	N	N	N	Y
9 Moakley	Y	N	N	N	N	N	Y
10 Delahunt	N	N	N	N	N	?	?
MICHIGAN							
1 Stupak	N	N	N	N	N	N	Y
2 ***Hoekstra***	Y	Y	N	N	N	N	Y
3 ***Ehlers***	Y	Y	N	N	N	N	Y
4 ***Camp***	Y	Y	N	N	N	N	Y
5 Barcia	Y	Y	N	N	N	N	Y
6 ***Upton***	Y	Y	N	N	N	N	Y
7 ***Smith***	Y	Y	N	N	?	N	Y
8 Stabenow	Y	Y	N	N	N	N	Y
9 Kildee	Y	N	N	N	N	N	Y
10 Bonior	Y	N	N	N	N	N	Y
11 ***Knollenberg***	Y	Y	N	N	N	N	Y
12 Levin	Y	N	N	N	N	N	Y
13 Rivers	Y	N	N	N	N	N	Y
14 Conyers	?	?	?	?	?	?	?
15 Kilpatrick	Y	N	N	N	?	N	Y
16 Dingell	Y	Y	Y	Y	?	N	Y
MINNESOTA							
1 ***Gutknecht***	N	N	Y	Y	Y	N	Y
2 Minge	N	N	Y	Y	Y	N	Y
3 ***Ramstad***	Y	Y	N	N	N	N	Y
4 Vento	Y	Y	N	N	N	N	Y
5 Sabo	Y	Y	N	N	N	N	Y
6 Luther	Y	N	N	N	Y	N	Y
7 Peterson	N	N	Y	Y	Y	N	N
8 Oberstar	N	N	Y	Y	Y	N	N
MISSISSIPPI							
1 ***Wicker***	Y	Y	N	N	N	N	Y
2 Thompson	N	N	N	N	N	N	Y
3 ***Pickering***	Y	Y	N	N	N	N	Y
4 Shows	Y	N	N	N	N	N	Y
5 Taylor	N	N	Y	Y	Y	N	Y
MISSOURI							
1 Clay	Y	?	?	N	N	N	Y
2 ***Talent***	Y	Y	N	N	N	N	Y
3 Gephardt	Y	Y	N	N	N	N	Y
4 Skelton	Y	Y	N	N	N	N	Y
5 McCarthy	Y	N	N	N	N	N	Y
6 Danner	Y	N	N	?	N	N	Y
7 ***Blunt***	Y	Y	N	N	N	N	Y
8 ***Emerson***	Y	Y	N	?	N	N	Y
9 ***Hulshof***	Y	Y	N	N	N	N	Y
MONTANA							
AL ***Hill***	Y	Y	N	N	N	N	Y
NEBRASKA							
1 ***Bereuter***	Y	Y	N	N	N	N	Y
2 ***Terry***	Y	Y	N	N	N	N	Y
3 ***Barrett***	Y	Y	N	N	N	N	Y
NEVADA							
1 Berkley	Y	Y	N	N	N	N	Y
2 ***Gibbons***	Y	Y	N	N	N	N	Y
NEW HAMPSHIRE							
1 ***Sununu***	Y	Y	N	N	N	N	Y
2 ***Bass***	Y	Y	N	N	N	N	Y
NEW JERSEY							
1 Andrews	Y	N	N	N	N	N	Y
2 ***LoBiondo***	Y	Y	N	N	N	N	Y
3 ***Saxton***	Y	Y	N	N	N	N	Y
4 ***Smith***	Y	Y	N	N	N	N	Y
5 ***Roukema***	Y	Y	N	N	?	N	Y
6 Pallone	N	N	N	N	N	N	Y
7 ***Franks***	?	?	N	N	N	N	Y
8 Pascrell	N	Y	N	N	N	N	Y
9 Rothman	Y	N	N	N	N	N	Y
10 Payne	N	Y	N	N	N	N	Y
11 ***Frelinghuysen***	Y	Y	N	N	N	N	Y
12 Holt	N	Y	N	N	N	N	Y
13 Menendez	Y	Y	N	N	N	N	Y
NEW MEXICO							
1 ***Wilson***	Y	Y	N	N	N	N	Y
2 ***Skeen***	Y	Y	N	N	N	N	Y
3 Udall	Y	N	N	N	N	N	Y
NEW YORK							
1 Forbes	N	N	N	N	N	Y	N
2 ***Lazio***	Y	Y	N	N	N	N	Y
3 ***King***	Y	Y	N	N	N	N	Y
4 McCarthy	Y	Y	N	N	N	N	Y
5 Ackerman	?	?	?	?	?	?	?
6 Meeks	N	N	N	N	N	N	Y
7 Crowley	N	N	N	N	N	N	Y
8 Nadler	Y	N	N	N	N	N	Y
9 Weiner	Y	N	N	N	N	N	Y
10 Towns	Y	N	Y	Y	Y	N	Y
11 Owens	N	N	N	N	N	N	Y
12 Velázquez	N	N	N	?	N	N	Y
13 ***Fossella***	Y	Y	N	N	N	N	Y
14 Maloney	Y	Y	N	N	N	N	Y
15 Rangel	Y	N	N	N	N	N	Y
16 Serrano	Y	N	N	N	N	N	Y
17 Engel	Y	Y	N	N	N	N	Y
18 Lowey	?	Y	N	N	N	N	Y
19 ***Kelly***	Y	Y	N	N	N	N	Y
20 ***Gilman***	Y	Y	N	N	N	N	Y
21 McNulty	Y	N	N	N	N	N	Y
22 ***Sweeney***	Y	Y	N	N	N	N	Y
23 ***Boehlert***	Y	Y	N	N	N	N	Y
24 ***McHugh***	Y	Y	N	N	N	N	Y
25 ***Walsh***	Y	Y	N	N	N	N	Y
26 Hinchey	Y	N	N	N	N	N	Y
27 ***Reynolds***	Y	Y	N	N	N	N	Y
28 Slaughter	Y	N	N	?	N	N	Y
29 LaFalce	Y	Y	N	N	N	N	Y
30 ***Quinn***	Y	Y	N	N	N	N	Y
31 ***Houghton***	Y	Y	N	N	N	N	Y
NORTH CAROLINA							
1 Clayton	Y	Y	N	?	N	N	Y
2 Etheridge	Y	N	N	N	N	N	Y
3 ***Jones***	Y	?	N	N	N	N	Y
4 Price	Y	Y	N	N	N	N	?
5 ***Burr***	Y	Y	N	N	N	N	Y
6 ***Coble***	Y	Y	N	N	N	N	Y
7 McIntyre	Y	Y	N	N	N	N	Y
8 ***Hayes***	Y	Y	N	N	N	N	Y
9 ***Myrick***	Y	Y	N	N	N	N	Y
10 ***Ballenger***	Y	Y	N	N	N	N	Y
11 ***Taylor***	Y	Y	N	N	N	N	Y
12 Watt	Y	N	N	N	?	N	Y
NORTH DAKOTA							
AL Pomeroy	Y	Y	N	N	N	N	Y
OHIO							
1 ***Chabot***	Y	Y	N	N	N	N	Y
2 ***Portman***	Y	Y	N	N	N	N	Y
3 Hall	Y	Y	N	N	N	N	Y
4 ***Oxley***	Y	Y	N	N	N	N	Y
5 ***Gillmor***	Y	Y	N	N	N	N	Y
6 Strickland	Y	Y	N	N	N	N	Y
7 ***Hobson***	Y	Y	N	N	N	N	Y
8 ***Boehner***	Y	Y	N	N	N	N	Y
9 Kaptur	Y	Y	N	N	N	N	Y
10 Kucinich	N	N	N	N	N	N	Y
11 Jones	Y	Y	N	N	N	N	?
12 ***Kasich***	Y	Y	N	N	N	N	Y
13 Brown	N	N	N	N	N	N	Y
14 Sawyer	Y	Y	N	N	N	N	Y
15 ***Pryce***	Y	Y	N	N	N	N	Y
16 ***Regula***	Y	Y	N	N	N	N	Y
17 Traficant	Y	Y	N	N	N	N	Y
18 ***Ney***	Y	Y	N	N	N	N	Y
19 ***LaTourette***	Y	Y	N	N	N	N	Y
OKLAHOMA							
1 ***Largent***	Y	Y	N	N	N	N	Y
2 ***Coburn***	Y	Y	N	N	N	N	N
3 ***Watkins***	Y	Y	N	N	N	N	Y
4 ***Watts***	Y	Y	N	?	N	N	Y
5 ***Istook***	Y	Y	N	N	N	N	Y
6 ***Lucas***	Y	Y	N	N	N	N	Y
OREGON							
1 Wu	Y	N	N	N	N	N	Y
2 ***Walden***	Y	Y	N	N	N	N	Y
3 Blumenauer	N	N	N	N	N	N	Y
4 DeFazio	N	Y	N	?	N	N	Y
5 Hooley	N	N	N	N	N	N	Y
PENNSYLVANIA							
1 Brady	N	Y	N	N	N	N	Y
2 Fattah	N	Y	N	N	N	N	Y
3 Borski	N	Y	N	N	N	N	Y
4 Klink	N	Y	N	N	N	N	Y
5 ***Peterson***	Y	Y	N	?	N	N	Y
6 Holden	Y	Y	N	N	N	N	Y
7 ***Weldon***	Y	Y	N	N	N	N	Y
8 ***Greenwood***	Y	Y	N	N	?	N	Y
9 ***Shuster***	Y	Y	N	N	N	N	Y
10 ***Sherwood***	Y	Y	N	N	N	N	Y
11 Kanjorski	Y	Y	N	N	N	N	Y
12 Murtha	Y	Y	N	?	?	N	Y
13 Hoeffel	N	N	N	N	N	N	Y
14 Coyne	N	N	N	N	N	N	Y
15 ***Toomey***	Y	Y	N	N	N	N	Y
16 ***Pitts***	Y	Y	N	N	N	N	Y
17 ***Gekas***	?	?	N	N	?	N	Y
18 Doyle	Y	N	N	?	?	N	Y
19 ***Goodling***	Y	Y	N	N	N	N	Y
20 Mascara	Y	N	N	N	N	N	Y
21 ***English***	Y	?	?	N	N	N	Y
RHODE ISLAND							
1 Kennedy	N	N	N	N	N	N	Y
2 Weygand	?	?	N	N	N	N	Y
SOUTH CAROLINA							
1 ***Sanford***	Y	Y	N	N	N	N	Y
2 ***Spence***	Y	Y	N	N	N	N	Y
3 ***Graham***	Y	Y	N	N	N	N	Y
4 ***DeMint***	Y	Y	N	N	N	N	Y
5 Spratt	Y	N	N	N	?	N	Y
6 Clyburn	N	N	N	N	N	N	?
SOUTH DAKOTA							
AL ***Thune***	Y	Y	N	N	N	N	Y
TENNESSEE							
1 ***Jenkins***	Y	Y	N	N	N	N	Y
2 ***Duncan***	Y	Y	N	N	N	N	Y
3 ***Wamp***	Y	Y	N	N	N	N	Y
4 ***Hilleary***	Y	Y	N	N	N	N	Y
5 Clement	Y	Y	N	N	N	N	Y
6 Gordon	Y	N	N	N	N	N	Y
7 ***Bryant***	Y	Y	N	N	N	N	Y
8 Tanner	Y	Y	N	N	N	N	Y
9 Ford	Y	Y	N	N	N	N	Y
TEXAS							
1 Sandlin	Y	N	N	N	N	N	Y
2 Turner	Y	Y	N	N	N	N	Y
3 ***Johnson, Sam***	Y	Y	N	?	N	?	Y
4 Hall	Y	Y	N	N	N	N	Y
5 ***Sessions***	Y	Y	N	N	N	N	Y
6 ***Barton***	?	Y	N	N	N	N	Y
7 ***Archer***	Y	Y	N	N	N	N	Y
8 ***Brady***	Y	Y	N	N	N	?	?
9 Lampson	Y	N	N	N	N	N	Y
10 Doggett	N	N	N	N	N	N	Y
11 Edwards	Y	N	N	N	N	N	Y
12 ***Granger***	Y	Y	N	N	N	N	Y
13 ***Thornberry***	Y	Y	N	N	N	N	Y
14 ***Paul***	Y	Y	N	N	N	N	N
15 Hinojosa	Y	N	N	N	N	N	Y
16 Reyes	Y	N	N	N	N	N	Y
17 Stenholm	N	N	N	N	N	N	Y
18 Jackson-Lee	N	N	N	N	N	N	Y
19 ***Combest***	Y	Y	N	N	N	N	Y
20 Gonzalez	Y	N	N	N	N	N	Y
21 ***Smith***	Y	Y	N	N	N	N	Y
22 ***DeLay***	Y	Y	N	N	N	N	Y
23 ***Bonilla***	Y	Y	N	N	N	N	Y
24 Frost	Y	N	N	?	?	N	Y
25 Bentsen	Y	N	N	N	N	N	Y
26 ***Armey***	Y	Y	N	N	N	N	Y
27 Ortiz	Y	N	N	N	N	N	Y
28 Rodriguez	Y	N	N	N	N	N	Y
29 Green	Y	N	N	N	N	N	Y
30 Johnson, E.B.	N	N	N	N	N	N	Y
UTAH							
1 ***Hansen***	?	Y	?	N	N	N	Y
2 ***Cook***	Y	Y	N	N	N	N	Y
3 ***Cannon***	Y	Y	N	?	N	N	Y
VERMONT							
AL *Sanders*	Y	Y	N	N	N	N	Y
VIRGINIA							
1 ***Bateman***	Y	Y	N	N	N	N	Y
2 Pickett	Y	Y	N	N	N	N	Y
3 Scott	Y	N	N	N	N	N	Y
4 Sisisky	Y	Y	N	N	N	N	Y
5 Goode	Y	Y	N	N	N	N	Y
6 ***Goodlatte***	Y	Y	N	N	N	N	Y
7 ***Bliley***	Y	Y	N	N	N	N	Y
8 Moran	Y	Y	N	?	?	N	Y
9 Boucher	Y	Y	N	?	N	N	Y
10 ***Wolf***	Y	Y	N	N	N	N	Y
11 ***Davis***	Y	Y	N	N	N	N	Y
WASHINGTON							
1 Inslee	N	N	N	N	N	N	Y
2 ***Metcalf***	Y	Y	N	N	N	N	Y
3 Baird	Y	Y	N	N	N	N	Y
4 ***Hastings***	Y	Y	N	N	N	N	Y
5 ***Nethercutt***	Y	Y	N	N	N	N	Y
6 Dicks	Y	Y	N	N	N	N	Y
7 McDermott	N	N	Y	Y	Y	N	Y
8 ***Dunn***	?	?	N	N	N	N	Y
9 Smith	Y	Y	N	N	N	N	Y
WEST VIRGINIA							
1 Mollohan	N	N	N	N	N	N	Y
2 Wise	N	N	Y	Y	Y	N	Y
3 Rahall	N	N	Y	Y	Y	N	Y
WISCONSIN							
1 ***Ryan***	N	N	Y	Y	Y	N	N
2 Baldwin	N	N	Y	Y	Y	N	N
3 Kind	N	N	Y	Y	Y	N	N
4 Kleczka	Y	N	N	Y	Y	N	Y
5 Barrett	N	N	Y	Y	Y	N	N
6 ***Petri***	Y	N	Y	?	Y	N	N
7 Obey	Y	N	Y	Y	Y	N	N
8 ***Green***	N	N	Y	Y	Y	N	N
9 ***Sensenbrenner***	N	N	Y	Y	Y	N	N
WYOMING							
AL ***Cubin***	Y	Y	N	N	N	N	Y

Southern states - Ala., Ark., Fla., Ga., Ky., La., Miss., N.C., Okla., S.C., Tenn., Texas, Va.

608. HR 3194. Fiscal 2000 Omnibus Appropriations/Rule. Adoption of the rule (H Res 386) to provide for House floor consideration of the conference report on the bill to provide $385 billion in spending and offsets to provide for the Departments of Labor, Health and Human Services, Education, Commerce, Justice, State, and Interior and the District of Columbia. Adopted 226-204: R 208-12; D 18-191 (ND 10-145, SD 8-46); I 0-1. Nov. 18, 1999.

609. HR 3194. Fiscal 2000 Omnibus Appropriations/Recommit. Obey, D-Wis., motion to recommit the conference report on the bill to provide almost $385 billion in new budget authority for those Cabinet departments and federal agencies whose fiscal 2000 appropriations bills were never enacted back to the conference committee, with instructions to the House managers to not agree to any provisions that would reduce appropriations for medical care for veterans. Motion rejected 212-219: R 4-217; D 207-2 (ND 153-2, SD 54-0); I 1-0. Nov. 18, 1999.

610. HR 3194. Fiscal 2000 Omnibus Appropriations/Conference Report. Adoption of the conference report on the bill to provide almost $385 billion in new budget authority for those Cabinet departments and federal agencies whose fiscal 2000 appropriations bills were never enacted. The measure would provide $435.8 million in federal funds for the District of Columbia. It also incorporates by reference four other appropriations bills: Labor-HHS-Education, Commerce-Justice-State, Interior and Foreign Operations. Also included are bills to reauthorize the State Department, permit satellite TV carriers to transmit local-to-local broadcasts, increase payments to Medicare health providers, and extend the Northeast Dairy Compact and block the administration's new milk pricing plan. The bill would also impose a 0.38 percent across-the-board spending cut, with flexibility for some accounts. Adopted (thus sent to the Senate) 296-135: R 170-51; D 125-84 (ND 91-64, SD 34-20); I 1-0. Nov. 18, 1999.

611. HR 1180. Working Disabled and Tax Extenders/Conference Report. Adoption of the conference report on the bill to allow disabled individuals to retain their federal health benefits after they return to work. The report would create a voucherlike system to permit disabled individuals receiving Social Security and Supplemental Security Income to purchase job training and rehabilitation services to prepare them to return to work. The conference report also would extend several tax provisions that would otherwise expire at the end of 1999, including the research tax credit and the work opportunity tax credit. The report also would delay for 90 days a proposed rule on organ transplants. Adopted (thus sent to the Senate) 418-2: R 212-0; D 205-2 (ND 152-1, SD 53-1); I 1-0. Nov. 18, 1999.

Key

- Y Voted for (yea).
- # Paired for.
- + Announced for.
- N Voted against (nay).
- X Paired against.
- – Announced against.
- P Voted "present."
- C Voted "present" to avoid possible conflict of interest.
- ? Did not vote or otherwise make a position known.

•

Democrats **_Republicans_**
Independents

	608	609	610	611
ALABAMA				
1 ***Callahan***	Y	N	Y	?
2 ***Everett***	Y	N	Y	?
3 ***Riley***	Y	N	Y	Y
4 ***Aderholt***	Y	N	Y	Y
5 Cramer	Y	Y	Y	Y
6 ***Bachus***	Y	N	Y	Y
7 Hilliard	N	Y	Y	Y
ALASKA				
AL ***Young***	Y	N	Y	Y
ARIZONA				
1 ***Salmon***	Y	N	N	Y
2 Pastor	Y	Y	N	Y
3 ***Stump***	Y	N	Y	Y
4 ***Shadegg***	Y	N	N	Y
5 ***Kolbe***	Y	N	Y	Y
6 ***Hayworth***	Y	N	Y	Y
ARKANSAS				
1 Berry	N	Y	N	N
2 Snyder	N	Y	Y	Y
3 ***Hutchinson***	Y	N	Y	Y
4 ***Dickey***	N	N	Y	Y
CALIFORNIA				
1 Thompson	N	Y	Y	Y
2 ***Herger***	Y	N	Y	Y
3 ***Ose***	Y	N	Y	Y
4 ***Doolittle***	Y	N	N	Y
5 Matsui	N	Y	Y	Y
6 Woolsey	N	Y	Y	Y
7 Miller, George	N	Y	N	Y
8 Pelosi	N	Y	Y	Y
9 Lee	N	Y	Y	Y
10 Tauscher	N	Y	Y	Y
11 ***Pombo***	Y	N	N	Y
12 Lantos	N	Y	Y	Y
13 Stark	N	Y	N	N
14 Eshoo	N	Y	Y	Y
15 ***Campbell***	Y	N	N	Y
16 Lofgren	N	Y	Y	Y
17 Farr	N	Y	Y	Y
18 Condit	N	Y	N	Y
19 ***Radanovich***	Y	N	Y	?
20 Dooley	N	Y	Y	Y
21 ***Thomas***	Y	N	Y	Y
22 Capps	?	?	?	?
23 ***Gallegly***	Y	N	Y	Y
24 Sherman	N	Y	Y	Y
25 ***McKeon***	Y	N	Y	Y
26 Berman	N	Y	Y	Y
27 ***Rogan***	Y	N	Y	Y
28 ***Dreier***	Y	N	Y	Y
29 Waxman	N	Y	Y	Y
30 Becerra	N	Y	N	Y
31 Martinez	N	Y	Y	Y
32 Dixon	N	Y	Y	Y
33 Roybal-Allard	N	Y	Y	Y
34 Napolitano	N	Y	N	Y
35 Waters	N	Y	N	Y
36 ***Kuykendall***	Y	N	Y	Y
37 Millender-McD.	N	Y	Y	Y
38 ***Horn***	Y	N	Y	Y
39 ***Royce***	Y	N	N	Y
40 ***Lewis***	Y	N	Y	Y
41 ***Miller***	Y	N	Y	Y
42 Baca	N	Y	Y	Y
43 ***Calvert***	Y	N	Y	Y
44 ***Bono***	Y	N	Y	Y
45 ***Rohrabacher***	Y	N	N	Y
46 Sanchez	N	Y	N	Y
47 ***Cox***	Y	N	N	Y
48 ***Packard***	Y	N	Y	Y
49 ***Bilbray***	Y	N	Y	Y
50 Filner	N	Y	N	Y
51 ***Cunningham***	Y	N	Y	Y
52 ***Hunter***	Y	N	Y	Y
COLORADO				
1 DeGette	N	Y	N	Y
2 Udall	N	Y	N	Y
3 ***McInnis***	Y	N	N	Y
4 ***Schaffer***	Y	N	N	Y
5 ***Hefley***	Y	N	N	Y
6 ***Tancredo***	Y	N	Y	Y
CONNECTICUT				
1 Larson	N	Y	N	Y
2 Gejdenson	N	Y	N	Y
3 DeLauro	N	Y	Y	Y
4 ***Shays***	Y	N	N	Y
5 Maloney	N	Y	N	Y
6 ***Johnson***	Y	N	Y	Y
DELAWARE				
AL ***Castle***	Y	N	Y	Y
FLORIDA				
1 ***Scarborough***	Y	N	N	Y
2 Boyd	N	Y	Y	Y
3 Brown	Y	Y	Y	Y
4 ***Fowler***	Y	N	Y	Y
5 Thurman	N	Y	N	Y
6 ***Stearns***	Y	N	N	Y
7 ***Mica***	Y	N	Y	Y
8 ***McCollum***	Y	N	Y	Y
9 ***Bilirakis***	Y	N	Y	Y
10 ***Young***	Y	N	Y	Y
11 Davis	N	Y	N	Y
12 ***Canady***	Y	N	Y	Y
13 ***Miller***	Y	N	Y	Y
14 ***Goss***	Y	N	Y	Y
15 ***Weldon***	Y	N	N	Y
16 ***Foley***	Y	N	Y	Y
17 Meek	Y	Y	Y	Y
18 ***Ros-Lehtinen***	Y	N	Y	Y
19 Wexler	?	?	?	?
20 Deutsch	N	Y	Y	Y
21 ***Diaz-Balart***	Y	N	Y	Y
22 ***Shaw***	Y	N	Y	Y
23 Hastings	N	Y	Y	Y
GEORGIA				
1 ***Kingston***	Y	N	Y	Y
2 Bishop	N	Y	Y	Y
3 ***Collins***	Y	N	Y	Y
4 McKinney	Y	Y	Y	Y
5 Lewis	N	Y	N	Y
6 ***Isakson***	Y	N	Y	Y
7 ***Barr***	Y	N	N	Y
8 ***Chambliss***	Y	N	Y	Y
9 ***Deal***	Y	N	Y	Y
10 ***Norwood***	Y	N	Y	Y
11 ***Linder***	Y	N	Y	Y
HAWAII				
1 Abercrombie	Y	N	Y	Y
2 Mink	N	Y	Y	Y
IDAHO				
1 ***Chenoweth-Hage***	Y	N	N	Y
2 ***Simpson***	Y	N	N	Y
ILLINOIS				
1 Rush	N	Y	Y	Y
2 Jackson	N	Y	N	Y
3 Lipinski	N	Y	N	Y
4 Gutierrez	N	Y	N	Y
5 Blagojevich	Y	Y	Y	Y
6 ***Hyde***	Y	N	Y	Y
7 Davis	N	Y	Y	Y
8 ***Crane***	Y	N	N	Y
9 Schakowsky	N	Y	N	Y
10 ***Porter***	Y	N	Y	Y
11 ***Weller***	Y	N	N	Y
12 Costello	N	Y	N	Y
13 ***Biggert***	Y	N	Y	Y
14 ***Hastert***		N	Y	Y

ND Northern Democrats SD Southern Democrats

	608	609	610	611
15 ***Ewing***	Y	N	Y	Y
16 ***Manzullo***	N	N	N	Y
17 Evans	N	Y	Y	Y
18 ***LaHood***	Y	N	Y	Y
19 Phelps	Y	Y	N	Y
20 ***Shimkus***	Y	N	Y	Y
INDIANA				
1 Visclosky	N	Y	N	Y
2 ***McIntosh***	Y	Y	Y	?
3 Roemer	N	Y	N	Y
4 ***Souder***	Y	N	Y	Y
5 ***Buyer***	Y	N	Y	Y
6 ***Burton***	Y	N	N	Y
7 ***Pease***	Y	N	Y	Y
8 ***Hostettler***	N	N	N	Y
9 Hill	N	Y	N	Y
10 Carson	N	Y	N	Y
IOWA				
1 ***Leach***	Y	N	Y	Y
2 ***Nussle***	N	N	Y	Y
3 Boswell	N	Y	N	Y
4 ***Ganske***	Y	N	Y	Y
5 ***Latham***	Y	N	Y	Y
KANSAS				
1 ***Moran***	Y	N	N	Y
2 ***Ryun***	Y	N	N	Y
3 Moore	N	Y	N	Y
4 ***Tiahrt***	Y	N	Y	Y
KENTUCKY				
1 ***Whitfield***	Y	N	Y	Y
2 ***Lewis***	Y	N	Y	Y
3 ***Northup***	Y	N	Y	Y
4 Lucas	N	Y	Y	Y
5 ***Rogers***	Y	N	Y	Y
6 ***Fletcher***	N	N	Y	?
LOUISIANA				
1 ***Vitter***	Y	N	Y	Y
2 Jefferson	N	Y	Y	Y
3 ***Tauzin***	Y	N	Y	Y
4 ***McCrery***	Y	N	Y	Y
5 ***Cooksey***	Y	N	Y	Y
6 ***Baker***	Y	N	Y	?
7 John	N	Y	Y	Y
MAINE				
1 Allen	N	Y	Y	Y
2 Baldacci	N	Y	Y	Y
MARYLAND				
1 ***Gilchrest***	Y	N	Y	Y
2 ***Ehrlich***	Y	N	Y	Y
3 Cardin	N	Y	Y	Y
4 Wynn	N	Y	Y	Y
5 Hoyer	N	Y	Y	Y
6 ***Bartlett***	Y	N	N	Y
7 Cummings	N	Y	Y	Y
8 ***Morella***	Y	N	Y	Y
MASSACHUSETTS				
1 Olver	N	Y	Y	Y
2 Neal	Y	Y	Y	Y
3 McGovern	N	Y	Y	Y
4 Frank	N	Y	Y	?
5 Meehan	N	Y	N	Y
6 Tierney	N	Y	Y	Y
7 Markey	N	Y	N	Y
8 Capuano	N	Y	N	Y
9 Moakley	N	Y	Y	Y
10 Delahunt	N	Y	N	Y
MICHIGAN				
1 Stupak	N	Y	Y	Y
2 ***Hoekstra***	Y	N	Y	Y
3 ***Ehlers***	Y	N	N	Y
4 ***Camp***	Y	N	Y	Y
5 Barcia	N	Y	N	Y
6 ***Upton***	Y	N	N	Y
7 ***Smith***	Y	N	Y	Y
8 Stabenow	N	Y	N	Y
9 Kildee	N	Y	N	Y
10 Bonior	N	Y	Y	Y
11 ***Knollenberg***	Y	N	Y	Y
12 Levin	N	Y	Y	Y
13 Rivers	N	Y	N	Y
14 Conyers	?	?	?	?
15 Kilpatrick	N	Y	Y	Y
16 Dingell	N	N	Y	Y

	608	609	610	611
MINNESOTA				
1 ***Gutknecht***	N	N	N	Y
2 Minge	N	Y	N	Y
3 ***Ramstad***	N	N	N	Y
4 Vento	N	Y	Y	Y
5 Sabo	N	Y	Y	Y
6 Luther	N	Y	N	Y
7 Peterson	N	Y	N	Y
8 Oberstar	N	Y	N	Y
MISSISSIPPI				
1 ***Wicker***	Y	N	Y	Y
2 Thompson	N	Y	N	Y
3 ***Pickering***	Y	N	Y	Y
4 Shows	N	Y	Y	Y
5 Taylor	N	Y	N	Y
MISSOURI				
1 Clay	N	Y	Y	Y
2 ***Talent***	Y	N	Y	Y
3 Gephardt	N	Y	Y	Y
4 Skelton	Y	Y	Y	Y
5 McCarthy	N	Y	N	Y
6 Danner	N	Y	Y	Y
7 ***Blunt***	Y	N	Y	Y
8 ***Emerson***	Y	N	Y	Y
9 ***Hulshof***	Y	N	Y	Y
MONTANA				
AL ***Hill***	Y	N	N	Y
NEBRASKA				
1 ***Bereuter***	Y	N	Y	Y
2 ***Terry***	Y	N	N	Y
3 ***Barrett***	Y	N	Y	Y
NEVADA				
1 Berkley	N	Y	N	Y
2 ***Gibbons***	Y	N	Y	Y
NEW HAMPSHIRE				
1 ***Sununu***	Y	N	Y	Y
2 ***Bass***	Y	N	Y	Y
NEW JERSEY				
1 Andrews	N	Y	Y	Y
2 ***LoBiondo***	Y	N	Y	Y
3 ***Saxton***	Y	N	Y	Y
4 ***Smith***	Y	N	Y	Y
5 ***Roukema***	Y	N	Y	Y
6 Pallone	N	Y	N	Y
7 ***Franks***	Y	N	Y	Y
8 Pascrell	N	Y	Y	Y
9 Rothman	N	Y	Y	Y
10 Payne	N	Y	Y	Y
11 ***Frelinghuysen***	Y	N	Y	Y
12 Holt	N	Y	N	Y
13 Menendez	N	Y	Y	Y
NEW MEXICO				
1 ***Wilson***	Y	N	Y	?
2 ***Skeen***	Y	N	Y	Y
3 Udall	N	Y	N	Y
NEW YORK				
1 Forbes	N	Y	Y	Y
2 ***Lazio***	Y	N	Y	Y
3 ***King***	Y	N	Y	Y
4 McCarthy	N	Y	Y	Y
5 Ackerman	N	Y	Y	Y
6 Meeks	N	Y	Y	Y
7 Crowley	N	Y	Y	Y
8 Nadler	N	Y	Y	Y
9 Weiner	N	Y	Y	Y
10 Towns	N	Y	Y	Y
11 Owens	N	Y	Y	Y
12 Velázquez	N	Y	Y	Y
13 ***Fossella***	Y	N	Y	Y
14 Maloney	N	Y	Y	Y
15 Rangel	N	Y	Y	Y
16 Serrano	N	Y	Y	?
17 Engel	N	Y	Y	Y
18 Lowey	N	Y	Y	Y
19 ***Kelly***	Y	N	Y	Y
20 ***Gilman***	Y	N	Y	Y
21 McNulty	N	Y	Y	Y
22 ***Sweeney***	Y	N	Y	Y
23 ***Boehlert***	Y	N	Y	Y
24 ***McHugh***	Y	N	Y	Y
25 ***Walsh***	Y	N	Y	Y
26 Hinchey	N	Y	Y	Y
27 ***Reynolds***	Y	N	Y	Y
28 Slaughter	N	Y	Y	Y
29 LaFalce	N	Y	Y	Y

	608	609	610	611
30 ***Quinn***	Y	N	Y	Y
31 ***Houghton***	Y	N	Y	Y
NORTH CAROLINA				
1 Clayton	N	Y	N	Y
2 Etheridge	N	Y	N	Y
3 ***Jones***	Y	N	N	Y
4 Price	N	Y	Y	Y
5 ***Burr***	Y	N	Y	Y
6 ***Coble***	Y	N	Y	Y
7 McIntyre	N	Y	N	Y
8 ***Hayes***	Y	N	Y	Y
9 ***Myrick***	Y	N	Y	Y
10 ***Ballenger***	Y	N	Y	Y
11 ***Taylor***	Y	N	Y	Y
12 Watt	N	Y	Y	Y
NORTH DAKOTA				
AL Pomeroy	N	Y	N	Y
OHIO				
1 ***Chabot***	Y	N	N	Y
2 ***Portman***	Y	N	Y	Y
3 Hall	N	Y	Y	Y
4 ***Oxley***	Y	N	N	Y
5 ***Gillmor***	Y	N	Y	Y
6 Strickland	N	Y	N	Y
7 ***Hobson***	Y	N	Y	Y
8 ***Boehner***	Y	N	Y	Y
9 Kaptur	N	Y	N	Y
10 Kucinich	N	Y	N	Y
11 Jones	N	Y	Y	Y
12 ***Kasich***	Y	N	Y	Y
13 Brown	N	Y	N	Y
14 Sawyer	N	Y	Y	Y
15 ***Pryce***	Y	N	Y	Y
16 ***Regula***	Y	N	Y	Y
17 Traficant	Y	Y	Y	Y
18 ***Ney***	Y	N	Y	Y
19 ***LaTourette***	Y	N	N	Y
OKLAHOMA				
1 ***Largent***	Y	N	Y	Y
2 ***Coburn***	N	N	N	Y
3 ***Watkins***	Y	N	N	Y
4 ***Watts***	Y	N	Y	Y
5 ***Istook***	Y	N	Y	Y
6 ***Lucas***	Y	N	N	Y
OREGON				
1 Wu	N	Y	Y	Y
2 ***Walden***	Y	N	Y	Y
3 Blumenauer	N	Y	N	Y
4 DeFazio	N	Y	N	Y
5 Hooley	N	Y	Y	Y
PENNSYLVANIA				
1 Brady	N	Y	Y	Y
2 Fattah	N	Y	Y	Y
3 Borski	N	Y	Y	Y
4 Klink	Y	Y	Y	Y
5 ***Peterson***	Y	N	Y	Y
6 Holden	N	Y	N	Y
7 ***Weldon***	Y	N	Y	Y
8 ***Greenwood***	Y	N	Y	Y
9 ***Shuster***	Y	N	Y	?
10 ***Sherwood***	Y	N	Y	Y
11 Kanjorski	N	Y	Y	Y
12 Murtha	Y	Y	Y	Y
13 Hoeffel	N	Y	N	Y
14 Coyne	N	Y	N	Y
15 ***Toomey***	Y	N	N	Y
16 ***Pitts***	Y	N	Y	Y
17 ***Gekas***	Y	N	Y	Y
18 Doyle	N	Y	Y	Y
19 ***Goodling***	Y	N	Y	Y
20 Mascara	N	Y	Y	Y
21 ***English***	Y	N	Y	Y
RHODE ISLAND				
1 Kennedy	N	Y	Y	Y
2 Weygand	N	Y	Y	Y
SOUTH CAROLINA				
1 ***Sanford***	Y	N	N	Y
2 ***Spence***	Y	N	N	Y
3 ***Graham***	Y	N	N	Y
4 ***DeMint***	Y	N	Y	Y
5 Spratt	N	Y	Y	Y
6 Clyburn	N	Y	Y	Y
SOUTH DAKOTA				
AL ***Thune***	Y	Y	Y	Y

	608	609	610	611
TENNESSEE				
1 ***Jenkins***	Y	N	Y	Y
2 ***Duncan***	Y	N	N	Y
3 ***Wamp***	Y	N	Y	Y
4 ***Hilleary***	Y	N	Y	Y
5 Clement	N	Y	N	Y
6 Gordon	N	Y	N	Y
7 ***Bryant***	Y	N	Y	Y
8 Tanner	N	Y	N	Y
9 Ford	N	Y	N	Y
TEXAS				
1 Sandlin	N	Y	Y	Y
2 Turner	N	Y	Y	Y
3 ***Johnson, Sam***	Y	N	N	Y
4 Hall	N	Y	N	Y
5 ***Sessions***	Y	N	Y	Y
6 ***Barton***	Y	N	Y	Y
7 ***Archer***	Y	N	Y	Y
8 ***Brady***	?	?	?	?
9 Lampson	N	Y	Y	Y
10 Doggett	N	Y	N	Y
11 Edwards	N	Y	N	Y
12 ***Granger***	Y	N	Y	Y
13 ***Thornberry***	Y	N	Y	Y
14 ***Paul***	Y	N	N	Y
15 Hinojosa	N	Y	Y	Y
16 Reyes	N	Y	N	Y
17 Stenholm	N	Y	Y	Y
18 Jackson-Lee	N	Y	N	Y
19 ***Combest***	Y	N	Y	Y
20 Gonzalez	N	Y	Y	Y
21 ***Smith***	Y	N	Y	Y
22 ***DeLay***	Y	N	Y	Y
23 ***Bonilla***	Y	N	Y	Y
24 Frost	N	Y	Y	Y
25 Bentsen	N	Y	Y	Y
26 ***Armey***	Y	N	Y	Y
27 Ortiz	Y	Y	Y	Y
28 Rodriguez	N	Y	Y	Y
29 Green	N	Y	N	Y
30 Johnson, E.B.	N	Y	Y	Y
UTAH				
1 ***Hansen***	Y	N	Y	Y
2 ***Cook***	Y	N	N	Y
3 ***Cannon***	Y	N	Y	Y
VERMONT				
AL *Sanders*	N	Y	Y	Y
VIRGINIA				
1 ***Bateman***	Y	N	Y	Y
2 Pickett	Y	Y	Y	Y
3 Scott	N	Y	Y	Y
4 Sisisky	Y	Y	Y	Y
5 Goode	N	Y	N	Y
6 ***Goodlatte***	Y	N	Y	Y
7 ***Bliley***	Y	N	Y	Y
8 Moran	N	Y	Y	Y
9 Boucher	Y	Y	Y	Y
10 ***Wolf***	Y	N	Y	Y
11 ***Davis***	Y	N	Y	Y
WASHINGTON				
1 Inslee	N	Y	N	Y
2 ***Metcalf***	Y	N	Y	Y
3 Baird	N	Y	N	Y
4 ***Hastings***	Y	N	Y	Y
5 ***Nethercutt***	Y	N	Y	?
6 Dicks	Y	Y	Y	Y
7 McDermott	N	Y	N	Y
8 ***Dunn***	Y	N	Y	Y
9 Smith	N	Y	Y	Y
WEST VIRGINIA				
1 Mollohan	N	Y	N	Y
2 Wise	N	Y	N	Y
3 Rahall	N	Y	N	Y
WISCONSIN				
1 ***Ryan***	N	Y	N	Y
2 Baldwin	N	Y	N	Y
3 Kind	N	Y	N	Y
4 Kleczka	N	Y	N	Y
5 Barrett	N	Y	N	Y
6 ***Petri***	N	N	N	Y
7 Obey	N	Y	N	Y
8 ***Green***	N	Y	N	Y
9 ***Sensenbrenner***	N	N	N	Y
WYOMING				
AL ***Cubin***	Y	N	Y	Y

Southern states - Ala., Ark., Fla., Ga., Ky., La., Miss., N.C., Okla., S.C., Tenn., Texas, Va.

House Roll Call Votes By Subject

A

B

C

D

E

F

Appendix S

SENATE ROLL CALL VOTES

Senate Roll Call Votes By Bill Number

Senate Bills

House Bills

Senate Vote 1

	1
ALABAMA	
Sessions	Y
Shelby	Y
ALASKA	
Murkowski	Y
Stevens	Y
ARIZONA	
Kyl	Y
McCain	Y
ARKANSAS	
Hutchinson	Y
Lincoln	Y
CALIFORNIA	
Boxer	Y
Feinstein	Y
COLORADO	
Allard	Y
Campbell	Y
CONNECTICUT	
Dodd	Y
Lieberman	Y
DELAWARE	
Roth	Y
Biden	Y
FLORIDA	
Mack	Y
Graham	Y
GEORGIA	
Coverdell	Y
Cleland	Y
HAWAII	
Akaka	Y
Inouye	Y
IDAHO	
Craig	Y
Crapo	Y
ILLINOIS	
Fitzgerald	Y
Durbin	Y
INDIANA	
Bayh	Y
Lugar	Y
IOWA	
Grassley	Y
Harkin	Y
KANSAS	
Brownback	Y
Roberts	Y
KENTUCKY	
Bunning	Y
McConnell	Y
LOUISIANA	
Breaux	Y
Landrieu	Y
MAINE	
Collins	Y
Snowe	Y
MARYLAND	
Mikulski	Y
Sarbanes	Y
MASSACHUSETTS	
Kennedy	Y
Kerry	Y
MICHIGAN	
Abraham	Y
Levin	Y
MINNESOTA	
Grams	Y
Wellstone	Y
MISSISSIPPI	
Cochran	Y
Lott	Y
MISSOURI	
Ashcroft	Y
Bond	Y
MONTANA	
Burns	Y
Baucus	Y
NEBRASKA	
Hagel	Y
Kerrey	Y
NEVADA	
Bryan	Y
Reid	Y
NEW HAMPSHIRE	
Gregg	Y
Smith	Y
NEW JERSEY	
Lautenberg	Y
Torricelli	Y
NEW MEXICO	
Domenici	Y
Bingaman	Y
NEW YORK	
Moynihan	Y
Schumer	Y
NORTH CAROLINA	
Helms	Y
Edwards	Y
NORTH DAKOTA	
Conrad	Y
Dorgan	Y
OHIO	
DeWine	Y
Voinovich	Y
OKLAHOMA	
Inhofe	Y
Nickles	Y
OREGON	
Smith	Y
Wyden	Y
PENNSYLVANIA	
Santorum	Y
Specter	Y
RHODE ISLAND	
Chafee	Y
Reed	Y
SOUTH CAROLINA	
Thurmond	Y
Hollings	Y
SOUTH DAKOTA	
Daschle	Y
Johnson	Y
TENNESSEE	
Frist	Y
Thompson	Y
TEXAS	
Gramm	Y
Hutchison	Y
UTAH	
Bennett	Y
Hatch	Y
VERMONT	
Jeffords	Y
Leahy	Y
VIRGINIA	
Warner	Y
Robb	Y
WASHINGTON	
Gorton	Y
Murray	Y
WEST VIRGINIA	
Byrd	Y
Rockefeller	Y
WISCONSIN	
Feingold	Y
Kohl	Y
WYOMING	
Enzi	Y
Thomas	Y

Key

- Y Voted for (yea).
- # Paired for.
- \+ Announced for.
- N Voted against (nay).
- X Paired against.
- – Announced against.
- P Voted "present."
- C Voted "present" to avoid possible conflict of interest.
- ? Did not vote or otherwise make a position known.

•

Democrats ***Republicans***
Independents

ND Northern Democrats SD Southern Democrats

Southern states - Ala., Ark., Fla., Ga., Ky., La., Miss., N.C., Okla., S.C., Tenn., Texas, Va.

1. Impeachment of President Clinton/Senate Trial Procedures. Adoption of the resolution (S Res 16) to establish procedures for the Senate trial of President Clinton. The House and the president's counsels have 24 hours each to present their respective cases. Senators then have 16 hours to question the parties. At that point, senators can consider a motion to dismiss. If the motion fails, the trial would continue and senators would have opportunities to vote on motions allowing the subpoena and examination of witnesses. Adopted 100-0: R 55-0; D 45-0 (ND 37-0, SD 8-0). Jan. 8, 1999.

Senate Votes 2, 3, 4, 5, 6, 7, 8

	2	3	4	5	6	7	8
ALABAMA							
Sessions	N	N	N	Y	N	N	Y
Shelby	N	N	N	Y	N	N	Y
ALASKA							
Murkowski	N	N	N	Y	N	N	Y
Stevens	N	N	N	Y	N	N	Y
ARIZONA							
Kyl	N	N	N	Y	N	N	Y
McCain	N	N	N	Y	N	N	Y
ARKANSAS							
Hutchinson	N	N	N	Y	N	N	Y
Lincoln	N	N	Y	N	Y	Y	N
CALIFORNIA							
Boxer	Y	Y	Y	N	Y	Y	N
Feinstein	Y	Y	Y	N	Y	Y	N
COLORADO							
Allard	N	N	N	Y	?	?	?
Campbell	N	N	N	Y	N	N	Y
CONNECTICUT							
Dodd	Y	Y	Y	N	Y	Y	N
Lieberman	Y	Y	Y	N	Y	Y	N
DELAWARE							
Roth	N	N	N	Y	N	N	Y
Biden	Y	Y	Y	N	Y	Y	N
FLORIDA							
Mack	N	N	N	Y	N	N	Y
Graham	Y	Y	Y	N	Y	Y	N
GEORGIA							
Coverdell	N	N	N	Y	N	N	Y
Cleland	Y	Y	Y	N	Y	Y	N
HAWAII							
Akaka	Y	Y	Y	N	Y	Y	N
Inouye	Y	Y	Y	N	Y	Y	N
IDAHO							
Craig	N	N	N	Y	N	N	Y
Crapo	N	N	N	Y	N	N	Y
ILLINOIS							
Fitzgerald	N	N	N	Y	N	N	Y
Durbin	Y	Y	Y	N	Y	Y	N
INDIANA							
Bayh	Y	Y	Y	N	Y	Y	N
Lugar	N	N	N	Y	N	N	Y
IOWA							
Grassley	N	N	N	Y	N	N	Y
Harkin	Y	Y	Y	N	Y	Y	N
KANSAS							
Brownback	N	N	N	Y	N	N	Y
Roberts	N	N	N	Y	N	N	Y
KENTUCKY							
Bunning	N	N	N	Y	N	N	Y
McConnell	N	N	N	Y	N	N	Y
LOUISIANA							
Breaux	Y	Y	Y	N	Y	Y	N
Landrieu	Y	N	Y	N	Y	Y	N
MAINE							
Collins	Y	Y	N	Y	N	N	Y
Snowe	N	N	N	Y	N	N	Y
MARYLAND							
Mikulski	Y	?	Y	N	+	+	–
Sarbanes	N	Y	Y	N	Y	Y	N
MASSACHUSETTS							
Kennedy	Y	Y	Y	N	Y	Y	N
Kerry	Y	N	Y	N	Y	Y	N
MICHIGAN							
Abraham	N	N	N	Y	N	N	Y
Levin	Y	Y	Y	N	Y	Y	N
MINNESOTA							
Grams	N	N	N	Y	N	N	Y
Wellstone	Y	Y	Y	N	Y	Y	N
MISSISSIPPI							
Cochran	N	N	N	Y	N	N	Y
Lott	N	N	N	Y	N	N	Y
MISSOURI							
Ashcroft	N	N	N	Y	N	N	Y
Bond	N	N	N	Y	N	N	Y
MONTANA							
Burns	N	N	N	Y	N	N	Y
Baucus	N	N	Y	N	Y	Y	N
NEBRASKA							
Hagel	N	N	N	Y	N	N	Y
Kerrey	Y	Y	Y	N	Y	Y	N
NEVADA							
Bryan	Y	Y	Y	N	Y	Y	N
Reid	Y	Y	Y	N	Y	Y	N
NEW HAMPSHIRE							
Gregg	N	N	N	Y	N	N	Y
Smith	N	N	N	Y	N	N	Y
NEW JERSEY							
Lautenberg	Y	Y	Y	N	Y	Y	N
Torricelli	Y	Y	Y	N	Y	Y	N
NEW MEXICO							
Domenici	N	N	N	Y	N	N	Y
Bingaman	Y	Y	Y	N	Y	Y	N
NEW YORK							
Moynihan	Y	Y	Y	N	Y	Y	N
Schumer	Y	Y	Y	N	Y	Y	N
NORTH CAROLINA							
Helms	N	N	N	Y	N	N	Y
Edwards	Y	Y	Y	N	Y	Y	N
NORTH DAKOTA							
Conrad	Y	Y	Y	N	Y	Y	N
Dorgan	Y	Y	Y	N	Y	Y	N
OHIO							
DeWine	N	N	N	Y	N	N	Y
Voinovich	N	N	N	Y	N	N	Y
OKLAHOMA							
Inhofe	N	N	N	Y	N	N	Y
Nickles	N	N	N	Y	N	N	Y
OREGON							
Smith	N	N	N	Y	N	N	Y
Wyden	Y	Y	Y	N	Y	Y	N
PENNSYLVANIA							
Santorum	N	N	N	Y	N	N	Y
Specter	Y	Y	N	Y	N	N	Y
RHODE ISLAND							
Chafee	N	N	N	Y	N	N	Y
Reed	Y	Y	Y	N	Y	Y	N
SOUTH CAROLINA							
Thurmond	N	N	N	Y	N	N	Y
Hollings	Y	Y	Y	N	Y	Y	N
SOUTH DAKOTA							
Daschle	Y	Y	Y	N	Y	Y	N
Johnson	Y	Y	Y	N	Y	Y	N
TENNESSEE							
Frist	N	N	N	Y	N	N	Y
Thompson	N	N	N	Y	N	N	Y
TEXAS							
Gramm	N	N	N	Y	N	N	Y
Hutchison	Y	Y	N	Y	N	N	Y
UTAH							
Bennett	N	N	N	Y	N	N	Y
Hatch	N	N	N	Y	N	N	Y
VERMONT							
Jeffords	N	N	N	Y	N	N	Y
Leahy	Y	Y	Y	N	Y	Y	N
VIRGINIA							
Warner	N	N	N	Y	N	N	Y
Robb	Y	Y	Y	N	Y	Y	N
WASHINGTON							
Gorton	N	N	N	Y	N	N	Y
Murray	Y	Y	Y	N	Y	Y	N
WEST VIRGINIA							
Byrd	N	N	Y	N	Y	Y	N
Rockefeller	N	N	Y	N	Y	Y	N
WISCONSIN							
Feingold	Y	Y	N	Y	Y	N	N
Kohl	Y	Y	Y	N	Y	Y	N
WYOMING							
Enzi	N	N	N	Y	N	N	Y
Thomas	N	N	N	Y	N	N	Y

ND Northern Democrats SD Southern Democrats

Southern states - Ala., Ark., Fla., Ga., Ky., La., Miss., N.C., Okla., S.C., Tenn., Texas, Va.

Key

- Y Voted for (yea).
- # Paired for.
- \+ Announced for.
- N Voted against (nay).
- X Paired against.
- – Announced against.
- P Voted "present."
- C Voted "present" to avoid possible conflict of interest.
- ? Did not vote or otherwise make a position known.

•

Democrats ***Republicans***
Independents

2. Impeachment of President Clinton/Allow Open Debate on Motion To Dismiss. Harkin, D-Iowa, motion to suspend the rules and allow open debate of the Byrd, D-W.Va., motion to dismiss impeachment proceedings against President Clinton. Motion rejected 43-57: R 3-52; D 40-5 (ND 33-4, SD 7-1). Jan. 25, 1999. (A two-thirds majority vote of those present and voting — 67 in this case — is required to adopt a motion proposing a change in Senate rules.)

3. Impeachment of President Clinton/Allow Open Debate on Motion To Issue Subpoenas and Depose Witnesses. Harkin, D-Iowa, motion to allow open debate of the motion to issue subpoenas and call witnesses in the impeachment trial of President Clinton. Motion rejected 41-58: R 3-52; D 38-6 (ND 32-4, SD 6-2). Jan. 26, 1999. (A two-thirds majority vote of those present and voting — 66 in this case — is required to adopt a motion proposing a change in Senate rules.)

4. Impeachment of President Clinton/Motion To Dismiss. Byrd, D-W.Va., motion to dismiss impeachment proceedings against President Clinton. Motion rejected 44-56: R 0-55; D 44-1 (ND 36-1, SD 8-0). Jan. 27, 1999.

5. Impeachment of President Clinton/Motion To Issue Subpoenas and Depose Witnesses. Motion to subpoena and depose witnesses in the impeachment trial of President Clinton. The motion allows House prosecutors to request Clinton's testimony and subpoena former White House intern Monica Lewinsky, Clinton confidant Vernon Jordan and White House aide Sidney Blumenthal. Motion agreed to 56-44: R 55-0; D 1-44 (ND 1-36, SD 0-8). Jan. 27, 1999.

6. S Res 30. Impeachment of President Clinton/Democratic Substitute for Deposition Procedures. Daschle, D-S.D., substitute amendment to the resolution outlining scheduling and procedures for deposing witnesses in the impeachment trial of President Clinton. The substitute would not allow videotaped depositions to be released to the public, would not allow House prosecutors to call additional witnesses later in the trial and would require final votes on the articles of impeachment on Feb. 12. Rejected 44-54: R 0-54; D 44-0 (ND 36-0, SD 8-0). Jan. 28, 1999.

7. S Res 30. Impeachment of President Clinton/Democratic Substitute for Trial Procedure. Daschle, D-S.D., substitute amendment to move immediately to a vote on articles of impeachment against President Clinton. Rejected 43-55: R 0-54; D 43-1 (ND 35-1, SD 8-0). Jan. 28, 1999.**8. S Res 30. Impeachment of President Clinton/Deposition and Trial Procedures.** Adoption of the resolution to outline the schedule for deposing witnesses and other trial procedures in the impeachment trial of President Clinton. The resolution provides for depositions to be videotaped and allows House prosecutors to move to admit the depositions into evidence. The resolution sets a goal of holding final votes on the articles of impeachment by Feb. 12 if no other business remains. Adopted 54-44: R 54-0; D 0-44 (ND 0-36, SD 0-8). Jan. 28, 1999.

8. S Res 30. Impeachment of President Clinton/Deposition and Trial Procedures. Adoption of the resolution to outline the schedule for deposing witnesses and other trial procedures in the impeachment trial of President Clinton. The resolution provides for depositions to be videotaped and allows House prosecutors to move to admit the depositions into evidence. The resolution sets a goal of holding final votes on the articles of impeachment by Feb. 12 if no other business remains. Adopted 54-44: R 54-0; D 0-44 (ND 0-36, SD 0-8). Jan. 28, 1999.

Senate Votes 9, 10, 11, 12, 13, 14

	9	10	11	12	13	14
ALABAMA						
Sessions	Y	N	N	Y	N	N
Shelby	Y	N	N	Y	N	N
ALASKA						
Murkowski	Y	Y	N	Y	N	N
Stevens	Y	N	N	Y	N	N
ARIZONA						
Kyl	Y	Y	N	Y	N	N
McCain	Y	Y	N	Y	N	N
ARKANSAS						
Hutchinson	Y	Y	N	Y	N	N
Lincoln	Y	N	Y	N	Y	Y
CALIFORNIA						
Boxer	Y	N	Y	N	Y	Y
Feinstein	Y	N	N	N	Y	Y
COLORADO						
Allard	Y	N	N	Y	N	N
Campbell	Y	N	Y	Y	N	N
CONNECTICUT						
Dodd	Y	N	Y	N	Y	Y
Lieberman	Y	N	N	Y	Y	Y
DELAWARE						
Roth	Y	N	N	Y	N	N
Biden	Y	N	Y	N	Y	Y
FLORIDA						
Mack	Y	Y	N	Y	N	N
Graham	Y	N	N	N	Y	Y
GEORGIA						
Coverdell	Y	N	N	Y	N	N
Cleland	Y	N	N	N	Y	Y
HAWAII						
Akaka	Y	N	Y	N	Y	Y
Inouye	Y	N	Y	N	Y	Y
IDAHO						
Craig	Y	Y	N	Y	N	N
Crapo	Y	Y	N	Y	N	N
ILLINOIS						
Fitzgerald	Y	Y	N	Y	N	N
Durbin	Y	N	N	N	Y	Y
INDIANA						
Bayh	Y	N	N	N	Y	Y
Lugar	Y	Y	N	Y	N	N
IOWA						
Grassley	Y	N	N	Y	N	N
Harkin	Y	N	Y	N	Y	Y
KANSAS						
Brownback	Y	N	N	Y	N	N
Roberts	Y	N	N	Y	N	N
KENTUCKY						
Bunning	Y	Y	N	Y	N	N
McConnell	Y	Y	N	Y	N	N
LOUISIANA						
Breaux	Y	N	N	Y	Y	Y
Landrieu	Y	N	Y	N	Y	Y
MAINE						
Collins	Y	N	N	Y	N	N
Snowe	Y	N	Y	N	N	N
MARYLAND						
Mikulski	Y	N	Y	N	Y	Y
Sarbanes	Y	N	Y	N	Y	Y
MASSACHUSETTS						
Kennedy	Y	N	Y	N	Y	Y
Kerry	Y	N	N	N	Y	Y
MICHIGAN						
Abraham	Y	Y	N	Y	N	N
Levin	Y	N	Y	N	Y	Y
MINNESOTA						
Grams	Y	Y	N	Y	N	N
Wellstone	Y	N	N	Y	Y	Y
MISSISSIPPI						
Cochran	Y	Y	N	Y	N	N
Lott	Y	Y	N	Y	N	N
MISSOURI						
Ashcroft	Y	Y	N	Y	N	N
Bond	Y	Y	N	Y	N	N
MONTANA						
Burns	Y	Y	N	Y	N	N
Baucus	Y	N	N	N	Y	Y
NEBRASKA						
Hagel	Y	Y	N	Y	N	N
Kerrey	Y	N	Y	N	Y	Y
NEVADA						
Bryan	Y	N	N	Y	Y	Y
Reid	Y	N	Y	N	Y	Y
NEW HAMPSHIRE						
Gregg	Y	N	N	Y	N	N
Smith	Y	Y	N	Y	N	N
NEW JERSEY						
Lautenberg	Y	N	Y	N	Y	Y
Torricelli	Y	N	Y	N	Y	Y
NEW MEXICO						
Domenici	Y	N	N	Y	N	N
Bingaman	Y	N	Y	N	Y	Y
NEW YORK						
Moynihan	Y	N	N	Y	Y	Y
Schumer	Y	N	N	N	Y	Y
NORTH CAROLINA						
Helms	Y	Y	N	Y	N	N
Edwards	Y	N	N	N	Y	Y
NORTH DAKOTA						
Conrad	Y	N	Y	N	Y	Y
Dorgan	Y	N	Y	N	Y	Y
OHIO						
DeWine	Y	Y	N	Y	N	N
Voinovich	Y	N	N	Y	N	N
OKLAHOMA						
Inhofe	Y	Y	N	Y	N	N
Nickles	Y	Y	N	Y	N	N
OREGON						
Smith	Y	N	N	Y	N	N
Wyden	Y	N	N	Y	Y	Y
PENNSYLVANIA						
Santorum	Y	Y	N	Y	N	N
Specter	Y	Y	N	Y	N	N
RHODE ISLAND						
Chafee	Y	N	N	Y	N	N
Reed	Y	N	Y	N	Y	Y
SOUTH CAROLINA						
Thurmond	Y	N	N	Y	N	N
Hollings	Y	N	N	Y	Y	Y
SOUTH DAKOTA						
Daschle	Y	N	Y	N	Y	Y
Johnson	Y	N	Y	N	Y	Y
TENNESSEE						
Frist	Y	Y	N	Y	N	N
Thompson	Y	Y	N	Y	N	N
TEXAS						
Gramm	Y	Y	N	Y	N	N
Hutchison	Y	N	N	Y	N	N
UTAH						
Bennett	Y	N	N	Y	N	N
Hatch	Y	Y	N	Y	N	N
VERMONT						
Jeffords	Y	N	N	N	N	Y
Leahy	Y	N	N	N	Y	Y
VIRGINIA						
Warner	Y	N	N	Y	N	N
Robb	Y	N	Y	N	Y	Y
WASHINGTON						
Gorton	Y	N	N	Y	N	N
Murray	Y	N	Y	N	Y	Y
WEST VIRGINIA						
Byrd	Y	N	N	Y	Y	Y
Rockefeller	Y	N	Y	N	Y	Y
WISCONSIN						
Feingold	Y	N	N	Y	N	Y
Kohl	Y	N	N	N	Y	Y
WYOMING						
Enzi	Y	N	N	Y	N	N
Thomas	Y	N	N	Y	N	N

Key

- Y Voted for (yea).
- # Paired for.
- + Announced for.
- N Voted against (nay).
- X Paired against.
- – Announced against.
- P Voted "present."
- C Voted "present" to avoid possible conflict of interest.
- ? Did not vote or otherwise make a position known.

•

Democrats ***Republicans***
Independents

ND Northern Democrats SD Southern Democrats

Southern states - Ala., Ark., Fla., Ga., Ky., La., Miss., N.C., Okla., S.C., Tenn., Texas, Va.

9. Impeachment of President Clinton/Admit Depositions into Evidence. Division I of the motion to admit and present evidence and authorize the appearance of witnesses in the impeachment trial of President Clinton. Division I would enter into evidence the transcripts and videotapes of the depositions of former White House intern Monica Lewinsky, Clinton confidant Vernon Jordan and White House aide Sidney Blumenthal. Motion agreed to 100-0: R 55-0; D 45-0 (ND 37-0, SD 8-0). Feb. 4, 1999.

10. Impeachment of President Clinton/Lewinsky Live Testimony. Division II of the motion to admit and present evidence and authorize the appearance of witnesses in the impeachment trial of President Clinton. Division II would issue a subpoena for former White House intern Monica Lewinsky to testify before the Senate for up to eight hours. Motion rejected 30-70: R 30-25; D 0-45 (ND 0-37, SD 0-8). Feb. 4, 1999.

11. Impeachment of President Clinton/Allow Use of Deposition Transcripts. Murray, D-Wash., substitute to Division III of the motion to admit and present evidence and authorize the appearance of witnesses in the impeachment trial of President Clinton. The Murray substitute would allow House prosecutors and White House attorneys to use excerpts from the written transcripts of the depositions of former White House intern Monica Lewinsky, Clinton confidant Vernon Jordan and White House aide Sidney Blumenthal, but not the videotapes. Motion rejected 27-73: R 2-53; D 25-20 (ND 22-15, SD 3-5). Feb. 4, 1999.

12. Impeachment of President Clinton/Allow Use of Deposition Videotapes. Division III of the motion to admit and present evidence and authorize the appearance of witnesses in the impeachment trial of President Clinton. Division III would allow House prosecutors and White House attorneys to present before the Senate up to six hours of excerpts from the videotapes of the depositions of former White House intern Monica Lewinsky, Clinton confidant Vernon Jordan and White House aide Sidney Blumenthal. Motion agreed to 62-38: R 53-2; D 9-36 (ND 7-30, SD 2-6). Feb. 4, 1999.

13. Impeachment of President Clinton/Motion To Move to Closing Arguments. Daschle, D-S.D., motion to proceed to closing arguments in the impeachment trial of President Clinton. The motion would allow for closing arguments, final deliberations and a vote on the articles of impeachment. Motion rejected 44-56: R 0-55; D 44-1 (ND 36-1, SD 8-0). Feb. 4, 1999.

14. Impeachment of President Clinton/Use of Deposition Videotape. Motion to require the House prosecutors to inform the White House attorneys by 2 p.m. on Feb. 5, 1999, which excerpts from the deposition videotapes they plan to use during their evidence presentation and closing arguments. Motion rejected 46-54: R 1-54; D 45-0 (ND 37-0, SD 8-0). Feb. 4, 1999.

Senate Votes 15, 16, 17, 18, 19

	15	16	17	18	19
ALABAMA					
Sessions	N	Y	Y	Y	Y
Shelby	N	Y	N	Y	Y
ALASKA					
Murkowski	N	Y	Y	Y	Y
Stevens	Y	Y	N	Y	Y
ARIZONA					
Kyl	Y	Y	Y	Y	Y
McCain	Y	Y	Y	Y	Y
ARKANSAS					
Hutchinson	N	Y	Y	Y	Y
Lincoln	Y	N	N	N	N
CALIFORNIA					
Boxer	Y	N	N	N	N
Feinstein	Y	N	N	N	N
COLORADO					
Allard	N	Y	Y	Y	Y
Campbell	N	Y	Y	Y	Y
CONNECTICUT					
Dodd	Y	N	N	N	N
Lieberman	Y	N	N	N	N
DELAWARE					
Roth	N	Y	Y	Y	N
Biden	Y	N	N	N	N
FLORIDA					
Mack	N	Y	Y	Y	Y
Graham	Y	N	N	N	N
GEORGIA					
Coverdell	N	Y	Y	Y	Y
Cleland	Y	N	N	N	N
HAWAII					
Akaka	Y	N	N	N	N
Inouye	Y	N	N	N	N
IDAHO					
Craig	N	Y	Y	Y	Y
Crapo	N	Y	Y	Y	Y
ILLINOIS					
Fitzgerald	N	Y	Y	Y	Y
Durbin	Y	N	N	N	N
INDIANA					
Bayh	Y	N	N	N	N
Lugar	Y	Y	Y	Y	N
IOWA					
Grassley	N	Y	Y	Y	Y
Harkin	Y	N	N	N	N
KANSAS					
Brownback	N	Y	Y	Y	Y
Roberts	N	Y	Y	Y	Y
KENTUCKY					
Bunning	N	Y	Y	Y	Y
McConnell	N	Y	Y	Y	N
LOUISIANA					
Breaux	Y	N	N	N	N
Landrieu	Y	N	N	N	N
MAINE					
Collins	Y	Y	N	N	N
Snowe	Y	Y	N	N	N
MARYLAND					
Mikulski	Y	N	N	N	N
Sarbanes	Y	N	N	N	N
MASSACHUSETTS					
Kennedy	Y	N	N	N	N
Kerry	Y	N	N	N	N
MICHIGAN					
Abraham	Y	Y	Y	Y	N
Levin	Y	N	N	N	N
MINNESOTA					
Grams	N	Y	Y	Y	Y
Wellstone	Y	N	N	N	N
MISSISSIPPI					
Cochran	N	Y	Y	Y	Y
Lott	N	Y	Y	Y	Y
MISSOURI					
Ashcroft	N	Y	Y	Y	Y
Bond	N	Y	Y	Y	Y
MONTANA					
Burns	N	Y	Y	Y	Y
Baucus	Y	N	N	N	N
NEBRASKA					
Hagel	Y	Y	Y	Y	Y
Kerrey	Y	N	N	N	N
NEVADA					
Bryan	Y	N	N	N	N
Reid	Y	N	N	N	N
NEW HAMPSHIRE					
Gregg	N	Y	Y	Y	Y
Smith	N	Y	Y	Y	Y
NEW JERSEY					
Lautenberg	Y	N	N	N	N
Torricelli	Y	N	N	N	N
NEW MEXICO					
Domenici	N	Y	Y	Y	?
Bingaman	Y	N	N	N	N
NEW YORK					
Moynihan	Y	N	N	N	N
Schumer	Y	N	N	N	N
NORTH CAROLINA					
Helms	N	Y	Y	Y	Y
Edwards	Y	N	N	N	N
NORTH DAKOTA					
Conrad	Y	N	N	N	N
Dorgan	Y	N	N	N	N
OHIO					
DeWine	Y	Y	Y	Y	Y
Voinovich	N	Y	Y	Y	Y
OKLAHOMA					
Inhofe	N	Y	Y	Y	Y
Nickles	N	Y	Y	Y	Y
OREGON					
Smith	Y	Y	Y	Y	N
Wyden	Y	N	N	N	N
PENNSYLVANIA					
Santorum	N	Y	Y	Y	Y
Specter	Y	N	N	N	Y
RHODE ISLAND					
Chafee	N	Y	N	N	N
Reed	Y	N	N	N	N
SOUTH CAROLINA					
Thurmond	N	Y	Y	Y	Y
Hollings	Y	N	N	N	N
SOUTH DAKOTA					
Daschle	Y	N	N	N	N
Johnson	Y	N	N	N	N
TENNESSEE					
Frist	N	Y	Y	Y	Y
Thompson	N	Y	N	Y	Y
TEXAS					
Gramm	N	Y	Y	Y	Y
Hutchison	Y	N	Y	Y	N
UTAH					
Bennett	N	Y	Y	Y	N
Hatch	N	Y	Y	Y	Y
VERMONT					
Jeffords	Y	Y	N	N	N
Leahy	Y	N	N	N	N
VIRGINIA					
Warner	N	Y	N	Y	Y
Robb	Y	N	N	N	N
WASHINGTON					
Gorton	Y	Y	N	Y	N
Murray	Y	N	N	N	N
WEST VIRGINIA					
Byrd	Y	N	N	N	Y
Rockefeller	Y	N	N	N	N
WISCONSIN					
Feingold	Y	N	N	N	N
Kohl	Y	N	N	N	N
WYOMING					
Enzi	N	Y	Y	Y	Y
Thomas	N	Y	Y	Y	Y

ND Northern Democrats SD Southern Democrats

Southern states - Ala., Ark., Fla., Ga., Ky., La., Miss., N.C., Okla., S.C., Tenn., Texas, Va.

Key

Y Voted for (yea).
\# Paired for.
\+ Announced for.
N Voted against (nay).
X Paired against.
– Announced against.
P Voted "present."
C Voted "present" to avoid possible conflict of interest.
? Did not vote or otherwise make a position known.

•

Democrats ***Republicans***
Independents

15. Impeachment of President Clinton/Allow Open Debate During Final Deliberations. Lott, R-Miss., motion to suspend the rules to allow open debate during final deliberations in the impeachment trial of President Clinton. Motion rejected 59-41: R 14-41; D 45-0 (ND 37-0, SD 8-0). Feb. 9, 1999. A two-thirds majority of those present and voting (67 in this case) is required to adopt a motion proposing a change in Senate rules.

16. Impeachment of President Clinton/Motion To Proceed into Closed Session. Lott, R-Miss., motion to proceed into closed session to begin final deliberations in the impeachment trial of President Clinton. Motion agreed to 53-47: R 53-2; D 0-45 (ND 0-37, SD 0-8). Feb. 9, 1999.

17. Impeachment of President Clinton/Article I/Grand Jury Perjury. Conviction on Article I, which would find President Clinton guilty of "perjurious, false and misleading testimony" during his Aug. 17, 1998, federal grand jury testimony about his relationship with former White House intern Monica Lewinsky, his prior testimony in the Paula Jones sexual harassment lawsuit and his attempts to influence others' testimony in both. Acquitted 45-55: R 45-10; D 0-45 (ND 0-37, SD 0-8). Feb. 12, 1999. A two-thirds majority of those present and voting (67 in this case) is required to convict the president and remove him from office. A "nay" was a vote in favor of the president's position.

18. Impeachment of President Clinton/Article II/Obstruction of Justice. Conviction on Article II, which would find President Clinton guilty of obstruction of justice, concealing evidence and delaying proceedings in the Paula Jones federal sexual harassment civil lawsuit. Acquitted 50-50: R 50-5; D 0-45 (ND 0-37, SD 0-8). Feb. 12, 1999. A two-thirds majority of those present and voting (67 in this case) is required to convict the president and remove him from office. A "nay" was a vote in support of the president's position.

19. Impeachment of President Clinton/Censure Resolution. Gramm, R-Texas, motion to postpone indefinitely the Feinstein, D-Calif., motion to suspend Senate rules to allow consideration of a resolution to censure President Clinton and "condemn his wrongful conduct in the strongest terms." Motion rejected 43-56: R 42-12; D 1-44 (ND 1-36, SD 0-8). Feb. 12, 1999. (Subsequently, the Feinstein motion to suspend the rules was withdrawn by unanimous consent because two-thirds of the Senate did not vote against the Gramm motion to postpone indefinitely.)

Senate Votes 20, 21, 22, 23, 24, 25, 26

	20	21	22	23	24	25	26
ALABAMA							
Sessions	N	Y	Y	Y	N	Y	Y
Shelby	?	Y	Y	Y	N	Y	Y
ALASKA							
Murkowski	Y	Y	Y	Y	N	Y	Y
Stevens	N	Y	Y	Y	N	Y	Y
ARIZONA							
Kyl	N	Y	N	Y	N	Y	Y
McCain	N	Y	N	Y	N	Y	Y
ARKANSAS							
Hutchinson	Y	Y	Y	Y	N	Y	Y
Lincoln	Y	Y	Y	Y	N	N	Y
CALIFORNIA							
Boxer	Y	Y	Y	Y	N	Y	Y
Feinstein	Y	Y	Y	Y	N	Y	Y
COLORADO							
Allard	Y	Y	Y	Y	N	Y	Y
Campbell	Y	Y	Y	Y	N	Y	Y
CONNECTICUT							
Dodd	N	Y	Y	Y	N	Y	N
Lieberman	Y	Y	Y	Y	N	Y	N
DELAWARE							
Roth	Y	Y	Y	Y	N	Y	Y
Biden	Y	Y	Y	Y	N	Y	Y
FLORIDA							
Mack	Y	Y	Y	Y	N	Y	Y
Graham	Y	Y	N	Y	N	N	N
GEORGIA							
Coverdell	Y	Y	Y	Y	N	Y	Y
Cleland	Y	Y	Y	Y	N	Y	Y
HAWAII							
Akaka	Y	Y	Y	Y	N	N	Y
Inouye	Y	Y	Y	Y	N	N	Y
IDAHO							
Craig	Y	Y	Y	Y	N	Y	Y
Crapo	Y	Y	Y	Y	N	Y	Y
ILLINOIS							
Fitzgerald	Y	Y	Y	Y	N	Y	Y
Durbin	Y	Y	Y	Y	N	Y	N
INDIANA							
Bayh	Y	Y	Y	Y	N	N	Y
Lugar	Y	Y	Y	Y	N	Y	Y
IOWA							
Grassley	N	Y	Y	Y	N	Y	Y
Harkin	Y	Y	Y	Y	N	N	Y
KANSAS							
Brownback	Y	Y	Y	Y	N	Y	Y
Roberts	Y	Y	Y	Y	N	Y	Y
KENTUCKY							
Bunning	Y	Y	N	Y	N	Y	Y
McConnell	Y	Y	Y	Y	N	Y	Y
LOUISIANA							
Breaux	Y	Y	Y	Y	N	Y	Y
Landrieu	Y	Y	Y	Y	N	Y	Y
MAINE							
Collins	Y	Y	Y	Y	N	Y	Y
Snowe	Y	Y	Y	Y	N	Y	Y
MARYLAND							
Mikulski	Y	Y	Y	Y	N	Y	Y
Sarbanes	Y	Y	Y	Y	N	Y	Y
MASSACHUSETTS							
Kennedy	Y	Y	Y	Y	N	N	Y
Kerry	Y	Y	Y	Y	N	Y	Y
MICHIGAN							
Abraham	Y	Y	Y	Y	N	Y	Y
Levin	Y	Y	Y	Y	N	N	Y
MINNESOTA							
Grams	N	Y	Y	Y	N	Y	Y
Wellstone	Y	Y	Y	Y	N	N	Y
MISSISSIPPI							
Cochran	Y	Y	Y	Y	N	Y	Y
Lott	Y	Y	Y	Y	N	Y	Y
MISSOURI							
Ashcroft	Y	Y	Y	Y	N	Y	Y
Bond	Y	Y	Y	Y	N	Y	Y
MONTANA							
Burns	Y	Y	Y	Y	N	Y	Y
Baucus	Y	Y	Y	Y	N	Y	Y
NEBRASKA							
Hagel	Y	Y	Y	Y	N	Y	Y
Kerrey	Y	Y	Y	Y	N	Y	Y
NEVADA							
Bryan	Y	Y	Y	Y	N	N	Y
Reid	Y	Y	Y	Y	N	Y	Y
NEW HAMPSHIRE							
Gregg	N	Y	N	Y	N	Y	N
Smith	Y	Y	N	Y	N	Y	Y
NEW JERSEY							
Lautenberg	Y	Y	Y	Y	N	Y	Y
Torricelli	Y	Y	Y	Y	N	N	Y
NEW MEXICO							
Domenici	Y	Y	Y	Y	N	Y	Y
Bingaman	Y	Y	Y	Y	N	Y	Y
NEW YORK							
Moynihan	Y	Y	Y	Y	N	N	+
Schumer	Y	Y	Y	Y	N	Y	Y
NORTH CAROLINA							
Helms	Y	Y	Y	Y	N	Y	Y
Edwards	Y	Y	Y	Y	N	Y	Y
NORTH DAKOTA							
Conrad	Y	Y	Y	Y	N	Y	Y
Dorgan	Y	Y	Y	Y	N	Y	Y
OHIO							
DeWine	Y	Y	Y	Y	N	Y	Y
Voinovich	Y	Y	Y	Y	N	Y	N
OKLAHOMA							
Inhofe	Y	Y	Y	Y	N	Y	Y
Nickles	N	Y	Y	Y	N	Y	N
OREGON							
Smith	Y	Y	Y	Y	N	Y	Y
Wyden	Y	Y	Y	Y	N	Y	Y
PENNSYLVANIA							
Santorum	Y	Y	Y	Y	N	Y	Y
Specter	Y	Y	Y	Y	N	Y	Y
RHODE ISLAND							
Chafee	Y	Y	Y	Y	N	Y	Y
Reed	Y	Y	Y	Y	N	N	Y
SOUTH CAROLINA							
Thurmond	Y	Y	Y	Y	N	Y	Y
Hollings	Y	Y	Y	Y	N	N	Y
SOUTH DAKOTA							
Daschle	Y	Y	Y	Y	N	N	Y
Johnson	Y	Y	Y	Y	N	N	Y
TENNESSEE							
Frist	Y	Y	Y	Y	N	Y	Y
Thompson	N	Y	Y	Y	N	Y	Y
TEXAS							
Gramm	Y	Y	Y	Y	N	Y	Y
Hutchison	Y	Y	Y	Y	N	Y	Y
UTAH							
Bennett	Y	Y	Y	Y	N	Y	Y
Hatch	Y	Y	Y	Y	N	Y	Y
VERMONT							
Jeffords	Y	Y	Y	Y	N	Y	Y
Leahy	Y	Y	Y	Y	N	Y	Y
VIRGINIA							
Warner	Y	Y	Y	Y	N	Y	Y
Robb	Y	Y	Y	Y	N	N	Y
WASHINGTON							
Gorton	P	Y	Y	Y	N	Y	Y
Murray	Y	Y	Y	Y	N	Y	Y
WEST VIRGINIA							
Byrd	Y	Y	Y	Y	N	Y	Y
Rockefeller	Y	Y	Y	Y	N	N	Y
WISCONSIN							
Feingold	N	Y	Y	Y	N	N	N
Kohl	Y	Y	Y	Y	N	N	Y
WYOMING							
Enzi	Y	Y	Y	Y	N	Y	Y
Thomas	Y	Y	Y	Y	N	Y	Y

ND Northern Democrats SD Southern Democrats

Southern states - Ala., Ark., Fla., Ga., Ky., La., Miss., N.C., Okla., S.C., Tenn., Texas, Va.

Key

- Y Voted for (yea).
- # Paired for.
- + Announced for.
- N Voted against (nay).
- X Paired against.
- – Announced against.
- P Voted "present."
- C Voted "present" to avoid possible conflict of interest.
- ? Did not vote or otherwise make a position known.

Democrats ***Republicans***
Independents

20. S 4. Military Pay Increase and Pension Revisions/Federal Workers. Crapo, R-Idaho, amendment that would repeal current law that reduces military pensions for personnel who work for the federal government after retiring from the military. Adopted 87-11: R 44-9; D 43-2 (ND 35-2, SD 8-0). Feb. 23, 1999.

21. S 4. Military Pay Increase and Pension Revisions/Health Care. Hutchison, R-Texas, amendment that would direct the Defense Department to ensure that health care coverage available through the TRICARE program is "substantially similar" to coverage available under similar plans offered through the Federal Employees Health Benefits program. The amendment also would ensure that military personnel transferred to other bases retain their health benefits and ensure that doctors are reimbursed at levels at least equal to Medicare when treating TRICARE enrollees. Adopted 100-0: R 55-0; D 45-0 (ND 37-0, SD 8-0). Feb. 23, 1999.

22. S 4. Military Pay Increase and Pension Revisions/Civilian Employee Pay. Sarbanes, D-Md., amendment that would express the sense of Congress that pay raises for civilian government employees should retain parity with military pay adjustments. Adopted 94-6: R 50-5; D 44-1 (ND 37-0, SD 7-1). Feb. 24, 1999.

23. S 4. Military Pay Increase and Pension Revisions/National Guard. Cleland, D-Ga., amendment that would allow National Guard and Reserve personnel to contribute to tax-free savings plans established for military members by the bill. Adopted 100-0: R 55-0; D 45-0 (ND 37-0, SD 8-0). Feb. 24, 1999.

24. S 4. Military Pay Increase and Pension Revisions/Medicare-Eligible Veterans. Warner, R-Va., motion to table (kill) the Rockefeller, D-W.Va., amendment that would authorize the Department of Veterans Affairs (VA) to establish a demonstration project at up to 10 sites where Medicare-eligible veterans could receive Medicare-covered services at a VA hospital. The Department of Health and Human Services would then reimburse the VA at a slightly reduced rate. Motion rejected 0-100: R 0-55; D 0-45 (ND 0-37, SD 0-8). Feb. 24, 1999. (Subsequently, the Rockefeller amendment was adopted by voice vote.)

25. S 4. Military Pay Increase and Pension Revisions/Revenue Provisions. Gramm, R-Texas, point of order that the Graham, D-Fla., amendment to pay for the bill by raising a projected $18 billion in revenue over 10 years is out of order because the Constitution requires revenue provisions to originate in the House. The Graham amendment would raise the revenue by extending superfund and oil spill liability taxes and by modifying foreign tax credits. Sustained 80-20: R 55-0; D 25-20 (ND 21-16, SD 4-4). Feb. 24, 1999. (The Graham amendment thus fell.)

26. S 4. Military Pay Increase and Pension Revisions/Passage. Passage of the bill to authorize a 4.8 percent military pay raise in fiscal 2000 and annual raises in following years. The bill also would revise military pay tables, increase pension benefits, authorize personnel to contribute to tax-free savings plans, expand Montgomery G.I. Bill benefits, establish allowances for personnel eligible for food stamps and increase health benefits. Passed 91-8: R 52-3; D 39-5 (ND 32-4, SD 7-1). Feb. 24, 1999.

Senate Vote 27

	27
ALABAMA	
Sessions	Y
Shelby	Y
ALASKA	
Murkowski	Y
Stevens	Y
ARIZONA	
Kyl	Y
McCain	Y
ARKANSAS	
Hutchinson	Y
Lincoln	Y
CALIFORNIA	
Boxer	Y
Feinstein	Y
COLORADO	
Allard	Y
Campbell	Y
CONNECTICUT	
Dodd	Y
Lieberman	Y
DELAWARE	
Roth	Y
Biden	Y
FLORIDA	
Mack	Y
Graham	Y
GEORGIA	
Coverdell	Y
Cleland	Y
HAWAII	
Akaka	Y
Inouye	Y
IDAHO	
Craig	Y
Crapo	Y
ILLINOIS	
Fitzgerald	Y
Durbin	Y
INDIANA	
Bayh	Y
Lugar	Y

	27
IOWA	
Grassley	Y
Harkin	Y
KANSAS	
Brownback	Y
Roberts	Y
KENTUCKY	
Bunning	Y
McConnell	Y
LOUISIANA	
Breaux	Y
Landrieu	Y
MAINE	
Collins	Y
Snowe	Y
MARYLAND	
Mikulski	Y
Sarbanes	Y
MASSACHUSETTS	
Kennedy	Y
Kerry	Y
MICHIGAN	
Abraham	Y
Levin	Y
MINNESOTA	
Grams	Y
Wellstone	Y
MISSISSIPPI	
Cochran	Y
Lott	Y
MISSOURI	
Ashcroft	Y
Bond	Y
MONTANA	
Burns	Y
Baucus	Y
NEBRASKA	
Hagel	Y
Kerrey	Y
NEVADA	
Bryan	Y
Reid	Y

	27
NEW HAMPSHIRE	
Gregg	Y
Smith	Y
NEW JERSEY	
Lautenberg	Y
Torricelli	?
NEW MEXICO	
Domenici	Y
Bingaman	Y
NEW YORK	
Moynihan	Y
Schumer	Y
NORTH CAROLINA	
Helms	Y
Edwards	Y
NORTH DAKOTA	
Conrad	Y
Dorgan	Y
OHIO	
DeWine	Y
Voinovich	Y
OKLAHOMA	
Inhofe	Y
Nickles	Y
OREGON	
Smith	Y
Wyden	Y
PENNSYLVANIA	
Santorum	Y
Specter	Y
RHODE ISLAND	
Chafee	Y
Reed	Y
SOUTH CAROLINA	
Thurmond	Y
Hollings	Y
SOUTH DAKOTA	
Daschle	Y
Johnson	Y
TENNESSEE	
Frist	Y
Thompson	Y

Key

Y Voted for (yea).
\# Paired for.
\+ Announced for.
N Voted against (nay).
X Paired against.
– Announced against.
P Voted "present."
C Voted "present" to avoid possible conflict of interest.
? Did not vote or otherwise make a position known.

Democrats ***Republicans***
Independents

	27
TEXAS	
Gramm	Y
Hutchison	Y
UTAH	
Bennett	Y
Hatch	Y
VERMONT	
Jeffords	Y
Leahy	Y
VIRGINIA	
Warner	Y
Robb	Y
WASHINGTON	
Gorton	Y
Murray	Y
WEST VIRGINIA	
Byrd	Y
Rockefeller	Y
WISCONSIN	
Feingold	Y
Kohl	Y
WYOMING	
Enzi	Y
Thomas	Y

ND Northern Democrats SD Southern Democrats

Southern states - Ala., Ark., Fla., Ga., Ky., La., Miss., N.C., Okla., S.C., Tenn., Texas, Va.

27. S Res 45. China Human Rights Abuses/Adoption. Adoption of the resolution to express the sense of the Senate that the United States should introduce and advocate a resolution at the U.N. Human Rights Commission calling on the Chinese government to end human rights abuses in China and Tibet. Adopted 99-0: R 55-0; D 44-0 (ND 36-0, SD 8-0). Feb. 25, 1999.

Senate Votes 28, 29

	28	29
ALABAMA		
Sessions	Y	Y
Shelby	Y	Y
ALASKA		
Murkowski	Y	Y
Stevens	Y	Y
ARIZONA		
Kyl	Y	Y
McCain	?	?
ARKANSAS		
Hutchinson	Y	Y
Lincoln	Y	Y
CALIFORNIA		
Boxer	Y	Y
Feinstein	Y	Y
COLORADO		
Allard	Y	N
Campbell	Y	Y
CONNECTICUT		
Dodd	Y	Y
Lieberman	Y	Y
DELAWARE		
Roth	Y	Y
Biden	Y	Y
FLORIDA		
Mack	Y	Y
Graham	Y	Y
GEORGIA		
Coverdell	Y	Y
Cleland	Y	Y
HAWAII		
Akaka	Y	Y
Inouye	Y	Y
IDAHO		
Craig	Y	Y
Crapo	Y	Y
ILLINOIS		
Fitzgerald	Y	Y
Durbin	Y	Y
INDIANA		
Bayh	Y	Y
Lugar	Y	Y
IOWA		
Grassley	Y	Y
Harkin	Y	Y
KANSAS		
Brownback	Y	Y
Roberts	Y	Y
KENTUCKY		
Bunning	Y	Y
McConnell	Y	Y
LOUISIANA		
Breaux	Y	Y
Landrieu	Y	Y
MAINE		
Collins	Y	Y
Snowe	Y	Y
MARYLAND		
Mikulski	Y	Y
Sarbanes	Y	Y
MASSACHUSETTS		
Kennedy	Y	Y
Kerry	Y	Y
MICHIGAN		
Abraham	Y	Y
Levin	Y	Y
MINNESOTA		
Grams	Y	Y
Wellstone	Y	Y
MISSISSIPPI		
Cochran	Y	Y
Lott	Y	Y
MISSOURI		
Ashcroft	Y	Y
Bond	Y	Y
MONTANA		
Burns	Y	Y
Baucus	Y	Y
NEBRASKA		
Hagel	Y	Y
Kerrey	Y	Y
NEVADA		
Bryan	Y	Y
Reid	Y	Y
NEW HAMPSHIRE		
Gregg	Y	N
Smith	Y	Y
NEW JERSEY		
Lautenberg	Y	Y
Torricelli	Y	Y
NEW MEXICO		
Domenici	Y	Y
Bingaman	Y	Y
NEW YORK		
Moynihan	Y	Y
Schumer	Y	Y
NORTH CAROLINA		
Helms	Y	N
Edwards	Y	Y
NORTH DAKOTA		
Conrad	Y	Y
Dorgan	Y	Y
OHIO		
DeWine	Y	Y
Voinovich	Y	Y
OKLAHOMA		
Inhofe	Y	Y
Nickles	Y	Y
OREGON		
Smith	Y	Y
Wyden	Y	Y
PENNSYLVANIA		
Santorum	Y	Y
Specter	Y	Y
RHODE ISLAND		
Chafee	Y	Y
Reed	Y	Y
SOUTH CAROLINA		
Thurmond	Y	Y
Hollings	Y	Y
SOUTH DAKOTA		
Daschle	Y	Y
Johnson	Y	Y
TENNESSEE		
Frist	Y	Y
Thompson	Y	Y
TEXAS		
Gramm	Y	N
Hutchison	Y	N
UTAH		
Bennett	Y	Y
Hatch	Y	Y
VERMONT		
Jeffords	Y	Y
Leahy	Y	Y
VIRGINIA		
Warner	Y	Y
Robb	Y	Y
WASHINGTON		
Gorton	Y	Y
Murray	Y	Y
WEST VIRGINIA		
Byrd	Y	?
Rockefeller	Y	Y
WISCONSIN		
Feingold	Y	Y
Kohl	Y	Y
WYOMING		
Enzi	Y	Y
Thomas	Y	N

Key

- Y Voted for (yea).
- # Paired for.
- \+ Announced for.
- N Voted against (nay).
- X Paired against.
- – Announced against.
- P Voted "present."
- C Voted "present" to avoid possible conflict of interest.
- ? Did not vote or otherwise make a position known.

•

Democrats ***Republicans***
Independents

ND Northern Democrats SD Southern Democrats

Southern states - Ala., Ark., Fla., Ga., Ky., La., Miss., N.C., Okla., S.C., Tenn., Texas, Va.

28. S 314. Year 2000 Small-Business Loans/Passage. Passage of the bill to require the Small Business Administration to establish a special loan guarantee program for small businesses to correct and prevent so-called Year 2000 computer problems, which will occur if computers mistake a two-digit code of "00" for 1900 instead of 2000. Passed 99-0: R 54-0; D 45-0 (ND 37-0, SD 8-0). March 2, 1999.

29. S Res 7. Year 2000 Committee Funding/Adoption. Adoption of the resolution to increase funding by $300,000 for the Senate's Special Committee on the Year 2000 Technology-Related Problems. Adopted 92-6: R 48-6; D 44-0 (ND 36-0, SD 8-0). March 2, 1999.

Senate Votes 30, 31, 32

	30	31	32
ALABAMA			
Sessions	Y	Y	Y
Shelby	Y	Y	Y
ALASKA			
Murkowski	Y	Y	Y
Stevens	Y	Y	Y
ARIZONA			
Kyl	Y	Y	Y
McCain	Y	Y	Y
ARKANSAS			
Hutchinson	Y	Y	Y
Lincoln	N	Y	Y
CALIFORNIA			
Boxer	N	Y	N
Feinstein	N	Y	N
COLORADO			
Allard	Y	Y	Y
Campbell	Y	Y	Y
CONNECTICUT			
Dodd	N	Y	N
Lieberman	N	Y	N
DELAWARE			
Roth	Y	Y	Y
Biden	?	Y	N
FLORIDA			
Mack	Y	Y	Y
Graham	N	Y	N
GEORGIA			
Coverdell	Y	Y	Y
Cleland	N	Y	N
HAWAII			
Akaka	N	Y	N
Inouye	N	Y	N
IDAHO			
Craig	Y	Y	Y
Crapo	Y	Y	Y
ILLINOIS			
Fitzgerald	Y	Y	Y
Durbin	N	Y	N
INDIANA			
Bayh	N	Y	N
Lugar	Y	Y	Y
IOWA			
Grassley	Y	Y	Y
Harkin	N	Y	N
KANSAS			
Brownback	Y	Y	Y
Roberts	Y	Y	Y
KENTUCKY			
Bunning	Y	Y	?
McConnell	Y	Y	Y
LOUISIANA			
Breaux	N	Y	N
Landrieu	N	Y	N
MAINE			
Collins	Y	Y	Y
Snowe	Y	Y	Y
MARYLAND			
Mikulski	N	Y	N
Sarbanes	N	Y	N
MASSACHUSETTS			
Kennedy	N	Y	N
Kerry	N	Y	N
MICHIGAN			
Abraham	Y	Y	Y
Levin	N	Y	N
MINNESOTA			
Grams	Y	Y	Y
Wellstone	N	Y	N
MISSISSIPPI			
Cochran	Y	Y	Y
Lott	Y	Y	Y
MISSOURI			
Ashcroft	Y	Y	Y
Bond	Y	Y	Y
MONTANA			
Burns	Y	Y	Y
Baucus	N	Y	N
NEBRASKA			
Hagel	Y	Y	Y
Kerrey	N	Y	N
NEVADA			
Bryan	N	Y	N
Reid	N	Y	N
NEW HAMPSHIRE			
Gregg	Y	Y	Y
Smith	Y	Y	Y
NEW JERSEY			
Lautenberg	N	Y	N
Torricelli	?	Y	N
NEW MEXICO			
Domenici	Y	Y	Y
Bingaman	N	Y	N
NEW YORK			
Moynihan	N	Y	N
Schumer	N	Y	N
NORTH CAROLINA			
Helms	Y	Y	Y
Edwards	N	Y	N
NORTH DAKOTA			
Conrad	N	Y	N
Dorgan	N	Y	?
OHIO			
DeWine	Y	Y	Y
Voinovich	Y	Y	Y
OKLAHOMA			
Inhofe	Y	Y	?
Nickles	Y	Y	Y
OREGON			
Smith	Y	Y	Y
Wyden	N	Y	N
PENNSYLVANIA			
Santorum	Y	Y	Y
Specter	Y	Y	Y
RHODE ISLAND			
Chafee	Y	Y	Y
Reed	N	Y	N
SOUTH CAROLINA			
Thurmond	Y	Y	Y
Hollings	N	Y	N
SOUTH DAKOTA			
Daschle	N	Y	N
Johnson	N	Y	N
TENNESSEE			
Frist	Y	Y	Y
Thompson	Y	Y	Y
TEXAS			
Gramm	Y	Y	Y
Hutchison	Y	Y	Y
UTAH			
Bennett	Y	Y	Y
Hatch	Y	Y	Y
VERMONT			
Jeffords	Y	Y	Y
Leahy	N	Y	N
VIRGINIA			
Warner	Y	Y	Y
Robb	N	Y	N
WASHINGTON			
Gorton	Y	Y	Y
Murray	N	Y	N
WEST VIRGINIA			
Byrd	?	Y	N
Rockefeller	N	Y	N
WISCONSIN			
Feingold	N	Y	N
Kohl	N	Y	N
WYOMING			
Enzi	Y	Y	Y
Thomas	Y	Y	Y

Key

- Y Voted for (yea).
- # Paired for.
- \+ Announced for.
- N Voted against (nay).
- X Paired against.
- – Announced against.
- P Voted "present."
- C Voted "present" to avoid possible conflict of interest.
- ? Did not vote or otherwise make a position known.

•

Democrats ***Republicans***
Independents

ND Northern Democrats SD Southern Democrats

Southern states - Ala., Ark., Fla., Ga., Ky., La., Miss., N.C., Okla., S.C., Tenn., Texas, Va.

30. S 280. Educational Flexibility/Aid to Disadvantaged Students. Jeffords, R-Vt., motion to table (kill) the Wellstone, D-Minn., amendment to the Health, Education, Labor and Pensions Committee substitute amendment. The Wellstone amendment would prohibit waiving requirements under Title I of the 1965 Elementary and Secondary Education Act, which provides aid to disadvantaged students. Motion agreed to 55-42: R 55-0; D 0-42 (ND 0-34, SD 0-8). March 3, 1999.

31. S 280. Educational Flexibility/Special Education Funding. Jeffords, R-Vt., amendment to the Bingaman, D-N.M., amendment to the Senate Health, Education, Labor and Pensions Committee substitute amendment. The Jeffords amendment would nullify the Bingaman amendment's authorization of $150 million to establish a drop-out prevention program and redirect the money to special education programs under the Individuals with Disabilities Education Act. Adopted 100-0: R 55-0; D 45-0 (ND 37-0, SD 8-0). March 4, 1999.

32. S 280. Educational Flexibility/Public Comment Requirements. Jeffords, R-Vt., motion to table (kill) the Jeffords amendment to the language that would be struck by the Health, Education, Labor and Pensions Committee substitute amendment. The Jeffords amendment would direct the Education Department to establish requirements on how states would provide for public comment and notice under the bill. Motion agreed to 54-43: R 53-0; D 1-43 (ND 0-36, SD 1-7). March 4, 1999.

Senate Votes 33, 34, 35, 36, 37, 38, 39, 40

	33	34	35	36	37	38	39	40
ALABAMA								
Sessions	–	Y	Y	N	Y	Y	N	Y
Shelby	N	Y	Y	N	Y	Y	N	Y
ALASKA								
Murkowski	N	Y	Y	N	Y	Y	N	Y
Stevens	N	Y	Y	N	Y	Y	N	Y
ARIZONA								
Kyl	–	Y	Y	N	Y	Y	N	Y
McCain	?	?	Y	N	Y	Y	N	Y
ARKANSAS								
Hutchinson	–	Y	Y	N	Y	Y	N	Y
Lincoln	N	N	N	Y	N	Y	Y	N
CALIFORNIA								
Boxer	N	N	N	Y	N	Y	Y	N
Feinstein	N	N	N	Y	N	Y	Y	N
COLORADO								
Allard	N	Y	Y	N	Y	Y	N	Y
Campbell	N	Y	Y	N	Y	Y	N	Y
CONNECTICUT								
Dodd	N	N	N	Y	N	Y	Y	N
Lieberman	N	N	N	Y	N	Y	Y	N
DELAWARE								
Roth	N	Y	Y	N	Y	Y	N	Y
Biden	N	N	?	Y	N	Y	Y	N
FLORIDA								
Mack	N	Y	Y	N	Y	Y	N	Y
Graham	N	?	?	Y	N	Y	Y	N
GEORGIA								
Coverdell	N	Y	Y	N	Y	Y	N	Y
Cleland	N	N	N	Y	N	Y	Y	N
HAWAII								
Akaka	N	N	N	Y	N	Y	Y	N
Inouye	N	N	N	Y	N	Y	Y	N
IDAHO								
Craig	N	Y	Y	N	Y	Y	N	Y
Crapo	N	Y	Y	N	Y	Y	N	Y
ILLINOIS								
Fitzgerald	P	Y	Y	N	Y	Y	N	Y
Durbin	N	N	N	Y	N	Y	Y	N
INDIANA								
Bayh	N	N	N	Y	N	Y	Y	N
Lugar	N	Y	Y	N	Y	Y	N	Y
IOWA								
Grassley	N	Y	Y	N	Y	Y	N	Y
Harkin	N	N	N	Y	N	Y	Y	N
KANSAS								
Brownback	N	Y	Y	N	Y	Y	N	Y
Roberts	N	Y	Y	N	Y	Y	N	Y
KENTUCKY								
Bunning	–	Y	Y	N	Y	Y	N	Y
McConnell	N	Y	Y	N	Y	Y	N	Y
LOUISIANA								
Breaux	N	N	N	Y	N	Y	N	N
Landrieu	N	?	N	Y	N	Y	Y	N
MAINE								
Collins	N	Y	Y	N	Y	Y	N	Y
Snowe	N	Y	Y	N	Y	Y	N	Y
MARYLAND								
Mikulski	?	N	N	Y	N	Y	Y	N
Sarbanes	N	N	N	Y	N	Y	Y	N
MASSACHUSETTS								
Kennedy	N	N	N	Y	N	Y	Y	N
Kerry	N	N	N	Y	N	Y	Y	N
MICHIGAN								
Abraham	N	Y	Y	N	Y	Y	N	Y
Levin	N	N	N	Y	N	Y	Y	N
MINNESOTA								
Grams	N	Y	Y	N	Y	Y	N	Y
Wellstone	N	N	?	Y	N	Y	Y	N
MISSISSIPPI								
Cochran	N	Y	Y	N	Y	Y	N	Y
Lott	N	Y	Y	N	Y	Y	N	Y
MISSOURI								
Ashcroft	N	Y	Y	N	Y	Y	N	Y
Bond	N	Y	Y	N	Y	Y	N	Y
MONTANA								
Burns	–	Y	Y	N	Y	Y	N	Y
Baucus	N	N	N	Y	N	Y	Y	N
NEBRASKA								
Hagel	N	Y	Y	N	Y	Y	N	Y
Kerrey	N	N	N	Y	N	Y	Y	N
NEVADA								
Bryan	N	N	N	Y	N	Y	Y	N
Reid	N	N	N	Y	N	Y	Y	N
NEW HAMPSHIRE								
Gregg	N	Y	Y	N	Y	Y	N	Y
Smith	N	Y	Y	N	Y	Y	N	Y
NEW JERSEY								
Lautenberg	N	?	N	Y	N	Y	Y	N
Torricelli	N	?	?	Y	N	Y	Y	N
NEW MEXICO								
Domenici	N	Y	Y	N	Y	Y	N	Y
Bingaman	N	N	N	Y	N	Y	Y	N
NEW YORK								
Moynihan	N	N	N	Y	N	Y	Y	N
Schumer	N	N	N	Y	N	Y	Y	N
NORTH CAROLINA								
Helms	N	Y	Y	N	Y	Y	N	Y
Edwards	N	N	N	Y	N	Y	Y	N
NORTH DAKOTA								
Conrad	–	N	N	Y	N	Y	N	Y
Dorgan	–	N	N	Y	N	Y	N	Y
OHIO								
DeWine	N	Y	Y	N	Y	Y	N	Y
Voinovich	N	Y	Y	N	Y	Y	N	Y
OKLAHOMA								
Inhofe	?	Y	Y	N	Y	Y	N	Y
Nickles	N	Y	Y	N	Y	Y	N	Y
OREGON								
Smith	N	Y	Y	N	Y	Y	N	Y
Wyden	N	N	N	Y	N	Y	Y	N
PENNSYLVANIA								
Santorum	N	Y	Y	N	Y	Y	N	Y
Specter	N	Y	Y	N	Y	Y	N	Y
RHODE ISLAND								
Chafee	N	Y	Y	N	Y	Y	N	Y
Reed	N	N	N	Y	N	Y	Y	N
SOUTH CAROLINA								
Thurmond	N	Y	Y	N	Y	Y	N	Y
Hollings	N	N	N	Y	N	Y	Y	N
SOUTH DAKOTA								
Daschle	N	N	N	Y	N	Y	Y	N
Johnson	N	N	N	Y	N	Y	N	Y
TENNESSEE								
Frist	N	Y	Y	N	Y	Y	N	Y
Thompson	N	Y	Y	N	Y	Y	N	Y
TEXAS								
Gramm	N	Y	Y	N	Y	Y	N	Y
Hutchison	N	Y	Y	N	Y	Y	N	Y
UTAH								
Bennett	N	Y	Y	N	Y	Y	N	Y
Hatch	N	Y	Y	N	Y	Y	N	Y
VERMONT								
Jeffords	N	Y	Y	N	Y	Y	N	Y
Leahy	N	N	N	Y	N	Y	N	Y
VIRGINIA								
Warner	N	Y	Y	N	Y	Y	N	Y
Robb	N	N	N	Y	N	Y	Y	N
WASHINGTON								
Gorton	N	Y	Y	N	Y	Y	N	Y
Murray	N	N	?	?	?	?	?	?
WEST VIRGINIA								
Byrd	N	N	N	Y	N	N	N	Y
Rockefeller	N	N	–	Y	N	Y	Y	N
WISCONSIN								
Feingold	N	N	N	Y	N	Y	Y	N
Kohl	N	N	N	Y	N	Y	Y	N
WYOMING								
Enzi	N	Y	Y	N	Y	Y	N	Y
Thomas	?	Y	Y	N	Y	Y	N	Y

Key

Y Voted for (yea).
Paired for.
+ Announced for.
N Voted against (nay).
X Paired against.
– Announced against.
P Voted "present."
C Voted "present" to avoid possible conflict of interest.
? Did not vote or otherwise make a position known.

•

Democrats ***Republicans***
Independents

ND Northern Democrats SD Southern Democrats

Southern states - Ala., Ark., Fla., Ga., Ky., La., Miss., N.C., Okla., S.C., Tenn., Texas, Va.

33. S 280. Educational Flexibility/Banking Regulation Implementation. Gramm, R-Texas, motion to table (kill) the Allard, R-Colo., amendment to the language that would be struck by the Health, Education, Labor and Pensions Committee substitute amendment. The Allard amendment would prohibit federal banking agencies from implementing so-called "know your customer" regulations under consideration by the agencies. Motion rejected 0-88: R 0-46; D 0-42 (ND 0-34, SD 0-8). March 5, 1999.

34. S 280. Educational Flexibility/Cloture. Motion to invoke cloture (thus limiting debate) on the committee substitute amendment that would allow states to waive certain federal rules normally required in order to use federal education funds. Motion rejected 54-41: R 54-0; D 0-41 (ND 0-35, SD 0-6). March 8, 1999. Three-fifths of the total Senate (60) is required to invoke cloture.

35. S 280. Educational Flexibility/Cloture. Motion to invoke cloture (thus limiting debate) on the committee substitute amendment that would allow states to waive certain federal rules normally required in order to use federal education funds. Motion rejected 55-39: R 55-0; D 0-39 (ND 0-32, SD 0-7). March 9, 1999. Three-fifths of the total Senate (60) is required to invoke cloture.

36. S 280. Educational Flexibility/New Teachers/Cloture. Motion to invoke cloture (thus limiting debate) on the Kennedy, D-Mass., motion to recommit the bill to the Health, Education, Labor and Pensions Committee with instructions to add language authorizing $11.4 billion over six years for hiring new teachers to reduce class size. Motion rejected 44-55: R 0-55; D 44-0 (ND 36-0, SD 8-0). March 10, 1999. Three-fifths of the total Senate (60) is required to invoke cloture.

37. S 280. Educational Flexibility/Special Education Funding/Cloture. Motion to invoke cloture (thus limiting debate) on the Jeffords, R-Vt., amendment to the Bingaman, D-N.M., amendment to the committee substitute. The Jeffords amendment would use $150 million, authorized for dropout prevention by the Bingaman amendment, for special education programs under the Individuals with Disabilities Education Act. Motion rejected 55-44: R 55-0; D 0-44 (ND 0-36, SD 0-8). March 10, 1999. Three-fifths of the total Senate (60) is required to invoke cloture. (Subsequently, all pending amendments except the substitute were withdrawn by voice vote.)

38. S Con Res 5. Palestinian Statehood/Adoption. Adoption of the concurrent resolution to express congressional opposition to a unilateral Palestinian declaration of statehood and urge the president to make clear that the United States would not recognize such a declared state. Adopted 98-1: R 55-0; D 43-1 (ND 35-1, SD 8-0). March 11, 1999.

39. S 280. Educational Flexibility/Special Education Funding. Kennedy, D-Mass., motion to table (kill) the Lott, R-Miss., amendment to the committee substitute amendment. The Lott amendment would allow local education agencies to redirect all or part of $1.2 billion previously appropriated for new teachers (PL 105-277) to special education programs under the Individuals with Disabilities Education Act. Motion rejected 38-61: R 0-55; D 38-6 (ND 31-5, SD 7-1). March 11, 1999. A "yea" was a vote in support of the president's position.

40. S 280. Educational Flexibility/Special Education Funding. Lott, R-Miss., amendment to the committee substitute amendment. The Lott amendment would allow local education agencies to redirect all or part of $1.2 billion previously appropriated (PL 105-277) for new teachers to special education programs under the Individuals with Disabilities Education Act. Adopted 60-39: R 55-0; D 5-39 (ND 5-31, SD 0-8). March 11, 1999.

Senate Votes 41, 42, 43, 44, 45, 46, 47, 48

	41	42	43	44	45	46	47	48
ALABAMA								
Sessions	Y	Y	Y	Y	Y	Y	Y	Y
Shelby	Y	Y	Y	Y	Y	Y	Y	Y
ALASKA								
Murkowski	Y	Y	Y	Y	Y	Y	Y	Y
Stevens	Y	Y	Y	Y	Y	Y	Y	Y
ARIZONA								
Kyl	Y	Y	Y	Y	Y	Y	Y	Y
McCain	Y	Y	Y	Y	Y	Y	Y	Y
ARKANSAS								
Hutchinson	Y	Y	Y	Y	Y	Y	Y	Y
Lincoln	N	N	N	N	Y	N	N	Y
CALIFORNIA								
Boxer	N	N	N	N	Y	N	N	Y
Feinstein	N	N	N	N	Y	N	N	Y
COLORADO								
Allard	Y	Y	Y	Y	Y	Y	Y	Y
Campbell	Y	Y	Y	Y	Y	Y	Y	Y
CONNECTICUT								
Dodd	N	N	N	N	N	N	N	Y
Lieberman	N	N	N	N	Y	N	N	Y
DELAWARE								
Roth	Y	Y	Y	Y	Y	Y	Y	Y
Biden	N	N	N	N	N	N	N	Y
FLORIDA								
Mack	Y	Y	Y	Y	Y	Y	Y	Y
Graham	N	N	N	N	N	Y	N	Y
GEORGIA								
Coverdell	Y	Y	Y	Y	Y	Y	Y	Y
Cleland	N	N	N	N	N	N	N	Y
HAWAII								
Akaka	N	N	N	N	N	N	N	Y
Inouye	N	N	N	N	N	N	N	Y
IDAHO								
Craig	Y	Y	Y	Y	Y	Y	Y	Y
Crapo	Y	Y	Y	Y	Y	Y	Y	Y
ILLINOIS								
Fitzgerald	Y	Y	Y	Y	Y	Y	Y	Y
Durbin	N	N	N	N	Y	N	N	Y
INDIANA								
Bayh	N	N	N	N	Y	N	N	Y
Lugar	Y	Y	Y	Y	Y	Y	Y	Y
IOWA								
Grassley	Y	Y	Y	Y	Y	Y	Y	Y
Harkin	N	N	N	N	N	N	N	Y
KANSAS								
Brownback	Y	Y	Y	Y	Y	Y	Y	Y
Roberts	Y	Y	Y	Y	Y	Y	Y	Y
KENTUCKY								
Bunning	Y	Y	Y	Y	Y	Y	Y	Y
McConnell	Y	Y	Y	Y	Y	Y	Y	Y
LOUISIANA								
Breaux	N	Y	N	N	Y	N	N	Y
Landrieu	N	Y	N	N	Y	N	Y	Y
MAINE								
Collins	Y	Y	Y	Y	Y	Y	Y	Y
Snowe	Y	Y	Y	Y	Y	Y	Y	Y
MARYLAND								
Mikulski	N	N	N	N	N	N	N	Y
Sarbanes	N	N	N	N	N	N	N	Y
MASSACHUSETTS								
Kennedy	N	N	N	N	N	N	N	Y
Kerry	N	N	N	N	N	N	N	Y
MICHIGAN								
Abraham	Y	Y	Y	Y	Y	Y	Y	Y
Levin	N	N	N	N	N	N	N	Y
MINNESOTA								
Grams	Y	Y	Y	Y	Y	Y	Y	Y
Wellstone	N	N	N	N	N	Y	N	N
MISSISSIPPI								
Cochran	Y	Y	Y	Y	Y	Y	Y	Y
Lott	Y	Y	Y	Y	Y	Y	Y	Y
MISSOURI								
Ashcroft	Y	Y	Y	Y	Y	Y	Y	Y
Bond	Y	Y	Y	Y	Y	Y	Y	Y
MONTANA								
Burns	Y	Y	Y	Y	Y	Y	Y	Y
Baucus	N	N	N	N	Y	N	N	Y
NEBRASKA								
Hagel	Y	Y	Y	Y	Y	Y	Y	Y
Kerrey	N	N	N	N	Y	N	N	Y
NEVADA								
Bryan	N	N	N	N	Y	N	N	Y
Reid	N	N	N	N	Y	N	N	Y
NEW HAMPSHIRE								
Gregg	Y	Y	Y	Y	Y	Y	Y	Y
Smith	Y	Y	Y	Y	Y	Y	Y	Y
NEW JERSEY								
Lautenberg	N	N	N	N	N	N	N	Y
Torricelli	N	N	N	N	Y	N	N	Y
NEW MEXICO								
Domenici	Y	Y	Y	Y	Y	Y	Y	Y
Bingaman	N	N	N	N	N	N	N	Y
NEW YORK								
Moynihan	N	N	N	N	N	N	N	Y
Schumer	N	N	N	N	Y	N	N	Y
NORTH CAROLINA								
Helms	Y	Y	Y	Y	Y	Y	Y	Y
Edwards	N	N	N	N	Y	N	N	Y
NORTH DAKOTA								
Conrad	N	Y	N	N	Y	N	N	Y
Dorgan	N	Y	N	N	Y	N	N	Y
OHIO								
DeWine	Y	Y	Y	Y	Y	Y	Y	Y
Voinovich	Y	Y	Y	Y	Y	Y	Y	Y
OKLAHOMA								
Inhofe	Y	Y	Y	Y	Y	Y	Y	Y
Nickles	Y	Y	Y	Y	Y	Y	Y	Y
OREGON								
Smith	Y	Y	Y	Y	Y	Y	Y	Y
Wyden	N	N	N	N	Y	N	N	Y
PENNSYLVANIA								
Santorum	Y	Y	Y	Y	Y	Y	Y	Y
Specter	Y	Y	Y	Y	Y	Y	Y	Y
RHODE ISLAND								
Chafee	Y	Y	Y	Y	Y	Y	Y	Y
Reed	N	N	N	N	N	N	N	Y
SOUTH CAROLINA								
Thurmond	Y	Y	Y	Y	Y	Y	Y	Y
Hollings	N	N	N	N	Y	N	N	Y
SOUTH DAKOTA								
Daschle	N	N	N	N	N	N	N	Y
Johnson	N	Y	N	N	Y	N	Y	Y
TENNESSEE								
Frist	Y	Y	Y	Y	Y	Y	Y	Y
Thompson	Y	Y	Y	Y	Y	Y	Y	Y
TEXAS								
Gramm	Y	Y	Y	Y	Y	Y	Y	Y
Hutchison	Y	Y	Y	Y	Y	Y	Y	Y
UTAH								
Bennett	Y	Y	Y	Y	Y	Y	Y	Y
Hatch	Y	Y	Y	Y	Y	Y	Y	Y
VERMONT								
Jeffords	Y	Y	Y	Y	Y	Y	Y	Y
Leahy	N	Y	N	N	N	Y	N	Y
VIRGINIA								
Warner	Y	Y	Y	Y	Y	Y	Y	Y
Robb	N	N	N	N	Y	N	N	Y
WASHINGTON								
Gorton	Y	Y	Y	Y	Y	Y	Y	Y
Murray	?	?	?	?	?	?	?	?
WEST VIRGINIA								
Byrd	N	N	N	N	Y	N	N	Y
Rockefeller	N	N	N	N	Y	N	N	Y
WISCONSIN								
Feingold	N	N	N	N	N	Y	N	Y
Kohl	N	N	N	N	N	N	N	Y
WYOMING								
Enzi	Y	Y	Y	Y	Y	Y	Y	Y
Thomas	Y	Y	Y	Y	Y	Y	Y	Y

ND Northern Democrats SD Southern Democrats

Southern states - Ala., Ark., Fla., Ga., Ky., La., Miss., N.C., Okla., S.C., Tenn., Texas, Va.

Key

- Y Voted for (yea).
- # Paired for.
- + Announced for.
- N Voted against (nay).
- X Paired against.
- – Announced against.
- P Voted "present."
- C Voted "present" to avoid possible conflict of interest.
- ? Did not vote or otherwise make a position known.

Democrats **_Republicans_** _Independents_

41. S 280. Educational Flexibility/New Teachers. Jeffords, R-Vt., motion to table (kill) the Murray, D-Wash., amendment to the committee substitute amendment. The Murray amendment would authorize $11.4 billion over six years to fund President Clinton's proposal to hire 100,000 new teachers to reduce class size. Motion agreed to 55-44: R 55-0; D 0-44 (ND 0-36, SD 0-8). March 11, 1999. A "nay" was a vote in support of the president's position.

42. S 280. Educational Flexibility/Special Education Funding. Lott, R-Miss., amendment to the committee substitute amendment. The Lott amendment would allow local education agencies to redirect all or part of $1.2 billion previously appropriated for new teachers (PL 105-277) to special education programs under the Individuals with Disabilities Education Act and would authorize an additional $150 million for special education programs. Adopted 61-38: R 55-0; D 6-38 (ND 4-32, SD 2-6). March 11, 1999.

43. S 280. Educational Flexibility/School Dropout Prevention. Jeffords, R-Vt., motion to table (kill) the Bingaman, D-N.M., amendment to the committee substitute amendment. The Bingaman amendment would authorize $150 million to establish a school dropout prevention program. Motion agreed to 55-44: R 55-0; D 0-44 (ND 0-36, SD 0-8). March 11, 1999.

44. S 280. Educational Flexibility/After-School Programs. Jeffords, R-Vt., motion to table (kill) the Boxer, D-Calif., amendment to the committee substitute amendment. The Boxer amendment would authorize $600 million per year for five years for after-school programs. Motion agreed to 55-44: R 55-0; D 0-44 (ND 0-36, SD 0-8). March 11, 1999.

45. S 280. Educational Flexibility/Special Education Funding. Lott, R-Miss., amendment to the committee substitute amendment. The Lott amendment would allow local education agencies to redirect all or part of $1.2 billion previously appropriated for new teachers (PL 105-277) to special education programs under the Individuals with Disabilities Education Act and authorize an additional $500 million for special education programs. The amendment also includes Ashcroft, R-Mo., language to expand language barring weapons on school property and Reed, D-R.I., language regarding the public comment period before an education waiver may be granted. Adopted 78-21: R 55-0; D 23-21 (ND 17-19, SD 6-2). March 11, 1999.

46. S 280. Educational Flexibility/Social Promotion. Jeffords, R-Vt., motion to table (kill) the Feinstein, D-Calif., amendment to the committee substitute. The Feinstein amendment would authorize $500 million per year for five years for remedial education grants to local agencies that bar social promotion. The Feinstein amendment includes Dorgan, D-N.D., language to require states and localities to issue annual report cards on their performance in such areas as school safety, class size and teacher qualifications. Motion agreed to 59-40: R 55-0; D 4-40 (ND 3-33, SD 1-7). March 11, 1999.

47. S 280. Educational Flexibility/Aid to Disadvantaged Students. Jeffords, R-Vt., motion to table (kill) the Wellstone, D-Minn., amendment to the committee substitute amendment. The Wellstone amendment would prohibit waiving portions of Title I of the 1965 Elementary and Secondary Education Act, concerning disadvantaged students. Motion agreed to 57-42: R 55-0; D 2-42 (ND 1-35, SD 1-7). March 11, 1999. (Subsequently, the committee substitute was adopted by voice vote.)

48. HR 800. Educational Flexibility/Passage. Passage of the bill that would allow a participating state to waive certain federal rules usually required to use federal education funds as long as the state meets certain accountability standards. Passed 98-1: R 55-0; D 43-1 (ND 35-1, SD 8-0). March 11, 1999. (Before passage, the Senate struck all after the enacting clause and inserted the text of S 280 as amended.)

Senate Votes 49, 50, 51, 52, 53, 54

	49	50	51	52	53	54
ALABAMA						
Sessions	Y	Y	Y	Y	Y	N
Shelby	Y	Y	Y	Y	Y	N
ALASKA						
Murkowski	Y	Y	Y	Y	N	Y
Stevens	Y	Y	Y	Y	N	Y
ARIZONA						
Kyl	Y	Y	Y	Y	Y	N
McCain	Y	Y	Y	Y	N	?
ARKANSAS						
Hutchinson	Y	Y	Y	Y	Y	N
Lincoln	Y	Y	Y	Y	Y	Y
CALIFORNIA						
Boxer	Y	Y	Y	Y	N	Y
Feinstein	?	?	Y	Y	Y	Y
COLORADO						
Allard	Y	Y	Y	Y	Y	Y
Campbell	Y	Y	Y	Y	Y	Y
CONNECTICUT						
Dodd	Y	Y	Y	Y	N	Y
Lieberman	Y	Y	Y	Y	Y	Y
DELAWARE						
Roth	Y	Y	Y	Y	Y	Y
Biden	Y	Y	Y	Y	Y	Y
FLORIDA						
Mack	Y	Y	Y	Y	Y	Y
Graham	Y	Y	Y	Y	Y	Y
GEORGIA						
Coverdell	Y	Y	Y	Y	Y	N
Cleland	Y	Y	Y	Y	N	Y
HAWAII						
Akaka	Y	Y	Y	Y	N	Y
Inouye	Y	Y	Y	Y	Y	Y
IDAHO						
Craig	Y	Y	Y	Y	Y	N
Crapo	Y	Y	Y	Y	Y	N
ILLINOIS						
Fitzgerald	Y	Y	Y	Y	Y	Y
Durbin	Y	Y	N	Y	N	Y
INDIANA						
Bayh	Y	Y	Y	Y	Y	Y
Lugar	Y	Y	Y	Y	Y	Y
IOWA						
Grassley	Y	Y	Y	Y	Y	N
Harkin	Y	Y	Y	Y	N	Y
KANSAS						
Brownback	Y	Y	Y	Y	Y	Y
Roberts	Y	Y	Y	Y	Y	Y
KENTUCKY						
Bunning	Y	Y	Y	Y	Y	N
McConnell	Y	Y	Y	Y	Y	Y
LOUISIANA						
Breaux	Y	Y	Y	Y	N	Y
Landrieu	Y	Y	Y	Y	N	Y
MAINE						
Collins	Y	Y	Y	Y	Y	N
Snowe	Y	Y	Y	Y	Y	N
MARYLAND						
Mikulski	Y	Y	Y	Y	N	Y
Sarbanes	Y	Y	Y	Y	N	Y
MASSACHUSETTS						
Kennedy	Y	Y	Y	Y	N	Y
Kerry	Y	Y	Y	Y	Y	Y
MICHIGAN						
Abraham	Y	Y	Y	Y	Y	Y
Levin	Y	Y	Y	Y	Y	Y
MINNESOTA						
Grams	Y	Y	Y	Y	Y	Y
Wellstone	Y	Y	N	Y	N	N
MISSISSIPPI						
Cochran	Y	Y	Y	Y	Y	Y
Lott	Y	Y	Y	Y	Y	N
MISSOURI						
Ashcroft	Y	Y	Y	Y	Y	N
Bond	Y	Y	Y	Y	Y	Y
MONTANA						
Burns	Y	Y	Y	Y	Y	N
Baucus	Y	Y	Y	Y	N	Y
NEBRASKA						
Hagel	Y	Y	Y	Y	Y	Y
Kerrey	Y	Y	Y	Y	Y	Y
NEVADA						
Bryan	Y	Y	Y	Y	Y	Y
Reid	Y	Y	Y	Y	N	Y
NEW HAMPSHIRE						
Gregg	Y	Y	Y	Y	Y	Y
Smith	Y	Y	Y	Y	Y	N
NEW JERSEY						
Lautenberg	Y	Y	Y	Y	N	Y
Torricelli	Y	Y	Y	Y	Y	N
NEW MEXICO						
Domenici	Y	Y	Y	Y	Y	Y
Bingaman	Y	Y	Y	Y	Y	Y
NEW YORK						
Moynihan	Y	Y	Y	Y	Y	Y
Schumer	Y	Y	Y	Y	Y	Y
NORTH CAROLINA						
Helms	Y	Y	Y	Y	Y	N
Edwards	Y	Y	Y	Y	Y	Y
NORTH DAKOTA						
Conrad	Y	Y	Y	Y	Y	N
Dorgan	Y	Y	Y	Y	Y	N
OHIO						
DeWine	Y	Y	Y	Y	N	N
Voinovich	Y	Y	Y	Y	Y	Y
OKLAHOMA						
Inhofe	Y	Y	Y	Y	Y	N
Nickles	Y	Y	Y	Y	Y	Y
OREGON						
Smith	Y	Y	Y	Y	Y	Y
Wyden	Y	Y	Y	Y	N	Y
PENNSYLVANIA						
Santorum	Y	Y	Y	Y	Y	N
Specter	Y	Y	Y	Y	N	N
RHODE ISLAND						
Chafee	Y	Y	Y	Y	N	Y
Reed	Y	Y	Y	Y	N	Y
SOUTH CAROLINA						
Thurmond	Y	Y	Y	Y	Y	N
Hollings	Y	Y	Y	Y	Y	N
SOUTH DAKOTA						
Daschle	Y	Y	Y	Y	N	Y
Johnson	Y	Y	Y	Y	Y	Y
TENNESSEE						
Frist	Y	Y	Y	Y	Y	Y
Thompson	Y	Y	Y	Y	Y	N
TEXAS						
Gramm	Y	Y	Y	Y	Y	Y
Hutchison	Y	Y	Y	Y	Y	Y
UTAH						
Bennett	Y	Y	Y	Y	Y	Y
Hatch	Y	Y	Y	Y	Y	N
VERMONT						
Jeffords	Y	Y	Y	Y	N	Y
Leahy	Y	Y	N	Y	Y	Y
VIRGINIA						
Warner	Y	Y	Y	Y	Y	Y
Robb	Y	Y	Y	Y	Y	Y
WASHINGTON						
Gorton	Y	Y	Y	Y	Y	Y
Murray	Y	Y	Y	Y	N	Y
WEST VIRGINIA						
Byrd	Y	Y	Y	Y	N	Y
Rockefeller	Y	Y	Y	Y	Y	Y
WISCONSIN						
Feingold	Y	Y	Y	Y	N	N
Kohl	Y	Y	Y	Y	N	Y
WYOMING						
Enzi	Y	Y	Y	Y	Y	N
Thomas	Y	Y	Y	Y	Y	Y

Key

- Y Voted for (yea).
- # Paired for.
- \+ Announced for.
- N Voted against (nay).
- X Paired against.
- – Announced against.
- P Voted "present."
- C Voted "present" to avoid possible conflict of interest.
- ? Did not vote or otherwise make a position known.

•

Democrats ***Republicans***
Independents

ND Northern Democrats SD Southern Democrats

Southern states - Ala., Ark., Fla., Ga., Ky., La., Miss., N.C., Okla., S.C., Tenn., Texas, Va.

49. S 257. Anti-Missile Defense/Funding Subject to Authorization and Appropriation. Cochran, R-Miss., amendment that would clarify that funding for an anti-missile defense program would occur through the annual authorization and appropriations process. Adopted 99-0: R 55-0; D 44-0 (ND 36-0, SD 8-0). March 16, 1999.

50. S 257. Anti-Missile Defense/Russian Nuclear Weapons. Landrieu, D-La., amendment that would state U.S. policy as seeking continued negotiated reductions of Russian nuclear forces. Adopted 99-0: R 55-0; D 44-0 (ND 36-0, SD 8-0). March 16, 1999.

51. S 257. Anti-Missile Defense/Passage. Passage of the bill to make it U.S. policy to deploy an "effective" national missile defense system "as soon as is technologically possible." The measure also would make it U.S. policy to seek continued negotiated reductions in Russian nuclear forces. Passed 97-3: R 55-0; D 42-3 (ND 34-3, SD 8-0). March 17, 1999.

52. S 643. Federal Aviation Administration Short-Term Extension/Passage. Passage of the bill to reauthorize programs and activities of the Federal Aviation Administration (FAA), including the Airport Improvement Program and the federal aviation war risk insurance program, through May 31, 1999. The measure also would release $30 million to the Metropolitan Washington Airports Authority for improvements at Washington Dulles and Ronald Reagan Washington National airports. Passed 100-0: R 55-0; D 45-0 (ND 37-0, SD 8-0). March 17, 1999. (Subsequently, the Senate called up HR 99, struck all after the enacting clause and inserted the text of S 643 as passed and then passed HR 99 by voice vote.)

53. S 544. Fiscal 1999 Supplemental Spending/Tobacco Settlement Money. Hutchison, R-Texas, motion to table (kill) the Specter, R-Pa., amendment that would waive the federal government's claim to a state's proceeds from the settlement reached between the states and tobacco companies if the state uses 20 percent of its settlement money for anti-smoking programs and 30 percent of the money for public health or tobacco farmer transition assistance programs. The underlying bill would prohibit the federal government from claiming any state tobacco settlement funds. Motion agreed to 71-29: R 48-7; D 23-22 (ND 18-19, SD 5-3). March 18, 1999.

54. S 544. Fiscal 1999 Supplemental Spending/China WTO Admission. Stevens, R-Alaska, motion to table (kill) the Hutchinson, R-Ark., amendment that would prohibit U.S. support for China's admission into the World Trade Organization (WTO) unless a joint resolution supporting such admission is enacted into law. Motion agreed to 69-30: R 30-24; D 39-6 (ND 32-5, SD 7-1). March 18, 1999.

Senate Votes 55, 56, 57, 58, 59, 60, 61, 62

	55	56	57	58	59	60	61	62
ALABAMA								
Sessions	Y	N	N	Y	N	Y	N	Y
Shelby	Y	N	Y	Y	N	Y	N	Y
ALASKA								
Murkowski	Y	N	N	Y	N	Y	N	Y
Stevens	Y	N	N	Y	N	Y	N	Y
ARIZONA								
Kyl	Y	N	N	Y	N	Y	N	Y
McCain	Y	N	Y	Y	N	Y	N	Y
ARKANSAS								
Hutchinson	Y	N	N	Y	N	Y	N	Y
Lincoln	N	N	Y	Y	Y	Y	Y	Y
CALIFORNIA								
Boxer	N	Y	Y	Y	Y	Y	Y	Y
Feinstein	N	Y	Y	Y	Y	Y	Y	Y
COLORADO								
Allard	Y	N	N	Y	N	Y	N	Y
Campbell	Y	N	N	Y	N	Y	N	Y
CONNECTICUT								
Dodd	N	Y	Y	Y	Y	Y	Y	Y
Lieberman	N	Y	Y	Y	Y	Y	Y	Y
DELAWARE								
Roth	Y	N	Y	Y	N	Y	N	Y
Biden	N	Y	Y	Y	Y	Y	Y	N
FLORIDA								
Mack	Y	N	Y	Y	N	Y	N	Y
Graham	N	Y	Y	Y	Y	Y	Y	Y
GEORGIA								
Coverdell	Y	N	N	Y	N	Y	N	Y
Cleland	N	Y	Y	Y	Y	Y	Y	Y
HAWAII								
Akaka	N	N	Y	Y	Y	Y	Y	Y
Inouye	N	N	Y	Y	Y	Y	Y	Y
IDAHO								
Craig	Y	N	N	Y	N	Y	N	Y
Crapo	Y	N	N	Y	N	Y	N	Y
ILLINOIS								
Fitzgerald	Y	N	N	Y	N	Y	N	Y
Durbin	N	Y	Y	Y	Y	Y	Y	Y
INDIANA								
Bayh	N	N	Y	Y	Y	Y	Y	Y
Lugar	Y	Y	Y	?	?	?	?	?
IOWA								
Grassley	Y	N	N	Y	N	Y	N	Y
Harkin	N	Y	Y	Y	Y	Y	Y	Y
KANSAS								
Brownback	Y	N	N	Y	N	Y	N	Y
Roberts	Y	N	N	Y	N	Y	N	Y
KENTUCKY								
Bunning	Y	N	N	Y	N	Y	N	Y
McConnell	Y	N	Y	Y	N	Y	N	Y
LOUISIANA								
Breaux	N	N	Y	Y	Y	Y	Y	Y
Landrieu	N	N	Y	Y	Y	Y	Y	Y
MAINE								
Collins	Y	Y	N	Y	N	Y	N	Y
Snowe	Y	Y	Y	Y	N	Y	N	Y
MARYLAND								
Mikulski	N	Y	Y	Y	Y	Y	Y	Y
Sarbanes	N	Y	Y	Y	Y	Y	Y	Y
MASSACHUSETTS								
Kennedy	N	Y	Y	Y	Y	Y	Y	Y
Kerry	N	Y	Y	Y	Y	Y	Y	Y
MICHIGAN								
Abraham	Y	N	Y	Y	N	Y	N	Y
Levin	N	Y	Y	Y	Y	Y	Y	Y
MINNESOTA								
Grams	Y	N	N	Y	N	Y	N	Y
Wellstone	N	Y	Y	Y	Y	Y	Y	Y
MISSISSIPPI								
Cochran	?	?	+	Y	N	Y	N	Y
Lott	Y	N	N	Y	N	Y	N	Y
MISSOURI								
Ashcroft	Y	N	N	Y	N	Y	N	Y
Bond	Y	N	N	Y	N	Y	N	Y
MONTANA								
Burns	Y	N	N	Y	N	Y	N	Y
Baucus	N	Y	Y	Y	Y	Y	Y	Y
NEBRASKA								
Hagel	Y	N	Y	Y	N	Y	N	Y
Kerrey	N	Y	Y	Y	Y	Y	Y	Y
NEVADA								
Bryan	N	Y	Y	Y	Y	Y	Y	Y
Reid	N	Y	Y	Y	Y	Y	Y	Y
NEW HAMPSHIRE								
Gregg	Y	N	N	Y	N	Y	N	Y
Smith	Y	N	N	Y	N	Y	N	Y
NEW JERSEY								
Lautenberg	N	Y	Y	Y	Y	Y	Y	Y
Torricelli	N	Y	Y	Y	Y	Y	Y	Y
NEW MEXICO								
Domenici	Y	N	N	Y	N	Y	N	Y
Bingaman	N	Y	N	Y	Y	Y	Y	Y
NEW YORK								
Moynihan	N	N	Y	Y	Y	Y	Y	Y
Schumer	N	Y	Y	Y	Y	Y	Y	N
NORTH CAROLINA								
Helms	Y	N	N	Y	N	Y	N	Y
Edwards	N	Y	Y	Y	Y	Y	Y	Y
NORTH DAKOTA								
Conrad	N	N	Y	Y	Y	Y	Y	Y
Dorgan	N	N	Y	Y	Y	Y	Y	Y
OHIO								
DeWine	Y	N	Y	Y	N	Y	N	Y
Voinovich	Y	N	N	Y	N	Y	N	Y
OKLAHOMA								
Inhofe	Y	N	N	Y	N	Y	N	Y
Nickles	Y	N	N	Y	N	Y	N	Y
OREGON								
Smith	Y	N	Y	Y	N	Y	N	Y
Wyden	N	Y	Y	Y	Y	Y	Y	Y
PENNSYLVANIA								
Santorum	Y	N	N	Y	N	Y	N	Y
Specter	Y	N	Y	Y	N	Y	N	Y
RHODE ISLAND								
Chafee	Y	Y	Y	Y	N	Y	N	Y
Reed	N	Y	Y	Y	Y	Y	Y	Y
SOUTH CAROLINA								
Thurmond	Y	N	N	Y	N	Y	N	Y
Hollings	N	N	N	Y	Y	Y	Y	Y
SOUTH DAKOTA								
Daschle	N	Y	Y	Y	Y	Y	Y	Y
Johnson	N	Y	Y	Y	Y	Y	Y	Y
TENNESSEE								
Frist	Y	N	N	Y	N	Y	N	Y
Thompson	Y	N	N	Y	N	Y	N	Y
TEXAS								
Gramm	Y	N	N	Y	N	Y	N	Y
Hutchison	Y	N	N	Y	N	Y	N	Y
UTAH								
Bennett	Y	N	N	Y	N	Y	N	Y
Hatch	Y	N	Y	Y	N	Y	N	Y
VERMONT								
Jeffords	Y	Y	Y	Y	N	Y	N	Y
Leahy	N	Y	Y	Y	Y	Y	Y	Y
VIRGINIA								
Warner	Y	Y	Y	Y	N	Y	N	Y
Robb	N	Y	Y	Y	Y	Y	Y	Y
WASHINGTON								
Gorton	Y	N	N	Y	N	Y	N	Y
Murray	N	Y	Y	Y	Y	Y	Y	Y
WEST VIRGINIA								
Byrd	N	N	Y	Y	Y	Y	Y	Y
Rockefeller	N	Y	Y	Y	Y	Y	Y	Y
WISCONSIN								
Feingold	Y	Y	N	Y	Y	Y	Y	Y
Kohl	N	Y	Y	Y	Y	Y	Y	Y
WYOMING								
Enzi	Y	N	N	Y	N	Y	N	Y
Thomas	Y	N	N	Y	N	Y	N	Y

ND Northern Democrats SD Southern Democrats

Southern states - Ala., Ark., Fla., Ga., Ky., La., Miss., N.C., Okla., S.C., Tenn., Texas, Va.

Key

- Y Voted for (yea).
- \# Paired for.
- \+ Announced for.
- N Voted against (nay).
- X Paired against.
- – Announced against.
- P Voted "present."
- C Voted "present" to avoid possible conflict of interest.
- ? Did not vote or otherwise make a position known.

•

Democrats ***Republicans*** *Independents*

55. S 544. Fiscal 1999 Supplemental Spending/U.S. Troops in Kosovo-Cloture. Motion to invoke cloture (thus limiting debate) on the Lott, R-Miss., amendment to the Hutchison, R-Texas, amendment. The Lott amendment would prohibit U.S. funding for military operations anywhere in Yugoslavia unless Congress enacted legislation specifically authorizing such action. The Hutchison amendment would prohibit deployment of U.S. troops to Kosovo until the warring parties agreed to a peace agreement and the president reported to Congress on a variety of issues, including the proposed rules of engagement and exit strategy. Motion rejected 55-44: R 54-0; D 1-44 (ND 1-36, SD 0-8). March 23, 1999. Three-fifths of the total Senate (60) is required to invoke cloture. (Subsequently, the Lott amendment fell when the Hutchison amendment was withdrawn.)

56. S 544. Fiscal 1999 Supplemental Spending/Glacier Bay Fishing. Reid, D-Nev., motion to table (kill) the Murkowski, R-Alaska, amendment that would prohibit the Interior Department from using funds to restrict commercial fishing or other marine activities in Glacier Bay National Park until Alaska's legal claim to ownership of affected areas was resolved. Motion rejected 40-59: R 6-48; D 34-11 (ND 30-7, SD 4-4). March 23, 1999. (Subsequently, the Murkowski amendment and the underlying $2 billion supplemental spending bill, which would provide money for disaster relief to victims of hurricanes Georges and Mitch and relief for U.S. farmers hurt by falling prices, were adopted by voice vote.)

57. S. Con Res 21. Air Operations Against Yugoslavia/Adoption. Adoption of the concurrent resolution to authorize President Clinton to conduct military air operations and missile strikes in cooperation with NATO against Yugoslavia. Adopted 58-41: R 16-38; D 42-3 (ND 35-2, SD 7-1). March 23, 1999.

58. S Con Res 20. Fiscal 2000 Budget Resolution/Social Security Off-Budget. Abraham, R-Mich., amendment to express the sense of Congress that Congress should pass legislation to reaffirm the off-budget status of the Social Security trust fund, require that Social Security surpluses be used only for Social Security or to reduce the debt, and establish a Senate point of order against any measure that would use the surpluses for other purposes. Adopted 99-0: R 54-0; D 45-0 (ND 37-0, SD 8-0). March 24, 1999.

59. S Con Res 20. Fiscal 2000 Budget Resolution/Social Security and Medicare Solvency. Lautenberg, D-N.J., motion to waive the Budget Act with respect to the Domenici, R-N.M., point of order against the Lautenberg amendment. The Lautenberg amendment would establish a Senate point of order against any measure that would increase spending or reduce taxes without offsets until Congress enacted legislation to ensure the long-term solvency of Social Security and extend the solvency of Medicare by at least 12 years. Motion rejected 45-54: R 0-54; D 45-0 (ND 37-0, SD 8-0). March 24, 1999. A three-fifths majority vote (60) of the total Senate is required to waive the Budget Act. (Subsequently, the chair upheld the point of order, and the amendment fell.)

60. S Con Res 20. Fiscal 2000 Budget Resolution/Social Security Stock Market Investment. Ashcroft, R-Mo., amendment that would express the sense of the Senate that the federal government should not invest Social Security funds in private financial markets. Adopted 99-0: R 54-0; D 45-0 (ND 37-0, SD 8-0). March 24, 1999.

61. S Con Res 20. Fiscal 2000 Budget Resolution/Medicare. Conrad, D-N.D., motion to waive the Budget Act with respect to the Domenici, R-N.M., point of order against the Conrad amendment. The Conrad amendment would reserve 40 percent of the non-Social Security budget surplus to ensure the solvency of Medicare through 2020 and would establish a Senate point of order against spending money reserved for Social Security or Medicare. Motion rejected 45-54: R 0-54; D 45-0 (ND 37-0, SD 8-0). March 24, 1999. A three-fifths majority vote (60) of the total Senate is required to waive the Budget Act. (Subsequently, the chair upheld the point of order, and the amendment fell.)

62. S Con Res 20. Fiscal 2000 Budget Resolution/Clinton Budget Proposal. Lautenberg, D-N.J., motion to table (kill) the Bond, R-Mo., amendment that would substitute President Clinton's budget proposal for the budget figures in the resolution. Motion agreed to 97-2: R 54-0; D 43-2 (ND 35-2, SD 8-0). March 24, 1999.

Senate Votes 63, 64, 65, 66, 67, 68, 69, 70

	63	64	65	66	67	68	69	70
ALABAMA								
Sessions	Y	N	Y	Y	Y	Y	N	Y
Shelby	Y	N	Y	Y	Y	Y	N	Y
ALASKA								
Murkowski	Y	N	Y	Y	Y	Y	N	Y
Stevens	Y	N	Y	Y	Y	Y	N	Y
ARIZONA								
Kyl	Y	N	Y	Y	Y	N	N	Y
McCain	Y	N	Y	Y	?	?	?	?
ARKANSAS								
Hutchinson	Y	N	Y	Y	Y	Y	N	Y
Lincoln	Y	N	N	N	Y	Y	Y	N
CALIFORNIA								
Boxer	Y	Y	N	N	Y	Y	Y	N
Feinstein	Y	Y	N	N	Y	Y	Y	N
COLORADO								
Allard	Y	N	Y	Y	Y	Y	N	Y
Campbell	Y	N	Y	Y	Y	Y	N	Y
CONNECTICUT								
Dodd	Y	Y	N	N	Y	Y	Y	N
Lieberman	Y	Y	N	N	Y	Y	Y	N
DELAWARE								
Roth	Y	N	Y	Y	Y	Y	N	Y
Biden	Y	Y	N	N	Y	Y	Y	N
FLORIDA								
Mack	Y	Y	Y	Y	Y	Y	N	Y
Graham	Y	Y	N	N	Y	Y	Y	N
GEORGIA								
Coverdell	Y	N	Y	Y	Y	Y	N	Y
Cleland	Y	Y	N	N	Y	Y	Y	N
HAWAII								
Akaka	Y	Y	N	N	Y	Y	Y	N
Inouye	Y	Y	N	N	Y	Y	Y	N
IDAHO								
Craig	Y	N	Y	Y	Y	Y	N	Y
Crapo	Y	N	Y	Y	Y	Y	N	Y
ILLINOIS								
Fitzgerald	Y	N	Y	Y	Y	Y	N	Y
Durbin	Y	Y	N	N	Y	Y	Y	N
INDIANA								
Bayh	Y	Y	N	N	Y	Y	Y	N
Lugar	?	?	?	?	?	?	N	Y
IOWA								
Grassley	Y	N	Y	Y	Y	Y	N	Y
Harkin	Y	Y	N	N	Y	Y	Y	N
KANSAS								
Brownback	Y	N	Y	Y	Y	Y	N	Y
Roberts	Y	N	Y	Y	Y	Y	N	Y
KENTUCKY								
Bunning	Y	N	Y	Y	Y	Y	N	Y
McConnell	Y	N	Y	Y	Y	Y	N	Y
LOUISIANA								
Breaux	Y	N	Y	N	Y	Y	Y	N
Landrieu	Y	N	N	N	Y	Y	Y	N
MAINE								
Collins	Y	Y	Y	Y	Y	Y	Y	Y
Snowe	Y	Y	Y	Y	Y	Y	Y	N
MARYLAND								
Mikulski	Y	Y	N	N	Y	Y	Y	N
Sarbanes	Y	Y	N	N	Y	Y	Y	N
MASSACHUSETTS								
Kennedy	Y	Y	N	N	Y	Y	Y	N
Kerry	Y	Y	N	N	Y	Y	Y	N
MICHIGAN								
Abraham	Y	Y	Y	Y	Y	Y	N	Y
Levin	Y	Y	N	N	Y	Y	Y	N
MINNESOTA								
Grams	Y	N	Y	Y	Y	Y	N	Y
Wellstone	Y	Y	N	N	Y	Y	Y	N
MISSISSIPPI								
Cochran	Y	N	Y	Y	Y	Y	N	Y
Lott	Y	N	Y	Y	Y	Y	N	Y
MISSOURI								
Ashcroft	Y	N	Y	Y	Y	Y	N	Y
Bond	Y	N	Y	Y	Y	Y	N	Y
MONTANA								
Burns	Y	N	Y	Y	Y	Y	N	Y
Baucus	Y	N	N	N	Y	Y	Y	N
NEBRASKA								
Hagel	Y	N	Y	Y	Y	Y	N	Y
Kerrey	Y	Y	Y	N	Y	Y	Y	Y
NEVADA								
Bryan	Y	Y	N	N	Y	Y	Y	N
Reid	Y	Y	N	N	Y	Y	Y	N
NEW HAMPSHIRE								
Gregg	Y	N	Y	Y	Y	Y	N	Y
Smith	Y	N	Y	Y	Y	Y	N	Y
NEW JERSEY								
Lautenberg	Y	Y	N	N	Y	Y	Y	N
Torricelli	Y	Y	N	N	Y	Y	Y	N
NEW MEXICO								
Domenici	Y	N	Y	Y	Y	Y	N	Y
Bingaman	Y	Y	N	N	Y	Y	Y	N
NEW YORK								
Moynihan	Y	Y	N	N	Y	Y	Y	N
Schumer	Y	Y	N	N	Y	Y	Y	N
NORTH CAROLINA								
Helms	Y	N	Y	Y	Y	Y	N	Y
Edwards	Y	N	N	N	Y	Y	Y	N
NORTH DAKOTA								
Conrad	Y	N	N	N	Y	Y	Y	N
Dorgan	Y	Y	N	N	Y	Y	Y	N
OHIO								
DeWine	Y	Y	Y	Y	Y	Y	N	Y
Voinovich	Y	N	Y	Y	Y	Y	N	Y
OKLAHOMA								
Inhofe	Y	N	Y	Y	Y	Y	N	Y
Nickles	Y	N	Y	Y	Y	Y	N	Y
OREGON								
Smith	Y	Y	Y	Y	Y	Y	N	Y
Wyden	Y	Y	N	N	Y	Y	Y	N
PENNSYLVANIA								
Santorum	Y	Y	Y	Y	Y	Y	N	Y
Specter	Y	Y	Y	N	Y	Y	N	N
RHODE ISLAND								
Chafee	Y	N	Y	Y	Y	Y	Y	N
Reed	Y	Y	N	N	Y	Y	Y	N
SOUTH CAROLINA								
Thurmond	Y	Y	Y	Y	Y	Y	N	Y
Hollings	Y	N	N	N	Y	Y	Y	N
SOUTH DAKOTA								
Daschle	Y	Y	N	N	Y	Y	Y	N
Johnson	Y	Y	N	N	Y	Y	Y	N
TENNESSEE								
Frist	Y	N	Y	Y	Y	Y	N	Y
Thompson	Y	N	Y	Y	Y	Y	N	Y
TEXAS								
Gramm	Y	N	Y	Y	Y	Y	N	Y
Hutchison	Y	N	Y	Y	Y	Y	N	Y
UTAH								
Bennett	Y	N	Y	Y	Y	Y	N	Y
Hatch	Y	N	Y	Y	Y	Y	N	Y
VERMONT								
Jeffords	Y	Y	Y	Y	Y	Y	Y	N
Leahy	Y	Y	N	N	Y	Y	Y	N
VIRGINIA								
Warner	Y	N	Y	Y	Y	Y	N	Y
Robb	Y	N	N	N	Y	Y	Y	Y
WASHINGTON								
Gorton	Y	N	Y	Y	Y	Y	N	Y
Murray	Y	Y	N	N	Y	Y	Y	N
WEST VIRGINIA								
Byrd	Y	Y	N	N	Y	Y	Y	N
Rockefeller	Y	Y	N	N	Y	Y	Y	N
WISCONSIN								
Feingold	Y	Y	N	N	Y	Y	Y	N
Kohl	Y	Y	N	N	Y	Y	Y	N
WYOMING								
Enzi	Y	N	Y	Y	Y	Y	N	Y
Thomas	Y	N	Y	Y	Y	Y	N	Y

ND Northern Democrats   SD Southern Democrats

Southern states - Ala., Ark., Fla., Ga., Ky., La., Miss., N.C., Okla., S.C., Tenn., Texas, Va.

Key

- Y Voted for (yea).
- # Paired for.
- + Announced for.
- N Voted against (nay).
- X Paired against.
- – Announced against.
- P Voted "present."
- C Voted "present" to avoid possible conflict of interest.
- ? Did not vote or otherwise make a position known.

•

Democrats ***Republicans***
Independents

63. S Con Res 20. Fiscal 2000 Budget Resolution/Veterans' Health Care. Johnson, D-S.D., amendment that would increase proposed fiscal 2000 funding for veterans' health care by $2 billion, offset by reducing all proposed discretionary funding except veterans and defense programs by the same amount. Adopted 99-0: R 54-0; D 45-0 (ND 37-0, SD 8-0). March 24, 1999.

64. S Con Res 20. Fiscal 2000 Budget Resolution/NIH Funding. Domenici, R-N.M., motion to waive the Budget Act with respect to the Bunning, R-Ky., point of order against the Specter, R-Pa., amendment. The Specter amendment would increase funding for National Institutes of Health biomedical research by $1.4 billion, offset by disallowing a federal income tax deduction for payments made to federal, state or local governments in connection with any tobacco litigation or settlement. Motion rejected 47-52: R 10-44; D 37-8 (ND 35-2, SD 2-6). March 25, 1999. A three-fifths majority vote (60) of the total Senate is required to waive the Budget Act. (Subsequently, the chair upheld the point of order, and the amendment fell.)

65. S Con Res 20. Fiscal 2000 Budget Resolution/Medicare. Roth, R-Del., amendment that would express the sense of the Senate that the budget resolution does not adopt President Clinton's Medicare proposals and that Congress should work in a "bipartisan fashion" to extend the program's solvency and should consider the Breaux, D-La., recommendations to the National Bipartisan Commission on the Future of Medicare. Adopted 56-43: R 54-0; D 2-43 (ND 1-36, SD 1-7). March 25, 1999.

66. S Con Res 20. Fiscal 2000 Budget Resolution/Tax Cuts. Domenici, R-N.M., motion to table (kill) the Kennedy, D-Mass., amendment that would strike the resolution's proposed $320 billion in tax cuts over 10 years and direct the funds to Medicare or debt reduction. Motion agreed to 53-46: R 53-1; D 0-45 (ND 0-37, SD 0-8). March 25, 1999.

67. S Res 57. Cuba Human Rights Abuses/Adoption. Adoption of the resolution that would express the sense of the Senate that the United States should introduce and advocate a resolution at the U.N. Human Rights Commission criticizing the Cuban government for its human rights abuses in Cuba. Adopted 98-0: R 53-0; D 45-0 (ND 37-0, SD 8-0). March 25, 1999.

68. S Con Res 20. Fiscal 2000 Budget Resolution/Farmland Protection Program. Santorum, R-Pa., amendment that would express the sense of the Senate that Congress should reauthorize the Farmland Protection Program this year. Adopted 97-1: R 52-1; D 45-0 (ND 37-0, SD 8-0). March 25, 1999.

69. S Con Res 20. Fiscal 2000 Budget Resolution/Community Development. Reed, D-R.I., motion to waive the Budget Act with respect to the Domenici, R-N.M., point of order against the Reed amendment. The Reed amendment would reduce the proposed tax cut and recommend increased funding for community and regional development. Motion rejected 49-50: R 4-50; D 45-0 (ND 37-0, SD 8-0). March 25, 1999. A three-fifths majority vote (60) of the total Senate is required to waive the Budget Act. (Subsequently, the chair upheld the point of order, and the amendment fell.)

70. S Con Res 20. Fiscal 2000 Budget Resolution/Mandatory Spending Offsets. Craig, R-Idaho, motion to waive the Budget Act with respect to the Lautenberg, D-N.J., point of order against the Craig amendment. The Craig amendment would modify pay-as-you-go rules to require that new mandatory spending programs be offset only by cuts in existing mandatory spending. Motion rejected 52-47: R 50-4; D 2-43 (ND 1-36, SD 1-7) March 25, 1999. A three-fifths majority vote (60) of the total Senate is required to waive the Budget Act. (Subsequently, the chair upheld the point of order, and the amendment fell.) March 25, 1999.

Senate Votes 71, 72, 73, 74, 75, 76, 77, 78

	71	72	73	74	75	76	77	78
ALABAMA								
Sessions	Y	Y	Y	?	Y	N	N	N
Shelby	Y	Y	Y	Y	Y	N	N	N
ALASKA								
Murkowski	Y	Y	Y	Y	Y	N	N	N
Stevens	Y	Y	N	Y	Y	N	N	N
ARIZONA								
Kyl	Y	Y	Y	Y	Y	N	N	N
McCain	?	?	?	?	?	?	?	?
ARKANSAS								
Hutchinson	Y	Y	Y	?	Y	N	N	N
Lincoln	Y	N	N	N	N	Y	Y	Y
CALIFORNIA								
Boxer	N	N	N	N	N	Y	Y	Y
Feinstein	N	N	N	N	N	Y	Y	N
COLORADO								
Allard	Y	Y	Y	Y	Y	N	N	N
Campbell	Y	Y	Y	N	Y	N	N	N
CONNECTICUT								
Dodd	N	N	N	N	N	Y	Y	Y
Lieberman	N	N	N	N	N	Y	Y	N
DELAWARE								
Roth	Y	Y	Y	Y	Y	N	N	N
Biden	Y	N	N	N	N	Y	Y	Y
FLORIDA								
Mack	Y	Y	Y	Y	Y	N	N	N
Graham	N	N	N	N	N	Y	N	Y
GEORGIA								
Coverdell	Y	Y	Y	Y	Y	N	N	N
Cleland	Y	N	N	N	N	Y	Y	N
HAWAII								
Akaka	N	N	N	N	N	Y	Y	Y
Inouye	N	N	N	N	N	Y	Y	Y
IDAHO								
Craig	Y	Y	Y	Y	Y	N	N	N
Crapo	Y	Y	Y	Y	Y	N	N	N
ILLINOIS								
Fitzgerald	Y	Y	Y	Y	Y	N	N	N
Durbin	N	N	N	N	N	Y	Y	N
INDIANA								
Bayh	Y	N	N	N	N	N	Y	N
Lugar	Y	Y	N	Y	Y	N	N	N
IOWA								
Grassley	Y	Y	Y	Y	Y	N	N	N
Harkin	N	N	N	N	N	Y	Y	Y
KANSAS								
Brownback	Y	Y	Y	Y	Y	N	N	N
Roberts	Y	Y	N	N	Y	N	N	N
KENTUCKY								
Bunning	Y	Y	Y	Y	Y	N	N	N
McConnell	Y	Y	Y	Y	Y	N	N	N
LOUISIANA								
Breaux	Y	N	N	N	N	Y	Y	Y
Landrieu	Y	N	N	N	N	Y	Y	N
MAINE								
Collins	Y	Y	N	N	Y	Y	N	N
Snowe	Y	Y	N	N	Y	Y	N	N
MARYLAND								
Mikulski	Y	N	N	N	N	Y	Y	Y
Sarbanes	N	N	N	N	N	Y	Y	N
MASSACHUSETTS								
Kennedy	N	N	N	N	N	Y	Y	N
Kerry	Y	N	N	N	N	Y	Y	N
MICHIGAN								
Abraham	Y	Y	Y	N	Y	Y	N	N
Levin	N	N	N	N	N	Y	Y	N
MINNESOTA								
Grams	Y	Y	Y	Y	Y	N	N	N
Wellstone	Y	N	N	N	N	Y	Y	N
MISSISSIPPI								
Cochran	Y	Y	Y	Y	Y	N	N	N
Lott	Y	Y	Y	Y	Y	N	N	N
MISSOURI								
Ashcroft	Y	Y	Y	Y	Y	N	N	N
Bond	Y	Y	N	Y	Y	N	N	N
MONTANA								
Burns	N	Y	Y	Y	Y	N	N	N
Baucus	N	N	N	N	N	Y	N	N
NEBRASKA								
Hagel	Y	Y	Y	Y	Y	N	N	N
Kerrey	Y	N	N	N	N	Y	Y	Y
NEVADA								
Bryan	Y	N	N	N	N	Y	Y	Y
Reid	N	N	N	N	N	Y	Y	Y
NEW HAMPSHIRE								
Gregg	Y	Y	Y	Y	Y	N	N	N
Smith	Y	Y	Y	Y	Y	N	N	N
NEW JERSEY								
Lautenberg	N	N	N	N	N	Y	Y	Y
Torricelli	Y	N	N	N	N	Y	Y	N
NEW MEXICO								
Domenici	Y	Y	N	Y	Y	N	N	N
Bingaman	Y	N	N	N	N	Y	Y	Y
NEW YORK								
Moynihan	N	N	N	N	N	Y	Y	N
Schumer	Y	N	N	N	N	Y	Y	N
NORTH CAROLINA								
Helms	Y	Y	Y	Y	Y	N	N	N
Edwards	Y	N	N	N	N	N	Y	N
NORTH DAKOTA								
Conrad	N	N	N	N	N	Y	Y	N
Dorgan	N	N	N	N	N	Y	Y	Y
OHIO								
DeWine	Y	Y	Y	N	Y	Y	N	N
Voinovich	N	Y	Y	Y	Y	N	N	Y
OKLAHOMA								
Inhofe	Y	Y	Y	Y	Y	N	N	N
Nickles	Y	Y	Y	Y	Y	N	N	N
OREGON								
Smith	Y	Y	N	Y	Y	Y	Y	N
Wyden	Y	N	N	N	N	Y	Y	N
PENNSYLVANIA								
Santorum	Y	Y	Y	Y	Y	Y	N	N
Specter	N	Y	N	N	Y	Y	Y	Y
RHODE ISLAND								
Chafee	N	Y	N	N	Y	Y	N	N
Reed	Y	N	N	N	N	Y	Y	N
SOUTH CAROLINA								
Thurmond	Y	Y	Y	Y	Y	N	N	N
Hollings	N	N	N	N	N	Y	Y	Y
SOUTH DAKOTA								
Daschle	N	N	N	N	N	Y	Y	N
Johnson	Y	N	N	N	N	Y	Y	N
TENNESSEE								
Frist	Y	Y	Y	N	Y	N	N	N
Thompson	Y	Y	Y	Y	Y	N	N	N
TEXAS								
Gramm	Y	Y	Y	Y	Y	N	N	N
Hutchison	Y	Y	Y	Y	Y	Y	N	N
UTAH								
Bennett	Y	Y	Y	Y	Y	Y	N	N
Hatch	Y	Y	Y	N	Y	Y	N	N
VERMONT								
Jeffords	N	Y	N	N	Y	Y	N	N
Leahy	N	N	N	N	N	Y	Y	Y
VIRGINIA								
Warner	Y	Y	Y	N	Y	N	N	N
Robb	N	N	N	N	N	N	Y	Y
WASHINGTON								
Gorton	Y	Y	N	Y	Y	N	N	N
Murray	N	N	N	N	N	Y	Y	N
WEST VIRGINIA								
Byrd	N	N	N	N	N	Y	Y	Y
Rockefeller	N	N	N	N	N	Y	Y	N
WISCONSIN								
Feingold	N	N	N	N	N	Y	Y	Y
Kohl	N	N	N	N	N	Y	Y	Y
WYOMING								
Enzi	Y	Y	Y	Y	Y	N	N	N
Thomas	Y	Y	Y	Y	?	?	?	?

Key

- Y Voted for (yea).
- # Paired for.
- + Announced for.
- N Voted against (nay).
- X Paired against.
- – Announced against.
- P Voted "present."
- C Voted "present" to avoid possible conflict of interest.
- ? Did not vote or otherwise make a position known.

Democrats ***Republicans*** *Independents*

ND Northern Democrats SD Southern Democrats

Southern states - Ala., Ark., Fla., Ga., Ky., La., Miss., N.C., Okla., S.C., Tenn., Texas, Va.

71. S Con Res 20. Fiscal 2000 Budget Resolution/Use Proposed Tax Cuts for Debt Reduction. Domenici, R-N.M., motion to table (kill) the Voinovich, R-Ohio, amendment that would strike the resolution's recommended tax cuts and redirect the funds for federal debt reduction. Motion agreed to 67-32: R 49-5; D 18-27 (ND 13-24, SD 5-3). March 25, 1999.

72. S Con Res 20. Fiscal 2000 Budget Resolution/Education Funding. Gregg, R-N.H., motion to table (kill) the Kennedy, D-Mass., amendment that would reduce the resolution's proposed tax cuts and redirect the revenue for President Clinton's plan to hire more teachers, as well as for increased funding for special education and other education programs. Motion agreed to 54-45: R 54-0; D 0-45 (ND 0-37, SD 0-8). March 25, 1999.

73. S Con Res 20. Fiscal 2000 Budget Resolution/Reserve Unexpected Surplus. Domenici, R-N.M., motion to waive the Budget Act with respect to the Lautenberg, D-N.J., point of order against the Crapo, R-Idaho, amendment. The Crapo amendment would propose that any non-Social Security budget surplus exceeding expectations outlined in the resolution be reserved for tax cuts or debt reduction. Motion rejected 42-57: R 42-12; D 0-45 (ND 0-37, SD 0-8). March 25, 1999. A three-fifths majority vote (60) of the total Senate is required to waive the Budget Act. (Subsequently, the chair upheld the point of order, and the amendment fell.)

74. S Con Res 20. Fiscal 2000 Budget Resolution/Child Care and Development. Domenici, R-N.M., motion to table (kill) the Dodd, D-Conn., amendment that would increase mandatory spending under the Child Care and Development Block Grant by $5 billion over five years and offset it by reducing tax cuts proposed in the resolution. Motion rejected 40-57: R 40-12; D 0-45 (ND 0-37, SD 0-8). March 25, 1999. (Subsequently, the Dodd amendment was adopted by voice vote.)

75. S Con Res 20. Fiscal 2000 Budget Resolution/Agriculture Funding. Domenici, R-N.M., motion to table (kill) the Dorgan, D-N.D., amendment that would increase proposed funding for agricultural programs by $30 billion over five years. Motion agreed to 53-45: R 53-0; D 0-45 (ND 0-37, SD 0-8). March 25, 1999.

76. S Con Res 20. Fiscal 2000 Budget Resolution/Tobacco Tax. Wyden, D-Ore., motion to waive the Budget Act with respect to the Bunning, R-Ky., point of order against the Snowe, R-Maine, amendment. The Snowe amendment would allow the Medicare prescription drug benefit program outlined in the resolution to be paid for by increased tobacco taxes. Motion rejected 54-44: R 12-41; D 42-3 (ND 36-1, SD 6-2). March 25, 1999. A three-fifths majority vote (60) of the total Senate is required to waive the Budget Act. (Subsequently, the chair upheld the point of order, and the amendment fell.)

77. S Con Res 20. Fiscal 2000 Budget Resolution/Minimum Wage Increase. Kennedy, D-Mass., motion to waive the Budget Act with respect to the Domenici, R-N.M., point of order against the Kennedy amendment. The Kennedy amendment would express the sense of the Senate that the minimum wage should be increased by $1 over two years. Motion rejected 45-53: R 2-51; D 43-2 (ND 36-1, SD 7-1). March 25, 1999. A three-fifths majority vote (60) of the total Senate is required to waive the Budget Act. (Subsequently, the chair upheld the point of order, and the amendment fell.)

78. S Con Res 20. Fiscal 2000 Budget Resolution/Current Services Baseline. Hollings, D-S.C., amendment that would replace funding levels in the resolution with the current services baseline levels in order to reduce the federal debt. Rejected 24-74: R 2-51; D 22-23 (ND 17-20, SD 5-3). March 25, 1999.

Senate Votes **79, 80, 81**

	79	80	81
ALABAMA			
Sessions	Y	N	Y
Shelby	Y	N	Y
ALASKA			
Murkowski	Y	N	Y
Stevens	Y	N	Y
ARIZONA			
Kyl	Y	N	Y
McCain	?	?	?
ARKANSAS			
Hutchinson	Y	N	Y
Lincoln	N	Y	N
CALIFORNIA			
Boxer	N	Y	N
Feinstein	N	Y	N
COLORADO			
Allard	Y	N	Y
Campbell	Y	N	Y
CONNECTICUT			
Dodd	N	Y	N
Lieberman	N	Y	N
DELAWARE			
Roth	Y	N	Y
Biden	N	Y	N
FLORIDA			
Mack	Y	N	Y
Graham	N	Y	N
GEORGIA			
Coverdell	Y	N	Y
Cleland	N	Y	N
HAWAII			
Akaka	N	Y	N
Inouye	N	Y	N
IDAHO			
Craig	Y	N	Y
Crapo	Y	N	Y
ILLINOIS			
Fitzgerald	Y	N	Y
Durbin	N	Y	N
INDIANA			
Bayh	N	Y	N
Lugar	Y	N	Y
IOWA			
Grassley	Y	N	Y
Harkin	N	Y	N
KANSAS			
Brownback	Y	N	Y
Roberts	Y	N	Y
KENTUCKY			
Bunning	Y	N	Y
McConnell	Y	N	Y
LOUISIANA			
Breaux	N	Y	Y
Landrieu	N	Y	N
MAINE			
Collins	Y	N	Y
Snowe	Y	N	Y
MARYLAND			
Mikulski	N	Y	N
Sarbanes	N	Y	N
MASSACHUSETTS			
Kennedy	N	Y	N
Kerry	N	Y	N
MICHIGAN			
Abraham	Y	N	Y
Levin	N	Y	N
MINNESOTA			
Grams	Y	N	Y
Wellstone	N	Y	N
MISSISSIPPI			
Cochran	Y	N	Y
Lott	Y	N	Y
MISSOURI			
Ashcroft	Y	N	Y
Bond	Y	N	Y
MONTANA			
Burns	Y	N	Y
Baucus	N	Y	N
NEBRASKA			
Hagel	Y	N	Y
Kerrey	N	Y	N
NEVADA			
Bryan	N	Y	N
Reid	N	Y	N
NEW HAMPSHIRE			
Gregg	Y	N	Y
Smith	Y	N	Y
NEW JERSEY			
Lautenberg	N	Y	N
Torricelli	N	Y	N
NEW MEXICO			
Domenici	Y	N	Y
Bingaman	N	Y	N
NEW YORK			
Moynihan	N	Y	N
Schumer	N	Y	N
NORTH CAROLINA			
Helms	Y	N	Y
Edwards	N	Y	N
NORTH DAKOTA			
Conrad	N	Y	N
Dorgan	N	Y	N
OHIO			
DeWine	Y	N	Y
Voinovich	Y	N	Y
OKLAHOMA			
Inhofe	Y	N	Y
Nickles	Y	N	Y
OREGON			
Smith	Y	N	Y
Wyden	N	Y	N
PENNSYLVANIA			
Santorum	Y	N	Y
Specter	Y	N	Y
RHODE ISLAND			
Chafee	Y	N	Y
Reed	N	Y	N
SOUTH CAROLINA			
Thurmond	Y	N	Y
Hollings	N	Y	N
SOUTH DAKOTA			
Daschle	N	Y	N
Johnson	N	Y	N
TENNESSEE			
Frist	Y	N	Y
Thompson	Y	N	Y
TEXAS			
Gramm	Y	N	Y
Hutchison	Y	N	Y
UTAH			
Bennett	Y	N	Y
Hatch	Y	N	Y
VERMONT			
Jeffords	Y	N	Y
Leahy	N	Y	N
VIRGINIA			
Warner	Y	N	Y
Robb	N	Y	N
WASHINGTON			
Gorton	Y	N	Y
Murray	N	Y	N
WEST VIRGINIA			
Byrd	N	Y	N
Rockefeller	N	Y	N
WISCONSIN			
Feingold	N	Y	N
Kohl	N	Y	N
WYOMING			
Enzi	Y	N	Y
Thomas	Y	N	Y

Key

- Y Voted for (yea).
- # Paired for.
- + Announced for.
- N Voted against (nay).
- X Paired against.
- – Announced against.
- P Voted "present."
- C Voted "present" to avoid possible conflict of interest.
- ? Did not vote or otherwise make a position known.

•

Democrats ***Republicans***
Independents

ND Northern Democrats SD Southern Democrats

Southern states - Ala., Ark., Fla., Ga., Ky., La., Miss., N.C., Okla., S.C., Tenn., Texas, Va.

79. S Con Res 20. Fiscal 2000 Budget Resolution/Medicare Prescription Drug Benefits. Domenici, R-N.M., motion to table (kill) the Kennedy, D-Mass., amendment that would establish a reserve fund to pay for Medicare prescription drug benefits. Motion agreed to 54-45: R 54-0; D 0-45 (ND 0-37, SD 0-8). March 25, 1999.

80. S Con Res 20. Fiscal 2000 Budget Resolution/One-Year Tax Cut Delay. Kerry, D-Mass., motion to waive the Budget Act with respect to the Domenici, R-N.M., point of order against the Kerry amendment. The Kerry amendment would require that new tax cuts be delayed for one year if in the year they are to take effect a budget deficit would result. Motion rejected 45-54: R 0-54; D 45-0 (ND 37-0, SD 8-0). March 25, 1999. A three-fifths majority vote (60) of the total Senate is required to waive the Budget Act. (Subsequently, the chair upheld the point of order, and the amendment fell.)

81. H Con Res 68. Fiscal 2000 Budget Resolution/Adoption. Adoption of the concurrent resolution to adopt a five-year budget plan that calls for tax cuts beginning in fiscal 2000 and increased spending for defense, education and agriculture. The resolution would dedicate Social Security surpluses for national debt reduction, but would rely on anticipated non-Social Security surpluses for tax cuts of $800 billion over 10 years. Adopted 55-44: R 54-0; D 1-44 (ND 0-37, SD 1-7). March 25, 1999. (Before passage, the Senate struck all after the enacting clause and inserted the text of S Con Res 20 as amended.)

Senate Votes 82, 83, 84

	82	83	84
ALABAMA			
Sessions	Y	Y	Y
Shelby	Y	Y	Y
ALASKA			
Murkowski	Y	Y	Y
Stevens	Y	Y	Y
ARIZONA			
Kyl	Y	Y	Y
McCain	Y	Y	Y
ARKANSAS			
Hutchinson	Y	Y	Y
Lincoln	Y	N	N
CALIFORNIA			
Boxer	Y	N	N
Feinstein	Y	N	N
COLORADO			
Allard	Y	Y	Y
Campbell	Y	Y	Y
CONNECTICUT			
Dodd	Y	N	N
Lieberman	Y	N	N
DELAWARE			
Roth	Y	Y	Y
Biden	Y	N	N
FLORIDA			
Mack	Y	Y	Y
Graham	Y	N	N
GEORGIA			
Coverdell	Y	Y	Y
Cleland	Y	N	N
HAWAII			
Akaka	Y	N	N
Inouye	Y	N	N
IDAHO			
Craig	Y	Y	Y
Crapo	Y	Y	Y
ILLINOIS			
Fitzgerald	Y	Y	Y
Durbin	Y	N	N
INDIANA			
Bayh	Y	N	N
Lugar	Y	Y	Y
IOWA			
Grassley	Y	Y	Y
Harkin	Y	N	N
KANSAS			
Brownback	Y	Y	Y
Roberts	Y	Y	Y
KENTUCKY			
Bunning	Y	Y	Y
McConnell	Y	Y	Y
LOUISIANA			
Breaux	Y	Y	N
Landrieu	Y	N	N
MAINE			
Collins	Y	Y	Y
Snowe	Y	Y	Y
MARYLAND			
Mikulski	Y	N	N
Sarbanes	Y	N	N
MASSACHUSETTS			
Kennedy	Y	N	N
Kerry	Y	N	N
MICHIGAN			
Abraham	Y	Y	Y
Levin	Y	N	N
MINNESOTA			
Grams	Y	Y	Y
Wellstone	Y	N	N
MISSISSIPPI			
Cochran	Y	Y	Y
Lott	Y	Y	Y
MISSOURI			
Ashcroft	Y	Y	Y
Bond	Y	Y	Y
MONTANA			
Burns	Y	Y	Y
Baucus	Y	N	N
NEBRASKA			
Hagel	Y	Y	Y
Kerrey	Y	Y	N
NEVADA			
Bryan	Y	N	N
Reid	Y	N	N
NEW HAMPSHIRE			
Gregg	Y	Y	Y
Smith	Y	Y	Y
NEW JERSEY			
Lautenberg	Y	N	N
Torricelli	Y	N	N
NEW MEXICO			
Domenici	Y	Y	Y
Bingaman	Y	N	N
NEW YORK			
Moynihan	+	–	–
Schumer	Y	N	N
NORTH CAROLINA			
Helms	Y	Y	Y
Edwards	Y	N	N
NORTH DAKOTA			
Conrad	Y	N	N
Dorgan	Y	N	N
OHIO			
DeWine	Y	Y	Y
Voinovich	Y	Y	Y
OKLAHOMA			
Inhofe	Y	Y	Y
Nickles	Y	Y	Y
OREGON			
Smith	Y	Y	Y
Wyden	Y	N	N
PENNSYLVANIA			
Santorum	Y	Y	Y
Specter	Y	Y	N
RHODE ISLAND			
Chafee	Y	Y	Y
Reed	Y	N	N
SOUTH CAROLINA			
Thurmond	Y	Y	Y
Hollings	Y	N	N
SOUTH DAKOTA			
Daschle	Y	N	N
Johnson	Y	N	N
TENNESSEE			
Frist	Y	Y	Y
Thompson	Y	Y	Y
TEXAS			
Gramm	Y	Y	Y
Hutchison	Y	Y	Y
UTAH			
Bennett	Y	Y	Y
Hatch	Y	Y	Y
VERMONT			
Jeffords	Y	Y	Y
Leahy	Y	N	N
VIRGINIA			
Warner	?	Y	Y
Robb	Y	N	N
WASHINGTON			
Gorton	Y	Y	Y
Murray	Y	N	N
WEST VIRGINIA			
Byrd	Y	N	N
Rockefeller	Y	N	N
WISCONSIN			
Feingold	Y	N	N
Kohl	Y	N	N
WYOMING			
Enzi	Y	Y	Y
Thomas	Y	Y	Y

Key

- Y Voted for (yea).
- # Paired for.
- + Announced for.
- N Voted against (nay).
- X Paired against.
- – Announced against.
- P Voted "present."
- C Voted "present" to avoid possible conflict of interest.
- ? Did not vote or otherwise make a position known.

•

Democrats ***Republicans***
Independents

ND Northern Democrats SD Southern Democrats

Southern states - Ala., Ark., Fla., Ga., Ky., La., Miss., N.C., Okla., S.C., Tenn., Texas, Va.

82. H Con Res 68. Fiscal 2000 Budget Resolution/Motion To Instruct-Social Security. Lautenberg, D-N.J., motion to instruct conferees to insist that the conference report include provisions to reserve all Social Security surpluses only for Social Security and not for other programs, including other retirement programs, or tax cuts. Motion agreed to 98-0: R 54-0; D 44-0 (ND 36-0, SD 8-0). April 13, 1999.

83. H Con Res 68. Fiscal 2000 Budget Resolution/Motion To Instruct-Medicare. Domenici, R-N.M., motion to instruct conferees to insist that the conference report include Senate-approved provisions to urge Congress to consider the Breaux, D-La., recommendations to the National Bipartisan Commission on the Future of Medicare and to make budgetary accommodations for the use of non-Social Security surpluses to establish a Medicare prescription-drug benefit program. Motion agreed to 57-42: R 55-0; D 2-42 (ND 1-35, SD 1-7). April 13, 1999.

84. H Con Res 68. Fiscal 2000 Budget Resolution/Motion To Instruct-Medicare. Domenici, R-N.M., motion to table (kill) the Kennedy, D-Mass., motion to instruct conferees to insist that the conference report include provisions that would allow tax relief for low- and middle-income working families and would reserve a portion of non-Social Security budget surpluses to extend the solvency of Medicare before using surpluses to provide tax relief or to increase spending. Motion agreed to 54-45: R 54-1; D 0-44 (ND 0-36, SD 0-8). April 13, 1999.

Senate Votes 85, 86, 87

Key

- Y Voted for (yea).
- # Paired for.
- + Announced for.
- N Voted against (nay).
- X Paired against.
- – Announced against.
- P Voted "present."
- C Voted "present" to avoid possible conflict of interest.
- ? Did not vote or otherwise make a position known.

•

Democrats ***Republicans***
Independents

	85	86	87
ALABAMA			
Sessions	N	Y	Y
Shelby	N	Y	Y
ALASKA			
Murkowski	N	Y	Y
Stevens	N	Y	Y
ARIZONA			
Kyl	N	Y	Y
McCain	Y	Y	Y
ARKANSAS			
Hutchinson	Y	?	?
Lincoln	Y	N	Y
CALIFORNIA			
Boxer	Y	N	?
Feinstein	Y	N	Y
COLORADO			
Allard	N	Y	Y
Campbell	Y	Y	?
CONNECTICUT			
Dodd	Y	N	Y
Lieberman	Y	N	Y
DELAWARE			
Roth	N	Y	Y
Biden	Y	N	Y
FLORIDA			
Mack	N	Y	Y
Graham	Y	N	Y
GEORGIA			
Coverdell	Y	Y	Y
Cleland	Y	N	Y
HAWAII			
Akaka	Y	N	Y
Inouye	Y	N	Y
IDAHO			
Craig	N	Y	Y
Crapo	N	Y	Y
ILLINOIS			
Fitzgerald	Y	Y	Y
Durbin	Y	N	Y
INDIANA			
Bayh	Y	N	Y
Lugar	Y	Y	Y
IOWA			
Grassley	Y	Y	Y
Harkin	Y	N	Y
KANSAS			
Brownback	N	Y	Y
Roberts	Y	Y	Y
KENTUCKY			
Bunning	N	Y	Y
McConnell	N	Y	Y
LOUISIANA			
Breaux	Y	N	Y
Landrieu	Y	N	Y
MAINE			
Collins	Y	Y	Y
Snowe	Y	Y	Y
MARYLAND			
Mikulski	Y	N	Y
Sarbanes	Y	N	Y
MASSACHUSETTS			
Kennedy	Y	N	Y
Kerry	Y	N	Y
MICHIGAN			
Abraham	Y	Y	Y
Levin	Y	N	Y
MINNESOTA			
Grams	N	Y	Y
Wellstone	Y	N	Y
MISSISSIPPI			
Cochran	N	Y	Y
Lott	N	Y	Y
MISSOURI			
Ashcroft	N	Y	Y
Bond	N	Y	Y
MONTANA			
Burns	N	Y	Y
Baucus	Y	N	Y
NEBRASKA			
Hagel	N	Y	Y
Kerrey	Y	N	Y
NEVADA			
Bryan	Y	N	Y
Reid	Y	N	Y
NEW HAMPSHIRE			
Gregg	N	Y	Y
Smith	N	Y	Y
NEW JERSEY			
Lautenberg	Y	N	Y
Torricelli	Y	N	Y
NEW MEXICO			
Domenici	Y	Y	Y
Bingaman	Y	N	Y
NEW YORK			
Moynihan	+	–	+
Schumer	Y	N	Y
NORTH CAROLINA			
Helms	N	Y	Y
Edwards	Y	N	Y
NORTH DAKOTA			
Conrad	Y	N	Y
Dorgan	Y	N	Y
OHIO			
DeWine	Y	Y	Y
Voinovich	Y	Y	Y
OKLAHOMA			
Inhofe	N	Y	Y
Nickles	N	Y	Y
OREGON			
Smith	Y	Y	Y
Wyden	Y	N	Y
PENNSYLVANIA			
Santorum	N	Y	Y
Specter	Y	Y	Y
RHODE ISLAND			
Chafee	Y	Y	Y
Reed	Y	N	Y
SOUTH CAROLINA			
Thurmond	N	Y	Y
Hollings	Y	N	Y
SOUTH DAKOTA			
Daschle	Y	N	Y
Johnson	Y	N	Y
TENNESSEE			
Frist	Y	Y	Y
Thompson	N	Y	Y
TEXAS			
Gramm	N	Y	Y
Hutchison	Y	Y	Y
UTAH			
Bennett	N	Y	Y
Hatch	Y	Y	Y
VERMONT			
Jeffords	Y	Y	Y
Leahy	Y	N	+
VIRGINIA			
Warner	Y	Y	Y
Robb	Y	N	Y
WASHINGTON			
Gorton	N	Y	Y
Murray	Y	N	Y
WEST VIRGINIA			
Byrd	Y	N	Y
Rockefeller	Y	N	Y
WISCONSIN			
Feingold	Y	N	Y
Kohl	Y	N	Y
WYOMING			
Enzi	N	Y	Y
Thomas	N	Y	Y

ND Northern Democrats SD Southern Democrats

Southern states - Ala., Ark., Fla., Ga., Ky., La., Miss., N.C., Okla., S.C., Tenn., Texas, Va.

85. H Con Res 68. Fiscal 2000 Budget Resolution/Motion To Instruct-Child Care. Dodd, D-Conn., motion to instruct conferees to insist that the conference report include the Senate-adopted Dodd amendment, which would increase mandatory spending under the Child Care and Development Block Grant program by $5 billion over five years and offset the cost by reducing the tax cuts proposed by the budget resolution. Motion agreed to 66-33: R 22-33; D 44-0 (ND 36-0, SD 8-0). April 13, 1999.

86. H Con Res 68. Fiscal 2000 Budget Resolution/Conference Report. Adoption of the conference report on the concurrent resolution to set broad spending and revenue targets for the next 10 years. For fiscal 2000, the resolution provides for $536.3 billion in discretionary spending, $290 billion of which would go to defense. It calls for $142 billion in tax cuts over five years and $778 billion over 10 years. The resolution recommends that Social Security surpluses be used only for retirement security purposes or to pay down the debt. Adopted 54-44: R 54-0; D 0-44 (ND 0-36, SD 0-8). April 15, 1999.

87. HR 1376. Tax Benefits for Troops/Passage. Passage of the bill to allow U.S. military personnel currently serving in Yugoslavia to receive hazard pay tax-free. The measure also would allow military personnel, reporters and relief workers a 180-day extension on the filing of their 1998 tax returns beginning when they return from Yugoslavia, and it would exempt personnel from the 3 percent excise tax on long-distance telephone calls. Passed (thus cleared for the president) 95-0: R 53-0; D 42-0 (ND 34-0, SD 8-0). April 15, 1999.

Senate Votes 88, 89, 90

	88	89	90
ALABAMA			
Sessions	Y	Y	Y
Shelby	?	Y	Y
ALASKA			
Murkowski	Y	Y	Y
Stevens	Y	Y	Y
ARIZONA			
Kyl	Y	Y	Y
McCain	?	Y	Y
ARKANSAS			
Hutchinson	Y	Y	Y
Lincoln	Y	Y	N
CALIFORNIA			
Boxer	Y	Y	N
Feinstein	Y	Y	N
COLORADO			
Allard	Y	Y	Y
Campbell	Y	Y	Y
CONNECTICUT			
Dodd	Y	Y	N
Lieberman	Y	Y	N
DELAWARE			
Roth	Y	Y	N
Biden	?	Y	N
FLORIDA			
Mack	Y	Y	Y
Graham	Y	Y	N
GEORGIA			
Coverdell	Y	Y	Y
Cleland	Y	Y	N
HAWAII			
Akaka	Y	Y	N
Inouye	Y	Y	N
IDAHO			
Craig	Y	Y	Y
Crapo	Y	Y	Y
ILLINOIS			
Fitzgerald	Y	Y	Y
Durbin	Y	Y	N
INDIANA			
Bayh	Y	Y	N
Lugar	Y	Y	Y

	88	89	90
IOWA			
Grassley	Y	Y	Y
Harkin	Y	Y	N
KANSAS			
Brownback	Y	Y	Y
Roberts	Y	Y	Y
KENTUCKY			
Bunning	Y	Y	Y
McConnell	Y	Y	Y
LOUISIANA			
Breaux	Y	Y	N
Landrieu	Y	Y	N
MAINE			
Collins	Y	Y	Y
Snowe	Y	Y	Y
MARYLAND			
Mikulski	?	Y	N
Sarbanes	?	Y	N
MASSACHUSETTS			
Kennedy	Y	Y	N
Kerry	?	Y	N
MICHIGAN			
Abraham	Y	Y	Y
Levin	Y	Y	N
MINNESOTA			
Grams	Y	Y	Y
Wellstone	Y	N	N
MISSISSIPPI			
Cochran	Y	Y	Y
Lott	Y	Y	Y
MISSOURI			
Ashcroft	Y	Y	Y
Bond	Y	Y	Y
MONTANA			
Burns	Y	Y	Y
Baucus	Y	Y	N
NEBRASKA			
Hagel	Y	Y	Y
Kerrey	Y	Y	N
NEVADA			
Bryan	Y	Y	N
Reid	Y	Y	N

	88	89	90
NEW HAMPSHIRE			
Gregg	?	Y	Y
Smith	Y	Y	Y
NEW JERSEY			
Lautenberg	?	Y	N
Torricelli	?	Y	N
NEW MEXICO			
Domenici	Y	Y	Y
Bingaman	Y	Y	N
NEW YORK			
Moynihan	+	+	–
Schumer	Y	Y	N
NORTH CAROLINA			
Helms	Y	Y	Y
Edwards	Y	Y	N
NORTH DAKOTA			
Conrad	Y	Y	N
Dorgan	Y	Y	N
OHIO			
DeWine	Y	Y	Y
Voinovich	Y	Y	Y
OKLAHOMA			
Inhofe	Y	Y	Y
Nickles	Y	Y	Y
OREGON			
Smith	Y	Y	Y
Wyden	Y	Y	N
PENNSYLVANIA			
Santorum	Y	Y	Y
Specter	Y	Y	Y
RHODE ISLAND			
Chafee	Y	Y	Y
Reed	+	Y	N
SOUTH CAROLINA			
Thurmond	Y	Y	Y
Hollings	Y	Y	N
SOUTH DAKOTA			
Daschle	Y	Y	N
Johnson	Y	Y	N
TENNESSEE			
Frist	?	Y	Y
Thompson	Y	Y	Y

Key

Y Voted for (yea).
\# Paired for.
\+ Announced for.
N Voted against (nay).
X Paired against.
– Announced against.
P Voted "present."
C Voted "present" to avoid possible conflict of interest.
? Did not vote or otherwise make a position known.

Democrats ***Republicans***
Independents

	88	89	90
TEXAS			
Gramm	Y	Y	Y
Hutchison	Y	Y	Y
UTAH			
Bennett	?	Y	Y
Hatch	Y	Y	Y
VERMONT			
Jeffords	?	Y	Y
Leahy	Y	Y	N
VIRGINIA			
Warner	Y	Y	Y
Robb	Y	Y	N
WASHINGTON			
Gorton	Y	Y	Y
Murray	Y	Y	N
WEST VIRGINIA			
Byrd	Y	Y	N
Rockefeller	Y	Y	N
WISCONSIN			
Feingold	Y	Y	N
Kohl	Y	Y	N
WYOMING			
Enzi	Y	Y	Y
Thomas	Y	Y	Y

ND Northern Democrats SD Southern Democrats

Southern states - Ala., Ark., Fla., Ga., Ky., La., Miss., N.C., Okla., S.C., Tenn., Texas, Va.

88. S 531. Rosa Parks Gold Medal/Passage. Passage of the bill to authorize the president to award a Congressional Gold Medal to Rosa Parks in recognition of her contributions to the nation. Passed 86-0: R 49-0; D 37-0 (ND 29-0, SD 8-0). April 19, 1999.

89. HR 800. Educational Flexibility/Conference Report. Adoption of the conference report on the bill to expand the Educational Flexibility Partnership Program by making all 50 states (plus the District of Columbia, Puerto Rico and other U.S. territories) eligible to participate in the program, instead of only the 12 states permitted under existing law. Under the bill, participating states could waive certain requirements of federal education programs. The agreement does not include a Senate provision that would have allowed states to use money appropriated for reducing class size for special education programs instead. Adopted (thus cleared for the president) 98-1: R 55-0; D 43-1 (ND 35-1, SD 8-0). April 21, 1999.

90. S 557. Budget Procedures/Social Security "Lockbox"-Cloture. Motion to invoke cloture (thus limiting debate) on the Abraham, R-Mich., amendment that would create a Social Security "lockbox," establish declining limits on the public debt and create a Senate point of order against any provision that would exceed the debt limit. The underlying bill would establish a Senate point of order against any emergency spending items that do not meet specific criteria. Motion rejected 54-45: R 54-1; D 0-44 (ND 0-36, SD 0-8). April 22, 1999. Three-fifths of the total Senate (60) is required to invoke cloture.

Senate Votes 91, 92, 93, 94, 95

	91	92	93	94	95
ALABAMA					
Sessions	Y	Y	Y	Y	Y
Shelby	Y	Y	Y	Y	N
ALASKA					
Murkowski	?	Y	Y	Y	Y
Stevens	Y	Y	Y	Y	Y
ARIZONA					
Kyl	Y	Y	Y	Y	Y
McCain	Y	Y	Y	Y	Y
ARKANSAS					
Hutchinson	Y	Y	Y	Y	Y
Lincoln	Y	Y	Y	N	N
CALIFORNIA					
Boxer	?	Y	Y	N	N
Feinstein	Y	Y	Y	N	N
COLORADO					
Allard	Y	Y	Y	Y	Y
Campbell	Y	Y	Y	Y	Y
CONNECTICUT					
Dodd	Y	Y	Y	N	N
Lieberman	Y	Y	Y	N	N
DELAWARE					
Roth	Y	Y	Y	Y	Y
Biden	?	Y	Y	N	N
FLORIDA					
Mack	Y	Y	Y	Y	Y
Graham	Y	Y	Y	N	N
GEORGIA					
Coverdell	Y	Y	Y	Y	Y
Cleland	Y	Y	Y	N	N
HAWAII					
Akaka	Y	Y	Y	N	N
Inouye	Y	Y	Y	N	N
IDAHO					
Craig	Y	Y	Y	Y	Y
Crapo	Y	Y	Y	Y	Y
ILLINOIS					
Fitzgerald	Y	Y	Y	Y	Y
Durbin	Y	Y	Y	N	N
INDIANA					
Bayh	Y	Y	Y	N	N
Lugar	Y	Y	Y	Y	Y
IOWA					
Grassley	Y	Y	Y	Y	Y
Harkin	Y	Y	Y	N	N
KANSAS					
Brownback	Y	Y	Y	Y	Y
Roberts	Y	Y	Y	Y	Y
KENTUCKY					
Bunning	Y	Y	Y	Y	Y
McConnell	Y	Y	Y	Y	Y
LOUISIANA					
Breaux	Y	Y	N	N	N
Landrieu	Y	Y	Y	N	N
MAINE					
Collins	Y	Y	Y	Y	Y
Snowe	Y	Y	Y	Y	Y
MARYLAND					
Mikulski	Y	Y	Y	N	N
Sarbanes	Y	Y	Y	N	N
MASSACHUSETTS					
Kennedy	Y	Y	Y	N	N
Kerry	Y	Y	Y	N	N
MICHIGAN					
Abraham	Y	Y	Y	Y	Y
Levin	Y	Y	Y	N	N
MINNESOTA					
Grams	Y	Y	Y	Y	Y
Wellstone	Y	Y	Y	N	N
MISSISSIPPI					
Cochran	Y	Y	Y	Y	N
Lott	Y	Y	Y	Y	Y
MISSOURI					
Ashcroft	Y	Y	Y	Y	Y
Bond	Y	Y	Y	Y	Y
MONTANA					
Burns	Y	Y	Y	Y	Y
Baucus	Y	Y	Y	N	N
NEBRASKA					
Hagel	Y	Y	Y	Y	Y
Kerrey	Y	Y	Y	N	N
NEVADA					
Bryan	Y	Y	Y	N	N
Reid	Y	Y	Y	N	N
NEW HAMPSHIRE					
Gregg	Y	Y	Y	Y	Y
Smith	Y	Y	Y	Y	Y
NEW JERSEY					
Lautenberg	?	Y	Y	N	N
Torricelli	Y	Y	Y	N	N
NEW MEXICO					
Domenici	Y	Y	Y	Y	Y
Bingaman	Y	Y	Y	N	N
NEW YORK					
Moynihan	+	+	?	–	–
Schumer	Y	Y	Y	N	N
NORTH CAROLINA					
Helms	Y	Y	Y	Y	Y
Edwards	Y	Y	Y	N	N
NORTH DAKOTA					
Conrad	Y	Y	Y	N	N
Dorgan	Y	Y	Y	N	N
OHIO					
DeWine	Y	Y	Y	Y	Y
Voinovich	Y	Y	Y	Y	Y
OKLAHOMA					
Inhofe	Y	Y	Y	Y	Y
Nickles	Y	Y	Y	Y	Y
OREGON					
Smith	Y	Y	Y	Y	Y
Wyden	Y	Y	Y	N	N
PENNSYLVANIA					
Santorum	Y	Y	Y	Y	Y
Specter	Y	Y	Y	Y	N
RHODE ISLAND					
Chafee	Y	Y	Y	Y	Y
Reed	Y	Y	Y	N	N
SOUTH CAROLINA					
Thurmond	Y	Y	Y	Y	Y
Hollings	Y	Y	Y	N	N
SOUTH DAKOTA					
Daschle	Y	Y	Y	N	N
Johnson	Y	Y	Y	N	N
TENNESSEE					
Frist	Y	Y	Y	Y	Y
Thompson	Y	Y	Y	Y	Y
TEXAS					
Gramm	Y	Y	Y	Y	Y
Hutchison	?	Y	Y	Y	Y
UTAH					
Bennett	Y	Y	Y	Y	Y
Hatch	Y	Y	Y	Y	Y
VERMONT					
Jeffords	Y	Y	Y	Y	Y
Leahy	Y	Y	Y	N	N
VIRGINIA					
Warner	Y	Y	Y	Y	Y
Robb	Y	Y	Y	N	N
WASHINGTON					
Gorton	Y	Y	Y	Y	Y
Murray	Y	Y	Y	N	N
WEST VIRGINIA					
Byrd	Y	Y	Y	N	N
Rockefeller	Y	Y	Y	N	N
WISCONSIN					
Feingold	Y	Y	Y	N	N
Kohl	Y	Y	Y	N	N
WYOMING					
Enzi	Y	Y	Y	Y	Y
Thomas	Y	Y	Y	Y	Y

Key

- Y Voted for (yea).
- # Paired for.
- + Announced for.
- N Voted against (nay).
- X Paired against.
- – Announced against.
- P Voted "present."
- C Voted "present" to avoid possible conflict of interest.
- ? Did not vote or otherwise make a position known.

Democrats *Republicans*
Independents

ND Northern Democrats SD Southern Democrats

Southern states - Ala., Ark., Fla., Ga., Ky., La., Miss., N.C., Okla., S.C., Tenn., Texas, Va.

91. S 96. Y2K Liability Limits/Cloture. Motion to invoke cloture (thus limiting debate) on the motion to proceed to the bill that would cap at $250,000, or three times the amount of actual damages, whichever is greater, the liability of businesses from damage caused by so-called Year 2000 computer problems. Motion agreed to 94-0: R 53-0; D 41-0 (ND 33-0, SD 8-0). April 26, 1999. Three-fifths of the total Senate (60) is required to invoke cloture.

92. H Con Res 92. Colorado School Shootings/Adoption. Adoption of the concurrent resolution to condemn the April 20 shootings at Columbine High School in Littleton, Colo., and offer condolences to families and friends of those killed. The measure also would praise the work of law enforcement officials and encourage a national dialogue on preventing school violence. Adopted 99-0: R 55-0; D 44-0 (ND 36-0, SD 8-0). April 27, 1999.

93. Procedural Motion. Lott, R-Miss., motion to instruct the sergeant-at-arms to request the attendance of absent senators. Motion agreed to 98-1: R 55-0; D 43-1 (ND 36-0, SD 7-1). April 28, 1999.

94. S 96. Y2K Liability Limits/Minimum Wage Increase. Lott, R-Miss., motion to table (kill) the Kennedy, D-Mass., motion to commit the bill to the Senate Health, Education, Labor & Pensions Committee with instructions to report it back with an amendment to increase the minimum wage by $1 over two years, to $5.65 an hour beginning Sept. 1, 1999, and to $6.15 an hour beginning Sept. 1, 2000. Motion agreed to 55-44: R 55-0; D 0-44 (ND 0-36, SD 0-8). April 28, 1999.

95. S 96. Y2K Liability Limits/Cloture. Motion to invoke cloture (thus limiting debate) on the McCain, R-Ariz., substitute amendment that would cap at $250,000, or three times the amount of actual damages, whichever is greater, the liability of small businesses from damage caused by so-called Year 2000 computer problems, which will occur if computers mistake a two-digit code of "00" for 1900 instead of 2000. Motion rejected 52-47: R 52-3; D 0-44 (ND 0-36, SD 0-8). April 29, 1999. Three-fifths of the total Senate (60) is required to invoke cloture.

Senate Votes 96, 97, 98, 99, 100

	96	97	98	99	100
ALABAMA					
Sessions	Y	Y	Y	P	Y
Shelby	Y	Y	Y	Y	Y
ALASKA					
Murkowski	Y	Y	Y	Y	Y
Stevens	?	?	Y	Y	Y
ARIZONA					
Kyl	Y	Y	Y	Y	Y
McCain	?	?	N	Y	Y
ARKANSAS					
Hutchinson	Y	Y	Y	Y	Y
Lincoln	N	Y	Y	Y	N
CALIFORNIA					
Boxer	N	Y	Y	Y	N
Feinstein	N	Y	Y	Y	N
COLORADO					
Allard	Y	Y	Y	Y	Y
Campbell	Y	Y	Y	Y	Y
CONNECTICUT					
Dodd	N	Y	N	Y	N
Lieberman	N	Y	N	Y	N
DELAWARE					
Roth	N	Y	Y	Y	Y
Biden	N	Y	N	Y	N
FLORIDA					
Mack	Y	Y	N	Y	Y
Graham	N	Y	N	Y	N
GEORGIA					
Coverdell	Y	Y	Y	Y	Y
Cleland	N	Y	N	Y	N
HAWAII					
Akaka	N	Y	Y	Y	N
Inouye	N	Y	N	Y	N
IDAHO					
Craig	Y	Y	Y	Y	Y
Crapo	Y	Y	Y	Y	Y
ILLINOIS					
Fitzgerald	Y	Y	Y	P	P
Durbin	N	Y	Y	Y	N
INDIANA					
Bayh	N	Y	N	Y	N
Lugar	Y	Y	N	Y	Y
IOWA					
Grassley	Y	Y	Y	Y	Y
Harkin	?	?	Y	Y	N
KANSAS					
Brownback	Y	Y	Y	Y	Y
Roberts	Y	Y	Y	Y	Y
KENTUCKY					
Bunning	?	?	Y	Y	Y
McConnell	Y	Y	N	Y	Y
LOUISIANA					
Breaux	N	Y	Y	Y	N
Landrieu	N	Y	N	+	–
MAINE					
Collins	Y	Y	Y	Y	Y
Snowe	Y	Y	Y	Y	Y
MARYLAND					
Mikulski	N	Y	Y	Y	N
Sarbanes	N	Y	Y	Y	N
MASSACHUSETTS					
Kennedy	N	Y	Y	Y	N
Kerry	N	Y	N	Y	N
MICHIGAN					
Abraham	Y	Y	Y	Y	Y
Levin	N	Y	Y	Y	N
MINNESOTA					
Grams	Y	Y	Y	Y	Y
Wellstone	N	Y	Y	Y	N
MISSISSIPPI					
Cochran	Y	Y	N	Y	Y
Lott	Y	Y	Y	Y	Y
MISSOURI					
Ashcroft	Y	Y	Y	Y	Y
Bond	Y	Y	Y	Y	Y
MONTANA					
Burns	Y	Y	Y	Y	Y
Baucus	N	Y	Y	Y	N
NEBRASKA					
Hagel	Y	Y	N	Y	Y
Kerrey	N	Y	Y	Y	N
NEVADA					
Bryan	N	Y	N	Y	N
Reid	N	Y	Y	Y	N
NEW HAMPSHIRE					
Gregg	Y	Y	Y	Y	Y
Smith	Y	Y	Y	Y	Y
NEW JERSEY					
Lautenberg	N	Y	N	Y	N
Torricelli	N	Y	Y	Y	N
NEW MEXICO					
Domenici	Y	Y	Y	Y	Y
Bingaman	N	Y	Y	Y	N
NEW YORK					
Moynihan	–	+	Y	?	N
Schumer	N	Y	Y	Y	N
NORTH CAROLINA					
Helms	Y	Y	Y	P	Y
Edwards	N	Y	Y	Y	N
NORTH DAKOTA					
Conrad	N	Y	Y	Y	N
Dorgan	N	Y	Y	+	?
OHIO					
DeWine	Y	Y	N	Y	Y
Voinovich	Y	Y	Y	Y	Y
OKLAHOMA					
Inhofe	Y	Y	Y	Y	Y
Nickles	Y	Y	Y	Y	Y
OREGON					
Smith	Y	Y	N	Y	Y
Wyden	N	Y	Y	Y	N
PENNSYLVANIA					
Santorum	Y	Y	Y	Y	Y
Specter	Y	Y	Y	Y	Y
RHODE ISLAND					
Chafee	Y	Y	Y	Y	Y
Reed	N	Y	Y	Y	N
SOUTH CAROLINA					
Thurmond	Y	Y	Y	Y	Y
Hollings	N	Y	Y	Y	N
SOUTH DAKOTA					
Daschle	N	Y	Y	Y	N
Johnson	N	Y	Y	Y	N
TENNESSEE					
Frist	Y	Y	Y	Y	Y
Thompson	Y	Y	Y	Y	Y
TEXAS					
Gramm	?	?	Y	Y	Y
Hutchison	Y	Y	Y	Y	Y
UTAH					
Bennett	Y	Y	Y	Y	Y
Hatch	?	?	N	Y	Y
VERMONT					
Jeffords	Y	Y	Y	Y	Y
Leahy	N	Y	N	Y	N
VIRGINIA					
Warner	Y	Y	Y	P	Y
Robb	N	Y	N	Y	N
WASHINGTON					
Gorton	Y	Y	Y	Y	Y
Murray	N	Y	Y	Y	N
WEST VIRGINIA					
Byrd	N	Y	Y	Y	N
Rockefeller	N	Y	Y	Y	N
WISCONSIN					
Feingold	N	Y	Y	Y	N
Kohl	N	Y	Y	Y	N
WYOMING					
Enzi	Y	Y	Y	Y	Y
Thomas	Y	Y	Y	P	Y

Key

- Y Voted for (yea).
- # Paired for.
- + Announced for.
- N Voted against (nay).
- X Paired against.
- – Announced against.
- P Voted "present."
- C Voted "present" to avoid possible conflict of interest.
- ? Did not vote or otherwise make a position known.

•

Democrats ***Republicans***
Independents

ND Northern Democrats SD Southern Democrats

Southern states - Ala., Ark., Fla., Ga., Ky., La., Miss., N.C., Okla., S.C., Tenn., Texas, Va.

96. S 557. Budget Procedures/Social Security 'Lockbox'-Cloture. Motion to invoke cloture (thus limiting debate) on the Abraham, R-Mich., amendment that would create a Social Security "lockbox," establish declining limits on the public debt and create a Senate point of order against any provision that would exceed the debt limit. The underlying bill would establish a Senate point of order against any emergency spending items that do not meet specific criteria. Motion rejected 49-44: R 49-1; D 0-43 (ND 0-35, SD 0-8). April 30, 1999. Three-fifths of the total Senate (60) is required to invoke cloture.

97. S Res 33. Military Appreciation Month/Adoption. Adoption of the resolution that would designate May 1999 as National Military Appreciation Month. Adopted 93-0: R 50-0; D 43-0 (ND 35-0, SD 8-0). April 30, 1999.

98. S J Res 20. U.S. Troops in Kosovo/Motion To Table. Lott, R-Miss., motion to table (kill) the joint resolution that would authorize the president to "use all necessary force and other means," in concert with U.S. allies, to accomplish U.S. and NATO objectives in Yugoslavia. Motion agreed to 78-22: R 46-9; D 32-13 (ND 28-9, SD 4-4). May 4, 1999.

99. S Res 94. Commend Jesse Jackson/Adoption. Adoption of the resolution to commend Jesse Jackson for his successful efforts to gain release of three U.S. soldiers held by the Yugoslav government. Adopted 92-0: R 50-0; D 42-0 (ND 35-0, SD 7-0). May 5, 1999.

100. S 900. Financial Services Overhaul/Democratic Substitute. Gramm, R-Texas, motion to table (kill) the Sarbanes, D-Md., substitute amendment that would remove bill language to exempt small, non-urban banks from the 1977 Community Reinvestment Act (PL 95-128), would alter language to allow certain banks to organize non-bank financial services as subsidiaries and would expand provisions regulating unitary thrifts. Motion agreed to 54-43: R 54-0; D 0-43 (ND 0-36, SD 0-7). May 5, 1999. A "nay" was a vote in support of the president's position.

Senate Votes 101, 102, 103, 104, 105

State	Senator	101	102	103	104	105
ALABAMA	***Sessions***	Y	Y	N	Y	Y
	Shelby	Y	Y	N	N	Y
ALASKA	***Murkowski***	Y	Y	N	Y	Y
	Stevens	Y	Y	Y	Y	Y
ARIZONA	***Kyl***	Y	Y	Y	Y	Y
	McCain	Y	Y	Y	Y	Y
ARKANSAS	***Hutchinson***	Y	Y	N	Y	Y
	Lincoln	N	Y	N	N	N
CALIFORNIA	Boxer	N	Y	N	N	N
	Feinstein	N	Y	N	N	N
COLORADO	***Allard***	Y	Y	Y	Y	Y
	Campbell	Y	Y	Y	N	Y
CONNECTICUT	Dodd	N	Y	Y	N	N
	Lieberman	N	Y	Y	N	N
DELAWARE	***Roth***	Y	Y	Y	Y	Y
	Biden	N	?	N	N	N
FLORIDA	***Mack***	Y	N	Y	Y	Y
	Graham	N	Y	N	N	N
GEORGIA	***Coverdell***	Y	Y	Y	Y	Y
	Cleland	N	Y	N	N	N
HAWAII	Akaka	N	Y	Y	N	N
	Inouye	N	Y	Y	N	N
IDAHO	***Craig***	Y	Y	N	Y	Y
	Crapo	Y	Y	N	Y	Y
ILLINOIS	***Fitzgerald***	P	P	P	P	P
	Durbin	N	Y	N	N	N
INDIANA	Bayh	N	Y	N	N	N
	Lugar	Y	Y	Y	Y	Y
IOWA	***Grassley***	Y	Y	N	Y	Y
	Harkin	N	Y	N	N	N
KANSAS	***Brownback***	Y	?	N	Y	Y
	Roberts	Y	Y	N	Y	Y
KENTUCKY	***Bunning***	Y	Y	Y	Y	Y
	McConnell	Y	Y	Y	Y	Y
LOUISIANA	Breaux	N	Y	Y	N	N
	Landrieu	–	Y	N	N	N
MAINE	***Collins***	Y	Y	N	Y	Y
	Snowe	Y	Y	N	Y	Y
MARYLAND	Mikulski	N	Y	N	N	N
	Sarbanes	N	Y	N	N	N
MASSACHUSETTS	Kennedy	N	Y	N	N	N
	Kerry	N	Y	N	N	N
MICHIGAN	***Abraham***	Y	Y	N	Y	Y
	Levin	N	Y	N	N	N
MINNESOTA	***Grams***	Y	Y	N	N	Y
	Wellstone	N	Y	N	Y	N
MISSISSIPPI	***Cochran***	Y	Y	Y	N	Y
	Lott	Y	Y	Y	Y	Y
MISSOURI	***Ashcroft***	Y	Y	N	Y	Y
	Bond	Y	Y	N	Y	Y
MONTANA	***Burns***	Y	Y	N	Y	Y
	Baucus	N	Y	N	N	N
NEBRASKA	***Hagel***	Y	Y	Y	N	Y
	Kerrey	N	Y	N	N	N
NEVADA	Bryan	N	Y	N	N	N
	Reid	N	Y	N	N	N
NEW HAMPSHIRE	***Gregg***	Y	Y	N	Y	Y
	Smith	Y	Y	Y	Y	Y
NEW JERSEY	Lautenberg	–	Y	N	N	N
	Torricelli	N	Y	N	N	N
NEW MEXICO	***Domenici***	Y	Y	Y	Y	Y
	Bingaman	N	Y	N	N	N
NEW YORK	Moynihan	N	Y	N	Y	N
	Schumer	N	Y	N	Y	N
NORTH CAROLINA	***Helms***	Y	Y	N	Y	Y
	Edwards	N	Y	N	N	N
NORTH DAKOTA	Conrad	N	Y	N	N	N
	Dorgan	N	Y	N	Y	N
OHIO	***DeWine***	Y	Y	N	Y	Y
	Voinovich	Y	Y	N	Y	Y
OKLAHOMA	***Inhofe***	Y	Y	N	Y	?
	Nickles	Y	N	Y	Y	Y
OREGON	***Smith***	Y	Y	Y	Y	Y
	Wyden	N	Y	N	N	N
PENNSYLVANIA	***Santorum***	Y	Y	N	Y	Y
	Specter	N	Y	N	Y	Y
RHODE ISLAND	***Chafee***	Y	Y	Y	Y	Y
	Reed	N	Y	Y	N	N
SOUTH CAROLINA	***Thurmond***	Y	Y	N	Y	Y
	Hollings	N	Y	N	N	Y
SOUTH DAKOTA	Daschle	N	Y	N	N	N
	Johnson	N	Y	N	N	N
TENNESSEE	***Frist***	Y	Y	N	Y	Y
	Thompson	Y	Y	N	Y	Y
TEXAS	***Gramm***	Y	Y	Y	Y	Y
	Hutchison	Y	Y	N	Y	Y
UTAH	***Bennett***	Y	Y	Y	N	Y
	Hatch	Y	Y	N	N	Y
VERMONT	***Jeffords***	N	Y	N	Y	Y
	Leahy	N	Y	N	N	N
VIRGINIA	***Warner***	Y	Y	Y	Y	Y
	Robb	N	Y	Y	N	N
WASHINGTON	***Gorton***	Y	Y	Y	Y	Y
	Murray	N	Y	Y	N	N
WEST VIRGINIA	Byrd	N	Y	N	Y	N
	Rockefeller	N	Y	N	N	N
WISCONSIN	Feingold	N	Y	N	Y	N
	Kohl	N	Y	N	N	N
WYOMING	***Enzi***	Y	Y	Y	Y	Y
	Thomas	Y	Y	N	Y	Y

ND Northern Democrats SD Southern Democrats

Southern states - Ala., Ark., Fla., Ga., Ky., La., Miss., N.C., Okla., S.C., Tenn., Texas, Va.

Key

- Y Voted for (yea).
- # Paired for.
- \+ Announced for.
- N Voted against (nay).
- X Paired against.
- – Announced against.
- P Voted "present."
- C Voted "present" to avoid possible conflict of interest.
- ? Did not vote or otherwise make a position known.

•

Democrats ***Republicans***
Independents

101. S 900. Financial Services Overhaul/Community Reinvestment. Gramm, R-Texas, motion to table (kill) the Bryan, D-Nev., amendment that would strike bill language to exempt small, non-urban banks from the 1977 Community Reinvestment Act (CRA), which requires banks to document their efforts to invest in all segments of their communities, and language to establish that if a bank has been in compliance with the CRA for three years a challenging group must provide substantial evidence to support its claim against the bank. The amendment would replace the language with a requirement that all banks within a holding company have and maintain "satisfactory" CRA ratings as a condition for using new financial powers created by the bill. Motion agreed to 52-45: R 52-2; D 0-43 (ND 0-36, SD 0-7). May 5, 1999.

102. S 900. Financial Services Overhaul/FICO Assessment and Financial Privacy. Gramm, R-Texas, amendment to strike language in the bill that would extend for three years an expiring 1996 provision under which banks and thrifts are assessed at different rates to help pay interest on bonds that financed part of the thrift bailout in the 1980s. The amendment also would prohibit attempts to obtain consumer information from a financial institution under false pretenses or by fraudulent means. Adopted 95-2: R 51-2; D 44-0 (ND 36-0, SD 8-0). May 6, 1999.

103. S 900. Financial Services Overhaul/Unitary Thrifts. Gorton, R-Wash., motion to table (kill) the Johnson, D-S.D., amendment that would prohibit the sale of unitary thrifts to other commercial businesses. Motion rejected 32-67: R 24-30; D 8-37 (ND 6-31, SD 2-6). May 6, 1999. (Subsequently, the amendment was adopted by voice vote.)

104. S 900. Financial Services Overhaul/Regulatory Oversight. Gramm, R-Texas, motion to table (kill) the Shelby, R-Ala., amendment that would allow national banks to conduct non-bank financial activities either through subsidiaries or bank holding company affiliates. The bill would allow only small rural banks that option, while requiring larger banks to conduct such operations only through holding companies that are separate from bank operations. Motion agreed to 53-46: R 47-7; D 6-39 (ND 6-31, SD 0-8). May 6, 1999.

105. S 900. Financial Services Overhaul/Passage. Passage of the bill that would eliminate current barriers erected by the 1933 Glass-Steagall Act and other laws that impede affiliations between banking, securities, insurance and other firms. The bill also would exempt small, non-urban banks from the 1977 Community Reinvestment Act (CRA), revise the Federal Home Loan Bank system and require that owners of automated teller machines (ATMs) provide notice on the ATM and on-screen of any charges imposed for the use of the terminal. Passed 54-44: R 53-0; D 1-44 (ND 0-37, SD 1-7). May 6, 1999. A "nay" was a vote in support of the president's position.

Senate Votes 106, 107, 108, 109, 110, 111

	106	107	108	109	110	111
ALABAMA						
Sessions	Y	Y	Y	Y	Y	Y
Shelby	Y	Y	Y	Y	Y	Y
ALASKA						
Murkowski	Y	Y	Y	Y	Y	Y
Stevens	Y	Y	Y	Y	Y	Y
ARIZONA						
Kyl	Y	Y	N	Y	Y	Y
McCain	Y	Y	Y	Y	Y	Y
ARKANSAS						
Hutchinson	Y	Y	Y	Y	Y	Y
Lincoln	Y	N	Y	N	Y	N
CALIFORNIA						
Boxer	Y	N	Y	N	Y	N
Feinstein	Y	N	Y	N	Y	N
COLORADO						
Allard	Y	Y	Y	Y	Y	Y
Campbell	Y	Y	Y	Y	Y	Y
CONNECTICUT						
Dodd	Y	N	Y	N	Y	N
Lieberman	Y	N	Y	N	Y	N
DELAWARE						
Roth	Y	Y	Y	Y	Y	Y
Biden	Y	N	Y	N	Y	N
FLORIDA						
Mack	Y	Y	Y	Y	Y	Y
Graham	Y	N	Y	N	Y	N
GEORGIA						
Coverdell	Y	Y	Y	Y	Y	Y
Cleland	Y	N	Y	N	Y	Y
HAWAII						
Akaka	Y	N	Y	N	Y	N
Inouye	Y	N	Y	N	?	?
IDAHO						
Craig	Y	Y	Y	Y	Y	Y
Crapo	Y	Y	Y	Y	Y	Y
ILLINOIS						
Fitzgerald	Y	Y	Y	Y	Y	N
Durbin	Y	N	Y	N	Y	N
INDIANA						
Bayh	Y	N	Y	N	Y	N
Lugar	Y	Y	Y	Y	Y	N
IOWA						
Grassley	Y	Y	Y	Y	Y	Y
Harkin	Y	N	Y	N	Y	N
KANSAS						
Brownback	Y	Y	Y	Y	Y	Y
Roberts	Y	Y	Y	Y	Y	Y
KENTUCKY						
Bunning	Y	Y	Y	Y	Y	Y
McConnell	Y	Y	Y	Y	Y	Y
LOUISIANA						
Breaux	Y	N	Y	N	Y	N
Landrieu	Y	N	Y	N	Y	N
MAINE						
Collins	Y	Y	Y	Y	Y	Y
Snowe	Y	Y	Y	Y	Y	Y
MARYLAND						
Mikulski	Y	N	Y	N	Y	N
Sarbanes	Y	N	Y	N	Y	N
MASSACHUSETTS						
Kennedy	Y	N	Y	N	Y	N
Kerry	Y	N	Y	N	Y	N
MICHIGAN						
Abraham	Y	Y	Y	Y	Y	Y
Levin	Y	N	Y	N	Y	N
MINNESOTA						
Grams	Y	Y	Y	Y	Y	Y
Wellstone	Y	N	Y	N	Y	N
MISSISSIPPI						
Cochran	Y	Y	Y	?	Y	Y
Lott	Y	Y	Y	Y	Y	Y
MISSOURI						
Ashcroft	Y	Y	Y	Y	Y	Y
Bond	Y	Y	Y	Y	Y	Y
MONTANA						
Burns	Y	Y	Y	Y	Y	Y
Baucus	Y	N	Y	N	Y	Y
NEBRASKA						
Hagel	Y	Y	Y	Y	Y	Y
Kerrey	Y	N	Y	N	Y	N
NEVADA						
Bryan	Y	N	Y	N	Y	N
Reid	Y	N	Y	N	Y	N
NEW HAMPSHIRE						
Gregg	Y	Y	Y	Y	Y	Y
Smith	Y	Y	Y	Y	Y	Y
NEW JERSEY						
Lautenberg	Y	N	Y	N	Y	N
Torricelli	Y	N	Y	N	Y	N
NEW MEXICO						
Domenici	Y	Y	Y	Y	Y	Y
Bingaman	Y	N	Y	N	Y	N
NEW YORK						
Moynihan	+	–	+	–	+	–
Schumer	Y	N	Y	N	Y	N
NORTH CAROLINA						
Helms	Y	Y	Y	Y	Y	Y
Edwards	Y	N	Y	N	Y	N
NORTH DAKOTA						
Conrad	Y	N	Y	N	Y	N
Dorgan	Y	N	Y	N	Y	N
OHIO						
DeWine	Y	Y	Y	Y	Y	N
Voinovich	N	Y	N	Y	Y	N
OKLAHOMA						
Inhofe	N	Y	Y	Y	Y	Y
Nickles	N	Y	Y	Y	Y	Y
OREGON						
Smith	Y	Y	Y	Y	Y	Y
Wyden	Y	N	Y	N	Y	N
PENNSYLVANIA						
Santorum	Y	Y	Y	Y	Y	Y
Specter	Y	Y	Y	Y	Y	Y
RHODE ISLAND						
Chafee	Y	Y	Y	Y	Y	N
Reed	Y	N	Y	N	Y	N
SOUTH CAROLINA						
Thurmond	Y	Y	Y	Y	Y	Y
Hollings	Y	N	Y	N	Y	N
SOUTH DAKOTA						
Daschle	Y	N	Y	N	Y	N
Johnson	Y	N	Y	N	Y	N
TENNESSEE						
Frist	Y	Y	Y	Y	Y	Y
Thompson	N	Y	N	Y	Y	Y
TEXAS						
Gramm	Y	Y	Y	Y	Y	Y
Hutchison	Y	Y	Y	Y	Y	Y
UTAH						
Bennett	Y	Y	Y	Y	Y	Y
Hatch	Y	Y	Y	Y	Y	Y
VERMONT						
Jeffords	Y	Y	Y	Y	Y	Y
Leahy	Y	N	Y	N	Y	N
VIRGINIA						
Warner	Y	Y	Y	Y	Y	N
Robb	Y	N	Y	N	Y	N
WASHINGTON						
Gorton	Y	Y	Y	Y	Y	Y
Murray	Y	N	Y	N	Y	N
WEST VIRGINIA						
Byrd	Y	N	Y	N	Y	N
Rockefeller	Y	N	Y	N	Y	N
WISCONSIN						
Feingold	Y	N	Y	N	Y	N
Kohl	Y	N	Y	N	Y	N
WYOMING						
Enzi	Y	Y	Y	Y	Y	Y
Thomas	N	Y	Y	Y	Y	Y

ND Northern Democrats SD Southern Democrats

Southern states - Ala., Ark., Fla., Ga., Ky., La., Miss., N.C., Okla., S.C., Tenn., Texas, Va.

Key

- Y Voted for (yea).
- # Paired for.
- \+ Announced for.
- N Voted against (nay).
- X Paired against.
- – Announced against.
- P Voted "present."
- C Voted "present" to avoid possible conflict of interest.
- ? Did not vote or otherwise make a position known.

Democrats ***Republicans***
Independents

106. S 254. Juvenile Crime/School Safety Grants. Gregg, R-N.H., amendment to the Hatch, R-Utah, amendment. The Gregg amendment would authorize $200 million in fiscal 2000, and additional funding in the four following years, for grants to local education and law enforcement agencies to implement school violence prevention and school safety programs. Adopted 94-5: R 50-5; D 44-0 (ND 36-0, SD 8-0). May 11, 1999.

107. S 254. Juvenile Crime/National Center for School Safety. Hatch, R-Utah, motion to table (kill) the Robb, D-Va., amendment to the Hatch amendment. The Robb amendment would authorize funding for a National Resource Center for School Safety and Youth Violence Prevention to support local education and law enforcement agencies. The amendment also would authorize funding for youth mental health programs and substance abuse and treatment programs. Motion agreed to 55-44: R 55-0; D 0-44 (ND 0-36, SD 0-8). May 11, 1999.

108. S 254. Juvenile Crime/Prevention Program Funding. Hatch, R-Utah, amendment to designate increased funding for prevention programs, such as drug treatment, school counseling and after-school programs. The amendment also would authorize a $50 million grant to states to hire prosecutors to prosecute juvenile offenders and would reauthorize the Violent Crime Reduction Trust Fund through fiscal 2005. Adopted 96-3: R 52-3; D 44-0 (ND 36-0, SD 8-0). May 11, 1999.

109. S 254. Juvenile Crime/Democratic Law Enforcement Amendment. Hatch, R-Utah, motion to table (kill) the Leahy, D-Vt., amendment that would increase authorization funding for law enforcement activities such as the Community Oriented Policing Services (COPS) program, increase penalties for drug sales to children and prohibit the transfer of assault weapons and high-capacity ammunition clips to juveniles. Motion agreed to 54-44: R 54-0; D 0-44 (ND 0-36, SD 0-8). May 12, 1999.

110. S 254. Juvenile Crime/Entertainment Industry Antitrust Exemption. Brownback, R-Kan., amendment that would provide a limited antitrust exemption to the entertainment industry to enable it to develop and disseminate voluntary code of conduct guidelines for television programs, video games, Internet content, movies and music. It also would require the Federal Trade Commission and the Justice Department to study whether the motion picture industry, recording industry and video game industry use violence or sex to market their products to minors and require the National Institutes of Health to study the impact of violent music, movies and video games on child development and youth violence. Adopted 98-0: R 55-0; D 43-0 (ND 35-0, SD 8-0). May 12, 1999.

111. S 254. Juvenile Crime/Gun Show Background Checks. Hatch, R-Utah, motion to table (kill) the Lautenberg, D-N.J., amendment that would require that all gun sales taking place at a gun show occur through a federally licensed gun dealer after the dealer has conducted a background check on the purchaser. It also would require that anyone planning, promoting or operating a gun show notify the Treasury Department, pay a fee and provide an updated list of all vendors. Motion agreed to 51-47: R 49-6; D 2-41 (ND 1-34, SD 1-7). May 12, 1999.

Senate Votes 112, 113, 114, 115, 116, 117

	112	113	114	115	116	117
ALABAMA						
Sessions	Y	Y	N	Y	N	N
Shelby	Y	Y	Y	Y	Y	N
ALASKA						
Murkowski	Y	Y	Y	Y	Y	N
Stevens	Y	Y	N	Y	Y	N
ARIZONA						
Kyl	Y	Y	Y	Y	Y	N
McCain	Y	Y	Y	Y	Y	N
ARKANSAS						
Hutchinson	Y	Y	Y	Y	N	N
Lincoln	N	Y	N	Y	N	N
CALIFORNIA						
Boxer	N	Y	Y	Y	N	N
Feinstein	N	Y	N	Y	N	N
COLORADO						
Allard	Y	Y	Y	Y	Y	N
Campbell	Y	Y	Y	Y	Y	N
CONNECTICUT						
Dodd	N	Y	Y	Y	N	N
Lieberman	N	Y	N	Y	N	N
DELAWARE						
Roth	N	Y	Y	Y	N	N
Biden	N	Y	N	Y	N	N
FLORIDA						
Mack	Y	Y	Y	Y	Y	N
Graham	N	Y	N	Y	N	N
GEORGIA						
Coverdell	Y	Y	N	Y	N	N
Cleland	Y	Y	Y	Y	N	N
HAWAII						
Akaka	N	Y	N	Y	N	N
Inouye	?	Y	?	?	?	?
IDAHO						
Craig	Y	Y	Y	Y	Y	N
Crapo	Y	Y	Y	Y	Y	N
ILLINOIS						
Fitzgerald	N	Y	Y	Y	N	N
Durbin	N	Y	N	Y	N	N
INDIANA						
Bayh	N	Y	Y	Y	N	N
Lugar	Y	Y	Y	Y	N	N
IOWA						
Grassley	Y	Y	N	Y	N	N
Harkin	N	Y	N	Y	N	N
KANSAS						
Brownback	Y	Y	Y	Y	Y	N
Roberts	Y	Y	Y	Y	Y	N
KENTUCKY						
Bunning	Y	Y	Y	Y	Y	N
McConnell	Y	Y	Y	Y	Y	N
LOUISIANA						
Breaux	N	Y	Y	Y	Y	N
Landrieu	N	Y	N	Y	N	N
MAINE						
Collins	Y	Y	Y	Y	N	N
Snowe	Y	Y	N	Y	Y	N
MARYLAND						
Mikulski	N	Y	N	Y	N	N
Sarbanes	N	Y	N	Y	N	N
MASSACHUSETTS						
Kennedy	N	Y	Y	Y	N	N
Kerry	N	Y	Y	Y	N	N
MICHIGAN						
Abraham	Y	Y	N	Y	N	N
Levin	N	Y	Y	Y	N	N
MINNESOTA						
Grams	Y	Y	Y	Y	Y	N
Wellstone	N	Y	N	Y	N	N
MISSISSIPPI						
Cochran	Y	Y	Y	Y	Y	N
Lott	Y	Y	Y	Y	Y	N
MISSOURI						
Ashcroft	Y	Y	N	Y	Y	N
Bond	Y	Y	N	Y	Y	N
MONTANA						
Burns	Y	Y	Y	Y	Y	N
Baucus	N	Y	Y	Y	Y	N
NEBRASKA						
Hagel	Y	Y	Y	Y	Y	N
Kerrey	N	Y	Y	Y	N	N
NEVADA						
Bryan	N	Y	N	Y	N	N
Reid	N	Y	N	Y	N	N
NEW HAMPSHIRE						
Gregg	Y	Y	N	Y	N	N
Smith	Y	Y	Y	N	Y	Y
NEW JERSEY						
Lautenberg	N	Y	N	Y	N	N
Torricelli	N	Y	Y	Y	N	N
NEW MEXICO						
Domenici	Y	Y	Y	Y	N	N
Bingaman	N	Y	N	Y	Y	N
NEW YORK						
Moynihan	–	Y	Y	+	–	–
Schumer	N	Y	Y	Y	N	N
NORTH CAROLINA						
Helms	Y	Y	N	Y	Y	N
Edwards	N	Y	N	Y	N	N
NORTH DAKOTA						
Conrad	N	Y	N	Y	N	N
Dorgan	N	Y	N	Y	N	N
OHIO						
DeWine	Y	Y	N	Y	N	N
Voinovich	Y	Y	Y	Y	N	N
OKLAHOMA						
Inhofe	Y	Y	Y	Y	Y	Y
Nickles	Y	Y	Y	Y	N	N
OREGON						
Smith	Y	Y	Y	Y	N	N
Wyden	N	Y	N	Y	N	N
PENNSYLVANIA						
Santorum	Y	Y	Y	Y	Y	N
Specter	Y	Y	Y	Y	Y	N
RHODE ISLAND						
Chafee	N	Y	Y	Y	N	N
Reed	N	Y	Y	Y	N	N
SOUTH CAROLINA						
Thurmond	Y	Y	N	Y	Y	N
Hollings	N	Y	N	Y	N	N
SOUTH DAKOTA						
Daschle	N	Y	Y	Y	N	N
Johnson	N	Y	N	Y	N	N
TENNESSEE						
Frist	Y	Y	Y	Y	N	N
Thompson	Y	Y	Y	Y	Y	N
TEXAS						
Gramm	Y	Y	Y	Y	Y	N
Hutchison	Y	Y	N	Y	Y	N
UTAH						
Bennett	Y	Y	Y	Y	N	N
Hatch	Y	Y	Y	Y	Y	N
VERMONT						
Jeffords	Y	Y	Y	Y	N	N
Leahy	N	Y	Y	Y	Y	N
VIRGINIA						
Warner	Y	Y	N	Y	N	N
Robb	N	Y	Y	Y	N	N
WASHINGTON						
Gorton	Y	Y	Y	Y	Y	N
Murray	N	Y	Y	Y	N	N
WEST VIRGINIA						
Byrd	N	Y	N	Y	N	N
Rockefeller	N	Y	N	Y	N	N
WISCONSIN						
Feingold	N	Y	Y	Y	N	N
Kohl	N	Y	N	Y	N	?
WYOMING						
Enzi	Y	Y	Y	N	Y	Y
Thomas	Y	Y	Y	Y	Y	N

ND Northern Democrats SD Southern Democrats

Southern states - Ala., Ark., Fla., Ga., Ky., La., Miss., N.C., Okla., S.C., Tenn., Texas, Va.

Key

- Y Voted for (yea).
- # Paired for.
- + Announced for.
- N Voted against (nay).
- X Paired against.
- – Announced against.
- P Voted "present."
- C Voted "present" to avoid possible conflict of interest.
- ? Did not vote or otherwise make a position known.

Democrats **•** ***Republicans*** *Independents*

112. S 254. Juvenile Crime/Voluntary Gun Show Background Checks. Craig, R-Idaho, amendment that would allow private gun sellers to access the national instant background check system to check the background of purchasers at gun shows. It also would provide civil liability immunity for certain future federal firearm violations. Adopted 53-45: R 52-3; D 1-42 (ND 0-35, SD 1-7). May 12, 1999.

113. S 254. Juvenile Crime/Internet Filtering. Hatch, R-Utah, amendment to require Internet service providers with more than 50,000 subscribers to provide to each customer computer software or other filtering technology to allow the subscriber to prevent minors from accessing unsuitable material. The technology would have to be provided either free or at cost. Adopted 100-0: R 55-0; D 45-0 (ND 37-0, SD 8-0). May 13, 1999.

114. S 254. Juvenile Crime/Violent Programming Restrictions. Hatch, R-Utah, motion to table (kill) the Hollings, D-S.C., amendment that would prohibit distribution of violent video programming to the public during hours when children are likely to make up a "substantial portion" of the audience. It would require the Federal Communications Commission to define violent programming and the appropriate hours and to issue regulations within nine months of enactment. Motion agreed to 60-39: R 41-14; D 19-25 (ND 16-20, SD 3-5). May 13, 1999.

115. S 254. Juvenile Crime/Youth Firearm Possession. Ashcroft, R-Mo., amendment to prohibit anyone under age 18 from possessing assault weapons or large capacity ammunition clips and increase penalties for juveniles caught with such weapons and individuals who transfer any weapon to a juvenile. Adopted 96-2: R 53-2; D 43-0 (ND 35-0, SD 8-0). May 13, 1999.

116. S 254. Juvenile Crime/Importation of Weapons. Smith, R-N.H., motion to table (kill) the Feinstein, D-Calif., amendment that would prohibit the importation of large-capacity ammunition feeding devices. Motion rejected 39-59: R 35-20; D 4-39 (ND 3-32, SD 1-7). May 13, 1999. (Subsequently, the Feinstein amendment was adopted by voice vote.)

117. S 254. Juvenile Crime/Republican Gun Proposals. McCain, R-Ariz., motion to table (kill) the Hatch, R-Utah, amendment that would increase mandatory minimum and maximum penalties for the illegal transfer or use of firearms, authorize funding for the hiring of additional prosecutors to prosecute drug cases and require anyone who attends a gun show with the intent of selling a firearm to obtain a background check on purchasers. Motion rejected 3-94: R 3-52; D 0-42 (ND 0-34, SD 0-8). May 13, 1999.

Senate Votes 118, 119, 120, 121, 122, 123, 124, 125

	118	119	120	121	122	123	124	125
ALABAMA								
Sessions	Y	Y	Y	Y	N	Y	Y	Y
Shelby	Y	Y	N	Y	N	Y	Y	Y
ALASKA								
Murkowski	Y	Y	Y	Y	Y	Y	Y	Y
Stevens	Y	Y	Y	Y	Y	Y	Y	Y
ARIZONA								
Kyl	Y	Y	Y	Y	Y	Y	Y	Y
McCain	Y	N	Y	Y	Y	Y	P	Y
ARKANSAS								
Hutchinson	Y	Y	Y	Y	Y	Y	Y	Y
Lincoln	N	Y	N	Y	Y	Y	Y	N
CALIFORNIA								
Boxer	N	N	N	N	Y	Y	N	N
Feinstein	N	N	N	Y	Y	Y	N	N
COLORADO								
Allard	Y	Y	Y	Y	N	Y	N	Y
Campbell	Y	Y	Y	Y	Y	Y	N	Y
CONNECTICUT								
Dodd	–	–	N	Y	Y	N	Y	N
Lieberman	N	N	N	Y	Y	Y	Y	N
DELAWARE								
Roth	Y	Y	Y	Y	Y	Y	N	Y
Biden	N	N	N	Y	Y	N	Y	N
FLORIDA								
Mack	Y	?	Y	Y	N	Y	N	Y
Graham	N	N	N	Y	Y	Y	Y	N
GEORGIA								
Coverdell	Y	Y	Y	Y	N	Y	Y	Y
Cleland	N	N	N	Y	Y	Y	Y	N
HAWAII								
Akaka	N	N	N	Y	Y	Y	Y	N
Inouye	?	?	N	Y	Y	N	Y	N
IDAHO								
Craig	Y	Y	Y	Y	N	Y	Y	Y
Crapo	Y	Y	Y	Y	N	Y	Y	Y
ILLINOIS								
Fitzgerald	N	N	Y	Y	Y	Y	Y	Y
Durbin	N	N	N	N	Y	Y	Y	N
INDIANA								
Bayh	N	Y	N	Y	Y	Y	N	N
Lugar	Y	N	Y	Y	Y	Y	Y	Y
IOWA								
Grassley	Y	Y	Y	Y	Y	Y	Y	Y
Harkin	N	N	N	N	Y	N	Y	N
KANSAS								
Brownback	Y	Y	?	?	?	?	?	Y
Roberts	Y	Y	Y	Y	Y	Y	Y	Y
KENTUCKY								
Bunning	Y	Y	Y	Y	N	Y	Y	Y
McConnell	Y	Y	Y	Y	Y	Y	Y	Y
LOUISIANA								
Breaux	?	?	N	Y	Y	Y	Y	N
Landrieu	N	Y	N	Y	Y	Y	N	N
MAINE								
Collins	Y	Y	Y	Y	Y	Y	N	Y
Snowe	Y	Y	Y	Y	Y	Y	Y	N
MARYLAND								
Mikulski	N	N	N	Y	Y	Y	Y	N
Sarbanes	N	N	N	Y	Y	Y	Y	N
MASSACHUSETTS								
Kennedy	N	N	N	Y	Y	N	Y	N
Kerry	N	N	N	Y	Y	Y	Y	N
MICHIGAN								
Abraham	Y	Y	Y	Y	Y	Y	Y	Y
Levin	N	N	N	N	Y	N	Y	N
MINNESOTA								
Grams	Y	Y	Y	Y	N	Y	Y	Y
Wellstone	N	N	N	N	Y	N	Y	N
MISSISSIPPI								
Cochran	Y	Y	Y	Y	Y	Y	Y	Y
Lott	Y	Y	Y	Y	Y	Y	Y	Y
MISSOURI								
Ashcroft	Y	Y	Y	Y	N	Y	Y	Y
Bond	Y	Y	Y	Y	N	Y	N	Y
MONTANA								
Burns	Y	Y	Y	Y	N	Y	Y	Y
Baucus	N	N	N	Y	Y	Y	Y	N
NEBRASKA								
Hagel	Y	Y	Y	Y	Y	Y	Y	Y
Kerrey	N	N	N	N	Y	Y	N	N
NEVADA								
Bryan	N	N	N	Y	Y	Y	Y	N
Reid	N	N	N	Y	Y	Y	Y	N
NEW HAMPSHIRE								
Gregg	Y	Y	Y	Y	Y	Y	Y	Y
Smith	N	Y	Y	Y	N	Y	Y	Y
NEW JERSEY								
Lautenberg	N	N	N	N	Y	N	Y	N
Torricelli	N	N	N	Y	Y	Y	N	N
NEW MEXICO								
Domenici	Y	Y	Y	Y	Y	Y	Y	Y
Bingaman	N	Y	N	N	Y	Y	N	N
NEW YORK								
Moynihan	–	–	–	–	+	+	–	–
Schumer	N	N	N	Y	Y	Y	Y	N
NORTH CAROLINA								
Helms	Y	Y	Y	Y	N	Y	Y	Y
Edwards	N	Y	N	Y	Y	Y	Y	N
NORTH DAKOTA								
Conrad	N	N	N	Y	Y	N	Y	N
Dorgan	N	N	N	Y	Y	N	Y	N
OHIO								
DeWine	Y	N	Y	Y	Y	Y	Y	Y
Voinovich	Y	N	Y	Y	Y	Y	Y	Y
OKLAHOMA								
Inhofe	?	?	Y	Y	N	Y	Y	Y
Nickles	Y	Y	Y	Y	N	Y	Y	Y
OREGON								
Smith	Y	Y	Y	Y	Y	Y	Y	Y
Wyden	N	N	N	Y	Y	Y	Y	N
PENNSYLVANIA								
Santorum	Y	Y	Y	Y	Y	Y	Y	Y
Specter	Y	Y	Y	Y	Y	Y	Y	Y
RHODE ISLAND								
Chafee	N	N	Y	Y	Y	Y	N	Y
Reed	N	N	N	N	Y	Y	N	N
SOUTH CAROLINA								
Thurmond	Y	Y	Y	Y	Y	Y	Y	Y
Hollings	N	N	N	N	Y	Y	Y	Y
SOUTH DAKOTA								
Daschle	N	N	N	Y	Y	Y	Y	N
Johnson	N	N	N	Y	Y	Y	Y	N
TENNESSEE								
Frist	Y	Y	Y	Y	Y	Y	Y	Y
Thompson	N	Y	Y	Y	N	N	Y	Y
TEXAS								
Gramm	Y	Y	Y	Y	N	Y	Y	Y
Hutchison	Y	Y	Y	Y	Y	Y	Y	Y
UTAH								
Bennett	Y	?	Y	Y	Y	Y	Y	Y
Hatch	Y	Y	Y	Y	Y	Y	Y	Y
VERMONT								
Jeffords	Y	Y	Y	Y	Y	Y	Y	Y
Leahy	N	N	N	N	Y	Y	N	N
VIRGINIA								
Warner	N	N	Y	Y	Y	Y	Y	Y
Robb	N	N	N	Y	Y	Y	Y	N
WASHINGTON								
Gorton	Y	Y	Y	Y	Y	Y	Y	Y
Murray	N	N	N	N	Y	N	N	N
WEST VIRGINIA								
Byrd	Y	N	N	Y	Y	Y	Y	N
Rockefeller	N	N	N	Y	Y	Y	Y	N
WISCONSIN								
Feingold	N	N	N	N	Y	N	Y	N
Kohl	N	N	N	Y	Y	Y	Y	N
WYOMING								
Enzi	N	Y	Y	Y	N	Y	Y	Y
Thomas	N	Y	Y	Y	N	Y	Y	Y

ND Northern Democrats SD Southern Democrats

Southern states - Ala., Ark., Fla., Ga., Ky., La., Miss., N.C., Okla., S.C., Tenn., Texas, Va.

Key

- Y Voted for (yea).
- # Paired for.
- + Announced for.
- N Voted against (nay).
- X Paired against.
- – Announced against.
- P Voted "present."
- C Voted "present" to avoid possible conflict of interest.
- ? Did not vote or otherwise make a position known.

Democrats ***Republicans***
Independents

118. S 254. Juvenile Crime/Republican Gun Proposals. Hatch, R-Utah, amendment that would increase mandatory minimum and maximum penalties for the illegal transfer or use of firearms, authorize funding to hire additional prosecutors to prosecute drug cases and require anyone who attends a gun show with the intent of selling a firearm to obtain a background check on purchasers. Adopted 48-47: R 47-7; D 1-40 (ND 1-33, SD 0-7). May 14, 1999.

119. S 254. Juvenile Crime/Internet Transfers. Hatch, R-Utah, motion to table (kill) the Schumer, D-N.Y., amendment that would allow only federally licensed and registered gun dealers to operate Internet Web sites designed to sell 10 or more guns. Motion agreed to 50-43: R 45-7; D 5-36 (ND 2-32, SD 3-4). May 14, 1999.

120. S 96. Y2K Liability Limits/Cloture. Motion to invoke cloture (thus limiting debate) on the motion to proceed to the bill that would cap at $250,000, or three times the amount of actual damages, whichever is greater, the liability of businesses from damage caused by so-called year 2000 computer problems, which will occur if computers mistake a two-digit code of "00" for 1900 instead of 2000. Motion rejected 53-45: R 53-1; D 0-44 (ND 0-36, SD 0-8). May 18, 1999. Three-fifths of the total Senate (60) is required to invoke cloture.

121. S 254. Juvenile Crime/School Memorials. Allard, R-Colo., amendment to state that Congress finds that it is not a violation of the First Amendment to include prayers or religious symbols in memorials or memorial services held at a public school to honor victims slain on the school campus. Adopted 85-13: R 54-0; D 31-13 (ND 24-12, SD 7-1). May 18, 1999.

122. S 254. Juvenile Crime/Handgun Safety Locks. Kohl, D-Wis., amendment that would prohibit the sale or transfer of handguns unless a secure gun storage or safety device is provided for each handgun. It also would provide civil liability exemptions for individuals who legally possess a handgun and use a secure gun storage or safety device, and would impose penalties of up to $2,500 and license suspension or revocation for manufacturers, dealers or importers who sell a handgun without the device. Adopted 78-20: R 34-20; D 44-0 (ND 36-0, SD 8-0). May 18, 1999.

123. S 254. Juvenile Crime/Gang Violence. Hatch, R-Utah, amendment that would increase sentences for gang offenders, prohibit violent felons from possessing body armor, authorize grants for purchasing bullet-resistant equipment and vehicle video cameras for law enforcement, and prohibit the teaching or distributing of bomb-making instructions if the information is intended to aid in a federal crime of violence. Adopted 85-13: R 53-1; D 32-12 (ND 24-12, SD 8-0). May 18, 1999.

124. S 254. Juvenile Crime/Interstate Liquor Sales. Byrd, D-W.Va., amendment that would allow a state to bring a civil action in federal district court against an individual charged with importing alcohol into the state in violation of state laws. Adopted 80-17: R 46-7; D 34-10 (ND 27-9, SD 7-1). May 18, 1999.

125. S 254. Juvenile Crime/Domestic Violence. Hatch, R-Utah, motion to table (kill) the Wellstone, D-Minn., amendment that would authorize grants to aid children who have witnessed domestic violence and to train adults how to work with them. Motion agreed to 55-44: R 54-1; D 1-43 (ND 0-36, SD 1-7). May 18, 1999.

Senate Votes 126, 127, 128, 129, 130, 131, 132, 133

	126	127	128	129	130	131	132	133
ALABAMA								
Sessions	N	Y	Y	N	Y	Y	Y	N
Shelby	N	Y	Y	Y	Y	Y	Y	N
ALASKA								
Murkowski	Y	Y	Y	Y	Y	Y	Y	Y
Stevens	N	Y	Y	Y	Y	N	Y	N
ARIZONA								
Kyl	N	Y	Y	Y	Y	Y	Y	Y
McCain	N	Y	Y	Y	Y	Y	Y	Y
ARKANSAS								
Hutchinson	Y	Y	Y	Y	Y	Y	Y	Y
Lincoln	N	N	N	Y	N	Y	N	Y
CALIFORNIA								
Boxer	N	N	N	Y	N	N	N	Y
Feinstein	N	N	N	Y	N	N	N	Y
COLORADO								
Allard	Y	Y	Y	Y	Y	Y	Y	N
Campbell	Y	Y	Y	Y	Y	Y	Y	N
CONNECTICUT								
Dodd	N	N	N	Y	N	Y	N	Y
Lieberman	N	Y	N	Y	N	Y	N	Y
DELAWARE								
Roth	N	Y	Y	Y	Y	Y	Y	Y
Biden	N	N	N	Y	N	Y	N	Y
FLORIDA								
Mack	N	Y	Y	Y	Y	Y	Y	Y
Graham	N	N	N	Y	N	N	N	Y
GEORGIA								
Coverdell	Y	Y	Y	Y	Y	Y	Y	N
Cleland	N	N	N	Y	N	N	N	Y
HAWAII								
Akaka	N	N	N	N	N	N	N	Y
Inouye	N	N	N	N	N	N	N	Y
IDAHO								
Craig	Y	Y	Y	Y	Y	Y	Y	N
Crapo	N	Y	Y	Y	Y	Y	Y	N
ILLINOIS								
Fitzgerald	Y	Y	Y	Y	Y	Y	Y	Y
Durbin	N	N	N	Y	N	N	N	Y
INDIANA								
Bayh	N	N	N	Y	N	Y	N	Y
Lugar	Y	Y	Y	N	Y	Y	Y	Y
IOWA								
Grassley	N	Y	Y	Y	Y	Y	Y	Y
Harkin	N	N	N	Y	N	Y	N	Y
KANSAS								
Brownback	N	Y	Y	Y	Y	Y	Y	Y
Roberts	N	Y	Y	?	Y	Y	Y	Y
KENTUCKY								
Bunning	Y	Y	Y	Y	Y	Y	Y	Y
McConnell	Y	Y	Y	Y	Y	Y	Y	Y
LOUISIANA								
Breaux	N	N	N	Y	N	Y	N	Y
Landrieu	N	N	N	Y	N	N	N	Y
MAINE								
Collins	N	Y	Y	Y	Y	Y	Y	Y
Snowe	N	Y	Y	Y	Y	Y	N	Y
MARYLAND								
Mikulski	N	N	N	Y	N	N	N	Y
Sarbanes	N	N	N	Y	N	N	N	Y
MASSACHUSETTS								
Kennedy	N	N	N	Y	N	Y	N	Y
Kerry	N	N	N	Y	N	Y	N	Y
MICHIGAN								
Abraham	Y	Y	Y	Y	Y	Y	Y	Y
Levin	N	N	N	N	N	N	N	Y
MINNESOTA								
Grams	N	Y	Y	Y	Y	Y	Y	N
Wellstone	N	N	N	N	N	N	N	Y
MISSISSIPPI								
Cochran	Y	Y	Y	N	Y	Y	Y	N
Lott	Y	Y	Y	Y	Y	Y	Y	N
MISSOURI								
Ashcroft	Y	Y	Y	Y	Y	Y	Y	Y
Bond	Y	Y	Y	N	Y	Y	Y	Y
MONTANA								
Burns	N	Y	Y	Y	Y	Y	Y	N
Baucus	N	N	N	Y	N	N	N	Y
NEBRASKA								
Hagel	N	Y	Y	N	Y	N	Y	N
Kerrey	N	N	Y	Y	N	N	N	Y
NEVADA								
Bryan	N	N	N	N	N	Y	N	Y
Reid	N	N	N	Y	N	N	N	Y
NEW HAMPSHIRE								
Gregg	N	Y	Y	Y	Y	Y	Y	Y
Smith	Y	Y	Y	Y	Y	Y	Y	N
NEW JERSEY								
Lautenberg	N	N	N	N	N	N	N	Y
Torricelli	N	N	N	Y	N	N	N	Y
NEW MEXICO								
Domenici	Y	Y	Y	Y	Y	Y	Y	Y
Bingaman	N	N	Y	Y	N	N	N	Y
NEW YORK								
Moynihan	–	–	–	+	N	N	N	Y
Schumer	N	N	N	Y	N	N	N	Y
NORTH CAROLINA								
Helms	Y	Y	Y	Y	Y	Y	Y	N
Edwards	N	N	N	Y	N	Y	N	Y
NORTH DAKOTA								
Conrad	N	N	Y	Y	N	Y	N	Y
Dorgan	N	N	Y	Y	N	Y	N	Y
OHIO								
DeWine	N	Y	Y	Y	Y	Y	Y	Y
Voinovich	N	Y	Y	Y	Y	N	Y	Y
OKLAHOMA								
Inhofe	Y	Y	Y	Y	Y	Y	Y	N
Nickles	N	Y	Y	Y	Y	N	Y	N
OREGON								
Smith	N	Y	Y	Y	Y	Y	Y	Y
Wyden	N	N	N	Y	N	Y	N	Y
PENNSYLVANIA								
Santorum	N	Y	Y	Y	Y	Y	Y	Y
Specter	N	Y	Y	Y	N	Y	N	Y
RHODE ISLAND								
Chafee	N	Y	Y	N	N	Y	Y	Y
Reed	N	N	N	Y	N	N	N	Y
SOUTH CAROLINA								
Thurmond	Y	Y	Y	Y	Y	Y	Y	Y
Hollings	N	N	Y	N	N	N	N	Y
SOUTH DAKOTA								
Daschle	N	N	N	Y	N	N	N	Y
Johnson	Y	N	N	Y	N	Y	N	Y
TENNESSEE								
Frist	Y	Y	Y	Y	Y	Y	Y	Y
Thompson	N	Y	Y	N	Y	N	Y	N
TEXAS								
Gramm	Y	Y	Y	Y	Y	Y	Y	N
Hutchison	Y	Y	Y	Y	Y	Y	Y	Y
UTAH								
Bennett	N	Y	Y	Y	Y	Y	Y	Y
Hatch	N	Y	Y	Y	Y	Y	Y	Y
VERMONT								
Jeffords	N	Y	Y	N	N	Y	Y	Y
Leahy	N	N	N	Y	N	N	N	Y
VIRGINIA								
Warner	Y	Y	Y	Y	Y	Y	Y	Y
Robb	N	N	N	Y	N	N	N	Y
WASHINGTON								
Gorton	N	Y	Y	Y	Y	Y	Y	Y
Murray	N	N	N	Y	N	N	N	Y
WEST VIRGINIA								
Byrd	Y	N	Y	Y	N	Y	N	Y
Rockefeller	N	N	N	N	N	N	N	Y
WISCONSIN								
Feingold	N	N	N	N	N	N	N	Y
Kohl	N	N	N	Y	N	N	N	Y
WYOMING								
Enzi	N	Y	Y	Y	Y	Y	Y	N
Thomas	N	Y	Y	Y	Y	Y	Y	N

ND Northern Democrats SD Southern Democrats

Southern states - Ala., Ark., Fla., Ga., Ky., La., Miss., N.C., Okla., S.C., Tenn., Texas, Va.

Key

- Y Voted for (yea).
- # Paired for.
- \+ Announced for.
- N Voted against (nay).
- X Paired against.
- – Announced against.
- P Voted "present."
- C Voted "present" to avoid possible conflict of interest.
- ? Did not vote or otherwise make a position known.

•

Democrats ***Republicans***
Independents

126. S 254. Juvenile Crime/Prosecution of Juveniles. Ashcroft, R-Mo., amendment that would provide financial incentives for states to try juveniles 14 or older as adults if they possess a firearm while committing a violent crime. Rejected 26-73: R 24-31; D 2-42 (ND 2-34, SD 0-8). May 18, 1999.

127. S 254. Juvenile Crime/Government Disclaimers. Sessions, R-Ala., amendment that would require a disclaimer on all printed material funded under the bill stating that it was printed or distributed at government expense and encouraging anyone who objects to the material to contact the attorney general. Adopted 56-43: R 55-0; D 1-43 (ND 1-35, SD 0-8). May 19, 1999.

128. S 254. Juvenile Crime/School Mental Health Providers. Hatch, R-Utah, motion to table (kill) the Wellstone, D-Minn., amendment that would authorize $340 million per year for five years for states and localities to recruit, train and hire 141,000 additional school-based mental health personnel. Motion agreed to 61-38: R 55-0; D 6-38 (ND 5-31, SD 1-7). May 19, 1999.

129. S 254. Juvenile Crime/Repeat Felons. Santorum, R-Pa., amendment that would require the federal government to reimburse a state for the costs of apprehending, prosecuting or imprisoning a person convicted of murder, rape or a sexual offense against a child in another state. The U.S. attorney general would transfer the money to the state apprehending the offender from the previous state's federal crime funding. Adopted 81-17: R 46-8; D 35-9 (ND 28-8, SD 7-1). May 19, 1999.

130. S 254. Juvenile Crime/Racial Disparity. Hatch, R-Utah, motion to table (kill) the Wellstone, D-Minn., amendment that would require states to address the disproportionate number of racial minorities in the juvenile justice system. Motion agreed to 52-48: R 52-3; D 0-45 (ND 0-37, SD 0-8). May 19, 1999.

131. S 254. Juvenile Crime/Federal Filming Guidelines. McConnell, R-Ky., amendment to require federal agencies to consider whether a movie or television show promotes violence when asked for permission to shoot scenes of the movie on federal property. Adopted 67-33: R 50-5; D 17-28 (ND 14-23, SD 3-5). May 19, 1999.

132. S 254. Juvenile Crime/After-School Programs. Hatch, R-Utah, motion to table (kill) the Boxer, D-Calif., amendment to authorize $600 million a year for fiscal 2000 through 2004 for state grants for after-school programs. Motion agreed to 53-47: R 53-2; D 0-45 (ND 0-37, SD 0-8). May 19, 1999.

133. S 254. Juvenile Crime/Pawn Shop Checks. Smith, R-Ore., amendment to require background checks on all purchasers of handguns at pawn shops, regardless of original ownership. Adopted 79-21: R 34-21; D 45-0 (ND 37-0, SD 8-0). May 20, 1999.

Senate Votes 134, 135, 136, 137, 138, 139, 140

	134	135	136	137	138	139	140
ALABAMA							
Sessions	N	N	N	Y	Y	N	Y
Shelby	N	Y	Y	Y	Y	N	N
ALASKA							
Murkowski	N	Y	N	Y	Y	N	Y
Stevens	N	Y	Y	Y	Y	N	Y
ARIZONA							
Kyl	N	N	Y	Y	Y	N	Y
McCain	N	N	N	?	?	?	?
ARKANSAS							
Hutchinson	N	N	Y	Y	N	N	N
Lincoln	Y	Y	Y	Y	N	Y	Y
CALIFORNIA							
Boxer	Y	Y	N	N	N	Y	Y
Feinstein	Y	Y	Y	Y	N	Y	Y
COLORADO							
Allard	N	N	N	Y	Y	N	Y
Campbell	N	Y	Y	Y	Y	N	N
CONNECTICUT							
Dodd	Y	Y	Y	Y	N	Y	Y
Lieberman	Y	Y	Y	Y	N	Y	Y
DELAWARE							
Roth	N	N	Y	Y	Y	Y	Y
Biden	Y	Y	Y	Y	N	Y	Y
FLORIDA							
Mack	N	Y	Y	Y	N	N	Y
Graham	Y	N	Y	Y	N	Y	Y
GEORGIA							
Coverdell	N	Y	Y	Y	Y	N	N
Cleland	Y	Y	N	N	N	Y	Y
HAWAII							
Akaka	Y	Y	Y	N	N	Y	Y
Inouye	Y	Y	Y	N	N	Y	Y
IDAHO							
Craig	N	Y	N	Y	Y	N	N
Crapo	N	N	N	N	Y	N	N
ILLINOIS							
Fitzgerald	Y	N	N	Y	Y	N	Y
Durbin	Y	Y	Y	N	N	Y	Y
INDIANA							
Bayh	Y	Y	N	Y	N	Y	Y
Lugar	Y	N	Y	Y	Y	N	Y
IOWA							
Grassley	N	Y	N	Y	Y	N	N
Harkin	Y	Y	Y	N	N	Y	Y
KANSAS							
Brownback	N	Y	Y	Y	N	N	N
Roberts	N	Y	Y	Y	Y	N	N
KENTUCKY							
Bunning	N	N	Y	Y	Y	N	N
McConnell	N	Y	Y	Y	Y	N	Y
LOUISIANA							
Breaux	Y	N	Y	Y	N	Y	Y
Landrieu	Y	Y	Y	Y	?	Y	Y
MAINE							
Collins	N	Y	Y	Y	N	N	Y
Snowe	N	Y	Y	Y	N	N	Y
MARYLAND							
Mikulski	Y	Y	Y	N	N	Y	Y
Sarbanes	Y	Y	Y	N	N	Y	Y
MASSACHUSETTS							
Kennedy	Y	Y	Y	N	N	Y	Y
Kerry	Y	Y	N	Y	N	Y	Y
MICHIGAN							
Abraham	N	N	Y	Y	N	Y	Y
Levin	Y	Y	Y	Y	N	Y	Y
MINNESOTA							
Grams	N	N	N	Y	N	N	Y
Wellstone	Y	Y	Y	N	N	Y	N
MISSISSIPPI							
Cochran	N	Y	Y	Y	Y	N	Y
Lott	N	Y	Y	Y	Y	N	Y
MISSOURI							
Ashcroft	N	N	N	Y	Y	N	Y
Bond	N	Y	Y	Y	Y	N	Y
MONTANA							
Burns	N	N	N	Y	Y	N	N
Baucus	N	Y	Y	Y	N	Y	Y
NEBRASKA							
Hagel	N	N	N	Y	N	N	Y
Kerrey	Y	Y	N	Y	N	Y	Y
NEVADA							
Bryan	Y	Y	N	Y	N	Y	Y
Reid	Y	Y	Y	N	N	Y	Y
NEW HAMPSHIRE							
Gregg	N	N	N	Y	N	N	N
Smith	N	N	N	Y	Y	N	N
NEW JERSEY							
Lautenberg	Y	Y	Y	N	N	Y	Y
Torricelli	Y	Y	N	Y	N	Y	Y
NEW MEXICO							
Domenici	N	Y	Y	Y	Y	N	Y
Bingaman	Y	Y	Y	Y	N	Y	Y
NEW YORK							
Moynihan	Y	Y	Y	N	N	Y	Y
Schumer	Y	Y	Y	N	N	Y	Y
NORTH CAROLINA							
Helms	N	Y	N	Y	Y	N	N
Edwards	Y	Y	N	N	N	Y	Y
NORTH DAKOTA							
Conrad	Y	Y	Y	Y	N	Y	Y
Dorgan	Y	Y	N	Y	N	Y	Y
OHIO							
DeWine	Y	Y	Y	Y	Y	N	Y
Voinovich	Y	N	Y	Y	N	N	N
OKLAHOMA							
Inhofe	N	N	N	Y	Y	N	N
Nickles	N	N	N	Y	N	N	N
OREGON							
Smith	N	Y	Y	Y	N	N	Y
Wyden	Y	Y	N	N	N	Y	Y
PENNSYLVANIA							
Santorum	N	N	N	Y	N	N	Y
Specter	N	Y	Y	Y	Y	Y	Y
RHODE ISLAND							
Chafee	Y	Y	Y	N	Y	N	Y
Reed	Y	Y	Y	N	N	Y	Y
SOUTH CAROLINA							
Thurmond	N	Y	Y	Y	Y	N	Y
Hollings	Y	Y	Y	N	?	?	?
SOUTH DAKOTA							
Daschle	Y	Y	Y	N	N	Y	Y
Johnson	Y	Y	Y	Y	N	Y	Y
TENNESSEE							
Frist	N	Y	Y	Y	Y	N	Y
Thompson	N	N	Y	Y	N	N	N
TEXAS							
Gramm	N	N	N	Y	N	N	N
Hutchison	N	N	Y	Y	Y	N	N
UTAH							
Bennett	N	Y	Y	Y	Y	N	Y
Hatch	N	Y	Y	Y	Y	N	Y
VERMONT							
Jeffords	N	Y	N	N	N	Y	Y
Leahy	Y	Y	Y	N	N	Y	Y
VIRGINIA							
Warner	Y	Y	Y	Y	Y	N	Y
Robb	Y	N	N	Y	N	Y	Y
WASHINGTON							
Gorton	N	Y	N	Y	Y	N	N
Murray	Y	Y	Y	N	N	Y	Y
WEST VIRGINIA							
Byrd	Y	Y	Y	Y	Y	Y	Y
Rockefeller	Y	Y	Y	Y	Y	Y	Y
WISCONSIN							
Feingold	Y	N	N	N	N	Y	N
Kohl	Y	Y	N	Y	Y	Y	Y
WYOMING							
Enzi	N	N	N	Y	Y	N	N
Thomas	N	N	N	Y	Y	N	N

ND Northern Democrats SD Southern Democrats

Southern states - Ala., Ark., Fla., Ga., Ky., La., Miss., N.C., Okla., S.C., Tenn., Texas, Va.

Key

Y Voted for (yea).
Paired for.
+ Announced for.
N Voted against (nay).
X Paired against.
– Announced against.
P Voted "present."
C Voted "present" to avoid possible conflict of interest.
? Did not vote or otherwise make a position known.

•

Democrats ***Republicans***
Independents

134. S 254. Juvenile Crime/Gun Show Checks. Lautenberg, D-N.J., amendment that would require criminal background checks on all gun sales at gun shows, prohibit non-federal licensees from participating in gun shows and direct the U.S. attorney general to hold background files collected on gun owners for 90 days. Adopted 51-50: R 6-49; D 44-1 (ND 36-1, SD 8-0), with Vice President Gore casting a "yea" vote, May 20, 1999. A "yea" was a vote in support of the president's position.

135. HR 1141. Fiscal 1999 Supplemental Appropriations/Budget Offsets. Domenici, R-N.M., motion to waive the Budget Act with respect to the Gramm, R-Texas, point of order against the conference report. Motion agreed to 70-30: R 29-26; D 41-4 (ND 36-1, SD 5-3). May 20, 1999. Three-fifths of the total Senate (60) is required to waive the Budget Act.

136. HR 1141. Fiscal 1999 Supplemental Appropriations/Conference Report. Adoption of the conference report on the $14.5 billion bill, which would provide $10.9 billion for the ongoing military operations in Kosovo and other defense needs, $1.9 billion for domestic and international disaster relief, $1 billion for humanitarian aid for Kosovo, $574 million for domestic agriculture relief and $100 million in aid for Jordan. Adopted (thus cleared for the president) 64-36: R 32-23; D 32-13 (ND 27-10, SD 5-3). May 20, 1999.

137. S 254. Juvenile Crime/Special Education. Frist, R-Tenn., amendment to allow local school officials to discipline federally defined special education students in the same manner as other students when they bring guns or bombs onto school grounds. Adopted 75-24: R 51-3; D 24-21 (ND 18-19, SD 6-2). May 20, 1999.

138. S 254. Juvenile Crime/Independent Film Commission. Bond, R-Mo., amendment that would authorize $1 million to create an independent panel to study the motion picture industry and make recommendations to promote industry accountability and to reduce juveniles' access to violence, pornography and other harmful material. Rejected 41-56: R 38-16; D 3-40 (ND 3-34, SD 0-6). May 20, 1999.

139. S 254. Juvenile Crime/Community Policing. Biden, D-Del., amendment that would authorize $1.15 billion a year for fiscal 2000 through 2005 to encourage and support community policing programs. Rejected 48-50: R 4-50; D 44-0 (ND 37-0, SD 7-0). May 20, 1999.

140. S 254. Juvenile Crime/Passage. Passage of the bill to authorize $5 billion over five years to states to help reduce juvenile crimes and punish juvenile offenders and allow federal prosecution of juvenile offenders age 14 and older. The bill would also tighten restrictions on gun sales. Passed 73-25: R 31-23; D 42-2 (ND 35-2, SD 7-0). May 20, 1999.

Senate Votes 141, 142, 143, 144

	141	142	143	144
ALABAMA				
Sessions	Y	N	Y	N
Shelby	Y	Y	Y	N
ALASKA				
Murkowski	?	Y	Y	N
Stevens	Y	N	Y	N
ARIZONA				
Kyl	Y	Y	N	N
McCain	?	?	?	?
ARKANSAS				
Hutchinson	+	N	Y	N
Lincoln	Y	Y	Y	Y
CALIFORNIA				
Boxer	Y	Y	N	Y
Feinstein	Y	Y	Y	Y
COLORADO				
Allard	Y	N	Y	N
Campbell	Y	Y	Y	Y
CONNECTICUT				
Dodd	Y	N	Y	Y
Lieberman	+	N	Y	Y
DELAWARE				
Roth	Y	Y	N	N
Biden	?	Y	N	Y
FLORIDA				
Mack	Y	N	Y	N
Graham	Y	N	Y	Y
GEORGIA				
Coverdell	Y	N	Y	N
Cleland	?	Y	Y	Y
HAWAII				
Akaka	Y	Y	Y	Y
Inouye	Y	Y	N	Y
IDAHO				
Craig	Y	N	Y	N
Crapo	Y	N	Y	N
ILLINOIS				
Fitzgerald	Y	N	Y	N
Durbin	Y	Y	N	Y
INDIANA				
Bayh	Y	Y	Y	Y
Lugar	Y	N	Y	N
IOWA				
Grassley	Y	Y	Y	N
Harkin	Y	Y	Y	Y
KANSAS				
Brownback	Y	N	Y	N
Roberts	Y	N	Y	N
KENTUCKY				
Bunning	Y	Y	Y	N
McConnell	Y	Y	Y	N
LOUISIANA				
Breaux	Y	Y	Y	Y
Landrieu	Y	Y	Y	Y
MAINE				
Collins	Y	Y	Y	N
Snowe	Y	N	Y	Y
MARYLAND				
Mikulski	Y	Y	Y	Y
Sarbanes	Y	Y	Y	Y
MASSACHUSETTS				
Kennedy	?	Y	Y	Y
Kerry	Y	Y	Y	Y
MICHIGAN				
Abraham	Y	Y	Y	N
Levin	Y	N	Y	Y
MINNESOTA				
Grams	Y	N	Y	N
Wellstone	Y	Y	Y	Y
MISSISSIPPI				
Cochran	Y	Y	Y	N
Lott	Y	Y	Y	N
MISSOURI				
Ashcroft	Y	N	Y	N
Bond	Y	N	Y	N
MONTANA				
Burns	Y	N	Y	N
Baucus	Y	Y	Y	Y
NEBRASKA				
Hagel	Y	Y	N	N
Kerrey	Y	N	Y	Y
NEVADA				
Bryan	Y	N	Y	Y
Reid	Y	N	Y	Y
NEW HAMPSHIRE				
Gregg	Y	N	Y	N
Smith	Y	Y	Y	N
NEW JERSEY				
Lautenberg	Y	Y	N	Y
Torricelli	?	Y	Y	Y
NEW MEXICO				
Domenici	Y	Y	Y	N
Bingaman	Y	Y	Y	Y
NEW YORK				
Moynihan	Y	N	N	Y
Schumer	Y	Y	Y	Y
NORTH CAROLINA				
Helms	Y	Y	Y	N
Edwards	Y	Y	Y	Y
NORTH DAKOTA				
Conrad	Y	N	Y	Y
Dorgan	Y	N	Y	Y
OHIO				
DeWine	Y	Y	Y	N
Voinovich	Y	Y	Y	N
OKLAHOMA				
Inhofe	Y	N	Y	N
Nickles	Y	N	Y	N
OREGON				
Smith	Y	N	N	N
Wyden	Y	Y	Y	Y
PENNSYLVANIA				
Santorum	Y	N	Y	N
Specter	Y	N	N	Y
RHODE ISLAND				
Chafee	Y	N	Y	Y
Reed	+	N	Y	Y
SOUTH CAROLINA				
Thurmond	Y	Y	Y	N
Hollings	Y	Y	Y	Y
SOUTH DAKOTA				
Daschle	Y	Y	Y	Y
Johnson	Y	Y	Y	Y
TENNESSEE				
Frist	Y	N	Y	N
Thompson	Y	N	Y	N
TEXAS				
Gramm	Y	N	Y	N
Hutchison	Y	N	Y	N
UTAH				
Bennett	Y	Y	Y	N
Hatch	Y	Y	Y	N
VERMONT				
Jeffords	Y	N	Y	N
Leahy	Y	Y	Y	Y
VIRGINIA				
Warner	Y	N	Y	N
Robb	Y	N	N	Y
WASHINGTON				
Gorton	Y	N	Y	N
Murray	Y	N	Y	Y
WEST VIRGINIA				
Byrd	Y	N	Y	Y
Rockefeller	Y	Y	Y	Y
WISCONSIN				
Feingold	+	N	Y	Y
Kohl	Y	N	Y	Y
WYOMING				
Enzi	Y	Y	Y	N
Thomas	Y	Y	Y	N

Key

- Y Voted for (yea).
- # Paired for.
- + Announced for.
- N Voted against (nay).
- X Paired against.
- – Announced against.
- P Voted "present."
- C Voted "present" to avoid possible conflict of interest.
- ? Did not vote or otherwise make a position known.

•

Democrats ***Republicans***
Independents

ND Northern Democrats SD Southern Democrats

Southern states - Ala., Ark., Fla., Ga., Ky., La., Miss., N.C., Okla., S.C., Tenn., Texas, Va.

141. S 1059. Fiscal 2000 Defense Authorization/War Crimes in Yugoslavia. Landrieu, D-La., amendment to express the sense of Congress that the United States, along with other U.N. contributors, should provide sufficient resources to investigate war crime allegations in Kosovo, should provide intelligence to aid evidence collection and should honor arrest warrants against all individuals regardless of their position. It also would urge NATO not to accept any diplomatic solution to the Kosovo conflict that would prevent the indictment and prosecution of war criminals. Adopted 90-0: R 52-0; D 38-0 (ND 31-0, SD 7-0). May 24, 1999.

142. S 1059. Fiscal 2000 Defense Authorization/Pearl Harbor Generals. Roth, R-Del., amendment that would urge President Clinton to posthumously advance the ranks of Rear Adm. Husband E. Kimmel and Maj. Gen. Walter C. Short to their highest ranks during World War II. Kimmel and Short were not retired at their highest wartime ranks because they were blamed for not preventing the Japanese attack at Pearl Harbor. Adopted 52-47: R 23-31; D 29-16 (ND 23-14, SD 6-2). May 25, 1999.

143. S 1059. Fiscal 2000 Defense Authorization/NATO Strategic Concept. Roberts, R-Kan., amendment to require the president to certify whether the Strategic Concept of NATO, adopted at the April 1999 NATO summit, imposes any new commitment or obligation on the United States. The amendment also would express the sense of the Senate that if it does, the president should submit the new policy to the Senate as a treaty for ratification. Adopted 87-12: R 49-5; D 38-7 (ND 31-6, SD 7-1). May 25, 1999.

144. S 1059. Fiscal 2000 Defense Authorization/Welfare Report. Wellstone, D-Minn., amendment to require the Health and Human Services Department to report on former welfare recipients' ability to achieve self-sufficiency. Rejected 49-50: R 4-50; D 45-0 (ND 37-0, SD 8-0). May 25, 1999.

Senate Votes 145, 146, 147, 148

Key

- Y Voted for (yea).
- # Paired for.
- + Announced for.
- N Voted against (nay).
- X Paired against.
- – Announced against.
- P Voted "present."
- C Voted "present" to avoid possible conflict of interest.
- ? Did not vote or otherwise make a position known.

•

Democrats ***Republicans***
Independents

State / Senator	145	146	147	148
ALABAMA				
Sessions	Y	Y	N	Y
Shelby	Y	Y	N	Y
ALASKA				
Murkowski	N	Y	N	Y
Stevens	N	Y	N	Y
ARIZONA				
Kyl	Y	Y	Y	Y
McCain	Y	Y	Y	Y
ARKANSAS				
Hutchinson	N	N	N	Y
Lincoln	Y	N	Y	N
CALIFORNIA				
Boxer	Y	N	N	N
Feinstein	Y	Y	N	N
COLORADO				
Allard	N	N	N	Y
Campbell	N	Y	N	Y
CONNECTICUT				
Dodd	Y	N	N	N
Lieberman	Y	N	Y	N
DELAWARE				
Roth	Y	Y	Y	Y
Biden	Y	Y	Y	N
FLORIDA				
Mack	Y	Y	N	Y
Graham	Y	Y	N	N
GEORGIA				
Coverdell	N	Y	N	Y
Cleland	N	N	N	N
HAWAII				
Akaka	Y	N	N	N
Inouye	Y	N	N	N
IDAHO				
Craig	N	Y	N	Y
Crapo	N	Y	N	Y
ILLINOIS				
Fitzgerald	N	Y	N	Y
Durbin	N	Y	N	N
INDIANA				
Bayh	Y	N	Y	N
Lugar	Y	N	Y	Y
IOWA				
Grassley	N	N	Y	Y
Harkin	Y	Y	Y	N
KANSAS				
Brownback	N	Y	N	Y
Roberts	N	Y	N	Y
KENTUCKY				
Bunning	N	N	N	Y
McConnell	Y	Y	N	Y
LOUISIANA				
Breaux	Y	N	N	Y
Landrieu	Y	N	Y	N
MAINE				
Collins	N	N	N	N
Snowe	N	Y	N	N
MARYLAND				
Mikulski	Y	N	N	N
Sarbanes	Y	N	N	N
MASSACHUSETTS				
Kennedy	Y	N	Y	N
Kerry	Y	N	Y	N
MICHIGAN				
Abraham	N	N	N	Y
Levin	Y	N	Y	N
MINNESOTA				
Grams	N	Y	Y	Y
Wellstone	N	N	Y	N
MISSISSIPPI				
Cochran	Y	Y	N	Y
Lott	Y	Y	N	Y
MISSOURI				
Ashcroft	N	Y	Y	Y
Bond	N	Y	Y	Y
MONTANA				
Burns	Y	Y	N	Y
Baucus	Y	N	N	N
NEBRASKA				
Hagel	Y	N	Y	Y
Kerrey	Y	Y	Y	N
NEVADA				
Bryan	Y	N	Y	N
Reid	Y	N	Y	Y
NEW HAMPSHIRE				
Gregg	N	Y	N	Y
Smith	N	N	N	Y
NEW JERSEY				
Lautenberg	Y	N	N	N
Torricelli	N	N	N	N
NEW MEXICO				
Domenici	N	Y	N	Y
Bingaman	Y	N	N	N
NEW YORK				
Moynihan	Y	N	Y	N
Schumer	Y	N	N	N
NORTH CAROLINA				
Helms	N	N	N	Y
Edwards	Y	N	N	N
NORTH DAKOTA				
Conrad	N	N	N	N
Dorgan	N	Y	N	N
OHIO				
DeWine	Y	Y	Y	Y
Voinovich	N	Y	Y	Y
OKLAHOMA				
Inhofe	N	N	N	Y
Nickles	N	Y	N	Y
OREGON				
Smith	Y	N	Y	Y
Wyden	Y	N	Y	N
PENNSYLVANIA				
Santorum	N	Y	Y	Y
Specter	N	Y	N	N
RHODE ISLAND				
Chafee	Y	Y	Y	N
Reed	Y	N	Y	N
SOUTH CAROLINA				
Thurmond	N	Y	N	Y
Hollings	N	Y	Y	N
SOUTH DAKOTA				
Daschle	Y	N	N	N
Johnson	N	N	N	N
TENNESSEE				
Frist	N	N	N	Y
Thompson	N	Y	Y	Y
TEXAS				
Gramm	N	N	Y	Y
Hutchison	N	Y	N	Y
UTAH				
Bennett	N	Y	N	Y
Hatch	Y	Y	N	Y
VERMONT				
Jeffords	N	Y	Y	N
Leahy	Y	N	Y	N
VIRGINIA				
Warner	Y	N	N	Y
Robb	Y	N	Y	N
WASHINGTON				
Gorton	N	Y	N	N
Murray	Y	N	N	N
WEST VIRGINIA				
Byrd	N	Y	Y	N
Rockefeller	Y	Y	Y	N
WISCONSIN				
Feingold	N	N	Y	N
Kohl	Y	Y	Y	N
WYOMING				
Enzi	N	N	N	Y
Thomas	N	N	N	Y

ND Northern Democrats SD Southern Democrats

Southern states - Ala., Ark., Fla., Ga., Ky., La., Miss., N.C., Okla., S.C., Tenn., Texas, Va.

145. S 1059. Fiscal 2000 Defense Authorization/Ground Troops in Kosovo. Warner, R-Va., motion to table (kill) the Specter, R-Pa., amendment that would prohibit the use of Defense Department funds for deployment of U.S. ground troops in Yugoslavia, except for peacekeeping personnel, unless Congress declares war or enacts a joint resolution authorizing the use of military force. Motion agreed to 52-48: R 17-38; D 35-10 (ND 29-8, SD 6-2). May 25, 1999. A "yea" was a vote in support of the president's position.

146. S 1059. Fiscal 2000 Defense Authorization/Defense Procurement. Gramm, R-Texas, amendment to strike language in the bill that would require the Defense Department to subject products made by federal prison labor to competition from products made by private companies. Rejected 49-51: R 38-17; D 11-34 (ND 9-28, SD 2-6). May 25, 1999. (At the conclusion of the vote, Gramm changed his position from "yea" to "nay" in order to preserve his right to offer a motion to reconsider at a later time.)

147. S 1059. Fiscal 2000 Defense Authorization/Military Base Closures. McCain, R-Ariz., amendment that would authorize a single round of military base closures and realignments in 2001. Rejected 40-60: R 17-38; D 23-22 (ND 19-18, SD 4-4). May 26, 1999. A "yea" was a vote in support of the president's position.

148. S 1059. Fiscal 2000 Defense Authorization/Overseas Military Hospital Abortions. Smith, R-N.H., motion to table (kill) the Murray, D-Wash., amendment to repeal current law prohibiting overseas U.S. military hospitals and medical facilities from performing privately funded abortions for U.S. service members and their dependents. Motion agreed to 51-49: R 49-6; D 2-43 (ND 1-36, SD 1-7). May 26, 1999.

Senate Votes 149, 150, 151, 152, 153, 154

	149	150	151	152	153	154
ALABAMA						
Sessions	Y	N	N	Y	Y	Y
Shelby	Y	N	Y	Y	Y	Y
ALASKA						
Murkowski	Y	Y	Y	Y	Y	Y
Stevens	Y	Y	Y	Y	Y	Y
ARIZONA						
Kyl	Y	Y	Y	Y	Y	Y
McCain	Y	Y	Y	?	Y	Y
ARKANSAS						
Hutchinson	Y	N	N	Y	Y	Y
Lincoln	Y	N	Y	Y	Y	Y
CALIFORNIA						
Boxer	N	N	Y	Y	N	Y
Feinstein	N	Y	Y	Y	Y	Y
COLORADO						
Allard	Y	N	N	Y	Y	Y
Campbell	Y	Y	Y	Y	Y	Y
CONNECTICUT						
Dodd	N	N	Y	Y	Y	Y
Lieberman	N	N	Y	Y	Y	Y
DELAWARE						
Roth	Y	Y	Y	Y	Y	Y
Biden	N	Y	Y	Y	Y	Y
FLORIDA						
Mack	Y	Y	Y	Y	Y	?
Graham	Y	Y	Y	Y	Y	Y
GEORGIA						
Coverdell	Y	Y	Y	Y	Y	Y
Cleland	N	N	N	Y	Y	Y
HAWAII						
Akaka	N	N	Y	Y	Y	Y
Inouye	N	N	Y	Y	Y	Y
IDAHO						
Craig	Y	Y	N	Y	Y	Y
Crapo	Y	Y	N	Y	Y	Y
ILLINOIS						
Fitzgerald	Y	Y	N	Y	Y	Y
Durbin	N	Y	Y	Y	Y	Y
INDIANA						
Bayh	Y	N	Y	Y	Y	Y
Lugar	Y	N	Y	Y	Y	?
IOWA						
Grassley	Y	N	N	Y	Y	Y
Harkin	N	N	Y	Y	N	Y
KANSAS						
Brownback	Y	Y	Y	Y	Y	Y
Roberts	Y	Y	Y	Y	Y	Y
KENTUCKY						
Bunning	Y	N	N	Y	Y	Y
McConnell	Y	Y	Y	Y	Y	Y
LOUISIANA						
Breaux	N	N	Y	Y	Y	Y
Landrieu	N	N	Y	Y	Y	Y
MAINE						
Collins	Y	Y	Y	Y	Y	Y
Snowe	Y	Y	Y	Y	Y	Y
MARYLAND						
Mikulski	N	N	Y	Y	Y	Y
Sarbanes	N	N	Y	Y	Y	Y
MASSACHUSETTS						
Kennedy	N	N	Y	Y	Y	Y
Kerry	N	N	Y	Y	Y	Y
MICHIGAN						
Abraham	Y	N	Y	Y	Y	Y
Levin	N	N	Y	Y	Y	Y
MINNESOTA						
Grams	Y	Y	Y	Y	Y	Y
Wellstone	N	N	Y	Y	N	N
MISSISSIPPI						
Cochran	Y	Y	Y	Y	Y	Y
Lott	Y	Y	Y	Y	Y	Y
MISSOURI						
Ashcroft	Y	Y	Y	Y	Y	Y
Bond	Y	Y	?	Y	Y	Y
MONTANA						
Burns	Y	Y	N	Y	Y	Y
Baucus	N	N	Y	Y	Y	Y
NEBRASKA						
Hagel	Y	Y	Y	Y	Y	Y
Kerrey	N	Y	Y	Y	Y	Y
NEVADA						
Bryan	N	N	Y	Y	Y	Y
Reid	N	N	Y	Y	N	Y
NEW HAMPSHIRE						
Gregg	Y	Y	N	Y	Y	Y
Smith	Y	N	N	Y	Y	Y
NEW JERSEY						
Lautenberg	N	N	Y	Y	?	?
Torricelli	N	Y	Y	Y	Y	Y
NEW MEXICO						
Domenici	Y	Y	Y	Y	Y	Y
Bingaman	N	N	Y	Y	Y	Y
NEW YORK						
Moynihan	N	N	+	Y	N	?
Schumer	N	N	Y	Y	N	Y
NORTH CAROLINA						
Helms	Y	Y	N	Y	Y	Y
Edwards	N	N	Y	Y	Y	Y
NORTH DAKOTA						
Conrad	N	N	Y	Y	Y	Y
Dorgan	N	Y	Y	Y	Y	Y
OHIO						
DeWine	Y	Y	Y	Y	Y	Y
Voinovich	Y	Y	N	Y	Y	Y
OKLAHOMA						
Inhofe	Y	N	N	Y	Y	Y
Nickles	Y	Y	N	Y	Y	Y
OREGON						
Smith	N	N	Y	Y	Y	Y
Wyden	N	N	Y	Y	N	Y
PENNSYLVANIA						
Santorum	Y	Y	N	Y	Y	Y
Specter	Y	Y	Y	?	?	Y
RHODE ISLAND						
Chafee	N	Y	Y	Y	Y	Y
Reed	N	N	Y	Y	Y	Y
SOUTH CAROLINA						
Thurmond	Y	Y	N	Y	Y	Y
Hollings	N	Y	Y	Y	Y	?
SOUTH DAKOTA						
Daschle	N	N	Y	Y	Y	Y
Johnson	N	N	Y	Y	N	Y
TENNESSEE						
Frist	Y	Y	Y	Y	Y	Y
Thompson	Y	Y	Y	Y	Y	Y
TEXAS						
Gramm	Y	Y	N	Y	Y	Y
Hutchison	Y	Y	Y	Y	Y	Y
UTAH						
Bennett	Y	Y	Y	Y	Y	Y
Hatch	Y	Y	Y	Y	Y	Y
VERMONT						
Jeffords	N	Y	Y	Y	N	Y
Leahy	N	N	Y	Y	Y	Y
VIRGINIA						
Warner	Y	N	Y	Y	Y	Y
Robb	N	N	Y	Y	Y	Y
WASHINGTON						
Gorton	Y	N	Y	Y	Y	Y
Murray	N	N	Y	Y	Y	Y
WEST VIRGINIA						
Byrd	Y	Y	Y	Y	Y	Y
Rockefeller	N	Y	Y	Y	Y	Y
WISCONSIN						
Feingold	N	N	N	Y	N	N
Kohl	N	Y	Y	Y	N	N
WYOMING						
Enzi	Y	N	N	Y	Y	Y
Thomas	Y	N	Y	Y	Y	Y

Key

- Y Voted for (yea).
- # Paired for.
- \+ Announced for.
- N Voted against (nay).
- X Paired against.
- – Announced against.
- P Voted "present."
- C Voted "present" to avoid possible conflict of interest.
- ? Did not vote or otherwise make a position known.

•

Democrats ***Republicans***
Independents

ND Northern Democrats SD Southern Democrats

Southern states - Ala., Ark., Fla., Ga., Ky., La., Miss., N.C., Okla., S.C., Tenn., Texas, Va.

149. S 1059. Fiscal 2000 Defense Authorization/Nuclear Weapons Reduction. Warner, R-Va., motion to table (kill) the Kerrey, D-Neb., amendment that would strike bill language requiring that U.S. strategic nuclear forces remain at START I levels through the end of fiscal 2000 unless Russia ratifies START II. Motion agreed to 56-44: R 52-3; D 4-41 (ND 2-35, SD 2-6). May 26, 1999.

150. S 1059. Fiscal 2000 Defense Authorization/Defense Procurement. Gramm, R-Texas, motion to reconsider the vote on the Gramm amendment to strike language in the bill that would require the Defense Department to subject products made by federal prison labor to competition from products made by private companies. Motion agreed to 51-49: R 40-15; D 11-34 (ND 9-28, SD 2-6). May 26, 1999. (Subsequently, the Gramm amendment was adopted by voice vote.)

151. S 1059. Fiscal 2000 Defense Authorization/Prohibit U.S. Action in Yugoslavia. Warner, R-Va., motion to table (kill) the Smith, R-N.H., amendment that would prohibit the use of Defense Department funds for U.S. military operations in Yugoslavia as of Oct. 1, 1999, unless Congress enacts legislation authorizing such operations. Motion agreed to 77-21: R 35-19; D 42-2 (ND 35-1, SD 7-1). May 26, 1999. A "yea" was a vote in support of the president's position.

152. S 1059. Fiscal 2000 Defense Authorization/Libya Sanctions. Kennedy, D-Mass., amendment that would express the sense of the Congress that the president should use all means, including the U.S. veto at the U.N. Security Council, to prevent the United Nations from lifting sanctions against Libya until Libya fulfills all the conditions in previous U.N. Security Council Resolutions. Adopted 98-0: R 53-0; D 45-0 (ND 37-0, SD 8-0). May 27, 1999.

153. S 1059. Fiscal 2000 Defense Authorization/Navy Aircraft Costs. Santorum, R-Pa., motion to table (kill) the Feingold, D-Wis., amendment that would cap funding for the Navy's F/A-18E and F aircraft program at $8.8 billion over five years. Motion agreed to 87-11: R 53-1; D 34-10 (ND 26-10, SD 8-0). May 27, 1999.

154. S 1059. Fiscal 2000 Defense Authorization/Passage. Passage of the bill to authorize $288.8 billion for defense-related activities in fiscal 2000, $8.3 billion more than President Clinton's request. The bill contains language that seeks to improve defense health coverage, authorize military pay increases and restrict China's ability to obtain U.S. weapons technology. Passed 92-3: R 53-0; D 39-3 (ND 32-3, SD 7-0). May 27, 1999.

Senate Votes 155, 156, 157, 158, 159, 160, 161, 162

	155	156	157	158	159	160	161	162
ALABAMA								
Sessions	Y	N	Y	Y	Y	N	N	N
Shelby	Y	N	Y	Y	N	N	Y	Y
ALASKA								
Murkowski	Y	N	Y	Y	Y	N	N	N
Stevens	Y	N	Y	Y	Y	N	?	?
ARIZONA								
Kyl	Y	Y	Y	Y	Y	N	N	N
McCain	?	Y	?	?	Y	N	N	N
ARKANSAS								
Hutchinson	Y	N	Y	Y	Y	N	N	N
Lincoln	Y	N	N	Y	Y	N	N	Y
CALIFORNIA								
Boxer	Y	N	N	N	N	Y	Y	Y
Feinstein	Y	N	N	Y	Y	N	N	N
COLORADO								
Allard	Y	Y	N	Y	Y	N	N	N
Campbell	Y	N	Y	Y	?	N	N	N
CONNECTICUT								
Dodd	?	N	Y	Y	Y	N	N	N
Lieberman	Y	N	Y	Y	Y	N	N	N
DELAWARE								
Roth	Y	N	Y	Y	N	N	N	N
Biden	?	?	?	?	N	?	Y	Y
FLORIDA								
Mack	Y	N	Y	Y	Y	N	N	N
Graham	Y	Y	N	Y	N	Y	Y	Y
GEORGIA								
Coverdell	Y	N	Y	Y	Y	N	N	N
Cleland	Y	N	Y	Y	N	Y	Y	Y
HAWAII								
Akaka	Y	N	Y	Y	N	Y	Y	Y
Inouye	Y	N	Y	Y	N	Y	?	?
IDAHO								
Craig	Y	N	Y	Y	Y	N	N	N
Crapo	?	?	?	?	?	?	N	N
ILLINOIS								
Fitzgerald	Y	N	Y	Y	Y	N	N	N
Durbin	Y	N	N	Y	N	Y	Y	Y
INDIANA								
Bayh	Y	Y	N	Y	N	N	Y	N
Lugar	Y	Y	Y	Y	Y	N	N	N
IOWA								
Grassley	Y	N	N	Y	Y	N	N	N
Harkin	Y	N	N	Y	N	Y	Y	Y
KANSAS								
Brownback	Y	Y	Y	Y	Y	N	N	N
Roberts	Y	N	Y	Y	Y	N	N	N
KENTUCKY								
Bunning	Y	N	Y	Y	Y	N	N	N
McConnell	Y	N	Y	Y	Y	N	N	N
LOUISIANA								
Breaux	Y	N	Y	Y	N	Y	Y	Y
Landrieu	Y	N	Y	Y	N	Y	Y	Y
MAINE								
Collins	Y	N	Y	Y	Y	N	N	N
Snowe	Y	N	Y	Y	Y	N	N	N
MARYLAND								
Mikulski	Y	N	N	Y	N	Y	Y	Y
Sarbanes	Y	N	N	Y	N	Y	Y	Y
MASSACHUSETTS								
Kennedy	Y	N	Y	Y	N	Y	Y	Y
Kerry	Y	Y	Y	Y	N	Y	Y	Y
MICHIGAN								
Abraham	Y	N	N	Y	Y	N	N	N
Levin	Y	N	N	Y	N	Y	Y	Y
MINNESOTA								
Grams	?	Y	N	Y	Y	N	N	N
Wellstone	Y	Y	N	N	N	Y	Y	Y
MISSISSIPPI								
Cochran	Y	N	Y	Y	Y	N	N	N
Lott	Y	N	Y	Y	Y	N	N	N
MISSOURI								
Ashcroft	Y	N	Y	Y	Y	N	N	N
Bond	Y	N	Y	Y	Y	N	N	N
MONTANA								
Burns	Y	N	Y	Y	Y	N	N	N
Baucus	Y	N	N	Y	Y	N	Y	N
NEBRASKA								
Hagel	Y	Y	Y	Y	Y	N	N	N
Kerrey	Y	N	Y	Y	N	N	Y	Y
NEVADA								
Bryan	Y	N	Y	Y	N	N	Y	Y
Reid	Y	N	Y	Y	N	Y	Y	Y
NEW HAMPSHIRE								
Gregg	Y	?	Y	Y	Y	?	N	N
Smith	Y	N	Y	Y	Y	N	N	N
NEW JERSEY								
Lautenberg	Y	N	N	Y	N	Y	Y	Y
Torricelli	?	Y	N	Y	N	Y	Y	Y
NEW MEXICO								
Domenici	Y	N	Y	Y	Y	N	N	N
Bingaman	Y	N	N	Y	N	N	Y	N
NEW YORK								
Moynihan	+	N	Y	Y	Y	N	N	N
Schumer	Y	N	N	Y	N	Y	Y	Y
NORTH CAROLINA								
Helms	Y	N	Y	Y	Y	N	N	N
Edwards	Y	Y	N	Y	N	Y	Y	Y
NORTH DAKOTA								
Conrad	Y	N	N	Y	N	Y	Y	Y
Dorgan	Y	N	Y	Y	N	Y	Y	Y
OHIO								
DeWine	Y	N	Y	Y	Y	N	N	N
Voinovich	Y	N	Y	Y	Y	N	N	N
OKLAHOMA								
Inhofe	Y	N	Y	Y	Y	N	N	N
Nickles	Y	N	Y	Y	Y	N	N	N
OREGON								
Smith	Y	N	Y	Y	Y	N	N	N
Wyden	Y	N	N	Y	Y	N	N	N
PENNSYLVANIA								
Santorum	Y	N	N	Y	Y	N	N	N
Specter	Y	N	Y	Y	N	N	Y	Y
RHODE ISLAND								
Chafee	Y	N	Y	Y	Y	N	N	N
Reed	Y	N	Y	Y	N	Y	Y	Y
SOUTH CAROLINA								
Thurmond	Y	N	Y	Y	Y	N	N	N
Hollings	Y	N	Y	Y	N	Y	Y	Y
SOUTH DAKOTA								
Daschle	Y	N	N	Y	N	Y	Y	Y
Johnson	Y	N	N	Y	N	Y	Y	Y
TENNESSEE								
Frist	Y	N	Y	Y	Y	N	N	N
Thompson	Y	N	Y	Y	Y	N	Y	N
TEXAS								
Gramm	Y	Y	Y	Y	Y	N	N	N
Hutchison	Y	N	Y	Y	Y	N	N	N
UTAH								
Bennett	Y	N	Y	Y	Y	N	N	N
Hatch	Y	N	Y	Y	Y	N	N	N
VERMONT								
Jeffords	Y	N	Y	Y	Y	N	N	N
Leahy	Y	N	Y	Y	N	Y	Y	Y
VIRGINIA								
Warner	Y	N	Y	Y	Y	N	N	N
Robb	Y	Y	N	Y	N	N	Y	N
WASHINGTON								
Gorton	Y	N	Y	Y	Y	N	N	N
Murray	Y	N	Y	Y	N	Y	Y	Y
WEST VIRGINIA								
Byrd	Y	N	N	Y	N	Y	Y	Y
Rockefeller	Y	N	N	Y	N	Y	Y	Y
WISCONSIN								
Feingold	Y	Y	N	N	N	Y	Y	Y
Kohl	Y	N	N	N	N	Y	Y	N
WYOMING								
Enzi	Y	N	Y	Y	Y	N	N	N
Thomas	Y	N	Y	Y	Y	N	N	N

Key

Y Voted for (yea).
Paired for.
\+ Announced for.
N Voted against (nay).
X Paired against.
– Announced against.
P Voted "present."
C Voted "present" to avoid possible conflict of interest.
? Did not vote or otherwise make a position known.

•

Democrats **_Republicans_**
Independents

ND Northern Democrats SD Southern Democrats

Southern states - Ala., Ark., Fla., Ga., Ky., La., Miss., N.C., Okla., S.C., Tenn., Texas, Va.

155. S 1122. Fiscal 2000 Defense Appropriations/Defense Department Disbursements. Grassley, R-Iowa, amendment to require the Defense Department to match disbursements with obligations for expenditures greater than $500,000. Approved 93-0: R 52-0; D 41-0 (ND 33-0, SD 8-0), June 8, 1999.

156. S 1122. Fiscal 2000 Defense Appropriations/Spending Reduction. McCain, R-Ariz., amendment to reduce the amount of spending for unrequested items by a total of $3.1 billion. Rejected 16-81: R 8-45; D 8-36 (ND 5-31, SD 3-5). June 8, 1999.

157. S 1122. Fiscal 2000 Defense Appropriations/Support Aircraft. Stevens, R-Alaska, motion to table the Boxer, D-Calif., amendment that would strike a provision to authorize the leasing of executive jets and instead require the Defense Department to study travel alternatives for top officers. Motion agreed to 66-31: R 48-5; D 18-26 (ND 14-22, SD 4-4). June 8, 1999.

158. S 1122. Fiscal 2000 Defense Appropriations/Passage. Passage of the bill to provide $264.7 billion in fiscal 2000 defense spending for the Department of Defense. Passed 93-4: R 53-0; D 40-4 (ND 32-4, SD 8-0). June 8, 1999.

159. S 96. Y2K Liability/Democratic Substitute. Hatch, R-Utah, motion to table (kill) the Kerry, D-Mass., amendment to require courts to determine proportionate liability, generally prohibit economic loss recovery and allow stronger state laws to take precedence. Motion agreed to 57-41: R 50-3; D 7-38 (ND 6-31, SD 1-7). June 9, 1999. A "nay" was a vote in support of the president's position.

160. S 96. Y2K Liability/Consumer Restitution. Leahy, D-Vt., amendment to exclude consumers from the act's restrictions on seeking compensation for harm caused by Y2K computer failures. Rejected 32-65: R 0-53; D 32-12 (ND 26-10, SD 6-2). June 9, 1999.

161. S 96. Y2K Liability/Lawsuit Application Expiration. Edwards, D-N.C., amendment to block the application of lawsuit protection for companies after 1999. Rejected 41-57: R 3-51; D 38-6 (ND 31-5, SD 7-1). June 10, 1999.

162. S 96. Y2K Liability/Lawsuit Dates. Edwards, D-N.C., amendment to allow liability protection against product failure only until January 1999. Rejected 36-62: R 2-52; D 34-10 (ND 27-9, SD 7-1). June 10, 1999.

Senate Votes 163, 164, 165, 166, 167, 168, 169, 170

	163	164	165	166	167	168	169	170
ALABAMA								
Sessions	Y	Y	Y	Y	Y	Y	Y	Y
Shelby	Y	Y	N	Y	Y	Y	Y	Y
ALASKA								
Murkowski	Y	Y	Y	Y	Y	Y	Y	Y
Stevens	Y	Y	Y	Y	Y	Y	Y	Y
ARIZONA								
Kyl	Y	Y	Y	Y	N	Y	Y	Y
McCain	?	Y	Y	Y	N	N	Y	Y
ARKANSAS								
Hutchinson	Y	Y	Y	Y	N	Y	Y	Y
Lincoln	Y	N	Y	N	Y	Y	Y	N
CALIFORNIA								
Boxer	N	N	N	N	Y	Y	Y	N
Feinstein	Y	N	Y	N	Y	Y	Y	N
COLORADO								
Allard	Y	Y	Y	Y	N	Y	Y	Y
Campbell	Y	Y	Y	Y	Y	Y	Y	Y
CONNECTICUT								
Dodd	Y	Y	Y	N	Y	Y	Y	N
Lieberman	Y	N	Y	N	Y	Y	Y	N
DELAWARE								
Roth	Y	Y	Y	N	N	Y	Y	Y
Biden	N	N	N	N	Y	Y	Y	N
FLORIDA								
Mack	Y	Y	Y	Y	N	Y	Y	Y
Graham	N	Y	N	N	Y	Y	Y	N
GEORGIA								
Coverdell	Y	Y	Y	Y	N	Y	Y	Y
Cleland	N	N	N	N	Y	Y	Y	N
HAWAII								
Akaka	N	N	N	N	Y	Y	Y	N
Inouye	N	N	N	N	Y	Y	Y	N
IDAHO								
Craig	Y	Y	Y	Y	Y	Y	Y	Y
Crapo	Y	Y	Y	Y	N	Y	Y	Y
ILLINOIS								
Fitzgerald	Y	Y	Y	Y	N	Y	Y	Y
Durbin	N	N	N	N	Y	Y	Y	N
INDIANA								
Bayh	Y	Y	N	N	Y	Y	Y	N
Lugar	Y	Y	Y	Y	Y	Y	Y	Y
IOWA								
Grassley	Y	Y	Y	Y	N	Y	Y	Y
Harkin	N	Y	N	N	Y	+	+	–
KANSAS								
Brownback	Y	Y	Y	Y	N	Y	Y	Y
Roberts	Y	Y	Y	Y	Y	Y	Y	Y
KENTUCKY								
Bunning	Y	Y	Y	Y	N	Y	Y	Y
McConnell	Y	Y	Y	Y	Y	Y	Y	Y
LOUISIANA								
Breaux	N	N	N	N	Y	Y	Y	N
Landrieu	Y	Y	N	N	Y	Y	Y	N
MAINE								
Collins	Y	Y	Y	Y	N	Y	Y	Y
Snowe	Y	Y	Y	Y	N	Y	Y	Y
MARYLAND								
Mikulski	N	N	N	N	Y	Y	Y	N
Sarbanes	N	N	N	N	Y	Y	Y	N
MASSACHUSETTS								
Kennedy	N	N	N	N	Y	Y	Y	N
Kerry	Y	Y	N	N	Y	Y	Y	N
MICHIGAN								
Abraham	Y	Y	Y	Y	Y	Y	Y	Y
Levin	N	N	N	N	Y	Y	Y	N
MINNESOTA								
Grams	Y	Y	Y	Y	N	Y	Y	Y
Wellstone	N	N	N	N	Y	Y	Y	N
MISSISSIPPI								
Cochran	Y	Y	N	Y	Y	Y	Y	Y
Lott	Y	Y	Y	Y	N	Y	Y	Y
MISSOURI								
Ashcroft	Y	Y	Y	Y	N	Y	Y	Y
Bond	Y	Y	Y	Y	Y	Y	Y	Y
MONTANA								
Burns	Y	Y	Y	Y	Y	Y	Y	Y
Baucus	Y	Y	Y	N	Y	Y	Y	N
NEBRASKA								
Hagel	Y	Y	Y	Y	N	Y	Y	Y
Kerrey	N	Y	N	N	Y	Y	Y	N
NEVADA								
Bryan	N	N	Y	N	Y	Y	Y	N
Reid	N	N	N	N	Y	Y	Y	N
NEW HAMPSHIRE								
Gregg	Y	Y	Y	Y	N	Y	Y	Y
Smith	Y	Y	Y	Y	N	Y	Y	Y
NEW JERSEY								
Lautenberg	N	N	N	N	Y	Y	Y	N
Torricelli	N	N	N	N	Y	Y	Y	N
NEW MEXICO								
Domenici	Y	Y	Y	Y	Y	Y	Y	Y
Bingaman	Y	Y	Y	N	Y	Y	Y	N
NEW YORK								
Moynihan	Y	Y	Y	N	Y	Y	Y	N
Schumer	N	Y	N	N	Y	Y	Y	N
NORTH CAROLINA								
Helms	Y	Y	Y	Y	Y	Y	Y	Y
Edwards	N	N	N	N	Y	Y	Y	N
NORTH DAKOTA								
Conrad	N	Y	N	N	Y	Y	Y	N
Dorgan	N	Y	N	N	Y	Y	Y	N
OHIO								
DeWine	Y	Y	Y	Y	Y	Y	Y	Y
Voinovich	Y	Y	Y	Y	N	Y	Y	Y
OKLAHOMA								
Inhofe	Y	Y	Y	Y	Y	Y	Y	Y
Nickles	Y	Y	Y	Y	N	Y	Y	Y
OREGON								
Smith	Y	Y	Y	Y	N	Y	Y	Y
Wyden	Y	N	Y	N	Y	Y	Y	N
PENNSYLVANIA								
Santorum	Y	Y	Y	Y	Y	Y	Y	Y
Specter	Y	Y	N	Y	Y	Y	Y	Y
RHODE ISLAND								
Chafee	Y	?	?	?	?	Y	Y	Y
Reed	N	N	N	N	Y	Y	Y	N
SOUTH CAROLINA								
Thurmond	Y	Y	Y	Y	Y	Y	Y	Y
Hollings	N	N	N	N	Y	Y	Y	N
SOUTH DAKOTA								
Daschle	N	N	N	N	Y	Y	Y	N
Johnson	N	N	N	N	Y	Y	Y	N
TENNESSEE								
Frist	Y	Y	Y	Y	N	Y	Y	Y
Thompson	Y	Y	N	Y	Y	Y	Y	Y
TEXAS								
Gramm	Y	Y	Y	Y	N	Y	Y	Y
Hutchison	Y	Y	Y	Y	Y	Y	Y	Y
UTAH								
Bennett	Y	Y	Y	Y	Y	Y	Y	Y
Hatch	Y	Y	Y	Y	Y	Y	Y	Y
VERMONT								
Jeffords	N	Y	Y	Y	Y	Y	Y	Y
Leahy	N	Y	N	N	Y	Y	Y	N
VIRGINIA								
Warner	Y	Y	Y	Y	N	Y	Y	Y
Robb	Y	Y	Y	N	Y	Y	Y	N
WASHINGTON								
Gorton	Y	Y	Y	Y	Y	Y	Y	Y
Murray	N	N	Y	N	Y	Y	Y	N
WEST VIRGINIA								
Byrd	N	N	Y	N	Y	Y	Y	N
Rockefeller	Y	Y	N	N	Y	Y	Y	N
WISCONSIN								
Feingold	N	N	N	N	Y	N	Y	N
Kohl	Y	Y	N	N	Y	Y	Y	N
WYOMING								
Enzi	Y	Y	Y	Y	N	Y	Y	Y
Thomas	?	Y	Y	Y	N	Y	Y	Y

ND Northern Democrats SD Southern Democrats

Southern states - Ala., Ark., Fla., Ga., Ky., La., Miss., N.C., Okla., S.C., Tenn., Texas, Va.

Key

- Y Voted for (yea).
- \# Paired for.
- \+ Announced for.
- N Voted against (nay).
- X Paired against.
- – Announced against.
- P Voted "present."
- C Voted "present" to avoid possible conflict of interest.
- ? Did not vote or otherwise make a position known.

Democrats ***Republicans***
Independents

163. S 96. Y2K Liability/Replacement Computers. Gorton, R-Wash., amendment to table (kill) the Boxer, D-Calif., amendment that would require computer manufacturers to repair or replace certain computers that are not Y2K-compliant. Motion agreed to 66-32: R 52-1; D 14-31 (ND 11-26, SD 3-5). June 10, 1999.

164. S 96. Y2K Liability Limits/Small Business Exemptions. Gregg, R-N.H., amendment that would exempt small businesses from certain civil penalties for first-time violations of federal regulations caused by Year 2000 computer failures. Adopted 71-28: R 54-0; D 17-28 (ND 14-23, SD 3-5). June 15, 1999.

165. HR 775. Y2K Liability Limits/Passage. Passage of the bill to cap at $250,000, or three times the amount of actual damages, whichever is less, the liability of small businesses from damage caused by so-called Year 2000 computer problems. Passed 62-37: R 50-4; D 12-33 (ND 10-27, SD 2-6). June 15, 1999. (Before passage, the Senate struck all after the enacting clause and inserted the text of S 96, as amended.) A "nay" was a vote in support of the president's position.

166. S 557. Budget Procedures/Social Security Lockbox-Cloture. Motion to invoke cloture (thus limiting debate) on the Lott, R-Miss., substitute amendment that would create a Social Security "lockbox," establish declining limits on the public debt and create a Senate point of order against any provision that would exceed the debt limit. The underlying bill would establish a Senate point of order against certain emergency spending items. Motion rejected 53-46: R 53-1; D 0-45 (ND 0-37, SD 0-8). June 15, 1999. Three-fifths of the total Senate (60) is required to invoke cloture.

167. HR 1664. Steel, Oil and Gas Loan Guarantee Program/Cloture. Motion to invoke cloture (thus limiting debate) on the motion to proceed to the bill to establish a $1 billion emergency loan guarantee program for the steel industry and a $500 million emergency loan guarantee program for the oil and gas industries, and to appropriate $270 million to cover loan defaults. Motion agreed to 71-28: R 26-28; D 45-0 (ND 37-0, SD 8-0). June 15, 1999. Three-fifths of the total Senate (60) is required to invoke cloture. (Subsequently, the motion to proceed was adopted by voice vote.)

168. S 1205. Fiscal 2000 Military Construction Appropriations/Passage. Passage of the bill to provide $8.3 billion for construction for bases and base closings, barracks, family housing and NATO infrastructure in fiscal 2000. Passed 97-2: R 54-1; D 43-1 (ND 35-1, SD 8-0). June 16, 1999.

169. S 331. Disability Work Incentives/Passage. Passage of the bill to amend the Social Security Act to expand the availability of health care coverage for disabled workers, to establish a program to help disabled individuals find and prepare for jobs, and to remove other disincentives that discourage the disabled from working. Passed 99-0: R 55-0; D 44-0 (ND 36-0, SD 8-0). June 16, 1999.

170. HR 1259. Social Security Lockbox/Cloture. Motion to invoke cloture (thus limiting debate) on a bill to reserve all of the Social Security surplus to be used only to guarantee the solvency of the Social Security and Medicare system. Motion rejected 55-44: R 55-0; D 0-44 (ND 0-36, SD 0-8). June 16, 1999. Three-fifths of the total Senate (60) is required to invoke cloture.

Senate Votes 171, 172, 173, 174, 175

	171	172	173	174	175
ALABAMA					
Sessions	Y	Y	Y	Y	Y
Shelby	Y	Y	Y	Y	Y
ALASKA					
Murkowski	Y	Y	Y	N	N
Stevens	Y	Y	Y	Y	Y
ARIZONA					
Kyl	Y	Y	Y	N	N
McCain	Y	Y	Y	N	?
ARKANSAS					
Hutchinson	Y	Y	Y	N	N
Lincoln	Y	Y	Y	Y	Y
CALIFORNIA					
Boxer	N	Y	Y	Y	Y
Feinstein	N	Y	Y	Y	Y
COLORADO					
Allard	Y	Y	Y	N	N
Campbell	Y	Y	Y	Y	N
CONNECTICUT					
Dodd	N	Y	Y	?	?
Lieberman	N	Y	Y	Y	Y
DELAWARE					
Roth	N	Y	Y	N	N
Biden	N	Y	Y	Y	Y
FLORIDA					
Mack	Y	Y	Y	N	N
Graham	Y	Y	Y	Y	Y
GEORGIA					
Coverdell	Y	Y	Y	N	N
Cleland	N	Y	Y	Y	Y
HAWAII					
Akaka	N	Y	Y	Y	N
Inouye	Y	Y	Y	Y	Y
IDAHO					
Craig	Y	Y	Y	N	N
Crapo	Y	Y	Y	N	N
ILLINOIS					
Fitzgerald	N	Y	Y	N	N
Durbin	N	Y	Y	Y	Y
INDIANA					
Bayh	N	Y	Y	Y	Y
Lugar	N	Y	Y	Y	Y
IOWA					
Grassley	N	Y	Y	N	N
Harkin	–	+	?	Y	Y
KANSAS					
Brownback	N	Y	Y	N	Y
Roberts	Y	Y	Y	Y	Y
KENTUCKY					
Bunning	Y	Y	Y	N	N
McConnell	Y	Y	Y	Y	N
LOUISIANA					
Breaux	Y	Y	Y	Y	Y
Landrieu	Y	Y	Y	Y	N
MAINE					
Collins	N	Y	Y	N	Y
Snowe	N	Y	Y	N	Y
MARYLAND					
Mikulski	Y	Y	Y	Y	Y
Sarbanes	Y	Y	Y	Y	Y
MASSACHUSETTS					
Kennedy	N	Y	Y	Y	Y
Kerry	N	Y	Y	Y	Y
MICHIGAN					
Abraham	Y	Y	Y	N	Y
Levin	N	Y	Y	Y	Y
MINNESOTA					
Grams	N	Y	Y	N	N
Wellstone	N	N	Y	Y	Y
MISSISSIPPI					
Cochran	Y	Y	Y	Y	Y
Lott	Y	Y	Y	N	N
MISSOURI					
Ashcroft	Y	Y	Y	N	N
Bond	Y	Y	Y	Y	N
MONTANA					
Burns	Y	Y	Y	N	N
Baucus	Y	Y	N	Y	Y
NEBRASKA					
Hagel	N	Y	Y	N	N
Kerrey	Y	Y	Y	Y	Y
NEVADA					
Bryan	N	Y	Y	Y	Y
Reid	Y	Y	Y	Y	Y
NEW HAMPSHIRE					
Gregg	N	Y	Y	N	Y
Smith	Y	Y	N	N	N
NEW JERSEY					
Lautenberg	Y	Y	Y	Y	Y
Torricelli	Y	Y	Y	Y	Y
NEW MEXICO					
Domenici	Y	Y	Y	Y	Y
Bingaman	N	Y	Y	Y	Y
NEW YORK					
Moynihan	Y	Y	Y	Y	Y
Schumer	N	Y	Y	Y	Y
NORTH CAROLINA					
Helms	Y	Y	Y	Y	N
Edwards	Y	Y	Y	Y	Y
NORTH DAKOTA					
Conrad	N	Y	N	Y	N
Dorgan	N	Y	Y	Y	Y
OHIO					
DeWine	Y	Y	Y	Y	Y
Voinovich	Y	Y	Y	N	N
OKLAHOMA					
Inhofe	Y	Y	Y	Y	N
Nickles	Y	Y	Y	N	N
OREGON					
Smith	N	Y	Y	N	Y
Wyden	N	Y	Y	Y	Y
PENNSYLVANIA					
Santorum	Y	Y	Y	?	?
Specter	Y	Y	Y	Y	N
RHODE ISLAND					
Chafee	N	Y	Y	N	Y
Reed	N	Y	Y	Y	Y
SOUTH CAROLINA					
Thurmond	Y	Y	Y	Y	N
Hollings	Y	Y	Y	Y	Y
SOUTH DAKOTA					
Daschle	Y	Y	Y	Y	Y
Johnson	N	Y	Y	Y	Y
TENNESSEE					
Frist	Y	Y	Y	N	N
Thompson	Y	Y	Y	N	N
TEXAS					
Gramm	Y	Y	N	N	N
Hutchison	Y	Y	Y	Y	N
UTAH					
Bennett	Y	Y	Y	Y	N
Hatch	Y	Y	Y	Y	N
VERMONT					
Jeffords	N	N	Y	Y	Y
Leahy	N	Y	Y	Y	Y
VIRGINIA					
Warner	N	Y	Y	N	Y
Robb	Y	Y	Y	Y	Y
WASHINGTON					
Gorton	Y	Y	Y	Y	Y
Murray	N	Y	Y	Y	Y
WEST VIRGINIA					
Byrd	Y	Y	Y	Y	Y
Rockefeller	N	Y	Y	Y	Y
WISCONSIN					
Feingold	N	Y	Y	Y	Y
Kohl	Y	Y	Y	Y	Y
WYOMING					
Enzi	Y	Y	Y	N	N
Thomas	Y	Y	Y	N	N

Key

- Y Voted for (yea).
- # Paired for.
- \+ Announced for.
- N Voted against (nay).
- X Paired against.
- – Announced against.
- P Voted "present."
- C Voted "present" to avoid possible conflict of interest.
- ? Did not vote or otherwise make a position known.

•

Democrats ***Republicans***
Independents

ND Northern Democrats SD Southern Democrats

Southern states - Ala., Ark., Fla., Ga., Ky., La., Miss., N.C., Okla., S.C., Tenn., Texas, Va.

171. S 1186. Fiscal 2000 Energy and Water Appropriations/Appeal Ruling of the Chair. Reid, D-Nev., motion to table (kill) the Jeffords, R-Vt., appeal of the ruling of the chair that the Jeffords motion-to recommit the bill to the committee with instructions to increase funding for renewable energy by $70 million-was out of order by virtue of a previous unanimous consent agreement. Motion agreed to 60-39: R 41-14; D 19-25 (ND 12-24, SD 7-1). June 16, 1999.

172. S 1186. Fiscal 2000 Energy and Water Appropriations/Passage. Passage of the bill to appropriate $21.7 billion for fiscal 2000 for energy and water resources development, including programs in the Army Corps of Engineers, the Bureau of Reclamation and the Department of Energy. Passed 97-2: R 54-1; D 43-1 (ND 35-1, SD 8-0). June 16, 1999.

173. HR 1905. Fiscal 2000 Legislative Branch Appropriations/Passage. Passage of the bill to appropriate $2.5 billion for fiscal 2000 legislative branch operations, including $489 million for the Senate and $739.9 million for the House. Passed 95-4: R 53-2; D 42-2 (ND 34-2, SD 8-0). June 16, 1999. (Before passage, the Senate struck certain provisions of the bill and substituted certain provisions of S 1206.)

174. HR 1664. Steel, Oil and Gas Loan Guarantee Program/Authorizations. Stevens, R-Alaska, motion to table (kill) the McCain, R-Ariz., amendment that would require the proper congressional committee to approve any authorizations contained in the bill before they can be funded. Motion agreed to 64-34: R 20-34; D 44-0 (ND 36-0, SD 8-0). June 17, 1999.

175. HR 1664. Steel, Oil and Gas Loan Guarantee Program/Glacier Bay National Park. Stevens, R-Alaska, motion to table (kill) the Murkowski, R-Alaska, amendment to prohibit the use of any funds appropriated in the bill by the Secretary of the Interior to close or otherwise restrict fishing in the non-wilderness waters of Glacier Bay National Park pending completion of an environmental impact study. Motion agreed to 59-38: R 18-35; D 41-3 (ND 34-2, SD 7-1). June 17, 1999.

Senate Votes 176, 177, 178, 179

	176	177	178	179
ALABAMA				
Sessions	Y	Y	Y	N
Shelby	Y	Y	Y	N
ALASKA				
Murkowski	N	?	N	N
Stevens	Y	Y	Y	N
ARIZONA				
Kyl	N	Y	N	N
McCain	?	?	?	?
ARKANSAS				
Hutchinson	N	Y	N	N
Lincoln	Y	Y	Y	Y
CALIFORNIA				
Boxer	Y	Y	Y	Y
Feinstein	Y	Y	N	N
COLORADO				
Allard	N	Y	N	N
Campbell	Y	Y	Y	N
CONNECTICUT				
Dodd	?	?	Y	N
Lieberman	Y	Y	N	N
DELAWARE				
Roth	N	Y	N	N
Biden	Y	Y	Y	N
FLORIDA				
Mack	N	Y	N	N
Graham	Y	Y	N	N
GEORGIA				
Coverdell	N	Y	N	N
Cleland	Y	Y	N	N
HAWAII				
Akaka	Y	Y	N	N
Inouye	Y	Y	N	N
IDAHO				
Craig	N	Y	N	N
Crapo	N	Y	N	N
ILLINOIS				
Fitzgerald	N	Y	N	Y
Durbin	Y	Y	Y	Y
INDIANA				
Bayh	Y	Y	Y	N
Lugar	Y	Y	N	N

	176	177	178	179
IOWA				
Grassley	N	Y	N	N
Harkin	Y	Y	Y	N
KANSAS				
Brownback	N	Y	N	N
Roberts	Y	Y	N	N
KENTUCKY				
Bunning	N	Y	N	N
McConnell	N	Y	N	N
LOUISIANA				
Breaux	Y	Y	N	N
Landrieu	Y	Y	N	N
MAINE				
Collins	N	Y	N	N
Snowe	N	Y	Y	N
MARYLAND				
Mikulski	Y	Y	Y	N
Sarbanes	Y	Y	Y	N
MASSACHUSETTS				
Kennedy	Y	?	N	N
Kerry	Y	Y	N	N
MICHIGAN				
Abraham	Y	Y	N	N
Levin	Y	Y	Y	N
MINNESOTA				
Grams	N	Y	N	Y
Wellstone	Y	Y	Y	Y
MISSISSIPPI				
Cochran	Y	Y	N	N
Lott	N	Y	N	N
MISSOURI				
Ashcroft	N	Y	N	N
Bond	Y	Y	N	N
MONTANA				
Burns	N	Y	Y	N
Baucus	Y	?	N	Y
NEBRASKA				
Hagel	N	Y	N	N
Kerrey	Y	Y	N	N
NEVADA				
Bryan	Y	Y	N	Y
Reid	Y	Y	Y	Y

	176	177	178	179
NEW HAMPSHIRE				
Gregg	N	Y	N	Y
Smith	N	Y	Y	Y
NEW JERSEY				
Lautenberg	Y	?	N	N
Torricelli	Y	Y	Y	N
NEW MEXICO				
Domenici	Y	Y	N	N
Bingaman	?	Y	N	Y
NEW YORK				
Moynihan	Y	Y	N	N
Schumer	Y	Y	Y	N
NORTH CAROLINA				
Helms	Y	Y	Y	Y
Edwards	Y	Y	Y	Y
NORTH DAKOTA				
Conrad	Y	Y	Y	N
Dorgan	Y	Y	Y	Y
OHIO				
DeWine	Y	Y	Y	N
Voinovich	N	Y	N	N
OKLAHOMA				
Inhofe	Y	?	Y	N
Nickles	N	?	N	Y
OREGON				
Smith	N	Y	N	N
Wyden	Y	Y	N	Y
PENNSYLVANIA				
Santorum	Y	?	Y	N
Specter	Y	Y	Y	Y
RHODE ISLAND				
Chafee	Y	?	N	N
Reed	Y	Y	Y	N
SOUTH CAROLINA				
Thurmond	Y	Y	Y	Y
Hollings	Y	Y	Y	Y
SOUTH DAKOTA				
Daschle	Y	Y	Y	N
Johnson	Y	Y	Y	Y
TENNESSEE				
Frist	N	Y	N	N
Thompson	N	Y	N	N

Key

- Y Voted for (yea).
- # Paired for.
- + Announced for.
- N Voted against (nay).
- X Paired against.
- – Announced against.
- P Voted "present."
- C Voted "present" to avoid possible conflict of interest.
- ? Did not vote or otherwise make a position known.

•

Democrats ***Republicans***
Independents

	176	177	178	179
TEXAS				
Gramm	N	Y	N	N
Hutchison	Y	Y	N	N
UTAH				
Bennett	Y	Y	Y	N
Hatch	Y	Y	Y	N
VERMONT				
Jeffords	N	Y	N	N
Leahy	Y	?	Y	N
VIRGINIA				
Warner	N	Y	N	N
Robb	Y	Y	Y	N
WASHINGTON				
Gorton	Y	Y	N	N
Murray	Y	Y	Y	N
WEST VIRGINIA				
Byrd	Y	Y	Y	N
Rockefeller	Y	Y	Y	N
WISCONSIN				
Feingold	N	Y	Y	Y
Kohl	Y	Y	N	Y
WYOMING				
Enzi	N	Y	N	N
Thomas	N	?	N	N

ND Northern Democrats SD Southern Democrats

Southern states - Ala., Ark., Fla., Ga., Ky., La., Miss., N.C., Okla., S.C., Tenn., Texas, Va.

176. HR 1664. Steel, Oil and Gas Loan Guarantee Program/Passage. Passage of a bill to establish a $1 billion emergency loan guarantee program for the steel industry and a $500 million emergency guarantee program for the oil and gas industries, and to appropriate $270 million to cover loan defaults and administrative costs. Passed 63-34: R 21-33; D 42-1 (ND 34-1, SD 8-0). June 18, 1999.

177. S 886. State Department Authorization/Grievance Filings. Sarbanes, D-Md., amendment to allow State Department employees two years to file a grievance (instead of one year as provided in the bill) and to limit the amount of time during which notice of an employee's suspension could be retained in the employee's file. Adopted 88-0: R 48-0; D 40-0 (ND 32-0, SD 8-0). June 21, 1999.

178. HR 975. Steel Import Quotas/Cloture. Motion to invoke cloture (thus limiting debate) on the bill to direct the president to take necessary steps — including imposing quotas, tariff surcharges or negotiated enforceable voluntary export restraints — to ensure that the monthly volume of imported steel products does not exceed the average monthly volume for the three-year period preceding July 1997. Motion failed 42-57: R 15-39; D 27-18 (ND 23-14, SD 4-4). June 22, 1999. Three-fifths of the total Senate (60) is required to invoke cloture. A "nay" was a vote in support of the president's position.

179. S 886. State Department Authorization/National Endowment for Democracy. Feingold, D-Wis., amendment that would require the National Endowment for Democracy to award a certain percentage of its grants on a competitive basis. Rejected 23-76: R 8-46; D 15-30 (ND 12-25, SD 3-5). June 22, 1999.

Senate Votes 180, 181, 182, 183

	180	181	182	183
ALABAMA				
Sessions	Y	N	Y	Y
Shelby	Y	N	Y	Y
ALASKA				
Murkowski	Y	N	Y	Y
Stevens	Y	N	Y	Y
ARIZONA				
Kyl	Y	N	Y	Y
McCain	?	N	Y	Y
ARKANSAS				
Hutchinson	Y	N	Y	Y
Lincoln	Y	Y	N	Y
CALIFORNIA				
Boxer	Y	Y	N	Y
Feinstein	Y	Y	N	Y
COLORADO				
Allard	Y	N	Y	Y
Campbell	Y	N	Y	Y
CONNECTICUT				
Dodd	Y	Y	N	Y
Lieberman	Y	Y	N	Y
DELAWARE				
Roth	Y	N	Y	Y
Biden	Y	Y	N	Y
FLORIDA				
Mack	Y	N	Y	Y
Graham	Y	Y	N	Y
GEORGIA				
Coverdell	Y	N	Y	Y
Cleland	Y	Y	N	Y
HAWAII				
Akaka	Y	Y	N	Y
Inouye	Y	Y	N	Y
IDAHO				
Craig	Y	N	Y	Y
Crapo	Y	N	Y	Y
ILLINOIS				
Fitzgerald	Y	N	N	Y
Durbin	Y	Y	N	Y
INDIANA				
Bayh	Y	Y	N	Y
Lugar	Y	N	Y	Y
IOWA				
Grassley	Y	N	Y	Y
Harkin	Y	Y	N	?
KANSAS				
Brownback	Y	N	Y	Y
Roberts	Y	N	Y	Y
KENTUCKY				
Bunning	Y	N	Y	Y
McConnell	Y	N	Y	Y
LOUISIANA				
Breaux	Y	Y	N	N
Landrieu	Y	Y	N	Y
MAINE				
Collins	Y	N	Y	Y
Snowe	Y	N	Y	Y
MARYLAND				
Mikulski	Y	Y	N	Y
Sarbanes	N	Y	N	Y
MASSACHUSETTS				
Kennedy	Y	Y	N	Y
Kerry	Y	Y	N	Y
MICHIGAN				
Abraham	Y	N	Y	Y
Levin	Y	Y	N	Y
MINNESOTA				
Grams	Y	N	Y	Y
Wellstone	Y	Y	N	Y
MISSISSIPPI				
Cochran	Y	N	Y	Y
Lott	Y	N	Y	Y
MISSOURI				
Ashcroft	Y	N	Y	Y
Bond	Y	N	Y	Y
MONTANA				
Burns	Y	N	Y	Y
Baucus	Y	Y	N	Y
NEBRASKA				
Hagel	Y	N	Y	Y
Kerrey	Y	Y	N	Y
NEVADA				
Bryan	Y	Y	N	Y
Reid	Y	Y	N	Y
NEW HAMPSHIRE				
Gregg	Y	N	Y	Y
Smith	N	N	Y	Y
NEW JERSEY				
Lautenberg	Y	Y	N	Y
Torricelli	Y	Y	N	Y
NEW MEXICO				
Domenici	Y	N	Y	Y
Bingaman	Y	Y	N	Y
NEW YORK				
Moynihan	Y	Y	N	Y
Schumer	Y	Y	N	Y
NORTH CAROLINA				
Helms	Y	N	Y	Y
Edwards	Y	Y	N	Y
NORTH DAKOTA				
Conrad	Y	Y	N	Y
Dorgan	Y	Y	N	Y
OHIO				
DeWine	Y	N	Y	Y
Voinovich	Y	N	Y	Y
OKLAHOMA				
Inhofe	Y	N	Y	Y
Nickles	Y	N	Y	Y
OREGON				
Smith	Y	N	Y	Y
Wyden	Y	Y	N	Y
PENNSYLVANIA				
Santorum	Y	N	Y	Y
Specter	Y	N	N	Y
RHODE ISLAND				
Chafee	Y	N	Y	Y
Reed	Y	Y	N	Y
SOUTH CAROLINA				
Thurmond	Y	N	Y	Y
Hollings	Y	Y	N	Y
SOUTH DAKOTA				
Daschle	Y	Y	N	Y
Johnson	Y	Y	N	Y
TENNESSEE				
Frist	Y	N	Y	Y
Thompson	Y	N	Y	Y
TEXAS				
Gramm	Y	N	Y	?
Hutchison	Y	N	Y	Y
UTAH				
Bennett	Y	N	Y	Y
Hatch	Y	N	Y	Y
VERMONT				
Jeffords	Y	N	Y	Y
Leahy	Y	Y	N	Y
VIRGINIA				
Warner	Y	N	Y	Y
Robb	Y	Y	N	Y
WASHINGTON				
Gorton	Y	N	Y	Y
Murray	Y	Y	N	Y
WEST VIRGINIA				
Byrd	Y	Y	N	Y
Rockefeller	Y	Y	N	Y
WISCONSIN				
Feingold	Y	Y	N	Y
Kohl	Y	Y	N	Y
WYOMING				
Enzi	Y	N	Y	Y
Thomas	Y	N	Y	Y

Key

- Y Voted for (yea).
- # Paired for.
- + Announced for.
- N Voted against (nay).
- X Paired against.
- – Announced against.
- P Voted "present."
- C Voted "present" to avoid possible conflict of interest.
- ? Did not vote or otherwise make a position known.

•

Democrats ***Republicans***
Independents

ND Northern Democrats SD Southern Democrats

Southern states - Ala., Ark., Fla., Ga., Ky., La., Miss., N.C., Okla., S.C., Tenn., Texas, Va.

180. S 886. State Department Authorization/Passage. Passage of the bill authorizing appropriations for fiscal 2000-2001 for the Department of State and other foreign operations-related programs. The bill would include provisions authorizing $819 million over three years to cover back U.S. debt to the United Nations and forgiving $107 million that the United Nations owes the United States. Passed 97-2: R 53-1; D 44-1 (ND 36-1, SD 8-0). June 22, 1999.

181. S 1233. Fiscal 2000 Agriculture Appropriations/Patients' Bill of Rights. Lott, R-Miss., motion to table (kill) the Lott amendment to the Dorgan, D-N.D., amendment that would attach the text of the Democrats' patients' rights bill (S 6) to the underlying appropriations bill. The Lott amendment would substitute the text of the Republicans' narrower patients' rights bill (S 326). Motion rejected 45-55: R 0-55; D 45-0 (ND 37-0, SD 8-0). June 22, 1999.

182. S 1233. Fiscal 2000 Agriculture Appropriations/Patients' Bill of Rights. Lott, R-Miss., motion to table (kill) the Dorgan, D-N.D., amendment to attach the text of the Democrats' patients' rights bill (S 6) to the underlying appropriations bill. Motion agreed to 53-47: R 53-2; D 0-45 (ND 0-37, SD 0-8). June 22, 1999.

183. Procedural Motion/Require Attendance. Lott, R-Miss., motion to instruct the sergeant at arms to request the attendance of absent senators. Motion agreed to 97-1: R 54-0; D 43-1 (ND 36-0, SD 7-1). June 24, 1999.

Senate Votes 184, 185, 186, 187, 188, 189, 190, 191

State / Senator	184	185	186	187	188	189	190	191
ALABAMA								
Sessions	Y	Y	Y	Y	Y	Y	Y	N
Shelby	Y	Y	Y	Y	Y	Y	Y	N
ALASKA								
Murkowski	?	?	?	?	Y	Y	Y	N
Stevens	Y	Y	Y	Y	Y	Y	Y	Y
ARIZONA								
Kyl	Y	Y	Y	Y	Y	Y	Y	N
McCain	Y	Y	Y	Y	?	Y	Y	N
ARKANSAS								
Hutchinson	?	?	?	?	Y	Y	Y	N
Lincoln	N	N	N	N	Y	N	Y	N
CALIFORNIA								
Boxer	?	?	?	?	Y	N	Y	Y
Feinstein	N	N	N	N	Y	N	Y	Y
COLORADO								
Allard	Y	Y	Y	Y	Y	Y	Y	N
Campbell	Y	Y	Y	Y	Y	Y	Y	Y
CONNECTICUT								
Dodd	–	N	N	N	Y	N	Y	N
Lieberman	–	–	–	–	Y	Y	Y	N
DELAWARE								
Roth	Y	Y	Y	Y	Y	Y	Y	N
Biden	N	N	N	N	Y	N	Y	Y
FLORIDA								
Mack	Y	Y	?	?	?	?	?	?
Graham	N	N	N	N	Y	Y	Y	Y
GEORGIA								
Coverdell	Y	Y	Y	Y	Y	Y	Y	N
Cleland	N	N	N	N	Y	N	Y	Y
HAWAII								
Akaka	N	N	N	N	Y	N	Y	Y
Inouye	N	N	N	N	Y	N	Y	Y
IDAHO								
Craig	Y	Y	Y	Y	Y	Y	Y	Y
Crapo	Y	Y	Y	Y	Y	Y	Y	N
ILLINOIS								
Fitzgerald	Y	Y	Y	Y	Y	Y	Y	Y
Durbin	N	N	N	N	Y	N	Y	Y
INDIANA								
Bayh	N	N	N	N	Y	Y	Y	Y
Lugar	Y	Y	Y	Y	Y	N	Y	N
IOWA								
Grassley	Y	Y	Y	Y	Y	Y	Y	Y
Harkin	N	N	N	N	Y	N	Y	Y
KANSAS								
Brownback	Y	Y	Y	Y	Y	Y	Y	N
Roberts	Y	Y	Y	Y	Y	N	Y	N
KENTUCKY								
Bunning	Y	Y	Y	Y	Y	Y	Y	Y
McConnell	Y	Y	Y	Y	Y	Y	Y	Y
LOUISIANA								
Breaux	N	N	N	N	Y	Y	Y	Y
Landrieu	N	N	N	N	Y	N	Y	N
MAINE								
Collins	Y	Y	Y	Y	Y	Y	Y	Y
Snowe	Y	Y	Y	Y	Y	Y	Y	N
MARYLAND								
Mikulski	N	N	N	N	Y	N	Y	Y
Sarbanes	N	N	N	N	Y	N	Y	Y
MASSACHUSETTS								
Kennedy	N	N	N	N	Y	N	Y	Y
Kerry	N	N	N	N	Y	N	Y	Y
MICHIGAN								
Abraham	Y	Y	Y	Y	Y	Y	Y	Y
Levin	N	N	N	N	Y	N	Y	Y
MINNESOTA								
Grams	Y	Y	Y	Y	Y	N	Y	N
Wellstone	?	N	N	N	Y	N	Y	Y
MISSISSIPPI								
Cochran	Y	Y	Y	Y	Y	Y	Y	N
Lott	Y	Y	Y	Y	Y	Y	Y	N
MISSOURI								
Ashcroft	Y	Y	Y	Y	Y	Y	Y	N
Bond	Y	Y	Y	Y	Y	N	Y	Y
MONTANA								
Burns	Y	Y	Y	Y	Y	Y	N	Y
Baucus	N	N	N	N	Y	N	Y	Y
NEBRASKA								
Hagel	Y	Y	Y	Y	Y	N	Y	N
Kerrey	N	N	N	N	Y	N	Y	Y
NEVADA								
Bryan	N	N	N	N	Y	Y	Y	Y
Reid	N	N	N	N	Y	Y	Y	Y
NEW HAMPSHIRE								
Gregg	Y	Y	Y	Y	Y	Y	Y	Y
Smith	Y	Y	N	N	Y	Y	N	N
NEW JERSEY								
Lautenberg	?	?	?	?	Y	N	Y	N
Torricelli	?	?	?	?	Y	Y	Y	Y
NEW MEXICO								
Domenici	Y	Y	Y	Y	Y	Y	Y	N
Bingaman	N	N	N	N	Y	N	Y	N
NEW YORK								
Moynihan	N	N	N	N	Y	N	Y	Y
Schumer	N	N	N	N	Y	N	Y	Y
NORTH CAROLINA								
Helms	Y	Y	Y	Y	Y	Y	N	N
Edwards	?	?	?	N	Y	Y	Y	Y
NORTH DAKOTA								
Conrad	N	N	N	N	Y	N	Y	N
Dorgan	N	N	N	N	Y	N	Y	N
OHIO								
DeWine	Y	Y	Y	Y	Y	Y	Y	Y
Voinovich	Y	Y	Y	Y	Y	?	?	?
OKLAHOMA								
Inhofe	?	?	?	?	Y	Y	Y	N
Nickles	Y	Y	Y	Y	Y	Y	Y	N
OREGON								
Smith	Y	Y	Y	Y	Y	Y	Y	N
Wyden	N	N	N	N	Y	N	Y	N
PENNSYLVANIA								
Santorum	Y	Y	Y	Y	Y	Y	Y	Y
Specter	Y	Y	Y	Y	Y	N	Y	Y
RHODE ISLAND								
Chafee	Y	N	Y	Y	Y	N	Y	N
Reed	N	N	N	N	Y	N	Y	Y
SOUTH CAROLINA								
Thurmond	Y	Y	Y	Y	Y	Y	Y	N
Hollings	N	N	N	N	Y	Y	Y	Y
SOUTH DAKOTA								
Daschle	N	N	N	N	Y	N	Y	Y
Johnson	N	N	N	N	Y	N	Y	Y
TENNESSEE								
Frist	Y	Y	Y	Y	Y	Y	Y	N
Thompson	Y	Y	Y	Y	Y	Y	Y	N
TEXAS								
Gramm	Y	Y	Y	Y	Y	Y	Y	N
Hutchison	Y	Y	Y	Y	Y	Y	Y	N
UTAH								
Bennett	Y	Y	Y	Y	Y	Y	Y	Y
Hatch	Y	Y	Y	Y	Y	Y	Y	Y
VERMONT								
Jeffords	?	?	?	?	Y	N	Y	N
Leahy	N	N	N	N	Y	N	Y	Y
VIRGINIA								
Warner	Y	N	Y	Y	Y	N	Y	N
Robb	N	N	N	N	Y	Y	Y	Y
WASHINGTON								
Gorton	?	?	?	?	Y	Y	Y	Y
Murray	N	N	N	N	Y	N	Y	N
WEST VIRGINIA								
Byrd	N	Y	Y	Y	Y	Y	Y	N
Rockefeller	N	N	N	N	Y	N	Y	Y
WISCONSIN								
Feingold	N	N	N	N	Y	N	Y	Y
Kohl	?	?	?	N	Y	Y	Y	Y
WYOMING								
Enzi	Y	Y	Y	Y	Y	N	N	Y
Thomas	Y	Y	Y	Y	Y	Y	Y	N

Key

- Y Voted for (yea).
- # Paired for.
- + Announced for.
- N Voted against (nay).
- X Paired against.
- – Announced against.
- P Voted "present."
- C Voted "present" to avoid possible conflict of interest.
- ? Did not vote or otherwise make a position known.

•

Democrats ***Republicans***
Independents

ND Northern Democrats SD Southern Democrats

Southern states - Ala., Ark., Fla., Ga., Ky., La., Miss., N.C., Okla., S.C., Tenn., Texas, Va.

184. S 1233. Fiscal 2000 Agriculture Appropriations/Cloture. Motion to invoke cloture (thus limiting debate) on the bill to provide $60.7 billion in new budget authority for the Agriculture Department, the Food and Drug Administration and rural development and nutrition programs in fiscal 2000. Motion rejected 50-37: R 50-0; D 0-37 (ND 0-30, SD 0-7). June 28, 1999. Three-fifths of the total Senate (60) is required to invoke cloture.

185. S 1143. Fiscal 2000 Transportation Appropriations/Cloture. Motion to invoke cloture (thus limiting debate) on the motion to proceed to the bill that would provide $49.5 billion in new budget authority for the Department of Transportation and related agencies in fiscal 2000. Motion rejected 49-40: R 48-2; D 1-38 (ND 1-31, SD 0-7). June 28, 1999. Three-fifths of the total Senate (60) is required to invoke cloture.

186. S 1217. Fiscal 2000 Commerce, Justice, State Appropriations/Cloture. Motion to invoke cloture (thus limiting debate) on the motion to proceed to the bill that would provide $35.3 billion in new budget authority for the departments of Commerce, Justice and State and the federal judiciary in fiscal 2000. Motion rejected 49-39: R 48-1; D 1-38 (ND 1-31, SD 0-7). June 28, 1999. Three-fifths of the total Senate (60) is required to invoke cloture.

187. S 1234. Fiscal 2000 Foreign Operations Appropriations/Cloture. Motion to invoke cloture (thus limiting debate) on the motion to proceed to the bill to provide $12.7 billion in new budget authority for foreign aid programs in fiscal 2000. Motion rejected 49-41: R 48-1; D 1-40 (ND 1-32, SD 0-8). June 28, 1999. Three-fifths of the total Senate (60) is required to invoke cloture.

188. S 1234. Fiscal 2000 Foreign Operations Appropriations/East Timor. Leahy, D-Vt., amendment that would direct administration officials to "immediately intensify their efforts" to persuade the Indonesian government and military to disarm and disband anti-independence militias in East Timor, grant human rights monitors full access to East Timor, and allow Timorese living in exile to return and release all political prisoners. Adopted 98-0: R 53-0; D 45-0 (ND 37-0, SD 8-0). June 30, 1999.

189. S 1234. Fiscal 2000 Foreign Operations Appropriations/Travel to Cuba. McConnell, R-Ky., motion to table (kill) the Dodd, D-Conn., amendment that would bar the president from regulating or prohibiting travel by U.S. citizens or legal residents to or from Cuba. Motion agreed to 55-43: R 43-10; D 12-33 (ND 7-30, SD 5-3). June 30, 1999.

190. District Judges/Confirmation. Confirmation of President Clinton's nominations of Keith P. Ellison of Texas to be U.S. District judge for the Southern District of Texas; Gary Allen Feess of California to be U.S. District judge for the Central District of California; Stefan R. Underhill of Connecticut to be U.S. District judge for the District of Connecticut; W. Allen Pepper Jr. of Mississippi to be U.S. District judge for the Northern District of Mississippi; and Karen E. Schreier of South Dakota to be U.S. District judge for the District of South Dakota. Confirmed 94-4: R 49-4; D 45-0 (ND 37-0, SD 8-0). June 30, 1999. A "yea" was a vote in support of the president's position.

191. S 1234. Fiscal 2000 Foreign Operations Appropriations/Azerbaijan Aid. McConnell, R-Ky., amendment to the Brownback, R-Kan., amendment. The McConnell amendment would strike language in the underlying amendment to allow the president to waive restrictions on certain U.S. aid to Azerbaijan. The Brownback amendment would expand U.S. aid to former Soviet Republics in the South Caucasus and Central Asia region. Adopted 53-45: R 19-34; D 34-11 (ND 28-9, SD 6-2). June 30, 1999. (Subsequently, the Brownback amendment as amended was adopted by voice vote.)

Senate Votes 192, 193, 194, 195, 196, 197

State	Senator	192	193	194	195	196	197
ALABAMA	***Sessions***	Y	Y	Y	Y	Y	N
	Shelby	Y	Y	Y	Y	N	N
ALASKA	***Murkowski***	Y	Y	Y	Y	?	?
	Stevens	Y	Y	N	Y	Y	Y
ARIZONA	***Kyl***	Y	Y	Y	Y	Y	N
	McCain	Y	Y	P	Y	Y	?
ARKANSAS	***Hutchinson***	Y	Y	Y	Y	Y	N
	Lincoln	Y	Y	Y	Y	Y	Y
CALIFORNIA	Boxer	Y	Y	N	Y	Y	Y
	Feinstein	Y	Y	N	Y	Y	Y
COLORADO	***Allard***	Y	Y	Y	N	Y	N
	Campbell	Y	Y	Y	Y	Y	Y
CONNECTICUT	Dodd	Y	Y	N	Y	Y	Y
	Lieberman	Y	Y	N	Y	Y	Y
DELAWARE	***Roth***	Y	N	N	Y	Y	N
	Biden	Y	Y	N	Y	N	N
FLORIDA	***Mack***	?	Y	Y	Y	Y	N
	Graham	Y	Y	Y	Y	Y	Y
GEORGIA	***Coverdell***	Y	Y	Y	Y	Y	N
	Cleland	Y	Y	N	Y	Y	Y
HAWAII	Akaka	Y	Y	N	Y	N	Y
	Inouye	Y	Y	?	?	Y	Y
IDAHO	***Craig***	Y	Y	Y	Y	Y	N
	Crapo	Y	Y	Y	Y	Y	N
ILLINOIS	***Fitzgerald***	Y	Y	Y	Y	Y	N
	Durbin	Y	Y	N	Y	N	Y
INDIANA	Bayh	Y	Y	N	Y	Y	Y
	Lugar	Y	Y	Y	Y	Y	N
IOWA	***Grassley***	Y	Y	Y	Y	Y	N
	Harkin	Y	Y	N	Y	Y	Y
KANSAS	***Brownback***	Y	Y	Y	Y	Y	N
	Roberts	Y	Y	Y	Y	Y	N
KENTUCKY	***Bunning***	Y	Y	Y	Y	Y	N
	McConnell	Y	Y	Y	Y	Y	N
LOUISIANA	Breaux	Y	Y	Y	Y	N	N
	Landrieu	Y	Y	N	Y	N	Y
MAINE	***Collins***	Y	Y	Y	Y	Y	Y
	Snowe	Y	Y	Y	Y	Y	Y
MARYLAND	Mikulski	Y	Y	N	Y	Y	Y
	Sarbanes	Y	Y	N	Y	N	Y
MASSACHUSETTS	Kennedy	Y	Y	N	Y	Y	Y
	Kerry	Y	Y	N	Y	Y	Y
MICHIGAN	***Abraham***	Y	Y	Y	Y	Y	N
	Levin	Y	Y	N	Y	N	Y
MINNESOTA	***Grams***	Y	Y	Y	Y	Y	N
	Wellstone	Y	Y	N	Y	N	Y
MISSISSIPPI	***Cochran***	Y	Y	Y	Y	Y	N
	Lott	Y	Y	Y	Y	Y	N
MISSOURI	***Ashcroft***	Y	Y	Y	Y	Y	N
	Bond	Y	Y	Y	Y	Y	N
MONTANA	***Burns***	Y	Y	Y	Y	Y	N
	Baucus	Y	Y	Y	Y	Y	Y
NEBRASKA	***Hagel***	Y	Y	Y	Y	Y	N
	Kerrey	Y	Y	Y	Y	Y	Y
NEVADA	Bryan	Y	Y	N	Y	Y	Y
	Reid	Y	Y	N	Y	N	N
NEW HAMPSHIRE	***Gregg***	Y	Y	Y	Y	Y	N
	Smith	N	Y	Y	N	Y	N
NEW JERSEY	Lautenberg	Y	Y	N	Y	Y	Y
	Torricelli	Y	Y	Y	Y	N	Y
NEW MEXICO	***Domenici***	Y	Y	Y	Y	Y	N
	Bingaman	Y	Y	N	Y	Y	Y
NEW YORK	Moynihan	Y	Y	N	Y	Y	Y
	Schumer	Y	Y	N	Y	Y	Y
NORTH CAROLINA	***Helms***	Y	Y	N	Y	Y	N
	Edwards	Y	Y	N	Y	N	Y
NORTH DAKOTA	Conrad	Y	Y	Y	Y	Y	N
	Dorgan	Y	Y	Y	Y	Y	N
OHIO	***DeWine***	Y	Y	N	Y	Y	N
	Voinovich	Y	Y	Y	Y	Y	N
OKLAHOMA	***Inhofe***	Y	Y	Y	Y	Y	N
	Nickles	Y	Y	Y	Y	Y	N
OREGON	***Smith***	Y	Y	Y	Y	Y	N
	Wyden	Y	Y	N	Y	Y	Y
PENNSYLVANIA	***Santorum***	Y	Y	Y	Y	Y	N
	Specter	Y	Y	N	Y	N	Y
RHODE ISLAND	***Chafee***	Y	Y	Y	Y	Y	Y
	Reed	Y	Y	N	Y	Y	Y
SOUTH CAROLINA	***Thurmond***	Y	Y	Y	Y	Y	N
	Hollings	Y	Y	N	Y	N	Y
SOUTH DAKOTA	Daschle	Y	Y	Y	Y	Y	Y
	Johnson	Y	Y	N	Y	N	Y
TENNESSEE	***Frist***	Y	Y	Y	Y	Y	N
	Thompson	Y	Y	Y	Y	Y	N
TEXAS	***Gramm***	Y	Y	Y	Y	Y	N
	Hutchison	Y	Y	N	Y	Y	N
UTAH	***Bennett***	Y	Y	Y	Y	Y	N
	Hatch	Y	Y	Y	Y	Y	N
VERMONT	***Jeffords***	Y	Y	Y	Y	Y	Y
	Leahy	Y	Y	N	Y	N	Y
VIRGINIA	***Warner***	Y	Y	Y	Y	Y	N
	Robb	Y	Y	Y	Y	Y	Y
WASHINGTON	***Gorton***	Y	Y	Y	Y	Y	N
	Murray	Y	Y	N	Y	Y	Y
WEST VIRGINIA	Byrd	N	Y	N	Y	Y	Y
	Rockefeller	Y	Y	N	Y	N	Y
WISCONSIN	Feingold	Y	Y	N	Y	N	Y
	Kohl	Y	Y	N	Y	Y	Y
WYOMING	***Enzi***	Y	Y	Y	Y	Y	N
	Thomas	Y	Y	Y	Y	Y	N

ND Northern Democrats   SD Southern Democrats

Southern states - Ala., Ark., Fla., Ga., Ky., La., Miss., N.C., Okla., S.C., Tenn., Texas, Va.

Key

- Y Voted for (yea).
- \# Paired for.
- \+ Announced for.
- N Voted against (nay).
- X Paired against.
- – Announced against.
- P Voted "present."
- C Voted "present" to avoid possible conflict of interest.
- ? Did not vote or otherwise make a position known.

Democrats   ***Republicans***
Independents

192. S 1234. Fiscal 2000 Foreign Operations Appropriations/Passage. Passage of the bill to provide $12.7 billion in new budget authority for foreign aid programs in fiscal 2000, $1.9 billion less than President Clinton's request. Passed 97-2: R 53-1; D 44-1 (ND 36-1, SD 8-0). June 30, 1999.

193. S 557. Budget Procedures/Cloture. Motion to invoke cloture (thus limiting debate) on the motion to proceed to the bill that would establish a Senate point of order against any emergency spending items that do not meet specific criteria. The motion to proceed is necessary to return to consideration of a Republican amendment that would create a Social Security "lockbox," establish declining limits on the public debt and create a Senate point of order against any provision that would exceed the debt limit. Motion agreed to 99-1: R 54-1; D 45-0 (ND 37-0, SD 8-0), July 1, 1999. Three-fifths of the total Senate (60) is required to invoke cloture. (Subsequently, the motion to proceed was adopted by voice vote.)

194. S 1282. Fiscal 2000 Treasury-Postal Service Appropriations/Alcohol Use by Minors. Campbell, R-Colo., motion to table (kill) the Lautenberg, D-N.J., amendment that would add alcohol use by minors to the topics addressed by the national anti-drug media campaign intended to reduce youth drug use. Motion agreed to 58-40: R 48-6; D 10-34 (ND 6-30, SD 4-4), July 1, 1999.

195. Summers Nomination/Confirmation. Confirmation of President Clinton's nomination of Lawrence H. Summers of Maryland to be Secretary of the Treasury. Confirmed 97-2: R 53-2; D 44-0 (ND 36-0, SD 8-0), July 1, 1999. A "yea" was a vote in support of the president's position.

196. HR 775. Y2K Liability Limits/Conference Report. Adoption of the conference report on the bill that would limit liability from so-called Year 2000 computer problems. The agreement would cap punitive damages for businesses with 50 or fewer employees at $250,000, or three times the amount of compensatory damages, whichever is less, would require a plaintiff to wait at least 30 days and up to 90 days before suing and would establish "proportional liability" to link defendants' share of liability to their degree of responsibility. Adopted (thus cleared for the president) 81-18: R 52-2; D 29-16 (ND 25-12, SD 4-4), July 1, 1999.

197. S 1282. Fiscal 2000 Treasury-Postal Service Appropriations/Abortion Coverage. Boxer, D-Calif., motion to table (kill) the DeWine, R-Ohio, amendment that would prohibit funding for abortions or for administrative expenses of federal health plans that provide coverage for abortions, except when the life of the mother is endangered or the pregnancy is the result of rape or incest. Motion rejected 47-51: R 7-46; D 40-5 (ND 33-4, SD 7-1), July 1, 1999. (Subsequently, the DeWine amendment was adopted and the $27.7 billion underlying bill was passed by voice vote.)

Senate Votes 198, 199, 200, 201, 202, 203, 204

	198	199	200	201	202	203	204
ALABAMA							
Sessions	N	Y	Y	N	Y	Y	N
Shelby	N	Y	Y	N	Y	Y	N
ALASKA							
Murkowski	N	Y	Y	N	Y	Y	N
Stevens	N	Y	Y	N	Y	Y	N
ARIZONA							
Kyl	N	Y	Y	N	Y	Y	N
McCain	N	Y	Y	N	Y	Y	Y
ARKANSAS							
Hutchinson	N	Y	Y	N	Y	Y	N
Lincoln	Y	N	N	Y	N	N	Y
CALIFORNIA							
Boxer	Y	N	N	Y	N	N	Y
Feinstein	Y	N	N	Y	N	N	Y
COLORADO							
Allard	N	Y	Y	N	Y	Y	N
Campbell	N	Y	Y	N	Y	Y	N
CONNECTICUT							
Dodd	Y	N	N	Y	N	N	Y
Lieberman	Y	N	N	Y	N	N	Y
DELAWARE							
Roth	N	Y	Y	N	Y	Y	N
Biden	Y	N	N	Y	N	N	Y
FLORIDA							
Mack	N	Y	Y	N	Y	Y	N
Graham	Y	N	N	Y	N	N	Y
GEORGIA							
Coverdell	N	Y	Y	N	Y	Y	N
Cleland	Y	N	N	Y	N	N	Y
HAWAII							
Akaka	Y	N	N	Y	N	N	Y
Inouye	Y	N	N	Y	N	N	Y
IDAHO							
Craig	N	Y	Y	N	Y	Y	N
Crapo	N	Y	Y	N	Y	Y	N
ILLINOIS							
Fitzgerald	N	N	N	N	Y	Y	N
Durbin	Y	N	N	Y	N	N	Y
INDIANA							
Bayh	Y	N	N	Y	N	N	Y
Lugar	N	Y	Y	N	Y	Y	N
IOWA							
Grassley	N	Y	Y	N	Y	Y	N
Harkin	Y	N	N	Y	N	N	Y
KANSAS							
Brownback	N	Y	Y	N	Y	Y	N
Roberts	N	Y	Y	N	Y	Y	N
KENTUCKY							
Bunning	N	Y	Y	N	Y	Y	N
McConnell	N	Y	Y	N	Y	Y	N
LOUISIANA							
Breaux	Y	N	N	Y	N	N	Y
Landrieu	Y	N	N	Y	N	N	Y
MAINE							
Collins	N	Y	Y	N	Y	Y	N
Snowe	N	Y	Y	N	Y	Y	N
MARYLAND							
Mikulski	Y	N	N	Y	N	N	Y
Sarbanes	Y	N	N	Y	N	N	Y
MASSACHUSETTS							
Kennedy	Y	N	N	Y	N	N	Y
Kerry	Y	N	N	Y	N	N	Y
MICHIGAN							
Abraham	N	N	Y	N	Y	Y	N
Levin	Y	N	N	Y	N	N	Y
MINNESOTA							
Grams	N	Y	Y	N	Y	Y	N
Wellstone	Y	N	N	Y	N	N	Y
MISSISSIPPI							
Cochran	N	Y	Y	N	Y	Y	N
Lott	N	Y	Y	N	Y	Y	N
MISSOURI							
Ashcroft	N	Y	Y	N	Y	Y	N
Bond	N	Y	Y	N	Y	Y	N
MONTANA							
Burns	N	Y	Y	N	Y	Y	N
Baucus	Y	N	N	Y	N	N	Y
NEBRASKA							
Hagel	N	Y	Y	N	Y	Y	N
Kerrey	Y	N	N	Y	N	N	Y
NEVADA							
Bryan	Y	N	N	Y	N	N	Y
Reid	Y	N	N	Y	N	N	Y
NEW HAMPSHIRE							
Gregg	N	Y	Y	N	Y	Y	N
Smith [1]	N	Y	Y	N	Y	Y	N
NEW JERSEY							
Lautenberg	Y	N	N	Y	N	N	Y
Torricelli	Y	N	N	Y	N	N	Y
NEW MEXICO							
Domenici	N	Y	Y	N	Y	Y	N
Bingaman	Y	N	N	Y	N	N	Y
NEW YORK							
Moynihan	Y	N	N	Y	N	N	Y
Schumer	Y	N	N	Y	N	N	Y
NORTH CAROLINA							
Helms	N	Y	Y	N	Y	Y	N
Edwards	Y	N	N	Y	N	N	Y
NORTH DAKOTA							
Conrad	Y	N	N	Y	N	N	Y
Dorgan	Y	N	N	Y	N	N	Y
OHIO							
DeWine	N	Y	Y	N	Y	Y	N
Voinovich	N	Y	Y	N	Y	Y	N
OKLAHOMA							
Inhofe	N	Y	Y	N	Y	Y	N
Nickles	N	Y	Y	N	Y	Y	N
OREGON							
Smith	N	Y	Y	N	Y	Y	N
Wyden	Y	N	N	Y	N	N	Y
PENNSYLVANIA							
Santorum	N	Y	Y	N	Y	Y	N
Specter	Y	Y	N	Y	N	Y	Y
RHODE ISLAND							
Chafee	Y	N	N	Y	N	Y	Y
Reed	Y	N	N	Y	N	N	Y
SOUTH CAROLINA							
Thurmond	N	Y	Y	N	Y	Y	N
Hollings	Y	N	N	Y	N	N	Y
SOUTH DAKOTA							
Daschle	Y	N	N	Y	N	N	Y
Johnson	Y	N	N	Y	N	N	Y
TENNESSEE							
Frist	N	Y	Y	N	Y	Y	N
Thompson	N	Y	Y	N	Y	Y	N
TEXAS							
Gramm	N	Y	Y	N	Y	Y	N
Hutchison	N	Y	Y	N	Y	Y	N
UTAH							
Bennett	N	Y	Y	N	Y	Y	N
Hatch	N	Y	Y	N	Y	Y	N
VERMONT							
Jeffords	N	Y	Y	N	Y	Y	N
Leahy	Y	N	N	Y	N	N	Y
VIRGINIA							
Warner	Y	Y	Y	N	Y	Y	N
Robb	Y	N	N	Y	N	N	Y
WASHINGTON							
Gorton	N	Y	Y	N	Y	Y	N
Murray	Y	N	N	Y	N	N	Y
WEST VIRGINIA							
Byrd	Y	N	N	Y	N	N	Y
Rockefeller	Y	N	N	Y	N	N	Y
WISCONSIN							
Feingold	Y	N	N	Y	N	N	Y
Kohl	Y	N	N	Y	N	N	Y
WYOMING							
Enzi	N	Y	Y	N	Y	Y	N
Thomas	N	Y	Y	N	Y	Y	N

Key

- Y Voted for (yea).
- # Paired for.
- + Announced for.
- N Voted against (nay).
- X Paired against.
- – Announced against.
- P Voted "present."
- C Voted "present" to avoid possible conflict of interest.
- ? Did not vote or otherwise make a position known.

Democrats ***Republicans*** *Independents*

ND Northern Democrats SD Southern Democrats

Southern states - Ala., Ark., Fla., Ga., Ky., La., Miss., N.C., Okla., S.C., Tenn., Texas, Va.

198. S 1344. Managed Care Revisions/Primary Physician. Robb, D-Va., amendment to strike the Nickles, R-Okla., amendment and replace it with language to allow women in group health plans to designate an obstetrician/gynecologist as their primary care physician, and to determine, with their physicians, using "generally accepted medical standards," the appropriate length of a hospital stay following a mastectomy, lumpectomy or lymph node dissection for the treatment of breast cancer. It also would allow self-employed individuals to fully deduct the cost of their health insurance on their federal taxes, with the cost offset by an extension of superfund taxes. Rejected 48-52: R 3-51; D 45-0 (ND 37-0, SD 8-0); I 0-1. July 13, 1999.

199. S 1344. Managed Care Revisions/Appeals Process and Medical Necessity. Frist, R-Tenn., amendment to the Nickles, R-Okla., amendment. The Frist amendment would strike the medical necessity provisions in the underlying bill, and replace the independent appeals provisions with language to establish a narrower internal and external appeals process. Adopted 52-48: R 51-3; D 0-45 (ND 0-37, SD 0-8); I 1-0. July 13, 1999.

200. S 1344. Managed Care Revisions/Cost Increases. Nickles, R-Okla., amendment to exempt from the bill's provisions any group health plan whose compliance would result in more than a 1 percent increase in premium costs in a plan year, or a 100,000-person decrease in any given plan year of the number of Americans with private health insurance. The amendment also includes the text of the previously adopted Frist, R-Tenn., amendment. Adopted 52-48: R 51-3; D 0-45 (ND 0-37, SD 0-8); I 1-0. July 13, 1999.

201. S 1344. Managed Care Revisions/Emergency Room Coverage. Graham, D-Fla., amendment to the Kennedy, D-Mass., amendment to the Daschle, D-S.D., substitute amendment. The Graham amendment would require group health plans to cover emergency room treatment and follow-up care for plan members without prior authorization if a "prudent layperson" determined that the member required immediate medical attention. Rejected 47-53: R 2-52; D 45-0 (ND 37-0, SD 8-0); I 0-1. July 13, 1999.

202. S 1344. Managed Care Revisions/Bill Scope, Deduction for Self-Employed. Santorum, R-Pa., amendment to the Kennedy, D-Mass., amendment to the Daschle, D-S.D., substitute amendment. The Santorum amendment would strike the Kennedy language to expand the scope of the substitute. Instead, it would allow the self-employed to fully deduct their health insurance costs on federal taxes, and express the sense of the Senate that states have primary responsibility for regulating health care. Adopted 53-47: R 52-2; D 0-45 (ND 0-37, SD 0-8); I 1-0. July 13, 1999. (Subsequently, the Kennedy amendment, as amended, was adopted by voice vote.)

203. S 1344. Managed Care Revisions/Cancer Treatments. Snowe, R-Maine, amendment to the Dodd, D-Conn., amendment to the Daschle, D-S.D., substitute amendment. The Snowe amendment would strike the Dodd amendment and replace it with language to allow all individuals in private health plans to determine, with their physicians, the length of hospital stay that is "medically necessary" following surgery for breast cancer. It also would allow all cancer patients to receive a second opinion on diagnoses or treatments. The Dodd amendment would require health plans to allow patients with life-threatening or serious illnesses, for whom standard treatments are ineffective, to participate in approved clinical trials. Adopted 55-45: R 54-0; D 0-45 (ND 0-37, SD 0-8); I 1-0. July 14, 1999. (Subsequently, the Dodd amendment, as amended, was adopted by voice vote.)

204. S 1344. Managed Care Revisions/Scope of Provisions. Kennedy, D-Mass., amendment to the Dodd, D-Conn., amendment to the Daschle, D-S.D., substitute amendment. The Kennedy amendment would apply the Daschle provisions to all individuals with private health insurance. Rejected 48-52: R 3-51; D 45-0 (ND 37-0, SD 8-0); I 0-1. July 14, 1999.

[1] *Robert C. Smith of New Hampshire changed his party affiliation from Republican to Independent on July 13, 1999.*

Senate Votes 205, 206, 207, 208, 209, 210

	205	206	207	208	209	210
ALABAMA						
Sessions	N	Y	Y	Y	N	Y
Shelby	N	Y	Y	Y	N	Y
ALASKA						
Murkowski	N	Y	Y	Y	N	Y
Stevens	N	Y	Y	Y	N	Y
ARIZONA						
Kyl	N	Y	Y	Y	N	Y
McCain	N	Y	Y	Y	N	Y
ARKANSAS						
Hutchinson	N	Y	Y	Y	N	Y
Lincoln	Y	N	N	N	Y	N
CALIFORNIA						
Boxer	Y	N	N	N	Y	N
Feinstein	Y	N	N	N	Y	N
COLORADO						
Allard	N	Y	Y	Y	N	Y
Campbell	N	Y	Y	Y	N	Y
CONNECTICUT						
Dodd	Y	N	N	N	Y	N
Lieberman	Y	N	N	N	Y	N
DELAWARE						
Roth	N	Y	Y	Y	N	Y
Biden	Y	N	N	N	Y	N
FLORIDA						
Mack	N	Y	Y	Y	N	Y
Graham	Y	N	N	N	Y	N
GEORGIA						
Coverdell	N	Y	Y	Y	N	Y
Cleland	Y	N	N	N	Y	N
HAWAII						
Akaka	Y	N	N	N	Y	N
Inouye	Y	N	N	N	Y	N
IDAHO						
Craig	N	Y	Y	Y	N	Y
Crapo	N	Y	Y	Y	N	Y
ILLINOIS						
Fitzgerald	N	N	Y	Y	N	N
Durbin	Y	N	N	N	Y	N
INDIANA						
Bayh	Y	N	N	N	Y	N
Lugar	N	Y	Y	Y	N	Y
IOWA						
Grassley	N	Y	Y	Y	N	Y
Harkin	Y	N	N	N	Y	N
KANSAS						
Brownback	N	Y	Y	Y	N	Y
Roberts	N	Y	Y	Y	N	Y
KENTUCKY						
Bunning	N	Y	Y	Y	N	Y
McConnell	N	Y	Y	Y	N	Y
LOUISIANA						
Breaux	Y	N	N	N	Y	N
Landrieu	Y	N	N	N	Y	N
MAINE						
Collins	N	Y	Y	Y	N	Y
Snowe	N	Y	Y	Y	Y	Y
MARYLAND						
Mikulski	Y	N	N	N	Y	N
Sarbanes	Y	N	N	N	Y	N
MASSACHUSETTS						
Kennedy	Y	N	N	N	Y	N
Kerry	Y	N	N	N	Y	N
MICHIGAN						
Abraham	N	Y	Y	Y	N	Y
Levin	Y	N	N	N	Y	N
MINNESOTA						
Grams	N	Y	Y	Y	N	Y
Wellstone	Y	N	N	N	Y	N
MISSISSIPPI						
Cochran	N	Y	Y	Y	N	Y
Lott	N	Y	Y	Y	N	Y
MISSOURI						
Ashcroft	N	Y	Y	Y	N	Y
Bond	N	Y	Y	Y	N	Y
MONTANA						
Burns	N	Y	Y	Y	N	Y
Baucus	Y	N	N	N	Y	N
NEBRASKA						
Hagel	N	Y	Y	Y	N	Y
Kerrey	Y	N	N	N	Y	N
NEVADA						
Bryan	Y	N	N	N	Y	N
Reid	Y	N	N	N	Y	N
NEW HAMPSHIRE						
Gregg	N	Y	Y	Y	N	Y
Smith	N	Y	Y	Y	N	Y
NEW JERSEY						
Lautenberg	Y	N	N	N	Y	N
Torricelli	Y	N	N	N	Y	N
NEW MEXICO						
Domenici	N	Y	Y	Y	N	Y
Bingaman	Y	N	N	N	Y	N
NEW YORK						
Moynihan	Y	N	N	N	Y	N
Schumer	Y	N	N	N	Y	N
NORTH CAROLINA						
Helms	N	Y	Y	Y	N	Y
Edwards	Y	N	N	N	Y	N
NORTH DAKOTA						
Conrad	Y	N	N	N	Y	N
Dorgan	Y	N	N	N	Y	N
OHIO						
DeWine	N	Y	Y	Y	N	Y
Voinovich	N	Y	Y	Y	N	Y
OKLAHOMA						
Inhofe	N	Y	Y	Y	N	Y
Nickles	N	Y	Y	Y	N	Y
OREGON						
Smith	N	Y	Y	Y	N	Y
Wyden	Y	N	N	N	Y	N
PENNSYLVANIA						
Santorum	N	Y	Y	Y	N	Y
Specter	Y	N	Y	Y	Y	Y
RHODE ISLAND						
Chafee	Y	Y	N	N	Y	N
Reed	Y	N	N	N	Y	N
SOUTH CAROLINA						
Thurmond	N	Y	Y	Y	N	Y
Hollings	Y	N	N	N	Y	N
SOUTH DAKOTA						
Daschle	Y	N	N	N	Y	N
Johnson	Y	N	N	N	Y	N
TENNESSEE						
Frist	N	Y	Y	Y	N	Y
Thompson	N	Y	Y	Y	N	Y
TEXAS						
Gramm	N	Y	Y	Y	N	Y
Hutchison	N	Y	Y	Y	N	Y
UTAH						
Bennett	N	Y	Y	Y	N	Y
Hatch	N	Y	Y	Y	N	Y
VERMONT						
Jeffords	N	Y	Y	Y	N	Y
Leahy	Y	N	N	N	Y	N
VIRGINIA						
Warner	N	Y	Y	Y	N	Y
Robb	Y	N	N	N	Y	N
WASHINGTON						
Gorton	N	Y	Y	Y	N	Y
Murray	Y	N	N	N	Y	N
WEST VIRGINIA						
Byrd	Y	N	N	N	Y	N
Rockefeller	Y	N	N	N	Y	N
WISCONSIN						
Feingold	Y	N	N	N	Y	N
Kohl	Y	N	N	N	Y	N
WYOMING						
Enzi	N	Y	Y	Y	N	Y
Thomas	N	Y	Y	Y	N	Y

Key

- Y Voted for (yea).
- # Paired for.
- + Announced for.
- N Voted against (nay).
- X Paired against.
- – Announced against.
- P Voted "present."
- C Voted "present" to avoid possible conflict of interest.
- ? Did not vote or otherwise make a position known.

•

Democrats ***Republicans***
Independents

ND Northern Democrats SD Southern Democrats

Southern states - Ala., Ark., Fla., Ga., Ky., La., Miss., N.C., Okla., S.C., Tenn., Texas, Va.

205. S 1344. Managed Care Revisions/Access to Specialists. Bingaman, D-N.M., amendment to the Collins, R-Maine, amendment to the Daschle, D-S.D., substitute amendment. The Bingaman amendment would have allowed patients in need of a specialist to visit one outside their plan network at no additional cost if the plan could not provide necessary care by a qualified provider within the network. Rejected 47-53: R 2-52; D 45-0 (ND 37-0, SD 8-0); I 0-1. July 14, 1999.

206. S 1344. Managed Care Revisions/Liability. Gregg, R-N.H., amendment to the Collins, R-Maine, amendment to the Daschle, D-S.D., substitute amendment. The Gregg amendment would strike language in the underlying bill that would allow patients to sue in state courts for damages if they are harmed by a plan's denial of treatment. Adopted 53-47: R 52-2; D 0-45 (ND 0-37, SD 0-8); I 1-0. July 15, 1999.

207. S 1344. Managed Care Revisions/Long-Term Care and Access. Collins, R-Maine, amendment that would allow individuals to deduct 100 percent of the costs of long-term care insurance and would revise the underlying bill's provisions concerning coverage of emergency room services, access to specialists, and obstetrician and gynecological care. The amendment also includes the Gregg, R-N.H., amendment. Adopted 54-46: R 53-1; D 0-45 (ND 0-37, SD 0-8); I 1-0. July 15, 1999.

208. S 1344. Managed Care Revisions/External Appeals and Clinical Trials. Ashcroft, R-Mo., amendment to the Wyden, D-Ore., amendment to the Daschle, D-S.D., substitute amendment. The Ashcroft amendment would strike the Wyden amendment and replace it with several revised Republican provisions concerning external appeals, approved clinical trials for cancer patients, exclusion of providers by plans, point of service options and continuing care for terminally ill patients. The Wyden amendment would, among other things, prevent plans from restricting what information physicians can give their patients or retaliating against doctors who aid patients in appealing plan decisions, and establish ombudsman programs for consumers. Adopted 54-46: R 53-1; D 0-45 (ND 0-37, SD 0-8); I 1-0. July 15, 1999.

209. S 1344. Managed Care Revisions/Continuing Care. Kerrey, D-Neb., amendment to the Wyden, D-Ore., amendment to the Daschle, D-S.D., substitute amendment. The Kerrey amendment would require plans to provide at least a 90-day extension of coverage for patients undergoing treatment if their plan changes or their doctor's contract with the plan is terminated. Rejected 48-52: R 3-51; D 45-0 (ND 37-0, SD 8-0); I 0-1. July 15, 1999. (Subsequently, the Wyden amendment as amended by the Ashcroft amendment was adopted by voice vote.)

210. S 1344. Managed Care Revisions/Passage. Passage of the bill to provide federal protections, such as access to emergency care, continuing care and approved clinical cancer trials, primarily for the 48 million Americans in self-insured health plans. The bill also would establish an internal and external appeals process, prohibit denials based on predictive genetic information, allow self-employed individuals to deduct the full cost of their health care and expand the availability of medical savings accounts. Passed 53-47: R 52-2; D 0-45 (ND 0-37, SD 0-8); I 1-0. July 15, 1999. (Before passage, the Senate adopted a Lott, R-Miss., substitute amendment by voice vote.) A "nay" was a vote in support of the president's position.

Senate Votes 211, 212, 213, 214, 215

	211	212	213	214	215
ALABAMA					
Sessions	Y	Y	Y	N	N
Shelby	Y	Y	N	N	N
ALASKA					
Murkowski	Y	Y	N	N	N
Stevens	Y	Y	N	N	N
ARIZONA					
Kyl	Y	Y	N	N	N
McCain	?	Y	N	N	N
ARKANSAS					
Hutchinson	Y	Y	Y	N	N
Lincoln	N	Y	N	N	Y
CALIFORNIA					
Boxer	?	Y	N	N	Y
Feinstein	N	Y	N	N	Y
COLORADO					
Allard	Y	Y	N	N	N
Campbell	Y	Y	N	Y	N
CONNECTICUT					
Dodd	?	Y	N	N	Y
Lieberman	N	Y	N	N	Y
DELAWARE					
Roth	N	Y	N	N	N
Biden	N	Y	N	N	Y
FLORIDA					
Mack	Y	Y	N	N	N
Graham	N	Y	N	N	Y
GEORGIA					
Coverdell	Y	Y	N	N	N
Cleland	N	Y	N	N	Y
HAWAII					
Akaka	N	Y	N	N	Y
Inouye	N	Y	N	N	Y
IDAHO					
Craig	Y	Y	N	N	?
Crapo	Y	Y	N	N	N
ILLINOIS					
Fitzgerald	Y	Y	N	N	N
Durbin	N	Y	N	N	Y
INDIANA					
Bayh	N	Y	N	N	Y
Lugar	Y	Y	N	N	N
IOWA					
Grassley	Y	Y	N	N	N
Harkin	N	Y	N	N	Y
KANSAS					
Brownback	Y	Y	N	N	N
Roberts	Y	Y	N	N	N
KENTUCKY					
Bunning	Y	Y	Y	N	N
McConnell	Y	Y	N	N	N
LOUISIANA					
Breaux	N	Y	N	N	Y
Landrieu	N	Y	N	N	Y
MAINE					
Collins	Y	Y	Y	N	N
Snowe	Y	Y	Y	N	N
MARYLAND					
Mikulski	N	Y	N	N	Y
Sarbanes	N	Y	N	N	Y
MASSACHUSETTS					
Kennedy	N	?	?	?	?
Kerry	?	Y	N	N	Y
MICHIGAN					
Abraham	Y	Y	N	N	N
Levin	N	Y	N	N	Y
MINNESOTA					
Grams	Y	Y	N	N	N
Wellstone	N	Y	Y	N	Y
MISSISSIPPI					
Cochran	Y	Y	N	N	N
Lott	Y	Y	N	N	N
MISSOURI					
Ashcroft	Y	Y	N	N	N
Bond	Y	Y	N	N	N
MONTANA					
Burns	+	Y	N	N	N
Baucus	N	Y	N	N	Y
NEBRASKA					
Hagel	Y	Y	N	N	N
Kerrey	N	Y	N	N	Y
NEVADA					
Bryan	N	Y	N	N	Y
Reid	N	Y	N	N	Y
NEW HAMPSHIRE					
Gregg	Y	Y	N	N	N
Smith	Y	Y	Y	Y	N
NEW JERSEY					
Lautenberg	N	Y	N	N	Y
Torricelli	N	Y	N	N	Y
NEW MEXICO					
Domenici	Y	Y	N	N	N
Bingaman	N	Y	N	N	Y
NEW YORK					
Moynihan	N	Y	N	N	Y
Schumer	N	Y	N	N	Y
NORTH CAROLINA					
Helms	Y	Y	Y	Y	N
Edwards	N	Y	N	N	Y
NORTH DAKOTA					
Conrad	N	Y	N	N	Y
Dorgan	N	Y	N	N	Y
OHIO					
DeWine	Y	Y	N	N	N
Voinovich	Y	Y	N	N	N
OKLAHOMA					
Inhofe	Y	Y	Y	N	N
Nickles	Y	Y	N	N	N
OREGON					
Smith	Y	Y	N	N	N
Wyden	N	Y	N	N	Y
PENNSYLVANIA					
Santorum	Y	Y	N	N	N
Specter	Y	Y	N	N	N
RHODE ISLAND					
Chafee	Y	Y	N	N	N
Reed	N	Y	N	N	Y
SOUTH CAROLINA					
Thurmond	Y	Y	N	N	N
Hollings	N	Y	Y	Y	Y
SOUTH DAKOTA					
Daschle	N	Y	N	N	Y
Johnson	N	Y	N	N	Y
TENNESSEE					
Frist	Y	Y	N	N	N
Thompson	Y	Y	N	N	N
TEXAS					
Gramm	Y	Y	N	N	N
Hutchison	Y	Y	N	N	N
UTAH					
Bennett	Y	Y	N	N	N
Hatch	Y	Y	N	N	N
VERMONT					
Jeffords	Y	Y	N	N	N
Leahy	N	Y	Y	N	Y
VIRGINIA					
Warner	Y	Y	N	N	N
Robb	N	Y	N	N	Y
WASHINGTON					
Gorton	Y	Y	N	N	N
Murray	N	Y	N	N	Y
WEST VIRGINIA					
Byrd	N	Y	N	N	Y
Rockefeller	N	Y	N	N	Y
WISCONSIN					
Feingold	N	Y	Y	Y	Y
Kohl	N	Y	N	N	Y
WYOMING					
Enzi	Y	Y	N	N	N
Thomas	Y	Y	N	N	N

Key

- Y Voted for (yea).
- # Paired for.
- + Announced for.
- N Voted against (nay).
- X Paired against.
- – Announced against.
- P Voted "present."
- C Voted "present" to avoid possible conflict of interest.
- ? Did not vote or otherwise make a position known.

•

Democrats ***Republicans***
Independents

ND Northern Democrats SD Southern Democrats

Southern states - Ala., Ark., Fla., Ga., Ky., La., Miss., N.C., Okla., S.C., Tenn., Texas, Va.

211. S 557. Budget Procedures/Social Security 'Lockbox'-Cloture. Motion to invoke cloture (thus limiting debate) on the Lott, R-Miss., amendment that would create a Social Security "lockbox," establish declining limits on the public debt and create a Senate point of order against any provision that would exceed the debt limit. Motion rejected 52-43: R 51-1; D 0-42 (ND 0-34, SD 0-8); I 1-0. July 16, 1999. Three-fifths of the total Senate (60) is required to invoke cloture.

212. HR 1555. Fiscal 2000 Intelligence Authorization/Cloture. Motion to invoke cloture (thus limiting debate) on the motion to proceed to the bill that would authorize intelligence programs for fiscal 2000. Motion agreed to 99-0: R 54-0; D 44-0 (ND 36-0, SD 8-0); I 1-0. July 20, 1999. Three-fifths of the total Senate (60) is required to invoke cloture.

213. S J Res 27. China Normal Trade Relations Denial/Discharge Motion. Smith, I-N.H., motion to discharge from the Finance Committee and bring to the Senate floor the joint resolution that would reverse President Clinton's June 3 decision to extend normal trade relations with China for one year. Motion rejected 12-87: R 7-47; D 4-40 (ND 3-33, SD 1-7); I 1-0. July 20, 1999.

214. S J Res 28. Vietnam Trade Relations Denial/Discharge Motion. Smith, I-N.H., motion to discharge from the Finance Committee and bring to the Senate floor the joint resolution that would disapprove President Clinton's June 3 decision to allow the United States to continue its trade with and provide other support to Vietnam. Motion rejected 5-94: R 2-52; D 2-42 (ND 1-35, SD 1-7); I 1-0. July 20, 1999.

215. HR 1555. Fiscal 2000 Intelligence Authorization/Energy Department Security. Levin, D-Mich., amendment to the Kyl, R-Ariz., amendment. The Levin amendment would require that the Energy secretary have responsibility for developing and implementing all department-wide security, counterintelligence and intelligence policies, while the director of the Agency for Nuclear Stewardship, a position that would be established by the Kyl amendment, would implement the secretary's policies within the new agency. Rejected 44-54: R 0-53; D 44-0 (ND 36-0, SD 8-0); I 0-1. July 21, 1999.

Senate Votes 216, 217, 218, 219, 220

	216	217	218	219	220
ALABAMA					
Sessions	Y	N	N	Y	Y
Shelby	Y	?	?	?	?
ALASKA					
Murkowski	Y	N	N	Y	Y
Stevens	Y	N	Y	Y	Y
ARIZONA					
Kyl	Y	N	N	Y	Y
McCain	?	?	?	?	?
ARKANSAS					
Hutchinson	Y	N	N	Y	Y
Lincoln	Y	Y	Y	N	N
CALIFORNIA					
Boxer	Y	Y	Y	N	N
Feinstein	Y	Y	Y	N	N
COLORADO					
Allard	Y	N	N	Y	N
Campbell	Y	N	Y	Y	Y
CONNECTICUT					
Dodd	Y	Y	N	N	N
Lieberman	Y	Y	N	Y	N
DELAWARE					
Roth	Y	Y	N	Y	N
Biden	Y	Y	Y	N	N
FLORIDA					
Mack	Y	N	Y	Y	N
Graham	Y	Y	Y	N	N
GEORGIA					
Coverdell	Y	N	N	Y	Y
Cleland	Y	Y	Y	N	N
HAWAII					
Akaka	Y	N	Y	N	N
Inouye	Y	Y	Y	N	N
IDAHO					
Craig	Y	N	N	Y	Y
Crapo	Y	N	N	Y	Y
ILLINOIS					
Fitzgerald	Y	N	N	Y	N
Durbin	Y	Y	N	N	N
INDIANA					
Bayh	Y	N	Y	N	N
Lugar	Y	N	N	Y	Y
IOWA					
Grassley	Y	Y	N	Y	N
Harkin	Y	Y	Y	N	N
KANSAS					
Brownback	Y	N	N	Y	Y
Roberts	Y	N	N	Y	Y
KENTUCKY					
Bunning	Y	N	N	Y	Y
McConnell	Y	N	N	Y	Y
LOUISIANA					
Breaux	Y	Y	Y	N	Y
Landrieu	Y	Y	Y	N	Y
MAINE					
Collins	Y	N	N	Y	N
Snowe	Y	N	Y	Y	N
MARYLAND					
Mikulski	Y	Y	Y	N	N
Sarbanes	Y	Y	Y	N	N
MASSACHUSETTS					
Kennedy	?	?	?	?	?
Kerry	Y	Y	Y	N	N
MICHIGAN					
Abraham	Y	N	N	Y	N
Levin	Y	Y	Y	N	N
MINNESOTA					
Grams	Y	N	N	Y	Y
Wellstone	Y	Y	Y	N	N
MISSISSIPPI					
Cochran	Y	N	N	Y	Y
Lott	Y	N	N	Y	Y
MISSOURI					
Ashcroft	Y	N	N	Y	Y
Bond	Y	N	N	Y	Y
MONTANA					
Burns	Y	N	N	Y	N
Baucus	Y	Y	Y	N	N
NEBRASKA					
Hagel	Y	N	Y	Y	Y
Kerrey	Y	Y	Y	N	N
NEVADA					
Bryan	Y	Y	Y	Y	N
Reid	Y	Y	Y	Y	N
NEW HAMPSHIRE					
Gregg	Y	N	N	Y	Y
Smith	Y	N	N	Y	N
NEW JERSEY					
Lautenberg	Y	Y	Y	N	N
Torricelli	Y	N	Y	N	N
NEW MEXICO					
Domenici	Y	N	N	Y	Y
Bingaman	Y	Y	Y	N	N
NEW YORK					
Moynihan	Y	Y	N	N	N
Schumer	Y	Y	Y	Y	N
NORTH CAROLINA					
Helms	Y	N	N	Y	Y
Edwards	Y	Y	Y	N	N
NORTH DAKOTA					
Conrad	Y	Y	Y	N	N
Dorgan	Y	Y	Y	N	N
OHIO					
DeWine	Y	N	Y	Y	N
Voinovich	Y	N	N	Y	Y
OKLAHOMA					
Inhofe	Y	N	N	Y	N
Nickles	Y	N	N	Y	Y
OREGON					
Smith	Y	N	N	Y	N
Wyden	N	Y	Y	N	N
PENNSYLVANIA					
Santorum	Y	N	N	Y	N
Specter	Y	Y	N	N	N
RHODE ISLAND					
Chafee	Y	N	N	Y	N
Reed	Y	Y	N	N	N
SOUTH CAROLINA					
Thurmond	Y	N	N	Y	N
Hollings	Y	Y	Y	N	N
SOUTH DAKOTA					
Daschle	Y	Y	Y	N	N
Johnson	Y	Y	Y	Y	N
TENNESSEE					
Frist	Y	N	N	Y	N
Thompson	Y	N	N	Y	Y
TEXAS					
Gramm	Y	N	N	?	Y
Hutchison	Y	Y	N	Y	Y
UTAH					
Bennett	Y	N	N	Y	Y
Hatch	Y	N	N	Y	Y
VERMONT					
Jeffords	?	Y	N	Y	N
Leahy	Y	Y	Y	N	?
VIRGINIA					
Warner	Y	N	N	Y	Y
Robb	Y	N	Y	N	N
WASHINGTON					
Gorton	Y	N	N	Y	Y
Murray	Y	Y	Y	N	N
WEST VIRGINIA					
Byrd	Y	Y	Y	N	N
Rockefeller	Y	Y	Y	N	N
WISCONSIN					
Feingold	Y	N	Y	N	N
Kohl	Y	N	Y	N	N
WYOMING					
Enzi	Y	N	N	Y	Y
Thomas	Y	N	N	Y	N

Key

- Y Voted for (yea).
- # Paired for.
- + Announced for.
- N Voted against (nay).
- X Paired against.
- – Announced against.
- P Voted "present."
- C Voted "present" to avoid possible conflict of interest.
- ? Did not vote or otherwise make a position known.

•

Democrats ***Republicans***
Independents

ND Northern Democrats SD Southern Democrats

Southern states - Ala., Ark., Fla., Ga., Ky., La., Miss., N.C., Okla., S.C., Tenn., Texas, Va.

216. HR 1555. Fiscal 2000 Intelligence Authorization/Energy Department Security. Kyl, R-Ariz., amendment to establish a semiautonomous Agency for Nuclear Stewardship within the Energy Department (DOE) to oversee all DOE activities related to national security, such as nuclear weapons, and all activities at DOE national security laboratories and nuclear weapons production facilities. The amendment would allow the new agency's director to bypass the Energy secretary and report security breaches directly to Congress and the president. Adopted 96-1: R 52-0; D 43-1 (ND 35-1, SD 8-0); I 1-0. July 21, 1999. (Subsequently, the underlying bill to authorize classified amounts in fiscal 2000 for intelligence agencies and intelligence-related activities of the U.S. government was passed by voice vote.)

217. S 1217. Fiscal 2000 Commerce, Justice, State Appropriations/Underage Drinking Media Campaign. Lautenberg, D-N.J., amendment that would provide $25 million for a media campaign to prevent alcohol use by individuals under 21 years old. Rejected 43-54: R 5-47; D 38-6 (ND 31-5, SD 7-1); I 0-1. July 22, 1999.

218. S 1217. Fiscal 2000 Commerce, Justice, State Appropriations/FCC Accounting Requirements. Hollings, D-S.C., motion to table (kill) the Enzi, R-Wyo., amendment that would prohibit the Federal Communications Commission from requiring the utilization of any accounting method that does not conform to "generally accepted accounting principles" established by the Financial Accounting Standards Board. Motion rejected 45-52: R 6-46; D 39-5 (ND 31-5, SD 8-0); I 0-1. July 22, 1999. (Subsequently, the Enzi amendment was adopted by voice vote.)

219. S 1217. Fiscal 2000 Commerce, Justice, State Appropriations/Prisoner Injunctive Relief. Gregg, R-N.H., motion to table (kill) the Wellstone, D-Minn., amendment that would exempt juveniles and the mentally ill from current laws that limit the power of federal courts to grant injunctive relief on the basis of prison conditions. Motion agreed to 56-40: R 50-1; D 5-39 (ND 5-31, SD 0-8); I 1-0. July 22, 1999.

220. S 1217. Fiscal 2000 Commerce, Justice, State Appropriations/Tuna Importation. Gregg, R-N.H., motion to table (kill) the Boxer, D-Calif., amendment that would prohibit importation of tuna from any nation in the Inter-American Tropical Tuna Commission in any year in which the nation has not paid a proportionate share of the commission's expenses. Motion rejected 35-61: R 33-19; D 2-41 (ND 0-35, SD 2-6); I 0-1. July 22, 1999. (Subsequently, the Boxer amendment was adopted and the $35.3 billion underlying bill was passed by voice vote.)

Senate Votes 221, 222, 223, 224

	221	222	223	224
ALABAMA				
Sessions	N	Y	Y	Y
Shelby	N	Y	Y	N
ALASKA				
Murkowski	N	Y	Y	Y
Stevens	N	Y	Y	Y
ARIZONA				
Kyl	N	Y	Y	N
McCain	?	?	N	Y
ARKANSAS				
Hutchinson	N	Y	Y	N
Lincoln	Y	N	Y	Y
CALIFORNIA				
Boxer	Y	N	N	Y
Feinstein	Y	N	N	Y
COLORADO				
Allard	N	Y	Y	N
Campbell	N	Y	Y	N
CONNECTICUT				
Dodd	Y	N	N	Y
Lieberman	Y	N	N	Y
DELAWARE				
Roth	Y	Y	N	Y
Biden	Y	N	?	Y
FLORIDA				
Mack	N	Y	Y	Y
Graham	Y	N	N	Y
GEORGIA				
Coverdell	N	Y	Y	N
Cleland	Y	N	N	Y
HAWAII				
Akaka	Y	N	N	Y
Inouye	Y	N	Y	Y
IDAHO				
Craig	N	Y	Y	N
Crapo	N	Y	Y	N
ILLINOIS				
Fitzgerald	N	Y	N	Y
Durbin	Y	N	N	Y
INDIANA				
Bayh	Y	N	N	Y
Lugar	N	Y	Y	Y

	221	222	223	224
IOWA				
Grassley	N	Y	Y	N
Harkin	Y	N	N	Y
KANSAS				
Brownback	N	Y	Y	N
Roberts	N	Y	Y	Y
KENTUCKY				
Bunning	N	Y	Y	N
McConnell	N	Y	Y	Y
LOUISIANA				
Breaux	Y	N	Y	Y
Landrieu	Y	N	N	Y
MAINE				
Collins	N	Y	N	Y
Snowe	N	Y	N	Y
MARYLAND				
Mikulski	Y	N	N	Y
Sarbanes	Y	N	N	Y
MASSACHUSETTS				
Kennedy	Y	N	?	Y
Kerry	Y	N	N	Y
MICHIGAN				
Abraham	N	Y	Y	Y
Levin	Y	N	N	Y
MINNESOTA				
Grams	N	Y	Y	N
Wellstone	Y	N	N	Y
MISSISSIPPI				
Cochran	N	Y	Y	Y
Lott	N	Y	?	Y
MISSOURI				
Ashcroft	N	Y	Y	Y
Bond	N	Y	Y	Y
MONTANA				
Burns	N	Y	Y	N
Baucus	Y	Y	N	Y
NEBRASKA				
Hagel	Y	Y	Y	Y
Kerrey	Y	N	N	Y
NEVADA				
Bryan	Y	N	Y	Y
Reid	Y	N	Y	Y

	221	222	223	224
NEW HAMPSHIRE				
Gregg	N	Y	N	Y
Smith	N	Y	Y	N
NEW JERSEY				
Lautenberg	Y	N	N	Y
Torricelli	Y	N	N	Y
NEW MEXICO				
Domenici	N	Y	Y	Y
Bingaman	Y	N	Y	Y
NEW YORK				
Moynihan	Y	Y	?	Y
Schumer	Y	N	N	Y
NORTH CAROLINA				
Helms	N	Y	Y	N
Edwards	Y	N	N	Y
NORTH DAKOTA				
Conrad	Y	N	Y	Y
Dorgan	Y	N	N	Y
OHIO				
DeWine	N	Y	Y	Y
Voinovich	?	?	N	?
OKLAHOMA				
Inhofe	N	Y	Y	N
Nickles	N	Y	Y	N
OREGON				
Smith	N	Y	Y	Y
Wyden	Y	N	N	Y
PENNSYLVANIA				
Santorum	N	Y	Y	N
Specter	N	N	N	Y
RHODE ISLAND				
Chafee	N	Y	Y	Y
Reed	Y	N	N	Y
SOUTH CAROLINA				
Thurmond	N	Y	Y	Y
Hollings	Y	N	Y	Y
SOUTH DAKOTA				
Daschle	Y	N	Y	Y
Johnson	Y	N	N	Y
TENNESSEE				
Frist	N	Y	Y	Y
Thompson	N	Y	Y	Y

Key

- Y Voted for (yea).
- # Paired for.
- + Announced for.
- N Voted against (nay).
- X Paired against.
- – Announced against.
- P Voted "present."
- C Voted "present" to avoid possible conflict of interest.
- ? Did not vote or otherwise make a position known.

•

Democrats ***Republicans***
Independents

	221	222	223	224
TEXAS				
Gramm	N	Y	Y	N
Hutchison	N	N	Y	N
UTAH				
Bennett	N	Y	Y	Y
Hatch	N	Y	Y	Y
VERMONT				
Jeffords	N	Y	N	Y
Leahy	Y	N	N	Y
VIRGINIA				
Warner	N	Y	Y	Y
Robb	Y	N	N	Y
WASHINGTON				
Gorton	N	Y	Y	Y
Murray	Y	N	N	Y
WEST VIRGINIA				
Byrd	Y	N	Y	Y
Rockefeller	Y	N	N	Y
WISCONSIN				
Feingold	Y	N	N	Y
Kohl	Y	N	N	Y
WYOMING				
Enzi	N	Y	Y	N
Thomas	N	Y	Y	N

ND Northern Democrats SD Southern Democrats

Southern states - Ala., Ark., Fla., Ga., Ky., La., Miss., N.C., Okla., S.C., Tenn., Texas, Va.

221. S Res 160. Legislating on Spending Bills/Conference Report Scope. Daschle, D-S.D., amendment that would reinstate all precedents of the Senate concerning Rule XXVIII that were in effect at the end of the 103rd Congress, thus re-establishing a Senate point of order against any conference report that contains provisions that were not in either the House- or Senate-passed bills. Rejected 47-51: R 2-50; D 45-0 (ND 37-0, SD 8-0); I 0-1. July 26, 1999.

222. S Res 160. Legislating on Spending Bills/Adoption. Adoption of the resolution to reapply all precedents of the Senate concerning Rule XVI that were in effect at the conclusion of the 103rd Congress, thus reinstating a Senate point of order against any amendment to an appropriations bill that contains authorizing language, known as a legislative "rider." Adopted 53-45: R 50-2; D 2-43 (ND 2-35, SD 0-8); I 1-0. July 26, 1999.

223. HR 2466. Fiscal 2000 Interior Appropriations/Mining Waste Disposal. Stevens, R-Alaska, motion to table (kill) the Murray, D-Wash., amendment that would remove bill language prohibiting implementation of a 1997 Interior Department ruling limiting mining waste disposal to a single, five-acre site for each mining operation. Motion agreed to 55-41: R 44-9; D 10-32 (ND 7-27, SD 3-5); I 1-0. July 27, 1999.

224. HR 1501. Juvenile Justice/Cloture. Motion to invoke cloture (thus limiting debate) on the Lott, R-Miss., substitute amendment that would authorize funding for programs designed to reduce youth violence. The amendment, the text of the Senate-passed juvenile crime measure (S 254), also contains several gun control provisions. Motion agreed to 77-22: R 32-21; D 45-0 (ND 37-0, SD 8-0); I 0-1. July 28, 1999. Three-fifths of the total Senate (60) is required to invoke cloture. (Subsequently, the Lott substitute amendment, the bill as amended and the procedural steps necessary for the Senate to proceed to a House-Senate conference were adopted by voice vote.)

Senate Votes 225, 226, 227, 228

	225	226	227	228
ALABAMA				
Sessions	Y	N	Y	N
Shelby	Y	N	Y	N
ALASKA				
Murkowski	Y	N	Y	N
Stevens	Y	N	Y	N
ARIZONA				
Kyl	Y	N	Y	N
McCain	Y	N	Y	N
ARKANSAS				
Hutchinson	Y	N	Y	N
Lincoln	N	Y	N	Y
CALIFORNIA				
Boxer	N	Y	N	Y
Feinstein	N	Y	N	Y
COLORADO				
Allard	Y	N	Y	N
Campbell	Y	N	Y	N
CONNECTICUT				
Dodd	N	Y	N	Y
Lieberman	N	N	N	Y
DELAWARE				
Roth	Y	N	N	N
Biden	N	Y	N	Y
FLORIDA				
Mack	Y	N	Y	N
Graham	N	Y	N	Y
GEORGIA				
Coverdell	Y	N	Y	N
Cleland	N	Y	N	Y
HAWAII				
Akaka	N	Y	N	Y
Inouye	N	Y	N	Y
IDAHO				
Craig	Y	N	Y	N
Crapo	Y	N	Y	N
ILLINOIS				
Fitzgerald	Y	N	Y	N
Durbin	N	Y	N	Y
INDIANA				
Bayh	N	N	N	Y
Lugar	Y	N	Y	N
IOWA				
Grassley	Y	N	Y	N
Harkin	N	Y	N	Y
KANSAS				
Brownback	Y	N	Y	N
Roberts	Y	N	Y	N
KENTUCKY				
Bunning	Y	N	Y	N
McConnell	Y	N	Y	N
LOUISIANA				
Breaux	N	Y	N	N
Landrieu	N	Y	N	Y
MAINE				
Collins	N	N	Y	N
Snowe	N	N	Y	N
MARYLAND				
Mikulski	N	Y	N	Y
Sarbanes	N	Y	N	Y
MASSACHUSETTS				
Kennedy	N	Y	N	Y
Kerry	N	Y	N	Y
MICHIGAN				
Abraham	Y	N	Y	N
Levin	N	Y	N	Y
MINNESOTA				
Grams	Y	N	Y	N
Wellstone	N	N	N	Y
MISSISSIPPI				
Cochran	Y	N	Y	N
Lott	Y	N	Y	N
MISSOURI				
Ashcroft	Y	N	Y	N
Bond	Y	N	Y	N
MONTANA				
Burns	Y	N	Y	N
Baucus	N	Y	N	Y
NEBRASKA				
Hagel	Y	N	Y	N
Kerrey	N	Y	N	N
NEVADA				
Bryan	N	Y	N	Y
Reid	N	Y	N	Y
NEW HAMPSHIRE				
Gregg	Y	N	Y	N
Smith	Y	N	Y	N
NEW JERSEY				
Lautenberg	N	Y	N	Y
Torricelli	N	N	N	Y
NEW MEXICO				
Domenici	Y	N	Y	N
Bingaman	N	Y	N	Y
NEW YORK				
Moynihan	N	Y	N	Y
Schumer	N	Y	N	Y
NORTH CAROLINA				
Helms	Y	N	Y	N
Edwards	N	N	N	Y
NORTH DAKOTA				
Conrad	N	Y	N	Y
Dorgan	N	Y	N	Y
OHIO				
DeWine	Y	N	Y	N
Voinovich	?	?	Y	N
OKLAHOMA				
Inhofe	Y	N	Y	N
Nickles	Y	N	Y	N
OREGON				
Smith	Y	N	Y	N
Wyden	N	Y	N	Y
PENNSYLVANIA				
Santorum	Y	N	Y	N
Specter	N	N	Y	N
RHODE ISLAND				
Chafee	Y	N	Y	N
Reed	N	Y	N	Y
SOUTH CAROLINA				
Thurmond	Y	N	Y	N
Hollings	N	Y	N	N
SOUTH DAKOTA				
Daschle	N	Y	N	Y
Johnson	N	Y	N	Y
TENNESSEE				
Frist	Y	N	Y	N
Thompson	Y	N	Y	N
TEXAS				
Gramm	Y	N	Y	N
Hutchison	Y	N	Y	N
UTAH				
Bennett	Y	N	Y	N
Hatch	Y	N	Y	N
VERMONT				
Jeffords	Y	N	Y	N
Leahy	N	Y	N	Y
VIRGINIA				
Warner	Y	N	Y	N
Robb	N	Y	N	Y
WASHINGTON				
Gorton	Y	N	Y	N
Murray	N	Y	N	Y
WEST VIRGINIA				
Byrd	N	N	N	Y
Rockefeller	N	Y	N	Y
WISCONSIN				
Feingold	N	Y	N	Y
Kohl	N	Y	N	Y
WYOMING				
Enzi	Y	N	Y	N
Thomas	Y	N	Y	N

Key

- Y Voted for (yea).
- # Paired for.
- + Announced for.
- N Voted against (nay).
- X Paired against.
- – Announced against.
- P Voted "present."
- C Voted "present" to avoid possible conflict of interest.
- ? Did not vote or otherwise make a position known.

Democrats • ***Republicans***
Independents

ND Northern Democrats SD Southern Democrats

Southern states - Ala., Ark., Fla., Ga., Ky., La., Miss., N.C., Okla., S.C., Tenn., Texas, Va.

225. S 1429. Tax Cuts/Sunset Entire Bill. Roth, R-Del., motion to waive the Budget Act with respect to the Lott, R-Miss., point of order against Section 1502 of the bill. The point of order states that the section violates the so-called Byrd rule because it would reduce revenues beyond fiscal 2009. Without the section, all bill provisions would sunset on Sept. 30, 2009. Motion rejected 51-48: R 50-3; D 0-45 (ND 0-37, SD 0-8); I 1-0. July 28, 1999. A three-fifths majority vote (60) of the total Senate is required to waive the Budget Act. (Subsequently, the chair upheld the point of order, and the section was struck.)

226. S 1429. Tax Cuts/Democratic Substitute. Moynihan, D-N.Y., substitute amendment to reduce federal taxes by $290 billion over 10 years. The amendment would increase the standard deduction for both single filers and married couples, set the standard deduction for married couples at twice the level of single filers to reduce the so-called marriage penalty, create a $1,000 long-term care credit and provide other tax relief. All bill provisions would sunset on Sept. 30, 2009. Rejected 39-60: R 0-53; D 39-6 (ND 32-5, SD 7-1); I 0-1. July 28, 1999.

227. S 1429. Tax Cuts/Social Security 'Lockbox.' Abraham, R-Mich., motion to waive the Budget Act with respect to the Reid, D-Nev., point of order against the Abraham amendment. The amendment would create a Social Security "lockbox," establish declining limits on the public debt and create a Senate point of order against any provision that would exceed the debt limit. Motion rejected 54-46: R 53-1; D 0-45 (ND 0-37, SD 0-8); I 1-0. July 29, 1999. A three-fifths majority vote (60) of the total Senate is required to waive the Budget Act. (Subsequently, the chair upheld the point of order, and the amendment fell.)

228. S 1429. Tax Cuts/Social Security and Medicare 'Lockbox.' Baucus, D-Mont., motion to waive the Budget Act with respect to the Domenici, R-N.M., point of order against the Baucus motion to recommit the bill to the Senate Finance Committee with instructions. The instructions would direct the committee to reduce the bill's tax cuts enough to allow reservation of the entire Social Security surplus for Social Security and one-third of the non-Social Security surplus for Medicare. Motion rejected 42-58: R 0-54; D 42-3 (ND 36-1, SD 6-2); I 0-1. July 29, 1999. A three-fifths majority vote (60) of the total Senate is required to waive the Budget Act. (Subsequently, the chair upheld the point of order, and the motion fell.)

Senate Votes 229, 230, 231

	229	230	231
ALABAMA			
Sessions	N	Y	N
Shelby	N	Y	N
ALASKA			
Murkowski	N	Y	N
Stevens	N	Y	N
ARIZONA			
Kyl	N	Y	N
McCain	N	Y	N
ARKANSAS			
Hutchinson	N	Y	N
Lincoln	Y	N	Y
CALIFORNIA			
Boxer	Y	N	Y
Feinstein	Y	N	Y
COLORADO			
Allard	N	Y	N
Campbell	N	Y	N
CONNECTICUT			
Dodd	Y	N	Y
Lieberman	Y	N	Y
DELAWARE			
Roth	N	N	N
Biden	Y	N	Y
FLORIDA			
Mack	N	Y	N
Graham	Y	N	Y
GEORGIA			
Coverdell	N	Y	N
Cleland	Y	N	Y
HAWAII			
Akaka	Y	N	Y
Inouye	Y	N	Y
IDAHO			
Craig	N	Y	N
Crapo	N	Y	N
ILLINOIS			
Fitzgerald	N	Y	N
Durbin	Y	N	Y
INDIANA			
Bayh	Y	N	Y
Lugar	N	Y	N
IOWA			
Grassley	N	Y	N
Harkin	Y	N	Y
KANSAS			
Brownback	N	Y	N
Roberts	N	Y	N
KENTUCKY			
Bunning	N	Y	N
McConnell	N	Y	N
LOUISIANA			
Breaux	N	N	N
Landrieu	Y	N	Y
MAINE			
Collins	N	N	N
Snowe	Y	N	N
MARYLAND			
Mikulski	Y	N	Y
Sarbanes	Y	N	Y
MASSACHUSETTS			
Kennedy	Y	N	Y
Kerry	Y	N	Y
MICHIGAN			
Abraham	N	Y	N
Levin	Y	N	Y
MINNESOTA			
Grams	N	Y	N
Wellstone	Y	N	Y
MISSISSIPPI			
Cochran	N	Y	N
Lott	N	Y	N
MISSOURI			
Ashcroft	N	Y	N
Bond	N	N	N
MONTANA			
Burns	N	Y	N
Baucus	Y	N	Y
NEBRASKA			
Hagel	N	Y	N
Kerrey	Y	N	Y
NEVADA			
Bryan	Y	N	Y
Reid	Y	N	Y
NEW HAMPSHIRE			
Gregg	N	Y	N
Smith	N	Y	N
NEW JERSEY			
Lautenberg	Y	N	Y
Torricelli	Y	N	Y
NEW MEXICO			
Domenici	N	N	N
Bingaman	Y	N	Y
NEW YORK			
Moynihan	Y	N	Y
Schumer	Y	N	Y
NORTH CAROLINA			
Helms	N	Y	N
Edwards	Y	N	Y
NORTH DAKOTA			
Conrad	Y	N	Y
Dorgan	Y	N	Y
OHIO			
DeWine	N	Y	N
Voinovich	Y	N	N
OKLAHOMA			
Inhofe	N	Y	N
Nickles	N	Y	N
OREGON			
Smith	N	Y	N
Wyden	Y	N	Y
PENNSYLVANIA			
Santorum	N	Y	N
Specter	N	N	Y
RHODE ISLAND			
Chafee	N	N	N
Reed	Y	N	Y
SOUTH CAROLINA			
Thurmond	N	Y	N
Hollings	Y	N	Y
SOUTH DAKOTA			
Daschle	Y	N	Y
Johnson	Y	N	Y
TENNESSEE			
Frist	N	Y	N
Thompson	N	Y	N
TEXAS			
Gramm	N	Y	N
Hutchison	N	Y	N
UTAH			
Bennett	N	Y	N
Hatch	N	Y	N
VERMONT			
Jeffords	N	N	N
Leahy	Y	N	Y
VIRGINIA			
Warner	N	Y	N
Robb	Y	N	Y
WASHINGTON			
Gorton	N	Y	N
Murray	Y	N	Y
WEST VIRGINIA			
Byrd	Y	N	Y
Rockefeller	Y	N	Y
WISCONSIN			
Feingold	Y	N	Y
Kohl	Y	N	Y
WYOMING			
Enzi	N	Y	N
Thomas	N	Y	N

Key

- Y Voted for (yea).
- # Paired for.
- + Announced for.
- N Voted against (nay).
- X Paired against.
- – Announced against.
- P Voted "present."
- C Voted "present" to avoid possible conflict of interest.
- ? Did not vote or otherwise make a position known.

Democrats ***Republicans***
Independents

ND Northern Democrats SD Southern Democrats

Southern states - Ala., Ark., Fla., Ga., Ky., La., Miss., N.C., Okla., S.C., Tenn., Texas, Va.

229. S 1429. Tax Cuts/Social Security and Medicare. Robb, D-Va., motion to waive the Budget Act with respect to the Thompson, R-Tenn., point of order against the Robb amendment. The amendment would prohibit the bill from taking effect until legislation has been enacted to extend the solvency of Social Security through 2075 and Medicare through 2027. Motion rejected 46-54: R 2-52; D 44-1 (ND 37-0, SD 7-1); I 0-1. July 29, 1999. A three-fifths majority vote (60) of the total Senate is required to waive the Budget Act. (Subsequently, the chair upheld the point of order, and the amendment fell.)

230. S 1429. Tax Cuts/Across-the-Board Cuts. Hutchison, R-Texas, motion to waive the Budget Act with respect to the Moynihan, D-N.Y., point of order against the Gramm, R-Texas, substitute amendment. The substitute would reduce taxes by $792 billion over 10 years by reducing income tax rates 10 percent, eliminating the so-called marriage penalty, repealing estate and gift taxes, reducing the capital gains tax and allowing self-employed individuals to fully deduct health insurance costs. Motion rejected 46-54: R 45-9; D 0-45 (ND 0-37, SD 0-8); I 1-0. July 29, 1999. A three-fifths majority vote (60) of the total Senate is required to waive the Budget Act. (Subsequently, the chair upheld the point of order, and the amendment fell.)

231. S 1429. Tax Cuts/Medicare Prescription Drug Benefits. Kennedy, D-Mass., motion to waive the Budget Act with respect to the Roth, R-Del., point of order against the Kennedy motion to recommit the bill to the Senate Finance Committee with instructions. The instructions would direct the committee to add language that would reduce the bill's tax cuts by an amount sufficient to allow establishment of a Medicare prescription drug benefit program. Motion rejected 45-55: R 1-53; D 44-1 (ND 37-0, SD 7-1); I 0-1. July 29, 1999. A three-fifths majority vote (60) of the total Senate is required to waive the Budget Act. (Subsequently, the chair upheld the point of order, and the motion fell.)

Senate Votes 232, 233, 234, 235, 236, 237, 238, 239

	232	233	234	235	236	237	238	239
ALABAMA								
Sessions	N	Y	N	Y	Y	Y	N	N
Shelby	N	Y	N	Y	Y	Y	Y	N
ALASKA								
Murkowski	N	Y	N	Y	Y	Y	N	N
Stevens	N	Y	N	Y	Y	Y	N	N
ARIZONA								
Kyl	N	Y	N	Y	Y	Y	Y	N
McCain	N	Y	N	Y	Y	Y	Y	N
ARKANSAS								
Hutchinson	N	Y	N	Y	Y	Y	Y	N
Lincoln	Y	Y	Y	N	N	N	N	Y
CALIFORNIA								
Boxer	Y	Y	Y	N	N	N	N	Y
Feinstein	Y	Y	Y	N	N	N	N	Y
COLORADO								
Allard	N	Y	N	Y	Y	Y	Y	N
Campbell	N	Y	N	Y	Y	Y	N	N
CONNECTICUT								
Dodd	Y	Y	Y	N	N	N	N	Y
Lieberman	Y	Y	Y	N	N	N	Y	Y
DELAWARE								
Roth	N	Y	N	Y	Y	Y	N	N
Biden	Y	Y	Y	N	N	N	Y	Y
FLORIDA								
Mack	N	Y	N	Y	Y	Y	N	N
Graham	Y	Y	N	N	N	N	N	N
GEORGIA								
Coverdell	N	Y	N	Y	Y	Y	N	N
Cleland	Y	Y	Y	N	N	N	N	Y
HAWAII								
Akaka	Y	Y	Y	N	N	N	N	Y
Inouye	Y	Y	Y	N	N	N	N	Y
IDAHO								
Craig	N	Y	N	Y	Y	Y	N	N
Crapo	N	Y	N	Y	Y	Y	N	N
ILLINOIS								
Fitzgerald	N	Y	N	Y	Y	Y	N	Y
Durbin	Y	Y	Y	N	N	N	N	Y
INDIANA								
Bayh	Y	Y	Y	N	N	Y	N	Y
Lugar	N	Y	N	Y	Y	Y	N	N
IOWA								
Grassley	N	Y	N	Y	Y	Y	N	N
Harkin	Y	Y	Y	N	N	N	N	Y
KANSAS								
Brownback	N	Y	N	Y	Y	Y	N	N
Roberts	N	Y	N	Y	Y	Y	N	N
KENTUCKY								
Bunning	N	Y	N	Y	Y	Y	N	N
McConnell	N	Y	N	Y	Y	Y	N	N
LOUISIANA								
Breaux	Y	Y	Y	N	N	Y	N	Y
Landrieu	Y	Y	Y	N	N	Y	N	Y
MAINE								
Collins	Y	Y	Y	Y	Y	Y	N	N
Snowe	Y	Y	Y	Y	Y	Y	N	N
MARYLAND								
Mikulski	Y	Y	Y	N	N	N	N	Y
Sarbanes	Y	Y	Y	N	N	N	N	Y
MASSACHUSETTS								
Kennedy	Y	Y	Y	N	N	Y	N	Y
Kerry	Y	Y	Y	N	N	Y	N	Y
MICHIGAN								
Abraham	N	Y	Y	Y	Y	Y	N	N
Levin	Y	Y	Y	N	N	N	N	Y
MINNESOTA								
Grams	N	Y	N	Y	Y	Y	N	N
Wellstone	Y	Y	Y	N	N	N	N	Y
MISSISSIPPI								
Cochran	N	Y	N	Y	Y	Y	N	N
Lott	N	Y	N	Y	Y	Y	N	N
MISSOURI								
Ashcroft	N	Y	N	Y	Y	Y	N	N
Bond	N	Y	N	Y	Y	Y	N	N
MONTANA								
Burns	N	Y	N	Y	Y	Y	N	N
Baucus	Y	Y	Y	N	N	N	N	Y
NEBRASKA								
Hagel	N	Y	N	Y	Y	Y	N	N
Kerrey	Y	Y	N	N	N	Y	N	Y
NEVADA								
Bryan	Y	Y	Y	N	N	N	N	Y
Reid	Y	Y	Y	N	N	N	N	Y
NEW HAMPSHIRE								
Gregg	N	Y	N	Y	Y	Y	Y	N
Smith	N	Y	N	Y	Y	Y	N	N
NEW JERSEY								
Lautenberg	Y	Y	Y	N	N	N	N	Y
Torricelli	Y	Y	Y	N	N	Y	N	Y
NEW MEXICO								
Domenici	N	Y	N	Y	Y	Y	N	N
Bingaman	Y	Y	Y	N	N	Y	N	Y
NEW YORK								
Moynihan	Y	Y	Y	N	N	N	Y	Y
Schumer	Y	Y	Y	N	N	Y	N	Y
NORTH CAROLINA								
Helms	N	Y	N	Y	Y	Y	N	N
Edwards	Y	Y	Y	N	N	N	N	Y
NORTH DAKOTA								
Conrad	Y	Y	Y	N	N	N	N	Y
Dorgan	Y	Y	Y	N	N	N	N	Y
OHIO								
DeWine	N	Y	N	Y	Y	Y	Y	N
Voinovich	N	N	N	N	Y	N	N	N
OKLAHOMA								
Inhofe	N	Y	N	Y	Y	Y	N	N
Nickles	N	Y	N	Y	Y	Y	N	N
OREGON								
Smith	N	Y	N	Y	Y	Y	N	N
Wyden	Y	Y	Y	N	N	Y	N	Y
PENNSYLVANIA								
Santorum	N	Y	N	Y	Y	Y	Y	N
Specter	Y	Y	Y	Y	Y	Y	Y	Y
RHODE ISLAND								
Chafee	N	Y	Y	Y	Y	Y	N	N
Reed	Y	Y	Y	N	N	N	N	Y
SOUTH CAROLINA								
Thurmond	N	Y	N	Y	Y	Y	N	N
Hollings	Y	N	Y	N	N	N	N	Y
SOUTH DAKOTA								
Daschle	Y	Y	Y	N	N	N	N	Y
Johnson	Y	Y	Y	N	N	N	N	Y
TENNESSEE								
Frist	N	Y	Y	Y	Y	Y	N	N
Thompson	N	Y	N	Y	Y	Y	Y	N
TEXAS								
Gramm	N	Y	N	Y	Y	Y	N	N
Hutchison	N	Y	Y	Y	Y	Y	N	N
UTAH								
Bennett	N	Y	N	Y	Y	Y	N	N
Hatch	N	Y	N	Y	Y	Y	N	N
VERMONT								
Jeffords	N	Y	N	Y	Y	Y	N	N
Leahy	Y	Y	Y	N	N	N	N	Y
VIRGINIA								
Warner	N	Y	N	Y	Y	Y	N	N
Robb	Y	Y	Y	N	N	N	N	Y
WASHINGTON								
Gorton	N	Y	N	Y	Y	Y	N	N
Murray	Y	Y	Y	N	N	N	N	Y
WEST VIRGINIA								
Byrd	Y	Y	Y	N	N	N	N	Y
Rockefeller	Y	Y	Y	N	N	N	N	Y
WISCONSIN								
Feingold	Y	Y	Y	N	N	N	N	Y
Kohl	Y	Y	Y	N	N	Y	N	Y
WYOMING								
Enzi	N	Y	N	Y	Y	Y	N	N
Thomas	N	Y	N	Y	Y	Y	N	N

Key

- Y Voted for (yea).
- # Paired for.
- \+ Announced for.
- N Voted against (nay).
- X Paired against.
- – Announced against.
- P Voted "present."
- C Voted "present" to avoid possible conflict of interest.
- ? Did not vote or otherwise make a position known.

•

Democrats ***Republicans***
Independents

ND Northern Democrats SD Southern Democrats

Southern states - Ala., Ark., Fla., Ga., Ky., La., Miss., N.C., Okla., S.C., Tenn., Texas, Va.

232. S 1429. Tax Reconciliation/Education Funding. Bingaman, D-N.M., motion to waive the Budget Act with respect to the Domenici, R-N.M., point of order against the Bingaman amendment. The amendment would express the sense of the Senate that $132 billion should be shifted from tax cuts for upper-income taxpayers to public education programs. Motion rejected 48-52: R 3-51; D 45-0 (ND 37-0, SD 8-0); I 0-1. July 30, 1999. A three-fifths majority vote (60) of the total Senate is required to waive the Budget Act. (Subsequently, the chair upheld the point of order, and the amendment fell.)

233. S 1429. Tax Reconciliation/Marriage Penalty. Hutchison, R-Texas, amendment that would move the starting date for relief from the so-called marriage penalty up to 2001, while pushing back the effective date for several other tax benefits in the bill, including the increase in the maximum income level for the new 14 percent tax rate. Adopted 98-2: R 53-1; D 44-1 (ND 37-0, SD 7-1); I 1-0. July 30, 1999.

234. S 1429. Tax Reconciliation/Health Care Providers. Kerry, D-Mass., motion to waive the Budget Act with respect to the Roth, R-Del., point of order against the Kerry motion to recommit the bill to the Senate Finance Committee with instructions to reserve $20 billion over 10 years by reducing or deferring tax cuts in the bill, in order to assist health care providers hurt unintentionally by the 1997 balanced-budget act (PL 104-33). Motion rejected 50-50: R 7-47; D 43-2 (ND 36-1, SD 7-1); I 0-1. July 30, 1999. A three-fifths majority vote (60) of the total Senate is required to waive the Budget Act. (Subsequently, the chair upheld the point of order, and the motion fell.)

235. S 1429. Tax Reconciliation/Medicare. Frist, R-Tenn., motion to waive the Budget Act with respect to the Baucus, D-Mont., point of order against the Frist amendment. The amendment would express the sense of the Senate that on-budget surpluses over the next 10 years are sufficient for Congress to modernize Medicare benefits, improve the program's solvency and provide prescription drug benefits. Motion rejected 54-46: R 53-1; D 0-45 (ND 0-37, SD 0-8); I 1-0. July 30, 1999. A three-fifths majority vote (60) of the total Senate is required to waive the Budget Act. (Subsequently, the chair upheld the point of order, and the amendment fell.)

236. S 1429. Tax Reconciliation/Social Security Surpluses. Domenici, R-N.M., motion to table (kill) the Lautenberg, D-N.J., motion to recommit the bill to the Senate Finance Committee with instructions to eliminate use of Social Security surpluses to fund tax reductions. Motion agreed to 55-45: R 54-0; D 0-45 (ND 0-37, SD 0-8); I 1-0. July 30, 1999.

237. S 1429. Tax Reconciliation/Defer Tax Reductions. Roth, R-Del., motion to table (kill) the Hollings, D-S.C., motion to recommit the bill to the Senate Finance Committee with instructions to defer tax reductions and instead use projected surpluses to reduce the national debt. Motion agreed to 65-35: R 53-1; D 11-34 (ND 9-28, SD 2-6); I 1-0. July 30, 1999.

238. S 1429. Tax Reconciliation/School Vouchers. McCain, R-Ariz., motion to waive the Budget Act with respect to the Reed, D-R.I., point of order against the McCain amendment. The amendment would authorize approximately $1.8 billion a year for three years to establish a pilot school voucher program, paid for by eliminating subsidies for ethanol, oil, gas and sugar. Motion rejected 13-87: R 10-44; D 3-42 (ND 3-34, SD 0-8); I 0-1. July 30, 1999. A three-fifths majority vote (60) of the total Senate is required to waive the Budget Act. (Subsequently, the chair upheld the point of order, and the amendment fell.)

239. S 1429. Tax Reconciliation/Minimum Wage Increase. Kennedy, D-Mass., motion to waive the Budget Act with respect to the Nickles, R-Okla., point of order against the Kennedy amendment, which would increase the minimum wage to $6.15 an hour. Motion rejected 46-54: R 2-52; D 44-1 (ND 37-0, SD 7-1); I 0-1. July 30, 1999. A three-fifths majority vote (60) of the total Senate is required to waive the Budget Act. (Subsequently, the chair upheld the point of order, and the amendment fell.)

Senate Votes 240, 241, 242, 243, 244, 245

	240	241	242	243	244	245
ALABAMA						
Sessions	Y	N	Y	N	N	N
Shelby	Y	N	Y	N	N	N
ALASKA						
Murkowski	Y	N	Y	N	N	N
Stevens	Y	N	Y	N	N	N
ARIZONA						
Kyl	Y	N	Y	N	N	N
McCain	Y	N	Y	Y	N	N
ARKANSAS						
Hutchinson	N	N	Y	Y	N	N
Lincoln	N	Y	N	Y	Y	Y
CALIFORNIA						
Boxer	N	Y	N	Y	Y	Y
Feinstein	N	Y	N	Y	Y	Y
COLORADO						
Allard	Y	N	Y	N	N	N
Campbell	Y	N	Y	N	N	N
CONNECTICUT						
Dodd	N	Y	N	Y	Y	Y
Lieberman	N	Y	N	Y	Y	Y
DELAWARE						
Roth	N	N	Y	N	N	N
Biden	N	Y	N	Y	Y	Y
FLORIDA						
Mack	Y	N	Y	N	N	N
Graham	N	Y	N	Y	Y	Y
GEORGIA						
Coverdell	Y	N	Y	N	N	N
Cleland	N	Y	N	Y	Y	Y
HAWAII						
Akaka	N	Y	N	Y	Y	Y
Inouye	N	Y	N	Y	Y	Y
IDAHO						
Craig	Y	N	Y	N	N	N
Crapo	Y	N	Y	N	N	N
ILLINOIS						
Fitzgerald	N	Y	Y	N	N	N
Durbin	N	Y	N	Y	Y	Y
INDIANA						
Bayh	N	Y	N	Y	Y	Y
Lugar	N	N	Y	N	N	N

	240	241	242	243	244	245
IOWA						
Grassley	Y	N	Y	N	N	Y
Harkin	N	Y	N	Y	Y	Y
KANSAS						
Brownback	Y	N	Y	N	N	N
Roberts	N	N	Y	N	N	N
KENTUCKY						
Bunning	N	N	Y	N	N	N
McConnell	Y	N	Y	N	N	N
LOUISIANA						
Breaux	N	Y	N	N	Y	Y
Landrieu	N	Y	N	Y	Y	Y
MAINE						
Collins	Y	Y	Y	Y	N	N
Snowe	N	Y	Y	Y	N	N
MARYLAND						
Mikulski	N	Y	N	Y	Y	Y
Sarbanes	N	Y	N	Y	Y	Y
MASSACHUSETTS						
Kennedy	N	Y	N	Y	Y	Y
Kerry	N	Y	N	Y	Y	Y
MICHIGAN						
Abraham	N	Y	Y	Y	Y	N
Levin	N	Y	N	Y	Y	Y
MINNESOTA						
Grams	N	N	Y	N	N	N
Wellstone	N	Y	N	Y	Y	Y
MISSISSIPPI						
Cochran	Y	N	Y	N	N	N
Lott	Y	N	Y	N	N	N
MISSOURI						
Ashcroft	N	N	Y	N	N	N
Bond	N	N	Y	N	N	N
MONTANA						
Burns	Y	N	Y	Y	N	N
Baucus	N	Y	N	Y	Y	Y
NEBRASKA						
Hagel	N	N	Y	N	N	N
Kerrey	N	Y	N	Y	Y	Y
NEVADA						
Bryan	N	Y	N	Y	Y	Y
Reid	Y	Y	N	Y	Y	Y

	240	241	242	243	244	245
NEW HAMPSHIRE						
Gregg	Y	N	Y	N	N	N
Smith	Y	N	Y	Y	N	N
NEW JERSEY						
Lautenberg	N	Y	N	Y	Y	Y
Torricelli	N	Y	N	Y	Y	Y
NEW MEXICO						
Domenici	N	N	Y	N	N	N
Bingaman	N	Y	N	Y	Y	Y
NEW YORK						
Moynihan	N	Y	N	Y	Y	Y
Schumer	N	Y	N	Y	Y	Y
NORTH CAROLINA						
Helms	Y	N	Y	N	N	N
Edwards	N	Y	N	Y	Y	Y
NORTH DAKOTA						
Conrad	N	Y	N	Y	Y	Y
Dorgan	N	Y	N	Y	Y	Y
OHIO						
DeWine	N	Y	Y	Y	N	N
Voinovich	N	N	Y	N	N	N
OKLAHOMA						
Inhofe	Y	N	Y	N	N	N
Nickles	Y	N	Y	N	N	N
OREGON						
Smith	N	Y	Y	N	N	N
Wyden	N	Y	N	Y	Y	Y
PENNSYLVANIA						
Santorum	N	Y	Y	Y	N	N
Specter	Y	Y	Y	Y	N	Y
RHODE ISLAND						
Chafee	N	N	Y	N	N	N
Reed	N	Y	N	Y	Y	Y
SOUTH CAROLINA						
Thurmond	Y	N	Y	N	N	N
Hollings	N	Y	N	Y	Y	Y
SOUTH DAKOTA						
Daschle	N	Y	N	Y	Y	Y
Johnson	N	Y	N	Y	Y	Y
TENNESSEE						
Frist	Y	N	Y	N	N	N
Thompson	Y	N	Y	N	N	N

Key

- Y Voted for (yea).
- # Paired for.
- \+ Announced for.
- N Voted against (nay).
- X Paired against.
- – Announced against.
- P Voted "present."
- C Voted "present" to avoid possible conflict of interest.
- ? Did not vote or otherwise make a position known.

•

Democrats ***Republicans***
Independents

	240	241	242	243	244	245
TEXAS						
Gramm	Y	N	Y	N	N	N
Hutchison	Y	N	Y	Y	N	N
UTAH						
Bennett	Y	N	Y	N	N	N
Hatch	Y	N	Y	N	N	N
VERMONT						
Jeffords	N	N	Y	Y	N	Y
Leahy	N	Y	N	Y	Y	Y
VIRGINIA						
Warner	N	N	Y	Y	N	N
Robb	N	Y	N	Y	Y	Y
WASHINGTON						
Gorton	Y	N	Y	N	N	N
Murray	N	Y	N	Y	Y	Y
WEST VIRGINIA						
Byrd	N	Y	N	Y	Y	Y
Rockefeller	N	Y	N	Y	Y	Y
WISCONSIN						
Feingold	N	Y	N	Y	Y	Y
Kohl	N	Y	N	Y	Y	Y
WYOMING						
Enzi	N	N	Y	N	N	N
Thomas	Y	N	Y	Y	N	N

ND Northern Democrats SD Southern Democrats

Southern states - Ala., Ark., Fla., Ga., Ky., La., Miss., N.C., Okla., S.C., Tenn., Texas, Va.

240. S 1429. Tax Reconciliation/Flat Tax. Specter, R-Pa., motion to waive the Budget Act with respect to the Baucus, D-Mont., point of order against the Specter substitute amendment. The amendment would create a flat, 20 percent individual income tax rate, with limited deductions for charitable contributions and home mortgages. Motion rejected 35-65: R 33-21; D 1-44 (ND 1-36, SD 0-8); I 1-0. July 30, 1999. A three-fifths majority vote (60) of the total Senate is required to waive the Budget Act. (Subsequently, the chair upheld the point of order, and the amendment fell.)

241. S 1429. Tax Reconciliation/Higher Education Tax Deduction. Schumer, D-N.Y., motion to waive the Budget Act with respect to the Roth, R-Del., point of order against the Schumer amendment, which would allow most individuals to deduct up to $12,000 in college tuition, and create a tax credit for student loan interest. Motion rejected 53-47: R 8-46; D 45-0 (ND 37-0, SD 8-0); I 0-1. July 30, 1999. A three-fifths majority vote (60) of the total Senate is required to waive the Budget Act. (Subsequently, the chair upheld the point of order, and the amendment fell.)

242. S 1429. Tax Reconciliation/School Construction. Nickles, R-Okla., motion to table (kill) the Robb, D-Va., motion to recommit the bill to the Senate Finance Committee with instructions to reduce or defer $5.7 billion in new tax cuts in order to allow for tax incentives for building and renovating schools. Motion agreed to 55-45: R 54-0; D 0-45 (ND 0-37, SD 0-8); I 1-0. July 30, 1999.

243. S 1429. Tax Reconciliation/Veterans' Health Care. Wellstone, D-Minn., motion to waive the Budget Act with respect to the Bond, R-Mo., point of order against the Wellstone motion to recommit the bill to the Senate Finance Committee with instructions to reserve $3 billion per year for five years for veterans' health care, offset by decreasing tax reductions for upper income taxpayers. Motion rejected 58-42: R 13-41; D 44-1 (ND 37-0, SD 7-1); I 1-0. July 30, 1999. A three-fifths majority vote (60) of the total Senate is required to waive the Budget Act. (Subsequently, the chair upheld the point of order, and the motion fell.)

244. S 1429. Tax Reconciliation/Technology Training Credits. Conrad, D-N.D., motion to waive the Budget Act with respect to the Nickles, R-Okla., point of order against the Conrad amendment. The amendment would allow businesses a partial tax credit for the costs of training workers in information technology skills. Motion rejected 46-54: R 1-53; D 45-0 (ND 37-0, SD 8-0); I 0-1. July 30, 1999. A three-fifths majority vote (60) of the total Senate is required to waive the Budget Act. (Subsequently, the chair upheld the point of order, and the amendment fell.)

245. S 1429. Tax Reconciliation/Pension Plans. Harkin, D-Iowa, motion to waive the Budget Act with respect to the Thompson, R-Tenn., point of order against the Harkin amendment. The amendment would prohibit employers from denying already accrued pension benefits after a company converts to a new pension plan. Motion rejected 48-52: R 3-51; D 45-0 (ND 37-0, SD 8-0); I 0-1. July 30, 1999. A three-fifths majority vote (60) of the total Senate is required to waive the Budget Act. (Subsequently, the chair upheld the point of order, and the amendment fell.)

Senate Votes 246, 247, 248, 249, 250, 251

	246	247	248	249	250	251
ALABAMA						
Sessions	N	Y	?	N	Y	N
Shelby	N	Y	?	N	Y	N
ALASKA						
Murkowski	N	Y	Y	N	Y	Y
Stevens	N	Y	Y	N	Y	Y
ARIZONA						
Kyl	Y	Y	Y	N	Y	Y
McCain	Y	Y	?	N	Y	Y
ARKANSAS						
Hutchinson	N	Y	Y	N	Y	N
Lincoln	N	N	Y	Y	N	N
CALIFORNIA						
Boxer	N	N	Y	Y	N	N
Feinstein	N	N	Y	Y	N	N
COLORADO						
Allard	Y	Y	Y	N	Y	N
Campbell	N	Y	Y	N	Y	N
CONNECTICUT						
Dodd	N	N	Y	Y	N	N
Lieberman	N	N	Y	Y	N	Y
DELAWARE						
Roth	N	Y	Y	N	Y	N
Biden	N	N	+	Y	N	N
FLORIDA						
Mack	N	Y	Y	N	Y	Y
Graham	N	N	Y	Y	Y	Y
GEORGIA						
Coverdell	N	Y	Y	N	Y	Y
Cleland	N	N	Y	Y	N	N
HAWAII						
Akaka	N	N	Y	Y	N	N
Inouye	N	N	Y	Y	N	N
IDAHO						
Craig	Y	Y	Y	N	Y	N
Crapo	Y	Y	Y	N	Y	N
ILLINOIS						
Fitzgerald	Y	Y	Y	N	Y	N
Durbin	Y	N	Y	Y	N	N
INDIANA						
Bayh	N	N	Y	Y	N	N
Lugar	N	Y	Y	N	Y	N
IOWA						
Grassley	N	Y	Y	N	Y	N
Harkin	N	N	Y	Y	N	N
KANSAS						
Brownback	Y	Y	Y	N	Y	N
Roberts	Y	Y	Y	N	Y	N
KENTUCKY						
Bunning	N	Y	Y	N	Y	Y
McConnell	N	Y	Y	N	Y	Y
LOUISIANA						
Breaux	N	Y	Y	Y	N	N
Landrieu	N	Y	Y	Y	N	N
MAINE						
Collins	N	Y	Y	N	Y	N
Snowe	N	Y	Y	N	Y	Y
MARYLAND						
Mikulski	N	N	Y	Y	N	N
Sarbanes	N	N	Y	Y	N	Y
MASSACHUSETTS						
Kennedy	N	N	Y	Y	N	?
Kerry	N	N	Y	Y	N	N
MICHIGAN						
Abraham	Y	Y	Y	N	Y	N
Levin	N	N	Y	Y	N	N
MINNESOTA						
Grams	N	Y	Y	N	Y	N
Wellstone	N	N	Y	Y	N	N
MISSISSIPPI						
Cochran	N	Y	Y	N	Y	N
Lott	N	Y	Y	N	Y	Y
MISSOURI						
Ashcroft	Y	Y	Y	N	Y	N
Bond	Y	Y	?	N	Y	N
MONTANA						
Burns	Y	Y	Y	N	N	N
Baucus	N	N	Y	Y	N	N
NEBRASKA						
Hagel	N	Y	Y	N	Y	N
Kerrey	N	Y	Y	Y	N	N
NEVADA						
Bryan	N	N	Y	Y	N	Y
Reid	N	N	Y	Y	N	Y
NEW HAMPSHIRE						
Gregg	Y	Y	Y	Y	Y	Y
Smith	Y	Y	Y	N	Y	Y
NEW JERSEY						
Lautenberg	N	N	Y	Y	N	Y
Torricelli	N	Y	Y	Y	N	Y
NEW MEXICO						
Domenici	N	Y	?	?	?	?
Bingaman	N	N	Y	Y	N	N
NEW YORK						
Moynihan	N	N	Y	Y	N	N
Schumer	N	N	Y	Y	N	N
NORTH CAROLINA						
Helms	N	Y	Y	N	Y	Y
Edwards	N	N	Y	Y	N	N
NORTH DAKOTA						
Conrad	N	N	Y	Y	N	N
Dorgan	N	N	Y	Y	N	N
OHIO						
DeWine	N	Y	Y	N	Y	Y
Voinovich	N	N	Y	N	Y	N
OKLAHOMA						
Inhofe	Y	Y	Y	N	Y	N
Nickles	Y	Y	Y	N	Y	N
OREGON						
Smith	N	Y	Y	N	Y	N
Wyden	Y	N	Y	Y	N	N
PENNSYLVANIA						
Santorum	N	Y	Y	Y	Y	Y
Specter	N	N	Y	N	Y	N
RHODE ISLAND						
Chafee	N	Y	Y	N	Y	N
Reed	N	N	Y	Y	N	N
SOUTH CAROLINA						
Thurmond	N	Y	Y	N	Y	Y
Hollings	N	N	Y	Y	N	N
SOUTH DAKOTA						
Daschle	N	N	Y	Y	N	N
Johnson	Y	N	Y	Y	N	N
TENNESSEE						
Frist	N	Y	Y	N	Y	N
Thompson	N	Y	Y	N	Y	Y
TEXAS						
Gramm	N	Y	Y	N	Y	Y
Hutchison	N	Y	Y	N	Y	N
UTAH						
Bennett	N	Y	Y	N	Y	N
Hatch	N	Y	+	–	?	N
VERMONT						
Jeffords	N	Y	Y	N	Y	N
Leahy	N	N	Y	Y	N	N
VIRGINIA						
Warner	N	Y	Y	N	Y	N
Robb	N	N	Y	Y	N	Y
WASHINGTON						
Gorton	Y	Y	Y	N	Y	N
Murray	N	N	Y	Y	N	N
WEST VIRGINIA						
Byrd	N	N	Y	Y	N	Y
Rockefeller	N	N	Y	Y	N	N
WISCONSIN						
Feingold	N	N	Y	Y	Y	N
Kohl	Y	N	Y	Y	N	Y
WYOMING						
Enzi	Y	Y	Y	N	Y	N
Thomas	Y	Y	Y	N	Y	N

Key

- Y Voted for (yea).
- # Paired for.
- + Announced for.
- N Voted against (nay).
- X Paired against.
- – Announced against.
- P Voted "present."
- C Voted "present" to avoid possible conflict of interest.
- ? Did not vote or otherwise make a position known.

Democrats ***Republicans*** *Independents*

ND Northern Democrats SD Southern Democrats

Southern states - Ala., Ark., Fla., Ga., Ky., La., Miss., N.C., Okla., S.C., Tenn., Texas, Va.

246. S 1429. Tax Reconciliation/Poultry Waste Conversion Credit. Ashcroft, R-Mo., amendment to strike bill language that would provide tax incentives for companies working to convert poultry waste into electricity. Rejected 23-77: R 18-36; D 4-41 (ND 4-33, SD 0-8); I 1-0. July 30, 1999.

247. S 1429. Tax Reconciliation/Passage. Passage of the bill to reduce federal taxes by $792 billion over 10 years. The measure would reduce the lowest income tax bracket from 15 percent to 14 percent beginning in 2001, increase the maximum income levels for the lowest bracket, provide relief from the so-called marriage penalty by allowing couples to calculate their taxes as individuals on the same form, reduce estate and gift taxes, increase the per year amount that may be transferred to an Individual Retirement Account, extend the research and development tax credit and allow taxpayers who pay 50 percent or more of their health insurance premiums to fully deduct the cost of the premiums. Passed 57-43: R 52-2; D 4-41 (ND 2-35, SD 2-6); I 1-0. July 30, 1999. A "nay" was a vote in support of the president's position. (Subsequently, the Senate took up HR 2488, struck all after the enacting clause, inserted the text of S 1429 and passed it by voice vote.)

248. S 335. Curb Deceptive Mailings/Passage. Passage of the bill that would establish new regulations and penalties to curtail deceptive mailings, such as certain sweepstakes, skill contests, matters designed to resemble checks and mailings made to look like government documents. The bill would require sweepstakes mailings to clearly disclose the game's rules and that the odds of winning are not improved by purchasing any products that are advertised, would prohibit the mailing from depicting an individual as a winner unless the person has actually won a prize and would implement stricter penalties for those who send mail that does not comply with federal standards, including fines ranging from $50,000 to $2 million, depending on the number of mailings sent. Passed 93-0: R 48-0; D 44-0 (ND 36-0, SD 8-0); I 1-0. Aug. 2, 1999.

249. S 1233. Fiscal 2000 Agriculture Appropriations/Republican Emergency Farm Aid Plan. Daschle, D-S.D., motion to table (kill) the Cochran, R-Miss., amendment to the Daschle amendment. The Cochran amendment would strike the Daschle language and instead provide $7 billion in emergency aid to farmers, mostly in supplemental market transition payments. Motion rejected 47-51: R 2-50; D 45-0 (ND 37-0, SD 8-0); I 0-1. Aug. 3, 1999. (Subsequently, the Cochran amendment was withdrawn.)

250. S 1233. Fiscal 2000 Agriculture Appropriations/Democratic Emergency Farm Aid Plan. Lott, R-Miss., motion to table (kill) the Harkin, D-Iowa, amendment to the Daschle, D-S.D., amendment. Both the Harkin and Daschle amendments would provide $10.8 billion in emergency aid to farmers and ranchers, including funds for disaster assistance, income loss payments and emergency trade provisions. Motion agreed to 54-44: R 51-1; D 2-43 (ND 1-36, SD 1-7); I 1-0. Aug. 3, 1999.

251. S 1233. Fiscal 2000 Agriculture Appropriations/Unilateral Food and Medicine Sanctions. Helms, R-N.C., motion to table (kill) the Ashcroft, R-Mo., amendment to the Daschle, D-S.D., amendment. The Ashcroft amendment would terminate U.S. unilateral sanctions on agricultural and medicinal goods and bar the president from imposing such sanctions against a country without congressional approval, with certain exceptions. Motion rejected 28-70: R 17-36; D 10-34 (ND 8-28, SD 2-6); I 1-0. Aug. 3, 1999. (Subsequently on Aug. 4, the Ashcroft amendment was adopted by voice vote.)

	252	253	254	255	256	257
ALABAMA						
Sessions	Y	Y	Y	Y	Y	Y
Shelby	Y	Y	Y	Y	Y	Y
ALASKA						
Murkowski	N	N	Y	Y	Y	Y
Stevens	Y	N	Y	Y	Y	Y
ARIZONA						
Kyl	N	N	N	Y	Y	Y
McCain	N	N	N	Y	Y	Y
ARKANSAS						
Hutchinson	Y	N	N	Y	Y	Y
Lincoln	Y	Y	Y	N	N	Y
CALIFORNIA						
Boxer	Y	Y	Y	N	N	Y
Feinstein	Y	Y	N	N	N	Y
COLORADO						
Allard	N	N	Y	Y	Y	Y
Campbell	N	N	Y	Y	N	Y
CONNECTICUT						
Dodd	Y	Y	Y	N	N	Y
Lieberman	Y	Y	Y	N	N	Y
DELAWARE						
Roth	Y	N	N	Y	Y	Y
Biden	Y	Y	N	N	N	Y
FLORIDA						
Mack	Y	?	?	Y	Y	N
Graham	Y	Y	Y	Y	Y	N
GEORGIA						
Coverdell	Y	Y	Y	Y	Y	Y
Cleland	Y	Y	Y	N	N	Y
HAWAII						
Akaka	N	Y	Y	N	N	Y
Inouye	N	Y	Y	N	N	Y
IDAHO						
Craig	N	N	Y	Y	Y	Y
Crapo	N	N	Y	?	?	?
ILLINOIS						
Fitzgerald	N	N	N	Y	Y	Y
Durbin	N	Y	Y	N	N	Y
INDIANA						
Bayh	N	Y	Y	N	N	Y
Lugar	N	Y	N	Y	Y	Y
IOWA						
Grassley	N	N	Y	Y	N	Y
Harkin	N	Y	Y	N	N	Y
KANSAS						
Brownback	N	N	N	Y	Y	Y
Roberts	N	N	Y	Y	Y	Y
KENTUCKY						
Bunning	Y	Y	Y	Y	Y	Y
McConnell	N	Y	Y	Y	Y	Y
LOUISIANA						
Breaux	Y	Y	Y	N	N	Y
Landrieu	Y	Y	Y	N	N	?
MAINE						
Collins	Y	N	N	Y	Y	Y
Snowe	Y	N	N	Y	Y	Y
MARYLAND						
Mikulski	Y	Y	N	N	N	Y
Sarbanes	Y	Y	N	N	N	Y
MASSACHUSETTS						
Kennedy	Y	Y	N	N	N	?
Kerry	Y	Y	N	N	N	Y
MICHIGAN						
Abraham	N	N	Y	Y	Y	Y
Levin	N	Y	Y	N	N	Y
MINNESOTA						
Grams	N	N	Y	Y	N	Y
Wellstone	N	Y	Y	N	N	Y
MISSISSIPPI						
Cochran	Y	Y	Y	Y	Y	Y
Lott	Y	Y	Y	Y	Y	Y
MISSOURI						
Ashcroft	Y	N	Y	Y	N	Y
Bond	Y	Y	Y	Y	Y	Y
MONTANA						
Burns	N	N	Y	N	N	Y
Baucus	N	Y	Y	N	N	Y
NEBRASKA						
Hagel	N	N	Y	Y	Y	Y
Kerrey	N	Y	Y	N	N	Y
NEVADA						
Bryan	N	Y	Y	N	N	Y
Reid	N	Y	Y	N	N	Y
NEW HAMPSHIRE						
Gregg	Y	Y	N	Y	Y	N
Smith	Y	N	N	Y	Y	N
NEW JERSEY						
Lautenberg	N	Y	N	N	N	Y
Torricelli	Y	Y	Y	N	Y	N
NEW MEXICO						
Domenici	N	Y	Y	Y	Y	Y
Bingaman	N	Y	Y	N	N	Y
NEW YORK						
Moynihan	Y	Y	N	N	N	Y
Schumer	Y	Y	N	N	N	Y
NORTH CAROLINA						
Helms	Y	Y	Y	Y	Y	Y
Edwards	Y	Y	Y	N	N	Y
NORTH DAKOTA						
Conrad	N	Y	Y	N	N	Y
Dorgan	N	Y	Y	N	N	Y
OHIO						
DeWine	N	N	N	Y	Y	Y
Voinovich	N	Y	N	Y	Y	N
OKLAHOMA						
Inhofe	Y	N	Y	Y	Y	Y
Nickles	N	N	N	Y	Y	Y
OREGON						
Smith	N	N	Y	Y	Y	Y
Wyden	N	Y	Y	N	N	Y
PENNSYLVANIA						
Santorum	Y	N	N	Y	Y	Y
Specter	Y	N	N	Y	Y	Y
RHODE ISLAND						
Chafee	Y	Y	N	Y	Y	Y
Reed	Y	Y	N	N	N	Y
SOUTH CAROLINA						
Thurmond	Y	Y	Y	Y	Y	Y
Hollings	Y	Y	Y	N	N	Y
SOUTH DAKOTA						
Daschle	N	Y	Y	N	N	Y
Johnson	N	Y	Y	N	N	Y
TENNESSEE						
Frist	Y	Y	N	Y	Y	Y
Thompson	Y	Y	N	Y	Y	Y
TEXAS						
Gramm	N	Y	Y	Y	Y	N
Hutchison	Y	Y	Y	Y	Y	Y
UTAH						
Bennett	N	N	Y	Y	Y	Y
Hatch	N	N	Y	Y	N	Y
VERMONT						
Jeffords	Y	Y	Y	Y	Y	Y
Leahy	Y	Y	Y	N	N	Y
VIRGINIA						
Warner	Y	Y	Y	Y	Y	Y
Robb	Y	Y	Y	N	N	Y
WASHINGTON						
Gorton	Y	N	N	Y	Y	Y
Murray	Y	Y	Y	N	N	Y
WEST VIRGINIA						
Byrd	Y	Y	N	N	N	Y
Rockefeller	Y	Y	Y	N	N	Y
WISCONSIN						
Feingold	N	Y	N	Y	Y	N
Kohl	N	Y	N	N	N	Y
WYOMING						
Enzi	N	N	Y	Y	Y	Y
Thomas	N	N	Y	Y	Y	Y

Key

- Y Voted for (yea).
- # Paired for.
- + Announced for.
- N Voted against (nay).
- X Paired against.
- – Announced against.
- P Voted "present."
- C Voted "present" to avoid possible conflict of interest.
- ? Did not vote or otherwise make a position known.

Democrats ***Republicans***
Independents

ND Northern Democrats SD Southern Democrats

Southern states - Ala., Ark., Fla., Ga., Ky., La., Miss., N.C., Okla., S.C., Tenn., Texas, Va.

252. S 1233. Fiscal 2000 Agriculture Appropriations/Milk Prices. Motion to invoke cloture (thus limiting debate) on the Lott, R-Miss., motion to recommit the bill to the Senate Appropriations Committee with Jeffords, R-Vt., instructions to add language to prohibit funding for the Agriculture Department to implement proposed changes in milk marketing orders in fiscal 2000. Motion rejected 53-47: R 27-27; D 25-20 (ND 17-20, SD 8-0); I 1-0. Aug. 4, 1999. Three-fifths of the total Senate (60) is required to invoke cloture.

253. S 1233. Fiscal 2000 Agriculture Appropriations/Emergency Farm Aid Plan. Cochran, R-Miss., motion to table (kill) the Roberts, R-Kan., amendment to the Daschle, D-S.D., amendment. The Roberts amendment would strike the Daschle language and instead provide $7.6 billion in emergency aid to farmers, mostly in supplemental market transition payments, but including $400 million for disaster assistance. The amendment also includes Ashcroft, R-Mo., language to require congressional approval before imposing U.S. unilateral sanctions that restrict agricultural and medicinal goods to a foreign country. Motion agreed to 66-33: R 21-32; D 45-0 (ND 37-0, SD 8-0); I 0-1. Aug. 4, 1999. (Subsequently, a modified Cochran amendment to strike the Daschle language and instead provide $7.4 billion in emergency aid to farmers was adopted by voice vote.)

254. S 1233. Fiscal 2000 Agriculture Appropriations/Sugar Program. Cochran, R-Miss., motion to table (kill) the McCain, R-Ariz., amendment to the Daschle, D-S.D., amendment. The McCain amendment would prohibit the Agriculture Department from using funds in the bill for the sugar program, which provides loans, import restrictions and price-supports for the industry. Motion agreed to 66-33: R 34-19; D 32-13 (ND 24-13, SD 8-0); I 0-1. Aug. 4, 1999.

255. S 1233. Fiscal 2000 Agriculture Appropriations/Democratic Emergency Farm Aid Plan. Cochran, R-Miss., motion to table (kill) the Dorgan, D-N.D., amendment to the Daschle, D-S.D., amendment. The Dorgan amendment would strike the Daschle language (as replaced by the Cochran amendment) and instead provide $9.8 billion in emergency aid to farmers and ranchers, including funds for disaster assistance, income loss payments and emergency trade provisions. Motion agreed to 55-44: R 52-1; D 2-43 (ND 1-36, SD 1-7); I 1-0. Aug. 4, 1999.

256. S 1233. Fiscal 2000 Agriculture Appropriations/Compromise Emergency Farm Aid Plan. Cochran, R-Miss., motion to table (kill) the Conrad, D-N.D., amendment to the Daschle, D-S.D., amendment. The Conrad amendment would provide $8.8 billion in emergency aid to farmers, mostly in supplemental market transition payments. Motion agreed to 51-48: R 47-6; D 3-42 (ND 2-35, SD 1-7); I 1-0. Aug. 4, 1999.

257. S 1233. Fiscal 2000 Agriculture Appropriations/Farm Aid and Unilateral Sanctions. Daschle, D-S.D., amendment (as replaced by the Cochran, R-Miss., and Ashcroft, R-Mo., amendments) that would provide $7.4 billion in emergency aid to farmers, mostly in supplemental market transition payments, and would prohibit the president from imposing any unilateral agricultural or medical sanctions against any nation unless Congress enacts legislation approving the act. Adopted 89-8: R 49-4; D 40-3 (ND 34-2, SD 6-1); I 0-1. Aug. 4, 1999.

Senate Votes 258, 259, 260, 261

	258	259	260	261
ALABAMA				
Sessions	N	N	N	Y
Shelby	N	Y	Y	Y
ALASKA				
Murkowski	N	Y	Y	Y
Stevens	N	Y	Y	Y
ARIZONA				
Kyl	N	N	N	Y
McCain	N	Y	N	Y
ARKANSAS				
Hutchinson	N	N	N	Y
Lincoln	N	Y	Y	N
CALIFORNIA				
Boxer	Y	Y	Y	N
Feinstein	Y	Y	Y	N
COLORADO				
Allard	N	N	?	Y
Campbell	N	Y	Y	Y
CONNECTICUT				
Dodd	Y	Y	Y	N
Lieberman	Y	Y	Y	N
DELAWARE				
Roth	N	Y	Y	Y
Biden	N	Y	Y	N
FLORIDA				
Mack	?	N	N	Y
Graham	Y	Y	Y	N
GEORGIA				
Coverdell	N	Y	Y	Y
Cleland	Y	Y	Y	N
HAWAII				
Akaka	Y	Y	Y	N
Inouye	Y	Y	Y	N
IDAHO				
Craig	N	N	Y	Y
Crapo	?	?	?	?
ILLINOIS				
Fitzgerald	Y	Y	N	Y
Durbin	Y	Y	Y	N
INDIANA				
Bayh	Y	Y	Y	N
Lugar	Y	Y	Y	Y
IOWA				
Grassley	Y	Y	Y	Y
Harkin	Y	Y	Y	N
KANSAS				
Brownback	Y	Y	N	Y
Roberts	Y	N	Y	Y
KENTUCKY				
Bunning	N	N	N	Y
McConnell	N	Y	Y	Y
LOUISIANA				
Breaux	N	Y	Y	N
Landrieu	?	+	?	N
MAINE				
Collins	Y	Y	Y	N
Snowe	Y	Y	Y	N
MARYLAND				
Mikulski	Y	Y	Y	N
Sarbanes	Y	Y	Y	N
MASSACHUSETTS				
Kennedy	?	Y	Y	N
Kerry	Y	Y	Y	N
MICHIGAN				
Abraham	Y	Y	Y	Y
Levin	Y	Y	Y	N
MINNESOTA				
Grams	Y	Y	Y	Y
Wellstone	Y	Y	Y	N
MISSISSIPPI				
Cochran	N	Y	Y	Y
Lott	N	N	Y	Y
MISSOURI				
Ashcroft	Y	Y	N	Y
Bond	Y	Y	Y	Y
MONTANA				
Burns	Y	Y	Y	Y
Baucus	Y	Y	Y	N
NEBRASKA				
Hagel	N	Y	N	Y
Kerrey	Y	Y	Y	N
NEVADA				
Bryan	Y	Y	Y	N
Reid	Y	Y	Y	N
NEW HAMPSHIRE				
Gregg	N	N	Y	Y
Smith	N	N	N	Y
NEW JERSEY				
Lautenberg	Y	Y	Y	N
Torricelli	Y	Y	Y	N
NEW MEXICO				
Domenici	N	Y	Y	Y
Bingaman	N	Y	Y	N
NEW YORK				
Moynihan	–	Y	Y	N
Schumer	Y	Y	Y	N
NORTH CAROLINA				
Helms	N	?	N	Y
Edwards	Y	Y	Y	N
NORTH DAKOTA				
Conrad	Y	Y	Y	N
Dorgan	Y	Y	Y	N
OHIO				
DeWine	Y	Y	Y	Y
Voinovich	N	Y	Y	N
OKLAHOMA				
Inhofe	N	N	N	Y
Nickles	N	N	N	Y
OREGON				
Smith	N	Y	Y	Y
Wyden	Y	Y	Y	N
PENNSYLVANIA				
Santorum	N	Y	Y	Y
Specter	N	Y	Y	N
RHODE ISLAND				
Chafee	N	Y	Y	Y
Reed	Y	Y	Y	N
SOUTH CAROLINA				
Thurmond	N	Y	N	Y
Hollings	Y	Y	Y	N
SOUTH DAKOTA				
Daschle	Y	Y	Y	N
Johnson	Y	Y	Y	N
TENNESSEE				
Frist	N	Y	Y	Y
Thompson	N	Y	Y	Y

Key

- Y Voted for (yea).
- # Paired for.
- + Announced for.
- N Voted against (nay).
- X Paired against.
- – Announced against.
- P Voted "present."
- C Voted "present" to avoid possible conflict of interest.
- ? Did not vote or otherwise make a position known.

•

Democrats ***Republicans***
Independents

	258	259	260	261
TEXAS				
Gramm	N	N	N	Y
Hutchison	N	N	Y	Y
UTAH				
Bennett	N	Y	Y	Y
Hatch	N	Y	Y	Y
VERMONT				
Jeffords	Y	Y	Y	Y
Leahy	Y	Y	Y	N
VIRGINIA				
Warner	N	Y	Y	Y
Robb	Y	Y	Y	N
WASHINGTON				
Gorton	N	Y	Y	Y
Murray	Y	Y	Y	N
WEST VIRGINIA				
Byrd	Y	Y	Y	N
Rockefeller	Y	Y	?	N
WISCONSIN				
Feingold	Y	Y	Y	N
Kohl	Y	Y	Y	N
WYOMING				
Enzi	N	N	Y	Y
Thomas	N	Y	Y	Y

ND Northern Democrats SD Southern Democrats

Southern states - Ala., Ark., Fla., Ga., Ky., La., Miss., N.C., Okla., S.C., Tenn., Texas, Va.

258. S 1233. Fiscal 2000 Agriculture Appropriations/Fuel Additive Effects on Health. Boxer, D-Calif., motion to table (kill) the Chafee, R-R.I., substitute amendment to the Boxer amendment. The Chafee amendment would express the sense of the Senate that the Environment and Public Works Committee should review EPA findings on the fuel additive methyl tertiary butyl ether (MTBE) and report to the Senate. The Boxer amendment would express the sense of the Senate that MTBE should be phased out in order to address the threats it poses to public health and the environment, and renewable ethanol should be promoted to replace MTBE. Motion agreed to 52-43: R 14-38; D 38-4 (ND 33-2, SD 5-2); I 0-1. Aug. 4, 1999. (Subsequently, the Boxer amendment was adopted and the underlying $70 billion bill was passed by voice vote.)

259. Holbrooke Nomination/Confirmation. Confirmation of President Clinton's nomination of Richard C. Holbrooke of New York to be the permanent U.S. representative to the United Nations. Confirmed 81-16: R 37-15; D 44-0 (ND 37-0, SD 7-0); I 0-1. Aug. 5, 1999. A "yea" was a vote in support of the president's position.

260. HR 2466. Fiscal 2000 Interior Appropriations/NEA Funding. Gorton, R-Wash., motion to table (kill) the Smith, I-N.H., amendment that would eliminate funding for the National Endowment for the Arts. Motion agreed to 80-16: R 37-15; D 43-0 (ND 36-0, SD 7-0); I 0-1. Aug. 5, 1999. A "yea" was a vote in support of the president's position.

261. HR 2488. Tax Reconciliation/Conference Report. Adoption of the conference report on the bill to reduce taxes by $792 billion over 10 years. The report would reduce each income tax rate by 1 percentage point and provide relief from the so-called marriage penalty by raising the standard deduction for joint filers to twice the level for single filers, phased in over five years. It also would phase out the estate tax, reduce capital gains tax rates from 10 percent and 20 percent to 8 percent and 18 percent, increase the per year amount that may be transferred to an Individual Retirement Account and allow taxpayers who pay 50 percent or more of their health insurance premiums to fully deduct the cost of the premiums. Adopted (thus cleared for the president) 50-49: R 49-4; D 0-45 (ND 0-37, SD 0-8); I 1-0. Aug. 5, 1999. A "nay" was a vote in support of the president's position.

Senate Votes 262, 263, 264, 265, 266, 267, 268, 269

	262	263	264	265	266	267	268	269
ALABAMA								
Sessions	Y	Y	Y	Y	N	N	Y	Y
Shelby	Y	Y	Y	Y	N	N	Y	Y
ALASKA								
Murkowski	?	?	?	?	X	?	?	?
Stevens	Y	Y	Y	Y	N	N	Y	Y
ARIZONA								
Kyl	Y	Y	Y	Y	N	N	Y	Y
McCain	?	?	?	?	?	?	?	?
ARKANSAS								
Hutchinson	Y	Y	Y	Y	N	N	Y	Y
Lincoln	Y	Y	N	N	N	N	Y	N
CALIFORNIA								
Boxer	Y	Y	N	N	Y	N	N	N
Feinstein	Y	Y	N	N	Y	N	N	Y
COLORADO								
Allard	Y	Y	Y	Y	N	N	Y	Y
Campbell	Y	Y	Y	Y	N	N	Y	Y
CONNECTICUT								
Dodd	Y	Y	N	N	Y	N	N	Y
Lieberman	Y	Y	N	N	Y	N	N	Y
DELAWARE								
Roth	Y	Y	Y	Y	#	N	N	Y
Biden	Y	Y	N	N	Y	N	N	N
FLORIDA								
Mack	Y	Y	Y	Y	N	N	Y	Y
Graham	Y	Y	N	N	Y	N	N	N
GEORGIA								
Coverdell	Y	Y	Y	Y	N	N	Y	Y
Cleland	Y	Y	N	N	Y	N	N	N
HAWAII								
Akaka	Y	Y	N	N	Y	N	N	N
Inouye	Y	Y	N	N	Y	N	Y	Y
IDAHO								
Craig	Y	Y	Y	Y	N	N	Y	Y
Crapo	Y	Y	N	Y	N	N	Y	Y
ILLINOIS								
Fitzgerald	Y	Y	Y	Y	N	N	N	Y
Durbin	Y	Y	N	N	Y	N	N	N
INDIANA								
Lugar	Y	Y	Y	Y	N	N	Y	Y
Bayh	Y	Y	N	N	Y	N	Y	N
IOWA								
Grassley	Y	Y	Y	Y	N	N	Y	Y
Harkin	Y	Y	N	N	Y	N	N	N
KANSAS								
Brownback	Y	Y	Y	Y	N	N	Y	Y
Roberts	Y	Y	Y	Y	N	N	Y	?
KENTUCKY								
Bunning	Y	Y	Y	Y	N	N	Y	Y
McConnell	Y	Y	Y	Y	N	N	Y	Y
LOUISIANA								
Breaux	Y	Y	N	N	N	N	Y	Y
Landrieu	Y	Y	N	N	N	N	Y	N
MAINE								
Collins	Y	Y	Y	Y	N	N	Y	N
Snowe	Y	Y	Y	Y	N	N	Y	N
MARYLAND								
Mikulski	?	?	N	N	Y	N	N	N
Sarbanes	?	?	N	N	Y	N	N	N
MASSACHUSETTS								
Kennedy	Y	Y	N	N	Y	N	N	N
Kerry	Y	Y	N	N	Y	N	N	N
MICHIGAN								
Abraham	Y	Y	Y	Y	N	N	Y	Y
Levin	Y	Y	N	N	Y	N	N	N
MINNESOTA								
Grams	Y	Y	Y	Y	N	N	Y	Y
Wellstone	Y	Y	N	N	Y	N	N	N
MISSISSIPPI								
Cochran	Y	Y	Y	Y	N	N	Y	Y
Lott	Y	Y	Y	Y	N	N	Y	Y
MISSOURI								
Ashcroft	Y	Y	Y	Y	N	N	Y	Y
Bond	Y	Y	Y	Y	N	N	Y	Y
MONTANA								
Burns	Y	Y	Y	Y	N	N	Y	Y
Baucus	Y	Y	N	N	Y	N	Y	Y
NEBRASKA								
Hagel	Y	Y	Y	Y	N	N	Y	Y
Kerrey	Y	Y	N	N	Y	N	Y	Y
NEVADA								
Bryan	Y	Y	N	N	Y	N	N	N
Reid	Y	Y	N	N	Y	N	N	N
NEW HAMPSHIRE								
Gregg	Y	Y	Y	Y	N	Y	Y	N
Smith	N	N	Y	Y	N	N	N	Y
NEW JERSEY								
Lautenberg	Y	Y	N	N	Y	N	N	N
Torricelli	Y	Y	N	N	Y	N	N	N
NEW MEXICO								
Domenici	Y	Y	Y	Y	N	N	Y	Y
Bingaman	Y	Y	N	N	Y	N	Y	N
NEW YORK								
Moynihan	Y	Y	N	N	Y	N	?	?
Schumer	Y	Y	N	N	Y	N	N	N
NORTH CAROLINA								
Helms	Y	Y	Y	Y	N	N	Y	Y
Edwards	Y	Y	N	N	Y	N	Y	N
NORTH DAKOTA								
Conrad	Y	Y	N	N	Y	N	Y	Y
Dorgan	Y	Y	N	N	Y	N	Y	Y
OHIO								
DeWine	Y	Y	Y	Y	N	N	Y	Y
Voinovich	?	?	N	Y	N	N	Y	Y
OKLAHOMA								
Inhofe	Y	Y	Y	Y	N	N	Y	Y
Nickles	Y	Y	Y	Y	N	N	Y	Y
OREGON								
Smith	Y	Y	Y	Y	N	N	N	Y
Wyden	Y	Y	N	N	Y	N	N	N
PENNSYLVANIA								
Santorum	Y	Y	Y	Y	N	N	Y	Y
Specter	Y	Y	Y	Y	Y	N	N	Y
RHODE ISLAND								
Chafee	Y	Y	N	Y	Y	N	?	?
Reed	Y	Y	N	N	Y	N	N	N
SOUTH CAROLINA								
Thurmond	Y	Y	Y	Y	N	N	Y	Y
Hollings	Y	Y	N	N	Y	N	Y	N
SOUTH DAKOTA								
Daschle	Y	Y	N	N	Y	N	Y	Y
Johnson	Y	Y	N	N	Y	N	Y	N
TENNESSEE								
Frist	Y	Y	Y	Y	N	N	Y	Y
Thompson	Y	Y	Y	Y	N	N	Y	Y
TEXAS								
Gramm	Y	Y	Y	Y	N	N	Y	Y
Hutchison	Y	Y	Y	Y	N	N	Y	Y
UTAH								
Bennett	Y	Y	Y	Y	N	N	Y	Y
Hatch	+	+	Y	Y	N	N	Y	Y
VERMONT								
Jeffords	Y	Y	Y	Y	Y	N	Y	N
Leahy	Y	Y	N	N	Y	N	Y	N
VIRGINIA								
Warner	Y	Y	N	Y	Y	N	Y	Y
Robb	Y	Y	N	N	Y	N	N	N
WASHINGTON								
Gorton	Y	Y	Y	Y	N	N	Y	Y
Murray	Y	Y	N	N	Y	N	N	N
WEST VIRGINIA								
Byrd	Y	Y	N	Y	N	Y	N	Y
Rockefeller	Y	Y	N	N	Y	N	N	N
WISCONSIN								
Feingold	Y	Y	N	N	Y	N	Y	N
Kohl	Y	Y	N	N	Y	N	Y	N
WYOMING								
Enzi	Y	Y	Y	Y	N	N	Y	Y
Thomas	Y	Y	Y	Y	N	N	Y	Y

Key

- Y Voted for (yea).
- \# Paired for.
- \+ Announced for.
- N Voted against (nay).
- X Paired against.
- – Announced against.
- P Voted "present."
- C Voted "present" to avoid possible conflict of interest.
- ? Did not vote or otherwise make a position known.

•

Democrats ***Republicans***
Independents

ND Northern Democrats SD Southern Democrats

Southern states - Ala., Ark., Fla., Ga., Ky., La., Miss., N.C., Okla., S.C., Tenn., Texas, Va.

262. Jordan Nomination/Confirmation. Confirmation of President Clinton's nomination of Adalberto Jose Jordan of Florida to be U.S. District judge for the Southern District of Florida. Confirmed 93-1: R 50-0; D 43-0 (ND 35-0, SD 8-0); I 0-1. Sept. 8, 1999. A "yea" was a vote in support of the president's position.

263. Pechman Nomination/Confirmation. Confirmation of President Clinton's nomination of Marsha J. Pechman of Washington to be U.S. District judge for the Western District of Washington. Confirmed 93-1: R 50-0; D 43-0 (ND 35-0, SD 8-0); I 0-1. Sept. 8, 1999. A "yea" was a vote in support of the president's position.

264. HR 2084. Fiscal 2000 Transportation Appropriations/Cloture. Motion to invoke cloture (thus limiting debate) on the motion to proceed to the fiscal 2000 appropriations bill for the Department of Transportation and related agencies. Motion rejected 49-49: R 48-4; D 0-45 (ND 0-37, SD 0-8); I 1-0. Sept. 9, 1999. Three-fifths of the total Senate (60) is required to invoke cloture.

265. HR 2466. Fiscal 2000 Interior Appropriations/Missouri Forest Mining. Lott, R-Miss., amendment that would require the Forest Service to assess the impact of lead and zinc mining in the Mark Twain National Forest in southern Missouri, prohibit the Interior Department from issuing new hard-rock mineral exploration prospecting permits and prohibit the department from segregating or withdrawing land in the forest. Adopted 54-44: R 52-0; D 1-44 (ND 1-36, SD 0-8); I 1-0. Sept. 9, 1999.

266. HR 2466. Fiscal 2000 Interior Appropriations/Resource Management Plans. Robb, D-Va., amendment to strike language in the bill that would give discretion to the secretaries of Agriculture and Interior as to whether new information concerning wildlife should be collected before revising resource management plans for national forests and Bureau of Land Management properties. Rejected 45-52: R 4-47; D 41-4 (ND 36-1, SD 5-3); I 0-1 Sept. 9, 1999.

267. HR 2466. Fiscal 2000 Interior Appropriations/Oil Royalty Valuation System. Nickles, R-Okla., motion to table (kill) the Hutchison, R-Texas, amendment that would prevent the Minerals Management Service from implementing a proposed new oil royalty valuation system for drilling on federal lands until Sept. 30, 2000. Motion rejected 2-96: R 1-51; D 1-44 (ND 1-36, SD 0-8); I 0-1. Sept. 9, 1999. (Subsequently, the Hutchison amendment was set aside.)

268. HR 2466. Fiscal 2000 Interior Appropriations/Jawed Leghold Traps. Stevens, R-Alaska, motion to table (kill) the Torricelli, D-N.J., amendment that would prevent the use of jawed leghold traps or neck snares in any part of the National Wildlife Refuge System, except for research, subsistence, conservation or facilities protection purposes. Motion agreed to 64-32: R 47-4; D 17-27 (ND 12-24, SD 5-3); I 0-1. Sept. 9, 1999.

269. HR 2466. Fiscal 2000 Interior Appropriations/Grazing Permits. Domenici, R-N.M., motion to table (kill) the Durbin, D-Ill., amendment to replace bill language that would require the Bureau of Land Management (BLM) to renew expiring grazing permits under the same terms and conditions as the old permit, with provisions to allow the BLM to modify conditions of grazing permits when they are up for renewal. Motion agreed to 58-37: R 46-4; D 11-33 (ND 10-26, SD 1-7); I 1-0. Sept. 9, 1999.

Senate Votes 270, 271, 272, 273, 274, 275, 276

	270	271	272	273	274	275	276
ALABAMA							
Sessions	?	?	Y	Y	Y	N	Y
Shelby	Y	Y	Y	Y	Y	N	Y
ALASKA							
Murkowski	Y	Y	Y	Y	N	N	Y
Stevens	Y	Y	Y	Y	Y	N	Y
ARIZONA							
Kyl	Y	Y	Y	Y	Y	N	Y
McCain	Y	Y	?	?	?	?	?
ARKANSAS							
Hutchinson	Y	Y	Y	Y	Y	N	Y
Lincoln	Y	Y	Y	Y	Y	N	Y
CALIFORNIA							
Boxer	Y	N	N	Y	N	Y	Y
Feinstein	Y	N	N	Y	N	Y	Y
COLORADO							
Allard	Y	Y	Y	Y	Y	N	Y
Campbell	Y	Y	Y	Y	Y	N	Y
CONNECTICUT							
Dodd	Y	N	N	Y	N	Y	Y
Lieberman	Y	N	N	Y	N	Y	Y
DELAWARE							
Roth	Y	Y	N	Y	Y	N	Y
Biden	Y	N	N	Y	N	N	Y
FLORIDA							
Mack	Y	Y	Y	Y	Y	N	Y
Graham	?	?	?	?	N	Y	Y
GEORGIA							
Coverdell	Y	Y	Y	Y	Y	N	Y
Cleland	Y	N	N	Y	Y	Y	Y
HAWAII							
Akaka	Y	N	N	N	N	Y	Y
Inouye	Y	Y	N	Y	Y	Y	Y
IDAHO							
Craig	Y	Y	Y	Y	Y	N	Y
Crapo	Y	Y	Y	Y	N	N	Y
ILLINOIS							
Fitzgerald	Y	Y	N	Y	Y	N	Y
Durbin	Y	N	N	Y	Y	Y	Y
INDIANA							
Lugar	Y	Y	Y	Y	Y	N	Y
Bayh	Y	N	N	Y	N	N	Y
IOWA							
Grassley	Y	Y	Y	Y	Y	N	Y
Harkin	Y	N	N	Y	Y	Y	Y
KANSAS							
Brownback	Y	Y	N	Y	Y	N	Y
Roberts	Y	Y	Y	Y	Y	N	Y
KENTUCKY							
Bunning	Y	Y	Y	Y	Y	N	Y
McConnell	Y	Y	Y	Y	Y	N	Y
LOUISIANA							
Breaux	Y	Y	Y	Y	?	?	?
Landrieu	Y	Y	Y	Y	Y	N	Y
MAINE							
Collins	Y	Y	Y	Y	Y	Y	Y
Snowe	Y	Y	Y	Y	Y	Y	Y
MARYLAND							
Mikulski	Y	N	N	Y	Y	N	Y
Sarbanes	Y	N	N	Y	N	Y	Y
MASSACHUSETTS							
Kennedy	Y	N	N	Y	N	Y	Y
Kerry	Y	N	N	Y	N	Y	Y
MICHIGAN							
Abraham	Y	Y	Y	Y	Y	N	Y
Levin	Y	N	N	Y	N	N	Y
MINNESOTA							
Grams	Y	Y	Y	Y	Y	N	Y
Wellstone	Y	N	Y	N	N	Y	+
MISSISSIPPI							
Cochran	Y	Y	Y	Y	Y	N	Y
Lott	Y	N	Y	Y	Y	N	Y
MISSOURI							
Ashcroft	Y	Y	Y	Y	Y	N	Y
Bond	Y	Y	Y	Y	N	N	Y
MONTANA							
Burns	Y	Y	Y	Y	N	N	Y
Baucus	Y	N	Y	Y	N	Y	Y
NEBRASKA							
Hagel	Y	Y	Y	Y	Y	N	Y
Kerrey	Y	N	N	Y	Y	Y	Y
NEVADA							
Bryan	Y	N	N	Y	Y	Y	Y
Reid	Y	N	N	Y	Y	Y	Y
NEW HAMPSHIRE							
Gregg	Y	Y	?	?	?	Y	Y
Smith	Y	Y	Y	Y	N	N	Y
NEW JERSEY							
Lautenberg	Y	N	N	Y	Y	Y	Y
Torricelli	Y	N	N	Y	Y	Y	Y
NEW MEXICO							
Domenici	Y	Y	Y	Y	Y	N	?
Bingaman	Y	Y	N	Y	N	Y	Y
NEW YORK							
Moynihan	Y	N	N	Y	Y	Y	Y
Schumer	Y	N	N	Y	N	Y	Y
NORTH CAROLINA							
Helms	?	?	Y	Y	Y	N	Y
Edwards	Y	N	N	Y	Y	Y	Y
NORTH DAKOTA							
Conrad	Y	N	N	Y	Y	N	Y
Dorgan	Y	N	N	Y	Y	Y	Y
OHIO							
DeWine	Y	Y	N	Y	Y	N	Y
Voinovich	Y	Y	Y	Y	N	N	Y
OKLAHOMA							
Inhofe	Y	Y	Y	Y	N	N	Y
Nickles	Y	Y	Y	Y	Y	N	Y
OREGON							
Smith	?	Y	Y	Y	N	Y	Y
Wyden	Y	N	N	Y	N	Y	Y
PENNSYLVANIA							
Santorum	Y	Y	Y	Y	Y	N	Y
Specter	Y	Y	N	Y	Y	N	Y
RHODE ISLAND							
Chafee	Y	Y	N	Y	N	#	?
Reed	Y	N	N	Y	N	Y	Y
SOUTH CAROLINA							
Thurmond	Y	Y	Y	Y	Y	N	Y
Hollings	Y	N	N	Y	N	Y	Y
SOUTH DAKOTA							
Daschle	Y	N	Y	Y	N	?	?
Johnson	Y	N	Y	Y	N	Y	Y
TENNESSEE							
Frist	Y	Y	Y	Y	Y	N	Y
Thompson	Y	Y	Y	Y	Y	N	Y
TEXAS							
Gramm	Y	Y	Y	Y	Y	N	Y
Hutchison	Y	Y	Y	Y	Y	N	Y
UTAH							
Bennett	?	?	Y	Y	Y	N	Y
Hatch	+	?	Y	Y	Y	N	Y
VERMONT							
Jeffords	Y	Y	N	Y	Y	Y	Y
Leahy	Y	N	N	Y	Y	Y	Y
VIRGINIA							
Warner	Y	Y	Y	Y	N	X	Y
Robb	Y	N	N	Y	N	Y	Y
WASHINGTON							
Gorton	Y	Y	Y	Y	Y	Y	Y
Murray	Y	N	N	Y	Y	Y	Y
WEST VIRGINIA							
Byrd	Y	N	Y	Y	Y	N	Y
Rockefeller	Y	N	N	Y	Y	Y	Y
WISCONSIN							
Feingold	Y	N	N	Y	N	Y	Y
Kohl	Y	N	N	Y	Y	N	Y
WYOMING							
Enzi	?	Y	Y	Y	N	N	Y
Thomas	Y	Y	Y	Y	N	N	Y

Key

Y Voted for (yea).
\# Paired for.
\+ Announced for.
N Voted against (nay).
X Paired against.
– Announced against.
P Voted "present."
C Voted "present" to avoid possible conflict of interest.
? Did not vote or otherwise make a position known.

•

Democrats **Republicans**
Independents

ND Northern Democrats SD Southern Democrats

Southern states - Ala., Ark., Fla., Ga., Ky., La., Miss., N.C., Okla., S.C., Tenn., Texas, Va.

270. S J Res 33. Clemency for Puerto Rican Nationalists/Cloture. Motion to invoke cloture (thus limiting debate) on the motion to proceed to the joint resolution that would state that President Clinton should not have granted clemency to members of a Puerto Rico independence group convicted of seditious conspiracy against the United States. Motion agreed to 93-0: R 48-0; D 44-0 (ND 37-0, SD 7-0); I 1-0. Sept. 13, 1999. Three-fifths of the total Senate (60) is required to invoke cloture.

271. HR 2466. Fiscal 2000 Interior Appropriations/Oil Royalty Valuation System/Cloture. Motion to invoke cloture (thus limiting debate) on the Hutchison, R-Texas, amendment to prevent the Minerals Management Service from implementing a proposed new oil royalty valuation system for drilling on federal lands until Sept. 30, 2000. Motion rejected 55-40: R 49-1; D 5-39 (ND 2-35, SD 3-4); I 1-0. Sept. 13, 1999. Three-fifths of the total Senate (60) is required to invoke cloture. (At the conclusion of the vote, Lott, R-Miss., entered a motion to reconsider the vote, to be voted on at a later time.)

272. HR 2466. Fiscal 2000 Interior Appropriations/Forest Service Programs. Craig, R-Idaho, motion to table (kill) the Bryan, D-Nev., amendment that would reduce funding for timber sales management and logging road construction by the Forest Service, redirecting the funds for road maintenance, wildlife and fisheries habitat management, and threatened and endangered species habitat management. Motion agreed to 54-43: R 45-7; D 8-36 (ND 5-32, SD 3-4); I 1-0. Sept. 14, 1999.

273. S J Res 33. Clemency for Puerto Rican Nationalists/Passage. Passage of the joint resolution that would state that President Clinton should not have granted clemency to members of a Puerto Rico independence group convicted of seditious conspiracy against the United States. Passed 95-2: R 52-0; D 42-2 (ND 35-2, SD 7-0); I 1-0. Sept. 14, 1999.

274. HR 2084. Fiscal 2000 Transportation Appropriations/Highway Funding Allocations. Judgment of the Senate on the germaneness of the highway funding allocation provisions in the Senate substitute (S 1143) to the House bill. The language would provide that additional revenue from revised receipt estimates from gas tax revenues be directed to each state's core highway programs. Chafee, R-R.I., had challenged the germaneness of the language. Ruled germane 62-35: R 41-11; D 21-23 (ND 17-20, SD 4-3); I 0-1. Sept. 15, 1999.

275. HR 2084. Fiscal 2000 Transportation Appropriations/Fuel Efficiency Standards. Gorton, R-Wash., amendment to express the sense of the Senate that the Department of Transportation should be allowed to study whether to raise the corporate average fuel economy (CAFE) standard for vehicles. It also would urge the Senate not to accept House-passed language that would prohibit an increase in CAFE standards. Rejected 40-55: R 6-45; D 34-9 (ND 29-7, SD 5-2); I 0-1. Sept. 15, 1999.

276. HR 2084. Fiscal 2000 Transportation Appropriations/Census Questionnaire. Helms, R-N.C., amendment to express the sense of the Senate that the Census Bureau should include marital status on the short-form census questionnaire to be used for the 2000 census. Adopted 94-0: R 51-0; D 42-0 (ND 35-0, SD 7-0); I 1-0. Sept. 15, 1999.

Senate Votes 277, 278, 279

	277	278	279
ALABAMA			
Sessions	N	Y	Y
Shelby	Y	Y	N
ALASKA			
Murkowski	Y	Y	Y
Stevens	Y	Y	Y
ARIZONA			
Kyl	Y	Y	Y
McCain	?	?	?
ARKANSAS			
Hutchinson	N	Y	Y
Lincoln	N	Y	N
CALIFORNIA			
Boxer	Y	Y	N
Feinstein	Y	Y	N
COLORADO			
Allard	N	Y	Y
Campbell	Y	Y	Y
CONNECTICUT			
Dodd	Y	Y	N
Lieberman	Y	Y	N
DELAWARE			
Roth	Y	Y	Y
Biden	?	Y	N
FLORIDA			
Mack	N	Y	Y
Graham	N	Y	N
GEORGIA			
Coverdell	Y	Y	Y
Cleland	N	Y	N
HAWAII			
Akaka	Y	Y	N
Inouye	?	?	?
IDAHO			
Craig	Y	Y	Y
Crapo	Y	Y	?
ILLINOIS			
Fitzgerald	N	Y	Y
Durbin	Y	Y	N
INDIANA			
Lugar	Y	Y	Y
Bayh	N	Y	N
IOWA			
Grassley	Y	Y	Y
Harkin	Y	Y	N
KANSAS			
Brownback	N	Y	Y
Roberts	N	Y	Y
KENTUCKY			
Bunning	N	Y	Y
McConnell	N	Y	Y
LOUISIANA			
Breaux	?	?	?
Landrieu	Y	Y	N
MAINE			
Collins	N	Y	Y
Snowe	N	Y	Y
MARYLAND			
Mikulski	Y	Y	N
Sarbanes	Y	Y	N
MASSACHUSETTS			
Kennedy	?	?	?
Kerry	Y	Y	?
MICHIGAN			
Abraham	N	Y	Y
Levin	Y	Y	N
MINNESOTA			
Grams	N	Y	Y
Wellstone	?	+	–
MISSISSIPPI			
Cochran	?	Y	Y
Lott	Y	Y	Y
MISSOURI			
Ashcroft	N	Y	Y
Bond	Y	Y	Y
MONTANA			
Burns	N	Y	Y
Baucus	N	Y	N
NEBRASKA			
Hagel	Y	Y	Y
Kerrey	N	Y	N
NEVADA			
Bryan	Y	Y	N
Reid	Y	Y	N
NEW HAMPSHIRE			
Gregg	Y	Y	Y
Smith	N	Y	Y
NEW JERSEY			
Lautenberg	Y	Y	N
Torricelli	Y	Y	N
NEW MEXICO			
Domenici	Y	Y	Y
Bingaman	N	Y	N
NEW YORK			
Moynihan	Y	Y	N
Schumer	N	Y	N
NORTH CAROLINA			
Helms	N	Y	Y
Edwards	N	Y	N
NORTH DAKOTA			
Conrad	Y	Y	Y
Dorgan	Y	Y	N
OHIO			
DeWine	N	Y	Y
Voinovich	Y	Y	Y
OKLAHOMA			
Inhofe	N	Y	Y
Nickles	Y	Y	Y
OREGON			
Smith	Y	Y	Y
Wyden	N	Y	N
PENNSYLVANIA			
Santorum	N	Y	Y
Specter	Y	Y	Y
RHODE ISLAND			
Chafee	Y	Y	?
Reed	Y	Y	N
SOUTH CAROLINA			
Thurmond	Y	Y	Y
Hollings	Y	Y	N
SOUTH DAKOTA			
Daschle	Y	Y	?
Johnson	Y	Y	N
TENNESSEE			
Frist	N	Y	Y
Thompson	Y	Y	Y
TEXAS			
Gramm	N	Y	Y
Hutchison	N	Y	Y
UTAH			
Bennett	Y	Y	Y
Hatch	Y	Y	Y
VERMONT			
Jeffords	Y	Y	N
Leahy	N	Y	N
VIRGINIA			
Warner	?	Y	Y
Robb	N	Y	N
WASHINGTON			
Gorton	Y	Y	Y
Murray	Y	Y	N
WEST VIRGINIA			
Byrd	Y	Y	Y
Rockefeller	Y	Y	N
WISCONSIN			
Feingold	N	Y	N
Kohl	Y	Y	N
WYOMING			
Enzi	N	Y	Y
Thomas	N	Y	Y

Key

- Y Voted for (yea).
- # Paired for.
- + Announced for.
- N Voted against (nay).
- X Paired against.
- – Announced against.
- P Voted "present."
- C Voted "present" to avoid possible conflict of interest.
- ? Did not vote or otherwise make a position known.

•

Democrats ***Republicans***
Independents

ND Northern Democrats SD Southern Democrats

Southern states - Ala., Ark., Fla., Ga., Ky., La., Miss., N.C., Okla., S.C., Tenn., Texas, Va.

277. HR 2490. Fiscal 2000 Treasury-Postal Appropriations/Conference Report. Adoption of the conference report on the bill to provide $28.2 billion for the Treasury Department, Postal Service, Executive Office of the President and other federal agencies in fiscal 2000. The measure would provide a 4.8 percent pay increase for federal civilian employees and includes House-passed language to double the president's annual salary to $400,000 when the next president takes office in 2001. It also would require federal employee health insurance plans that offer prescription drug coverage to include contraceptive coverage. Adopted (thus cleared for the president) 54-38: R 27-24; D 27-13 (ND 25-8, SD 2-5); I 0-1. Sept. 16, 1999.

278. HR 2084. Fiscal 2000 Transportation Appropriations/Passage. Passage of the bill to provide $49.5 billion in new budget authority for the Department of Transportation and related programs in fiscal 2000. Passed 95-0: R 53-0; D 41-0 (ND 34-0, SD 7-0); I 1-0. Sept. 16, 1999.

279. HR 2587. Fiscal 2000 District of Columbia Appropriations/Conference Report. Adoption of the conference report on the bill to provide $429.1 million in federal payments to the District of Columbia and approve the District's $6.8 billion budget. The measure would provide $17 million for a program to allow D.C. students to pay in-state tuition rates at colleges not in the District, and contains legislative provisions to prohibit the District from spending federal, local or private funds on needle-exchange programs or to legalize marijuana or reduce marijuana penalties. Adopted (thus cleared for the president) 52-39: R 49-2; D 2-37 (ND 2-30, SD 0-7); I 1-0. Sept. 16, 1999.

Senate Votes 280, 281, 282, 283

	280	281	282	283
ALABAMA				
Sessions	Y	Y	N	N
Shelby	Y	Y	N	N
ALASKA				
Murkowski	Y	Y	N	N
Stevens	Y	Y	N	N
ARIZONA				
Kyl	Y	Y	N	N
McCain	?	?	?	?
ARKANSAS				
Hutchinson	Y	Y	N	N
Lincoln	N	N	Y	Y
CALIFORNIA				
Boxer	N	N	Y	Y
Feinstein	N	N	Y	Y
COLORADO				
Allard	Y	Y	N	N
Campbell	Y	Y	N	N
CONNECTICUT				
Dodd	N	N	Y	Y
Lieberman	N	N	Y	Y
DELAWARE				
Roth	Y	Y	N	N
Biden	N	N	Y	Y
FLORIDA				
Mack	Y	Y	N	N
Graham	N	N	Y	Y
GEORGIA				
Coverdell	Y	Y	N	N
Cleland	N	N	Y	Y
HAWAII				
Akaka	N	N	Y	Y
Inouye	N	N	Y	Y
IDAHO				
Craig	Y	Y	N	N
Crapo	Y	Y	N	N
ILLINOIS				
Fitzgerald	P	Y	N	N
Durbin	N	N	Y	Y
INDIANA				
Lugar	Y	Y	N	N
Bayh	N	N	Y	Y
IOWA				
Grassley	Y	Y	N	N
Harkin	N	N	Y	Y
KANSAS				
Brownback	Y	Y	N	N
Roberts	Y	Y	N	N
KENTUCKY				
Bunning	Y	Y	N	N
McConnell	Y	Y	N	N
LOUISIANA				
Breaux	N	N	Y	Y
Landrieu	N	N	Y	Y
MAINE				
Collins	Y	Y	N	N
Snowe	Y	Y	N	N
MARYLAND				
Mikulski	N	N	Y	Y
Sarbanes	N	N	Y	Y
MASSACHUSETTS				
Kennedy	N	N	Y	Y
Kerry	N	N	Y	Y
MICHIGAN				
Abraham	Y	Y	N	N
Levin	N	N	Y	Y
MINNESOTA				
Grams	Y	Y	N	N
Wellstone	N	N	Y	Y
MISSISSIPPI				
Cochran	Y	Y	N	N
Lott	Y	Y	N	N
MISSOURI				
Ashcroft	Y	Y	N	N
Bond	Y	Y	N	N
MONTANA				
Burns	Y	Y	N	N
Baucus	N	N	Y	Y
NEBRASKA				
Hagel	Y	Y	N	N
Kerrey	N	N	Y	Y
NEVADA				
Bryan	N	N	Y	Y
Reid	N	N	Y	Y
NEW HAMPSHIRE				
Gregg	Y	Y	N	N
Smith	Y	Y	N	N
NEW JERSEY				
Lautenberg	N	N	Y	Y
Torricelli	N	N	Y	Y
NEW MEXICO				
Domenici	Y	Y	N	N
Bingaman	N	N	Y	Y
NEW YORK				
Moynihan	N	Y	Y	Y
Schumer	N	N	Y	Y
NORTH CAROLINA				
Helms	Y	Y	N	?
Edwards	N	N	Y	Y
NORTH DAKOTA				
Conrad	N	N	Y	Y
Dorgan	N	N	Y	Y
OHIO				
DeWine	Y	Y	N	N
Voinovich	Y	Y	N	N
OKLAHOMA				
Inhofe	Y	Y	N	N
Nickles	Y	Y	N	N
OREGON				
Smith	Y	Y	N	N
Wyden	N	N	Y	Y
PENNSYLVANIA				
Santorum	Y	Y	N	N
Specter	Y	Y	N	N
RHODE ISLAND				
Chafee	Y	Y	N	N
Reed	N	N	Y	Y
SOUTH CAROLINA				
Thurmond	Y	Y	N	N
Hollings	N	N	Y	Y
SOUTH DAKOTA				
Daschle	N	N	Y	Y
Johnson	N	N	Y	Y
TENNESSEE				
Frist	Y	Y	N	N
Thompson	Y	Y	N	N
TEXAS				
Gramm	Y	Y	N	N
Hutchison	Y	Y	N	N
UTAH				
Bennett	Y	Y	N	N
Hatch	Y	Y	N	N
VERMONT				
Jeffords	Y	Y	N	N
Leahy	N	N	Y	Y
VIRGINIA				
Warner	Y	Y	N	N
Robb	N	N	Y	Y
WASHINGTON				
Gorton	Y	Y	N	N
Murray	N	N	Y	Y
WEST VIRGINIA				
Byrd	N	N	Y	Y
Rockefeller	N	N	Y	Y
WISCONSIN				
Feingold	N	N	Y	Y
Kohl	N	N	Y	Y
WYOMING				
Enzi	Y	Y	N	N
Thomas	Y	Y	N	N

Key

- Y Voted for (yea).
- # Paired for.
- + Announced for.
- N Voted against (nay).
- X Paired against.
- – Announced against.
- P Voted "present."
- C Voted "present" to avoid possible conflict of interest.
- ? Did not vote or otherwise make a position known.

Democrats ***Republicans***
Independents

ND Northern Democrats SD Southern Democrats

Southern states - Ala., Ark., Fla., Ga., Ky., La., Miss., N.C., Okla., S.C., Tenn., Texas, Va.

280. S 625. Bankruptcy Overhaul/Cloture. Motion to invoke cloture (thus limiting debate) on the bill that would revise bankruptcy laws to make it easier for courts to move debtors from Chapter 7 of the bankruptcy code, which allows most debts to be discharged, to Chapter 13, which requires a reorganization of debts under a repayment plan. Motion rejected 53-45: R 52-0; D 0-45 (ND 0-37, SD 0-8); I 1-0. Sept. 21, 1999. Three-fifths of the total Senate (60) is required to invoke cloture.

281. Stewart Nomination/Cloture. Motion to invoke cloture (thus limiting debate) on President Clinton's nomination of Brian Theadore Stewart of Utah to be U.S. District judge for the District of Utah. Motion rejected 55-44: R 53-0; D 1-44 (ND 1-36, SD 0-8); I 1-0. Sept. 21, 1999. Three-fifths of the total Senate (60) is required to invoke cloture.

282. Berzon Nomination/MotionTo Proceed. Motion to proceed to executive session to consider President Clinton's nomination of Marsha L. Berzon of California to be a judge for the 9th U.S. Circuit Court of Appeals. Motion rejected 45-54: R 0-53; D 45-0 (ND 37-0, SD 8-0); I 0-1. Sept. 21, 1999.

283. Paez Nomination/Motion To Proceed. Motion to proceed to executive session to consider President Clinton's nomination of Richard A. Paez of California to be a judge for the 9th U.S. Circuit Court of Appeals. Motion rejected 45-53: R 0-52; D 45-0 (ND 37-0, SD 8-0); I 0-1. Sept. 21, 1999.

Senate Votes 284, 285, 286, 287

	284	285	286	287
ALABAMA				
Sessions	Y	N	N	Y
Shelby	Y	N	N	Y
ALASKA				
Murkowski	Y	N	N	Y
Stevens	Y	N	Y	Y
ARIZONA				
Kyl	Y	N	N	Y
McCain	?	?	?	Y
ARKANSAS				
Hutchinson	Y	Y	N	Y
Lincoln	Y	N	Y	Y
CALIFORNIA				
Boxer	N	Y	Y	N
Feinstein	Y	N	Y	N
COLORADO				
Allard	Y	N	N	Y
Campbell	Y	Y	Y	Y
CONNECTICUT				
Dodd	Y	Y	Y	N
Lieberman	Y	Y	Y	N
DELAWARE				
Roth	Y	N	N	Y
Biden	Y	Y	Y	N
FLORIDA				
Mack	Y	N	N	Y
Graham	Y	N	Y	N
GEORGIA				
Coverdell	Y	N	N	Y
Cleland	Y	Y	Y	N
HAWAII				
Akaka	Y	Y	Y	N
Inouye	Y	N	Y	Y
IDAHO				
Craig	Y	N	N	Y
Crapo	Y	N	N	Y
ILLINOIS				
Fitzgerald	Y	N	N	Y
Durbin	Y	Y	Y	N
INDIANA				
Lugar	Y	N	N	Y
Bayh	Y	N	Y	N
IOWA				
Grassley	Y	Y	Y	Y
Harkin	N	Y	Y	N
KANSAS				
Brownback	Y	N	N	Y
Roberts	Y	N	Y	Y
KENTUCKY				
Bunning	Y	N	N	Y
McConnell	Y	N	Y	Y
LOUISIANA				
Breaux	Y	N	Y	Y
Landrieu	Y	N	Y	Y
MAINE				
Collins	Y	Y	Y	Y
Snowe	Y	Y	N	Y
MARYLAND				
Mikulski	Y	N	Y	N
Sarbanes	Y	N	Y	N
MASSACHUSETTS				
Kennedy	Y	Y	Y	N
Kerry	Y	Y	Y	N
MICHIGAN				
Abraham	Y	N	N	Y
Levin	Y	N	Y	N
MINNESOTA				
Grams	Y	N	N	Y
Wellstone	N	Y	Y	N
MISSISSIPPI				
Cochran	Y	N	Y	Y
Lott	Y	N	N	Y
MISSOURI				
Ashcroft	Y	N	N	Y
Bond	Y	N	Y	Y
MONTANA				
Burns	Y	N	N	Y
Baucus	Y	Y	Y	N
NEBRASKA				
Hagel	Y	N	Y	Y
Kerrey	Y	Y	Y	N
NEVADA				
Bryan	Y	N	Y	N
Reid	Y	Y	Y	N
NEW HAMPSHIRE				
Gregg	Y	N	N	Y
Smith	Y	Y	N	Y
NEW JERSEY				
Lautenberg	Y	N	Y	N
Torricelli	Y	N	Y	N
NEW MEXICO				
Domenici	Y	N	N	Y
Bingaman	Y	Y	Y	Y
NEW YORK				
Moynihan	Y	N	Y	–
Schumer	Y	Y	Y	N
NORTH CAROLINA				
Helms	Y	N	N	Y
Edwards	Y	N	Y	N
NORTH DAKOTA				
Conrad	Y	Y	Y	N
Dorgan	Y	Y	Y	N
OHIO				
DeWine	Y	N	Y	Y
Voinovich	Y	N	N	Y
OKLAHOMA				
Inhofe	Y	N	N	Y
Nickles	Y	N	N	Y
OREGON				
Smith	Y	Y	N	Y
Wyden	Y	Y	Y	N
PENNSYLVANIA				
Santorum	Y	Y	Y	Y
Specter	Y	Y	Y	Y
RHODE ISLAND				
Chafee	Y	N	Y	Y
Reed	Y	Y	Y	N
SOUTH CAROLINA				
Thurmond	Y	N	N	Y
Hollings	Y	N	Y	N
SOUTH DAKOTA				
Daschle	Y	Y	Y	N
Johnson	Y	Y	Y	N
TENNESSEE				
Frist	Y	N	N	Y
Thompson	Y	N	N	Y
TEXAS				
Gramm	Y	N	N	Y
Hutchison	Y	N	N	Y
UTAH				
Bennett	Y	N	Y	Y
Hatch	Y	N	Y	Y
VERMONT				
Jeffords	Y	Y	Y	Y
Leahy	Y	Y	Y	N
VIRGINIA				
Warner	Y	N	N	Y
Robb	Y	Y	Y	N
WASHINGTON				
Gorton	C	N	N	Y
Murray	Y	Y	Y	N
WEST VIRGINIA				
Byrd	Y	N	Y	N
Rockefeller	Y	Y	Y	N
WISCONSIN				
Feingold	N	N	Y	N
Kohl	N	N	Y	N
WYOMING				
Enzi	Y	N	N	Y
Thomas	Y	N	N	Y

ND Northern Democrats SD Southern Democrats

Southern states - Ala., Ark., Fla., Ga., Ky., La., Miss., N.C., Okla., S.C., Tenn., Texas, Va.

Key

- Y Voted for (yea).
- # Paired for.
- + Announced for.
- N Voted against (nay).
- X Paired against.
- – Announced against.
- P Voted "present."
- C Voted "present" to avoid possible conflict of interest.
- ? Did not vote or otherwise make a position known.

•

Democrats ***Republicans***
Independents

284. S 1059. Fiscal 2000 Defense Authorization/Conference Report. Adoption of the conference report on the bill to authorize $288.8 billion in funds for defense programs. The conference report also would establish a semi-autonomous agency within the Energy Department that would be responsible for nuclear weapons development, naval nuclear propulsion, defense nuclear non-proliferation and fissile material disposition, and would establish security, intelligence and counterintelligence offices. The conference report includes $3.1 billion for development and production of the F-22 fighter. Adopted (thus cleared for the president) 93-5: R 52-0; D 40-5 (ND 32-5, SD 8-0); I 1-0. Sept. 22, 1999.

285. HR 2684. Fiscal 2000 VA-HUD Appropriations/Veterans' Medical Care. Wellstone, D-Minn., motion to waive the Budget Act with respect to the Bond, R-Mo., point of order against the Wellstone amendment. The Wellstone amendment would increase funding for veterans' medical care by $1.3 billion. Motion rejected 36-63: R 9-44; D 26-19 (ND 24-13, SD 2-6); I 1-0. Sept. 22, 1999. A three-fifths majority vote (60) of the total Senate is required to waive the Budget Act. (Subsequently, the chair upheld the point of order, and the amendment fell.)

286. HR 2684. Fiscal 2000 VA-HUD Appropriations/Veterans' Benefits, AmeriCorps. Bond, R-Mo., motion to table (kill) the Smith, I-N.H., amendment that would reduce funding for the AmeriCorps national service program by $225 million and reallocate $210 million for veterans' medical benefits, $5 million for homeless veterans and $10 million for construction of veterans' extended care facilities. Motion agreed to 61-38: R 16-37; D 45-0 (ND 37-0, SD 8-0); I 0-1. Sept. 22, 1999.

287. HR 2466. Fiscal 2000 Interior Appropriations/Oil Royalty Valuation System/Proceed. Motion to proceed to the Lott, R-Miss., motion to reconsider the cloture vote (vote 271) on the Hutchison, R-Texas, amendment that would prevent the Minerals Management Service from implementing a proposed new oil royalty valuation system for drilling on federal lands until Sept. 30, 2000. Motion agreed to 60-39: R 54-0; D 5-39 (ND 2-34, SD 3-5); I 1-0. Sept. 23, 1999.

Senate Votes 288, 289, 290, 291

	288	289	290	291
ALABAMA				
Sessions	Y	Y	Y	Y
Shelby	Y	Y	Y	Y
ALASKA				
Murkowski	Y	Y	Y	Y
Stevens	Y	Y	Y	Y
ARIZONA				
Kyl	Y	Y	Y	Y
McCain	Y	Y	–	?
ARKANSAS				
Hutchinson	Y	Y	Y	Y
Lincoln	Y	Y	Y	Y
CALIFORNIA				
Boxer	N	N	N	N
Feinstein	N	N	N	Y
COLORADO				
Allard	Y	Y	Y	Y
Campbell	Y	Y	Y	Y
CONNECTICUT				
Dodd	N	N	N	Y
Lieberman	N	N	N	Y
DELAWARE				
Roth	Y	Y	N	Y
Biden	N	N	N	N
FLORIDA				
Mack	Y	Y	Y	Y
Graham	N	N	N	N
GEORGIA				
Coverdell	Y	Y	Y	Y
Cleland	N	N	N	Y
HAWAII				
Akaka	N	N	N	Y
Inouye	Y	Y	Y	Y
IDAHO				
Craig	Y	Y	Y	Y
Crapo	Y	Y	Y	Y
ILLINOIS				
Fitzgerald	Y	Y	Y	Y
Durbin	N	N	N	Y
INDIANA				
Lugar	Y	Y	Y	Y
Bayh	N	N	N	Y
IOWA				
Grassley	Y	Y	Y	Y
Harkin	N	N	N	Y
KANSAS				
Brownback	Y	Y	Y	Y
Roberts	Y	Y	Y	Y
KENTUCKY				
Bunning	Y	Y	Y	Y
McConnell	Y	Y	Y	Y
LOUISIANA				
Breaux	Y	Y	Y	Y
Landrieu	Y	Y	Y	Y
MAINE				
Collins	Y	Y	N	Y
Snowe	Y	Y	N	Y
MARYLAND				
Mikulski	N	N	N	Y
Sarbanes	N	N	N	Y
MASSACHUSETTS				
Kennedy	N	N	N	Y
Kerry	N	N	N	Y
MICHIGAN				
Abraham	Y	Y	Y	Y
Levin	N	N	N	Y
MINNESOTA				
Grams	Y	Y	Y	Y
Wellstone	N	N	N	N
MISSISSIPPI				
Cochran	Y	Y	Y	Y
Lott	Y	Y	Y	Y
MISSOURI				
Ashcroft	Y	Y	Y	N
Bond	Y	Y	Y	Y
MONTANA				
Burns	Y	Y	Y	Y
Baucus	N	N	N	Y
NEBRASKA				
Hagel	Y	Y	Y	Y
Kerrey	N	N	N	Y
NEVADA				
Bryan	N	N	N	Y
Reid	N	N	N	Y
NEW HAMPSHIRE				
Gregg	Y	Y	N	Y
Smith	Y	Y	Y	Y
NEW JERSEY				
Lautenberg	N	N	N	N
Torricelli	N	N	N	Y
NEW MEXICO				
Domenici	Y	Y	Y	Y
Bingaman	Y	Y	Y	Y
NEW YORK				
Moynihan	–	–	N	Y
Schumer	N	N	N	Y
NORTH CAROLINA				
Helms	Y	Y	Y	Y
Edwards	N	N	N	Y
NORTH DAKOTA				
Conrad	N	N	N	Y
Dorgan	N	N	N	Y
OHIO				
DeWine	Y	Y	Y	Y
Voinovich	Y	Y	Y	N
OKLAHOMA				
Inhofe	Y	Y	Y	Y
Nickles	Y	Y	Y	Y
OREGON				
Smith	Y	Y	N	Y
Wyden	N	N	N	N
PENNSYLVANIA				
Santorum	Y	Y	Y	Y
Specter	Y	Y	N	Y
RHODE ISLAND				
Chafee	Y	Y	Y	Y
Reed	N	N	N	Y
SOUTH CAROLINA				
Thurmond	Y	Y	Y	Y
Hollings	N	N	N	Y
SOUTH DAKOTA				
Daschle	N	N	N	Y
Johnson	N	N	N	Y
TENNESSEE				
Frist	Y	Y	Y	Y
Thompson	Y	Y	Y	Y
TEXAS				
Gramm	Y	Y	Y	Y
Hutchison	Y	Y	Y	Y
UTAH				
Bennett	Y	Y	Y	Y
Hatch	Y	Y	Y	Y
VERMONT				
Jeffords	Y	Y	N	Y
Leahy	N	N	N	Y
VIRGINIA				
Warner	Y	Y	P	Y
Robb	N	N	N	Y
WASHINGTON				
Gorton	Y	Y	Y	Y
Murray	N	N	N	N
WEST VIRGINIA				
Byrd	N	N	N	Y
Rockefeller	N	N	N	Y
WISCONSIN				
Feingold	N	N	N	N
Kohl	N	N	N	Y
WYOMING				
Enzi	Y	Y	Y	Y
Thomas	Y	Y	Y	Y

Key

- Y Voted for (yea).
- # Paired for.
- + Announced for.
- N Voted against (nay).
- X Paired against.
- – Announced against.
- P Voted "present."
- C Voted "present" to avoid possible conflict of interest.
- ? Did not vote or otherwise make a position known.

Democrats **_Republicans_**
Independents

ND Northern Democrats SD Southern Democrats

Southern states - Ala., Ark., Fla., Ga., Ky., La., Miss., N.C., Okla., S.C., Tenn., Texas, Va.

288. HR 2466. Fiscal 2000 Interior Appropriations/Oil Royalty Valuation System/Reconsider. Lott, R-Miss., motion to reconsider the cloture vote (vote 271) on the Hutchison, R-Texas, amendment that would prevent the Minerals Management Service from implementing a proposed new oil royalty valuation system for drilling on federal lands until Sept. 30, 2000. Motion agreed to 60-39: R 54-0; D 5-39 (ND 2-34, SD 3-5); I 1-0. Sept. 23, 1999.

289. HR 2466. Fiscal 2000 Interior Appropriations/Oil Royalty Valuation System/Cloture. Motion to invoke cloture (thus limiting debate) on the Hutchison, R-Texas, amendment that would prevent the Minerals Management Service from implementing a proposed new oil royalty valuation system for drilling on federal lands until Sept. 30, 2000. Motion agreed to 60-39: R 54-0; D 5-39 (ND 2-34, SD 3-5); I 1-0. Sept. 23, 1999. Three-fifths of the total Senate (60) is required to invoke cloture.

290. HR 2466. Fiscal 2000 Interior Appropriations/Oil Royalty Valuation System. Hutchison, R-Texas, amendment that would prevent the Minerals Management Service from implementing a proposed new oil royalty valuation system for drilling on federal lands until Sept. 30, 2000. Adopted 51-47: R 45-7; D 5-40 (ND 2-35, SD 3-5); I 1-0. Sept. 23, 1999.

291. HR 2466. Fiscal 2000 Interior Appropriations /Passage. Passage of the bill to provide $14.1 billion for the Department of Interior, related agencies and cultural programs and agencies in fiscal 2000. Passed 89-10: R 51-2; D 37-8 (ND 30-7, SD 7-1); I 1-0. Sept. 23, 1999.

Senate Votes 292, 293, 294, 295, 296, 297, 298

	292	293	294	295	296	297	298
ALABAMA							
Sessions	Y	Y	N	Y	Y	Y	Y
Shelby	N	Y	N	Y	Y	Y	Y
ALASKA							
Murkowski	N	Y	N	Y	Y	Y	Y
Stevens	Y	Y	N	Y	Y	Y	Y
ARIZONA							
Kyl	N	Y	N	Y	Y	Y	Y
McCain	?	?	?	?	?	?	?
ARKANSAS							
Hutchinson	Y	Y	N	Y	Y	Y	Y
Lincoln	Y	N	Y	Y	Y	N	N
CALIFORNIA							
Boxer	Y	N	Y	Y	Y	N	N
Feinstein	Y	N	Y	Y	Y	N	N
COLORADO							
Allard	N	Y	N	Y	Y	Y	Y
Campbell	N	Y	N	Y	Y	Y	Y
CONNECTICUT							
Dodd	Y	N	Y	Y	Y	N	N
Lieberman	Y	N	Y	N	Y	N	N
DELAWARE							
Roth	Y	Y	N	Y	Y	Y	Y
Biden	Y	N	Y	Y	Y	N	N
FLORIDA							
Mack	?	Y	N	Y	Y	Y	Y
Graham	Y	N	Y	Y	Y	N	N
GEORGIA							
Coverdell	Y	Y	N	Y	Y	Y	Y
Cleland	Y	N	Y	Y	Y	N	N
HAWAII							
Akaka	Y	N	Y	Y	Y	N	N
Inouye	?	N	Y	Y	Y	N	N
IDAHO							
Craig	Y	Y	N	Y	Y	Y	Y
Crapo	Y	Y	N	Y	Y	Y	Y
ILLINOIS							
Fitzgerald	Y	Y	N	Y	Y	Y	Y
Durbin	Y	N	Y	Y	Y	N	N
INDIANA							
Lugar	Y	Y	N	Y	Y	Y	Y
Bayh	Y	N	Y	Y	Y	N	N
IOWA							
Grassley	Y	Y	N	Y	Y	Y	Y
Harkin	Y	N	Y	Y	Y	N	N
KANSAS							
Brownback	Y	Y	N	Y	Y	Y	Y
Roberts	Y	Y	N	Y	Y	Y	Y
KENTUCKY							
Bunning	Y	?	?	Y	Y	Y	Y
McConnell	N	Y	N	Y	Y	Y	Y
LOUISIANA							
Breaux	Y	N	Y	Y	Y	N	N
Landrieu	Y	N	Y	Y	Y	N	N
MAINE							
Collins	Y	Y	N	Y	Y	Y	Y
Snowe	Y	Y	N	Y	Y	Y	Y
MARYLAND							
Mikulski	Y	N	Y	Y	Y	N	N
Sarbanes	Y	N	Y	Y	Y	N	N
MASSACHUSETTS							
Kennedy	Y	N	Y	Y	Y	N	N
Kerry	Y	N	Y	Y	Y	N	N
MICHIGAN							
Abraham	Y	Y	N	Y	Y	Y	Y
Levin	Y	N	Y	Y	Y	–	–
MINNESOTA							
Grams	Y	Y	N	Y	Y	Y	Y
Wellstone	Y	N	Y	N	Y	N	N
MISSISSIPPI							
Cochran	N	Y	N	Y	Y	Y	Y
Lott	N	Y	N	Y	Y	Y	Y
MISSOURI							
Ashcroft	Y	Y	N	Y	N	Y	Y
Bond	N	Y	N	Y	Y	Y	Y
MONTANA							
Burns	Y	Y	N	Y	Y	Y	Y
Baucus	Y	N	Y	Y	Y	N	N
NEBRASKA							
Hagel	Y	?	?	Y	Y	Y	Y
Kerrey	Y	N	Y	Y	Y	N	N
NEVADA							
Bryan	Y	N	Y	Y	Y	N	N
Reid	Y	N	Y	Y	Y	N	N
NEW HAMPSHIRE							
Gregg	N	Y	N	Y	Y	Y	Y
Smith	Y	Y	N	Y	Y	Y	Y
NEW JERSEY							
Lautenberg	Y	N	Y	Y	Y	N	N
Torricelli	Y	?	?	Y	Y	N	N
NEW MEXICO							
Domenici	Y	Y	N	Y	Y	Y	Y
Bingaman	Y	N	Y	Y	Y	N	N
NEW YORK							
Moynihan	Y	N	Y	Y	Y	N	N
Schumer	Y	N	Y	Y	Y	N	N
NORTH CAROLINA							
Helms	N	Y	N	Y	Y	Y	Y
Edwards	Y	N	Y	Y	Y	N	N
NORTH DAKOTA							
Conrad	Y	N	Y	Y	Y	N	N
Dorgan	Y	N	Y	Y	Y	N	N
OHIO							
DeWine	Y	Y	N	Y	Y	Y	Y
Voinovich	N	Y	N	Y	Y	N	Y
OKLAHOMA							
Inhofe	?	Y	N	Y	Y	Y	Y
Nickles	?	Y	N	Y	Y	Y	Y
OREGON							
Smith	Y	Y	N	Y	Y	Y	Y
Wyden	Y	N	Y	Y	Y	N	N
PENNSYLVANIA							
Santorum	Y	Y	N	Y	Y	Y	Y
Specter	Y	Y	N	Y	Y	Y	Y
RHODE ISLAND							
Chafee	N	?	?	Y	Y	Y	Y
Reed	Y	N	Y	Y	Y	N	N
SOUTH CAROLINA							
Thurmond	N	Y	N	Y	Y	Y	Y
Hollings	Y	N	Y	Y	Y	N	N
SOUTH DAKOTA							
Daschle	Y	N	Y	Y	Y	N	N
Johnson	Y	N	Y	Y	Y	N	N
TENNESSEE							
Frist	Y	Y	N	Y	Y	Y	Y
Thompson	Y	Y	N	Y	Y	Y	Y
TEXAS							
Gramm	N	Y	N	Y	Y	Y	Y
Hutchison	Y	Y	N	Y	Y	Y	Y
UTAH							
Bennett	Y	Y	N	Y	Y	Y	Y
Hatch	Y	Y	N	Y	Y	Y	Y
VERMONT							
Jeffords	Y	Y	N	N	Y	Y	Y
Leahy	Y	+	+	Y	Y	N	N
VIRGINIA							
Warner	Y	Y	N	Y	Y	Y	Y
Robb	Y	N	Y	Y	Y	N	N
WASHINGTON							
Gorton	N	Y	N	Y	Y	Y	Y
Murray	Y	N	Y	Y	Y	N	N
WEST VIRGINIA							
Byrd	Y	N	N	Y	Y	N	N
Rockefeller	?	N	Y	Y	Y	N	N
WISCONSIN							
Feingold	Y	N	Y	Y	Y	N	N
Kohl	Y	?	?	Y	Y	N	N
WYOMING							
Enzi	N	Y	N	Y	Y	Y	Y
Thomas	N	Y	N	Y	Y	Y	Y

ND Northern Democrats SD Southern Democrats

Southern states - Ala., Ark., Fla., Ga., Ky., La., Miss., N.C., Okla., S.C., Tenn., Texas, Va.

Key

- Y Voted for (yea).
- # Paired for.
- + Announced for.
- N Voted against (nay).
- X Paired against.
- – Announced against.
- P Voted "present."
- C Voted "present" to avoid possible conflict of interest.
- ? Did not vote or otherwise make a position known.

•

Democrats ***Republicans***
Independents

292. HR 2684. Fiscal 2000 VA-HUD Appropriations/"Atomic Veterans" Benefits. Wellstone, D-Minn., amendment to express the sense of the Senate that lung cancer, colon cancer, and brain and central nervous system cancer, afflictions developed by some veterans who were exposed to radiation at Hiroshima, Nagasaki and nuclear test sites, should be added to the list of radiogenic diseases that are presumed by the Department of Veterans Affairs to be service-connected disabilities. Adopted 76-18: R 32-18; D 43-0 (ND 35-0, SD 8-0); I 1-0, Sept. 24, 1999. (Subsequently, the underlying bill was passed by voice vote.)

293. S Res 186. Republican Education Funding Resolution/Adoption. Adoption of the resolution to express the sense of the Senate that the 106th Congress has taken "strong steps" to revise the U.S. educational system and allow states and localities more flexibility and authority over education, and that the reauthorization of the Elementary and Secondary Education Act will enable Congress to "continue its efforts to send decision-making back to states, local schools and families." Adopted 51-42: R 50-0; D 0-42 (ND 0-34, SD 0-8); I 1-0. Sept. 27, 1999.

294. S Res 187. Democratic Education Funding Resolution/Adoption. Adoption of the resolution to express the sense of the Senate that the Senate should increase federal funding for education programs, including programs to reduce class sizes, recruit and train teachers, increase after-school programs and help schools use technology more effectively in classrooms. The resolution also would urge the Senate to remain within discretionary spending caps and not tap the Social Security surplus when drafting the fiscal 2000 Labor-HHS-Education spending bill. Rejected 41-52: R 0-50; D 41-1 (ND 33-1, SD 8-0); I 0-1. Sept. 27, 1999.

295. HR 2605. Fiscal 2000 Energy and Water Appropriations/Conference Report. Adoption of the conference report on the bill to provide $21.3 billion in funding for energy and water resources development, including programs of the Army Corps of Engineers, the Energy Department and some Interior Department programs. Adopted (thus cleared for the president) 96-3: R 52-1; D 43-2 (ND 35-2, SD 8-0); I 1-0. Sept. 28, 1999.

296. H J Res 68. Fiscal 2000 Continuing Appropriations/Passage. Passage of the joint resolution to provide continuing appropriations through Oct. 21 for agencies covered by the 12 fiscal 2000 spending bills not yet enacted. The continuing resolution would set spending levels at the fiscal 1999 levels. Passed (thus cleared for the president) 98-1: R 52-1; D 45-0 (ND 37-0, SD 8-0); I 1-0. Sept. 28, 1999.

297. S 1650. Fiscal 2000 Labor-HHS-Education Appropriations/Republican Teacher Hiring Plan. Gorton, R-Wash., amendment that would provide $1.2 billion for a teacher assistance initiative once the program is authorized. If the initiative is not authorized by July 1, 2000, school districts could use the funds to hire new teachers or for other activities to improve students' academic achievement. Adopted 53-45: R 52-1; D 0-44 (ND 0-36, SD 0-8); I 1-0. Sept. 29, 1999.

298. S 1650. Fiscal 2000 Labor-HHS-Education Appropriations/Democratic Teacher Hiring Plan. Specter, R-Pa., motion to table (kill) the Murray, D-Wash., amendment that would specify that $1.4 billion of the funds provided in the bill be used for President Clinton's initiative to hire 100,000 new teachers to reduce class size. Motion agreed to 54-44: R 53-0; D 0-44 (ND 0-36, SD 0-8); I 1-0. Sept. 29, 1999. A "nay" is a vote in support of the president's position.

Senate Votes 299, 300, 301

	299	300	301
ALABAMA			
Sessions	Y	N	Y
Shelby	Y	N	Y
ALASKA			
Murkowski	Y	N	Y
Stevens	Y	Y	Y
ARIZONA			
Kyl	Y	N	Y
McCain	?	?	?
ARKANSAS			
Hutchinson	Y	N	Y
Lincoln	N	Y	N
CALIFORNIA			
Boxer	N	Y	N
Feinstein	N	Y	N
COLORADO			
Allard	Y	N	Y
Campbell	Y	N	Y
CONNECTICUT			
Dodd	N	Y	N
Lieberman	N	Y	N
DELAWARE			
Roth	Y	N	Y
Biden	N	Y	N
FLORIDA			
Mack	Y	N	?
Graham	N	Y	N
GEORGIA			
Coverdell	Y	N	Y
Cleland	N	Y	Y
HAWAII			
Akaka	N	Y	N
Inouye	N	Y	N
IDAHO			
Craig	Y	N	Y
Crapo	Y	N	Y
ILLINOIS			
Fitzgerald	Y	Y	Y
Durbin	N	Y	N
INDIANA			
Lugar	Y	N	Y
Bayh	N	Y	N
IOWA			
Grassley	Y	N	Y
Harkin	N	Y	N
KANSAS			
Brownback	Y	N	Y
Roberts	Y	N	Y
KENTUCKY			
Bunning	Y	N	Y
McConnell	Y	N	Y
LOUISIANA			
Breaux	N	Y	N
Landrieu	N	Y	N
MAINE			
Collins	Y	N	Y
Snowe	N	N	Y
MARYLAND			
Mikulski	N	Y	N
Sarbanes	N	Y	N
MASSACHUSETTS			
Kennedy	N	Y	N
Kerry	N	Y	N
MICHIGAN			
Abraham	Y	N	Y
Levin	N	Y	N
MINNESOTA			
Grams	Y	N	Y
Wellstone	N	Y	N
MISSISSIPPI			
Cochran	Y	N	Y
Lott	Y	N	Y
MISSOURI			
Ashcroft	Y	N	Y
Bond	Y	N	Y
MONTANA			
Burns	Y	N	Y
Baucus	N	Y	N
NEBRASKA			
Hagel	Y	N	Y
Kerrey	N	Y	N
NEVADA			
Bryan	N	Y	N
Reid	N	Y	N
NEW HAMPSHIRE			
Gregg	Y	N	Y
Smith	Y	N	Y
NEW JERSEY			
Lautenberg	N	Y	N
Torricelli	N	Y	N
NEW MEXICO			
Domenici	Y	N	Y
Bingaman	N	Y	N
NEW YORK			
Moynihan	N	Y	N
Schumer	N	Y	N
NORTH CAROLINA			
Helms	Y	N	Y
Edwards	N	Y	N
NORTH DAKOTA			
Conrad	N	Y	N
Dorgan	N	Y	N
OHIO			
DeWine	Y	N	?
Voinovich	Y	N	Y
OKLAHOMA			
Inhofe	Y	N	Y
Nickles	Y	N	Y
OREGON			
Smith	Y	N	Y
Wyden	N	Y	N
PENNSYLVANIA			
Santorum	Y	N	Y
Specter	Y	Y	Y
RHODE ISLAND			
Chafee	Y	Y	?
Reed	N	Y	N
SOUTH CAROLINA			
Thurmond	Y	N	Y
Hollings	N	Y	N
SOUTH DAKOTA			
Daschle	N	Y	N
Johnson	N	Y	N
TENNESSEE			
Frist	Y	N	Y
Thompson	Y	N	Y
TEXAS			
Gramm	Y	N	Y
Hutchison	Y	N	Y
UTAH			
Bennett	Y	N	Y
Hatch	Y	N	Y
VERMONT			
Jeffords	Y	Y	N
Leahy	N	Y	N
VIRGINIA			
Warner	Y	N	Y
Robb	N	Y	N
WASHINGTON			
Gorton	Y	N	Y
Murray	N	Y	N
WEST VIRGINIA			
Byrd	N	Y	N
Rockefeller	N	Y	N
WISCONSIN			
Feingold	Y	Y	Y
Kohl	N	Y	N
WYOMING			
Enzi	Y	N	Y
Thomas	Y	N	?

Key

- Y Voted for (yea).
- # Paired for.
- + Announced for.
- N Voted against (nay).
- X Paired against.
- – Announced against.
- P Voted "present."
- C Voted "present" to avoid possible conflict of interest.
- ? Did not vote or otherwise make a position known.

•

Democrats ***Republicans***
Independents

ND Northern Democrats SD Southern Democrats

Southern states - Ala., Ark., Fla., Ga., Ky., La., Miss., N.C., Okla., S.C., Tenn., Texas, Va.

299. S 1650. Fiscal 2000 Labor-HHS-Education Appropriations/After-School Programs. Specter, R-Pa., motion to table (kill) the Boxer, D-Calif., amendment that would provide $200 million for after-school programs. Motion agreed to 54-45: R 52-1; D 1-44 (ND 1-36, SD 0-8); I 1-0. Sept. 30, 1999. A "nay" was a vote in support of the president's position.

300. S 1650. Fiscal 2000 Labor-HHS-Education Appropriations/NLRB and Health Center Funding. Specter, R-Pa., motion to table (kill) the Hutchinson, R-Ark., amendment to the Hutchinson amendment. Both Hutchinson amendments would transfer $25.5 million from the National Labor Relations Board (NLRB) and redirect the funds to community health centers. Motion agreed to 50-49: R 5-48; D 45-0 (ND 37-0, SD 8-0); I 0-1. Sept. 30, 1999. (Subsequently, the underlying Hutchinson amendment was rejected by voice vote.)

301. S 1650. Fiscal 2000 Labor-HHS-Education Appropriations/Public Broadcasting. Specter, R-Pa., motion to table (kill) the Reid, D-Nev., amendment that would increase funding for the Corporation for Public Broadcasting by $125 million to $475 million. Motion agreed to 51-44: R 48-1; D 2-43 (ND 1-36, SD 1-7); I 1-0. Sept. 30, 1999.

Senate Votes 302, 303, 304

	302	303	304
ALABAMA			
Sessions	Y	Y	N
Shelby	Y	Y	N
ALASKA			
Murkowski	Y	Y	N
Stevens	Y	Y	N
ARIZONA			
Kyl	Y	Y	N
McCain	?	?	?
ARKANSAS			
Hutchinson	N	Y	N
Lincoln	N	N	Y
CALIFORNIA			
Boxer	N	N	Y
Feinstein	N	N	Y
COLORADO			
Allard	Y	Y	N
Campbell	Y	N	Y
CONNECTICUT			
Dodd	N	N	Y
Lieberman	N	N	Y
DELAWARE			
Roth	N	N	N
Biden	N	N	Y
FLORIDA			
Mack	?	?	?
Graham	N	N	Y
GEORGIA			
Coverdell	Y	Y	N
Cleland	N	N	Y
HAWAII			
Akaka	N	N	Y
Inouye	N	N	Y
IDAHO			
Craig	Y	Y	N
Crapo	Y	Y	N
ILLINOIS			
Fitzgerald	Y	Y	N
Durbin	N	N	Y
INDIANA			
Lugar	Y	Y	N
Bayh	N	N	Y
IOWA			
Grassley	N	Y	N
Harkin	N	N	Y
KANSAS			
Brownback	Y	Y	N
Roberts	Y	Y	N
KENTUCKY			
Bunning	Y	Y	N
McConnell	Y	Y	N
LOUISIANA			
Breaux	N	N	N
Landrieu	N	N	N
MAINE			
Collins	N	N	N
Snowe	N	N	N
MARYLAND			
Mikulski	N	N	Y
Sarbanes	N	N	Y
MASSACHUSETTS			
Kennedy	N	N	?
Kerry	N	N	Y
MICHIGAN			
Abraham	N	N	N
Levin	N	N	Y
MINNESOTA			
Grams	Y	Y	N
Wellstone	N	N	Y
MISSISSIPPI			
Cochran	Y	Y	N
Lott	Y	Y	N
MISSOURI			
Ashcroft	Y	Y	N
Bond	Y	?	N
MONTANA			
Burns	Y	Y	N
Baucus	N	N	Y
NEBRASKA			
Hagel	Y	Y	N
Kerrey	N	N	Y
NEVADA			
Bryan	N	N	Y
Reid	N	N	Y
NEW HAMPSHIRE			
Gregg	Y	Y	N
Smith	Y	Y	N
NEW JERSEY			
Lautenberg	N	N	Y
Torricelli	N	N	Y
NEW MEXICO			
Domenici	Y	Y	N
Bingaman	N	N	Y
NEW YORK			
Moynihan	N	N	Y
Schumer	N	N	Y
NORTH CAROLINA			
Helms	Y	Y	N
Edwards	N	N	Y
NORTH DAKOTA			
Conrad	N	N	Y
Dorgan	N	N	Y
OHIO			
DeWine	N	N	N
Voinovich	Y	Y	N
OKLAHOMA			
Inhofe	Y	Y	N
Nickles	Y	Y	N
OREGON			
Smith	N	N	N
Wyden	N	N	Y
PENNSYLVANIA			
Santorum	N	Y	N
Specter	Y	Y	Y
RHODE ISLAND			
Chafee	?	?	?
Reed	N	N	Y
SOUTH CAROLINA			
Thurmond	Y	Y	N
Hollings	N	N	Y
SOUTH DAKOTA			
Daschle	N	N	Y
Johnson	N	N	Y
TENNESSEE			
Frist	Y	Y	N
Thompson	Y	Y	N
TEXAS			
Gramm	Y	Y	N
Hutchison	N	Y	N
UTAH			
Bennett	N	N	N
Hatch	N	N	N
VERMONT			
Jeffords	N	N	N
Leahy	N	N	Y
VIRGINIA			
Warner	Y	N	N
Robb	N	N	Y
WASHINGTON			
Gorton	Y	Y	N
Murray	N	N	Y
WEST VIRGINIA			
Byrd	N	Y	Y
Rockefeller	N	N	Y
WISCONSIN			
Feingold	Y	Y	Y
Kohl	N	N	Y
WYOMING			
Enzi	Y	Y	N
Thomas	?	?	?

Key

- Y Voted for (yea).
- # Paired for.
- \+ Announced for.
- N Voted against (nay).
- X Paired against.
- – Announced against.
- P Voted "present."
- C Voted "present" to avoid possible conflict of interest.
- ? Did not vote or otherwise make a position known.

Democrats ***Republicans***
Independents

ND Northern Democrats SD Southern Democrats

Southern states - Ala., Ark., Fla., Ga., Ky., La., Miss., N.C., Okla., S.C., Tenn., Texas, Va.

302. S 1650. Fiscal 2000 Labor-HHS-Education Appropriations/Social Services Block Grants. Coverdell, R-Ga., motion to table (kill) the Graham, D-Fla., amendment that would increase funding for social services block grants in areas such as child care, child welfare and services for the disabled, by $1.3 billion to $2.4 billion. Motion rejected 39-57: R 37-13; D 1-44 (ND 1-36, SD 0-8); I 1-0. Sept. 30, 1999. (Subsequently, the Graham amendment as amended was adopted by voice vote.)

303. S 1650. Fiscal 2000 Labor-HHS-Education Appropriations/Child Care Block Grants. Specter, R-Pa., motion to table (kill) the Dodd, D-Conn., amendment that would increase funding for the Child Care and Development Block Grant program by $817 million to $2 billion. Motion rejected 41-54: R 38-11; D 2-43 (ND 2-35, SD 0-8); I 1-0. Sept. 30, 1999. (Subsequently, the Dodd amendment was adopted by voice vote.)

304. S 1650. Fiscal 2000 Labor-HHS-Education Appropriations/OSHA Compliance Assistance. Specter, R-Pa., motion to table (kill) the Coverdell, R-Ga., amendment to the Enzi, R-Wyo., amendment. Both amendments would redirect $17 million from Occupational Safety and Health Administration (OSHA) workplace inspections to OSHA compliance assistance programs. Motion rejected 44-51: R 2-48; D 42-2 (ND 36-0, SD 6-2); I 0-1. Sept. 30, 1999. (Subsequently, the Coverdell amendment and the Enzi amendment as amended were adopted by voice vote.)

Senate Votes 305, 306, 307, 308, 309, 310, 311, 312

	305	306	307	308	309	310	311	312
ALABAMA								
Sessions	Y	Y	N	Y	N	N	N	Y
Shelby	Y	Y	N	Y	N	N	N	Y
ALASKA								
Murkowski	Y	Y	N	Y	N	N	N	Y
Stevens	Y	Y	N	Y	Y	N	N	Y
ARIZONA								
Kyl	Y	Y	N	Y	Y	N	N	Y
McCain	?	–	N	Y	Y	N	N	Y
ARKANSAS								
Hutchinson	Y	Y	N	Y	N	N	N	Y
Lincoln	Y	Y	Y	Y	Y	Y	Y	N
CALIFORNIA								
Boxer	?	Y	Y	N	Y	N	Y	N
Feinstein	Y	Y	Y	Y	Y	N	Y	N
COLORADO								
Allard	Y	Y	N	Y	N	N	N	Y
Campbell	Y	Y	N	Y	N	N	N	Y
CONNECTICUT								
Dodd	Y	Y	Y	Y	Y	Y	Y	N
Lieberman	Y	Y	Y	Y	Y	Y	Y	N
DELAWARE								
Roth	Y	Y	N	Y	Y	N	N	Y
Biden	Y	Y	Y	Y	Y	Y	N	N
FLORIDA								
Mack	?	?	?	?	?	?	?	Y
Graham	Y	Y	Y	Y	Y	Y	N	N
GEORGIA								
Coverdell	Y	Y	N	Y	N	N	N	Y
Cleland	Y	Y	Y	Y	Y	N	Y	N
HAWAII								
Akaka	Y	Y	Y	Y	Y	N	N	N
Inouye	Y	Y	Y	Y	Y	Y	N	N
IDAHO								
Craig	Y	Y	N	Y	N	N	N	Y
Crapo	Y	Y	N	Y	N	N	N	Y
ILLINOIS								
Fitzgerald	Y	Y	N	Y	Y	Y	N	Y
Durbin	Y	Y	Y	Y	Y	Y	N	N
INDIANA								
Lugar	?	Y	N	Y	Y	N	N	Y
Bayh	Y	Y	Y	Y	Y	Y	N	N
IOWA								
Grassley	Y	Y	N	Y	Y	N	N	Y
Harkin	Y	Y	Y	Y	Y	N	Y	N
KANSAS								
Brownback	Y	Y	N	Y	N	N	N	Y
Roberts	Y	Y	N	Y	N	N	N	Y
KENTUCKY								
Bunning	Y	Y	N	Y	N	N	N	Y
McConnell	Y	Y	N	Y	N	N	N	Y
LOUISIANA								
Breaux	Y	Y	Y	Y	Y	N	N	N
Landrieu	Y	Y	Y	Y	Y	N	N	N
MAINE								
Collins	Y	Y	N	Y	Y	Y	N	Y
Snowe	Y	Y	N	Y	Y	Y	Y	Y
MARYLAND								
Mikulski	Y	Y	Y	N	Y	Y	Y	N
Sarbanes	Y	Y	Y	Y	Y	Y	Y	N
MASSACHUSETTS								
Kennedy	Y	?	Y	Y	Y	Y	Y	N
Kerry	Y	Y	Y	Y	Y	Y	Y	N
MICHIGAN								
Abraham	Y	Y	N	Y	Y	N	N	Y
Levin	+	Y	Y	Y	Y	Y	Y	N
MINNESOTA								
Grams	Y	Y	N	Y	N	N	N	Y
Wellstone	Y	Y	Y	N	Y	Y	Y	N
MISSISSIPPI								
Cochran	Y	Y	N	Y	Y	N	N	Y
Lott	Y	Y	N	Y	N	N	N	Y
MISSOURI								
Ashcroft	Y	Y	N	Y	Y	N	N	Y
Bond	Y	Y	N	Y	Y	N	N	Y
MONTANA								
Burns	Y	Y	N	Y	N	N	N	Y
Baucus	Y	Y	Y	?	?	N	Y	N
NEBRASKA								
Hagel	Y	N	N	Y	N	N	N	N
Kerrey	Y	Y	Y	Y	Y	N	Y	N
NEVADA								
Bryan	Y	Y	Y	Y	Y	N	Y	N
Reid	Y	Y	Y	Y	Y	N	N	N
NEW HAMPSHIRE								
Gregg	Y	Y	N	Y	N	Y	N	Y
Smith	Y	Y	N	Y	N	Y	N	N
NEW JERSEY								
Lautenberg	Y	Y	Y	Y	Y	Y	Y	N
Torricelli	Y	Y	Y	Y	Y	Y	Y	N
NEW MEXICO								
Domenici	Y	Y	N	Y	Y	N	N	Y
Bingaman	Y	Y	Y	Y	Y	N	N	N
NEW YORK								
Moynihan	Y	Y	Y	Y	Y	Y	Y	N
Schumer	Y	Y	Y	Y	Y	Y	N	N
NORTH CAROLINA								
Helms	Y	Y	N	Y	N	N	N	Y
Edwards	Y	Y	Y	Y	Y	Y	N	N
NORTH DAKOTA								
Conrad	Y	N	Y	Y	Y	Y	Y	N
Dorgan	Y	Y	Y	Y	Y	Y	N	N
OHIO								
DeWine	Y	Y	N	Y	Y	Y	N	Y
Voinovich	Y	Y	N	Y	Y	N	N	N
OKLAHOMA								
Inhofe	Y	Y	N	Y	N	N	N	Y
Nickles	Y	Y	N	Y	N	N	N	Y
OREGON								
Smith	Y	?	N	Y	Y	N	N	N
Wyden	?	Y	Y	Y	Y	N	Y	N
PENNSYLVANIA								
Santorum	Y	Y	N	Y	N	N	N	Y
Specter	Y	Y	N	Y	Y	N	Y	Y
RHODE ISLAND								
Chafee	Y	Y	N	Y	Y	?	?	Y
Reed	Y	+	Y	Y	Y	Y	Y	N
SOUTH CAROLINA								
Thurmond	Y	Y	N	Y	Y	N	N	Y
Hollings	Y	?	Y	Y	Y	Y	Y	N
SOUTH DAKOTA								
Daschle	Y	?	Y	Y	Y	Y	N	N
Johnson	Y	Y	Y	N	Y	Y	Y	N
TENNESSEE								
Frist	Y	Y	N	Y	Y	N	N	Y
Thompson	Y	Y	N	Y	N	N	N	Y
TEXAS								
Gramm	Y	Y	N	Y	N	N	N	Y
Hutchison	Y	Y	N	Y	N	Y	N	Y
UTAH								
Bennett	Y	Y	N	Y	Y	N	N	Y
Hatch	Y	?	N	Y	Y	N	N	Y
VERMONT								
Jeffords	Y	Y	N	Y	Y	Y	Y	Y
Leahy	Y	Y	Y	Y	Y	Y	Y	N
VIRGINIA								
Warner	Y	Y	N	Y	N	Y	N	Y
Robb	Y	Y	Y	Y	Y	Y	N	N
WASHINGTON								
Gorton	Y	Y	N	Y	Y	N	N	Y
Murray	Y	Y	Y	Y	Y	Y	N	N
WEST VIRGINIA								
Byrd	Y	Y	Y	Y	Y	N	Y	N
Rockefeller	Y	Y	Y	Y	Y	N	N	N
WISCONSIN								
Feingold	Y	Y	Y	N	Y	N	Y	N
Kohl	Y	Y	Y	Y	Y	N	N	N
WYOMING								
Enzi	Y	N	N	Y	N	N	N	Y
Thomas	?	?	N	Y	N	N	N	Y

ND Northern Democrats SD Southern Democrats

Southern states - Ala., Ark., Fla., Ga., Ky., La., Miss., N.C., Okla., S.C., Tenn., Texas, Va.

Key

Y Voted for (yea).
Paired for.
\+ Announced for.
N Voted against (nay).
X Paired against.
– Announced against.
P Voted "present."
C Voted "present" to avoid possible conflict of interest.
? Did not vote or otherwise make a position known.

•

Democrats ***Republicans***
Independents

305. S 1650. Fiscal 2000 Labor-HHS-Education Appropriations/ Diabetes Research. Collins, R-Maine, amendment to express the sense of the Senate that the National Institutes of Health should increase research funding for diabetes research by $827 million in fiscal 2000. Adopted 93-0: R 50-0; D 42-0 (ND 34-0, SD 8-0); I 1-0. Oct. 1, 1999.

306. HR 2084. Fiscal 2000 Transportation Appropriations/Conference Report. Adoption of the conference report on the bill to appropriate $50.2 billion for transportation programs in fiscal 2000. The measure would provide $27.7 billion for highways, $5.8 billion for mass transit programs, $10.1 billion for the Federal Aviation Administration (FAA), $4 billion for the Coast Guard and $571 million for Amtrak. The conference report includes Senate-passed language to fund the FAA entirely out of the Airport and Airway Trust Fund. Adopted (thus cleared for the president) 88-3: R 47-2; D 40-1 (ND 33-1, SD 7-0); I 1-0. Oct. 4, 1999.

307. White Nomination/Confirmation. Confirmation of President Clinton's nomination of Ronnie L. White of Missouri to be U.S. District judge for the Eastern District of Missouri. Rejected 45-54: R 0-53; D 45-0 (ND 37-0, SD 8-0); I 0-1. Oct. 5, 1999. A "yea" was a vote in support of the president's position.

308. Stewart Nomination/Confirmation. Confirmation of President Clinton's nomination of Brian Theadore Stewart of Utah to be U.S. District judge for the District of Utah. Confirmed 93-5: R 53-0; D 39-5 (ND 31-5, SD 8-0); I 1-0. Oct. 5, 1999. A "yea" was a vote in support of the president's position.

309. Fisher Nomination/Confirmation. Confirmation of President Clinton's nomination of Raymond C. Fisher of California to be a judge for the 9th U.S. Circuit Court of Appeals. Confirmed 69-29: R 25-28; D 44-0 (ND 36-0, SD 8-0); I 0-1. Oct. 5, 1999. A "yea" was a vote in support of the president's position.

310. S 82. Federal Aviation Administration Reauthorization/Additional Flights at Reagan National Airport. Robb, D-Va., amendment to the Gorton, R-Wash., amendment. The Robb amendment would strike language in the Gorton amendment that would allow an additional 24 flights a day into and out of Ronald Reagan Washington National Airport. Rejected 37-61: R 8-44; D 28-17 (ND 23-14, SD 5-3); I 1-0. Oct. 5, 1999. (Subsequently, the Gorton amendment was adopted by voice vote.)

311. S 82. Federal Aviation Administration Reauthorization/Airline Overbooking. Lautenberg, D-N.J., amendment to require airlines to refund tickets to passengers who are bumped involuntarily from flights on which they have paid reservations. Rejected 30-68: R 3-49; D 27-18 (ND 24-13, SD 3-5); I 0-1. Oct. 5, 1999. (Subsequently, the Senate took up HR 1000, struck all after the enacting clause, inserted the text of S 82 and passed the measure to authorize $45 billion over four years for the Federal Aviation Administration by voice vote.)

312. HR 2606. Fiscal 2000 Foreign Operations Appropriations/ Conference Report. Adoption of the conference report on the bill to provide $12.7 billion for foreign aid programs in fiscal 2000, $1.9 billion less than requested by President Clinton. The final bill does not include House-passed abortion-related restrictions on aid to international family planning groups. Adopted (thus cleared for the president) 51-49: R 51-3; D 0-45 (ND 0-37, SD 0-8); I 0-1. Oct. 6, 1999. A "nay" was a vote in support of the president's position.

Senate Votes 313, 314, 315, 316

	313	314	315	316
ALABAMA				
Sessions	Y	Y	Y	Y
Shelby	Y	Y	Y	Y
ALASKA				
Murkowski	Y	Y	Y	Y
Stevens	Y	Y	Y	Y
ARIZONA				
Kyl	Y	Y	Y	Y
McCain	N	Y	?	?
ARKANSAS				
Hutchinson	Y	Y	Y	Y
Lincoln	N	N	N	N
CALIFORNIA				
Boxer	N	N	N	N
Feinstein	N	N	N	N
COLORADO				
Allard	Y	Y	Y	Y
Campbell	Y	Y	Y	Y
CONNECTICUT				
Dodd	N	N	N	N
Lieberman	N	N	N	N
DELAWARE				
Roth	Y	Y	Y	Y
Biden	N	N	N	N
FLORIDA				
Mack	Y	Y	Y	Y
Graham	N	N	N	N
GEORGIA				
Coverdell	Y	Y	Y	Y
Cleland	N	N	N	N
HAWAII				
Akaka	N	N	N	N
Inouye	N	N	N	N
IDAHO				
Craig	Y	Y	Y	Y
Crapo	Y	Y	Y	Y
ILLINOIS				
Fitzgerald	Y	Y	Y	Y
Durbin	N	N	N	N
INDIANA				
Lugar	Y	Y	Y	Y
Bayh	N	N	N	N
IOWA				
Grassley	Y	Y	Y	Y
Harkin	N	N	N	N
KANSAS				
Brownback	Y	Y	Y	Y
Roberts	Y	Y	Y	Y
KENTUCKY				
Bunning	Y	Y	Y	Y
McConnell	Y	Y	Y	Y
LOUISIANA				
Breaux	N	N	N	N
Landrieu	N	N	N	N
MAINE				
Collins	Y	Y	Y	N
Snowe	Y	N	Y	N
MARYLAND				
Mikulski	N	N	N	N
Sarbanes	N	N	N	N
MASSACHUSETTS				
Kennedy	N	N	N	N
Kerry	N	N	N	N
MICHIGAN				
Abraham	Y	Y	Y	Y
Levin	N	N	N	N
MINNESOTA				
Grams	Y	Y	Y	Y
Wellstone	N	N	N	N
MISSISSIPPI				
Cochran	Y	Y	Y	Y
Lott	Y	Y	Y	Y
MISSOURI				
Ashcroft	Y	Y	Y	Y
Bond	Y	Y	Y	Y
MONTANA				
Burns	Y	Y	Y	Y
Baucus	N	N	N	N
NEBRASKA				
Hagel	Y	Y	Y	Y
Kerrey	N	N	N	N
NEVADA				
Bryan	N	N	N	N
Reid	N	N	N	N
NEW HAMPSHIRE				
Gregg	Y	Y	Y	Y
Smith	Y	Y	Y	Y
NEW JERSEY				
Lautenberg	N	N	N	N
Torricelli	N	N	N	N
NEW MEXICO				
Domenici	Y	Y	Y	Y
Bingaman	N	N	N	N
NEW YORK				
Moynihan	N	N	N	N
Schumer	N	N	N	N
NORTH CAROLINA				
Helms	Y	Y	Y	Y
Edwards	N	Y	N	N
NORTH DAKOTA				
Conrad	N	N	Y	N
Dorgan	N	N	N	N
OHIO				
DeWine	Y	Y	Y	N
Voinovich	Y	Y	Y	Y
OKLAHOMA				
Inhofe	Y	Y	Y	Y
Nickles	Y	Y	Y	Y
OREGON				
Smith	Y	Y	Y	Y
Wyden	N	N	N	N
PENNSYLVANIA				
Santorum	Y	Y	Y	Y
Specter	Y	Y	Y	N
RHODE ISLAND				
Chafee	Y	Y	Y	Y
Reed	N	N	N	N
SOUTH CAROLINA				
Thurmond	Y	Y	Y	Y
Hollings	N	N	N	N
SOUTH DAKOTA				
Daschle	N	N	N	N
Johnson	N	N	N	N
TENNESSEE				
Frist	Y	Y	Y	Y
Thompson	Y	Y	Y	Y
TEXAS				
Gramm	Y	Y	Y	Y
Hutchison	Y	Y	Y	Y
UTAH				
Bennett	Y	Y	Y	Y
Hatch	Y	Y	Y	Y
VERMONT				
Jeffords	Y	N	Y	Y
Leahy	N	N	N	N
VIRGINIA				
Warner	Y	Y	Y	Y
Robb	N	N	N	N
WASHINGTON				
Gorton	Y	Y	Y	Y
Murray	N	N	N	N
WEST VIRGINIA				
Byrd	N	N	N	N
Rockefeller	N	N	N	N
WISCONSIN				
Feingold	N	N	Y	N
Kohl	N	N	N	N
WYOMING				
Enzi	Y	Y	Y	Y
Thomas	Y	Y	Y	Y

Key

- Y Voted for (yea).
- # Paired for.
- + Announced for.
- N Voted against (nay).
- X Paired against.
- – Announced against.
- P Voted "present."
- C Voted "present" to avoid possible conflict of interest.
- ? Did not vote or otherwise make a position known.

•

Democrats ***Republicans***
Independents

ND Northern Democrats SD Southern Democrats

Southern states - Ala., Ark., Fla., Ga., Ky., La., Miss., N.C., Okla., S.C., Tenn., Texas, Va.

313. S 1650. Fiscal 2000 Labor-HHS-Education Appropriations/Across-the-Board Spending Cuts. Nickles, R-Okla., amendment to the Nickles amendment. Both amendments would express the sense of the Senate that Congress should adopt an across-the-board cut in all discretionary funding if failure to do so would result in tapping the Social Security surplus to provide fiscal 2000 spending. Adopted 54-46: R 53-1; D 0-45 (ND 0-37, SD 0-8); I 1-0. Oct. 6, 1999.

314. S 1650. Fiscal 2000 Labor-HHS-Education Appropriations/Closing Tax 'Loopholes.' Nickles, R-Okla., motion to table (kill) the Lautenberg, D-N.J., amendment to the Nickles amendment. The Lautenberg amendment would express the sense of the Senate that Congress should close "special-interest tax loopholes" in order to avoid spending the Social Security surplus in fiscal 2000, rather than adopting across-the-board cuts in discretionary spending. Motion agreed to 54-46: R 52-2; D 1-44 (ND 0-37, SD 1-7); I 1-0. Oct. 6, 1999. (Subsequently, the Nickles amendment was withdrawn by voice vote.)

315. S 1650. Fiscal 2000 Labor-HHS-Education Appropriations/Teacher Training Funds. Specter, R-Pa., motion to table (kill) the Kennedy, D-Mass., amendment that would provide $300 million for teacher preparation and recruitment. Motion agreed to 56-43: R 53-0; D 2-43 (ND 2-35, SD 0-8); I 1-0. Oct. 6, 1999.

316. S 1650. Fiscal 2000 Labor-HHS-Education Appropriations/Education Exemption from Across-the-Board Spending Cuts. Nickles, R-Okla., motion to table (kill) the Kennedy, D-Mass., amendment that would exempt education funding from any across-the-board spending reductions. Motion agreed to 50-49: R 49-4; D 0-45 (ND 0-37, SD 0-8); I 1-0. Oct. 6, 1999.

Senate Votes 317, 318, 319, 320, 321

	317	318	319	320	321
ALABAMA					
Sessions	Y	Y	N	N	N
Shelby	Y	Y	N	Y	Y
ALASKA					
Murkowski	Y	Y	N	Y	Y
Stevens	Y	Y	N	Y	Y
ARIZONA					
Kyl	Y	Y	N	N	N
McCain	?	Y	N	N	N
ARKANSAS					
Hutchinson	Y	Y	N	N	Y
Lincoln	N	Y	N	Y	Y
CALIFORNIA					
Boxer	N	Y	N	Y	Y
Feinstein	N	Y	N	Y	Y
COLORADO					
Allard	Y	Y	N	N	N
Campbell	Y	Y	N	Y	Y
CONNECTICUT					
Dodd	?	?	?	?	?
Lieberman	N	Y	N	Y	Y
DELAWARE					
Roth	Y	Y	N	N	Y
Biden	N	Y	N	Y	Y
FLORIDA					
Mack	Y	Y	N	N	Y
Graham	N	Y	N	Y	N
GEORGIA					
Coverdell	Y	Y	N	N	Y
Cleland	N	Y	N	Y	Y
HAWAII					
Akaka	N	Y	N	Y	Y
Inouye	N	Y	N	Y	Y
IDAHO					
Craig	Y	Y	N	N	N
Crapo	Y	Y	N	N	N
ILLINOIS					
Fitzgerald	Y	Y	N	Y	N
Durbin	N	Y	N	Y	Y
INDIANA					
Lugar	N	Y	N	N	Y
Bayh	N	Y	N	Y	N
IOWA					
Grassley	Y	Y	N	N	Y
Harkin	N	Y	N	Y	Y
KANSAS					
Brownback	Y	Y	N	N	N
Roberts	Y	Y	N	N	Y
KENTUCKY					
Bunning	Y	Y	N	N	N
McConnell	Y	Y	N	N	Y
LOUISIANA					
Breaux	N	Y	N	Y	Y
Landrieu	N	Y	N	Y	Y
MAINE					
Collins	Y	Y	N	N	Y
Snowe	Y	Y	N	Y	Y
MARYLAND					
Mikulski	N	Y	N	Y	Y
Sarbanes	N	Y	N	Y	Y
MASSACHUSETTS					
Kennedy	N	Y	N	Y	Y
Kerry	N	Y	N	Y	Y
MICHIGAN					
Abraham	Y	Y	N	Y	Y
Levin	N	Y	N	Y	Y
MINNESOTA					
Grams	Y	Y	N	N	N
Wellstone	N	Y	N	Y	Y
MISSISSIPPI					
Cochran	Y	Y	N	N	Y
Lott	Y	Y	N	N	Y
MISSOURI					
Ashcroft	Y	Y	N	N	N
Bond	Y	Y	N	N	Y
MONTANA					
Burns	Y	Y	N	N	Y
Baucus	N	Y	N	Y	Y
NEBRASKA					
Hagel	Y	Y	N	N	N
Kerrey	N	Y	N	Y	Y
NEVADA					
Bryan	N	Y	N	Y	Y
Reid	N	Y	N	Y	Y
NEW HAMPSHIRE					
Gregg	Y	Y	N	N	Y
Smith	Y	Y	N	N	N
NEW JERSEY					
Lautenberg	N	Y	N	Y	Y
Torricelli	N	Y	N	Y	Y
NEW MEXICO					
Domenici	Y	Y	N	Y	Y
Bingaman	N	Y	N	Y	Y
NEW YORK					
Moynihan	N	Y	N	Y	Y
Schumer	N	Y	N	Y	?
NORTH CAROLINA					
Helms	Y	Y	N	N	N
Edwards	N	Y	N	Y	N
NORTH DAKOTA					
Conrad	N	Y	N	Y	N
Dorgan	N	Y	N	Y	Y
OHIO					
DeWine	Y	Y	N	Y	Y
Voinovich	Y	Y	N	Y	N
OKLAHOMA					
Inhofe	Y	Y	N	N	N
Nickles	Y	Y	N	N	N
OREGON					
Smith	Y	Y	N	Y	Y
Wyden	N	Y	N	Y	Y
PENNSYLVANIA					
Santorum	Y	Y	N	Y	Y
Specter	Y	Y	Y	Y	Y
RHODE ISLAND					
Chafee	Y	Y	N	N	Y
Reed	N	Y	N	Y	Y
SOUTH CAROLINA					
Thurmond	Y	Y	N	N	Y
Hollings	N	Y	N	Y	Y
SOUTH DAKOTA					
Daschle	N	Y	N	Y	Y
Johnson	N	Y	N	Y	Y
TENNESSEE					
Frist	Y	Y	N	N	Y
Thompson	Y	Y	N	N	Y
TEXAS					
Gramm	Y	Y	N	N	N
Hutchison	Y	Y	N	N	Y
UTAH					
Bennett	Y	Y	N	N	Y
Hatch	Y	Y	N	N	Y
VERMONT					
Jeffords	Y	Y	Y	Y	Y
Leahy	N	Y	N	Y	Y
VIRGINIA					
Warner	Y	Y	N	N	Y
Robb	N	Y	N	Y	Y
WASHINGTON					
Gorton	Y	Y	N	Y	Y
Murray	N	Y	N	Y	Y
WEST VIRGINIA					
Byrd	N	Y	N	Y	Y
Rockefeller	N	Y	N	Y	Y
WISCONSIN					
Feingold	N	Y	N	Y	N
Kohl	N	Y	N	Y	Y
WYOMING					
Enzi	Y	N	N	N	N
Thomas	Y	Y	N	N	N

ND Northern Democrats SD Southern Democrats

Southern states - Ala., Ark., Fla., Ga., Ky., La., Miss., N.C., Okla., S.C., Tenn., Texas, Va.

Key

- Y Voted for (yea).
- # Paired for.
- \+ Announced for.
- N Voted against (nay).
- X Paired against.
- – Announced against.
- P Voted "present."
- C Voted "present" to avoid possible conflict of interest.
- ? Did not vote or otherwise make a position known.

•

Democrats **Republicans**
Independents

317. S 1650. Fiscal 2000 Labor-HHS-Education Appropriations/ Education Accountability. Coverdell, R-Ga., motion to table (kill) the Bingaman, D-N.M., amendment that would direct $200 million of the education funds in the bill for states and local school districts to implement accountability provisions of the Elementary and Secondary Education Act by providing support to schools. Motion agreed to 53-45: R 52-1; D 0-44 (ND 0-36, SD 0-8); I 1-0. Oct. 7, 1999.

318. S 1650. Fiscal 2000 Labor-HHS-Education Appropriations/Report on Former Welfare Recipients. Wellstone, D-Minn., amendment that would express the sense of the Senate that Congress should study the economic status of former welfare recipients who lost their assistance under the 1996 welfare law (PL 104-193). Adopted 98-1: R 53-1; D 44-0 (ND 36-0, SD 8-0); I 1-0. Oct. 7, 1999.

319. S 1650. Fiscal 2000 Labor-HHS-Education Appropriations/ Ergonomics Regulations. Specter, R-Pa., motion to table (kill) the Bond, R-Mo., amendment to the Bond amendment. The second-degree Bond amendment would prohibit the Labor Department and the Occupational Safety and Health Administration from issuing any standard, regulation or guideline regarding ergonomics prior to Sept. 30, 2000. The underlying amendment is similar. Motion rejected 2-97: R 2-52; D 0-44 (ND 0-36, SD 0-8); I 0-1. Oct. 7, 1999. (Subsequently, the underlying Bond amendment was withdrawn by voice vote.)

320. S 1650. Fiscal 2000 Labor-HHS-Education Appropriations/ Prevailing Wage Requirement for Rebuilding Disaster Areas. Specter, R-Pa., motion to table (kill) the Smith, I-N.H., amendment that would prohibit the applicability of the 1931 Davis-Bacon Act in locations declared federal disaster areas by the president. Davis-Bacon requires that any workers on a federal project be paid prevailing wages. Motion agreed to 59-40: R 15-39; D 44-0 (ND 36-0, SD 8-0); I 0-1. Oct. 7, 1999.

321. S 1650. Fiscal 2000 Labor-HHS-Education Appropriations/ Passage. Passage of the bill to provide approximately $93 billion in discretionary spending for the departments of Labor, Health and Human Services, and Education, and for related agencies and programs. Passed 73-25: R 35-19; D 38-5 (ND 32-3, SD 6-2); I 0-1. Oct. 7, 1999.

Senate Votes 322, 323, 324

	322	323	324
ALABAMA			
Sessions	Y	Y	Y
Shelby	Y	Y	Y
ALASKA			
Murkowski	Y	Y	Y
Stevens	Y	Y	Y
ARIZONA			
Kyl	Y	N	Y
McCain	Y	N	Y
ARKANSAS			
Hutchinson	Y	Y	Y
Lincoln	Y	Y	N
CALIFORNIA			
Boxer	Y	Y	N
Feinstein	Y	Y	N
COLORADO			
Allard	Y	Y	Y
Campbell	Y	Y	Y
CONNECTICUT			
Dodd	?	N	N
Lieberman	N	N	N
DELAWARE			
Roth	N	N	Y
Biden	N	N	N
FLORIDA			
Mack	Y	Y	Y
Graham	Y	N	N
GEORGIA			
Coverdell	Y	Y	Y
Cleland	Y	Y	N
HAWAII			
Akaka	Y	Y	N
Inouye	Y	Y	N
IDAHO			
Craig	Y	Y	Y
Crapo	Y	Y	Y
ILLINOIS			
Fitzgerald	Y	Y	Y
Durbin	Y	Y	N
INDIANA			
Lugar	Y	Y	Y
Bayh	Y	Y	N
IOWA			
Grassley	Y	Y	Y
Harkin	Y	Y	N
KANSAS			
Brownback	Y	Y	Y
Roberts	Y	Y	Y
KENTUCKY			
Bunning	Y	Y	Y
McConnell	Y	Y	Y
LOUISIANA			
Breaux	Y	Y	N
Landrieu	Y	Y	N
MAINE			
Collins	N	N	Y
Snowe	N	N	Y
MARYLAND			
Mikulski	N	N	N
Sarbanes	N	N	N
MASSACHUSETTS			
Kennedy	Y	Y	N
Kerry	Y	Y	N
MICHIGAN			
Abraham	Y	Y	Y
Levin	Y	Y	N
MINNESOTA			
Grams	Y	Y	Y
Wellstone	Y	Y	N
MISSISSIPPI			
Cochran	Y	Y	Y
Lott	Y	Y	Y
MISSOURI			
Ashcroft	Y	Y	Y
Bond	Y	Y	Y
MONTANA			
Burns	Y	Y	Y
Baucus	Y	Y	N
NEBRASKA			
Hagel	Y	Y	Y
Kerrey	Y	Y	N
NEVADA			
Bryan	Y	Y	N
Reid	Y	Y	N
NEW HAMPSHIRE			
Gregg	N	N	Y
Smith	N	N	Y
NEW JERSEY			
Lautenberg	N	N	N
Torricelli	N	N	N
NEW MEXICO			
Domenici	Y	Y	Y
Bingaman	Y	Y	N
NEW YORK			
Moynihan	N	N	N
Schumer	N	N	N
NORTH CAROLINA			
Helms	Y	Y	Y
Edwards	Y	Y	N
NORTH DAKOTA			
Conrad	Y	Y	N
Dorgan	Y	Y	N
OHIO			
DeWine	Y	Y	Y
Voinovich	Y	N	Y
OKLAHOMA			
Inhofe	Y	Y	Y
Nickles	N	N	Y
OREGON			
Smith	Y	Y	Y
Wyden	Y	Y	N
PENNSYLVANIA			
Santorum	N	N	Y
Specter	N	N	Y
RHODE ISLAND			
Chafee	N	N	Y
Reed	N	N	N
SOUTH CAROLINA			
Thurmond	Y	Y	Y
Hollings	Y	Y	N
SOUTH DAKOTA			
Daschle	Y	Y	N
Johnson	Y	Y	N
TENNESSEE			
Frist	Y	Y	Y
Thompson	Y	Y	Y
TEXAS			
Gramm	Y	Y	Y
Hutchison	Y	Y	Y
UTAH			
Bennett	Y	Y	Y
Hatch	Y	Y	Y
VERMONT			
Jeffords	N	N	Y
Leahy	N	N	N
VIRGINIA			
Warner	Y	Y	Y
Robb	Y	Y	N
WASHINGTON			
Gorton	Y	Y	Y
Murray	Y	Y	N
WEST VIRGINIA			
Byrd	Y	Y	N
Rockefeller	Y	Y	N
WISCONSIN			
Feingold	Y	N	N
Kohl	Y	Y	N
WYOMING			
Enzi	Y	Y	Y
Thomas	Y	Y	Y

Key

- Y Voted for (yea).
- # Paired for.
- + Announced for.
- N Voted against (nay).
- X Paired against.
- – Announced against.
- P Voted "present."
- C Voted "present" to avoid possible conflict of interest.
- ? Did not vote or otherwise make a position known.

•

Democrats ***Republicans***
Independents

ND Northern Democrats SD Southern Democrats

Southern states - Ala., Ark., Fla., Ga., Ky., La., Miss., N.C., Okla., S.C., Tenn., Texas, Va.

322. HR 1906. Fiscal 2000 Agriculture Appropriations/Conference Report/Cloture. Motion to invoke cloture (thus limiting debate) on the conference report on the bill to provide $69 billion for agriculture programs, the Food and Drug Administration and rural development programs in fiscal 2000. The measure would allocate $8.7 billion in emergency aid to farmers, but does not contain provisions on milk prices or Senate-passed language to lift unilateral sanctions on food and medicine exports. Motion agreed to 79-20: R 45-9; D 34-10 (ND 26-10, SD 8-0); I 0-1. Three-fifths of the total Senate (60) is required to invoke cloture. Oct. 12, 1999.

323. HR 1906. Fiscal 2000 Agriculture Appropriations/Conference Report. Adoption of the conference report on the bill to provide $69 billion for agriculture programs, the Food and Drug Administration and rural development programs in fiscal 2000. The measure would allocate $8.7 billion in emergency aid to farmers, but does not contain provisions on milk prices or Senate-passed language to lift unilateral sanctions on food and medicine exports. Adopted (thus cleared for the president) 74-26: R 42-12; D 32-13 (ND 25-12, SD 7-1); I 0-1. Oct. 13, 1999.

324. Nuclear Test Ban Treaty/Motion to Proceed. Motion to proceed to executive session to consider the Comprehensive Nuclear Test Ban Treaty (Treaty Doc 105-28), which would ban all nuclear weapons testing six months after the pact is ratified by the 44 nations that have either nuclear power plants or nuclear research reactors. Motion agreed to 55-45: R 54-0; D 0-45 (ND 0-37, SD 0-8); I 1-0. Oct. 13, 1999.

	325	326	327
ALABAMA			
Sessions	N	Y	Y
Shelby	N	Y	Y
ALASKA			
Murkowski	N	Y	N
Stevens	N	Y	N
ARIZONA			
Kyl	N	Y	N
McCain	N	N	Y
ARKANSAS			
Hutchinson	N	Y	N
Lincoln	Y	Y	Y
CALIFORNIA			
Boxer	Y	N	Y
Feinstein	Y	Y	Y
COLORADO			
Allard	N	Y	Y
Campbell	N	Y	Y
CONNECTICUT			
Dodd	Y	Y	Y
Lieberman	Y	Y	Y
DELAWARE			
Roth	N	Y	Y
Biden	Y	Y	Y
FLORIDA			
Mack	N	Y	Y
Graham	Y	N	Y
GEORGIA			
Coverdell	N	Y	N
Cleland	Y	Y	Y
HAWAII			
Akaka	Y	Y	Y
Inouye	Y	Y	Y
IDAHO			
Craig	N	Y	Y
Crapo	N	Y	Y
ILLINOIS			
Fitzgerald	N	N	Y
Durbin	Y	Y	Y
INDIANA			
Lugar	N	Y	Y
Bayh	Y	N	Y
IOWA			
Grassley	N	Y	Y
Harkin	Y	N	Y
KANSAS			
Brownback	N	Y	Y
Roberts	N	Y	Y
KENTUCKY			
Bunning	N	Y	Y
McConnell	N	Y	Y
LOUISIANA			
Breaux	Y	Y	Y
Landrieu	Y	Y	Y
MAINE			
Collins	N	Y	N
Snowe	N	Y	N
MARYLAND			
Mikulski	Y	Y	Y
Sarbanes	Y	Y	Y
MASSACHUSETTS			
Kennedy	Y	+	?
Kerry	Y	?	?
MICHIGAN			
Abraham	N	Y	Y
Levin	Y	Y	Y
MINNESOTA			
Grams	N	Y	Y
Wellstone	Y	N	Y
MISSISSIPPI			
Cochran	N	Y	N
Lott	N	Y	N
MISSOURI			
Ashcroft	N	Y	Y
Bond	N	Y	N
MONTANA			
Burns	N	Y	Y
Baucus	Y	Y	Y
NEBRASKA			
Hagel	N	Y	N
Kerrey	Y	Y	Y
NEVADA			
Bryan	Y	Y	Y
Reid	Y	Y	Y
NEW HAMPSHIRE			
Gregg	N	Y	N
Smith	N	Y	N
NEW JERSEY			
Lautenberg	Y	Y	Y
Torricelli	Y	Y	Y
NEW MEXICO			
Domenici	N	Y	Y
Bingaman	Y	Y	Y
NEW YORK			
Moynihan	Y	Y	Y
Schumer	Y	Y	Y
NORTH CAROLINA			
Helms	N	Y	Y
Edwards	Y	Y	Y
NORTH DAKOTA			
Conrad	Y	Y	Y
Dorgan	Y	Y	Y
OHIO			
DeWine	N	Y	Y
Voinovich	N	N	N
OKLAHOMA			
Inhofe	N	Y	N
Nickles	N	Y	N
OREGON			
Smith	Y	Y	Y
Wyden	Y	Y	Y
PENNSYLVANIA			
Santorum	N	Y	Y
Specter	Y	Y	Y
RHODE ISLAND			
Chafee	Y	Y	?
Reed	Y	Y	Y
SOUTH CAROLINA			
Thurmond	N	Y	N
Hollings	Y	Y	Y
SOUTH DAKOTA			
Daschle	Y	Y	Y
Johnson	Y	Y	Y
TENNESSEE			
Frist	N	Y	Y
Thompson	N	Y	N
TEXAS			
Gramm	N	Y	N
Hutchison	N	Y	Y
UTAH			
Bennett	N	Y	Y
Hatch	N	Y	Y
VERMONT			
Jeffords	Y	Y	Y
Leahy	Y	Y	Y
VIRGINIA			
Warner	N	Y	Y
Robb	Y	N	Y
WASHINGTON			
Gorton	N	Y	Y
Murray	Y	Y	Y
WEST VIRGINIA			
Byrd	P	Y	Y
Rockefeller	Y	Y	Y
WISCONSIN			
Feingold	Y	N	Y
Kohl	Y	N	Y
WYOMING			
Enzi	N	Y	N
Thomas	N	Y	Y

Key

- Y Voted for (yea).
- # Paired for.
- \+ Announced for.
- N Voted against (nay).
- X Paired against.
- – Announced against.
- P Voted "present."
- C Voted "present" to avoid possible conflict of interest.
- ? Did not vote or otherwise make a position known.

•

Democrats ***Republicans***
Independents

ND Northern Democrats SD Southern Democrats

Southern states - Ala., Ark., Fla., Ga., Ky., La., Miss., N.C., Okla., S.C., Tenn., Texas, Va.

325. Nuclear Test Ban Treaty/Adoption. Adoption of the resolution of ratification of the Comprehensive Nuclear Test Ban Treaty (Treaty Doc 105-28), which would ban nuclear weapons testing six months after the pact is ratified by the 44 nations that have either nuclear power plants or nuclear research reactors. Rejected 48-51: R 4-50; D 44-0 (ND 36-0, SD 8-0); I 0-1. A two-thirds majority of those present and voting (66 in this case) is required for adoption of resolutions of ratification. Oct. 13, 1999. A "yea" was a vote in support of the president's position.

326. HR 2561. Fiscal 2000 Defense Appropriations/Conference Report. Adoption of the conference report on the bill to appropriate $267.8 billion in defense spending for fiscal 2000. The report includes $1 billion of the $1.9 billion requested by the administration for the F-22 jet fighter program and would designate $7.2 billion of the bill's total budget authority as emergency spending. Adopted (thus cleared for the president) 87-11: R 51-3; D 35-8 (ND 29-6, SD 6-2); I 1-0. Oct. 14, 1999.

327. S 1593. Campaign Finance Revisions/Contribution Disclosure. McCain, R-Ariz., amendment that would require national political parties to disclose transfers of funds to state and local parties. The amendment would require state and local parties to file with the Federal Election Commission (FEC) all disclosure reports required by state or local law. It also would require electronic filing of all disclosure reports and FEC notification within 24 hours of every donation received in the last 90 days of a campaign. Adopted 77-20: R 34-19; D 43-0 (ND 35-0, SD 8-0); I 0-1. Oct. 14, 1999.

Senate Votes 328, 329, 330, 331, 332, 333

	328	329	330	331	332	333
ALABAMA						
Sessions	Y	N	N	N	Y	Y
Shelby	Y	N	N	N	Y	Y
ALASKA						
Murkowski	Y	N	N	N	Y	Y
Stevens	Y	N	N	N	Y	Y
ARIZONA						
Kyl	N	N	N	N	Y	Y
McCain	N	N	Y	Y	N	N
ARKANSAS						
Hutchinson	Y	N	N	Y	Y	Y
Lincoln	Y	N	Y	Y	N	N
CALIFORNIA						
Boxer	Y	N	Y	Y	N	N
Feinstein	Y	N	Y	Y	N	N
COLORADO						
Allard	Y	N	N	N	Y	Y
Campbell	Y	N	N	N	Y	Y
CONNECTICUT						
Dodd	+	–	Y	Y	N	N
Lieberman	Y	N	Y	Y	N	N
DELAWARE						
Roth	Y	?	N	Y	N	N
Biden	Y	?	Y	Y	N	N
FLORIDA						
Mack	Y	N	N	N	Y	Y
Graham	Y	N	Y	Y	N	N
GEORGIA						
Coverdell	Y	N	N	N	Y	Y
Cleland	Y	N	Y	Y	N	N
HAWAII						
Akaka	Y	N	Y	Y	N	N
Inouye	Y	N	Y	Y	N	N
IDAHO						
Craig	Y	N	N	N	Y	Y
Crapo	Y	N	N	N	Y	Y
ILLINOIS						
Fitzgerald	Y	N	N	N	Y	Y
Durbin	Y	N	Y	Y	N	N
INDIANA						
Lugar	Y	N	N	N	Y	Y
Bayh	N	N	Y	Y	N	N
IOWA						
Grassley	Y	N	N	N	Y	Y
Harkin	Y	N	Y	Y	N	N
KANSAS						
Brownback	Y	N	N	Y	Y	Y
Roberts	Y	N	N	N	Y	Y
KENTUCKY						
Bunning	Y	N	N	N	Y	Y
McConnell	Y	N	N	N	Y	Y
LOUISIANA						
Breaux	Y	N	Y	Y	Y	Y
Landrieu	Y	N	Y	Y	Y	Y
MAINE						
Collins	Y	N	Y	Y	N	N
Snowe	Y	N	Y	Y	N	N
MARYLAND						
Mikulski	Y	N	Y	Y	N	N
Sarbanes	Y	N	Y	Y	N	N
MASSACHUSETTS						
Kennedy	+	N	Y	Y	N	N
Kerry	Y	N	Y	Y	N	N
MICHIGAN						
Abraham	Y	N	N	N	Y	Y
Levin	Y	N	Y	Y	N	N
MINNESOTA						
Grams	Y	N	N	N	Y	Y
Wellstone	Y	N	Y	Y	N	N
MISSISSIPPI						
Cochran	Y	N	N	N	Y	Y
Lott	Y	N	N	N	Y	Y
MISSOURI						
Ashcroft	Y	N	N	N	Y	Y
Bond	Y	N	N	N	Y	Y
MONTANA						
Burns	Y	N	N	N	Y	Y
Baucus	Y	N	Y	Y	N	N
NEBRASKA						
Hagel	Y	N	N	N	Y	Y
Kerrey	Y	N	Y	Y	N	N
NEVADA						
Bryan	Y	N	Y	Y	N	N
Reid	Y	N	Y	Y	N	N
NEW HAMPSHIRE						
Gregg	Y	N	N	N	Y	Y
Smith	Y	N	N	N	Y	Y
NEW JERSEY						
Lautenberg	Y	?	Y	Y	N	N
Torricelli	Y	N	Y	Y	N	N
NEW MEXICO						
Domenici	Y	N	N	N	Y	Y
Bingaman	Y	?	Y	Y	N	N
NEW YORK						
Moynihan	Y	N	Y	Y	N	N
Schumer	Y	N	Y	Y	N	N
NORTH CAROLINA						
Helms	Y	N	N	N	Y	Y
Edwards	Y	N	Y	Y	N	N
NORTH DAKOTA						
Conrad	Y	N	Y	Y	N	N
Dorgan	Y	N	Y	Y	N	N
OHIO						
DeWine	Y	N	N	N	Y	Y
Voinovich	N	N	N	N	Y	Y
OKLAHOMA						
Inhofe	Y	N	N	N	Y	Y
Nickles	Y	N	N	N	Y	Y
OREGON						
Smith	Y	?	N	N	Y	Y
Wyden	Y	N	Y	Y	N	N
PENNSYLVANIA						
Santorum	Y	N	N	N	Y	Y
Specter	Y	N	Y	N	Y	Y
RHODE ISLAND						
Chafee	Y	N	Y	N	N	N
Reed	Y	N	Y	Y	N	N
SOUTH CAROLINA						
Thurmond	Y	N	N	N	Y	Y
Hollings	Y	Y	Y	Y	Y	Y
SOUTH DAKOTA						
Daschle	Y	N	Y	Y	N	N
Johnson	Y	N	Y	Y	N	N
TENNESSEE						
Frist	Y	N	N	N	Y	Y
Thompson	Y	N	Y	Y	Y	Y
TEXAS						
Gramm	Y	N	N	N	Y	Y
Hutchison	Y	N	N	N	N	Y
UTAH						
Bennett	Y	N	N	N	Y	Y
Hatch	Y	N	N	N	Y	Y
VERMONT						
Jeffords	Y	N	Y	Y	N	N
Leahy	Y	N	Y	Y	N	N
VIRGINIA						
Warner	Y	N	N	N	Y	Y
Robb	Y	N	Y	Y	N	N
WASHINGTON						
Gorton	Y	N	N	N	Y	Y
Murray	Y	N	Y	Y	N	N
WEST VIRGINIA						
Byrd	Y	N	Y	Y	Y	Y
Rockefeller	Y	N	Y	Y	N	N
WISCONSIN						
Feingold	N	N	Y	Y	N	N
Kohl	Y	?	Y	Y	N	N
WYOMING						
Enzi	Y	N	N	N	Y	Y
Thomas	Y	N	N	N	Y	Y

Key

- Y Voted for (yea).
- # Paired for.
- + Announced for.
- N Voted against (nay).
- X Paired against.
- – Announced against.
- P Voted "present."
- C Voted "present" to avoid possible conflict of interest.
- ? Did not vote or otherwise make a position known.

•

Democrats ***Republicans***
Independents

ND Northern Democrats SD Southern Democrats

Southern states - Ala., Ark., Fla., Ga., Ky., La., Miss., N.C., Okla., S.C., Tenn., Texas, Va.

328. HR 2684. Fiscal 2000 VA-HUD Appropriations/Conference Report. Adoption of the conference report on the bill to provide $99.5 billion for the departments of Veterans Affairs (VA), Housing and Urban Development (HUD), and 17 independent agencies. The bill would provide $44.3 billion in VA funding and $26 billion for HUD. The conference report total includes $4.2 billion in advance funding for HUD's Section 8 rental subsidy program for 2001, and $2.5 billion in emergency funding for the Federal Emergency Management Agency. Adopted (thus cleared for the president) 93-5: R 51-3; D 41-2 (ND 33-2, SD 8-0); I 1-0. Oct. 15, 1999.

329. S 1593. Campaign Finance Revisions/Soft Money Donations and Union Dues. McCain, R-Ariz., motion to table (kill) the Reid, D-Nev., amendment to the Daschle, D-S.D., substitute amendment. The Reid amendment would prohibit national party committees from collecting "soft money" donations, which currently are unlimited and unregulated, and would prohibit unions from using the dues of non-union workers for political purposes without the workers' consent. The Daschle amendment would substitute the text of the broader campaign finance bill (HR 417) passed by the House on Sept. 14. Motion rejected 1-92: R 0-52; D 1-39 (ND 0-32, SD 1-7); I 0-1. Oct. 18, 1999.

330. S 1593. Campaign Finance Revisions/Shays-Meehan Substitute/ Cloture. Motion to invoke cloture (thus limiting debate) on the Daschle, D-S.D., substitute amendment, which would insert text similar to the campaign finance bill (HR 417) passed by the House on Sept. 14. The amendment would ban all contributions of "soft money," or money used for party-building activities as opposed to supporting a specific candidate, and impose restrictions on issue advocacy communications. It also would raise individual aggregate contribution limits and the amount that may be given to state political parties. Motion rejected 52-48: R 7-47; D 45-0 (ND 37-0, SD 8-0); I 0-1. Three-fifths of the total Senate (60) is required to invoke cloture. Oct. 19, 1999. A "yea" was a vote in support of the president's position.

331. S 1593. Campaign Finance Revisions/Soft Money Donations and Union Dues/Cloture. Motion to invoke cloture (thus limiting debate) on the Reid, D-Nev., amendment to the Daschle, D-S.D., substitute amendment. The Reid amendment would prohibit national party committees from collecting "soft money" donations, which currently are unlimited and unregulated, and would prohibit unions from using the dues of non-union workers for political purposes without the workers' consent. It includes the previously adopted McCain, R-Ariz., amendment on disclosure requirements. Motion rejected 53-47: R 8-46; D 45-0 (ND 37-0, SD 8-0); I 0-1. Three-fifths of the total Senate (60) is required to invoke cloture. Oct. 19, 1999.

332. S 1692. Abortion Procedure Ban/Motion to Proceed. Motion to proceed to the bill that would ban a certain late-term abortion procedure, in which the physician partially delivers the fetus before completing the abortion. Anyone convicted of performing such an abortion would be subject to a fine and up to two years in prison. Motion agreed to 52-48: R 47-7; D 4-41 (ND 1-36, SD 3-5); I 1-0. Oct. 20, 1999.

333. S 1692. Abortion Procedure Ban/Procedural Motion. Coverdell, R-Ga., motion to table (kill) the Lott, R-Miss., motion to reconsider the vote (#332) on the motion to proceed to the bill that would ban a certain late-term abortion procedure, in which the physician partially delivers the fetus before completing the abortion. Motion agreed to 53-47: R 48-6; D 4-41 (ND 1-36, SD 3-5); I 1-0. Oct. 20, 1999.

Senate Votes 334, 335, 336, 337, 338, 339, 340

State / Senator	334	335	336	337	338	339	340
ALABAMA							
Sessions	N	Y	Y	N	Y	N	Y
Shelby	N	Y	Y	N	Y	N	Y
ALASKA							
Murkowski	N	Y	Y	N	Y	Y	Y
Stevens	N	Y	N	Y	N	N	Y
ARIZONA							
Kyl	N	Y	Y	N	Y	N	Y
McCain	?	?	?	?	Y	N	Y
ARKANSAS							
Hutchinson	N	Y	Y	N	Y	N	Y
Lincoln	Y	N	N	Y	N	Y	Y
CALIFORNIA							
Boxer	Y	Y	N	Y	N	Y	N
Feinstein	Y	Y	N	Y	N	Y	N
COLORADO							
Allard	N	Y	Y	N	Y	N	Y
Campbell	N	Y	N	Y	Y	N	Y
CONNECTICUT							
Dodd	Y	N	N	Y	N	Y	N
Lieberman	Y	N	N	Y	N	Y	N
DELAWARE							
Roth	N	Y	Y	N	N	N	Y
Biden	N	N	N	Y	N	Y	Y
FLORIDA							
Mack	N	Y	Y	N	?	?	?
Graham	Y	N	N	Y	N	N	N
GEORGIA							
Coverdell	N	Y	Y	N	Y	N	Y
Cleland	Y	N	N	Y	N	Y	N
HAWAII							
Akaka	Y	N	N	Y	N	Y	N
Inouye	Y	Y	N	Y	N	N	N
IDAHO							
Craig	N	Y	Y	N	Y	N	Y
Crapo	N	Y	Y	N	Y	N	Y
ILLINOIS							
Fitzgerald	N	Y	Y	N	Y	N	Y
Durbin	Y	N	N	Y	N	Y	N
INDIANA							
Lugar	N	Y	Y	N	Y	Y	Y
Bayh	N	N	N	Y	N	N	Y
IOWA							
Grassley	N	Y	Y	N	Y	N	Y
Harkin	Y	N	N	Y	N	Y	N
KANSAS							
Brownback	N	Y	Y	N	Y	N	Y
Roberts	N	Y	Y	N	Y	N	Y
KENTUCKY							
Bunning	N	Y	Y	N	Y	N	Y
McConnell	N	Y	Y	N	Y	N	Y
LOUISIANA							
Breaux	N	N	Y	N	Y	Y	Y
Landrieu	N	N	N	Y	N	Y	Y
MAINE							
Collins	Y	N	N	Y	N	N	N
Snowe	Y	N	N	Y	N	Y	N
MARYLAND							
Mikulski	Y	N	N	Y	N	Y	N
Sarbanes	Y	N	N	Y	N	Y	N
MASSACHUSETTS							
Kennedy	Y	N	N	Y	N	Y	N
Kerry	Y	N	N	Y	N	N	N
MICHIGAN							
Abraham	N	Y	Y	N	Y	Y	Y
Levin	Y	N	N	Y	N	Y	N
MINNESOTA							
Grams	N	Y	Y	N	Y	N	Y
Wellstone	Y	N	N	Y	N	Y	N
MISSISSIPPI							
Cochran	N	Y	Y	N	Y	N	Y
Lott	N	Y	Y	N	Y	N	Y
MISSOURI							
Ashcroft	N	Y	Y	N	Y	N	Y
Bond	N	Y	Y	N	Y	N	Y
MONTANA							
Burns	N	Y	Y	N	Y	N	Y
Baucus	Y	N	N	Y	N	Y	N
NEBRASKA							
Hagel	N	Y	Y	N	Y	N	Y
Kerrey	Y	N	N	Y	N	N	N
NEVADA							
Bryan	Y	N	N	Y	N	Y	N
Reid	N	N	Y	N	N	Y	Y
NEW HAMPSHIRE							
Gregg	N	Y	Y	?	?	?	?
Smith	N	Y	Y	N	Y	N	Y
NEW JERSEY							
Lautenberg	Y	Y	N	Y	N	Y	N
Torricelli	Y	N	N	Y	N	Y	N
NEW MEXICO							
Domenici	N	Y	Y	N	Y	N	Y
Bingaman	Y	N	N	Y	N	N	N
NEW YORK							
Moynihan	N	N	N	Y	N	Y	Y
Schumer	Y	Y	N	Y	N	Y	N
NORTH CAROLINA							
Helms	N	Y	Y	N	Y	N	Y
Edwards	Y	N	N	Y	N	N	N
NORTH DAKOTA							
Conrad	N	Y	N	Y	N	Y	Y
Dorgan	N	Y	N	Y	N	Y	Y
OHIO							
DeWine	N	Y	Y	N	Y	Y	Y
Voinovich	N	Y	Y	N	Y	Y	Y
OKLAHOMA							
Inhofe	N	Y	Y	N	Y	N	Y
Nickles	N	Y	Y	N	Y	N	Y
OREGON							
Smith	N	Y	Y	N	Y	Y	Y
Wyden	Y	N	N	Y	N	Y	N
PENNSYLVANIA							
Santorum	N	Y	Y	N	Y	Y	Y
Specter	N	N	N	Y	N	Y	Y
RHODE ISLAND							
Chafee	Y	Y	N	Y	?	?	?
Reed	Y	Y	N	Y	N	Y	N
SOUTH CAROLINA							
Thurmond	N	Y	Y	N	Y	N	Y
Hollings	N	Y	N	Y	N	Y	Y
SOUTH DAKOTA							
Daschle	N	N	N	Y	N	Y	Y
Johnson	N	N	N	Y	N	N	Y
TENNESSEE							
Frist	N	Y	Y	N	Y	N	Y
Thompson	N	Y	Y	N	Y	N	Y
TEXAS							
Gramm	N	Y	Y	N	Y	N	Y
Hutchison	N	Y	Y	N	Y	Y	Y
UTAH							
Bennett	N	Y	Y	N	Y	N	Y
Hatch	N	Y	Y	N	Y	Y	Y
VERMONT							
Jeffords	Y	Y	N	Y	N	Y	N
Leahy	N	N	N	Y	N	Y	Y
VIRGINIA							
Warner	N	Y	N	Y	N	N	Y
Robb	Y	N	N	Y	N	N	N
WASHINGTON							
Gorton	N	Y	Y	N	Y	N	Y
Murray	Y	Y	N	Y	N	Y	N
WEST VIRGINIA							
Byrd	N	N	N	Y	N	N	Y
Rockefeller	Y	N	N	Y	N	N	N
WISCONSIN							
Feingold	Y	N	N	Y	N	Y	N
Kohl	Y	N	N	Y	N	Y	N
WYOMING							
Enzi	N	Y	Y	N	Y	N	Y
Thomas	N	Y	Y	N	Y	N	Y

Key

- Y Voted for (yea).
- \# Paired for.
- \+ Announced for.
- N Voted against (nay).
- X Paired against.
- – Announced against.
- P Voted "present."
- C Voted "present" to avoid possible conflict of interest.
- ? Did not vote or otherwise make a position known.

•

Democrats ***Republicans***
Independents

ND Northern Democrats SD Southern Democrats

Southern states - Ala., Ark., Fla., Ga., Ky., La., Miss., N.C., Okla., S.C., Tenn., Texas, Va.

334. S 1692. **Abortion Procedure Ban/Sense of Congress.** Boxer, D-Calif., motion to table (kill) the Santorum, R-Pa., amendment to the instructions of the Santorum motion to commit the bill to the Senate Health, Education, Labor and Pensions Committee. The amendment would express the sense of Congress that the procedure opponents call "partial birth" abortion should be banned. Motion rejected 36-63: R 4-49; D 32-13 (ND 27-10, SD 5-3); I 0-1. (Subsequently, the motion to commit was withdrawn, and the amendment was adopted by voice vote.) Oct. 20, 1999.

335. S 1692. **Abortion Procedure Ban/Post-Viability Abortions.** Santorum, R-Pa., motion to table (kill) the Durbin, D-Ill., substitute amendment that would prohibit doctors from aborting viable fetuses unless the physician certified that the act was necessary because the life of the mother was in danger or continuing the pregnancy would risk grievous injury to her health. Motion agreed to 61-38: R 50-3; D 10-35 (ND 9-28, SD 1-7); I 1-0. Oct. 20, 1999.

336. S 1692. **Abortion Procedure Ban/*Roe v. Wade*.** Santorum, R-Pa., motion to table (kill) the Harkin, D-Iowa, amendment to the Boxer, D-Calif., amendment. The Harkin amendment would express the sense of Congress that the Supreme Court's 1973 *Roe v. Wade* decision was appropriate, secures an important constitutional right and should not be overturned. The Boxer amendment would express the sense of Congress that lawmakers must protect a woman's life and health in any reproductive health legislation Congress passes. Motion rejected 48-51: R 45-8; D 2-43 (ND 1-36, SD 1-7); I 1-0. Oct. 21, 1999.

337. S 1692. **Abortion Procedure Ban/*Roe v. Wade*.** Harkin, D-Iowa, amendment to the Boxer, D-Calif., amendment. The Harkin amendment would express the sense of Congress that the Supreme Court's 1973 *Roe v. Wade* decision was appropriate, secures an important constitutional right and should not be overturned. The Boxer amendment would express the sense of Congress that lawmakers must protect a woman's life and health in any reproductive health legislation Congress passes. Adopted 51-47: R 8-44; D 43-2 (ND 36-1, SD 7-1); I 0-1. (Subsequently, the Boxer amendment as amended was adopted by voice vote.) Oct. 21, 1999.

338. S 1692. **Abortion Procedure Ban/Fetal Tissue Disclosure.** Smith, I-N.H., amendment to require anyone receiving fetal tissue obtained as a result of an abortion to disclose to the government various information, including what medical procedure was used to abort the fetus, how old it was, what the tissue is to be used for, the names of anyone involved in the transfer of the tissue and whether any money was exchanged as a result of the transfer. Rejected 46-51: R 44-7; D 1-44 (ND 0-37, SD 1-7); I 1-0. Oct. 21, 1999.

339. S 1692. **Abortion Procedure Ban/Special Needs Children.** Landrieu, D-La., amendment to express the sense of Congress that the federal government should fully cover educational, medical and respite care expenses of families with special needs children. Rejected 46-51: R 12-39; D 34-11 (ND 29-8, SD 5-3); I 0-1. Oct. 21, 1999.

340. S 1692. **Abortion Procedure Ban/Passage.** Passage of the bill that would ban a certain late-term abortion procedure, in which the physician partially delivers the fetus before completing the abortion. Anyone convicted of performing such an abortion would be subject to a fine and up to two years in prison. The penalties would not apply if the abortion is necessary to save the mother's life. Passed 63-34: R 48-3; D 14-31 (ND 10-27, SD 4-4); I 1-0. Oct. 21, 1999. A "nay" was a vote in support of the president's position.

Senate Vote 341

	341
ALABAMA	
Sessions	Y
Shelby	Y
ALASKA	
Murkowski	Y
Stevens	Y
ARIZONA	
Kyl	Y
McCain	?
ARKANSAS	
Hutchinson	Y
Lincoln	Y
CALIFORNIA	
Boxer	Y
Feinstein	Y
COLORADO	
Allard	Y
Campbell	Y
CONNECTICUT	
Dodd	Y
Lieberman	Y
DELAWARE	
Roth	Y
Biden	Y
FLORIDA	
Mack	Y
Graham	Y
GEORGIA	
Coverdell	Y
Cleland	N
HAWAII	
Akaka	Y
Inouye	Y
IDAHO	
Craig	Y
Crapo	Y
ILLINOIS	
Fitzgerald	Y
Durbin	Y
INDIANA	
Lugar	Y
Bayh	Y
IOWA	
Grassley	Y
Harkin	Y
KANSAS	
Brownback	Y
Roberts	Y
KENTUCKY	
Bunning	N
McConnell	Y
LOUISIANA	
Breaux	Y
Landrieu	Y
MAINE	
Collins	N
Snowe	N
MARYLAND	
Mikulski	Y
Sarbanes	Y
MASSACHUSETTS	
Kennedy	Y
Kerry	Y
MICHIGAN	
Abraham	Y
Levin	Y
MINNESOTA	
Grams	Y
Wellstone	Y
MISSISSIPPI	
Cochran	Y
Lott	Y
MISSOURI	
Ashcroft	Y
Bond	Y
MONTANA	
Burns	Y
Baucus	Y
NEBRASKA	
Hagel	Y
Kerrey	Y
NEVADA	
Bryan	Y
Reid	Y
NEW HAMPSHIRE	
Gregg	Y
Smith	N
NEW JERSEY	
Lautenberg	Y
Torricelli	Y
NEW MEXICO	
Domenici	Y
Bingaman	Y
NEW YORK	
Moynihan	Y
Schumer	Y
NORTH CAROLINA	
Helms	N
Edwards	Y
NORTH DAKOTA	
Conrad	Y
Dorgan	Y
OHIO	
DeWine	Y
Voinovich	Y
OKLAHOMA	
Inhofe	Y
Nickles	Y
OREGON	
Smith	Y
Wyden	Y
PENNSYLVANIA	
Santorum	Y
Specter	Y
RHODE ISLAND	
Vacant *	
Reed	Y
SOUTH CAROLINA	
Thurmond	N
Hollings	Y
SOUTH DAKOTA	
Daschle	Y
Johnson	Y
TENNESSEE	
Frist	Y
Thompson	Y
TEXAS	
Gramm	Y
Hutchison	Y
UTAH	
Bennett	Y
Hatch	Y
VERMONT	
Jeffords	Y
Leahy	Y
VIRGINIA	
Warner	Y
Robb	Y
WASHINGTON	
Gorton	Y
Murray	Y
WEST VIRGINIA	
Byrd	N
Rockefeller	Y
WISCONSIN	
Feingold	Y
Kohl	Y
WYOMING	
Enzi	Y
Thomas	Y

Key

- Y Voted for (yea).
- # Paired for.
- + Announced for.
- N Voted against (nay).
- X Paired against.
- – Announced against.
- P Voted "present."
- C Voted "present" to avoid possible conflict of interest.
- ? Did not vote or otherwise make a position known.

•

Democrats ***Republicans***
Independents

ND Northern Democrats SD Southern Democrats

Southern states - Ala., Ark., Fla., Ga., Ky., La., Miss., N.C., Okla., S.C., Tenn., Texas, Va.

341\. **HR 434. Trade with Sub-Saharan Africa/Cloture.** Motion to invoke cloture (thus limiting debate) on the motion to proceed to the bill that would extend certain trade preferences to the nations of sub-Saharan Africa and seek to promote private investment in the region. The bill would grant duty-free status to many products, including textiles and apparel, if the president certified that the origin nations had met several conditions. Motion agreed to 90-8: R 47-5; D 43-2 (ND 36-1, SD 7-1); I 0-1. Three-fifths of the total Senate (60) is required to invoke cloture. Oct. 26, 1999.

* *Sen. John H. Chafee, R-R.I., died Oct. 24.*

Senate Votes 342, 343, 344, 345, 346, 347, 348

	342	343	344	345	346	347	348
ALABAMA							
Sessions	Y	Y	Y	Y	N	Y	Y
Shelby	Y	Y	Y	N	Y	Y	Y
ALASKA							
Murkowski	Y	Y	Y	Y	Y	Y	Y
Stevens	Y	Y	Y	Y	Y	Y	Y
ARIZONA							
Kyl	Y	Y	Y	Y	Y	Y	Y
McCain	?	–	?	?	?	?	?
ARKANSAS							
Hutchinson	Y	Y	Y	Y	Y	Y	Y
Lincoln	N	N	Y	N	Y	Y	Y
CALIFORNIA							
Boxer	?	N	N	N	N	N	N
Feinstein	N	N	Y	N	Y	N	Y
COLORADO							
Allard	Y	Y	Y	Y	Y	Y	Y
Campbell	N	Y	N	N	N	Y	N
CONNECTICUT							
Dodd	N	N	Y	Y	N	Y	Y
Lieberman	N	N	Y	Y	Y	Y	Y
DELAWARE							
Roth	Y	Y	Y	Y	Y	Y	Y
Biden	N	N	Y	N	N	N	Y
FLORIDA							
Mack	Y	Y	Y	Y	Y	Y	Y
Graham	N	N	Y	Y	Y	Y	Y
GEORGIA							
Coverdell	Y	Y	Y	Y	Y	Y	Y
Cleland	N	N	N	N	N	N	N
HAWAII							
Akaka	N	N	Y	N	N	N	N
Inouye	?	N	N	N	N	N	N
IDAHO							
Craig	Y	Y	Y	Y	Y	Y	Y
Crapo	Y	Y	Y	Y	Y	Y	Y
ILLINOIS							
Fitzgerald	Y	N	Y	Y	Y	Y	Y
Durbin	N	N	Y	N	N	N	N
INDIANA							
Lugar	Y	Y	Y	Y	Y	Y	Y
Bayh	N	N	Y	N	Y	N	Y
IOWA							
Grassley	Y	Y	Y	Y	Y	Y	Y
Harkin	N	N	Y	N	N	N	Y
KANSAS							
Brownback	Y	Y	Y	Y	Y	Y	Y
Roberts	Y	Y	Y	Y	Y	Y	Y
KENTUCKY							
Bunning	N	Y	N	Y	N	Y	N
McConnell	Y	Y	Y	Y	Y	Y	Y
LOUISIANA							
Breaux	N	N	Y	Y	Y	Y	Y
Landrieu	N	N	Y	Y	N	Y	Y
MAINE							
Collins	N	Y	N	N	N	N	N
Snowe	N	Y	N	N	N	N	N
MARYLAND							
Mikulski	N	N	Y	N	N	N	N
Sarbanes	N	N	N	N	N	N	N
MASSACHUSETTS							
Kennedy	?	N	N	N	N	N	N
Kerry	N	N	Y	N	N	N	Y
MICHIGAN							
Abraham	Y	N	Y	Y	Y	Y	Y
Levin	N	N	N	N	N	N	N
MINNESOTA							
Grams	Y	Y	Y	Y	Y	Y	Y
Wellstone	N	N	N	N	N	N	Y
MISSISSIPPI							
Cochran	Y	Y	Y	Y	Y	Y	Y
Lott	Y	Y	Y	Y	Y	Y	Y
MISSOURI							
Ashcroft	Y	N	Y	Y	Y	Y	Y
Bond	Y	Y	Y	Y	Y	Y	Y
MONTANA							
Burns	Y	Y	Y	Y	Y	Y	Y
Baucus	N	N	Y	Y	Y	Y	Y
NEBRASKA							
Hagel	Y	Y	Y	Y	Y	Y	Y
Kerrey	N	N	Y	Y	Y	Y	Y
NEVADA							
Bryan	N	N	Y	N	N	N	Y
Reid	N	N	N	N	N	N	Y
NEW HAMPSHIRE							
Gregg	Y	?	?	?	?	?	?
Smith[1]	N	Y	N	Y	N	Y	N
NEW JERSEY							
Lautenberg	?	N	Y	N	N	N	N
Torricelli	N	N	N	N	N	N	N
NEW MEXICO							
Domenici	Y	Y	Y	Y	Y	Y	Y
Bingaman	N	N	Y	N	N	N	Y
NEW YORK							
Moynihan	N	N	Y	Y	Y	Y	Y
Schumer	N	N	Y	N	N	N	Y
NORTH CAROLINA							
Helms	?	Y	N	N	N	N	N
Edwards	N	N	N	N	N	N	N
NORTH DAKOTA							
Conrad	N	N	N	N	N	N	Y
Dorgan	?	N	N	N	N	N	N
OHIO							
DeWine	Y	Y	Y	Y	Y	Y	Y
Voinovich	Y	N	Y	Y	Y	Y	Y
OKLAHOMA							
Inhofe	Y	Y	Y	Y	N	Y	Y
Nickles	Y	Y	Y	Y	Y	Y	Y
OREGON							
Smith	Y	Y	Y	Y	Y	Y	Y
Wyden	N	N	Y	N	Y	N	Y
PENNSYLVANIA							
Santorum	Y	N	Y	Y	Y	Y	Y
Specter	Y	Y	Y	Y	N	Y	Y
RHODE ISLAND							
Reed	N	N	N	N	N	N	N
Vacant							
SOUTH CAROLINA							
Thurmond	N	Y	N	N	N	N	N
Hollings	N	N	N	N	N	N	N
SOUTH DAKOTA							
Daschle	N	N	Y	N	Y	N	Y
Johnson	N	N	Y	N	N	N	N
TENNESSEE							
Frist	Y	Y	Y	Y	Y	Y	Y
Thompson	Y	Y	Y	Y	Y	Y	Y
TEXAS							
Gramm	Y	Y	Y	Y	Y	Y	Y
Hutchison	Y	Y	Y	Y	N	Y	Y
UTAH							
Bennett	Y	Y	Y	Y	Y	Y	Y
Hatch	+	Y	Y	Y	Y	Y	Y
VERMONT							
Jeffords	Y	Y	Y	Y	Y	Y	Y
Leahy	N	N	Y	N	N	N	Y
VIRGINIA							
Warner	Y	Y	Y	Y	Y	Y	Y
Robb	N	Y	Y	N	N	N	N
WASHINGTON							
Gorton	Y	Y	Y	Y	Y	Y	Y
Murray	N	N	Y	N	Y	N	Y
WEST VIRGINIA							
Byrd	N	Y	N	N	N	N	N
Rockefeller	N	N	Y	N	N	N	N
WISCONSIN							
Feingold	N	N	N	N	N	N	Y
Kohl	N	N	Y	N	N	N	N
WYOMING							
Enzi	Y	Y	Y	Y	Y	Y	Y
Thomas	Y	Y	Y	Y	Y	Y	Y

ND Northern Democrats SD Southern Democrats

Southern states - Ala., Ark., Fla., Ga., Ky., La., Miss., N.C., Okla., S.C., Tenn., Texas, Va.

Key

- Y Voted for (yea).
- # Paired for.
- \+ Announced for.
- N Voted against (nay).
- X Paired against.
- – Announced against.
- P Voted "present."
- C Voted "present" to avoid possible conflict of interest.
- ? Did not vote or otherwise make a position known.

•

Democrats ***Republicans***
Independents

342. HR 434. Trade with Sub-Saharan Africa and the Caribbean/Cloture. Motion to invoke cloture (thus limiting debate) on the Roth, R-Del., substitute amendment that would extend certain trade preferences to the nations of sub-Saharan Africa and seek to promote private investment in the region, expand U.S. trade with the Caribbean, reauthorize the General System of Preferences through June 30, 2004, and reauthorize the Trade Adjustment Assistance Act (PL 93-618) through Sept. 30, 2001. Motion rejected 45-46: R 45-5; D 0-40 (ND 0-32, SD 0-8); I 0-1. Oct. 29, 1999. Three-fifths of the total Senate (60) is required to invoke cloture.

343. HR 3064. Fiscal 2000 District of Columbia, Labor-HHS-Education Appropriations/Conference Report. Adoption of the conference report on the bill to provide $317.1 billion in budget authority for the departments of Labor, Health and Human Services and Education, and for related agencies. The conference report would provide $429.1 million in federal funds for the District of Columbia. The conference report also includes a 0.97 percent across-the-board budget cut that would reduce fiscal 2000 outlays by $3.5 billion. Adopted (thus cleared for the president) 49-48: R 47-5; D 2-43 (ND 1-36, SD 1-7). Nov. 2, 1999. A "nay" was a vote in support of the president's position.

344. HR 434. Trade with Sub-Saharan Africa and the Caribbean/Cloture. Motion to invoke cloture (thus limiting debate) on the Roth, R-Del., substitute amendment that would extend certain trade preferences to the nations of sub-Saharan Africa and seek to promote private investment in the region, expand U.S. trade with the Caribbean, extend the General System of Preferences through June 30, 2004, and reauthorize the Trade Adjustment Assistance Act (PL 93-618) through Sept. 30, 2001. Motion agreed to 74-23: R 45-7; D 29-16 (ND 24-13, SD 5-3). Nov. 2, 1999. Three-fifths of the total Senate (60) is required to invoke cloture.

345. HR 434. Trade with Sub-Saharan Africa and the Caribbean/Labor Standards. Roth, R-Del., motion to table (kill) the Hollings, D-S.C., amendment that would require the president to negotiate a side agreement with each nation on labor standards and submit the agreement to Congress before that nation could receive the bill's trade preferences. Motion agreed to 54-43: R 46-6; D 8-37 (ND 5-32, SD 3-5). Nov. 2, 1999.

346. HR 434. Trade with Sub-Saharan Africa and the Caribbean/Transshipment. Roth, R-Del., motion to table (kill) the Feingold, D-Wis., amendment that would require U.S. businesses importing textile and apparel goods to certify that they have attempted to verify the actual country of origin and that the goods do not violate applicable trademark, copyright or patent laws. The amendment also would specify that the president could extend the bill's preferences only to nations that take action against groups that engage in trans-shipment, the practice of falsifying information about where the good was made in order to receive trade preferences. The U.S. importer and the final retail seller could be held liable for false statements or omissions designed to evade the requirements. Motion agreed to 53-44: R 41-11; D 12-33 (ND 9-28, SD 3-5). Nov. 2, 1999.

347. HR 434. Trade with Sub-Saharan Africa and the Caribbean/Environmental Side Agreements. Moynihan, D-N.Y., motion to table (kill) the Hollings, D-S.C., amendment that would require the president to negotiate a side agreement on the environment with each nation before that nation could receive the bill's trade preferences. Motion agreed to 57-40: R 48-4; D 9-36 (ND 5-32, SD 4-4). Nov. 2, 1999.

348. HR 434. Trade with Sub-Saharan Africa and the Caribbean/Reciprocal Trade Agreements. Roth, R-Del., motion to table (kill) the Hollings, D-S.C., amendment to require that before any nation could receive the bill's trade preferences, the president must negotiate and implement a reciprocal trade agreement with that country. Motion agreed to 70-27: R 45-7; D 25-20 (ND 21-16, SD 4-4). Nov. 2, 1999.

[1] *Robert C. Smith of New Hampshire changed his party affiliation from Independent to Republican on Nov. 1, 1999.*

Senate Votes 349, 350, 351, 352, 353, 354

	349	350	351	352	353	354
ALABAMA						
Sessions	Y	N	Y	Y	Y	Y
Shelby	Y	N	Y	Y	Y	N
ALASKA						
Murkowski	Y	Y	Y	Y	Y	Y
Stevens	Y	Y	Y	Y	Y	Y
ARIZONA						
Kyl	Y	Y	Y	Y	Y	Y
McCain	?	?	?	?	+	?
ARKANSAS						
Hutchinson	Y	Y	Y	Y	Y	Y
Lincoln	Y	Y	Y	Y	Y	Y
CALIFORNIA						
Boxer	N	Y	Y	N	N	N
Feinstein	Y	Y	Y	Y	Y	Y
COLORADO						
Allard	Y	Y	Y	Y	Y	Y
Campbell	N	N	Y	N	Y	Y
CONNECTICUT						
Dodd	Y	Y	Y	Y	Y	Y
Lieberman	Y	Y	Y	Y	Y	Y
DELAWARE						
Roth	Y	Y	Y	Y	Y	Y
Biden	Y	N	Y	N	Y	Y
FLORIDA						
Mack	Y	Y	Y	Y	Y	Y
Graham	Y	Y	Y	Y	Y	Y
GEORGIA						
Coverdell	Y	Y	Y	Y	Y	Y
Cleland	N	N	Y	N	N	Y
HAWAII						
Akaka	N	N	Y	N	N	Y
Inouye	?	?	?	?	?	Y
IDAHO						
Craig	Y	N	Y	Y	Y	Y
Crapo	Y	N	Y	Y	Y	Y
ILLINOIS						
Fitzgerald	Y	Y	Y	Y	Y	C
Durbin	N	N	Y	N	Y	Y
INDIANA						
Lugar	Y	Y	Y	Y	Y	Y
Bayh	Y	N	Y	Y	Y	Y
IOWA						
Grassley	Y	Y	Y	Y	Y	Y
Harkin	N	Y	Y	N	Y	N
KANSAS						
Brownback	Y	Y	Y	Y	Y	Y
Roberts	Y	Y	Y	Y	Y	Y
KENTUCKY						
Bunning	Y	N	Y	Y	N	Y
McConnell	Y	Y	Y	Y	Y	Y
LOUISIANA						
Breaux	Y	Y	Y	Y	Y	Y
Landrieu	Y	Y	Y	Y	Y	Y
MAINE						
Collins	N	N	Y	N	N	Y
Snowe	N	N	Y	N	N	Y
MARYLAND						
Mikulski	N	N	Y	N	Y	N
Sarbanes	N	N	Y	N	N	Y
MASSACHUSETTS						
Kennedy	N	–	+	–	–	Y
Kerry	N	Y	Y	N	Y	Y
MICHIGAN						
Abraham	Y	Y	Y	Y	Y	Y
Levin	N	N	Y	N	Y	Y
MINNESOTA						
Grams	Y	Y	Y	Y	Y	Y
Wellstone	N	N	Y	N	N	N
MISSISSIPPI						
Cochran	Y	Y	Y	Y	Y	Y
Lott	Y	Y	Y	Y	Y	Y
MISSOURI						
Ashcroft	Y	Y	Y	Y	Y	Y
Bond	Y	Y	Y	Y	Y	Y
MONTANA						
Burns	Y	N	Y	Y	Y	Y
Baucus	N	N	Y	Y	Y	Y
NEBRASKA						
Hagel	Y	Y	Y	Y	Y	Y
Kerrey	Y	Y	Y	Y	Y	Y
NEVADA						
Bryan	Y	Y	Y	N	Y	N
Reid	N	Y	Y	N	N	Y
NEW HAMPSHIRE						
Gregg	Y	Y	Y	Y	Y	Y
Smith	Y	N	Y	Y	N	Y
NEW JERSEY						
Lautenberg	N	Y	Y	N	Y	Y
Torricelli	N	N	Y	N	Y	Y
NEW MEXICO						
Domenici	Y	Y	Y	Y	Y	Y
Bingaman	Y	Y	Y	Y	Y	Y
NEW YORK						
Moynihan	Y	Y	Y	Y	Y	Y
Schumer	N	Y	Y	N	Y	Y
NORTH CAROLINA						
Helms	Y	N	Y	Y	N	Y
Edwards	Y	N	Y	N	N	Y
NORTH DAKOTA						
Conrad	N	N	Y	Y	Y	Y
Dorgan	N	N	Y	N	N	N
OHIO						
DeWine	Y	N	Y	Y	Y	Y
Voinovich	Y	Y	Y	Y	Y	Y
OKLAHOMA						
Inhofe	Y	N	Y	Y	Y	Y
Nickles	Y	Y	Y	Y	Y	Y
OREGON						
Smith	Y	Y	Y	Y	Y	Y
Wyden	Y	Y	Y	Y	Y	Y
PENNSYLVANIA						
Santorum	Y	N	Y	Y	?	Y
Specter	N	N	Y	N	Y	Y
RHODE ISLAND						
Reed	N	N	Y	N	N	Y
Chafee, L.[1]						Y
SOUTH CAROLINA						
Thurmond	Y	N	Y	Y	N	Y
Hollings	N	N	Y	N	N	Y
SOUTH DAKOTA						
Daschle	Y	Y	Y	Y	Y	Y
Johnson	N	N	Y	N	Y	Y
TENNESSEE						
Frist	Y	Y	Y	Y	Y	Y
Thompson	Y	Y	Y	Y	Y	Y
TEXAS						
Gramm	Y	Y	Y	Y	Y	Y
Hutchison	Y	N	Y	Y	Y	Y
UTAH						
Bennett	Y	Y	Y	Y	Y	Y
Hatch	Y	N	Y	Y	Y	Y
VERMONT						
Jeffords	N	N	Y	N	Y	Y
Leahy	N	N	Y	N	N	Y
VIRGINIA						
Warner	Y	Y	Y	Y	Y	Y
Robb	Y	N	Y	Y	Y	Y
WASHINGTON						
Gorton	Y	Y	Y	Y	Y	Y
Murray	Y	Y	Y	Y	Y	Y
WEST VIRGINIA						
Byrd	N	N	Y	N	N	Y
Rockefeller	N	N	Y	Y	Y	Y
WISCONSIN						
Feingold	N	N	Y	N	N	N
Kohl	N	N	Y	?	Y	Y
WYOMING						
Enzi	Y	Y	Y	Y	Y	Y
Thomas	Y	Y	Y	Y	Y	Y

Key

- Y Voted for (yea).
- # Paired for.
- + Announced for.
- N Voted against (nay).
- X Paired against.
- – Announced against.
- P Voted "present."
- C Voted "present" to avoid possible conflict of interest.
- ? Did not vote or otherwise make a position known.

•

Democrats ***Republicans***
Independents

ND Northern Democrats SD Southern Democrats

Southern states - Ala., Ark., Fla., Ga., Ky., La., Miss., N.C., Okla., S.C., Tenn., Texas, Va.

349. HR 434. Trade with Sub-Saharan Africa and the Caribbean/ Human Rights and Worker Rights. Moynihan, D-N.Y., motion to table (kill) the Wellstone, D-Minn., amendment that would require that Caribbean nations receiving the bill's trade benefits not engage in significant human rights violations and that they provide effective enforcement of internationally recognized worker rights. Motion agreed to 66-31: R 48-5; D 18-26 (ND 12-24, SD 6-2). Nov. 3, 1999.

350. HR 434. Trade with Sub-Saharan Africa and the Caribbean/ Dumping. Roth, R-Del., motion to table (kill) the Specter, R-Pa., amendment that would allow anyone financially hurt by the sale in the United States of an imported good at less than foreign market value or construction costs to file a civil action against the relevant manufacturer, producer, exporter or importer. Motion agreed to 54-42: R 34-19; D 20-23 (ND 16-19, SD 4-4). Nov. 3, 1999.

351. HR 434. Trade with Sub-Saharan Africa and the Caribbean/Child Labor. Harkin, D-Iowa, amendment that would prohibit nations that do not effectively enforce the child labor standards established by the International Labor Organization from receiving benefits under the bill. Adopted 96-0: R 53-0; D 43-0 (ND 35-0, SD 8-0). Nov. 3, 1999.

352. HR 434. Trade with Sub-Saharan Africa and the Caribbean/ Africa Trade Alternative. Moynihan, D-N.Y., motion to table (kill) the Feingold, D-Wis., amendment that would revise the bill's Africa trade provisions by strengthening the standards a sub-Saharan African nation would have to achieve to receive the trade benefits, increasing prohibitions on trans-shipment of products and increasing the list of products eligible for preferential tariff treatment. Motion agreed to 66-29: R 48-5; D 18-24 (ND 13-21, SD 5-3). Nov. 3, 1999.

353. HR 434. Trade with Sub-Saharan Africa and the Caribbean/ Passage. Passage of the bill to extend certain trade preferences to the nations of sub-Saharan Africa and seek to promote private investment in the region, expand U.S. trade with the Caribbean, extend the Generalized System of Preferences through June 30, 2004, and reauthorize the Trade Adjustment Assistance Act (PL 93-618) through Sept. 30, 2001. Passed 76-19: R 46-6; D 30-13 (ND 25-10, SD 5-3). (Before passage, the Senate adopted the Roth, R-Del., substitute amendment containing the amended texts of S 1386, S 1387, S 1388 and S 1389 by voice vote.) Nov. 3, 1999. A "yea" was a vote in support of the president's position.

354. S 900. Financial Services Overhaul/Conference Report. Adoption of the conference report on the bill that would eliminate current barriers erected by the 1933 Glass-Steagall Act and other laws that impede affiliations between banking, securities, insurance and other firms. The bill also would require that owners of automated teller machines (ATMs) provide notice on the ATM and on-screen of any charges imposed for the use of the terminal. Adopted (thus sent to the House) 90-8: R 52-1; D 38-7 (ND 30-7, SD 8-0). Nov. 4, 1999.

[1] *John H. Chafee, R-R.I., died Oct. 24, 1999. The last vote for which he was eligible was Vote 340. Lincoln Chafee, R-R.I., was sworn in on Nov. 4, 1999, to fill his father's unexpired term. The first vote for which he was eligible was Vote 354.*

Senate Votes 355, 356, 357, 358, 359, 360

	355	356	357	358	359	360
ALABAMA						
Sessions	Y	Y	Y	Y	Y	Y
Shelby	Y	Y	Y	Y	Y	Y
ALASKA						
Murkowski	Y	Y	Y	Y	Y	Y
Stevens	Y	Y	Y	Y	N	Y
ARIZONA						
Kyl	Y	Y	Y	Y	Y	Y
McCain	Y	+	+	?	?	
ARKANSAS						
Hutchinson	Y	Y	Y	Y	Y	Y
Lincoln	Y	N	N	N	Y	N
CALIFORNIA						
Boxer	Y	N	N	N	N	N
Feinstein	Y	N	N	N	N	N
COLORADO						
Allard	Y	Y	Y	Y	Y	Y
Campbell	Y	Y	Y	Y	N	Y
CONNECTICUT						
Dodd	Y	N	N	N	N	N
Lieberman	Y	N	N	N	N	Y
DELAWARE						
Roth	Y	Y	Y	Y	Y	Y
Biden	Y	N	N	N	Y	N
FLORIDA						
Mack	Y	Y	Y	Y	Y	Y
Graham	Y	N	N	N	N	N
GEORGIA						
Coverdell	Y	Y	Y	Y	Y	Y
Cleland	Y	N	Y	N	Y	N
HAWAII						
Akaka	Y	N	N	N	N	N
Inouye	Y	N	N	N	N	N
IDAHO						
Craig	Y	Y	Y	Y	Y	N
Crapo	Y	Y	Y	Y	Y	N
ILLINOIS						
Fitzgerald	C	Y	Y	C	C	Y
Durbin	Y	N	N	N	N	N
INDIANA						
Lugar	Y	Y	Y	Y	Y	Y
Bayh	Y	N	N	N	N	N

	355	356	357	358	359	360
IOWA						
Grassley	Y	Y	Y	N	Y	Y
Harkin	Y	N	N	N	N	N
KANSAS						
Brownback	Y	Y	Y	Y	Y	Y
Roberts	Y	Y	Y	Y	Y	Y
KENTUCKY						
Bunning	Y	Y	Y	Y	Y	Y
McConnell	Y	Y	Y	Y	Y	Y
LOUISIANA						
Breaux	Y	N	N	N	N	N
Landrieu	Y	N	N	N	N	N
MAINE						
Collins	Y	Y	Y	Y	Y	N
Snowe	Y	N	Y	Y	Y	Y
MARYLAND						
Mikulski	Y	N	N	N	N	N
Sarbanes	Y	N	N	N	N	N
MASSACHUSETTS						
Kennedy	Y	N	N	N	N	N
Kerry	Y	N	N	N	N	N
MICHIGAN						
Abraham	Y	Y	Y	Y	Y	Y
Levin	Y	N	N	N	N	N
MINNESOTA						
Grams	Y	Y	Y	Y	Y	Y
Wellstone	Y	N	N	N	N	N
MISSISSIPPI						
Cochran	Y	Y	Y	Y	Y	Y
Lott	Y	Y	Y	Y	Y	Y
MISSOURI						
Ashcroft	Y	Y	Y	Y	Y	Y
Bond	Y	Y	Y	Y	Y	Y
MONTANA						
Burns	Y	Y	Y	Y	Y	Y
Baucus	Y	N	N	N	N	N
NEBRASKA						
Hagel	Y	Y	Y	Y	Y	Y
Kerrey	Y	N	N	N	N	N
NEVADA						
Bryan	Y	N	N	N	Y	N
Reid	Y	N	N	N	N	N

	355	356	357	358	359	360
NEW HAMPSHIRE						
Gregg	Y	Y	Y	Y	Y	Y
Smith	Y	Y	Y	Y	Y	Y
NEW JERSEY						
Lautenberg	?	N	N	N	N	N
Torricelli	Y	N	N	N	Y	N
NEW MEXICO						
Domenici	Y	Y	Y	Y	Y	Y
Bingaman	Y	N	N	N	N	N
NEW YORK						
Moynihan	+	N	N	N	N	N
Schumer	Y	N	N	N	N	N
NORTH CAROLINA						
Helms	Y	Y	Y	Y	Y	Y
Edwards	Y	N	N	N	N	N
NORTH DAKOTA						
Conrad	Y	N	N	N	N	Y
Dorgan	Y	N	N	N	N	N
OHIO						
DeWine	Y	Y	Y	Y	Y	Y
Voinovich	Y	Y	N	Y	Y	Y
OKLAHOMA						
Inhofe	Y	Y	Y	Y	Y	Y
Nickles	Y	Y	Y	Y	Y	Y
OREGON						
Smith	Y	Y	Y	Y	Y	Y
Wyden	Y	N	N	N	N	N
PENNSYLVANIA						
Santorum	Y	Y	Y	Y	Y	Y
Specter	Y	N	Y	N	Y	N
RHODE ISLAND						
Chafee	Y	N	Y	Y	Y	N
Reed	Y	N	N	N	N	N
SOUTH CAROLINA						
Thurmond	Y	Y	Y	Y	Y	Y
Hollings	?	?	?	?	?	N
SOUTH DAKOTA						
Daschle	Y	N	N	N	N	N
Johnson	Y	N	N	Y	Y	N
TENNESSEE						
Frist	Y	Y	Y	Y	Y	Y
Thompson	Y	Y	Y	Y	Y	Y

Key

- Y Voted for (yea).
- # Paired for.
- + Announced for.
- N Voted against (nay).
- X Paired against.
- – Announced against.
- P Voted "present."
- C Voted "present" to avoid possible conflict of interest.
- ? Did not vote or otherwise make a position known.

•

Democrats ***Republicans***
Independents

	355	356	357	358	359	360
TEXAS						
Gramm	?	Y	Y	Y	Y	Y
Hutchison	Y	Y	Y	Y	Y	Y
UTAH						
Bennett	Y	Y	Y	Y	Y	Y
Hatch	Y	Y	Y	Y	Y	Y
VERMONT						
Jeffords	Y	N	Y	N	N	N
Leahy	+	N	N	N	N	N
VIRGINIA						
Warner	Y	Y	Y	Y	Y	Y
Robb	Y	N	N	N	Y	N
WASHINGTON						
Gorton	Y	Y	Y	Y	Y	N
Murray	Y	N	N	N	N	N
WEST VIRGINIA						
Byrd	Y	N	N	N	N	Y
Rockefeller	Y	N	N	N	N	N
WISCONSIN						
Feingold	Y	N	N	N	Y	N
Kohl	Y	N	N	N	Y	N
WYOMING						
Enzi	Y	Y	Y	Y	Y	Y
Thomas	Y	Y	Y	Y	Y	Y

ND Northern Democrats SD Southern Democrats

Southern states - Ala., Ark., Fla., Ga., Ky., La., Miss., N.C., Okla., S.C., Tenn., Texas, Va.

355. S 625. **Bankruptcy Overhaul/Health Care Facility Bankruptcies.** Grassley, R-Iowa, amendment that would establish a set of protections for patients of hospitals and nursing care facilities when the facility files for bankruptcy. The proposal also would require the attorney general and the Health and Human Services Department to establish a policy and protocols for coordinating a response to bankruptcies of health care facilities. Adopted 94-0: R 53-0; D 41-0 (ND 34-0, SD 7-0). Nov. 8, 1999.

356. S 625. **Bankruptcy Overhaul/Democratic Minimum Wage Increase.** Domenici, R-N.M., motion to table (kill) the Kennedy, D-Mass., amendment that would increase the minimum wage by $1 an hour over two years, to $5.65 an hour beginning Jan. 1, 2000, and to $6.15 an hour beginning Jan. 1, 2001. The amendment also would provide $9.5 billion in tax cuts over five years, offset by extending the Superfund tax and eliminating some corporate tax breaks. Motion agreed to 50-48: R 50-4; D 0-44 (ND 0-37, SD 0-7). Nov. 9, 1999. A "nay" was a vote in support of the president's position.

357. S 625. **Bankruptcy Overhaul/Republican Minimum Wage Increase.** Domenici, R-N.M., amendment that would increase the minimum wage by $1 an hour over three years, to $5.50 an hour beginning March 1, 2000, to $5.85 an hour beginning March 1, 2001, and to $6.15 an hour beginning March 1, 2002. The amendment also would provide $18.4 billion in tax cuts over five years. Adopted 54-44: R 53-1; D 1-43 (ND 0-37, SD 1-6). Nov. 9, 1999. A "nay" was a vote in support of the president's position.

358. S 625. **Bankruptcy Overhaul/Predatory Lending.** Gramm, R-Texas, motion to table (kill) the Durbin, D-Ill., amendment that would invalidate claims against borrowers if the creditor has committed material violations of the Truth in Lending Act, such as lending based on home equity without regard to the borrower's ability to repay or imposing illegal fees such as prepayment penalties. Motion agreed to 51-46: R 50-3; D 1-43 (ND 1-36, SD 0-7). Nov. 9, 1999.

359. S 625. **Bankruptcy Overhaul/College-Age Credit Card Consumers.** Hatch, R-Utah, motion to table (kill) the Dodd, D-Conn., amendment that would prohibit credit card issuers from issuing a card to any consumer under age 21 unless the consumer provides either parental consent or financial information indicating an independent means of repaying debt that may arise from the issuance. Motion agreed to 59-38: R 50-3; D 9-35 (ND 6-31, SD 3-4). Nov. 9, 1999.

360. S 625. **Bankruptcy Overhaul/Drug Penalties.** Hatch, R-Utah, amendment that would increase penalties for manufacturing amphetamines and methamphetamines and authorize funds for law enforcement efforts to reduce such activities. The amendment also would increase penalties for a variety of offenses, including possession of more than 50 grams of powder cocaine, distributing drugs to minors and drug trafficking near a school. Adopted 50-49: R 47-7; D 3-42 (ND 3-34, SD 0-8). Nov. 10, 1999. A "nay" was a vote in support of the president's position.

Senate Votes 361, 362, 363, 364, 365

	361	362	363	364	365
ALABAMA					
Sessions	Y	Y	N	Y	N
Shelby	Y	Y	Y	Y	N
ALASKA					
Murkowski	Y	Y	N	Y	N
Stevens	Y	Y	Y	Y	N
ARIZONA					
Kyl	+	Y	N	Y	N
McCain	?	?	?	?	?
ARKANSAS					
Hutchinson	Y	Y	N	Y	N
Lincoln	Y	Y	N	Y	Y
CALIFORNIA					
Boxer	Y	Y	N	Y	?
Feinstein	Y	Y	N	Y	Y
COLORADO					
Allard	Y	Y	Y	N	N
Campbell	Y	Y	Y	Y	N
CONNECTICUT					
Dodd	Y	Y	N	Y	Y
Lieberman	Y	Y	N	Y	Y
DELAWARE					
Roth	Y	Y	N	Y	N
Biden	Y	Y	N	Y	N
FLORIDA					
Mack	Y	Y	Y	N	N
Graham	Y	Y	Y	N	Y
GEORGIA					
Coverdell	Y	Y	N	Y	N
Cleland	Y	Y	N	Y	Y
HAWAII					
Akaka	Y	Y	N	Y	Y
Inouye	Y	Y	N	Y	Y
IDAHO					
Craig	Y	Y	Y	N	N
Crapo	Y	Y	Y	N	N
ILLINOIS					
Fitzgerald	N	Y	C	C	C
Durbin	Y	Y	N	Y	Y
INDIANA					
Lugar	Y	Y	N	Y	N
Bayh	Y	Y	N	Y	Y
IOWA					
Grassley	Y	Y	N	Y	N
Harkin	Y	Y	N	Y	Y
KANSAS					
Brownback	Y	Y	Y	N	Y
Roberts	Y	Y	Y	N	N
KENTUCKY					
Bunning	Y	Y	Y	Y	N
McConnell	Y	Y	N	Y	N
LOUISIANA					
Breaux	Y	Y	N	Y	Y
Landrieu	Y	Y	N	Y	Y
MAINE					
Collins	Y	Y	N	Y	N
Snowe	Y	Y	N	Y	N
MARYLAND					
Mikulski	Y	Y	N	Y	Y
Sarbanes	Y	Y	N	Y	Y
MASSACHUSETTS					
Kennedy	Y	Y	N	Y	Y
Kerry	Y	Y	N	Y	Y
MICHIGAN					
Abraham	Y	Y	N	Y	N
Levin	Y	Y	N	Y	Y
MINNESOTA					
Grams	Y	Y	Y	N	N
Wellstone	Y	Y	N	Y	Y
MISSISSIPPI					
Cochran	Y	Y	N	Y	N
Lott	Y	Y	N	Y	N
MISSOURI					
Ashcroft	Y	Y	N	Y	N
Bond	Y	Y	N	Y	N
MONTANA					
Burns	Y	N	Y	Y	N
Baucus	Y	Y	N	Y	Y
NEBRASKA					
Hagel	Y	Y	Y	N	N
Kerrey	Y	Y	N	Y	Y
NEVADA					
Bryan	Y	Y	N	Y	Y
Reid	Y	Y	N	Y	Y
NEW HAMPSHIRE					
Gregg	Y	Y	Y	N	N
Smith	Y	Y	Y	N	N
NEW JERSEY					
Lautenberg	Y	Y	Y	N	Y
Torricelli	Y	Y	Y	N	Y
NEW MEXICO					
Domenici	Y	Y	Y	Y	N
Bingaman	Y	Y	N	Y	Y
NEW YORK					
Moynihan	Y	Y	N	Y	Y
Schumer	Y	Y	N	Y	Y
NORTH CAROLINA					
Helms	N	Y	Y	N	N
Edwards	Y	Y	N	Y	Y
NORTH DAKOTA					
Conrad	Y	Y	N	Y	Y
Dorgan	Y	Y	N	Y	Y
OHIO					
DeWine	Y	Y	N	Y	N
Voinovich	Y	Y	N	Y	Y
OKLAHOMA					
Inhofe	Y	Y	Y	Y	N
Nickles	Y	Y	Y	N	N
OREGON					
Smith	Y	Y	N	Y	N
Wyden	Y	Y	N	Y	Y
PENNSYLVANIA					
Santorum	Y	Y	N	Y	?
Specter	Y	N	Y	N	N
RHODE ISLAND					
Chafee	Y	Y	N	Y	N
Reed	Y	Y	N	Y	Y
SOUTH CAROLINA					
Thurmond	Y	Y	Y	N	N
Hollings	Y	Y	N	Y	Y
SOUTH DAKOTA					
Daschle	Y	Y	N	Y	Y
Johnson	Y	Y	N	Y	Y
TENNESSEE					
Frist	Y	Y	N	Y	N
Thompson	Y	Y	Y	N	N
TEXAS					
Gramm	Y	Y	Y	N	N
Hutchison	Y	Y	Y	N	N
UTAH					
Bennett	Y	Y	Y	N	N
Hatch	Y	Y	N	Y	N
VERMONT					
Jeffords	Y	Y	N	Y	Y
Leahy	Y	Y	N	Y	Y
VIRGINIA					
Warner	Y	Y	N	Y	N
Robb	Y	Y	N	Y	N
WASHINGTON					
Gorton	Y	Y	N	Y	N
Murray	Y	Y	N	Y	Y
WEST VIRGINIA					
Byrd	Y	Y	N	Y	Y
Rockefeller	Y	N	N	Y	Y
WISCONSIN					
Feingold	Y	Y	N	Y	Y
Kohl	Y	Y	N	Y	Y
WYOMING					
Enzi	Y	Y	N	Y	N
Thomas	Y	Y	Y	N	N

Key

- Y Voted for (yea).
- # Paired for.
- + Announced for.
- N Voted against (nay).
- X Paired against.
- – Announced against.
- P Voted "present."
- C Voted "present" to avoid possible conflict of interest.
- ? Did not vote or otherwise make a position known.

•

Democrats ***Republicans***
Independents

ND Northern Democrats SD Southern Democrats

Southern states - Ala., Ark., Fla., Ga., Ky., La., Miss., N.C., Okla., S.C., Tenn., Texas, Va.

361. Moseley-Braun Nomination/Confirmation. Confirmation of President Clinton's nomination of former Democratic Sen. Carol Moseley-Braun of Illinois to be U.S. ambassador to New Zealand and Samoa. Confirmed 96-2: R 51-2; D 45-0 (ND 37-0, SD 8-0). A "yea" was a vote in support of the president's position. Nov. 10, 1999.

362. Morgan Nomination/Confirmation. Confirmation of President Clinton's nomination of Linda Joan Morgan of Maryland to be a member of the Surface Transportation Board. Confirmed 96-3: R 52-2; D 44-1 (ND 36-1, SD 8-0). A "yea" was a vote in support of the president's position. Nov. 10, 1999.

363. S 625. Bankruptcy Overhaul/Homestead Exemption Cap. Hutchison, R-Texas, amendment to the Kohl, D-Wis., amendment. The Hutchison amendment would allow states to opt out of the homestead exemption cap proposed by the Kohl amendment. Rejected 29-69: R 26-27; D 3-42 (ND 2-35, SD 1-7). Nov. 10, 1999.

364. S 625. Bankruptcy Overhaul/Homestead Exemption Cap. Kohl, D-Wis., amendment that would prohibit a debtor from exempting more than $100,000 in equity, adjusted for changes in the cost of living, in real or personal property that the debtor uses as a residence. The amendment would not apply to the primary residence of a family farmer. Adopted 76-22: R 34-19; D 42-3 (ND 35-2, SD 7-1). Nov. 10, 1999.

365. S 625. Bankruptcy Overhaul/Family-Related Debtor Expenses. Dodd, D-Conn., amendment that would include health care costs, alimony, child and spousal support payments, adoption expenses and other family-related items on the list of allowable expenses for a debtor. The amendment also would allow debtors to keep domestic support payments and household goods, as well as items worth less than $400, though items worth more than $400, if purchased within 70 days of bankruptcy, could be kept if the creditor could not prove at a hearing that the items were not reasonably necessary for the maintenance or support of the debtor. Rejected 45-51: R 3-49; D 42-2 (ND 35-1, SD 7-1). Nov. 10, 1999.

Senate Votes 366, 367, 368, 369, 370, 371

	366	367	368	369	370	371
ALABAMA						
Sessions	N	Y	Y	Y	Y	Y
Shelby	N	Y	Y	Y	Y	Y
ALASKA						
Murkowski	N	Y	Y	Y	Y	Y
Stevens	N	Y	Y	Y	Y	Y
ARIZONA						
Kyl	N	Y	Y	Y	Y	Y
McCain	?	?	?	?	?	?
ARKANSAS						
Hutchinson	N	Y	N	Y	Y	Y
Lincoln	N	N	Y	Y	N	Y
CALIFORNIA						
Boxer	Y	N	Y	?	?	?
Feinstein	N	N	Y	Y	N	Y
COLORADO						
Allard	N	Y	N	Y	Y	Y
Campbell	N	Y	Y	Y	Y	Y
CONNECTICUT						
Dodd	Y	N	Y	Y	Y	Y
Lieberman	N	N	Y	Y	N	Y
DELAWARE						
Roth	N	Y	Y	Y	N	Y
Biden	N	Y	Y	Y	N	Y
FLORIDA						
Mack	N	Y	N	Y	Y	Y
Graham	N	N	Y	Y	N	Y
GEORGIA						
Coverdell	N	Y	N	Y	Y	Y
Cleland	N	N	Y	Y	Y	Y
HAWAII						
Akaka	Y	N	Y	Y	N	Y
Inouye	Y	N	Y	Y	Y	Y
IDAHO						
Craig	N	Y	Y	Y	Y	Y
Crapo	N	Y	Y	Y	Y	Y
ILLINOIS						
Fitzgerald	N	C	C	N	N	Y
Durbin	N	N	Y	Y	N	Y
INDIANA						
Lugar	N	Y	Y	Y	N	Y
Bayh	N	N	Y	Y	Y	Y
IOWA						
Grassley	Y	Y	Y	Y	Y	Y
Harkin	Y	N	Y	Y	N	Y
KANSAS						
Brownback	N	Y	N	Y	N	Y
Roberts	N	Y	Y	Y	Y	Y
KENTUCKY						
Bunning	N	Y	N	?	?	+
McConnell	N	Y	Y	Y	Y	Y
LOUISIANA						
Breaux	N	N	Y	Y	Y	Y
Landrieu	N	N	Y	Y	N	Y
MAINE						
Collins	N	Y	Y	Y	N	Y
Snowe	N	N	Y	Y	N	Y
MARYLAND						
Mikulski	N	N	Y	Y	Y	Y
Sarbanes	Y	N	Y	Y	N	Y
MASSACHUSETTS						
Kennedy	Y	N	Y	Y	N	Y
Kerry	Y	N	Y	Y	N	Y
MICHIGAN						
Abraham	N	Y	Y	Y	Y	Y
Levin	Y	N	Y	Y	Y	Y
MINNESOTA						
Grams	N	Y	Y	N	Y	Y
Wellstone	Y	N	Y	N	N	Y
MISSISSIPPI						
Cochran	N	Y	Y	Y	Y	Y
Lott	N	Y	N	Y	Y	Y
MISSOURI						
Ashcroft	N	Y	N	?	?	?
Bond	N	Y	Y	?	?	?
MONTANA						
Burns	N	Y	Y	Y	Y	Y
Baucus	Y	N	Y	Y	N	Y
NEBRASKA						
Hagel	N	Y	N	Y	Y	Y
Kerrey	Y	N	Y	Y	N	Y
NEVADA						
Bryan	Y	N	Y	Y	Y	Y
Reid	Y	N	Y	Y	Y	Y
NEW HAMPSHIRE						
Gregg	N	Y	Y	Y	Y	Y
Smith	N	Y	N	Y	Y	Y
NEW JERSEY						
Lautenberg	Y	N	Y	?	?	?
Torricelli	N	Y	Y	Y	N	Y
NEW MEXICO						
Domenici	N	Y	Y	Y	Y	Y
Bingaman	N	N	Y	Y	N	Y
NEW YORK						
Moynihan	Y	N	Y	?	?	?
Schumer	N	N	Y	?	N	Y
NORTH CAROLINA						
Helms	N	Y	Y	Y	Y	Y
Edwards	N	N	Y	Y	Y	Y
NORTH DAKOTA						
Conrad	Y	N	Y	N	Y	Y
Dorgan	Y	N	Y	N	Y	Y
OHIO						
DeWine	N	Y	Y	Y	Y	Y
Voinovich	?	?	Y	Y	Y	N
OKLAHOMA						
Inhofe	N	Y	N	Y	Y	Y
Nickles	N	Y	Y	Y	Y	Y
OREGON						
Smith	N	Y	Y	?	?	?
Wyden	N	N	Y	Y	N	Y
PENNSYLVANIA						
Santorum	N	Y	Y	Y	Y	Y
Specter	N	Y	N	Y	Y	Y
RHODE ISLAND						
Chafee	N	N	Y	Y	N	Y
Reed	N	N	Y	Y	N	Y
SOUTH CAROLINA						
Thurmond	N	Y	Y	Y	Y	Y
Hollings	Y	N	Y	Y	Y	Y
SOUTH DAKOTA						
Daschle	Y	N	Y	Y	N	Y
Johnson	Y	Y	Y	Y	N	Y
TENNESSEE						
Frist	N	Y	Y	?	?	?
Thompson	N	Y	N	Y	Y	Y
TEXAS						
Gramm	N	Y	N	Y	Y	Y
Hutchison	N	Y	Y	?	?	?
UTAH						
Bennett	N	Y	Y	Y	Y	Y
Hatch	N	Y	Y	Y	Y	Y
VERMONT						
Jeffords	N	Y	Y	Y	N	Y
Leahy	Y	N	Y	Y	N	Y
VIRGINIA						
Warner	N	Y	Y	Y	Y	Y
Robb	N	Y	Y	Y	Y	Y
WASHINGTON						
Gorton	N	Y	Y	?	?	?
Murray	N	N	Y	Y	N	Y
WEST VIRGINIA						
Byrd	Y	N	Y	N	Y	Y
Rockefeller	Y	N	Y	Y	Y	Y
WISCONSIN						
Feingold	Y	N	Y	N	N	Y
Kohl	Y	N	Y	N	Y	Y
WYOMING						
Enzi	N	Y	N	Y	Y	Y
Thomas	N	Y	N	Y	Y	Y

Key

- Y Voted for (yea).
- \# Paired for.
- \+ Announced for.
- N Voted against (nay).
- X Paired against.
- – Announced against.
- P Voted "present."
- C Voted "present" to avoid possible conflict of interest.
- ? Did not vote or otherwise make a position known.

•

Democrats ***Republicans***
Independents

ND Northern Democrats SD Southern Democrats

Southern states - Ala., Ark., Fla., Ga., Ky., La., Miss., N.C., Okla., S.C., Tenn., Texas, Va.

366. S 625. Bankruptcy Overhaul/Agribusiness Mergers. Wellstone, D-Minn., amendment that would impose a moratorium on mergers and acquisitions between any agribusiness company whose total assets are more than $100 million with an agribusiness company whose assets are more than $10 million for 18 months or until Congress enacts legislation addressing the problem of market concentration in the agricultural sector, whichever comes first. The amendment also would establish a commission to review such mergers and to make legislative recommendations. Rejected 27-71: R 1-52; D 26-19 (ND 25-12, SD 1-7). Nov. 17, 1999.

367. S 625. Bankruptcy Overhaul/Lower-Income Debtors. Grassley, R-Iowa, motion to table (kill) the Moynihan, D-N.Y., amendment that would exempt individuals and families with monthly incomes below the national or applicable state median monthly income from the bill's expansion of circumstances under which transactions prior to bankruptcy are considered fraudulent. Individuals and families exempted from the expansion would be subject to current non-dischargeability requirements. Motion agreed to 54-43: R 50-2; D 4-41 (ND 3-34, SD 1-7). Nov. 17, 1999.

368. S 625. Bankruptcy Overhaul/Indiscriminate Credit Lending. Feinstein, D-Calif., amendment that would express the sense of Congress that certain lenders sometimes offer credit indiscriminately, without checking the consumer's ability to repay, and that the resulting debt may be a major contributing factor to consumer insolvency. The amendment would require the Federal Reserve Board of Governors to study and report on consumer credit industry practices such as extending credit indiscriminately and gauge the effect of such practices on consumer debt and insolvency. Adopted 82-16: R 37-16; D 45-0 (ND 37-0, SD 8-0). Nov. 17, 1999.

369. HR 3194. Fiscal 2000 Omnibus Appropriations/Conference Report/Motion to Proceed. Motion to proceed to the conference report on the bill to provide almost $385 billion in new budget authority for those Cabinet departments and federal agencies whose fiscal 2000 appropriations bills were never enacted. The measure would provide $435.8 million in federal funds for the District of Columbia. It also incorporates by reference four other appropriations bills: Labor-HHS-Education, Commerce-Justice-State, Interior and Foreign Operations. Also included are bills to reauthorize the State Department, permit satellite TV carriers to transmit local-to-local broadcasts, increase payments to Medicare health providers, and extend the Northeast Dairy Compact and block the administration's new milk pricing plan. The bill would also impose a 0.38 percent across-the-board spending cut, with flexibility for some accounts. Motion agreed to 80-8: R 45-2; D 35-6 (ND 27-6, SD 8-0). Nov. 18, 1999.

370. H J Res 82. Fiscal 2000 Continuing Appropriations/Coal Mining Practices. Byrd, D-W.Va., amendment to impose a two-year moratorium on an Oct. 20, 1999, federal court ruling challenging the legality of certain coal mining practices. Adopted 56-33: R 39-8; D 17-25 (ND 12-22, SD 5-3). Nov. 18, 1999.

371. H J Res 82. Fiscal 2000 Continuing Appropriations/North Carolina Disaster Relief. Helms, R-N.C., amendment to provide $81 million for loan forgiveness to North Carolina farmers who were victims of Hurricane Floyd. Adopted 88-1: R 46-1; D 42-0 (ND 34-0, SD 8-0). (Subsequently, the underlying joint resolution to provide continuing appropriations at fiscal 1999 levels through Nov. 23, 1999, for agencies covered by the fiscal 2000 spending bills not yet enacted was passed by voice vote.) Nov. 18, 1999.

Senate Votes 372, 373, 374

	372	373	374
ALABAMA			
Sessions	Y	Y	N
Shelby	Y	Y	N
ALASKA			
Murkowski	Y	Y	Y
Stevens	Y	Y	Y
ARIZONA			
Kyl	Y	Y	Y
McCain	?	?	N
ARKANSAS			
Hutchinson	Y	Y	Y
Lincoln	Y	Y	Y
CALIFORNIA			
Boxer	Y	Y	N
Feinstein	Y	Y	Y
COLORADO			
Allard	Y	Y	N
Campbell	Y	Y	Y
CONNECTICUT			
Dodd	Y	Y	Y
Lieberman	Y	Y	Y
DELAWARE			
Roth	Y	Y	Y
Biden	Y	Y	Y
FLORIDA			
Mack	Y	Y	Y
Graham	Y	N	N
GEORGIA			
Coverdell	Y	Y	Y
Cleland	Y	Y	Y
HAWAII			
Akaka	Y	Y	Y
Inouye	Y	Y	Y
IDAHO			
Craig	Y	Y	Y
Crapo	Y	Y	Y
ILLINOIS			
Fitzgerald	Y	N	N
Durbin	Y	N	Y
INDIANA			
Lugar	Y	Y	Y
Bayh	Y	Y	N
IOWA			
Grassley	Y	Y	Y
Harkin	Y	Y	Y
KANSAS			
Brownback	Y	Y	Y
Roberts	Y	Y	Y
KENTUCKY			
Bunning	Y	Y	Y
McConnell	Y	Y	Y
LOUISIANA			
Breaux	Y	Y	Y
Landrieu	Y	Y	Y
MAINE			
Collins	Y	Y	Y
Snowe	Y	Y	Y
MARYLAND			
Mikulski	Y	Y	Y
Sarbanes	Y	Y	Y
MASSACHUSETTS			
Kennedy	Y	Y	Y
Kerry	Y	Y	Y
MICHIGAN			
Abraham	Y	Y	Y
Levin	Y	Y	N
MINNESOTA			
Grams	Y	N	N
Wellstone	Y	N	N
MISSISSIPPI			
Cochran	Y	Y	Y
Lott	Y	Y	Y
MISSOURI			
Ashcroft	Y	Y	Y
Bond	Y	Y	Y
MONTANA			
Burns	Y	Y	Y
Baucus	Y	Y	N
NEBRASKA			
Hagel	Y	Y	N
Kerrey	Y	Y	Y
NEVADA			
Bryan	Y	Y	Y
Reid	Y	Y	Y
NEW HAMPSHIRE			
Gregg	Y	Y	Y
Smith	Y	Y	N
NEW JERSEY			
Lautenberg	Y	Y	Y
Torricelli	Y	Y	Y
NEW MEXICO			
Domenici	Y	Y	Y
Bingaman	Y	Y	Y
NEW YORK			
Moynihan	Y	Y	Y
Schumer	Y	Y	Y
NORTH CAROLINA			
Helms	Y	Y	Y
Edwards	Y	Y	N
NORTH DAKOTA			
Conrad	Y	N	N
Dorgan	Y	N	N
OHIO			
DeWine	Y	Y	Y
Voinovich	N	Y	N
OKLAHOMA			
Inhofe	Y	Y	N
Nickles	Y	Y	Y
OREGON			
Smith	+	+	+
Wyden	Y	Y	Y
PENNSYLVANIA			
Santorum	Y	Y	Y
Specter	Y	Y	Y
RHODE ISLAND			
Chafee	Y	Y	Y
Reed	Y	Y	Y
SOUTH CAROLINA			
Thurmond	Y	Y	Y
Hollings	Y	Y	Y
SOUTH DAKOTA			
Daschle	Y	Y	Y
Johnson	Y	Y	Y
TENNESSEE			
Frist	Y	Y	Y
Thompson	Y	Y	Y
TEXAS			
Gramm	Y	Y	Y
Hutchison	Y	Y	Y
UTAH			
Bennett	Y	Y	Y
Hatch	Y	Y	Y
VERMONT			
Jeffords	Y	Y	Y
Leahy	Y	Y	Y
VIRGINIA			
Warner	Y	Y	Y
Robb	Y	Y	Y
WASHINGTON			
Gorton	–	?	Y
Murray	?	?	?
WEST VIRGINIA			
Byrd	Y	Y	N
Rockefeller	Y	Y	Y
WISCONSIN			
Feingold	Y	N	N
Kohl	Y	N	N
WYOMING			
Enzi	Y	Y	N
Thomas	Y	Y	N

Key

- Y Voted for (yea).
- # Paired for.
- + Announced for.
- N Voted against (nay).
- X Paired against.
- – Announced against.
- P Voted "present."
- C Voted "present" to avoid possible conflict of interest.
- ? Did not vote or otherwise make a position known.

Democrats **_Republicans_**
Independents

ND Northern Democrats SD Southern Democrats

Southern states - Ala., Ark., Fla., Ga., Ky., La., Miss., N.C., Okla., S.C., Tenn., Texas, Va.

372. HR 1180. Working Disabled and Tax Extenders/Conference Report. Adoption of the conference report on the bill to allow disabled individuals to retain their federal health benefits after they return to work. The report would create a voucherlike system to permit disabled individuals receiving Social Security and Supplemental Security Income to purchase job training and rehabilitation services to prepare them to return to work. The conference report also would extend several tax provisions that would otherwise expire at the end of 1999, including the research tax credit and the work opportunity tax credit. The report also would delay for 90 days a proposed rule on organ transplants. Adopted (thus cleared for the president) 95-1: R 51-1; D 44-0 (ND 36-0, SD 8-0). Nov. 19, 1999.

373. HR 3194. Fiscal 2000 Omnibus Appropriations/Conference Report/Cloture. Motion to invoke cloture (thus limiting debate) on the conference report on legislation principally to provide almost $385 billion in new budget authority for those Cabinet departments and federal agencies whose fiscal 2000 appropriations bills had not yet been enacted. The measure would provide $435.8 million in federal funds for the District of Columbia. It also incorporates by reference four other appropriations bills: Labor-HHS-Education (HR 3424), Commerce-Justice-State (HR 3421), Interior (HR 3423) and foreign operations (HR 3422). Also included by reference is a bill (HR 3425) that would impose a 0.38 percent across-the-board spending cut, with flexibility for some accounts, and legislation to reauthorize the State Department (HR 3427), permit satellite TV carriers to transmit local-to-local broadcasts (S 1948), increase payments to Medicare health providers (HR 3426), and extend the Northeast Dairy Compact and block the administration's new milk pricing plan (HR 3428). Motion agreed to 87-9: R 50-2; D 37-7 (ND 30-6, SD 7-1). Nov. 19, 1999. Three-fifths of the total Senate (60) is required to invoke cloture.

374. HR 3194. Fiscal 2000 Omnibus Appropriations/Conference Report. Adoption of the conference report on legislation principally to provide almost $385 billion in new budget authority for those Cabinet departments and federal agencies whose fiscal 2000 appropriations bills had not yet been enacted. The measure would provide $435.8 million in federal funds for the District of Columbia. It also incorporates by reference four other appropriations bills: Labor-HHS-Education (HR 3424), Commerce-Justice-State (HR 3421), Interior (HR 3423) and foreign operations (HR 3422). Also included by reference is a bill (HR 3425) that would impose a 0.38 percent across-the-board spending cut, with flexibility for some accounts, and legislation to reauthorize the State Department (HR 3427), permit satellite TV carriers to transmit local-to-local broadcasts (S 1948), increase payments to Medicare health providers (HR 3426), and extend the Northeast Dairy Compact and block the administration's new milk pricing plan (HR 3428). Adopted (thus cleared for the president) 74-24: R 42-12; D 32-12 (ND 26-10, SD 6-2). A "yea" was a vote in support of the president's position. Nov. 19, 1999.

Senate Roll Call Votes By Subject

Appendix I

GENERAL INDEX

General Index

General Index

B

General Index

G

L

N

P

Q

R

S